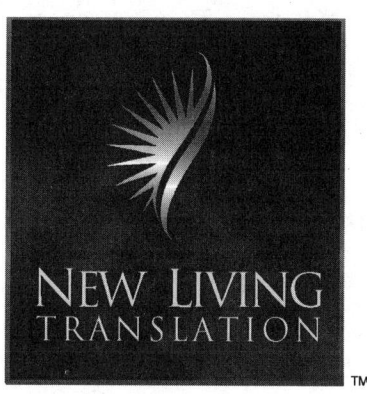

NEW LIVING
TRANSLATION ™

Complete
Concordance

John R. Kohlenberger III
and
James A. Swanson

Tyndale House Publishers, Inc.
Wheaton, Illinois

Library of Congress Cataloging-in-Publication Data

Kohlenberger, John R., and James A. Swanson

New Living Translation complete concordance / John R. Kohlenberger III; James Swanson
p. cm.
ISBN 0-8423-3274-X (hardcover : alk. paper)
1. Bible—Concordances, English—New Living Translation. I. Swanson, James A. II. Title.
BS425.K6445 1996
220.5'208—dc20 96–26072
CIP

Printed in the United States of America

00 99 98 97 96
8 7 6 5 4 3 2 1

CONTENTS

ACKNOWLEDGMENTS

Thanks to Dr. Philip Comfort of Tyndale House Publishers for inviting us to do this book and for his valuable editorial input.

Thanks to Tim Botts of Tyndale House Publishers for his input on page layout and design.

Thanks to Roger Green and Tim Hare of Telios Systems for their work in developing the programing to analyze, sort, and set the contexts for this concordance.

Special thanks to our wives and children—Carolyn, Sarah, and Joshua Kohlenberger, and Sandra, Jon, David, and Natanya Lee Swanson—for their encouragement and patience.

DEDICATION

To Dr. Kenneth N. Taylor

For his courage and innovation as a Bible translator
and his integrity and creativity as a Bible publisher

INTRODUCTION

Funk and Wagnalls defines *concordance* as "an alphabetical index of the important words in a book as they occur in context." As such, a biblical concordance is an essential tool for studying the Bible. It is therefore not surprising that concordances regularly appear on Christian bookstore best-seller lists. It is also not surprising that most of the best-selling English Bible translations have at least one official concordance in print.

What may seem surprising is the lack of an offical concordance to *The Living Bible*, one of the most successful versions of the twentieth century, with more than 40 million copies in print. However, *The Living Bible* was not a rigorous translation of the Bible intended for meticulous study; it was one man's paraphrase or explanatory restatement of the Bible intended "to simplify the deep and often complex thoughts of the Word of God," to make "the Bible easier to understand and follow."

A quarter century after the release of *Living Letters*, Kenneth N. Taylor and ninety biblical scholars have produced the New Living Translation (NLT), a genuine translation, suitable for study and thus meriting an official concordance. And because Tyndale House Publishers was committed to producing this essential reference work, they commissioned the concordance before the release of the NLT. As a result, *The New Living Translation Complete Concordance* is the first biblical concordance to be published in the same year as the version it indexes.

FEATURES OF THE NLT COMPLETE CONCORDANCE

The New Living Translation Complete Concordance (*NLTCC*) is "complete" or exhaustive in terms of vocabulary. The NLT contains a total of 740,104 words, with a vocabulary of 14,912 words. The main concordance indexes 333,022 occurrences of 14,753 major words, while the "Index of Articles, Conjunctions, Particles, Prepositions, and Pronouns" indexes 409,031 occurrences of 169 highly frequent words. The third section, the "Selected Index to the Footnotes of the NLT" indexes 17,498 occurrences of 2,753 significant words from the 3,420 footnotes to the NLT.

THE MAIN CONCORDANCE

Following is a typical entry from the main concordance:

AARON'S (45) [AARON]
AARON'S...DESCENDANTS (6) Ex 40:15; Lev 6:18; Nu 10:8; 1Ch 24:1,3; Ps 118:3
AARON'S SON(S) (17) Ex 28:4,40; 40:31; Lev 1:5,8,11; 2:2; 3:2; 6:14; 8:13,24; 10:1,16; 16:1; Nu 3:2,32; 20:28
Ex 7:12 But then **A** snake swallowed up their snakes.
15:20 **A** sister, took a tambourine and led all the women
28: 4 They will also make special garments for **A** sons to

The heading consists of:
(1) the indexed word: **AARON'S**;
(2) the frequency count in parentheses: (45);
(3) the list of related words in brackets: [AARON].

The phrase-index subheadings consist of:
(1) the indexed phrase: **AARON'S SON(S)**
(2) the frequency count in parentheses: (17);
(3) the index of book-chapter-verse references: Ex 28:4, etc.

The context lines consist of:
(1) the book-chapter-verse references: Ex 7:12, etc.
(2) the context for the indexed word;
(3) the boldfaced first letter of the indexed word: **A**.

Headings

There are four kinds of headings: (1) NLT word headings, (2) phrase-index subheadings, (3) NLT "See" references, and (4) KJV "See" references.

NLT Word Headings

The simplest heading is a word and its frequency count:

ABAGTHA (1)

The frequency count lists the total number of times the word appears in the NLT, which is also the number of contexts listed in the concordance.

The headings show the indexed words exactly as they are spelled in the NLT. (The sole exceptions are two headings each for GOD, LORD, and LORD'S, discussed in the last paragraph of this section.) If the word occurs in other forms or spellings, these words are listed in square brackets following the frequency count:

ABANDON (47) [ABANDONED, ABANDONING, ABANDONS]

ABANDONED (77) [ABANDON]

ABANDONING (4) [ABANDON]

ABANDONS (6) [ABANDON]

Rather than listing all related words after each indexed word, the editors chose one indexed word to act as the "group heading," for example, ABANDON. All related words are listed at the group heading, and each related word points back to the group heading.

Proper names and place names composed of more than one word in the original languages are usually hyphenated in the NLT, for example, Abel-beth-maacah and Beth-shan. Note that according to standard computer alphabetical order, apostrophe (') comes before hyphen (-), and hyphen before the letters of the alphabet. Thus the following alphabetized list:

BAAL

BAAL'S

BAAL-BERITH

BAALAH

Compound or double names that are not hyphenated in the NLT, such as Simon Peter or Pontius Pilate, are indexed under their component words. Thus, there is no heading for SIMON PETER, but each name points to the other:

PETER (191) [CEPHAS, PETER'S, SIMON]

SIMON (73) [PETER, SIMON'S]

As mentioned above, there are two headings each for GOD, LORD, and LORD'S. LORD* and LORD'S* represent the proper name of God, *Yahweh*, which is typeset in the NLT as "LORD" and "LORD's." The other Hebrew and Greek words translated "Lord" or "lord" are indexed under LORD, and those translated "Lord's" or "lord's" are indexed under LORD'S. Three times in Isaiah the Hebrew *Yah Yahweh* or *Yah Yah* is translated "LORD GOD." These special occurrences of GOD are indexed under GOD*, while all other occurrences of "God" or "god" are indexed under GOD.

Phrase-Index Subheadings

In addition to indexing every word of the NLT, the *NLTCC* indexes 968 frequent phrases under 242 key words. Under both MAN and SON, for example, are indexes of the 176 occurrences of "Son of Man."

An ellipsis (...) in the phrase subhead allows for variations in wording. For example, ALL...NATIONS accounts for "all nations" as well as "all the nations" and "all of the nations." If there is only one variation in wording, the alternate letter or word is in parentheses, as in SON(S) OF AARON and GLORY OF (THE) GOD. The front slash (/) separates different forms of a word used in a phrase, as in GAVE/GIVE/GIVING...GLORY.

NLT "See" References

One hundred sixty-four words occur a total of 408,676 times—more than half the bulk of the NLT. These words are exhaustively indexed in their own section: The "Index of Articles, Conjunctions, Particles, Prepositions, Pronouns, and Other Highly Frequent Words." These words are also represented by headings in the main concordance, with a "see" reference to this special index:

A (9213) [AN] See Index of Articles, Etc.

Ten of these 164 words have a selected listing of contexts in the main concordance.

HAD, HAS, HAVE, and HAVING are most often used as auxiliary verbs to indicate the English perfect tense, as in the phrase "I **have** given you." This usage is not indexed in the main concordance. These words are indexed when they are primary verbs, expressing the ideas of ownership, "I **have** more than enough"; childbirth, "Sarah will **have** a son"; causation, "**Have** them wash their clothing"; and obligation, "The owner will **have** to pay."

Though neither I nor AM is indexed in the main concordance, 61 occurrences of the phrase "I am" are indexed. These references list significant instances of the self-revelation of God, such as in Exodus 3:14, "**I AM THE ONE WHO ALWAYS IS**," and Revelation 1:8, "**I am** the Alpha and the Omega."

MINE is indexed in the main concordance when it is not a pronoun (2 of 81 occurrences). ON and SO are each indexed once as proper names. When WILL means a testament or volition, as in "the will of God," it is indexed in the main concordance (71 of 11,210 occurrences).

KJV "See" References

The King James, or Authorized, Version has had a profound impact on the English language in general and on theological vocabulary in particular, because it has been the dominant English Bible translation for nearly four centuries. To show the relationship of familiar KJV words to NLT terms, 1,251 KJV "see" references point to 2,267 NLT words. These include such headings as:

COMFORTER [KJV] See COUNSELOR

ELIAS [KJV] See ELIJAH

(HOLY) GHOST [KJV] See (HOLY) SPIRIT

Note that multiple-word "see" references, such as (HOLY) SPIRIT, do not refer to multiple-word headings. References to Holy Spirit can be looked up under either HOLY or SPIRIT.

Context Lines

As mentioned above, *Funk and Wagnalls* defines *concordance* as "an alphabetical index of the important words in a book as they occur in context." The context is a snippet of a verse that gives the reader a better idea of how the word is used and helps to locate specific verses that contain the word.

For word study or any other kind of Bible study, a concordance context is rarely enough to work with. Sometimes a short sentence or a whole verse fits on one line, as in John 14:15: "If you love me, obey my commandments." But this is the exception rather than the rule.

Taken by themselves, context lines can and do misrepresent the teaching of Scripture by taking statements out of the larger context. "There is no God" is a direct quote of Psalm 14:1. Of course the Bible does not teach this! The fuller context makes it clear that "Only fools say in their hearts, 'There is no God.' "

The editors, programmer, and proofreaders of the *NLTCC* have taken great care to create contexts that are informative and accurate. But the reader should *always* check word contexts by looking them up in the NLT itself.

Context Lines: General Format

Context lines present three items of information. First is the location of the indexed word by book, chapter, and verse. Second is the context itself. Third is the indexed word, abbreviated by its first letter and in bold type (see below for exceptions). If a word occurs more than once in a context, it is abbreviated and bold each time. For example, under the heading HOLY:

Rev 3: 7 This is the message from the one who is **h**
4: 8 "**H**, **h**, **h** is the Lord God Almighty—

Note in the example above that the book abbreviation is only used at the first occurrence. This makes it easier to scan columns of the concordance to see how often a word is used in a book. A table of book abbreviations precedes page 1 of the main concordance. It also includes special verse designations discussed below.

Context Lines: Special Formats

Special Typefaces. Some words and phrases are set in italic type in the NLT. these include *Interlude* (72 times in the Psalms) and *The Book of the History of the Kings* (34 times in Kings and Esther). Small caps are used in phrases such as "I AM THE ONE WHO ALWAYS IS" (Exodus 3:14). These typefaces are reflected in the context lines:

Ex 3:14 God replied, "I AM THE ONE WHO **A** IS.

2Ki 1:18 in *The **B** of the History of the Kings of Israel.*

Line Breaks and Columns. Line breaks and tabular columns are used in the NLT to format poetry and lists. In the *NLTCC* line breaks are indicated by a front slash (/) and column breaks by a vertical bar (|), as under JUDAH:

Rev 7: 5 from **J** | 12,000 / from Reuben | 12,000

Books of One Chapter. Five biblical books have only one chapter: Obadiah, Philemon, 2 John, 3 John, and Jude. Though some reference works index these books by verse only (e.g., Jude 17), in the *NLTCC* all five books are indexed by chapter 1 and the verse number (e.g., Jude 1:17).

Psalm Titles. There are 116 psalms that have superscripts or titles that have no verse numbers in the NLT. The letter T is used as the verse designation for these titles (e.g., Psalm 2:T).

The Shorter Ending of Mark. The oldest manuscripts of Mark conclude with 16:8. The NLT includes "two of the more noteworthy endings" that are found in later manuscripts. The traditional "Longer Ending of Mark" has verses numbered 9 through 20. The "Shorter Ending of Mark" has no verse numbers, but is indexed as Mark 16:S in the concordance.

Two Verses Translated as One. Twenty-four pairs of verses in Numbers 1 and 2 as well as Hebrews 13:20–21 are translated as a single verse. In the main concordance, these verse ranges are indexed by the first verse, with the second verse in brackets, as under NUMBER:

Nu 1:20[-21] This is the **n** of men twenty years old or older

THE INDEX OF ARTICLES, CONJUNCTIONS, PARTICLES, PREPOSITIONS, PRONOUNS, AND OTHER HIGHLY FREQUENT WORDS

The main concordance indexes 333,022 references to 14,753 NLT words. The "Index of Articles, etc." indexes 409,031 references to 169 NLT words. These include words that occur more than 1,000 times, such as "I," "me," and "my," and less frequent words that are related to them, such as "I'd" and "mine."

The format of the "Index of Articles, etc." is very simple. Each of the 164 words has a heading and frequency count, followed by an exhaustive index of occurrences. Books and chapters are in bold for easier location:

A (9213)
Ge 1:2; **2:**7, 7, 8, 10, 18, 19, 21, 22, 23, 24; **3:**13, 17, 17, 24; **4:**1, 2, 2,

SELECTED INDEX TO THE FOOTNOTES OF THE NLT

The NLT has 3,420 footnotes. Most offer alternate or more "literal" translations or discuss variant readings in ancient texts and versions. Most alternate translations can be located under the heading OR. More precise translations can be located under the headings ARAMAIC, GREEK, and HEBREW. Variant readings are listed under such heads as MANUSCRIPTS and VERSIONS. Parallel passages and New Testament citations of the Old Testament are listed under book abbreviations, such as GEN and PS.

As in the main concordance, each footnote word is indexed under a heading with a frequency count. The context is preceded by a word or phrase from the NLT text enclosed in braces { }. The context is usually the entire footnote. Abridged footnotes are marked with ellipses (…). For example:

ADAR (10)
Ezr 6:15 {on March 12} Aramaic *on the third day of the month* **A**, of the Hebrew calendar.…
Est 9:17 {the following day} Hebrew *on the fourteenth day,* of the Hebrew month of **A**.

Unlike the main concordance, The "Selected Index to the Footnotes of the NLT" does not index every occurrence of every word, but only those words that differ from the NLT text. For example, the footnote to "your good eye" in Matthew 5:29 reads "Greek *your right eye.*" This footnote is indexed under RIGHT, but not under EYE.

FEATURES OF THE MAIN CONCORDANCE

NLT WORD HEADING
The indexed word as spelled in the NLT (see the introduction, page vii).

FREQUENCY COUNT
Total number of occurrences in the NLT (see the introduction, page vii).

RELATED WORD LIST
Other forms and related words in the NLT (see the introduction, page viii).

JUDAH (816) [JUDAH'S, JUDEA, JUDEAN, JUDEANS, OHOLIBAH]
KINGS OF JUDAH (31) 1Sa 27:6; 1Ki 14:29; 15:7,23; 22:45; 2Ki 8:23; 12:18,19; 14:18;

PHRASE-INDEX SUBHEADING
Identifies (and totals) frequent phrases involving frequent words (see the introduction, page viii).

PHRASE INDEX
Lists all occurrences of the phrase (see the introduction, page viii).

Ge 49:9 **J** is a young lion / that has finished eating its prey.

BIBLICAL REFERENCE
See the abbreviations below. Brackets [] indicate a verse range (see page ix).

INDEXED WORD
Abbreviated by its first letter, usually **bold** (see the introduction, page ix).

NLT LINE FORMATS
Front slash (/) indicates a line break; vertical bar (|) indicates a column break (see the introduction, page ix).

Nu 2:3[-4] **J** | Nahshon son of Amminadab | 74,600

1Ki 14:29 in *The Book of the History of the Kings of **J**.*

ITALIC TYPEFACE
Italicized text in the NLT is reflected in the context lines (see the introduction, page ix).

A (9213) [AN] See Index of Articles, Etc.

NRSV "See" REFERENCES
Refers to an index in another location (see the introduction, page viii).

SELAH [KJV] See INTERLUDE

KJV "See" REFERENCES
Cross-references key words to NLT vocabulary (see the introduction, page viii).

ABBREVIATIONS

BOOKS OF THE BIBLE

1Ch	1 Chronicles
1Co	1 Corinthians
1Jn	1 John
1Ki	1 Kings
1Pe	1 Peter
1Sa	1 Samuel
1Th	1 Thessalonians
1Ti	1 Timothy
2Ch	2 Chronicles
2Co	2 Corinthians
2Jn	2 John
2Ki	2 Kings
2Pe	2 Peter
2Sa	2 Samuel
2Th	2 Thessalonians
2Ti	2 Timothy
3Jn	3 John
Ac	Acts
Am	Amos
Col	Colossians
Da	Daniel
Dt	Deuteronomy
Ecc	Ecclesiastes
Eph	Ephesians
Est	Esther
Ex	Exodus
Eze	Ezekiel
Ezr	Ezra
Gal	Galatians
Ge	Genesis
Hab	Habakkuk
Hag	Haggai
Heb	Hebrews
Hos	Hosea
Isa	Isaiah
Jas	James
Jdg	Judges
Jer	Jeremiah
Jn	John
Jnh	Jonah
Job	Job
Joel	Joel
Jos	Joshua
Jude	Jude
La	Lamentations
Lev	Leviticus
Lk	Luke
Mal	Malachi
Mic	Micah
Mk	Mark
Mt	Matthew
Na	Nahum
Ne	Nehemiah
Nu	Numbers
Ob	Obadiah
Phm	Philemon
Php	Philippians
Pr	Proverbs
Ps	Psalms
Rev	Revelation
Ro	Romans
Ru	Ruth
SS	Song of Songs
Tit	Titus
Zec	Zechariah
Zep	Zephaniah

OTHER

S	Shorter Endingof Mark
T	Psalm Titles

The
New Living Translation Complete Concordance

A

A (9213) [AN] See Index of Articles, Etc.

AARON (323) [AARON'S]

AARON AND MOSES (6) Ex 5:3; 6:20,26,26; Nu 3:1; 1Ch 23:13

AARON THE PRIEST (18) Ex 31:10; 38:21; 39:41; Lev 1:7; 13:2; Nu 3:6; 4:16,28,33; 7:8; 16:37; 18:28; 25:7,11; 26:1; 33:38; Jos 21:13; Jdg 20:28

DESCENDANT(S) OF AARON (17) Lev 21:21; Nu 16:40; Jos 21:4,10,13,19; 1Ch 6:50,54,57,60; 23:28; 24:31; 2Ch 13:10; 29:21; 31:19; Ne 10:38; 12:47

MOSES AND AARON (69) Ex 4:29,31; 5:1,20; 6:13; 7:6,8,10,20,22; 8:8,12,15,17,25; 9:8,27; 10:3,8,16; 11:10; 12:1,28,31,43,50; 16:2,6; 40:31; Lev 9:23; 11:1; 13:1; 14:33; 15:1; Nu 1:17,44; 2:1; 3:39; 4:1,17,37,41,45; 9:6; 14:2,5,26; 16:3,18,19,20,22,41,42,43,45; 19:1; 20:2,6,12,23; 26:9,64; 33:1; Jos 24:5; 1Sa 12:6,8; Ps 77:20; 99:6

SON(S) OF AARON (18) Ex 6:25; 38:21; Lev 1:7; 3:5,8,13; Nu 4:16,28,33; 7:8; 16:37; 26:1; Jos 24:33; 1Ch 6:3; 24:1; 2Ch 26:18; Ezr 7:5,5

Ex 4:14 he said. "What about your brother, **A** the Levite?
4:16 **A** will be your spokesman to the people, and you
4:27 Now the LORD had said to **A**, "Go out into the
4:27 So **A** traveled to the mountain of God, where he
4:28 then told **A** everything the LORD had
4:29 So Moses and **A** returned to Egypt and called the
4:30 **A** told them everything the LORD had told
4:31 convinced that the LORD had sent Moses and **A**.
5: 1 Israel's leaders, Moses and **A** went to see Pharaoh.
5: 3 But **A** and Moses persisted. "The God of the
5:20 they left Pharaoh's court, they met Moses and **A**,
6:13 LORD ordered Moses and **A** to return to Pharaoh,
6:20 sister Jochebed, and she bore him **A** and Moses.
6:23 **A** married Elisheba, the daughter of Amminadab
6:25 Eleazar son of **A** married one of the daughters of
6:26 The **A** and Moses named in this list are the same **A**
7: 1 Your brother, **A**, will be your prophet; he will
7: 2 Tell **A** everything I say to you and have him
7: 6 and **A** did just as the LORD had commanded
7: 7 and **A** was eighty-three at the time they made their
7: 8 Then the LORD said to Moses and **A**,
7: 9 When he makes this demand, say to **A**,
7:10 So Moses and **A** went to see Pharaoh, and they
7:10 **A** threw down his staff before Pharaoh and his
7:19 "Tell **A** to point his staff toward the waters of
7:20 and **A** did just as the LORD had commanded
7:22 He refused to listen to Moses and **A**, just as the
8: 5 "Tell **A** to point his shepherd's staff toward all the
8: 6 **A** did so, and frogs covered the whole land of
8: 8 Pharaoh summoned Moses and **A** and begged,
8:12 So Moses and **A** left Pharaoh, and Moses pleaded
8:15 He refused to listen to Moses and **A**, just as the
8:16 to Moses, "Tell **A** to strike the dust with his staff.
8:17 and **A** did just as the LORD had commanded
8:25 Pharaoh hastily called for Moses and **A**.
9: 8 Then the LORD said to Moses and **A**, "Take soot
9:27 Then Pharaoh urgently sent for Moses and **A**.
10: 3 So Moses and **A** went to Pharaoh and said,
10: 8 So Moses and **A** were brought back to Pharaoh.
10:16 Pharaoh quickly sent for Moses and **A**. "I confess
11:10 and **A** did these miracles in Pharaoh's presence,
12: 1 and **A** while they were still in the land of Egypt:
12:28 LORD had commanded through Moses and **A**.
12:31 Pharaoh sent for Moses and **A** during the night.
12:43 Then the LORD said to Moses and **A**, "These are
12:50 all the LORD's instructions to Moses and **A**.
16: 2 of Israel spoke bitterly against Moses and **A**.
16: 6 and **A** called a meeting of all the people of Israel
16: 9 Then Moses said to **A**, "Say this to the entire
16:10 And as **A** spoke to the people, they looked out
16:33 Moses said to **A**, "Get a container and put two
16:34 **A** did this, just as the LORD had commanded
17:10 Meanwhile Moses, **A**, and Hur went to the top of a
17:12 So **A** and Hur found a stone for him to sit on.
18:12 **A** and the leaders of Israel came out to meet him.
19:24 "Go down anyway and bring **A** back with you.
24: 1 up here to me, and bring along **A**, Nadab, Abihu,
24: 9 Then Moses, **A**, Nadab, Abihu, and seventy of the
24:14 consult with **A** and Hur, who are here with you."
27:21 **A** and his sons will keep the lamps burning in the
28: 1 **A**, and his sons, Nadab, Abihu, Eleazar,
28: 2 Make special clothing for **A** to show his separation
28: 3 garments that will set **A** apart from everyone else,
28:12 **A** will carry these names before the LORD as a
28:29 **A** will carry the names of the tribes of Israel on the
28:30 **A** will always carry the objects used to determine
28:35 **A** will wear this robe whenever he enters the Holy
28:38 **A** will wear it on his forehead, thus bearing the
28:41 Clothe **A** and his sons with these garments, and
28:43 These must be worn whenever **A** and his sons enter
28:43 This law is permanent for **A** and his descendants.
29: 1 "This is the ceremony for the dedication of **A**
29: 4 "Present **A** and his sons at the entrance of the
29: 9 In this way, you will ordain **A** and his sons.
29:10 and **A** and his sons will lay their hands on its head.
29:15 "Next **A** and his sons must lay their hands on the
29:19 "Now take the other ram and have **A** and his sons
29:20 some of it on the tip of the right earlobes of **A**
29:21 Sprinkle it on **A** and his sons and on their clothes.
29:22 "Since this is the ram for the ordination of **A**
29:24 Put all these in the hands of **A** and his sons to be
29:27 the parts of the ordination ram that belong to **A**
29:28 these parts will be the regular share of **A** and his
29:30 Whoever is the next high priest after **A** will wear
29:32 **A** and his sons are to eat this meat, along with the
29:35 "This is how you will ordain **A** and his sons to
29:44 and I will set apart **A** and his sons as holy,
30: 7 "Every morning when **A** trims the lamps, he must
30:10 "Once a year **A** must purify the altar by placing on
30:19 **A** and his sons will wash their hands and feet there
30:21 This is a permanent law for **A** and his descendants,
30:30 Use this oil also to anoint **A** and his sons,
31:10 beautifully stitched, holy garments for **A** the priest,
32: 1 the mountain right away, the people went to **A**.
32: 2 So **A** said, "Tell your wives and sons
32: 3 All the people obeyed **A** and brought him their
32: 4 Then **A** took the gold, melted it down, and molded
32: 5 When **A** saw how excited the people were about it,
32:21 After that, he turned to **A**. "What did the people
32:22 "Don't get upset, sir," **A** replied. "You yourself
32:25 When Moses saw that **A** had let the people get
32:35 because they had worshiped the calf **A** had made.
34:30 And when **A** and the people of Israel saw the
34:31 But Moses called to them and asked **A**
35:19 the sacred garments for **A** and his sons to wear
38:21 and Ithamar son of **A** the priest served as recorder.
39:26 This robe was to be worn when **A** ministered to the
39:27 Tunics were then made for **A** and his sons from
39:41 the holy garments for **A** the priest and for his sons
40:12 "Bring **A** and his sons to the entrance of the
40:13 Clothe **A** with the holy garments and anoint him,
40:31 Moses and **A** and Aaron's sons washed their hands
Lev 1: 7 the sons of **A** the priest will build a wood fire on
2: 3 The rest of the flour will be given to **A** and his
2:10 The rest of the grain offering will be given to **A**
3: 5 The sons of **A** will burn these on the altar on top of
3: 8 The sons of **A** will then sprinkle the sheep's blood
3:13 Then the sons of **A** will sprinkle the goat's blood
6: 9 "Give **A** and his sons the following instructions
6:16 the rest of the flour will belong to **A** and his sons
6:20 "On the day **A** and his sons are anointed,
6:25 "Give **A** and his sons these further instructions
7:31 but the breast will belong to **A** and his sons.
7:35 It has been set apart for **A** and his descendants
8: 2 "Now bring **A** and his sons, along with their
8: 6 Then he presented **A** and his sons and washed
8: 7 He clothed **A** with the embroidered tunic and tied
8: 8 Then Moses placed the chestpiece on **A** and put the
8:14 and **A** and his sons laid their hands on its head
8:18 and **A** and his sons laid their hands on its head
8:22 **A** and his sons laid their hands on its head
8:27 He gave all of these to **A** and his sons, and he
8:30 and he sprinkled them on **A** and his clothing
8:30 he made **A** and his sons and their clothing holy.
8:31 Then Moses said to **A** and his sons, "Boil the rest
8:36 So **A** and his sons did everything the LORD had
9: 1 Moses called together **A** and his sons
9: 2 He said to **A**, "Take a young bull for a sin offering
9: 7 Then Moses said to **A**, "Approach the altar
9: 8 So **A** went to the altar and slaughtered the calf as a
9:12 Next **A** slaughtered the animal for the whole burnt
9:15 Next **A** presented the sacrifices for the people.
9:18 Then **A** slaughtered the bull and the ram for the
9:21 **A** then lifted up the breasts and right thighs as an
9:22 **A** raised his hands toward the people and blessed
9:23 Next Moses and **A** went into the Tabernacle,
10: 3 Then Moses said to **A**, "This is what the LORD
10: 3 before all the people.' " And **A** was silent.
10: 6 Then Moses said to **A** and his sons Eleazar
10: 8 Then the LORD said to **A**,
10:12 Then Moses said to **A** and his remaining sons,
10:19 Then **A** answered Moses on behalf of his sons.
11: 1 Then the LORD said to Moses and **A**,
13: 1 The LORD said to Moses and **A**,
13: 2 they must be brought to **A** the priest or to one of
14:33 Then the LORD said to Moses and **A**,
15: 1 The LORD said to Moses and **A**,
16: 2 "Warn your brother **A** not to enter the Most Holy
16: 3 "When **A** enters the sanctuary area, he must
16: 6 "**A** will present the bull as a sin offering, to make
16: 9 LORD will be presented by **A** as a sin offering.
16:11 "Then **A** will present the young bull as a sin
16:15 "Then **A** must slaughter the goat as a sin offering
16:17 **A** goes in to make atonement for the Most Holy
16:18 "Then **A** will go out to make atonement for the
16:20 "When **A** has finished making atonement for the
16:23 "As **A** enters the Tabernacle, he must take off the
16:27 whose blood **A** brought into the Most Holy Place
16:32 high priest who serves in place of his ancestor **A**.
17: 2 "Give **A** and his sons and all the Israelites these
21:17 "Tell **A** that in all future generations,
21:21 Even though he is a descendant of **A**, his physical
21:24 So Moses gave these instructions to **A** and his sons
22: 2 "Tell **A** and his sons to treat the sacred gifts that
22:18 "Give **A** and his sons and all the Israelites these
24: 3 **A** will set it up outside the inner curtain of the
24: 9 The loaves of bread belong to **A** and his male
Nu 1: 3 to go to war. You and **A** are to direct the project,
1:17 Now Moses and **A** and the chosen leaders
1:44 by Moses and **A** and the twelve leaders of Israel,
2: 1 LORD gave these instructions to Moses and **A**:
3: 1 This is the family line of **A** and Moses as it was
3: 4 and Ithamar to serve as priests with their father, **A**.

3: 6 and present them to **A** the priest as his assistants.
3: 7 They will serve **A** and the whole community,
3: 9 Assign the Levites to **A** and his sons as their
3:10 Appoint **A** and his sons to carry out the duties of
3:38 for the tents of Moses and of **A** and his sons,
3:39 by Moses and **A** at the LORD's command,
3:48 Give the silver to **A** and his sons as the redemption
3:51 And Moses gave the redemption money to **A**
4: 1 Then the LORD said to Moses and **A**,
4: 5 **A** and his sons must enter the Tabernacle first to
4:11 "**A** and his sons must also spread a dark blue cloth
4:15 When **A** and his sons have finished covering the
4:16 "Eleazar son of **A** the priest will be responsible for
4:17 Then the LORD said to Moses and **A**,
4:19 **A** and his sons must always go in with them
4:27 **A** and his sons will direct the Gershonites
4:28 directly responsible to Ithamar son of **A** the priest.
4:33 They are directly responsible to Ithamar son of **A**
4:34 So Moses, **A**, and the other leaders of the
4:37 Moses and **A** counted them, just as the LORD
4:41 Moses and **A** counted them, just as the LORD
4:45 Moses and **A** counted them, just as the LORD
4:46 So Moses, **A**, and the leaders of Israel counted all
6:23 "Instruct **A** and his sons to bless the people of
6:27 This is how **A** and his sons will designate the
7: 8 under the leadership of Ithamar son of **A** the priest.
8: 2 "Tell **A** that when he sets up the seven lamps in
8: 3 So **A** did this. He set up the seven lamps so they
8:11 **A** must present the Levites to the LORD as a
8:13 Then have the Levites stand in front of **A** and his
8:19 I have assigned the Levites to **A** and his sons.
8:20 So Moses, **A**, and the whole community of Israel
8:21 and **A** presented them to the LORD as a special
8:22 to perform their duties, helping **A** and his sons.
9: 6 that day. So they came to Moses and **A** that day
12: 1 Miriam and **A** criticized Moses because he had
12: 4 **A**, and Miriam and said, "Go out to the
12: 5 "**A** and Miriam!" he called, and they stepped
12:10 with leprosy. When **A** saw what had happened,
13:26 to Moses, **A**, and the people of Israel at Kadesh in
14: 2 a great chorus of complaint against Moses and **A**.
14: 5 and **A** fell face down on the ground before the
14:26 Then the LORD said to Moses and **A**,
15:33 He was apprehended and taken before Moses, **A**,
16: 3 They went to Moses and **A** and said, "You have
16:11 And who is **A** that you are complaining about
16:16 with all your followers. **A** will also be here.
16:17 the LORD. **A** will also bring his incense burner."
16:18 the entrance of the Tabernacle with Moses and **A**.
16:19 up the entire community against Moses and **A**,
16:20 and the LORD said to Moses and **A**,
16:22 But Moses and **A** fell face down on the ground.
16:37 "Tell Eleazar son of **A** the priest to pull all the
16:40 no one who was not a descendant of **A**—
16:41 began muttering again against Moses and **A**,
16:42 As the people gathered to protest to Moses and **A**,
16:43 Moses and **A** came and stood at the entrance of the
16:45 But Moses and **A** fell face down on the ground.
16:46 And Moses said to **A**, "Quick, take an incense
16:47 **A** did as Moses told him and ran out among the
16:47 but **A** burned the incense and made atonement for
16:50 **A** returned to Moses at the entrance of the
17: 6 tribal leaders, including **A**, brought Moses a staff.
18: 1 The LORD now said to **A**: "You, your sons,
18: 8 The LORD gave these further instructions to **A**:
18:20 And the LORD said to **A**, "You priests will
18:28 must present the LORD's portion to **A** the priest.
19: 1 The LORD said to Moses and **A**,
20: 2 at that place, so they rebelled against Moses and **A**.
20: 6 Moses and **A** turned away from the people
20: 8 "You and **A** must take the staff and assemble the
20:10 Then he and **A** summoned the people to come
20:12 But the LORD said to Moses and **A**,
20:23 and **A** at Mount Hor on the border of the land of
20:24 "The time has come for **A** to join his ancestors in
20:25 Now take **A** and his son Eleazar up Mount Hor.
20:26 his son. **A** will die there and join his ancestors."
20:28 Moses removed the priestly garments from **A**
20:28 Then **A** died there on top of the mountain,
20:29 When the people realized that **A** had died, all Israel
25: 7 of Eleazar and grandson of **A** the priest saw this,
25:11 and grandson of **A** the priest has turned my anger
26: 1 the LORD said to Moses and to Eleazar son of **A**,
26: 9 who conspired with Korah against Moses and **A**,
26:59 Amram and Jochebed became the parents of **A**,
26:60 To **A** were born Nadab, Abihu, Eleazar,
26:64 and **A** counted in this census had been among
27:13 have seen it, you will die as **A** your brother did,
33: 1 out of Egypt under the leadership of Moses and **A**.
33:38 **A** the priest was directed by the LORD to go up
33:39 **A** was 123 years old when he died there on Mount
Dt 9:20 so angry with **A** that he wanted to destroy him.
9:20 But I prayed for **A**, and the LORD spared him.
10: 6 traveled to Moserah, where **A** died and was buried.
32:50 just as **A**, your brother, died on Mount Hor
Jos 21: 4 The descendants of **A**, who were members of the
21:10 to the descendants of **A**, who were members of the
21:13 were given to the descendants of **A** the priest:
21:19 were given to the priests, the descendants of **A**.
24: 5 "Then I sent Moses and **A**, and I brought terrible
24:33 Eleazar son of **A** also died. He was buried in the
Jdg 20:28 son of Eleazar and grandson of **A** was the priest.)
1Sa 2:28 I chose your ancestor **A** from among all his
12: 6 was the LORD who appointed Moses and **A**,"
12: 8 he sent Moses and **A** to rescue them from Egypt
1Ch 6: 3 The children of Amram were **A**, Moses,
6: 3 The sons of **A** were Nadab, Abihu, Eleazar,
6:49 Only **A** and his descendants served as priests.
6:50 The descendants of **A** were Eleazar, Phinehas,
6:54 of **A** who were from the clan of Kohath.
6:57 So the descendants of **A** were given the following
6:60 thirteen towns was given to the descendants of **A**.
12:27 This included Jehoiada, leader of the family of **A**,
23:13 The sons of Amram were **A** and Moses. **A** and his descendants were set apart to dedicate
23:28 the descendants of **A**, as they served at the house
24: 1 The sons of **A** were Nadab, Abihu, Eleazar,
24:19 **A** in obedience to the commands of the LORD,
24:31 Like the descendants of **A**, they were assigned to
27:17 son of Kemuel / **A** (the priests) | Zadok
2Ch 13:10 Only the descendants of **A** serve the LORD as
26:18 the sons of **A** who are set apart for this work.
29:21 the priests, who were descendants of **A**,
31:19 As for the priests, the descendants of **A**, who were
Ezr 7: 5 son of Eleazar, son of **A** the high priest.
Ne 10:38 A priest—a descendant of **A**—will be with the
12:47 they received to the priests, the descendants of **A**.
Ps 77:20 of sheep, / with Moses and **A** as their shepherds.
99: 6 Moses and **A** were among his priests;
105:26 his servant, / along with **A**, whom he had chosen.
106:16 and envious of **A**, the LORD's holy priest.
115:10 O priests of **A**, trust the LORD! / He is your
115:12 people of Israel / and the family of **A**, the priests.
135:19 the LORD! / O priests of **A**, praise the LORD!
Mic 6: 4 I sent Moses, **A**, and Miriam to help you.
Lk 1: 5 Elizabeth, was also from the priestly line of **A**.
Ac 7:40 They told **A**, 'Make us some gods who can lead us,
Heb 5: 4 to be called by God for this work, just as **A** was.
7:11 instead of from the line of Levi and **A**?

AARON'S (45) [AARON]

AARON'S...DESCENDANTS (6) Ex 40:15; Lev 6:18; Nu 10:8; 1Ch 24:1,3; Ps 118:3

AARON'S SON(S) (17) Ex 28:4,40; 40:31; Lev 1:5,8,11; 2:2; 3:2; 6:14; 8:13,24; 10:1,16; 16:1; Nu 3:2,32; 20:28

Ex 7:12 But then **A** snake swallowed up their snakes.
15:20 **A** sister, took a tambourine and led all the women
28: 4 They will also make special garments for **A** sons to
28:30 to be carried over **A** heart when he goes into the
28:32 with an opening for **A** head in the middle of it.
28:37 This medallion will be attached to the front of **A**
28:39 "Weave **A** patterned tunic from fine linen cloth.
28:40 "Then for **A** sons, make tunics, sashes,
29: 5 Then put **A** tunic on him, along with the
29:26 Then take the breast of **A** ordination ram, and lift it
29:29 "**A** sacred garments must be preserved for his
39: 1 This same cloth was used for **A** sacred garments,
39:23 with an opening for **A** head in the middle of it.
40:15 **A** descendants are set apart for the priesthood
40:31 Moses and Aaron and **A** sons washed their hands
Lev 1: 5 in the LORD's presence, and **A** sons, the priests,
1: 8 **A** sons will then put the pieces of the animal,
1:11 **A** sons, the priests, will sprinkle its blood against
2: 2 Bring this offering to one of **A** sons, and he will
3: 2 **A** sons, the priests, will then sprinkle the animal's
6:14 **A** sons must present this offering to the LORD in
6:18 Any of **A** male descendants, from generation to
8: 9 He placed on **A** head the turban with the gold
8:12 Then he poured some of the anointing oil on **A**
8:13 Next Moses presented **A** sons and clothed them in
8:23 of its blood and put it on the lobe of **A** right ear,
8:24 Next he presented **A** sons and put some of the
10: 1 **A** sons Nadab and Abihu put coals of fire in their
10: 4 Moses called for Mishael and Elzaphan, **A** cousins, the sons of **A** uncle Uzziel.
10:16 angry with Eleazar and Ithamar, **A** remaining sons.
16: 1 The LORD spoke to Moses after the death of **A**
Nu 3: 2 **A** sons were Nadab (the firstborn), Abihu, Eleazar,
3:32 Eleazar the priest, **A** son, was the chief
10: 8 Only the priests, **A** descendants, are allowed to
17: 3 Inscribe **A** name on the staff of the tribe of Levi,
17: 8 he found that **A** staff, representing the tribe of
17:10 "Place **A** staff permanently before the Ark of the
20:26 There you will remove **A** priestly garments and put
20:28 from Aaron and put them on Eleazar, **A** son.
1Ch 24: 1 This is how **A** descendants, the priests,
24: 3 David divided **A** descendants into groups
Ps 118: 3 Let **A** descendants, the priests, repeat:
133: 2 that was poured over **A** head, / that ran down his
Heb 9: 4 some manna, **A** staff that sprouted leaves,

AARONITES [KJV] See AARON

ABADDON (1) [DESTROY]

Rev 9:11 his name in Hebrew is ***A***, and in Greek,

ABAGTHA (1)

Est 1:10 Biztha, Harbona, Bigtha, **A**, Zethar, and Carcas,

ABANA (1)

2Ki 5:12 Aren't the **A** River and Pharpar River of Damascus

ABANDON (47) [ABANDONED, ABANDONING, ABANDONS]

Nu 14:43 The LORD will **a** you because you have
Dt 4:31 he will not **a** you or destroy you or forget the
31:16 They will **a** me and break the covenant I have
31:17 I will **a** them, hiding my face from them, and they
32:20 He said, 'I will **a** them; / I will see to their end!
Jos 1: 5 as I was with Moses. I will not fail you or **a** you.
10: 6 to Joshua at Gilgal, "Don't **a** your servants now!"
1Sa 12:22 The LORD will not **a** his chosen people, for that
2Sa 18:13 did it—you yourself would be the first to **a** me."
1Ki 9: 6 "But if you or your descendants **a** me and disobey
14:16 He will **a** Israel because Jeroboam sinned
2Ch 7:19 "But if you **a** me and disobey the laws
15: 2 find him. But if you **a** him, he will **a** you.
24:18 They decided to **a** the Temple of the LORD,
Ezr 8:22 but his fierce anger rages against those who **a**
9: 9 but in his unfailing love our God did not **a** us in
Ne 9:17 of unfailing love and mercy. You did not **a** them,
9:19 But in your great mercy you did not **a** them to die
9:31 did not destroy them completely or **a** them forever.
Ps 27: 9 Don't leave me now; don't **a** me, / O God of my
27:10 Even if my father and mother **a** me, / the LORD
35:22 Do not stay silent. / Don't **a** me now, O Lord.
37:28 loves justice, / and he will never **a** the godly.
38:21 Do not **a** me, LORD. / Do not stand at a distance,
71: 9 me aside. / Don't **a** me when my strength is failing.
71:18 Now that I am old and gray, / do not **a** me, O God.
73:27 him will perish, / for you destroy those who **a** you.
94:14 he will not **a** his own special possession.
119:39 Help me **a** my shameful ways; / your laws are all I
119:87 me off, / but I refused to **a** your commandments.
138: 8 endures forever. / Don't **a** me, for you made me.
Pr 27:10 Never **a** a friend—either yours or your father's.
Isa 2:20 They will **a** their gold and silver idols to the moles
58: 2 was a righteous nation that would never **a** its God.
Jer 14: 9 are known as your people. Please don't **a** us now!"
14:21 the sake of your own name, LORD, do not **a** us.
22:24 surely as I live," says the LORD, "I will **a** you,
23:33 are the burden! The LORD says he will **a** you!'
33:26 I will never **a** the descendants of Jacob or David,
51: 9 but nothing can save her now. Let her go; **a** her.
La 3:31 For the Lord does not **a** anyone forever.
Eze 27:29 All the oarsmen **a** their ships; the sailors
Jn 14:18 No, I will not **a** you as orphans—I will come to
Ac 7:19 and forced parents to **a** their newborn babies
7:21 When at last they had to **a** him, Pharaoh's daughter
27:30 Then the sailors tried to **a** the ship; they lowered

ABANDONED (77) [ABANDON]

Nu 14:43 abandon you because you have **a** the LORD."
Dt 32:15 Then they **a** the God who had made them;
Jdg 2:12 They **a** the LORD, the God of their ancestors,
2:13 They **a** the LORD to serve Baal and the images of
6:13 But now the LORD has **a** us and handed us over
10: 6 but they **a** the LORD and no longer served him at
10:10 against you because we have **a** you as our God
10:13 Yet you have **a** me and served other gods. So I will
1Sa 7: 2 because it seemed that the LORD had **a** them.
31: 7 his sons were dead, they **a** their towns and fled.
2Sa 5:21 The Philistines had **a** their idols there, so David
22:23 before me; / I have never **a** his principles.
1Ki 11:33 For Solomon has **a** me and worshiped Ashtoreth,
15:21 he **a** his project of fortifying Ramah and withdrew
2Ki 21:22 He **a** the LORD, the God of his ancestors, and he
22:17 For my people have **a** me and worshiped pagan
25: 5 of Jericho, for by then his men had all **a** him.
1Ch 10: 7 his sons were dead, they **a** their towns and fled.
14:12 The Philistines had **a** their idols there, so David
2Ch 7:22 answer will be, 'Because his people **a** the LORD,
11:14 The Levites even **a** their homes and property
12: 1 and strong, he **a** the law of the LORD,
12: 5 You have **a** me, so I am abandoning you to
13:10 the LORD is our God, and we have not **a** him.
13:11 of the LORD our God, but you have **a** him.
16: 5 he **a** his project of fortifying Ramah.
21:10 because Jehoram had **a** the LORD, the God of his
24:20 You have **a** the LORD, and now he has **a** you!"
24:24 The people of Judah had **a** the LORD, the God of
28: 6 of Judah's troops because they had **a** the LORD,
29: 6 They **a** the LORD and his Temple; they turned
30: 7 your ancestors and relatives who **a** the LORD,
34:25 For the people of Judah have **a** me and worshiped
Ezr 5:12 he **a** them to King Nebuchadnezzar of Babylon,
Job 5: 4 Their children are **a** far from help, with no one to
15:28 They will live in **a** houses that are ready to tumble
18: 4 out in anger, but will that cause the earth to be **a**?
Ps 9:10 have never **a** anyone who searches for you.
18:22 before me; / I have never **a** his principles.
71:11 They say, "God has **a** him. / Let's go and get him,
78:48 He **a** their cattle to the hail, / their livestock to
78:60 Then he **a** his dwelling at Shiloh, / the Tabernacle
88: 5 They have **a** me to death, / and I am as good as
Pr 2:17 She has **a** her husband and ignores the covenant
Isa 1: 8 Jerusalem stands **a** like a watchman's shelter in a
16: 8 Weep for the **a** farms of Heshbon
17: 5 Israel will be **a** like the grainfields in the valley of
17: 9 They will become like the cities the Amorites **a**
24:19 Everything is lost, **a**, and confused.
27:10 cities will be silent and empty, the houses **a**,
49:19 "Even the most desolate parts of your **a** land will
54: 6 as though you were a young wife **a** by her
54: 7 "For a brief moment I **a** you, but with great
Jer 4:29 All the cities have been **a**—not a person remains!
8:19 "Has the LORD **a** Jerusalem?" the people ask.
9:13 because my people have **a** the instructions I gave
12: 7 "I have **a** my people, my special possession.
16:11 worshiped other gods and served them. They **a** me.
17:16 I have not **a** my job as a shepherd for your people.
33: 5 I have **a** them because of all their wickedness.
33:24 LORD chose Judah and Israel and then **a** them!'
51:62 will remain here. She will lie empty and **a** forever.'
52: 8 of Jericho, for by then his men had all **a** him.
Eze 34: 8 you **a** my flock and left them to be attacked by

44:10 And the men of the tribe of Levi who a me when
44:15 faithfully in the Temple when Israel a me for idols.
Joel 1:17 The barns and granaries stand empty and a.
Mic 5: 3 The people of Israel will be a to their enemies until
Zep 2: 7 They will lie down to rest in the a houses in
Mal 2:14 You cry out, "Why has the LORD a us?" I'll tell
Mk 6:11 It is a sign that you have a that village to its fate."
Lk 9: 5 It is a sign that you have a that village to its fate."
Ro 1:26 That is why God a them to their shameful desires.
1:28 he a them to their evil minds and let them do
Gal 2:14 make these Gentiles obey the Jewish laws you a?
2Ti 4:16 no one was with me. Everyone had a me.

ABANDONING (4) [ABANDON]
Ge 26:22 A that one, he dug another well, and the local
2Ki 7: 7 a their tents, horses, donkeys, and everything else,
2Ch 12: 5 have abandoned me, so I am a you to Shishak."
Eze 23:11 a herself to her lust and prostitution.

ABANDONS (6) [ABANDON]
Nu 32:15 him like this and he a them again in the wilderness,
Job 12:23 He makes nations expand, and he a them.
Pr 15:10 Whoever a the right path will be severely
Jer 14: 5 The deer a her newborn fawn because there is no
Zec 11:17 Doom is certain for this worthless shepherd who a
2Co 4: 9 We are hunted down, but God never a us. We get

ABASE(D), ABASING [KJV] See HUMBLE, HUMBLED

ABATED [KJV] See RECEDE

ABBA (1)
Mk 14:36 "A, Father," he said, "everything is possible for

ABDA (2)
1Ki 4: 6 Adoniram son of A was in charge of the labor
Ne 11:17 and A son of Shammua, son of Galal, son of

ABDEEL (2)
Ge 25:13 was Nebaioth, followed by Kedar, A, Mibsam,
Jer 36:26 and Shelemiah son of A to arrest Baruch

ABDI (3)
1Ch 6:44 was traced back through Kishi, A, Malluch,
2Ch 29:12 Kish son of A and Azariah son of Jehallelel.
Ezr 10:26 Mattaniah, Zechariah, Jehiel, A, Jeremoth,

ABDIEL (1)
1Ch 5:15 Ahi son of A, son of Guni, was the leader of their

ABDON (7)
Jos 19:28 A, Rehob, Hammon, Kanah, and as far as Greater
21:30 From the tribe of Asher they received Mishal, A,
Jdg 12:13 After Elon died, A son of Hillel, from Pirathon,
1Ch 6:74 the territory of Asher, they received Mashal, A,
8:23 A, Zicri, Hanan,
8:30 and his oldest son was named A. Jeiel's other sons
9:36 and his oldest son was named A. Jeiel's other sons

ABEDNEGO (14)
Da 1: 7 was called Meshach. / Azariah was called A.
2:49 and A to be in charge of all the affairs of the
3:12 some Jews—Shadrach, Meshach, and A—
3:13 Meshach, and A to be brought before him.
3:14 to them, "Is it true, Shadrach, Meshach, and A,
3:16 Shadrach, Meshach, and A replied,
3:19 and A that his face became distorted with rage.
3:20 and A and throw them into the blazing furnace.
3:23 So Shadrach, Meshach, and A, securely tied,
3:26 "Shadrach, Meshach, and A, servants of the Most
3:26 Meshach, and A stepped out of the fire.
3:28 "Praise to the God of Shadrach, Meshach, and A!
3:29 Meshach, and A, they will be torn limb from limb,
3:30 and A to even higher positions in the province of

ABEL (12) [ABEL'S]
Ge 4: 2 she gave birth to a second son and named him A.
4: 2 When they grew up, A became a shepherd,
4: 4 while A brought several choice lambs from the
4: 8 to his brother, A, "Let's go out into the fields."
4: 9 Where is A?" "I don't know!" Cain retorted.
4:25 "God has granted me another son in place of A,
2Sa 20:18 to settle an argument, ask advice at the city of A.'
Mt 23:35 from righteous A to Zechariah son of Barachiah,
Lk 11:51 from the murder of A to the murder of Zechariah,
Heb 11: 4 It was by faith that A brought a more acceptable
11: 4 And although A is long dead, he still speaks to us
12:24 of crying out for vengeance as the blood of A did.

ABEL'S (2) [ABEL]
Ge 4: 4 best of his flock. The LORD accepted A offering,
Heb 11: 4 God accepted A offering to show that he was a

ABEL-BETH-MAACAH (5) [MAACAH]
2Sa 20:14 to mobilize his own clan of Bicri at the city of A.
20:15 they attacked A and built a ramp against the city
1Ki 15:20 Dan, A, and all Kinnereth, with all the land of
2Ki 15:29 the towns of Ijon, A, Janoah, Kedesh, and Hazor.
2Ch 16: 4 of Ijon, Dan, A, and all the store cities in Naphtali.

ABEL-KERAMIM (1)
Jdg 11:33 twenty towns—and as far away as A.

ABEL-MEHOLAH (3)
Jdg 7:22 near Zererah and to the border of A near Tabbath.
1Ki 4:12 and all the territory from Beth-shan to A and over
19:16 and anoint Elisha son of Shaphat from A to replace

ABEL-MIZRAIM (1)
Ge 50:11 the Canaanites, renamed the place A, for they said,

ABEL-SHITTIM (1)
Nu 33:49 Beth-jeshimoth as far as A on the plains of Moab.

ABEZ [KJV] See EBEZ

ABHOR (2) [ABHORRED]
Job 19:19 My close friends a me. Those I loved have turned
Ps 119:163 I hate and a all falsehood, / but I love your law.

ABHORRED (1) [ABHOR]
Ps 106:40 his people, / and he a his own special possession.

ABI-ALBON (2)
2Sa 23:31 A the Arbathite; / Azmaveth from Bahurim;
1Ch 11:32 Hurai from near Nahale-gaash; / A the Arbathite;

ABIA, ABIAH [KJV] See ABIJAH

ABIASAPH (4)
Ex 6:24 of Korah included Assir, Elkanah, and A.
1Ch 6:23 Elkanah, A, Assir,
6:37 Tahath, Assir, A, Korah,
9:19 a descendant of A, from the clan of Korah.

ABIATHAR (27) [ABIATHAR'S]
1Sa 22:20 Only A, one of the sons of Ahimelech, escaped
23: 6 A the priest went to Keilah with David,
23: 9 Saul's plan and told A the priest to bring the ephod
30: 7 Then he said to A the priest, "Bring me the ephod!" So A brought it.
2Sa 8:17 and Ahimelech son of A were the priests.
15:24 A and Zadok and the Levites took the Ark of the
15:27 and A should return quietly to the city with your
15:29 and A took the Ark of God back to the city
15:35 Zadok and A, the priests, are there. Tell them the
17:15 Then Hushai reported to Zadok and A, the priests,
19:11 Then King David sent Zadok and A, the priests,
20:25 the court secretary. Zadok and A were the priests.
1Ki 1: 7 son of Zeruiah and A the priest into his confidence,
1:19 has invited all your sons and A the priest and Joab,
1:25 the commander of the army, and A the priest.
1:42 still speaking, Jonathan son of A the priest arrived.
2:22 and that he has A the priest and Joab son of
2:26 Then the king said to A the priest, "Go back to
2:27 So Solomon deposed A from his position as priest
2:35 he installed Zadok the priest to take the place of A.
4: 4 of the army. / Zadok and A were the priests.
1Ch 15:11 the priests, Zadok and A, and these Levite leaders:
18:16 and Ahimelech son of A were the priests.
24: 6 Zadok the priest, Ahimelech son of A,
27:34 succeeded by Jehoiada son of Benaiah and by A.
Mk 2:26 of God (during the days when A was high priest),

ABIATHAR'S (1) [ABIATHAR]
2Sa 15:27 city with your son Ahimaaz and A son Jonathan.

ABIDA (2)
Ge 25: 4 sons were Ephah, Epher, Hanoch, A, and Eldaah.
1Ch 1:33 were Ephah, Epher, Hanoch, A, and Eldaah.

ABIDAN (5)
Nu 1:11 Benjamin | A son of Gideoni
2:22[-23] Benjamin | A son of Gideoni | 35,400
7:60 On the ninth day A son of Gideoni, leader of the
7:65 This was the offering brought by A son of Gideoni.
10:24 The tribe of Benjamin was led by A son of

ABIDE(TH), ABIDING [KJV] See ENDURE, KEEP, LIVE, REMAIN, STAND, STAY

ABIEL (2)
1Sa 9: 1 He was the son of A and grandson of Zeror,
14:51 Kish, were brothers; both were sons of A.

ABIEZER (10)
Jos 17: 2 A, Helek, Asriel, Shechem, Hepher, and Shemida.
Jdg 6:11 which belonged to Joash of the clan of A.
6:24 in Ophrah in the land of the clan of A to this day.
6:34 to arms, and the men of the clan of A came to him.
8: 2 better than the entire crop of my little clan of A?
8:32 Joash, at Ophrah in the land of the clan of A.
2Sa 23:27 A from Anathoth; / Sibbecai from Hushah;
1Ch 7:18 gave birth to Ishhod, A, and Mahlah.
11:28 Ira son of Ikkesh from Tekoa; / A from Anathoth;
27:12 A from Anathoth in the territory of Benjamin was

ABIGAIL (16)
1Sa 25: 3 and his wife, A, was a sensible and beautiful
25:14 one of Nabal's servants went to A and told her,
25:18 A lost no time. She quickly gathered two hundred
25:23 When A saw David, she quickly got off her
25:32 David replied to A, "Praise the LORD, the God
25:36 When A arrived home, she found that Nabal had
25:39 messengers to A to ask her to become his wife.
25:40 the messengers arrived at Carmel, they told A,
27: 3 Ahinoam of Jezreel and A of Carmel,
30: 5 David's two wives, Ahinoam of Jezreel and A,
2Sa 2: 2 David's wives were Ahinoam from Jezreel and A,
3: 3 The second was Kileab, whose mother was A,
17:25 His mother, A daughter of Nahash, was the sister
1Ch 2:16 Their sisters were named Zeruiah and A.
2:17 A married a man named Jether, an Ishmaelite,
3: 1 was Kileab, whose mother was A from Carmel.

ABIHAIL (5)
Nu 3:35 leader of the Merarite clans was Zuriel son of A.
1Ch 2:29 of Abishur and his wife A were Ahban and Molid.
5:14 These were all descendants of A son of Huri,
2Ch 11:18 the daughter of David's son Jerimoth and of A,
Est 9:29 Then Queen Esther, the daughter of A, along with

ABIHU (13)
Ex 6:23 and she bore him Nadab, A, Eleazar, and Ithamar.
24: 1 up here to me, and bring along Aaron, Nadab, A,
24: 9 Then Moses, Aaron, Nadab, A, and seventy of the
28: 1 and his sons, Nadab, A, Eleazar, and Ithamar,
Lev 10: 1 and A put coals of fire in their incense burners
10: 6 your relatives, may mourn for Nadab and A,
Nu 3: 2 Nadab (the firstborn), A, Eleazar, and Ithamar.
3: 4 and A died in the LORD's presence in the
26:60 Aaron were born Nadab, A, Eleazar, and Ithamar.
26:61 and A died when they burned before the LORD a
1Ch 6: 3 of Aaron were Nadab, A, Eleazar, and Ithamar.
24: 1 of Aaron were Nadab, A, Eleazar, and Ithamar.
24: 2 But Nadab and A died before their father did,

ABIHUD (1)
1Ch 8: 3 The sons of Bela were Addar, Gera, A,

ABIJAH (27) [ABIJAH'S]
1Sa 8: 2 Joel and A, his oldest sons, held court in
1Ki 14: 1 At that time Jeroboam's son A became very sick.
2Ki 18: 2 His mother was A, the daughter of Zechariah.
1Ch 2:24 his wife A gave birth to a son named Ashhur (the
3:10 of Solomon were Rehoboam, A, Asa, Jehoshaphat,
6:28 Samuel were Joel (the older) and A (the second).
7: 8 Joash, Eliezer, Elioenai, Omri, Jeremoth, A,
24:10 lot fell to Hakkoz. / The eighth lot fell to A.
2Ch 11:20 Maacah gave birth to A, Attai, Ziza,
11:22 Rehoboam made Maacah's son A chief among the
12:16 of David. Then his son A became the next king.
13: 1 A began to rule over Judah in the eighteenth year
13: 2 Then war broke out between A and Jeroboam.
13: 3 Judah, led by King A, fielded 400,000 seasoned
13: 4 A stood on Mount Zemaraim and shouted to
13:15 and the Israelite army and routed them before A
13:17 A and his army inflicted heavy losses on them;
13:19 A and his army pursued Jeroboam's troops
13:21 A of Judah grew more and more powerful.
14: 1 When A died, he was buried in the City of David.
29: 1 His mother was A, the daughter of Zechariah.
Ne 10: 7 Meshullam, A, Mijamin,
12: 4 Iddo, Ginnethon, A,
12:17 Zicri was leader of the family of A. / There was
Mt 1: 7 Rehoboam was the father of A. / A was the father of Asaph.
Lk 1: 5 Zechariah was a member of the priestly order of A.

ABIJAH'S (2) [ABIJAH]
2Ch 13:20 Israel never regained his power during A lifetime,
13:22 The rest of the events of A reign, including his

ABIJAM (6) [ABIJAM'S]
1Ki 14:31 Then his son A became the next king.
15: 1 A began to rule over Judah in the eighteenth year
15: 4 and he gave A a son to rule after him in Jerusalem.
15: 6 There was war between A and Jeroboam
15: 7 *of Judah.* There was constant war between A
15: 8 When A died, he was buried in the City of David.

ABIJAM'S (2) [ABIJAM]
1Ki 15: 6 between Abijam and Jeroboam throughout A reign.
15: 7 The rest of the events in A reign and all his deeds

ABILENE (1)
Lk 3: 1 and Traconitis; Lysanias was ruler over A.

ABILITIES (3) [ABLE]
Mt 25:15 dividing it in proportion to their a—and then left
1Co 12: 1 I will write about the special a the Holy Spirit
14: 1 but also desire the special a the Spirit gives,

ABILITY (20) [ABLE]
Ex 35:34 the tribe of Dan, the a to teach their skills to others.
Lev 27: 8 go to the priest and he will evaluate your a to pay.
1Ch 26: 6 Obed-edom's son Shemaiah had sons with great a
Job 39:20 Did you give it the a to leap forward like a locust?
Da 1:17 And God gave Daniel special a in understanding
6: 3 Because of his great a, the king made plans to
Ac 2: 4 as the Holy Spirit gave them this a.

Ro 12: 6 God has given each of us the **a** to do certain things
12: 6 So if God has given you the **a** to prophesy,
12: 8 If God has given you leadership **a**,
1Co 12: 8 To one person the Spirit gives the **a** to give wise
12:10 perform miracles, and to another the **a** to prophesy.
12:10 He gives someone else the **a** to know whether it is
12:10 Still another person is given the **a** to speak in
12:10 and another is given the **a** to interpret what is being
12:30 Does God give all of us the **a** to speak in unknown
14: 2 For if your gift is the **a** to speak in tongues,
2Co 1:21 along with you, the **a** to stand firm for Christ.
Php 3: 9 on my own goodness or my **a** to obey God's law,
1Ti 3:10 in the church as a test of their character and **a**.

ABIMAEL (2)

Ge 10:28 Obal, **A**, Sheba,
1Ch 1:22 Obal, **A**, Sheba,

ABIMELECH (59) [ABIMELECH'S]

Ge 20: 2 So King **A** sent for her and had her brought to him
20: 3 But one night God came to **A** in a dream and told
20: 4 But **A** had not slept with her yet, so he said,
20: 8 **A** got up early the next morning and hastily called
20: 9 Then **A** called for Abraham. "What is this you
20:14 Then **A** took sheep and oxen and servants—
20:15 a place where you would like to live," **A** told him.
20:17 prayed to God, and God healed **A**, his wife,
20:18 a warning to **A** for having taken Abraham's wife.
21:22 About this time, **A** came with Phicol, his army
21:22 that God helps you in everything you do," **A** said.
21:25 Then Abraham complained to **A** about a well that
21:26 "This is the first I've heard of it," **A** said. "And I
21:27 Then Abraham gave sheep and oxen to **A**, and they
21:29 **A** asked, "Why are you doing that?"
21:32 **A** left with Phicol, the commander of his army,
26: 1 to Gerar, where **A**, king of the Philistines, lived.
26: 8 But some time later, **A**, king of the Philistines,
26: 9 **A** called for Isaac and exclaimed, "She is
26:10 "How could you treat us this way!" **A** exclaimed.
26:11 Then **A** made a public proclamation:
26:16 And **A** asked Isaac to leave the country.
26:26 King **A** arrived with his adviser, Ahuzzath,
Jdg 8:31 in Shechem, who bore him a son named **A**.
9: 1 One day Gideon's son **A** went to Shechem to visit
9: 3 they decided in favor of **A** because he was their
9: 6 the pillar at Shechem and made **A** their king.
9:16 and in good faith by making **A** your king,
9:18 **A**, to be your king just because he is your relative.
9:19 and his descendants, then may you find joy in **A**,
9:20 then may fire come out from **A** and devour the
9:20 of Shechem and Beth-millo and devour **A**!"
9:21 in Beer because he was afraid of his brother **A**.
9:22 After **A** had ruled over Israel for three years,
9:23 God stirred up trouble between **A** and the people of
9:24 God punished **A** and the men of Shechem for
9:25 The people of Shechem set an ambush for **A** on the
9:25 that way. But someone warned **A** about their plot.
9:27 wine flowed freely, and everyone began cursing **A**.
9:28 "Who is **A**?" Gaal shouted. "He's not a true
9:28 true descendants. Why should we serve **A**?
9:29 If I were in charge, I would get rid of **A**. I would
9:31 He sent messengers to **A** in Arumah, telling him,
9:34 So **A** and his men went by night and split into four
9:35 Gaal was standing at the city gates when **A** and his
9:38 "Wasn't it you that said, 'Who is **A**, and why
9:39 then led the men of Shechem into battle against **A**,
9:41 **A** stayed in Arumah, and Zebul drove Gaal and his
9:42 out into the fields to battle. When **A** heard about it,
9:43 When **A** saw the people coming out of the city,
9:44 **A** and his group stormed the city gate to keep the
9:45 The battle went on all day before **A** finally
9:47 Someone reported to **A** that the people were
9:50 Then **A** attacked the city of Thebez and captured it.
9:52 **A** followed them to attack the tower. But as he
9:54 Don't let it be said that a woman killed **A**!"
9:56 God punished **A** for the evil he had done against
2Sa 11:21 Wasn't Gideon's son **A** killed at Thebez by a
Ps 34: T the time he pretended to be insane in front of **A**,

ABIMELECH'S (8) [ABIMELECH]

Ge 21:25 **A** servants had taken violently from Abraham's
Jdg 9: 3 So **A** uncles spoke to all the people of Shechem on
9:28 Why should we be **A** servants? He's merely the
9:44 while **A** other two groups cut them down in the
9:49 cut down some branches, following **A** example.
9:53 roof threw down a millstone that landed on **A** head
9:55 When **A** men saw that he was dead, they disbanded
10: 1 After **A** death, Tola, the son of Puah

ABINADAB (10) [ABINADAB'S]

1Sa 7: 1 They took it to the hillside home of **A** and ordained
16: 8 Then Jesse told his son **A** to step forward and walk
17:13 three oldest sons—Eliab, **A**, and Shammah—
31: 2 three of his sons—Jonathan, **A**, and Malkishua.
2Sa 6: 3 and brought it from the hillside home of **A**.
1Ch 2:13 was Eliab, his second was **A**, his third was Shimea,
8:33 the father of Jonathan, Malkishua, **A**, and Eshbaal.
9:39 the father of Jonathan, Malkishua, **A**, and Eshbaal.
10: 2 three of his sons—Jonathan, **A**, and Malkishua.
13: 7 the Ark of God from the house of **A** on a new cart,

ABINADAB'S (1) [ABINADAB, BEN-ABINADAB]

2Sa 6: 3 Uzzah and Ahio, **A** sons, were guiding the cart

ABINOAM (4)

Jdg 4: 6 One day she sent for Barak son of **A**, who lived in
4:12 When Sisera was told that Barak son of **A** had
5: 1 day Deborah and Barak son of **A** sang this song:
5:12 Barak! / Lead your captives away, son of **A**!

ABIRAM (11)

Nu 16: 1 conspired with Dathan and **A**, the sons of Eliab,
16:12 Then Moses summoned Dathan and **A**, the sons of
16:24 get away from the tents of Korah, Dathan, and **A**."
16:25 and rushed over to the tents of Dathan and **A**,
16:27 stood back from the tents of Korah, Dathan, and **A**.
16:27 Then Dathan and **A** came out and stood at the
26: 9 Eliab was the father of Nemuel, Dathan, and **A**.
26: 9 and **A** are the same community leaders who
Dt 11: 6 see what he did to Dathan and **A** (the sons of Eliab,
1Ki 16:34 he laid the foundations, his oldest son, **A**, died.
Ps 106:17 and buried **A** and the other rebels.

ABISHAG (5)

1Ki 1: 3 and they found **A** from Shunem and brought her to
1:15 was very old now, and **A** was taking care of him.
2:17 Ask him to give me **A**, the girl from Shunem,
2:21 "Then let your brother Adonijah marry **A**, the girl
2:22 "How can you possibly ask me to give **A** to

ABISHAI (29)

1Sa 26: 6 asked Ahimelech the Hittite and **A** son of Zeruiah,
26: 6 Joab's brother. "I'll go with you," **A** replied.
26: 7 So David and **A** went right into Saul's camp
26: 8 **A** whispered to David. "Let me thrust that spear
26:12 and **A** got away without anyone seeing them
2Sa 2:18 Joab, **A**, and Asahel, the three sons of Zeruiah,
2:24 When Joab and **A** found out what had happened,
3:30 So Joab and his brother **A** killed Abner
3:39 these two sons of Zeruiah—Joab and **A**—
10:10 of the army under the command of his brother **A**,
10:14 they ran from **A** and retreated into the city.
16: 9 **A** son of Zeruiah demanded. "Let me go over
16:11 Then David said to **A** and the other officers,
18: 2 one-third under Joab's brother **A** son of Zeruiah,
18: 5 the king gave this command to Joab, **A**, and Ittai:
18:12 "We all heard the king say to you and **A** and Ittai,
19:21 Then **A** son of Zeruiah said, "Shimei should die,
20: 6 Then David said to **A**, "That troublemaker Sheba
20: 7 So **A** and Joab set out after Sheba with an elite
20:10 Joab and his brother **A** left him lying there
21:17 But **A** son of Zeruiah came to his rescue and killed
23:18 **A** son of Zeruiah, the brother of Joab,
23:19 **A** was the most famous of the Thirty and was their
1Ch 2:16 Zeruiah had three sons named **A**, Joab, and Asahel.
11:20 **A**, the brother of Joab, was the leader of the Thirty.
11:21 **A** was the most famous of the Thirty and was their
18:12 **A** son of Zeruiah destroyed eighteen thousand
19:11 of the army under the command of his brother **A**,
19:15 they ran from **A** and retreated into the city.

ABISHUA (5)

1Ch 6: 4 father of Phinehas. / Phinehas was the father of **A**.
6: 5 **A** was the father of Bukki. / Bukki was the father
6:50 descendants of Aaron were Eleazar, Phinehas, **A**,
8: 4 **A**, Naaman, Ahoah,
Ezr 7: 5 son of **A**, son of Phinehas, son of Eleazar, son of

ABISHUR (2)

1Ch 2:28 The sons of Shammai were Nadab and **A**.
2:29 The sons of **A** and his wife Abihail were Ahban

ABITAL (2)

2Sa 3: 4 The fifth was Shephatiah, whose mother was **A**.
1Ch 3: 3 The fifth was Shephatiah, whose mother was **A**.

ABITUB (1)

1Ch 8:11 wife Hushim had already given birth to **A**

ABIUD (2)

Mt 1:13 Zerubbabel was the father of **A**. / **A** was the father

ABJECTS [KJV] See PEOPLE

ABLAZE (3) [BLAZE]

Ps 83:14 through a forest / and as a flame sets mountains **a**,
Isa 30:33 the LORD, like fire from a volcano, will set it **a**.
Zec 12: 6 clans of Judah like a brazier that sets a woodpile **a**

ABLE (181) [ABILITIES, ABILITY, ENABLED]

Ge 1:25 each **a** to reproduce more of its own kind.
11: 7 Then they won't be **a** to understand each other."
11:30 Now Sarai was not **a** to have any children.
26:22 has made room for us, and we will be **a** to thrive."
27:20 "How were you **a** to find it so quickly, my son?"
30: 2 "He is the only one **a** to give you children!"
47:17 But at least they were **a** to purchase food for that
Ex 7:18 The Egyptians will not be **a** to drink any water
8: 7 But the magicians were **a** to do the same thing with
10: 2 You will be **a** to tell wonderful stories to your
10: 5 so many that you won't be **a** to see the ground.
16:32 later generations will be **a** to see the bread that the
17: 6 Then the people will be **a** to drink." Moses did just
17:13 and his troops were **a** to crush the army of Amalek.
18:23 to do so, then you will be **a** to endure the pressures,
21:19 If the injured person is later **a** to walk again,
31: 4 He is **a** to create beautiful objects from gold,
32:30 Perhaps I will be **a** to obtain forgiveness for you."
35:32 He is **a** to create beautiful objects from gold,
40:35 Moses was no longer **a** to enter the Tabernacle
Lev 14:30 whichever the person was **a** to afford.
17: 6 That way the priest will be **a** to sprinkle the blood
26: 6 in the land, and you will be **a** to sleep without fear.
Nu 1: 3 twenty years old or older who are **a** to go to war.
1:20[-21] years old or older who were **a** to go to war,
1:45 were twenty years old or older and **a** to go to war.
5:28 be unharmed and will still be **a** to have children.
14:16 'The LORD was not **a** to bring them into the land
22: 6 Then perhaps I will be **a** to conquer them and drive
22:11 Perhaps then I will be **a** to conquer them and drive
32:27 all who are **a** to bear arms will cross over to fight
32:29 and Reuben who are **a** to fight the LORD's
Dt 4:10 and they will be **a** to teach my laws to their
7:24 No one will be **a** to stand against you, and you will
9:28 because he wasn't **a** to bring them to the land he
11:25 No one will be **a** to stand against you,
16:17 All must give as they are **a**, according to the
19: 6 an enraged avenger might be **a** to chase down
31: 2 now 120 years old and am no longer **a** to lead you.
Jos 1: 5 No one will be **a** to stand their ground against you
10: 8 Not a single one of them will be **a** to stand up to
22:27 Then your descendants will not be **a** to say to ours,
23: 9 for you, and no one has yet been **a** to defeat you.
24:19 "You are not **a** to serve the LORD, for he is a
Jdg 2:14 and they were no longer **a** to resist them.
1Sa 6:20 "Who is **a** to stand in the presence of the LORD,
17: 9 If your man is **a** to kill me, then we will be your
2Sa 2:22 I will never be **a** to face your brother Joab if I have
3:21 Then you will be **a** to rule over everything your
1Ki 3: 9 For who by himself is **a** to govern this great nation
5: 3 was not **a** to build a Temple to honor the name of
2Ki 7: 2 see it happen, but you won't be **a** to eat any of it!"
7:19 see it happen, but you won't be **a** to eat any of it!"
9:27 He was **a** to go on as far as Megiddo, but he died
9:37 so that no one will be **a** to recognize her.' "
18:29 He will never be **a** to rescue you from my power.
18:35 What god of any nation has ever been **a** to save its
1Ch 9:13 They were heads of clans and very **a** men.
12:21 and **a** warriors who became commanders in his
21:30 But David was not **a** to go there to inquire of God,
2Ch 1:10 for who is **a** to govern this great nation of yours?"
14: 6 he was **a** to build up the fortified cities throughout
20:20 LORD your God, and you will be **a** to stand firm.
25: 9 "The LORD is **a** to give you much more than
30: 9 and they will be **a** to return to this land.
32:13 Were any of the gods of those nations **a** to rescue
32:14 anywhere, was **a** to rescue his people from me!
32:15 no god of any nation has ever yet been **a** to rescue
34:25 against this place, and nothing will be **a** to stop it.'
Ezr 6:10 Then they will be **a** to offer acceptable sacrifices to
9: 9 so that we were **a** to rebuild the Temple of our God
Ne 6:13 Then they would be **a** to accuse and discredit me.
Job 13:20 two things I beg of you, and I will be **a** to face you.
25: 3 Who is **a** to count his heavenly army? Does his
38:31 Are you **a** to restrain the Pleiades or Orion?
Ps 129: 2 but they have never been **a** to finish me off.
Pr 27:11 to be wise! Then I will be **a** to answer my critics.
Ecc 8: 1 to be wise, to be **a** to analyze and interpret things.
Isa 1:31 the straw on fire, and no one will be **a** to put it out.
22:22 will open doors, and no one will be **a** to shut them;
22:22 close doors, and no one will be **a** to open them.
36:14 deceive you. He will never be **a** to rescue you.
36:20 What god of any nation has ever been **a** to save its
40:13 Who is **a** to advise the Spirit of the LORD?
47:11 and you won't be **a** to charm it away.
47:11 upon you, and you won't be **a** to buy your way out.
48:11 the pagan nations will not be **a** to claim that their
Jer 1:18 or people of Judah will be **a** to stand against you.
10:23 is not his own. No one is **a** to plan his own course.
13:19 their gates, and no one will be **a** to open them.
17:27 and no one will be **a** to put out the roaring
26: 3 Then I will be **a** to withhold the disaster I am ready
36: 3 Then I will be **a** to forgive their sins
49:11 too, will be **a** to depend on me for help."
Eze 1: 9 The living beings were **a** to fly in any direction
3:26 of your mouth so you won't be **a** to pray for them,
4: 8 so you won't be **a** to turn from side to side until the
20: 9 That way the surrounding nations wouldn't be **a** to
20:14 of Egypt wouldn't be **a** to claim I destroyed them
33:22 so I would be **a** to speak when this man arrived the
34:25 Then my people will be **a** to camp safely in the
36:30 and never again will the surrounding nations be **a**
Da 2:47 for you have been **a** to reveal this secret."
3:15 What god will be **a** to rescue you from my power
3:17 the God whom we serve is **a** to save us.
4:37 and he is **a** to humble those who are proud."
6:20 **a** to rescue you from the lions?"
11:15 The best troops of the south will not be **a** to stand
11:16 onward unopposed; none will be **a** to stop him.
Hos 2: 7 her lovers, she won't be **a** to catch up with them.
2:10 No one will be **a** to rescue her from my hands.
Joel 2:14 give you so much that you will be **a** to offer grain
Am 2:15 Even warriors on horses won't be **a** to outrun the
5: 6 Your gods in Bethel certainly won't be **a** to quench
Mic 2: 3 your evil with evil; you won't be **a** to escape!
Zep 3: 9 so that everyone will be **a** to worship the LORD
Mal 3: 2 "But who will be **a** to endure it when he comes?
3: 2 Who will be **a** to stand and face him when he
Mt 15:31 Those who hadn't been **a** to speak were talking,
20:22 Are you **a** to drink from the bitter cup of sorrow I
20:22 to drink?" "Oh yes," they replied, "we are **a**!"
26:61 'I am **a** to destroy the Temple of God and rebuild

Mk 4:33 the people as much as they were a to understand.
9:39 in my name will soon be a to speak evil of me.
10:38 Are you a to drink from the bitter cup of sorrow I
10:38 Are you a to be baptized with the baptism of
10:39 "Oh yes," they said, "we are a!" And Jesus said,
16:18 They will be a to handle snakes with safety,
16:18 They will be a to place their hands on the sick
Lk 1:20 you won't be a to speak until the child is born.
14:32 If he is not a, then while the enemy is still far
17:21 You won't be a to say, 'Here it is!' or 'It's over
17:22 of the Son of Man, but you won't be a to," he said.
21:15 that none of your opponents will be a to reply!
Jn 7:34 And you won't be a to come where I am."
7:36 and 'You won't be a to come where I am'?"
9:32 Never since the world began has anyone been a to
21:18 you were a to do as you liked and go wherever you
Ac 5:39 But if it is of God, you will not be a to stop them.
6:10 None of them was a to stand against the wisdom
15:10 that neither we nor our ancestors were a to bear?
19:35 At last the mayor was a to quiet them down
20:32 his message that is a to build you up and give you
Ro 4:19 his wife, had never been a to have children.
4:21 He was absolutely convinced that God was a to do
6:11 and a to live for the glory of God through Christ
8:39 nothing in all creation will ever be a to separate us
15:14 so well that you are a to teach others all about
15:32 I will be a to come to you with a happy heart,
16:25 God is a to make you strong, just as the Good
1Co 6:3 So you should surely be a to resolve ordinary
7:5 so that Satan won't be a to tempt them because of
12:3 and no one is a to say, "Jesus is Lord," except by
14:2 to people, since they won't be a to understand you.
14:5 but even more I wish you were all a to prophesy.
15:50 These perishable bodies of ours are not a to live
2Co 1:4 we will be a to give them the same comfort God
2:7 so discouraged that he won't be a to recover.
8:12 it isn't important how much you are a to give.
10:16 Then we will be a to go and preach the Good News
Eph 3:20 he is a to accomplish infinitely more than we
6:11 so that you will be a to stand firm against all
Col 2:4 so that no one will be a to deceive you with
1Ti 3:2 having guests in his home and must be a to teach.
5:14 Then the enemy will not be a to say anything
2Ti 1:12 and I am sure that he is a to guard what I have
2:2 people who are a to pass them on to others.
2:24 They must be a to teach effectively and be patient
Tit 1:9 then he will be a to encourage others with right
Heb 2:18 he is a to help us when we are being tempted.
5:2 he is human, he is a to deal gently with the people,
7:25 Therefore he is a, once and forever, to save
9:9 and sacrifices that the priests offer are not a to
10:1 but they were never a to provide perfect cleansing
11:11 together with Abraham was a to have a child,
11:19 God was a to bring him back to life again.
Jude 1:24 to God, who is a to keep you from stumbling,
Rev 3:18 buy ointment for your eyes so you will be a to see.
5:3 on earth or under the earth was a to open the scroll
6:17 wrath has come, and who will be a to survive?"
13:4 they exclaimed. "Who is a to fight against him?"

ABNER (55) [ABNER'S]

1Sa 14:50 The commander of Saul's army was his cousin A,
17:55 he asked A, the general of his army, "A, whose son is he?" "I really don't know," A said.
17:57 A brought him to Saul with the Philistine's head
20:25 Jonathan sitting opposite him and A beside him.
26:5 Saul and his general, A son of Ner, were sleeping
26:7 A and the warriors were lying asleep around him.
26:14 Then he shouted down to A and Saul, "Wake up, A!" "Who is it?" A demanded.
26:15 "Well, A, you're a great man, aren't you?"
2Sa 2:8 But A son of Ner, the commander of Saul's army,
2:12 One day A led some of Ishbosheth's troops from
2:13 and they met A at the pool of Gibeon.
2:14 Then A suggested to Joab, "Let's have a few of
2:17 and by the end of the day A and the men of Israel
2:19 and he began chasing A. He was relentless
2:20 When A looked back and saw him coming,
2:21 "Go fight someone else!" A warned. "Take on
2:21 But Asahel refused and kept right on chasing A.
2:22 Again A shouted to him, "Get away from here!
2:23 so A thrust the butt end of his spear through
2:24 found out what had happened, they set out after A.
2:26 A shouted down to Joab, "Must we always solve
2:29 All that night A and his men retreated through the
3:6 A became a powerful leader among those who
3:7 accused A of sleeping with one of his father's
3:8 A became furious. "Am I a Judean dog to be
3:11 because he was afraid of what A might do.
3:12 Then A sent messengers to David, saying,
3:16 Then A told him, "Go back home!" So Palti
3:17 A had consulted with the leaders of Israel.
3:19 A also spoke with the leaders of the tribe of
3:20 When A came to Hebron with his twenty men,
3:21 Then A said to David, "Let me go and call all the
3:21 heart desires." So David sent A safely on his way.
3:22 But just after A left, Joab and some of David's
3:23 When Joab was told that A had just been there
3:24 "What do you mean by letting A get away?
3:26 left David and sent messengers to catch up with A.
3:27 When A arrived at Hebron, Joab took him aside at
3:27 and killed A in revenge for killing his brother
3:28 my people are innocent of this crime against A.
3:30 So Joab and his brother Abishai killed A
3:30 because A had killed their brother Asahel at the
3:31 put on sackcloth. Go into deep mourning for A."
3:32 They buried A in Hebron, and the king and all the
3:33 Then the king sang this funeral song for A: / "Should A have died as fools die?
3:34 a wicked plot." / All the people wept again for A.
1Ki 2:5 A son of Ner and Amasa son of Jether.
2:32 For my father was no party to the deaths of A son
1Ch 26:28 Saul son of Kish, A son of Ner, and Joab son of
27:21 son of Zechariah / Benjamin | Jaasiel son of A

ABNER'S (6) [ABNER]

1Sa 14:51 A father, Ner, and Saul's father, Kish,
2Sa 2:25 A troops from the tribe of Benjamin regrouped
2:31 But three hundred and sixty of A men, all from the
3:37 knew that David was not responsible for A death.
4:1 When Ishbosheth heard about A death at Hebron,
4:12 and buried it in A tomb in Hebron.

ABOARD (6) [BOARD]

Ge 7:7 and he went a the boat to escape—he and his wife
Jn 21:11 So Simon Peter went a and dragged the net to the
Ac 21:6 Then we went a, and they returned home.
27:16 where with great difficulty we hoisted a the
27:31 "You will all die unless the sailors stay a."
27:37 us began eating—for that is the number we had a.

ABODEST [KJV] See SIT

ABOLISH (3) [ABOLISHED]

Eze 36:29 you good crops, and I will a famine in the land.
Mic 5:14 I will a your pagan shrines with their Asherah
Mt 5:17 I did not come to a the law of Moses

ABOLISHED (1) [ABOLISH]

Isa 2:18 Idols will be utterly a and destroyed.

ABOMINABLE (3) [ABOMINATION]

Jer 7:30 "They have set up their a idols right in my own
13:27 and your a idol worship out in the fields and on the
32:34 They have set up their a idols right in my own

ABOMINATION (2) [ABOMINABLE]

Pr 3:32 Such wicked people are an a to the LORD,
Lk 16:15 What this world honors is an a in the sight of God.

ABOUND (1)

Eze 47:9 Fish will a in the Dead Sea, for its waters will be

ABOUNDED, ABOUNDETH [KJV] See BOUNTIFUL, GROWING, MORE, OVERFLOWED, SHOWERED

ABOUT (1212) See Index of Articles, Etc.

ABOVE (114)

Ge 1:7 God made this space to separate the waters a from
7:17 the ground and lifting the boat high a the earth.
7:18 As the waters rose higher and higher a the ground,
7:20 standing more than twenty-two feet a the highest
49:25 bless you / with the blessings of the heavens a,
Ex 25:20 atonement cover with their wings spread out a it.
25:22 and talk to you from a the atonement cover
28:28 securely to the ephod a the beautiful sash.
36:14 A the Tabernacle, a roof covering was made from
37:9 and their wings were stretched out a the atonement
39:21 the chestpiece was held securely to the ephod a the
Lev 26:19 spirit by making the skies a as unyielding as iron
Nu 7:89 between the two cherubim a the Ark's cover—
9:22 Whether the cloud stayed a the Tabernacle for two
11:31 were quail flying about three feet a the ground.
12:10 As the cloud moved from a the Tabernacle,
14:10 appeared to all the Israelites from a the Tabernacle.
Dt 7:14 You will be blessed a all the nations of the earth.
10:15 chose you, their descendants, a every other nation,
11:21 so that as long as the sky remains a the earth,
14:1 or shave the hair a your foreheads for the sake of
17:20 and acting as if he is a his fellow citizens.
28:1 the LORD your God will exalt you a all the
28:23 The skies a will be as unyielding as bronze,
33:24 "May Asher be blessed a other sons; / may he be
Jos 2:11 your God is the supreme God of the heavens a
13:19 Sibmah, Zereth-shahar on the hill a the valley,
15:8 Then it went west to the top of the mountain a the
Jdg 5:24 May she be blessed a all women who live in tents.
1Sa 9:22 the table, honoring them a the thirty special guests.
10:23 and he stood head and shoulders a anyone else.
13:18 and the third moved toward the border a the valley
2Sa 6:21 who chose me a your father and his family!
1Ki 7:29 A and below the lions and oxen were wreath
7:31 It projected 1-1/2 feet a the cart's top like a round
2Ki 23:12 built on the palace roof a the upper room of Ahaz.
1Ch 6:65 of Judah, Simeon, and Benjamin, mentioned a,
16:25 worthy of praise! / He is to be revered a all gods.
Job 18:6 The lamp hanging a them will be quenched.
28:18 trying to get it. The price of wisdom is far a pearls.
31:2 What has God a chosen for us? What is our
35:5 up into the sky and see the clouds high a you.
Ps 7:7 before you. / Sit on your throne high a them.
27:6 my head high, / a my enemies who surround me.
29:3 The voice of the LORD echoes a the sea.
47:8 God reigns a the nations, / sitting on his holy
57:5 Be exalted, O God, a the highest heavens!
57:11 Be exalted, O God, a the highest heavens.
80:1 O God, enthroned a the cherubim, / display your
93:4 the shore—/ the LORD a is mightier than these!
95:3 LORD is a great God, / the great King a all gods.
96:4 of praise! / He is to be revered a all the gods.
97:9 over all the earth; / you are exalted far a all gods.
99:2 majesty in Jerusalem, / supreme a all the nations.
101:6 Only those who are a reproach / will be allowed to
103:11 is as great as the height of the heavens a the earth.
105:39 The LORD spread out a cloud a them as a
108:5 Be exalted, O God, a the highest heavens.
113:4 For the LORD is high a the nations; / his glory is
148:4 Praise him, skies a! / Praise him, vapors high a the clouds!
Pr 4:23 A all else, guard your heart, for it affects
8:28 I was there when he set the clouds a, when he
15:24 The path of the wise leads to life a; they leave the
Isa 13:10 The heavens will be black a them. No light will
14:13 ascend to heaven and set my throne a God's stars.
34:4 The heavens a will melt away and disappear like a
40:22 It is God who sits a the circle of the earth.
48:13 palm of my right hand spread out the heavens a.
49:11 The highways will be raised a the valleys.
51:6 Look up to the skies a, and gaze down on the earth
Jer 35:4 directly a the room of Maaseiah son of Shallum,
La 3:54 The water flowed a my head, and I cried out,
Eze 1:22 There was a surface spread out a them like the sky.
1:25 a voice spoke from beyond the crystal surface a
1:26 A the surface over their heads was what looked
1:26 And high a this throne was a figure whose
8:11 so there was a thick cloud of incense a their heads.
10:1 a the crystal surface over the heads of the
10:4 Then the glory of the LORD rose up from a the
10:18 door of the Temple and hovered a the cherubim.
10:19 And the glory of the God of Israel hovered a them.
11:22 and the glory of the God of Israel hovered a them.
11:23 the city and stopped a the mountain to the east.
19:11 soon became very tall, / towering a all the others.
27:7 finest linen, and they flew as a banner a you.
29:15 never again great enough to rise a its neighbors.
31:5 This great tree towered a all the other trees around
31:10 and because it set itself so high a the others,
32:8 Even the brightest stars will become dark a you.
41:6 one a the other, with thirty rooms on each level.
41:16 walls of the Temple were paneled with wood a
41:17 The space a the door leading into the Most Holy
Da 12:6 dressed in linen, who was now standing a the river,
12:7 man dressed in linen, who was standing a the river,
Na 2:3 with a forest of spears waving a them.
Zec 9:14 The LORD will appear a his people; his arrows
Mt 1:17 All those listed a include fourteen generations
27:37 A signboard was fastened to the cross a Jesus'
Mk 2:4 so they dug through the clay roof a his head.
15:26 A signboard was fastened to the cross a Jesus'
Lk 1:42 "You are blessed by God a all other women,
23:38 A signboard was nailed to the cross a him with
Jn 3:31 "He has come from a and is greater than anyone
8:23 said to them, "You are from below; I am from a.
19:11 over me at all unless it were given to you from a.
Ac 2:2 roaring of a mighty windstorm in the skies a them,
2:19 And I will cause wonders in the heavens a
Ro 8:39 Whether we are high a the sky or in the deepest
Eph 1:21 Now he is far a any ruler or authority or power
Php 2:9 and gave him a name that is a every other name,
Heb 9:5 The glorious cherubim were a the Ark.
Jas 1:17 is good and perfect comes to us from God a,
2Pe 1:20 A all, you must understand that no prophecy in

ABRAHAM (261) [ABRAHAM'S, ABRAM, ABRAM'S]

DESCENDANT(S) OF ABRAHAM (11) Ge 25:4; 50:24; Jer 33:26; Mt 3:9; Lk 3:8; Jn 8:33,37; Ro 9:7; 11:1; 2Co 11:22; Heb 2:16

FATHER ABRAHAM (4) Lk 16:24,27,30; Jn 8:53

GOD OF ABRAHAM (12) Ex 3:6,15,16; 4:5; 1Ki 18:36; 2Ch 30:6; Ps 47:9; Mt 22:32; Mk 12:26; Lk 20:37; Ac 3:13; 7:32

SON(S) OF ABRAHAM (8) Ge 21:9; 25:12,19; 1Ch 1:28,33; Lk 3:34; 19:9; Ac 13:26

Ge 17:5 now you will be known as A, for you will be the
17:9 "Your part of the agreement," God told A, "is to
17:17 Then A bowed down to the ground, but he laughed
17:18 And A said to God, "Yes, may Ishmael enjoy your
17:22 That ended the conversation, and God left A.
17:23 On that very day A took his son Ishmael and every
17:24 A was ninety-nine years old at that time,
18:1 The LORD appeared again to A while he was
18:1 as A was sitting at the entrance to his tent,
18:6 So A ran back to the tent and said to Sarah,
18:7 Then A ran out to the herd and chose a fat calf
18:8 they ate, A waited on them there beneath the trees.
18:9 they asked him. "In the tent," A replied.
18:11 And since A and Sarah were both very old,
18:13 Then the LORD said to A, "Why did Sarah
18:16 toward Sodom. A went with them part of the way.
18:17 "Should I hide my plan from A?" the LORD
18:18 "For A will become a great and mighty nation,
18:20 So the LORD told A, "I have heard that the
18:22 but the LORD remained with A for a while.
18:23 A approached him and said, "Will you destroy
18:27 Then A spoke again. "Since I have begun, let me
18:29 Then A pressed his request further.
18:30 "Please don't be angry, my Lord," A pleaded.
18:31 Then A said, "Since I have dared to speak to the
18:32 Finally, A said, "Lord, please do not get angry;

18:33 when he had finished his conversation with **A**, and **A** returned to his tent.
19:27 The next morning **A** was up early and hurried out
20: 1 Now **A** moved south to the Negev and settled for a
20: 2 **A** told people there that his wife, Sarah, was his
20: 5 **A** told me, 'She is my sister,' and she herself said,
20: 9 Then Abimelech called for **A**. "What is this you
20:11 "Well," **A** said, "I figured this to be a godless
20:14 and gave them to **A**, and he returned his wife,
20:17 Then **A** prayed to God, and God healed
21: 2 and she gave a son to **A** in his old age.
21: 3 And **A** named his son Isaac.
21: 4 **A** circumcised him as God had commanded.
21: 5 **A** was one hundred years old at the time.
21: 7 a baby? Yet I have given **A** a son in his old age!"
21: 8 **A** gave a big party to celebrate the happy occasion.
21: 9 the son of **A** and her Egyptian servant Hagar—
21:10 So she turned to **A** and demanded, "Get rid of that
21:11 This upset **A** very much because Ishmael was his
21:12 But God told **A**, "Do not be upset over the boy
21:14 So **A** got up early the next morning, prepared food
21:22 came with Phicol, his army commander, to visit **A**.
21:24 **A** replied, "All right, I swear to it!"
21:25 Then **A** complained to Abimelech about a well that
21:27 Then **A** gave sheep and oxen to Abimelech,
21:28 But when **A** took seven additional ewe lambs
21:30 **A** replied, "They are my gift to you as a public
21:33 Then **A** planted a tamarisk tree at Beersheba,
21:34 And **A** lived in Philistine country for a long time.
22: 1 "**A**!" God called. "Yes," he replied. "Here I
22: 3 The next morning **A** got up early. He saddled his
22: 4 day of the journey, **A** saw the place in the distance.
22: 5 here with the donkey," **A** told the young men.
22: 6 **A** placed the wood for the burnt offering on Isaac's
22: 7 Isaac said, "Father?" "Yes, my son," **A** replied.
22: 8 "God will provide a lamb, my son," **A** answered.
22: 9 arrived at the place where God had told **A** to go,
22:10 And **A** took the knife and lifted it up to kill his son
22:11 of the LORD shouted to him from heaven, "**A**! **A**!"
22:13 Then **A** looked up and saw a ram caught by its
22:14 **A** named the place "The LORD Will Provide."
22:15 Then the angel of the LORD called again to **A**
22:19 to Beersheba, where **A** lived for quite some time.
22:20 Soon after this, **A** heard that Milcah, his brother
23: 2 of Canaan. There **A** mourned and wept for her.
23: 5 The Hittites replied to **A**,
23: 7 Then **A** bowed low before them and said,
23:10 and he answered **A** as the others listened,
23:11 "No, sir," he said to **A**, "please listen to me.
23:12 **A** bowed again to the people of the land,
23:16 So **A** paid Ephron the amount he had suggested,
23:19 So **A** buried Sarah there in Canaan, in the cave of
23:20 and the cave were sold to **A** by the Hittites as a
24: 1 **A** was now a very old man, and the LORD had
24: 2 One day **A** said to the man in charge of his
24: 6 "No!" **A** warned. "Be careful never to take my
24:12 me success and show kindness to my master, **A**.
24:27 to the LORD, the God of my master, **A**," he said.
24:27 "The LORD has been so kind and faithful to **A**,
24:42 'O LORD, the God of my master, **A**, if you are
24:48 I praised the LORD, the God of my master, **A**,
25: 1 Now **A** married again. Keturah was his new wife,
25: 4 These were all descendants of **A** through Keturah.
25: 5 **A** left everything he owned to his son Isaac.
25: 7 **A** lived for 175 years,
25:10 This was the field **A** had purchased from the
25:12 the son of **A** through Hagar, Sarah's Egyptian
25:19 is the history of the family of Isaac, the son of **A**.
26: 3 just as I solemnly promised **A**, your father.
26: 5 I will do this because **A** listened to me and obeyed
26:15 that had been dug by the servants of his father, **A**.
26:18 renamed them, using the names **A** had given them.
26:24 "I am the God of your father, **A**," he said.
26:24 I will do this because of my promise to **A**,
28: 4 your descendants the blessings he promised to **A**.
28: 4 we now are foreigners, for God gave it to **A**."
28:13 the God of your grandfather **A** and the God of your
31:42 the God of my grandfather **A**, the awe-inspiring
31:53 the God of your grandfather **A** and the God of my
32: 9 "O God of my grandfather **A** and my father,
35:12 And I will pass on to you the land I gave to **A**
35:27 (now called Hebron), where **A** had also lived.
48:15 the God before whom my grandfather **A** and my
48:16 and the names of my grandfather **A** and my father,
49:30 which **A** bought from Ephron the Hittite for a
49:31 There **A** and his wife Sarah are buried. There Isaac
49:32 It is the cave that my grandfather **A** bought from
50:13 This is the cave that **A** had bought for a permanent
50:24 the land he vowed to give to the descendants of **A**,
Ex 2:24 and remembered his covenant promise to **A**,
3: 6 the God of **A**, the God of Isaac, and the God of
3:15 the God of **A**, the God of Isaac, and the God of
3:16 your ancestors—the God of **A**, Isaac, and Jacob—
4: 5 the God of **A**, the God of Isaac, and the God of
6: 3 I appeared to **A**, to Isaac, and to Jacob as God
6: 8 I will bring you into the land I swore to give to **A**,
32:13 covenant with your servants—**A**, Isaac, and Jacob.
33: 1 lead them to the land I solemnly promised **A**,
Lev 26:42 with Isaac, and with **A**, and I will remember the
Nu 32:11 will ever see the land I solemnly promised to **A**,
Dt 1: 8 the LORD swore to give to your ancestors **A**,
6:10 into the land he swore to give your ancestors **A**,
9: 5 fulfill the oath he had sworn to your ancestors **A**,
9:27 but remember instead your servants **A**, Isaac,
29:13 and as he swore to your ancestors **A**, Isaac,
30:20 land the LORD swore to give your ancestors **A**,
34: 4 "This is the land I promised on oath to **A**, Isaac,
Jos 24: 2 including Terah, the father of **A** and Nahor,
24: 3 But I took your ancestor **A** from the land beyond
1Ki 18:36 "O LORD, God of **A**, Isaac, and Jacob,
2Ki 13:23 He pitied them because of his covenant with **A**,
1Ch 1:27 and Abram, later known as **A**.
1:28 The sons of **A** were Isaac and Ishmael.
1:33 All these were sons of **A** by his concubine
1:34 **A** was the father of Isaac. The sons of Isaac were
16:16 This is the covenant he made with **A** / and the oath
29:18 the God of our ancestors **A**, Isaac, and Israel,
2Ch 20: 7 land forever to the descendants of your friend **A**?
30: 6 to the LORD, the God of **A**, Isaac, and Israel,
Ne 9: 7 him from Ur of the Chaldeans and renamed him **A**.
Ps 47: 9 They join us in praising the God of **A**. / For all the
105: 6 O children of **A**, God's servant, / O descendants of
105: 9 This is the covenant he made with **A** / and the oath
105:42 remembered his sacred promise / to **A** his servant.
Isa 29:22 That is why the LORD, who redeemed **A**, says to
41: 8 my chosen one, descended from my friend **A**,
51: 2 Yes, think about your ancestors **A** and Sarah,
51: 2 whom you came. **A** was alone when I called him.
63:16 Even if **A** and Jacob would disown us, LORD,
Jer 33:26 descendants will rule the descendants of **A**,
Eze 33:24 '**A** was only one man, and yet he gained
Mic 7:20 as you promised with an oath to our ancestors **A**
Mt 1: 1 the Messiah, a descendant of King David and of **A**:
1: 2 **A** was the father of Isaac. / Isaac was the father of
1:17 fourteen generations from **A** to King David,
3: 9 'We're safe—we're the descendants of **A**.'
3: 9 can change these stones here into children of **A**.
8:11 come from all over the world and sit down with **A**,
22:31 Long after **A**, Isaac, and Jacob had died, God said,
22:32 'I am the God of **A**, the God of Isaac, and the God
Mk 12:26 Long after **A**, Isaac, and Jacob had died, God said to Moses, 'I am the God of **A**, the God of Isaac,
Lk 1:55 he promised our ancestors—**A** and his children—
1:73 the covenant he gave to our ancestor **A**.
3: 8 'We're safe—we're the descendants of **A**.'
3: 8 can change these stones here into children of **A**.
3:34 Isaac was the son of **A**. / **A** was the son of Terah.
13:28 gnashing of teeth, for you will see **A**, Isaac, Jacob,
16:22 and was carried by the angels to be with **A**.
16:23 he saw Lazarus in the far distance with **A**.
16:24 rich man shouted, 'Father **A**, have some pity!
16:25 "But **A** said to him, 'Son, remember that during
16:27 "Then the rich man said, 'Please, Father **A**,
16:29 "But **A** said, 'Moses and the prophets have warned
16:30 "The rich man replied, 'No, Father **A**! But if
16:31 "But **A** said, 'If they won't listen to Moses
19: 9 for this man has shown himself to be a son of **A**.
20:37 Long after **A**, Isaac, and Jacob had died,
20:37 he referred to the Lord as 'the God of **A**, the God
Jn 7:22 is older than the law of Moses; it goes back to **A**.)
8:33 "But we are descendants of **A**," they said.
8:37 Yes, I realize that you are descendants of **A**.
8:39 "Our father is **A**," they declared. "No,"
8:39 Jesus replied, "for if you were children of **A**,
8:40 trying to kill me. **A** wouldn't do a thing like that.
8:52 Even **A** and the prophets died, but you say that
8:53 Are you greater than our father **A**, who died?
8:56 Your ancestor **A** rejoiced as he looked forward to
8:57 years old. How can you say you have seen **A**?"
8:58 "The truth is, I existed before **A** was even born!"
Ac 3:13 For it is the God of **A**, the God of Isaac, the God of
3:25 For God said to **A**, 'Through your descendants all
7: 2 Our glorious God appeared to our ancestor **A** in
7: 4 So **A** left the land of the Chaldeans and lived in
7: 5 eventually the whole country would belong to **A**
7: 8 God also gave **A** the covenant of circumcision at
7:16 and buried in the tomb **A** had bought from the sons
7:17 near when God would fulfill his promise to **A**,
7:32 your ancestors—the God of **A**, Isaac, and Jacob.'
13:26 you sons of **A**, and also all of you devout Gentiles
Ro 4: 1 **A** was, humanly speaking, the founder of our
4: 2 But from God's point of view **A** had no basis at all
4: 3 For the Scriptures tell us, "**A** believed God,
4: 9 or is it for Gentiles, too? Well, what about **A**?
4:11 The circumcision ceremony was a sign that **A**
4:11 So **A** is the spiritual father of those who have faith
4:12 And **A** is also the spiritual father of those who
4:12 but only if they have the same kind of faith **A** had
4:13 that God's promise to give the whole earth to **A**
4:16 For **A** is the father of all who believe.
4:17 because **A** believed in the God who brings the dead
4:18 When God promised **A** that he would become the father of many nations, **A** believed him.
4:20 **A** never wavered in believing God's promise.
9: 7 Just the fact that they are descendants of **A** doesn't
9: 7 be counted," though **A** had other children, too.
11: 1 a descendant of **A** and a member of the tribe of
11:16 And since **A** and the other patriarchs were holy,
11:17 you also receive the blessing God has promised **A**
11:28 his chosen people because of his promises to **A**,
2Co 11:22 So am I. And they are descendants of **A**? So am I.
Gal 3: 6 In the same way, "**A** believed God, so God
3: 7 The real children of **A**, then, are all those who put
3: 8 God promised this good news to **A** long ago when
3: 9 faith in Christ share the same blessing **A** received
3:14 Gentiles with the same blessing he promised to **A**,
3:16 God gave the promise to **A** and his child.
3:17 The agreement God made with **A** could not be
3:18 God's promise. But God gave it to **A** as a promise.
3:20 acted on his own when he made his promise to **A**.
3:29 belong to Christ, you are the true children of **A**.
4:22 The Scriptures say that **A** had two sons, one from
Heb 2:16 know that Jesus came to help the descendants of **A**,
6:13 For example, there was God's promise to **A**.
6:15 Then **A** waited patiently, and he received what
7: 1 When **A** was returning home after winning a great
7: 2 Then **A** took a tenth of all he had won in the battle
7: 4 Even **A**, the great patriarch of Israel,
7: 6 not even related to Levi, collected a tenth from **A**.
7: 6 And Melchizedek placed a blessing upon **A**,
7: 9 a tithe to Melchizedek through their ancestor **A**.
11: 8 It was by faith that **A** obeyed when God called him
11:10 **A** did this because he was confidently looking
11:11 It was by faith that Sarah together with **A** was able
11:11 **A** believed that God would keep his promise.
11:12 **A**, who was too old to have any children—
11:17 It was by faith that **A** offered Isaac as a sacrifice
11:17 **A**, who had received God's promises, was ready to
11:19 **A** assumed that if Isaac died, God was able to
11:19 a sense, **A** did receive his son back from the dead.
Jas 2:21 Don't you remember that our ancestor **A** was
2:23 "**A** believed God, so God declared him to be
1Pe 3: 6 For instance, Sarah obeyed her husband, **A**,

ABRAHAM'S (30) [ABRAHAM]

Ge 19:29 But God had listened to **A** request and kept Lot
20:18 a warning to Abimelech for having taken **A** wife.
21:25 servants had taken violently from **A** servants.
22: 1 Later on God tested **A** faith and obedience.
22:19 Then they returned to **A** young men and traveled
23:18 They became **A** permanent possession by the
24: 9 a solemn oath that he would follow **A** instructions.
24:10 He loaded ten of **A** camels with gifts and set out,
24:10 and went to the village where **A** brother Nahor had
24:15 who was the son of **A** brother Nahor and his wife,
24:33 But **A** servant said, "I don't want to eat until I
24:34 "I am **A** servant," he explained.
24:52 **A** servant bowed to the ground and worshiped the
24:59 and sent her away with **A** servant and his men.
24:61 mounted the camels and left with **A** servant.
25:11 After **A** death, God poured out rich blessings on
26: 1 struck the land, as had happened before in **A** time.
26:18 which the Philistines had filled in after **A** death.
28: 9 of Nebaioth and the daughter of Ishmael, **A** son.
1Ch 1:32 **A** concubine, were Zimran, Jokshan, Medan,
Ac 7: 8 And so Isaac, **A** son, was circumcised when he was
Ro 4:16 we follow Jewish customs, if we have faith like **A**.
4:19 And **A** faith did not weaken, even though he knew
4:22 And because of **A** faith, God declared him to be
4:23 him to be righteous—wasn't just for **A** benefit.
9: 7 of Abraham doesn't make them truly **A** children.
9: 8 This means that **A** physical descendants are not
9: 8 the promise who are considered to be **A** children.
11:17 But some of these branches from **A** tree, some of
Heb 7:10 the seed from which he came was in **A** loins when

ABRAM (65) [ABRAHAM]

Ge 11:26 he became the father of **A**, Nahor, and Haran.
11:27 Terah was the father of **A**, Nahor, and Haran;
11:29 Meanwhile, **A** married Sarai, and his brother
11:31 Terah took his son **A**, his daughter-in-law Sarai,
12: 1 Then the LORD told **A**, "Leave your country,
12: 4 So **A** departed as the LORD had instructed him,
12: 4 **A** was seventy-five years old when he left Haran.
12: 7 Then the LORD appeared to **A** and said, "I am
12: 7 And **A** built an altar there to commemorate the
12: 8 **A** traveled southward and set up camp in the hill
12: 9 Then **A** traveled south by stages toward the Negev.
12:10 in the land, so **A** went down to Egypt to wait it out.
12:11 **A** said to Sarai, "You are a very beautiful woman.
12:16 Then Pharaoh gave **A** many gifts because of her—
12:18 So Pharaoh called for **A** and accused him sharply.
12:20 **A** and his wife, with all their household
13: 1 **A** with his wife and Lot and all that they owned,
13: 2 for **A** was very rich in livestock, silver, and gold.
13: 4 This was the place where **A** had built the altar,
13: 5 Now Lot, who was traveling with **A**, was also very
13: 6 But the land could not support both **A** and Lot with
13: 7 an argument broke out between the herdsmen of **A**
13: 8 Then **A** talked it over with Lot. "This arguing
13:11 and servants and parted company with his uncle **A**.
13:12 So while **A** stayed in the land of Canaan,
13:14 After Lot was gone, the LORD said to **A**,
13:18 Then **A** moved his camp to the oak grove owned
14:13 the men who escaped came and told **A** the Hebrew,
14:14 When **A** learned that Lot had been captured,
14:15 but **A** chased them to Hobah, north of Damascus.
14:16 **A** and his allies recovered everything—the goods
14:17 As **A** returned from his victory over Kedorlaomer
14:19 Melchizedek blessed **A** with this blessing: "Blessed be **A** by God Most High, / Creator of
14:20 Then **A** gave Melchizedek a tenth of all the goods
14:22 **A** replied, "I have solemnly promised the LORD,
14:23 you might say, 'I am the one who made **A** rich!'
15: 1 Afterward the LORD spoke to **A** in a vision and said to him, "Do not be afraid, **A**,
15: 2 But **A** replied, "O Sovereign LORD, what good
15: 5 Then the LORD brought **A** outside beneath the
15: 6 And **A** believed the LORD, and the LORD
15: 8 But **A** replied, "O Sovereign LORD, how can I
15:10 **A** took all these and killed them. He cut each one
15:11 to eat the carcasses, but **A** chased them away.
15:12 the sun was going down, **A** fell into a deep sleep.
15:13 Then the LORD told **A**, "You can be sure that
15:17 **A** saw a smoking firepot and a flaming torch pass
15:18 So the LORD made a covenant with **A** that day
16: 2 and gave her to **A** so she could bear his children.
16: 2 me from having any children," Sarai said to **A**.
16: 2 I can have children through her." And **A** agreed.
16: 3 the Egyptian servant and gave her to **A** as a wife.

16: 3 (This happened ten years after A first arrived in the
16: 4 So A slept with Hagar, and she became pregnant.
16: 5 Then Sarai said to A, "It's all your fault! Now this
16: 6 A replied, "Since she is your servant, you may
16:15 So Hagar gave A a son, and A named him Ishmael.
16:16 A was eighty-six years old at that time.
17: 1 When A was ninety-nine years old, the LORD
17: 3 At this, A fell face down in the dust. Then God
17: 5 It will no longer be A; now you will be known as
1Ch 1:27 and A, later known as Abraham.
Ne 9: 7 who chose A and brought him from Ur of the

ABRAM'S (6) [ABRAHAM]

Ge 12:17 Pharaoh's household because of Sarai, A wife.
14:12 captured Lot—A nephew who lived in Sodom—
14:13 and his relatives, Eshcol and Aner, were A allies.
14:16 A nephew Lot with his possessions, and all the
16: 1 But Sarai, A wife, had no children. So Sarai took
16: 3 So Sarai, A wife, took Hagar the Egyptian servant

ABROAD (3)

Dt 33:18 people of Zebulun prosper in their expeditions a.
Job 15:23 They wander a for bread, saying, 'Where is it?'
Mt 10:27 in the darkness, shout a when daybreak comes.

ABRONAH (2)

Nu 33:34 They left Jotbathah and camped at A.
33:35 They left A and camped at Ezion-geber.

ABRUPTLY (1)

Ac 27:14 But the weather changed a, and a wind of typhoon

ABSALOM (90) [ABSALOM'S]

2Sa 3: 3 The third was A, whose mother was Maacah,
13: 1 David's son A had a beautiful sister named Tamar.
13:20 Her brother A saw her and asked, "Is it true that
13:22 And though A never spoke to Amnon about it,
13:23 A invited all the king's sons to come to a feast.
13:25 A pressed him, but the king wouldn't come,
13:26 "Well, then," A said, "if you can't come,
13:27 But A kept on pressing the king until he finally
13:28 A told his men, "Wait until Amnon gets drunk;
13:30 "A has killed all your sons; not one is left alive!"
13:32 A has been plotting this ever since Amnon raped
13:34 Meanwhile A escaped. Then the watchman on the
13:37 A fled to his grandfather, Talmai son of Ammihud,
13:39 longed to be reunited with his son A.
14: 1 Joab realized how much the king longed to see A.
14:21 "All right, go and bring back the young man A."
14:23 went to Geshur and brought A back to Jerusalem.
14:24 "A may go to his own house, but he must never
14:24 into my presence." So A did not see the king.
14:25 Now no one in Israel was as handsome as A.
14:28 A lived in Jerusalem for two years without getting
14:29 Then A sent for Joab to ask him to intercede for
14:29 A sent for him a second time, but again Joab
14:30 So A said to his servants, "Go and set fire to
14:30 So they set his field on fire, as A had commanded.
14:31 Then Joab came to A and demanded, "Why did
14:32 And A replied, "Because I wanted you to ask the
14:33 So Joab told the king what A had said. Then at last
14:33 and A came and bowed low before the king,
15: 1 After this, A bought a chariot and horses, and he
15: 2 A would ask where they were from, and they
15: 3 Then A would say, "You've really got a strong
15: 5 tried to bow before him, A wouldn't let them.
15: 6 A stole the hearts of all the people of Israel.
15: 7 After four years, A said to the king, "Let me go to
15: 9 and fulfill your vow." So A went to Hebron.
15:10 "you will know that A has been crowned king in
15:12 Soon many others also joined A,
15:13 "All Israel has joined A in a conspiracy against
15:19 Go on back with your men to King A, for you are a
15:31 that his adviser Ahithophel was now backing A,
15:31 let Ahithophel give A foolish advice!"
15:34 Return to Jerusalem and tell A, 'I will now be your
15:37 to Jerusalem, getting there just as A arrived.
16: 8 and now the LORD has given it to your son A.
16:15 Meanwhile, A and his men arrived at Jerusalem,
16:16 the Arkite arrived, he went immediately to see A.
16:17 A asked him. "Why aren't you with him?"
16:20 Then A turned to Ahithophel and asked him,
16:22 and A went into the tent to sleep with his father's
16:23 A followed Ahithophel's advice, just as David had
17: 1 Now Ahithophel urged A, "Let me choose twelve
17: 4 This plan seemed good to A and to all the other
17: 5 But then A said, "Bring in Hushai the Arkite.
17: 6 A told him what Ahithophel had said.
17:14 Then A and all the leaders of Israel said,
17:14 better plan, so that he could bring disaster upon A!
17:18 En-rogel to go to David, and he told A about it.
17:23 Ahithophel was publicly disgraced when A refused
17:24 A had mobilized the entire army of Israel and was
17:25 A had appointed Amasa as commander of his
17:26 A and the Israelite army set up camp in the land of
18: 5 "For my sake, deal gently with young A."
18: 9 A came unexpectedly upon some of David's men.
18:10 and told Joab, "I saw A dangling in a tree."
18:12 'For my sake, please don't harm young A.'
18:15 armor bearers then surrounded A and killed him.
18:18 A had built a monument to himself in the King's
18:19 the LORD has saved him from his enemy A."
18:29 "What about young A?" the king demanded.
18:32 "What about young A?" the king demanded.
18:33 he cried, "O my son A! My son, my son A!
18:33 have died instead of you! O A, my son, my son."
19: 1 that the king was weeping and mourning for A.
19: 4 weeping, "O my son A! O A, my son, my son!"
19: 6 If A had lived and all of us had died, you would be
19: 8 the Israelites who supported A had fled to their
19: 9 but A chased him out of the country.
19:10 Now A, whom we anointed to rule over us, is dead.
20: 6 Sheba is going to hurt us more than A did.
1Ki 1: 6 handsome man and had been born next after A.
2: 7 took care of me when I fled from your brother A.
2:28 Although he had not followed A earlier, Joab had
15: 2 His mother was Maacah, the daughter of A.
15:10 His grandmother was Maacah, the daughter of A.
1Ch 3: 2 The third was A, whose mother was Maacah,
2Ch 11:20 another cousin, Maacah, the daughter of A.
Ps 3: T regarding the time David fled from his son A.

ABSALOM'S (10) [ABSALOM]

2Sa 13: 4 told him, "I am in love with Tamar, A sister."
13:20 So Tamar lived as a desolate woman in A house.
13:23 when A sheep were being sheared at Baal-hazor
13:29 So at A signal they murdered Amnon.
17:20 When A men arrived, they asked her, "Have you
17:20 A men looked for them without success
18: 3 of us die—it will make no difference to A troops;
18:14 and plunged them into A heart as he dangled from
18:17 They threw A body into a deep pit in the forest
18:18 and it is known as A Monument to this day.

ABSENCE (1) [ABSENT]

2Ki 8: 6 of any crops that had been harvested during her a.

ABSENT (2) [ABSENCE]

Jdg 21: 8 "Was anyone a when we presented ourselves to
Isa 23:16 Long a from her lovers, she will take a harp,

ABSOLUTE (4) [ABSOLUTELY]

Ps 147: 5 How great is our Lord! His power is a!
Eze 43:12 And this is the basic law of the Temple: a holiness!
1Co 7: 6 only my suggestion. It's not meant to be an a rule.
1Ti 2: 7 this is the a truth—as a preacher and apostle to

ABSOLUTELY (10) [ABSOLUTE]

Dt 4:23 for the LORD your God has a forbidden this.
2Ki 14:26 in Israel, and how they had a no one to help them.
Job 9:30 and cleanse my hands with lye to make them a
15:15 Even the heavens cannot be a pure in his sight.
Jer 26:15 For it is a true that the LORD sent me to speak
Mk 5:42 walked around! Her parents were a overwhelmed.
Jn 5:30 And my judgment is a just, because it is according
Ac 3:10 often at the Beautiful Gate, they were a astounded!
Ro 4:21 He was a convinced that God was able to do
Gal 3:21 between God's law and God's promises? A not!

ABSOLVED (1)

Dt 21: 8 Then they will be a of the guilt of this person's

ABSORBED (1)

Job 14:22 They are a in their own pain and grief."

ABSTAIN (3)

Ex 19:15 And until then, a from having sexual intercourse."
Ac 15:20 and tell them to a from eating meat sacrificed to
15:29 You must a from eating food offered to idols,

ABSURD (1)

Ecc 5:10 How a to think that wealth brings true happiness!

ABUNDANCE (18) [ABUNDANT]

Ge 27:37 I have guaranteed him an a of grain and wine—
Dt 28:11 "The LORD will give you an a of good things in
33:15 and the a from the everlasting hills;
2Ch 29:35 There was an a of burnt offerings, along with the
Ne 9:25 and vineyards and olive groves and orchards in a.
9:36 to our ancestors! We are slaves among all this a!
Est 1: 7 and there was an a of royal wine, just as the king
Job 29: 6 In those days my cows produced milk in a, and my
36:31 acts he governs the people, giving them food in a.
Ps 36: 8 You feed them from the a of your own house,
65:11 even the hard pathways overflow with a.
66:12 But you brought us to a place of great a.
Isa 33:16 be supplied to them, and they will have water in a.
35: 2 there will be an a of flowers and singing and joy!
Jer 31:14 I will supply the priests with an a of offerings.
Zec 9:17 and women will thrive on the a of grain and new
Mt 13:12 be given, and they will have an a of knowledge.
25:29 even more will be given, and they will have an a.

ABUNDANT (18) [ABUNDANCE, ABUNDANTLY]

Ge 4:12 No longer will it yield a crops for you, no matter
Dt 8: 9 is as common as stone, and copper is a in the hills.
28:11 many children, numerous livestock, and a crops.
28:47 and enthusiasm for the a benefits you have
30: 9 and your fields will produce a harvests,
Job 20:17 He will never again enjoy a streams of olive oil
Ps 4: 7 than those who have a harvests of grain and wine.
65:10 the earth with showers / and bless its a crops.
68: 9 You sent a rain, O God, / to refresh the weary
72: 7 May there be a prosperity until the end of time.
72:16 May there be a crops throughout the land,
Isa 44: 3 For I will give you a water to quench your thirst
Eze 19:10 It had lush, green foliage / because of the a water.
31: 4 so a that there was enough for all the trees nearby.
31: 7 and beautiful, for its roots went deep into a water.
Mal 3:11 Your crops will be a, for I will guard them from
Jn 16:24 and you will receive, and you will have a joy.
Ro 5:20 God's wonderful kindness became more a.

ABUNDANTLY (1) [ABUNDANT]

Isa 55: 7 Yes, turn to our God, for he will a pardon.

ABUSE (5) [ABUSED, ABUSERS, ABUSIVE]

1Sa 17:26 and putting an end to his a of Israel?"
Jer 23:10 For the prophets do evil and a their power.
Mt 27:39 And the people passing by shouted a, shaking their
Mk 15:29 And the people passing by shouted a, shaking their
1Co 4:12 who curse us. We are patient with those who a us.

ABUSED (3) [ABUSE]

Jdg 19:25 The men of the town a her all night, taking turns
Job 31:21 If my arm has a an orphan because I thought I
Eze 34:22 and they will no longer be a and destroyed.

ABUSERS (1) [ABUSE]

1Co 6:10 thieves, greedy people, drunkards, a,

ABUSIVE (2) [ABUSE]

1Co 5:11 or is a, or a drunkard, or a swindler.
Eph 4:29 Don't use foul or a language. Let everything you

ACACIA (33) [ACACIAS]

Ex 25: 5 ram skins and fine goatskin leather; a wood;
25:10 "Make an Ark of a wood—a sacred chest 3-3/4
25:13 Make poles from a wood, and overlay them with
25:23 "Then make a table of a wood, 3 feet long,
25:28 Make these poles from a wood and overlay them
26:15 Tabernacle will consist of frames made of a wood.
26:26 "Make crossbars of a wood to run across the
26:32 gold hooks set into four posts made from a wood
26:37 gold hooks set into five posts made from a wood
27: 1 "Using a wood, make a square altar 7-1/2 feet
27: 6 For moving the altar, make poles from a wood,
30: 1 "Then make a small altar out of a wood for
30: 5 The poles are to be made of a wood and overlaid
35: 7 ram skins and fine goatskin leather; a wood;
35:24 the LORD. And those who had a wood brought it.
36:20 they made frames of a wood standing on end.
36:31 Then they made five crossbars from a wood to tie
36:36 to four gold hooks set into four posts of a wood.
37: 1 Next Bezalel made the Ark out of a wood. It was
37: 4 Then he made poles from a wood and overlaid
37:10 Then he made a table out of a wood, 3 feet long,
37:15 He made the carrying poles of a wood and overlaid
37:25 The incense altar was made of a wood. It was
37:28 The carrying poles were made of a wood and were
38: 1 animal sacrifices also was constructed of a wood.
38: 6 The carrying poles themselves were made of a
Nu 25: 1 While the Israelites were camped at A, some of the
Dt 10: 3 "So I made a chest of a wood and cut two stone
Jos 2: 1 sent out two spies from the Israelite camp at A.
3: 1 next morning Joshua and all the Israelites left A
Isa 41:19 cedar, a, myrtle, olive, cypress, fir, and pine—
Hos 5: 2 You have dug a deep pit to trap them at A.
Mic 6: 5 And remember your journey from A to Gilgal,

ACACIAS (1) [ACACIA]

Joel 3:18 LORD's Temple, watering the arid valley of a.

ACBOR (7)

Ge 36:38 Shaul died, Baal-hanan son of A became king.
2Ki 22:12 Ahikam son of Shaphan, A son of Micaiah,
22:14 So Hilkiah the priest, Ahikam, A, Shaphan,
1Ch 1:49 Shaul died, Baal-hanan son of A became king.
2Ch 34:20 Ahikam son of Shaphan, A son of Micaiah,
Jer 26:22 Then King Jehoiakim sent Elnathan son of A to
36:12 Elnathan son of A, Gemariah son of Shaphan,

ACCENT (2) [ACCENTED]

Jdg 18: 3 Noticing the young Levite's a, they took him aside
Mt 26:73 be one of them; we can tell by your Galilean a."

ACCENTED (1) [ACCENT]

SS 1:10 stately is your neck, a with a long string of jewels.

ACCEPT (101) [ACCEPTABLE, ACCEPTANCE, ACCEPTED, ACCEPTING, ACCEPTS]

Ge 4: 5 but he did not a Cain's. This made Cain very angry
14:24 All I'll a is what these young men of mine have
33:10 "No, please a them," Jacob said, "for what a
Ex 2:21 Moses was happy to a the invitation, and he settled
3:18 "The leaders of the people of Israel will a your
21:30 the dead person's relatives may a a payment from
22:11 The owner must a the neighbor's word, and no
22:16 pay the customary dowry and a her as his wife.
25: 3 Here is a list of items you may a on my behalf:
28:38 always wear it so the LORD will a the people.
34: 9 our sins. A us as your own special possession."
34:16 And you will a their daughters, who worship other
Lev 1: 4 its head so the LORD will a it as your substitute,
19: 7 it will be contaminated, and I will not a it.

22:25 You must never **a** mutilated or defective animals
Nu 16:15 and said to the LORD, "Do not **a** their offerings!
30: 8 But if her husband refuses to **a** her vow
30:12 But if her husband refuses to **a** it on the day he
32:30 then they must **a** land with the rest of you in the
35:31 you must never **a** a ransom payment for the life of
35:32 And never **a** a ransom payment from someone who
Dt 16:19 Never **a** a bribe, for bribes blind the eyes of the
20:11 If they **a** your terms and open the gates to you,
24:17 and you must never **a** a widow's garment in pledge
33: 3 They follow in your steps / and **a** your instruction.
33:11 the Levites, O LORD, / and **a** all their work.
Jos 2:21 "I **a** your terms," she replied. And she sent them
1Sa 10: 4 offer you two of the loaves, which you are to **a**.
18:22 Why don't you **a** the king's offer and become his
18:26 David was delighted to **a** the offer. So before the
25:24 and said, "I **a** all blame in this matter, my lord.
26:19 you up against me, then let him **a** my offering.
2Sa 24:23 and may the LORD your God **a** your sacrifice."
2Ki 5:15 the world except in Israel. Now please **a** my gifts."
5:16 whom I serve, I will not **a** any gifts."
Ne 10:29 They vowed to **a** the curse of God if they failed to
Job 2:10 Should we **a** only good things from the hand of
42: 8 pray for you, and I will **a** his prayer on your behalf.
Ps 15: 5 and who refuse to **a** bribes to testify against the
51:16 I brought you a burnt offering, / you would not **a** it.
119:108 LORD, **a** my grateful thanks / and teach me your
141: 2 **A** my prayer as incense offered to you, / and my
Pr 10:17 People who **a** correction are on the pathway to life,
13:14 those who **a** it avoid the snares of death.
13:18 if you **a** criticism, you will be honored.
17:23 The wicked **a** secret bribes to pervert justice.
29: 1 Whoever stubbornly refuses to **a** criticism will
29:18 When people do not **a** divine guidance, they run
Ecc 5:19 To enjoy your work and **a** your lot in life—that is
Isa 29:24 and those who constantly complain will **a**
56: 7 I will **a** their burnt offerings and sacrifices,
Jer 6:20 I cannot **a** your burnt offerings.
14:10 Now I will no longer **a** you as my people.
14:12 and grain offerings to me, I will not **a** them.
25:28 And if they refuse to **a** the cup, tell them,
La 3:30 strike them. Let them **a** the insults of their enemies.
Eze 20:40 Israel will someday worship me, and I will **a** them.
24:17 or **a** any food brought to you by consoling
39:26 They will **a** responsibility for their past shame
43:27 Then I will **a** you, says the Sovereign LORD."
Am 5:22 I will not **a** your burnt offerings and grain
Zec 6:11 **A** their gifts and make a crown from the silver
Mal 1:10 "and I will not **a** your offerings.
1:13 Should I **a** from you such offerings as these?"
2:13 and he doesn't **a** them with pleasure.
3: 4 Then once more the LORD will **a** the offerings
Mt 10:10 Don't hesitate to **a** hospitality, because those who
11:14 And if you are willing to **a** what I say, he is Elijah,
13:22 represents those who hear and **a** the Good News,
13:23 the hearts of those who truly **a** God's message
18:17 but the other person won't **a** it, treat that person as
19:11 "Not everyone can **a** this statement," Jesus said.
19:12 of Heaven. Let anyone who can, **a** this statement."
27: 6 "since it's against the law to **a** money paid for
Mk 4:18 represents those who hear and **a** the Good News,
4:20 and **a** God's message and produce a huge harvest
Lk 1:17 and he will change disobedient minds to **a** a godly
1:38 and I am willing to **a** whatever he wants.
8:14 represents those who hear and **a** the message,
10: 7 Don't hesitate to **a** hospitality, because those who
Jn 5:43 even though you readily **a** others who represent
6:60 is very hard to understand. How can anyone **a** it?"
Ac 28:28 also available to the Gentiles, and they will **a** it."
Ro 11:12 the world will share when the Jews finally **a** it.
12: 1 be a living and holy sacrifice—the kind he will **a**.
14: 1 **A** Christians who are weak in faith, and don't
15: 7 So **a** each other just as Christ has accepted you;
15:31 be willing to **a** the donation I am bringing them.
1Co 6: 7 Why not just **a** the injustice and leave it at that?
7:17 You must **a** whatever situation the Lord has put
10:27 go ahead; **a** the invitation if you want to.
Gal 3: 8 to this time when God would **a** the Gentiles,
1Ti 4: 9 This is true, and everyone should **a** it.
Jas 1:21 and humbly **a** the message God has planted in your
1Pe 2:13 For the Lord's sake, **a** all authority—the king as
2:18 You who are slaves must **a** the authority of your
3: 1 you wives must **a** the authority of your husbands,
even those who refuse to **a** the Good News.
5: 5 You younger men, **a** the authority of the elders.
1Jn 1: 8 only fooling ourselves and refusing to **a** the truth.
3Jn 1: 7 and **a** nothing from those who are not Christians.

ACCEPTABLE (14) [ACCEPT]

Lev 22:27 it will be **a** as an offering given to the LORD by
27: 9 one that is **a** as an offering to the LORD—
27:11 one that is not **a** as an offering to the LORD—
Ezr 6:10 Then they will be able to offer **a** sacrifices to the
Isa 66: 3 an ox, it is no more **a** than a human sacrifice.
Mal 3: 3 so that they may once again offer **a** sacrifices to
Mk 7:19 he showed that every kind of food is **a**.)
Ac 10:15 "If God says something is **a**, don't say it isn't."
11: 9 'If God says something is **a**, don't say it isn't.'
1Co 1:30 He is the one who made us **a** to God. He made us
7:39 but this must be a marriage **a** to the Lord.
Gal 4:31 of the free woman, **a** to God because of our faith.
Php 4:18 They are a sweet-smelling sacrifice that is **a** to God
Heb 11: 4 It was by faith that Abel brought a more **a** offering

ACCEPTANCE (1) [ACCEPT]

Ro 11:15 how much more wonderful their **a** will be.

ACCEPTED (55) [ACCEPT]

Ge 4: 4 best of his flock. The LORD **a** Abel's offering,
4: 7 You will be **a** if you respond in the right way.
17:11 be a sign that you and they have **a** this covenant.
33:11 Jacob continued to insist, so Esau finally **a** them.
Lev 1: 3 of the Tabernacle so it will be **a** by the LORD.
7:18 on the third day, it will not be **a** by the LORD.
19: 5 offer it properly so it will be **a** on your behalf.
22:19 it will be **a** only if it is a male animal with no
22:20 because it won't be **a** on your behalf.
22:25 Such animals will not be **a** on your behalf
22:29 sacrificed properly so it will be **a** on your behalf.
23:11 before the LORD so it may be **a** on your behalf.
Nu 31:54 and Eleazar the priest **a** the gifts from the military
Jdg 13:23 he wouldn't have **a** our burnt offering and grain
1Sa 8: 3 for money. They **a** bribes and perverted justice.
25:35 Then David **a** her gifts and told her, "Return home
2Ch 25:16 you have done this and have not **a** my counsel."
Ezr 8:30 and the Levites **a** the task of transporting these
Est 2:15 she **a** the advice of Hegai, the eunuch in charge of
Job 33:26 When he prays to God, he will be **a**. And God will
42: 9 commanded them, and the LORD **a** Job's prayer.
Isa 56: 6 Sabbath day of rest, and who have **a** his covenant.
66: 3 their sins, are cursed. Their offerings will not be **a**.
Mt 28:15 So the guards **a** the bribe and said what they were
Lk 4:24 the truth is, no prophet is **a** in his own hometown.
7:36 so Jesus **a** the invitation and sat down to eat.
Jn 1:11 own land and among his own people, he was not **a**.
1:12 But to all who believed him and **a** him, he gave the
8:17 agree about something, their witness is **a** as fact.
17: 8 and they **a** them and know that I came from you,
Ac 5:40 The council **a** his advice. They called in the
8:14 that the people of Samaria had **a** God's message,
9:28 Then the apostles **a** Saul, and after that he was
12:23 because he **a** the people's worship instead of
16:14 opened her heart, and she **a** what Paul was saying.
Ro 3:27 that we have done anything to be **a** by God?
3:30 and there is only one way of being **a** by him.
4: 2 Was it because of his good deeds that God **a** him?
4:10 The answer is that God **a** him first, and then he
4:11 and that God had already **a** him and declared him
5:16 but we have the free gift of being **a** by God,
14: 3 not condemn those who do, for God has **a** them.
15: 7 So accept each other just as Christ has **a** you;
Gal 2: 9 and they **a** Barnabas and me as their co-workers.
2:16 that we might be **a** by God because of our faith in
Col 2: 6 And now, just as you **a** Christ Jesus as your Lord,
1Th 2:13 You **a** what we said as the very word of God—
2Th 3: 8 We never **a** food from anyone without paying for
Heb 10:34 you owned was taken from you, you **a** it with joy.
11: 4 God **a** Abel's offering to show that he was a
1Pe 1:22 your sins when you **a** the truth of the Good News.
3: 5 trusted God and **a** the authority of their husbands.
Rev 14:11 and his statue and have **a** the mark of his name.
19:20 miracles that deceived all who had **a** the mark of
20: 4 nor **a** his mark on their forehead or their hands.

ACCEPTING (5) [ACCEPT]

Nu 18:32 You will not be considered guilty for **a** the
2Ki 5:20 have let this Aramean get away without **a** his gifts.
Lk 10:16 "Anyone who accepts your message is also **a** me.
2Co 11: 8 I "robbed" other churches by **a** their contributions
Gal 3:18 then it would not be the result of **a** God's promise.

ACCEPTS (7) [ACCEPT]

Dt 27:25 'Cursed is anyone who **a** payment to kill an
Pr 13: 1 A wise child **a** a parent's discipline; a young
Lk 10:16 "Anyone who **a** your message is also accepting
Ac 10:35 In every nation he **a** those who fear him and do
15: 8 confirmed that he **a** Gentiles by giving them the
Heb 12: 6 and he punishes those he **a** as his children."
Rev 14: 9 or who **a** his mark on the forehead or the hand

ACCESS (2)

Jdg 3:23 the latrine and escaped through the sewage **a**.
Eze 28:14 You had **a** to the holy mountain of God

ACCESSORIES (8)

Ex 25:39 pounds of pure gold for the lampstand and its **a**.
30:27 the lampstand and all its **a**, the incense altar,
31: 8 the gold lampstand and all its **a**; the incense altar;
35:14 the lampstand and its **a**; the lamp cups and the oil
37:24 The entire lampstand, along with its **a**, was made
39:37 the gold lampstand and its **a**; the lamp cups
Nu 4:26 the necessary cords, and all the altar's **a**.
4:32 pegs, cords, **a**, and everything else related to their

ACCHO [KJV] See ACCO

ACCIDENT (3) [ACCIDENTAL, ACCIDENTALLY]

Ex 21:13 But if it is an **a** and God allows it to happen,
Dt 19: 6 no death sentence and the first death had been an **a**.
Jos 20: 6 high priest who was in office at the time of the **a**.

ACCIDENTAL (3) [ACCIDENT]

Jos 20: 4 the one who caused the **a** death will appear before
20: 5 release the accused to them, for the death was **a**.
20: 6 because the death was **a** must continue to live in

ACCIDENTALLY (10) [ACCIDENT]

Nu 35: 6 where a person who has **a** killed someone can flee
35:11 for people to flee to if they have killed someone **a**.
35:15 Anyone who **a** kills someone may flee there for
35:23 or **a** drops a stone on someone, though they were
Dt 4:42 where anyone who had **a** killed someone without
19: 4 "If someone **a** kills a neighbor without harboring
Jos 20: 9 Anyone who **a** killed another person could take
21:13 Hebron (a city of refuge for those who **a** killed
21:21 Shechem (a city of refuge for those who **a** killed
Mt 23:24 strain your water so you won't **a** swallow a gnat,

ACCO (1) [UMMAH]

Jdg 1:31 of Asher also failed to drive out the residents of **A**,

ACCOMPANIED (53) [ACCOMPANY]

Ge 31:27 with joyful singing **a** by tambourines and harps.
50: 9 number of chariots, cavalry, and people **a** Joseph.
50:14 and all who had **a** him to his father's funeral.
Lev 7:12 the usual animal sacrifice must be **a** by various
7:13 This peace offering of thanksgiving must also be **a**
Nu 22:39 Then Balaam **a** Balak to Kiriath-huzoth,
28: 9 They must be **a** by a grain offering of three quarts
28:12 These will be **a** by grain offerings of choice flour
28:20 These will be **a** by grain offerings of choice flour
28:28 These will be **a** by grain offerings of choice flour
29: 3 These must be **a** by grain offerings of choice flour
29: 9 These offerings must be **a** by the prescribed grain
29:14 Each of these offerings must be **a** by a grain
29:18 and lambs must be **a** by the prescribed grain
29:21 and lambs must be **a** by the prescribed grain
29:24 and lambs must be **a** by the prescribed grain
29:27 and lambs must be **a** by the prescribed grain
29:30 and lambs must be **a** by the prescribed grain
29:33 and lambs must be **a** by the prescribed grain
29:37 Each of these offerings must be **a** by the prescribed
Jos 8:10 and started toward Ai, **a** by the leaders of Israel.
Ru 1:22 **a** by her daughter-in-law Ruth, the young Moabite
1Sa 28: 8 the woman's home at night, **a** by two of his men.
2Sa 16:15 and his men arrived at Jerusalem, **a** by Ahithophel.
2Ch 5:13 **A** by trumpets, cymbals, and other instruments,
7: 6 They **a** the singing with music from the
29:27 **a** by the trumpets and other instruments of David,
30:21 priests sang to the LORD, **a** by loud instruments.
Ps 4: T A psalm of David, to be **a** by stringed instruments.
5: T A psalm of David, to be **a** by the flute.
6: T of David, to be **a** by an eight-stringed instrument.
8: T A psalm of David, to be **a** by a stringed instrument.
12: T of David, to be **a** by an eight-stringed instrument.
45:14 she is led to the king, / **a** by her bridesmaids.
54: T David is hiding." To be **a** by stringed instruments.
55: T A psalm of David, to be **a** by stringed instruments.
61: T A psalm of David, to be **a** by stringed instruments.
67: T A psalm, to be **a** by stringed instruments. A song.
76: T A psalm of Asaph, to be **a** by stringed instruments.
81: T psalm of Asaph, to be **a** by a stringed instrument.
84: T of Korah, to be **a** by a stringed instrument.
92: 3 **a** by the harp and lute / and the harmony of the
147: 7 the LORD; / sing praises to our God, **a** by harps.
149: 3 his name with dancing, / **a** by tambourine and harp.
Jer 41: 1 the royal family, arrived in Mizpah **a** by ten men.
Hab 3:19 This prayer is to be **a** by stringed instruments.)
Lk 22:39 Then, **a** by the disciples, Jesus left the upstairs
Ac 10:23 with them, **a** by some other believers from Joppa.
11:12 These six brothers here **a** me, and we soon arrived
15: 2 **a** by some local believers, to talk to the apostles
20:38 see him again. Then they **a** him down to the ship.
21:16 Some believers from Caesarea **a** us, and they took
25:23 **a** by military officers and prominent men of the

ACCOMPANIES (1) [ACCOMPANY]

Job 30:31 plays sad music, and my flute **a** those who weep.

ACCOMPANIMENT (3) [ACCOMPANY]

1Ch 15:16 and musicians to sing joyful songs to the **a** of lyres,
25: 1 and Jeduthun to proclaim God's messages to the **a**
25: 3 who proclaimed God's messages to the **a** of the

ACCOMPANY (8) [ACCOMPANIED, ACCOMPANIES, ACCOMPANIMENT, ACCOMPANYING]

Lev 23:13 A grain offering must **a** it consisting of three quarts
23:38 the offerings you make to **a** your vows, and any
Nu 15:11 "These are the instructions for what is to **a** each
1Ch 16:42 and other instruments to **a** the songs of praise to
Ezr 8:22 and horsemen to **a** us and protect us from enemies
Mk 16:17 These signs will **a** those who believe: They will
Jn 18: 3 of Roman soldiers and Temple guards to **a** him.
2Co 8:19 He was appointed by the churches to **a** us as we

ACCOMPANYING (14) [ACCOMPANY]

Lev 23:18 together with the **a** grain offerings and drink
Nu 15: 9 then the grain offering **a** it must include five quarts
28:10 daily burnt offering and its **a** drink offering.
28:15 daily burnt offering and its **a** drink offering.
28:31 regular daily burnt offering and its **a** grain offering.
29:11 with its grain offering, and their **a** drink offerings.
29:16 daily burnt offering with its **a** grain offering
29:19 daily burnt offering with its **a** grain offering
29:22 daily burnt offering with its **a** grain offering
29:25 daily burnt offering with its **a** grain offering
29:28 daily burnt offering with its **a** grain offering
29:31 daily burnt offering with its **a** grain offering
29:34 daily burnt offering with its **a** grain offering
29:38 daily burnt offering with its **a** grain offering

ACCOMPLISH (15) [ACCOMPLISHED, ACCOMPLISHES]

Ge 11: 6 "If they can **a** this when they have just begun to
24:12 Abraham. Help me to **a** the purpose of my journey.
Jos 11:18 waging war for a long time to **a** this.
2Ki 8:13 "How could a nobody like me ever **a** such a great
Job 35: 6 If you sin, what do you **a** against him? Even if you
Ecc 2:11 I looked at everything I had worked so hard to **a**,
4: 9 Two people can **a** more than twice as much as one;
Isa 10:12 After the Lord has used the king of Assyria to **a** his
55:11 It will **a** all I want it to, and it will prosper
Jer 48:30 "but her boasts are false; they **a** nothing.
Eze 25:14 By the hand of my people of Israel, I will **a** this.
Da 11: 3 a vast kingdom and **a** everything he sets out to do.
Mic 2: 1 any of the wicked schemes you have power to **a**.
Lk 13:32 and the third day I will **a** my purpose.
Eph 3:20 he is able to **a** infinitely more than we would ever

ACCOMPLISHED (15) [ACCOMPLISH]

Dt 12: 7 and you will rejoice in all you have **a**
Jdg 15:18 "You have **a** this great victory by the strength of
1Ch 25: 7 and each of them—288 in all—was an **a** musician.
2Ch 29:36 the people, for everything had been **a** so quickly.
Job 22:28 Whatever you decide to do will be **a**, and light will
Isa 25: 1 planned them long ago, and now you have **a** them.
26:12 us peace, / for all we have **a** is really from you.
53:11 When he sees all that is **a** by his anguish, he will
Da 9:26 One will be killed, appearing to have **a** nothing,
Lk 12:50 of me, and I am under a heavy burden until it is **a**.
Ac 21:19 had **a** among the Gentiles through his ministry.
Ro 1:17 This is **a** from start to finish by faith.
8: 4 so that the requirement of the law would be fully **a**
10: 4 For Christ has **a** the whole purpose of the law.
1Co 4: 7 why boast as though you have **a** something on your

ACCOMPLISHES (1) [ACCOMPLISH]

Jn 6:63 who gives eternal life. Human effort **a** nothing.

ACCORDANCE (3) [ACCORDING]

Jos 14: 2 in **a** with the LORD's command through Moses.
14: 5 So the distribution of the land was in strict **a** with
Ac 7:44 It was constructed in exact **a** with the plan shown

ACCORDING (87) [ACCORDANCE]

Ge 10:20 identified **a** to their tribes, languages, territories,
10:31 identified **a** to their tribes, languages, territories,
10:32 listed nation by nation **a** to their lines of descent.
25:16 listed **a** to the places they settled and camped.
Ex 6:16 of Levi, listed **a** to their family groups.
6:19 clans of the Levites, listed **a** to their genealogies.
6:25 of the Levite clans, listed **a** to their family groups.
16:21 morning by morning, each family **a** to its need.
21:23 then the offender must be punished **a** to the injury.
25: 9 and its furnishings exactly **a** to the plans I will
25:40 "Be sure that you make everything **a** to the pattern
26:30 "Set up this Tabernacle **a** to the design you were
Lev 24:19 person must be dealt with **a** to the injury inflicted
Nu 1:18 All the people were registered **a** to their ancestry
1:20[-21] each listed **a** to his own clan and family:
1:44 of Israel, all listed **a** to their ancestral descent.
3:20 the Levite clans, listed **a** to their family groups.
7: 5 Distribute them among the Levites **a** to the work
8: 4 It was built **a** to the exact design the LORD had
26:57 for the Levites who were counted **a** to their clans:
28: 2 appointed times and offered **a** to my instructions.
Dt 10:12 to live **a** to his will, to love and worship him with
16:17 **a** to the blessings given to them by the LORD
32: 8 of the peoples / **a** to the number of angelic beings.
Jos 8:33 This was all done **a** to the instructions Moses,
22: 9 the territory that belonged to them **a** to the
2Sa 7:21 For the sake of your promise and **a** to your will,
1Ki 16:34 This all happened **a** to the message from the
2Ki 24: 3 These disasters happened to Judah **a** to the
1Ch 6:19 the Levite clans, listed **a** to their ancestral descent:
7: 9 **A** to their family genealogy, there were 20,200
17:19 For my sake, O LORD, and **a** to your will,
23:27 It was **a** to David's final instructions that all the
24: 3 David divided Aaron's descendants into groups **a**
24:19 **a** to the procedures established by their ancestor
26:31 who was the leader of the Hebronites **a** to the
2Ch 4: 7 then cast ten gold lampstands **a** to the
8:13 The number of sacrifices varied from day to day **a**
17:14 His army was enrolled **a** to ancestral clans.
24:13 They restored the Temple of God **a** to its original
30:16 They took their places at the Temple **a** to the
31:17 or older who were listed **a** to their jobs and their
35: 4 Report for duty **a** to the family divisions of your
35:10 organized by their divisions, **a** to the king's orders.
35:12 so they could offer them to the LORD **a** to the
35:26 and his acts of devotion done **a** to the written law
Ne 6: 6 the wall. **A** to his reports, you plan to be their king
13:22 Have compassion on me **a** to your great
Job 34:11 He repays people **a** to their deeds. He treats people
a to their ways.
Ps 26: 3 unfailing love, / and I have lived **a** to your truth.
62:12 you judge all people / **a** to what they have done.
81:12 and stubborn way, / living **a** to their own desires.
86:11 O LORD, / that I may live **a** to your truth!
Pr 24:12 And he will judge all people **a** to what they have
Isa 14:24 have planned. It will come about **a** to my purposes.
63: 7 which he has granted **a** to his mercy and love.
Jer 17:10 their due rewards, **a** to what their actions deserve."
32:19 all people, and you reward them **a** to their deeds.
La 3:32 he also shows compassion **a** to the greatness of his
Eze 18:30 each of you, O people of Israel, **a** to your actions,
33:20 But I will judge each of you **a** to your deeds."
Da 6:15 "Your Majesty knows that **a** to the law of the
Mt 16:27 and will judge all people **a** to their deeds.
Lk 2:24 So they offered a sacrifice **a** to what was required
Jn 5:30 because it is **a** to the will of God who sent me;
Ac 4:28 everything they did occurred **a** to your eternal will
13:36 for after David had served his generation **a** to the
18:18 Paul had shaved his head **a** to Jewish custom,
Ro 2: 6 will judge all people **a** to what they have done.
8:28 love God and are called **a** to his purpose for them.
9:11 (This message proves that God chooses **a** to his
9:12 not **a** to our good or bad works.) She was told,
1Co 3: 8 rewarded individually, **a** to their own hard work.
8: 5 **A** to some people, there are many so-called gods
2Co 8:11 Give whatever you can **a** to what you have.
Gal 5:16 So I advise you to live **a** to your new life in the
Eph 1: 9 designed long ago **a** to his good pleasure.
4: 7 he has given each one of us a special gift **a** to the
Heb 8: 5 "Be sure that you make everything **a** to the design
9:22 In fact, we can say that **a** to the law of Moses,
1Pe 1:17 He will judge or reward you **a** to what you do.
4:19 So if you are suffering **a** to God's will, keep on
Rev 20:12 And the dead were judged **a** to the things written
in the books, **a** to what they had done.
20:13 in them. They were all judged **a** to their deeds.
22:12 my reward is with me, to repay all **a** to their deeds.

ACCOUNT (23) [ACCOUNTABLE, ACCOUNTED, ACCOUNTING, ACCOUNTS]

Ge 2: 4 This is the **a** of the creation of the heavens
Ex 32:34 But when I call the people to **a**, I will certainly
Dt 31:18 At that time I will hide my face from them on **a** of
1Ki 9:15 This is the **a** of the forced labor that Solomon
2Ki 4:24 Don't slow down on my **a** unless I tell you to."
22: 7 supervisors to keep **a** of the money they receive,
2Ch 33:19 the **a** of the way God answered him,
33:19 and an **a** of all his sins and unfaithfulness are
Est 6: 2 In those records he discovered an **a** of how
10: 2 and the full **a** of the greatness of Mordecai,
Ps 10:13 can they think, "God will never call us to **a**"?
Ecc 11: 9 But remember that you must give an **a** to God for
Eze 7: 3 I will call you to **a** for all your disgusting behavior.
12:19 because their land will be stripped bare on **a** of
16:14 Your fame soon spread throughout the world on **a**
Hos 2: 2 "But now, call Israel to **a**, for she is no longer my
8:13 I will call my people to **a** for their sins, and I will
Mt 12:36 that you must give an **a** on judgment day of every
25:19 and called them to give an **a** of how they had used
Jn 19:35 report is from an eyewitness giving an accurate **a**;
21:24 And we all know that his **a** of these things is
Ac 21:19 Paul gave a detailed **a** of the things God had
Ro 14:12 each of us will have to give a personal **a** to God.

ACCOUNTABLE (8) [ACCOUNT]

Nu 5:31 but his wife will be held **a** for her sin.' "
Jos 24:22 "You are **a** for this decision," Joshua said.
24:22 the LORD." "Yes," they replied, "we are **a**."
2Ch 24:22 see what they are doing and hold them **a**!"
Isa 47: 8 You say, 'I'm self-sufficient and not **a** to anyone!
47:10 'I am self-sufficient and not **a** to anyone!'
Eze 33: 6 die in their sins, but I will hold the watchman **a**.
Heb 13:17 over your souls, and they know they are **a** to God.

ACCOUNTED (2) [ACCOUNT]

Nu 31:49 we have **a** for all the men who went out to battle
Ezr 8:34 Everything was **a** for by number and weight,

ACCOUNTING (2) [ACCOUNT]

2Ki 12:15 No **a** was required from the construction
Job 14: 3 on such a frail creature and demand an **a** from me?

ACCOUNTS (5) [ACCOUNT]

1Sa 15: 2 'I have decided to settle **a** with the nation of
1Ch 29:30 These **a** include the mighty deeds of his reign
Mt 18:23 **a** up to date with servants who had borrowed
Lk 1: 1 Many people have written **a** about the events that
1: 3 Having carefully investigated all of these **a** from

ACCUMULATE (1) [ACCUMULATED]

Dt 17:17 And he must not **a** vast amounts of wealth in silver

ACCUMULATED (2) [ACCUMULATE]

Mt 23:36 all the **a** judgment of the centuries will break upon
Jas 5: 3 This treasure you have **a** will stand as evidence

ACCURACY (1) [ACCURATE]

Ac 18:25 to others with great enthusiasm and **a** about Jesus.

ACCURATE (6) [ACCURACY, ACCURATELY]

Lev 19:36 Your scales and weights must be **a**.
19:36 for measuring dry goods or liquids must be **a**.
Dt 25:13 "You must use **a** scales when you weigh out
Pr 22:21 and bring an **a** report to those who sent you.
Jn 19:35 This report is from an eyewitness giving an **a**
21:24 we all know that his account of these things is **a**.

ACCURATELY (1) [ACCURATE]

Ac 18:26 him aside and explained the way of God more **a**.

ACCUSATION (3) [ACCUSE]

Ezr 4: 6 the enemies of Judah wrote him a letter of **a**
Job 31:36 I would face the **a** proudly. I would treasure it like
Ac 7:54 The Jewish leaders were infuriated by Stephen's **a**,

ACCUSATIONS (19) [ACCUSE]

Dt 22:20 "But suppose the man's **a** are true, and her
Job 13:26 "You write bitter **a** against me and bring up all the
Ps 4: 2 How long will you make these groundless **a**?
Pr 3:30 Don't make **a** against someone who hasn't
Isa 58: 9 oppressing the helpless and stop making false **a**
Jer 26:11 and prophets presented their **a** to the officials
Mic 1: 2 The Sovereign LORD has made **a** against you;
Zec 3: 2 said to Satan, "I, the LORD, reject your **a**, Satan.
Mt 27:12 and other leaders made their **a** against him,
Lk 23:10 of religious law stood there shouting their **a**.
Ac 7: 1 the high priest asked Stephen, "Are these **a** true?"
21:30 population of the city was rocked by these **a**,
24: 8 You can find out the truth of our **a** by examining
25: 2 met with him and made their **a** against Paul.
25: 5 has done anything wrong, you can make your **a**."
25: 7 and made many serious **a** they couldn't prove.
25:18 But the **a** made against him weren't at all what I
26: 2 against all these **a** made by the Jewish leaders,
1Pe 2:15 silence those who make foolish **a** against you.

ACCUSE (27) [ACCUSATION, ACCUSATIONS, ACCUSED, ACCUSER, ACCUSERS, ACCUSES, ACCUSING]

Ge 44: 7 think we are, that you **a** us of such a terrible thing?
1Sa 12: 5 "that you can never **a** me of robbing you."
22:15 Please don't **a** me and my family in this matter,
1Ki 21:10 Find two scoundrels who will **a** him of cursing
Ne 6:13 Then they would be able to **a** and discredit me.
Ps 27:12 For they **a** me of things I've never done
31:18 those proud and arrogant lips that **a** the godly.
35:11 They **a** me of things I don't even know about.
71:13 Bring disgrace and destruction on those who **a** me.
103: 9 He will not constantly **a** us, / nor remain angry
Pr 25:10 or others may **a** you of gossip. Then you will never
Jer 2:29 Why do you **a** me of doing wrong? You are the
Eze 22: 9 People **a** others falsely and send them to their
23:36 you must **a** Oholah and Oholibah of all their awful
Zep 3: 8 soon when I will stand up and **a** these evil nations.
Mt 22:15 into saying something for which they could **a** him.
Lk 3:14 and don't **a** people of things you know they didn't
Jn 5:45 "Yet it is not I who will **a** you of this before the
5:45 Moses will **a** you! Yes, Moses, on whom you set
7: 7 but it does hate me because I **a** it of sin and evil.
8:46 Which of you can truthfully **a** me of sin?
Ac 24:13 These men certainly cannot prove the things they **a**
Ro 2:15 for their own consciences either **a** them or tell
8:33 Who dares **a** us whom God has chosen for his
1Ti 5:19 unless there are two or three witnesses to **a** him.
1Pe 2:12 Even if they **a** you of doing wrong, they will see
Jude 1: 9 did not dare **a** Satan of blasphemy, but simply said,

ACCUSED (19) [ACCUSE]

Ge 12:18 So Pharaoh called for Abram and **a** him sharply.
Dt 19:17 the accuser and **a** must appear before the priests
19:19 will receive the punishment intended for the **a**.
22:17 He has **a** her of shameful things, claiming that she
22:19 pieces of silver, for he falsely **a** a virgin of Israel.
Jos 20: 4 They must allow the **a** to enter the city and live
20: 5 the leaders must not release the **a** to them,
2Sa 3: 7 **a** Abner of sleeping with one of his father's
1Ki 8:32 between your servants—the accuser and the **a**.
21:13 Then two scoundrels **a** him before all the people of
2Ch 6:23 between your servants—the accuser and the **a**.
Job 6:14 but you have **a** me without the slightest fear of the
Da 6:24 to arrest the men who had maliciously **a** Daniel.
Mk 13: 9 You will be **a** before governors and kings of being
15: 3 Then the leading priests **a** him of many crimes,
Lk 21:12 and you will be **a** before kings and governors of
Ac 18:13 They **a** Paul of "persuading people to worship
Php 3: 6 so carefully that I was never **a** of any fault.
Rev 12:10 the one who **a** our brothers and sisters before our

ACCUSER (11) [ACCUSE]

Dt 19:17 then both the **a** and accused must appear before the
19:18 and if the **a** is found to be lying,
19:19 the **a** will receive the punishment intended for the
1Ki 8:32 between your servants—the **a** and the accused.
2Ch 6:23 between your servants—the **a** and the accused.
Job 1: 6 the LORD, and Satan the **A** came with them.
2: 1 the LORD, and Satan the **A** came with them.
31:35 Let my **a** write out the charges against me.
Ps 109: 6 to turn on him. / Send an **a** to bring him to trial.
Lk 12:58 If you are on the way to court and you meet your **a**,
Rev 12:10 For the **A** has been thrown down to earth—the one

ACCUSERS (13) [ACCUSE]

2Sa 22:44 "You gave me victory over my **a**. / You preserved
Ps 18:43 You gave me victory over my **a**. / You appointed
109:20 curses become the LORD's punishment for my **a**
109:29 obvious to all; / clothe my **a** with disgrace.
127: 5 to shame when he confronts his **a** at the city gates.
Jn 8: 9 When the **a** heard this, they slipped away one by
8:10 stood up again and said to her, "Where are your **a**?
18:28 His **a** didn't go in themselves because it would
Ac 18:14 Gallio turned to Paul's **a** and said, "Listen,
23:30 I have told his **a** to bring their charges before
23:35 "I will hear your case myself when your **a** arrive,"

24:18 My a saw me in the Temple as I was completing a
25:16 to defend themselves face to face with their a.

ACCUSES (4) [ACCUSE]
Dt 19:16 witness comes forward and a someone of a crime,
22:14 and falsely a her of having slept with another man.
Job 22: 4 Is it because of your reverence for him that he a
31:38 "If my land a me and all its furrows weep

ACCUSING (6) [ACCUSE]
Ps 31:20 shelter them in your presence, / far from a tongues.
Jer 2: 9 bring my case against you and will keep on a you,
Da 6: 5 "Our only chance of finding grounds for a Daniel
Zec 3: 1 at the angel's right hand, a Jeshua of many things.
Mt 23:31 you are a yourselves of being the descendants of
Lk 23:14 brought this man to me, a him of leading a revolt.

ACCUSTOMED (2) [CUSTOM]
Hos 10:11 "Israel is like a trained heifer a to treading out the
1Co 8: 7 Some are a to thinking of idols as being real,

ACELDAMA [KJV] See AKELDAMA

ACHAIA (4)
Ac 18:12 But when Gallio became governor of A, some Jews
18:27 Apollos had been thinking about going to A,
18:27 They wrote to the believers in A, asking them to
19:21 to Macedonia and A before returning to Jerusalem.

ACHAICUS (1)
1Co 16:17 that Stephanas, Fortunatus, and A have come here.

ACHAN (12)
Jos 7: 1 A man named A had stolen some of these things,
7: 1 A was the son of Carmi, of the family of Zimri,
7:18 forward person by person, and A was singled out.
7:19 Then Joshua said to A, "My son, give glory to the
7:20 A replied, "I have sinned against the LORD,
7:22 just as A had said, with the silver buried beneath
7:24 Then Joshua and all the Israelites took A,
7:25 Then Joshua said to A, "Why have you brought
7:25 And all the Israelites stoned A and his family
7:26 They piled a great heap of stones over A,
22:20 Didn't God punish all the people of Israel when A,
1Ch 2: 7 A son of Carmi, one of Zerah's descendants,

ACHAZ [KJV] See AHAZ

ACHE (1) [ACHES, ACHING, TOOTHACHE]
2Co 6:10 Our hearts a, but we always have joy. We are poor,

ACHES (1) [ACHE]
Isa 21: 3 My stomach a and burns with pain. Sharp pangs of

ACHIEVED (5) [ACHIEVEMENTS]
Pr 5: 9 to merciless people everything you have a in life.
Ecc 5: 6 and he might wipe out everything you have a.
Mt 5:18 of God's law will remain until its purpose is a.
Php 3:12 I don't mean to say that I have already a these
Heb 7:11 if the priesthood of Levi could have a God's

ACHIEVEMENTS (6) [ACHIEVED]
1Ki 10: 6 "Everything I heard in my country about your a
2Ki 10:34 and a are recorded in *The Book of the History of*
2Ch 9: 5 "Everything I heard in my country about your a
Est 10: 2 His great a and the full account of the greatness of
2Co 11:18 And since others boast about their human a,
Jas 1:11 wealthy people will fade away with all of their a.

ACHING (1) [ACHE]
Job 33:19 and pain, with ceaseless a in their bones.

ACHISH (16) [ACHISH'S]
1Sa 21:10 escaped from Saul and went to King A of Gath.
21:12 and was afraid of what King A might do to him.
21:14 Finally, King A said to his men, "Must you bring
27: 2 to live at Gath under the protection of King A.
27: 5 One day David said to A, "If it is all right with
27: 6 So A gave him the town of Ziklag (which still
27: 9 and clothing before returning home to see King A.
27:10 A would ask. And David would reply,
27:12 A believed David and thought to himself,
28: 1 King A told David, "You and your men will be
28: 2 Then A told David, "I will make you my personal
29: 2 and his men marched at the rear with King A.
29: 3 And A told them, "This is David, the man who ran
29: 6 So A finally summoned David and his men.
29: 9 But A insisted, "As far as I'm concerned,
1Ki 2:39 two of Shimei's slaves escaped to King A of Gath.

ACHISH'S (1) [ACHISH]
1Sa 21:11 But A officers weren't happy about his being there.

ACHMETHA [KJV] See ECBATANA

ACHOR (3)
Jos 7:24 he had, and they brought them to the valley of A.
15: 7 From that point it went through the valley of A to
Isa 65:10 and the valley of A will be a place to pasture herds.

ACHSA [KJV] See ACSAH

ACKNOWLEDGE (16) [ACKNOWLEDGED, ACKNOWLEDGES]
Dt 26: 3 'With this gift I a that the LORD your God has
Jdg 2:10 another generation grew up who did not a the
Job 24:13 They refuse to a its ways. They will not stay in its
31:34 so that I refused to a my sin and would not go
Ps 22:27 The whole earth will a the LORD and return to
100: 3 A that the LORD is God! / He made us, and we
Pr 14: 9 of guilt, but the godly a it and seek reconciliation.
Isa 33:13 far away! And you that are near, a my might!"
Jer 3:13 Only a your guilt. Admit that you rebelled against
13:16 A him before he brings darkness upon you,
Mt 10:32 I will openly a that person before my Father in
Lk 12: 8 will openly a that person in the presence of God's
Ro 1:28 When they refused to a God, he abandoned them
1Jn 4: 3 If a prophet does not a Jesus, that person is not
3Jn 1: 9 loves to be the leader, does not a our authority.
Rev 3: 9 your feet. They will a that you are the ones I love.

ACKNOWLEDGED (1) [ACKNOWLEDGE]
Ezr 10:19 and they each a their guilt by offering a ram as a

ACKNOWLEDGES (3) [ACKNOWLEDGE]
Mt 10:32 "If anyone a me publicly here on earth, I will
Lk 12: 8 If anyone a me publicly here on earth, I, the Son of
1Jn 4: 2 If a prophet a that Jesus Christ became a human

ACQUAINTED (5)
Job 24:16 sleep in the daytime. They are not a with the light.
Isa 53: 3 a man of sorrows, a with bitterest grief.
Jn 18:15 That other disciple was a with the high priest,
Ac 18: 2 There he became a with a Jew named Aquila,
28:20 you to come here today so we could get a and

ACQUIRE (3) [ACQUIRED]
Ge 34:10 with us. You are free to a property among us."
Ne 5:16 to working on the wall and refused to a any land.
Pr 19: 8 To a wisdom is to love oneself; people who

ACQUIRED (9) [ACQUIRE]
Ge 26:14 He a large flocks of sheep and goats, great herds of
31:18 all the livestock he had a at Paddan-aram—
46: 6 and all the belongings they had a in the land of
Dt 3:14 a the whole Argob region in Bashan all the way to
Ru 4:10 And with the land I have a Ruth, the Moabite
1Ki 10:28 the king's traders a them from Cilicia at the
2Ch 1:16 the king's traders a them from Cilicia at the
32:29 He built many towns and a vast flocks and herds,
Mic 4:13 Then you will give all the wealth they a as

ACQUIT (3) [ACQUITTAL, ACQUITTED]
1Ki 8:32 the guilty party and a the one who is innocent.
2Ch 6:23 the guilty party, and a the one who is innocent.
Pr 17:15 The LORD despises those who a the guilty

ACQUITTAL (1) [ACQUIT]
Ro 3:27 because our a is not based on our good deeds.

ACQUITTED (1) [ACQUIT]
Job 23: 7 can reason with him, so I would be a by my Judge.

ACRE (1) [ACRES]
1Sa 14:14 their bodies were scattered over about half an a.

ACRES (1) [ACRE]
Isa 5:10 Ten a of vineyard will not produce even six

ACRID (1)
Isa 65: 5 in my nostrils, an a smell that never goes away.

ACROSS (184) [CROSS]
Ge 8: 1 He sent a wind to blow a the waters, and the floods
9:19 came all the people now scattered a the earth.
11: 9 many languages, thus scattering them a the earth.
19:28 He looked out a the plain to Sodom and Gomorrah
25:18 Ishmael's descendants were scattered a the country
32:22 and eleven sons a the Jabbok River.
Ex 8: 2 I will send vast hordes of frogs a your entire land
14: 9 the shore near Pi-hahiroth, a from Baal-zephon.
14:23 followed them a the bottom of the sea.
26:26 "Make crossbars of acacia wood to run a the
26:31 "A the inside of the Tabernacle hang a special
26:35 and lampstand a the room from each other outside
39:10 Four rows of gemstones were set a it. In the first
40:24 He set the lampstand in the Tabernacle a from the
Nu 4:26 and altar, the curtain a the courtyard entrance,
22: 1 camped east of the Jordan River, a from Jericho.
26: 3 of Moab beside the Jordan River, a from Jericho.
26:63 of Moab beside the Jordan River, a from Jericho.
31:12 of Moab beside the Jordan River, a from Jericho.
32: 5 instead of giving us land a the Jordan River."
32: 6 want to stay back here while your brothers go a
32: 7 going a to the land the LORD has given them?
33:48 of Moab beside the Jordan River, a from Jericho.
34:15 the east side of the Jordan River, a from Jericho."
35: 1 a from Jericho, the LORD said to Moses,
36:13 of Moab beside the Jordan River, a from Jericho.
Dt 2: 1 and set out a the wilderness toward the Red Sea,
3:20 your God is giving them a the Jordan River,
3:28 for he will lead the people a the Jordan.
32:49 and climb Mount Nebo, which is a from Jericho.
32:49 Look out a the land of Canaan, the land I am
33:26 He rides a the heavens to help you, / a the skies in majestic splendor.
34: 1 and climbed Pisgah Peak, which is a from Jericho.
Jos 1: 2 you must lead my people a the Jordan River into
1:14 must lead the other tribes a the Jordan to help them
3: 6 of the Covenant and lead the people a the river."
3:11 the whole earth, will lead you a the Jordan River!
4: 1 When all the people were safely a the river,
4: 7 when the Ark of the LORD's covenant went a.'
4:10 Meanwhile, the people hurried a the riverbed.
4:12 and the half-tribe of Manasseh led the Israelites a
4:23 your eyes, and he kept it dry until you were all a,
7: 7 why did you bring us a the Jordan River if you are
8:14 When the king of Ai saw the Israelites a the valley,
13:32 plains of Moab, a the Jordan River, east of Jericho.
15: 7 which is a from the slopes of Adummim on the
17: 5 the land of Gilead and Bashan a the Jordan River,
18:17 and on to Geliloth (which is a from the slopes of
19:33 and extended a to Adami-nekeb, Jabneel, and as
19:46 also Rakkon along with the territory a from Joppa.
20: 8 the east side of the Jordan River, a from Jericho,
Jdg 3:28 of the shallows of the Jordan River a from Moab,
5: 4 and marched a the fields of Edom, / the earth
11:26 spread a the land from Heshbon to Aroer and in all
12: 5 a fugitive from Ephraim tried to go back a,
16: 3 and carried them all the way to the top of the hill a
1Sa 5:11 and great fear was sweeping a the city.
14: 6 "Let's go a to see those pagans," Jonathan said to
17: 8 Goliath stood and shouted a to the Israelites,
17:40 and sling, he started a to fight Goliath.
30:16 the Amalekites were spread out a the fields,
2Sa 4: 7 they fled a the Jordan Valley through the night.
5:18 and spread out a the valley of Rephaim.
5:22 and again spread out a the valley of Rephaim.
17:16 He must go a at once into the wilderness beyond.
17:22 and all the people with him went a the Jordan
17:24 and was leading his troops a the Jordan River.
18: 8 The battle raged all a the countryside, and more
18:23 Then Ahimaaz took a shortcut a the plain of the
19:15 to Gilgal to meet him and escort him a the river.
19:16 hurried a with the men of Judah to welcome King
19:18 and worked hard ferrying the king's household a
19:31 from Rogelim to conduct the king a the Jordan.
19:33 "Come a with me and live in Jerusalem," the king
19:36 Just to go a the river with you is all the honor I
19:40 and half the army of Israel escorted him a the river.
20:14 Sheba had traveled a Israel to mobilize his own
1Ki 6: 3 running a the entire width of the Temple.
7:23 cast a large round tank, 15 feet a from rim to rim;
7:31 a round pedestal, and its opening was 2-1/4 feet a;
7:38 Each basin was 6 feet a and could hold 220 gallons
19:19 over to him and threw his cloak a his shoulders
22:24 walked up to Micaiah and slapped him a the face.
2Ki 2: 8 and the two of them went a on dry ground!
2:14 Then the river divided, and Elisha went a.
3:22 the sun was shining a the water, making it look as
19:24 rivers of Egypt / so that my armies could go a!"
25: 4 They made a dash a the fields, in the direction of
1Ch 1:10 who was known a the earth as a heroic warrior.
5:11 A from the Reubenites in the land of Bashan lived
2Ch 3: 4 running a the entire width of the Temple.
3:14 A the entrance of the Most Holy Place,
4: 2 cast a large round tank, 15 feet a from rim to rim;
18:23 walked up to Micaiah and slapped him a the face.
Est 5: 1 court of the palace, just a from the king's hall.
Job 1: 7 "I have been going back and forth a the earth,
2: 2 "I have been going back and forth a the earth,
8:16 the sunshine, its branches spreading a the garden.
15:29 and their possessions will no longer spread a the
37: 3 It rolls a the heavens, and his lightning flashes out
38:32 of the Bear with her cubs a the heavens?
Ps 44:15 shame is written a our faces.
66: 6 the Red Sea, / and his people went a on foot.
66:12 You sent troops to ride a our broken bodies.
68:33 Sing to the one who rides a the ancient heavens,
97: 4 His lightning flashes out a the world. / The earth
105:31 on the Egyptians, / and gnats swarmed a Egypt.
106: 9 He led Israel a the sea bottom that was as dry as a
147:14 He sends peace a your nation / and satisfies you
Ecc 8:16 I tried to observe everything that goes on all a the
SS 4: 1 like flocks of goats frisking a the slopes of Gilead.
6: 5 Your hair, as it falls a your face, is like a flock of
Isa 7:19 come in vast hordes, spreading a the whole land.
15: 7 they can carry and flee a the Ravine of Willows.
30: 6 Look at the animals moving slowly a the terrible
37:25 rivers of Egypt / so that my armies could go a!"
41:18 Rivers fed by springs will flow a the dry,
50: 3 I am the one who sends darkness out a the skies,
Jer 8:19 of my people; it can be heard all a the land.
9:22 "Bodies will be scattered a the fields like dung,
25:22 and Sidon, and the kings of the regions a the sea.
31:39 stretched out over the hill of Gareb and a to Goah.
46:12 Your mightiest warriors will stumble a each other
48:34 can be heard from Heshbon clear a to Elealeh
52: 7 They made a dash a the fields, in the direction of
Eze 5: 2 Scatter another third a your map and slash at it
31:12 Its branches were scattered a the mountains
32: 8 I will bring darkness everywhere a your land.
34: 6 the mountains and hills, a the face of the earth,
37: 2 They were scattered everywhere a the ground.
37: 7 I spoke, there was a rattling noise all a the valley.
40: 2 From there I could see what appeared to be a city a
40:19 Then the man measured a the Temple's outer

42: 3 built three levels high and stood a from each other.
47: 3 along the stream for 1,750 feet and told me to go a.
47: 4 off another 1,750 feet and told me to go a again.
48: 1 Dan's territory extends all the way a the land of
48:23 and it extends a the entire land of Israel from east
48:24 also extending a the land from east to west.
48:26 which also extends a the land from east to west.
Da 4:30 As he looked out a the city, he said, "Just look at
Joel 2: 2 Suddenly, like dawn spreading a the mountains,
2: 5 like the roar of a fire sweeping a a field,
Am 7:10 is intolerable. It will lead to rebellion all a the land.
9: 8 I will uproot it and scatter its people a the earth.
Ob 1:18 The fire will roar a the field, devouring everything
Na 3:18 Your people are scattered a the mountains.
Hab 1: 6 and violent nation who will march a the world
3: 3 moving a the deserts from Edom and Mount Paran.
3:12 You marched a the land in awesome anger
Zec 6: 7 eager to be off, to patrol back and forth a the earth.
14: 5 flee through this valley, for it will reach a to Azal.
Mt 8:23 the boat and started a the lake with his disciples.
9: 1 a boat and went back a the lake to his own town.
13: 4 As he scattered it a his field, some seeds fell on a
27:32 they came a a man named Simon, who was from
27:45 darkness fell a the whole land until three o'clock.
27:60 Then he rolled a great stone a the entrance as he
Mk 4: 4 As he scattered it a his field, some seed fell on a
5:21 When Jesus went back a to the other side of the
6:45 into the boat and head out a the lake to Bethsaida,
13: 3 Jesus sat on the slopes of the Mount of Olives a the
15:33 darkness fell a the whole land until three o'clock.
Lk 7:17 spread all over Judea and even out a its borders.
8: 5 As he scattered it a his field, some seed fell on a
8:23 On the way a, Jesus lay down for a nap, and while
8:26 the land of the Gerasenes, a the lake from Galilee.
17:24 It will be as evident as the lightning that flashes a
23:44 and darkness fell a the whole land until three
24:17 They stopped short, sadness written a their faces.
Jn 6:17 and headed out a the lake toward Capernaum.
6:22 The next morning, back a the lake, crowds began
6:24 and went a to Capernaum to look for him.
11:38 It was a cave with a stone rolled a its entrance.
Ac 5:15 so that Peter's shadow might fall a some of them
13: 6 Afterward they preached from town to town a the
16:11 and sailed straight a to the island of Samothrace,
27:17 The sailors were afraid of being driven a to the
27:27 as we were being driven a the Sea of Adria,
28:13 From there we sailed a to Rhegium. A day later a
Rev 1:13 He was wearing a long robe with a gold sash a his
12:10 Then I heard a loud voice shouting a the heavens,
15: 6 clothed in spotless white linen with gold belts a

ACSAH (7)

Jos 15:16 "I will give my daughter A in marriage to the one
15:17 one who conquered it, so A became Othniel's wife.
15:18 When A married Othniel, she urged him to ask her
Jdg 1:12 "I will give my daughter A in marriage to the one
1:13 one who conquered it, so A became Othniel's wife.
1:14 When A married Othniel, she urged him to ask her
1Ch 2:49 and Gibea). Caleb also had a daughter named A.

ACSHAPH (3)

Jos 11: 1 of Madon; the king of Shimron; the king of A;
12:20 The king of Shimron-meron / The king of A
19:25 included these towns: Helkath, Hali, Beten, A,

ACT (60) [ACTED, ACTING, ACTION, ACTIONS, ACTIVELY, ACTIVITIES, ACTIVITY, ACTS, ENACTED]

Ge 44: 4 'Why have you repaid an a of kindness with such
Ex 22: 2 "If a thief is caught in the a of breaking into a
Lev 18: 3 So do not a like the people in Egypt, where you
20:13 They have committed a detestable a and are guilty
20:14 and her mother, such an a is terribly wicked.
20:21 marries his brother's wife, it is an a of impurity.
20:27 "Men and women among you who a as mediums
Nu 5:13 is no witness since she was not caught in the a.
16: 3 What right do you have to a as though you are
23:19 Has he ever spoken and failed to a? / Has he ever
Dt 13:14 and can prove that such a detestable a has occurred
17:13 will hear about it and be afraid to a so arrogantly.
22:28 "If a man is caught in the a of raping a young
24:13 the LORD your God will count it as a righteous a.
32: 5 when they a like that, are they really his children?
2Sa 6:21 So I am willing to a like a fool in order to show my
14: 2 A like a woman who has been in deep sorrow for a
19: 5 Yet you a like this, making us feel ashamed,
1Ki 1:21 If you do not a, my son Solomon and I will be
2: 5 He pretended that it was an a of war, but it was
2Ch 19: 9 "You must always a in the fear of the LORD,
23: 1 Athaliah's reign, Jehoiada the priest decided to a.
24: 5 not delay!" But the Levites did not a right away.
Ezr 10:14 Let our leaders a on behalf of us all. Everyone who
Ne 5:15 because of my fear of God, I did not a that way.
7: 3 Appoint the residents of Jerusalem to a as guards,
Ps 2:10 Now then, you kings, a wisely! / Be warned,
36: 3 They refuse to a wisely or do what is good.
37: 7 of the LORD, / and wait patiently for him to a.
37:34 Don't be impatient for the LORD to a!
119:126 LORD, it is time for you to a, / for these evil
Pr 13:16 Wise people think before they a; fools don't
20:11 Even children are known by the way they a,
21:24 and haughty; they a with boundless arrogance.
Ecc 6: 8 and knowing how to a in front of others?
Isa 1:10 You a just like the rulers and people of Sodom
42:20 and understand what is right but refuse to a on it.
58: 2 Yet they a so pious! They come to the Temple
63:19 Why do you a as though we had never been known
Jer 10: 2 "Do not a like other nations who try to read their
17: 1 "My people a as though their evil ways are laws to
Da 9:19 hear. O Lord, forgive. O Lord, listen and a!
Hos 8:12 they a as if those laws don't apply to them.
12: 6 A on the principles of love and justice, and always
Zep 2: 2 A now, before the fierce fury of the LORD falls
Mal 3:17 "On the day when I a, they will be my own special
4: 3 On the day when I a, you will tread upon the
Mt 7:16 You can detect them by the way they a, just as you
Jn 8: 3 a woman they had caught in the a of adultery.
8: 4 "this woman was caught in the very a of adultery.
8:41 you are obeying your real father when you a that
Ro 5:18 but Christ's one a of righteousness makes all
12:16 Don't try to a important, but enjoy the company of
1Co 10:18 all who eat the sacrifices are united by that a.
2Co 6: 3 hindered from finding the Lord by the way we a,
10: 2 those who think we a from purely human motives.
12:11 You have made me a like a fool—boasting like
Eph 5:17 Don't a thoughtlessly, but try to understand what
2Ti 3: 5 They will a as if they are religious, but they will
Heb 2: 2 violation of the law and every a of disobedience.

ACTED (21) [ACT]

Ge 20: 5 he is my brother.' I a in complete innocence!"
31:28 tell them good-bye? You have a very foolishly!
Lev 20:12 They have a contrary to nature and are guilty of a
Dt 32: 5 "But they have a corruptly toward him;
Jdg 9:16 "Now make sure you have a honorably and in
9:19 If you have a honorably and in good faith toward
9:20 But if you have not a in good faith, then may fire
1Ki 8:47 'We have sinned, done evil, and a wickedly.'
1Ch 24: 6 a as secretary and wrote down the names
2Ch 6:37 'We have sinned, done evil, and a wickedly.'
Ps 26: 1 O LORD, / for I have a with integrity;
99: 4 have established fairness. / You have a with justice
106: 6 We have done wrong! We have a wickedly!
136:12 He a with a strong hand and powerful arm.
Eze 20: 9 do it, for I a to protect the honor of my name.
25:15 The people of Philistia have a against Judah out of
39:23 for sin, for they a in treachery against their God.
Ob 1:11 You a as though you were one of Israel's enemies.
Ac 17:14 The believers a at once, sending Paul on to the
2Co 1:12 That is how we have a toward everyone,
Gal 3:20 but God a on his own when he made his promise to

ACTING (15) [ACT]

Ge 34:19 and Shechem lost no time in a on this request,
Dt 17:20 and a as if he is above his fellow citizens.
1Sa 2: 3 "Stop a so proud and haughty! / Don't speak with
2Sa 11:11 I swear that I will never be guilty of a like that."
Ne 13:27 and a unfaithfully toward God by marrying foreign
Eze 5: 2 After a out the siege, burn it there. Scatter another
16:30 such things as these, a like a shameless prostitute.
18:24 turn to sinful ways and start a like other sinners,
Mt 5:45 you will be a as true children of your Father in
Lk 6:35 and you will truly be a as children of the Most
Ro 14:15 by what you eat, you are not a in love if you eat it.
14:23 They would be condemned for not a in faith before
1Co 3: 3 You are a like people who don't belong to the
3: 4 aren't you a like those who are not Christians?
2Co 11:17 something the Lord wants, but I am a like a fool.

ACTION (17) [ACT]

Jos 8: 4 in ambush close behind the city and be ready for a.
Ezr 10:15 Jahzeiah son of Tikvah opposed this course of a,
Est 3: 7 to determine the best day and month to take a.
Ps 36: 4 sinful plots. / Their course of a is never good.
107:24 They, too, observed the LORD's power in a,
Pr 2: 9 know how to find the right course of a every time.
Ecc 12:11 A wise teacher's words spur students to a
Isa 48: 3 Then suddenly I took a, and all my predictions
58: 2 to me and asking me to take a on their behalf.
Eze 33: 4 Then if those who hear the alarm refuse to take a—
38: 8 A long time from now you will be called into a.
Zec 2:13 for he is springing into a from his holy dwelling."
Mt 2:17 Herod's brutal a fulfilled the prophecy of
Ac 7:22 and he became mighty in both speech and a.
18:12 some Jews rose in concerted a against Paul
2Co 8: 5 for their first a was to dedicate themselves to the
Php 2:12 to put into a God's saving work in your lives,

ACTIONS (40) [ACT]

Ge 8:21 and a are bent toward evil from childhood.
Job 22: 2 "Can a person's a be of benefit to God? Can even
Ps 14: 1 They are corrupt, and their a are evil; / no one does
53: 1 They are corrupt, and their a are evil; / no one does
67: 4 and direct the a of the whole world. / *Interlude*
119: 5 Oh, that my a would consistently / reflect your
Pr 21: 4 Haughty eyes, a proud heart, and evil a are all sin.
Ecc 7:23 my best to let wisdom guide my thoughts and a.
9: 1 Even though the a of godly and wise people are in
Isa 43:13 can oppose what I do. No one can reverse my a."
45:13 my righteous purpose, and I will guide all his a.
47: 7 or think about the consequences of your a.
59: 5 energy spinning evil plans that end up in deadly a.
Jer 4:18 "Your own a have brought this upon you.
17:10 due rewards, according to what their a deserve."
44:25 of Heaven, and you have proved it by your a.
Eze 12: 6 All of these a will be a sign for the people of
12:10 These a contain a message for Zedekiah in
12:11 Then explain that your a are a demonstration of
18:30 of you, O people of Israel, according to your a,
20: 4 Make them realize how loathsome the a of their
21:24 whatever you do, all your a are filled with sin.
24:14 will be judged on the basis of all your wicked a,
37:18 When your people ask you what your a mean,
Hos 9:15 drive them from my land because of their evil a.
Am 6: 3 but your a only bring the day of judgment closer.
Zec 11:11 the LORD was speaking to them through my a.
Mal 1:12 "But you dishonor my name with your a.
Lk 10:29 The man wanted to justify his a, so he asked Jesus,
23:51 the decision and a of the other religious leaders.
Jn 3:19 darkness more than the light, for their a were evil.
Col 1:21 separated from him by your evil thoughts and a,
Jas 1:15 evil desires lead to evil a, and evil a lead to death.
2:14 you have faith if you don't prove it by your a?
2:22 faith was made complete by what he did—by his a.
2:25 She was made right with God by her a—when she
1Jn 3:18 we love each other; let us really show it by our a.
3:19 It is by our a that we know we are living in the
Rev 15: 3 "Great and marvelous are your a, / Lord God

ACTIVELY (1) [ACT]

Lk 22: 2 and teachers of religious law were a plotting

ACTIVITIES (8) [ACT]

Lev 18:27 "All these detestable a are practiced by the people
18:30 and do not practice any of these detestable a.
2Ch 27: 7 of Jotham's reign, including his wars and other a,
Ne 11:23 under royal orders, which determined their daily a.
La 3:63 In all their a, they constantly mock me with their
Eze 22: 9 and people who take part in lewd a.
Mk 4:27 and then he went on with his other a. As the days
Gal 5:20 idolatry, participation in demonic a, hostility,

ACTIVITY (3) [ACT]

Ecc 3: 1 for everything, / a season for every a under heaven.
8:16 I discovered that there is ceaseless a, day
Isa 59: 6 they do is productive; all their a is filled with sin.

ACTS (30) [ACT]

Ex 6: 6 you with mighty power and great a of judgment.
7: 4 the forces of Israel out with great a of judgment.
32:11 land of Egypt with such great power and mighty a?
Lev 20:13 "The penalty for homosexual a is death to both
Nu 33: 4 gods of Egypt that night with great a of judgment!
Dt 4:34 wonders, war, awesome power, and terrifying a?
12:31 These nations have committed many detestable a
32:16 they provoked his fury with detestable a.
34:12 and terrifying a in the sight of all Israel.
1Ki 11:41 are recorded in *The Book of the A of Solomon.*
2Ch 32:32 and his a of devotion are recorded in *The Vision*
35:26 and his a of devotion done according to the written
Job 36:31 By his mighty a he governs the people,
Ps 21:13 and singing we celebrate your mighty a.
22:31 His righteous a will be told to those yet unborn.
64: 9 stand in awe, / proclaiming the mighty a of God,
77: 2 pleading. / There can be no joy for me until he a.
103:12 He has removed our rebellious a / as far away from
106: 7 They soon forgot his many a of kindness to them.
107:22 and sing joyfully about his glorious a.
141: 4 don't let me participate in a of wickedness.
145: 4 each generation tell its children / of your mighty a.
Isa 52: 4 For the oppressive a of ruthless people are like a
Jer 23:11 I have seen their despicable a right here in my own
Eze 16:16 where you carried out your a of prostitution.
16:43 your disgusting sins, you have added these lewd a.
35:11 I will punish you for all your a of anger, envy,
Da 4:37 All his a are just and true, and he is able to humble
Mt 6: 2 and streets to call attention to their a of charity!
Rev 18: 9 rulers of the world who took part in her immoral a

ACTUALLY (25)

Ge 37:10 your brothers, and I a come and bow before you?"
38:29 and the other baby was a the first to be born.
Ex 37: 8 so they were a a part of the atonement cover—
Lev 25:16 the person selling the land is a selling you a certain
1Sa 23:11 And will Saul a come as I have heard? O LORD,
2Ki 8:10 But the LORD has shown me that he will a die!"
Ezr 9:13 But we have a been punished far less than we
Jer 11:15 their destruction? They a rejoice in doing evil!
Eze 22:27 They a destroy people's lives for profit!
Mt 12:30 and anyone who isn't working with me is a
Lk 11:23 and anyone who isn't working with me is a
Jn 7:22 (A, this tradition of circumcision is older than the
16: 7 But it is a best for you that I go away, because if I
17: 6 A, they were always yours, and you gave them to
Ac 1: 3 and proved to them in many ways that he was a
7:47 But it was Solomon who a built it.
Ro 3: 5 punish us?" (That is a the way some people talk.)
10:18 Have they a heard the message? Yes, they have:
1Co 2:12 And God has a given us his Spirit (not the world's
6:15 Don't you realize that your bodies are a parts of
2Co 12: 6 highly of me than what they can a see in my life
Gal 4: 1 even though they a own everything their father
Eph 5:28 For a man is a loving himself when he loves his
1Jn 1: 3 We are telling you about what we ourselves have a
5:10 Those who don't believe this are a calling God a

ACZIB (4)

Jos 15:44 Keilah, A, and Mareshah—nine towns with their
19:29 at Hosah. The territory also included Mehebel, A,
Jdg 1:31 Sidon, Ahlab, A, Helbah, Aphik, and Rehob.
Mic 1:14 The town of A has deceived the kings of Israel,

ADADAH (1)
Jos 15:22 Kinah, Dimonah, A,

ADAH (8)
Ge 4:19 Lamech married two women—A and Zillah.
4:20 A gave birth to a baby named Jabal. He became the
4:23 One day Lamech said to A and Zillah, "Listen to
36: 2 A, the daughter of Elon the Hittite;
36: 4 Esau and A had a son named Eliphaz. Esau
36:10 sons were Eliphaz, the son of Esau's wife A;
36:12 These were all grandchildren of Esau's wife A.
36:16 descended from Eliphaz, the son of Esau and A.

ADAIAH (9)
2Ki 22: 1 was Jedidah, the daughter of A from Bozkath.
1Ch 6:41 Ethni, Zerah, A,
8:21 A, Beraiah, and Shimrath were the sons of Shimei.
9:12 Other returning priests were A son of Jeroham,
2Ch 23: 1 Azariah son of Obed, Maaseiah son of A,
Ezr 10:29 Meshullam, Malluch, A, Jashub, Sheal,
10:39 Shelemiah, Nathan, A,
Ne 11: 5 son of Hazaiah, son of A, son of Joiarib, son of
11:12 Also, there was A son of Jeroham, son of Pelaliah,

ADALIA (1)
Est 9: 8 Poratha, A, Aridatha,

ADAM (37) [ADAM'S]
Ge 2:19 He brought them to A to see what he would call them, and A chose a name for each one.
2:21 So the LORD God caused A to fall into a deep
2:22 made a woman from the rib and brought her to A.
2:23 "At last!" A exclaimed. "She is part of my own
2:25 Now, although A and his wife were both naked,
3: 9 The LORD God called to A, "Where are you?"
3:12 "Yes," A admitted, "but it was the woman you
3:17 And to A he said, "Because you listened to your
3:20 Then A named his wife Eve, because she would be
3:21 God made clothing from animal skins for A
3:23 So the LORD God banished A and his wife from
3:23 and he sent A out to cultivate the ground from
4: 1 Now A slept with his wife, Eve, and she became
4:25 A slept with his wife again, and she gave birth to
5: 1 This is the history of the descendants of A.
5: 3 When A was 130 years old, his son Seth was born,
5: 4 A lived another 800 years, and he had other sons
Jos 3:16 water began piling up at a town upstream called A,
1Ch 1: 1 The descendants of A were Seth, Enosh,
Hos 6: 7 "But like A, you broke my covenant and rebelled
Lk 3:38 Seth was the son of A. / A was the son of God.
Ro 5:12 When A sinned, sin entered the entire human race.
5:14 an explicit commandment of God, as A did.
5:14 What a contrast between A and Christ, who was
5:15 For this one man, A, brought death to many
5:17 The sin of this one man, A, caused death to rule
1Co 15:21 as death came into the world through a man, A,
15:22 Everyone dies because all of us are related to A,
15:45 The Scriptures tell us, "The first man, A, became a
15:45 But the last A—that is, Christ—is a life-giving
15:47 A, the first man, was made from the dust of the
15:49 Just as we are now like A, the man of the earth,
1Ti 2:13 For God made A first, and afterward he made Eve.
2:14 And it was the woman, not A, who was deceived
Jude 1:14 Now Enoch, who lived seven generations after A,

ADAM'S (5) [ADAM]
Ge 2:21 He took one of A ribs and closed up the place from
Ro 5:12 A sin brought death, so death spread to everyone,
5:16 For A sin led to condemnation, but we have the
5:18 A one sin brought condemnation upon everyone,
1Co 15:48 Every human being has an earthly body just like A,

ADAMAH (1)
Jos 19:36 A, Ramah, Hazor,

ADAMANT [KJV] See HARD

ADAMI-NEKEB (1)
Jos 19:33 and extended across to A, Jabneel, and as far as

ADBEEL (1)
1Ch 1:29 were Nebaioth (the oldest), Kedar, A, Mibsam,

ADD (20) [ADDED, ADDING, ADDITION, ADDITIONAL, ADDS]
Lev 2:12 You may a yeast and honey to the offerings
2:13 Never forget to a salt to your grain offerings.
6:12 Each morning the priest will a fresh wood to the
Dt 4: 2 Do not a to or subtract from these commands I am
12:32 I give you. Do not a to them or subtract from them.
2Ki 20: 6 I will a fifteen years to your life, and I will rescue
1Ch 22:14 for the walls, though you may need to a more.
2Ch 28:13 "We cannot afford to a to our sins and guilt.
Ne 2: 9 The king, I should a, had sent along army officers
Job 29:22 And after I spoke, they had nothing to a, for my
Ps 61: 6 A many years to the life of the king! / May his
69:26 those you have punished, they a insult to injury;
Pr 9:11 will multiply your days and a years to your life.
30: 6 Do not a to his words, or he may rebuke you,
Isa 38: 5 seen your tears. I will a fifteen years to your life,
Mal 2: 3 and I will a you to the dung heap.
Mt 6:27 Can all your worries a a single moment to your
Lk 12:25 Can all your worries a a single moment to your
Gal 2: 6 there had nothing to a to what I was preaching.
Rev 22:18 God will a to that person the plagues described in

ADDAN (2)
Ezr 2:59 of Tel-melah, Tel-harsha, Kerub, A, and Immer.
Ne 7:61 of Tel-melah, Tel-harsha, Kerub, A, and Immer.

ADDAR (2) [ATAROTH-ADDAR, HAZAR-ADDAR]
Jos 15: 3 Then it went up to A, where it turned toward
1Ch 8: 3 The sons of Bela were A, Gera, Abihud,

ADDED (36) [ADD]
Ge 16:10 The angel a, "I will give you more descendants
17:15 Then God a, "Regarding Sarai, your wife—
30:40 Jacob a them to his own flock, thus separating the
Lev 5:16 paying for the loss, plus an a penalty of 20 percent.
22:14 the amount eaten, plus an a penalty of 20 percent.
Nu 36: 4 their inheritance of land will be a to that of the new
Dt 32:46 he a: "Take to heart all the words I have given you
Ru 3:17 and she a, "He gave me these six scoops of barley
1Sa 12:19 "For now we have a to our sins by asking for a
1Ki 22: 5 Then Jehoshaphat a, "But first let's find out what
22:28 Then he a to those standing around, "Take note of
2Ch 18: 4 Then Jehoshaphat a, "But first let's find out what
18:27 Then he a to those standing around, "Take note of
Ezr 10:13 Then they a, "This isn't something that can be
Est 5:12 Then Haman a, "And that's not all! Queen Esther
5:13 Then he a, "But all this is meaningless as long as I
Job 34:37 For now you have a rebellion and blasphemy
Ecc 3:14 is final. Nothing can be a to it or taken from it.
Jer 36:32 burned in the fire. Only this time, he a much more!
44:19 "And," the women a, "do you suppose that we
45: 3 And now the LORD has a more! I am weary of
Eze 3:10 Then he a, "Son of man, let all my words sink
8:13 Then he a, "Come, and I will show you greater
16:26 Then you a lustful Egypt to your lovers,
16:29 You a to your lovers by embracing that great
16:43 your disgusting sins, you have a these lewd acts.
42: 8 This wall a length to the outer block of rooms,
Mt 9:13 Then he a, "Now go and learn the meaning of this
13:52 Then he a, "Every teacher of religious law who
Mk 7:20 And then he a, "It is the thought-life that defiles
Lk 6: 5 And Jesus a, "I, the Son of Man, am master even
21:10 Then he a, "Nations and kingdoms will proclaim
Ac 2:41 what Peter said were baptized and a to the church—
2:47 And each day the Lord a to their group those who
Heb 10: 9 Then he a, "Look, I have come to do your will."
Rev 19: 9 And he a, "These are true words that come from

ADDER [KJV] See VIPER

ADDI (2)
Lk 3:28 Melki was the son of A. / A was the son of Cosam.

ADDING (4) [ADD]
Lev 25: 8 years times seven, a up to forty-nine years in all.
Nu 5: 7 a a penalty of 20 percent and returning it to the
2Ch 32: 5 and by a to the fortifications and constructing a
Lk 3:20 put John in prison, a this sin to his many others.

ADDITION (55) [ADD]
Ge 22:24 In a to his eight sons from Milcah, Nahor had four
28: 9 in a to the wives he already had.
Lev 9:17 the altar, in a to the regular morning burnt offering.
14:17 right foot, in a to the blood of the guilt offering.
14:28 right foot, in a to the blood of the guilt offering.
23: 4 In a to the Sabbath, the LORD has established
23:38 These festivals must be observed in a to the
23:38 And these offerings must be given in a to your
25: 8 "In a, you must count off seven Sabbath years,
Nu 16:49 in a to those who had died in the incident
28:10 in a to the regular daily burnt offering and its
28:15 This is in a to the regular daily burnt offering
28:23 You will present these offerings in a to your
28:24 These will be offered in a to the regular whole
28:31 are in a to the regular daily burnt offering and its
29: 5 In a, you must sacrifice a male goat as a sin
29: 6 These special sacrifices are in a to your regular
29:11 This is in a to the sin offering of atonement
29:16 in a to the regular daily burnt offering with its
29:19 in a to the regular daily burnt offering with its
29:22 in a to the regular daily burnt offering with its
29:25 in a to the regular daily burnt offering with its
29:28 in a to the regular daily burnt offering with its
29:31 in a to the regular daily burnt offering with its
29:34 in a to the regular daily burnt offering with its
29:38 in a to the regular daily burnt offering with its
29:39 These are in a to the sacrifices and offerings you
35: 6 for safety. In a, give them forty-two other towns.
Dt 29: 1 in a to the covenant he had made with them at
Jos 15:58 In a, there were Halhul, Beth-zur, Gedor,
17: 5 in a to the land of Gilead and Bashan across the
Jdg 1:18 In a, Judah captured the cities of Gaza, Ashkelon,
1Sa 11: 8 300,000 men of Israel, in a to 30,000 from Judah.
15: 4 There were 200,000 troops in a to 10,000 men
2Sa 2:30 only nineteen men were missing, in a to Asahel.
7:19 Sovereign LORD, in a to everything else,
2Ki 21:16 This was in a to the sin that he caused the people
1Ch 7: 9 among their descendants, in a to their clan leaders.
17:17 And now, O God, in a to everything else,
29: 3 This is in a to the building materials I have already
2Ch 31: 4 In a, he required the people in Jerusalem to bring
Ezr 1: 6 They gave them many choice gifts in a to all the
2:65 in a to 7,337 servants and 200 singers, both men
Ne 3:11 of the Ovens, in a to another section of the wall.
7:67 in a to 7,337 servants and 245 singers, both men
10:32 "In a, we promise to obey the command to pay the
Est 9:30 In a, letters wishing peace and security were sent
Isa 54: 2 "Enlarge your house; build an a; spread out your
Eze 16:23 In a to all your other wickedness,
44: 7 Thus, in a to all your other disgusting sins,
Mt 14:21 five loaves, in a to all the women and children!
15:38 fed that day, in a to all the women and children.
Jn 5:18 In a to disobeying the Sabbath rules, he had
2Co 7:13 In a to our own encouragement, we were
Heb 7: 9 In a, we might even say that Levi's descendants,

ADDITIONAL (18) [ADD]
Ge 21:28 But when Abraham took seven a ewe lambs
29:30 He then stayed and worked the a seven years.
43:22 We also have a money to buy more grain. We have
Ex 36: 3 the sanctuary. A gifts were brought each morning.
Dt 19: 9 you must designate three a cities of refuge.
Jos 15:18 she urged him to ask her father for an a field.
Jdg 1:14 she urged him to ask her father for an a field.
2Sa 5: 9 He built a fortifications around the city, starting at
10:16 they were joined by a Aramean troops summoned
1Ki 10:15 This did not include the a revenue he received
1Ch 19:16 so they summoned a Aramean troops from the
2Ch 9:14 This did not include the a revenue he received
17: 2 and he assigned a garrisons to the land of Judah
Ne 3:20 who repaired an a section from the buttress to the
Ecc 2:10 in hard work, an a reward for all my labors.
Eze 41:13 including its walls, was an a 175 feet in length.
45: 2 An a strip of land 87-1/2 feet wide is to be left
48:15 "An a strip of land 8-1/3 miles long by 1-2/3 miles

ADDRESS (4) [ADDRESSED]
Dt 20: 5 "Then the officers of the army will a the troops
2Ch 32: 6 Then Hezekiah encouraged them with this a:
Mt 23: 9 And don't a anyone here on earth as 'Father,'
Ac 24: 2 against Paul in the following a to the governor:

ADDRESSED (15) [ADDRESS]
Ge 34:11 Then Shechem a Dinah's father and brothers.
Dt 1: 5 So Moses a the people of Israel while they were in
27: 9 and the Levitical priests a all Israel as follows:
1Sa 12: 1 Then Samuel a the people again: "I have done as
1Ch 13: 2 Then he a the entire assembly of Israel as follows:
28: 2 and stood before them and a them as follows:
Jer 28: 1 a me publicly in the Temple while all the priests
Ac 1:15 Peter stood up and a them as follows:
3:12 Peter saw his opportunity and a the crowd.
5:35 Then he a his colleagues as follows: "Men of
9: 2 He requested letters a to the synagogues in
15: 7 long discussion, Peter stood and a them as follows:
17:22 standing before the Council, a them as follows:
19:25 employed in related trades, and a them as follows:
21:40 and he a them in their own language, Aramaic.

ADDS (3) [ADD]
Pr 10:22 makes a person rich, and he a no sorrow with it.
Heb 10:17 Then he a, / "I will never again remember
Rev 22:18 If anyone a anything to what is written here,

ADEQUATE (1)
2Co 2:16 And who is a for such a task as this?

ADER [KJV] See EDER

ADIEL (3)
1Ch 4:36 Jeshohaiah, Asaiah, A, Jesimiel, Benaiah,
9:12 of Malkijah, and Maasai son of A, son of Jahzerah,
27:25 Azmaveth son of A was in charge of the palace

ADIN (4)
Ezr 2:15 The family of A | 454
8: 6 From the family of A: Ebed son of Jonathan
Ne 7:20 The family of A | 655
10:16 Adonijah, Bigvai, A,

ADINA (1)
1Ch 11:42 A son of Shiza, the Reubenite leader who had

ADITHAIM (1)
Jos 15:36 Shaaraim, A, Gederah, and Gederothaim. In all,

ADJACENT (2)
Nu 21:13 in the wilderness a to the territory of the Amorites.
Eze 45: 6 "A to the larger sacred area will be a section of

ADJOURNED (1)
Ac 24:22 a the hearing and said, "Wait until Lysias,

ADJURE [KJV] See COMMAND, DEMAND

ADLAI (1)
1Ch 27:29 Shaphat son of A was responsible for the cattle in

ADMAH (6)
Ge 10:19 to Sodom, Gomorrah, **A**, and Zeboiim, near Lasha.
14: 2 King Birsha of Gomorrah, King Shinab of **A**,
14: 3 The kings of Sodom, Gomorrah, **A**, Zeboiim,
14: 8 Gomorrah, **A**, Zeboiim, and Bela (now called
Dt 29:23 be just like Sodom and Gomorrah, **A** and Zeboiim,
Hos 11: 8 How can I destroy you like **A** and Zeboiim?

ADMATHA (1)
Est 1:14 Shethar, **A**, Tarshish, Meres, Marsena,

ADMIN (2)
Lk 3:33 Amminadab was the son of **A**. / **A** was the son of

ADMINISTER (1) [ADMINISTERING, ADMINISTRATION, ADMINISTRATIVE, ADMINISTRATOR, ADMINISTRATORS]
Ex 18:26 These men were constantly available to **a** justice.

ADMINISTERING (1) [ADMINISTER]
Ac 6: 2 the word of God, not **a** a food program," they said.

ADMINISTRATION (2) [ADMINISTER]
Ne 2:16 the officials, or anyone else in the **a**.
11:24 was the king's agent in all matters of public **a**.

ADMINISTRATIVE (3) [ADMINISTER]
Ge 39: 6 So Potiphar gave Joseph complete **a** responsibility
1Ch 29: 6 and the king's **a** officers all gave willingly.
Jer 36:12 in the palace where the **a** officials were meeting.

ADMINISTRATOR (9) [ADMINISTER]
Nu 3:32 Aaron's son, was the chief **a** over all the Levites,
Jdg 9:28 He's merely the son of Gideon, and Zebul is his **a**.
2Ki 18:18 Eliakim son of Hilkiah, the palace **a**,
18:37 the palace **a**, Shebna the court secretary, and Joah
19: 2 And he sent Eliakim the palace **a**, Shebna the court
Isa 22:15 told me to confront Shebna, the palace **a**,
36: 3 Eliakim son of Hilkiah, the palace **a**,
36:22 the palace **a**, Shebna the court secretary, and Joah
37: 2 And he sent Eliakim the palace **a**, Shebna the court

ADMINISTRATORS (9) [ADMINISTER]
2Ki 10: 5 So the palace and city **a**, together with the other
1Ch 26:29 and his sons were appointed to serve as public **a**
2Ch 35: 8 Zechariah, and Jehiel, the **a** of God's Temple,
Est 3: 9 I will give 375 tons of silver to the government **a**
Da 6: 2 and two others as **a** to supervise the princes
6: 3 proved himself more capable than all the other **a**
6: 4 Then the other **a** and princes began searching for
6: 6 So the **a** and princes went to the king and said,
6: 7 We **a**, prefects, princes, advisers, and other

ADMIRABLE (1) [ADMIRE]
Php 4: 8 Think about things that are pure and lovely and **a**.

ADMIRATION (1) [ADMIRE]
2Ki 5: 1 The king of Aram had high **a** for Naaman,

ADMIRE (2) [ADMIRABLE, ADMIRATION, ADMIRED, ADMIRES]
Mt 6:16 so people will **a** them for their fasting.
Lk 16: 8 "The rich man had to **a** the dishonest rascal for

ADMIRED (2) [ADMIRE]
Est 2:15 and she was **a** by everyone who saw her.
Mt 6: 1 to be **a**, because then you will lose the reward from

ADMIRES (1) [ADMIRE]
Pr 12: 8 Everyone **a** a person with good sense, but a warped

ADMIT (13) [ADMITTED, ADMITTING]
Ge 26: 7 He was afraid to **a** that she was his wife.
Ex 9:27 and Aaron. "I finally **a** my fault," he confessed.
Job 32: 2 because Job refused to **a** that he had sinned
Isa 41:26 else predicted this, making you **a** that he was right?
48: 6 and seen them fulfilled, but you refuse to **a** it.
Jer 3:13 **A** that you rebelled against the LORD your God
Hos 5:15 Then I will return to my place until they **a** their
Mic 3: 7 And you will **a** that your messages were not from
Jn 12:42 But they wouldn't **a** it to anyone because of their
Ac 24:14 "But I **a** that I follow the Way, which they call a
26: 5 If they would **a** it, they know that I have been a
2Co 12:16 Some of you **a** I was not a burden to you. But they
Jas 4:10 before the Lord and **a** your dependence on him,

ADMITTED (7) [ADMIT]
Ge 3:12 "Yes," Adam **a**, "but it was the woman you gave
38:26 Judah **a** that they were his and said, "She is more
Nu 22:30 ever done anything like this before?" "No," he **a**.
1Sa 14:43 of Jonathan. "I tasted a little honey," Jonathan **a**.
15:15 spared the best of the sheep and cattle," Saul **a**.
15:24 Then Saul finally **a**, "Yes, I have sinned. I have
Eze 44: 5 Take careful note of who may be **a** to the Temple

ADMITTING (1) [ADMIT]
Jdg 17: 2 "The LORD bless you for **a** it," his mother

ADNA (2)
Ezr 10:30 **A**, Kelal, Benaiah, Maaseiah, Mattaniah, Bezalel,
Ne 12:15 **A** was leader of the family of Harim. / Helkai was

ADNAH (2)
1Ch 12:20 **A**, Jozabad, Jediael, Michael, Jozabad, Elihu,
2Ch 17:14 in units of one thousand, under the command of **A**.

ADO [KJV] See COMMOTION

ADONI-BEZEK (3) [BEZEK]
Jdg 1: 5 While at Bezek they encountered King **A**
1: 6 **A** escaped, but the Israelites soon captured him
1: 7 **A** said, "I once had seventy kings with thumbs

ADONI-ZEDEK (2)
Jos 10: 1 Now **A**, king of Jerusalem, heard that Joshua had
10: 3 So King **A** of Jerusalem sent messengers to several

ADONIJAH (25) [ADONIJAH'S]
2Sa 3: 4 The fourth was **A**, whose mother was Haggith.
1Ki 1: 5 About that time David's son **A**, whose mother was
1: 6 **A** was a very handsome man and had been born
1: 7 **A** took Joab son of Zeruiah and Abiathar the priest
1: 8 and refused to support **A** were Zadok the priest,
1: 9 **A** went to the stone of Zoheleth near the spring of
1:11 **A**, has made himself king and that our lord David
1:13 upon your throne? Then why has **A** become king?'
1:18 But instead, **A** has become the new king, and you
1:24 have you decided that **A** will be the next king
1:25 with him and shouting, 'Long live King **A**!'
1:41 **A** and his guests heard the celebrating
1:42 "Come in," **A** said to him, "for you are a good
1:50 **A** himself was afraid of Solomon, so he rushed to
1:51 Word soon reached Solomon that **A** had seized the
1:53 So King Solomon summoned **A**, and they brought
2:13 One day **A**, whose mother was Haggith, came to
2:21 "Then let your brother **A** marry Abishag, the girl
2:22 can you possibly ask me to give Abishag to **A**?"
2:23 "May God strike me dead if **A** has not sealed his
2:24 as the LORD lives, **A** will die this very day!"
2:25 Jehoiada to execute him, and **A** was put to death.
1Ch 3: 2 The fourth was **A**, whose mother was Haggith.
2Ch 17: 8 Asahel, Shemiramoth, Jehonathan, **A**, Tobijah,
Ne 10:16 **A**, Bigvai, Adin,

ADONIJAH'S (4) [ADONIJAH]
1Ki 1:49 Then all of **A** guests jumped up in panic from the
2:19 So Bathsheba went to King Solomon to speak on **A**
2:28 Absalom earlier, Joab had also joined **A** revolt.
2:28 When Joab heard about **A** death, he ran to the

ADONIKAM (3)
Ezr 2:13 The family of **A** | 666
8:13 From the family of **A**, who came later: Eliphelet,
Ne 7:18 The family of **A** | 667

ADONIRAM (5)
2Sa 20:24 **A** was in charge of the labor force.
1Ki 4: 6 **A** son of Abda was in charge of the labor force.
5:14 at home. **A** was in charge of this labor force.
12:18 King Rehoboam sent **A**, who was in charge of the
2Ch 10:18 King Rehoboam sent **A**, who was in charge of the

ADOPT (2) [ADOPTED, ADOPTING]
Gal 4: 5 so that he could **a** us as his very own children.
Eph 1: 5 His unchanging plan has always been to **a** us into

ADOPTED (6) [ADOPT]
Ex 2:10 him back to the princess, who **a** him as her son.
Est 2: 7 Mordecai **a** her into his family and raised her as his
9:23 So the Jews **a** Mordecai's suggestion and began
Ps 106:35 among the pagans / and **a** their evil customs.
Zec 9: 7 worship our God and be **a** as a new clan in Judah.
Ro 8:15 like God's very own children, **a** into his family—

ADOPTING (1) [ADOPT]
Ge 48: 5 Now I am **a** as my own sons these two boys of

ADORAIM (1)
2Ch 11: 9 **A**, Lachish, Azekah,

ADORATION (1) [ADORE]
2Th 2: 4 and tear down every object of **a** and worship.

ADORE (1) [ADORATION]
1Ch 29:11 We **a** you as the one who is over all things.

ADORNED (1)
Eze 28:13 Your clothing was **a** with every precious stone—

ADRAMMELECH (3)
2Ki 17:31 even burned their own children as sacrifices to **A**
19:37 his sons **A** and Sharezer killed him with their
Isa 37:38 his sons **A** and Sharezer killed him with their

ADRAMYTTIUM (1)
Ac 27: 2 We left on a boat whose home port was **A**; it was

ADRIA (1)
Ac 27:27 as we were being driven across the Sea of **A**,

ADRIEL (2)
1Sa 18:19 Saul gave Merab in marriage to **A**, a man from
2Sa 21: 8 the wife of **A** son of Barzillai from Meholah.

ADRIFT (1)
2Co 11:25 Once I spent a whole night and a day **a** at sea.

ADULLAM (9) [ADULLAMITE]
Ge 38: 1 About this time, Judah left home and moved to **A**,
Jos 12:15 The king of Libnah / The king of **A**
15:35 Jarmuth, **A**, Socoh, Azekah,
1Sa 22: 1 So David left Gath and escaped to the cave of **A**.
2Sa 23:13 when David was at the cave of **A**,
1Ch 11:15 when David was at the rock near the cave of **A**,
2Ch 11: 7 Beth-zur, Soco, **A**,
Ne 11:30 Zanoah, and **A** with their villages. They were also
Mic 1:15 your town. And the leaders of Israel will go to **A**.

ADULLAMITE (2) [ADULLAM]
Ge 38:12 and his friend Hirah the **A** went to Timnah to
38:20 Judah asked his friend Hirah the **A** to take the

ADULTERER (1) [ADULTERY]
Job 24:15 The **a** waits for the twilight, for he says, 'No one

ADULTERERS (7) [ADULTERY]
Ps 50:18 you help him, / and you spend your time with **a**.
Isa 57: 3 you offspring of **a** and prostitutes!
Eze 33:26 Murderers! Idolaters! **A**! Should the land belong to
Hos 7: 4 They are all **a**, always aflame with lust. They are
Mal 3: 5 ready witness against all sorcerers and **a** and liars.
1Co 6: 9 idol worshipers, **a**, male prostitutes, homosexuals,
Jas 4: 4 You **a**! Don't you realize that friendship with this

ADULTERESSES (1) [ADULTERY]
Eze 23:45 cities for what they really are—**a** and murderers.

ADULTERIES (1) [ADULTERY]
Jer 3: 2 land where you have not been defiled by your **a**?

ADULTEROUS (11) [ADULTERY]
Pr 2:16 immoral woman, from the flattery of the **a** woman.
5:20 or embrace the breasts of an **a** woman?
6:24 from the smooth tongue of an **a** woman.
7: 5 from listening to the flattery of an **a** woman.
23:27 prostitute is a deep pit; an **a** woman is treacherous.
27:13 if someone guarantees the debt of an **a** woman.
30:20 Equally amazing is how an **a** woman can satisfy
Jer 9: 2 in the desert, for they are all **a** and treacherous.
Eze 16:32 you are an **a** wife who takes in strangers instead of
43: 7 name any longer by their **a** worship of other gods
Mk 8:38 of me and my message in these **a** and sinful days,

ADULTERY (63) [ADULTERER, ADULTERERS, ADULTERESSES, ADULTERIES, ADULTEROUS]
Ex 20:14 "Do not commit **a**.
34:15 committing **a** against me by sacrificing to their
34:16 Then they will cause your sons to commit **a** against
Lev 20:10 "If a man commits **a** with another man's wife,
Dt 5:18 " 'Do not commit **a**.
22:22 "If a man is discovered committing **a**, both he
Ps 51: T him after David had committed **a** with Bathsheba.
106:39 and their love of idols was **a** in the LORD's sight.
Pr 6:32 But the man who commits **a** is an utter fool,
Isa 57: 7 You have committed **a** on the mountaintops by
57: 8 This is **a**, for you are loving these idols instead of
Jer 3: 6 Like a wife who commits **a**, Israel has worshiped
3: 9 she thought nothing of committing **a** by
3:13 and committed **a** against him by worshiping idols
5: 7 But they thanked me by committing **a** and lining
7: 9 murder, commit **a**, lie, and worship Baal and all
13:27 I am keenly aware of your **a** and lust, and your
23:10 For the land is full of **a**, and it lies under a curse.
23:14 They commit **a**, and they love dishonesty.
29:23 They have committed **a** with their neighbors'
Eze 16:17 and worshiped them, which is **a** against me.
16:22 In all your years of **a** and loathsome sin, you have
16:38 I will punish you for your murder and **a**. I will
18: 6 And suppose he does not commit **a** or have
18:11 worships idols on the mountains, commits **a**,
18:15 idols on the mountains, does not commit **a**,
22:11 Within your walls live men who commit **a** with
23:17 So they came and committed **a** with her,
23:37 They have committed both **a** and murder—
23:37 **a** by worshiping idols and murder by burning their
Hos 1: 2 openly committing **a** against the LORD by
2: 4 are not my children! They were conceived in **a**.
3: 1 back to you and love her, even though she loves **a**.
4: 2 You curse and lie and kill and steal and commit **a**.
4:13 and your daughters-in-law commit **a**.
Mt 5:27 that the law of Moses says, 'Do not commit **a**.'
5:28 eye has already committed **a** with her in his heart.
5:32 she has been unfaithful, causes her to commit **a**.
5:32 anyone who marries a divorced woman commits **a**.
15:19 murder, **a**, all other sexual immorality, theft,
19: 9 divorces his wife and marries another commits **a**—
19:18 " 'Do not murder. Do not commit **a**. Do not steal.

Mk 7:22 **a**, greed, wickedness, deceit, eagerness for lustful
10:11 and marries someone else commits **a** against her.
10:12 her husband and remarries, she commits **a**."
10:19 'Do not murder. Do not commit **a**. Do not steal.
Lk 16:18 his wife and marries someone else commits **a**,
16:18 who marries a divorced woman commits **a**."
18:11 For I never cheat, I don't sin, I don't commit **a**,
18:20 'Do not commit **a**. Do not murder. Do not steal.
Jn 8:3 brought a woman they had caught in the act of **a**.
8:4 "this woman was caught in the very act of **a**.
Ro 2:22 You say it is wrong to commit **a**, but do you do it?
7:3 she would be committing **a** if she married another
7:3 and does not commit **a** when she remarries.
13:9 For the commandments against **a** and murder
13:13 or in **a** and immoral living, or in fighting
Heb 13:4 people who are immoral and those who commit **a**.
Jas 2:11 "Do not commit **a**," also said, "Do not murder."
2:11 broken the entire law, even if you do not commit **a**.
2Pe 2:14 They commit **a** with their eyes, and their lust is
Rev 2:22 and she will suffer greatly with all who commit **a**
18:3 The rulers of the world have committed **a** with her,

ADULTS (1)
Isa 65:20 No longer will **a** die before they have lived a full

ADUMMIM (2)
Jos 15:7 which is across from the slopes of **A** on the south
18:17 to Geliloth (which is across from the slopes of **A**).

ADVANCE (12) [ADVANCED, ADVANCING]
Lev 25:36 Do not demand an **a** or charge interest on the
Jdg 20:32 But the Israelites had agreed in **a** to run away
Job 19:12 His troops **a**. They build up roads to attack me.
Isa 43:9 of them predict something even a single day in **a**?
Jer 46:3 "Buckle on your armor and **a** into battle!
49:28 This is what the LORD says: "**A** against Kedar!
Da 11:10 assemble a mighty army that will **a** like a flood
Joel 2:10 The earth quakes as they **a**, and the heavens
3:9 Let all your fighting men **a** for the attack!
Hab 1:9 Their hordes **a** like a wind from the desert,
Ro 8:29 For God knew his people in **a**, and he chose them
1Pe 1:11 when he told them in **a** about Christ's suffering

ADVANCED (8) [ADVANCE]
Jdg 20:20 Then they **a** toward Gibeah to attack the men of
20:34 and **a** against Benjamin from behind. The fighting
1Sa 7:7 at Mizpah, they mobilized their army and **a**.
2Ki 6:18 As the Aramean army **a** toward them,
2Ch 12:4 fortified cities and then **a** to attack Jerusalem.
14:9 hundred chariots. They **a** to the city of Mareshah,
Ps 48:4 of the earth joined forces / and **a** against the city.
Lk 5:12 Jesus met a man with an **a** case of leprosy.

ADVANCING (2) [ADVANCE]
Isa 19:1 The LORD is **a** against Egypt, riding on a swift
Mt 11:12 the Kingdom of Heaven has been forcefully **a**,

ADVANTAGE (24) [ADVANTAGES]
Ge 11:6 just begun to take **a** of their common language
Ex 17:11 up the staff with his hands, the Israelites had the **a**.
Lev 19:14 deaf with respect and by not taking **a** of the blind.
25:14 sell property, you must never take **a** of each other.
25:17 Show your fear of God by not taking **a** of each
Dt 24:14 "Never take **a** of poor laborers, whether fellow
Ne 5:15 Even their assistants took **a** of the people. But
Job 17:5 They denounce their companions for their own **a**,
24:21 For they have taken **a** of the childless who have no
Ecc 3:19 So people have no real **a** over the animals.
5:11 So what is the **a** of wealth—except perhaps to
6:8 do wise people really have any **a** over fools?
Isa 3:5 People will take **a** of each other—man against
3:14 You have taken **a** of the poor, filling your barns
Jer 9:4 They all take **a** of one another and spread their
Da 11:2 Using his wealth for political **a**, he will stir up
Ro 3:1 Then what's the **a** of being a Jew? Is there any
7:8 But sin took **a** of this law and aroused all kinds of
7:11 Sin took **a** of the law and fooled me; it took the
2Co 7:2 led anyone astray. We have not taken **a** of anyone.
11:20 take **a** of you, put on airs, and slap you in the face.
12:16 think I was sneaky and took **a** of you by trickery.
12:17 Did any of the men I sent to you take **a** of you?
12:18 other brother with him, did Titus take **a** of you?

ADVANTAGES (1) [ADVANTAGE]
Ro 3:2 Yes, being a Jew has many **a**. First of all, the Jews

ADVERSARIES (2) [ADVERSARY]
Dt 32:27 that their **a** might misunderstand and say,
Ps 89:23 I will beat down his **a** before him / and destroy

ADVERSARY (1) [ADVERSARIES, ADVERSITY]
Job 27:7 be punished like the wicked, my **a** like evil men.

ADVERSITIES [KJV] See ANGUISH

ADVERSITY (2) [ADVERSARY]
Job 36:15 who suffer. For he gets their attention through **a**.
Isa 30:20 Though the Lord gave you **a** for food and affliction

ADVERTISE [KJV] See TELL, SPEAK

ADVICE (70) [ADVISE]
Ex 18:19 Now let me give you a word of **a**, and may God be
18:23 If you follow this **a**, and if God directs you to do
18:24 Moses listened to his father-in-law's **a**
Nu 31:16 are the very ones who followed Balaam's **a**
1Sa 8:6 with their request and went to the LORD for **a**.
2Sa 15:31 let Ahithophel give Absalom foolish **a**!"
15:34 Then you can frustrate and counter Ahithophel's **a**.
16:23 Absalom followed Ahithophel's **a**, just as David
17:6 Should we follow Ahithophel's **a**? If not,
17:14 "Hushai's **a** is better than Ahithophel's."
17:23 publicly disgraced when Absalom refused his **a**.
20:18 to settle an argument, ask **a** at the city of Abel.'
20:22 the woman went to the people with her wise **a**,
1Ki 12:6 his father, Solomon. "What is your **a**?" he asked.
12:8 But Rehoboam rejected the **a** of the elders
12:9 "What is your **a**?" he asked them. "How should I
12:13 for he rejected the **a** of the older counselors
12:28 So on the **a** of his counselors, the king made two
2Ch 10:6 his father, Solomon. "What is your **a**?" he asked.
10:8 But Rehoboam rejected the **a** of the elders
10:9 "What is your **a**?" he asked them. "How should I
10:13 for he rejected the **a** of the older counselors
22:5 Following their evil **a**, Ahaziah made an alliance
24:17 and persuaded the king to listen to their **a**.
25:16 and said, "Since when have I asked your **a**?
25:19 your conquest of Edom, but my **a** is to stay home.
Ezr 10:3 We will follow the **a** given by you and by the
Est 1:13 and customs, for he always asked their **a**.
2:4 This **a** was very appealing to the king, so he put
2:15 she accepted the **a** of Hegai, the eunuch in charge
Job 5:8 "My **a** to you is this: Go to God and present your
29:21 "Everyone listened to me and valued my **a**.
Ps 1:1 of those / who do not follow the **a** of the wicked,
119:24 Your decrees please me; / they give me wise **a**.
Pr 1:25 You ignored my **a** and rejected the correction I
1:30 They rejected my **a** and paid no attention when I
7:1 Follow my **a**, my son; always treasure my
8:8 My **a** is wholesome and good. There is nothing
8:14 Good **a** and success belong to me. Insight
10:21 The godly give good **a**, but fools are destroyed by
10:31 The godly person gives wise **a**, but the tongue that
12:5 godly are just; the **a** of the wicked is treacherous.
12:15 Fools think they need no **a**, but the wise listen to
12:26 The godly give good **a** to their friends; the wicked
13:10 leads to arguments; those who take **a** are wise.
13:13 People who despise **a** will find themselves in
13:14 The **a** of the wise is like a life-giving fountain;
15:7 Only the wise can give good **a**; fools cannot do so.
15:22 Plans go wrong for lack of **a**; many counselors
18:13 what folly, to give **a** before listening to the facts!
19:20 Get all the **a** and instruction you can, and be wise
20:5 Though good **a** lies deep within a person's heart,
20:18 don't go to war without the **a** of others.
22:20 thirty sayings for you, filled with **a** and knowledge.
23:9 breath on fools, for they will despise the wisest **a**.
25:11 Timely **a** is as lovely as golden apples in a silver
Ecc 4:13 to be an old and foolish king who refuses all **a**.
Isa 40:14 Has the LORD ever needed anyone's **a**? Does he
44:25 I cause wise people to give bad **a**, thus proving
Jer 18:18 him to teach the law and give us **a** and prophecies.
38:15 And if I give you **a**, you won't listen to me
Eze 14:7 and who then come to a prophet asking for my **a**.
14:10 evil people who claim to want my **a**—
Da 1:20 the king found the **a** of these young men to be ten
Zec 10:2 Household gods give false **a**, fortune-tellers predict
Lk 14:7 sit near the head of the table, he gave them this **a**:
Jn 8:38 But you are following the **a** of your father."
Ac 5:38 "So my **a** is, leave these men alone. If they are
5:40 The council accepted his **a**. They called in the
1Co 12:8 person the Spirit gives the ability to give wise **a**;

ADVISE (7) [ADVICE, ADVISED, ADVISER, ADVISERS]
Dt 1:22 They will **a** us on the best route to take and decide
Ps 32:8 for your life. / I will **a** you and watch over you.
Pr 6:22 you wake up in the morning, they will **a** you.
Isa 40:13 Who is able to **a** the Spirit of the LORD?
Gal 5:16 So I **a** you to live according to your new life in the
1Ti 5:14 So I **a** these younger widows to marry again,
Rev 3:18 I **a** you to buy gold from me—gold that has been

ADVISED (3) [ADVISE]
2Sa 17:21 And they told him how Ahithophel had **a** that he
1Ki 20:8 to any more demands," the leaders and people **a**.
Pr 21:30 Human plans, no matter how wise or well **a**,

ADVISER (11) [ADVISE]
Ge 26:26 King Abimelech arrived with his **a**, Ahuzzath,
2Sa 15:31 When someone told David that his **a** Ahithophel
15:34 and tell Absalom, 'I will now be your **a**,
15:34 just as I was your father's **a** in the past.'
1Ki 4:5 son of Nathan, a priest, was a trusted **a** to the king.
2Ki 22:12 court secretary, and Asaiah the king's personal **a**:
1Ch 27:33 Ahithophel was the royal **a**. Hushai the Arkite was
2Ch 34:20 court secretary, and Asaiah the king's personal **a**:
Job 12:20 He silences the trusted **a**, and he removes the
Jer 39:3 the king's **a**, and many others.
39:13 a chief officer, and Nergal-sharezer, the king's **a**,

ADVISERS (39) [ADVISE]
Ge 41:37 were well received by Pharaoh and his **a**.
50:4 Joseph approached Pharaoh's **a** and asked them to
50:7 a great number of Pharaoh's counselors and **a**—
1Sa 28:7 Saul then said to his **a**, "Find a woman who is a
28:7 His **a** replied, "There is a medium at Endor."
2Sa 10:3 Hanun's **a** said to their master, "Do you really
12:18 David's **a** were afraid to tell him. "He was
12:21 His **a** were amazed. "We don't understand you,"
13:31 His **a** also tore their clothes in horror and sorrow.
15:15 "We are with you," his **a** replied. "Do what you
1Ki 1:2 So his **a** told him, "We will find a young virgin
1:23 The king's **a** told him, "Nathan the prophet is here
12:8 had grown up with him and who were now his **a**.
12:14 and followed the counsel of his younger **a**. He told
2Ki 12:21 and Jehozabad son of Shomer—both trusted **a**.
24:12 along with his **a**, nobles, and officials,
25:19 of the Judean army, five of the king's personal **a**,
1Ch 19:3 Hanun's **a** said to him, "Do you really think these
2Ch 10:8 had grown up with him and who were now his **a**.
10:14 and followed the counsel of his younger **a**. He told
22:4 members of Ahab's family became his **a**, and they
25:17 After consulting with his **a**, King Amaziah of
32:3 he consulted with his officials and military **a**,
Est 1:13 He immediately consulted with his **a**, who knew all
Ps 105:22 king's aides as he pleased / and teach the king's **a**.
Pr 25:1 collected by the **a** of King Hezekiah of Judah.
29:12 If a ruler honors liars, all his **a** will be wicked.
Isa 3:3 honorable citizens, **a**, skilled magicians,
47:13 You have more than enough **a**, astrologers,
Jer 52:25 of the Judean army, seven of the king's personal **a**,
Da 1:5 then some of them would be made his **a** in the
1:19 So they were appointed to his regular staff of **a**.
3:2 prefects, governors, **a**, counselors, judges,
3:24 jumped up in amazement and exclaimed to his **a**,
3:27 and **a** crowded around them and saw that the fire
4:36 My **a** and officers sought me out, and I was
6:7 We administrators, prefects, princes, **a**, and other
Mt 14:2 he said to his **a**, "This must be John the Baptist
Ac 25:12 Festus conferred with his **a** and then replied,

ADVOCATE (4)
1Sa 24:15 He is my **a**, and he will rescue me from your
Job 16:19 my witness is in heaven. My **a** is there on high.
Gal 6:13 And even those who **a** circumcision don't really
Heb 9:24 heaven itself to appear now before God as our **A**.

AENEAS (3)
Ac 9:33 There he met a man named **A**, who had been
9:34 Peter said to him, "**A**, Jesus Christ heals you!
9:35 and Sharon turned to the Lord when they saw **A**

AENON (1)
Jn 3:23 At this time John the Baptist was baptizing at **A**,

AFAR (1) [FAR]
Pr 31:14 like a merchant's ship; she brings her food from **a**.

AFFAIR (4) [AFFAIRS]
1Ki 15:5 except in the **a** concerning Uriah the Hittite.
Ezr 10:13 many of us are involved in this extremely sinful **a**.
10:14 may be turned away from us concerning this **a**."
Pr 7:5 Let them hold you back from an **a** with an immoral

AFFAIRS (14) [AFFAIR]
Ge 39:5 All his household **a** began to run smoothly, and his
2Sa 17:23 set his **a** in order, and hanged himself.
1Ki 4:6 Ahishar was manager of palace **a**. / Adoniram son
2Ki 20:1 Set your **a** in order, for you are going to die.
Isa 38:1 Set your **a** in order, for you are going to die.
41:4 directing the **a** of the human race as each new
Da 2:49 and Abednego to be in charge of all the **a** of the
6:4 some fault in the way Daniel was handling his **a**,
Lk 16:1 "A rich man hired a manager to handle his **a**,
Ac 7:10 and put him in charge of all the **a** of the palace.
24:10 that you have been a judge of Jewish **a** for many
Php 2:4 Don't think only about your own **a**, but be
2Ti 2:4 do not let yourself become tied up in the **a** of this
1Pe 4:15 making trouble, or prying into other people's **a**.

AFFECT (2) [AFFECTED, AFFECTS]
Job 35:8 No, your sins **a** only people like yourself, and your good deeds **a** only other people.

AFFECTED (30) [AFFECT]
Lev 13:3 then examine the **a** area of a person's skin.
13:3 If the hair in the **a** area has turned white
13:4 "But if the **a** area of the skin is white but does not
13:5 If the **a** area has not changed or spread on the skin,
13:6 If the **a** area has faded and not spread, the priest
13:10 and an open sore appears in the **a** area,
13:17 the **a** areas have indeed turned completely white,
13:20 and if the hair in the **a** area has turned white,
13:21 priest sees that there is no white hair in the **a** area,
13:22 If during that time the **a** area spreads on the skin,
13:25 If the hair in the **a** area turns white and the problem
13:26 discovers that there is no white hair in the **a** area
13:27 If at the end of that time the **a** area has spread on
13:28 But if the **a** area has not moved or spread on the
13:30 and fine yellow hair is found in the **a** area,
13:31 and there is no black hair in the **a** area,
13:32 If at the end of that time the **a** area has not spread
13:33 shave off all hair except the hair on the **a** area.
13:37 and black hair has grown in the **a** area,
13:39 the priest must examine the **a** area. If the patch is
13:49 If the **a** area in the clothing, the animal hide,
13:50 After examining the **a** spot, the priest will put it

13:51 If the **a** area has spread, the material is clearly
13:53 and the **a** spot has not spread in the clothing,
13:55 If he sees that the **a** area has not changed
13:56 But if the priest sees that the **a** area has faded after
14:44 If he sees that the **a** areas have spread, the walls
14:48 and finds that the **a** areas have not reappeared after
1Co 5:6 is allowed to go on sinning, soon all will be **a**?
Eph 2:11 even though it **a** only their bodies and not their

AFFECTION (6) [AFFECTIONATELY, AFFECTIONS]

Ge 29:34 "Surely now my husband will feel **a** for me,
34:3 for Dinah was strong, and he tried to win her **a**.
Ex 20:5 am a jealous God who will not share your **a** with
Dt 5:9 am a jealous God who will not share your **a** with
Ro 12:10 Love each other with genuine **a**, and take delight in
2Co 9:14 And they will pray for you with deep **a** because of

AFFECTIONATELY (1) [AFFECTION]

Ge 33:4 to meet him and embraced him **a** and kissed him.

AFFECTIONS (1) [AFFECTION]

Ps 26:2 and cross-examine me. / Test my motives and **a**.

AFFECTS (2) [AFFECT]

Pr 4:23 guard your heart, for it **a** everything you do.
1Co 6:18 No other sin so clearly **a** the body as this one does.

AFFINITY [KJV] See ALLIANCE, ARRANGED

AFFIRM (1) [AFFIRMATION, REAFFIRM]

Dt 27:26 'Cursed is anyone who does not **a** the terms of this

AFFIRMATION (1) [AFFIRM]

2Co 1:19 to you, and he is the divine Yes—God's **a**.

AFFLICT (2) [AFFLICTED, AFFLICTING, AFFLICTION, AFFLICTIONS]

Dt 28:27 "The LORD will **a** you with the boils of Egypt
1Sa 5:6 Then the LORD began to **a** the people of Ashdod

AFFLICTED (6) [AFFLICT]

1Sa 5:12 Those who didn't die were **a** with tumors;
Job 36:6 not let the wicked live but gives justice to the **a**.
36:8 come upon them and they are enslaved and **a**,
Ps 74:19 your doves. / Don't forget your **a** people forever.
Isa 51:21 But now listen to this, you **a** ones, who sit in a
La 1:3 has been led away into captivity, **a** and enslaved.

AFFLICTING (2) [AFFLICT]

1Sa 5:9 the LORD began **a** its people, young and old,
6:5 Perhaps then he will stop **a** you, your gods,

AFFLICTION (3) [AFFLICT]

Job 30:27 and restless. Days of **a** have come upon me.
Ps 88:T to be sung to the tune "The Suffering of **A**."
Isa 30:20 Lord gave you adversity for food and **a** for drink,

AFFLICTIONS (1) [AFFLICT]

La 3:1 I am the one who has seen the **a** that come from

AFFORD (12)

Lev 5:7 "If any of them cannot **a** to bring a sheep,
5:11 "If any of the people cannot **a** to bring young
12:8 "If a woman cannot **a** to bring a sheep, she must
14:21 "But anyone who cannot **a** two lambs must bring
14:22 or two young pigeons, whichever the person can **a**.
14:30 whichever the person was able to **a**.
14:32 but who cannot **a** to bring the sacrifices normally
25:28 But if the original owner cannot **a** to redeem it,
27:8 a vow but cannot **a** to pay the prescribed amount,
1Sa 18:23 "How can a poor man from a humble family **a** the
2Ch 28:13 "We cannot **a** to add to our sins and guilt.
2Co 8:3 testify that they gave not only what they could **a**

AFFRIGHT [KJV] See TERRIFY

AFIRE (1) [FIRE]

SS 1:10 are your cheeks, with your earrings setting them **a**!

AFLAME (1) [FLAME]

Hos 7:4 They are all adulterers, always **a** with lust.

AFOREHAND [KJV] See AHEAD

AFRAID (223) [FEAR]

Ge 3:10 heard you, so I hid. I was **a** because I was naked."
9:2 and all the birds and fish will be **a** of you.
15:1 in a vision and said to him, "Do not be **a**, Abram,
18:15 Sarah was **a**, so she denied that she had laughed.
19:30 Lot left Zoar because he was **a** of the people there,
21:17 from the sky, "Hagar, what's wrong? Do not be **a**!
26:7 He was **a** to admit that she was his wife.
26:9 "Because I was **a** someone would kill me to get
26:24 "Do not be **a**, for I am with you and will bless
28:17 He was **a** and said, "What an awesome place this
31:31 "I rushed away because I was **a**," Jacob answered.
32:11 I am **a** that he is coming to kill me, along with my
35:17 the midwife finally exclaimed, "Don't be **a**—
38:11 to do this because he was **a** Shelah would also die,
46:3 Do not be **a** to go down to Egypt, for I will see to it
50:15 their father was dead, Joseph's brothers became **a**.
50:19 But Joseph told them, "Don't be **a** of me. Am I
50:21 No, don't be **a**. Indeed, I myself will take care of
Ex 3:6 face in his hands because he was **a** to look at God.
4:19 said to him, "Do not be **a** to return to Egypt,
14:13 But Moses told the people, "Don't be **a**. Just stand
20:20 "Don't be **a**," Moses said, "for God has come in
34:30 of Moses' face, they were **a** to come near him.
Nu 12:8 as he is. Should you not be **a** to criticize him?"
14:9 and don't be **a** of the people of the land.
14:9 but the LORD is with us! Don't be **a** of them!"
21:34 The LORD said to Moses, "Do not be **a** of him,
Dt 1:17 Don't be **a** of how they will react, for you are
1:21 of your ancestors, has promised you. Don't be **a**!
1:29 "But I said to you, 'Don't be **a**!
1:39 You were **a** they would be captured, but they will
3:2 But the LORD told me, 'Do not be **a** of him,
3:22 Do not be **a** of the nations there, for the LORD
5:5 for you were **a** of the fire and did not climb the
7:18 But don't be **a** of them! Just remember what the
7:21 "No, do not be **a** of those nations, for the LORD
13:11 Then all Israel will hear about it and be **a**, and such
17:13 will hear about it and be **a** to act so arrogantly.
19:20 Those who hear about it will be **a** to do such an
20:1 and an army greater than your own, do not be **a**.
20:3 Do not be **a** as you go out to fight today! Do not
21:21 and all Israel will hear about it and be **a**.
31:6 Be strong and courageous! Do not be **a** of them!
31:8 Do not be **a** or discouraged, for the LORD is the
Jos 1:9 and courageous! Do not be **a** or discouraged.
2:9 this land," she told them. "We are all **a** of you.
6:1 because the people were **a** of the Israelites.
8:1 said to Joshua, "Do not be **a** or discouraged.
10:2 and his people became very **a** when they heard all
10:8 "Do not be **a** of them," the LORD said to
10:25 "Don't ever be **a** or discouraged," Joshua told his
11:6 the LORD said to Joshua, "Do not be **a** of them.
Jdg 4:18 "Come into my tent, sir. Come in. Don't be **a**."
6:23 LORD replied. "Do not be **a**. You will not die."
6:27 because he was **a** of the other members of his
7:3 'Whoever is timid or **a** may leave and go
7:10 But if you are **a** to attack, go down to the camp
8:20 draw his sword, for he was only a boy and was **a**.
9:21 because he was **a** of his brother Abimelech.
1Sa 3:15 He was **a** to tell Eli what the LORD had said to
4:20 "Don't be **a**," they said. "You have a baby boy!"
11:7 And the LORD made the people **a** of Saul's
12:12 "But when you were **a** of Nahash, the king of
12:20 "Don't be **a**," Samuel reassured them. "You have
15:24 for I was **a** of the people and did what they
16:4 at Bethlehem, the leaders of the town became **a**.
18:12 for Saul was **a** of him, and he was jealous
18:15 recognized this, he became even more **a** of him.
18:29 he became even more **a** of him, and he remained
21:12 and was **a** of what King Achish might do to him.
23:3 David's men said, "We're **a** even here in Judah.
23:17 "Don't be **a**," Jonathan reassured him.
28:13 "Don't be **a**!" the king told her. "What do you
29:9 But my commanders are **a** to have you with them
31:4 But his armor bearer was **a** and would not do it.
2Sa 1:14 "Were you not **a** to kill the LORD's anointed
3:11 because he was **a** of what Abner might do.
6:9 David was now **a** of the LORD and asked,
9:7 But David said, "Don't be **a**! I've asked you to
10:19 the Arameans were **a** to help the Ammonites.
12:18 David's advisers were **a** to tell him. "He was
13:28 gets drunk; then at my signal, kill him! Don't be **a**.
1Ki 1:50 Adonijah himself was **a** of Solomon, so he rushed
17:13 But Elijah said to her, "Don't be **a**! Go ahead
19:3 Elijah was **a** and fled for his life. He went to
2Ki 1:15 angel of the LORD said to Elijah, "Don't be **a**.
6:16 "Don't be **a**!" Elisha told him. "For there are
25:26 for they were **a** of what the Babylonians would do
1Ch 10:4 But his armor bearer was **a** and would not do it.
13:12 David was now **a** of God and asked, "How can I
22:13 and courageous; do not be **a** or lose heart!
28:20 Don't be **a** or discouraged by the size of the task,
2Ch 20:15 This is what the LORD says: Do not be **a**!
20:17 and Jerusalem. Do not be **a** or discouraged.
32:7 Don't be **a** of the king of Assyria or his mighty
Ezr 3:3 Even though the people were **a** of the local
Ne 4:14 and said to them, "Don't be **a** of the enemy!
Est 9:2 a stand against them, for everyone was **a** of them.
Job 6:21 You have seen my calamity, and you are **a**.
33:7 So you don't need to be **a** of me. I am not some great person to make you nervous and **a**.
41:25 When it rises, the mighty are **a**, gripped by terror.
Ps 3:6 I am not **a** of ten thousand enemies / who surround
23:4 through the dark valley of death, / I will not be **a**,
27:1 and my salvation— / so why should I be **a**?
31:11 even my friends are **a** to come near me.
40:9 I have not been **a** to speak out, / as you, O LORD,
56:3 But when I am **a**, / I put my trust in you.
56:4 your word. / I trust in God, so why should I be **a**?
56:11 I trust in God, so why should I be **a**? / What can
78:53 He kept them safe so they were not **a**; / but the sea
91:5 Do not be **a** of the terrors of the night, / nor fear
118:6 The LORD is for me, so I will not be **a**.
Pr 3:25 You need not be **a** of disaster or the destruction
Ecc 12:5 You will be **a** of heights and of falling,
Isa 8:12 Do not be **a** that some plan conceived behind
10:24 do not be **a** of the Assyrians when they oppress
12:2 come to save me. / I will trust in him and not be **a**.
13:8 and are **a**. Fear grips them with terrible pangs,
35:4 Say to those who are **a**, "Be strong, and do not
40:9 Shout louder to Jerusalem—do not be **a**.
41:10 Don't be **a**, for I am with you. Do not be dismayed,
41:13 And I say to you, 'Do not be **a**. I am here to help
41:14 you are, O Israel, don't be **a**, for I will help you.
43:1 "Do not be **a**, for I have ransomed you. I have
43:5 "Do not be **a**, for I am with you. I will gather you
44:2 O Jacob, my servant, do not be **a**. O Israel,
44:8 Do not tremble; do not be **a**. Have I not proclaimed
51:7 Do not be **a** of people's scorn or their slanderous
51:12 So why are you **a** of mere humans, who wither like
57:11 Why were you more **a** of them than of me? How is
Jer 1:8 And don't be **a** of the people, for I will be with you
1:17 Do not be **a** of them, or I will make you look
10:2 Do not be **a** of their predictions, even though other
10:5 Do not be **a** of such gods, for they can neither
14:4 The farmers are **a**; they, too, cover their heads.
22:25 to kill you, of whom you are so desperately **a**—
23:4 to care for them, and they will never be **a** again.
30:10 "So do not be **a**, Jacob, my servant; do not be
30:10 in their own land, and no one will make them **a**.
35:11 we were **a** of the Babylonian and Aramean armies.
38:19 "But I am **a** to surrender," the king said,
41:18 They were **a** of what the Babylonians would do
46:27 "But do not be **a**, Jacob, my servant; do not be
46:27 and quiet, and nothing will make them **a**.
Eze 2:6 Don't be **a** even though their threats are sharp as
3:9 So don't be **a** of them or fear their angry looks,
34:28 will live in safety, and no one will make them **a**.
39:26 then no one will bother them or make them **a**.
Da 1:10 I am **a** the king will have me beheaded for
5:10 live the king! Don't be so pale and **a** about this.
10:12 Then he said, "Don't be **a**, Daniel. Since the first
10:19 "Don't be **a**," he said, "for you are deeply loved
Joel 2:21 Don't be **a**, my people! Be glad now and rejoice
2:22 Don't be **a**, you animals of the field! The pastures
Zep 3:13 in safety; there will be no one to make them **a**."
3:16 to Jerusalem will be, "Cheer up, Zion! Don't be **a**!
Hag 2:5 when you came out of Egypt. So do not be **a**.
Zec 8:13 So don't be **a** or discouraged, but instead get on
8:15 and the people of Judah. So don't be **a**.
Mt 1:20 "do not be **a** to go ahead with your marriage to
2:22 new ruler was Herod's son Archelaus, he was **a**.
8:26 And Jesus answered, "Why are you **a**? You have
10:26 But don't be **a** of those who threaten you.
10:28 "Don't be **a** of those who want to kill you.
10:31 So don't be **a**; you are more valuable to him than a
14:5 would have executed John, but he was **a** of a riot,
14:27 "It's all right," he said. "I am here! Don't be **a**."
17:7 touched them. "Get up," he said, "don't be **a**."
21:46 but they were **a** to try because the crowds
25:25 I was **a** I would lose your money, so I hid it in the
28:5 "Don't be **a**!" he said. "I know you are looking
28:10 Then Jesus said to them, "Don't be **a**! Go tell my
Mk 4:40 And he asked them, "Why are you so **a**? Do you
5:36 their comments and said to Jairus, "Don't be **a**.
6:50 "It's all right," he said. "I am here! Don't be **a**."
9:6 know what to say, for they were all terribly **a**.
9:32 and they were **a** to ask him what he meant.
11:18 But they were **a** of him because the people were
11:32 For they were **a** that the people would start a riot,
12:12 But they were **a** to touch him because of the
Lk 1:13 But the angel said, "Don't be **a**, Zechariah!
2:10 the angel reassured them. "Don't be **a**!" he said.
5:10 also amazed. Jesus replied to Simon, "Don't be **a**!
8:35 clothed and sane. And the whole crowd was **a**.
8:50 what had happened, he said to Jairus, "Don't be **a**.
9:45 understand it, and they were **a** to ask him about it.
12:4 don't be **a** of those who want to kill you.
12:7 So don't be **a**; you are more valuable to him than a
12:32 "So don't be **a**, little flock. For it gives your
19:21 I was **a** because you are a hard man to deal with,
20:19 But they were **a** there would be a riot if they
Jn 6:20 he called out to them, "I am here! Don't be **a**."
7:13 for they were **a** of getting in trouble with the
9:22 said this because they were **a** of the Jewish leaders,
12:15 "Don't be **a**, people of Israel. / Look, your King is
14:27 peace the world gives. So don't be troubled or **a**.
20:19 because they were **a** of the Jewish leaders.
Ac 5:26 for they were **a** the people would kill them if they
9:26 meet with the believers, but they were all **a** of him.
18:9 to Paul in a vision and told him, "Don't be **a**!
19:40 I am **a** we are in danger of being charged with
27:17 The sailors were **a** of being driven across to the
27:24 and he said, 'Don't be **a**, Paul, for you will surely
27:29 At this rate they were **a** we would soon be driven
Ro 13:4 of course you should be **a**, for you will be
2Co 12:20 For I am **a** that when I come to visit you I won't
12:20 I am **a** that I will find quarreling, jealousy,
12:21 Yes, I am **a** that when I come, God will humble me
Gal 2:12 because he was **a** of what these legalists would
4:11 I am **a** that all my hard work for you was worth
1Th 3:5 I was **a** that the Tempter had gotten the best of you
1Ti 5:15 For I am **a** that some of them have already gone
2Ti 4:5 Don't be **a** of suffering for the Lord. Work at
Heb 11:23 and they were not **a** of what the king might do.
11:27 He was not **a** of the king. Moses kept right on
13:6 "The Lord is my helper, / so I will not be **a**.
1Pe 3:14 reward you for it. So don't be **a** and don't worry.
1Jn 4:17 So we will not be **a** on the day of judgment,
4:18 If we are **a**, it is for fear of judgment, and this
Rev 1:17 he laid his right hand on me and said, "Don't be **a**!
2:10 Don't be **a** of what you are about to suffer.
12:11 of their testimony. And they were not **a** to die.

AFRESH (1) [FRESH]

La 3:23 is his faithfulness; his mercies begin **a** each day.

AFRESH [KJV] See also AGAIN

AFRICAN (1)

Ac 27:17 across to the sandbars of Syrtis off the **A** coast,

AFTER (788) [AFTERWARD]

Ge 1:27 in his own image; / God patterned them **a** himself;
3:24 **A** banishing them from the garden, the LORD
4:17 Cain founded a city, he named it Enoch **a** his son.
5: 4 **A** the birth of Seth, Adam lived another 800 years,
5: 7 **A** the birth of Enosh, Seth lived another 807 years,
5:10 **A** the birth of Kenan, Enosh lived another 815
5:13 **A** the birth of Mahalalel, Kenan lived another 840
5:16 **A** the birth of Jared, Mahalalel lived 830 years,
5:19 **A** the birth of Enoch, Jared lived another 800
5:22 **A** the birth of Methuselah, Enoch lived another
5:26 **A** the birth of Lamech, Methuselah lived another
5:30 **A** the birth of Noah, Lamech lived 595 years,
8: 3 the flood gradually began to recede. **A** 150 days,
8: 6 **A** another forty days, Noah opened the window he
8:13 years old, ten and a half months **a** the flood began,
9:20 **A** the Flood, Noah became a farmer and planted a
9:28 Noah lived another 350 years **a** the Flood.
10: 1 Many children were born to them **a** the Flood.
10:32 with the people of these nations **a** the Flood.
11:10 was born. This happened two years **a** the Flood.
11:11 **A** the birth of Arphaxad, Shem lived another 500
11:13 **A** the birth of Shelah, Arphaxad lived another 403
11:15 **A** the birth of Eber, Shelah lived another 403 years
11:17 **A** the birth of Peleg, Eber lived another 430 years
11:19 **A** the birth of Reu, Peleg lived another 209 years
11:21 **A** the birth of Serug, Reu lived another 207 years
11:23 **A** the birth of Nahor, Serug lived another 200
11:25 **A** the birth of Terah, Nahor lived another 119
12: 8 **A** that, Abram traveled southward and set up camp
13: 8 to stop," he said. "**A** all, we are close relatives!
13:14 **A** Lot was gone, the LORD said to Abram,
14:14 He chased a Kedorlaomer's army until he caught
15:16 **A** four generations your descendants will return
16: 3 (This happened ten years **a** Abram first arrived in
17: 7 covenant between us, generation **a** generation.
17: 7 your God and the God of your descendants **a** you.
17:12 must be circumcised on the eighth day **a** his birth.
19: 3 with fresh bread made without yeast. **A** the meal,
21: 4 Eight days **a** Isaac was born, Abraham circumcised
21:32 **A** making their covenant, Abimelech left with
22:20 Soon **a** this, Abraham heard that Milcah,
24:67 and she was a special comfort to him **a** the death of
25:11 **A** Abraham's death, God poured out rich blessings
26:18 which the Philistines had filled in **a** Abraham's
29: 3 **A** watering them, the stone would be rolled back
29:14 **A** Jacob had been there about a month,
29:28 A week **a** Jacob had married Leah, Laban gave
30:25 Soon **a** Joseph was born to Rachel, Jacob said to
32:23 **A** they were on the other side, he sent over all his
35: 8 Soon **a** this, Rebekah's old nurse, Deborah, died.
35: 9 he arrived at Bethel **a** traveling from Paddan-aram.
35:17 **A** a very hard delivery, the midwife finally
36:30 The Horite clans are named **a** their clan leaders,
37:12 Soon **a** this, Joseph's brothers went to pasture their
37:27 responsible for his death; **a** all, he is our brother!"
38:12 **A** the time of mourning was over, Judah and his
38:29 break out first?" And ever **a**, he was called Perez.
39:10 She kept putting pressure on him day **a** day,
39:19 **A** hearing his wife's story, Potiphar was furious!
39:23 The chief jailer had no more worries **a** that,
41:14 **A** a quick shave and change of clothes, he went in
41:49 **A** seven years, the granaries were filled to
43:20 to him, "Sir, **a** our first trip to Egypt to buy food,
44: 4 household manager, "Chase **a** them and stop them.
45:24 his brothers off, and as they left, he called **a** them,
47:28 Jacob lived for seventeen years **a** his arrival in
48: 1 One day not long **a** this, word came to Joseph that
50: 5 **A** his burial is complete, I will return without
Ex 2: 5 Soon **a** this, one of Pharaoh's daughters came
2:12 **A** looking around to make sure no one was
4: 9 "And if they do not believe you even **a** these two
4:10 and I'm not now, even **a** you have spoken to me.
4:26 **A** that, the LORD left him alone.
5: 1 **A** this presentation to Israel's leaders, Moses
7: 4 **a** which I will lead the forces of Israel out with
9: 7 But even **a** he found it to be true, his heart
10:12 and eat all the crops still left **a** the hailstorm."
11: 1 **A** that, Pharaoh will let you go. In fact, he will be
13: 9 **A** all, it was the LORD who rescued you from
14: 4 harden Pharaoh's heart, and he will chase **a** you.
14: 4 **A** this, the Egyptians will know that I am the
14: 5 were not planning to return to Egypt **a** three days,
14: 8 and he chased **a** the people of Israel who had
15:27 **A** leaving Marah, they came to Elim, where there
16: 1 They arrived there a month **a** leaving Egypt.
17:16 be at war with Amalek generation **a** generation."
18:27 Soon **a** this, Moses said good-bye to his
19: 1 of Sinai exactly two months **a** they left Egypt.
19: 2 **A** breaking camp at Rephidim, they came to the
21: 6 **A** that, the slave will belong to his master forever.
21:21 If the slave recovers **a** a couple of days, however,
29:30 Whoever is the next high priest **a** Aaron will wear
29:37 **A** that, the altar will be exceedingly holy,
30:29 **A** this, whatever touches them will become holy.
32: 6 **A** this, they celebrated with feasting and drinking,
32:21 **A** that, he turned to Aaron. "What did the people
Lev 6:10 **a** dressing in his special linen clothing
6:16 **A** burning this handful, the rest of the flour will
8:21 **A** washing the internal organs and the legs with
9: 1 **A** the ordination ceremony, on the eighth day,
9:22 **A** that, Aaron raised his hands toward the people
9:22 Then, **a** presenting the sin offering, the whole
10:12 "Take what is left of the grain offering **a** the
11:32 **A** that, it will be ceremonially clean and may be
11:44 **A** all, I, the LORD, am your God. You must be
12: 7 Then she will be ceremonially clean again **a** her
12: 7 These are the instructions to be followed **a** the
13: 6 So **a** washing the clothes, the person will be
13: 7 But if the rash continues to spread **a** this
13:12 "Now suppose the priest discovers **a** his
13:17 If, **a** another examination, the affected areas have
13:34 **A** washing clothes, that person will be clean.
13:35 But if the infection begins to spread **a** the person is
13:50 **A** examining the affected spot, the priest will put it
13:55 area has not changed appearance **a** being washed,
13:56 that the affected area has faded **a** being washed,
13:58 But if the spot disappears **a** the object is washed,
14:19 **A** that, the priest will slaughter the whole burnt
14:43 "But if the mildew reappears **a** all these things
14:48 areas have not reappeared **a** the fresh plastering,
14:52 **A** he has purified the house in this way,
15:18 **A** having sexual intercourse, both the man
15:28 seven days. **A** that, she will be ceremonially clean.
16: 1 The LORD spoke to Moses **a** the death of
16:11 **A** he has slaughtered this bull for the sin offering,
16:12 **a** filling both his hands with fragrant incense,
16:17 No one may enter until he comes out again **a**
16:22 **A** the man sets it free in the wilderness, the goat
17: 7 law for them, to be kept generation **a** generation.
17:15 until evening; **a** that, you will be considered clean.
21: 6 **A** all, they are the ones who present the offerings
22: 7 **A** all, this food has been set aside for them.
23: 6 Then the day **a** the Passover celebration,
23:11 On the day **a** the Sabbath, the priest will lift it up
23:14 or fresh kernels on that day until **a** you have
23:15 "From the day **a** the Sabbath, the day the bundle
23:16 Keep counting until the day **a** the seventh Sabbath,
23:27 on the ninth day **a** the Festival of Trumpets.
23:34 Shelters on the fifth day **a** the Day of Atonement.
23:39 **a** you have harvested all the produce of the land,
24:23 **A** Moses gave all these instructions to the
25:16 **A** all, the person selling the land is actually selling
25:27 **A** buying it back, the original owner may
25:29 has the right to redeem it for a full year **a** its sale.
25:33 **A** all, the cities reserved for the Levites are the
26:27 "If **a** this you still refuse to listen and still remain
27:18 But if the field is dedicated **a** the Year of Jubilee,
Nu 1: 1 during the second year **a** Israel's departure from
6:19 **A** each Nazirite's head has been shaved, the priest
6:20 **A** this ceremony the Nazirites may again drink
7:88 This was the dedication offering for the altar **a** it
8:15 **A** this, they may go in and out of the Tabernacle to
8:26 **A** retirement they may assist their fellow Levites
9: 1 during the second year **a** Israel's departure from
10:11 during the second year **a** Israel's departure from
10:33 They marched for three days **a** leaving the
11: 3 **A** that, the area was known as Taberah—
11: 6 and day **a** day we have nothing to eat but this
12:14 camp for seven days, and **a** that she may return."
13:25 **A** exploring the land for forty days, the men
14:11 even **a** all the miraculous signs I have done among
19:12 they will continue to be unclean even **a** the seventh
21:32 **A** Moses sent men to explore the Jazer area,
25: 8 and rushed **a** the man into his tent. Phinehas thrust
26: 1 **A** the plague had ended, the LORD said to Moses
26: 5 The Hanochite clan, named **a** its ancestor Hanoch.
26: 5 The Palluite clan, named **a** its ancestor Pallu.
26: 6 The Hezronite clan, named **a** its ancestor Hezron.
26: 6 The Carmite clan, named **a** its ancestor Carmi.
26:12 The Nemuelite clan, named **a** its ancestor Nemuel.
26:12 The Jaminite clan, named **a** its ancestor Jamin.
26:12 The Jakinite clan, named **a** its ancestor Jakin.
26:13 The Zerahite clan, named **a** its ancestor Zerah.
26:13 The Shaulite clan, named **a** its ancestor Shaul.
26:15 The Zephonite clan, named **a** its ancestor Zephon.
26:15 The Haggite clan, named **a** its ancestor Haggi.
26:15 The Shunite clan, named **a** its ancestor Shuni.
26:16 The Oznite clan, named **a** its ancestor Ozni.
26:16 The Erite clan, named **a** its ancestor Eri.
26:17 The Arodite clan, named **a** its ancestor Arodi.
26:17 The Arelite clan, named **a** its ancestor Areli.
26:20 The Shelanite clan, named **a** its ancestor Shelah.
26:20 The Perezite clan, named **a** its ancestor Perez.
26:20 The Zerahite clan, named **a** its ancestor Zerah.
26:21 The Hezronites, named **a** their ancestor Hezron.
26:21 The Hamulites, named **a** their ancestor Hamul.
26:23 The Tolaite clan, named **a** its ancestor Tola.
26:23 The Puite clan, named **a** its ancestor Puah.
26:24 The Jashubite clan, named **a** its ancestor Jashub.
26:24 Shimronite clan, named **a** its ancestor Shimron.
26:26 The Seredite clan, named **a** its ancestor Sered.
26:26 The Elonite clan, named **a** its ancestor Elon.
26:26 The Jahleelite clan, named **a** its ancestor Jahleel.
26:29 The Makirite clan, named **a** its ancestor Makir.
26:29 named **a** its ancestor Gilead, Makir's son.
26:30 The Iezerites, named **a** their ancestor Iezer.
26:30 The Helekites, named **a** their ancestor Helek.
26:31 The Asrielites, named **a** their ancestor Asriel.
26:31 named **a** their ancestor Shechem.
26:32 The Shemidaites, named **a** their ancestor Shemida.
26:32 The Hepherites, named **a** their ancestor Hepher.
26:35 Shuthelahite clan, named **a** its ancestor Shuthelah.
26:35 The Bekerite clan, named **a** its ancestor Beker.
26:35 The Tahanite clan, named **a** its ancestor Tahan.
26:36 The Eranites, named **a** their ancestor Eran.
26:38 The Belaite clan, named **a** its ancestor Bela.
26:38 The Ashbelite clan, named **a** its ancestor Ashbel.
26:38 The Ahiramite clan, named **a** its ancestor Ahiram.
26:39 Shuphamite clan, named **a** its ancestor Shupham.
26:39 Huphamite clan, named **a** its ancestor Hupham.
26:40 The Ardites, named **a** their ancestor Ard.
26:40 The Naamites, named **a** their ancestor Naaman.
26:42 The Shuhamite clan, named **a** its ancestor Shuham.
26:44 The Imnite clan, named **a** its ancestor Imnah.
26:44 The Ishvite clan, named **a** its ancestor Ishvi.
26:44 The Beriite clan, named **a** its ancestor Beriah.
26:45 The Heberites, named **a** their ancestor Heber.
26:45 The Malkielites, named **a** their ancestor Malkiel.
26:48 The Jahzeelite clan, named **a** its ancestor Jahzeel.
26:48 The Gunite clan, named **a** its ancestor Guni.
26:49 The Jezerite clan, named **a** its ancestor Jezer.
26:49 The Shillemite clan, named **a** its ancestor Shillem.
26:57 Gershonite clan, named **a** its ancestor Gershon.
26:57 The Kohathite clan, named **a** its ancestor Kohath.
26:57 The Merarite clan, named **a** its ancestor Merari.
27:13 **A** you have seen it, you will die as Aaron your
31: 2 **A** that, you will die and join your ancestors."
31:11 **A** they had gathered the plunder and captives,
32: 9 **A** they went up to the valley of Eshcol and scouted
32:42 and he renamed that area Nobah **a** himself.
33: 3 **a** the first Passover celebration in early spring.
33: 5 **A** leaving Rameses, the Israelites set up camp at
33:38 during the fortieth year **a** Israel's departure from
35:28 But **a** the death of the high priest, the slayer may
Dt 1: 3 But forty years **a** the Israelites left Mount Sinai,
1: 4 This was **a** he had defeated King Sihon of the
1:32 But even **a** all he did, you refused to trust the
3:14 Jair renamed this region **a** himself, calling it the
9: 4 "**A** the LORD your God has done this for you,
11:12 He watches over it day **a** day throughout the year!
15:17 the door. **A** that, he will be your servant for life.
16:13 **a** the grain has been threshed and the grapes have
17:11 **A** they have interpreted the law and reached a
21:13 her father and mother. **A** that you may marry her.
22:13 **a** sleeping with her, changes his mind about her
24:21 Do not glean the vines **a** they are picked, but leave
28:14 I am giving you today to follow **a** other gods
31:16 **A** you are gone, these people will begin
31:27 How much more rebellious will you be **a** my
31:29 I know that **a** my death you will become utterly
Jos 1: 1 **A** the death of Moses the LORD's servant,
2:11 No one has the courage to fight **a** hearing such
5: 5 but none of those born **a** the Exodus,
5: 8 **A** all the males had been circumcised, they rested
6: 8 **A** Joshua spoke to the people, the seven priests
8:16 the men in the city were called out to chase **a** them.
8:17 or Bethel who did not chase **a** the Israelites,
10:21 **A** that, no one dared to speak a word against Israel.
10:36 **A** leaving Eglon, they attacked Hebron,
14:15 It had been named **a** Arba, a great hero of the
15:13 which had been named **a** Anak's ancestor.
19:47 They renamed the city Dan **a** their ancestor.
19:49 **A** all the land was divided among the tribes,
20: 6 **A** that, the one found innocent is free to return
22:17 even **a** the plague that struck the entire assembly of
24: 6 the Egyptians chased **a** you with chariots
24:29 Soon **a** this, Joshua son of Nun, the servant of the
Jdg 1: 1 **A** Joshua died, the Israelites asked the LORD,
2: 6 **A** Joshua sent the people away, each of the tribes
2:10 **A** that generation died, another generation grew up
2:12 They chased **a** other gods, worshiping the gods of
3:18 **A** delivering the payment, Ehud sent home those
3:24 **A** Ehud was gone, the king's servants returned
3:25 But when the king didn't come out **a** a long delay,
3:31 **A** Ehud, Shamgar son of Anath rescued Israel.
4: 1 **A** Ehud's death, the Israelites again did what was
6:29 And **a** asking around and making a careful search,
7:19 It was just **a** midnight, **a** the changing of the guard,
7:23 who joined in the chase **a** the fleeing army of
8: 7 "**A** the LORD gives me victory over Zebah
8: 9 "**A** I return in victory, I will tear down this
8:13 **A** this, Gideon returned by way of Heres Pass.
9: 3 And **a** listening to their proposal, they decided in
9:22 **A** Abimelech had ruled over Israel for three years,
10: 1 **A** Abimelech's death, Tola, the son of Puah
10: 3 **A** Tola died, a man from Gilead named Jair judged
11:16 their journey from Egypt **a** crossing the Red Sea,
11:26 But now **a** three hundred years you make an issue
12: 8 **A** Jephthah, Ibzan became Israel's judge. He lived
12:11 **A** him, Elon from Zebulun became Israel's judge.
12:13 **A** Elon died, Abdon son of Hillel, from Pirathon,
16:16 So day **a** day she nagged him until he couldn't
18:22 and some of his neighbors came chasing **a** them.
18:23 these men together and chased **a** us like this?"
18:29 They renamed the town Dan **a** their ancestor,
19: 2 father's home in Bethlehem. **A** about four months,
19:21 **A** they washed their feet, they had supper together.
20:42 but the Israelites chased **a** them and killed them.
21: 9 For **a** they counted all the people, no one from
Ru 3: 7 **A** Boaz had finished his meal and was in good
3:10 now than ever by not running **a** a younger man,
4: 4 because I am next in line to redeem it **a** you."
1Sa 1: 7 Year **a** year it was the same—Peninnah would
1: 9 Hannah went over to the Tabernacle **a** supper to
1:25 **A** sacrificing the bull, they took the child to Eli.
4: 3 **A** the battle was over, the army of Israel retreated
5: 1 **A** the Philistines captured the Ark of God,
6: 3 you will know that God didn't send the plague **a**
9:25 **A** the feast, when they had returned to the town,
9:27 **A** the servant was gone, Samuel said, "Stay here,
10: 7 **A** these signs take place, do whatever you think is
13: 3 Soon **a** this, Jonathan attacked and defeated the
13:14 for the LORD has sought out a man **a** his own

14:27 the honey. **A** he had eaten it, he felt much better.
14:37 Saul asked God, "Should we go **a** the Philistines?
17:35 I go **a** it with a club and take the lamb from its
17:52 great shout of triumph and rushed **a** the Philistines,
17:57 **A** David had killed Goliath, Abner brought him to
18: 1 **A** David had finished talking with Saul, he met
18: 6 was returning home **a** David had killed Goliath.
18:21 "I have a way for you to become my son-in-law **a**
19: 8 War broke out shortly **a** that, and David led his
20:19 The day **a** tomorrow, toward evening, go to the
23:13 David had escaped, so he didn't go to Keilah **a** all.
23:14 Saul hunted him day **a** day, but God didn't let him
23:25 in the wilderness of Maon. But Saul kept **a** him.
24: 1 **A** Saul returned from fighting the Philistines,
24: 7 **A** Saul had left the cave and gone on his way,
24: 8 David came out and shouted **a** him, "My lord the
26: 9 For who can remain innocent **a** attacking the
30: 8 And the LORD told him, "Yes, go **a** them.
2Sa 1: 1 **A** the death of Saul, David returned from his
1: 2 On the third day **a** David's return, a man arrived
2: 1 **A** this, David asked the LORD, "Should I move
2:24 out what had happened, they set out **a** Abner.
3: 8 "**A** all I have done for you and your father by not
3:22 But just **a** Abner left, Joab and some of David's
5:13 **A** moving from Hebron to Jerusalem,
5:22 But **a** a while the Philistines returned and again
6:13 **A** the men who were carrying it had gone six steps,
8: 1 **A** this, David subdued and humbled the Philistines
8:13 **A** his return he destroyed eighteen thousand
10: 1 Some time **a** this, King Nahash of the Ammonites
10:14 **A** the battle was over, Joab returned to Jerusalem.
10:19 **A** that, the Arameans were afraid to help the
11: 2 Late one afternoon David got out of bed **a** taking a
11: 4 (She had just completed the purification rites **a**
11: 8 David even sent a gift to Uriah **a** he had left the
11:10 Why didn't you go home last night **a** being away
12:15 **A** Nathan returned to his home, the LORD made
12:20 **A** that, he returned to the palace and ate.
13: 4 of a king look so dejected morning **a** morning?"
15: 1 **A** this, Absalom bought a chariot and horses,
15: 7 **A** four years, Absalom said to the king, "Let me
17: 1 "Let me choose twelve thousand men to start out **a**
17: 3 **A** all, it is only this man's life that you seek.
17:29 and thirsty **a** your long march through the
18:18 He named the monument **a** himself, and it is
19:39 **A** David had blessed and embraced him,
20: 6 and chase **a** him before he gets into a fortified city
20: 7 and Joab set out **a** Sheba with an elite guard from
20:10 left him lying there and continued **a** Sheba.
21:14 **A** that, God ended the famine in the land of Israel.
21:17 **A** that, David's men declared, "You are not going
21:18 **A** this, there was another battle against the
22: 1 David sang this song to the LORD **a** the LORD
23: 5 He will constantly look **a** my safety and success.
24:10 But **a** he had taken the census, David's conscience
1Ki 1: 6 handsome man and had been born next **a** Absalom.
1:20 your decision as to who will become king **a** you.
6: 1 This was 480 years **a** the people of Israel were
6: 9 **A** completing the Temple structure, Solomon put
6:36 so that there was one layer of cedar beams **a** every
7:12 so that there was one layer of cedar beams **a** every
8:66 **A** the festival was over, Solomon sent the people
9:24 **A** Solomon moved his wife, Pharaoh's daughter,
10: 8 privilege for your officials to stand here day **a** day,
10:25 Year **a** year, everyone who came to visit brought
11:24 **A** David conquered Hadadezer, Rezon and his men
13:14 he rode **a** the man of God and found him sitting
13:23 Now **a** the man of God had finished eating
13:33 But even **a** this, Jeroboam did not turn from his
15: 4 and he gave Abijam a son to rule **a** him in
17: 7 But **a** a while the brook dried up, for there was no
18: 1 **A** many months passed, in the third year of the
18:33 the offering and the wood." **A** they had done this,
19:11 **A** the wind there was an earthquake,
19:12 And **a** the earthquake there was a fire,
19:12 And **a** the fire there was the sound of a gentle
19:20 ran **a** Elijah, and said to him, "First let me go
20:23 **A** their defeat, Ben-hadad's officers said to him,
22:32 Jehoshaphat in his royal robes, they went **a** him.
2Ki 1: 1 **A** King Ahab's death, the nation of Moab declared
3: 5 But **a** Ahab's death, the king of Moab rebelled
4: 5 many jars to her, and she filled one **a** another.
4:40 But **a** the men had eaten a bite or two they cried
5:20 I will chase **a** him and get something from him."
5:21 So Gehazi set off **a** him. When Naaman saw him
running **a** him, he climbed
6:23 **A** that, the Aramean raiders stayed away from the
6:25 **A** a while even a donkey's head sold for two
7: 8 they went into one tent **a** another, eating,
8: 3 **A** the famine ended she returned to the land of
9:27 Jehu rode **a** him, shouting, "Shoot him, too!"
10:15 **A** they had greeted each other, Jehu said to him,
13: 3 and his son Ben-hadad to defeat them time **a** time.
14:17 King Amaziah of Judah lived on for fifteen years **a**
14:19 But his enemies sent assassins **a** him, and they
14:22 **A** his father's death, Uzziah rebuilt the town of
17:29 In town **a** town where they lived, they placed their
18: 5 in the land of Judah, either before or **a** his time.
19: 5 **A** King Hezekiah's officials delivered the king's
19:14 **A** Hezekiah received the letter and read it, he went
20:12 Soon **a** this, Merodach-baladan son of Baladan,
22:20 disaster against this city until **a** you have died
24: 7 The king of Egypt never returned **a** that,
25: 5 But the Babylonians chased **a** them and caught the
1Ch 2:19 **A** Azubah died, Caleb married Ephrathah, and they
2:24 Soon **a** Hezron died in the town of
6:31 at the house of the LORD **a** he put the Ark there.
8: 8 **A** Shaharaim divorced his wives Hushim
12:19 **A** much discussion, they sent them back, for they
12:22 Day **a** day more men joined David until he had a
14:13 But **a** a while, the Philistines returned and raided
18: 1 **A** this, David subdued and humbled the Philistines
19: 1 Some time **a** this, King Nahash of the Ammonites
19:19 **A** that, the Arameans were no longer willing to
20: 4 **A** this, war broke out with the Philistines at Gezer.
23: 6 **a** the clans descended from the three sons of Levi
2Ch 5:10 with the people of Israel **a** they left Egypt.
9: 7 privilege for your officials to stand here day **a** day,
9:24 Year **a** year, everyone who came to visit brought
15:15 Eagerly they sought **a** God, and they found him.
18:31 Jehoshaphat in his royal robes, they went **a** him.
20: 1 **A** this, the armies of the Moabites, Ammonites,
20:21 **A** consulting the leaders of the people, the king
20:23 **A** they had finished off the army of Seir,
21:18 It was **a** this that the LORD struck Jehoram with
22: 4 **A** the death of his father, members of Ahab's
23: 8 Jehoiada the priest did not let anyone go home **a**
24:11 This went on day **a** day, and a large amount of
24:17 But **a** Jehoiada's death, the leaders of Judah came
25:17 **A** consulting with his advisers, King Amaziah of
25:25 King Amaziah of Judah lived on for fifteen years **a**
25:27 **A** Amaziah turned away from the LORD,
25:27 But his enemies sent assassins **a** him, and they
26: 2 **A** his father's death, Uzziah rebuilt the town of
26:17 Azariah the high priest went in **a** him with eighty
31: 1 **A** this, the Israelites returned to their own towns
32: 1 **A** Hezekiah had faithfully carried out this work,
33:14 It was **a** this that Manasseh rebuilt the outer wall of
34: 8 **a** he had purified the land and the Temple,
34:28 and its people until **a** you have died and been
35:20 **A** Josiah had finished restoring the Temple,
36:17 young men, even chasing **a** them into the Temple.
Ezr 3: 8 during the second year **a** they arrived in Jerusalem.
8:22 **A** all, we had told the king, "Our God protects all
8:33 On the fourth day **a** our arrival, the silver, gold,
9:10 O our God, what can we say **a** all of this?
Ne 2:11 Three days **a** my arrival at Jerusalem,
3:14 **A** rebuilding it, he hung the doors and installed the
3:23 **A** them, Benjamin, Hasshub, and Azariah son of
5: 7 **A** thinking about the situation, I spoke out against
6:15 just fifty-two days **a** we had begun.
7: 1 **A** the wall was finished and I had hung the doors
11: 8 and **a** him there were Gabbai and Sallai, and a total
Est 2: 1 But **a** Xerxes' anger had cooled, he began thinking
2: 4 **A** that, the young woman who pleases you most
2:19 Even **a** all the young women had been transferred
3: 4 They spoke to him day **a** day, but still he refused to
Job 19:26 And **a** my body has decayed, yet in my body I will
20:21 Nothing is left **a** he finishes gorging himself;
21: 3 let me speak. **A** I have spoken, you may mock me.
22: 8 **A** all, you think the land belongs to the powerful
29:18 'Surely I will die surrounded by my family **a** a
29:22 And **a** I spoke, they had nothing to add, for my
30: 5 and people shout **a** them as if they were thieves.
34:34 **A** all, bright people will tell me, and wise people
36:14 They die young **a** wasting their lives in immoral
42: 7 **A** the LORD had finished speaking to Job,
42:16 Job lived 140 years **a** that, living to see four
Ps 10:15 Go **a** them until the last one is destroyed!
16: 4 Those who chase **a** other gods will be filled with
19: 2 Day **a** day they continue to speak; / night **a** night
they make him known.
19: 5 **a** his wedding. / It rejoices like a great athlete
49:11 They may name their estates **a** themselves,
51: T **a** David had committed adultery with Bathsheba.
61: 8 to your name / as I fulfill my vows day **a** day.
71:18 your mighty miracles to all who come **a** me.
84: 6 where pools of blessing collect **a** the rains!
88: 7 anger lies heavy on me; / wave **a** wave engulfs me.
102: 8 My enemies taunt me day **a** day. / They mock
145:13 You rule generation **a** generation. / The LORD is
Pr 19: 7 The poor call **a** them, but they are gone.
20: 7 with integrity; blessed are their children **a** them.
27:25 **A** the hay is harvested, the new crop appears,
Ecc 2: 3 **A** much thought, I decided to cheer myself with
6:12 And who can tell what will happen in the future **a**
7:27 "I came to this result **a** looking into the matter
10:11 It does no good to charm a snake **a** it has bitten
Isa 1: 8 shelter in a vineyard or field **a** the harvest is over.
7:10 Not long **a** this, the LORD sent this message to
9:13 For **a** all this punishment, the people will still not
10:12 **A** the Lord has used the king of Assyria to
13:20 Generation **a** generation will come and go,
17: 5 grainfields in the valley of Rephaim **a** the harvest.
17: 6 like the stray olives left on the tree **a** the harvest.
21: 8 "Day **a** day I have stood on the watchtower,
21: 8 Night **a** night I have remained at my post.
23:17 **a** seventy years the LORD will revive Tyre.
24:13 the tree or the few grapes left on the vine **a** harvest,
28:19 morning **a** morning, day and night, until you are
29: 1 Year **a** year you offer your many sacrifices.
37: 5 **A** King Hezekiah's officials delivered the king's
37:14 **A** Hezekiah received the letter and read it, he went
39: 1 Soon **a** this, Merodach-baladan son of Baladan,
40:26 He brings them out one **a** another, calling each by
44:15 And **a** his care, he uses part of the wood to make a
64:12 **A** all this, LORD, must you still refuse to help
Jer 2:25 Why do you refuse to turn from all this running **a**
3: 7 I thought that **a** she had done all this she would
3:15 And I will give you leaders **a** my own heart,
8: 9 the word of the LORD. Are they so wise **a** all?
9:22 like dung, or like bundles of grain **a** the harvest.
21: 7 the LORD, even **a** King Zedekiah, his officials,
24: 1 **A** King Nebuchadnezzar of Babylon exiled
25:12 "Then, **a** the seventy years of captivity are over,
25:26 northern countries, far and near, one **a** the other—
25:32 "Look! Disaster will fall upon nation **a** nation!
29: 2 This was **a** King Jehoiachin, the queen mother,
32:16 Then **a** I had given the papers to Baruch, I prayed
32:33 Day **a** day, year **a** year, I taught them right from
34: 8 This message came to Jeremiah from the LORD **a**
34:14 Hebrew slave must be freed **a** serving six years.
35:15 I have sent you prophet **a** prophet to tell you to
36:27 **A** the king had burned Jeremiah's scroll,
39:12 "Look **a** him well, and give him anything he
40: 1 The LORD gave a message to Jeremiah **a**
40:13 Soon **a** this, Johanan son of Kareah and the other
45: 1 **a** Baruch had written down everything Jeremiah
52: 8 But the Babylonians chased **a** them and caught
Eze 4: 6 **A** that, turn over and lie on your right side for 40
5: 2 **A** acting out the siege, burn it there.
7: 5 With one blow **a** another I will bring total disaster!
12:14 to the four winds and send the sword **a** them.
15: 5 useless both before and **a** being put into the fire!
16:28 And **a** your prostitution there you still were not
17:18 For the king of Israel broke his treaty **a** swearing to
18:28 They will live, because **a** thinking it over,
20:36 in the wilderness **a** bringing them out of Egypt,
22:18 the worthless slag that remains **a** silver is smelted.
23: 5 "Then Oholah lusted **a** other lovers instead of me,
23:20 She lusted **a** lovers whose attentions were gross
23:38 Then **a** doing these terrible things, they defiled my
33:31 their mouths, but their hearts seek only **a** money.
37:25 and their grandchildren **a** them will live there
forever, generation **a** generation.
38: 8 which will be lying in peace **a** her recovery from
38: 8 and **a** the return of her people from many lands.
39:26 and treachery against me **a** they come home to live
40: 1 fourteen years **a** the fall of Jerusalem—the LORD
41: 1 **A** that, the man brought me into the Holy Place,
43: 1 **A** this, the man brought me back around to the east
44:26 to his Temple duties **a** being ritually cleansed
44:31 or that dies **a** being attacked by another animal.
47: 4 **A** another 1,750 feet, it was up to my waist.
48:31 be three gates, each one named **a** a tribe of Israel.
Da 1:11 appointed by the chief official to look **a** Daniel,
1:16 So **a** that, the attendant fed them only vegetables
2:39 "But **a** your kingdom comes to an end,
2:39 **A** that kingdom has fallen, yet a third great
4: 8 (He was named Belteshazzar **a** my god,
4:34 "**A** this time had passed, I, Nebuchadnezzar,
9:26 "**A** this period of sixty-two sets of seven,
9:27 but **a** half this time, he will put an end to the
11:12 **A** the enemy army is swept away, the king of the
11:18 "**A** this, he will turn his attention to the coastal
11:20 but **a** a very brief reign, he will die, though neither
Hos 1: 8 **A** Gomer had weaned Lo-ruhamah, she again
2: 5 'I'll run **a** other lovers and sell myself to them for
2: 7 When she runs **a** her lovers, she won't be able to
4: 2 is violence everywhere, with one murder **a** another.
4:12 Longing **a** idols has made them foolish. They have
6:10 My people have defiled themselves by chasing **a**
7: 7 They kill their kings one **a** another, and no one
8: 3 is good, and now their enemies will chase **a** them.
12: 1 the wind; they chase **a** the east wind all day long.
14: 8 I am the one who looks **a** you and cares for you.
Joel 1: 4 **A** the cutting locusts finished eating the crops,
1: 4 **A** them came the hopping locusts, and
2:28 "Then **a** I have poured out my rains again, I will
Am 5:19 **A** escaping the bear, he leans his hand against a
7: 1 This was **a** the king's share had been harvested
9: 3 I will send the great sea serpent **a** them to bite
Jnh 1: 6 So the captain went down **a** him. "How can you
Mic 2: 3 **A** I am through with you, none of you will ever
3: 4 **A** all the evil you have done, he won't even look at
7: 1 I feel like the fruit picker **a** the harvest who can
7: 9 But **a** that, he will take up my case and punish my
Na 2: 2 land of Israel lies empty and broken **a** your attacks,
Zec 2: 8 "**A** a period of glory, the LORD Almighty sent
10: 3 For the LORD Almighty has arrived to look **a** his
11:16 nor look **a** the young, nor heal the injured, nor feed
Mt 1:12 **A** the Babylonian exile: / Jehoiachin was the father
2: 9 **A** this interview the wise men went their way.
2:13 **A** the wise men were gone, an angel of the Lord
3:16 **A** his baptism, as Jesus came up out of the water,
7:28 **A** Jesus finished speaking, the crowds were
9:27 **A** Jesus left the girl's home, two blind men
14:22 Immediately **a** this, Jesus made his disciples get
14:34 **A** they had crossed the lake, they landed at
16: 5 Later, **a** they crossed to the other side of the lake,
17:22 One day **a** they had returned to Galilee, Jesus told
19: 1 **A** Jesus had finished saying these things, he left
21:41 will give him his share of the crop **a** each harvest."
22:23 a group of Jews who say there is no resurrection **a**
22:31 Long **a** Abraham, Isaac, and Jacob had died,
22:46 And **a** that, no one dared to ask him any more
24:29 "Immediately **a** those horrible days end, / the sun
25:19 "**A** a long time their master returned from his trip
26:32 But **a** I have been raised from the dead, I will go
27: 7 **A** some discussion they finally decided to buy the
27:35 **A** they had nailed him to the cross, the soldiers
27:53 **a** Jesus' resurrection. They left the cemetery,
27:63 '**A** three days I will be raised from the dead.'
Mk 1:14 Later on, **a** John was arrested by Herod Antipas,
1:29 **A** Jesus and his disciples left the synagogue,
6:45 Immediately **a** this, Jesus made his disciples get
8: 9 that day, and he sent them home **a** they had eaten.
8:10 Immediately **a** this, he got into a boat with his
9:33 **A** they arrived at Capernaum, Jesus and his
10:34 and kill him, but **a** three days he will rise again."
12:18 a group of Jews who say there is no resurrection **a**

12:26 Long a Abraham, Isaac, and Jacob had died,
12:34 And a that, no one dared to ask him any more
13:24 "At that time, a those horrible days end, / the sun
14:28 But a I am raised from the dead, I will go ahead of
16:14 to believe those who had seen him a he had risen.
Lk 1:48 servant girl, / and now generation a generation
1:59 They wanted to name him Zechariah, a his father.
2:22 as required by the law of Moses a the birth of a
2:43 A the celebration was over, they started home to
4:38 A leaving the synagogue that day, Jesus went to
7:24 A they left, Jesus talked to the crowd about John.
7:42 Who do you suppose loved him more a that?"
9:36 what they had seen until long a this happened.
9:37 The next day, a they had come down the mountain,
14:22 A the servant had done this, he reported, 'There is
15:30 Yet when this son of yours comes back a
19:14 and sent a delegation a him to say they did not
19:28 A telling this story, Jesus went on toward
19:47 A that, he taught daily in the Temple,
20:27 a group of Jews who say there is no resurrection a
20:31 And so it went, one a the other, until each of the
20:37 Long a Abraham, Isaac, and Jacob had died,
22:20 A supper he took another cup of wine and said,
22:58 A a while someone else looked at him and said,
23: 9 He asked Jesus question a question, but Jesus
Jn 1:16 he brought to us—one gracious blessing a another!
2:12 A the wedding he went to Capernaum for a few
2:22 A he was raised from the dead, the disciples
3: 1 A dark one evening, a Jewish religious leader
4:13 "People soon become thirsty again a drinking this
4:54 miraculous sign in Galilee a coming from Judea.
6: 1 A this, Jesus crossed over the Sea of Galilee,
6:31 A all, our ancestors ate manna while they
7: 1 A this, Jesus stayed in Galilee, going from village
7:10 But a his brothers had left for the festival,
7:31 "A all," they said, "would you expect the
10: 4 A he has gathered his own flock, he walks ahead of
11: 7 Finally a two days, he said to his disciples,
12:16 But a Jesus entered into his glory,
12:19 Look, the whole world has gone a him!"
12:36 A saying these things, Jesus went away and was
13:12 A washing their feet, he put on his robe again
14: 9 I am, even a all the time I have been with you?
16:16 Then, just a little while a that, you will see me
16:19 Then, just a little while a that, you will see me
18: 1 A saying these things, Jesus crossed the Kidron
21:15 A breakfast Jesus said to Simon Peter, "Simon son
Ac 1: 2 until the day he ascended to heaven a giving his
1: 3 During the forty days a his crucifixion,
1: 9 It was not long a he said this that he was taken up
2: 1 of Pentecost, seven weeks a Jesus' resurrection,
4:31 A this prayer, the building where they were
5: 4 And a selling it, the money was yours to give
5:30 from the dead a you killed him by crucifying him.
5:37 A him, at the time of the census, there was Judas of
8:25 A testifying and preaching the word of the Lord in
9:23 A a while the Jewish leaders decided to kill him.
9:28 and a that he was constantly with them in
10:37 beginning in Galilee a John the Baptist began
10:41 and drank with him a he rose from the dead.
11:19 a Stephen's death traveled as far as Phoenicia,
12: 4 to bring Peter out for public trial a the Passover.
12:12 A a little thought, he went to the home of Mary,
13: 3 So a more fasting and prayer, the men laid their
13:15 A the usual readings from the books of Moses
13:20 A that, judges ruled until the time of Samuel the
13:22 'David son of Jesse is a man a my own heart,
13:36 for a David had served his generation according to
14:21 A preaching the Good News in Derbe and making
15: 7 a a long discussion, Peter stood and addressed
15:36 A some time Paul said to Barnabas, "Let's return
16:18 This went on day a day until Paul got
17: 9 and the other believers a they had posted bail.
17:11 They searched the Scriptures day a day to check up
17:27 all of this was that the nations should seek a God
18: 5 And a Silas and Timothy came down from
18: 7 A that he stayed with Titius Justus, a Gentile who
18:18 Paul stayed in Corinth for some time a that and
18:23 A spending some time in Antioch, Paul went back
19:21 "And a that," he said, "I must go on to Rome!"
20:23 except that the Holy Spirit has told me in city a
20:29 vicious wolves, will come in among you a I leave,
21: 1 A saying farewell to the Ephesian elders, we sailed
21: 7 The next stop a leaving Tyre was Ptolemais,
21:19 A greetings were exchanged, Paul gave a detailed
21:20 A hearing this, they praised God. But then they
22:17 "One day a I returned to Jerusalem, I was praying
24:17 "A several years away, I returned to Jerusalem
25: 1 Three days a Festus arrived in Caesarea to take
25:26 King Agrippa, so that a we examine him,
27: 7 and a great difficulty we finally neared Cnidus.
27:38 A eating, the crew lightened the ship further by
28:11 It was three months a the shipwreck that we set
28:17 Three days a Paul's arrival, he called together the
28:25 But a they had argued back and forth among
Ro 2: 7 seeking a the glory and honor and immortality that
3:29 A all, God is not the God of the Jews only, is he?
4:10 Was he declared righteous only a he had been
15:23 and a all these long years of waiting, I am eager to
15:24 And a I have enjoyed your fellowship for a little
1Co 9:27 I fear that a preaching to others I myself might be
10: 5 Yet a all this, God was not pleased with most of
11:25 he took the cup of wine a supper, saying,
11:34 I'll give you instructions about the other matters a
14:31 one a the other, so that everyone will learn and be
15: 6 A that, he was seen by more than five hundred of
15: 8 Last of all, I saw him, too, long a the others,
15: 9 and I am not worthy to be called an apostle a the
15:24 A that the end will come, when he will turn the
16: 5 I am coming to visit you a I have been to
2Co 9: 4 only to find that you still weren't ready a all I had
10: 6 disobedient a the rest of you became loyal
11:19 A all, you, who think you are so wise,
Gal 1:21 Then a this visit, I went north into the provinces of
3: 2 for the Holy Spirit came upon you only a you
3: 3 A starting your Christian lives in the Spirit,
Eph 6:13 so that a the battle you will still be standing firm.
Php 3:17 Dear friends, pattern your lives a mine, and learn
Col 4:16 A you have read this letter, pass it on to the church
1Th 2:17 a we were separated from you for a little while
2:19 A all, what gives us hope and joy, and what is our
1Ti 6: 7 A all, we didn't bring anything with us when we
Tit 3:10 A that, have nothing more to do with that person.
Heb 1: 3 A he died to cleanse us from the stain of sin,
4:10 just as God rested a creating the world.
7: 1 When Abraham was returning home a winning a
7:28 But a the law was given, God appointed his Son
9:17 The will goes into effect only a the death of the
9:19 For a Moses had given the people all of God's
9:25 Place year a year to offer the blood of an animal.
9:27 person dies only once and a that comes judgment,
10: 1 system were repeated again and again, year a year,
10: 3 sacrifices reminded them of their sins year a year.
10:11 the priest stands before the altar day a day,
10:26 if we deliberately continue sinning a we have
12: 4 A all, you have not yet given your lives in your
12: 8 are illegitimate and are not really his children a all.
12:15 Look a each other so that none of you will miss out
1Pe 1: 7 So if your faith remains strong a being tried by
4: 2 spend the rest of your life chasing a evil desires,
5:10 A you have suffered a little while, he will restore,
2Pe 1:15 I want you to remember them long a I am gone.
2: 8 by the wickedness he saw and heard day a day.
Jude 1:14 Now Enoch, who lived seven generations a Adam,
Rev 4: 1 and I will show you what must happen a these
4: 8 Day a day and night a night they keep on saying,
7: 9 A this I saw a vast crowd, too great to count,
11:11 But a three and a half days, the spirit of life from
14:17 A that, another angel came from the Temple in
18: 1 A all this I saw another angel come down from
19: 1 A this, I heard the sound of a vast crowd in heaven

AFTERBIRTH (1)

Dt 28:57 She will hide from them the a and the new baby

AFTERNOON (14)

Ge 24:42 "So this a when I came to the spring I prayed this
Jdg 19: 8 to eat; then you can leave some time this a."
19: 9 That a, as he and his concubine and servant were
2Sa 11: 2 Late one a David got out of bed after taking a nap
1Ki 18:29 They raved all a until the time of the evening
Mk 6:35 Late in the a his disciples came to him and said,
11:11 and then he left because it was late in the a.
Lk 9:12 Late in the a the twelve disciples came to him
23:54 This was done late on Friday a, the day of
Jn 1:39 It was about four o'clock in the a when they went
4:52 "Yesterday a at one o'clock his fever suddenly
Ac 3: 1 and John went to the Temple one a to take part in
10: 3 One a about three o'clock, he had a vision in
10:30 I was praying in my house at three o'clock in the a.

AFTERWARD (83) [AFTER]

Ge 4: 9 A the LORD asked Cain, "Where is your
6: 4 In those days, and even a, giants lived on the earth,
15: 1 A the LORD spoke to Abram in a vision and said
19:30 A Lot left Zoar because he was afraid of the people
31:54 to a feast. A they spent the night there in the hills.
34:30 A Jacob said to Levi and Simeon, "You have
38:19 A she went home, took off her veil, and put on her
41:21 but a they were still as ugly and gaunt as before!
41:30 But a there will be seven years of famine so great
Ex 21: 3 when he became your slave and then married a,
29:25 A take the bread from their hands, and burn it on
29:26 as a special gift to him. A keep it for yourself.
29:36 A make an offering to cleanse the altar.
33:11 A Moses would return to the camp, but the young
34:35 A he would put the veil on again until he returned
Nu 19: 7 A he may return to the camp, though he will
19:21 the water of purification must a wash their clothes,
Dt 25:10 Ever a his family will be referred to as 'the family
26:11 A go and celebrate because of all the good things
Jos 24: 5 on Egypt; and a I brought you out as a free people.
Jdg 6:33 Soon a the armies of Midian, Amalek,
7:25 A the Israelites brought the heads of Oreb
16:10 A Delilah said to him, "You made fun of me
1Sa 19: 7 A Jonathan called David and told him what had
1Ki 13:31 A the prophet said to his sons, "When I die,
14:27 A Rehoboam made bronze shields as substitutes,
17:13 A there will still be enough food for you and your
20:22 A the prophet said to King Ahab, "Get ready for
2Ki 9:34 A he said, "Someone go and bury this cursed
19: 9 Soon a King Sennacherib received word that King
1Ch 7:23 A Ephraim slept with his wife, and she became
2Ch 35:14 A the Levites prepared a meal for themselves
Est 6:12 A Mordecai returned to the palace gate, but Haman
Pr 5:11 A you will groan in anguish when disease
Ecc 9:15 But a no one thought any more about him.
Isa 1:26 A I will give you good judges and wise counselors
37: 9 Soon a King Sennacherib received word that King
Jer 12:15 But a I will return and have compassion on all of
13: 6 A long time a, the LORD said to me, "Go back
28:12 Soon a the LORD gave this message to Jeremiah:
46:26 But a the land will recover from the ravages of
49: 6 But a I will restore the fortunes of the
Eze 11:24 A the Spirit of God carried me back again to
43:27 On the eighth day, and on each day a, the priests
Da 7:20 and the little horn that came up a and destroyed
8:27 A I got up and performed my duties for the king,
11: 8 For some years a he will leave the king of the
Hos 3: 5 But a the people will return to the LORD their
Mt 14:23 A he went up into the hills by himself to pray.
17:19 A the disciples asked Jesus privately,
Mk 3:13 A Jesus went up on a mountain and called the ones
4:34 but a when he was alone with his disciples,
6:46 A he went up into the hills by himself to pray.
8:19 many baskets of leftovers did you pick up a?"
9:28 A, when Jesus was alone in the house with his
16:12 A he appeared to two who were walking from
16: S A Jesus himself sent them out from east to west
Lk 1:24 Soon a his wife, Elizabeth, became pregnant
6:12 One day soon a Jesus went to a mountain to pray,
7:11 Soon a Jesus went with his disciples to the village
8: 1 Not long a Jesus began a tour of the nearby cities
Jn 3:22 A Jesus and his disciples left Jerusalem, but they
5: 1 A Jesus returned to Jerusalem for one of the Jewish
5:14 But a Jesus found him in the Temple and told him,
6:11 out to the people. A he did the same with the fish.
19:38 A Joseph of Arimathea, who had been a secret
Ac 9:19 A he ate some food and was strengthened.
10:48 A Cornelius asked him to stay with them for
12:19 A Herod left Judea to stay in Caesarea for a while.
13: 6 A they preached from town to town across the
15:16 'A I will return, / and I will restore the fallen
19:21 A Paul felt impelled by the Holy Spirit to go over
21:15 Shortly a we packed our things and left for
1Co 7: 5 A they should come together again so that Satan
Gal 2:12 But a, when some Jewish friends of James came,
1Ti 2:13 For God made Adam first, and a he made Eve.
Heb 12: 2 because of the joy he knew would be his a.
12:11 But a there will be a quiet harvest of right living
12:17 And a, when he wanted his father's blessing,
Jas 1:12 A they will receive the crown of life that God has
1Pe 1:11 about Christ's suffering and his great glory a.
4:13 and a you will have the wonderful joy of sharing
Rev 20: 3 A he would be released again for a little while.

AGABUS (2)

Ac 11:28 One of them named A stood up in one of the
21:10 During our stay of several days, a man named A,

AGAG (6) [AGAG'S, AGAGITE]

Nu 24: 7 Their king will be greater than A; / their kingdom
1Sa 15: 8 He captured A, the Amalekite king, but completely
15:20 I brought back King A, but I destroyed everyone
15:32 Then Samuel said, "Bring King A to me."
15:32 A arrived full of smiles, for he thought,
15:33 And Samuel cut A to pieces before the LORD at

AGAG'S (1) [AGAG]

1Sa 15: 9 Saul and his men spared A life and kept the best of

AGAGITE (3) [AGAG]

Est 3: 1 son of Hammedatha the A to prime minister,
3:10 giving it to Haman son of Hammedatha the A—
9:24 Haman son of Hammedatha the A, the enemy of

AGAIN (892)

Ge 4:25 Adam slept with his wife a, and she gave birth to
8:10 Seven days later, Noah released the dove a.
8:12 A week later, he released the dove a, and this time
8:21 and said to himself, "I will never a curse the earth,
9:15 Never a will there be a flood that will destroy all
13: 4 the altar, and there he a worshiped the LORD.
18: 1 The LORD appeared a to Abraham while he was
18:27 Then Abraham spoke a. "Since I have begun,
19: 2 as early as you like and be on your way a."
19:33 He was unaware of her lying down or getting up a.
19:34 Let's get him drunk with wine a tonight, and you
19:35 So that night they got him drunk a,
19:35 he was unaware of her lying down or getting up a.
22:15 Then the angel of the LORD called a to Abraham
22:19 young men and traveled home a to Beersheba,
23:12 Abraham bowed a to the people of the land,
24:16 down to the spring, filled her jug, and came up a.
24:20 the watering trough and ran down to the well a.
25: 1 Now Abraham married a. Keturah was his new
26:21 dug another well, but a there was a fight over it.
26:31 Then Isaac sent them home a in peace.
29:33 She soon became pregnant a and had another son.
29:34 A she became pregnant and had a son. She named
29:35 Once a she became pregnant and had a son.
30: 7 Then Bilhah became pregnant a and gave Jacob a
30:17 She became pregnant a and gave birth to her fifth
30:19 Then she became pregnant a and had a sixth son.
30:31 Laban asked a. Jacob replied, "Don't give me
31: 7 breaking his wage agreement with me a and a.
32: 1 As Jacob and his household started on their way a,
35: 5 When they set out a, terror from God came over
35: 9 God appeared to Jacob once a when he arrived at
37: 1 So Jacob settled a in the land of Canaan, where his
38:11 not to marry a at that time but to return to her
38:23 laughingstock of the village if we went back a."
38:26 son Shelah." But Judah never slept with Tamar a.
41: 5 Soon he fell asleep a and had a second dream.
41: 7 Then Pharaoh woke up a and realized it was a
43: 2 said to his sons, "Go a and buy us a little food."

43: 3 couldn't see him a unless Benjamin came along.
43:21 in our sacks. Here it is; we have brought it back a.
43:28 is alive and well." Then they bowed a before him.
44:13 loaded the donkeys a, and returned to the city.
44:23 'You may not see me a unless your youngest
44:25 when he said, 'Go back a and buy us a little food,'
45: 4 And he said a, "I am Joseph, your brother whom
46: 4 to Egypt, and I will bring your descendants back a.
47:10 Then Jacob blessed Pharaoh a before he left.
47:15 of money, they came to Joseph crying a for food.
47:18 The next year they came a and said, "Our money
48:11 said to Joseph, "I never thought I would see you a,
48:21 will be with you and will bring you a to Canaan,
Ex 2:13 next day, as Moses was out visiting his people a,
4: 1 But Moses protested a, "Look, they won't believe
4: 4 and grabbed it, and it became a shepherd's staff a.
4: 6 Moses did so, and when he took it out a, his hand
4: 7 "Now put your hand back into your robe a,"
4:13 But Moses a pleaded, "Lord, please!
7:22 But a the magicians of Egypt used their secret arts,
8: 1 "Go to Pharaoh once a and tell him, 'This is what
8:29 don't change your mind a and refuse to let the
8:32 But Pharaoh hardened his heart a and refused to let
9: 4 But the LORD will a make a distinction between
9:34 and his officials sinned yet a by stubbornly
10: 1 "Return to Pharaoh and a make your demands.
10:14 and there has never a been one like it.
10:20 But the LORD made Pharaoh stubborn once a,
10:28 "Don't ever let me see you a! The day you do,
10:29 Moses replied. "I will never see you a."
11: 6 been such wailing before and there never will be a.
12:16 first day of the festival, and a on the seventh day,
13:16 A I say, this ceremony will be like a mark branded
14: 4 And once a I will harden Pharaoh's heart, and he
14:13 Egyptians that you see today will never be seen a.
14:26 said to Moses, "Raise your hand over the sea a.
21: 8 bought her, he may allow her to be bought back a.
21:19 If the injured person is later able to walk a,
24: 7 They all responded a, "We will do everything the
30: 8 he must a burn incense in the LORD's presence.
34:34 he removed the veil until he came out a.
34:35 Afterward he would put the veil on a until he
37:17 made the lampstand, a using pure, hammered gold.
40:37 the cloud stayed, they would stay until it moved a.
Lev 9:23 they came back out, they blessed the people a,
11:32 it will be ceremonially clean and may be used a.
12: 7 Then she will be ceremonially clean a after her
13: 6 The priest will examine the skin a on the seventh
13: 7 the infected person must return to be examined a.
13:34 and he will examine the infection a on the seventh
13:51 On the seventh day the priest must inspect it a.
13:53 "But if the priest examines it a and the affected
13:55 Then the priest must inspect the object a. If he sees
13:58 after the object is washed, it must be washed a;
14: 9 seventh day, they must a shave off all their hair,
14:19 and a perform the atonement ceremony for the
14:44 the priest must return and inspect the house a.
16:17 No one may enter until he comes out a after
22: 7 they will be clean a and may eat the sacred
22:13 her father's home, she may eat her father's food a.
23: 8 the people must a stop all their regular work to
23:36 you must gather a for a sacred assembly
26: 5 harvest will extend until it is time to plant grain a.
27:15 20 percent. Then the house will a belong to you.
27:19 20 percent. Then the field will a belong to you.
Nu 1:51 the Levites will take it down and set it up a.
3:14 The LORD spoke a to Moses, there in the
6:11 vow that day and let their hair begin to grow a.
6:20 After this ceremony the Nazirites may a drink
12:15 until she was brought back before they traveled a.
14:22 but a and a they tested me by refusing to listen.
16: 8 Then Moses spoke a to Korah: "Now listen,
16:41 community began muttering a against Moses
18: 5 the LORD's anger will never a blaze against the
22:15 Then Balak tried a. This time he sent a larger
22:25 foot against the wall. So Balaam beat the donkey a.
22:27 In a fit of rage Balaam beat it a with his staff.
23:29 Balaam a told Balak, "Build me seven altars
32:15 like this and he abandons them a in the wilderness,
32:31 The tribes of Gad and Reuben said a, "Sir, we will
Dt 1:31 saw how the LORD your God cared for you a and a here in the wilderness,
1:43 you a rebelled against the LORD's command
4:29 From there you will search a for the LORD your
5:25 If the LORD our God speaks to us a, we will
6: 7 Repeat them a and a to your children.
6: 7 you are lying down and when you are getting up a.
9: 6 I will say it a: The LORD your God is not giving
9:19 was ready to destroy you. But a he listened to me.
10: 4 The LORD a wrote the terms of the covenant—
10:10 And once a the LORD yielded to my pleas
11:19 you are lying down and when you are getting up a.
13:11 and such wickedness will never a be done among
18:16 You begged that you might never a have to listen
19:20 about it will be afraid to do such an evil thing a.
24: 4 the former husband may not marry her a, for she
28:68 a journey I promised you would never a make.
30: 4 God will go and find you and bring you back a.
30: 5 to your ancestors, and you will possess that land a.
30: 8 Then you will a obey the LORD and keep all the
33: 7 the cry of Judah / and bring them a to their people.
33:11 strike down their foes so they never rise a."
Jos 5: 2 to make the Israelites a circumcised people a."
5:12 manna appeared that day, and it was never seen a.
6:12 and the priests a carried the Ark of the LORD.
Jdg 3:12 Once a the Israelites did what was evil in the
4: 1 the Israelites a did what was evil in the LORD's
4:19 gave him some milk to drink and covered him a.
6: 1 A the Israelites did what was evil in the LORD's
9:37 But a Gaal said, "No, people are coming down
10: 6 A the Israelites did evil in the LORD's sight.
13: 1 A the Israelites did what was evil in the LORD's
13: 8 please let the man of God come back to us a
13: 9 and the angel of God appeared once a to his wife
13:10 man who appeared to me the other day is here a!"
13:21 The angel did not appear a to Manoah and his
16:12 room as before, and a Delilah cried out, "Samson!
16:14 it with the loom shuttle. A she cried out, "Samson!
16:28 the LORD, "Sovereign LORD, remember me a.
18:21 They started on their way a, placing their children,
19: 8 On the morning of the fifth day he was up early a,
19: 8 ready to leave, and a the woman's father said,
20:23 we fight against our relatives from Benjamin a?"
20:28 we fight against our relatives from Benjamin a
Ru 1: 6 his people in Judah by giving them good crops a.
1:12 your parents' homes, for I am too old to marry a.
1:14 And a they wept together, and Orpah kissed her
2:15 When Ruth went back to work a, Boaz ordered his
4:17 women said, "Now at last Naomi has a son a!"
1Sa 1:18 Then she went back and began to eat a, and she
3: 6 Then the LORD called out a, "Samuel!" A Samuel jumped up and ran to Eli.
3: 9 So he said to Samuel, "Go and lie down a, and if someone calls a, say, 'Yes, LORD,
4:10 fought desperately, and Israel was defeated a.
5: 3 the Ark of the LORD! So they set the idol up a.
5: 4 fallen face down before the Ark of the LORD a.
5:11 So the people summoned the rulers a and begged
7:13 and didn't invade Israel a for a long time.
10:25 the LORD. Then Samuel sent the people home a.
12: 1 Then Samuel addressed the people a: "I have done
12:10 "Then they cried to the LORD a and confessed,
13: 4 So the entire Israelite army mobilized a and met
15:11 been loyal to me and has a refused to obey me."
15:30 Then Saul pleaded a, "I know I have sinned.
15:35 Samuel never went to meet with Saul a, but he
16:16 will quiet you, and you will soon be well a."
17:39 "I'm not used to them." So he took them off a.
19: 9 spirit from the LORD suddenly came upon him a.
20:17 made David reaffirm his vow of friendship a,
20:27 But when David's place was empty a the next day,
23: 4 David asked the LORD a, and a the LORD replied,
23:12 A David asked, "Will these men of Keilah really
23:22 and check a to be sure of where he is staying
23:27 Saul that the Philistines were raiding Israel a.
27:11 This happened a and a while he was living among
2Sa 2:22 A Abner shouted to him, "Get away from here!
3:34 a wicked plot." / All the people wept a for Abner.
5:22 and a spread out across the valley of Rephaim.
5:23 And once a David asked the LORD what to do.
10:18 But a the Arameans fled from the Israelites.
11:13 home to his wife. A he slept at the palace entrance.
12:21 have stopped your mourning and are eating a."
12:23 Can I bring him back a? I will go to him one day,
14:10 I can assure you they will never complain a!"
14:14 out on the ground, which cannot be gathered up a.
14:17 Yes, the king will give us peace of mind a.' I know
14:29 for him a second time, but a Joab refused to come.
15:25 bring me back to see the Ark and the Tabernacle a.
19:10 Let's ask David to come back and be our king a."
19:22 for celebration! I am once a the king of Israel!"
19:30 "I am content just to have you back a, my lord!"
19:37 Then let me return a to die in my own town,
19:43 to speak of bringing him back to be our king a."
20:10 Joab did not need to strike a, and Amasa soon
20:23 Joab once a became the commander of David's
21: 3 so that the LORD will bless his people a."
21:15 Once a the Philistines were at war with Israel.
21:17 men declared, "You are not going out to battle a!
24: 1 Once a the anger of the LORD burned against
1Ki 1:31 Then Bathsheba bowed low before him a
2:19 When he sat down on his throne a, he ordered that
8:47 they may turn to you a in repentance and pray,
10:10 Never a were so many spices brought in as those
12:27 they will a give their allegiance to King Rehoboam
13: 6 ask the LORD your God to restore my hand a!"
13: 6 the LORD, and the king's hand became normal a.
13:24 and the man of God started off a. But as he was
17:14 the LORD sends rain and the crops grow a!"
18:34 he said, "Do the same thing a!" And when they
19: 6 a jar of water! So he ate and drank and lay down a.
19: 7 Then the angel of the LORD came a and touched
19:14 He replied a, "I have zealously served the LORD
19:19 his cloak across his shoulders and walked away a.
20: 5 Soon Ben-hadad's messengers returned a and said,
2Ki 1:12 And a the fire of God fell from heaven and killed
2: 4 But Elisha replied a, "As surely as the LORD
2: 5 "Quiet!" he answered a. "Of course I know it."
2: 6 But a Elisha replied, "As surely as the LORD
4:15 "Call her back a," Elisha told him.
4:34 And the child's body began to grow warm a!
4:35 Then he stretched himself out a on the child.
5: 7 He is only trying to find an excuse to invade us a."
5:17 From now on I will never a offer any burnt
5:19 in peace," Elisha said. So Naaman started home a.
6:22 and drink and send them home a to their master."
8: 8 tell him to ask the LORD if I will get well a."
9:19 A Jehu answered, "What do you know about
13: 5 Then Israel lived in safety a as they had in former
15:29 King Tiglath-pileser of Assyria attacked Israel a,
17:13 A and a the LORD had sent his prophets
19:30 will take root a in your own soil, and you will
23:10 so no one could ever a use it to sacrifice a son
1Ch 14:13 the Philistines returned and raided the valley a.
14:14 And once a David asked God what to do. "Do not
19:18 But a the Arameans fled from the Israelites.
29:22 And a they crowned David's son Solomon as their
2Ch 1:12 king has ever had before you or will ever have a!"
6:37 they may turn to you a in repentance and pray,
24:11 and took the chest back to the Temple a.
28:17 The armies of Edom had a invaded Judah
32:15 I say it a—no god of any nation has ever yet been
Ezr 9:10 For once a we have ignored your commands!
9:14 But now we are a breaking your commands
Ne 2:15 I turned back and entered a at the Valley Gate.
4: 2 they are pulling out of the rubbish and using a!"
4:12 lived near the enemy came and told us a and a,
5: 8 but you are selling them back into slavery a.
9:28 all was going well, your people turned to sin a,
9:28 Yet whenever your people cried to you a for help,
9:30 So once a you allowed the pagan inhabitants of the
13:11 Then I called all the Levites back a and restored
13:21 the wall? If you do this a, I will arrest you!"
Est 2:14 never going to the king a unless he had especially
5:12 me to dine with her and the king a tomorrow!"
7: 2 the king a asked her, "Tell me what you want,
8: 4 A the king held out the gold scepter to Esther.
9:13 give the Jews in Susa permission to do a tomorrow
9:15 more people, though a they took no plunder.
Job 2: 1 One day the angels came a to present themselves
3: 6 never a to be counted among the days of the year, never a to appear among the months.
5:19 He will rescue you a and a so that no evil can
6: 1 Then Job spoke a:
7: 7 a breath, and I will never a experience pleasure.
7:10 gone forever from their home—never to be seen a.
9: 1 Then Job spoke a:
10:17 A and a you witness against me. You pour out
12: 1 Then Job spoke a:
14: 7 there is hope that it will sprout a and grow new
14: 9 water it may bud and sprout a like a new seedling.
14:12 people lie down and do not rise a.
14:13 But mark your calendar to think of me a!
14:14 If mortals die, can they live a? This thought would
16: 1 Then Job spoke a:
16:14 A and a he smashed me, charging at me like a
17:10 "As for all of you, come back and try a! But I will
19: 1 Then Job spoke a:
20: 9 his friends nor his family will ever see him a.
20:17 He will never a enjoy abundant streams of olive oil
21: 1 Then Job spoke a:
21:17 "Yet the wicked get away with it time and time a.
23: 1 Then Job spoke a:
26: 1 Then Job spoke a:
33:14 But God speaks a and a, though people do not
33:25 as healthy as a child's, firm and youthful a.
34:15 would cease, and humanity would turn a to dust.
35: 6 Even if you sin a and a, what effect will it
41: 8 the battle that follows, and you will never try it a!
Ps 36:12 They have been thrown down, never to rise a.
37:36 But when I looked a, they were gone! / Though I
39:13 Spare me so I can smile a / before I am gone
41:10 on me. / Make me well a, so I can pay them back!
42: 5 in God! / I will praise him a—/ my Savior and
42:11 I will praise him a—/ my Savior and my God!
43: 5 I will praise him a—/ my Savior and my God!
49:19 before them / and never a see the light of day.
51: 8 Oh, give me back my joy a; / you have broken
51:12 Restore to me a the joy of your salvation,
51:19 and bulls will a be sacrificed on your altar.
71:20 much hardship, / but you will restore me to life a
71:21 me to even greater honor / and comfort me once a.
77: 7 me forever? / Will he never a show me favor?
78:41 A and a they tested God's patience
80: 3 Turn us a to yourself, O God. / Make your face
80: 7 Turn us a to yourself, O God Almighty.
80:18 Then we will never forsake you a. / Revive us
80:19 Turn us a to yourself, O LORD God Almighty.
85: 4 Now turn to us a, O God of our salvation.
85: 6 Won't you revive us a, / so your people can rejoice
90:16 Let us see your miracles a; / let our children see
94: 8 Think a, you fools! / When will you finally catch
94:15 Judgment will come a for the righteous, / and those
104: 9 the seas, / so they would never a cover the earth.
104:23 they labor until the evening shadows fall a.
104:29 take away their breath, they die / and turn a to dust.
106:43 A and a he delivered them, / but they
107:12 they fell, and no one helped them rise a.
107:26 and sank a to the depths; / the sailors cringed in
116: 7 Now I can rest a, / for the LORD has been
119:106 I've promised it once, and I'll promise a: / I will
119:107 restore my life a, just as you promised.
Pr 19:19 If you rescue them once, you will have to do it a.
24:16 trip seven times, but each time they will rise a.
Ecc 1: 5 The sun rises and sets and hurries around to rise a.
1: 7 water returns a to the rivers and flows a to the sea.
4: 1 A I observed all the oppression that takes place in
4:16 So a, it is all meaningless, like chasing the wind.
SS 1: 2 "Kiss me a and a, for your love is sweeter
5: 3 Should I get dressed a? I have washed my feet.
6:13 come back, that we may see you once a."
Isa 1:26 Then Jerusalem will a be called the Home of
6:13 survive, it will be invaded a and burned.
6:13 the stump will be a holy seed that will grow a."
8: 1 A the LORD said to me, "Make a large
8: 5 Then the LORD spoke to me a and said,
8:15 of them will stumble and fall, never to rise a.
9: 3 Israel will a be great, and its people will rejoice as
9: 5 Never a will uniforms be bloodstained by war.
13:20 Babylon will never rise a. Generation after
13:20 and go, but the land will never a be lived in.

14: 1 of Jacob. Israel will be his special people once a.
14: 1 He will bring them back to settle once a in their
14: 7 the land is at rest and is quiet. Finally it can sing a!
17: 8 They will never a bow down to their Asherah poles
21:12 If you wish to ask a, then come back and ask."
23:12 He says, "Never a will you rejoice, O daughter of
23:12 were a lovely city, but you will never a be strong.
23:16 sing her songs, so that she will a be remembered.
23:17 She will return a to all her evil ways around the
24:20 It falls and will not rise a, for its sins are very
26:14 are dead and gone. / Never a will they return!
26:19 belong to God will live; / their bodies will rise a!
28:10 He tells us everything over and over a, a line at a
28:13 the LORD will spell out his message for them a,
28:16 build on. Whoever believes need never run away a.
28:19 A and a that flood will come, morning after
29:17 of Lebanon will be a fertile field once a.
37:31 will take root a in your own soil, and you will
38: 9 When King Hezekiah was well a, he wrote this
38:11 I said, "Never a will I see the LORD GOD
38:11 land of the living. / Never a will I see my friends
42: 9 has come true, and now I will prophesy a.
43:25 for my own sake and will never think of them a.
44:26 and the towns of Judah will be lived in once a,
45: 1 gates will be opened, never a to shut against him.
45:17 They will never a be humiliated and disgraced
47: 1 never a will you be the lovely princess, tender
47: 5 Never a will you be known as the queen of
47:12 you strike terror into the hearts of people once a.
48: 3 and a I warned you about what was going to
49: 8 land of Israel and reassign it to its own people a.
51: 3 The LORD will comfort Israel a and make her
52: 5 the LORD. "Why are my people enslaved a?
52:15 And he will a startle many nations. Kings will
54: 9 that I would never a let a flood cover the earth
54: 9 so now I swear that I will never a pour out my
62: 4 Never a will you be called the Godforsaken City
62: 8 "I will never a hand you over to your enemies.
62: 8 Never a will foreign warriors come and take away
63: 8 Surely they will not be false a." And he became
65:10 the plain of Sharon will a be filled with flocks,
Jer 1:13 Then the LORD spoke to me a and asked,
3: 1 marries someone else, he is not to take her back a,
3:12 come home to me a, for I am merciful.
3:14 I will bring you a to the land of Israel—one from
3:19 I thought you would never turn away from me a.
6: 9 the few who remain in Israel will be gleaned a,
7:10 only to go right back to all those evils a?
8: 2 Their bones will not be gathered up a or buried
8: 4 When people fall down, don't they get up a?
10:20 have been taken away, and I will never see them a.
11: 7 out of Egypt, repeating over and over a to this day:
11: 9 A the LORD spoke to me and said, "I have
12:15 I will bring them home to their own lands a,
18: 4 squashed the jar into a lump of clay and started a.
22:10 For he will never return to see his native land a.
22:12 in a distant land and never a see his own country."
22:27 You will never a return to the land of your desire.
23: 4 to care for them, and they will never be afraid a.
24: 6 are well treated, and I will bring them back here a.
25: 4 "A and a, the LORD has sent you his
26: 5 for I sent them a and a to warn you, but you
27:22 someday I will bring them back to Jerusalem a."
28:11 And Hananiah said a to the crowd that had
29:10 I have promised, and I will bring you home a.
29:14 sent you and bring you home a to your own land."
30: 3 and they will possess it and live here a.
30:10 For I will bring you home a from distant lands,
30:18 When I bring you home a from your captivity
30:21 They will have their own ruler a, and he will not
31: 2 I will a come to give rest to the people of Israel."
31: 4 You will a be happy and dance merrily with
31: 5 A you will plant your vineyards on the mountains
31:17 "Your children will come a to their own land.
31:18 Turn me a to you and restore me, for you alone are
31:21 Come back a, my virgin Israel; return to your cities
31:23 "When I bring them back a, the people of Judah
and its cities will a say,
31:34 and will never a remember their sins."
31:40 The city will never a be captured or destroyed."
32:15 Someday people will a own property here in this
32:37 I will surely bring my people back a from all the
32:43 "Fields will a be bought and sold in this land
32:44 Yes, fields will once a be bought and sold—
33:11 voices of bridegrooms and brides will be heard a,
33:13 Once a their flocks will prosper in the towns of the
34:11 the people they had freed, making them slaves a.
34:16 women you had freed, making them slaves once a.
34:22 I will call the Babylonian armies back a. They will
35:14 But I have spoken to you a and a, and you
36:28 and write everything a just as you did on the scroll
36:32 and dictated a to his secretary Baruch.
42:18 And you will never see your homeland a.'
44: 4 "A and a I sent my servants, the prophets,
46:27 For I will bring you home a from distant lands,
47: 6 sword of the LORD, when will you be at rest a?
48: 2 No one will ever brag about Moab a, for there is a
50: 3 such destruction that no one will live in her a.
50: 5 the way to Jerusalem and will start back home a.
50: 5 an eternal covenant that will never a be broken.
50: 8 land of the Babylonians. Lead my people home a.
50:19 And I will bring Israel home a to her own land,
50:34 He will defend them and give them rest a in Israel.
50:39 Never a will people live there; it will lie desolate
51:26 Even your stones will never a be used for building.
51:39 fall asleep, never a to waken," says the LORD.
51:57 "They will fall asleep and never wake up a!"
51:64 and her people will sink, never a to rise,
La 3:40 Let us turn a in repentance to the LORD.
5:21 Restore us, O LORD, and bring us back to you a!
Eze 5: 9 than I have punished anyone before or ever will a.
6: 1 A a message came to me from the LORD:
11:17 and I will give you the land of Israel once a.
11:24 Afterward the Spirit of God carried me back a to
12: 1 A a message came to me from the LORD:
12:12 and his eyes will never see his homeland a.
12:21 A a message came to me from the LORD:
13: 9 and they will never a see their own land.
16: 8 And when I passed by and saw you a, you were
17:14 so Israel would not become strong a and revolt.
17:17 when the king of Babylon lays siege to Jerusalem a
19: 9 in captivity, / so his voice could never a be heard
20:14 But a I held back in order to protect the honor of
20:21 So a I threatened to pour out my fury on them in
21:24 A and a your guilt cries out against you,
22:23 A a message came to me from the LORD:
23:27 You will never a cast longing eyes on those things
26:20 Never a will you be given a position of respect
28:25 The people of Israel will a live in their own land,
29:13 a from the nations to which they have been
29:15 never a great enough to rise above its neighbors.
32:13 Never a will people or animals disturb those
32:14 Then I will let the waters of Egypt become calm a,
33: 1 Once a a message came to me from the LORD:
33:16 None of their past sins will be brought up a,
33:18 For a I say, when righteous people turn to evil,
34:16 strayed away, and I will bring them safely home a.
34:29 so my people will never a go hungry or be shamed
35: 1 A a message came to me from the LORD:
36: 8 and they will be coming home a soon!
36:11 of Israel, I will bring people to live on you once a.
36:12 I will cause my people to walk on you once a,
36:12 You will never a devour their children.
36:14 But you will never a devour your people
36:22 I am bringing you back a but not because you
36:24 all the nations and bring you home a to your land.
36:30 and never a will the surrounding nations be able to
36:34 a shock to all who passed by—will a be farmed.
37: 3 of man, can these bones become living people a?"
37: 5 am going to breathe into you and make you live a!
37: 9 into these dead bodies so that they may live a.' "
37:12 open your graves of exile and cause you to rise a.
37:15 A a message came to me from the LORD:
38:12 I will go to those once-desolate cities that are a
39:14 and to bury them, so the land will be made clean a.
39:29 And I will never a turn my back on them, for I will
40:27 And here a, directly opposite the outer gateway,
43:22 Then cleanse and make atonement for the altar a,
44: 2 gate must remain closed; it will never a be opened.
47: 4 off another 1,750 feet and told me to go across a.
Da 2: 7 They said a, "Please, Your Majesty. Tell us the
4:26 back a when you have learned that heaven rules.
9:17 Lord, smile a on your desolate sanctuary.
10:18 Then the one who looked like a man touched me a,
11: 8 When he returns a to Egypt, he will carry back
11:29 "Then at the appointed time he will once a invade
12:13 you will rise a to receive the inheritance set aside
Hos 1: 6 Soon Gomer became pregnant a and gave birth to a
1: 8 she a became pregnant and gave birth to a second
1:11 when God will a plant his people in his land.
2:14 "But then I will win her back once a. I will lead
3: 1 the LORD said to me, "Go and get your wife a.
11:11 And I will bring them home a," says the LORD.
12: 9 And I will make you live in tents a, as you do each
14: 3 Never a will we call the idols we have made 'our
14: 7 My people will return a to the safety of their land.
Joel 2: 2 have not been seen before and never will be seen a.
2:22 The trees will a be filled with luscious fruit;
2:24 The threshing floors will a be piled high with
2:26 Once a you will have all the food you want,
2:26 Never a will my people be disgraced like this.
2:27 My people will never a be disgraced like this.
2:28 "Then after I have poured out my rains a, I will
3: 7 But I will bring them back a from all these places
3:17 and foreign armies will never conquer her a.
Am 1: 3 "The people of Damascus have sinned a and a,
1: 6 "The people of Gaza have sinned a and a,
1: 9 "The people of Tyre have sinned a and a,
1:11 "The people of Edom have sinned a and a,
1:13 "The people of Ammon have sinned a and a,
2: 1 "The people of Moab have sinned a and a,
2: 4 "The people of Judah have sinned a and a,
2: 6 "The people of Israel have sinned a and a,
5: 2 "The virgin Israel has fallen, / never to rise a!
8: 2 I will not delay their punishment a.
8: 8 the Nile River at floodtime, toss about, and sink a.
8:14 and Beersheba will fall down, never to rise a."
9: 5 like the Nile River at floodtime, and then it sinks a.
9:14 will rebuild their ruined cities and live in them a.
9:15 your God. "Then they will never be uprooted a."
Jnh 1:12 the sea," Jonah said, "and it will become calm a.
2: 4 How will I ever a see your holy Temple?'
Mic 1:16 be snatched away, and you will never see them a.
2: 3 none of you will ever a walk proudly in the
2:12 I will bring you together a like sheep in a fold,
2:12 your land will a be filled with noisy crowds!
4: 7 but I will make them strong a, a mighty nation.
4: 8 royal might and power will come back to you a.
5:13 so you will never a worship the work of your own
7: 8 my enemies! For though I fall, I will rise a.
7:19 Once a you will have compassion on us. You will
Na 1:12 already punished you once, and I will not do it a.
1:15 from Nineveh will never invade your land a.
2: 2 but the LORD will restore its honor and power a.
2:13 Never a will you bring back plunder from
2:13 Never a will the voices of your proud messengers
3: 3 over them, scramble to their feet, and fall a.
Hab 3: 2 begin a to help us, as you did in years gone by.
Zep 2: 7 people in kindness and restore their prosperity a.
3: 7 listen to my warnings, so I won't need to strike a.'
3:20 I will gather you together and bring you home a.
Hag 2: 6 In just a little while I will a shake the heavens
Zec 1:12 How long will it be until you a show mercy to
1:17 The towns of Israel will a overflow with
1:17 and the LORD will a comfort Zion and choose
2: 1 When I looked around me a, I saw a man with a
2:12 and he will once a choose Jerusalem to be his own
5: 1 I looked up a and saw a scroll flying through the
5: 8 her back into the basket and closed the heavy lid a.
6: 1 Then I looked up a and saw four chariots coming
8: 4 Once a old men and women will walk Jerusalem's
8: 8 I will bring them home a to live safely in
9: 8 No foreign oppressor will ever a overrun my
10: 8 their population will grow a to its former size.
10: 9 they will survive and come home a to Israel.
11:15 "Go a and play the part of a worthless shepherd.
13: 3 If anyone begins prophesying a, his own father
14:11 safe at last, never a to be cursed and destroyed.
Mal 1: 4 may try to rebuild, but I will demolish them a!
3: 3 so that they may once a offer acceptable sacrifices
3:18 Then you will a see the difference between the
Mt 2: 9 Once a the star appeared to them, guiding them to
5:13 Can you make it useful a? It will be thrown out
5:26 I assure you that you won't be free a until you
5:33 "A, you have heard that the law of Moses says,
6: 7 answered only by repeating their words a and a.
8: 2 "if you want to, you can make me well a."
9:18 "but you can bring her back to life a if you just
13:44 he hid it a and sold everything he owned to get
13:45 "A, the Kingdom of Heaven is like a pearl
13:47 "A, the Kingdom of Heaven is like a fishing net
14: 2 must be John the Baptist come back to life a!
15:25 But she came and worshiped him and pleaded a,
15:31 and those who had been blind could see a!
16:11 So a I say, 'Beware of the yeast of the Pharisees
18:16 take one or two others with you and go back a,
19:24 I say it a—it is easier for a camel to go through the
20: 5 and a around three o'clock he did the same thing.
20: 6 At five o'clock that evening he was in town a
21:19 Then he said to it, "May you never bear fruit a!"
23:39 tell you this, you will never see me a until you say,
24:21 anything the world has ever seen or will ever see a.
25:14 "A, the Kingdom of Heaven can be illustrated by
26:29 I will not drink wine a until the day I drink it new
26:42 A he left them and prayed, "My Father! If this cup
26:43 He returned to them a and found them sleeping,
26:44 back to pray a third time, saying the same things a.
26:72 A Peter denied it, this time with an oath. "I don't
27: 1 and other leaders met a to discuss how to persuade
27:21 So when the governor asked a, "Which of these
27:31 took off the robe and put his own clothes on him a.
27:40 can destroy the Temple and build it a in three days,
27:50 Then Jesus shouted out a, and he gave up his spirit.
Mk 1:40 you want to, you can make me well a," he said.
2:13 Then Jesus went out to the lakeshore a and taught
3: 1 Jesus went into the synagogue a and noticed a man
3: 5 man reached out his hand, and it became normal a!
3:20 the crowds began to gather a, and soon he and his
4: 1 Once a Jesus began teaching by the lakeshore.
5:10 Then the spirits begged him a and a not to send
6:14 must be John the Baptist come back to life a.
7:19 through the stomach and then comes out a."
7:37 A and a they said, "Everything he does is
8: 1 had gathered, and the people ran out of food a.
8:25 Then Jesus placed his hands over the man's eyes a.
8:31 be killed, and three days later he would rise a.
9:25 to come out of this child and never enter him a!"
9:50 if it loses its flavor, how do you make it salty a?
10:10 in the house, they brought up the subject a.
10:24 But Jesus said a, "Dear children, it is very hard to
10:34 and kill him, but after three days he will rise a."
11:14 to the tree, "May no one ever eat your fruit a!"
11:27 By this time they had arrived in Jerusalem a.
13:19 God created the world. And it will never happen a.
14:25 I solemnly declare that I will not drink wine a until
14:39 Then Jesus left them a and prayed, repeating his
14:40 A he returned to them and found them sleeping,
14:70 Peter denied it a. A little later some other
15:20 the purple robe and put his own clothes on him a.
Lk 1:64 Instantly Zechariah could speak a, and he began
5: 5 catch a thing. But if you say so, we'll try a."
5:12 "if you want to, you can make me well a."
5:26 And they praised God, saying over and over a,
6:10 man reached out his hand, and it became normal a!
7:45 but she has kissed my feet a and a from the time I
9: 7 "This is John the Baptist come back to life a."
12:59 you won't be free a until you have paid the last
13: 5 No, and I tell you a that unless you repent, you will
13: 6 and came a and a to see if there was any fruit on it,
13:35 And you will never see me a until you say,
14: 6 A they had no answer.
14:34 if it loses its flavor, how do you make it salty a?
17: 4 a day and each time turns a and asks forgiveness,
17:22 Later he talked a about this with his disciples.
18:33 and kill him, but on the third day he will rise a."
20: 9 Now Jesus turned to the people a and told them
20:36 And they will never die a. In these respects they
22:16 For I tell you now that I won't eat it a until it
22:18 For I will not drink wine a until the Kingdom of
22:32 So when you have repented and turned to me a,
22:45 At last he stood up a and returned to the disciples,

24: 7 and that he would rise **a** the third day?"
24:12 then he went home **a**, wondering what had
24:46 and die and rise **a** from the dead on the third day.
Jn 1:35 John was **a** standing with two of his disciples.
3: 3 Jesus replied, "I assure you, unless you are born **a**,
3: 4 go back into his mother's womb and be born **a**?"
3: 7 surprised at my statement that you must be born **a**.
3:13 have come to earth and will return to heaven **a**.
4:13 "People soon become thirsty **a** after drinking this
4:15 Then I'll never be thirsty **a**, and I won't have to
5:29 and they will rise **a**. Those who have done good
6:35 No one who comes to me will ever be hungry **a**.
6:53 So Jesus said **a**, "I assure you, unless you eat the
6:62 if you see me, the Son of Man, return to heaven **a**?
8: 2 but early the next morning he was back **a** at the
8: 7 so he stood up **a** and said, "All right, stone her.
8: 8 Then he stooped down **a** and wrote in the dust.
8:10 Then Jesus stood up **a** and said to her, "Where are
8:21 Later Jesus said to them **a**, "I am going away.
9:17 Then the Pharisees once **a** questioned the man who
9:27 Didn't you listen? Why do you want to hear it **a**?
10:17 I lay down my life that I may have it back **a**.
10:18 when I want to and also the power to take it **a**.
10:19 the people were **a** divided in their opinions about
10:31 Once **a** the Jewish leaders picked up stones to kill
10:39 Once **a** they tried to arrest him, but he got away
11: 7 he said to his disciples, "Let's go to Judea **a**."
11: 8 were trying to kill you. Are you going there **a**?"
11:23 Jesus told her, "Your brother will rise **a**."
11:25 though they die like everyone else, will live **a**.
11:38 And **a** Jesus was deeply troubled. Then they came
12:28 have already brought it glory, and I will do it **a**."
13:12 he put on his robe **a** and sat down and asked,
14:19 In just a little while the world will not see me **a**,
14:19 but you will. For I will live **a**, and you will, too.
14:20 When I am raised to life **a**, you will know that I am
14:28 I am going away, but I will come back to you **a**.
16:16 just a little while after that, you will see me **a**."
16:19 just a little while after that, you will see me **a**.
16:20 suddenly turn to wonderful joy when you see me **a**.
16:22 You have sorrow now, but I will see you **a**;
18: 7 And **a** they replied, "Jesus of Nazareth."
18:25 they asked him **a**, "Aren't you one of his
18:27 **A** Peter denied it. And immediately a rooster
18:38 Then he went out **a** to the people and told them,
19: 4 Pilate went outside **a** and said to the people,
19: 9 He took Jesus back into the headquarters **a**
19:13 they said this, Pilate brought Jesus out to them **a**.
20:21 He spoke to them **a** and said, "Peace be with you.
20:26 Eight days later the disciples were together **a**,
21: 1 Later Jesus appeared **a** to the disciples beside the
Ac 1:20 And **a**, 'Let his position be given to someone else.'
2:24 the horrors of death and raised him back to life **a**,
3:20 and he will send Jesus your Messiah to you **a**.
4:17 them not to speak to anyone in Jesus' name **a**."
4:18 and told them never **a** to speak or teach about
5:28 "Didn't we tell you never **a** to teach in this man's
5:40 Then they ordered them never **a** to speak in the
7:26 "The next day he visited them **a** and saw two men
8:39 The eunuch never saw him **a** but went on his way
9:12 and laying his hands on him so that he can see **a**."
10:15 The voice spoke **a**, "If God says something is
10:16 Then the sheet was pulled up **a** to heaven.
11: 9 "But the voice from heaven came **a**, 'If God says
13:34 to raise him from the dead, never **a** to die.
13:42 the people asked them to return **a** and speak about
14:21 Paul and Barnabas returned **a** to Lystra, Iconium,
14:25 They preached **a** in Perga, then went on to Attalia.
16: 7 but **a** the Spirit of Jesus did not let them go.
19:34 they started shouting **a** and kept it up for two
20:25 I have preached the Kingdom will ever see me **a**.
20:38 he had said that they would never see him **a**.
23:15 commander to bring Paul back to the council **a**,"
24:25 "When it is more convenient, I'll call for you **a**."
27:28 A little later they sounded **a** and found only 90
Ro 6: 9 Christ rose from the dead, and he will never die **a**.
10: 7 place of the dead" (to bring Christ back to life **a**).
11:23 God will graft them back into the tree **a**.
14: 9 Christ died and rose **a** for this very purpose,
15:11 And yet **a**, / "Praise the Lord, all you Gentiles;
15:24 for a little while, you can send me on my way **a**.
1Co 3:20 And **a**, / "The Lord knows the thoughts of the
4:18 become arrogant, thinking I will never visit you **a**.
7: 5 Afterward they should come together **a** so that
7:40 it will be better for her if she doesn't marry **a**,
8:13 I will never eat meat **a** as long as I live—
11:26 are announcing the Lord's death until he comes **a**.
15:20 a great harvest of those who will be raised to life **a**.
15:29 Why do it unless the dead will someday rise **a**?
2Co 1:14 on the day when our Lord Jesus comes back **a**.
1:16 on my way to Macedonia and **a** on my return trip.
3: 1 Are we beginning **a** to tell you how good we are?
4: 9 knocked down, but we get up **a** and keep going.
5:12 Are we trying to pat ourselves on the back **a**?
8: 4 They begged us **a** and **a** for the gracious privilege
8:17 He welcomed our request that he visit you **a**.
11: 6 this by now, for we have proved it **a** and **a**.
11:16 Once **a**, don't think that I have lost my wits to talk
11:21 I'm talking like a fool **a**—I can boast about it,
11:23 without number, and faced death **a** and **a**.
12:21 I come, God will humble me **a** because of you.
13: 2 Now I **a** warn them and all others, just as I did
Gal 1: 9 I will say it **a**: If anyone preaches any other gospel
2: 1 fourteen years later I went back to Jerusalem **a**,
3: 5 I ask you **a**, does God give you the Holy Spirit
4: 9 why do you want to go back **a** and become slaves
4:19 feel as if I am going through labor pains for you **a**,
5: 1 and don't get tied up **a** in slavery to the law.
5: 3 I'll say it **a**. If you are trying to find favor with
5:21 Let me tell you **a**, as I have before, that anyone
Eph 5:33 So **a** I say, each man must love his wife as he loves
Php 1: 6 on that day when Christ Jesus comes back **a**.
1:27 whether I come and see you **a** or only hear about
2:26 Now I am sending him home **a**, for he has been
3:18 often before, and I say it **a** with tears in my eyes,
4: 4 be full of joy in the Lord. I say it **a**—rejoice!
4:10 praise the Lord that you are concerned about me **a**.
1Th 2:17 because of our intense longing to see you **a**.
2:18 and I, Paul, tried **a** and **a**, but Satan prevented
2:19 before our Lord Jesus when he comes back **a**.
3:10 asking God to let us see you **a** to fill up anything
4:14 we believe that Jesus died and was raised to life **a**,
5:23 until that day when our Lord Jesus Christ comes **a**.
2Th 2: 1 let us tell you about the coming **a** of our Lord Jesus
1Ti 5:14 So I advise these younger widows to marry **a**,
2Ti 1: 4 I long to see you **a**, for I remember your tears as
1: 4 I will be filled with joy when we are together **a**.
2:23 **A** I say, don't get involved in foolish,
Heb 1: 5 And **a** God said, / "I will be his Father, / and he
5:12 you need someone to teach you **a** the basic things a
6: 1 stop going over the basics of Christianity **a** and **a**.
6: 1 Surely we don't need to start all over **a** with the
6: 6 is impossible to bring such people to repentance **a**
6: 6 the Son of God to the cross **a** by rejecting him,
8:12 and I will never **a** remember their sins."
9:25 Nor did he enter heaven to offer himself **a** and **a**,
9:26 he would have had to die **a** and **a**,
9:28 He will come **a** but not to deal with our sins **a**.
10: 1 under the old system were repeated **a** and **a**,
10:17 Then he adds, / "I will never **a** remember
10:25 especially now that the day of his coming back **a** is
11:19 God was able to bring him back to life **a**.
11:35 Women received their loved ones back **a** from
12:26 "Once **a** I will shake not only the earth
13:20[-21] who brought **a** from the dead our Lord Jesus,
Jas 4: 4 I say it **a**, that if your aim is to enjoy this world,
5:18 grass turned green, and the crops began to grow **a**.
5:19 away from the truth and is brought back **a**,
1Pe 1: 3 that God has given us the privilege of being born **a**.
1: 3 because Jesus Christ rose **a** from the dead.
1:23 For you have been born **a**. Your new life did not
2Pe 1:16 power of our Lord Jesus Christ and his coming **a**.
2:20 get tangled up with sin and become its slave **a**,
Rev 2: 5 Turn back to me **a** and work as you did at first.
3: 3 believed at first; hold to it firmly and turn to me **a**.
5:11 Then I looked **a**, and I heard the singing of
7:16 They will never **a** be hungry or thirsty, and they
10: 8 Then the voice from heaven called to me **a**: "Go
10:11 "You must prophesy **a** about many peoples,
18:14 that you prized so much will never be yours **a**.
18:22 Never **a** will the sound of music be heard there—
19: 3 **A** and **a** their voices rang, "Hallelujah!
19: 6 Then I heard **a** what sounded like the shout of a
20: 3 Afterward he would be released **a** for a little while.
20: 4 They came to life **a**, and they reigned with Christ
22: 9 But **a** he said, "No, don't worship me. I am a

AGAINST (1132) See Index of Articles, Etc.

AGAR [KJV] See HAGAR

AGATE (3)

Ex 28:19 row will contain a jacinth, an **a**, and an amethyst.
39:12 the third row were a jacinth, an **a**, and an amethyst.
Rev 21:19 second sapphire, the third **a**, the fourth emerald,

AGE (66) [AGE-OLD, AGED, AGES, WELL-AGED]

AGE TO COME (2) Lk 20:35; Heb 6:5

END OF THE AGE (2) Mt 28:20; Heb 9:26

OLD AGE (19) Ge 15:15; 21:2,7; 25:8; 35:29; 37:3; 44:20; Ru 4:15; 1Sa 2:31; 26:10; 1Ki 11:4; 15:23; 1Ch 29:28; 2Ch 24:15; Job 5:26; 21:7; Ps 71:9; 92:14; Lk 1:36

THIS AGE (1) 1Co 10:11

Ge 5: 5 He died at the **a** of 930.
5: 8 He died at the **a** of 912.
5:11 He died at the **a** of 905.
5:14 He died at the **a** of 910.
5:17 He died at the **a** of 895.
5:20 He died at the **a** of 962.
5:27 He died at the **a** of 969.
5:31 He died at the **a** of 777.
15:15 (But you will die in peace, at a ripe old **a**.)
17:17 "How could I become a father at the **a** of one
18:11 and Sarah was long past the **a** of having children,
21: 2 and she gave a son to Abraham in his old **a**.
21: 7 Yet I have given Abraham a son in his old **a**!"
25: 8 and he died at a ripe old **a**, joining his ancestors in
25:17 Ishmael finally died at the **a** of 137 and joined his
26:34 At the **a** of forty, Esau married a young woman
35:29 and he died at a ripe old **a**, joining his ancestors in
37: 3 because Joseph had been born to him in his old **a**.
44:20 have a father, an old man, and a child of his old **a**,
48:10 half blind because of his **a** and could hardly see.
50:26 So Joseph died at the **a** of 110. They embalmed
Lev 27: 4 a woman of that **a** is valued at thirty pieces of
27: 5 a girl of that **a** is valued at ten pieces of silver.
27: 6 a girl of that **a** is valued at three pieces of silver.
Nu 4:35 and fifty years of **a** who were eligible for service in
4:39 and fifty years of **a** who were eligible for service in
4:43 and fifty years of **a** who were eligible for service in
4:47 and fifty years of **a** who were eligible for service in
8:24 They must begin serving in the Tabernacle at the **a**
8:25 and they must retire at the **a** of fifty.
26: 2 out how many of each family are of military **a**."
Dt 2:16 "When all the men of fighting **a** had died,
Jos 24:29 the servant of the LORD, died at the **a** of 110.
Jdg 2: 8 the servant of the LORD, died at the **a** of 110.
Ru 4:15 restore your youth and care for you in your old **a**.
1Sa 2:31 die before their time. None will live to a ripe old **a**.
26:10 down someday, or he will die in battle or of old **a**.
2Sa 24: 9 There were 800,000 men of military **a** in Israel
1Ki 11: 4 In Solomon's old **a**, they turned his heart to
15:23 *of Judah*. In his old **a** his feet became diseased.
1Ch 8: 1 The sons of Benjamin, in order of **a**, included Bela
21: 5 There were 1,100,000 men of military **a** in Israel,
24:31 means of sacred lots, without regard to **a** or rank.
26:13 without regard to **a** or training, for it was all
27:23 those who were younger than twenty years of **a**,
29:28 He died at a ripe old **a**, having enjoyed long life,
2Ch 24:15 Jehoiada lived to a very old **a**, finally dying at 130.
Job 5:26 You will live to a good old **a**. You will not be
21: 7 "The truth is that the wicked live to a good old **a**.
32: 7 are older should speak, for wisdom comes with **a**.'
Ps 71: 9 And now, in my old **a**, don't set me aside.
92:14 Even in old **a** they will still produce fruit;
Ecc 12: 3 Your limbs will tremble with **a**, and your strong
Isa 46: 4 your lifetime—until your hair is white with **a**.
Da 1:10 and thin compared to the other youths your **a**,
5:31 Mede took over the kingdom at the **a** of sixty-two.
Mt 28:20 I am with you always, even to the end of the **a**."
Lk 1:36 Elizabeth has become pregnant in her old **a**!
20:35 But that is not the way it will be in the **a** to come.
21:24 and trampled down by the Gentiles until the **a** of
Ro 4:19 was too old to be a father at the **a** of one hundred
1Co 10:11 who live at the time when this **a** is drawing to a
Gal 1:14 I was one of the most religious Jews of my own **a**,
4: 2 until they reach whatever **a** their father set.
Heb 6: 5 the word of God and the power of the **a** to come—
9:26 He came once for all time, at the end of the **a**,

AGE-OLD (3) [AGE]

Ps 119:52 I meditate on your **a** laws; / O LORD,
Mt 15: 2 "Why do your disciples disobey our **a** traditions?"
Mk 7: 5 "Why don't your disciples follow our **a** customs?

AGED (8) [AGE]

Lev 19:32 of elderly people and showing respect for the **a**.
Dt 32:25 and young women, / both infants and the **a**.
1Ki 1: 5 decided to make himself king in place of his **a**
Job 12:12 Wisdom belongs to the **a**, and understanding to
15:10 On our side are **a**, gray-haired men much older
29: 8 and even the **a** rose in respect at my coming.
32: 9 Sometimes the **a** do not understand justice.
Pr 17: 6 Grandchildren are the crowning glory of the **a**;

AGEE (1)

2Sa 23:11 Next in rank was Shammah son of **A** from Harar.

AGENT (2) [AGENTS]

Ne 11:24 was the king's **a** in all matters of public
Eze 27:12 "Tarshish was your **a**, trading your wares in

AGENTS (5) [AGENT]

Ezr 4: 5 They bribed **a** to work against them and to frustrate
Est 2: 3 Let the king appoint **a** in each province to bring
Ps 132: 9 Your priests will be **a** of salvation; / may your
132:16 I will make its priests the **a** of salvation; / its godly
Lk 20:20 the leaders sent secret **a** pretending to be honest

AGES (17) [AGE]

Ge 43:33 he seated them in the order of their **a**,
Lev 27: 3 A man between the **a** of twenty and sixty is valued
27: 6 A boy between the **a** of one month and five years
Nu 4: 3 Count all the men between the **a** of thirty and fifty
4:23 Count all the men between the **a** of thirty and fifty
4:30 Count all the men between the **a** of thirty and fifty
Ps 25: 6 which you have shown from long **a** past.
41:13 of Israel, / who lives forever from eternal **a** past.
74:12 You, O God, are my king from **a** past,
102:25 In **a** past you laid the foundation of the earth,
Pr 8:23 I was appointed in **a** past, at the very first,
Isa 44: 8 Have I not proclaimed from **a** past what my
45:17 and disgraced throughout everlasting **a**.
63:16 be our Father. You are our Redeemer from **a** past.
Jer 23:40 your name will be infamous throughout the **a**.' "
Gal 1: 5 glory belongs to God through all the **a** of eternity.
Eph 3:21 in Christ Jesus forever and ever through endless **a**.

AGGRAVATE (1) [AGGRAVATED]

Col 3:21 Fathers, don't **a** your children. If you do, they will

AGGRAVATED (1) [AGGRAVATE]

Nu 11:10 became extremely angry. Moses was also very **a**.

AGHAST (2)

Da 4:19 for a time, **a** at the meaning of the dream.
Na 2:10 The people stand **a**, their faces pale and trembling.

AGITATED (1)

Pr 29: 8 Mockers can get a whole town **a**, but those who are

AGLOW (2)

Ex 34:35 and the people would see his face **a**. Afterward he
SS 5:14 His body is like bright ivory, **a** with sapphires.

AGO (84)

Ge 41:10 "Some time **a**, you were angry with the chief
42:21 because of what we did to Joseph long **a**.
Ex 13:11 the land he swore to give your ancestors long **a**,
33: 1 I told them long **a** that I would give this land to
Dt 5: 3 The LORD did not make this covenant long **a**
32: 7 Remember the days of long **a**; / think about the
1Sa 1:26 "I am the woman who stood here several years **a**
9:20 about those donkeys that were lost three days **a**,
30:13 "My master left me behind three days **a** because I
2Ki 19:25 It was I, the LORD, who decided this long **a**.
19:25 Long **a** I planned what I am now causing to
Ezr 5:11 built here many years **a** by a great king of Israel.
Ne 12:46 and thanks to God began long **a** in the days of
Ps 44: 1 of all you did in other days, / in days long **a**:
77:11 I remember your wonderful deeds of long **a**.
Ecc 1:10 How do you know it didn't already exist long **a**?
6:10 It was known long **a** what each person would be.
Isa 10:24 they oppress you just as the Egyptians did long **a**.
11:16 just as he did for Israel long **a** when they returned
17: 9 abandoned when the Israelites came here so long **a**.
22:11 for help. He is the one who planned this long **a**.
25: 1 You planned them long **a**, and now you have
37:26 It was I, the LORD, who decided this long **a**.
37:26 Long **a** I planned what I am now causing to
41:22 "Let them try to tell us what happened long **a**
45:21 Who made these things known long **a**?
52: 4 "Long **a** my people went to live as resident
61: 4 the ancient ruins, repairing cities long **a** destroyed.
64: 3 When you came down long **a**, you did awesome
Jer 2: 2 you were to please me as a young bride long **a**,
2:20 Long **a** I broke your yoke and tore away the chains
30:20 Their children will prosper as they did long **a**.
31: 3 Long **a** the LORD said to Israel: "I have loved
34:13 I made a covenant with your ancestors long **a** when
La 2:17 fulfilled the promises of disaster he made long **a**.
Eze 16:22 you have not once thought of the days long **a** when
26:20 to lie there with those who descended there long **a**.
36:28 live in Israel, the land I gave your ancestors long **a**.
38:17 You are the one I was talking about long **a**, when I
Hos 2:15 to me there, as she did long **a** when she was young,
9: 9 are as depraved as what they did in Gibeah long **a**.
Am 4:10 you like the plagues I sent against Egypt long **a**.
Mic 7:14 pastures of Bashan and Gilead as they did long **a**.
7:20 oath to our ancestors Abraham and Jacob long **a**.
Zec 7: 7 through the prophets years **a** when Jerusalem
Mt 11:21 people would have sat in deep repentance long **a**,
26:24 must die, as the Scriptures declared long **a**.
Mk 14:21 must die, as the Scriptures declared long **a**.
Lk 1:70 as he promised / through his holy prophets long **a**.
10:13 people would have sat in deep repentance long **a**,
11:47 for the very prophets your ancestors killed long **a**.
24:21 to rescue Israel. That all happened three days **a**.
24:46 it was written long **a** that the Messiah must suffer
Jn 11: 8 "only a few days **a** the Jewish leaders in Judea
Ac 1:16 This was predicted long **a** by the Holy Spirit,
2:16 was predicted centuries **a** by the prophet Joel:
3:21 as God promised long **a** through his prophets.
4:25 you spoke long **a** by the Holy Spirit through our
5:36 Some time **a** there was that fellow Theudas,
10:30 "Four days **a** I was praying in my house at three
15: 7 among you some time **a** to preach to the Gentiles
15:18 he who made these things known long **a**.'
21:38 you the Egyptian who led a rebellion some time **a**
24:11 **a** that I arrived in Jerusalem to worship at the
Ro 1: 2 This Good News was promised long **a** by God
3:21 but by the way promised in the Scriptures long **a**.
15: 4 Such things were written in the Scriptures long **a** to
1Co 10: 1 happened to our ancestors in the wilderness long **a**.
2Co 8:10 I suggest that you finish what you started a year **a**,
9: 2 in Greece were ready to send an offering a year **a**.
12: 2 caught up into the third heaven fourteen years **a**.
Gal 3: 8 God promised this good news to Abraham long **a**
6:14 of that cross, my interest in this world died long **a**,
Eph 1: 4 Long **a**, even before he made the world, God loved
1: 9 designed long **a** according to his good pleasure.
1:11 and all things happen just as he decided long **a**.
1:13 you the Holy Spirit, whom he promised long **a**.
2:10 can do the good things he planned for us long **a**.
Heb 1: 1 Long **a** God spoke many times and in many ways
1Pe 1: 2 God the Father chose you long **a**, and the Spirit has
3:20 those who disobeyed God long **a** when God waited
2Pe 2: 3 But God condemned them long **a**, and their
3: 2 and understand what the holy prophets said long **a**
Jude 1: 4 The fate of such people was determined long **a**,

AGONE [KJV] See AGO

AGONIZED (2) [AGONY]

Col 2: 1 I want you to know how much I have **a** for you
4:13 I can assure you that he has **a** for you and also for

AGONY (5) [AGONIZED]

2Ch 21:19 caused his bowels to come out, and he died in **a**.
Ps 6: 2 am weak. / Heal me, LORD, for my body is in **a**.
Isa 26:18 we, too, writhe in **a**, / but nothing comes of our
Lk 22:44 and he was in such a **a** of spirit that his sweat fell to
Rev 9: 5 but to torture them for five months with **a** like the

AGREE (21) [AGREED, AGREEING, AGREEMENT, AGREES]

Ge 34:23 let's **a** to this so they will settle here among us."
1Sa 11: 3 will come to save us, we will **a** to your terms."
1Ki 22:13 Be sure that you **a** with them and promise
2Ch 18:12 Be sure that you **a** with them and promise
Ne 10:36 We **a** to give to God our oldest sons
Job 22:21 If you **a** with him, you will have peace at last,
41: 4 Will it **a** to work for you? Can you make it be your
Eze 14:23 you will **a** that these things are not being done to
Mt 18:19 If two of you **a** down here on earth concerning
20:13 Didn't you **a** to work all day for the usual wage?
Lk 11:48 You **a** with your ancestors that what they did was
Jn 8:17 Your own law says that if two people **a** about
Ac 16:15 "If you **a** that I am faithful to the Lord," she said,
23:21 are ready, expecting you to **a** to their request."
Ro 7:16 and my bad conscience shows that I **a** that the law
1Co 8: 1 You think that everyone should **a** with your perfect
Gal 2: 3 And they did **a**. They did not even demand that my
Php 3:15 I hope all of you who are mature Christians will **a**
1Jn 5: 8 the water, and the blood—and all three **a**.
Rev 17:13 They will all **a** to give their power and authority to
17:17 They will mutually **a** to give their authority to the

AGREED (64) [AGREE]

Ge 16: 2 I can have children through her." And Abram **a**.
23: 9 full price, of course, whatever is publicly **a** upon,
23:16 four hundred pieces of silver, as was publicly **a**.
29:19 "**A**!" Laban replied. "I'd rather give her to you
29:28 So Jacob **a** to work seven more years. A week after
34:18 Hamor and Shechem gladly **a**,
34:24 So all the men **a** and were circumcised.
37:27 after all, he is our brother!" And his brothers **a**.
42:20 If you are, I will spare you." To this they **a**.
50: 6 Pharaoh **a** to Joseph's request. "Go and bury your
Dt 1:14 "You **a** that my plan was a good one.
Jos 2:14 lives as a guarantee for your safety," the men **a**.
Jdg 9: 4 which he used to hire some soldiers who **a** to
14:13 "All right," they **a**, "let's hear your riddle."
17:11 The Levite **a** to this and became like one of
20:32 But the Israelites had **a** in advance to run away
1Sa 1:23 "Whatever you think is best," Elkanah **a**.
8:22 a king." Then Samuel **a** and sent the people home.
9:10 "All right," Saul **a**, "let's try it!" So they started
14:40 and all of you stand over there." And the people **a**.
15:31 So Samuel finally **a** and went with him, and Saul
20:35 The next morning, as **a**, Jonathan went out into the
22: 4 The king **a**, and David's parents stayed in Moab
28: 2 "Very well!" David **a**. "Now you will see for
2Sa 2:14 of hand-to-hand combat." "All right," Joab **a**.
13: 7 So David **a** and sent Tamar to Amnon's house to
13:27 the king until he finally **a** to let all his sons attend,
18: 4 that's the best plan, I'll do it," the king finally **a**.
19:38 "Good," the king **a**. "Kimham will go with me,
1Ki 1: 7 and they **a** to help him become king.
15:20 Ben-hadad **a** to King Asa's request and sent his
18:24 to the wood is the true God!" And all the people **a**.
20: 7 I already **a** when he sent the message demanding
22:12 All the other prophets **a**. "Yes," they said, "go up
2Ki 12: 8 So the priests **a** not to collect any more money
12: 8 and they also **a** not to undertake the repairs of the
1Ch 12:38 In fact, all Israel **a** that David should be their king.
13: 4 The whole assembly **a** to this, for the people could
2Ch 15:13 They **a** that anyone who refused to seek the
16: 4 Ben-hadad **a** to King Asa's request and sent his
18:11 All the other prophets **a**. "Yes," they said, "go up
28:12 **a** with this and confronted the men returning from
Ne 2: 6 So the king **a**, and I set a date for my departure.
Est 3:10 The king **a**, confirming his decision by removing
9:14 So the king **a**, and the decree was announced in
9:27 the Jews throughout the realm **a** to inaugurate this
Jer 38: 5 So King Zedekiah **a**. "All right," he said. "Do as
Da 1:14 So the attendant **a** to Daniel's suggestion
6: 7 and other officials have unanimously **a** that Your
Mt 20: 2 He **a** to pay the normal daily wage and sent them
26: 5 the Passover," they **a**, "or there will be a riot."
26:60 But even though they found many who **a** to give
Mk 14: 2 the Passover," they **a**, "or there will be a riot."
Lk 7:29 unjust tax collectors, **a** that God's plan was right,
9:59 The man **a**, but he said, "Lord, first let me return
15:12 So his father **a** to divide his wealth between his
23:51 but he had not **a** with the decision and actions of
Ac 5: 2 the full amount. His wife had **a** to this deception.
15:25 good to us, having unanimously **a** on our decision,
15:37 Barnabas **a** and wanted to take along John Mark.
21:26 So Paul **a** to their request, and the next day he went
21:40 The commander **a**, so Paul stood on the stairs
26:31 As they talked it over they **a**, "This man hasn't
Heb 11:13 They **a** that they were no more than foreigners

AGREEING (4) [AGREE]

Nu 30:14 nothing on the day he hears of it, then he is **a** to it.
Am 3: 3 Can two people walk together without **a** on the
Ac 22:20 witness Stephen was killed, I was standing there **a**.
Php 2: 2 Then make me truly happy by **a** wholeheartedly

AGREEMENT (17) [AGREE]

Ge 17: 9 "Your part of the **a**," God told Abraham, "is to
23:18 **a** made in the presence of the Hittite elders at the
31: 7 breaking his wage **a** with me again and again.
31:48 will stand as a witness to remind us of our **a**,"
Lev 25:14 "When you make an **a** with a neighbor to buy
Jos 9:15 and the leaders of Israel ratified their **a** with a
24:26 As a reminder of their **a**, he took a huge stone
Jdg 18: 4 He told them about his **a** with Micah and that he
2Sa 3:12 messengers to David, saying, "Let's make an **a**,
23: 5 His **a** is eternal, final, sealed. / He will constantly
Ps 89: 3 "I have made a solemn **a** with David,
Pr 6: 2 if you have trapped yourself by your **a** and are
Lk 22:20 an **a** sealed with the blood I will pour out for you.
1Co 7: 5 The only exception to this rule would be the **a** of
Gal 3:15 as no one can set aside or amend an irrevocable **a**,
3:17 The **a** God made with Abraham could not be
3:20 a mediator is needed if two people enter into an **a**,

AGREES (2) [AGREE]

Ac 15:15 And this conversion of Gentiles **a** with what the
1Co 1:22 because they believe only what **a** with their own

AGRIPPA (14)

Ac 12: 1 About that time King Herod **A** began to persecute
12:19 Herod **A** ordered a thorough search for him.
25:13 A few days later King **A** arrived with his sister,
25:22 "I'd like to hear the man myself," **A** said.
25:23 So the next day **A** and Bernice arrived at the
25:24 Then Festus said, "King **A** and all present, this is
25:26 and especially you, King **A**, so that after we
26: 1 Then **A** said to Paul, "You may speak in your
26: 2 "I am fortunate, King **A**, that you are the one
26:19 "And so, O King **A**, I was not disobedient to that
26:26 And King **A** knows about these things. I speak
26:27 King **A**, do you believe the prophets? I know you
26:28 **A** interrupted him. "Do you think you can make
26:32 And **A** said to Festus, "He could be set free if he

AGROUND (1) [GROUND]

Ac 27:41 But the ship hit a shoal and ran **a**. The bow of the

AGUE [KJV] See FEVERS

AGUR (1)

Pr 30: 1 The message of **A** son of Jakeh. An oracle. I am

AH (3) [AHA]

2Ki 6: 5 "**A**, my lord!" he cried. "It was a borrowed ax!"
6:15 "**A**, my lord, what will we do now?" he cried out
SS 2: 8 "**A**, I hear him—my lover! Here he comes,

AHA (5) [AH]

Ps 35:21 "**A**," they say. "**A**! / With our own eyes we
40:15 be horrified by their shame, / for they said, "**A**!
70: 3 be horrified by their shame, / for they said, "**A**!
Eze 36: 2 Your enemies have taunted you, saying, '**A**!

AHAB (100) [AHAB'S]

1Ki 16:28 in Samaria. Then his son **A** became the next king.
16:29 **A** son of Omri began to rule over Israel in the
16:30 But **A** did what was evil in the LORD's sight,
17: 1 told King **A**, "As surely as the LORD, the God of
18: 1 said to Elijah, "Go and present yourself to King **A**.
18: 2 So Elijah went to appear before **A**. Meanwhile,
18: 3 So **A** summoned Obadiah, who was in charge of
18: 5 **A** said to Obadiah, "We must check every spring
18: 6 **A** went one way by himself, and Obadiah went
18: 9 you are sending me to my death at the hands of **A**?
18:10 King **A** forced the king of that nation to swear to
18:12 When **A** comes and cannot find you, he will kill
18:15 I stand, that I will present myself to **A** today."
18:16 So Obadiah went to tell **A** that Elijah had come,
and **A** went out to meet him.
18:17 **A** asked when he saw him.
18:20 So **A** summoned all the people and the prophets to
18:41 Then Elijah said to **A**, "Go and enjoy a good meal!
18:42 So **A** prepared a feast. But Elijah climbed to the
18:44 Then Elijah shouted, "Hurry to **A** and tell him,
18:45 a terrific rainstorm, and **A** left quickly for Jezreel.
19: 1 When **A** got home, he told Jezebel what Elijah had
20: 2 the city to relay this message to King **A** of Israel:
20: 4 "All right, my lord," **A** replied. "All that I have is
20: 7 Then **A** summoned all the leaders of the land
20: 9 So **A** told the messengers from Ben-hadad,
20:10 Then Ben-hadad sent this message to **A**:
20:13 Then a prophet came to see King **A** and told him,
20:14 **A** asked, "How will he do it?" And the prophet
20:14 **A** asked. "Yes," the prophet answered.
20:15 So **A** mustered the troops of the 232 provincial
20:22 Afterward the prophet said to King **A**, "Get ready
20:31 our heads. Then perhaps King **A** will let you live."
20:33 **A** invited him up into his chariot!
20:34 Then **A** said, "I will let you go under these
21: 1 King **A** had a palace in Jezreel, and near the palace
21: 2 One day **A** said to Naboth, "Since your vineyard is
21: 4 So **A** went home angry and sullen because of
21: 6 or to trade it, and he refused!" **A** told her.
21:15 When Jezebel heard the news, she said to **A**,
21:16 So **A** immediately went down to the vineyard to
21:18 "Go down to meet King **A**, who rules in Samaria.
21:20 **A** exclaimed to Elijah. "Yes," Elijah answered,
21:25 to what was evil in the LORD's sight as did **A**,
21:27 When **A** heard this message, he tore his clothing,
21:29 "Do you see how **A** has humbled himself before
22: 2 King Jehoshaphat of Judah went to visit King **A** of
22: 3 During the visit, **A** said to his officials, "Do you
22: 4 And Jehoshaphat replied to King **A**, "Why,
22: 6 So King **A** summoned his prophets, about four
22: 8 King **A** replied, "There is still one prophet of the
22:10 King **A** of Israel and King Jehoshaphat of Judah,

22:15 arrived before the king, **A** asked him, "Micaiah,
22:20 'Who can entice **A** to go into battle against
22:26 King **A** of Israel then ordered, "Arrest Micaiah
22:30 Now King **A** said to Jehoshaphat, "As we go into
22:30 So **A** disguised himself, and they went into battle.
22:34 of here!" **A** groaned to the driver of his chariot.
22:35 and **A** was propped up in his chariot facing the
22:40 When **A** died, he was buried among his ancestors.
22:49 At that time Ahaziah son of **A** proposed to
22:51 Ahaziah son of **A** began to rule over Israel in the
2Ki 8:16 Joram's reign in Israel. Joram was the son of **A**.
8:18 of the kings of Israel and was as wicked as King **A**,
8:25 reign in Israel. King Joram was the son of **A**.
8:27 he was related by marriage to the family of **A**.
9:7 You are to destroy the family of **A**, your master.
9:8 The entire family of **A** must be wiped out—
9:9 I will destroy the family of **A** as I destroyed the
9:25 and I were riding along behind his father, **A**?
10:1 Now **A** had seventy sons living in the city of
10:11 So **A** was left without a single survivor.
10:13 We are going to visit the sons of King **A**
10:18 "**A** hardly worshiped Baal at all compared to the
10:30 my instructions to destroy the family of **A**.
21:3 an Asherah pole, just as King **A** of Israel had done.
21:13 by the same measure I used for the family of **A**.
2Ch 18:1 his son to marry the daughter of King **A** of Israel.
18:2 A few years later, he went to Samaria to visit **A**,
18:2 Then **A** enticed Jehoshaphat to join forces with
18:3 **A** asked. And Jehoshaphat replied, "Why,
18:5 So King **A** summoned his prophets, four hundred
18:7 King **A** replied, "There is still one prophet of the
18:9 King **A** of Israel and King Jehoshaphat of Judah,
18:14 arrived before the king, **A** asked him, "Micaiah,
18:19 'Who can entice King **A** of Israel to go into battle
18:25 King **A** of Israel then ordered, "Arrest Micaiah
18:29 Now King **A** said to Jehoshaphat, "As we go into
18:29 So **A** disguised himself, and they went into battle.
18:33 of here!" **A** groaned to the driver of his chariot.
18:34 and **A** propped himself up in his chariot facing the
21:6 of the kings of Israel and was as wicked as King **A**,
21:13 Judah to worship idols, just as King **A** did in Israel.
22:4 was evil in the LORD's sight, just as **A** had done.
22:5 with King Joram, the son of King **A** of Israel.
22:7 the LORD had appointed to end the dynasty of **A**.
22:8 was executing judgment against the family of **A**,
Jer 29:21 **A** son of Kolaiah and Zedekiah son of Maaseiah—
29:22 'May the LORD make you like Zedekiah and **A**,
Mic 6:16 only example you follow is that of wicked King **A**!

AHAB'S (25) [AHAB]

1Ki 18:46 and ran ahead of **A** chariot all the way to the
20:12 This reply of **A** reached Ben-hadad and the other
20:19 But by now **A** provincial commanders had led the
21:8 So she wrote letters in **A** name, sealed them with
22:10 All of **A** prophets were prophesying there in front
22:22 go out and inspire all **A** prophets to speak lies.'
22:39 The rest of the events in **A** reign and the story of
22:41 Judah in the fourth year of King **A** reign in Israel.
2Ki 1:1 After King **A** death, the nation of Moab declared
3:1 **A** son Joram began to rule over Israel in the
3:5 But after **A** death, the king of Moab rebelled
8:18 King Ahab, for he had married one of **A** daughters.
8:27 Ahaziah followed the evil example of King **A**
9:10 Dogs will eat **A** wife, Jezebel, at the plot of land in
10:1 of the people, and to the guardians of King **A** sons.
10:3 select the best qualified of King **A** sons to be your king, and prepare to fight for **A** dynasty."
10:10 that was spoken concerning **A** family will not fail.
10:11 Then Jehu killed all of **A** relatives living in Jezreel
10:17 he killed everyone who was left there from **A**
2Ch 18:9 All of **A** prophets were prophesying there in front
18:21 go out and inspire all **A** prophets to speak lies.'
21:6 King Ahab, for he had married one of **A** daughters.
22:3 Ahaziah also followed the evil example of King **A**
22:4 members of **A** family became his advisers,

AHARAH (1)

1Ch 8:1 order of age, included Bela (the oldest), Ashbel, **A**,

AHARHEL (1)

1Ch 4:8 Zobebah, and all the families of **A** son of Harum.

AHASAI [KJV] See AHZAI

AHASBAI (1)

2Sa 23:34 Eliphelet son of **A** from Maacah; / Eliam son of

AHASUERUS (1)

Da 9:1 the son of **A**, who became king of the Babylonians.

AHAVA (3)

Ezr 8:15 I assembled the exiles at the **A** Canal, and we
8:21 And there by the **A** Canal, I gave orders for all of
8:31 We broke camp at the **A** Canal on April 19

AHAZ (40)

2Ki 15:38 of David. Then his son **A** became the next king.
16:1 **A** son of Jotham began to rule over Judah in the
16:2 **A** was twenty years old when he became king,
16:5 and King Pekah of Israel declared war on **A**.
16:7 King **A** sent messengers to King Tiglath-pileser of
16:8 Then **A** took the silver and gold from the Temple
16:10 King **A** then went to Damascus to meet with King
16:14 Then King **A** removed the old bronze altar from
16:16 Uriah the priest did just as King **A** instructed him.
16:20 When **A** died, he was buried with his ancestors in
18:1 Hezekiah son of **A** began to rule over Judah in the
20:11 to move ten steps backward on the sundial of **A**!
23:12 built on the palace roof above the upper room of **A**.
1Ch 3:13 **A**, Hezekiah, Manasseh,
8:35 was the father of Pithon, Melech, Tahrea, and **A**.
8:36 **A** was the father of Jadah. / Jadah was the father of
9:41 of Micah were Pithon, Melech, Tahrea, and **A**.
9:42 **A** was the father of Jadah. / Jadah was the father of
2Ch 27:9 City of David, and his son **A** became the next king.
28:1 **A** was twenty years old when he became king,
28:5 his God allowed the king of Aram to defeat **A**
28:5 The armies of Israel also defeated **A** and inflicted
28:16 About that time King **A** of Judah asked the king of
28:19 was humbling Judah because of King **A** of Judah,
28:20 he oppressed King **A** instead of helping him.
28:21 **A** took valuable items from the LORD's Temple,
28:22 And when trouble came to King **A**, he became
28:27 When King **A** died, he was buried in Jerusalem
29:19 utensils taken by King **A** when he was unfaithful
Isa 1:1 the reigns of Uzziah, Jotham, **A**, and Hezekiah—
7:1 During the reign of **A** son of Jotham and grandson
7:3 "Go out to meet King **A**, you and your son
7:10 after this, the LORD sent this message to King **A**:
7:11 "Ask me for a sign, **A**, to prove that I will crush
14:28 This message came to me the year King **A** died:
38:8 **A**!' " So the shadow on the sundial moved
Hos 1:1 Jotham, **A**, and Hezekiah were kings of Judah,
Mic 1:1 **A**, and Hezekiah were kings of Judah.
Mt 1:9 Jotham was the father of **A**. / **A** was the father of Hezekiah.

AHAZ'S (3)

2Ki 16:19 The rest of the events in **A** reign and his deeds are
17:1 Israel in the twelfth year of King **A** reign in Judah.
2Ch 28:26 The rest of the events of **A** reign and all his

AHAZIAH (38) [AHAZIAH'S]

1Ki 22:40 Then his son **A** became the next king.
22:49 At that time **A** son of Ahab proposed to
22:51 **A** son of Ahab began to rule over Israel in the
2Ki 1:2 One day Israel's new king, **A**, fell through the
1:17 So **A** died, just as the LORD had promised
1:17 Since **A** did not have a son to succeed him,
8:24 of David. Then his son **A** became the next king.
8:25 **A** son of Jehoram began to rule over Judah in the
8:26 **A** was twenty-two years old when he became king,
8:27 **A** followed the evil example of King Ahab's
8:28 **A** joined King Joram of Israel in his war against
8:29 was there, King **A** of Judah went to visit him.
9:16 King **A** of Judah was there, too, for he had gone to
9:21 and King **A** of Judah rode out in their chariots to
9:23 and fled, shouting to King **A**, "Treason, **A**!"
9:27 When King **A** of Judah saw what was happening,
9:27 So they shot **A** in his chariot at the Ascent of Gur,
10:13 he met some relatives of King **A** of Judah.
10:13 And they replied, "We are relatives of King **A**.
11:1 When Athaliah, the mother of King **A** of Judah,
12:18 Jehoram, and **A**, the previous kings of Judah,
1Ch 3:11 Jehoram, **A**, Joash,
2Ch 20:35 of Judah made an alliance with King **A** of Israel,
20:37 "Because you have allied yourself with King **A**,
21:17 his wives. Only his youngest son, **A**, was spared.
22:1 Then the people of Jerusalem made **A**,
22:1 So **A** son of Jehoram reigned as king of Judah.
22:2 **A** was twenty-two years old when he became king,
22:3 **A** also followed the evil example of King Ahab's
22:5 evil advice, **A** made an alliance with King Joram,
22:6 and King **A** of Judah went to Jezreel to visit him.
22:7 a fatal mistake, for God had decided to punish **A**.
22:7 It was during this visit that **A** went out with Joram
22:8 and Ahaziah's relatives who were attending **A**.
22:9 Then Jehu's men searched for **A**, and they found
22:9 **A** was given a decent burial because the people
22:10 When Athaliah, the mother of King **A** of Judah,

AHAZIAH'S (8) [AHAZIAH]

2Ki 1:18 The rest of the events in **A** reign are recorded in
9:29 **A** reign over Judah had begun in the eleventh year
11:2 But **A** sister Jehosheba, the daughter of King Jehoram, took **A** infant son, Joash,
2Ch 22:8 and **A** relatives who were attending Ahaziah.
22:9 None of the surviving members of **A** family was
22:11 But **A** sister Jehosheba, the daughter of King Jehoram, took **A** infant son, Joash,

AHBAN (1)

1Ch 2:29 of Abishur and his wife Abihail were **A** and Molid.

AHEAD (178) [HEAD]

Ge 23:15 that between friends? Go **a** and bury your dead."
24:7 He will send his angel **a** of you, and he will see to
29:26 marry off a younger daughter **a** of the firstborn,"
31:16 So go **a** and do whatever God has told you."
32:16 He told his servants to lead them on **a**, each group
32:21 So the presents were sent on **a**, and Jacob spent
33:3 Then Jacob went on **a**. As he approached his
33:14 So go on **a** of us. We will follow at our own pace
45:5 He sent me here **a** of you to preserve your lives.
45:11 for there are still five years of famine **a** of us.
46:28 Jacob sent Judah on **a** to meet Joseph and get
48:20 In this way, Jacob put Ephraim **a** of Manasseh.
Ex 8:25 Go **a** and offer sacrifices to your God," he said.
8:28 "All right, go **a**," Pharaoh replied. "I will let you
17:5 of the leaders of Israel and walk on **a** of the people.
23:28 I will send hornets **a** of you to drive out the
23:31 in the land, and you will drive them out **a** of you.
Lev 19:16 "Do not try to get **a** at the cost of your neighbor's
Nu 10:33 with the Ark of the LORD's covenant moving **a**
14:44 But the people pushed **a** toward the hill country of
32:24 Go **a** and build towns for your families
32:30 if they refuse to cross over and march **a** of you,
Dt 7:1 he will clear away many nations **a** of you:
7:22 will drive those nations out **a** of you little by little.
9:3 But the LORD your God will cross over **a** of you
9:5 your God will drive these nations out **a** of you only
11:25 your God will send fear and dread **a** of you,
18:12 the LORD your God will drive them out **a** of you.
31:3 But the LORD your God himself will cross over **a**
31:6 of them! The LORD your God will go **a** of you.
Jos 3:14 carrying the Ark of the Covenant went **a** of them.
6:4 Seven priests will walk **a** of the Ark, each carrying
9:15 Then Joshua went **a** and signed a peace treaty with
24:12 And I sent hornets **a** of you to drive out the two
Jdg 4:14 over Sisera, for the LORD is marching **a** of you."
18:6 "For the LORD will go **a** of you on your
Ru 2:2 And Naomi said, "All right, my daughter, go **a**."
1Sa 9:19 "Go on up the hill **a** of me to the place of sacrifice,
9:24 it before Saul. "Go **a** and eat it," Samuel said.
9:27 of town, Samuel told Saul to send his servant on **a**.
10:8 Then go down to Gilgal **a** of me and wait for me
12:2 I have selected him **a** of my own sons, and I stand
17:7 An armor bearer walked **a** of him carrying a huge
17:37 Saul finally consented. "All right, go **a**," he said.
17:41 out toward David with his shield bearer **a** of him,
20:22 the arrows are still **a** of you,' then it will mean that
20:37 Jonathan shouted, "The arrow is still **a** of you.
23:24 So the men of Ziph returned home **a** of Saul.
25:19 "Go on **a**. I will follow you shortly." But she
30:20 up all the flocks and herds and drove them on **a**.
2Sa 3:10 I should just go **a** and give David the rest of Saul's
5:19 over to me?" The LORD replied, "Yes, go **a**.
5:24 is moving **a** of you to strike down the Philistines."
7:3 "Go **a** and do what you have in mind,
14:12 of you!" she said. "Go **a**," he urged. "Speak!"
15:1 and he hired fifty footmen to run **a** of him.
18:23 he begged. Joab finally said, "All right, go **a**."
18:23 and got to Mahanaim **a** of the man from Cush.
19:17 They rushed down to the Jordan to arrive **a** of the
1Ki 14:24 had driven from the land **a** of the Israelites.
17:13 Go **a** and cook that 'last meal,' but bake me a little
18:46 and ran **a** of Ahab's chariot all the way to the
19:7 some more, for there is a long journey **a** of you."
19:19 There were eleven teams of oxen **a** of him, and he
21:26 had driven from the land **a** of the Israelites.
22:6 or not?" They all replied, "Go right **a**!
22:15 or not?" And Micaiah replied, "Go right **a**!
22:22 will succeed,' said the LORD. 'Go **a** and do it.'
2Ki 4:31 Gehazi hurried on **a** and laid the staff on the
4:41 and said, "Now it's all right; go **a** and eat."
6:2 us to meet." "All right," he told them, "go **a**."
16:3 had driven from the land **a** of the Israelites.
17:11 the LORD had driven from the land **a** of them.
21:2 had driven from the land **a** of the Israelites.
1Ch 14:10 The LORD replied, "Yes, go **a**. I will give you
14:15 That will be the signal that God is moving **a** of you
17:2 "Go **a** with what you have in mind,
29:1 The work **a** of him is enormous, for the Temple he
2Ch 14:7 So they went **a** with these projects and brought
18:5 They all replied, "Go **a**, for God will give you a
18:14 or not?" And Micaiah replied, "Go right **a**!
18:21 will succeed,' said the LORD. 'Go **a** and do it.'
20:21 the king appointed singers to walk **a** of the army,
28:3 had driven from the land **a** of the Israelites.
33:2 had driven from the land **a** of the Israelites.
Ne 4:7 and Ashdodites heard that the work was going **a**
Est 3:11 "but go **a** and do as you like with these people."
8:8 Now go **a** and send a message to the Jews in the
9:5 But the Jews went **a** on the appointed day
Job 22:28 and light will shine on the road **a** of you.
33:32 But if you have anything to say, go **a**. I want to
34:33 not mine. Go **a**, share your wisdom with us.
Ps 92:7 there is only eternal destruction **a** of them.
105:17 Then he sent someone to Egypt **a** of them—
139:3 You chart the path **a** of me / and tell me where to
Pr 4:25 Look straight **a**, and fix your eyes on what lies
6:23 and this teaching are a lamp to light the way **a** of
14:8 The wise look **a** to see what is coming, but fools
14:16 fools plunge **a** with great confidence.
22:3 A prudent person foresees the danger **a** and takes
22:16 A person who gets **a** by oppressing the poor
23:18 For surely you have a future **a** of you; your hope
27:12 A prudent person foresees the danger **a** and takes
Ecc 9:3 no hope. There is nothing **a** but death anyway.
9:7 So go **a**. Eat your food and drink your wine with a
11:2 for you do not know what risks might lie **a**.
Isa 21:2 Go **a**, you Elamites and Medes, take part in the
26:7 of justice, / and you smooth out the road **a** of them.
29:9 Then go **a** and be blind if you must. You are
41:23 If you are gods, tell what will occur in the days **a**.
42:16 and smooth out the road **a** of them. / Yes, I will
44:7 can tell you what is going to happen in the days **a**?
48:5 That is why I told you **a** of time what I was going
52:12 For the LORD will go **a** of you, and the God of
65:24 their needs, I will go **a** and answer their prayers!
Jer 44:25 Then go **a** and carry out your promises and vows
La 2:8 for their destruction, then he went **a** and did it.
Eze 10:22 and they traveled straight **a**, just as the others had.
20:39 go right **a** and worship your idols, but then don't

Joel 2: 3 A of them the land lies as fair as the Garden of
Am 4: 4 "Go a and offer your sacrifices to the idols at
Hab 1: 9 the desert, sweeping captives a of them like sand.
Mal 1: 9 "Go a, beg God to be merciful to you! But when
Mt 1:20 "do not be afraid to go a with your marriage to
2: 9 It went a of them and stopped over the place where
21: 1 the Mount of Olives. Jesus sent two of them on a.
21: 8 Most of the crowd spread their coats on the road a
23:32 Go a. Finish what they started.
24: 3 And will there be any sign a of time to signal your
26:32 I will go a of you to Galilee and meet you there."
26:36 and he said, "Sit here while I go on a to pray."
26:50 go a and do what you have come for."
28: 7 from the dead, and he is going a of you to Galilee.
Mk 6:33 and people from many towns ran a along the shore
10:32 to Jerusalem, and Jesus was walking a of them.
11: 1 the Mount of Olives. Jesus sent two of them on a.
11: 8 Many in the crowd spread their coats on the road a
13: 4 And will there be any sign a of time to show us
14: 8 and has anointed my body for burial a of time.
14:15 is the place; go a and prepare our supper there."
14:16 So the two disciples went on a into the city
14:28 I will go a of you to Galilee and meet you there."
16: 7 including Peter: Jesus is going a of you to Galilee.
Lk 7:40 "All right, Teacher," Simon replied, "go a."
9:52 He sent messengers a to a Samaritan village to
10: 1 and sent them on a in pairs to all the towns
12:50 There is a terrible baptism a of me, and I am under
18:39 The crowds a of Jesus tried to hush the man,
19: 4 So he ran a and climbed a sycamore tree beside the
19:28 on toward Jerusalem, walking a of his disciples.
19:29 on the Mount of Olives, he sent two disciples a.
19:36 spread out their coats on the road a of Jesus.
19:41 came closer to Jerusalem and Jesus saw the city a,
21: 7 take place? And will there be any sign a of time?"
22: 8 Jesus sent Peter and John a and said, "Go
22:12 is the place. Go a and prepare our supper there."
Jn 5: 7 to get there, someone else always gets in a of me."
7:23 you go a and do it, so as not to break the law of
10: 4 he walks a of them, and they follow him
12:27 Should I pray, 'Father, save me from what lies a'?
Ac 19:22 on a to Macedonia while he stayed awhile longer
20: 5 They went a and waited for us at Troas.
20:13 for us to join him, and we went on a by ship.
20:23 me in city after city that jail and suffering lie a.
27:10 he said, "I believe there is trouble a if we go on—
Ro 1:24 So God let them go a and do whatever shameful
1:32 yet they go right a and do them anyway.
15: 1 but we cannot just go a and do them to please
1Co 7: 9 control themselves, they should go a and marry.
10: 1 by sending a cloud that moved along a of them,
10:27 isn't a Christian asks you home for dinner, go a;
2Co 9: 5 So I thought I should send these brothers a of me
Php 3:13 the past and looking forward to what lies a,
1Th 4:15 rise to meet him a of those who are in their graves.
Heb 11:26 for he was looking a to the great reward that God
Jas 5: 1 because of all the terrible troubles a of you.
1Pe 1: 6 There is wonderful joy a, even though it is
2Pe 3:17 I am warning you a of time, dear friends, so that

AHER (1)
1Ch 7:12 and Huppim. Hushim was the son of A.

AHI (2)
1Ch 5:15 A son of Abdiel, son of Guni, was the leader of
7:34 The sons of Shomer were A, Rohgah, Hubbah,

AHIAH (1)
Ne 10:26 A, Hanan, Anan,

AHIAM (2)
2Sa 23:33 Shagee from Harar; / A son of Sharar from Harar;
1Ch 11:35 A son of Sharar from Harar; / Eliphal son of Ur;

AHIAN (1)
1Ch 7:19 The sons of Shemida were A, Shechem, Likhi,

AHIEZER (6)
Nu 1:12 Dan | A son of Ammishaddai
2:25[-26] Dan | A son of Ammishaddai | 62,700
7:66 On the tenth day A son of Ammishaddai, leader of
7:71 This was the offering brought by A son of
10:25 under the leadership of A son of Ammishaddai.
1Ch 12: 3 Their leader was A son of Shemaah from Gibeah;

AHIHUD (2)
Nu 34:27 Asher | A son of Shelomi
1Ch 8: 7 Gera, the father of Uzza and A, led them when

AHIJAH (24) [AHIJAH'S]
1Sa 14: 3 (Among Saul's men was A the priest, who was
14: 3 A was the son of Ahitub, Ichabod's brother.
14:18 Then Saul shouted to A, "Bring the ephod here!"
14:18 For at that time A was wearing the ephod in front
14:19 So Saul said to A, "Never mind; let's get going!"
1Ki 4: 3 Elihoreph and A, the sons of Shisha, were court
11:29 the prophet A from Shiloh met him on the road,
11:30 and A took the new cloak he was wearing and tore
12:15 son of Nebat through the prophet A from Shiloh.
14: 2 Then go to the prophet A at Shiloh—the man who
14: 5 But the LORD had told A, "Jeroboam's wife will
14: 6 So when A heard her footsteps at the door,
14:12 Then A said to Jeroboam's wife, "Go on home,
14:18 the LORD had promised through the prophet A.
15:27 Then Baasha son of A, from the tribe of Issachar,
15:29 Jeroboam by the prophet A from Shiloh.
21:22 son of Nebat and the family of Baasha son of A,
2Ki 9: 9 of Jeroboam son of Nebat and of Baasha son of A.
1Ch 2:25 were Ram (the oldest), Bunah, Oren, Ozem, and A.
8: 7 Ehud's sons were Naaman, A, and Gera. Gera,
11:36 Hepher from Mekerah; / A from Pelon;
26:20 Other Levites, led by A, were in charge of the
2Ch 9:29 and in *The Prophecy of A from Shiloh,*
10:15 son of Nebat by the prophet A from Shiloh.

AHIJAH'S (1) [AHIJAH]
1Ki 14: 4 So Jeroboam's wife went to A home at Shiloh.

AHIKAM (9)
2Ki 22:12 A son of Shaphan, Acbor son of Micaiah,
22:14 So Hilkiah the priest, A, Acbor, Shaphan,
25:22 Nebuchadnezzar appointed Gedaliah son of A
2Ch 34:20 A son of Shaphan, Acbor son of Micaiah,
Jer 26:24 A son of Shaphan also stood with Jeremiah
39:14 They put him under the care of Gedaliah son of A
40: 5 then return to Gedaliah son of A and grandson of
40: 6 So Jeremiah returned to Gedaliah son of A at
40: 7 A as governor over the poor people who were left

AHILUD (5)
2Sa 8:16 Jehoshaphat son of A was the royal historian.
20:24 Jehoshaphat son of A was the royal historian.
1Ki 4: 3 Jehoshaphat son of A was the royal historian.
4:12 Baana son of A, in Taanach and Megiddo, all of
1Ch 18:15 Jehoshaphat son of A was the royal historian.

AHIMAAZ (16)
1Sa 14:50 Saul's wife was Ahinoam, the daughter of A.
2Sa 15:27 should return quietly to the city with your son A
15:36 and they will send their sons A and Jonathan to
17:17 Jonathan and A had been staying at En-rogel
17:20 they asked her, "Have you seen A and Jonathan?"
18:19 Then Zadok's son A said, "Let me run to the king
18:22 But A continued to plead with Joab,
18:23 Then A took a shortcut across the plain of the
18:27 "The first man runs like A son of Zadok,"
18:28 Then A cried out to the king, "All is well!"
18:29 A replied, "When Joab told me to come, there was
18:30 the king told him. So A stepped aside.
1Ki 4:15 A, in Naphtali. (He was married to Basemath,
1Ch 6: 8 the father of Zadok. / Zadok was the father of A.
6: 9 A was the father of Azariah. / Azariah was the
6:53 Zadok, and A.

AHIMAN (4)
Nu 13:22 arrived at Hebron, where A, Sheshai, and Talmai—
Jos 15:14 Sheshai, A, and Talmai—descendants of Anak.
Jdg 1:10 defeating the forces of Sheshai, A, and Talmai.
1Ch 9:17 Akkub, Talmon, A, and their relatives.

AHIMELECH (17)
1Sa 21: 1 David went to the city of Nob to see A the priest.
21: 1 A trembled when he saw him. "Why are you
21: 8 David asked A, "Do you have a spear or sword?
22: 9 he said, "I saw David talking to A the priest.
22:10 A consulted the LORD to find out what David
22:11 King Saul immediately sent for A and all his
22:12 son of Ahitub!" "What is it, my king?" A asked.
22:14 "But sir," A replied, "is there anyone among all
22:16 "You will surely die, A, along with your entire
22:20 one of the sons of A, escaped and fled to David.
26: 6 David asked A the Hittite and Abishai son of
2Sa 8:17 of Ahitub and A son of Abiathar were the priests.
1Ch 18:16 of Ahitub and A son of Abiathar were the priests.
24: 3 who was a descendant of Eleazar, and of A,
24: 6 Zadok the priest, A son of Abiathar, and the family
24:31 Zadok, A, and the family leaders of the priests
Ps 52: T told Saul that A had given refuge to David.

AHIMOTH (1)
1Ch 6:25 The descendants of Elkanah were Amasai, A,

AHINADAB (1)
1Ki 4:14 A son of Iddo, in Mahanaim.

AHINOAM (7)
1Sa 14:50 Saul's wife was A, the daughter of Ahimaaz.
25:43 David also married A from Jezreel, making both of
27: 3 A of Jezreel and Abigail of Carmel,
30: 5 David's two wives, A of Jezreel and Abigail,
2Sa 2: 2 David's wives were A from Jezreel and Abigail,
3: 2 was Amnon, whose mother was A of Jezreel.
1Ch 3: 1 was Amnon, whose mother was A of Jezreel.

AHIO (6)
2Sa 6: 3 Uzzah and A, Abinadab's sons, were guiding the
6: 4 with the Ark of God on it, with A walking in front.
1Ch 8:14 A, Shashak, Jeremoth,
8:31 Gedor, A, Zechariah,
9:37 Gedor, A, Zechariah, and Mikloth.
13: 7 on a new cart, with Uzzah and A guiding it.

AHIRA (5)
Nu 1:15 Naphtali | A son of Enan
2:29[-30] Naphtali | A son of Enan | 53,400
7:78 On the twelfth day A son of Enan, leader of the
7:83 This was the offering brought by A son of Enan.
10:27 The tribe of Naphtali was led by A son of Enan.

AHIRAM (1) [AHIRAMITE]
Nu 26:38 The Ahiramite clan, named after its ancestor A.

AHIRAMITE (1) [AHIRAM]
Nu 26:38 The A clan, named after its ancestor Ahiram.

AHISAMACH (3)
Ex 31: 6 "And I have appointed Oholiab son of A,
35:34 LORD has given both him and Oholiab son of A,
38:23 He was assisted by Oholiab son of A, of the tribe

AHISHAHAR (1)
1Ch 7:10 Ehud, Kenaanah, Zethan, Tarshish, and A.

AHISHAR (1)
1Ki 4: 6 A was manager of palace affairs. / Adoniram son

AHITHOPHEL (17) [AHITHOPHEL'S]
2Sa 15:12 While he was offering the sacrifices, he sent for A,
15:31 When someone told David that his adviser A was
15:31 "O LORD, let A give Absalom foolish advice!"
16:15 his men arrived at Jerusalem, accompanied by A.
16:20 Then Absalom turned to A and asked him,
16:21 A told him, "Go and sleep with your father's
16:23 For every word A spoke seemed as wise as though
17: 1 Now A urged Absalom, "Let me choose twelve
17: 6 Absalom told him what A had said.
17: 7 "this time I think A has made a mistake.
17:14 LORD had arranged to defeat the counsel of A,
17:15 what A had said and what he himself had
17:21 And they told him how A had advised that he be
17:23 A was publicly disgraced when Absalom refused
23:34 from Maacah; / Eliam son of A from Giloh;
1Ch 27:33 A was the royal adviser. Hushai the Arkite was the
27:34 A was succeeded by Jehoiada son of Benaiah

AHITHOPHEL'S (4) [AHITHOPHEL]
2Sa 15:34 Then you can frustrate and counter A advice.
16:23 Absalom followed A advice, just as David had
17: 6 Should we follow A advice? If not, speak up."
17:14 of Israel said, "Hushai's advice is better than A."

AHITUB (13)
1Sa 14: 3 Ahijah was the son of A, Ichabod's brother.
14: 3 A was the son of Phinehas and the grandson of Eli,
22:12 shouted at him, "Listen to me, you son of A!"
2Sa 8:17 Zadok son of A and Ahimelech son of Abiathar
1Ch 6: 7 father of Amariah. / Amariah was the father of A.
6: 8 A was the father of Zadok. / Zadok was the father
6:11 father of Amariah. / Amariah was the father of A.
6:12 A was the father of Zadok. / Zadok was the father
6:52 Meraioth, Amariah, A,
9:11 son of Zadok, son of Meraioth, son of A.
18:16 Zadok son of A and Ahimelech son of Abiathar
Ezr 7: 2 son of Shallum, son of Zadok, son of A,
Ne 11:11 son of Zadok, son of Meraioth, son of A,

AHLAB (1)
Jdg 1:31 Sidon, A, Aczib, Helbah, Aphik, and Rehob.

AHLAI (2)
1Ch 2:31 was Sheshan. Sheshan had a descendant named A.
11:41 Uriah the Hittite; / Zabad son of A;

AHOAH (6)
2Sa 23: 9 was Eleazar son of Dodai, a descendant of A.
23:28 Zalmon from A; / Maharai from Netophah;
1Ch 8: 4 Abishua, Naaman, A,
11:12 was Eleazar son of Dodai, a descendant of A.
11:29 Sibbecai from Hushah; / Zalmon from A;
27: 4 Dodai, a descendant of A, was commander of the

AHOLAH [KJV] See OHOLAH

AHOLIAB [KJV] See OHOLIAB

AHOLIBAH [KJV] See OHOLIBAH

AHOLIBAMAH [KJV] See OHOLIBAMAH

AHUMAI (1)
1Ch 4: 2 Jahath was the father of A and Lahad. These were

AHUZZAM (1)
1Ch 4: 6 Naarah gave birth to A, Hepher, Temeni,

AHUZZATH (1)
Ge 26:26 A, and also Phicol, his army commander.

AHZAI (1)
Ne 11:13 son of A, son of Meshillemoth, son of Immer;

AI (30)
Ge 12: 8 between Bethel on the west and A on the east.
13: 3 and A where they had camped before.

Jos 7: 2 of his men from Jericho to spy out the city of **A**,
7: 4 but they were soundly defeated. The men of **A**
8: 1 Take the entire army and attack **A**, for I have given to you the king of **A**, his people,
8: 3 and the army of Israel set out to attack **A**.
8: 5 the men of **A** will come out to fight as they did
8: 9 in ambush between Bethel and the west side of **A**.
8:10 Joshua roused his men and started toward **A**,
8:11 They camped on the north side of **A**, with a valley
8:12 men to lie in ambush between Bethel and **A**,
8:14 When the king of **A** saw the Israelites across the
8:17 There was not a man left in **A** or Bethel who did
8:18 "Point your spear toward **A**, for I will give you the
8:20 When the men of **A** looked behind them,
8:21 the city, they turned and attacked the men of **A**.
8:22 So the men of **A** were caught in a trap, and all of
8:23 Only the king of **A** was taken alive and brought to
8:25 So the entire population of **A** was wiped out that
8:26 who had lived in **A** was completely destroyed.
8:28 So **A** became a permanent mound of ruins,
8:29 Joshua hung the king of **A** on a tree and left him
9: 3 Gibeon heard what had happened to Jericho and **A**,
10: 1 and completely destroyed **A** and killed its king,
10: 2 as large as the royal cities and larger than **A**.
12: 9 The king of Jericho / The king of **A**, near Bethel
Ezr 2:28 The peoples of Bethel and **A** | 223
Ne 7:32 The peoples of Bethel and **A** | 123
Jer 49: 3 O Heshbon, for the town of **A** is destroyed.

AIAH (3)
Ge 36:24 The sons of Zibeon were **A** and Anah. This is the
2Sa 21: 8 whose mother was Rizpah daughter of **A**.
1Ch 1:40 and Onam. The sons of Zibeon were **A** and Anah.

AIATH (1)
Isa 10:28 are coming! They are now at **A**, now at Migron.

AID (9)
Ex 2:17 This time, however, Moses came to their **a**,
Ps 22:19 You are my strength; come quickly to my **a**!
35: 2 your shield. / Prepare for battle, and come to my **a**.
70: 5 am poor and needy; / please hurry to my **a**, O God.
86: 5 so full of unfailing love for all who ask your **a**.
101: 2 a blameless life—/ when will you come to my **a**?
Isa 30: 6 camels loaded with treasure to pay for Egypt's **a**.
60:10 your cities. Kings and rulers will send you **a**.
Ac 24:17 I returned to Jerusalem with money to **a** my people

AIDES (3)
Ps 105:22 He could instruct the king's **a** as he pleased
Mt 22:13 Then the king said to his **a**, 'Bind him hand
Mk 6:21 and he gave a party for his palace **a**, army officers,

AIJA (1)
Ne 11:31 Micmash, **A**, and Bethel with its surrounding

AIJALON (10)
Jos 10:12 and the moon over the valley of **A**."
19:42 Shaalabbin, **A**, Ithlah,
21:24 **A**, and Gath-rimmon—four towns.
Jdg 1:35 **A**, and Shaalbim, but when the descendants of
12:12 When he died, he was buried at **A** in Zebulun.
1Sa 14:31 killed the Philistines all day from Micmash to **A**,
1Ch 6:69 **A**, and Gath-rimmon.
8:13 They were the leaders of the clans living in **A**,
2Ch 11:10 Zorah, **A**, and Hebron. These became the fortified
28:18 **A**, Gederoth, Soco with its villages, Timnah with

AIM (5) [AIMED, AIMLESSLY, AIMS]
Ps 64: 3 they wield; / bitter words are the arrows they **a**.
Jer 9: 8 For their tongues **a** lies like poisoned arrows.
Ro 15: 2 let us **a** for harmony in the church and try to build
2Co 5: 9 So our **a** is to please him always, whether we are
Jas 4: 4 I say it again, that if your **a** is to enjoy this world,

AIMED (3) [AIM]
Ps 21:12 and run / when they see your arrows **a** at them.
La 3:12 He bent his bow and **a** it squarely at me.
Eph 6:16 shield to stop the fiery arrows **a** at you by Satan.

AIMLESSLY (1) [AIM]
Ge 21:14 out into the wilderness of Beersheba, wandering **a**.

AIMS (1) [AIM]
Ezr 4: 5 to work against them and to frustrate their **a**.

AIN (6)
Nu 34:11 then down to Riblah on the east side of **A**.
Jos 15:32 Lebaoth, Shilhim, **A**, and Rimmon. In all,
19: 7 It also included **A**, Rimmon, Ether, and Ashan—
21:16 **A**, Juttah, and Beth-shemesh—nine towns from
1Ch 4:32 lived in Etam, **A**, Rimmon, Token, and Ashan—
6:59 **A**, Juttah, and Beth-shemesh.

AIR (24) [AIRS]
Ex 9:10 Pharaoh watched, Moses tossed the soot into the **a**,
2Sa 16:13 stones at David and tossing dust into the **a**.
18: 9 His mule kept going and left him dangling in the **a**.
Job 2:12 and threw dust into the **a** over their heads to
41:16 are close together so no **a** can get between them.
Ps 62: 9 on the scales, / they are lighter than a puff of **a**.
144: 4 For we are like a breath of **a**; / our days are like a
Pr 18: 2 they only want to **a** their own opinions.
Ecc 3:19 For humans and animals both breathe the same **a**,
Isa 3:16 who walk around with their noses in the **a**,
41:16 You will toss them in the **a**, and the wind will blow
51: 3 Lovely songs of thanksgiving will fill the **a**.
Eze 1:21 When the living beings flew into the **a**, the wheels
10:16 When they rose into the **a**, the wheels stayed
11:22 and rose into the **a** with their wheels beside them,
Am 4:10 all your horses. The stench of death filled the **a**!
Zep 1: 3 Even the birds of the **a** and the fish in the sea will
Zec 5: 1 up again and saw a scroll flying through the **a**.
Ac 22:23 their coats, and tossed handfuls of dust into the **a**.
Eph 2: 2 the mighty prince of the power of the **a**.
1Th 4:17 caught up in the clouds to meet the Lord in the **a**
Rev 8:13 single eagle crying loudly as it flew through the **a**,
9: 2 the sunlight and **a** were darkened by the smoke.
16:17 the seventh angel poured out his bowl into the **a**.

AIRS (1) [AIR]
2Co 11:20 take advantage of you, put on **a**, and slap you in

AJAH [KJV] See AIAH

AJALON [KJV] See AIJALON

AKAN (2)
Ge 36:27 The sons of Ezer were Bilhan, Zaavan, and **A**.
1Ch 1:42 The sons of Ezer were Bilhan, Zaavan, and **A**.

AKELDAMA (1) [FIELD, BLOOD]
Ac 1:19 and they gave the place the Aramaic name ***A***,

AKIM (2)
Mt 1:14 Zadok was the father of **A**. / **A** was the father of

AKKAD (1)
Ge 10:10 with the cities of Babel, Erech, **A**, and Calneh.

AKKUB (8)
1Ch 3:24 Eliashib, Pelaiah, **A**, Johanan, Delaiah,
9:17 **A**, Talmon, Ahiman, and their relatives.
Ezr 2:42 Ater, Talmon, **A**, Hatita, and Shobai | 139
2:45 Lebanah, Hagabah, **A**,
Ne 7:45 Ater, Talmon, **A**, Hatita, and Shobai | 138
8: 7 Jeshua, Bani, Sherebiah, Jamin, **A**, Shabbethai,
11:19 **A**, Talmon, and 172 of their associates,
12:25 and **A** were the gatekeepers in charge of the

ALAMMELECH [KJV] See ALLAMMELECH

ALARM (14) [ALARMED, ALARMS]
Nu 10: 9 you must sound the **a** with these trumpets
Ne 4:18 The trumpeter stayed with me to sound the **a**.
Jer 4: 5 Tell them to sound the **a** throughout the land:
6: 1 Flee from Jerusalem! Sound the **a** in Tekoa!
Eze 33: 3 enemy coming, he blows the **a** to warn the people.
33: 4 Then if those who hear the **a** refuse to take action
33: 6 and doesn't sound the **a** to warn the people,
Da 11:44 then news from the east and the north will **a** him,
Hos 5: 8 Sound the **a** in Ramah! Raise the battle cry in
8: 1 "Sound the **a**! The enemy descends like an eagle
Joel 2: 1 Sound the **a** on my holy mountain! Let everyone
Na 2: 1 Sound the **a**! Man the ramparts! Muster your
Zep 1:10 "a cry of **a** will come from the Fish Gate and echo
2Co 7:11 such indignation, such **a**, such longing to see me,

ALARMED (7) [ALARM]
Ex 1:12 The Egyptians soon became **a**
2Ch 20: 3 Jehoshaphat was **a** by this news and sought the
Da 1:10 But he was **a** by Daniel's suggestion. "My lord the
4:19 don't be **a** by the dream and what it means."
5: 9 So the king grew even more **a**, and his face turned
Am 3: 6 the war trumpet blares, shouldn't the people be **a**?
Ac 16:38 the city officials were **a** to learn that Paul and Silas

ALARMS (1) [ALARM]
Jer 42:14 you think you will be free from war, famine, and **a**,

ALAS (4)
Ex 32:31 So Moses returned to the LORD and said, "**A**,
Nu 24:23 "**A**, who can survive when God does this?
Jer 34: 5 They will weep for you and say, "**A**, our king is
Eze 6:11 hands in horror, and stamp your feet. Cry out, '**A**!'

ALCOHOL (1) [ALCOHOLIC]
Hos 4:11 "**A** and prostitution have robbed my people of

ALCOHOLIC (5) [ALCOHOL]
Lev 10: 9 or any other **a** drink before going into the
Nu 6: 3 they must give up wine and other **a** drinks.
Jdg 13: 4 You must not drink wine or any other **a** drink
13: 7 You must not drink wine or any other **a** drink
13:14 or raisins, drink wine or any other **a** drink,

ALCOVES (13)
Eze 40: 7 There were guard **a** on each side built into the
40: 7 Each of these **a** was 10-1/2 feet square, with a
40:10 There were three guard **a** on each side of the
40:12 In front of each of the guard **a** was a 21-inch curb.
40:12 The **a** themselves were 10-1/2 feet square.
40:13 distance between the back walls of facing guard **a**;
40:16 narrowed inward through the walls of the guard **a**
40:21 Here, too, there were three guard **a** on each side,
40:21 wide between the back walls of facing guard **a**.
40:25 wide between the back walls of facing guard **a**.
40:29 Its guard **a**, dividing walls, and foyer were the
40:33 Its guard **a**, dividing walls, and foyer were the
40:36 The guard **a**, dividing walls, and foyer of this

ALEMETH (4) [ALMON]
1Ch 6:60 Geba, **A**, and Anathoth, each with its pasturelands.
7: 8 Omri, Jeremoth, Abijah, Anathoth, and **A**.
8:36 Jadah was the father of **A**, Azmaveth, and Zimri.
9:42 Jadah was the father of **A**, Azmaveth, and Zimri.

ALERT (8)
Isa 21: 7 Tell him to sound the **a** when he sees chariots
Mt 24:43 exactly when a burglar was coming would stay **a**
26:41 Keep **a** and pray. Otherwise temptation will
Mk 13:33 when they will happen, stay **a** and keep watch.
14:38 Keep **a** and pray. Otherwise, temptation will
Eph 6:18 Stay **a** and be persistent in your prayers for all
Col 4: 2 Devote yourselves to prayer with an **a** mind
1Th 5: 6 not asleep like the others. Stay **a** and be sober.

ALEXANDER (5)
Mk 15:21 Jesus' cross. (Simon is the father of **A** and Rufus.)
Ac 4: 6 priest was there, along with Caiaphas, John, **A**,
19:33 **A** was thrust forward by some of the Jews,
1Ti 1:20 Hymenaeus and **A** are two examples of this.
2Ti 4:14 **A** the coppersmith has done me much harm,

ALEXANDRIA (3) [ALEXANDRIAN]
Ac 6: 9 from Cyrene, **A**, Cilicia, and the province of Asia.
18:24 had just arrived in Ephesus from **A** in Egypt.
27: 6 There the officer found an Egyptian ship from **A**

ALEXANDRIAN (1) [ALEXANDRIA]
Ac 28:11 an **A** ship with the twin gods as its figurehead.

ALIENS (1)
1Pe 2:11 and sisters, you are foreigners and **a** here.

ALIKE (48) [LIKE]
Ge 6:20 of bird and each kind of animal, large and small **a**,
18:23 "Will you destroy both innocent and guilty **a**?
19:25 eliminating all life—people, plants, and animals **a**.
Ex 9: 9 boils to break out on people and animals **a**."
9:25 was destroyed—people, animals, and crops **a**.
11: 3 by Pharaoh's officials and the Egyptian people **a**.)
Nu 5: 3 This applies to men and women **a**. Remove them
18:11 male and female **a**, may eat of these offerings.
Dt 1:17 those who are rich; be fair to lowly and great **a**.
3: 6 town we conquered—men, women, and children **a**.
Jos 8:33 foreigners and citizens **a**—along with the leaders,
1Sa 18: 5 was applauded by the fighting men and officers **a**.
30:24 We share and share **a**—those who go to battle
1Ki 7:37 water carts were the same size and were made **a**,
14:10 your dynasty and kill all your sons, slave or free **a**.
21:21 male descendants, slave or free **a**, survive in Israel!
2Ki 9: 8 wiped out—every male, slave and free **a**, in Israel.
2Ch 31:15 dividing the gifts fairly among young and old **a**.
Job 3:19 Rich and poor are there **a**, and the slave is free
21:26 Both **a** are buried in the same dust, both eaten by
Ps 36: 6 You care for people and animals **a**, O LORD.
139:12 as day. / Darkness and light are both **a** to you.
Isa 10:33 vast army of Assyria—officers and high officials **a**.
Jer 2:26 officials, priests, and prophets—all are **a** in this.
8:16 the land and everything in it—cities and people **a**.'
31:24 and shepherds **a** will live together in peace
44:20 men and women **a**, who had given him that
47: 2 the land and everything in it—cities and people **a**.
51: 3 Young and old **a** will be completely destroyed.
Eze 13:18 the souls of my people, both young and old **a**.
14:13 a famine to destroy both people and animals **a**.
14:19 and the plague killed people and animals **a**.
18: 4 are mine to judge—both parents and children **a**.
20:47 every tree will be burned—green and dry trees **a**.
21: 3 your people—the righteous and the wicked **a**.
Joel 2:29 out my Spirit even on servants, men and women **a**.
Mic 7: 3 Officials and judges **a** demand bribes. The people
Zep 1: 3 "I will sweep away both people and animals **a**.
Mt 22:10 good and bad **a**, and the banquet hall was filled
Jn 4:36 joy awaits both the planter and the harvester **a**!
Ac 2:18 upon all my servants, men and women **a**,
18: 4 trying to convince the Jews and Greeks **a**.
19:17 quickly all through Ephesus, to Jews and Greeks **a**.
20:21 I have had one message for Jews and Gentiles **a**—
26:23 from the dead as a light to Jews and Gentiles **a**."
Ro 1:14 in other cultures, to the educated and uneducated **a**.
14: 5 than another day, while others think every day is **a**.
1Co 4: 9 to the entire world—to people and angels **a**.

ALIVE (97) [LIVE]
Ge 6:19 into the boat with you to keep them **a** during the
6:20 and small alike, will come to you to be kept **a**.
7:23 They were all destroyed, and only Noah was left **a**,
37:22 his blood? Let's just throw him **a** into this pit here.
43:27 the old man you spoke about? Is he still **a**?"
43:28 "Yes," they replied. "He is **a** and well."
45: 3 he said to his brothers. "Is my father still **a**?"
45: 7 has sent me here to keep you and your families **a**

45:26 "Joseph is still **a**!" they told him. "And he is ruler
45:28 My son Joseph is **a**! I will go and see him before I
46:30 you with my own eyes and know you are still **a**."
Ex 4:18 I don't even know whether they are still **a**."
8: 9 only the frogs in the Nile River will remain **a**."
22: 4 or a donkey or a sheep and it is recovered **a**,
Lev 16:10 the scapegoat will be presented to the LORD **a**.
26:39 Those still left **a** will rot away in enemy lands
Nu 14:38 the land, only Joshua and Caleb remained **a**.
16:30 and they go down **a** into the grave,
16:33 So they went down **a** into the grave, along with
Dt 4: 4 faithful to the LORD your God are still **a** today.
5: 3 our ancestors, but with all of us who are **a** today.
Jos 8:23 Only the king of Ai was taken **a** and brought to
10:28 the king. Not one person in the city was left **a**.
10:37 the entire population. Not one person was left **a**.
11: 8 of Mizpah, until not one enemy warrior was left **a**.
14:10 the LORD has kept me **a** and well as he promised
Jdg 4:16 all of Sisera's warriors. Not a single one was left **a**.
1Sa 2:33 Those who are left **a** will live in sadness and grief,
20:31 As long as that son of Jesse is **a**, you'll never be
25:22 of his household is still **a** tomorrow morning!"
25:34 not one of Nabal's men would be **a** tomorrow
27: 9 David didn't leave one person **a** in the villages he
27:11 No one was left **a** to come to Gath and tell where
2Sa 9: 1 wondering if anyone in Saul's family was still **a**,
9: 3 asked him, "Is anyone still **a** from Saul's family?
9: 3 "Yes, one of Jonathan's sons is still **a**,
12:22 "I fasted and wept while the child was **a**, for I
13:30 has killed all your sons; not one is left **a**!"
17:12 to the ground, so that not one of his men is left **a**.
18:14 Absalom's heart as he dangled from the oak still **a**.
1Ki 1:48 to sit on my throne while I am still **a** to see it.' "
11:12 David, I will not do this while you are still **a**.
17:23 him to his mother. "Look, your son is **a**!" he said.
20:18 "Take them **a**," Ben-hadad commanded,
20:32 The king of Israel responded, "Is he still **a**?
2Ki 7:12 and then they will take us **a** and capture the city."
10:14 "Take them **a**!" Jehu shouted to his men.
Job 4:20 They are **a** in the morning, but by evening they are
Ps 33:19 from death / and keeps them **a** in times of famine.
35:25 have what we wanted! / Now we will eat him **a**!"
41: 2 and keeps them **a**. / He gives them prosperity
54: 4 my helper. / The Lord is the one who keeps me **a**!
55:15 by surprise; / let the grave swallow them **a**,
124: 3 they would have swallowed us **a** / because of their
Pr 1:12 Let's swallow them **a** as the grave swallows its
Isa 4: 1 In that day few men will be left **a**. Seven women
13:12 Few will be left **a** when I have finished my work.
16:14 will be ended, and few of its people will be left **a**."
24: 6 left desolate, destroyed by fire. Few will be left **a**.
51:18 Not one of your children is left **a** to help you
Jer 5:10 and destroy them, but leave a scattered few **a**.
29:22 and Ahab, whom the king of Babylon burned **a**!'
La 1:11 They have sold their treasures for food to stay **a**.
Eze 32:27 brought terror to everyone while they were still **a**.
Da 2:10 "There isn't a man **a** who can tell Your Majesty
Am 5: 3 town sends a hundred, only ten will come back **a**."
Jnh 4: 3 I'd rather be dead than **a** because nothing I
Mic 3: 2 You skin my people **a** and tear the flesh off their
Mt 27:63 what that deceiver once said while he was still **a**:
Mk 16:11 But when she told them that Jesus was **a** and she
Lk 20:38 of the living, not the dead. They are all **a** to him."
24: 5 are you looking in a tomb for someone who is **a**?
24:23 and they had seen angels who told them Jesus is **a**!
Jn 4:51 servants met him with the news that his son was **a**
21:22 "If I want him to remain **a** until I return,
21:23 only said, "If I want him to remain **a** until I return,
Ac 1: 3 to them in many ways that he was actually **a**.
9:41 the believers, and he showed them that she was **a**.
20:10 into his arms. "Don't worry," he said, "he's **a**!"
25:19 called Jesus who died, but whom Paul insists is **a**.
26:22 so that I am still **a** today to tell these facts to
Ro 7: 2 the law binds her to her husband as long as he is **a**.
7: 3 So while her husband is **a**, she would be
8:10 your spirit is **a** because you have been made right
14: 9 so that he might be Lord of those who are **a** and of
1Co 15: 6 most of whom are still **a**, though some have died
2Co 6: 9 We live close to death, but here we are, still **a**.
Col 2:13 Then God made you **a** with Christ. He forgave all
1Th 4:17 we who are still **a** and remain on the earth will be
5:10 whether we are dead or **a** at the time of his return.
Heb 9:17 While the person is still **a**, no one can use the will
Rev 1:18 Look, I am **a** forever and ever! And I hold the keys
2: 8 who is the First and the Last, who died and is **a**:
3: 1 and that you have a reputation for being **a**—
17: 8 The beast you saw was **a** but isn't now. And yet he
17:11 The scarlet beast that was **a** and then died is the
19:20 and his false prophet were thrown **a** into the lake

ALL (5051) [ALL-CONSUMING, ALL-POWERFUL] See Index of Articles, Etc.

ALL THE DAYS (2) Ps 23:6; 27:4

ALL THE EARTH (46) Ge 9:13; 18:25; Ex 9:14; 19:5; 34:10; Jos 3:13; 23:14; 1Sa 2:8; 1Ki 10:23; 1Ch 16:30; 2Ch 9:22; Job 1:8; 2:3; 25:3,4; Ps 19:4; 47:2,7; 57:5,11; 66:1; 83:18; 96:9; 97:5,9; 98:4; 108:5; 138:4; Ecc 7:20; Isa 40:28; 54:5; Jer 6:19; 50:23; La 2:15; 4:12; Mic 4:13; Na 3:5; Hab 2:14,20; Zep 3:8; Zec 4:14; 6:5; 14:9; Jn 17:2; Rev 11:4; 13:12

ALL THE FIRSTBORN (16) Ex 11:5; 12:12,29; 13:2,15,15; Nu 3:12,13,13,13,40; 8:16,17,17,18; Dt 15:19

ALL...GENERATIONS (13) Ex 3:15; 16:33; 27:21; Lev 10:9; 21:17; 23:41; 24:3; Dt 29:15; Ps 90:1; Isa 45:25; 60:15; Da 4:3; Joel 3:20

ALL ISRAEL (84) Lev 25:33; Nu 20:29; 25:11; Dt 13:11; 21:21; 27:9; 31:7; 34:12; Jos 6:18; 22:22; 1Sa 7:2,7; 10:24; 11:2; 18:16; 25:1; 26:15; 28:3; 30:25; 2Sa 5:5; 6:15; 8:15; 10:17; 12:12; 15:13; 16:21; 17:10; 19:11,20; 1Ki 1:20; 3:28; 4:1,7; 5:13; 8:62,63,65; 11:42; 12:1,16,18,20; 14:13; 22:17; 2Ki 10:21; 1Ch 9:1; 11:1,4,10; 12:38; 13:6,8; 14:8; 15:28; 18:14; 19:17; 28:4,8; 29:23,26; 2Ch 1:2; 7:6; 9:30; 10:1,3,16,16; 12:1; 18:16; 28:23; 29:24,24; 30:1,5; Ne 7:73; 13:26; Isa 65:8; Eze 5:13; Da 9:7,11; Am 3:13; Zec 12:12; Mal 4:4; Ro 11:26

ALL (THE) JEWS (10) Est 3:6,13; 4:8,16; Ac 10:22; 18:2,28; 21:21; 22:12; Ro 11:5

ALL JUDAH (7) 2Ki 22:13; 2Ch 31:20; 32:33; 34:9; 35:24; Jer 4:5; 18:11

ALL MY/YOUR HEART (29) Dt 4:29; 6:5; 10:12; 11:13; 13:3; 30:6,10; Jos 22:5; 1Sa 12:20; 1Ch 22:19; Ps 9:1; 28:7; 86:12; 111:1; 119:34,58,69,145; 138:1; Pr 3:5; Zep 3:14; Mt 22:37; Mk 12:30,33; Lk 10:27; Ro 1:9; 6:17; 7:22; Eph 6:6

ALL THE ISRAELITES (30) Ex 14:26; Lev 16:17; 17:2; 21:24; 22:18; Nu 3:8; 8:19; 14:10; 36:8; Dt 29:2; Jos 3:1,7; 4:14; 7:23,24,25; 8:33; 22:33; Jdg 8:27; 10:8; 14:3; 20:1,11,26; 1Sa 2:14; 11:15; 1Ch 13:2; 15:3; 2Ch 11:3; 35:17

ALL THE...KINGDOMS (19) Dt 3:21; 28:25; 1Ki 4:21,24; 2Ki 19:15,19; 1Ch 29:30; 2Ch 17:10; 20:6; 36:23; Ezr 1:2; Isa 37:16,20; Jer 10:7,7; 15:4; 25:26; Da 7:27; Lk 4:5

ALL THE KINGS (9) Jos 9:1; 11:2,17; 1Ki 10:15; 2Ch 9:14,26; Ps 47:9; 135:11; Jer 25:20

ALL THE LAND (35) Ge 2:6; 41:19; 45:9,20,26; 47:20; Ex 9:23; 10:19; Dt 3:8; 7:18; 19:8; 34:2,2; Jos 1:4,6; 11:22; 12:1; 13:4,6; 19:49; 21:43; 23:4; Jdg 11:21; 2Sa 9:7; 1Ki 4:10; 15:20; Job 42:15; Ps 44:2; Isa 7:22; 33:9; Jer 46:7; Eze 25:5; Zec 14:10; Mt 8:10; Lk 7:9

ALL THE MEN (34) Ge 19:4; 34:24; 39:14; Ex 34:23; 38:26; Nu 1:2,45; 4:3,23,30,35,39,43,47; 26:2,4; 31:7,49; 32:29; Dt 2:14,16; 21:21; 29:10; Jos 5:4,6; 8:16,24; Jdg 8:17; 2Ch 16:6; 20:13; Ezr 10:17; Est 1:11; Jer 32:12; 44:15

ALL...NATIONS (118) Ge 18:18; 22:18; 26:4; 49:10; Ex 19:5; Lev 26:45; Nu 24:8; Dt 7:7,14,16; 11:23; 14:2; 28:1,10,37,64; 30:3; Jos 4:24; 1Sa 8:5; 10:18; 1Ki 4:31; 8:53; 2Ki 19:17; 1Ch 14:17; 16:31; 2Ch 32:17; Ps 9:17; 22:28; 59:8; 67:3,5; 72:11,17; 82:8; 86:9; 96:10,13; 99:2; 117:1; Isa 2:4; 8:9; 21:2; 29:7; 37:18; 40:15; 42:6; 52:10; 56:7; 60:1,2,3; 62:10; 66:18; Jer 3:17; 6:18; 9:26; 12:14; 25:15,17,29,31; 27:7; 28:11,14; 33:9; 34:17; 44:8; 50:14; Eze 5:8,15; 20:23,41; 25:8; 29:15; 31:6,17,18; 32:16; 36:24; 38:16,23; Da 3:4; 5:19; 7:14; 9:16; Joel 3:11; Am 9:12; Mic 4:3; 5:15; 7:16; Zep 3:20; Hag 2:7,7; Zec 11:10; 12:2,6,9; 14:2,12,14; Mal 3:12; Mt 24:14,30; 25:32; 28:19; Mk 11:17; Lk 21:24; 24:47; Ac 14:16; 17:26; Gal 3:8; Rev 1:7; 2:26; 11:9; 12:5; 15:4; 18:3; 21:26

ALL PEOPLE (37) Ge 3:20; Dt 2:25; Ps 62:12; 65:2; 148:11; Pr 8:4; 24:12; Ecc 6:7; Isa 2:17; 40:5; 57:16; Jer 4:2; 9:1; 10:14; 17:10; 31:30; 32:19; 51:17; Eze 18:4; 32:26; Joel 2:28; Zep 3:9; Mt 7:21; 16:27; Lk 2:31; 3:6; Ac 2:17; Ro 2:6; 3:9; 5:18,20,21; 11:32; 1Ti 2:1; 4:10; Tit 2:11; Heb 12:23

ALL...PEOPLES (6) Dt 4:19; Est 8:9; Ps 96:10; Isa 66:18; Jer 32:27; Rev 11:9

ALL...SERVANTS (12) Ge 20:8; Dt 12:12; 16:11; 29:2; 34:11; 1Sa 22:14; 2Ki 9:7; 1Ch 21:3; Est 2:18; Ps 134:1; Ac 2:18; Rev 19:5

ALL THINGS (16) 1Ch 29:11; Ps 8:6; Isa 44:24; Ac 3:21; 1Co 15:27,27,28,28; Eph 1:11,22; 3:9; Heb 2:8,8; 1Jn 2:27; Rev 8:9; 21:5

ALL THESE THINGS (34) Lev 9:5; 14:43; Nu 16:28; Dt 30:1; 2Ki 23:4; 2Ch 4:16; Ps 106:29; Ecc 2:9; Isa 8:16; Jer 16:10; 25:30; 35:8; La 1:16; Eze 27:14; Da 4:28; 12:7; Zec 8:17; Mt 24:34; Lk 2:51; 21:6,28; 24:26,48; Jn 17:1; Ac 3:18; Ro 8:37; 2Co 4:15; Php 3:7; 2Th 2:15; 2Ti 2:7; Heb 9:5; Rev 2:19; 22:8,20

ALL THE TRIBES (14) Ex 28:10; Nu 2:17; 10:25; Dt 12:5; 29:21; Jdg 20:2; 2Sa 5:1; 1Ki 8:1; 11:32; 14:21; 2Ch 5:2; 7:8; 12:13; Rev 7:4

ALL THE WORDS (3) Dt 9:10; 32:44,46

ALL THE WORK (5) Dt 28:12; 1Ch 28:20; 2Ch 5:1; 8:16; Lk 10:40

ALL THE WORLD (36) 2Sa 7:26; 1Ki 3:13; 10:20; 2Ki 5:15; 1Ch 17:24; 2Ch 9:19; Ps 19:4; 50:12; Isa 11:10; 18:3; 42:5,19; 45:6,22; 49:26; La 2:13,15; 4:12; Eze 16:57; 20:48; 21:5; 23:29,32; Da 4:11,12,20; Zep 2:15; Mt 12:21; Mk 16:15; Ro 2:5; 10:18; Heb 2:9; 1Pe 4:13; 1Jn 2:2; Rev 13:3; 18:18

AT ALL TIMES (11) Lev 6:13; Dt 1:16; 2Ki 11:8; 1Ch 23:31; 2Ch 23:7; Ne 4:23; Ps 34:1; 62:8; 2Co 13:8; Eph 6:18; Jas 3:17

FOR ALL TIME (11) Nu 25:13; Dt 4:40; 2Sa 7:16; 1Ch 17:14; Heb 9:12,26; 10:2,10,12; 1Pe 3:18; Jude 1:3

ALL-CONSUMING (1) [ALL]

Isa 33:14 "can live here in the presence of this **a** fire?"

ALL-POWERFUL (1) [ALL]

Job 36:22 "Look, God is **a**. Who is a teacher like him?

ALLAMMELECH (1)

Jos 19:26 **A**, Amad, and Mishal. The boundary on the west

ALLEGIANCE (11) [ALLY]

1Ki 12:27 they will again give their **a** to King Rehoboam of
2Ki 25:11 and the troops who had declared their **a** to the king
Ne 6:18 For many in Judah had sworn **a** to him because his
Isa 45:23 and every tongue will confess **a** to my name."
Jer 52:15 and the troops who had declared their **a** to the king
Mt 10:22 everyone will hate you because of your **a** to me.
24: 9 hated all over the world because of your **a** to me.
Mk 13:13 everyone will hate you because of your **a** to me.
Lk 21:17 everyone will hate you because of your **a** to me.
Ac 17: 7 for they profess **a** to another king, Jesus."
Ro 14:11 and every tongue will confess **a** to God.' "

ALLEGING [KJV] See PROVING

ALLELUIA [KJV] See HALLELUJAH

ALLEYS (2)

Ps 10: 8 They lurk in dark **a**, / murdering the innocent who
Lk 14:21 the streets and **a** of the city and invite the poor,

ALLIANCE (10) [ALLY]

Ge 14: 3 and Bela formed an **a** and mobilized their armies in
Jdg 6:33 and the people of the east formed an **a** against
1Ki 3: 1 Solomon made an **a** with Pharaoh, the king of
5:12 and Solomon made a formal **a** of peace.
2Ch 20:35 King Jehoshaphat of Judah made an **a** with King
22: 5 evil advice, Ahaziah made an **a** with King Joram,
Isa 16: 1 to Jerusalem as a token of **a** with the king of Judah.
Da 11: 6 an **a** will be formed between the king of the north
11: 6 in marriage to the king of the north to secure the **a**,
11:17 and will form an **a** with the king of the south.

ALLIANCES (5) [ALLY]

Isa 2: 6 because they have made **a** with foreigners from the
Jer 2:18 "What have you gained by your **a** with Egypt
Da 2:43 forming **a** with each other through intermarriage.
11:23 making deceitful promises, he will make various **a**.
Hos 12: 1 they make **a** with Assyria and cut deals with the

ALLIED (8) [ALLY]

Jos 13:21 princes living in the region who were **a** with Sihon.
Jdg 8:10 all that remained of the **a** armies of the east—
1Ki 20: 1 by the chariots and horses of thirty-two **a** kings.
20:16 and the thirty-two **a** kings were still in their tents
2Ch 20:37 "Because you have **a** yourself with King Ahaziah,
Ps 83: 8 too, / and is **a** with the descendants of Lot.
Isa 7: 2 "Aram is **a** with Israel against us!" So the hearts
Eze 37:16 'This stick represents Judah and its **a** tribes.'

ALLIES (39) [ALLY]

Ge 14: 5 One year later, Kedorlaomer and his **a** arrived.
14:13 his relatives, Eshcol and Aner, were Abram's **a**.
14:16 Abram and his **a** recovered everything—the goods
14:17 from his victory over Kedorlaomer and his **a**,
14:24 But give a share of the goods to my **a**—Aner,
Jos 10: 1 had made peace with Israel and were now their **a**.
Jdg 18: 7 a great distance from Sidon and had no **a** nearby.
18:28 a great distance from Sidon and had no **a** nearby.
1Sa 22:17 for they are **a** and conspirators with David!
2Sa 10:19 and his Aramean **a** realized they had been defeated
2Ki 18:20 Which of your **a** will give you any military
1Ch 5:20 So the Hagrites and all their **a** were defeated.
2Ch 20:23 and Ammon turned against their **a** from Mount
Ps 83: 5 They signed a treaty as **a** against you—
Isa 20: 5 power of Ethiopia and boasted of their **a** in Egypt!
31: 2 who are wicked, and he will crush their **a**, too.
36: 5 Which of your **a** will give you any military
60:12 For the nations that refuse to be your **a** will be
Jer 4:30 you no good! Your **a** despise you and will kill you.
13:21 the LORD sets your foreign **a** over you as rulers?
22:20 Weep, for your **a** are all gone. Search for them in
22:22 And now your **a** have all disappeared with a puff
30:14 All your **a** have left you and do not care about you
46: 9 Come, all you **a** from Ethiopia, Libya, and Lydia
47: 4 along with their **a** from Tyre and Sidon.
50:37 her **a** from other lands will become as weak as
La 1:19 "I begged my **a** for help, but they betrayed me.
4:17 We looked in vain for our **a** to come and save us,
Eze 16:37 I will gather together all your **a**—these lovers of
30: 5 Libya, Lydia, and Arabia, with all their other **a**,
30: 6 All of Egypt's **a** will fall, and the pride of their
30: 8 I have set Egypt on fire and destroyed all their **a**.
31:17 Its **a**, too, were all destroyed and had passed away.
32:21 leaders will mockingly welcome Egypt and its **a**,
32:23 of the pit, and they are surrounded by their **a**.
38: 9 You and all your **a**—a vast and awesome horde—
39: 6 and on all your **a** who live safely on the coasts.
Ob 1: 7 "All your **a** will turn against you. They will help
Na 1:12 "Even though the Assyrians have many **a**,

ALLON (1)

1Ch 4:37 son of **A**, son of Jedaiah, son of Shimri, son of

ALLON-BACHUTH [KJV] See OAK (OF WEEPING)

ALLOTMENT (12) [ALLOTMENTS, ALLOTTED]

Jos 16: 1 The **a** to the descendants of Joseph extended from
17: 1 The next **a** of land was given to the half-tribe of
18:11 The first **a** of land went to the families of the tribe

19: 1 The second a of land went to the families of the
19:10 The third a of land went to the families of the tribe
19:17 The fourth a of land went to the families of the
19:24 The fifth a of land went to the families of the tribe
19:32 The sixth a of land went to the families of the tribe
19:40 and last a of land went to the families of the tribe
Jer 13:25 This is your a, that which is due you,"
Eze 45: 8 These sections of land will be the prince's a.
45: 8 of the land to the people, giving an a to each tribe.

ALLOTMENTS (3) [ALLOTMENT]

Jos 13:32 These are the a Moses had made while he was on
2Ch 31:18 Food a were also given to all the families listed in
Eze 48:29 These are the a that will be set aside for each

ALLOTTED (23) [ALLOTMENT]

Nu 18: 9 You are a the portion of the most holy offerings
33:54 A larger inheritance of land will be a to each of the
33:54 and a smaller inheritance will be a to each of the
36: 7 of every tribe must remain fixed as it was first a.
36: 9 each tribe of Israel must hold on to its a
Jos 12: 7 (Joshua a this land to the tribes of Israel as their
14: 1 inherited land in Canaan as a by Eleazar the priest,
17: 2 Land on the west side of the Jordan was a to the
18: 2 tribes who had not yet been a their inheritance.
21: 5 The other families of the Kohathite clan were a ten
21:20 clan from the tribe of Levi was a these towns
21:23 and pasturelands were a to the priests from the
21:25 The half-tribe of Manasseh a the following towns
21:33 and their pasturelands were a to the clan of
21:40 So twelve towns were a to the clan of Merari.
23: 4 I have a to you as an inheritance all the land of the
24:32 This land was located in the territory a to the tribes
Jdg 1: 3 the Canaanites living in the territory a to us.
2: 6 tribes left to take possession of the land a to them.
Eze 48:13 The land a to the Levites will be the same size
48:15 the sacred Temple area, will be a for public use—
48:22 everything between the territories a to Judah
48:23 "These are the territories a to the rest of the tribes.

ALLOW (39) [ALLOWANCE, ALLOWED, ALLOWING, ALLOWS]

Ge 34:14 They said to them, "We couldn't possibly a this,
Ex 1:16 as they are born. A only the baby girls to live."
21: 8 bought her, he may a her to be bought back again.
23: 7 I will not a anyone guilty of this to go free.
23:12 It will also a the people of your household,
Lev 13:45 tear their clothing and a their hair to hang loose.
25:35 a resident foreigner and a them to live with you.
25:53 You must not a a resident foreigner to treat any of
Nu 16: 5 The LORD will a those who are chosen to enter
20:21 Because Edom refused to a Israel to pass through
Dt 2:30 But King Sihon refused to a you to pass through,
18:10 or sorcery, or a them to interpret omens,
Jos 9:26 Joshua did not a the people of Israel to kill them.
20: 4 They must a the accused to enter the city and live
Jdg 2:23 the nations out or a Joshua to conquer them all.
Ru 1:17 May the LORD punish me severely if I a
1Sa 4: 3 "Why did the LORD a us to be defeated by the
13:19 The Philistines wouldn't a them for fear they
21: 5 "I never a my men to be with women when they
2Ki 5:17 but please a me to load two of my mules with earth
18:31 Then I will a each of you to continue eating from
2Ch 11:14 and his sons would not a them to serve the LORD
Ps 16:10 the dead / or a your godly one to rot in the grave.
44:10 from our enemies / and a them to plunder our land.
74:10 O God, will you a our enemies to mock you?
101: 7 I will not a deceivers to serve me, / and liars will
104:14 You a them to produce food from the earth—
Isa 13:20 and shepherds will not a their sheep to stay
26: 2 to all who are righteous; / a the faithful to enter.
36:16 Then I will a each of you to continue eating from
Eze 25: 4 I will a nomads from the eastern deserts to overrun
36:15 I will not a those foreign nations to sneer at you,
42: 5 because the upper levels had to a a space for
Hab 1:13 But will you, who cannot a sin in any form,
Mt 18:18 and whatever you a on earth is allowed in heaven.
Mk 1:34 who he was, he refused to a the demons to speak.
Ac 2:27 the dead / or a your Holy One to rot in the grave.
13:35 'You will not a your Holy One to rot in the grave.'
24:23 and a his friends to visit him and take care of his

ALLOWANCE (6) [ALLOW]

2Ki 25:30 The Babylonian king also gave him a regular a to
Ne 5:14 I nor my officials drew on our official food a.
5:18 Yet I refused to claim the governor's food a
Jer 52:34 The Babylonian king also gave him a regular a to
Eph 4: 2 making a for each other's faults because of your
Col 3:13 You must make a for each other's faults

ALLOWED (94) [ALLOW]

Ge 3: 3 at the center of the garden that we are not a to eat.
31: 7 But God has not a him to do me any harm.
43: 5 'You won't be a to come and see me unless your
44:26 We won't be a to see the man in charge of the
Ex 1:17 refused to obey the king and a the boys to live,
1:18 he demanded. "Why have you a the boys to live?"
7: 2 He will demand that the people of Israel be a to
12:22 no one is a to leave the house until morning.
12:43 No foreigners are a to eat the Passover lamb.
21: 8 But he is not a to sell her to foreigners, since he is
22:18 "A sorceress must not be a to live.
24: 2 Moses, are a to come near to the LORD.
24: 2 none of the other people are a to climb on the
34: 3 In fact, no one is a anywhere on the mountain.
34:20 No one is a to appear before me without a gift.
Lev 16:17 No one else is a inside the Tabernacle while Aaron
20:18 the source of her flow, and she a him to do it.
22:13 only members of the priests' families are a to eat
25: 7 and the wild animals will also be a to eat of the
25:20 since we are not a to plant or harvest crops that
26:35 it will take the rest you never a it to take every
27:33 it is good or bad, and no substitutions will be a.
Nu 6: 4 they are not a to eat or drink anything that comes
10: 8 Aaron's descendants, are a to blow the trumpets.
Dt 2:29 The descendants of Esau at Mount Seir a us to go
22:29 violated her, and he will never be a to divorce her.
34: 4 I have now a you to see it, but you will not enter
Jos 6: 1 of the Israelites. No one was a to go in or out.
1Sa 14:30 If the men had been a to eat freely from the food
17:26 that he is a to defy the armies of the living God?"
1Ki 13:16 "I am not a to eat any food or drink any water here
15: 4 the LORD his God a his dynasty to continue,
2Ki 13: 3 and he a King Hazael of Aram and his son
23: 9 not a to serve at the LORD's altar in Jerusalem,
23: 9 but they were a to eat unleavened bread with the
25:12 But the captain of the guard a some of the poorest
25:29 and a him to dine at the king's table for the rest of
2Ch 28: 5 That is why the LORD his God a the king of
30:18 and they were a to eat the Passover meal anyway,
34:11 They restored what earlier kings of Judah had a to
Ezr 2:62 so they were not a to serve as priests.
9: 8 for the LORD our God has a a few of us to
9:13 have a some of us to survive as a remnant.
Ne 7:64 so they were not a to serve as priests.
9:30 So once again you a the pagan inhabitants of the
Est 4: 2 for no one was a to enter while wearing clothes of
8:11 They were a to kill, slaughter, and annihilate
Job 21:30 are spared in times of calamity and are a to escape.
24:11 They press out olive oil without being a to taste it,
24:23 They may be a to live in security, but God is
Ps 5: 5 the proud will not be a to stand in your presence,
71:20 You have a me to suffer much hardship, / but you
78:61 He a the Ark of his might to be captured;
79:10 Why should pagan nations be a to scoff, / asking,
94: 3 How long will the wicked be a to gloat?
101: 6 who are above reproach / will be a to serve me.
101: 7 and liars will not be a to enter my presence.
Pr 21:28 cut off, but an attentive witness will be a to speak.
27:18 Workers who tend a fig tree are a to eat its fruit.
Isa 38:16 have restored my health / and have a me to live!
42:24 Who a Israel to be robbed and hurt? Was it not the
63:17 why have you a us to turn from your path?
Jer 20: 7 you persuaded me, and I a myself to be persuaded.
27:11 a to stay in their own country to farm the land as
48:11 in peace. She is like wine that has been a to settle.
50: 7 enemies said, 'We are a to attack them freely,
52:16 But Nebuzaradan a some of the poorest people to
52:33 and a him to dine at the king's table for the rest of
Eze 18:24 acting like other sinners, should they be a to live?
20:26 and I a them to give their firstborn children as
23: 3 they a themselves to be fondled and caressed.
23:21 when you first a yourself to be fondled
Da 7:12 but they were a to live for a while longer.
Hos 9: 4 you will not be a to pour out wine as a sacrifice to
Mt 18:18 and whatever you allow on earth is a in heaven.
19: 3 "Should a man be a to divorce his wife for any
Mk 10: 2 "Should a man be a to divorce his wife?"
Jn 18:15 so he was a to enter the courtyard with Jesus.
18:28 and they wouldn't be a to celebrate the Passover
Ac 10:40 to life three days later. Then God a him to appear,
11: 6 reptiles, and birds that we are not a to eat.
1Co 5: 6 Don't you realize that if even one person is a to go
6:12 You may say, "I am a to do anything." But I
6:12 And even though "I am a to do anything," I must
9: 7 of sheep and isn't a to drink some of the milk?
10:23 You say, "I am a to do anything"—but not
10:23 You say, "I am a to do anything"—but not
Heb 3:19 So we see that they were not a to enter his rest
Rev 11: 9 stare at their bodies. No one will be a to bury them.
12:14 This a her to fly to a place prepared for her in the
13: 5 Then the beast was a to speak great blasphemies
13: 7 And the beast was a to wage war against God's
13:14 And with all the miracles he was a to perform on
21:27 Nothing evil will be a to enter—no one who

ALLOWING (2) [ALLOW]

Lev 22:16 by a unauthorized people to eat them.
Nu 35:32 a the slayer to return to his property before the

ALLOWS (4) [ALLOW]

Ex 21:13 But if it is an accident and God a it to happen,
Ecc 3:18 Then I realized that God a people to continue in
1Jn 3: 1 for he a us to be called his children, and we really
Jude 1: 4 saying that God's forgiveness a us to live immoral

ALLY (5) [ALLEGIANCE, ALLIANCE, ALLIANCES, ALLIED, ALLIES]

Job 24:17 They a themselves with the terrors of the darkness.
Ps 144: 2 He is my loving a and my fortress, / my tower of
Isa 19:24 And Israel will be their a. The three will be
48:14 and listen: 'The LORD has chosen Cyrus as his a.
Jer 2:36 you flit from one a to another asking for help.

ALMIGHTY (346) [MIGHT]

GOD ALMIGHTY (37) Ge 17:1; 28:3; 35:11; 43:14; 48:3; Ex 6:3; 2Sa 5:10; 1Ki 19:10,14; Ps 59:5; 80:4,7,14,19; 84:8; 89:8; Jer 5:14; 15:16; 35:17; 38:17; 44:7; Eze 10:5; Hos 12:5; Am 3:13; 4:13; 5:14,15,16,27; 6:8,14; Rev 4:8; 11:17; 15:3; 16:7,14; 21:22

LORD ALMIGHTY (3) Ro 9:29; 2Co 6:18; Jas 5:4

LORD* ALMIGHTY (260) 1Sa 1:3,11; 4:4; 15:2; 17:45; 2Sa 6:2,18; 7:8,26,27; 1Ki 18:15; 2Ki 3:14; 19:31; 1Ch 11:9; 17:7,24; Ps 24:10; 46:7,11; 48:8; 69:6; 84:1,3,12; Isa 1:9,24; 2:12; 3:1,15; 5:7,9,16,24; 6:3,5; 8:13,18; 9:7,13,19; 10:16,23,24,26,33; 13:4,13; 14:22,23,24,27; 17:3; 18:7,7; 19:4,12,16,17,18,20,25; 21:10; 22:5,12,14,14,15,25; 23:9; 24:23; 25:6; 28:5,22,29; 29:6; 31:4,5; 37:16,32; 39:5; 44:6; 45:13; 47:4; 48:2; 51:15; 54:5; Jer 2:19; 6:6,9; 7:3,21; 8:3; 9:7,15,17; 10:16; 11:17,20,22; 16:9; 19:3,11,15; 20:12; 23:15,16,36; 25:8,27,28,29,32; 26:18; 27:4,18,19,21; 28:2,14; 29:4,8,17,21,25; 30:8; 31:23,35; 32:14,15,18; 33:11,12; 35:13,18,19; 39:16; 42:15,18; 43:10; 44:2,11,25; 46:10,10,18,25; 48:1,15; 49:5,7,26,35; 50:18,25,31,33,34; 51:5,14,19,33,57,58; Am 9:5; Mic 4:4; Na 2:13; 3:5; Hab 2:13; Zep 2:9,10; Hag 1:2,5,7,9,14; 2:4,6,7,8,9,9,11,23,23; Zec 1:3,3,4,6,12,14,16,17; 2:8,9,11; 3:7,9,10; 4:6,9; 5:4; 6:12,15; 7:3,4,9,12,12,13; 8:1,2,3,4,6,6,7,9,9,11,14,14,18,19,20,21,22,23; 9:15; 10:3; 12:5; 13:2,7; 14:16,17,21,21; Mal 1:4,6,8,9,10,11,13,14; 2:2,4,7,8,12,16; 3:1,5,7,10,11,12,14,17; 4:1,3

LORD GOD ALMIGHTY (5) Rev 4:8; 11:17; 15:3; 16:7; 21:22

LORD* GOD ALMIGHTY (21) 2Sa 5:10; 1Ki 19:10,14; Ps 59:5; 80:4,19; 84:8; 89:8; Jer 5:14; 15:16; 35:17; 38:17; 44:7; Hos 12:5; Am 3:13; 4:13; 5:14,15,16; 6:8,14

Ge 17: 1 LORD appeared to him and said, "I am God A;
28: 3 May God A bless you and give you many children.
35:11 Then God said, "I am God A. Multiply and fill the
43:14 May God A give you mercy as you go before the
48: 3 "God A appeared to me at Luz in the land of
49:25 of your ancestors help you; / may the A bless you
Ex 6: 3 to Abraham, to Isaac, and to Jacob as God A,
Nu 24: 4 the words of God, / who sees a vision from the A,
24:16 the Most High, / who sees a vision from the A,
Ru 1:20 for the A has made life very bitter for me.
1:21 me to suffer and the A has sent such tragedy?"
1Sa 1: 3 and sacrifice to the LORD A at the Tabernacle.
1:11 "O LORD A, if you will look down upon my
4: 4 back the Ark of the Covenant of the LORD A,
15: 2 This is what the LORD A says: 'I have decided to
17:45 but I come to you in the name of the LORD A—
2Sa 5:10 because the LORD God A was with him.
6: 2 which bears the name of the LORD A, who is
6:18 blessed the people in the name of the LORD A.
7: 8 servant David, 'This is what the LORD A says:
7:26 will say, 'The LORD A is God over Israel!'
7:27 "O LORD A, God of Israel, I have been bold
1Ki 18:15 But Elijah said, "I swear by the LORD A,
19:10 "I have zealously served the LORD God A.
19:14 "I have zealously served the LORD God A.
2Ki 3:14 "As surely as the LORD A lives, whom I serve,
19:31 The passion of the LORD A will make this
1Ch 11: 9 because the LORD A was with him.
17: 7 servant David, 'This is what the LORD A says:
17:24 will say, 'The LORD A is God over Israel!'
Job 5:17 Do not despise the chastening of the A when you
6: 4 For the A has struck me down with his arrows.
6:14 accused me without the slightest fear of the A.
8: 3 God twist justice? Does the A twist what is right?
8: 5 But if you pray to God and seek the favor of the A,
11: 7 discover everything there is to know about the A?
13: 3 Oh, how I long to speak directly to the A. I want to
15:25 clenched their fists against God, defying the A.
21:15 Who is the A, and why should we obey him?
21:20 Let them drink deeply of the anger of the A.
22: 3 Is it any pleasure to the A if you are righteous?
22:17 'Leave us alone! What can the A do for us?'
22:23 If you return to the A and clean up your life,
22:25 Then the A himself will be your treasure. He will
22:26 "Then you will delight yourself in the A and look
23:16 has made my heart faint; the A has terrified me.
24: 1 "Why doesn't the A open the court and bring
27: 2 my rights, by the A who has embittered my soul.
27:10 Can they take delight in the A? Can they call to
27:11 I will not conceal anything that concerns the A.
27:13 from God; this is their inheritance from the A.
29: 5 The A was still with me, and my children were
31: 2 What is our inheritance from the A on high?
31:35 to my defense. Let the A show me that I am wrong.
32: 8 the breath of the A within them, that makes them
33: 4 has made me, and the breath of the A gives me life.
34:10 that God doesn't sin! The A can do no wrong.
34:12 God will not do wrong. The A cannot twist justice.
34:17 Are you going to condemn the a Judge?
35:13 God doesn't listen, to say the A isn't concerned.
37:23 We cannot imagine the power of the A, yet he is
40: 2 "Do you still want to argue with the A? You are
Ps 24:10 The LORD A—/ he is the King of glory.
46: 7 The LORD A is here among us; / the God of
46:11 The LORD A is here among us; / the God of
48: 8 have seen it ourselves—/ the city of the LORD A.
59: 5 O LORD God A, the God of Israel, / rise up to
68:14 The A scattered the enemy kings / like a blowing
69: 6 because of me, / O Sovereign LORD A.
80: 4 O LORD God A, / how long will you be angry
80: 7 Turn us again to yourself, O God A. / Make your
80:14 Come back, we beg you, O God A. / Look down
80:19 Turn us again to yourself, O LORD God A.
84: 1 How lovely is your dwelling place, / O LORD A.
84: 3 your altar, / O LORD A, my King and my God!
84: 8 O LORD God A, hear my prayer. / Listen, O God
84:12 O LORD A, / happy are those who trust in you.

89: 8 O LORD God A! / Where is there anyone as
91: 1 Most High / will find rest in the shadow of the A.
Isa 1: 9 If the LORD A had not spared a few of us,
1:24 Therefore, the Lord, the LORD A, the Mighty
2:12 In that day the LORD A will punish the proud,
3: 1 The Lord, the LORD A, will cut off the supplies
3:15 dust like that!" demands the Lord, the LORD A.
5: 7 They are the vineyard of the LORD A. / Israel
5: 9 But the LORD A has sealed your awful fate.
5:16 But the LORD A is exalted by his justice.
5:24 for they have rejected the law of the LORD A.
6: 3 they sang, "Holy, holy, holy is the LORD A!
6: 5 Yet I have seen the King, the LORD A!"
8:13 Do not fear anything except the LORD A.
8:18 reveal the plans the LORD A has for his people.
9: 7 The passionate commitment of the LORD A will
9:13 will still not repent and turn to the LORD A.
9:19 land is blackened by the fury of the LORD A.
10:16 of all your evil boasting, the Lord, the LORD A,
10:23 Yes, the Lord, the LORD A, has already decided
10:24 So this is what the Lord, the LORD A, says:
10:26 The LORD A will beat them with his whip,
10:33 The Lord, the LORD A, will chop down the
13: 4 The LORD A has brought them here to form an
13: 6 time has arrived—the time for the A to destroy.
13:13 I, the LORD A, will show my fury and fierce
14:22 This is what the LORD A says: "I, myself,
14:23 of destruction. I, the LORD A, have spoken!"
14:24 The LORD A has sworn this oath: "It will all
14:27 The LORD A has spoken—who can change his
17: 3 of Israel's departed glory," says the LORD A.
18: 7 But the time will come when the LORD A will
18: 7 They will bring the gifts to the LORD A in
19: 4 to a fierce king," says the Lord, the LORD A.
19:12 let them tell you what the LORD A is going to do
19:16 in fear beneath the upraised fist of the LORD A.
19:17 for the LORD A has laid out his plans against
19:18 five of Egypt's cities will follow the LORD A.
19:20 and a witness to the LORD A in the land of
19:25 For the LORD A will say, "Blessed be Egypt,
21:10 I have told you everything the LORD A,
22: 5 of confusion and terror the Lord, the LORD A,
22:12 The Lord, the LORD A, called you to weep
22:14 The LORD A has revealed to me that this sin will
22:14 That is the judgment of the Lord, the LORD A.
22:15 Furthermore, the Lord, the LORD A, told me to
22:25 The LORD A says: "When that time comes,
23: 9 The LORD A has done it to destroy your pride
24:23 Then the LORD A will mount his throne on
25: 6 the LORD A will spread a wonderful feast for
28: 5 Then at last the LORD A will himself be Israel's
28:22 For the Lord, the LORD A, has plainly told me
28:29 The LORD A is a wonderful teacher, and he
29: 6 In an instant, I, the LORD A, will come against
31: 4 the LORD A will come and fight on Mount Zion.
31: 5 The LORD A will hover over Jerusalem as a bird
37:16 "O LORD A, God of Israel, you are enthroned
37:32 The passion of the LORD A will make this
39: 5 "Listen to this message from the LORD A:
44: 6 Israel's King and Redeemer, the LORD A, says:
45:13 not for a reward! I, the LORD A, have spoken!"
47: 4 Our Redeemer, whose name is the LORD A,
48: 2 on the God of Israel, whose name is the LORD A.
51:15 its waves to roar. My name is the LORD A.
54: 5 The LORD A is his name! He is your Redeemer,
Jer 2:19 of him. I, the Lord, the LORD A, have spoken!
5:14 Therefore, this is what the LORD God A says:
6: 6 This is what the LORD A says: "Cut down the
6: 9 This is what the LORD A says: "Disaster will
7: 3 The LORD A, the God of Israel, says: Even now,
7:21 This is what the LORD A, the God of Israel,
8: 3 I will send them. I, the LORD A, have spoken!
9: 7 Therefore, the LORD A says, "See, I will melt
9:15 So now, listen to what the LORD A, the God of
9:17 This is what the LORD A says: "Think about
10:16 special possession. / The LORD A is his name!
11:17 I, the LORD A, who planted this olive tree,
11:20 O LORD A, you are just, and you examine the
11:22 So this is what the LORD A says about them:
15:16 for I bear your name, O LORD God A.
16: 9 For the LORD A, the God of Israel, says: In your
19: 3 This is what the LORD A, the God of Israel,
19:11 say to them, 'This is what the LORD A says:
19:15 "This is what the LORD A, the God of Israel,
20:12 O LORD A! You know those who are righteous,
23:15 this is what the LORD A says concerning the
23:16 is my warning to my people," says the LORD A.
23:36 words of our God, the living God, the LORD A.
25: 8 And now the LORD A says: Because you have
25:27 "Now tell them, 'The LORD A, the God of
25:28 to accept the cup, tell them, 'The LORD A says:
25:29 of the earth. I, the LORD A, have spoken!'
25:32 This is what the LORD A says: "Look!
26:18 people of Judah, 'This is what the LORD A says:
27: 4 'This is what the LORD A, the God of Israel,
27:18 let them pray to the LORD A about the gold
27:19 "For this is what the LORD A says about the
27:21 Yes, this is what the LORD A, the God of Israel,
28: 2 "The LORD A, the God of Israel, says: I will
28:14 The LORD A, the God of Israel, says: I have put
29: 4 The LORD A, the God of Israel, sends this
29: 8 The LORD A, the God of Israel, says, "Do not
29:17 This is what the LORD A says: "I will send war,
29:21 This is what the LORD A, the God of Israel,
29:25 "This is what the LORD A, the God of Israel,
30: 8 "For in that day, says the LORD A, I will break
31:23 This is what the LORD A, the God of Israel,
31:35 His name is the LORD A, and this is what he
32:14 "The LORD A, the God of Israel, says:
32:15 For the LORD A, the God of Israel, says:
32:18 are the great and powerful God, the LORD A.
33:11 'Give thanks to the LORD A, for the LORD is
33:12 "This is what the LORD A says: This land—
35:13 "The LORD A, the God of Israel, says: Go
35:17 "Therefore, the LORD God A, the God of Israel,
35:18 and said, "This is what the LORD A,
35:19 I, the LORD A, the God of Israel, have spoken!"
38:17 "The LORD God A, the God of Israel, says:
39:16 'The LORD A, the God of Israel, says:
42:15 The LORD A, the God of Israel, says: 'If you
42:18 "For the LORD A, the God of Israel, says:
43:10 of Judah, 'The LORD A, the God of Israel, says:
44: 2 "This is what the LORD A, the God of Israel,
44: 7 "And now the LORD God A, the God of Israel,
44:11 "Therefore, the LORD A, the God of Israel,
44:25 The LORD A, the God of Israel, says: You
46:10 For this is the day of the Lord, the LORD A,
46:10 The Lord, the LORD A, will receive a sacrifice
46:18 says the King, whose name is the LORD A,
46:25 The LORD A, the God of Israel, says: "I will
48: 1 This is what the LORD A, the God of Israel,
48:15 says the King, whose name is the LORD A.
49: 5 terror upon you," says the Lord, the LORD A.
49: 7 This is what the LORD A says: "Where are all
49:26 warriors will all be killed," says the LORD A.
49:35 This is what the LORD A says: "I will destroy
50:18 Therefore, the LORD A, the God of Israel,
50:25 will be the work of the Sovereign LORD A.
50:31 O proud people," says the Lord, the LORD A.
50:33 And now the LORD A says this: "The people of
50:34 His name is the LORD A. He will defend them
51: 5 For the LORD A has not forsaken Israel
51:14 The LORD A has taken this vow and has sworn
51:19 special possession. / The LORD A is his name!
51:33 For the LORD A, the God of Israel, says:
51:57 says the King, whose name is the LORD A.
51:58 This is what the LORD A says: "The wide walls
Eze 1:24 or like the voice of the A, or like the shouting of a
10: 5 of the cherubim sounded like the voice of God A
Hos 12: 5 the LORD God A, the LORD is his name!
Joel 1:15 the day when destruction comes from the A.
Am 3:13 all Israel," says the Lord, the LORD God A.
4:13 under his feet. The LORD God A is his name!
5:14 Then the LORD God A will truly be your helper,
5:15 Perhaps even yet the LORD God A will have
5:16 this is what the Lord, the LORD God A, says:
5:27 says the LORD, whose name is God A.
6: 8 and this is what he, the LORD God A, says:
6:14 nation against you," says the LORD God A.
9: 5 The Lord, the LORD A, touches the land and it
Mic 4: 4 nothing to fear. The LORD A has promised this!
Na 2:13 "I am your enemy!" says the LORD A.
3: 5 declares the LORD A. "And now I will lift your
Hab 2:13 Has not the LORD A promised that the wealth of
Zep 2: 9 says the LORD A, the God of Israel, "Moab
2:10 they have scoffed at the people of the LORD A.
Hag 1: 2 "This is what the LORD A says: The people are
1: 5 This is what the LORD A says: Consider how
1: 7 "This is what the LORD A says: Consider how
1: 9 my house lies in ruins, says the LORD A,
1:14 began their work on the house of the LORD A,
2: 4 and work, for I am with you, says the LORD A.
2: 6 "For this is what the LORD A says: In just a little
2: 7 I will fill this place with glory, says the LORD A.
2: 8 is mine, and the gold is mine, says the LORD A.
2: 9 be greater than its past glory, says the LORD A.
2: 9 I will bring peace. I, the LORD A, have spoken!"
2:11 "This is what the LORD A says! Ask the priests
2:23 this happens, says the LORD A, I will honor you,
2:23 chosen you. I, the LORD A, have spoken!"
Zec 1: 3 to the people, 'This is what the LORD A says:
1: 3 and I will return to you, says the LORD A.'
1: 4 said to them, 'This is what the LORD A says:
1: 6 received what we deserved from the LORD A.
1:12 "O LORD A, for seventy years now you have
1:14 'This is what the LORD A says: My love for
1:16 My Temple will be rebuilt, says the LORD A,
1:17 Say this also: 'This is what the LORD A says:
2: 8 the LORD A sent me against the nations who
2: 9 Then you will know that the LORD A has sent
2:11 and you will know that the LORD A sent me to
3: 7 "This is what the LORD A says: If you follow
3: 9 engrave an inscription on it, says the LORD A,
3:10 And on that day, says the LORD A, each of you
4: 6 by strength, but by my Spirit, says the LORD A.
4: 9 Then you will know that the LORD A has sent
5: 4 And this is what the LORD A says: I am sending
6:12 Tell him that the LORD A says: Here is the man
6:15 know my messages have been from the LORD A.
7: 3 and of the priests at the Temple of the LORD A:
7: 4 The LORD A sent me this message:
7: 9 "This is what the LORD A says: Judge fairly
7:12 or the messages that the LORD A had sent them
7:12 That is why the LORD A was so angry with
7:13 listen when they called to me, says the LORD A.
8: 1 another message came to me from the LORD A:
8: 2 "This is what the LORD A says: My love for
8: 3 the mountain of the LORD A will be called the
8: 4 This is what the LORD A says: Once again old
8: 6 "This is what the LORD A says: All this may
8: 6 you think this is impossible for me, the LORD A?
8: 7 This is what the LORD A says: You can be sure
8: 9 "This is what the LORD A says: Take heart
8: 9 the LORD A ever since the foundation was laid.
8:11 as I treated them before, says the LORD A.
8:14 "For this is what the LORD A says: I did not
8:14 and I promised to punish them, says the LORD A.
8:18 message that came to me from the LORD A.
8:19 "This is what the LORD A says: The traditional
8:20 "This is what the LORD A says: People from
8:21 the LORD to bless us and to seek the LORD A.
8:22 will come to Jerusalem to seek the LORD A
8:23 "This is what the LORD A says: In those days
9:15 The LORD A will protect his people, and they
10: 3 For the LORD A has arrived to look after his
12: 5 of Jerusalem have found strength in the LORD A,
13: 2 "And on that day, says the LORD A, I will get
13: 7 the man who is my partner, says the LORD A.
14:16 the LORD A, and to celebrate the Festival of
14:17 the King, the LORD A, will have no rain.
14:21 Judah will be set apart as holy to the LORD A.
14:21 longer be traders in the Temple of the LORD A.
Mal 1: 4 But this is what the LORD A says: "They may
1: 6 The LORD A says to the priests: "A son honors
1: 8 and see how pleased he is!" says the LORD A.
1: 9 he show you any favor at all?" asks the LORD A.
1:10 not at all pleased with you," says the LORD A,
1:11 is great among the nations," says the LORD A.
1:13 your noses at his commands," says the LORD A.
1:14 For I am a great king," says the LORD A,
2: 2 Honor my name," says the LORD A, "or I will
2: 4 the Levites may continue," says the LORD A.
2: 7 for the priests are the messengers of the LORD A.
2: 8 I made with the Levites," says the LORD A.
2:12 and yet brings an offering to the LORD A.
2:16 a victim's bloodstained coat," says the LORD A.
3: 1 so eagerly, is surely coming," says the LORD A.
3: 5 these people do not fear me," says the LORD A.
3: 7 and I will return to you," says the LORD A.
3:10 If you do," says the LORD A, "I will open the
3:11 shrivel before they are ripe," says the LORD A.
3:12 land will be such a delight," says the LORD A.
3:14 or by trying to show the LORD A that we are
3:17 "They will be my people," says the LORD A.
4: 1 The LORD A says, "The day of judgment is
4: 3 were dust under your feet," says the LORD A.
Ro 9:29 And Isaiah said in another place, / "If the Lord A
2Co 6:18 will be my sons and daughters, / says the Lord A."
1Ti 6:15 from heaven by the blessed and only a God,
Jas 5: 4 of the reapers have reached the ears of the Lord A.
Rev 1: 8 always was, and who is still to come, the A One."
4: 8 on saying, / "Holy, holy, holy is the Lord God A—
11:17 they said, / "We give thanks to you, Lord God A,
15: 3 and marvelous are your actions, / Lord God A.
16: 7 "Yes, Lord God A, your punishments are true
16:14 the Lord on that great judgment day of God A.
19: 6 "Hallelujah! For the Lord our God, the A, reigns.
19:15 and he trod the winepress of the fierce wrath of a
21:22 for the Lord God A and the Lamb are its temple.

ALMODAD (2)
Ge 10:26 Joktan was the ancestor of A, Sheleph,
1Ch 1:20 Joktan was the ancestor of A, Sheleph,

ALMON (1) [ALEMETH]
Jos 21:18 Anathoth, and A—four towns.

ALMON-DIBLATHAIM (2) [BETH-DIBLATHAIM]
Nu 33:46 They left Dibon-gad and camped at A.
33:47 They left A and camped in the mountains east of

ALMOND (6) [ALMONDS]
Ge 30:37 a, and plane trees and peeled off strips of the bark
Ex 25:33 branches will hold a cup shaped like an a blossom,
25:34 lampstand will be decorated with four a blossoms,
37:19 six branches held a cup shaped like an a blossom,
37:20 was also decorated with four a blossoms.
Jer 1:11 And I replied, "I see a branch from an a tree."

ALMONDS (2) [ALMOND]
Ge 43:11 balm, honey, spices, myrrh, pistachio nuts, and a.
Nu 17: 8 of Levi, had sprouted, blossomed, and produced a!

ALMOST (23)
Ge 8:11 Noah now knew that the water was a gone.
27: 1 When Isaac was old and a blind, he called for
27:30 and a before Jacob had left his father,
43: 2 When the grain they had brought from Egypt was a
1Sa 3: 2 One night Eli, who was a blind by now, had just
20:37 When the boy had a reached the arrow,
2Sa 23:22 These are some of the deeds that made Benaiah a
1Ch 29: 7 they gave a 188 tons of gold, 10,000 gold coins,
2Ch 8:18 and brought back to Solomon a seventeen tons of
Ps 73: 2 the cliff! / My feet were slipping, and I was a gone.
119:87 They a finished me off, / but I refused to abandon
Ecc 4: 5 Foolish people refuse to work and a starve.
7:12 Wisdom or money can get you a anything, but it's
Isa 58: 2 You would a think this was a righteous nation that
Jer 38: 9 of hunger, for a all the bread in the city is gone."
Eze 30: 3 for the terrible day is a here—the day of the
Hos 9: 7 has come; the day of payment is a here.
Jn 11:55 It was now a time for the celebration of Passover,
Ac 13:44 The following week a the entire city turned out to
21:27 The seven days were a ended when some Jews
Ro 13:12 The night is a gone; the day of salvation will soon
Php 2:27 And he surely was ill; in fact, he a died. But God
4:12 I know how to live on a nothing or with

ALMSDEEDS [KJV] See HELPING

ALMUG (6)

1Ki 10:11 they also brought rich cargoes of a wood
10:12 The king used the a wood to make railings for the
10:12 or since has there been such a supply of beautiful a
2Ch 2:8 send me cedar, cypress, and a logs from Lebanon,
9:10 they also brought rich cargoes of a wood
9:11 The king used the a wood to make steps for the

ALOES (5)

Nu 24:6 They are like a planted by the LORD,
Ps 45:8 Your robes are perfumed with myrrh, a, and cassia.
Pr 7:17 perfumed my bed with myrrh, a, and cinnamon.
SS 4:14 and saffron, calamus and cinnamon, myrrh and a,
Jn 19:39 of embalming ointment made from myrrh and a.

ALOFT (1)

Dt 32:11 to take them in / and carried them a on his pinions.

ALONE (208) [LONE, LONELY]

Ge 2:18 God said, "It is not good for the man to be a.
7:1 of the earth, I consider you a to be righteous.
19:8 Do with them as you wish, but leave these men a,
26:22 and the local people finally left him a.
32:24 This left Jacob all a in the camp, and a man came
42:38 is dead, and he a is left of his mother's children.
44:20 is dead, and he a is left of his mother's children,
45:1 He wanted to be a with his brothers when he told
Ex 4:26 After that, the LORD left him a.
14:12 Didn't we tell you to leave us a while we were still
18:14 he said, "Why are you trying to do all this a?
24:2 You a, Moses, are allowed to come near to the
29:33 They a may eat the meat and bread used for their
32:10 Now leave me a so my anger can blaze against
Nu 11:17 along with you, so you will not have to carry it a.
18:1 and your sons a will be held liable for violations
23:3 to me." So Balaam went a to the top of a hill,
31:23 that burns must be purified by the water a.
Dt 2:37 LORD our God had commanded us to leave a.
6:4 O Israel! The LORD is our God, the LORD a.
9:14 Leave me a so I may destroy them and erase their
10:20 cling to him. Your oaths must be in his name a.
13:4 Serve only the LORD your God and fear him a.
32:12 The LORD a guided them; / they lived without
Jos 22:22 "The LORD a is God! The LORD a is God!
24:14 Euphrates River and in Egypt. Serve the LORD a.
24:18 will serve the LORD, for he a is our God."
24:24 serve the LORD our God. We will obey him a."
Jdg 3:20 Ehud walked over to Eglon as he was sitting a in a
Ru 1:5 This left Naomi a, without her husband or sons.
1Sa 2:9 in darkness. / No one will succeed by strength a.
12:10 and you a if you will rescue us from our enemies.'
21:1 "Why are you a?" he asked. "Why is no one with
2Sa 16:11 Leave him a and let him curse, for the LORD has
18:25 and the king replied, "If he is a, he has news."
1Ki 3:18 We were a; there were only two of us in the house.
8:39 they deserve, for you a know the human heart.
11:29 a new cloak. The two of them were a in a field,
15:19 King Baasha of Israel so that he will leave me a."
19:4 Then he went on a into the desert, traveling all
19:10 I a am left, and now they are trying to kill me,
19:14 I a am left, and now they are trying to kill me,
2Ki 4:27 her away, but the man of God said, "Leave her a.
4:33 He went in a and shut the door behind him
17:36 and bow before him; offer sacrifices to him a.
19:15 You a are God of all the kingdoms of the earth. You a created the heavens and the earth.
19:19 all the kingdoms of the earth will know that you a,
23:18 Josiah replied, "Leave it a. Don't disturb his
1Ch 29:12 Riches and honor come from you a, for you rule
2Ch 6:30 they deserve, for you a know the human heart.
13:10 and the Levites a may help them in their work.
14:11 Help us, O LORD our God, for we trust in you a.
16:3 King Baasha of Israel so that he will leave me a."
20:6 our ancestors, you a are the God who is in heaven.
26:18 That is the work of the priests a, the sons of Aaron
32:12 altar at the Temple and to make sacrifices on it a.
33:13 Manasseh had finally realized that the LORD a is
Ezr 4:3 We a will build the Temple for the LORD,
Ne 9:6 You a are the LORD. You made the skies
Est 3:6 it was not enough to lay hands on Mordecai a.
9:12 killed five hundred people in the fortress of Susa a
Job 7:16 Oh, leave me a for these few remaining days.
7:19 Why won't you leave me a—even for a moment?
9:8 He a has spread out the heavens and marches on
10:20 I have only a little time left, so leave me a—
13:13 "Be silent now and leave me a. Let me speak—
22:17 For they said to God, 'Leave us a! What can the
Ps 4:8 for you a, O LORD, will keep me safe.
16:5 LORD, you a are my inheritance, my cup of
24:6 They a may enter God's presence / and worship
25:15 for he a can rescue me from the traps of my
25:16 mercy on me, / for I am a and in deep distress.
31:4 enemies set for me, / for I find protection in you a.
33:20 We depend on the LORD a to save us. / Only he
33:22 surround us, LORD, / for our hope is in you a.
51:4 Against you, and you a, have I sinned; / I have
62:2 He a is my rock and my salvation, / my fortress
62:6 He a is my rock and my salvation, / my fortress
62:7 My salvation and my honor come from God a.
71:5 O Lord, you a are my hope. / I've trusted you,
71:16 I will tell everyone that you a are just and good.
72:18 God of Israel, / who a does such wonderful things.
75:7 It is God a who judges; / he decides who will rise
83:18 until they learn that you a are called the LORD,
83:18 that you a are the Most High, supreme over all the
86:10 and perform great miracles. / You a are God.
91:2 He a is my refuge, my place of safety; / he is my
136:4 Give thanks to him who a does mighty miracles.
142:3 and you a know the way I should turn.
Pr 21:9 It is better to live a in the corner of an attic than
21:19 It is better to live a in the desert than with a
25:24 It is better to live a in the corner of an attic than
Ecc 4:8 This is the case of a man who is all a, without a
4:10 But people who are a when they fall are in real
4:11 from each other. But how can one be warm a?
4:12 A person standing a can be attacked and defeated,
Isa 2:11 be brought low and the LORD a will be exalted.
2:17 will lie in the dust. The LORD a will be exalted!
5:8 built on great estates so you can be a in the land.
8:13 He a is the Holy One. If you fear him, you need
22:4 Leave me a to weep; do not try to comfort me.
26:13 others have ruled us, / but we worship you a.
37:16 You a are God of all the kingdoms of the earth. You a created the heavens and the earth.
37:20 all the kingdoms of the earth will know that you a,
41:4 the LORD, the First and the Last. I a am he."
43:10 believe in me, and understand that I a am God.
43:25 "I—yes, I a—am the one who blots out your sins
44:24 who made all things. I a stretched out the heavens.
46:9 For I am God—I a! I am God, and there is no one
48:12 my chosen one! I a am God, the First and the Last.
49:21 I was left here all a. Who bore these children?
51:2 you came. Abraham was a when I called him.
63:3 "I have trodden the winepress a; no one was there
63:5 So I executed vengeance a; unaided, I passed down
Jer 3:2 You sit a like a nomad in the desert. You have
4:2 and if you will swear by my name a, and begin to
7:29 head in mourning, and weep a on the mountains.
9:24 Let them boast in this a: that they truly know me
10:7 O King of nations? That title belongs to you a!
13:17 to listen, I will weep a because of your pride.
15:17 I sat a because your hand was on me. I burst with
17:14 O LORD, you a can heal me; you a can save. My praises are for you a!
17:17 me now! You a are my hope in the day of disaster.
31:18 and restore me, for you a are the LORD my God.
49:31 "They live a in the desert without walls or gates.
La 1:1 broken with grief, she sits a in her mourning.
3:28 Let them sit a in silence beneath the LORD's
Eze 6:10 They will know that I a am the LORD and that I
6:13 then they will know that I a am the LORD.
9:8 they were carrying out their orders, I was all a.
14:16 Those three a would be saved, but the land would
14:18 could not save the people. They a would be saved.
14:20 They a would be saved by their righteousness.
20:26 and show them that I a am the LORD.
29:16 Then Israel will know that I a am the Sovereign
32:31 he will be relieved to find that he is not a in having
37:3 I replied, "you a know the answer to that."
40:46 for they a of all the Levites may approach the
44:28 will not have any, for I a am their inheritance.
Da 2:20 and ever, / for he a has all wisdom and power.
10:8 So I was left there all a to watch this amazing
11:8 afterward he will leave the king of the north a.
Hos 4:16 She will stand a and unprotected, like a helpless
4:17 Leave her a because she is married to idolatry.
5:6 he has withdrawn from them, and they are now a.
9:12 be a terrible day when I turn away and leave you a.
14:3 No, in you a do the orphans find mercy."
Joel 2:27 of Israel and that I a am the LORD your God.
Am 3:2 among all the families on the earth, I chose you a.
Jnh 2:9 For my salvation comes from the LORD a."
Zec 14:9 be one LORD—his name a will be worshiped.
Mt 8:34 but they begged him to go away and leave them a.
12:4 they ate the special bread reserved for the priests a.
14:13 off by himself in a boat to a remote area to be a.
14:23 by himself to pray. Night fell while he was there a.
27:19 "Leave that innocent man a, because I had a
27:49 But the rest said, "Leave him a. Let's see whether
Mk 1:35 and went out a into the wilderness to pray.
2:26 ate the special bread reserved for the priests a,
4:10 when Jesus was a with the twelve disciples
4:34 but afterward when he was a with his disciples,
5:17 pleading with Jesus to go away and leave them a.
6:47 in the middle of the lake, and Jesus was a on land.
9:28 when Jesus was a in the house with his disciples,
10:10 when he was a with his disciples in the house,
14:6 But Jesus replied, "Leave her a. Why berate her
15:36 to him on a stick so he could drink. "Leave him a.
Lk 6:4 ate the special bread reserved for the priests a,
8:37 region begged Jesus to go away and leave them a,
9:18 One day as Jesus was a, praying, he came over to
9:36 When the voice died away, Jesus was there a.
9:39 and injuring him. It hardly ever leaves him a.
10:23 Then when they were a, he turned to the disciples
Jn 4:8 He was a at the time because his disciples had
5:44 don't care about the honor that comes from God a.
6:10 all of them—the men a numbered five thousand—
6:15 make him king, so he went higher into the hills a.
6:68 we go? You a have the words that give eternal life.
8:16 be correct in every respect because I am not a—
11:48 If we leave him a, the whole nation will follow
12:7 Jesus replied, "Leave her a. She did it in
12:24 the soil. Unless it dies it will be a—a single seed.
16:32 each one going his own way, leaving me a.
16:32 Yet I am not a because the Father is with me.
Ac 5:38 "So my advice is, leave these men a. If they are
Ro 11:3 I a am left, and now they are trying to kill me,
16:27 To God, who a is wise, be the glory forever
1Co 1:30 God a made it possible for you to be in Christ
2:11 anyone else is really thinking except that person a,
12:11 He a decides which gift each person should have.
Gal 5:11 preaching salvation through the cross of Christ a.
6:12 for teaching that the cross of Christ a can save.
1Th 3:1 we decided that I should stay a in Athens,
1Ti 1:17 the unseen one who never dies; he a is God.
5:5 one who is truly a in this world, has placed her
5:16 the church can care for widows who are truly a.
6:16 He a can never die, and he lives in light so brilliant
Jas 2:24 made right with God by what we do, not by faith a.
4:12 God a, who made the law, can rightly judge among
4:12 He a has the power to save or to destroy.
Jude 1:25 All glory to him, who a is God our Savior,
Rev 15:4 For you a are holy. / All nations will come
19:1 is from our God. Glory and power belong to him a.

ALONG (479) [ALONGSIDE]

Ge 3:14 dust as long as you live, crawling a on your belly.
7:2 Take a seven pairs of each animal that I have
7:8 a with all the birds and other small animals.
7:14 a with birds and flying insects of every kind.
7:23 a with those who were with him in the boat.
16:7 Hagar beside a desert spring a the road to Shur.
17:27 a with all the other men and boys of the household,
19:25 a with the other cities and villages of the plain,
19:26 But Lot's wife looked back as she was following a
22:3 two of his servants with him, a with his son Isaac.
24:45 I saw Rebekah coming a with her water jug on her
24:48 because he had led me a the right path to find a
24:59 been Rebekah's childhood nurse went a with her.
30:32 or spotted, a with all the dark-colored sheep.
32:7 a with the flocks and herds and camels, into two
32:11 coming to kill me, a with my wives and children.
32:12 become as numerous as the sands a the seashore—
37:14 how your brothers and the flocks are getting a,"
37:28 and the Ishmaelite traders took him a to Egypt.
41:2 up out of the river and began grazing a its bank.
41:18 up out of the river and began grazing a its bank.
42:5 So Jacob's sons arrived in Egypt a with others to
43:3 couldn't see him again unless Benjamin came a.
43:27 He asked them how they had been getting a,
44:2 youngest brother's sack, a with his grain money."
45:24 he called after them, "Don't quarrel a the way!"
46:15 to Leah in Paddan-aram, a with their sister, Dinah.
49:17 beside the road, / a poisonous viper a the path,
Ex 2:3 and laid it among the reeds a the edge of the Nile
2:5 and her servant girls walked a the riverbank.
4:17 And be sure to take your shepherd's staff a so you
7:15 Be sure to take a the shepherd's staff that turned
7:24 Then the Egyptians dug wells a the riverbank to
10:8 "But tell me, just whom do you want to take a?"
10:10 to be with you if you try to take your little ones a!
12:38 went with them, a with the many flocks and herds.
13:18 So God led them a a route through the wilderness
14:2 Camp there a the shore, opposite Baal-zephon.
14:7 a with the rest of the chariots of Egypt, each with a
18:8 him about the problems they had faced a the way
23:1 "Do not pass a false reports. Do not cooperate
24:1 up here to me, and bring a Aaron, Nadab, Abihu,
26:4 Put loops of blue yarn a the edge of the last sheet
26:5 The fifty loops a the edge of one set are to match the fifty loops a the edge of the other.
26:10 Put fifty loops a the edge of the last sheet in each
26:23 a with an extra frame at each corner.
29:3 a with the young bull and the two rams.
29:5 a with the embroidered robe of the ephod,
29:32 a with the bread in the basket, at the Tabernacle
29:41 a with the same offerings of flour and wine as in
33:3 But I will not travel a with you, for you are a
33:3 I would be tempted to destroy you a the way."
36:2 a with all those who were specially gifted by the
36:11 Fifty blue loops were placed a the edge of the last
36:12 The fifty loops a the edge of the first set of sheets
36:12 matched the loops a the edge of the second set.
36:17 Then they made fifty loops a the edge of the last
36:24 a with forty silver bases, two for each frame.
36:26 a with forty silver bases, two for each frame.
36:30 a with sixteen silver bases, two for each frame.
36:33 a each side, running from one end to the other.
37:12 A rim about 3 inches wide was attached a the
37:24 The entire lampstand, a with its accessories,
39:25 between the pomegranates a the hem of the robe,
40:22 a the north side of the Holy Place, just outside the
Lev 5:2 or an animal that scurries a the ground—
8:2 and his sons, a with their special clothing,
8:7 in the robe of the ephod, a with the ephod itself,
8:25 two kidneys with their fat, a with the right thigh.
8:31 and eat it a with the bread that is in the basket of
9:19 a with the kidneys and the lobe of the liver.
10:15 a with the fat of the offerings given by fire.
11:20 all swarming insects that walk a the ground.
11:41 "Consider detestable any animal that scurries a the
11:42 This includes all animals that slither a on their
11:44 any of these animals that scurry a the ground.
14:4 a with some cedarwood, a scarlet cloth, and a
14:6 a with the cedarwood, the scarlet cloth,
14:10 a with five quarts of choice flour mixed with olive
14:11 a with the offerings, before the LORD at the
14:20 and offer it on the altar a with the grain offering.
14:21 a with two quarts of choice flour mixed with olive
14:24 the lamb for the guilt offering, a with the olive oil,
14:31 to be presented a with the grain offering.
19:9 do not harvest the grain a the edges of your fields,
20:5 a with all those who commit prostitution by
23:13 A with this sacrifice, you must also offer one quart

23:18 A with this bread, present seven one-year-old
23:22 do not harvest the grain a the edges of your fields,
Nu 1:50 a with its furnishings and equipment.
4: 9 a with its lamps, lamp snuffers, trays, and special
5: 8 be given to the priest, a with a ram for atonement.
6:15 a with their prescribed grain offerings and drink
6:17 a with the basket of bread made without yeast.
6:20 a with the breast and thigh pieces that were lifted
7: 1 a with all its furnishings and the altar with its
7:87 a with their prescribed grain offerings.
8: 8 a with a second young bull for a sin offering.
11:17 They will bear the burden of the people a with you,
13:29 The Canaanites live a the coast of the
Mediterranean Sea and a the Jordan Valley."
15:24 and it must be offered a with the prescribed grain
16:32 a with their households and the followers who
16:33 down alive into the grave, a with their belongings.
20: 4 into this wilderness to die, a with all our livestock?
21: 4 of Edom. But the people grew impatient a the way,
22:22 As Balaam and two servants were riding a,
24: 8 up from Egypt, / drawing them a like a wild ox.
27: 4 Give us property a with the rest of our relatives."
27: 7 You must give them an inheritance of land a with
28: 7 A with it you must present the proper drink
28:31 special burnt offerings, a with their drink offerings,
31: 6 They carried a the holy objects of the sanctuary
33: 2 identified by the different places they stopped a the
33:49 A the Jordan River they camped from
34: 3 from the wilderness of Zin, a the edge of Edom.
34:11 From there the boundary will run down a the
34:12 and then a the Jordan River to the Dead Sea.
35: 2 to live in, a with the surrounding pasturelands.
Dt 2: 8 "Then as we traveled northward a the desert route
2:35 a with anything of value from the towns we
2:37 we stayed away from the Ammonites a the Jabbok
3:12 I gave the territory beyond Aroer a the Arnon
8:13 and gold have multiplied a with everything else,
11: 6 a with their households and tents and every living
Jos 2: 7 So the king's men went looking for the spies a the
2:13 a with my father and mother, my brothers
2:22 chasing them had searched everywhere a the road,
5: 1 and all the Canaanite kings who lived a the
6:22 and bring her out, a with all her family."
7:15 a with everything he has, for he has broken the
8:33 a with the leaders, officers, and judges,
9: 1 and a the coast of the Mediterranean Sea as far
9: 5 And they took a dry, moldy bread for provisions.
10:10 Then the Israelites chased the enemy a the road to
10:10 at Azekah and Makkedah, killing them a the way.
11: 4 a with a vast array of horses and chariots,
13:21 and was killed by Moses a with the chiefs of
15: 5 The eastern boundary extended a the Dead Sea to
15: 8 a the southern slopes of the Jebusites,
15:10 passed a to the town of Kesalon on the northern
15:21 The towns of Judah situated a the borders of Edom
15:47 of Egypt and a the coast of the Mediterranean Sea.
17: 4 us an inheritance a with the men of our tribe."
17: 4 So Joshua gave them an inheritance a with their
17: 6 an inheritance a with the male descendants.
18:14 then ran south a the western edge of the hill facing
18:18 From there it passed a the north side of the slope
19:46 also Rakkon a with the territory across from Joppa.
21:11 of Judah, a with its surrounding pasturelands.
24: 1 a with their elders, leaders, judges, and officers.
24:32 which the Israelites had brought a with them when
Jdg 1:18 and Ekron, a with their surrounding territories.
4: 7 a with his chariots and warriors, to the Kishon
5:10 And you who must walk a the road, listen!
11:18 They traveled a Moab's eastern border and camped
11:26 to Aroer and in all the towns a the Arnon River.
14: 9 of the honey into his hands and ate it a the way.
18:20 so he took a the sacred ephod, the household idols,
20:31 and a the roads leading to Bethel and Gibeah.
20:32 so that the men of Benjamin would chase them a
20:45 but Israel killed five thousand of them a the road.
21:19 a the east side of the road that goes from Bethel to
1Sa 1:24 They brought a a three-year-old bull for our god Dagon."
5: 7 We will all be destroyed a with our god Dagon."
6: 3 God of Israel back, a with a gift," they were told.
6:12 the cows went straight a the road toward
7:11 to Beth-car, slaughtering them all a the way.
7:14 a with the rest of the territory that the Philistines
13: 5 and as many warriors as the grains of sand a the
16:20 a with a young goat and a donkey loaded down
17:18 See how your brothers are getting a, and bring me
17:52 and wounded Philistines were strewn all a the road
18: 6 Women came out from all the towns a the way to
22:16 surely die, Ahimelech, a with your entire family!"
25:42 she took a five of her servant girls as attendants,
26: 3 Saul camped a the road beside the hill of Hakilah,
27: 3 David brought his two wives a with him—
27: 8 near Shur, a the road to Egypt, since ancient times.
2Sa 2:24 near Giah, a the road to the wilderness of Gibeon.
3:16 Palti followed a behind her as far as Bahurim,
5:11 a with carpenters and stonemasons to build him a
8: 3 out to strengthen his control a the Euphrates River.
8: 8 a with a large amount of bronze from Hadadezer's
8:11 a with the silver and gold he had set apart from the
11: 7 asked him how Joab and the army were getting a
11:17 And Uriah was killed a with several other Israelite
13:34 from the Horonaim road a the side of the hill."
15:18 David from Gath, a with the king's bodyguard.
15:22 and his six hundred men and their families went a.
16:14 and all who were with him grew weary a the way,
22:34 a deer, / leading me safely a the mountain heights.
1Ki 2:26 and you suffered right a with him through all his
5: 9 We will float them a the coast to whatever place
8: 4 a with the Tabernacle and all its sacred utensils,
9:26 in the land of Edom, a the shore of the Red Sea.
13:24 But as he was traveling a, a lion came out
14:16 and made all of Israel sin a with him."
14:28 the guards would carry them a and then return
15:18 who was ruling in Damascus, a with this message:
18: 7 As Obadiah was walking a, he saw Elijah coming
2Ki 1: 9 the king has commanded you to come a with us."
2:11 As they were walking a and talking, suddenly a
2:23 As he was walking a the road, a group of boys
3: 9 and all three armies traveled a a roundabout route
3:21 and old, and stationed themselves a their border.
4:29 my staff and go! Don't talk to anyone a the way.
6:26 One day as the king of Israel was walking a the
6:30 And as the king walked a the wall, the people
9:25 when you and I were riding a behind his father,
9:27 was happening, he fled a the road to Beth-haggan.
10:12 A the way, while he was at Beth-eked of the
10:16 to the LORD." So Jehonadab rode a with him.
12:18 a with what he himself had dedicated.
12:18 a with all the gold in the treasuries of the
15:25 assassinated the king, a with Argob and Arieh,
16:10 to Uriah the priest, a with its design in full detail.
17: 6 a the banks of the Habor River in Gozan,
18:11 in Halah, a the banks of the Habor River in Gozan,
24:12 a with his advisers, nobles, and officials,
24:15 a with his wives and officials, the queen mother,
25:11 a with the rest of the people and the troops who
1Ch 5:10 Then they moved into the Hagrite settlements all a
5:12 a with Janai and Shaphat.
6:33 These are the men who served, a with their sons:
7:29 A the border of Manasseh were the towns of
14: 1 a with stonemasons and carpenters to build him a
18: 3 out to strengthen his control a the Euphrates River.
18: 8 a with a large amount of bronze from Hadadezer's
18:11 a with the silver and gold he had taken from the
24:25 a with Isshiah, the brother of Micah.
2Ch 2:15 "Send a the wheat, barley, olive oil, and wine that
4: 8 five a the south wall ad five a the north wall.
5: 5 a with the special tent and all its sacred utensils.
8:17 in the land of Edom, a the shore of the Red Sea.
12:11 the guards would carry them a and then return
13:19 and Ephron, a with their surrounding villages.
15: 9 a with the people of Ephraim, Manasseh,
16: 2 who was ruling in Damascus, a with this message:
17: 8 He sent Levites a with them, including Shemaiah,
25:24 a with hostages, and then returned to Samaria.
29:35 of burnt offerings, a with the usual drink offerings,
Ezr 3: 7 and floated a the coast of the Mediterranean Sea to
8:15 that not one Levite had volunteered to come a.
8:18 a with eighteen of his sons and brothers.
8:22 and protect us from enemies a the way.
8:31 and saved us from enemies and bandits a the way.
8:33 a with Jozabad son of Jeshua and Noadiah son of
Ne 2: 9 had sent a army officers and horsemen to protect
4: 3 collapse if even a fox walked a the top of it!"
4:19 and we are widely separated from each other a the
7: 2 a with Hananiah, the commander of the fortress,
7: 5 a with the ordinary citizens, for registration.
7:73 the Temple servants, a with some of the people—
12:31 One of the choirs proceeded southward a the top of
12:33 a with Azariah, Ezra, Meshullam,
12:38 a the top of the wall past the Tower of the Ovens
Est 2: 6 a with King Jehoiachin of Judah and many others.
2: 8 Esther, a with many other young women,
9:29 the daughter of Abihail, a with Mordecai the Jew,
Job 11:10 If God comes a and puts a person in prison, or if he
42:15 And their father put them into his will a with their
Ps 1: 3 They are like trees planted a the riverbank,
17: 4 which have kept me from going a with cruel
18:33 a deer, / leading me safely a the mountain heights.
23: 3 renews my strength. / He guides me a right paths,
26: 4 not spend time with liars / or go a with hypocrites.
26: 9 of sinners. / Don't condemn me a with murderers.
27:11 O LORD. / Lead me a the path of honesty,
32: 8 "I will guide you a the best pathway for your life.
37:34 Travel steadily a his path. / He will honor you,
40: 2 on solid ground / and steadied me as I walked a.
77:20 You led your people a that road like a flock of
78:27 birds as plentiful as the sands a the seashore!
89:41 Everyone who comes a has robbed him / while his
104:26 See the ships sailing a, / and Leviathan, which you
105:26 his servant, / a with Aaron, whom he had chosen.
106:15 they asked for, / but he sent a plague a with it.
110: 7 But he himself will be refreshed from brooks a the
119:35 Make me walk a the path of your commands,
119:95 Though the wicked hide a the way to kill me,
119:110 The wicked have set their traps for me a your path,
132: 8 a with the Ark, the symbol of your power.
139:24 and lead me a the path of everlasting life.
140: 5 out a net; / they have placed traps all a the way.
Pr 1:15 Don't go a with them, my child! Stay far away
1:21 She calls out to the crowds a the main street,
Ecc 7:23 All a I have tried my best to let wisdom guide my
8:15 That way they will experience some happiness a
12: 5 dragging a without any sexual desire.
12: 5 the mourners will walk a the streets.
SS 3: 6 the deserts like a cloud of smoke a the ground?
Isa 9: 1 which lies a the road that runs between the Jordan
9:12 a with Arameans from the east and Philistines
10: 4 You will stumble a as prisoners or lie among the
15: 5 Their crying can be heard all a the road to
18: 1 of the Nile. Its winged sailboats glide a the river,
19: 7 All the greenery a the riverbank will wither
23: 3 you grain from Egypt and harvests from a the Nile.
35: 9 Lions will not lurk a its course, and there will be
41: 7 the anvil. "Good," they say. "It's coming a fine."
42:16 a new path, / guiding them a an unfamiliar way.
44:11 the LORD in shame, a with all these craftsmen—
46: 4 I will care for you. I will carry you a and save you.
48:17 and leads you a the paths you should follow.
48:19 become as numerous as the sands a the seashore—
59:10 wonder we grope like blind people and stumble a.
Jer 8: 5 Then why do these people keep going a their
11:13 to your god Baal—are a every street in Jerusalem.
15: 8 widows than the grains of sand a the seashore.
17: 8 They are like trees planted a a riverbank,
18:22 a pit for me, and they have hidden traps a my path.
23:34 I will punish that person a with his entire family.
23:39 a with this city that I gave to you and your
24: 1 to Babylon a with the princes of Judah and all the
25:20 a with all the foreigners living in that land. So did
26:22 to Egypt a with several other men to capture Uriah.
27:20 a with all the other important people of Judah
33:11 a with the joyous songs of people bringing
36:12 a with Delaiah son of Shemaiah, Elnathan son of
38:10 king told Ebed-melech, "Take a thirty of my men,
41: 5 and had brought a grain offerings and incense.
47: 4 a with their allies from Tyre and Sidon.
47: 7 and the people living a the sea must be
49: 3 for your god Molech will be exiled a with his
52:15 a with the rest of the craftsmen and the troops who
Eze 5:17 And a with the famine, wild animals will attack
16:15 "But you thought you could get a without me,
16:15 yourself as a prostitute to every man who came a.
17: 7 eagle with broad wings and full plumage came a.
24: 5 pot to a boil, and cook the bones a with the meat.
27:35 All who live a the coastlands / are appalled at your
30:22 his arms—the good arm a with the broken one—
31:14 They will land in the pit a with all the proud
34:10 the flock, a with their right to feed themselves.
38: 6 a with the armies of Beth-togarmah from the
40: 7 with a distance between them of 8-3/4 feet a the
40:14 He measured the dividing walls all a the inside of
40:17 A stone pavement ran a the walls of the courtyard,
40:25 It had windows a the walls as the others did,
40:26 and there were palm tree decorations a the dividing
40:29 It also had windows a its walls and in the foyer
40:33 and there were windows a the walls and in the
41: 5 There was a row of rooms a the outside wall;
41:10 and the row of rooms a the outer wall of the inner
41:19 The figures were carved all a the inside of the
45:25 and the grain offering, a with the required olive oil.
46:23 A the inside of these walls was a ledge of stone
47: 3 he led me a the stream for 1,750 feet and told me
47: 6 I had seen, then he led me back a the riverbank.
47:10 Fishermen will stand a the shores of the Dead Sea,
47:12 All kinds of fruit trees will grow a both sides of the
47:18 and runs southward a the Jordan River between
48:18 and 3-1/3 miles to the west a the border of the
Da 2:18 so they would not be executed a with the other
6:24 into the lions' den, a with their wives and children.
11: 6 She will be given up a with her supporters.
11: 8 with him, a with priceless gold and silver dishes.
Hos 2:18 the birds and the animals that scurry a the ground
5: 7 religion will devour them, a with their wealth.
6: 9 Gangs of priests murder travelers a the road to
11: 3 Israel how to walk, leading him a by the hand.
11: 4 I led Israel a with my ropes of kindness and love.
12:11 their altars are lined up like the heaps of stone a
13: 7 like a lion, or like a leopard that lurks a the road.
14: 9 in them. But sinners stumble and fall a the way.
Joel 2: 5 Look at them as they leap a the mountaintops!
2: 9 They swarm over the city and run a its walls.
Jnh 1: 4 But as the ship was sailing a, suddenly the LORD
Na 2: 4 The chariots race recklessly a the streets
Zep 1: 3 a with the rest of humanity," says the LORD.
2: 5 it will be for you Philistines who live a the coast
Zec 3: 7 and out of my presence a with these others
7: 2 sent Sharezer and Regemmelech, a with their men,
12:12 of David will mourn, a with the family of Nathan,
Mt 4:18 One day as Jesus was walking a the shore beside
8: 4 him examine you. Don't talk to anyone a the way.
8: 4 Take a the offering required in the law of Moses
9:10 a with his fellow tax collectors and many other
9:27 two blind men followed a behind him, shouting,
13:21 At first they get a fine, but they wilt as soon as
15:32 them away hungry, or they will faint a the road."
22:16 a with the supporters of Herod, to ask him this
25: 4 but the other five were wise enough to take a extra
Mk 1:16 One day as Jesus was walking a the shores of the
1:44 him examine you. Don't talk to anyone a the way.
1:44 Take a the offering required in the law of Moses
2:14 As he walked a, he saw Levi son of Alphaeus
2:15 a with his fellow tax collectors and many other
4: 1 There was such a large crowd a the shore that he
4:17 At first they get a fine, but they wilt as soon as
6:33 and people from many towns ran ahead a the shore
8: 3 without feeding them, they will faint a the road.
8:27 As they were walking a, he asked them, "Who do
11: 8 branches in the fields and spread them a the way.
14:51 There was a young man following a behind,
15: 7 convicted a with others for murder during an
Lk 1:18 old man now, and my wife is also well a in years."
2:38 She came a just as Simeon was talking with Mary
5:14 Take a the offering required in the law of Moses
8: 2 a with some women he had healed and from whom
9: 3 "Don't even take a a walking stick," he instructed
9:57 As they were walking a, someone said to Jesus,
10: 4 Don't take a any money, or a traveler's bag,
10:31 "By chance a Jewish priest came a; but when he
10:33 "Then a despised Samaritan came a, and when he
19:37 began to shout and sing as they walked a,
19:40 the stones a the road would burst into cheers!"

23:13 and other religious leaders, **a** with the people,
23:27 Great crowds trailed **a** behind, including many
24:14 As they walked **a** they were talking about
24:15 Jesus himself came **a** and joined them and began
24:35 appeared to them as they were walking **a** the road
Jn 8:48 Didn't we say all **a** that you were possessed by a
9: 1 As Jesus was walking **a**, he saw a man who had
18:15 Simon Peter followed **a** behind, as did another of
Ac 1:14 **a** with Mary the mother of Jesus, several other
4: 6 priest was there, **a** with Caiaphas, John, Alexander,
5:21 the high council, **a** with all the elders of Israel.
8:25 And they stopped in many Samaritan villages **a** the
8:29 "Go over and walk **a** beside the carriage."
8:36 As they rode **a**, they came to some water,
8:40 and in every city **a** the way until he came to
14: 5 A mob of Gentiles and Jews, **a** with their leaders,
15: 3 and they stopped **a** the way in Phoenicia
15:23 This is the letter they took **a** with them:
15:25 **a** with our beloved Barnabas and Paul,
15:36 to see how the new believers are getting **a**."
15:37 Barnabas agreed and wanted to take **a** John Mark.
16:15 She was baptized **a** with other members of her
16:17 She followed **a** behind us shouting, "These men
16:31 you will be saved, **a** with your entire household."
17:23 for as I was walking **a** I saw your many altars.
19:25 **a** with others employed in related trades,
19:29 dragging **a** Gaius and Aristarchus,
20: 2 **A** the way, he encouraged the believers in all the
23:21 There are more than forty men hiding **a** the way
27: 2 it was scheduled to make several stops at ports **a**
27: 5 We passed **a** the coast of the provinces of Cilicia
27: 8 We struggled **a** the coast with great difficulty
27:13 they pulled up anchor and sailed **a** close to shore.
27:29 would soon be driven against the rocks **a** the shore,
Ro 10: 3 to keep the law. They won't go **a** with God's way.
13: 3 So do what they say, and you will get **a** well.
15:10 O you Gentiles, / **a** with his people, the Jews."
1Co 7: 7 I wish everyone could get **a** without marrying,
9: 5 Don't we have the right to bring a Christian wife **a**
10: 1 by sending a cloud that moved **a** ahead of them,
12: 2 and swept **a** in worshiping speechless idols.
14:16 who don't understand you praise God **a** with you?
16: 4 And if it seems appropriate for me also to go **a**,
16:11 to seeing him soon, **a** with the other believers.
16:12 I urged him to visit you **a** with the other believers,
16:19 **a** with Aquila and Priscilla and all the others who
2Co 1:21 It is God who gives us, **a** with you, the ability to
2:14 and leads us **a** in Christ's triumphal procession.
4:14 us with Jesus and present us to himself **a** with you.
11:28 the daily burden of how the churches are getting **a**.
Gal 2: 1 this time with Barnabas; and Titus came **a**, too.
5: 7 You were getting **a** so well. Who has interfered
Eph 1: 8 on us, **a** with all wisdom and understanding.
2: 6 For he raised us from the dead **a** with Christ,
2:19 You are citizens **a** with all of God's holy people.
6:21 will tell you all about how I am getting **a**.
Php 2:19 cheer me up by telling me how you are getting **a**.
4:11 for I have learned how to get **a** happily whether I
Col 4: 7 loved brother, will tell you how I am getting **a**.
2Th 1:12 of you, and you will be honored **a** with him.
1Ti 6:11 **a** with faith, love, perseverance, and gentleness.
2Ti 2: 3 Endure suffering **a** with me, as a good soldier of
Heb 5:13 And a person who is living on milk isn't very far **a**
9:19 took the blood of calves and goats, **a** with water,
10:34 You suffered **a** with those who were thrown into
2Pe 2:12 and they will be destroyed **a** with them.
3:12 should look forward to that day and hurry it **a**—
1Jn 2:17 world is fading away, **a** with everything it craves.
Rev 20: 8 a mighty host, as numberless as sand **a** the shore.

ALONGSIDE (3) [ALONG]

Ex 29:17 Set them **a** the head and the other pieces of the
Ru 2:23 So Ruth worked **a** the women in Boaz's fields
1Ki 5: 6 Let my men work **a** yours, and I will pay your men

ALOOF (2)

Ps 109: 1 O God, whom I praise, / don't stand silent and **a**
Ob 1:11 You stood **a**, refusing to lift a finger to help when

ALOTH (1)

1Ki 4:16 Baana son of Hushai, in Asher and in **A**.

ALOUD (15) [LOUD]

Ge 45: 2 Then he broke down and wept **a**. His sobs could be
Nu 14: 1 Then all the people began weeping **a**, and they
Ezr 3:12 and they wept **a** when they saw the new Temple's
Ne 8: 3 and read **a** to everyone who could understand.
9: 3 their God was read **a** to them for about three hours.
Job 23: 2 is still a bitter one, and I try hard not to groan **a**.
Ps 55:17 Morning, noon, and night / I plead **a** in my distress,
66: 8 whole world bless our God / and sing **a** his praises.
119:13 I have recited **a** / all the laws you have given us.
Pr 8: 3 entrance to the city, at the city gates, she cries **a**,
Jer 51:61 get to Babylon, read **a** everything on this scroll.
La 2:18 Cry **a** before the Lord, O walls of Jerusalem!
Zep 3:14 Sing, O daughter of Zion; shout **a**, O Israel!
Ac 8:28 he was reading **a** from the book of the prophet
20:37 They wept **a** as they embraced him in farewell,

ALPHA (3)

Rev 1: 8 "I am the **A** and the Omega—the beginning
21: 6 I am the **A** and the Omega—the Beginning
22:13 I am the **A** and the Omega, the First and the Last,

ALPHAEUS (5)

Mt 10: 3 Matthew (the tax collector), / James (son of **A**),
Mk 2:14 he saw Levi son of **A** sitting at his tax-collection
3:18 Matthew, / Thomas, / James (son of **A**),
Lk 6:15 Matthew, / Thomas, / James (son of **A**),
Ac 1:13 Bartholomew, / Matthew, / James (son of **A**),

ALREADY (143) [READY]

Ge 14:24 is what these young men of mine have **a** eaten.
27:33 I have **a** eaten it, and I blessed him with an
28: 9 in addition to the wives he **a** had.
Ex 1: 5 Joseph was **a** down in Egypt. In all, Jacob had
19:23 Moses protested. "You **a** told them not to.
21:16 of their victims or have **a** sold them as slaves.
32: 8 They have **a** turned from the way I commanded
36: 6 You have **a** given more than enough."
Lev 27:26 because the firstborn of these animals **a** belong to
Nu 10:21 the Tabernacle would **a** be set up at its new
12:12 let her be like a stillborn baby, **a** decayed at birth."
16:46 is blazing among them—the plague has **a** begun."
16:47 The plague indeed had **a** begun, but Aaron burned
34:14 and half the tribe of Manasseh have **a** received
Dt 9:12 They have **a** turned from the way I commanded
Jos 13: 8 and Gad had **a** received their inheritance on the
14: 3 Moses had **a** given an inheritance of land to the
17: 1 and Bashan on the east side of the Jordan had **a**
18: 7 for they have **a** received their inheritance,
23: 4 as well as the land of those we have **a** conquered—
Jdg 8:10 armies of the east—for 120,000 had **a** been killed.
1Sa 2:25 for the LORD was **a** planning to put them to
5:11 For the plague from God had **a** begun, and great
12:12 even though the LORD your God was **a** your
13:14 The LORD has **a** chosen him to be king over his
17:13 had **a** joined Saul's army to fight the Philistines.
21:15 We **a** have enough of them around here!
2Sa 2: 8 had **a** gone to Mahanaim with Saul's son
13:16 greater wrong than what you have **a** done to me."
17: 9 He has probably **a** hidden in some pit or cave.
1Ki 6:10 As **a** stated, there was a complex of rooms on three
20: 5 'I have **a** demanded that you give me your silver,
20: 7 I **a** agreed when he sent the message demanding
20:11 should not boast like a warrior who has **a** won."
1Ch 8:11 Shaharaim's wife Hushim had **a** given birth to
29: 3 materials I have **a** collected for his holy Temple.
29:14 and we give you only what you have **a** given us!
2Ch 1: 4 David had **a** moved the Ark of God from
20: 2 They are **a** at Hazazon-tamar." (This was another
28:13 Our guilt is **a** great, and the LORD's fierce anger is
a turned against
28:18 They had **a** captured Beth-shemesh, Aijalon,
Ezr 4:12 They have **a** laid the foundation for its walls
Ne 5: 4 "We have **a** borrowed to the limit on our fields
5: 5 We have **a** sold some of our daughters, and we are
5: 5 and vineyards are **a** mortgaged to others."
5:18 because the people were **a** having a difficult time.
9:25 with cisterns **a** dug and vineyards and olive groves
Job 40: 5 I have said too much **a**. I have nothing more to
Ecc 1:10 How do you know it didn't **a** exist long ago?
3:15 and whatever will exist in the future has **a** existed
6:10 Everything has **a** been decided. It was known long
Isa 10:23 LORD Almighty, has **a** decided to consume them.
16:13 The LORD has **a** said this about Moab in the past.
43:19 See, I have **a** begun! Do you not see it?
Jer 31:34 to the greatest, will **a** know me," says the LORD.
33: 5 The men of this city are **a** as good as dead, for I
45: 3 with trouble! Haven't I had enough pain **a**?
Eze 17: 8 The vine did this even though it was **a** planted in
35: 5 when I had **a** punished them for all their sins.
Da 8: 1 following the one that had **a** appeared to me.
Mic 6: 8 O people, the LORD has **a** told you what is good,
Na 1:12 O my people, I have **a** punished you once, and I
2: 1 Nineveh, you are **a** surrounded by enemy armies!
Mal 2: 2 Indeed, I have **a** cursed them, because you have
3: 6 That is why you descendants of Jacob are not **a**
Mt 5:28 eye has **a** committed adultery with her in his heart.
6:32 Your heavenly Father **a** knows all your needs,
9:13 not those who think they are **a** good enough."
17:12 But I tell you, he has **a** come, but he wasn't
Mk 2:17 not those who think they are **a** good enough."
4:36 He was **a** in the boat, so they started out,
5: 8 For Jesus had **a** said to the spirit, "Come out of the
9:13 But I tell you, Elijah has **a** come, and he was badly
14:15 He will take you upstairs to a large room that is **a**
15:44 Pilate couldn't believe that Jesus was **a** dead,
16: 4 a very large one—had **a** been rolled aside.
Lk 1:36 say she was barren, but she's **a** in her sixth month.
5:32 with those who think they are **a** good enough."
8:29 For Jesus had **a** commanded the evil spirit to come
12:30 most people, but your Father **a** knows your needs.
12:49 and I wish that my task were **a** completed!
19:25 master,' they said, 'that servant has enough **a**!'
22:12 He will take you upstairs to a large room that is **a**
Jn 1: 1 In the beginning the Word **a** existed. He was with
3:18 But those who do not trust him have **a** been judged
4:23 and is **a** here when true worshipers will worship
4:38 others had **a** done the work, and you will gather the
5:24 but they have **a** passed from death into life.
6: 6 for he **a** knew what he was going to do.
6:47 anyone who believes in me **a** has eternal life.
10:25 Jesus replied, "I have **a** told you, and you don't
11:17 he was told that Lazarus had **a** been in his grave
12:28 saying, "I have **a** brought it glory, and I will do it
13: 2 and the Devil had **a** enticed Judas, son of Simon
15: 3 You have **a** been pruned for greater fruitfulness by
16:11 because the prince of this world has **a** been judged.
16:32 But the time is coming—in fact, it is **a** here—
19:33 they saw that he was dead **a**, so they didn't break
Ac 4: 3 They arrested them and, since it was **a** evening,
21:25 all we ask of them is what we **a** told them in a
28:20 the hope of Israel—the Messiah—has **a** come."
Ro 3: 9 not at all, for we have **a** shown that all people,
4:11 ceremony was a sign that Abraham **a** had faith
4:11 and that God had **a** accepted him and declared him
8:24 For if you **a** have something, you don't need to
10: 8 is the message we preach—is **a** within easy reach.
15:20 rather than where a church has **a** been started by
1Co 3:11 lay any other foundation than the one we **a** have—
4: 8 You think you **a** have everything you need! You
are **a** rich! Without us you have become kings! I
wish you really were on your thrones **a**, for
5: 3 one who has done this, I have **a** passed judgment
2Co 3: 7 even though the brightness was **a** fading away.
13: 2 I have **a** warned those who had been sinning when
Gal 1: 6 You are **a** following a different way
2:18 I make myself guilty if I rebuild the old system I **a**
Eph 3: 2 As you **a** know, God has given me this special
Php 3:12 I don't mean to say that I have **a** achieved these
things or that I have **a** reached perfection!
3:16 must be sure to obey the truth we have learned **a**.
1Th 4: 1 You are doing this **a**, and we encourage you to do
4:10 your love is **a** strong toward all the Christians in all
5:11 and build each other up, just as you are **a** doing.
2Th 2: 2 who say that the day of the Lord has **a** begun.
2: 7 For this lawlessness is **a** at work secretly, and it
1Ti 5:15 For I am afraid that some of them have **a** gone
2Ti 2:18 lie that the resurrection of the dead has **a** occurred;
4: 6 my life has **a** been poured out as an offering to
Tit 1:11 they have **a** turned whole families away from the
Heb 4: 7 David a long time later in the words **a** quoted:
6:20 Jesus has **a** gone in there for us. He has become
7: 6 the one who had **a** received the promises of God.
8: 4 since there **a** are priests who offer the gifts
8:11 from the least to the greatest, / will **a** know me.
2Pe 1: 9 They have **a** forgotten that God has cleansed them
1:12 even though you **a** know them and are standing
1Jn 2: 8 is disappearing and the true light is **a** shining.
2:18 and **a** many such antichrists have appeared.
3: 2 Yes, dear friends, we are **a** God's children, and we
4: 3 is going to come into the world, and he is **a** here.
4: 4 You have **a** won your fight with these false
Rev 17:10 Five kings have **a** fallen, the sixth now reigns,

ALSO (763) See Index of Articles, Etc.

ALTAR (417) [ALTAR'S, ALTARS]

Ge 8:20 Then Noah built an **a** to the LORD and sacrificed
12: 7 And Abram built an **a** there to commemorate the
12: 8 There he built an **a** and worshiped the LORD.
13: 4 This was the place where Abram had built the **a**,
13:18 is at Hebron. There he built an **a** to the LORD.
22: 9 to go, he built an **a** and placed the wood on it.
22: 9 tied Isaac up and laid him on the **a** over the wood.
22:13 and sacrificed it as a burnt offering on the **a** in
26:25 Then Isaac built an **a** there and worshiped the
33:20 And there he built an **a** and called it
35: 1 Build an **a** there to worship me—the God who
35: 3 where I will build an **a** to the God who answered
35: 7 Jacob built an **a** there and named it El-bethel,
Ex 17:15 Moses built an **a** there and called it "The LORD
20:26 And you may not approach my **a** by steps. If you
21:14 then the slayer must be dragged even from my **a**
24: 4 Early the next morning he built an **a** at the foot of
24: 4 He also set up twelve pillars around the **a**, one for
24: 6 The other half he splashed against the **a**.
27: 1 make a square **a** 7-1/2 feet wide, 7-1/2 feet long,
27: 2 Make a horn at each of the four corners of the **a** so
the horns and **a** are all one piece. Overlay the **a**
27: 6 For moving the **a**, make poles from acacia wood,
27: 7 put the poles into the rings at two sides of the **a**.
27: 8 The **a** must be hollow, made from planks.
28:43 or approach the **a** in the Holy Place to perform
29:12 Smear some of its blood on the horns of the **a** with
29:12 and pour out the rest at the base of the **a**.
29:13 two kidneys with their fat, and burn them on the **a**.
29:16 be collected and sprinkled on the sides of the **a**.
29:18 and burn them all on the **a**. This is a burnt offering
29:20 Sprinkle the rest of the blood on the sides of the **a**.
29:21 Then take some of the blood from the **a** and mix it
29:25 and burn it on the **a** as a burnt offering that will be
29:36 Afterward make an offering to cleanse the **a**.
29:36 Purify the **a** by making atonement for it; make it
29:37 Make atonement for the **a** every day for seven
29:37 After that, the **a** will be exceedingly holy,
29:38 "This is what you are to offer on the **a**. Offer two
29:44 I will make the Tabernacle and the **a** most holy,
30: 1 "Then make a small **a** out of acacia wood for
30: 2 carved from the same piece of wood as the **a**.
30: 3 the top, sides, and horns of the **a** with pure gold,
30: 3 and run a gold molding around the entire **a**.
30: 4 Beneath the molding, on opposite sides of the **a**,
30: 6 Place the incense **a** just outside the inner curtain,
30: 7 the lamps, he must burn fragrant incense on the **a**.
30: 9 Do not offer any unholy incense on this **a**, or any
30:10 "Once a year Aaron must purify the **a** by placing
30:10 for this is the LORD's supremely holy **a**."
30:18 Put it between the Tabernacle and the **a**, and fill it
30:20 and before they approach the **a** to burn offerings to
30:27 the lampstand and all its accessories, the incense **a**,
30:28 the **a** of burnt offering with all its utensils,
31: 8 lampstand with all its accessories; the incense **a**;
31: 9 the **a** of burnt offering with all its utensils,
32: 5 he built an **a** in front of the calf and announced,

35:15 the incense **a** and its carrying poles; the anointing
35:16 the **a** of burnt offering; the bronze grating of the **a**
37:25 The incense **a** was made of acacia wood. It was
37:25 made from the same piece of wood as the **a** itself.
37:26 and horns of the **a** with pure gold and ran a gold
38: 1 The **a** for burning animal sacrifices also was
38: 2 with the rest. This **a** was overlaid with bronze.
38: 3 all the bronze utensils to be used with the **a**—
38: 7 were inserted into the rings at the side of the **a**.
38: 7 The **a** was hollow and was made from planks.
38:30 the bronze **a** with its bronze grating and **a** utensils.
39:38 the gold **a**; the anointing oil; the fragrant incense;
39:39 the bronze **a**; the bronze grating; its poles
40: 5 "Place the incense **a** just outside the inner curtain,
40: 6 Place the **a** of burnt offering in front of the
40: 7 the Tabernacle and the **a** and fill it with water.
40:10 Sprinkle the anointing oil on the **a** of burnt offering
40:10 Then the **a** will become most holy.
40:26 He also placed the incense **a** in the Tabernacle,
40:29 and he placed the **a** of burnt offering near the
40:30 large washbasin between the Tabernacle and the **a**.
40:32 Whenever they walked past the **a** to enter the
40:33 the courtyard around the Tabernacle and the **a**.
Lev 1: 5 sides of the **a** that stands in front of the Tabernacle.
1: 7 of Aaron the priest will build a wood fire on the **a**.
1: 9 the priests will burn the entire sacrifice on the **a**.
1:11 Slaughter the animal on the north side of the **a** in
1:11 will sprinkle its blood against the sides of the **a**.
1:12 the head and fat, on top of the wood fire on the **a**.
1:13 the priests will burn the entire sacrifice on the **a**.
1:15 The priest will take the bird to the **a**, twist off its head, and burn the head on the **a**.
1:15 let its blood drain out against the sides of the **a**.
1:16 and throw them to the east side of the **a** among the
1:17 he will burn it on top of the wood fire on the **a**.
2: 2 and burn this token portion on the **a** fire.
2: 8 bring it to the priests who will present it at the **a**.
2: 9 and burn it on the **a** as an offering made by fire,
2:12 but these must never be burned on the **a** as an
3: 2 the animal's blood against the sides of the **a**.
3: 5 The sons of Aaron will burn these on the **a** on top
3: 8 the sheep's blood against the sides of the **a**.
3:11 The priest will burn them on the **a** as food,
3:13 sprinkle the goat's blood against the sides of the **a**.
3:16 The priest will burn them on the **a** as food,
4: 7 **a** that stands in the LORD's presence in the
4: 7 **a** of burnt offerings at the entrance of the
4:10 Then he must burn them on the **a** of burnt
4:18 **a** that stands in the LORD's presence in the
4:18 then be poured out at the base of the **a** of burnt
4:19 remove all the animal's fat and burn it on the **a**,
4:25 put it on the horns of the **a** of burnt offerings,
4:25 pour out the rest of the blood at the base of the **a**.
4:26 He must burn all the goat's fat on the **a**, just as is
4:30 put the blood on the horns of the **a** of burnt
4:30 pour out the rest of the blood at the base of the **a**.
4:31 Then the priest will burn the fat on the **a**, and it
4:34 put it on the horns of the **a** of burnt offerings,
4:34 pour out the rest of the blood at the base of the **a**.
4:35 Then the priest will burn the fat on the **a** on top of
5: 9 blood of the sin offering against the sides of the **a**,
5: 9 and the rest will be drained out at the base of the **a**.
5:12 He will burn this flour on the **a** just like any other
6: 9 The burnt offering must be left on the **a** until the
6: 9 and the **a** fire must be kept burning all night.
6:10 of the burnt offering and put them beside the **a**.
6:12 Meanwhile, the fire on the **a** must be kept burning;
6:13 the fire must be kept burning on the **a** at all times.
6:14 this offering to the LORD in front of the **a**.
6:15 He will burn this token portion on the **a**, and it will
7: 2 and its blood sprinkled against the sides of the **a**.
7: 3 The priest will then offer all its fat on the **a**,
7: 5 The priests will burn these parts on the **a** as an
7:14 then belong to the priest who sprinkles the **a** with
7:31 Then the priest will burn the fat on the **a**,
8:11 He sprinkled the **a** seven times, anointing it and all
8:15 he put it on the four horns of the **a** to purify it.
8:15 poured out the rest of the blood at the base of the **a**.
8:15 he set the **a** apart as holy and made atonement for
8:16 and their fat, and he burned them all on the **a**.
8:19 and sprinkled it against the sides of the **a**.
8:20 the head, some of its pieces, and the fat on the **a**.
8:21 Moses burned the entire ram on the **a** as a whole
8:24 the rest of the blood against the sides of the **a**.
8:28 and burned them on the **a** on top of the burnt
8:30 and some of the blood that was on the **a**,
9: 7 "Approach the **a** and present your sin offering
9: 8 So Aaron went to the **a** and slaughtered the calf as
9: 9 his finger into it and put it on the horns of the **a**.
9: 9 poured out the rest of the blood at the base of the **a**.
9:10 Then he burned on the **a** the fat, the kidneys,
9:12 and he sprinkled it against the sides of the **a**.
9:13 the head, and he burned each part on the **a**.
9:14 and also burned them on the **a** as a whole burnt
9:17 burning a handful of the flour on the **a**,
9:18 and he sprinkled it against the sides of the **a**.
9:20 of these animals and then burned them on the **a**.
9:22 the peace offering, he stepped down from the **a**.
9:24 consumed the burnt offering and the fat on the **a**.
10:12 in it, and eat it beside the **a**, for it is most holy.
14:20 and offer it on the **a** along with the grain offering.
16:12 coals from the **a** that stands before the LORD.
16:18 **a** that stands before the LORD by smearing some
16:19 the blood and sprinkle it seven times over the **a**.
16:20 the Tabernacle, and the **a**, he must bring the living
16:25 also burn all the fat of the sin offering on the **a**.
16:33 the Tabernacle, the **a**, the priests, and the entire
17: 6 and burn the fat on the LORD's **a** at the entrance
21:23 go behind the inner curtain or come near the **a**,
22:22 never be offered to the LORD by fire on the **a**.
Nu 3:26 courtyard that surrounded the Tabernacle and **a**,
4:11 must also spread a dark blue cloth over the gold **a**
4:11 Then they are to attach the carrying poles to the **a**.
4:13 "The ashes must be removed from the **a**,
4:13 and the **a** must then be covered with a purple cloth.
4:14 All the **a** utensils—the firepans, hooks, shovels,
4:26 walls that surround the Tabernacle and **a**,
5:25 lift it up before the LORD, and carry it to the **a**.
5:26 a handful as a token portion and burn it on the **a**.
7: 1 with all its furnishings and the **a** with its utensils.
7:10 gifts for the **a** at the time it was anointed.
7:10 They each placed their gifts before the **a**.
7:11 gift on a different day for the dedication of the **a**."
7:84 So this was the dedication offering for the **a**,
7:88 This was the dedication offering for the **a** after it
16:38 incense burners into a sheet as a covering for the **a**,
16:38 The **a** covering will then serve as a warning to the
16:39 hammered out into a sheet of metal to cover the **a**.
16:46 and place burning coals on it from the **a**.
18: 3 not to touch any of the sacred objects or the **a**.
18: 5 the sacred duties within the sanctuary and at the **a**.
18: 7 handle all the sacred service associated with the **a**
18:11 the **a** also belong to you as your regular share.
18:17 Sprinkle their blood on the **a**, and burn their fat as
18:18 that are presented by lifting them up before the **a**.
23: 2 them sacrificed a young bull and a ram on each **a**.
23: 4 have sacrificed a young bull and a ram on each **a**."
23:14 and offered a young bull and a ram on each **a**.
23:30 and offered a young bull and a ram on each **a**.
28: 2 The offerings you present to me by fire on the **a**
Dt 12:27 and blood of your burnt offerings on the **a** of the
12:27 poured out beside the **a** of the LORD your God,
16:21 pole beside the **a** of the LORD your God.
26: 4 and set it before the **a** of the LORD your God.
27: 5 Then build an **a** there to the LORD your God,
27: 6 On the **a** you must offer burnt offerings to the
33:10 and offer whole burnt offerings on the **a**.
Jos 8:30 Then Joshua built an **a** to the LORD, the God of
8:31 "Make me an **a** from stones that are uncut
8:31 Then on the **a** they presented burnt offerings
8:32 copied the law of Moses onto the stones of the **a**.
9:27 the people of Israel and for the **a** of the LORD—
13:14 from the offerings burned on the **a** to the LORD,
22:10 and the half-tribe of Manasseh built a very large **a**
22:11 When the rest of Israel heard they had built the **a** at
22:16 and build an **a** in rebellion against him?
22:19 If you need the **a** because your land is defiled,
22:19 rebellion by building another **a** for yourselves.
22:19 There is only one true **a** of the LORD our God.
22:22 We have not built the **a** in rebellion against the
22:23 that we have not built an **a** for ourselves to turn
22:24 "We have built this **a** because we fear that in the
22:26 So we decided to build the **a**, not for burnt
22:28 'Look at this copy of the LORD's **a** that our
22:29 or turn away from him by building our own **a** for
22:29 Only the **a** of the LORD our God that stands in
22:34 of Reuben and Gad named the **a** "Witness,"
Jdg 6:24 And Gideon built an **a** to the LORD there
6:24 The **a** remains in Ophrah in the land of the clan of
6:25 Pull down your father's **a** to Baal, and cut down
6:26 Then build an **a** to the LORD your God here on
6:26 Sacrifice the bull as a burnt offering on the **a**,
6:28 someone discovered that the **a** of Baal had been
6:28 In their place a new **a** had been built, and it had the
6:30 "He must die for destroying the **a** of Baal and for
6:31 and destroy the one who knocked down his **a**!"
6:32 because he knocked down Baal's **a**.
13:20 As the flames from the **a** shot up toward the sky,
21: 4 Early the next morning the people built an **a**
1Sa 2:15 before the animal's fat had been burned on the **a**.
2:28 to offer sacrifices on my **a**, to burn incense, and to
7:17 And Samuel built an **a** to the LORD at Ramah.
10: 5 of prophets coming down from the **a** on the hill.
10:13 finished prophesying, he climbed the hill to the **a**.
14:35 And Saul built an **a** to the LORD, the first one he
2Sa 24:18 and build an **a** to the LORD on the threshing floor
24:21 and to build an **a** to the LORD there,
24:22 and ox yokes for wood to build a fire on the **a**.
24:25 David built an **a** there to the LORD and offered
1Ki 1:50 sacred tent and caught hold of the horns of the **a**.
1:51 that Adonijah had seized the horns of the **a**
1:53 and they brought him down from the **a**.
2:28 the LORD and caught hold of the horns of the **a**.
2:31 "Kill him there beside the **a** and bury him.
6:20 pure gold. He also overlaid the **a** made of cedar.
6:22 including the **a** that belonged to the Most Holy
7:48 the gold **a**, / the gold table for the Bread of the
8:22 **a** of the LORD in front of the entire community
8:31 oath of innocence in front of the **a** at this Temple,
8:54 he stood up in front of the **a** of the LORD,
8:64 because the bronze **a** in the LORD's presence
8:65 seven days for the dedication of the **a** and seven
9:25 and peace offerings to the LORD on the **a** he had
12:33 Jeroboam offered sacrifices on the **a** at Bethel.
12:33 for Israel, and he went up to the **a** to burn incense.
13: 1 was approaching the **a** to offer a sacrifice.
13: 2 the LORD's command, he shouted, "O **a**, **a**!
13: 3 This **a** will split apart, and its ashes will be poured
13: 4 with the man of God for speaking against the **a**.
13: 5 At the same time a wide crack appeared in the **a**,
13:32 told him to proclaim against the **a** in Bethel
16:32 he built a temple and an **a** for Baal in Samaria.
18:23 cut it into pieces and lay it on the wood of their **a**,
18:23 the other bull and lay it on the wood on the **a**,
18:26 prepared one of the bulls and placed it on the **a**.
18:26 Then they danced wildly around the **a** they had
18:30 They all crowded around him as he repaired the **a**
18:32 and he used the stones to rebuild the LORD's **a**.
18:32 Then he dug a trench around the **a** large enough to
18:33 He piled wood on the **a**, cut the bull into pieces,
18:35 and the water ran around the **a** and even
18:36 Elijah the prophet walked up to the **a** and prayed,
2Ki 11:11 around to the north side and all around the **a**.
12: 9 and set it on the right-hand side of the **a** at the
16:10 While he was there, he noticed an unusual **a**.
16:10 So he sent a model of the **a** to Uriah the priest,
16:11 Uriah built an **a** just like it by following the king's
16:12 he inspected the **a** and made offerings on it.
16:14 Then King Ahaz removed the old bronze **a** from
16:14 had stood between the entrance and the new **a**,
16:14 and placed it on the north side of the new **a**.
16:15 "Use the new **a** for the morning sacrifices of burnt
16:15 and sacrifices should be sprinkled over the new **a**.
16:15 The old bronze **a** will be only for my personal
18:22 and make everyone in Judah worship only at the **a**
23: 9 allowed to serve at the LORD's **a** in Jerusalem,
23:10 Then the king defiled the **a** of Topheth in the
23:15 The king also tore down the **a** at Bethel, the pagan
23:16 and he burned them on the **a** at Bethel to desecrate
23:16 God as Jeroboam stood beside the **a** at the festival.
23:17 things that you have just done to the **a** at Bethel!"
1Ch 6:49 They presented the offerings on the **a** of burnt offering and the **a** of incense,
16:40 and evening on the **a** set aside for that purpose,
21:18 **a** to the LORD at the threshing floor of Araunah
21:22 Then I will build an **a** to the LORD there, so that
21:23 threshing tools for wood to build a fire on the **a**.
21:26 David built an **a** there to the LORD and sacrificed
21:26 fire from heaven to burn up the offering on the **a**.
21:29 and the **a** that Moses made in the wilderness were
22: 1 and the place of the **a** for Israel's burnt offerings!"
28:18 he designated the amount of refined gold for the **a**
2Ch 1: 5 But the bronze **a** made by Bezalel son of Uri
1: 6 Solomon went up to the bronze **a** in the LORD's
4: 1 Solomon also made a bronze **a** 30 feet long,
4:19 the gold **a**; / the tables for the Bread of the
5:12 and stood at the east side of the **a** playing cymbals,
6:12 **a** of the LORD in front of the entire community
6:22 oath of innocence in front of the **a** at this Temple,
7: 7 because the bronze **a** he had built could not handle
7: 9 for they had celebrated the dedication of the **a** for
8:12 **a** he had built in front of the foyer of the Temple.
15: 8 And he repaired the **a** of the LORD, which stood
23:10 around to the north side and all around the **a**.
26:16 and personally burning incense on the **a**.
26:19 before the incense **a** in the LORD's Temple,
29:18 the **a** of burnt offering with all its utensils,
29:19 They are now in front of the **a** of the LORD,
29:21 to sacrifice the animals on the **a** of the LORD.
29:22 the priests took the blood and sprinkled it on the **a**.
29:22 killed the rams and sprinkled their blood on the **a**.
29:24 and sprinkled their blood on the **a** to make
29:27 ordered that the burnt offering be placed on the **a**.
30:16 blood to the priests, who then sprinkled it on the **a**.
32:12 and Jerusalem to worship at only the one **a** at the
33:16 Then he restored the **a** of the LORD
35:11 who sprinkled the blood on the **a** while the Levites
35:16 All the burnt offerings were sacrificed on the **a** of
Ezr 3: 2 family began to rebuild the **a** of the God of Israel
3: 3 the local residents, they rebuilt the **a** at its old site.
3: 3 to sacrifice burnt offerings on the **a** to the LORD.
7:17 all of which will be offered on the **a** of the Temple
Ne 10:34 to be burned on the **a** of the LORD our God,
13:31 I also made sure that the supply of wood for the **a**
Ps 26: 6 my innocence. / I come to your **a**, O LORD,
43: 4 There I will go to the **a** of God, / to God—
50: 8 or the burnt offerings you constantly bring to my **a**.
51:19 and bulls will again be sacrificed on your **a**.
84: 3 and raises her young—/ at a place near your **a**,
118:27 Bring forward the sacrifice and put it on the **a**.
Isa 6: 6 Then one of the seraphim flew over to the **a**,
19:19 In that day there will be an **a** to the LORD in the
27: 9 be an Asherah pole or incense **a** left standing.
29: 2 her name Ariel means—an **a** covered with blood.
36: 7 and make everyone in Judah worship only at the **a**
66: 3 bad as putting a dog or the blood of a pig on the **a**!
La 2: 7 The Lord has rejected his own **a**; he despises his
Eze 8: 5 the north, beside the entrance to the gate of the **a**,
8:16 the entrance, between the foyer and the bronze **a**,
9: 2 Temple courtyard and stood beside the bronze **a**.
40:38 sacrifices was washed before being taken to the **a**.
40:46 inner gate is for the priests in charge of the **a**—
40:47 The **a** stood there in the courtyard in front of the
41:22 There was an **a** made of wood, 3-1/2 feet square
43:13 "These are the measurements of the **a**: There is a gutter all around the **a** 21 inches wide
43:13 around its edge. And this is the height of the **a**:
43:14 From the gutter the **a** rises 3-1/2 feet to a ledge that surrounds the **a**;
43:14 From the lower ledge the **a** rises 7 feet to the upper
43:15 The top of the **a**, the hearth, rises still 7 feet higher,
43:16 The top of the **a** is square, measuring 21 feet by 21
43:17 There are steps going up the east side of the **a**."
43:18 and the sprinkling of blood when the **a** is built.
43:20 of its blood and smear it on the four horns of the **a**,
43:20 This will cleanse and make atonement for the **a**.
43:22 Then cleanse and make atonement for the **a** again,
43:26 days to cleanse and make atonement for the **a**,
43:27 the priests will sacrifice on the **a** the burnt
45:19 the four corners of the upper ledge on the **a**,
47: 1 then passed to the right of the **a** on its south side.

Joel 1:13 Wail, you who serve before the **a**! Come,
2:17 will stand between the people and the **a**, weeping.
Am 3:14 The horns of the **a** will be cut off and fall to the
9:1 I saw a vision of the Lord standing beside the **a**.
Zec 9:15 drenched with blood like the corners of the **a**.
14:20 will be as sacred as the basins used beside the **a**.
Mal 1:7 my name by offering defiled sacrifices on my **a**.
1:7 "You defile them by saying the **a** of the LORD
2:13 You cover the LORD's **a** with tears, weeping
Mt 5:23 "So if you are standing before the **a** in the Temple,
5:24 leave your sacrifice there beside the **a**. Go and be
23:18 And you say that to take an oath 'by the **a**' can be
23:18 but to swear 'by the gifts on the **a**' is binding!
23:19 gift on the **a**, or the **a** that makes the gift sacred?
23:20 When you swear 'by the **a**,' you are swearing by it
23:35 whom you murdered in the Temple between the **a**
Lk 1:11 standing to the right of the incense **a**.
11:51 who was killed between the **a** and the sanctuary.
1Co 9:13 And those who serve at the **a** get a share of the
Heb 7:13 whose members do not serve at the **a**.
9:4 In that room were a gold incense **a** and a wooden
10:6 you were not pleased with animals burned on the **a**
10:8 or grain offerings or animals burned on the **a**
10:11 the priest stands before the **a** day after day,
13:10 We have an **a** from which the priests in the Temple
Jas 2:21 he did when he offered his son Isaac on the **a**?
Rev 6:9 I saw under the **a** the souls of all who had been
8:3 with a gold incense burner came and stood at the **a**.
8:3 to be offered on the gold **a** before the throne.
8:4 ascended up to God from the **a** where the angel
8:5 angel filled the incense burner with fire from the **a**
9:13 of the gold **a** that stands in the presence of God.
11:1 "Go and measure the Temple of God and the **a**,
16:7 And I heard a voice from the **a** saying, "Yes,

ALTAR'S (2) [ALTAR]

Lev 16:18 from the bull and the goat on each of the **a** horns.
Nu 4:26 the necessary cords, and all the **a** accessories.

ALTARS (77) [ALTAR]

Ex 20:24 "The **a** you make for me must be simple **a** of
20:24 Offer on such **a** your sacrifices to me—your burnt
20:24 Build **a** in the places where I remind you who I
20:25 If you build **a** from stone, use only uncut stones.
34:13 Instead, you must break down their pagan **a**,
Lev 26:30 your pagan shrines and cut down your incense **a**.
Nu 3:31 the table, the lampstand, the **a**, the various utensils
23:1 said to King Balak, "Build me seven **a** here,
23:4 "I have prepared seven **a** and have sacrificed a
23:14 He built seven **a** there and offered a young bull
23:29 "Build me seven **a** and prepare me seven young
Dt 7:5 you must break down their pagan **a** and shatter
12:3 Break down their **a** and smash their sacred pillars.
Jdg 2:2 in this land; instead, you were to destroy their **a**.
1Ki 3:2 people of Israel sacrificed their offerings at local **a**,
3:3 offered sacrifices and burned incense at the local **a**.
3:4 The most important of these **a** was at Gibeon,
19:10 torn down your **a**, and killed every one of your
19:14 torn down your **a**, and killed every one of your
2Ki 11:18 They demolished the **a** and smashed the idols to
11:18 killed Mattan the priest of Baal in front of the **a**.
18:22 Didn't Hezekiah tear down his shrines and **a**
21:3 He constructed **a** for Baal and set up an Asherah
21:4 He even built pagan **a** in the Temple of the
21:5 He built these **a** for all the forces of heaven in both
23:12 Josiah tore down the **a** that the kings of Judah had
23:12 The king destroyed the **a** that Manasseh had built
23:20 the priests of the pagan shrines on their own **a**,
23:20 and he burned human bones on the **a** to desecrate
2Ch 14:3 He removed the pagan **a** and the shrines.
14:5 as well as the incense **a** from every one of Judah's
23:17 They demolished the **a** and smashed the idols,
23:17 killed Mattan the priest of Baal in front of the **a**.
28:24 then set up **a** to pagan gods in every corner of
30:14 to work and removed the pagan **a** from Jerusalem.
30:14 They took away all the incense **a** and threw them
31:1 and removed the pagan shrines and **a**.
32:12 who destroyed all the LORD's shrines and **a**.
33:3 He constructed **a** for the images of Baal and set up
33:4 He even built pagan **a** in the Temple of the
33:5 He put these **a** for the stars of heaven in both
33:15 He tore down all the **a** he had built on the hill
33:15 Temple stood and all the **a** that were in Jerusalem,
34:4 He saw to it that the **a** for the images of Baal and
their incense **a** were torn down.
34:5 the bones of the pagan priests on their own **a**,
34:7 He destroyed the pagan **a** and the Asherah poles,
34:7 He cut down the incense **a** throughout the land of
Ps 78:58 They made God angry by building **a** to other gods;
Isa 17:8 Asherah poles or burn incense on the **a** they built.
27:9 all the pagan **a** will be crushed to dust.
36:7 Didn't Hezekiah tear down his shrines and **a**
60:7 and the rams of Nebaioth will be brought for my **a**.
Jer 11:13 Your **a** of shame—**a** for burning incense to your
17:1 or with an iron chisel on the corners of their **a**.
17:2 Even their children go to worship at their sacred **a**
Eze 6:4 All your **a** will be demolished, and your incense **a**
will be smashed.
6:5 of your idols and scatter your bones around your **a**.
6:6 your **a**, your idols, your incense **a**,
6:13 their dead lie scattered among their idols and **a**,
16:24 and put **a** to idols in every town square.
16:31 street corner and your **a** to idols in every square.
16:39 down your pagan shrines and the **a** to your idols.
23:37 by burning their children as sacrifices on their **a**.
43:8 They put their idol **a** right next to mine with only a

Hos 8:11 "Israel has built many **a** to take away sin, but these
very **a** became places for sinning!
10:1 the more they poured it on the **a** of their foreign
10:2 The LORD will break down their foreign **a**
12:11 their **a** are lined up like the heaps of stone along
Am 3:14 for its sins, I will destroy the pagan **a** at Bethel.
Ac 17:23 for as I was walking along I saw your many **a**.
Ro 11:3 have killed your prophets and torn down your **a**.

ALTERED (1)

Jn 10:35 And you know that the Scriptures cannot be **a**.

ALTERNATE (1) [ALTERNATING]

Ex 28:34 and pomegranates are to **a** all the way around the

ALTERNATING (1) [ALTERNATE]

Ex 39:26 with bells and pomegranates **a** all around the hem.

ALTHOUGH (24) [THOUGH]

Ge 2:25 Now, **a** Adam and his wife were both naked,
31:34 So **a** Laban searched all the tents, he couldn't find
Ex 11:10 **A** Moses and Aaron did these miracles in
Dt 3:18 '**A** the LORD your God has given you this land
1Sa 15:17 told him, "**A** you may think little of yourself,
1Ki 2:28 **A** he had not followed Absalom earlier, Joab had
15:14 **A** the pagan shrines were not completely removed,
2Ch 15:17 **A** the pagan shrines were not completely removed
24:24 **A** the Arameans attacked with only a small army,
Job 10:7 **A** you know I am not guilty, no one can rescue me
Ps 21:11 **A** they plot against you, / their evil schemes will
35:7 **A** I did them no wrong, / they laid a trap for me.
35:7 **A** I did them no wrong, / they dug a pit for me.
92:7 **A** the wicked flourish like weeds, / and evildoers
Eze 11:16 **A** I have scattered you in the countries of the
Mk 4:36 leaving the crowds behind (**a** other boats
Jn 1:10 But **a** the world was made through him, the world
11:5 **A** Jesus loved Martha, Mary, and Lazarus,
Ro 8:23 **a** we have the Holy Spirit within us as a foretaste
1Co 11:12 For **a** the first woman came from man, all men
2Co 13:4 **A** he died on the cross in weakness, he now lives
Heb 7:10 For **a** Levi wasn't born yet, the seed from which he
11:4 And **a** Abel is long dead, he still speaks to us
1Pe 4:6 so that **a** their bodies were punished with death,

ALTOGETHER (3) [TOGETHER]

Ge 46:27 So **a**, there were seventy members of Jacob's
SS 5:16 His mouth is **a** sweet; he is lovely in every way.
Jn 4:14 But the water I give them takes away thirst **a**.

ALUSH (2)

Nu 33:13 They left Dophkah and camped at **A**.
33:14 They left **A** and camped at Rephidim, where there

ALVAH (2)

Ge 36:40 in the places named for them: Timna, **A**, Jetheth,
1Ch 1:51 The clan leaders of Edom were Timna, **A**, Jetheth,

ALVAN (2)

Ge 36:23 The sons of Shobal were **A**, Manahath, Ebal,
1Ch 1:40 The sons of Shobal were **A**, Manahath, Ebal,

ALWAYS (253)

Ge 17:7 And I will **a** be your God and the God of your
26:29 We have **a** treated you well, and we sent you away
27:28 May God **a** give you plenty of dew for healthy
Ex 3:14 God replied, "I AM THE ONE WHO **A** IS.
3:15 it has **a** been my name, and it will be used
13:9 Let it remind you **a** to keep the LORD's
13:15 except that the firstborn sons are **a** redeemed.'
19:9 Then they will **a** have confidence in you."
23:8 A bribe **a** hurts the cause of the person who is in
25:30 You must **a** keep the special Bread of the Presence
28:30 Aaron will **a** carry the objects used to determine
28:38 He must **a** wear it so the LORD will accept the
30:20 They must **a** wash before ministering in these
30:31 of Israel, 'This will **a** be my holy anointing oil.
Lev 7:33 The right thigh must **a** be given to the priest who
11:11 and they will **a** be forbidden to you. You must
19:3 and you must **a** observe my Sabbath days of rest,
19:13 rob anyone. "**A** pay your hired workers promptly.
19:15 "**A** judge your neighbors fairly, neither favoring
25:32 "The Levites **a** have the right to redeem any house
Nu 4:19 Aaron and his sons must **a** go in with them
18:15 But you must **a** redeem your firstborn sons
22:30 "But I am the same donkey you **a** ride on,"
35:31 to execution; murderers must **a** be put to death.
Dt 5:29 Oh, that they would **a** have hearts like this,
8:18 **A** remember that it is the LORD your God who
14:23 The purpose of tithing is to teach you **a** to fear the
15:11 There will **a** be some among you who are poor.
16:1 **a** celebrate the Passover at the proper time in early
17:6 There must **a** be at least two or three witnesses.
17:10 make at the place the LORD chooses will **a** stand.
17:19 He must **a** keep this copy of the law with him
19:9 if you **a** love the LORD your God and walk in his
24:18 **A** remember that you were slaves in Egypt and that
28:13 not the tail, and you will **a** have the upper hand.
1Sa 2:30 branch of the tribe of Levi would **a** be my priests.
19:4 He has **a** helped you in any way he could.
20:2 for he **a** tells me everything he's going to do,
20:5 I've **a** eaten with your father on this occasion,
2Sa 2:26 "Must we **a** solve our differences with swords?
7:6 My home has **a** been a tent, moving from one place

10:2 his father, Nahash, was **a** completely loyal to me."
16:4 "I will **a** do whatever you want me to do."
1Ki 2:4 one of them will **a** sit on the throne of Israel.'
2:45 and may one of David's descendants **a** sit on this
5:1 King Hiram of Tyre had **a** been a loyal friend of
8:25 as you have done, they will **a** reign over Israel.'
8:29 May you **a** hear the prayers I make toward this
8:61 his people, **a** be faithful to the LORD our God.
8:61 May you **a** obey his laws and commands, just as
9:3 there forever. I will **a** watch over it and care for it.
9:4 **a** obeying my commands and keeping my laws
11:38 as my servant David did, then I will **a** be with you.
12:7 they will **a** be your loyal subjects."
14:8 his heart and **a** did whatever I wanted him to do.
17:14 There will **a** be plenty of flour and oil left in your
17:16 there was **a** enough left in the containers,
2Ki 20:3 how I have **a** tried to be faithful to you and do
20:10 "The shadow **a** moves forward,"
1Ch 16:15 He **a** stands by his covenant—/ the commitment he
17:5 My home has **a** been a tent, moving from one place
19:2 his father, Nahash, was **a** completely loyal to me."
23:25 has given us peace, and he will **a** live in Jerusalem.
29:18 and Israel, make your people **a** want to obey you.
2Ch 6:16 as you have done, they will **a** reign over Israel.'
6:20 May you **a** hear the prayers I make toward this
7:16 My eyes and my heart will **a** be here.
10:7 to please them, they will **a** be your loyal subjects."
19:6 "**A** think carefully before pronouncing judgment.
19:9 "You must **a** act in the fear of the LORD,
Ne 4:21 to sunset. And half the men were **a** on guard.
9:8 you promised, for you are **a** true to your word.
10:35 "We promise **a** to bring the first part of every
Est 1:13 and customs, for he **a** asked their advice.
Job 1:10 You have **a** protected him and his home and his
3:25 What I **a** feared has happened to me. What I
14:20 You **a** overpower them, and then they pass from
20:20 He was **a** greedy but never satisfied. Of all the
24:23 to live in security, but God is **a** watching them.
Ps 9:18 the hopes of the poor will not **a** be crushed.
10:8 They are **a** searching / for some helpless victim.
16:8 I know the LORD is **a** with me. / I will not be
25:15 My eyes are **a** looking to the LORD for help,
27:9 You have **a** been my helper. / Don't leave me now;
31:1 to shame. / Rescue me, for you **a** do what is right.
37:26 The godly **a** give generous loans to others,
46:1 and strength, / **a** ready to help in times of trouble.
56:5 They are **a** twisting what I say; / they spend their
61:8 Then I will **a** sing praises to your name / as I fulfill
71:3 protecting rock of safety, / where I am **a** welcome.
71:6 cared for me. / No wonder I am **a** praising you!
72:2 in the right way; / let the poor **a** be treated fairly.
72:15 May the people **a** pray for him / and bless him all
75:9 as for me, I will **a** proclaim what God has done;
84:4 can live in your house, / **a** singing your praises.
85:5 Will you be angry with us **a**? / Will you prolong
102:27 But you are **a** the same; / your years never end.
105:8 He **a** stands by his covenant—/ the commitment he
106:3 who deal justly with others / and **a** do what is right.
109:15 May these sins **a** remain before the LORD,
111:5 who trust him; / he **a** remembers his covenant.
119:99 my teachers, / for I am **a** thinking of your decrees.
119:144 Your decrees are **a** fair; / help me to understand
131:3 put your hope in the LORD—/ now and **a**.
Pr 5:19 a graceful deer. Let her breasts satisfy you **a**. May
you **a** be captivated by her love.
6:21 Keep their words **a** in your heart. Tie them around
7:1 my advice, my son; **a** treasure my commands.
8:30 his constant delight, rejoicing **a** in his presence.
17:17 A friend is **a** loyal, and a brother is born to help in
18:15 Intelligent people are **a** open to new ideas. In fact,
21:26 They are **a** greedy for more, while the godly love
22:18 sayings deep within yourself, **a** ready on your lips.
23:7 They are **a** thinking about how much it costs.
23:17 envy sinners, but **a** continue to fear the LORD.
23:29 Who is **a** fighting? Who is **a** complaining?
24:2 and their words are **a** stirring up trouble.
Ecc 5:12 But the rich are **a** worrying and seldom get a good
7:20 is not a single person in all the earth who is **a** good
7:24 Wisdom is **a** distant and very difficult to find.
9:11 The fastest runner doesn't **a** win the race,
9:11 and the strongest warrior doesn't **a** win the battle.
9:11 And those who are educated don't **a** lead
Isa 16:5 will reign, one who **a** does what is just and right.
26:4 Trust in the LORD **a**, / for the LORD GOD is
28:24 Does a farmer **a** plow and never sow? Is he forever
38:3 how I have **a** tried to be faithful to you and do
48:16 I have **a** told you plainly what would happen
54:15 Your enemies will **a** be defeated because I am on
55:11 with my word. I send it out, and it **a** produces fruit.
57:16 against you forever; I will not **a** show my anger.
66:22 and earth will remain, so will you **a** be my people,
Jer 3:25 and our ancestors have **a** sinned against the
12:1 you **a** give me justice when I bring a case before
13:23 Neither can you start doing good, for you **a** do evil.
15:6 I am tired of **a** giving you another chance.
17:25 There will **a** be a descendant of David sitting on
17:25 and their officials will **a** ride among the people of
22:4 there will **a** be a descendant of David sitting on the
28:8 **a** warning of war, famine, and disease.
33:18 And there will **a** be Levitical priests to offer burnt
35:7 or plant crops or vineyards, but **a** live in tents.
35:19 Jehonadab son of Recab will **a** have descendants
44:17 and princes have **a** done in the towns of Judah
49:9 Those who harvest grapes **a** leave a few for the
Eze 12:25 For I am the LORD! What I threaten **a** happens.
44:2 of Israel, entered here. Thus, it must **a** remain shut.
46:9 came in; they must **a** use the opposite gateway.

47:12 and fall, and there will a be fruit on their branches.
Da 6: 4 He was faithful and honest and a responsible.
6:10 just as he had a done, giving thanks to his God.
9: 4 You a fulfill your promises of unfailing love to
Hos 7: 4 They are all adulterers, a aflame with lust.
7:16 They are like a crooked bow that a misses its
12: 6 and a live in confident dependence on your God.
14: 8 I am like a tree that is a green, giving my fruit to
Am 3: 7 "But a, first of all, I warn you through my servants
4: 1 and who are a asking your husbands for another
Ob 1: 5 Those who harvest grapes a leave a few for the
Mal 2:16 "So guard yourself; a remain loyal to your wife."
Mt 13:10 "Why do you a tell stories when you talk to the
13:34 Jesus a used stories and illustrations like these
18:10 For I tell you that in heaven their angels are a in
26:11 You will a have the poor among you, but I will not
28:20 I am with you a, even to the end of the age."
Mk 10: 1 As a there were the crowds, and as usual he taught
14: 7 You will a have the poor among you, and you can
Lk 5:33 "John the Baptist's disciples a fast and pray,"
5:33 of the Pharisees. Why are yours a feasting?"
9:39 foams at the mouth. It is a hitting and injuring him.
13: 6 was any fruit on it, but he was a disappointed.
13:22 as he went, a pressing on toward Jerusalem.
14: 8 to a wedding feast, don't a head for the best seat.
17: 1 his disciples, "There will a be temptations to sin,
Jn 5: 7 to get there, someone else a gets in ahead of me."
8:25 "I am the one I have a claimed to be.
8:29 For I a do those things that are pleasing to him."
8:44 from the beginning and has a hated the truth.
11:27 "I have a believed you are the Messiah, the Son of
11:42 You a hear me, but I said it out loud for the sake of
12: 8 You will a have the poor among you, but I will not
14: 3 get you, so that you will a be with me where I am.
17: 6 Actually, they were a yours, and you gave them to
Ac 2:25 'I know the Lord is a with me. / I will not be
6:13 "This man is a speaking against the Temple
9:36 She was a doing kind things for others and helping
14:17 There were a his reminders, such as sending you
23: 1 I have a lived before God in all good conscience!"
24:16 I a try to maintain a clear conscience before God
Ro 1:10 One of the things I a pray for is the opportunity,
8: 7 For the sinful nature is a hostile to God. It never
12:12 for you. Be patient in trouble, and a be prayerful.
15:20 My ambition has a been to preach the Good News
1Co 1: 9 do this for you, for he a does just what he says,
11: 2 that you a keep me in your thoughts and you are
13: 7 never gives up, never loses faith, is a hopeful,
15:58 and steady, a enthusiastic about the Lord's work,
2Co 5: 6 So we are a confident, even though we know that
5: 9 So our aim is to please him a, whether we are here
6:10 Our hearts ache, but we a have joy. We are poor,
7:14 I have a told you the truth, and now my boasting to
9: 8 Then you will a have everything you need
Gal 5:15 of showing love among yourselves you are a biting
6: 7 get away with it. You will a reap what you sow!
Eph 1: 5 His unchanging plan has a been to adopt us into
2: 7 so God can a point to us as examples of the
4: 3 A keep yourselves united in the Holy Spirit,
5:20 And you will a give thanks for everything to God
Php 1: 4 I a pray for you, and I make my requests with a
1:11 May you a be filled with the fruit of your
1:20 but that I will a be bold for Christ, as I have been
1:20 and that my life will a honor Christ, whether I live
2:12 you were a so careful to follow my instructions
4: 4 A be full of joy in the Lord. I say it again—rejoice!
4:10 I know you have a been concerned for me, but for
Col 1: 3 We a pray for you, and we give thanks to God the
1:10 Then the way you live will a honor and please the
1:12 a thanking the Father, who has enabled you to
3:15 are all called to live in peace. And a be thankful.
3:20 You children must a obey your parents, for this is
4:12 He a prays earnestly for you, asking God to make
1Th 1: 2 We a thank God for all of you and pray for you
5:15 but a try to do good to each other and to everyone
5:16 A be joyful.
5:18 No matter what happens, a be thankful, for this is
2Th 1: 3 and sisters, we a thank God for you, as is right,
2:13 As for us, we a thank God for you, dear brothers
3: 4 the things we commanded you, and that you a will.
3:16 May the Lord of peace himself a give you his
1Ti 1:19 faith in Christ, and a keep your conscience clear.
5:10 are in trouble? Has she a been ready to do good?
6: 5 These people a cause trouble. Their minds are
6:18 a being ready to share with others whatever God
Tit 3: 1 should be obedient, a ready to do what is good.
Phm 1: 4 I a thank God when I pray for you, Philemon,
Heb 1:12 But you are a the same; / you will never grow
2: 2 The message God delivered through angels has a
3:10 and I said, / 'Their hearts a turn away from me.
7: 7 the person who has the power to bless is a greater
7:20 God took an oath that Christ would a be a priest,
9: 7 and only once a year, and a with blood, which he
12:10 But God's discipline is a right and good for us
Jas 3:17 good deeds. It shows no partiality and is a sincere.
1Pe 2:23 his case in the hands of God, who a judges fairly.
3:15 about your Christian hope, a be ready to explain it.
1Jn 2: 7 for it is an old one you have a had, right from the
2:29 Since we know that God is a right, we also know
Rev 1: 4 one who is, who a was, and who is still to come;
1: 8 "I am the one who is, who a was, and who is still
4: 8 the one who a was, who is, and who is still to
11:17 God Almighty, / the one who is and who a was,
16: 5 this judgment, O Holy One, who is and who a was.

AM (1318) [BE] See Index of Articles, Etc.

AMAD (1)
Jos 19:26 Allammelech, A, and Mishal. The boundary on the

AMAL (1)
1Ch 7:35 Helem were Zophah, Imna, Shelesh, and A.

AMALEK (18) [AMALEKITE, AMALEKITES]
Ge 36:12 Eliphaz had another son named A, born to Timna,
36:16 Korah, Gatam, and A. These clans in the land of
Ex 17: 8 the warriors of A came to fight against them.
17: 9 the Israelites to arms, and fight the army of A.
17:10 He led his men out to fight the army of A.
17:13 and his troops were able to crush the army of A.
17:14 I will blot out every trace of A from under
17:16 so now the LORD will be at war with A
Nu 24:20 Then Balaam looked over at the people of A
24:20 this prophecy: / "A was the greatest of nations,
Jdg 6: 3 planted their crops, marauders from Midian, A,
6:33 Soon afterward the armies of Midian, A,
7:12 The armies of Midian, A, and the people of the
1Sa 15: 2 A for opposing Israel when they came from Egypt.
15: 5 Then Saul went to the city of A and lay in wait in
2Sa 8:12 Edom, Moab, Ammon, Philistia, and A—and from
1Ch 1:36 Omar, Zepho, Gatam, Kenaz, and A, who was born
18:11 Edom, Moab, Ammon, Philistia, and A.

AMALEKITE (8) [AMALEK]
1Sa 15: 3 and completely destroy the entire A nation—
15: 8 He captured Agag, the A king, but completely
30:13 am an Egyptian—the slave of an A," he replied.
30:16 So the Egyptian led them to the A encampment.
2Sa 1: 8 said to me, 'Who are you?' I replied, 'I am an A.'
1:10 "So I killed him," the A told David, "for I knew
1:13 And he replied, "I am a foreigner, an A, who lives
1:15 So the man thrust his sword into the A and killed

AMALEKITES (25) [AMALEK]
Ge 14: 7 and destroyed the A, and also the Amorites living
Ex 17:11 he lowered his hands, the A gained the upper hand.
Nu 13:29 The A live in the Negev, and the Hittites,
14:25 and don't go on toward the land where the A
14:43 When you face the A and Canaanites in battle,
14:45 Then the A and the Canaanites who lived in those
Dt 25:17 "Never forget what the A did to you as you came
25:19 you are to destroy the A and erase their memory
Jdg 3:13 Together with the Ammonites and A,
5:14 from Ephraim—a land that once belonged to the A,
10:12 the Sidonians, the A, and the Maonites? When they
12:15 at Pirathon in Ephraim, in the hill country of the A.
1Sa 14:48 He did great deeds and conquered the A,
15: 6 "Move away from where the A live or else you
15: 7 Then Saul slaughtered the A from Havilah all the
15:18 destroy the sinners, the A, until they are all dead.'
27: 8 raiding the Geshurites, the Girzites, and the A—
28:18 you did not obey his instructions concerning the A.
30: 1 they found that the A had made a raid into the
30:16 the A were spread out across the fields, eating
30:17 None of the A escaped except four hundred young
30:18 David got back everything the A had taken, and he
2Sa 1: 1 David returned from his victory over the A
1Ch 4:43 They destroyed the few A who had survived,
Ps 83: 7 Gebalites, Ammonites, and A, / and people from

AMAM (1)
Jos 15:26 A, Shema, Moladah,

AMANA (1)
SS 4: 8 Come down from the top of Mount A, from Mount

AMARIAH (16)
1Ch 6: 7 Meraioth was the father of A. / A was the father of
6:11 Azariah was the father of A. / A was the father of
6:52 Meraioth, A, Ahitub,
23:19 A (the second), Jahaziel (the third), and Jekameam
24:23 A was second-in-command, Jahaziel was third,
2Ch 19:11 "A the high priest will have final say in all cases
31:15 Miniamin, Jeshua, Shemaiah, A, and Shecaniah.
Ezr 7: 3 son of A, son of Azariah, son of Meraioth,
10:42 Shallum, A, and Joseph.
Ne 10: 3 Pashhur, A, Malkijah,
11: 4 son of Zechariah, son of A, son of Shephatiah,
12: 2 A, Malluch, Hattush,
12:13 of Ezra. / Jehohanan was leader of the family of A.
Zep 1: 1 son of Gedaliah, son of A, son of Hezekiah.

AMASA (15) [AMASA'S]
2Sa 17:25 Absalom had appointed A as commander of his
17:25 (A was Joab's cousin. His father was Jether,
19:13 And David told them to tell A, "Since you are my
19:14 Then A convinced all the leaders of Judah,
20: 4 Then the king instructed A to mobilize the army of
20: 5 So A went out to notify the troops, but it took him
20: 8 A met them, coming from the opposite direction.
20: 8 As he stepped forward to greet A, he secretly
20:10 A didn't notice the dagger in his left hand,
20:10 Joab did not need to strike again, and A soon died.
20:12 But A lay in his blood in the middle of the road,
1Ki 2: 5 Abner son of Ner and A son of Jether.
2:32 of the army of Israel, and A son of Jether,
1Ch 2:17 an Ishmaelite, and they had a son named A.
2Ch 28:12 Jehizkiah son of Shallum, and A son of Hadlai—

AMASA'S (2) [AMASA]
2Sa 20:11 One of Joab's young officers shouted to A troops,
20:13 With A body out of the way, everyone went on

AMASAI (5)
1Ch 6:25 The descendants of Elkanah were A, Ahimoth,
6:35 Zuph, Elkanah, Mahath, A,
12:18 Then the Spirit came upon A, who later became a
15:24 Joshaphat, Nethanel, A, Zechariah, Benaiah,
2Ch 29:12 Mahath son of A and Joel son of Azariah.

AMASHSAI (1)
Ne 11:13 There were also A son of Azarel, son of Ahzai,

AMASIAH (1)
2Ch 17:16 Next was A son of Zicri, who volunteered for the

AMASSED (1)
Eze 28: 4 and understanding you have a a great wealth—

AMAZE (1) [AMAZED, AMAZEMENT, AMAZING]
Pr 30:18 There are three things that a me—no, four things I

AMAZED (43) [AMAZE]
Ex 3: 2 Moses was a because the bush was engulfed in
2Sa 12:21 His advisers were a. "We don't understand you,"
1Ki 10: 5 She was also a at the food on his tables,
2Ch 9: 4 She was also a at the food on his tables,
Ps 52: 6 The righteous will see it and be a. / They will
Isa 29: 9 Are you a and incredulous? Do you not believe it?
52:14 Many were a when they saw him—beaten
59:16 He was a to see that no one intervened to help the
63: 5 I was a and appalled at what I saw. So I executed
Mic 7:16 All the nations of the world will stand a at what the
Hab 1: 5 LORD replied, "Look at the nations and be a!
Mt 7:28 the crowds were a at his teaching,
8:10 When Jesus heard this, he was a. Turning to the
12:23 The crowd was a. "Could it be that Jesus is the
15:31 The crowd was a! Those who hadn't been able to
21:20 The disciples were a when they saw this
22:22 His reply a them, and they went away.
Mk 1:22 They were a at his teaching, for he taught as one
5:20 for him; and everyone was a at what he told them.
6: 6 And he was a at their unbelief. / Then Jesus went
7:37 for they were completely a. Again and again they
10:24 This a them. But Jesus said again, "Dear children,
12:17 be given to God." This reply completely a them.
Lk 2:33 and Mary were a at what was being said about
2:47 And all who heard him were a at his understanding
4:22 and were a by the gracious words that fell from his
4:32 There, too, the people were a at the things he said,
4:36 A, the people exclaimed, "What authority
5:10 James and John, the sons of Zebedee, were also a.
7: 9 When Jesus heard this, he was a. Turning to the
11:14 the man's voice returned to him. The crowd was a,
11:38 His host was a to see that he sat down to eat
20:26 Instead, they were a by his answer, and they were
Ac 2:12 They stood there a and perplexed. "What can this
4:13 The members of the council were a when they saw
8:13 and he was a by the great miracles and signs Philip
9:21 All who heard him were a. "Isn't this the same
10:45 The Jewish believers who came with Peter were a
12:16 finally went out and opened the door, they were a.
13:41 'Look you mockers, / be a and die! / For I am
Rev 17: 6 witnesses for Jesus. I stared at her completely a.
17: 7 "Why are you so a?" the angel asked. "I will tell
17: 8 will be a at the reappearance of this beast who had

AMAZEMENT (6) [AMAZE]
Ge 43:33 and to their a, he seated them in the order of their
Isa 41:23 Or perform a mighty miracle that will fill us with a
Jer 18:16 and shake their heads in a at its utter desolation.
Da 3:24 Nebuchadnezzar jumped up in a and exclaimed to
Mk 1:27 A gripped the audience, and they began to discuss
Lk 8:25 your faith?" And they were filled with awe and a.

AMAZIAH (40) [AMAZIAH'S]
2Ki 12:21 of David. Then his son A became the next king.
13:12 of his power and his war with King A of Judah,
14: 1 A son of Joash began to rule over Judah in the
14: 2 A was twenty-five years old when he became king,
14: 3 A did what was pleasing in the LORD's sight,
14: 4 A did not destroy the pagan shrines,
14: 5 When A was well established as king, he executed
14: 7 It was A who killed ten thousand Edomites in the
14: 8 One day A sent this challenge to Israel's king
14: 9 But King Jehoash of Israel replied to King A of
14:11 But A refused to listen, so King Jehoash of Israel mobilized his army against King A of Judah.
14:13 King Jehoash of Israel captured King A of Judah at
14:15 of his power and his war with King A of Judah,
14:17 King A of Judah lived on for fifteen years after the
15: 1 Uzziah son of A began to rule over Judah in the
15: 3 the LORD's sight, just as his father, A, had done.
1Ch 3:12 A, Uzziah, Jotham,
4:34 included Meshobab, Jamlech, Joshah son of A,
6:45 Hashabiah, A, Hilkiah,
2Ch 24:27 When Joash died, his son A became the next king.
25: 1 A was twenty-five years old when he became king,
25: 2 A did what was pleasing in the LORD's sight,
25: 3 When A was well established as king, he executed

25: 5 Another thing A did was to organize the army,
25: 9 A asked the man of God, "But what should I do
25:10 So A discharged the hired troops and sent them
25:11 Then A summoned his courage and led his army to
25:13 the hired troops that A had sent home raided
25:14 When King A returned from defeating the
25:17 King A of Judah sent this challenge to Israel's king
25:18 But King Jehoash of Israel replied to King A of
25:20 But A would not listen, for God was arranging to
25:21 Israel mobilized his army against King A of Judah.
25:23 King Jehoash of Israel captured King A of Judah at
25:25 King A of Judah lived on for fifteen years after the
25:27 After A turned away from the LORD, there was a
26: 4 the LORD's sight, just as his father, A, had done.
Am 7:10 But when A, the priest of Bethel, heard what Amos
7:12 Then A sent orders to Amos: "Get out of here,

AMAZIAH'S (6) [AMAZIAH]

2Ki 14:18 The rest of the events in A reign are recorded in
14:19 There was a conspiracy against A life in Jerusalem,
14:21 of Judah then crowned A sixteen-year-old son,
14:23 in the fifteenth year of King A reign in Judah.
2Ch 25:26 The rest of the events of A reign, from beginning
26: 1 of Judah then crowned A sixteen-year-old son,

AMAZING (22) [AMAZE]

Ex 3: 3 "A!" Moses said to himself. "Why isn't that bush
Dt 5:15 LORD your God brought you out with a power
6:21 but the LORD brought us out of Egypt with a
7: 8 That is why the LORD rescued you with such a
7:19 and the a power he used when he brought you out
26: 8 So the LORD brought us out of Egypt with a
29: 3 the miraculous signs, and the a wonders.
Jdg 13:19 and his wife watched, the LORD did an a thing.
1Ch 16:24 Tell everyone about the a things he does.
Job 40:19 It is a prime example of God's a handiwork.
Ps 64: 9 acts of God, / realizing all the a things he does.
85: 1 you have poured out a blessings on your land!
96: 3 Tell everyone about the a things he does.
111: 2 How a are the deeds of the LORD! / All who
126: 2 "What a things the LORD has done for them."
126: 3 Yes, the LORD has done a things for us!
Pr 30:20 Equally a is how an adulterous woman can satisfy
Da 10: 8 So I was left there all alone to watch this a vision.
Hab 3: 2 and I am filled with awe by the a things you have
Lk 5:26 and over again, "We have seen a things today."
24:22 this morning, and they came back with an a report.
Ac 6: 8 performed a miracles and signs among the people.

AMBASSADOR (3) [AMBASSADORS]

Jer 49:14 I have heard a message from the LORD that an a
Ob 1: 1 the LORD that an a was sent to the nations to say,
Eph 6:20 chains now for preaching this message as God's a.

AMBASSADORS (20) [AMBASSADOR]

Nu 20:14 he sent a to the king of Edom with this message:
21:21 The Israelites now sent a to King Sihon of the
Dt 2:26 "Then from the wilderness of Kedemoth I sent a
Jos 9: 4 They sent a to Joshua, loading their donkeys with
2Sa 10: 2 So David sent a to express sympathy to Hanun
10: 2 But when David's a arrived in the land of Ammon,
10: 4 So Hanun seized David's a and shaved off half of
1Ki 4:34 And kings from every nation sent their a to listen
5: 1 king of Israel, Hiram sent a to congratulate him.
1Ch 19: 2 So David sent a to express sympathy to Hanun
19: 2 But when David's a arrived in the land of Ammon,
19: 4 So Hanun seized David's a and shaved their
2Ch 32:31 when a arrived from Babylon to ask about the
35:21 But King Neco sent a to Josiah with this message:
Isa 18: 2 and a are sent in fast boats down the Nile.
33: 7 But now your a weep in bitter disappointment,
Jer 27: 3 and Sidon through their a to King Zedekiah in
29: 3 when they went to Babylon as King Zedekiah's a
Eze 17:15 sending a to Egypt to request a great army
2Co 5:20 We are Christ's a, and God is using us to speak to

AMBASSAGE [KJV] See DELEGATION

AMBER (3)

Eze 1: 4 The fire inside the cloud glowed like gleaming a.
1:27 From his waist up, he looked like gleaming a,
8: 2 From the waist up he looked like gleaming a.

AMBITION (10)

Pr 11: 6 the a of treacherous people traps them.
Mt 16:24 you must put aside your selfish a, shoulder your
Mk 8:34 he told them, "you must put aside your selfish a,
Lk 9:23 you must put aside your selfish a, shoulder your
Ro 15:20 My a has always been to preach the Good News
Gal 5:20 jealousy, outbursts of anger, selfish a, divisions,
Php 1:17 They preach with selfish a, not sincerely,
1Th 4:11 This should be your a: to live a quiet life,
Jas 3:14 bitterly jealous and there is selfish a in your hearts,
3:16 For wherever there is jealousy and selfish a,

AMBUSH (22) [AMBUSHES]

Jos 8: 2 the cattle for yourselves. Set an a behind the city."
8: 4 "Hide in a close behind the city and be ready for
8: 7 Then you will jump up from your a and take
8: 9 So they left that night and lay in a between Bethel
8:12 sent five thousand men to lie in a between Bethel
8:13 army north of the city and the a west of the city.
8:14 But he didn't realize there was an a behind the
8:19 the men in a jumped up and poured into the city.
8:21 and the other Israelites saw that the a had
Jdg 9:25 The people of Shechem set an a for Abimelech on
9:43 his men into three groups and set an a in the fields.
20:29 So the Israelites set an a all around Gibeah.
20:33 Then the Israelites hiding in a west of Gibeah
20:36 to give those hiding in a more room to maneuver.
2Ch 13:13 army around behind the men of Judah to a them.
Ps 59: 3 They have set an a for me. / Fierce enemies are out
64: 4 They shoot from a at the innocent,
Pr 1:11 Let's hide and kill someone! Let's a the innocent!
1:18 They set an a for themselves; they booby-trap their
12: 6 The words of the wicked are like a murderous a,
Jer 51:12 Prepare an a, for the LORD will fulfill all his
Hos 6: 9 are bands of robbers, lying in a for their victims.

AMBUSHES (1) [AMBUSH]

Dt 19:11 and deliberately a and murders that neighbor

AMEN (52)

Dt 27:15 the LORD.' / And all the people will reply, 'A.'
27:16 or mother.' / And all the people will reply, 'A.'
27:17 And all the people will reply, 'A.'
27:18 on the road.' / And all the people will reply, 'A.'
27:19 and widows.' / And all the people will reply, 'A.'
27:20 his father.' / And all the people will reply, 'A.'
27:21 an animal.' / And all the people will reply, 'A.'
27:22 or his mother.' / And all the people will reply, 'A.'
27:23 And all the people will reply, 'A.'
27:24 in secret.' / And all the people will reply, 'A.'
27:25 And all the people will reply, 'A.'
27:26 obeying them.' / And all the people will reply, 'A.'
1Ki 1:36 "A!" Benaiah son of Jehoiada replied.
1Ch 16:36 And all the people shouted "A!" and praised the
Ne 5:13 "A," and they praised the LORD.
8: 6 the great God, and all the people chanted, "A! A!"
Ps 41:13 lives forever from eternal ages past. / A and a!
72:19 whole earth be filled with his glory. / A and a!
89:52 Blessed be the LORD forever! / A and a!
106:48 Let all the people say, "A!" / Praise the LORD!
Jer 28: 6 He said, "A! May your prophecies come true!
Mk 16: S message of salvation that gives eternal life. A.
Ro 1:25 Creator himself, who is to be praised forever. A.
9: 5 over everything and is worthy of eternal praise! A.
11:36 for his glory. To him be glory evermore. A.
15:33 who gives us his peace, be with you all. A.
16:27 be the glory forever through Jesus Christ. A.
2Co 1:20 That is why we say "A" when we give glory to
Gal 1: 5 belongs to God through all the ages of eternity. A.
6:18 grace of our Lord Jesus Christ be with you all. A.
Eph 3:21 Jesus forever and ever through endless ages. A.
Php 4:20 glory be to God our Father forever and ever. A.
1Ti 1:17 the unseen one who never dies; he alone is God. A.
6:16 ever will. To him be honor and power forever. A.
2Ti 4:18 To God be the glory forever and ever. A.
Heb 13:20[-21] To him be glory forever and ever. A.
1Pe 4:11 and power belong to him forever and ever. A.
5:11 All power is his forever and ever. A.
2Pe 3:18 all glory and honor, both now and forevermore. A.
Jude 1:25 to him, in the beginning, now, and forevermore. A.
Rev 1: 6 everlasting glory! He rules forever and ever! A!
1: 7 of the earth will weep because of him. Yes! A!
3:14 This is the message from the one who is the A—
5:14 And the four living beings said, "A!"
7:12 They said, / "A! Blessing and glory and wisdom
7:12 belong to our God forever and forever. A!"
19: 4 on the throne. They cried out, "A! Hallelujah!"
22:20 "Yes, I am coming soon!" A! Come, Lord Jesus!

AMEND (1) [AMENDS]

Gal 3:15 no one can set aside or a an irrevocable agreement,

AMENDS (2) [AMEND]

2Sa 21: 3 asked them, "What can I do for you to make a?
Pr 18:19 It's harder to make a with an offended friend than

AMERCE [KJV] See FINE

AMETHYST (3)

Ex 28:19 third row will contain a jacinth, an agate, and an a.
39:12 In the third row were a jacinth, an agate, and an a.
Rev 21:20 the eleventh jacinth, the twelfth a.

AMI (2)

Ezr 2:57 Shephatiah, Hattil, Pokereth-hazzebaim, and A.
Ne 7:59 Shephatiah, Hattil, Pokereth-hazzebaim, and A.

AMIABLE [KJV] See LOVELY

AMINADAB [KJV] See AMMINADAB

AMISS (1)

Ps 17: 3 You have scrutinized me and found nothing a,

AMISS [KJV] See also WRONG

AMITTAI (2)

2Ki 14:25 of Israel, had promised through Jonah son of A,
Jnh 1: 1 The LORD gave this message to Jonah son of A:

AMMAH (1)

2Sa 2:24 down as they arrived at the hill of A near Giah,

AMMI (1)

Hos 2: 1 In that day you will call your brothers A—

AMMIEL (5) [ELIAM]

Nu 13:12 Dan | A son of Gemalli
2Sa 9: 4 Ziba told him, "at the home of Makir son of A."
17:27 an Ammonite, and by Makir son of A of Lo-debar,
1Ch 3: 5 Bathsheba, the daughter of A, was the mother of
26: 5 A (the sixth), Issachar (the seventh), and Peullethai

AMMIHUD (10)

Nu 1:10 Ephraim son of Joseph | Elishama son of A
2:18[-19] Ephraim | Elishama son of A | 40,500
7:48 On the seventh day Elishama son of A, leader of
7:53 was the offering brought by Elishama son of A.
10:22 under the leadership of Elishama son of A.
34:20 Simeon | Shemuel son of A
34:28 Naphtali | Pedahel son of A
2Sa 13:37 Talmai son of A, the king of Geshur.
1Ch 7:26 Ladan, A, Elishama,
9: 4 family that returned was that of Uthai son of A,

AMMINADAB (17)

Ex 6:23 the daughter of A and sister of Nahshon,
Nu 1: 7 Judah | Nahshon son of A
2: 3[-4] Judah | Nahshon son of A | 74,600
7:12 On the first day Nahshon son of A, leader of the
7:17 was the offering brought by Nahshon son of A.
10:14 under the leadership of Nahshon son of A.
Ru 4:19 was the father of Ram. / Ram was the father of A.
4:20 A was the father of Nahshon. / Nahshon was the
1Ch 2:10 Ram was the father of A. / A was the father of
6:22 The descendants of Kohath were A, Korah, Assir,
15:10 112 descendants of Uzziel, with A as their leader.
15:11 Uriel, Asaiah, Joel, Shemaiah, Eliel, and A.
Mt 1: 4 Ram was the father of A. / A was the father of
Lk 3:33 Nahshon was the son of A. / A was the son of

AMMINADIB [KJV] See PRINCELY

AMMISHADDAI (5)

Nu 1:12 Dan | Ahiezer son of A
2:25[-26] Dan | Ahiezer son of A | 62,700
7:66 On the tenth day Ahiezer son of A, leader of the
7:71 This was the offering brought by Ahiezer son of A.
10:25 under the leadership of Ahiezer son of A.

AMMIZABAD (1)

1Ch 27: 6 as the Thirty. His son A was his chief officer.

AMMON (45) [AMMONITE, AMMONITES]

Dt 2:19 and enter the land of A. But do not bother the
2:19 I have given the land of A to them as their
Jos 13:10 and extended as far as the borders of A.
13:25 all the towns of Gilead, and half of the land of A,
Jdg 10: 6 the gods of Aram, Sidon, Moab, A, and Philistia.
10:17 At that time the armies of A had gathered for war
11:12 Then Jephthah sent messengers to the king of A,
11:13 The king of A answered Jephthah's messengers,
11:15 Israel did not steal any land from Moab or A.
11:27 decide today which of us is right—Israel or A."
11:28 But the king of A paid no attention to Jephthah's
12: 1 didn't you call for us to help you fight against A?
12: 2 "You failed to help us in our struggle against A.
1Sa 11: 1 King Nahash of A led his army against the Israelite
12:12 the king of A, you came to me and said that you
14:47 against Moab, A, Edom, the kings of Zobah,
2Sa 8:12 Edom, Moab, A, Philistia, and Amalek—and from
10: 2 David's ambassadors arrived in the land of A,
10: 6 Now the people of A realized how seriously they
12:26 ending their siege of Rabbah, the capital of A.
23:37 Zelek from A; / Naharai from Beeroth (Joab's
1Ki 11: 1 A, Edom, Sidon, and from among the Hittites.
1Ch 11:39 Zelek from A; / Naharai from Beeroth (Joab's
18:11 Edom, Moab, A, Philistia, and Amalek.
19: 2 David's ambassadors arrived in the land of A,
19: 6 Now the people of A realized how seriously they
2Ch 12:13 mother was Naamah, a woman from A.
20:10 "And now see what the armies of A, Moab,
20:22 the LORD caused the armies of A, Moab,
20:23 and A turned against their allies from Mount Seir
Ne 13:23 had married women from Ashdod, A, and Moab.
Isa 11:14 will occupy all the lands of Edom, Moab, and A.
Jer 25:21 Then I went to the nations of Edom, Moab, and A,
27: 3 messages to the kings of Edom, Moab, A, Tyre,
40:11 When the Judeans in Moab, A, Edom,
40:14 said to him, "Did you know that Baalis, king of A,
41:10 with him, he started back toward the land of A.
41:15 his men escaped from Johanan into the land of A.
Eze 21:20 one road going to A and its capital, Rabbah,
25: 2 look toward the land of A and prophesy against its
25:10 from the eastern deserts, just as I handed over A.
Da 11:41 Edom, and the best part of A will escape.
Am 1:13 "The people of A have sinned again and again,
Zep 2: 8 have heard the taunts of the people of Moab and A,
2: 9 and A will be destroyed as completely as Sodom

AMMONITE (17) [AMMON]

Nu 21:24 They went only as far as the A border
Dt 3:11 It can still be seen in the A city of Rabbah.)
3:16 all the way to the Jabbok River on the A frontier.
Jdg 11:14 Jephthah sent this message back to the A king:
2Sa 10: 8 The A troops drew up their battle lines at the

12:31 That is how he dealt with the people of all the **A**
17:27 an **A**, and by Makir son of Ammiel of Lo-debar,
1Ki 14:21 Rehoboam's mother was Naamah, an **A** woman.
14:31 His mother was Naamah, an **A** woman. Then his
2Ki 24: 2 Moabite, and **A** raiders against Judah to destroy it,
1Ch 19: 7 where they were joined by the **A** troops that Hanun
19: 9 The **A** troops drew up their battle lines at the gate
20: 3 That is how he dealt with the people of all the **A**
2Ch 24:26 the son of an **A** woman named Shimeath,
Ne 2:10 and Tobiah the **A** official heard of my arrival,
4: 3 Tobiah the **A**, who was standing beside him,
13: 1 the people found a statement which said that no **A**

AMMONITES (56) [AMMON]

Ge 19:38 the ancestor of the nation now known as the **A**.
Nu 21:24 because the boundary of the **A** was fortified.
Dt 2:19 But do not bother the **A**, the descendants of Lot,
2:20 though the **A** referred to them as Zamzummites.
2:21 destroyed them so the **A** could occupy their land.
2:37 we stayed away from the **A** along the Jabbok River
23: 3 "No **A** or Moabites, or any of their descendants
23: 6 try to help the **A** or the Moabites in any way.
Jos 12: 2 which serves as a boundary for the **A**.
Jdg 3:13 Together with the **A** and Amalekites,
10: 7 he handed them over to the Philistines and the **A**,
10: 9 The **A** also crossed to the west side of the Jordan
10:11 the Egyptians, the Amorites, the **A**, the Philistines,
10:18 "Whoever attacks the **A** first will become ruler
11: 4 this time, the **A** began their war against Israel.
11: 5 When the **A** attacked, the leaders of Gilead sent for
11: 6 and be our commander! Help us fight the **A**!"
11: 8 "If you will lead us in battle against the **A**, we will
11: 9 and if the LORD gives me victory over the **A**,
11:29 Mizpah in Gilead, and led an army against the **A**.
11:30 He said, "If you give me victory over the **A**,
11:32 So Jephthah led his army against the **A**,
11:33 He thoroughly defeated the **A** from Aroer to an
11:33 away as Abel-keramim. Thus Israel subdued the **A**.
11:36 given you a great victory over your enemies, the **A**.
12: 3 and the LORD gave me victory over the **A**.
1Sa 11:11 He launched a surprise attack against the **A**
2Sa 10: 1 Some time after this, King Nahash of the **A** died,
10:10 of his brother Abishai, who was to attack the **A**.
10:11 "And if the **A** are too strong for you, I will come
10:14 And when the **A** saw the Arameans running,
10:19 After that, the Arameans were afraid to help the **A**.
11: 1 sent Joab and the Israelite army to destroy the **A**.
1Ki 11: 5 and Molech, the detestable god of the **A**.
11: 7 another for Molech, the detestable god of the **A**.
11:33 the god of Moab; and Molech, the god of the **A**.
2Ki 23:13 and for Molech, the detestable god of the **A**.
1Ch 19: 1 Some time after this, King Nahash of the **A** died,
19: 6 and the **A** sent thirty-eight tons of silver to hire
19:11 of his brother Abishai, who was to attack the **A**.
19:12 "And if the **A** are too strong for you, I will help
19:15 And when the **A** saw the Arameans running,
19:19 the Arameans were no longer willing to help the **A**.
20: 1 attacks against the towns and villages of the **A**.
2Ch 20: 1 After this, the armies of the Moabites, **A**, and some
27: 5 Jotham waged war against the **A** and conquered
Ezr 9: 1 Hittites, Perizzites, Jebusites, **A**, Moabites,
Ne 4: 7 But when Sanballat and Tobiah and the Arabs, **A**,
Ps 83: 7 Gebalites, **A**, and Amalekites, / and people from
Jer 9:26 the Egyptians, Edomites, **A**, Moabites, the people
49: 1 This message was given concerning the **A**. This is
49: 6 But afterward I will restore the fortunes of the **A**,"
Eze 21:28 prophesy concerning the **A** and their mockery.
25: 3 Give the **A** this message from the Sovereign
25: 5 and all the land of the **A** into an enclosure for
25:10 the **A** will no longer be counted among the nations.

AMNON (25) [AMNON'S]

2Sa 3: 2 The oldest was **A**, whose mother was Ahinoam of
13: 1 And **A**, her half brother, fell desperately in love
13: 2 **A** became so obsessed with Tamar that he became
13: 3 Now **A** had a very crafty friend—his cousin
13: 4 One day Jonadab said to **A**, "What's the trouble?
13: 4 So **A** told him, "I am in love with Tamar,
13: 6 So **A** pretended to be sick. And when the king
came to see him, **A** asked him,
13: 9 "Everyone get out of here," **A** told his servants.
13:14 But **A** wouldn't listen to her, and since he was
13:16 already done to me." But **A** wouldn't listen to her.
13:20 and asked, "Is it true that **A** has been with you?
13:22 And though Absalom never spoke to **A** about it,
13:22 he hated **A** deeply because of what he had done to
13:26 about sending my brother **A** instead?" "Why **A**?"
13:27 agreed to let all his sons attend, including **A**.
13:28 Absalom told his men, "Wait until **A** gets drunk;
13:29 So at Absalom's signal they murdered **A**.
13:32 not all your sons have been killed! It was only **A**!
13:32 Absalom has been plotting this ever since **A** raped
13:33 No, your sons aren't all dead! It was only **A**."
13:37 And David mourned many days for his son **A**.
1Ch 3: 1 The oldest was **A**, whose mother was Ahinoam of
4:20 The sons of Shimon were **A**, Rinnah, Ben-hanan,

AMNON'S (4) [AMNON]

2Sa 13: 7 and sent Tamar to **A** house to prepare some food
13: 8 When Tamar arrived at **A** house, she went to the
13:15 Then suddenly **A** love turned to hate, and he hated
13:39 And David, now reconciled to **A** death, longed to

AMOK (2)

Ne 12: 7 Sallu, **A**, Hilkiah, and Jedaiah. These were the
12:20 of Sallu. / Eber was leader of the family of **A**.

AMON (13) [AMON'S]

1Ki 22:26 "Arrest Micaiah and take him back to **A**,
2Ki 21:18 of Uzza. Then his son **A** became the next king.
21:19 **A** was twenty-two years old when he became king,
21:24 killed all those who had conspired against King **A**,
1Ch 3:14 **A**, and Josiah.
2Ch 18:25 "Arrest Micaiah and take him back to **A**,
33:20 at his palace. Then his son **A** became the next king.
33:21 **A** was twenty-two years old when he became king,
33:23 before the LORD. Instead, **A** sinned even more.
33:25 killed all those who had conspired against King **A**,
Jer 25: 3 from the thirteenth year of Josiah son of **A**, king of
46:25 "I will punish **A**, the god of Thebes, and all the
Zep 1: 1 when Josiah son of **A** was king of Judah.

AMON'S (3) [AMON]

2Ki 21:23 Then **A** own servants plotted against him
21:25 The rest of the events in **A** reign and all his deeds
2Ch 33:24 At last **A** own officials plotted against him

AMONG (722)

Ge 3: 8 in the garden, so they hid themselves **a** the trees.
7: 1 for **a** all the people of the earth, I consider you
13:12 to a place near Sodom, **a** the cities of the plain.
17: 6 will represent many nations. Kings will be **a** them!
17:10 must keep: Each male **a** you must be circumcised;
17:16 many nations. Kings will be **a** her descendants!"
17:20 Twelve princes will be **a** his descendants.
19: 9 We let you settle **a** us, and now you are trying to
23: 6 "Certainly, for you are an honored prince **a** us.
23:10 Ephron was sitting there **a** the others, and he
24: 5 then take Isaac there to live **a** your relatives?"
24:40 you must get a wife for my son from **a** my
30:32 Let me go out **a** your flocks today and remove all
34:10 And you may live **a** us; the land is open to you!
34:10 with us. You are free to acquire property **a** us."
34:15 If every man **a** you will be circumcised like we are,
34:21 "Let's invite them to live here **a** us and ply their
34:23 let's agree to this so they will settle here **a** us."
34:30 "You have made me stink **a** all the people of this
land—**a** all the Canaanites and Perizzites.
35:11 many nations. Kings will be **a** your descendants!
36:10 **A** Esau's sons were Eliphaz, the son of Esau's wife
42:21 Speaking **a** themselves, they said, "This has all
42:24 He then chose Simeon from **a** them and had him
49:14 a strong beast of burden, / resting **a** the sheepfolds.
49:26 the head of Joseph, / who is a prince **a** his brothers.
Ex 2: 3 and laid it **a** the reeds along the edge of the Nile
2: 5 When the princess saw the little basket **a** the reeds,
10: 1 my power by performing miraculous signs **a** them.
10: 2 **a** the Egyptians to prove that I am the LORD."
10:26 for the LORD our God from **a** these animals.
11: 7 But **a** the Israelites it will be so peaceful that not
12:19 living with you, as if they had been born **a** you.
12:48 "If there are foreigners living **a** you who want to
12:48 They will be treated just as if they had been born **a**
12:49 or a foreigner who has settled **a** you."
15:11 "Who else **a** the gods is like you, O LORD?
19: 5 you will be my own special treasure from **a** all the
20:10 your livestock, and any foreigners living **a** you.
23: 9 "Do not oppress the foreigners living **a** you.
23:11 Then let the poor **a** you harvest any volunteer crop
23:26 will be no miscarriages or infertility **a** your people,
23:33 Do not even let them live **a** you! If you do,
25: 8 me a sacred residence where I can live **a** them.
29:45 I will live **a** the people of Israel and be their God,
29:46 them out of Egypt so that I could live **a** them.
30:12 Then there will be no plagues **a** the people as you
33: 5 If I were there **a** you for even a moment, I would
Lev 1:16 and throw them to the east side of the altar **a** the
7:10 are to be shared **a** all the priests and their sons.
10: 3 **a** those who are near me. / I will be glorified
15:31 defiling my Tabernacle that is right there **a** them.
16:29 by birth, as well as to the foreigners living **a** you.
17: 8 both to Israelites and to the foreigners living **a** you.
17:10 whether an Israelite or a foreigner living **a** you,
17:12 and the foreigners who live **a** you must never eat
17:13 both to Israelites and to the foreigners living **a** you.
17:15 both to Israelites and the foreigners living **a** you.
18:26 by birth and to the foreigners living **a** you.
19:10 for the poor and the foreigners who live **a** you,
19:16 "Do not spread slanderous gossip **a** your people.
20: 2 by birth as well as to the foreigners living **a** you.
20: 2 If any **a** them devote their children as burnt
20: 6 "If any **a** the people are unfaithful by consulting
20:14 to death to wipe out such wickedness from **a** you.
20:27 "Men and women **a** you who act as mediums
21: 4 As a husband **a** his relatives, he must not defile
21:15 that he may not dishonor his descendants **a** the
22:18 by birth as well as to the foreigners living **a** you.
23:22 it for the poor and the foreigners living **a** you.
23:30 And I will destroy anyone **a** you who does any
24:16 or foreigner **a** you who blasphemes the LORD's
24:22 to Israelites by birth and foreigners who live **a** you.
25:44 female slaves from **a** the foreigners who live **a** you.
26:11 I will live **a** you, and I will not despise you.
26:12 I will walk **a** you; I will be your God, and you will
26:33 I will scatter you **a** the nations and attack you with
26:38 You will die **a** the foreign nations and be devoured
Nu 1:16 own families, were chosen from **a** all the people.
3:12 "I have chosen the Levites from **a** the Israelites as
3:22 one month old or older **a** these Gershonite clans.
3:28 one month old or older **a** these Kohathite clans.
3:34 one month old or older **a** these Merarite clans.
3:39 So **a** the Levite clans counted by Moses and Aaron
4:18 "Don't let the Kohathite clans be destroyed from **a**
5: 3 they will not defile the camp, where I live **a** you."
5:27 and her name will become a curse word **a** her
7: 5 Distribute them **a** the Levites according to the
8:17 For all the firstborn males **a** the people of Israel are
9:14 And if foreigners living **a** you want to celebrate the
9:14 both to you and to the foreigners living **a** you.' "
11: 1 Fire from the LORD raged **a** them and destroyed
11: 3 because fire from the LORD had burned **a** them
11:20 who is here **a** you, and you have complained to
11:26 They were listed **a** the leaders but had not gone out
11:33 and he caused a severe plague to break out **a** them.
13:32 discouraging reports about the land **a** the Israelites:
14: 4 Then they plotted **a** themselves, "Let's choose a
14:11 even after all the miraculous signs I have done **a**
14:39 the Israelites, there was much sorrow **a** the people.
15:14 And if any foreigners living **a** you want to present
15:16 both to you and to the foreigners living **a** you."
15:26 including the foreigners living **a** you, for the entire
15:29 to native Israelites and the foreigners living **a** you.
16: 3 anyone else **a** all these people of the LORD?"
16: 9 **a** all the people of Israel to be near him as you
16:46 and carry it quickly **a** the people to make
16:46 The LORD's anger is blazing **a** them—the plague
16:47 did as Moses told him and ran out **a** the people.
18: 6 I myself have chosen your fellow Levites from **a**
18:20 of land or share of property **a** the people of Israel.
18:23 offenses against it. This is a permanent law **a** you.
18:23 will receive no inheritance of land **a** the Israelites,
18:24 receive no inheritance of land **a** the Israelites."
19:10 of Israel and any foreigners who live **a** them.
20:13 and where he demonstrated his holiness **a** them.
21: 6 So the LORD sent poisonous snakes **a** them,
25:11 by displaying passionate zeal **a** them on my behalf.
26:53 "Divide the land **a** the tribes in proportion to their
26:56 Each inheritance must be assigned by lot **a** the
26:59 of Levi, born **a** the Levites in the land of Egypt.
26:62 of land when it was divided **a** the Israelites.
26:64 and Aaron counted in this census had been **a** those
27: 3 "But he was not **a** Korah's followers, who rebelled
33:54 You must distribute the land **a** the clans by sacred
33:54 the land will be divided **a** your ancestral tribes.
34:13 "This is the territory you are to divide **a**
34:13 commands that the land be divided up **a** the nine
34:17 "These are the men who are to divide the land **a**
34:29 dividing of the land of Canaan **a** the Israelites."
35:34 the LORD, who lives **a** the people of Israel.' "
36: 2 divide the land by sacred lot **a** the people of Israel.
Dt 1:16 but also to the foreigners living **a** you.
4:27 For the LORD will scatter you **a** the nations,
5:14 other livestock, and any foreigners living **a** you.
6:15 your God, who lives **a** you, is a jealous God.
7:21 for the LORD your God is **a** you, and he is a great
10: 9 or inheritance reserved for them **a** the other
10:18 He shows love to the foreigners living **a** you
12: 5 from **a** all the tribes for his name to be honored.
13: 1 "Suppose there are prophets **a** you, or those who
13: 5 you must execute them to remove the evil from **a**
13:11 and such wickedness will never again be done **a**
13:13 that some worthless rabble **a** you have led their
13:14 prove that such a detestable act has occurred **a** you,
14:21 You may give it to a foreigner living **a** you, or you
14:29 it to the Levites, who have no inheritance **a** you,
14:29 as well as to the foreigners living **a** you,
15: 3 not to the foreigners living **a** you.
15: 4 There should be no poor **a** you, for the LORD
15:11 There will always be some **a** you who are poor.
16:11 orphans, and widows who live **a** you.
17: 2 "Suppose a man or woman **a** you, in one of your
17: 7 In this way, you will purge all evil from **a** you.
18: 2 They will have no inheritance of their own **a** the
18:15 a prophet like me from **a** your fellow Israelites,
18:18 I will raise up a prophet like you from **a** their
19:19 In this way, you will cleanse such evil from **a** you.
21:11 And suppose you see **a** the captives a beautiful
21:21 In this way, you will cleanse this evil from **a** you,
22:21 Such evil must be cleansed from **a** you.
23: 7 and you lived as foreigners **a** the Egyptians.
23:14 He must not see any shameful thing **a** you, or he
23:16 Let them live **a** you in whatever town they choose,
24: 7 must die. You must cleanse the evil from **a** you.
24:17 "True justice must be given to foreigners living **a**
26:11 and the foreigners living **a** you in the celebration.
28:21 The LORD will send diseases **a** you until none of
28:37 and a mockery **a** all the nations to which the
28:43 The foreigners living **a** you will become stronger
28:46 and warning **a** you and your descendants forever.
28:54 The most tenderhearted man **a** you will have no
28:56 The most tender and delicate woman **a** you—
28:64 For the LORD will scatter you **a** all the nations
28:65 There **a** those nations you will find no place of
29:11 and the foreigners living **a** you who chop your
29:18 or tribe **a** you would turn away from the LORD
29:18 and so that no root **a** you would bear bitter
30: 1 and you meditate on them as you are living **a** the
31:17 have come because God is no longer **a** us!'
32:51 For both of you broke faith with me **a** the Israelites
33:16 crowning the brow of the prince **a** his brothers.
Jos 3: 5 for tomorrow the LORD will do great wonders **a**
3:10 Today you will know that the living God is **a** you.
4: 7 These stones will stand as a permanent memorial **a**
6:25 And she lives **a** the Israelites to this day.
7:11 about it and hidden the things **a** their belongings.
7:12 the things **a** you that were set apart for destruction.
7:13 Hidden **a** you, O Israel, are things set apart for the

8: 9 But Joshua remained a the people in the camp that
8:35 and the foreigners who lived a the Israelites.
9:22 live in a distant land when you live right here a us?
11:23 special possession, dividing the land a the tribes.
13: 7 when you divide the land a the nine tribes
13:13 so they continue to live a the Israelites to this day.
15:63 so the Jebusites live there a the people of Judah to
16:10 so the people of Gezer live as slaves a the people
19:49 After all the land was divided a the tribes,
20: 4 the accused to enter the city and live there a them.
20: 9 Israelites as well as the foreigners living a them.
22:19 where the LORD lives a us in his Tabernacle,
22:31 "Today we know the LORD is a us because you
23:12 the survivors of these nations remaining a you,
24:17 As we traveled through the wilderness a our
24:23 right then," Joshua said, "destroy the idols a you,
Jdg 1:16 They settled a the people there, near the town of
1:21 So to this day the Jebusites live in Jerusalem a the
1:29 so the Canaanites continued to live there a them.
1:30 and Nahalol, who continued to live a them.
3: 5 So Israel lived a the Canaanites, Hittites, Amorites,
5: 8 could be seen / a forty thousand warriors in Israel!
5:16 Why did you sit at home a the sheepfolds—
14: 3 in our tribe or a all the Israelites you could marry?
18: 2 So the men of Dan chose five warriors from a their
20:12 "What a terrible thing has been done a you!
21:12 A the residents of Jabesh-gilead they found four
Ru 2:11 and your own land to live here a complete
2:15 "Let her gather grain right a the sheaves without
1Sa 2:24 The reports I hear a the LORD's people are not
2:28 I chose your ancestor Aaron from a all his relatives
2:36 'give us jobs a the priests so we will have enough
8:15 and distribute it a his officers and attendants.
10:21 And finally Saul son of Kish was chosen from a
10:22 the LORD replied, "He is hiding a the baggage."
13: 3 The news spread quickly a the Philistines that
14: 3 (A Saul's men was Ahijah the priest, who was
14:30 eat freely from the food they found a our enemies,
14:34 Then go out a the troops and tell them,
14:41 and I guilty, or is the sin a the others?"
16:13 So as David stood there a his brothers,
22:14 "is there anyone a all your servants who is as
25: 7 While your shepherds stayed a us near Carmel,
26:19 so I can no longer live a the LORD's people
27: 7 and they lived there a the Philistines for a year
27:11 and again while he was living a the Philistines.
30: 5 widow of Nabal of Carmel, were a those captured.
30:17 David and his men rushed in a them
30:22 But some troublemakers a David's men said,
2Sa 2:18 sons of Zeruiah, were a David's forces that day.
3: 6 Abner became a powerful leader a those who were
14:20 and you understand everything that happens a us!"
17: 8 He won't be spending the night a the troops.
17: 9 of your men fall, there will be panic a your troops,
19:28 but instead you have honored me a those who eat
22:50 For this, O LORD, I will praise you a the nations;
23: 8 the three greatest warriors a David's men.
23: 9 Next in rank a the Three was Eleazar son of Dodai,
23:13 The Three (who were a the Thirty—an elite group
a David's fighting men) went down
1Ki 1: 8 But a those who remained loyal to David
3: 8 And here I am a your own chosen people, a nation
5: 6 there is no one a us who can cut timber like you
6:13 I will live a the people of Israel and never forsake
8:16 I have never chosen a city a the tribes of Israel as
8:53 a all the nations of the earth to be your own special
9: 7 an object of mockery and ridicule a the nations.
11: 1 Ammon, Edom, Sidon, and from a the Hittites.
11:20 who was brought up in Pharaoh's palace a
14:21 the city the LORD had chosen from a all the
14:31 he was buried a his ancestors in the City of David.
22:40 When Ahab died, he was buried a his ancestors.
2Ki 5: 2 and a their captives was a young girl who had been
11: 2 and stole him away from a the rest of the king's
17: 6 River in Gozan, and a the cities of the Medes.
17:25 the LORD sent lions a them to kill some of them.
17:26 He has sent lions a them to destroy them
17:32 but they appointed from a themselves priests to
17:34 And this is still going on a them today.
18:11 River in Gozan, and a the cities of the Medes.
21: 7 the city I have chosen from a all the other tribes of
1Ch 7: 4 military service a their descendants was 36,000,
7: 7 military service a their descendants was 22,034.
7: 9 available for military service a their descendants,
7:40 a the descendants listed in their tribal genealogy.
9:10 A the priests who returned were Jedaiah, Jehoiarib,
11:11 the three greatest warriors a David's men.
11:12 Next in rank a the Three was Eleazar son of Dodai,
11:15 The Three (who were a the Thirty—an elite group
a David's fighting men) went down
11:26 These were also included a David's mighty men:
12: 1 They were a the warriors who fought beside David
12: 4 a famous warrior and leader a the Thirty;
12:14 The weakest a them could take on a hundred
12:18 who later became a leader a the Thirty, and he
16:24 Publish his glorious deeds a the nations.
16:35 Gather and rescue us from a the nations,
24: 4 for there were more family leaders a the
24: 5 sanctuary from a the descendants of both Eleazar
26:10 appointed Shimri as the leader a his sons,
26:32 There were twenty-seven hundred capable men a
28: 4 has chosen me from a all my father's family to be
28: 4 and from a the families of Judah, he chose my
28: 4 And from a my father's sons, the LORD was
28: 5 And from a my sons—for the LORD has given
2Ch 6: 5 I have never chosen a city a the tribes of Israel as
6:18 "But will God really live on earth a people?
7:13 devour your crops, or I might send plagues a you.
7:20 I will make it a spectacle of contempt a the
11:13 and Levites living a the northern tribes of Israel
11:22 Rehoboam made Maacah's son Abijah chief a the
12:13 the city the LORD had chosen from a all the
13:17 there were 500,000 casualties a Israel's finest
15: 9 Manasseh, and Simeon who had settled a them.
19: 4 lived in Jerusalem, but he went out a the people,
20:22 and Mount Seir to start fighting a themselves.
22:11 and stole him away from a the rest of the king's
24:16 He was buried a the kings in the City of David,
31:15 They distributed the gifts a the families of priests
31:15 dividing the gifts fairly a young and old alike.
31:19 to distribute portions to every male a the priests
32:23 then on King Hezekiah became highly respected a
33: 7 the city I have chosen from a all the other tribes of
35:12 They divided the burnt offerings a the people by
Ne 1: 8 'If you sin, I will scatter you a the nations.
9:36 our ancestors! We are slaves a all this abundance!
Est 4: 3 there was great mourning a the Jews.
9:28 These days would never cease to be celebrated a
9:28 of what happened ever die out a their descendants.
10: 3 He was very great a the Jews, who held him in
Job 2: 8 with a piece of broken pottery as he sat a the ashes.
3: 6 never again to be counted a the days of the year,
3: 6 of the year, never again to appear a the months.
17: 6 "God has made a mockery of me a the people;
17:10 and try again! But I will not find a wise man a you.
28:13 where to find it, for it is not found a the living.
29: 7 city gate and took my place a the honored leaders.
29:25 I lived as a king a his troops and as one who
30: 6 in frightening ravines and in caves and a the rocks.
30: 7 They sound like animals as they howl a the bushes;
40:22 The lotus plants give it shade a the willows beside
Ps 1: 5 Sinners will have no place a the godly.
16:10 For you will not leave my soul a the dead
18:49 For this, O LORD, I will praise you a the nations;
22:18 They divide my clothes a themselves / and throw
22:22 and sisters. / I will praise you a all your people.
22:25 I will praise you a all the people; / I will fulfill my
42: 4 used to be: / I walked a the crowds of worshipers,
44:11 you have scattered us a the nations.
45: 9 Kings' daughters are a your concubines. / At your
46: 7 The LORD Almighty is here a us; / the God of
46:11 The LORD Almighty is here a us; / the God of
57: 9 the people. / I will sing your praises a the nations.
67: 2 your saving power a people everywhere.
68:13 Though they lived a the sheepfolds, / now they are
68:18 Now the LORD God will live a us here.
68:30 the reeds, / this herd of bulls a the weaker calves.
69:28 of Life; / don't let them be counted a the righteous.
77:14 You demonstrate your awesome power a the
78:60 the Tabernacle where he had lived a the people.
86: 8 Nowhere a the pagan gods is there a god like you,
87: 4 record Egypt and Babylon a those who know me—
96: 3 Publish his glorious deeds a the nations.
99: 6 Moses and Aaron were a his priests; / Samuel also
104:12 the streams / and sing a the branches of the trees.
105:27 They performed miraculous signs a the Egyptians,
105:37 there were no sick or feeble people a them.
106:27 that he would scatter their descendants a the
106:29 all these things, / so a plague broke out a them.
106:35 Instead, they mingled a the pagans / and adopted
106:47 save us! / Gather us back from a the nations,
108: 3 the people. / I will sing your praises a the nations.
113: 8 He sets them a princes, / even the princes of his
120: 5 How I suffer a these scoundrels of Meshech!
120: 6 I am tired of living here / a people who hate peace.
146: 9 The LORD protects the foreigners a us.
Pr 6:19 out lies, / a person who sows discord a brothers.
14:33 understanding heart; wisdom is not found a fools.
15:31 you will be at home a the wise.
21:15 a joy to the godly, but it causes dismay a evildoers.
25: 6 with the king or push for a place a the great.
30:26 but they make their homes a the rocky cliffs.
Ecc 11: 2 Divide your gifts a many, for you do not know
12: 2 and there is no silver lining left a the clouds.
SS 1: 7 For why should I wander like a prostitute a the
2: 2 other women, my beloved is like a lily a thorns."
2:16 lover is mine, and I am his. He feeds a the lilies!
4: 5 like twin fawns of a gazelle, feeding a the lilies.
6: 3 and my lover is mine. He grazes a the lilies!"
7:11 the fields and spend the night a the wildflowers.
Isa 1:31 The strongest a you will disappear like burning
2:21 and hide a the jagged rocks at the tops of cliffs.
3: 8 They have offended his glorious presence a them.
3:16 Their eyes rove a the crowds, flirting with the men.
5:13 The great and honored a them will starve,
5:17 In those days flocks will feed a the ruins; lambs
10: 4 will stumble along as prisoners or lie a the dead.
10:16 will send a plague a your proud troops,
11: 6 Calves and yearlings will be safe a lions, and a
11: 7 The cattle will graze a bears. Cubs and calves will
11: 8 Babies will crawl safely a poisonous snakes.
11:12 He will raise a flag a the nations for Israel to rally
12: 6 For great is the Holy One of Israel who lives a
13:21 Ostriches will live a the ruins, and wild goats will
16: 4 Let our outcasts stay a you. Hide them from our
29:14 of this, I will do wonders a these hypocrites.
31: 3 and fall a those they are trying to help.
32: 4 Even the hotheads a them will be full of sense
33:14 The sinners a my people shake with fear.
34:14 Wild goats will bleat at one another a the ruins,
50:10 Who a you fears the LORD and obeys his
53: 8 But who a the people realized that he was dying
53:12 He was counted a those who were sinners. He bore
55: 4 by being my witness and a leader a the nations.
61: 9 will be known and honored a the nations.
63:11 Where is the one who sent his Holy Spirit to be a
65: 4 At night they go out a the graves and secret places
65: 8 "For just as good grapes are found a a cluster of
65:15 Your name will be a curse word a my people,
66:19 I will perform a sign a them. And I will send those
Jer 4: 3 your hearts! Do not waste your good seed a thorns.
5:26 "A my people are wicked men who lie in wait for
6:15 Therefore, they will lie a the slaughtered.
6:26 dress yourselves in sackcloth, and sit a the ashes.
7:28 Truth has vanished from a them; it is no longer
8:12 Therefore, they will lie a the slaughtered.
8:17 "I will send these enemy troops a you like
10: 7 A all the wise people of the earth and in all the
11: 9 "I have discovered a conspiracy against me a the
12:16 then they will be given a place a my people.
14: 9 to save us? You are right here a us, LORD.
17:25 and their officials will always ride a the people of
18:13 heard of such a thing, even a the pagan nations?
29:23 For these men have done terrible things a my
29:27 who pretends to be a prophet a you?
34: 5 but will die peacefully a your people. They will
39:14 So Jeremiah stayed in Judah a his own people.
40: 1 He had found Jeremiah bound in chains a the
44: 7 or child a you who has come here from Judah,
46:16 and fall over each other and say a themselves,
49:11 But I will preserve the orphans who remain a you.
49:15 "I will cut you down to size a the nations, Edom.
49:16 Though you live a the peaks with the eagles,
50:23 and shattered. Babylon is desolate a the nations!
La 1: 2 A all her lovers, there is no one left to help her.
1: 3 She lives a foreign nations and has no place of rest.
3:45 discarded us as refuse and garbage a the nations.
4:15 distant lands and wandered there a foreign nations,
Eze 1:13 lightning was flashing back and forth a them.
2: 5 at least they will know they have had a prophet a
3:15 I sat there a them for seven days, overwhelmed.
3:25 with ropes so you cannot go out a the people.
6: 8 and they will be scattered a the nations of the
6: 9 Then when they are exiled a the nations, they will
6:13 When their dead lie scattered a their idols
10: 7 and took some live coals from the fire burning a
11: 1 A them were Jaazaniah son of Azzur and Pelatiah
11: 1 son of Benaiah, who were leaders a the people.
12: 2 you live a rebels who could see the truth if they
12:15 And when I scatter them a the nations, they will
15: 6 like grapevines growing a the trees of the forest.
18:18 doing what was clearly wrong a his people.
19: 2 A lioness a lions! / She lay down a the young lions
19: 6 He prowled a the other lions / and became a leader
a them. / He learned to catch
20:22 a the nations who had seen my power in bringing
20:23 I vowed I would scatter them a all the nations
22:15 I will scatter you a the nations and purge you of
22:16 And when you have been dishonored a the nations,
22:26 so that my holy name is greatly dishonored a them.
25: 4 They will set up their camps a you and pitch their
25:10 the Ammonites will no longer be counted a the
26:13 No more will the sound of harps be heard a your
28:14 mountain of God and walked a the stones of fire.
28:16 from your place a the stones of fire.
28:22 against you and reveal my holiness a you,
28:25 the nations of the world my holiness a my people.
30:11 He and his armies—ruthless a the nations—
30:26 I will scatter the Egyptians a the nations.
31: 3 deep forest shade with its top high a the clouds.
31:13 and the wild animals lay a its branches.
31:18 You will lie there a the outcasts who have died by
32: 2 You think of yourself as a strong young lion a the
32:19 So go down to the pit and lie there a the outcasts.'
32:21 they lie a the outcasts, all victims of the sword.'
32:25 They have a resting place a the slaughtered,
32:28 Egypt, will lie crushed and broken a the outcasts,
32:29 they were, they also lie a those killed by the sword,
32:32 and his hordes will lie there a the outcasts who
33:24 the scattered remnants of Judah living a the ruined
33:33 then they will know a prophet has been a them."
34:13 home to their own land of Israel from a the peoples
34:24 and my servant David will be a prince a my
36:20 But when they were scattered a the nations,
36:22 which you dishonored while you were scattered a
36:23 name is—the name you dishonored a the nations.
37: 2 He led me around a the old, dry bones that covered
37:21 I will gather the people of Israel from a the
37:26 and I will put my Temple a them forever.
37:27 I will make my home a them. I will be their God,
37:28 And since my Temple will remain a them forever,
39: 7 I will make known my holy name a my people of
39:21 "Thus, I will demonstrate my glory a the nations.
43: 7 remain here forever, living a the people of Israel.
43: 9 to honor their kings, and I will live a them forever.
44: 9 including those who live a the people of Israel,
44:22 They may choose their wives only from a the
44:24 judges to resolve any disagreements a my people.
45: 1 "When you divide the land a the tribes of Israel,
47:21 "Divide the land within these boundaries a the
47:22 joined you and are raising their families a you.
47:22 and they will receive an inheritance a the tribes.
Da 2:11 you your dream, and they do not live a people."
4:15 and let him live like an animal a the plants of the
4:35 a the angels of heaven / and with those who live on
5:21 of an animal, and he lived a the wild donkeys.
7: 8 suddenly another small horn appeared a them.
11:14 Lawless ones a your own people will join them in
11:24 distribute a his followers the plunder and wealth of
11:39 and dividing the land a them as their reward.
Hos 8: 8 they lie a the nations like an old pot that no one

9:17 They will be wanderers, homeless **a** the nations.
10: 4 So perverted justice springs up **a** them like
10:14 Now the terrors of war will rise **a** your people.
11: 9 I am the Holy One living **a** you, and I will not
Joel 2:19 You will no longer be an object of mockery **a** the
2:27 Then you will know that I am here **a** my people of
2:32 These will be **a** the survivors whom the LORD
3: 2 for scattering my inheritance **a** the nations, and for
Am 2:14 get away. The strongest **a** you will become weak.
3: 2 "From **a** all the families on the earth, I chose you
Ob 1: 2 "I will cut you down to size **a** the nations, Edom;
1: 4 as high as eagles and build your nest **a** the stars,
Mic 3:11 to us," you say, "for the LORD is here **a** us."
5: 7 Then the few left in Israel will go out **a** the nations.
5: 8 The remnant of Israel will go out **a** the nations
6:12 The rich **a** you have become wealthy through
7:18 who pardons the sins of the survivors **a** his people?
Zep 2:14 Owls of many kinds will live **a** the ruins of its
3:11 all the proud and arrogant people from **a** you.
3:15 the King of Israel, will live **a** you!
3:17 For the LORD your God has arrived to live **a** you.
3:20 a name of distinction **a** all the nations of the earth.
Hag 2: 5 My Spirit remains **a** you, just as I promised when
Zec 1: 8 was standing **a** some myrtle trees in a small valley.
1:10 So the man standing **a** the myrtle trees explained,
1:11 who was standing **a** the myrtle trees, "We have
2:10 O Jerusalem, for I am coming to live **a** you.
2:11 I will live **a** you, and you will know that the
7:14 I scattered them as with a whirlwind **a** the distant
8:12 I am planting seeds of peace and prosperity **a** you.
8:13 **A** the nations, Judah and Israel had become
10: 9 Though I have scattered them like seeds **a** the
12: 6 or like a burning torch **a** sheaves of grain.
12: 8 the weakest **a** them will be as mighty as King
14: 2 and half will be left **a** the ruins of the city.
Mal 1:10 "I wish that someone **a** you would shut the
1:11 For my name is great **a** the nations,"
1:14 "and my name is feared **a** the nations!
3: 5 or who deprive the foreigners living **a** you of
Mt 9: 3 some of the teachers of religious law said **a**
10:16 "Look, I am sending you out as sheep **a** wolves.
12:15 followed him. He healed all the sick **a** them,
12:28 then the Kingdom of God has arrived **a** you.
13: 7 Other seeds fell **a** thorns that shot up and choked
13:25 his enemy came and planted weeds **a** the wheat.
13:39 The enemy who planted the weeds **a** the wheat is
13:56 All his sisters live right here **a** us. What makes him
13:57 in his own hometown and **a** his own family."
18: 2 a small child over to him and put the child **a** them.
18:20 because they are mine, I am there **a** them."
20:26 But **a** you it should be quite different.
20:26 Whoever wants to be a leader **a** you must be your
21:25 merely human?" They talked it over **a** themselves.
23:11 The greatest **a** you must be a servant.
24:30 and there will be deep mourning **a** all the nations
26:11 You will always have the poor **a** you, but I will not
27:56 **A** them were Mary Magdalene, Mary (the mother
28:15 Their story spread widely **a** the Jews, and they still
Mk 1:13 He was out **a** the wild animals, and angels took
2: 8 Jesus knew what they were discussing **a**
2:15 (There were many people of this kind **a** the crowds
4: 7 Other seed fell **a** thorns that shot up and choked
4:41 they were filled with awe and said **a** themselves,
5: 3 This man lived **a** the tombs and could not be
5: 5 and throughout the night he would wander **a** the
6: 3 and Simon. And his sisters live right here **a** us."
6: 4 and **a** his relatives and his own family."
6: 5 he couldn't do any mighty miracles **a** them except
9:36 Then he put a little child **a** them. Taking the child
9:50 You must have the qualities of salt **a** yourselves
10:43 But **a** you it should be quite different.
10:43 Whoever wants to be a leader **a** you must be your
11:31 They talked it over **a** themselves. "If we say it was
14: 7 You will always have the poor **a** you, and you can
Lk 1: 1 accounts about the events that took place **a** us.
1: 2 the reports circulating **a** us from the early disciples
2: 9 Suddenly, an angel of the Lord appeared **a** them,
2:44 because they assumed he was with friends **a** the
2:44 they started to look for him **a** their relatives
2:46 was in the Temple, sitting **a** the religious teachers,
7:16 saying, "A mighty prophet has risen **a** us,"
7:49 The men at the table said **a** themselves,
8: 2 **A** them were Mary Magdalene, from whom he had
8: 7 Other seed fell **a** thorns that shot up and choked
9:46 Then there was an argument **a** them as to which of
9:48 Whoever is the least **a** you is the greatest."
10: 3 that I am sending you out as lambs **a** wolves.
10:19 and you can walk **a** snakes and scorpions and crush
11:20 then the Kingdom of God has arrived **a** you.
13:19 the birds come and find shelter **a** its branches."
17:21 over there!' For the Kingdom of God is **a** you."
19:39 But some of the Pharisees **a** the crowd said,
20: 5 They talked it over **a** themselves. "If we say it was
22:17 he said, "Take this and share it **a** yourselves.
22:21 "But here at this table, sitting **a** us as a friend,
22:24 And they began to argue **a** themselves as to who
22:26 But **a** you, those who are the greatest should take
22:37 'He was counted **a** those who were rebels.' Yes,
22:38 they replied, "we have two swords **a** us."
24:36 Jesus himself was suddenly standing there **a** them.
Jn 1:11 Even in his own land and **a** his own people, he was
1:14 Word became human and lived here on earth **a** us.
7:12 There was a lot of discussion about him **a** the
7:25 who lived there in Jerusalem said **a** themselves,
7:31 Many **a** the crowds at the Temple believed in him.
9:16 So there was a deep division of opinion **a** them.
11:54 Jesus stopped his public ministry **a** the people
12: 8 You will always have the poor **a** you, but I will not
15:24 If I hadn't done such miraculous signs **a** them that
19:23 they divided his clothes **a** the four of them.
19:24 "They divided my clothes **a** themselves and threw
20:19 Suddenly, Jesus was standing there **a** them!
20:26 but suddenly, as before, Jesus was standing **a** them.
21:20 and asked, "Lord, who **a** us will betray you?"
21:23 So the rumor spread **a** the community of believers
Ac 1:10 two white-robed men suddenly stood there **a** them.
1:19 The news of his death spread rapidly **a** all the
2:27 For you will not leave my soul **a** the dead
2:29 and was buried, and his tomb is still here **a** us.
2:31 He was saying that the Messiah would not be left **a**
3:22 raise up a Prophet like me from **a** your own people.
4:14 had been healed was standing right there **a** them,
4:15 the council chamber and conferred **a** themselves.
4:34 There was no poverty **a** them, because people who
5:12 many miraculous signs and wonders **a** the people.
6: 3 "Now look around **a** yourselves, friends,
6: 8 amazing miracles and signs **a** the people.
7:37 'God will raise up a Prophet like me from **a** your
12:18 there was a great commotion **a** the soldiers about
13: 1 **A** the prophets and teachers of the church at
14: 2 stirred up distrust **a** the Gentiles against Paul
14:14 their clothing in dismay and ran out **a** the people,
15: 7 you all know that God chose me from **a** you some
15:12 and wonders God had done through them **a** the
17:34 **A** them were Dionysius, a member of the Council,
20:29 vicious wolves, will come in **a** you after I leave,
21:19 accomplished **a** the Gentiles through his ministry.
21:32 his soldiers and officers and ran down **a** the crowd.
26: 4 from my earliest childhood **a** my own people
26:18 for their sins and be given a place **a** God's people,
28:25 after they had argued back and forth **a** themselves,
Ro 1: 6 You are **a** those who have been called to belong to
1:13 I want to work **a** you and see good results, just as I
have done **a** other Gentiles.
15: 9 "I will praise you **a** the Gentiles; / I will sing
16: 7 They are respected **a** the apostles and became
1Co 1:10 the Lord Jesus Christ to stop arguing **a** yourselves.
2: 4 but the Holy Spirit was powerful **a** you.
2: 6 Yet when I am **a** mature Christians, I do speak
5: 1 report about the sexual immorality going on **a** you,
5: 7 Remove this wicked person from **a** you so that you
5:13 "You must remove the evil person from **a** you."
6: 2 can't you decide these little things **a** yourselves?
9:11 We have planted good spiritual seed **a** you. Is it too
11:11 But in relationships **a** the Lord's people,
11:18 I hear that there are divisions **a** you when you meet
11:19 there must be divisions **a** you so that those of you
12:25 This makes for harmony **a** the members, so that all
14:25 declaring, "God is really here **a** you."
2Co 3: 2 can read it and recognize our good work **a** you.
6:16 in them / and walk **a** them. / I will be their God,
10: 8 put to shame by having my work **a** you destroyed.
10:15 and that our work **a** you will be greatly enlarged.
12:12 did many signs and wonders and miracles **a** you.
13: 3 his dealings with you; he is a mighty power **a** you.
13: 5 If you cannot tell that Jesus Christ is **a** you,
Gal 3: 5 give you the Holy Spirit and work miracles **a** you
5: 9 But it takes only one wrong person **a** you to infect
5:15 But if instead of showing love **a** yourselves you are
Eph 5: 3 be no sexual immorality, impurity, or greed **a** you.
5: 3 Such sins have no place **a** God's people.
5:19 and hymns and spiritual songs **a** yourselves,
Col 4: 5 Live wisely **a** those who are not Christians,
4:11 These are the only Jewish Christians **a** my
1Th 1: 5 And you know that the way we lived **a** you was
2: 7 but we were as gentle **a** you as a mother feeding
2: 9 and sisters, how hard we worked **a** you?
2: 9 there as we preached God's Good News **a** you.
4: 9 love that should be shown **a** God's people.
5:12 They work hard **a** you and warn you against all
2Th 1:10 And you will be **a** those praising him on that day,
2:13 We are thankful that God chose you to be **a** the
Tit 3:10 If anyone is causing divisions **a** you, give a first
Heb 2:12 and sisters. / I will praise you **a** all your people."
12:15 Watch out that no bitter root of unbelief rises up **a**
Jas 1: 1 It is written to Jewish Christians scattered **a** the
4: 1 What is causing the quarrels and fights **a** you?
4:12 who made the law, can rightly judge **a** us.
5:13 Are any **a** you suffering? They should keep on
5:14 Are any **a** you sick? They should call for the elders
5:19 if anyone **a** you wanders away from the truth
1Pe 2:12 Be careful how you live **a** your unbelieving
4:17 and it must begin first **a** God's own children.
2Pe 1:10 work hard to prove that you really are **a** those God
2: 1 in Israel, just as there will be false teachers **a** you.
2:13 They are a disgrace and a stain **a** you. They revel
1Jn 2: 8 commandment is true in Christ and is true **a** you,
Jude 1: 4 godless people have wormed their way in **a** you,
1:19 and they are the ones who are creating divisions **a**
Rev 2: 1 the one who walks **a** the seven gold lampstands:
2: 5 and remove your lampstand from its place **a** the
2:13 was martyred **a** you by Satan's followers.
2:14 You tolerate some **a** you who are like Balaam,
2:15 the same way, you have some Nicolaitans **a** you—
5: 6 the four living beings and **a** the twenty-four elders.
6: 6 And a voice from **a** the four living beings said,
6:15 in the caves and **a** the rocks of the mountains.
7:15 And he who sits on the throne will live **a** them
14: 4 They have been purchased from **a** the people on
21: 3 "Look, the home of God is now **a** his people!

AMORITE (14) [AMORITES]

Ge 14:13 at the oak grove belonging to Mamre the **A**.
Nu 21:29 and his daughters as captives of Sihon, the **A** king.
Dt 2:24 Look, I will help you defeat Sihon the **A**, king of
3: 8 "We now possessed all the land of the two **A**
4:47 Og of Bashan—the two **A** kings east of the Jordan.
Jos 2:10 and Og, the two **A** kings east of the Jordan River,
5: 1 When all the **A** kings west of the Jordan and all the
9:10 We have also heard what he did to the two **A** kings
10: 5 So these five **A** kings combined their armies for a
10: 6 For all the **A** kings who live in the hill country
10: 9 from Gilgal and took the **A** armies by surprise.
13:21 Sihon was the **A** king who had reigned in Heshbon
Eze 16: 3 Your father was an **A** and your mother a Hittite!
16:45 must have been a Hittite and your father an **A**.

AMORITES (77) [AMORITE]

Ge 10:16 Jebusites, **A**, Girgashites,
14: 7 and also the **A** living in Hazazon-tamar.
15:16 when the sin of the **A** has run its course."
15:21 **A**, Canaanites, Girgashites, and Jebusites."
48:22 the portion that I took from the **A** with my sword
Ex 3: 8 Hittites, **A**, Perizzites, Hivites, and Jebusites live.
3:17 Hittites, **A**, Perizzites, Hivites, and Jebusites—
13: 5 the Canaanites, Hittites, **A**, Hivites, and Jebusites.
23:23 go before you and bring you into the land of the **A**,
33: 2 **A**, Hittites, Perizzites, Hivites, and Jebusites.
34:11 the **A**, Canaanites, Hittites, Perizzites, Hivites,
Nu 13:29 Jebusites, and **A** live in the hill country.
21:13 in the wilderness adjacent to the territory of the **A**.
21:13 the boundary line between the Moabites and the **A**.
21:21 to King Sihon of the **A** with this message:
21:25 So Israel captured all the towns of the **A**
21:26 had been the capital of King Sihon of the **A**.
21:31 the people of Israel occupied the territory of the **A**.
21:32 in the region and drove out the **A** who lived there.
21:34 the same to him as you did to King Sihon of the **A**,
22: 2 knew what the Israelites had done to the **A**.
32:33 son of Joseph the territory of King Sihon of the **A**
32:39 and conquered it, and they drove out the **A**,
Dt 1: 4 was after he had defeated King Sihon of the **A**,
1: 7 Go to the hill country of the **A** and to all the
1:19 and headed toward the hill country of the **A**.
1:27 us here from Egypt to be slaughtered by these **A**.
1:44 But the **A** who lived there came out against you
3: 2 Treat him just as you treated King Sihon of the **A**,
3: 9 called Sirion by the Sidonians; the **A** call it Senir.)
4:46 (This land was formerly occupied by the **A** under
7: 1 Girgashites, **A**, Canaanites, Perizzites, Hivites,
20:17 **A**, Canaanites, Perizzites, Hivites, and Jebusites,
31: 4 as he destroyed Sihon and Og, the kings of the **A**.
Jos 3:10 Hittites, Hivites, Perizzites, Girgashites, **A**,
7: 7 Jordan River if you are going to let the **A** kill us?
9: 1 **A**, Canaanites, Perizzites, Hivites, and Jebusites,
10:11 As the **A** retreated down the road from Beth-horon,
10:12 the LORD gave the Israelites victory over the **A**,
11: 3 of Canaan, both east and west; the kings of the **A**;
12: 2 King Sihon of the **A**, who lived in Heshbon,
12: 8 the **A**, the Canaanites, the Perizzites, the Hivites,
13: 4 northward to Aphek on the border of the **A**;
13:10 also included all the towns of King Sihon of the **A**,
24: 8 I brought you into the land of the **A** on the east
24:11 including the **A**, the Perizzites, the Canaanites,
24:12 ahead of you to drive out the two kings of the **A**.
24:15 Or will it be the gods of the **A** in whose land you
24:18 It was the LORD who drove out the **A**
Jdg 1:34 the **A** forced them into the hill country and would
1:35 The **A** were determined to stay in Mount Heres,
1:35 they forced the **A** to work as slaves.
1:36 The boundary of the **A** ran from Scorpion Pass to
3: 5 Hittites, **A**, Perizzites, Hivites, and Jebusites,
6:10 You must not worship the gods of the **A**, in whose
10: 8 of the Jordan River in the land of the **A** (that is,
10:11 the **A**, the Ammonites, the Philistines,
11:19 Israel sent messengers to King Sihon of the **A**,
11:21 So Israel took control of all the land of the **A**,
11:23 who took away the land from the **A** and gave it to
1Sa 7:14 also peace between Israel and the **A** in those days.
2Sa 21: 2 but were all that was left of the nation of the **A**.
1Ki 4:19 including the territories of King Sihon of the **A**
9:20 including **A**, Hittites, Perizzites, Hivites,
21:26 because he worshiped idols just as the **A** had
2Ki 21:11 He is even more wicked than the **A**, who lived in
1Ch 1:14 Jebusites, **A**, Girgashites,
2Ch 8: 7 **A**, Perizzites, Hivites, and Jebusites.
Ezr 9: 1 Ammonites, Moabites, Egyptians, and **A**.
Ne 9: 8 Hittites, **A**, Perizzites, Jebusites, and Girgashites.
Ps 135:11 Sihon king of the **A**, / Og king of Bashan, / and all
136:19 Sihon king of the **A**, / His faithful love endures
Isa 17: 9 They will become like the cities the **A** abandoned
28:21 at Mount Perazim and against the **A** at Gibeon.
Am 2: 9 I destroyed the **A** before my people arrived in the
2: 9 The **A** were as tall as cedar trees and strong as
2:10 forty years so you could possess the land of the **A**.

AMOS (11)

Am 1: 1 This message was given to **A**, a shepherd from the
7: 8 the LORD said to me, "**A**, what do you see?"
7:10 the priest of Bethel, heard what **A** was saying,
7:10 "**A** is hatching a plot against you right here on
7:12 Then Amaziah sent orders to **A**: "Get out of here,
7:14 But **A** replied, "I'm not one of your professional
8: 2 "What do you see, **A**?" he asked. I replied,
Mt 1:10 Manasseh was the father of **A**. / **A** was the father
of Josiah.
Lk 3:25 Mattathias was the son of **A**. / **A** was the son of
Nahum. / Nahum was the son of

AMOUNT (43) [AMOUNTED, AMOUNTS]
Ge 23:16 So Abraham paid Ephron the **a** he had suggested,
41:49 that the people could not keep track of the **a**.
Ex 21:22 damages in the **a** the woman's husband demands
38:25 The **a** of silver that was given was about 7,545
Lev 6: 5 they must restore the principal **a** plus a penalty of
22:14 realizing it must pay the priest for the **a** eaten,
25:52 then they will repay a relatively small **a** for their
27: 8 a vow but cannot afford to pay the prescribed **a**,
27: 8 You will then pay the **a** decided by the priest.
27:16 its value will be assessed by the **a** of seed required
1Sa 30:16 because of the vast **a** of plunder they had taken
2Sa 8: 8 along with a large **a** of bronze from Hadadezer's
12:30 David took a vast **a** of plunder from the city.
2Ki 18:15 To gather this **a**, King Hezekiah used all the silver
1Ch 18: 8 along with a large **a** of bronze from Hadadezer's
20: 2 David took a vast **a** of plunder from the city.
28:15 He told Solomon the **a** of gold needed for the gold
28:15 and the **a** of silver for the silver lampstands
28:16 He designated the **a** of gold for the table on which
28:16 would be placed and the **a** of silver for other tables.
28:17 David also designated the **a** of gold for the solid
28:17 and dishes, as well as the **a** of silver for every dish.
28:18 he designated the **a** of refined gold for the altar of
2Ch 2: 9 An immense **a** of timber will be needed,
24:11 after day, and a large **a** of money was collected.
Job 6:25 are painful, but what do your criticisms **a** to?
Isa 13:17 and no **a** of silver or gold will buy them off.
Jer 2:22 No **a** of soap or lye can make you clean. You are
22:30 David to rule in Judah. His life will **a** to nothing."
Eze 46: 5 and whatever **a** of flour he chooses to go with each
46: 7 And with each lamb he is to bring whatever **a** of
Da 8:24 He will cause a shocking **a** of destruction
Mt 13:33 Even though she used a large **a** of flour, the yeast
25:20 bags of gold to invest and I have doubled the **a**.'
25:21 You have been faithful in handling this small **a**,
25:22 bags of gold to invest, and I have doubled the **a**.'
25:23 You have been faithful in handling this small **a**,
Lk 13:21 Even though she used a large **a** of flour, the yeast
19:16 ten times as much as the original **a**!
19:18 reported a good gain—five times the original **a**.
19:20 servant brought back only the original **a** of money
Ac 5: 2 to the apostles, but he claimed it was the full **a**.
1Co 16: 2 each of you should put aside some **a** of money in

AMOUNTED (1) [AMOUNT]
Nu 31:43 **a** to 337,500 sheep,

AMOUNTS (11) [AMOUNT]
Ge 47:12 and brothers in **a** appropriate to the number of their
Ex 30:34 weighing out the same **a** of each.
Dt 17:17 And he must not accumulate vast **a** of wealth in
1Ch 22: 3 David provided large **a** of iron for the nails that
22: 4 and Sidon had brought vast **a** of cedar to David.
22: 5 So David collected vast **a** of building materials
2Ch 20:25 They found vast **a** of equipment, clothing,
28: 8 from Judah and took tremendous **a** of plunder,
Isa 29:13 And their worship of me **a** to nothing more than
Eze 38:12 I will capture vast **a** of plunder and take many
Mk 12:41 in their money. Many rich people put in large **a**.

AMOZ (13)
2Ki 19: 2 in sackcloth, to the prophet Isaiah son of **A**.
19:20 Then Isaiah son of **A** sent this message to
20: 1 and the prophet Isaiah son of **A** went to visit him.
2Ch 26:22 are recorded by the prophet Isaiah son of **A**.
32:20 and the prophet Isaiah son of **A** cried out in prayer
32:32 *The Vision of the Prophet Isaiah Son of* **A**,
Isa 1: 1 and Jerusalem came to Isaiah son of **A** during the
2: 1 This is another vision that Isaiah son of **A** saw
13: 1 Isaiah son of **A** received this message concerning
20: 2 the LORD told Isaiah son of **A**, "Take off all
37: 2 in sackcloth, to the prophet Isaiah son of **A**.
37:21 Then Isaiah son of **A** sent this message to
38: 1 and the prophet Isaiah son of **A** went to visit him.

AMPHIPOLIS (1)
Ac 17: 1 and Silas traveled through the towns of **A**

AMPHITHEATER (2)
Ac 19:29 Everyone rushed to the **a**, dragging along Gaius
19:31 begging him not to risk his life by entering the **a**.

AMPLIATUS (1)
Ro 16: 8 Say hello to **A**, whom I love as one of the Lord's

AMRAM (16) [AMRAM'S]
Ex 6:18 The descendants of Kohath included **A**, Izhar,
6:20 **A** married his father's sister Jochebed, and she
6:20 and Moses. (**A** lived to be 137 years old.)
Nu 3:19 of his descendants, **A**, Izhar, Hebron, and Uzziel.
3:27 were composed of the clans descended from **A**,
26:58 of the Levites. Now Kohath was the ancestor of **A**,
26:59 **A** and Jochebed became the parents of Aaron,
1Ch 6: 2 The descendants of Kohath were **A**, Izhar, Hebron,
6: 3 The children of **A** were Aaron, Moses,
6:18 The descendants of Kohath included **A**, Izhar,
23:12 The descendants of Kohath included **A**, Izhar,
23:13 The sons of **A** were Aaron and Moses. Aaron
24:20 From the descendants of **A**, the leader was
26:23 These are the leaders that descended from **A**,
26:24 From the clan of **A**, Shebuel was a descendant of
Ezr 10:34 From the family of Bani: Maadai, **A**, Uel,

AMRAM'S (1) [AMRAM]
Nu 26:59 and **A** wife was named Jochebed. She also was a

AMRAPHEL (1)
Ge 14: 1 King **A** of Babylonia, King Arioch of Ellasar,

AMUSEMENT (1)
Ex 32:25 of control—and much to the **a** of their enemies—

AMZI (2)
1Ch 6:46 **A**, Bani, Shemer,
Ne 11:12 son of Pelaliah, son of **A**, son of Zechariah, son of

AN (1130) [A] See Index of Articles, Etc.

ANAB (2)
Jos 11:21 Debir, **A**, and the entire hill country of Judah
15:50 **A**, Eshtemoh, Anim,

ANAH (11)
Ge 36: 2 the daughter of **A** and granddaughter of Zibeon the
36:14 the daughter of **A** and granddaughter of Zibeon.
36:18 from Esau's wife Oholibamah, the daughter of **A**.
36:20 to the land of Seir: Lotan, Shobal, Zibeon, **A**,
36:24 The sons of Zibeon were Aiah and **A**. This is the **A** who discovered the hot springs in the
36:25 The son of **A** was Dishon, and Oholibamah was his
36:29 of the Horite clans were Lotan, Shobal, Zibeon, **A**,
1Ch 1:38 Shobal, Zibeon, **A**, Dishon, Ezer, and Dishan.
1:40 and Onam. The sons of Zibeon were Aiah and **A**.
1:41 The son of **A** was Dishon. The sons of Dishon

ANAHARATH (1)
Jos 19:19 Hapharaim, Shion, **A**,

ANAIAH (2)
Ne 8: 4 Shema, **A**, Uriah, Hilkiah, and Maaseiah.
10:22 Pelatiah, Hanan, **A**,

ANAK (8) [ANAK'S, ANAKITE, ANAKITES]
Nu 13:22 Sheshai, and Talmai—all descendants of **A**—lived.
13:28 We also saw the descendants of **A** who are living
13:33 We even saw giants there, the descendants of **A**.
Dt 1:28 even seen giants there—the descendants of **A**!'
Jos 11:21 Joshua destroyed all the descendants of **A**,
15:14 Sheshai, Ahiman, and Talmai—descendants of **A**.
21:11 (Arba was an ancestor of **A**.)
Jdg 1:20 who were descendants of the three sons of **A**.

ANAK'S (1) [ANAK]
Jos 15:13 Hebron), which had been named after **A** ancestor.

ANAKIMS [KJV] See ANAK

ANAKITE (1) [ANAK]
Dt 9: 2 and tall—descendants of the famous **A** giants.

ANAKITES (7) [ANAK]
Dt 2:10 They were as tall as the **A**, another race of giants.
2:11 and the **A** are often referred to as the Rephaites,
2:21 a numerous and powerful race, as tall as the **A**.
9: 2 heard the saying, 'Who can stand up to the **A**?'
Jos 14:12 You will remember that as scouts we found the **A**
14:15 had been named after Arba, a great hero of the **A**.)
15:14 Caleb drove out the three **A**—Sheshai, Ahiman,

ANALYZE (1)
Ecc 8: 1 to be wise, to be able to **a** and interpret things.

ANAMITES (2)
Ge 10:13 ancestor of the Ludites, **A**, Lehabites, Naphtuhites,
1Ch 1:11 ancestor of the Ludites, **A**, Lehabites, Naphtuhites,

ANAMMELECH (1)
2Ki 17:31 own children as sacrifices to Adrammelech and **A**.

ANAN (1)
Ne 10:26 Ahiah, Hanan, **A**,

ANANI (1)
1Ch 3:24 Pelaiah, Akkub, Johanan, Delaiah, and **A**—

ANANIAH (2)
Ne 3:23 and grandson of **A** repaired the sections next to
11:32 They were also in Anathoth, Nob, **A**,

ANANIAS (11)
Ac 5: 1 There was also a man named **A** who, with his wife,
5: 3 Then Peter said, "**A**, why has Satan filled your
5: 5 As soon as **A** heard these words, he fell to the floor
9:10 Now there was a believer in Damascus named **A**.
9:10 The Lord spoke to him in a vision, calling, "**A**!"
9:12 I have shown him a vision of a man named **A**
9:13 "But Lord," exclaimed **A**, "I've heard about the
9:17 So **A** went and found Saul. He laid his hands on
22:12 A man named **A** lived there. He was a godly man
23: 2 Instantly **A** the high priest commanded those close
24: 1 Five days later **A**, the high priest, arrived with

ANARCHY (2)
Isa 3: 4 children to rule over them, and **a** will prevail.
Eze 30:13 left in Egypt; **a** will prevail throughout the land!

ANATH (2) [BETH-ANATH]
Jdg 3:31 After Ehud, Shamgar son of **A** rescued Israel.
5: 6 "In the days of Shamgar son of **A**, and in the days

ANATHEMA [KJV] See CURSED

ANATHOTH (20)
Jos 21:18 **A**, and Almon—four towns.
2Sa 23:27 Abiezer from **A**; / Sibbecai from Hushah;
1Ki 2:26 Abiathar the priest, "Go back to your home in **A**.
1Ch 6:60 Geba, Alemeth, and **A**, each with its pasturelands.
7: 8 Eliezer, Elioenai, Omri, Jeremoth, Abijah, **A**,
11:28 Ira son of Ikkesh from Tekoa; / Abiezer from **A**;
12: 3 sons of Azmaveth; / Beracah and Jehu from **A**;
27:12 Abiezer from **A** in the territory of Benjamin was
Ezr 2:23 The people of **A** | 128
Ne 7:27 The people of **A** | 128
10:19 Hariph, **A**, Nebai,
11:32 They were also in **A**, Nob, Ananiah,
Isa 10:30 mighty army comes. Poor **A**, what a fate is yours!
Jer 1: 1 one of the priests from **A**, a town in the land of
11:21 The men of **A** wanted me dead. They said they
11:23 Not one of these plotters from **A** will survive,
29:27 have you done nothing to stop Jeremiah from **A**,
32: 7 will come and say to you, 'Buy my field at **A**.
32: 8 "Buy my field at **A** in the land of Benjamin.
32: 9 So I bought the field at **A**, paying Hanamel

ANCESTOR (122) [ANCESTORS, ANCESTORS', ANCESTRAL, ANCESTRY]
Ge 9:18 with their father. (Ham is the **a** of the Canaanites.)
10:13 Mizraim was the **a** of the Ludites, Anamites,
10:15 oldest son was Sidon, the **a** of the Sidonians.
10:15 Canaan was also the **a** of the Hittites,
10:21 Shem was the **a** of all the descendants of Eber.
10:26 Joktan was the **a** of Almodad, Sheleph,
19:37 He became the **a** of the nation now known as the
19:38 He became the **a** of the nation now known as the
36:43 names of the clans of Esau, the **a** of the Edomites,
Ex 6:17 and Shimei, each of whom is the **a** of a clan.
Lev 16:32 high priest who serves in place of his **a** Aaron.
Nu 26: 5 The Hanochite clan, named after its **a** Hanoch.
26: 5 The Palluite clan, named after its **a** Pallu.
26: 6 The Hezronite clan, named after its **a** Hezron.
26: 6 The Carmite clan, named after its **a** Carmi.
26: 8 Pallu was the **a** of Eliab,
26:12 The Nemuelite clan, named after its **a** Nemuel.
26:12 The Jaminite clan, named after its **a** Jamin.
26:12 The Jakinite clan, named after its **a** Jakin.
26:13 The Zerahite clan, named after its **a** Zerah.
26:13 The Shaulite clan, named after its **a** Shaul.
26:15 The Zephonite clan, named after its **a** Zephon.
26:15 The Haggite clan, named after its **a** Haggi.
26:15 The Shunite clan, named after its **a** Shuni.
26:16 The Oznite clan, named after its **a** Ozni. / The Erite
26:16 The Erite clan, named after its **a** Eri.
26:17 The Arodite clan, named after its **a** Arodi.
26:17 The Arelite clan, named after its **a** Areli.
26:20 The Shelanite clan, named after its **a** Shelah.
26:20 The Perezite clan, named after its **a** Perez.
26:20 The Zerahite clan, named after its **a** Zerah.
26:21 The Hezronites, named after their **a** Hezron.
26:21 The Hamulites, named after their **a** Hamul.
26:23 The Tolaite clan, named after its **a** Tola.
26:23 The Puite clan, named after its **a** Puah.
26:24 The Jashubite clan, named after its **a** Jashub.
26:24 The Shimronite clan, named after its **a** Shimron.
26:26 The Seredite clan, named after its **a** Sered.
26:26 The Elonite clan, named after its **a** Elon.
26:26 The Jahleelite clan, named after its **a** Jahleel.
26:29 The Makirite clan, named after its **a** Makir.
26:29 named after its **a** Gilead, Makir's son.
26:30 The Iezerites, named after their **a** Iezer.
26:30 The Helekites, named after their **a** Helek.
26:31 The Asrielites, named after their **a** Asriel.
26:31 The Shechemites, named after their **a** Shechem.
26:32 The Shemidaites, named after their **a** Shemida.
26:32 The Hepherites, named after their **a** Hepher.
26:35 The Shuthelahite clan, named after its **a** Shuthelah.
26:35 The Bekerite clan, named after its **a** Beker.
26:35 The Tahanite clan, named after its **a** Tahan.
26:36 The Eranites, named after their **a** Eran.
26:38 The Belaite clan, named after its **a** Bela.
26:38 The Ashbelite clan, named after its **a** Ashbel.
26:38 The Ahiramite clan, named after its **a** Ahiram.
26:39 The Shuphamite clan, named after its **a** Shupham.
26:39 The Huphamite clan, named after its **a** Hupham.
26:40 The Ardites, named after their **a** Ard.
26:40 The Naamites, named after their **a** Naaman.
26:42 The Shuhamite clan, named after its **a** Shuham.
26:44 The Imnite clan, named after its **a** Imnah.
26:44 The Ishvite clan, named after its **a** Ishvi.
26:44 The Beriite clan, named after its **a** Beriah.
26:45 The Heberites, named after their **a** Heber.
26:45 The Malkielites, named after their **a** Malkiel.
26:48 The Jahzeelite clan, named after its **a** Jahzeel.
26:48 The Gunite clan, named after its **a** Guni.
26:49 The Jezerite clan, named after its **a** Jezer.

26:49 The Shillemite clan, named after its **a** Shillem.
26:57 The Gershonite clan, named after its **a** Gershon.
26:57 The Kohathite clan, named after its **a** Kohath.
26:57 The Merarite clan, named after its **a** Merari.
26:58 of the Levites. Now Kohath was the **a** of Amram,
Dt 26: 5 'My **a** Jacob was a wandering Aramean who went
Jos 15:13 Hebron), which had been named after Anak's **a**.
19:47 They renamed the city Dan after their **a**.
21:11 (Arba was an **a** of Anak.)
24: 3 But I took your **a** Abraham from the land beyond
Jdg 18:29 They renamed the town Dan after their **a**.
Ru 4:12 woman who will be like those of our **a** Perez,
4:18 This is their family line beginning with their **a**
1Sa 2:28 I chose your **a** Aaron from among all his relatives
1Ki 15: 3 his God, as the heart of his **a** David had been.
15:11 in the LORD's sight, as his **a** David had done.
2Ki 14: 3 in the LORD's sight, but not like his **a** David.
16: 2 of the LORD his God, as his **a** David had done.
18: 3 the LORD's sight, just as his **a** David had done.
20: 5 what the LORD, the God of your **a** David, says:
22: 2 and followed the example of his **a** David.
1Ch 1:10 Cush was also the **a** of Nimrod, who was known
1:11 Mizraim was the **a** of the Ludites, Anamites,
1:13 oldest son was Sidon, the **a** of the Sidonians.
1:13 Canaan was also the **a** of the Hittites,
1:20 Joktan was the **a** of Almodad, Sheleph,
4: 4 (the firstborn of Ephrathah), the **a** of Bethlehem.
4: 8 and Koz, who became the **a** of Anub, Zobebah,
24:19 **a** Aaron in obedience to the commands of the
29:10 "O LORD, the God of our **a** Israel, may you be
2Ch 21:12 what the LORD, the God of your **a** David, says:
28: 1 the sight of the LORD, as his **a** David had done.
29: 2 the LORD's sight, just as his **a** David had done.
34: 2 and followed the example of his **a** David.
34: 3 Josiah began to seek the God of his **a** David.
Isa 9: 7 and justice from the throne of his **a** David.
38: 5 what the LORD, the God of your **a** David, says:
58:14 of the inheritance I promised to Jacob, your **a**.
Jer 35: 6 son of Recab, our **a**, gave us this command:
35:10 obeyed all the commands of Jehonadab, our **a**.
35:14 because their **a** Jehonadab told them not to.
35:16 The families of Recab have obeyed their **a**
35:18 You have obeyed your **a** Jehonadab in every
Mal 1: 2 "I showed my love for you by loving your **a**
Mk 11:10 Bless the coming kingdom of our **a** David!
Lk 1:32 And the Lord God will give him the throne of his **a**
1:73 the covenant he gave to our **a** Abraham.
Jn 4:12 are you greater than our **a** Jacob who gave us this
8:56 Your **a** Abraham rejoiced as he looked forward to
Ac 4:25 ago by the Holy Spirit through our **a** King David,
7: 2 Our glorious God appeared to our **a** Abraham in
Ro 9:10 This son was our **a** Isaac. When he grew up,
Heb 7: 9 paid a tithe to Melchizedek through their **a**
Jas 2:21 Don't you remember that our **a** Abraham was

ANCESTORS (338) [ANCESTOR]

Ge 25: 8 and he died at a ripe old age, joining his **a** in death.
25:17 died at the age of 137 and joined his **a** in death.
31:53 I call on the God of our **a**—the God of your
35:29 and he died at a ripe old age, joining his **a** in death.
43:23 "Your God, the God of your **a**, must have put it
46:34 as our **a** have been for many generations.'
47: 3 And they replied, "We are shepherds like our **a**.
47: 9 but I am still not nearly as old as many of my **a**."
47:30 take me out of Egypt and bury me beside my **a**."
48:21 will bring you again to Canaan, the land of your **a**.
49:25 May the God of your **a** help you;
49:26 May the blessings of your **a** / be greater than the
Ex 3: 6 Then he said, "I am the God of your **a**—the God
3:13 tell them, 'The God of your **a** has sent me to you,'
3:15 "Tell them, 'The LORD, the God of your **a**—
3:16 Tell them, 'The LORD, the God of your **a**—
4: 5 will realize that the LORD, the God of their **a**—
6:14 These are the **a** of clans from some of Israel's
6:25 These are the **a** of the Levite clans,
13: 5 This is the land he swore to give your **a**—a land
13:11 you into the land he swore to give your **a** long ago,
Lev 23:43 **a** had to live in shelters when I rescued them from
25:10 of you returns to the lands that belonged to your **a**
25:13 must return to the lands that belonged to your **a**.
26:39 because of their sins and the sins of their **a**.
26:40 and the sins of their **a** for betraying me and being
26:45 I will remember my ancient covenant with their **a**,
Nu 11:12 a baby—to the land you swore to give their **a**?
14:23 will never even see the land I swore to give their **a**.
20:15 and that our **a** went down to Egypt. We lived there
20:24 "The time has come for Aaron to join his **a** in
20:26 his son. Aaron will die there and join his **a**."
31: 2 After that, you will die and join your **a**."
32: 8 This is what your **a** did when I sent them from
Dt 1: 8 land the LORD swore to give to your **a** Abraham,
1:11 And may the LORD, the God of your **a**,
1:21 the LORD, the God of your **a**, has promised you.
1:35 live to see the good land I swore to give your **a**,
4: 1 land the LORD, the God of your **a**, is giving you.
4:31 forget the solemn covenant he made with your **a**.
4:37 Because he loved your **a**, he chose to bless their
5: 3 did not make this covenant long ago with our **a**,
6: 3 as the LORD, the God of your **a**, promised you.
6:10 into the land he swore to give your **a** Abraham,
6:18 that the LORD solemnly promised to give your **a**.
6:23 this land he had solemnly promised to give our **a**.
7: 8 he was keeping the oath he had sworn to your **a**.
7:12 love with you, as he solemnly promised your **a**.
7:13 you arrive in the land he swore to give your **a**,
8: 1 occupy the land the LORD swore to give your **a**.
8: 3 a food previously unknown to you and your **a**.
8:16 in the wilderness, a food unknown to your **a**.
8:18 does it to fulfill the covenant he made with your **a**.
9: 5 and to fulfill the oath he had sworn to your **a**
10:11 the people into the land I swore to give their **a**,
10:15 Yet the LORD chose your **a** as the objects of his
10:22 When your **a** went down into Egypt, there were
11: 9 life in the land the LORD swore to give to your **a**
11:21 in the land the LORD swore to give your **a**.
12: 1 land the LORD, the God of your **a**, is giving you.
13: 6 gods that neither you nor your **a** have known.
13:17 great nation, just as he solemnly promised your **a**.
19: 8 as he solemnly promised your **a**, and gives you all
19:14 markers your **a** set up to mark their property.
26: 3 brought me into the land he swore to give our **a**.'
26: 7 we cried out to the LORD, the God of our **a**.
26:15 and honey—just as you solemnly promised our **a**.'
27: 3 as the LORD, the God of your **a**, promised you.
28:11 good things in the land he swore to give your **a**—
28:36 crowned to a nation unknown to you and your **a**.
28:64 gods that neither you nor your **a** have known,
29:13 and as he swore to your **a** Abraham, Isaac,
29:25 the God of their **a**, when he brought them out of
30: 5 will return you to the land that belonged to your **a**,
30: 5 even more prosperous and numerous than your **a**!
30: 9 delight in being good to you as he was to your **a**.
30:20 land the LORD swore to give your **a** Abraham,
31: 7 into the land that the LORD swore to give their **a**.
31:16 to Moses, "You are about to die and join your **a**.
31:20 bring them into the land I swore to give their **a**—
32:17 recently arrived, / to gods their **a** had never feared.
32:50 must die there on the mountain and join your **a**,
32:50 your brother, died on Mount Hor and joined his **a**.
Jos 1: 6 to possess all the land I swore to give their **a**.
18: 3 the LORD, the God of your **a**, has given to you?
21:43 to Israel all the land he had sworn to give their **a**,
21:44 just as he had solemnly promised their **a**.
22:28 'Look at this copy of the LORD's altar that our **a**
24: 2 Your **a**, including Terah, the father of Abraham
24: 6 But when your **a** arrived at the Red Sea,
24:14 Put away forever the idols your **a** worshiped when
24:15 Would you prefer the gods your **a** served beyond
24:17 and our **a** from slavery in the land of Egypt.
Jdg 2: 1 of Egypt into this land that I swore to give your **a**,
2:12 They abandoned the LORD, the God of their **a**,
2:17 quickly they turned away from the path of their **a**,
2:20 have violated the covenant I made with their **a**
2:22 or not they would obey the LORD as their **a** did."
3: 4 the LORD had given to their **a** through Moses.
6:13 And where are all the miracles our **a** told us about?
1Sa 2:27 "Didn't I reveal myself to your **a** when the people
12: 6 "He brought your **a** out of the land of Egypt.
12: 7 things the LORD has done for you and your **a**.
12:15 will be as heavy upon you as it was upon your **a**.
1Ki 8:21 with our **a** when he brought them out of Egypt."
8:34 and return them to this land you gave their **a**.
8:40 as long as they live in the land you gave to our **a**.
8:48 and pray toward the land you gave to their **a**,
8:53 For when you brought our **a** out of Egypt,
8:57 LORD our God be with us as he was with our **a**;
8:58 laws, and regulations that he gave our **a**.
9: 9 who brought their **a** out of Egypt, and they
13:22 body will not be buried in the grave of your **a**."
14:15 of Israel from this good land that he gave their **a**
14:22 their sin, for it was even worse than that of their **a**.
14:31 he was buried among his **a** in the City of David.
15:12 the land and removed all the idols his **a** had made.
15:24 he was buried with his **a** in the City of David.
19: 4 "Take my life, for I am no better than my **a**."
21: 3 the inheritance that was passed down by my **a**."
22:40 When Ahab died, he was buried among his **a**.
22:50 he was buried with his **a** in the City of David.
2Ki 8:24 he was buried with his **a** in the City of David.
9:28 where they buried him with his **a** in the City of
10:35 Jehu died, he was buried with his **a** in Samaria.
12:21 Joash was buried with his **a** in the City of David.
13: 9 he was buried in Samaria with his **a**.
13:13 Jehoash died, he was buried with his **a** in Samaria.
14:16 Jehoash died, he was buried with his **a** in Samaria.
14:20 and he was buried with his **a** in the City of David.
14:29 he was buried with his **a**, the kings of Israel.
15: 7 he was buried near his **a** in the City of David.
15: 9 was evil in the LORD's sight, as his **a** had done.
15:38 he was buried with his **a** in the City of David.
16:20 he was buried with his **a** in the City of David.
17:13 in the whole law that I commanded your **a**
17:14 They were as stubborn as their **a** and refused to
17:15 and the covenant he had made with their **a**,
20:17 all the treasures stored up by your **a**—will be
21: 8 them into exile from this land that I gave their **a**."
21:15 and have angered me ever since their **a** came out of
21:22 He abandoned the LORD, the God of his **a**,
22:13 because our **a** have not obeyed the words in this
23:32 evil in the LORD's sight, just as his **a** had done.
23:37 evil in the LORD's sight, just as his **a** had done.
1Ch 5:25 and violated their covenant with the God of their **a**.
9:19 just as their **a** had guarded the Tabernacle in the
9:22 David and Samuel the seer had appointed their **a**
12:17 then may the God of our **a** see and judge you."
28: 9 my son, get to know the God of your **a**.
29:15 and strangers in the land as our **a** were before us.
29:18 the God of our **a** Abraham, Isaac, and Israel,
29:20 the God of their **a**, and they bowed low and knelt
2Ch 6:25 and return them to this land you gave their **a**.
6:31 as long as they live in the land you gave to our **a**.
6:38 and pray toward the land you gave to their **a**,
7:22 the God of their **a**, who brought them out of Egypt,
11:16 offer sacrifices to the LORD, the God of their **a**.
13:12 the God of your **a**, for you will not succeed!"
13:18 they trusted in the LORD, the God of their **a**.
14: 4 the God of their **a**, and to obey his law and his
15:12 the God of their **a**, with all their heart and soul.
19: 4 people to return to the LORD, the God of their **a**.
20: 6 He prayed, "O LORD, God of our **a**, you alone
20:10 You would not let our **a** invade those nations when
20:33 themselves to following the God of their **a**.
21: 1 he was buried with his **a** in the City of David.
21:10 had abandoned the LORD, the God of his **a**.
21:19 honor him at his funeral as they had done for his **a**.
24:18 the God of their **a**, and they worshiped Asherah
24:24 the God of their **a**, so judgment was executed
25:28 and he was buried with his **a** in the City of David.
28: 6 had abandoned the LORD, the God of their **a**.
28: 9 and said, "The LORD, the God of your **a**,
28:25 aroused the anger of the LORD, the God of his **a**.
29: 5 the Temple of the LORD, the God of your **a**.
29: 6 Our **a** were unfaithful and did what was evil in the
30: 7 Do not be like your **a** and relatives who abandoned
30: 7 the God of their **a**, and became an object of
30:19 decide to follow the LORD, the God of their **a**,
30:22 their sins to the LORD, the God of their **a**.
32:15 been able to rescue his people from me or my **a**.
33: 8 them into exile from this land that I gave their **a**."
33:12 his God and cried out humbly to the God of his **a**.
34:21 because our **a** have not obeyed the word of the
34:32 their covenant with God, the God of their **a**.
34:33 not turn away from the LORD, the God of their **a**.
35: 4 duty according to the family divisions of your **a**,
36:15 The LORD, the God of their **a**, repeatedly sent his
Ezr 5:12 But because our **a** angered the God of heaven,
7:27 Praise the LORD, the God of our **a**, who made
8:28 freewill offering to the LORD, the God of our **a**.
10:11 the God of your **a**, and do what he demands.
Ne 2: 3 For the city where my **a** are buried is in ruins,
2: 5 send me to Judah to rebuild the city where my **a**
9: 2 confessed their own sins and the sins of their **a**.
9: 9 saw the sufferings and sorrows of our **a** in Egypt,
9:12 You led our **a** by a pillar of cloud during the day
9:16 But our **a** were a proud and stubborn lot, and they
9:22 "Then you helped our **a** conquer great kingdoms
9:23 them into the land you had promised to their **a**.
9:25 Our **a** captured fortified cities and fertile land.
9:32 and **a** from the days when the kings of Assyria first
9:34 and **a** did not obey your law or listen to your
9:36 here in the land of plenty that you gave to our **a**!
13:18 Wasn't it enough that your **a** did this sort of thing,
Job 8: 8 Pay attention to the experience of our **a**.
Ps 22: 4 Our **a** trusted in you, / and you rescued them.
39:12 traveler passing through, / as my **a** were before me.
44: 1 heard it with our own ears—/ our **a** have told us
44: 2 and gave all the land to our **a**; / you crushed their
enemies, / setting our **a** free.
78: 3 and know, / stories our **a** handed down to us.
78: 5 he gave his law to Israel. / He commanded our **a**
78: 8 Then they will not be like their **a**—/ stubborn,
78:12 the miracles he did for their **a** in Egypt,
95: 9 For there your **a** tried my patience; / they courted
106: 6 Both we and our **a** have sinned. / We have done
106: 7 Our **a** in Egypt / were not impressed by the
106:28 Then our **a** joined in the worship of Baal at Peor;
109:14 May the LORD never forget the sins of his **a**;
Pr 22:28 the ancient boundary markers set up by your **a**.
Isa 19:11 dare tell Pharaoh about their long line of wise **a**?
39: 6 all the treasures stored up by your **a**—will be
43:27 the very beginning, your **a** sinned against me—
51: 2 Yes, think about your **a** Abraham and Sarah,
64:11 beautiful Temple where our **a** praised you has been
65: 7 both for their own sins and for those of their **a**,"
Jer 2: 5 "What sin did your **a** find in me that led them to
3:18 They will return to the land I gave their **a** as an
3:24 we have watched as everything our **a** worked for—
3:25 and our **a** have always sinned against the LORD
7: 7 in this land that I gave to your **a** to keep forever.
7:14 for help, this place that I gave to you and your **a**.
7:22 When I led your **a** out of Egypt, it was not burnt
7:25 From the day your **a** left Egypt until now, I have
7:26 been stubborn and sinful—even worse than their **a**.
9:14 the images of Baal, as their **a** taught them.
11: 4 For I said to your **a** when I brought them out of
11: 5 so I could keep my promise to your **a** to give you a
11: 6 and say, 'Remember the covenant your **a** made,
11: 7 For I solemnly warned your **a** when I brought them
11: 8 But your **a** did not pay any attention; they would
11:10 have both broken the covenant I made with their **a**.
14:20 we confess our wickedness and that of our **a**,
16:11 It is because your **a** were unfaithful to me.
16:12 And you are even worse than your **a**!
16:13 land where you and your **a** have never been.
16:15 will bring them back to this land that I gave their **a**.
16:19 will come to you and say, "Our **a** were foolish,
17:22 make it a holy day. I gave this command to your **a**,
19: 4 by their **a**, or by the kings of Judah.
23:27 just as their **a** did by worshiping the idols of Baal.
23:39 along with this city that I gave to you and your **a**.
24:10 land of Israel, which I gave to them and their **a**."
25: 5 that the LORD gave to you and your **a** forever.
30: 3 bring them home to this land that I gave to their **a**,
31:32 I made with their **a** when I took them by the hand
32:22 land that you had promised their **a** long before—
32:23 Our **a** came and conquered it and lived in it,
34: 5 in your memory, just as they did for your **a**.
34:13 I made a covenant with your **a** long ago when I
35:15 in peace here in the land I gave to you and your **a**.
44: 3 gods that neither they nor you nor any of your **a**

44: 9 Have you forgotten the sins of your a, the sins of
44:10 the decrees I gave to you and your a before you.
44:17 just as we and our a did before us, and as our kings
44:21 the LORD did not know that you and your a,
50: 7 the LORD, their place of rest, the hope of their a.'
La 5: 7 It was our a who sinned, but they died before the
Eze 2: 3 Their a have rebelled against me from the
20: 4 how loathsome the actions of their a really were.
20:24 Sabbath days and longing for the idols of their a.
20:27 Your a continued to blaspheme and betray me,
20:30 Do you plan to pollute yourselves just as your a
20:36 I will judge you there just as I did your a in the
20:42 brought you home to the land I promised your a,
36:28 will live in Israel, the land I gave your a long ago.
37:25 They will live in the land of Israel where their a
47:14 I swore that I would give this land to your a,
Da 2:23 I thank and praise you, God of my a, / for you have
9: 6 and princes and a and to all the people of the land.
9: 8 and a are covered with shame because we have
9:16 because of our sins and the sins of our a.
11:37 He will have no regard for the gods of his a,
11:38 a god his a never knew—and lavish on him gold,
Hos 9:10 When I saw your a, it was like seeing the first ripe
Am 2: 4 led astray by the same lies that deceived their a.
7: 9 The pagan shrines of your a and the temples of
Mic 7:20 as you promised with an oath to our a Abraham
Zec 1: 2 "I, the LORD, was very angry with your a.
1: 4 Do not be like your a who would not listen when
1: 5 "Your a and their prophets are now long dead.
1: 6 my servants the prophets happened to your a,
7:11 "Your a would not listen to this message.
8:14 I did not change my mind when your a angered me
Mal 2:10 to each other, violating the covenant of our a?
3: 7 Ever since the days of your a, you have scorned
Mt 1: 1 This is a record of the a of Jesus the Messiah,
23:29 For you build tombs for the prophets your a killed
23:29 and decorate the graves of the godly people your a
Lk 1:55 For he promised our a—Abraham and his
1:72 He has been merciful to our a / by remembering
6:23 prophets were also treated that way by your a.
6:26 the crowds, / for their a also praised false prophets.
11:47 For you build tombs for the very prophets your a
11:48 You agree with your a that what they did was
Jn 4:20 here at Mount Gerizim, where our a worshiped?"
6:31 our a ate manna while they journeyed through the
6:49 Your a ate manna in the wilderness, but they all
6:58 bread will live forever and not die as your a did,
Ac 3:13 the God of all our a who has brought glory to his
3:25 included in the covenant God promised to your a.
5:30 The God of our a raised Jesus from the dead after
7:11 There was great misery for our a, as they ran out of
7:32 'I am the God of your a—the God of Abraham,
7:39 "But our a rejected Moses and wanted to return to
7:44 "Our a carried the Tabernacle with them through
7:51 the Holy Spirit? But your a did, and so do you!
7:52 Name one prophet your a didn't persecute!
13:17 "The God of this nation of Israel chose our a
13:32 God's promise to our a has come true in our own
15:10 a yoke that neither we nor our a were able to bear?
22:14 'The God of our a has chosen you to know his will
23: 6 "Brothers, I am a Pharisee, as were all my a!
24:14 I worship the God of our a, and I firmly believe the
26: 6 to the fulfillment of God's promise made to our a.
28:17 nothing against our people or the customs of our a.
28:25 "The Holy Spirit was right when he said to our a
Ro 9: 5 Their a were great people of God, and Christ
15: 8 that God is true to the promises he made to their a.
1Co 10: 1 what happened to our a in the wilderness long ago.
2Ti 1: 3 I serve with a clear conscience, just as my a did.
Heb 1: 1 and in many ways to our a through the prophets.
3: 9 There your a tried my patience, / even though they
7: 3 no record of his father or mother or any of his a—
8: 9 I made with their a / when I took them by the hand
1Pe 1:18 you from the empty life you inherited from your a.

ANCESTORS' (2) [ANCESTOR]

Ex 28:10 naming all the tribes in the order of their a births.
Ezr 4:15 We suggest that you search your a records,

ANCESTRAL (20) [ANCESTOR]

Lev 25:34 may never be sold. It is their permanent a property.
25:41 and they will return to their clan and a property.
27:16 "If you dedicate to the LORD a piece of your a
27:22 but which is not part of your a property,
Nu 1:44 of Israel, all listed according to their a descent.
13: 2 Send one leader from each of the twelve a tribes."
17: 2 wooden staffs, one from each of Israel's a tribes,
17: 3 for there must be one staff for the leader of each a
26:55 and define the inheritance of each a tribe by means
33:54 the land will be divided among your a tribes.
36: 4 causing it to be lost forever to our a tribe."
36: 6 they like, as long as it is within their own a tribe.
36: 8 so that all the Israelites will keep their a property.
36:12 their inheritance of land remained within their a
1Ch 6:19 the Levite clans, listed according to their a descent:
7: 2 Each of them was the leader of an a clan.
7:40 descendants of Asher was the head of an a clan.
8:28 These were the leaders of the a clans, and they
2Ch 17:14 His army was enrolled according to a clans.
Jer 48:45 a fire comes from Heshbon, King Sihon's a home,

ANCESTRY (2) [ANCESTOR]

Nu 1:18 All the people were registered according to their a
Ne 13: 3 all those of mixed a were immediately expelled

ANCHOR (3) [ANCHORED, ANCHORS]

Ac 27:13 So they pulled up a and sailed along close to shore.
27:17 so they lowered the sea a and were thus driven
Heb 6:19 is like a strong and trustworthy a for our souls.

ANCHORED (2) [ANCHOR]

Ps 119:61 to drag me into sin, / but I am firmly a to your law.
Mk 6:53 on the other side of the lake, they a the boat

ANCHORS (3) [ANCHOR]

Ac 27:29 so they threw out four a from the stern and prayed
27:30 though they were going to put out a from the prow.
27:40 So they cut off the a and left them in the sea.

ANCIENT (38)

Lev 26:45 I will remember my a covenant with their
Nu 13:22 (The a town of Hebron was founded seven years
21:27 For this reason the a poets wrote this about him:
Dt 33:15 with the finest crops of the a mountains,
Jdg 5:21 River swept them away—/ that a river, the Kishon.
1Sa 27: 8 near Shur, along the road to Egypt, since a times.
1Ch 4:22 These names all come from a records.
Est 9:26 because it is the a word for casting lots.)
Ps 24: 7 Open up, a gates! / Open up, a doors,
24: 9 Open up, a gates! / Open up, a doors,
68:33 Sing to the one who rides across the a heavens,
74: 2 Remember that we are the people you chose in a
Pr 22:28 the a boundary markers set up by your ancestors.
23:10 orphans by moving the a boundary markers,
Isa 44: 7 Let them do as I have done since a times.
61: 4 They will rebuild the a ruins, repairing cities long
Jer 5:15 "It is a mighty nation, an a nation, a people whose
18:15 They have stumbled off the a highways of good,
28: 8 The a prophets who preceded you and me spoke
La 1: 7 Jerusalem remembers her a splendor.
Eze 29:21 "And the day will come when I will cause the a
36: 2 saying, 'Aha! Now the a heights belong to us!'
Da 7: 9 were put in place and the A One sat down to judge.
7:13 He approached the A One and was led into his
7:22 until the A One came and judged in favor of the
Mt 5:12 the a prophets were persecuted, too.
Mk 6:15 Others thought Jesus was the a prophet Elijah.
7: 3 cupped hands, as required by their a traditions.
Lk 2: 4 had to go to Bethlehem in Judea, David's a home.
6:23 the a prophets were also treated that way by your
9: 8 or some other a prophet risen from the dead."
9:19 and others say you are one of the other a prophets
18:31 all the predictions of the a prophets concerning the
Ac 15: 1 "Unless you keep the a Jewish custom of
2Pe 2: 5 And God did not spare the a world—except for
Rev 12: 9 the a serpent called the Devil, or Satan, the one

ANCLE, ANCLES [KJV] See ANKLE, ANKLES

AND (27934) See Index of Articles, Etc.

ANDREW (13) [ANDREW'S]

Mt 4:18 Simon, also called Peter, and A—fishing with a
10: 2 (also called Peter), / then A (Peter's brother),
Mk 1:16 he saw Simon and his brother, A, fishing with a
3:18 A, / Philip, / Bartholomew, / Matthew, / Thomas,
13: 3 and A came to him privately and asked him,
Lk 6:14 (he also called him Peter), / A (Peter's brother),
Jn 1:40 A, Simon Peter's brother, was one of these men
1:41 The first thing A did was to find his brother,
1:42 Then A brought Simon to meet Jesus.
1:44 was from Bethsaida, A and Peter's hometown.
6: 8 Then A, Simon Peter's brother, spoke up.
12:22 Philip told A about it, and they went together to
Ac 1:13 Peter, / John, / James, / A, / Philip, / Thomas,

ANDREW'S (1) [ANDREW]

Mk 1:29 they went over to Simon and A home, and James

ANDRONICUS (1)

Ro 16: 7 Then there are A and Junia, my relatives,

ANEM (1)

1Ch 6:73 Ramoth, and A, with their pasturelands.

ANER (3)

Ge 14:13 Mamre and his relatives, Eshcol and A,
14:24 the goods to my allies—A, Eshcol, and Mamre."
1Ch 6:70 A and Bileam, each with its pasturelands.

ANETHOTHITE, ANETOTHITE [KJV] See ANATHOTH

ANEW (2) [NEW]

Ps 78: 7 So each generation can set its hope a on God,
Eph 2:10 He has created us a in Christ Jesus, so that we can

ANGEL (232) [ANGEL'S, ANGELIC, ANGELS, ARCHANGEL, ARCHANGELS]

ANGEL OF GOD (10) Ge 21:17; 31:11; Ex 14:19; Jdg 6:20; 13:9; 1Sa 29:9; 2Sa 14:17,20; 19:27; Ac 10:3

ANGEL OF THE LORD (11) Mt 1:20,24; 2:13,19; 28:2; Lk 1:11; 2:9; Ac 5:19; 8:26; 12:7,23

ANGEL OF THE LORD* (52) Ge 16:7,9; 22:11,15; Ex 3:2; Nu 22:22,23,24,25,26,31,32,34,35; Jdg 2:1,4; 5:23; 6:11,12,21,21,22,22; 13:3,13,15,16,16,17,18,20,21; 2Sa 24:16; 1Ki 19:7; 2Ki 1:3,15; 19:35; 1Ch 21:12,15,16,18,30; Ps 34:7; 35:5,6; Isa 37:36; Zec 1:11,12; 3:1,5,6; 12:8

Ge 16: 7 The a of the LORD found Hagar beside a desert
16: 8 The a said to her, "Hagar, Sarai's servant,
16: 9 Then the a of the LORD said, "Return to your
16:10 The a added, "I will give you more descendants
16:11 And the a also said, "You are now pregnant
19:21 "All right," the a said, "I will grant your request.
21:17 and the a of God called to Hagar from the sky,
22:11 At that moment the a of the LORD shouted to
22:12 "Lay down the knife," the a said. "Do not hurt
22:15 Then the a of the LORD called again to Abraham
24: 7 He will send his a ahead of you, and he will see to
24:40 will send his a with you and will make your
31:11 in my dream, the a of God said to me, 'Jacob!'
31:12 The a said, 'Look, and you will see that only the
48:16 and the a who has kept me from all harm—may he
Ex 3: 2 the a of the LORD appeared to him as a blazing
14:19 Then the a of God, who had been leading the
23:20 I am sending my a before you to lead you safely to
23:23 For my a will go before you and bring you into the
32:34 Look! My a will lead the way before you!
33: 2 And I will send an a before you to drive out the
Nu 20:16 and sent an a who brought us out of Egypt.
22:22 so he sent the a of the LORD to stand in the road
22:23 Balaam's donkey suddenly saw the a of the
22:24 Then the a of the LORD stood at a place where
22:25 When the donkey saw the a of the LORD
22:26 Then the a of the LORD moved farther down the
22:27 This time when the donkey saw the a, it lay down
22:31 and he saw the a of the LORD standing in the
22:32 the a of the LORD demanded. "I have come to
22:34 Then Balaam confessed to the a of the LORD,
22:35 But the a of the LORD told him, "Go with these
Jdg 2: 1 The a of the LORD went up from Gilgal to
2: 4 When the a of the LORD finished speaking,
5:23 of Meroz be cursed,' said the a of the LORD.
6:11 Then the a of the LORD came and sat beneath the
6:12 The a of the LORD appeared to him and said,
6:19 he brought them out and presented them to the a,
6:20 The a of God said to him, "Place the meat
6:21 Then the a of the LORD touched the meat
6:21 had brought. And the a of the LORD disappeared.
6:22 When Gideon realized that it was the a of the
6:22 I have seen the a of the LORD face to face!"
13: 3 The a of the LORD appeared to Manoah's wife
13: 9 and the a of God appeared once again to his wife
13:13 The a of the LORD replied, "Be sure your wife
13:15 Then Manoah said to the a of the LORD,
13:16 "I will stay," the a of the LORD replied, "but I
13:16 (Manoah didn't realize it was the a of the
13:17 Then Manoah asked the a of the LORD,
13:18 you ask my name?" the a of the LORD replied.
13:20 the sky, the a of the LORD ascended in the fire.
13:21 The a did not appear again to Manoah and his
13:21 Manoah finally realized it was the a of the
1Sa 29: 9 as I'm concerned, you're as perfect as an a of God.
2Sa 14:17 I know that you are like an a of God and can
14:20 But you are as wise as an a of God, and you
19:27 But I know that you are like an a of God, so do
22:11 Mounted on a mighty a, he flew, / soaring on the
24:16 But as the death a was preparing to destroy
24:16 the LORD relented and said to the a, "Stop!
24:16 At that moment the a of the LORD was by the
24:17 When David saw the a, he said to the LORD,
1Ki 13:18 And an a gave me this message from the LORD:
19: 5 an a touched him and told him, "Get up and eat!"
19: 7 Then the a of the LORD came again and touched
2Ki 1: 3 But the a of the LORD told Elijah, who was from
1:15 Then the a of the LORD said to Elijah, "Don't be
19:35 That night the a of the LORD went out to the
1Ch 21:12 or three days of severe plague as the a of the
21:15 And God sent an a to destroy Jerusalem. But just as the a was preparing to destroy it,
21:15 the LORD relented and said to the death a,
21:15 At that moment the a of the LORD was standing
21:16 and saw the a of the LORD standing between
21:18 Then the a of the LORD told Gad to instruct
21:20 wheat at the time, turned and saw the a there.
21:27 Then the LORD spoke to the a, who put the
21:30 by the drawn sword of the a of the LORD.
2Ch 32:21 And the LORD sent an a who destroyed the
Ps 18:10 Mounted on a mighty a, he flew, / soaring on the
34: 7 For the a of the LORD guards all who fear him,
35: 5 in the wind—/ a wind sent by the a of the LORD.
35: 6 with the a of the LORD pursuing them.
89: 6 What mightiest a is anything like the LORD?
Isa 37:36 That night the a of the LORD went out to the
Da 3:28 He sent his a to rescue his servants who trusted in
6:22 My God sent his a to shut the lions' mouths
Hos 12: 4 Yes, he wrestled with the a and won. He wept
Zec 1: 9 I asked the a who was talking with me, "My lord,
1: 9 horses for?" "I will show you," the a replied.
1:11 Then the other riders reported to the a of the
1:12 the a of the LORD prayed this prayer:
1:13 and comforting words to the a who talked with me.
1:14 Then the a said to me, "Shout this message for all
1:19 I asked the a who was talking with me. He replied,
1:21 The a replied, "The blacksmiths have come to
2: 3 Then the a who was with me went to meet a
2: 3 to meet a second a who was coming toward him.
2: 4 The other a said, "Hurry, and say to that young
3: 1 Then the a showed me Jeshua the high priest

3: 1 high priest standing before the **a** of the LORD.
3: 3 clothing was filthy as he stood there before the **a**.
3: 4 So the **a** said to the others standing there,
3: 5 and dressed him in new clothes while the **a** of the
3: 6 Then the **a** of the LORD spoke very solemnly to
4: 1 Then the **a** who had been talking with me returned
4: 4 Then I asked the **a**, "What are these, my lord?
4: 5 the **a** asked. "No, my lord," I replied.
4: 11 Then I asked the **a**, "What are these two olive
5: 2 "What do you see?" the **a** asked. "I see a flying
5: 5 Then the **a** who was talking with me came forward
5: 8 The **a** said, "The woman's name is Wickedness,"
5: 10 "Where are they taking the basket?" I asked the **a**.
6: 4 my lord?" I asked the **a** who was talking with me.
12: 8 like the **a** of the LORD who goes before them!
Mt 1: 20 and an **a** of the Lord appeared to him in a dream.
1: 20 "Joseph, son of David," the **a** said, "do not be
1: 24 he did what the **a** of the Lord commanded.
2: 13 an **a** of the Lord appeared to Joseph in a dream.
2: 13 Egypt with the child and his mother," the **a** said.
2: 19 an **a** of the Lord appeared in a dream to Joseph in
28: 2 because an **a** of the Lord came down from heaven
28: 5 Then the **a** spoke to the women. "Don't be
Mk 16: 6 but the **a** said, "Do not be so surprised. You are
Lk 1: 11 Zechariah was in the sanctuary when an **a** of the
1: 13 But the **a** said, "Don't be afraid, Zechariah!
1: 18 Zechariah said to the **a**, "How can I know this will
1: 19 Then the **a** said, "I am Gabriel! I stand in the very
1: 26 God sent the **a** Gabriel to Nazareth, a village in
1: 29 Mary tried to think what the **a** could mean.
1: 30 "Don't be frightened, Mary," the **a** told her,
1: 34 Mary asked the **a**, "But how can I have a baby?
1: 35 The **a** replied, "The Holy Spirit will come upon
1: 38 you have said come true." And then the **a** left.
2: 9 Suddenly, an **a** of the Lord appeared among them,
2: 10 but the **a** reassured them. "Don't be afraid!"
2: 13 the **a** was joined by a vast host of others—
2: 17 and what the **a** had said to them about this child.
2: 20 they had seen the child, just as the **a** had said.
2: 21 the name given him by the **a** even before he was
22: 43 Then an **a** from heaven appeared and strengthened
Jn 12: 29 while others declared an **a** had spoken to him.
Ac 5: 19 But an **a** of the Lord came at night,
7: 30 an **a** appeared to Moses in the flame of a burning
7: 35 Through the **a** who appeared to him in the burning
7: 38 and the **a** who gave him life-giving words on
8: 26 As for Philip, an **a** of the Lord said to him,
10: 3 he had a vision in which he saw an **a** of God
coming toward him. "Cornelius!" the **a** said.
10: 4 "What is it, sir?" he asked the **a**. And the **a** replied,
10: 7 As soon as the **a** was gone, Cornelius called two of
10: 22 A holy **a** instructed him to send for you so you can
11: 13 He told us how an **a** had appeared to him in his
12: 7 in the cell, and an **a** of the Lord stood before Peter.
12: 7 The **a** tapped him on the side to awaken him
12: 8 Then the **a** told him, "Get dressed and put on your
coat and follow me," the **a** ordered.
12: 9 So Peter left the cell, following the **a**. But all the
12: 10 down the street, and then the **a** suddenly left him.
12: 11 "The Lord has sent his **a** and saved me from
12: 15 she insisted, they decided, "It must be his **a**."
12: 23 an **a** of the Lord struck Herod with a sickness,
23: 9 "Perhaps a spirit or an **a** spoke to him."
27: 23 For last night an **a** of the God to whom I belong
1Co 10: 10 for that is why God sent his **a** of death to destroy
2Co 11: 14 Even Satan can disguise himself as an **a** of light.
Gal 1: 8 Even if an **a** comes from heaven and preaches any
4: 14 and cared for me as though I were an **a** from God
Heb 1: 5 For God never said to any **a** what he said to Jesus:
1: 13 And God never said to an **a**, as he did to his Son,
11: 28 so that the **a** of death would not kill their firstborn
Rev 1: 1 An **a** was sent to God's servant John so that John
2: 1 "Write this letter to the **a** of the church in Ephesus.
2: 8 "Write this letter to the **a** of the church in Smyrna.
2: 12 "Write this letter to the **a** of the church in
2: 18 "Write this letter to the **a** of the church in
3: 1 "Write this letter to the **a** of the church in Sardis.
3: 7 "Write this letter to the **a** of the church in
3: 14 "Write this letter to the **a** of the church in
5: 2 And I saw a strong **a**, who shouted with a loud
7: 2 And I saw another **a** coming from the east,
8: 3 Then another **a** with a gold incense burner came
8: 4 ascended up to God from the altar where the **a** had
8: 5 Then the **a** filled the incense burner with fire from
8: 7 The first **a** blew his trumpet, and hail and fire
8: 8 Then the second **a** blew his trumpet, and a great
8: 10 Then the third **a** blew his trumpet, and a great
8: 12 Then the fourth **a** blew his trumpet, and one-third
9: 1 Then the fifth **a** blew his trumpet, and I saw a star
9: 11 Their king is the **a** from the bottomless pit;
9: 13 Then the sixth **a** blew his trumpet, and I heard a
9: 14 And the voice spoke to the sixth **a** who held the
10: 1 Then I saw another mighty **a** coming down from
10: 5 Then the mighty **a** standing on the sea and on the
10: 7 But when the seventh **a** blows his trumpet,
10: 8 and take the unrolled scroll from the **a** who is
10: 10 So I took the little scroll from the hands of the **a**,
11: 15 Then the seventh **a** blew his trumpet, and there
14: 6 And I saw another **a** flying through the heavens,
14: 8 Then another **a** followed him through the skies,
14: 9 Then a third **a** followed them, shouting,
14: 15 Then an **a** came from the Temple and called out in
14: 17 another **a** came from the Temple in heaven,
14: 18 Then another **a**, who has power to destroy the
14: 18 world with fire, shouted to the **a** with the sickle,
14: 19 So the **a** swung his sickle on the earth and loaded
16: 2 So the first **a** left the Temple and poured out his
16: 3 Then the second **a** poured out his bowl on the sea,
16: 4 Then the third **a** poured out his bowl on the rivers
16: 5 And I heard the **a** who had authority over all water
16: 8 Then the fourth **a** poured out his bowl on the sun,
16: 10 Then the fifth **a** poured out his bowl on the throne
16: 12 Then the sixth **a** poured out his bowl on the great
16: 17 Then the seventh **a** poured out his bowl into the
17: 3 So the **a** took me in spirit into the wilderness.
17: 7 "Why are you so amazed?" the **a** asked. "I will
17: 15 And the **a** said to me, "The waters where the
18: 1 After all this I saw another **a** come down from
18: 21 Then a mighty **a** picked up a boulder as large as a
19: 9 And the **a** said, "Write this: Blessed are those who
19: 17 Then I saw an **a** standing in the sun, shouting to
20: 1 Then I saw an **a** come down from heaven with the
20: 3 The **a** threw him into the bottomless pit, which he
21: 15 The **a** who talked to me held in his hand a gold
21: 17 and found them to be 216 feet thick (the **a** used a
22: 1 And the **a** showed me a pure river with the water
22: 6 Then the **a** said to me, "These words are
22: 6 has sent his **a** to tell you what will happen
22: 8 I fell down to worship the **a** who showed them to
22: 16 have sent my **a** to give you this message for the

ANGEL'S (3) [ANGEL]

Zec 3: 1 Satan was there at the **a** right hand,
Mt 28: 8 to find the disciples to give them the **a** message.
Ac 6: 15 because his face became as bright as an **a**.

ANGELIC (4) [ANGEL]

Ge 3: 24 the LORD God stationed mighty **a** beings to the
Dt 32: 8 the peoples / according to the number of **a** beings.
Ps 89: 7 The highest **a** powers stand in awe of God.
Eze 28: 14 and anointed you as the mighty **a** guardian.

ANGELS (110) [ANGEL]

Ge 19: 1 That evening the two **a** came to the entrance of the
19: 10 But the two **a** reached out and pulled Lot in
19: 12 the **a** asked. "Get them out of this place—
19: 15 At dawn the next morning the **a** became insistent.
19: 16 the **a** seized his hand and the hands of his wife
19: 17 "Run for your lives!" the **a** warned. "Do not stop
28: 12 And he saw the **a** of God going up and down on it.
32: 1 on their way again, **a** of God came to meet him.
Dt 32: 43 O heavens, / and let all the **a** of God worship him,
Jdg 13: 6 He was like one of God's **a**, terrifying to look at.
Ne 9: 6 to everything, and all the **a** of heaven worship you.
Job 1: 6 One day the **a** came to present themselves before
2: 1 One day the **a** came again to present themselves
4: 18 "If God cannot trust his own **a** and has charged
5: 1 You may turn to the **a**, but they give you no help.
15: 15 Why, God doesn't even trust the **a**!
33: 22 are at death's door; the **a** of death wait for them.
38: 7 stars sang together and all the **a** shouted for joy?
Ps 29: 1 Give honor to the LORD, you **a**; / give honor to
78: 25 They ate the food of **a**! / God gave them all they
78: 49 dispatched against them / a band of destroying **a**.
89: 5 myriads of **a** will praise you for your faithfulness.
91: 11 For he orders his **a** / to protect you wherever you
103: 20 Praise the LORD, you **a** of his, / you mighty
103: 21 Yes, praise the LORD, you armies of **a**
148: 2 Praise him, all his **a**! / Praise him, all the armies of
Isa 24: 21 In that day the LORD will punish the fallen **a** in
Da 4: 35 among the **a** of heaven / and with those who live
7: 10 Millions of **a** ministered to him, and a hundred
Mt 4: 6 Scriptures say, / 'He orders his **a** to protect you.
4: 11 Devil went away, and **a** came and cared for Jesus.
13: 39 the end of the world, and the harvesters are the **a**.
13: 41 I, the Son of Man, will send my **a**, and they will
13: 49 The **a** will come and separate the wicked people
16: 27 will come in the glory of my Father with his **a**
18: 10 For I tell you that in heaven their **a** are always in
22: 30 be married. They will be like the **a** in heaven.
24: 31 And he will send forth his **a** with the sound of a
24: 36 not even the **a** in heaven or the Son himself.
25: 31 and all the **a** with him, then he will sit upon his
26: 53 ask my Father for thousands of **a** to protect us,
Mk 1: 13 among the wild animals, and **a** took care of him.
8: 38 I return in the glory of my Father with the holy **a**."
12: 25 be married. They will be like the **a** in heaven.
13: 27 And he will send forth his **a** to gather together his
13: 32 not even the **a** in heaven or the Son himself.
Lk 2: 15 When the **a** had returned to heaven, the shepherds
2: 20 and praising God for what the **a** had told them,
4: 10 'He orders his **a** to protect and guard you.
9: 26 and in the glory of the Father and the holy **a**.
12: 8 that person in the presence of God's **a**.
12: 9 on earth, I will deny that person before God's **a**.
15: 10 there is joy in the presence of God's **a** when even
16: 22 and was carried by the **a** to be with Abraham.
20: 36 never die again. In these respects they are like **a**.
24: 23 and they had seen **a** who told them Jesus is alive!
Jn 1: 51 will all see heaven open and the **a** of God going up
20: 12 She saw two white-robed **a** sitting at the head
20: 13 "Why are you crying?" the **a** asked her.
Ac 7: 53 though you received it from the hands of **a**."
23: 8 say there is no resurrection or **a** or spirits,
Ro 8: 38 and life can't. The **a** can't, and the demons can't.
1Co 4: 9 to the entire world—to people and **a** alike.
6: 3 Don't you realize that we Christians will judge **a**?
11: 10 as a sign of authority because the **a** are watching.
Gal 3: 19 God gave his laws to **a** to give to Moses, who was
Col 2: 18 And don't let anyone say you must worship **a**,
2Th 1: 7 from heaven. He will come with his mighty **a**,
1Ti 3: 16 He was seen by **a** / and was announced to the
5: 21 and the holy **a** to obey these instructions without
Heb 1: 4 This shows that God's Son is far greater than the **a**,
1: 6 God said, "Let all the **a** of God worship him."
1: 7 God calls his **a** / "messengers swift as the wind,
1: 14 But **a** are only servants. They are spirits sent from
2: 2 The message God delivered through **a** has always
2: 5 we are talking about will not be controlled by **a**.
2: 7 For a little while you made him lower than the **a**,
2: 9 "for a little while was made lower than the **a**"
2: 16 help the descendants of Abraham, not to help the **a**.
12: 22 and to thousands of **a** in joyful assembly.
13: 2 for some who have done this have entertained **a**
1Pe 1: 12 so wonderful that even the **a** are eagerly watching
3: 22 and all the **a** and authorities and powers are
2Pe 2: 4 For God did not spare even the **a** when they
2: 11 But the **a**, even though they are far greater in
Jude 1: 6 And I remind you of the **a** who did not stay within
1: 9 But even Michael, one of the mightiest of the **a**,
Rev 1: 20 The seven stars are the **a** of the seven churches,
3: 5 before my Father and his **a** that they are mine.
5: 11 and millions of **a** around the throne and the living
7: 1 Then I saw four **a** standing at the four corners of
7: 2 And he shouted out to those four **a** who had been
7: 11 And all the **a** were standing around the throne
8: 2 And I saw the seven **a** who stand before God,
8: 6 Then the seven **a** with the seven trumpets prepared
8: 13 because of what will happen when the last three **a**
9: 14 "Release the four **a** who are bound at the great
9: 15 And the four **a** who had been prepared for this
12: 7 and the **a** under his command fought the dragon
and his **a**.
12: 9 was thrown down to the earth with all his **a**.
14: 10 and burning sulfur in the presence of the holy **a**
15: 1 Seven **a** were holding the seven last plagues,
15: 6 The seven **a** who were holding the bowls of the
15: 7 **a** a gold bowl filled with the terrible wrath of God,
15: 8 No one could enter the Temple until the seven **a**
16: 1 voice shouting from the Temple to the seven **a**,
17: 1 One of the seven **a** who had poured out the seven
21: 9 Then one of the seven **a** who held the seven bowls
21: 12 and high, with twelve gates guarded by twelve **a**.

ANGER (301) [ANGERED, ANGRIER, ANGRILY, ANGRY]

Ge 49: 6 For in their **a** they murdered men, / and they
49: 7 Cursed be their **a**, for it is fierce; / cursed be their
Ex 11: 8 Then, burning with **a**, Moses left Pharaoh's
15: 7 Your **a** flashed forth; / it consumed them as fire
22: 24 My **a** will blaze forth against you, and I will kill
32: 10 leave me alone so my **a** can blaze against them
32: 12 face of the earth.' Turn away from your fierce **a**.
32: 19 In terrible **a**, he threw the stone tablets to the
34: 6 I am slow to **a** and rich in unfailing love
Nu 1: 53 of Israel protection from the LORD's fierce **a**.
11: 1 The LORD heard them, his **a** blazed against them.
11: 33 the **a** of the LORD blazed against the people,
14: 18 'The LORD is slow to **a** and rich in unfailing
16: 46 The LORD's **a** is blazing among them—
18: 5 the LORD's **a** will never again blaze against the
25: 3 causing the LORD's **a** to blaze against his people.
25: 4 so his fierce **a** will turn away from the people of
25: 11 and grandson of Aaron the priest has turned my **a**
25: 11 all Israel as I had intended to do in my **a**.
Dt 4: 25 of the LORD your God and will arouse his **a**.
6: 15 His **a** will flare up against you and wipe you from
7: 4 Then the **a** of the LORD will burn against you,
11: 17 If you do, the LORD's **a** will burn against you.
13: 17 Then the LORD will turn from his fierce **a**
29: 20 His **a** and jealousy will burn against them.
29: 23 and Zeboiim, which the LORD destroyed in his **a**.
29: 27 That is why the LORD's **a** burned against this
29: 28 In great **a** and fury the LORD uprooted his people
31: 17 Then my **a** will blaze forth against them. I will
32: 19 He was provoked to **a** by his own sons
32: 22 For my **a** blazes forth like fire / and burns to the
Jos 23: 16 and serving other gods, his **a** will burn against you,
Jdg 2: 14 This made the LORD burn with **a** against Israel,
2: 20 So the LORD burned with **a** against Israel.
3: 8 Then the LORD burned with **a** against Israel,
10: 7 So the LORD burned with **a** against Israel,
1Sa 11: 7 the LORD made the people afraid of Saul's **a**,
20: 34 Jonathan left the table in fierce **a** and refused to eat
2Sa 6: 7 Then the LORD's **a** blazed out against Uzzah for
6: 8 because the LORD's **a** had blazed out against
22: 8 the heavens shook; / they quaked because of his **a**.
24: 1 Once again the **a** of the LORD burned against
24: 17 Let your **a** fall against me and my family."
1Ki 14: 22 arousing his **a** with their sin, for it was even worse
15: 30 because Jeroboam had aroused the **a** of the
16: 2 You have aroused my **a** by causing my people to
16: 7 arousing him to **a** by his sins, just like the family
16: 13 arousing the **a** of the LORD, the God of Israel,
16: 26 Thus, he aroused the **a** of the LORD, the God of
16: 33 He did more to arouse the **a** of the LORD,
22: 53 arousing the **a** of the LORD, the God of Israel,
2Ki 3: 27 As a result, the **a** against Israel was great, so they
17: 11 done many evil things, arousing the LORD's **a**.
17: 17 sold themselves to evil, arousing the LORD's **a**.
21: 6 that was evil in the LORD's sight, arousing his **a**.
22: 13 The LORD's **a** is burning against us because our
22: 17 My **a** is burning against this place, and it will not
23: 26 the LORD's **a** burned against Judah because of
23: 26 and he did not hold back his fierce **a** from them.
24: 20 So the LORD, in his **a**, finally banished the
1Ch 13: 10 Then the LORD's **a** blazed out against Uzzah,
13: 11 because the LORD's **a** had blazed out against

15:13 the **a** of the LORD our God burst out against us.
21:17 my God, let your **a** fall against me and my family,
27:24 because the **a** of God broke out against Israel.
2Ch 12:7 I will not use Shishak to pour out my **a** on
12:12 humbled himself, the LORD's **a** was turned aside,
19:2 "What you have done has brought the LORD's **a**
19:10 so that his **a** will not come against you and them.
24:18 Then the **a** of God burned against Judah
28:11 because now the LORD's fierce **a** has been
28:13 and the LORD's fierce **a** is already turned against
28:25 In this way, he aroused the **a** of the LORD,
29:8 That is why the LORD's **a** has fallen upon Judah
29:10 so that his fierce **a** will turn away from us.
30:8 so that his fierce **a** will turn away from you.
32:25 So the LORD's **a** came against him and against
32:26 So the LORD's **a** did not come against them
33:6 that was evil in the LORD's sight, arousing his **a**.
34:21 The LORD's **a** has been poured out against us
34:25 My **a** will be poured out against this place,
36:16 They scoffed at the prophets until the LORD's **a**
Ezr 7:23 for why should we risk bringing God's **a** against
8:22 but his fierce **a** rages against those who abandon
9:14 Surely your **a** will destroy us until even this little
10:14 so that the fierce **a** of our God may be turned away
Ne 4:5 for they have provoked you to **a** here in the
Est 1:12 This made the king furious, and he burned with **a**.
1:18 end to the contempt and **a** throughout your realm.
2:1 But after Xerxes' **a** had cooled, he began thinking
7:10 set up for Mordecai, and the king's **a** was pacified.
Job 4:9 a breath from God. They vanish in a blast of his **a**.
9:5 he moves the mountains, overturning them in his **a**.
9:13 And God does not restrain his **a**. The mightiest
10:17 You pour out an ever-increasing volume of **a** upon
14:13 and forget me there until your **a** has passed.
18:4 You may tear your hair out in **a**, but will that cause
20:23 of trouble. May God rain down his **a** upon him.
20:28 his house. God's **a** will descend on him in torrents.
21:17 skips them when he distributes sorrows in his **a**.
21:20 Let them drink deeply of the **a** of the Almighty.
35:15 out against him because he does not respond in **a**?
36:33 his presence; the storm announces his indignant **a**.
40:11 Give vent to your **a**. Let it overflow against the
Ps 2:5 Then in **a** he rebukes them, / terrifying them with
2:12 your pursuits—/ for his **a** can flare up in an instant.
4:4 Don't sin by letting **a** gain control over you.
6:1 O LORD, do not rebuke me in your **a**
7:6 Arise, O LORD, in **a**! / Stand up against the fury
18:7 mountains shook; / they quaked because of his **a**.
21:9 The LORD will consume them in his **a**;
27:9 yourself from me. / Do not reject your servant in **a**.
30:5 His **a** lasts for a moment, / but his favor lasts a
37:8 Stop your **a**! / Turn from your rage! / Do not envy
38:1 O LORD, don't rebuke me in your **a**!
38:3 Because of your **a**, my whole body is sick;
55:3 bring trouble on me, / hunting me down in their **a**.
56:7 in your **a**, O God, throw them to the ground.
59:13 Destroy them in your **a**! / Wipe them out
69:24 fury on them; / consume them with your burning **a**.
74:1 Why is your **a** so intense against the sheep of your
76:7 Who can stand before you when your **a** explodes?
78:21 against Jacob. / Yes, his **a** rose against Israel,
78:31 the **a** of God rose against them, / and he killed their
78:38 destroy them all. / Many a time he held back his **a**
78:49 He loosed on them his fierce **a**—/ all his fury,
78:50 He turned his **a** against them; / he did not spare the
85:3 your fury. / You have ended your blazing **a**.
85:4 God of our salvation. / Put aside your **a** against us.
88:7 Your **a** lies heavy on me; / wave after wave
88:16 Your fierce **a** has overwhelmed me. / Your terrors
89:46 How long will your **a** burn like fire?
90:7 We wither beneath your **a**; / we are overwhelmed
90:11 Who can comprehend the power of your **a**?
95:11 So in my **a** I made a vow: / 'They will never enter
102:10 because of your **a** and wrath. / For you have picked
106:23 He begged him to turn from his **a** and not destroy
106:40 That is why the LORD's **a** burned against his
110:5 He will strike down many kings in the day of his **a**.
112:10 They will grind their teeth in **a**; / they will slink
124:3 us alive / because of their burning **a** against us.
138:7 you will preserve me against the **a** of my enemies.
Pr 14:29 Those who control their **a** have great
15:1 turns away wrath, but harsh words stir up **a**.
16:14 The **a** of the king is a deadly threat; the wise do
19:11 People with good sense restrain their **a**; they earn
19:12 The king's **a** is like a lion's roar, but his favor is
20:2 like a lion's roar; to rouse his **a** is to risk your life.
21:14 A secret gift calms **a**; a secret bribe pacifies fury.
24:18 with you and will turn his **a** away from them.
25:23 north brings rain, so a gossiping tongue causes **a**!
27:4 **A** is cruel, and wrath is like a flood, but who can
29:8 town agitated, but those who are wise will calm **a**.
29:11 A fool gives full vent to **a**, but a wise person
30:33 to the nose causes bleeding, so **a** causes quarrels.
Ecc 7:9 be quick-tempered, for **a** is the friend of fools.
Isa 5:25 That is why the **a** of the LORD burns against his
5:25 But even then the LORD's **a** will not be satisfied.
7:4 Tell him he doesn't need to fear the fierce **a** of
9:12 But even then the LORD's **a** will not be satisfied.
9:17 But even then the LORD's **a** will not be satisfied.
9:21 But even then the LORD's **a** will not be satisfied.
10:4 But even then the LORD's **a** will not be satisfied.
10:5 is certain for Assyria, the whip of my **a**.
10:25 In a little while my **a** against you will end, and
then my **a** will rise up to destroy them."
13:3 I am exalted. I have called them to satisfy my **a**."
13:5 they carry his **a** with them and will destroy the
13:9 is coming—the terrible day of his fury and fierce **a**.
13:13 will show my fury and fierce **a**."
26:20 Hide until the LORD's **a** against your enemies
27:4 My **a** against Israel will be gone. If I find briers
28:21 The LORD will come suddenly and in **a**, as he
30:27 burning with **a**, surrounded by a thick,
30:28 His **a** pours out like a flood on his enemies,
48:9 I will hold back my **a** and not wipe you out.
51:13 Will you continue to fear the **a** of your enemies
54:8 In a moment of **a** I turned my face away for a little
54:9 swear that I will never again pour out my **a** on you.
57:16 against you forever; I will not always show my **a**.
60:10 For though I have destroyed you in my **a**, I will
61:2 with it, the day of God's **a** against their enemies.
63:3 In my **a** I have trampled my enemies as if they
63:6 I crushed the nations in my **a** and made them
64:5 We are constant sinners, so your **a** is heavy on us.
65:16 For I will put aside my **a** and forget the evil of
66:14 on his people—and his **a** against his enemies.
66:15 He will bring punishment with the fury of his **a**
Jer 4:4 or my **a** will burn like an unquenchable fire
4:8 for the fierce **a** of the LORD is still upon us.
4:26 lay in ruins, crushed by the LORD's fierce **a**.
6:15 They will be humbled beneath my punishing **a**,"
7:20 be consumed by the unquenchable fire of my **a**."
10:10 The whole earth trembles at his **a**.
10:18 troubles upon you. At last you will feel my **a**."
10:24 be gentle. Do not correct me in **a**, for I would die.
11:17 provoking my **a** by offering incense to Baal."
12:13 for the fierce **a** of the LORD is upon them."
15:14 For my **a** blazes forth like fire, and it will consume
17:4 For you have kindled my **a** into a roaring fire that
18:20 for them and tried to protect them from your **a**.
18:23 Let them die before you. Deal with them in your **a**.
21:12 or my **a** will burn like an unquenchable fire
23:19 The LORD's **a** bursts out like a storm,
23:20 The **a** of the LORD will not diminish until it has
25:15 my hand this cup filled to the brim with my **a**,
25:17 So I took the cup of **a** from the LORD and made
25:26 himself drank from the cup of the LORD's **a**.
25:27 God of Israel, says: Drink from this cup of my **a**.
25:37 turned into a wasteland by the LORD's fierce **a**.
25:38 the sword of the enemy and the LORD's fierce **a**.
30:23 The LORD's **a** bursts out like a storm, a driving
30:24 The fierce **a** of the LORD will not diminish until
32:31 it has done nothing but **a** me, so I am determined
32:32 the priests, and the prophets—stir up my **a**.
33:5 I have determined to destroy them in my terrible **a**.
36:7 For the LORD's terrible **a** has been pronounced
42:18 'Just as my **a** and fury were poured out on the
44:3 all their wickedness, my **a** rose high against them.
44:8 Why arouse my **a** by burning incense to the idols
49:37 My fierce **a** will bring great disaster upon the
50:13 Because of the LORD's **a**, Babylon will become a
51:45 Save yourselves! Run from the LORD's fierce **a**.
52:3 So the LORD, in his **a**, finally banished the
La 1:12 LORD brought on me in the day of his fierce **a**.
2:1 The Lord in his **a** has cast a dark shadow over
2:2 In his **a** he has broken down the fortress walls of
2:6 Kings and priests fall together before his **a**.
2:21 You have killed them in your **a**, slaughtering them
2:22 In the day of the LORD's **a**, no one has escaped
3:1 that come from the rod of the LORD's **a**.
3:43 "You have engulfed us with your **a**, chased us
3:66 Chase them down in your **a**, destroying them from
4:11 But now the **a** of the LORD is satisfied. His fiercest
a has now been poured out.
4:21 too, must drink from the cup of the LORD's **a**.
Eze 5:13 Then at last my **a** will be spent, and I will be
5:13 the LORD, have spoken to them in my jealous **a**.
7:3 hope remains, for I will unleash my **a** against you.
7:12 for all of them will fall under my terrible **a**.
7:19 their deliverance in that day of the LORD's **a**.
13:13 with a great flood of **a**, and with hailstones of fury.
13:15 At last my **a** against the wall and those who
16:26 fanning the flames of my **a** with your increasing
16:42 you will be spent, and my jealous **a** will subside.
20:8 them to satisfy my **a** while they were still in Egypt.
20:33 I will rule you with an iron fist in great **a** and with
21:31 fury on you and blow on you with the fire of my **a**.
22:21 you together and blow the fire of my **a** upon you,
22:31 fury on them, consuming them in the fire of my **a**.
23:25 I will turn my jealous **a** against you, and they will
24:8 her blood on a rock as an open expression of my **a**
30:14 and they will lie in ruins, burned up by my **a**.
35:11 I will punish you for all your acts of **a**, envy,
36:5 My jealous **a** is on fire against these nations,
38:19 For in my jealousy and blazing **a**, I promise a
43:8 by such wickedness, so I consumed them in my **a**.
Da 3:22 And because the king, in his **a**, had demanded such
9:16 please turn your furious **a** away from your city of
11:11 Then the king of the south, in great **a**, will rally
11:30 But he will vent his **a** against the people of the
11:44 and he will set out in great **a** to destroy many as he
Hos 5:10 So I will pour my **a** down on them like a waterfall.
11:9 I will not punish you as much as my burning **a** tells
13:11 In my **a** I gave you kings, and in my fury I took
14:4 know no bounds, for my **a** will be gone forever!
Am 1:11 them no mercy and were unrelenting in their **a**.
Jnh 3:9 and hold back his fierce **a** from destroying us."
Na 1:6 Who can stand before his fierce **a**? Who can
Hab 2:7 Suddenly, your debtors will rise up in **a**. They will
3:2 to save us. And in your **a**, remember your mercy.
3:8 Was it in **a**, LORD, that you struck the rivers
3:12 You marched across the land in awesome **a**
Zep 1:15 It is a day when the LORD's **a** will be poured out.
1:18 be of no use to you on that day of the LORD's **a**.
2:2 and the terrible day of the LORD's **a** begins.
2:3 protect you from his **a** on that day of destruction.
3:8 and pour out my fiercest **a** and fury on them.
Zec 6:8 "Those who went north have vented the **a** of my
10:3 "My **a** burns against your shepherds, and I will
Ac 19:28 At this their **a** boiled, and they began shouting,
Ro 1:18 But God shows his **a** from heaven against all
2:8 But he will pour out his **a** and wrath on those who
3:25 for our sins and to satisfy God's **a** against us.
2Co 11:29 Who is led astray, and I do not burn with **a**?
12:20 jealousy, outbursts of **a**, selfishness, backstabbing,
Gal 5:20 hostility, quarreling, jealousy, outbursts of **a**,
Eph 2:3 and we were under God's **a** just like everyone else.
4:26 And "don't sin by letting **a** gain control over
4:27 for **a** gives a mighty foothold to the Devil.
4:31 of all bitterness, rage, **a**, harsh words, and slander,
5:6 for the terrible **a** of God comes upon all those who
Col 3:6 God's terrible **a** will come upon those who do such
3:8 But now is the time to get rid of **a**, rage,
1Th 2:16 But the **a** of God has caught up with them at last.
5:9 our Lord Jesus Christ, not to pour out his **a** on us.
1Ti 2:8 lifted up to God, free from **a** and controversy.
Heb 3:11 So in my **a** I made a vow: / 'They will never enter
4:3 didn't believe, God said, / "In my **a** I made a vow:
Jas 1:20 Your **a** can never make things right in God's sight.
Rev 12:12 For the Devil has come down to you in great **a**,

ANGERED (12) [ANGER]

Jdg 2:12 the people around them. And they **a** the LORD.
2Sa 10:6 Ammon realized how seriously they had **a** David,
1Ki 14:15 for they have **a** the LORD by worshiping Asherah
2Ki 21:15 and have **a** me ever since their ancestors came out
1Ch 19:6 Ammon realized how seriously they had **a** David,
Ezr 5:12 But because our ancestors **a** the God of heaven,
Ps 106:29 They **a** the LORD with all these things, / so a
106:32 At Meribah, too, they **a** the LORD,
Jer 8:19 why have they **a** me with their carved idols
Eze 16:43 but have **a** me by doing all these evil things,
Joel 2:13 for he is gracious and merciful. He is not easily **a**.
Zec 8:14 I did not change my mind when your ancestors **a**

ANGLE (2)

2Ch 26:9 at the Valley Gate, and at the **a** in the wall.
Ecc 7:27 after looking into the matter from every possible **a**.

ANGRIER (1) [ANGER]

Nu 32:14 You are making the LORD even **a** with Israel.

ANGRILY (7) [ANGER]

Ge 30:15 But Leah **a** replied, "Wasn't it enough that you
34:31 treat our sister like a prostitute?" they retorted **a**.
Nu 24:10 He **a** clapped his hands and shouted, "I called you
35:21 Or if someone **a** hits another person with a fist
Job 16:9 God hates me and tears **a** at my flesh. He gnashes
32:5 saw that they had no further reply, he spoke out **a**.
Mk 3:5 He looked around at them **a**, because he was

ANGRY (148) [ANGER]

Ge 4:5 accept Cain's. This made Cain very **a** and dejected.
4:6 "Why are you so **a**?" the LORD asked him.
18:30 "Please don't be **a**, my Lord," Abraham pleaded.
18:32 Finally, Abraham said, "Lord, please do not get **a**;
31:36 Then Jacob became very **a**. "What did you find?"
40:2 Pharaoh became very **a** with these officials,
41:10 time ago, you were **a** with the chief baker and me,
45:5 But don't be **a** with yourselves that you did this to
Ex 4:14 Then the LORD became **a** with Moses.
16:20 a terrible smell. And Moses was very **a** with them.
32:11 so **a** with your own people whom you brought
Lev 10:6 and the LORD will be **a** with the whole
10:16 he became very **a** with Eleazar and Ithamar,
Nu 11:10 and the LORD became extremely **a**.
16:15 Then Moses became very **a** and said to the
16:22 "Must you be **a** with all the people when only one
Dt 1:34 heard your complaining, he became very **a**.
1:37 "And the LORD was also **a** with me because of
3:26 "But the LORD was **a** with me because of you,
4:21 "But the LORD was very **a** with me because of
9:7 "Remember how **a** you made the LORD your
9:8 Remember how **a** you made the LORD at Mount
9:18 what the LORD hated, thus making him very **a**.
9:20 so **a** with Aaron that he wanted to destroy him.
9:22 "You also made the LORD **a** at Taberah,
29:24 LORD done this to his land? Why was he so **a**?'
31:29 for you will make the LORD very **a** by doing
Jos 7:1 so the LORD was very **a** with the Israelites.
7:26 ever since. So the LORD was no longer **a**.
9:20 for God would be **a** with us if we broke our oath.
22:18 he will be **a** with all of us tomorrow.
Jdg 6:39 Gideon said to God, "Please don't be **a** with me,
8:3 heard Gideon's answer, they were no longer **a**.
18:25 and they might get **a** and kill you and your
1Sa 11:6 came mightily upon Saul, and he became very **a**.
17:28 Eliab, heard David talking to the men, he was **a**.
18:8 This made Saul very **a**. "What's this?" he said.
20:7 But if he is **a** and loses his temper, then you will
20:10 will I know whether or not your father is **a**?"
20:13 But if he is **a** and wants you killed,
29:4 But the Philistine commanders were **a**. "Send him
2Sa 6:8 David was **a** because the LORD's anger had
11:20 But he might get **a** and ask, 'Why did the troops go
13:21 David heard what had happened, he was very **a**.
19:42 Why should this make you **a**? We have charged
1Ki 8:46 you may become **a** with them and let their enemies
11:9 The LORD was very **a** with Solomon, for his

13: 4 King Jeroboam was very **a** with the man of God
20:43 So the king of Israel went home to Samaria **a**
21: 4 So Ahab went home **a** and sullen because of
21:22 for you have made him very **a** and have led all of
2Ki 5:11 But Naaman became **a** and stalked away.
13: 3 So the LORD was very **a** with Israel, and he
13:19 But the man of God was **a** with him. "You should
17:18 And because the LORD was **a**, he swept them
22:17 and I am very **a** with them for everything they
23:19 kings of Israel and had made the LORD very **a**.
1Ch 13:11 David was **a** because the LORD's anger had
2Ch 6:36 you may become **a** with them and let their enemies
16:10 so **a** with Hanani for saying this that he threw him
25:10 This made them **a** with Judah, and they returned
25:15 This made the LORD very **a**, and he sent a
28: 9 was **a** with Judah and let you defeat them.
34:25 and I am very **a** with them for everything they
Ne 2:10 they were very **a** that someone had come who was
4: 1 Sanballat was very **a** when he learned that we were
5: 6 When I heard their complaints, I was very **a**.
9:17 gracious and merciful, slow to become **a**, and full
Est 2:21 became **a** at King Xerxes and plotted to assassinate
Job 14: 6 us a little rest, won't you? Turn away your **a** stare.
32: 2 Barakel the Buzite, of the clan of Ram, became **a**.
32: 2 He was **a** because Job refused to admit that he had
32: 3 He was also **a** with Job's three friends
42: 7 "I am **a** with you and with your two friends,
Ps 2:12 Submit to God's royal son, or he will become **a**,
7:11 perfectly fair. / He is **a** with the wicked every day.
60: 1 You have been **a** with us; now restore us to your
78:21 When the LORD heard them, he was **a**. / The fire
78:58 They made God **a** by building altars to other gods;
78:59 When God heard them, he was very **a**, / and he
78:62 because he was so **a** with his own people—
79: 5 O LORD, how long will you be **a** with us?
80: 4 how long will you be **a** and reject our prayers?
85: 5 Will you be **a** with us always? / Will you prolong
86:15 are a merciful and gracious God, / slow to get **a**,
89:38 Why are you so **a** with the one you chose as king?
95:10 For forty years I was **a** with them, and I said,
103: 8 he is slow to get **a** and full of unfailing love.
103: 9 not constantly accuse us, / nor remain **a** forever.
106:33 They made Moses **a**, / and he spoke foolishly.
138: 7 You will clench your fist against my **a** enemies!
145: 8 and merciful, / slow to get **a**, full of unfailing love.
Pr 14:35 are doing; he is **a** with those who cause trouble.
19: 3 own foolishness and then are **a** at the LORD.
22:24 Keep away from **a**, short-tempered people,
Ecc 5: 6 That would make God **a**, and he might wipe out
5:17 live under a cloud—frustrated, discouraged, and **a**.
10: 4 If your boss is **a** with you, don't quit! A quiet spirit
SS 1: 6 My brothers were **a** with me and sent me out to
Isa 12: 1 "Praise the LORD! / He was **a** with me,
14: 6 blows of rage and held the nations in your **a** grip.
30:30 With **a** indignation he will bring down his mighty
41:11 "See, all your **a** enemies lie there, confused
45:24 And all who were **a** with him will come to him
47: 6 For I was **a** with my chosen people and began their
57:17 I was **a** and punished these greedy people.
64: 9 Oh, don't be so **a** with us, LORD. Please don't
Jer 2:35 Surely he isn't **a** with me!' Now I will punish you
3: 5 Surely you won't be **a** about such a little thing!
3:12 for I am merciful. I will not be **a** with you forever.
7:18 No wonder I am so **a**! Watch how the children
21: 5 fight against you with great power, for I am very **a**.
25: 6 Do not make me **a** by worshiping the idols you
La 5:22 you utterly rejected us? Are you **a** with us still?
Eze 3: 9 So don't be afraid of them or fear their **a** looks,
8: 3 is a large idol that has made the LORD very **a**.
8: 5 stood the idol that had made the LORD so **a**.
16:42 I will be calm and will not be **a** with you anymore.
35:11 I will pay back your **a** deeds with mine.
Da 6:14 the king was very **a** with himself for signing the
Jnh 4: 1 of plans upset Jonah, and he became very **a**.
4: 2 slow to get **a** and filled with unfailing love.
4: 4 "Is it right for you to be **a** about this?"
4: 9 "Is it right for you to be **a** because the plant
4: 9 "Yes," Jonah retorted, "even **a** enough to die!"
Mic 7:18 You cannot stay **a** with your people forever,
Na 1: 3 The LORD is slow to get **a**, but his power is
Zec 1: 2 the LORD, was very **a** with your ancestors.
1:12 for seventy years now you have been **a** with
1:15 But I am very **a** with the other nations that enjoy
1:15 I was only a little **a** with my people, but the nations
7:12 is why the LORD Almighty was so **a** with them.
Mal 1: 4 People with Whom the LORD Is Forever **A**.'
Mt 5:22 But I say, if you are **a** with someone, you are
18:34 Then the **a** king sent the man to prison until he had
20:15 my money? Should you be **a** because I am kind?'
Lk 14:21 His master was **a** and said, 'Go quickly into the
15:28 "The older brother was **a** and wouldn't go in.
Ac 12:20 Now Herod was very **a** with the people of Tyre
Ro 10:19 I will make you **a** by blessing the foolish
2Co 6: 5 have been beaten, been put in jail, faced **a** mobs,
Eph 4:26 Don't let the sun go down while you are still **a**,
6: 4 Don't make your children **a** by the way you treat
Heb 3:10 So I was **a** with them, and I said, / 'Their hearts
3:17 And who made God **a** for forty years? Wasn't it
Jas 1:19 be quick to listen, slow to speak, and slow to get **a**.
Rev 11:18 The nations were **a** with you, / but now the time of
12:17 Then the dragon became **a** at the woman, and he

ANGUISH (49) [ANGUISHED]

Ge 37:29 he tore his clothes in **a** and frustration.
42:21 We saw his terror and **a** and heard his pleadings,
43:14 And if I must bear the **a** of their deaths, then
Ex 15:14 and tremble; / **a** will grip the people of Philistia.
Jdg 11:35 When he saw her, he tore his clothes in **a**.
1Sa 1:10 Hannah was in deep **a**, crying bitterly as she
1:16 For I have been praying out of great **a**
Job 7:11 cannot keep from speaking. I must express my **a**.
15:24 They live in distress and **a**, like a king preparing
19:22 as God does? Why aren't you satisfied with my **a**?
Ps 13: 2 How long must I struggle with **a** in my soul,
31: 7 my troubles, / and you care about the **a** of my soul.
55: 4 My heart is in **a**. / The terror of death overpowers
Pr 1:27 and when **a** and distress overwhelm you.
5:11 Afterward you will groan in **a** when disease
23:29 Who has **a**? Who has sorrow? Who is always
Isa 8:22 there will be trouble and **a** and dark despair.
16:12 On the hilltops the people of Moab will pray in **a**
38:15 throughout my years / because of this **a** I have felt.
38:17 Yes, it was good for me to suffer this **a**, / for you
53:11 When he sees all that is accomplished by his **a**,
Jer 15: 8 I will cause **a** and terror to come upon them
22:23 of Lebanon, but soon you will cry and groan in **a**—
22:23 **a** like that of a woman about to give birth.
31:15 "A cry of **a** is heard in Ramah—mourning
49:24 Fear, **a**, and pain have gripped her as they do a
La 1:18 look upon my **a** and despair, for my sons
1:20 "LORD, see my **a**! My heart is broken and my
2:13 of Jerusalem, to what can I compare your **a**?
3: 5 and surrounded me with **a** and distress.
Eze 7: 7 It will ring with shouts of **a**, not shouts of joy.
21: 6 Groan before them with bitter **a** and a broken
21:12 pound your thighs in **a**, for that sword will
23:34 In deep **a** you will drain that cup of terror to the
23:34 will smash it to pieces and beat your breast in **a**.
27:31 They weep for you with bitter **a** and deep
Da 6:20 When he got there, he called out in **a**, "Daniel,
12: 1 Then there will be a time of **a** greater than any
Mic 1:10 roll in the dust to show your **a** and despair.
Zep 1:15 It is a day of terrible distress and **a**, a day of ruin
Mt 2:18 "A cry of **a** is heard in Ramah—/ weeping
26:37 and he began to be filled with **a** and deep distress.
Lk 16:24 cool my tongue, because I am in **a** in these flames.'
16:25 now he is here being comforted, and you are in **a**.
Jn 13:21 Now Jesus was in great **a** of spirit, and he
16:21 her **a** gives place to joy because she has brought a
Ac 7:10 and delivered him from his **a**. And God gave him
Jas 5: 1 weep and groan with **a** because of all the terrible
Rev 16:10 And his subjects ground their teeth in **a**,

ANGUISHED (1) [ANGUISH]

Ps 38: 8 My groans come from an **a** heart.

ANIAM (1)

1Ch 7:19 of Shemida were Ahian, Shechem, Likhi, and **A**.

ANIM (1)

Jos 15:50 Anab, Eshtemoh, **A**,

ANIMAL (131) [ANIMAL'S, ANIMALS, ANIMALS']

Ge 1:24 "Let the earth bring forth every kind of **a**—
2:19 LORD God formed from the soil every kind of **a**
3:21 And the LORD God made clothing from **a** skins
6:19 Bring a pair of every kind of **a**—a male and a
6:20 Pairs of each kind of bird and each kind of **a**,
7: 2 Take along seven pairs of each **a** that I have
7:14 the boat were pairs of every kind of breathing **a**—
31:39 You made me pay for every **a** stolen from the
37:20 We can tell our father that a wild **a** has eaten him.
37:33 son's robe. A wild **a** has attacked and eaten him.
44:28 doubtless torn to pieces by some wild **a**.
Ex 9: 6 but the Israelites didn't lose a single **a** from their
9:19 or **a** left outside will die beneath the hail.' "
12: 5 This **a** must be a one-year-old male, either a sheep
13: 2 firstborn sons of Israel and every firstborn male **a**.
21:34 owner of the well must pay in full for the dead **a**
22: 5 "If an **a** is grazing in a field or vineyard
22:10 ox, sheep, or any other **a**, but it dies or is injured
22:12 But if the **a** or property was stolen, payment must
22:13 If it was attacked by a wild **a**, the carcass must be
22:14 "If someone borrows an **a** from a neighbor and it
22:15 And no payment is required if the **a** was rented
22:19 "Anyone who has sexual relations with an **a** must
22:30 Leave the newborn **a** with its mother for seven
22:31 do not eat any **a** that has been attacked and killed
by a wild **a**.
38: 1 The altar for burning **a** sacrifices also was
Lev 1: 5 Then slaughter the **a** in the LORD's presence,
1: 6 When the **a** has been skinned and cut into pieces,
1: 8 Aaron's sons will then put the pieces of the **a**,
1:11 Slaughter the **a** on the north side of the altar in the
1:12 Then you must cut the **a** in pieces, and the priests
3: 1 The **a** you offer to the LORD must have no
5: 2 such as the dead body of an **a** that is ceremonially
5: 2 whether a wild **a**, a domesticated **a**, or an **a** that
scurries along the ground—
5:15 The **a** must have no physical defects, and it must
5:18 The **a** must have no physical defects, and it must
6:25 The **a** given as a sin offering is most holy and must
7: 2 The **a** sacrificed as a guilt offering must be
7: 7 the meat of the sacrificed **a** belongs to the priest in
7: 8 the hide of the sacrificed **a** also belongs to the
7:12 the usual **a** sacrifice must be accompanied by
7:14 sprinkles the altar with blood from the sacrificed **a**.
7:21 whether it is human defilement or an unclean **a**,
7:24 The fat of an **a** found dead or killed by a wild **a**
may never be eaten,
7:26 you must never eat the blood of any bird or **a**.
7:30 Bring the fat of the **a**, together with the breast,
9:12 Next Aaron slaughtered the **a** for the whole burnt
9:13 They handed the **a** to him piece by piece,
11:12 any marine **a** that does not have both fins
11:25 If you move the dead body of an unclean **a**,
11:26 "Any **a** that has divided but unsplit hooves or that
11:26 If you touch the dead body of such an **a**, you will
11:27 If you touch the dead body of such an **a**, you will
11:31 If you touch the dead body of such an **a**, you will
11:32 If such an **a** dies and falls on something,
11:33 "If such an **a** dies and falls into a clay pot,
11:35 Any object on which the dead body of such an **a**
11:36 if the dead body of such an **a** falls into a spring
11:39 "If an **a** that is permitted for eating dies and you
11:41 "Consider detestable any **a** that scurries along the
13:48 some woolen or linen fabric, the hide of an **a**,
13:49 affected area in the clothing, the **a** hide, the fabric,
17:13 If you go hunting and kill an **a** or bird that is
17:14 drink it, for the life of any bird or **a** is in the blood.
17:15 If you eat from the carcass of an **a** that died a
natural death or was killed by a wild **a**,
18:23 himself by having sexual intercourse with an **a**,
18:23 to a male **a** in order to have intercourse with it;
20:15 "If a man has sexual intercourse with an **a**,
20:15 he must be put to death, and the **a** must be killed.
20:16 If a woman approaches a male **a** to have
20:16 with it, she and the **a** must both be put to death.
20:25 You must not defile yourselves by eating any **a**
22: 8 The priests may never eat an **a** that has died a
22:19 it will be accepted only if it is a male **a** with no
22:20 Do not bring an **a** with physical defects, because it
22:21 you must offer an **a** that has no physical defects of
22:22 An **a** that is blind, injured, mutilated, or that has a
22:24 If an **a** has damaged testicles or is castrated,
22:28 But you must never slaughter a mother **a** and her
22:30 Eat the entire sacrificial **a** on the day it is
24:18 "Anyone who kills another person's **a** must pay it
back in full—a live **a** for the **a** that was killed.
24:21 "Whoever kills an **a** must make full restitution,
27: 9 "If your vow involves giving a clean **a**—one that
27:10 The **a** should never be exchanged or substituted for
27:10 neither a good **a** for a bad one nor a bad **a** for
27:10 then both the original **a** and the substitute will be
27:11 But if your vow involves an unclean **a**—one that is
27:11 then you must bring the **a** to the priest.
27:13 If you want to redeem the **a**, you must pay the
27:27 if it is the firstborn of a ceremonially unclean **a**,
27:28 whether a person, an **a**, or an inherited field—
27:32 The LORD also owns every tenth **a** counted off
27:33 The tenth **a** must not be selected on the basis of
27:33 then both the original **a** and the substituted one will
Nu 15: 3 the sacrifice must be an **a** from your flocks of
18:15 firstborn of every mother, whether human or **a**,
19: 8 The man who burns the **a** must also wash his
Dt 4:17 an **a** or a bird,
14: 6 "Any **a** that has split hooves and chews the cud
14: 7 but if the **a** doesn't have both, it may not be eaten.
15:21 But if this firstborn **a** has any defect, such as being
27:21 is anyone who has sexual intercourse with an **a**.'
1Sa 2:13 While the meat of the sacrificed **a** was still boiling,
17:35 If the **a** turns on me, I catch it by the jaw and club
2Ki 14: 9 But just then a wild **a** came by and stepped on the
2Ch 25:18 But just then a wild **a** came by and stepped on the
Job 28: 8 No wild **a** has ever walked upon those treasures;
Ps 73:22 I must have seemed like a senseless **a** to you.
Jer 27: 5 have made the earth and all its people and every **a**.
Eze 4:14 now I have never eaten any **a** that died of sickness
21:21 They will inspect the livers of their **a** sacrifices.
34: 5 a shepherd. They are easy prey for any wild **a**.
34: 8 and left them to be attacked by every wild **a**.
44:31 meat from any bird or **a** that dies a natural death
44:31 or that dies after being attacked by another **a**.
Da 4:15 and let him live like an **a** among the plants of the
4:16 let him have the mind of an **a** instead of a human.
5:21 He was given the mind of an **a**, and he lived
Zec 1:18 Then I looked up and saw four **a** horns.
Heb 9:25 Place year after year to offer the blood of an **a**.
10: 5 "You did not want **a** sacrifices and grain offerings.
10: 8 "You did not want **a** sacrifices or grain offerings
12:20 "If even an **a** touches the mountain, it must be

ANIMAL'S (10) [ANIMAL]

Ex 22: 5 then the **a** owner must pay damages in the form of
Lev 3: 2 Lay your hand on the **a** head, and slaughter it at the
3: 2 then sprinkle the **a** blood against the sides of the
4: 5 then take some of the **a** blood into the Tabernacle,
4:19 The priest must remove all the **a** fat and burn it on
6: 6 physical defects or the **a** equivalent value in silver.
6:30 people's sins, none of that **a** meat may be eaten.
7:15 The **a** meat must be eaten on the same day it is
10:18 Since the **a** blood was not taken into the Holy
1Sa 2:15 even before the **a** fat had been burned on the altar.

ANIMALS (242) [ANIMAL]

Ge 1:24 kind of animal—livestock, small **a**, and wildlife."
1:25 made all sorts of wild **a**, livestock, and small **a**,
1:26 and all the livestock, wild **a**, and small **a**."
1:28 Be masters over the fish and birds and all the **a**."
1:30 and other green plants to the **a** and birds for their
2:20 gave names to all the livestock, birds, and wild **a**.
3:14 and wild **a** of the whole earth to be cursed.
6: 7 Yes, and I will destroy all the **a** and birds, too.
6:21 enough food for your family and for all the **a**."

7: 8 With them were all the various kinds of **a**—
7: 8 along with all the birds and other small **a**.
7:21 birds, domestic **a**, wild **a**, all kinds of small **a**,
7:23 people, **a** both large and small, and birds.
8: 1 God remembered Noah and all the **a** in the boat.
8:17 Release all the **a** and birds so they can breed
8:19 And all the various kinds of **a** and birds came out,
8:20 an altar to the LORD and sacrificed on it the **a**
9: 2 All the wild **a**, large and small, and all the birds
9: 4 But you must never eat **a** that still have their
9: 5 **A** that kill people must die, and any person who
9:10 and with the **a** you brought with you—all these birds and livestock and wild **a**.
13: 6 There were too many **a** for the available
19:25 eliminating all life—people, plants, and **a** alike.
31: 8 For if he said the speckled **a** were mine, the whole
31:39 If any were attacked and killed by wild **a**, did I
32:16 each group of **a** by itself, separated by a distance in
32:17 Whose servants are you? Whose **a** are these?'
41:19 I've never seen such ugly **a** in all the land of
45:17 "Tell your brothers to load their pack **a** and return
Ex 8:17 the entire land, covering the Egyptians and their **a**.
8:18 And the gnats covered all the people and **a**.
9: 7 it was true that none of the Israelites' **a** were dead.
9: 9 causing boils to break out on people and **a** alike."
9:10 broke out on the people and **a** throughout Egypt.
9:22 on the people, the **a**, and the crops."
9:25 fields was destroyed—people, **a**, and crops alike.
10:26 for the LORD our God from among these **a**.
11: 5 lowliest slave. Even the firstborn of the **a** will die.
12:12 and firstborn male **a** in the land of Egypt.
13:12 and firstborn male **a** must be presented to the
13:15 throughout the land of Egypt, both people and **a**.
19:13 or **a** that cross the boundary must be stoned to
20: 4 any kind, whether in the shape of birds or **a** or fish.
23:11 Leave the rest for the **a** to eat. The same applies to
23:29 and the wild **a** would become too many to control.
24: 6 Moses took half the blood from these **a** and drew it
Lev 1: 2 you must bring **a** from your flocks and herds.
9:20 these fat parts on top of the breasts of these **a**
11: 2 to the Israelites: The **a** you may use for food
11: 4 eat the **a** named here because they either have split
11: 8 You may not eat the meat of these **a** or touch their
11: 9 "As for marine **a**, you may eat whatever has both
11:10 eat marine **a** that do not have both fins and scales.
11:27 Of the **a** that walk on all fours, those that have
11:29 "Of the small **a** that scurry or creep on the ground,
11:31 All these small **a** are unclean for you. If you touch
11:41 along the ground; such **a** may never be eaten.
11:42 This includes all **a** that slither along on their
11:42 All such **a** are to be considered detestable.
11:43 Never defile yourselves by touching such **a**.
11:44 any of these **a** that scurry along the ground.
11:46 "These are the instructions regarding the land **a**,
17: 5 This rule will stop the Israelites from sacrificing **a**
19:19 "Do not breed your cattle with other kinds of **a**.
20:25 between ceremonially clean and unclean **a**,
22: 8 a natural death or has been torn apart by wild **a**,
22:25 or defective **a** from foreigners to be offered as a
22:25 Such **a** will not be accepted on your behalf
25: 7 and the wild **a** will also be allowed to eat of the
26: 6 I will remove the wild **a** from your land
26:22 I will release wild **a** that will kill your children
27:26 because the firstborn of these **a** already belong to
Nu 3:13 myself all the firstborn in Israel of both men and **a**.
8:17 the people of Israel are mine, both people and **a**.
18:15 and the firstborn males of ritually unclean **a**.
18:18 The meat of these **a** will be yours, just like the
28:31 Be sure that all the **a** you sacrifice have no
31:11 the plunder and captives, both people and **a**,
31:26 taken in the battle, including the people and **a**.
31:47 Moses took one of every fifty prisoners and **a**
Dt 5: 8 any kind, whether in the shape of birds or **a** or fish.
7:13 and give fertility to your land and your **a**.
7:22 the wild **a** would multiply too quickly for you.
12: 6 and your offerings of the firstborn **a** of your flocks
12:15 "But you may butcher **a** for meat in any town,
12:15 You may eat as many **a** as the LORD your God
14: 3 "You must not eat **a** that are ceremonially unclean.
14: 4 These are the **a** you may eat: the ox, the sheep,
14: 8 All these **a** are ceremonially unclean for you.
14: 8 not eat or even touch the dead bodies of such **a**.
14: 9 "As for marine **a**, you may eat whatever has both
14:10 eat marine **a** that do not have both fins and scales.
15:20 and your family must eat these **a** in the presence of
28:26 dead bodies will be food for the birds and wild **a**,
1Sa 14:34 in it.' " So that night all the troops brought their **a**
17:44 and I'll give your flesh to the birds and wild **a**!"
17:46 dead bodies of your men to the birds and wild **a**,
2Sa 21:10 and stopped wild **a** from eating them at night.
1Ki 4:33 He could also speak about **a**, birds, reptiles,
2Ki 3: 9 But there was no water for the men or their pack **a**.
3:17 for yourselves and for your cattle and your other **a**.
2Ch 15:11 of the **a** they had taken as plunder in the battle—
29:21 to sacrifice the **a** on the altar of the LORD.
31: 3 The king also made a personal contribution of **a** for
35:11 blood on the altar while the Levites prepared the **a**.
Ne 2:12 We took no pack **a** with us, except the donkey that
Job 1:15 They stole all the **a** and killed all the farmhands.
5:22 and famine; wild **a** will not terrify you.
5:23 the field, and its wild **a** will be at peace with you.
12: 7 "Ask the **a**, and they will teach you. Ask the birds
30: 7 They sound like **a** as they howl among the bushes;
35:11 Where is the one who makes us wiser than the **a**
37: 8 The wild **a** hide in the rocks or in their dens.
39:15 crush them or that wild **a** might destroy them.
40:20 offer it their best food, where all the wild **a** play.
Ps 8: 7 the sheep and the cattle / and all the wild **a**,
36: 6 You care for people and **a** alike, O LORD.
49:12 long despite their riches—/ they will die like the **a**.
49:20 don't understand / that they will die like the **a**.
50:10 For all the **a** of the forest are mine, / and I own the
50:11 and all the **a** of the field belong to me.
68:30 enemy nations—/ these wild **a** lurking in the reeds,
74:14 heads of Leviathan / and let the desert **a** eat him.
79: 2 your godly ones / has become food for the wild **a**.
80:13 the forest devours us, / and the wild **a** feed on us.
104:11 They provide water for all the **a**, / and the wild
104:20 becomes night, / when all the forest **a** prowl about.
135: 8 in each Egyptian home, / both people and **a**.
147: 9 He feeds the wild **a**, / and the young ravens cry to
148:10 wild **a** and all livestock, / reptiles and birds,
Pr 12:10 The godly are concerned for the welfare of their **a**,
30:30 the lion, king of **a**, who won't turn aside for
Ecc 3:18 see for themselves that they are no better than **a**.
3:19 For humans and **a** both breathe the same air,
3:19 So people have no real advantage over the **a**.
3:21 and the spirit of **a** goes downward into the earth?
Isa 1: 3 Even the **a**—the donkey and the ox—know their
1:11 I don't want the fat from your rams or other **a**.
5: 5 will break down its walls / and let the **a** trample it.
13:21 Wild **a** of the desert will move into the ruined city.
18: 6 the fields for the mountain birds and wild **a** to eat.
18: 6 The wild **a** will gnaw at bones all winter.
22:13 you slaughter sacrificial **a**, feast on meat, and drink
30: 6 Look at the **a** moving slowly across the terrible
34:14 Wild **a** of the desert will mingle there with hyenas,
34:16 Not one of these birds and **a** will be missing,
40:16 All Lebanon's sacrificial **a** would not make an
43:20 The wild **a** in the fields will thank me, the jackals
56: 9 wild **a** of the field! Come, wild **a** of the forest!
Jer 7:20 Its people, **a**, trees, and crops will be consumed by
7:33 my people will be food for the vultures and wild **a**,
9:10 heard no more; the birds and wild **a** all have fled.
12: 4 The wild **a** and birds have disappeared because of
15: 3 to devour, and the wild **a** to finish up what is left.
16: 4 bodies will be food for the vultures and wild **a**.
19: 7 the dead bodies as food for the vultures and wild **a**.
21: 6 upon this city, and both people and **a** will die.
27: 6 put everything, even the wild **a**, under his control.
28:14 even the wild **a**, under his control.' "
32:43 a land where people and **a** have all disappeared.'
33:10 and the people and **a** have all disappeared.'
33:12 and the people and **a** have all disappeared—
34:20 bodies will be food for the vultures and wild **a**.
50: 3 will be gone; both people and **a** will flee.
50:39 It will be a home for the wild **a** of the desert.
51:62 so that neither people nor **a** will remain here.
Eze 4:14 And I have never eaten any of the **a** that our laws
5:17 And along with the famine, wild **a** will attack you,
14:13 a famine to destroy both people and **a** alike.
14:15 invasion of dangerous wild **a** to devastate the land
14:19 the land, and the plague killed people and **a** alike.
14:21 and plague—destroying all her people and **a**.
29: 5 for I have given you as food to the wild **a**
29: 8 O Egypt, and destroy both people and **a**.
29:11 not a soul will pass that way, neither people nor **a**.
31: 6 and in its shade all the wild **a** gave birth to their
31:13 fallen trunk, and the wild **a** lay among its branches.
32: 4 and the wild **a** of the whole earth will gorge
32:13 or **a** disturb those waters with their feet.
33:27 living in the open fields will be eaten by wild **a**.
34: 3 the milk, wear the wool, and butcher the best **a**,
34:25 and drive away the dangerous **a** from the land.
34:28 and wild **a** will no longer attack them.
38:20 living things—all the fish, birds, **a**, and people—
39: 4 I will give you as food to the vultures and wild **a**.
39:17 son of man, call all the birds and wild **a**,
40:39 where the sacrificial **a** were slaughtered for the
40:42 and other implements and the sacrificial **a**.
43:25 None of these **a** may have physical defects of any
44:11 and they may still slaughter the **a** brought for burnt
Da 2:38 and has put even the **a** and birds under your
4:12 Wild **a** lived in its shade, and birds nested in its
4:14 Chase the **a** from its shade and the birds from its
4:21 Wild **a** lived in its shade, and birds nested in its
4:23 Let him eat grass with the **a** of the field for seven
4:25 and you will live in the fields with the wild **a**.
4:32 You will live in the fields with the wild **a**, and you
Hos 2:12 where only wild **a** will eat the fruit.
2:18 that time I will make a covenant with all the wild **a**
2:18 the birds and the **a** that scurry along the ground
4: 3 Even the **a**, birds, and fish have begun to
Joel 1:18 How the **a** moan with hunger! The cattle wander
1:20 Even the wild **a** cry out to you because they have
2:22 Don't be afraid, you **a** of the field! The pastures
Jnh 3: 7 not even the **a**, may eat or drink anything at all.
4:11 in spiritual darkness, not to mention all the **a**.
Hab 2:17 You terrified the wild **a** you caught in your traps.
Zep 1: 3 "I will sweep away both people and **a** alike.
2:14 and cattle. All sorts of wild **a** will settle there.
2:15 it has become an utter ruin, a place where **a** live!
Zec 8:10 were no jobs and no wages for either people or **a**.
14:15 donkeys, and all the other **a** in the enemy camps.
Mal 1: 8 When you give blind **a** as sacrifices, isn't that
1: 8 And isn't it wrong to offer **a** that are crippled
1:13 **A** that are stolen and mutilated, crippled and sick—
Mt 21: 7 They brought the **a** to him and threw their
Mk 1:13 He was out among the wild **a**, and angels took care
Ac 10:12 In the sheet were all sorts of **a**, reptiles, and birds.
11: 6 I saw all sorts of small **a**, wild **a**, reptiles,
15:20 consuming blood or eating the meat of strangled **a**.
15:29 consuming blood or eating the meat of strangled **a**,
21:25 nor consume blood, nor eat meat from strangled **a**,
Ro 1:23 look like mere people, or birds and **a** and snakes.
1Co 15:39 of flesh—whether of humans, **a**, birds, or fish.
Tit 1:12 are all liars; they are cruel **a** and lazy gluttons."
Heb 9:23 in heaven—had to be purified by the blood of **a**.
9:23 with far better sacrifices than the blood of **a**.
10: 6 you were not pleased with **a** burned on the altar
10: 8 or grain offerings or **a** burned on the altar or other
13:11 the high priest brought the blood of **a** into the Holy
13:11 but the bodies of the **a** were burned outside the
Jas 3: 7 People can tame all kinds of **a** and birds
2Pe 2:12 These false teachers are like unthinking **a**,
Jude 1:10 Like **a**, they do whatever their instincts tell them,
Rev 6: 8 with the sword and famine and disease and wild **a**.

ANIMALS' (1) [ANIMAL]

Lev 16:27 This includes the **a** hides, the internal organs,

ANISE [KJV] See TINIEST PART OF YOUR INCOME

ANKLE (1) [ANKLEBONES, ANKLES]

Isa 3:20 **a** chains, sashes, perfumes, and charms;

ANKLEBONES (1) [ANKLE]

Ac 3: 7 the man's feet and **a** were healed and strengthened.

ANKLES (2) [ANKLE]

Isa 3:16 noses in the air, with tinkling ornaments on their **a**.
Eze 47: 3 go across. At that point the water was up to my **a**.

ANNA (1)

Lk 2:36 **A**, a prophet, was also there in the Temple.

ANNAS (4)

Lk 3: 2 **A** and Caiaphas were the high priests. At this time
Jn 18:13 First they took him to **A**, the father-in-law of
18:24 Then **A** bound Jesus and sent him to Caiaphas,
Ac 4: 6 **A** the high priest was there, along with Caiaphas,

ANNIHILATE (2) [ANNIHILATED]

Est 7: 4 sold to those who would kill, slaughter, and **a** us.
8:11 and **a** anyone of any nationality or province who

ANNIHILATED (2) [ANNIHILATE]

Est 3:13 must be killed, slaughtered, and **a** on a single day.
9: 5 They killed and **a** their enemies and did as they

ANNIVERSARY (4)

Ex 13: 4 This day in early spring will be the **a** of your
23:15 for that is the **a** of your exodus from Egypt.
Dt 16: 6 Sacrifice it there as the sun goes down on the **a** of
Zec 7: 3 and fast each summer on the **a** of the Temple's

ANNOUNCE (25) [ANNOUNCED, ANNOUNCEMENT, ANNOUNCES, ANNOUNCING]

Ex 7: 2 I say to you and have him **a** it to Pharaoh.
12: 3 **A** to the whole community that on the tenth day of
17:14 down as a permanent record, and **a** it to Joshua:
Nu 23: 7 'curse Jacob for me! / Come and **a** Israel's doom.'
27: 8 Moreover **a** this to the people of Israel: 'If a man
Dt 20: 9 they will **a** the names of the unit commanders.
2Sa 1:20 Don't **a** the news in Gath, / or the Philistines will
Isa 61: 1 and to **a** that captives will be released
Jer 4:16 "Warn the surrounding nations and **a** to Jerusalem:
18: 7 If I **a** that a certain nation or kingdom is to be
18: 9 And if I **a** that I will build up and plant a certain
51:10 let us **a** in Jerusalem everything the LORD our
Eze 22:28 And your prophets **a** false visions and speak false
33: 8 If I **a** that some wicked people are sure to die
Joel 1:14 **A** a time of fasting; call the people together for a
2:15 **A** a time of fasting; call the people together for a
Am 3: 9 **A** this to the leaders of Philistia and Egypt:
3:13 and **a** it throughout all Israel," says the Lord,
Jnh 1: 2 **A** my judgment against it because I have seen how
Mt 10: 7 and **a** to them that the Kingdom of Heaven is near.
Lk 8: 1 and villages to **a** the Good News concerning the
Tit 1: 3 revealed this Good News, and we **a** it to everyone.
1Jn 1: 2 and **a** to you that he is the one who is eternal life.
1: 5 This is the message he has given us to **a** to you:
Rev 3: 5 but I will **a** before my Father and his angels that

ANNOUNCED (28) [ANNOUNCE]

Ge 37: 6 "Listen to this dream," he **a**.
Ex 9: 5 The LORD **a** that he would send the plague the
11: 4 So Moses **a** to Pharaoh, "This is what the LORD
24: 3 When Moses had **a** to the people all the teachings
32: 5 he built an altar in front of the calf and **a**,
Lev 8: 5 Moses **a** to them, "The LORD has commanded
1Sa 13: 4 He **a** that the Philistine garrison at Geba had been
2Ch 35: 1 Then Josiah **a** that the Passover of the LORD
Est 9:14 So the king agreed, and the decree was **a** in Susa.
Ps 98: 2 The LORD has **a** his victory / and has revealed
Jer 4:15 country of Ephraim, your destruction has been **a**.
25:13 all the penalties **a** by Jeremiah against the nations.
26:13 he will cancel this disaster that he has **a** against
Eze 38:17 when I **a** through Israel's prophets that in future
Am 4:12 bring upon you all these further disasters I have **a**.
Mk 1: 7 He **a**: "Someone is coming soon who is far greater
1:15 "At last the time has come!" he **a**. "The Kingdom

Lk 3:18 John used many such warnings as he **a** the Good
23:14 and he **a** his verdict. "You brought this man to me,
Jn 9:22 who had **a** that anyone saying Jesus was the
11:57 and Pharisees had publicly **a** that anyone seeing
Ac 21:26 Then he publicly **a** the date when their vows would
1Ti 3:16 He was seen by angels / and was **a** to the nations.
Heb 2: 3 salvation that was **a** by the Lord Jesus himself?
4: 2 of rest—has been **a** to us just as it was to them.
4: 7 God **a** this through David a long time later in the
1Pe 1:12 And now this Good News has been **a** by those who
Rev 10: 7 It will happen just as he **a** it to his servants the

ANNOUNCEMENT (5) [ANNOUNCE]

Jer 5:20 "Make this **a** to Israel and to Judah:
26: 2 and make an **a** to the people who have come there
Zep 3:16 On that day the **a** to Jerusalem will be, "Cheer up,
Lk 10:11 town from our feet as a public **a** of your doom.
Rev 9:16 I heard an **a** of how many there were.

ANNOUNCES (3) [ANNOUNCE]

Job 36:33 The thunder **a** his presence; the storm **a** his indignant anger.
Ps 68:11 The Lord **a** victory, / and throngs of women shout

ANNOUNCING (6) [ANNOUNCE]

Isa 63: 1 "It is I, the LORD, **a** your salvation! It is I,
Mt 9:35 and **a** the Good News about the Kingdom.
27:37 cross above Jesus' head, **a** the charge against him.
Mk 15:26 cross above Jesus' head, **a** the charge against him.
1Co 11:26 you are **a** the Lord's death until he comes again.
Eph 3: 2 God has given me this special ministry of **a** his

ANNOYING (1) [ANNOYS]

Pr 27:15 A nagging wife is as **a** as the constant dripping on

ANNOYS (1) [ANNOYING]

Pr 19:13 a father; a nagging wife **a** like a constant dripping.

ANNUAL (34)

Ex 13: 9 This **a** festival will be a visible reminder to you,
23:15 This festival will be an **a** event at the appointed
30:10 be a regular, **a** event from generation to generation,
Lev 23:37 "These are the LORD's appointed **a** festivals.
23:44 So Moses gave these instructions regarding the **a**
Nu 10:10 sounding them at your **a** festivals and at the
15: 3 or a special sacrifice at any of the **a** festivals,
29:39 these offerings to the LORD at your **a** festivals.
Jdg 9:27 During the **a** harvest festival at Shechem, held in
21:19 Then they thought of the **a** festival of the LORD
1Sa 1:21 and their children went on their **a** trip to offer a
20: 6 to go home to Bethlehem for an **a** family sacrifice.
1Ki 5:11 In return Solomon sent him an **a** payment of
8: 2 They all assembled before the king at the **a**
12:32 similar to the **a** Festival of Shelters in Judah.
2Ki 3: 4 They used to pay the king of Israel an **a** tribute of
17: 3 so Israel was forced to pay heavy **a** tribute to
17: 4 and by refusing to pay the **a** tribute to Assyria.
2Ch 5: 3 They all assembled before the king at the **a**
8:13 new moon festivals, and at the three **a** festivals—
24: 5 towns of Judah and collect the required **a** offerings,
26: 8 The Meunites paid **a** tribute to him, and his fame
27: 5 he received from them an **a** tribute of 7,500 pounds
31: 3 and for the other **a** festivals as required in the law
Ezr 3: 5 and the other **a** festivals to the LORD.
Ne 10:32 we promise to obey the command to pay the **a**
10:33 the new moon celebrations, and the **a** festivals;
Est 9:19 living in unwalled villages celebrate an **a** festival
9:21 encouraging them to celebrate an **a** festival on
9:23 Mordecai's suggestion and began this **a** custom.
9:31 an **a** celebration of these days at the appointed
Hos 2:11 I will put an end to her **a** festivals, her new moon
Jn 2:13 It was time for the **a** Passover celebration,
6: 4 (It was nearly time for the **a** Passover celebration.)

ANOINT (18) [ANOINTED, ANOINTING]

Ex 28:41 with these garments, and then **a** and ordain them.
30:26 Use this scented oil to **a** the Tabernacle, the Ark of
30:30 Use this oil also to **a** Aaron and his sons,
40:11 Next **a** the large washbasin and its pedestal to
40:13 Clothe Aaron with the holy garments and **a** him,
40:15 **A** them as you did their father, so they may serve
1Sa 9:16 **A** him to be the leader of my people, Israel.
16: 3 and I will show you which of his sons to **a** for
16:12 And the LORD said, "This is the one; **a** him."
1Ki 1:34 and Nathan the prophet are to **a** him king over
19:15 you arrive there, **a** Hazael to be king of Aram.
19:16 Then **a** Jehu son of Nimshi to be king of Israel,
19:16 and **a** Elisha son of Shaphat from Abel-meholah to
2Ki 9: 3 I **a** you to be the king over Israel.' Then open the
9: 6 I **a** you king over the LORD's people, Israel.
Da 9:24 the prophetic vision, and to **a** the Most Holy Place.
Mic 6:15 your olives but not get enough oil to **a** yourselves.
Lk 7:46 You neglected the courtesy of olive oil to **a** my

ANOINTED (70) [ANOINT]

LORD'S* ANOINTED (10) 1Sa 16:6; 24:6,10; 26:9,16,23; 2Sa 1:14,16; 19:21; La 4:20

Ge 31:13 the place where you **a** the pillar of stone and made
35:14 an offering to God and **a** the pillar with olive oil.
Ex 29:29 so they can be **a** and ordained in them.
Lev 6:20 "On the day Aaron and his sons are **a**, they must
6:22 offering this same sacrifice on the day they are **a**.
8:10 and **a** the Tabernacle and everything in it,
16:32 **a** high priest who serves in place of his ancestor
Nu 3: 3 They were **a** and set apart to minister as priests.
7: 1 he **a** it and set it apart as holy, along with all its
7:10 dedication gifts for the altar at the time it was **a**.
7:84 brought by the leaders of Israel at the time it was **a**:
7:88 the dedication offering for the altar after it was **a**.
1Sa 2:10 to his king; / he increases the might of his **a** one."
2:35 and his family will be priests to my **a** kings
10:16 But Saul didn't tell his uncle that Samuel had **a**
12: 3 as I stand before the LORD and before his **a** one—
12: 5 "The LORD and his **a** one are my witnesses,"
15: 1 "I **a** you king of Israel because the LORD told
15:17 of Israel? The LORD has **a** you king of Israel.
16: 6 and thought, "Surely this is the LORD's **a**!"
24: 6 "It is a serious thing to attack the LORD's **a** one,
24:10 'I will never harm him—he is the LORD's **a** one.'
26: 9 innocent after attacking the LORD's **a** one?
26:11 LORD forbid that I should kill the one he has **a**!
26:16 you failed to protect your master, the LORD's **a**!
26:23 you in my power, for you are the LORD's **a** one.
2Sa 1:14 "Were you not afraid to kill the LORD's **a** one?"
1:16 confessed that you killed the LORD's **a** one."
1:21 the shield of Saul will no longer be **a** with oil.
2: 7 of Judah, who have **a** me as their new king."
3:39 And even though I am the **a** king, these two sons
5: 3 before the LORD. And they **a** him king of Israel.
5:17 When the Philistines heard that David had been **a**
12: 7 'I **a** you king of Israel and saved you from the
19:10 Now Absalom, whom we **a** to rule over us, is dead.
19:21 should die, for he cursed the LORD's **a** king!"
22:51 to your king; / you show unfailing love to your **a**,
23: 1 David, the man **a** by the God of Jacob,
1Ki 1:45 and Zadok and Nathan have **a** him as the new king.
2Ki 9:12 and that at the LORD's command he had been **a**
11:12 They **a** him, and all the people clapped their hands
23:30 Then the people **a** his son Jehoahaz and made him
1Ch 11: 3 They **a** him king of Israel, just as the LORD had
14: 8 When the Philistines heard that David had been **a**
29:22 They **a** him before the LORD as their leader, and they **a** Zadok as their priest.
2Ch 6:42 O LORD God, do not reject your **a** one.
23:11 Then they **a** him, and everyone shouted,
Ps 2: 2 against the LORD / and against his **a** one.
18:50 to your king; / you show unfailing love to your **a**,
20: 6 Now I know that the LORD saves his **a** king.
28: 8 his people / and gives victory to his **a** king.
45: 7 is wrong. / Therefore, God—your God—has **a** you,
84: 9 our protector! / Have mercy on the one you have **a**.
89:20 my servant David. / I have **a** him with my holy oil.
89:51 O LORD; / they mock the one you **a** as king.
132:17 of David; / my **a** one will be a light for my people.
Isa 45: 1 his **a** one, whose right hand he will empower.
La 4:20 Our king, the LORD's **a**, the very life of our
Eze 28:14 and **a** you as the mighty angelic guardian.
Da 9:25 given to rebuild Jerusalem until the **A** One comes.
9:26 the **A** One will be killed, appearing to have
Hab 3:13 to rescue your chosen people, to save your **a** ones.
Zec 4:14 "They represent the two **a** ones who assist the
Mk 14: 8 and has **a** my body for burial ahead of time.
Lk 7:46 my head, but she has **a** my feet with rare perfume.
Jn 12: 3 and she **a** Jesus' feet with it and wiped his feet
Ac 4:27 against Jesus, your holy servant, whom you **a**.
10:38 And no doubt you know that God **a** Jesus of
Heb 1: 9 is wrong. / Therefore God, your God, has **a** you,

ANOINTING (30) [ANOINT]

Ex 25: 6 spices for the **a** oil and the fragrant incense;
29: 7 Then take the **a** oil and pour it over his head.
29:21 from the altar and mix it with some of the **a** oil.
29:36 atonement for it; make it holy by **a** it with oil.
30:25 Blend these ingredients into a holy **a** oil.
30:31 of Israel, 'This will always be my holy **a** oil.
31:11 the **a** oil; and the special incense for the Holy
35: 8 spices for the **a** oil and the fragrant incense;
35:15 its carrying poles; the **a** oil and fragrant incense;
35:28 oil for the light, the **a** oil, and the fragrant incense.
37:29 Then he made the sacred oil for **a** the priests
39:38 the gold altar; the **a** oil; the fragrant incense;
40: 9 "Take the **a** oil and sprinkle it on the Tabernacle
40:10 Sprinkle the **a** oil on the altar of burnt offering
40:15 With this **a**, Aaron's descendants are set apart for
Lev 7:36 their regular share from the time of the priests' **a**.
8: 2 the **a** oil, the bull for the sin offering, the two rams,
8:10 Then Moses took the **a** oil and anointed the
8:11 **a** it and all its utensils and the washbasin and its
8:12 Then he poured some of the **a** oil on Aaron's head,
8:12 thus **a** him and making him holy for his work.
8:30 Next Moses took some of the **a** oil and some of the
10: 7 of death, for the **a** oil of the LORD is upon you."
21:10 who has had the **a** oil poured on his head and has
21:12 because he has been made holy by the **a** oil of his
Nu 4:16 the daily grain offering, and the **a** oil.
Ps 23: 5 You welcome me as a guest, / **a** my head with oil.
133: 2 For harmony is as precious as the fragrant **a** oil
Mk 6:13 healed many sick people, **a** them with olive oil.
Jas 5:14 over them, **a** them with oil in the name of the Lord.

ANON [KJV] See RIGHT (AWAY)

ANOTHER (418)

LOVE ONE ANOTHER (7) 1Th 4:9; 1Jn 2:7; 3:11,23; 4:7; 2Jn 1:5,6

ONE ANOTHER (37) Ge 25:18; 42:1; Lev 19:11; Isa 13:8; 34:14; 41:6; Jer 9:4,20; 22:8; Eze 4:17; 24:23; Zep 3:13; Zec 7:9; Mt 21:38; Mk 12:7; Lk 8:25; Jn 10:41; 13:35; 1Co 3:3; Gal 5:13,15,15,26,26; Eph 4:32; 5:21; Php 2:2; 1Th 4:9; Heb 10:24; 13:4; 1Pe 3:8; 1Jn 2:7; 3:11,23; 4:7; 2Jn 1:5,6

Ge 4:25 with his wife again, and she gave birth to **a** son.
4:25 "God has granted me **a** son in place of Abel,
5: 4 Adam lived **a** 800 years, and he had other sons
5: 7 Seth lived **a** 807 years, and he had other sons
5:10 Enosh lived **a** 815 years, and he had other sons
5:13 Kenan lived **a** 840 years, and he had other sons
5:19 Jared lived **a** 800 years, and he had other sons
5:22 Enoch lived **a** 300 years in close fellowship with
5:26 Methuselah lived **a** 782 years, and he had other
8: 6 After **a** forty days, Noah opened the window he
9: 6 you must execute anyone who murders **a** person,
9:11 I solemnly promise never to send **a** flood to kill all
9:28 Noah lived **a** 350 years after the Flood.
11:11 Shem lived **a** 500 years and had other sons
11:13 Arphaxad lived **a** 403 years and had other sons
11:15 Shelah lived **a** 403 years and had other sons
11:17 Eber lived **a** 430 years and had other sons
11:19 Peleg lived **a** 209 years and had other sons
11:21 Reu lived **a** 207 years and had other sons
11:23 Serug lived **a** 200 years and had other sons
11:25 Nahor lived **a** 119 years and had other sons
13: 9 to stay in this area, then I'll move on to **a** place."
25:18 descended from Ishmael camped close to one **a**.
26:21 Isaac's men then dug **a** well, but again there was a
26:22 Abandoning that one, he dug **a** well, and the local
29:27 if you promise to work **a** seven years for me."
29:33 She soon became pregnant again and had **a** son.
29:33 heard that I was unloved and has given me **a** son."
30:10 Soon Zilpah presented him with **a** son.
30:24 she said, "May the LORD give me yet **a** son."
35:17 "Don't be afraid—you have **a** son!"
36:12 Eliphaz had **a** son named Amalek, born to Timna,
37: 9 Then Joseph had **a** dream and told his brothers
38: 4 Then Judah's wife had **a** son, and she named him
40:23 all about Joseph, never giving him **a** thought.
41:22 "A little later I had **a** dream. This time there were
42: 1 "Why are you standing around looking at one **a**?
43: 6 "Why did you ever tell him you had **a** brother?"
43: 7 and he asked us if we had **a** brother so we told him.
Ex 12: 4 let them share the lamb with **a** family in the
21:10 If he himself marries her and then takes **a** wife,
21:14 if someone deliberately attacks and kills **a** person,
22: 6 gets out of control and goes into **a** person's field,
26:36 "Make **a** curtain from fine linen for the entrance of
36:32 They made **a** five for the north side and five for the
36:37 Then they made **a** curtain for the entrance to the
Lev 12: 5 then wait **a** sixty-six days to be purified from the
13: 5 On the seventh day the priest will make **a**
13:17 If, after **a** examination, the affected areas have
13:33 must put the person in quarantine for **a** seven days,
13:36 the priest must do **a** examination. If the infection
14:39 On the seventh day the priest must return for **a**
19:11 "Do not steal. "Do not cheat one **a**. "Do not lie.
20:10 "If a man commits adultery with **a** man's wife,
23:36 and present **a** offering to the LORD by fire.
24:17 "Anyone who takes **a** person's life must be put to
24:18 "Anyone who kills **a** person's animal must pay it
24:19 "Anyone who injures **a** person must be dealt with
24:20 Whatever anyone does to hurt **a** person must be
24:21 but whoever kills **a** person must be put to death.
27:10 should never be exchanged or substituted for **a**—
Nu 5: 6 betray the LORD by doing wrong to **a** person,
5:13 Suppose she sleeps with **a** man, but there is no
5:20 and defiled yourself by sleeping with **a** man"—
19: 2 "Here is **a** ritual law required by the LORD:
23:13 King Balak told him, "Come with me to **a** place.
23:27 to Balaam, "Come, I will take you to yet **a** place.
28:25 On the seventh day of the festival you must call **a**
29: 7 you must call **a** holy assembly of all the people.
29:12 you must call yet **a** holy assembly of all the people,
29:35 the festival, call all the people to **a** holy assembly.
32:41 The people of Jair, **a** clan of the tribe of Manasseh,
35:16 and kills **a** person with a piece of iron,
35:17 and kills **a** person with a large stone,
35:18 and kills **a** person with a wooden weapon.
35:20 So if in premeditated hostility someone pushes **a**
35:21 Or if someone angrily hits **a** person with a fist
35:22 " 'But suppose someone pushes **a** person without
35:22 or throws something that unintentionally hits **a**
36: 3 But if any of them marries **a** man from **a** tribe,
36: 9 No inheritance may pass from one tribe to **a**;
Dt 2:10 They were as tall as the Anakites, **a** race of giants.
4:34 himself by rescuing it from **a** by means of trials,
16:13 "**A** celebration, the Festival of Shelters, must be
18:20 prophet who claims to give a message from **a** god
22:14 and falsely accuses her of having slept with **a** man.
22:24 man must die because he violated **a** man's wife.
24: 2 If she then leaves and marries **a** man
27:24 'Cursed is anyone who kills **a** person in secret.'
28:30 be engaged to a woman, but **a** man will ravish her.
29:28 people from their land and exiled them to **a** land,
34:10 There has never been **a** prophet like Moses,
Jos 4: 9 Joshua also built **a** memorial of twelve stones in
20: 3 Anyone who kills **a** person unintentionally can run
20: 9 Anyone who accidentally killed **a** person could
21:27 of Gershon, **a** clan within the tribe of Levi,
22:19 or draw us into your rebellion by building **a** altar
Jdg 2:10 **a** generation grew up who did not acknowledge the
9:37 And **a** group is coming down the road past the
19: 8 this afternoon." So they had **a** day of feasting.
20:25 but the men of Benjamin killed **a** eighteen
20:45 They continued the chase until they had killed **a**
Ru 1: 9 May the LORD bless you with the security of **a**
3:12 there is **a** man who is more closely related to you

1Sa 2: 7 The LORD makes one poor and **a** rich; / he brings one down and lifts **a** up.
2:25 If someone sins against **a** person, God can mediate
10: 3 young goats, **a** will have three loaves of bread,
13:18 **a** went west to Beth-horon, and the third moved
17:20 So David left the sheep with **a** shepherd and set out
18:11 and escaped. This happened **a** time, too,
18:21 "Here's **a** chance to see him killed by the
28: 1 mustered their armies for **a** war with Israel.
2Sa 3:11 Ishbosheth didn't dare say **a** word because he was
7: 6 always been a tent, moving from one place to **a**.
7:22 We have never even heard of **a** god like you!
8:14 This was **a** example of how the LORD made
11:25 David said. "The sword kills one as well as **a**!
12:11 I will give your wives to **a** man, and he will go to
18:26 the watchman saw **a** man running toward them.
18:26 He shouted down, "Here comes **a** one!" The king
21:18 there was **a** battle against the Philistines at Gob.
21:18 Hushah killed Saph, **a** descendant of the giants.
21:19 In still **a** battle at Gob, Elhanan son of Jair from
21:20 In **a** battle with the Philistines at Gath, a huge man
23:20 **A** time he chased a lion down into a pit. Then,
23:21 **A** time, armed only with a club, he killed a great
1Ki 4:15 married to Basemath, **a** of Solomon's daughters.)
6: 8 and **a** flight of stairs between the second and third
8:31 "If someone wrongs **a** person and is required to
11: 7 the detestable god of Moab, and **a** for Molech,
11:26 **A** rebel leader was Jeroboam son of Nebat, one of
13:10 So he left Bethel and went home **a** way.
18: 6 by himself, and Obadiah went **a** way by himself.
20:22 "Get ready for **a** attack by the king of Aram next
20:25 Recruit **a** army like the one you lost. Give us the
20:30 but the wall fell on them and killed **a** 27,000.
20:35 one of the group of prophets to say to **a** man,
20:37 Then the prophet turned to **a** man and said,
21:28 Then **a** message from the LORD came to Elijah,
2Ki 1:11 So the king sent **a** captain with fifty men.
4: 5 brought many jars to her, and she filled one after **a**.
4: 6 "Bring me **a** jar," she said to one of her sons.
7: 8 they went into one tent after **a**, eating,
11: 6 **A** third of you are to stand guard at the Sur Gate.
18: 5 There was never **a** king like him in the land of
18:32 Then I will arrange to take you to **a** land like this
19:37 and **a** son, Esarhaddon, became the next king of
23:34 then installed Eliakim, **a** of Josiah's sons,
1Ch 2:48 **A** of Caleb's concubines, Maacah, gave birth to
3: 4 to Jerusalem, where he reigned **a** thirty-three years.
4:19 and **a** was the father of Eshtemoa the Maacathite.
11:22 **A** time he chased a lion down into a pit. Then,
11:23 **A** time, armed with only a club, he killed an
16:20 forth between nations, / from one kingdom to **a**.
17: 5 always been a tent, moving from one place to **a**.
17:20 We have never even heard of **a** god like you!
18:13 This was **a** example of how the LORD made
20: 5 During **a** battle with the Philistines, Elhanan son of
20: 6 In **a** battle with the Philistines at Gath, a huge man
23: 5 and **a** four thousand will praise the LORD with
29: 1 the Temple he will build is not just **a** building—
2Ch 3:15 each topped by a capital extending upward **a** 7-1/2
6:22 "If someone wrongs **a** person and is required to
11:20 Later Rehoboam married **a** cousin, Maacah,
20: 2 (This was **a** name for En-gedi.)
23: 5 **A** third will go over to the royal palace,
25: 5 **A** thing Amaziah did was to organize the army,
25:12 They captured **a** ten thousand and took them to the
29:17 of the LORD itself, which took **a** eight days.
30:23 then decided to continue the festival **a** seven days, so they celebrated joyfully for **a** week.
35:24 out of his chariot and placed him in **a** chariot.
Ezr 2:59 **A** group returned to Jerusalem at this time from the
Ne 3:11 of the Ovens, in addition to **a** section of the wall.
3:19 repaired **a** section of wall opposite the armory by
3:21 and grandson of Hakkoz rebuilt **a** section of the
3:24 who rebuilt **a** section of the wall from Azariah's
3:27 who repaired **a** section opposite the great
3:30 the sixth son of Zalaph, repaired **a** section,
7:61 "**A** group returned to Jerusalem at this time from
9: 1 On October 31 the people returned for **a**
Est 1:19 and that you choose **a** queen more worthy than she.
2:14 the care of Shaashgaz, **a** of the king's eunuchs.
9:29 wrote **a** letter putting the queen's full authority
Job 1:16 still speaking, **a** messenger arrived with this news:
1:18 still speaking, **a** messenger arrived with this news:
21:25 **A** person dies in bitter poverty, never having tasted
31:10 then may my wife belong to **a** man; may other men
Ps 75: 6 even from the wilderness—/ can raise **a** person up.
105:13 forth between nations, / from one kingdom to **a**.
Pr 6:26 and sleeping with **a** man's wife may cost you your
6:29 So it is with the man who sleeps with **a** man's
17: 9 Disregarding **a** person's faults preserves love;
22:26 Do not co-sign **a** person's note or put up **a**
23:28 looking for **a** victim who will be unfaithful to his
23:35 When will I wake up so I can have **a** drink?"
Ecc 4: 7 I observed yet **a** example of meaninglessness in
5:13 There is **a** serious problem I have seen in the
6: 1 There is **a** serious tragedy I have seen in our world.
9:13 Here is **a** bit of wisdom that has impressed me as I
10: 5 There is **a** evil I have seen as I have watched the
Isa 2: 1 This is **a** vision that Isaiah son of Amoz saw
13: 8 They look helplessly at one **a** as the flames of the
34:14 Wild goats will bleat at one **a** among the ruins,
36:17 Then I will arrange to take you to **a** land like this
37:38 and **a** son, Esarhaddon, became the next king of
40:26 He brings them out one after **a**, calling each by its
41: 6 They encourage one **a** with the words,
65:15 destroy you and call his true servants by **a** name.
Jer 2: 1 The LORD gave me **a** message. He said,
2:11 Has any nation ever exchanged its gods for **a** god,
2:36 you flit from one ally to **a** asking for help.
7: 1 The LORD gave **a** message to Jeremiah. He said,
9: 4 They all take advantage of one **a** and spread their
9:20 your daughters to wail; teach one **a** how to lament.
11: 1 The LORD gave **a** message to Jeremiah. He said,
13: 3 Then the LORD gave me **a** message:
15: 6 I am tired of always giving you **a** chance.
16: 1 The LORD gave me **a** message. He said,
18: 1 The LORD gave **a** message to Jeremiah. He said,
22: 8 will pass by the ruins of this city and say to one **a**,
30: 1 The LORD gave **a** message to Jeremiah. He said,
33:23 The LORD gave **a** message to Jeremiah. He said,
36:27 the LORD gave Jeremiah **a** message.
36:28 "Get **a** scroll, and write everything again just as
36:32 Then Jeremiah took **a** scroll and dictated again to
43: 8 the LORD gave **a** message to Jeremiah.
La 3:38 it not the Most High who helps one and harms **a**?
Eze 4:17 so scarce that the people will look at one **a** in
5: 2 Scatter **a** third across your map and slash at it with
7: 5 With one blow after **a** I will bring total disaster!
15: 7 if they escape from one fire, they will fall into **a**.
16: 1 Then **a** message came to me from the LORD:
17: 7 But then **a** great eagle with broad wings and full
18: 1 Then **a** message came to me from the LORD:
19: 5 hopes for him were gone, / she took **a** of her cubs
28:20 Then **a** message came to me from the LORD:
30: 1 This is **a** message that came to me from the
32:17 **a** message came to me from the LORD:
34:17 I will judge between one sheep and **a**,
34:22 And I will judge between one sheep and **a**.
37:16 Then take **a** stick and carve these words on it:
38: 1 This is **a** message that came to me from the
40:23 there was **a** gateway leading to the Temple's inner
40:27 was **a** gateway that led into the inner courtyard.
42: 3 **A** block of rooms looked out onto the pavement of
42:12 and **a** on the east at the end of the interior
43:23 offer **a** young bull that has no defects and a perfect
44:31 or that dies after being attacked by **a** animal.
46: 7 With the ram he must bring **a** half bushel of flour.
46:11 **a** half bushel of flour with each ram, and as much
47: 4 He measured off **a** 1,750 feet and told me to go
47: 4 After **a** 1,750 feet, it was up to my waist.
47: 5 Then he measured **a** 1,750 feet, and the river was
Da 2:39 **a** great kingdom, inferior to yours, will rise to take
7: 8 suddenly **a** small horn appeared among them.
7:24 Then **a** king will arise, different from the other ten,
8: 1 of King Belshazzar's reign, I, Daniel, saw **a** vision,
10: 1 Daniel (also known as Belteshazzar) had **a** vision.
11:18 But **a** commander from a land will put an end to
Hos 4: 2 is violence everywhere, with one murder after **a**.
7: 7 They kill their kings one after **a**, and no one cries
Am 4: 1 and who are always asking your husbands for **a**
4: 7 I sent rain on one town but withheld it from **a**.
4: 7 Rain fell on one field, while **a** field withered away.
4: 8 People staggered from one town to **a** for a drink of
7: 4 Then the Sovereign LORD showed me **a** vision.
7: 7 Then he showed me **a** vision. I saw the Lord
8: 1 Then the Sovereign LORD showed me **a** vision.
Mic 7:18 Where is **a** God like you, who pardons the sins of
Zep 3:13 to each other, never telling lies or deceiving one **a**.
Hag 2: 1 the LORD sent **a** message through the prophet
Zec 1: 7 the LORD sent **a** message to the prophet
4: 8 Then **a** message came to me from the LORD:
6: 9 Then I received **a** message from the LORD:
7: 1 **a** message came to Zechariah from the LORD.
7: 9 and show mercy and kindness to one **a**.
8: 1 Then **a** message came to me from the LORD
8:18 Here is **a** message that came to me from the
8:21 The people of one city will say to the people in **a**,
Mal 2:13 Here is **a** thing you do. You cover the LORD's
Mt 2:12 when it was time to leave, they went home **a** way,
2:22 Then, in **a** dream, he was warned to go to Galilee.
8:21 **A** of his disciples said, "Lord, first let me return
13:24 Here is **a** story Jesus told: "The Kingdom of
13:31 Here is **a** illustration Jesus used: "The Kingdom of
15:14 and if one blind person guides **a**, they will both fall
18:15 "If **a** believer sins against you, go privately
19: 9 divorces his wife and marries **a** commits adultery
21:33 vineyard to tenant farmers and moved to **a** country.
21:35 his servants, beat one, killed one, and stoned **a**.
21:38 they said to one **a**, 'Here comes the heir to this
22: 5 about their business, one to his farm, **a** to his store.
24: 2 that not one stone will be left on top of **a**!"
25:15 two bags of gold to **a**, and one bag of gold to the
26:71 **a** servant girl noticed him and said to those
Mk 4:26 "Here is **a** illustration of what the Kingdom of
8: 1 About this time **a** great crowd had gathered,
9:26 and threw the boy into **a** violent convulsion
12: 1 vineyard to tenant farmers and moved to **a** country.
12: 4 "The owner then sent **a** servant, but they beat him
12: 7 "But the farmers said to one **a**, 'Here comes the
13: 2 that not one stone will be left on top of **a**."
14:58 and in three days I will build **a**, made without
15:37 Then Jesus uttered **a** loud cry and breathed his last.
Lk 6: 6 On **a** Sabbath day, a man with a deformed right
6:39 "What good is it for one blind person to lead **a**?
8:25 They said to one **a**, "Who is this man, that even
9:56 So they went on to **a** village.
9:59 He said to **a** person, "Come, be my disciple."
9:61 **A** said, "Yes, Lord, I will follow you, but first let
13: 8 Leave it **a** year, and I'll give it special attention
14:19 **A** said he had just bought five pair of oxen
14:20 **A** had just been married, so he said he couldn't
16: 6 that bill and write **a** one for four hundred gallons.'
17: 3 If **a** believer sins, rebuke him; then if he repents,
20: 9 and moved to **a** country to live for several years.
20:11 So the owner sent **a** servant, but the same thing
21: 6 that not one stone will be left on top of **a**."
22:20 After supper he took **a** cup of wine and said,
Jn 1:16 he brought to us—one gracious blessing after **a**!
10:41 didn't do miracles," they remarked to one **a**,
11:15 because this will give you **a** opportunity to believe
13:35 Your love for one **a** will prove to the world that
14:16 ask the Father, and he will give you **a** Counselor,
18:15 followed along behind, as did **a** of the disciples.
Ac 12:17 he said. And then he went to **a** place.
13:35 **A** psalm explains more fully, saying, 'You will not
17: 7 for they profess allegiance to **a** king, Jesus."
19:32 were all shouting, some one thing and some **a**.
21:34 Some shouted one thing and some **a**. He couldn't
28:11 set sail on **a** ship that had wintered at the island—
Ro 7: 3 she would be committing adultery if she married **a**
7:23 But there is **a** law at work within me that is at war
9:21 one jar for decoration and **a** to throw garbage into?
9:29 And Isaiah said in **a** place, / "If the Lord Almighty
13:11 **A** reason for right living is that you know how late
14: 2 But **a** believer who has a sensitive conscience will
14: 5 some think one day is more holy than **a** day,
14:10 So why do you condemn **a** Christian? Why do you look down on **a** Christian?
14:13 you will not put an obstacle in **a** Christian's path.
14:15 And if **a** Christian is distressed by what you eat,
14:20 But it is wrong to eat anything if it makes **a** person
14:21 or do anything else if it might cause **a** Christian to
15:10 And in **a** place it is written, / "Rejoice, O you
1Co 3: 3 You are jealous of one **a** and quarrel with each
3: 4 follower of Paul," and **a** says, "I prefer Apollos,"
4: 6 brag about one of your leaders at the expense of **a**.
6: 1 When you have something against **a** Christian,
6: 6 But instead, one Christian sues **a**—right in front of
8:13 If what I eat is going to make **a** Christian sin,
8:13 for I don't want to make **a** Christian stumble.
12: 8 to **a** he gives the gift of special knowledge.
12: 9 The Spirit gives special faith to **a**, and to someone
12:10 perform miracles, and to **a** the ability to prophesy.
12:10 really the Spirit of God or **a** spirit that is speaking.
12:10 Still **a** person is given the ability to speak in
12:10 and **a** is given the ability to interpret what is being
14:26 When you meet, one will sing, **a** will teach,
14:26 **a** will tell some special revelation God has given,
14:26 while **a** will interpret what is said.
14:30 and **a** person receives a revelation from the Lord,
15:21 from the dead has begun through **a** man,
15:41 while the moon and stars each have **a** kind.
2Co 2: 1 I won't make them unhappy with **a** painful visit."
8:18 We are also sending **a** brother with Titus. He is
8:22 And we are also sending with them **a** brother who
11: 9 who came from Macedonia brought me **a** gift.
Gal 3:24 Let me put it **a** way. The law was our guardian
5:13 sinful nature, but freedom to serve one **a** in love.
5:15 you are always biting and devouring one **a**,
5:15 watch out! Beware of destroying one **a**.
5:26 or irritate one **a**, or be jealous of one **a**.
Eph 4:32 kind to each other, tenderhearted, forgiving one **a**,
5:21 you will submit to one **a** out of reverence for
Php 2: 2 loving one **a**, and working together with one heart
1Th 4: 6 Never cheat **a** Christian in this matter by taking his
4: 9 For God himself has taught you to love one **a**.
1Ti 5:18 And in **a** place, "Those who work deserve their
6: 2 because you are helping **a** believer by your efforts.
Heb 4: 7 So God set **a** time for entering his place of rest,
4: 8 God would not have spoken later about **a** day of
5: 6 And in **a** passage God said to him, / "You are a
7:23 **A** difference is that there were many priests under
7:23 When one priest died, **a** had to take his place.
10:24 Think of ways to encourage one **a** to outbursts of
11: 8 and go to **a** land that God would give him as his
12:26 shook the earth, but now he makes **a** promise:
13: 4 and remain faithful to one **a** in marriage.
Jas 2: 2 and **a** comes in who is poor and dressed in shabby
2:25 Rahab the prostitute is **a** example of this. She was
1Pe 3: 8 loving one **a** with tender hearts and humble minds.
1Jn 2: 7 This commandment—to love one **a**—is the same
2: 9 but rejects **a** Christian is still in darkness.
3:11 heard from the beginning: We should love one **a**.
3:15 Anyone who hates **a** Christian is really a murderer
3:23 Jesus Christ, and love one **a**, just as he commanded
4: 7 Dear friends, let us continue to love one **a**, for love
4:20 "I love God," but hates **a** Christian,
2Jn 1: 5 to urge you, dear lady, that we should love one **a**.
1: 6 and he has commanded us to love one **a**, just as
Rev 6: 4 And **a** horse appeared, a red one. Its rider was
7: 2 And I saw **a** angel coming from the east,
8: 3 Then **a** angel with a gold incense burner came
10: 1 Then I saw **a** mighty angel coming down from
12: 3 I witnessed in heaven **a** significant event.
13:11 Then I saw **a** beast come up out of the earth.
14: 6 And I saw **a** angel flying through the heavens,
14: 8 Then **a** angel followed him through the skies,
14:17 **a** angel came from the Temple in heaven,
14:18 Then **a** angel, who has power to destroy the world
15: 1 Then I saw in heaven **a** significant event, and it
18: 1 After all this I saw **a** angel come down from
18: 4 Then I heard **a** voice calling from heaven,
18:18 "Where in all the world is there **a** city like this?"

ANSWER (151) [ANSWERED, ANSWERING, ANSWERS]

Ex 19: 8 So Moses brought the people's **a** back to the
Lev 7:18 if you eat it, you will have to **a** for your sin.
19: 8 you will **a** for the sin of profaning what is holy to
25:21 The **a** is, 'I will order my blessing for you in the

Jdg 8: 3 When the men of Ephraim heard Gideon's **a**,
8: 8 to Peniel and asked for food, but he got the same **a**.
14: 15 "Get the **a** to the riddle from your husband,
14: 16 people a riddle, but you haven't told me the **a**."
14: 16 "I haven't even given the **a** to my father
14: 17 he told her the **a** because of her persistent nagging.
14: 17 Then she gave the **a** to the young men.
14: 18 the men of the town came to Samson with their **a**:
14: 18 you wouldn't have found the **a** to my riddle!"
19: 28 He said, "Get up! Let's go!" But there was no **a**.
1Sa 1: 11 my sorrow and **a** my prayer and give me a son,
2: 1 Now I have an **a** for my enemies, / as I delight in
4: 20 But she did not **a** or respond in any way.
17: 30 them the same thing and received the same **a**.
28: 6 but the LORD refused to **a** him, either by dreams
2Sa 22: 42 cried to the LORD, but he refused to **a** them.
24: 13 and let me know what **a** to give the LORD."
1Ki 8: 52 Hear and **a** them whenever they cry out to you.
9: 9 And the **a** will be, 'Because his people forgot the
12: 5 Then come back for my **a**." So the people went
12: 6 he asked. "How should I **a** these people?"
12: 7 the people today and give them a favorable **a**,
12: 9 "How should I **a** these people who want me to
14: 5 You must give her the **a** that I give you."
18: 26 of Baal all morning, shouting, "O Baal, **a** us!"
18: 29 but still there was no reply, no voice, no **a**.
18: 37 O LORD, **a** me! **A** me so these people will know
20: 11 The king of Israel sent back this **a**: "A warrior still
21: 4 home angry and sullen because of Naboth's **a**.
2Ki 18: 36 But the people were silent and did not **a**
1Ch 21: 12 and let me know what **a** to give the LORD."
2Ch 7: 22 And the **a** will be, 'Because his people abandoned
10: 5 "Come back in three days for my **a**."
10: 6 he asked. "How should I **a** these people?"
10: 9 "How should I **a** these people who want me to
Ezr 5: 11 "This was their **a**: 'We are the servants of the God
Job 6: 24 "All I want is a reasonable **a**—then I will keep
9: 3 would it be possible to **a** him even once in a
9: 14 that I should try to **a** God or even reason with him?
11: 2 "Shouldn't someone **a** this torrent of words?
12: 4 I am a man who calls on God and receives an **a**.
13: 22 Now summon me, and I will **a**! Or let me speak to
14: 15 You would call and I would **a**, and you would
15: 17 will listen, I will **a** you from my own experience.
18: 2 you stop talking? Speak sense if you want us to **a**!
30: 20 "I cry to you, O God, but you don't **a** me. I stand
32: 3 God by their inability to **a** Job's arguments.
32: 14 with me, I would not **a** with that kind of logic!
33: 5 **A** me, if you can; make your case and take your
35: 4 "I will **a** you and all your friends, too.
35: 12 "And if they do cry out and God does not **a**,
38: 3 have some questions for you, and you must **a** them.
40: 7 have some questions for you, and you must **a** them.
42: 4 some questions for you, and you must **a** them.'
Ps 4: 1 **A** me when I call, / O God who declares me
4: 3 The LORD will **a** when I call to him.
6: 9 has heard my plea; / the LORD will **a** my prayer.
13: 3 Turn and **a** me, O LORD my God!
17: 6 I am praying to you because I know you will **a**,
18: 41 cried to the LORD, but he refused to **a** them.
20: 5 our God. / May the LORD **a** all your prayers.
20: 6 He will **a** him from his holy heaven / and rescue
22: 2 Every day I call to you, my God, but you do not **a**.
27: 7 my pleading, O LORD. / Be merciful and **a** me!
28: 1 Please help me; don't refuse to **a** me. / For if you
38: 15 O LORD. / You must **a** for me, O Lord my God.
55: 2 Please listen and **a** me, / for I am overwhelmed by
65: 2 for you **a** our prayers, / and to you all people will
65: 5 You faithfully **a** our prayers with awesome deeds,
69: 13 O God, / **a** my prayer with your sure salvation.
69: 16 **A** my prayers, O LORD, / for your unfailing love
69: 17 **a** me quickly, for I am in deep trouble!
86: 1 and hear my prayer; / **a** me, for I need your help.
86: 7 you whenever trouble strikes, / and you will **a** me.
91: 15 When they call on me, I will **a**; / I will be with
102: 2 your ear / and **a** me quickly when I call to you,
119: 42 Then I will have an **a** for those who taunt me,
119: 145 I pray with all my heart; **a** me, LORD! / I will
138: 3 When I pray, you **a** me; / you encourage me by
143: 1 **A** me because you are faithful and righteous.
143: 7 Come quickly, LORD, and **a** me, / for my
Pr 1: 28 "I will not **a** when they cry for help. Even though
15: 1 A gentle **a** turns away wrath, but harsh words stir
16: 1 our thoughts, but the LORD gives the right **a**.
18: 23 The poor plead for mercy; the rich **a** with insults.
26: 4 arguing with fools, don't **a** their foolish arguments,
26: 5 with fools, be sure to **a** their foolish arguments,
27: 11 out to be wise! Then I will be able to **a** my critics.
Ecc 2: 20 It was not the **a** to my search for satisfaction in this
Isa 36: 21 But the people were silent and did not **a**
37: 21 This is my **a** to your prayer concerning King
41: 17 from thirst, then I, the LORD, will **a** them.
41: 28 told you this. Not one gave any **a** when I asked.
46: 7 And when someone prays to it, there is no **a**.
58: 9 Then when you call, the LORD will **a**. 'Yes,
65: 12 the executioner, for when I called, you did not **a**.
65: 24 I will **a** them before they even call to me.
65: 24 their needs, I will go ahead and **a** their prayers!
66: 4 For when I called, they did not **a**. When I spoke,
Jer 7: 13 not listen. I called out to you, but you refused to **a**.
22: 9 And the **a** will be, 'Because they violated their
23: 35 keep asking each other, 'What is the LORD's **a**?'
23: 37 'What is the LORD's **a**?' or 'What is the LORD
35: 17 Because you refuse to listen or **a** when I call,
44: 20 and women alike, who had given him that **a**,
Eze 37: 3 I replied, "you alone know the **a** to that."
Da 10: 12 heard in heaven. I have come in **a** to your prayer.
Hos 2: 21 "I will **a** the pleading of the sky for clouds,
2: 21 which will pour down water on the earth in **a** to its
2: 22 Then the earth will **a** the thirsty cries of the grain,
Am 6: 10 And the person will **a**, "No!" Then he will say,
Mic 6: 3 Tell me why your patience is exhausted! **A** me!
Hab 2: 1 will say to me and how he will **a** my complaint.
2: 2 "Write my **a** in large, clear letters on a tablet,
Zec 13: 9 They will call on my name, and I will **a** them.
Mt 19: 17 But to **a** your question, you can receive eternal life
21: 24 authority to do these things if you **a** one question,"
21: 27 "Then I won't **a** your question either."
22: 46 No one could **a** him. And after that, no one dared
25: 45 And he will **a**, 'I assure you, when you refused to
26: 62 "Well, aren't you going to **a** these charges?
Mk 3: 4 or to destroy it?" But they wouldn't **a** him.
7: 29 "Good **a**!" he said. "And because you have
9: 34 But they didn't **a**, because they had been arguing
11: 29 authority to do these things if you **a** one question,"
11: 30 from heaven or was it merely human? **A** me!"
11: 33 "Then I won't **a** your question either."
14: 60 "Well, aren't you going to **a** these charges?
Lk 14: 4 When they refused to **a**, Jesus touched the sick
14: 6 Again they had no **a**.
20: 8 "Then I won't **a** your question either."
20: 26 Instead, they were amazed by his **a**, and they were
21: 14 So don't worry about how to **a** the charges against
22: 68 And if I ask you a question, you won't **a**.
23: 9 question after question, but Jesus refused to **a**.
Jn 1: 22 Tell us, so we can give an **a** to those who sent us.
8: 7 They kept demanding an **a**, so he stood up again
18: 22 "Is that the way to **a** the high priest?"
19: 9 "Where are you from?" But Jesus gave no **a**.
Ro 4: 10 The **a** is that God accepted him first, and then he
7: 25 Thank God! The **a** is in Jesus Christ our Lord.
1Co 9: 3 This is my **a** to those who question my authority as
2Co 5: 12 so you can **a** those who brag about having a
Col 4: 6 so that you will have the right **a** for everyone.
Phm 1: 22 for I am hoping that God will **a** your prayers
Jas 1: 6 ask him, be sure that you really expect him to **a**,

ANSWERED (100) [ANSWER]

Ge 22: 8 "God will provide a lamb, my son," Abraham **a**.
22: 11 "Abraham! Abraham!" "Yes," he **a**.
23: 10 and he **a** Abraham as the others listened,
23: 14 "Well," Ephron **a**,
25: 21 So the LORD **a** Isaac's prayer, and his wife
27: 18 "Yes, my son," he **a**. "Who is it—Esau
30: 17 And God **a** her prayers. She became pregnant
30: 22 and **a** her prayers by giving her a child.
31: 31 "I rushed away because I was afraid," Jacob **a**.
33: 9 "Brother, I have plenty," Esau **a**. "Keep what you
35: 3 where I will build an altar to the God who **a** my
Ex 24: 3 the LORD had given him, they **a** in unison,
Lev 10: 19 Then Aaron **a** Moses on behalf of his sons.
Nu 9: 8 Moses **a**, "Wait here until I have received
13: 31 other men who had explored the land with him **a**,
20: 19 The Israelites **a**, "We will stay on the main road.
22: 18 But Balaam **a** them, "Even if Balak were to give
22: 30 same donkey you always ride on," the donkey **a**.
Jos 1: 16 They **a** Joshua, "We will do whatever you
9: 9 They **a**, "We are from a very distant country.
10: 14 when the LORD **a** such a request from a human
22: 21 and the half-tribe of Manasseh **a** these high
24: 21 But the people **a** Joshua, saying, "No, we are
Jdg 1: 2 The LORD **a**, "Judah, for I have given them
6: 18 The LORD **a**, "I will stay here until you return."
11: 13 The king of Ammon **a** Jephthah's messengers,
13: 9 God **a** his prayer, and the angel of God appeared
14: 19 and gave their clothing to the men who had **a** his
20: 18 The LORD **a**, "Judah is to go first."
1Sa 7: 9 with the LORD to help Israel, and the LORD **a**.
2Sa 1: 6 The young man **a**, "I happened to be on Mount
24: 25 And the LORD **a** his prayer, and the plague was
1Ki 2: 30 But Joab **a**, "No, I will die here." So Benaiah
10: 3 Solomon **a** all her questions; nothing was too hard
13: 18 But the old prophet **a**, "I am a prophet, too,
20: 14 attack first?" Ahab asked. "Yes," the prophet **a**.
21: 20 "Yes," Elijah **a**, "I have come because you have
2Ki 2: 3 "Quiet!" Elisha **a**. "Of course I know it."
2: 5 "Quiet!" he **a** again. "Of course I know it."
8: 13 But Elisha **a**, "The LORD has shown me that you
9: 19 Again Jehu **a**, "What do you know about peace?
1Ch 5: 20 and he **a** their prayer because they trusted in him.
21: 26 the LORD **a** him by sending fire from heaven to
21: 28 When David saw that the LORD had **a** his prayer,
2Ch 9: 2 Solomon **a** all her questions; nothing was too hard
33: 19 the account of the way God **a** him,
Ezr 10: 12 Then the whole assembly raised their voices and **a**,
Est 1: 16 Memucan **a** the king and his princes,
Job 1: 7 And Satan **a** the LORD, "I have been going back
2: 2 And Satan **a** the LORD, "I have been going back
32: 12 not one of you has refuted Job or **a** his arguments.
38: 1 Then the LORD **a** Job from the whirlwind:
40: 6 Then the LORD **a** Job from the whirlwind:
Ps 3: 4 the LORD, / and he **a** me from his holy mountain.
31: 22 heard my cry for mercy / and **a** my call for help.
34: 4 I prayed to the LORD, and he **a** me, / freeing me
81: 7 and I saved you; / I **a** out of the thundercloud.
99: 6 They cried to the LORD for help, / and he **a** them.
99: 8 O LORD our God, you **a** them. / You were a
118: 5 and the LORD **a** me and rescued me.
119: 26 I told you my plans, and you **a**. / Now teach me
120: 1 I cried out to him, and he **a** my prayer.
Jer 44: 15 the southern region of Egypt—**a** Jeremiah,
Da 2: 4 Then the astrologers **a** the king in Aramaic,
5: 17 Daniel **a** the king, "Keep your gifts or give them
6: 21 Daniel **a**, "Long live the king!
Am 7: 8 "Amos, what do you see?" I **a**, "A plumb line."
Jnh 1: 9 And Jonah **a**, "I am a Hebrew, and I worship the
2: 2 to the LORD in my great trouble, and he **a** me.
Hag 2: 13 will it be defiled?" And the priests **a**, "Yes."
Zec 4: 2 I **a**, "I see a solid gold lampstand with a bowl of
Mt 6: 7 They think their prayers are **a** only by repeating
8: 26 And Jesus **a**, "Why are you afraid? You have
12: 11 And he **a**, "If you had one sheep, and it fell into a
16: 16 Simon Peter **a**, "You are the Messiah, the Son of
20: 13 "He **a** one of them, 'Friend, I haven't been unfair!
21: 29 The son **a**, 'No, I won't go,' but later he changed
Mk 7: 29 "And because you have **a** so well, I have healed
10: 38 But Jesus **a**, "You don't know what you are
12: 28 He realized that Jesus had **a** well, so he asked,
Lk 3: 16 John **a** their questions by saying, "I baptize with
5: 31 Jesus **a** them, "Healthy people don't need a
7: 40 Then Jesus spoke up and **a** his thoughts. "Simon,"
7: 43 Simon **a**, "I suppose the one for whom he
10: 27 The man **a**, " 'You must love the Lord your God
13: 8 "The gardener **a**, 'Give it one more chance.
17: 6 the Lord **a**, "you could say to this mulberry tree,
23: 7 When they **a** that he was, Pilate sent him to Herod
Jn 8: 19 Jesus **a**, "Since you don't know who I am,
8: 54 Jesus **a**, "If I am merely boasting about myself,
8: 58 Jesus **a**, "The truth is, I existed before Abraham
9: 3 because of his sins or his parents' sins," Jesus **a**.
9: 34 "You were born in sin!" they **a**. "Are you trying
9: 36 The man **a**, "Who is he, sir, because I would like
13: 38 Jesus **a**, "Die for me? No, before the rooster crows
18: 36 Then Jesus **a**, "I am not an earthly king. If I were,
Ac 11: 18 all their objections were **a** and they began praising
23: 34 what province he was from. "Cilicia," Paul **a**.
2Co 1: 11 many people's prayers for our safety have been **a**.
Rev 10: 3 And when he shouted, the seven thunders **a**.

ANSWERING (1) [ANSWER]

Ps 118: 21 I thank you for **a** my prayer / and saving me!

ANSWERS (8) [ANSWER]

1Sa 23: 6 taking the ephod with him to get **a** for David from
1Ki 18: 24 The god who **a** by setting fire to the wood is the
Job 32: 20 I must speak to find relief, so let me give my **a**.
40: 2 You are God's critic, but do you have the **a**?"
40: 4 "I am nothing—how could I ever find the **a**?
Ps 116: 1 the LORD because he hears / and **a** my prayers.
Lk 2: 47 him were amazed at his understanding and his **a**.
1Co 8: 2 Anyone who claims to know all the **a** doesn't

ANTELOPE (1) [ANTELOPES]

Dt 14: 5 the roebuck, the wild goat, the ibex, the **a**,

ANTELOPES (1) [ANTELOPE]

Isa 51: 20 and lie in the streets, helpless as **a** caught in a net.

ANTHOTHIJAH (1)

1Ch 8: 24 Hananiah, Elam, **A**,

ANTICHRIST (3) [ANTICHRISTS]

1Jn 2: 18 You have heard that the **A** is coming, and already
4: 3 from God. Such a person has the spirit of the **A**.
2Jn 1: 7 a real body. Such a person is a deceiver and an **a**.

ANTICHRISTS (2) [ANTICHRIST]

1Jn 2: 18 and already many such **a** have appeared.
2: 22 Such people are **a**, for they have denied the Father

ANTICIPATES (1) [ANTICIPATION]

Ro 8: 21 All creation **a** the day when it will join God's

ANTICIPATION (2) [ANTICIPATES]

Isa 5: 14 The grave is licking its chops in **a** of Jerusalem,
1Th 1: 3 and your continual **a** of the return of our Lord

ANTIOCH (25)

Ac 6: 5 and Nicolas of **A** (a Gentile convert to the Jewish
11: 19 as far as Phoenicia, Cyprus, and **A** of Syria.
11: 20 some of the believers who went to **A** from Cyprus
11: 22 heard what had happened, they sent Barnabas to **A**.
11: 26 When he found him, he brought him back to **A**.
11: 26 (It was there at **A** that the believers were first
11: 27 some prophets traveled from Jerusalem to **A**.
11: 29 So the believers in **A** decided to send relief to the
12: 25 they returned to **A**, taking John Mark with them.
13: 1 and teachers of the church at **A** of Syria were
13: 14 and Paul traveled inland to **A** of Pisidia.
14: 19 Now some Jews arrived from **A** and Iconium
14: 21 again to Lystra, Iconium, and **A** of Pisidia,
14: 26 Finally, they returned by ship to **A** of Syria,
14: 27 Upon arriving in **A**, they called the church together
14: 28 And they stayed there with the believers in **A** for a
15: 1 While Paul and Barnabas were at **A** of Syria,
15: 22 and they sent them to **A** of Syria with Paul
15: 23 It is written to the Gentile believers in **A**, Syria,
15: 30 The four messengers went at once to **A**, where they
15: 35 and Barnabas stayed in **A** to assist many others
18: 22 the church at Jerusalem and then went back to **A**.
18: 23 After spending some time in **A**, Paul went back to
Gal 2: 11 But when Peter came to **A**, I had to oppose him
2Ti 3: 11 You know all about how I was persecuted in **A**,

ANTIPAS (11)
Mt 14: 1 When Herod **A** heard about Jesus,
Mk 1:14 Later on, after John was arrested by Herod **A**,
6:14 Herod **A**, the king, soon heard about Jesus,
Lk 3: 1 over Judea; Herod **A** was ruler over Galilee;
3:19 John also publicly criticized Herod **A**, ruler of
9: 7 When reports of Jesus' miracles reached Herod **A**,
13:31 want to live, because Herod **A** wants to kill you!"
23: 7 answered that he was, Pilate sent him to Herod **A**,
Ac 4:27 For Herod **A**, Pontius Pilate the governor,
13: 1 (the childhood companion of King Herod **A**),
Rev 2:13 And you refused to deny me even when **A**,

ANTIPATRIS (1)
Ac 23:31 as ordered, the soldiers took Paul as far as **A**.

ANTIQUITY [KJV] See HISTORY

ANTOTHIJAH [KJV] See ANTHOTHIJAH

ANTOTHITE [KJV] See ANATHOTH

ANTS (2)
Pr 6: 6 Take a lesson from the **a**, you lazybones.
30:25 **A**—they aren't strong, / but they store up food for

ANUB (1)
1Ch 4: 8 and Koz, who became the ancestor of **A**, Zobebah,

ANVIL (1)
Isa 41: 7 the goldsmith, and the molder helps at the **a**.

ANXIETY (1) [ANXIOUS]
Ps 116:11 In my **a** I cried out to you, / "These people are all

ANXIOUS (9) [ANXIETY, ANXIOUSLY]
Ex 6: 1 so **a** to get rid of them that he will force them to
11: 1 so **a** to get rid of you that he will practically force
Job 33:32 I want to hear it, for I am **a** to see you justified.
Mk 15:15 So Pilate, **a** to please the crowd, released Barabbas
Lk 22:15 **a** to eat this Passover meal with you before my
2Co 8:20 for we are **a** that no one should find fault with the
Gal 4:17 so **a** to win your favor are not doing it for your
Php 2:28 So I am all the more **a** to send him back to you,
1Pe 4: 2 but you will be **a** to do the will of God.

ANXIOUSLY (5) [ANXIOUS]
Ps 127: 2 until late at night, / **a** working for food to eat;
Pr 1:28 Even though they **a** search for me, they will not
Jer 48:19 The people of Aroer stand **a** beside the road to
Mic 1:12 The people of Maroth **a** wait for relief, but only
Ro 8:23 wait **a** for that day when God will give us our full

ANY (600) [ANYBODY, ANYMORE, ANYONE, ANYONE'S, ANYTHING, ANYTIME, ANYWAY, ANYWHERE]
Ge 2: 5 the earth, for the LORD God had not sent **a** rain.
2:16 "You may freely eat **a** fruit in the garden
2:25 were both naked, neither of them felt **a** shame.
3: 1 "Did God really say you must not eat **a** of the fruit
6: 2 human race and took **a** they wanted as their wives.
9: 5 and **a** person who murders must be killed.
11:30 Now Sarai was not able to have **a** children.
13: 9 Take your choice of **a** section of the land you want,
16: 2 "The LORD has kept me from having **a**
19:12 "Do you have **a** other relatives here in the city?"
20:16 for **a** embarrassment I may have caused you.
20:16 This will settle **a** claim against me in this matter."
22:12 "Do not hurt the boy in **a** way, for now I know
24:23 "Would your father have **a** room to put us up for
28: 1 "Do not marry **a** of these Canaanite women.
30: 1 When Rachel saw that she wasn't having **a**
30:33 If you find in my flock **a** white sheep or goats that
30:35 were speckled and spotted with **a** white patches,
31: 7 But God has not allowed him to do me **a** harm.
31:39 If **a** were attacked and killed by wild animals,
37: 3 Now Jacob loved Joseph more than **a** of his other
43:34 five times as much as to **a** of the others.
44: 9 If you find his cup with **a** one of us, let that one
44:29 brother from me, too, and **a** harm comes to him,
47: 6 choose **a** place you like for them to live. Give them
47: 6 And if **a** of them have special skills, put them in
49:16 will govern his people / like **a** other tribe in Israel.
Ex 3: 5 "Do not come **a** closer," God told him. "Take off
5: 7 "Do not supply the people with **a** more straw for
7:18 The Egyptians will not be able to drink **a** water
9:18 a hailstorm worse than **a** in all of Egypt's history.
12:10 Do not leave **a** of it until the next day. Whatever is
12:15 Anyone who eats bread made with yeast at **a** time
12:16 No work of **a** kind may be done on these days
12:44 But **a** slave who has been purchased may eat it if
12:46 You must not carry **a** of its meat outside, and you may not break **a** of its bones.
13: 3 (Remember, you are not to use **a** yeast.)
16:19 Moses told them, "Do not keep **a** of it overnight."
17:12 became too tired to hold up the staff **a** longer.
19:13 **A** people or animals that cross the boundary must
20: 3 "Do not worship **a** other gods besides me.
20: 4 "Do not make idols of **a** kind, whether in the
20: 5 who will not share your affection with **a** other god!
20:10 On that day no one in your household may do **a**
20:10 your livestock, and **a** foreigners living among you.
21:11 If he fails in **a** of these three ways, she may leave as a free woman without making **a**
21:23 But if **a** harm results, then the offender must be
22:10 ox, sheep, or **a** other animal, but it dies or is
22:20 "Anyone who sacrifices to **a** god other than the
22:21 "Do not oppress foreigners in **a** way. Remember,
22:31 do not eat **a** animal that has been attacked
23:11 Then let the poor among you harvest **a** volunteer
23:13 never pray to or swear by **a** other gods.
23:24 gods of these other nations or serve them in **a** way,
24:14 If there are **a** problems while I am gone,
28:38 thus bearing the guilt connected with **a** errors
29:34 If **a** of the ordination meat or bread remains until
30: 9 Do not offer **a** unholy incense on this altar, or **a** burnt offerings, grain offerings, or drink
30:32 and you must never make **a** of it for yourselves.
30:33 or puts **a** of it on someone who is not a priest will
34:10 before anywhere in all the earth or in **a** nation.
34:15 "Do not make treaties of **a** kind with the people
Lev 2: 4 flour mixed with olive oil but without **a** yeast.
2:11 "Do not use yeast in **a** of the grain offerings you
3:17 "You must never eat **a** fat or blood. This is a
4:27 "If **a** of the citizens of Israel do something
4:32 "If **a** of the people bring a sheep as their sin
5: 1 "If **a** of the people are called to testify about
5: 3 "Or if they come into contact with **a** source of
5: 4 "Or if they make a rash vow of **a** kind, whether its
5: 5 "When **a** of the people become aware of their guilt in **a** of these ways,
5: 7 "If **a** of them cannot afford to bring a sheep,
5:11 "If **a** of the people cannot afford to bring young
5:11 not mix it with olive oil or put **a** incense on it.
5:12 He will burn this flour on the altar just like **a** other
5:15 "If **a** of the people sin by unintentionally defiling
5:17 "If **a** of them sin by doing something forbidden by
6: 3 under oath, or they commit **a** other similar sin.
6: 4 If they have sinned in **a** of these ways and are
6:18 **A** of Aaron's male descendants, from generation to
7: 9 **A** grain offering that has been baked in an oven,
7:18 If **a** of the meat from this peace offering is eaten on
7:24 though it may be used for **a** other purpose.
7:26 you must never eat the blood of **a** bird or animal.
8:32 **A** meat or bread that is left over must then be
10: 9 or **a** other alcoholic drink before going into the
10:14 and thigh that were lifted up may be eaten in **a**
11:12 **a** marine animal that does not have both fins
11:24 If you touch **a** of their dead bodies, you will be
11:26 "**A** animal that has divided but unsplit hooves
11:34 used to cleanse an unclean object touches **a** food,
11:34 And **a** beverage that is in such an unclean
11:35 **A** object on which the dead body of such an animal
11:40 If you eat **a** of its meat or carry away its carcass,
11:41 "Consider detestable **a** animal that scurries along
11:44 So do not defile yourselves by touching **a** of these
13:14 But if **a** open sores appear, the infected person will
13:45 "Those who suffer from **a** contagious skin disease
14:57 when dealing with **a** contagious skin disease
15: 2 **A** man who has a genital discharge is ceremonially
15: 4 **A** bedding on which he lies and anything on which
15: 9 **A** blanket on which the man rides will be defiled.
15:12 **A** clay pot touched by the man with the discharge
15:17 **A** clothing or leather that comes in contact with the
15:23 whether it is her bedding or **a** piece of furniture.
15:24 and **a** bed on which he lies will be defiled.
15:33 who has had a bodily discharge of **a** kind;
16:29 you must spend the day fasting and not do **a** work.
17: 3 If **a** Israelite sacrifices a bull or a lamb or a goat
17:10 among you, who eats or drinks blood in **a** form.
17:11 for the life of **a** creature is in its blood. I have
17:14 for the life of **a** bird or animal is in the blood.
18: 8 Do not have sexual intercourse with **a** of your
18:11 with the daughter of **a** of your father's wives;
18:21 "Do not give **a** of your children as a sacrifice to
18:24 "Do not defile yourselves in **a** of these ways,
18:26 and you must not do **a** of these detestable things.
18:29 Whoever does **a** of these detestable things will be
18:30 and do not practice **a** of these detestable activities.
18:30 Do not defile yourselves by doing **a** of them,
19: 6 **A** leftovers that remain until the third day must be
19: 7 If **a** of the offering is eaten on the third day,
19:17 "Do not nurse hatred in your heart for **a** of your
20: 2 If **a** among them devote their children as burnt
20: 6 "If **a** among the people are unfaithful by
20:25 You must not defile yourselves by eating **a** animal
22: 3 Remind them that if **a** of their descendants are
22: 4 "If **a** of the priests have a contagious skin disease
22: 4 or **a** kind of discharge that makes them
22: 4 If **a** of the priests become unclean by touching a
22: 5 someone who is ceremonially unclean for **a** reason,
22: 6 They must not eat **a** of the sacred offerings until
22:21 an animal that has no physical defects of **a** kind.
22:30 Don't leave **a** of it until the second day. I am the
23:14 Do not eat **a** bread or roasted grain or fresh kernels
23:30 And I will destroy anyone among you who does **a**
23:38 and **a** freewill offerings that you present to the
24:16 **A** Israelite or foreigner among you who
25: 6 and **a** foreigners who live with you may eat the
25:11 do not plant **a** seeds or store away **a** of the crops
25:24 stipulation that the land can be redeemed at **a** time.
25:25 If **a** of your Israelite relatives go bankrupt and are
25:31 Such a house may be redeemed at **a** time and must
25:32 "The Levites always have the right to redeem **a**
25:33 And **a** property that can be redeemed by the
25:35 "If **a** of your Israelite relatives fall into poverty
25:39 "If **a** of your Israelite relatives go bankrupt
25:53 You must not allow a resident foreigner to treat **a**
25:54 If **a** Israelites have not been redeemed by the time
27:33 If **a** exchange is in fact made, then both the
Nu 5: 6 If **a** of the people—men or women—
5:31 The husband will be innocent of **a** guilt in this
6:21 If **a** Nazirites have vowed to give the LORD
9:10 'If **a** of the people now or in future generations are
9:12 They must not leave **a** of the lamb until the next
9:12 and they must not break **a** of its bones.
11:23 said to Moses, "Is there **a** limit to my power?
12: 3 Now Moses was more humble than **a** other person
13:32 "The land we explored will swallow up **a** who go
15: 3 a burnt offering or **a** other offering given by fire,
15: 3 or a special sacrifice at **a** of the annual festivals,
15:14 And if **a** foreigners living among you want to
17:10 against me and prevent **a** further deaths."
18: 1 responsible for **a** offenses related to the sanctuary.
18: 3 they must be careful not to touch **a** of the sacred
18: 7 **A** other person who comes too near the sanctuary
18:11 **A** member of your family who is ceremonially
18:13 **A** member of your family who is ceremonially
18:23 and they will be held responsible for **a** offenses
19:10 of Israel and **a** foreigners who live among them.
19:15 **A** container in the tent that was not covered with a
20:19 If **a** of our livestock drinks your water, we will pay
23:23 no sorcery has **a** power against Israel.
27: 3 died in the wilderness without leaving **a** sons,"
30:13 her husband may either confirm or nullify **a** vows
32:17 so they will be safe from **a** attacks by the local
32:19 But we do not want **a** of the land on the other side
36: 3 But if **a** of them marries a man from another tribe,
Dt 1:17 Bring me **a** cases that are too difficult for you,
2: 5 and I will not give you **a** of their land.
2: 9 and I will not give you **a** of their land.' "
2:19 and I will not give you **a** of their land.' "
3:24 Is there a god in heaven or on earth who can
4:16 by making a physical image in **a** form—
4:23 You will break it if you make idols of **a** shape
4:25 do not corrupt yourselves by making idols of **a**
4:33 Has **a** nation ever heard the voice of God speaking
4:34 Has **a** other god taken one nation for himself by
4:42 having **a** previous hostility could flee for safety.
5: 7 " 'Do not worship **a** other gods besides me.
5: 8 " 'Do not make idols of **a** kind, whether in the
5: 9 who will not share your affection with **a** other god!
5:14 On that day no one in your household may do **a**
5:14 other livestock, and **a** foreigners living among you.
5:26 Can **a** living thing hear the voice of the living God
6:14 "You must not worship **a** of the gods of
7:26 Do not bring **a** detestable objects into your home,
12:15 "But you may butcher animals for meat in **a** town,
12:21 you may butcher **a** of the cattle or sheep the
14: 6 "**A** animal that has split hooves and chews the cud
14:11 "You may eat **a** bird that is ceremonially clean.
14:20 But you may eat **a** winged creature that is
15: 7 "But if there are **a** poor people in your towns
15:21 But if this firstborn animal has **a** defect, such as
16: 4 Let no yeast be found in **a** house throughout your
16: 4 And do not let **a** of the meat of the Passover lamb
17: 3 the sun, the moon, or **a** of the forces of heaven,
17:11 must be fully executed; do not modify it in **a** way.
18: 6 "**A** Levite who so desires may come from any
18: 6 so desires may come from **a** town in Israel,
18:20 But **a** prophet who claims to give a message from
19: 4 a neighbor without harboring **a** previous hatred,
19: 4 the slayer may flee to **a** of these cities and be safe.
20: 6 planted a vineyard but not yet eaten **a** of its fruit?
22: 9 "Do not plant **a** other crop between the rows of
23: 3 or **a** of their descendants for ten generations,
23: 6 to help the Ammonites or the Moabites in **a** way.
23:10 "**A** man who becomes ceremonially defiled
23:14 He must not see **a** shameful thing among you,
23:18 God **a** offering from the earnings of a prostitute,
23:24 but do not take **a** away in a basket.
24: 5 the army or given **a** other special responsibilities.
24:21 but leave **a** remaining grapes for the foreigners,
26:13 not violated or forgotten **a** of your commands.
26:14 I have not eaten **a** of it while in mourning; I have
26:14 and I have not offered **a** of it to the dead.
26:19 he will make you greater than **a** other nation.
28:14 You must not turn away from **a** of the commands I
32:12 guided them; / they lived without **a** foreign gods.
Jos 2:19 be killed—not a hand will be laid on **a** of them.
2:20 however, we are not bound by this oath in **a** way."
3: 4 and the Ark. Make sure you don't come **a** closer."
6:10 "Not a single word from **a** of you until I tell you to
6:18 Do not take **a** of the things set apart for
7:12 I will not remain with you **a** longer unless you
11:13 Joshua did not burn **a** of the cities built on mounds
13:14 Moses did not assign **a** land to the tribe of Levi.
18: 7 However, the Levites will not receive **a** land.
18: 7 and the half-tribe of Manasseh won't receive **a**
19:50 For the LORD had said he could have **a** town he
23: 6 Law of Moses. Do not deviate from them in **a** way.
Jdg 2: 2 you were not to make **a** covenants with the people
8:35 Nor did they show **a** loyalty to the family of
11: 2 "You will not get **a** of our father's inheritance,"
11:15 Israel did not steal **a** land from Moab or Ammon.
11:25 Are you **a** better than Balak son of Zippor, king of
13: 4 or **a** other alcoholic drink or eat **a** forbidden food.
13: 7 or **a** other alcoholic drink or eat **a** forbidden food.
13:14 or **a** other alcoholic drink, or eat **a** forbidden food."
16:16 she nagged him until he couldn't stand it **a** longer.
21: 5 "Was **a** tribe of Israel not represented when we
Ru 2: 8 when you gather grain; don't go to **a** other fields.
1Sa 4:20 But she did not answer or respond in **a** way.
5: 7 "We can't keep the Ark of the God of Israel here **a**
8: 7 They don't want me to be their king **a** longer.

12: 3 have I stolen? Have I ever cheated a of you?
12: 4 "you have never cheated or oppressed us in a way,
12:20 and that you don't turn your back on him in a way.
16:10 to Jesse, "The LORD has not chosen a of these."
19: 4 He has always helped you in a way he could.
20: 2 "I'm sure he's not planning a such thing, for he
21: 4 "We don't have a regular bread," the priest
21: 4 men have not slept with a women recently."
22:15 for I knew nothing of a plot against you."
25: 8 Please give us a provisions you might have on
25:15 to us, and we never suffered a harm from them.
25:25 please don't pay a attention to him.
25:28 Please forgive me if I have offended in a way.
29: 4 Is there a better way for him to reconcile himself
30:22 go with us, so they can't have a of the plunder.
2Sa 6:20 He exposed himself to the servant girls like a
9: 3 I want to show God's kindness to them in a way I
12: 5 "a man who would do such a thing deserves to
14: 2 and don't bathe or wear a perfume.
21: 5 to keep us from having a place at all in Israel.
22:30 crush an army; / with my God I can scale a wall.
1Ki 1: 6 King David, had never disciplined him at a time,
1:27 Has my lord really done this without letting a of
6: 7 ax, or a other iron tool at the building site.
9:22 But Solomon did not conscript a of the Israelites
10:23 and wiser than a other king in all the earth.
13: 8 would not eat a food or drink a water in this place.
13: 9 must not eat a food or drink a water while you are
13:16 "I am not allowed to eat a food or drink a water
13:17 'You must not eat a food or drink a water while
16:25 even more than a of the kings before him.
16:30 even more than a of the kings before him.
16:33 than a of the other kings of Israel before him.
18:26 answer us!" But there was no reply of a kind.
20: 8 "Don't give in to a more demands," the leaders
20:39 if for a reason he gets away, you will either die
2Ki 4: 6 "There aren't a more!" he told her. And
5:16 whom I serve, I will not accept a gifts."
5:17 From now on I will never again offer a burnt
5:17 or sacrifices to a other god except the LORD.
6:33 Why should I wait a longer for the LORD?"
7: 2 see it happen, but you won't be able to eat a of it!"
7:19 see it happen, but you won't be able to eat a of it!"
8: 6 including the value of a crops that had been
10:19 A of Baal's worshipers who fail to come will be
11: 8 A unauthorized person who approaches you must
12: 7 Don't use a more gifts for your own needs.
12: 8 So the priests agreed not to collect a more money
12:12 and they paid a other expenses related to the
17:35 "Do not worship a other gods or bow before them
17:37 wrote for you. You must not worship a other gods.
18:20 Which of your allies will give you a military
18:33 Have the gods of a other nations ever saved their
18:35 What god of a nation has ever been able to save its
19:11 stood in their way! Why should you be a different?
1Ch 4: 9 who was more distinguished than a of his brothers.
9:28 They checked them in and out to avoid a loss.
2Ch 2: 5 our God is an awesome God, greater than a other.
2:14 an engraver and can follow a design given to him.
8: 9 But Solomon did not conscript a of the Israelites
8:15 Solomon did not deviate in a way from David's
9:22 and wiser than a other king in all the earth.
11:21 Rehoboam loved Maacah more than a of his other
17: 1 He strengthened Judah to stand against a attack
20: 9 'Whenever we are faced with a calamity such as
23: 7 A unauthorized person who enters the Temple
26:13 They were prepared to assist the king against a
29:11 dear Levites, do not neglect your duties a longer!
32:13 Were a of the gods of those nations able to rescue
32:14 Name just one time when a god, anywhere,
32:14 What makes you think your God can do a better?
32:15 no god of a nation has ever yet been able to rescue
Ezr 1: 4 Those who live in a place where Jewish survivors
6:11 "Those who violate this decree in a way will have
6:12 as the place to honor his name destroy a king
7:13 "I decree that a of the people of Israel in my
7:16 "Moreover you are to take a silver and gold which
7:18 A money that is left over may be used in whatever
7:20 for your God's Temple or for a similar needs,
7:24 of God will be required to pay taxes of a kind.'
9:12 and not to help those nations in a way.
10: 6 the night there, but he did not eat a food or drink.
Ne 5:16 working on the wall and refused to acquire a land.
6: 8 are lying. There is no truth in a part of your story."
10:31 the people of the land should bring a merchandise
10:31 to be sold on the Sabbath or on a other holy day,
10:31 And we promise not to do a work every seventh
11:20 inheritance was located in a of the towns of Judah.
13:26 "There was no king from a nation who could
Est 2:17 the king loved her more than a of the other young
3: 8 Their laws are different from those of a other
8:11 and annihilate anyone of a nationality or province
9:10 of the Jews. But they did not take a plunder.
9:16 who hated them. But they did not take a plunder.
Job 6:13 I am utterly helpless, without a chance of success.
6:22 Have I begged you to use a of your wealth on my
11:12 An empty-headed person won't become wise a
11:17 A darkness will be as bright as morning.
15:19 those to whom the land was given long before a
18:19 nor a survivor in their home country.
22: 3 Is it a pleasure to the Almighty if you are
22: 3 Would it be a gain to him if you were perfect?
24:10 The poor must go about naked, without a clothing.
27:10 in the Almighty? Can they call to God at a time?
31: 7 my eyes have seen, or if I am guilty of a other sin,
33:12 yourself have said, 'God is greater than a person.'
34:19 and he doesn't pay a more attention to the rich
34:27 They have no respect for a of his ways.
Ps 18:29 crush an army; / with my God I can scale a wall.
34:10 but those who trust in the LORD will never lack a
34:12 Do a of you want to live / a life that is long
69:14 me out of the mud; / don't let me sink a deeper!
77:13 ways are holy. / Is there a god as mighty as you?
82: 7 You will fall as a prince, / for all must die.' "
87: 2 city of Jerusalem / more than a other city in Israel.
119:101 I have refused to walk on a path of evil, / that I
119:133 your word, / so I will not be overcome by a evil.
135: 5 that our Lord is greater than a other god.
147:20 He has not done this with a other nation; / they do
Pr 14:34 exalts a nation, but sin is a disgrace to a people.
18:17 A story sounds true until someone sets the record
22:29 Do you see a truly competent workers? They will
26: 1 Honor doesn't go with fools a more than snow
Ecc 1:16 I am wiser than a of the kings who ruled in
1:16 greater wisdom and knowledge than a of them."
2: 7 more than a of the kings who lived in Jerusalem
2: 9 So I became greater than a of the kings who ruled
2:10 I took. I did not restrain myself from a joy.
6: 8 do wise people really have a advantage over fools?
7:10 for you don't know whether they were a better
9:15 But afterward no one thought a more about him.
12: 5 dragging along without a sexual desire.
SS 1: 1 song of songs, more wonderful than a other.
Isa 1: 6 without a ointments or bandages.
1:11 "Don't bring me a more burnt offerings!
3: 7 "I can't help. I don't have a extra food or clothes.
17:11 but you will never pick a grapes from them.
19:15 or poor, important or unknown, can offer a help.
30: 9 to pay a attention to the LORD's instructions.
30:10 We don't want a more of your reports." They say,
36: 5 Which of your allies will give you a military
36:18 Have the gods of a other nations ever saved their
36:20 What god of a nation has ever been able to save its
37:11 stood in their way! Why should you be a different?
41:28 told you this. Not one gave a answer when I asked.
43: 9 Can a of them predict something even a single day
44: 8 You are my witnesses—is there a other God?
48: 1 You don't follow through on a of your promises,
48:14 "Have a of your idols ever told you this? Come,
54:15 If a nation comes to fight you, it will not be
Jer 2:11 Has a nation ever exchanged its gods for another
2:23 you say that? Go and look in a valley in the land!
5: 6 tearing apart a who dare to venture out.
10: 5 for they can neither harm you nor do you a good."
11: 8 But your ancestors did not pay a attention;
12:17 But a nation who refuses to obey me will be
14:14 tell them to speak. I did not give them a messages.
14:22 Can a of the foreign gods send us rain? Does it fall
18:21 Let their wives become widows without a
23:34 If a prophet, priest, or anyone else says, 'I have a
27: 8 I will punish a nation that refuses to be his slave,
27:11 But the people of a nation that submits to the king
30:13 You are beyond the help of a medicine.
31:16 "Do not weep a longer, for I will reward you.
36:24 Neither the king nor his officials showed a signs of
37:14 "I had no intention of doing a such thing."
37:17 "Do you have a messages from the LORD?"
37:21 every day as long as there was a left in the city.
40:10 Settle in a town you wish, and live off the land.
40:16 said to Johanan, "I forbid you to do a such thing,
42:21 but you will not obey the LORD your God a
44: 3 gods that neither they nor you nor a of your
44:26 that my name will no longer be spoken by a of the
La 1:12 and see if there is a suffering like mine,
1:16 a who might encourage me are far away.
4: 4 cry for bread, but no one has a to give them.
4:20 we could hold our own against a nation on earth!
Eze 1: 9 The living beings were able to fly in a direction
1:17 The beings could move forward in a of the four
3: 7 but they won't listen to you a more than they listen
4:14 I have never eaten a animal that died of sickness
4:14 And I have never eaten a of the animals that our
7:13 And if a merchants should survive, they will never
7:15 A who leave the city walls will be killed by enemy
9:10 So I will not spare them or have a pity on them.
10:11 The cherubim could move forward in a of the four
23:25 and a survivors will then be slaughtered by the
24:16 Yet you must not show a sorrow. Do not weep;
24:17 or accept a food brought to you by consoling
31: 8 This tree became taller than a of the other cedars in
34: 5 a shepherd. They are easy prey for a wild animal.
35: 7 killing off all who try to escape and a who return.
39:14 will be appointed to search the land for a skeletons
43: 7 and their kings will not defile my holy name a
43:25 these animals may have physical defects of a kind.
44:13 They may not touch a of my holy things
44:24 "They will serve as judges to resolve a
44:28 "As to property, the priests will not have a,
44:31 The priests may never eat meat from a bird
45:23 young bulls and seven rams without a defects.
46:18 for I do not want a of my people unjustly evicted
Da 2:10 has ever asked such a thing of a magician,
2:30 because I am wiser than a living person that I
3:28 than serve or worship a god except their own God.
3:29 If a people, whatever their race or nation
7: 7 It was different from a of the other beasts, and it
11:37 for the god beloved of women, nor for a other god,
12: 1 Then there will be a time of anguish greater than a
Hos 1: 7 from their enemies without a help from weapons
8: 7 And if there is a grain, foreigners will eat it.
Am 1: 3 I will not let them go unpunished a longer!
1: 6 I will not let them go unpunished a longer!
1: 9 I will not let them go unpunished a longer!
1:11 I will not let them go unpunished a longer!
1:13 I will not let them go unpunished a longer!
2: 1 I will not let them go unpunished a longer!
2: 4 I will not let them go unpunished a longer!
2: 6 I will not let them go unpunished a longer!
Mic 2: 1 and hurry to carry out a of the wicked schemes you
Na 3: 8 Are you a better than Thebes, surrounded by
Hab 1:13 But will you, who cannot allow sin in a form,
Hag 2:12 or stew, wine or oil, or a other kind of food,
2:13 then brushes against a of the things mentioned,
Zec 11: 9 I told them, "I won't be your shepherd a longer.
14:17 And a nation anywhere in the world that refuses to
14:21 All who come to worship will be free to use a of
Mal 1: 9 why should he show you a favor at all?"
Mt 5:34 But I say, don't make a vows! If you say,
10: 9 "Don't take a money with you.
12:25 "A kingdom at war with itself is doomed.
16: 5 discovered they had forgotten to bring a food.
16: 7 saying this because they hadn't brought a bread.
16:17 to you. You did not learn this from a human being.
16:24 "If a of you wants to be my follower,
19: 3 man be allowed to divorce his wife for a reason?"
21:19 He went over to see if there were a figs on it,
22:46 no one dared to ask him a more questions.
24: 3 And will there be a sign ahead of time to signal
24:23 or 'There he is,' don't pay a attention.
Mk 3:28 "I assure you that a sin can be forgiven,
6: 5 he couldn't do a mighty miracles among them
8:12 I will not give this generation a such sign."
8:14 discovered they had forgotten to bring a food,
8:16 saying this because they hadn't brought a bread.
8:34 "If a of you wants to be my follower," he told
9: 3 far whiter than a earthly process could ever make
11:13 so he went over to see if he could find a figs on it.
12:34 no one dared to ask him a more questions.
13: 4 And will there be a sign ahead of time to show us
13:19 For those will be days of greater horror than at a
13:21 or, 'There he is,' don't pay a attention.
Lk 4:26 Yet Elijah was not sent to a of them. He was sent
9:23 the crowd, "If a of you wants to be my follower,
10: 4 Don't take along a money, or a traveler's bag,
11:17 he said, "A kingdom at war with itself is doomed.
12: 4 only kill the body; they cannot do a more to you.
12:24 And you are far more valuable to him than a birds!
12:42 And the Lord replied, "I'm talking to a faithful,
13: 6 and again to see if there was a fruit on it,
20:40 ended their questions; no one dared to ask a more.
21: 7 And will there be a sign ahead of time?"
21:29 "Notice the fig tree, or a other tree.
Jn 10:33 They replied, "Not for a good work, but for
14: 5 "We haven't a idea where you are going, so how
15: 7 you may ask a request you like, and it will be
17:16 They are not part of this world a more than I am.
18:38 and told them, "He is not guilty of a crime.
20:27 in my side. Don't be faithless a longer. Believe!"
21: 5 He called out, "Friends, have you caught a fish?"
Ac 3: 6 But Peter said, "I don't have a money for you.
8:16 The Holy Spirit had not yet come upon a of them,
9: 2 asking their cooperation in the arrest of a followers
13:15 if you have a word of encouragement for us,
17:27 find him—though he is not far from a one of us.
19:12 and a evil spirits within them came out.
23: 5 'Do not speak evil of a one who rules over
24:12 nor did I incite a riot in a synagogue or on the
26: 8 Why does it seem incredible to a of you that God
Ro 3: 1 Is there a value in the Jewish ceremony of
6: 9 die again. Death no longer has a power over him.
6:13 Do not let a part of your body become a tool of
13: 9 and coveting—and a other commandment—
16:19 what is right and to stay innocent of a wrong.
1Co 1:13 Were a of you baptized in the name of Paul?
1:14 I thank God that I did not baptize a of you except
3:11 For no one can lay a other foundation than the one
9:15 Yet I have never used a of these rights. And I am
10:20 I don't want a of you to be partners with
10:25 You may eat a meat that is sold in the marketplace.
10:27 is offered to you and don't ask a questions about it.
12:15 that does not make it a less a part of the body.
12:16 would that make it a less a part of the body?
12:31 And in a event, you should desire the most helpful
12:31 about something else that is better than a of them!
13: 1 If I could speak in a language in heaven or on earth
14:35 If they have a questions to ask, let them ask their
2Co 7: 9 to have, so you were not harmed by us in a way.
8:20 By traveling together we will guard against a
11: 9 I have never yet asked you for a support, and I
12:17 Did a of the men I sent to you take advantage of
Gal 1: 1 I was not appointed by a group or by human
1: 8 who preaches a other message than the one we told
1: 8 comes from heaven and preaches a other message,
1: 9 If anyone preaches a other gospel than the one you
6:15 It doesn't make a difference now whether we have
Eph 1:21 Now he is far above a ruler or authority or power
5:27 without a spot or wrinkle or a other blemish.
Php 2: 1 Is there a encouragement from belonging to
2: 1 A comfort from his love? A fellowship together in
3: 6 so carefully that I was never accused of a fault.
1Th 2: 3 So you can see that we were not preaching with a
2Th 3: 6 Stay away from a Christian who lives in idleness
3: 8 so that we would not be a burden to a of you.
1Ti 4: 4 God created is good, we should not reject a of it.
5: 3 The church should care for a widow who has no
Phm 1:18 If he has harmed you in a way or stolen anything
Heb 1: 5 For God never said to a angel what he said to
6:16 And without a question that oath is binding.
7: 3 of his father or mother or a of his ancestors—
7:20 be a priest, but he never did this for a other priest.
9:17 no one can use the will to get a of the things

10:18 there is no need to offer a more sacrifices.
11:12 Abraham, who was too old to have a children—
Jas 2:16 but then you don't give that person a food
5:13 Are a among you suffering? They should keep on
5:14 Are a among you sick? They should call for the
1Pe 1:14 ways of doing evil; you didn't know a better then.
3:1 Your godly lives will speak to them better than a
1Jn 5:16 If you see a Christian sinning in a way that does
2Jn 1:10 him into your house or encourage him in a way.
Rev 18:22 There will be no industry of a kind, and no more
22:19 And if anyone removes a of the words of this

ANYBODY (2) [ANY]

Jdg 4:20 "If a comes and asks you if there is anyone here,
1Co 13:2 it move, without love I would be no good to a.

ANYMORE (30) [ANY]

Ge 30:9 Leah realized that she wasn't getting pregnant a,
Ex 6:9 the LORD had said, but they wouldn't listen a.
6:12 "My own people won't listen to me a.
Jdg 10:13 and served other gods. So I will not rescue you a.
Ps 39:10 Please, don't punish me a! / I am exhausted by the
Isa 11:13 will end. They will not fight against each other a.
33:8 Your roads are deserted; no one travels them a.
34:10 generation to generation. No one will live there a.
49:10 and scorching desert winds will not reach them a.
59:2 your sin, he has turned away and will not listen a.
65:17 that no one will even think about the old ones a.
Jer 2:15 the cities are now in ruins. No one lives in them a.
2:31 We won't have anything to do with him a!'
14:11 said to me, "Do not pray for these people a.
30:14 allies have left you and do not care about you a.
42:11 Do not fear the king of Babylon a,
49:18 says the LORD. "No one will live there a.
49:33 will be desolate forever. No one will live there a."
50:40 says the LORD. "No one will live there a.
Eze 16:42 I will be calm and will not be angry with you a.
18:3 you will not say this proverb a in Israel.
39:7 I will not let it be desecrated a. And the nations,
Lk 22:51 But Jesus said, "Don't resist a." And he touched
Jn 16:16 little while I will be gone, and you won't see me a.
16:19 little while I will be gone, and you won't see me a.
Ro 14:13 So don't condemn each other a. Decide instead to
2Co 5:17 They are not the same a, for the old life is gone.
Gal 2:12 Peter wouldn't eat with the Gentiles a because he
Eph 4:19 They don't care a about right and wrong, and they
Rev 20:3 so Satan could not deceive the nations a until the

ANYONE (480) [ANY]

Ge 4:15 for I will give seven times your punishment to a
4:15 Then the LORD put a mark on Cain to warn a
4:24 If a who kills Cain is to be punished seven times,
4:24 a who takes revenge against me will be punished
9:6 you must execute a who murders another person,
17:14 A who refuses to be circumcised will be cut off
19:12 this place—sons-in-law, sons, daughters, or a else.
26:11 "A who harms this man or his wife will die!"
Ex 12:15 A who eats bread made with yeast at any time
12:19 A who eats anything made with yeast during this
21:12 "A who hits a person hard enough to cause death
21:15 "A who strikes father or mother must be put to
21:17 "A who curses father or mother must be put to
22:1 "A fine must be paid by a who steals an ox
22:16 "If a man seduces a virgin who is not engaged to a
22:19 "A who has sexual relations with an animal must
22:20 "A who sacrifices to any god other than the
22:28 not blaspheme God or curse a who rules over you.
23:7 "Keep far away from falsely charging a with evil.
23:7 to death. I will not allow a guilty of this to go free.
30:33 A who blends scented oil like it or puts any of it
31:14 A who desecrates it must die; a who works on that day will be cut off from the
31:15 a who works on the Sabbath must be put to death.
33:16 how will a ever know that your people and I have
33:19 I will show kindness to a I choose, and I will show mercy to a I choose.
35:2 to the LORD. A who works on that day will die.
Lev 6:18 A or anything that touches this food will become
6:27 or a who touches the sacrificial meat will become
7:20 A who is ceremonially unclean but eats meat from
7:21 If a touches anything that is unclean, whether it is
7:25 A who eats fat from an offering given to the
7:27 A who eats blood must be cut off from the
11:36 But a who removes the dead body will be defiled.
13:9 "A who develops a contagious skin disease must
13:18 "If a has had a boil on the skin that has started to
13:24 "If a has suffered a burn on the skin
13:29 "If a, whether a man or woman, has an open sore
13:38 "If a, whether a man or woman, has shiny white
14:21 "But a who cannot afford two lambs must bring
14:46 A who enters the house while it is closed will be
15:33 for dealing with a, man or woman, who has had a
17:10 "And I will turn against a, whether an Israelite
19:13 "Do not cheat or rob a. "Always pay your hired
19:18 "Never seek revenge or bear a grudge against a,
22:14 "A who eats the sacred offerings without realizing
23:29 A who does not spend that day in humility will be
23:30 And I will destroy a among you who does any kind
24:16 A who blasphemes the LORD's name must be
24:17 "A who takes another person's life must be put to
24:18 "A who kills another person's animal must pay it
24:19 "A who injures another person must be dealt with
24:20 Whatever a does to hurt another person must be
25:29 "A who sells a house inside a walled city has the
25:49 a nephew, or a else who is closely related.
Nu 1:51 A else who goes too near the Tabernacle will be
3:10 A else who comes too near the sanctuary must be
3:38 A other than a priest or Levite who came too near
5:2 "Command the people of Israel to remove a from
16:3 a else among all these people of the LORD?"
16:40 If a did, the same thing would happen to him as
19:18 on a who was in the tent, or a who has touched a
19:21 and a who touches the water of purification will
19:22 and a that a defiled person touches will be
31:19 And all of you who have killed a or touched a dead
35:15 A who accidentally kills someone may flee there
36:6 Let them marry a they like, as long as it is within
Dt 4:42 where a who had accidentally killed someone
12:22 A, whether ceremonially clean or unclean, may eat
15:22 A may eat it, whether ceremonially clean
15:22 or unclean, just as a may eat a gazelle or deer.
17:12 A arrogant enough to reject the verdict of the judge
18:12 A who does these things is an object of horror
18:19 I will personally deal with a who will not listen to
19:3 so that a who has killed someone can flee there for
19:15 "Never convict a of a crime on the testimony of
20:5 'Has a just built a new house but not yet dedicated
20:6 Has a just planted a vineyard but not yet eaten any
20:7 Has a just become engaged? Well, go home
20:8 Then the officers will also say, 'Is a terrified?
20:8 If you are, go home before you frighten a else.'
21:23 same day, for a hanging on a tree is cursed of God.
24:7 "If a kidnaps a fellow Israelite and treats him as a
27:15 'Cursed is a who carves or casts idols and secretly
27:16 'Cursed is a who despises father or mother.'
27:17 'Cursed is a who steals property from a neighbor
27:18 'Cursed is a who leads a blind person astray on the
27:19 'Cursed is a who is unjust to foreigners, orphans,
27:20 'Cursed is a who has sexual intercourse with his
27:21 'Cursed is a who has sexual intercourse with an
27:22 'Cursed is a who has sexual intercourse with his
27:23 'Cursed is a who has sexual intercourse with his
27:24 'Cursed is a who kills another person in secret.'
27:25 'Cursed is a who accepts payment to kill an
27:26 'Cursed is a who does not affirm the terms of this
Jos 1:18 A who rebels against your word and does not obey
6:26 "May the curse of the LORD fall on a / who tries
20:3 A who kills another person unintentionally can run
20:9 A who accidentally killed another person could
Jdg 3:28 across from Moab, preventing a from crossing.
4:20 "If anybody comes and asks you if there is a here,
16:7 not yet been dried, I will be as weak as a else."
16:11 have never been used, I will be as weak as a else."
16:13 with the loom shuttle, I will be as weak as a else."
16:17 leave me, and I would become as weak as a else."
21:5 vowing that a who refused to come must die.
21:8 "Was a absent when we presented ourselves to the
21:18 because we have sworn with a solemn oath that a
Ru 2:2 leftover grain behind a who will let me do it."
4:7 In those days it was the custom in Israel for a
1Sa 2:13 Whenever a offered a sacrifice, Eli's sons would
5:5 a who enters the temple of Dagon will step on its
9:2 head and shoulders taller than a else in the land.
10:12 matter who his father is; a can become a prophet."
10:23 and he stood head and shoulders above a else.
11:7 "This is what will happen to the oxen of a who
14:24 "Let a curse fall on a who eats before evening—
14:28 oath that a who eats food today will be cursed.
17:25 reward the king has offered to a who kills him?
21:2 "He told me not to tell a why I am here.
22:14 "is there a among all your servants who is as
26:6 "Will a volunteer to go in there with me?"
26:12 and Abishai got away without a seeing them
26:15 "Where in all Israel is there a as mighty?
30:2 and everyone else but without killing a.
30:24 Do you think a will listen to you when you talk
2Sa 9:1 One day David began wondering if a in Saul's
9:3 asked him, "Is a still alive from Saul's family?
14:10 the king said. "If a objects, bring them to me.
14:11 you won't let a take vengeance against my son.
15:3 It's too bad the king doesn't have a to hear it.
1Ki 4:31 He was wiser than a else, including Ethan the
13:33 A who wanted to could become a priest for the
15:17 and fortified Ramah in order to prevent a from
19:17 A who escapes from Hazael will be killed by Jehu,
2Ki 4:29 my staff and go! Don't talk to a along the way.
7:9 is wonderful news, and we aren't sharing it with a!
9:15 don't let a escape to Jezreel to report what we have
10:5 We will not make a king; do whatever you think is
10:23 Don't let a in who worships the LORD!"
10:24 and had warned them, "If you let a escape,
11:15 of the Temple, and kill a who tries to rescue her.
1Ch 16:21 Yet he did not let a oppress them. / He warned
2Ch 7:18 then I will not let a take away your throne. This is
13:9 You let a become a priest these days!
15:13 They agreed that a who refused to seek the
16:1 and fortified Ramah in order to prevent a from
23:8 Jehoiada the priest did not let a go home after their
23:14 of the Temple, and kill a who tries to rescue her.
Ezr 7:26 A who refuses to obey the law of your God
Ne 2:12 I had not told a about the plans God had put in my
2:16 for I had not yet said anything to a about my plans.
2:16 the officials, or a else in the administration.
Est 2:10 Esther had not told a of her nationality and family
4:11 "The whole world knows that a who appears
8:11 and annihilate a of any nationality or province who
9:2 themselves against a who might try to harm them.
Job 17:15 But where then is my hope? Can a find it?
24:25 "Can a claim otherwise? Who can prove me
28:4 a mine shaft into the earth far from where a lives.
31:5 "Have I lied to a or deceived a?
31:30 No, I have never cursed a or asked for revenge.
32:21 I won't play favorites or try to flatter a.
34:24 He brings the mighty to ruin without asking a,
36:5 "God is mighty, yet he does not despise a! He is
36:29 Can a really understand the spreading of the clouds
Ps 5:2 and my God, / for I will never pray to a but you.
9:10 have never abandoned a who searches for you.
45:7 pouring out the oil of joy on you more than on a
88:12 Can a in the land of forgetfulness talk about your
89:8 Where is there a as mighty as you, LORD?
105:14 Yet he did not let a oppress them. / He warned
119:63 A who fears you is my friend—/ a who obeys your
Pr 4:22 and radiant health to a who discovers their
5:16 of your springs in public, having sex with just a?
8:9 My words are plain to a with understanding,
9:7 A who rebukes a mocker will get a smart retort.
9:7 A who rebukes the wicked will get hurt.
17:19 A who loves to quarrel loves sin; a who speaks boastfully invites disaster.
20:16 Be sure to get collateral from a who guarantees the
22:11 A who loves a pure heart and gracious speech is
22:23 their defender. He will injure a who injures them.
25:9 the matter with them privately. Don't tell a else,
27:13 Be sure to get collateral from a who guarantees the
Ecc 2:12 and a else would come to the same conclusions I
Isa 2:22 are as frail as breath. How can they be of help to a?
9:19 are fuel for the fire, and no one spares a else.
13:15 A who is captured will be run through with a
33:8 made before witnesses. They have no respect for a.
41:11 and ashamed. A who opposes you will die.
41:24 A who chooses you becomes filthy, just like you!
42:8 that is my name! I will not give my glory to a else.
46:7 no answer. It has no power to get a out of trouble.
47:8 'I'm self-sufficient and not accountable to a!
47:10 'I am self-sufficient and not accountable to a!'
53:9 He had done no wrong, and he never deceived a.
55:1 "Is a thirsty? Come and drink—even if you have
56:3 for the eunuchs. They are as much mine as a else.
59:15 and a who tries to live a godly life is soon
Jer 2:10 See if a has ever heard of anything as strange as
8:6 Is a sorry for sin? Does a say, "What a terrible
11:3 Cursed is a who does not obey the terms of my
18:13 LORD said, "Has a ever heard of such a thing,
23:24 Can a hide from me? Am I not everywhere in all
23:34 If any prophet, priest, or a else says, 'I have a
27:5 I can give these things of mine to a I choose.
29:26 You are responsible to put a who claims to be a
30:20 before me, and I will punish a who hurts them.
32:7 the right to buy it before it is offered to a else.' "
32:8 have the right to buy it before it is offered to a else,
36:19 told Baruch. "Don't tell a where you are!"
38:24 "Don't tell a you told me this, or you will die!
41:4 before a had heard about Gedaliah's murder,
La 3:31 For the Lord does not abandon a forever.
Eze 5:9 you more severely than I have punished a before
6:12 And a who survives will be killed by famine.
9:6 little children. But do not touch a with the mark.
18:9 A who does these things is just and will surely live,
44:29 Whatever a sets apart for the LORD will belong
45:6 This will be set aside to be a city where a in Israel
45:20 of the new year for a who has sinned through error
Da 3:6 A who refuses to obey will immediately be thrown
4:17 of the world and gives them to a he chooses—
4:25 of the world and gives them to a he chooses.
4:32 of the world and gives them to a he chooses."
5:21 and appoints a he desires to rule over them.
6:7 that for the next thirty days a who prays to a,
6:12 that for the next thirty days a who prays to a,
8:26 for a long time, so do not tell a about them yet."
Hos 3:3 you will not have sexual intercourse with a,
Joel 2:32 And a who calls on the name of the LORD will
Am 6:10 ask the last survivor, "Is there a else with you?"
Mic 3:5 but you declare war on a who refuses to pay you.
7:5 Don't trust a—not your best friend or even your
Na 3:19 Where can a be found who has not suffered from
Hag 2:3 Is there a who can remember this house—
Zec 2:8 'A who harms you harms my most precious
13:3 If a begins prophesying again, his own father
Mt 5:19 But a who obeys God's laws and teaches them will
5:28 a who even looks at a woman with lust in his eye
5:32 And a who marries a divorced woman commits
5:47 to your friends, how are you different from a else?
7:24 "A who listens to my teaching and obeys me is
7:26 But a who hears my teaching and ignores it is
8:4 him examine you. Don't talk to a along the way.
9:30 sternly warned them, "Don't tell a about this."
10:32 "If a acknowledges me publicly here on earth,
10:33 But if a denies me here on earth, I will deny that
10:40 "A who welcomes you is welcoming me,
10:40 and a who welcomes me is welcoming the Father
11:15 A who is willing to hear should listen
12:30 A who isn't helping me opposes me, and a who isn't working with me is actually
12:32 A who blasphemes against me, the Son of Man,
12:50 A who does the will of my Father in heaven is my
13:9 A who is willing to hear should listen
13:43 A who is willing to hear should listen
15:4 and 'A who speaks evil of father or mother must
16:20 Then he sternly warned them not to tell a that he
17:9 "Don't tell a what you have seen until I, the Son
18:4 a who becomes as humble as this little child is the
18:5 And a who welcomes a little child like this on my
18:6 But if a causes one of these little ones who trusts in
18:7 "How terrible it will be for a who causes others to
19:12 of Heaven. Let a who can, accept this statement."
21:3 If a asks what you are doing, just say, 'The Lord
21:44 A who stumbles over that stone will be broken to pieces, and it will crush a on whom it falls."

23: 8 Don't ever let **a** call you 'Rabbi,' for you have
23: 9 And don't address **a** here on earth as 'Father,'
23:10 And don't let **a** call you 'Master,' for there is only
24: 4 Jesus told them, "Don't let **a** mislead you.
24:23 "Then if **a** tells you, 'Look, here is the Messiah,'
27:15 during the Passover celebration—**a** the people wanted.
Mk 1:44 him examine you. Don't talk to **a** along the way.
3:29 but **a** who blasphemes against the Holy Spirit will
3:35 **A** who does God's will is my brother and sister
4: 9 "**A** who is willing to hear should listen
4:21 "Would **a** light a lamp and then put it under a
4:23 **A** who is willing to hear should listen
5:37 and wouldn't let **a** go with him except Peter
5:43 Jesus commanded them not to tell **a** what had
7:10 and '**A** who speaks evil of father or mother must
7:36 Jesus told the crowd not to tell **a**, but the more he
8:30 But Jesus warned them not to tell **a** about him.
9: 9 he told them not to tell **a** what they had seen until
9:35 "**A** who wants to be the first must take last place
9:37 "**A** who welcomes a little child like this on my
9:37 and **a** who welcomes me welcomes my Father who
9:40 **A** who is not against us is for us.
9:41 If **a** gives you even a cup of water because you
9:42 "But if **a** causes one of these little ones who trusts
10:15 **a** who doesn't have their kind of faith will never
11: 3 If **a** asks what you are doing, just say, 'The Lord
11:25 first forgive **a** you are holding a grudge against,
13: 5 Jesus replied, "Don't let **a** mislead you,
13:21 "And then if **a** tells you, 'Look, here is the
15: 6 year at Passover time—**a** the people requested.
16: 8 saying nothing to **a** because they were too
16:16 **A** who believes and is baptized will be saved.
16:16 But **a** who refuses to believe will be condemned.
Lk 4: 6 because they are mine to give to **a** I please.
5:14 Then Jesus instructed him not to tell **a** what had
6:30 Give what you have to **a** who asks you for it;
6:49 But **a** who listens and doesn't obey is like a person
7: 4 "If **a** deserves your help, it is he," they said,
8: 8 "**A** who is willing to hear should listen
8:51 Jesus wouldn't let **a** go in with him except Peter,
8:56 but Jesus insisted that they not tell **a** what had
9:21 Jesus warned them not to tell **a** about this.
9:36 They didn't tell **a** what they had seen until long
9:48 "**A** who welcomes a little child like this on my
9:48 and **a** who welcomes me welcomes my Father who
9:50 stop him! **A** who is not against you is for you."
9:62 "**A** who puts a hand to the plow and then looks
10: 4 of sandals. And don't stop to greet **a** on the road.
10:16 "**A** who accepts your message is also accepting
10:16 And **a** who rejects you is rejecting me.
10:16 And **a** who rejects me is rejecting God who sent
11:23 "**A** who isn't helping me opposes me, and **a** who
12: 8 If **a** acknowledges me publicly here on earth,
12: 9 But if **a** denies me here on earth, I will deny that
12:10 but **a** who speaks blasphemies against the Holy
14:23 behind the hedges and urge **a** you find to come,
14:35 **A** who is willing to hear should listen
16:18 "**A** who divorces his wife and marries someone
16:18 and **a** who marries a divorced woman commits
16:26 **A** who wanted to cross over to you from here is
18:17 **a** who doesn't have their kind of faith will never
19:31 If **a** asks what you are doing, just say, 'The Lord
20:18 to pieces, and it will crush **a** on whom it falls."
21: 8 He replied, "Don't let **a** mislead you. For many
Jn 3:31 has come from above and is greater than **a** else.
4:23 The Father is looking for **a** who will worship him
5:21 He will even raise from the dead **a** he wants to,
6:46 (Not that **a** has ever seen the Father; only I,
6:47 **a** who believes in me already has eternal life.
6:51 **A** who eats this bread will live forever; this bread
6:58 **A** who eats this bread will live forever and not die
6:60 is very hard to understand. How can **a** accept it?"
7:11 at the festival and kept asking if **a** had seen him.
7:17 **A** who wants to do the will of God will know
7:46 "We have never heard **a** talk like this!" the guards
8:15 all your human limitations, but I am not judging **a**.
8:33 "We have never been slaves to **a** on earth.
8:47 **A** whose Father is God listens gladly to the words
8:51 **a** who obeys my teaching will never die!"
9:22 who had announced that **a** saying Jesus was the
9:32 Never since the world began has **a** been able to
10: 1 **a** who sneaks over the wall of a sheepfold,
10:29 them to me, and he is more powerful than **a** else.
11:57 and Pharisees had publicly announced that **a** seeing
12:42 But they wouldn't admit it to **a** because of their
12:47 If **a** hears me and doesn't obey me, I am not his
13:20 **a** who welcomes my messenger is welcoming me,
13:20 and **a** who welcomes me is welcoming the Father
14: 9 **A** who has seen me has seen the Father! So why
14:12 **a** who believes in me will do the same works I
14:24 **A** who doesn't love me will not do what I say.
15: 6 **A** who parts from me is thrown away like a useless
15:23 **A** who hates me hates my Father, too.
16:30 and don't need **a** to tell you anything.
19:12 **A** who declares himself a king is a rebel against
Ac 2:21 And **a** who calls on the name of the Lord / will be
3:23 '**A** who will not listen to that Prophet will be cut
4:17 We'll warn them not to speak to **a** in Jesus' name
10:28 shown me that I should never think of **a** as impure.
10:47 "Can **a** object to their being baptized, now that
24:12 I didn't argue with **a** in the Temple, nor did I incite
25:11 neither you nor **a** else has a right to turn me over to
28:21 from Judea or reports from **a** who has arrived here.
Ro 2: 2 in his justice, will punish **a** who does such things.
9:15 said to Moses, / "I will show mercy to **a** I choose,
9:15 and I will show compassion to **a** I choose."
9:16 hard for it. God will show mercy to **a** he chooses.
9:33 But **a** who believes in him / will not be
10:11 "**A** who believes in him will not be disappointed."
10:13 For "**A** who calls on the name of the Lord will be
10:15 And how will **a** go and tell them without being
12:17 Never pay back evil for evil to **a**. Do things in such
13:10 Love does no wrong to **a**, so love satisfies all of
1Co 1:16 of Stephanas. I don't remember baptizing **a** else.)
2:11 No one can know what **a** else is really thinking
3:12 Now **a** who builds on that foundation may use
3:17 God will bring ruin upon **a** who ruins this temple.
4: 3 it matters very little what you or **a** else thinks.
4: 7 What makes you better than **a** else? What do you
5:11 **a** who claims to be a Christian yet indulges in
6: 5 Isn't there **a** in all the church who is wise enough
7:30 or wealth should not keep **a** from doing God's
8: 2 **A** who claims to know all the answers doesn't
9: 1 Do I not have as much freedom as **a** else? Am I not
9:18 preaching the Good News without expense to **a**,
11:16 But if **a** wants to argue about this, all I can say is
11:27 So if **a** eats this bread or drinks this cup of the
14:13 So **a** who has the gift of speaking in tongues
16:11 Don't let **a** despise him. Send him on his way with
16:22 If **a** does not love the Lord, that person is cursed.
2Co 3:16 But whenever **a** turns to the Lord, then the veil is
4: 2 We do not try to trick **a**, and we do not distort the
4: 3 If the Good News we preach is veiled from **a**,
7: 2 We have not done wrong to **a**. We have not led **a**
astray. We have not taken advantage of **a**.
8:23 If **a** asks about Titus, say that he is my partner who
11: 4 You seem to believe whatever **a** tells you, even if
12: 6 I don't want **a** to think more highly of me than
Gal 1: 8 Let God's curse fall on **a**, including myself,
1: 9 If **a** preaches any other gospel than the one you
1:16 to me, I did not rush out to consult with **a** else;
5:21 that **a** living that sort of life will not inherit the
6: 4 and you won't need to compare yourself to **a** else.
6:17 now on, don't let **a** trouble me with these things.
Php 3: 4 Yet I could have confidence in myself if **a** could.
Col 2: 8 Don't let **a** lead you astray with empty philosophy
2:16 So don't let **a** condemn you for what you eat
2:18 Don't let **a** condemn you by insisting on
2:18 And don't let **a** say you must worship angels,
1Th 2: 6 we have never asked for it from you or **a** else.
2: 9 so that our expenses would not be a burden to **a**
4: 8 **A** who refuses to live by these rules is not
2Th 3: 8 We never accepted food from **a** without paying for
1Ti 4:12 Don't let **a** think less of you because you are
5:20 **A** who sins should be rebuked in front of the whole
5:21 without taking sides or showing special favor to **a**.
6: 4 **A** who teaches anything different is both conceited
Tit 2:15 so don't let **a** ignore you or disregard what you
3: 2 They must not speak evil of **a**, and they must avoid
3:10 If **a** is causing divisions among you, give a first
Heb 1: 9 pouring out the oil of joy on you more than on **a**
4:11 For **a** who disobeys God, as the people of Israel
10:28 **A** who refused to obey the law of Moses was put to
10:38 But I will have no pleasure in **a** who turns away."
11: 6 **A** who wants to come to him must believe that
Jas 1:13 to do wrong, and he never tempts **a** else either.
2:14 it by your actions? That kind of faith can't save **a**.
5:15 And **a** who has committed sins will be forgiven.
5:19 if **a** among you wanders away from the truth
1Pe 2: 6 a chosen cornerstone, / and **a** who believes in him
2:22 He never sinned, and he never deceived **a**.
2Pe 3: 4 Why, as far back as **a** can remember,
3: 9 He does not want **a** to perish, so he is giving more
1Jn 2: 9 **A** who says, "I am in the light" but rejects another
2:10 But **a** who loves other Christians is walking in the
2:10 in the light and does not cause **a** to stumble.
2:23 **A** who denies the Son doesn't have the Father
2:23 But **a** who confesses the Son has the Father also.
2:27 so you don't need **a** to teach you what is true.
3: 7 Dear children, don't let **a** deceive you about this:
3:10 **A** who does not obey God's commands and does
3:15 **A** who hates another Christian is really a murderer
4: 7 **A** who loves is born of God and knows God.
4: 8 But **a** who does not love does not know God—
2Jn 1:11 **A** who encourages him becomes a partner in his
Rev 2: 7 "**A** who is willing to hear should listen to the
2:11 "**A** who is willing to hear should listen to the
2:17 "**A** who is willing to hear should listen to the
2:29 **A** who is willing to hear should listen to the Spirit
3: 6 **A** who is willing to hear should listen to the Spirit
3:13 **A** who is willing to hear should listen to the Spirit
3:22 **A** who is willing to hear should listen to the Spirit
11: 5 If **a** tries to harm them, fire flashes from the
11: 5 This is how **a** who tries to harm them must die.
13: 4 "Is there **a** as great as the beast?" they exclaimed.
13: 9 **A** who is willing to hear should listen
13:15 Then the statue commanded that **a** refusing to
14: 9 "**A** who worships the beast and his statue or who
20:15 And **a** whose name was not found recorded in the
22:17 Let the thirsty ones come—**a** who wants to.
22:18 If **a** adds anything to what is written here, God will
22:19 And if **a** removes any of the words of this

ANYONE'S (5) [ANY]

Lev 6:27 and if the sacrificial blood splatters **a** clothing,
Isa 40:14 Has the LORD ever needed **a** advice? Does he
Eze 46:18 And the prince may never take **a** property by force.
Jn 20:23 If you forgive **a** sins, they are forgiven. If you
Ac 20:33 "I have never coveted **a** money or fine clothing.

ANYTHING (207) [ANY]

Ge 18:14 Is **a** too hard for the LORD? About a year from
30:31 Jacob replied, "Don't give me **a** at all. Just do one
31:32 If you find **a** that belongs to you, I swear before all
42:38 If **a** should happen to him, you would bring my
Ex 12:19 Anyone who eats **a** made with yeast during this
12:20 during those days you must not eat **a** made with
18:22 **A** that is too important or too complicated can be
20:17 ox or donkey, or **a** else your neighbor owns."
22: 9 donkey, sheep, article of clothing, or **a** else.
22:29 "Do not hold **a** back when you give me the tithe of
Lev 4: 2 by doing **a** forbidden by the LORD's commands.
6: 5 or **a** gained by swearing falsely. When they realize
6:18 or **a** that touches this food will become holy."
6:27 **A** or anyone who touches the sacrificial meat will
7:17 But **a** left over until the third day must be
7:19 "Meat that touches **a** ceremonially unclean may
7:21 If anyone touches **a** that is unclean, whether it is
12: 4 of purification, she must not touch **a** that is holy.
13:48 the hide of an animal, or **a** made of leather.
13:59 or linen clothing or fabric, or in **a** made of leather.
15: 4 he lies and **a** on which he sits will be defiled.
15:10 If you touch or carry **a** that was under him,
15:20 **A** on which she lies or sits during that time will be
15:26 **A** on which she lies or sits during that time will be
15:27 If you touch her bed or **a** on which she sits,
25:37 do not charge your relatives interest on **a** you lend
27:28 "However, **a** specially set apart by the LORD—
27:28 **A** devoted in this way has been set apart for the
Nu 6: 4 to eat or drink **a** that comes from a grapevine,
6:21 If any Nazirites have vowed to give the LORD **a**
16:26 and don't touch **a** that belongs to them.
19:22 **A** and anyone that a defiled person touches will be
22:16 Please don't let **a** stop you from coming.
22:17 I will pay you well and do **a** you ask of me.
22:18 I would be powerless to do **a** against the will of the
22:19 night to see if the LORD has **a** else to say to me."
22:30 "Have I ever done **a** like this before?" "No,"
22:38 "I have come, but I have no power to say just **a**.
23:12 "Can I say **a** except what the LORD tells me?"
24:13 I am powerless to do **a** against the will of the
31:22 **A** made of gold, silver, bronze, iron, tin, or lead—
Dt 2:35 along with **a** of value from the towns we
4:32 See if **a** as great as this has ever happened before.
5:21 ox or donkey, or **a** else your neighbor owns.'
14:21 "Do not eat **a** that has died a natural death.
14:26 you arrive, use the money to buy **a** you want—
15:21 as being lame or blind, or if **a** else is wrong with it,
22: 3 clothing, or **a** else your neighbor loses.
23:19 food, or **a** else that may be loaned with interest.
24:10 "If you lend **a** to your neighbor, do not enter your
28:29 the darkness, and you will not succeed at **a** you do.
Jdg 13:16 angel of the LORD replied, "but I will not eat **a**.
19:20 old man said. "I will give you **a** you might need.
Ru 1:17 May the LORD punish me severely if I allow **a**
1Sa 3:17 And may God punish you if you hide **a** from me!"
3:18 Samuel told Eli everything; he didn't hold **a** back.
4: 7 We have never had to face **a** like this before!
9: 7 "But we don't have **a** to offer him," Saul replied.
19: 4 "He's never done **a** to harm you.
20:26 Saul didn't say **a** about it that day, for he said to
21: 3 Give me five loaves of bread or **a** else you have."
25:36 so she didn't tell him **a** about her meeting with
30:12 because he hadn't had **a** to eat or drink for three
30:19 son or daughter, or **a** else that had been taken.
2Sa 3:35 David had refused to eat **a** the day of the funeral,
3:35 "May God kill me if I eat **a** before sundown."
14:19 Nobody can hide **a** from you. Yes, Joab sent me
14:32 if he finds me guilty of **a**, then let him execute
19:35 eighty years old today, and I can no longer enjoy **a**.
1Ki 2:17 on my behalf, for I know he will do **a** you request.
18:43 he returned to Elijah and said, "I didn't see **a**."
22: 8 He never prophesies **a** but bad news for me!
22:18 He never prophesies **a** but bad news for me."
2Ki 10: 5 "We are your servants and will do **a** you tell us.
1Ch 29:14 who are my people, that we could give **a** to you?
2Ch 18: 7 He never prophesies **a** but bad news for me!
18:17 He never prophesies **a** but bad news for me."
Ezr 7:20 If you run short of money for **a** necessary for your
Ne 2:16 for I had not yet said **a** to anyone about my plans.
5: 5 and we are helpless to do **a** about it, for our fields
Job 2:10 things from the hand of God and never **a** bad?"
27:11 I will not conceal **a** that concerns the Almighty.
33:32 But if you have **a** to say, go ahead. I want to hear
42: 2 "I know that you can do **a**, and no one can stop
Ps 73:25 but you? / I desire you more than **a** on earth.
89: 6 What mightiest angel is **a** like the LORD?
101: 3 I will refuse to look at / **a** vile and vulgar. / I hate
139:24 Point out **a** in me that offends you, / and lead me
Pr 8:22 me from the beginning, before he created **a** else.
30:30 king of animals, who won't turn aside for **a**,
Ecc 2:10 **A** I wanted, I took. I did not restrain myself from
2:25 For who can eat or enjoy **a** apart from him?
6: 8 Do poor people gain **a** by being wise and knowing
7:12 Wisdom or money can get you almost **a**, but it's
9: 6 They no longer have a part in **a** here on earth.
11: 4 for perfect conditions, you will never get **a** done.
Isa 7:11 Ask for **a** you like, and make it as difficult as you
8:13 Do not fear **a** except the LORD Almighty.
55: 8 "And my ways are far beyond **a** you could
57:13 Let's see if your idols can do **a** for you when you
66: 8 Who has ever seen or heard of **a** as strange as this?
Jer 2:10 See if anyone has ever heard of **a** as strange as this.
2:31 We won't have **a** to do with him anymore!'
2:35 And yet you say, 'I haven't done **a** wrong.
12: 4 Yet the people say, "The LORD won't do **a**!"
20:10 And they say, "If you say **a**, we will report it."
32:27 all the peoples of the world. Is **a** too hard for me?
39:12 "Look after him well, and give him **a** he wants."
La 3:37 Can **a** happen without the Lord's permission?

4: 5 foods now beg in the streets for **a** they can get.
Eze 13: 7 Can your visions be **a** but false if you claim,
14: 3 them into sin. Why should I let them ask me **a**?
44:18 They must not wear **a** that would cause them to
Da 5:23 gods that neither see nor hear nor know **a** at all.
6: 4 his affairs, but they couldn't find **a** to criticize.
Joel 1: 2 your history, has **a** like this ever happened before?
Jnh 3: 7 not even the animals, may eat or drink **a** at all.
4: 5 as he waited to see if **a** would happen to the city.
Zep 3: 2 No one can tell it **a**; it refuses all correction.
Mt 14: 7 so he promised with an oath to give her **a** she
15:17 "**A** you eat passes through the stomach and
16:26 in the process? Is **a** worth more than your soul?
18:19 agree down here on earth concerning **a** you ask,
24:21 For that will be a time of greater horror than **a** the
25:42 I was thirsty, and you didn't give me **a** to drink.
Mk 2:12 "We've never seen **a** like this before!"
6:22 "Ask me for **a** you like," the king said to the girl,
8:18 can't you hear?' Don't you remember **a** at all?
8:23 hands on him and asked, "Can you see **a** now?"
8:37 Is **a** worth more than your soul?
9:23 Jesus asked. "**A** is possible if a person believes."
11:24 You can pray for **a**, and if you believe, you will
16:18 and if they drink **a** poisonous, it won't hurt them.
Lk 9:53 The people of the village refused to have **a** to do
15:16 pigs looked good to him. But no one gave him **a**.
22:35 a traveler's bag, or extra clothing, did you lack **a**?"
23:41 our evil deeds, but this man hasn't done **a** wrong."
24:41 Then he asked them, "Do you have **a** here to eat?"
Jn 1:46 "Can **a** good come from there?" "Just come
4: 9 for Jews refuse to have **a** to do with Samaritans.
9:29 but as for this man, we don't know **a** about him."
9:30 my eyes, and yet you don't know **a** about him!
14:13 You can ask for **a** in my name, and I will do it,
14:14 Yes, ask **a** in my name, and I will do it!
16:23 At that time you won't need to ask me for **a**.
16:30 and don't need anyone to tell you **a**.
18:23 Jesus replied, "If I said **a** wrong, you must give
Ac 10:14 "I have never in all my life eaten **a** forbidden by
11: 8 'I have never eaten **a** forbidden by our Jewish
19:36 no matter what is said. Don't do **a** rash.
24:19 be here to bring charges if they have **a** against me!
25: 5 If Paul has done **a** wrong, you can make your
26:31 "This man hasn't done **a** worthy of death
27:19 and **a** else they could lay their hands on.
Ro 3:27 that we have done **a** to be accepted by God?
4:21 convinced that God was able to do **a** he promised.
8:35 Can **a** ever separate us from Christ's love? Does it
9:11 were born, before they had done **a** good or bad,
14: 2 one person believes it is all right to eat **a**.
14: 3 Those who think it is all right to eat **a** must not
14:20 But it is wrong to eat **a** if it makes another person
14:21 or do **a** else if it might cause another Christian to
14:23 If you do **a** you believe is not right, you are
15:18 I dare not boast of **a** else. I have brought the
1Co 3: 2 solid food, because you couldn't handle **a** stronger.
6:12 You may say, "I am allowed to do **a**." But I reply,
6:12 And even though "I am allowed to do **a**," I must
not become a slave to **a**.
8: 8 We don't miss out on **a** if we don't eat it, and we
don't gain **a** if we do.
9:12 We would rather put up with **a** than put an obstacle
10:23 You say, "I am allowed to do **a**"—but not
10:23 You say, "I am allowed to do **a**"—but not
11: 7 A man should not wear **a** on his head when
12:17 were just one big ear, how could you smell **a**?
2Co 3: 5 It is not that we think we can do **a** of lasting value
11: 7 Good News to you without expecting **a** in return?
13: 7 We pray to God that you will not do **a** wrong.
Gal 6:14 God forbid that I should boast about **a** except the
Eph 1:21 or power or leader or **a** else in this world
Php 1:20 and hope that I will never do **a** that causes me
4: 6 Don't worry about **a**; instead, pray about
Col 1:15 He existed before God made **a** at all and is
1Th 3:10 asking God to let us see you again to fill up **a** that
1Ti 1:10 and for those who do **a** else that contradicts the
5:14 Then the enemy will not be able to say **a** against
6: 4 Anyone who teaches **a** different is both conceited
6: 7 we didn't bring **a** with us when we came into the
6: 7 and we certainly cannot carry **a** with us when we
2Ti 2:10 I am willing to endure **a** if it will bring salvation
2:22 Run from **a** that stimulates youthful lust.
2:22 Follow **a** that makes you want to do right.
Tit 1:16 and disobedient, worthless for doing **a** good.
2: 8 because they won't have **a** bad to say about us.
Phm 1:14 But I didn't want to do **a** without your consent.
1:18 has harmed you in any way or stolen **a** from you,
Heb 9:16 no one gets **a** until it is proved that the person who
11: 3 that what we now see did not come from **a** that can
Jas 1: 4 you will be strong in character and ready for **a**.
1: 7 People like that should not expect to receive **a**
5:12 never take an oath, by heaven or earth or **a** else.
1Jn 5:14 us whenever we ask him for **a** in line with his will.
5:21 keep away from **a** that might take God's place in
Jude 1:11 Like Balaam, they will do **a** for money. And like
Rev 13:17 And no one could buy or sell **a** without that mark,
22: 3 No longer will **a** be cursed. For the throne of God
22:18 If anyone adds **a** to what is written here, God will

ANYTIME (2) [ANY]

Lk 16:29 Your brothers can read their writings **a** they want
Jn 7: 6 But you can go **a**, and it will make no difference.

ANYWAY (25) [ANY]

Ge 31:14 none of our father's wealth will come to us **a**.
Ex 16:27 Some of the people went out **a** to gather food,
19:24 "Go down **a** and bring Aaron back with you.
1Sa 17:26 "Who is this pagan Philistine **a**, that he is allowed
17:28 was angry. "What are you doing around here **a**?"
24:14 Who is the king of Israel trying to catch **a**?
2Sa 13:20 Since he's your brother **a**, don't worry about it."
16:19 "And **a**, why shouldn't I serve you? I helped your
18:23 "Yes, but let me go **a**," he begged. Joab finally
1Ki 11: 2 their gods. Yet Solomon insisted on loving them **a**.
2Ki 7: 4 But if they kill us, we would have died **a**."
2Ch 30:18 and they were allowed to eat the Passover meal **a**,
Ecc 9: 3 have no hope. There is nothing ahead but death **a**.
Isa 57:18 I have seen what they do, but I will heal them **a**!
Jer 38:15 if I give you advice, you won't listen to me **a**."
Eze 14: 9 if a prophet is deceived and gives a message **a**,
Hos 10: 3 the difference? What could a king do for us **a**?"
Mt 21:29 but later he changed his mind and went **a**.
Jn 7:49 what do they know about it? A curse on them **a**!"
20:29 are those who haven't seen me and believe **a**."
Ac 13:28 but they asked Pilate to have him killed **a**.
Ro 1:32 yet they go right ahead and do them **a**.
5:14 they all died **a**—even though they did not disobey
7:19 I don't. And when I try not to do wrong, I do it **a**.
2Co 12:14 And **a**, little children don't pay for their parents'

ANYWHERE (27) [ANY]

Ge 19:17 the angels warned. "Do not stop **a** in the valley.
19:31 "There isn't a man **a** in this entire area for us to
38:22 to Judah and told him that he couldn't find her **a**
Ex 13: 7 or **a** within the borders of your land during this
34: 3 In fact, no one is allowed **a** on the mountain.
34:10 that have never been done before **a** in all the earth
Lev 17: 3 or a lamb or a goat **a** inside or outside the camp
Nu 18:31 and your families may eat this food **a** you wish,
Dt 12:13 careful not to sacrifice your burnt offerings just **a**.
1Sa 9: 4 of Benjamin, but they couldn't find the donkeys **a**.
1Ki 2:36 But don't step outside the city to go **a** else.
2:42 by the LORD and warn you not to go **a** else,
17: 7 dried up, for there was no rainfall **a** in the land.
2Ki 5:25 Gehazi?" "I haven't been **a**," he replied.
2Ch 32:14 Name just one time when any god, **a**, was able to
Job 41:33 There is nothing else so fearless **a** on earth.
Ps 84:10 in your courts / is better than a thousand **a** else!
Ecc 2:11 the wind. There was nothing really worthwhile **a**.
SS 3: 3 'Have you seen him **a**, this one I love so much?'
5: 6 I searched for him, but I couldn't find him **a**.
Isa 58: 4 This kind of fasting will never get you **a** with me.
Jer 3: 2 Is there **a** in the entire land where you have not
Eze 20: 6 with milk and honey, the best of all lands **a**.
Na 3: 7 Yet no one **a** will regret your destruction."
Zec 14:17 And any nation **a** in the world that refuses to come
Mt 27:24 Pilate saw that he wasn't getting **a** and that a riot
Mk 1:45 Jesus that he couldn't enter a town **a** publicly.

APACE [KJV] See CAME, FLEE

APART (132) [PART]

Ex 12:21 slaughter the lamb they have set **a** for the Passover.
20: 9 Six days a week are set **a** for your daily duties
20:11 blessed the Sabbath day and set it **a** as holy.
28: 1 will be set **a** from the common people.
28: 3 garments that will set Aaron **a** from everyone else,
28:36 these words: SET **A** AS HOLY TO THE LORD.
28:41 Set them **a** as holy so they can serve as my priests.
29:21 and their clothing will be set **a** as holy to the
29:33 not eat them, for these things are set **a** and holy.
29:44 and I will set **a** Aaron and his sons as holy,
39:30 these words: SET **A** AS HOLY TO THE LORD.
40:13 anoint him, setting him **a** to serve me as a priest.
40:15 Aaron's descendants are set **a** for the priesthood
Lev 1:17 the priest will tear the bird **a**, though not
7:35 It has been set **a** for Aaron and his descendants
8:15 he set the altar **a** as holy and made atonement for
20: 7 So set yourselves **a** to be holy, for I, the LORD,
20:24 your God, who has set you **a** from all other people.
20:26 I have set you **a** from all other people to be my
21: 6 They must be set **a** to God as holy and must never
21: 7 for the priests must be set **a** to God as holy.
22: 2 gifts that the Israelites set **a** for me with great care,
22: 8 a natural death or has been torn **a** by wild animals,
25:10 This year will be set **a** as holy, a time to proclaim
27:21 will be holy, a field specially set **a** for the LORD.
27:28 anything specially set **a** by the LORD—
27:28 Anything devoted in this way has been set **a** for the
27:29 A person specially set **a** by the LORD for
27:30 to the LORD and must be set **a** to him as holy.
27:32 and flocks. They are set **a** to him as holy.
Nu 3: 3 They were anointed and set **a** to minister as priests.
3:13 I set **a** for myself all the firstborn in Israel of both
6: 2 setting themselves **a** to the LORD in a special
6: 5 for they are holy and set **a** to the LORD.
6: 8 This applies as long as they are set **a** to the
7: 1 he anointed it and set it **a** as holy, along with all its
8: 6 "Now set the Levites **a** from the rest of the people
8:14 you will set the Levites **a** from the rest of the
8:17 I set them **a** for myself on the night I killed all the
16: 3 Everyone in Israel has been set **a** by the LORD,
18:14 "Whatever is specially set **a** for the LORD also
18:17 They are holy and have been set **a** for the LORD.
18:24 which have been set **a** as offerings to the LORD.
23: 9 who live by themselves, / set **a** from other nations.
31:28 Set **a** one out of every five hundred as the
Dt 4:41 Then Moses set **a** three cities of refuge east of the
5:13 Six days a week are set **a** for your daily duties
7:26 then you will be set **a** for destruction just like
7:26 such things, for they are set **a** for destruction.
10: 8 At that time the LORD set **a** the tribe of Levi to
13:17 Keep none of the plunder that has been set **a** for
14: 2 You have been set **a** as holy to the LORD your
14:21 for you are set **a** as holy to the LORD your God.
19: 2 Then you must set **a** three cities of refuge in the
Jos 6:18 Do not take any of the things set **a** for destruction,
7: 1 concerning the things set **a** for the LORD.
7:11 the things that I commanded to be set **a** for me.
7:12 For now Israel has been set **a** for destruction.
7:12 things among you that were set **a** for destruction.
7:13 O Israel, are things set **a** for the LORD.
7:15 The one who has stolen what was set **a** for
20: 9 These cities were set **a** for Israelites as well as the
22:20 sinned by stealing the things set **a** for the LORD?
Jdg 14: 6 and he ripped the lion's jaws **a** with his bare hands.
2Sa 8:11 and gold he had set **a** from the other nations he had
1Ki 5: 9 Then we will break the rafts **a** and deliver the
9: 3 I have set **a** this Temple you have built so that my
9: 7 I will reject this Temple that I have set **a** to honor
13: 3 This altar will split **a**, and its ashes will be poured
2Ki 24:13 They cut **a** all the gold vessels that King Solomon
1Ch 2: 7 taking plunder that had been set **a** for the LORD.
23:13 and his descendants were set **a** to dedicate the most
2Ch 2: 4 It will be a place set **a** to burn incense and sweet
7:16 this Temple and set it **a** to be my home forever.
7:20 I will reject this Temple that I have set **a** to honor
23: 6 Temple of the LORD, for they are set **a** as holy.
26:18 the sons of Aaron who are set **a** for this work.
30: 8 Come to his Temple which he has set **a** as holy
30:17 lambs for them, to set them **a** for the LORD.
35: 3 who had been set **a** to serve the LORD and were
Ezr 8:28 and these treasures have been set **a** as holy to the
Job 16:12 "I was living quietly until he broke me **a**. He took
28: 9 People know how to tear **a** flinty rocks
Ps 4: 3 The LORD has set **a** the godly for himself.
17:12 They are like hungry lions, eager to tear me **a**—
50:22 all of you who ignore me, / or I will tear you **a**,
107:16 prison gates of bronze; / he cut **a** their bars of iron.
124: 6 the LORD, / who did not let their teeth tear us **a**!
Pr 11:11 it prosper, but the talk of the wicked tears it **a**.
Ecc 2:25 For who can eat or enjoy anything **a** from him?
Isa 38:13 all night, / but I was torn **a** as though by lions.
41:15 You will tear all your enemies **a**, making chaff of
Jer 1: 5 Before you were born I set you **a** and appointed
5: 6 their towns, tearing **a** any who dare to venture out.
13: 7 But now it was mildewed and falling **a**. The belt
34:18 I will cut you **a** just as you cut **a** the calf when
34:19 Yes, I will cut you **a**, whether you are officials of
Eze 20:12 them that I, the LORD, had set them **a** to be holy,
22:27 leaders are like wolves, who tear **a** their victims.
30:16 will be racked with pain; Thebes will be torn **a**;
37:28 have set Israel **a** for myself to be holy."
43:26 for the altar, thus setting it **a** for holy use.
44:24 and they will see to it that the Sabbath is set **a** as a
44:29 Whatever anyone sets **a** for the LORD will
45: 7 "Two special sections of land will be set **a** for the
48:14 for it belongs to the LORD; it is set **a** as holy.
Da 6:24 and tore them **a** before they even hit the floor of
11: 4 his kingdom will be broken **a** and divided into four
Hos 5:14 will tear at Israel and Judah as a lion rips **a** its prey.
13: 8 I will tear you **a** and devour you like a hungry lion.
Zec 12:14 will mourn separately, husbands and wives **a**.
14: 4 And the Mount of Olives will split **a**, making a
14:20 these words: SET **A** AS HOLY TO THE LORD.
14:21 and Judah will be set **a** as holy to the LORD
Mt 7:15 but are really wolves that will tear you **a**.
24:51 He will tear the servant **a** and banish him with the
27:51 from top to bottom. The earth shook, rocks split **a**,
Lk 12:46 He will tear the servant **a** and banish him with the
12:52 From now on families will be split **a**, three in favor
23:45 the thick veil hanging in the Temple was torn **a**.
Jn 15: 4 the vine, and you cannot be fruitful **a** from me.
15: 5 much fruit. For **a** from me you can do nothing.
Ac 20:32 inheritance with all those he has set **a** for himself.
23:10 the commander, fearing they would tear him **a**,
26:18 among God's people, who are set **a** by faith in me.'
27:41 by the force of the waves and began to break **a**.
Ro 14:20 Don't tear **a** the work of God over what you eat.
1Co 6:11 washed away, and you have been set **a** for God.
7:14 a godly influence, but now they are set **a** for him.
Eph 2:12 In those days you were living **a** from Christ.
Heb 7:26 He has now been set **a** from sinners, and he has

APELLES (1)

Ro 16:10 Give my greetings to **A**, a good man whom Christ

APES (2)

1Ki 10:22 down with gold, silver, ivory, **a**, and peacocks.
2Ch 9:21 down with gold, silver, ivory, **a**, and peacocks.

APHARSACHITES, APHARSATHCHITES

[KJV] See LOCAL LEADERS

APHARSITES [KJV] See PERSIANS

APHEK (8)

Jos 12:18 The king of **A** / The king of Lasharon
13: 4 stretching northward to **A** on the border of the
19:30 Ummah, **A**, and Rehob—twenty-two towns with
1Sa 4: 1 near Ebenezer, and the Philistines were at **A**.
29: 1 The entire Philistine army now mobilized at **A**,
1Ki 20:26 and marched out against Israel, this time at **A**.
20:30 The rest fled behind the walls of **A**, but the wall
2Ki 13:17 you will completely conquer the Arameans at **A**.

APHEKAH (1)
Jos 15:53 Janim, Beth-tappuah, **A**,

APHIAH (1)
1Sa 9: 1 from the family of Becorath and the clan of **A**.

APHIK (1)
Jdg 1:31 Sidon, Ahlab, Aczib, Helbah, **A**, and Rehob.

APHRAH [KJV] See BETH-LEAPHRAH

APHSES [KJV] See HAPPIZZEZ

APOLLONIA (1)
Ac 17: 1 of Amphipolis and **A** and came to Thessalonica,

APOLLOS (12)
Ac 18:24 Meanwhile, a Jew named **A**, an eloquent speaker
18:27 **A** had been thinking about going to Achaia,
19: 1 While **A** was in Corinth, Paul traveled through the
1Co 1:12 Others are saying, "I follow **A**," or "I follow
3: 4 follower of Paul," and another says, "I prefer **A**,"
3: 5 Who is **A**, and who is Paul, that we should be the
3: 6 and **A** watered it, but it was God, not we,
3:22 Paul and **A** and Peter; the whole world and life
4: 1 So look at **A** and me as mere servants of Christ
4: 6 I have used **A** and myself to illustrate what I've
16:12 Now about our brother **A**—I urged him to visit you
Tit 3:13 can to help Zenas the lawyer and **A** with their trip.

APOLLYON (1)
Rev 9:11 name in Hebrew is *Abaddon,* and in Greek, ***A***—

APOLOGIZED (1)
Ac 16:39 They came to the jail and **a** to them. Then they

APOSTLE (25) [APOSTLES, APOSTLES']
Ac 1:25 as an **a** to replace Judas the traitor in this ministry,
1:26 was chosen and became an **a** with the other eleven.
12: 2 He had the **a** James (John's brother) killed with a
Ro 1: 1 chosen by God to be an **a** and sent out to preach
11:13 God has appointed me as the **a** to the Gentiles.
1Co 1: 1 chosen by the will of God to be an **a** of Christ
9: 1 as much freedom as anyone else? Am I not an **a**?
9: 2 Even if others think I am not an **a**, I certainly am to
9: 2 for you are living proof that I am the Lord's **a**.
9: 3 answer to those who question my authority as an **a**.
12:29 Is everyone an **a**? Of course not. Is everyone a
15: 9 and I am not worthy to be called an **a** after the way
2Co 1: 1 appointed by God to be an **a** of Christ Jesus,
12:12 certainly gave you every proof that I am truly an **a**,
Gal 1: 1 This letter is from Paul, an **a**. I was not appointed
1:19 And the only other **a** I met at that time was James,
Eph 1: 1 chosen by God to be an **a** of Christ Jesus.
Col 1: 1 chosen by God to be an **a** of Christ Jesus,
1Ti 1: 1 This letter is from Paul, an **a** of Christ Jesus,
2: 7 and **a** to teach the Gentiles about faith and truth.
2Ti 1: 1 is from Paul, an **a** of Christ Jesus by God's will,
1:11 a preacher, an **a**, and a teacher of this Good News.
Tit 1: 1 from Paul, a slave of God and an **a** of Jesus Christ.
1Pe 1: 1 This letter is from Peter, an **a** of Jesus Christ.
2Pe 1: 1 is from Simon Peter, a slave and **a** of Jesus Christ.

APOSTLES (75) [APOSTLE]
Mt 10: 2 Here are the names of the twelve **a**: / first Simon
Mk 3:14 them to be his regular companions, calling them **a**.
6:30 The **a** returned to Jesus from their ministry tour
6:31 that Jesus and his **a** didn't even have time to eat.
Lk 6:13 of his disciples and chose twelve of them to be **a**.
9: 1 One day Jesus called together his twelve **a**
9:10 When the **a** returned, they told Jesus everything
11:49 'I will send prophets and **a** to them, and they will
17: 5 One day the **a** said to the Lord, "We need more
22:14 and the twelve **a** sat down together at the table.
24:10 several others. They told the **a** what had happened,
Ac 1: 2 chosen **a** further instructions from the Holy Spirit.
1: 3 he appeared to the **a** from time to time and proved
1: 6 When the **a** were with Jesus, they kept asking him,
1:12 The **a** were at the Mount of Olives when this
2:14 Then Peter stepped forward with the eleven other **a**
2:37 and they said to him and to the other **a**, "Brothers,
2:43 and the **a** performed many miraculous signs
4:18 So they called the **a** back in and told them never
4:33 And the **a** gave powerful witness to the
4:35 and brought the money to the **a** to give to others in
4:36 the one the **a** nicknamed Barnabas (which means
4:37 and brought the money to the **a** for those in need.
5: 2 He brought part of the money to the **a**, but he
5:12 the **a** were performing many miraculous signs
5:18 They arrested the **a** and put them in the jail.
5:21 So the **a** entered the Temple about daybreak
5:21 Then they sent for the **a** to be brought for trial.
5:26 would kill them if they treated the **a** roughly.
5:27 Then they brought the **a** in before the council.
5:29 But Peter and the **a** replied, "We must obey God
5:34 and ordered that the **a** be sent outside the council
5:40 They called in the **a** and had them flogged.
5:41 The **a** left the high council rejoicing that God had
6: 2 "We **a** should spend our time preaching
6: 6 These seven were presented to the **a**, who prayed
8: 1 and all the believers except the **a** fled into Judea
8:14 When the **a** back in Jerusalem heard that the
8:18 when the **a** placed their hands upon people's heads,
9:27 Then Barnabas brought him to the **a** and told them
9:28 Then the **a** accepted Saul, and after that he was
10:39 "And we **a** are witnesses of all he did throughout
11: 1 Soon the news reached the **a** and other believers in
14: 3 The **a** stayed there a long time, preaching boldly
14: 4 Some sided with the Jews, and some with the **a**.
14: 6 When the **a** learned of it, they fled for their lives.
14:13 and they prepared to sacrifice to the **a** at the city
15: 2 to talk to the **a** and elders about this question.
15: 4 by the whole church, including the **a** and elders.
15: 6 So the **a** and church elders got together to decide
15:22 Then the **a** and elders and the whole church in
15:23 "This letter is from the **a** and elders, your brothers
16: 4 as decided by the **a** and elders in Jerusalem.
Ro 16: 7 They are respected among the **a** and became
1Co 4: 9 But sometimes I think God has put us **a** on display,
12:28 first are **a**, / second are prophets, / third are
15: 5 He was seen by Peter and then by the twelve **a**.
15: 7 Then he was seen by James and later by all the **a**.
15: 9 For I am the least of all the **a**, and I am not worthy
15:10 For I have worked harder than all the other **a**,
15:15 And we **a** would all be lying about God, for we
2Co 11: 5 But I don't think I am inferior to these "super **a**."
11:13 These people are false **a**. They have fooled you by disguising themselves as **a** of Christ.
12:11 for I am not at all inferior to these "super **a**,"
Gal 1:17 to consult with those who were **a** before I was.
Eph 2:20 built on the foundation of the **a** and the prophets.
3: 5 he has revealed it by the Holy Spirit to his holy **a**
4:11 the **a**, the prophets, the evangelists, and the pastors
1Th 2: 7 As **a** of Christ we certainly had a right to make
2Pe 3: 2 our Lord and Savior commanded through your **a**.
Jude 1:17 must remember what the **a** of our Lord Jesus Christ
Rev 2: 2 examined the claims of those who say they are **a**
18:20 O holy people of God and **a** and prophets!
21:14 written the names of the twelve **a** of the Lamb.

APOSTLES' (2) [APOSTLE]
Ac 2:42 and devoted themselves to the **a** teaching
5:15 As a result of the **a** work, sick people were brought

APOTHECARIES, APOTHECARY [KJV] See PERFUMES, INCENSE

APOTHECARIES' [KJV] See PERFUMED

APPAIM (2)
1Ch 2:30 The sons of Nadab were Seled and **A**. Seled died
2:31 but **A** had a son named Ishi. The son of Ishi was

APPALLED (7) [APPALLING]
Ezr 9: 4 And I sat there utterly **a** until the time of the
Job 18:20 People in the west are **a** at their fate; people in the
Isa 63: 5 I was amazed and **a** at what I saw. So I executed
Jer 19: 8 All who pass by will be **a** and will gasp at the
49:17 All who pass by will be **a** and will gasp at the
Eze 27:35 are **a** at your terrible fate. / Their kings are filled
28:19 All who knew you are **a** at your fate. You have

APPALLING (2) [APPALLED]
1Ki 9: 8 it will become an **a** sight for all who pass by.
2Ch 7:21 it will become an **a** sight to all who pass by.

APPAREL [KJV] See CLOTHES, DRESS, GARMENT, ROBES

APPARENTLY (1)
Ac 14:19 and dragged him out of the city, **a** dead.

APPEAL (9) [APPEALED, APPEALING, APPEALS]
2Ki 8: 5 the mother of the boy walked in to make her **a** to
Ac 25:11 me over to these men to kill me. I **a** to Caesar!"
28:19 the decision, I felt it necessary to **a** to Caesar,
Ro 16:17 And now I make one more **a**, my dear brothers
1Co 1:10 I **a** to you by the authority of the Lord Jesus Christ
2Th 3:12 In the name of the Lord Jesus Christ we **a** to such
1Ti 5: 1 but **a** to him respectfully as though he were your
1Pe 3:21 it is an **a** to God from a clean conscience.
5: 1 he returns. As a fellow elder, this is my **a** to you:

APPEALED (6) [APPEAL]
Ex 10: 7 court officials now came to Pharaoh and **a** to him.
1Sa 15: 9 and lambs—everything, in fact, that **a** to them.
Ac 25:12 You have **a** to Caesar, and to Caesar you shall
25:21 But Paul **a** to the emperor. So I ordered him back
25:25 However, he **a** his case to the emperor, and I
26:32 "He could be set free if he hadn't **a** to Caesar!"

APPEALING (2) [APPEAL]
Est 2: 4 This advice was very **a** to the king, so he put the
Lk 18: 3 **a** for justice against someone who had harmed her.

APPEALS (1) [APPEAL]
1Co 2: 6 and not the kind that **a** to the rulers of this world,

APPEAR (37) [APPEARANCE, APPEARED, APPEARING, APPEARS, REAPPEARANCE, REAPPEARED, REAPPEARS]
Ge 1: 9 be gathered into one place so dry ground may **a**."
1:14 "Let bright lights **a** in the sky to separate the day
8: 5 to go down, other mountain peaks began to **a**.
Ex 3:11 "But who am I to **a** before Pharaoh?"
19: 3 Then Moses climbed the mountain to **a** before
23:17 every man in Israel must **a** before the Sovereign
30:20 before they go into the Tabernacle to **a** before the
34:20 No one is allowed to **a** before me without a gift.
34:23 Three times each year all the men of Israel must **a**
34:24 and conquer your land when you go to **a** before the
Lev 9: 4 because the LORD will **a** to them today."
9: 6 the glorious presence of the LORD will **a** to
13: 4 is white but does not **a** to be more than skin-deep,
13:14 But if any open sores **a**, the infected person will be
13:21 and if it doesn't **a** to be more than skin-deep
13:32 and if the infection does not **a** to be more than
Dt 16:16 They must **a** before the LORD your God at the
19:17 the accuser and accused must **a** before the priests
Jos 20: 4 the one who caused the accidental death will **a**
Jdg 13:21 The angel did not **a** again to Manoah and his wife.
1Sa 3:21 The LORD continued to **a** at Shiloh and gave
1Ki 18: 2 So Elijah went to **a** before Ahab. Meanwhile,
Est 1:17 that Queen Vashti has refused to **a** before the king.
Job 3: 6 of the year, never again to **a** among the months.
38:12 "Have you ever commanded the morning to **a**
38:35 Can you make lightning **a** and cause it to strike as
Ps 21: 9 when you **a**. / The LORD will consume them in
84: 7 and each of them will **a** before God in Jerusalem.
102:16 will rebuild Jerusalem. / He will **a** in his glory.
Isa 50: 8 me now? Where are my enemies? Let them **a**!
Zec 9:14 The LORD will **a** above his people; his arrows
Mt 24:11 And many false prophets will **a** and will lead many
24:30 the sign of the coming of the Son of Man will **a** in
Jn 7:27 When the Messiah comes, he will simply **a**;
Ac 10:40 to life three days later. Then God allowed him to **a**,
26:16 and about other times I will **a** to you.
Heb 9:24 For Christ has entered into heaven itself to **a** now

APPEARANCE (18) [APPEAR]
Lev 13:55 If he sees that the affected area has not changed **a**
Nu 9:16 at night the cloud changed to the **a** of fire.
1Sa 16: 7 "Don't judge by his **a** or height, for I have rejected
16: 7 People judge by outward **a**, but the LORD looks
2Sa 10: 5 for they were very embarrassed by their **a**.
1Ch 19: 5 for they were very embarrassed by their **a**.
Isa 11: 3 He will never judge by **a**, false evidence,
53: 2 was nothing beautiful or majestic about his **a**,
Eze 1:26 And high above this throne was a figure whose **a**
43:10 Tell them its **a** and its plan so they will be ashamed
Mt 17: 2 Jesus' **a** changed so that his face shone like the
Mk 9: 2 was there. As the men watched, Jesus' **a** changed,
16:12 him at first because he had changed his **a**.
Lk 9:29 And as he was praying, the **a** of his face changed,
12:56 You know how to interpret the **a** of the earth
2Co 10: 7 is that you make your decisions on the basis of **a**.
1Ti 2: 9 And I want women to be modest in their **a**.
Jas 1:23 in a mirror but doing nothing to improve your **a**.

APPEARED (95) [APPEAR]
GOD...APPEARED (17) Ge 31:24,29; 35:1,7,9; 48:3; Ex 4:5; 6:2,3; Jdg 13:6,9,9; 1Ki 11:9; 2Ch 1:7; Eze 43:2; Ac 7:2; 13:30

THE LORD*...APPEARED (21) Ge 12:7; 17:1; 18:1; 26:2,24; Ex 3:2; 4:1; Lev 9:23; Nu 14:10; 16:19,42; 20:6; Dt 31:15; Jdg 6:12; 13:3; 1Ki 3:5; 9:2; 11:9; 2Ch 3:1; 7:12; Eze 1:28

Ge 12: 7 Then the LORD **a** to Abram and said, "I am
17: 1 the LORD **a** to him and said, "I am God
18: 1 The LORD **a** again to Abraham while he was
26: 2 The LORD **a** to him there and said, "Do not go
26:24 where the LORD **a** to him on the night of his
31:24 But the previous night God had **a** to Laban in a
31:29 but the God of your father **a** to me last night
31:42 That is why he **a** to you last night and vindicated
34:20 and he **a** with his father before the town leaders to
35: 1 the God who **a** to you when you fled from your
35: 7 because God had **a** to him there at Bethel when he
35: 9 God **a** to Jacob once again when he arrived at
38:28 thread around the wrist of the child who **a** first,
41: 6 Then suddenly, seven more heads **a** on the stalk,
48: 3 "God Almighty **a** to me at Luz in the land of
Ex 3: 2 the angel of the LORD **a** to him as a blazing fire
3:16 Isaac, and Jacob—**a** to me in a burning bush.
4: 1 They'll just say, 'The LORD never **a** to you.' "
4: 5 and the God of Jacob—really has **a** to you."
6: 3 I **a** to Abraham, to Isaac, and to Jacob as God
Lev 9:23 and the glorious presence of the LORD **a** to the
13:32 area has not spread and no yellow hair has **a**,
Nu 9:15 cloud over the Tabernacle **a** to be a pillar of fire.
14:10 Then the glorious presence of the LORD **a** to all
14:14 that you have **a** in full view of your people in the
16:19 Then the glorious presence of the LORD **a** to the
16:42 and the glorious presence of the LORD **a**.
20: 6 Then the glorious presence of the LORD **a** to
Dt 31:15 And the LORD **a** to them in a pillar of cloud at
33:16 and the favor of the one who **a** in the burning bush.
Jos 5:12 No manna **a** that day, and it was never seen again.
Jdg 6:12 The angel of the LORD **a** to him and said,
13: 3 The angel of the LORD **a** to Manoah's wife
13: 6 and told her husband, "A man of God **a** to me!
13: 9 and the angel of God **a** once again to his wife as

13:10 "The man who a to me the other day is here
13:23 He wouldn't have a to us and told us this
1Ki 3:5 That night the LORD a to Solomon in a dream,
9:2 Then the LORD a to Solomon a second time,
11:9 the God of Israel, who had a to him twice.
13:5 At the same time a wide crack a in the altar,
2Ki 2:11 and talking, suddenly a chariot of fire a,
3:20 morning sacrifice was offered, water suddenly a!
2Ch 1:7 That night God a to Solomon in a dream and said,
3:1 where the LORD had a to Solomon's father,
7:12 Then one night the LORD a to Solomon and said,
Ne 2:1 I had never a sad in his presence before this time.
Ps 33:9 he spoke, the world began! / It a at his command.
106:9 the Red Sea to divide, and a dry path a.
Jer 37:5 Hophra of Egypt a at the southern border of Judah.
Eze 1:28 This was the way the glory of the LORD a to me.
8:2 I saw a figure that a to be a man. From the waist
9:2 Six men soon a from the upper gate that faces
10:1 I saw what a to be a throne of blue sapphire above
40:2 From there I could see what a to be a city across
43:2 the glory of the God of Israel a from the east.
Da 7:6 Then the third of these strange beasts a, and it
7:8 suddenly another small horn a among them.
8:1 following the one that had already a to me.
8:5 suddenly a male goat a from the west,
Mt 1:20 and an angel of the Lord a to him in a dream.
2:9 Once again the star a to them, guiding them to
2:13 an angel of the Lord a to Joseph in a dream.
2:16 because the wise men had told him the star first a
2:19 an angel of the Lord a in a dream to Joseph in
17:3 Moses and Elijah a and began talking with Jesus.
27:53 the holy city of Jerusalem, and a to many people.
Mk 9:4 Then Elijah and Moses a and began talking with
9:26 The boy lay there motionless, and he a to be dead.
16:12 Afterward he a to two who were walking from
16:14 Still later he a to the eleven disciples as they were
Lk 1:11 was in the sanctuary when an angel of the Lord a,
1:28 Gabriel a to her and said, "Greetings,
2:9 Suddenly, an angel of the Lord a among them,
9:30 Moses and Elijah, a and began talking with Jesus.
22:43 Then an angel from heaven a and strengthened
24:4 Suddenly, two men a to them, clothed in dazzling
24:34 "The Lord has really risen! He a to Peter!"
24:35 had a to them as they were walking along the road
Jn 21:1 Later Jesus a again to the disciples beside the Sea
21:14 This was the third time Jesus had a to his disciples
Ac 1:3 he a to the apostles from time to time and proved
2:3 what looked like flames or tongues of fire a
7:2 Our glorious God a to our ancestor Abraham in
7:30 an angel a to Moses in the flame of a burning bush.
7:35 Through the angel who a to him in the burning
9:17 who a to you on the road, has sent me so that you
11:13 He told us how an angel had a to him in his home
13:31 And he a over a period of many days to those who
23:11 That night the Lord a to Paul and said,
26:16 For I have a to you to appoint you as my servant
Php 2:7 humble position of a slave and a in human form.
1Ti 3:16 great mystery of our faith: / Christ a in the flesh
1Jn 2:18 and already many such antichrists have a.
Rev 6:4 And another horse a, a red one. Its rider was given

APPEARING (2) [APPEAR]

Da 9:26 will be killed, a to have accomplished nothing,
Zec 5:5 and said, "Look up! Something is a in the sky."

APPEARS (18) [APPEAR]

Lev 13:3 has turned white and a to be more than skin-deep,
13:10 and an open sore a in the affected area,
13:25 and the problem a to be no more than skin-deep,
13:26 and the problem a to be no more than skin-deep
13:30 If it a to be more than skin-deep and fine yellow
13:34 has not spread and a to be no more than skin-deep,
13:37 But if it a that the infection has stopped spreading
13:42 if a reddish white infection a on the front
14:37 and the contamination a to go deeper than the
Est 4:11 "The whole world knows that anyone who a
Pr 27:25 After the hay is harvested, the new crop a,
Eze 21:27 And it will not be restored until the one a who has
Joel 2:2 spreading across the mountains, a mighty army a!
Zec 5:2 "It a to be about thirty feet long and fifteen feet
Mal 3:2 Who will be able to stand and face him when he a?
2Th 1:7 and also for us when the Lord Jesus a from heaven.
2Ti 4:1 and the dead when he a to set up his Kingdom:
2Pe 1:19 until the day Christ a and his brilliant light shines

APPEASE (2)

Ge 32:20 a Esau with the presents before meeting him face
Pr 16:14 is a deadly threat; the wise do what they can to a it.

APPETITE (6) [APPETITES]

Job 6:7 My a disappears when I look at it; I gag at the
33:20 They lose their a and do not care for even the most
Ps 102:4 is sick, withered like grass, / and I have lost my a.
Pr 16:26 It is good for workers to have an a; an empty
30:20 how an adulterous woman can satisfy her sexual a,
Php 3:19 Their god is their a, they brag about shameful

APPETITES (3) [APPETITE]

Nu 11:6 But now our a are gone, and day after day we have
Job 38:39 prey for a lioness and satisfy the young lions' a
Ps 107:18 Their a were gone, / and death was near.

APPHIA (1)

Phm 1:2 and to our sister A and to Archippus, a fellow

APPIAN (1)

Ac 28:15 and they came to meet us at the Forum on the A

APPLAUDED (1) [APPLAUDS]

1Sa 18:5 an appointment that was a by the fighting men

APPLAUDS (1) [APPLAUDED]

Ps 49:18 and the world loudly a their success.

APPLE (4) [APPLES]

Ps 17:8 Guard me as the a of your eye. / Hide me in the
SS 2:3 my lover is like the finest a tree in the orchard.
8:5 "I aroused you under the a tree, where your
Joel 1:12 The pomegranate trees, palm trees, and a trees—

APPLES (3) [APPLE]

Pr 25:11 Timely advice is as lovely as golden a in a silver
SS 2:5 me with your love—your 'raisins' and your 'a'—
7:8 grape clusters, and the scent of your breath like a.

APPLIED (2) [APPLY]

Ps 119:94 For I have a myself to obey your commandments.
Eze 13:12 will cry out, 'Where is the whitewash you a?'

APPLIES (23) [APPLY]

Ge 17:12 This a not only to members of your family,
Ex 12:49 This law a to everyone, whether a native-born
21:31 "The same principle a if the bull gores a boy
23:11 The same a to your vineyards and olive groves.
Lev 7:36 This regulation a throughout the generations to
15:3 This defilement a whether the discharge continues
15:22 The same a if you touch an object on which she
16:29 and it a to those who are Israelites by birth,
17:8 which a both to Israelites and to the foreigners
17:13 "And this command a both to Israelites and to the
17:15 "And this command also a both to Israelites
18:26 This a both to you who are Israelites by birth
Nu 5:3 This a to men and women alike. Remove them
6:8 This a as long as they are set apart to the LORD.
15:29 This same law a both to native Israelites
19:14 "This is the ritual law that a when someone dies in
Dt 14:23 This a to your tithes of grain, new wine, olive oil,
15:3 however, a only to your fellow Israelites—
24:21 This also a to the grapes in your vineyard. Do not
Eze 7:13 For what God has said a to everyone—it will not
Ro 3:19 the law a to those to whom it was given,
7:1 don't you know that the law a only to a person
Heb 6:9 like this, we really don't believe that it a to you.

APPLY (17) [APPLIED, APPLIES]

Ex 12:19 These same regulations a to the foreigners living
Lev 15:7 The same instructions a if you touch the man who
20:2 which a to those who are Israelites by birth as well
22:18 which a to those who are Israelites by birth as well
24:22 "These same regulations a to Israelites by birth
27:17 Year of Jubilee, then the entire assessment will a.
Nu 5:30 and the priest will a this entire ritual law to her.
9:14 The same laws a both to you and to the foreigners
15:16 and regulations will a both to you
Dt 20:15 But these instructions a only to distant towns,
Job 5:27 is true. Listen to my counsel, and a it to yourself."
Pr 22:17 words of the wise; a your heart to my instruction.
Isa 42:23 Will not even one of you a these lessons from the
Hos 8:12 my laws, they act as if those laws don't a to them.
Ac 13:40 Be careful! Don't let the prophets' words a to you.
Ro 7:2 if he dies, the laws of marriage no longer a to her.
2Pe 1:5 So make every effort to a the benefits of these

APPOINT (26) [APPOINTED, APPOINTING, APPOINTMENT, APPOINTMENTS, APPOINTS]

Ge 41:34 Let Pharaoh a officials over the land, and let them
41:40 I hereby a you to direct this project. You will
Ex 18:21 A them as judges over groups of one thousand,
21:13 I will a a place where the slayer can run for safety.
Nu 3:10 A Aaron and his sons to carry out the duties of the
27:16 please a a new leader for the community.
Dt 1:13 good reputation, and I will a them as your leaders.'
16:18 "A judges and officials for each of your tribes in
17:15 You must a a fellow Israelite, not a foreigner.
2Sa 19:13 may God strike me dead if I do not a you as
1Ch 15:16 David also ordered the Levite leaders to a a choir
Ezr 7:25 are to use the wisdom God has given you to a
Ne 7:3 A the residents of Jerusalem to act as guards,
Est 2:3 Let the king a agents in each province to bring
Ps 61:7 A your unfailing love and faithfulness to watch
Isa 3:4 Then he will a children to rule over them,
66:21 "And I will a some of those who return to be my
Jer 1:10 Today I a you to stand up against nations
23:4 Then I will a responsible shepherds to care for
23:32 I did not send or a them, and they have no message
49:19 from its land, and I will a the leader of my choice.
50:44 from its land, and I will a the leader of my choice.
51:27 A a leader, and bring a multitude of horses!
Mic 5:5 we will a seven rulers to watch over us,
Ac 26:16 For I have appeared to you to a you as my servant
Tit 1:5 and a elders in each town as I instructed you.

APPOINTED (133) [APPOINT]

APPOINTED FESTIVALS (5) Lev 23:2; 1Ch 23:31; 2Ch 2:4; Hos 2:11; Zep 3:18

APPOINTED TIME(S) (10) Ex 13:10; 23:15; 34:18; Nu 28:2; Est 9:27,31; Da 11:27,29,35; Mt 8:29

Ge 24:14 let her be the one you have a as Isaac's wife.
41:38 As they discussed who should be a for the job,
Ex 2:14 "Who a you to be our prince and judge?
13:10 "So celebrate this festival at the a time each year.
16:23 "The LORD has a tomorrow as a day of rest,
23:15 This festival will be an annual event at the a time
31:6 "And I have a Oholiab son of Ahisamach,
34:18 at the a time each year in early spring,
Lev 7:35 time they were a to serve the LORD as priests.
16:29 "On the a day in early autumn, you must spend the
23:2 instructions regarding the LORD's a festivals,
23:5 which begins at twilight on its a day in early
23:24 "On the a day in early autumn, you are to
23:37 "These are the LORD's a annual festivals.
Nu 9:3 at twilight on the a day in early spring. Be sure to
9:5 in the wilderness of Sinai as twilight fell on the a
9:11 sacrifice one month later, at twilight on the a day.
28:2 See to it that they are brought at the a times
28:16 "On the a day in early spring, you must celebrate
29:1 celebrated on the a day in early autumn each year.
34:29 These are the men the LORD has a to oversee the
Dt 1:15 and a them to serve as judges and officials over
Jdg 18:30 and they a Jonathan son of Gershom, a descendant
1Sa 8:1 grew old, he a his sons to be judges over Israel.
10:1 because the LORD has a you to be the leader of
12:6 "It was the LORD who a Moses and Aaron,"
18:13 and a him commander over only a thousand men,
2Sa 6:21 He a me as the leader of Israel, the people of the
7:11 from the time I a judges to rule my people. And I
17:25 Absalom had a Amasa as commander of his army,
18:1 David now a generals and captains to lead his
1Ki 1:35 for I have a him to be ruler over Israel and Judah."
2:35 Then the king a Benaiah to command the army in
9:23 He also a 550 of them to supervise the various
12:32 And it was at Bethel that he a priests for the pagan
12:33 So on the a day in midautumn, a day that he
2Ki 7:17 The king a his officer to control the traffic at the
17:32 but they a from among themselves priests to offer
23:5 who had been a by the previous kings of Judah,
25:22 Then King Nebuchadnezzar a Gedaliah son of
25:23 the king of Babylon had a Gedaliah as governor,
1Ch 6:48 were a to various other tasks in the Tabernacle,
9:22 David and Samuel the seer had a their ancestors
15:17 So the Levites a Heman son of Joel, Asaph son of
16:4 David a the following Levites to lead the people in
16:41 David also a Heman, Jeduthun, and the others
16:42 And the sons of Jeduthun were a as gatekeepers.
17:10 from the time I a judges to rule my people. And I
23:1 he a his son Solomon to be king over Israel.
23:31 at new moon celebrations, and at all the a festivals.
25:1 then a men from the families of Asaph,
25:8 The musicians were a to their particular term of
26:10 Merari clan, a Shimri as the leader among his sons,
26:29 and his sons were a to serve as public
2Ch 2:4 and at the other a festivals of the LORD our God.
2:14 with your craftsmen and those a by my lord David,
8:10 King Solomon also a 250 of them to supervise the
11:15 Jeroboam a his own priests to serve at the pagan
13:9 and the Levites and have a your own priests,
19:5 He a judges throughout the nation in all the
19:8 Jehoshaphat a some of the Levites and priests
20:21 the king a singers to walk ahead of the army,
22:7 whom the LORD had a to end the dynasty of
30:15 On the a day in midspring, the people slaughtered
31:19 men were a to distribute portions to every male
32:6 He a military officers over the people and asked
34:8 and the Temple, Josiah a Shaphan son of Azaliah,
35:1 in Jerusalem on the a day in early spring.
35:5 Then stand in your a holy places and help the
36:4 The king of Egypt a Eliakim, the brother of
36:10 And Nebuchadnezzar a Jehoiachin's uncle,
36:23 He has a me to build him a Temple at Jerusalem in
Ezr 1:2 He has a me to build him a Temple at Jerusalem in
5:14 whom King Cyrus a as governor of Judah.
8:24 I a twelve leaders of the priests—Sherebiah,
Ne 6:7 He also reports that you have a prophets to
7:1 the gatekeepers, singers, and Levites were a.
9:17 and a a leader to take them back to their slavery in
12:44 On that day men were a to be in charge of the
13:4 who had been a as supervisor of the storerooms of
13:13 And I a Hanan son of Zaccur and grandson of
Est 3:14 they would be ready to do their duty on the a day.
4:5 one of the king's eunuchs who had been a as her
8:2 And Esther a Mordecai to be in charge of Haman's
9:5 But the Jews went ahead on the a day and struck
9:27 these two prescribed days at the a time each year.
9:31 an annual celebration of these days at the a time,
Ps 18:43 my accusers. / You a me as the ruler over nations;
Pr 8:23 I was a in ages past, at the very first,
Isa 61:1 because the LORD has a me to bring good news
Jer 1:5 and a you as my spokesman to the world."
25:9 of Babylon, whom I have a as my deputy.
29:26 'The LORD has a you to replace Jehoiada as the
37:1 He was a by King Nebuchadnezzar of Babylon.
40:5 He has been a governor of Judah by the king of
40:7 a Gedaliah son of Ahikam as governor over the
41:2 whom the king of Babylon had a governor.
41:18 the governor a by the Babylonian king.
Eze 3:17 of man, I have a you as a watchman for Israel.
9:1 "Bring on the men a to punish the city!
39:14 special crews will be a to search the land for any
43:21 and burn it at the a place outside the Temple area.
Da 1:11 been a by the chief official to look after Daniel,
1:19 So they were a to his regular staff of advisers.

2:48 Then the king **a** Daniel to a high position and gave
2:49 Daniel's request, the king **a** Shadrach, Meshach,
6:1 and he **a** a prince to rule over each province.
11:27 for an end will still come at the **a** time.
11:29 "Then at the **a** time he will once again invade the
11:35 the time of the end, for the **a** time is still to come.
Hos 2:11 and her Sabbath days—all her **a** festivals.
8:4 The people have **a** kings and princes, but not with
Zep 3:18 "I will gather you who mourn for the **a** festivals;
Mt 8:29 You have no right to torture us before God's **a**
Lk 4:18 for he has **a** me to preach Good News to the poor.
Jn 15:16 I **a** you to go and produce fruit that will last,
Ac 7:10 so that Pharaoh **a** him governor over all of Egypt
13:48 and all who were **a** to eternal life became
14:23 Paul and Barnabas also **a** elders in every church
17:31 judging the world with justice by the man he has **a**,
20:28 over whom the Holy Spirit has **a** you as elders.
Ro 9:17 "I have **a** you for the very purpose of displaying
11:13 God has **a** me as the apostle to the Gentiles.
2Co 1:1 **a** by God to be an apostle of Christ Jesus,
8:19 He was **a** by the churches to accompany us as we
Gal 1:1 I was not **a** by any group or by human authority.
Col 1:23 and I, Paul, have been **a** by God to proclaim it.
1Ti 1:1 **a** by the command of God our Savior and by Christ
3:10 Before they are **a** as deacons, they should be given
Heb 3:2 For he was faithful to God, who **a** him, just as
7:28 the law was given, God **a** his Son with an oath,
1Pe 2:14 and the officials he has **a**. For the king has sent
Rev 17:12 they will be **a** to their kingdoms for one brief

APPOINTING (3) [APPOINT]
Da 11:39 **a** them to positions of authority and dividing the
1Ti 1:12 considering me trustworthy and **a** me to serve him,
5:22 Never be in a hurry about **a** an elder. Do not

APPOINTMENT (2) [APPOINT]
1Sa 18:5 an **a** that was applauded by the fighting men
Ac 12:21 and an **a** with Herod was granted. When the day

APPOINTMENTS (1) [APPOINT]
2Ch 31:13 These **a** were made by King Hezekiah

APPOINTS (2) [APPOINT]
Da 5:21 and **a** anyone he desires to rule over them.
Jn 3:27 "God in heaven **a** each person's work.

APPRECIATE (3) [APPRECIATED, APPRECIATION]
2Ki 4:13 "Tell her that we **a** the kind concern she has
Pr 28:23 In the end, people **a** frankness more than flattery.
Isa 1:3 know their owner and **a** his care, but not my people

APPRECIATED (2) [APPRECIATE]
Pr 16:21 and instruction is **a** if it's well presented.
Ecc 9:16 they are poor. What they say will not be **a** for long.

APPRECIATION (1) [APPRECIATE]
Pr 23:8 and you will have to take back your words of **a** for

APPREHEND [KJV] See CATCH

APPREHENDED (1)
Nu 15:33 He was **a** and taken before Moses, Aaron,

APPROACH (17) [APPROACHED, APPROACHES, APPROACHING]
Ex 20:26 And you may not **a** my altar by steps. If you do,
28:43 or **a** the altar in the Holy Place to perform their
30:20 and before they **a** the altar to burn offerings to the
Lev 9:7 "**A** the altar and present your sin offering and your
22:3 they **a** the sacred food presented by the Israelites,
Nu 4:19 and not die when they **a** the most sacred objects.
4:20 Otherwise they must not **a** the sanctuary and look
8:19 so no plague will strike them when they **a** the
Dt 20:10 "As you **a** a town to attack it, first offer its people
2Sa 22:12 in darkness, / veiling his **a** with dense rain clouds.
Ps 18:11 in darkness, / veiling his **a** with dense rain clouds.
Jer 8:16 The whole land trembles at the **a** of the terrible
30:21 I will invite him to **a** me, says the LORD, for who
Eze 40:46 for they alone of all the Levites may **a** the LORD
44:13 They may not **a** me to minister as priests.
44:16 enter my sanctuary and **a** my table to serve me.
1Ti 6:16 lives in light so brilliant that no human can **a** him.

APPROACHED (33) [APPROACH]
Ge 18:23 Abraham **a** him and said, "Will you destroy both
33:3 As he **a** his brother, he bowed low seven times
50:4 Joseph **a** Pharaoh's advisers and asked them to
Ex 2:7 Then the baby's sister **a** the princess. "Should I go
14:10 As Pharaoh and his army **a**, the people of Israel
Jos 5:13 As Joshua **a** the city of Jericho, he looked up
1Sa 9:18 Just then Saul **a** Samuel at the gateway and asked,
2Sa 14:4 When the woman **a** the king, she fell with her face
20:17 As he **a**, the woman asked, "Are you Joab?"
1Ki 2:1 As the time of King David's death **a**, he gave this
20:17 As they **a**, Ben-hadad's scouts reported to him,
22:21 until finally a spirit **a** the LORD and said, 'I can
2Ki 4:25 As she **a** the man of God at Mount Carmel,
2Ch 18:20 until finally a spirit **a** the LORD and said, 'I can
Ezr 4:2 So they **a** Zerubbabel and the other leaders
Est 3:8 Then Haman **a** King Xerxes and said, "There is a
5:2 gold scepter to her. So Esther **a** and touched its tip.
Pr 7:10 The woman **a** him, dressed seductively and sly of
Jer 42:1 and all the people, from the least to the greatest, **a**
Da 7:13 He **a** the Ancient One and was led into his
7:16 So I **a** one of those standing beside the throne
8:17 As Gabriel **a** the place where I was standing,
Mt 8:2 Suddenly, a man with leprosy **a** Jesus. He knelt
21:1 As Jesus and the disciples **a** Jerusalem, they came
27:57 As evening **a**, Joseph, a rich man from Arimathea
Mk 11:1 As Jesus and his disciples **a** Jerusalem, they came
15:42 the day before the Sabbath. As evening **a**,
Lk 7:12 A funeral procession was coming out as he **a** the
18:35 As they **a** Jericho, a blind beggar was sitting beside
22:47 But even as he said this, a mob **a**, led by Judas,
Jn 1:47 As they **a**, Jesus said, "Here comes an honest
Ac 3:2 As they **a** the Temple, a man lame from birth was
Rev 10:9 So I **a** him and asked him to give me the little

APPROACHES (6) [APPROACH]
Lev 20:16 If a woman **a** a male animal to have intercourse
2Ki 11:8 Any unauthorized person who **a** you must be
Job 38:14 the features of the earth take shape as the light **a**,
Ps 50:3 Our God **a** with the noise of thunder. / Fire devours
Hab 2:3 surely, the time **a** when the vision will be fulfilled.
Jn 14:30 to talk to you, because the prince of this world **a**.

APPROACHING (10) [APPROACH]
Ge 12:11 As he was **a** the borders of Egypt, Abram said to
Nu 21:1 heard that the Israelites were **a** on the road to
33:40 heard that the people of Israel were **a** his land.
1Sa 7:7 when they learned that the Philistines were **a**.
1Ki 13:1 and he arrived there just as Jeroboam was **a** the
2Ki 7:6 of horses and the sounds of a great army **a**.
9:17 the tower of Jezreel saw Jehu and his company **a**,
1Ch 21:21 When Araunah saw the king **a**, he left his threshing
Jer 37:11 army left Jerusalem because of Pharaoh's **a** army,
51:46 panic when you hear the first rumor of **a** forces.

APPROPRIATE (9) [APPROPRIATELY]
Ge 47:12 and brothers in amounts **a** to the number of their
49:28 Each received a blessing that was **a** to him.
Nu 2:17 each in position under the **a** family banner.
Dt 25:2 presence with the number of lashes **a** to the crime.
Ezr 7:17 and the **a** grain offerings and drink offerings,
1Co 16:4 And if it seems **a** for me also to go along, then we
Gal 6:9 for we will reap a harvest of blessing at the **a** time.
1Ti 2:9 They should wear decent and **a** clothing and not
Tit 2:3 teach the older women to live in a way that is **a** for

APPROPRIATELY (1) [APPROPRIATE]
2Ch 32:25 But Hezekiah did not respond **a** to the kindness

APPROVAL (14) [APPROVE]
Ge 41:44 a foot in the entire land of Egypt without your **a**."
2Sa 14:22 "At last I know that I have gained your **a**,
Job 29:24 at them. My look of **a** was precious to them.
Ps 90:17 And may the Lord our God show us his **a**
Pr 8:35 finds me finds life and wins **a** from the LORD.
Mt 27:43 let God show his **a** by delivering him!
Mk 6:19 but without Herod's **a** she was powerless.
Jn 5:41 "Your **a** or disapproval means nothing to me,
Ro 2:13 is not merely knowing the law that brings God's **a**.
6:16 or you can choose to obey God and receive his **a**.
1Co 8:8 It's true that we can't win God's **a** by what we eat.
Gal 2:19 keep the law, I realized I could never earn God's **a**.
Heb 11:2 God gave his **a** to people in days of old because of
11:39 these people we have mentioned received God's **a**

APPROVE (5) [APPROVAL, APPROVED, APPROVES]
Ex 21:22 the woman's husband demands and the judges **a**.
1Ch 13:2 "If you **a** and if it is the will of the LORD our
Ro 13:13 we do, so that everyone can **a** of our behavior.
14:18 please God. And other people will **a** of you, too.
2Ti 2:15 Work hard so God can **a** you. Be a good worker,

APPROVED (10) [APPROVE]
Ge 7:2 Take along seven pairs of each animal that I have **a**
7:8 those **a** for eating and sacrifice and those that were
8:20 and birds that had been **a** for that purpose.
Lev 10:19 Would the LORD have **a** if I had eaten the sin
10:20 And when Moses heard this, he **a**.
17:13 and kill an animal or bird that is **a** for eating,
2Co 13:6 that we have passed the test and are **a** by God.
Eph 6:4 with the discipline and instruction **a** by the Lord.
1Th 2:4 For we speak as messengers who have been **a** by
Heb 11:5 he was taken up, he was **a** as pleasing to God.

APPROVES (3) [APPROVE]
Pr 12:2 The LORD **a** of those who are good, but he
Ecc 9:7 your wine with a happy heart, for God **a** of this!
Ro 16:10 greetings to Apelles, a good man whom Christ **a**.

APPROXIMATELY (1)
Jos 7:4 So **a** three thousand warriors were sent, but they

APRIL (10)
2Ki 25:27 and released him from prison on **A** 2 of that year.
Ezr 6:19 On **A** 21 the returned exiles celebrated Passover.
7:9 He had left Babylon on **A** 8 and came to Jerusalem
8:31 We broke camp at the Ahava Canal on **A** 19
Est 3:7 So in the month of **A**, during the twelfth year of
3:12 On **A** 17 Haman called in the king's secretaries
Eze 29:17 On **A** 26, during the twenty-seventh year of King
30:20 On **A** 29, during the eleventh year of King
40:1 On **A** 28, during the twenty-fifth year of our
Da 10:4 On **A** 23, as I was standing beside the great Tigris

APRON (1)
Lk 12:37 put on an **a**, and serve them as they sit and eat!

APTITUDE (1)
Da 1:17 God gave these four young men an unusual **a** for

AQUEDUCT (3)
2Ki 18:17 The Assyrians stopped beside the **a** that feeds
Isa 7:3 You will find the king at the end of the **a** that feeds
36:2 The Assyrians stopped beside the **a** that feeds

AQUILA (6)
Ac 18:2 There he became acquainted with a Jew named **A**,
18:18 the coast of Syria, taking Priscilla and **A** with him.
18:26 and **A** heard him preaching boldly in the
Ro 16:3 Greet Priscilla and **A**. They have been co-workers
1Co 16:19 along with **A** and Priscilla and all the others who
2Ti 4:19 Give my greetings to Priscilla and **A** and those

AR (7)
Nu 21:15 which extend as far as the settlement of **A** on the
21:28 the city of Sihon. / It burned the city of **A** in Moab;
Dt 2:9 I have given them **A** as their property, and I will
2:10 called the Emites had once lived in the area of **A**.
2:18 'Today you will cross the border of Moab at **A**
2:29 and so did the Moabites, who live in **A**.
Isa 15:1 In one night your cities of **A** and Kir will be

ARA (1)
1Ch 7:38 The sons of Jether were Jephunneh, Pispah, and **A**.

ARAB (3) [ARABIA, ARABIANS, ARABS]
Jos 15:52 Also included were the towns of **A**, Dumah,
Ne 2:19 Tobiah, and Geshem the **A** heard of our plan,
6:1 When Sanballat, Tobiah, Geshem the **A**,

ARABAH (3) [BETH-ARABAH]
Dt 2:8 and avoided the road through the **A** Valley that
1Sa 23:24 of Maon in the **A** Valley south of Jeshimon.
Am 6:14 from Lebo-hamath in the north to the **A** Valley in

ARABIA (9) [ARAB]
1Ki 10:15 from merchants and traders, all the kings of **A**,
2Ch 9:14 All the kings of **A** and the governors of the land
Isa 21:13 This message came to me concerning **A**:
21:13 O caravans from Dedan, hide in the deserts of **A**.
Jer 25:24 I went to the kings of **A**, the kings of the nomadic
Eze 30:5 Ethiopia, Libya, Lydia, and **A**, with all their other
Joel 3:8 and they will sell them to the peoples of **A**,
Gal 1:17 I went away into **A** and later returned to the city of
4:25 And now Jerusalem is just like Mount Sinai in **A**,

ARABIANS (2) [ARAB]
Eze 27:21 "The **A** and the princes of Kedar brought lambs
Ac 2:11 Cretans, and **A**. And we all hear these people

ARABS (5) [ARAB]
2Ch 17:11 and the **A** brought seventy-seven hundred rams
21:16 the LORD stirred up the Philistines and the **A**,
22:1 The marauding bands of **A** had killed all the older
26:7 but also in his battles with the **A** of Gur and in his
Ne 4:7 But when Sanballat and Tobiah and the **A**,

ARAD (5)
Nu 21:1 The Canaanite king of **A**, who lived in the Negev,
33:40 It was then that the Canaanite king of **A**, who lived
Jos 12:14 The king of Hormah / The king of **A**
Jdg 1:16 the people there, near the town of **A** in the Negev.
1Ch 8:15 Zebadiah, **A**, Eder,

ARAH (4)
1Ch 7:39 The sons of Ulla were **A**, Hanniel, and Rizia.
Ezr 2:5 The family of **A** | 775
Ne 6:18 because his father-in-law was Shecaniah son of **A**
7:10 The family of **A** | 652

ARAM (61) [ARAM-MAACAH, ARAM-NAHARAIM, ARAM-ZOBAH, ARAMAIC, ARAMEAN, ARAMEANS, PADDAN-ARAM]
Ge 10:22 Shem were Elam, Asshur, Arphaxad, Lud, and **A**.
10:23 The descendants of **A** were Uz, Hul, Gether,
22:21 was Buz, followed by Kemuel (the father of **A**),
Nu 23:7 "Balak summoned me to come from **A**;
Jdg 3:10 went to war against King Cushan-rishathaim of **A**,
10:6 and the gods of **A**, Sidon, Moab, Ammon,
1Ki 10:29 to the kings of the Hittites and the kings of **A**.
11:25 hated Israel intensely and continued to reign in **A**.
15:18 and grandson of Hezion, the king of **A**,
19:15 you arrive there, anoint Hazael to be king of **A**.
20:1 Now King Ben-hadad of **A** mobilized his army,
20:22 "Get ready for another attack by the king of **A**
22:1 For three years there was no war between **A**

22:31 Now the king of A had issued these orders to his
2Ki 5: 1 The king of A had high admiration for Naaman,
5: 1 because through him the LORD had given A
6: 8 When the king of A was at war with Israel,
6:11 The king of A became very upset over this.
6:14 So one night the king of A sent a great army with
6:24 King Ben-hadad of A mobilized his entire army
7: 6 For the Lord had caused the whole army of A to
8: 7 Now Elisha went to Damascus, the capital of A,
8: 9 and said, "Your servant Ben-hadad, the king of A,
8:13 shown me that you are going to be the king of A."
8:15 he died. Then Hazael became the next king of A.
8:28 war against King Hazael of A at Ramoth-gilead.
9:14 Israel against the forces of King Hazael of A.
12:17 About this time King Hazael of A went to war
13: 3 and he allowed King Hazael of A and his son
13: 4 The LORD could see how terribly the king of A
13: 7 The king of A had killed the others like they were
13:17 is the LORD's arrow, full of victory over A,
13:19 "Then you would have beaten A until they were
13:22 King Hazael of A had oppressed Israel during the
13:24 King Hazael of A died, and his son Ben-hadad
15:37 days the LORD began to send King Rezin of A
16: 5 Then King Rezin of A and King Pekah of Israel
16: 7 and rescue me from the attacking armies of A
1Ch 1:17 Shem were Elam, Asshur, Arphaxad, Lud, and A.
1:17 The descendants of A were Uz, Hul, Gether,
2:23 (Later Geshur and A captured the Towns of Jair
7:34 of Shomer were Ahi, Rohgah, Hubbah, and A.
2Ch 1:17 to the kings of the Hittites and the kings of A.
16: 2 He sent it to King Ben-hadad of A, who was ruling
16: 7 "Because you have put your trust in the king of A
16: 7 your chance to destroy the army of the king of A.
18:30 Now the king of A had issued these orders to his
22: 5 They went out to fight King Hazael of A at
28: 5 his God allowed the king of A to defeat Ahaz
28:23 for he said, "These gods helped the kings of A,
Isa 7: 1 Jerusalem was attacked by King Rezin of A
7: 2 "A is allied with Israel against us!" So the hearts
7: 4 King Rezin of A and Pekah son of Remaliah.
7: 5 the kings of A and Israel are coming against you.
7: 8 because A is no stronger than its capital,
7:16 you fear so much—the kings of Israel and A—
17: 3 The few left in A will share the fate of Israel's
Eze 27:16 "A sent merchants to buy your wares. They traded
Hos 12:12 Jacob fled to the land of A and earned a wife by
Am 1: 5 and the people of A will return to Kir as slaves.
Zec 9: 1 the message from the LORD against the land of A

ARAM-MAACAH (1) [ARAM]

1Ch 19: 6 and troops from Aram-naharaim, A, and Zobah.

ARAM-NAHARAIM (5) [ARAM]

Ge 24:10 He traveled to A and went to the village where
Dt 23: 4 Balaam son of Beor from Pethor in A to curse you.
Jdg 3: 8 handed them over to King Cushan-rishathaim of A.
1Ch 19: 6 tons of silver to hire chariots and troops from A,
Ps 60: T regarding the time David fought A

ARAM-ZOBAH (1) [ARAM]

Ps 60: T the time David fought Aram-naharaim and A,

ARAMAIC (7) [ARAM]

2Ki 18:26 "Please speak to us in A, for we understand it
Ezr 4: 7 sent a letter to Artaxerxes in the A language,
Isa 36:11 "Please speak to us in A, for we understand it
Da 2: 4 Then the astrologers answered the king in A,
Ac 1:19 and they gave the place the A name *Akeldama,*
21:40 and he addressed them in their own language, A.
26:14 and I heard a voice saying to me in A, 'Saul,

ARAMEAN (31) [ARAM]

Ge 25:20 the daughter of Bethuel the A from Paddan-aram
28: 5 his mother's brother, the son of Bethuel the A.
Dt 26: 5 'My ancestor Jacob was a wandering A who went
2Sa 8: 6 the A capital, and the Arameans became David's
10: 6 so they hired twenty thousand A mercenaries from
10:16 they were joined by additional A troops summoned
10:19 and his A allies realized they had been defeated by
1Ki 20:20 Each Israelite soldier killed his A opponent,
20:20 and suddenly the entire A army panicked and fled.
20:26 The following spring he called up the A army
20:27 to the vast A forces that filled the countryside!
20:29 The Israelites killed 100,000 A foot soldiers in one
22:32 So when the A charioteers saw Jehoshaphat in his
22:34 An A soldier, however, randomly shot an arrow at
2Ki 5: 2 Now groups of A raiders had invaded the land of
5:20 "My master should not have let this A get away
6:18 As the A army advanced toward them,
6:23 the A raiders stayed away from the land of Israel.
7: 4 might as well go out and surrender to the A army.
7:10 that they had gone out to the A camp and no one
7:14 scouts to see what had happened to the A army.
7:16 of Samaria rushed out and plundered the A camp.
16: 9 So the Assyrians attacked the A capital of
24: 2 the LORD sent bands of Babylonian, A, Moabite,
1Ch 7:14 born to his A concubine, were Asriel and Makir.
18: 6 the A capital, and the Arameans became David's
19:16 so they summoned additional A troops from the
2Ch 18:31 So when the A charioteers saw Jehoshaphat in his
18:33 An A soldier, however, randomly shot an arrow at
24:23 of the year, the A army marched against Joash.
Jer 35:11 we were afraid of the Babylonian and A armies.

ARAMEANS (39) [ARAM]

2Sa 8: 5 When A from Damascus arrived to help
8: 6 and the A became David's subjects and brought
10: 8 while the A from Zobah and Rehob and the men
10: 9 and led them out to fight the A in the fields.
10:11 "If the A are too strong for me, then come over
10:13 and his troops attacked, the A began to run away.
10:14 And when the Ammonites saw the A running,
10:15 The A now realized that they were no match for
10:17 The A positioned themselves there in battle
10:18 But again the A fled from the Israelites. This time
10:19 the A were afraid to help the Ammonites.
1Ki 20:21 and the A were killed in a great slaughter.
20:28 The A have said that the LORD is a god of the
22: 3 "Do you realize that the A are still occupying our
22:11 With these horns you will gore the A to death!"
22:35 Ahab was propped up in his chariot facing the A.
2Ki 6: 9 for the A are planning to mobilize their troops
7: 5 that evening they went out to the camp of the A,
7:12 The A know we are starving, so they have left their
7:15 and equipment that the A had thrown away in their
13: 5 to rescue the Israelites from the tyranny of the A.
13:17 for you will completely conquer the A at Aphek.
1Ch 18: 5 When A from Damascus arrived to help
18: 6 and the A became David's subjects and brought
19:10 and led them out to fight the A in the fields.
19:12 "If the A are too strong for me, then come over
19:14 and his troops attacked, the A began to run away.
19:15 And when the Ammonites saw the A running,
19:16 The A now realized that they were no match for
19:18 But again the A fled from the Israelites. This time
19:19 the A were no longer willing to help the
2Ch 18:10 With these horns you will gore the A to death!"
18:34 up in his chariot facing the A until evening.
22: 5 and the A wounded Joram in the battle.
24:24 Although the A attacked with only a small army,
24:25 The A withdrew, leaving Joash severely wounded.
Isa 9:12 along with A from the east and Philistines from the
22: 6 Elamites are the archers; A drive the chariots.
Am 9: 7 the Philistines from Crete and led the A out of Kir.

ARAMITESS [KJV] See ARAMEAN

ARAN (2)

Ge 36:28 The sons of Dishan were Uz and A.
1Ch 1:42 and Akan. The sons of Dishan were Uz and A.

ARARAT (4)

Ge 8: 4 the boat came to rest on the mountains of A.
2Ki 19:37 They then escaped to the land of A, and another
Isa 37:38 They then escaped to the land of A, and another
Jer 51:27 Bring out the armies of A, Minni, and Ashkenaz.

ARAUNAH (15) [ARAUNAH'S]

2Sa 24:16 was by the threshing floor of A the Jebusite.
24:18 LORD on the threshing floor of A the Jebusite."
24:20 When A saw the king and his men coming toward
24:21 "Why have you come, my lord?" A asked.
24:22 my lord, and use it as you wish," A said to David.
24:24 But the king replied to A, "No, I insist on buying
1Ch 21:15 standing by the threshing floor of A the Jebusite.
21:18 the LORD at the threshing floor of A the Jebusite.
21:20 A, who was busy threshing wheat at the time,
21:21 When A saw the king approaching, he left his
21:22 David said to A, "Let me buy this threshing floor
21:23 my lord, and use it as you wish," A said to David.
21:24 But the king replied to A, "No, I insist on paying
21:25 So David gave A six hundred pieces of gold in
2Ch 3: 1 The Temple was built on the threshing floor of A

ARAUNAH'S (1) [ARAUNAH]

1Ch 21:28 he offered sacrifices there at A threshing floor.

ARBA (4) [KIRIATH-ARBA]

Jos 14:15 It had been named after A, a great hero of the
15:13 So Caleb was given the city of A (that is, Hebron),
21:11 (A was an ancestor of Anak.)
2Sa 23:35 Hezro from Carmel; / Paarai from A;

ARBAH [KJV] See KIRIATH-ARBA

ARBATHITE (2)

2Sa 23:31 Abi-albon the A; / Azmaveth from Bahurim;
1Ch 11:32 Hurai from near Nahale-gaash; / Abi-albon the A;

ARCHANGEL (2) [ANGEL]

Da 12: 1 the a who stands guard over your nation, will arise.
1Th 4:16 with the call of the a, and with the trumpet call of

ARCHANGELS (1) [ANGEL]

Da 10:13 Then Michael, one of the a, came to help me,

ARCHELAUS (1)

Mt 2:22 he learned that the new ruler was Herod's son A,

ARCHER (2) [ARCHERS]

Ge 21:20 in the wilderness of Paran. He became an expert a,
Pr 26:10 or a bystander is like an a who shoots recklessly.

ARCHERS (16) [ARCHER]

Ge 49:23 He has been attacked by a, / who shot at him
1Sa 31: 3 and the Philistine a caught up with him
2Sa 11:24 the a on the wall shot arrows at us. Some of our
1Ch 8:40 of Ulam were all skilled warriors and expert a.
10: 3 and the Philistine a caught up with him
12: 2 All of them were expert a, and they could shoot
2Ch 35:23 But the enemy a hit King Josiah with their arrows
Job 16:13 His a surrounded me, and his arrows pierced me
Isa 21:17 Only a few of its courageous a will survive.
22: 6 Elamites are the a; Arameans drive the chariots.
66:19 to the Libyans and Lydians (who are famous as a),
Jer 49:35 "I will destroy the a of Elam—the best of their
50:14 Let your a shoot at her. Spare no arrows, for she
50:29 "Send out a call for a to come to Babylon.
51: 3 Don't let the a put on their armor or draw their
Am 2:15 The a will fail to stand their ground. The swiftest

ARCHES [KJV] See FOYER

ARCHEVITES [KJV] See ERECH

ARCHIPPUS (2)

Col 4:17 And say to A, "Be sure to carry out the work the
Phm 1: 2 and to our sister Apphia and to A, a fellow soldier

ARCHITECT (1)

Pr 8:30 I was the a at his side. I was his constant delight,

ARCHIVES (2)

Ezr 5:17 we request that you search in the royal a of
6: 1 orders that a search be made in the Babylonian a,

ARCTURUS [KJV] See BEAR

ARD (2) [ARDITES]

Ge 46:21 Naaman, Ehi, Rosh, Muppim, Huppim, and A.
Nu 26:40 The Ardites, named after their ancestor A.

ARDITES (1) [ARD]

Nu 26:40 The A, named after their ancestor Ard.

ARDON (1)

1Ch 2:18 Azubah's sons were named Jesher, Shobab, and A.

ARE (4398) [BE] See Index of Articles, Etc.

AREA (130) [AREAS]

Ge 10:30 The descendants of Joktan lived in the a extending
12: 6 At that time, the a was inhabited by Canaanites.
13: 9 If you want that a over there, then I'll stay here.
13: 9 If you want to stay in this a, then I'll move on to
13:10 The whole a was well watered everywhere,
13:13 The people of this a were unusually wicked
19:31 "There isn't a man anywhere in this entire a for us
34: 1 visit some of the young women who lived in the a.
35: 5 came over the people in all the towns of that a,
36:43 each clan giving its name to the a it occupied.
Lev 10:17 didn't you eat the sin offering in the sanctuary a?"
10:18 you should have eaten the meat in the sanctuary a
13: 3 then examine the affected a of a person's skin.
13: 3 If the hair in the affected a has turned white
13: 4 "But if the affected a of the skin is white but does
13: 5 If the affected a has not changed or spread on the
13: 6 If the affected a has faded and not spread,
13:10 and an open sore appears in the affected a,
13:20 and if the hair in the affected a has turned white,
13:21 sees that there is no white hair in the affected a,
13:22 If during that time the affected a spreads on the
13:23 But if the a grows no larger and does not spread,
13:24 a burn on the skin and the burned a changes color,
13:25 If the hair in the affected a turns white
13:26 that there is no white hair in the affected a
13:27 If at the end of that time the affected a has spread
13:28 But if the affected a has not moved or spread on
13:30 and fine yellow hair is found in the affected a,
13:31 and there is no black hair in the affected a,
13:32 If at the end of that time the affected a has not
13:33 shave off all hair except the hair on the affected a.
13:37 and black hair has grown in the affected a,
13:39 the priest must examine the affected a. If the patch
13:49 If the affected a in the clothing, the animal hide,
13:51 If the affected a has spread, the material is clearly
13:55 If he sees that the affected a has not changed
13:56 But if the priest sees that the affected a has faded
14:13 then slaughter the lamb there in the sacred a at the
14:40 then be thrown into an a outside the town
14:56 in a swollen a of skin, in a skin rash, or in a shiny
16: 3 "When Aaron enters the sanctuary a, he must
27:16 fifty pieces of silver for an a that produces five
Nu 1:52 designated camping a with its own family banner.
2: 2 "Each tribe will be assigned its own a in the camp,
3:23 They were assigned the a to the west of the
3:29 They were assigned the a south of the Tabernacle
3:35 They were assigned the a north of the Tabernacle
3:38 The a in front of the Tabernacle in the east toward
11: 3 After that, the a was known as Taberah—
21:14 speaks of "the town of Waheb in the a of Suphah,
21:32 After Moses sent men to explore the Jazer a,
32: 4 the LORD has conquered this whole a for the
32:42 and he renamed that a Nobah after himself.
35: 5 This a will serve as the larger pastureland for the
36: 3 the total a of our tribal land will be reduced.
Dt 2:10 called the Emites had once lived in the a of Ar.
2:20 (That a, too, was once considered the land of the

2:23 who had lived in villages in the **a** of Gaza.)
2:36 town in the gorge, and the whole **a** as far as Gilead.
3:16 and Gad I gave the **a** extending from Gilead to the
4:48 So Israel conquered all the **a** from Aroer at the
23:12 "Mark off an **a** outside the camp for a latrine.
Jos 12: 2 This territory included half of the present **a** of
13: 4 In the north, this **a** has not yet been conquered:
13: 5 and all of the Lebanon mountain **a** to the east,
13:15 Moses had assigned the following **a** to the families
13:23 and villages in this **a** were given as an inheritance
13:24 Moses had assigned the following **a** to the families
13:28 and villages in this **a** were given as an inheritance
13:29 Moses had assigned the following **a** to the families
Jdg 11:33 the Ammonites from Aroer to an **a** near Minnith—
17: 8 arrived in that **a** of Ephraim, looking for a good
19: 1 living in a remote **a** of the hill country of Ephraim.
19:18 "We are on our way home to a remote **a** in the hill
1Sa 9: 4 the land of Shalishah, the Shaalim **a**, and the entire
23:23 And if he is in the **a** at all, I'll track him down,
1Ki 8:64 That same day the king dedicated the central **a** of
9:13 So Hiram called that **a** Cabul—"worthless"—
2Ki 10:33 He conquered the **a** from the town of Aroer by the
24: 7 for the king of Babylon occupied the entire **a**
1Ch 5: 8 These Reubenites lived in the **a** that stretches from
6:62 Naphtali, and from the Bashan **a** of Manasseh,
9:16 son of Elkanah, who lived in the **a** of Netophah.
11: 8 the city from the Millo to the surrounding **a**,
26:30 of the LORD and the service of the king in that **a**.
2Ch 7: 7 then dedicated the central **a** of the courtyard in
14:14 were at Gerar, they attacked all the towns in that **a**,
26: 6 Then he built new towns in the Ashdod **a** and in
32:33 he was buried in the upper **a** of the royal cemetery,
Ne 12:29 from Beth-gilgal and the **a** of Geba and Azmaveth,
Job 1: 3 He was, in fact, the richest person in that entire **a**.
Jer 28:11 of Babylon." At that, Jeremiah left the Temple **a**.
31:40 And the entire **a**—including the graveyard and ash
Eze 40: 5 see a wall completely surrounding the Temple **a**.
41: 9 This left an open **a** between these side rooms
41:10 This open **a** measured 35 feet in width, and it went
42:15 the east gateway to measure the entire Temple **a**.
42:20 So the **a** was 875 feet on each side with a wall all
43:21 burn it at the appointed place outside the Temple **a**.
45: 1 6-2/3 miles wide. The entire **a** will be holy ground.
45: 3 Within the larger sacred **a**, measure out a portion
45: 4 This **a** will be a holy land, set aside for the priests
45: 5 will be a living **a** for the Levites who work at the
45: 6 "Adjacent to the larger sacred **a** will be a section
48: 9 "The **a** set aside for the LORD's Temple will be
48:11 This **a** is set aside for the ordained priests,
48:15 south of the sacred Temple **a**, will be allotted for
48:18 Outside the city there will be a farming **a** that
48:18 miles to the west along the border of the sacred **a**.
48:20 This entire **a**—including the sacred lands
Zep 1:11 all you who live in the market **a**, for all who buy
2: 6 The coastal **a** will become a pasture, a place of
Mt 3:12 Then he will clean up the threshing **a**,
8:28 so dangerous that no one could go through that **a**.
9:35 traveled through all the cities and villages of that **a**,
12:15 He left that **a**, and many people followed him.
14:13 he went off by himself in a boat to a remote **a** to be
14:35 quickly throughout the whole surrounding **a**,
19: 1 of Judea and into the **a** east of the Jordan River.
Mk 1:28 spread quickly through that entire **a** of Galilee.
6:55 and they ran throughout the whole **a** and began
10: 1 of Judea and into the **a** east of the Jordan River.
11:27 As Jesus was walking through the Temple **a**,
Lk 3:17 Then he will clean up the threshing **a**,
6:17 level **a**, surrounded by many of his followers
Jn 2:14 In the Temple **a** he saw merchants selling cattle,
Ac 5:12 Temple in the **a** known as Solomon's Colonnade.
14: 6 cities of Lystra and Derbe and the surrounding **a**,
16: 3 In deference to the Jews of the **a**, he arranged for
16: 6 and Silas traveled through the **a** of Phrygia

AREAS (17) [AREA]

Lev 13:17 the affected **a** have indeed turned completely
14:40 the priest must order that the stones from those **a**
14:44 If he sees that the affected **a** have spread, the walls
14:48 and finds that the affected **a** have not reappeared
Nu 4:24 "The duties of the Gershonites will be in the **a** of
Jos 19:15 The towns in these **a** included Kattath, Nahalal,
1Ch 6:56 and outlying **a** were given to Caleb son of
2Ch 27: 4 constructed fortresses and towers in the wooded **a**.
Ne 4:13 the lowest parts of the wall in the exposed **a**.
Isa 7:19 They will settle in the fertile **a** and also in the
Eze 45: 7 the eastern and western boundaries of the tribal **a**.
48:21 "The **a** that remain, to the east and to the west of
48:21 Each of these **a** will be 8-1/3 miles wide,
48:22 except for the **a** set aside for the sacred lands
Da 11:24 Without warning he will enter the richest **a** of the
Zec 7: 7 and the foothills of Judah were populated **a**?' "
Ac 2:10 Egypt, and the **a** of Libya toward Cyrene,

ARELI (2) [ARELITE]

Ge 46:16 Haggi, Shuni, Ezbon, Eri, Arodi, and **A**.
Nu 26:17 The Arelite clan, named after its ancestor **A**.

ARELITE (1) [ARELI]

Nu 26:17 The **A** clan, named after its ancestor Areli.

AREN'T (51) [BE, NOT]

Ge 34:14 possibly allow this, because you **a** circumcised.
Nu 23:25 "If you **a** going to curse them, at least don't bless
Jdg 8: 2 **A** the last grapes of Ephraim's harvest better than
11: 7 "**A** you the ones who hated me and drove me from
1Sa 1: 8 "Why **a** you eating? Why be so sad just
26:15 "Well, Abner, you're a great man, **a** you?"
2Sa 13:33 No, your sons **a** all dead! It was only Amnon."
16:17 Absalom asked him. "Why **a** you with him?"
2Ki 4: 6 "There **a** any more!" he told her. And
5:12 **A** the Abana River and Pharpar River of Damascus
7: 9 wonderful news, and we **a** sharing it with anyone!
10: 9 "You **a** to blame," he told them. "I am the one
Ne 2: 2 "Why are you so sad? You **a** sick, are you?
Job 19:22 God does? Why **a** you satisfied with my anguish?
Ps 73: 5 They **a** troubled like other people / or plagued with
Pr 30:25 Ants—they **a** strong, / but they store up food for
30:26 Rock badgers—they **a** powerful, / but they make
Isa 7:13 of David! You **a** satisfied to exhaust my patience.
58: 3 before you!' they say. 'Why **a** you impressed?'
Jer 37: 9 that the Babylonians are gone for good. They **a**!
Da 3:25 around in the fire. They **a** even hurt by the flames!
Hos 5: 7 honor of the LORD, bearing children that **a** his.
Mt 12: 7 But you would not have condemned those who **a**
15:15 "Explain what you meant when you said people **a**
22: 8 and the guests I invited **a** worthy of the honor.
26:62 "Well, **a** you going to answer these charges?
Mk 14:60 "Well, **a** you going to answer these charges?
15: 4 Pilate asked him, "**A** you going to say something?
Jn 1:25 "If you **a** the Messiah or Elijah or the Prophet,
4:18 and you **a** even married to the man you're living
8:47 Since you don't, it proves you **a** God's children."
8:57 The people said, "You **a** even fifty years old.
10:12 He will leave the sheep because they **a** his and he
18:17 asked Peter, "**A** you one of Jesus' disciples?"
18:25 asked him again, "**A** you one of his disciples?"
Ac 19:26 many people that handmade gods **a** gods at all.
21:38 "**A** you the Egyptian who led a rebellion some
Ro 3:20 the clearer it becomes that we **a** obeying it.
1Co 2:14 But people who **a** Christians can't understand these
3: 2 handle anything stronger. And you still **a** ready,
3: 4 **a** you acting like those who are not Christians?
3: 7 ones who do the planting or watering **a** important,
5: 2 Why **a** you mourning in sorrow and shame?
7: 8 I say to those who **a** married and to widows—
10:16 **a** we sharing in the benefits of the blood of Christ?
10:16 **a** we sharing in the benefits of the body of Christ?
1Th 5: 4 But you **a** in the dark about these things,
Jas 2: 5 **A** they the ones who will inherit the kingdom God
2: 7 **A** they the ones who slander Jesus Christ,
Jude 1:23 but be careful that you **a** contaminated by their
Rev 2: 9 but they really **a** because theirs is a synagogue of

ARETAS (1)

2Co 11:32 the governor under King **A** kept guards at the city

ARGOB (5)

Dt 3: 4 the entire **A** region in his kingdom of Bashan.
3:13 (The **A** region of Bashan used to be known as the
3:14 acquired the whole **A** region in Bashan all the way
1Ki 4:13 in Gilead, and in the **A** region of Bashan,
2Ki 15:25 assassinated the king, along with **A** and Arieh,

ARGUE (24) [ARGUED, ARGUING, ARGUMENT, ARGUMENTS]

Jdg 6:31 are you defending Baal? Will you **a** his case?
Job 9:32 like me, so I cannot **a** with him or take him to trial.
13: 3 I want to **a** my case with God himself.
13: 8 in his favor? Will you **a** God's case for him?
13:15 I cannot wait. I am going to **a** my case with him.
13:19 Who can **a** with me over this? If you could prove
23: 6 Would he merely **a** with me in his greatness?
40: 2 "Do you still want to **a** with the Almighty?
Ps 119:154 **A** my case; take my side! / Protect my life as you
Isa 1:18 "Come now, let us **a** this out," says the LORD.
45: 9 "Destruction is certain for those who **a** with their
45: 9 Does a clay pot ever **a** with its maker?
45:21 Consult together, **a** your case, and state your
Hab 1: 3 I am surrounded by people who love to **a** and fight.
Mk 8:11 that Jesus had arrived, they came to **a** with him.
Lk 22:24 And they began to **a** among themselves as to who
Ac 11:17 in the Lord Jesus Christ, who was I to **a**?"
23: 9 Pharisees jumped up to **a** that Paul was all right.
24:12 I didn't **a** with anyone in the Temple, nor did I
Ro 3: 7 "But," some might still **a**, "how can God judge
10: 1 and don't **a** with them about what they think is
1Co 11:16 But if anyone wants to **a** about this, all I can say is
Tit 2: 8 Then those who want to **a** will be ashamed
Jas 2:18 Now someone may **a**, "Some people have faith;

ARGUED (12) [ARGUE]

Ge 26:20 they said, and they **a** over it with Isaac's herdsmen.
26:20 because they had **a** about it with him.
Ex 6:30 This is the same Moses who had **a** with the
17: 7 because the people of Israel **a** with Moses
Nu 20:13 because it was where the people of Israel **a** with
Jdg 8: 1 And they **a** heatedly with Gideon.
1Ki 3:22 And so they **a** back and forth before the king.
Lk 23:20 Pilate **a** with them, because he wanted to release
Ac 13:45 they slandered Paul and **a** against whatever he said.
15: 2 disagreeing with them, **a** forcefully and at length.
22:19 " 'But Lord,' I **a**, 'they certainly know that I
28:25 But after they had **a** back and forth among

ARGUING (18) [ARGUE]

Ge 13: 8 "This **a** between our herdsmen has got to stop,"
Ex 17: 2 Moses replied. "Why are you **a** with me?
17: 7 of testing"—and Meribah—"the place of **a**"—
Job 32:14 If Job had been **a** with me, I would not answer
Pr 26: 4 When **a** with fools, don't answer their foolish
26: 5 When **a** with fools, be sure to answer their foolish
Ecc 6:10 So there's no use **a** with God about your destiny.
Mk 9:14 as some teachers of religious law were **a** with
9:16 "What is all this **a** about?" he asked.
9:34 because they had been **a** about which of them was
Jn 6:52 Then the people began **a** with each other about
Ac 19: 8 **a** persuasively about the Kingdom of God.
Ro 10:21 but they kept disobeying me and **a** with me."
1Co 1:10 the Lord Jesus Christ to stop **a** among yourselves.
Php 2:14 you do, stay away from complaining and **a**,
1Ti 1: 6 and spend their time **a** and talking foolishness.
4: 7 Do not waste time **a** over godless ideas and old
Jude 1: 9 (This took place when Michael was **a** with Satan

ARGUMENT (12) [ARGUE]

Ge 13: 7 So an **a** broke out between the herdsmen of Abram
26:20 So Isaac named the well "**A**," because they had
Ex 18:16 When an **a** arises, I am the one who settles the
2Sa 19: 9 Israel there was much discussion and **a** going on.
19:43 The **a** continued back and forth, and the men of
20:18 used to be a saying, 'If you want to settle an **a**,
1Ki 3:16 two prostitutes came to the king to have an **a**
Pr 26:17 ears is as foolish as interfering in someone else's **a**.
Lk 9:46 Then there was an **a** among them as to which of
Jn 3:25 At that time a certain Jew began an **a** with John's
2Co 10: 5 With these weapons we break down every proud **a**
2Pe 3: 4 This will be their **a**: "Jesus promised to come

ARGUMENTS (21) [ARGUE]

Job 13: 6 Listen to my charge; pay attention to my **a**.
13: 7 defending God by means of lies and dishonest **a**?
23: 4 I would lay out my case and present my **a**.
32: 3 God by their inability to answer Job's **a**.
32:11 all this time, listening very carefully to your **a**,
32:12 not one of you has refuted Job or answered his **a**.
37:19 to God. We are too ignorant to make our own **a**.
Pr 13:10 Pride leads to **a**; those who take advice are wise.
18:18 Casting lots can end **a** and settle disputes between
18:19 **A** separate friends like a gate locked with iron
26: 4 arguing with fools, don't answer their foolish **a**,
26: 5 with fools, be sure to answer their foolish **a**,
Isa 41: 1 Bring your strongest **a**. Come now and speak.
Ac 18:28 He refuted all the Jews with powerful **a** in public
1Co 1:11 of Chloe's household have told me about your **a**,
6: 5 the church who is wise enough to decide these **a**?
Col 2: 4 one will be able to deceive you with persuasive **a**.
1Ti 1: 4 For these things only cause **a**; they don't help
6: 4 This stirs up **a** ending in jealousy, fighting, slander,
2Ti 2:14 Such **a** are useless, and they can ruin those who
2:23 in foolish, ignorant **a** that only start fights.

ARID (1)

Joel 3:18 watering the **a** valley of acacias.

ARIDAI (1)

Est 9: 9 Parmashta, Arisai, **A**, and Vaizatha—

ARIDATHA (1)

Est 9: 8 Poratha, Adalia, **A**,

ARIEH (1)

2Ki 15:25 assassinated the king, along with Argob and **A**,

ARIEL (3) [JERUSALEM]

Ezr 8:16 **A**, Shemaiah, Elnathan, Jarib, Elnathan, Nathan,
Isa 29: 1 "Destruction is certain for **A**, the City of David.
29: 2 For Jerusalem will become as her name **A** means—

ARIMATHEA (4)

Mt 27:57 a rich man from **A** who was one of Jesus'
Mk 15:43 Joseph from **A** (who was waiting for the Kingdom
Lk 23:51 He was from the town of **A** in Judea, and he had
Jn 19:38 Afterward Joseph of **A**, who had been a secret

ARIOCH (6)

Ge 14: 1 King **A** of Ellasar, King Kedorlaomer of Elam,
Da 2:14 When **A**, the commander of the king's guard,
2:15 He asked **A**, "Why has the king issued such a
2:15 So **A** told him all that had happened.
2:24 Then Daniel went in to see **A**, who had been
2:25 Then **A** quickly took Daniel to the king and said,

ARISAI (1)

Est 9: 9 Parmashta, **A**, Aridai, and Vaizatha—

ARISE (24) [RISE]

Nu 10:35 the Ark set out, Moses would cry, "**A**, O LORD,
Dt 32:38 Let those gods **a** and help you! / Let them provide
Jdg 5:12 Wake up, wake up, and sing a song! / **A**, Barak!
2Ch 6:41 **a** and enter this resting place of yours,
Est 4:14 deliverance for the Jews will **a** from some other
Ps 3: 7 **A**, O LORD! / Rescue me, my God! / Slap all my
7: 6 **A**, O LORD, in anger! / Stand up against the fury
9:19 **A**, O LORD! / Do not let mere mortals defy you!
10:12 **A**, O LORD! / Punish the wicked, O God!
17:13 **A**, O LORD! / Stand against them and bring them
68: 1 **A**, O God, and scatter your enemies. / Let those
73:20 is gone when they awake. / When you **a**, O Lord,
74:22 **A**, O God, and defend your cause.
94: 2 **A**, O judge of the earth. / Sentence the proud to the
102:13 You will **a** and have mercy on Jerusalem—

132: 8 A, O LORD, and enter your sanctuary,
SS 2:13 A, my beloved, my fair one, and come away.' "
Isa 47:11 A catastrophe will a so fast that you won't know
60: 1 "A, Jerusalem! Let your light shine for all the
Da 7:17 represent four kingdoms that will a from the earth.
7:24 Then another king will a, different from the other
9:26 and a ruler will a whose armies will destroy the
12: 1 who stands guard over your nation, will a.
Hos 13:15 a blast from the LORD—will a in the desert.

ARISES (2) [RISE]

Ex 18:16 When an argument a, I am the one who settles the
Dt 17: 8 "Suppose a case a in a local court that is too hard

ARISING (1) [RISE]

SS 6:10 'Who is this,' they ask, 'a like the dawn, as fair as

ARISTARCHUS (5)

Ac 19:29 to the amphitheater, dragging along Gaius and A,
20: 4 A and Secundus, from Thessalonica; Gaius,
27: 2 And A, a Macedonian from Thessalonica, was also
Col 4:10 A, who is in prison with me, sends you his
Phm 1:24 So do Mark, A, Demas, and Luke, my co-workers.

ARISTOBULUS (1)

Ro 16:10 best regards to the members of the household of A.

ARK (196) [ARK'S]

ARK OF THE/HIS COVENANT (61) Ex 16:34; 25:22; 26:33,34; 30:6,26,36; 31:7; 39:35; 40:3,5,21; Lev 16:13; Nu 4:5; 7:89; 10:33; 14:44; 17:4,10; Dt 10:2,5,8; 31:9,25,26; Jos 3:3,6,8,11,14,17; 4:7,9,16,18; 6:6,8; 8:33; Jdg 20:27; 1Sa 4:3, 4,5; 2Sa 15:24; 1Ki 3:15; 6:19; 8:1,6; 1Ch 15:25,26,28,29; 16:37; 17:1; 22:19; 28:2,18; 2Ch 5:2,7; Jer 3:16; Heb 9:4; Rev 11:19

ARK OF...GOD (41) Jdg 20:27; 1Sa 3:3; 4:4,11,13,17,19, 21,22; 5:1,2,7,8,8,10,10,11; 6:3; 2Sa 6:2,3,4,6,7,12; 7:2; 15:24,25,29; 1Ch 13:3,5,6,7,12,14; 15:1,2,15,24; 16:1; 2Ch 1:4; Rev 11:19

ARK OF THE LORD* (34) Jos 3:13; 4:5,11; 6:7,11,12, 13,13; 7:6; 1Sa 4:6; 5:3,4; 6:1,2,8,11,15,18,19,21; 7:1; 2Sa 6:9,10,11,15,16,17; 1Ki 8:4; 1Ch 15:2,3,12,14; 16:4; 2Ch 8:11

Ex 16:34 He eventually placed it for safekeeping in the A of
25:10 "Make an A of acacia wood—a sacred chest 3-3/4
25:14 Fit the poles into the rings at the sides of the A to
25:16 When the A is finished, place inside it the stone
25:21 Place inside the A the stone tablets inscribed with
25:21 Then put the atonement cover on top of the A.
25:22 cherubim that hover over the A of the Covenant.
26:33 is in place, put the A of the Covenant behind it.
26:34 on top of the A of the Covenant inside the Most
30: 6 of atonement—that rests on the A of the Covenant.
30:26 oil to anoint the Tabernacle, the A of the Covenant,
30:36 and put some of it in front of the A of the
31: 7 the A of the Covenant; the Ark's cover—
35:12 the A and its poles; the Ark's cover—the place of
35:12 the inner curtain to enclose the A in the Most Holy
37: 1 Next Bezalel made the A out of acacia wood.
37: 5 He put the poles into the rings at the sides of the A
39:35 the A of the Covenant and its carrying poles;
40: 3 Place the A of the Covenant inside, and install the inner curtain to enclose the A within
40: 5 the inner curtain, opposite the A of the Covenant.
40:20 He placed inside the A the stone tablets inscribed
40:21 Then he brought the A of the Covenant into the
Lev 16:13 of atonement—that rests on the A of the Covenant.
16:14 and then seven times against the front of the A.
16:15 the atonement cover and against the front of the A,
Nu 3:31 four clans were responsible for the care of the A,
4: 5 and cover the A of the Covenant with it.
4: 6 they must put the carrying poles of the A in place.
7:89 of atonement—that rests on the A of the Covenant.
10:33 with the A of the LORD's covenant moving
10:35 And whenever the A set out, Moses would cry,
10:36 And when the A was set down, he would say,
14:44 despite the fact that neither Moses nor the A of the
17: 4 Put these staffs in the Tabernacle in front of the A
17:10 "Place Aaron's staff permanently before the A of
Dt 10: 2 tablets in the sacred chest—the A of the Covenant.'
10: 5 and placed the tablets in the A of the Covenant,
10: 5 And the tablets are still there in the A.
10: 8 of Levi to carry the A of the LORD's covenant,
31: 9 who carried the A of the LORD's covenant,
31:25 who carried the A of the LORD's covenant:
31:26 and place it beside the A of the Covenant of the
Jos 3: 3 "When you see the Levitical priests carrying the A
3: 4 keeping a clear distance between you and the A.
3: 6 "Lift up the A of the Covenant and lead the people
3: 8 the priests who are carrying the A of the Covenant:
3:11 The A of the Covenant, which belongs to the Lord
3:13 The priests will be carrying the A of the LORD,
3:14 the priests who were carrying the A of the
3:15 the A touched the water at the river's edge,
3:17 the priests who were carrying the A of the
4: 5 in front of the A of the LORD your God.
4: 7 the A of the LORD's covenant went across.'
4: 9 at the place where the priests who carried the A of
4:10 The priests who were carrying the A stood in the
4:11 the priests crossed over with the A of the LORD.
4:16 "Command the priests carrying the A of the
4:18 And as soon as the priests carrying the A of the
6: 4 Seven priests will walk ahead of the A,
6: 6 and said, "Take up the A of the Covenant,
6: 7 will lead the way in front of the A of the LORD."
6: 8 And the priests carrying the A of the LORD's
6: 9 both in front of the priests and behind the A,
6:11 So the A of the LORD was carried around the
6:12 and the priests again carried the A of the LORD.
6:13 horns marched in front of the A of the LORD,
6:13 with the horns and behind the A of the LORD.
7: 6 and bowed down facing the A of the LORD until
8:33 priests carrying the A of the LORD's covenant.
Jdg 20:27 (In those days the A of the Covenant of God was in
1Sa 3: 3 was sleeping in the Tabernacle near the A of God.
4: 3 "Let's bring the A of the Covenant of the LORD
4: 4 So they sent men to Shiloh to bring back the A of
4: 4 helped carry the A of God to where the battle was
4: 5 When the Israelites saw the A of the Covenant of
4: 6 it was because the A of the LORD had arrived,
4:11 The A of God was captured, and Hophni
4:13 his heart trembled for the safety of the A of God
4:17 too. And the A of God has been captured."
4:18 messenger mentioned what had happened to the A,
4:19 When she heard that the A of God had been
4:21 because the A of God had been captured and
4:22 from Israel, for the A of God has been captured."
5: 1 After the Philistines captured the A of God,
5: 2 They carried the A of God into the temple of
5: 3 face to the ground in front of the A of the LORD!
5: 4 the idol had fallen face down before the A of the
5: 7 "We can't keep the A of the God of Israel here
5: 8 "What should we do with the A of the God of
5: 8 So they moved the A of the God of Israel to Gath.
5: 9 But when the A arrived at Gath, the LORD began
5:10 So they sent the A of God to the city of Ekron,
5:10 "They are bringing the A of the God of Israel here
5:11 "Please send the A of the God of Israel back to its
6: 1 The A of the LORD remained in Philistine
6: 2 "What should we do about the A of the LORD?
6: 3 "Send the A of the God of Israel back, along with
6: 8 Put the A of the LORD on the cart, and beside it
6:11 Then the A of the LORD and the chest containing
6:13 and when they saw the A, they were overjoyed!
6:15 Several men of the tribe of Levi lifted the A of the
6:18 where they set the A of the LORD,
6:19 because they looked into the A of the LORD.
6:20 cried out. "Where can we send the A from here?"
6:21 "The Philistines have returned the A of the
7: 1 So the men of Kiriath-jearim came to get the A of
7: 2 The A remained in Kiriath-jearim for a long time
2Sa 6: 2 to Baalah of Judah to bring home the A of God,
6: 3 They placed the A of God on a new cart
6: 4 with the A of God on it, with Ahio walking in
6: 6 and Uzzah put out his hand to steady the A of God.
6: 7 and God struck him dead beside the A of God.
6: 9 "How can I ever bring the A of the LORD back
6:10 So David decided not to move the A of the
6:11 The A of the LORD remained there with the
6:12 and everything he has because of the A of God."
6:12 and brought the A to the City of David with a great
6:15 and all Israel brought up the A of the LORD with
6:16 But as the A of the LORD entered the City of
6:17 The A of the LORD was placed inside the special
7: 2 cedar palace, but the A of God is out in a tent!"
11:11 "The A and the armies of Israel and Judah are
15:24 and the Levites took the A of the Covenant of God
15:25 David instructed Zadok to take the A of God back
15:25 "he will bring me back to see the A
15:29 and Abiathar took the A of God back to the city
1Ki 2:26 because you carried the A of the Sovereign
3:15 and stood before the A of the Lord's covenant,
6:19 where the A of the LORD's covenant would be
8: 1 They were to bring the A of the LORD's
8: 3 of Israel arrived, the priests picked up the A.
8: 4 the priests and Levites took the A of the LORD,
8: 5 and oxen before the A in such numbers that no one
8: 6 Then the priests carried the A of the LORD's
8: 7 The cherubim spread their wings over the A,
8: 7 forming a canopy over the A and its carrying
8: 9 Nothing was in the A except the two stone tablets
8:21 And I have prepared a place there for the A,
1Ch 6:31 at the house of the LORD after he put the A there.
13: 3 It is time to bring back the A of our God, for we
13: 5 to join in bringing the A of God from
13: 6 to bring back the A of God, which bears the name
13: 7 They transported the A of God from the house of
13: 9 and Uzzah put out his hand to steady the A.
13:10 him dead because he had laid his hand on the A.
13:12 "How can I ever bring the A of God back into my
13:13 So David decided not to move the A into the City
13:14 The A of God remained there with the family of
15: 1 He also prepared a place for the A of God and set
15: 2 "When we transport the A of God this time,
15: 2 The LORD has chosen them to carry the A of the
15: 3 A of the LORD to the place he had prepared for
15:12 so you can bring the A of the LORD, the God of
15:13 Because you Levites did not carry the A the first
15:14 themselves in order to bring the A of the LORD,
15:15 Then the Levites carried the A of God on their
15:23 Berekiah and Elkanah were chosen to guard the A.
15:24 trumpets as they marched in front of the A of God.
15:24 and Jehiah were chosen to guard the A.
15:25 A of the LORD's covenant up to Jerusalem with a
15:26 as they carried the A of the LORD's covenant,
15:27 as were the Levites who carried the A, the singers,
15:28 So all Israel brought up the A of the LORD's
15:29 But as the A of the LORD's covenant entered the
16: 1 So they brought the A of God into the special tent
16: 4 the A of the LORD by asking for his blessings
16: 6 played the trumpets regularly before the A of
16:37 regularly before the A of the LORD's covenant,
17: 1 but the A of the LORD's covenant is out in a
22:19 so that you can bring the A of the LORD's
28: 2 It was my desire to build a temple where the A of
28:18 whose wings were stretched out over the A of the
2Ch 1: 4 David had already moved the A of God from
5: 2 They were to bring the A of the LORD's
5: 4 leaders of Israel arrived, the Levites moved the A,
5: 6 and oxen before the A in such numbers that no one
5: 7 Then the priests carried the A of the LORD's
5: 8 The cherubim spread their wings out over the A,
5: 8 forming a canopy over the A and its carrying
5:10 Nothing was in the A except the two stone tablets
6:11 There I have placed the A, and in the A is the covenant that the LORD made
6:41 where your magnificent A has been placed.
8:11 for the A of the LORD has been there, and it is
35: 3 "Since the A is now in Solomon's Temple and you
Ps 78:61 He allowed the A of his might to be captured;
132: 6 We heard that the A was in Ephrathah; / then we
132: 8 along with the A, the symbol of your power.
Jer 3:16 you possessed the A of the LORD's covenant.
3:16 and there will be no need to rebuild the A.
Heb 9: 4 and a wooden chest called the A of the Covenant,
9: 4 Inside the A were a gold jar containing some
9: 5 The glorious cherubim were above the A.
11: 7 It was by faith that Noah built an a to save his
Rev 11:19 and the A of his Covenant could be seen inside the

ARK'S (14) [ARK]

Ex 25:17 "Then make the A cover—the place of
26:34 "Then put the A cover—the place of atonement—
30: 6 outside the inner curtain, opposite the A cover—
31: 7 the A cover—the place of atonement;
35:12 the Ark and its poles; the A cover—the place of
37: 6 Then, from pure gold, he made the A cover—
39:35 the Covenant and its carrying poles; the A cover—
40:20 and then he attached the A carrying poles.
40:20 He also set the A cover—the place of atonement—
Lev 16: 2 For the A cover—the place of atonement—is there,
16:13 so that a cloud of incense will rise over the A
Nu 7:89 between the two cherubim above the A cover—
1Ch 28:11 and the inner sanctuary where the A cover—
Heb 9: 5 Their wings were stretched out over the A cover,

ARKITE (4) [ARKITES]

2Sa 15:32 David found Hushai the A waiting for him.
16:16 When David's friend Hushai the A arrived,
17: 5 then Absalom said, "Bring in Hushai the A.
1Ch 27:33 royal adviser. Hushai the A was the king's friend.

ARKITES (3) [ARKITE]

Ge 10:17 Hivites, A, Sinites,
Jos 16: 2 it ran over to Ataroth in the territory of the A.
1Ch 1:15 Hivites, A, Sinites,

ARM (28) [ARMBANDS, ARMED, ARMFUL, ARMIES, ARMOR, ARMORY, ARMPIT, ARMPITS, ARMRESTS, ARMS, ARMY]

Nu 32:17 Then we will a ourselves and lead our fellow
32:20 and a yourselves for the LORD's battles,
Dt 33:20 poised there like a lion / to tear off an a or a head.
2Ki 5:18 god Rimmon to worship there and leans on my a,
Job 31:21 If my a has abused an orphan because I thought I
31:22 out of place! Let my a be torn from its socket!
38:15 and it stops the a that is raised in violence.
Ps 60: 5 Use your strong right a to save us, / and rescue
89:10 You scattered your enemies with your mighty a.
89:13 Powerful is your a! / Strong is your hand!
108: 6 Use your strong right a to save me, / and rescue
118:15 The strong right a of the LORD has done glorious
118:16 The strong right a of the LORD is raised in
118:16 The strong right a of the LORD has done glorious
136:12 He acted with a strong hand and powerful a.
SS 8: 6 like a seal over your heart, or like a seal on your a.
Isa 13: 7 Every a is paralyzed with fear. Even the strongest
30:30 he will bring down his mighty a on his enemies.
Eze 4: 7 Lie there with your a bared and prophesy her
17: 9 it won't take a strong a or a large army to do it.
30:21 "Son of man, I have broken the a of Pharaoh,
30:21 His a has not been put in a cast so that it may heal.
30:22 his arms—the good a along with the broken one—
Zec 11:17 The sword will cut his a and pierce his right eye!
11:17 His a will become useless, and his right eye
Lk 1:51 His mighty a does tremendous things! / How he
Ac 23:19 The commander took him by the a, led him aside,
1Pe 4: 1 you must a yourselves with the same attitude he

ARMAGEDDON (1)

Rev 16:16 and their armies to a place called *A* in Hebrew.

ARMBANDS (1) [ARM]

Nu 31:50 a, bracelets, rings, earrings, and necklaces.

ARMED (48) [ARM]

Ge 12:20 then sent them out of the country under a escort—
Nu 31: 5 a total of twelve thousand men a for battle.
32:32 We will cross the Jordan into Canaan fully a to
Dt 3:18 a and ready to protect your Israelite relatives.
Jos 1:14 side of the Jordan River, but your warriors, fully a,
4:12 The a warriors from the tribes of Reuben, Gad,
6: 7 and the a men will lead the way in front of the Ark
6: 9 A guards marched both in front of the priests

6:13 A guards marched both in front of the priests with
Jdg 20:2 tribes of Israel—400,000 warriors a with swords—
20:15 Twenty-six thousand of their warriors a with
20:17 Israel had 400,000 warriors a with swords,
1Sa 17:40 Then, a only with his shepherd's staff and sling,
2Sa 21:16 seven pounds, and he was a with a new sword.
22:40 You have a me with strength for the battle;
23:7 One must be a to chop them down; / they will be
23:21 Another time, a only with a club, he killed a great Egyptian warrior who was a with
1Ch 5:18 They were all skilled in combat and a with shields,
11:23 Another time, a with only a club, he killed an
12:23 These are the numbers of a warriors who joined
12:24 there were 6,800 warriors a with shields
12:33 They were fully a and prepared for battle
12:34 and 37,000 warriors a with shields and spears.
12:37 there were 120,000 troops a with every kind of
2Ch 14:8 the tribe of Judah, a with large shields and spears.
14:8 tribe of Benjamin, a with small shields and bows.
17:18 was Jehozabad, who commanded 180,000 a men.
Ne 4:13 So I placed a guards behind the lowest parts of the
4:13 by families, a with swords, spears, and bows.
Ps 18:39 You have a me with strength for the battle;
65:6 your power / and a yourself with mighty strength.
78:9 The warriors of Ephraim, though fully a,
93:1 LORD is robed in majesty and a with strength.
Pr 6:11 a bandit; scarcity will attack you like an a robber.
24:34 a bandit; scarcity will attack you like an a robber.
Jer 6:23 They are fully a for slaughter. They are cruel
50:42 They are fully a for slaughter. They are cruel
Eze 23:24 every side, surrounding you with men a for battle.
38:4 and make you a vast and mighty horde, all fully a.
Mt 26:47 arrived with a mob that was a with swords
26:55 that you have come a with swords and clubs to
Mk 14:43 arrived with a mob that was a with swords
14:48 that you come a with swords and clubs to arrest
Lk 11:21 For when Satan, who is completely a, guards his
22:52 "that you have come a with swords and clubs to
Ac 26:12 a with the authority and commission of the leading
Rev 9:7 The locusts looked like horses a for battle.

ARMENIA [KJV] See ARARAT

ARMFUL (1) [ARM]

Ac 28:3 As Paul gathered an a of sticks and was laying

ARMIES (129) [ARM]

Ge 14:3 and mobilized their a in Siddim Valley (that is,
Ex 14:4 great glory at the expense of Pharaoh and his a.
14:17 great glory at the expense of Pharaoh and his a,
15:4 Pharaoh's chariots and a, / he has thrown into the
Lev 26:25 I will send a against you to carry out these
Dt 11:4 They didn't see what the LORD did to the a of
28:51 Its a will devour your livestock and crops, and you
Jos 9:2 These kings quickly combined their a to fight
10:5 So these five Amorite kings combined their a for a
10:6 country have come out against us with their a."
10:9 from Gilgal and took the Amorite a by surprise.
10:20 and wiped out the five a except for a tiny remnant
11:4 Their combined a, along with a vast array of
12:7 and the Israelite a defeated on the west side of the
Jdg 6:33 Soon afterward the a of Midian, Amalek,
7:1 The a of Midian were camped north of them in the
7:12 The a of Midian, Amalek, and the people of the
7:14 victory over all the a united with Midian!"
8:10 all that remained of the allied a of the east—
10:17 At that time the a of Ammon had gathered for war
1Sa 17:10 I defy the a of Israel! Send me a man who will
17:26 that he is allowed to defy the a of the living God?"
17:36 too, for he has defied the a of the living God!
17:45 the God of the a of Israel, whom you have defied.
28:1 About that time the Philistines mustered their a for
28:4 and Saul and the a of Israel camped at Gilboa.
2Sa 2:17 The two a then began to fight each other, and by
11:11 "The Ark and the a of Israel and Judah are living
1Ki 12:21 he mobilized the a of Judah and Benjamin—
15:20 King Asa's request and sent his a to attack Israel.
20:29 The two a camped opposite each other for seven
22:19 on his throne with all the a of heaven around him,
22:29 and King Jehoshaphat of Judah led their a against
2Ki 3:9 and all three a traveled along a roundabout route
3:21 when the people of Moab heard about the three a
3:23 "The three a have attacked and killed each other!
14:11 The two a drew up their battle lines at
16:7 and rescue me from the attacking a of Aram
19:24 rivers of Egypt / so that my a could go across!"
19:32 His a will not enter Jerusalem to shoot their
1Ch 5:18 There were 44,760 skilled warriors in the a of
11:6 Jebusites will become the commander of my a!"
11:6 so he became the commander of David's a.
2Ch 11:1 he mobilized the a of Judah and Benjamin—
14:8 Both a were composed of courageous fighting
14:10 so Asa deployed his a for battle in the valley north
16:4 King Asa's request and sent his a to attack Israel.
18:18 on his throne with all the a of heaven on his right
18:28 and King Jehoshaphat of Judah led their a against
20:1 After this, the a of the Moabites, Ammonites,
20:10 "And now see what the a of Ammon, Moab,
20:22 the LORD caused the a of Ammon, Moab,
20:23 The a of Moab and Ammon turned against their
25:21 The two a drew up their battle lines at
28:5 The a of Israel also defeated Ahaz and inflicted
28:8 The a of Israel captured 200,000 women
28:17 The a of Edom had again invaded Judah and taken
33:11 So the LORD sent the Assyrian a, and they took
Job 10:17 of anger upon me and bring fresh a against me.
Ps 20:7 Some nations boast of their a and weapons,
44:9 in dishonor. / You no longer lead our a to battle.
60:10 O God? / Will you no longer march with our a?
68:12 Enemy kings and their a flee, / while the women of
103:21 Yes, praise the LORD, you a of angels
108:11 O God? / Will you no longer march with our a?
137:7 on the day the a of Babylon captured Jerusalem.
148:2 all his angels! / Praise him, all the a of heaven!
Isa 8:7 the king of Assyria and all his mighty a.
10:28 Look, the mighty a of Assyria are coming!
13:3 the LORD, have assigned this task to these a,
13:4 Listen, as the a march! It is the noise and the shout
13:18 The attacking a will shoot down the young people
17:12 The a rush forward like waves thundering toward
34:2 His fury is against all their a. He will completely
37:25 rivers of Egypt / so that my a could go across!"
37:33 His a will not enter Jerusalem to shoot their
41:2 He puts entire a to the sword. He scatters them in
48:14 empire of Babylon, destroying the Babylonian a.'
54:16 And I have created the a that destroy.
Jer 1:15 I am calling the a of the kingdoms of the north to
4:29 At the noise of marching a, the people flee in terror
6:26 For suddenly, the destroying a will be upon you!
10:22 Hear the terrifying roar of great a as they roll down
12:12 Destroying a plunder the land. The sword of the
13:20 See the a marching down from the north! Where is
13:22 you have been raped and destroyed by invading a.
19:7 and Jerusalem and let invading a slaughter them.
21:2 he will force Nebuchadnezzar to withdraw his a."
25:9 I will gather together all the a of the north under
34:1 came with all the a from the kingdoms he ruled,
34:22 I will call the Babylonian a back again. They will
35:11 we were afraid of the Babylonian and Aramean a.
51:21 With you I will shatter a, destroying the horse
51:27 Bring out the a of Ararat, Minni, and Ashkenaz.
51:28 Bring against her the a of the kings of the Medes
51:28 and the a of all the countries they rule.
51:48 for out of the north will come destroying a against
51:56 Destroying a come against Babylon. Her mighty
Eze 14:17 and I told enemy a to come and destroy
19:8 Then the a of the nations attacked him,
30:11 He and his a—ruthless among the nations—
38:6 along with the a of Beth-togarmah from the distant
38:7 Keep all the a around you mobilized, and take
Da 1:1 came to Jerusalem and besieged it with his a.
8:10 to the heavens where it attacked the heavenly a,
8:11 He even challenged the Commander of heaven's a
8:13 will the Temple and heaven's a be trampled on?"
9:26 and a ruler will arise whose a will destroy the city
11:22 Before him great a will be swept away, including a
Hos 1:7 enemies without any help from weapons or a."
10:10 I will call out the a of the nations to punish you for
10:13 believing that great a could make your nation safe!
Joel 2:20 I will remove these a from the north and send them
3:2 "I will gather the a of the world into the valley of
3:17 and foreign a will never conquer her again.
Ob 1:1 everyone! Let's assemble our a and attack Edom!"
Mic 6:9 "The a of destruction are coming; the LORD is
Na 2:1 Nineveh, you are already surrounded by enemy a!
Zep 3:15 of judgment and will disperse the a of your enemy.
Zec 9:8 guard my Temple and protect it from invading a.
12:2 nations that send their a to besiege Jerusalem.
Lk 2:13 host of others—the a of heaven—praising God:
21:20 "And when you see Jerusalem surrounded by a,
Heb 11:34 became strong in battle and put whole a to flight.
Rev 16:12 so that the kings from the east could march their a
16:16 and their a to a place called *Armageddon* in
19:14 The a of heaven, dressed in pure white linen,
19:19 and their a in order to fight against the one sitting
20:9 But fire from heaven came down on the attacking a

ARMONI (1)

2Sa 21:8 But he gave them Saul's two sons A

ARMOR (40) [ARM]

Jdg 9:54 He said to his young a bearer, "Draw your sword
1Sa 14:1 Jonathan said to the young man who carried his a,
14:6 to see those pagans," Jonathan said to his a bearer.
14:12 right behind me," Jonathan said to his a bearer,
14:13 and his a bearer killed them right and left.
14:17 found that Jonathan and his a bearer were gone.
16:21 and David became one of Saul's a bearers.
17:7 An a bearer walked ahead of him carrying a huge
17:38 Then Saul gave David his own a—a bronze helmet
17:54 but he stored the Philistine's a in his own tent.)
31:4 Saul groaned to his a bearer, "Take your sword
31:4 But his a bearer was afraid and would not do it.
31:5 When his a bearer realized that Saul was dead,
31:6 So Saul, three of his sons, his a bearer, and his
31:9 So they cut off Saul's head and stripped off his a.
31:10 They placed his a in the temple of the Ashtoreths,
2Sa 18:15 Ten of Joab's young a bearers then surrounded
23:37 Naharai from Beeroth (Joab's a bearer);
1Ki 22:34 hit the king of Israel between the joints of his a.
1Ch 10:4 Saul groaned to his a bearer, "Take your sword
10:4 But his a bearer was afraid and would not do it.
10:5 When his a bearer realized that Saul was dead,
10:9 So they stripped off Saul's a and cut off his head.
10:10 They placed his a in the temple of their gods,
11:39 Naharai from Beeroth (Joab's a bearer);
2Ch 18:33 hit the king of Israel between the joints of his a.
Job 41:13 and who can penetrate its double layer of a?
Ps 35:2 Put on your a, and take up your shield.
91:4 His faithful promises are your a and protection.
Isa 59:17 He put on righteousness as his body a and placed
Jer 46:3 "Buckle on your a and advance into battle!
46:4 sharpen your spears, and prepare your a.
51:3 Don't let the archers put on their a or draw their
Ro 13:12 Clothe yourselves with the a of right living,
Eph 6:11 Put on all of God's a so that you will be able to
6:13 Use every piece of God's a to resist the enemy in
6:14 of truth and the body a of God's righteousness.
1Th 5:8 protected by the body a of faith and love,
Rev 9:9 They wore a made of iron, and their wings roared
9:17 The riders wore a that was fiery red and sky blue

ARMORY (5) [ARM]

2Ki 20:13 He also took them to see his a and showed them all
Ne 3:19 repaired another section of wall opposite the a by
Isa 22:8 stripped away. You run to the a for your weapons.
39:2 He also took them to see his a and showed them all
Jer 50:25 "The LORD has opened his a and brought out

ARMOURBEARER [KJV] See ARMOR BEARER

ARMOURY [KJV] See ARMORY

ARMPIT (1) [ARM]

Eze 29:7 you splintered and stabbed her in the a.

ARMPITS (1) [ARM]

Jer 38:12 "Put these rags under your a to protect you from

ARMRESTS (2) [ARM]

1Ki 10:19 On both sides of the seat were a, with the figure of
2Ch 9:18 On both sides of the seat were a, with the figure of

ARMS (50) [ARM]

Ge 48:14 But Jacob crossed his a as he reached out to lay his
49:24 remained strong, / and his a were strengthened
Ex 17:9 commanded Joshua, "Call the Israelites to a,
17:12 Moses' a finally became too tired to hold up the
Nu 11:12 that why you have told me to carry them in my a—
32:27 all who are able to bear a will cross over to fight
Dt 33:27 your refuge, / and his everlasting a are under you.
Jos 5:4 because all the men who were old enough to bear a
5:6 enough to bear a when they left Egypt had died.
Jdg 3:27 hill country of Ephraim, Ehud sounded a call to a.
6:34 He blew a ram's horn as a call to a, and the men of
15:14 and he snapped the ropes on his a as if they were
16:12 But Samson snapped the ropes from his a as if they
1Sa 13:3 so Saul sounded the call to a throughout Israel.
2Sa 12:3 his cup. He cuddled it in his a like a baby daughter.
1Ki 1:2 She will lie in your a and keep you warm."
3:20 She laid her dead child in my a and took mine to
2Ki 4:16 this time you will be holding a son in your a!"
Ps 10:15 Break the a of these wicked, evil people! / Go after
18:32 God a me with strength; / he has made my way
28:9 like a shepherd, / and carry them forever in your a.
68:19 For each day he carries us in his a. / *Interlude*
Pr 7:13 She threw her a around him and kissed him,
31:20 hand to the poor and opens her a to the needy.
SS 5:14 His a are like round bars of gold, set with
Isa 40:11 He will carry the lambs in his a, holding them
49:22 will carry your little sons back to you in their a;
65:2 "I opened my a to my own people all day long,
66:12 her breasts, carried in her a, and treated with love.
Jer 44:7 here from Judah, not even the babies in your a.
48:25 and her a have been broken," says the LORD.
La 2:12 they cry, and then collapse in their mothers' a.
Eze 13:20 I will tear them from your a, setting my people free
30:22 I will break both of his a—the good arm along
30:24 I will strengthen the a of Babylon's king and put
30:24 But I will break the a of Pharaoh, king of Egypt,
30:25 I will strengthen the a of the king of Babylon,
30:25 while the a of Pharaoh fall useless to his sides.
Da 2:32 its chest and a were of silver, its belly and thighs
10:6 His a and feet shone like polished bronze, and his
Joel 3:12 "Let the nations be called to a. Let them march to
Na 3:3 and glittering spears in the upraised a of the
Mt 23:5 On their a they wear extra wide prayer boxes with
Mk 9:36 Taking the child in his a, he said to them,
10:16 Then he took the children into his a and placed his
Lk 2:28 He took the child in his a and praised God, saying,
8:40 of the lake the crowds received Jesus with open a
14:2 because there was a man there whose a and legs
Ac 20:10 went down, bent over him, and took him into his a.
Ro 10:21 God said, / "All day long I opened my a to them,

ARMY (420) [ARM]

Ge 14:8 But now the a of the kings of Sodom, Gomorrah,
14:10 And as the a of the kings of Sodom and Gomorrah
14:14 He chased after Kedorlaomer's a until he caught
14:15 Kedorlaomer's a fled, but Abram chased them to
21:22 with Phicol, his a commander, to visit Abraham.
21:32 left with Phicol, the commander of his a.
26:26 Ahuzzath, and also Phicol, his a commander.
32:6 to meet Jacob—with an a of four hundred men!
36:35 He was the one who destroyed the Midianite a in
Ex 12:36 So, like a victorious a, they plundered the
13:18 and the Israelites left Egypt like a marching a.
14:9 All the forces in Pharaoh's a—all his horses,
14:10 As Pharaoh and his a approached, the people of
14:18 When I am finished with Pharaoh and his a,
14:24 the LORD looked down on the Egyptian a from
14:28 and charioteers—the entire a of Pharaoh.
17:9 the Israelites to arms, and fight the a of Amalek.
17:10 He led his men out to fight the a of Amalek.

17:13 and his troops were able to crush the **a** of Amalek.
Nu 20:18 out of my land or I will meet you with an **a**!"
20:20 With that he mobilized his **a** and marched out to
21:23 he mobilized his entire **a** and attacked Israel in the
21:34 I have given you victory over Og and his entire **a**,
31:9 Then the Israelite **a** captured the Midianite women
31:28 donkeys, sheep, and goats that belong to the **a**.
Dt 3:1 where King Og and his **a** attacked us at Edrei.
3:2 for I have given you victory over Og and his **a**,
20:1 and chariots and an **a** greater than your own,
20:5 "Then the officers of the **a** will address the troops
24:5 newly married man must not be drafted into the **a**
Jos 5:14 "I am commander of the LORD's **a**." At this,
5:15 The commander of the LORD's **a** replied,
6:3 Your entire **a** is to march around the city once a
8:1 Take the entire **a** and attack Ai, for I have given to
8:3 So Joshua and the **a** of Israel set out to attack Ai.
8:5 When our main **a** attacks, the men of Ai will come
8:13 So they stationed the main **a** north of the city
8:14 and all his **a** hurriedly went out early the next
8:15 and the Israelite **a** fled toward the wilderness as
8:24 When the Israelite **a** finished killing all the men
10:7 So Joshua and the entire Israelite **a** left Gilgal
10:15 and the Israelite **a** returned to their camp at Gilgal.
10:20 and the Israelite **a** continued the slaughter
10:24 Joshua told the captains of his **a**, "Come and put
10:33 King Horam of Gezer had arrived with his **a** to
10:33 Joshua's men killed him and destroyed his entire **a**.
10:34 Then Joshua and the Israelite **a** went to Eglon
10:43 and the Israelite **a** returned to their camp at Gilgal.
Jdg 4:2 The commander of his **a** was Sisera, who lived in
4:7 I will lure Sisera, commander of Jabin's **a**,
7:1 and his **a** got up early and went as far as the spring
7:23 who joined in the chase after the fleeing **a** of
8:3 and Zeeb, the generals of the Midianite **a**.
8:11 and Jogbehah, taking the Midianite **a** by surprise.
9:32 Come by night with an **a** and hide out in the fields.
9:35 when Abimelech and his **a** came out of hiding.
10:17 in Gilead, preparing to attack Israel's **a** at Mizpah.
11:11 and he became their ruler and commander of the **a**.
11:20 he mobilized his **a** at Jahaz and attacked them.
11:29 in Gilead, and led an **a** against the Ammonites.
11:32 So Jephthah led his **a** against the Ammonites,
12:1 Then the tribe of Ephraim mobilized its **a**
12:4 So Jephthah called out his **a** and attacked the men
1Sa 4:1 The Israelite **a** was camped near Ebenezer,
4:2 Philistines attacked and defeated the **a** of Israel,
4:3 the **a** of Israel retreated to their camp, and their
7:7 at Mizpah, they mobilized their **a** and advanced.
8:11 "The king will draft your sons into his **a** and make
11:1 King Nahash of Ammon led his **a** against the
11:11 having divided his **a** into three detachments.
11:11 The remnant of their **a** was so badly scattered that
12:9 the general of Hazor's **a**, and by the Philistines
13:2 three thousand special troops from the **a** of Israel
13:4 So the entire Israelite **a** mobilized again and met
13:5 The Philistines mustered a mighty **a** of three
13:15 the rest of the troops went with Saul to meet the **a**.
13:23 been secured by a contingent of the Philistine **a**.
14:15 Suddenly, panic broke out in the Philistine **a**,
14:16 the vast **a** of Philistines began to melt away in
14:21 who had gone over to the Philistine **a** revolted
14:28 "Your father made the **a** take a strict oath that
14:38 I want all my **a** commanders to come here.
14:46 Then Saul called back the **a** from chasing the
14:50 The commander of Saul's **a** was his cousin Abner,
14:52 was brave and strong, he drafted him into his **a**.
15:4 So Saul mobilized his **a** at Telaim. There were
15:15 "It's true that the **a** spared the best of the sheep
17:1 The Philistines now mustered their **a** for battle
17:8 "Do you need a whole **a** to settle this?
17:13 had already joined Saul's **a** to fight the Philistines.
17:14 Since David's three oldest brothers were in the **a**,
17:16 Philistine giant strutted in front of the Israelite **a**.
17:19 with Saul and the Israelite **a** at the valley of Elah,
17:20 **a** was leaving for the battlefield with shouts
17:21 forces stood facing each other, **a** against **a**.
17:23 shouting his challenge to the **a** of Israel.
17:24 As soon as the Israelite **a** saw him, they began to
17:33 and he has been in the **a** since he was a boy!"
17:53 Then the Israelite **a** returned and plundered the
17:55 he asked Abner, the general of his **a**, "Abner,
18:5 So Saul made him a commander in his **a**,
18:6 **a** was returning home after David had killed
18:30 Whenever the Philistine **a** attacked, David was
22:7 he promised to make you commanders in his **a**?
23:3 to go to Keilah to fight the whole Philistine **a**!"
23:8 So Saul mobilized his entire **a** to march to Keilah
28:5 When Saul saw the vast Philistine **a**, he became
28:19 and the **a** of Israel over to the Philistines
28:19 The LORD will bring the entire **a** of Israel down
29:1 The entire Philistine **a** now mobilized at Aphek,
29:11 while the Philistine **a** went on to Jezreel.
31:7 and beyond the Jordan saw that their **a** had been
2Sa 1:4 The man replied, "Our entire **a** fled. Many men
1:12 and for the LORD's **a** and the nation of Israel,
2:8 But Abner son of Ner, the commander of Saul's **a**,
8:6 Then he placed several **a** garrisons in Damascus,
8:9 heard that David had destroyed the **a** of Hadadezer,
8:14 He placed **a** garrisons throughout Edom, and all
8:16 Joab son of Zeruiah was commander of the **a**.
10:7 he sent Joab and the entire Israelite **a** to fight them.
10:9 on two fronts, he chose the best troops in his **a**.
10:10 He left the rest of the **a** under the command of his
10:17 crossed the Jordan River, and led the **a** to Helam.
10:18 including Shobach, the commander of their **a**.
11:1 and the Israelite **a** to destroy the Ammonites.
11:7 asked him how Joab and the **a** were getting along
11:12 "and tomorrow you may return to the **a**."
12:26 and the Israelite **a** was successfully ending their
12:28 Now bring the rest of the **a** and finish the job,
12:29 So David led the rest of his **a** to Rabbah
12:31 Then David and his **a** returned to Jerusalem.
17:11 "I suggest that you mobilize the entire **a** of Israel,
17:11 That way you will have an **a** as numerous as the
17:13 you will have the entire **a** of Israel there at your
17:16 Otherwise he will die and his entire **a** with him."
17:24 Absalom had mobilized the entire **a** of Israel
17:25 had appointed Amasa as commander of his **a**,
17:26 and the Israelite **a** set up camp in the land of
18:16 and his men returned from chasing the **a** of Israel.
18:17 over it. And the **a** of Israel fled to their homes.
19:13 you as commander of my **a** in place of Joab."
19:40 All the **a** of Judah and half the **a** of Israel escorted him across the
20:4 Then the king instructed Amasa to mobilize the **a**
20:7 out after Sheba with an elite guard from Joab's **a**
20:23 once again became the commander of David's **a**.
22:30 In your strength I can crush an **a**; / with my God I
23:9 the Philistines when the entire Israelite **a** had fled.
23:10 The rest of the **a** did not return until it was time to
23:11 in a field full of lentils. The Israelite **a** fled,
23:13 the Philistine **a** was camped in the valley of
24:2 So the king said to Joab, the commander of his **a**,
1Ki 1:19 the priest and Joab, the commander of the **a**.
1:25 He also invited Joab, the commander of the **a**,
2:5 son of Zeruiah murdered my two **a** commanders,
2:32 commander of the **a** of Israel, and Amasa son of Jether, commander of the **a** of Judah.
2:35 Benaiah to command the **a** in place of Joab,
4:4 Benaiah son of Jehoiada was commander of the **a**.
9:22 government officials, officers in his **a**,
11:15 had gone to Edom with Joab, his **a** commander,
11:15 the Israelite **a** had killed nearly every male in
11:16 Joab and the **a** had stayed there for six months,
12:21 to fight against the **a** of Israel and to restore the
15:27 and the Israelite **a** were laying siege to the
16:15 When the **a** of Israel, which was then engaged in
16:16 they chose Omri, commander of the **a**, as their new
16:17 So Omri led the **a** of Israel away from Gibbethon
20:1 Now King Ben-hadad of Aram mobilized his **a**,
20:15 Then he called out the rest of his **a** of seven
20:19 provincial commanders had led the **a** out to fight.
20:20 and suddenly the entire Aramean **a** panicked
20:25 Recruit another **a** like the one you lost. Give us the
20:26 The following spring he called up the Aramean **a**
20:27 Israel then mustered its **a**, set up supply lines,
20:27 But the Israelite **a** looked like two little flocks of
20:28 of the plains. So I will help you defeat this vast **a**.
2Ki 1:9 Then he sent an **a** captain with fifty soldiers to
3:6 So King Joram mustered the **a** of Israel
3:18 for he will make you victorious over the **a** of
3:24 the **a** of Israel rushed out and attacked the
3:24 The **a** of Israel chased them into the land of Moab,
4:13 for her to the king or to the commander of the **a**?"
5:1 admiration for Naaman, the commander of his **a**,
6:14 So one night the king of Aram sent a great **a** with
6:18 As the Aramean **a** advanced toward them,
6:24 King Ben-hadad of Aram mobilized his entire **a**
7:4 as well go out and surrender to the Aramean **a**.
7:6 For the Lord had caused the whole **a** of Aram to
7:6 of horses and the sounds of a great **a** approaching.
7:14 scouts to see what had happened to the Aramean **a**.
8:21 Jehoram's **a**, however, deserted him and fled.
9:5 he found Jehu sitting in a meeting with the other **a**
9:14 (Now Joram had been with the **a** at Ramoth-gilead,
13:7 Jehoahaz's **a** was reduced to fifty mounted troops,
14:11 so King Jehoash of Israel mobilized his **a** against
14:12 Judah was routed by the **a** of Israel, and its **a** scattered and fled for home.
14:13 Then Jehoash ordered his **a** to demolish six
15:25 the commander of Pekahiah's **a**, conspired against
18:17 a huge **a** to confront King Hezekiah in Jerusalem.
18:23 can find two thousand horsemen in your entire **a**,
18:24 With your tiny **a**, how can you think of challenging
19:9 of Ethiopia was leading an **a** to fight against him.
23:29 King Josiah marched out with his **a** to fight him,
25:1 King Nebuchadnezzar of Babylon led his entire **a**
25:10 **a** as they tore down the walls of Jerusalem.
25:19 he took an officer of the Judean **a**, five of the
25:19 the **a** commander's chief secretary, who was in
25:23 When all the **a** commanders and their men learned
25:26 as well as the **a** commanders, fled in panic to
1Ch 1:46 He was the one who destroyed the Midianite **a** in
10:7 the Jezreel Valley saw that their **a** had been routed
11:13 in a field full of barley, and the Israelite **a** fled.
11:15 the Philistine **a** was camped in the valley of
12:14 These warriors from Gad were **a** commanders.
12:19 men from Manasseh defected from the Israelite **a**
12:21 able warriors who became commanders in his **a**.
12:22 David until he had a great **a**, like the **a** of God.
13:1 including the generals and captains of his **a**.
14:16 and he struck down the Philistine **a** all the way
15:25 and the generals of the **a** went to the home of
18:6 Then he placed several **a** garrisons in Damascus,
18:9 had destroyed the **a** of King Hadadezer of Zobah,
18:13 He placed **a** garrisons throughout Edom, and all
18:15 Joab son of Zeruiah was commander of the **a**.
19:7 the support of the king of Maacah and his **a**.
19:10 on two fronts, he chose the best troops in his **a**.
19:11 He left the rest of the **a** under the command of his
19:18 including Shobach, the commander of their **a**.
20:1 Joab led the Israelite **a** in successful attacks against
20:3 Then David and his **a** returned to Jerusalem.
25:1 David and the **a** commanders then appointed men
26:26 and captains and other officers of the **a**.
27:1 who served the king by supervising the **a** divisions
27:3 and was in charge of all the **a** officers for the first
27:34 Joab was commander of the Israelite **a**.
28:1 the commanders of the twelve **a** divisions,
29:6 tribes of Israel, the generals and captains of the **a**,
29:24 All the royal officials, the **a** commanders,
2Ch 1:2 the generals and captains of the **a**, the judges,
8:9 officers in his **a**, commanders of his chariots,
11:1 to fight against the **a** of Israel and to restore the
12:3 and a countless **a** of foot soldiers,
13:3 When the **a** of Judah arrived in the hill country of
13:4 and shouted to Jeroboam and the Israelite **a**:
13:8 Your **a** is vast indeed, but with you are those gold
13:13 Jeroboam had secretly sent part of his **a** around
13:15 God defeated Jeroboam and the Israelite **a**
13:15 and routed them before Abijah and the **a** of Judah.
13:16 The Israelite **a** fled from Judah, and God handed
13:17 Abijah and his **a** inflicted heavy losses on them;
13:19 Abijah and his **a** pursued Jeroboam's troops
14:8 King Asa had an **a** of 300,000 warriors from the
14:8 He also had an **a** of 280,000 warriors from the tribe
14:9 Zerah attacked Judah with an **a** of a million men
14:12 in the presence of Asa and the **a** of Judah,
14:13 Asa and his **a** pursued them as far as Gerar, and
14:13 They were destroyed by the LORD and his **a**,
14:13 and the **a** of Judah carried off vast quantities of
16:7 you missed your chance to destroy the **a** of the
16:8 to the Ethiopians and Libyans and their vast **a**,
17:13 and stationed an **a** of seasoned troops at Jerusalem.
17:14 His **a** was enrolled according to ancestral clans.
20:2 "A vast **a** from Edom is marching against you
20:12 We are powerless against this mighty **a** that is
20:15 Don't be discouraged by this mighty **a**,
20:20 Early the next morning the **a** of Judah went out
20:21 the king appointed singers to walk ahead of the **a**,
20:23 After they had finished off the **a** of Seir,
20:24 So when the **a** of Judah arrived at the lookout point
21:9 So Jehoram went to attack Edom with his full **a**
23:1 and made a pact with five **a** commanders:
24:23 of the year, the Aramean **a** marched against Joash.
24:24 the Arameans attacked with only a small **a**,
24:24 helped them conquer the much larger **a** of Judah.
25:5 Another thing Amaziah did was to organize the **a**,
25:5 and found that he had an **a** of 300,000 men twenty
25:9 I do about the silver I paid to hire the **a** of Israel?"
25:11 his courage and led his **a** to the Valley of Salt,
25:21 So King Jehoash of Israel mobilized his **a** against
25:22 Judah was routed by the **a** of Israel, and its **a** scattered and fled for home.
25:23 Then Jehoash ordered his **a** to demolish six
26:11 Uzziah had an **a** of well-trained warriors, ready to
26:11 This great **a** of fighting men had been mustered
26:11 the secretary of the **a**, and his assistant, Maaseiah.
26:13 The **a** consisted of 307,500 men, all elite troops.
26:14 Uzziah provided the entire **a** with shields, spears,
28:5 and inflicted many casualties on his **a**.
28:9 in Samaria when the **a** of Israel returned home.
32:1 giving orders for his **a** to break through their walls.
32:7 be afraid of the king of Assyria or his mighty **a**,
32:8 He may have a great **a**, but they are just men.
32:21 destroyed the Assyrian **a** with all its commanders
35:20 King Neco of Egypt led his **a** up from Egypt to do
35:20 and Josiah and his **a** marched out to fight him.
35:22 he led his **a** into battle on the plain of Megiddo.
36:19 Then his **a** set fire to the Temple of God,
Ne 2:9 had sent along **a** officers and horsemen to protect
4:2 in front of his friends and the Samarian **a** officers,
Job 25:3 Who is able to count his heavenly **a**? Does his light
Ps 18:29 In your strength I can crush an **a**; / with my God I
27:3 Though a mighty **a** surrounds me, / my heart will
33:16 The best-equipped **a** cannot save a king, / nor is
136:15 but he hurled Pharaoh and his **a** into the sea.
Pr 30:27 have no king, / but they march like an **a** in ranks.
30:31 the male goat, / a king as he leads his **a**.
Ecc 9:14 and a great king came with his **a** and besieged it.
SS 6:4 You are as majestic as an **a** with banners!
6:10 as the sun, as majestic as an **a** with banners?'
Isa 3:3 **a** officers, honorable citizens, advisers,
7:17 king of Assyria will come with his great **a**!"
7:18 In that day the LORD will whistle for the **a** of Upper Egypt and for the **a** of Assyria.
9:4 just as he did when he destroyed the **a** of Midian
10:18 Assyria's vast **a** is like a glorious forest, yet it will
10:19 Only a few from all that mighty **a** will survive—
10:26 staff was raised to drown the Egyptian **a** in the sea.
10:30 out a warning to Laishah, for the mighty **a** comes.
10:33 He will destroy all that vast **a** of Assyria—officers
13:4 Almighty has brought them here to form an **a**.
14:31 A powerful **a** is coming out of the north.
18:6 Your mighty **a** will be left dead in the fields for the
28:2 For the Lord will send the mighty Assyrian **a**
33:4 so Jerusalem will strip the fallen **a** of Assyria!
36:2 **a** from Lachish to confront King Hezekiah in
36:8 can find two thousand horsemen in your entire **a**,
36:9 With your tiny **a**, how can you think of challenging
37:9 of Ethiopia was leading an **a** to fight against him.
43:14 "For your sakes I will send an invading **a** against
43:17 I called forth the mighty **a** of Egypt with all its
Jer 6:1 Warn everyone that a powerful **a** is coming from
6:22 "See a great **a** marching from the north!
6:23 the noise of their **a** is like a roaring sea.
8:16 land trembles at the approach of the terrible **a**,
15:20 They will fight against you like an attacking **a**,
22:25 of Babylon and the mighty Babylonian **a**.
26:21 When King Jehoiakim and the **a** officers

32: 2 Jerusalem was under siege from the Babylonian **a**,
34: 7 At this time the Babylonian **a** was besieging
34:21 and his officials to the **a** of the king of Babylon.
37: 5 At this time the **a** of Pharaoh Hophra of Egypt
37: 5 When the Babylonian **a** heard about it,
37: 7 that Pharaoh's **a** is about to return to Egypt,
37:10 if you were to destroy the entire Babylonian **a**,
37:11 When the Babylonian **a** left Jerusalem because of Pharaoh's approaching **a**,
38: 3 be handed over to the **a** of the king of Babylon,
38:22 and given to the officers of the Babylonian **a**.
39: 1 and his **a** returned to besiege Jerusalem.
39: 3 All the officers of the Babylonian **a** came in
42: 1 Then all the **a** officers, including Johanan son of
42: 8 for Johanan son of Kareah and the **a** officers,
43: 4 So Johanan and all the **a** officers and all the people
46: 2 and his **a** were defeated beside the Euphrates River
46: 5 But look! The Egyptian **a** flees in terror.
46: 8 It is the Egyptian **a**, boasting that it will cover the
46:22 The invading **a** marches in; they come against her
46:26 to King Nebuchadnezzar of Babylon and his **a**.
47: 1 of Gaza, before it was captured by the Egyptian **a**.
50: 9 I am raising up an **a** of great nations from the
50:41 "Look! A great **a** is marching from the north!
50:42 the noise of their **a** is like a roaring sea.
51:32 The fortifications are burning, and the **a** is in panic.
52: 4 King Nebuchadnezzar of Babylon led his entire **a**
52:14 **a** as they tore down the walls of Jerusalem.
52:25 he took an officer of the Judean **a**, seven of the
52:25 the **a** commander's chief secretary, who was in
La 1:15 At his command a great **a** has come to crush my
Eze 1:24 of the Almighty, or like the shouting of a mighty **a**.
7:14 "The trumpets call Israel's **a** to mobilize, but no
17: 9 it won't take a strong arm or a large **a** to do it.
17:15 sending ambassadors to Egypt to request a great **a**
17:17 and all his mighty **a** will fail to help Israel when
23:24 wagons, and a great **a** fully prepared for attack.
23:46 Bring an **a** against them and hand them over to be
26: 7 against Tyre with his cavalry, chariots, and great **a**.
27:10 Lydia, and Libya served in your great **a**.
28: 7 I will bring against you an enemy **a**, the terror of
29: 8 I will bring an **a** against you, O Egypt, and destroy
29:18 the **a** of King Nebuchadnezzar of Babylon fought
29:18 and his **a** won no plunder to compensate them for
29:19 plundering everything they have to pay his **a**.
31:12 A foreign **a**—the terror of the nations—cut it down
32:31 that he is not alone in having his entire **a** killed,
33: 2 When I bring an **a** against a country, the people of
37:10 and stood up on their feet—a great **a** of them.
38:15 north with your vast cavalry and your mighty **a**,
Da 3:20 Then he ordered some of the strongest men of his **a**
8:12 But the **a** of heaven was restrained from destroying
11: 7 he will raise an **a** and enter the fortress of the king
11:10 assemble a mighty **a** that will advance like a flood
11:12 After the enemy **a** is swept away, the king of the
11:13 a fully equipped **a** far greater than the one he lost.
11:25 and raise a great **a** against the king of the south.
11:25 king of the south will go to battle with a mighty **a**,
11:26 His **a** will be swept away, and many will be killed.
11:31 His **a** will take over the Temple fortress,
Hos 13:16 They will be killed by an invading **a**, their little
Joel 1: 6 A vast **a** of locusts has invaded my land. It is a terrible **a**, too numerous to count! Its teeth
2: 2 across the mountains, a mighty **a** appears!
2: 5 a field, or like a mighty **a** moving into battle.
2:11 This is his mighty **a**, and they follow his orders.
2:25 It was I who sent this great destroying **a** against
Mt 22: 7 He sent out his **a** to destroy the murderers and burn
Mk 6:21 **a** officers, and the leading citizens of Galilee.
Lk 14:31 and discussing whether his **a** of ten thousand is
Jn 11:48 and then the Roman **a** will come and destroy both
Ac 10: 1 In Caesarea there lived a Roman **a** officer named
27: 1 placed in the custody of an **a** officer named Julius,
2Ti 2: 4 satisfy the one who has enlisted you in his **a**.
Jas 4: 1 Isn't it the whole **a** of evil desires at war within
Rev 9: 9 and their wings roared like an **a** of chariots rushing
9:16 They led an **a** of 200 million mounted troops—
19:19 fight against the one sitting on the horse and his **a**.
19:21 Their entire **a** was killed by the sharp sword that

ARNAN (1) [ARNAN'S]

1Ch 3:21 Rephaiah's son was **A**. Arnan's son was Obadiah.

ARNAN'S (1) [ARNAN]

1Ch 3:21 Rephaiah's son was Arnan. **A** son was Obadiah.

ARNI (2)

Lk 3:33 Admin was the son of **A**. / **A** was the son of

ARNON (26)

Nu 21:13 Then they moved to the far side of the **A** River,
21:13 The **A** is the boundary line between the Moabites
21:14 area of Suphah, and the ravines; and the **A** River
21:24 and occupied their land from the **A** River to the
21:26 and seized all his land as far as the **A** River.
21:28 in Moab; / it destroyed the rulers of the **A** heights.
22:36 town on the **A** River at the border of his land.
Dt 2:24 "Then the LORD said, 'Now cross the **A** Gorge!
2:36 us conquer Aroer on the edge of the **A** Gorge,
3: 8 from the **A** Gorge to Mount Hermon.
3:12 I gave the territory beyond Aroer along the **A**
3:16 from Gilead to the middle of the **A** Gorge,
4:48 Aroer at the edge of the **A** Gorge to Mount Sirion,
Jos 12: 1 Their territory extended from the **A** Gorge to
12: 2 included Aroer, on the edge of the **A** Gorge,
12: 2 and extended from the middle of the **A** Gorge to
13: 9 **A** Gorge (including the town in the middle of the
13:16 **A** Gorge (including the town in the middle of the
Jdg 11:13 they stole my land from the **A** River to the Jabbok
11:18 and camped on the other side of the **A** River.
11:18 But they never once crossed the **A** River into
11:22 from the **A** River to the Jabbok River, and from the
11:26 to Aroer and in all the towns along the **A** River.
2Ki 10:33 of Aroer by the **A** Gorge to as far north as Gilead
Isa 16: 2 birds at the shallow crossings of the **A** River.
Jer 48:20 and wail! Tell it by the banks of the **A** River:

ARODI (2) [ARODITE]

Ge 46:16 Haggi, Shuni, Ezbon, Eri, **A**, and Areli.
Nu 26:17 The Arodite clan, named after its ancestor **A**.

ARODITE (1) [ARODI]

Nu 26:17 The **A** clan, named after its ancestor Arodi.

AROER (17)

Nu 32:34 of Gad built the towns of Dibon, Ataroth, **A**,
Dt 2:36 "The LORD our God helped us conquer **A** on the
3:12 I gave the territory beyond **A** along the Arnon
4:48 So Israel conquered all the area from **A** at the edge
Jos 12: 2 His kingdom included **A**, on the edge of the Arnon
13: 9 Their territory extended from **A** on the edge of the
13:16 Their territory extended from **A** on the edge of the
13:25 as far as the town of **A** just west of Rabbah.
Jdg 11:26 spread across the land from Heshbon to **A** and in
11:33 He thoroughly defeated the Ammonites from **A** to
1Sa 30:28 **A**, Siphmoth, Eshtemoa,
2Sa 24: 5 First they crossed the Jordan and camped at **A**,
2Ki 10:33 He conquered the area from the town of **A** by the
1Ch 5: 8 lived in the area that stretches from **A** to Nebo
11:44 Shama and Jeiel, the sons of Hotham, from **A**;
Isa 17: 2 The cities of **A** will be deserted. Sheep will graze
Jer 48:19 The people of **A** stand anxiously beside the road to

AROMA (2) [AROMATIC]

Ge 27:17 with its rich **a**, and some freshly baked bread.
Ps 66:15 to you—/ the best of my rams as a pleasing **a**.

AROMATIC (3) [AROMA]

Ge 2:12 **a** resin and onyx stone are also found there.
2Ki 20:13 the silver, the gold, the spices, and the **a** oils.
Isa 39: 2 the silver, the gold, the spices, and the **a** oils.

AROSE (4) [RISE]

Jdg 5: 7 of Israel—/ until Deborah **a** as a mother for Israel.
Mt 2: 2 We have seen his star as it **a**, and we have come to
Mk 4:37 But soon a fierce storm **a**. High waves began to
Ac 23: 9 So a great clamor **a**. Some of the teachers of

AROUND (404) [ROUNDABOUT]

Ge 2:11 which flows **a** the entire land of Havilah,
2:13 the Gihon, which flows **a** the entire land of Cush.
3: 7 So they strung fig leaves together **a** their hips to
6:16 Construct an opening all the way **a** the boat,
14: 7 Then they swung **a** to En-mishpat (now called
27:16 and she fastened a strip of the goat's skin **a** his
37: 7 and then your bundles all gathered **a** and bowed
37:15 a man noticed him wandering **a** the countryside.
38:28 and the midwife tied a scarlet thread **a** the wrist of
39:11 no one else was **a** when he was doing his work
39:14 Soon all the men **a** the place came running.
39:17 "That Hebrew slave you've had **a** here tried to
42: 1 "Why are you standing **a** looking at one another?
49: 1 called together all his sons and said, "Gather **a** me,
Ex 2:12 After looking **a** to make sure no one was watching,
14:19 and the pillar of cloud also moved **a** behind them.
16:13 The next morning the desert all **a** the camp was
19:23 You told me to set boundaries **a** the mountain
24: 4 He also set up twelve pillars **a** the altar, one for
25:11 with pure gold, and put a molding of gold all **a** it.
25:24 it with pure gold and run a molding of gold **a** it.
25:25 Put a rim about three inches wide **a** the top edge, and put a gold molding all **a** the rim.
25:27 close to the rim **a** the top. These rings will support
27:17 All the posts **a** the courtyard must be connected by
28:34 and pomegranates are to alternate all the way **a** the
30: 3 and run a gold molding **a** the entire altar.
34:10 And all the people **a** you will see the power of the
37: 2 and out, and it had a molding of gold all the way **a**.
37:11 with pure gold, with a gold molding all **a** the edge.
37:12 of the table, and a gold molding ran **a** the rim.
37:26 with pure gold and ran a gold molding **a** the edge.
38:31 posts that supported the curtains **a** the courtyard,
39:26 and pomegranates alternating all **a** the hem.
40: 8 Then set up the courtyard **a** the outside of the tent,
40:33 Then he hung the curtains forming the courtyard **a**
Lev 3: 3 by fire. This includes the fat **a** the internal organs,
3: 4 the two kidneys with the fat **a** them near the loins,
3: 9 off near the backbone, the fat **a** the internal organs,
3:10 the two kidneys with the fat **a** them near the loins,
3:14 This part includes the fat **a** the internal organs,
3:15 the two kidneys with the fat **a** them near the loins,
4: 8 The priest must remove all the fat **a** the bull's
4: 9 the two kidneys with the fat **a** them near the loins,
7: 3 the fat from the tail, the fat **a** the internal organs,
7: 4 the two kidneys with the fat **a** them near the loins,
8: 7 the embroidered tunic and tied the sash **a** his waist.
8:16 He took all the fat **a** the internal organs, the lobe of
8:25 the fat **a** the internal organs, the lobe of the liver,
9:19 fat from the tail and from **a** the internal organs—
13:43 and if he finds swelling **a** the reddish white sore,
16: 4 He must tie the linen sash **a** his waist and put the
25:34 The strip of pastureland **a** each of the Levitical
Nu 1:50 you travel, and they must care for it and camp **a** it.
1:53 But the Levites will camp **a** the Tabernacle of the
1:53 The Levites are responsible to stand guard **a** the
3: 7 their sacred duties in and **a** the Tabernacle.
11:24 and stationed them **a** the Tabernacle.
11:31 the sea and let them fall into the camp and all **a** it!
14:25 Now turn **a** and don't go on toward the land where
20:21 through their country, Israel was forced to turn **a**.
21: 4 taking the road to the Red Sea to go **a** the land of
35: 4 The pastureland assigned to the Levites **a** these
Dt 1:40 turn **a** now and go on back through the wilderness
2: 1 "Then we turned **a** and set out across the
2: 1 and we wandered **a** Mount Seir for a long time.
2: 3 'You have been wandering **a** in this hill country
2: 5 for I have given them all the hill country **a** Mount
17:14 'We ought to have a king like the other nations **a**
22: 8 "Every new house you build must have a barrier **a**
23:14 for the LORD your God moves **a** in your camp to
28:29 You will grope **a** in broad daylight, just like a blind
28:34 You will go mad because of all the tragedy **a** you.
28:67 your terror at the awesome horrors you see **a** you.
Jos 2: 1 side of the Jordan River, especially **a** Jericho."
6: 3 Your entire army is to march **a** the city once a day
6: 4 On the seventh day you are to march **a** the city
6: 7 "March **a** the city, and the armed men will lead the
6:11 So the Ark of the LORD was carried **a** the city
6:14 On the second day they marched **a** the city once
6:15 and marched **a** the city as they had done before.
6:15 But this time they went **a** the city seven times.
6:16 The seventh time **a**, as the priests sounded the long
11: 5 They established their camp **a** the water near
17:16 and the Canaanites in the lowlands **a** Beth-shan
Jdg 2:12 worshiping the gods of the people **a** them.
2:14 He sold them to their enemies all **a**, and they were
6:29 And after asking **a** and making a careful search,
6:39 remain dry while the ground **a** it is wet with dew."
7:21 Each man stood at his position **a** the camp
7:21 and watched as all the Midianites rushed **a** in a
8:11 Gideon circled **a** by the caravan route east of
8:26 the kings, or the chains **a** the necks of their camels.
9:34 into four groups, stationing themselves **a** Shechem.
10: 4 His thirty sons rode **a** on thirty donkeys, and they
11:18 they went **a** Edom and Moab through the
18:14 The five men who had scouted out the land **a** Laish
18:23 The men of Dan turned **a** and said, "What do you
18:26 them for him to attack, he turned **a** and went home.
20:29 So the Israelites set an ambush all **a** Gibeah.
Ru 3: 8 **A** midnight, Boaz suddenly woke up and turned
4: 9 said to the leaders and to the crowd standing **a**,
1Sa 7:16 Each year he traveled **a**, setting up his court first at
8:20 "We want to be like the nations **a** us. Our king
14: 2 of Gibeah, **a** the pomegranate tree at Migron.
17:28 was angry. "What are you doing **a** here anyway?"
21:15 We already have enough of them **a** here!
24: 8 And when Saul looked **a**, David bowed low before
26: 5 slipped over to Saul's camp one night to look **a**.
26: 7 Abner and the warriors were lying asleep **a** him.
26:16 your master, the LORD's anointed! Look **a**!
31: 3 The fighting grew very fierce **a** Saul,
2Sa 3: 8 "Am I a Judean dog to be kicked **a** like this?"
4: 5 went to Ishbosheth's home **a** noon as he was taking
5: 9 He built additional fortifications **a** the city,
5:23 circle **a** behind them and attack them near the
14:26 then only because it was too heavy to carry **a**.
20:12 saw that a crowd was gathering **a** to stare at him.
22: 6 The grave wrapped its ropes **a** me; / death itself
24: 6 of Tahtim-hodshi and to Dan-jaan and **a** to Sidon.
1Ki 3: 1 the Temple of the LORD and the wall **a** the city.
3: 7 I am like a little child who doesn't know his way **a**.
6: 5 all the way **a** the sides and rear of the building.
7:20 two hundred pomegranates in two rows **a** them,
7:24 There were about six gourds per foot all the way **a**,
7:35 **A** the top of each cart there was a rim 9 inches
7:36 there was room, and there were wreaths all **a**.
7:42 that were hung **a** the capitals on top of the pillars),
8:14 Then the king turned **a** to the entire community of
18:26 Then they danced wildly **a** the altar they had made.
18:30 They all crowded **a** him as he repaired the altar of
18:32 Then he dug a trench **a** the altar large enough to
18:35 and the water ran **a** the altar and even overflowed
19: 6 He looked **a** and saw some bread baked on hot
19:21 He passed **a** the meat to the other plowmen,
22: 7 "Isn't there a prophet of the LORD **a**, too?
22:19 on his throne with all the armies of heaven **a** him,
22:28 Then he added to those standing **a**, "Take note of
2Ki 1: 8 hairy man, and he wore a leather belt **a** his waist."
2:24 Elisha turned **a** and looked at them, and he cursed
4:20 held him on her lap. But **a** noontime he died.
6:17 he saw that the hillside **a** Elisha was filled with
7:10 all in order, but there was not a single person **a**.
9:22 witchcraft of your mother, Jezebel, are all **a** us?"
9:23 Then King Joram reined the chariot horses **a**
10: 9 and spoke to the crowd that had gathered **a** them.
11:11 The guards stationed themselves **a** the king,
11:11 the south side of the Temple **a** to the north side and all **a** the altar.
17:15 They followed the example of the nations **a** them,
23:16 Then as Josiah was looking **a**, he noticed several
25:17 a network of bronze pomegranates all the way **a**.
1Ch 9:27 They would spend the night **a** the house of God,
10: 3 The fighting grew very fierce **a** Saul,
14:14 circle **a** behind them and attack them near the
2Ch 4: 3 There were about six oxen per foot all the way **a**,

4:13 that were hung **a** the capitals on top of the pillars),
6:3 Then the king turned **a** to the entire community of
13:13 Jeroboam had secretly sent part of his army **a**
17:9 and traveled **a** through all the towns of Judah,
18:6 "Isn't there a prophet of the LORD **a**, too?
18:27 Then he added to those standing **a**, "Take note of
20:10 so they went **a** them and did not destroy them.
23:10 He stationed the guards **a** the king, with their
23:10 the south side of the Temple **a** to the north side and all **a** the altar.
29:26 then took their positions **a** the Temple with the
31:19 who were living in the open villages **a** the towns,
33:14 and continuing **a** the hill of Ophel, where it was
Ne 4:6 to half its original height **a** the entire city,
12:29 for the singers had built their own villages **a**
12:38 The second choir went northward **a** the other way
13:21 are you doing out here, camping **a** the wall?
Job 12:18 With ropes **a** their waist, they are led away.
18:9 grabs them by the heel. A noose tightens **a** them.
19:12 up roads to attack me. They camp all **a** my tent.
21:29 But I tell you to ask those who have been **a**,
23:17 Darkness is all **a** me; thick, impenetrable darkness
29:5 was still with me, and my children were **a** me.
36:30 See how he spreads the lightning **a** him and how it
37:12 The clouds turn **a** and **a** under his direction.
41:1 a crocodile with a hook or put a noose **a** its jaw?
Ps 1:1 the advice of the wicked, / or stand **a** with sinners,
3:3 But you, O LORD, are a shield **a** me, / my glory,
18:5 The grave wrapped its ropes **a** me; / death itself
36:11 trample me; / don't let the wicked push me **a**.
39:1 curb my tongue / when the ungodly are **a** me."
43:2 Why must I wander **a** in darkness, / oppressed by
44:13 an object of scorn and derision to the nations **a** us.
48:12 of Jerusalem. / Walk **a** and count the many towers.
50:3 in his way, / and a great storm rages **a** him.
50:20 You sit **a** and slander a brother—/ your own
78:28 to fall within their camp / and all **a** their tents.
79:3 Blood has flowed like water all **a** Jerusalem;
79:4 an object of scorn and derision to those **a** us.
81:11 people wouldn't listen. / Israel did not want me **a**.
88:17 They swirl **a** me like floodwaters all day long.
91:7 at your side, / though ten thousand are dying **a** you,
109:3 They are all **a** me with their hateful words,
109:19 like clothing; / may they be tied **a** him like a belt.
116:3 Death had its hands **a** my throat; / the terrors of the
118:12 They swarmed **a** me like bees; / they blazed
128:3 There they sit **a** your table / as vigorous
139:11 to hide me / and the light **a** me to become night—
142:7 so I can thank you. / The godly will crowd **a** me,
Pr 6:21 words always in your heart. Tie them **a** your neck.
7:13 She threw her arms **a** him and kissed him, and with
11:13 A gossip goes **a** revealing secrets, but those who
20:19 so don't hang **a** with someone who talks too much.
28:19 have plenty of food; playing **a** brings poverty.
29:3 but if he hangs **a** with prostitutes, his wealth is
Ecc 1:5 The sun rises and sets and hurries **a** to rise again.
Isa 3:16 who walk **a** with their noses in the air,
6:2 Hovering **a** him were mighty seraphim, each with
7:18 They will swarm **a** you like flies. Like bees,
11:12 raise a flag among the nations for Israel to rally **a**.
12:5 Make known his praise **a** the world.
20:2 as he was told and walked **a** naked and barefoot.
20:3 "My servant Isaiah has been walking **a** naked
23:17 She will return again to all her evil ways **a** the
25:6 spread a wonderful feast for everyone **a** the world.
29:3 I will build siege towers **a** it and will destroy it.
30:21 "This is the way; turn **a** and walk here."
31:5 hover over Jerusalem as a bird hovers **a** its nest.
32:9 Listen, you women who lie **a** in lazy ease.
33:1 who have destroyed everything **a** you but have
45:20 What fools they are who carry **a** their wooden idols
46:7 They carry it **a** on their shoulders, and when they
56:10 They love to lie **a**, sleeping and dreaming.
58:10 and the darkness **a** you will be as bright as day.
60:5 for merchants from **a** the world will come to you.
60:11 Your gates will stay open **a** the clock to receive the
Jer 3:2 "Look all **a** you. Is there anywhere in the entire
6:3 They will set up camp **a** the city and divide your
9:16 I will scatter them **a** the world, and they will be
13:1 "Go and buy a linen belt and put it **a** your waist,
13:2 as the LORD directed me and put it **a** my waist.
16:19 Nations from **a** the world will come to you
17:26 And from all **a** Jerusalem, from the towns of Judah
21:14 forests that will burn up everything **a** you.' "
29:18 and disease, and I will scatter them **a** the world.
31:26 At this, I woke up and looked **a**. My sleep had
32:20 to do great miracles in Israel and all **a** the world.
46:14 sword of destruction will devour everyone **a** you.
49:36 They will be exiled to countries **a** the world.
50:32 of Babylon that will burn everything **a** them."
50:46 and her cry of despair will be heard **a** the world.
52:22 a network of bronze pomegranates all the way **a**.
52:23 and a total of one hundred on the network **a** the
La 1:12 Look **a** and see if there is any suffering like mine,
2:22 "You have invited terrors from all **a** as though you
Eze 1:9 were able to fly in any direction without turning **a**.
1:12 forward in all directions without having to turn **a**.
1:18 and they were covered with eyes all **a** the edges.
1:28 All **a** him was a glowing halo, like a rainbow
5:15 You will be a warning to all the nations **a** you.
6:5 of your idols and scatter your bones **a** your altars.
9:4 and sigh because of the sins they see **a** them."
11:12 you have copied the sins of the nations **a** you."
12:6 into the night. Cover your face and don't look **a**.
13:4 these prophets of yours are like jackals digging **a**
13:5 to strengthen the breaks in the walls **a** the nation.
16:8 So I wrapped my cloak **a** you to cover your
20:32 "You say, 'We want to be like the nations all **a** us,
20:39 but then don't turn **a** and bring gifts to me.
26:17 their naval power, / once spread fear **a** the world.
31:5 This great tree towered above all the other trees **a**
32:2 heaving **a** in your own rivers, stirring up mud with
34:26 and their homes **a** my holy hill to be a blessing.
36:36 Then the nations all **a**—all those still left—
37:2 He led me **a** among the old, dry bones that covered
38:4 I will turn you **a** and put hooks into your jaws to
38:7 Keep all the armies **a** you mobilized, and take
38:12 and they think the whole world revolves **a** them!'
40:24 Then the man took me **a** to the south gateway
40:35 Then he took me **a** to the north gateway leading to
41:10 feet in width, and it went all the way **a** the Temple.
41:13 The courtyard **a** the building, including its walls,
42:20 **a** it to separate the holy places from the common.
43:1 the man brought me back **a** to the east gateway.
43:13 There is a gutter all **a** the altar 21 inches wide
43:13 inches deep, with a curb 9 inches wide **a** its edge.
43:17 and a 10-1/2-inch curb all **a** the edge.
43:20 the upper ledge, and the curb that runs **a** that ledge.
45:2 of land 87-1/2 feet wide is to be left empty all **a** it.
46:23 stone with fireplaces under the ledge all the way **a**.
47:2 north gateway and led me **a** to the eastern entrance.
48:35 "The distance **a** the entire city will be six miles.
Da 3:25 "I see four men, unbound, walking **a** in the fire.
3:27 and advisers crowded **a** them and saw that the fire
5:7 royal honor and will wear a gold chain **a** his neck.
5:16 and you will wear a gold chain **a** your neck.
5:29 in purple robes, a gold chain was hung **a** his neck,
10:5 linen clothing, with a belt of pure gold **a** his waist.
Hos 7:2 Their sinful deeds are all **a** them; I see them all!
10:8 Thorns and thistles will grow up **a** them.
Am 2:8 they lounge **a** in clothing stolen from their debtors.
3:9 "Take your seats now on the hills **a** Samaria,
Jnh 2:5 The waters closed in **a** me, and seaweed wrapped itself **a** my head.
Mic 1:8 I will walk **a** naked and barefoot in sorrow
2:2 No one's family or inheritance is safe with you **a**!
3:6 Now the night will close **a** you, cutting off all your
4:5 Even though the nations **a** us worship idols,
5:4 for he will be highly honored all **a** the world.
7:16 will stand in silent awe, deaf to everything **a** them.
Hab 1:3 Must I forever see this sin and misery all **a** me?
Zep 2:11 Then people from nations **a** the world will worship
Zec 2:1 When I looked **a** me again, I saw a man with a
2:5 For I, myself, will be a wall of fire **a** Jerusalem,
4:2 **A** the bowl are seven lamps, each one having
4:10 eyes of the LORD that search all **a** the world."
8:20 and cities **a** the world will travel to Jerusalem.
8:23 and languages **a** the world will clutch at the hem of
Mal 1:11 All **a** the world they offer sweet incense and pure
Mt 2:16 and **a** Bethlehem who were two years old
9:22 Jesus turned **a** and said to her, "Daughter,
14:30 But when he looked **a** at the high waves, he was
15:31 crippled were made well, the lame were walking **a**,
18:6 into the sea with a large millstone tied **a** the neck.
20:3 and saw some people standing **a** doing nothing.
20:5 and again **a** three o'clock he did the same thing.
20:6 town again and saw some more people standing **a**.
21:9 and the crowds all **a** him were shouting,
21:33 landowner planted a vineyard, built a wall **a** it,
26:71 girl noticed him and said to those standing **a**,
27:36 Then they sat **a** and kept guard as he hung there.
Mk 2:13 and taught the crowds that gathered **a** him.
3:5 He looked **a** at them angrily, because he was
3:9 Jesus instructed his disciples to bring **a** a boat
3:10 a result, many sick people were crowding **a** him,
3:32 There was a crowd **a** Jesus, and someone said,
3:34 Then he looked at those **a** him and said,
4:10 and with the others who were gathered **a**,
5:15 A crowd soon gathered **a** Jesus, but they were
5:21 a large crowd gathered **a** him on the shore.
5:30 so he turned **a** in the crowd and asked,
5:31 said to him, "All this crowd is pressing **a** you.
5:32 But he kept on looking **a** to see who had done it.
5:42 years old, immediately stood up and walked **a**!
8:24 The man looked **a**. "Yes," he said, "I see people,
8:24 very clearly. They look like trees walking **a**."
9:8 Suddenly they looked **a**, and Moses and Elijah
9:42 into the sea with a large millstone tied **a** the neck.
10:23 Jesus looked **a** and said to his disciples,
11:9 and the crowds all **a** him were shouting,
11:11 He looked **a** carefully at everything, and then he
12:1 "A man planted a vineyard, built a wall **a** it,
14:18 As they were sitting **a** the table eating, Jesus said,
Lk 4:44 So he continued to travel **a**, preaching in
5:8 leave me—I'm too much of a sinner to be **a** you."
6:10 He looked **a** at them one by one and then said to
7:15 dead boy sat up and began to talk to those **a** him!
7:49 does this man think he is, going **a** forgiving sins?"
8:35 A crowd soon gathered **a** Jesus, for they wanted to
10:7 enter a town, don't move **a** from home to home.
12:52 favor of me, and two against—or the other way **a**.
14:17 he sent his servant **a** to notify the guests that it was
14:25 following Jesus. He turned **a** and said to them,
16:1 but soon a rumor went **a** that the manager was
17:2 **a** the neck than to face the punishment in store for
18:31 Gathering the twelve disciples **a** him, Jesus told
22:6 arrest him quietly when the crowds weren't **a**.
22:25 world the kings and great men order their people **a**,
22:55 The guards lit a fire in the courtyard and sat **a** it,
Jn 1:38 Jesus looked **a** and saw them following. "What do
4:35 Look **a** you! Vast fields are ripening all **a** us and
6:3 into the hills and sat down with his disciples **a** him.
11:52 of all the children of God scattered **a** the world.
13:4 took off his robe, wrapped a towel **a** his waist,
13:5 and to wipe them with the towel he had **a** him.
18:18 and the household servants were standing **a** a
21:20 Peter turned **a** and saw the disciple Jesus loved
Ac 5:16 Crowds came in from the villages **a** Jerusalem,
6:3 "Now look **a** among yourselves, friends,
9:35 to the Lord when they saw Aeneas walking **a**.
10:38 Then Jesus went **a** doing good and healing all who
13:11 and he began wandering **a** begging for someone to
13:18 forty years of wandering **a** in the wilderness.
14:20 But as the believers stood **a** him, he got up
16:25 **A** midnight, Paul and Silas were praying
19:27 the province of Asia and all **a** the world—
22:6 bright light from heaven suddenly shone **a** me.
24:18 There was no crowd **a** me and no rioting.
25:7 the Jewish leaders from Jerusalem gathered **a**
2Co 4:5 We don't go **a** preaching about ourselves;
12:14 It's the other way **a**; parents supply food for their
Tit 2:3 They must not go **a** speaking evil of others
Heb 11:30 It was by faith that the people of Israel marched **a**
Jas 3:3 We can make a large horse turn **a** and go wherever
1Pe 5:8 He prowls **a** like a roaring lion, looking for some
2Pe 1:4 the decadence all **a** you caused by evil desires
2:7 sick of all the immorality and wickedness **a** him.
3:11 Since everything **a** us is going to melt away,
3:16 and unstable have twisted his letters **a** to mean
1Jn 5:19 and that the world **a** us is under the power
Rev 4:6 the center and **a** the throne were four living beings,
5:11 and millions of angels **a** the throne and the living
6:8 of its rider, who was followed **a** by the Grave.
7:11 And all the angels were standing **a** the throne
7:11 and **a** the elders and the four living beings.
16:19 and cities **a** the world fell into heaps of rubble.

AROUSE (4) [ROUSE]

Nu 24:9 and lies down; / like a lioness, who dares to **a** her?
Dt 4:25 sight of the LORD your God and will **a** his anger.
1Ki 16:33 He did more to **a** the anger of the LORD, the God
Jer 44:8 Why **a** my anger by burning incense to the idols

AROUSED (9) [ROUSE]

1Ki 15:30 because Jeroboam had **a** the anger of the LORD,
16:2 You have **a** my anger by causing my people to sin.
16:26 Thus, he **a** the anger of the LORD, the God of
2Ch 28:25 In this way, he **a** the anger of the LORD, the God
Job 17:8 see me. The innocent are **a** against the ungodly.
Ps 78:65 like a mighty man **a** from a drunken stupor.
SS 8:5 "I **a** you under the apple tree, where your mother
Ro 7:5 and the law **a** these evil desires that produced
7:8 and **a** all kinds of forbidden desires within me!

AROUSING (8) [ROUSE]

1Ki 14:22 **a** his anger with their sin, for it was even worse
16:7 **a** him to anger by his sins, just like the family of
16:13 **a** the anger of the LORD, the God of Israel,
22:53 **a** the anger of the LORD, the God of Israel,
2Ki 17:11 had done many evil things, **a** the LORD's anger.
17:17 and sold themselves to evil, **a** the LORD's anger.
21:6 that was evil in the LORD's sight, **a** his anger.
2Ch 33:6 that was evil in the LORD's sight, **a** his anger.

ARPAD (6)

2Ki 18:34 What happened to the gods of Hamath and **A**?
19:13 happened to the king of Hamath and the king of **A**?
Isa 10:9 Hamath will fall before us as **A** did.
36:19 What happened to the gods of Hamath and **A**?
37:13 happened to the king of Hamath and the king of **A**?
Jer 49:23 "The towns of Hamath and **A** are struck with fear,

ARPHAXAD (11)

Ge 10:22 of Shem were Elam, Asshur, **A**, Lud, and Aram.
10:24 **A** was the father of Shelah, and Shelah was the
11:10 Shem was 100 years old, his son **A** was born.
11:11 After the birth of **A**, Shem lived another 500 years
11:12 When **A** was 35 years old, his son Shelah was
11:13 **A** lived another 403 years and had other sons
1Ch 1:17 of Shem were Elam, Asshur, **A**, Lud, and Aram.
1:18 **A** was the father of Shelah. Shelah was the father
1:24 the family line descended from Shem: **A**, Shelah,
Lk 3:36 Cainan was the son of **A**. / **A** was the son of Shem.

ARRANGE (10) [ARRANGED, ARRANGEMENT, ARRANGEMENTS, ARRANGES, ARRANGING, PREARRANGED]

Ex 40:4 Then bring in the table, and **a** the utensils on it.
Lev 6:12 the fire and **a** the daily whole burnt offering on it.
24:3 and must **a** to have the lamps tended continually,
24:6 and **a** the loaves in two rows, with six in each row.
1Ki 2:9 and you will know how to **a** a bloody death for
2Ki 18:32 Then I will **a** to take you to another land like this
Ps 109:6 **A** for an evil person to turn on him. / Send an
Isa 36:17 Then I will **a** to take you to another land like this
Mk 14:10 went to the leading priests to **a** to betray Jesus to
Ac 25:21 So I ordered him back to jail until I could **a** to send

ARRANGED (15) [ARRANGE]

Ge 21:21 and his mother **a** a marriage for him with a young
33:2 Jacob now **a** his family into a column, with his two
38:6 Judah **a** his marriage to a young woman named
Ex 40:23 And he **a** the Bread of the Presence on the table
2Sa 17:14 For the LORD had **a** to defeat the counsel of
1Ki 4:7 Each of them **a** provisions for one month of the

7:39 He **a** five water carts on the south side of the
1Ch 16:37 David **a** for Asaph and his fellow Levites to
2Ch 11:23 and **a** for each of them to have several wives.
18: 1 and he **a** for his son to marry the daughter of King
Eze 42:10 These rooms were **a** just like the rooms on the
Jnh 1:17 Now the LORD had **a** for a great fish to swallow
4: 6 And the LORD God **a** for a leafy plant to grow
Ac 16: 3 he **a** for Timothy to be circumcised before they
20:13 land to Assos, where he had **a** for us to join him,

ARRANGEMENT (1) [ARRANGE]

Jos 9:27 choose to build it. That **a** continues to this day.

ARRANGEMENTS (4) [ARRANGE]

Jdg 14:10 As his father was making final **a** for the marriage,
2Sa 17:17 **A** had been made for a servant girl to bring them
Eze 40:36 as in the others and the same window **a**.
Mk 14:13 sent two of them into Jerusalem to make the **a**.

ARRANGES (1) [ARRANGE]

Ex 21: 9 And if the slave girl's owner **a** for her to marry his

ARRANGING (1) [ARRANGE]

2Ch 25:20 for God was **a** to destroy him for worshiping the

ARRAY (2) [ARRAYED]

Jos 11: 4 along with a vast **a** of horses and chariots,
1Ch 12:38 All these men came in battle **a** to Hebron with the

ARRAYED (2) [ARRAY]

Job 6: 4 my spirit. All God's terrors are **a** against me.
Ps 110: 3 will serve you willingly. / **A** in holy garments,

ARREST (31) [ARRESTED]

1Sa 19:14 When the troops came to **a** David, she told them he
1Ki 22:26 "**A** Micaiah and take him back to Amon,
2Ki 1: 9 sent an army captain with fifty soldiers to **a** him.
2Ch 18:25 "**A** Micaiah and take him back to Amon,
Ne 13:21 the wall? If you do this again, I will **a** you!"
Jer 36:26 and Shelemiah son of Abdeel to **a** Baruch
37:13 The sentry making the **a** was Irijah son of
Da 6:24 Then the king gave orders to **a** the men who had
Mt 21:46 They wanted to **a** him, but they were afraid to try
26:48 "You will know which one to **a** when I go over
26:55 have come armed with swords and clubs to **a** me?
Why didn't you **a** me in the Temple?
Mk 6:17 For Herod had sent soldiers to **a** and imprison John
12:12 The Jewish leaders wanted to **a** him for using this
14:44 "You will know which one to **a** when I go over
14:48 you come armed with swords and clubs to **a** me?
14:49 Why didn't you **a** me in the Temple? I was there
Lk 20:19 they wanted to **a** Jesus immediately because they
20:20 to the Roman governor so he would **a** Jesus.
22: 6 so they could **a** him quietly when the crowds
22:52 have come armed with swords and clubs to **a** me?
22:53 Why didn't you **a** me in the Temple? I was there
Jn 7:30 Then the leaders tried to **a** him; but no one laid a
7:32 and the leading priests sent Temple guards to **a**
7:45 The Temple guards who had been sent to **a** him
10:39 Once again they tried to **a** him, but he got away
11:57 must report him immediately so they could **a** him.
Ac 1:16 who guided the Temple police to **a** Jesus.
9: 2 asking their cooperation in the **a** of any followers
9:14 leading priests to **a** every believer in Damascus."
9:21 "And we understand that he came here to **a** them

ARRESTED (35) [ARREST]

Ex 2:15 he gave orders to have Moses **a** and killed.
2Ki 17: 4 he **a** him and put him in prison for his rebellion.
Jer 20: 2 So he **a** Jeremiah the prophet and had him whipped
37:13 a sentry **a** him and said, "You are defecting to the
Da 6:16 So at last the king gave orders for Daniel to be **a**
Mt 4:12 When Jesus heard that John had been **a**, he left
10:19 When you are **a**, don't worry about what to say in
14: 3 For Herod had **a** and imprisoned John as a favor to
18:30 He had the man **a** and jailed until the debt could be
24: 9 "Then you will be **a**, persecuted, and killed.
26:50 Then the others grabbed Jesus and **a** him.
26:57 Then the people who had **a** Jesus led him to the
27:18 (He knew very well that the Jewish leaders had **a**
Mk 1:14 Later on, after John was **a** by Herod Antipas,
12:13 into saying something for which he could be **a**.
13:11 But when you are **a** and stand trial, don't worry
14:46 Then the others grabbed Jesus and **a** him.
15:10 that the leading priests had **a** Jesus out of envy.)
Lk 20:19 But they were afraid there would be a riot if they **a**
22:54 So they **a** him and led him to the high priest's
24:20 leading priests and other religious leaders **a** him
Jn 7:44 And some wanted him **a**, but no one touched him.
8:20 But he was not **a**, because his time had not yet
18:12 and the Temple guards **a** Jesus and tied him up.
18:36 my followers would have fought when I was **a** by
Ac 4: 3 They **a** them and, since it was already evening,
5:18 They **a** the apostles and put them in the jail.
5:26 captain went with his Temple guards and **a** them,
6:12 So they **a** Stephen and brought him before the high
12: 3 he **a** Peter during the Passover celebration
21:33 The commander **a** him and ordered him bound
24: 6 he was trying to defile the Temple when we **a** him.
26:21 Some Jews **a** me in the Temple for preaching this,
28:17 I was **a** in Jerusalem and handed over to the
Rev 13:10 The people who are destined for prison will be **a**

ARRIVAL (24) [ARRIVE]

Ge 26:24 the LORD appeared to him on the night of his **a**.
29:13 As soon as Laban heard about Jacob's **a**, he rushed
41:50 before the **a** of the first of the famine years,
43:25 so they prepared their gifts for Joseph's **a** at noon.
47:28 Jacob lived for seventeen years after his **a** in
Ru 1:19 the entire town was stirred by their **a**.
1Sa 22: 6 The news of his **a** in Judah soon reached Saul.
26: 3 David was hiding. But David knew of Saul's **a**,
1Ch 12:39 had been made by their relatives for their **a**.
Ezr 8:33 On the fourth day after our **a**, the silver, gold,
Ne 2:10 and Tobiah the Ammonite official heard of my **a**,
2:11 Three days after my **a** at Jerusalem,
Isa 14: 9 place of the dead there is excitement over your **a**.
Hos 6: 3 Then he will respond to us as surely as the **a** of
Mt 14:35 The news of their **a** spread quickly throughout the
17:24 On their **a** in Capernaum, the tax collectors for the
Mk 2: 1 and the news of his **a** spread quickly through the
7:24 he couldn't. As usual, the news of his **a** spread fast.
Lk 1:17 coming of the Lord, preparing the people for his **a**.
9:52 ahead to a Samaritan village to prepare for his **a**.
Jn 12: 9 When all the people heard of Jesus' **a**,
Ac 25: 7 On Paul's **a** in court, the Jewish leaders from
28:17 Three days after Paul's **a**, he called together the
2Co 7: 6 are discouraged, encouraged us by the **a** of Titus.

ARRIVE (34) [ARRIVAL, ARRIVED, ARRIVES, ARRIVING]

Ge 29: 3 for all the flocks to **a** before removing the stone.
Ex 4:21 "When you **a** back in Egypt, go to Pharaoh
12:25 When you **a** in the land the LORD has promised
Lev 14:34 "When you **a** in Canaan, the land I am giving you
23:10 "When you **a** in the land I am giving you and you
Nu 10: 9 "When you **a** in your own land and go to war
15:18 When you **a** in the land where I am taking you,
Dt 4: 5 and regulations when you **a** in the land you are
7:13 When you **a** in the land he swore to give your
12: 9 when you **a** in the place of rest the LORD your
14:26 When you **a**, use the money to buy anything you
15: 7 **a** in the land the LORD your God is giving you,
17:14 "You will soon **a** in the land the LORD your God
18: 9 "When you **a** in the land the LORD your God is
19:14 "When you **a** in the land the LORD your God is
26: 1 "When you **a** in the land the LORD your God is
32:35 their feet will slip. / Their day of disaster will **a**,
1Sa 10: 5 "When you **a** at Gibeah of God,
10: 8 When I **a**, I will give you further instructions."
13:11 and you didn't **a** when you said you would,
2Sa 19:17 They rushed down to the Jordan to **a** ahead of the
1Ki 19:15 When you **a** there, anoint Hazael to be king of
Pr 18: 3 When the wicked **a**, contempt, shame, and disgrace
Isa 13:22 are numbered; its time of destruction will soon **a**.
Da 11:34 these persecutions are going on, a little help will **a**.
Joel 3:14 It is there that the day of the LORD will soon **a**.
Zec 6:10 As soon as they **a**, meet them at the home of Josiah
Mt 24:30 And they will see the Son of Man **a** on the clouds
Mk 9: 1 you see the Kingdom of God **a** in great power!"
13:26 Then everyone will see the Son of Man **a** on the
Lk 21:27 Then everyone will see the Son of Man **a** on the
Ac 9:11 of Judas. When you **a**, ask for Saul of Tarsus.
23:35 will hear your case myself when your accusers **a**,"
1Co 11:34 you instructions about the other matters after I **a**.

ARRIVED (275) [ARRIVE]

Ge 12: 5 his household at Haran—and finally **a** in Canaan.
12:14 And sure enough, when they **a** in Egypt,
14: 5 One year later, Kedorlaomer and his allies **a**.
16: 3 (This happened ten years after Abram first **a** in the
19: 1 city of Sodom, and Lot was sitting there as they **a**.
22: 9 When they **a** at the place where God had told
24:15 a young woman named Rebekah **a** with a water jug
25:29 Esau **a** home exhausted and hungry from a hunt.
26:26 King Abimelech **a** with his adviser, Ahuzzath,
28:11 At sundown he **a** at a good place to set up camp
29: 9 Rachel **a** with her father's sheep, for she was a
33:18 Then they **a** safely at Shechem, in Canaan,
34: 7 He **a** just as Jacob's sons were coming in from the
35: 6 Finally, they **a** at Luz (now called Bethel)
35: 9 God appeared to Jacob once again when he **a** at
37:15 When he **a** there, a man noticed him wandering
37:23 So when Joseph **a**, they pulled off his beautiful
38:27 In due season the time of Tamar's delivery **a**,
39: 1 Now when Joseph **a** in Egypt with the Ishmaelite
42: 5 So Jacob's sons **a** in Egypt along with others to
43:19 As the brothers **a** at the entrance to the palace,
44:14 was still at home when Judah and his brothers **a**,
46: 6 Jacob and his entire family **a** in Egypt—
46:28 to the land of Goshen. And when they all **a** there,
46:29 As soon as Joseph **a**, he embraced his father
48: 2 When Jacob heard that Joseph had **a**, he gathered
48: 5 who were born here in the land of Egypt before I **a**.
50:10 When they **a** at the threshing floor of Atad,
Ex 2:15 When Moses **a** in Midian, he sat down beside a
10:13 When morning **a**, the east wind had brought the
16: 1 They **a** there a month after leaving Egypt.
16:13 That evening vast numbers of quail **a** and covered
16:35 for forty years until they **a** in the land of Canaan,
18: 5 They **a** while Moses and the people were camped
19: 1 The Israelites **a** in the wilderness of Sinai exactly
Nu 10:13 When the time to move **a**, the LORD gave the
10:21 When they **a** at the next camp, the Tabernacle
13:22 passed first through the Negev and **a** at Hebron,
13:27 "We **a** in the land you sent us to see, and it is
20: 1 In early spring the people of Israel **a** in the
20:22 Israel left Kadesh as a group and **a** at Mount Hor.
22: 5 "A vast horde of people has **a** from Egypt.
Dt 1:19 of the Amorites. When we **a** at Kadesh-barnea,
2:14 **a** at Kadesh-barnea until we finally crossed Zered
11: 5 cared for you in the wilderness until you **a** here.
15: 2 or relatives, for the LORD's time of release has **a**.
32:17 had not known before, / to gods only recently **a**,
Jos 3: 1 left Acacia and **a** at the banks of the Jordan River,
9: 6 When they **a** at the camp of Israel at Gilgal,
10:33 King Horam of Gezer had **a** with his army to help
22:15 When they **a** in the land of Gilead, they said to the
24: 6 But when your ancestors **a** at the Red Sea,
Jdg 3:27 When he **a** in the hill country of Ephraim,
6: 5 **a** on droves of camels too numerous to count.
11:16 When the people of Israel **a** at Kadesh on their
14: 7 When Samson **a** in Timnah, he talked with the
15:14 As Samson **a** at Lehi, the Philistines came shouting
17: 8 **a** in that area of Ephraim, looking for a good place
18: 2 When these warriors **a** in the hill country of
19: 3 When he **a** at her father's house, she took him
20:15 **a** in Gibeah to join the seven hundred warriors who
Ru 1:22 They **a** in Bethlehem at the beginning of the barley
2: 4 Boaz **a** from Bethlehem and greeted the harvesters.
1Sa 4: 6 told it was because the Ark of the LORD had **a**,
4:12 the battlefront and **a** at Shiloh later that same day.
4:13 When the messenger **a** and told what had
5: 9 But when the Ark **a** at Gath, the LORD began
7:10 the burnt offering, the Philistines **a** for battle.
9:12 He has just **a** to take part in a public sacrifice up on
10:10 When Saul and his servant **a** at Gibeah, they saw
11: 9 there was throughout the city when that message **a**!
11:11 But before dawn the next morning, Saul **a**,
13:10 was finishing with the burnt offering, Samuel **a**.
15:32 Agag **a** full of smiles, for he thought,
16: 4 When he **a** at Bethlehem, the leaders of the town
16: 6 When they **a**, Samuel took one look at Eliab
17:20 He **a** at the outskirts of the camp just as the
19:20 But when they **a** and saw Samuel and the other
19:22 went to Ramah and **a** at the great well in Secu.
22:12 When they **a**, Saul shouted at him, "Listen to me,
25:36 When Abigail **a** home, she found that Nabal had
25:40 When the messengers **a** at Carmel, they told
30: 1 and his men **a** home at their town of Ziklag,
30:16 When David and his men **a**, the Amalekites were
30:26 When he **a** at Ziklag, David sent part of the
2Sa 1: 2 a man **a** from the Israelite battlefront.
2:24 The sun was just going down as they **a** at the hill
2:29 and they did not stop until they **a** at Mahanaim.
3:27 When Abner **a** at Hebron, Joab took him aside at
4: 8 They **a** at Hebron and presented Ishbosheth's head
5:18 The Philistines **a** and spread out across the valley
6: 6 But when they **a** at the threshing floor of Nacon,
8: 5 When Arameans from Damascus **a** to help
10: 2 But when David's ambassadors **a** in the land of
10:16 These troops **a** at Helam under the command of
11: 7 When Uriah **a**, David asked him how Joab
12: 4 One day a guest **a** at the home of the rich man.
13: 8 When Tamar **a** at Amnon's house, she went to the
13:32 **a** and said, "No, not all your sons have been
13:36 They soon **a**, weeping and sobbing, and the king
15:13 A messenger soon **a** in Jerusalem to tell King
15:20 You **a** only yesterday, and now should I force you
15:37 to Jerusalem, getting there just as Absalom **a**.
16:15 Meanwhile, Absalom and his men **a** at Jerusalem,
16:16 When David's friend Hushai the Arkite **a**, he went
17: 6 When Hushai **a**, Absalom told him what
17:20 When Absalom's men **a**, they asked her,
17:24 David soon **a** at Mahanaim. By now, Absalom had
17:27 When David **a** at Mahanaim, he was warmly
18:31 Then the man from Cush **a** and said, "I have good
19:15 And when he **a** at the Jordan River, the people of
19:24 **a** from Jerusalem to meet the king.
19:31 Barzillai the Gileadite now **a** from Rogelim to
20: 3 When the king **a** at his palace in Jerusalem,
20: 8 As they **a** at the great stone in Gibeon, Amasa met
20:15 When Joab's forces **a**, they attacked
1Ki 1:22 still speaking with the king, Nathan the prophet **a**.
1:42 Jonathan son of Abiathar the priest **a**.
8: 3 When all the leaders of Israel **a**, the priests picked
10: 2 She **a** in Jerusalem with a large group of attendants
10: 7 I didn't believe it until I **a** here and saw it with my
12:21 When Rehoboam **a** at Jerusalem, he mobilized the
13: 1 and he **a** there just as Jeroboam was approaching
17:10 As he **a** at the gates of the village, he saw a widow
20:33 And when Ben-hadad **a**, Ahab invited him up into
22:15 When Micaiah **a** before the king, Ahab asked him,
22:35 to the floor of his chariot, and as evening **a** he died.
2Ki 3:24 When they **a** at the Israelite camp, the army of
4:12 the woman I want to speak to her." When she **a**,
4:32 When Elisha **a**, the child was indeed dead,
5:22 from the hill country of Ephraim have just **a**.
5:24 But when they **a** at the hill, Gehazi took the gifts
6: 4 When they **a** at the Jordan, they began cutting
6:32 But before the messenger **a**, Elisha said to the
6:33 While Elisha was still saying this, the messenger **a**.
7: 8 When the lepers **a** at the edge of the camp,
9: 5 When he **a** there, he found Jehu sitting in a
10: 7 When the letter **a**, the leaders killed all seventy of
10:17 When Jehu **a** in Samaria, he killed everyone who
17:25 did not worship the LORD when they first **a**,
24:11 Nebuchadnezzar himself **a** at the city during the
25: 8 an official of the Babylonian king, **a** in Jerusalem.
1Ch 13: 9 But when they **a** at the threshing floor of Nacon,
14: 9 The Philistines had **a** in the valley of Rephaim
18: 5 When Arameans from Damascus **a** to help
19: 2 But when David's ambassadors **a** in the land of
19:16 These troops **a** under the command of Shobach,
20: 2 When David **a** at Rabbah, he removed the crown

2Ch 5: 4 When all the leaders of Israel **a**, the Levites moved
9: 1 She **a** with a large group of attendants and a great
9: 6 I didn't believe it until I **a** here and saw it with my
11: 1 When Rehoboam **a** at Jerusalem, he mobilized the
13: 4 When the army of Judah **a** in the hill country of
18: 14 When Micaiah **a** before the king, Ahab asked him,
19: 1 When King Jehoshaphat of Judah **a** safely home to
20: 7 those who lived in this land when your people **a**?
20: 24 So when the army of Judah **a** at the lookout point
28: 20 So when King Tiglath-pileser of Assyria **a**,
32: 23 and many gifts for the LORD **a** at Jerusalem,
32: 31 when ambassadors **a** from Babylon to ask about
Ezr 2: 68 When they **a** at the Temple of the LORD in
3: 8 during the second year after they **a** in Jerusalem.
5: 3 and their colleagues soon **a** in Jerusalem
7: 8 Ezra **a** in Jerusalem in August of that year.
8: 15 the lists of the people and the priests who had **a**.
8: 32 So at last we **a** safely in Jerusalem, where we
Ne 1: 2 with some other men who had just **a** from Judah.
13: 7 When I **a** back in Jerusalem and learned the extent
Est 6: 4 Haman had just **a** in the outer court of the palace to
6: 14 the king's eunuchs **a** to take Haman to the banquet
8: 17 and province, wherever the king's decree **a**,
Job 1: 14 a messenger **a** at Job's home with this news:
1: 16 still speaking, another messenger **a** with this news:
1: 17 still speaking, a third messenger **a** with this news:
1: 18 still speaking, another messenger **a** with this news:
15: 19 the land was given long before any foreigners **a**.
Ps 105: 23 Then Israel **a** in Egypt; / Jacob lived as a foreigner
Isa 13: 6 Scream in terror, for the LORD's time has **a**—
Jer 25: 34 The time of your slaughter has **a**; you will fall
35: 11 But when King Nebuchadnezzar of Babylon **a** in
39: 4 so they fled when the darkness of night **a**.
41: 1 **a** in Mizpah accompanied by ten men.
41: 5 eighty men **a** from Shechem, Shiloh, and Samaria.
50: 31 LORD Almighty. "Your day of reckoning has **a**.
52: 12 an official of the Babylonian king, **a** in Jerusalem.
Eze 7: 6 The end has come! It has finally **a**! Your final
23: 40 Then when they **a**, you bathed yourselves,
33: 22 so I would be able to speak when this man **a** the
Da 3: 3 When all these officials had **a** and were standing
7: 22 Then the time **a** for the holy people to take over the
Am 2: 9 I destroyed the Amorites before my people **a** in the
Zep 3: 17 For the LORD your God has **a** to live among you.
Zec 10: 3 For the LORD Almighty has **a** to look after his
Mt 2: 1 some wise men from eastern lands **a** in Jerusalem,
8: 5 When Jesus **a** in Capernaum, a Roman officer
8: 14 When Jesus **a** at Peter's house,
8: 28 When Jesus **a** on the other side of the lake in the
9: 23 When Jesus **a** at the official's home, he noticed the
12: 28 then the Kingdom of God has **a** among you.
15: 1 and teachers of religious law now **a** from
17: 14 When they **a** at the foot of the mountain, a huge
26: 47 **a** with a mob that was armed with swords
Mk 2: 3 Four men **a** carrying a paralyzed man on a mat.
3: 22 But the teachers of religious law who had **a** from
3: 31 and brothers **a** at the house where he was teaching.
5: 1 So they **a** at the other side of the lake, in the land
5: 35 messengers **a** from Jairus' home with the message,
6: 53 When they **a** at Gennesaret on the other side of the
7: 1 and teachers of religious law **a** from Jerusalem to
7: 30 And when she **a** home, her little girl was lying
8: 11 When the Pharisees heard that Jesus had **a**,
8: 22 When they **a** at Bethsaida, some people brought a
9: 33 After they **a** at Capernaum, Jesus and his disciples
11: 15 When they **a** back in Jerusalem, Jesus entered the
11: 27 By this time they had **a** in Jerusalem again.
14: 17 In the evening Jesus **a** with the twelve disciples.
14: 43 **a** with a mob that was armed with swords
14: 45 As soon as they **a**, Judas walked up to Jesus.
16: 4 But when they **a**, they looked up and saw that the
Lk 7: 6 But just before they **a** at the house, the officer sent
8: 26 So they **a** in the land of the Gerasenes,
8: 49 a messenger **a** from Jairus' home with the
8: 51 When they **a** at the house, Jesus wouldn't let
11: 6 'A friend of mine has just **a** for a visit, and I have
11: 20 then the Kingdom of God has **a** among you.
15: 6 When you **a**, you would call together your friends
21: 20 you will know that the time of its destruction has **a**.
22: 7 Now the Festival of Unleavened Bread **a**,
24: 33 When they **a**, they were greeted with the report,
Jn 4: 27 Just then his disciples **a**. They were astonished to
4: 46 he **a** at the town of Cana, where he had turned the
6: 21 and immediately the boat **a** at their destination!
6: 25 When they **a** and found him, they asked, "Teacher,
11: 17 When Jesus **a** at Bethany, he was told that Lazarus
11: 32 When Mary **a** and saw Jesus, she fell down at his
11: 55 and many people from the country **a** in Jerusalem
12: 1 Jesus **a** in Bethany, the home of Lazarus—
18: 3 lanterns, and weapons, they **a** at the olive grove.
20: 6 Then Simon Peter **a** and went inside. He also
Ac 5: 21 When the high priest and his officials **a**,
5: 25 Then someone **a** with the news that the men they
8: 15 As soon as they **a**, they prayed for these new
9: 26 When Saul **a** in Jerusalem, he tried to meet with
9: 39 and as soon as he **a**, they took him to the upstairs
10: 24 They **a** in Caesarea the following day.
11: 2 But when Peter **a** back in Jerusalem, some of the
11: 11 then three men who had been sent from Caesarea **a**
11: 12 and we soon **a** at the home of the man who had
11: 23 When he **a** and saw this proof of God's favor,
12: 21 When the day **a**, Herod put on his royal robes,
14: 19 Now some Jews **a** from Antioch and Iconium
15: 1 some men from Judea **a** and began to teach the
15: 4 When they **a** in Jerusalem, Paul and Barnabas were
17: 10 When they **a** there, they went to the synagogue.
18: 2 who had recently **a** from Italy with his wife,
18: 19 When they **a** at the port of Ephesus, Paul left the
18: 24 had just **a** in Ephesus from Alexandria in Egypt.
18: 27 When he **a** there, he proved to be of great benefit
20: 6 in Macedonia and five days later **a** in Troas,
20: 15 island of Samos. And a day later we **a** at Miletus.
20: 18 When they **a** he declared, "You know that from
21: 10 who also had the gift of prophecy, **a** from Judea.
23: 27 and they were about to kill him when I **a** with the
23: 33 When they **a** in Caesarea, they presented Paul
24: 1 **a** with some of the Jewish leaders and the lawyer
24: 11 ago that I **a** in Jerusalem to worship at the Temple.
25: 1 Three days after Festus **a** in Caesarea to take over
25: 13 A few days later King Agrippa **a** with his sister,
25: 23 and Bernice **a** at the auditorium with great pomp,
27: 8 with great difficulty and finally **a** at Fair Havens,
28: 16 When we **a** in Rome, Paul was permitted to have
28: 21 from Judea or reports from anyone who has **a** here.
2Co 2: 13 because my dear brother Titus hadn't yet **a** with a
7: 5 When we **a** in Macedonia there was no rest for us.
Gal 2: 12 When he first **a**, he ate with the Gentile Christians,

ARRIVES (16) [ARRIVE]

Lev 25: 54 been redeemed by the time the Year of Jubilee **a**,
1Sa 9: 13 The guests won't start until he **a** to bless the
16: 11 "We will not sit down to eat until he **a**."
2Sa 15: 14 If we get out of the city before he **a**, both we
2Ki 6: 32 When he **a**, shut the door and keep him out.
Job 6: 17 But when the hot weather **a**, the water disappears.
Eze 24: 27 And when he **a**, your voice will suddenly return
32: 31 "When Pharaoh **a**, he will be relieved to find that
Joel 2: 31 before that great and terrible day of the LORD **a**.
Zec 9: 16 When that day **a**, the LORD their God will rescue
Mal 4: 5 before the great and dreadful day of the LORD **a**.
Mk 13: 36 Don't let him find you sleeping when he **a** without
Lk 12: 36 and let him in the moment he **a** and knocks.
Ac 2: 20 before that great and glorious day of the Lord **a**.
24: 22 "Wait until Lysias, the garrison commander, **a**.
Tit 3: 12 As soon as one of them **a**, do your best to meet me

ARRIVING (2) [ARRIVE]

Ge 29: 1 Jacob hurried on, finally **a** in the land of the east.
Ac 14: 27 Upon **a** in Antioch, they called the church together

ARROGANCE (13) [ARROGANT]

1Sa 2: 3 so proud and haughty! / Don't speak with such **a**!
2Ki 19: 28 And because of your **a** against me, / which I have
Ps 75: 5 at the heavens / or speak with rebellious **a**.' "
94: 4 Hear their **a**! / How these evildoers boast!
Pr 8: 13 I hate pride, **a**, corruption, and perverted speech.
21: 24 are proud and haughty; they act with boundless **a**.
Isa 2: 17 The **a** of all people will be brought low.
9: 9 will soon discover it. In their pride and **a** they say,
13: 11 I will crush the **a** of the proud and the haughtiness
37: 29 And because of your **a** against me, / which I have
Jer 48: 29 know of her loftiness, her **a**, and her haughty heart.
Hos 5: 5 "The **a** of Israel testifies against her; she will
7: 10 His **a** testifies against him, yet he doesn't return to

ARROGANT (26) [ARROGANCE, ARROGANTLY]

Lev 26: 19 I will break down your **a** spirit by making the skies
Dt 17: 12 Anyone **a** enough to reject the verdict of the judge
Job 34: 7 "Has there ever been a man as **a** as Job, with his
Ps 31: 18 those proud and **a** lips that accuse the godly.
31: 23 to him, / but he harshly punishes all who are **a**.
73: 12 Look at these **a** people—/ enjoying a life of ease
83: 2 Don't you see what your **a** enemies are doing?
119: 69 **A** people have made up lies about me, / but in truth
119: 78 Bring disgrace upon the **a** people who lied about
119: 85 These **a** people who hate your law / have dug deep
119: 122 for me. / Don't let those who are **a** oppress me!
123: 4 scoffing of the proud / and the contempt of the **a**.
Isa 5: 15 In that day the **a** will be brought down to the dust;
10: 12 of Assyria and punish him—for he is proud and **a**.
26: 5 the proud / and brings the **a** city to the dust.
Eze 31: 10 Because it became proud and **a**, and because it set
33: 28 her pride. Her **a** power will come to an end.
Hab 2: 5 Wealth is treacherous, and the **a** are never at rest.
Zep 3: 4 Its prophets are **a** liars seeking their own gain.
3: 11 all the proud and **a** people from among you.
Mal 3: 15 From now on we will say, "Blessed are the **a**."
4: 1 The **a** and the wicked will be burned up like straw
1Co 4: 18 I know that some of you have become **a**, thinking I
4: 19 then I'll find out whether these **a** people are just
Tit 1: 7 He must not be **a** or quick-tempered; he must not
2Pe 2: 10 These people are proud and **a**, daring even to scoff

ARROGANTLY (6) [ARROGANT]

Dt 1: 43 and **a** went into the hill country to fight.
17: 13 will hear about it and be afraid to act so **a**.
Ne 9: 10 for you knew how **a** the Egyptians were treating
Ps 55: 12 bear that. / It is not my foes who so **a** insult me—
Da 7: 8 like human eyes and a mouth that was boasting **a**.
7: 20 had human eyes and a mouth that was boasting **a**.

ARROW (15) [ARROWHEAD, ARROWS]

1Sa 20: 36 the boy ran, and Jonathan shot an **a** beyond him.
20: 37 When the boy had almost reached the **a**,
20: 37 Jonathan shouted, "The **a** is still ahead of you.
1Ki 22: 34 however, randomly shot an **a** at the Israelite troops,
22: 34 and the **a** hit the king of Israel between the joints
2Ki 9: 24 The **a** pierced his heart, and he sank down dead in
13: 17 Then Elisha proclaimed, "This is the LORD's **a**,
2Ch 18: 33 however, randomly shot an **a** at the Israelite troops,
18: 33 and the **a** hit the king of Israel between the joints
Job 20: 24 He will try to escape, but God's **a** will pierce him.
20: 25 The **a** is pulled from his body, and the arrowhead
Pr 7: 23 awaiting the **a** that would pierce its heart. He was
25: 18 with a sword, or shooting them with a sharp **a**.
Isa 49: 2 of his hand. I am like a sharp **a** in his quiver.
Zec 9: 13 Judah is my bow, and Israel is my **a**! Jerusalem is

ARROWHEAD (1) [ARROW]

Job 20: 25 from his body, and the **a** glistens with blood.

ARROWS (54) [ARROW]

Ge 27: 3 and a quiver full of **a** out into the open country,
Ex 19: 13 boundary must be stoned to death or shot with **a**.
Nu 24: 8 their bones in pieces, / shooting them with **a**.
Dt 32: 23 upon them / and shoot them down with my **a**.
32: 42 I will make my **a** drunk with blood, / and my
1Sa 20: 20 and shoot three **a** to the side of the stone pile as
20: 21 Then I will send a boy to bring the **a** back. If you
20: 22 the **a** are still ahead of you,' then it will mean that
20: 35 and took a young boy with him to gather his **a**.
20: 36 the boy, "so you can find the **a** as I shoot them."
20: 38 So the boy quickly gathered up the **a** and ran back
20: 40 Then Jonathan gave his bow and **a** to the boy
2Sa 11: 24 the archers on the wall shot **a** at us. Some of our
22: 15 He shot his **a** and scattered his enemies;
2Ki 13: 15 Elisha told him, "Get a bow and some **a**."
13: 18 Now pick up the other **a** and strike them against
19: 32 armies will not enter Jerusalem to shoot their **a**.
1Ch 12: 2 and they could shoot **a** or sling stones with their
2Ch 26: 15 designed by brilliant men to shoot **a** and hurl
35: 23 But the enemy archers hit King Josiah with their **a**
Job 6: 4 For the Almighty has struck me down with his **a**.
6: 4 He has sent his poisoned **a** deep within my spirit.
16: 13 and his **a** pierced me without mercy.
39: 23 The **a** rattle against it, and the spear and javelin
41: 28 **A** cannot make it flee. Stones shot from a sling are
Ps 7: 13 his deadly weapons / and ignite his flaming **a**.
11: 2 their bows / and setting their **a** in the bowstrings.
18: 14 He shot his **a** and scattered his enemies;
21: 12 and run / when they see your **a** aimed at them.
38: 2 Your **a** have struck deep, / and your blows are
45: 5 Your **a** are sharp, / piercing your enemies' hearts.
57: 4 whose teeth pierce like spears and **a**,
64: 3 they wield; / bitter words are the **a** they aim.
64: 7 them down. / Suddenly, his **a** will pierce them.
76: 3 There he breaks the **a** of the enemy, / the shields
77: 17 crackled in the sky. / Your **a** of lightning flashed.
120: 4 You will be pierced with sharp **a** / and burned with
127: 4 a young man / are like sharp **a** in a warrior's hands.
144: 6 your enemies! / Release your **a** and confuse them!
Isa 5: 28 Their **a** will be sharp and their bows ready for
13: 18 armies will shoot down the young people with **a**.
21: 15 drawn swords and sharp **a** and the terrors of war.
37: 33 armies will not enter Jerusalem to shoot their **a**.
Jer 9: 8 For their tongues aim lies like poisoned **a**.
50: 9 The enemies' **a** will go straight to the mark;
50: 14 Spare no **a**, for she has sinned against the LORD.
51: 11 Sharpen the **a**! Lift up the shields! For the LORD
La 3: 13 He shot his **a** deep into my heart.
Eze 5: 16 "I will shower you with the deadly **a** of famine to
21: 21 They will cast lots by shaking **a** from the quiver.
39: 9 and large shields, bows and **a**, javelins and spears,
Hab 3: 11 obscured by brilliance from your **a** and the flashing
Zec 9: 14 above his people; his **a** will fly like lightning!
Eph 6: 16 shield to stop the fiery **a** aimed at you by Satan.

ARTAXERXES (14) [ARTAXERXES']

Ezr 4: 7 And even later during the reign of King **A** of
4: 7 sent a letter to **A** in the Aramaic language,
4: 8 telling King **A** about the situation in Jerusalem.
4: 11 "To **A**, from your loyal subjects in the province
4: 17 Then **A** made this reply: / "To Rehum the
4: 23 When this letter from King **A** was read to Rehum,
6: 14 by Cyrus, Darius, and **A**, the kings of Persia.
7: 1 years later, during the reign of King **A** of Persia,
7: 11 King **A** had presented a copy of this letter to Ezra,
7: 12 "Greetings from **A**, the king of kings, to Ezra the
7: 21 "I, **A** the king, hereby send this decree to all the
8: 1 with me from Babylon during the reign of King **A**:
Ne 5: 14 the thirty-second year of the reign of King **A**—
13: 6 year of the reign of King **A** of Babylon,

ARTAXERXES' (3) [ARTAXERXES]

Ezr 7: 7 with him in the seventh year of King **A** reign.
Ne 1: 1 In late autumn of the twentieth year of King **A**
2: 1 during the twentieth year of King **A** reign,

ARTEMAS (1)

Tit 3: 12 I am planning to send either **A** or Tychicus to you.

ARTEMIS (7)

Ac 19: 24 silver shrines of the Greek goddess **A**.
19: 27 great goddess **A** will lose its influence and that **A**
19: 28 began shouting, "Great is **A** of the Ephesians!"
19: 34 for two hours: "Great is **A** of the Ephesians! Great
is **A** of the Ephesians!"
19: 35 is the official guardian of the temple of the great **A**,

ARTFUL (1) [ARTS]

Isa 3: 18 The Lord will strip away their **a** beauty—

ARTICLE (1) [ARTICLES]
Ex 22: 9 donkey, sheep, a of clothing, or anything else.

ARTICLES (9) [ARTICLE]
Ex 11: 2 and women to ask their Egyptian neighbors for a
12:35 the Egyptians for clothing and a of silver and gold.
27:19 "All the a used in the work of the Tabernacle,
39:40 all the a used in the operation of the Tabernacle;
2Ki 12:13 or other a of gold or silver for the Temple of the
2Ch 24:12 who made a of iron and bronze for the LORD's
Ezr 8:27 2 fine a of polished bronze, as precious as gold.
Jer 27:18 Let them pray that these remaining a will not be
27:19 bronze water carts, and all the other ceremonial a.

ARTIFICER(S) [KJV] See CRAFTSMAN, CARPENTER, MAGICIAN

ARTILLERY [KJV] See BOW AND ARROWS

ARTS (4) [ARTFUL]
Ex 7:11 and they did the same thing with their secret a.
7:22 again the magicians of Egypt used their secret a,
8: 7 were able to do the same thing with their secret a.
8:18 tried to do the same thing with their secret a,

ARUBBOTH (1)
1Ki 4:10 Ben-hesed, in A, including Socoh and all the land

ARUMAH (2)
Jdg 9:31 He sent messengers to Abimelech in A,
9:41 Abimelech stayed in A, and Zebul drove Gaal

ARVAD (2) [ARVADITES]
Eze 27: 8 "Your oarsmen came from Sidon and A;
27:11 Men from A and from Helech stood on your walls

ARVADITES (2) [ARVAD]
Ge 10:18 A, Zemarites, and Hamathites.
1Ch 1:16 A, Zemarites, and Hamathites.

ARZA (1)
1Ki 16: 9 Elah was getting drunk at the home of A,

AS (4872) See Index of Articles, Etc.

ASA (41) [ASA'S]
1Ki 15: 8 of David. Then his son A became the next king.
15: 9 A began to rule over Judah in the twentieth year of
15:11 A did what was pleasing in the LORD's sight,
15:14 A remained faithful to the LORD throughout his
15:16 There was constant war between King A of Judah
15:18 A responded by taking all the silver and gold that
15:22 Then King A sent an order throughout Judah,
15:22 A used these materials to fortify the town of Geba
15:24 When A died, he was buried with his ancestors in
15:32 There was constant war between A and King
22:41 Jehoshaphat son of A began to rule over Judah in
22:43 good king, following the example of his father, A.
22:46 their practices from the days of his father, A.
1Ch 3:10 Solomon were Rehoboam, Abijah, A, Jehoshaphat,
9:16 and Berekiah son of A, son of Elkanah, who lived
2Ch 14: 1 of David. Then his son A became the next king.
14: 2 for A did what was pleasing and good in the sight
14: 5 A also removed the pagan shrines, as well as the
14: 7 A told the people of Judah, "Let us build towns
14: 8 King A had an army of 300,000 warriors from the
14:10 so A deployed his armies for battle in the valley
14:11 Then A cried out to the LORD his God,
14:12 defeated the Ethiopians in the presence of A
14:13 A and his army pursued them as far as Gerar,
15: 2 and he went out to meet King A as he was
15: 2 "Listen to me, A!" he shouted. "Listen, all you
15: 8 When A heard this message from Azariah the
15: 9 Then A called together all the people of Judah
15:16 King A even deposed his grandmother Maacah
15:17 A remained fully committed to the LORD
16: 2 A responded by taking the silver and gold from the
16: 6 Then King A called out all the men of Judah to
16: 6 A used these materials to fortify the towns of Geba
16: 7 At that time Hanani the seer came to King A
16:10 A became so angry with Hanani for saying this that
16:10 A also began to oppress some of his people.
16:12 of his reign, A developed a serious foot disease.
17: 2 of Ephraim that his father, A, had conquered.
20:32 a good king, following the ways of his father, A.
21:12 Jehoshaphat, or your grandfather King A of Judah.
Jer 41: 9 A when he fortified Mizpah to protect himself

ASA'S (20) [ASA]
1Ki 15:17 from entering or leaving King A territory in Judah.
15:20 Ben-hadad agreed to King A request and sent his
15:23 The rest of the events in A reign, the extent of his
15:25 Israel in the second year of King A reign in Judah.
15:28 Baasha killed Nadab in the third year of King A
15:33 Israel in the third year of King A reign in Judah.
16: 8 in the twenty-sixth year of King A reign in Judah.
16:10 the twenty-seventh year of King A reign in Judah.
16:15 the twenty-seventh year of King A reign in Judah,
16:23 in the thirty-first year of King A reign in Judah.
16:29 in the thirty-eighth year of King A reign in Judah.
2Ch 14: 5 So A kingdom enjoyed a period of peace.
15: 9 Many had moved to Judah during A reign when
15:10 in late spring, during the fifteenth year of A reign.
15:19 no more war until the thirty-fifth year of A reign.
16: 1 In the thirty-sixth year of A reign, King Baasha of
16: 1 from entering or leaving King A territory in Judah.
16: 4 Ben-hadad agreed to King A request and sent his
16:11 The rest of the events of A reign, from beginning
17: 1 Then Jehoshaphat, A son, became the next king.

ASAHEL (17) [ASAHEL'S]
2Sa 2:18 Joab, Abishai, and A, the three sons of Zeruiah,
2:18 David's forces that day. A could run like a deer,
2:20 saw him coming, he called out, "Is that you, A?"
2:21 But A refused and kept right on chasing Abner.
2:23 But A would not give up, so Abner thrust the butt
2:23 and stood still when they saw A lying there.
2:30 only nineteen men were missing, in addition to A.
3:27 killed Abner in revenge for killing his brother A.
3:30 because Abner had killed their brother A at the
23:24 of the Thirty included: / A, Joab's brother;
1Ch 2:16 had three sons named Abishai, Joab, and A.
11:26 A, Joab's brother; / Elhanan son of Dodo from
27: 7 A, the brother of Joab, was commander of the
27: 7 his division. A was succeeded by his son Zebadiah.
2Ch 17: 8 Nethaniah, Zebadiah, A, Shemiramoth,
31:13 Azaziah, Nahath, A, Jerimoth, Jozabad, Eliel,
Ezr 10:15 Only Jonathan son of A and Jahzeiah son of

ASAHEL'S (2) [ASAHEL]
2Sa 2:23 so Abner thrust the butt end of his spear through A
2:32 Joab and his men took A body to Bethlehem

ASAIAH (8)
2Ki 22:12 court secretary, and A the king's personal adviser:
22:14 and A went to the newer Mishneh section of
1Ch 4:36 Jaakobah, Jeshohaiah, A, Adiel, Jesimiel, Benaiah,
6:30 Shimea, Haggiah, and A.
9: 5 from the Shilonite clan, including A (the oldest)
15: 6 220 from the clan of Merari, with A as their leader.
15:11 Uriel, A, Joel, Shemaiah, Eliel, and Amminadab.
2Ch 34:20 court secretary, and A the king's personal adviser:

ASAPH (45) [ASAPH'S]
2Ki 18:18 and Joah son of A, the royal historian.
18:37 and Joah son of A, the royal historian, went back
1Ch 6:39 Heman's first assistant was A from the clan of
9:15 Mattaniah son of Mica, son of Zicri, son of A;
15:17 appointed Heman son of Joel, A son of Berekiah,
15:19 Heman, A, and Ethan were chosen to sound the
16: 5 A, the leader of this group, sounded the cymbals.
16: 7 That day David gave to A and his fellow Levites
16:37 David arranged for A and his fellow Levites to
25: 1 then appointed men from the families of A,
25: 2 From the sons of A, there were Zaccur, Joseph,
25: 2 They worked under the direction of their father, A,
25: 6 A, Jeduthun, and Heman reported directly to the
25: 9 The first lot fell to Joseph of the A clan and twelve
26: 1 was Meshelemiah son of Kore, of the family of A.
2Ch 5:12 A, Heman, Jeduthun, and all their sons
20:14 of Mattaniah, a Levite who was a descendant of A.
29:13 Shimri and Jeiel. / From the family of A:
29:30 LORD with the psalms of David and A the seer.
35:15 The musicians, descendants of A, were in their
35:15 A, Heman, and Jeduthun, the king's seer.
Ezr 2:41 The singers of the family of A | 128
3:10 And the Levites, descendants of A, clashed their
Ne 2: 8 And please send a letter to A, the manager of the
7:44 The singers of the family of A | 148
11:17 son of Mica, son of Zabdi, a descendant of A,
11:22 son of Mattaniah, son of Mica, a descendant of A,
12:35 son of Micaiah, son of Zaccur, a descendant of A.
12:46 to God began long ago in the days of David and A.
Ps 50: T A psalm of A.
73: T A psalm of A.
74: T A psalm of A.
75: T A psalm of A, to be sung to the tune "Do Not
76: T A psalm of A, to be accompanied by stringed
77: T For Jeduthun, the choir director: A psalm of A.
78: T A psalm of A.
79: T A psalm of A.
80: T A psalm of A, to be sung to the tune "Lilies of the
81: T A psalm of A, to be accompanied by a stringed
82: T A psalm of A.
83: T A psalm of A. A song.
Isa 36: 3 and Joah son of A, the royal historian.
36:22 and Joah son of A, the royal historian, went back
Mt 1: 7 the father of Abijah. / Abijah was the father of A.
1: 8 A was the father of Jehoshaphat. / Jehoshaphat was

ASAPH'S (1) [ASAPH]
1Ch 6:39 A genealogy was traced back through Berekiah,

ASAREL (1)
1Ch 4:16 sons of Jehallelel were Ziph, Ziphah, Tiria, and A.

ASARELAH (2)
1Ch 25: 2 there were Zaccur, Joseph, Nethaniah, and A.
25:14 The seventh lot fell to A and twelve of his sons

ASCEND (2) [ASCENDED, ASCENDING, ASCENDS, ASCENT]
Isa 14:13 'I will a to heaven and set my throne above God's
Rev 18:18 They will weep as they watch the smoke a,

ASCENDED (13) [ASCEND]
Jdg 13:20 the sky, the angel of the LORD a in the fire.
2Ki 25:27 Evil-merodach a to the Babylonian throne.
Ps 47: 5 God has a with a mighty shout. / The LORD has a with trumpets blaring.
68:18 When you a to the heights, / you led a crowd of
Jer 52:31 Evil-merodach a to the Babylonian throne.
Jn 20:17 Jesus said, "for I haven't yet a to the Father.
Ac 1: 2 until the day he a to heaven after giving his chosen
2:34 For David himself never a into heaven, yet he said,
Eph 4: 8 the Scriptures say, / "When he a to the heights,
4: 9 Notice that it says "he a." This means that Christ
4:10 The same one who came down is the one who a
Rev 8: 4 a up to God from the altar where the angel had

ASCENDING (1) [ASCEND]
Jn 20:17 and tell them that I am a to my Father and your

ASCENDS (1) [ASCEND]
Rev 19: 3 The smoke from that city a forever and forever!"

ASCENT (18) [ASCEND]
2Ki 9:27 So they shot Ahaziah in his chariot at the A of Gur,
2Ch 20:16 You will find them coming up through the a of Ziz
Ne 12:37 on the a of the city wall toward the City of David.
Ps 120: T A song for the a to Jerusalem.
121: T A song for the a to Jerusalem.
122: T A song for the a to Jerusalem. A psalm of David.
123: T A song for the a to Jerusalem.
124: T A song for the a to Jerusalem. A psalm of David.
125: T A song for the a to Jerusalem.
126: T A song for the a to Jerusalem.
127: T A song for the a to Jerusalem. A psalm of
128: T A song for the a to Jerusalem.
129: T A song for the a to Jerusalem.
130: T A song for the a to Jerusalem.
131: T A song for the a to Jerusalem. A psalm of David.
132: T A song for the a to Jerusalem.
133: T A song for the a to Jerusalem. A psalm of David.
134: T A song for the a to Jerusalem.

ASENATH (3)
Ge 41:45 a young woman named A, the daughter of
41:50 two sons were born to Joseph and his wife, A,
46:20 Their mother was A, daughter of Potiphera,

ASER [KJV] See ASHER

ASH (4) [ASHES]
Ex 27: 3 The a buckets, shovels, basins, meat hooks,
38: 3 the a buckets, shovels, basins, meat hooks,
Lev 4:12 He will burn it all on a wood fire in the a heap.
Jer 31:40 including the graveyard and a dump in the valley,

ASHAMED (52) [SHAME]
2Sa 19: 3 They crept back into the city as though they were a
19: 5 Yet you act like this, making us feel a, as though
2Ch 30:15 Then the priests and Levites became a, so they
Ezr 8:22 For I was a to ask the king for soldiers
9: 6 I prayed, "O my God, I am utterly a; I blush to lift
Job 11: 3 you mock God, shouldn't someone make you a?
19: 3 You should be a of dealing with me so harshly.
Ps 83:17 Let them be a and terrified forever. / Make them
119:46 to kings about your decrees, / and I will not be a.
119:80 your principles; / then I will never have to be a.
Isa 3: 9 They are not one bit a. How terrible it will be for
26:11 Perhaps then they will be a. / Let your fire
29:22 "My people will no longer pale with fear or be a.
41:11 all your angry enemies lie there, confused and a.
45:24 were angry with him will come to him and be a.
65:13 You will be sad and a, but they will rejoice.
Jer 6:15 Are they a when they do these disgusting things?
8:12 Are they a when they do these disgusting things?
22:22 at last you will see your wickedness and be a.
31:19 I was thoroughly a of all I did in my younger
48:13 At last Moab will be a of her idol Chemosh,
48:13 as Israel was a of her gold calf at Bethel.
51:51 "We are a," the people say. "We are insulted
Eze 16:39 leaving you completely naked and a.
16:52 You should be deeply a because your sins are
16:54 Then you will be truly a of everything you have
21:24 cries out against you, for you are not a of your sin.
36:32 you should be utterly a of all you have done!
43:10 and its plan so they will be a of all their sins.
43:11 And if they are a of what they have done,
Mic 1:11 of Shaphir, go as captives into exile—naked and a.
7:10 They will be a that they taunted me, saying,
Zep 3:11 then you will no longer need to be a of yourselves,
Mk 8:38 If a person is a of me and my message in these
8:38 will be a of that person when I return in the glory
Lk 9:26 If a person is a of me and my message, I, the Son
9:26 will be a of that person when I return in my glory
Ro 1:16 For I am not a of this Good News about Christ.
6:21 since now you are a of the things you used to do,
12:20 and they will be a of what they have done to you."
2Co 11:21 I'm a to say that we were not strong enough to do
2Th 3:14 this letter. Stay away from them so they will be a.
2Ti 1: 8 So you must never be a to tell others about our
1: 8 And don't be a of me, either, even though I'm in
1:12 But I am not a of it, for I know the one in whom I
1:16 He was never a of me because I was in prison.
2:15 one who does not need to be a and who correctly
Tit 2: 8 Then those who want to argue will be a

Heb 2:11 That is why Jesus is not **a** to call them his brothers
11:16 That is why God is not **a** to be called their God,
1Pe 3:16 they will be **a** when they see what a good life you
Rev 16:15 so they will not need to walk naked and **a**."

ASHAN (3) [BOR-ASHAN]

Jos 15:42 Besides these, there were Libnah, Ether, **A**,
19:7 It also included Ain, Rimmon, Ether, and **A**—
1Ch 4:32 also lived in Etam, Ain, Rimmon, Token, and **A**—

ASHBEL (3) [ASHBELITE]

Ge 46:21 Beker, **A**, Gera, Naaman, Ehi, Rosh, Muppim,
Nu 26:38 The Ashbelite clan, named after its ancestor **A**.
1Ch 8:1 order of age, included Bela (the oldest), **A**, Aharah,

ASHBELITE (1) [ASHBEL]

Nu 26:38 The **A** clan, named after its ancestor Ashbel.

ASHCHENAZ [KJV] See ASHKENAZ

ASHDOD (17) [ASHDODITES]

Jos 11:22 though some still remained in Gaza, Gath, and **A**.
13:4 cities of Gaza, **A**, Ashkelon, Gath, and Ekron.
15:46 and included the towns near **A** with their
15:47 It also included **A** with its towns and villages
1Sa 5:1 from the battleground at Ebenezer to the city of **A**.
5:3 But when the citizens of **A** went to see it the next
5:6 Then the LORD began to afflict the people of **A**
6:17 to the LORD were gifts from the rulers of **A**,
2Ch 26:6 and broke down the walls of Gath, Jabneh, and **A**.
26:6 Then he built new towns in the **A** area and in other
Ne 13:23 of the men of Judah had married women from **A**,
13:24 half their children spoke in the language of **A**
Isa 20:1 Sargon of Assyria captured the Philistine city of **A**,
Jer 25:20 of Ashkelon, Gaza, Ekron, and what remains of **A**.
Am 1:8 I will slaughter the people of **A** and destroy the
Zep 2:4 Gaza, Ashkelon, **A**, Ekron—these Philistine cities,
Zec 9:6 Foreigners will occupy the city of **A**. Thus, I will

ASHDODITES (1) [ASHDOD]

Ne 4:7 and **A** heard that the work was going ahead

ASHDOTHPISGAH [KJV] See PISGAH

ASHEN (1) [ASHEN-FACED]

Da 5:9 even more alarmed, and his face turned **a** white.

ASHEN-FACED (1) [ASHEN]

Jer 30:6 Then why do they stand there, **a**, hands pressed

ASHER (43) [ASHER'S]

Ge 30:13 and Leah named him **A**, for she said, "What joy is
35:26 sons of Zilpah, Leah's servant, were Gad and **A**.
46:17 The sons of **A** were Imnah, Ishvah, Ishvi,
49:20 "**A** will produce rich foods, / food fit for kings.
Ex 1:4 Dan, Naphtali, Gad, and **A**.
Nu 1:13 **A** | Pagiel son of Ocran
1:40[-41] **A** | 41,500
2:25[-26] "The divisions of Dan, **A**, and Naphtali are to
2:27[-28] **A** | Pagiel son of Ocran | 41,500
7:72 leader of the tribe of **A**, presented his offering.
10:26 The tribe of **A** was led by Pagiel son of Ocran.
13:13 **A** | Sethur son of Michael
26:44 were the clans descended from the sons of **A**:
26:46 **A** also had a daughter named Serah.
26:47 The men from all the clans of **A** numbered 53,400.
34:27 **A** | Ahihud son of Shelomi
Dt 27:13 And the tribes of Reuben, Gad, **A**, Zebulun, Dan,
33:24 Moses said this about the tribe of **A**: / "May **A** be blessed above other sons; / may he be
Jos 17:7 extended from the border of **A** to Micmethath,
17:10 North of Manasseh was the territory of **A**, and to
17:11 of Issachar and **A** were given to Manasseh:
19:24 of land went to the families of the tribe of **A**.
19:31 the inheritance of the families of the tribe of **A**.
19:34 the boundary of **A** on the west, and the Jordan
21:6 **A**, Naphtali, and the half-tribe of Manasseh in
21:30 From the tribe of **A** they received Mishal, Abdon,
Jdg 1:31 The tribe of **A** also failed to drive out the residents
1:32 dominated the land where the people of **A** lived.
5:17 did he stay home? / **A** sat unmoved at the seashore,
6:35 **A**, Zebulun, and Naphtali, summoning their
7:23 sent for the warriors of Naphtali, **A**, and Manasseh,
1Ki 4:16 Baana son of Hushai, in **A** and in Aloth.
1Ch 2:2 Dan, Joseph, Benjamin, Naphtali, Gad, and **A**.
6:62 **A**, Naphtali, and from the Bashan area of
6:74 From the territory of **A**, they received Mashal,
7:30 The sons of **A** were Imnah, Ishvah, Ishvi,
7:40 Each of these descendants of **A** was the head of an
12:36 From the tribe of **A**, there were 40,000 trained
2Ch 30:11 However, some from **A**, Manasseh, and Zebulun
Eze 48:34 the gates will be named for Gad, **A**, and Naphtali.
Lk 2:36 of Phanuel, of the tribe of **A**, and was very old.
Rev 7:6 from **A** | 12,000 / from Naphtali | 12,000

ASHER'S (2) [ASHER]

Eze 48:2 **A** territory lies south of Dan's and also extends
48:3 Naphtali's land lies south of **A**, also extending

ASHERAH (39)

Dt 7:5 Cut down their **A** poles and burn their idols.
12:3 Burn their **A** poles and cut down their carved idols.
16:21 "You must never set up an **A** pole beside the altar
Jdg 3:7 worshiped the images of Baal and the **A** poles.
6:25 and cut down the **A** pole standing beside it.
6:26 using as fuel the wood of the **A** pole you cut
6:28 and that the **A** pole beside it was gone.
6:30 the altar of Baal and for cutting down the **A** pole."
1Ki 14:15 have angered the LORD by worshiping **A** poles.
14:23 set up sacred pillars and **A** poles on every high hill
15:13 because she had made an obscene **A** pole.
16:33 Then he set up an **A** pole. He did more to arouse
18:19 all 450 prophets of Baal and the 400 prophets of **A**,
2Ki 13:6 They even set up an **A** pole in Samaria.
17:10 sacred pillars and **A** poles at the top of every hill
17:16 They set up an **A** pole and worshiped Baal and all
18:4 the sacred pillars, and knocked down the **A** poles.
21:3 constructed altars for Baal and set up an **A** pole,
21:7 Manasseh even took an **A** pole he had made
23:4 to worship Baal, **A**, and all the forces of heaven.
23:6 The king removed the **A** pole from the LORD's
23:7 where the women wove coverings for the **A** pole.
23:14 the sacred pillars and cut down the **A** poles.
23:15 crushed the stones to dust and burned the **A** pole.
2Ch 14:3 the sacred pillars and cut down the **A** poles.
15:16 because she had made an obscene **A** pole.
17:6 down the pagan shrines and destroyed the **A** poles.
19:3 for you have removed the **A** poles throughout the
24:18 and they worshiped **A** poles and idols instead!
31:1 cut down the **A** poles, and removed the pagan
33:3 altars for the images of Baal and set up **A** poles.
33:19 and set up **A** poles and idols before he repented.
34:3 the **A** poles, and the carved idols and cast images.
34:4 He also made sure that the **A** poles, the carved
34:7 He destroyed the pagan altars and the **A** poles,
Isa 17:8 They will never again bow down to their **A** poles
27:9 There won't be an **A** pole or incense altar left
Jer 17:2 go to worship at their sacred altars and **A** poles,
Mic 5:14 I will abolish your pagan shrines with their **A** poles

ASHES (37) [ASH]

Ge 18:27 to my Lord, even though I am but dust and **a**.
Lev 1:16 them to the east side of the altar among the **a**.
4:12 outside the camp, the place where the **a** are thrown.
6:10 the priest on duty must clean out the **a** of the burnt
6:11 and carry the **a** outside the camp to a place that is
Nu 4:13 "The **a** must be removed from the altar,
19:9 clean will gather up the **a** of the heifer
19:10 The man who gathers up the **a** of the heifer must
19:17 put some of the **a** from the burnt purification
1Sa 2:8 lifts the poor from the dust—/ yes, from a pile of **a**!
2Sa 13:19 now Tamar tore her robe and put **a** on her head.
1Ki 13:3 and its **a** will be poured out on the ground."
13:5 crack appeared in the altar, and the **a** poured out,
2Ki 23:4 and he carried the **a** away to Bethel.
Est 4:1 he tore his clothes, put on sackcloth and **a**,
4:3 and many people lay in sackcloth and **a**.
Job 2:8 a piece of broken pottery as he sat among the **a**.
13:12 Your statements have about as much value as **a**.
30:19 me into the mud. I have become as dust and **a**.
42:6 and I sit in dust and **a** to show my repentance."
Ps 102:9 I eat **a** instead of my food. / My tears run down
147:16 he scatters frost upon the ground like **a**.
Isa 44:20 The poor, deluded fool feeds on **a**. He is trusting
58:5 dress in sackcloth and cover yourselves with **a**.
61:3 he will give beauty for **a**, joy instead of mourning,
Jer 6:26 dress yourselves in sackcloth, and sit among the **a**.
21:10 by the king of Babylon, and he will reduce it to **a**.'
Eze 27:30 as they throw dust on their heads and roll in **a**.
28:18 I let it burn you to **a** on the ground in the sight of
Da 9:3 wore rough sackcloth and sprinkled myself with **a**.
Am 2:1 tomb of Edom's king and burned his bones to **a**.
Jnh 3:6 dressed himself in sackcloth and sat on a heap of **a**.
Hab 2:13 promised that the wealth of nations will turn to **a**?
Mt 11:21 and throwing **a** on their heads to show their
Lk 10:13 and throwing **a** on their heads to show their
Heb 9:13 and the **a** of a young cow could cleanse people's
2Pe 2:6 the cities of Sodom and Gomorrah into heaps of **a**

ASHHUR (2)

1Ch 2:24 his wife Abijah gave birth to a son named **A** (the
4:5 **A** (the father of Tekoa) had two wives,

ASHIMA (1)

2Ki 17:30 god Nergal. And those from Hamath worshiped **A**.

ASHKELON (13)

Jos 13:4 cities of Gaza, Ashdod, **A**, Gath, and Ekron.
Jdg 1:18 Judah captured the cities of Gaza, **A**, and Ekron,
14:19 He went down to the town of **A**, killed thirty men,
1Sa 6:17 the rulers of Ashdod, Gaza, **A**, Gath, and Ekron.
2Sa 1:20 will rejoice. / Don't proclaim it in the streets of **A**,
Jer 25:20 of Uz and the kings of the Philistine cities of **A**,
47:5 city of Gaza will be demolished; **A** will lie in ruins.
47:7 For the city of **A** and the people living along the
Am 1:8 the people of Ashdod and destroy the king of **A**.
Zep 2:4 Gaza, **A**, Ashdod, Ekron—these Philistine cities,
2:7 will lie down to rest in the abandoned houses in **A**.
Zec 9:5 The city of **A** will see Tyre fall and will be filled
9:5 its king killed, and **A** will be completely deserted.

ASHKENAZ (3)

Ge 10:3 The descendants of Gomer were **A**, Riphath,
1Ch 1:6 The descendants of Gomer were **A**, Riphath,
Jer 51:27 Bring out the armies of Ararat, Minni, and **A**.

ASHNAH (2)

Jos 15:33 were also given to Judah: Eshtaol, Zorah, **A**,
15:43 Iphtah, **A**, Nezib,

ASHORE (6) [SHORE]

Jnh 1:13 the sailors tried even harder to row the boat **a**.
Jn 21:7 for work), jumped into the water, and swam **a**.
Ac 21:4 We went **a**, found the local believers, and stayed
27:3 kind to Paul and let him go **a** to visit with friends
27:42 kill the prisoners to make sure they didn't swim **a**
27:44 the broken ship. So everyone escaped safely **a**!

ASHPENAZ (1)

Da 1:3 Then the king ordered **A**, who was in charge of the

ASHRIEL [KJV] See ASRIEL

ASHTAROTH (7) [BE-ESHTERAH]

Dt 1:4 King Og of Bashan, who had ruled in **A** and Edrei.
Jos 9:10 and King Og of Bashan (who lived in **A**).
12:4 the last of the Rephaites, lived at **A** and Edrei.
13:12 Og of Bashan, who had reigned in **A** and Edrei.
13:31 and King Og's royal cities of **A** and Edrei.
1Ch 6:71 with its pasturelands and **A** with its pasturelands.
11:44 Uzzia from **A**; / Shama and Jeiel, the sons of

ASHTEROTH-KARNAIM (1)

Ge 14:5 They conquered the Rephaites in **A**, the Zuzites in

ASHTORETH (8) [ASHTORETHS]

Jdg 2:13 the LORD to serve Baal and the images of **A**.
10:6 They worshiped images of Baal and **A**,
1Sa 7:3 get rid of your foreign gods and your images of **A**.
7:4 of Baal and **A** and worshiped only the LORD.
12:10 and worshiping the images of Baal and **A**.
1Ki 11:5 Solomon worshiped **A**, the goddess of the
11:33 For Solomon has abandoned me and worshiped **A**,
2Ki 23:13 King Solomon of Israel had built shrines for **A**,

ASHTORETHS (1) [ASHTORETH]

1Sa 31:10 They placed his armor in the temple of the **A**,

ASHUR [KJV] See ASHHUR

ASHURBANIPAL (1)

Ezr 4:10 and noble **A** had deported and relocated in Samaria

ASHURITES (1)

2Sa 2:9 Jezreel, Ephraim, Benjamin, the land of the **A**,

ASHVATH (1)

1Ch 7:33 The sons of Japhlet were Pasach, Bimhal, and **A**.

ASIA (18)

Ac 2:9 Judea, Cappadocia, Pontus, the province of **A**,
6:9 Alexandria, Cilicia, and the province of **A**.
16:6 them not to go into the province of **A** at that time.
19:10 so that people throughout the province of **A**—
19:22 while he stayed awhile longer in the province of **A**.
19:27 goddess worshiped throughout the province of **A**
20:4 and Trophimus, who were from the province of **A**.
20:16 want to spend further time in the province of **A**.
20:18 the day I set foot in the province of **A** until now
21:27 from the province of **A** saw Paul in the Temple
24:19 some Jews from the province of **A** were there—
27:2 stops at ports along the coast of the province of **A**.
Ro 16:5 person to become a Christian in the province of **A**.
1Co 16:19 The churches here in the province of **A** greet you
2Co 1:8 the trouble we went through in the province of **A**.
2Ti 1:15 here from the province of **A** have deserted me;
1Pe 1:1 Galatia, Cappadocia, the province of **A**,
Rev 1:4 John to the seven churches in the province of **A**.

ASIDE (71) [SIDE]

Ex 16:23 want today, and set **a** what is left for tomorrow."
29:27 "Set **a** as holy the parts of the ordination ram that
34:21 "Six days are set **a** for work, but on the Sabbath
Lev 22:7 After all, this food has been set **a** for them.
Nu 15:19 But you must set some **a** as a gift to the LORD.
15:20 the first of the flour you grind and set it **a** as a gift,
18:29 Be sure to set **a** the best portions of the gifts given
Dt 14:22 "You must set **a** a tithe of your crops—
15:19 "You must set **a** for the LORD your God all the
19:7 That is why I am commanding you to set **a** three
Jdg 10:16 Then the Israelites put **a** their foreign gods
18:3 they took him **a** and asked him, "Who brought you
1Sa 9:23 the piece that had been set **a** for the guest of honor.
18:11 But David jumped **a** and escaped. This happened
2Sa 3:27 Joab took him **a** at the gateway as if to speak with
18:30 the king told him. So Ahimaaz stepped **a**.
2Ki 4:4 into the jars, setting the jars **a** as they are filled."
22:2 He did not turn **a** from doing what was right.
1Ch 16:40 and evening on the altar set **a** for that purpose,
2Ch 12:12 the LORD's anger was turned **a**,
34:2 He did not turn **a** from doing what was right.
35:22 He laid **a** his royal robes so the enemy would not
Ne 13:5 and the special portion set **a** for the priests.
Job 6:18 The caravans turn **a** to be refreshed, but there is
23:11 I have followed his ways and not turned **a**.
24:4 The poor are kicked **a**; the needy must hide
29:8 The young stepped **a** when they saw me, and even

34:27 For they turned a from following him. They have
Ps 43: 2 my only safe haven. / Why have you tossed me a?
44: 9 But now you have tossed us a in dishonor.
71: 9 And now, in my old age, don't set me a.
85: 4 God of our salvation. / Put a your anger against us.
109:23 I am falling like a grasshopper that is brushed a.
Pr 30:30 king of animals, who won't turn a for anything,
Isa 65:16 For I will put a my anger and forget the evil of
Jer 12: 3 to be butchered! Set them a to be slaughtered!
Eze 10:11 in which their heads were turned, never turning a.
15: 6 they are useless, I have set them a to be burned!
45: 1 you must set a a section of it for the LORD as his
45: 2 875 feet by 875 feet, will be set a for the Temple.
45: 4 set a for the priests who minister to the LORD in
45: 6 This will be set a to be a city where anyone in
48: 8 "South of Judah is the land set a for a special
48: 9 "The area set a for the LORD's Temple will be
48:11 This area is set a for the ordained priests,
48:22 except for the areas set a for the sacred lands
48:29 These are the allotments that will be set a for each
Da 12:13 you will rise again to receive the inheritance set a
Mt 16:22 But Peter took him a and corrected him.
16:24 you must put a your selfish ambition,
20:17 he took the twelve disciples a privately and told
28: 2 from heaven and rolled a the stone and sat on it.
Mk 8:32 Peter took him a and told him he shouldn't say
8:34 told them, "you must put a your selfish ambition,
10:32 Taking the twelve disciples a, Jesus once more
10:50 Bartimaeus threw a his coat, jumped up, and came
16: 4 a very large one—had already been rolled a.
Lk 9:23 you must put a your selfish ambition,
24: 2 the stone covering the entrance had been rolled a.
Jn 11:28 She called Mary a from the mourners and told her,
11:39 "Roll the stone a," Jesus told them. But Martha,
11:41 So they rolled the stone a. Then Jesus looked up to
Ac 7:27 "But the man in the wrong pushed Moses a
18:26 they took him a and explained the way of God
22:20 I kept the coats they laid a as they stoned him.'
23:19 led him a, and asked, "What is it you want to tell
1Co 16: 2 each of you should put a some amount of money in
2Co 3:11 which has been set a, was full of glory,
Gal 3:15 Just as no one can set a or amend an irrevocable
Heb 7:18 the old requirement about the priesthood was set a
8:13 It is now out of date and ready to be put a.

ASIEL (1)

1Ch 4:35 Jehu son of Joshibiah, son of Seraiah, son of A,

ASK (276) [ASKED, ASKING, ASKS]

Ge 23: 8 you feel, be so kind as to a Ephron son of Zohar
24:14 I will a one of them for a drink. If she says, 'Yes,
24:57 "we'll call Rebekah and a her what she thinks."
25:22 So she went to a the LORD about it. "Why is this
31:39 and a you to reduce the count of your flock?
32:17 you meet Esau, he will a, 'Where are you going?
32:29 asked him. "Why do you a?" the man replied.
40:14 me to Pharaoh, and a him to let me out of here.
44: 4 A them, 'Why have you repaid an act of kindness
Ex 3:13 They will a, 'Which god are you talking about?
3:22 The Israelite women will a for silver and gold
6:27 They are the ones who went to Pharaoh to a
8:29 "I will a the LORD to cause the swarms of flies
11: 2 and women to a their Egyptian neighbors for
12:26 Then your children will a, 'What does all this
13:14 "And in the future, your children will a you,
Lev 25:20 But you might a, 'What will we eat during the
Nu 22:17 I will pay you well and do anything you a of me.
Dt 6:20 "In the future your children will a you, 'What is
29:24 The surrounding nations will a, 'Why has the
30:12 It is not up in heaven, so distant that you must a,
30:13 is not beyond the sea, so far away that you must a,
32: 7 A your father and he will inform you. / Inquire of
32:37 Then he will a, 'Where are their gods, / the rocks
Jos 4: 6 In the future, your children will a, 'What do these
4:21 "In the future, your children will a, 'What do these
9: 6 "We have come from a distant land to a you to
9:11 our people to be their servants, and a for peace.'
15:18 she urged him to a her father for an additional
Jdg 1:14 she urged him to a her father for an additional
8:21 said to Gideon, "Don't a a boy to do a man's job!
9: 2 "A the people of Shechem whether they want to
12: 5 they would a. If the man said, "No, I'm not,"
13: 6 I didn't a where he was from, and he didn't tell me
13:18 "Why do you a my name?" the angel of the
18: 5 "A God whether or not our journey will be
Ru 1:16 "Don't a me to leave you and turn back.
1Sa 1: 8 "What's the matter, Hannah?" Elkanah would a.
8: 9 Do as they a, but solemnly warn them about how a
9: 9 they would say, "Let's go and a the seer,"
10:14 So we went to the prophet Samuel to a him where
12:17 I will a the LORD to send thunder and rain today.
14:36 is best." But the priest said, "Let's a God first."
19: 3 I'll a my father to go out there with me, and I'll
23: 9 the ephod and a the LORD what he should do.
25: 8 A your own servants, and they will tell you this is
25:39 messengers to Abigail to a her to become his wife.
25:40 "David has sent us to a if you will marry him."
27:10 Achish would a. And David would reply,
28: 7 is a medium, so I can go and a her what to do."
28:16 "Why a me if the LORD has left you and has
2Sa 2: 7 I a you to be my strong and loyal subjects like the
11:20 But he might get angry and a, 'Why did the troops
13: 5 a him to let Tamar come and prepare some food
14:12 "Please let me a one more thing of you!" she said.
14:29 Then Absalom sent for Joab to a him to intercede
14:32 "Because I wanted you to a the king why he
15: 2 Absalom would a where they were from, and they
19:10 Let's a David to come back and be our king
20:18 to settle an argument, a advice at the city of Abel.'
1Ki 2:14 In fact, I have a favor to a of you." "What is it?"
2:16 So now I have just one favor to a of you.
2:17 A him to give me Abishag, the girl from Shunem,
2:22 "How can you possibly a me to give Abishag to
3: 5 "What do you want? A, and I will give it to you!"
3:13 And I will also give you what you did not a for—
5: 6 and I will pay your men whatever wages you a.
8:43 where you live, and grant what they a of you.
9: 8 They will scoff and a, 'Why did the LORD do
13: 6 "Please a the LORD your God to restore my
14: 3 of honey, and a him what will happen to the boy."
14: 5 She will a you about her son, for he is very sick.
22: 7 too? I would like to a him the same question."
2Ki 1: 2 the god of Ekron, to a whether he would recover.
1: 3 the messengers of the king of Samaria and a them,
1: 3 god of Ekron, to a whether the king will get well?
1: 6 god of Ekron, to a whether the king will get well?
1:16 the god of Ekron, to a whether you will get well?
3:11 If there is, we can a the LORD what to do."
4:13 Now a her what we can do for her. Does she want
4:26 Run out to meet her and a her, 'Is everything all
8: 8 Then tell him to a the LORD if I will get well
8: 9 of Aram, has sent me to a you if he will recover."
22:13 A him about the words written in this scroll that
1Ch 15:13 We failed to a God how to move it in the proper
2Ch 1: 7 "What do you want? A, and I will give it to you!"
1:11 and you did not a for personal wealth and honor
6:33 where you live, and grant what they a of you.
7:21 They will a, 'Why has the LORD done such
18: 6 too? I would like to a him the same question."
25:15 the LORD very angry, and he sent a prophet to a,
32:31 when ambassadors arrived from Babylon to a
34:21 A him about the words written in this scroll that
Ezr 8:17 to a him and his relatives and the Temple servants
8:22 For I was ashamed to a the king for soldiers
Ne 1:11 Please grant me success now as I go to a the king
Est 2:11 near the courtyard of the harem to a about Esther
5:14 and in the morning a the king to hang Mordecai on
6: 4 a the king to hang Mordecai from the gallows he
Job 8: 8 "Just a the former generation. Pay attention to the
9:12 Who dares to a him, 'What are you doing?'
12: 7 "A the animals, and they will teach you.
12: 7 A the birds of the sky, and they will tell you.
20: 7 Those who knew him will a, 'Where is he?'
21:29 But I tell you to a those who have been around,
35: 3 Yet you also a, 'What's the use of living a
35:10 Yet they don't a, 'Where is God my Creator,
42: 3 You a, 'Who is this that questions my wisdom
Ps 2: 8 Only a, and I will give you the nations as your
27: 4 The one thing I a of the LORD—/ the thing I seek
41: 5 "How soon will he die and be forgotten?" they a.
64: 5 set their traps. / "Who will ever notice?" they a.
73:11 "Does God realize what is going on?" they a.
86: 5 so full of unfailing love for all who a your aid.
139:11 I could a the darkness to hide me / and the light
Pr 27:10 you won't have to a your relatives for assistance.
SS 6:10 'Who is this,' they a, 'arising like the dawn,
Isa 3: 7 extra food or clothes. Don't a me to get involved!"
7:11 "A me for a sign, Ahaz, to prove that I will crush
7:11 A for anything you like, and make it as difficult as
8:19 the future from the dead? Why not a your God?
14:16 Everyone there will stare at you and a, 'Can this be
17: 8 They will no longer a their idols for help
21:12 If you wish to a again, then come back and a."
22:11 are to no avail because you never a God for help.
30:19 no more. He will be gracious if you a for help.
43:22 my dear people, you refuse to a for my help.
44:20 Yet he cannot bring himself to a, "Is this thing,
45:19 And I did not tell the people of Israel to a me for
47:12 A them to help you strike terror into the hearts of
Jer 2: 6 They did not a, 'Where is the LORD who brought
2: 8 The priests did not a, 'Where is the LORD?'
5:19 "And when your people a, 'Why is the LORD
8:19 the people a. "Is her King no longer there?"
10:21 follow the LORD or a what he wants of them.
13:22 You may a yourself, "Why is all this happening to
15: 5 for you? Who will even bother to a how you are?
15:11 Your enemies will a you to plead on their behalf in
16:10 you tell the people all these things, they will a,
19: 1 Then a some of the leaders of the people and of the
21: 2 "Please a the LORD to help us.
30: 6 Now let me a you a question: Do men give birth to
33: 3 A me and I will tell you some remarkable secrets
36: 7 and a the LORD's forgiveness before it is too
36:14 to a Baruch to come and read the messages to
37: 3 the priest, son of Maaseiah, to a Jeremiah,
37: 7 who sent you to a me what is going to happen,
38:14 "I want to a you something," the king said.
50: 5 They will a the way to Jerusalem and will start
Eze 14: 3 into sin. Why should I let them a me anything?
18:19 " 'What?' you a. 'Doesn't the child pay for the
20: 3 How dare you come to a for my help? As surely as
21: 7 When they a you why, tell them, 'I groan
37:18 When your people a you what your actions mean,
38:13 and Dedan and the merchants of Tarshish will a,
Da 2:18 He urged them to a the God of heaven to show
9:18 We do not a because we deserve help, but
Hos 9:14 I will a for wombs that don't give birth and breasts
Am 6:10 he will a the last survivor, "Is there anyone else
6:12 Stupid even to a—but that's how stupid you are
Ob 1: 3 up here?' you a boastfully. Don't fool yourselves!
Hab 2:19 You a speechless stone images to tell you what to
Zep 1: 6 They no longer a for the LORD's guidance
Hag 2:11 A the priests this question about the law:
Zec 7: 3 They were to a this question of the prophets
8:21 'Let us go to Jerusalem to a the LORD to bless us
8:22 and to a the LORD to bless them.
10: 1 A the LORD for rain in the spring, and he will
Mal 1: 6 "But you a, 'How have we ever despised your
1: 7 "Then you a, 'How have we defiled the
2:17 "Wearied him?" you a. "How have we wearied
3: 7 "But you a, 'How can we return when we have
3: 8 cheated me! "But you a, 'What do you mean?
Mt 5:42 Give to those who a, and don't turn away from
6: 8 exactly what you need even before you a him!
7: 7 on asking, and you will be given what you a for.
7: 9 if your children a for a loaf of bread, do you give
7:10 Or if they a for a fish, do you give them a snake?
7:11 Father give good gifts to those who a him.
9:38 a him to send out more workers for his fields."
11: 2 was doing. So he sent his disciples to a Jesus,
12:39 faithless generation would a for a miraculous sign;
16: 4 faithless generation would a for a miraculous sign,
18:19 down here on earth concerning anything you a,
19:17 "Why a me about what is good?" Jesus replied.
20:20 with her sons. She knelt respectfully to a a favor.
21:22 you will receive whatever you a for in prayer."
21:25 from heaven, he will a why we didn't believe him.
22:16 the supporters of Herod, to a him this question:
22:34 they thought up a fresh question of their own to a
22:46 no one dared to a him any more questions.
26:22 one by one they began to a him, "I'm not the one,
26:53 Don't you realize that I could a my Father for
27:20 and other leaders persuaded the crowds to a for
Mk 5:31 How can you a, 'Who touched me?' "
6:22 "A me for anything you like," the king said to the
6:23 he promised, "I will give you whatever you a,
6:24 and asked her mother, "What should I a for?"
6:24 mother told her, "A for John the Baptist's head!"
9:32 and they were afraid to a him what he meant.
11:31 from heaven, he will a why we didn't believe him.
12:34 no one dared to a him any more questions.
14:19 one by one they began to a him, "I'm not the one,
15:43 his courage and went to Pilate to a for Jesus' body.
Lk 7: 3 he sent some respected Jewish leaders to a him to
7:19 and he sent them to the Lord to a him, "Are you
7:20 and said to him, "John the Baptist sent us to a,
9:45 and they were afraid to a him about it.
10: 2 and a him to send out more workers for his fields.
11: 9 on asking, and you will be given what you a for.
11:11 if your children a for a fish, do you give them a
11:12 Or if they a for an egg, do you give them a
11:13 Father give the Holy Spirit to those who a him."
20: 3 "Let me a you a question first," he replied.
20: 5 from heaven, he will a why we didn't believe him.
20:40 ended their questions; no one dared to a any more.
22:23 Then the disciples began to a each other which of
22:68 And if I a you a question, you won't answer.
Jn 1:19 and Temple assistants from Jerusalem to a John
4:10 God has for you and who I am, you would a me,
9:21 He is old enough to speak for himself. A him."
9:23 "He is old enough to speak for himself. A him."
11:22 I know that God will give you whatever you a."
12:22 Andrew about it, and they went together to a Jesus.
13:24 Simon Peter motioned to him to a who would do
14:13 You can a for anything in my name, and I will do
14:14 Yes, a anything in my name, and I will do it!
14:16 And I will a the Father, and he will give you
15: 7 you may a any request you like, and it will be
15:16 so that the Father will give you whatever you a for,
16:19 Jesus realized they wanted to a him, so he said,
16:23 At that time you won't need to a me for anything.
16:23 you can go directly to the Father and a him,
16:24 A, using my name, and you will receive, and you
16:26 Then you will a in my name. I'm not saying I will
a the Father on your behalf,
18:21 A those who heard me. They know what I said."
21:12 And no one dared a him if he really was the Lord
Ac 9:11 of Judas. When you arrive, a for Saul of Tarsus.
10: 6 lives near the shore. A him to come and visit you."
21:25 all we a of them is what we already told them in a
23:20 "Some Jews are going to a you to bring Paul before
24:20 A these men here what wrongdoing the Jewish
Ro 10:12 who generously gives his riches to all who a for
11: 1 I a, then, has God rejected his people, the Jews?
12: 1 of what he has done for you, is this too much to a?
1Co 4:16 So I a you to follow my example and do as I do.
6: 1 a lawsuit and a a secular court to decide the matter,
9:11 Is it too much to a, in return, for mere food
10:25 Don't a whether or not it was offered to idols,
10:27 offered to you and don't a any questions about it.
14:12 a God for those that will be of real help to the
14:35 If they have any questions to a, let them a their
husbands at home,
15:35 But someone may a, "How will the dead be
2Co 3: 1 or a you to write letters of recommendation for
11: 9 have enough to live on, I did not a you to help me.
Gal 3: 2 Let me a you this one question: Did you receive
3: 5 I a you again, does God give you the Holy Spirit
Eph 3:20 infinitely more than we would ever dare to a
6:19 A God to give me the right words as I boldly
Php 4: 3 And I a you, my true teammate, to help these
Col 1: 9 We a God to give you a complete understanding of
1: 9 and we a him to make you wise with spiritual
2Th 3: 1 dear brothers and sisters, I a you to pray for us.
3: 9 It wasn't that we didn't have the right to a you to
Phm 1: 9 but because of our love, I prefer just to a you.
1:21 as I write this letter that you will do what I a
Jas 1: 5 you to do—a him, and he will gladly tell you.
1: 6 But when you a him, be sure that you really expect
4: 2 have what you want is that you don't a God for it.

4: 3 And even when you do **a**, you don't get it
1Jn 5:14 we **a** him for anything in line with his will.
5:15 we can be sure that he will give us what we **a** for.
Rev 2:24 of Satan, really). I will **a** nothing more of you

ASKED (618) [ASK]

Ge 3: 1 "Really?" he **a** the woman. "Did God really say
3:11 you that you were naked?" the LORD God **a**.
3:13 Then the LORD God **a** the woman, "How could
4: 6 "Why are you so angry?" the LORD **a** him.
4: 9 Afterward the LORD **a** Cain, "Where is your
17:20 I will bless him also, just as you have **a**.
18: 9 "Where is Sarah, your wife?" they **a** him.
18:17 I hide my plan from Abraham?" the LORD **a**.
19:12 the angels **a**. "Get them out of this place—
21:29 Abimelech **a**, "Why are you doing that?"
24: 5 The servant **a**, "But suppose I can't find a young
24:17 Running over to her, the servant **a**, "Please give
24:23 "Whose daughter are you?" he **a**. "Would your
24:39 woman willing to come back with me?' I **a** him.
24:47 When I **a** her whose daughter she was, she told me,
24:58 they **a** her. And she replied, "Yes, I will go."
24:65 she **a** the servant. And he replied, "It is my
25:22 about it. "Why is this happening to me?" she **a**.
26: 7 And when the men there **a** him about Rebekah,
26:16 And Abimelech **a** Isaac to leave the country.
26:27 "Why have you come?" Isaac **a** them. "This is
27:20 Isaac **a**, "How were you able to find it so quickly,
27:24 son Esau?" he **a**. "Yes, of course," Jacob replied.
27:32 But Isaac **a** him, "Who are you?" "Why, it's me,
29: 4 Jacob went over to the shepherds and **a** them,
29: 6 Jacob **a**. "He's well and prosperous. Look,
29: 7 Jacob **a**. "They'll be hungry if you stop so early in
30: 2 Jacob flew into a rage. "Am I God?" he **a**. "He is
30:31 Laban **a** again. Jacob replied, "Don't give me
32:27 is your name?" the man **a**. He replied, "Jacob."
32:29 Jacob **a** him. "Why do you ask?" the man replied.
33: 5 Esau looked at the women and children and **a**,
33: 8 Esau **a**. Jacob replied, "They are gifts, my lord,
37:10 his father **a**. "Will your mother, your brothers,
37:15 "What are you looking for?" he **a**.
37:32 robe to their father and **a** him to identify it.
38:16 "How much will you pay me?" Tamar **a**.
38:17 give me so I can be sure you will send it?" she **a**.
38:20 Judah **a** his friend Hirah the Adullamite to take the
38:21 So he **a** the men who lived there, "Where can I
40: 7 "Why do you look so worried today?" he **a**.
42:22 Reuben **a**. "But you wouldn't listen. And now we
43: 7 "But the man specifically **a** us about our family,"
43: 7 and he **a** us if we had another brother so we told
43:27 He **a** them how they had been getting along,
43:29 Joseph **a**, "Is this your youngest brother, the one
44:19 "You **a** us, my lord, if we had a father or a brother.
47: 3 Pharaoh **a** them, "What is your occupation?"
47: 8 "How old are you?" Pharaoh **a** him.
48: 8 over at the two boys. "Are these your sons?" he **a**.
50: 4 and **a** them to speak to Pharaoh on his behalf.
Ex 2: 7 Hebrew women to nurse the baby for you?" she **a**.
2:18 When the girls returned to Reuel, their father, he **a**,
2:20 "Well, where is he then?" their father **a**. "Did you
3:11 am I to appear before Pharaoh?" Moses **a** God.
4: 2 Then the LORD **a** him, "What do you have there
4:11 the LORD **a** him. "Who makes people so they
8:30 and **a** the LORD to remove all the flies.
8:31 And the LORD did as Moses **a** and caused the
12:35 and **a** the Egyptians for clothing and articles of
12:36 and they gave the Israelites whatever they **a** for.
14: 5 we done, letting all these slaves get away?" they **a**.
16:15 "What is it?" they **a**. And Moses told them,
16:22 people came and **a** Moses why this had happened.
16:28 and instructions?" the LORD **a** Moses.
18: 7 They **a** about each other's health and then went to
33:17 "I will indeed do what you have **a**, for you have
34:31 But Moses called to them and **a** Aaron
Nu 22: 9 That night God came to Balaam and **a** him,
22:28 your beating me these three times?" it **a** Balaam.
22:37 didn't you come right away?" Balak **a** Balaam.
23:17 "What did the LORD say?" Balak **a** eagerly.
32: 6 Moses **a** the Reubenites and Gadites.
Jos 5:13 Joshua went up to him and **a**, "Are you friend
15:18 got down off her donkey, Caleb **a** her, "What is it?
17:14 The descendants of Joseph came to Joshua and **a**,
18: 3 Then Joshua **a** them, "How long are you going to
24: 9 He **a** Balaam son of Beor to curse you,
Jdg 1: 1 After Joshua died, the Israelites **a** the LORD,
1:14 got down off her donkey, Caleb **a** her, "What is it?
5:25 Sisera **a** for water, / and Jael gave him milk.
6:40 So that night God did as Gideon **a**. The fleece was
8: 1 Then the people of Ephraim **a** Gideon, "Why have
8: 5 reached Succoth, Gideon **a** the leaders of the town,
8: 8 there Gideon went up to Peniel and **a** for food,
8:18 Then Gideon **a** Zebah and Zalmunna, "The men
11:17 Then they **a** the king of Moab for similar
13:11 Manoah ran back with his wife and **a**, "Are you
13:12 So Manoah **a** him, "When your words come true,
13:17 Then Manoah **a** the angel of the LORD, "What is
15:10 The men of Judah **a** the Philistines, "Why have
17: 9 Micah **a** him. And he replied, "I am a Levite from
18: 3 they took him aside and **a** him, "Who brought you
18: 8 to Zorah and Eshtaol, their relatives **a** them,
19:17 he **a** them where they were from and where they
20: 3 then **a** how this terrible crime had happened.
20:18 the battle the Israelites went to Bethel and **a** God,
20:23 Then they **a** the LORD, "Should we fight against
20:28 The Israelites **a** the LORD, "Should we fight
21: 8 So they **a**, "Was anyone absent when we presented
21:16 So the Israelite leaders **a**, "How can we find wives
Ru 1:19 their arrival. "Is it really Naomi?" the women **a**.
2: 5 Then Boaz **a** his foreman, "Who is that girl over
2: 7 She **a** me this morning if she could gather grain
2:10 "Why are you being so kind to me?" she **a**.
3:16 Naomi **a**, "What happened, my daughter?"
4: 2 from the town and **a** them to sit as witnesses.
1Sa 1:17 May the God of Israel grant the request you have **a**
1:20 for she said, "I **a** the LORD for him."
1:26 "Sir, do you remember me?" Hannah **a**. "I am the
1:27 I **a** the LORD to give me this child, and he has
4: 3 Israel retreated to their camp, and their leaders **a**,
4: 6 "What's going on?" the Philistines **a**. "What's all
4:14 "What is all the noise about?" Eli **a**.
6: 2 the rulers of the five Philistine cities and **a**,
6: 2 called in their priests and diviners and **a** them,
6: 4 they **a**. And they were told, "Since the plague has
9:11 So Saul and his servant **a**, "Is the seer here
9:18 then Saul approached Samuel at the gateway and **a**,
10:14 Saul's uncle **a** him. "We went to look for the
10:15 "Oh? And what did he say?" his uncle **a**.
10:22 So they **a** the LORD, "Where is he?"
11: 1 But the citizens of Jabesh **a** for peace. "Make a
11: 5 he returned to town, he **a**, "What's the matter?
12: 1 "I have done as you **a** and given you a king.
12:13 You **a** for him, and the LORD has granted your
13:12 and I haven't even **a** for the LORD's help!'
14:37 So Saul **a** God, "Should we go after the
15:16 told me last night!" "What was it?" Saul **a**.
16: 2 But Samuel **a**, "How can I do that? If Saul hears
16: 4 "What's wrong?" they **a**. "Do you come in
16:11 Then Samuel **a**, "Are these all the sons you
17:26 he **a** them. "Who is this pagan Philistine anyway,
17:30 and **a** them the same thing and received the same
17:55 he **a** Abner, the general of his army, "Abner,
18: 5 Whatever Saul **a** David to do, David did it
20: 6 tell him I **a** permission to go home to Bethlehem
20:10 Then David **a**, "How will I know whether or not
20:27 was empty again the next day, Saul **a** Jonathan,
20:28 "David earnestly **a** me if he could go to
21: 1 "Why are you alone?" he **a**. "Why is no one with
21: 8 David **a** Ahimelech, "Do you have a spear
21:11 "Isn't this David, the king of the land?" they **a**.
22: 3 where he **a** the king, "Would you let my father
22:12 of Ahitub!" "What is it, my king?" Ahimelech **a**.
23: 2 David **a** the LORD, "Should I go and attack
23: 4 So David **a** the LORD again, and again the
23:12 Again David **a**, "Will these men of Keilah really
26: 6 David **a** Ahimelech the Hittite and Abishai son of
28: 6 He **a** the LORD what he should do,
28:14 "What does he look like?" Saul **a**. "He is an old
28:15 Samuel **a**. "Because I am in deep trouble,"
30: 8 Then David **a** the LORD, "Should I chase them?
30:13 David **a** him. "I am an Egyptian—the slave of an
30:15 David **a**. The young man replied, "If you swear by
2Sa 1: 3 "Where have you come from?" David **a**.
1: 7 for me to come to him. 'How can I help?' I **a** him.
1:14 to kill the LORD's anointed one?" David **a**.
2: 1 After this, David **a** the LORD, "Should I move
2: 1 Then David **a**, "Which town should I go to?"
5:19 So David **a** the LORD, "Should I go out to fight
5:23 And once again David **a** the LORD what to do.
6: 9 David was now afraid of the LORD and **a**,
7: 7 I have never **a** them, "Why haven't you built me a
9: 2 the king **a**. "Yes sir, I am," Ziba replied.
9: 3 The king then **a** him, "Is anyone still alive from
9: 4 the king **a**. "In Lo-debar," Ziba told him,
9: 7 I've **a** you to come so that I can be kind to you
11: 7 David **a** him how Joab and the army were getting
11:10 he summoned him and **a**, "What's the matter with
12:19 "Is the baby dead?" he **a**. "Yes," they replied.
13: 6 when the king came to see him, Amnon **a** him,
13:20 Her brother Absalom saw her and **a**, "Is it true that
13:26 Amnon instead?" "Why Amnon?" the king **a**.
14: 5 the king **a**. "I am a widow," she replied.
14:18 the king replied. "Yes, my lord?" she **a**.
15:19 turned to Ittai, the captain of the Gittites, and **a**,
16: 2 the king **a** Ziba. And Ziba replied, "The donkeys
16: 3 the king **a** him. "He stayed in Jerusalem,"
16:17 Absalom **a** him. "Why aren't you with him?"
16:20 Then Absalom turned to Ahithophel and **a** him,
17: 6 Then he **a**, "What is your opinion? Should we
17:20 they **a** her, "Have you seen Ahimaaz
19:25 come with me, Mephibosheth?" the king **a** him.
20:17 As he approached, the woman **a**, "Are you Joab?"
21: 1 for three years, so David **a** the LORD about it.
21: 3 David **a** them, "What can I do for you to make
21: 4 David **a**. "Just tell me and I will do it for you."
21:12 and **a** for the bones of Saul and his son Jonathan.
24:13 So Gad came to David and **a** him, "Will you
24:21 "Why have you come, my lord?" Araunah **a**.
1Ki 1:11 Solomon's mother, and **a** her, "Did you realize
1:16 before him. "What can I do for you?" he **a** her.
1:24 He **a**, "My lord, have you decided that Adonijah
1:41 the sound of trumpets, he **a**, "What's going on?
2:13 she **a** him. "No," he said, "I come in peace.
2:14 I have a favor to ask of you." "What is it?" she **a**.
2:16 Please don't turn me down." "What is it?" she **a**.
2:20 "What is it, my mother?" he **a**. "You know I
3:10 and was glad that he had **a** for wisdom.
3:11 "Because you have **a** for wisdom in governing my
3:11 and have not **a** for a long life or riches for yourself
3:12 I will give you what you **a** for! I will give you a
5: 8 and I will do as you have **a** concerning the timber.
7:13 then **a** for a man named Huram to come from Tyre,
9:13 "What kind of towns are these, my brother?" he **a**.
10:13 gave the queen of Sheba whatever she **a** for,
11:22 "Why?" Pharaoh **a** him. "What do you lack here?
12: 6 his father, Solomon. "What is your advice?" he **a**.
12: 8 and instead **a** the opinion of the young men who
12: 9 "What is your advice?" he **a** them. "How should
13:12 The old prophet **a** them, "Which way did he go?"
13:14 The old prophet **a** him, "Are you the man of God
17:10 he saw a widow gathering sticks, and he **a** her,
18: 7 "Is it really you, my lord Elijah?" he **a**.
18:17 Israel's troublemaker?" Ahab **a** when he saw him.
20: 9 'I will give you everything you **a** for the first time,
20:14 Ahab **a**, "How will he do it?" And the prophet
20:14 Ahab **a**. "Yes," the prophet answered.
21: 5 his wife, Jezebel, **a** him. "What has made you
21: 6 "I **a** Naboth to sell me his vineyard or to trade it,
21: 7 Jezebel **a**. "Get up and eat and don't worry about
22: 4 Then he turned to Jehoshaphat and **a**, "Will you
22: 6 about four hundred of them, and **a** them,
22: 7 But Jehoshaphat **a**, "Isn't there a prophet of the
22:15 arrived before the king, Ahab **a** him, "Micaiah,
22:22 the LORD **a**. "And the spirit replied, 'I will go
2Ki 1: 5 he **a** them, "Why have you returned so soon?"
2: 3 of prophets from Bethel came to Elisha and **a** him,
2: 5 of prophets from Jericho came to Elisha and **a** him,
2:10 "You have **a** a difficult thing," Elijah replied.
2:18 they returned. "Didn't I tell you not to go?" he **a**.
3: 8 Then Jehoshaphat **a**, "What route will we take?"
3:11 But King Jehoshaphat of Judah **a**, "Is there no
4: 2 Elisha **a**. "Tell me, what do you have in the
4:14 Later Elisha **a** Gehazi, "What do you think we can
4:23 "Why today?" he **a**. "It is neither a new moon
5:21 to meet him. "Is everything all right?" Naaman **a**.
5:25 Elisha **a** him, "Where have you been, Gehazi?"
5:26 But Elisha **a** him, "Don't you realize that I was
6: 6 "Where did it fall?" the man of God **a**. When he
6:18 them blind." And the LORD did as Elisha **a**.
6:28 But then the king **a**, "What is the matter?"
7: 3 we sit here waiting to die?" they **a** each other.
8: 6 "Is this true?" the king **a** her. And she told him
8:12 "What's the matter, my lord?" Hazael **a** him.
8:14 When Hazael went back, the king **a** him,
9: 5 Jehu **a**. "For you, Commander," he replied.
9:11 and one of them **a** him, "What did that crazy
10:13 "Who are you?" he **a** them. And they replied,
12: 7 for Jehoiada and the other priests and **a** them,
20:11 So Isaiah **a** the LORD to do this, and he caused
20:14 the prophet went to King Hezekiah and **a** him,
20:15 Isaiah **a**. "They saw everything,"
23:17 Josiah **a**. And the people of the town told him,
1Ch 13:12 David was now afraid of God and **a**, "How can I
14:10 So David **a** God, "Should I go out to fight the
14:14 And once again David **a** God what to do. "Do not
17: 6 I have never **a** them, "Why haven't you built me a
2Ch 1:11 but rather you **a** for wisdom and knowledge to
9:12 gave the queen of Sheba whatever she **a** for—
10: 6 his father, Solomon. "What is your advice?" he **a**.
10: 8 and instead **a** the opinion of the young men who
10: 9 "What is your advice?" he **a** them. "How should
18: 3 Ahab **a**. And Jehoshaphat replied, "Why,
18: 5 his prophets, four hundred of them, and **a** them,
18: 6 But Jehoshaphat **a**, "Isn't there a prophet of the
18:14 arrived before the king, Ahab **a** him, "Micaiah,
18:20 do it!' " 'How will you do this?' the LORD **a**.
19: 2 love those who hate the LORD?" he **a** the king.
24: 6 king called for Jehoiada the high priest and **a** him,
25: 9 Amaziah **a** the man of God, "But what should I do
25:16 and said, "Since when have I **a** your advice?
28:16 About that time King Ahaz of Judah **a** the king of
30: 1 He **a** everyone to come to the Temple of the
31: 9 come from?" Hezekiah **a** the priests and Levites.
32: 6 and **a** them to assemble before him in the square at
Ezr 5: 3 their colleagues soon arrived in Jerusalem and **a**,
5: 4 They also **a** for a list of the names of all the people
5: 9 We **a** the leaders, 'Who gave you permission to
7: 6 and the king gave him everything he **a** for,
Ne 1: 2 I **a** them about the Jews who had survived the
2: 2 So the king **a** me, "Why are you so sad?
2: 4 The king **a**, "Well, how can I help you?" With a
2: 6 beside him, **a**, "How long will you be gone?
2:19 rebelling against the king like this?" they **a**.
5:17 I **a** for nothing, even though I regularly fed 150
8: 1 They **a** Ezra the scribe to bring out the Book of the
12:27 the Levites throughout the land were **a** to come to
Est 1:13 and customs, for he always **a** their advice.
2:15 She **a** for nothing except what he suggested,
3: 3 Then the palace officials at the king's gate **a**
4: 8 of all Jews, and he **a** Hathach to show it to Esther.
4: 8 He also **a** Hathach to explain it to her and to urge
5: 3 Then the king **a** her, "What do you want,
6: 3 the king **a**. His attendants replied, "Nothing has
7: 2 the king again **a** her, "Tell me what you want,
Job 1: 7 have you come from?" the LORD **a** Satan.
1: 8 Then the LORD **a** Satan, "Have you noticed my
2: 2 have you come from?" the LORD **a** Satan.
2: 3 Then the LORD **a** Satan, "Have you noticed my
6:22 But why? Have I ever **a** you for a gift? Have I
6:23 Have I ever **a** you to rescue me from my enemies?
6:23 Have I **a** you to save me from ruthless people?
31:30 I have never cursed anyone or **a** for revenge.
Ps 21: 4 He **a** you to preserve his life, / and you have
105:40 They **a** for meat, and he sent them quail; / he gave
106:15 So he gave them what they **a** for, / but he sent a
Isa 8: 2 I **a** Uriah the priest and Zechariah son of
38:22 And Hezekiah had **a**, "What sign will prove that I
39: 3 the prophet went to King Hezekiah and **a** him,
39: 4 **a** Isaiah. "They saw everything,"
40: 6 voice said, "Shout!" I **a**, "What should I shout?"
41:28 told you this. Not one gave any answer when I **a**.

Jer 1:13 Then the LORD spoke to me again and **a**,
37:17 where the king **a** him, "Do you have any messages
37:18 Then Jeremiah **a** the king, "What crime have I
38:27 and **a** him why the king had called for him.
40:15 we let him come and murder you?" Johanan **a**.
Eze 8:15 "Have you seen this?" he **a**. "But I will show you
8:17 "Have you seen this, son of man?" he **a**. "Is it
12:9 people of Israel, have **a** you what all this means.
24:19 Then the people **a**, "What does all this mean?
37:3 Then he **a** me, "Son of man, can these bones
Da 1:8 He **a** the chief official for permission to eat other
2:10 has ever **a** such a thing of any magician, enchanter,
2:15 He **a** Arioch, "Why has the king issued such a
2:23 and strength. / You have told me what we **a** of you
5:13 The king **a** him, "Are you Daniel, who was exiled
7:16 beside the throne and **a** him what it all meant.
7:20 I also **a** about the ten horns on the fourth beast's
12:6 One of them **a** the man dressed in linen, who was
12:8 So I **a**, "How will all this finally end, my lord?"
Hos 13:10 the land? You **a** for them, now let them save you!
Am 8:2 "What do you see, Amos?" he **a**. I replied,
Jnh 1:11 they **a** him, "What should we do to you to stop
Hag 2:13 Then Haggai **a**, "But if someone becomes
Zec 1:9 I **a** the angel who was talking with me, "My lord,
1:19 I **a** the angel who was talking with me. He replied,
1:21 I **a**. The angel replied, "The blacksmiths have
2:2 I **a**. He replied, "I am going to measure Jerusalem,
4:2 he **a**. I answered, "I see a solid gold lampstand
4:4 Then I **a** the angel, "What are these, my lord?
4:5 you know?" the angel **a**. "No, my lord," I replied.
4:11 Then I **a** the angel, "What are these two olive trees
4:13 you know?" he **a**. "No, my lord," I replied.
5:2 "What do you see?" the angel **a**. "I see a flying
5:6 I **a**. He replied, "It is a basket for measuring grain,
5:10 "Where are they taking the basket?" I **a** the angel.
6:4 my lord?" I **a** the angel who was talking with me.
Mt 2:4 say the Messiah would be born?" he **a** them.
8:27 "Who is this?" they **a** themselves.
9:4 Jesus knew what they were thinking, so he **a** them,
9:11 teacher eat with such scum?" they **a** his disciples.
9:14 of John the Baptist came to Jesus and **a** him,
9:28 and Jesus **a** them, "Do you believe I can make you
12:10 The Pharisees **a** Jesus, "Is it legal to work by
12:48 Jesus **a**, "Who is my mother? Who are my
13:10 His disciples came and **a** him, "Why do you
13:28 " 'Shall we pull out the weeds?' they **a**.
14:8 At her mother's urging, the girl **a**, "I want the
14:19 toward heaven, and **a** God's blessing on the food.
15:12 Then the disciples came to him and **a**, "Do you
15:15 Then Peter **a** Jesus, "Explain what you meant
15:16 "Don't you understand?" Jesus **a** him.
15:34 Jesus **a**, "How many loaves of bread do you
16:13 he **a** his disciples, "Who do people say that the
16:15 Then he **a** them, "Who do you say I am?"
17:10 His disciples **a**, "Why do the teachers of religious
17:19 Afterward the disciples **a** Jesus privately,
17:24 for the Temple tax came to Peter and **a** him,
17:25 to speak, Jesus **a** him, "What do you think, Peter?
18:1 About that time the disciples came to Jesus and **a**,
18:21 Then Peter came to him and **a**, "Lord, how often
19:7 letter of divorce and send her away?" they **a**.
19:18 "Which ones?" the man **a**. And Jesus replied:
19:25 "Then who in the world can be saved?" they **a**.
20:6 He **a** them, 'Why haven't you been working
20:21 he **a**. She replied, "In your Kingdom, will you let
20:24 other disciples heard what James and John had **a**,
21:10 was stirred as he entered. "Who is this?" they **a**.
21:16 and **a** Jesus, "Do you hear what these children are
21:20 disciples were amazed when they saw this and **a**,
21:40 the owner of the vineyard returns," Jesus **a**,
21:42 Then Jesus **a** them, "Didn't you ever read this in
22:12 'Friend,' he **a**, 'how is it that you are here without
22:20 he **a**, "Whose picture and title are stamped on it?"
22:41 by the Pharisees, Jesus **a** them a question:
24:3 His disciples came to him privately and **a**,
25:8 Then the five foolish ones **a** the others,
26:15 and **a**, "How much will you pay me to betray
26:17 the disciples came to Jesus and **a**,
26:25 also **a**, "Teacher, I'm not the one, am I?"
26:26 took a loaf of bread and **a** God's blessing on it.
27:11 the governor **a** him. Jesus replied, "Yes, it is as
27:17 he **a** them, "Which one do you want me to release
27:21 So when the governor **a** again, "Which of these
27:22 "But if I release Barabbas," Pilate **a** them,
27:58 went to Pilate and **a** for Jesus' body. And Pilate
Mk 1:27 they **a** excitedly. "It has such authority! Even evil
2:18 One day some people came to Jesus and **a**,
3:4 Then he turned to his critics and **a**, "Is it legal to
4:10 they **a** him, "What do your stories mean?"
4:21 Then Jesus **a** them, "Would anyone light a lamp
4:30 Jesus **a**, "How can I describe the Kingdom of
4:40 And he **a** them, "Why are you so afraid? Do you
5:9 Then Jesus **a**, "What is your name?"
5:30 so he turned around in the crowd and **a**,
5:39 "Why all this weeping and commotion?" he **a**.
6:2 They **a**, "Where did he get all his wisdom
6:24 She went out and **a** her mother, "What should I
6:37 "You feed them." "With what?" they **a**.
6:38 he **a**. "Go and find out." They came back
6:41 toward heaven, and **a** God's blessing on the food.
7:5 the Pharisees and teachers of religious law **a** him,
7:17 and his disciples **a** him what he meant by the
7:18 "Don't you understand either?" he **a**. "Can't you
8:4 for them here in the wilderness?" his disciples **a**.
8:5 bread do you have?" he **a**. "Seven," they replied.
8:21 "Don't you understand even yet?" he **a** them.
8:23 on the man's eyes, he laid his hands on him and **a**,
8:27 As they were walking along, he **a** them, "Who do
8:29 Then Jesus **a**, "Who do you say I am?"
9:10 but they often **a** each other what he meant by
9:16 "What is all this arguing about?" he **a**.
9:18 So I **a** your disciples to cast out the evil spirit,
9:21 Jesus **a** the boy's father. He replied, "Since he was
9:23 "What do you mean, 'If I can'?" Jesus **a**.
9:28 they **a** him, "Why couldn't we cast out that evil
9:33 Jesus **a** them, "What were you discussing out on
10:3 did Moses say about divorce?" Jesus **a** them.
10:17 up to Jesus, knelt down, and **a**, "Good Teacher,
10:18 call me good?" Jesus **a**. "Only God is truly good.
10:26 "Then who in the world can be saved?" they **a**.
10:36 "What is it?" he **a**.
10:41 disciples discovered what James and John had **a**,
10:51 Jesus **a**. "Teacher," the blind man said, "I want to
12:9 Jesus **a**. "I'll tell you—he will come and kill them
12:16 he **a**, "Whose picture and title are stamped on it?"
12:28 so he **a**, "Of all the commandments, which is the
12:35 Jesus was teaching the people in the Temple, he **a**,
13:3 and Andrew came to him privately and **a** him,
14:4 was this expensive perfume wasted?" they **a**.
14:12 Jesus' disciples **a** him, "Where do you want us to
14:22 took a loaf of bread and **a** God's blessing on it.
14:48 Jesus **a** them, "Am I some dangerous criminal,
14:60 high priest stood up before the others and **a** Jesus,
14:61 Then the high priest **a** him, "Are you the Messiah,
15:2 Pilate **a** Jesus, "Are you the King of the Jews?"
15:4 and Pilate **a** him, "Aren't you going to say
15:9 I give you the King of the Jews?" Pilate **a**.
15:12 "But if I release Barabbas," Pilate **a** them,
15:44 for the Roman military officer in charge and **a** him.
Lk 1:34 Mary **a** the angel, "But how can I have a baby?
1:62 So they **a** the baby's father, communicating to him
1:66 who heard about it reflected on these events and **a**,
2:49 "But why did you need to search?" he **a**.
3:10 The crowd **a**, "What should we do?"
3:12 corrupt tax collectors came to be baptized and **a**,
3:14 **a** some soldiers. John replied, "Don't extort
4:22 "How can this be?" they **a**. "Isn't this Joseph's
5:3 Jesus **a** Simon, its owner, to push it out into the
5:22 Jesus knew what they were thinking, so he **a** them,
5:34 Jesus **a**, "Do wedding guests fast while celebrating
7:31 Jesus **a**. "With what will I compare them?
7:36 One of the Pharisees **a** Jesus to come to his home
8:9 His disciples **a** him what the story meant.
8:25 Then he **a** them, "Where is your faith?" And they
8:30 Jesus **a**. "Legion," he replied—for the man was
8:45 Jesus **a**. Everyone denied it, and Peter said,
9:16 toward heaven, and **a** God's blessing on the food.
9:18 praying, he came over to his disciples and **a** them,
9:20 Then he **a** them, "Who do you say I am?"
10:29 so he **a** Jesus, "And who is my neighbor?"
10:36 to the man who was attacked by bandits?" Jesus **a**.
11:16 others **a** for a miraculous sign from heaven to see
12:41 Peter **a**, "Lord, is this illustration just for us
13:2 from Galilee?" he **a**. "Is that why they suffered?
13:20 He also **a**, "What else is the Kingdom of God like?
13:23 Someone **a** him, "Lord, will only a few be
14:3 Jesus **a** the Pharisees and experts in religious law,
14:5 Then he turned to them and **a**, "Which of you
14:18 and wanted to inspect it, so he **a** to be excused.
15:26 and he **a** one of the servants what was going on.
16:5 He **a** the first one, 'How much do you owe him?'
16:7 he **a** the next man. 'A thousand bushels of wheat,'
17:17 Jesus **a**, "Didn't I heal ten men? Where are the
17:20 One day the Pharisees **a** Jesus, "When will the
17:37 the disciples **a**. Jesus replied, "Just as the
18:18 Once a religious leader **a** Jesus this question:
18:19 me good?" Jesus **a** him. "Only God is truly good.
18:36 of a crowd going past, he **a** what was happening.
18:41 Then Jesus **a** the man, "What do you want me to
19:33 as they were untying it, the owners **a** them,
20:13 " 'What will I do?' the owner **a** himself. 'I know!
20:15 of the vineyard will do to those farmers?" Jesus **a**.
20:41 "Why is it," he **a**, "that the Messiah is said to be
21:7 "Teacher," they **a**, "when will all this take place?
22:9 "Where do you want us to go?" they **a** him.
22:31 "Simon, Simon, Satan has **a** to have all of you,
22:35 Then Jesus **a** them, "When I sent you out to
22:46 he **a**. "Get up and pray. Otherwise, temptation will
22:52 "Am I some dangerous criminal," he **a**, "that you
22:64 They blindfolded him, then they hit him and **a**,
23:3 So Pilate **a** him, "Are you the King of the Jews?"
23:6 "Oh, is he a Galilean?" Pilate **a**.
23:9 He **a** Jesus question after question, but Jesus
23:52 He went to Pilate and **a** for Jesus' body.
24:5 Then the men **a**, "Why are you looking in a tomb
24:19 "What things?" Jesus **a**. "The things that
24:30 **a** God's blessing on it, broke it, then gave it to
24:38 "Why are you frightened?" he **a**. "Why do you
24:41 Then he **a** them, "Do you have anything here to
Jn 1:21 "Well then, who are you?" they **a**. "Are you
1:25 **a** him, "If you aren't the Messiah or Elijah
1:38 he **a** them. They replied, "Rabbi" (which means
1:48 Nathanael **a**. And Jesus replied, "I could see you
1:50 Jesus **a** him, "Do you believe all this just because I
2:4 "How does that concern you and me?" Jesus **a**.
3:9 "What do you mean?" Nicodemus **a**.
4:27 but none of them **a** him why he was doing it
4:33 brought it to him?" the disciples **a** each other.
4:48 Jesus **a**, "Must I do miraculous signs and wonders
4:52 He **a** them when the boy had begun to feel better,
5:6 been ill, he **a** him, "Would you like to get well?"
6:5 Turning to Philip, he **a**, "Philip, where can we buy
6:25 they arrived and found him, they **a**, "Teacher,
6:52 can this man give us his flesh to eat?" they **a**.
6:67 Then Jesus turned to the Twelve and **a**, "Are you
7:15 hasn't studied everything we've studied?" they **a**.
7:35 "Where is he planning to go?" they **a**. "Maybe he
7:51 convict a man before he is given a hearing?" he **a**.
8:19 they **a**. Jesus answered, "Since you don't know
8:22 The Jewish leaders **a**, "Is he planning to commit
9:2 "Teacher," his disciples **a** him, "why was this
9:8 and others who knew him as a blind beggar **a** each
9:10 They **a**, "Who healed you? What happened?"
9:12 is he now?" they **a**. "I don't know," he replied.
9:15 The Pharisees **a** the man all about it. So he told
9:19 They **a** them, "Is this your son? Was he born
9:26 "But what did he do?" they **a**. "How did he heal
9:40 who were standing there heard him and **a**,
10:24 The Jewish leaders surrounded him and **a**,
11:34 he **a** them. They told him, "Lord, come and see."
11:47 "What are we going to do?" they **a** each other.
11:56 they **a** each other, "What do you think?
12:34 "Die?" **a** the crowd. "We understood from
13:12 he put on his robe again and sat down and **a**,
13:25 Leaning toward Jesus, he **a**, "Lord, who is it?"
13:37 "But why can't I come now, Lord?" he **a**. "I am
16:5 and none of you has **a** me where I am going.
16:17 The disciples **a** each other, "What does he mean
16:31 Jesus **a**, "Do you finally believe?
18:4 to meet them, he **a**, "Whom are you looking for?"
18:7 Once more he **a** them, "Whom are you searching
18:17 The woman **a** Peter, "Aren't you one of Jesus'
18:25 they **a** him again, "Aren't you one of his
18:26 relative of the man whose ear Peter had cut off, **a**,
18:29 So Pilate, the governor, went out to them and **a**,
18:33 "Are you the King of the Jews?" he **a** him.
18:35 "Am I a Jew?" Pilate **a**. "Your own people
18:38 "What is truth?" Pilate **a**. Then he went out again
19:9 Jesus back into the headquarters again and **a** him,
19:15 Pilate **a**. "We have no king but Caesar,"
19:31 so they **a** Pilate to hasten their deaths by ordering
19:38 **a** Pilate for permission to take Jesus' body down.
20:13 "Why are you crying?" the angels **a** her.
20:15 "Why are you crying?" Jesus **a** her. "Who are
21:17 Once more he **a** him, "Simon son of John, do you
21:17 Peter was grieved that Jesus **a** the question a third
21:20 who had leaned over to Jesus during supper and **a**,
21:21 Peter **a** Jesus, "What about him, Lord?"
Ac 2:12 "What can this mean?" they **a** each other.
3:3 John about to enter, he **a** them for some money.
4:16 should we do with these men?" they **a** each other.
5:8 Peter **a** her, "Was this the price you and your
7:1 Then the high priest **a** Stephen, "Are these
7:27 'Who made you a ruler and judge over us?' he **a**.
7:46 and **a** for the privilege of building a permanent
8:30 so he **a**, "Do you understand what you are
8:34 The eunuch **a** Philip, "Was Isaiah talking about
9:5 "Who are you, sir?" Saul **a**. And the voice
9:21 they **a**. "And we understand that he came here to
9:40 But Peter **a** them all to leave the room; then he
10:4 "What is it, sir?" he **a** the angel. And the angel
10:18 They **a** if this was the place where Simon Peter
10:46 in tongues and praising God. Then Peter **a**,
10:48 Afterward Cornelius **a** him to stay with them for
13:25 As John was finishing his ministry he **a**, 'Do you
13:28 but they **a** Pilate to have him killed anyway.
13:42 the people **a** them to return again and speak about
16:15 of her household, and she **a** us to be her guests.
16:30 He brought them out and **a**, "Sirs, what must I do
18:20 They **a** him to stay longer, but he declined.
19:2 he **a** them. "No," they replied, "we don't know
19:3 he **a**. And they replied, "The baptism of John."
21:33 Then he **a** the crowd who he was and what he had
21:37 you know Greek?" the commander **a**, surprised.
22:8 " 'Who are you, sir?' I **a**. And he replied, 'I am
22:26 The officer went to the commander and **a**,
22:27 So the commander went over and **a** Paul,
23:18 me over and **a** me to bring this young man to you
23:19 led him aside, and **a**, "What is it you want to tell
23:34 and then **a** Paul what province he was from.
25:3 They **a** Festus as a favor to transfer Paul to
25:9 Then Festus, wanting to please the Jews, **a** him,
25:15 charges against him and **a** me to sentence him.
25:20 and I **a** him whether he would be willing to stand
26:15 " 'Who are you, sir?' I **a**. "And the Lord replied,
28:20 I **a** you to come here today so we could get
1Co 7:1 Now about the questions you **a** in your letter.
16:20 The other believers here have **a** me to greet you for
2Co 11:9 I have never yet **a** you for any support, and I never
1Th 2:6 we have never **a** for it from you or anyone else.
1Pe 3:15 And if you are **a** about your Christian hope,
Rev 7:13 Then one of the twenty-four elders **a** me,
10:9 and **a** him to give me the little scroll.
17:7 "Why are you so amazed?" the angel **a**. "I will

ASKELON [KJV] See ASHKELON

ASKING (65) [ASK]

Ge 27:6 to her son Jacob, "I overheard your father **a** Esau
Jos 11:20 and caused them to fight the Israelites instead of **a**
14:12 So I'm **a** you to give me the hill country that the
Jdg 6:29 And after **a** around and making a careful search,
11:17 they sent messengers to the king of Edom **a** for
11:19 **a** for permission to cross through his land to get to
1Sa 10:2 and that your father is worried about you and is **a**,
12:17 you have been in **a** the LORD for a king!"
12:19 "For now we have added to our sins by **a** for a
16:22 Then Saul sent word to Jesse **a**, "Please let David
17:25 "Have you seen the giant?" the men were **a**.
17:29 David replied. "I was only **a** a question!"

1Ki 1: 6 at any time, even by **a**, "What are you doing?"
2:22 "You might as well be **a** me to give him the
2Ki 17: 4 **a** King So of Egypt to help him shake free of
1Ch 10:14 instead of **a** the LORD for guidance.
16: 4 the Ark of the LORD by **a** for his blessings
Ne 6: 2 and Geshem sent me a message **a** me to meet them
Job 34:24 He brings the mighty to ruin without **a** anyone,
Ps 79:10 be allowed to scoff, / **a**, "Where is their God?"
Pr 18: 6 get into constant quarrels; they are **a** for a beating.
Isa 6: 8 Then I heard the Lord **a**, "Whom should I send as
58: 2 to me and **a** me to take action on their behalf.
65: 1 before inquired about me are now **a** about me.
Jer 2:36 you flit from one ally to another **a** for help.
23:35 You should keep **a** each other, 'What is the
Eze 14: 4 fall into sin and then come to a prophet **a** for help.
14: 7 and who then come to a prophet **a** for my advice.
16:15 who came along. Your beauty was theirs for the **a**!
Da 6:11 and found him praying and **a** for God's help.
Hos 4:12 They are **a** a piece of wood to tell them what to do!
Am 4: 1 and who are always **a** your husbands for another
Mal 2:17 You have wearied him by **a**, "Where is the God of
Mt 2: 1 men from eastern lands arrived in Jerusalem, **a**,
2: 7 message to the wise men, **a** them to come see him.
7: 7 "Keep on **a**, and you will be given what you ask
16: 1 and Sadducees came to test Jesus' claims by **a** him
20:22 Jesus told them, "You don't know what you are **a**!
Mk 1:37 They said, "Everyone is **a** for you."
3:32 your brothers and sisters are outside, **a** for you."
9:11 Now they began **a** him, "Why do the teachers of
10:38 Jesus answered, "You don't know what you are **a**!
15: 8 toward Pilate, **a** him to release a prisoner as usual.
Lk 10:25 law stood up to test Jesus by **a** him this question:
11: 9 "And so I tell you, keep on **a**, and you will be
11:29 and this evil generation keeps **a** me to show them a
Jn 4: 9 Why are you **a** me for a drink?"
7:11 at the festival and kept **a** if anyone had seen him.
14: 9 has seen the Father! So why are you **a** to see him?
16:19 so he said, "Are you **a** yourselves what I meant?
17:15 I'm not **a** you to take them out of the world,
18:19 the high priest began **a** Jesus about his followers
18:21 Why are you **a** me this question? Ask those who
18:39 But you have a custom of **a** me to release someone
Ac 1: 6 they kept **a** him, "Lord, are you going to free
9: 2 **a** their cooperation in the arrest of any followers of
18:27 to the believers in Achaia, **a** them to welcome him.
20:17 at Ephesus, **a** them to come down to meet him.
Ro 10:20 showed myself to those / who were not **a** for me."
2Co 1:17 You may be **a** why I changed my plan. Hadn't I
Eph 1:17 **a** God, the glorious Father of our Lord Jesus
Col 4:12 for you, **a** God to make you strong and perfect,
1Th 3:10 **a** God to let us see you again to fill up anything
Phm 1: 8 That is why I am boldly **a** a favor of you. I could
Jas 1: 5 he will gladly tell you. He will not resent your **a**.

ASKS (45) [ASK]

Ge 46:33 calls for you and **a** you about your occupation,
Ex 19: 8 "We will certainly do everything the LORD **a** of
22:10 "Now suppose someone **a** a neighbor to care for a
Jdg 4:20 anybody comes and **a** you if there is anyone here,
1Sa 20: 6 If your father **a** where I am, tell him I asked
Ecc 4: 8 But then he **a** himself, "Who am I working for?
SS 8: 8 What will we do if someone **a** to marry her?
Isa 40:25 compare me? Who is my equal?" **a** the Holy One.
50: 1 The LORD **a**, "Did I sell you as slaves to my
52: 5 And now, what is this?" **a** the LORD. "Why are
66: 9 and then not deliver it?" **a** the LORD. "No!
Jer 5: 9 Should I not punish them for this?" **a** the LORD.
5:29 Should I not punish them for this?" **a** the LORD.
7:19 **a** the LORD. "Most of all, they hurt themselves,
8:19 carved idols and worthless gods?" **a** the LORD.
9: 9 Should I not punish them for this?" **a** the LORD.
22:16 that what it means to know me?" **a** the LORD.
23:23 I a God who is only in one place?" **a** the LORD.
23:24 in all the heavens and earth?" **a** the LORD.
23:29 Does not my word burn like fire?" **a** the LORD.
23:33 the people or one of the prophets or priests **a** you,
31:20 still my son, my darling child?" **a** the LORD.
44: 7 LORD God Almighty, the God of Israel, **a** you:
Eze 17: 9 "So now the Sovereign LORD **a**: Should I let this
18:23 "Do you think, **a** the Sovereign LORD, that I like
33:11 So now the Sovereign LORD **a**: What chance do
Hos 6: 4 what should I do with you?" **a** the LORD.
Am 2:11 deny this, my people of Israel?" **a** the LORD.
9: 7 **a** the LORD. "I brought you out of Egypt,
Zec 13: 6 And if someone **a**, 'Then what are those scars on
Mal 1: 9 you any favor at all?" **a** the LORD Almighty.
1:13 from you such offerings as these?" **a** the LORD.
Mt 7: 8 For everyone who **a**, receives. Everyone who
21: 3 If anyone **a** what you are doing, just say,
Mk 11: 3 If anyone **a** what you are doing, just say,
14:14 house he enters, say to the owner, 'The Teacher **a**,
Lk 6:30 Give what you have to anyone who **a** you for it;
11:10 For everyone who **a**, receives. Everyone who
17: 4 and each time turns again and **a** forgiveness,
19:31 If anyone **a** what you are doing, just say,
22:11 say to the owner, 'The Teacher **a**, Where is the
Ac 7:49 **a** the Lord. / 'Could you build a dwelling place for
1Co 10:27 If someone who isn't a Christian **a** you home for
2Co 8:23 If anyone **a** about Titus, say that he is my partner
1Ti 5: 5 Night and day she **a** God for help and spends much

ASLEEP (25) [SLEEP]

Ge 41: 5 Soon he fell **a** again and had a second dream.
Jdg 4:21 But when Sisera fell **a** from exhaustion,
1Sa 26: 7 went right into Saul's camp and found him **a**,
26: 7 Abner and the warriors were lying **a** around him.
2Sa 4: 6 had been sifting wheat, became drowsy and fell **a**.
1Ki 3:20 and took my son from beside me while I was **a**.
18:27 on a trip, or he is **a** and needs to be wakened!"
Job 3:13 at birth, I would be at peace now, **a** and at rest.
Jer 51:39 I will make them drink until they fall **a**,
51:57 "They will fall **a** and never wake up again!"
Jnh 1: 5 And all this time Jonah was sound **a** down in the
Zec 4: 1 me returned and woke me, as though I had been **a**.
Mt 1:20 As he considered this, he fell **a**, and an angel of the
9:24 "Go away, for the girl isn't dead; she's only **a**."
26:40 he returned to the disciples and found them **a**.
Mk 5:39 he asked. "The child isn't dead; she is only **a**."
14:37 Then he returned and found the disciples **a**.
14:37 "Simon!" he said to Peter. "Are you **a**?
Lk 8:52 "Stop the weeping! She isn't dead; she is only **a**."
9:32 and the others were very drowsy and had fallen **a**.
17:34 That night two people will be **a** in one bed;
22:45 only to find them **a**, exhausted from grief.
Jn 11:11 Then he said, "Our friend Lazarus has fallen **a**,
Ac 12: 6 he was **a**, chained between two soldiers,
1Th 5: 6 So be on your guard, not **a** like the others.

ASNAH (1)

Ezr 2:50 **A**, Meunim, Nephusim,

ASNAPPER [KJV] See ASHURBANIPAL

ASP(S) [KJV] See SNAKE(S), VIPER

ASPATHA (1)

Est 9: 7 They also killed Parshandatha, Dalphon, **A**,

ASPHALT (1)

Ge 11: 3 burnt brick and collect natural **a** to use as mortar.

ASRIEL (3) [ASRIELITES]

Nu 26:31 The Asrielites, named after their ancestor **A**.
Jos 17: 2 Abiezer, Helek, **A**, Shechem, Hepher,
1Ch 7:14 to his Aramean concubine, were **A** and Makir.

ASRIELITES (1) [ASRIEL]

Nu 26:31 The **A**, named after their ancestor Asriel.

ASS(ES), ASS'S [KJV] See DONKEY

ASSAILANT (2)

Ex 21:19 even with a crutch, the **a** will be innocent.
21:19 the **a** must pay for time lost because of the injury

ASSASSINATE (4) [ASSASSINATED, ASSASSINATION, ASSASSINS]

1Sa 19: 1 urged his servants and his son Jonathan to **a** David.
Est 2:21 became angry at King Xerxes and plotted to **a** him.
6: 2 private quarters. They had plotted to **a** the king.
Jer 40:14 has sent Ishmael son of Nethaniah to **a** you?"

ASSASSINATED (13) [ASSASSINATE]

1Ki 15:27 plotted against Nadab and **a** him while he
16:16 heard that Zimri had **a** the king, they chose Omri,
2Ki 12:20 and **a** him at Beth-millo on the road to Silla.
14: 5 as king, he executed the men who had **a** his father.
15:10 **a** him in public, and became the next king.
15:14 of Gadi went to Samaria from Tirzah and **a** him,
15:25 Pekah **a** the king, along with Argob and Arieh,
15:30 son of Elah conspired against Pekah and **a** him.
21:23 plotted against him and **a** him in his palace.
25:25 ten men and **a** Gedaliah and everyone with him,
2Ch 24:25 They **a** him as he lay in bed. Then he was buried in
25: 3 as king, he executed the men who had **a** his father.
33:24 plotted against him and **a** him in his palace.

ASSASSINATION (1) [ASSASSINATE]

Est 7: 9 the man who saved the king from **a**."

ASSASSINS (7) [ASSASSINATE]

2Ki 12:21 The **a** were Jozacar son of Shimeath
14: 6 However, he did not kill the children of the **a**,
14:19 But his enemies sent **a** after him, and they killed
2Ch 24:26 The **a** were Jozacar, the son of an Ammonite
25: 4 However, he did not kill the children of the **a**,
25:27 But his enemies sent **a** after him, and they killed
Ac 21:38 and took four thousand members of the **A** out into

ASSAULT (2) [ASSAULTED]

Dt 17: 8 or a case involving different kinds of **a**.
Est 7: 8 "Will he even **a** the queen right here in the palace,

ASSAULTED (1) [ASSAULT]

Nu 25:18 because they **a** you with deceit by tricking you into

ASSEMBLE (15) [ASSEMBLED, ASSEMBLIES, ASSEMBLY]

Lev 23: 3 day of complete rest, a holy day to **a** for worship.
Nu 8: 9 Then **a** the whole community of Israel and present
10: 2 silver to be used for summoning the people to **a**
20: 8 must take the staff and **a** the entire community.
21:16 "**A** the people, and I will give them water."
Dt 16: 8 On the seventh day the people must **a** before the
31:11 **a** before the LORD your God at the place he
Jdg 4: 6 **A** ten thousand warriors from the tribes of Naphtali
1Ki 8: 1 the tribes and families of Israel to **a** in Jerusalem.
2Ch 5: 2 the tribes and families of Israel to **a** in Jerusalem.
32: 6 and asked them to **a** before him in the square at the
Isa 4: 5 provide shade for Jerusalem and all who **a** there.
Da 11:10 the sons of the king of the north will **a** a mighty
Ob 1: 1 everyone! Let's **a** our armies and attack Edom!"
1Ti 2: 8 So wherever you **a**, I want men to pray with holy

ASSEMBLED (18) [ASSEMBLE]

Lev 8: 4 and all the people **a** at the Tabernacle entrance.
Nu 16:19 and they all **a** at the Tabernacle entrance.
Dt 10: 4 of the fire on the mountain as you were **a** below.
18:16 your God when you were **a** at Mount Sinai.
33: 5 king in Israel—/ when the leaders of the people **a**,
33:21 to them. / When the leaders of the people were **a**,
Jdg 20:22 and **a** at the same place they had fought the
20:30 on the third day and **a** at the same place as before.
1Ki 8: 2 They all **a** before the king at the annual Festival of
2Ch 5: 3 They all **a** before the king at the annual Festival of
30: 3 and the people had not yet **a** at Jerusalem.
30:13 so a huge crowd **a** at Jerusalem in midspring to
Ezr 3: 1 all the people **a** together as one person in
8:15 I **a** the exiles at the Ahava Canal, and we camped
Ne 8: 1 all the people **a** together as one person at the
Da 11:11 will rally against the vast forces **a** by the king of
Lk 22:66 At daybreak all the leaders of the people **a**,
Ac 10:27 and went inside where the others were **a**.

ASSEMBLIES (2) [ASSEMBLE]

Lev 23:37 Celebrate them by gathering in sacred **a** to present
Am 5:21 hypocrisy of your religious festivals and solemn **a**.

ASSEMBLY (63) [ASSEMBLE]

ASSEMBLY OF THE FAITHFUL (1) Ps 149:1

ASSEMBLY OF ISRAEL (5) Dt 31:30; 33:4; Jdg 21:24; 1Ki 12:3; 1Ch 13:2

ASSEMBLY OF THE LORD* (5) Dt 23:1,2,3,8; Jos 22:17

SOLEMN ASSEMBLY (3) Nu 29:1; 2Ki 10:20; Ne 8:18

WHOLE ASSEMBLY (7) Jos 22:12; 1Ki 12:3; 1Ch 13:4; 29:10,20; Ezr 10:12; Ne 5:13

Ge 28: 3 And may your descendants become a great **a** of
Lev 23: 7 stop their regular work and gather for a sacred **a**.
23: 8 stop all their regular work to hold a sacred **a**."
23:21 all your regular work and gather for a sacred **a**.
23:24 You will call the people to a sacred **a**—the Festival
23:27 you must humble yourselves, gather for a sacred **a**,
23:35 It will begin with a sacred **a** on the first day,
23:36 you must gather again for a sacred **a** and present
23:36 This will be a solemn closing **a**, and no regular
Nu 10: 7 But when you call the people to an **a**,
16: 2 250 other prominent leaders, all members of the **a**.
25: 7 the priest saw this, he jumped up and left the **a**.
28:18 the festival you must call a sacred **a** of the people.
28:25 festival you must call another holy **a** of the people.
28:26 the LORD, you must call a holy **a** of the people.
29: 1 You must call a solemn **a** of all the people on that
29: 7 you must call another holy **a** of all the people.
29:12 you must call yet another holy **a** of all the people,
29:35 of the festival, call all the people to another holy **a**.
35:24 the **a** must follow these regulations in making a
Dt 23: 1 he may not be included in the **a** of the LORD.
23: 2 may not be included in the **a** of the LORD.
23: 3 may be included in the **a** of the LORD.
23: 8 you from Egypt may enter the **a** of the LORD.
31:30 So Moses recited this entire song to the **a** of Israel:
33: 4 the law, / the special possession of the **a** of Israel.
Jos 8:35 Moses had ever given was read to the entire **a**,
18: 1 the entire Israelite **a** gathered at Shiloh and set up
22:12 the whole **a** gathered at Shiloh and prepared to go
22:17 even after the plague that struck the entire **a** of the
Jdg 20: 1 came together in one large **a** and stood in the
20: 2 took their positions in the **a** of the people of God.
21:13 The Israelite **a** sent a peace delegation to the little
21:24 So the **a** of Israel departed by tribes and families,
1Ki 12: 3 and the whole **a** of Israel went to speak with
12:20 they called an **a** and made him king over all Israel.
2Ki 10:20 "Prepare a solemn **a** to worship Baal!"
1Ch 13: 2 Then he addressed the entire **a** of Israel as follows:
13: 4 The whole **a** agreed to this, for the people could
28: 8 give you this charge for all Israel, the LORD's **a**:
29: 1 Then King David turned to the entire **a** and said,
29:10 praised the LORD in the presence of the whole **a**:
29:20 Then David said to the whole **a**, "Give praise to
29:20 And the entire **a** praised the LORD, the God of
2Ch 1: 3 Then Solomon led the entire **a** to the hill at Gibeon
6:13 He stood on the platform before the entire **a**,
29:23 then brought before the king and the **a** of people,
29:28 The entire **a** worshiped the LORD as the singers
30:23 The entire **a** then decided to continue the festival
30:25 The entire **a** of Judah rejoiced,
Ezr 10: 8 and be expelled from the **a** of the exiles.
10:12 Then the whole **a** raised their voices and answered,
Ne 5:13 The whole **a** responded, "Amen," and they
8: 2 the priest brought the scroll of the law before the **a**,
8:18 Then on October 15 they held a solemn **a**,
13: 1 or Moabite should ever be permitted to enter the **a**
13: 3 ancestry were immediately expelled from the **a**.
Ps 40:10 saving power. / I have told everyone in the great **a**
149: 1 new song. / Sing his praises in the **a** of the faithful.
Ac 7:38 Moses was with the **a** of God's people in the
19:39 about other matters, they can be settled in a legal **a**.

Heb 12:22 and to thousands of angels in joyful **a**.
12:23 You have come to the **a** of God's firstborn

ASSENT [KJV] See AGREE

ASSESS (4) [ASSESSED, ASSESSMENT, ASSESSMENTS]
Lev 27:12 He will **a** its value, and his assessment will be
27:14 to the LORD, the priest must come to **a** its value.
27:18 the priest must **a** the land's value in proportion to
27:23 the priest must **a** its value based on the years until

ASSESSED (4) [ASSESS]
Lev 27:16 its value will be **a** by the amount of seed required
27:19 you must pay the land's value as **a** by the priest,
27:23 then give the **a** value of the land as a sacred
27:27 the priest may sell it to someone else for its **a**

ASSESSMENT (5) [ASSESS]
Lev 27:12 He will assess its value, and his **a** will be final.
27:14 to assess its value. The priest's **a** will be final.
27:17 in the Year of Jubilee, then the entire **a** will apply.
27:27 you may redeem it by paying the priest's **a** of its
2Ki 12:4 whether it is a regular **a**, a payment of vows,

ASSESSMENTS (1) [ASSESS]
Lev 27:25 All the value **a** must be measured in terms of the

ASSHUR (5) [ASSHURITES]
Ge 2:14 branch is the Tigris, which flows to the east of **A**.
10:22 of Shem were Elam, **A**, Arphaxad, Lud, and Aram.
25:18 which is east of Egypt in the direction of **A**.
1Ch 1:17 of Shem were Elam, **A**, Arphaxad, Lud, and Aram.
Eze 27:23 Haran, Canneh, Eden, Sheba, **A**, and Kilmad came

ASSHURITES (1) [ASSHUR]
Ge 25:3 Dedan's descendants were the **A**, Letushites,

ASSIGN (13) [ASSIGNED, ASSIGNING, ASSIGNMENTS, REASSIGN]
Ge 45:18 'Pharaoh will **a** to you the very best territory in the
Nu 3:9 **A** the Levites to Aaron and his sons as their
4:19 and **a** a specific duty or load to each person.
4:27 They must **a** the Gershonites the loads they are to
4:32 You must **a** the various loads to each man by
8:26 This is how you will **a** duties to the Levites."
26:55 Make sure you **a** the land by lot, and define the
27:7 **A** them the property that would have been given to
Jos 6:6 and **a** seven priests to walk in front of it,
13:14 Moses did not **a** any land to the tribe of Levi.
15:13 The LORD instructed Joshua to **a** some of
18:8 and I will **a** the land to the tribes by casting sacred
Eze 45:8 they will **a** the rest of the land to the people,

ASSIGNED (71) [ASSIGN]
Ge 40:4 and Potiphar **a** Joseph to take care of them.
47:11 So Joseph **a** the best land of Egypt—the land of
47:22 for they were **a** food from Pharaoh and didn't need
Nu 2:2 "Each tribe will be **a** its own area in the camp,
3:23 They were **a** the area to the west of the Tabernacle
3:29 They were **a** the area south of the Tabernacle for
3:35 They were **a** the area north of the Tabernacle for
4:28 So these are the duties **a** to the Gershonites at the
4:49 Each man was **a** his task and told what to carry,
8:19 I have **a** the Levites to Aaron and his sons.
26:56 Each inheritance must be **a** by lot among the larger
32:33 So Moses **a** to the tribes of Gad, Reuben, and half
35:4 The pastureland **a** to the Levites around these
Dt 2:12 from the land that the LORD had **a** to Israel.)
32:8 When the Most High **a** lands to the nations,
33:21 for themselves; / a leader's share was **a** to them.
Jos 13:8 of the LORD, had previously **a** this land to them.
13:15 Moses had **a** the following area to the families of
13:24 Moses had **a** the following area to the families of
13:29 Moses had **a** the following area to the families of
15:1 The land **a** to the families of the tribe of Judah
18:6 God to decide which section will be **a** to each tribe.
18:11 It lay between the territory previously **a** to the
21:4 were given thirteen towns that were originally **a** to
21:8 and **a** these towns and pasturelands to the Levites
Jdg 18:1 out the people who lived in the land **a** to them.
1Sa 2:28 And I **a** the sacrificial offerings to you priests.
2Sa 11:16 So Joab **a** Uriah to a spot close to the city wall
1Ki 4:27 and his court, each during his **a** month.
7:40 had **a** him to make for the Temple of the LORD:
9:22 Instead, he **a** them to serve as fighting men,
2Ki 22:5 Entrust this money to the men **a** to supervise the
1Ch 6:31 David **a** the following men to lead the music at the
6:54 and territory **a** by means of sacred lots to the
6:64 So the people of Israel **a** all these towns
6:65 were also **a** by means of sacred lots.
6:70 The remaining descendants of Kohath were **a** these
9:28 Some of the gatekeepers were **a** to care for the
22:2 and he **a** them the task of preparing blocks of stone
24:5 All tasks were **a** to the various groups by means of
24:31 they were **a** to their duties by means of sacred lots,
26:13 They were **a** by families for guard duty at the
26:14 The north gate was **a** to his son Zechariah, a man
26:16 Shuppim and Hosah were **a** the west gate
26:17 Six Levites were **a** each day to the east gate,
26:18 Six were **a** each day to the west gate, four to the
2Ch 4:11 had **a** him to make for the Temple of God:
7:6 The priests took their **a** positions, and so did the
8:9 Instead, he **a** them to serve as fighting men,
8:14 He also **a** the Levites to lead the people in praise
8:14 And he **a** the gatekeepers to their gates by their
17:2 and he **a** additional garrisons to the land of Judah
34:10 He entrusted the money to the men **a** to supervise
34:16 "Your officials are doing everything they were **a**
35:2 Josiah also **a** the priests to their duties
35:5 and help the families **a** to you as they bring their
35:15 descendants of Asaph, were in their **a** places,
Ne 13:30 and **a** tasks to the priests and Levites,
Est 2:9 He also **a** her seven maids specially chosen from
Job 7:3 I, too, have been **a** months of futility, long
Isa 13:3 the LORD, have **a** this task to these armies,
43:28 and **a** Israel a future of complete destruction
Jer 35:4 and we went into the room **a** to the sons of Hanan
39:10 and he **a** them fields and vineyards to care for.
Eze 46:19 and led me to the sacred rooms **a** to the priests,
Da 1:5 The king **a** them a daily ration of the best food
1:15 men who had been eating the food **a** by the king.
Jn 5:36 They have been **a** to me by the Father, and they
9:4 All of us must quickly carry out the tasks **a** us by
Ac 20:24 use it for doing the work **a** me by the Lord Jesus—
1Pe 5:3 Don't lord it over the people **a** to your care,

ASSIGNING (2) [ASSIGN]
2Ch 8:14 In **a** the priests to their duties, Solomon followed
25:5 **a** leaders to each clan from Judah and Benjamin.

ASSIGNMENTS (1) [ASSIGN]
1Ch 24:6 down the names and **a** in the presence of the king,

ASSIR (4)
Ex 6:24 The descendants of Korah included **A**, Elkanah,
1Ch 6:22 of Kohath were Amminadab, Korah, **A**,
6:23 Elkanah, Abiasaph, **A**,
6:37 Tahath, **A**, Abiasaph, Korah,

ASSIST (11) [ASSISTANCE, ASSISTANT, ASSISTANTS, ASSISTED, ASSISTING]
Nu 8:26 After retirement they may **a** their fellow Levites by
18:2 "Bring your relatives of the tribe of Levi to **a** you
1Ch 22:17 Then David ordered all the leaders of Israel to **a**
23:28 The work of the Levites was to **a** the priests,
2Ch 8:14 in praise and to **a** the priests in their daily duties.
19:11 The Levites will **a** you in making sure that justice
26:13 They were prepared to **a** the king against any
Ne 12:27 asked to come to Jerusalem to **a** in the ceremonies.
Pr 29:24 If you **a** a thief, you are only hurting yourself.
Zec 4:14 "They represent the two anointed ones who **a** the
Ac 15:35 and Barnabas stayed in Antioch to **a** many others

ASSISTANCE (1) [ASSIST]
Pr 27:10 of need, you won't have to ask your relatives for **a**.

ASSISTANT (17) [ASSIST]
Ex 24:13 and his **a** Joshua climbed up the mountain of God.
31:6 son of Ahisamach, of the tribe of Dan, to be his **a**.
Nu 11:28 who had been Moses' personal **a** since his youth,
Dt 1:38 Instead, your **a**, Joshua son of Nun, will lead the
Jos 1:1 the LORD spoke to Joshua son of Nun, Moses' **a**.
1Ki 19:21 and they all ate. Then he went with Elijah as his **a**.
2Ki 3:11 is here. He used to be Elijah's personal **a**."
25:18 his **a** Zephaniah, and the three chief gatekeepers.
1Ch 6:39 Heman's first **a** was Asaph from the clan of
6:44 Heman's second **a** was Ethan from the clan of
2Ch 26:11 the secretary of the army, and his **a**, Maaseiah.
Ne 11:17 Bakbukiah, who was Mattaniah's **a**; and Abda son
13:13 of Zaccur and grandson of Mattaniah as their **a**.
Jer 52:24 his **a** Zephaniah, and the three chief gatekeepers.
Lk 10:32 A Temple **a** walked over and looked at him lying
Ac 12:20 made friends with Blastus, Herod's personal **a**,
13:5 of God. (John Mark went with them as their **a**.)

ASSISTANTS (13) [ASSIST]
Nu 3:6 and present them to Aaron the priest as his **a**.
3:9 Assign the Levites to Aaron and his sons as their **a**.
18:6 from among the Israelites to be your special **a**.
1Ch 9:2 came some of the priests, Levites, and Temple **a**.
15:18 The following men were chosen as their **a**:
16:5 His **a** were Zechariah (the second), then Jeiel,
18:17 David's sons served as the king's chief **a**.
2Ch 31:15 His faithful **a** were Eden, Miniamin, Jeshua,
Ezr 8:20 The Temple servants were **a** to the Levites—
Ne 5:15 Even their **a** took advantage of the people. But
Eze 46:24 **a** to boil the sacrifices offered by the people."
Jn 1:19 and Temple **a** from Jerusalem to ask John whether
Ac 19:22 He sent his two **a**, Timothy and Erastus, on ahead

ASSISTED (10) [ASSIST]
Ex 33:11 but the young man who **a** him, Joshua son of Nun,
38:23 He was **a** by Oholiab son of Ahisamach,
Nu 1:4 **a** by one family leader from each tribe."
1Sa 2:11 the LORD's helper, for he **a** Eli the priest.
2:22 women who **a** at the entrance of the Tabernacle.
1Ch 23:31 They **a** with the burnt offerings that were presented
2Ch 31:12 Levite was put in charge, **a** by his brother Shimei.
34:13 Still others **a** as secretaries, officials,
Ezr 1:6 And all their neighbors **a** by giving them vessels of
Ne 11:9 who was **a** by Judah son of Hassenuah,

ASSISTING (2) [ASSIST]
1Sa 3:1 the boy Samuel was serving the LORD by **a** Eli.
2Ki 7:2 The officer **a** the king said to the man of God,

ASSOCIATE (4) [ASSOCIATED, ASSOCIATES, ASSOCIATING]
Jos 23:7 Make sure you do not **a** with the other people still
Pr 24:21 the LORD and the king, and don't **a** with rebels.
1Co 5:9 I told you not to **a** with people who indulge in
5:11 What I meant was that you are not to **a** with

ASSOCIATED (1) [ASSOCIATE]
Nu 18:7 must personally handle all the sacred service **a**

ASSOCIATES (9) [ASSOCIATE]
Ne 11:12 together with 822 of their **a**, who worked at the
11:13 and 242 of his **a**, who were heads of their families.
11:14 and 128 of his outstanding **a**. Their chief officer
11:19 Akkub, Talmon, and 172 of their **a**, who guarded
12:7 of the priests and their **a** in the days of Jeshua.
12:8 who with his **a** was in charge of the songs of
12:9 Their **a**, Bakbukiah and Unni, stood opposite them
12:24 Sherebiah, Jeshua, Binnui, Kadmiel, and other **a**,
Est 1:14 They were his closest **a** and held the highest

ASSOCIATING (1) [ASSOCIATE]
Lk 15:2 that he was **a** with such despicable people—

ASSOS (1)
Ac 20:13 Paul went by land to **A**, where he had arranged for

ASSUMED (9) [ASSUMING]
Dt 22:27 it must be **a** that she screamed, but there was no
Mt 20:10 to get their pay, they **a** they would receive more.
Lk 2:44 because they **a** he was with friends among the
Jn 11:31 they **a** she was going to Lazarus's grave to weep.
Ac 7:25 Moses **a** his brothers would realize that God had
16:27 He **a** the prisoners had escaped, so he drew his
21:29 and they **a** Paul had taken him into the Temple.)
Heb 11:19 Abraham **a** that if Isaac died, God was able to
Rev 11:17 always was, / for now you have **a** your great power

ASSUMING (1) [ASSUMED]
Job 6:29 Stop **a** my guilt, for I am righteous. Don't be

ASSUR [KJV] See ASSYRIA

ASSURANCE (6) [ASSURE]
Job 24:22 They may rise high, but they have no **a** in life.
Isa 26:19 Yet we have this **a**: / Those who belong to God
Col 1:23 Don't drift away from the **a** you received when
1:27 and this is your **a** that you will share in his glory.
1Th 1:5 for the Holy Spirit gave you full **a** that what we
Heb 11:1 It is the confident **a** that what we hope for is going

ASSURANCES (2) [ASSURE]
Jer 6:14 They give **a** of peace when all is war.
8:11 They give **a** of peace when all is war.

ASSURE (60) [ASSURANCE, ASSURANCES, ASSURED, ASSURES, ASSURING, REASSURE, REASSURED, REASSURING]
Dt 8:19 "But I **a** you of this: If you ever forget the LORD
2Sa 14:10 I can **a** you they will never complain again!"
Mt 5:18 I **a** you, until heaven and earth disappear,
5:26 I **a** you that you won't be free again until you have
6:2 I **a** you, they have received all the reward they will
6:5 I **a** you, that is all the reward they will ever get.
6:16 I **a** you, that is the only reward they will ever get.
10:15 I **a** you, the wicked cities of Sodom and Gomorrah
10:23 I **a** you that I, the Son of Man, will return before
11:11 "I **a** you, of all who have ever lived, none is
11:22 I **a** you, Tyre and Sidon will be better off on the
11:24 I **a** you, Sodom will be better off on the judgment
13:17 I **a** you, many prophets and godly people have
16:28 And I **a** you that some of you standing here right
17:20 "I **a** you, even if you had faith as small as a
18:3 Then he said, "I **a** you, unless you turn from your
19:28 "I **a** you that when I, the Son of Man,
21:21 "I **a** you, if you have faith and don't doubt,
21:31 "I **a** you, corrupt tax collectors and prostitutes will
23:36 I **a** you, all the accumulated judgment of the
24:2 I **a** you, they will be so completely demolished that
24:34 I **a** you, this generation will not pass from the
24:47 I **a** you, the master will put that servant in charge
25:40 And the King will tell them, 'I **a** you, when you
25:45 And he will answer, 'I **a** you, when you refused to
26:13 I **a** you, wherever the Good News is preached
Mk 3:28 "I **a** you that any sin can be forgiven,
8:12 I **a** you, I will not give this generation any such
9:1 "I **a** you that some of you standing here right now
9:41 the Messiah, I **a** you, that person will be rewarded.
10:15 I **a** you, anyone who doesn't have their kind of
10:29 "I **a** you that everyone who has given up house
11:23 I **a** you that you can say to this mountain,
12:43 He called his disciples to him and said, "I **a** you,
13:30 I **a** you, this generation will not pass from the
14:9 I **a** you, wherever the Good News is preached
Lk 9:27 And I **a** you that some of you standing here right
12:8 "And I **a** you of this: If anyone acknowledges me

12:44 I **a** you, the master will put that servant in charge
18:17 I **a** you, anyone who doesn't have their kind of
18:29 "Yes," Jesus replied, "and I **a** you, everyone who
21:3 "I **a** you," he said, "this poor widow has given
21:32 I **a** you, this generation will not pass from the
23:43 And Jesus replied, "I **a** you, today you will be
Jn 3:3 Jesus replied, "I **a** you, unless you are born again,
3:11 I **a** you, I am telling you what we know and have
5:19 Jesus replied, "I **a** you, the Son can do nothing by
5:24 "I **a** you, those who listen to my message
5:25 "And I **a** you that the time is coming, in fact it is
5:32 and I can **a** you that everything he says about me is
6:32 Jesus said, "I **a** you, Moses didn't give them bread
6:47 "I **a** you, anyone who believes in me already has
6:53 So Jesus said again, "I **a** you, unless you eat the
8:34 "I **a** you that everyone who sins is a slave of sin.
8:51 I **a** you, anyone who obeys my teaching will never
10:1 "I **a** you, anyone who sneaks over the wall of a
10:7 "I **a** you, I am the gate for the sheep," he said.
Gal 1:11 I solemnly **a** you that the Good News of salvation
Col 4:13 I can **a** you that he has agonized for you and also
1Pe 5:12 and **a** you that the grace of God is with you no

ASSURED (4) [ASSURE]

Pr 16:5 be **a** that the proud will be punished.
Jer 26:15 rest **a** that you will be killing an innocent man!
40:9 Gedaliah **a** them that it would be safe for them to
Eph 3:12 into God's presence, **a** of his glad welcome.

ASSURES (1) [ASSURE]

Heb 10:39 seal their fate. We have faith that **a** our salvation.

ASSURING (2) [ASSURE]

Jer 5:24 each spring and fall, **a** us of plentiful harvests.'
Ro 4:24 **a** us that God will also declare us to be righteous if

ASSWAGE [KJV] See TAKE (AWAY)

ASSYRIA (129) [ASSYRIA'S, ASSYRIAN, ASSYRIANS]

Ge 10:11 From there he extended his reign to **A**, where he
Nu 24:22 will be destroyed / when **A** takes you captive."
24:24 of Cyprus; / they will oppress both **A** and Eber,
2Ki 15:19 Then King Tiglath-pileser of **A** invaded the land.
15:20 So the king of **A** turned from attacking Israel
15:29 King Tiglath-pileser of **A** attacked Israel again,
15:29 and he took the people to **A** as captives.
16:7 to King Tiglath-pileser of **A** with this message:
16:10 Damascus to meet with King Tiglath-pileser of **A**.
16:18 In deference to the king of **A**, he also removed the
17:3 King Shalmaneser of **A** attacked and defeated King
17:3 Israel was forced to pay heavy annual tribute to **A**.
17:4 Then Hoshea conspired against the king of **A** by
17:4 and by refusing to pay the annual tribute to **A**.
17:4 When the king of **A** discovered this treachery,
17:5 Then the king of **A** invaded the entire land, and for
17:6 and the people of Israel were exiled to **A**.
17:23 So Israel was carried off to the land of **A**,
17:24 And the king of **A** transported groups of people
17:26 So a message was sent to the king of **A**:
17:27 The king of **A** then commanded, "Send one of the
18:7 He revolted against the king of **A** and refused to
18:9 King Shalmaneser of **A** attacked Israel and began a
18:11 that time the king of **A** deported the Israelites to **A**
18:13 King Sennacherib of **A** came to attack the fortified
18:14 King Hezekiah sent this message to the king of **A**
18:14 The king of **A** then demanded a settlement of more
18:17 Nevertheless the king of **A** sent his commander in
18:19 "This is what the great king of **A** says: What are
18:20 will give you any military backing against **A**?
18:23 My master, the king of **A**, will strike a bargain
18:28 "Listen to this message from the great king of **A**!
18:31 These are the terms the king of **A** is offering:
18:33 nations ever saved their people from the king of **A**?
19:7 and the king will receive a report from **A** telling
19:10 Jerusalem will not be captured by the king of **A**.
19:11 You know perfectly well what the kings of **A** have
19:12 The former kings of **A** destroyed them all!
19:17 that the kings of **A** have destroyed all these
19:20 heard your prayer about King Sennacherib of **A**.
19:32 this is what the LORD says about the king of **A**:
19:36 Then King Sennacherib of **A** broke camp
19:37 Esarhaddon, became the next king of **A**.
20:6 I will rescue you and this city from the king of **A**.
23:29 went to the Euphrates River to help the king of **A**.
1Ch 5:6 taken into captivity by King Tiglath-pileser of **A**.
5:26 So the God of Israel caused King Pul of **A** (also
2Ch 28:16 asked the king of **A** for help against his enemies.
28:20 So when King Tiglath-pileser of **A** arrived,
28:21 and gave them to the king of **A** as tribute.
32:1 this work, King Sennacherib of **A** invaded Judah.
32:4 "Why should the kings of **A** come here and find
32:7 Don't be afraid of the king of **A** or his mighty
32:9 Then King Sennacherib of **A**, while still besieging
32:10 "This is what King Sennacherib of **A** says:
32:11 our God will rescue us from the king of **A**.'
32:13 and the other kings of **A** before me have done to all
32:22 people of Jerusalem from King Sennacherib of **A**
Ezr 4:2 since King Esarhaddon of **A** brought us here."
6:22 changed the attitude of the king of **A** toward them,
Ne 9:32 and ancestors from the days when the kings of **A**
Ps 83:8 **A** has joined them, too, / and is allied with the
Isa 7:17 The mighty king of **A** will come with his great
7:18 the army of Upper Egypt and for the army of **A**.
8:4 the king of **A** will invade both Damascus
8:7 the king of **A** and all his mighty armies.
10:5 "Destruction is certain for **A**, the whip of my
10:6 **A** will enslave my people, who are a godless
10:7 But the king of **A** will not know that it is I who
10:12 After the Lord has used the king of **A** to
10:12 he will turn against the king of **A** and punish him
10:16 Listen now, king of **A**! Because of all your evil
10:28 Look, the mighty armies of **A** are coming!
10:33 He will destroy all that vast army of **A**—officers
11:11 returning them to the land of Israel from **A**,
11:16 He will make a highway from **A** for the remnant
19:23 day Egypt and **A** will be connected by a highway.
19:25 my people. Blessed be **A**, the land I have made.
20:1 In the year when King Sargon of **A** captured the
20:4 For the king of **A** will take away the Egyptians
20:6 on Egypt to protect us from the king of **A**.' "
27:13 Many who were dying in exile in **A** and Egypt will
33:4 so Jerusalem will strip the fallen army of **A**!
33:7 for **A** has refused their petition for peace.
36:1 King Sennacherib of **A** came to attack the fortified
36:2 Then the king of **A** sent his personal representative
36:4 "This is what the great king of **A** says: What are
36:5 will give you any military backing against **A**?
36:8 My master, the king of **A**, will strike a bargain
36:13 "Listen to this message from the great king of **A**!
36:16 These are the terms the king of **A** is offering:
36:18 nations ever saved their people from the king of **A**?
37:7 from **A** telling him that he is needed at home.
37:10 Jerusalem will not be captured by the king of **A**.
37:11 You know perfectly well what the kings of **A** have
37:12 The former kings of **A** destroyed them all!
37:18 that the kings of **A** have destroyed all these
37:21 to your prayer concerning King Sennacherib of **A**.
37:33 this is what the LORD says about the king of **A**:
37:37 Then King Sennacherib of **A** broke camp
37:38 Esarhaddon, became the next king of **A**.
38:6 I will rescue you and this city from the king of **A**.
52:4 they have been oppressed without cause by **A**.
Jer 2:18 you gained by your alliances with Egypt and **A**?
2:36 in Egypt will let you down, just as **A** did before.
50:17 First the king of **A** ate them up. Then King
50:18 and his land, just as I punished the king of **A**.
La 5:6 to Egypt and **A** to get enough food to survive.
Eze 23:7 herself with the most desirable men of **A**,
31:3 You are as **A** was—a great and mighty nation.
31:3 **A**, too, was once like a cedar of Lebanon, full of
31:15 When **A** went down into the grave, I made the
32:22 "**A** lies there surrounded by the graves of all its
Hos 5:13 Israel turned to **A**, to the great king there,
7:11 first calling to Egypt, then flying to **A**.
8:9 looking for a mate, they have gone up to **A**.
9:3 You will be carried off to Egypt and **A**, where you
9:6 Even if you escape destruction from **A**, you will be
10:6 away with them when they go as captives to **A**,
11:5 go back to Egypt and will be forced to serve **A**.
11:11 Flying like doves, they will return from **A**.
12:1 they make alliances with **A** and cut deals with the
14:3 **A** cannot save us, nor can our strength in battle.
Mic 5:6 They will rule **A** with drawn swords and enter the
7:12 from **A** all the way to the towns of Egypt, and from
Zep 2:13 He will destroy **A** and make its great capital,
Zec 10:10 and **A** and resettle them in Gilead and Lebanon.
10:11 The pride of **A** will be crushed, and the rule of

ASSYRIA'S (5) [ASSYRIA]

2Ki 17:4 So of Egypt to help him shake free of **A** power
19:29 that the LORD will protect this city from **A** king.
Isa 10:18 **A** vast army is like a glorious forest, yet it will be
10:18 The LORD will completely destroy **A** warriors,
37:30 that the LORD will protect this city from **A** king.

ASSYRIAN (29) [ASSYRIA]

2Ki 16:8 palace treasury and sent it as a gift to the **A** king.
18:16 overlaid with gold, and he gave it all to the **A** king.
18:19 Then the **A** king's personal representative sent this
18:30 This city will never be handed over to the **A** king.'
18:37 and told him what the **A** representative had said.
19:4 But perhaps the LORD your God has heard the **A**
19:6 speech against me from the **A** king's messengers.
19:8 the **A** representative left Jerusalem and went to
19:35 the angel of the LORD went out to the **A** camp and killed 185,000 **A** troops.
2Ch 30:6 us who have survived the conquest of the **A** kings.
32:18 The **A** officials who brought the letters shouted
32:21 who destroyed the **A** army with all its commanders
33:11 So the LORD sent the **A** armies, and they took
Isa 28:2 For the Lord will send the mighty **A** army against
30:33 of burning—has long been ready for the **A** king;
33:18 **A** officers outside your walls counted your towers
36:4 Then the **A** king's personal representative sent this
36:15 This city will never be handed over to the **A** king.'
36:22 and told him what the **A** representative had said.
37:4 But perhaps the LORD your God has heard the **A**
37:6 speech against me from the **A** king's messengers.
37:8 the **A** representative left Jerusalem and went to
37:36 the angel of the LORD went out to the **A** camp and killed 185,000 **A** troops.
Eze 23:9 And so I handed her over to her **A** lovers,
23:12 She fawned over her **A** neighbors, those handsome
Na 1:13 your chains and release you from **A** oppression."
3:18 O **A** king, your princes lie dead in the dust.

ASSYRIANS (32) [ASSYRIA]

2Ki 16:9 So the **A** attacked the Aramean capital of
17:24 So the **A** took over Samaria and the other towns of
18:17 The **A** stopped beside the aqueduct that feeds
19:18 But of course the **A** could destroy them!
19:35 When the surviving **A** woke up the next morning,
1Ch 5:26 The **A** exiled them to Halah, Habor, Hara,
Isa 7:20 these **A** you have hired to protect you—and use it
8:9 "The **A** will cry, 'Do your best to defend
9:11 bringing Rezin's enemies, the **A**, against them—
10:17 night he will burn those thorns and briers, the **A**.
10:20 They will no longer depend on the **A**, who would
10:24 do not be afraid of the **A** when they oppress you
14:25 I will break the **A** when they are in Israel; I will
19:23 and **A** will move freely between their lands,
23:13 The **A** have handed Babylon over to the wild
28:15 You say, "The **A** can never touch us, for we have
30:31 the LORD's command, the **A** will be shattered.
31:8 "The **A** will be destroyed, but not by the swords of
31:8 The strong young **A** will be taken away as
33:1 Destruction is certain for you **A**, who have
33:8 The **A** have broken their peace pact and care
33:11 You **A** will gain nothing by all your efforts.
36:2 The **A** stopped beside the aqueduct that feeds
37:19 But of course the **A** could destroy them!
37:36 When the surviving **A** woke up the next morning,
Eze 16:28 You have prostituted yourselves with the **A**,
23:5 and she gave her love to the **A**, her neighbors.
23:23 And all the **A** will come with them—
Mic 5:5 When the **A** invade our land and break through our
5:6 They will rescue us from the **A** when they pour
Na 1:12 "Even though the **A** have many allies, they will be
1:14 And this is what the LORD says concerning the **A**

ASTAROTH [KJV] See ASHTAROTH

ASTONISHED (9)

Job 17:8 The upright are **a** when they see me. The innocent
Jer 18:16 All who pass by will be **a** and shake their heads in
Mt 13:54 everyone was **a** and said, "Where does he get his
Mk 6:2 the synagogue, and many who heard him were **a**.
6:51 the wind stopped. They were **a** at what they saw.
Lk 2:18 All who heard the shepherds' story were **a**,
Jn 4:27 They were **a** to find him talking to a woman,
5:20 healing this man. You will be **a** at what he does.
Ac 13:12 and was **a** at what he learned about the Lord.

ASTOUNDED (5) [ASTOUNDING]

Ps 40:3 Many will see what he has done and be **a**.
Hab 1:5 and be amazed! Watch and be **a** at what I will do!
Mt 19:25 The disciples were **a**. "Then who in the world can
Mk 10:26 The disciples were **a**. "Then who in the world can
Ac 3:10 often at the Beautiful Gate, they were absolutely **a**!

ASTOUNDING (3) [ASTOUNDED]

Ac 3:12 of Israel," he said, "what is so **a** about this?
2Co 12:4 and heard things so **a** that they cannot be told.
Rev 13:13 He did **a** miracles, such as making fire flash down

ASTRAY (26) [STRAY]

Nu 5:12 'Suppose a man's wife goes **a** and is unfaithful to
5:20 But if you have gone **a** while under your husband's
Dt 13:5 or dreamers who try to lead you **a** must be put to
13:13 **a** by encouraging them to worship foreign gods.
27:18 'Cursed is anyone who leads a blind person **a** on
Ps 25:8 he shows the proper path to those who go **a**.
Pr 10:17 to life, but those who ignore it will lead others **a**.
12:26 advice to their friends; the wicked lead them **a**.
20:1 Whoever is led **a** by drink cannot be wise.
Jer 4:1 away your detestable idols and go **a** no more,
50:6 Their shepherds have led them **a** and turned them
Eze 48:11 and did not go **a** when the people of Israel
Am 2:4 They have been led **a** by the same lies that
Mic 3:5 "You are leading my people **a**! You promise peace
Mt 24:5 saying, 'I am the Messiah.' They will lead many **a**.
24:11 prophets will appear and will lead many people **a**.
Mk 13:6 claiming to be the Messiah. They will lead many **a**.
Jn 7:47 "Have you been led **a**, too?" the Pharisees
Ac 2:40 yourselves from this generation that has gone **a**!"
1Co 12:2 that when you were still pagans you were led **a**
2Co 7:2 done wrong to anyone. We have not led anyone **a**.
11:29 Who is led **a**, and I do not burn with anger?
Col 2:8 Don't let anyone lead you **a** with empty
1Ti 5:15 I am afraid that some of them have already gone **a**
1Jn 2:26 need to be aware of those who want to lead you **a**.
Rev 2:20 who calls herself a prophet—to lead my servants **a**.

ASTROLOGER (1) [ASTROLOGERS]

Da 2:10 such a thing of any magician, enchanter, or **a**!

ASTROLOGERS (9) [ASTROLOGER]

Isa 47:13 have more than enough advisers, **a**, and stargazers.
Da 2:2 in his magicians, enchanters, sorcerers, and **a**,
2:4 Then the **a** answered the king in Aramaic,
2:5 But the king said to the **a**, "I am serious about this.
2:10 The **a** replied to the king, "There isn't a man alive
3:8 But some of the **a** went to the king and informed
4:7 When all the magicians, enchanters, **a**,
5:7 The king shouted for the enchanters, **a**,
5:11 enchanters, **a**, and fortune-tellers of Babylon.

ASTUTE (1)

Ezr 8:18 He was a very **a** man and a descendant of Mahli,

ASUPPIM [KJV] See STOREHOUSES

ASWAN (2)
Eze 29:10 from Migdol to **A**, as far south as the border of
30:6 From Migdol to **A** they will be slaughtered by the

ASYNCRITUS (1)
Ro 16:14 And please give my greetings to **A**, Phlegon,

AT (2475) See Index of Articles, Etc.

ATAD (1)
Ge 50:10 When they arrived at the threshing floor of **A**,

ATARAH (1)
1Ch 2:26 Jerahmeel had a second wife named **A**. She was

ATAROTH (4) [ATAROTH-ADDAR]
Nu 32:3 "**A**, Dibon, Jazer, Nimrah, Heshbon, Elealeh,
32:34 people of Gad built the towns of Dibon, **A**, Aroer,
Jos 16:2 it ran over to **A** in the territory of the Arkites.
16:7 From Janoah it turned southward to **A** and Naarah,

ATAROTH-ADDAR (2) [ATAROTH]
Jos 16:5 eastern boundary of their inheritance began at **A**.
18:13 and proceeded down to **A** to the top of the hill

ATE (78) [EAT]
Ge 3:6 make her so wise! So she **a** some of the fruit.
3:6 her husband, who was with her. Then he **a** it, too.
3:12 you gave me who brought me the fruit, and I **a** it."
3:13 tricked me," she replied. "That's why I **a** it."
3:17 to your wife and **a** the fruit I told you not to eat,
18:8 As they **a**, Abraham waited on them there beneath
25:34 Esau **a** and drank and went on about his business,
26:30 and they **a** and drank in preparation for the treaty
27:25 took the food over to his father, and Isaac **a** it.
40:17 for Pharaoh, but the birds came and **a** them."
41:4 Then the thin, ugly cows **a** the fat ones! At this
41:20 ugly cows **a** up the seven fat ones that had come
43:32 Joseph **a** by himself, and his brothers were served
Ex 10:15 They **a** all the plants and all the fruit on the trees
16:35 So the people of Israel **a** manna for forty years
34:28 forty nights. In all that time he neither **a** nor drank.
Dt 9:9 and all that time I **a** nothing and drank no water.
32:38 are those gods, / who **a** the fat of their sacrifices
Jos 5:12 So from that time on the Israelites **a** from the crops
Jdg 14:9 of the honey into his hands and **a** it along the way.
14:9 gave some to his father and mother, and they **a** it.
1Sa 9:24 I invited these others!" So Saul **a** with Samuel.
14:24 on my enemies." So no one **a** a thing all day,
14:27 a stick into a piece of honeycomb and **a** the honey.
14:32 but they **a** them without draining the blood.
28:25 the meal to Saul and his men, and they **a** it.
2Sa 9:11 that time on, Mephibosheth **a** regularly with David,
12:3 It **a** from the man's own plate and drank from his
12:20 After that, he returned to the palace and **a**.
1Ki 13:19 and the man of God **a** some food and drank some
13:22 You came back to this place and **a** food and drank
19:6 of water! So he **a** and drank and lay down again.
19:8 So he got up and **a** and drank, and the food gave
19:21 the meat to the other plowmen, and they all **a**.
2Ki 6:29 So we cooked my son and **a** him. Then the next
9:34 Then Jehu went into the palace and **a** and drank.
Ezr 6:22 They **a** the Passover meal and celebrated the
Ne 9:25 So they **a** until they were full and grew fat
Ps 78:25 They **a** the food of angels! / God gave them all
78:29 The people **a** their fill. / He gave them what they
105:35 They **a** up everything green in the land,
106:28 they even **a** sacrifices offered to the dead!
Jer 50:17 First the king of Assyria **a** them up. Then King
La 4:5 The people who once **a** only the richest foods now
Eze 3:3 And when I **a** it, it tasted as sweet as honey.
16:13 You **a** the finest foods—fine flour, honey,
Da 4:33 He **a** grass like a cow, and he was drenched with
5:21 He **a** grass like a cow, and he was drenched with
Am 7:2 In my vision the locusts **a** everything in sight that
Jnh 4:7 The next morning at dawn the worm **a** through the
Mt 4:2 For forty days and forty nights he **a** nothing
12:4 and they **a** the special bread reserved for the priests
13:4 fell on a footpath, and the birds came and **a** them.
14:20 They all **a** as much as they wanted, and they
15:37 They all **a** until they were full, and when the scraps
Mk 2:26 **a** the special bread reserved for the priests alone,
4:4 seed fell on a footpath, and the birds came and **a** it.
6:42 They all **a** as much as they wanted,
8:8 They **a** until they were full, and when the scraps
Lk 4:2 He **a** nothing all that time and was very hungry.
6:1 off the husks in their hands, and **a** the grains.
6:4 **a** the special bread reserved for the priests alone,
8:5 it was stepped on, and the birds came and **a** it.
9:17 They all **a** as much as they wanted, and they
13:26 You will say, 'But we **a** and drank with you,
24:43 and he **a** it as they watched.
Jn 6:11 with the fish. And they all **a** until they were full.
6:31 our ancestors **a** manna while they journeyed
6:49 Your ancestors **a** manna in the wilderness, but they
6:58 ancestors did, even though they **a** the manna."
Ac 9:19 Afterward he **a** some food and was strengthened.
10:41 We were those who **a** and drank with him after he
11:3 the home of Gentiles and even **a** with them!"
20:11 back upstairs and **a** the Lord's Supper together.
27:35 God before them all, and broke off a piece and **a** it.
1Co 10:3 And all of them **a** the same miraculous food,
Gal 2:12 he first arrived, he **a** with the Gentile Christians,
Rev 10:10 little scroll from the hands of the angel, and I **a** it!

ATER (5)
Ezr 2:16 The family of **A** (descendants of Hezekiah) | 98
2:42 **A**, Talmon, Akkub, Hatita, and Shobai | 139
Ne 7:21 The family of **A** (descendants of Hezekiah) | 98
7:45 **A**, Talmon, Akkub, Hatita, and Shobai | 138
10:17 **A**, Hezekiah, Azzur,

ATHACH (1)
1Sa 30:30 Hormah, Bor-ashan, **A**,

ATHAIAH (1)
Ne 11:4 **A** son of Uzziah, son of Zechariah, son of

ATHALIAH (17) [ATHALIAH'S]
2Ki 8:26 His mother was **A**, a granddaughter of King Omri
11:1 When **A**, the mother of King Ahaziah of Judah,
11:2 and his nurse in a bedroom to hide him from **A**,
11:3 LORD for six years while **A** ruled over the land.
11:13 When **A** heard all the noise made by the guards
11:14 When **A** saw all this, she tore her clothes in despair
11:20 because **A** had been killed at the king's palace.
1Ch 8:26 Shamsherai, Shehariah, **A**,
2Ch 22:2 His mother was **A**, a granddaughter of King Omri
22:10 When **A**, the mother of King Ahaziah of Judah,
22:11 hid the child so that **A** could not murder him.
22:12 of God for six years while **A** ruled over the land.
23:12 When **A** heard the noise of the people running
23:13 When **A** saw all this, she tore her clothes in despair
23:21 the city was peaceful because **A** had been killed.
24:7 the followers of wicked **A** had broken into the
Ezr 8:7 of Elam: Jeshaiah son of **A** and 70 other men.

ATHALIAH'S (2) [ATHALIAH]
2Ki 11:4 In the seventh year of **A** reign, Jehoiada the priest
2Ch 23:1 In the seventh year of **A** reign, Jehoiada the priest

ATHARIM (1)
Nu 21:1 the Israelites were approaching on the road to **A**.

ATHENIANS (1) [ATHENS]
Ac 17:21 (It should be explained that all the **A** as well as the

ATHENS (6) [ATHENIANS]
Ac 17:15 Those escorting Paul went with him to **A**,
17:16 While Paul was waiting for them in **A**, he was
17:21 **A** seemed to spend all their time discussing the
17:22 "Men of **A**, I notice that you are very religious,
18:1 Then Paul left **A** and went to Corinth.
1Th 3:1 we decided that I should stay alone in **A**,

ATHLAI (1)
Ezr 10:28 of Bebai: Jehohanan, Hananiah, Zabbai, and **A**.

ATHLETE (3) [ATHLETES]
Ps 19:5 after his wedding. / It rejoices like a great **a**
1Co 9:27 I discipline my body like an **a**, training it to do
2Ti 2:5 just as an **a** either follows the rules or is

ATHLETES (1) [ATHLETE]
1Co 9:25 All **a** practice strict self-control. They do it to win

ATONE (1) [ATONEMENT]
Da 9:24 to bring an end to sin, to **a** for guilt, to bring in

ATONEMENT (108) [ATONE]
Ex 25:17 the Ark's cover—the place of **a**—out of pure gold.
25:18 and place them at the two ends of the **a** cover.
25:19 Attach the cherubim to each end of the **a** cover,
25:20 looking down on the **a** cover with their wings
25:21 to you. Then put the **a** cover on top of the Ark.
25:22 and talk to you from above the **a** cover between the
26:34 "Then put the Ark's cover—the place of **a**—
29:33 and bread used for their **a** in the ordination
29:36 a young bull as an offering for the **a** of sin.
29:36 Purify the altar by making **a** for it; make it holy by
29:37 Make **a** for the altar every day for seven days.
30:6 opposite the Ark's cover—the place of **a**—
30:10 the blood from the offering made for the **a** of sin.
30:15 is given to the LORD to make **a** for yourselves,
30:16 and it will make **a** for your lives."
31:7 of the Covenant; the Ark's cover—the place of **a**;
35:12 and its poles; the Ark's cover—the place of **a**;
37:6 he made the Ark's cover—the place of **a**.
37:7 and placed them at the two ends of the **a** cover.
37:8 so they were actually a part of the **a** cover—
37:9 each other as they looked down on the **a** cover,
37:9 and their wings were stretched out above the **a**
39:35 its carrying poles; the Ark's cover—the place of **a**;
40:20 set the Ark's cover—the place of **a**—on top of it.
Lev 1:4 accept it as your substitute, thus making **a** for you.
4:20 In this way, the priest will make **a** for the people,
4:26 this way, the priest will make **a** for the leader's sin,
4:31 In this way, the priest will make **a** for them,
4:35 In this way, the priest will make **a** for them,
5:6 their sin, and the priest will make **a** for them.
5:10 the priest will make **a** for those who are guilty,
5:13 the priest will make **a** for those who are guilty,
5:16 he will make **a** for them with the ram sacrificed as
5:18 the priest will make **a** for those who are guilty,
6:7 then make **a** for them before the LORD,
6:30 to make **a** in the Holy Place for the people's sins,
7:7 belongs to the priest in charge of the **a** ceremony.
8:15 he set the altar apart as holy and made **a** for it.
8:34 by the LORD in order to make **a** for you.
9:7 and your whole burnt offering to make **a** for
9:7 Then present the offerings to make **a** for the
10:17 and for making **a** for the people before the
12:7 present them to the LORD and make **a** for her.
12:8 priest will sacrifice them, thus making **a** for her,
14:18 the priest will make **a** before the LORD for the
14:19 and again perform the **a** ceremony for the person
14:20 the priest will make **a** for the person being
14:21 thus making **a** for the person being cleansed.
14:29 the priest will make **a** for the person being
14:31 the priest will make **a** before the LORD for the
14:53 In this way, the priest will make **a** for the house,
15:15 the priest will make **a** for the man before the
15:30 the priest will make **a** for her before the LORD
16:2 the place of **a**—is there, and I myself am present in the cloud over the **a**
16:6 sin offering, to make **a** for himself and his family.
16:10 into the wilderness, it will make **a** for the people.
16:13 the place of **a**—that rests on the Ark of the
16:14 and sprinkle it on the front of the **a** cover and
16:15 There he will sprinkle the blood on the **a** cover
16:16 this way, he will make **a** for the Most Holy Place,
16:17 Aaron goes in to make **a** for the Most Holy Place.
16:17 he comes out again after making **a** for himself,
16:18 "Then Aaron will go out to make **a** for the altar
16:20 "When Aaron has finished making **a** for the Most
16:24 he will make **a** for himself and for the people.
16:27 into the Most Holy Place to make **a** for Israel,
16:30 On this day, **a** will be made for you, and you will
16:32 the **a** ceremony will be performed by the anointed
16:33 and make **a** for the Most Holy Place,
16:34 to make **a** for the Israelites once each year."
17:11 you the blood so you can make **a** for your sins.
17:11 It is the blood, representing life, that brings you **a**.
19:22 then make **a** for him before the LORD with the
23:27 "Remember that the Day of **A** is to be celebrated
23:28 during that entire day because it is the Day of **A**,
23:28 when **a** will be made for you before the LORD
23:32 fasting will begin the evening before the Day of **A**
23:34 of Shelters on the fifth day after the Day of **A**.
25:9 Then on the Day of **A** of the fiftieth year,
Nu 5:8 must be given to the priest, along with a ram for **a**.
6:11 he will make **a** for the guilt they incurred from the
7:89 the place of **a**—that rests on the Ark of the
8:12 for a burnt offering, to make **a** for the Levites.
8:19 on behalf of the Israelites and make **a** for them
8:21 then performed the rite of **a** over them to purify
15:25 With it the priest will make **a** for the whole
15:28 The priest will make **a** for the guilty person before
16:46 and carry it quickly among the people to make **a**
16:47 but Aaron burned the incense and made **a** for them.
25:13 for his God and made **a** for the people of Israel."
28:22 goat as a sin offering, to make **a** for yourselves.
28:30 offer one male goat to make **a** for yourselves.
29:5 goat as a sin offering, to make **a** for yourselves.
29:7 On that day, the Day of **A**, the people must go
29:11 This is in addition to the sin offering of **a**
31:50 This will make **a** for our lives before the LORD."
35:33 And no **a** can be made for murder except by the
1Ch 6:49 They made **a** for Israel by following all the
28:11 the Ark's cover—the place of **a**—would be kept.
2Ch 29:24 and sprinkled their blood on the altar to make **a** for
Ne 10:33 and for the sin offerings to make **a** for Israel.
Eze 43:20 This will cleanse and make **a** for the altar.
43:22 Then cleanse and make **a** for the altar again,
43:26 for seven days to cleanse and make **a** for the altar,
45:15 and peace offerings that will make **a** for the people
45:20 In that way, you will make **a** for the Temple.
Heb 9:5 stretched out over the Ark's cover, the place of **a**.

ATROTH-BETH-JOAB (1) [JOAB]
1Ch 2:54 the Netophathites, **A**, the other half of the

ATROTH-SHOPHAN (1)
Nu 32:35 **A**, Jazer, Jogbehah,

ATTACH (14) [ATTACHED, ATTACHING]
Ex 25:12 and **a** them to its four feet, two rings on each side.
25:19 **A** the cherubim to each end of the atonement
28:22 "To **a** the chestpiece to the ephod, make braided
28:23 and **a** them to the top corners of the chestpiece.
28:26 and **a** them to the two lower inside corners of the
28:27 gold rings and **a** them to the ephod near the sash.
28:28 Then **a** the bottom rings of the chestpiece to the
28:33 and scarlet yarn, and **a** them to the hem of the robe,
30:4 **a** two gold rings to support the carrying poles.
39:15 To **a** the chestpiece to the ephod, they made
39:21 Blue cords were used to **a** the bottom rings of the
Nu 4:11 Then they are to **a** the carrying poles to the altar.
15:38 and **a** the tassels at each corner with a blue cord.
21:8 of a poisonous snake and **a** it to the top of a pole.

ATTACHED (28) [ATTACH]
Ex 26:24 and firmly **a** at the top with a single ring,
27:10 The curtains will be held up with silver hooks **a** to the silver rods that are **a** to the posts.
27:16 It will be **a** to four posts that fit into four bases.
28:14 and two cords made of pure gold will be **a** to the
28:17 Four rows of gemstones will be **a** to it. The first
28:37 This medallion will be **a** to the front of Aaron's

36:18 so the two sets of sheets were firmly **a** to each
36:29 and firmly **a** at the top with a single ring,
36:36 then **a** to four gold hooks set into four posts of
37:12 A rim about 3 inches wide was **a** along the edges
37:13 four rings of gold and **a** them to the four table legs
39:4 which were **a** to its corners so it could be tied
39:6 onyx stones, **a** to the shoulder-pieces of the ephod,
39:16 and **a** them to the top corners of the chestpiece.
39:19 Two more gold rings were **a** to the lower inside
39:20 Then two gold rings were **a** to the ephod near the
39:24 Pomegranates were **a** to the bottom edge of the
40:20 and then he **a** the Ark's carrying poles.
40:28 He **a** the curtain at the entrance of the Tabernacle,
Lev 8:7 and **a** the ephod with its decorative sash.
Nu 21:9 a snake out of bronze and **a** it to the top of a pole.
1Ki 6:10 **a** to the Temple walls by cedar timbers.
2Ch 3:16 decorative pomegranates and **a** them to the chains.
9:18 six steps, and there was a footstool of gold **a** to it.
Eze 37:7 and **a** themselves as they had been before.
Ac 13:7 He had **a** himself to the governor, Sergius Paulus,
1Co 7:31 good use of them without becoming **a** to them,

ATTACHING (1) [ATTACH]

Ex 40:18 and **a** the crossbars and raising the posts.

ATTACK (143) [ATTACKED, ATTACKERS, ATTACKING, ATTACKS]

Ge 4:7 Sin is waiting to **a** and destroy you, and you must
Ex 34:24 No one will **a** and conquer your land when you go
Lev 26:33 the nations and **a** you with my own weapons.
Nu 25:17 "**A** the Midianites and destroy them,
Dt 1:42 'Tell them not to **a**, for I will not go with them.
2:24 you his land. **A** him and begin to occupy the land.
13:15 you must **a** that town and completely destroy all its
20:10 "As you approach a town to **a** it, first offer its
20:12 and prepare to fight, you must **a** the town.
28:7 will conquer your enemies when they **a** you.
28:7 They will **a** you from one direction, but they will
28:25 You will **a** your enemies from one direction,
28:52 They will **a** all the towns in the land the LORD
Jos 2:3 spies sent here to discover the best way to **a** us."
8:1 Take the entire army and **a** Ai, for I have given to
8:3 So Joshua and the army of Israel set out to **a** Ai.
9:18 But the Israelites did not **a** the towns, for their
10:5 kings combined their armies for a united **a**.
10:33 During the **a** on Lachish, King Horam of Gezer
Jdg 1:1 "Which tribe should **a** the Canaanites first?"
6:3 Amalek, and the people of the east would **a** Israel,
7:10 But if you are afraid to **a**, go down to the camp
7:11 Then you will be eager to **a**." So Gideon took
7:24 saying, "Come down to **a** the Midianites.
9:52 Abimelech followed them to **a** the tower. But as he
10:17 in Gilead, preparing to **a** Israel's army at Mizpah.
18:9 The men replied, "Let's **a**! We have seen the land,
18:26 saw that there were too many of them for him to **a**,
20:9 we will draw lots to decide who will **a** Gibeah.
20:11 and they gathered together to **a** the town.
20:18 "Which tribe should lead the **a** against the people
20:20 Then they advanced toward Gibeah to **a** the men of
20:31 When the warriors of Benjamin came out to **a**,
20:33 reached Baal-tamar, they turned and prepared to **a**.
20:39 for the Israelites to turn and **a** Benjamin's warriors.
1Sa 11:11 He launched a surprise **a** against the Ammonites
17:48 As Goliath moved closer to **a**, David quickly ran
22:13 to revolt against me and to come here and **a** me?"
23:2 asked the LORD, "Should I go and **a** them?"
23:8 army to march to Keilah and **a** David and his men.
24:6 "It is a serious thing to **a** the LORD's anointed
2Sa 5:23 "Do not **a** them straight on," the LORD replied.
5:23 behind them and **a** them near the balsam trees.
5:24 marching feet in the tops of the balsam trees, **a**!
10:10 his brother Abishai, who was to **a** the Ammonites.
20:22 the trumpet and called his troops back from the **a**,
1Ki 13:26 has fulfilled his word by causing the lion to **a**
15:20 King Asa's request and sent his armies to **a** Israel.
16:17 army of Israel away from Gibbethon to **a** Tirzah,
20:12 "Prepare to **a**!" Ben-hadad commanded his
20:12 his officers. So they prepared to **a** the city.
20:14 "Should we **a** first?" Ahab asked. "Yes,"
20:22 "Get ready for another **a** by the king of Aram next
22:31 "**A** only the king of Israel!"
2Ki 3:8 "We will **a** from the wilderness of Edom,"
3:25 Kir-hareseth was left, but even that came under **a**.
7:6 has hired the Hittites and Egyptians to **a** us!"
8:21 So Jehoram went with all his chariots to **a** the town
12:17 and captured it. Then he turned to **a** Jerusalem.
12:18 So Hazael called off his **a** on Jerusalem.
15:37 of Aram and King Pekah of Israel to **a** Judah.
18:13 King Sennacherib of Assyria came to **a** the
19:9 Before leaving to meet the **a**, he sent this message
1Ch 11:6 "Whoever leads the **a** against the Jebusites will
11:6 the son of David's sister Zeruiah, led the **a**,
14:14 "Do not **a** them straight on," God replied.
14:14 behind them and **a** them near the balsam trees.
14:15 marching feet in the tops of the balsam trees, **a**!
19:11 his brother Abishai, who was to **a** the Ammonites.
2Ch 12:4 fortified cities and then advanced to **a** Jerusalem.
16:4 King Asa's request and sent his armies to **a** Israel.
17:1 He strengthened Judah to stand against any **a** from
18:2 to join forces with him to **a** Ramoth-gilead.
18:30 to his charioteers: "**A** only the king of Israel!"
18:31 and God helped him by turning the **a** away from
20:12 against this mighty army that is about to **a** us.
21:9 So Jehoram went to **a** Edom with his full army
21:16 who lived near the Ethiopians, to **a** Jehoram.
32:2 that Sennacherib also intended to **a** Jerusalem,
Ne 4:12 "They will come from all directions and **a** us!"
Est 8:11 or province who might **a** them or their children
Job 15:21 and even on good days they fear the **a** of the
15:24 and anguish, like a king preparing for an **a**.
19:12 His troops advance. They build up roads to **a** me.
Ps 17:9 Protect me from wicked people who **a** me,
27:2 to destroy me, / when my enemies and foes **a** me,
27:3 no fear. / Even if they **a** me, / I remain confident.
31:21 He kept me safe when my city was under **a**.
56:1 troops press in on me. / My foes **a** me all day long.
60:4 who honor you—/ a rallying point in the face of **a**.
69:4 are doing so without cause. / They **a** me with lies,
94:21 They **a** the righteous / and condemn the innocent to
109:28 When they **a** me, they will be disgraced! / But I,
119:150 Those lawless people are coming near to **a** me;
Pr 6:11 a bandit; scarcity will **a** you like an armed robber.
24:34 a bandit; scarcity will **a** you like an armed robber.
SS 3:8 ready to defend the king against an **a** during the
Isa 7:1 The city withstood the **a**, however, and was not
8:10 develop your strategies, prepare your plans of **a**—
11:14 Together they will **a** and plunder the nations to the
16:3 Protect us from their relentless **a**. Do not betray us.
18:5 Even before you begin your **a**, while your plans are
36:1 King Sennacherib of Assyria came to **a** the
37:9 Before leaving to meet the **a**, he sent this message
Jer 1:15 They will **a** its walls and all the other towns of
5:6 So now a lion from the forest will **a** them; a wolf
6:4 They shout, 'Prepare for battle and **a** at noon!
6:5 So let us **a** by night and destroy her palaces!' "
21:2 King Nebuchadnezzar of Babylon has begun his **a**
30:16 and those who **a** you will be attacked.
37:19 told you the king of Babylon would not **a** you?
46:13 about King Nebuchadnezzar's plans to **a** Egypt.
49:31 and **a** those self-sufficient nomadic tribes,"
50:3 For a nation will **a** her from the north and bring
50:7 enemies said, 'We are allowed to **a** them freely,
50:9 I will bring them against Babylon to **a** her, and she
50:14 "Yes, prepare to **a** Babylon, all you nations round
La 3:10 He hid like a bear or a lion, waiting to **a** me.
Eze 4:3 and demonstrate how the enemy will **a** Jerusalem.
5:17 along with the famine, wild animals will **a** you,
21:21 uncertain whether to **a** Jerusalem or Rabbah.
21:23 of their rebellion. Then he will **a** and capture them.
23:24 wagons, and a great army fully prepared for **a**.
24:2 of Babylon is beginning his **a** against Jerusalem.
26:8 Then he will **a** you by building a siege wall,
26:19 will sink beneath the terrible waves of enemy **a**.
28:23 The **a** will come from every direction, and your
34:28 and wild animals will no longer **a** them.
Da 11:39 god's help, he will **a** the strongest fortresses.
11:40 time of the end, the king of the south will **a** him,
Hos 10:10 Now I will **a** you, too, for your rebellion
13:7 So now I will **a** you like a lion, or like a leopard
Joel 3:9 Let all your fighting men advance for the **a**!
Am 1:8 Then I will turn to **a** Ekron, and the few Philistines
Ob 1:1 Let's assemble our armies and **a** Edom!"
Na 2:1 and keep a sharp watch for the enemy **a** to begin!
2:3 The **a** begins! See their scarlet uniforms!
Mt 7:6 They will trample the pearls, then turn and **a** you.
11:12 been forcefully advancing, and violent people **a** it.
Ac 14:5 with their leaders, decided to **a** and stone them.
2Co 6:7 as our weapon, both to **a** and to defend ourselves.
2Ti 4:18 and the Lord will deliver me from every evil **a**
Rev 9:4 but to **a** all the people who did not have the seal of

ATTACKED (102) [ATTACK]

Ge 4:8 were together there, Cain **a** and killed his brother.
4:23 I have killed a youth who **a** and wounded me.
14:15 and **a** during the night from several directions.
31:39 If any were **a** and killed by wild animals, did I
35:5 in all the towns of that area, and no one **a** them.
37:33 my son's robe. A wild animal has **a** and eaten him.
49:23 He has been **a** by archers, / who shot at him
Ex 9:15 I could have **a** you with a plague that would have
22:13 If it was **a** by a wild animal, the carcass must be
22:31 do not eat any animal that has been **a** and killed by
Nu 14:45 and **a** them and chased them as far as Hormah.
21:1 So he **a** the Israelites and took some of them as
21:23 his entire army and **a** Israel in the wilderness,
21:33 Og of Bashan and all his people **a** them at Edrei.
31:7 They **a** Midian just as the LORD had commanded
Dt 3:1 where King Og and his army **a** us at Edrei.
20:19 the trees. They are not enemies that need to be **a**!
25:18 They **a** you when you were exhausted and weary,
Jos 8:14 and **a** the Israelites at a place overlooking the
8:21 from the city, they turned and **a** the men of Ai.
10:5 moved all their troops into place and **a** Gibeon.
10:10 and **a** them at Azekah and Makkedah,
10:29 and the Israelites went to Libnah and **a** it.
10:31 Joshua and the Israelites went to Lachish and **a** it.
10:34 and the Israelite army went to Eglon and **a** it.
10:36 After leaving Eglon, they **a** Hebron,
10:38 Then they turned back and **a** Debir.
11:7 traveled to the water near Merom and **a** suddenly.
13:12 for Moses had **a** them and driven them out.
Jdg 1:4 When the men of Judah **a**, the LORD gave them
1:8 The men of Judah **a** Jerusalem and captured it,
1:22 The descendants of Joseph **a** the town of Bethel,
3:13 Eglon **a** Israel and took possession of Jericho.
3:29 They **a** the Moabites and killed about ten thousand
4:15 When Barak **a**, the LORD threw Sisera and all his
9:43 jumped up from their hiding places and **a** them.
9:50 Then Abimelech **a** the city of Thebez and captured
10:9 crossed to the west side of the Jordan and **a** Judah,
11:5 When the Ammonites **a**, the leaders of Gilead sent
11:12 demanding to know why Israel was being **a**.
11:20 he mobilized his army at Jahaz and **a** them.
12:4 and **a** the men of Ephraim and defeated them.
14:5 a young lion **a** Samson near the vineyards of
15:8 So he **a** the Philistines with great fury and killed
15:10 asked the Philistines, "Why have you **a** us?"
18:27 They **a** and killed all the people and burned the
20:41 the Israelites turned and **a**. At this point
1Sa 4:2 The Philistines **a** and defeated the army of Israel,
13:3 Jonathan **a** and defeated the garrison of Philistines
18:30 Whenever the Philistine army **a**, David was more
19:8 He **a** them with such fury that they all ran away.
27:9 didn't leave one person alive in the villages he **a**.
31:1 Now the Philistines **a** Israel, forcing the Israelites
2Sa 10:13 When Joab and his troops **a**, the Arameans began
10:17 there in battle formation and then **a** David.
20:15 they **a** Abel-beth-maacah and built a ramp against
22:19 They **a** me at a moment when I was weakest,
23:11 at Lehi and **a** the Israelites in a field full of lentils.
1Ki 9:16 (The king of Egypt had **a** and captured Gezer,
13:28 for the lion had not eaten the body nor **a** the
14:25 King Shishak of Egypt came up and **a** Jerusalem.
20:36 when he had gone, a lion **a** and killed him.
2Ki 3:23 "The three armies have **a** and killed each other!
3:24 the army of Israel rushed out and **a** the Moabites,
15:29 King Tiglath-pileser of Assyria **a** Israel again,
16:9 So the Assyrians **a** the Aramean capital of
17:3 King Shalmaneser of Assyria **a** and defeated King
18:9 King Shalmaneser of Assyria **a** Israel and began a
1Ch 10:1 Now the Philistines **a** Israel, forcing the Israelites
19:14 When Joab and his troops **a**, the Arameans began
2Ch 12:2 King Shishak of Egypt **a** Jerusalem in the fifth year
13:14 When Judah realized that they were being **a** from
14:9 Once an Ethiopian named Zerah **a** Judah with an
14:14 were at Gerar, they **a** all the towns in that area,
14:15 They also **a** the camps of herdsmen and captured
24:24 Although the Arameans **a** with only a small army,
Ps 18:18 They **a** me at a moment when I was weakest,
35:15 I am **a** by people I don't even know; / they hurl
81:5 a decree for Israel / when he **a** Egypt to set us free.
118:11 Yes, they surrounded and **a** me, / but I destroyed
Ecc 4:12 A person standing alone can be **a** and defeated,
Isa 7:1 Jerusalem was **a** by King Rezin of Aram and King
14:29 you Philistines, that the king who **a** you is dead.
21:5 and prepare for battle! You are being **a**!
26:14 You **a** them and destroyed them, / and they are
59:15 and anyone who tries to live a godly life is soon **a**.
Jer 30:16 be plundered, and those who attack you will be **a**.
49:28 which were **a** by King Nebuchadnezzar of
La 3:5 He has **a** me and surrounded me with anguish
Eze 19:8 Then the armies of the nations **a** him,
34:8 and left them to be **a** by every wild animal.
36:3 Your enemies have **a** you from all directions,
44:31 or that dies after being **a** by another animal.
Da 8:10 His power reached to the heavens where it **a** the
Hos 10:9 it not right that the wicked men of Gibeah were **a**?
Joel 3:19 because they **a** Judah and killed her innocent
Am 1:13 When they **a** Gilead to extend their borders,
Lk 10:30 Jerusalem to Jericho, and he was **a** by bandits.
10:36 was a neighbor to the man who was **a** by bandits?"
20:10 But the farmers **a** the servant, beat him up,
Ac 17:5 They **a** the home of Jason, searching for Paul
19:16 and **a** them with such violence that they fled from

ATTACKERS (3) [ATTACK]

2Ki 17:20 He punished them by handing them over to their **a**
Jer 50:10 Babylonia will be plundered until the **a** are glutted
Joel 2:7 The **a** march like warriors and scale city walls like

ATTACKING (22) [ATTACK]

Jdg 11:27 Rather, you have wronged me by **a** me.
1Sa 26:9 For who can remain innocent after **a** the LORD's
1Ki 16:15 then engaged in **a** the Philistine town of
2Ki 15:20 So the king of Assyria turned from **a** Israel and did
16:7 Come up and rescue me from the **a** armies of Aram
19:8 his king, who had left Lachish and was **a** Libnah.
Ps 22:13 Like roaring lions **a** their prey, / they come at me
35:1 oppose me. / Declare war on those who are **a** me.
54:3 For strangers are **a** me; / violent men are trying to
56:2 hound me constantly, / and many are boldly **a** me.
64:4 at the innocent, / **a** suddenly and fearlessly.
Pr 28:15 is as dangerous to the poor as a lion or bear **a** them.
Isa 10:7 He will merely think he is **a** my people as part of
13:16 be sacked and their wives raped by the **a** hordes.
13:18 The **a** armies will shoot down the young people
29:3 your enemy, surrounding Jerusalem and **a** its walls.
29:7 Those who are **a** her walls will vanish like a vision
37:8 his king, who had left Lachish and was **a** Libnah.
Jer 15:20 They will fight against you like an **a** army, but I
21:4 of Babylon and the Babylonians who are **a** you.
Na 3:11 a drunkard. You will hide for fear of the **a** enemy.
Rev 20:9 But fire from heaven came down on the **a** armies

ATTACKS (22) [ATTACK]

Ge 32:8 He thought, "If Esau **a** one group,
Ex 21:14 if someone deliberately **a** and kills another person,
Nu 32:17 so they will be safe from any **a** by the local people.
Dt 22:26 This case is similar to that of someone who **a**
Jos 8:5 When our main army **a**, the men of Ai will come
15:16 my daughter Acsah in marriage to the one who **a**
Jdg 1:12 my daughter Acsah in marriage to the one who **a**
10:18 "Whoever **a** the Ammonites first will become
2Sa 17:9 And when he comes out and **a** and a few of your
1Ki 8:37 or crop disease, or **a** of locusts or caterpillars,
20:1 the Israelite capital, and launched **a** against it.

1Ch 20: 1 Joab led the Israelite army in successful a against
2Ch 6:28 or crop disease, or a of locusts or caterpillars,
Job 9:17 For he a me without reason, and he multiplies my
Ps 35:17 and do nothing? / Rescue me from their fierce a.
Isa 13: 2 "See the flags waving as the enemy a. Cheer them
Jer 1:18 For see, today I have made you immune to their a.
La 2: 3 Lord has withdrawn his protection as the enemy a.
Na 2: 2 land of Israel lies empty and broken after your a,
Lk 11:22 until someone who is stronger a and overpowers
Jn 10:12 And so the wolf a them and scatters the flock.
1Pe 5: 8 Watch out for a from the Devil, your great enemy.

ATTAI (4)

1Ch 2:35 be the wife of Jarha, and they had a son named A.
2:36 A was the father of Nathan. / Nathan was the father
12:11 A was sixth. / Eliel was seventh.
2Ch 11:20 gave birth to Abijah, A, Ziza, and Shelomith.

ATTAIN (1)

Pr 13:19 but fools will not turn from evil to a them.

ATTALIA (1)

Ac 14:25 They preached again in Perga, then went on to A.

ATTEMPT (5) [ATTEMPTED, ATTEMPTING, ATTEMPTS]

1Sa 19:10 Saul hurled his spear at David in an a to kill him.
2Ki 3:26 a to break through the enemy lines near the king of
Ps 36: 4 is never good. / They make no a to turn from evil.
2Co 10: 9 Now this is not just an a to frighten you by my
Gal 4:23 The son of the slave-wife was born in a human a to

ATTEMPTED (1) [ATTEMPT]

Ezr 4:15 against the kings and countries who a to control it.

ATTEMPTING (1) [ATTEMPT]

Da 11:27 at the conference table, a to deceive each other.

ATTEMPTS (1) [ATTEMPT]

Job 41: 9 The hunter who a it will be thrown down.

ATTEND (8) [ATTENDANT, ATTENDANTS, ATTENDED, ATTENDING]

Lev 21:12 of his God by leaving it to a his parents' funeral,
Nu 25: 2 These women invited them to a sacrifices to their
2Sa 13:27 the king until he finally agreed to let all his sons a,
1Ki 1:25 and he has invited your sons to a the celebration.
Jer 36: 9 People from all over Judah came to a the services
Da 7:10 to him, and a hundred million stood to a him.
Zec 14:18 And if the people of Egypt refuse to a the festival,
Jn 12:20 Some Greeks who had come to Jerusalem to a the

ATTENDANT (6) [ATTEND]

Est 4: 5 king's eunuchs who had been appointed as her a.
6: 1 so he ordered an a to bring the historical records of
Da 1:11 Daniel talked it over with the a who had been
1:14 So the a agreed to Daniel's suggestion and tested
1:16 the a fed them only vegetables instead of the rich
Lk 4:20 up the scroll, handed it back to the a, and sat down.

ATTENDANTS (14) [ATTEND]

Ge 45: 1 no longer. "Out, all of you!" he cried out to his a.
1Sa 8:15 and distribute it among his officers and a.
25:42 she took along five of her servant girls as a,
1Ki 10: 2 She arrived in Jerusalem with a large group of a
10:13 Then she and all her a left and returned to their
2Ch 9: 1 She arrived with a large group of a and a great
9:12 Then she and all her a left and returned to their
Est 2: 2 So his a suggested, "Let us search the empire to
5: 5 The king turned to his a and said, "Tell Haman to
6: 3 His a replied, "Nothing has been done."
6: 5 So the a replied to the king, "Haman is out there."
7: 8 his a covered Haman's face, signaling his doom.
Ps 89:14 Unfailing love and truth walk before you as a.
Ac 10: 7 and a devout soldier, one of his personal a.

ATTENDED (4) [ATTEND]

Jdg 21: 8 discovered that no one from Jabesh-gilead had a.
2Ch 31: 1 the Israelites who a went to all the towns of Judah,
Est 1:10 Zethar, and Carcas, the seven eunuchs who a him,
Lk 2:42 was twelve years old, they a the festival as usual.

ATTENDING (1) [ATTEND]

2Ch 22: 8 and Ahaziah's relatives who were a Ahaziah.

ATTENTION (70) [ATTENTIONS, ATTENTIVE]

Ex 3: 4 the LORD saw that he had caught Moses' a,
7: 1 the LORD said to Moses, "Pay close a to this.
23:21 Pay a to him, and obey all of his instructions.
30:16 It will bring you, the Israelites, to the LORD's a,
Jdg 5: 3 "Listen, you kings! / Pay a, you mighty rulers!
11:28 But the king of Ammon paid no a to Jephthah's
1Sa 25:25 ill-tempered man; please don't pay any a to him.
1Ki 12:15 So the king paid no a to the people's demands.
2Ch 8: 2 Solomon now turned his a to rebuilding the towns
10:15 So the king paid no a to the people's demands.
Ne 8: 3 All the people paid close a to the Book of the Law.
Job 8: 8 Pay a to the experience of our ancestors.
13: 6 Listen to my charge; pay a to my arguments.
34: 2 you wise men. Pay a, you who have knowledge.
34:19 and he doesn't pay any more a to the rich than to
34:28 they cause the poor to cry out, catching God's a.
36:10 He gets their a and says they must turn away from
36:15 who suffer. For he gets their a through adversity.
Ps 5: 1 hear me as I pray; / pay a to my groaning.
17: 1 Listen to my cry for help. / Pay a to my prayer,
49: 1 all you people! / Pay a, everyone in the world!
54: 2 O God, listen to my prayer. / Pay a to my plea.
66:19 But God did listen! / He paid a to my prayer.
119:71 for it taught me to pay a to your principles.
130: 2 Hear my cry, O Lord. / Pay a to my prayer.
Pr 1:24 I reached out to you, but you paid no a.
1:30 my advice and paid no a when I corrected them.
4: 1 to your father's instruction. Pay a and grow wise,
4:20 Pay a, my child, to what I say. Listen carefully.
5: 1 My son, pay a to my wisdom; listen carefully to
5:13 Why didn't I pay a to those who gave me
7:24 Listen to me, my sons, and pay a to my words.
17: 4 to wicked talk; liars pay a to destructive words.
23: 1 dining with a ruler, pay a to what is put before you.
Isa 30: 9 refuse to pay any a to the LORD's instructions.
31: 4 it pays no a to the shepherd's shouts and noise.
44:21 "Pay a, O Israel, for you are my servant. I,
49: 7 "Kings will stand at a when you pass by.
Jer 3: 8 she paid no a. She saw that I had divorced faithless
5: 3 You struck your people, but they paid no a.
6:17 But you replied, 'No! We won't pay a!'
11: 8 But your ancestors did not pay any a; they would
14:12 When they fast in my presence, I will pay no a.
17:23 They stubbornly refused to pay a and would not
22: 5 But if you refuse to pay a to this warning, I swear
Eze 20:19 'Follow my laws, pay a to my instructions,
40: 4 and listen. Pay close a to everything I show you.
Da 6:13 from Judah, is paying no a to you or your law.
11:18 he will turn his a to the coastal cities and conquer
Mic 1: 2 A! Let all the people of the world listen!
Mal 2:13 because he pays no a to your offerings,
Mt 6: 2 and streets to call a to their acts of charity!
23: 7 They enjoy the a they get on the streets, and they
24:15 standing in the holy place"—reader, pay a!
24:23 is the Messiah,' or 'There he is,' don't pay any a.
Mk 4:24 And be sure to pay a to what you hear. The more
13:14 standing where it should not be"—reader, pay a!
13:21 is the Messiah,' or, 'There he is,' don't pay any a.
Lk 8:18 So be sure to pay a to what you hear. To those who
13: 8 and I'll give it special a and plenty of fertilizer.
Ac 13: 8 and urged the governor to pay no a to what Saul
18:17 right there in the courtroom. But Gallio paid no a.
24: 4 kindly give me your a for only a moment as I
1Co 4: 6 If you pay a to the Scriptures, you won't brag
Gal 4:17 off from me so that you will pay more a to them.
1Ti 2: 9 and not draw a to themselves by the way they fix
4:15 Give your complete a to these matters.
Jas 2: 3 If you give special a and a good seat to the rich
2: 9 But if you pay special a to the rich, you are
2Pe 1:19 Pay close a to what they wrote, for their words are

ATTENTIONS (1) [ATTENTION]

Eze 23:20 She lusted after lovers whose a were gross

ATTENTIVE (2) [ATTENTION]

2Ch 6:40 be a to all the prayers made to you in this place.
Pr 21:28 cut off, but an a witness will be allowed to speak.

ATTIC (2)

Pr 21: 9 It is better to live alone in the corner of an a than
25:24 It is better to live alone in the corner of an a than

ATTIRE [KJV] See DRESS(ED), TURBANS

ATTITUDE (8) [ATTITUDES]

Ge 31: 2 a considerable cooling in Laban's a toward him.
Ezr 6:22 because the LORD had changed the a of the king
Job 19:29 yourselves are in danger of punishment for your a.
Pr 14:30 A relaxed a lengthens life; jealousy rots it away.
Ro 14:18 If you serve Christ with this a, you will please
15: 5 each with the a of Christ Jesus toward the other.
Php 2: 5 Your a should be the same that Christ Jesus had.
1Pe 4: 1 you must arm yourselves with the same a he had,

ATTITUDES (1) [ATTITUDE]

Eph 4:23 must be a spiritual renewal of your thoughts and a.

ATTORNEY (1)

Isa 3:13 He is the great prosecuting a, presenting his case

ATTRACT (1) [ATTRACTED, ATTRACTIVE]

Isa 53: 2 about his appearance, nothing to a us to him.

ATTRACTED (2) [ATTRACT]

Dt 21:11 and you are a to her and want to marry her.
Heb 13: 9 So do not be a by strange, new ideas.

ATTRACTIVE (4) [ATTRACT]

Pr 19:22 Loyalty makes a person a. And it is better to be
Eze 23: 6 They were all a young men, captains
1Ti 2:10 make themselves a by the good things they do.
Tit 2:10 the teaching about God our Savior a in every way.

ATTUNE (1)

Pr 23:12 a your ears to hear words of knowledge.

AUDIENCE (3)

Pr 25: 6 Don't demand an a with the king or push for a
Mk 1:27 Amazement gripped the a, and they began to
Ac 26:29 and everyone here in this a might become the same

AUDITORIUM (1)

Ac 25:23 and Bernice arrived at the a with great pomp,

AUGMENT [KJV] See EVEN

AUGUST (7)

2Ki 25: 8 On A 14 of that year, which was the nineteenth
Ezr 7: 8 Ezra arrived in Jerusalem in A of that year.
7: 9 Babylon on April 8 and came to Jerusalem on A 4,
Jer 1: 3 In A of that year, the people of Jerusalem were
52:12 On A 17 of that year, which was the nineteenth
Eze 20: 1 On A 14, during the seventh year of King
Hag 1: 1 On A 29 of the second year of King Darius's

AUGUSTUS (1)

Lk 2: 1 At that time the Roman emperor, A, decreed that a

AUL [KJV] See AWL

AUNT (5)

Ge 29:12 cousin on her father's side, her a Rebekah's son.
Lev 18:12 Do not have intercourse with your a, your father's
18:13 Do not have sexual intercourse with your a,
18:14 sexual intercourse with his wife; she also is your a.
20:19 "If a man has sexual intercourse with his a,

AUTHOR (1)

Ac 3:15 You killed the a of life, but God raised him to life.

AUTHORITIES (10) [AUTHORITY]

Lk 12:11 to trial in the synagogues and before rulers and a,
Ac 16:19 and dragged them before the a at the marketplace.
Ro 13: 3 For the a do not frighten people who are doing
13: 4 The a are sent by God to help you. But if you are
13: 4 The a are established by God for that very purpose,
Eph 3:10 to all the rulers and a in the heavenly realms.
6:12 against the evil rulers and a of the unseen world,
Col 1:16 we can't see—kings, kingdoms, rulers, and a.
2:15 In this way, God disarmed the evil rulers and a.
1Pe 3:22 and all the angels and a and powers are bowing

AUTHORITY (128) [AUTHORITIES, AUTHORIZED, AUTHORIZING]

Ge 16: 9 "Return to your mistress and submit to her a."
39: 9 No one here has more a than I do! He has held
41:42 signet ring on Joseph's finger as a symbol of his a.
Nu 5:20 have gone astray while under your husband's a
27:20 Transfer your a to him so the whole community of
Jdg 5:14 from Zebulun came those who carry the rod of a.
1Ki 4:33 He could speak with a about all kinds of plants,
2Ki 11:14 king standing in his place of a by the pillar,
23: 3 The king took his place of a beside the pillar
1Ch 26: 6 ability who earned positions of great a in the clan.
2Ch 23:13 his place of a by the pillar at the Temple entrance.
34:31 The king took his place of a beside the pillar
Est 8:11 The king's decree gave the Jews in every city a to
9:29 wrote another letter putting the queen's full a
10: 3 with a next to that of King Xerxes himself.
Ps 8: 6 everything you made, / giving us a over all things
Pr 29: 2 When the godly are in a, the people rejoice.
29:16 When the wicked are in a, sin increases.
Ecc 10: 6 if they give foolish people great a, and if they fail
Isa 3: 5 Young people will revolt against a, and nobodies
22:21 will have your royal robes, your title, and your a.
Jer 5:13 are windbags full of words with no divine a.
23:36 For people are using it to give a to their own ideas,
29:25 You wrote a letter on your own a to Zephaniah son
Da 7: 6 it had four heads. Great a was given to this beast.
7:12 the other three beasts, their a was taken from them,
7:14 He was given a, honor, and royal power over all
11: 4 nor will the kingdom hold the a it once had.
11:39 appointing them to positions of a and dividing the
Zec 3: 7 then you will be given a over my Temple and its
10:12 and they will go wherever they wish by my a.
Mt 7:29 for he taught as one who had real a—quite unlike
8: 9 because I am under the a of my superior officers
and I have a over my soldiers.
9: 6 Son of Man, have the a on earth to forgive sins."
9: 8 praised God for sending a man with such great a.
10: 1 and gave them a to cast out evil spirits and to heal
11:27 "My Father has given me a over everything.
21:23 "By whose a did you drive out the merchants from
the Temple? Who gave you such a?"
21:24 "I'll tell you who gave me the a to do these things
28:18 "I have been given complete a in heaven and on
Mk 1:22 his teaching, for he taught as one who had real a—
1:27 they asked excitedly. "It has such a! Even evil
2:10 Son of Man, have the a on earth to forgive sins."
3:15 and he gave them a to cast out demons.
6: 7 them out two by two, with a to cast out evil spirits.
11:28 "By whose a did you drive out the merchants from
the Temple? Who gave you such a?"
11:29 "I'll tell who gave me a to do these things if you
Lk 4: 6 you the glory of these kingdoms and a over them—
4:32 at the things he said, because he spoke with a.
4:36 "What a and power this man's words possess!
5:24 Son of Man, have the a on earth to forgive sins."

7: 8 because I am under the a of my superior officers, and I have a over my soldiers.
9: 1 and gave them power and a to cast out demons
10:19 And I have given you a over all the power of the
10:22 "My Father has given me a over everything.
20: 2 "By whose a did you drive out the merchants from the Temple? Who gave you such a?"
24:47 With my a, take this message of repentance to all
Jn 2:18 "If you have this a from God, show us a
3:35 his Son, and he has given him a over everything.
5:27 And he has given him a to judge all mankind
12:49 I don't speak on my own a. The Father who sent
13: 3 Jesus knew that the Father had given him a over
17: 2 For you have given him a over everyone in all the
Ac 4: 2 and John were claiming, on the a of Jesus,
5:29 "We must obey God rather than human a.
8:27 a eunuch of great a under the queen of Ethiopia.
25: 5 So he said, "Those of you in a can return with me.
26:12 armed with the a and commission of the leading
Ro 1: 5 and a to tell Gentiles everywhere what God has
14:14 and am perfectly sure on the a of the Lord Jesus
1Co 1:10 I appeal to you by the a of the Lord Jesus Christ to
7: 4 The wife gives a over her body to her husband,
7: 4 and the husband also gives a over his body to his
9: 3 This is my answer to those who question my a as
11:10 should wear a covering on her head as a sign of a
15:27 "God has given him a over all things."
15:27 (Of course, when it says "a over all things,"
15:27 not include God himself, who gave Christ his a.)
15:28 so that God, who gave his Son a over all things,
2Co 2:10 I do so with Christ's a for your benefit,
2:17 God's message with sincerity and with Christ's a.
10: 8 I may seem to be boasting too much about the a
10: 8 But this a is to build you up, not to tear you down.
10:13 But we will not boast of a we do not have.
10:14 We are not going too far when we claim a over
13:10 For I want to use the a the Lord has given me to
Gal 1: 1 I was not appointed by any group or by human a.
Eph 1:10 bring everything together under the a of Christ—
1:21 or a or power or leader or anything else in this
1:22 And God has put all things under the a of Christ,
1:22 and he gave him this a for the benefit of the
4:17 With the Lord's a let me say this: Live no longer
Col 2:10 is the Lord over every ruler and a in the universe.
2Th 3: 6 we give you this command with the a of our Lord
1Ti 2: 2 Pray this way for kings and all others who are in a,
2:12 I do not let women teach men or have a over them.
Tit 2:15 You have the a to do this, so don't let anyone
Heb 2: 8 You gave him a over all things." Now when it
1Pe 2:13 For the Lord's sake, accept all a—the king as head
2:18 You who are slaves must accept the a of your
3: 1 you wives must accept the a of your husbands,
3: 5 trusted God and accepted the a of their husbands.
5: 5 You younger men, accept the a of the elders.
2Pe 2:10 their own evil, lustful desires and who despise a.
3Jn 1: 9 loves to be the leader, does not acknowledge our a.
Jude 1: 6 did not stay within the limits of a God gave them
1: 8 who claim a from their dreams, live immoral lives, defy a,
1:25 Yes, glory, majesty, power, and a belong to him,
Rev 2:26 to the very end, I will give a over all the nations.
2:28 They will have the same a I received from my
6: 4 and the a to remove peace from the earth.
6: 8 They were given a over one-fourth of the earth,
12:10 and kingdom of our God, and the a of his Christ!
13: 2 gave him his own power and throne and great a.
13: 5 And he was given a to do what he wanted for
13: 7 And he was given a to rule over every tribe
13:12 He exercised all the a of the first beast. And he
16: 5 And I heard the angel who had a over all water
17:13 will all agree to give their power and a to him.
17:17 They will mutually agree to give their a to the
18: 1 angel come down from heaven with great a,
20: 4 sitting on them had been given the a to judge.

AUTHORIZED (2) [AUTHORITY]
Ac 9:14 And we hear that he is a by the leading priests to
26:10 A by the leading priests, I caused many of the

AUTHORIZING (1) [AUTHORITY]
Ac 22: 5 a me to bring the Christians from there to

AUTUMN (16)
Lev 16:29 "On the appointed day in early a, you must spend
23:24 "On the appointed day in early a, you are to
Nu 29: 1 on the appointed day in early a each year.
1Ki 8: 2 king at the annual Festival of Shelters in early a.
2Ch 5: 3 king at the annual Festival of Shelters in early a.
31: 7 and the heaps continued to grow until early a.
Ezr 3: 1 Now in early a, when the Israelites had settled in
Ne 1: 1 In late a of the twentieth year of King Artaxerxes'
Isa 18: 4 or as the dew forms on an a morning during the
64: 6 Like a leaves, we wither and fall. And our sins,
Jer 36: 9 on the day of sacred fasting held in late a,
36:22 It was late a, and the king was in a winterized part
Eze 45:25 of Shelters, which occurs every year in early a,
Joel 2:23 Once more the a rains will come, as well as the
Zec 7: 5 in the summer and at the festival in early a,
8:19 midsummer, a, and winter are now ended.

AVA [KJV] See AVVA

AVAIL (3)
Isa 22:11 But all your feverish plans are to no a because you
29: 8 conquest over Jerusalem, but all to no a."
Da 11:25 but to no a, for plots against him will succeed.

AVAILABLE (21)
Ge 13: 6 There were too many animals for the a
42: 1 When Jacob heard that there was grain a in Egypt,
Ex 18:26 These men were constantly a to administer justice.
Nu 2: 3[-4] their leaders, and the number of their a troops:
2:10[-11] leaders, and the number of their a troops:
2:18[-19] leaders, and the number of their a troops:
2:25[-26] leaders, and the number of their a troops:
1Sa 21: 6 So, since there was no other food a, the priest gave
1Ch 7: 2 the total number of men a for military service from
7: 4 The total number of men a for military service
7: 5 The total number of men a for military service
7: 7 The total number of men a for military service
7: 9 there were 20,200 men a for military service
7:11 and their descendants included 17,200 men a for
7:40 There were 26,000 men a for military service
22:15 and craftsmen of every kind a to you.
SS 6: 8 and unnumbered virgins a to me.
Jn 16:10 Righteousness is a because I go to the Father,
Ac 28:28 this salvation from God is also a to the Gentiles,
Ro 11:11 His purpose was to make his salvation a to the
Eph 3: 8 about the endless treasures a to them in Christ.

AVEN (2) [BETH-AVEN]
Hos 10: 8 And the pagan shrines of A, the place of Israel's
Am 1: 5 slaughter its people all the way to the valley of A.

AVENGE (13) [VENGEANCE]
Nu 35:12 a dead person's relatives who want to a the death.
Dt 32:43 for he will a the blood of his servants.
Jos 20: 3 for the relatives may seek to a the killing.
20: 5 If the relatives of the victim come to a the killing,
2Ki 9: 7 I will a the murder of my prophets and all the
Isa 63: 4 For the time has come for me to a my people,
Jer 5: 9 "Should I not a myself against a nation such as
5:29 "Should I not a myself against a nation such as
9: 9 "Should I not a myself against a nation such as
51:36 be your lawyer to plead your case, and I will a you.
Hos 1: 4 for I am about to punish King Jehu's dynasty to a
Ro 12:19 Dear friends, never a yourselves. Leave that to
Rev 6:10 When will you a our blood against these people?"

AVENGED (3) [VENGEANCE]
Ps 58:10 The godly will rejoice when they see injustice a.
Ac 7:24 So Moses came to his defense and a him,
Rev 19: 2 and he has a the murder of his servants."

AVENGER (5) [VENGEANCE]
Nu 35:19 When they meet, the a must execute the murderer.
35:24 making a judgment between the slayer and the a,
35:25 They must protect the slayer from the a, and they
Dt 19: 6 an enraged a might be able to chase down and kill
19:12 and handed over to the dead person's a to be

AVENGES (2) [VENGEANCE]
Ps 9:12 For he who a murder cares for the helpless.
1Th 4: 6 for the Lord a all such sins, as we have solemnly

AVENGING (2) [VENGEANCE]
Ex 15: 9 I will divide the plunder, / a myself against them.
Eze 25:12 The people of Edom have sinned greatly by a

AVERT (1)
Jer 11:15 Can their sacrifices a their destruction?

AVIM, AVIMS [KJV] See AVVIM, AVVITES

AVITES [KJV] See AVVITES

AVITH (2)
Ge 36:35 Bedad became king and ruled from the city of A.
1Ch 1:46 Bedad became king and ruled from the city of A.

AVOID (21) [AVOIDED, AVOIDING]
Lev 21: 1 "Tell the priests to a making themselves
1Ch 9:28 They checked them in and out to a any loss.
Ne 5: 9 God in order to a being mocked by enemy nations?
Pr 4:15 A their haunts. Turn away and go somewhere else,
4:24 A all perverse talk; stay far from corrupt speech.
13:14 those who accept it a the snares of death.
14:16 The wise are cautious and a danger; fools plunge
19: 7 how much more will their friends a them.
24:12 Don't try to a responsibility by saying you didn't
Ecc 8: 3 Don't try to a doing your duty, and don't take a
8: 7 how can people a what they don't know is going to
Isa 28:15 You boast that you have struck a bargain to a death
28:18 I will cancel the bargain you made to a death,
Eze 46:20 They will do it here to a carrying the sacrifices
Hos 4:15 Israel is a prostitute, may Judah a such guilt.
Mk 9:30 through Galilee. Jesus tried to a all publicity
Ro 4:15 (The only way to a breaking the law is to have no
1Co 5:10 You would have to leave this world to a people
1Ti 6:20 A godless, foolish discussions with those who
2Ti 2:16 A godless, foolish discussions that lead to more
Tit 3: 2 speak evil of anyone, and they must a quarreling.

AVOIDED (6) [AVOID]
Ge 43:11 said to them, "If it can't be a, then at least do this.
Dt 2: 8 and a the road through the Arabah Valley that
Jdg 5: 6 and in the days of Jael, / people a the main roads,
Ezr 9:12 You promised that if we a these things, we would
Pr 16: 6 cover sin; evil is a by fear of the LORD.
Ac 27:21 You would have a all this injury and loss.

AVOIDING (1) [AVOID]
Pr 20: 3 A a fight is a mark of honor; only fools insist on

AVVA (1)
2Ki 17:24 Cuthah, A, Hamath, and Sepharvaim and resettled

AVVIM (1)
Jos 18:23 A, Parah, Ophrah,

AVVITES (3)
Dt 2:23 from Crete invaded and destroyed the A,
Jos 13: 4 The land of the A in the south also remains to be
2Ki 17:31 The A worshiped their gods Nibhaz and Tartak.

AWAIT (7) [WAIT]
Ps 65: 4 What joys a us / inside your holy Temple.
Mt 11:21 "What horrors a you, Korazin and Bethsaida!
Lk 6:24 "What sorrows a you who are rich, / for you have
6:25 What sorrows a you who are satisfied
6:25 What sorrows a you who laugh carelessly,
6:26 What sorrows a you who are praised by the
10:13 "What horrors a you, Korazin and Bethsaida!

AWAITED (2) [WAIT]
La 2:16 Long have we a this day, and it is finally here!"
Rev 12: 2 and she cried out in the pain of labor as she a her

AWAITING (5) [WAIT]
Ps 10: 5 They do not see your punishment a them.
Pr 7:23 a the arrow that would pierce its heart. He was like
Jer 42:17 That is the fate a every one of you who insists on
Mk 14:35 the awful hour a him might pass him by.
Jn 3:18 "There is no judgment a those who trust him.

AWAITS (11) [WAIT]
Job 20:29 This is the fate that a the wicked. It is the
Ecc 9: 2 The same destiny ultimately a everyone,
Isa 42:23 lessons from the past and see the ruin that a you?
Eze 7:10 "The day of judgment is here; your destruction a!
Mic 1:12 but only bitterness a them as the LORD's
Mt 5:12 Be very glad! For a great reward a you in heaven.
Lk 6:23 leap for joy! For a great reward a you in heaven.
Jn 4:36 What joy a both the planter and the harvester alike!
Ac 20:22 by the Holy Spirit, not knowing what a me,
2Ti 4: 8 And now the prize a me—the crown of
1Pe 4:17 what terrible fate a those who have never believed

AWAKE (14) [WAKE]
Ps 17:15 I will see you. / When I a, I will be fully satisfied,
36: 4 They lie a at night, hatching sinful plots.
63: 6 I lie a thinking of you, / meditating on you through
73:20 that is gone when they a. / When you arise,
102: 7 I lie a, / lonely as a solitary bird on the roof.
119:148 I stay a through the night, / thinking about your
SS 4:16 "A, north wind! Come, south wind! Blow on my
Isa 21: 4 at night is now a faint memory. I lie a, trembling.
Mic 2: 1 How terrible it will be for you who lie a at night,
Zec 13: 7 "A, O sword, against my shepherd, the man who
Mt 25:13 "So stay a and be prepared, because you do not
26:40 "Couldn't you stay a and watch with me even one
Mk 14:37 Couldn't you stay a and watch with me even one
Eph 5:14 This is why it is said, / "A, O sleeper, / rise up

AWAKEN (4) [WAKE]
SS 2: 7 of the wild, not to a love until the time is right.
3: 5 of the wild, not to a love until the time is right."
8: 4 of Jerusalem, not to a love until the time is right."
Ac 12: 7 The angel tapped him on the side to a him

AWAKENED (1) [WAKE]
SS 5: 2 night as I was sleeping, my heart a in a dream.

AWARE (22) [AWARENESS]
Ge 28:16 LORD is in this place, and I wasn't even a of it."
38:14 Tamar was a that Shelah had grown up, but they
Ex 3: 7 harsh slave drivers. Yes, I am a of their suffering.
34:29 he wasn't a that his face glowed because he had
Lev 4:23 When he becomes a of his sin, he must bring as his
4:28 When they become a of their sin, they must bring
5: 3 considered guilty as soon as they become a of it.
5: 4 not fully a of what they were doing at the time.
5: 5 "When any of the people become a of their guilt
5:17 When they become a of their guilt,
Nu 14:14 who are well a that you are with this people.
1Sa 2:22 but he was a of what his sons were doing to the
23:17 and I will be next to you, as my father is well a."
Job 39: 2 Are you a of the time of their delivery?
Ps 26: 3 For I am constantly a of your unfailing love,
73:11 "Is the Most High even a of what is happening?"
Jer 13:27 I am keenly a of your adultery and lust, and your
32:19 You are very a of the conduct of all people,
Lk 12:48 "But people who are not a that they are doing
Ac 26: 4 "As the Jewish leaders are well a, I was given a
Ro 1:32 They are fully a of God's death penalty for those
1Jn 2:26 because you need to be a of those who want to lead

AWARENESS (1) [AWARE]

Hab 2:14 fill the sea, with an a of the glory of the LORD.

AWAY (879)

Ge 15:11 to eat the carcasses, but Abram chased them a.
15:14 and in the end they will come a with great wealth.
16: 6 So Sarai treated her harshly, and Hagar ran a.
16: 8 "I am running a from my mistress," she replied.
21:14 He sent her a with their son, and she walked out
21:16 and sat down by herself about a hundred yards a.
24:59 and sent her a with Abraham's servant and his
25: 6 and sent them off to the east, a from Isaac.
26:29 you well, and we sent you a from us in peace.
27:35 he tricked me. He has carried a your blessing."
28: 5 So Isaac sent Jacob a, and he went to Paddan-aram
29: 8 "We don't roll a the stone and begin the watering
29:10 Jacob went over to the well and rolled a the stone
31:19 Laban was some distance a, shearing his sheep.
31:26 of war, that you have stolen them a like this?
31:27 Why did you slip a secretly? I would have given
31:31 "I rushed a because I was afraid,"
35:16 began while they were still some distance a.
36: 6 of Canaan—and moved a from his brother, Jacob.
39:12 Joseph tore himself a, but as he did, his shirt came
40:19 Then birds will come and peck a at your flesh."
41:35 and store it a so there will be food in the cities.
44:28 and that one of them went a and never returned—
44:29 If you take a his brother from me, too, and any
45: 9 all the land of Egypt. Come down to me right a!
49: 6 O my soul, stay a from them. / May I never be a
Ex 2:17 often come and chase the girls and their flocks a.
4: 3 Moses was terrified, so he turned and ran a.
8: 8 "Plead with the LORD to take the frogs a from
8:28 But don't go too far a. Now hurry, and pray for
10:17 and plead with the LORD your God to take a this
12:31 "Go a, all of you! Go and serve the LORD as
14: 5 have we done, letting all these slaves get a?"
15:22 Then Moses led the people of Israel a from the
19:13 The people must stay a from the mountain until
22:10 any other animal, but it dies or is injured or gets a,
23: 4 your enemy's ox or donkey that has strayed a,
23: 7 "Keep far a from falsely charging anyone with
32: 1 failed to come back down the mountain right a,
32:12 face of the earth.' Turn a from your fierce anger.
Lev 4:12 must be carried a to a ceremonially clean place
10: 4 and carry the bodies of your relatives a from the
11:40 If you eat any of its meat or carry a its carcass,
13:50 affected spot, the priest will put it a for seven days.
14: 7 living bird free so it can fly a into the open fields.
16:10 When it is sent a into the wilderness, it will make
25: 5 And don't store a the crops that grow naturally
25:11 or store a any of the crops that grow naturally,
26:16 causing your eyes to fail and your life to ebb a.
26:36 demoralize you in the land of your enemies far a.
26:39 Those still left alive will rot a in enemy lands
Nu 9:13 who are ceremonially clean and not a on a trip,
16:21 "Get a from these people so that I may instantly
16:24 "Then tell all the people to get a from the tents of
16:26 "Get a from the tents of these wicked men,
16:45 "Get a from these people so that I can instantly
18:22 and Levites are to stay a from the Tabernacle.
20: 6 Moses and Aaron turned a from the people
21: 7 Pray that the LORD will take a the snakes."
21:30 wiped them out / as far a as Nophah and Medeba."
22:33 Three times the donkey saw me and shied a;
22:37 Why didn't you come right a?" Balak asked
25: 4 so his fierce anger will turn a from the people of
25:11 a from the Israelites by displaying passionate zeal
32:15 If you turn a from him like this and he abandons
Dt 2:37 we stayed a from the Ammonites along the Jabbok
6: 7 you are at home and when you are a on a journey,
7: 1 he will clear a many nations ahead of you:
7: 4 They will lead your young people a from me to
7:22 You will not clear them a all at once, for if you
11:16 "But do not let your heart turn a from the LORD
11:19 you are at home and when you are a on a journey,
13:10 because they have tried to draw you a from the
15:13 a male servant, do not send him a empty-handed.
17:17 because they will lead him a from the LORD.
17:20 It will also prevent him from turning a from these
22: 1 you see your neighbor's ox or sheep wandering a,
23: 9 your enemies, stay a from everything impure.
23:10 emission must leave the camp and stay a all day.
23:14 thing among you, or he might turn a from you.
23:24 but do not take any a in a basket.
24: 1 a letter of divorce, gives it to her, and sends her a.
28:14 You must not turn a from any of the commands I
28:26 and no one will be there to chase them a.
28:31 Your donkey will be driven a, never to be returned.
28:32 as your sons and daughters are taken a as slaves.
28:41 not keep them, for they will be led a into captivity.
29:18 or tribe among you would turn a from the LORD
30:13 It is not beyond the sea, so far a that you must ask,
30:17 But if your heart turns a and you refuse to listen,
30:17 and if you are drawn a to serve and worship other
32:34 these things, / sealing them a within my treasury.
Jos 1: 7 Do not turn a from them, and you will be
5: 9 "Today I have rolled a the shame of your slavery
7: 5 at this turn of events, and their courage melted a.
8: 5 as they did before, and we will run a from them.
8: 6 'The Israelites are running a from us as they did
8:16 In this way, they were lured a from the city.
22: 7 As Joshua sent them a, he blessed them
22:16 How could you turn a from the LORD and build
22:18 And yet today you are turning a from following the
22:23 an altar for ourselves to turn a from the LORD.
22:29 or turn a from him by building our own altar for
23:12 "But if you turn a from him and intermarry with
24:14 Put a forever the idols your ancestors worshiped
24:28 Then Joshua sent the people a, each to his own
Jdg 2: 6 After Joshua sent the people a, each of the tribes
2:17 How quickly they turned a from the path of their
4:11 had moved a from the other members of his tribe
5:12 Barak! / Lead your captives a, son of Abinoam!
5:21 The Kishon River swept them a—/ that ancient
6: 4 in the land and destroying crops as far a as Gaza.
6:18 Don't go a until I come back and bring my
7:22 Those who were not killed fled to places as far a as
9:40 but he was defeated and ran a. Many of Shechem's
11:23 who took a the land from the Amorites and gave it
11:33 twenty towns—and as far a as Abel-keramim.
11:38 And he let her go a for two months. She and her
11:40 for young Israelite women to go a for four days
15:13 with two new ropes and led him a from the rock.
15:17 he finished speaking, he threw a the jawbone;
16:14 and yanked his hair a from the loom and the fabric.
18:24 "You've taken a all my gods and my priest,
20:31 out to attack, they were drawn a from the town.
20:32 But the Israelites had agreed in advance to run a
20:32 along the roads and be drawn a from the town.
Ru 1:21 I went a full, but the LORD has brought me home
4: 4 But if you don't want it, let me know right a,
1Sa 1:14 he demanded. "Throw a your wine!"
4:20 but before she passed a the midwives tried to
6: 7 the cart, but shut their calves a from them in a pen.
8:14 He will take a the best of your fields and vineyards
9: 3 One day Kish's donkeys strayed a, and he told
12:10 'We have sinned by turning a from the LORD
13: 8 realized that his troops were rapidly slipping a.
14:16 the vast army of Philistines began to melt a in
14:22 the chase when they saw the Philistines running a.
15: 6 "Move a from where the Amalekites live or else
16:23 feel better, and the tormenting spirit would go a.
17:24 army saw him, they began to run a in fright.
19: 8 He attacked them with such fury that they all ran a.
19:11 warned him, "If you don't get a tonight,
19:18 So David got a and went to Ramah to see Samuel,
20: 3 But I swear to you that I am only a step a from
20:22 for the LORD is sending you a.
22:17 They knew he was running a from me, but they
24:19 Who else would let his enemy get a when he had
25:10 There are lots of servants these days who run a
26:12 and Abishai got a without anyone seeing them
26:25 Then David went a, and Saul returned home.
29: 3 the man who ran a from King Saul of Israel.
2Sa 2:22 Again Abner shouted to him, "Get a from here!
3:15 So Ishbosheth took Michal a from her husband
3:23 visiting the king and had been sent a in safety,
3:24 "What do you mean by letting Abner get a?
10:13 his troops attacked, the Arameans began to run a.
11:10 Why didn't you go home last night after being a
13:19 with her face in her hands, she went a crying.
14:14 He does not sweep a the lives of those he cares
17: 2 and his troops will panic, and everyone will run a.
17:11 bringing them from as far a as Dan and Beersheba.
23: 6 But the godless are like thorns to be thrown a,
1Ki 8:65 A large crowd had gathered from as far a as
11: 3 sure enough, they led his heart a from the LORD.
11: 9 for his heart had turned a from the LORD,
11:11 I will surely tear the kingdom a from you and give
11:12 still alive. I will take the kingdom a from your son.
11:35 But I will take the kingdom a from his son
12: 5 come back for my answer." So the people went a.
14: 8 I ripped the kingdom a from the family of David
15:22 help to carry a the building stones and timbers that
16:17 So Omri led the army of Israel a from Gibbethon
18:12 the Spirit of the LORD will carry you a to who
18:27 Or maybe he is a on a trip, or he is asleep
19:19 his cloak across his shoulders and walked a again.
20: 6 They will take a everything you consider
20:39 if for any reason he gets a, you will either die
21:21 is going to bring disaster to you and sweep you a.
2Ki 1:11 the king says that you must come down right a."
2: 3 is going to take your master a from you today?"
2: 5 is going to take your master a from you today?"
2: 9 "What can I do for you before I am taken a?"
2:23 "Go a, you baldhead!" they chanted. "Go a, you baldhead!"
4:27 Gehazi began to push her a, but the man of God
5:11 But Naaman became angry and stalked a.
5:12 So Naaman turned and went a in a rage.
5:20 let this Aramean get a without accepting his gifts.
6:23 the Aramean raiders stayed a from the land of
7:15 and equipment that the Arameans had thrown a in
9: 2 Call him into a back room a from his friends,
11: 2 and stole him a from among the rest of the king's
16: 9 of Damascus and led its population a as captives,
17:21 For when the LORD tore Israel a from the
17:21 Then Jeroboam drew Israel a from following the
17:23 until the LORD finally swept them a, just as all
18:14 tribute money you demand if you will only go a."
20:18 Some of your own descendants will be taken a into
21:13 I will wipe a the people of Jerusalem as one wipes
23: 4 and he carried the ashes a to Bethel.
23: 5 He did a with the pagan priests, who had been
24:13 Nebuchadnezzar carried a all the treasures from
24:15 Nebuchadnezzar led King Jehoiachin a as a captive
25: 7 him in bronze chains, and led him a to Babylon.
25:13 and they carried all the bronze a to Babylon.
1Ch 4:33 and their surrounding villages as far a as Baalath.
5:22 So they lived in their land until they were taken a
5:26 to invade the land and lead a the people of Reuben,
12:40 And people from as far a as Issachar, Zebulun,
19:14 his troops attacked, the Arameans began to run a.
21:20 His four sons, who were with him, ran a and hid.
2Ch 7: 8 They came from as far a as Lebo-hamath in the
7:18 then I will not let anyone take a your throne.
10: 5 three days for my answer." So the people went a.
12: 9 and took a all the treasures of the Temple of the
13: 9 And you have chased a the priests of the LORD
16: 6 all the men of Judah to carry a the building stones
18:31 and God helped him by turning the attack a from
21:17 and carried a everything of value in the royal
22:11 and stole him a from among the rest of the king's
24: 5 Do not delay!" But the Levites did not act right a.
25:27 After Amaziah turned a from the LORD,
29:10 so that his fierce anger will turn a from us.
30: 8 so that his fierce anger will turn a from you.
30:14 They took a all the incense altars and threw them
33:11 him in bronze chains, and led him a to Babylon.
34:33 they did not turn a from the LORD, the God of
36: 6 Jehoiakim in chains and led him a to Babylon.
36:20 The few who survived were taken a to Babylon,
Ezr 6: 6 west of the Euphrates: / "Stay a from there!
10: 3 and to send them a with their children.
10:14 so that the fierce anger of our God may be turned a
Ne 6:11 "Should someone in my position run a from
8:12 So the people went a to eat and drink at a festive
9:26 They threw a your law, they killed the prophets
12:43 joy of the people of Jerusalem could be heard far a.
Est 4:17 So Mordecai went a and did as Esther told him.
Job 1: 1 He feared God and stayed a from evil.
1:11 But take a everything he has, and he will surely
1:21 everything I had, / and the LORD has taken it a.
2: 5 But take a his health, and he will surely curse you
7:21 Why not just pardon my sin and take a my guilt?
9:12 If he sends death to snatch someone a, who can
9:25 swiftly than a runner. It flees a, filled with tragedy.
12:17 He leads counselors a stripped of good judgment;
12:18 With ropes around their waist, they are led a.
12:19 He leads priests a stripped of status; he overthrows
12:24 He takes a the understanding of kings, and he
13:24 Why do you turn a from me? Why do you consider
13:28 I waste a like rotting wood, like a moth-eaten coat.
14: 6 us a little rest, won't you? Turn a your angry stare.
14:19 wears a the stones and floods wash a the soil,
14:20 You disfigure them in death and send them a.
16: 5 that helps you. I would try to take a your grief.
19:13 "My relatives stay far a, and my friends have
20: 7 he will perish forever, thrown a like his own dung.
20:28 A flood will sweep a his house. God's anger will
21:14 All this, even though they say to God, 'Go a.
21:17 "Yet the wicked get a with it time and time again.
21:18 Are they carried a by the storm? Not at all!
22: 9 You must have sent widows a without helping
22:16 They were snatched a in the prime of life,
22:16 and the foundations of their lives were washed a
24:22 "God, in his power, drags a the rich. They may
27: 2 vow by the living God, who has taken a my rights,
27: 8 when God cuts them off and takes a their life?
27:16 and they may store a mounds of clothing.
27:20 and they are blown a in the storms of the night.
27:21 The east wind carries them a, and they are gone. It sweeps them a.
31:21 an orphan because I thought I could get a with it,
31:32 I have never turned a a stranger but have opened
32:22 if I tried, my Creator would soon do a with me.
33:21 They waste a to skin and bones.
34: 5 'I am innocent, but God has taken a my rights.
34:20 At midnight they all pass a; the mighty are
36:10 their attention and says they must turn a from evil.
36:16 "God has led you a from danger, giving you
37:21 in the sky when the wind clears a the clouds.
39:11 Can you go a and trust the ox to do your work?
40:24 it off guard or put a ring in its nose and lead it a.
Ps 4: 1 Take a my distress. / Have mercy on me and hear
5:10 Drive them a because of their many sins, / for they
6: 8 Go a, all you who do evil, / for the LORD has
9: 3 My enemies turn a in retreat; / they are overthrown
10: 1 O LORD, why do you stand so far a? / Why do
10: 9 they capture their victims / and drag them a in nets.
10:13 Why do the wicked get a with cursing God?
14: 3 But no, all have turned a from God; / all have
22:19 O LORD, do not stay a! / You are my strength;
22:24 He has not turned and walked a. / He has listened
28: 3 Don't drag me a with the wicked—/ with those
30: 7 Then you turned a from me, and I was shattered.
30:11 You have taken a my clothes of mourning
31: 9 of my tears. / My body and soul are withering a.
31:10 drained my strength; / I am wasting a from within.
34: T be insane in front of Abimelech, who sent him a.
34:14 Turn a from evil and do good. / Work hard at
35: 5 Blow them a like chaff in the wind—/ a wind sent
37: 2 For like grass, they soon fade a. / Like springtime
38:11 My loved ones and friends stay a, fearing my
39: 4 days are numbered, / and that my life is fleeing a.
44:20 If we had turned a from worshiping our God
45:10 Forget your people and your homeland far a.
48: 5 they were stunned; / they were terrified and ran a.
53: 3 But no, all have turned a from God; / all have
55: 6 wings like a dove; / then I would fly a and rest!
55: 7 I would fly far a / to the quiet of the wilderness.
55: 8 far a from this wild storm of hatred.
56: 7 Don't let them get a with their wickedness;
58: 9 God will sweep them a, both young and old,
71:12 O God, don't stay a. / My God, please hurry to
73:19 an instant they are destroyed, / swept a by terrors.
80: 8 you drove a the pagan nations and transplanted us
83:13 O my God, blow them a like whirling dust,
88: 8 my friends to loathe me; / you have sent them all a.

88:14 reject me? / Why do you turn your face **a** from me?
88:18 You have taken **a** my companions and loved ones;
90:5 You sweep people **a** like dreams that disappear
95:10 'They are a people whose hearts turn **a** from me.
101:4 reject perverse ideas / and stay **a** from every evil.
102:2 Don't turn **a** from me / in my time of distress.
102:26 change them like a garment, / and they will fade **a**.
103:12 as far **a** from us as the east is from the west.
104:7 water fled; / at the sound of your thunder, it fled **a**.
104:29 But if you turn **a** from them, they panic. / When you take **a** their breath, they die
112:10 in anger; / they will slink **a**, their hopes thwarted.
114:3 The water of the Jordan River turned **a**.
114:5 What happened, Jordan River, that you turned **a**?
119:51 utter contempt, / but I do not turn **a** from your law.
119:102 I haven't turned **a** from your laws, / for you have
119:176 I have wandered **a** like a lost sheep; / come
125:5 O LORD. / Take them **a** with those who do evil.
137:2 We put **a** our lyres, / hanging them on the branches
139:2 You know my every thought when far **a**.
139:7 your spirit! / I can never get **a** from your presence!
143:7 Don't turn **a** from me, / or I will die.
Pr 1:15 with them, my child! Stay far **a** from their paths.
1:17 When a bird sees a trap being set, it stays **a**.
1:32 For they are simpletons who turn **a** from me—
3:3 Never let loyalty and kindness get **a** from you!
4:2 good guidance. Don't turn **a** from my teaching.
4:5 Don't forget or turn **a** from my words.
4:15 Avoid their haunts. Turn **a** and go somewhere else,
7:19 for my husband is not home. He's **a** on a long trip.
7:25 Don't let your hearts stray **a** toward her.
10:5 a youth who sleeps **a** the hour of opportunity
10:7 the godly, but the name of a wicked person rots **a**.
10:25 strikes like a cyclone, whirling the wicked **a**,
12:11 work means prosperity; only fools idle **a** their time.
13:23 produce much food, but injustice sweeps it all **a**.
14:7 Stay **a** from fools, for you won't find knowledge
14:30 A relaxed attitude lengthens life; jealousy rots it **a**.
15:1 A gentle answer turns **a** wrath, but harsh words stir
15:12 who rebuke them, so they stay **a** from the wise.
16:17 The path of the upright leads **a** from evil;
19:4 makes many "friends"; poverty drives them **a**.
19:26 or chase **a** their mother are a public disgrace
20:30 Physical punishment cleanses **a** evil;
22:5 treacherous road; whoever values life will stay **a**.
22:15 with foolishness, but discipline will drive it **a**.
22:24 Keep **a** from angry, short-tempered people,
24:18 with you and will turn his anger **a** from them.
25:25 Good news from far **a** is like cold water to the
27:10 go to a neighbor than to a relative who lives far **a**.
28:1 The wicked run **a** when no one is chasing them,
Ecc 2:26 God takes the wealth **a** and gives it to those who
3:5 A time to embrace and a time to turn **a**.
3:6 to lose. / A time to keep and a time to throw **a**.
5:16 for the wind, and everything will be swept **a**.
SS 2:10 'Rise up, my beloved, my fair one, and come **a**.
2:13 Arise, my beloved, my fair one, and come **a**.' "
2:17 Before the dawn comes and the shadows flee **a**,
4:6 Before the dawn comes and the shadows flee **a**,
6:5 Look **a**, for your eyes overcome me! Your hair,
Isa 1:4 and corrupt children who have turned **a** from the
1:20 But if you keep turning **a** and refusing to listen,
1:30 You will wither **a** like an oak or garden without
3:9 The very look on their faces gives them **a**
3:18 The Lord will strip **a** their artful beauty—
5:13 So I will send my people into exile far **a**
5:26 He will send a signal to the nations far **a**. He will
6:12 Do not stop until the LORD has sent everyone **a**
8:4 and Samaria and carry **a** their riches."
8:17 though he has turned **a** from the people of Israel.
8:21 My people will be led **a** as captives, weary
10:18 and they will waste **a** like sick people in a plague.
13:5 They came from countries far **a**. They are the
14:13 I will preside on the mountain of the gods far **a** in
15:4 cities of Heshbon and Elealeh will be heard far **a**,
17:2 There will be no one to chase them **a**.
19:7 along the riverbank will wither and blow **a**.
20:4 For the king of Assyria will take **a** the Egyptians
22:3 The people try to slip **a**, but they are captured,
22:8 Judah's defenses have been stripped **a**. You run to
22:17 the LORD is about to seize you and hurl you **a**.
22:18 you up into a ball and toss you **a** into a distant,
24:23 of the sun and moon will seem to fade **a**.
25:8 The Sovereign LORD will wipe **a** all tears.
27:3 day and night I will watch to keep enemies **a**.
27:8 He has exiled her from her land as though blown **a**
27:9 The LORD did this to purge **a** Israel's sin.
27:11 for its people have turned **a** from God.
28:16 Whoever believes need never run **a** again.
28:17 the enemy will come like a flood to sweep it **a**.
28:19 day and night, until you are carried **a**."
29:5 your ruthless enemies will be driven **a** like chaff
29:13 honor me with their lips, but their hearts are far **a**.
30:24 its chaff having been blown **a** by the wind.
30:27 The LORD is coming from far **a**, burning with
30:28 like a flood on his enemies, sweeping them all **a**.
31:4 fight on Mount Zion. He will not be frightened **a**!
31:7 when every one of you will throw **a** the gold idols
31:8 The strong young Assyrians will be taken **a** as
33:13 Listen to what I have done, you nations far **a**!
33:15 a profit by fraud, who stay far **a** from bribes,
34:4 The heavens above will melt **a** and disappear like a
38:12 My life has been blown **a** / like a shepherd's tent in
39:7 Some of your own descendants will be taken **a** into
40:6 "Shout that people are like the grass that dies **a**.
40:26 them to see that none are lost or have strayed **a**.
41:3 He chases them **a** and goes on safely, though he is
41:9 For I have chosen you and will not throw you **a**.
41:16 them in the air, and the wind will blow them all **a**;
42:17 them their gods—/ they will be turned **a** in shame.
44:22 I have swept **a** your sins like the morning mists.
46:1 Bel and Nebo, are being hauled **a** on ox carts.
47:10 and 'knowledge' have caused you to turn **a** from
47:11 you suddenly, and you won't be able to charm it **a**.
47:15 will slip **a** and disappear, unable to help.
49:12 See, my people will return from far **a**, from lands
49:17 and all who are trying to destroy you will go **a**.
49:19 Your enemies who enslaved you will be far **a**.
49:21 were killed, and the rest were carried **a** into exile.
50:1 mother gone because I divorced her and sent her **a**?
50:1 you went **a** as captives because of your sins.
50:5 to me, and I have listened. I do not rebel or turn **a**.
51:8 The worm will eat **a** at them as it eats wool.
53:6 All of us have strayed **a** like sheep. We have left
53:8 From prison and trial they led him **a** to his death.
54:8 In a moment of anger I turned my face **a** for a little
54:14 Your enemies will stay far **a**; you will live in
57:1 The righteous pass **a**; the godly often die before
57:14 Clear **a** the rocks and stones so my people can
57:16 If I did, all people would pass **a**—all the souls I
59:2 he has turned **a** and will not listen anymore.
59:11 We look to be rescued, but it is far **a** from us.
62:8 warriors come and take **a** your grain and wine.
64:6 and fall. And our sins, like the wind, sweep us **a**.
64:7 you have turned **a** from us and turned us over to
65:5 in my nostrils, an acrid smell that never goes **a**.
65:8 (and someone will say, 'Don't throw them all **a**—
Jer 1:3 the people of Jerusalem were taken **a** as captives.
2:14 of slaves? Why has she been carried **a** as plunder?
2:20 your yoke and tore **a** the chains of your slavery,
2:22 You are stained with guilt that cannot be washed **a**.
3:8 that I had divorced faithless Israel and sent her **a**.
3:19 and I thought you would never turn **a** from me
4:1 "If you will throw **a** your detestable idols and go
4:25 were gone. All the birds of the sky had flown **a**.
7:21 "**A** with your burnt offerings and sacrifices!
7:33 and no one will be left to scare them **a**.
8:13 I will take **a** their rich harvests of figs and grapes.
9:2 that I could go **a** and forget them and live in a
10:20 My children have been taken **a**, and I will never
12:3 Drag these people **a** like helpless sheep to be
13:9 This illustrates how I will rot **a** the pride of Judah
13:17 because the LORD's flock will be led **a** into
13:19 The people of Judah will be taken **a** as captives.
13:23 Can a leopard take **a** its spots? Neither can you
15:1 these people, I wouldn't help them. **A** with them!
15:3 to kill, the dogs to drag **a**, the vultures to devour,
15:7 of your cities and take **a** everything you hold dear.
16:5 I have taken **a** my unfailing love and my mercy.
17:4 and I will send you **a** as captives to a foreign land.
17:5 and turn their hearts **a** from the LORD.
17:13 all who turn **a** from you will be disgraced
22:10 Instead, weep for the captive king being led **a**!
22:11 King Josiah, and was taken **a** as a captive:
22:22 All your friends have been taken **a** as captives.
23:14 evil instead of turning them **a** from their sins.
25:10 I will take **a** your happy singing and laughter.
27:10 drive you from your land and send you far **a** to die.
27:18 articles will not be carried **a** with you to Babylon!
27:22 They will all be carried **a** to Babylon and will stay
29:6 many grandchildren. Multiply! Do not dwindle **a**!
31:19 I turned **a** from God, but then I was sorry. I kicked
31:36 Israel as I am to do **a** with the laws of nature!
31:37 so I will not consider casting them **a** forever for
33:8 I will cleanse **a** their sins against me, and I will
39:7 him in chains, and sent him **a** to exile in Babylon.
40:10 and summer fruits and olives, and store them **a**."
41:8 barley, oil, and honey that they had hidden **a**.
41:16 and his officers led **a** all the people they had
43:12 all their idols and carrying **a** the people as captives.
46:15 because the LORD has driven them **a**.
46:16 Let's get **a** from the sword of the enemy!'
46:22 Silent as a serpent gliding **a**, Egypt flees.
48:9 Oh, that Moab had wings so she could fly **a**,
48:44 I will see to it that you do not get **a**, for the time of
48:46 and daughters have been taken **a** as captives.
49:29 their household goods and camels will be taken **a**.
50:16 all those who plant crops; send all the harvesters **a**.
51:2 will come and winnow her, blowing her **a** as chaff.
52:11 him in bronze chains, and led him **a** to Babylon.
52:17 and they carried all the bronze **a** to Babylon.
La 1:3 Judah has been led **a** into captivity, afflicted
1:5 have been captured and taken **a** to distant lands.
1:8 so she has been tossed **a** like a filthy rag.
1:16 any who might encourage me are far **a**.
1:17 Let them be thrown **a** like a filthy rag!"
2:12 Their lives ebb **a** like the life of a warrior wounded
3:17 Peace has been stripped **a**, and I have forgotten
4:9 who die of hunger, wasting **a** for want of food.
4:15 "Get **a**!" the people shouted at them. "You are
5:13 The young men are led **a** to work at millstones,
Eze 3:14 The Spirit lifted me up and took me **a**. I went in
4:17 and they will waste **a** under their punishment.
6:12 Disease will strike down those who are far **a** in
7:4 I will turn my eyes **a** and show no pity,
7:11 will survive. All their wealth will be swept **a**.
7:19 "They will throw **a** their money, tossing it out like
11:15 saying, 'They are far **a** from the LORD, so now
11:19 I will take **a** their hearts of stone and give them
12:6 pack to your shoulders and walk **a** into the night.
12:11 be driven from their homes and sent **a** into exile.
13:13 I will sweep **a** your whitewashed wall with a storm
13:19 You turn my people **a** from me for a few handfuls
14:6 Repent and turn **a** from your idols, and stop all
17:4 Then he carried it **a** to a city filled with merchants,
17:10 it will wither **a** completely when the east wind
17:12 took **a** her king and princes, and brought them to
17:15 break her sworn treaties like that and get **a** with it?
18:8 stays **a** from injustice, is honest and fair when
18:21 But if wicked people turn **a** from all their sins
18:27 And if wicked people turn **a** from their
19:4 They led him **a** in chains / to the land of Egypt.
23:10 killed her and took **a** her children as their slaves.
23:22 those very nations from which you turned **a** in
23:25 Your children will be taken **a** as captives,
24:11 Now set the empty pot on the coals to scorch **a** the
24:16 of man, I am going to take **a** your dearest treasure.
24:23 or weep, but you will waste **a** because of your sins.
24:25 "Son of man, on the day I take **a** their stronghold—
24:25 I will also take **a** their sons and daughters.
25:3 and laughed at Judah as she went **a** into exile,
26:4 I will scrape **a** its soil and make it a bare rock!
26:18 The islands are dismayed as you pass **a**.'
27:34 and your crew / have passed **a** with you.
30:4 Their wealth will be carried **a** and their
30:17 in battle, and the women will be taken **a** as slaves.
30:18 and its daughters will be led **a** as captives.
31:12 All those who lived beneath its shadow went **a**
31:17 Its allies, too, were all destroyed and had passed **a**.
32:20 Egypt will be dragged **a** to its judgment.
33:10 'Our sins are heavy upon us; we are wasting **a**!
34:4 not gone looking for those who have wandered **a**
34:10 I will take **a** their right to feed the flock, along with
34:16 I will search for my lost ones who strayed **a**,
34:25 and drive **a** the dangerous animals from the land.
36:25 Your filth will be washed **a**, and you will no longer
37:1 and I was carried **a** by the Spirit of the LORD to a
38:13 Who are you to drive **a** their cattle and seize their
39:23 then know why Israel was sent **a** to exile—
39:24 I turned my face **a** and punished them in
39:28 responsible for sending them **a** to exile
43:9 Now let them put **a** their idols and the sacred
44:10 **a** from me to worship idols must bear the
Da 2:35 and the wind blew them all **a** without a trace.
7:26 and all his power will be taken **a** and completely
9:11 All Israel has disobeyed your law and turned **a**,
9:16 please turn your furious anger **a** from your city of
10:7 but they were suddenly terrified and ran **a** to hide.
11:12 After the enemy army is swept **a**, the king of the
11:22 Before him great armies will be swept **a**,
11:26 His army will be swept **a**, and many will be killed.
12:11 "From the time the daily sacrifice is taken **a**
Hos 2:9 I will take **a** the linen and wool clothing I gave her
4:19 So a mighty wind will sweep them **a**. They will die
8:11 "Israel has built many altars to take **a** sin,
9:11 The glory of Israel will fly **a** like a bird, for your
9:12 It will be a terrible day when I turn **a** and leave you
10:5 wail for it, because its glory will be stripped **a**.
10:6 so much will be carted **a** with them when they go
13:8 to pieces like a bear whose cubs have been taken **a**.
13:11 I gave you kings, and in my fury I took them **a**.
13:12 have been collected and stored **a** for punishment.
13:15 thing they have will be plundered and carried **a**.
14:8 "O Israel, stay **a** from idols! I am the one who
Joel 2:20 these armies from the north and send them far **a**.
3:8 sell them to the peoples of Arabia, a nation far **a**.
Am 2:14 Your fastest runners will not get **a**. The strongest
4:2 "The time will come when you will be led **a** with
4:2 Every last one of you will be dragged **a** like a fish
4:7 fell on one field, while another field withered **a**.
5:23 **A** with your hymns of praise! They are only noise
6:3 You push **a** every thought of coming disaster,
6:7 you will be the first to be led **a** as captives.
6:10 goes into the house to carry **a** a dead body, he will
7:11 and the people of Israel will be sent **a** into
7:15 But the LORD called me **a** from my flock
Jnh 1:3 and went in the opposite direction in order to get **a**
1:3 hoping that by going **a** to the west he could escape
1:10 Then he told them that he was running **a** from the
4:2 do this, LORD? That is why I ran **a** to Tarshish!
4:7 of the plant, so that it soon died and withered **a**.
Mic 1:7 and they will now be carried **a** to pay prostitutes
1:11 very foundations of their city have been swept **a**.
1:16 for the children you love will be snatched **a**,
3:3 cut **a** their skin, and break their bones.
Na 1:5 presence the mountains quake, and the hills melt **a**;
1:8 But he sweeps **a** his enemies in an overwhelming
2:8 The people are slipping **a**. "Stop, stop!"
3:10 Thebes fell, and her people were led **a** as captives.
3:16 swarm of locusts, they strip the land and then fly **a**.
3:17 But like locusts that fly **a** when the sun comes up
3:17 the earth, all of them will fly **a** and disappear.
Hab 1:17 Will you let them get **a** with this forever? Will they
2:3 But these things I plan won't happen right **a**.
Zep 1:2 "I will sweep **a** everything in all your land,"
1:3 "I will sweep **a** both people and animals alike.
2:2 and your opportunity is blown **a** like chaff.
3:19 I will bring together those who were chased **a**.
Hag 1:9 when you brought your harvest home, I blew it **a**.
Zec 2:6 The LORD says, "Come **a**! Flee from the north,
2:7 Come **a**! Escape to Jerusalem, you who are exiled
3:4 to Jeshua he said, "See, I have taken **a** your sins,
7:11 They turned stubbornly **a** and put their fingers in
9:4 But now the Lord will strip **a** Tyre's possessions
14:2 Half the population will be taken **a** into captivity,
14:12 become like walking corpses, their flesh rotting **a**.
Mal 3:3 of silver, watching closely as the dross is burned **a**.
3:7 'How can we return when we have never gone **a**?'
Mt 4:11 Then the Devil went **a**, and angels came and cared
4:24 soon coming to be healed from as far **a** as Syria.
5:29 causes you to lust, gouge it out and throw it **a**.

5:30 causes you to sin, cut it off and throw it **a**.
5:42 and don't turn **a** from those who want to borrow.
6: 6 But when you pray, go **a** by yourself, shut the door
7:23 Go **a**; the things you did were unauthorized.'
8:34 but they begged him to go **a** and leave them alone.
9:16 the patch shrinks and pulls **a** from the old cloth,
9:24 He said, "Go **a**, for the girl isn't dead; she's only
13:12 even what they have will be taken **a** from them.
13:19 and snatches the seed **a** from their hearts.
13:48 the good fish into crates, and throw the bad ones **a**.
14:15 Send the crowds **a** so they can go to the villages
14:24 the disciples were in trouble far **a** from land,
15: 8 me with their words, / but their hearts are far **a**.
15:23 a word. Then his disciples urged him to send her **a**.
15:32 I don't want to send them **a** hungry, or they will
16: 4 prophet Jonah." Then Jesus left them and went **a**.
16:23 turned to Peter and said, "Get **a** from me, Satan!
18: 8 or foot causes you to sin, cut it off and throw it **a**.
18: 9 eye causes you to sin, gouge it out and throw it **a**.
18:12 and one wanders **a** and is lost, what will he do?
18:13 than over the ninety-nine that didn't wander **a**!
19: 7 write an official letter of divorce and send her **a**?"
19:22 he went sadly **a** because he had many possessions.
21:43 that the Kingdom of God will be taken **a** from you
22:22 His reply amazed them, and they went **a**.
24:10 And many will turn **a** from me and betray and hate
24:39 happen until the Flood came and swept them all **a**.
25:29 even what little they have will be taken **a**.
25:41 will turn to those on the left and say, '**A** with you,
25:46 And they will go **a** into eternal punishment,
26:39 let this cup of suffering be taken **a** from me.
26:42 If this cup cannot be taken **a** until I drink it,
26:52 "Put **a** your sword," Jesus told him. "Those who
26:75 me three times." And he went **a**, crying bitterly.
27:31 on him again. Then they led him **a** to be crucified.
Mk 1:30 a high fever. They told Jesus about her right **a**.
2:20 But someday he will be taken **a** from them, and
2:21 new patch shrinks and pulls **a** from the old cloth,
3: 6 At once the Pharisees went **a** and met with the
3: 8 and even from as far **a** as Tyre and Sidon.
4:15 then Satan comes at once and takes it **a** from them.
4:25 even what they have will be taken **a** from them."
5: 6 When Jesus was still some distance **a**, the man saw
5:17 and the crowd began pleading with Jesus to go **a**
6:31 "Let's get **a** from the crowds for a while
6:36 Send the crowds **a** so they can go to the nearby
7: 7 honor me with their lips, / but their hearts are far **a**.
7:17 Then Jesus went into a house to get **a** from the
7:25 Right **a** a woman came to him whose little girl was
7:33 Jesus led him to a private place **a** from the crowd.
8:33 said to Peter very sternly, "Get **a** from me, Satan!
10: 4 wife an official letter of divorce and send her **a**."
10:22 and he went sadly **a** because he had many
12:12 of the crowds. So they left him and went **a**.
14:36 Please take this cup of suffering **a** from me. Yet I
14:44 Then you can take him **a** under guard."
14:50 all his disciples deserted him and ran **a**.
14:52 off his clothes, but he escaped and ran **a** naked.
14:65 even the guards were hitting him as they led him **a**.
15:20 on him again. Then they led him **a** to be crucified.
16: 3 roll the stone **a** from the entrance to the tomb.
Lk 1:25 "He has taken **a** my disgrace of having no
1:53 good things / and sent the rich **a** with empty hands.
4:30 but he slipped **a** through the crowd and left them.
4:34 "Go **a**! Why are you bothering us, Jesus of
5:35 Someday he will be taken **a** from them, and
6:30 and when things are taken **a** from you, don't try to
8:12 but then the Devil comes and steals it **a**
8:18 even what they think they have will be taken **a**
8:37 all the people in that region begged Jesus to go **a**
9:10 Then he slipped quietly **a** with them toward the
9:12 "Send the crowds **a** to the nearby villages
9:36 When the voice died **a**, Jesus was there alone.
9:53 But they were turned **a**. The people of the village
10:42 has discovered it—and I won't take it **a** from her."
12:19 you have enough stored **a** for years to come.
13:27 I don't know you. Go **a**, all you who do evil.'
14: 4 the sick man and healed him and sent him **a**.
14:32 If he is not able, then while the enemy is still far **a**,
14:35 It is thrown **a**. Anyone who is willing to hear
15: 4 and one of them strayed **a** and was lost in the
15: 7 others who are righteous and haven't strayed **a**!
15:20 And while he was still a long distance **a**, his father
17:34 one will be taken **a**, and the other will be left.
19:11 that the Kingdom of God would begin right **a**.
19:12 "A nobleman was called **a** to a distant empire to
19:26 even what little they have will be taken **a**.
20:11 treated shamefully, and he went **a** empty-handed.
20:12 He, too, was wounded and chased **a**.
21:24 or sent **a** as captives to all the nations of the world.
22:41 He walked **a**, about a stone's throw, and knelt
22:42 please take this cup of suffering **a** from me.
23:26 As they led Jesus **a**, Simon of Cyrene, who was
23:55 As his body was taken **a**, the women from Galilee
Jn 1:29 There is the Lamb of God who takes **a** the sin of
3:20 They stay **a** from the light for fear their sins will be
4:14 But the water I give them takes **a** thirst altogether.
6:66 At this point many of his disciples turned **a**
8: 9 they slipped **a** one by one, beginning with the
8:21 Later Jesus said to them again, "I am going **a**.
9:15 my eyes, and when it was washed **a**, I could see!"
10:13 The hired hand runs **a** because he is merely hired
10:28 never perish. No one will snatch them **a** from me,
10:39 they tried to arrest him, but he got **a** and left them.
12:36 Jesus went **a** and was hidden from them.
13:33 how brief are these moments before I must go **a**
14:28 I am going **a**, but I will come back to you again.
15: 6 Anyone who parts from me is thrown **a** like a
16: 1 have told you these things so that you won't fall **a**.
16: 5 "But now I am going **a** to the one who sent me,
16: 7 But it is actually best for you that I go **a**, because if
16: 7 If I do go **a**, he will come because I will send him
18:31 "Then take him **a** and judge him by your own
19:15 "**A** with him," they yelled. "**A** with him—crucify
19:16 to be crucified. / So they took Jesus and led him **a**.
19:38 gave him permission, he came and took the body **a**.
20: 1 and found that the stone had been rolled **a** from the
20:13 "Because they have taken **a** my Lord,"
20:15 "Sir," she said, "if you have taken him **a**, tell me
Ac 1:11 Jesus has been taken **a** from you into heaven.
5: 4 And after selling it, the money was yours to give **a**.
7:42 Then God turned **a** from them and gave them up to
7:43 I will send you into captivity / far **a** in Babylon.'
8:39 of the water, the Spirit of the Lord caught Philip **a**.
13: 8 He was trying to turn the governor **a** from the
17:30 everyone everywhere to turn **a** from idols
21:25 and they should stay **a** from all sexual
22:16 and be baptized, and have your sins washed **a**,
22:21 for I will send you far **a** to the Gentiles!'"
22:22 one voice they shouted, "**A** with such a fellow!
23:10 ordered his soldiers to take him **a** from them
23:22 warned the young man as he sent him **a**.
24:17 "After several years **a**, I returned to Jerusalem
24:25 Felix was terrified. "Go **a** for now," he replied.
Ro 1:18 wicked people who push the truth **a** from
3:12 All have turned **a** from God; / all have gone wrong.
3:22 when we trust in Jesus Christ to take **a** our sins.
3:24 Christ Jesus, who has freed us by taking **a** our sins.
8:38 even the powers of hell can't keep God's love **a**.
11: 5 for not all the Jews have turned **a** from God.
11:27 my covenant with them / and take **a** their sins."
16:17 to what you have been taught. Stay **a** from them.
1Co 6:11 but now your sins have been washed **a**, and you
6:13 though someday God will do **a** with both of them.
6:18 Run **a** from sexual sin! No other sin so clearly
7:31 for this world and all it contains will pass **a**.
9:25 They do it to win a prize that will fade **a**, but we do
13:11 But when I grew up, I put **a** childish things.
2Co 3: 7 even though the brightness was already fading **a**.
3:13 people of Israel would not see the glory fading **a**.
3:16 anyone turns to the Lord, then the veil is taken **a**.
5: 8 and we would rather be **a** from these bodies,
5: 9 we are here in this body or **a** from this body.
7:10 use sorrow in our lives to help us turn **a** from sin
11: 3 But I fear that somehow you will be led **a** from
11:33 a window in the city wall, and that's how I got **a**!
12: 8 Three different times I begged the Lord to take it **a**.
Gal 1: 6 I am shocked that you are turning **a** so soon from
1:17 I went **a** into Arabia and later returned to the city
3: 4 was it? Are you now going to just throw it all **a**?
4:14 to you, you did not reject me and turn me **a**.
5: 4 from Christ! You have fallen **a** from God's grace.
6: 7 that you can't ignore God and get **a** with it.
Eph 2:13 Though you once were far **a** from God, now you
2:17 of peace to you Gentiles who were far **a** from him,
4:18 they are far **a** from the life of God because they
4:25 So put **a** all falsehood and "tell your neighbor the
5: 2 and gave himself as a sacrifice to take **a** your sins.
Php 2:12 And now that I am **a** you must be even more
2:14 you do, stay **a** from complaining and arguing,
2:30 the things you couldn't do because you were far **a**.
Col 1:21 includes you who were once so far **a** from God.
1:23 Don't drift **a** from the assurance you received
2: 5 For though I am far **a** from you, my heart is with
2:11 the cutting **a** of your sinful nature.
2:13 because your sinful nature was not yet cut **a**.
3:25 For God has no favorites who can get **a** with evil.
1Th 1: 9 and how you turned **a** from idols to serve the true
5:22 Keep **a** from every kind of evil.
2Th 3: 6 Stay **a** from any Christian who lives in idleness
3:14 Stay **a** from them so they will be ashamed.
1Ti 1: 6 They have turned **a** from these things and spend
4: 1 last times some will turn **a** from what we believe;
2Ti 2:19 to the Lord must turn **a** from all wickedness."
3: 5 them godly. You must stay **a** from people like that.
3: 9 But they won't get **a** with this for long.
Tit 1:11 they have already turned whole families **a** from the
3: 5 He washed **a** our sins and gave us a new life
3:11 For people like that have turned **a** from the truth.
Phm 1:15 Onesimus ran **a** for a little while so you could have
Heb 1:12 They will fade **a** like old clothing. / But you are
2: 1 the truth we have heard, or we may drift **a** from it.
2:17 then could offer a sacrifice that would take **a** the
3:10 and I said, / 'Their hearts always turn **a** from me.
3:12 turning you **a** from the living God.
6: 1 with the importance of turning **a** from evil deeds
6: 6 and who then turn **a** from God. It is impossible to
9:28 as a sacrifice to take **a** the sins of many people.
10: 4 for the blood of bulls and goats to take **a** sins.
10:11 offering sacrifices that can never take **a** sins.
10:35 Do not throw **a** this confident trust in the Lord,
10:38 I will have no pleasure in anyone who turns **a**."
13: 5 Stay **a** from the love of money; be satisfied with
Jas 1:10 They will fade **a** like a flower in the field.
1:11 the flower withers, and its beauty fades **a**.
1:11 wealthy people will fade **a** with all of their
1:24 You see yourself, walk **a**, and forget what you look
2:25 and sent them safely **a** by a different road.
4: 2 so you fight and quarrel to take it **a** from them.
5: 2 Your wealth is rotting **a**, and your fine clothes are
5: 3 The very wealth you were counting on will eat **a**
5:19 if anyone among you wanders **a** from the truth
1Pe 1:24 prophet says, / "People are like grass that dies **a**;
1:24 The grass withers, / and the flowers fall **a**.
2:11 So I warn you to keep **a** from evil desires
2:24 He personally carried **a** our sins in his own body
3:11 Turn **a** from evil and do good. / Work hard at
2Pe 1:10 Doing this, you will never stumble or fall **a**.
2:17 of water or as clouds blown **a** by the wind—
3:10 Then the heavens will pass **a** with a terrible noise,
3:11 Since everything around us is going to melt **a**,
3:12 on fire and the elements will melt **a** in the flames.
3:17 and not be carried **a** by the errors of these wicked
1Jn 2: 2 He takes **a** not only our sins but the sins of all the
2:17 And this world is fading **a**, along with everything it
3: 5 And you know that Jesus came to take **a** our sins,
4:10 and sent his Son as a sacrifice to take **a** our sins.
5:21 keep **a** from anything that might take God's place
Rev 2:17 eat of the manna that has been hidden **a** in heaven.
2:21 but she would not turn **a** from her immorality.
2:22 unless they turn **a** from all their evil deeds.
3:11 you have, so that no one will take **a** your crown.
6:14 And the sky was rolled up like a scroll and taken **a**.
7:17 And God will wipe **a** all their tears."
9: 6 find it. They will long to die, but death will flee **a**!
12: 5 And the child was snatched **a** from the dragon
13:10 are destined for prison will be arrested and taken **a**.
18: 4 from heaven, "Come **a** from her, my people.
18:21 down as violently as I have thrown **a** this stone,
21: 8 But cowards who turn **a** from me, and unbelievers,

AWE (24) [AWE-INSPIRING, AWED, AWESOME, AWESOMELY, AWESTRUCK]

Dt 28:10 by the LORD, and they will stand in **a** of you.
1Ch 29:25 so the entire nation of Israel stood in **a** of him,
Ps 5: 7 with deepest **a** I will worship at your Temple.
33: 8 the LORD, / and let everyone stand in **a** of him.
64: 9 Then everyone will stand in **a**,
65: 8 the ends of the earth / stand in **a** of your wonders.
89: 7 The highest angelic powers stand in **a** of God.
Isa 29:23 of Israel. They will stand in **a** of the God of Israel.
Jer 5:24 'Let us live in **a** of the LORD our God, for he
33: 9 good I do for my people and will tremble with **a**!
Hos 3: 5 They will come trembling in **a** to the LORD,
Mic 7:16 They will stand in silent **a**, deaf to everything
Hab 3: 2 and I am filled with **a** by the amazing things you
Mal 2: 5 greatly revered me and stood in **a** of my name.
Mt 8:27 The disciples just sat there in **a**. "Who is this?"
Mk 4:41 And they were filled with **a** and said among
9:15 The crowd watched Jesus in **a** as he came toward
Lk 5:26 Everyone was gripped with great wonder and **a**.
8:25 And they were filled with **a** and amazement.
9:43 **A** gripped the people as they saw this display of
Ac 2:43 A deep sense of **a** came over them all,
3:11 Everyone stood there in **a** of the wonderful thing
Heb 12:28 God by worshiping him with holy fear and **a**.
Rev 13: 3 at this miracle and followed the beast in **a**.

AWE-INSPIRING (4) [AWE]

Ge 31:42 the **a** God of my father, Isaac—
Ps 45: 4 and justice. / Go forth to perform **a** deeds!
111: 9 with them forever. / What a holy, **a** name he has!
145: 6 Your **a** deeds will be on every tongue; / I will

AWED (1) [AWE]

1Ki 3:28 and the people were **a** as they realized the great

AWESOME (48) [AWE]

Ge 28:17 He was afraid and said, "What an **a** place this is!
31:53 So Jacob took an oath before the **a** God of his
Ex 15:11 is glorious in holiness like you—/ so **a** in splendor,
16:10 they could see the **a** glory of the LORD.
20:20 "for God has come in this way to show you his **a**
24:17 The Israelites at the foot of the mountain saw an **a**
24: 7 The **a** glory of the LORD on the mountaintop
34:10 the **a** power I will display through you.
40:35 and the Tabernacle was filled with the **a** glory of
Dt 4:34 miraculous signs, wonders, war, **a** power,
5:25 will certainly die and be consumed by this **a** fire.
7:21 God is among you, and he is a great and **a** God.
10:17 He is the great God, mighty and **a**, who shows no
11: 2 your God or seen his greatness and **a** power.
28:58 the glorious and **a** name of the LORD your God,
28:67 because of your terror at the **a** horrors you see
2Sa 7:23 You performed **a** miracles and drove out the
1Ch 17:21 You performed **a** miracles and drove out the
2Ch 2: 5 magnificent Temple because our God is an **a** God,
Ne 1: 5 and **a** God who keeps his covenant of unfailing
9:32 our God, the great and mighty and **a** God,
Job 10:16 like a lion and display your **a** power against me.
13:21 and don't terrify me with your **a** presence.
Ps 47: 2 For the LORD Most High is **a**. / He is the great
65: 5 You faithfully answer our prayers with **a** deeds,
66: 3 Say to God, "How **a** are your deeds!
66: 5 has done, / what **a** miracles he does for his people!
68:35 God is **a** in his sanctuary. / The God of Israel gives
76:11 Let everyone bring tribute to the **A** One.
77:14 You demonstrate your **a** power among the nations.
89: 7 He is far more **a** than those who surround his
90:11 Your wrath is as **a** as the fear you deserve.
99: 3 Let them praise your great and **a** name.
106:22 things in that land, / such **a** deeds at the Red Sea.
131: 1 myself with matters too great / or **a** for me.
Isa 21: 2 I see an **a** vision: I see you plundered
40:10 He will rule with **a** strength. See, he brings his
64: 3 you did **a** things beyond our highest expectations.
La 2: 1 In his day of **a** fury, the Lord has shown no mercy
Eze 20:33 with an iron fist in great anger and with **a** power.

38: 9 You and all your allies—a vast and **a** horde—
Da 2:31 of a man, shining brilliantly, frightening and **a**.
9: 4 "O Lord, you are a great and **a** God!
Joel 2:11 The day of the LORD is an **a**, terrible thing.
Hab 3: 4 flash from his hands. He rejoices in his **a** power.
3:12 You marched across the land in **a** anger
Zep 1: 7 for the **a** day of the LORD's judgment has come.
Heb 12:19 For they heard an **a** trumpet blast and a voice with

AWESOMELY (1) [AWE]
Eze 1:18 The rims of the four wheels were **a** tall, and they

AWESTRUCK (2) [AWE]
Jnh 1:16 The sailors were **a** by the LORD's great power,
Lk 5: 9 For he was **a** by the size of their catch, as were the

AWFUL (13)
Ps 74: 3 Walk through the **a** ruins of the city; / see how the
Isa 5: 9 But the LORD Almighty has sealed your **a** fate.
Jer 2:23 valley in the land! Face the **a** sins you have done.
48:34 their **a** cries of terror can be heard from Heshbon
La 3:20 I will never forget this **a** time, as I grieve over my
Eze 23:33 You will reel like a drunkard beneath the **a** blows
23:36 accuse Oholah and Oholibah of all their **a** deeds.
Hos 10: 9 "O Israel, ever since that **a** night in Gibeah,
Joel 1: 3 Pass the **a** story down from generation to
Jnh 1: 8 "What have you done to bring this **a** storm down
Mk 14:35 the **a** hour awaiting him might pass him by.
Lk 6:25 for a time of **a** hunger is before you.
1Co 7:22 the Lord has now set you free from the **a** power of

AWHILE (6) [WHILE]
Ge 18: 5 Please stay **a** before continuing on your journey."
Jdg 19: 4 Her father urged him to stay **a**, so he stayed three
Ac 13:11 and you will be stricken **a** with blindness."
19:22 on ahead to Macedonia while he stayed **a** longer in
1Co 16: 6 It could be that I will stay **a** with you, perhaps all
16: 7 I want to come and stay **a**, if the Lord will let me.

AWL (2)
Ex 21: 6 to the door and publicly pierce his ear with an **a**.
Dt 15:17 take an **a** and push it through his earlobe into the

AWNINGS (1)
Eze 27: 7 and purple **a** made bright with dyes from the coasts

AWOKE (1) [WAKE]
Mk 1:35 The next morning Jesus **a** long before daybreak

AX (15) [AXES, BATTLE-AX]
Dt 19: 5 And suppose one of them swings an **a** and the **a** head flies off the handle,
Jdg 9:48 He took an **a** and chopped some branches from a
1Sa 13:21 and an eighth of an ounce for sharpening an **a**,
1Ki 6: 7 **a**, or any other iron tool at the building site.
2Ki 6: 5 them was chopping, his **a** head fell into the river.
6: 5 my lord!" he cried. "It was a borrowed **a**!"
6: 6 Then the **a** head rose to the surface and floated.
Pr 25:18 others is as harmful as hitting them with an **a**,
Ecc 10: 9 there is danger with each stroke of your **a**!
10:10 Since a dull **a** requires great strength,
Isa 10:15 Can the **a** boast greater power than the person who
10:34 The Mighty One will cut down the enemy as an **a**
Mt 3:10 Even now the **a** of God's judgment is poised,
Lk 3: 9 Even now the **a** of God's judgment is poised,

AXES (5) [AX]
1Sa 13:20 picks, **a**, or sickles, they had to take them to a
2Sa 12:31 picks, and **a**, and to work in the brick kilns.
1Ch 20: 3 and forced them to labor with saws, picks, and **a**.
Ps 74: 6 With **a** and picks, / they smashed the carved
Jer 46:22 they come against her with **a** like woodsmen.

AXLES (3)
1Ki 7:30 of these carts had four bronze wheels and bronze **a**.
7:32 to **a** that had been cast as one unit with the cart.
7:33 The **a**, spokes, rims, and hubs were all cast from

AXLETREES [KJV] See AXLES

AYYAH (1)
1Ch 7:28 and its surrounding villages to the north as far as **A**

AZAL (1)
Zec 14: 5 through this valley, for it will reach across to **A**.

AZALIAH (2)
2Ki 22: 3 King Josiah sent Shaphan son of **A** and grandson
2Ch 34: 8 the Temple, Josiah appointed Shaphan son of **A**,

AZANIAH (1)
Ne 10: 9 The Levites who signed were Jeshua son of **A**,

AZAREL (5)
1Ch 12: 6 Elkanah, Isshiah, **A**, Joezer, and Jashobeam,
27:22 Dan | **A** son of Jeroham These were the leaders of
Ezr 10:41 **A**, Shelemiah, Shemariah,
Ne 11:13 There were also Amashsai son of **A**, son of Ahzai,
12:36 **A**, Milalai, Gilalai, Maai, Nethanel, Judah,

AZARIAH (38) [AZARIAH'S]
1Ki 4: 2 his high officials: / **A** son of Zadok was the priest.
4: 5 **A** son of Nathan presided over the district
1Ch 2: 8 The son of Ethan was **A**.
2:38 was the father of Jehu. / Jehu was the father of **A**.
2:39 **A** was the father of Helez. / Helez was the father of
6: 9 Ahimaaz was the father of **A**. / **A** was the father of
6:10 Johanan was the father of **A**, the high priest at the
6:11 **A** was the father of Amariah. / Amariah was the
6:13 the father of Hilkiah. / Hilkiah was the father of **A**.
6:14 **A** was the father of Seraiah. / Seraiah was the
6:36 Elkanah, Joel, **A**, Zephaniah,
9:11 **A** son of Hilkiah, son of Meshullam, son of Zadok,
9:11 **A** was the chief officer of the house of God.
2Ch 15: 1 Then the Spirit of God came upon **A** son of Oded,
15: 8 When Asa heard this message from **A** the prophet,
21: 2 were **A**, Jehiel, Zechariah, Azariahu, Michael,
23: 1 **A** son of Jeroham, Ishmael son of Jehohanan,
23: 1 **A** son of Obed, Maaseiah son of Adaiah,
26:17 **A** the high priest went in after him with eighty
26:20 When **A** and the other priests saw the leprosy,
28:12 **A** son of Jehohanan, Berekiah son of
29:12 Mahath son of Amasai and Joel son of **A**.
29:12 Kish son of Abdi and **A** son of Jehallelel.
31:10 And **A** the high priest, from the family of Zadok,
31:13 appointments were made by King Hezekiah and **A**,
Ezr 7: 1 was the son of Seraiah, son of **A**, son of Hilkiah,
7: 3 son of Amariah, son of **A**, son of Meraioth,
Ne 3:23 and **A** son of Maaseiah and grandson of Ananiah
8: 7 Hodiah, Maaseiah, Kelita, **A**, Jozabad, Hanan,
10: 2 Seraiah, **A**, Jeremiah,
12:33 along with **A**, Ezra, Meshullam,
Jer 43: 2 **A** son of Hoshaiah and Johanan son of Kareah
Da 1: 6 and **A** were four of the young men chosen,
1: 7 was called Meshach. / **A** was called Abednego.
1:11 to look after Daniel, Hananiah, Mishael, and **A**.
1:19 him as much as Daniel, Hananiah, Mishael, and **A**.
2:17 Mishael, and **A** what had happened.

AZARIAH'S (1) [AZARIAH]
Ne 3:24 who rebuilt another section of the wall from **A**

AZARIAHU (1)
2Ch 21: 2 were Azariah, Jehiel, Zechariah, **A**, Michael,

AZAZ (1)
1Ch 5: 8 and Bela son of **A**, son of Shema, son of Joel.

AZAZIAH (3)
1Ch 15:21 Jeiel, and **A** were chosen to play the harps.
27:20 Ephraim | Hoshea son of **A** / Manasseh (west)
2Ch 31:13 **A**, Nahath, Asahel, Jerimoth, Jozabad, Eliel,

AZBUK (1)
Ne 3:16 Next to him was Nehemiah son of **A**, the leader of

AZEKAH (7)
Jos 10:10 and attacked them at **A** and Makkedah,
10:11 hailstorm that continued until they reached **A**.
15:35 Jarmuth, Adullam, Socoh, **A**,
1Sa 17: 1 between Socoh in Judah and **A** at Ephes-dammim.
2Ch 11: 9 Adoraim, Lachish, **A**,
Ne 11:30 nearby fields and **A** with its surrounding villages.
Jer 34: 7 army was besieging Jerusalem, Lachish, and **A**—

AZEL (6) [AZEL'S]
1Ch 8:37 the father of Eleasah. / Eleasah was the father of **A**.
8:38 **A** had six sons: Azrikam, Bokeru, Ishmael,
8:38 Obadiah, and Hanan. These were the sons of **A**.
9:43 son was Eleasah. / Eleasah's son was **A**.
9:44 **A** had six sons, and their names were Azrikam,
9:44 Obadiah, and Hanan. These were the sons of **A**.

AZEL'S (1) [AZEL]
1Ch 8:39 **A** brother Eshek had three sons: Ulam (the oldest),

AZEM [KJV] See EZEM

AZGAD (4)
Ezr 2:12 The family of **A** | 1,222
8:12 From the family of **A**: Johanan son of Hakkatan
Ne 7:17 The family of **A** | 2,322
10:15 Bunni, **A**, Bebai,

AZIEL (1) [JAAZIEL]
1Ch 15:20 Zechariah, **A**, Shemiramoth, Jehiel, Unni, Eliab,

AZIZA (1)
Ezr 10:27 Eliashib, Mattaniah, Jeremoth, Zabad, and **A**.

AZMAVETH (7) [BETH-AZMAVETH]
2Sa 23:31 Abi-albon the Arbathite; / **A** from Bahurim;
1Ch 8:36 Jadah was the father of Alemeth, **A**, and Zimri.
9:42 Jadah was the father of Alemeth, **A**, and Zimri.
11:33 **A** from Bahurim; / Eliahba from Shaalbon;
12: 3 Jeziel and Pelet, sons of **A**; / Beracah and Jehu
27:25 **A** son of Adiel was in charge of the palace
Ne 12:29 came from Beth-gilgal and the area of Geba and **A**,

AZMON (3)
Nu 34: 4 from which it will go to Hazar-addar, and on to **A**.
34: 5 From **A** the boundary will turn toward the brook of
Jos 15: 4 From there it passed to **A**, until it finally reached

AZNOTH-TABOR (1) [TABOR]
Jos 19:34 The western boundary ran past **A**, then to Hukkok,

AZOR (2)
Mt 1:13 father of Eliakim. / Eliakim was the father of **A**.
1:14 **A** was the father of Zadok. / Zadok was the father

AZOTUS (1)
Ac 8:40 Philip found himself farther north at the city of **A**!

AZRIEL (3)
1Ch 5:24 Epher, Ishi, Eliel, **A**, Jeremiah, Hodaviah,
27:19 son of Obadiah / Naphtali | Jeremoth son of **A**
Jer 36:26 commanded his son Jerahmeel, Seraiah son of **A**,

AZRIKAM (6)
1Ch 3:23 sons of Neariah were Elioenai, Hizkiah, and **A**—
8:38 **A**, Bokeru, Ishmael, Sheariah, Obadiah,
9:14 son of **A**, son of Hashabiah, a descendant of
9:44 and their names were **A**, Bokeru, Ishmael,
2Ch 28: 7 **A**, the king's palace commander; and Elkanah,
Ne 11:15 son of **A**, son of Hashabiah, son of Bunni;

AZUBAH (4)
1Ki 22:42 His mother was **A**, the daughter of Shilhi.
1Ch 2:18 Hezron's son Caleb had two wives named **A**
2:19 After **A** died, Caleb married Ephrathah, and they
2Ch 20:31 His mother was **A**, the daughter of Shilhi.

AZUBAH'S (1)
1Ch 2:18 **A** sons were named Jesher, Shobab, and Ardon.

AZUR [KJV] See AZZUR

AZZAH [KJV] See GAZA

AZZAN (1)
Nu 34:26 Issachar | Paltiel son of **A**

AZZUR (3)
Ne 10:17 Ater, Hezekiah, **A**,
Jer 28: 1 Hananiah son of **A**, a prophet from Gibeon,
Eze 11: 1 Among them were Jaazaniah son of **A** and

B

BAAL (86) [BAAL'S, BAAL-BERITH, BAAL-GAD, BAAL-HAMON, BAAL-HANAN, BAAL-HAZOR, BAAL-HERMON, BAAL-MEON, BAAL-PEOR, BAAL-PERAZIM, BAAL-SHALISHAH, BAAL-TAMAR, BAAL-ZEBUB, BAAL-ZEPHON, BAMOTH-BAAL, KIRIATH-BAAL]
Nu 25: 3 Before long Israel was joining in the worship of **B**
25: 5 everyone who had joined in worshiping **B** of Peor.
25:18 deceit by tricking you into worshiping **B** of Peor,
Dt 4: 3 everyone who had worshiped the god **B** of Peor.
Jdg 2:11 the LORD's sight and worshiped the images of **B**.
2:13 They abandoned the LORD to serve **B**
3: 7 and they worshiped the images of **B**
6:25 Pull down your father's altar to **B**, and cut down
6:28 someone discovered that the altar of **B** had been
6:30 "He must die for destroying the altar of **B** and for
6:31 shouted to the mob, "Why are you defending **B**?
6:31 If **B** truly is a god, let him defend himself
6:32 which means "Let **B** defend himself,"
8:33 themselves by worshiping the images of **B**,
10: 6 They worshiped images of **B** and Ashtoreth,
10:10 you as our God and have served the images of **B**."
1Sa 7: 4 So the Israelites destroyed their images of **B**
12:10 and worshiping the images of **B** and Ashtoreth.
1Ki 16:31 of the Sidonians, and he began to worship **B**.
16:32 he built a temple and an altar for **B** in Samaria.
18:18 and have worshiped the images of **B** instead.
18:19 with all 450 prophets of **B** and the 400 prophets of
18:21 follow him! But if **B** is God, then follow him!"
18:22 of the LORD who is left, but **B** has 450 prophets.
18:23 The prophets of **B** may choose whichever one they
18:25 Then Elijah said to the prophets of **B**, "You go
18:26 Then they called on the name of **B** all morning, shouting, "O **B**, answer us!"
18:40 Elijah commanded, "Seize all the prophets of **B**.

19: 1 and that he had slaughtered the prophets of **B**.
19:18 others in Israel who have never bowed to **B**
22:53 He served **B** and worshiped him,
2Ki 3: 2 He at least tore down the sacred pillar of **B** that his
10:18 "Ahab hardly worshiped **B** at all compared to the
10:19 Summon all the prophets and worshipers of **B**,
10:19 for I am going to offer a great sacrifice to **B**.
10:19 Jehu's plan was to destroy all the worshipers of **B**.
10:20 "Prepare a solemn assembly to worship **B**!"
10:21 all Israel summoning those who worshiped **B**.
10:21 and filled the temple of **B** from one end to the
10:22 "Be sure that every worshiper of **B** wears one of
10:23 Then Jehu went into the temple of **B** with
10:23 Jehu said to the worshipers of **B**, "Make sure that only those who worship **B** are
10:25 men went into the fortress of the temple of **B**.
10:26 out the sacred pillar used in the worship of **B**
10:27 They broke down the sacred pillar of **B** and wrecked the temple of **B**,
10:28 Jehu destroyed every trace of **B** worship from
11:18 the people of the land went over to the temple of **B**
11:18 and they killed Mattan the priest of **B** in front of
17:16 and worshiped **B** and all the forces of heaven.
21: 3 He constructed altars for **B** and set up an Asherah
23: 4 all the utensils that were used to worship **B**,
23: 5 They had also offered incense to **B**, and to the sun,
1Ch 5: 5 Micah, Reaiah, **B**,
8:30 Jeiel's other sons were Zur, Kish, **B**, Ner, Nadab,
9:36 Jeiel's other sons were Zur, Kish, **B**, Ner, Nadab,
2Ch 17: 3 early years and did not worship the images of **B**.
23:17 And all the people went over to the temple of **B**
23:17 and they killed Mattan the priest of **B** in front of
24: 7 Temple of the LORD to worship the images of **B**.
28: 2 of Israel and cast images for the worship of **B**.
33: 3 He constructed altars for the images of **B** and set
34: 4 He saw to it that the altars for the images of **B**
Ps 106:28 Then our ancestors joined in the worship of **B** at
Jer 2: 8 and the prophets spoke in the name of **B**,
2:23 not true! We haven't worshiped the images of **B**!'
7: 9 and worship **B** and all those other new gods of
9:14 their own desires and worshiped the images of **B**,
11:13 altars for burning incense to your god **B**—
11:17 provoking my anger by offering incense to **B**."
12:16 they taught my people to swear by the name of **B**),
19: 5 They have built pagan shrines to **B**, and there they burn their sons as sacrifices to **B**.
23:13 for they prophesied by **B** and led my people of
23:27 as their ancestors did by worshiping the idols of **B**.
32:29 to rise by offering incense to **B** on the rooftops
32:35 They have built pagan shrines to **B** in the valley of
Hos 2: 8 and silver she used in worshiping the god **B** were
2:13 when she burned incense to her images of **B**,
2:17 I will cause you to forget your images of **B**;
11: 2 offering sacrifices to the images of **B** and burning
13: 1 But the people of Ephraim sinned by worshiping **B**
Zep 1: 4 and destroy every last trace of their **B** worship.
Ro 11: 4 others who have never bowed down to **B**!"

BAAL'S (2) [BAAL]

Jdg 6:32 because he knocked down **B** altar.
2Ki 10:19 Any of **B** worshipers who fail to come will be put

BAAL-BERITH (3) [BAAL]

Jdg 8:33 the images of Baal, making **B** their god.
9: 4 him seventy silver coins from the temple of **B**,
9:46 took refuge within the walls of the temple of **B**.

BAAL-GAD (3) [BAAL, GAD]

Jos 11:17 to **B** at the foot of Mount Hermon in the valley of
12: 7 from **B** in the valley of Lebanon to Mount Halak,
13: 5 from **B** beneath Mount Hermon to Lebo-hamath;

BAAL-HAMON (1) [BAAL]

SS 8:11 "Solomon has a vineyard at **B**, which he rents to

BAAL-HANAN (5) [BAAL]

Ge 36:38 When Shaul died, **B** son of Acbor became king.
36:39 When **B** died, Hadad became king and ruled from
1Ch 1:49 When Shaul died, **B** son of Acbor became king.
1:50 When **B** died, Hadad became king and ruled from
27:28 **B** from Geder was in charge of the king's olive

BAAL-HAZOR (1) [BAAL, HAZOR]

2Sa 13:23 when Absalom's sheep were being sheared at **B**

BAAL-HERMON (2) [BAAL, HERMON]

Jdg 3: 3 of Lebanon from Mount **B** to Lebo-hamath.
1Ch 5:23 spread through the land from Bashan to **B**,

BAAL-MEON (3) [BAAL]

Nu 32:38 Nebo, **B**, and Sibmah. They changed the names of
1Ch 5: 8 the area that stretches from Aroer to Nebo and **B**.
Eze 25: 9 frontier cities—Beth-jeshimoth, **B**, and Kiriathaim.

BAAL-PEOR (2) [BAAL]

Dt 4: 3 You saw what the LORD did to you at **B**,
Hos 9:10 But then they deserted me for **B**, giving themselves

BAAL-PERAZIM (4) [BAAL]

2Sa 5:20 So David went to **B** and defeated the Philistines
5:20 So David named that place **B** (which means
1Ch 14:11 So David and his troops went to **B** and defeated the
14:11 So that place was named **B** (which means

BAAL-SHALISHAH (1) [BAAL, SHALISHAH]

2Ki 4:42 One day a man from **B** brought the man of God a

BAAL-TAMAR (1) [BAAL, TAMAR]

Jdg 20:33 the main group of Israelite warriors reached **B**,

BAAL-ZEBUB (4) [BAAL]

2Ki 1: 2 So he sent messengers to the temple of **B**, the god
1: 3 and ask them, 'Why are you going to **B**,
1: 6 He said, 'Why are you going to **B**, the god of
1:16 Why did you send messengers to **B**, the god of

BAAL-ZEPHON (3) [BAAL, ZEPHON]

Ex 14: 2 the sea. Camp there along the shore, opposite **B**.
14: 9 beside the shore near Pi-hahiroth, across from **B**.
Nu 33: 7 opposite **B**, and camped near Migdol.

BAALAH (6) [BALAH, BILHAH, KIRIATH-JEARIM]

Jos 15: 9 Then it turned toward **B** (that is, Kiriath-jearim).
15:10 The border circled west of **B** to Mount Seir,
15:11 where it turned toward Shikkeron and Mount **B**.
15:29 **B**, Iim, Ezem,
2Sa 6: 2 He led them to **B** of Judah to bring home the Ark
1Ch 13: 6 and all Israel went to **B** of Judah (also called

BAALATH (4) [BAALATH-BEER]

Jos 19:44 Eltekeh, Gibbethon, **B**,
1Ki 9:18 **B**, and Tamar in the desert, within his land.
1Ch 4:33 and their surrounding villages as far away as **B**.
2Ch 8: 6 He also rebuilt **B** and other supply centers at this

BAALATH-BEER (1) [BAALATH, BEER]

Jos 19: 8 including all the villages as far south as **B** (also

BAALIS (1)

Jer 40:14 to him, "Did you know that **B**, king of Ammon,

BAANA (3)

1Ki 4:12 **B** son of Ahilud, in Taanach and Megiddo, all of
4:16 **B** son of Hushai, in Asher and in Aloth.
Ne 3: 4 grandson of Meshezabel, and then Zadok son of **B**.

BAANAH (9)

2Sa 4: 2 Now there were two brothers, **B** and Recab,
4: 5 One day Recab and **B**, the sons of Rimmon from
4: 6 So Recab and **B** slipped past the doorkeeper,
4: 9 But David said to Recab and **B**, "As surely as the
23:29 Heled son of **B** from Netophah; / Ithai son of Ribai
1Ch 11:30 from Netophah; / Heled son of **B** from Netophah;
Ezr 2: 2 Mordecai, Bilshan, Mispar, Bigvai, Rehum, and **B**.
Ne 7: 7 Mordecai, Bilshan, Mispar, Bigvai, Rehum, and **B**.
10:27 Malluch, Harim, and **B**.

BAARA (1)

1Ch 8: 8 Shaharaim divorced his wives Hushim and **B**,

BAASEIAH (1)

1Ch 6:40 Michael, **B**, Malkijah,

BAASHA (26) [BAASHA'S]

1Ki 15:16 between King Asa of Judah and King **B** of Israel.
15:17 King **B** of Israel invaded Judah and fortified
15:19 Break your treaty with King **B** of Israel so that he
15:21 As soon as **B** of Israel heard what was happening,
15:22 and timbers that **B** had been using to fortify
15:27 Then **B** son of Ahijah, from the tribe of Issachar,
15:28 **B** killed Nadab in the third year of King Asa's
15:32 constant war between Asa and King **B** of Israel.
15:33 **B** began to rule over Israel in the third year of King
15:33 in Judah. **B** reigned in Tirzah twenty-four years.
16: 1 to King **B** by the prophet Jehu son of Hanani:
16: 6 When **B** died, he was buried in Tirzah. Then his
16: 7 from the LORD had been spoken against **B**
16: 7 because **B** had done what was evil in the LORD's
16: 7 because **B** had destroyed the family of Jeroboam.
16: 8 Elah son of **B** began to rule over Israel from Tirzah
16:11 immediately killed the entire royal family of **B**,
16:12 So Zimri destroyed the dynasty of **B** as the LORD
16:13 This happened because of the sins of **B** and his son
21:22 son of Nebat and the family of **B** son of Ahijah,
2Ki 9: 9 of Jeroboam son of Nebat and of **B** son of Ahijah.
2Ch 16: 1 King **B** of Israel invaded Judah and fortified
16: 3 Break your treaty with King **B** of Israel so that he
16: 5 As soon as **B** of Israel heard what was happening,
16: 6 and timbers that **B** had been using to fortify
Jer 41: 9 Mizpah to protect himself against King **B** of Israel.

BAASHA'S (1) [BAASHA]

1Ki 16: 5 The rest of the events in **B** reign and the extent of

BABBLE (2) [BABBLER, BABBLES, BABBLING]

Job 11: 3 Should I remain silent while you **b** on? When you
Mt 6: 7 don't **b** on and on as people of other religions do.

BABBLER (1) [BABBLE]

Ac 17:18 "This **b** has picked up some strange ideas."

BABBLES (1) [BABBLE]

2Ki 9:11 "You know the way such a man **b** on,"

BABBLING (2) [BABBLE]

Pr 10: 8 to be instructed, but **b** fools fall flat on their faces.
10:14 but the **b** of a fool invites trouble.

BABBLINGS [KJV] See DISCUSSIONS

BABE(S) [KJV] See BABY, CHILD, PERSON

BABEL (2) [BABYLON]

Ge 10:10 with the cities of **B**, Erech, Akkad, and Calneh.
11: 9 That is why the city was called **B**, because it was

BABIES (19) [BABY]

Ex 1:19 They have their **b** so quickly that we cannot get
1Sa 15: 3 men, women, children, **b**, cattle, sheep, camels,
22:19 men and women, children and **b**, and all the cattle,
2Ch 31:18 including the little **b**, the wives, and the sons
Ps 137: 9 Happy is the one who takes your **b** / and smashes
Isa 11: 8 **B** will crawl safely among poisonous snakes.
13:18 They will have no mercy on helpless **b** and will
65:20 "No longer will **b** die when only a few days old.
Jer 30: 6 Do men give birth to **b**? Then why do they stand
44: 7 here from Judah, not even the **b** in your arms.
La 2:11 Little children and tiny **b** are fainting and dying in
Joel 2:16 the elders, the children, and even the **b**.
Na 3:10 Her **b** were dashed to death against the stones of
Mt 24:19 and for mothers nursing their **b** in those days.
Mk 13:17 and for mothers nursing their **b** in those days.
Lk 21:23 pregnant women and for mothers nursing their **b**.
Ac 7:19 and forced parents to abandon their newborn **b**
1Co 14:20 Be innocent as **b** when it comes to evil, but be
Heb 5:12 You are like **b** who drink only milk and cannot eat

BABY (51) [BABIES, BABY'S]

Ge 4:20 Adah gave birth to a **b** named Jabal. He became
17:17 Sarah is ninety; how could she have a **b**?"
18:12 could a worn-out woman like me have a **b**?"
18:13 did she say, 'Can an old woman like me have a **b**?'
21: 7 would have dreamed that I would ever have a **b**?
38: 9 from having a **b** who would belong to his brother.
38:29 and the other **b** was actually the first to be born.
38:30 Then the **b** with the scarlet thread on his wrist was
Ex 1:16 as they are born. Allow only the **b** girls to live."
1:22 the Nile River. But you may spare the **b** girls."
2: 2 She saw what a beautiful **b** he was and kept him
2: 3 She put the **b** in the basket and laid it among the
2: 6 As the princess opened it, she found the **b** boy.
2: 7 and find one of the Hebrew women to nurse the **b**
2: 9 So the baby's mother took her **b** home and nursed
2:22 Later they had a **b** boy, and Moses named him
Nu 11:12 like a nurse carries a **b**—to the land you swore to
12:12 Don't let her be like a stillborn **b**, already decayed
Dt 28:57 them the afterbirth and the new **b** she has borne,
Ru 4:16 Naomi took care of the **b** and cared for him as if he
1Sa 1:22 She told her husband, "Wait until the **b** is weaned.
1:23 So she stayed home and nursed the **b**.
4:20 be afraid," they said. "You have a **b** boy!"
2Sa 12: 3 He cuddled it in his arms like a **b** daughter.
12:15 the LORD made Bathsheba's **b** deathly ill.
12:18 Then on the seventh day the **b** died.
12:18 "He was so broken up about the **b** being sick,"
12:19 "Is the **b** dead?" he asked. "Yes," they replied.
12:21 "While the **b** was still living, you wept
12:21 But now that the **b** is dead, you have stopped your
1Ki 3:17 I gave birth to a **b** while she was with me in the
3:18 Three days later, she also had a **b**. We were alone;
3:19 But her **b** died during the night when she rolled
3:27 but give the **b** to the woman who wants him to
Job 3:16 like a **b** who never lives to see the light?
24: 9 her breast; they take the **b** as a pledge for a loan.
Ecc 11: 5 and as mysterious as a tiny **b** being formed in a
Isa 45:10 How terrible it would be if a newborn **b** said to its
66: 8 Jerusalem's birth pains begin, the **b** will be born;
Lk 1:34 Mary asked the angel, "But how can I have a **b**?
1:35 So the **b** born to you will be holy, and he will be
1:44 my **b** jumped for joy the instant I heard your voice!
1:57 Now it was time for Elizabeth's **b** to be born,
1:59 When the **b** was eight days old, all the relatives
2: 6 they were there, the time came for her **b** to be born.
2:12 You will find a **b** lying in a manger,
2:16 And there was the **b**, lying in the manger.
2:21 Eight days later, when the **b** was circumcised,
2:27 and Joseph came to present the **b** Jesus to the Lord
1Pe 2: 2 Cry out for this nourishment as a **b** cries for milk,
Rev 12: 4 ready to devour the **b** as soon as it was born.

BABY'S (6) [BABY]

Ge 35:18 the **b** father, however, called him Benjamin.
Ex 2: 4 The **b** sister then stood at a distance, watching to
2: 7 Then the **b** sister approached the princess.
2: 8 So the girl rushed home and called the **b** mother.
2: 9 So the **b** mother took her baby home and nursed
Lk 1:62 So they asked the **b** father, communicating to him

BABYLON (283) [BABEL, BABYLON'S, BABYLONIA, BABYLONIAN, BABYLONIANS]

KING OF BABYLON (65) 2Ki 20:12; 24:7,17,20; 25:6,7,11,20,21,23,24; 2Ch 36:17; Isa 14:4; 39:1; Jer 20:4;

21:4,10; 25:11,12,26; 27:9,11,12,14,17; 28:2,4; 29:22; 32:3,4,28,36; 34:2,3,21; 36:29; 37:17,19; 38:3,23; 39:5; 40:5,7,9,11; 41:2; 42:11; 43:10; 50:18,43; 52:3,9,10,15,26,27; Eze 17:12,17; 19:9; 21:21,23; 24:2; 29:19; 30:25; 32:11

Jos 7:21 For I saw a beautiful robe imported from **B**,
2Ki 17:24 of Assyria transported groups of people from **B**,
17:30 Those from **B** worshiped idols of their god
20:12 king of **B**, sent Hezekiah his best wishes and a gift,
20:14 "They came from the distant land of **B**."
20:17 up by your ancestors—will be carried off to **B**.
24:1 King Nebuchadnezzar of **B** invaded the land of
24:7 for the king of **B** occupied the entire area formerly
24:10 the officers of King Nebuchadnezzar of **B** came up
24:15 led King Jehoiachin away as a captive to **B**,
24:17 Then the king of **B** installed Mattaniah,
24:20 Then Zedekiah rebelled against the king of **B**.
25:1 King Nebuchadnezzar of **B** led his entire army
25:6 They brought him to the king of **B** at Riblah,
25:7 The king of **B** made Zedekiah watch as all his sons
25:7 him in bronze chains, and led him away to **B**.
25:11 who had declared their allegiance to the king of **B**.
25:13 and they carried all the bronze away to **B**.
25:20 took them all to the king of **B** at Riblah.
25:21 of Hamath, the king of **B** had them all put to death.
25:23 and their men learned that the king of **B** had
25:24 "Live in the land and serve the king of **B**, and all
25:27 thirty-seventh year of King Jehoiachin's exile in **B**,
25:28 treatment over all the other exiled kings in **B**.
1Ch 9:1 The people of Judah were exiled to **B** because they
2Ch 32:31 when ambassadors arrived from **B** to ask about the
33:11 him in bronze chains, and led him away to **B**.
36:6 Then King Nebuchadnezzar of **B** came to
36:6 bound Jehoiakim in chains and led him away to **B**.
36:7 the LORD, and he placed them in his palace in **B**.
36:10 Jehoiachin was summoned to **B** by King
36:10 of the LORD were taken to **B** at that time.
36:17 So the LORD brought the king of **B** against them.
36:18 The king also took home to **B** all the utensils,
36:20 The few who survived were taken away to **B**,
Ezr 1:11 Jerusalem when the exiles returned there from **B**.
2:1 They had been deported to **B** by King
4:12 to Jerusalem from **B** are rebuilding this rebellious
5:12 he abandoned them to King Nebuchadnezzar of **B**.
5:13 However, King Cyrus of **B**, during the first year of
5:14 in Jerusalem and had placed in the temple of **B**.
5:17 **B** to discover whether King Cyrus ever issued a
6:5 which were taken to **B** by Nebuchadnezzar from
7:6 He came up to Jerusalem from **B**, and the king
7:9 He had left **B** on April 8 and came to Jerusalem on
7:16 which you may obtain from the province of **B**,
8:1 me from **B** during the reign of King Artaxerxes:
Ne 7:6 They had been deported to **B** by King
13:6 year of the reign of King Artaxerxes of **B**,
Est 2:6 He had been exiled from Jerusalem to **B** by King
Ps 87:4 record Egypt and **B** among those who know me—
137:1 Beside the rivers of **B**, we sat and wept / as we
137:7 on the day the armies of **B** captured Jerusalem.
137:8 O **B**, you will be destroyed. / Happy is the one who
Isa 13:1 this message concerning the destruction of **B**:
13:2 Wave to them as they march against **B** to destroy
13:17 For I will stir up the Medes against **B**, and no
13:19 **B**, the most glorious of kingdoms, the flower of
13:20 **B** will never rise again. Generation after generation
14:4 you will taunt the king of **B**. You will say,
14:23 I will make **B** into a desolate land, a place of
21:2 **B** will fall, and the groaning of all the nations she
21:9 Then the watchman said, "**B** is fallen!
21:9 All the idols of **B** lie broken on the ground!"
23:13 The Assyrians have handed **B** over to the wild
39:1 king of **B**, sent Hezekiah his best wishes and a gift.
39:3 "They came from the distant land of **B**."
39:6 up by your ancestors—will be carried off to **B**.
43:14 your sakes I will send an invading army against **B**.
46:1 The idols of **B**, Bel and Nebo, are being hauled
47:1 "Come, **B**, unconquered one, sit in the dust.
47:6 But you, **B**, showed them no mercy. You have
48:14 He will use him to put an end to the empire of **B**,
48:20 Leave **B** and the Babylonians, singing as you go!
52:11 Put **B** behind you, with everything it represents,
Jer 20:4 hand the people of Judah over to the king of **B**.
20:4 He will take them captive to **B** or run them through
20:5 and silver of your kings—will be carried off to **B**.
20:6 and all your household will go as captives to **B**.
21:2 King Nebuchadnezzar of **B** has begun his attack on
21:4 make your weapons useless against the king of **B**
21:7 will hand them over to King Nebuchadnezzar of **B**.
21:10 It will be captured by the king of **B**, and he will
22:25 to King Nebuchadnezzar of **B** and the mighty
24:1 After King Nebuchadnezzar of **B** exiled Jehoiachin
24:1 to **B** along with the princes of Judah and all the
25:1 when King Nebuchadnezzar of **B** began his reign.
25:9 of the north under King Nebuchadnezzar of **B**,
25:11 and her neighboring lands will serve the king of **B**
25:12 I will punish the king of **B** and his people for their
25:26 the king of **B** himself drank from the cup of the
27:6 give your countries to King Nebuchadnezzar of **B**,
27:7 and great kings will conquer and rule over **B**.
27:8 and disease upon that nation until **B** has conquered
27:9 who say, "The king of **B** will not conquer you."
27:11 **B** will be allowed to stay in their own country to
27:12 submit to the king of **B** and his people," I said.
27:14 telling you, 'The king of **B** will not conquer you.'
27:16 taken from my Temple will be returned from **B**.
27:17 Surrender to the king of **B**, and you will live.
27:18 articles will not be carried away with you to **B**!
27:20 King Nebuchadnezzar of **B** left them here when he
27:20 king of Judah, to **B**, along with all the other
27:22 They will all be carried away to **B** and will stay
28:2 I will remove the yoke of the king of **B** from your
28:3 that King Nebuchadnezzar carried off to **B**.
28:4 and all the other captives that were taken to **B**.
28:4 I will surely break the yoke that the king of **B** has
28:6 I hope he does bring back from **B** the treasures of
28:11 now subject to King Nebuchadnezzar of **B**."
28:14 into slavery under King Nebuchadnezzar of **B**.
29:1 and all the people who had been exiled to **B** by
29:3 when they went to **B** as King Zedekiah's
29:4 all the captives he has exiled to **B** from Jerusalem:
29:7 And work for the peace and prosperity of **B**.
29:7 are held captive, for if **B** has peace, so will you."
29:8 and mediums who are there in **B** trick you.
29:10 "The truth is that you will be in **B** for seventy
29:15 the LORD has raised up prophets for you in **B**.
29:16 your relatives who were not exiled to **B**.
29:20 from the LORD, all you captives there in **B**.
29:22 and Ahab, whom the king of **B** burned alive!'
29:24 this message to Shemaiah the Nehelamite in **B**:
29:28 Jeremiah sent a letter here to **B**, predicting that our
29:31 "Send an open letter to all the exiles in **B**.
32:3 I am about to hand this city over to the king of **B**.
32:4 and taken to the king of **B** to be judged
32:5 I will take Zedekiah to **B** and will deal with him
32:28 king of **B**, and he will capture it.
32:36 'It will fall to the king of **B** through war, famine,
34:1 King Nebuchadnezzar of **B** came with all the
34:2 I am about to hand this city over to the king of **B**,
34:3 You will stand before the king of **B** to be judged
34:3 and sentenced. Then you will be exiled to **B**.'
34:21 and his officials to the army of the king of **B**.
35:11 But when King Nebuchadnezzar of **B** arrived in
36:29 because it said the king of **B** would destroy this
37:1 He was appointed by King Nebuchadnezzar of **B**.
37:17 "You will be defeated by the king of **B**."
37:19 who told you the king of **B** would not attack you?
38:3 surely be handed over to the army of the king of **B**,
38:17 If you surrender to **B**, you and your family will
38:23 You will be seized by the king of **B**, and this city
39:5 They took him to King Nebuchadnezzar of **B**,
39:5 There the king of **B** pronounced judgment upon
39:7 him in chains, and sent him away to exile in **B**.
39:9 sent to **B** the remnant of the population as well as
40:1 and Judah who were being sent to exile in **B**.
40:4 If you want to come with me to **B**, you are
40:5 appointed governor of Judah by the king of **B**.
40:7 **B** had appointed Gedaliah son of Ahikam as
40:7 in Judah, and that he hadn't exiled everyone to **B**.
40:9 "Stay here, and serve the king of **B**," he said,
40:11 that the king of **B** had left a few people in Judah
41:2 whom the king of **B** had appointed governor.
42:11 Do not fear the king of **B** anymore,
43:10 servant Nebuchadnezzar, king of **B**, here to Egypt.
44:30 of Judah over to King Nebuchadnezzar of **B**.
46:2 Euphrates River by King Nebuchadnezzar of **B**.
46:26 to King Nebuchadnezzar of **B** and his army.
49:28 were attacked by King Nebuchadnezzar of **B**.
49:30 for King Nebuchadnezzar of **B** has plotted against
50:1 Jeremiah the prophet this message concerning **B**
50:2 signal flag so everyone will know that **B** will fall!
50:8 "But now, flee from **B**! Leave the land of the
50:9 I will bring them against **B** to attack her, and she
50:13 **B** will become a deserted wasteland.
50:14 "Yes, prepare to attack **B**, all you nations round
50:16 Lead from **B** all those who plant crops; send all the
50:17 Then King Nebuchadnezzar of **B** cracked their
50:18 "Now I will punish the king of **B** and his land,
50:21 Yes, march against **B**, the land of rebels, a land
50:23 **B**, the mightiest hammer in all the earth,
50:23 and shattered. **B** is desolate among the nations!
50:24 Listen, **B**, for I have set a trap for you. You are
50:27 For the time has come for **B** to be devastated.
50:28 Listen to the people who have escaped from **B**,
50:29 "Send out a call for archers to come to **B**.
50:32 For I will light a fire in the cities of **B** that will
50:34 But the people of **B**—there will be no rest for
50:35 "It will strike the people of **B**—her princes
50:39 "Soon this city of **B** will be inhabited by ostriches
50:42 are marching in battle formation to destroy you, **B**.
50:43 The king of **B** has received reports about the
50:44 I will chase **B** from its land, and I will appoint the
50:45 Listen to the LORD's plans against **B**
51:1 "I will stir up a destroyer against **B** and the people
51:6 Flee from **B**! Save yourselves! Don't get trapped in
51:7 **B** has been like a golden cup in the LORD's
51:8 But now suddenly, **B**, too, has fallen. Weep for
51:11 spirit of the kings of the Medes to march against **B**
51:12 Raise the battle flag against **B**! Reinforce the guard
51:12 for the LORD will fulfill all his plans against **B**.
51:24 I will repay **B** and the people of Babylonia for all
51:27 Signal many nations to mobilize for war against **B**.
51:29 **B** trembles and writhes in pain, for everything the
51:29 **B** will be left desolate without a single inhabitant.
51:33 "**B** is like wheat on a threshing floor, about to be
51:34 "King Nebuchadnezzar of **B** has eaten and crushed
51:35 May **B** be repaid for all the violence she did to
51:37 and **B** will become a heap of rubble, haunted by
51:38 their drunken feasts, the people of **B** roar like lions.
51:41 "How **B** is fallen—great **B**, praised throughout the earth!
51:42 The sea has risen over **B**; she is covered by its
51:44 And I will punish Bel, the god of **B**, and pull from
51:44 and worship him. The wall of **B** has fallen.
51:45 "Listen, my people, flee from **B**. Save yourselves!
51:48 the north will come destroying armies against **B**,"
51:49 "Just as **B** killed the people of Israel and others
51:53 Though **B** reaches as high as the heavens,
51:54 Hear the cry of **B**, the sound of great destruction
51:55 For the LORD is destroying **B**. He will silence
51:56 Destroying armies come against **B**. Her mighty
51:56 and he is giving **B** all she deserves.
51:58 "The wide walls of **B** will be leveled to the
51:59 when he went to **B** with King Zedekiah of Judah.
51:60 the terrible disasters that would soon come upon **B**.
51:61 He said to Seraiah, "When you get to **B**,
51:62 you have said that you will destroy **B** so that
51:64 'In this same way **B** and her people will sink,
52:3 Then Zedekiah rebelled against the king of **B**.
52:4 King Nebuchadnezzar of **B** led his entire army
52:9 They brought him to the king of **B** at Riblah,
52:10 the king of **B** made Zedekiah watch as all his sons
52:11 him in bronze chains, and led him away to **B**.
52:15 who had declared their allegiance to the king of **B**.
52:17 and they carried all the bronze away to **B**.
52:26 took them all to the king of **B** at Riblah.
52:27 of Hamath, the king of **B** had them all put to death.
52:28 The number of captives taken to **B** in the seventh
52:31 thirty-seventh year of King Jehoiachin's exile in **B**,
52:32 treatment over all the other exiled kings in **B**.
Eze 1:1 with the Judean exiles beside the Kebar River in **B**,
12:13 I will bring him to **B**, the land of the Babylonians,
14:22 and they will come here to join you as exiles in **B**.
17:12 The king of **B** came to Jerusalem, took away her king and princes, and brought them to **B**.
17:14 Only by keeping her treaty with **B** could Israel
17:15 this man of Israel's royal family rebelled against **B**,
17:16 Sovereign LORD, the king of Israel will die in **B**,
17:17 when the king of **B** lays siege to Jerusalem again
17:20 I will bring him to **B** and deal with him there for
19:9 and brought him before the king of **B**. / They held
21:19 Put a signpost on the road that comes out of **B**
21:21 The king of **B** now stands at the fork,
21:23 But the king of **B** will remind the people of their
24:2 because on this very day the king of **B** is beginning
24:26 a refugee from Jerusalem will come to you in **B**
26:7 I will bring King Nebuchadnezzar of **B**—the king
29:18 the army of King Nebuchadnezzar of **B** fought
29:19 the land of Egypt to Nebuchadnezzar, king of **B**.
30:10 Through King Nebuchadnezzar of **B**, I will destroy
30:25 I will strengthen the arms of the king of **B**,
32:11 The sword of the king of **B** will come against you.
Da 1:1 King Nebuchadnezzar of **B** came to Jerusalem
1:2 When Nebuchadnezzar returned to **B**, he took with
1:3 who had been brought to **B** as captives.
2:12 he sent out orders to execute all the wise men of **B**.
2:18 be executed along with the other wise men of **B**.
2:24 had been ordered to execute the wise men of **B**.
2:48 made Daniel ruler over the whole province of **B**,
2:49 be in charge of all the affairs of the province of **B**,
3:1 set it up on the plain of Dura in the province of **B**.
3:12 whom you have put in charge of the province of **B**.
3:30 to even higher positions in the province of **B**.
4:6 I issued an order calling in all the wise men of **B**,
4:29 a walk on the flat roof of the royal palace in **B**.
4:30 the city, he said, "Just look at this great city of **B**!
5:7 He said to these wise men of **B**, "Whoever can
5:11 enchanters, astrologers, and fortune-tellers of **B**.
7:1 the first year of King Belshazzar's reign in **B**,
Mic 4:10 You will soon be sent into exile in distant **B**.
Zec 2:7 Escape to Jerusalem, you who are exiled in **B**!"
6:10 gifts of silver and gold from the Jews exiled in **B**.
Mt 1:11 and his brothers (born at the time of the exile to **B**).
Ac 7:43 So I will send you into captivity / far away in **B**.'
Rev 14:8 him through the skies, shouting, "**B** is fallen—
16:19 The great city of **B** split into three pieces,
17:5 "**B** the Great, Mother of All Prostitutes
18:2 He gave a mighty shout, "**B** is fallen—that great
18:10 "How terrible, how terrible for **B**, that great city!
18:21 He threw it into the ocean and shouted, "**B**,

BABYLON'S (14) [BABYLON]

2Ki 20:18 eunuchs who will serve in the palace of **B** king."
Isa 13:22 **B** days are numbered; its time of destruction will
39:7 eunuchs who will serve in the palace of **B** king."
Jer 27:8 So you must submit to **B** king and serve him; put your neck under **B** yoke!
27:13 every nation that refuses to submit to **B** king?
34:21 And though **B** king has left this city for a while,
39:13 the king's adviser, and the other officers of **B** king
50:46 The earth will shake with the noise of **B** fall,
51:52 "but the time is coming when **B** idols will be
Eze 21:19 and trace two routes on it for the sword of **B** king
30:24 I will strengthen the arms of **B** king and put my
30:25 And when I put my sword in the hand of **B** king
Rev 16:19 And so God remembered all of **B** sins, and he

BABYLONIA (20) [BABYLON]

Ge 10:10 built the foundation for his empire in the land of **B**,
11:2 they found a plain in the land of **B** and settled
14:1 King Amraphel of **B**, King Arioch of Ellasar,
14:9 of Elam and the kings of Goiim, **B**, and Ellasar—
Ezr 5:12 destroyed this Temple and exiled the people to **B**.
Isa 11:11 Upper Egypt, Ethiopia, Elam, **B**, Hamath,
21:1 message came to me concerning the land of **B**:
23:13 Look at the land of **B**—the people of that land are
47:1 O daughter of **B**, never again will you be the lovely
47:5 "O daughter of **B**, sit now in darkness and silence.
Jer 50:10 **B** will be plundered until the attackers are glutted
51:1 a destroyer against Babylon and the people of **B**.
51:24 and the people of **B** for all the wrong they have
51:35 "May the people of **B** be paid in full for all the

Eze 11:24 the Spirit of God carried me back again to **B**,
16:29 by embracing that great merchant land of **B**—
23:15 dressed like chariot officers from the land of **B**.
23:16 so she sent messengers to **B** to invite them to come
Da 1: 2 in the treasure-house of his god in the land of **B**.
Zec 5:11 "To the land of **B** where they will build a temple

BABYLONIAN (32) [BABYLON]

2Ki 20:13 Hezekiah welcomed the **B** envoys and showed
24: 2 Then the LORD sent bands of **B**, Aramean,
25: 8 captain of the guard, an official of the **B** king,
25:10 **B** army as they tore down the walls of Jerusalem.
25:24 Gedaliah vowed to them that the **B** officials meant
25:27 Evil-merodach ascended to the **B** throne.
25:30 The **B** king also gave him a regular allowance to
Ezr 6: 1 orders that a search be made in the **B** archives,
Isa 39: 2 Hezekiah welcomed the **B** envoys and showed
48:14 the empire of Babylon, destroying the **B** armies.'
Jer 22:25 of Babylon and the mighty **B** army.
32: 2 Jerusalem was under siege from the **B** army,
34: 7 At this time the **B** army was besieging Jerusalem,
34:22 I will call the **B** armies back again. They will fight
35:11 we were afraid of the **B** and Aramean armies.
37: 5 When the **B** army heard about it, they withdrew
37:10 Even if you were to destroy the entire **B** army,
37:11 When the **B** army left Jerusalem because of
38:22 and given to the officers of the **B** army.
39: 3 All the officers of the **B** army came in and sat in
41: 3 and **B** soldiers who were with Gedaliah at Mizpah.
41:18 the governor appointed by the **B** king.
52:12 captain of the guard, an official of the **B** king,
52:14 **B** army as they tore down the walls of Jerusalem.
52:31 Evil-merodach ascended to the **B** throne.
52:34 The **B** king also gave him a regular allowance to
Eze 23:14 pictures of **B** military officers, outfitted in striking
Da 1: 7 The chief official renamed them with these **B**
5:30 That very night Belshazzar, the **B** king, was killed.
Mt 1:12 After the **B** exile: / Jehoiachin was the father of
1:17 and fourteen from David's time to the **B** exile, and fourteen from the **B** exile to the Messiah.

BABYLONIANS (57) [BABYLON]

2Ki 24:12 and the queen mother, surrendered to the **B**.
25: 4 But since the city was surrounded by the **B**,
25: 5 But the **B** chased after them and caught the king on
25:13 The **B** broke up the bronze pillars, the bronze
25:25 and everyone with him, both Judeans and **B**.
25:26 for they were afraid of what the **B** would do to
1Ch 3:17 who was taken prisoner by the **B**, were Shealtiel,
2Ch 36:17 The **B** killed Judah's young men, even chasing
Ezr 4: 9 the people of Tarpel, the Persians, the **B**,
Isa 43:14 And the **B** will be forced to flee in those ships they
48:20 Leave Babylon and the **B**, singing as you go!
Jer 21: 4 king of Babylon and the **B** who are attacking you.
21: 9 those who go out and surrender to the **B** will live.
24: 5 the exiles I sent from Judah to the land of the **B**.
25:12 I will make the country of the **B** an everlasting
25:14 Many nations and great kings will enslave the **B**,
32: 4 King Zedekiah will be captured by the **B** and taken
32: 5 If you fight against the **B**, you will never
32:24 the city has been handed over to the **B**,
32:25 even though the city will soon belong to the **B**."
32:28 I will hand this city over to the **B** and to
32:29 The **B** outside the walls will come in and set fire to
32:43 'It has been ravaged by the **B**, a land where people
33: 5 the **B** will still enter. The men of this city are
37: 8 Then the **B** will come back and capture this city
37: 9 Do not fool yourselves that the **B** are gone for
37:13 and said, "You are defecting to the **B**!"
38: 2 but those who surrender to the **B** will live.
38:18 This city will be handed over to the **B**, and they
38:19 "for the **B** will hand me over to the Judeans who
38:23 your wives and children will be led out to the **B**,
39: 2 on July 18, the **B** broke through the wall,
39: 4 and his royal guard saw the **B** in the city gate,
39: 5 But the **B** chased the king and caught him on the
39: 8 Meanwhile, the **B** burned Jerusalem,
40: 9 that it would be safe for them to surrender to the **B**.
40:10 I will stay at Mizpah to represent you before the **B**
41:18 They were afraid of what the **B** would do when
43: 3 so we will stay here and be killed by the **B** or be
50: 1 message concerning Babylon and the land of the **B**.
50: 8 flee from Babylon! Leave the land of the **B**.
50:25 The terror that falls upon the **B** will be the work of
50:35 "The sword of destruction will strike the **B**,"
50:45 plans against Babylon and the land of the **B**.
51: 4 They will fall dead in the land of the **B**, slashed to
51:54 sound of great destruction from the land of the **B**.
52: 7 But since the city was surrounded by the **B**,
52: 8 But the **B** chased after them and caught King
52:17 The **B** broke up the bronze pillars, the bronze
Eze 1: 3 there beside the Kebar River in the land of the **B**,
12:13 the land of the **B**, though he will never see it,
21:23 it is a mistake, because of their treaty with the **B**.
23:23 For the **B** will come with all the Chaldeans from
Da 1: 4 young men the language and literature of the **B**."
9: 1 the son of Ahasuerus, who became king of the **B**.
Hab 1: 6 I am raising up the **B** to be a new power on the
1:12 you have decreed the rise of these **B** to punish

BACHRITES [KJV] See BEKERITE

BACK (727) [BACK-TO-BACK, BACKBONE, BACKED, BACKGROUND, BACKING, BACKS, BACKSLIDERS, BACKSLIDING, BACKSTABBERS, BACKSTABBING, BACKWARD]

Ge 3:24 And a flaming sword flashed **b** and forth,
8: 7 and released a raven that flew **b** and forth until the
8: 9 Noah held out his hand and drew the dove **b** inside.
8:12 the dove again, and this time it did not come **b**.
8:13 the flood began, Noah lifted **b** the cover to look.
14:21 told him, "Give **b** my people who were captured.
18: 6 So Abraham ran **b** to the tent and said to Sarah,
19: 9 "Stand **b**!" they shouted. "Who do you think you
19:17 And don't look **b**! Escape to the mountains,
19:26 But Lot's wife looked **b** as she was following
22: 5 worship there, and then we will come right **b**."
24: 8 If she is unwilling to come **b** with you, then you
24:38 I was told to bring **b** a young woman from here to
24:39 find a young woman willing to come **b** with me?'
24:54 next morning, he said, "Send me **b** to my master."
24:56 and I want to report **b** to my master."
27:31 Then he said, "I'm **b**, Father, and I have the wild
28:15 I will someday bring you safely **b** to this land.
28:21 and if he will bring me **b** safely to my father,
29: 3 the stone would be rolled **b** over the mouth of the
29: 7 you water the flocks so they can get **b** to grazing?"
30:25 Jacob said to Laban, "I want to go **b** home.
30:31 Just do one thing, and I'll go **b** to work for you.
31:32 relatives of ours, I will give it **b** without question."
33:16 So Esau started **b** to Seir that same day.
37:14 Jacob said. "Then come **b** and bring me word."
37:22 and then he would bring him **b** to his father.
37:30 Then he went **b** to his brothers and lamented,
38:20 the Adullamite to take the young goat **b** to her
38:23 laughingstock of the village if we went **b** again."
38:29 But then he drew **b** his hand, and the other baby
39: 9 He has held **b** nothing from me except you,
40:14 And please have some pity on me when you are **b**
42:20 But bring your youngest brother **b** to me. In this
42:34 But bring your youngest brother **b** to me. Then I
42:34 what you say, then I will give you **b** your brother,
42:37 my two sons if I don't bring Benjamin **b** to you.
43: 9 If I don't bring him **b** to you, then let me bear the
43:13 Then take your brother and go **b** to the man.
43:21 in our sacks. Here it is; we have brought it **b** again.
44: 1 and put each man's money **b** into his sack.
44: 8 Didn't we bring **b** the money we found in our
44:25 when he said, 'Go **b** again and buy us a little food,'
44:30 I cannot go **b** to my father without the boy.
44:32 I told him, 'If I don't bring him **b** to you, I will
46: 4 and I will bring your descendants **b** again.
49:33 he lay **b** in the bed, breathed his last, and died.
50: 5 take my body **b** to the land of Canaan, and bury me
50:15 "Now Joseph will pay us **b** for all the evil we did
50:24 He will bring you **b** to the land he vowed to give to
50:25 he said, "When God comes to lead us **b** to Canaan, you must take my body **b** with you."
Ex 2:10 the child's mother brought him **b** to the princess,
4: 7 "Now put your hand **b** into your robe again,"
4:18 Then Moses went **b** home and talked it over with
4:18 "I would like to go **b** to Egypt to visit my family.
4:20 on a donkey, and headed **b** to the land of Egypt.
4:21 "When you arrive **b** in Egypt, go to Pharaoh
5: 4 the people from their tasks? Get **b** to work!
5:18 Now, get **b** to work! No straw will be given to you,
5:22 So Moses went **b** to the LORD and protested,
6:11 "Go **b** to Pharaoh, and tell him to let the people of
9: 1 "Go **b** to Pharaoh," the LORD commanded
10: 8 So Moses and Aaron were brought **b** to Pharaoh.
14:26 Then the waters will rush **b** over the Egyptian
14:27 The water roared **b** into its usual place,
16: 3 "Oh, that we were **b** in Egypt," they moaned.
19: 8 So Moses brought the people's answer **b** to the
19:21 "Go **b** down and warn the people not to cross the
19:24 "Go down anyway and bring Aaron **b** with you.
21: 8 bought her, he may allow her to be bought **b** again.
22:29 "Do not hold anything **b** when you give me the
23: 4 that has strayed away, take it **b** to its owner.
24:14 "Stay here and wait for us until we come **b**.
26:12 will be left to hang over the **b** of the Tabernacle,
28: 7 It will consist of two pieces, front and **b**, joined at
32: 1 When Moses failed to come **b** down the mountain
32:15 They were inscribed on both sides, front and **b**.
32:27 Go **b** and forth from one end of the camp to the
Lev 6: 4 they must give **b** whatever they have taken by theft
6:11 Then he must change **b** into his normal clothing
8:28 Moses then took all the offerings **b** and burned
9:23 and when they came **b** out, they blessed the people
13:42 infection appears on the front or the **b** of his head,
21:20 or has a humped **b** or is a dwarf, or has a defective
24:18 kills another person's animal must pay it **b** in full
24:20 does to hurt another person must be paid **b** in kind.
25:25 a kinsman redeemer, may buy it **b** for them.
25:26 sold it manages to get enough money to buy it **b**,
25:27 After buying it **b**, the original owner may
25:29 that time, the seller retains the right to buy it **b**.
25:48 They may be bought **b** by a close relative—
Nu 12:15 and the people waited until she was brought **b**
13:20 and bring **b** samples of the crops you see."
14: 4 "Let's choose a leader and go **b** to Egypt!"
16:27 So all the people stood **b** from the tents of Korah,
20:28 and Moses and Eleazar went **b** down.
22:23 but Balaam beat it and turned it **b** onto the road.
22:34 I will go **b** home if you are against my going."
23: 5 "Go **b** to Balak and tell him what I told you."
23:16 "Go **b** to Balak and give him this message."
24:11 Now get out of here! Go **b** home! I had planned to
32: 6 "Do you mean you want to stay **b** here while your
33: 7 They left Etham and turned **b** toward Pi-hahiroth,
35:25 and they must send the slayer **b** to live in a city of
Dt 1:25 picked some of its fruit and brought it **b** to us.
1:40 and go on **b** through the wilderness toward the Red
11:17 He will shut up the sky and hold **b** the rain,
16: 7 Then go **b** to your tents the next morning.
19:12 the murderer brought **b** from the city of refuge
22: 1 don't pretend not to see it. Take it **b** to its owner.
24:19 of grain from your field, don't go **b** to get it.
28:68 Then the LORD will send you **b** to Egypt in
30: 3 and gather you **b** from all the nations where he has
30: 4 God will go and find you and bring you **b** again.
Jos 8:24 they went **b** and finished off everyone inside.
10:19 Don't let them get **b** to their cities, for the LORD
10:38 Then they turned **b** and attacked Debir.
11:10 Joshua then turned **b** and captured Hazor
22: 8 "Share with your relatives **b** home the great
22: 9 They started the journey **b** to their own land of
24:27 against you if you go **b** on your word to God."
Jdg 1: 7 Now God has paid me **b** for what I did to them."
3:19 the stone carvings near Gilgal, he turned **b**.
6:18 Don't go away until I come **b** and bring my
9: 9 just to wave **b** and forth over the trees?'
9:11 I quit producing my sweet fruit just to wave **b**
9:13 just to wave **b** and forth over the trees?'
9:44 gate to keep the men of Shechem from getting **b** in,
11:13 the Jordan. Now then, give **b** the land peaceably."
11:14 Jephthah sent this message **b** to the Ammonite
11:35 made a vow to the LORD and cannot take it **b**."
12: 5 a fugitive from Ephraim tried to go **b** across,
13: 8 please let the man of God come **b** to us again
13:11 Manoah ran **b** with his wife and asked, "Are you
14:19 and he went **b** home to live with his father
15:10 We have come to pay him **b** for what he did to
15:11 "I only paid them **b** for what they did to me."
16:14 But Samson woke up, pulled **b** the loom shuttle,
16:18 "Come **b** one more time," she said, "for he has
16:22 But before long his hair began to grow **b**.
16:28 so that I may pay **b** the Philistines for the loss of
16:31 They took him **b** home and buried him between
19: 3 donkey to Bethlehem to persuade her to come **b**.
Ru 1: 7 and they took the road that would lead them **b** to
1: 8 "Go **b** to your mothers' homes instead of coming
1:15 "your sister-in-law has gone **b** to her people
1:16 "Don't ask me to leave you and turn **b**.
2: 6 "She is the young woman from Moab who came **b**
2:15 When Ruth went **b** to work again, Boaz ordered
2:18 She carried it **b** into town and showed it to her
2:21 Boaz even told me to come **b** and stay with his
3:15 barley into the cloak and helped her put it on her **b**.
3:16 When Ruth went **b** to her mother-in-law,
3:17 'Don't go **b** to your mother-in-law
4: 3 "You know Naomi, who came **b** from Moab.
1Sa 1:11 and give me a son, then I will give him **b** to you.
1:18 Then she went **b** and began to eat again, and she
3: 5 Eli replied. "Go on **b** to bed." So he did.
3: 6 call you, my son," Eli said. "Go on **b** to bed."
3: 9 your servant is listening.' " So Samuel went **b** to
3:18 told Eli everything; he didn't hold anything **b**.
4: 4 So they sent men to Shiloh to bring **b** the Ark of
5:11 "Please send the Ark of the God of Israel **b** to its
6: 3 "Send the Ark of the God of Israel **b**, along with a
11: 9 So Saul sent the messengers **b** to Jabesh-gilead to
12:20 and that you don't turn your **b** on him in any way.
12:21 Don't go **b** to worshiping worthless idols that
14:13 and the Philistines fell **b** as Jonathan and his armor
14:46 Then Saul called **b** the army from chasing the
15:20 I brought **b** King Agag, but I destroyed everyone
15:27 Saul grabbed at him to try to hold him **b** and tore
17: 6 and he slung a bronze javelin over his **b**.
17:15 But David went **b** and forth between working for
17:18 getting along, and bring me **b** a letter from them."
18:24 When Saul's men reported this **b** to the king,
19:15 lies there!" And he sent them **b** to David's house.
20:21 Then I will send a boy to bring the arrows **b**.
20:38 gathered up the arrows and ran **b** to his master.
20:40 to the boy and told him to take them **b** to the city.
23:23 and come **b** with a more definite report.
24:10 For the LORD placed you at my mercy **b** there in
24:16 Saul called **b**, "Is that really you, my son David?"
24:22 But David and his men went **b** to their stronghold.
25:39 who has paid **b** Nabal and kept me from doing it
26: 1 Now some messengers from Ziph came **b** to Saul
26:21 Come **b** home, my son, and I will no longer try to
28:15 "Why have you disturbed me by calling me **b**?"
28:22 so you can regain your strength for the trip **b**."
29: 4 "Send him **b**!" they demanded. "He can't go into
29: 7 Please don't upset them, but go **b** quietly."
29:11 So David headed **b** into the land of the Philistines,
30:14 We were on our way **b** from raiding the Kerethites
30:15 you will not kill me or give me **b** to my master,
30:18 David got **b** everything the Amalekites had taken,
30:19 that had been taken. David brought everything **b**.
2Sa 2: 1 asked the LORD, "Should I move **b** to Judah?"
2:20 When Abner looked **b** and saw him coming,
2:23 and the spear came out through his **b**.
3:13 with you unless you bring **b** my wife Michal,
3:14 "Give me **b** my wife Michal, for I bought her with
3:16 Then Abner told him, "Go **b** home!" So Palti
3:26 at the pool of Sirah and brought him **b** with them.
6: 9 "How can I ever bring the Ark of the LORD **b**
7:17 So Nathan went **b** to David and told him
10: 4 at the buttocks, and sent them **b** to David in shame.
11:15 is fiercest. Then pull **b** so that he will be killed."
11:23 "And as we chased them **b** to the city gates,
12:23 Can I bring him **b** again? I will go to him one day,
13: 5 what to do. Go **b** to bed and pretend you are sick.
13:30 As they were on the way **b** to Jerusalem, this report

14:14 That is why God tries to bring us **b** when we have
14:21 go and bring **b** the young man Absalom."
14:23 to Geshur and brought Absalom **b** to Jerusalem.
14:32 me **b** from Geshur if he didn't intend to see me.
15:8 in Hebron if he would bring me **b** to Jerusalem."
15:19 Go on **b** with your men to King Absalom, for you
15:20 Go on **b** and take your troops with you, and may
15:25 David instructed Zadok to take the Ark of God **b**
15:25 "he will bring me **b** to see the Ark
15:29 and Abiathar took the Ark of God **b** to the city
16:3 'Today I will get **b** the kingdom of my grandfather
16:8 "The LORD is paying you **b** for murdering Saul
17:3 and I will bring all the people **b** to you as a bride
18:7 and the Israelite troops were beaten **b** by David's
19:3 They crept **b** into the city as though they were
19:10 Let's ask David to come **b** and be our king again."
19:12 Why are you the last ones to welcome me **b**?"
19:14 to us, and bring **b** all those who are with you."
19:15 So the king started **b** to Jerusalem. And when he
19:30 "I am content just to have you **b** again, my lord!"
19:43 we were the first to speak of bringing him **b** to be
19:43 The argument continued **b** and forth, and the men
20:4 within three days and to report **b** at that time.
20:22 the trumpet and called his troops **b** from the attack,
22:48 He is the God who pays **b** those who harm me;
23:12 in the middle of the field and beat **b** the Philistines.
23:16 water from the well, and brought it **b** to David.
1Ki 1:28 So she came **b** in and stood before the king.
1:35 When you bring him **b** here, he will sit on my
2:26 the priest, "Go **b** to your home in Anathoth.
2:40 he had found them, he took them **b** to Jerusalem.
3:22 And so they argued **b** and forth before the king.
5:2 Then Solomon sent this message **b** to Hiram:
6:34 and each door was hinged to fold **b** upon itself.
9:28 and brought **b** to Solomon some sixteen tons of
10:19 The throne had six steps and a rounded **b**. On both
12:5 Then come **b** for my answer." So the people went
12:24 Go **b** home, for what has happened is my
13:4 paralyzed in that position, and he couldn't pull it **b**.
13:19 So they went **b** together, and the man of God ate
13:22 You came **b** to this place and ate food and drank
13:29 and took it **b** to the city to mourn over him
14:9 And since you have turned your **b** on me,
17:22 the life of the child returned, and he came **b** to life!
18:37 and that you have brought them **b** to yourself."
18:44 tell him, 'Climb into your chariot and go **b** home.
19:15 the LORD told him, "Go **b** the way you came,
19:20 then I will go with you!" Elijah replied, "Go on **b**!
20:11 The king of Israel sent **b** this answer: "A warrior
20:34 "I will give **b** the towns my father took from your
22:26 "Arrest Micaiah and take him **b** to Amon,
2Ki 1:6 and told us to go **b** to the king with a message from
4:15 "Call her **b** again," Elisha told him.
4:22 I can hurry to the man of God and come right **b**."
4:35 Elisha got up and walked **b** and forth in the room a
4:39 and came **b** with a pocketful of wild gourds.
5:15 and his entire party went **b** to find the man of God.
5:17 from this place, and I will take it **b** home with me.
5:24 took the gifts from the servants and sent the men **b**.
6:13 And the report came **b**: "Elisha is at Dothan."
7:4 and we will starve if we go **b** into the city.
7:9 let's go **b** and tell the people at the palace."
7:10 So they went **b** to the city and told the gatekeepers
8:1 told the woman whose son he had brought **b** to life,
8:3 and she went to see the king about getting **b** her
8:5 about the time Elisha had brought a boy **b** to life.
8:5 is her son—the very one Elisha brought **b** to life!"
8:14 When Hazael went **b**, the king asked him,
9:2 Call him into a **b** room away from his friends,
9:11 Jehu went **b** to his fellow officers, and one of them
9:17 they are coming in peace," King Joram shouted **b**.
14:20 They brought him **b** to Jerusalem on a horse,
17:27 "Send one of the exiled priests from Samaria **b** to
18:37 of Asaph, the royal historian, went **b** to Hezekiah.
19:9 he sent this message **b** to Hezekiah in Jerusalem:
20:5 "Go **b** to Hezekiah, the leader of my people.
22:20 place.' " So they took her message **b** to the king.
23:8 Josiah brought **b** to Jerusalem all the priests of the
23:26 and he did not hold **b** his fierce anger from them.
23:30 Josiah's officers took his body **b** in a chariot from
1Ch 6:33 His genealogy was traced **b** through Joel, Samuel,
6:39 Asaph's genealogy was traced **b** through Berekiah,
6:44 Ethan's genealogy was traced **b** through Kishi,
10:12 the bodies of Saul and his three sons **b** to Jabesh.
11:14 in the middle of the field and beat **b** the Philistines.
11:18 water from the well, and brought it **b** to David.
12:19 much discussion, they sent them **b**, for they said,
13:3 It is time to bring **b** the Ark of our God, for we
13:6 to bring **b** the Ark of God, which bears the name of
13:12 "How can I ever bring the Ark of God **b** into my
16:20 They wandered **b** and forth between nations,
17:15 So Nathan went **b** to David and told him
19:4 at the buttocks, and sent them **b** to David in shame.
21:27 to the angel, who put the sword **b** into its sheath.
2Ch 8:18 and brought **b** to Solomon almost seventeen tons
10:5 "Come **b** in three days for my answer."
11:4 Go **b** home, for what has happened is my
18:25 "Arrest Micaiah and take him **b** to Amon,
24:11 and took the chest **b** to the Temple again.
24:19 The LORD sent prophets to bring them **b** to him,
24:23 Then they sent all the plunder **b** to their king in
25:10 the hired troops and sent them **b** to Ephraim.
25:23 at Beth-shemesh and brought him **b** to Jerusalem.
25:28 They brought him **b** to Jerusalem on a horse,
28:8 amounts of plunder, which they took **b** to Samaria.
28:15 and took all the prisoners **b** to their own land—
34:28 place.' " So they took her message **b** to the king.
35:3 and you do not need to carry it **b** and forth on your
35:22 God had indeed spoken, and he would not turn **b**.
35:24 Then they brought him **b** to Jerusalem, where he
Ezr 1:11 **b** to Jerusalem when the exiles returned there from
6:5 will be taken **b** to Jerusalem and put into God's
Ne 1:9 I will bring you **b** to the place I have chosen for
2:15 inspecting the wall before I turned **b** and entered
4:4 May their scoffing fall **b** on their own heads,
5:8 but you are selling them **b** into slavery again.
5:12 "We will give **b** everything and demand nothing
6:7 "You can be very sure that this report will get **b** to
6:17 many letters went **b** and forth between Tobiah
9:17 and appointed a leader to take them **b** to their
13:7 When I arrived **b** in Jerusalem and learned the
13:9 and I brought **b** the utensils for God's Temple,
13:11 Then I called all the Levites **b** again and restored
Est 4:10 Then Esther told Hathach to go **b** and relay this
4:13 Mordecai sent **b** this reply to Esther: "Don't think
8:2 which he had taken **b** from Haman—and gave it to
Job 1:7 "I have been going **b** and forth across the earth,
2:2 "I have been going **b** and forth across the earth,
7:6 days are swifter than a weaver's shuttle flying **b**
7:9 and vanishes, those who die will not come **b**.
10:9 made of dust—will you turn me **b** to dust so soon?
12:15 If he holds **b** the rain, the earth becomes a desert.
17:10 "As for all of you, come **b** and try again! But I
20:10 the poor, for he must give **b** his ill-gotten wealth.
28:4 They descend on ropes, swinging **b** and forth.
32:6 so I held **b** and did not dare to tell you what I
34:14 If God were to take **b** his spirit and withdraw his
36:21 Turn **b** from evil, for it was to prevent you from
38:31 "Can you hold **b** the movements of the stars?
41:15 The overlapping scales on its **b** make a shield.
42:6 I take **b** everything I said, and I sit in dust
Ps 6:10 and terrified. / May they suddenly turn **b** in shame.
9:13 hate me. / Snatch me **b** from the jaws of death.
18:47 He is the God who pays **b** those who harm me;
21:2 you have held **b** nothing that he requested.
21:3 You welcomed him **b** with success and prosperity.
28:4 Pay them **b** for all their evil deeds!
35:4 those trying to kill me; / turn them **b** in confusion.
40:11 don't hold **b** your tender mercies from me.
40:14 take delight in my trouble / be turned **b** in disgrace.
41:10 on me. / Make me well again, so I can pay them **b**!
44:5 Only by your power can we push **b** our enemies;
51:8 Oh, give me **b** my joy again; / you have broken
69:4 demanding that I give **b** what I didn't steal.
70:2 take delight in my trouble / be turned **b** in disgrace.
74:11 Why do you hold **b** your strong right hand?
77:1 I cry out to God without holding **b**. / Oh, that God
78:38 destroy them all. / Many a time he held **b** his anger
78:57 They turned **b** and were as faithless as their parents
80:14 Come **b**, we beg you, O God Almighty.
89:34 I will not take **b** a single word I said.
90:3 You turn people **b** to dust, saying, / "Return to
90:13 O LORD, come **b** to us! / How long will you
94:23 God will make the sins of evil people fall **b** upon
104:22 At dawn they slink **b** / into their dens to rest.
105:13 They wandered **b** and forth between nations,
106:47 save us! / Gather us **b** from among the nations,
119:156 is your mercy; / in your justice, give me **b** my life.
119:159 Give **b** my life because of your unfailing love.
129:3 My **b** is covered with cuts, / as if a farmer had
129:5 hate Jerusalem / be turned **b** in shameful defeat.
132:11 swore to David / a promise he will never take **b**:
137:8 be destroyed. / Happy is the one who pays you **b**
147:2 and bringing the exiles **b** to Israel.
Pr 1:10 if sinners entice you, turn your **b** on them!
3:7 Instead, fear the LORD and turn your **b** on evil.
3:28 "Come **b** tomorrow, and then I'll help you."
4:6 Don't turn your **b** on wisdom, for she will protect
6:31 it means selling everything in his house to pay it **b**.
7:5 Let them hold you **b** from an affair with an
17:10 than a hundred lashes on the **b** of a fool.
19:27 my child, you have turned your **b** on knowledge.
23:8 and you will have to take **b** your words of
24:11 sentenced to death; don't stand **b** and let them die.
24:29 "Now I can pay them **b** for all their meanness to
26:3 with a bridle, and a fool with a rod to his **b**!
26:14 As a door turns **b** and forth on its hinges,
26:27 down on others, it will roll **b** and crush you.
29:11 vent to anger, but a wise person quietly holds it **b**.
30:4 but God goes up to heaven and comes **b** down?
Ecc 1:6 and north, here and there, twisting **b** and forth,
3:15 in the past. For God calls each event **b** in its turn.
3:22 No one will bring them **b** from death to enjoy life
8:8 None of us can hold **b** our spirit from departing.
SS 2:17 the shadows flee away, come **b** to me, my love.
5:5 fingers with lovely myrrh, as I pulled **b** the bolt.
6:13 Come **b**, come **b**, that we may see you once
Isa 11:11 In that day the Lord will bring **b** a remnant of his
13:14 rushing **b** to their own lands like hunted deer,
14:1 He will bring them **b** to settle once again in their
21:12 If you wish to ask again, then come **b** and ask."
23:15 But then the city will come **b** to life and sing sweet
33:18 You will think **b** to this time of terror when the
34:8 the year when Edom will be paid **b** for all it did to
36:22 of Asaph, the royal historian, went **b** to Hezekiah.
37:9 he sent this message **b** to Hezekiah in Jerusalem:
38:5 "Go **b** to Hezekiah and tell him, 'This is what the
41:9 I have called you **b** from the ends of the earth
43:6 and daughters **b** to Israel from the distant corners
45:23 my own name, and I will never go **b** on my word:
48:9 I will hold **b** my anger and not wipe you out.
49:5 me to bring his people of Israel **b** to him.
49:17 Soon your descendants will come **b**, and all who
49:18 and see, for all your children will come **b** to you.
49:22 They will carry your little sons **b** to you in their
50:6 I give my **b** to those who beat me and my cheeks
54:6 For the LORD has called you **b** from your grief—
54:7 but with great compassion I will take you **b**.
56:8 who brings **b** the outcasts of Israel, says:
59:20 "to buy **b** those in Israel who have turned from
65:7 insulted me on the hills. I will pay them **b** in full!
66:20 They will bring the remnant of your people **b** from
Jer 2:12 at such a thing and shrink **b** in horror and dismay,
3:1 marries someone else, he is not to take her **b** again,
3:1 Yet I am still calling you to come **b** to me.
3:7 But she did not come **b**. And though her faithless
3:22 says the LORD, "come **b** to me,
4:1 "O Israel, come **b** to me," says the LORD.
7:10 only to go right **b** to all those evils again?
8:4 and discover their mistake, don't they turn **b**?
8:5 refusing to turn **b**, even though I have warned
13:6 "Go **b** to the Euphrates and get the linen belt that I
14:1 explaining why he was holding **b** the rain:
15:6 You have forsaken me and turned your **b** on me,"
15:7 because they refuse to turn **b** to me from all their
16:15 who brought the people of Israel **b** to their own
16:15 For I will bring them **b** to this land that I gave their
18:17 And in all their trouble I will turn my **b** on them
21:3 "Go **b** to King Zedekiah and tell him,
23:3 I will bring them **b** into their own fold, and they
23:8 who brought the people of Israel **b** to their own
24:6 are well treated, and I will bring them **b** here again.
26:18 "Think **b** to the days when Micah of Moresheth
26:19 Then the LORD held **b** the terrible disaster he had
26:23 and brought him **b** to King Jehoiakim.
27:22 But someday I will bring them **b** to Jerusalem
28:3 I will bring **b** all the Temple treasures that King
28:4 And I will bring **b** Jehoiachin son of Jehoiakim,
28:6 I hope he does bring **b** from Babylon the treasures
30:17 I will give you **b** your health and heal your
31:16 Your children will come **b** to you from the distant
31:21 Come **b** again, my virgin Israel; return to your
31:23 "When I bring them **b** again, the people of Judah
32:37 I will surely bring my people **b** again from all the
32:37 I will bring them **b** to this very city and let them
34:11 They took **b** the people they had freed,
34:16 and defiled my name by taking **b** the men
34:22 I will call the Babylonian armies **b** again.
36:2 Begin with the first message **b** in the days of
37:8 Then the Babylonians will come **b** and capture this
37:20 Don't send me **b** to the dungeon in the house of
38:26 just tell them you begged me not to send you **b** to
39:14 of Shaphan, who was to take him **b** to his home.
41:10 with him, he started **b** toward the land of Ammon.
44:5 would not listen or turn **b** from their wicked ways.
46:16 let's go **b** to our homeland where we were born.
47:6 rest again? Go **b** into your sheath; rest and be still!
48:10 who hold **b** their swords from shedding blood!
48:20 "And the reply comes **b**, 'Moab lies in ruins;
49:2 will come and take **b** the land you took from her,"
50:2 "Tell the whole world, and keep nothing **b**!
50:5 the way to Jerusalem and will start **b** home again.
50:6 and cannot remember how to get **b** to the fold.
50:16 sword of the enemy and rush **b** to their own lands.
La 1:13 He has placed a trap in my path and turned me **b**.
2:14 They did not try to hold you **b** from exile by
3:64 Pay them **b**, LORD, for all the evil they have
5:21 O LORD, and bring us **b** to you again! Give us **b**
the joys we once had!
Eze 1:10 on the left side, and the face of an eagle at the **b**.
1:13 and it looked as though lightning was flashing **b**
7:11 Their violence will fall **b** on them as punishment
9:11 who carried the writer's case, reported **b** and said,
11:17 will gather you **b** from the nations where you are
11:24 Afterward the Spirit of God carried me **b** again to
12:3 Pack whatever you can carry on your **b** and leave
18:32 says the Sovereign LORD. Turn **b** and live!
20:14 But again I held **b** in order to protect the honor of
20:17 and held **b** from destroying them in the wilderness.
20:43 You will look **b** at all your sins and hate
23:35 you have forgotten me and turned your **b** on me,
24:14 The time has come and I won't hold **b**; I will not
29:7 you gave way, and her **b** was thrown out of joint.
29:14 and bring its people **b** to the land of Pathros in
33:15 they might give **b** a borrower's pledge,
33:30 of man, your people are whispering behind your **b**.
34:13 I will bring them **b** home to their own land of
35:11 I will pay **b** your angry deeds with mine.
36:22 I am bringing you **b** again but not because you
36:35 And when I bring you **b**, people will say,
37:12 Then I will bring you **b** to the land of Israel.
39:23 I turned my **b** on them and let their enemies
39:29 And I will never again turn my **b** on them, for I
40:13 measuring the distance between the **b** walls of
40:21 and 43-3/4 feet wide between the **b** walls of facing
40:25 and 43-3/4 feet wide between the **b** walls of facing
42:6 each of the upper levels was set **b** from the level
43:1 the man brought me **b** around to the east gateway.
44:1 Then the man brought me **b** to the east gateway in
46:2 and then go **b** out the way he came.
46:21 Then he brought me **b** to the outer courtyard
47:1 Then the man brought me **b** to the entrance of the
47:6 I had seen, then he led me **b** along the riverbank.
Da 4:26 This means that you will receive your kingdom **b**
6:12 So they went **b** to the king and reminded him about
7:6 It had four wings like birds' wings on its **b**, and it
11:8 he will carry **b** their idols with him, along with
Hos 2:9 "But now I will take **b** the wine and ripened grain
2:14 "But then I will win her **b** once again. I will lead
3:1 Bring her **b** to you and love her, even though she
3:2 So I bought her **b** for fifteen pieces of silver

8:13 I will punish them. They will go **b** down to Egypt.
11: 5 they will go **b** to Egypt and will be forced to serve
12: 6 So now, come **b** to your God! Act on the principles
Joel 2:20 I will drive them **b** into the parched wastelands,
2:25 "I will give you **b** what you lost to the stripping
3: 4 and pay you **b** for everything you have done.
3: 7 But I will bring them **b** again from all these places
3: 7 and I will pay you **b** for all you have done.
Am 5: 3 town sends a hundred, only ten will come **b** alive."
5: 4 to the family of Israel: "Come **b** to me and live!
5: 6 Come **b** to the LORD and live! If you don't,
7:12 Go on **b** to the land of Judah and do your
8: 5 to end so you can get **b** to cheating the helpless.
9:14 I will bring my exiled people of Israel **b** from
Ob 1:15 All your evil deeds will fall **b** on your own heads.
1:17 And the people of Israel will come **b** to reclaim
Jnh 3: 9 and hold **b** his fierce anger from destroying us."
Mic 2:13 of your cities of captivity, **b** to your own land.
4: 8 royal might and power will come **b** to you again.
5: 7 rain falling on the grass, which no one can hold **b**.
Na 2:13 Never again will you bring **b** plunder from
3: 7 All who see you will shrink **b** in horror and say,
Zec 5: 8 and he pushed her **b** into the basket and closed the
6: 7 to be off, to patrol **b** and forth across the earth.
9:12 Come **b** to the place of safety, all you prisoners,
10:10 I will bring them **b** from Egypt and Assyria
10:11 of distress, for the waves of the sea will be held **b**.
Mt 2: 8 come **b** and tell me so that I can go and worship
2:20 the child and his mother **b** to the land of Israel,
9: 1 and went **b** across the lake to his own town.
9:18 "but you can bring her **b** to life again if you just
10:13 your blessing stand; if it is not, take **b** the blessing.
11: 4 "Go **b** to John and tell him about what you have
14: 2 "This must be John the Baptist come **b** to life
14: 9 because he didn't want to **b** down in front of his
14:22 Jesus made his disciples get **b** into the boat
14:32 And when they climbed **b** into the boat, the wind
18:15 and confesses it, you have won that person **b**.
18:16 take one or two others with you and go **b** again,
24:48 and thinks, 'My master won't be **b** for a while,'
25:12 But he called **b**, 'I don't know you!'
26:44 So he went **b** to pray a third time, saying the same
26:64 of power and coming **b** on the clouds of heaven."
27: 3 So he took the thirty pieces of silver **b** to the
27:21 the crowd shouted **b** their reply: "Barabbas!"
27:25 And all the people yelled **b**, "We will take
27:64 and then telling everyone he came **b** to life!
Mk 4:38 Jesus was sleeping at the **b** of the boat with his
5:18 When Jesus got **b** into the boat, the man who had
5:21 When Jesus went **b** across to the other side of the
6:14 "This must be John the Baptist come **b** to life
6:16 the man I beheaded, has come **b** from the dead."
6:25 So the girl hurried **b** to the king and told him,
6:38 They came **b** and reported, "We have five loaves
6:45 Jesus made his disciples get **b** into the boat
7:31 then **b** to the Sea of Galilee and the region of the
8:13 So he got **b** into the boat and left them, and he
8:26 "Don't go **b** into the village on your way home."
11:15 When they arrived **b** in Jerusalem, Jesus entered
12: 3 beat him up, and sent him **b** empty-handed.
13:15 A person outside the house must not go **b** into the
14:62 of power and coming **b** on the clouds of heaven."
15:13 They shouted **b**, "Crucify him!"
16:13 they rushed **b** to tell the others, but no one believed
Lk 1:56 three months and then went **b** to her own home.
2:20 The shepherds went **b** to their fields and flocks,
2:45 they went **b** to Jerusalem to search for him there.
4:20 handed it **b** to the attendant, and sat down.
6:30 are taken away from you, don't try to get them **b**.
6:37 Stop criticizing others, or it will all come **b** on you.
6:38 it will be used to measure what is given **b** to you."
7: 1 finished saying all this, he went **b** to Capernaum.
7:15 around him! And Jesus gave him **b** to his mother.
7:22 "Go **b** to John and tell him what you have seen
8:37 and left, crossing **b** to the other side of the lake.
8:39 go **b** to your family and tell them all the wonderful
9: 7 "This is John the Baptist come **b** to life again."
9:42 healed the boy. Then he gave him **b** to his father.
9:62 then looks **b** is not fit for the Kingdom of God."
12:19 And I'll sit **b** and say to myself, My friend,
12:45 servant thinks, 'My master won't be **b** for a while,'
14:12 For they will repay you by inviting you **b**.
15:27 'Your brother is **b**,' he was told, 'and your father
15:30 Yet when this son of yours comes **b** after
15:32 For your brother was dead and has come **b** to life!
17:15 came **b** to Jesus, shouting, "Praise God,
19: 8 I will give them **b** four times as much!"
19:20 "But the third servant brought **b** only the original
20:10 beat him up, and sent him **b** empty-handed.
23:11 put a royal robe on him and sent him **b** to Pilate.
23:15 came to the same conclusion and sent him **b** to us.
24: 6 Don't you remember what he told you **b** in Galilee,
24: 9 So they rushed **b** to tell his eleven disciples—
24:22 and they came **b** with an amazing report.
24:33 And within the hour they were on their way **b** to
Jn 3: 4 "How can an old man go **b** into his mother's
4:28 and went **b** to the village and told everyone,
4:50 Then Jesus told him, "Go **b** home. Your son will
6:17 But as darkness fell and Jesus still hadn't come **b**,
6:22 The next morning, **b** across the lake, crowds began
7:22 than the law of Moses; it goes **b** to Abraham.)
8: 2 but early the next morning he was **b** again at the
9: 7 So the man went and washed, and came **b** seeing!
10:17 because I lay down my life that I may have it **b**
12:17 Lazarus **b** to life were telling others all about it.
14:28 I am going away, but I will come **b** to you again.
17: 1 Glorify your Son so he can give glory **b** to you.
17:10 and you have given them **b** to me, so they are my
18:11 said to Peter, "Put your sword **b** into its sheath.
18:33 Then Pilate went **b** inside and called for Jesus to be
18:40 But they shouted **b**, "No! Not this man,
19: 9 He took Jesus **b** into the headquarters again
19:15 no king but Caesar," the leading priests shouted **b**.
Ac 1:12 so they walked the half mile **b** to Jerusalem.
2:24 the horrors of death and raised him **b** to life again,
3:26 to bless you by turning each of you **b** from your
4:18 So they called the apostles **b** in and told them
7:35 so God sent **b** the same man his people had
7:36 and **b** and forth through the wilderness for forty
8:14 When the apostles **b** in Jerusalem heard that the
9: 2 both men and women—**b** to Jerusalem in chains.
9:17 has sent me so that you may get your sight **b**
11: 2 But when Peter arrived **b** in Jerusalem, some of the
11:10 and all it contained was pulled **b** up to heaven.
11:26 When he found him, he brought him **b** to Antioch.
12:14 the door, she ran **b** inside and told everyone,
14:20 around him, he got up and went **b** into the city.
14:24 Then they traveled **b** through Pisidia to Pamphylia.
15:33 then Judas and Silas were sent **b** to Jerusalem,
18:21 So he left, saying, "I will come **b** later,
18:22 church at Jerusalem and then went **b** to Antioch.
18:23 Paul went **b** to Galatia and Phrygia, visiting all the
20: 3 He was preparing to sail **b** to Syria when he
20:11 Then they all went **b** upstairs and ate the Lord's
23:10 away from them and bring him **b** to the fortress.
23:15 commander to bring Paul **b** to the council again,"
25:21 So I ordered him **b** to jail until I could arrange to
28:25 But after they had argued **b** and forth among
Ro 4:17 believed in the God who brings the dead **b** to life
4:24 who brought Jesus our Lord **b** from the dead.
10: 7 place of the dead" (to bring Christ **b** to life again).
11:23 God will graft them **b** into the tree again.
11:24 he will be far more eager to graft the Jews **b** into
11:35 give him so much that he would have to pay it **b**?
12:17 Never pay **b** evil for evil to anyone. Do things in
1Co 7:11 let her remain single or else go **b** to him.
15:23 then when Christ comes **b**, all his people will be
2Co 1:14 Then on the day when our Lord Jesus comes **b**
5:12 Are we trying to pat ourselves on the **b** again?
5:18 who brought us **b** to himself through what Christ
Gal 2: 1 Then fourteen years later I went **b** to Jerusalem
4: 9 why do you want to go **b** again and become slaves
5: 7 Who has interfered with you to hold you **b** from
5:10 I am trusting the Lord to bring you **b** to believing
6: 1 and humbly help that person **b** onto the right path.
Php 1: 6 on that day when Christ Jesus comes **b** again.
2:19 Then when he comes **b**, he can cheer me up by
2:25 I thought I should send Epaphroditus **b** to you.
2:28 So I am all the more anxious to send him **b** to you,
Col 1:22 yet now he has brought you **b** as his friends.
3:25 you will be paid **b** for the wrong you have done.
1Th 2:17 we tried very hard to come **b** because of our
2:19 before our Lord Jesus when he comes **b** again.
4:14 God will bring **b** with Jesus all the Christians who
5:15 See that no one pays **b** evil for evil, but always try
2Th 2: 6 And you know what is holding him **b**, for he can
2: 7 the one who is holding it **b** steps out of the way.
Tit 2: 9 do their best to please them. They must not talk **b**
Phm 1:12 I am sending him **b** to you, and with him comes
1:15 for a little while so you could have him **b** forever.
Heb 8: 9 so I turned my **b** on them, says the Lord.
10:25 especially now that the day of his coming **b** again
11:15 came from, they would have found a way to go **b**.
11:19 God was able to bring him **b** to life again.
11:19 Abraham did receive his son **b** from the dead.
11:35 Women received their loved ones **b** again from
12:20 They staggered **b** under God's command: "If even
13:19 prayers right now so that I can come **b** to you soon.
Jas 1: 8 They waver **b** and forth in everything they do.
5: 4 The wages you held **b** cry out against you.
5:19 away from the truth and is brought **b** again,
5:20 that person **b** will save that sinner from death
1Pe 1:14 Don't slip **b** into your old ways of doing evil;
3: 9 Instead, pay them **b** with a blessing. That is what
2Pe 2:18 they lure **b** into sin those who have just escaped
3: 4 "Jesus promised to come **b**, did he? Then where is
3: 4 Why, as far **b** as anyone can remember,
1Jn 2:28 of courage and not shrink **b** from him in shame.
Rev 2: 5 Turn **b** to me again and work as you did at first.
3: 3 Go **b** to what you heard and believed at first;
4: 6 living beings, each covered with eyes, front and **b**.
7: 1 holding **b** the four winds from blowing upon the
13:14 who was fatally wounded and then came **b** to life.
20: 5 (The rest of the dead did not come **b** to life until

BACK-TO-BACK (1) [BACK]

Ecc 4:12 and defeated, but two can stand **b** and conquer.

BACKBITER, BACKBITING(S) [KJV] See BACKSTABBERS, BACKSTABBING, GOSSIPING

BACKBONE (1) [BACK, BONE]

Lev 3: 9 includes the fat of the entire tail cut off near the **b**,

BACKED (2) [BACK]

Ps 138: 2 and faithfulness, / because your promises are **b**
Ecc 8: 4 The king's command is **b** by great power. No one

BACKFIRE (1) [BACKFIRES]

Est 9:25 he issued a decree causing Haman's evil plot to **b**,

BACKFIRES (1) [BACKFIRE]

Ps 7:16 They make trouble, / but it **b** on them. / They plan

BACKGROUND (2) [BACK]

Est 2:10 not told anyone of her nationality and family **b**,
2:20 to keep her nationality and family **b** a secret.

BACKING (3) [BACK]

2Sa 15:31 that his adviser Ahithophel was now **b** Absalom,
2Ki 18:20 Which of your allies will give you any military **b**
Isa 36: 5 Which of your allies will give you any military **b**

BACKS (24) [BACK]

Ge 44:11 They quickly took their sacks from the **b** of their
Dt 33:29 low before you, / and you will trample on their **b**!"
2Ki 16:17 He also removed the Sea from the **b** of the bronze
2Ch 29: 6 and his Temple; they turned their **b** on him.
Ne 9:29 They stubbornly turned their **b** on you and refused
Job 19:18 When I stand to speak, they turn their **b** on me.
Ps 66:11 your net / and laid the burden of slavery on our **b**.
78: 9 turned their **b** and fled when the day of battle
Pr 14: 3 The talk of fools is a rod for their **b**, but the words
19:29 will be punished, and the **b** of fools will be beaten.
Isa 51:23 trampled you into the dust and walked on your **b**."
53: 3 We turned our **b** on him and looked the other way
59:13 We have turned our **b** on God. We know how
Jer 2:27 They turn their **b** on me, but in times of trouble
32:33 My people have turned their **b** on me and have
Eze 8:16 about twenty-five men were standing with their **b**
10:12 including their hands, their **b**, and their wings.
Jnh 2: 8 Those who worship false gods turn their **b** on all
Mic 2: 8 You steal the shirts right off the **b** of those who
Ac 21:21 Gentile world to turn their **b** on the laws of Moses.
Ro 11:10 and let their **b** grow weaker and weaker."
Tit 1:14 of people who have turned their **b** on the truth.
Heb 10:39 But we are not like those who turn their **b** on God
11:36 and their **b** were cut open with whips.

BACKSLIDERS (1) [BACK]

Pr 14:14 **B** get what they deserve; good people receive their

BACKSLIDING (1) [BACK]

Eze 37:23 other sins, for I will save them from their sinful **b**.

BACKSTABBERS (1) [BACK]

Ro 1:30 They are **b**, haters of God, insolent, proud,

BACKSTABBING (2) [BACK]

2Co 12:20 outbursts of anger, selfishness, **b**, gossip, conceit,
1Pe 2: 1 Be done with hypocrisy and jealousy and **b**.

BACKWARD (11) [BACK]

Ge 9:23 held it over their shoulders, walked **b** into the tent,
1Sa 4:18 to the Ark, Eli fell **b** from his seat beside the gate.
2Ki 20: 9 the sundial to go forward ten steps or **b** ten steps?"
20:10 Hezekiah replied. "Make it go **b** instead."
20:11 and he caused the shadow to move ten steps **b** on
Isa 38: 8 I will cause the sun's shadow to move ten steps **b**
38: 8 So the shadow on the sundial moved **b** ten steps.
Jer 7:24 their evil hearts. They went **b** instead of forward.
46: 5 The bravest of its fighting men run without a **b**
47: 3 without a **b** glance at their helpless children.
Jn 18: 6 as he said, "I am he," they all fell **b** to the ground!

BAD (57) [BADLY]

Ge 37: 2 But Joseph reported to his father some of the **b**
Lev 5: 4 of any kind, whether its purpose is for good or **b**,
27:10 neither a good animal for a **b** one nor a **b** animal
27:33 be selected on the basis of whether it is good or **b**,
Nu 13:19 Is it good or **b**? Do their towns have walls or are
1Sa 15:23 Rebellion is as **b** as the sin of witchcraft, and
stubbornness is as **b** as worshiping idols.
28:10 nothing **b** will happen to you for doing this."
2Sa 15: 3 It's too **b** the king doesn't have anyone to hear it.
1Ki 14: 6 Then he told her, "I have **b** news for you.
21:19 Isn't killing Naboth **b** enough? Must you rob him,
22: 8 He never prophesies anything but **b** news for me!
22:18 He never prophesies anything but **b** news for me."
2Ki 2:19 But the water is **b**, and the land is unproductive."
2Ch 18: 7 He never prophesies anything but **b** news for me!
18:17 He never prophesies anything but **b** news for me."
Job 2:10 from the hand of God and never anything **b**?"
10:15 If I am guilty, too **b** for me. And even if I'm
Ps 10: 6 to themselves, "Nothing **b** will ever happen to us!
25:17 My problems go from **b** to worse. / Oh, save me
112: 7 They do not fear **b** news; / they confidently trust
Pr 18: 9 A lazy person is as **b** as someone who destroys
20: 8 the evidence, distinguishing the **b** from the good.
25:20 is as **b** as stealing someone's jacket in cold weather
Ecc 3:17 both good and **b**, for all their deeds."
9: 2 whether they are righteous or wicked, good or **b**,
12:14 including every secret thing, whether good or **b**.
Isa 41:23 and fear. Do something, whether good or **b**!
44:25 I cause wise people to give **b** advice, thus proving
45: 7 I am the one who sends good times and **b** times.
65: 8 as good grapes are found among a cluster of **b** ones
66: 3 it is as **b** as putting a dog or the blood of a pig on
Jer 9: 3 And they only go from **b** to worse! They care
17: 9 desperately wicked. Who really knows how **b** it is?
24: 3 "Figs, some very good and some very **b**."
29:17 and make them like rotting figs—too **b** to eat.
Eze 3:20 If good people turn **b** and don't listen to my

Hos 5:10 "The leaders of Judah have become as **b** as
Am 9:10 all those who say, 'Nothing **b** will happen to us.'
Mt 7:17 good fruit, and an unhealthy tree produces **b** fruit.
7:18 A good tree can't produce **b** fruit, and a **b** tree can't produce good fruit.
12:33 Make a tree **b**, and its fruit will be **b**.
13:48 good fish into crates, and throw the **b** ones away.
22:10 good and **b** alike, and the banquet hall was filled
Lk 6:43 "A good tree can't produce **b** fruit, and a **b** tree can't produce good fruit.
Ro 2: 1 But you are just as **b**, and you have no excuse!
7:16 and my **b** conscience shows that I agree that the
9:11 before they had done anything good or **b**,
9:12 not according to our good or **b** works.) She was
1Co 15:33 for "**b** company corrupts good character."
2Co 10:10 person he is weak, and his speeches are really **b**!"
Tit 2: 8 because they won't have anything **b** to say about
3Jn 1:11 Dear friend, don't let this **b** example influence you.

BADGER (2) [BADGERS]
Lev 11: 5 The same is true of the rock **b**
Dt 14: 7 you may not eat the camel, the hare, or the rock **b**.

BADGERS (2) [BADGER]
Ps 104:18 and the rocks form a refuge for rock **b**.
Pr 30:26 Rock **b**—they aren't powerful, / but they make

BADGERS' SKINS [KJV] See GOATSKIN, LEATHER

BADLY (15) [BAD]
Ge 43:18 They were **b** frightened when they saw where they
Ex 2:14 Moses was **b** frightened because he realized that
Jos 8:15 the wilderness as though they were **b** beaten,
1Sa 7: 7 The Israelites were **b** frightened when they learned
11:11 so **b** scattered that no two of them were left
1Ki 22:34 driver of his chariot. "I have been **b** wounded!"
2Ch 18:33 driver of his chariot. "I have been **b** wounded!"
35:23 "Take me from the battle, for I am **b** wounded!"
Ne 2: 2 man with deep troubles." Then I was **b** frightened,
Jer 8: 8 when your teachers have twisted it so **b**?
36:16 had finished reading, they were **b** frightened.
Mt 17:12 but he wasn't recognized, and he was **b** mistreated.
Mk 9:13 Elijah has already come, and he was **b** mistreated,
Ac 19:16 that they fled from the house, naked and **b** injured.
1Th 2: 2 You know how **b** we had been treated at Philippi

BAFFLED (1)
Job 32:15 You sit there **b**, with no further response.

BAG (13) [BAGGAGE, BAGS]
Ge 42:35 there at the top of each one was the **b** of money
1Sa 17:40 from a stream and put them in his shepherd's **b**.
17:49 Reaching into his shepherd's **b** and taking out a
Jer 10:17 "Pack your **b** and prepare to leave; the siege is
Mt 10:10 Don't carry a traveler's **b** with an extra coat
25:15 of gold to another, and one **b** of gold to the last—
25:18 But the servant who received the one **b** of gold dug
25:24 "Then the servant with the one **b** of gold came
Mk 6: 8 walking stick—no food, no traveler's **b**, no money.
Lk 9: 3 "nor a traveler's **b**, nor food, nor money.
10: 4 Don't take along any money, or a traveler's **b**,
22:35 a traveler's **b**, or extra clothing, did you lack
22:36 he said, "take your money and a traveler's **b**.

BAGGAGE (2) [BAG]
1Sa 10:22 the LORD replied, "He is hiding among the **b**."
Eze 12: 4 Bring your **b** outside during the day so they can

BAGS (12) [BAG]
Ge 43:11 Fill your **b** with the best products of the land.
2Ki 5:23 two sets of clothing, tied up the money in two **b**,
12:10 brought to the LORD's Temple and put it into **b**.
Mt 25:15 He gave five **b** of gold to one, two **b** of gold to another, and one bag of gold to
25:16 The servant who received the five **b** of gold began
25:17 The servant with two **b** of gold also went right to
25:20 The servant to whom he had entrusted the five **b** of
25:20 you gave me five **b** of gold to invest and I have
25:22 the servant who had received the two **b** of gold,
25:22 'Sir, you gave me two **b** of gold to invest,
25:28 and give it to the one with the ten **b** of gold.

BAHURIM (7)
2Sa 3:16 Palti followed along behind her as far as **B**,
16: 5 As David and his party passed **B**, a man came out
17:18 Meanwhile, they escaped to **B**, where a man hid
19:16 son of Gera the Benjaminite, the man from **B**,
23:31 Abi-albon the Arbathite; / Azmaveth from **B**;
1Ki 2: 8 Shimei son of Gera, the Benjaminite from **B**.
1Ch 11:33 Azmaveth from **B**; / Eliahba from Shaalbon;

BAIL (1)
Ac 17: 9 and the other believers after they had posted **b**.

BAIT (2)
Am 3: 5 Does a bird ever get caught in a trap that has no **b**?
2Pe 2:18 With lustful desire as their **b**, they lure back into

BAJITH [KJV] See TEMPLE

BAKBAKKAR (1)
1Ch 9:15 **B**; Heresh; Galal; Mattaniah son of Mica, son of

BAKBUK (2)
Ezr 2:51 **B**, Hakupha, Harhur,
Ne 7:53 **B**, Hakupha, Harhur,

BAKBUKIAH (3)
Ne 11:17 **B**, who was Mattaniah's assistant; and Abda son of
12: 9 Their associates, **B** and Unni, stood opposite them
12:25 This included Mattaniah, **B**, and Obadiah.

BAKE (10) [BAKED, BAKER, BAKERY, BAKING, HALF-BAKED, SUNBAKED]
Ge 18: 6 measures of your best flour, and **b** some bread."
Ex 16:23 So **b** or boil as much as you want today, and set
Lev 24: 5 "You must **b** twelve loaves of bread from choice
1Sa 8:13 and force them to cook and **b** and make perfumes
1Ki 17:13 that 'last meal,' but **b** me a little loaf of bread first.
Isa 44:15 to make a fire to warm himself and **b** his bread.
44:19 and used it to **b** my bread and roast my meat.
Eze 4:12 **b** it over a fire using dried human dung as fuel
4:15 "You may **b** your bread with cow dung instead of
46:20 and **b** the flour from the grain offerings into bread.

BAKED (11) [BAKE]
Ge 27:17 with its rich aroma, and some freshly **b** bread.
Ex 12:39 they **b** bread from the yeastless dough they had
Lev 2: 4 "When you present some kind of **b** bread as a
6:16 be **b** without yeast and eaten in a sacred place
7: 9 Any grain offering that has been **b** in an oven,
23:17 These loaves must be **b** from three quarts of choice
Jdg 6:19 and with half a bushel of flour he **b** some bread
1Sa 28:24 She kneaded dough and **b** unleavened bread.
2Sa 13: 8 Then she **b** some special bread for him.
1Ki 19: 6 looked around and saw some bread **b** on hot stones
La 5:10 our skin has been blackened as though **b** in an

BAKER (9) [BAKE]
Ge 40: 1 chief cup-bearer and chief **b** offended him.
40: 5 night the cup-bearer and the **b** each had a dream,
40:16 When the chief **b** saw that the first dream had such
40:20 He sent for his chief cup-bearer and chief **b**,
40:22 but he sentenced the chief **b** to be impaled on a
41:10 time ago, you were angry with the chief **b** and me,
41:11 One night the chief **b** and I each had a dream,
41:13 and the chief **b** was executed and impaled on a
Hos 7: 4 hot even while the **b** is still kneading the dough.

BAKERY (1) [BAKE]
Ge 40:17 In the top basket were all kinds of **b** goods for

BAKING (1) [BAKE]
1Ch 9:31 was entrusted with **b** the bread used in the

BALAAM (73) [BALAAM'S]
Nu 22: 5 sent messengers to **B** son of Beor, who was living
22: 5 He sent this message to request that **B** come to
22: 7 and took money with them to pay **B** to curse Israel.
22: 7 They went to **B** and urgently explained to him
22: 8 "Stay here overnight," **B** said. "In the morning I
22: 8 So the officials from Moab stayed there with **B**.
22: 9 That night God came to **B** and asked him,
22:10 So **B** said to God, "Balak son of Zippor, king of
22:12 "Do not go with them," God told **B**. "You are not
22:13 The next morning **B** got up and told Balak's
22:14 and reported, "**B** refused to come with us."
22:16 They went to **B** and gave him this message:
22:18 But **B** answered them, "Even if Balak were to give
22:20 That night God came to **B** and told him,
22:21 So the next morning **B** saddled his donkey
22:22 But God was furious that **B** was going, so he sent
22:22 his way. As **B** and two servants were riding along,
22:23 but **B** beat it and turned it back onto the road.
22:25 foot against the wall. So **B** beat the donkey again.
22:27 the donkey saw the angel, it lay down under **B**.
22:27 In a fit of rage **B** beat it again with his staff.
22:28 your beating me these three times?" it asked **B**.
22:29 **B** shouted. "If I had a sword with me, I would kill
22:31 **B** fell face down on the ground before him.
22:34 Then **B** confessed to the angel of the LORD,
22:35 you to say." So **B** went on with Balak's officials.
22:36 When King Balak heard that **B** was on the way,
22:37 didn't you come right away?" Balak asked **B**.
22:38 **B** replied, "I have come, but I have no power to
22:39 Then **B** accompanied Balak to Kiriath-huzoth,
22:40 He sent portions of the meat to **B** and the officials
22:41 The next morning Balak took **B** up to
23: 1 **B** said to King Balak, "Build me seven altars here,
23: 3 Then **B** said to Balak, "Stand here by your burnt
23: 3 to me." So **B** went alone to the top of a hill,
23: 4 **B** said to him, "I have prepared seven altars
23: 5 Then the LORD gave **B** a message for King
23: 6 When **B** returned, the king was standing beside his
23: 7 This was the prophecy **B** delivered:
23:11 Then King Balak demanded of **B**, "What have you
23:12 But **B** replied, "Can I say anything except what
23:14 So Balak took **B** to the plateau of Zophim on
23:15 Then **B** said to the king, "Stand here by your burnt
23:16 So the LORD met **B** and gave him a message.
23:17 So **B** returned to the place where the king
23:18 This was the prophecy **B** delivered: / "Rise up,
23:25 Then Balak said to **B**, "If you aren't going to curse
23:26 But **B** replied, "Didn't I tell you that I must do
23:27 Then King Balak said to **B**, "Come, I will take you
23:28 So Balak took **B** to the top of Mount Peor,
23:29 **B** again told Balak, "Build me seven altars
23:30 So Balak did as **B** ordered and offered a young bull
24: 1 By now **B** realized that the LORD intended to
24: 3 "This is the prophecy of **B** son of Beor,
24:10 King Balak flew into a rage against **B**. He angrily
24:12 **B** told Balak, "Don't you remember what I told
24:15 This is the prophecy **B** delivered: / "This is the message of **B** son of Beor,
24:20 Then **B** looked over at the people of Amalek
24:23 **B** concluded his prophecies by saying: / "Alas,
24:25 Then **B** and Balak returned to their homes.
31: 8 They also killed **B** son of Beor with the sword.
Dt 23: 4 they tried to hire **B** son of Beor from Pethor in
23: 5 (But the LORD your God would not listen to **B**.
Jos 13:22 The Israelites also killed **B** the magician, the son of
24: 9 He asked **B** son of Beor to curse you,
24:10 I made **B** bless you, and so I rescued you from
Ne 13: 2 Instead, they hired **B** to curse them, though our
Mic 6: 5 and how **B** son of Beor blessed you instead?
2Pe 2:15 right road and followed the way of **B** son of Beor,
2:16 But **B** was stopped from his mad course when his
Jude 1:11 Like **B**, they will do anything for money. And like
Rev 2:14 You tolerate some among you who are like **B**,

BALAAM'S (4) [BALAAM]
Nu 22:23 **B** donkey suddenly saw the angel of the LORD
22:25 to squeeze by and crushed **B** foot against the wall.
22:31 Then the LORD opened **B** eyes, and he saw the
31:16 "These are the very ones who followed **B** advice

BALAC [KJV] See BALAK

BALADAN (2)
2Ki 20:12 Soon after this, Merodach-baladan son of **B**,
Isa 39: 1 Soon after this, Merodach-baladan son of **B**,

BALAH (1) [BAALAH]
Jos 19: 3 Hazar-shual, **B**, Ezem,

BALAK (38) [BALAK'S]
Nu 22: 2 **B** son of Zippor, the Moabite king, knew what the
22: 4 like an ox devours grass!" So **B**, king of Moab,
22: 7 and urgently explained to him what **B** wanted.
22:10 said to God, "**B** son of Zippor, king of Moab,
22:14 So the Moabite officials returned to King **B**
22:15 Then **B** tried again. This time he sent a larger
22:16 this message: / "This is what **B** son of Zippor says:
22:18 "Even if **B** were to give me a palace filled with
22:36 When King **B** heard that Balaam was on the way,
22:37 didn't you come right away?" **B** asked Balaam.
22:39 Then Balaam accompanied **B** to Kiriath-huzoth,
22:41 The next morning **B** took Balaam up to
23: 1 Balaam said to King **B**, "Build me seven altars
23: 2 **B** followed his instructions, and the two of them
23: 3 Then Balaam said to **B**, "Stand here by your burnt
23: 5 the LORD gave Balaam a message for King **B**
23: 5 "Go back to **B** and tell him what I told you."
23: 7 "**B** summoned me to come from Aram;
23:11 Then King **B** demanded of Balaam, "What have
23:13 Then King **B** told him, "Come with me to another
23:14 So **B** took Balaam to the plateau of Zophim on
23:16 "Go back to **B** and give him this message."
23:17 "What did the LORD say?" **B** asked eagerly.
23:18 "Rise up, **B**, and listen! / Hear me, son of Zippor.
23:25 Then **B** said to Balaam, "If you aren't going to
23:27 Then King **B** said to Balaam, "Come, I will take
23:28 So **B** took Balaam to the top of Mount Peor,
23:29 Balaam again told **B**, "Build me seven altars
23:30 So **B** did as Balaam ordered and offered a young
24:10 King **B** flew into a rage against Balaam. He angrily
24:12 Balaam told **B**, "Don't you remember what I told
24:13 'Even if **B** were to give me a palace filled with
24:25 Then Balaam and **B** returned to their homes.
Jos 24: 9 Then **B** son of Zippor, king of Moab, started a war
24:10 Balaam bless you, and so I rescued you from **B**.
Jdg 11:25 Are you any better than **B** son of Zippor, king of
Mic 6: 5 how King **B** of Moab tried to have you cursed
Rev 2:14 who showed **B** how to trip up the people of Israel.

BALAK'S (4) [BALAK]
Nu 22: 7 **B** messengers, officials of both Moab and Midian,
22:13 next morning Balaam got up and told **B** officials,
22:35 you to say." So Balaam went on with **B** officials.
23:17 and the officials of Moab were standing beside **B**

BALANCE (1) [BALANCED, BALANCES]
Ps 119:109 My life constantly hangs in the **b**, / but I will not

BALANCED (1) [BALANCE]
Da 1:20 In all matters requiring wisdom and **b** judgment,

BALANCES (2) [BALANCE]
Job 37:16 Do you understand how he **b** the clouds with
Da 5:27 you have been weighed on the **b** and have failed

BALD (5) [BALDHEAD]
Lev 11:22 all varieties, crickets, **b** locusts, and grasshoppers.
13:40 "If a man loses his hair and his head becomes **b**,

13:41 hair on his forehead, he simply has a **b** forehead;
Isa 3:17 the LORD will make them **b** for all to see!
Mic 1:16 Make yourselves as **b** as an eagle, for your little

BALDHEAD (2) [BALD]
2Ki 2:23 "Go away, you **b**!" they chanted. "Go away, you **b**!"

BALL (1)
Isa 22:18 He will crumple you up into a **b** and toss you away

BALM (3)
Ge 37:25 taking spices, **b**, and myrrh from Gilead to Egypt.
43:11 **b**, honey, spices, myrrh, pistachio nuts,
Eze 27:17 wheat from Minnith, early figs, honey, oil, and **b**.

BALSAM (4)
2Sa 5:23 behind them and attack them near the **b** trees.
5:24 sound like marching feet in the tops of the **b** trees,
1Ch 14:14 behind them and attack them near the **b** trees.
14:15 sound like marching feet in the tops of the **b** trees,

BAMAH (1)
Eze 20:29 (This idol shrine has been called **B**—'high place'

BAMOTH (1) [BAMOTH-BAAL]
Nu 21:19 Nahaliel, and **B**.

BAMOTH-BAAL (2) [BAMOTH]
Nu 22:41 The next morning Balak took Balaam up to **B**.
Jos 13:17 towns on the plain—Dibon, **B**, Beth-baal-meon,

BAND (11) [BANDED, BANDS]
Jdg 3:27 Then he led a **b** of Israelites down from the hills.
11: 3 Soon he had a large **b** of rebels following him.
1Sa 10: 5 you will meet a **b** of prophets coming down from
10:26 a **b** of men whose hearts God had touched became
25:11 and give it to a **b** of outlaws who come from who
2Ki 13:21 burying a man, they spied a **b** of these raiders.
Ps 78:49 dispatched against them / a **b** of destroying angels.
Isa 9: 4 the army of Midian with Gideon's little **b**.
Eze 16:40 They will **b** together in a mob to stone you and run
Da 4:15 bound with a **b** of iron and bronze and surrounded
4:23 bound with a **b** of iron and bronze and surrounded

BANDAGE (3) [BANDAGED, BANDAGES]
1Ki 20:38 having placed a **b** over his eyes to disguise
20:41 Then the prophet pulled the **b** from his eyes,
Hos 6: 1 He has injured us; now he will **b** our wounds.

BANDAGED (1) [BANDAGE]
Lk 10:34 soothed his wounds with medicine and **b** them.

BANDAGES (2) [BANDAGE]
Job 5:18 For though he wounds, he also **b**. He strikes,
Isa 1: 6 and infected wounds—without any ointments or **b**.

BANDED (1) [BAND]
Ac 27:17 Then we **b** the ship with ropes to strengthen the

BANDIT (2) [BANDITS]
Pr 6:11 and poverty will pounce on you like a **b**;
24:34 and poverty will pounce on you like a **b**;

BANDITS (4) [BANDIT]
Ezr 8:31 and saved us from enemies and **b** along the way.
Hos 7: 1 Samaria is filled with liars, thieves, and **b**!
Lk 10:30 Jerusalem to Jericho, and he was attacked by **b**.
10:36 a neighbor to the man who was attacked by **b**?"

BANDS (9) [BAND]
Ge 49:19 "Gad will be plundered by marauding **b**, / but he
Ex 36:38 their decorated tops and **b** were overlaid with gold.
2Ki 24: 2 Then the LORD sent **b** of Babylonian, Aramean,
1Ch 12:21 They helped David chase down **b** of raiders,
2Ch 22: 1 The marauding **b** of Arabs had killed all the older
Job 1:17 "Three **b** of Chaldean raiders have stolen your
Isa 52: 2 Remove the slave **b** from your neck, O captive
Jer 40: 7 The leaders of the Judean guerrilla **b** in the
Hos 6: 9 Its citizens are **b** of robbers, lying in ambush for

BANI (16)
2Sa 23:36 Igal son of Nathan from Zobah; / **B** from Gad;
1Ch 6:46 Amzi, **B**, Shemer,
9: 4 son of Omri, son of Imri, son of **B**, a descendant of
Ezr 2:10 The family of **B** | 642
8:10 From the family of **B**: Shelomith son of Josiphiah
10:29 From the family of **B**: Meshullam, Malluch,
10:34 From the family of **B**: Maadai, Amram, Uel,
Ne 3:17 working under the supervision of Rehum son of **B**.
7:15 The family of **B** | 648
8: 7 Jeshua, **B**, Sherebiah, Jamin, Akkub, Shabbethai,
9: 4 **B**, Kadmiel, Shebaniah, Bunni, Sherebiah, **B**,
9: 5 Jeshua, Kadmiel, **B**, Hashabneiah, Sherebiah,
10:13 Hodiah, **B**, and Beninu.
10:14 signed were Parosh, Pahath-moab, Elam, Zattu, **B**,
11:22 of the Levites in Jerusalem was Uzzi son of **B**,

BANISH (9) [BANISHED, BANISHING, BANISHMENT]
Nu 12:14 **B** her from the camp for seven days, and after that
2Ki 23:27 I will **b** the people from my presence and reject my
Ps 51:11 Do not **b** me from your presence, / and don't take
125: 5 But **b** those who turn to crooked ways, O LORD.
Ecc 11:10 So **b** grief and pain, but remember that youth,
Isa 55: 7 Let them **b** from their minds the very thought of
Eze 4:13 bread in the Gentile lands, where I will **b** them!"
Mt 24:51 the servant apart and **b** him with the hypocrites.
Lk 12:46 the servant apart and **b** him with the unfaithful.

BANISHED (16) [BANISH]
Ge 3:23 So the LORD God **b** Adam and his wife from the
4:11 You are hereby **b** from the ground you have
4:14 You have **b** me from my land and from your
2Sa 14:13 you have refused to bring home your own **b** son.
1Ki 15:12 He **b** the shrine prostitutes from the land
22:46 He **b** from the land the rest of the shrine
2Ki 13:23 destroyed them or **b** them from his presence.
24:20 finally **b** the people of Jerusalem and Judah from
Ne 13:28 the Horonite, so I **b** him from my presence.
Est 1:19 It should order that Queen Vashti be forever **b**
Isa 24:11 its lowest ebb. Gladness has been **b** from the land.
Jer 52: 3 finally **b** the people of Jerusalem and Judah from
Eze 13: 9 and they will be **b** from the community of Israel.
28:16 So I **b** you from the mountain of God. I expelled
Zec 5: 3 One side says that those who steal will be **b** from
5: 3 those who swear falsely will be **b** from the land.

BANISHING (1) [BANISH]
Ge 3:24 After **b** them from the garden, the LORD God

BANISHMENT (1) [BANISH]
Ezr 7:26 **b**, confiscation of goods, or imprisonment."

BANK (9) [BANKERS, BANKRUPT, BANKS]
Ge 41: 1 Pharaoh dreamed that he was standing on the **b** of
41: 2 up out of the river and began grazing along its **b**.
41:17 "I was standing on the **b** of the Nile River,"
41:18 up out of the river and began grazing along its **b**.
Dt 4:49 And they took the eastern **b** of the Jordan Valley as
2Sa 17:22 and they were all on the other **b** before dawn.
2Ki 2:13 and returned to the **b** of the Jordan River.
Mt 25:27 you should at least have put my money into the **b**
Lk 19:23 why didn't you deposit the money in the **b** so I

BANKERS (1) [BANK]
Isa 24: 2 and sellers, lenders and borrowers, **b** and debtors—

BANKRUPT (3) [BANK]
Lev 25:25 If any of your Israelite relatives go **b** and are
25:39 "If any of your Israelite relatives go **b** and sell
25:47 and if some of your Israelite relatives go **b** and sell

BANKS (14) [BANK]
Dt 3:17 including the Jordan River and its eastern **b**,
Jos 3: 1 left Acacia and arrived at the **b** of the Jordan River,
3: 8 'When you reach the **b** of the Jordan River, take a
3:15 and the Jordan was overflowing its **b**.
4:18 the Jordan River flooded its **b** as before.
2Ki 17: 6 along the **b** of the Habor River in Gozan,
18:11 in Halah, along the **b** of the Habor River in Gozan,
19:32 their shields and build **b** of earth against its walls.
1Ch 12:15 living in the lowlands on both the east and west **b**.
Job 6:15 a seasonal brook that overflows its **b** in the spring
Isa 15: 6 The grassy **b** are scorched, and the tender plants
37:33 their shields and build **b** of earth against its walls.
Jer 48:20 and wail! Tell it by the **b** of the Arnon River:
Da 12: 5 and saw two others standing on opposite **b** of the

BANNED (2)
1Sa 18:13 Saul **b** him from his presence and appointed him
28: 3 And Saul had **b** all mediums and psychics from the

BANNER (10) [BANNERS]
Ex 17:15 altar there and called it "The LORD Is My **B**."
Nu 1:52 a designated camping area with its own family **b**.
2:17 each in position under the appropriate family **b**.
10:14 camped with Judah headed the march with their **b**,
10:18 that camped with Reuben set out with their **b**,
10:22 that camped with Ephraim set out with their **b**,
10:25 tribes that camped with Dan set out under their **b**.
Ps 60: 4 But you have raised a **b** for those who honor you—
Isa 11:10 In that day the heir to David's throne will be a **b** of
Eze 27: 7 finest linen, and they flew as a **b** above you.

BANNERS (9) [BANNER]
Nu 2: 2 various groups will camp beneath their family **b**.
2: 3[-4] side of the Tabernacle, beneath their family **b**.
2:10[-11] of the Tabernacle, beneath their family **b**.
2:18[-19] of the Tabernacle, beneath their family **b**.
2:25[-26] of the Tabernacle, beneath their family **b**.
2:34 and marched under their **b** exactly as the LORD
Ps 20: 5 hear of your victory, / flying **b** to honor our God.
SS 6: 4 You are as majestic as an army with **b**!
6:10 bright as the sun, as majestic as an army with **b**?'

BANQUET (26) [BANQUETS]
Ge 40:20 and he gave a **b** for all his officials and household
1Ki 1:41 and shouting just as they were finishing their **b**.
1:49 guests jumped up in panic from the **b** table
3:15 Then he invited all his officials to a great **b**.
2Ch 18: 2 who prepared a great **b** for him and his officials.
Est 1: 3 he gave a **b** for all his princes and officials.
1: 5 the king gave a special **b** for all the palace servants
1: 9 Queen Vashti gave a **b** for the women of the palace
2:18 he gave a **b** in Esther's honor for all his princes
5: 4 and Haman come today to a **b** I have prepared for
5: 5 and said, "Tell Haman to come quickly to a **b**,
5: 5 So the king and Haman went to Esther's **b**.
5: 8 please come with Haman tomorrow to the **b** I will
5: 9 What a happy man Haman was as he left the **b**!
5:12 and the king himself to the **b** she prepared for us.
5:14 you can go on your merry way to the **b** with the
6:14 the king's eunuchs arrived to take Haman to the **b**
7: 1 So the king and Haman went to Queen Esther's **b**.
Pr 9: 2 She has prepared a great **b**, mixed the wines,
SS 2: 4 He brings me to the **b** hall, so everyone can see
Eze 39:20 Feast at my **b** table—feast on horses, riders,
Da 5:10 what was happening, she hurried to the **b** hall.
Mt 22: 3 guests were invited, and when the **b** was ready,
22:10 and bad alike, and the **b** hall was filled with guests.
Lk 5:29 Soon Levi held a **b** in his home with Jesus as the
Rev 19:17 Gather together for the great **b** God has prepared.

BANQUETS (5) [BANQUET]
Mt 23: 6 And how they love to sit at the head table at **b**
24:38 the people were enjoying **b** and parties
Mk 12:39 love the seats of honor in the synagogues and at **b**.
Lk 17:27 the people enjoyed **b** and parties and weddings
20:46 love the seats of honor in the synagogues and at **b**.

BAPTISM (21) [BAPTIZE]
Mt 3:16 After his **b**, as Jesus came up out of the water,
21:25 "Did John's **b** come from heaven or was it merely
Mk 10:38 Are you able to be baptized with the **b** of suffering
10:39 drink from my cup and be baptized with my **b**,
11:30 "Did John's **b** come from heaven or was it merely
Lk 3: 7 of John's preaching to the crowds that came for **b**:
7:30 God's plan for them, for they had refused John's **b**.
12:50 There is a terrible **b** ahead of me, and I am under a
20: 4 "Did John's **b** come from heaven, or was it merely
Jn 3:23 water there and people kept coming to him for **b**.
Ac 18:25 However, he knew only about John's **b**.
19: 3 "Then what **b** did you experience?" he asked. And they replied, "The **b** of John."
19: 4 "John's **b** was to demonstrate a desire to turn from
Ro 6: 4 For we died and were buried with Christ by **b**.
Gal 3:27 And all who have been united with Christ in **b**
Eph 4: 5 There is only one Lord, one faith, one **b**,
5:26 her holy and clean, washed by **b** and God's word.
1Pe 3:21 And this is a picture of **b**, which now saves you by
3:21 **B** is not a removal of dirt from your body; it is an
1Jn 5: 6 Christ was revealed as God's Son by his **b** in water

BAPTISMS (1) [BAPTIZE]
Heb 6: 2 You don't need further instruction about **b**,

BAPTIST (26) [BAPTIZE]
Mt 3: 1 In those days John the **B** began preaching in the
9:14 One day the disciples of John the **B** came to Jesus
11: 2 John the **B**, who was now in prison, heard about all
11:11 have ever lived, none is greater than John the **B**.
11:12 And from the time John the **B** began preaching
11:18 For John the **B** didn't drink wine and he often
14: 2 "This must be John the **B** come back to life again!
14: 8 "I want the head of John the **B** on a tray!"
16:14 "Well," they replied, "some say John the **B**,
17:13 realized he had been speaking of John the **B**.
21:32 For John the **B** came and showed you the way to
Mk 1: 4 This messenger was John the **B**. He lived in the
6:14 "This must be John the **B** come back to life again.
6:25 "I want the head of John the **B**, right now, on a
8:28 "Well," they replied, "some say John the **B**,
Lk 7:18 The disciples of John the **B** told John about
7:20 and said to him, "John the **B** sent us to ask,
7:33 For John the **B** didn't drink wine and he often
9: 7 "This is John the **B** come back to life again."
9:19 "Well," they replied, "some say John the **B**,
16:16 "Until John the **B** began to preach, the laws of
Jn 1: 6 God sent John the **B**
3:23 At this time John the **B** was baptizing at Aenon,
5:33 In fact, you sent messengers to listen to John the **B**,
Ac 10:37 beginning in Galilee after John the **B** began
13:24 John the **B** preached the need for everyone in Israel

BAPTIST'S (2) [BAPTIZE]
Mk 6:24 Her mother told her, "Ask for John the **B** head!"
Lk 5:33 "John the **B** disciples always fast and pray,"

BAPTIZE (13) [BAPTISM, BAPTISMS, BAPTIST, BAPTIST'S, BAPTIZED, BAPTIZES, BAPTIZING]
Mt 3:11 "I **b** with water those who turn from their sins
3:11 He will **b** you with the Holy Spirit and with fire.
3:14 But John didn't want to **b** him. "I am the one who
Mk 1: 8 I **b** you with water, but he will **b** you with the Holy Spirit!"
Lk 3:16 their questions by saying, "I **b** with water;
3:16 He will **b** you with the Holy Spirit and with fire.
Jn 1:25 or the Prophet, what right do you have to **b**?"
1:26 John told them, "I **b** with water, but right here in
1:33 but when God sent me to **b** with water, he told me,

4: 2 (though Jesus himself didn't **b** them—his disciples
1Co 1:14 I thank God that I did not **b** any of you except
1:17 For Christ didn't send me to **b**, but to preach the

BAPTIZED (47) [BAPTIZE]
Mt 3: 6 confessed their sins, he **b** them in the Jordan River.
3: 7 many Pharisees and Sadducees coming to be **b**,
3:13 from Galilee to the Jordan River to be **b** by John.
3:14 "I am the one who needs to be **b** by you," he said,
3:15 do everything that is right." So then John **b** him.
Mk 1: 4 and was preaching that people should be **b** to show
1: 5 confessed their sins, he **b** them in the Jordan River.
1: 9 and he was **b** by John in the Jordan River.
10:38 Are you able to be **b** with the baptism of suffering I must be **b** with?"
10:39 drink from my cup and be **b** with my baptism,
16:16 Anyone who believes and is **b** will be saved.
Lk 3: 3 preaching that people should be **b** to show that
3:12 Even corrupt tax collectors came to be **b**
3:21 One day when the crowds were being **b**, Jesus himself was **b**.
7:29 God's plan was right, for they had been **b** by John.
Jn 3:22 but they stayed in Judea for a while and **b** there.
Ac 1: 5 John **b** with water, but in just a few days you will be **b** with the Holy
1:22 from the time he was **b** by John until the day he
2:38 and be **b** in the name of Jesus Christ for the
2:41 Those who believed what Peter said were **b**
8:12 As a result, many men and women were **b**.
8:13 Then Simon himself believed and was **b**. He began
8:16 for they had only been **b** in the name of the Lord
8:36 "Look! There's some water! Why can't I be **b**?"
8:38 they went down into the water, and Philip **b** him.
9:18 he regained his sight. Then he got up and was **b**.
10:47 "Can anyone object to their being **b**, now that they
10:48 So he gave orders for them to be **b** in the name of
11:16 'John **b** with water, but you will be **b** with the Holy Spirit.'
13:24 in Israel to turn from sin and turn to God and be **b**.
16:15 She was **b** along with other members of her
16:33 everyone in his household were immediately **b**.
18: 8 in Corinth also became believers and were **b**.
19: 5 they were **b** in the name of the Lord Jesus.
22:16 Get up and be **b**, and have your sins washed away,
Ro 6: 3 and were **b** to become one with Christ Jesus,
1Co 1:13 for you? Were any of you **b** in the name of Paul?
1:15 for now no one can say they were **b** in my name.
1:16 (Oh yes, I also **b** the household of Stephanas.
10: 2 of Moses, they were all **b** in the cloud and the sea.
12:13 But we have all been **b** into Christ's body by one
15:29 then what point is there in people being **b** for those
Col 2:12 For you were buried with Christ when you were **b**.

BAPTIZES (1) [BAPTIZE]
Jn 1:33 He is the one who **b** with the Holy Spirit.'

BAPTIZING (9) [BAPTIZE]
Mt 11:12 John the Baptist began preaching and **b** until now,
28:19 **b** them in the name of the Father and the Son
Jn 1:28 village east of the Jordan River, where John was **b**.
1:31 but I have been **b** with water in order to point him
3:23 At this time John the Baptist was **b** at Aenon,
3:26 the one you said was the Messiah, is also **b** people.
4: 1 "Jesus is **b** and making more disciples than John"
10:40 River to stay near the place where John was first **b**.
1Co 1:16 of Stephanas. I don't remember **b** anyone else.)

BAR (6) [BARRED, BARS]
Jos 7:21 and a **b** of gold weighing more than a pound.
7:24 the silver, the robe, the **b** of gold, his sons,
Jdg 16: 3 and lifted them, **b** and all, right out of the ground.
Ne 7: 3 are still on duty, have them shut and **b** the doors.
Jer 15:12 break a **b** of iron from the north, or a **b** of bronze?

BAR-JESUS (1)
Ac 13: 6 met a Jewish sorcerer, a false prophet named **B**.

BARABBAS (15)
Mt 27:16 a notorious criminal in prison, a man named **B**.
27:17 to you—**B**, or Jesus who is called the Messiah?"
27:20 persuaded the crowds to ask for **B** to be released
27:21 the crowd shouted back their reply: "**B**!"
27:22 "But if I release **B**," Pilate asked them,
27:26 So Pilate released **B** to them. He ordered Jesus
Mk 15: 7 One of the prisoners at that time was **B**,
15:11 mob to demand the release of **B** instead of Jesus.
15:12 "But if I release **B**," Pilate asked them,
15:15 anxious to please the crowd, released **B** to them.
Lk 23:18 they shouted, "Kill him, and release **B** to us!"
23:19 (**B** was in prison for murder and for taking part in
23:25 As they had requested, he released **B**, the man in
Jn 18:40 they shouted back, "No! Not this man, but **B**!" (**B** was a criminal.)

BARACHIAH (1)
Mt 23:35 people from righteous Abel to Zechariah son of **B**,

BARAK (16)
Jdg 4: 6 One day she sent for **B** son of Abinoam, who lived
4: 8 **B** told her, "I will go, but only if you go with
4: 9 of a woman." So Deborah went with **B** to Kedesh.
4:10 **B** called together the tribes of Zebulun
4:12 When Sisera was told that **B** son of Abinoam had
4:14 Then Deborah said to **B**, "Get ready!
4:14 So **B** led his ten thousand warriors down the slopes
4:15 When **B** attacked, the LORD threw Sisera and all
4:16 **B** chased the enemy and their chariots all the way
4:22 When **B** came looking for Sisera, Jael went out to
5: 1 and **B** son of Abinoam sang this song:
5:12 Wake up, wake up, and sing a song! / Arise, **B**!
5:15 The princes of Issachar were with Deborah and **B**.
5:15 They followed **B**, rushing into the valley.
1Sa 12:11 **B**, Jephthah, and Samuel to save you, and you
Heb 11:32 **B**, Samson, Jephthah, David, Samuel, and all the

BARAKEL (2)
Job 32: 2 Then Elihu son of **B** the Buzite, of the clan of
32: 6 Elihu son of **B** the Buzite said, "I am young

BARBARIANS [KJV] See BARBARIC

BARBARIC (1)
Col 3:11 or uncircumcised, **b**, uncivilized, slave, or free.

BARBED (1)
Eze 2: 6 their threats are sharp as thorns and **b** like briers,

BARE (21) [BARED, BAREFOOT, BARELY, BARREN]
Jdg 6: 5 And they stayed until the land was stripped **b**.
14: 6 and he ripped the lion's jaws apart with his **b**
2Sa 12:16 without food and lay all night on the **b** ground.
15:30 and his feet were **b** as a sign of mourning.
22:16 and the foundations of the earth were laid **b**.
2Ki 9:13 They quickly spread out their cloaks on the **b** steps
Ps 18:15 and the foundations of the earth were laid **b**.
29: 9 and strips the forests **b**. / In his Temple everyone
Isa 17: 6 Yes, Israel will be stripped **b** of people,"
49: 9 green pastures and on hills that were previously **b**.
Jer 14: 6 The wild donkeys stand on the **b** hills panting like
48:32 the Dead Sea, but the destroyer has stripped you **b**!
49:10 But I will strip **b** the land of Edom, and there will
Eze 13:14 because their land will be stripped **b** on account of
23:29 rob you of all you own, leaving you naked and **b**.
26: 4 I will scrape away its soil and make it a **b** rock!
26:14 I will make your island a **b** rock, a place for
29:18 Tyre that the warriors' heads were rubbed **b**
Joel 1: 7 their bark and leaving the branches white and **b**.
Hab 3:13 the wicked and laid **b** their bones from head to toe.
1Co 14:25 As they listen, their secret thoughts will be laid **b**,

BARED (2) [BARE]
Isa 9:12 With **b** fangs, they will devour Israel. But even
Eze 4: 7 Lie there with your arm **b** and prophesy her

BAREFOOT (4) [BARE, FOOT]
Isa 20: 2 did as he was told and walked around naked and **b**.
20: 3 around naked and **b** for the last three years.
20: 4 He will make them walk naked and **b**, both young
Mic 1: 8 walk around naked and **b** in sorrow and shame.

BARELY (5) [BARE]
Ge 44: 4 But when they were **b** out of the city, Joseph said
Ecc 4: 6 better to be lazy and **b** survive than to work hard,
Isa 28: 9 Are we little children, **b** old enough to talk?
40:24 They hardly get started, **b** taking root, when he
1Pe 4:18 And / "If the righteous are **b** saved, / what chance

BARGAIN (5) [BARGAINS]
2Ki 18:23 the king of Assyria, will strike a **b** with you.
Pr 20:14 "It's worthless," then brags about getting a **b**!
Isa 28:15 You boast that you have struck a **b** to avoid death
28:18 I will cancel the **b** you made to avoid death,
36: 8 the king of Assyria, will strike a **b** with you.

BARGAINS (2) [BARGAIN]
Pr 31:18 She watches for **b**; her lights burn late into the
Eze 7:12 There is no reason for buyers to rejoice over the **b**

BARIAH (1)
1Ch 3:22 and his sons, Hattush, Igal, **B**, Neariah,

BARK (3)
Ge 30:37 and peeled off strips of the **b** to make white streaks
Ex 11: 7 it will be so peaceful that not even a dog will **b**.
Joel 1: 7 stripping their **b** and leaving the branches white

BARKOS (2)
Ezr 2:53 **B**, Sisera, Temah,
Ne 7:55 **B**, Sisera, Temah,

BARLEY (37)
Ex 9:31 All the flax and **b** were destroyed because the **b** was ripe
Lev 27:16 for an area that produces five bushels of **b** seed.
Nu 5:15 two quarts of **b** flour to be presented on her behalf.
Dt 8: 8 It is a land of wheat and **b**, of grapevines, fig trees,
Jdg 7:13 and in my dream a loaf of **b** bread came tumbling
Ru 1:22 in Bethlehem at the beginning of the **b** harvest.
2:16 And pull out some heads of **b** from the bundles
2:17 So Ruth gathered **b** there all day, and when she
2:23 and gathered grain with them until the end of the **b**
3: 2 Tonight he will be winnowing **b** at the threshing
3:15 He measured out six scoops of **b** into the cloak
3:17 "He gave me these six scoops of **b** and said,
2Sa 14:30 "Go and set fire to Joab's **b** field, the field next to
17:28 wheat and **b** flour, roasted grain, beans, lentils,
21: 9 died together at the beginning of the **b** harvest.
1Ki 4:28 They also brought the necessary **b** and straw for
2Ki 4:42 and twenty loaves of **b** bread made from the first
7: 1 and ten quarts of **b** grain will cost only half an
7:16 and ten quarts of **b** grain were sold for half an
7:18 and ten quarts of **b** grain will cost half an ounce of
1Ch 11:13 The battle took place in a field full of **b**,
2Ch 2:10 100,000 bushels of **b**, 110,000 gallons of wine,
2:15 "Send along the wheat, **b**, olive oil, and wine that
27: 5 50,000 bushels of wheat, and 50,000 bushels of **b**.
Job 31:40 land instead of wheat and weeds instead of **b**."
Isa 28:25 cummin, wheat, **b**, and spelt, each in its own
Jer 41: 8 **b**, oil, and honey that they had hidden away.
Eze 4: 9 get some wheat, **b**, beans, lentils, millet, and spelt,
4:12 Each day prepare your bread as you would **b**
13:19 my people away from me for a few handfuls of **b**
45:13 bushel of wheat or **b** for every sixty you harvest,
Hos 3: 2 and about five bushels of **b** and a measure of wine.
Joel 1:11 Weep, because the wheat and **b**—yes, all the field
Jn 6: 9 "There's a young boy here with five **b** loaves
6:13 There were only five **b** loaves to start with,
Rev 6: 6 of wheat bread or three loaves of **b** for a day's pay.

BARN (4) [BARNS]
Hag 2:19 you a promise now while the seed is still in the **b**,
Mt 3:12 storing the grain in his **b** but burning the chaff with
13:30 and burn them and to put the wheat in the **b**.' "
Lk 3:17 storing the grain in his **b** but burning the chaff with

BARNABAS (43) [BARNABAS'S, JOSEPH]
Ac 4:36 the one the apostles nicknamed **B** (which means
9:27 Then **B** brought him to the apostles and told them
9:27 **B** also told them what the Lord had said to Saul
11:22 heard what had happened, they sent **B** to Antioch.
11:24 **B** was a good man, full of the Holy Spirit
11:25 Then **B** went on to Tarsus to find Saul.
11:30 entrusting their gifts to **B** and Saul to take to the
12:25 When **B** and Saul had finished their mission in
13: 1 teachers of the church at Antioch of Syria were **B**,
13: 2 "Dedicate **B** and Saul for the special work I have
13: 4 and **B** went down to the seaport of Seleucia and
13: 7 The governor invited **B** and Saul to visit him,
13: 8 to pay no attention to what Saul and **B** said.
13:14 But **B** and Paul traveled inland to Antioch of
13:32 "And now **B** and I are here to bring you this Good
13:42 As Paul and **B** left the synagogue that day,
13:43 worshiped at the synagogue followed Paul and **B**,
13:46 Then Paul and **B** spoke out boldly and declared,
13:50 mob against Paul and **B** and ran them out of town.
14: 1 Paul and **B** went together to the synagogue
14: 2 up distrust among the Gentiles against Paul and **B**,
14: 8 Paul and **B** came upon a man with crippled feet.
14:12 They decided that **B** was the Greek god Zeus
14:14 But when **B** and Paul heard what was happening,
14:18 and **B** could scarcely restrain the people from
14:20 into the city. The next day he left with **B** for Derbe.
14:21 Paul and **B** returned again to Lystra, Iconium,
14:23 and **B** also appointed elders in every church
15: 1 While Paul and **B** were at Antioch of Syria,
15: 2 Paul and **B**, disagreeing with them,
15: 2 Finally, Paul and **B** were sent to Jerusalem,
15: 4 and **B** were welcomed by the whole church,
15:12 and everyone listened as **B** and Paul told about the
15:22 of Syria with Paul and **B** to report on this decision.
15:25 along with our beloved **B** and Paul,
15:35 and **B** stayed in Antioch to assist many others who
15:36 After some time Paul said to **B**, "Let's return to
15:37 **B** agreed and wanted to take along John Mark.
15:39 **B** took John Mark with him and sailed for Cyprus.
1Co 9: 6 Or is it only **B** and I who have to work to support
Gal 2: 1 I went back to Jerusalem again, this time with **B**;
2: 9 and they accepted **B** and me as their co-workers.
2:13 and even **B** was influenced to join them in their

BARNABAS'S (1) [BARNABAS]
Col 4:10 you his greetings, and so does Mark, **B** cousin.

BARNS (9) [BARN]
Ps 50: 9 But I want no more bulls from your **b**; / I want no
Pr 3:10 Then he will fill your **b** with grain, and your vats
Isa 3:14 filling your **b** with grain extorted from helpless
Joel 1:17 The **b** and granaries stand empty and abandoned.
Hab 3:17 flocks die in the fields, and the cattle **b** are empty,
Mt 6:26 They don't need to plant or harvest or put food in **b**
Lk 12:17 In fact, his **b** were full to overflowing.
12:18 I'll tear down my **b** and build bigger ones.
12:24 They don't need to plant or harvest or put food in **b**

BARRACKS (1)
Jer 51:30 They stay in their **b**. Their courage is gone.

BARRAGE (1)
Job 18:15 will disappear beneath a fiery **b** of burning sulfur.

BARRED (4) [BAR]
Dt 3: 5 were all fortified cities with high walls and **b** gates.
1Ki 4:13 including sixty great fortified cities with gates **b**
2Ch 8: 5 rebuilding their walls and installing **b** gates.
Job 38:10 For I locked it behind **b** gates, limiting its shores.

BARREL(S) [KJV] See JAR

BARREN (20) [BARE]
Dt 28:18 You will be cursed with few children and **b** fields.
1Sa 2: 5 now full. / The **b** woman now has seven children;
Job 3: 7 Let that night be **b**. Let it have no joy.
15:34 For the godless are **b**. Their homes,
38:26 Who makes the rain fall on **b** land, in a desert
Ps 105:41 to form a river through the dry and **b** land.
113: 9 He gives the **b** woman a home, / so that she
Pr 30:16 the grave, / the **b** womb, / the thirsty desert,
Isa 22:18 into a ball and toss you away into a distant, **b** land.
41:19 myrtle, olive, cypress, fir, and pine—on **b** land.
51: 3 Her **b** wilderness will become as beautiful as
Jer 2: 2 and followed me even through the **b** wilderness.
2: 6 out of Egypt and led us through the **b** wilderness—
12:10 and turning all its beauty into a **b** wilderness.
17: 6 They will live in the **b** wilderness, on the salty flats
Hos 2: 3 of thirst, as in a desert or a dry and **b** wilderness.
Hab 3:17 the olive crop fails, and the fields lie empty and **b**;
Lk 1: 7 They had no children because Elizabeth was **b**,
1:36 People used to say she was **b**, but she's already in
Heb 11:11 even though they were too old and Sarah was **b**.

BARRICADED (1)
Jdg 9:51 They **b** themselves in and climbed up to the roof of

BARRIER (2)
Dt 22: 8 "Every new house you build must have a **b** around
Jos 22:25 The LORD has placed the Jordan River as a **b**

BARS (13) [BAR]
2Ch 14: 7 and fortify them with walls, towers, gates, and **b**.
Ne 3: 3 hung the doors, and put the bolts and **b** in place.
3: 6 set up the doors, and installed the bolts and **b**.
3:13 hung its doors, and installed the bolts and **b**.
3:14 he hung the doors and installed the bolts and **b**.
3:15 hung its doors, and installed its bolts and **b**.
Job 40:18 bones are tubes of bronze. Its limbs are **b** of iron.
Ps 107:16 gates of bronze; / he cut apart their **b** of iron.
147:13 For he has fortified the **b** of your gates
Pr 18:19 separate friends like a gate locked with iron **b**.
SS 5:14 His arms are like round **b** of gold, set with
Isa 45: 2 down gates of bronze and cut through **b** of iron.
La 2: 9 All their locks and **b** are destroyed, for he has

BARSABBAS (2)
Ac 1:23 Joseph called **B** (also known as Justus)
15:22 church leaders—Judas (also called **B**) and Silas.

BARTER (1) [BARTERED]
Eze 27: 9 Ships came with goods from every land to **b** for

BARTERED (1) [BARTER]
Eze 27:19 cassia, and calamus were **b** for your wares.

BARTHOLOMEW (4)
Mt 10: 3 Philip, / **B**, / Thomas, / Matthew (the tax collector),
Mk 3:18 Andrew, / Philip, / **B**, / Matthew, / Thomas,
Lk 6:14 (Peter's brother), / James, / John, / Philip, / **B**,
Ac 1:13 John, / James, / Andrew, / Philip, / Thomas, / **B**,

BARTIMAEUS (3) [TIMAEUS]
Mk 10:46 A blind beggar named **B** (son of Timaeus)
10:47 When **B** heard that Jesus from Nazareth was
10:50 **B** threw aside his coat, jumped up, and came to

BARUCH (26)
Ne 3:20 Next to him was **B** son of Zabbai, who repaired an
10: 6 Daniel, Ginnethon, **B**,
11: 5 and Maaseiah son of **B**, son of Col-hozeh, son of
Jer 32:12 and I handed them to **B** son of Neriah
32:13 Then I said to **B** as they all listened,
32:16 Then after I had given the papers to **B**, I prayed to
36: 4 So Jeremiah sent for **B** son of Neriah, and as
36: 4 **B** wrote down all the prophecies that the LORD
36: 5 Then Jeremiah said to **B**, "I am a prisoner here
36: 8 **B** did as Jeremiah told him and read these
36:10 **B** read Jeremiah's words to all the people from the
36:13 When Micaiah told them about the messages **B**
36:14 to ask **B** to come and read the messages to them,
36:14 So **B** took the scroll and went to them.
36:15 the officials said, and **B** did as they requested.
36:16 By the time **B** had finished reading, they were
36:18 So **B** explained, "Jeremiah dictated them to me
36:19 Jeremiah should both hide," the officials told **B**.
36:26 and Shelemiah son of Abdeel to arrest **B**
36:32 another scroll and dictated again to his secretary **B**.
43: 3 **B** son of Neriah has convinced you to say this,
43: 6 Also included were the prophet Jeremiah and **B**.
45: 1 The prophet Jeremiah gave a message to **B** son of
45: 1 after **B** had written down everything Jeremiah had
45: 2 is what LORD, the God of Israel, says to you, **B**:
45: 4 "**B**, this is what the LORD says: I will destroy

BARZILLAI (12)
2Sa 17:27 of Lo-debar, and by **B** the Gileadite from Rogelim.
19:31 **B** the Gileadite now arrived from Rogelim to
19:33 with me and live in Jerusalem," the king said to **B**.
19:39 and embraced him, **B** returned to his own home.
21: 8 the wife of Adriel son of **B** from Meholah.
1Ki 2: 7 "Be kind to the sons of **B** from Gilead. Make them
Ezr 2:61 families of priests—Hobaiah, Hakkoz, and **B**—
2:61 (This **B** had married one of the daughters of
2:61 had married one of the daughters of **B** from Gilead
Ne 7:63 Hobaiah, Hakkoz, and **B**—also returned to
7:63 (This **B** had married one of the daughters of
7:63 had married one of the daughters of **B** from Gilead

BASE (21) [BASED, BASES, BASIC, BASICS, BASIS]
Ex 19: 2 they came to the **b** of Mount Sinai and set up camp
25:31 the **b**, center stem, lamp cups, buds, and blossoms.
29:12 and pour out the rest at the **b** of the altar.
37:17 Its **b**, center stem, lamp cups, blossoms, and buds
38:10 were twenty posts, each with its own bronze **b**,
38:17 Each post had a bronze **b**, and all the hooks
38:27 pounds of silver, about 75 pounds for each **b**.
Lev 4: 7 **b** of the altar of burnt offerings at the entrance of
4:18 then be poured out at the **b** of the altar of burnt
4:25 and pour out the rest of the blood at the **b** of the
4:30 and pour out the rest of the blood at the **b** of the
4:34 and pour out the rest of the blood at the **b** of the
5: 9 and the rest will be drained out at the **b** of the altar.
8:15 He poured out the rest of the blood at the **b** of the
9: 9 He poured out the rest of the blood at the **b** of the
Nu 8: 4 from its **b** to its decorative blossoms,
Jos 18:16 and down to the **b** of the mountain beside the
1Ki 7:25 The Sea rested on a **b** of twelve bronze oxen,
2Ch 4: 4 The Sea rested on a **b** of twelve bronze oxen,
Ecc 10:13 Since fools **b** their thoughts on foolish premises,
Eze 41:22 Its corners, **b**, and sides were all made of wood.

BASED (18) [BASE]
Lev 25:15 the price of the land should be **b** on the number of
25:27 The price of the land will be **b** on the number of
25:50 The price of their freedom will be **b** on the number
27:23 the priest must assess its value **b** on the years until
Ezr 7:14 in Judah and Jerusalem, **b** on your God's law,
Job 15: 5 what to say. Your words are **b** on clever deception.
Ps 89:17 glorious strength. / Our power is **b** on your favor.
Isa 59: 4 being fair and honest. Their lawsuits are **b** on lies.
Eze 44:24 Their decisions must be **b** on my regulations.
Mt 22:40 and all the demands of the prophets are **b** on these
Jn 3:19 Their judgment is **b** on this fact: The light from
Ro 3:27 because our acquittal is not **b** on our good deeds. It is **b** on our faith.
4:13 and his descendants was not **b** on obedience to
Gal 1:11 which I preach is not **b** on mere human reasoning
1Ti 1:18 **b** on the prophetic words spoken about you earlier.
Heb 7:11 it was that priesthood on which the law was **b**—
8: 6 a better covenant with God, **b** on better promises.

BASEMATH (7)
Ge 26:34 He also married **B**, the daughter of Elon the Hittite.
36: 3 He also married his cousin **B**, who was the
36: 4 Esau and **B** had a son named Reuel.
36:10 wife Adah; and Reuel, the son of Esau's wife **B**.
36:13 These were all grandchildren of Esau's wife **B**.
36:17 descended from Reuel, the son of Esau and **B**.
1Ki 4:15 (He was married to **B**, another of Solomon's

BASER [KJV] See WORTHLESS

BASES (39) [BASE]
Ex 26:19 will fit into forty silver **b**—two **b** under each frame.
26:21 with their forty silver **b**, two **b** for each frame.
26:25 of the Tabernacle, supported by sixteen silver **b**—two **b** under each frame.
26:32 overlaid with gold. The posts will fit into silver **b**.
26:37 with gold. The posts will fit into five bronze **b**.
27:10 twenty bronze posts that fit into twenty bronze **b**.
27:11 held up by twenty posts fitted into bronze **b**,
27:12 75 feet long, supported by ten posts set into ten **b**.
27:14 feet long, supported by three posts set into three **b**.
27:15 feet long, supported by three posts set into three **b**.
27:16 It will be attached to four posts that fit into four **b**.
27:17 The posts are to be set in solid bronze **b**.
27:18 The **b** supporting its walls will be made of bronze.
35:11 the clasps, frames, crossbars, posts, and **b**;
35:17 for the walls of the courtyard; the posts and their **b**;
36:24 along with forty silver **b**, two for each frame.
36:26 along with forty silver **b**, two for each frame.
36:30 along with sixteen silver **b**, two for each frame.
36:36 were overlaid with gold and set into four silver **b**.
36:38 with gold. The five **b** were molded from bronze.
38:11 bronze posts and **b** and with silver hooks and rods.
38:12 by ten posts and **b** and with silver hooks and rods.
38:14 and was supported by three posts set into three **b**.
38:15 and was supported by three posts set into three **b**.
38:19 was supported by four posts set into four bronze **b**.
38:27 The 100 **b** for the frames of the sanctuary walls
38:30 which was used for casting the **b** for the posts at
38:31 Bronze was also used to make the **b** for the posts
38:31 the **b** for the curtain at the entrance of the
39:33 the clasps, frames, crossbars, posts, and **b**;
39:40 the courtyard and the posts and **b** holding them up;
40:18 put it together by setting its frames into their **b**
Nu 3:36 the crossbars, the pillars, the **b**, and all the
3:37 for the posts of the courtyard and all their **b**,
4:31 the crossbars, the pillars with their **b**,
4:32 the posts for the courtyard walls with their **b**,

BASEST [KJV] See LOWLIEST, UNIMPORTANT

BASHAN (55)
Nu 21:33 Then they turned and marched toward **B**, but King Og of **B** and all his people attacked them
32:33 of the Amorites and the land of King Og of **B**—
Dt 1: 4 who had ruled in Heshbon, and King Og of **B**,
3: 1 "Next we headed for the land of **B**, where King
3: 4 the entire Argob region in his kingdom of **B**.
3: 6 We completely destroyed the kingdom of **B**,
3:10 and **B** as far as the towns of Salecah and Edrei, which were part of Og's kingdom in **B**.
3:11 King Og of **B** was the last of the giant Rephaites.
3:13 Then I gave the rest of Gilead and all of **B**—
3:13 (The Argob region of **B** used to be known as the
3:14 acquired the whole Argob region in **B** all the way
4:43 tribe of Gad; Golan in **B** for the tribe of Manasseh.
4:47 conquered his land and that of King Og of **B**—
29: 7 and King Og of **B** came out to fight against us,
32:14 He gave them choice rams and goats from **B**,
33:22 "Dan is a lion's cub, / leaping out from **B**."
Jos 9:10 and King Og of **B** (who lived in Ashtaroth).
12: 4 King Og of **B**, the last of the Rephaites, lived at
12: 5 to Salecah in the north and to all of **B** in the east,
13:11 all of Mount Hermon, all of **B** as far as Salecah,
13:12 and all the territory of King Og of **B**, who had
13:30 including all of **B**, all the former kingdom of King Og, and the sixty towns of Jair in **B**.
17: 1 and **B** on the east side of the Jordan had already
17: 5 the land of Gilead and **B** across the Jordan River,
20: 8 and Golan in **B**, in the land of the tribe of
21: 6 Naphtali, and the half-tribe of Manasseh in **B**.
21:27 Golan in **B** (a city of refuge) and Be-eshterah.
22: 7 Now Moses had given the land of **B** to the
1Ki 4:13 in Gilead, and in the Argob region of **B**,
4:19 of King Sihon of the Amorites and King Og of **B**.
2Ki 10:33 the Arnon Gorge to as far north as Gilead and **B**.
1Ch 5:11 Across from the Reubenites in the land of **B** lived
5:12 Joel was the leader in the land of **B**, and Shapham
5:16 in **B** and its villages, and throughout the Sharon
5:23 spread through the land from **B** to Baal-hermon,
6:62 Asher, Naphtali, and from the **B** area of Manasseh,
6:71 the town of Golan in **B** with its pasturelands
Ne 9:22 Sihon of Heshbon and the land of King Og of **B**.
Ps 22:12 of bulls; / fierce bulls of **B** have hemmed me in!
68:15 The majestic mountains of **B** / stretch high into the
68:22 Lord says, "I will bring my enemies down from **B**;
135:11 Sihon king of the Amorites, / Og king of **B**,
136:20 and Og king of **B**. / His faithful love endures
Isa 2:13 tall cedars of Lebanon and the mighty oaks of **B**.
33: 9 a wilderness. **B** and Carmel have been plundered.
Jer 22:20 Search for them in Lebanon. Shout for them at **B**.
50:19 her own land, to feed in the fields of Carmel and **B**,
Eze 27: 6 They carved oars for you from the oaks of **B**.
39:18 were rams, lambs, goats, and fat young bulls of **B**!
Mic 7:14 Let them enjoy the fertile pastures of **B** and Gilead
Na 1: 4 dry up, the lush pastures of **B** and Carmel fade,
Zec 11: 2 Weep, you oaks of **B**, as you watch the thickest

BASHANHAVOTHJAIR [KJV] See JAIR, TOWNS

BASHEMATH [KJV] See BASEMATH

BASIC (2) [BASE]
Eze 43:12 And this is the **b** law of the Temple:
Heb 5:12 you need someone to teach you again the **b** things

BASICS (1) [BASE]
Heb 6: 1 So let us stop going over the **b** of Christianity

BASIN (18) [BASINS, WASHBASIN]
Ex 12:22 Drain each lamb's blood into a **b**. Then take a
40:31 Aaron's sons washed their hands and feet in the **b**.
Nu 7:13 3-1/4 pounds and a silver **b** of about 1-3/4 pounds.
7:19 3-1/4 pounds and a silver **b** of about 1-3/4 pounds.
7:25 3-1/4 pounds and a silver **b** of about 1-3/4 pounds.
7:31 3-1/4 pounds and a silver **b** of about 1-3/4 pounds.
7:37 3-1/4 pounds and a silver **b** of about 1-3/4 pounds.
7:43 3-1/4 pounds and a silver **b** of about 1-3/4 pounds.
7:49 3-1/4 pounds and a silver **b** of about 1-3/4 pounds.
7:55 3-1/4 pounds and a silver **b** of about 1-3/4 pounds.
7:61 3-1/4 pounds and a silver **b** of about 1-3/4 pounds.
7:67 3-1/4 pounds and a silver **b** of about 1-3/4 pounds.
7:73 3-1/4 pounds and a silver **b** of about 1-3/4 pounds.
7:79 3-1/4 pounds and a silver **b** of about 1-3/4 pounds.
7:85 for each platter and 1-3/4 pounds for each **b**.
1Ki 7:31 The top of each cart had a circular frame for the **b**.
7:38 Each **b** was 6 feet across and could hold 220
Jn 13: 5 and poured water into a **b**. Then he began to wash

BASINS (26) [BASIN]
Ex 24: 6 blood from these animals and drew it off into **b**.
24: 8 Then Moses sprinkled the blood from the **b** over
27: 3 The ash buckets, shovels, **b**, meat hooks,
38: 3 ash buckets, shovels, **b**, meat hooks, and firepans.
Nu 4:14 the firepans, hooks, shovels, **b**, and all the
7:84 twelve silver platters, twelve silver **b**, and twelve
1Ki 7:30 of the carts were supporting posts for the bronze **b**;
7:38 Huram also made ten bronze **b**, one for each cart.
7:40 He also made the necessary pots, shovels, and **b**.
7:43 the ten water carts holding the ten **b**,
7:45 the pots, the shovels, and the **b**. All these utensils
7:50 the cups, lamp snuffers, **b**, dishes, and firepans,
2Ki 12:13 lamp snuffers, **b**, trumpets, or other articles of gold

16:17 the side panels and **b** from the portable water carts.
25:15 captain of the guard, also took the firepans and **b**,
1Ch 28:17 used to handle the sacrificial meat and for the **b**,
2Ch 4: 6 He also made ten **b** for water to wash the offerings,
4: 6 the Sea itself, and not the **b**, for their own washing.
4: 8 north wall. Then he molded one hundred gold **b**.
4:11 also made the necessary pots, shovels, and **b**.
4:14 the water carts holding the **b**,
4:22 **b**, dishes, and firepans, all of pure gold;
Ne 7:70 gold coins, 50 gold **b**, and 530 robes for the priests.
Jer 52:18 took all the pots, shovels, lamp snuffers, **b**, dishes,
52:19 small bowls, firepans, **b**, pots, lampstands, dishes,
Zec 14:20 will be as sacred as the **b** used beside the altar.

BASIS (7) [BASE]

Lev 25:23 the land must never be sold on a permanent **b**
25:53 must treat them as servants hired on a yearly **b**.
27:33 The tenth animal must not be selected on the **b** of
Eze 24:14 You will be judged on the **b** of all your wicked
Ro 4: 2 But from God's point of view Abraham had no **b**
2Co 10: 7 you make your decisions on the **b** of appearance.
Gal 3: 8 accept the Gentiles, too, on the **b** of their faith.

BASKET (32) [BASKETS]

Ge 40:17 In the top **b** were all kinds of bakery goods for
Ex 2: 3 she got a little **b** made of papyrus reeds
2: 3 She put the baby in the **b** and laid it among the
2: 5 When the princess saw the little **b** among the
29: 3 Place these various kinds of bread in a single **b**,
29:23 and one wafer from the **b** of yeastless bread that
29:32 along with the bread in the **b**, at the Tabernacle
Lev 8: 2 the two rams, and the **b** of unleavened bread
8:26 All these were taken from the **b** of bread made
8:31 and eat it along with the bread that is in the **b** of
Nu 6:15 a **b** of bread made without yeast—cakes of choice
6:17 along with the **b** of bread made without yeast.
Dt 23:24 but do not take any away in a **b**.
26: 2 of the first produce from each harvest into a **b**
26: 4 The priest will then take the **b** from your hand
Jdg 6:19 carrying the meat in a **b** and the broth in a pot,
Pr 25:11 advice is as lovely as golden apples in a silver **b**.
Jer 24: 2 One **b** was filled with fresh, ripe figs,
Am 8: 1 another vision. In it I saw a **b** filled with ripe fruit.
8: 2 he asked. I replied, "A **b** full of ripe fruit."
Zec 5: 6 He replied, "It is a **b** for measuring grain, and it is
5: 7 When the heavy lead cover was lifted off the **b**,
5: 8 and he pushed her back into the **b** and closed the
5: 9 and they picked up the **b** and flew with it into the
5:10 "Where are they taking the **b**?" I asked the angel.
5:11 Babylonia where they will build a temple for the **b**.
5:11 is ready, they will set the **b** there on its pedestal."
Mt 5:15 Don't hide your light under a **b**! Instead, put it on a
Mk 4:21 anyone light a lamp and then put it under a **b**
Lk 11:33 lights a lamp and then hides it or puts it under a **b**.
Ac 9:25 in a large **b** through an opening in the city wall.
2Co 11:33 But I was lowered in a **b** through a window in the

BASKETS (16) [BASKET]

Ge 40:16 "there were three **b** of pastries on my head.
40:18 Joseph told him. "The three **b** mean three days.
Dt 28: 5 You will be blessed with **b** overflowing with fruit,
28:17 You will be cursed with **b** empty of fruit, and with
2Ki 10: 7 They placed their heads in **b** and presented them to
Jer 24: 1 I saw two **b** of figs placed in front of the LORD's
Mt 14:20 and they picked up twelve **b** of leftovers.
15:37 there were seven large **b** of food left over!
16: 9 five loaves, and the **b** of food that were left over?
16:10 I fed with seven loaves, with **b** of food left over?
Mk 6:43 and they picked up twelve **b** of leftover bread
8: 8 there were seven large **b** of food left over!
8:19 How many **b** of leftovers did you pick up
8:20 how many large **b** of leftovers did you pick up?"
Lk 9:17 and they picked up twelve **b** of leftovers!
Jn 6:13 but twelve **b** were filled with the pieces of bread

BASMATH [KJV] See BASEMATH

BASON(S) [KJV] See BASIN, DISH

BASTARD(S) [KJV] See ILLEGITIMATE (BIRTH), FOREIGNERS

BAT (2) [BATS]

Lev 11:19 herons of all kinds, the hoopoe, and the **b**.
Dt 14:18 herons of all kinds, the hoopoe, and the **b**.

BATCH (1)

Gal 5: 9 a little yeast spreads quickly through the whole **b**

BATH (3) [BATHE]

Ru 3: 3 take a **b** and put on perfume and dress in your
2Sa 11: 2 he noticed a woman of unusual beauty taking a **b**.
Eze 45:11 and the **b** will each measure one-tenth of a homer.

BATH-RABBIM (1)

SS 7: 4 the sparkling pools in Heshbon by the gate of **B**.

BATHE (21) [BATH, BATHED, BATHING]

Ex 2: 5 one of Pharaoh's daughters came down to **b** in the
Lev 14: 9 and wash their clothes and **b** themselves in water.
15: 5 be required to wash your clothes and **b** in water,
15: 6 be required to wash your clothes and **b** in water.
15:10 be required to wash your clothes and **b** in water,
15:11 be required to wash your clothes and **b** in water,
15:13 must wash his clothes and **b** in fresh springwater.
15:18 both the man and the woman must **b**,
15:21 you must wash your clothes and **b** in water,
15:27 be required to wash your clothes and **b** in water,
16:24 Then he must **b** his entire body with water in a
16:26 a scapegoat must wash his clothes and **b** in water.
16:28 and **b** himself in water before returning to the
17:15 must wash your clothes and **b** yourselves in water.
17:16 But if you do not wash your clothes and **b**,
Nu 19: 7 must wash his clothes and **b** himself in water.
19: 8 animal must also wash his clothes and **b** in water,
19:19 cleansed must wash their clothes and **b** themselves,
Dt 23:11 Toward evening he must **b** himself, and at sunset
33:24 by his brothers; / may he **b** his feet in olive oil.
2Sa 14: 2 and don't **b** or wear any perfume.

BATHED (4) [BATHE]

1Ki 22:38 where the prostitutes **b**, and dogs came and licked
Eze 16: 9 "Then I **b** you and washed off your blood, and I
23:40 you **b** yourselves, painted your eyelids,
Jn 13:10 "A person who has **b** all over does not need to

BATHING (1) [BATHE]

Lev 14: 8 off all their hair, and **b** themselves in water.

BATHSHEBA (15) [BATHSHEBA'S]

2Sa 11: 3 and he was told, "She is **B**, the daughter of Eliam
11: 5 When **B** discovered that she was pregnant, she sent
11:26 When **B** heard that her husband was dead,
12:24 Then David comforted **B**, his wife, and slept with
1Ki 1:11 Then Nathan the prophet went to **B**,
1:15 So **B** went into the king's bedroom. He was very
1:16 **B** bowed low before him. "What can I do for
1:28 "Call **B**," David said. So she came back in
1:31 Then **B** bowed low before him again
2:13 was Haggith, came to see **B**, Solomon's mother.
2:18 "All right," **B** replied. "I will speak to the king
2:19 So **B** went to King Solomon to speak on
1Ch 3: 5 **B**, the daughter of Ammiel, was the mother of
Ps 51: T to him after David had committed adultery with **B**.
Mt 1: 6 was the father of Solomon (his mother was **B**,

BATHSHEBA'S (1) [BATHSHEBA]

2Sa 12:15 to his home, the LORD made **B** baby deathly ill.

BATHSHUA (1)

1Ch 2: 3 Judah had three sons through **B**, a Canaanite

BATS (1) [BAT]

Isa 2:20 their gold and silver idols to the moles and **b**.

BATTALION (3)

Mt 27:27 into their headquarters and called out the entire **b**.
Mk 15:16 into their headquarters and called out the entire **b**.
Jn 18: 3 and Pharisees had given Judas a **b** of Roman

BATTER (1) [BATTERED, BATTERING, STORM-BATTERED]

Ac 27:18 as gale-force winds continued to **b** the ship,

BATTERED (2) [BATTER]

Dt 1:44 and **b** you all the way from Seir to Hormah.
Isa 24:12 The city is left in ruins, with its gates **b** down.

BATTERING (5) [BATTER]

2Sa 20:15 a ramp against the city wall and began **b** it down.
Jer 6: 6 Almighty says: "Cut down the trees for **b** rams.
Eze 4: 2 Surround it with enemy camps and **b** rams.
21:22 With **b** rams they will go against the gates,
26: 9 He will pound your walls with **b** rams

BATTLE (237) [BATTLE-AX, BATTLEFIELD, BATTLEFRONT, BATTLEGROUND, BATTLEMENTS, BATTLES]

Ge 14: 8 prepared for **b** in the valley of the Dead Sea
Ex 13:17 God said, "If the people are faced with a **b**,
Lev 26:37 over each other in flight, as though fleeing in **b**.
Nu 14: 3 taking us to this country only to have us die in **b**?
14:43 you face the Amalekites and Canaanites in **b**,
21:23 in the wilderness, engaging them in **b** at Jahaz.
27:17 Give them someone who will lead them into **b**,
31: 4 tribe of Israel, send one thousand men into **b**."
31: 5 a total of twelve thousand men armed for **b**.
31: 6 Phinehas son of Eleazar the priest led them into **b**.
31: 8 Evi, Rekem, Zur, Hur, and Reba—died in the **b**.
31:14 military commanders who had returned from the **b**.
31:21 the priest said to the men who were in the **b**,
31:26 are to make a list of all the plunder taken in the **b**,
31:27 and give half to the men who fought the **b** and half
31:49 all the men who went out to **b** under our command;
32:17 and lead our fellow Israelites into **b** until we have
Dt 2:14 old enough to fight in **b** had died in the wilderness.
20: 2 Before you go into **b**, the priest will come forward
20: 5 You might be killed in the **b**, and someone else
20: 6 You might die in **b**, and someone else would eat
20: 7 You might die in the **b**, and someone else would
Jos 4:13 were ready for **b**, and they crossed over to the
10:16 During the **b**, the five kings escaped and hid in a
Jdg 2:15 Every time Israel went out to **b**, the LORD fought
3: 2 of Israelites who had no experience in **b**.
4:14 warriors down the slopes of Mount Tabor into **b**.
5:19 but they carried off no treasures of **b**.
9:39 then led the men of Shechem into **b** against
9:42 people of Shechem went out into the fields to **b**.
9:45 The **b** went on all day before Abimelech finally
11: 8 "If you will lead us in **b** against the Ammonites,
12: 3 So I risked my life and went to **b** without you,
20:18 Before the **b** the Israelites went to Bethel
20:32 "We're defeating them as we did in the first **b**!"
20:39 "We're defeating them as we did in the first **b**!"
20:44 Benjamin's greatest warriors died in that day's **b**.
1Sa 4: 3 After the **b** was over, the army of Israel retreated to
4: 3 If we carry it into **b** with us, it will save us from
4: 4 helped carry the Ark of God to where the **b** was
4:13 waiting beside the road to hear the news of the **b**,
7:10 the burnt offering, the Philistines arrived for **b**.
8:20 Our king will govern us and lead us into **b**."
11: 7 who refuses to follow Saul and Samuel into **b**!"
13:11 and the Philistines are at Micmash ready for **b**.
14: 6 He can win a **b** whether he has many warriors
14:20 and his six hundred men rushed out to the **b**
14:23 and the **b** continued to rage even out beyond
14:32 That evening they flew upon the **b** plunder
17: 1 The Philistines now mustered their army for **b**
17:20 leaving for the battlefield with shouts and **b** cries.
17:28 and dishonesty. You just want to see the **b**!"
17:47 It is his **b**, not ours. The LORD will give you to
18:13 but David faithfully led his troops into **b**.
18:16 he was so successful at leading his troops into **b**.
26:10 down someday, or he will die in **b** or of old age.
28: 1 and your men will be expected to join me in **b**."
29: 4 they demanded. "He can't go into the **b** with us.
29: 4 himself with his master than by turning on us in **b**?
29: 9 are afraid to have you with them in the **b**.
30:24 those who go to **b** and those who guard the
2Sa 1: 4 "Tell me how the **b** went." The man replied,
1:22 they did not return from **b** empty-handed.
1:25 How the mighty heroes have fallen in **b**!
3:30 had killed their brother Asahel at the **b** of Gibeon.
4: 4 and Jonathan were killed at the **b** of Jezreel.
4: 4 When news of the **b** reached the capital, the child's
10: 8 The Ammonite troops drew up their **b** lines at the
10:14 After the **b** was over, Joab returned to Jerusalem.
10:17 The Arameans positioned themselves there in **b**
11:15 "Station Uriah on the front lines where the **b** is
11:18 Then Joab sent a **b** report to David.
11:19 "Report all the news of the **b** to the king.
18: 6 So the **b** began in the forest of Ephraim,
18: 8 The **b** raged all across the countryside, and more
18: 9 During the **b**, Absalom came unexpectedly upon
19: 3 they were ashamed and had been beaten in **b**.
21:12 and Jonathan had died in a **b** with the Philistines,
21:15 when David and his men were in the thick of **b**,
21:17 men declared, "You are not going out to **b** again!
21:18 there was another **b** against the Philistines at Gob.
21:19 In still another **b** at Gob, Elhanan son of Jair from
21:20 In another **b** with the Philistines at Gath, a huge
22:35 He prepares me for **b**; / he strengthens me to draw
22:40 You have armed me with strength for the **b**;
23: 8 to kill eight hundred enemy warriors in a single **b**.
23:18 to kill three hundred enemy warriors in a single **b**.
1Ki 11:15 to bury some Israelites who had died in **b**.
20:11 "A warrior still dressing for **b** should not boast
20:27 its army, set up supply lines, and moved into the **b**.
20:29 seven days, and on the seventh day the **b** began.
20:39 the prophet called out to him, "Sir, I was in the **b**,
22:20 'Who can entice Ahab to go into **b** against
22:27 and water until I return safely from the **b**!' "
22:30 "As we go into **b**, I will disguise myself so no one
22:30 So Ahab disguised himself, and they went into **b**.
22:35 The **b** raged all that day, and Ahab was propped up
2Ki 3:26 the king of Moab saw that he was losing the **b**,
8:28 When King Joram was wounded in the **b**,
14: 8 and grandson of Jehu: "Come and meet me in **b**!"
14:11 The two armies drew up their **b** lines at
1Ch 5:10 of Saul, the Reubenites defeated the Hagrites in **b**.
5:20 They cried out to God during the **b**, and he
5:22 Many of the Hagrites were killed in the **b**
11:11 to kill three hundred enemy warriors in a single **b**.
11:13 He was with David in the **b** against the Philistines
11:13 The **b** took place in a field full of barley,
11:20 to kill three hundred enemy warriors in a single **b**.
12: 1 among the warriors who fought beside David in **b**.
12:33 They were fully armed and prepared for **b**
12:35 there were 28,600 warriors, all prepared for **b**.
12:36 were 40,000 trained warriors, all prepared for **b**.
12:38 All these men came in **b** array to Hebron with the
19: 9 The Ammonite troops drew up their **b** lines at the
19:17 and positioned his troops in **b** formation.
19:17 Then he engaged the enemy troops in **b**, and they
20: 5 During another **b** with the Philistines, Elhanan son
20: 6 In another **b** with the Philistines at Gath, a huge
26:27 gained in **b** to maintain the house of the LORD.
2Ch 13:12 blow their trumpets and lead us into **b** against you.
13:15 At the sound of their **b** cry, God defeated
14:10 so Asa deployed his armies for **b** in the valley
15: 2 to meet King Asa as he was returning from the **b**.
15:11 of the animals they had taken as plunder in the **b**—
18: 3 to command. We will certainly join you in **b**."
18:19 'Who can entice King Ahab of Israel to go into **b**
18:26 and water until I return safely from the **b**!' "
18:29 "As we go into **b**, I will disguise myself so no one
18:29 So Ahab disguised himself, and they went into **b**.
18:34 The **b** raged all that day, and Ahab propped
20:15 this mighty army, for the **b** is not yours, but God's.

22: 5 and the Arameans wounded Joram in the **b**.
25: 8 If you let them go with your troops into **b**, you will
25:17 and grandson of Jehu: "Come and meet me in **b**!"
25:21 The two armies drew up their **b** lines at
26:11 ready to march into **b**, unit by unit.
28:12 with this and confronted the men returning from **b**.
29: 9 Our fathers have been killed in **b**, and our sons
35:20 to do **b** at Carchemish on the Euphrates River,
35:22 he led his army into **b** on the plain of Megiddo.
35:23 He cried out to his men, "Take me from the **b**,
Job 36:12 they will perish in **b** and die from lack of
38:23 it for the time of trouble, for the day of **b** and war.
39:24 and rushes forward into **b** when the trumpet blows.
39:25 the **b** even at a distance. It quivers at the noise of **b**
41: 8 hand on it, you will never forget the **b** that follows,
Ps 2: 2 The kings of the earth prepare for **b**; / the rulers
18:34 He prepares me for **b**; / he strengthens me to draw
18:39 You have armed me with strength for the **b**;
24: 8 strong and mighty, / the LORD, invincible in **b**.
35: 2 your shield. / Prepare for **b**, and come to my aid.
44: 9 in dishonor. / You no longer lead our armies to **b**.
55:18 and keeps me safe / from the **b** waged against me,
74: 4 **b** cries; / there they set up their **b** standards.
78: 9 their backs and fled when the day of **b** came.
89:43 sword useless / and have refused to help him in **b**.
110: 3 In that day of **b**, / your people will serve you
140: 7 strong savior, / you protected me on the day of **b**.
144: 1 He gives me strength for war / and skill for **b**.
Pr 21:31 The horses are prepared for **b**, but the victory
Ecc 8: 8 There is no escaping that obligation, that dark **b**.
9:11 and the strongest warrior doesn't always win the **b**.
Isa 3:25 The men of the city will die in **b**.
5:28 arrows will be sharp and their bows ready for **b**.
8: 9 all you nations. Prepare for **b**—and die! Yes, die!
9: 5 that day of peace, **b** gear will no longer be issued.
14:19 dumped into a mass grave with those killed in **b**.
18: 3 When I raise my **b** flag on the mountain, let all the
21: 5 Quick! Grab your shields and prepare for **b**!
30:16 They will give us swift horses for riding into **b**.'
31: 9 with terror and flee when they see the **b** flags,"
42:13 full of fury. / He will shout his thundering **b** cry,
42:25 out such fury on them and destroyed them in **b**.
Jer 4:16 raising a **b** cry against the towns of Judah.
4:19 of enemy trumpets and the roar of their **b** cries.
6: 4 They shout, 'Prepare for **b** and attack at noon!
6:23 They are marching in **b** formation to destroy you,
8: 6 the path of sin as swiftly as a horse rushing into **b**!
11:22 Their young men will die in **b**, and their little boys
18:21 in a plague, and let their young men be killed in **b**!
19: 7 For I will upset the **b** plans of Judah and Jerusalem
20:16 Terrify him all day long with **b** shouts,
46: 2 on the occasion of the **b** of Carchemish when
46: 3 "Buckle on your armor and advance into **b**!
46:14 Mobilize for **b**, for the sword of destruction will
48: 3 then the roar of **b** will surge against Horonaim,
49:14 a coalition against Edom, and prepare for **b**!"
50:22 "Let the **b** cry be heard in the land, a shout of
50:42 They are marching in **b** formation to destroy you,
51:12 Raise the **b** flag against Babylon!
51:27 Sound the **b** cry! Bring out the armies of Ararat,
51:55 against her; the noise of **b** rings through the city.
La 2:12 ebb away like the life of a warrior wounded in **b**.
Eze 9: 2 that faces north, each carrying a **b** club in his hand.
13: 5 They have not helped it to stand firm in **b** on the
17:21 all the best warriors of Israel will be killed in **b**,
23:24 every side, surrounding you with men armed for **b**.
30:17 men of Heliopolis and Bubastis will die in **b**,
Da 8:25 He will even take on the Prince of princes in **b**,
11:10 and carry the **b** as far as the enemy's fortress.
11:20 he will die, though neither in **b** nor open conflict.
11:25 The king of the south will go to **b** with a mighty
Hos 5: 8 Raise the **b** cry in Beth-aven! Lead on into **b**,
14: 3 Assyria cannot save us, nor can our strength in **b**.
Joel 2: 5 a field, or like a mighty army moving into **b**.
Am 1:14 There will be wild shouts during the **b**,
2: 2 The people will fall in the noise of **b**,
5: 3 one of your cities sends a thousand men to **b**,
9: 1 Then those who survive will be slaughtered in **b**.
Mic 2: 8 ragged as men who have just come home from **b**.
Na 2:13 The finest of your youth will be killed in **b**.
Zep 1:16 trumpet calls, and **b** cries. Down go the walled
Zec 9:10 I will remove the **b** chariots from Israel
9:10 and I will destroy all the weapons used in **b**.
9:15 They will shout in **b** as though drunk with wine,
10: 3 and glorious, like a proud warhorse in **b**.
10: 4 the tent peg, the **b** bow, and all the rulers.
10: 5 They will be like mighty warriors in **b**,
Ac 4:26 The kings of the earth prepared for **b**; / the rulers
1Co 14: 8 will the soldiers know they are being called to **b**?
Eph 6:13 so that after the **b** you will still be standing firm.
6:16 In every **b** you will need faith as your shield to
Heb 7: 1 home after winning a great **b** against many kings,
7: 2 Abraham took a tenth of all he had won in the **b**
7: 4 by giving him a tenth of what he had taken in **b**.
11:34 They became strong in **b** and put whole armies to
1Jn 2:13 because you have won your **b** with Satan.
2:14 your hearts, and you have won your **b** with Satan.
5: 5 And the ones who win this **b** against the world are
Rev 9: 7 The locusts looked like horses armed for **b**.
9: 9 roared like an army of chariots rushing into **b**.
12: 8 And the dragon lost the **b** and was forced out of
16:14 **b** against the Lord on that great judgment day of
20: 8 He will gather them together for **b**—a mighty host,

BATTLE-AX (1) [AX, BATTLE]

Jer 51:20 "You are my **b** and sword," says the LORD.

BATTLEFIELD (4) [BATTLE, FIELD]

Jdg 5:18 Zebulun risked his life, / as did Naphtali, on the **b**.
1Sa 4:17 "Thousands of Israelite troops are dead on the **b**.
17:20 the Israelite army was leaving for the **b** with shouts
2Sa 1: 4 Many men are dead and wounded on the **b**,

BATTLEFRONT (3) [BATTLE]

1Sa 4:12 A man from the tribe of Benjamin ran from the **b**
4:16 He said to Eli, "I have just come from the **b**—
2Sa 1: 2 David's return, a man arrived from the Israelite **b**.

BATTLEGROUND (1) [BATTLE]

1Sa 5: 1 they took it from the **b** at Ebenezer to the city of

BATTLEMENT [KJV] See EDGE

BATTLEMENTS (1) [BATTLE]

Zep 1:16 Down go the walled cities and strongest **b**!

BATTLES (10) [BATTLE]

Nu 32:20 your word and arm yourselves for the LORD's **b**,
32:29 and Reuben who are able to fight the LORD's **b**
1Sa 18:17 to be a real warrior by fighting the LORD's **b**."
25:28 for you are fighting the LORD's **b**.
1Ch 22: 8 'You have killed many men in the great **b** you
2Ch 26: 7 but also in his **b** with the Arabs of Gur and in his
32: 8 our God to help us and to fight our **b** for us!"
Ac 7:45 when Joshua led the **b** against the Gentile nations
1Ti 1:18 you the confidence to fight well in the Lord's **b**.
Rev 6: 2 He rode out to win many **b** and gain the victory.

BAVAI [KJV] See BINNUI

BAY (4)

Jos 15: 2 The southern boundary began at the south **b** of the
15: 5 The northern boundary began at the **b** where the
18:19 and ended at the north **b** of the Dead Sea,
Ac 27:39 but they saw a **b** with a beach and wondered if they

BAZLUTH (2)

Ezr 2:52 **B**, Mehida, Harsha,
Ne 7:54 **B**, Mehida, Harsha,

BDELLIUM [KJV] See RESIN

BE (5584) [AM, ARE, AREN'T, BEEN, BEING, HE'S, SHE'S, THERE'S, THEY'RE, WAS, WE'RE, WELL-BEING, WERE, WHAT'S] See Index of Articles, Etc.

BE-ESHTERAH (1) [ASHTAROTH]

Jos 21:27 Golan in Bashan (a city of refuge) and **B**.

BEACH (5)

Isa 17:13 But though they roar like breakers on a **b**, God will
Jnh 2:10 LORD ordered the fish to spit up Jonah on the **b**,
Mk 3: 9 to have it ready in case he was crowded off the **b**.
Jn 21: 4 At dawn the disciples saw Jesus standing on the **b**,
Ac 27:39 but they saw a bay with a **b** and wondered if they

BEACON (1)

Ro 2:19 and a **b** light for people who are lost in darkness

BEACON [KJV] See also FLAGPOLE

BEAD (1) [BEADS]

SS 4: 9 of your eyes, by a single **b** of your necklace.

BEADS (1) [BEAD]

SS 1:11 make earrings of gold for you and **b** of silver."

BEAK (1)

Ge 8:11 bird returned to him with a fresh olive leaf in its **b**.

BEALIAH (1)

1Ch 12: 5 Eluzai, Jerimoth, **B**, Shemariah, and Shephatiah

BEALOTH (1)

Jos 15:24 Ziph, Telem, **B**,

BEAM (5) [BEAMED, BEAMS]

1Sa 17: 7 his spear was as heavy and thick as a weaver's **b**,
2Sa 21:19 handle of his spear was as thick as a weaver's **b**!
1Ch 11:23 and whose spear was as thick as a weaver's **b**.
20: 5 of Lahmi's spear was as thick as a weaver's **b**!
Ezr 6:11 in any way will have a **b** pulled from their house.

BEAMED (1) [BEAM]

Ac 9: 3 a brilliant light from heaven suddenly **b** down

BEAMS (14) [BEAM]

1Ki 6: 6 by **b** resting on ledges built out from the wall.
6: 6 So the **b** were not inserted into the walls
6: 9 Solomon put in a ceiling made of **b** and planks of
6:36 so that there was one layer of cedar **b** after every
7: 2 The great cedar ceiling **b** rested on four rows of
7:11 also cut to measure, and cedar **b** were also used.
7:12 so that there was one layer of cedar **b** after every
2Ch 3: 7 All the walls, **b**, doors, and thresholds throughout
34:11 stone for the walls and timber for the rafters and **b**.
Ne 2: 8 I will need it to make **b** for the gates of the Temple
3: 3 laid the **b**, hung the doors, and put the bolts
3: 6 They laid the **b**, set up the doors, and installed the
Jer 22: 7 They will tear out all your fine cedar **b** and throw
Hab 2:11 and the **b** in the ceilings echo the complaint.

BEANS (2)

2Sa 17:28 wheat and barley flour, roasted grain, **b**, lentils,
Eze 4: 9 get some wheat, barley, **b**, lentils, millet, and spelt,

BEAR (68) [AFTERBIRTH, BEAR'S, BEARER, BEARERS, BEARING, BEARS, BIRTH, BIRTHDAY, BIRTHDAYS, BIRTHRIGHT, BIRTHS, BORE, BORN, BORNE, CHILDBEARING, CHILDBIRTH, CUP-BEARER, CUP-BEARERS, FIRSTBORN, FREEBORN, NATIVE-BORN, NEWBORN, REBIRTH, REBORN, SEED-BEARING, STILLBORN]

Ge 3:16 "You will **b** children with intense pain
4:13 "My punishment is too great for me to **b**!
16: 2 and gave her to Abram so she could **b** his children.
17:13 Your bodies will thus **b** the mark of my everlasting
17:19 God replied, "Sarah, your wife, will **b** you a son.
30: 3 Bilhah, and she will **b** children for me."
43: 9 him back to you, then let me **b** the blame forever.
43:14 And if I must **b** the anguish of their deaths, then
44:32 bring him back to you, I will **b** the blame forever.'
44:34 I cannot **b** to see what this would do to him."
Lev 19:18 seek revenge or **b** a grudge against anyone,
26:20 will yield no crops, and your trees will **b** no fruit.
Nu 11:17 They will **b** the burden of the people along with
32:27 all who are able to **b** arms will cross over to fight
Dt 7:14 be childless, and all your livestock will **b** young.
29:18 and so that no root among you would **b** bitter
Jos 5: 4 because all the men who were old enough to **b**
5: 6 enough to **b** arms when they left Egypt had died.
Ru 1:12 and I were to get married tonight and **b** sons,
1Sa 17:34 a lion or a **b** comes to steal a lamb from the flock,
17:37 and the **b** will save me from this Philistine!"
2Sa 17: 8 as a mother **b** who has been robbed of her cubs.
Job 9: 9 the **B**, Orion, the Pleiades, and the constellations of
11:12 more than a wild donkey can **b** human offspring!
21: 3 **B** with me, and let me speak. After I have spoken,
21:10 to breed. Their cows **b** calves without miscarriage.
38:32 or guide the constellation of the **B** with her cubs
Ps 38: 4 overwhelms me—/ it is a burden too heavy to **b**.
55:12 It is not an enemy who taunts me—/ I could **b** that.
119:143 As pressure and stress **b** down on me, / I find joy
Pr 11:30 The godly are like trees that **b** life-giving fruit,
12:12 each other's loot, while the godly **b** their own fruit.
17:12 It is safer to meet a **b** robbed of her cubs than to
18:14 sick body, but who can **b** it if the spirit is crushed?
28:15 dangerous to the poor as a lion or **b** attacking them.
31:27 and does not have to **b** the consequences of
Isa 53:11 to be counted righteous, for he will **b** all their sins.
54: 1 For the woman who could **b** no children now has
Jer 10:19 is great. My sickness is incurable, but I must **b** it.
15:16 for I **b** your name, O LORD God Almighty.
44:22 because the LORD could no longer **b** all the evil
La 3:10 He hid like a **b** or a lion, waiting to attack me.
5: 1 that has happened to us. See all the sorrows we **b**!
Eze 4: 4 You are to **b** their sins for the number of days you
4: 5 You will **b** Israel's sins for 390 days—one day for
23:35 you must **b** the consequences of all your lewdness
44:10 must **b** the consequences of their unfaithfulness.
44:12 and taken an oath that they must **b** the
44:13 for they must **b** the shame of all the sins they have
Da 7: 5 Then I saw a second beast, and it looked like a **b**.
9:19 for your people and your city **b** your name."
Hos 9:16 Their roots are dried up; they will **b** no more fruit.
13: 8 I will rip you to pieces like a **b** whose cubs have
13:16 The people of Samaria must **b** the consequences of
Am 5:19 like a man who runs from a lion—only to meet a **b**.
5:19 After escaping the **b**, he leans his hand against a
Mt 21:19 Then he said to it, "May you never **b** fruit again!"
Lk 1:13 and your wife, Elizabeth, will **b** you a son!
Jn 15: 2 and he prunes the branches that do **b** fruit so they
16:12 more I want to tell you, but you can't **b** it now.
Ac 15:10 that neither we nor our ancestors were able to **b**?
2Co 3: 7 people of Israel could not **b** to look at Moses' face.
11: 1 as I keep on talking like a fool. Please **b** with me.
Gal 4:27 For the woman who could **b** no children / now has
6:17 For I **b** on my body the scars that show I belong to
1Th 3: 5 That is why, when I could **b** it no longer, I sent
Heb 13:13 him outside the camp and **b** the disgrace he bore.
Jas 2: 7 slander Jesus Christ, whose noble name you **b**?

BEAR'S (1) [BEAR]

Rev 13: 2 like a leopard, but it had **b** feet and a lion's mouth!

BEARD (9) [BEARDS]

Lev 14: 9 including the hair of the **b** and eyebrows, and wash
1Sa 21:13 scratching on doors and drooling down his **b**.
2Sa 10: 4 and shaved off half of each man's **b**,
19:24 or clothes nor trimmed his **b** since the day the king
20: 9 and took him by the **b** with his right hand as
Ezr 9: 3 tore my clothing, pulled hair from my head and **b**,

Ps 133: 2 poured over Aaron's head, / that ran down his **b**
Isa 50: 6 and my cheeks to those who pull out my **b**.
Eze 5: 1 and use it as a razor to shave your head and **b**.

BEARDS (8) [BEARD]

Lev 19:27 hair on your temples or clip the edges of your **b**.
21: 5 trim the edges of their **b**, or cut their bodies.
2Sa 10: 5 the men to stay at Jericho until their **b** grew out,
1Ch 19: 4 seized David's ambassadors and shaved their **b**,
19: 5 the men to stay at Jericho until their **b** grew out,
Isa 15: 2 will shave their heads in sorrow and cut off their **b**.
Jer 41: 5 They had shaved off their **b**, torn their clothes,
48:37 They shave their heads and **b** in mourning.

BEARER (16) [BEAR]

Jdg 9:54 He said to his young armor **b**, "Draw your sword
1Sa 14: 6 to see those pagans," Jonathan said to his armor **b**.
14:12 right behind me," Jonathan said to his armor **b**,
14:13 and his armor **b** killed them right and left.
14:17 found that Jonathan and his armor **b** were gone.
17: 7 An armor **b** walked ahead of him carrying a huge
17:41 Goliath walked out toward David with his shield **b**
31: 4 Saul groaned to his armor **b**, "Take your sword
31: 4 But his armor **b** was afraid and would not do it.
31: 5 When his armor **b** realized that Saul was dead,
31: 6 So Saul, three of his sons, his armor **b**, and his
2Sa 23:37 Naharai from Beeroth (Joab's armor **b**);
1Ch 10: 4 Saul groaned to his armor **b**, "Take your sword
10: 4 But his armor **b** was afraid and would not do it.
10: 5 When his armor **b** realized that Saul was dead,
11:39 Naharai from Beeroth (Joab's armor **b**);

BEARERS (3) [BEAR]

1Sa 16:21 and David became one of Saul's armor **b**.
2Sa 18:15 Ten of Joab's young armor **b** then surrounded
Lk 7:14 to the coffin and touched it, and the **b** stopped.

BEARING (6) [BEAR]

Ex 28:38 thus **b** the guilt connected with any errors
Ps 1: 3 the riverbank, / **b** fruit each season without fail.
SS 4:13 You are like a lovely orchard **b** precious fruit,
Isa 11: 1 yes, a new Branch **b** fruit from the old root.
Hos 5: 7 the honor of the LORD, **b** children that aren't his.
Rev 22: 2 **b** twelve crops of fruit, with a fresh crop each

BEARS (13) [BEAR]

Ex 23:21 your sins. He is my representative—he **b** my name.
Dt 25: 6 The first son she **b** to him will be counted as the
1Sa 17:36 I have done this to both lions and **b**, and I'll do it
2Sa 6: 2 which **b** the name of the LORD Almighty,
1Ki 8:43 will know that this Temple I have built **b** your
2Ki 2:24 Then two **b** came out of the woods and mauled
1Ch 13: 6 which **b** the name of the LORD who is enthroned
2Ch 6:33 will know that this Temple I have built **b** your
Ps 74: 7 They utterly defiled the place that **b** your holy
Isa 11: 7 The cattle will graze among **b**. Cubs and calves
59:11 We growl like hungry **b**; we moan like mournful
Heb 6: 7 that falls on it and **b** a good crop for the farmer,
6: 8 But if a field **b** thistles and thorns, it is useless.

BEAST (48) [BEAST'S, BEASTS, BESTIAL]

Ge 49:14 "Issachar is a strong **b** of burden, / resting among
Da 7: 4 The first **b** was like a lion with eagles' wings.
7: 5 Then I saw a second **b**, and it looked like a bear.
7: 6 had four heads. Great authority was given to this **b**.
7: 7 I saw a fourth **b**, terrifying, dreadful, and very
7:11 I kept watching until the fourth **b** was killed
7:19 I wanted to know the true meaning of the fourth **b**,
7:23 "This fourth **b** is the fourth world power that will
Rev 11: 7 the **b** that comes up out of the bottomless pit will
13: 1 And now in my vision I saw a **b** rising up out of
13: 2 This **b** looked like a leopard, but it had bear's feet
13: 3 I saw that one of the heads of the **b** seemed
13: 3 marveled at this miracle and followed the **b** in awe.
13: 4 They worshiped the dragon for giving the **b** such power, and they worshiped the **b**.
13: 4 "Is there anyone as great as the **b**?"
13: 5 Then the **b** was allowed to speak great blasphemies
13: 7 And the **b** was allowed to wage war against God's
13: 8 people who belong to this world worshiped the **b**.
13:11 Then I saw another **b** come up out of the earth.
13:12 He exercised all the authority of the first **b**.
13:12 who belong to this world to worship the first **b**,
13:14 he was allowed to perform on behalf of the first **b**,
13:14 of the world to make a great statue of the first **b**,
13:17 which was either the name of the **b** or the number
13:18 who has understanding solve the number of the **b**,
14: 9 "Anyone who worships the **b** and his statue
14:11 for they have worshiped the **b** and his statue
15: 2 all the people who had been victorious over the **b**
16: 2 broke out on everyone who had the mark of the **b**
16:10 angel poured out his bowl on the throne of the **b**,
16:13 mouth of the dragon, the **b**, and the false prophet.
17: 3 There I saw a woman sitting on a scarlet **b** that had
17: 7 and of the **b** with seven heads and ten horns.
17: 8 The **b** you saw was alive but isn't now. And yet he
17: 8 will be amazed at the reappearance of this **b** who
17: 9 The seven heads of the **b** represent the seven hills
17:11 The scarlet **b** that was alive and then died is the
17:12 for one brief moment to reign with the **b**.
17:16 The scarlet **b** and his ten horns—which represent
17:17 agree to give their authority to the scarlet **b**,
19:19 Then I saw the **b** gathering the kings of the earth
19:20 And the **b** was captured, and with him the false
19:20 who did mighty miracles on behalf of the **b**—
19:20 deceived all who had accepted the mark of the **b**
19:20 Both the **b** and his false prophet were thrown alive
20: 4 the souls of those who had not worshiped the **b**
20:10 with sulfur, joining the **b** and the false prophet.

BEAST'S (1) [BEAST]

Da 7:20 I also asked about the ten horns on the fourth **b**

BEASTS (14) [BEAST]

Dt 32:24 They will be troubled by the fangs of wild **b**,
Job 41:34 the creatures, it is the proudest. It is the king of **b**."
Ps 74:19 Don't let these wild **b** destroy your doves.
Isa 23:13 Assyrians have handed Babylon over to the wild **b**.
46: 1 But look! The **b** are staggering under the weight!
Jer 12: 9 Bring on the wild **b** to pick their corpses clean!
Eze 14:21 war, famine, **b**, and plague—destroying all her
Da 7: 3 Then four huge **b** came up out of the water,
7: 6 Then the third of these strange **b** appeared, and it
7: 7 It was different from any of the other **b**, and it had
7:12 As for the other three **b**, their authority was taken
7:17 "These four huge **b** represent four kingdoms that
1Co 15:32 And what value was there in fighting wild **b**—
Rev 18: 2 a nest for filthy buzzards, and a den for dreadful **b**.

BEAT (37) [BEATEN, BEATING, BEATINGS, BEATS]

Ex 30:36 **B** some of it very fine and put some of it in front of
Nu 22:23 but Balaam **b** it and turned it back onto the road.
22:25 against the wall. So Balaam **b** the donkey again.
22:27 In a fit of rage Balaam **b** it again with his staff.
22:32 "Why did you **b** your donkey those three times?"
Dt 24:20 When you **b** the olives from your olive trees,
Ru 2:17 and when she **b** out the grain that evening, it came
2Sa 23:12 the middle of the field and **b** back the Philistines.
1Ki 20:23 they won. But we can **b** them easily on the plains.
20:25 There's not a shadow of a doubt that we will **b**
1Ch 11:14 the middle of the field and **b** back the Philistines.
Ne 13:25 I **b** some of them and pulled out their hair.
Ps 81: 2 Sing! **B** the tambourine. / Play the sweet lyre
89:23 I will **b** down his adversaries before him
Pr 23:35 feel it. I didn't even know it when they **b** me up.
Isa 2: 4 All the nations will **b** their swords into plowshares
10:26 The LORD Almighty will **b** them with his whip,
32:12 **B** your breasts in sorrow for your bountiful farms
50: 6 I give my back to those who **b** me and my cheeks
Eze 23:34 smash it to pieces and **b** your breast in anguish.
Joel 3:10 **B** your plowshares into swords and your pruning
Am 1: 3 They **b** down my people in Gilead as grain is
Jnh 4: 8 The sun **b** down on his head until he grew faint
Mic 4: 3 All the nations will **b** their swords into plowshares
Na 2: 7 like doves; watch them **b** their breasts in sorrow.
Mt 7:25 and the winds **b** against that house,
7:27 floods come and the winds **b** against that house,
21:35 his servants, **b** one, killed one, and stoned another.
27:30 grabbed the stick and **b** him on the head with it.
Mk 10:34 spit on him, **b** him with their whips, and kill him,
12: 3 **b** him up, and sent him back empty-handed.
12: 4 but they **b** him over the head and treated him
15:19 And they **b** him on the head with a stick, spit on
Lk 10:30 stripped him of his clothes and money, **b** him up,
18:13 Instead, he **b** his chest in sorrow, saying, 'O God,
20:10 **b** him up, and sent him back empty-handed.
Ac 22:19 and **b** those in every synagogue who believed on

BEATEN (30) [BEAT]

Ex 5:16 We are **b** for something that isn't our fault!
21:20 "If a male or female slave is **b** and dies, the owner
Nu 8: 4 to its decorative blossoms, was made of **b** gold.
10: 2 "Make two trumpets of **b** silver to be used for
Dt 25: 2 and be **b** in his presence with the number of lashes
Jos 8:15 toward the wilderness as though they were badly **b**,
Jdg 20:36 Then the Benjaminites saw that they were **b**.
2Sa 18: 7 and the Israelite troops were **b** back by David's
19: 3 they were ashamed and had been **b** in battle.
2Ki 13:19 "Then you would have **b** Aram until they were
Pr 19:29 will be punished, and the backs of fools will be **b**.
Isa 28:27 never used on dill; rather, it is **b** with a light stick.
28:27 on cummin; instead, it is **b** softly with a flail.
52:14 **b** and bloodied, so disfigured one would scarcely
53: 5 He was **b** that we might have peace. He was
Jer 10: 9 They bring **b** sheets of silver from Tarshish
Mic 4:12 know that he is gathering them together to be **b**
Mt 10:17 handed over to the courts and **b** in the synagogues.
Mk 12: 5 Others who were sent were either **b** or killed,
13: 9 handed over to the courts and **b** in the synagogues.
Lk 20:11 he was **b** up and treated shamefully, and he went
Ac 16:22 ordered them stripped and **b** with wooden rods.
16:23 They were severely **b**, and then they were thrown
16:37 "They have publicly **b** us without trial and jailed
18:17 and had **b** him right there in the courtroom.
2Co 6: 5 We have been **b**, been put in jail, faced angry
6: 9 We have been **b** within an inch of our lives.
11:25 Three times I was **b** with rods. Once I was stoned.
Heb 10:33 you were exposed to public ridicule and were **b**
1Pe 2:20 you get no credit for being patient if you are **b** for

BEATING (11) [BEAT]

Ex 2:11 he saw an Egyptian **b** one of the Hebrew slaves.
39: 3 A skilled craftsman made gold thread by **b** gold
Nu 22:28 "What have I done to you that deserves your **b** me
Jdg 19:22 They began **b** at the door and shouting to the old
Job 9:34 The mediator could make God stop **b** me, and I
Ps 89:32 sin with the rod, / and their disobedience with **b**.
Pr 18: 6 get into constant quarrels; they are asking for a **b**.
30:33 As the **b** of cream yields butter, and a blow to the
Isa 25: 4 of ruthless people are like a storm **b** against a wall,
Lk 22:63 in charge of Jesus began mocking and **b** him.
Ac 21:32 and the troops coming, they stopped **b** Paul.

BEATINGS (1) [BEAT]

1Co 4:11 We have endured many **b**, and we have no homes

BEATS (1) [BEAT]

Ps 38:10 My heart **b** wildly, my strength fails, / and I am

BEAUTIFUL (122) [BEAUTY]

Ge 2: 9 the garden—**b** trees that produced delicious fruit.
6: 2 the sons of God saw the **b** women of the human
12:11 Abram said to Sarai, "You are a very **b** woman.
13:10 the garden of the LORD or the **b** land of Egypt.
24:16 Now Rebekah was very **b**, and she was a virgin;
26: 7 would kill him to get her, because she was very **b**.
29:17 but Rachel was **b** in every way, with a lovely face
37: 3 So one day he gave Joseph a special gift—a **b** robe.
37:23 So when Joseph arrived, they pulled off his **b** robe
37:32 They took the **b** robe to their father and asked him
41:42 He dressed him in **b** clothing and placed the royal
Ex 2: 2 She saw what a **b** baby he was and kept him
27:16 and decorate it with **b** embroidery in blue, purple,
28: 2 **b** garments that will lend dignity to his work.
28:28 chestpiece securely to the ephod above the **b** sash.
31: 4 He is able to create **b** objects from gold, silver,
35:32 He is able to create **b** objects from gold, silver,
39: 1 the craftsmen made **b** garments of blue, purple,
39:21 was held securely to the ephod above the **b** sash.
Nu 24: 5 How **b** are your tents, O Jacob; / how lovely are
Dt 3:25 the **b** hill country and the Lebanon mountains.'
21:11 And suppose you see among the captives a **b**
Jos 7:21 For I saw a **b** robe imported from Babylon,
Jdg 15: 2 But look, her sister is more **b** than she is.
1Sa 25: 3 and his wife, Abigail, was a sensible and **b** woman.
2Sa 7: 2 "Here I am living in this **b** cedar palace,
7: 7 "Why haven't you built me a **b** cedar temple?" '
13: 1 David's son Absalom had a **b** sister named Tamar.
13:18 She was wearing a long, **b** robe, as was the custom
14:27 daughter's name was Tamar, and she was very **b**.
1Ki 1: 3 So they searched throughout the country for a **b**
1: 4 The girl was very **b**, and she waited on the king
10:12 or since has there been such a supply of **b** almug
2Ki 2:19 "This town is located in **b** natural surroundings,
1Ch 17: 1 "Here I am living in this **b** cedar palace,
17: 6 "Why haven't you built me a **b** cedar temple?" '
2Ch 3: 6 The walls of the Temple were decorated with **b**
9:11 Never before had there been such **b** instruments in
Est 1:11 to gaze on her beauty, for she was a very **b** woman.
2: 2 "Let us search the empire to find **b** young virgins
2: 3 these **b** young women into the royal harem at Susa.
2: 7 This man had a **b** and lovely young cousin,
Job 26:13 His Spirit made the heavens **b**, and his power
Ps 45: 1 My heart overflows with a **b** thought! / I will recite
45:14 In her **b** robes, she is led to the king,
Pr 4: 9 your head; she will present you with a **b** crown."
11:16 **B** women obtain wealth, and violent men get rich.
11:22 A woman who is **b** but lacks discretion is like a
Ecc 2: 4 homes for myself and by planting **b** vineyards.
2: 8 both men and women, and had many **b** concubines.
3:11 God has made everything **b** for its own time.
SS 1: 5 "I am dark and **b**, O women of Jerusalem,
1: 8 "If you don't know, O most **b** woman,
1:15 "How **b** you are, my beloved, how **b**!
4: 1 "How **b** you are, my beloved, how **b**!
4: 3 are like a ribbon of scarlet. Oh, how **b** your mouth!
4: 7 You are so **b**, my beloved, so perfect in every part.
6: 1 "O rarest of **b** women, where has your lover gone?
6: 4 you are as **b** as the lovely town of Tirzah.
6: 4 Yes, as **b** as Jerusalem! You are as majestic as an
7: 1 "How **b** are your sandaled feet, O queenly maiden.
Isa 4: 2 will be lush and **b**, and the fruit of the land will be
5: 9 "Many **b** homes will stand deserted, the owners
22: 7 They fill your **b** valleys and crowd against your
22:16 you are, building a **b** tomb for yourself in the rock?
25: 2 **B** palaces in distant lands disappear and will never
51: 3 Her barren wilderness will become as **b** as Eden—
52: 1 Put on your **b** clothes, O holy city of Jerusalem,
52: 7 How **b** on the mountains are the feet of those who
53: 2 There was nothing **b** or majestic about his
60:15 and rebuffed by all, you will be **b** forever.
64:11 **b** Temple where our ancestors praised you has
Jer 3:19 I wanted nothing more than to give you this **b**
4:30 Why do you dress up in your most **b** clothing
6: 2 O Jerusalem, you are my **b** and delicate daughter—
11:16 a thriving olive tree, **b** to see and full of good fruit.
13:20 Where is your flock—your **b** flock—that he gave
22:15 "But a **b** palace does not make a great king!
22:23 It may be nice to live in a **b** palace lined with
48:17 scepter is broken, how the **b** staff is shattered!
La 2: 4 His fury is poured out like fire on **b** Jerusalem.
2:15 "Is this the city called 'Most **B** in All the World,'
Eze 16: 7 You grew up and became a **b** jewel. Your breasts
16:11 you lovely jewelry, bracelets, and **b** necklaces,
16:13 And so you were made **b** with gold and silver.
16:13 and olive oil—and became more **b** than ever.
16:39 They will strip you and take your **b** jewels,
20:15 with milk and honey, the most **b** place on earth.
23:26 They will strip you of your **b** clothes and jewels.
23:42 on your wrists and **b** crowns on your heads.
26:16 and take off their royal robes and **b** clothing.
31: 7 It was strong and **b**, for its roots went deep into

31:16 trees of Eden, the most **b** and the best of Lebanon,
33:32 like someone who sings love songs with a **b** voice
Da 4:30 have built this **b** city as my royal residence and as
Hos 9:13 I have watched Israel become as **b** and pleasant as
10: 1 the more **b** the statues and idols they built.
14: 6 Its branches will spread out like those of **b** olive
Am 3:15 And I will destroy the **b** homes of the wealthy—
5:11 you will never live in the **b** stone houses you are
6: 8 and false glory of Israel, and I hate their **b** homes.
8:13 **B** girls and fine young men will grow faint
Na 3: 4 All this because Nineveh, the **b** and faithless city,
Zec 9:17 How wonderful and **b** they will be! The young
11: 2 the tallest and most **b** of them are fallen.
Mt 23:27 **b** on the outside but filled on the inside with dead
26: 7 a woman came in with a **b** jar of expensive
Mk 14: 3 a woman came in with a **b** jar of expensive
Lk 7:25 people who wear **b** clothes and live in luxury are
7:37 and brought a **b** jar filled with expensive perfume.
21: 5 Some of his disciples began talking about the **b**
Ac 3: 2 beside the Temple gate, the one called the **B** Gate,
3:10 lame beggar they had seen so often at the **B** Gate,
7:20 time Moses was born—a **b** child in God's eyes.
Ro 10:15 "How **b** are the feet of those who bring good
1Pe 3: 3 fancy hairstyles, expensive jewelry, or **b** clothes.
3: 5 way the holy women of old made themselves **b**.
Rev 17: 4 and **b** jewelry made of gold and precious gems
18:16 She was so **b**—like a woman clothed in finest
21: 2 coming down from God out of heaven like a **b**

BEAUTIFULLY (12) [BEAUTY]

Ex 31:10 the **b** stitched, holy garments for Aaron the priest,
35:19 the **b** stitched clothing for the priests to wear while
39:41 the **b** crafted garments to be worn while
Jdg 5:30 and colorful, **b** embroidered robes for me.'
Est 1: 6 The courtyard was decorated with **b** woven white
Eze 16:10 clothing of linen and silk, **b** embroidered,
16:13 were made of fine linen and were **b** embroidered.
16:18 You used the **b** embroidered clothes I gave you to
23:41 You sat with them on a **b** embroidered couch
28:13 all **b** crafted for you and set in the finest gold.
Mt 6:29 yet Solomon in all his glory was not dressed as **b**
Lk 12:27 yet Solomon in all his glory was not dressed as **b**

BEAUTIFY (3) [BEAUTY]

Ezr 7:27 who made the king want to **b** the Temple of the
Ps 144:12 be like graceful pillars, / carved to **b** a palace.
Isa 60:13 of cypress, fir, and pine—to **b** my sanctuary.

BEAUTY (43) [BEAUTIFUL, BEAUTIFULLY, BEAUTIFY]

Ge 12:14 they arrived in Egypt, everyone spoke of her **b**.
2Sa 11: 2 he noticed a woman of unusual **b** taking a bath.
1Ch 16:27 surround him; / strength and **b** are in his dwelling.
Est 1:11 He wanted all the men to gaze on her **b**, for she
2: 3 will see that they are all given **b** treatments.
2: 9 menu for her and provided her with **b** treatments.
2:12 she was given the prescribed twelve months of **b**
2:13 or jewelry she wanted to enhance her **b**.
Ps 45:11 For your royal husband delights in your **b**;
50: 2 From Mount Zion, the perfection of **b**,
96: 6 surround him; / strength and **b** are in his sanctuary.
Pr 6:25 Don't lust for her **b**. Don't let her coyness seduce
31:30 Charm is deceptive, and **b** does not last; but a
SS 5: 9 "O woman of rare **b**, what is it about your loved
Isa 3:18 The Lord will strip away their artful **b**—
3:24 Their **b** will be gone. Only shame will be left to
28: 1 but its glorious **b** will suddenly disappear.
28: 4 but its glorious **b** will suddenly disappear.
40: 6 Their **b** fades as quickly as the **b** of flowers in
61: 3 he will give **b** for ashes, joy instead of mourning,
64:11 burned down, and all the things of **b** are destroyed.
Jer 12:10 and turning all its **b** into a barren wilderness.
La 1: 6 All the **b** and majesty of Jerusalem are gone.
Eze 16:14 spread throughout the world on account of your **b**,
16:14 the splendor I bestowed on you perfected your **b**,
16:15 so you trusted instead in your fame and **b**.
16:15 who came along. Your **b** was theirs for the asking!
16:25 On every street corner you defiled your **b**,
27: 3 You claimed, O Tyre, to be perfect in **b**.
28:12 You were the perfection of wisdom and **b**.
28:17 heart was filled with pride because of all your **b**.
31: 8 No tree in the garden of God came close to it in **b**.
Joel 2: 3 land lies as fair as the Garden of Eden in all its **b**.
Na 3: 4 of deadly charms, enticed the nations with her **b**.
1Co 15:40 bodies is different from the **b** of the earthly bodies.
15:41 And even the stars differ from each other in their **b**
Jas 1:11 the grass; the flower withers, and its **b** fades away.
1Pe 1:24 their **b** fades as quickly as the **b** of
3: 3 Don't be concerned about the outward **b** that
3: 4 You should be known for the **b** that comes from
3: 4 the unfading **b** of a gentle and quiet spirit, which is

BEBAI (6)

Ezr 2:11 The family of **B** | 623
8:11 From the family of **B**: Zechariah son of **B** and 28 other men.
10:28 From the family of **B**: Jehohanan, Hananiah,
Ne 7:16 The family of **B** | 628
10:15 Bunni, Azgad, **B**,

BECAME (405) [BECOME]

Ge 2: 7 it the breath of life. And the man **b** a living person.
4: 1 Adam slept with his wife, Eve, and she **b** pregnant.
4: 2 When they grew up, Abel **b** a shepherd, while Cain
4:17 Then Cain's wife **b** pregnant and gave birth to a
4:20 He **b** the first of the herdsmen who live in tents.
6: 4 they gave birth to children who **b** the heroes
9:20 the Flood, Noah **b** a farmer and planted a vineyard.
9:21 One day he **b** drunk on some wine he had made
10: 5 Their descendants **b** the seafaring peoples in
10: 8 descendants was Nimrod, who **b** a heroic warrior.
10: 9 His name **b** proverbial, and people would speak of
11:26 he **b** the father of Abram, Nahor, and Haran.
15:17 As the sun went down and it **b** dark, Abram saw a
16: 4 So Abram slept with Hagar, and she **b** pregnant.
19:15 At dawn the next morning the angels **b** insistent.
19:26 along behind him, and she **b** a pillar of salt.
19:36 So both of Lot's daughters **b** pregnant by their
19:37 He **b** the ancestor of the nation now known as the
19:38 He **b** the ancestor of the nation now known as the
21: 2 Sarah **b** pregnant, and she gave a son to Abraham
21:20 in the wilderness of Paran. He **b** an expert archer,
22:23 Bethuel **b** the father of Rebekah.
23:18 They **b** Abraham's permanent possession by the
24:67 Rebekah into his mother's tent, and she **b** his wife.
25:16 These twelve sons of Ishmael **b** the founders of
25:21 Isaac's prayer, and his wife **b** pregnant with twins.
25:27 As the boys grew up, Esau **b** a skillful hunter,
26:13 He **b** a rich man, and his wealth only continued to
26:14 Soon the Philistines **b** jealous of him,
29:32 So Leah **b** pregnant and had a son. She named him
29:33 She soon **b** pregnant again and had another son.
29:34 Again she **b** pregnant and had a son. She named
29:35 Once again she **b** pregnant and had a son.
30: 1 having any children, she **b** jealous of her sister.
30: 5 Bilhah **b** pregnant and presented him with a son.
30: 7 Then Bilhah **b** pregnant again and gave Jacob a
30:17 She **b** pregnant again and gave birth to her fifth
30:19 Then she **b** pregnant again and had a sixth son.
30:23 She **b** pregnant and gave birth to a son. "God has
30:43 and he **b** very wealthy, with many servants,
31:36 Then Jacob **b** very angry. "What did you find?"
36:15 and grandchildren **b** the leaders of different clans.
36:15 **b** the leaders of the clans of Teman, Omar, Zepho,
36:17 The sons of Esau's son Reuel **b** the leaders of the
36:18 and his wife Oholibamah **b** the leaders of the clans
36:33 Bela died, Jobab son of Zerah from Bozrah **b** king.
36:34 Husham from the land of the Temanites **b** king.
36:35 Hadad son of Bedad **b** king and ruled from the city
36:36 Samlah from the city of Masrekah **b** king.
36:37 city of Rehoboth on the Euphrates River **b** king.
36:38 When Shaul died, Baal-hanan son of Acbor **b** king.
36:39 Hadad **b** king and ruled from the city of Pau.
38: 3 She **b** pregnant and had a son, and Judah named
38:18 then let him sleep with her, and she **b** pregnant.
39: 4 So Joseph naturally **b** quite a favorite with him.
40: 2 Pharaoh **b** very angry with these officials,
41: 8 Pharaoh **b** very concerned as to what the dreams
47:13 Meanwhile, the famine **b** worse and worse,
47:21 all the people of Egypt **b** servants to Pharaoh.
50:15 their father was dead, Joseph's brothers **b** afraid.
Ex 1:12 The Egyptians soon **b** alarmed
2: 2 The woman **b** pregnant and gave birth to a son.
4: 3 So Moses threw it down, and it **b** a snake!
4: 4 and grabbed it, and it **b** a shepherd's staff again.
4:14 Then the LORD **b** angry with Moses.
6:14 Their descendants **b** the clans of Reuben.
6:15 Their descendants **b** the clans of Simeon.
6:24 Their descendants **b** the clans of Korah.
7:10 staff before Pharaoh and his court, and it **b** a snake.
7:12 Their staffs **b** snakes, too! But then Aaron's snake
7:21 and the water **b** so foul that the Egyptians couldn't
14:20 But the cloud **b** darkness to the Egyptians,
15: 8 a wall; / in the middle of the sea the waters **b** hard.
16:21 And as the sun **b** hot, the food they had not picked
16:31 In time, the food **b** known as manna. It was white
17:12 Moses' arms finally **b** too tired to hold up the staff
21: 3 If he was single when he **b** your slave and
21: 3 But if he was married before he **b** a slave, then his
Lev 10:16 a result, he **b** very angry with Eleazar and Ithamar,
Nu 11:10 tents weeping, and the LORD **b** extremely angry.
12:10 Miriam suddenly **b** white as snow with leprosy.
16:15 Then Moses **b** very angry and said to the LORD,
26:59 Amram and Jochebed **b** the parents of Aaron,
Dt 1:34 LORD heard your complaining, he **b** very angry.
10: 6 His son Eleazar **b** the high priest in his place.
26: 5 but in Egypt they **b** a mighty and numerous nation.
32:15 But Israel soon **b** fat and unruly; / the people grew
33: 5 The LORD **b** king in Israel—/ when the leaders
Jos 6:27 and his name **b** famous throughout the land.
8:28 So Ai **b** a permanent mound of ruins, desolate to
10: 2 and his people **b** very afraid when they heard all
15:17 one who conquered it, so Acsah **b** Othniel's wife.
17:13 however, when the Israelites **b** strong enough,
Jdg 1:13 one who conquered it, so Acsah **b** Othniel's wife.
1:35 but when the descendants of Joseph **b** stronger,
3:10 LORD came upon him, and he **b** Israel's judge.
3:25 after a long delay, they **b** concerned and got a key.
4:24 And from that time on Israel **b** stronger
8:27 and it **b** a trap for Gideon and his family.
11:11 and he **b** their ruler and commander of the army.
12: 8 After Jephthah, Ibzan **b** Israel's judge. He lived in
12:11 After him, Elon from Zebulun **b** Israel's judge.
12:13 son of Hillel, from Pirathon, **b** Israel's judge.
17:11 agreed to this and **b** like one of Micah's sons.
20:41 warriors realized disaster was near and **b** terrified.
Ru 4:17 He **b** the father of Jesse and the grandfather of
1Sa 2:11 And the boy **b** the LORD's helper, for he assisted
7: 6 So it was at Mizpah that Samuel **b** Israel's judge.
10:26 a band of men whose hearts God had touched **b** his
11: 6 came mightily upon Saul, and he **b** very angry.
13: 1 Saul was thirty years old when he **b** king, and he
16: 4 at Bethlehem, the leaders of the town **b** afraid.
16:21 and David **b** one of Saul's armor bearers.
18: 1 love between them, and they **b** the best of friends.
18:15 Saul recognized this, he **b** even more afraid of him.
18:29 he **b** even more afraid of him, and he remained
18:30 So David's name **b** very famous throughout the
25:42 with David's messengers. And so she **b** his wife.
28: 5 saw the vast Philistine army, he **b** frantic with fear.
2Sa 2:10 Ishbosheth was forty years old when he **b** king,
3: 1 As time passed David **b** stronger and stronger,
3: 1 while Saul's dynasty **b** weaker and weaker.
3: 6 Abner **b** a powerful leader among those who were
3: 8 Abner **b** furious. "Am I a Judean dog to be kicked
4: 4 as she was running, and he **b** crippled as a result.)
4: 6 had been sifting wheat, **b** drowsy and fell asleep.
5:10 And David **b** more and more powerful,
7:24 people forever, and you, O LORD, **b** their God.
8: 2 The Moabites who were spared **b** David's servants
8: 6 and the Arameans **b** David's subjects and brought
8:13 So David **b** very famous. After his return he
8:14 and all the Edomites **b** David's subjects.
10: 1 of the Ammonites died, and his son Hanun **b** king.
10:19 they surrendered to them and **b** their subjects.
11:27 her to the palace, and she **b** one of his wives.
12:24 She **b** pregnant and gave birth to a son, and they
13: 2 Amnon **b** so obsessed with Tamar that he **b** ill.
20:23 Joab once again **b** the commander of David's
21:15 in the thick of battle, David **b** weak and exhausted.
23:18 It was by such feats that he **b** as famous as the
1Ki 10:23 So King Solomon **b** richer and wiser than any
11:24 and his men fled to Damascus, where he **b** king.
11:43 David. Then his son Rehoboam **b** the next king.
12:25 in the hill country of Ephraim, and it **b** his capital.
12:30 This **b** a great sin, for the people worshiped them,
13: 4 But instantly the king's hand **b** paralyzed in that
13: 6 the LORD, and the king's hand **b** normal again.
13:34 This **b** a great sin and resulted in the destruction of
14: 1 At that time Jeroboam's son Abijah **b** very sick.
14:20 Jeroboam died, his son Nadab **b** the next king.
14:21 He was forty-one years old when he **b** king,
14:31 Then his son Abijam **b** the next king.
15: 8 City of David. Then his son Asa **b** the next king.
15:23 *Kings of Judah*. In his old age his feet **b** diseased.
15:24 Then his son Jehoshaphat **b** the next king.
15:28 reign in Judah, and he **b** the next king of Israel.
16: 6 in Tirzah. Then his son Elah **b** the next king.
16:10 Asa's reign in Judah. Then Zimri **b** the next king.
16:22 So Tibni was killed, and Omri **b** the next king.
16:28 in Samaria. Then his son Ahab **b** the next king.
17:17 Some time later, the woman's son **b** sick. He grew
22:40 Then his son Ahaziah **b** the next king.
22:42 He was thirty-five years old when he **b** king,
22:50 of David. Then his son Jehoram **b** the next king.
2Ki 1:17 to succeed him, his brother Joram **b** the next king.
4:17 But sure enough, the woman soon **b** pregnant.
5:11 But Naaman **b** angry and stalked away. "I thought
5:14 And his flesh **b** as healthy as a young child's,
6:11 The king of Aram **b** very upset over this. He called
8:11 at Hazael with a fixed gaze until Hazael **b** uneasy.
8:15 he died. Then Hazael **b** the next king of Aram.
8:17 Jehoram was thirty-two years old when he **b** king,
8:24 of David. Then his son Ahaziah **b** the next king.
8:26 Ahaziah was twenty-two years old when he **b** king,
10:35 in Samaria. Then his son Jehoahaz **b** the next king.
11:21 Joash was seven years old when he **b** king.
12:10 Whenever the chest **b** full, the court secretary
12:21 of David. Then his son Amaziah **b** the next king.
13: 9 Then his son Jehoash **b** the next king.
13:13 Then his son Jeroboam II **b** the next king.
13:24 Aram died, and his son Ben-hadad **b** the next king.
14: 2 Amaziah was twenty-five years old when he **b**
14:16 Then his son Jeroboam II **b** the next king.
14:29 of Israel. Then his son Zechariah **b** the next king.
15: 2 He was sixteen years old when he **b** king, and he
15: 7 of David. Then his son Jotham **b** the next king.
15:10 assassinated him in public, and **b** the next king.
15:14 and assassinated him, and he **b** the next king.
15:22 Menahem died, his son Pekahiah **b** the next king.
15:25 at Samaria. Pekah then **b** the next king of Israel.
15:33 He was twenty-five years old when he **b** king,
15:38 City of David. Then his son Ahaz **b** the next king.
16: 2 Ahaz was twenty years old when he **b** king, and he
16:20 of David. Then his son Hezekiah **b** the next king.
17:15 worthless idols and **b** worthless themselves.
18: 2 He was twenty-five years old when he **b** king,
19:37 Esarhaddon, **b** the next king of Assyria.
20: 1 About that time Hezekiah **b** deathly ill,
20:21 Hezekiah died, his son Manasseh **b** the next king.
21: 1 Manasseh was twelve years old when he **b** king,
21:18 of Uzza. Then his son Amon **b** the next king.
21:19 Amon was twenty-two years old when he **b** king,
21:26 of Uzza. Then his son Josiah **b** the next king.
22: 1 Josiah was eight years old when he **b** king, and he
23:31 Jehoahaz was twenty-three years old when he **b**
23:36 Jehoiakim was twenty-five years old when he **b**
24: 6 Jehoiakim died, his son Jehoiachin **b** the next king.
24: 8 Jehoiachin was eighteen years old when he **b** king,
24:18 Zedekiah was twenty-one years old when he **b**
1Ch 1:44 Bela died, Jobab son of Zerah from Bozrah **b** king.
1:45 Husham from the land of the Temanites **b** king.
1:46 Hadad son of Bedad **b** king and ruled from the city
1:47 Samlah from the city of Masrekah **b** king.
1:48 city of Rehoboth on the Euphrates River **b** king.
1:49 When Shaul died, Baal-hanan son of Acbor **b** king.
1:50 Hadad **b** king and ruled from the city of Pau.
4: 8 and Koz, who **b** the ancestor of Anub, Zobebah,

4:17 who **b** the mother of Miriam, Shammai,
4:18 who **b** the mother of Jered (the father of Gedor),
4:27 So Simeon's tribe never **b** as large as the tribe of
5:2 It was the descendants of Judah that **b** the most
7:3 and Isshiah. These five **b** the leaders of clans.
7:23 and she **b** pregnant and gave birth to a son.
8:10 and Mirmah. These sons all **b** the leaders of clans.
11:6 so he **b** the commander of David's armies.
11:9 And David **b** more and more powerful,
11:20 It was by such feats that he **b** as famous as the
12:18 who later **b** a leader among the Thirty, and he said,
12:21 and able warriors who **b** commanders in his army.
18:2 and the Moabites **b** David's subjects and brought
18:6 and the Arameans **b** David's subjects and brought
18:13 and all the Edomites **b** David's subjects.
19:1 of the Ammonites died, and his son Hanun **b** king.
19:19 they surrendered to David and **b** his subjects.
2Ch 9:22 So King Solomon **b** richer and wiser than any
9:31 David. Then his son Rehoboam **b** the next king.
11:10 These **b** the fortified cities of Judah and Benjamin.
12:13 He was forty-one years old when he **b** king,
12:16 of David. Then his son Abijah **b** the next king.
13:6 of David's son Solomon, **b** a traitor to his master.
14:1 City of David. Then his son Asa **b** the next king.
16:10 Asa **b** so angry with Hanani for saying this that he
16:12 Even when the disease **b** life threatening, he did
17:1 Then Jehoshaphat, Asa's son, **b** the next king.
17:5 so he **b** very wealthy and highly esteemed.
17:12 So Jehoshaphat **b** more and more powerful
20:31 He was thirty-five years old when he **b** king,
21:1 of David. Then his son Jehoram **b** the next king.
21:3 Jehoram **b** king because he was the oldest.
21:5 Jehoram was thirty-two years old when he **b** king,
21:20 Jehoram was thirty-two years old when he **b** king,
22:2 Ahaziah was twenty-two years old when he **b** king,
22:4 members of Ahab's family **b** his advisers, and they
24:1 Joash was seven years old when he **b** king, and he
24:11 Whenever the chest **b** full, the Levites carried it to
24:27 When Joash died, his son Amaziah **b** the next king.
25:1 Amaziah was twenty-five years old when he **b**
26:3 Uzziah was sixteen when he **b** king, and he reigned
26:15 for the LORD helped him wonderfully until he **b**
26:16 he also **b** proud, which led to his downfall.
26:23 to the kings. Then his son Jotham **b** the next king.
27:1 Jotham was twenty-five years old when he **b** king,
27:6 King Jotham **b** powerful because he was careful to
27:8 He was twenty-five years old when he **b** king,
27:9 City of David, and his son Ahaz **b** the next king.
28:1 Ahaz was twenty years old when he **b** king, and he
28:22 he **b** even more unfaithful to the LORD.
28:27 Then his son Hezekiah **b** the next king.
29:1 Hezekiah was twenty-five years old when he **b** the
30:7 and **b** an object of derision, as you yourselves can
30:15 Then the priests and Levites **b** ashamed, so they
32:23 then on King Hezekiah **b** highly respected among
32:24 About that time, Hezekiah **b** deathly ill. He prayed
32:25 to the kindness shown him, and he **b** proud.
32:33 his death. Then his son Manasseh **b** the next king.
33:1 Manasseh was twelve years old when he **b** king,
33:20 at his palace. Then his son Amon **b** the next king.
33:21 Amon was twenty-two years old when he **b** king,
34:1 Josiah was eight years old when he **b** king, and he
36:2 Jehoahaz was twenty-three years old when he **b**
36:5 Jehoiakim was twenty-five years old when he **b**
36:8 *and Judah.* Then his son Jehoiachin **b** the next
36:9 Jehoiachin was eighteen years old when he **b** king,
36:11 Zedekiah was twenty-one years old when he **b**
36:14 and the people **b** more and more unfaithful.
36:20 and they **b** servants to the king and his sons until
Ne 4:7 in the wall were being repaired, they **b** furious.
9:29 but they **b** proud and obstinate and disobeyed your
13:8 I **b** very upset and threw all of Tobiah's belongings
Est 2:21 **b** angry at King Xerxes and plotted to assassinate
8:17 And many of the people of the land **b** Jews
9:4 spread throughout all the provinces as he **b** more
9:27 it on to their descendants and to all who **b** Jews.
10:3 Mordecai the Jew **b** the prime minister,
Job 32:2 of Barakel the Buzite, of the clan of Ram, **b** angry.
Ps 105:21 he **b** ruler over all the king's possessions.
105:24 of Israel / until they **b** too mighty for their enemies.
114:2 the land of Judah **b** God's sanctuary, / and Israel **b** his kingdom.
Ecc 2:9 So I **b** greater than any of the kings who ruled in
Isa 8:3 with my wife, and she **b** pregnant and had a son.
37:38 Esarhaddon, **b** the next king of Assyria.
38:1 About that time Hezekiah **b** deathly ill,
51:2 But when I blessed him, he **b** a great nation."
63:8 will not be false again." And he **b** their Savior.
63:10 That is why he **b** their enemy and fought against
Jer 52:1 Zedekiah was twenty-one years old when he **b**
Eze 16:7 You grew up and **b** a beautiful jewel. Your breasts **b** full, and your hair grew,
16:8 says the Sovereign LORD, and you **b** mine.
16:13 and olive oil—and **b** more beautiful than ever.
19:3 to catch and devour prey, / and he **b** a man-eater.
19:6 and **b** a leader among them. / He learned to catch
19:6 and devour prey, / and he, too, **b** a man-eater.
19:11 Its branches **b** very strong, / strong enough to be a
19:11 It soon **b** very tall, / towering above all the others.
23:3 They **b** prostitutes in Egypt. Even as young girls,
23:17 she **b** disgusted with them and broke off their
23:18 "So I **b** disgusted with Oholibah, just as I was with
31:8 This tree **b** taller than any of the other cedars in the
31:10 Because it **b** proud and arrogant, and because it set
Da 2:35 But the rock that knocked the statue down **b** a
3:19 and Abednego that his face **b** distorted with rage.
8:4 its victims. It did as it pleased and **b** very great.
8:8 The goat **b** very powerful. But at the height of its
8:17 I **b** so terrified that I fell to the ground.
9:1 son of Ahasuerus, who **b** king of the Babylonians.
Hos 1:3 and she **b** pregnant and gave Hosea a son.
1:6 Soon Gomer **b** pregnant again and gave birth to a
1:8 she again **b** pregnant and gave birth to a second
2:5 and **b** pregnant in a shameful way.
8:11 away sin, but these very altars **b** places for sinning!
9:10 Soon they **b** as vile as the god they worshiped.
12:3 when he **b** a man, he even fought with God.
13:6 were satisfied, then you **b** proud and forgot me.
Jnh 4:1 change of plans upset Jonah, and he **b** very angry.
Zec 7:14 Their land **b** so desolate that no one even traveled
7:14 The land that had been so pleasant **b** a desert."
11:8 But I **b** impatient with these sheep—this nation—
Mt 1:18 still a virgin, she **b** pregnant by the Holy Spirit.
4:2 and forty nights he ate nothing and **b** very hungry.
12:13 his hand, and it **b** normal, just like the other one.
17:2 like the sun, and his clothing **b** dazzling white.
22:7 "Then the king **b** furious. He sent out his army to
Mk 3:5 man reached out his hand, and it **b** normal again!
9:3 and his clothing **b** dazzling white, far whiter than
Lk 1:24 **b** pregnant and went into seclusion for five
1:80 John grew up and **b** strong in spirit. Then he lived
4:14 Soon he **b** well known throughout the surrounding
6:10 man reached out his hand, and it **b** normal again!
9:29 face changed, and his clothing **b** dazzling white.
15:16 The boy **b** so hungry that even the pods he was
18:23 man heard this, he **b** sad because he was very rich.
23:5 Then they **b** desperate. "But he is causing riots
23:12 who had been enemies before, **b** friends that day.
Jn 1:14 So the Word **b** human and lived here on earth
Ac 1:26 was chosen and **b** an apostle with the other eleven.
6:15 because his face **b** as bright as an angel's.
7:8 Isaac **b** the father of Jacob, and Jacob was the
7:22 and he **b** mighty in both speech and action.
9:22 Saul's preaching **b** more and more powerful,
9:37 About this time she **b** ill and died. Her friends
13:48 and all who were appointed to eternal life **b**
17:4 Some of those who listened were persuaded and **b** converts,
17:34 but some joined him and **b** believers. Among them
18:2 There he **b** acquainted with a Jew named Aquila,
18:8 Many others in Corinth also **b** believers and were
18:12 But when Gallio **b** governor of Achaia, some Jews
19:18 Many who **b** believers confessed their sinful
20:9 sitting on the windowsill, **b** very drowsy.
22:3 I **b** very zealous to honor God in everything I did,
Ro 1:21 The result was that their minds **b** dark
1:22 Claiming to be wise, they **b** utter fools instead.
1:29 Their lives **b** full of every kind of wickedness,
5:19 one person disobeyed God, many people **b** sinners.
5:20 God's wonderful kindness **b** more abundant.
6:3 Or have you forgotten that when we **b** Christians
16:7 among the apostles and **b** Christians before I did.
1Co 4:15 For I **b** your father in Christ Jesus when I preached
7:18 a man who was circumcised before he **b** a believer
7:18 And the man who was uncircumcised when he **b** a
7:24 whatever situation you were in when you **b** a
15:45 tell us, "The first man, Adam, **b** a living person."
2Co 8:9 he was very rich, yet for your sakes he **b** poor,
10:6 remained disobedient after the rest of you **b** loyal
Gal 4:24 represents Mount Sinai where people first **b**
1Th 1:7 you yourselves **b** an example to all the Christians
Tit 3:3 and **b** slaves to many wicked desires and evil
Phm 1:10 because he **b** a believer as a result of my ministry
Heb 2:14 Jesus also **b** flesh and blood by being born in
5:9 and he **b** the source of eternal salvation for all
7:16 He **b** a priest, not by meeting the old requirement
11:34 They **b** strong in battle and put whole armies to
Jas 1:18 out of all creation, **b** his choice possession.
1Jn 4:2 If a prophet acknowledges that Jesus Christ **b** a
Rev 6:12 The sun **b** as dark as black cloth, and the moon **b** as red as blood.
7:1 in the trees, and the sea **b** as smooth as glass.
8:8 And one-third of the water in the sea **b** blood.
8:12 and one-third of the stars, and they **b** dark.
12:17 Then the dragon **b** angry at the woman, and he
16:3 bowl on the sea, and it **b** like the blood of a corpse.
16:4 bowl on the rivers and springs, and they **b** blood.
18:15 The merchants who **b** wealthy by selling her these

BECAUSE (1291) See Index of Articles, Etc.

BECHORATH [KJV] See BECORATH

BECOME (377) [BECAME, BECOMES, BECOMING]

Ge 3:5 You will **b** just like God, knowing everything,
3:22 "The people have **b** as we are,
6:11 Now the earth had **b** corrupt in God's sight, and it
12:2 I will cause you to **b** the father of a great nation.
17:16 and she will **b** the mother of many nations.
17:17 "How could I **b** a father at the age of one
17:20 I will cause him to multiply and **b** a great nation.
18:18 "For Abraham will **b** a great and mighty nation,
22:14 This name has now **b** a proverb: "On the mountain
24:35 has blessed my master richly; he has **b** a great man.
24:60 "Our sister, may you **b** / the mother of many
25:23 "The sons in your womb will **b** two rival nations.
26:4 I will cause your descendants to **b** as numerous as
26:16 "for you have **b** too rich and powerful for us."
26:24 many descendants, and they will **b** a great nation.
27:29 May many nations **b** your servants. May you be
28:3 And may your descendants **b** a great assembly of
28:22 This memorial pillar will **b** a place for worshiping
32:12 and to multiply my descendants until they **b** as
34:16 and live here and unite with you to **b** one people.
34:23 do this, all their flocks and possessions will **b** ours.
35:11 fill the earth! **B** a great nation, even many nations.
42:9 have come to see how vulnerable our land has **b**."
45:7 families alive so that you will **b** a great nation.
46:3 for I will see to it that you **b** a great nation there.
47:19 for food; we will then **b** servants to Pharaoh.
47:19 and so the land will not **b** empty and desolate."
48:16 Isaac. And may they **b** a mighty nation."
48:19 "Manasseh, too, will **b** a great people, but his younger brother will **b** even greater.
48:19 His descendants will **b** a multitude of nations!"
Ex 6:9 They had **b** too discouraged by the increasing
7:9 your shepherd's staff,' and it will **b** a snake."
15:2 is my strength and my song; / he has **b** my victory.
22:24 Your wives will **b** widows, and your children will **b** fatherless.
23:29 in one year because the land would **b** a wilderness,
23:29 and the wild animals would **b** too many to control.
26:11 In this way, the two sets will **b** a single unit.
29:37 and whatever touches it will **b** holy.
30:29 After this, whatever touches them will **b** holy.
40:10 sanctifying them. Then the altar will **b** most holy.
Lev 4:28 When they **b** aware of their sin, they must bring as
5:3 they will be considered guilty as soon as they **b**
5:5 "When any of the people **b** aware of their guilt in
5:17 held responsible. When they **b** aware of their guilt,
6:18 or anything that touches this food will **b** holy."
6:27 or anyone who touches the sacrificial meat will **b**
11:35 It has **b** defiled, and it will remain that way.
18:25 As a result, the entire land has **b** defiled. That is
18:27 where I am taking you, and the land has **b** defiled.
19:20 girl who is committed to **b** someone else's wife,
22:4 If any of the priests **b** unclean by touching a
24:12 the LORD's will in the matter should **b** clear.
25:30 then the house within the walled city will **b** the
26:33 Your land will **b** desolate, and your cities will lie
27:21 the LORD. It will **b** the property of the priests.
Nu 5:27 She will **b** infertile, and her name will **b** a curse word among her
9:7 "We have **b** ceremonially unclean by touching a
16:38 for these burners have **b** holy because they were
19:20 "But those who **b** defiled and do not purify
30:5 then all her vows and pledges will **b** invalid.
Dt 4:20 the burning furnace of Egypt to **b** his own people
7:25 Do not take it or it will **b** a snare to you, for it is
8:12 For when you have **b** full and prosperous and have
8:13 and herds have **b** very large and your silver
8:14 Do not **b** proud at that time and forget the LORD
8:18 LORD your God who gives you power to **b** rich,
9:12 because the people you led out of Egypt have **b**
20:7 Has anyone just **b** engaged? Well, go home and get
23:17 or woman may ever **b** a temple prostitute.
27:9 Today you have **b** the people of the LORD your
28:37 You will **b** an object of horror, a proverb and a
28:43 The foreigners living among you will **b** stronger and stronger, while you **b** weaker and weaker.
30:16 If you do this, you will live and **b** a great nation,
31:20 There they will **b** prosperous; they will eat all the food they want and **b** well nourished.
31:29 I know that after my death you will **b** utterly
Jos 14:4 The tribe of Joseph had **b** two separate tribes—
Jdg 4:4 was a prophet who had **b** a judge in Israel.
10:18 "Whoever attacks the Ammonites first will **b** ruler
11:39 she died a virgin. So it has **b** a custom in Israel
13:2 His wife was unable to **b** pregnant, and they had no
13:3 you will soon **b** pregnant and give birth to a son.
13:5 You will **b** pregnant and give birth to a son,
13:7 'You will **b** pregnant and give birth to a son.
16:17 leave me, and I would **b** as weak as anyone else."
Ru 4:13 with her, the LORD enabled her to **b** pregnant,
1Sa 2:29 and they have **b** fat from the best offerings of my
4:9 we will **b** the Hebrews' slaves just as they have
10:11 a prophet? How did the son of Kish **b** a prophet?"
10:12 matter who his father is; anyone can **b** a prophet."
18:21 "I have a way for you to **b** my son-in-law after
18:22 you accept the king's offer and **b** his son-in-law?"
25:39 messengers to Abigail to ask her to **b** his wife.
25:41 I am even willing to **b** a slave to David's
28:16 if the LORD has left you and has **b** your enemy?
2Sa 16:2 you into the wilderness for those who **b** faint."
1Ki 1:7 his confidence, and they agreed to help him **b** king.
1:13 your throne? Then why has Adonijah **b** king?'
1:18 But instead, Adonijah has **b** the new king, and you
1:20 for your decision as to who will **b** king after you.
8:20 for I have **b** king in my father's place.
8:46 you may **b** angry with them and let their enemies
9:8 it will **b** an appalling sight for all who pass by.
11:24 and had **b** the leader of a gang of rebels.
13:33 Anyone who wanted to could **b** a priest for the
14:2 at Shiloh—the man who told me I would **b** king.
18:2 the famine had **b** very severe in Samaria.
2Ki 2:9 "Please let me **b** your rightful successor."
2:15 they exclaimed, "Elisha has **b** Elijah's successor!"
18:27 The people will **b** so hungry and thirsty that they
20:18 They will **b** eunuchs who will serve in the palace
22:19 that this land would be cursed and **b** desolate.
25:3 the famine in the city had **b** very severe,
1Ch 11:6 Jebusites will **b** the commander of my armies!"
12:23 They were all eager to see David **b** king instead of
12:31 for the express purpose of helping David **b** king.
17:22 and you, O LORD, have **b** their God.
2Ch 6:10 for I have **b** king in my father's place.
6:36 you may **b** angry with them and let their enemies
7:21 it will **b** an appalling sight to all who pass by.
8:1 It was now twenty years since Solomon had **b**
12:8 But they will **b** his subjects, so that they can learn

13: 9 You let anyone **b** a priest these days!
13: 9 and seven rams can **b** a priest of these so-called
21: 4 But when Jehoram had **b** solidly established as
26: 8 spread even to Egypt, for he had **b** very powerful.
26:16 But when he had **b** powerful, he also became
35:25 These songs of sorrow have **b** a tradition and are
Ezr 9: 2 So the holy race has **b** polluted by these mixed
9:12 these things, we would **b** a prosperous nation.
Ne 4: 4 and may they themselves **b** captives in a foreign
9:17 gracious and merciful, slow to **b** angry, and full of
Est 2:19 and Mordecai had **b** a palace official,
Job 11:12 An empty-headed person won't **b** wise any more
17: 9 and those with pure hearts will **b** stronger
30:19 me into the mud. I have **b** as dust and ashes.
30:21 You have **b** cruel toward me. You persecute me
31:29 to ruin or **b** excited when harm came their way?
33:25 Then his body will **b** as healthy as a child's,
Ps 2: 7 'You are my son. / Today I have **b** your Father.
2:12 Submit to God's royal son, or he will **b** angry,
14: 3 have turned away from God; / all have **b** corrupt.
45:16 Your sons will **b** kings like their father. / You will
49:16 grow rich, / and their homes **b** ever more splendid.
53: 3 have turned away from God; / all have **b** corrupt.
60: 8 Moab will **b** my lowly servant, / and Edom will be
63:10 will die by the sword / and **b** the food of jackals.
69:22 Let the bountiful table set before them **b** a snare, / and let their security **b** a trap.
69:25 May their homes **b** desolate / and their tents be
73:21 Then I realized how bitter I had **b**, / how pained I
79: 2 your godly ones / has **b** food for the wild animals.
84: 6 it will **b** a place of refreshing springs,
87: 4 They have all **b** citizens of Jerusalem!
87: 5 of Jerusalem, / "Everyone has **b** a citizen here."
87: 6 will say, "This one has **b** a citizen of Jerusalem."
107:39 When they decrease in number and **b** impoverished
108: 9 Moab will **b** my lowly servant, / and Edom will be
109: 9 May his children **b** fatherless, / and may his wife **b** a widow.
109:20 May those curses **b** the LORD's punishment for
118:14 is my strength and my song; / he has **b** my victory.
118:22 by the builders / has now **b** the cornerstone.
139:11 to hide me / and the light around me to **b** night—
Pr 1: 5 are wise listen to these proverbs and **b** even wiser.
9:12 If you **b** wise, you will be the one to benefit.
11:24 It is possible to give freely and **b** more wealthy,
12:24 Work hard and **b** a leader; be lazy and **b** a slave.
13:20 Whoever walks with the wise will **b** wise;
17:18 to **b** responsible for a neighbor's debts.
21:17 Those who love pleasure **b** poor; wine and luxury
23:15 My child, how I will rejoice if you **b** wise.
26: 4 or you will **b** as foolish as they are.
26: 5 or they will **b** wise in their own estimation.
29:21 is pampered from childhood will later **b** a rebel.
Ecc 4:14 He might even **b** king, though he was born in
4:16 He might **b** the leader of millions and be very
12:12 them can go on forever and **b** very exhausting!
Isa 1:21 how Jerusalem, once so faithful, has **b** a prostitute.
1:22 like pure silver, you have **b** like worthless slag.
2: 2 the Temple of the LORD in Jerusalem will **b** the
7:23 pieces of silver, will **b** patches of briers and thorns.
12: 2 and my song; / he has **b** my salvation."
14: 1 join them there and **b** a part of the people of Israel.
17: 1 Damascus will disappear! It will **b** a heap of ruins.
17: 9 They will **b** like the cities the Amorites abandoned
19: 6 and the streams of Egypt will **b** foul with rotting
29: 2 For Jerusalem will **b** as her name Ariel means—
29:17 And the fertile fields will **b** a lush and fertile
32:15 Then the wilderness will **b** a fertile field,
32:15 and the fertile field will **b** a lush and fertile forest.
34:13 The ruins will **b** a haunt for jackals and a home for
35: 2 The deserts will **b** as green as the mountains of
35: 7 The parched ground will **b** a pool, and springs of
36:12 The people will **b** so hungry and thirsty that they
39: 7 They will **b** eunuchs who will serve in the palace
40:30 Even youths will **b** exhausted, and young men will
48:19 Then you would have **b** as numerous as the sands
51: 3 Her barren wilderness will **b** as beautiful as Eden
51: 4 and my justice will **b** a light to the nations.
60:22 The tiniest group will **b** a mighty nation. I,
Jer 2: 5 foolish idols, only to **b** foolish themselves.
2:14 "Why has Israel **b** a nation of slaves? Why has she
4:26 I looked, and the fertile fields had **b** a wilderness.
10:22 will be destroyed and will **b** a haunt for jackals.
12: 9 My chosen people have **b** as disgusting to me as a
13:10 Therefore, they will **b** like this linen belt—good for
17:11 at the end of their lives, will **b** poor old fools.
18:16 Therefore, their land will **b** desolate, a monument
18:21 Let their wives **b** widows without any children!
19:12 I will cause this city to **b** defiled like Topheth.
19:13 the palace of Judah's kings, will **b** like Topheth—
22: 5 that this palace will **b** a pile of rubble.' "
25:11 This entire land will **b** a desolate wasteland.
29:22 Their terrible fate will **b** proverbial, so that
42:18 You will **b** an object of damnation, horror, cursing,
46:21 Egypt's famed mercenaries have **b** like fattened
48:39 She has **b** an object of ridicule, an example of ruin
49: 2 It will **b** a desolate heap, and the neighboring
49:13 "that Bozrah will **b** an object of horror and a heap
49:24 Damascus has **b** feeble, and all her people turn to
50:12 You will **b** the least of nations—a wilderness,
50:13 Babylon will **b** a deserted wasteland.
50:36 it strikes her wise counselors, they will **b** fools!
50:37 her allies from other lands will **b** as weak as
51:30 courage is gone. They have **b** as fearful as women.
51:37 and Babylon will **b** a pile of rubble, haunted by
52: 6 the famine in the city had **b** very severe,
La 1: 5 Her oppressors have **b** her masters, and her
4: 1 has lost its luster! Even the finest gold has **b** dull.
5: 8 Slaves have now **b** our masters; there is no one left
Eze 5:15 You will **b** an object of mockery and taunting
5:16 The famine will **b** more and more severe until
17:14 so Israel would not **b** strong again and revolt.
17:23 It will **b** a noble cedar, sending forth its branches
19: 3 to **b** a strong young lion. / He learned to catch
21: 7 strong knees will tremble and **b** as weak as water.
22:24 you will **b** like an uncleared wilderness or a desert
26: 2 Because she has been destroyed, I will **b** wealthy!'
26: 5 The island of Tyre will **b** uninhabited. It will be a
26: 5 Tyre will **b** the prey of many nations,
29: 9 The land of Egypt will **b** a desolate wasteland,
32: 8 Even the brightest stars will **b** dark above you.
32:14 Then I will let the waters of Egypt **b** calm again,
37: 3 of man, can these bones **b** living people again?"
37:11 They are saying, 'We have **b** old, dry bones—
Da 1:10 "If you **b** pale and thin compared to the other
5: 7 He will **b** the third highest ruler in the kingdom!"
5:16 You will **b** the third highest ruler in the kingdom."
8:24 He will **b** very strong, but not by his own power.
11: 5 but one of this king's own officials will **b** more
11:23 With a mere handful of followers, he will **b** strong.
Hos 1:10 come when Israel will prosper and **b** a great nation.
5: 9 of punishment comes, you will **b** a heap of rubble.
5:10 "The leaders of Judah have **b** as bad as thieves.
7: 8 Now they have **b** as worthless as a half-baked
7: 9 unaware of how weak and old he has **b**.
7:11 "The people of Israel have **b** like silly,
9:13 I have watched Israel **b** as beautiful and pleasant as
Joel 2:17 to you, so don't let them **b** an object of mockery.
2:17 Don't let their name **b** a proverb of unbelieving
3:19 Egypt will **b** a wasteland and Edom a wilderness,
Am 2:14 get away. The strongest among you will **b** weak.
7:17 your wife will **b** a prostitute in this city, and your
7:17 And the people of Israel will certainly **b** captives in
Ob 1:17 "But Jerusalem will **b** a refuge for those who
Jnh 1:12 the sea," Jonah said, "and it will **b** calm again.
Mic 4: 1 the Temple of the LORD in Jerusalem will **b** the
6:12 The rich among you have **b** wealthy through
7:13 But the land will **b** empty and desolate because of
Hab 1: 4 The law has **b** paralyzed and useless, and there is
Zep 2: 6 The coastal area will **b** a pasture, a place of
2: 9 Their land will **b** a place of stinging nettles,
2:14 so proud will **b** a pasture for sheep and cattle.
2:15 But now, look how it has **b** an utter ruin, a place
Hag 2:12 or any other kind of food, will it also **b** holy?"
Zec 8:13 and Israel had **b** symbols of what it means to be
8:19 They will **b** festivals of joy and celebration for the
10: 7 The people of Israel will **b** like mighty warriors,
10:11 And the waters of the Nile will **b** dry. The pride of
11:17 His arm will **b** useless, and his right eye
14:10 south of Jerusalem, will **b** one vast plain.
14:12 Their people will **b** like walking corpses,
Mt 6:20 where they will never **b** moth-eaten or rusty
13:52 "Every teacher of religious law who has **b** a
18: 3 you turn from your sins and **b** as little children,
20:27 and whoever wants to be first must **b** your slave.
21:42 has now **b** the cornerstone. / This is the Lord's
23:26 of the cup, and then the outside will **b** clean, too.
23:35 you will **b** guilty of murdering all the godly people
24:32 When its buds **b** tender and its leaves begin to
Mk 4:32 it grows to **b** one of the largest of plants, with long
9:18 foam at the mouth and grind his teeth and **b** rigid.
12:10 by the builders / has now **b** the cornerstone.
13:28 When its buds **b** tender and its leaves begin to
Lk 1:31 You will **b** pregnant and have a son, and you are to
1:36 your relative Elizabeth has **b** pregnant in her old
6:40 But the student who works hard will **b** like the
14:33 So no one can **b** my disciple without giving up
19: 2 tax-collecting business, and he had **b** very rich.
20:17 by the builders / has now **b** the cornerstone.'
Jn 1:12 he gave the right to **b** children of God.
3:30 He must **b** greater and greater, and I must **b** less and less.
4:13 "People soon **b** thirsty again after drinking this
7: 4 "You can't **b** a public figure if you hide like this!
9:27 it again? Do you want to **b** his disciples, too?"
12:36 is still time; then you will **b** children of the light."
Ac 1:20 where it says, 'Let his home **b** desolate, with no
4:11 you builders rejected / has now **b** the cornerstone.'
6: 5 to the Jewish faith, who had now **b** a Christian).
7:40 for we don't know what has **b** of this Moses,
13:33 'You are my Son. / Today I have **b** your Father.'
22:24 He wanted to find out why the crowd had **b**
26:29 and everyone here in this audience might **b** the
Ro 4:18 When God promised Abraham that he would **b** the
6: 3 and were baptized to **b** one with Christ Jesus,
6:13 Do not let any part of your body **b** a tool of
6:18 and you have **b** slaves to your new master,
6:19 be slaves of righteousness so that you will **b** holy.
6:22 from the power of sin and have **b** slaves of God.
8:29 in advance, and he chose them to **b** like his Son,
11: 9 when he said, / "Let their bountiful table **b** a snare,
16: 5 He was the very first person to **b** a Christian in the
1Co 3:18 you will have to **b** a fool so you can **b** wise by God's standards.
4: 8 are already rich! Without us you have **b** kings!
4: 9 We have **b** a spectacle to the entire world—
4:18 I know that some of you have **b** arrogant,
6:12 to do anything," I must not **b** a slave to anything.
9:19 yet I have **b** a servant of everyone so that I can
9:20 I **b** one of them so that I can bring them to Christ.
15:20 He has **b** the first of a great harvest of those who
16:15 and his household were the first to **b** Christians in
2Co 2: 7 Otherwise he may **b** so discouraged that he won't
3:18 we **b** more and more like him and reflect his glory
5:17 that those who **b** Christians **b** new persons.
12:13 do in the other churches, was to **b** a burden to you.
Gal 2:16 And yet we Jewish Christians know that we **b** right
3: 3 why are you now trying to **b** perfect by your own
4: 6 And because you Gentiles have **b** his children,
4: 9 go back again and **b** slaves once more to the weak
4:12 these things, for I have **b** like you Gentiles were—
4:16 Have I now **b** your enemy because I am telling you
5:26 Let us not **b** conceited, or irritate one another,
Php 1:14 and **b** more bold in telling others about Christ.
3: 9 and **b** one with him. I no longer count on my own
Col 3:21 If you do, they will **b** discouraged and quit trying.
1Ti 5:13 they are likely to **b** lazy and spend their time
2Ti 2: 4 do not let yourself **b** tied up in the affairs of this
Heb 1: 5 "You are my Son. / Today I have **b** your Father."
5: 4 And no one can **b** a high priest simply because he
5: 5 That is why Christ did not exalt himself to **b** High
5: 5 "You are my Son. / Today I have **b** your Father."
6: 1 go on instead and **b** mature in our understanding.
6:12 Then you will not **b** spiritually dull and indifferent.
6:20 He has **b** our eternal High Priest in the line of
9:11 So Christ has now **b** the High Priest over all the
12: 3 to him, so that you don't **b** weary and give up.
12:13 will not stumble and fall but will **b** strong.
Jas 3: 1 not many of you should **b** teachers in the church,
5: 3 Your gold and silver have **b** worthless. The very
1Pe 2: 7 by the builders / has now **b** the cornerstone."
2Pe 1: 8 the more you will **b** productive and useful in your
2:20 then get tangled up with sin and **b** its slave again,
1Jn 5:18 We know that those who have **b** part of God's
3Jn 1: 8 so that we may **b** partners with them for the truth.
Rev 3:12 All who are victorious will **b** pillars in the Temple
5:10 And you have caused them to **b** God's kingdom
11:15 "The whole world has now **b** the kingdom of our
18: 2 She has **b** the hideout of demons and evil spirits,

BECOMES (34) [BECOME]

Ge 37:20 Then we'll see what **b** of all his dreams!"
Lev 4:23 When he **b** aware of his sin, he must bring as his
12: 2 When a woman **b** pregnant and gives birth to a
13:40 "If a man loses his hair and his head **b** bald,
21: 9 If a priest's daughter **b** a prostitute, defiling her
22:13 But if she **b** a widow or is divorced and has no
25:47 "If a resident foreigner **b** rich, and if some of your
Nu 5:14 If her husband **b** jealous and suspicious of his wife,
Dt 15:12 Israelite man or woman voluntarily **b** your servant
23:10 "Any man who **b** ceremonially defiled because of
Job 11:20 They have no escape. Their hope **b** despair."
12:15 If he holds back the rain, the earth **b** a desert.
Ps 65:12 The wilderness **b** a lush pasture, / and the hillsides
104:20 You send the darkness, and it **b** night, / when all
113: 9 woman a home, / so that she **b** a happy mother.
Pr 24: 3 built by wisdom and **b** strong through good sense.
26: 7 of a fool, a proverb **b** as limp as a paralyzed leg.
30:22 a slave who **b** a king, / an overbearing fool who
Ecc 2:26 But if a sinner **b** wealthy, God takes the wealth
Isa 41:24 Anyone who chooses you **b** filthy, just like you!
Eze 12:24 "Then you will see what **b** of all the false visions
Da 11: 7 But when one of her relatives **b** king of the south,
Hag 2:13 "But if someone **b** ceremonially unclean by
Zec 10: 1 showers of rain so that every field **b** a lush pasture.
Mt 13:32 but it **b** the largest of garden plants and grows into
18: 4 anyone who **b** as humble as this little child is the
Lk 13:19 it grows and **b** a tree, and the birds come and find
Jn 4:14 It **b** a perpetual spring within them, giving them
Ro 3:20 the clearer it **b** that we aren't obeying it.
6:16 that whatever you choose to obey **b** your master?
1Co 6:16 himself to a prostitute, he **b** one body with her?
6:17 But the person who is joined to the Lord **b** one
Eph 5:13 shines on them, it **b** clear how evil these things are.
2Jn 1:11 Anyone who encourages him **b** a partner in his evil

BECOMING (14) [BECOME]

Ex 1: 9 "These Israelites are **b** a threat to us because there
Lev 13:24 **b** either a shiny reddish white or white,
Dt 17:20 This regular reading will prevent him from **b** proud
Ne 4:10 began to complain that the workers were **b** tired.
Isa 59: 1 is not too weak to save you, and he is not **b** deaf.
Hos 4: 3 and all living things are **b** sick and dying.
Ac 27: 9 The weather was **b** dangerous for long voyages by
Ro 1: 8 Let me say first of all that your faith in God is **b**
1Co 7:31 make good use of them without **b** attached to them,
10:13 He will keep the temptation from **b** so strong that
Gal 3:23 was shown to us as the way of **b** right with God,
Eph 2:21 joined together, **b** a holy temple for the Lord.
4:15 **b** more and more in every way like Christ, who is
1Th 3: 3 and to keep you from **b** disturbed by the troubles

BECORATH (1)

1Sa 9: 1 from the family of **B** and the clan of Aphiah.

BED (69) [BEDDING, BEDRIDDEN, BEDROOM, BEDROOMS, BEDS, BEDSIDE, BEDSPREADS, SICKBED]

Ge 24:32 gave him straw to **b** them down, fed them,
48: 2 gathered his strength and sat up in **b** to greet him.
49: 4 of my wives; / you dishonored me in my own **b**.
49:33 he lay back in the **b**, breathed his last, and died.
Lev 15:21 If you touch her **b**, you must wash your clothes
15:24 and any **b** on which he lies will be defiled.
15:27 If you touch her **b** or anything on which she sits,
Dt 3:11 His iron **b** was more than thirteen feet long and six
Jdg 16: 3 But Samson stayed in **b** only until midnight.
1Sa 3: 2 who was almost blind by now, had just gone to **b**.

3: 5 Eli replied. "Go on back to **b**." So he did.
3: 6 call you, my son," Eli said. "Go on back to **b**."
3: 9 servant is listening.' " So Samuel went back to **b**.
3:15 Samuel stayed in **b** until morning, then got up
9:25 roof of the house and prepared a **b** for him there.
19:13 Then she took an idol and put it in his **b**, covered it
19:14 told them he was sick and couldn't get out of **b**.
19:15 "Then bring him to me in his **b**," Saul ordered,
19:16 they discovered that it was only an idol in the **b**
25:37 he had a stroke, and he lay on his **b** paralyzed.
2Sa 4: 7 they cut off his head as he lay there on his **b**.
4:11 innocent man in his own house and on his own **b**?
11: 2 Late one afternoon David got out of **b** after taking
12:11 and he will go to **b** with them in public view.
13: 5 what to do. Go back to **b** and pretend you are sick.
13:11 grabbed her and demanded, "Come to **b** with me,
1Ki 1:47 king bowed his head in worship as he lay in his **b**,
17:19 where he lived, and laid the body on his **b**.
21: 4 The king went to **b** with his face to the wall
2Ki 1: 4 You will never leave the **b** on which you are lying,
1: 6 you will never leave the **b** on which you are lying,
1:16 you will never leave the **b** on which you are lying,
4:10 room for him on the roof and furnish it with a **b**,
4:21 She carried him up to the **b** of the man of God,
4:32 was indeed dead, lying there on the prophet's **b**.
7:12 The king got out of **b** in the middle of the night
20: 5 and three days from now you will get out of **b**
2Ch 16:14 He was laid on a **b** perfumed with sweet spices
24:25 They assassinated him as he lay in **b**. Then he was
Est 2:12 each young woman was taken to the king's **b**,
Job 7: 4 When I go to **b**, I think, 'When will it be
7:13 If I think, 'My **b** will comfort me, and I will try to
17:13 might go to the grave and make my **b** in darkness.
27:19 "The wicked go to **b** rich but wake up to find that
33:15 when deep sleep falls on people as they lie in **b**.
Ps 6: 6 out from sobbing. / Every night tears drench my **b**;
41: 8 they say. / "He will never get out of that **b**!"
Pr 7:16 My **b** is spread with colored sheets of finest linen
7:17 I've perfumed my **b** with myrrh, aloes,
22:27 even your **b** will be snatched from under you.
26:14 on its hinges, so the lazy person turns over in **b**.
SS 3: 1 "One night as I lay in **b**, I yearned deeply for my
6:12 I found myself in my princely **b** with my beloved
Isa 28:20 the **b** you have made is too short to lie on.
57: 8 You have climbed right into **b** with these
Eze 23:17 adultery with her, defiling her in the **b** of love.
Da 2:28 and the visions you saw as you lay on your **b**.
4: 5 I saw visions that terrified me as I lay in my **b**.
4:10 " 'While I was lying in my **b**, this is what I
7: 1 had a dream and saw visions as he lay in his **b**.
Mt 8: 6 "Lord, my young servant lies in **b**, paralyzed
8:14 Peter's mother-in-law was in **b** with a high fever.
Mk 1:30 Simon's mother-in-law was sick in **b** with a high
4:21 it under a basket or under a **b** to shut out the light?
7:30 her little girl was lying quietly in **b**, and the demon
Lk 8:16 a lamp and then cover it up or put it under a **b**.
11: 7 door is locked for the night, and we are all in **b**.
17:34 That night two people will be asleep in one **b**;
Ac 9:34 Jesus Christ heals you! Get up and make your **b**!"

BEDAD (2)
Ge 36:35 Hadad son of **B** became king and ruled from the
1Ch 1:46 Hadad son of **B** became king and ruled from the

BEDAN (1)
1Ch 7:17 The son of Ulam was **B**. All these were considered

BEDCHAMBER [KJV] See BEDROOM

BEDDING (3) [BED]
Lev 15: 4 Any **b** on which he lies and anything on which he
15: 5 "So if you touch the man's **b**, you will be required
15:23 whether it is her **b** or any piece of furniture.

BEDEIAH (1)
Ezr 10:35 Benaiah, **B**, Keluhi,

BEDRIDDEN (1) [BED]
Ac 9:33 who had been paralyzed and **b** for eight years.

BEDROOM (11) [BED, ROOM]
2Sa 4: 6 went into Ishbosheth's **b**, and stabbed him in the
13:10 "Now bring the food into my **b** and feed it to me
1Ki 1:15 So Bathsheba went into the king's **b**. He was very
2Ki 6:12 the words you speak in the privacy of your **b**!"
11: 2 and his nurse in a **b** to hide him from Athaliah,
2Ch 22:11 She put Joash and his nurse in a **b**. In this way,
Pr 7:27 is the road to the grave. Her **b** is the den of death.
SS 1: 4 let's run! Bring me into your **b**, O my king."
3: 4 into my mother's **b**, where I had been conceived.
5: 2 He was knocking at my **b** door. 'Open to me,
Lk 11: 7 He would call out from his **b**, 'Don't bother me.

BEDROOMS (1) [BED, ROOM]
Ex 8: 3 your houses, even into your **b** and onto your beds!

BEDS (6) [BED]
Ex 8: 3 even into your bedrooms and onto your **b**!
Ps 149: 5 Let them sing for joy as they lie on their **b**.
SS 5:13 His cheeks are like sweetly scented **b** of spices.
6: 2 to his spice **b**, to graze and to gather the lilies.
Am 6: 4 who sprawl on ivory **b** surrounded with luxury,
Ac 5:15 sick people were brought out into the streets on **b**

BEDSIDE (2) [BED]
Mk 1:31 He went to her **b**, and as he took her by the hand
Lk 4:39 Standing at her **b**, he spoke to the fever,

BEDSPREADS (1) [BED]
Pr 31:22 She quilts her own **b**. She dresses like royalty in

BEEF (1)
Isa 25: 6 with clear, well-aged wine and choice **b**.

BEEN (1007) [BE] See Index of Articles, Etc.

BEER (5) [BAALATH-BEER, BEER-LAHAIROI, BEER-ELIM]
Nu 21:16 From there the Israelites traveled to **B**, which is the
Dt 14:26 you want—an ox, a sheep, some wine, or **b**.
Jdg 9:21 Then Jotham escaped and lived in **B** because he
Isa 28: 7 and prophets reel and stagger from **b** and wine.
29: 9 but not from wine! You stagger, but not from **b**!

BEER-ELIM (1) [BEER]
Isa 15: 8 from one end to the other—from Eglaim to **B**.

BEER-LAHAIROI (3) [BEER]
Ge 16:14 Later that well was named **B**, and it can still be
24:62 home was in the Negev, had returned from **B**.
25:11 on Isaac, who settled near **B** in the Negev.

BEERA (1)
1Ch 7:37 Bezer, Hod, Shamma, Shilshah, Ithran, and **B**.

BEERAH (2) [BEERAH'S]
1Ch 5: 6 and **B**. / **B** was the leader of the Reubenites

BEERAH'S (1) [BEERAH]
1Ch 5: 7 **B** relatives are listed in their genealogy by their

BEERI (2)
Ge 26:34 woman named Judith, the daughter of **B** the Hittite.
Hos 1: 1 to Hosea son of **B** during the years when Uzziah,

BEEROTH (10)
Jos 9:17 were Gibeon, Kephirah, **B**, and Kiriath-jearim.
18:25 Also Gibeon, Ramah, **B**,
2Sa 4: 2 sons of Rimmon, who was a Benjaminite from **B**.
4: 2 The town of **B** is now part of Benjamin
4: 3 because the original people of **B** fled to Gittaim,
4: 5 and Baanah, the sons of Rimmon from **B**,
23:37 Naharai from **B** (Joab's armor bearer);
1Ch 11:39 Naharai from **B** (Joab's armor bearer);
Ezr 2:25 peoples of Kiriath-jearim, Kephirah, and **B** | 743
Ne 7:29 peoples of Kiriath-jearim, Kephirah, and **B** | 743

BEERSHEBA (30)
Ge 21:14 and she walked out into the wilderness of **B**,
21:31 So ever since, that place has been known as **B**—
21:33 Then Abraham planted a tamarisk tree at **B**,
22:19 young men and traveled home again to **B**,
26:23 From there Isaac moved to **B**,
26:33 the town that grew up there has been called **B**—
28:10 Jacob left **B** and traveled toward Haran.
46: 1 And when he came to **B**, he offered sacrifices to
46: 5 So Jacob left **B**, and his sons brought him to Egypt.
Jos 15:28 Hazar-shual, **B**, Biziothiah,
19: 2 Simeon's inheritance included **B**, Sheba, Moladah,
Jdg 20: 1 from Dan to **B** and from the land of Gilead,
1Sa 8: 2 Joel and Abijah, his oldest sons, held court in **B**.
2Sa 3:10 king over Israel as well as Judah, from Dan to **B**."
17:11 bringing them from as far away as Dan and **B**.
24: 2 land—from Dan in the north to **B** in the south—
24: 7 Finally, they went south to Judah as far as **B**.
1Ki 4:25 And from Dan to **B**, each family had its own home
19: 3 He went to **B**, a town in Judah, and he left his
2Ki 12: 1 forty years. His mother was Zibiah, from **B**.
23: 8 where they had burned incense, from Geba to **B**.
1Ch 4:28 They lived in **B**, Moladah, Hazar-shual,
21: 2 from **B** in the south to Dan in the north—and bring
2Ch 19: 4 traveling from **B** to the hill country of Ephraim,
24: 1 forty years. His mother was Zibiah, from **B**.
30: 5 all Israel, from **B** in the south to Dan in the north,
Ne 11:27 Hazar-shual, **B** with its villages,
11:30 living all the way from **B** to the valley of Hinnom.
Am 5: 5 go to worship the idols of Bethel, Gilgal, or **B**.
8:14 Dan, and **B** will fall down, never to rise again."

BEES (4)
Dt 1:44 lived there came out against you like a swarm of **b**.
Jdg 14: 8 And he found that a swarm of **b** had made some
Ps 118:12 They swarmed around me like **b**; / they blazed
Isa 7:18 you like flies. Like **b**, they will sting and kill.

BEESH-TERAH [KJV] See BE-ESHTERAH

BEETLE [KJV] See BALD LOCUSTS

BEEVES [KJV] See BULL, CATTLE, HERD

BEFALLS (1)
Pr 12:21 No real harm **b** the godly, but the wicked have

BEFORE (1022) [BEFOREHAND] See Index of Articles, Etc.

BEFOREHAND (4) [BEFORE]
2Ki 24:13 As the LORD had said **b**,
Ac 3:18 the prophets had declared about the Messiah **b**—
10:41 but to us whom God had chosen **b** to be his
17:26 He decided **b** which should rise and fall, and he

BEG (33) [BEGGAR, BEGGARS, BEGGED, BEGGING, BEGS]
Ge 50:17 of the God of your father, **b** you to forgive us."
Ex 9:28 Please **b** the LORD to end this terrifying thunder
11: 8 bowing low. 'Please leave!' they will **b**. 'Hurry!
Nu 12:13 out to the LORD, "Heal her, O God, I **b** you!"
1Sa 8:18 you will **b** for relief from this king you are
Est 4: 8 and to urge her to go to the king to **b** for mercy
Job 13:20 "O God, there are two things I **b** of you, and I will
20:10 His children will **b** from the poor, for he must give
41: 3 Will it **b** you for mercy or implore you for pity?
Ps 80:14 Come back, we **b** you, O God Almighty.
88: 9 my tears. / Each day I **b** for your help, O LORD;
Pr 6: 3 your pride; go and **b** to have your name erased.
19: 6 Many **b** favors from a prince; everyone is the
30: 7 O God, I **b** two favors from you before I die.
Isa 27: 5 if they surrender and **b** for peace and protection."
Jer 7:16 or pray for them, and don't **b** me to help them,
11:11 Though they **b** for mercy, I will not listen to their
37:20 Listen, my lord the king, I **b** you. Don't send me
42: 3 **B** the LORD your God to show us what to do
La 4: 5 now **b** in the streets for anything they can get.
Hos 10: 8 They will **b** the mountains to bury them
Mic 3: 4 Then you **b** the LORD for help in times of
Hab 2:19 How terrible it will be for you who **b** lifeless
Zep 2: 3 **B** the LORD to save you—all you who are
Mal 1: 9 "Go ahead, **b** God to be merciful to you! But when
Lk 8:28 High God? Please, I **b** you, don't torture me!"
16: 3 to go out and dig ditches, and I'm too proud to **b**.
23:30 People will **b** the mountains to fall on them
Ac 3: 2 so he could **b** from the people going into the
9:38 so they sent two men to **b** him, "Please come as
2Co 6: 1 we **b** you not to reject this marvelous message of
Eph 4: 1 **b** you to lead a life worthy of your calling,
1Th 4:10 we **b** you to love them more and more.

BEGAN (304) [BEGIN]
Ge 4:26 It was during his lifetime that people first **b** to
6: 1 When the human population **b** to grow rapidly on
8: 1 across the waters, and the floods **b** to disappear.
8: 3 So the flood gradually **b** to recede. After 150 days,
8: 4 exactly five months from the time the flood **b**,
8: 5 to go down, other mountain peaks **b** to appear.
8:13 years old, ten and a half months after the flood **b**,
11: 3 They **b** to talk about construction projects.
14:11 and Gomorrah and **b** their long journey home,
16: 4 she **b** to treat her mistress Sarai with contempt.
19: 9 they lunged at Lot and **b** breaking down the door.
27:33 Isaac **b** to tremble uncontrollably and said,
31: 2 And Jacob **b** to notice a considerable cooling in
31: 8 the whole flock **b** to produce speckled lambs.
35:16 But Rachel's pains of childbirth **b** while they were
39: 5 the LORD **b** to bless Potiphar for Joseph's sake.
39: 5 All his household affairs **b** to run smoothly,
39: 7 Potiphar's wife **b** to desire him and invited him to
39:14 she **b** screaming. Soon all the men around the
40:10 It had three branches that **b** to bud and blossom,
41: 2 up out of the river and **b** grazing along its bank.
41:18 up out of the river and **b** grazing along its bank.
41:54 Then the seven years of famine **b**, just as Joseph
41:55 Throughout the land of Egypt the people **b** to
44:12 Joseph's servant **b** searching the oldest brother's
45:14 embraced Benjamin, and Benjamin also **b** to weep.
45:15 over them, and then they **b** talking freely with him.
47:27 And before long, they **b** to prosper there, and their
Ex 9: 6 morning all the livestock of the Egyptians **b** to die,
12:51 And that very day the LORD **b** to lead the people
14:10 The people **b** to panic, and they cried out to the
14:25 Their chariot wheels **b** to come off, making their
14:27 So as the sun **b** to rise, Moses raised his hand over
Nu 11: 1 The people soon **b** to complain to the LORD
11: 4 the Israelites **b** to crave the good things of Egypt,
11: 4 and the people of Israel also **b** to complain.
14: 1 Then all the people **b** weeping aloud, and they
14:10 But the whole community **b** to talk about stoning
16:41 But the very next morning the whole community **b**
21: 5 and they **b** to murmur against God and Moses.
Dt 1: 5 Jordan River. He **b** to explain the law as follows:
Jos 3:16 the water **b** piling up at a town upstream called
5:11 The very next day they **b** to eat unleavened bread
15: 2 The southern boundary **b** at the south bay of the
15: 5 The northern boundary **b** at the bay where the
16: 5 The eastern boundary of their inheritance **b** at
16: 6 The northern boundary **b** at the Mediterranean,
18:12 The northern boundary **b** at the Jordan River,
18:15 The southern boundary **b** at the outskirts of
Jdg 6:28 next morning, as the people of the town **b** to stir,
9:27 flowed freely, and everyone **b** cursing Abimelech.
10: 8 who **b** to oppress them that year. For eighteen
11: 4 this time, the Ammonites **b** their war against Israel.
13:25 the Spirit of the LORD **b** to take hold of him.
16:22 But before long his hair **b** to grow back.
19:22 They **b** beating at the door and shouting to the old
20:31 they had done before, they **b** to kill the Israelites.
1Sa 1:18 Then she went back and **b** to eat again, and she

4:19 were dead, her labor pains suddenly **b**.
5:6 Then the LORD **b** to afflict the people of Ashdod
5:9 the LORD **b** afflicting its people, young and old,
10:10 God came upon Saul, and he, too, **b** to prophesy.
14:16 the vast army of Philistines **b** to melt away in
17:24 army saw him, they **b** to run away in fright.
18:10 and he **b** to rave like a madman.
18:10 David **b** to play the harp, as he did whenever this
19:20 upon Saul's men, and they also **b** to prophesy.
19:23 God came upon Saul, and he, too, **b** to prophesy!
20:24 and when the new moon festival **b**, the king sat
22:2 Then others **b** coming—men who were in trouble
23:13 left Keilah and **b** roaming the countryside.
23:26 Just as Saul and his men **b** to close in on David
24:5 But then David's conscience **b** bothering him
24:16 that really you, my son David?" Then he **b** to cry.
30:6 and children, and they **b** to talk of stoning him.
2Sa 2:17 The two armies then **b** to fight each other, and by
2:19 and he **b** chasing Abner. He was relentless
5:4 David was thirty years old when he **b** to reign,
9:1 One day David **b** wondering if anyone in Saul's
10:13 his troops attacked, the Arameans **b** to run away.
18:6 So the battle **b** in the forest of Ephraim,
20:15 ramp against the city wall and **b** battering it down.
24:10 the census, David's conscience **b** to bother him.
1Ki 3:17 "Please, my lord," one of them **b**, "this woman
6:1 that he **b** the construction of the Temple of the
15:1 Abijam **b** to rule over Judah in the eighteenth year
15:9 Asa **b** to rule over Judah in the twentieth year of
15:25 Nadab son of Jeroboam **b** to rule over Israel in the
15:33 Baasha **b** to rule over Israel in the third year of
16:8 Elah son of Baasha **b** to rule over Israel from
16:15 Zimri **b** to rule over Israel from Tirzah in the
16:23 Omri **b** to rule over Israel in the thirty-first year of
16:29 Ahab son of Omri **b** to rule over Israel in the
16:31 Ethbaal of the Sidonians, and he **b** to worship Baal.
18:27 About noontime Elijah **b** mocking them.
20:29 for seven days, and on the seventh day the battle **b**.
22:41 Jehoshaphat son of Asa **b** to rule over Judah in the
22:51 Ahaziah son of Ahab **b** to rule over Israel in the
2Ki 2:23 a group of boys from the town **b** mocking
3:1 Ahab's son Joram **b** to rule over Israel in the
4:27 Gehazi **b** to push her away, but the man of God
4:34 And the child's body **b** to grow warm again!
6:4 arrived at the Jordan, they **b** cutting down trees.
8:16 Jehoram son of King Jehoshaphat of Judah **b** to
8:25 Ahaziah son of Jehoram **b** to rule over Judah in the
10:32 At about that time the LORD **b** to reduce the size
12:1 Joash **b** to rule over Judah in the seventh year of
13:1 Jehoahaz son of Jehu **b** to rule over Israel in the
13:10 Jehoash son of Jehoahaz **b** to rule over Israel in the
14:1 Amaziah son of Joash **b** to rule over Judah in the
14:23 **b** to rule over Israel in the fifteenth year of King
15:1 Uzziah son of Amaziah **b** to rule over Judah in the
15:8 Zechariah son of Jeroboam II **b** to rule over Israel
15:13 Shallum son of Jabesh **b** to rule over Israel in the
15:17 Menahem son of Gadi **b** to rule over Israel in the
15:23 Pekahiah son of Menahem **b** to rule over Israel in
15:27 Pekah son of Remaliah **b** to rule over Israel in the
15:30 He **b** to rule over Israel in the twentieth year of
15:32 Jotham son of Uzziah **b** to rule over Judah in the
15:37 In those days the LORD **b** to send King Rezin of
16:1 Ahaz son of Jotham **b** to rule over Judah in the
17:1 Hoshea son of Elah **b** to rule over Israel in the
18:1 Hezekiah son of Ahaz **b** to rule over Judah in the
18:9 and **b** a siege on the city of Samaria.
1Ch 19:14 his troops attacked, the Arameans **b** to run away.
27:24 Joab **b** the census but never finished it
2Ch 3:1 So Solomon **b** to build the Temple of the LORD
3:2 The construction **b** in midspring, during the fourth
13:1 Abijah **b** to rule over Judah in the eighteenth year
13:15 and the men of Judah **b** to shout. At the sound of
16:10 Asa also **b** to oppress some of his people.
20:22 At the moment they **b** to sing and give praise,
29:15 Then they **b** to purify the Temple of the LORD,
29:17 The work **b** on a day in early spring, and in eight
31:10 "Since the people **b** bringing their gifts to the
34:3 Josiah **b** to seek the God of his ancestor David.
34:3 twelfth year, he **b** to purify Judah and Jerusalem,
Ezr 3:2 and Zerubbabel son of Shealtiel with his family **b**
3:3 Then they immediately **b** to sacrifice burnt
3:6 Fifteen days before the Festival of Shelters **b**,
3:8 The construction of the Temple of God **b** in
4:6 Years later when Xerxes **b** his reign, the enemies
Ne 2:18 Let's rebuild the wall!" So they **b** the good work.
4:10 Then the people of Judah **b** to complain that the
12:46 and thanks to God **b** long ago in the days of David
13:12 And once more all the people of Judah **b** bringing
Est 2:1 he **b** thinking about Vashti and what she had done
9:23 Mordecai's suggestion and **b** this annual custom.
Ps 33:9 For when he spoke, the world **b**! / It appeared at
39:3 and **b** to burn, / igniting a fire of words:
Pr 8:23 in ages past, at the very first, before the earth **b**.
Isa 40:21 of God—the words he gave before the world **b**?
47:6 and **b** their punishment by letting them fall into
64:4 For since the world **b**, no ear has heard and no eye
Jer 25:1 King Nebuchadnezzar of Babylon **b** his reign.
40:12 they **b** to return to Judah from the places to which
41:14 from Mizpah escaped and **b** to help Johanan.
Eze 9:6 So they **b** by killing the seventy leaders.
37:10 the wind entered the bodies, and they **b** to breathe.
Da 6:4 and princes **b** searching for some fault in the way
7:10 Then the court **b** its session, and the books were
9:23 The moment you **b** praying, a command was
10:12 Since the first day you **b** to pray for understanding
10:16 my lips, and I opened my mouth and **b** to speak.
Hos 1:2 When the LORD first **b** speaking to Israel
9:15 LORD says, "All their wickedness **b** at Gilgal;
there I **b** to hate them.
Hab 3:11 The lofty sun and moon **b** to fade, obscured by
Hag 1:14 and **b** their work on the house of the LORD
2:15 **b** to lay the foundation of the LORD's Temple.
Zec 8:10 Before the work on the Temple **b**, there were no
Mt 3:1 In those days John the Baptist **b** preaching in the
4:17 From then on, Jesus **b** to preach, "Turn from your
8:29 They **b** screaming at him, "Why are you bothering
11:7 had gone, Jesus **b** talking about him to the crowds.
11:12 And from the time John the Baptist **b** preaching
11:20 Then Jesus **b** to denounce the cities where he had
12:1 so they **b** breaking off heads of wheat and eating
13:26 When the crop **b** to grow and produce grain,
14:30 at the high waves, he was terrified and **b** to sink.
16:21 then on Jesus **b** to tell his disciples plainly that he
17:3 and Elijah appeared and **b** talking with Jesus.
20:30 they **b** shouting, "Lord, Son of David, have mercy
21:12 and **b** to drive out the merchants and their
21:23 When Jesus returned to the Temple and **b** teaching,
25:16 The servant who received the five bags of gold **b**
26:16 Judas **b** looking for the right time and place to
26:22 one by one they **b** to ask him, "I'm not the one,
26:37 and he **b** to be filled with anguish and deep
Mk 1:24 and he **b** shouting, "Why are you bothering us,
1:27 and they **b** to discuss what had happened.
2:23 his disciples **b** breaking off heads of wheat.
3:20 the crowds **b** to gather again, and soon he and his
4:1 Once again Jesus **b** teaching by the lakeshore.
4:2 He **b** to teach the people by telling many stories
4:37 High waves **b** to break into the boat until it was
5:17 and the crowd **b** pleading with Jesus to go away
5:20 and **b** to tell everyone about the great things Jesus
6:2 The next Sabbath he **b** teaching in the synagogue,
6:55 and **b** carrying sick people to him on mats.
8:31 Then Jesus **b** to tell them that he, the Son of Man,
9:4 and Moses appeared and **b** talking with Jesus.
9:11 Now they **b** asking him, "Why do the teachers of
10:28 Then Peter **b** to mention all that he and the other
10:32 Jesus once more **b** to describe everything that was
10:47 he **b** to shout out, "Jesus, Son of David,
11:15 and **b** to drive out the merchants and their
11:18 Jesus had done, they **b** planning how to kill him.
12:1 Then Jesus **b** telling them stories: "A man planted
14:11 So he **b** looking for the right time and place to
14:19 one by one they **b** to ask him, "I'm not the one,
14:33 and he **b** to be filled with horror and deep distress.
14:65 Then some of them **b** to spit at him, and they
14:69 saw him standing there and **b** telling the others,
14:70 A little later some other bystanders **b** saying to
15:8 The mob **b** to crowd in toward Pilate, asking him
Lk 1:64 could speak again, and he **b** praising God.
1:80 Then he lived out in the wilderness until he **b** his
2:38 with Mary and Joseph, and she **b** praising God.
3:23 Jesus was about thirty years old when he **b** his
4:33 a man possessed by a demon **b** shouting at Jesus,
5:6 And this time their nets were so full they **b** to tear!
6:11 with rage and **b** to discuss what to do with him.
7:15 dead boy sat up and **b** to talk to those around him!
8:1 Not long afterward Jesus **b** a tour of the nearby
8:6 This seed **b** to grow, but soon it withered and died
8:23 and while he was sleeping the wind **b** to rise.
8:47 she **b** to tremble and fell to her knees before him.
9:6 So they **b** their circuit of the villages,
9:30 and Elijah, appeared and **b** talking with Jesus.
14:18 But they all **b** making excuses. One said he had
15:14 famine swept over the land, and he **b** to starve.
15:24 He was lost, but now he is found.' So the party **b**.
16:16 "Until John the Baptist **b** to preach, the laws of
18:38 So he **b** shouting, "Jesus, Son of David,
19:37 all of his followers **b** to shout and sing as they
19:41 and Jesus saw the city ahead, he **b** to cry.
19:45 and **b** to drive out the merchants from their stalls.
19:47 and the other leaders of the people **b** planning how
21:5 Some of his disciples **b** talking about the beautiful
22:6 So he **b** looking for an opportunity to betray Jesus
22:23 Then the disciples **b** to ask each other which of
22:24 And they **b** to argue among themselves as to who
22:56 noticed him in the firelight and **b** staring at him.
22:63 Now the guards in charge of Jesus **b** mocking
23:2 They **b** at once to state their case: "This man has
23:11 Now Herod and his soldiers **b** mocking
24:15 and joined them and **b** walking beside them.
Jn 3:25 At that time a certain Jew **b** an argument with
5:9 was healed! He rolled up the mat and **b** walking!
5:16 So the Jewish leaders **b** harassing Jesus for
6:22 crowds **b** gathering on the shore, waiting to see
6:41 Then the people **b** to murmur in disagreement
6:52 Then the people **b** arguing with each other about
7:14 Jesus went up to the Temple and **b** to teach.
9:32 Never since the world **b** has anyone been able to
11:53 So from that time on the Jewish leaders **b** to plot
11:55 the cleansing ceremony before the Passover **b**.
12:1 Six days before the Passover ceremonies **b**,
13:5 Then he **b** to wash the disciples' feet and to wipe
17:5 me into the glory we shared before the world **b**.
17:24 because you loved me even before the world **b**!
18:19 the high priest **b** asking Jesus about his followers
19:6 the leading priests and Temple guards **b** shouting,
Ac 1:1 first book I told you about everything Jesus **b** to do
2:4 the Holy Spirit and **b** speaking in other languages,
3:8 He jumped up, stood on his feet, and **b** to walk!
5:21 about daybreak and immediately **b** teaching.
7:58 dragged him out of the city and **b** to stone him.
8:1 A great wave of persecution **b** that day,
8:13 He **b** following Philip wherever he went, and he
8:35 So Philip **b** with this same Scripture and then used
9:20 And immediately he **b** preaching about Jesus in the
10:37 beginning in Galilee after John the Baptist **b**
11:15 "Well, I **b** telling them the Good News, but just as
11:18 objections were answered and they **b** praising God.
11:20 and Cyrene **b** preaching to Gentiles about the Lord
12:1 About that time King Herod Agrippa **b** to
13:11 and he **b** wandering around begging for someone
15:1 from Judea arrived and **b** to teach the Christians:
19:9 Then he **b** preaching daily at the lecture hall of
19:24 It **b** with Demetrius, a silversmith who had a large
19:28 At this their anger boiled, and they **b** shouting,
19:29 A crowd **b** to gather, and soon the city was filled
23:1 Gazing intently at the high council, Paul **b**:
25:6 and on the following day Paul's trial **b**.
27:13 When a light wind **b** blowing from the south,
27:18 the ship, the crew **b** throwing the cargo overboard.
27:37 and all 276 of us **b** eating—for that is the number
27:41 by the force of the waves and **b** to break apart.
28:13 A day later a south wind **b** blowing,
28:23 He **b** lecturing in the morning and went on into the
Ro 1:21 And they **b** to think up foolish ideas of what God
1Co 2:7 he made it for our benefit before the world **b**.
2Co 3:7 yet it **b** with such glory that the people of Israel
8:11 to completion just as enthusiastically as you **b** it.
Php 1:6 sure that God, who **b** the good work within you,
Col 1:17 He existed before everything else **b**, and he holds
2Ti 1:9 that was his plan long before the world **b**—
Tit 1:2 which God promised them before the world **b**—
Heb 9:26 had to die again and again, ever since the world **b**.
Jas 5:18 grass turned green, and the crops **b** to grow again.
1Pe 1:20 chose him for this purpose long before the world **b**,
Rev 17:8 in the Book of Life from before the world **b**,

BEGAT, BEGET, BEGETTEST, BEGETTETH
[KJV] See FATHER

BEGGAR (8) [BEG]

Mk 10:46 A blind **b** named Bartimaeus (son of Timaeus)
Lk 16:20 At his door lay a diseased **b** named Lazarus.
16:22 the **b** died and was carried by the angels to be with
18:35 a blind **b** was sitting beside the road.
Jn 9:8 and others who knew him as a blind **b** asked each
other, "Is this the same man—that **b**?"
9:9 And the **b** kept saying, "I am the same man!"
Ac 3:10 When they realized he was the lame **b** they had

BEGGARS (1) [BEG]

Ps 109:10 May his children wander as **b**; / may they be

BEGGED (53) [BEG]

Ge 19:7 "Please, my brothers," he **b**, "don't do such a
19:18 "Oh no, my lords, please," Lot **b**.
27:34 and bitter cry. "O my father, bless me, too!" he **b**.
30:14 Leah. Rachel **b** Leah to give some of them to her.
34:11 kind to me, and let me have her as my wife," he **b**.
Ex 5:15 with him. "Please don't treat us like this," they **b**.
8:8 Then Pharaoh summoned Moses and Aaron and **b**,
Dt 18:16 You **b** that you might never again have to listen to
1Sa 5:11 the people summoned the rulers again and **b** them,
7:8 to save us from the Philistines!" they **b** Samuel.
2Sa 1:9 Then he **b** me, 'Come over here and put me out of
3:35 day of the funeral, and now everyone **b** him to eat.
12:16 David **b** God to spare the child. He went without
18:23 "Yes, but let me go anyway," he **b**. Joab finally
1Ki 20:32 and ropes and went to the king of Israel and **b**,
Job 6:22 Have I **b** you to use any of your wealth on my
Ps 30:8 O LORD. / I **b** the Lord for mercy, saying,
106:23 He **b** him to turn from his anger and not destroy
Jer 21:1 the priest, to speak with him. They **b** Jeremiah,
26:19 the LORD. They **b** him to have mercy on them.
36:25 and Gemariah **b** the king not to burn the scroll,
38:26 just tell them you **b** me not to send you back to
La 1:19 "I **b** my allies for help, but they betrayed me.
Mt 8:31 so the demons **b**, "If you cast us out, send us into
8:34 but they **b** him to go away and leave them alone.
14:36 The sick **b** him to let them touch even the fringe of
18:26 But the man fell down before the king and **b** him,
18:29 fell down before him and **b** for a little more time.
Mk 5:10 Then the spirits **b** him again and again not to send
5:12 "Send us into those pigs," the evil spirits **b**.
5:18 the man who had been demon possessed **b** to go,
6:56 The sick **b** him to let them at least touch the fringe
7:26 She **b** him to release her child from the demon's
7:32 and the people **b** Jesus to lay his hands on the man
8:22 to Jesus, and they **b** him to touch and heal the man.
Lk 4:38 with a high fever. "Please heal her," everyone **b**.
4:42 finally found him, they **b** him not to leave them.
7:4 So they earnestly **b** Jesus to come with them
8:37 And all the people in that region **b** Jesus to go
8:38 The man who had been demon possessed **b** to go,
9:40 I **b** your disciples to cast the spirit out, but they
15:28 and wouldn't go in. His father came out and **b** him,
24:29 but they **b** him to stay the night with them, since it
Jn 4:40 out to see him, they **b** him to stay at their village.
4:47 and **b** him to come to Capernaum with him to heal
Ac 8:31 And he **b** Philip to come up into the carriage
13:21 Then the people **b** for a king, and God gave them
16:39 they brought them out and **b** them to leave the city.
21:12 local believers, **b** Paul not to go on to Jerusalem.
27:33 to the early morning light, Paul **b** everyone to eat.
2Co 8:4 They **b** us again and again for the gracious
12:8 Three different times I **b** the Lord to take it away.
Heb 12:19 so terrible that they **b** God to stop speaking.

BEGGING (11) [BEG]
1Sa 2:36 bow before his descendants, **b** for money and food.
Est 8: 3 and **b** him with tears to stop Haman's evil plot
Ps 37:25 nor seen their children **b** for bread.
Hos 7:14 **b** foreign gods for crops and prosperity.
Mt 15:23 they said. "She is bothering us with all her **b**."
Mk 1:40 and knelt in front of Jesus, **b** to be healed.
Lk 5:12 the ground, face down in the dust, **b** to be healed.
8:31 The demons kept **b** Jesus not to send them into the
8:41 at Jesus' feet, **b** him to come home with him.
Ac 13:11 and he began wandering around **b** for someone to
19:31 **b** him not to risk his life by entering the

BEGIN (63) [BEGAN, BEGINNER, BEGINNING, BEGINNINGS, BEGINS, BEGUN]
Ge 7: 4 One week from today I will **b** forty days and forty
29: 8 and **b** the watering until all the flocks
31:16 father are legally ours and our children's to **b** with.
37:35 for my son," he would say, and then **b** to weep.
Ex 36: 2 So Moses told Bezalel and Oholiab to **b** the work,
Lev 23:32 and fasting will **b** the evening before the Day of
23:34 "Tell the Israelites to **b** the Festival of Shelters on
23:35 It will **b** with a sacred assembly on the first day,
23:39 you will **b** to celebrate this seven-day festival to
Nu 6:11 vow that day and let their hair **b** to grow again.
8:24 They must **b** serving in the Tabernacle at the age
28:17 following day a joyous, seven-day festival will **b**,
34: 3 The southern boundary will **b** on the east at the
34: 7 "Your northern boundary will **b** at the
Dt 2:24 you his land. Attack him and **b** to occupy the land.
2:31 to you. **B** now to conquer and occupy his land.'
17:14 Then you may **b** to think, 'We ought to have a king
30: 2 and your children **b** wholeheartedly to obey all the
31:16 these people will **b** worshiping foreign gods,
31:20 Then they will **b** to worship other gods; they will
32:41 my flashing sword / and **b** to carry out justice,
Jos 3: 7 "Today I will **b** to make you great in the eyes of
1Ch 22: 5 So I will **b** making preparations for it now."
22:16 Now **b** the work, and may the LORD be with
Est 1:17 Women everywhere will **b** to despise their
Job 8:12 not ready to be cut, they **b** to wither.
Pr 9: 6 Leave your foolish ways behind, and **b** to live;
Ecc 10:18 lets the roof leak, and soon the rafters **b** to rot.
Isa 5:11 Destruction is certain for you who get up early to **b**
18: 5 Even before you **b** your attack, while your plans
19:18 They will even **b** to speak the Hebrew language.
32:10 a year—you careless ones will suddenly **b** to care.
66: 7 "Before the birth pains even **b**, Jerusalem gives
66: 8 But by the time Jerusalem's birth pains **b**, the baby
Jer 4: 2 and **b** to live good, honest lives and uphold justice,
9:18 Quick! **B** your weeping! Let the tears flow from
10:17 and prepare to leave; the siege is about to **b**,"
26:13 your sinning and **b** to obey the LORD your God,
36: 2 **B** with the first message back in the days of Josiah,
51:33 In just a little while her harvest will **b**."
La 3:23 is his faithfulness; his mercies **b** afresh each day.
Eze 9: 6 the mark. **B** your task right here at the Temple."
12: 4 just as captives do when they **b** a long march to
18:21 and **b** to obey my laws and do what is just
Joel 3:16 and the earth and heavens will **b** to shake.
Na 2: 1 and keep a sharp watch for the enemy attack to **b**!
Hab 3: 2 **b** again to help us, as you did in years gone by.
Zec 4:10 for the LORD rejoices to see the work **b**,
Mt 24:32 its buds become tender and its leaves **b** to sprout,
Mk 13: 9 But when these things **b** to happen, watch out!
13:28 its buds become tender and its leaves **b** to sprout,
Lk 14:28 "But don't **b** until you count the cost. For who would **b** construction of a building
19:11 that the Kingdom of God would **b** right away.
21:28 So when all these things **b** to happen, stand straight
Jn 1:27 who will soon **b** his ministry. I am not even worthy
4:35 Do you think the work of harvesting will not **b**
2Co 8:10 and you were the first to **b** doing something about
9: 2 that stirred up many of them to **b** helping.
Eph 1:19 I pray that you will **b** to understand the incredible
4:28 **B** using your hands for honest work, and then give
1Th 5: 3 birth pains **b** when her child is about to be born.
1Pe 4:17 and it must **b** first among God's own children.

BEGINNER (1) [BEGIN]
Heb 5:12 basic things a **b** must learn about the Scriptures.

BEGINNING (74) [BEGIN]
Ge 1: 1 In the **b** God created the heavens and the earth.
31: 1 But Jacob soon learned that Laban's sons were **b** to
Ex 29:30 seven days before **b** to minister in the Tabernacle
Nu 10:10 and at the **b** of each month to rejoice over your
29:12 It is the **b** of the Festival of Shelters, a seven-day
Dt 2:25 **B** today I will make all people throughout the earth
16: 9 "Count off seven weeks from the **b** of your grain
Jdg 12: 2 "I summoned you at the **b** of the dispute, but you
Ru 1:22 They arrived in Bethlehem at the **b** of the barley
4:18 This is their family line **b** with their ancestor
2Sa 3: 1 That was the **b** of a long war between those who
21: 9 So all seven of them died together at the **b** of the
1Ch 12:15 during its seasonal flooding at the **b** of the year
29:29 the events of King David's reign, from **b** to end,
2Ch 9:29 of the events of Solomon's reign, from **b** to end,
12:15 of the events of Rehoboam's reign, from **b** to end,
16:11 rest of the events of Asa's reign, from **b** to end,
20:34 of the events of Jehoshaphat's reign, from **b** to end,
24:23 At the **b** of the year, the Aramean army marched
25:26 of the events of Amaziah's reign, from **b** to end,
26:22 rest of the events of Uzziah's reign, from **b** to end,
28:26 of Ahaz's reign and all his dealings, from **b** to end,
35:27 from **b** to end, are recorded in *The Book of the*
Ezr 5: 2 and Jeshua son of Jehozadak responded by **b** the
Job 42:12 the second half of his life even more than in the **b**.
Ps 90: 2 and the world, / you are God, without **b** or end.
Pr 1: 7 Fear of the LORD is the **b** of knowledge.
8:22 "The LORD formed me from the **b**, before he
9:10 Fear of the LORD is the **b** of wisdom.
17:14 **B** a quarrel is like opening a floodgate, so drop the
Ecc 3:11 see the whole scope of God's work from **b** to end.
Isa 43:27 From the very **b**, your ancestors sinned against
Jer 49:34 at the **b** of the reign of King Zedekiah of Judah.
La 4:22 But Edom, your punishment is just **b**; soon your
Eze 2: 3 ancestors have rebelled against me from the **b**,
24: 2 because on this very day the king of Babylon is **b**
Mt 19: 4 "They record that from the **b** 'God made them
20: 8 and pay them, **b** with the last workers first.
24: 8 But all this will be only the **b** of the horrors to
24:33 when you see the events I've described **b** to
Mk 10: 6 But God's plan was seen from the **b** of creation,
13: 8 But all this will be only the **b** of the horrors to
13:29 when you see the events I've described **b** to
Lk 1: 3 investigated all of these accounts from the **b**,
12:54 "When you see clouds **b** to form in the west,
24:47 of repentance to all the nations, **b** in Jerusalem:
Jn 1: 1 In the **b** the Word already existed. He was with
1: 2 He was in the **b** with God.
6:64 (For Jesus knew from the **b** who didn't believe,
8: 9 they slipped away one by one, **b** with the oldest,
8:44 He was a murderer from the **b** and has always
15:27 because you have been with me from the **b**.
Ac 10:37 **b** in Galilee after John the Baptist began preaching.
11:15 Spirit fell on them, just as he fell on us at the **b**.
Ro 11: 2 his own people, whom he chose from the very **b**.
16:25 you Gentiles, a plan kept secret from the **b** of time.
2Co 3: 1 Are we **b** again to tell you how good we are?
Eph 1:11 inheritance from God, for he chose us from the **b**,
3: 9 Creator of all things, had kept secret from the **b**.
Heb 1:10 in the **b** you laid the foundation of the earth,
7: 3 or any of his ancestors—no **b** or end to his life.
1Jn 1: 1 The one who existed from the **b** is the one we have
2: 7 an old one you have always had, right from the **b**.
2:13 you know Christ, the one who is from the **b**.
2:14 you know Christ, the one who is from the **b**.
2:24 faithful to what you have been taught from the **b**.
3: 8 to the Devil, who has been sinning since the **b**.
3:11 This is the message we have heard from the **b**:
2Jn 1: 5 a new commandment, but one we had from the **b**.
1: 6 to love one another, just as you heard from the **b**.
Jude 1:25 belong to him, in the **b**, now, and forevermore.
Rev 1: 8 the **b** and the end," says the Lord God.
21: 6 am the Alpha and the Omega—the **B** and the End.
22:13 the First and the Last, the **B** and the End."

BEGINNINGS (1) [BEGIN]
Zec 4:10 Do not despise these small **b**, for the LORD

BEGINS (17) [BEGIN]
Lev 13:35 But if the infection **b** to spread after the person is
23: 5 which **b** at twilight on its appointed day in early
23: 6 the Festival of Unleavened Bread **b**.
Isa 30:26 So it will be when the LORD **b** to heal his people
Eze 47:20 border to the point where the northern border **b**,
Na 2: 3 The attack **b**! See their scarlet uniforms!
Zep 2: 2 before judgment **b** and your opportunity is blown
2: 2 and the terrible day of the LORD's anger **b**.
Zec 13: 3 If anyone **b** prophesying again, his own father
Mt 24:49 and **b** oppressing the other servants, partying,
26: 2 the Passover celebration **b** in two days, and I,
Mk 1: 1 Here **b** the Good News about Jesus the Messiah,
Lk 1: 5 It all **b** with a Jewish priest, Zechariah, who lived
12:45 and **b** oppressing the other servants, partying,
22: 1 which **b** with the Passover celebration,
22:15 this Passover meal with you before my suffering **b**.
1Co 14:36 Do you think that the knowledge of God's word **b**

BEGONE (2) [GO]
Isa 30:22 filthy rags. "Ugh!" you will say to them. "**B**!"
Mic 2:10 Up! **B**! This is no longer your land and home,

BEGRUDGING (1) [GRUDGE]
Dt 15:10 Give freely without **b** it, and the LORD your God

BEGS (1) [BEG]
2Sa 3:29 or who dies by the sword or who **b** for food!"

BEGUILE(D), BEGUILING [KJV] See DECEIVE, DISQUALIFY, ENTICE, TRICK

BEGUN (25) [BEGIN]
Ge 11: 6 "If they can accomplish this when they have just **b**
18:27 "Since I have **b**, let me go on and speak further to
Ex 5:23 You have not even **b** to rescue them!"
Nu 16:46 blazing among them—the plague has already **b**."
16:47 The plague indeed had already **b**, but Aaron
Dt 2:31 I have **b** to hand King Sihon and his land over to
3:24 You have only **b** to show me your greatness
1Sa 5:11 For the plague from God had already **b**, and great
2Ki 15: 1 Ahaziah's reign over Judah had **b** in the eleventh
18: 4 because the people of Israel had **b** to worship it by
2Ch 29:27 songs of praise to the LORD were **b**,
Ezr 3: 6 the priests had **b** to sacrifice burnt offerings to the
Ne 6:15 finished—just fifty-two days after we had **b**.
Job 33: 2 Now that I have **b** to speak, let me continue.
Isa 43:19 See, I have already **b**! Do you not see it?
Jer 21: 2 King Nebuchadnezzar of Babylon has **b** his attack
25:29 I have **b** to punish Jerusalem, the city where my
Da 8: 3 even though it had **b** to grow later than the shorter
Hos 4: 3 the animals, birds, and fish have **b** to disappear.
Jn 4:52 He asked them when the boy had **b** to feel better,
Ac 14:26 where their journey had **b** and where they had been
1Co 15:21 now the resurrection from the dead has **b** through
2Co 5:17 for the old life is gone. A new life has **b**!
2Th 2: 2 who say that the day of the Lord has already **b**.
Rev 11:17 assumed your great power / and have **b** to reign.

BEHALF (40)
Ge 50: 4 and asked them to speak to Pharaoh on his **b**.
Ex 25: 3 Here is a list of items you may accept on my **b**:
Lev 10:19 Then Aaron answered Moses on **b** of his sons.
19: 5 offer it properly so it will be accepted on your **b**.
22:20 because it won't be accepted on your **b**.
22:25 Such animals will not be accepted on your **b**
22:29 so it will be accepted on your **b**.
23:11 the LORD so it may be accepted on your **b**.
24: 8 **b** of the Israelites as a continual part of the
Nu 3: 8 serving in the Tabernacle on **b** of all the Israelites.
3:38 for the sanctuary on **b** of the people of Israel.
3:50 The silver collected on **b** of these firstborn sons of
5:15 two quarts of barley flour to be presented on her **b**.
8:19 They will serve in the Tabernacle on **b** of the
25:11 displaying passionate zeal among them on my **b**.
Dt 18:19 to the messages the prophet proclaims on my **b**.
Jdg 9: 3 uncles spoke to all the people of Shechem on his **b**.
1Ki 2:17 He replied, "Speak to King Solomon on my **b**,
2:19 went to King Solomon to speak on Adonijah's **b**.
1Ch 16:21 oppress them. / He warned kings on their **b**:
29:21 and many other sacrifices on **b** of Israel.
Ezr 10:14 Let our leaders act on **b** of us all. Everyone who
Ne 3:17 who supervised the building of the wall on **b** of his
Job 6:22 I begged you to use any of your wealth on my **b**?
16:18 do not conceal my blood. Let it cry out on my **b**.
42: 8 for you, and I will accept his prayer on your **b**.
Ps 105:14 oppress them. / He warned kings on their **b**:
Isa 58: 2 to me and asking me to take action on their **b**.
63:15 and the might you used to show on our **b**?
Jer 15:11 Your enemies will ask you to plead on their **b** in
Mt 18: 5 a little child like this on my **b** is welcoming me.
Mk 9:37 a little child like this on my **b** welcomes me,
Lk 9:48 a little child like this on my **b** welcomes me,
Jn 5:31 "If I were to testify on my own **b**, my testimony
16:26 I'm not saying I will ask the Father on your **b**,
Phm 1:13 and he would have helped me on your **b**.
Heb 7:25 He lives forever to plead with God on their **b**.
Rev 13:14 he was allowed to perform on **b** of the first beast,
18:20 For at last God has judged her on your **b**.
19:20 who did mighty miracles on **b** of the beast—

BEHAVE (1) [BEHAVED, BEHAVING, BEHAVIOR]
Ro 8:15 You should **b** instead like God's very own

BEHAVED (2) [BEHAVE]
Job 36: 9 He shows them their sins, for they have **b** proudly.
Eze 5: 7 and have **b** even worse than your neighbors,

BEHAVING (1) [BEHAVE]
Jdg 2:19 **b** worse than those who had lived before them.

BEHAVIOR (18) [BEHAVE]
1Sa 20:34 for he was crushed by his father's shameful **b**
1Ki 8:25 'If your descendants guard their **b** as you have
2Ch 6:16 'If your descendants guard their **b** and obey my
Eze 7: 3 I will call you to account for all your disgusting **b**.
7: 8 your punishment for all your disgusting **b**.
14:23 When you meet them and see their **b**, you will
36:29 I will cleanse you of your filthy **b**. I will give you
Mic 2: 7 Will the LORD have patience with such **b**?
Ro 1:29 envy, murder, fighting, deception, malicious **b**,
12: 2 Don't copy the **b** and customs of this world,
13:13 we do, so that everyone can approve of our **b**.
2Co 12:20 backstabbing, gossip, conceit, and disorderly **b**.
Eph 4:31 and slander, as well as all types of malicious **b**.
5: 8 of light from the Lord, and your **b** should show it!
Col 3: 8 rage, malicious **b**, slander, and dirty language.
1Pe 2: 1 So get rid of all malicious **b** and deceit. Don't just
2:12 they will see your honorable **b**, and they will
3: 2 by watching your pure, godly **b**.

BEHEADED (6)
Da 1:10 I am afraid the king will have me **b** for neglecting
Mt 14:10 So John was **b** in the prison,
Mk 6:16 "John, the man I **b**, has come back from the
6:27 bring it to him. The soldier **b** John in the prison,
Lk 9: 9 "I **b** John," Herod said, "so who is this man about
Rev 20: 4 And I saw the souls of those who had been **b** for

BEHIND (130)
Ge 19: 6 outside to talk to them, shutting the door **b** him.
19:26 looked back as she was following along **b** him,
32:18 for his master Esau! He is coming right **b** us.' "
32:20 'Your servant Jacob is right **b** us.' " Jacob's plan
39:15 my loud cries, he ran and left his shirt **b** with me."
39:18 by my screams. He ran out, leaving his shirt **b**!"
Ex 10:26 property must go with us; not a hoof can be left **b**.

14:19 the people of Israel, moved to a position **b** them,
14:19 and the pillar of cloud also moved around **b** them.
26:33 is in place, put the Ark of the Covenant **b** it.
33:11 son of Nun, stayed **b** in the Tent of Meeting.
33:23 will remove my hand, and you will see me from **b**.
Lev 16: 2 Place **b** the inner curtain whenever he chooses;
16:12 carry the burner and incense **b** the inner curtain.
16:15 the people and bring its blood **b** the inner curtain.
21:23 he must never go **b** the inner curtain or come near
Dt 3:19 may stay **b** in the towns I have given you.
25:18 and they struck down those who were lagging **b**.
Jos 3: 4 Stay about a half mile **b** them, keeping a clear
6: 8 Ark of the LORD's covenant followed **b** them.
6: 9 marched both in front of the priests and **b** the Ark,
6:13 with the horns and **b** the Ark of the LORD.
8: 2 cattle for yourselves. Set an ambush **b** the city."
8: 4 "Hide in ambush close **b** the city and be ready for
8:14 But he didn't realize there was an ambush **b** the
8:20 When the men of Ai looked **b** them, smoke from
Jdg 20:34 and advanced against Benjamin from **b**.
20:40 But when the warriors of Benjamin looked **b** them
Ru 2: 2 leftover grain **b** anyone who will let me do it."
2: 3 So Ruth went out to gather grain **b** the harvesters.
2: 7 morning if she could gather grain **b** the harvesters.
2: 8 Stay right **b** the women working in my field.
1Sa 14:12 "Come on, climb right **b** me," Jonathan said to his
21: 9 "It is wrapped in a cloth **b** the ephod.
25:13 and two hundred remained **b** to guard their
30:13 "My master left me **b** three days ago because I
2Sa 3:16 Palti followed along **b** her as far as Bahurim,
3:31 And King David himself walked **b** the procession
5:23 circle around **b** them and attack them near the
11: 1 city of Rabbah. But David stayed **b** in Jerusalem.
13:17 "Throw this woman out, and lock the door **b** her!"
15:16 He left no one **b** except ten of his concubines to
1Ki 7: 8 living quarters surrounded a courtyard **b** this hall;
11:27 This is the story **b** his rebellion. Solomon was
20:30 The rest fled **b** the walls of Aphek, but the wall fell
2Ki 4: 4 your house with your sons and shut the door **b** you.
4:33 He went in alone and shut the door **b** him
9:18 "What do you know about peace? Get **b** me!"
9:19 "What do you know about peace? Get **b** me!"
9:25 when you and I were riding along **b** his father,
11: 6 And the final third must stand guard **b** the palace
25: 4 and fled through the gate between the two walls **b**
25:12 people to stay **b** in Judah to care for the vineyards
1Ch 14:14 circle around **b** them and attack them near the
20: 1 destroyed it. But David had stayed **b** in Jerusalem.
2Ch 13:13 army around **b** the men of Judah to ambush them.
Ne 4:13 So I placed armed guards **b** the lowest parts of the
4:16 The officers stationed themselves **b** the people of
Est 7: 7 But Haman stayed **b** to plead for his life with
9:29 **b** Mordecai's letter to establish the Festival of
Job 11:14 Get rid of your sins and leave all iniquity **b** you.
38:10 For I locked it **b** barred gates, limiting its shores.
Ps 49:10 and senseless, / leaving all their wealth **b**.
63: 8 I follow close **b** you; / your strong right hand holds
68:25 Singers are in front, musicians are **b**; / with them
Pr 9: 6 Leave your foolish ways **b**, and begin to live;
15:24 the wise leads to life above; they leave the grave **b**.
SS 2: 9 or a young deer. Look, there he is **b** the wall!
2:14 "My dove is hiding **b** some rocks, **b** an outcrop on the cliff.
4: 1 Your eyes **b** your veil are like doves.
4: 3 Your cheeks **b** your veil are like pomegranate
6: 7 Your cheeks **b** your veil are like pomegranate
Isa 5:18 is certain for those who drag their sins **b** them,
8:12 Do not be afraid that some plan conceived **b** closed
15: 9 both those who try to run and those who remain **b**.
52:11 Put Babylon **b** you, with everything it represents,
52:12 and the God of Israel will protect you from **b**.
57: 8 **B** closed doors, you have set up your idols
58: 8 the glory of the LORD will protect you from **b**.
Jer 39: 4 a gate between the two walls **b** the king's garden
40: 7 over the poor people who were left **b** in Judah,
42:16 and famine you fear will follow close **b** you,
52: 7 and fled through the gate between the two walls **b**
52:16 people to stay **b** in Judah to care for the vineyards
Eze 3:12 me up, and I heard a loud rumbling sound **b** me.
18:31 Put all your rebellion **b** you, and get for yourselves
23: 8 she did not leave her spirit of prostitution **b**.
26:10 through your broken gates, pulling chariots **b** them.
33:30 of man, your people are whispering **b** your back.
39:28 them home. I will leave none of my people **b**.
46:12 he entered, and the gateway will be shut **b** him.
Joel 2: 3 **B** them is nothing but desolation; not one thing
Hab 3: 5 marches before him; plague follows close **b**.
Zec 1: 8 **B** him were red, brown, and white horses,
Mt 4:22 followed him, leaving the boat and their father **b**.
6: 6 go away by yourself, shut the door **b** you,
9:20 had a hemorrhage for twelve years came up **b** him.
9:27 two blind men followed along **b** him, shouting,
20:29 left the city of Jericho, a huge crowd followed **b**.
26:58 Peter was following far **b** and eventually came to
Mk 4:36 leaving the crowds **b** (although other boats
5:24 Jesus went with him, and the crowd thronged **b**.
5:27 so she came up **b** him through the crowd
10:28 all that he and the other disciples had left **b**.
10:32 and the people following **b** were overwhelmed
14:51 There was a young man following along **b**,
14:54 Peter followed far **b** and then slipped inside the
Lk 2:43 home to Nazareth, but Jesus stayed **b** in Jerusalem.
7:38 Then she knelt **b** him at his feet, weeping.
8:44 She came up **b** Jesus and touched the fringe of his
12: 3 and what you have whispered **b** closed doors will
14:23 'Go out into the country lanes and **b** the hedges
22:54 priest's residence, and Peter was following far **b**.
23:27 Great crowds trailed along **b**, including many
Jn 2:14 and he saw money changers **b** their counters.
6:22 disciples had gone off in their boat, leaving him **b**.
17:11 the world; I am leaving them **b** and coming to you.
18:15 Simon Peter followed along **b**, as did another of
20:14 over her shoulder and saw someone standing **b** her.
20:19 the disciples were meeting **b** locked doors
Ac 16:17 She followed along **b** us shouting, "These men are
17:14 to the coast, while Silas and Timothy remained **b**.
18:19 at the port of Ephesus, Paul left the others **b**.
21:30 and immediately the gates were closed **b** him.
21:36 And the crowd followed **b** shouting, "Kill him,
27:16 We sailed **b** a small island named Cauda,
27:16 aboard the lifeboat that was being towed **b** us.
Heb 9: 3 and **b** the curtain was the second room called the
Rev 1:10 Suddenly, I heard a loud voice **b** me, a voice that

BEHOVED [KJV] See MUST, NECESSARY

BEING (232) [BE, BEINGS]

HUMAN BEING (9) Jos 10:14; Da 7:4; Mt 16:17; Ac 10:26; Ro 9:20; 1Co 15:48; 2Co 5:16; Heb 2:14; 1Jn 4:2

LIVING BEING (6) Ge 9:6; Eze 1:9,23; Rev 6:3,5,7

Ge 9: 6 for to kill a person is to kill a living **b** made in
10: 9 and people would speak of someone as **b** "like
38:28 As they were **b** born, one of them reached out his
43:18 when they saw where they were **b** taken.
Lev 2: 8 has been prepared before **b** offered to the LORD,
13:55 area has not changed appearance after **b** washed,
13:56 that the affected area has faded after **b** washed,
14: 7 blood seven times over the person **b** purified,
14: 8 "The people **b** purified must complete the
14:18 before the LORD for the person **b** cleansed.
14:20 the priest will make atonement for the person **b**
14:21 thus making atonement for the person **b** cleansed.
14:22 The person **b** cleansed must also bring two
14:23 the person **b** cleansed must bring the offerings to
14:29 the priest will make atonement for the person **b**
14:31 before the LORD for the person **b** cleansed.
26:40 for betraying me and **b** hostile toward me.
Nu 5:19 and you have not defiled yourself by **b** unfaithful,
5:27 If she has defiled herself by **b** unfaithful to her
5:29 If a woman defiles herself by **b** unfaithful to her
19:19 Then on the seventh day the people **b** cleansed
35:12 The slayer must not be killed before **b** tried by the
Dt 10:16 cleanse your sinful hearts and stop **b** stubborn.
15:21 such as **b** lame or blind, or if anything else is
22:21 **b** promiscuous while living in her parents' home.
30: 9 for the LORD will delight in **b** good to you as he
Jos 10:14 LORD answered such a request from a human **b**.
15: 1 with the wilderness of Zin **b** its southernmost
20: 9 they could escape **b** killed in revenge prior to
22:31 you have rescued Israel from **b** destroyed by the
Jdg 8:24 (The enemies, **b** Ishmaelites, all wore gold
11:12 demanding to know why Israel was **b** attacked.
Ru 2:10 "Why are you **b** so kind to me?" she asked.
1Sa 4: 4 the Ark of God to where the battle was **b** fought.
15:23 of the LORD, he has rejected you from **b** king."
15:26 he has rejected you from **b** the king of Israel."
21:11 But Achish's officers weren't happy about his **b**
26:23 his own reward for doing good and for **b** loyal,
2Sa 2: 5 "May the LORD bless you for **b** so loyal to your
11:10 Why didn't you go home last night after **b** away
12:18 "He was so broken up about the baby **b** sick,"
13:23 when Absalom's sheep were **b** sheared at
15:35 Tell them the plans that are **b** made to capture me,
16:12 And perhaps the LORD will see that I am **b**
17: 9 will start shouting that your men are **b** slaughtered.
1Ki 6: 6 the bottom floor **b** 7-1/2 feet wide, the second floor
6:24 cherubim was 15 feet, each wing **b** 7-1/2 feet long.
2Ki 3:15 While the harp was **b** played, the power of the
10: 6 Now the seventy sons of the king were **b** cared for
2Ch 13:14 When Judah realized that they were **b** attacked
Ezr 5: 8 It is **b** rebuilt with specially prepared stones, and timber is **b** laid in its walls.
9:13 "Now we are **b** punished because of our
Ne 4: 4 "Hear us, O our God, for we are **b** mocked.
4: 7 and that the gaps in the wall were **b** repaired,
5: 9 God in order to avoid **b** mocked by enemy nations?
8: 8 and clearly explained the meaning of what was **b**
9:33 Every time you punished us you were **b** just.
13: 1 that same day, as the Book of Moses was **b** read,
Est 4:11 **b** invited is doomed to die unless the king holds
Job 24:11 They press out olive oil without **b** allowed to taste
39: 9 "Will the wild ox consent to **b** tamed? Will it stay
Ps 21: 6 You have given him the joy of **b** in your presence.
44:22 killed every day; / we are **b** slaughtered like sheep.
48: 7 of Tarshish / **b** shattered by a powerful east wind.
49:13 though they will be remembered as **b** so wise.
51: 6 so you can teach me to be wise in my inmost **b**.
84: 2 of the LORD. / With my whole **b**, body and soul,
139:15 You watched me as I was **b** formed in utter
148: 5 for he issued his command, and they came into **b**.
Pr 1:17 When a bird sees a trap **b** set, it stays away.
1:22 "How long will you go on **b** simpleminded?
3:26 He will keep your foot from **b** caught in a trap.
17:26 It is wrong to fine the godly for **b** good or to punish nobles for **b** honest!
22: 1 for **b** held in high esteem is better than having
27:21 and gold, but a person is tested by **b** praised.
30:32 If you have been a fool by **b** proud or plotting evil,
Ecc 1:13 and to explore by wisdom everything **b** done in the
5: 3 Just as **b** too busy gives you nightmares, **b** a fool makes you a blabbermouth.
5: 8 If you see a poor person **b** oppressed by the
5: 8 and justice **b** miscarried throughout the land,
6: 8 Do poor people gain anything by **b** wise
7:11 **B** wise is as good as **b** rich; in fact, it is better.
9:11 by chance, by **b** at the right place at the right time.
11: 5 and as mysterious as a tiny baby **b** formed in a
Isa 21: 5 and prepare for battle! You are **b** attacked!
22: 4 Let me cry for my people as I watch them **b**
28: 7 Now, however, Israel is **b** led by drunks!
46: 1 Bel and Nebo, are **b** hauled away on ox carts.
48:13 the heavens above. I spoke, and they came into **b**.
52: 5 My name is **b** blasphemed all day long.
55: 4 He displayed my power by **b** my witness and a
59: 4 No one cares about **b** fair and honest.
65: 1 I am **b** found by people who were not looking for
66: 5 and throw you out for **b** loyal to my name.
66: 9 I would never keep this nation from **b** born,"
Jer 22:10 Instead, weep for the captive king **b** led away!
40: 1 and Judah who were **b** sent to exile in Babylon.
48: 2 they say, 'we will cut her off from **b** a nation.'
48: 4 for all Moab is **b** destroyed. Her little ones will cry
La 5:12 Our princes are **b** hanged by their thumbs,
Eze 1: 9 The wings of each living **b** touched the wings of
1:23 Beneath this surface the wings of each living **b**
2: 8 Do not join them in **b** a rebel. Open your mouth,
11: 2 for the wicked counsel **b** given in this city.
14:23 you will agree that these things are not **b** done to
15: 5 are useless both before and after **b** put into the fire!
18:18 for **b** cruel and robbing close relatives, doing what
18:25 "Yet you say, 'The Lord isn't **b** just!' Listen to
18:26 When righteous people turn from **b** good and start
21: 9 the LORD: A sword is **b** sharpened and polished.
21:10 It is **b** prepared for terrible slaughter; it will flash
21:11 the sword is now **b** sharpened and polished; it is **b** prepared for the executioner!
25: 7 I will cut you off from **b** a nation and destroy you
40:38 sacrifices was washed before **b** taken to the altar.
44:25 A priest must never defile himself by **b** in the
44:26 return to his Temple duties after **b** ritually cleansed
44:31 or that dies after **b** attacked by another animal.
Da 3:25 the flames! And the fourth looks like a divine **b**!"
4:27 Break from your wicked past by **b** merciful to the
7: 4 its two hind feet on the ground, like a human **b**.
Hos 4: 6 My people are **b** destroyed because they don't
13:13 but they are like a child who resists **b** born.
Zec 11: 2 as you watch the thickest forests **b** felled.
Mt 1:19 Joseph, her fiancé, **b** a just man, decided to break
5:22 you are in danger of **b** brought before the court.
10:37 than you love me, you are not worthy of **b** mine;
10:37 more than me, you are not worthy of **b** mine.
10:38 and follow me, you are not worthy of **b** mine.
11: 5 and the Good News is **b** preached to the poor.
16:17 to you. You did not learn this from any human **b**.
23: 7 get on the streets, and they enjoy **b** called 'Rabbi.'
23:31 you are accusing yourselves of **b** the descendants
24:32 you know without **b** told that summer is near.
Mk 1:13 He was there for forty days, **b** tempted by Satan.
13: 9 before governors and kings of **b** my followers.
13:28 you know without **b** told that summer is near.
15:32 Even the two criminals who were **b** crucified with
Lk 1:10 While the incense was **b** burned, a great crowd
2:33 and Mary were amazed at what was **b** said about
3:21 One day when the crowds were **b** baptized,
7:22 and the Good News is **b** preached to the poor.
8:12 and prevents them from believing and **b** saved.
10:42 There is really only one thing worth **b** concerned
15:19 and I am no longer worthy of **b** called your son.
15:21 and I am no longer worthy of **b** called your son.'
16: 8 rich man had to admire the dishonest rascal for **b**
16:25 So now he is here **b** comforted, and you are in
20:35 For those worthy of **b** raised from the dead won't
21:12 before kings and governors of **b** my followers.
21:30 you know without **b** told that summer is near.
Jn 3: 5 no one can enter the Kingdom of God without **b**
17:23 I in them and you in me, all **b** perfected into one.
Ac 2: 6 their own languages **b** spoken by the believers.
2:47 Lord added to their group those who were **b** saved.
3: 2 a man lame from birth was **b** carried in.
4: 9 are we **b** questioned because we've done a good
6: 1 saying that their widows were **b** discriminated
10:10 But while lunch was **b** prepared, he fell into a
10:26 and said, "Stand up! I'm a human **b** like you!"
10:47 "Can anyone object to their **b** baptized, now that
11:12 with them and not to worry about their **b** Gentiles.
15: 3 that the Gentiles, too, were **b** converted.
15:32 Then Judas and Silas, both **b** prophets,
19:40 I am afraid we are in danger of **b** charged with
27:16 aboard the lifeboat that was **b** towed behind us.
27:17 The sailors were afraid of **b** driven across to the
27:27 as we were **b** driven across the Sea of Adria,
Ro 2:26 them all the rights and honors of **b** his own people?
3: 1 Then what's the advantage of **b** a Jew? Is there any
3: 2 Yes, **b** a Jew has many advantages. First of all,
3:21 But now God has shown us a different way of **b**
3:25 God was **b** entirely fair and just when he did not
3:30 and there is only one way of **b** accepted by him.
4: 1 concerning this question of **b** saved by faith?
5:16 but we have the free gift of **b** accepted by God,
8:36 every day; we are **b** slaughtered like sheep.")
9:14 can we say? Was God **b** unfair? Of course not!
9:20 Who are you, a mere human **b**, to criticize God?
9:32 and **b** good instead of by depending on faith.
10:15 how will anyone go and tell them without **b** sent?
11: 5 A few are **b** saved as a result of God's kindness in
11:18 But you must be careful not to brag about **b** grafted
13: 5 to keep from **b** punished and to keep a clear
1Co 1:18 But we who are **b** saved recognize this message as
2: 6 rulers of this world, who are **b** brought to nothing.

8: 7 Some are accustomed to thinking of idols as **b** real,
12: 10 is given the ability to interpret what is **b** said.
14: 8 how will the soldiers know they are **b** called to
15: 29 then what point is there in people **b** baptized for
15: 48 Every human **b** has an earthly body just like
16: 1 Now about the money **b** collected for the
2Co 2: 15 fragrance is perceived differently by those **b** saved
2: 16 But to those who are **b** saved we are a life-giving
3: 14 to this day whenever the old covenant is **b** read,
4: 16 are dying, our spirits are **b** renewed every day.
5: 16 that way, as though he were merely a human **b**.
10: 16 Then there will be no question about **b** in someone
Gal 1: 7 You are **b** fooled by those who twist and change
5: 3 If you are trying to find favor with God by **b**
5: 11 The fact that I am still **b** persecuted proves that I
Php 1: 18 the fact remains that the message about Christ is **b**
Col 3: 10 that is continually **b** renewed as you learn more
1Th 2: 13 you didn't think of the words we spoke as **b** just
2Th 1: 7 And God will provide rest for you who are **b**
1Ti 3: 6 because he might be proud of **b** chosen so soon,
6: 2 is a Christian, that is no excuse for **b** disrespectful.
6: 18 always **b** ready to share with others whatever God
Heb 2: 14 became flesh and blood by **b** born in human form.
2: 14 For only as a human **b** could he die, and only by
2: 18 he is able to help us when we are **b** tempted.
13: 3 Share the sorrow of those **b** mistreated, as though
Jas 3: 14 ambition in your hearts, don't brag about **b** wise.
1Pe 1: 3 that God has given us the privilege of **b** born again.
1: 7 It is **b** tested as fire tests and purifies gold—
1: 7 So if your faith remains strong after **b** tried by
2: 20 you get no credit for **b** patient if you are beaten for
4: 14 Be happy if you are insulted for **b** a Christian.
4: 16 But it is no shame to suffer for **b** a Christian.
4: 16 Praise God for the privilege of **b** called by his
2Pe 3: 9 The Lord isn't really **b** slow about his promise to
3: 9 people think. No, he is **b** patient for your sake.
1Jn 4: 2 acknowledges that Jesus Christ became a human **b**,
Rev 3: 1 and that you have a reputation for **b** alive—
6: 3 I heard the second living **b** say, "Come!"
6: 5 third seal, I heard the third living **b** say, "Come!"
6: 7 I heard the fourth living **b** say, "Come!"
6: 9 the word of God and for **b** faithful in their witness.

BEINGS (40) [BEING]

HUMAN BEINGS (3) Ac 14:15; Heb 2:14; 5:1

LIVING BEINGS (30) Eze 1:5,9,11,13,14,19,20,20,21,21,21,21; 3:13; 10:15,17,20; Rev 4:6,7,8,9; 5:6,8,11,14; 6:1,6; 7:11; 14:3; 15:7; 19:4

Ge 3: 24 the LORD God stationed mighty angelic **b** to the
Dt 32: 8 the peoples / according to the number of angelic **b**.
Eze 1: 5 From the center of the cloud came four living **b**
1: 9 being touched the wings of the two **b** beside it.
1: 9 The living **b** were able to fly in any direction
1: 11 touch the wings of the living **b** on either side of it,
1: 13 The living **b** looked like bright coals of fire
1: 14 And the living **b** darted to and fro like flashes of
1: 15 As I looked at these **b**, I saw four wheels on the
1: 17 The **b** could move forward in any of the four
1: 19 When the four living **b** moved, the wheels moved
1: 20 The spirit of the four living **b** was in the wheels.
1: 20 spirit went, the wheels and the living **b** went, too.
1: 21 When the living **b** moved, the wheels moved.
1: 21 When the living **b** stopped, the wheels stopped.
1: 21 When the living **b** flew into the air, the wheels rose
1: 21 For the spirit of the living **b** was in the wheels.
3: 13 It was the sound of the wings of the living **b** as
10: 15 These were the same living **b** I had seen beside the
10: 17 for the spirit of the living **b** was in the wheels.
10: 20 These were the same living **b** I had seen beneath
10: 22 were just like the faces of the **b** I had seen at the
Da 8: 10 throwing some of the heavenly **b** and stars to the
Ac 14: 15 We are merely human **b** like yourselves!
Heb 2: 14 Because God's children are human **b**—made of
5: 1 other human **b** in their dealings with God.
Rev 4: 6 and around the throne were four living **b**,
4: 7 The first of these living **b** had the form of a lion;
4: 8 Each of these living **b** had six wings, and their
4: 9 Whenever the living **b** give glory and honor
5: 6 and the four living **b** and among the twenty-four
5: 8 the four living **b** and the twenty-four elders fell
5: 11 around the throne and the living **b** and the elders.
5: 14 And the four living **b** said, "Amen!"
6: 1 Then one of the four living **b** called out with a
6: 6 And a voice from among the four living **b** said,
7: 11 and around the elders and the four living **b**.
14: 3 and before the four living **b** and the twenty-four
15: 7 And one of the four living **b** handed each of the
19: 4 and the four living **b** fell down and worshiped

BEKER (4) [BEKERITE]

Ge 46: 21 **B**, Ashbel, Gera, Naaman, Ehi, Rosh, Muppim,
Nu 26: 35 The Bekerite clan, named after its ancestor **B**.
1Ch 7: 6 of Benjamin's sons were Bela, **B**, and Jediael.
7: 8 The sons of **B** were Zemirah, Joash, Eliezer,

BEKERITE (1) [BEKER]

Nu 26: 35 The **B** clan, named after its ancestor Beker.

BEL (3)

Isa 46: 1 The idols of Babylon, **B** and Nebo, are being
Jer 50: 2 Her gods **B** and Marduk will be utterly disgraced.
51: 44 And I will punish **B**, the god of Babylon, and pull

BELA (14) [BELAITE, BELAITES, ZOAR]

Ge 14: 2 of Zeboiim, and the king of **B** (now called Zoar).
14: 3 and **B** formed an alliance and mobilized their
14: 8 Admah, Zeboiim, and **B** (now called Zoar)
36: 32 **B** son of Beor, who ruled from his city of
36: 33 When **B** died, Jobab son of Zerah from Bozrah
46: 21 Benjamin's sons were **B**, Beker, Ashbel, Gera,
Nu 26: 38 The Belaite clan, named after its ancestor **B**.
1Ch 1: 43 **B** son of Beor, who ruled from his city of
1: 44 When **B** died, Jobab son of Zerah from Bozrah
5: 8 and **B** son of Azaz, son of Shema, son of Joel.
7: 6 Three of Benjamin's sons were **B**, Beker,
7: 7 The sons of **B** were Ezbon, Uzzi, Uzziel, Jerimoth,
8: 1 of age, included **B** (the oldest), Ashbel, Aharah,
8: 3 The sons of **B** were Addar, Gera, Abihud,

BELAITE (1) [BELA]

Nu 26: 38 The **B** clan, named after its ancestor Bela.

BELAITES (1) [BELA]

Nu 26: 40 These were the subclans descended from the **B**:

BELCH [KJV] See FILTH

BELIEF (3) [BELIEVE]

1Th 2: 14 because of their **b** in Christ Jesus, suffered from
2Th 2: 13 who makes you holy and by your **b** in the truth.
Tit 1: 9 and steadfast **b** in the trustworthy message he was

BELIEVE (218) [BELIEF, BELIEVED, BELIEVER, BELIEVERS, BELIEVES, BELIEVING]

Ge 45: 26 Jacob was stunned at the news—he couldn't **b** it.
Ex 3: 13 ancestors has sent me to you,' they won't **b** me.
4: 1 Moses protested again, "Look, they won't **b** me!
4: 5 "Perform this sign, and they will **b** you,"
4: 8 "If they do not **b** the first miraculous sign,
4: 8 they will **b** the second," the LORD said.
4: 9 "And if they do not **b** you even after these two
Nu 14: 11 Will they never **b** me, even after all the miraculous
22: 37 "Didn't you **b** me when I said I would reward you
Dt 28: 66 with no reason to **b** that you will see the morning
2Sa 20: 20 And Joab replied, "**B** me, I don't want to destroy
1Ki 10: 7 I didn't **b** it until I arrived here and saw it with my
2Ki 17: 14 and refused to **b** in the LORD their God.
2Ch 9: 6 I didn't **b** it until I arrived here and saw it with my
20: 20 **B** in the LORD your God, and you will be able
20: 20 **B** in his prophets, and you will succeed."
Job 4: 6 Shouldn't you **b** that God will care for those who
Ps 78: 22 for they did not **b** God / or trust him to care for
78: 32 on sinning. / They refused to **b** in his miracles.
106: 24 for they wouldn't **b** his promise to care for them.
119: 66 I **b** in your commands; / now teach me good
Pr 14: 15 Only simpletons **b** everything they are told!
26: 24 may sound pleasant enough, but don't **b** them.
Isa 7: 9 its king, Pekah son of Remaliah. You do not **b** me?
7: 9 you want me to protect you, learn to **b** what I say."
29: 9 Do you not **b** it? Then go ahead and be blind if you
29: 24 Those in error will then **b** the truth, and those who
43: 10 You have been chosen to know me, **b** in me,
Jer 28: 15 has not sent you, but the people **b** your lies.
40: 14 assassinate you?" But Gedaliah refused to **b** them.
51: 41 The world can scarcely **b** its eyes at her fall!
Hab 1: 5 something you wouldn't **b** even if someone told
2: 9 You **b** your wealth will buy security, putting your
2: 18 your own hands! What fools you are to **b** such lies!
Mt 9: 28 asked them, "Do you **b** I can make you see?"
13: 21 or are persecuted because they **b** the word.
13: 57 they were deeply offended and refused to **b** in him.
17: 17 How long must I be with you until you **b**?
21: 22 If you **b**, you will receive whatever you ask for in
21: 25 was from heaven, he will ask why we didn't **b** him.
21: 32 and you didn't **b** him, while tax collectors
21: 32 you refused to turn from your sins and **b** him.
24: 26 and look. Or, 'Look, he is hiding here,' don't **b** it!
27: 42 come down from the cross, and we will **b** in him!
Mk 1: 15 Turn from your sins and **b** this Good News!"
4: 17 or are persecuted because they **b** the word.
6: 3 were deeply offended and refused to **b** in him.
6: 52 for their hearts were hard and they did not **b**.
9: 19 How long must I be with you until you **b**?
9: 24 "I do **b**, but help me not to doubt!"
11: 23 All that's required is that you really **b** and do not
11: 24 pray for anything, and if you **b**, you will have it.
11: 31 was from heaven, he will ask why we didn't **b** him.
15: 32 down from the cross so we can see it and **b** him!"
15: 44 Pilate couldn't **b** that Jesus was already dead,
16: 11 was alive and she had seen him, they didn't **b** her.
16: 14 their stubborn refusal to **b** those who had seen him
16: 16 But anyone who refuses to **b** will be condemned.
16: 17 These signs will accompany those who **b**:
Lk 1: 20 And now, since you didn't **b** what I said,
8: 13 They **b** for a while, but they wilt when the hot
17: 23 Don't **b** such reports or go out to look for him.
20: 5 was from heaven, he will ask why we didn't **b** him.
21: 8 'The time has come!' But don't **b** them.
22: 67 But he replied, "If I tell you, you won't **b** me.
24: 11 the story sounded like nonsense, so they didn't **b** it.
24: 25 so hard to **b** all that the prophets wrote in the
Jn 1: 7 so that everyone might **b** because of his testimony.
1: 50 "Do you **b** all this just because I told you I had
3: 11 we know and have seen, and yet you won't **b** us.
3: 12 But if you don't even **b** me when I tell you about
3: 12 how can you possibly **b** if I tell you what is going
3: 32 and heard, but how few **b** what he tells them!
3: 33 Those who **b** him discover that God is true.
3: 36 And all who **b** in God's Son have eternal life.
4: 21 Jesus replied, "**B** me, the time is coming when it
4: 41 for many of them to hear his message and **b**.
4: 42 "Now we **b** because we have heard him ourselves,
4: 48 and wonders before you people will **b** in me?"
5: 24 and **b** in God who sent me have eternal life.
5: 38 message in your hearts, because you do not **b** me—
5: 39 because you **b** they give you eternal life.
5: 44 No wonder you can't **b**! For you gladly honor each
5: 47 And since you don't **b** what he wrote, how will
you **b** what I say?"
6: 29 God wants you to do: **B** in the one he has sent."
6: 30 us a miraculous sign if you want us to **b** in you.
6: 35 hungry again. Those who **b** in me will never thirst.
6: 40 see his Son and **b** in him should have eternal life—
6: 64 But some of you don't **b** me." (For Jesus knew
from the beginning who didn't **b**,
6: 69 We **b** them, and we know you are the Holy One of
7: 5 For even his brothers didn't **b** in him.
7: 38 If you **b** in me, come and drink! For the Scriptures
8: 24 for unless you **b** that I am who I say I am, you will
8: 45 when I tell the truth, you just naturally don't **b** me!
8: 46 I am telling you the truth, why don't you **b** me?
9: 18 The Jewish leaders wouldn't **b** he had been blind,
9: 35 the man and said, "Do you **b** in the Son of Man?"
9: 38 "Yes, Lord," the man said, "I **b**!" And he
10: 25 "I have already told you, and you don't **b** me.
10: 26 But you don't **b** me because you are not part of my
10: 37 Don't **b** me unless I carry out my Father's work.
10: 38 But if I do his work, **b** in what I have done, even if
you don't **b** me.
11: 15 because this will give you another opportunity to **b**
11: 25 Those who **b** in me, even though they die like
11: 26 and will never perish. Do you **b** this, Martha?"
11: 40 I tell you that you will see God's glory if you **b**?"
11: 42 people standing here, so they will **b** you sent me."
12: 36 **B** in the light while there is still time; then you will
12: 37 he had done, most of the people did not **b** in him.
12: 39 But the people couldn't **b**, for as Isaiah also said,
13: 19 so that when it happens you will **b** I am the
14: 10 Don't you **b** that I am in the Father and the Father
14: 11 Just **b** that I am in the Father and the Father is in
14: 11 Or at least **b** because of what you have seen me do.
14: 29 so that you will **b** when they do happen.
16: 27 because you love me and **b** that I came from God.
16: 30 From this we **b** that you came from God."
16: 31 Jesus asked, "Do you finally **b**?
17: 8 that I came from you, and they **b** you sent me.
17: 20 but also for all who will ever **b** in me because of
17: 21 will be in us, and the world will **b** you sent me.
19: 35 it is presented so that you also can **b**.
20: 25 "I won't **b** it unless I see the nail wounds in his
20: 27 in my side. Don't be faithless any longer. **B**!"
20: 29 Jesus told him, "You **b** because you have seen me.
20: 29 are those who haven't seen me and **b** anyway."
20: 31 so that you may **b** that Jesus is the Messiah,
Ac 13: 41 in your own day, / something you wouldn't **b**
15: 7 so that they could hear the Good News and **b**.
15: 11 We **b** that we are all saved the same way,
16: 31 "**B** on the Lord Jesus and you will be saved,
19: 4 John himself told the people to **b** in Jesus, the one
22: 18 for the people here won't **b** you when you give
23: 8 or spirits, but the Pharisees **b** in all of these.
24: 14 and I firmly **b** the Jewish law and everything
24: 21 because I **b** in the resurrection of the dead!' "
26: 9 "I used to **b** that I ought to do everything I could
26: 27 King Agrippa, do you **b** the prophets? I know you
27: 10 he said, "I **b** there is trouble ahead if we go on—
27: 25 So take courage! For I **b** God. It will be just as he
28: 20 this chain because I **b** that the hope of Israel—
28: 22 But we want to hear what you **b**, for the only thing
Ro 1: 5 so that they will **b** and obey him, bringing glory to
1: 25 truth about God, they deliberately chose to **b** lies.
3: 25 We are made right with God when we **b** that Jesus
3: 26 to be right in his sight because they **b** in Jesus.
4: 16 For Abraham is the father of all who **b**.
4: 24 will also declare us to be righteous if we **b** in God,
10: 4 the law. All who **b** in him are made right with God.
10: 9 and **b** in your heart that God raised him from the
10: 14 they call on him to save them unless they **b** in him?
10: 14 And how can they **b** in him if they have never
11: 20 were broken off because they didn't **b** God, and
you are there because you do **b**.
14: 22 You may have the faith to **b** that there is nothing
14: 23 If you do anything you **b** is not right, you are
15: 13 keep you happy and full of peace as you **b** in him.
16: 26 so that they might **b** and obey Christ.
1Co 1: 21 has used our foolish preaching to save all who **b**.
1: 22 because they **b** only what agrees with their own
3: 5 only servants. Through us God caused you to **b**.
5: 1 I can hardly **b** the report about the sexual
8: 12 them to do something they **b** is wrong.
11: 18 you meet as a church, and to some extent I **b** it.
15: 2 this Good News that saves you if you firmly **b** it—
16: 13 Be on guard. Stand true to what you **b**.
2Co 4: 4 has blinded the minds of those who don't **b**,
5: 14 Since we **b** that Christ died for everyone, we also
b that we have all died to the old life we
11: 4 You seem to **b** whatever anyone tells you, even if
Gal 1: 20 You must **b** what I am saying, for I declare before
3: 5 because you **b** the message you heard about Christ.
3: 22 so the only way to receive God's promise is to **b** in
Eph 1: 19 greatness of his power for us who **b** him.
2: 21 We who **b** are carefully joined together,
4: 14 forever changing our minds about what we **b**
Php 1: 1 who **b** in Christ Jesus, and to the elders

3:15 on some point, I **b** God will make it plain to you.
Col 1:23 But you must continue to **b** this truth and stand in
1Th 2:13 And this word continues to work in you who **b**.
4:14 For since we **b** that Jesus died and was raised to life again, we also **b** that when Jesus comes,
2Th 2:2 or a letter supposedly from us, don't **b** them.
2:10 because they refuse to **b** the truth that would save
2:11 deception upon them, and they will **b** all these lies.
1Ti 1:15 This is a true saying, and everyone should **b** it:
1:16 that they, too, can **b** in him and receive eternal life.
4:1 the last times some will turn away from what we **b**;
4:3 thanksgiving by people who know and **b** the truth.
4:10 and suffer much in order that people will **b** the
4:10 of all people, and particularly of those who **b**.
5:8 in the same household, have denied what we **b**.
6:12 Fight the good fight for what we **b**. Hold tightly to
2Ti 2:25 those people's hearts, and they will **b** the truth.
Heb 4:2 no good because they didn't **b** what God told them.
4:3 For only we who **b** can enter his place of rest.
4:3 As for those who didn't **b**, God said, / "In my
6:9 like this, we really don't **b** that it applies to you.
11:6 Anyone who wants to come to him must **b** that
Jas 2:19 Do you still think it's enough just to **b** that there is
2:19 Well, even the demons **b** this, and they tremble in
1Pe 2:7 Yes, he is very precious to you who **b**. But for
2:12 and they will **b** and give honor to God when he
2Pe 1:13 I **b** I should keep on reminding you of these things
1Jn 3:3 And all who **b** this will keep themselves pure,
3:23 We must **b** in the name of his Son, Jesus Christ,
4:1 do not **b** everyone who claims to speak by the
5:5 are the ones who **b** that Jesus is the Son of God.
5:9 Since we **b** human testimony, surely we can **b** the testimony that comes from
5:10 All who **b** in the Son of God know that this is true.
5:10 Those who don't **b** this are actually calling God a
5:10 because they don't **b** what God has testified about
5:13 I write this to you who **b** in the Son of God,
2Jn 1:7 They do not **b** that Jesus Christ came to earth in a

BELIEVED (71) [BELIEVE]

Ge 15:6 And Abram **b** the LORD, and the LORD
Ex 9:20 Some of Pharaoh's officials **b** what the LORD
1Sa 27:12 Achish **b** David and thought to himself, "By now
Ps 106:12 Then at last his people **b** his promises. / Then they
116:10 I **b** in you, so I prayed, / "I am deeply troubled,
Isa 53:1 Who has **b** our message? To whom will the
La 4:12 would have **b** an enemy could march through the
Jnh 3:5 The people of Nineveh **b** God's message, and from
Mt 8:13 "Go on home. What you have **b** has happened."
14:5 because all the people **b** John was a prophet.
Mk 16:13 rushed back to tell the others, but no one **b** them.
Lk 1:45 because you **b** that the Lord would do what he
Jn 1:12 But to all who **b** him and accepted him, he gave
2:11 display of his glory. And his disciples **b** in him.
2:22 said this. And they **b** both Jesus and the Scriptures.
4:39 Many Samaritans from the village **b** in Jesus
4:50 And the man **b** Jesus' word and started home.
4:53 And the officer and his entire household **b** in Jesus.
5:46 But if you had **b** Moses, you would have **b** me because he wrote about me.
6:36 But you haven't **b** in me even though you have
7:31 Many among the crowds at the Temple **b** in him.
8:30 Then many who heard him say these things **b** in
8:31 Jesus said to the people who **b** in him, "You are
10:42 And many **b** in him there.
11:27 "I have always **b** you are the Messiah, the Son of
11:45 Many of the people who were with Mary **b** in
12:11 of the people had deserted them and **b** in Jesus.
12:38 "Lord, who has **b** our message? / To whom will
12:42 including some of the Jewish leaders, **b** in him.
20:8 the other disciple also went in, and he saw and **b**—
Ac 2:41 Those who **b** what Peter said were baptized
4:4 But many of the people who heard their message **b**
5:14 And more and more people **b** and were brought to
8:12 But now the people **b** Philip's message of Good
8:13 Then Simon himself **b** and was baptized. He began
9:42 through the whole town, and many **b** in the Lord.
11:17 gift he gave us when we **b** in the Lord Jesus Christ,
11:21 and large numbers of these Gentiles **b** and turned
13:12 he **b** and was astonished at what he learned about
14:1 that a great number of both Jews and Gentiles **b**.
16:34 household rejoiced because they all **b** in God.
17:12 As a result, many Jews **b**, as did some of the
18:8 the synagogue, and all his household **b** in the Lord.
18:27 great benefit to those who, by God's grace, had **b**.
19:2 "Did you receive the Holy Spirit when you **b**?"
21:20 how many thousands of Jews have also **b**,
22:19 and beat those in every synagogue who **b** on you.
28:24 Some **b** and some didn't.
Ro 4:3 For the Scriptures tell us, "Abraham **b** God,
4:17 because Abraham **b** in the God who brings the
4:18 the father of many nations, Abraham **b** him.
10:16 the prophet said, "Lord, who has **b** our message?"
13:11 our salvation is nearer now than when we first **b**.
1Co 15:2 you **b** something that was never true in the first
15:11 The important thing is that you **b** what we
2Co 4:13 had when he said, "I **b** in God, and so I speak."
11:4 or a different kind of gospel than the one you **b**.
Gal 2:16 So we have **b** in Christ Jesus, that we might be
3:2 for the Holy Spirit came upon you only after you **b**
3:6 In the same way, "Abraham **b** God, so God
Eph 1:13 And when you **b** in Christ, he identified you as his
2:8 God saved you by his special favor when you **b**.
3:6 Both groups have **b** the Good News, and both are
2Th 1:10 on that day, for you **b** what we testified about him.
1Ti 3:16 He was **b** on in the world / and was taken up into
Heb 3:14 trusting God just as firmly as when we first **b**,
11:11 Abraham **b** that God would keep his promise.
Jas 2:23 "Abraham **b** God, so God declared him to be
1Pe 4:17 what terrible fate awaits those who have never **b**
Rev 3:3 Go back to what you heard and **b** at first; hold to it

BELIEVER (14) [BELIEVE]

Mt 18:15 "If another **b** sins against you, go privately
Lk 17:3 If another **b** sins, rebuke him; then if he repents,
Ac 9:10 Now there was a **b** in Damascus named Ananias.
9:14 the leading priests to arrest every **b** in Damascus."
9:26 They thought he was only pretending to be a **b**!
9:36 There was a **b** in Joppa named Tabitha (which in
16:1 a young disciple whose mother was a Jewish **b**,
Ro 14:2 But another **b** who has a sensitive conscience will
1Co 7:18 a man who was circumcised before he became a **b**
7:18 he became a **b** should not be circumcised now.
7:24 situation you were in when you became a **b**,
2Co 6:15 How can a **b** be a partner with an unbeliever?
1Ti 6:2 because you are helping another **b** by your efforts.
Phm 1:10 because he became a **b** as a result of my ministry

BELIEVERS (88) [BELIEVE]

Jn 21:23 So the rumor spread among the community of **b**
Ac 1:15 on a day when about 120 **b** were present,
2:1 the **b** were meeting together in one place.
2:6 to hear their own languages being spoken by the **b**.
2:42 They joined with the other **b** and devoted
2:44 And all the **b** met together constantly and shared
4:4 so that the number of **b** totaled about five thousand
4:23 Peter and John found the other **b** and told them
4:24 Then all the **b** were united as they lifted their
4:32 All the **b** were of one heart and mind, and they felt
5:12 And the **b** were meeting regularly at the Temple in
6:1 But as the **b** rapidly multiplied, there were
6:2 So the Twelve called a meeting of all the **b**.
6:7 The number of **b** greatly increased in Jerusalem,
8:1 and all the **b** except the apostles fled into Judea
8:4 But the **b** who had fled Jerusalem went everywhere
8:17 Then Peter and John laid their hands upon these **b**,
9:13 things this man has done to the **b** in Jerusalem!
9:19 Saul stayed with the **b** in Damascus for a few days.
9:25 some of the other **b** let him down in a large basket
9:26 he tried to meet with the **b**, but they were all afraid
9:30 When the **b** heard about it, however, they took him
9:31 The **b** were walking in the fear of the Lord and in
9:32 Peter traveled from place to place to visit the **b**,
9:41 Then he called in the widows and all the **b**, and he
10:23 accompanied by some other **b** from Joppa.
10:45 The Jewish **b** who came with Peter were amazed
11:1 and other **b** in Judea that the Gentiles had received
11:2 in Jerusalem, some of the Jewish **b** criticized him.
11:19 the **b** who had fled from Jerusalem during the
11:20 some of the **b** who went to Antioch from Cyprus
11:23 and he encouraged the **b** to stay true to the Lord.
11:26 (It was there at Antioch that the **b** were first called
11:29 So the **b** in Antioch decided to send relief to the **b** in Judea,
12:1 Agrippa began to persecute some **b** in the church.
12:24 spreading rapidly, and there were many new **b**.
13:48 all who were appointed to eternal life became **b**.
13:52 And the **b** were filled with joy and with the Holy
14:20 But as the **b** stood around him, he got up and went
14:22 where they strengthened the **b**. They encouraged
14:28 And they stayed there with the **b** in Antioch for a
15:2 accompanied by some local **b**, to talk to the
15:3 the way in Phoenicia and Samaria to visit the **b**.
15:10 **b** with a yoke that neither we nor our ancestors
15:23 It is written to the Gentile **b** in Antioch, Syria,
15:36 the Lord, to see how the new **b** are getting along."
15:40 Paul chose Silas, and the **b** sent them off,
16:2 Timothy was well thought of by the **b** in Lystra
16:40 where they met with the **b** and encouraged them
17:6 dragged out Jason and some of the other **b** instead
17:9 and the other **b** after they had posted bail.
17:10 That very night the **b** sent Paul and Silas to Berea.
17:14 The **b** acted at once, sending Paul on to the coast,
17:34 but some joined him and became **b**. Among them
18:8 Many others in Corinth also became **b** and were
18:23 went back to Galatia and Phrygia, visiting all the **b**,
18:27 They wrote to the **b** in Achaia, asking them to
19:1 he came to Ephesus, where he found several **b**.
19:9 so Paul left the synagogue and took the **b** with him.
19:18 Many who became **b** confessed their sinful
19:30 Paul wanted to go in, but the **b** wouldn't let him.
20:1 all over, Paul sent for the **b** and encouraged them.
20:2 he encouraged the **b** in all the towns he passed
21:4 We went ashore, found the local **b**, and stayed with
21:7 where we greeted the **b** but stayed only one day.
21:12 were traveling with him, as well as the local **b**,
21:16 Some **b** from Caesarea accompanied us, and they
21:17 All the **b** in Jerusalem welcomed us cordially.
26:10 I caused many of the **b** in Jerusalem to be sent to
28:14 There we found some **b**, who invited us to stay
28:15 The **b** in Rome had heard we were coming,
Ro 8:27 for the Spirit pleads for us **b** in harmony with
15:26 the **b** in Greece have eagerly taken up an offering
16:15 to Olympas and all the other **b** who are with them.
1Co 14:22 in tongues is a sign, not for **b**, but for unbelievers;
14:22 prophecy, however, is for the benefit of **b**,
16:11 forward to seeing him soon, along with the other **b**.
16:12 I urged him to visit you along with the other **b**,
16:20 The other **b** here have asked me to greet you for
1Th 2:10 and honest and faultless toward all of you **b**.
2:14 you imitated the **b** in God's churches in Judea
1Ti 4:12 Be an example to all **b** in what you teach,
4:13 the church, encouraging the **b**, and teaching them.
Tit 1:6 and his children must be **b** who are not wild
3:15 Please give my greetings to all of the **b** who love
Heb 13:24 to all your leaders and to the other **b** there.
Rev 19:10 and other **b** who testify of their faith in Jesus.

BELIEVES (18) [BELIEVE]

Isa 28:16 to build on. Whoever **b** need never run away again.
Mk 9:23 Jesus asked. "Anything is possible if a person **b**."
16:16 Anyone who **b** and is baptized will be saved.
Jn 3:15 so that everyone who **b** in me will have eternal life.
3:16 so that everyone who **b** in him will not perish
6:47 anyone who **b** in me already has eternal life.
7:48 single one of us rulers or Pharisees who **b** in him?
14:12 anyone who **b** in me will do the same works I have
Ac 10:43 saying that everyone who **b** in him will have their
13:39 Everyone who **b** in him is freed from all guilt
Ro 1:16 power of God at work, saving everyone who **b**—
9:33 But anyone who **b** in him / will not be
10:11 "Anyone who **b** in him will not be disappointed."
14:2 one person **b** it is all right to eat anything.
14:14 But if someone **b** it is wrong, then for that person it
2Th 3:2 and evil people, for not everyone **b** in the Lord.
1Pe 2:6 a chosen cornerstone, / and anyone who **b** in him
1Jn 5:1 Everyone who **b** that Jesus is the Christ is a child

BELIEVING (15) [BELIEVE]

Jer 29:31 not send him and has tricked you into **b** his lies,
Hos 10:13 **b** that great armies could make your nation safe!
Lk 8:12 it away and prevents them from **b** and being saved.
Jn 3:18 been judged for not **b** in the only Son of God.
7:39 who would be given to everyone **b** in him.
11:26 They are given eternal life for **b** in me and will
20:31 of God, and that by **b** in him you will have life.
Ro 1:25 Instead of **b** what they knew was the truth about
4:20 Abraham never wavered in **b** God's promise.
10:10 For it is by **b** in your heart that you are made right
1Co 15:18 all who have died **b** in Christ have perished!
2Co 3:14 And this veil can be removed only by **b** in Christ.
5:7 That is why we live by **b** and not by seeing.
Gal 5:10 I am trusting the Lord to bring you back to **b** as I
2Th 2:12 Then they will be condemned for not **b** the truth

BELITTLE (1)

Pr 11:12 It is foolish to **b** a neighbor; a person with good

BELLIES (1) [BELLY]

Lev 11:42 includes all animals that slither along on their **b**,

BELLOWS (1)

Jer 6:29 The **b** blow fiercely. The refining fire grows hotter.

BELLS (6)

Ex 28:33 to the hem of the robe, with gold **b** between them.
28:34 The gold **b** and pomegranates are to alternate all
28:35 and the **b** will tinkle as he goes in and out of the
39:25 **B** of pure gold were placed between the
39:26 with **b** and pomegranates alternating all around the
Zec 14:20 On that day even the harness **b** of the horses will

BELLY (10) [BELLIES, BELLYFUL]

Ge 3:14 dust as long as you live, crawling along on your **b**.
Jdg 3:21 to his right thigh, and plunged it into the king's **b**.
Job 40:16 See its powerful loins and the muscles of its **b**.
41:30 Its **b** is covered with scales as sharp as glass.
Pr 13:25 but the **b** of the wicked goes hungry.
SS 7:2 Your **b** is lovely, like a heap of wheat set about
Jer 51:34 a great monster and filled his **b** with our riches.
Da 2:32 were of silver, its **b** and thighs were of bronze,
2:39 represented by the bronze **b** and thighs,
Mt 12:40 For as Jonah was in the **b** of the great fish for three

BELLYFUL (1) [BELLY]

Job 20:23 May God give him a **b** of trouble. May God rain

BELONG (124) [BELONGED, BELONGING, BELONGINGS, BELONGS]

Ge 32:18 You should reply, 'These **b** to your servant Jacob.
38:9 from having a baby who would **b** to his brother.
47:24 harvest it, a fifth of your crop will **b** to Pharaoh.
Ex 21:4 but his wife and children will still **b** to his master.
21:6 After that, the slave will **b** to his master forever.
29:27 holy the parts of the ordination ram that **b** to Aaron
Lev 5:13 The rest of the flour will **b** to the priest, just as
6:16 the rest of the flour will **b** to Aaron and his sons
7:14 then **b** to the priest who sprinkles the altar with
7:31 but the breast will **b** to Aaron and his sons.
10:15 Then they will **b** to you and your descendants
23:20 are holy to the LORD and will **b** to the priests.
24:9 The loaves of bread **b** to Aaron and his male
25:28 then it will **b** to the new owner until the next Year
27:15 20 percent. Then the house will again **b** to you.
27:19 plus 20 percent. Then the field will again **b** to you.
27:26 because the firstborn of these animals already **b** to
Nu 5:9 that the Israelites bring to a priest will **b** to him.
8:14 the people of Israel, and the Levites will **b** to me.
18:11 before the altar also **b** to you as your regular share.
18:13 that the people present to the LORD **b** to you.
31:28 donkeys, sheep, and goats that **b** to the army.
31:54 to the LORD that the people of Israel **b** to him.
Dt 7:6 are a holy people, who **b** to the LORD your God.
10:14 and everything in it all **b** to the LORD your God.

22: 2 If it does not **b** to someone nearby or you don't
29:29 "There are secret things that **b** to the LORD,
29:29 but the revealed things **b** to us and our descendants
32: 9 For the people of Israel **b** to the LORD; / Jacob is
1Sa 1:28 and he will **b** to the LORD his whole life."
30:13 "To whom do you **b**, and where do you come
30:20 "These all **b** to David as his reward!" they said.
Ne 5: 5 We **b** to the same family, and our children are just
Job 31:10 then may my wife **b** to another man; may other
Ps 24: 1 in it. / The world and all its people **b** to him.
47: 9 For all the kings of the earth **b** to God. / He is
50:11 and all the animals of the field **b** to me.
73:23 Yet I still **b** to you; / you are holding my right
74:16 Both day and night **b** to you; / you made the
82: 8 and judge the earth, / for all the nations **b** to you.
115:16 The heavens **b** to the LORD, / but he has given
Pr 8:14 Good advice and success **b** to me. Insight
Isa 26:19 Those who **b** to God will live; / their bodies will
44: 5 Some will proudly claim, 'I **b** to the LORD.'
Jer 5:10 from the vine, for they do not **b** to the LORD.
6:13 they trick others to get what does not **b** to them.
8:10 they trick others to get what does not **b** to them.
32:25 even though the city will soon **b** to the
Eze 33:26 Idolaters! Adulterers! Should the land **b** to you?
36: 2 saying, 'Aha! Now the ancient heights **b** to us!'
44:29 Whatever anyone sets apart for the LORD will **b**
46:16 it will **b** to him and his descendants forever.
48:21 the sacred lands and the city, will **b** to the prince.
Joel 2:17 They **b** to you, so don't let them become an object
Mt 5: 5 and lowly, / for the whole earth will **b** to them.
13:38 The weeds are the people who **b** to the evil one.
Mk 9:41 even a cup of water because you **b** to the Messiah,
Jn 13: 8 "But if I don't wash you, you won't **b** to me."
15:21 of the world will hate you because you **b** to me,
17: 9 those you have given me, because they **b** to you.
17:10 And all of them, since they are mine, **b** to you;
17:14 hates them because they do not **b** to the world,
Ac 7: 5 that eventually the whole country would **b** to
18:10 because many people here in this city **b** to me."
27:23 For last night an angel of the God to whom I **b**
Ro 1: 6 You are among those who have been called to **b** to
8: 1 So now there is no condemnation for those who **b**
11:24 to graft the Jews back into the tree where they **b**.
12: 5 we **b** to each other, and each of us needs all the
14: 8 the Lord. So in life and in death, we **b** to the Lord.
1Co 1: 4 he has given you, now that you **b** to Christ Jesus.
3: 3 You are acting like people who don't **b** to the
3: 9 We work together as partners who **b** to God.
3:23 and you **b** to Christ, and Christ belongs to God.
6:19 given to you by God? You do not **b** to yourself,
2Co 10: 7 You must recognize that we **b** to Christ just as
10: 7 as those who proudly declare that they **b** to Christ.
Gal 3:29 And now that you **b** to Christ, you are the true
3:29 and now all the promises God gave to him **b** to
5:24 Those who **b** to Christ Jesus have nailed the
6:17 For I bear on my body the scars that show I **b** to
Eph 1: 3 in the heavenly realms because we **b** to Christ.
1: 6 out on us because we **b** to his dearly loved Son.
2:13 But now you **b** to Christ Jesus. Though you once
4:25 neighbor the truth" because we **b** to each other.
6: 1 obey your parents because you **b** to the Lord,
Php 4: 2 Please, because you **b** to the Lord, settle your
Col 3:18 as is fitting for those who **b** to the Lord.
1Th 1: 1 you who **b** to God the Father and the Lord Jesus
3:13 our Lord Jesus comes with all those who **b** to him.
5: 5 and of the day; we don't **b** to darkness and night.
5:18 for this is God's will for you who **b** to Christ Jesus.
2Th 1: 1 you who **b** to God our Father and the Lord Jesus
1Ti 6:11 But you, Timothy, **b** to God; so run from all these
2Ti 2:19 and "Those who claim they **b** to the Lord must
Heb 3: 1 dear friends who **b** to God and are bound for
1Pe 3:16 what a good life you live because you **b** to Christ.
4:11 All glory and power **b** to him forever and ever.
1Jn 2: 3 And how can we be sure that we **b** to him?
2: 4 If someone says, "I **b** to God," but doesn't obey
2:19 they left us, it proved that they do not **b** with us.
3: 1 But the people who **b** to this world don't know
3: 8 keep on sinning, it shows they **b** to the Devil,
3:10 and does not love other Christians does not **b** to
4: 4 But you **b** to God, my dear children. You have
4: 5 These people **b** to this world, so they speak from
4: 6 But we **b** to God; that is why those who know God
4: 6 If they do not **b** to God, they do not listen to us.
Jude 1:25 glory, majesty, power, and authority **b** to him,
Rev 3: 9 I will force those who **b** to Satan—those liars who
3:10 the whole world to test those who **b** to this world.
5:13 and power / **b** to the one sitting on the throne
6:10 who **b** to this world for what they have done to us?
7:12 **b** to our God forever and forever. Amen!"
8:13 terror to all who **b** to this world because of what
11:10 All the people who **b** to this world will give
12:17 and confess that they **b** to Jesus.
13: 8 And all the people who **b** to this world worshiped
13:12 and those who **b** to this world to worship the first
13:14 he deceived all the people who **b** to this world.
14: 6 News to preach to the people who **b** to this world
17: 2 and the people who **b** to this world have been
17: 8 And the people who **b** to this world, whose names
19: 1 is from our God. Glory and power **b** to him alone.

BELONGED (32) [BELONG]

Ge 30:42 so the weaker lambs **b** to Laban, and the stronger
47:20 so severe, and their land then **b** to Pharaoh.
Lev 25:10 when each of you returns to the lands that **b** to
25:13 must return to the lands that **b** to your ancestors.
Dt 11: 6 and tents and every living thing that **b** to them.
30: 5 He will return you to the land that **b** to your
Jos 17: 8 (The land surrounding Tappuah **b** to Manasseh,
17: 8 of Manasseh's territory, **b** to the tribe of Ephraim.)
17: 9 (Several towns in Manasseh's territory **b** to the
17:10 The land south of the ravine **b** to Ephraim,
17:10 and the land north of the ravine **b** to Manasseh,
22: 9 the territory that **b** to them according to the
Jdg 5:14 a land that once **b** to the Amalekites,
6:11 at Ophrah, which **b** to Joash of the clan of Abiezer.
Ru 2: 3 she found herself working in a field that **b** to Boaz,
4: 3 She is selling the land that **b** to our relative
2Sa 9: 7 I will give you all the land that once **b** to your
9: 9 your master's grandson everything that **b** to Saul
1Ki 6:22 including the altar that **b** to the Most Holy Place.
2Ki 9:21 They met him at the field that had **b** to Naboth of
11:10 and shields that had once **b** to King David
14:28 both Damascus and Hamath, which had **b** to Judah,
1Ch 5: 2 a ruler for the nation, but the birthright **b** to Joseph.
2Ch 23: 9 and shields that had once **b** to King David
Ne 13: 5 Moses had decreed that these offerings **b** to the
Isa 63:19 why do you treat us as though we never **b** to you?
Jer 38: 6 It **b** to Malkijah, a member of the royal family.
Jn 15:19 The world would love you if you **b** to it, but you
1Co 7:32 I had to talk as though you **b** to this world or as
1Jn 2:19 our churches because they never really **b** with us;
3:12 who **b** to the evil one and killed his brother.
Jude 1: 6 God gave them but left the place where they **b**.

BELONGING (17) [BELONG]

Ge 14:13 who was camped at the oak grove **b** to Mamre the
18: 1 he was camped near the oak grove **b** to Mamre.
23:17 He bought the plot of land **b** to Ephron at
47:22 The only land he didn't buy was that **b** to the
Lev 25:32 house they have sold within the cities **b** to them.
Nu 17: 5 Buds will sprout on the staff **b** to the man I choose.
31:42 The half of the plunder **b** to the people of Israel,
31:42 which Moses had separated from the half **b** to the
Dt 2: 4 "You will be passing through the country **b** to
9: 1 River to occupy the land **b** to nations much greater
Jos 18:14 one of the towns **b** to the tribe of Judah.
2Ch 26:23 he was buried nearby in a burial field **b** to the
Eze 1:15 on the ground beneath them, one wheel **b** to each.
48:13 the same size and shape as that **b** to the priests—
Ac 28: 7 Near the shore where we landed was an estate **b** to
Php 2: 1 Is there any encouragement from **b** to Christ?
Heb 7:16 not by meeting the old requirement of **b** to the tribe

BELONGINGS (10) [BELONG]

Ge 12:20 and his wife, with all their household and **b**.
45:20 Don't worry about your **b**, for the best of all the
46: 6 and all the **b** they had acquired in the land of
Nu 16:30 opens up and swallows them and all their **b**,
16:33 went down alive into the grave, along with their **b**.
Jos 7:11 lied about it and hidden the things among their **b**.
Jdg 14:19 town of Ashkelon, killed thirty men, took their **b**,
Ne 13: 8 and threw all of Tobiah's **b** from the room.
Lk 11:22 strips him of his weapons, and carries off his **b**.
15:13 few days later this younger son packed all his **b**

BELONGS (61) [BELONG]

Ge 27: 4 Then I will pronounce the blessing that **b** to you,
28:13 Isaac. The ground you are lying on **b** to you.
31:32 If you find anything that **b** to you, I swear before
31:37 Now show me what you have found that **b** to you!
49:10 until the coming of the one to whom it **b**,
Ex 9:29 This will prove to you that the earth **b** to the
12:42 the land of Egypt, so this same night now **b** to him.
19: 5 the nations of the earth; for all the earth **b** to me.
34:19 "Every firstborn male **b** to me—of both cattle
35: 2 a day of total rest, a holy day that **b** to the LORD.
Lev 3:16 Remember, all the fat **b** to the LORD.
7: 7 the meat of the sacrificed animal **b** to the priest in
7: 8 the hide of the sacrificed animal also **b** to the
7: 9 or cooked on a griddle **b** to the priest who presents
25:23 on a permanent basis because it really **b** to me.
27:30 **b** to the LORD and must be set apart to him as
Nu 5: 8 it **b** to the LORD and must be given to the priest,
16: 5 morning the LORD will show us who **b** to him
16:26 and don't touch anything that **b** to them.
18: 9 that portion **b** to you and your sons.
18:14 is specially set apart for the LORD also **b** to you.
31:30 and goats in the half that **b** to the people of Israel.
Jos 3:11 which **b** to the Lord of the whole earth,
7:14 will point out the tribe to which the guilty man **b**.
13: 3 territory that **b** to the Canaanites. This land extends
13: 4 including Mearah (which **b** to the Sidonians),
14:14 Hebron still **b** to the descendants of Caleb son of
1Sa 27: 6 (which still **b** to the kings of Judah to this day),
2Sa 20:19 Why do you want to destroy what **b** to the
1Ki 3:23 and each says that the dead child **b** to the other.
1Ch 29:16 your holy name come from you! It all **b** to you!
Job 12:12 Wisdom **b** to the aged, and understanding to those
22: 8 you think the land **b** to the powerful and that those
Ps 62:11 heard it many times: / Power, O God, **b** to you;
65: 1 What mighty praise, O God, / **b** to you in Zion.
94: 1 O LORD, the God to whom vengeance **b**,
95: 5 The sea **b** to him, for he made it. / His hands
Pr 21:31 for battle, but the victory **b** to the LORD.
Jer 10: 7 O King of nations? That title **b** to you alone!
Eze 48:14 or traded or used by others, for it **b** to the LORD;
Mt 19:14 For the Kingdom of Heaven **b** to such as these."
22:21 he said, "give to Caesar what **b** to him.
22:21 But everything that **b** to God must be given to
Mk 10:14 For the Kingdom of God **b** to such as these.
12:17 Jesus said, "give to Caesar what **b** to him.
12:17 But everything that **b** to God must be given to
Lk 18:16 For the Kingdom of God **b** to such as these.
20:25 he said, "give to Caesar what **b** to him.
20:25 But everything that **b** to God must be given to
Ac 1:25 for he has deserted us and gone where he **b**."
1Co 2: 6 but not the kind of wisdom that **b** to this world,
3:21 following a particular leader. Everything **b** to you:
3:22 the present and the future. Everything **b** to you,
3:23 and you belong to Christ, and Christ **b** to God.
6:15 which **b** to Christ, and join it to a prostitute?
Gal 1: 5 That is why all glory **b** to God through all the ages
4: 7 since you are his child, everything he has **b** to you.
Col 1:12 who has enabled you to share the inheritance that **b**
Heb 3:14 first believed, we will share in all that **b** to Christ.
7:13 For the one we are talking about **b** to a different
Rev 13: 8 which **b** to the Lamb who was killed before the

BELOVED (44) [LOVE]

BELOVED SON (8) Ge 22:12,16; Mt 3:17; 17:5; Mk 1:11; 9:7; Lk 3:22; 2Pe 1:17

MY BELOVED (23) SS 1:9,15; 2:2,10,13; 4:T,7; 5:8; 6:4,12; 7:6; 8:13; Isa 5:1; Jer 11:15; Mt 3:17; 12:18; 17:5; Mk 1:11; 9:7; Lk 3:22; 1Co 4:14,17; 2Pe 1:17

YOUR BELOVED (4) Ge 22:12,16; Ps 60:5; 108:6

Ge 22:12 You have not withheld even your **b** son from me."
22:16 obeyed me and have not withheld even your **b** son,
Dt 13: 6 "Suppose your brother, son, daughter, **b** wife,
28:54 own brother, his **b** wife, and his surviving children.
2Sa 1:23 How **b** and gracious were Saul and Jonathan!
12:25 "**b** of the LORD"—because the LORD loved
Ps 60: 5 right arm to save us, / and rescue your **b** people.
108: 6 right arm to save me, / and rescue your **b** people.
Pr 7: 4 a sister; make insight a **b** member of your family.
SS 1: 9 What a lovely filly you are, my **b** one!
1:15 "How beautiful you are, my **b**, how beautiful!
2: 2 to other women, my **b** is like a lily among thorns."
2:10 'Rise up, my **b**, my fair one, and come away.
2:13 Arise, my **b**, my fair one, and come away.' "
4: 1 "How beautiful you are, my **b**, how beautiful!
4: 7 You are so beautiful, my **b**, so perfect in every
5: 1 "Oh, lover and **b**, eat and drink! Yes, drink deeply
5: 8 If you find my **b** one, tell him that I am sick with
6: 4 "O my **b**, you are as beautiful as the lovely town
6: 9 my perfect one, the only **b** daughter of her mother!
6:12 I found myself in my princely bed with my **b**
7: 6 "Oh, how delightful you are, my **b**; how pleasant
8:13 "O my **b**, lingering in the gardens, how wonderful
Isa 5: 1 My **b** has a vineyard / on a rich and fertile hill.
Jer 11:15 What right do my **b** people have to come to my
22: 6 "You are as **b** to me as fruitful Gilead
La 1:15 The Lord has trampled his **b** city as grapes are
Da 11:37 nor for the god **b** of women, nor for any other god,
Hos 9:16 if they give birth, I will slaughter their **b** children."
Mal 2:11 for the men of Judah have defiled the LORD's **b**
Mt 3:17 And a voice from heaven said, "This is my **b** Son,
12:18 my Servant, / whom I have chosen. / He is my **B**,
17: 5 a voice from the cloud said, "This is my **b** Son,
Mk 1:11 "You are my **b** Son, and I am fully pleased with
9: 7 a voice from the cloud said, "This is my **b** Son.
Lk 3:22 a voice from heaven said, "You are my **b** Son,
Ac 15:25 along with our **b** Barnabas and Paul,
Ro 16: 9 our co-worker in Christ, and **b** Stachys.
1Co 4:14 to shame you, but to warn you as my **b** children.
4:17 For he is my **b** and trustworthy child in the Lord.
Phm 1:16 just a slave; he is a **b** brother, especially to me.
2Pe 1:17 called down from heaven, "This is my **b** Son;
3:15 This is just as our **b** brother Paul wrote to you with
Rev 20: 9 and surrounded God's people and the **b** city.

BELOW (31)

Ge 1: 7 to separate the waters above from the waters **b**.
6:16 all the way around the boat, 18 inches **b** the roof.
35: 8 She was buried beneath the oak tree in the valley **b**
Ex 32:17 heard the noise of the people shouting **b** them,
Nu 22:41 he could see the people of Israel spread out **b** him.
Dt 4:49 far south as the Dead Sea, **b** the slopes of Pisgah.)
9:16 There **b** me I could see the gold calf you had made
10: 4 the fire on the mountain as you were assembled **b**.
Jos 2:11 supreme God of the heavens above and the earth **b**.
3:16 And the water **b** that point flowed on to the Dead
Jdg 7: 8 Now the Midianite camp was in the valley just **b**
1Ki 4:12 all of Beth-shan near Zarethan **b** Jezreel,
7:24 The Sea was encircled just **b** its rim by two rows of
7:29 Above and **b** the lions and oxen were wreath
2Ch 4: 3 The Sea was encircled just **b** its rim by two rows of
25:12 them off, dashing them to pieces on the rocks **b**.
Job 28: 5 but **b** the surface the earth is melted as by fire.
Ps 113: 6 Far **b** him are the heavens and the earth.
Isa 40:22 The people **b** must seem to him like grasshoppers!
Jer 48: 5 while cries of terror rise from Horonaim **b**.
Eze 32:18 For I will send them down to the world **b** in
32:24 hordes who descended as outcasts to the world **b**.
41: 7 Each level was wider than the one **b** it,
41:16 were paneled with wood above and **b** the windows.
Am 9: 1 so the roof will crash down on the people **b**.
Mic 1: 6 roll the stones of her walls down into the valley **b**,
Mk 14:66 Meanwhile, Peter was **b** in the courtyard. One of
Jn 8:23 Then he said to them, "You are from **b**; I am from
Ac 2:19 and signs on the earth **b**—/ blood and fire
20: 9 a deep sleep and fell three stories to his death **b**.
Rev 16:21 pounds fell from the sky onto the people **b**.

BELSHAZZAR (5) [BELSHAZZAR'S]

Da 5: 1 King **B** gave a great feast for a thousand of his

5: 2 While **B** was drinking, he gave orders to bring in
5: 10 She said to **B**, "Long live the king! Don't be
5: 22 are his successor, O **B**, and you knew all this,
5: 30 That very night **B**, the Babylonian king, was killed.

BELSHAZZAR'S (3) [BELSHAZZAR]

Da 5: 29 Then at **B** command, Daniel was dressed in purple
7: 1 during the first year of King **B** reign in Babylon,
8: 1 During the third year of King **B** reign, I, Daniel,

BELT (21) [BELTED, BELTS]

1Sa 18: 4 by giving him his robe, tunic, sword, bow, and **b**.
2Sa 18: 11 you with ten pieces of silver and a hero's **b**!"
20: 8 his uniform with a dagger strapped to his **b**.
1Ki 2: 5 staining his **b** and sandals with the blood of war.
18: 46 He tucked his cloak into his **b** and ran ahead of
2Ki 1: 8 and he wore a leather **b** around his waist."
Ps 109: 19 may they be tied around him like a **b**.
Isa 5: 27 Not a **b** will be loose, not a sandal thong broken.
Jer 13: 1 "Go and buy a linen **b** and put it around your
13: 2 So I bought the **b** as the LORD directed me
13: 4 "Take the linen **b** you are wearing, and go to the
13: 6 and get the linen **b** that I told you to hide there."
13: 7 was mildewed and falling apart. The **b** was useless.
13: 10 Therefore, they will become like this linen **b**—
13: 11 As a **b** clings to a person's waist, so I created
Da 10: 5 with a **b** of pure gold around his waist.
Mt 3: 4 woven from camel hair, and he wore a leather **b**;
Mk 1: 6 woven from camel hair, and he wore a leather **b**;
Ac 21: 11 he took Paul's **b** and bound his own feet and hands
21: 11 'So shall the owner of this **b** be bound by the
Eph 6: 14 putting on the sturdy **b** of truth and the body armor

BELTED (2) [BELT]

Ne 4: 18 All the builders had a sword **b** to their side.
Pr 31: 24 She makes **b** linen garments and sashes to sell to

BELTESHAZZAR (10) [DANIEL]

Da 1: 7 Daniel was called **B**. / Hananiah was called
2: 26 The king said to Daniel (also known as **B**), "Is this
4: 8 (He was named **B** after my god, and the spirit of
4: 9 "I said to him, 'O **B**, master magician, I know that
4: 18 " 'O **B**, that was the dream that I,
4: 19 Upon hearing this, Daniel (also known as **B**)
4: 19 Finally, the king said to him, "**B**, don't be alarmed
4: 19 **B** replied, "Oh, how I wish the events
5: 12 whom the king named **B**, has a sharp mind and is
10: 1 of King Cyrus of Persia, Daniel (also known as **B**)

BELTS (2) [BELT]

Eze 23: 15 Handsome **b** encircled their waists, and flowing
Rev 15: 6 clothed in spotless white linen with gold **b** across

BEMOAN(ED), BEMOANING [KJV] See also MOURN, PLEADING, SYMPATHY

BEN-ABINADAB (1) [ABINADAB]

1Ki 4: 11 **B**, in Naphoth-dor. (He was married to Taphath,

BEN-AMMI (1)

Ge 19: 38 daughter gave birth to a son, she named him **B**.

BEN-DEKER (1)

1Ki 4: 9 **B**, in Makaz, Shaalbim, Beth-shemesh,

BEN-GEBER (1) [GEBER]

1Ki 4: 13 **B**, in Ramoth-gilead, including the Towns of Jair

BEN-HADAD (32) [BEN-HADAD'S, HADAD]

1Ki 15: 18 He sent it with some of his officials to **B** son of
15: 20 **B** agreed to King Asa's request and sent his armies
20: 1 Now King **B** of Aram mobilized his army,
20: 2 **B** sent messengers into the city to relay this
20: 2 to King Ahab of Israel: "This is what **B** says:
20: 5 returned again and said, "This is what **B** says:
20: 9 So Ahab told the messengers from **B**, "Say this to
20: 9 So the messengers returned to **B** with the response.
20: 10 Then **B** sent this message to Ahab: "May the gods
20: 12 This reply of Ahab's reached **B** and the other kings
20: 12 "Prepare to attack!" **B** commanded his officers.
20: 16 as **B** and the thirty-two allied kings were still in
20: 18 "Take them alive," **B** commanded, "whether they
20: 20 but King **B** and a few others escaped on horses.
20: 25 will beat them." So King **B** did as they suggested.
20: 30 **B** fled into the city and hid in a secret room.
20: 32 king of Israel and begged, "Your servant **B** says,
20: 33 of hope, and they replied, "Yes, your brother **B**!"
20: 33 And when **B** arrived, Ahab invited him up into his
20: 34 **B** told him, "I will give back the towns my father
20: 34 So they made a treaty, and **B** was set free.
2Ki 6: 24 King **B** of Aram mobilized his entire army
8: 7 the capital of Aram, where King **B** lay sick.
8: 9 He went in to him and said, "Your servant **B**,
13: 3 and his son **B** to defeat them time after time.
13: 24 of Aram died, and his son **B** became the next king.
13: 25 Then Jehoash son of Jehoahaz recaptured from **B**
13: 25 Jehoash defeated **B** on three occasions, and
2Ch 16: 2 He sent it to King **B** of Aram, who was ruling in
16: 4 **B** agreed to King Asa's request and sent his armies
Jer 49: 27 of Damascus that will burn up the palaces of **B**."
Am 1: 4 and the fortresses of King **B** will be destroyed.

BEN-HADAD'S (4) [BEN-HADAD]

1Ki 20: 5 Soon **B** messengers returned again and said,
20: 17 As they approached, **B** scouts reported to him,
20: 23 After their defeat, **B** officers said to him,
20: 31 **B** officers said to him, "Sir, we have heard that the

BEN-HAIL (1)

2Ch 17: 7 These officials included **B**, Obadiah, Zechariah,

BEN-HANAN (1) [HANAN]

1Ch 4: 20 of Shimon were Amnon, Rinnah, **B**, and Tilon.

BEN-HESED (1)

1Ki 4: 10 **B**, in Arubboth, including Socoh and all the land of

BEN-HINNOM (1) [HINNOM]

2Ki 23: 10 king defiled the altar of Topheth in the valley of **B**,

BEN-HUR (1) [HUR]

1Ki 4: 8 **B**, in the hill country of Ephraim.

BEN-ONI (1) [BENJAMIN]

Ge 35: 18 to die, but with her last breath she named him **B**;

BEN-ZOHETH (1)

1Ch 4: 20 The descendants of Ishi were Zoheth and **B**.

BENAIAH (44)

2Sa 8: 18 **B** son of Jehoiada was captain of the king's
20: 23 **B** son of Jehoiada was commander of the king's
23: 20 There was also **B** son of Jehoiada, a valiant warrior
23: 21 **B** wrenched the spear from the Egyptian's hand
23: 22 These are some of the deeds that made **B** almost as
23: 30 **B** from Pirathon; / Hurai from Nahale-gaash;
1Ki 1: 8 **B** son of Jehoiada, Nathan the prophet, Shimei,
1: 10 or **B**, or the king's bodyguard, or his brother
1: 26 Zadok the priest, **B** son of Jehoiada, nor Solomon.
1: 32 Nathan the prophet, and **B** son of Jehoiada."
1: 36 "Amen!" **B** son of Jehoiada replied.
1: 38 the priest, Nathan the prophet, **B** son of Jehoiada,
1: 44 Nathan the prophet, and **B** son of Jehoiada,
2: 25 So King Solomon ordered **B** son of Jehoiada to
2: 29 he sent **B** son of Jehoiada to execute him.
2: 30 **B** went into the sacred tent of the LORD and said
2: 30 So **B** returned to the king and told him what Joab
2: 34 So **B** son of Jehoiada returned to the sacred tent
2: 35 Then the king appointed **B** to command the army
2: 46 **B** son of Jehoiada took Shimei outside and killed
4: 4 **B** son of Jehoiada was commander of the army.
1Ch 4: 36 Jaakobah, Jeshohaiah, Asaiah, Adiel, Jesimiel, **B**,
11: 22 There was also **B** son of Jehoiada, a valiant warrior
11: 23 **B** wrenched the spear from the Egyptian's hand
11: 24 These are some of the deeds that made **B** as
11: 31 (from the tribe of Benjamin); / **B** from Pirathon;
15: 18 Jehiel, Unni, Eliab, **B**, Maaseiah, Mattithiah,
15: 20 Maaseiah, and **B** were chosen to play the lyres.
15: 24 Joshaphat, Nethanel, Amasai, Zechariah, **B**,
16: 5 Jehiel, Mattithiah, Eliab, **B**, Obed-edom, and Jeiel.
16: 6 The priests, **B** and Jahaziel, played the trumpets
18: 17 **B** son of Jehoiada was captain of the king's
27: 5 **B** son of Jehoiada the priest was commander of the
27: 6 This was the **B** who commanded David's elite
27: 14 **B** from Pirathon in Ephraim was commander of the
27: 34 Ahithophel was succeeded by Jehoiada son of **B**
2Ch 20: 14 son of **B**, son of Jeiel, son of Mattaniah,
31: 13 Jerimoth, Jozabad, Eliel, Ismakiah, Mahath, and **B**.
Ezr 10: 25 Malkijah, Mijamin, Eleazar, Hashabiah, and **B**.
10: 30 Adna, Kelal, **B**, Maaseiah, Mattaniah, Bezalel,
10: 35 **B**, Bedeiah, Keluhi,
10: 43 Mattithiah, Zabad, Zebina, Jaddai, Joel, and **B**.
Eze 11: 1 were Jaazaniah son of Azzur and Pelatiah son of **B**,
11: 13 was still speaking, Pelatiah son of **B** suddenly died.

BEND (8) [BENDS, BENT]

Ge 49: 15 the land, / he will **b** his shoulder to the task
Ps 7: 12 sharpen his sword; / he will **b** and string his bow.
17: 6 will answer, O God. / **B** down and listen as I pray.
31: 2 **B** down and listen to me; / rescue me quickly.
86: 1 **B** down, O LORD, and hear my prayer;
102: 2 from me / in my time of distress. / **B** down your ear
144: 5 **B** down the heavens, LORD, and come down.
Jer 9: 3 "My people **b** their tongues like bows to shoot

BENDS (2) [BEND]

Ps 116: 2 Because he **b** down and listens, / I will pray as
La 2: 4 He **b** his bow against his people as though he were

BENE-BERAK (1)

Jos 19: 45 Jehud, **B**, Gath-rimmon,

BENE-JAAKAN (2) [JAAKAN]

Nu 33: 31 They left Moseroth and camped at **B**.
33: 32 They left **B** and camped at Hor-haggidgad.

BENEATH (120) [UNDERNEATH]

Ge 1: 9 "Let the waters **b** the sky be gathered into one
15: 5 Then the LORD brought Abram outside **b** the
18: 8 Abraham waited on them there **b** the trees.
35: 4 and he buried them **b** the tree near Shechem.
35: 8 She was buried **b** the oak tree in the valley below
49: 25 of the heavens above, / blessings of the earth **b**,
Ex 2: 23 But the Israelites still groaned **b** their burden of
9: 19 or animal left outside will die **b** the hail.' "
23: 5 someone who hates you struggling **b** a heavy load,
25: 35 One blossom will be set **b** each pair of branches
30: 4 **B** the molding, on opposite sides of the altar,
37: 21 One blossom was set **b** each pair of branches,
37: 27 **b** the molding, to hold the carrying poles.
Lev 26: 8 All your enemies will fall **b** the blows of your
26: 19 as iron and the earth **b** as hard as bronze.
Nu 2: 2 and the various groups will camp **b** their family
2: 3[-4] side of the Tabernacle, **b** their family banners.
2: 10[-11] of the Tabernacle, **b** their family banners.
2: 18[-19] of the Tabernacle, **b** their family banners.
2: 25[-26] of the Tabernacle, **b** their family banners.
6: 18 and put it on the fire **b** the peace-offering sacrifice.
16: 31 when the ground suddenly split open **b** them.
Dt 28: 23 as bronze, and the earth **b** will be as hard as iron.
33: 13 from the heavens, / and water from **b** the earth;
Jos 2: 6 up to the roof and hidden them **b** piles of flax.)
7: 21 They are hidden in the ground **b** my tent,
7: 22 as Achan had said, with the silver buried **b** the rest.
13: 5 from Baal-gad **b** Mount Hermon to Lebo-hamath;
24: 26 and rolled it **b** the oak tree beside the Tabernacle
Jdg 3: 22 so deep that the handle disappeared **b** the king's
6: 11 the LORD came and sat **b** the oak tree at Ophrah,
1Sa 22: 6 the king was sitting **b** a tamarisk tree on the hill at
31: 13 and buried them **b** the tamarisk tree at Jabesh,
2Sa 18: 9 but as he rode **b** the thick branches of a great oak,
22: 10 came down; / dark storm clouds were **b** his feet.
22: 39 so they could not get up; / they fell **b** my feet.
1Ki 8: 6 and placed it **b** the wings of the cherubim.
2Ki 18: 21 you will find it to be a stick that breaks **b** your
1Ch 10: 12 Then they buried their remains **b** the oak tree at
2Ch 5: 7 and placed it **b** the wings of the cherubim.
Ne 9: 11 the sea. They sank like stones **b** the mighty waters.
Job 9: 13 The mightiest forces against him are crushed **b** his
18: 15 The home of the wicked will disappear **b** a fiery
26: 5 "The dead tremble in their place **b** the waters.
30: 7 they huddle together for shelter **b** the nettles.
35: 9 "The oppressed cry out **b** the wrongs that are done
35: 9 to them. They groan **b** the power of the mighty.
Ps 10: 10 they fall **b** the strength of the wicked.
18: 9 came down; / dark storm clouds were **b** his feet.
18: 38 so they could not get up; / they fell **b** my feet.
45: 5 nations fall before you, / lying down **b** your feet.
47: 3 nations before us, / putting our enemies **b** our feet.
57: 1 I will hide **b** the shadow of your wings
61: 4 your sanctuary, / safe **b** the shelter of your wings!
90: 7 We wither **b** your anger; / we are overwhelmed by
90: 9 We live our lives **b** your wrath. / We end our lives
145: 14 the fallen / and lifts up those bent **b** their loads.
146: 8 The LORD lifts the burdens of those bent **b** their
Pr 11: 5 by their honesty; the wicked fall **b** their load of sin.
Isa 10: 6 plunder them, trampling them like dirt **b** its feet.
19: 16 They will cower in fear **b** the upraised fist of the
24: 18 you from the heavens. The world is shaken **b** you.
26: 16 We were bowed **b** the burden of your discipline.
27: 11 and used for kindling **b** the cooking pots.
28: 3 of Israel—will be trampled **b** its enemies' feet.
36: 6 you will find it to be a stick that breaks **b** your
40: 7 and the flowers fade **b** the breath of the LORD.
43: 17 I drew them **b** the waves, and they drowned,
51: 6 to the skies above, and gaze down on the earth **b**.
54: 16 I have created the blacksmith who fans the coals **b**
57: 5 You worship your idols with great passion **b** every
Jer 6: 15 They will be humbled **b** my punishing anger,"
17: 2 **b** every green tree and on every high hill.
38: 11 and went to a room in the palace **b** the treasury,
52: 20 and the Sea with the twelve bulls **b** it was too great
La 2: 3 All the strength of Israel vanishes **b** his fury.
3: 28 Let them sit alone in silence **b** the LORD's
3: 66 destroying them from **b** the LORD's heavens.
Eze 1: 8 **B** each of their wings I could see human hands.
1: 15 I saw four wheels on the ground **b** them,
1: 23 **B** this surface the wings of each living being
3: 13 and the rumbling of their wheels **b** them.
10: 2 "Go in between the whirling wheels **b** the
10: 8 looked like human hands hidden **b** their wings.)
10: 20 These were the same living beings I had seen **b** the
17: 6 up toward the eagle, and its roots grew down **b** it.
17: 23 sort will nest in it, finding shelter **b** its branches.
21: 10 Those far stronger than you have fallen **b** its
23: 33 You will reel like a drunkard **b** the awful blows of
24: 5 from the flock and heap fuel on the fire **b** the pot.
24: 9 of murderers! I myself will pile up the fuel **b** her.
26: 19 You will sink **b** the terrible waves of enemy attack.
26: 20 Your city will lie in ruins, buried **b** the earth,
27: 7 You stood **b** blue and purple awnings made bright
31: 12 All those who lived **b** its shadow went away
32: 27 their bodies, and their swords **b** their heads.
42: 5 levels of rooms was narrower than the one **b** it
42: 6 of the upper levels was set back from the level **b** it.
47: 1 There I saw a stream flowing eastward from **b** the
Da 5: 6 knocked together and his legs gave way **b** him.
7: 7 iron teeth and trampled what was left **b** its feet.
7: 19 and it trampled what was left **b** its feet.
Jnh 2: 3 I was buried **b** your wild and stormy waves.
2: 5 "I sank **b** the waves, and death was very near.
Mic 1: 4 They melt **b** his feet and flow into the valleys like
Na 1: 3 The billowing clouds are the dust **b** his feet.
Hab 3: 16 My legs gave way **b** me, and I shook in terror.
Mt 13: 6 but they soon wilted **b** the hot sun and died
15: 27 to eat crumbs that fall **b** their master's table."
20: 25 and officials lord it over the people **b** them.
22: 44 until I humble your enemies **b** your feet.'
23: 37 together as a hen protects her chicks **b** her wings,

Mk 4: 6 but it soon wilted **b** the hot sun and died
10:42 and officials lord it over the people **b** them.
12:36 until I humble your enemies **b** your feet.'
Lk 11:46 For you crush people **b** impossible religious
13:34 together as a hen protects her chicks **b** her wings,
1Co 15:25 reign until he humbles all his enemies **b** his feet.
1Pe 2:20 suffer for doing right and are patient **b** the blows,
Rev 12: 1 clothed with the sun, with the moon **b** her feet,

BENEFICIAL (2) [BENEFIT]

1Co 10:23 allowed to do anything"—but not everything is **b**.
Tit 3: 8 These things are good and **b** for everyone.

BENEFIT (32) [BENEFICIAL, BENEFITED, BENEFITS]

Dt 33:19 sacrifices there. / They **b** from the riches of the sea
Job 22: 2 "Can a person's actions be of **b** to God? Can even
35: 3 use of living a righteous life? How will it **b** me?'
Pr 9:12 If you become wise, you will be the one to **b**.
Isa 57:12 so righteous. None of them will **b** or save you.
Mt 16:26 And how do you **b** if you gain the whole world
Mk 2:27 said to them, "The Sabbath was made to **b** people, and not people to **b** the Sabbath.
8:36 And how do you **b** if you gain the whole world
Lk 9:25 And how do you **b** if you gain the whole world
16: 9 use your worldly resources to **b** others and make
Jn 12:30 told them, "The voice was for your **b**, not mine.
Ac 18:27 he proved to be of great **b** to those who, by God's
Ro 4:23 him to be righteous—wasn't just for Abraham's **b**.
11:28 But this has been to your **b**, for God has given his
16: 6 to Mary, who has worked so hard for your **b**.
1Co 1:30 For our **b** God made Christ to be wisdom itself.
2: 7 though he made it for our **b** before the world
7:35 I am saying this for your **b**, not to place restrictions
9:14 News should be supported by those who **b** from it.
11: 9 And man was not made for woman's **b**, but woman
14:22 prophecy, however, is for the **b** of believers,
2Co 1: 6 down with troubles, it is for your **b** and salvation!
2:10 I do so with Christ's authority for your **b**,
4:15 All of these things are for your **b**. And as God's
5:13 And if we are in our right minds, it is for your **b**.
12:19 Everything we do, dear friends, is for your **b**.
Gal 2: 8 for the **b** of the Jews worked through me for the **b** of the Gentiles.
Eph 1:22 and he gave him this authority for the **b** of the
Heb 11:40 better things in mind for us that would also **b** them,
13:17 That would certainly not be for your **b**.

BENEFITED (2) [BENEFIT]

Jn 1:16 We have all **b** from the rich blessings he brought to
5:35 shone brightly for a while, and you **b** and rejoiced.

BENEFITS (7) [BENEFIT]

Dt 28:47 and enthusiasm for the abundant **b** you have
Job 36:28 down from the clouds, and everyone **b** from it.
Pr 12:14 the work of their hands also gives them many **b**.
Isa 54:17 These **b** are enjoyed by the servants of the
1Co 10:16 aren't we sharing in the **b** of the blood of Christ?
10:16 aren't we sharing in the **b** of the body of Christ?
2Pe 1: 5 So make every effort to apply the **b** of these

BENINU (1)

Ne 10:13 Hodiah, Bani, and **B**.

BENJAMIN (160) [BENJAMIN'S, BENJAMINITE, BENJAMINITES]

JUDAH AND BENJAMIN (18) 1Ki 12:21,23; 2Ch 11:1,3,10,12,23; 15:2,8,9; 25:5; Ezr 1:5; 4:1; 10:9; Ne 11:1,4; Jer 17:26; Eze 48:22

TRIBE OF BENJAMIN (37) Nu 7:60; 10:24; Dt 33:12; Jos 18:11,20,21,28; 21:17; Jdg 1:21; 3:15; 20:12,46; 21:1,16; 1Sa 4:12; 9:1; 10:20,21; 2Sa 2:25,31; 3:19; 19:17; 23:29; 1Ch 9:7,9; 11:31; 12:2,29; 2Ch 14:8; Ne 11:7,36; Est 2:5; Ps 7:T; 68:27; Ac 13:21; Ro 11:1; Php 3:5

Ge 35:18 the baby's father, however, called him **B**.
35:24 The sons of Rachel were Joseph and **B**.
42: 4 **B**, go with them, however, for fear some harm
42:36 Simeon is gone, and now you want to take **B**, too.
42:37 "You may kill my two sons if I don't bring **B** back
43: 3 we couldn't see him again unless **B** came along.
43: 5 But if you don't let **B** go, we may as well stay at
43:14 that he might release Simeon and return **B**.
43:15 So they took **B** and the gifts and double the money
43:16 When Joseph saw that **B** was with them, he said to
43:29 Looking at his brother **B**, Joseph asked, "Is this
43:34 He gave the largest serving to **B**—five times as
45:12 and so can my brother **B**, that I really am Joseph!
45:14 Weeping with joy, he embraced **B**, and **B** also began to weep.
45:22 but to **B** he gave five changes of clothes and three
46:19 sons of Jacob's wife Rachel were Joseph and **B**.
49:27 "**B** is a wolf that prowls. / He devours his enemies
Ex 1: 3 Issachar, Zebulun, **B**,
Nu 1:11 **B** | Abidan son of Gideoni
1:36[-37] **B** | 35,400
2:18[-19] and **B** are to camp on the west side of the
2:22[-23] **B** | Abidan son of Gideoni | 35,400
7:60 leader of the tribe of **B**, presented his offering.
10:24 The tribe of **B** was led by Abidan son of Gideoni.
13: 9 **B** | Palti son of Raphu
26:38 were the clans descended from the sons of **B**:
26:41 The men from all the clans of **B** numbered 45,600.
34:21 **B** | Elidad son of Kislon
Dt 27:12 and **B** must stand on Mount Gerizim to proclaim a
33:12 Moses said this about the tribe of **B**: / "The people of **B** are loved by the LORD
Jos 18:11 of land went to the families of the tribe of **B**.
18:20 the inheritance for the families of the tribe of **B**.
18:21 the towns given to the families of the tribe of **B**.
18:28 inheritance given to the families of the tribe of **B**.
21: 4 assigned to the tribes of Judah, Simeon, and **B**.
21:17 From the tribe of **B** the priests were given the
Jdg 1:21 The tribe of **B**, however, failed to drive out the
1:21 Jebusites live in Jerusalem among the people of **B**.
3:15 of Gera, of the tribe of **B**, who was left-handed.
5:14 to the Amalekites, / and **B** also followed you.
10: 9 of the Jordan and attacked Judah, **B**, and Ephraim.
19:14 as they came to Gibeah, a town in the land of **B**,
19:16 but he was living in Gibeah in the territory of **B**.
20: 3 (Word soon reached the land of **B** that the other
20: 4 a town in the land of **B**, to spend the night.
20:12 The Israelites sent messengers to the tribe of **B**,
20:13 of this evil." But the people of **B** would not listen.
20:18 should lead the attack against the people of **B**?"
20:20 advanced toward Gibeah to attack the men of **B**.
20:23 "Should we fight against our relatives from **B**
20:24 So they went out to fight against the warriors of **B**,
20:25 but the men of **B** killed another eighteen thousand
20:28 "Should we fight against our relatives from **B**
20:31 When the warriors of **B** came out to attack,
20:32 Then the warriors of **B** shouted, "We're defeating
20:32 so that the men of **B** would chase them along the
20:34 and advanced against **B** from behind. The fighting
20:34 so heavy that **B** didn't realize the impending
20:35 So the LORD helped Israel defeat **B**, and that day
20:40 But when the warriors of **B** looked behind them
20:46 So the tribe of **B** lost twenty-five thousand brave
21: 1 daughters in marriage to a man from the tribe of **B**.
21: 6 The Israelites felt deep sadness for **B** and said,
21:13 of **B** who were living at the rock of Rimmon.
21:14 Then the men of **B** returned to their homes,
21:15 The people felt sorry for **B** because the LORD
21:16 since all the women of the tribe of **B** are dead?
21:20 They told the men of **B** who still needed wives,
21:23 So the men of **B** did as they were told.
1Sa 4:12 A man from the tribe of **B** ran from the battlefront
9: 1 was a rich, influential man from the tribe of **B**.
9: 4 the Shaalim area, and the entire land of **B**,
9:16 I will send you a man from the land of **B**.
9:21 Saul replied, "But I'm only from **B**, the smallest
10: 2 Rachel's tomb at Zelzah, on the border of **B**.
10:20 before the LORD, and the tribe of **B** was chosen.
10:21 Then he brought each family of the tribe of **B**
13: 2 Saul's son Jonathan to Gibeah in the land of **B**.
13:15 went up from Gilgal to Gibeah in the land of **B**.
13:16 staying at Geba, near Gibeah, in the land of **B**.
22: 7 "Listen here, you men of **B**!" Saul shouted when
2Sa 2: 9 Jezreel, Ephraim, **B**, the land of the Ashurites,
2:25 Abner's troops from the tribe of **B** regrouped there
2:31 all from the tribe of **B**, had been killed.
3:19 Abner also spoke with the leaders of the tribe of **B**.
3:19 that all the people of Israel and **B** supported him.
4: 2 The town of Beeroth is now part of **B**
19:17 A thousand men from the tribe of **B** were with him,
21:14 Saul's father, at the town of Zela in the land of **B**.
23:29 son of Ribai from Gibeah (from the tribe of **B**);
1Ki 4:18 Shimei son of Ela, in **B**.
12:21 he mobilized the armies of Judah and **B**—
12:23 king of Judah, and to all the people of Judah and **B**,
15:22 these materials to fortify the town of Geba in **B**
1Ch 2: 2 Dan, Joseph, **B**, Naphtali, Gad, and Asher.
6:60 And from the territory of **B** they were given
6:65 of Judah, Simeon, and **B**, mentioned above,
7:10 **B**, Ehud, Kenaanah, Zethan, Tarshish,
8: 1 The sons of **B**, in order of age, included Bela (the
8:40 150 in all. All these were descendants of **B**.
9: 3 **B**, Ephraim, and Manasseh came and settled in
9: 7 From the tribe of **B** came Sallu son of Meshullam,
9: 9 In all, 956 families from the tribe of **B** returned.
11:31 son of Ribai from Gibeah (from the tribe of **B**);
12: 2 They were all relatives of Saul from the tribe of **B**.
12:16 Others from **B** and Judah came to David at the
12:29 From the tribe of **B**, Saul's relatives, there were
21: 6 tribes of Levi and **B** in the census because he was
27:12 Abiezer from Anathoth in the territory of **B** was
27:21 Iddo son of Zechariah / **B** | Jaasiel son of Abner
2Ch 11: 1 he mobilized the armies of Judah and **B**—
11: 3 of Judah, and to all the Israelites in Judah and **B**:
11:10 These became the fortified cities of Judah and **B**.
11:12 So only Judah and **B** remained under his control.
11:23 fortified cities throughout the land of Judah and **B**.
14: 8 an army of 280,000 warriors from the tribe of **B**,
15: 2 "Listen, all you people of Judah and **B**!
15: 8 removed all the idols in the land of Judah and **B**
15: 9 Asa called together all the people of Judah and **B**,
17:17 From **B**, there were 200,000 troops equipped with
25: 5 assigning leaders to each clan from Judah and **B**.
31: 1 **B**, Ephraim, and Manasseh, and they smashed the
34: 9 as well as from all Judah, **B**, and the people of
34:32 and the people of **B** to make a similar pledge.
Ezr 1: 5 and **B** to return to Jerusalem to rebuild the Temple
4: 1 and **B** heard that the exiles were rebuilding a
10: 9 people of Judah and **B** had gathered in Jerusalem.
10:32 **B**, Malluch, and Shemariah.
Ne 3:23 After them, **B**, Hasshub, and Azariah son of
11: 1 and **B** were chosen by sacred lots to live there,
11: 4 people from Judah and **B** resettled in Jerusalem.
11: 7 From the tribe of **B**: Sallu son of Meshullam,
11:31 Some of the people of **B** lived at Geba, Micmash,
11:36 lived in Judah were sent to live with the tribe of **B**.
12:34 Judah, **B**, Shemaiah, Jeremiah,
Est 2: 5 He was from the tribe of **B** and was a descendant
Ps 7: T to the LORD concerning Cush of the tribe of **B**.
68:27 Look, the little tribe of **B** leads the way.
80: 2 to Ephraim, **B**, and Manasseh. / Show us your
Jer 1: 1 the priests from Anathoth, a town in the land of **B**.
6: 1 "Run for your lives, you people of **B**! Flee from
17:26 from the towns of Judah and **B**, from the western
20: 2 and put in stocks at the **B** Gate of the LORD's
32: 8 "Buy my field at Anathoth in the land of **B**.
32:44 in the land of **B** and here in Jerusalem, in the towns
33:13 the foothills of Judah, the Negev, the land of **B**,
37:12 started to leave the city on his way to the land of **B**,
37:13 But as he was walking through the **B** Gate, a sentry
38: 7 At that time the king was holding court at the **B**
Eze 48:22 between the territories allotted to Judah and **B**,
48:32 the gates will be named for Joseph, **B**, and Dan.
Hos 5: 8 in Beth-aven! Lead on into battle, O warriors of **B**!
Ob 1:19 And the people of **B** will occupy the land of
Zec 14:10 and will be inhabited all the way from the **B** Gate
Ac 13:21 a man of the tribe of **B**, who reigned for forty
Ro 11: 1 of Abraham and a member of the tribe of **B**.
Php 3: 5 Jewish family that is a branch of the tribe of **B**.
Rev 7: 8 from Joseph | 12,000 / from **B** | 12,000.

BENJAMIN'S (14) [BENJAMIN]

Ge 44:12 line to the youngest. The cup was found in **B** sack!
46:21 **B** sons were Bela, Beker, Ashbel, Gera, Naaman,
Jdg 20:16 Seven hundred of **B** warriors were left-handed,
20:17 armed with swords, not counting **B** warriors.
20:21 But **B** warriors, who were defending the town,
20:35 and that day the Israelites killed 25,100 of **B**
20:36 The Israelites had retreated from **B** warriors in
20:39 for the Israelites to turn and attack **B** warriors.
20:39 By that time **B** warriors had killed about thirty
20:41 At this point **B** warriors realized disaster was near
20:44 Eighteen thousand of **B** greatest warriors died in
1Ch 7: 6 Three of **B** sons were Bela, Beker, and Jediael.
Eze 48:23 **B** territory lies just south of the prince's lands,
48:24 South of **B** territory lies that of Simeon,

BENJAMINITE (4) [BENJAMIN]

2Sa 4: 2 were sons of Rimmon, who was a **B** from Beeroth.
19:16 Then Shimei son of Gera the **B**, the man from
20: 1 a **B**, blew a trumpet and shouted, "We have
1Ki 2: 8 Shimei son of Gera, the **B** from Bahurim.

BENJAMINITES (3) [BENJAMIN]

Jdg 20:36 Then the **B** saw that they were beaten.
20:43 The Israelites surrounded the **B** and were relentless
1Ch 12:29 Most of the **B** had remained loyal to Saul until this

BENO (2)

1Ch 24:26 From the descendants of Jaaziah, the leader was **B**.
24:27 the leaders were **B**, Shoham, Zaccur, and Ibri.

BENT (9) [BEND]

Ge 8:21 and actions are **b** toward evil from childhood.
Ps 38: 6 I am **b** over and racked with pain. / My days are
145:14 the fallen / and lifts up those **b** beneath their loads.
146: 8 The LORD lifts the burdens of those **b** beneath
La 3:12 He **b** his bow and aimed it squarely at me.
Eze 22: 6 Israel who lives within your walls is **b** on murder.
Hab 1: 9 "On they come, all of them **b** on violence.
Lk 13:11 She had been **b** double for eighteen years and was
Ac 20:10 Paul went down, **b** over him, and took him into his

BEON (1)

Nu 32: 3 Nimrah, Heshbon, Elealeh, Sebam, Nebo, and **B**—

BEOR (11)

Ge 36:32 Bela son of **B**, who ruled from his city of
Nu 22: 5 sent messengers to Balaam son of **B**, who was
24: 3 "This is the prophecy of Balaam son of **B**,
24:15 "This is the message of Balaam son of **B**,
31: 8 They also killed Balaam son of **B** with the sword.
Dt 23: 4 they tried to hire Balaam son of **B** from Pethor in
Jos 13:22 also killed Balaam the magician, the son of **B**.
24: 9 He asked Balaam son of **B** to curse you,
1Ch 1:43 Bela son of **B**, who ruled from his city of
Mic 6: 5 and how Balaam son of **B** blessed you instead?
2Pe 2:15 and followed the way of Balaam son of **B**,

BERA (1)

Ge 14: 2 fought against King **B** of Sodom, King Birsha of

BERACAH (1)

1Ch 12: 3 sons of Azmaveth; / **B** and Jehu from Anathoth;

BERACHIAH [KJV] See BEREKIAH

BERAIAH (1)

1Ch 8:21 Adaiah, **B**, and Shimrath were the sons of Shimei.

BERATE (2)

Mt 26:10 "Why **b** her for doing such a good thing to me?
Mk 14: 6 Why **b** her for doing such a good thing to me?

BEREA (5)

Ac 17:10 very night the believers sent Paul and Silas to **B**.

17:11 And the people of **B** were more open-minded than
17:13 that Paul was preaching the word of God in **B**,
17:15 then they returned to **B** with a message for Silas
20: 4 They were Sopater of **B**, the son of Pyrrhus;

BEREAVE (1)
Eze 36:14 never again devour your people or **b** your nation,

BERED (2)
Ge 16:14 and it can still be found between Kadesh and **B**.
1Ch 7:20 were Shuthelah, **B**, Tahath, Eleadah, Tahath,

BEREKIAH (11)
1Ch 3:20 Ohel, **B**, Hasadiah, and Jushab-hesed.
6:39 Asaph's genealogy was traced back through **B**,
9:16 and **B** son of Asa, son of Elkanah, who lived in the
15:17 appointed Heman son of Joel, Asaph son of **B**,
15:23 **B** and Elkanah were chosen to guard the Ark.
2Ch 28:12 **B** son of Meshillemoth, Jehizkiah son of Shallum,
Ne 3: 4 Beside him were Meshullam son of **B**
3:30 while Meshullam son of **B** rebuilt the wall next to
6:18 married to the daughter of Meshullam son of **B**.
Zec 1: 1 this message to the prophet Zechariah son of **B**
1: 7 another message to the prophet Zechariah son of **B**

BERI (1)
1Ch 7:36 of Zophah were Suah, Harnepher, Shual, **B**, Imrah,

BERIAH (9) [BERIAH'S, BERIITE, BERIITES]
Ge 46:17 sons of Asher were Imnah, Ishvah, Ishvi, and **B**.
Nu 26:44 The Beriite clan, named after its ancestor **B**.
1Ch 7:23 Ephraim named him **B** because of the tragedy his
7:30 sons of Asher were Imnah, Ishvah, Ishvi, and **B**.
7:31 The sons of **B** were Heber and Malkiel (the father
8:13 **B**, and Shema. They were the leaders of the clans
8:16 Michael, Ishpah, and Joha were the sons of **B**.
23:10 of Shimei were Jahath, Ziza, Jeush, and **B**.
23:11 Jeush and **B** were counted as a single family

BERIAH'S (1) [BERIAH]
Ge 46:17 was named Serah. **B** sons were Heber and Malkiel.

BERIITE (1) [BERIAH]
Nu 26:44 The **B** clan, named after its ancestor Beriah.

BERIITES (1) [BERIAH]
Nu 26:45 These were the subclans descended from the **B**:

BERITH [KJV] See BAAL-BERITH

BERNICE (3)
Ac 25:13 with his sister, **B**, to pay their respects to Festus.
25:23 and **B** arrived at the auditorium with great pomp,
26:30 Then the king, the governor, **B**, and all the others

BERODACHBALADAN [KJV] See MERODACH-BALADAN

BEROTHAH (1)
Eze 47:16 then it will run to **B** and Sibraim, which are on the

BEROTHAI (1) [CUN]
2Sa 8: 8 of bronze from Hadadezer's cities of Tebah and **B**.

BERRIES [KJV] See OLIVES

BERYL (4)
Ex 28:20 The fourth row will contain a **b**, an onyx, and a
39:13 In the fourth row were a **b**, an onyx, and a jasper.
Eze 28:13 **b**, onyx, jasper, sapphire, turquoise, and emerald—
Rev 21:20 the eighth **b**, the ninth topaz, the tenth chrysoprase,

BESAI (2)
Ezr 2:49 Uzza, Paseah, **B**,
Ne 7:52 **B**, Meunim, Nephusim,

BESEECH(ING), BESOUGHT [KJV] See APPEAL, ASKING, BEG, ENTREAT, IMPLORE, PLEAD, PLEASE, PRAY, URGE

BESIDE (161) [BESIDES, SIDE]
Ge 12: 6 near Shechem and set up camp **b** the oak at Moreh.
16: 7 The angel of the LORD found Hagar **b** a desert
24:11 There the servant made the camels kneel down **b** a
24:13 See, here I am, standing **b** this spring,
24:30 where the man was still standing **b** his camels.
24:43 Here I am, standing **b** this spring. I will say to
29: 2 flocks of sheep lying in an open field **b** a well,
30:38 Then he set up these peeled branches **b** the
31:46 then sat down **b** the pile of stones to share a meal.
38:14 Then she sat **b** the road at the entrance to the
38:21 "Where can I find the prostitute who was sitting **b**
41: 3 These cows went over and stood **b** the fat cows.
47:30 me out of Egypt and bury me **b** my ancestors."
48: 7 So with great sorrow I buried her there **b** the road
49:17 He will be a snake **b** the road, / a poisonous viper
49:22 is a fruitful tree, / a fruitful tree **b** a fountain.
Ex 2:15 Moses arrived in Midian, he sat down **b** a well.
14: 9 as they were camped **b** the shore near Pi-hahiroth,
15:27 palm trees. They camped there **b** the springs.
33:21 LORD continued, "Stand here on this rock **b** me.
Lev 6:10 ashes of the burnt offering and put them **b** the altar.
10:12 yeast in it, and eat it **b** the altar, for it is most holy.
26:30 I will leave your corpses piled up **b** your lifeless
Nu 6: 9 because someone suddenly falls dead **b** them,
23: 6 the king was standing **b** his burnt offerings with all
23:17 and the officials of Moab were standing **b** Balak's
24: 6 planted by the LORD, / like cedars **b** the waters.
26: 3 camped on the plains of Moab **b** the Jordan River,
26:63 and Eleazar the priest on the plains of Moab **b** the
31:12 which was camped on the plains of Moab **b** the
33:10 They left Elim and camped **b** the Red Sea.
33:48 and camped on the plains of Moab **b** the Jordan
35: 1 While Israel was camped **b** the Jordan on the
36:13 camped on the plains of Moab **b** the Jordan River,
Dt 12:27 be poured out **b** the altar of the LORD your God,
16:21 "You must never set up an Asherah pole **b** the
31:26 and place it **b** the Ark of the Covenant of the
33:12 and live in safety **b** him. / He surrounds them
Jos 18:16 and down to the base of the mountain **b** the valley
24:26 and rolled it beneath the oak tree **b** the Tabernacle
Jdg 6:25 and cut down the Asherah pole standing **b** it.
6:28 and that the Asherah pole **b** it was gone.
9: 6 and Beth-millo called a meeting under the oak **b**
Ru 3: 7 he lay down **b** the heap of grain and went to sleep.
1Sa 1: 9 Eli the priest was sitting at his customary place **b**
4:13 Eli was waiting **b** the road to hear the news of the
4:18 the Ark, Eli fell backward from his seat **b** the gate.
5: 2 temple of Dagon and placed it **b** the idol of Dagon.
6: 8 and **b** it place a chest containing the gold rats
6:14 of a man named Joshua and stopped **b** a large rock.
10: 2 you will see two men **b** Rachel's tomb at Zelzah,
20:25 Jonathan sitting opposite him and Abner **b** him.
26: 3 Saul camped along the road **b** the hill of Hakilah,
26: 7 with his spear stuck in the ground **b** his head.
26:16 and the jug of water that were **b** his head?"
31: 5 he fell on his own sword and died **b** the king.
2Sa 2:32 to Bethlehem and buried him there **b** his father.
4:12 and hung their bodies **b** the pool in Hebron.
6: 7 and God struck him dead **b** the Ark of God.
15:24 of the Covenant of God and set it down **b** the road.
17:23 He died there and was buried **b** his father.
1Ki 2:31 "Kill him there **b** the altar and bury him.
3:20 and took my son from **b** me while I was asleep.
3:20 child in my arms and took mine to sleep **b** her.
7:20 **b** the rounded surface next to the latticework.
13:24 with the donkey and the lion standing **b** it.
13:25 body lying in the road and the lion standing **b** it,
13:28 The donkey and lion were still standing there **b** it,
13:31 man of God is buried. Lay my bones **b** his bones.
17: 5 LORD had told him and camped **b** Kerith Brook.
20:38 The prophet waited for the king **b** the road,
22:38 Then his chariot was washed **b** the pool of
2Ki 2: 7 as Elijah and Elisha stopped **b** the Jordan River.
11: 8 must be killed. Stay right **b** the king at all times."
18:17 The Assyrians stopped **b** the aqueduct that feeds
23: 3 The king took his place of authority **b** the pillar
23:16 God as Jeroboam stood **b** the altar at the festival.
1Ch 12: 1 They were among the warriors who fought **b**
2Ch 23: 7 must be killed. Stay right **b** the king at all times."
34:31 The king took his place of authority **b** the pillar
Ne 2: 6 The king, with the queen sitting **b** him, asked,
3: 4 **B** him were Meshullam son of Berekiah
3:10 Next Jedaiah son of Harumaph repaired the wall **b**
3:25 from the king's house **b** the court of the guard.
4: 3 the Ammonite, who was standing **b** him, remarked,
9: 9 and you heard their cries from **b** the Red Sea.
Job 1:14 were plowing, with the donkeys feeding **b** them,
40:22 The lotus plants give it shade among the willows **b**
Ps 16: 8 I will not be shaken, for he is right **b** me.
23: 2 green meadows; / he leads me **b** peaceful streams.
23: 4 I will not be afraid, / for you are close **b** me.
78:13 The water stood up like walls **b** them!
104:12 The birds nest **b** the streams / and sing among the
109:31 For he stands **b** the needy, / ready to save them
121: 5 The LORD stands **b** you as your protective shade.
137: 1 **B** the rivers of Babylon, we sat and wept / as we
SS 5:12 His eyes are like doves **b** brooks of water; they are
Isa 36: 2 The Assyrians stopped **b** the aqueduct that feeds
49:10 For the LORD in his mercy will lead them **b** cool
Jer 3: 2 You sit like a prostitute **b** the road waiting for a
20:11 But the LORD stands **b** me like a great warrior.
31: 9 They will walk **b** quiet streams and not stumble.
46: 2 and his army were defeated **b** the Euphrates River
46:10 will receive a sacrifice today in the north country **b**
48:19 The people of Aroer stand anxiously **b** the road to
Eze 1: 1 while I was with the Judean exiles **b** the Kebar
1: 3 there **b** the Kebar River in the land of the
1: 9 being touched the wings of the two beings **b** it.
3:15 of Judean exiles in Tel-abib, **b** the Kebar River.
8: 5 to the north, **b** the entrance to the gate of the altar,
9: 2 the Temple courtyard and stood **b** the bronze altar.
10: 6 So the man went in and stood **b** one of the wheels.
10: 9 Each of the four cherubim had a wheel **b** him,
10:15 These were the same living beings I had seen **b** the
10:16 they rose into the air, the wheels stayed **b** them,
11:22 and rose into the air with their wheels **b** them,
17: 5 of its seedlings in fertile ground **b** a broad river,
32:13 all your flocks and herds that graze **b** the streams.
39:15 a marker will be set up **b** them so the burial crews
40: 3 shone like bronze standing **b** a gateway entrance.
40:44 one **b** the north gateway, facing south,
40:44 and the other **b** the south gateway, facing north.
40:45 "The building **b** the north inner gate is for the
40:46 The building **b** the south inner gate is for the
43: 6 who had been measuring was still standing **b** me.)
46:19 Then the man brought me through the entrance **b**
Da 7:16 So I approached one of those standing **b** the throne
8: 2 in the province of Elam, standing **b** the Ulai River.
8: 3 me a ram with two long horns standing **b** the river.
8: 6 ram that I had seen standing **b** the river.
10: 4 as I was standing **b** the great Tigris River,
11: 1 I have been standing **b** Michael as his support
Am 7: 7 I saw the Lord standing **b** a wall that had been built
9: 1 Then I saw a vision of the Lord standing **b** the
Zec 14:20 will be as sacred as the basins used **b** the altar.
Mt 4:13 he went to Capernaum, **b** the Sea of Galilee,
4:15 of Naphtali, / **b** the sea, beyond the Jordan River—
4:18 One day as Jesus was walking along the shore **b**
5:24 leave your sacrifice there **b** the altar. Go and be
20:30 Two blind men were sitting **b** the road. When they
21: 2 you will see a donkey tied there, with its colt **b** it.
21:19 and he noticed a fig tree **b** the road. He went over
Mk 10:46 was sitting **b** the road as Jesus was going by.
Lk 10:30 beat him up, and left him half dead **b** the road.
10:34 Kneeling **b** him, the Samaritan soothed his wounds
18:35 a blind beggar was sitting **b** the road.
19: 4 ran ahead and climbed a sycamore tree **b** the road,
23:39 One of the criminals hanging **b** him scoffed,
24:15 and joined them and began walking **b** them.
Jn 4: 6 long walk, sat wearily **b** the well about noontime.
4:28 The woman left her water jar **b** the well and went
19:26 When Jesus saw his mother standing there **b** the
21: 1 Later Jesus appeared again to the disciples **b** the
Ac 2: 7 They were **b** themselves with wonder. "How can
2:25 I will not be shaken, for he is right **b** me.
3: 2 Each day he was put **b** the Temple gate, the one
5:10 they carried her out and buried her **b** her husband.
8:29 "Go over and walk along **b** the carriage."
22:13 He came to me and stood **b** me and said,
27:23 to whom I belong and whom I serve stood **b** me,
Heb 12: 2 Now he is seated in the place of highest honor **b**

BESIDES (21) [BESIDE]
Ge 17:17 "**B**, Sarah is ninety; how could she have a baby?"
20:12 **B**, she is my sister—we both have the same father,
Ex 20: 3 "Do not worship any other gods **b** me.
33:13 **B**, don't forget that this nation is your very own
Dt 5: 7 " 'Do not worship any other gods **b** me.
Jos 15:42 **B** these, there were Libnah, Ether, Ashan,
15:55 **B** these, there were Maon, Carmel, Ziph, Juttah,
1Sa 2: 2 There is no one **b** you; / there is no Rock like our
1Ki 10:13 **b** all the other customary gifts he had
11: 1 **B** Pharaoh's daughter, he married women from
2Ch 17:19 **b** those Jehoshaphat stationed in the fortified cities
Ne 5:15 daily ration of food and wine, **b** a pound of silver.
5:17 at my table, **b** all the visitors from other lands!
Ps 94: 7 they say, / "and **b**, the God of Israel doesn't care."
Isa 56: 8 I will bring others, too, **b** my people Israel."
Mk 4:24 the more you will understand—and even more, **b**.
Lk 16:26 And **b**, there is a great chasm separating us.
Jn 4:12 And **b**, are you greater than our ancestor Jacob
20:30 miraculous signs **b** the ones recorded in this book.
2Co 11:28 Then, **b** all this, I have the daily burden of how the
1Ti 5:13 **B**, they are likely to become lazy and spend their

BESIEGE (4) [SIEGE]
Dt 20:20 Use them to make the equipment you need to **b** the
1Ki 20: 1 They went to **b** Samaria, the Israelite capital,
Jer 39: 1 and his army returned to **b** Jerusalem.
Zec 12: 2 nations that send their armies to **b** Jerusalem.

BESIEGED (6) [SIEGE]
2Ki 6:24 of Aram mobilized his entire army and **b** Samaria.
16: 5 on Ahaz. They **b** Jerusalem but did not conquer it.
17: 5 the entire land, and for three years he **b** Samaria.
24:10 of Babylon came up against Jerusalem and **b** it.
Ecc 9:14 and a great king came with his army and **b** it.
Da 1: 1 came to Jerusalem and **b** it with his armies.

BESIEGING (5) [SIEGE]
Dt 20:19 "When you are **b** a town and the war drags on,
1Ki 8:37 or if your people's enemies are in the land **b** their
2Ch 6:28 or if your people's enemies are in the land **b** their
32: 9 of Assyria, while still **b** the town of Lachish,
Jer 34: 7 At this time the Babylonian army was **b** Jerusalem,

BESODEIAH (1)
Ne 3: 6 by Joiada son of Paseah and Meshullam son of **B**.

BESOM [KJV] See BROOM

BESOR (2)
1Sa 30: 9 men set out, and they soon came to **B** Brook.
30:21 When they reached **B** Brook and met the two

BEST (120) [GOOD]
Ge 4: 4 several choice lambs from the **b** of his flock.
18: 6 Get three measures of your **b** flour, and bake some
24:10 taking with him the **b** of everything his master
27:15 Then she took Esau's **b** clothes, which were there
38:23 "We tried our **b** to send her the goat.
43:11 Fill your bags with the **b** products of the land.
45:18 'Pharaoh will assign to you the very **b** territory in
45:20 for the **b** of all the land of Egypt is yours."
47: 6 Give them the **b** land of Egypt—the land of
47:11 So Joseph assigned the **b** land of Egypt—the land
Ex 14: 7 He took with him six hundred of Egypt's **b**

15: 4 into the sea. / The very **b** of Pharaoh's officers
34:26 You must bring the **b** of the first of each year's
Nu 18:12 the **b** of the olive oil, wine, and grain.
18:29 Be sure to set aside the **b** portions of the gifts given
18:30 'When you present the **b** part, it will be considered
18:32 tithes if you give the **b** portion to the priests.
Dt 1:22 They will advise us on the **b** route to take
1:33 who goes before you looking for the **b** places to
33:16 with the **b** gifts of the earth and its fullness,
33:21 The people of Gad took the **b** land for themselves;
Jos 2: 3 They are spies sent here to discover the **b** way to
Jdg 6:25 "Take the second **b** bull from your father's herd,
14:20 who had been Samson's **b** man at the wedding.
15: 2 "so I gave her in marriage to your **b** man.
15: 6 gave Samson's wife to be married to his **b** man."
1Sa 1:23 "Whatever you think is **b**," Elkanah agreed.
2:29 and they have become fat from the **b** offerings of
3:18 Eli replied. "Let him do what he thinks **b**."
8:14 He will take away the **b** of your fields
10: 7 do whatever you think is **b**, for God will be with
14: 7 "Do what you think is **b**," the youth replied.
14:36 men replied, "We'll do whatever you think is **b**."
15: 9 Agag's life and kept the **b** of the sheep and cattle,
15:15 "It's true that the army spared the **b** of the sheep
15:21 Then my troops brought in the **b** of the sheep
18: 1 between them, and they became the **b** of friends.
26: 2 So Saul took three thousand of his **b** troops
27: 1 The **b** thing for me to do is escape to the
2Sa 10: 9 on two fronts, he chose the **b** troops in his army.
15:15 his advisers replied. "Do what you think is **b**."
15:26 with me, then let him do what seems **b** to him."
18: 4 "If you think that's the **b** plan, I'll do it," the king
19:27 are like an angel of God, so do what you think is **b**.
1Ki 2: 6 Do with him what you think **b**, but don't let him
20: 3 and so are the **b** of your wives and children!' "
2Ki 3:19 You will conquer the **b** of their cities,
10: 3 select the **b** qualified of King Ahab's sons to be
10: 5 make anyone king; do whatever you think is **b**."
20:12 of Babylon, sent Hezekiah his **b** wishes and a gift,
24:14 including all the princes and the **b** of the soldiers,
24:16 He also took seven thousand of the **b** troops
1Ch 12:32 the times and knew the **b** course for Israel to take.
19:10 on two fronts, he chose the **b** troops in his army.
2Ch 10: 7 show them kindness and do your **b** to please them,
Ne 10:37 We will bring the **b** of our flour and other grain
offerings, the **b** of our fruit, and the **b** of our new
wine and olive oil.
Est 2: 9 and her maids into the **b** place in the harem.
3: 7 to determine the **b** day and month to take action.
Job 40:20 The mountains offer it their **b** food, where all the
Ps 32: 8 "I will guide you along the **b** pathway for your
41: 9 Even my **b** friend, the one I trusted completely,
66:15 to you—/ the **b** of my rams as a pleasing aroma.
81:16 But I would feed you with the **b** of foods. / I would
89:22 His enemies will not get the **b** of him, / nor will the
90:10 But even the **b** of these years are filled with pain
118:13 You did your **b** to kill me, O my enemy,
119:10 I have tried my **b** to find you—/ don't let me
122: 9 I will seek what is **b** for you, O Jerusalem.
Pr 3: 9 and with the **b** part of everything your land
9:17 is refreshing; food eaten in secret tastes the **b**!"
16:28 seeds of strife; gossip separates the **b** of friends.
Ecc 6:12 who knows how our days can **b** be spent?
7:23 All along I have tried my **b** to let wisdom guide my
SS 7: 9 May your kisses be as exciting as the **b** wine,
Isa 8: 9 will cry, 'Do your **b** to defend yourselves,
19:11 Their **b** counsel to the king of Egypt is stupid
39: 1 of Babylon, sent Hezekiah his **b** wishes and a gift.
40:14 need instruction about what is good or what is **b**?
60:16 and mighty nations will bring the **b** of their goods
Jer 2:21 I chose a vine of the purest stock—the very **b**.
26:14 and in your power—do with me as you think **b**.
49:35 the archers of Elam—the **b** of their marksmen.
Eze 17:21 And all the **b** warriors of Israel will be killed in
20: 6 with milk and honey, the **b** of all lands anywhere.
24: 5 Use only the **b** sheep from the flock and heap fuel
31:16 of Eden, the most beautiful and the **b** of Lebanon,
34: 3 the milk, wear the wool, and butcher the **b** animals,
34:18 Is it not enough for you to keep the **b** of the
34:18 Is it not enough for you to take the **b** water for
Da 1: 5 The king assigned them a daily ration of the **b** food
11:15 The **b** troops of the south will not be able to stand
11:41 Edom, and the **b** part of Ammon will escape.
Joel 3: 9 "Get ready for war! Call out your **b** warriors!
Jnh 4:10 to put it there. And a plant is only, at **b**, short lived.
Mic 7: 4 Even the **b** of them is like a brier; the straightest is
7: 5 trust anyone—not your **b** friend or even your wife!
Mt 27:65 "Take guards and secure it the **b** you can."
Lk 14: 8 a wedding feast, don't always head for the **b** seat.
22: 4 and captains of the Temple guard to discuss the **b**
Jn 2:10 "Usually a host serves the **b** wine first," he said.
2:10 But you have kept the **b** until now!"
5:34 But the **b** testimony about me is not from a man,
16: 7 But it is actually **b** for you that I go away,
Ro 12:21 Don't let evil get the **b** of you, but conquer evil by
16:10 And give my **b** regards to the members of the
1Co 7:26 I think it is **b** to remain just as you are.
7:35 you to do whatever will help you serve the Lord **b**,
10:24 Think of other Christians and what is **b** for them.
10:33 I don't just do what I like or what is **b** for me,
10:33 but what is **b** for them so they may be saved.
2Co 8: 5 **B** of all, they went beyond our highest hopes,
12: 9 you need. My power works **b** in your weakness."
Gal 1:13 the Christians. I did my **b** to get rid of them.
1Th 3: 5 I was afraid that the Tempter had gotten the **b** of
Tit 2: 9 obey their masters and do their **b** to please them.
3:12 do your **b** to meet me at Nicopolis as quickly as
Heb 4:11 Let us do our **b** to enter that place of rest.
12:10 us for a few years, doing the **b** they knew how.

BEST-EQUIPPED (1) [GOOD, EQUIP]

Ps 33:16 The **b** army cannot save a king, / nor is great

BESTIAL (1) [BEAST]

Eze 23:20 after lovers whose attentions were gross and **b**.

BESTOWED (2)

Job 29:20 New honors are constantly **b** on me, and my
Eze 16:14 because the splendor I **b** on you perfected your

BETEN (1)

Jos 19:25 included these towns: Helkath, Hali, **B**, Acshaph,

BETH-ANATH (3) [ANATH]

Jos 19:38 Yiron, Migdal-el, Horem, **B**, and Beth-shemesh—
Jdg 1:33 to drive out the residents of Beth-shemesh and **B**.
1:33 and **B** were sometimes forced to work as slaves for

BETH-ANOTH (1)

Jos 15:59 Maarath, **B**, and Eltekon—six towns with their

BETH-ARABAH (3) [ARABAH]

Jos 15: 6 then proceeded north of **B** to the stone of Bohan.
15:61 In the wilderness there were the towns of **B**,
18:22 **B**, Zemaraim, Bethel,

BETH-ARBEL (1)

Hos 10:14 just as they did when Shalman destroyed **B**.

BETH-ASHBEA (1)

1Ch 4:21 of Mareshah), the families of linen workers at **B**,

BETH-AVEN (7) [AVEN]

Jos 7: 2 to spy out the city of Ai, east of Bethel, near **B**.
18:12 through the hill country and the wilderness of **B**.
1Sa 13: 5 the seashore! They camped at Micmash east of **B**.
14:23 the battle continued to rage even out beyond **B**.
Hos 4:15 who worship me insincerely at Gilgal and at **B**.
5: 8 Raise the battle cry in **B**! Lead on into battle,
10: 5 people of Samaria tremble for their calf idol at **B**.

BETH-AZMAVETH (2) [AZMAVETH]

Ezr 2:24 The people of **B** | 42
Ne 7:28 The people of **B** | 42

BETH-BAAL-MEON (1) [BAAL-MEON, BETH-MEON]

Jos 13:17 other towns on the plain—Dibon, Bamoth-baal, **B**,

BETH-BARAH (1)

Jdg 7:24 them off at the shallows of the Jordan River at **B**."

BETH-BIRI (1) [BETH-LEBAOTH]

1Ch 4:31 Beth-marcaboth, Hazar-susim, **B**, and Shaaraim.

BETH-CAR (1)

1Sa 7:11 The men of Israel chased them from Mizpah to **B**,

BETH-DAGON (2) [DAGON]

Jos 15:41 Gederoth, **B**, Naamah, and Makkedah—
19:27 turned east toward **B**, and ran as far as Zebulun in

BETH-DIBLATHAIM (1) [ALMON-DIBLATHAIM]

Jer 48:22 and on Dibon and Nebo and **B**,

BETH-EDEN (1) [EDEN]

Am 1: 5 I will destroy the ruler in **B**, and the people of

BETH-EKED (2)

2Ki 10:12 the way, while he was at **B** of the Shepherds,
10:14 forty-two of them and killed them at the well of **B**.

BETH-EMEK (1)

Jos 19:27 valley of Iphtah-el, running north to **B** and Neiel.

BETH-EZEL (1)

Mic 1:11 The people of **B** mourn because the very

BETH-GADER (1)

1Ch 2:51 father of Bethlehem), and Hareph (the father of **B**).

BETH-GAMUL (1) [GAMUL]

Jer 48:23 and on Kiriathaim and **B** and Beth-meon,

BETH-GILGAL (1) [GILGAL]

Ne 12:29 They also came from **B** and the area of Geba

BETH-HAGGAN (1)

2Ki 9:27 what was happening, he fled along the road to **B**.

BETH-HAKKEREM (2)

Ne 3:14 Malkijah son of Recab, the leader of the **B** district.
Jer 6: 1 Sound the alarm in Tekoa! Send up a signal at **B**!

BETH-HARAM (1)

Jos 13:27 In the valley were **B**, Beth-nimrah, Succoth,

BETH-HARAN (1) [HARAN]

Nu 32:36 Beth-nimrah, and **B**. These were all fortified cities

BETH-HOGLAH (3) [HOGLAH]

Jos 15: 6 crossed to **B**, then proceeded north of Beth-arabah
18:19 ran past the north slope of **B**, and ended at the
18:21 of the tribe of Benjamin. / Jericho, **B**, Emek-keziz,

BETH-HORON (14) [HORONITE]

Jos 10:10 the Israelites chased the enemy along the road to **B**
10:11 As the Amorites retreated down the road from **B**,
16: 3 to the territory of the Japhletites as far as Lower **B**,
16: 5 at Ataroth-addar. From there it ran to Upper **B**,
18:13 to the top of the hill south of Lower **B**.
18:14 south along the western edge of the hill facing **B**,
21:22 Kibzaim, and **B**—four towns.
1Sa 13:18 another went west to **B**, and the third moved
1Ki 9:17 of Gezer.) He also built up the towns of Lower **B**,
1Ch 6:68 Jokmeam, **B**,
7:24 towns of Lower and Upper **B** and Uzzen-sheerah.
2Ch 8: 5 He fortified the cities of Upper **B** and Lower **B**,
25:13 of the towns of Judah between Samaria and **B**,

BETH-JESHIMOTH (4)

Nu 33:49 Along the Jordan River they camped from **B** as far
Jos 12: 3 as the Dead Sea, from **B** to the slopes of Pisgah.
13:20 Beth-peor, the slopes of Pisgah, and **B**,
Eze 25: 9 frontier cities—**B**, Baal-meon, and Kiriathaim.

BETH-LEAPHRAH (1)

Mic 1:10 You people in **B**, roll in the dust to show your

BETH-LEBAOTH (1) [BETH-BIRI]

Jos 19: 6 **B**, and Sharuhen—thirteen towns with their

BETH-MARCABOTH (2)

Jos 19: 5 Ziklag, **B**, Hazar-susah,
1Ch 4:31 **B**, Hazar-susim, Beth-biri, and Shaaraim.

BETH-MEON (1) [BAAL-MEON, BETH-BAAL-MEON]

Jer 48:23 and on Kiriathaim and Beth-gamul and **B**,

BETH-MILLO (4) [MILLO]

Jdg 9: 6 and **B** called a meeting under the oak beside the
9:20 and devour the people of Shechem and **B**;
9:20 of Shechem and **B** and devour Abimelech!"
2Ki 12:20 and assassinated him at **B** on the road to Silla.

BETH-NIMRAH (2) [NIMRAH]

Nu 32:36 **B**, and Beth-haran. These were all fortified cities
Jos 13:27 the valley were Beth-haram, **B**, Succoth, Zaphon,

BETH-PAZZEZ (1)

Jos 19:21 Remeth, En-gannim, En-haddah, and **B**.

BETH-PELET (2) [PELET]

Jos 15:27 Hazar-gaddah, Heshmon, **B**,
Ne 11:26 They also lived in Jeshua, Moladah, **B**,

BETH-PEOR (4) [PEOR]

Dt 3:29 So we stayed in the valley near **B**.
4:46 and as they camped in the valley near **B** east of the
34: 6 He was buried in a valley near **B** in Moab, but to
Jos 13:20 **B**, the slopes of Pisgah, and Beth-jeshimoth.

BETH-RAPHA (1) [RAPHA]

1Ch 4:12 Eshton was the father of **B**, Paseah, and Tehinnah.

BETH-REHOB (2) [REHOB]

Jdg 18:28 allies nearby. This happened in the valley near **B**.
2Sa 10: 6 Aramean mercenaries from the lands of **B**

BETH-SHAN (9)

Jos 17:11 **B**, Ibleam, Dor (that is, Naphoth-dor), Endor,
17:16 and the Canaanites in the lowlands around **B**
Jdg 1:27 Manasseh failed to drive out the people living in **B**,
1Sa 31:10 they fastened his body to the wall of the city of **B**.
31:12 their warriors traveled all night to **B** and took the
2Sa 21:12 from the public square of the Philistine city of **B**.)
1Ki 4:12 and Megiddo, all of **B** near Zarethan below Jezreel,
4:12 and all the territory from **B** to Abel-meholah
1Ch 7:29 the border of Manasseh were the towns of **B**,

BETH-SHEMESH (20)

Jos 15:10 and went down to **B** and on to Timnah.
19:22 Shahazumah, and **B**, ending at the Jordan River—
19:38 Yiron, Migdal-el, Horem, Beth-anath, and **B**—
21:16 Ain, Juttah, and **B**—nine towns from these two
Jdg 1:33 Naphtali also failed to drive out the residents of **B**

1:33 the people of **B** and Beth-anath were sometimes
1Sa 6: 9 If they cross the border of our land and go to **B**,
6:12 the cows went straight along the road toward **B**,
6:12 rulers followed them as far as the border of **B**.
6:13 The people of **B** were harvesting wheat in the
6:15 offered to the LORD that day by the people of **B**.
6:18 The large rock at **B**, where they set the Ark of the
6:19 But the LORD killed seventy men from **B**
1Ki 4: 9 Ben-deker, in Makaz, Shaalbim, **B**,
2Ki 14:11 The two armies drew up their battle lines at **B** in
14:13 of Israel captured King Amaziah of Judah at **B**
1Ch 6:59 Ain, Juttah, and **B**.
2Ch 25:21 The two armies drew up their battle lines at **B** in
25:23 of Israel captured King Amaziah of Judah at **B**
28:18 They had already captured **B**, Aijalon, Gederoth,

BETH-SHITTAH (1)

Jdg 7:22 killed fled to places as far away as **B** near Zererah

BETH-TAPPUAH (1) [TAPPUAH]

Jos 15:53 Janim, **B**, Aphekah,

BETH-TOGARMAH (1) [TOGARMAH]

Eze 38: 6 along with the armies of **B** from the distant north

BETH-ZUR (4) [ZUR]

Jos 15:58 In addition, there were Halhul, **B**, Gedor,
1Ch 2:45 of Shammai was Maon. Maon was the father of **B**.
2Ch 11: 7 **B**, Soco, Adullam,
Ne 3:16 son of Azbuk, the leader of half the district of **B**.

BETHANY (13)

Mt 21:17 Then he returned to **B**, where he stayed overnight.
26: 6 Meanwhile, Jesus was in **B** at the home of Simon,
Mk 11: 1 they came to the towns of Bethphage and **B**,
11:11 Then he went out to **B** with the twelve disciples.
11:12 The next morning as they were leaving **B**,
14: 3 Meanwhile, Jesus was in **B** at the home of Simon,
Lk 19:29 As they came to the towns of Bethphage and **B**,
24:50 Then Jesus led them to **B**, and lifting his hands to
Jn 1:28 This incident took place at **B**, a village east of the
11: 1 He lived in **B** with his sisters, Mary and Martha.
11:17 When Jesus arrived at **B**, he was told that Lazarus
11:18 **B** was only a few miles down the road from
12: 1 Jesus arrived in **B**, the home of Lazarus—

BETHARAM [KJV] See BETH-HARAM

BETHEL (77) [EL-BETHEL, LUZ]

Ge 12: 8 and set up camp in the hill country between **B** on
13: 3 Then they continued traveling by stages toward **B**,
13: 3 to the place between **B** and Ai where they had
28:19 He named the place **B**—"house of God"—
31:13 I am the God you met at **B**, the place where you
35: 1 said to Jacob, "Now move on to **B** and settle there.
35: 3 We are now going to **B**, where I will build an altar
35: 6 Finally, they arrived at Luz (now called **B**)
35: 7 because God had appeared to him there at **B** when
35: 8 buried beneath the oak tree in the valley below **B**.
35: 9 he arrived at **B** after traveling from Paddan-aram.
35:15 Jacob called the place **B**—"house of God"—
35:16 Leaving **B**, they traveled on toward Ephrath (that
Jos 7: 2 to spy out the city of Ai, east of **B**, near Beth-aven.
8: 9 they left that night and lay in ambush between **B**
8:12 sent five thousand men to lie in ambush between **B**
8:17 in Ai or **B** who did not chase after the Israelites,
12: 9 The king of Jericho / The king of Ai, near **B**
12:16 The king of Makkedah / The king of **B**
16: 1 the wilderness and into the hill country of **B**.
16: 2 From **B** (that is, Luz) it ran over to Ataroth in the
18:13 there the boundary went south to Luz (that is, **B**)
18:22 Beth-arabah, Zemaraim, **B**,
Jdg 1:22 The descendants of Joseph attacked the town of **B**,
1:23 They sent spies to **B** (formerly known as Luz),
4: 5 and **B** in the hill country of Ephraim,
20:18 Before the battle the Israelites went to **B** and asked
20:23 (For they had gone up to **B** and wept in the
20:26 Then all the Israelites went up to **B** and wept in the
20:27 days the Ark of the Covenant of God was in **B**,
20:31 and along the roads leading to **B** and Gibeah.
21: 2 And the people went to **B** and sat in the presence
21:19 between Lebonah and **B**, along the east side of the road that goes from **B** to
1Sa 7:16 setting up his court first at **B**, then at Gilgal,
10: 3 you who are on their way to worship God at **B**.
13: 2 with him to Micmash and the hill country of **B**.
30:27 and his men had been: **B**, Ramoth-negev, Jattir,
1Ki 12:29 and northern ends of Israel—in **B** and in Dan.
12:32 Jeroboam also instituted a religious festival in **B**,
12:32 There at **B** he himself offered sacrifices to the
12:32 And it was at **B** that he appointed priests for the
12:33 Jeroboam offered sacrifices on the altar at **B**.
13: 1 a man of God from Judah went to **B**,
13:10 So he left **B** and went home another way.
13:11 it happened, there was an old prophet living in **B**,
13:11 and told him what the man of God had done in **B**
13:25 and they went and reported it in **B**, where the old
13:32 LORD told him to proclaim against the altar in **B**
16:34 his reign that Hiel, a man from **B**, rebuilt Jericho.
2Ki 2: 2 for the LORD has told me to go to **B**."
2: 2 never leave you!" So they went on together to **B**.
2: 3 The group of prophets from **B** came to Elisha
2:23 Elisha left Jericho and went up to **B**. As he was
10:29 however, destroy the gold calves at **B** and Dan,
17:28 who had been exiled from Samaria returned to **B**
23: 4 Kidron Valley, and he carried the ashes away to **B**.
23:15 The king also tore down the altar at **B**, the pagan
23:16 and he burned them on the altar at **B** to desecrate
23:17 things that you have just done to the altar at **B**!"
23:19 in the towns of Samaria, just as he had done at **B**.
1Ch 7:28 of Ephraim lived in the territory that included **B**
2Ch 13:19 of his towns, including **B**, Jeshanah, and Ephron,
Ezr 2:28 The peoples of **B** and Ai | 223
Ne 7:32 The peoples of **B** and Ai | 123
11:31 Aija, and **B** with its surrounding villages.
Jer 48:13 as Israel was ashamed of her gold calf at **B**.
Hos 10:15 You will share that fate, **B**, because of your great
12: 4 There at **B** he met God face to face, and God spoke
Am 3:14 for its sins, I will destroy the pagan altars at **B**.
4: 4 and offer your sacrifices to the idols at **B**
5: 5 Don't go to worship the idols of **B**, Gilgal,
5: 5 and the people of **B** will come to nothing."
5: 6 Your gods in **B** certainly won't be able to quench
7:10 But when Amaziah, the priest of **B**, heard what
7:13 Don't bother us here in **B** with your prophecies,
Zec 7: 2 The people of **B** had sent Sharezer

BETHESDA (1)

Jn 5: 2 the city, near the Sheep Gate, was the pool of **B**,

BETHLEHEM (52) [EPHRATH]

Ge 35:16 they traveled on toward Ephrath (that is, **B**).
35:19 and was buried on the way to Ephrath (that is, **B**).
48: 7 just a short distance from Ephrath (that is, **B**).
Jos 19:15 Nahalal, Shimron, Idalah, and **B**—
Jdg 12: 8 Ibzan became Israel's judge. He lived in **B**,
12:10 When he died, he was buried at **B**.
17: 7 One day a young Levite from **B** in Judah
17: 9 And he replied, "I am a Levite from **B** in Judah,
19: 1 One day he brought home a woman from **B** in
19: 2 to him and returned to her father's home in **B**.
19: 3 and an extra donkey to **B** to persuade her to come
19:18 "We have been in **B** in Judah," the man replied.
Ru 1: 1 a man from **B** in Judah left the country because of
1: 2 They were Ephrathites from **B** in the land of Judah.
1:19 When they came to **B**, the entire town was stirred
1:22 They arrived in **B** at the beginning of the barley
2: 1 a wealthy and influential man in **B** named Boaz,
2: 4 Boaz arrived from **B** and greeted the harvesters.
4:11 May you be great in Ephrathah and famous in **B**.
1Sa 16: 1 Now fill your horn with olive oil and go to **B**.
16: 4 When he arrived at **B**, the leaders of the town
17:12 an Ephrathite from **B** in the land of Judah.
17:15 for Saul and helping his father with the sheep in **B**.
17:58 "His name is Jesse, and we live in **B**."
20: 6 tell him I asked permission to go home to **B** for an
20:28 "David earnestly asked me if he could go to **B**.
2Sa 2:32 Joab and his men took Asahel's body to **B**
21:19 Elhanan son of Jair from **B** killed the brother of
23:14 Philistine detachment had occupied the town of **B**.
23:15 love some of that good water from the well in **B**,
23:24 Joab's brother; / Elhanan son of Dodo from **B**;
1Ch 2:51 Salma (the father of **B**), and Hareph (the father of
2:54 The descendants of Salma were **B**,
4: 4 Hur (the firstborn of Ephrathah), the ancestor of **B**.
11:16 Philistine detachment had occupied the town of **B**.
11:17 love some of that good water from the well in **B**,
11:26 Joab's brother; / Elhanan son of Dodo from **B**;
2Ch 11: 6 He built up **B**, Etam, Tekoa,
Ezr 2:21 The people of **B** | 123
Ne 7:26 The peoples of **B** and Netophah | 188
Jer 41:17 them all to the village of Geruth-kimham near **B**,
Mic 5: 2 But you, O **B** Ephrathah, are only a small village in
Mt 2: 1 Jesus was born in the town of **B** in Judea,
2: 5 "In **B**," they said, "for this is what the prophet
2: 6 'O **B** of Judah, / you are not just a lowly village in
2: 8 "Go to **B** and search carefully for the child.
2: 9 again the star appeared to them, guiding them to **B**.
2:16 and around **B** who were two years old and under,
Lk 2: 4 he had to go to **B** in Judea, David's ancient home.
2:11 has been born tonight in **B**, the city of David!
2:15 said to each other, "Come on, let's go to **B**!
Jn 7:42 in **B**, the village where King David was born."

BETHPHAGE (3)

Mt 21: 1 they came to the town of **B** on the Mount of
Mk 11: 1 they came to the towns of **B** and Bethany,
Lk 19:29 As they came to the towns of **B** and Bethany,

BETHSAIDA (7)

Mt 11:21 "What horrors await you, Korazin and **B**! For if
Mk 6:45 into the boat and head out across the lake to **B**,
8:22 When they arrived at **B**, some people brought a
Lk 9:10 quietly away with them toward the town of **B**.
10:13 "What horrors await you, Korazin and **B**! For if
Jn 1:44 Philip was from **B**, Andrew and Peter's hometown.
12:21 paid a visit to Philip, who was from **B** in Galilee.

BETHUEL (10) [BETHUL]

Ge 22:22 Kesed, Hazo, Pildash, Jidlaph, and **B**.
22:23 **B** became the father of Rebekah.
24:15 Her father was **B**, who was the son of Abraham's
24:24 "My father is **B**," she replied. "My grandparents
24:47 she told me, 'My father is **B**, the son of Nahor
24:50 Then Laban and **B** replied, "The LORD has
25:20 the daughter of **B** the Aramean from Paddan-aram
28: 2 to the house of your grandfather **B**,
28: 5 his mother's brother, the son of **B** the Aramean.
1Ch 4:30 **B**, Hormah, Ziklag,

BETHUL (1) [BETHUEL]

Jos 19: 4 Eltolad, **B**, Hormah,

BETIMES [KJV] See EARLY, FAVOR, PROMPT, REPEATEDLY

BETONIM (1)

Jos 13:26 extended from Heshbon to Ramath-mizpeh and **B**,

BETRAY (36) [BETRAYED, BETRAYER, BETRAYING]

Nu 5: 6 **b** the LORD by doing wrong to another person,
Jos 2:14 "If you don't **b** us, we will keep our promise when
2:20 If you **b** us, however, we are not bound by this
1Sa 20: 8 your father. But please don't **b** me to him!"
23:12 "Will these men of Keilah really **b** me and my
23:12 And the LORD replied, "Yes, they will **b** you."
1Ch 12:17 But if you have come to **b** me to my enemies when
Isa 16: 3 Protect us from their relentless attack. Do not **b** us.
33: 1 to you, while you **b** your promises to them.
Eze 20:27 Your ancestors continued to blaspheme and **b** me,
Mt 10:21 "Brother will **b** brother to death, fathers will **b** their own children,
24:10 will turn away from me and **b** and hate each other.
26:15 "How much will you pay me to **b** Jesus to you?"
26:16 looking for the right time and place to **b** Jesus.
26:21 he said, "The truth is, one of you will **b** me."
26:23 "One of you who is eating with me now will **b** me.
26:25 Judas, the one who would **b** him, also asked,
Mk 13:12 "Brother will **b** brother to death, fathers will **b** their own children,
14:10 went to the leading priests to arrange to **b** Jesus to
14:11 looking for the right time and place to **b** Jesus.
14:18 Jesus said, "The truth is, one of you will **b** me,
Lk 21:16 brothers, relatives, and friends—will **b** you.
22: 4 guard to discuss the best way to **b** Jesus to them.
22: 6 So he began looking for an opportunity to **b** Jesus
22:21 among us as a friend, is the man who will **b** me.
22:48 But Jesus said, "Judas, how can you **b** me, the Son
Jn 6:64 didn't believe, and he knew who would **b** him.)
6:71 one of the Twelve, who would **b** him.
12: 4 of his disciples—the one who would **b** him—said,
13: 2 of Simon Iscariot, to carry out his plan to **b** Jesus.
13:11 For Jesus knew who would **b** him. That is what he
13:21 "The truth is, one of you will **b** me!"
21:20 and asked, "Lord, who among us will **b** you?"
2Ti 3: 4 They will **b** their friends, be reckless, be puffed up

BETRAYED (28) [BETRAY]

1Sa 23:19 Ziph went to Saul in Gibeah and **b** David to him.
2Sa 18:13 And if I had **b** the king by killing his son—
Ps 7: 4 if I have **b** a friend / or plundered my enemy
55:20 As for this friend of mine, he **b** me; / he broke his
Isa 33: 1 to them. Now you, too, will be **b** and destroyed!
Jer 3:20 But you have **b** me, you people of Israel! You have
38:22 friends you have! They have **b** and misled you.
La 1: 2 All her friends have **b** her; they are now her
1:19 "I begged my allies for help, but they **b** me.
Hos 5: 7 For they have **b** the honor of the LORD,
Mic 2: 4 He has given our fields / to those who **b** us."
Mt 10: 4 (the Zealot), / Judas Iscariot (who later **b** him).
17:22 Jesus told them, "The Son of Man is going to be **b**.
20:18 "the Son of Man will be **b** to the leading priests
26: 2 and I, the Son of Man, will be **b** and crucified."
26:45 the Son of Man, am **b** into the hands of sinners.
27: 3 When Judas, who had **b** him, realized that Jesus
27: 4 he declared, "for I have **b** an innocent man."
Mk 3:19 Judas Iscariot (who later **b** him).
9:31 said to them, "The Son of Man is going to be **b**.
10:33 "the Son of Man will be **b** to the leading priests
14:41 the Son of Man, am **b** into the hands of sinners.
Lk 6:16 (son of James), / Judas Iscariot (who later **b** him).
9:44 what I say. The Son of Man is going to be **b**."
24: 7 that the Son of Man must be **b** into the hands of
Ac 7:52 the Messiah whom you **b** and murdered.
1Co 11:23 On the night when he was **b**, the Lord Jesus took a
Rev 20:10 Then the Devil, who **b** them, was thrown into the

BETRAYER (6) [BETRAY]

Mt 26:24 long ago. But how terrible it will be for my **b**.
26:46 Up, let's be going. See, my **b** is here!"
Mk 14:21 long ago. But how terrible it will be for my **b**.
14:42 Up, let's be going. See, my **b** is here!"
Lk 22:22 God's plan. But how terrible it will be for my **b**!"
Jn 18: 2 Judas, the **b**, knew this place, because Jesus had

BETRAYING (3) [BETRAY]

Lev 26:40 and the sins of their ancestors for **b** me and being
Jos 22:16 demands to know why you are **b** the God of Israel.
2Sa 3: 8 for you and your father by not **b** you to David,

BETTER (168) [GOOD]

Ge 41:38 Pharaoh said, "Who could do it **b** than Joseph?
Ex 14:12 Our Egyptian slavery was far **b** than dying out here
16: 3 "It would have been **b** if the LORD had killed us
Nu 11:18 had meat to eat! Surely we were **b** off in Egypt!"
Jdg 8: 2 Aren't the last grapes of Ephraim's harvest **b** than
11:25 Are you any **b** than Balak son of Zippor, king of
18:19 Isn't it **b** to be a priest for an entire tribe of Israel
Ru 4:15 and who has been **b** to you than seven sons!"
1Sa 1: 8 You have me—isn't that **b** than having ten sons?"

14:27 ate the honey. After he had eaten it, he felt much **b**.
14:29 See how much **b** I feel now that I have eaten this
15:22 to his voice? Obedience is far **b** than sacrifice.
15:22 Listening to him is much **b** than offering the fat of
15:28 given it to someone else—one who is **b** than you.
16:23 Then Saul would feel **b**, and the tormenting spirit
24:17 he said to David, "You are a **b** man than I am,
25:17 You'd **b** think fast, for there is going to be trouble
29:4 Is there any **b** way for him to reconcile himself
2Sa 13:5 for you. Tell him you'll feel **b** if she feeds you."
17:14 "Hushai's advice is **b** than Ahithophel's."
17:14 which really was the **b** plan, so that he could bring
18:3 and it is **b** that you stay here in the city and send us
1Ki 2:32 two men who were more righteous and **b** than he.
19:4 "Take my life, for I am no **b** than my ancestors."
21:2 I will give you a **b** vineyard in exchange, or if you
2Ki 5:12 and Pharpar River of Damascus **b** than all the
7:4 If they let us live, so much the **b**. But if they kill
7:13 "We had **b** send out scouts to check into this.
2Ch 12:8 so that they can learn how much **b** it is to serve me
21:13 your own brothers, men who were **b** than you.
32:14 What makes you think your God can do any **b**?
Job 5:14 they see no **b** in the daytime than at night.
12:3 a few things myself—and you're no **b** than I am.
13:2 I know as much as you do. You are no **b** than I am.
31:23 That would be **b** than facing the judgment sent by
Ps 4:6 Many people say, "Who will show us **b** times?"
37:16 It is **b** to be godly and have little / than to be evil
63:3 Your unfailing love is **b** to me than life itself;
84:10 your courts / is **b** than a thousand anywhere else!
118:8 It is **b** to trust the LORD / than to put confidence
118:9 It is **b** to trust the LORD / than to put confidence
Pr 3:14 For the profit of wisdom is **b** than silver, and her wages are **b** than gold.
8:19 My gifts are **b** than the purest gold, my wages **b** than sterling silver!
11:15 is dangerous; it is **b** to refuse than to suffer later.
12:9 It is **b** to be a nobody with a servant than to be
15:16 It is **b** to have little with fear for the LORD than
15:17 A bowl of soup with someone you love is **b** than
16:8 It is **b** to be poor and godly than rich
16:16 How much **b** to get wisdom than gold,
16:19 It is **b** to live humbly with the poor than to share
16:32 It is **b** to be patient than powerful; it is **b** to have self-control than to conquer a city.
17:1 A dry crust eaten in peace is **b** than a great feast
19:1 It is **b** to be poor and honest than to be a fool
19:22 And it is **b** to be poor than dishonest.
21:9 It is **b** to live alone in the corner of an attic than
21:19 It is **b** to live alone in the desert than with a crabby,
22:1 for being held in high esteem is **b** than having
25:7 It is **b** to wait for an invitation than to be sent to the
25:24 It is **b** to live alone in the corner of an attic than
27:5 An open rebuke is **b** than hidden love!
27:6 Wounds from a friend are **b** than many kisses from
27:10 It is **b** to go to a neighbor than to a relative who
28:6 It is **b** to be poor and honest than rich and crooked.
Ecc 2:13 than foolishness, just as light is **b** than darkness.
2:24 So I decided there is nothing **b** than to enjoy food
3:12 So I concluded that there is nothing **b** for people
3:18 they can see for themselves that they are no **b** than
3:22 So I saw that there is nothing **b** for people than to
4:2 So I concluded that the dead are **b** off than the
4:6 They feel it is **b** to be lazy and barely survive than
4:9 as much as one; they get a **b** return for their labor.
4:12 Three are even **b**, for a triple-braided cord is not
4:13 It is **b** to be a poor but wise youth than to be an old
5:5 It is **b** to say nothing than to promise something
6:3 I say he would have been **b** off born dead.
7:1 the day you die is **b** than the day you are born.
7:2 It is **b** to spend your time at funerals than at
7:3 Sorrow is **b** than laughter, for sadness has a
7:5 It is **b** to be criticized by a wise person than to be
7:8 Finishing is **b** than starting. Patience is **b** than pride.
7:10 for you don't know whether they were any **b** than
7:11 Being wise is as good as being rich; in fact, it is **b**.
8:12 I know that those who fear God will be **b** off.
8:15 because there is nothing **b** for people to do in this
9:4 "It is **b** to be a live dog than a dead lion!"
9:16 Then I realized that though wisdom is **b** than
9:17 the quiet words of a wise person are **b** than the
SS 4:10 my bride! How much **b** it is than wine!
5:10 is dark and dazzling, **b** than ten thousand others!
Isa 9:10 in ruins now, but we will rebuild it **b** than before.
40:20 Or is a poor person's wooden idol **b**? Can God be
56:12 this go on and on, and tomorrow will be even **b**."
Jer 42:21 but you will not obey the LORD your God any **b**
La 4:9 Those killed by the sword are far **b** off than those
Eze 14:22 then you will feel **b** about what I have done to
Da 1:15 and **b** nourished than the young men who had been
1:20 men to be ten times **b** than that of all the magicians
Hos 2:7 because I was **b** off with him than I am now.'
Am 6:2 You are no **b** than they were, and look at how they
Jnh 4:8 "Death is certainly **b** than this!" he exclaimed.
Na 3:8 Are you any **b** than Thebes, surrounded by rivers,
Mt 5:20 unless you obey God **b** than the teachers of
5:29 It is **b** for you to lose one part of your body than
5:30 It is **b** for you to lose one part of your body than
10:15 and Gomorrah will be **b** off on the judgment day
11:22 and Sidon will be **b** off on the judgment day than
11:24 Sodom will be **b** off on the judgment day than
18:6 it would be **b** for that person to be thrown into the
18:8 It is **b** to enter heaven crippled or lame than to be
18:9 It is **b** to enter heaven half blind than to have two
19:10 then said to him, "Then it is **b** not to marry!"
26:24 Far **b** for him if he had never been born!"
Mk 5:26 she had to pay them, but she had gotten no **b**.
9:42 it would be **b** for that person to be thrown into the
9:43 It is **b** to enter heaven with only one hand than to
9:45 It is **b** to enter heaven with only one foot than to be
9:47 It is **b** to enter the Kingdom of God half blind than
14:21 Far **b** for him if he had never been born!"
Lk 5:39 the fresh and the new. 'The old is **b**,' they say."
10:12 even wicked Sodom will be **b** off than such a town
10:14 and Sidon will be **b** off on the judgment day than
14:10 'Friend, we have a **b** place than this for you!'
17:2 It would be **b** to be thrown into the sea with a large
Jn 4:12 How can you offer **b** water than he and his sons
4:52 He asked them when the boy had begun to feel **b**,
11:12 if he is sleeping, that means he is getting **b**!"
18:14 Jewish leaders, "**B** that one should die for all."
Ro 2:25 you are no **b** off than an uncircumcised Gentile.
2:27 be much **b** off than you Jews who are circumcised
3:8 you might as well say that the more we sin the **b** it
3:9 Well then, are we Jews **b** than others? No, not at
1Co 4:7 What makes you **b** than anyone else? What do you
7:8 to widows—it's **b** to stay unmarried, just as I am.
7:9 and marry. It's **b** to marry than to burn with lust.
7:38 and the person who doesn't marry does even **b**.
7:40 But in my opinion it will be **b** for her if she doesn't
12:31 let me tell you about something else that is **b** than
Gal 4:1 those children are not much **b** off than slaves until
Php 1:21 For to me, living is for Christ, and dying is even **b**.
1:22 service for Christ. I really don't know which is **b**.
1:23 and be with Christ. That would be far **b** for me,
1:24 but it is **b** for you that I live.
2:3 Be humble, thinking of others as **b** than yourself.
Col 1:10 the while, you will learn to know God **b** and **b**.
Heb 6:9 We are confident that you are meant for **b** things,
7:19 and now a **b** hope has taken its place.
7:22 guarantees the effectiveness of this **b** covenant.
8:6 for he is the one who guarantees for us a **b** covenant with God, based on **b** promises.
9:23 with far **b** sacrifices than the blood of animals.
10:34 You knew you had **b** things waiting for you in
11:16 But they were looking for a **b** place, a heavenly
11:26 He thought it was **b** to suffer for the sake of the
11:35 They placed their hope in the resurrection to a **b**
11:40 For God had far **b** things in mind for us that would
1Pe 1:14 ways of doing evil; you didn't know any **b** then.
3:1 Your godly lives will speak to them **b** than any
3:17 Remember, it is **b** to suffer for doing good, if that
2Pe 1:2 to know Jesus, our God and Lord, **b** and **b**.
1:3 As we know Jesus **b**, his divine power gives us
1:5 A life of moral excellence leads to knowing God **b**.
2:21 It would be **b** if they had never known the right

BETWEEN (226)

Ge 1:6 And God said, "Let there be space **b** the waters,
9:16 I will remember the eternal covenant **b** God
10:12 city of the empire, located **b** Nineveh and Calah.
12:8 and set up camp in the hill country **b** Bethel on the
13:3 to the place **b** Bethel and Ai where they had
13:7 So an argument broke out **b** the herdsmen of
13:8 "This arguing **b** our herdsmen has got to stop,"
15:17 and a flaming torch pass **b** the halves of the
16:14 and it can still be found **b** Kadesh and Bered.
17:7 "I will continue this everlasting covenant **b** us,
17:7 It will continue **b** me and your offspring forever.
20:1 and settled for a while **b** Kadesh and Shur at a
23:15 hundred pieces of silver, but what is that **b** friends?
26:28 decided we should have a treaty, a covenant **b** us.
31:49 "May the LORD keep watch **b** us to make sure
31:52 stand **b** us as a witness of our vows. I will not cross
32:16 of animals by itself, separated by a distance in **b**.
Ex 8:23 I will make a clear distinction **b** your people
9:4 But the LORD will again make a distinction **b** the
11:7 the LORD makes a distinction **b** the Egyptians
14:2 "Tell the people to march toward Pi-hahiroth **b**
14:3 They are trapped **b** the wilderness and the sea!'
14:20 The cloud settled **b** the Israelite and Egyptian
16:1 into the Sin Desert, **b** Elim and Mount Sinai.
21:35 sell the live bull and divide the money **b** them.
22:9 "Suppose there is a dispute **b** two people as to
25:22 and talk to you from above the atonement cover **b**
28:33 to the hem of the robe, with gold bells **b** them.
30:18 Put it **b** the Tabernacle and the altar, and fill it with
31:13 for the Sabbath is a sign of the covenant **b** me
39:25 Bells of pure gold were placed **b** the pomegranates
40:7 Set the large washbasin **b** the Tabernacle
40:30 Next he placed the large washbasin **b** the
Lev 10:10 You are to distinguish **b** what is holy and what is
11:47 so you can distinguish **b** what is unclean and may
20:25 therefore make a distinction **b** ceremonially clean
20:25 unclean animals, and **b** clean and unclean birds.
27:3 A man **b** the ages of twenty and sixty is valued at
27:5 A boy **b** five and twenty is valued at twenty pieces
27:6 A boy **b** the ages of one month and five years is
Nu 4:3 Count all the men **b** the ages of thirty and fifty who
4:23 Count all the men **b** the ages of thirty and fifty who
4:30 Count all the men **b** the ages of thirty and fifty who
4:35 The count included all the men **b** thirty and fifty
4:39 The count included all the men **b** thirty and fifty
4:43 The count included all the men **b** thirty and fifty
4:47 All the men **b** thirty and fifty years of age who
7:89 he heard the voice speaking to him from **b** the two
13:23 it took two of them to carry it on a pole **b** them!
16:48 He stood **b** the living and the dead until the plague
18:19 This is an unbreakable covenant **b** the LORD
21:13 The Arnon is the boundary line **b** the Moabites
22:24 where the road narrowed **b** two vineyard walls.
30:16 gave Moses concerning relationships **b** a man
30:16 and **b** a father and a young daughter who still lives
35:24 regulations in making a judgment **b** the slayer
Dt 1:1 **b** Paran on one side and Tophel, Laban, Hazeroth,
5:5 I stood as an intermediary **b** you and the LORD,
11:26 "Today I am giving you the choice **b** a blessing
22:9 "Do not plant any other crop **b** the rows of your
30:15 Today I am giving you a choice **b** prosperity and disaster, **b** life and death.
30:19 "Today I have given you the choice **b** life and death, **b** blessings and curses.
Jos 3:4 keeping a clear distance **b** you and the Ark.
8:9 So they left that night and lay in ambush **b** Bethel
8:11 north side of Ai, with a valley **b** them and the city.
8:12 sent five thousand men to lie in ambush **b** Bethel
8:33 and **b** them stood the Levitical priests carrying the
18:11 It lay **b** the territory previously assigned to the
22:25 placed the Jordan River as a barrier **b** our people
22:34 "It is a witness **b** us and them that the LORD is
24:7 I put darkness **b** you and the Egyptians.
24:25 and binding contract **b** themselves
Jdg 4:5 which stood **b** Ramah and Bethel in the hill
9:23 God stirred up trouble **b** Abimelech and the people
13:25 which is located **b** the towns of Zorah and Eshtaol,
16:25 of the temple, **b** the two pillars supporting the roof.
16:31 back home and buried him **b** Zorah and Eshtaol,
21:19 **b** Lebonah and Bethel, along the east side of the
1Sa 4:4 who is enthroned **b** the cherubim.
7:12 and placed it **b** the towns of Mizpah and Jeshanah.
7:14 And there was also peace **b** Israel and the Amorites
14:4 Jonathan had to go down **b** two rocky cliffs that
14:42 Saul said, "Now choose **b** me and Jonathan."
17:1 and camped **b** Socoh in Judah and Azekah at
17:3 other on opposite hills, with the valley **b** them.
17:15 But David went back and forth **b** working for Saul
18:1 There was an immediate bond of love **b** them,
24:12 The LORD will decide **b** us. Perhaps the LORD
2Sa 3:1 That was the beginning of a long war **b** those who
6:2 who is enthroned **b** the cherubim.
8:10 and there had been many wars **b** them.
19:29 and Ziba will divide your land equally **b** you."
1Ki 3:9 and know the difference **b** right and wrong.
3:26 will be neither yours nor mine; divide him **b** us!"
6:8 and another flight of stairs **b** the second and third
7:46 cast in clay molds in the Jordan Valley **b** Succoth
8:32 then hear from heaven and judge **b** your servants—
14:30 There was constant war **b** Rehoboam
15:6 There was war **b** Abijam and Jeroboam throughout
15:7 *Kings of Judah*. There was constant war **b** Abijam
15:16 There was constant war **b** King Asa of Judah
15:19 "Let us renew the treaty that existed **b** your father
15:32 There was constant war **b** Asa and King Baasha of
18:6 So they divided the land **b** them. Ahab went one
18:21 "How long are you going to waver **b** two
22:1 For three years there was no war **b** Aram
22:34 and the arrow hit the king of Israel **b** the joints of
2Ki 2:11 It drove **b** them, separating them, and Elijah was
9:24 Jehu drew his bow and shot Joram **b** the shoulders.
11:17 Then Jehoiada made a covenant **b** the LORD
11:17 He also made a covenant **b** the king
14:25 Jeroboam II recovered the territories of Israel **b**
16:14 which had stood **b** the entrance and the new altar,
19:15 you are enthroned **b** the mighty cherubim!
25:4 and fled through the gate **b** the two walls behind
1Ch 13:6 of the LORD who is enthroned **b** the cherubim.
16:20 They wandered back and forth **b** nations,
18:10 and there had been many wars **b** them.
21:16 and saw the angel of the LORD standing **b**
2Ch 4:17 cast in clay molds in the Jordan Valley **b** Succoth
6:23 then hear from heaven and judge **b** your servants—
13:2 Then war broke out **b** Abijah and Jeroboam.
16:3 "Let us renew the treaty that existed **b** your father
18:33 and the arrow hit the king of Israel **b** the joints of
23:16 Then Jehoiada made a covenant **b** himself
25:13 raided several of the towns of Judah **b** Samaria
Ne 6:17 many letters went back and forth **b** Tobiah
Job 6:30 Don't I know the difference **b** right and wrong?
16:21 that someone would mediate **b** God and me, as a person mediates **b** friends.
41:16 They are close together so no air can get **b** them.
Ps 99:1 He sits on his throne **b** the cherubim.
105:13 They wandered back and forth **b** nations,
106:23 chosen one, stepped **b** the LORD and the people.
Pr 18:18 and settle disputes **b** powerful opponents.
SS 1:13 My lover is like a sachet of myrrh lying **b** my
6:13 she moves so gracefully **b** two lines of dancers?"
Isa 9:1 which lies along the road that runs **b** the Jordan
11:13 Then at last the jealousy **b** Israel and Judah will
19:23 and Assyrians will move freely **b** their lands,
22:11 **B** the city walls, you build a reservoir for water
37:16 you are enthroned **b** the mighty cherubim!
Jer 23:28 There is a difference **b** chaff and wheat!
34:18 you walked **b** its halves to solemnize your vows.
38:27 No one had overheard the conversation **b** Jeremiah
39:4 They went out through a gate **b** the two walls
43:9 bury large rocks **b** the pavement stones at the
52:7 and fled through the gate **b** the two walls behind
Eze 4:3 take an iron griddle and place it **b** you and the city.
8:16 At the entrance, **b** the foyer and the bronze altar,
9:3 Then the glory of the God of Israel rose up from **b**
10:2 "Go in **b** the whirling wheels beneath the
10:6 "Go **b** the cherubim and take some burning coals from **b** the wheels."
20:12 them my Sabbath days of rest as a sign **b** them
22:26 To them there is no difference **b** what is holy
22:26 And they do not teach my people the difference **b**
34:17 I will judge **b** one sheep and another,
34:20 I will surely judge **b** the fat sheep and the scrawny

34:22 And I will judge **b** one sheep and another.
40: 7 with a distance **b** them of 8-3/4 feet along the
40:13 measuring the distance **b** the back walls of facing
40:19 across the Temple's outer courtyard **b** the outer
40:21 and 43-3/4 feet wide **b** the back walls of facing
40:23 The distance **b** the two gateways was 175 feet.
40:25 and 43-3/4 feet wide **b** the back walls of facing
40:27 The distance **b** the two gateways was 175 feet.
41: 9 This left an open area **b** these side rooms
41:18 and there was a palm tree carving **b** each of the
42: 4 **B** the two blocks of rooms ran a walkway 17-1/2
42:10 just south of the inner courtyard **b** the Temple
42:11 There was a walkway **b** the two blocks of rooms
43: 8 altars right next to mine with only a wall **b** them
44:23 They will teach my people the difference **b** what is
47:16 which are on the border **b** Damascus and Hamath,
47:17 on the border **b** Hamath to the north and Damascus
47:18 "The eastern border starts at a point **b** Hauran
47:18 and runs southward along the Jordan River **b** Israel
48:22 So the prince's land will include everything **b** the
Da 7: 5 and it had three ribs in its mouth **b** its teeth.
8: 5 which had one very large horn **b** its eyes,
8:21 and the large horn **b** its eyes represents the first
11: 6 an alliance will be formed **b** the king of the north
11:45 He will halt **b** the glorious holy mountain
Joel 2:17 will stand **b** the people and the altar, weeping.
Zec 6: 1 and saw four chariots coming from **b** two bronze
6:13 and there will be perfect harmony **b** the two.
11:14 to show that the bond of unity **b** Judah and Israel
Mal 3:18 Then you will again see the difference **b** the
3:18 **b** those who serve God and those who do not."
Mt 23:35 whom you murdered in the Temple **b** the altar
26:28 which seals the covenant **b** God and his people.
Mk 14:24 sealing the covenant **b** God and his people.
Lk 11:51 who was killed **b** the altar and the sanctuary.
12:53 There will be a division **b** father and son, mother
15:12 So his father agreed to divide his wealth **b** his sons.
17:11 he reached the border **b** Galilee and Samaria.
Jn 19:18 with him, one on either side, with Jesus **b** them.
Ac 7:38 He was the mediator **b** the people of Israel
12: 6 he was asleep, chained **b** two soldiers, with others
15: 9 He made no distinction **b** us and them, for he also
27: 4 so we sailed north of Cyprus **b** the island
27:39 and wondered if they could get **b** the rocks and get
Ro 2:17 You boast that all is well **b** yourself and God.
5:14 What a contrast **b** Adam and Christ, who was yet
5:15 And what a difference **b** our sin and God's
14:22 you are doing, but keep it **b** yourself and God.
1Co 11:25 "This cup is the new covenant **b** God and you,
2Co 1:13 and there is nothing written **b** the lines and nothing
1:19 the Son of God, never wavers **b** yes and no.
6:12 If there is a problem **b** us, it is not because of a
6:15 What harmony can there be **b** Christ
6:16 And what union can there be **b** God's temple
Gal 3:19 who was the mediator **b** God and the people.
3:21 is there a conflict **b** God's law and God's
Eph 2:14 For Christ himself has made peace **b** us Jews
2:15 His purpose was to make peace **b** Jews
Php 1:23 I'm torn **b** two desires: Sometimes I want to live,
Heb 5:14 themselves to recognize the difference **b** right
9: 1 Now in that first covenant **b** God and Israel,
9:15 is the one who mediates the new covenant **b** God
12:24 the one who mediates the new covenant **b** God
1Jn 2:21 but because you know the difference **b** truth
Rev 5: 6 but was now standing **b** the throne and the four

BEVERAGE (1)

Lev 11:34 And any **b** that is in such an unclean container will

BEWAIL(ED) [KJV] See GRIEF-STRICKEN, GRIEVE, MOURN, WAIL, WAILING, WEEP

BEWARE (18) [WARY]

Dt 8:11 **B** that in your plenty you do not forget the LORD
Jer 7:32 So **b**, for the time is coming," says the LORD,
9: 4 "**B** of your neighbor! **B** of your brother!
19: 6 So **b**, for the time is coming, says the LORD,
Mt 7:15 "**B** of false prophets who come disguised as
10:17 But **b**! For you will be handed over to the courts
16: 6 "**B** of the yeast of the Pharisees and Sadducees."
16:11 '**B** of the yeast of the Pharisees
18:10 "**B** that you don't despise a single one of these
Mk 8:15 "**B** of the yeast of the Pharisees and of Herod."
12:38 "**B** of these teachers of religious law! For they
Lk 12: 1 "**B** of the yeast of the Pharisees—**b** of their hypocrisy.
12:15 Then he said, "**B**! Don't be greedy for what you
20:46 "**B** of these teachers of religious law! For they
Ac 20:28 "And now **b**! Be sure that you feed and shepherd
Gal 5:15 watch out! **B** of destroying one another.

BEWILDERED (2)

Mk 16: 8 trembling and **b**, saying nothing to anyone
Ac 2: 6 and they were **b** to hear their own languages being

BEWRAY(ETH) [KJV] See BETRAY

BEYOND (63)

Ge 35:21 then traveled on and camped **b** the tower of Eder.
41:16 "It is **b** my power to do this," Joseph replied.
48:22 And I give you an extra portion **b** what I have
Lev 15:25 continues for many days **b** the normal period,
Nu 6:21 **b** what is required by their normal Nazirite vow,
33: 8 and crossed the Red Sea into the wilderness **b**.
Dt 3:12 I gave the territory **b** Aroer along the Arnon
30:13 It is not **b** the sea, so far away that you must ask,
Jos 13: 9 the gorge) to the plain **b** Medeba, as far as Dibon.
13:16 in the middle of the gorge) to the plain **b** Medeba.
21:12 But the fields **b** the city and the surrounding
24: 2 and Nahor, lived **b** the Euphrates River,
24: 3 But I took your ancestor Abraham from the land **b**
24:14 worshiped when they lived **b** the Euphrates River
24:15 Would you prefer the gods your ancestors served **b**
1Sa 14:23 and the battle continued to rage even out **b**
20:36 So the boy ran, and Jonathan shot an arrow **b** him.
31: 7 and **b** the Jordan saw that their army had been
2Sa 16:21 you have insulted him **b** hope of reconciliation,
17:16 He must go across at once into the wilderness **b**.
22:49 You hold me safe **b** the reach of my enemies;
1Ki 14:15 and will scatter them **b** the Euphrates River,
2Ch 20: 2 is marching against you from **b** the Dead Sea.
Ne 3: 2 next to them, and **b** them was Zaccur son of Imri.
3: 8 **B** him was Hananiah, a manufacturer of perfumes.
3:29 and **b** him was Shemaiah son of Shecaniah,
Job 36:26 "Look, God is exalted **b** what we can understand.
Ps 18:48 You hold me safe **b** the reach of my enemies;
36: 5 your faithfulness reaches **b** the clouds.
105:34 and hordes of locusts came—/ locusts **b** number.
145: 3 worthy of praise! / His greatness is **b** discovery!
147: 5 His understanding is **b** comprehension!
Pr 6:15 destroyed suddenly, broken **b** all hope of healing.
8:29 so they would not spread **b** their boundaries.
29: 1 accept criticism will suddenly be broken **b** repair.
30:13 They are proud **b** description and disdainful.
Isa 41: 1 "Listen in silence before me, you lands **b** the sea.
41: 5 The lands **b** the sea watch in fear. Remote lands
42: 4 Even distant lands **b** the sea will wait for his
55: 8 "And my ways are far **b** anything you could
64: 3 you did awesome things **b** our highest
66:19 and to all the lands **b** the sea that have not heard of
Jer 8:18 My grief is **b** healing; my heart is broken.
19:11 people of Judah and Jerusalem **b** all hope of repair.
30:13 your injury. You are **b** the help of any medicine.
La 3:19 my suffering and homelessness is bitter **b** words.
Eze 1:25 a voice spoke from **b** the crystal surface above
Hab 2: 9 putting your families **b** the reach of danger.
Zep 3:10 My scattered people who live **b** the rivers of
Zec 1:15 but the nations punished them far **b** my intentions.
Mal 1: 5 the LORD's great power reaches far **b** our
Mt 4:15 of Naphtali, / beside the sea, **b** the Jordan River—
4:24 News about him spread far **b** the borders of Galilee
Lk 2:40 He was filled with wisdom **b** his years, and God
17:24 Son of Man returns, you will know it **b** all doubt.
Jn 10:40 He went **b** the Jordan River to stay near the place
Ro 11:11 Did God's people stumble and fall **b** recovery?
2Co 8: 5 Best of all, they went **b** our highest hopes, for their
10:16 the Good News in other places that are far **b** you,
1Th 1: 8 even **b** Greece, for wherever we go we find people
1Pe 1: 4 and undefiled, **b** the reach of change and decay.
2Jn 1: 9 For if you wander **b** the teaching of Christ,
Rev 13: 3 heads of the beast seemed wounded **b** recovery—

BEZAI (3)

Ezr 2:17 The family of **B** | 323
Ne 7:23 The family of **B** | 324
10:18 Hodiah, Hashum, **B**,

BEZALEL (10)

Ex 31: 2 "Look, I have chosen **B** son of Uri, grandson of
35:30 "The LORD has chosen **B** son of Uri,
35:31 The LORD has filled **B** with the Spirit of God,
36: 1 "**B**, Oholiab, and the other craftsmen whom the
36: 2 So Moses told **B** and Oholiab to begin the work,
37: 1 Next **B** made the Ark out of acacia wood. It was
38:22 **B** son of Uri, grandson of Hur, of the tribe of
1Ch 2:20 Hur was the father of Uri. Uri was the father of **B**.
2Ch 1: 5 But the bronze altar made by **B** son of Uri
Ezr 10:30 Kelal, Benaiah, Maaseiah, Mattaniah, **B**, Binnui,

BEZEK (3) [ADONI-BEZEK]

Jdg 1: 4 ten thousand enemy warriors at the town of **B**.
1: 5 While at **B** they encountered King Adoni-bezek
1Sa 11: 8 When Saul mobilized them at **B**, he found that

BEZER (5)

Dt 4:43 **B** on the wilderness plateau for the tribe of
Jos 20: 8 **B**, in the wilderness plain of the tribe of Reuben;
21:36 From the tribe of Reuben they received **B**, Jahaz,
1Ch 6:78 they received **B** (a desert town), Jahaz,
7:37 **B**, Hod, Shamma, Shilshah, Ithran, and Beera.

BICRI (3)

2Sa 20: 1 Then a troublemaker named Sheba son of **B**,
20:14 his own clan of **B** at the city of Abel-beth-maacah.
20:21 All I want is a man named Sheba son of **B** from the

BID(DEN), BIDDETH [KJV] See also CALLED, INVITE, PROCLAIM, SAID, SAY, SAYING, TEACH, WELCOME

BIDDING (1)

Isa 46:11 from a distant land who will come and do my **b**.

BIDKAR (1)

2Ki 9:25 Jehu said to **B**, his officer, "Throw him into the

BIG (19) [BIGGER]

Ge 21: 8 Abraham gave a **b** party to celebrate the happy
43:16 this noon. Take them inside and prepare a **b** feast."
Ex 29:20 their right thumbs and the **b** toes of their right feet.
Lev 8:23 of his right hand, and the **b** toe of his right foot.
8:24 their right hands, and the **b** toe of their right feet.
14:14 of the right hand, and on the **b** toe of the right foot.
14:17 of the right hand, and on the **b** toe of the right foot,
14:25 of the right hand, and on the **b** toe of the right foot.
14:28 of the right hand, and on the **b** toe of the right foot,
Jdg 1: 6 captured him and cut off his thumbs and **b** toes.
1: 7 had seventy kings with thumbs and **b** toes cut off,
9:38 "Now where is that **b** mouth of yours?"
1Sa 25:36 she found that Nabal had thrown a **b** party and was
Pr 23: 2 If you are a **b** eater, put a knife to your throat,
Isa 30:14 left that is **b** enough to carry coals from a fireplace
Hos 4:10 Though they do a **b** business as prostitutes,
Lk 10:40 But Martha was worrying over the **b** dinner she
1Co 4:19 out whether these arrogant people are just **b** talkers
12:17 Or if your whole body were just one **b** ear,

BIGGER (4) [BIG]

Mt 9:16 the old cloth, leaving an even **b** hole than before.
Mk 2:21 the old cloth, leaving an even **b** hole than before.
Lk 12:18 'I know! I'll tear down my barns and build **b** ones.
12:26 like that, what's the use of worrying over **b** things?

BIGTHA (1)

Est 1:10 Biztha, Harbona, **B**, Abagtha, Zethar, and Carcas,

BIGTHANA (2)

Est 2:21 two of the king's eunuchs, **B** and Teresh—
6: 2 of how Mordecai had exposed the plot of **B**

BIGVAI (6)

Ezr 2: 2 Reelaiah, Mordecai, Bilshan, Mispar, **B**, Rehum,
2:14 The family of **B** | 2,056
8:14 From the family of **B**: Uthai, Zaccur, and 70 other
Ne 7: 7 Nahamani, Mordecai, Bilshan, Mispar, **B**, Rehum,
7:19 The family of **B** | 2,067
10:16 Adonijah, **B**, Adin,

BILDAD (5)

Job 2:11 **B** the Shuhite, and Zophar the Naamathite.
8: 1 Then **B** the Shuhite replied to Job:
18: 1 Then **B** the Shuhite replied:
25: 1 Then **B** the Shuhite replied:
42: 9 So Eliphaz the Temanite, **B** the Shuhite,

BILEAM (1)

1Ch 6:70 Aner and **B**, each with its pasturelands.

BILGAH (3)

1Ch 24:14 The fifteenth lot fell to **B**. / The sixteenth lot fell to
Ne 12: 5 Miniamin, Moadiah, **B**,
12:18 Shammua was leader of the family of **B**.

BILGAI (1)

Ne 10: 8 Maaziah, **B**, and Shemaiah. These were the priests.

BILHAH (11) [BAALAH]

Ge 29:29 Laban gave Rachel a servant, **B**, to be her maid.
30: 3 Then Rachel told him, "Sleep with my servant, **B**,
30: 4 So Rachel gave him **B** to be his wife, and Jacob
30: 5 **B** became pregnant and presented him with a son.
30: 7 Then **B** became pregnant again and gave Jacob a
35:22 While he was there, Reuben slept with **B**,
35:25 The sons of **B**, Rachel's servant, were Dan
37: 2 the sons of his father's wives **B** and Zilpah.
46:25 seven were the descendants of Jacob through **B**,
1Ch 4:29 **B**, Ezem, Tolad,
7:13 They were all descendants of Jacob's wife **B**.

BILHAN (4)

Ge 36:27 The sons of Ezer were **B**, Zaavan, and Akan.
1Ch 1:42 The sons of Ezer were **B**, Zaavan, and Akan.
7:10 The son of Jediael was **B**. The sons of **B** were Jeush, Benjamin, Ehud,

BILL (3) [BILLS]

Lk 10:35 'If his **b** runs higher than that,' he said, 'I'll pay the
16: 6 'Tear up that **b** and write another one for four
16: 7 'take your **b** and replace it with one for only eight

BILLOW (1) [BILLOWED, BILLOWING]

Ps 144: 5 Touch the mountains so they **b** smoke.

BILLOWED (2) [BILLOW]

Ex 19:18 The smoke **b** into the sky like smoke from a
Rev 9:17 and smoke and burning sulfur **b** from their mouths.

BILLOWING (2) [BILLOW]

Ex 20:18 the lightning and the smoke **b** from the mountain,
Na 1: 3 The **b** clouds are the dust beneath his feet.

BILLS (1) [BILL]

Lk 14:28 to see if there is enough money to pay the **b**?

BILSHAN (2)

Ezr 2: 2 Reelaiah, Mordecai, **B**, Mispar, Bigvai, Rehum,
Ne 7: 7 Nahamani, Mordecai, **B**, Mispar, Bigvai, Rehum,

BIMHAL (1)

1Ch 7:33 The sons of Japhlet were Pasach, **B**, and Ashvath.

BIND (10) [BINDER, BINDING, BINDS, BOUND]

Ps 129: 4 he has cut the cords used by the ungodly to **b** me.
149: 8 to **b** their kings with shackles / and their leaders
Ecc 7:26 Her passion is a trap, and her soft hands will **b** you.
Isa 9: 4 For God will break the chains that **b** his people
Jer 30:13 There is no one to help you or **b** up your injury.
50: 5 They will **b** themselves to the LORD with an
Eze 34:16 I will **b** up the injured and strengthen the weak.
Da 3:20 of the strongest men of his army to **b** Shadrach,
Mt 22:13 '**B** him hand and foot and throw him out into the
Eph 4: 3 Holy Spirit, and **b** yourselves together with peace.

BINDER (1) [BIND]

Ps 129: 7 ignored by the harvester, / despised by the **b**.

BINDING (7) [BIND]

Jos 9:15 of Israel ratified their agreement with a **b** oath.
24:25 and **b** contract between themselves
Ps 147: 3 He heals the brokenhearted, / **b** up their wounds.
Mt 23:16 then you say that it is **b** to swear 'by the gold in the
23:18 but to swear 'by the gifts on the altar' is **b**!
Ac 22: 4 **b** and delivering both men and women to prison.
Heb 6:16 them to it. And without any question that oath is **b**.

BINDS (2) [BIND]

Ro 7: 2 the law **b** her to her husband as long as he is alive.
Col 3:14 Love is what **b** us all together in perfect harmony.

BINEA (3) [BINEA'S]

1Ch 8:37 Moza was the father of **B**. / **B** was the father of Rephaiah.
9:43 Moza was the father of **B**. / Binea's son was

BINEA'S (1) [BINEA]

1Ch 9:43 **B** son was Rephaiah. / Rephaiah's son was

BINNUI (8)

Ezr 8:33 Jozabad son of Jeshua and Noadiah son of **B**—
10:30 Kelal, Benaiah, Maaseiah, Mattaniah, Bezalel, **B**,
10:38 From the family of **B**: Shimei,
Ne 3:18 Next down the line were his countrymen led by **B**
3:24 Next was **B** son of Henadad, who rebuilt another
10: 9 **B** from the family of Henadad, Kadmiel,
12: 8 **B**, Kadmiel, Sherebiah, Judah, and Mattaniah,
12:24 Hashabiah, Sherebiah, Jeshua, **B**, Kadmiel,

BIRD (41) [BIRD'S, BIRDS, BIRDS']

Ge 1:21 and every sort of fish and every kind of **b**.
2:19 formed from the soil every kind of animal and **b**.
6:20 Pairs of each kind of **b** and each kind of animal,
7: 3 Then select seven pairs of every kind of **b**.
8:11 the **b** returned to him with a fresh olive leaf in its
Lev 1:14 "If you bring a **b** as a burnt offering to the
1:15 The priest will take the **b** to the altar, twist off its
1:17 Then, grasping the **b** by its wings, the priest will tear the **b** apart, though not
5:10 The priest will offer the second **b** as a whole burnt
7:26 you must never eat the blood of any **b** or animal.
14: 6 He will then dip the living **b**, along with the
14: 6 hyssop branch, into the blood of the slaughtered **b**.
14: 7 the priest will set the living **b** free so it can fly
14:51 the living **b** into the blood of the slaughtered **b**,
14:53 he will release the living **b** in the open fields
17:13 and kill an animal or **b** that is approved for eating,
17:14 for the life of any **b** or animal is in the blood.
20:25 or **b** or creeping creature that I have forbidden.
Dt 4:17 an animal or a **b**,
14:11 "You may eat any **b** that is ceremonially clean.
Job 28: 7 treasures that no **b** of prey can see, no falcon's eye
41: 5 Can you make it a pet like a **b**, or give it to your
Ps 50:11 Every **b** of the mountains / and all the animals of
102: 7 I lie awake, / lonely as a solitary **b** on the roof.
124: 7 We escaped like a **b** from a hunter's trap.
Pr 1:17 When a **b** sees a trap being set, it stays away.
6: 5 escaping from a hunter, like a **b** fleeing from a net.
7:23 He was like a **b** flying into a snare, little knowing
23: 5 can disappear as though they had the wings of a **b**!
27: 8 A person who strays from home is like a **b** that
Ecc 10:20 A little **b** may tell them what you have said.
Isa 31: 5 hover over Jerusalem as a **b** hovers around its nest.
46:11 I will call a swift **b** of prey from the east—a leader
Jer 17:11 Like a **b** that hatches eggs she has not laid, so are
La 3:52 whom I have never harmed, chased me like a **b**.
Eze 44:31 The priests may never eat meat from any **b**
Hos 7:12 and bring them down like a **b** from the sky.
9:11 The glory of Israel will fly away like a **b**, for your
Am 3: 5 Does a **b** ever get caught in a trap that has no bait?

BIRD'S (2) [BIRD]

Lev 14: 7 The priest will also sprinkle the dead **b** blood
Dt 22: 6 "If you find a **b** nest on the ground or in a tree

BIRDS (88) [BIRD]

Ge 1:20 Let the skies be filled with **b** of every kind."
1:22 the oceans. Let the **b** increase and fill the earth."
1:26 the fish in the sea, the **b** in the sky, and all the
1:28 masters over the fish and **b** and all the animals."
1:30 green plants to the animals and **b** for their food."
2:20 names to all the livestock, **b**, and wild animals.
6: 7 and I will destroy all the animals and **b**, too.
7: 8 along with all the **b** and other small animals.
7:14 along with **b** and flying insects of every kind.
7:21 **b**, domestic animals, wild animals, all kinds of
7:23 people, animals both large and small, and **b**.
8:17 Release all the animals and **b** so they can breed
8:19 all the various kinds of animals and **b** came out,
8:20 and **b** that had been approved for that purpose.
9: 2 and all the **b** and fish will be afraid of you.
9:10 all these **b** and livestock and wild animals.
15:10 by side. He did not, however, divide the **b** in half.
40:17 goods for Pharaoh, but the **b** came and ate them."
40:19 Then **b** will come and peck away at your flesh."
Ex 20: 4 whether in the shape of **b** or animals or fish.
Lev 5: 7 One of the **b** will be a sin offering, and the other
5: 8 who will offer one of the **b** as the sin offering.
11:13 "These are the **b** you must never eat because they
11:46 the **b**, and all the living things that move through
14: 4 using two wild **b** of a kind permitted for food,
14: 5 The priest will order one of the **b** to be slaughtered
14:49 To purify the house the priest will need two **b**,
14:50 He will slaughter one of the **b** over a clay pot that
20:25 unclean animals, and between clean and unclean **b**.
Nu 6:11 The priest will offer one of the **b** for a sin offering
Dt 5: 8 whether in the shape of **b** or animals or fish.
14:12 These are the **b** you may not eat: the eagle,
28:26 Your dead bodies will be food for the **b** and wild
1Sa 17:44 and I'll give your flesh to the **b** and wild animals!"
17:46 I will give the dead bodies of your men to the **b**
1Ki 4:33 also speak about animals, **b**, reptiles, and fish.
Job 12: 7 Ask the **b** of the sky, and they will tell you.
28:21 Even the sharp-eyed **b** in the sky cannot discover
35:11 one who makes us wiser than the animals and **b**?'
Ps 8: 8 the **b** in the sky, the fish in the sea,
78:27 **b** as plentiful as the sands along the seashore!
78:28 He caused the **b** to fall within their camp / and all
79: 2 as food for the **b** of heaven. / The flesh of your
104:12 The **b** nest beside the streams / and sing among the
104:17 There the **b** make their nests, / and the storks make
148:10 wild animals and all livestock, / reptiles and **b**,
Ecc 9:12 Like fish in a net or **b** in a snare, people are often
12: 4 Even the chirping of **b** will wake you up. But you
SS 2:12 springing up, and the time of singing **b** has come,
Isa 16: 2 The women of Moab are left like homeless **b** at the
18: 6 will be left dead in the fields for the mountain **b**
34:16 Not one of these **b** and animals will be missing,
Jer 4:25 were gone. All the **b** of the sky had flown away.
5:27 Like a cage filled with **b**, their homes are filled
9:10 no more; the **b** and wild animals all have fled.
12: 4 The wild animals and **b** have disappeared
Eze 13:20 which you use to ensnare my people like **b**.
13:20 setting my people free like **b** set free from a cage.
17:23 **B** of every sort will nest in it, finding shelter
29: 5 I have given you as food to the wild animals and **b**.
31: 6 The **b** nested in its branches, and in its shade all
31:13 The **b** roosted on its fallen trunk, and the wild
32: 4 All the **b** of the heavens will land on you,
38:20 living things—all the fish, **b**, animals, and people
39:17 son of man, call all the **b** and wild animals,
Da 2:38 has put even the animals and **b** under your control.
4:12 lived in its shade, and **b** nested in its branches.
4:14 animals from its shade and the **b** from its branches.
4:21 lived in its shade, and **b** nested in its branches.
Hos 2:18 and the **b** and the animals that scurry along the
4: 3 Even the animals, **b**, and fish have begun to
11:11 Like a flock of **b**, they will come from Egypt.
Zep 1: 3 Even the **b** of the air and the fish in the sea will
Mt 6:26 Look at the **b**. They don't need to plant or harvest
8:20 and **b** have nests, but I, the Son of Man, have no
13: 4 fell on a footpath, and the **b** came and ate them.
13:32 and grows into a tree where **b** can come and find
Mk 4: 4 seed fell on a footpath, and the **b** came and ate it.
4:32 with long branches where **b** can come and find
Lk 8: 5 where it was stepped on, and the **b** came and ate it.
9:58 and **b** have nests, but I, the Son of Man, have no
12:24 And you are far more valuable to him than any **b**!
13:19 and the **b** come and find shelter among its
Ac 10:12 the sheet were all sorts of animals, reptiles, and **b**.
11: 6 reptiles, and **b** that we are not allowed to eat.
Ro 1:23 like mere people, or **b** and animals and snakes.
1Co 15:39 of flesh—whether of humans, animals, **b**, or fish.
Jas 3: 7 all kinds of animals and **b** and reptiles and fish,

BIRDS' (2) [BIRD]

Da 4:33 as eagles' feathers and his nails were like **b** claws.
7: 6 It had four wings like **b** wings on its back, and it

BIRSHA (1)

Ge 14: 2 King **B** of Gomorrah, King Shinab of Admah,

BIRTH (145) [BEAR]

Ge 4: 1 the time came, she gave **b** to Cain, and she said,
4: 2 Later she gave **b** to a second son and named him
4:17 Cain's wife became pregnant and gave **b** to a son,
4:20 Adah gave **b** to a baby named Jabal. He became
4:25 with his wife again, and she gave **b** to another son.
5: 4 After the **b** of Seth, Adam lived another 800 years,
5: 7 After the **b** of Enosh, Seth lived another 807 years,
5:10 After the **b** of Kenan, Enosh lived another 815
5:13 After the **b** of Mahalalel, Kenan lived another 840
5:16 After the **b** of Jared, Mahalalel lived 830 years,
5:19 After the **b** of Enoch, Jared lived another 800
5:22 After the **b** of Methuselah, Enoch lived another
5:26 After the **b** of Lamech, Methuselah lived another
5:30 After the **b** of Noah, Lamech lived 595 years,
6: 4 they gave **b** to children who became the heroes
11:11 After the **b** of Arphaxad, Shem lived another 500
11:13 After the **b** of Shelah, Arphaxad lived another 403
11:15 After the **b** of Eber, Shelah lived another 403 years
11:17 After the **b** of Peleg, Eber lived another 430 years
11:19 After the **b** of Reu, Peleg lived another 209 years
11:21 After the **b** of Serug, Reu lived another 207 years
11:23 After the **b** of Nahor, Serug lived another 200
11:25 After the **b** of Terah, Nahor lived another 119
11:28 he died in Ur of the Chaldeans, the place of his **b**.
16:11 "You are now pregnant and will give **b** to a son.
17:12 must be circumcised on the eighth day after his **b**.
19:37 When the older daughter gave **b** to a son,
19:38 When the younger daughter gave **b** to a son,
24:36 was very old, she gave **b** to my master's son,
25:25 The first was very red at **b**. He was covered with
30:17 became pregnant again and gave **b** to her fifth son.
30:21 Later she gave **b** to a daughter and named her
30:23 She became pregnant and gave **b** to a son.
38: 5 At the time of Shelah's **b**, they were living at
Ex 1:16 "When you help the Hebrew women give **b**,
1:19 They are not slow in giving **b** like Egyptian
2: 2 The woman became pregnant and gave **b** to a son.
18: 4 for Moses had said at his **b**, "The God of my
Lev 12: 2 a woman becomes pregnant and gives **b** to a son,
12: 5 If a woman gives **b** to a daughter, she will be
12: 7 the instructions to be followed after the **b** of a son
16:29 and it applies to those who are Israelites by **b**,
18:26 This applies both to you who are Israelites by **b**
20: 2 which apply to those who are Israelites by **b** as
22:18 which apply to those who are Israelites by **b** as
23:42 all of you who are Israelites by **b** must live in
24:22 "These same regulations apply to Israelites by **b**
Nu 12:12 her be like a stillborn baby, already decayed at **b**."
Dt 23: 2 "Those of illegitimate **b** and their descendants for
32:18 you forgot the God who had given you **b**.
Jdg 13: 3 will soon become pregnant and give **b** to a son.
13: 5 You will become pregnant and give **b** to a son,
13: 5 he will be dedicated to God as a Nazirite from **b**.
13: 7 'You will become pregnant and give **b** to a son.
13: 7 the moment of his **b** until the day of his death.' "
16:17 "for I was dedicated to God as a Nazirite from **b**.
Ru 1:11 Can I still give **b** to other sons who could grow up
4:13 her to become pregnant, and she gave **b** to a son.
1Sa 1:20 and in due time she gave **b** to a son. She named
2Sa 11:27 became one of his wives. Then she gave **b** to a son.
12:24 She became pregnant and gave **b** to a son, and they
1Ki 3:17 I gave **b** to a baby while she was with me in the
1Ch 2:24 his wife Abijah gave **b** to a son named Ashhur (the
2:46 Caleb's concubine Ephah gave **b** to Haran, Moza,
2:48 Maacah, gave **b** to Sheber and Tirhanah.
2:49 She also gave **b** to Shaaph (the father of
4: 6 Naarah gave **b** to Ahuzzam, Hepher, Temeni,
4: 7 Helah gave **b** to Zereth, Izhar, Ethnan,
4: 9 him Jabez because his **b** had been so painful.
7:16 Maacah, gave **b** to a son whom she named Peresh.
7:18 Makir's sister Hammoleketh gave **b** to Ishhod,
7:23 and she became pregnant and gave **b** to a son.
8: 9 new wife, gave **b** to Jobab, Zibia, Mesha, Malcam,
8:11 Shaharaim's wife Hushim had already given **b** to
2Ch 11:20 Maacah gave **b** to Abijah, Attai, Ziza,
11:21 and they gave **b** to twenty-eight sons and sixty
Job 3: 1 At last Job spoke, and he cursed the day of his **b**.
3: 3 "Cursed be the day of my **b**, and cursed be the
3:11 "Why didn't I die at **b** as I came from the womb?
3:13 For if I had died at **b**, I would be at peace now,
10:18 mother's womb? Why didn't you let me die at **b**?
15:35 and evil, and their hearts give **b** only to deceit."
38:29 Who gives **b** to the frost from the heavens?
39: 1 "Do you know when the mountain goats give **b**?
39: 3 They crouch down to give **b** to their young
Ps 7:14 they are pregnant with trouble / and give **b** to lies.
22:10 I was thrust upon you at my **b**. / You have been my
58: 3 even from **b** they have lied and gone their own
71: 6 Yes, you have been with me from **b**; / from my
Pr 23:25 parents joy! May she who gave you **b** be happy.
Ecc 6: 4 I realize that his **b** would have been meaningless
SS 8: 5 the apple tree, where your mother gave you **b**,
Isa 7:14 She will give **b** to a son and will call him
13: 8 like those of a woman about to give **b**.
21: 3 are upon me, like the pangs of a woman giving **b**.
26:17 We were like a woman about to give **b**, / writhing
42:14 I will gasp and pant like a woman giving **b**.
49: 1 The LORD called me before my **b**; from within
54: 1 even though you never gave **b** to a child.
66: 7 "Before the **b** pains even begin, Jerusalem gives **b** to a son.
66: 8 But by the time Jerusalem's **b** pains begin,
66: 9 Would I ever bring this nation to the point of **b**
Jer 4:31 like that of a woman giving **b** to her first child.
6:24 gripped us, like that of a woman about to give **b**.
13:21 You will writhe in pain like a woman giving **b**!
15:10 is mine, my mother. Oh, that I had died at **b**!
20:14 I was born! May the day of my **b** not be blessed.
20:17 for he did not kill me at **b**. Oh, that I had died in
22:23 anguish like that of a woman about to give **b**.
30: 6 Do men give **b** to babies? Then why do they stand
30: 6 against their sides like women about to give **b**?
31: 8 the expectant mothers and women about to give **b**.
48:41 will be as frightened as a woman about to give **b**.

49:22 will be as frightened as a woman about to give **b**.
49:24 have gripped her as they do a woman giving **b**.
50:43 gripped him, like that of a woman about to give **b**.
Eze 21:30 you in your own country, the land of your **b**.
31: 6 and in its shade all the wild animals gave **b** to their
Hos 1: 6 became pregnant again and gave **b** to a daughter.
1: 8 again became pregnant and gave **b** to a second son.
9:11 for your children will die at **b** or perish in the
9:14 I will ask for wombs that don't give **b** and breasts
9:16 And if they give **b**, I will slaughter their beloved
13:13 The people have been offered new **b**, but they are
Mic 5: 3 time when the woman in labor gives **b** to her son.
Mt 1:23 will conceive a child! / She will give **b** to a son,
Lk 1:14 and many will rejoice with you at his **b**,
1:15 be filled with the Holy Spirit, even before his **b**.
2: 7 She gave **b** to her first child, a son. She wrapped
2:22 as required by the law of Moses after the **b** of a
Jn 1:13 This is not a physical **b** resulting from human
9: 1 he saw a man who had been blind from **b**.
Ac 3: 2 a man lame from **b** was being carried in.
14: 8 He had been that way from **b**, so he had never
22:28 it cost me plenty!" "But I am a citizen by **b**!"
Ro 9:10 he married Rebekah, who gave **b** to twins.
Gal 2:14 "Since you, a Jew by **b**, have discarded the Jewish
2:15 You and I are Jews by **b**, not 'sinners' like the
4:27 even though you never gave **b** to a child.
Eph 2:11 forget that you Gentiles used to be outsiders by **b**.
1Th 5: 3 **b** pains begin when her child is about to be born.
Rev 12: 4 the woman as she was about to give **b** to her child,
12: 5 She gave **b** to a boy who was to rule all nations
12:13 he pursued the woman who had given **b** to the

BIRTHDAY (4) [BEAR]
Ge 40:20 Pharaoh's **b** came three days later, and he gave a
Ex 30:14 All who have reached their twentieth **b** must give
Mt 14: 6 But at a **b** party for Herod, Herodias' daughter
Mk 6:21 It was Herod's **b**, and he gave a party for his

BIRTHDAYS (1) [BEAR]
Job 1: 4 Every year when Job's sons had **b**, they invited

BIRTHRIGHT (7) [BEAR]
Ge 25:31 "All right, but trade me your **b** for it."
25:32 said Esau. "What good is my **b** to me now?"
25:34 indifferent to the fact that he had given up his **b**.
27:36 first taking my **b** and now stealing my blessing.
1Ch 5: 1 his **b** was given to the sons of his brother Joseph.
5: 2 a ruler for the nation, but the **b** belonged to Joseph.
Heb 12:16 He traded his **b** as the oldest son for a single meal.

BIRTHS (1) [BEAR]
Ex 28:10 all the tribes in the order of their ancestors' **b**.

BIRZAITH (1)
1Ch 7:31 Beriah were Heber and Malkiel (the father of **B**).

BISHLAM (1)
Ezr 4: 7 of Judah, led by **B**, Mithredath, and Tabeel,

BISHOPRICK [KJV] See POSITION

BIT (11) [BITS]
1Sa 14:29 I feel now that I have eaten this little **b** of honey.
14:43 "It was only a little **b** on the end of a stick.
Ps 32: 9 that needs a **b** and bridle to keep it under control."
142: 4 help me; / no one cares a **b** what happens to me.
Ecc 9:13 Here is another **b** of wisdom that has impressed me
Isa 3: 9 They are not one **b** ashamed. How terrible it will
30: 5 He will not help you even one little **b**."
44:10 his own god—an idol that cannot help him one **b**!
Eze 5: 3 Keep just a **b** of the hair and tie it up in your robe.
2Co 11:15 In the end they will get every **b** of punishment
Jas 3: 3 and go wherever we want by means of a small **b** in

BITE (6) [BITES, BITING, BITTEN, SNAKEBITES]
Dt 2:28 We will pay for every **b** of food we eat and all the
28:31 your eyes, but you won't get a single **b** of the meat.
1Ki 17:11 he called to her, "Bring me a **b** of bread, too."
2Ki 4:40 But after the men had eaten a **b** or two they cried
Jer 8:17 what you do, they will **b** you, and you will die."
Am 9: 3 I will send the great sea serpent after them to **b**

BITES (2) [BITE]
Ge 49:17 viper along the path, / that **b** the horse's heels
Pr 23:32 For in the end it **b** like a poisonous serpent;

BITHIAH (1)
1Ch 4:18 Mered's Egyptian wife was named **B**, and she was

BITHYNIA (2)
Ac 16: 7 of Mysia, they headed for the province of **B**,
1Pe 1: 1 Galatia, Cappadocia, the province of Asia, and **B**.

BITING (1) [BITE]
Gal 5:15 showing love among yourselves you are always **b**

BITS (3) [BIT]
2Ki 23:12 He smashed them to **b** and scattered the pieces in
Da 2:34 the feet of iron and clay, smashing them to **b**.

Hos 8: 6 It is not God! Therefore, it must be smashed to **b**.

BITTEN (6) [BITE]
Nu 21: 6 among them, and many of them were **b** and died.
21: 8 Those who are **b** will live if they simply look at
21: 9 Whenever those who were **b** looked at the bronze
Ecc 10: 8 demolish an old wall, you could be **b** by a snake.
10:11 It does no good to charm a snake after it has **b** you.
Am 5:19 against a wall in his house—and is **b** by a snake.

BITTER (53) [BITTEREST, BITTERLY, BITTERNESS, EMBITTERED]
Ge 27:34 When Esau understood, he let out a loud and **b** cry.
Ex 1:13 and decided to make their slavery more **b** still.
12: 8 That evening everyone must eat roast lamb with **b**
15:23 But the people couldn't drink it because it was **b**.
15:23 the place was called Marah, which means "**b**.")
Nu 5:18 holding the jar of **b** water that brings a curse to
5:19 may you be immune from the effects of this **b**
5:23 of leather and wash them off into the **b** water.
5:24 He will then make the woman drink the **b** water,
5:24 on the curse and cause **b** suffering in cases of guilt.
5:27 the water that brings the curse will cause **b**
9:11 They must eat the lamb at that time with **b** herbs
Dt 4:30 "When those **b** days have come upon you far in
29:18 and so that no root among you would bear **b**
32:32 Their grapes are poison, / and their clusters are **b**.
Ru 1:13 Things are far more **b** for me than for you,
1:20 for the Almighty has made life very **b** for me.
1Sa 30: 6 because his men were very **b** about losing their
1Ki 11:25 Rezon was Israel's **b** enemy for the rest of
2Ki 14:26 For the LORD saw the **b** suffering of everyone in
Est 4: 1 out into the city, crying with a loud and **b** wail.
Job 9:18 my breath, but fills me instead with **b** sorrows.
13:26 "You write **b** accusations against me and bring up
21:25 Another person dies in **b** poverty, never having
23: 2 "My complaint today is still a **b** one, and I try hard
Ps 64: 3 they wield; / **b** words are the arrows they aim.
73:21 Then I realized how **b** I had become, / how pained
Pr 1:31 That is why they must eat the **b** fruit of living their
5: 4 But the result is as **b** as poison, sharp as a
27: 7 is full, but even **b** food tastes sweet to the hungry.
30:23 a **b** woman who finally gets a husband, / a servant
Ecc 7:26 I discovered that a seductive woman is more **b** than
Isa 5:20 and light is dark; that **b** is sweet and sweet is **b**.
24: 9 and song; strong drink now turns **b** in the mouth.
33: 7 But now your ambassadors weep in **b**
Jer 2:19 **b** thing it is to forsake the LORD your God,
4:18 This punishment is a **b** dose of your own medicine.
La 3:19 my suffering and homelessness is **b** beyond words.
Eze 21: 6 Groan before them with **b** anguish and a broken
27:31 They weep for you with **b** anguish and deep
Am 5: 7 making it a **b** pill for the poor and oppressed.
6:12 and make **b** the sweet fruit of righteousness.
8:10 only son had died. How very **b** that day will be!
Mt 20:22 Are you able to drink from the **b** cup of sorrow I
27:34 The soldiers gave him wine mixed with **b** gall,
Mk 10:38 Are you able to drink from the **b** cup of sorrow I
Ro 9: 2 My heart is filled with **b** sorrow and unending
Heb 12:15 Watch out that no **b** root of unbelief rises up
12:17 late for repentance, even though he wept **b** tears.
Jas 3:11 bubble out with both fresh water and **b** water?
Rev 8:11 It made one-third of the water **b**, and many people died because the water was so **b**.

BITTEREST (1) [BITTER]
Isa 53: 3 a man of sorrows, acquainted with **b** grief.

BITTERLY (22) [BITTER]
Ge 27:36 Esau said **b**, "No wonder his name is Jacob,
Ex 16: 2 the whole community of Israel spoke **b** against
Jdg 21: 2 until evening, raising their voices and weeping **b**.
1Sa 1:10 crying **b** as she prayed to the LORD.
27:12 "By now the people of Israel must hate him **b**.
2Sa 13:36 and the king and his officials wept **b** with them.
2Ki 20: 3 in your sight." Then he broke down and wept **b**.
Ezr 10: 1 and children—gathered and wept **b** with him.
Job 17: 2 by mockers. I watch how **b** they taunt me.
Isa 38: 3 in your sight." Then he broke down and wept **b**.
Jer 6:26 Mourn and weep **b**, as for the loss of an only son.
48: 5 refugees will climb the hills of Luhith, weeping **b**,
La 1: 4 women are crying—how **b** Jerusalem weeps!
Eze 27:30 They weep **b** as they throw dust on their heads
Hos 12:14 But the people of Israel have **b** provoked the
Am 6:14 "It will oppress you **b** throughout your land—
Zep 1:14 it comes—a day when strong men will cry **b**.
Zec 12:10 They will grieve **b** for him as for a firstborn son
Mt 26:75 me three times." And he went away, crying **b**.
Lk 5:30 and their teachers of religious law complained **b** to
22:62 And Peter left the courtyard, crying **b**.
Jas 3:14 But if you are **b** jealous and there is selfish

BITTERN [KJV] See PORCUPINES, HAWK, OWLS

BITTERNESS (14) [BITTER]
2Sa 2:26 Don't you realize the only thing we will gain is **b**
Job 7:11 express my anguish. I must complain in my **b**.
10: 1 complain freely. I will speak in the **b** of my soul.
Pr 14:10 Each heart knows its own **b**, and no one else can
17:25 child brings grief to a father and **b** to a mother.
Jer 9:15 I will feed them with **b** and give them poison to
23:15 "I will feed them with **b** and give them poison to
La 3:15 He has filled me with **b**. He has given me a cup of
Eze 3:14 I went in **b** and turmoil, but the LORD's hold on
Mic 1:12 but only **b** awaits them as the LORD's judgment
Ac 8:23 for I can see that you are full of **b** and held captive
Ro 3:14 "Their mouths are full of cursing and **b**."
Eph 4:31 Get rid of all **b**, rage, anger, harsh words,
Rev 8:11 The name of the star was **B**. It made one-third of

BIZIOTHIAH (1)
Jos 15:28 Hazar-shual, Beersheba, **B**,

BIZTHA (1)
Est 1:10 **B**, Harbona, Bigtha, Abagtha, Zethar, and Carcas,

BLABBERMOUTH (1) [MOUTH]
Ecc 5: 3 gives you nightmares, being a fool makes you a **b**.

BLACK (18) [BLACKENED, BLACKER, BLACKEST, BLACKNESS]
Ex 10:15 of the whole country, making the ground look **b**.
Lev 13:31 and there is no **b** hair in the affected area,
13:37 and **b** hair has grown in the affected area,
Dt 4:11 the sky, shrouded in **b** clouds and deep darkness.
1Ki 18:45 And sure enough, the sky was soon **b** with clouds.
Job 3: 5 Let a **b** cloud overshadow it, and let the darkness
24:17 The **b** night is their morning. They ally themselves
SS 5:11 head is the finest gold, and his hair is wavy and **b**.
Isa 13:10 The heavens will be **b** above them. No light will
60: 2 Darkness as **b** as night will cover all the nations of
Jer 4:28 earth will mourn, the heavens will be draped in **b**,
Eze 31:15 I clothed Lebanon in **b** and caused the trees of the
Zec 6: 2 was pulled by red horses, the second by **b** horses,
6: 6 The chariot with **b** horses is going north,
Mt 5:36 my head!' for you can't turn one hair white or **b**.
Ac 13: 1 Simeon (called "the **b** man"), Lucius (from
Rev 6: 5 And I looked up and saw a **b** horse, and its rider
6:12 The sun became as dark as **b** cloth, and the moon

BLACKENED (2) [BLACK]
Isa 9:19 The land is **b** by the fury of the LORD Almighty.
La 5:10 our skin has been **b** as though baked in an oven.

BLACKER (1) [BLACK]
La 4: 8 But now their faces are **b** than soot. No one even

BLACKEST (1) [BLACK]
2Pe 2:17 They are doomed to **b** darkness.

BLACKNESS (2) [BLACK]
Joel 2: 2 and gloom, a day of thick clouds and deep **b**.
Zep 1:15 a day of darkness and gloom, of clouds, **b**,

BLACKSMITH (3) [SMITHS]
1Sa 13:20 or sickles, they had to take them to a Philistine **b**.
Isa 44:12 The **b** stands at his forge to make a sharp tool,
54:16 I have created the **b** who fans the coals beneath the

BLACKSMITHS (3) [SMITHS]
1Sa 13:19 There were no **b** in the land of Israel in those days.
Zec 1:20 Then the LORD showed me four **b**.
1:21 "The **b** have come to terrify the four horns that

BLADE (5) [BLADES]
Dt 29:23 and nothing growing, not even a **b** of grass.
Job 39: 8 where it searches for every **b** of grass.
Ecc 10:10 a dull ax requires great strength, sharpen the **b**.
Isa 58: 5 bowing your heads like a **b** of grass in the wind.
Mk 4:28 First a leaf **b** pushes through, then the heads of

BLADES (3) [BLADE]
Mt 13: 7 thorns that shot up and choked out the tender **b**.
Mk 4: 7 and choked out the tender **b** so that it produced no
Lk 8: 7 thorns that shot up and choked out the tender **b**.

BLAINS [KJV] See BOILS

BLAME (11) [BLAMED, BLAMELESS, BLAMING]
Ge 43: 9 him back to you, then let me bear the **b** forever.
44:32 bring him back to you, I will bear the **b** forever.'
1Sa 25:24 and said, "I accept all **b** in this matter, my lord.
2Ki 10: 9 "You aren't to **b**," he told them. "I am the one
Eze 18:13 person live? No! He must die and must take full **b**.
Hos 4: 4 your finger at someone else and try to pass the **b**!
Mic 1: 5 Who is to **b** for Israel's rebellion? Samaria,
Ac 5:28 about Jesus, and you intend to **b** us for his death!"
Ro 9:19 "Why does God **b** people for not listening?
1Co 1: 8 and he will keep you free from all **b** on the great
Php 2:15 so that no one can speak a word of **b** against you.

BLAMED (3) [BLAME]
Nu 20: 3 The people **b** Moses and said, "We wish we had
Jdg 15: 3 "This time I cannot be **b** for everything I am going
Ac 20:26 been faithful. No one's damnation can be **b** on me,

BLAMELESS (21) [BLAME]
Ge 6: 9 the only **b** man living on earth at the time.
17: 1 serve me faithfully and live a **b** life.
Dt 18:13 You must be **b** before the LORD your God.

2Sa 22:24 I am **b** before God; / I have kept myself from sin.
Job 1: 1 He was **b**, a man of complete integrity. He feared
9:20 Though I am **b**, it would prove me wicked.
9:22 I say, 'He destroys both the **b** and the wicked.'
12: 4 I am a just and **b** man, yet they laugh at me.
Ps 15: 2 Those who lead **b** lives / and do what is right,
18:23 I am **b** before God; / I have kept myself from sin.
101: 2 I will be careful to live a **b** life—/ when will you
119:80 May I be **b** in keeping your principles; / then I will
Eze 28:15 "You were **b** in all you did from the day you were
Php 1:10 you may live pure and **b** lives until Christ returns.
Col 1:22 and **b** as you stand before him without a single
1Th 3:13 As a result, Christ will make your hearts strong, **b**,
5:23 and body be kept **b** until that day when our Lord
Tit 1: 7 An elder must live a **b** life because he is God's
Heb 7:26 of high priest we need because he is holy and **b**,
2Pe 3:14 make every effort to live a pure and **b** life.
Rev 14: 5 falsehood can be charged against them; they are **b**.

BLAMING (1) [BLAME]
Job 1:22 In all of this, Job did not sin by **b** God.

BLANKET (5) [BLANKETED, BLANKETS]
Lev 15: 9 Any **b** on which the man rides will be defiled.
Jdg 4:18 went into her tent, and she covered him with a **b**.
2Ki 8:15 But the next day Hazael took a **b**, soaked it in
Ecc 4:11 two under the same **b** can gain warmth from each
Isa 14:11 Now maggots are your sheet and worms your **b**.'

BLANKETED (1) [BLANKET]
Ps 105:28 The LORD **b** Egypt in darkness, / for they had

BLANKETS (5) [BLANKET]
Jdg 5:10 on fine donkeys / and sit on fancy saddle **b**, listen!
1Sa 19:13 took an idol and put it in his bed, covered it with **b**,
1Ki 1: 1 and no matter how many **b** covered him, he could
Isa 28:20 short to lie on. The **b** are too narrow to cover you.
Eze 27:20 Dedan traded their expensive saddle **b** with you.

BLARE (1) [BLARES, BLARING]
Am 2: 2 of battle, as the warriors shout and the trumpets **b**.

BLARES (1) [BLARE]
Am 3: 6 When the war trumpet **b**, shouldn't the people be

BLARING (2) [BLARE]
2Ch 15:14 their oath of loyalty to the LORD with trumpets **b**
Ps 47: 5 The LORD has ascended with trumpets **b**.

BLASPHEME (8) [BLASPHEMED, BLASPHEMER, BLASPHEMES, BLASPHEMIES, BLASPHEMING, BLASPHEMOUS, BLASPHEMY]
Ex 22:28 "Do not **b** God or curse anyone who rules over
Lev 24:15 Those who **b** God will suffer the consequences of
Nu 15:30 native Israelites or foreigners, **b** the LORD,
2Sa 12:14 LORD great opportunity to despise and **b** him,
Ps 139:20 They **b** you; / your enemies take your name in
Eze 20:27 Your ancestors continued to **b** and betray me,
Ac 6:11 saying, "We heard him **b** Moses, and even God."
1Ti 1:20 over to Satan so they would learn not to **b** God.

BLASPHEMED (3) [BLASPHEME]
Lev 24:11 this son of an Israelite woman **b** the LORD's
Isa 52: 5 in exultation. My name is being **b** all day long.
Rev 13: 1 And written on each head were names that **b** God.

BLASPHEMER (2) [BLASPHEME]
Lev 24:14 "Take the **b** outside the camp, and tell all those
24:23 they led the **b** outside the camp and stoned him to

BLASPHEMES (5) [BLASPHEME]
Lev 24:16 Anyone who **b** the LORD's name must be stoned
24:16 or foreigner among you who **b** the LORD's name
Mt 12:32 Anyone who **b** against me, the Son of Man, can be
Mk 3:29 but anyone who **b** against the Holy Spirit will
Ro 2:24 "The world **b** the name of God because of you."

BLASPHEMIES (5) [BLASPHEME]
Ne 9:18 of Egypt!' They sinned and committed terrible **b**.
9:26 to return to you, and they committed terrible **b**.
Lk 12:10 but anyone who speaks **b** against the Holy Spirit
Rev 13: 5 Then the beast was allowed to speak great **b**
17: 3 and ten horns, written all over with **b** against God.

BLASPHEMING (2) [BLASPHEME]
1Sa 3:13 because his sons are **b** God and he hasn't
Da 11:36 than every god there is, even **b** the God of gods.

BLASPHEMOUS (2) [BLASPHEME]
2Ki 19: 6 Do not be disturbed by this **b** speech against me
Isa 37: 6 Do not be disturbed by this **b** speech against me

BLASPHEMY (17) [BLASPHEME]
Job 34:37 and **b** against God to your other sins."
Mt 9: 3 "**B**! This man talks like he is God!" some of the
12:31 "Every sin or **b** can be forgiven—except **b** against the Holy Spirit, which can never
12:32 but **b** against the Holy Spirit will never be
26:65 tore his clothing to show his horror, shouting, '**B**!
26:65 we need other witnesses? You have all heard his **b**.
Mk 2: 7 This is **b**! Who but God can forgive sins!"
2: 8 so he said to them, "Why do you think this is **b**?
3:28 you that any sin can be forgiven, including **b**;
14:64 You have all heard his **b**. What is your verdict?"
Lk 5:21 "This is **b**! Who but God can forgive sins?"
5:22 so he asked them, "Why do you think this is **b**?
Jn 10:33 good work, but for **b**, because you, a mere man,
10:36 why do you call it **b** when the Holy One who was
Jude 1: 9 did not dare accuse Satan of **b**, but simply said,
Rev 13: 6 And he spoke terrible words of **b** against God,

BLAST (23) [BLASTS]
Ex 15: 8 At the **b** of your breath, the waters piled up!
15:10 But with a **b** of your breath, / the sea covered them.
19:13 until they hear one long **b** from the ram's horn.
19:16 There was a long, loud **b** from a ram's horn,
19:19 As the horn **b** grew louder and louder,
20:18 heard the thunder and the loud **b** of the horn,
Jos 6: 5 When you hear the priests give one long **b** on the
6:16 as the priests sounded the long **b** on their horns,
2Sa 22:16 command of the LORD, / at the **b** of his breath,
1Ki 19:11 It was such a terrible **b** that the rocks were torn
Ne 4:20 When you hear the **b** of the trumpet, rush to
Job 4: 9 a breath from God. They vanish in a **b** of his anger.
Ps 18:15 O LORD, / at the **b** of your breath,
150: 3 Praise him with a **b** of the trumpet; / praise him
Isa 58: 1 "Shout with the voice of a trumpet **b**. Tell my
Jer 4:12 It is a roaring **b** sent by me! Now I will pronounce
4:19 For I have heard the **b** of enemy trumpets
Hos 13:15 but the east wind—a **b** from the LORD—
Mt 24:31 his angels with the sound of a mighty trumpet **b**,
Heb 12:19 For they heard an awesome trumpet **b** and a voice
Rev 1:10 behind me, a voice that sounded like a trumpet **b**.
4: 1 spoke to me with the sound of a mighty trumpet **b**.
16: 9 Everyone was burned by this **b** of heat, and they

BLASTS (3) [BLAST]
Lev 23:24 Festival of Trumpets—with loud **b** from a trumpet.
Nu 10: 6 You must sound short **b** to signal moving on.
Rev 8: 6 seven trumpets prepared to blow their mighty **b**.

BLASTUS (1)
Ac 12:20 They made friends with **B**, Herod's personal

BLAZE (8) [ABLAZE, BLAZED, BLAZES, BLAZING]
Ex 22:24 My anger will **b** forth against you, and I will kill
32:10 leave me alone so my anger can **b** against them
Nu 18: 5 the LORD's anger will never again **b** against the
21:28 forth from Heshbon, / a **b** from the city of Sihon.
25: 3 causing the LORD's anger to **b** against his
Dt 31:17 Then my anger will **b** forth against them. I will
Pr 16:27 hunt for scandal; their words are a destructive **b**.
Hos 7: 6 Their hearts **b** like a furnace with intrigue.

BLAZED (11) [BLAZE]
Lev 9:24 Fire **b** forth from the LORD's presence
10: 2 So fire **b** forth from the LORD's presence
Nu 11: 1 the LORD heard them, his anger **b** against them.
11:33 the anger of the LORD **b** against the people,
16:35 Then fire **b** forth from the LORD and burned up
2Sa 6: 7 Then the LORD's anger **b** out against Uzzah for
6: 8 because the LORD's anger had **b** out against
22:13 shone before him, / and bolts of lightning **b** forth.
1Ch 13:10 Then the LORD's anger **b** out against Uzzah,
13:11 because the LORD's anger had **b** out against
Ps 118:12 like bees; / they **b** against me like a roaring flame.

BLAZES (4) [BLAZE]
Dt 32:22 For my anger **b** forth like fire / and burns to the
Isa 62: 1 the dawn, and her salvation **b** like a burning torch.
Jer 15:14 For my anger **b** forth like fire, and it will consume
Na 1: 6 His rage **b** forth like fire, and the mountains

BLAZING (18) [BLAZE]
Ex 3: 2 the angel of the LORD appeared to him as a **b** fire
Nu 16:46 The LORD's anger is **b** among them—the plague
Dt 5:23 while the mountain was **b** with fire, all your tribal
18:16 your God or see this **b** fire for fear you would die.
Jdg 7:20 They held the **b** torches in their left hands
Ps 11: 6 He rains down **b** coals on the wicked,
85: 3 your fury. / You have ended your **b** anger.
Pr 30:16 the barren womb, / the thirsty desert, / the **b** fire.
Eze 38:19 For in my jealousy and **b** anger, I promise a mighty
Da 3: 6 will immediately be thrown into a **b** furnace."
3:11 refuse to obey must be thrown into a **b** furnace.
3:15 you will be thrown immediately into the **b** furnace.
3:17 If we are thrown into the **b** furnace, the God whom
3:20 and Abednego and throw them into the **b** furnace.
7: 9 He sat on a fiery throne with wheels of **b** fire,
Mal 3: 2 For he will be like a **b** fire that refines metal
Jn 18: 3 Now with **b** torches, lanterns, and weapons,
Jas 3: 6 It can turn the entire course of your life into a **b**

BLEACHED (3)
2Ki 18:17 near the road leading to the field where cloth is **b**.
Isa 7: 3 near the road leading to the field where cloth is **b**.
36: 2 near the road leading to the field where cloth is **b**.

BLEAT (2) [BLEATING]
Isa 34:14 Wild goats will **b** at one another among the ruins,
Joel 1:18 is no pasture for them. The sheep **b** in misery.

BLEATING (1) [BLEAT]
1Sa 15:14 "Then what is all the **b** of sheep and lowing of

BLEEDING (4) [BLOOD]
Lev 12: 7 ceremonially clean again after her **b** at childbirth.
Pr 30:33 and a blow to the nose causes **b**, so anger causes
Mk 5:29 Immediately the **b** stopped, and she could feel that
Lk 8:44 the fringe of his robe. Immediately, the **b** stopped.

BLEMISH (3)
Lev 21:21 Since he has a **b**, he may not offer food to his God.
1Sa 25:31 don't let this be a **b** on your record. Then you
Eph 5:27 church without a spot or wrinkle or any other **b**.

BLEND (1) [BLENDS]
Ex 30:25 **B** these ingredients into a holy anointing oil.

BLENDS (1) [BLEND]
Ex 30:33 Anyone who **b** scented oil like it or puts any of it

BLESS (145) [BLESSED, BLESSES, BLESSING, BLESSINGS]
BLESS THE LORD* (8) Jdg 5:2,9; Ps 16:7; 41:13; 72:18; 134:1,2; 144:1
BLESS YOU (50) Ge 12:2,3; 22:17; 26:3,24; 27:10,29; 28:3; 49:25; Ex 20:24; 23:25; Nu 6:24; Dt 1:11; 7:13; 14:29; 15:4,6,10,18; 23:20; 24:13,19; 28:8; 30:16; Jos 24:10; Jdg 17:2; Ru 1:9; 2:4; 3:10; 1Sa 15:13; 23:21; 25:33; 2Sa 2:5; Ps 118:26; 128:5; 129:8; 134:3; 145:2,10; Isa 30:23; Jer 31:23; Hag 2:19; Lk 1:30; Ac 3:26; Heb 6:14; Jas 1:25; 2:16; 1Pe 3:9; 2Pe 1:2; Jude 1:21
THE LORD* BLESS (11) Nu 6:24; Jdg 17:2; Ru 1:9; 2:4,19,20; 3:10; 1Sa 15:13; 23:21; 2Sa 2:5; Jer 31:23
Ge 12: 2 I will **b** you and make you famous, and I will make
12: 3 I will **b** those who **b** you and curse those who
17:16 And I will **b** her and give you a son from her!
17:16 Yes, I will **b** her richly, and she will become the
17:20 As for Ishmael, I will **b** him also, just as you have
22:17 I will **b** you richly. I will multiply your
26: 3 this land. If you do, I will be with you and **b** you.
26:24 not be afraid, for I am with you and will **b** you.
27: 7 He wants to **b** Esau in the LORD's presence
27:10 eat it and **b** you instead of Esau before he dies."
27:29 you are cursed, and all who **b** you are blessed."
27:34 bitter cry. "O my father, **b** me, too!" he begged.
27:38 O my father, **b** me, too!" Then Esau broke down
28: 3 May God Almighty **b** you and give you many
32:26 "I will not let you go unless you **b** me."
39: 5 the LORD began to **b** Potiphar for Joseph's sake.
48: 9 "Bring them over to me, and I will **b** them."
48:16 has kept me from all harm—may he **b** these boys.
48:20 "The people of Israel will use your names to **b**
49:25 your ancestors help you; / may the Almighty **b** you
Ex 20:24 you who I am, and I will come and **b** you there.
23:25 If you do, I will **b** you with food and water, and I
Nu 6:23 and his sons to **b** the people of Israel with this
6:24 'May the LORD **b** you / and protect you.
6:27 Israelites as my people, and I myself will **b** them."
22: 6 I know that blessings fall on the people you **b**.
23:20 I received a command to **b**; / he has blessed,
23:25 aren't going to curse them, at least don't **b** them!"
24: 1 realized that the LORD intended to **b** Israel,
Dt 1:11 a thousand times more and **b** you as he promised!
4:37 he chose to **b** their descendants and personally
7:13 He will love you and **b** you and make you into a
14:29 Then the LORD your God will **b** you in all your
15: 4 for the LORD your God will greatly **b** you in the
15: 6 The LORD your God will **b** you as he has
15:10 and the LORD your God will **b** you in everything
15:18 and the LORD your God will **b** you in all you do.
23:20 so the LORD your God may **b** you in everything
24:13 so your neighbor can sleep in it and **b** you.
24:19 Then the LORD your God will **b** you in all you
26:15 and **b** your people Israel and the land you have
28: 8 "The LORD will **b** everything you do and will
28: 8 The LORD your God will **b** you in the land he is
28:12 treasury in the heavens to **b** all the work you do.
30:16 and the LORD your God will **b** you and the land
33:11 **B** the Levites, O LORD, / and accept all their
Jos 24:10 I made Balaam **b** you, and so I rescued you from
Jdg 5: 2 and the people gladly follow—/ **b** the LORD!
5: 9 and to those who gladly followed. / **B** the LORD!
17: 2 "The LORD **b** you for admitting it," his mother
17:13 "I know the LORD will **b** me now," Micah said,
Ru 1: 9 May the LORD **b** you with the security of another
2: 4 he said. "The LORD **b** you!" the harvesters
2:19 May the LORD **b** the one who helped you!"
2:20 "May the LORD **b** him!" Naomi told her
3:10 "The LORD **b** you, my daughter!"
1Sa 2:20 Eli would **b** Elkanah and his wife and say,
2:35 I will **b** his descendants, and his family will be
9:13 The guests won't start until he arrives to **b** the
15:13 him cheerfully. "May the LORD **b** you," he said.
23:21 "The LORD **b** you," Saul said. "At last
25:33 **B** you for keeping me from murdering the man
2Sa 2: 5 "May the LORD **b** you for being so loyal to your
6:20 When David returned home to **b** his family,
7:29 may it please you to **b** me and my family so that

16:12 and will **b** me because of these curses."
21: 3 so that the LORD will **b** his people again."
1Ch 4:10 "Oh, that you would **b** me and extend my lands!
16:43 and David returned home to **b** his family.
17:27 it has pleased you to **b** me and my family so that
Ne 5:19 that I have done for these people, and **b** me for it.
Job 2: 4 for skin—he blesses you only because you **b** him.
Ps 5:12 For you **b** the godly, O LORD,
16: 7 I will **b** the LORD who guides me; / even at night
28: 9 your people! / **B** Israel, your special possession!
41:13 **B** the LORD, the God of Israel, / who lives
65:10 the earth with showers / and **b** its abundant crops.
66: 8 Let the whole world **b** our God / and sing aloud his
67: 1 May God be merciful and **b** us. / May his face
67: 6 its harvests, / and God, our God, will richly **b** us.
67: 7 Yes, God will **b** us, / and people all over the world
72:15 always pray for him / and **b** him all day long.
72:18 **B** the LORD God, the God of Israel, / who alone
72:19 **B** his glorious name forever! / Let the whole earth
87: 5 And the Most High will personally **b** this city.
96: 2 Sing to the LORD; **b** his name. / Each day
100: 4 with praise. / Give thanks to him and **b** his name.
109:17 He never blessed others; / now don't you **b** him.
109:28 let them curse me if they like, / but you will **b** me!
115:12 LORD remembers us, / and he will surely **b** us.
115:12 He will **b** the people of Israel / and the family of
115:13 He will **b** those who fear the LORD, / both great
115:14 May the LORD richly **b** / both you and your
118:26 **B** the one who comes in the name of the LORD.
118:26 We **b** you from the house of the LORD.
128: 5 May the LORD continually **b** you from Zion.
129: 8 be upon you; / we **b** you in the LORD's name."
134: 1 Oh, **b** the LORD, all you servants of the LORD,
134: 2 Lift your hands in holiness, / and **b** the LORD.
134: 3 made heaven and earth, / **b** you from Jerusalem.
144: 1 **B** the LORD, who is my rock. / He gives me
145: 1 and King, / and **b** your name forever and ever.
145: 2 I will **b** you every day, / and I will praise you
145:10 LORD, / and your faithful followers will **b** you.
145:21 and everyone on earth will **b** his holy name.
Pr 11:11 Upright citizens **b** a city and make it prosper,
11:26 but they **b** the one who sells to them in their time
31:28 Her children stand and **b** her. Her husband praises
Isa 30:23 Then the LORD will **b** you with rain at planting
32:20 God will greatly **b** his people. Wherever they plant
56: 6 "I will also **b** the Gentiles who commit themselves
66: 2 "I will **b** those who have humble and contrite
Jer 18:10 I will not **b** that nation as I had said I would.
31:23 and its cities will again say, 'The LORD **b** you—
Eze 44:30 to the priests so the LORD will **b** your homes.
Hos 4: 6 laws of your God, I will forget to **b** your children.
Hag 2:19 their crops. From this day onward I will **b** you."
Zec 4: 7 will shout: 'May God **b** it! May God **b** it!' "
8:15 Neither will I change my decision to **b** Jerusalem
8:21 'Let us go to Jerusalem to ask the LORD to **b** us
8:22 and to ask the LORD to **b** them.
Mt 21: 9 **B** the one who comes in the name of the Lord!
23:39 '**B** the one who comes in the name of the
Mk 10:13 to Jesus so he could touch them and **b** them,
11: 9 **B** the one who comes in the name of the Lord!
11:10 **B** the coming kingdom of our ancestor David!
Lk 1:30 the angel told her, "for God has decided to **b** you!
11:27 in the crowd called out, "God **b** your mother—
13:35 '**B** the one who comes in the name of the
18:15 to Jesus so he could touch them and **b** them,
19:38 "**B** the King who comes in the name of the Lord!
Jn 12:13 **B** the one who comes in the name of the Lord!
Ac 3:26 to **b** you by turning each of you back from your
Ro 12:14 don't curse them; pray that God will **b** them.
1Co 4:12 We **b** those who curse us. We are patient with
10:16 When we **b** the cup at the Lord's Table, aren't we
Heb 6:14 "I will certainly **b** you richly, / and I will multiply
7: 7 the person who has the power to **b** is always
Jas 1:25 what you heard, then God will **b** you for doing it.
2:16 and you say, "Well, good-bye and God **b** you;
1Pe 3: 9 what God wants you to do, and he will **b** you for it.
2Pe 1: 2 May God **b** you with his special favor
Jude 1:21 Live in such a way that God's love can **b** you as

BLESSED (165) [BLESS]

BLESSED BE (17) Ge 14:19,20; 2Sa 18:28; 22:47; 1Ki 1:48; 8:15; 1Ch 16:36; 2Ch 2:12; 6:4; Ps 18:46; 89:52; 106:48; 113:2; 124:6; Isa 19:25,25,25

BLESSED (BE)...GOD (13) Ge 9:26; 14:19,20; 2Sa 18:28; 1Ki 1:48; 8:15; 1Ch 16:36; 2Ch 2:12; 6:4; Ps 106:48; Mk 14:61; 1Ti 1:11; 6:15

BLESSED BE THE LORD* (9) 2Sa 18:28; 1Ki 1:48; 8:15; 1Ch 16:36; 2Ch 2:12; 6:4; Ps 89:52; 106:48; 124:6

THE LORD* BLESSED (6) Ge 26:12; Ex 20:11; Jdg 13:24; 2Sa 6:11; 1Ch 13:14; Job 42:12

Ge 1:22 Then God **b** them, saying, "Let the fish multiply
1:28 God **b** them and told them, "Multiply and fill the
2: 3 And God **b** the seventh day and declared it holy,
5: 2 and he **b** them and called them "human."
9: 1 God **b** Noah and his sons and told them, "Multiply
9:26 "May Shem be **b** by the LORD my God;
12: 3 All the families of the earth will be **b** through
14:19 Melchizedek **b** Abram with this blessing:
14:19 "**B** be Abram by God Most High, / Creator of
14:20 And **b** be God Most High, / who has helped you
18:18 and all the nations of the earth will be **b** through
22:18 all the nations of the earth will be **b**—
24: 1 old man, and the LORD had **b** him in every way.
24:31 and stay with us, you who are **b** by the LORD.
24:35 "And the LORD has **b** my master richly; he has
24:60 They **b** her with this blessing as she parted:
26: 4 descendants all the nations of the earth will be **b**.
26:12 more grain than he planted, for the LORD **b** him.
26:29 And now look how the LORD has **b** you!"
27:27 he was finally convinced, and he **b** his son.
27:27 smell of the open fields that the LORD has **b**.
27:29 curse you are cursed, and all who bless you are **b**."
27:30 As soon as Isaac had **b** Jacob, and almost before
27:33 and I **b** him with an irrevocable blessing before
28: 1 So Isaac called for Jacob, **b** him, and said, "Do not
28: 6 Esau heard that his father had **b** Jacob and sent him
28:14 All the families of the earth will be **b** through you
30:27 learned by divination that the LORD has **b** me
30:30 The LORD has **b** you from everything I do!
31:55 kissed his daughters and grandchildren and **b** them.
32:29 you ask?" the man replied. Then he **b** Jacob there.
35: 9 after traveling from Paddan-aram. God **b** him
39: 2 and **b** him greatly as he served in the home of his
47: 7 presented him to Pharaoh, and Jacob **b** Pharaoh.
47:10 Then Jacob **b** Pharaoh again before he left.
48: 3 to me at Luz in the land of Canaan and **b** me.
48:15 Then he **b** Joseph and said, "May God, the God
48:20 So Jacob **b** the boys that day with this blessing:
49:28 and these are the blessings with which Jacob **b** his
Ex 1:20 So God **b** the midwives, and the Israelites
20:11 That is why the LORD **b** the Sabbath day and set
39:43 Moses inspected all their work and **b** them
Lev 9:22 raised his hands toward the people and **b** them.
9:23 when they came back out, they **b** the people again,
Nu 22:12 are not to curse these people, for I have **b** them!"
23:11 to curse my enemies. Instead, you have **b** them!"
23:20 to bless; / he has **b**, and I cannot reverse it!
24: 9 **B** is everyone who blesses you, O Israel,
24:10 my enemies! Instead, you have **b** them three times.
Dt 2: 7 The LORD your God has **b** everything you have
7:14 You will be **b** above all the nations of the earth.
11:27 You will be **b** if you obey the commands of the
12: 7 because the LORD your God has **b** you.
15:14 with which the LORD your God has **b** you.
28: 3 You will be **b** in your towns and in the country.
28: 4 You will be **b** with many children and productive
28: 4 You will be **b** with fertile herds and flocks.
28: 5 You will be **b** with baskets overflowing with fruit,
28: 6 You will be **b** wherever you go, both in coming
33:13 of Joseph: / "May their land be **b** by the LORD
33:20 "**B** is the one who enlarges Gad's territory!
33:24 "May Asher be **b** above other sons; / may he be
33:29 How **b** you are, O Israel! / Who else is like you,
Jos 14:13 So Joshua **b** Caleb son of Jephunneh and gave
22: 6 So Joshua **b** them and sent them home.
22: 7 the Jordan. As Joshua sent them away, he **b** them
Jdg 5:24 "Most **b** is Jael, / the wife of Heber the Kenite.
5:24 May she be **b** above all women who live in tents.
13:24 And the LORD **b** him as he grew up.
Ru 1: 6 Then Naomi heard in Moab that the LORD had **b**
1Sa 2: 1 in the LORD! / Oh, how the LORD has **b** me!
2Sa 6:11 and the LORD **b** him and his entire household.
6:12 "The LORD has **b** Obed-edom's home
6:18 David **b** the people in the name of the LORD
14:22 to the ground before the king and **b** him and said,
18:28 the ground and said, "**B** be the LORD your God,
19:39 After David had **b** and embraced him,
22:47 **B** be my rock! / May God, the rock of my
1Ki 1:48 '**B** be the LORD, the God of Israel, who today
8:15 "**B** be the LORD, the God of Israel, who has kept
8:66 They **b** the king as they went, and they were all
1Ch 13:14 and the LORD **b** him and his entire household.
16: 2 David **b** the people in the name of the LORD.
16:36 **B** be the LORD, the God of Israel,
26: 5 (the eighth). God had richly **b** Obed-edom.
2Ch 2:12 **B** be the LORD, the God of Israel, who made the
6: 4 "**B** be the LORD, the God of Israel, who has kept
30:27 Then the Levitical priests stood and **b** the people,
31:10 plenty to spare, for the LORD has **b** his people."
Job 3:22 It is a **b** relief when they finally die, when they
29:13 I helped those who had lost hope, and they **b** me.
36:11 then they will be **b** with prosperity throughout their
42:12 So the LORD **b** Job in the second half of his life
Ps 18:46 The LORD lives! **B** be my rock! / May the God
37:22 Those **b** by the LORD will inherit the land,
45: 2 from your lips. / God himself has **b** you forever.
72:17 May all nations be **b** through him / and bring him
89:52 **B** be the LORD forever! / Amen and amen!
106:48 **B** be the LORD, the God of Israel,
109:17 now you curse him. / He never **b** others;
112: 2 an entire generation of godly people will be **b**.
113: 2 **B** be the name of the LORD / forever and ever.
115:15 May you be **b** by the LORD, / who made heaven
119:12 **B** are you, O LORD; / teach me your principles.
124: 6 **B** be the LORD, / who did not let their teeth tear
147:13 bars of your gates / and **b** your children within you.
Pr 14:21 one's neighbors; **b** are those who help the poor.
20: 7 walk with integrity; **b** are their children after them.
22: 9 **B** are those who are generous, because they feed
28:14 **B** are those who have a tender conscience,
Isa 19:25 "**B** be Egypt, my people. **B** be Assyria, the land I
have made. **B** be Israel, my special possession!"
30:18 **B** are those who wait for him to help them.
32: 8 be generous to others and will be **b** for all they do.
51: 2 But when I **b** him, he became a great nation."
56: 2 **B** are those who are careful to do this. **B** are those
who honor my Sabbath days of rest by
56: 2 And **b** are those who keep themselves from doing
61: 9 realize that they are a people the LORD has **b**."
65:23 For they are people **b** by the LORD, and their
65:23 by the LORD, and their children, too, will be **b**.
66: 3 they burn incense, it is as if they had **b** an idol.
Jer 17: 7 "But **b** are those who trust in the LORD and have
20:14 day I was born! May the day of my birth not be **b**.
22:15 right in all his dealings. That is why God **b** him.
Da 12:12 And **b** are those who wait and remain until the end
Mic 6: 5 and how Balaam son of Beor **b** you instead?
Mal 3:12 "Then all nations will call you **b**, for your land
3:15 From now on we will say, '**B** are the arrogant.'
Mt 13:16 "But **b** are your eyes, because they see; and your
16:17 Jesus replied, "You are **b**, Simon son of John,
19:15 his hands on their heads and **b** them before he left.
25:34 on the right, 'Come, you who are **b** by my Father,
Mk 8: 7 so Jesus also **b** these and told the disciples to pass
10:16 and placed his hands on their heads and **b** them.
14:61 "Are you the Messiah, the Son of the **b** God?"
Lk 1:42 "You are **b** by God above all other women, and
your child is **b**.
1:45 You are **b**, because you believed that the Lord
1:48 now generation after generation / will call me **b**.
2:34 Then Simeon **b** them, and he said to Mary,
11:28 "But even more **b** are all who hear the word of
24:50 and lifting his hands to heaven, he **b** them.
Jn 6:23 near the place where the Lord had **b** the bread
20:29 **B** are those who haven't seen me and believe
Ac 3:25 descendants all the families on earth will be **b**.'
20:35 'It is more **b** to give than to receive.' "
Ro 14:22 **B** are those who do not condemn themselves by
Gal 3: 8 he said, "All nations will be **b** through you."
3:14 God has **b** the Gentiles with the same blessing he
Eph 1: 3 who has **b** us with every spiritual blessing in the
1Ti 1:11 glorious Good News entrusted to me by our **b** God.
6:15 time Christ will be revealed from heaven by the **b**
Heb 7: 1 many kings, Melchizedek met him and **b** him.
7: 7 to bless is always greater than the person who is **b**.
11:20 It was by faith that Isaac **b** his two sons, Jacob
11:21 **b** each of Joseph's sons and bowed in worship as
Rev 14:13 **B** are those who die in the Lord from now on.
14:13 Yes, says the Spirit, they are **b** indeed, for they will
16:15 **B** are all who are watching for me, who keep their
19: 9 **B** are those who are invited to the wedding feast of
20: 6 **B** and holy are those who share in the first
22: 7 **B** are those who obey the prophecy written in this
22:14 **B** are those who wash their robes so they can enter

BLESSES (24) [BLESS]

Nu 24: 9 Blessed is everyone who **b** you, O Israel,
Dt 16:15 gives you bountiful harvests and **b** all your work.
Jdg 9: 9 'Should I quit producing the olive oil that **b** both
Job 2: 4 for skin—he **b** you only because you bless him.
Ps 29:11 people strength. / The LORD **b** them with peace.
107:38 How he **b** them! / They raise large families there,
Mt 5: 3 "God **b** those who realize their need for him,
5: 4 God **b** those who mourn, / for they will be
5: 5 God **b** those who are gentle and lowly,
5: 6 God **b** those who are hungry and thirsty for justice,
5: 7 God **b** those who are merciful, / for they will be
5: 8 God **b** those whose hearts are pure, / for they will
5: 9 God **b** those who work for peace, / for they will be
5:10 God **b** those who are persecuted because they live
5:11 "God **b** you when you are mocked and persecuted
11: 6 'God **b** those who are not offended by me.' "
Lk 6:20 his disciples and said, / "God **b** you who are poor,
6:21 God **b** you who are hungry now, / for you will be
satisfied. / God **b** you who weep now,
6:22 God **b** you who are hated and excluded
7:23 'God **b** those who are not offended by me.' "
Jas 1:12 God **b** the people who patiently endure testing.
Rev 1: 3 God **b** the one who reads this prophecy to the
1: 3 and he **b** all who listen to it and obey what it says.

BLESSING (105) [BLESS]

Ge 12: 2 you famous, and I will make you a **b** to others.
14:19 Melchizedek blessed Abram with this **b**:
17:18 to God, "Yes, may Ishmael enjoy your special **b**!"
24:60 They blessed her with this **b** as she parted:
27: 4 Then I will pronounce the **b** that belongs to you,
27:12 and then he'll curse me instead of **b** me."
27:19 Sit up and eat it so you can give me your **b**."
27:23 like Esau's. So Isaac pronounced his **b** on Jacob.
27:25 I will eat it, and then I will give you my **b**."
27:31 Sit up and eat it so you can give me your **b**."
27:33 and I blessed him with an irrevocable **b** before you
27:35 and he tricked me. He has carried away your **b**."
27:36 first taking my birthright and now stealing my **b**.
27:36 Oh, haven't you saved even one **b** for me?"
27:38 Esau pleaded, "Not one **b** left for me? O my
27:41 Esau hated Jacob because he had stolen his **b**,
48:20 So Jacob blessed the boys that day with this **b**:
49:28 Each received a **b** that was appropriate to him.
Ex 4:18 are still alive." "Go with my **b**," Jethro replied.
12:32 and be gone. Go, but give me a **b** as you leave."
32:29 Because of this, he will now give you a great **b**."
Lev 25:21 'I will order my **b** for you in the sixth year,
Nu 6:23 to bless the people of Israel with this special **b**:
Dt 11:26 "Today I am giving you the choice between a **b**
11:29 you must pronounce a **b** from Mount Gerizim
15: 5 You will receive this **b** if you carefully obey the
23: 5 He turned the intended curse into a **b**
27:12 on Mount Gerizim to proclaim a **b** over the people.
32:21 Now I will rouse their jealousy by **b** other nations;
32:21 I will provoke their fury by **b** the foolish Gentiles.
33: 1 This is the **b** that Moses, the man of God, gave to
33:17 This is my **b** for the multitudes of Ephraim
Jos 8:33 the LORD, had given for **b** the people of Israel.
15:19 She said, "Give me a further **b**. You have been
Jdg 1:15 She said, "Give me a further **b**. You have been
2Sa 7:29 For when you grant a **b** to your servant,

7:29 O Sovereign LORD, it is an eternal **b**!"
1Ki 8:14 of Israel standing before him and gave this **b**:
8:55 and shouted this **b** over the entire community of
1Ch 17:27 when you grant a **b**, O LORD, it is an eternal **b**!"
2Ch 6:3 of Israel standing before him and gave this **b**:
20:26 On the fourth day they gathered in the Valley of **B**,
20:26 It is still called the Valley of **B** today.
Ne 13:2 though our God turned the curse into a **b**.
Ps 16:5 you alone are my inheritance, my cup of **b**.
24:5 They will receive the LORD's **b** / and have right
31:19 for protection, / **b** them before the watching world.
37:26 loans to others, / and their children are a **b**.
84:6 where pools of **b** collect after the rains!
107:30 What a **b** was that stillness / as he brought them
119:122 Please guarantee a **b** for me. / Don't let those who
129:8 may those who pass by refuse to give them this **b**:
133:3 And the LORD has pronounced his **b**, / even life
139:5 follow me. / You place your hand of **b** on my head.
Pr 3:33 the wicked, but his **b** is on the home of the upright.
5:18 Let your wife be a fountain of **b** for you. Rejoice in
10:22 The **b** of the LORD makes a person rich, and he
20:21 An inheritance obtained early in life is not a **b** in
Isa 19:24 will be together, and Israel will be a **b** to them.
54:10 My covenant of **b** will never be broken,"
65:16 All who invoke a **b** or take an oath will do so by
Jer 4:2 then you will be a **b** to the nations of the world,
Eze 34:26 and their homes around my holy hill to be a **b**.
Hos 12:4 and won. He wept and pleaded for a **b** from him.
Joel 2:14 sending you a **b** instead of this terrible curse.
Zec 8:13 and make you both a symbol and a source of **b**!
Mal 3:10 I will pour out a **b** so great you won't have enough
Mt 10:12 are invited into someone's home, give it your **b**.
10:13 it turns out to be a worthy home, let your **b** stand; if it is not, take back the **b**.
14:19 up toward heaven, and asked God's **b** on the food.
26:26 Jesus took a loaf of bread and asked God's **b** on it.
Mk 6:41 up toward heaven, and asked God's **b** on the food.
14:22 Jesus took a loaf of bread and asked God's **b** on it.
Lk 9:16 up toward heaven, and asked God's **b** on the food.
10:5 "Whenever you enter a home, give it your **b**.
10:6 If those who live there are worthy, the **b** will stand; if they are not, the **b** will return to you.
24:30 asked God's **b** on it, broke it, then gave it to them.
24:51 While he was **b** them, he left them and was taken
Jn 1:16 he brought to us—one gracious **b** after another!
13:17 these things—now do them! That is the path of **b**.
Ro 1:11 so I can share a spiritual **b** with you that will help
1:12 In this way, each of us will be a **b** to the other.
4:9 Now then, is this **b** only for the Jews, or is it for
10:19 "I will rouse your jealousy by **b** other nations.
10:19 I will make you angry by **b** the foolish Gentiles."
11:12 think how much greater a **b** the world will share
11:17 So now you also receive the **b** God has promised
15:29 when I come, Christ will give me a great **b** for you.
2Co 1:15 and trust, I wanted to give you a double **b**.
Gal 3:9 All who put their faith in Christ share the same **b**
3:14 God has blessed the Gentiles with the same **b** he
6:9 for we will reap a harvest of **b** at the appropriate
Eph 1:3 who has blessed us with every spiritual **b** in the
6:3 and mother, "you will live a long life, full of **b**."
Heb 6:7 a good crop for the farmer, it has the **b** of God.
7:6 And Melchizedek placed a **b** upon Abraham,
12:17 And afterward, when he wanted his father's **b**,
Jas 3:10 And so **b** and cursing come pouring out of the
1Pe 3:9 Instead, pay them back with a **b**. That is what God
Rev 5:12 and strength / and honor and glory and **b**."
5:13 also sang: / "**B** and honor and glory and power
7:12 They said, / "Amen! **B** and glory and wisdom

BLESSINGS (59) [BLESS]

Ge 15:2 what good are all your **b** when I don't even have a
25:11 Abraham's death, God poured out rich **b** on Isaac,
28:4 and your descendants the **b** he promised to
49:25 bless you / with the **b** of the heavens above, / **b** of the earth beneath, / and **b** of the breasts and womb.
49:26 May the **b** of your ancestors / be greater than the **b** of the eternal mountains,
49:26 These **b** will fall on the head of Joseph, / who is a
49:28 and these are the **b** with which Jacob blessed his
Nu 22:6 the land. I know that **b** fall on the people you bless.
Dt 10:8 the LORD, and to pronounce **b** in his name.
16:10 Bring him a freewill offering in proportion to the **b**
16:17 according to the **b** given to them by the LORD
21:5 and to pronounce **b** in the LORD's name.
28:2 You will experience all these **b** if you obey the
30:1 happen to you—the **b** and the curses I have listed
30:19 between life and death, between **b** and curses.
33:16 May these **b** rest on Joseph's head,
33:23 you are rich in favor / and full of the LORD's **b**;
Jos 8:34 Joshua then read to them all the **b** and curses
1Sa 26:25 And Saul said to David, "**B** on you, my son David.
1Ki 2:45 But may I receive the LORD's rich **b**, and may
1Ch 16:4 before the Ark of the LORD by asking for his **b**
23:13 and to pronounce **b** in his name forever.
Ne 9:25 and grew fat and enjoyed themselves in all your **b**.
Ps 3:8 O LORD. / May your **b** rest on your people.
21:6 You have endowed him with eternal **b**. / You have
23:5 my head with oil. / My cup overflows with **b**.
31:19 You have stored up great **b** for those who honor
77:10 that the **b** of the Most High have changed to
85:1 you have poured out amazing **b** on your land!
85:12 Yes, the LORD pours down his **b**. / Our land will
119:58 With all my heart I want your **b**. / Be merciful just
129:8 "The LORD's **b** be upon you; / we bless you in
Pr 10:6 The godly are showered with **b**; evil people cover
13:21 chases sinners, while **b** chase the righteous!
24:25 But **b** are showered on those who convict the
Isa 29:23 when they see their many children and material **b**,
44:3 will pour out my Spirit and my **b** on your children.
56:3 "And my **b** are for Gentiles, too, when they
56:3 And my **b** are also for the eunuchs. They are as
Jer 5:25 wickedness has deprived you of these wonderful **b**.
Eze 34:26 And I will send showers, showers of **b**, which will
36:37 I am ready to hear Israel's prayers for these **b**,
Zep 1:6 ask for the LORD's guidance or seek my **b**."
Zec 8:12 remnant in Judah and Israel the heirs of these **b**.
Mal 2:2 I will curse even the **b** you receive. Indeed, I have
Jn 1:16 We have all benefited from the rich **b** he brought
Ac 13:34 'I will give you the sacred **b** I promised to David.'
15:33 with the **b** of the Christians, to those who had sent
Ro 11:9 all is well. / Let their **b** cause them to stumble.
15:27 **b** of the Good News from the Jewish Christians,
1Co 9:23 the Good News, and in doing so I enjoy its **b**.
16:11 Send him on his way with your **b** when he returns
Eph 3:6 and enjoy together the promise of **b** through Christ
Php 1:7 We have shared together the **b** of God, both when I
1Pe 1:13 Look forward to the special **b** that will come to
Rev 21:7 All who are victorious will inherit all these **b**,

BLEW (24) [BLOW]

Ex 10:19 west wind that **b** the locusts out into the Red Sea.
14:21 The wind **b** all that night, turning the seabed into
Jdg 6:34 He **b** a ram's horn as a call to arms, and the men of
7:19 they **b** the horns and broke their clay jars.
7:20 Then all three groups **b** their horns and broke their
7:22 When the three hundred Israelites **b** their horns,
2Sa 2:28 So Joab **b** his trumpet, and his men stopped
18:16 Then Joab **b** the trumpet, and his men returned
20:1 a Benjaminite, **b** a trumpet and shouted, "We have
20:22 So he **b** the trumpet and called his troops back
2Ki 9:13 out their cloaks on the bare steps and **b** a trumpet,
2Ch 7:6 the priests **b** the trumpets, while all Israel stood.
13:14 LORD for help. Then the priests **b** the trumpets,
29:28 the LORD as the singers sang and the trumpets **b**,
Da 2:35 and the wind **b** them all away without a trace.
Hag 1:9 when you brought your harvest home, I **b** it away.
Ac 27:14 they called it) caught the ship and **b** it out to sea.
Rev 8:7 The first angel **b** his trumpet, and hail and fire
8:8 Then the second angel **b** his trumpet, and a great
8:10 Then the third angel **b** his trumpet, and a great
8:12 Then the fourth angel **b** his trumpet, and one-third
9:1 Then the fifth angel **b** his trumpet, and I saw a star
9:13 Then the sixth angel **b** his trumpet, and I heard a
11:15 Then the seventh angel **b** his trumpet, and there

BLIGHT (4)

Dt 28:22 and drought, and with **b** and mildew.
Isa 42:15 and hills / and bring a **b** on all their greenery.
Am 4:9 your farms and vineyards with **b** and mildew.
Hag 2:17 I sent **b** and mildew and hail to destroy all the

BLIND (98) [BLINDED, BLINDFOLDED, BLINDING, BLINDLY, BLINDNESS, BLINDS]

Ge 27:1 When Isaac was old and almost **b**, he called for
48:10 Now Jacob was half **b** because of his age
Lev 19:14 with respect and by not taking advantage of the **b**.
21:18 whether he is **b** or lame, stunted or deformed,
22:22 An animal that is **b**, injured, mutilated, or that has
Dt 15:21 such as being lame or **b**, or if anything else is
16:19 for bribes **b** the eyes of the wise and corrupt the
27:18 'Cursed is anyone who leads a **b** person astray on
28:29 just like a **b** person groping in the darkness,
1Sa 3:2 One night Eli, who was almost **b** by now, had just
4:15 who was ninety-eight years old and **b**.
2Sa 5:6 "Even the **b** and lame could keep you out!"
5:8 the city and destroy those 'lame' and '**b**' Jebusites.
5:8 "The **b** and the lame may not enter the house."
2Ki 6:18 Elisha prayed, "O LORD, please make them **b**."
Job 5:14 They grope in the daylight as though they were **b**;
29:15 I served as eyes for the **b** and feet for the lame.
Ps 36:2 In their **b** conceit, / they cannot see how wicked
38:10 beats wildly, my strength fails, / and I am going **b**.
69:23 Let their eyes go **b** so they cannot see, / and let
81:12 So I let them follow their **b** and stubborn way,
94:9 ears deaf? / Is the one who formed your eyes **b**?
146:8 The LORD opens the eyes of the **b**. / The LORD
Ecc 2:14 For the wise person sees, while the fool is **b**.
12:3 be too few to do their work, and you will be **b**, too.
Isa 29:9 Then go ahead and be **b** if you must. You are
29:18 and **b** people will see through the gloom
35:5 he will open the eyes of the **b** and unstop the ears
42:7 You will open the eyes of the **b** and free the
42:16 I will lead **b** Israel down a new path,
42:18 "Oh, how deaf and **b** you are toward me!
42:19 Who in all the world is as **b** as my own people,
42:19 Who is as **b** as my chosen people, the servant of
43:8 Bring out the people who have eyes but are **b**,
56:10 his shepherds—are **b** to every danger.
59:10 No wonder we grope like **b** people and stumble
Jer 5:26 lie in wait for victims like a hunter hiding in a **b**.
31:8 I will not forget the **b** and lame, the expectant
Zep 1:17 I will make you as helpless as a **b** man searching
Zec 11:17 become useless, and his right eye completely **b**!"
12:4 of Judah, but I will **b** the horses of her enemies.
Mal 1:8 When you give **b** animals as sacrifices, isn't that
Mt 9:27 two **b** men followed along behind him, shouting,
11:5 the **b** see, the lame walk, the lepers are cured,
12:22 who was both **b** and unable to talk, was brought to
15:14 They are **b** guides leading the **b**, and if one **b** person guides another, they will both
15:30 crowd brought him the lame, **b**, crippled, mute,
15:31 and those who had been **b** could see again!
18:9 It is better to enter heaven half **b** than to have two
20:30 Two **b** men were sitting beside the road.
21:14 The **b** and the lame came to him, and he healed
23:16 "**B** guides! How terrible it will be for you! For you
23:17 **B** fools! Which is greater, the gold, or the Temple
23:19 How **b**! For which is greater, the gift on the altar,
23:24 **B** guides! You strain your water so you won't
23:26 **B** Pharisees! First wash the inside of the cup,
Mk 8:22 some people brought a **b** man to Jesus, and they
8:23 Jesus took the **b** man by the hand and led him out
9:47 It is better to enter the Kingdom of God half **b** than
10:46 A **b** beggar named Bartimaeus (son of Timaeus)
10:49 So they called the **b** man. "Cheer up," they said.
10:51 "Teacher," the **b** man said, "I want to see!"
10:52 healed you." And instantly the **b** man could see!
Lk 4:18 that captives will be released, / that the **b** will see,
6:39 "What good is it for one **b** person to lead another?
7:21 he cast out evil spirits and restored sight to the **b**.
7:22 the **b** see, the lame walk, the lepers are cured,
14:13 invite the poor, the crippled, the lame, and the **b**.
14:21 invite the poor, the crippled, the lame, and the **b**.'
18:35 a **b** beggar was sitting beside the road.
Jn 5:3 **b**, lame, or paralyzed—lay on the porches.
9:1 he saw a man who had been **b** from birth.
9:2 disciples asked him, "why was this man born **b**?
9:3 "He was born **b** so the power of God could be
9:6 and smoothed the mud over the **b** man's eyes.
9:8 and others who knew him as a **b** beggar asked each
9:17 once again questioned the man who had been **b**
9:18 Jewish leaders wouldn't believe he had been **b**,
9:19 your son? Was he born **b**? If so, how can he see?"
9:20 "We know this is our son and that he was born **b**,
9:24 second time they called in the man who had been **b**
9:25 "But I know this: I was **b**, and now I can see!"
9:32 been able to open the eyes of someone born **b**.
9:39 I have come to give sight to the **b** and to show those who think they see that they are **b**."
9:40 heard him and asked, "Are you saying we are **b**?"
9:41 "If you were **b**, you wouldn't be guilty,"
10:21 a demon! Can a demon open the eyes of the **b**?"
11:37 But some said, "This man healed a **b** man.
Ac 9:8 himself up off the ground, he found that he was **b**.
9:9 He remained there **b** for three days. And all that
Ro 2:19 You are convinced that you are a guide for the **b**
11:10 Let their eyes go **b** so they cannot see, / and let
2Pe 1:9 But those who fail to develop these virtues are **b**
1Jn 2:11 they are going, for the darkness has made them **b**.
Rev 3:17 and miserable and poor and **b** and naked.

BLINDED (8) [BLIND]

Ge 19:11 Then they **b** the men of Sodom so they couldn't
Ex 21:26 a male or female slave in the eye and the eye is **b**,
Ps 88:9 My eyes are **b** by my tears. / Each day I beg for
Isa 21:3 I hear what God is planning; I am **b** with dismay.
62:2 your righteousness. Kings will be **b** by your glory.
Jn 12:40 "The Lord has **b** their eyes / and hardened their
Ac 22:11 "I was **b** by the intense light and had to be led into
2Co 4:4 has **b** the minds of those who don't believe,

BLINDFOLDED (2) [BLIND]

Mk 14:65 and they **b** him and hit his face with their fists.
Lk 22:64 They **b** him, then they hit him and asked,

BLINDING (1) [BLIND]

Am 5:9 With **b** speed and power he destroys the strong,

BLINDLY (3) [BLIND]

Pr 22:3 the simpleton goes **b** on and suffers the
27:12 The simpleton goes **b** on and suffers the
La 4:14 They wandered **b** through the streets, so defiled by

BLINDNESS (2) [BLIND]

Dt 28:28 will strike you with madness, **b**, and panic.
Ac 13:11 upon you, and you will be stricken awhile with **b**."

BLINDS (1) [BLIND]

Job 9:24 and God **b** the eyes of the judges and lets them be

BLINKING (1)

1Co 15:52 It will happen in a moment, in the **b** of an eye,

BLISTER (2) [BLISTERED]

Dt 8:4 didn't wear out, and your feet didn't **b** or swell.
Pr 6:28 Can he walk on hot coals and not **b** his feet?

BLISTERED (1) [BLISTER]

Eze 29:18 rubbed bare and their shoulders were raw and **b**.

BLOCK (14) [BLOCKED, BLOCKS]

Nu 22:22 of the LORD to stand in the road to **b** his way.
22:32 "I have come to **b** your way because you are
22:34 I did not realize you were standing in the road to **b**
Job 30:13 They **b** my road and do everything they can to
Ps 35:3 and javelin / and **b** the way of my enemies.
Isa 44:13 wood-carver measures and marks out a **b** of wood,
44:19 never stops to reflect, "Why, it's just a **b** of wood!
Eze 42:3 One **b** of rooms overlooked the 35-foot width of
42:3 Another **b** of rooms looked out onto the pavement
42:8 This wall added length to the outer **b** of rooms,
42:8 extended for only 87-1/2 feet, while the inner **b**—

42:12 the wall facing the doors of the inner **b** of rooms,
Hos 2:6 I will **b** the road to make her lose her way.
Zep 2:14 Rubble will **b** all the doorways, and the cedar

BLOCKED (6) [BLOCK]

2Ch 32:30 He **b** up the upper spring of Gihon and brought the
Job 19:8 God has **b** my way and plunged my path into
Jer 51:32 All the escape routes are **b**. The fortifications are
La 3:9 He has **b** my path with a high stone wall. He has
Eze 39:11 The path of those who travel there will be **b** by this
Da 10:13 spirit prince of the kingdom of Persia **b** my way.

BLOCKS (8) [BLOCK]

1Ki 5:17 and shaped costly **b** of stone for the foundation of
7:9 costly **b** of stone, cut and trimmed to exact
7:11 The costly **b** of stone used in the walls were also
1Ch 22:2 and he assigned them the task of preparing **b** of
Eze 42:3 The two **b** were built three levels high and stood
42:4 Between the two **b** of rooms ran a walkway 17-1/2
42:10 On the south side of the Temple there were two **b**
42:11 There was a walkway between the two **b** of rooms

BLOOD (289) [AKELDAMA, BLEEDING, BLOOD-SMEARED, BLOODBATH, BLOODIED, BLOODRED, BLOODSHED, BLOODSHOT, BLOODSTAINED, BLOODSTAINS, BLOODTHIRSTY, BLOODY, LIFEBLOOD, PURE-BLOODED]

FLESH AND BLOOD (7) Ge 29:14; Jdg 9:2; 2Sa 19:12; 1Co 15:50; Eph 6:12; Heb 2:14,14

Ge 4:10 your brother's **b** cries out to me from the ground!
4:11 the ground you have defiled with your brother's **b**.
29:14 "Just think, my very own flesh and **b**!"
37:22 "Why should we shed his **b**? Let's just throw him
37:31 brothers killed a goat and dipped the robe in its **b**.
Ex 4:9 the dry ground. When you do, it will turn into **b**."
7:17 the Nile with this staff, and the river will turn to **b**.
7:19 Everywhere in Egypt the water will turn into **b**,
7:20 of the Nile. Suddenly, the whole river turned to **b**!
7:21 There was **b** everywhere throughout the land of
7:22 their secret arts, and they, too, turned water into **b**.
7:25 time the LORD turned the water of the Nile to **b**.
12:7 They are to take some of the lamb's **b** and smear it
12:13 The **b** you have smeared on your doorposts will
12:13 as a sign. When I see the **b**, I will pass over you.
12:22 Drain each lamb's **b** into a basin. Then take a
12:22 of hyssop branches and dip it into the lamb's **b**.
12:22 and sides of the doorframe, staining it with the **b**.
12:23 But when he sees the **b** on the top and sides of the
23:18 "Sacrificial **b** must never be offered together with
24:6 Moses took half the **b** from these animals and drew
24:8 Then Moses sprinkled the **b** from the basins over
24:8 "This **b** confirms the covenant the LORD has
29:12 Smear some of its **b** on the horns of the altar with
29:16 Its **b** will be collected and sprinkled on the sides of
29:20 Collect the **b** and place some of it on the tip of the
29:20 Sprinkle the rest of the **b** on the sides of the altar.
29:21 Then take some of the **b** from the altar and mix it
30:10 **b** from the offering made for the atonement of sin.
Lev 1:5 will present the **b** by sprinkling it against the sides
1:11 will sprinkle its **b** against the sides of the altar.
1:15 then let its **b** drain out against the sides of the altar.
3:2 then sprinkle the animal's **b** against the sides of the
3:8 then sprinkle the sheep's **b** against the sides of the
3:13 Then the sons of Aaron will sprinkle the goat's **b**
3:17 "You must never eat any fat or **b**. This is a
4:5 then take some of the animal's **b** into the
4:6 dip his finger into the **b**, and sprinkle it seven times
4:7 The priest will put some of the **b** on the horns of
4:7 The rest of the bull's **b** must be poured out at the
4:16 The priest will bring some of its **b** into the
4:17 dip his finger into the **b**, and sprinkle it seven times
4:18 then put some of the **b** on the horns of the incense
4:18 The rest of the **b** must then be poured out at the
4:25 Then the priest will dip his finger into the **b** of the
4:25 and pour out the rest of the **b** at the base of the
4:30 The priest will then dip his finger into the **b**,
4:30 put the **b** on the horns of the altar of burnt
4:30 and pour out the rest of the **b** at the base of the
4:34 The priest will then dip his finger into the **b**,
4:34 and pour out the rest of the **b** at the base of the
5:9 Then he will sprinkle some of the **b** of the sin
6:27 and if the sacrificial **b** splatters anyone's clothing,
6:30 the **b** of a sin offering has been taken into the
7:2 and its **b** sprinkled against the sides of the altar.
7:14 the altar with **b** from the sacrificed animal.
7:26 you must never eat the **b** of any bird or animal.
7:27 Anyone who eats **b** must be cut off from the
7:33 always be given to the priest who sprinkles the **b**
8:15 Moses took some of the **b**, and with his finger he
8:15 He poured out the rest of the **b** at the base of the
8:19 Then Moses took the ram's **b** and sprinkled it
8:23 Then Moses took some of its **b** and put it on the
8:24 and put some of the **b** on the lobe of their right
8:24 then sprinkled the rest of the **b** against the sides of
8:30 and some of the **b** that was on the altar,
9:9 His sons brought him the **b**, and he dipped his
9:9 He poured out the rest of the **b** at the base of the
9:12 His sons brought him the **b**, and he sprinkled it
9:18 His sons brought him the **b**, and he sprinkled it
10:18 Since the animal's **b** was not taken into the Holy
12:4 purification from the **b** of childbirth is completed.
12:5 days to be purified from the **b** of childbirth.
14:6 hyssop branch, into the **b** of the slaughtered bird.
14:7 The priest will also sprinkle the dead bird's **b**
14:14 then take some of the **b** from the guilt offering
14:17 right foot, in addition to the **b** of the guilt offering.
14:25 and put some of its **b** on the tip of the person's
14:28 right foot, in addition to the **b** of the guilt offering.
14:51 and the living bird into the **b** of the slaughtered
15:25 "If the menstrual flow of **b** continues for many
15:25 or if she discharges **b** unrelated to her
16:14 Then he must dip his finger into the **b** of the bull
16:15 the people and bring its **b** behind the inner curtain.
16:15 There he will sprinkle the **b** on the atonement
16:15 front of the Ark, just as he did with the bull's **b**.
16:18 LORD by smearing some of the **b** from the bull
16:19 Then he must dip his finger into the **b** and sprinkle
16:27 whose **b** Aaron brought into the Most Holy Place
17:4 Such a person has shed **b** and must be cut off from
17:6 That way the priest will be able to sprinkle the **b**
17:10 among you, who eats or drinks **b** in any form.
17:11 for the life of any creature is in its **b**. I have given
you the **b** so you can make atonement
17:11 It is the **b**, representing life, that brings you
17:12 who live among you must never eat or drink **b**.'
17:13 you must drain out the **b** and cover it with earth.
17:14 The life of every creature is in the **b**. That is why I
17:14 for the life of any bird or animal is in the **b**.
17:14 So whoever eats or drinks **b** must be cut off.
19:26 "Never eat meat that has not been drained of its **b**.
Nu 18:17 Sprinkle their **b** on the altar, and burn their fat as
19:4 Eleazar will take some of its **b** on his finger
19:5 heifer must be burned—its hide, meat, **b**, and dung.
23:24 on prey, / drinking the **b** of the slaughtered!"
Dt 12:16 The only restriction is that you are not to eat the **b**.
12:23 The only restriction is never to eat the **b**,
12:23 for the **b** is the life, and you must not eat the life
12:24 Instead, pour out the **b** on the ground like water.
12:25 Do not eat the **b**; then all will go well with you
12:27 and **b** of your burnt offerings on the altar of the
12:27 The **b** of your other sacrifices must be poured out
15:23 But do not eat the **b**. You must pour it out on the
21:7 they must say, 'Our hands did not shed this **b**,
21:8 will be absolved of the guilt of this person's **b**.
32:42 I will make my arrows drunk with **b**, / and my
32:42 the **b** of the slaughtered and the captives,
32:43 for he will avenge the **b** of his servants.
Jdg 9:2 And remember, I am your own flesh and **b**!"
1Sa 14:32 but they ate them without draining the **b**.
14:33 the LORD by eating meat that still has **b** in it."
14:34 and sheep here to kill them and drain the **b**.
14:34 by eating meat with the **b** still in it.' "
2Sa 19:12 my relatives, my own tribe, my own flesh and **b**!
20:12 But Amasa lay in his **b** in the middle of the road,
23:17 "This water is as precious as the **b** of these men
1Ki 2:5 staining his belt and sandals with the **b** of war.
2:37 will surely die; your **b** will be on your own head."
18:28 with knives and swords until the **b** gushed out.
21:19 dogs will lick your **b** outside the city just as they
licked the **b** of Naboth!' "
22:35 The **b** from his wound ran down to the floor of his
22:38 and dogs came and licked the king's **b**,
2Ki 3:22 across the water, making it look as red as **b**.
3:23 "It's **b**!" the Moabites exclaimed. "The three
9:33 and some of her **b** spattered against the wall
16:13 over it, and sprinkled the **b** of peace offerings on it.
16:15 The **b** from the burnt offerings and sacrifices
21:16 filled from one end to the other with innocent **b**.
24:4 He had filled Jerusalem with innocent **b**,
1Ch 11:19 "This water is as precious as the **b** of these men
22:8 And since you have shed so much **b** before me,
28:3 for you are a warrior and have shed much **b**.'
2Ch 29:22 and the priests took the **b** and sprinkled it on the
29:22 killed the rams and sprinkled their **b** on the altar.
29:24 and sprinkled their **b** on the altar to make
30:16 The Levites brought the sacrificial **b** to the priests,
35:11 Passover lambs and presented the **b** to the priests,
35:11 who sprinkled the **b** on the altar while the Levites
Job 16:13 me without mercy. The ground is wet with my **b**.
16:18 "O earth, do not conceal my **b**. Let it cry out on
20:25 from his body, and the arrowhead glistens with **b**.
39:30 Its nestlings gulp down **b**, for it feeds on the
Ps 50:13 bulls you sacrifice; / I don't need the **b** of goats.
51:14 Forgive me for shedding **b**, O God who saves;
58:10 They will wash their feet in the **b** of the wicked.
68:23 You, my people, will wash your feet in their **b**,
78:44 For he turned their rivers into **b**, / so no one could
79:3 **B** has flowed like water all around Jerusalem;
79:10 for they have spilled the **b** of your servants.
105:29 He turned the nation's water into **b**, / poisoning all
106:38 They shed innocent **b**, / the **b** of their sons and
daughters.
Isa 1:11 I don't want to see the **b** from your offerings of
1:15 For your hands are covered with the **b** of your
15:9 The stream near Dibon runs red with **b**, but I am
29:2 as her name Ariel means—an altar covered with **b**.
34:3 fill the land. The mountains will flow with their **b**.
34:6 The sword of the LORD is drenched with **b**.
34:7 The land will be soaked with **b** and the soil
49:26 They will be drunk with rivers of their own **b**.
63:3 my foes. It is their **b** that has stained my clothes.
66:3 bad as putting a dog or the **b** of a pig on the altar!
Jer 2:34 Your clothing is stained with the **b** of the innocent
18:21 children starve! Let the sword pour out their **b**!
19:4 And they have filled this place with the **b** of
46:10 devour until it is satisfied, yes, drunk with your **b**!
48:10 who hold back their swords from shedding **b**!
51:35 be paid in full for all the **b** they spilled,"
La 4:13 who defiled the city by shedding innocent **b**.
4:14 so defiled by **b** that no one dared to touch them.
Eze 3:18 hold you responsible, demanding your **b** for theirs.
3:20 hold you responsible, demanding your **b** for theirs.
16:6 you there, helplessly kicking about in your own **b**.
16:9 "Then I bathed you and washed off your **b**, and I
16:22 lay naked in a field, kicking about in your own **b**.
16:38 I will cover you with **b** in my jealous fury.
21:32 and your **b** will be spilled in your own land.
24:7 leaving **b** on the rocks for all to see.
24:8 So I will splash her **b** on a rock as an open
28:23 against you, and **b** will be spilled in your streets.
32:6 I will drench the earth with your gushing **b** all the
33:25 You eat meat with **b** in it, you worship idols,
35:6 since you show no distaste for **b**,
39:17 of Israel, and there eat the flesh and drink the **b**!
39:18 and drink the **b** of princes as though they were
39:19 until you are glutted; drink **b** until you are drunk.
43:18 and the sprinkling of **b** when the altar is built.
43:20 You will take some of its **b** and smear it on the
44:7 offered me my food, the fat and **b** of sacrifices.
44:15 and offer the fat and **b** of the sacrifices,
45:19 The priest will take some of the **b** of this sin
Hos 6:8 is a city of sinners, tracked with footprints of **b**.
Joel 2:30 and on the earth—**b** and fire and pillars of smoke.
Mic 4:11 calling for your **b**, eager to gloat over your
Zep 1:17 Your **b** will be poured out into the dust, and your
Zec 9:7 They will no longer eat meat with **b** in it or feed on
9:11 of the covenant I made with you, sealed with **b**,
9:15 drunk with wine, shedding the **b** of their enemies.
9:15 They will be filled with **b** like a bowl,
9:15 drenched with **b** like the corners of the altar.
Mt 26:28 for this is my **b**, which seals the covenant between
27:8 That is why the field is still called the Field of **B**.
27:24 saying, "I am innocent of the **b** of this man.
Mk 14:24 And he said to them, "This is my **b**, poured out for
Lk 22:20 an agreement sealed with the **b** I will pour out for
22:44 his sweat fell to the ground like great drops of **b**.
Jn 6:53 eat the flesh of the Son of Man and drink his **b**,
6:54 who eat my flesh and drink my **b** have eternal life,
6:55 flesh is the true food, and my **b** is the true drink.
6:56 All who eat my flesh and drink my **b** remain in me,
19:34 his side with a spear, and **b** and water flowed out.
Ac 1:19 name *Akeldama,* which means "Field of **B**.")
2:19 the earth below—/ **b** and fire and clouds of smoke.
15:20 and from consuming **b** or eating the meat of
15:29 from consuming **b** or eating the meat of strangled
18:6 and said, "Your **b** be upon your own heads—
20:28 God's flock—his church, purchased with his **b**—
21:25 nor consume **b**, nor eat meat from strangled
Ro 3:25 with God when we believe that Jesus shed his **b**,
5:9 been made right in God's sight by the **b** of Christ,
1Co 10:16 aren't we sharing in the benefits of the **b** of Christ?
11:25 and you, sealed by the shedding of my **b**.
11:27 of sinning against the body and the **b** of the Lord.
15:50 and **b** cannot inherit the Kingdom of God.
Eph 1:7 purchased our freedom through the **b** of his Son,
2:13 brought near to him because of the **b** of Christ.
6:12 not fighting against people made of flesh and **b**,
Col 1:14 God has purchased our freedom with his **b** and has
1:20 and on earth by means of his **b** on the cross.
Heb 2:14 made of flesh and **b**—Jesus also became flesh and
b by being born in human form.
9:7 and only once a year, and always with **b**, which he
9:12 Once for all time he took **b** into that Most Holy
Place, but not the **b** of goats and calves. He took
his own **b**, and with it he secured our
9:13 the **b** of goats and bulls and the ashes of a young
9:14 Just think how much more the **b** of Christ will
9:18 That is why **b** was required under the first
9:19 he took the **b** of calves and goats, along with
9:20 "This **b** confirms the covenant God has made with
9:21 he sprinkled **b** on the sacred tent and on everything
9:22 everything was purified by sprinkling with **b**.
9:22 Without the shedding of **b**, there is no forgiveness
9:23 in heaven—had to be purified by the **b** of animals.
9:23 with far better sacrifices than the **b** of animals.
9:25 Place year after year to offer the **b** of an animal.
10:4 For it is not possible for the **b** of bulls and goats to
10:19 Most Holy Place because of the **b** of Jesus.
10:22 been sprinkled with Christ's **b** to make us clean,
10:29 and have treated the **b** of the covenant as if it were
11:28 and to sprinkle **b** on the doorposts so that the angel
12:24 between God and people, and to the sprinkled **b**,
12:24 of crying out for vengeance as the **b** of Abel did.
13:11 the high priest brought the **b** of animals into the
13:12 to make his people holy by shedding his own **b**.
13:20[-21] by an everlasting covenant, signed with his **b**.
1Pe 1:2 obeyed Jesus Christ and are cleansed by his **b**.
1Jn 1:7 and the **b** of Jesus, his Son, cleanses us from every
5:6 in water and by shedding his **b** on the cross—not
by water only, but by water and **b**.
5:8 the Spirit, the water, and the **b**—and all three
Rev 1:5 and has freed us from our sins by shedding his **b**
5:9 and your **b** has ransomed people for God
6:10 When will you avenge our **b** against these
6:12 as black cloth, and the moon became as red as **b**.
7:14 They washed their robes in the **b** of the Lamb
8:7 and fire mixed with **b** were thrown down upon the
8:8 And one-third of the water in the sea became **b**.
11:6 have the power to turn the rivers and oceans into **b**,
12:11 because of the **b** of the Lamb and because of their
14:20 and **b** flowed from the winepress in a stream about
16:3 on the sea, and it became like the **b** of a corpse.
16:4 bowl on the rivers and springs, and they became **b**.
16:6 and their **b** was poured out on the earth.
16:6 So you have given their murderers **b** to drink.
17:6 drunk with the **b** of God's holy people who were

18:24 In her streets the **b** of the prophets was spilled.
19:13 He was clothed with a robe dipped in **b**, and his

BLOOD-SMEARED (2) [BLOOD]
Ex 4:25 and said, "What a **b** bridegroom you are to me!"
4:26 (When she called Moses a "**b** bridegroom,"

BLOODBATH (1) [BLOOD]
Eze 35:6 distaste for blood, I will give you a **b** of your own.

BLOODGUILTINESS [KJV] See BLOOD

BLOODIED (2) [BLOOD]
Isa 52:14 beaten and **b**, so disfigured one would scarcely
Eze 7:23 for my people, for the land is **b** by terrible crimes.

BLOODRED (2) [BLOOD]
Joel 2:31 and the moon will turn **b** before that great
Ac 2:20 be turned into darkness, / and the moon will turn **b**,

BLOODSHED (6) [BLOOD]
Dt 22:8 That way you will not bring the guilt of **b** on your
1Sa 25:31 conscience the staggering burden of needless **b**
2Sa 14:11 I want no more **b**." "As surely as the LORD
Isa 5:7 to yield a crop of justice, / but instead he found **b**.
Eze 22:13 in indignation over your dishonest gain and **b**.
38:22 punish you and your hordes with disease and **b**;

BLOODSHOT (1) [BLOOD]
Pr 23:29 Who has unnecessary bruises? Who has **b** eyes?

BLOODSTAINED (2) [BLOOD]
Isa 9:5 Never again will uniforms be **b** by war. All such
Mal 2:16 "It is as cruel as putting on a victim's **b** coat,"

BLOODSTAINS (1) [BLOOD]
Isa 4:4 He will cleanse Jerusalem of its **b** by a spirit of

BLOODTHIRSTY (1) [BLOOD]
Pr 29:10 The **b** hate the honest, but the upright seek out the

BLOODY (2) [BLOOD]
1Ki 2:9 and you will know how to arrange a **b** death for
Eze 36:17 To me their conduct was as filthy as a **b** rag.

BLOOM (2) [BLOOMS]
Ex 9:31 because the barley was ripe and the flax was in **b**.
Ps 103:15 are like grass; / like wildflowers, we **b** and die.

BLOOMS (1) [BLOOM]
Ps 90:6 In the morning it **b** and flourishes, / but by evening

BLOSSOM (18) [BLOSSOMED, BLOSSOMING, BLOSSOMS]
Ge 40:10 It had three branches that began to bud and **b**,
Ex 25:33 branches will hold a cup shaped like an almond **b**,
25:35 One **b** will be set beneath each pair of branches
37:19 six branches held a cup shaped like an almond **b**,
37:21 One **b** was set beneath each pair of branches,
1Ki 7:26 its rim flared out like a cup and resembled a lily **b**.
2Ch 4:5 its rim flared out like a cup and resembled a lily **b**.
Job 14:2 Like a flower, we **b** for a moment and then wither.
Ps 65:12 a lush pasture, / and the hillsides **b** with joy.
92:7 flourish like weeds, / and evildoers **b** with success,
SS 2:13 fig trees are budding, and the grapevines are in **b**.
2:15 of your love, for the grapevines are all in **b**."
Isa 17:11 so well that they **b** on the very morning you plant
27:6 Israel will bud and **b** and fill the whole earth with
35:1 in those days. The desert will **b** with flowers.
51:3 will comfort Israel again and make her deserts **b**.
Hos 14:5 It will **b** like the lily; it will send roots deep into
14:7 They will flourish like grain and **b** like grapevines.

BLOSSOMED (1) [BLOSSOM]
Nu 17:8 of Levi, had sprouted, **b**, and produced almonds!

BLOSSOMING (1) [BLOSSOM]
SS 6:11 budding yet, or whether the pomegranates were **b**.

BLOSSOMS (8) [BLOSSOM]
Ex 25:31 the base, center stem, lamp cups, buds, and **b**.
25:34 lampstand will be decorated with four almond **b**,
37:17 Its base, center stem, lamp cups, **b**, and buds were
37:20 lampstand was also decorated with four almond **b**.
Nu 8:4 entire lampstand, from its base to its decorative **b**,
Job 15:33 like an olive tree that sheds its **b** so the fruit cannot
SS 7:12 the vines have budded, whether the **b** have opened,
Hab 3:17 Even though the fig trees have no **b**, and there are

BLOT (12) [BLOTS, BLOTTED, BLOTTING]
Ex 17:14 I will **b** out every trace of Amalek from under
32:32 then **b** me out of the record you are keeping."
32:33 "I will **b** out whoever has sinned against me.
2Ki 14:27 because the LORD had not said he would **b** out
Ne 4:5 Do not **b** out their sins, for they have provoked you
Ps 51:1 your great compassion, / **b** out the stain of my sins.
Isa 5:30 hover over Israel. The clouds will **b** out the light.
Jer 5:18 "Yet even in those days I will not **b** you out
18:23 Don't forgive their crimes and **b** out their sins.
49:28 against Kedar! **B** out the warriors from the East!
Eze 13:9 I will **b** their names from Israel's record books,
32:7 When I **b** you out, I will veil the heavens

BLOTS (1) [BLOT]
Isa 43:25 am the one who **b** out your sins for my own sake

BLOTTED (3) [BLOT]
Job 3:6 Let that night be **b** off the calendar, never again to
Ps 109:13 May his family name be **b** out in a single
La 2:6 The LORD has **b** out all memory of the holy

BLOTTING (1) [BLOT]
Ac 27:20 **b** out the sun and the stars, until at last all hope

BLOW (34) [BLEW, BLOWING, BLOWN, BLOWS, DEATHBLOW]
Ge 8:1 He sent a wind to **b** across the waters,
Ex 10:13 and the LORD caused an east wind to **b** all that
Lev 25:9 **b** the trumpets loud and long throughout the land.
Nu 10:7 **b** the trumpets using a different signal.
10:8 are allowed to **b** the trumpets.
10:10 **B** the trumpets in times of gladness, too,
Jdg 7:18 those of you on the other sides of the camp **b** your
1Ki 1:34 Then **b** the trumpets and shout, 'Long live King
1Ch 15:24 were chosen to **b** the trumpets as they marched in
2Ch 13:12 His priests **b** their trumpets and lead us into battle
21:14 your wives, and all that is yours with a heavy **b**.
Ezr 3:10 and took their places to **b** their trumpets.
Job 28:25 He made the winds **b** and determined how much
Ps 35:5 **B** them away like chaff in the wind—/ a wind sent
83:13 O my God, **b** them away like whirling dust,
Pr 30:33 and a **b** to the nose causes bleeding, so anger
SS 4:16 **B** on my garden and waft its lovely perfume to my
Isa 18:3 the world take notice. When I **b** the trumpet, listen!
19:7 along the riverbank will wither and **b** away.
41:16 them in the air, and the wind will **b** them all away;
Jer 6:29 The bellows **b** fiercely. The refining fire grows
Eze 7:5 With one **b** after another I will bring total disaster!
7:9 know that it is I, the LORD, who is striking the **b**.
21:31 on you and **b** on you with the fire of my anger.
22:21 you together and **b** the fire of my anger upon you,
Hos 5:8 "**B** the ram's horn in Gibeah! Sound the alarm in
13:15 It will **b** hard against the people of Ephraim,
Joel 2:1 **B** the trumpet in Jerusalem! Sound the alarm on
2:15 **B** the trumpet in Jerusalem! Announce a time of
Jnh 4:8 God sent a scorching east wind to **b** on Jonah.
Na 1:9 He will destroy you with one **b**; he won't need to
Lk 8:13 but they wilt when the hot winds of testing **b**.
Rev 8:6 seven trumpets prepared to **b** their mighty blasts.
8:13 when the last three angels **b** their trumpets."

BLOWING (18) [BLOW]
Jos 6:4 the city seven times, with the priests **b** the horns.
6:8 of the LORD, **b** the horns as they marched.
6:9 the Ark, with the priests continually **b** the horns.
6:13 in front of the Ark of the LORD, **b** their horns.
2Sa 6:15 the LORD with much shouting and **b** of trumpets.
2Ki 11:14 all over the land were rejoicing and **b** trumpets.
1Ch 15:28 the **b** of horns and trumpets, the crashing of
2Ch 23:13 all over the land were rejoicing and **b** trumpets.
Ps 68:14 like a **b** snowstorm on Mount Zalmon.
Jer 4:11 "A burning wind is **b** in from the desert.
13:24 just as chaff is scattered by the winds **b** in from the
51:2 will come and winnow her, **b** her away as chaff.
Da 7:2 with strong winds **b** from every direction.
Mt 6:2 **b** trumpets in the synagogues and streets to call
Ac 27:13 When a light wind began **b** from the south,
28:13 A day later a south wind began **b**, so the following
Jude 1:12 They are like clouds **b** over dry land without
Rev 7:1 holding back the four winds from **b** upon the earth.

BLOWN (13) [BLOW]
Nu 10:3 When both trumpets are **b**, the people will know
10:4 But if only one is **b**, then only the leaders of the
1Ki 1:39 Then the trumpets were **b**, and all the people
Job 13:25 Would you terrify a leaf that is **b** by the wind?
27:20 and they are **b** away in the storms of the night.
Ps 68:2 Drive them off like smoke **b** by the wind.
Isa 27:8 He has exiled her from her land as though **b** away
30:24 its chaff having been **b** away by the wind.
38:12 My life has been **b** away / like a shepherd's tent in
Hos 13:3 like chaff **b** by the wind, like smoke from a
Zep 2:2 and your opportunity is **b** away like chaff.
1Co 15:52 the blinking of an eye, when the last trumpet is **b**.
2Pe 2:17 springs of water or as clouds **b** away by the wind—

BLOWS (16) [BLOW]
Lev 26:8 All your enemies will fall beneath the **b** of your
Dt 6:22 dealing terrifying **b** against Egypt and Pharaoh
Jdg 7:18 As soon as my group **b** the rams' horns, those of
Job 39:24 and rushes forward into battle when the trumpet **b**.
Ps 38:2 have struck deep, / and your **b** are crushing me.
39:10 I am exhausted by the **b** from your hand.
103:16 The wind **b**, and we are gone—/ as though we had
Ecc 1:6 The wind **b** south and north, here and there,
Isa 14:6 You persecuted the people with unceasing **b** of
40:24 when he **b** on them and their work withers.
Eze 17:10 away completely when the east wind **b** against it.
23:33 You will reel like a drunkard beneath the awful **b**
33:3 enemy coming, he **b** the alarm to warn the people.
Lk 12:55 When the south wind **b**, you say, 'Today will be a
1Pe 2:20 suffer for doing right and are patient beneath the **b**,
Rev 10:7 But when the seventh angel **b** his trumpet,

BLUE (51)
Ex 25:4 **b**, purple, and scarlet yarn; fine linen; goat hair for
26:1 These sheets are to be decorated with **b**, purple,
26:4 Put loops of **b** yarn along the edge of the last sheet
26:31 skillfully embroidered into the cloth using **b**,
26:36 designs into it, using **b**, purple, and scarlet yarn.
27:16 and decorate it with beautiful embroidery in **b**,
28:5 and embroidered with gold thread and **b**,
28:6 and skillfully embroidered with gold thread and **b**,
28:8 linen cloth embroidered with gold thread and **b**,
28:15 linen cloth embroidered with gold thread and **b**,
28:28 chestpiece to the rings on the ephod with **b** cords.
28:31 "Make the robe of the ephod entirely of **b** cloth,
28:33 Make pomegranates out of **b**, purple, and scarlet
28:37 the front of Aaron's turban by means of a **b** cord.
35:6 **b**, purple, and scarlet yarn; fine linen; goat hair for
35:23 Others brought **b**, purple, and scarlet yarn,
35:25 were skilled in sewing and spinning prepared **b**,
35:35 designers, weavers, and embroiderers in **b**, purple,
36:8 One of the craftsmen then embroidered **b**, purple,
36:11 Fifty **b** loops were placed along the edge of the last
36:35 were skillfully embroidered into it with **b**,
36:37 made of fine linen cloth and embroidered with **b**,
38:18 made of fine linen cloth and embroidered with **b**,
38:23 designing, and embroidering **b**, purple,
39:1 the craftsmen made beautiful garments of **b**,
39:2 and embroidered with gold thread and **b**,
39:3 then embroidered it into the linen with the **b**,
39:5 fine linen cloth; **b**, purple, and scarlet yarn;
39:8 and embroidered with gold thread and **b**,
39:21 **B** cords were used to attach the bottom rings of the
39:22 The robe of the ephod was woven entirely of **b**
39:24 These were finely crafted of **b**, purple, and scarlet
39:29 made of fine linen cloth and embroidered with **b**,
39:31 This medallion was tied to the turban with a **b**
Nu 4:6 and the goatskin leather with a dark **b** cloth.
4:7 "Next they must spread a **b** cloth over the table,
4:9 they must cover the lampstand with a dark **b** cloth,
4:11 and his sons must also spread a dark **b** cloth over
4:12 of the sanctuary must be wrapped in a dark **b** cloth,
15:38 and attach the tassels at each corner with a **b** cord.
2Ch 2:7 who is expert at dyeing purple, scarlet, and **b** cloth;
2:14 **b**, and scarlet cloth and in working with linen.
3:14 Solomon hung a curtain made of fine linen and **b**,
Est 1:6 beautifully woven white and **b** linen hangings,
8:15 Then Mordecai put on the royal robe of **b**
Eze 1:26 was what looked like a throne made of **b** sapphire.
10:1 I saw what appeared to be a throne of **b** sapphire
23:6 captains and commanders dressed in handsome **b**,
27:7 You stood beneath **b** and purple awnings made
27:24 **b** cloth, embroidery, and many-colored carpets
Rev 9:17 armor that was fiery red and sky **b** and yellow.

BLURRED (2)
Ps 6:7 My vision is **b** by grief; / my eyes are worn out
31:9 My sight is **b** because of my tears. / My body

BLURTED (2)
Mt 17:4 Peter **b** out, "Lord, this is wonderful! If you want
Lk 9:33 he was saying, **b** out, "Master, this is wonderful!

BLUSH (4)
Ezr 9:6 I am utterly ashamed; I **b** to lift up my face to you.
Isa 1:29 You will **b** when you think of all the sins you
Jer 6:15 No, not at all—they don't even **b**! Therefore,
8:12 No, not at all—they don't even **b**! Therefore,

BLUSTERING (1)
Job 8:2 will you go on like this? Your words are a **b** wind.

BOAR (1)
Ps 80:13 The **b** from the forest devours us, / and the wild

BOARD (4) [ABOARD, BOARDED]
Eze 27:27 everyone on **b** sinks into the depths of the sea.
Jnh 1:3 He bought a ticket and went on **b**, hoping that by
Ac 27:6 that was bound for Italy, and he put us on **b**.
28:10 people put on **b** all sorts of things we would need

BOARDED (3) [BOARD]
Ac 16:11 We **b** a boat at Troas and sailed straight across to
20:6 we **b** a ship at Philippi in Macedonia and five days
21:2 There we **b** a ship sailing for the Syrian province

BOAST (52) [BOASTED, BOASTFUL, BOASTFULLY, BOASTING, BOASTS]
Jdg 7:2 the Israelites will **b** to me that they saved
1Ki 20:11 "A warrior still dressing for battle should not **b**
Ps 20:7 Some nations **b** of their armies and weapons, / but we **b** in the LORD our God.
34:2 I will **b** only in the LORD; / let all who are
49:6 They trust in their wealth / and **b** of great riches.
49:20 People who **b** of their wealth don't understand
52:1 do you? / Why **b** about this crime of yours,
73:9 They **b** against the very heavens, / and their words
94:4 Hear their arrogance! / How these evildoers **b**!
Isa 5:22 who **b** about all the liquor they can hold.
10:15 Can the ax **b** greater power than the person who
19:11 and wrong. Will they still **b** of their wisdom?

28:15 You **b** that you have struck a bargain to avoid
45:25 of Israel will be justified, and in him they will **b**.
61: 6 treasures of the nations and will **b** in their riches.
Jer 9:24 Let them **b** in this alone: that they truly know me
48:14 "You used to **b**, 'We are heroes, mighty men of
La 2:17 enemies to rejoice over her and **b** of their power.
Eze 28: 2 not a god, though you **b** that you are like a god.
28: 9 Will you then **b**, 'I am a god!' to those who kill
Da 11:37 for he will **b** that he is greater than them all.
Am 6:13 You **b**, "Didn't we take Karnaim by our own
Ro 2:17 You **b** that all is well between yourself and God.
3:27 Can we **b**, then, that we have done anything to be
4: 2 If so, he would have had something to **b** about.
15:18 I dare not **b** of anything else. I have brought the
1Co 1:29 so that no one can ever **b** in the presence of God.
1:31 the Scriptures say, / "The person who wishes to **b** should **b** only of what the Lord has done."
4: 7 why **b** as though you have accomplished
5: 6 How terrible that you should **b** about your
9:16 the Good News is not something I can **b** about.
13: 3 and even sacrificed my body, I could **b** about it;
2Co 10:13 But we will not **b** of authority we do not have.
10:17 the Scriptures say, / "The person who wishes to **b** should **b** only of what the Lord has done."
10:18 When people **b** about themselves, it doesn't count
11:12 feet of those who **b** that their work is just like ours.
11:16 would to a foolish person, while I also **b** a little.
11:18 And since others **b** about their human
11:21 But whatever they dare to **b** about—I'm talking like a fool again—I can **b** about it, too.
11:30 If I must **b**, I would rather **b** about the things that show how
12: 5 do it. I am going to **b** only about my weaknesses.
12: 6 I have plenty to **b** about and would be no fool in
12: 9 So now I am glad to **b** about my weaknesses,
Gal 6:14 God forbid that I should **b** about anything except
Eph 2: 9 things we have done, so none of us can **b** about it.
Php 1:26 you will have even more reason to **b** about what
3: 3 we **b** about what Christ Jesus has done for us.

BOASTED (6) [BOAST]

Est 5:11 and **b** to them about his great wealth and his many
Isa 20: 5 power of Ethiopia and **b** of their allies in Egypt!
Jer 48:42 be a nation, for she has **b** against the LORD.
La 4:20 We had foolishly **b** that under his protection we
Eze 35:13 In saying that, you **b** proudly against me, and I
Zep 2:15 all the world there is no city as great as I," it **b**.

BOASTFUL (5) [BOAST]

Isa 25: 5 So the **b** songs of ruthless people are stilled.
Da 7:11 because I could hear the little horn's **b** speech.
Ro 1:30 haters of God, insolent, proud, and **b**.
1Co 13: 4 and kind. Love is not jealous or **b** or proud
2Ti 3: 2 They will be **b** and proud, scoffing at God,

BOASTFULLY (2) [BOAST]

Pr 17:19 loves sin; anyone who speaks **b** invites disaster.
Ob 1: 3 us way up here?' you ask **b**. Don't fool yourselves!

BOASTING (20) [BOAST]

Ps 17:10 They are without pity. / Listen to their **b**.
75: 4 "I warned the proud, 'Stop your **b**!' / I told the
Isa 10:16 Because of all your evil **b**, the Lord, the LORD
Jer 46: 8 **b** that it will cover the earth like a flood,
Da 7: 8 human eyes and a mouth that was **b** arrogantly.
7:20 human eyes and a mouth that was **b** arrogantly.
Zec 13: 4 "No one will be **b** then of a prophetic gift! No one
Jn 8:54 Jesus answered, "If I am merely **b** about myself,
2Co 7:14 and now my **b** to Titus has also proved true!
8:24 and prove to all the churches that our **b** about you
9: 2 and I have been **b** to our friends in Macedonia that
9: 3 I don't want it to turn out that I was wrong in my **b**
10: 8 I may seem to be **b** too much about the authority
11:10 I will never stop **b** about this all over Greece.
12: 1 This **b** is all so foolish, but let me go on. Let me
12: 5 That experience is something worth **b** about,
12:11 You have made me act like a fool—**b** like this.
Jas 4:16 Otherwise you will be **b** about your own plans, and all such **b** is evil.
2Pe 2:18 They brag about themselves with empty, foolish **b**.

BOASTS (5) [BOAST]

Isa 10:13 He **b**, "By my own power and wisdom I have won
Jer 21:13 I will fight against this city of Jerusalem that **b**,
48:30 says the LORD, "but her **b** are false;
Hos 12: 8 Israel **b**, "I am rich, and I've gotten it all by
Rev 18: 7 and sorrows. She **b**, 'I am queen on my throne.

BOAT (70) [BOATS, LIFEBOAT, SAILBOATS]

Ge 6:14 "Make a **b** from resinous wood and seal it with tar,
6:16 Construct an opening all the way around the **b**,
6:16 Then put three decks inside the **b**—bottom, middle,
6:18 But I solemnly swear to keep you safe in the **b**,
6:19 into the **b** with you to keep them alive during the
7: 1 "Go into the **b** with all your family, for among all
7: 7 and he went aboard the **b** to escape—he and his
7: 9 They came into the **b** in pairs, male and female,
7:13 But Noah had gone into the **b** that very day with
7:14 With them in the **b** were pairs of every kind of
7:15 Two by two they came into the **b**,
7:17 the ground and lifting the **b** high above the earth.
7:18 the ground, the **b** floated safely on the surface.
7:23 along with those who were with him in the **b**.
8: 1 remembered Noah and all the animals in the **b**.
8: 4 the **b** came to rest on the mountains of Ararat.
8: 6 Noah opened the window he had made in the **b**
8: 9 So it returned to the **b**, and Noah held out his hand
8:16 "Leave the **b**, all of you.
8:18 his wife, and his sons and their wives left the **b**.
Job 9:26 It disappears like a swift **b**, like an eagle that
Jnh 1:13 the sailors tried even harder to row the **b** ashore.
Mt 4:21 and John, sitting in a **b** with their father, Zebedee,
4:22 leaving the **b** and their father behind.
8:23 Then Jesus got into the **b** and started across the
8:24 storm came up, with waves breaking into the **b**.
9: 1 Jesus climbed into a **b** and went back across the
13: 2 He got into a **b**, where he sat and taught as the
14:13 he went off by himself in a **b** to a remote area to be
14:14 A vast crowd was there as he stepped from the **b**,
14:22 Jesus made his disciples get back into the **b**
14:29 So Peter went over the side of the **b** and walked on
14:32 And when they climbed back into the **b**, the wind
15:39 and he got into a **b** and crossed over to the region
24:38 weddings right up to the time Noah entered his **b**.
Mk 1:19 James and John, in a **b** mending their nets.
1:20 in the **b** with the hired men and went with him.
3: 9 Jesus instructed his disciples to bring around a **b**
4: 1 a large crowd along the shore that he got into a **b**
4:36 He was already in the **b**, so they started out,
4:37 High waves began to break into the **b** until it was
4:38 Jesus was sleeping at the back of the **b** with his
5: 2 Just as Jesus was climbing from the **b**, a man
5:18 When Jesus got back into the **b**, the man who had
6:32 They left by **b** for a quieter spot.
6:34 A vast crowd was there as he stepped from the **b**,
6:45 Jesus made his disciples get back into the **b**
6:47 the disciples were in their **b** out in the middle of
6:51 Then he climbed into the **b**, and the wind stopped.
6:53 on the other side of the lake, they anchored the **b**
8:10 he got into a **b** with his disciples and crossed over
8:13 So he got back into the **b** and left them, and he
8:14 was only one loaf of bread with them in the **b**.
Lk 5: 3 So he sat in the **b** and taught the crowds from
5: 7 shout for help brought their partners in the other **b**,
8:22 of the lake." So they got into a **b** and started out.
8:27 As Jesus was climbing out of the **b**, a man who
8:37 So Jesus returned to the **b** and left, crossing back to
17:27 weddings right up to the time Noah entered his **b**
Jn 6:17 they got into the **b** and headed out across the lake
6:19 they saw Jesus walking on the water toward the **b**.
6:21 and immediately the **b** arrived at their destination!
6:22 and that the disciples had gone off in their **b**,
21: 3 So they went out in the **b**, but they caught nothing
21: 6 out your net on the right-hand side of the **b**,
21: 8 The others stayed with the **b** and pulled the loaded
Ac 16:11 We boarded a **b** at Troas and sailed straight across
27: 2 We left on a **b** whose home port was Adramyttium;
27:32 So the soldiers cut the ropes and let the **b** fall off.
1Pe 3:20 waited patiently while Noah was building his **b**.

BOATS (8) [BOAT]

Isa 2:16 trading ships and all the small **b** in the harbor.
18: 2 and ambassadors are sent in fast **b** down the Nile.
Mk 4:36 leaving the crowds behind (although other **b**
Lk 5: 2 He noticed two empty **b** at the water's edge,
5: 3 Stepping into one of the **b**, Jesus asked Simon,
5: 7 and soon both **b** were filled with fish and on the
Jn 6:23 Several **b** from Tiberias landed near the place
6:24 they got into the **b** and went across to Capernaum

BOAZ (38) [BOAZ'S]

Ru 2: 1 and influential man in Bethlehem named **B**,
2: 3 found herself working in a field that belonged to **B**,
2: 4 **B** arrived from Bethlehem and greeted the
2: 5 Then **B** asked his foreman, "Who is that girl over
2: 8 **B** went over and said to Ruth, "Listen,
2:11 "Yes, I know," **B** replied. "But I also know about
2:14 At lunchtime **B** called to her, "Come over here
2:14 she sat with his harvesters, and **B** gave her food—
2:15 back to work again, **B** ordered his young men,
2:19 "The man I worked with today is named **B**."
2:21 **B** even told me to come back and stay with his
3: 2 **B** is a close relative of ours, and he's been very
3: 3 but don't let **B** see you until he has finished his
3: 7 After **B** had finished his meal and was in good
3: 8 **B** suddenly woke up and turned over.
3:10 LORD bless you, my daughter!" **B** exclaimed.
3:14 For **B** said, "No one must know that a woman was
3:15 **B** also said to her, "Bring your cloak and spread it
3:15 her put it on her back. Then **B** returned to the town.
3:16 Ruth told Naomi everything **B** had done for her,
4: 1 So **B** went to the town gate and took a seat there.
4: 1 **B** called out to him, "Come over here, friend.
4: 2 Then **B** called ten leaders from the town and asked
4: 3 And **B** said to the family redeemer, "You know
4: 5 Then **B** told him, "Of course, your purchase of the
4: 8 redeemer drew off his sandal as he said to **B**,
4: 9 Then **B** said to the leaders and to the crowd
4:13 So **B** married Ruth and took her home to live with
4:21 Salmon was the father of **B**. / **B** was the father of Obed.
1Ki 7:21 one on the south Jakin, and the one on the north **B**.
1Ch 2:11 the father of Salmon. / Salmon was the father of **B**.
2:12 **B** was the father of Obed. / Obed was the father of
2Ch 3:17 one on the south Jakin, and the one on the north **B**.
Mt 1: 5 Salmon was the father of **B** (his mother was
1: 5 **B** was the father of Obed (his mother was Ruth).
Lk 3:32 Obed was the son of **B**. / **B** was the son of Salmon.

BOAZ'S (2) [BOAZ]

Ru 2:23 So Ruth worked alongside the women in **B** fields
3:14 So Ruth lay at **B** feet until the morning, but she got

BODIES (128) [BODY]

Ge 17:13 Your **b** will thus bear the mark of my everlasting
47:18 are yours. We have nothing left but our **b** and land.
Ex 14:30 And the Israelites could see the **b** of the Egyptians
28:42 to be worn next to their **b**, reaching from waist to
Lev 10: 4 and carry the **b** of your relatives away from the
11: 8 eat the meat of these animals or touch their dead **b**.
11:11 never eat their meat or even touch their dead **b**.
11:24 If you touch any of their dead **b**, you will be
19:28 "Never cut your **b** in mourning for the dead
21: 5 trim the edges of their beards, or cut their **b**.
22: 6 until they have purified their **b** with water.
Nu 14:32 as for you, your dead **b** will fall in this wilderness.
Dt 4:19 The LORD your God designated these heavenly **b**
14: 8 not eat or even touch the dead **b** of such animals.
28:26 Your dead **b** will be food for the birds and wild
Jos 7:25 stoned Achan and his family and burned their **b**.
10:27 Joshua gave instructions for the **b** of the kings to
Jdg 9:40 and the ground was covered with dead **b** all the
1Sa 14:14 and their **b** were scattered over about half an acre.
17:46 then I will give the dead **b** of your men to the birds
17:52 The **b** of the dead and wounded Philistines were
31: 8 they found the **b** of Saul and his three sons on
31:12 and took the **b** of Saul and his sons down from the
31:12 brought them to Jabesh, where they burned the **b**.
2Sa 4:12 and hung their **b** beside the pool in Hebron.
21:10 She prevented vultures from tearing at their **b**
21:12 **b** from the public square of the Philistine city of
2Ki 10:25 and the guards and officers dragged their **b** outside.
1Ch 10: 8 they found the **b** of Saul and his sons on Mount
10:12 their warriors went out and brought the **b** of Saul
2Ch 20:24 there were dead **b** lying on the ground for as far as
Est 9:13 and have the **b** of Haman's ten sons hung from the
9:14 They also hung the **b** of Haman's ten sons from the
Ps 49:14 Their **b** will rot in the grave, / far from their grand
66:12 You sent troops to ride across our broken **b**.
69:23 and let their **b** grow weaker and weaker.
73: 4 a painless life; / their **b** are so healthy and strong.
79: 2 They have left the **b** of your servants / as food for
Isa 5:25 and the rotting **b** of his people are thrown as
22: 2 **B** are lying everywhere, killed by famine
26:19 belong to God will live; / their **b** will rise again!
34: 3 and the stench of rotting **b** will fill the land.
66:24 they will see the dead **b** of those who have rebelled
Jer 7:32 so many **b** in Topheth that there won't be room for
9:22 "**B** will be scattered across the fields like dung,
14:16 their **b** will be thrown out into the streets of
14:18 I see the **b** of people slaughtered by the enemy.
16: 4 and their **b** will be food for the vultures and wild
19: 7 The enemy will leave the dead **b** as food for the
19:11 They will bury the **b** in Topheth until there is no
25:33 mourn for them or gather up their **b** to bury them.
34:20 Your **b** will be food for the vultures and wild
41: 7 but ten of them and threw their **b** into a cistern.
41: 9 The cistern where Ishmael dumped the **b** of the
Eze 9: 7 "Fill its courtyards with the **b** of those you kill!
10:12 The cherubim had eyes all over their **b**,
32:27 their shields covering their **b**, and their swords
37: 8 Then skin formed to cover their **b**, but they still
37: 9 Breathe into these dead **b** so that they may live
37:10 and the wind entered the **b**, and they began to
39:12 of Israel to cleanse the land by burying the **b**.
Da 12: 2 Many of those whose **b** lie dead and buried will
Joel 2:20 The stench of their rotting **b** will rise over the
Am 8: 3 Dead **b** will be scattered everywhere. They will be
Na 3: 3 the streets—dead **b**, heaps of **b**, everywhere.
Zep 1:17 and your **b** will lie there rotting on the ground."
Mt 27:52 The **b** of many godly men and women who had
Lk 24:39 because ghosts don't have **b**, as you see that I do!"
Jn 19:31 legs be broken. Then their **b** could be taken down.
Ac 14:11 local dialect, "These men are gods in human **b**!"
Ro 1:24 did vile and degrading things with each other's **b**.
8:23 including the new **b** he has promised us.
12: 1 I plead with you to give your **b** to God.
12: 4 Just as our **b** have many parts and each part has a
1Co 6:13 But our **b** were not made for sexual immorality.
6:13 made for the Lord, and the Lord cares about our **b**.
6:14 And God will raise our **b** from the dead by his
6:15 Don't you realize that your **b** are actually parts of
12:18 But God made our **b** with many parts, and he has
15:35 dead be raised? What kind of **b** will they have?"
15:40 There are **b** in the heavens, and there are **b** on earth.
15:40 The glory of the heavenly **b** is different from the beauty of the earthly **b**.
15:42 Our earthly **b**, which die and decay, will be
15:43 Our **b** now disappoint us, but when they are raised,
15:44 They are natural human **b** now, but when they are raised, they will be spiritual **b**. For just as there are natural **b**, so also there are spiritual **b**.
15:48 but our heavenly **b** will be just like Christ's.
15:50 These perishable **b** of ours are not able to live
15:52 who have died will be raised with transformed **b**.
15:53 For our perishable earthly **b** must be transformed into heavenly **b** that will never die.
15:54 when our perishable earthly **b** have been transformed into heavenly **b** that will never die—
2Co 4: 7 in perishable containers, that is, in our weak **b**.
4:10 these **b** of ours constantly share in the death of
4:10 so that the life of Jesus may also be seen in our **b**.
4:11 the life of Jesus will be obvious in our dying **b**.
4:16 Though our **b** are dying, our spirits are being

5: 1 when we die and leave these **b**—we will have a
5: 2 We grow weary in our present **b**, and we long for
5: 2 we will put on our heavenly **b** like new clothing.
5: 3 For we will not be spirits without **b**, but we will put on new heavenly **b**.
5: 4 Our dying **b** make us groan and sigh, but it's not that we want to die and have no **b** at all. We want to slip into our new **b** so that these dying **b** will be swallowed up by
5: 6 live in these **b** we are not at home with the Lord.
5: 8 and we would rather be away from these **b**, for
5: 10 deserve for the good or evil we have done in our **b**.
Eph 2: 11 even though it affected only their **b** and not their
5: 28 ought to love their wives as they love their own **b**.
Php 3: 21 He will take these weak mortal **b** of ours
3: 21 and change them into glorious **b** like his own,
Heb 3: 17 people who sinned, whose **b** fell in the wilderness?
9: 13 could cleanse people's **b** from ritual defilement.
10: 22 and our **b** have been washed with pure water.
13: 3 as though you feel their pain in your own **b**.
13: 11 but the **b** of the animals were burned outside the
1Pe 4: 6 so that although their **b** were punished with death,
Rev 11: 8 And their **b** will lie in the main street of Jerusalem,
11: 9 languages, and nations will come to stare at their **b**.
19: 21 of the sky gorged themselves on the dead **b**.

BODILY (2) [BODY]

Lev 15: 33 or woman, who has had a **b** discharge of any kind;
Col 2: 23 strong devotion, humility, and severe **b** discipline.

BODY (238) [BODIES, BODILY]

ONE BODY (9) Ro 12:5,5; 1Co 6:16; 10:17; 12:12,20; Eph 2:16; 4:4; Col 3:15

WHOLE BODY (9) Ps 38:3; 63:1; Mt 5:29,30; Ro 6:13; 1Co 12:17,17; Eph 4:16,16

Ge 2: 7 And the LORD God formed a man's **b** from the
9: 23 into the tent, and covered their father's naked **b**.
23: 3 Then, leaving her **b**, he went to the Hittite elders
40: 19 will cut off your head and impale your **b** on a pole.
50: 2 Then Joseph told his morticians to embalm the **b**.
50: 5 take my **b** back to the land of Canaan, and bury me
50: 13 They carried his **b** to the land of Canaan
50: 25 to Canaan, you must take my **b** back with you."
50: 26 and his **b** was placed in a coffin in Egypt.
Ex 4: 7 out this time, it was as healthy as the rest of his **b**.
29: 17 alongside the head and the other pieces of the **b**,
30: 32 It must never be poured on the **b** of an ordinary
Lev 5: 2 such as the dead **b** of an animal that is
5: 8 its neck but without severing its head from the **b**.
11: 25 If you move the dead **b** of an unclean animal,
11: 26 If you touch the dead **b** of such an animal, you will
11: 27 If you touch the dead **b** of such an animal, you will
11: 31 If you touch the dead **b** of such an animal, you will
11: 35 Any object on which the dead **b** of such an animal
11: 36 if the dead **b** of such an animal falls into a spring
11: 36 But anyone who removes the dead **b** will be
11: 37 If the dead **b** falls on seed grain to be planted in the
11: 38 But if the seed is wet when the dead **b** falls on it,
13: 12 someone's skin, covering the **b** from head to foot.
13: 13 person to see if the disease covers the entire **b**.
15: 16 an emission of semen, he must wash his entire **b**,
16: 4 Then he must wash his entire **b** and put on his
16: 4 and the undergarments worn next to his **b**.
16: 24 Then he must bathe his entire **b** with water in a
Nu 5: 22 may this water that brings the curse enter your **b**
6: 6 And they may not go near a dead **b** during the
6: 11 for the guilt they incurred from the dead **b**.
8: 7 And have them shave their entire **b** and wash their
9: 10 at Passover time because of touching a dead **b**,
19: 11 "All those who touch a dead human **b** will be
19: 13 All those who touch a dead **b** and do not purify
25: 8 thrust the spear all the way through the man's **b**
31: 19 or touched a dead **b** must stay outside the camp for
Dt 4: 8 and regulations as fair as this **b** of laws that I am
21: 2 judges must determine which town is nearest the **b**.
21: 6 "The leaders of the town nearest the **b** must wash
21: 23 the **b** must never remain on the tree overnight.
21: 23 You must bury the **b** that same day, for anyone
31: 24 writing down this entire **b** of law in a book,
Jos 8: 29 At sunset the Israelites took down the **b** and threw
Jdg 16: 31 and other relatives went down to get his **b**.
19: 28 So he put her **b** on his donkey and took her home.
19: 29 and cut his concubine's **b** into twelve pieces.
20: 6 So I cut her **b** into twelve pieces and sent the
1Sa 5: 4 Only the trunk of his **b** was left intact.
31: 10 and they fastened his **b** to the wall of the city of
2Sa 2: 32 Joab and his men took Asahel's **b** to Bethlehem
18: 17 They threw Absalom's **b** into a deep pit in the
20: 13 With Amasa's **b** out of the way, everyone went on
1Ki 13: 22 your **b** will not be buried in the grave of your
13: 24 His **b** lay there on the road, with the donkey
13: 25 People came by and saw the **b** lying in the road
13: 28 and he went out and found the **b** lying in the road.
13: 28 for the lion had not eaten the **b** nor attacked the
13: 29 So the prophet laid the **b** of the man of God on the
13: 30 He laid the **b** in his own grave, crying out in grief,
17: 19 And he took the boy's **b** from her, carried him up
17: 19 where he lived, and laid the **b** on his bed.
21: 23 that the dogs of Jezreel will eat the **b** of your wife,
22: 37 and his **b** was taken to Samaria and buried there.
2Ki 4: 34 Then he lay down on the child's **b**, placing his
4: 34 And the child's **b** began to grow warm again!
9: 33 And Jehu trampled her **b** under his horses' hooves.
9: 37 Her **b** will be scattered like dung on the field of
13: 21 So they hastily threw the **b** they were burying into
13: 21 But as soon as the **b** touched Elisha's bones,
23: 30 Josiah's officers took his **b** back in a chariot from
Job 6: 12 strength as hard as stone? Is my **b** made of bronze?
19: 26 after my **b** has decayed, yet in my **b** I will see God!
20: 25 The arrow is pulled from his **b**, and the arrowhead
21: 6 about what I am saying, I shudder. My **b** trembles.
21: 33 Many pay their respects as the **b** is laid to rest
24: 5 spend all their time just getting enough to keep **b**
33: 25 Then his **b** will become as healthy as a child's,
Ps 6: 2 am weak. / Heal me, LORD, for my **b** is in agony.
16: 9 mouth shouts his praises! / My **b** rests in safety.
22: 17 I can count every bone in my **b**. / My enemies stare
31: 9 of my tears. / My **b** and soul are withering away.
38: 3 Because of your anger, my whole **b** is sick;
63: 1 My soul thirsts for you; / my whole **b** longs for you
84: 2 of the LORD. / With my whole being, **b** and soul,
139: 13 You made all the delicate, inner parts of my **b**
Pr 5: 11 groan in anguish when disease consumes your **b**,
16: 24 sweet to the soul and healthy for the **b**.
18: 14 The human spirit can endure a sick **b**, but who can
SS 5: 14 His **b** is like bright ivory, aglow with sapphires.
Isa 14: 19 but your **b** is thrown from the grave like a
59: 17 He put on righteousness as his **b** armor and placed
Jer 9: 25 I will punish all those who are circumcised in **b**
20: 17 my mother's womb, that her **b** had been my grave!
36: 30 His dead **b** will be thrown out to lie unburied—
Eze 1: 11 on either side of it, and the other pair covered its **b**.
1: 23 and each had two wings covering its **b**.
16: 25 offering your **b** to every passerby in an endless
37: 7 The bones of each **b** came together and attached
Da 7: 11 beast was killed and its **b** was destroyed by fire.
10: 6 His **b** looked like a dazzling gem. From his face
Am 6: 10 goes into the house to carry away a dead **b**, he will
Mal 2: 15 In **b** and spirit you are his. And what does he
Mt 5: 29 It is better for you to lose one part of your **b** than for your whole **b** to be thrown into hell.
5: 30 It is better for you to lose one part of your **b** than for your whole **b** to be thrown into hell.
6: 22 "Your eye is a lamp for your **b**. A pure eye lets
10: 28 They can only kill your **b**; they cannot touch your
10: 28 only God, who can destroy both soul and **b** in hell.
14: 12 John's disciples came for his **b** and buried it.
15: 17 through the stomach and then goes out of the **b**.
26: 12 this perfume on me to prepare my **b** for burial.
26: 26 saying, "Take it and eat it, for this is my **b**."
26: 41 though the spirit is willing enough, the **b** is weak!"
27: 58 went to Pilate and asked for Jesus' **b**. And Pilate
27: 59 Joseph took the **b** and wrapped it in a long linen
27: 64 and stealing his **b** and then telling everyone he
28: 6 would happen. Come, see where his **b** was lying.
28: 13 night while we were sleeping, and they stole his **b**.'
Mk 6: 29 they came for his **b** and buried it in a tomb.
12: 8 murdered him and threw his **b** out of the vineyard.
14: 8 and has anointed my **b** for burial ahead of time.
14: 22 the disciples, saying, "Take it, for this is my **b**."
14: 38 though the spirit is willing enough, the **b** is weak."
15: 43 his courage and went to Pilate to ask for Jesus' **b**.
15: 45 the fact, and Pilate told Joseph he could have the **b**.
15: 46 and taking Jesus' **b** down from the cross,
15: 47 the mother of Joseph saw where Jesus' **b** was laid.
16: 1 and purchased burial spices to put on Jesus' **b**.
16: 6 from the dead! Look, this is where they laid his **b**.
Lk 11: 34 Your eye is a lamp for your **b**. A pure eye lets
12: 4 They can only kill the **b**; they cannot do any more
22: 19 the disciples, saying, "This is my **b**, given for you.
23: 52 He went to Pilate and asked for Jesus' **b**.
23: 53 Then he took the **b** down from the cross
23: 55 As his **b** was taken away, the women from Galilee
23: 55 and saw the tomb where they placed his **b**.
24: 3 but they couldn't find the **b** of the Lord Jesus.
24: 23 They said his **b** was missing, and they had seen
24: 24 and sure enough, Jesus' **b** was gone, just as the
Jn 2: 21 But by "this temple," Jesus meant his **b**.
19: 38 asked Pilate for permission to take Jesus' **b** down.
19: 38 him permission, he came and took the **b** away.
19: 40 Together they wrapped Jesus' **b** in a long linen
20: 2 "They have taken the Lord's **b** out of the tomb,
20: 12 and foot of the place where the **b** of Jesus had been
Ac 2: 26 my mouth shouts his praises! / My **b** rests in hope.
2: 31 the dead and that his **b** would not rot in the grave.
9: 40 Turning to the **b** he said, "Get up, Tabitha."
13: 36 of God, he died and was buried, and his **b** decayed.
13: 37 whom God raised and whose **b** did not decay.
Ro 2: 29 And true circumcision is not a cutting of the **b**
6: 13 Do not let any part of your **b** become a tool of
6: 13 And use your whole **b** as a tool to do what is right
8: 3 He sent his own Son in a human **b** like ours,
8: 10 even though your **b** will die because of sin,
8: 11 he will give life to your mortal **b** by this same
12: 5 so it is with Christ's **b**. We are all parts of his one **b**, and each of us has
12: 5 And since we are all one **b** in Christ, we belong to
1Co 6: 15 Should a man take his **b**, which belongs to Christ,
6: 16 himself to a prostitute, he becomes one **b** with her?
6: 18 other sin so clearly affects the **b** as this one does.
6: 18 For sexual immorality is a sin against your own **b**.
6: 19 Or don't you know that your **b** is the temple of the
6: 20 a high price. So you must honor God with your **b**.
7: 4 The wife gives authority over her **b** to her husband,
7: 4 and the husband also gives authority over his **b** to
7: 34 been married can be more devoted to the Lord in **b**
9: 27 I discipline my **b** like an athlete, training it to do
10: 16 aren't we sharing in the benefits of the **b** of Christ?
10: 17 all eat from one loaf, showing that we are one **b**.
11: 24 he broke it and said, "This is my **b**, which is given
11: 27 that person is guilty of sinning against the **b**
11: 29 not honoring the **b** of Christ, you are eating
12: 12 The human **b** has many parts, but the many parts make up only one **b**. So it is with the **b** of Christ.
12: 13 But we have all been baptized into Christ's **b** by
12: 14 Yes, the **b** has many different parts, not just one
12: 15 "I am not a part of the **b** because I am not a
12: 15 that does not make it any less a part of the **b**.
12: 16 "I am not part of the **b** because I am only an ear
12: 16 would that make it any less a part of the **b**?
12: 17 Suppose the whole **b** were an eye—then how
12: 17 Or if your whole **b** were just one big ear,
12: 19 What a strange thing a **b** would be if it had only
12: 20 Yes, there are many parts, but only one **b**.
12: 24 So God has put the **b** together in such a way that
12: 27 Now all of you together are Christ's **b**, and each
12: 28 members that God has placed in the **b** of Christ:
13: 3 I have to the poor and even sacrificed my **b**,
15: 38 Then God gives it a new **b**—just the kind he wants
15: 46 What came first was the natural **b**, then the spiritual **b** comes later.
15: 48 Every human being has an earthly **b** just like
2Co 5: 1 an eternal **b** made for us by God himself and not
5: 9 whether we are here in this **b** or away from this **b**.
7: 1 ourselves from everything that can defile our **b**
12: 3 Whether my **b** was there or just my spirit, I don't
Gal 2: 20 So I live my life in this earthly **b** by trusting in the
6: 17 For I bear on my **b** the scars that show I belong to
Eph 1: 23 And the church is his **b**; it is filled by Christ,
2: 16 Together as one **b**, Christ reconciled both groups to
3: 6 and both are part of the same **b** and enjoy together
4: 4 We are all one **b**, we have the same Spirit, and we
4: 12 his work and build up the church, the **b** of Christ,
4: 15 like Christ, who is the head of his **b**, the church.
4: 16 the whole **b** is fitted together perfectly.
4: 16 so that the whole **b** is healthy and growing and full
5: 23 the head of his wife as Christ is the head of his **b**,
5: 29 No one hates his own **b** but lovingly cares for it,
5: 29 just as Christ cares for his **b**, which is the church.
5: 30 And we are his **b**.
6: 14 of truth and the **b** armor of God's righteousness.
Col 1: 18 Christ is the head of the church, which is his **b**.
1: 22 through his death on the cross in his own human **b**.
1: 24 I am glad when I suffer for you in my **b**, for I am
1: 24 what remains of Christ's sufferings for his **b**,
2: 9 in Christ the fullness of God lives in a human **b**,
2: 19 they are not connected to Christ, the head of the **b**.
2: 19 For we are joined together in his **b** by his strong
3: 15 For as members of one **b** you are all called to live
1Th 4: 4 Then each of you will control your **b** and live in
5: 8 protected by the **b** armor of faith and love,
5: 23 and **b** be kept blameless until that day when our
Heb 10: 5 But you have given me a **b** so that I may obey you.
10: 10 sacrifice of the **b** of Jesus Christ once for all time.
Jas 2: 26 Just as the **b** is dead without a spirit, so also faith is
1Pe 2: 24 He personally carried away our sins in his own **b**
3: 21 Baptism is not a removal of dirt from your **b**;
2Jn 1: 7 believe that Jesus Christ came to earth in a real **b**.
3Jn 1: 2 and that your **b** is as healthy as I know your soul is.
Jude 1: 9 Michael was arguing with Satan about Moses' **b**.)

BODYGUARD (16) [GUARD]

1Sa 22: 14 he is the captain of your **b** and a highly honored
28: 2 "I will make you my personal **b** for life."
2Sa 8: 18 son of Jehoiada was captain of the king's **b**.
15: 18 with David from Gath, along with the king's **b**.
20: 7 elite guard from Joab's army and the king's own **b**.
20: 23 son of Jehoiada was commander of the king's **b**.
23: 23 And David made him commander of his **b**.
1Ki 1: 8 the prophet, Shimei, Rei, and David's personal **b**.
1: 10 or Benaiah, or the king's **b**, or his brother
1: 38 and the king's **b** took Solomon down to Gihon
1: 44 Benaiah son of Jehoiada, protected by the king's **b**.
2Ki 11: 8 Form a **b** for the king and keep your weapons in
1Ch 11: 25 And David made him commander of his **b**.
18: 17 son of Jehoiada was captain of the king's **b**.
2Ch 12: 10 entrusted them to the care of the captain of his **b**.
23: 7 form a **b** for the king and keep your weapons in

BODYGUARDS (1) [GUARD]

1Sa 22: 17 And he ordered his **b**, "Kill these priests of the

BOHAN (4)

Jos 15: 6 proceeded north of Beth-arabah to the stone of **B**. (**B** was Reuben's son.)
18: 17 Then it went down to the stone of **B**. (**B** was Reuben's son.)

BOIL (18) [BOILED, BOILING, BOILS]

Ex 16: 23 So bake or **b** as much as you want today, and set
29: 31 and **b** its meat in a sacred place.
Lev 6: 28 If a clay pot is used to **b** the sacrificial meat,
8: 31 "**B** the rest of the meat at the Tabernacle entrance,
13: 18 "If anyone has had a **b** on the skin that has started
13: 20 skin disease that has broken out in the **b**.
13: 23 does not spread, it is merely the scar from the **b**,
Dt 14: 21 "Do not **b** a young goat in its mother's milk.
2Ki 20: 7 an ointment from figs and spread it over the **b**."
Job 41: 31 "The crocodile makes the water **b** with its
Isa 38: 21 an ointment from figs and spread it over the **b**,
64: 2 As fire causes wood to burn and water to **b**,
Jer 1: 14 "for terror from the north will **b** out on the people
Eze 24: 3 Put a pot of water on the fire to **b**.
24: 5 Bring the pot to a **b**, and cook the bones along with
24: 10 on the wood! Let the fire roar to make the pot **b**.
46: 24 to **b** the sacrifices offered by the people."
Zec 14: 21 be free to use any of these pots to **b** their sacrifices.

BOILED (8) [BOIL]
Ex 12: 9 The meat must never be eaten raw or **b**; roast it all,
Nu 6:19 the priest will take for each of them the **b** shoulder
11: 8 Then they **b** it in a pot and made it into flat cakes.
1Sa 2:15 He would demand raw meat before it had been **b**
20:30 Saul **b** with rage at Jonathan. "You stupid son of a
2Ch 35:13 and they **b** the holy offerings in pots, kettles,
Jer 44: 6 And so my fury **b** over and fell like fire on the
Ac 19:28 At this their anger **b**, and they began shouting,

BOILING (3) [BOIL]
1Sa 2:13 While the meat of the sacrificed animal was still **b**,
Job 41:20 like steam from a **b** pot on a fire of dry rushes.
Jer 1:13 And I replied, "I see a pot of **b** water, tipping from

BOILS (6) [BOIL]
Ex 9: 9 causing **b** to break out on people and animals
9:10 and terrible **b** broke out on the people and animals
9:11 because the **b** had broken out on them, too.
Dt 28:27 "The LORD will afflict you with the **b** of Egypt
28:35 will cover you from head to foot with incurable **b**.
Job 2: 7 and he struck Job with a terrible case of **b** from

BOISTEROUS (1)
Zep 2:15 This is the fate of that **b** city, once so secure.

BOKERU (2)
1Ch 8:38 Azrikam, **B**, Ishmael, Sheariah, Obadiah,
9:44 **B**, Ishmael, Sheariah, Obadiah, and Hanan.

BOKIM (1)
Jdg 2: 1 The angel of the LORD went up from Gilgal to **B**

BOLD (14) [BOLDEST, BOLDLY, BOLDNESS]
2Sa 7:27 I have been **b** enough to pray this prayer
1Ch 17:25 I have been **b** enough to pray this prayer
Ps 32: 7 and grow more and more **b** in their wickedness."
Pr 10:10 cause trouble, but a **b** reproof promotes peace.
21:29 The wicked put up a **b** front, but the upright
28: 1 one is chasing them, but the godly are as **b** as lions.
Isa 45:19 I publicly proclaim **b** promises. I do not whisper
Ro 15:15 I have been **b** enough to emphasize some of these
2Co 3:12 gives us such confidence, we can be very **b**.
10: 1 even though some of you say I am **b** in my letters
10: 2 but when I come I may have to be very **b** with
Php 1:14 and become more **b** in telling others about Christ.
1:20 but that I will always be **b** for Christ, as I have
1Jn 3:21 is clear, we can come to God with **b** confidence.

BOLDEST (1) [BOLD]
Eze 21: 7 When it comes true, the **b** heart will melt with fear;

BOLDLY (17) [BOLD]
Nu 13:20 Enter the land **b**, and bring back samples of the
Ps 56: 2 me constantly, / and many are **b** attacking me.
Eze 23:39 they **b** came into my Temple to worship!
24: 7 She murders **b**, leaving blood on the rocks for all
Ac 9:27 and how he **b** preached in the name of Jesus in
9:28 in Jerusalem, preaching **b** in the name of the Lord.
13:46 Then Paul and Barnabas spoke out **b** and declared,
14: 3 long time, preaching **b** about the grace of the Lord.
18:26 and Aquila heard him preaching **b** in the
19: 8 and preached **b** for the next three months,
Ro 10:20 And later Isaiah spoke **b** for God: / "I was found
Eph 6:19 Ask God to give me the right words as I **b** explain
6:20 But pray that I will keep on speaking **b** for him,
1Th 2: 2 us the courage to declare his Good News to you **b**,
Phm 1: 8 That is why I am **b** asking a favor of you. I could
Heb 4:16 So let us come **b** to the throne of our gracious God.
10:19 we can **b** enter heaven's Most Holy Place

BOLDNESS (5) [BOLD]
Na 2:11 full of fight and **b**, where the old and feeble
Ac 4:13 council were amazed when they saw the **b** of Peter
4:29 and give your servants great **b** in their preaching.
4:31 And they preached God's message with **b**.
28:31 proclaiming the Kingdom of God with all **b**

BOLSTER [KJV] See HEAD

BOLT (2) [BOLTED, BOLTS]
Ne 6:10 inside the Temple of God and **b** the doors shut.
SS 5: 5 fingers with lovely myrrh, as I pulled back the **b**.

BOLTED (2) [BOLT]
Ge 19:10 reached out and pulled Lot in and **b** the door.
Nu 22:23 The donkey **b** off the road into a field, but Balaam

BOLTS (11) [BOLT]
Dt 33:25 May the **b** of your gates be of iron and bronze;
2Sa 22:13 shone before him, / and **b** of lightning blazed forth.
Ne 3: 3 hung the doors, and put the **b** and bars in place.
3: 6 set up the doors, and installed the **b** and bars.
3:13 hung its doors, and installed the **b** and bars.
3:14 he hung the doors and installed the **b** and bars.
3:15 hung its doors, and installed its **b** and bars.
Job 36:32 He fills his hands with lightning **b**. He hurls each
Ps 29: 7 The voice of the LORD strikes with lightning **b**.
78:48 cattle to the hail, / their livestock to **b** of lightning.
144: 6 Release your lightning **b** and scatter your enemies!

BOND (2) [BONDAGE, BONDS]
1Sa 18: 1 There was an immediate **b** of love between them,
Zec 11:14 to show that the **b** of unity between Judah

BONDAGE (3) [BOND]
Isa 10:27 In that day the LORD will end the **b** of his
Jer 34: 9 No one was to keep a fellow Judean in **b**.
Lk 13:16 to free this dear woman from the **b** in which Satan

BONDMAID(S) [KJV] See SLAVE, SLAVES, SLAVE-WIFE

BONDMAN, BONDMEN [KJV] See SLAVE, SLAVES

BONDS (2) [BOND]
Ps 116:16 and you have freed me from my **b**!
Isa 52:11 Go now, leave your **b** and slavery. Put Babylon

BONDSERVANT [KJV] See SLAVE

BONDWOMAN, BONDWOMEN [KJV] See SERVANT, SLAVE, SLAVES, SLAVE-WIFE

BONE (5) [BACKBONE, BONES]
Ge 2:23 "She is part of my own flesh and **b**!
Nu 19:16 or if someone touches a human **b** or a grave,
19:18 in the tent, or anyone who has touched a human **b**,
Job 22: 6 you as a pledge. Yes, you stripped him to the **b**.
Ps 22:17 I can count every **b** in my body. / My enemies

BONES (65) [BONE]
Ex 12:46 meat outside, and you may not break any of its **b**.
13:19 Moses took the **b** of Joseph with him, for Joseph
13:19 his **b** with them when God led them out of Egypt—
Nu 9:12 next morning, and they must not break any of its **b**.
24: 8 that oppose him, / breaking their **b** in pieces,
Jos 24:32 The **b** of Joseph, which the Israelites had brought
2Sa 21:12 and asked for the **b** of Saul and his son Jonathan.
21:13 So David brought the **b** of Saul and Jonathan,
21:13 as well as the **b** of the men the Gibeonites had
1Ki 13: 2 and human **b** will be burned on you."
13:31 man of God is buried. Lay my **b** beside his **b**.
2Ki 13:21 But as soon as the body touched Elisha's **b**,
23:14 these places by scattering human **b** over them.
23:16 He ordered that the **b** be brought out, and he
23:18 "Leave it alone. Don't disturb his **b**."
23:18 So they did not burn his **b** or those of the old
23:20 and he burned human **b** on the altars to desecrate
2Ch 34: 5 Then he burned the **b** of the pagan priests on their
Job 10:11 and flesh, and you knit my **b** and sinews together.
16: 8 You have reduced me to skin and **b**—as proof,
19:20 I have been reduced to skin and **b** and have
20:11 was just a young man, but his **b** will lie in the dust.
30:17 something were relentlessly gnawing at my **b**.
30:30 skin has turned dark, and my **b** burn with fever.
33:19 and pain, with ceaseless aching in their **b**.
33:21 They waste away to skin and **b**.
40:18 Its **b** are tubes of bronze. Its limbs are bars of iron.
Ps 22:14 out like water, / and all my **b** are out of joint.
34:20 from harm—/ not one of their **b** will be broken!
53: 5 God will scatter the **b** of your enemies. / You will
102: 3 like smoke, / and my **b** burn like red-hot coals.
102: 5 of my groaning, / I am reduced to skin and **b**.
109:24 knees are weak from fasting, / and I am skin and **b**.
141: 7 so the **b** of the wicked will be scattered without a
Isa 18: 6 The wild animals will gnaw at **b** all winter.
Jer 8: 2 They will dig out their **b** and spread them out on
8: 2 Their **b** will not be gathered up again or buried
20: 9 It's like a fire in my **b**! I am weary of holding it in!
50:17 Nebuchadnezzar of Babylon cracked their **b**."
La 1:13 "He has sent fire from heaven that burns in my **b**.
3: 4 my skin and flesh grow old. He has broken my **b**.
4: 8 Their skin sticks to their **b**; it is as dry and hard as
Eze 6: 5 of your idols and scatter your **b** around your altars.
24: 5 pot to a boil, and cook the **b** along with the meat.
24:10 many spices. Then empty the pot and burn the **b**.
32: 5 with your flesh and fill the valleys with your **b**.
34: 4 have not tended the sick or bound up the broken **b**.
37: 1 the Spirit of the LORD to a valley filled with **b**.
37: 2 among the old, dry **b** that covered the valley floor.
37: 3 of man, can these **b** become living people again?"
37: 4 said to me, "Speak to these **b** and say, 'Dry **b**,
37: 7 The **b** of each body came together and attached
37: 8 as I watched, muscles and flesh formed over the **b**.
37:11 of man, these **b** represent the people of Israel.
37:11 They are saying, 'We have become old, dry **b**—
39:15 Whenever some **b** are found, a marker will be set
Am 2: 1 tomb of Edom's king and burned his **b** to ashes.
Mic 3: 2 skin my people alive and tear the flesh off their **b**.
3: 3 cut away their skin, and break their **b**.
Hab 3:13 the wicked and laid bare their **b** from head to toe.
Mt 23:27 but filled on the inside with dead people's **b**
Jn 19:36 that say, "Not one of his **b** will be broken,"
Heb 11:22 so sure of it that he commanded them to carry his **b**

BONFIRE (1) [FIRE]
Ac 19:19 incantation books and burned them at a public **b**.

BONNETS [KJV] See HEADDRESSES, SCARVES, TURBANS

BOOBY-TRAP (1) [TRAP]
Pr 1:18 an ambush for themselves; they **b** their own lives!

BOOK (116) [BOOKS]
BOOK OF THE COVENANT (4) Ex 24:7; 2Ki 23:2,21; 2Ch 34:30
BOOK OF THE HISTORY (35) 1Ki 14:19,29; 15:7,23,31; 16:5,14,20,27; 22:39,45; 2Ki 1:18; 8:23; 10:34; 12:19; 13:8,12; 14:15,18,28; 15:6,11,15,21,26,31,36; 16:19; 20:20; 21:17,25; 23:28; 24:5; Est 2:23; 10:2
BOOK OF THE KINGS (11) 1Ch 9:1; 2Ch 16:11; 20:34; 24:27; 25:26; 27:7; 28:26; 32:32; 33:18; 35:27; 36:8
BOOK OF THE LAW (22) Dt 28:61; 29:21; 30:10; 31:26; Jos 1:8; 8:31,34; 23:6; 24:26; 2Ki 14:6; 22:8,11; 2Ch 17:9; 25:4; 34:14,15; Ne 8:1,3,8,18; 9:3; Gal 3:10
BOOK OF LIFE (8) Ps 69:28; Php 4:3; Rev 3:5; 13:8; 17:8; 20:12,15; 21:27
BOOK OF MOSES (3) 2Ch 35:12; Ezr 6:18; Ne 13:1

Ex 24: 7 Then he took the **B** of the Covenant and read it to
Nu 21:14 For this reason *The* **B** *of the Wars of the LORD*
Dt 1: 1 This **b** records the words that Moses spoke to all
28:58 all the terms of this law that are written in this **b**,
28:61 even those not mentioned in this **B** of the Law,
29:20 All the curses written in this **b** will come down on
29:21 the covenant curses recorded in this **B** of the Law.
29:27 down on it all the curses recorded in this **b**.
30:10 and laws written in this **B** of the Law,
31:24 writing down this entire body of law in a **b**,
31:26 "Take this **B** of the Law and place it beside the
Jos 1: 8 Study this **B** of the Law continually. Meditate on it
8:31 LORD's servant had written in the **B** of the Law:
8:34 and curses Moses had written in the **B** of the Law.
10:13 Is this event not recorded in *The* **B** *of Jashar*?
23: 6 instructions written in the **B** of the Law of Moses.
24:26 Joshua recorded these things in the **B** of the Law of
2Sa 1:18 the Bow, and it is recorded in *The* **B** *of Jashar.*
1Ki 11:41 are recorded in *The* **B** *of the Acts of Solomon.*
14:19 are recorded in *The* **B** *of the History of the Kings*
14:29 and all his deeds are recorded in *The* **B** *of the*
15: 7 and all his deeds are recorded in *The* **B** *of the*
15:23 **B** *of the History of the Kings of Judah.* In his old
15:31 and all his deeds are recorded in *The* **B** *of the*
16: 5 and the extent of his power are recorded in *The* **B**
16:14 and all his deeds are recorded in *The* **B** *of the*
16:20 and his conspiracy are recorded in *The* **B** *of the*
16:27 and all his deeds are recorded in *The* **B** *of the*
22:39 and the cities he built are recorded in *The* **B** *of*
22:45 and the wars he waged are recorded in *The* **B** *of*
2Ki 1:18 in *The* **B** *of the History of the Kings of Israel.*
8:23 and all his deeds are recorded in *The* **B** *of the*
10:34 and achievements are recorded in *The* **B** *of the*
12:19 and all his deeds are recorded in *The* **B** *of the*
13: 8 are recorded in *The* **B** *of the History of the Kings*
13:12 are recorded in *The* **B** *of the History of the Kings*
14: 6 the LORD written in the **B** of the Law of Moses:
14:15 are recorded in *The* **B** *of the History of the Kings*
14:18 in *The* **B** *of the History of the Kings of Judah.*
14:28 are recorded in *The* **B** *of the History of the Kings*
15: 6 and all his deeds are recorded in *The* **B** *of the*
15:11 in *The* **B** *of the History of the Kings of Israel.*
15:15 are recorded in *The* **B** *of the History of the Kings*
15:21 and all his deeds are recorded in *The* **B** *of the*
15:26 and all his deeds are recorded in *The* **B** *of the*
15:31 and all his deeds are recorded in *The* **B** *of the*
15:36 and all his deeds are recorded in *The* **B** *of the*
16:19 and his deeds are recorded in *The* **B** *of the*
20:20 are recorded in *The* **B** *of the History of the Kings*
21:17 are recorded in *The* **B** *of the History of the Kings*
21:25 and all his deeds are recorded in *The* **B** *of the*
22: 8 "I have found the **B** of the Law in the LORD's
22:11 When the king heard what was written in the **B** of
23: 2 There the king read to them the entire **B** of the
23:21 as it is written in the **B** of the Covenant."
23:28 and all his deeds are recorded in *The* **B** *of the*
24: 5 and all his deeds are recorded in *The* **B** *of the*
1Ch 9: 1 record in *The* **B** *of the Kings of Israel.*
2Ch 16:11 are recorded in *The* **B** *of the Kings of Judah*
17: 9 They took copies of the **B** of the Law of the
20:34 is included in *The* **B** *of the Kings of Israel.*
24:27 *on the* **B** *of the Kings.* When Joash died,
25: 4 the LORD written in the **B** of the Law of Moses:
25:26 are recorded in *The* **B** *of the Kings of Judah*
27: 7 are recorded in *The* **B** *of the Kings of Israel*
28:26 are recorded in *The* **B** *of the Kings of Judah*
32:32 which is included in *The* **B** *of the Kings of Judah*
33:18 are recorded in *The* **B** *of the Kings of Israel.*
34:14 he found the **B** of the Law of the LORD as it had
34:15 "I have found the **B** of the Law in the LORD's
34:30 There the king read to them the entire **B** of the
35:12 to the instructions recorded in the **B** of Moses.
35:25 and are recorded in *The* **B** *of Laments.*
35:27 are recorded in *The* **B** *of the Kings of Israel*
36: 8 are recorded in *The* **B** *of the Kings of Israel*
Ezr 6:18 following all the instructions recorded in the **B** of
Ne 8: 1 They asked Ezra the scribe to bring out the **B** of
8: 3 All the people paid close attention to the **B** of the
8: 5 When they saw him open the **b**, they all rose to
8: 8 They read from the **B** of the Law of God
8:18 Ezra read from the **B** of the Law of God on each of
9: 3 The **B** of the Law of the LORD their God was
12:23 in *The* **B** *of History* down to the days of Johanan,
13: 1 that same day, as the **B** of Moses was being read,
Est 2:23 This was all duly recorded in *The* **B** *of the*

10: 2 are recorded in *The **B** of the History of the Kings*
Ps 56: 8 You have recorded each one in your **b**.
69:28 Erase their names from the **B** of Life; / don't let
139:16 Every day of my life was recorded in your **b**.
Isa 29:11 All these future events are a sealed **b** to them.
29:18 that day deaf people will hear words read from a **b**,
34:16 Search the **b** of the LORD, and see what he will
Jer 25:13 them all the terrors I have promised in this **b**—
Da 10:21 I will tell you what is written in the **B** of Truth.
12: 1 whose name is written in the **b** will be rescued.
12: 4 a secret; seal up the **b** until the time of the end.
Mk 1: 2 In the **b** of the prophet Isaiah, God said, / "Look,
Lk 20:42 For David himself wrote in the **b** of Psalms:
Jn 20:30 signs besides the ones recorded in this **b**.
Ac 1: 1 In my first **b** I told you about everything Jesus
1:20 "This was predicted in the **b** of Psalms, where it
7:42 as their gods! In the **b** of the prophets it is written,
8:28 he was reading aloud from the **b** of the prophet
Gal 3:10 that are written in God's **B** of the Law."
Php 4: 3 whose names are written in the **B** of Life.
Heb 9:19 and sprinkled both the **b** of God's laws and all the
Rev 3: 5 I will never erase their names from the **B** of Life,
13: 8 whose names were not written in the **B** of Life,
17: 8 whose names were not written in the **B** of Life
20:12 the books were opened, including the **B** of Life.
20:15 in the **B** of Life was thrown into the lake of fire.
21:27 whose names are written in the Lamb's **B** of Life.
22:18 everyone who hears the prophetic words of this **b**:
22:18 add to that person the plagues described in this **b**.
22:19 removes any of the words of this prophetic **b**,
22:19 and in the holy city that are described in this **b**.

BOOKS (12) [BOOK]

Eze 13: 9 I will blot their names from Israel's record **b**,
Da 7:10 the court began its session, and the **b** were opened.
Jn 21:25 the whole world could not contain the **b**.
Ac 13:15 After the usual readings from the **b** of Moses
19:19 been practicing magic brought their incantation **b**
19:19 The value of the **b** was several million dollars.
24:14 and everything written in the **b** of prophecy.
28:23 from the five **b** of Moses and the **b** of the prophets.
2Ti 4:13 Also bring my **b**, and especially my papers.
Rev 20:12 And the **b** were opened, including the Book of
20:12 judged according to the things written in the **b**,

BOOMERANGS (1)

Pr 21: 7 do what is just, their violence **b** and destroys them.

BOOTH (3)

Mt 9: 9 he saw Matthew sitting at his tax-collection **b**.
Mk 2:14 Levi son of Alphaeus sitting at his tax-collection **b**.
Lk 5:27 collector named Levi sitting at his tax-collection **b**.

BOOZ [KJV] See BOAZ

BOR-ASHAN (1)

1Sa 30:30 Hormah, **B**, Athach,

BORDER (60) [BORDERS]

Ge 15:18 all the way from the **b** of Egypt to the great
Ex 8: 2 across your entire land from one **b** to the other.
10:14 swarmed over the land of Egypt from **b** to **b**.
Nu 20:16 camped at Kadesh, a town on the **b** of your land.
20:17 leave it until we have crossed the opposite **b**."
20:23 and Aaron at Mount Hor on the **b** of the land of
21:11 in the wilderness on the eastern **b** of Moab.
21:15 as far as the settlement of Ar on the **b** of Moab."
21:24 They went only as far as the Ammonite **b**
22:36 town on the Arnon River at the **b** of his land.
33:37 and camped at Mount Hor, at the **b** of Edom.
33:44 and camped at Iye-abarim on the **b** of Moab.
Dt 2:18 'Today you will cross the **b** of Moab at Ar
Jos 13: 4 stretching northward to Aphek on the **b** of the
13:27 The Jordan River was the western **b**, extending as
15: 1 tribe of Judah reached southward to the **b** of Edom,
15: 7 From there the **b** extended to the springs at
15: 9 From there the **b** extended from the top of the
15:10 The **b** circled west of Baalah to Mount Seir,
16: 8 From Tappuah the **b** extended westward,
17: 7 extended from the **b** of Asher to Micmethath,
17: 8 town of Tappuah, on the **b** of Manasseh's territory,
17: 9 the **b** of Manasseh followed the northern side of
17:10 Mediterranean Sea forming Manasseh's western **b**.
18:18 The **b** then went down into the valley,
19:12 the boundary line went east from Sarid to the **b** of
Jdg 7:22 and to the **b** of Abel-meholah near Tabbath.
11:18 They traveled along Moab's eastern **b** and camped
1Sa 6: 9 If they cross the **b** of our land and go to
6:12 The Philistine rulers followed them as far as the **b**
10: 2 Rachel's tomb at Zelzah, on the **b** of Benjamin.
13:18 and the third moved toward the **b** above the valley
1Ki 4:21 of the Philistines, as far south as the **b** of Egypt.
2Ki 3:21 and old, and stationed themselves along their **b**.
1Ch 7:29 Along the **b** of Manasseh were the towns of
2Ch 9:26 to the land of the Philistines and the **b** of Egypt.
Ps 78:54 He brought them to the **b** of his holy land, / to this
133: 2 ran down his beard / and onto the **b** of his robe.
Isa 19:19 there will be a monument to the LORD at its **b**.
Jer 37: 5 of Egypt appeared at the southern **b** of Judah.
Eze 29:10 Migdol to Aswan, as far south as the **b** of Ethiopia.
45: 7 One section will share a **b** with the east side of the
45: 7 and the second section will share a **b** on the west
47:15 "The northern **b** will run from the Mediterranean
47:16 which are on the **b** between Damascus
47:16 and finally to Hazer-hatticon, on the **b** of Hauran.
47:17 So the northern **b** will run from the Mediterranean
47:17 on the **b** between Hamath to the north
47:18 "The eastern **b** starts at a point between Hauran
47:18 as far south as Tamar. This will be the eastern **b**.
47:19 "The southern **b** will go west from Tamar to the
47:19 to the Mediterranean. This will be the southern **b**.
47:20 your **b** from the southern **b** to the point where the
northern **b** begins,
48: 1 then runs on to Hazar-enan on the **b** of Damascus,
48:18 and 3-1/3 miles to the west along the **b** of the
48:28 The southern **b** of Gad runs from Tamar to the
Lk 17:11 he reached the **b** between Galilee and Samaria.

BORDERS (20) [BORDER]

Ge 12:11 As he was approaching the **b** of Egypt, Abram said
49:13 be a harbor for ships; / his **b** will extend to Sidon.
Ex 13: 7 or anywhere within the **b** of your land during this
Dt 3:14 in Bashan all the way to the **b** of the Geshurites
Jos 13:10 and extended as far as the **b** of Ammon.
15:21 The towns of Judah situated along the **b** of Edom
Isa 26:15 made our nation great; / you have extended our **b**!
Eze 11:10 You will be slaughtered all the way to the **b** of
11:11 safe inside. I will judge you even to the **b** of Israel,
45: 7 and western **b** of the prince's lands will line up
48:21 directions to the eastern and western **b** of Israel.
48:27 is just south of Zebulun with the same **b** to the east
Am 1:13 When they attacked Gilead to extend their **b**,
Mic 5: 6 when they pour over the **b** to invade our land.
7:11 cities will be rebuilt, and your **b** will be extended.
Zep 2: 8 mocking my people and invading their **b**.
Mal 1: 5 great power reaches far beyond our **b**!' "
Mt 4:24 News about him spread far beyond the **b** of Galilee
Lk 7:17 day spread all over Judea and even out across its **b**.
Ac 16: 7 Then coming to the **b** of Mysia, they headed for

BORE (13) [BEAR]

Ge 25: 2 and she **b** him Zimran, Jokshan, Medan, Midian,
25:16 the founders of twelve tribes that **b** their names,
Ex 6:20 sister Jochebed, and she **b** him Aaron and Moses.
6:23 and she **b** him Nadab, Abihu, Eleazar, and Ithamar.
6:25 of the daughters of Putiel, and she **b** him Phinehas.
Jdg 8:31 in Shechem, who **b** him a son named Abimelech.
1Ki 11:20 She **b** him a son, Genubath, who was brought up in
Isa 49:21 I was left here all alone. Who **b** these children?
53:12 He **b** the sins of many and interceded for sinners.
La 2:22 The enemy has killed all the children I **b**
Eze 23: 4 I married them, and they **b** me sons and daughters.
Ac 24: 4 But lest I **b** you, kindly give me your attention for
Heb 13:13 to him outside the camp and bear the disgrace he **b**.

BORED (1)

2Ki 12: 9 Then Jehoiada the priest **b** a hole in the lid of a

BORN (176) [BEAR]

Ge 4:22 To Lamech's other wife, Zillah, was **b** Tubal-cain.
5: 3 Adam was 130 years old, his son Seth was **b**,
5: 6 Seth was 105 years old, his son Enosh was **b**.
5: 9 Enosh was 90 years old, his son Kenan was **b**.
5:12 Kenan was 70 years old, his son Mahalalel was **b**.
5:15 Mahalalel was 65 years old, his son Jared was **b**.
5:18 Jared was 162 years old, his son Enoch was **b**.
5:21 Enoch was 65 years old, his son Methuselah was **b**.
5:25 was 187 years old, his son Lamech was **b**.
5:28 Lamech was 182 years old, his son Noah was **b**.
10: 1 Many children were **b** to them after the Flood.
10:21 Sons were also **b** to Shem, the older brother of
11:10 Shem was 100 years old, his son Arphaxad was **b**.
11:12 Arphaxad was 35 years old, his son Shelah was **b**.
11:14 Shelah was 30 years old, his son Eber was **b**.
11:16 When Eber was 34 years old, his son Peleg was **b**.
11:18 When Peleg was 30 years old, his son Reu was **b**.
11:20 When Reu was 32 years old, his son Serug was **b**.
11:22 Serug was 30 years old, his son Nahor was **b**.
11:24 Nahor was 29 years old, his son Terah was **b**.
14:14 he called together the men **b** into his household,
17:12 but also to the servants **b** in your household
17:21 who will be **b** to you and Sarah about this time
17:27 whether they were **b** there or bought as servants.
21: 4 Eight days after Isaac was **b**, Abraham circumcised
25:24 And when the time came, the twins were **b**.
25:26 Then the other twin was **b** with his hand grasping
25:26 Isaac was sixty years old when the twins were **b**.
30:25 Soon after Joseph was **b** to Rachel, Jacob said to
31: 8 streaked ones, then all the lambs were **b** streaked.
35:26 These were the sons **b** to Jacob at Paddan-aram.
36: 5 All these sons were **b** to Esau in the land of
36:12 son named Amalek, **b** to Timna, his concubine.
37: 3 because Joseph had been **b** to him in his old age.
38:28 As they were being **b**, one of them reached out his
38:29 and the other baby was actually the first to be **b**.
38:30 the baby with the scarlet thread on his wrist was **b**,
41:50 two sons were **b** to Joseph and his wife, Asenath,
46:15 These are the sons of Jacob who were **b** to Leah in
46:20 Joseph's sons, **b** in the land of Egypt,
46:27 Joseph also had two sons who had been **b** in Egypt.
48: 5 who were **b** here in the land of Egypt before I
48: 6 But the children **b** to you in the future will be your
Ex 1:16 give birth, kill all the boys as soon as they are **b**.
12:19 living with you, as if they had been **b** among you.
12:48 They will be treated just as if they had been **b**
18: 3 for Moses had said when the boy was **b**, "I have
21:22 a pregnant woman so her child is **b** prematurely.
Lev 22:27 "When a bull or a ram or a male goat is **b**, it must
25:45 including those who have been **b** in your land.
Nu 26:59 of Levi, **b** among the Levites in the land of Egypt.
26:60 To Aaron were **b** Nadab, Abihu, Eleazar,
Jos 5: 5 but none of those **b** after the Exodus,
Jdg 13: 8 more instructions about this son who is to be **b**."
13:24 When her son was **b**, they named him Samson.
2Sa 3: 2 These were the sons who were **b** to David in
3: 5 These sons were all **b** to David in Hebron.
5:14 These are the names of David's sons who were **b**
1Ki 1: 6 handsome man and had been **b** next after Absalom.
13: 2 A child named Josiah will be **b** into the dynasty of
2Ki 19: 3 It is like when a child is ready to be **b**,
1Ch 1:36 Gatam, Kenaz, and Amalek, who was **b** to Timna.
3: 1 These were the sons who were **b** to David in
3: 4 These six sons were **b** to David in Hebron,
3: 5 The sons **b** to David in Jerusalem included Shimea,
7:14 **b** to his Aramean concubine, were Asriel
14: 4 These are the names of David's sons who were **b**
Job 3:10 for letting me be **b** to all this trouble.
5: 7 People are **b** for trouble as predictably as sparks fly
8: 9 For we were **b** but yesterday and know so little.
14: 4 Who can create purity in one **b** impure? No one!
15: 7 "Were you the first person ever **b**? Were you **b**
before the hills were made?
38:21 For you were **b** before it was all created, and you
39: 1 Have you watched as the wild deer are **b**?
Ps 22:10 You have been my God from the moment I was **b**.
22:29 Let all mortals—those **b** to die—bow down in his
33: 6 He breathed the word, / and all the stars were **b**.
51: 5 For I was **b** a sinner—/ yes, from the moment my
58: 3 These wicked people are **b** sinners; / even from
78: 6 might know them—/ even the children not yet **b**—
104:30 When you send your Spirit, new life is **b**
127: 4 Children **b** to a young man / are like sharp arrows
139:16 You saw me before I was **b**. / Every day of my life
Pr 8:24 I was **b** before the oceans were created,
8:25 the mountains and the hills were formed, I was **b**—
17:17 and a brother is **b** to help in time of need.
Ecc 2: 7 and women, and others were **b** into my household.
3: 2 A time to be **b** and a time to die. / A time to plant
4: 3 most fortunate of all are those who were never **b**.
4:14 even become king, though he was **b** in poverty.
5:15 and empty-handed as on the day they were **b**.
6: 3 I say he would have been better off **b** dead.
7: 1 the day you die is better than the day you are **b**.
Isa 9: 6 For a child is **b** to us, a son is given to us.
14:29 From that snake a poisonous snake will be **b**,
26:18 no one has been **b** to populate the earth.
37: 3 It is like when a child is ready to be **b**,
45:10 baby said to its father and mother, 'Why was I **b**?
46: 3 and have cared for you since before you were **b**.
48: 1 the name of Israel and **b** into the family of Judah.
49:20 The generations **b** in exile will return and say,
66: 8 Has a nation ever been **b** in a single day?
66: 8 Jerusalem's birth pains begin, the baby will be **b**;
66: 9 I would never keep this nation from being **b**,"
Jer 1: 5 Before you were **b** I set you apart and appointed
16: 3 LORD says about the children **b** here in this city
20:14 Yet I curse the day I was **b**! May the day of my
20:18 Why was I ever **b**? My entire life has been filled
46:16 let's go back to our homeland where we were **b**.
Eze 16: 4 When you were **b**, no one cared about you.
16: 5 On the day you were **b**, you were dumped in a
Hos 1: 2 so some of her children will be **b** to you from other
2: 3 strip her as naked as she was on the day she was **b**.
12: 3 Before Jacob was **b**, he struggled with his brother;
13:13 but they are like a child who resists being **b**.
Mt 1:11 and his brothers (**b** at the time of the exile to
1:18 Now this is how Jesus the Messiah was **b**.
1:25 but she remained a virgin until her son was **b**.
2: 1 Jesus was **b** in the town of Bethlehem in Judea,
2: 4 did the prophets say the Messiah would be **b**?"
19:12 Some are **b** as eunuchs, some have been made that
26:24 Far better for him if he had never been **b**!"
Mk 7:26 Since she was a Gentile, **b** in Syrian Phoenicia,
14:21 Far better for him if he had never been **b**!"
Lk 1:20 you won't be able to speak until the child is **b**.
1:35 So the baby **b** to you will be holy, and he will be
1:57 Now it was time for Elizabeth's baby to be **b**,
2: 6 were there, the time came for her baby to be **b**.
2:11 has been **b** tonight in Bethlehem, the city of David!
Jn 3: 3 "I assure you, unless you are **b** again,
3: 4 go back into his mother's womb and be **b** again?"
3: 5 the Kingdom of God without being **b** of water
3: 7 at my statement that you must be **b** again.
3: 8 so you can't explain how people are **b** of the
7:42 the Messiah will be **b** of the royal line of David,
7:42 the village where King David was **b**."
8:41 They replied, "We were not **b** out of wedlock!
8:58 truth is, I existed before Abraham was even **b**!"
9: 2 disciples asked him, "why was this man **b** blind?
9: 3 "He was **b** blind so the power of God could be
9:19 your son? Was he **b** blind? If so, how can he see?"
9:20 "We know this is our son and that he was **b** blind,
9:32 been able to open the eyes of someone **b** blind.
9:34 "You were **b** in sin!" they answered. "Are you
16:21 When her child is **b**, her anguish gives place to joy
18:37 are right," Jesus said. "I was **b** for that purpose.
Ac 2: 8 the languages of the lands where we were **b**!
7:20 "At that time Moses was **b**—a beautiful child in
7:29 in the land of Midian, where his two sons were **b**.
18: 2 **b** in Pontus, who had recently arrived from Italy
22: 3 "I am a Jew, **b** in Tarsus, a city in Cilicia, and I
Ro 1: 3 as a man, **b** into King David's royal family line.
2:28 Jew just because you were **b** of Jewish parents or
9: 6 for not everyone **b** into a Jewish family is truly a
9:11 But before they were **b**, before they had done
1Co 11:12 all men have been **b** from women ever since,

15: 8 as though I had been **b** at the wrong time.
Gal 1:15 to choose me and call me, even before I was **b**!
4: 4 God sent his Son, **b** of a woman, subject to the
4:23 The son of the slave-wife was **b** in a human
4:23 But the son of the freeborn wife was **b** as God's
4:29 And we who are **b** of the Holy Spirit are
Eph 2: 3 We were **b** with an evil nature, and we were under
Php 3: 5 having been **b** into a pure-blooded Jewish family
1Th 5: 3 birth pains begin when her child is about to be **b**.
2Ti 2: 8 Never forget that Jesus Christ was a man **b** into
Heb 2:14 became flesh and blood by being **b** in human form.
7:10 For although Levi wasn't **b** yet, the seed from
1Pe 1: 3 God has given us the privilege of being **b** again.
1:23 For you have been **b** again. Your new life did not
2Pe 2:12 of instinct, who are **b** to be caught and killed.
1Jn 3: 9 Those who have been **b** into God's family do not
3: 9 keep on sinning, because they have been **b** of God.
4: 7 Anyone who loves is **b** of God and knows God.
Rev 12: 4 ready to devour the baby as soon as it was **b**.

BORNE (5) [BEAR]

Ge 22:20 his brother Nahor's wife, had **b** Nahor eight sons.
Dt 28:57 them the afterbirth and the new baby she has **b**,
Isa 49:15 Can she feel no love for a child she has **b**?
Eze 16:20 and daughters—the children you had **b** to me—
Lk 23:29 the wombs that have not **b** a child and the breasts

BORROW (7) [BORROWED, BORROWER, BORROWER'S, BORROWERS, BORROWS]

Dt 15: 6 money to many nations but will never need to **b**!
28:12 but you will never need to **b** from them.
2Ki 4: 3 "**B** as many empty jars as you can from your
Ne 5: 7 by charging them interest when they **b** money!"
Ps 37:21 The wicked **b** and never repay, / but the godly are
Mt 5:42 and don't turn away from those who want to **b**.
Lk 11: 5 at midnight, wanting to **b** three loaves of bread.

BORROWED (4) [BORROW]

Ex 22:14 at the time, the person who **b** it must pay for it.
2Ki 6: 5 "Ah, my lord!" he cried. "It was a **b** ax!"
Ne 5: 4 "We have already **b** to the limit on our fields
Mt 18:23 to date with servants who had **b** money from him.

BORROWER (2) [BORROW]

Pr 22: 7 rich rule the poor, so the **b** is servant to the lender.
Jer 15:10 to foreclose nor a **b** who refuses to pay—

BORROWER'S (1) [BORROW]

Eze 33:15 For instance, they might give back a **b** pledge,

BORROWERS (1) [BORROW]

Isa 24: 2 and sellers, lenders and **b**, bankers and debtors—

BORROWS (1) [BORROW]

Ex 22:14 "If someone **b** an animal from a neighbor and it is

BOSCATH [KJV] See BOZKATH

BOSS (1)

Ecc 10: 4 If your **b** is angry with you, don't quit! A quiet

BOTH (319)

Ge 2:25 Now, although Adam and his wife were **b** naked,
3: 5 like God, knowing everything, **b** good and evil."
3:22 as we are, knowing everything, **b** good and evil.
7:23 people, animals **b** large and small, and birds.
13: 6 But the land could not support **b** Abram and Lot
17:26 **B** were circumcised the same day,
18:11 And since Abraham and Sarah were **b** very old,
18:23 "Will you destroy **b** innocent and guilty alike?
19:36 So **b** of Lot's daughters became pregnant by their
20:12 we **b** have the same father, though different
20:14 and oxen and servants—**b** men and women—
22: 8 Abraham answered. And they **b** went on together.
27:45 for you. Why should I lose **b** of you in one day?"
32: 5 goats, and many servants, **b** men and women.
32:28 because you have struggled with **b** God and men
33: 4 and kissed him. **B** of them were in tears.
34:28 **b** inside the town and outside in the fields.
36: 7 There was not enough land to support them **b**
40: 8 And they replied, "We **b** had dreams last night,
41:25 "**B** dreams mean the same thing," Joseph told
41:26 and the seven plump heads of grain **b** represent
Ex 4:15 I will help **b** of you to speak clearly, and I will tell
13:15 the land of Egypt, **b** people and animals.
14:29 as the water stood up like a wall on **b** sides.
15: 1 he has thrown **b** horse and rider into the sea.
15:21 he has thrown **b** horse and rider into the sea."
22: 9 **B** parties must come before God for a decision,
26:24 **B** of these corner frames will be made the same
32:15 They were inscribed on **b** sides, front and back.
34:19 male belongs to me—of **b** cattle and sheep.
35:22 **B** men and women came, all whose hearts were
35:34 And the LORD has given **b** him and Oholiab son
Lev 7: 7 "For **b** the sin offering and the guilt offering,
9: 2 **b** with no physical defects, and present them to the
10:19 "Today my sons presented **b** their sin offering
11: 4 either have split hooves or chew the cud, but not **b**.
11: 9 you may eat whatever has **b** fins and scales,
11:10 eat marine animals that do not have **b** fins
11:12 any marine animal that does not have **b** fins
15:18 **b** the man and the woman must bathe,
16:12 after filling **b** his hands with fragrant incense,
16:21 He is to lay **b** of his hands on the goat's head
17: 8 which applies **b** to Israelites and to the foreigners
17:13 "And this command applies **b** to Israelites and to
17:15 "And this command also applies **b** to Israelites
18:17 "Do not have sexual intercourse with **b** a woman
18:17 and her daughter or marry **b** a woman and her
18:26 This applies **b** to you who are Israelites by birth
20:10 **b** the man and the woman must be put to death.
20:11 **b** the man and the woman must die, for they are
20:12 with his daughter-in-law, **b** must be put to death.
20:13 "The penalty for homosexual acts is death to **b**
20:14 If a man has intercourse with **b** a woman and her
20:16 with it, she and the animal must **b** be put to death.
20:16 **B** must die, for they are guilty of a capital offense.
20:17 **B** of them must be publicly cut off from the
20:18 **b** of them must be cut off from the community,
20:19 **B** parties are guilty of a capital offense.
20:20 **B** the man and woman involved are guilty of a
27:10 then **b** the original animal and the substitute will be
27:33 then **b** the original animal and the substituted one
Nu 3:13 I set apart for myself all the firstborn in Israel of **b**
7:13 These were **b** filled with grain offerings of choice
7:19 These were **b** filled with grain offerings of choice
7:25 These were **b** filled with grain offerings of choice
7:31 These were **b** filled with grain offerings of choice
7:37 These were **b** filled with grain offerings of choice
7:43 These were **b** filled with grain offerings of choice
7:49 These were **b** filled with grain offerings of choice
7:55 These were **b** filled with grain offerings of choice
7:61 These were **b** filled with grain offerings of choice
7:67 These were **b** filled with grain offerings of choice
7:73 These were **b** filled with grain offerings of choice
7:79 These were **b** filled with grain offerings of choice
8:17 people of Israel are mine, **b** people and animals.
9:14 The same laws apply **b** to you and to the
10: 3 When **b** trumpets are blown, the people will know
14:22 and the miraculous signs I performed **b** in Egypt
15:16 and regulations will apply **b** to you
15:29 This same law applies **b** to native Israelites
18: 3 or the altar. If they do, **b** you and they will die.
22: 7 officials of **b** Moab and Midian, set out and took
24:24 of Cyprus; / they will oppress **b** Assyria and Eber,
27:14 for you **b** rebelled against my instructions in the
31:11 the plunder and captives, **b** people and animals,
Dt 2:11 **B** the Emites and the Anakites are often referred to
4:39 The LORD is God **b** in heaven and on earth,
14: 7 but if the animal doesn't have **b**, it may not be
14: 9 you may eat whatever has **b** fins and scales.
14:10 eat marine animals that do not have **b** fins
19:17 then **b** the accuser and accused must appear before
21:15 and not the other, and **b** have given him sons.
22:22 **b** he and the other man's wife must be killed.
22:24 you must take **b** of them to the gates of the town
23:18 for **b** are detestable to the LORD your God.
28: 6 wherever you go, **b** in coming and in going.
28:19 cursed wherever you go, **b** in coming and in going.
28:59 then the LORD will overwhelm **b** you and your
29:22 **b** your own descendants and the foreigners who
32:25 **b** young men and young women, / **b** infants and the aged.
32:51 For **b** of you broke faith with me among the
Jos 6: 9 Armed guards marched **b** in front of the priests
6:13 Armed guards marched **b** in front of the priests
11: 3 the kings of Canaan, **b** east and west; the kings of
22:28 it is a reminder of the relationship **b** of us have
Jdg 8:21 So Gideon killed them **b** and took the royal
9: 9 'Should I quit producing the olive oil that blesses **b**
9:13 'Should I quit producing the wine that cheers **b**
Ru 1: 5 **b** Mahlon and Kilion died. This left Naomi alone,
1Sa 2: 6 The LORD brings **b** death and life; / he brings
6: 4 "Since the plague has struck **b** you and your five
14:13 So they climbed up using **b** hands and feet,
14:15 **b** in the camp and in the field, including even the
14:51 Kish, were brothers; **b** were sons of Abiel.
17:36 I have done this to **b** lions and bears, and I'll do it
20:41 **B** of them were in tears as they embraced each
22:23 own life, for the same person wants to kill us **b**."
25:43 from Jezreel, making **b** of them his wives.
2Sa 1:22 **B** Saul and Jonathan killed their strongest foes;
9:13 And Mephibosheth, who was crippled in **b** feet,
15:14 **b** we and the city of Jerusalem will be spared from
18:32 **b** now and in the future, be as that young man is!"
1Ki 3:23 **B** of you claim the living child is yours, and each
5: 8 I can supply you with **b** cedar and cypress.
6:30 The floor in **b** rooms was overlaid with gold.
7:29 **B** the panels and the crossbars were decorated with
8:29 May you watch over this Temple **b** day and night,
10:19 On **b** sides of the seat were armrests,
11:21 that David and his commander Joab were **b** dead,
2Ki 12:21 and Jehozabad son of Shomer—**b** trusted advisers.
14:28 and how he recovered for Israel **b** Damascus
17:13 his prophets and seers to warn **b** Israel and Judah:
21: 5 of heaven in **b** courtyards of the LORD's Temple.
23:24 **b** in Jerusalem and throughout the land of Judah.
25:25 everyone with him, **b** Judeans and Babylonians.
1Ch 12: 8 They were expert with **b** shield and spear, as fierce
12:15 all the people living in the lowlands on **b** the east
24: 5 from among the descendants of **b** Eleazar
2Ch 3:13 So the wingspan of **b** cherubim together was 30
3:13 They **b** stood and faced out toward the main room
6:20 May you watch over this Temple **b** day and night,
9:18 On **b** sides of the seat were armrests,
14: 8 **B** armies were composed of courageous fighting
19: 8 for cases concerning **b** the law of the LORD
26:10 **b** on the hillsides and in the fertile valleys.
33: 5 He put these altars for the stars of heaven in **b**
36:17 killing **b** young and old, men and women, healthy
36:18 and the treasures from **b** the LORD's Temple
Ezr 2:65 7,337 servants and 200 singers, **b** men and women.
8:33 Noadiah son of Binnui—**b** of whom were Levites.
10: 9 They were trembling **b** because of the seriousness
Ne 7:67 7,337 servants and 245 singers, **b** men and women.
Est 9:31 decreed by **b** Mordecai the Jew and Queen Esther.
Job 9:22 'He destroys **b** the blameless and the wicked.'
12:16 deceivers and deceived are **b** in his power.
21:26 **B** alike are buried in the same dust, **b** eaten by the same worms.
31:15 For God created **b** me and my servants. He created us **b**.
36: 5 He is mighty in **b** power and understanding.
Ps 11: 5 The LORD examines **b** the righteous
58: 9 God will sweep them away, **b** young and old,
74:16 **B** day and night belong to you; / you made the
74:17 of the earth, / and you make **b** summer and winter.
104:25 with life of every kind, / **b** great and small.
106: 6 **B** we and our ancestors have sinned. / We have
115:13 those who fear the LORD, / **b** great and small.
115:14 the LORD richly bless / **b** you and your children.
115:18 **b** now and forever! / Praise the LORD!
121: 8 over you as you come and go, / **b** now and forever.
125: 2 and protects his people, **b** now and forever.
135: 8 in each Egyptian home, / **b** people and animals.
139: 5 You **b** precede and follow me. / You place your
139:12 as day. / Darkness and light are **b** alike to you.
Pr 3: 4 Then you will find favor with **b** God and people,
15: 3 keeping his eye on **b** the evil and the good.
20:12 and eyes to see—**b** are gifts from the LORD.
22: 2 have this in common: The LORD made them **b**.
27: 3 the resentment caused by a fool is heavier than **b**.
29:13 the LORD gives light to the eyes of **b**.
Ecc 2: 7 I bought slaves, **b** men and women, and others
2: 8 I hired wonderful singers, **b** men and women,
2:15 **B** of them die. Just as the fool will die, so will I.
2:16 For the wise person and the fool **b** die, and in the days to come, **b** will be forgotten.
3:17 **b** good and bad, for all their deeds."
3:19 For humans and animals **b** breathe the same air, and **b** die.
3:20 **B** go to the same place—the dust from which they
7:14 hard times strike, realize that **b** come from God.
Isa 7:16 the kings of Israel and Aram—will **b** be dead.
8: 2 son of Jeberekiah, **b** known as honest men,
8: 4 the king of Assyria will invade **b** Damascus
9:14 the LORD will destroy **b** the head and the tail,
9:21 will feed on Manasseh, and **b** will devour Judah.
15: 9 **b** those who try to run and those who remain
20: 4 them walk naked and barefoot, **b** young and old,
46: 2 **B** the idols and the ones carrying them are bowed
57:19 May they have peace, **b** near and far, for I will heal
65: 7 **b** for their own sins and for those of their
66: 2 My hands have made **b** heaven and earth, and they
Jer 6:21 Fathers and sons will **b** fall over them. Neighbors
11:10 and Judah have **b** broken the covenant I made with
16: 6 **B** the great and the lowly will die in this land.
21: 6 upon this city, and **b** people and animals will die.
32:14 Take **b** this sealed deed and the unsealed copy,
34: 9 to free their Hebrew slaves—**b** men and women.
36:19 "You and Jeremiah should **b** hide," the officials
48: 8 **b** on the plateaus and in the valleys,
50: 3 will be gone; **b** people and animals will flee.
Eze 2:10 and I saw that **b** sides were covered with funeral
10:12 **B** the cherubim and the wheels were covered with
13:15 and those who whitewashed it are **b** gone.
13:18 the souls of my people, **b** young and old alike.
14: 7 **b** Israelites and foreigners, who reject me and set
14:13 and sending a famine to destroy **b** people
15: 5 Vine branches are useless **b** before and after being
16:37 **b** those you loved and those you hated—
18: 4 are mine to judge—**b** parents and children alike.
22: 4 you are guilty of **b** murder and idolatry. Your day
22: 5 you will be mocked by people **b** far and near.
23:37 They have committed **b** adultery and murder—
29: 8 O Egypt, and destroy **b** people and animals.
29:10 I am now the enemy of **b** you and your river.
30:22 I will break **b** of his arms—the good arm along
41:23 **B** the Holy Place and the Most Holy Place had
41:26 On **b** sides of the foyer there were recessed
47: 7 many trees were now growing on **b** sides of the
47:12 All kinds of fruit trees will grow along **b** sides of
Da 8: 7 at the ram and struck it, breaking off **b** its horns.
12: 7 raised **b** his hands toward heaven and took this
Hos 4: 9 So now I will punish **b** priests and people for all
8:14 But they have **b** forgotten their Maker. Therefore,
Am 2: 7 **B** father and son sleep with the same woman,
6:11 homes **b** great and small will be smashed to pieces.
Mic 1: 1 The messages concerned **b** Samaria and Jerusalem,
7: 3 They go about their evil deeds with **b** hands.
Zep 1: 3 "I will sweep away **b** people and animals alike.
Hag 1:11 a drought to starve **b** you and your cattle and to
Zec 8:13 Now I will rescue you and make you **b** a symbol
14: 8 flowing continuously **b** in summer and in winter.
Mt 5:45 For he gives his sunlight to **b** the evil and the good,
6:24 the other. You cannot serve **b** God and money.
9:17 That way **b** the wine and the wineskins are
10:28 only God, who can destroy **b** soul and body in hell.
12:22 who was **b** blind and unable to talk, was brought to
12:22 healed the man so that he could **b** speak and see.
13:30 Let **b** grow together until the harvest. Then I will
15:14 guides another, they will **b** fall into a ditch."
17:27 a coin. Take the coin and pay the tax for **b** of us."
18: 8 into the unquenchable fire with **b** of your hands
27:61 **B** Mary Magdalene and the other Mary were
Lk 1: 7 was barren, and now they were **b** very old.

2:52 So Jesus grew **b** in height and in wisdom, and he
3: 3 Then John went from place to place on **b** sides of
5: 7 and soon **b** boats were filled with fish and on the
7:42 so he kindly forgave them **b**, canceling their debts.
15:18 "Father, I have sinned against **b** heaven and you,
15:21 'Father, I have sinned against **b** heaven and you,
16:13 the other. You cannot serve **b** God and money."
23:32 Two others, **b** criminals, were led out to be
24:19 highly regarded by **b** God and all the people.
Jn 2:22 And they believed **b** Jesus and the Scriptures.
4:36 What joy awaits **b** the planter and the harvester
11:48 and destroy **b** our Temple and our nation."
15:24 they saw all that I did and yet hated **b** of us—
Ac 2:10 visitors from Rome (**b** Jews and converts to
2:36 made this Jesus whom you crucified to be **b** Lord
5:14 to the Lord—crowds of **b** men and women.
7:22 and he became mighty in **b** speech and action.
8: 3 dragging out **b** men and women to throw them into
9: 2 He wanted to bring them—**b** men and women—
11:26 **B** of them stayed there with the church for a full
13:50 Then the Jewish leaders stirred up **b** the influential
14: 1 with such power that a great number of **b** Jews
15:32 Then Judas and Silas, **b** being prophets,
19:10 **b** Jews and Greeks—heard the Lord's message.
22: 4 binding and delivering **b** men and women to
23:10 and the men were tugging at Paul from **b** sides,
24:15 that he will raise **b** the righteous and the ungodly.
25:24 this is the man whose death is demanded **b** by the
26:17 And I will protect you from **b** your own people
26:29 I pray to God that **b** you and everyone here in this
Ro 9:24 he selected, **b** from the Jews and from the Gentiles.
11:22 Notice how God is **b** kind and severe. He is severe
1Co 1:24 **b** Jews and Gentiles, Christ is the mighty power of
6:13 though someday God will do away with **b** of them.
7: 5 to this rule would be the agreement of **b** husband
8: 5 and many lords, **b** in heaven and on earth.
14:15 Well then, what shall I do? I will do **b**. I will pray
2Co 6: 7 as our weapon, **b** to attack and to defend ourselves.
12:18 For we **b** have the same Spirit and walk in each
Eph 2:16 Christ reconciled **b** groups to God by means of his
2:18 Now all of us, **b** Jews and Gentiles, may come to
3: 6 **B** groups have believed the Good News, and **b** are
part of the same body and enjoy together
6: 9 remember, you **b** have the same Master in heaven,
Php 1: 7 **b** when I was in prison and when I was out,
1Th 1: 6 In this way, you imitated **b** us and the Lord.
2Th 2:15 grip on everything we taught you **b** in person
1Ti 4: 8 for it promises a reward in **b** this life and the next.
5:17 especially those who work hard at **b** preaching
6: 4 Anyone who teaches anything different is **b**
Phm 1:11 in the past, but now he is very useful to **b** of us.
1:16 to you, **b** as a slave and as a brother in the Lord.
Heb 5: 3 **b** for their sins and for his own sins.
6:18 So God has given us **b** his promise and his oath.
9:19 and sprinkled **b** the book of God's laws and all the
Jas 3:11 Does a spring of water bubble out with **b** fresh
1Pe 4: 5 who will judge everyone, **b** the living and the dead.
2Pe 3: 1 and in **b** of them I have tried to stimulate your
3:18 be all glory and honor, **b** now and forevermore.
2Jn 1: 9 you will have fellowship with **b** the Father
Rev 1:19 **b** the things that are now happening and the things
19:18 of all humanity, **b** free and slave, small and great."
19:20 **B** the beast and his false prophet were thrown alive
20:12 I saw the dead, **b** great and small, standing before
22:16 I am **b** the source of David and the heir to his

BOTHER (21) [BOTHERED, BOTHERING]

Dt 2: 5 Don't **b** them, for I have given them all the hill
2: 9 'Do not **b** the Moabites, the descendants of Lot,
2:19 But do not **b** the Ammonites, the descendants of
Ru 2: 9 I have warned the young men not to **b** you.
2Sa 24:10 the census, David's conscience began to **b** him.
2Ki 3:14 I would not **b** with you except for my respect for
Job 30:20 I stand before you, and you don't **b** to look.
Ps 119:155 for they do not **b** with your principles.
Pr 9: 8 So don't **b** rebuking mockers; they will only hate
Jer 5:12 about the LORD and have said, 'He won't **b** us!
15: 5 for you? Who will even **b** to ask how you are?
22:21 I warned you, but you replied, 'Don't **b** me.'
Eze 23:19 But that didn't **b** her. She turned to even greater
39:26 And then no one will **b** them or make them afraid.
Am 7:13 Don't **b** us here in Bethel with your prophecies,
Mt 19:13 for them. The disciples told them not to **b** him.
24:26 is out in the desert,' don't **b** to go and look.
Mk 10:13 but the disciples told them not to **b** him.
Lk 11: 7 He would call out from his bedroom, 'Don't **b** me.
18:15 but the disciples told them not to **b** him.
Gal 2:12 Gentile Christians, who don't **b** with circumcision.

BOTHERED (3) [BOTHER]

Jer 17: 8 Such trees are not **b** by the heat or worried by long
1Co 10:25 to idols, and then your conscience won't be **b**.
10:27 about it. Your conscience should not be **b** by this.

BOTHERING (9) [BOTHER]

1Sa 16:16 for you whenever the tormenting spirit is **b** you.
24: 5 But then David's conscience began **b** him
Isa 27: 4 If I find briers and thorns **b** her, I will burn them
Mt 8:29 at him, "Why are you **b** us, Son of God?
15:23 they said. "She is **b** us with all her begging."
Mk 1:24 "Why are you **b** us, Jesus of Nazareth?
5: 7 shrieking, "Why are you **b** me, Jesus,
Lk 4:34 "Go away! Why are you **b** us, Jesus of Nazareth?
8:28 screaming, "Why are you **b** me, Jesus, Son of the

BOTTLE (3)

Ps 56: 8 You have collected all my tears in your **b**.
Ecc 10: 1 Dead flies will cause even a **b** of perfume to stink!
Jer 48:38 For I have smashed Moab like an old, unwanted **b**.

BOTTOM (27) [BOTTOMLESS]

Ge 6:16 **b**, middle, and upper—and put a door in the side.
Ex 14:23 followed them across the **b** of the sea.
15: 5 covered them; / they sank to the **b** like a stone.
26:24 These corner frames will be connected at the **b**
28:28 Then attach the **b** rings of the chestpiece to the
36:29 These corner frames were connected at the **b**
36:29 a single ring, forming a single unit from top to **b**.
39:21 Blue cords were used to attach the **b** rings of the
39:24 Pomegranates were attached to the **b** edge of the
Jdg 6:11 **b** of a winepress to hide the grain from the
2Sa 22:16 blast of his breath, / the **b** of the sea could be seen,
1Ki 6: 6 the **b** floor being 7-1/2 feet wide, the second floor
6: 8 The entrance to the **b** floor was on the south side of
17:12 in the jar and a little cooking oil in the **b** of the jug.
Ps 18:15 of your breath, / the **b** of the sea could be seen,
35:10 I will praise him from the **b** of my heart:
106: 9 He led Israel across the sea **b** that was as dry as a
Isa 63:13 Where is the one who led them through the **b** of
Jer 38: 6 but there was a thick layer of mud at the **b**,
Eze 23:34 you will drain that cup of terror to the very **b**.
27:32 such a city as Tyre, / now silent at the **b** of the sea?
27:34 are a wrecked ship, / broken at the **b** of the sea.
41: 7 A stairway led up from the **b** level through the
Am 9: 3 Even if they hide at the **b** of the ocean, I will send
Jnh 1: 4 violent storm that threatened to send them to the **b**.
Mt 27:51 in the Temple was torn in two, from top to **b**.
Mk 15:38 in the Temple was torn in two, from top to **b**.

BOTTOMLESS (7) [BOTTOM]

Lk 8:31 kept begging Jesus not to send them into the **B** Pit.
Rev 9: 1 and he was given the key to the shaft of the **b** pit.
9:11 Their king is the angel from the **b** pit; his name in
11: 7 the beast that comes up out of the **b** pit will declare
17: 8 And yet he will soon come up out of the **b** pit
20: 1 come down from heaven with the key to the **b** pit
20: 3 The angel threw him into the **b** pit, which he

BOUGHS (2)

Dt 24:20 from your olive trees, don't go over the **b** twice.
Eze 31: 8 equal to it; no plane tree had **b** to compare.

BOUGHT (43) [BUY]

Ge 17:27 whether they were born there or **b** as servants.
23:17 He **b** the plot of land belonging to Ephron at
33:19 Jacob **b** the land he camped on from the family of
47:20 So Joseph **b** all the land of Egypt for Pharaoh.
47:23 "See, I have **b** you and your land for Pharaoh.
49:30 which Abraham **b** from Ephron the Hittite for a
49:32 It is the cave that my grandfather Abraham **b** from
50:13 This is the cave that Abraham had **b** for a
Ex 21: 8 If she does not please the man who **b** her, he may
allow her to be **b** back again.
Lev 25:27 has the right to redeem it from the one who **b** it.
25:48 They may be **b** back by a close relative—
Jos 24:32 in the parcel of ground Jacob had **b** from the sons
Ru 4: 9 "You are witnesses that today I have **b** from
2Sa 3:14 for I **b** her with the lives of one hundred
15: 1 After this, Absalom **b** a chariot and horses, and he
1Ki 10:29 and horses could be **b** for 150 pieces of silver.
16:24 Then Omri **b** the hill now known as Samaria from
2Ch 1:17 and horses could be **b** for 150 pieces of silver.
Ezr 3: 7 and **b** cedar logs from the people of Tyre
Job 28:15 "It cannot be **b** for gold or silver.
Ecc 2: 7 I **b** slaves, both men and women, and others were
Jer 13: 2 So I **b** the belt as the LORD directed me and put
32: 9 So I **b** the field at Anathoth, paying Hanamel
32:43 "Fields will again be **b** and sold in this land about
32:44 Yes, fields will once again be **b** and sold—
37:12 the land of Benjamin, to see the property he had **b**.
Hos 3: 2 So I **b** her back for fifteen pieces of silver
Jnh 1: 3 He **b** a ticket and went on board, hoping that by
Mic 1: 7 These things were **b** with the money earned by her
Zec 11:11 Those who **b** and sold sheep were watching me,
Mt 13:46 great value, he sold everything he owned and **b** it!
Mk 7: 4 they eat nothing **b** from the market unless they
15:46 Joseph **b** a long sheet of linen cloth, and taking
Lk 14:18 One said he had just **b** a field and wanted to
14:19 Another said he had just **b** five pair of oxen
Ac 1:18 (Judas **b** a field with the money he received for his
7:16 and buried in the tomb Abraham had **b** from the
8:20 perish with you for thinking God's gift can be **b**!
1Co 6:20 for God **b** you with a high price. So you must
2Pe 2: 1 and even turn against their Master who **b** them.
Rev 18:12 She **b** great quantities of gold, silver, jewels,
18:13 She also **b** cinnamon, spice, incense, myrrh,

BOULDER (2) [BOULDERS]

Pr 26:27 If you roll a **b** down on others, it will roll back
Rev 18:21 Then a mighty angel picked up a **b** as large as a

BOULDERS (1) [BOULDER]

Isa 62:10 Smooth out the road; pull out the **b**; raise a flag for

BOUNCED (1)

La 2:20 little children, those they once **b** on their knees?

BOUND (38) [BIND]

Ge 42:16 I'll keep the rest of you here, **b** in prison.
44:30 the boy. Our father's life is **b** up in the boy's life.
Nu 6: 4 As long as they are **b** by their Nazirite vow,
Jos 2:20 however, we are not **b** by this oath in any way."
Jdg 16:21 where he was **b** with bronze chains and made to
2Sa 3:34 Your hands were not **b**; / your feet were not
2Ki 25: 7 **b** him in bronze chains, and led him away to
2Ch 33:11 **b** him in bronze chains, and led him away to
36: 6 and he **b** Jehoiakim in chains and led him away to
Ne 10:29 now all heartily **b** themselves with an oath.
Jer 39: 7 he gouged out Zedekiah's eyes, **b** him in chains,
40: 1 He had found Jeremiah **b** in chains among the
52:11 **b** him in bronze chains, and led him away to
La 3: 7 and I cannot escape. He has **b** me in heavy chains.
Eze 3:25 There you will be **b** with ropes so you cannot go
27:24 and many-colored carpets **b** with cords and made
30:21 Neither has it been **b** up with a splint to make it
34: 4 have not tended the sick or **b** up the broken bones.
Da 4:15 **b** with a band of iron and bronze and surrounded
4:23 **b** with a band of iron and bronze and surrounded
Na 3:10 as servants. All their leaders were **b** in chains.
Mt 27: 2 Then they **b** him and took him to Pilate, the Roman
Mk 15: 1 They **b** Jesus and took him to Pilate, the Roman
Jn 11:44 And Lazarus came out, **b** in graveclothes, his face
18:24 Then Annas **b** Jesus and sent him to Caiaphas,
Ac 21:11 Paul's belt and **b** his own feet and hands with it.
21:11 'So shall the owner of this belt be **b** by the Jewish
21:33 arrested him and ordered him **b** with two chains.
22:29 because he had ordered him **b** and whipped.
23:12 and **b** themselves with an oath to neither eat nor
23:14 "We have **b** ourselves under oath to neither eat nor
27: 6 Egyptian ship from Alexandria that was **b** for Italy,
28:20 so I could tell you that I am **b** with this chain
1Co 9:19 This means I am not **b** to obey people just
Heb 3: 1 friends who belong to God and are **b** for heaven,
6:17 God also **b** himself with an oath, so that those who
Rev 9:14 "Release the four angels who are **b** at the great
20: 2 Satan—and **b** him in chains for a thousand years.

BOUNDARIES (27) [BOUNDARY]

Ex 19:12 Do not go up on the mountain or even touch its **b**.
19:21 back down and warn the people not to cross the **b**.
19:23 You told me to set **b** around the mountain and to
19:24 or the people cross the **b** to come up here.
23:31 And I will fix your **b** from the Red Sea to the
34:24 that stand in your way and will enlarge your **b**.
Nu 34: 2 you as your special possession, these will be the **b**.
34:12 to the Dead Sea. These are the **b** of your land."
Dt 32: 8 human race, / he established the **b** of the peoples
Jos 12: 5 and westward to the **b** of the kingdoms of Geshur
15:12 These are the **b** for the families of the tribe of
19:18 Its **b** included the following towns: Jezreel,
19:25 Its **b** included these towns: Helkath, Hali, Beten,
Job 26:10 separated the waters; he set the **b** for day and night.
38: 8 "Who defined the **b** of the sea as it burst from the
Ps 33: 7 He gave the sea its **b** / and locked the oceans in
74:17 You set the **b** of the earth, / and you make both
Pr 8:29 the seas, so they would not spread beyond their **b**.
Eze 16:27 why I struck you with my fist and reduced your **b**.
27: 4 You extended your **b** into the sea. Your builders
45: 7 with the eastern and western **b** of the tribal areas.
47:21 "Divide the land within these **b** among the tribes
48: 7 all of whose **b** extend from east to west.
48:25 of Issachar with the same eastern and western **b**.
Mic 2: 5 Others will set your **b** then, and the LORD's
Ac 17:26 should rise and fall, and he determined their **b**.
2Co 10:13 Our goal is to stay within the **b** of God's plan for

BOUNDARY (54) [BOUNDARIES, BOUNDLESS, BOUNDS]

Ge 31:53 God of his father, Isaac, to respect the **b** line.
Ex 19:12 Set **b** lines that the people may not pass.
19:13 or animals that cross the **b** must be stoned to death
Nu 21:13 The Arnon is the **b** line between the Moabites
21:24 because the **b** of the Ammonites was fortified.
34: 3 The southern **b** will begin on the east at the Dead
34: 5 From Azmon the **b** will turn toward the brook of
34: 6 "Your western **b** will be the coastline of the
34: 7 "Your northern **b** will begin at the Mediterranean
34: 9 to Hazar-enan. This will be your northern **b**.
34:10 "The eastern **b** will start at Hazar-enan and run
34:11 From there the **b** will run down along the eastern
Dt 19:14 never steal someone's land by moving the **b**
27:17 property from a neighbor by moving a **b** marker.'
Jos 12: 2 which serves as a **b** for the Ammonites.
13: 3 on the **b** of Egypt, northward to the **b** of Ekron,
13:23 The Jordan River marked the western **b** for the
15: 2 The southern **b** began at the south bay of the Dead
15: 4 the Mediterranean Sea. This was their southern **b**.
15: 5 The eastern **b** extended along the Dead Sea to the
15: 5 The northern **b** began at the bay where the Jordan
15: 8 The **b** then passed through the valley of the son of
15:11 The **b** line then proceeded to the slope of the hill
15:12 The western **b** was the shoreline of the
15:46 From Ekron the **b** extended west and included the
16: 5 The eastern **b** of their inheritance began at
16: 6 The northern **b** began at the Mediterranean,
17: 7 The **b** of the tribe of Manasseh extended from the
17: 7 Then the **b** went south from Micmethath to the
18:12 The northern **b** began at the Jordan River,
18:13 From there the **b** went south to Luz (that is, Bethel)
18:14 The **b** then ran south along the western edge of the
18:14 to the tribe of Judah. This was the western **b**.
18:15 The southern **b** began at the outskirts of

18:17 From En-rogel the **b** proceeded northeast to
18:20 The eastern **b** was the Jordan River. This was the
19:10 The **b** of Zebulun's inheritance started at Sarid.
19:12 the **b** line went east from Sarid to the border of
19:14 The northern **b** of Zebulun passed Hannathon
19:22 The **b** also touched Tabor, Shahazumah,
19:26 The **b** on the west went from Carmel to
19:29 Then the **b** turned toward Ramah and the fortified
19:33 Its **b** ran from Heleph, from the oak at Zaanannim,
19:34 The western **b** ran past Aznoth-tabor, then to
19:34 and touched the **b** of Zebulun in the south,
19:34 the **b** of Asher on the west, and the Jordan River
Jdg 1:36 The **b** of the Amorites ran from Scorpion Pass to
Job 24: 2 Evil people steal land by moving the **b** markers.
Ps 104: 9 Then you set a firm **b** for the seas, / so they would
Pr 22:28 the ancient **b** markers set up by your ancestors.
23:10 orphans by moving the ancient **b** markers,
Jer 5:22 an everlasting **b** that the waters cannot cross.
Eze 48: 1 Its **b** line follows the Hethlon road to Lebo-hamath

BOUNDING (1)

SS 2: 8 leaping on the mountains and **b** over the hills.

BOUNDLESS (2) [BOUNDARY]

Pr 21:24 are proud and haughty; they act with **b** arrogance.
1Pe 1: 3 for it is by his **b** mercy that God has given us the

BOUNDS (3) [BOUNDARY]

Ge 49:26 reaching to the utmost **b** of the everlasting hills.
Jer 5:22 and roar, but they can never pass the **b** I set.
Hos 14: 4 and faithlessness, and my love will know no **b**,

BOUNTIFUL (12) [BOUNTY]

Dt 16:15 for it is the LORD your God who gives you **b**
2Ki 18:32 a country with **b** harvests of grain and wine,
Ps 65: 9 not run dry; / they provide a **b** harvest of grain,
65:11 You crown the year with a **b** harvest;
68:10 finally settled, / and with a **b** harvest, O God,
69:22 Let the **b** table set before them become a snare,
85:12 his blessings. / Our land will yield its **b** crops.
Isa 32:12 Beat your breasts in sorrow for your **b** farms that
32:20 Wherever they plant seed, **b** crops will spring up.
36:17 a country with **b** harvests of grain and wine,
Ro 5:15 brought forgiveness to many through God's **b** gift.
11: 9 when he said, / "Let their **b** table become a snare,

BOUNTY (5) [BOUNTIFUL]

Lev 25: 7 animals will also be allowed to eat of the land's **b**.
Dt 15:14 Share with him some of the **b** with which the
33:14 grow in the sun, / and the **b** produced each month;
Jer 2: 7 I brought you into a fruitful land to enjoy its **b**
31:14 I will satisfy my people with my **b**. I, the LORD,

BOUQUET (1)

SS 1:14 He is like a **b** of flowers in the gardens of

BOUTS (2)

Isa 5:11 begin long drinking **b** that last late into the night.
Hos 4:18 The men of Israel finish up their drinking **b** and off

BOW (74) [BOWED, BOWING, BOWS, BOWSTRINGS]

Ge 27: 3 Take your **b** and a quiver full of arrows out into the
27:29 May all your mother's sons **b** low before you.
37:10 and I actually come and **b** before you?"
48:22 I took from the Amorites with my sword and **b**."
49: 8 All your relatives will **b** before you.
49:24 But his **b** remained strong, / and his arms were
Ex 20: 5 You must never worship or **b** down to them,
33:10 would stand and **b** low at their tent entrances.
Dt 5: 9 You must never worship or **b** down to them,
33:29 Your enemies will **b** low before you,
1Sa 2:36 Then all of your descendants will **b** before his
18: 4 by giving him his robe, tunic, sword, **b**, and belt.
20:40 Then Jonathan gave his **b** and arrows to the boy
2Sa 1:18 It is known as the Song of the **B**, and it is recorded
15: 5 And when people tried to **b** before him,
22:35 he strengthens me to draw a **b** of bronze.
2Ki 5:18 may the LORD pardon me when I **b**, too."
9:24 Then Jehu drew his **b** and shot Joram between the
13:15 Elisha told him, "Get a **b** and some arrows."
13:16 told the king of Israel to put his hand on the **b**,
17:35 or **b** before them or serve them or offer sacrifices
17:36 You must worship him and **b** before him;
Est 3: 2 All the king's officials would **b** down before
3: 2 But Mordecai refused to **b** down or show him
3: 5 When Haman saw that Mordecai would not **b**
Ps 7:12 sharpen his sword; / he will bend and string his **b**.
18:34 he strengthens me to draw a **b** of bronze.
22:27 People from every nation will **b** down before him.
22:29 those born to die—**b** down in his presence.
44: 6 I do not trust my **b**; / I do not count on my sword
46: 9 He breaks the **b** and snaps the spear in two;
68:31 let Ethiopia **b** in submission to God.
72: 9 Desert nomads will **b** before him; / his enemies
72:11 All kings will **b** before him, / and all nations will
78:57 had been. / They were as useless as a crooked **b**.
81: 9 you must not **b** down before a false god.
86: 9 each one—/ will come and **b** before you, Lord;
95: 6 Come, let us worship and **b** down. / Let us kneel
97: 7 worthless gods—/ for every god must **b** to him.
99: 5 our God! / **B** low before his feet, for he is holy!
132: 7 place of the LORD; / let us **b** low before him.
138: 2 I **b** before your holy Temple as I worship. / I will
Pr 14:19 Evil people will **b** before good people; the wicked
will **b** at the gates of the godly.
Isa 2: 8 The people **b** down and worship these things they
17: 8 They will never again **b** down to their Asherah
41: 2 the sword. He scatters them in the wind with his **b**.
44:19 Should I **b** down to worship a chunk of wood?"
45:23 Every knee will **b** to me, and every tongue will
46: 6 a god from it. Then they **b** down and worship it!
49: 7 Princes will **b** low because the LORD has chosen
49:23 They will **b** to the earth before you and lick the
60:14 of your tormentors will come and **b** before you.
65:12 All of you will **b** before the executioner, for when I
Jer 46: 9 and Lydia who are skilled with the shield and **b**!
La 2: 4 He bends his **b** against his people as though he
3:12 He bent his **b** and aimed it squarely at me.
Da 3: 5 **b** to the ground to worship King Nebuchadnezzar's
3:10 You issued a decree requiring all the people to **b**
3:15 If you **b** down and worship the statue I have made
Hos 7:16 They are like a crooked **b** that always misses its
Mic 6: 6 Should we **b** before God with offerings of yearling
Zep 1: 5 For they go up to their roofs and **b** to the sun,
Zec 9:13 Judah is my **b**, and Israel is my arrow! Jerusalem is
10: 4 the tent peg, the battle **b**, and all the rulers.
Mk 12:38 and to have everyone **b** to them as they walk in the
Lk 4: 7 I will give it all to you if you will **b** down
20:46 and to have everyone **b** to them as they walk in the
Ac 27:41 The **b** of the ship stuck fast, while the stern was
Ro 14:11 as I live,' says the Lord, / 'every knee will **b** to me
Php 2:10 so that at the name of Jesus every knee will **b**,
Jas 4:10 When you **b** down before the Lord and admit your
Rev 3: 9 but are not—to come and **b** down at your feet.
6: 2 Its rider carried a **b**, and a crown was placed on his

BOWED (57) [BOW]

Ge 17:17 Then Abraham **b** down to the ground, but he
19: 1 Then he welcomed them and **b** low to the ground.
23: 7 Then Abraham **b** low before them and said,
23:12 Abraham **b** again to the people of the land,
24:48 "Then I **b** my head and worshiped the LORD.
24:52 Abraham's servant **b** to the ground and worshiped
33: 3 his brother, he **b** low seven times before him.
33: 6 forward with their children and **b** low before him.
33: 7 Leah came with her children, and they **b** down.
37: 7 bundles all gathered around and **b** low before it!"
37: 9 moon, and eleven stars **b** low before me!"
42: 6 They **b** low before him, with their faces to the
43:26 they gave him their gifts and **b** low before him.
43:28 is alive and well." Then they **b** again before him.
47:31 and Jacob **b** in worship as he leaned on his staff.
48:12 their grandfather's knees, and he **b** low to him.
50:18 Then his brothers came and **b** low before him.
Ex 4:31 for them, they all **b** their heads and worshiped.
12:27 and did not destroy us.' " Then all the people **b**
18: 7 He **b** to him respectfully and greeted him warmly.
Jos 7: 6 and **b** down facing the Ark of the LORD until
1Sa 20:41 Then David **b** to Jonathan with his face to the
24: 8 when Saul looked around, David **b** low before him.
25:23 quickly got off her donkey and **b** low before him.
25:41 She **b** low to the ground and responded, "Yes,
2Sa 9: 6 he **b** low in great fear and said, "I am your
14:33 and Absalom came and **b** low before the king,
18:21 king what you have seen." The man **b** and ran off.
18:28 He **b** low with his face to the ground and said,
24:20 and **b** before the king with his face to the ground.
1Ki 1:16 Bathsheba **b** low before him. "What can I do for
1:23 Nathan went in and **b** low before the king.
1:31 Then Bathsheba **b** low before him again
1:47 Then the king **b** his head in worship as he lay in
1:53 He came and **b** low before the king, and Solomon
2:19 his throne to meet her, and he **b** down before her.
19:18 thousand others in Israel who have never **b** to Baal
2Ki 2:15 they went to meet him and **b** down before him.
21: 3 He also **b** before all the forces of heaven
1Ch 21:21 threshing floor and **b** to the ground before David.
29:20 and they **b** low and knelt before the LORD
2Ch 20:18 Then King Jehoshaphat **b** down with his face to the
24:17 the leaders of Judah came and **b** before King Joash
25:14 them up as his own gods, **b** down in front of them,
29:29 and everyone with him **b** down in worship.
29:30 they offered joyous praise and **b** down in worship.
33: 3 He also **b** before all the stars of heaven
Ne 8: 6 Then they **b** down and worshiped the LORD with
Ps 106:19 they **b** before an image made of gold.
Isa 26:16 We were **b** beneath the burden of your discipline.
46: 2 the idols and the ones carrying them are **b** down.
Da 2:46 Then King Nebuchadnezzar **b** to the ground before
3: 7 **b** to the ground and worshiped the statue that King
Lk 24: 5 The women were terrified and **b** low before them.
Jn 19:30 Then he **b** his head and gave up his spirit.
Ro 11: 4 I have seven thousand others who have never **b**
Heb 11:21 and **b** in worship as he leaned on his staff.

BOWELS (3)

Jdg 3:22 Ehud left the dagger in, and the king's **b** emptied.
2Ch 21:15 disease until it causes your **b** to come out."
21:19 the disease caused his **b** to come out, and he died

BOWING (8) [BOW]

Ge 18: 2 welcoming them by **b** low to the ground.
Ex 11: 8 officials of Egypt will come running to me, **b** low.
Dt 8:19 follow other gods, worshiping and **b** down to them,
Jdg 2:17 themselves to other gods, **b** down to them.
2:19 other gods, worshiping and **b** down to them.
Isa 58: 5 **b** your heads like a blade of grass in the wind.
Jer 2:20 you have prostituted yourselves by **b** down to
1Pe 3:22 and authorities and powers are **b** before him.

BOWL (17) [BOWL-SHAPED, BOWLFUL, BOWLS]

Jdg 5:25 and Jael gave him milk. / In a **b** fit for kings,
2Ki 2:20 Elisha said, "Bring me a new **b** with salt in it."
Pr 15:17 A **b** of soup with someone you love is better than
Ecc 12: 6 silver cord of life snaps and the golden **b** is broken.
Zec 4: 2 "I see a solid gold lampstand with a **b** of oil on top
4: 2 Around the **b** are seven lamps, each one having
4: 3 I see two olive trees, one on each side of the **b**."
9:15 They will be filled with blood like a **b**,
Mt 27:24 So he sent for a **b** of water and washed his hands
Rev 15: 7 a gold **b** filled with the terrible wrath of God,
16: 2 left the Temple and poured out his **b** over the earth,
16: 3 Then the second angel poured out his **b** on the sea,
16: 4 Then the third angel poured out his **b** on the rivers
16: 8 Then the fourth angel poured out his **b** on the sun,
16:10 Then the fifth angel poured out his **b** on the throne
16:12 Then the sixth angel poured out his **b** on the great
16:17 Then the seventh angel poured out his **b** into the

BOWL-SHAPED (2) [BOWL]

1Ki 7:41 two pillars, / two **b** capitals on top of the pillars,
2Ch 4:12 two pillars, / two **b** capitals on top of the pillars,

BOWLFUL (2) [BOWL]

Jdg 6:38 the fleece and wrung out a whole **b** of water.
Am 6: 6 You drink wine by the **b**, and you perfume

BOWLS (20) [BOWL]

Ex 7:19 even the water stored in wooden **b** and stone pots
8: 3 will fill even your ovens and your kneading **b**.
12:34 They wrapped their kneading **b** in their spare
25:29 and **b** to be used in pouring out drink offerings.
37:16 using pure gold, he made the plates, dishes, **b**,
Nu 4: 7 and place the dishes, spoons, **b**, cups,
Dt 28: 5 with fruit, and with kneading **b** filled with bread.
28:17 of fruit, and with kneading **b** empty of bread.
2Sa 17:28 cooking pots, serving **b**, wheat and barley flour,
Ezr 1:10 gold **b** | 30 / silver **b** | 410
8:25 the gold, the gold **b**, and the other items that the
8:27 20 gold **b**, equal in value to 1,000 gold coins,
Jer 52:19 also took the small **b**, firepans, basins, pots,
52:19 lampstands, dishes, **b** used for drink offerings,
Rev 5: 8 a harp, and they held gold **b** filled with incense—
15: 6 The seven angels who were holding the **b** of the
16: 1 and empty out the seven **b** of God's wrath on the
17: 1 angels who had poured out the seven **b** came over
21: 9 Then one of the seven angels who held the seven **b**

BOWS (17) [BOW]

Ge 33: 7 Finally, Rachel and Joseph came and made their **b**.
Jos 24:12 was not your swords or **b** that brought you victory.
1Ch 5:18 in combat and armed with shields, swords, and **b**.
2Ch 14: 8 tribe of Benjamin, armed with small shields and **b**.
17:17 there were 200,000 troops equipped with **b**
26:14 spears, helmets, coats of mail, **b**, and sling stones.
Ne 4:13 by families, armed with swords, spears, and **b**.
4:16 guard with spears, shields, **b**, and coats of mail.
Ps 11: 2 The wicked are stringing their **b** / and setting their
37:14 and string their **b** / to kill the poor
37:15 with their own swords, / and their **b** will be broken.
Isa 5:28 arrows will be sharp and their **b** ready for battle.
44:15 He makes an idol and **b** down and praises it!
Jer 9: 3 "My people bend their tongues like **b** to shoot lies.
51: 3 let the archers put on their armor or draw their **b**.
Eze 39: 9 large shields, **b** and arrows, javelins and spears,
Hos 2:18 all swords and **b**, so you can live unafraid in peace

BOWSTRINGS (4) [BOW]

Jdg 16: 7 "If I am tied up with seven new **b** that have not yet
16: 8 the Philistine leaders brought Delilah seven new **b**,
16: 9 But Samson snapped the **b** as if they were string
Ps 11: 2 their bows / and setting their arrows in the **b**.

BOX (2) [BOXES, FIREBOX]

Mk 12:41 Jesus went over to the collection **b** in the Temple
Lk 21: 1 rich people putting their gifts into the collection **b**.

BOX [KJV] See also JAR, PINE, VIAL

BOXER (1)

1Co 9:26 I am not like a **b** who misses his punches.

BOXES (1) [BOX]

Mt 23: 5 On their arms they wear extra wide prayer **b** with

BOY (73) [BOY'S, BOYHOOD, BOYS, BOYS']

Ge 21:12 "Do not be upset over the **b** and your servant wife.
21:15 was gone, she left the **b** in the shade of a bush.
21:16 "I don't want to watch the **b** die," she said,
21:19 filled her water container and gave the **b** a drink.
21:20 And God was with the **b** as he grew up in the
22: 5 "The **b** and I will travel a little farther. We will
22: 7 "We have the wood and the fire," said the **b**,
22:12 "Do not hurt the **b** in any way, for now I know
37:30 back to his brothers and lamented, "The **b** is gone!
38: 3 and had a son, and Judah named the **b** Er.
43: 8 Judah said to his father, "Send the **b** with me,
44:22 said to you, 'My lord, the **b** cannot leave his father,

44:30 I cannot go back to my father without the **b**.
44:31 When he sees that the **b** is not with us, our father
44:32 pledge to my father that I would take care of the **b**.
44:33 here as a slave instead of the **b**, and let the **b** return
44:34 For how can I return to my father if the **b** is not
48:14 hand was on the head of Ephraim, the younger **b**,
Ex 2: 6 As the princess opened it, she found the baby **b**.
2:22 Later they had a baby **b**, and Moses named him
18: 3 for Moses had said when the **b** was born, "I have
21:31 "The same principle applies if the bull gores a **b**
Lev 12: 3 On the eighth day, the **b** must be circumcised.
27: 5 A **b** between five and twenty is valued at twenty
27: 6 A **b** between the ages of one month and five years
Jdg 8:20 his sword, for he was only a **b** and was afraid.
8:21 said to Gideon, "Don't ask a **b** to do a man's job!
1Sa 2:11 And the **b** became the LORD's helper, for he
2:18 Now Samuel, though only a **b**, was the LORD's
3: 1 the **b** Samuel was serving the LORD by assisting
3: 8 realized it was the LORD who was calling the **b**.
4:20 be afraid," they said. "You have a baby **b**!"
12: 2 I have served as your leader since I was a **b**.
17:33 You are only a **b**, and he has been in the army since he was a **b**!"
17:42 sneering in contempt at this ruddy-faced **b**.
17:58 "Tell me about your father, my **b**," Saul said.
20:21 Then I will send a **b** to bring the arrows back.
20:35 and took a young **b** with him to gather his arrows.
20:36 "Start running," he told the **b**, "so you can
20:36 So the **b** ran, and Jonathan shot an arrow beyond
20:37 When the **b** had almost reached the arrow,
20:38 So the **b** quickly gathered up the arrows and ran
20:40 Then Jonathan gave his bow and arrows to the **b**
20:41 As soon as the **b** was gone, David came out from
2Sa 7: 8 my people Israel when you were just a shepherd **b**,
17:18 But a **b** saw them leaving En-rogel to go to David,
1Ki 14: 3 of honey, and ask him what will happen to the **b**."
2Ki 4:35 This time the **b** sneezed seven times and opened
8: 5 about the time Elisha had brought a **b** back to life.
8: 5 the mother of the **b** walked in to make her appeal
1Ch 17: 7 my people Israel when you were just a shepherd **b**,
Mt 17:17 long must I put up with you? Bring the **b** to me."
17:18 Then Jesus rebuked the demon in the **b**, and it left him. From that moment the **b** was well.
21:28 A man with two sons told the older **b**, 'Son,
Mk 9:19 long must I put up with you? Bring the **b** to me."
9:20 So they brought the **b**. But when the evil spirit saw
9:26 and threw the **b** into another violent convulsion
9:26 The **b** lay there motionless, and he appeared to be
Lk 1:57 for Elizabeth's baby to be born, and it was a **b**.
2:23 of the Lord says, "If a woman's first child is a **b**,
7:12 The **b** who had died was the only son of a widow,
7:15 Then the dead **b** sat up and began to talk to those
9:38 "Teacher, look at my **b**, who is my only son.
9:42 As the **b** came forward, the demon knocked him to
9:42 But Jesus rebuked the evil spirit and healed the **b**.
15:16 The **b** became so hungry that even the pods he was
Jn 4:49 "Lord, please come now before my little **b** dies."
4:52 He asked them when the **b** had begun to feel better,
6: 9 "There's a young **b** here with five barley loaves
Rev 12: 5 She gave birth to a **b** who was to rule all nations

BOY'S (7) [BOY]

Ge 21:17 Then God heard the **b** cries, and the angel of God
21:17 God has heard the **b** cries from the place where
44:30 the boy. Our father's life is bound up in the **b** life.
Jdg 13:12 what kind of rules should govern the **b** life
1Ki 17:19 And he took the **b** body from her, carried him up to
2Ki 4:30 But the **b** mother said, "As surely as the LORD
Mk 9:21 Jesus asked the **b** father. He replied, "Since he was

BOYHOOD (1) [BOY]

Lk 4:16 he came to the village of Nazareth, his **b** home,

BOYS (20) [BOY]

Ge 17:27 with all the other men and **b** of the household,
25:27 As the **b** grew up, Esau became a skillful hunter,
48: 5 Now I am adopting as my own sons these two **b** of
48: 8 Then Jacob looked over at the two **b**. "Are these
48:10 So Joseph brought the **b** close to him, and Jacob
48:12 Joseph took the **b** from their grandfather's knees,
48:13 Then he positioned the **b** so Ephraim was at
48:16 has kept me from all harm—may he bless these **b**.
48:20 So Jacob blessed the **b** that day with this blessing:
Ex 1:16 give birth, kill all the **b** as soon as they are born.
1:17 refused to obey the king and allowed the **b** to live,
1:18 "Why have you allowed the **b** to live?"
1:22 "Throw all the newborn Israelite **b** into the Nile
Nu 31:17 Now kill all the **b** and all the women who have
2Ki 2:23 a group of **b** from the town began mocking
Jer 11:22 die in battle, and their little **b** and girls will starve.
La 2:21 young and old, **b** and girls, killed by the swords of
Joel 3: 3 They traded young **b** for prostitutes and little girls
Zec 8: 5 And the streets of the city will be filled with **b**
Mt 2:16 He sent soldiers to kill all the **b** in and around

BOYS' (1) [BOY]

Ge 48:14 as he reached out to lay his hands on the **b** heads.

BOZEZ (1)

1Sa 14: 4 down between two rocky cliffs that were called **B**

BOZKATH (2)

Jos 15:39 Lachish, **B**, Eglon,
2Ki 22: 1 was Jedidah, the daughter of Adaiah from **B**.

BOZRAH (8)

Ge 36:33 Jobab son of Zerah from **B** became king.
1Ch 1:44 Jobab son of Zerah from **B** became king.
Isa 34: 6 will offer a great sacrifice in the rich city of **B**.
63: 1 from the city of **B**, with his clothing stained red?
Jer 48:24 and on Kerioth and **B**—all the cities of Moab,
49:13 "that **B** will become an object of horror and a heap
49:22 as an eagle, and he will spread his wings against **B**.
Am 1:12 and the fortresses of **B** will be destroyed."

BRACE (2) [BRACED]

Job 38: 3 **B** yourself, because I have some questions for you,
40: 7 "**B** yourself, because I have some questions for

BRACED (1) [BRACE]

1Ki 7:28 They were constructed with side panels **b** with

BRACELETS (8)

Ge 24:22 for her nose and two large gold **b** for her wrists.
24:30 saw the nose-ring and the **b** on his sister's wrists,
24:47 his wife, Milcah.' So I gave her the ring and the **b**.
Nu 31:50 armbands, **b**, rings, earrings, and necklaces.
2Sa 1:10 Then I took his crown and one of his **b** so I could
Isa 3:19 their earrings, **b**, and veils of shimmering gauze.
Eze 16:11 you lovely jewelry, **b**, and beautiful necklaces,
23:42 who put **b** on your wrists and beautiful crowns on

BRAG (15) [BRAGGART, BRAGGARTS, BRAGGED, BRAGGING, BRAGS]

Ps 10: 3 For they **b** about their evil desires; / they praise the
97: 7 all who **b** about their worthless gods—
Pr 13:16 before they act; fools don't and even **b** about it!
27: 1 Don't **b** about tomorrow, since you don't know
30:32 by being proud or plotting evil, don't **b** about it—
Jer 48: 2 No one will ever **b** about Moab again, for there is a
Am 4: 5 so you can **b** about it everywhere!
Ro 11:18 But you must be careful not to **b** about being
1Co 4: 6 you won't **b** about one of your leaders at the
2Co 5:12 so you can answer those who **b** about having a
Gal 6:13 so they can **b** about it and claim you as their
Php 3:19 god is their appetite, they **b** about shameful things,
Jas 3:13 And if you don't **b** about the good you do,
3:14 ambition in your hearts, don't **b** about being wise.
2Pe 2:18 They **b** about themselves with empty,

BRAGGART (1) [BRAG]

Isa 9: 8 The Lord has spoken out against that **b** Israel,

BRAGGARTS (1) [BRAG]

Jude 1:16 They are loudmouthed **b**, and they flatter others to

BRAGGED (1) [BRAG]

Est 5:11 He **b** about the honors the king had given him

BRAGGING (5) [BRAG]

Isa 9:11 The LORD will reply to their **b** by bringing
47: 8 **b** as if you were the greatest in the world!
Am 6:13 And just as stupid is this **b** about your conquest of
Ro 11:25 so that you will not feel proud and start **b**.
2Co 11:17 Such **b** is not something the Lord wants, but I am

BRAGS (1) [BRAG]

Pr 20:14 "It's worthless," then **b** about getting a bargain!

BRAIDED (2) [BRAIDS, TRIPLE-BRAIDED]

Ex 28:22 to the ephod, make **b** cords of pure gold.
39:15 to the ephod, they made **b** cords of pure gold.

BRAIDS (2) [BRAIDED]

Jdg 16:13 "If you weave the seven **b** of my hair into the
16:13 Delilah wove the seven **b** of his hair into the fabric

BRAINS (1)

Hos 4:11 and prostitution have robbed my people of their **b**.

BRAMBLE (1) [BRAMBLES]

Lk 6:44 never grow on thornbushes or grapes on **b** bushes.

BRAMBLE [KJV] See also THORNBUSH

BRAMBLES (1) [BRAMBLE]

Hos 9: 6 your treasures of silver; **b** will fill your homes.

BRANCH (29) [BRANCHES]

Ge 2:13 The second **b** is the Gihon, which flows around the
2:14 The third **b** is the Tigris, which flows to the east of Asshur. The fourth **b** is the Euphrates.
Ex 15:25 LORD for help, and the LORD showed him a **b**.
15:25 Moses took the **b** and threw it into the water.
Lev 14: 4 some cedarwood, a scarlet cloth, and a hyssop **b**.
14: 6 the cedarwood, the scarlet cloth, and the hyssop **b**,
14:49 some cedarwood, a scarlet cloth, and a hyssop **b**.
14:51 dip the cedarwood, the hyssop **b**, the scarlet cloth,
Nu 19: 6 a hyssop **b**, and scarlet thread and throw them into
19:18 who is ceremonially clean must take a hyssop **b**
1Sa 2:30 I had promised that your **b** of the tribe of Levi
Isa 4: 2 But in the future, Israel—the **b** of the LORD—
9:14 both the head and the tail, the palm **b** and the reed.
11: 1 yes, a new **B** bearing fruit from the old root.
14:19 body is thrown from the grave like a discarded **b**.
Jer 1:11 And I replied, "I see a **b** from an almond tree."
23: 5 "when I will place a righteous **B** on King David's
Eze 17: 3 He took hold of the highest **b** of a cedar tree
Da 1: 4 "Make sure they are well versed in every **b** of
Zec 3: 8 Soon I am going to bring my servant, the **B**.
6:12 Here is the man called the **B**. He will **b** out where he is and build the Temple of
Jn 15: 2 He cuts off every **b** that doesn't produce fruit,
15: 4 For a **b** cannot produce fruit if it is severed from
15: 6 who parts from me is thrown away like a useless **b**
19:29 put it on a hyssop **b**, and held it up to his lips.
Ro 11:18 Remember, you are just a **b**, not the root.
Php 3: 5 Jewish family that is a **b** of the tribe of Benjamin.

BRANCHES (84) [BRANCH]

Ge 2:10 watering the garden and then dividing into four **b**.
2:11 One of these **b** is the Pishon, which flows around
30:38 Then he set up these peeled **b** beside the watering
30:39 the flocks mated in front of the white-streaked **b**,
30:41 to mate, Jacob set up the peeled **b** in front of them.
40:10 It had three **b** that began to bud and blossom,
40:12 Joseph said. "The three **b** mean three days.
49:22 tree beside a fountain. / His **b** reach over the wall.
Ex 12:22 Then take a cluster of hyssop **b** and dip it into the
25:32 It will have six **b**, three **b** going out from each side
25:33 Each of the six **b** will hold a cup shaped like an
25:35 One blossom will be set beneath each pair of **b**
25:36 and **b** must all be one piece with the stem,
37:18 The lampstand had six **b**, three going out from
37:19 Each of the six **b** held a cup shaped like an almond
37:21 One blossom was set beneath each pair of **b**,
37:22 and **b** were all one piece with the stem,
Lev 23:40 and collect palm fronds and other leafy **b**
Jdg 9:48 He took an ax and chopped some **b** from a tree,
9:49 So each of them cut down some **b**,
9:49 They piled the **b** against the walls of the temple
2Sa 18: 9 but as he rode beneath the thick **b** of a great oak,
Ne 8:15 telling the people to go to the hills to get **b** from
8:15 They were to use these **b** to make shelters in which
8:16 So the people went out and cut **b** and used them to
Job 8:16 in the sunshine, its **b** spreading across the garden.
14: 7 is hope that it will sprout again and grow new **b**.
18:16 Their roots will dry up, and their **b** will wither.
27:18 as a spiderweb, as flimsy as a shelter made of **b**.
29:19 the water, whose **b** are refreshed with the dew.
Ps 80:10 the mighty cedars were covered with our **b**.
80:11 We spread our **b** west to the Mediterranean Sea,
104:12 the streams / and sing among the **b** of the trees.
137: 2 hanging them on the **b** of the willow trees.
SS 7: 8 climb up into the palm tree and take hold of its **b**.'
Isa 17: 6 Only two or three remain in the highest **b**, four
18: 5 with pruning shears. He will snip your spreading **b**.
27:10 Cattle will graze there, chewing on twigs and **b**.
27:11 The people are like the dead **b** of a tree, broken off
Jer 5:10 Strip the **b** from the vine, for they do not belong to
Eze 15: 5 Vine **b** are useless both before and after being put
17: 6 Its **b** turned up toward the eagle, and its roots grew
17: 6 It soon produced strong **b** and luxuriant leaves.
17: 7 vine sent its roots and **b** out toward him for water.
17:23 sending forth its **b** and producing seed.
17:23 sort will nest in it, finding shelter beneath its **b**.
19:11 Its **b** became very strong, / strong enough to be a
19:11 of its height / and because of its many lush **b**.
19:12 and tore off its **b**. / Its stem was destroyed by fire.
19:14 A fire has come from its **b** / and devoured its fruit.
31: 3 full of thick **b** that cast deep forest shade with its
31: 5 It prospered and grew long thick **b** because of all
31: 6 The birds nested in its **b**, and in its shade all the
31: 8 No cypress had **b** equal to it; no plane tree had
31:12 Its **b** were scattered across the mountains
31:13 fallen trunk, and the wild animals lay among its **b**.
47:12 and fall, and there will always be fruit on their **b**.
Da 4:12 animals lived in its shade, and birds nested in its **b**.
4:14 "Cut down the tree; lop off its **b**!
4:14 the animals from its shade and the birds from its **b**.
4:21 animals lived in its shade, and birds nested in its **b**.
Hos 14: 6 Its **b** will spread out like those of beautiful olive
Joel 1: 7 their bark and leaving the **b** white and bare.
Zec 4:12 and what are the two olive **b** that pour out golden
Mt 13:32 where birds can come and find shelter in its **b**."
21: 8 and others cut **b** from the trees and spread them on
Mk 4:32 with long **b** where birds can come and find
11: 8 and others cut leafy **b** in the fields and spread them
Lk 13:19 and the birds come and find shelter among its **b**."
Jn 12:13 took palm **b** and went down the road to meet him.
15: 2 and he prunes the **b** that do bear fruit so they will
15: 5 "Yes, I am the vine; you are the **b**. Those who
15: 6 Such **b** are gathered into a pile to be burned.
Ro 11:16 if the roots of the tree are holy, the **b** will be, too.
11:17 But some of these **b** from Abraham's tree, some of
11:17 who were **b** from a wild olive tree, were grafted in.
11:18 grafted in to replace the **b** that were broken off.
11:19 "those **b** were broken off to make room for me."
11:20 those **b**, the Jews, were broken off because they
11:21 For if God did not spare the **b** he put there in the
11:24 **b** from a wild olive tree and graft you into his own
Heb 9:19 using **b** of hyssop bushes and scarlet wool.
Rev 7: 9 clothed in white and held palm **b** in their hands.

BRAND (1) [BRAND-NEW]

Isa 48: 7 They are **b** new, not things from the past. So you

BRAND-NEW (3) [BRAND, NEW]

Jdg 16:11 "If I am tied up with **b** ropes that have never been

Isa 43:19 For I am about to do a **b** thing. See, I have already
Col 3:10 In its place you have clothed yourselves with a **b**

BRANDED (2)

Ex 13: 9 like a mark **b** on your hands or your forehead.
13:16 this ceremony will be like a mark **b** on your hands

BRANDISH (3) [BRANDISHED]

Eze 21:14 Then take the sword and **b** it twice, even three
32:10 They will shudder in fear for their lives as I **b** my
Zec 9:13 and like a warrior, I will **b** it against the Greeks.

BRANDISHED (1) [BRANDISH]

Pr 26: 9 is as dangerous as a thornbush **b** by a drunkard.

BRASEN [KJV] See METAL, BRONZE

BRASH (2)

Pr 7:11 She was the **b**, rebellious type who never stays at
9:13 The woman named Folly is loud and **b**. She is

BRASS [KJV] See BRONZE

BRAVE (7) [BRAVELY, BRAVEST]

Jdg 20:46 lost twenty-five thousand **b** warriors that day,
1Sa 14:52 So whenever Saul saw a young man who was **b**
16:18 he is **b** and strong and has good judgment.
1Ch 12: 8 Some **b** and experienced warriors from the tribe of
12:21 for they were all **b** and able warriors who became
2Ch 26:17 with eighty other priests of the LORD, all **b** men.
Ps 27:14 Be **b** and courageous. / Yes, wait patiently for the

BRAVELY (2) [BRAVE]

2Sa 10:12 Let us fight **b** to save our people and the cities of
1Ch 19:13 Let us fight **b** to save our people and the cities of

BRAVERY [KJV] See ARTFUL

BRAVEST (4) [BRAVE]

Jdg 3:29 ten thousand of their strongest and **b** warriors.
2Sa 17:10 Then even the **b** of them, though they have the
Isa 15: 4 The **b** warriors of Moab will cry out in utter terror.
Jer 46: 5 The **b** of its fighting men run without a backward

BRAWLS (1)

Pr 20: 1 Wine produces mockers; liquor leads to **b**.

BRAY (1)

Job 6: 5 Wild donkeys **b** when they find no green grass,

BRAZEN (1) [BRAZENLY]

Pr 7:13 and kissed him, and with a **b** look she said,

BRAZENLY (1) [BRAZEN]

Nu 15:30 "But those who **b** violate the LORD's will,

BRAZIER (1)

Zec 12: 6 clans of Judah like a **b** that sets a woodpile ablaze

BREACHED (1)

Ps 144:14 May there be no **b** walls, no forced exile,

BREAD (231) [BREADS]

UNLEAVENED BREAD (21) Ex 12:17; 23:15; 34:18; Lev 8:2,26,26; 23:6; Dt 16:16; Jos 5:11; Jdg 6:20; 1Sa 28:24; 2Ki 23:9; 2Ch 30:13,21; 35:17; Ezr 6:22; Mt 26:17; Mk 14:1,12; Lk 22:1,7

Ge 14:18 priest of God Most High, brought him **b** and wine.
18: 6 measures of your best flour, and bake some **b**."
19: 3 complete with fresh **b** made without yeast.
25:34 Then Jacob gave Esau some **b** and lentil stew.
27:17 with its rich aroma, and some freshly baked **b**.
47:15 "Our money is gone," they said, "but give us **b**.
Ex 12: 8 lamb with bitter herbs and **b** made without yeast.
12:15 you may eat only **b** made without yeast.
12:15 Anyone who eats **b** made with yeast at any time
12:17 "Celebrate this Festival of Unleavened **B**, for it
12:18 Only **b** without yeast may be eaten from the
12:20 you live, eat only **b** that has no yeast in it."
12:34 The Israelites took with them their **b** dough made
12:39 they baked **b** from the yeastless dough they had
12:39 out of Egypt and had no time to wait for **b** to rise.
13: 6 For seven days you will eat only **b** without yeast.
13: 7 Eat only **b** without yeast during those seven days.
16: 8 meat to eat in the evening and **b** in the morning,
16:12 and in the morning you will be filled with **b**.
16:32 later generations will be able to see the **b** that the
23:15 The first is the Festival of Unleavened **B**.
23:15 For seven days you are to eat **b** made without
23:18 be offered together with **b** that has yeast in it.
25:30 You must always keep the special **B** of the
29: 2 fine wheat flour and no yeast, make loaves of **b**,
29: 3 Place these various kinds of **b** in a single basket,
29:23 Then take one loaf of **b**, one cake mixed with olive
29:23 and one wafer from the basket of yeastless **b** that
29:25 Afterward take the **b** from their hands, and burn it
29:32 along with the **b** in the basket, at the Tabernacle
29:33 and **b** used for their atonement in the ordination
29:34 the ordination meat or **b** remains until the morning,
34:18 "Be sure to celebrate the Festival of Unleavened **B**
34:25 "You must not offer **b** made with yeast as a
35:13 and all of its utensils; the **B** of the Presence;
39:36 the table and all its utensils; the **B** of the Presence;
40:23 And he arranged the **B** of the Presence on the table
Lev 2: 4 "When you present some kind of baked **b** as a
7:12 must be accompanied by various kinds of **b**—
7:13 must also be accompanied by loaves of yeast **b**.
7:14 One of each kind of **b** must be presented as a gift
7:14 This **b** will then belong to the priest who sprinkles
8: 2 the two rams, and the basket of unleavened **b**
8:26 On top of these he placed a loaf of unleavened **b**,
8:26 a cake of unleavened **b** soaked with olive oil,
8:26 All these were taken from the basket of **b** made
8:31 and eat it along with the **b** that is in the basket of
8:32 Any meat or **b** that is left over must then be burned
23: 6 the Festival of Unleavened **B** begins.
23: 6 and during that time all the **b** you eat must be made
23:14 Do not eat any **b** or roasted grain or fresh kernels
23:17 bring two loaves of **b** to be lifted up before the
23:18 Along with this **b**, present seven one-year-old
24: 5 "You must bake twelve loaves of **b** from choice
24: 6 Place the **b** in the LORD's presence on the pure
24: 7 to be burned in place of the **b** as an offering given
24: 8 Every Sabbath day this **b** must be laid out before
24: 9 The loaves of **b** belong to Aaron and his male
26:26 so the **b** from one oven will have to be stretched to
Nu 4: 7 where the **B** of the Presence is displayed, and place
4: 7 spoons, bowls, cups, and the special **b** on the cloth.
6:15 a basket of **b** made without yeast—cakes of choice
6:17 along with the basket of **b** made without yeast.
9:11 time with bitter herbs and **b** made without yeast.
28:17 will begin, but no **b** made with yeast may be eaten.
Dt 8: 3 He did it to teach you that people need more than **b**
9:18 the LORD, neither eating **b** nor drinking water.
16: 3 Eat it with **b** made without yeast. For seven days
eat only **b** made without yeast,
16: 3 Eat this **b**—the **b** of suffering—so that you will
16: 8 For the next six days you may not eat **b** made with
16:16 the Festival of Unleavened **B**, the Festival of
28: 5 with fruit, and with kneading bowls filled with **b**.
28:17 of fruit, and with kneading bowls empty of **b**.
29: 6 You had no **b** or wine or other strong drink,
Jos 5:11 The very next day they began to eat unleavened **b**
9: 5 And they took along dry, moldy **b** for provisions.
9:12 "This **b** was hot from the ovens when we left.
9:14 So the Israelite leaders examined their **b**, but they
Jdg 6:19 and with half a bushel of flour he baked some **b**
6:20 "Place the meat and the unleavened **b** on this rock,
6:21 touched the meat and **b** with the staff in his hand,
7:13 and in my dream a loaf of barley **b** came tumbling
19:19 and plenty of **b** and wine for ourselves."
Ru 2:14 You can dip your **b** in the wine if you like."
1Sa 10: 3 young goats, another will have three loaves of **b**,
17:17 and these ten loaves of **b** to your brothers.
21: 3 Give me five loaves of **b** or anything else you
21: 4 "We don't have any regular **b**," the priest replied.
21: 4 "But there is the holy **b**, which I guess you can
21: 6 food available, the priest gave him the holy **b**—
21: 6 the **B** of the Presence that was placed before the
21: 6 It had just been replaced that day with fresh **b**.
25:11 Should I take my **b** and water and the meat I've
25:18 She quickly gathered two hundred loaves of **b**,
28:24 She kneaded dough and baked unleavened **b**.
30:11 They gave him some **b** to eat and some water to
2Sa 6:19 a loaf of **b**, a cake of dates, and a cake of raisins.
13: 8 Then she baked some special **b** for him.
16: 1 two donkeys loaded with two hundred loaves of **b**,
16: 2 and the **b** and summer fruit are for the young men
1Ki 7:48 the gold table for the **B** of the Presence,
14: 3 Take him a gift of ten loaves of **b**, some cakes,
17: 6 The ravens brought him **b** and meat each morning
17:11 he called to her, "Bring me a bite of **b**, too."
17:12 that I don't have a single piece of **b** in the house.
17:13 that 'last meal,' but bake me a little loaf of **b** first.
19: 6 looked around and saw some **b** baked on hot stones
22:27 and feed him nothing but **b** and water until I return
2Ki 4:42 and twenty loaves of barley **b** made from the first
18:32 harvests of grain and wine, **b** and vineyards,
23: 9 but they were allowed to eat unleavened **b** with the
1Ch 9:31 was entrusted with baking the **b** used in the
9:32 the **b** to be set on the table each Sabbath day.
16: 3 a loaf of **b**, a cake of dates, and a cake of raisins.
23:29 They were in charge of the sacred **b** that was set
28:16 on which the **B** of the Presence would be placed
2Ch 2: 4 before him, to display the special sacrificial **b**,
4:19 the gold altar; / the tables for the **B** of the Presence;
13:11 They place the **B** of the Presence on the holy table,
18:26 and feed him nothing but **b** and water until I return
29:18 and the table of the **B** of the Presence with all its
30:13 and the Festival of Unleavened **B**.
30:21 of Unleavened **B** for seven days with great joy.
35:17 and the Festival of Unleavened **B** for seven days.
Ezr 6:22 and celebrated the Festival of Unleavened **B** for
Ne 9:15 "You gave them **b** from heaven when they were
9:20 and you did not stop giving them **b** from heaven
10:33 This will provide for the **B** of the Presence;
Job 15:23 They wander abroad for **b**, saying, 'Where is it?'
28: 5 **B** comes from the earth, but below the surface the
Ps 14: 4 evil never learn? / They eat up my people like **b**;
37:25 nor seen their children begging for **b**.
53: 4 evil never learn? / They eat up my people like **b**;
78:20 but he can't give his people **b** and meat."
78:24 for them to eat. / He gave them **b** from heaven.
104:15 lotion for their skin, / and **b** to give them strength.
105:40 them quail; / he gave them manna—**b** from heaven.
Pr 20:17 Stolen **b** tastes sweet, but it turns to gravel in the
28:21 do wrong for something as small as a piece of **b**.
Isa 28:28 **B** grain is easily crushed, so he doesn't keep on
36:17 harvests of grain and wine, **b** and vineyards—
44:15 to make a fire to warm himself and bake his **b**.
44:19 and used it to bake my **b** and roast my meat.
55:10 seed for the farmer and **b** for the hungry.
Jer 5:17 They will eat your harvests and your children's **b**,
37:21 **b** every day as long as there was any left in the
38: 9 of hunger, for almost all the **b** in the city is gone."
La 1:11 Her people groan as they search for **b**. They have
4: 4 The children cry for **b**, but no one has any to give
Eze 4: 9 Use this food to make **b** for yourself during the
4:12 Each day prepare your **b** as you would barley
4:12 using dried human dung as fuel and then eat the **b**.
4:13 Israel will eat defiled **b** in the Gentile lands,
4:15 "You may bake your **b** with cow dung instead of
13:19 me for a few handfuls of barley or a piece of **b**.
45:21 Only **b** without yeast may be eaten during that
46:20 and bake the flour from the grain offerings into **b**.
Am 4: 5 Present your **b** made with yeast as an offering of
8:11 not a famine of **b** or water but of hearing the words
Hag 2:12 and happens to brush against some **b** or stew,
Mt 4: 3 Son of God, change these stones into loaves of **b**."
4: 4 'People need more than **b** for their life;
7: 9 if your children ask for a loaf of **b**, do you give
12: 4 and they ate the special **b** reserved for the priests
13:33 Heaven is like yeast used by a woman making **b**.
14:17 "We have only five loaves of **b** and two fish!"
14:19 he gave some of the **b** and fish to each disciple,
15:34 "How many loaves of **b** do you have?"
16: 7 was saying this because they hadn't brought any **b**.
16:12 or **b** but about the false teaching of the Pharisees
26:17 On the first day of the Festival of Unleavened **B**,
26:26 Jesus took a loaf of **b** and asked God's blessing on
Mk 2:26 ate the special **b** reserved for the priests alone,
6:38 "We have five loaves of **b** and two fish."
6:41 he kept giving the **b** and fish to the disciples to
6:43 and they picked up twelve baskets of leftover **b**
8: 5 "How many loaves of **b** do you have?" he asked.
8: 6 to his disciples, who distributed the **b** to the crowd.
8:14 so there was only one loaf of **b** with them in the
8:16 was saying this because they hadn't brought any **b**.
8:19 the five thousand men I fed with five loaves of **b**?
14: 1 and the Festival of Unleavened **B**.
14:12 On the first day of the Festival of Unleavened **B**
14:22 Jesus took a loaf of **b** and asked God's blessing on
Lk 4: 3 the Son of God, change this stone into a loaf of **b**."
4: 4 'People need more than **b** for their life.' "
6: 4 ate the special **b** reserved for the priests alone,
9:13 "We have only five loaves of **b** and two fish.
9:16 he kept giving the **b** and fish to the disciples to
11: 5 at midnight, wanting to borrow three loaves of **b**.
13:21 It is like yeast used by a woman making **b**.
22: 1 The Festival of Unleavened **B**, which begins with
22: 7 Now the Festival of Unleavened **B** arrived,
22:19 Then he took a loaf of **b**; and when he had thanked
24:30 As they sat down to eat, he took a small loaf of **b**,
24:35 they had recognized him as he was breaking the **b**.
Jn 6: 5 where can we buy **b** to feed all these people?"
6:13 but twelve baskets were filled with the pieces of **b**
6:23 near the place where the Lord had blessed the **b**
6:31 'Moses gave them **b** from heaven to eat.' "
6:32 assure you, Moses didn't give them **b** from heaven.
6:32 And now he offers you the true **b** from heaven.
6:33 The true **b** of God is the one who comes down
6:34 they said, "give us that **b** every day of our lives."
6:35 Jesus replied, "I am the **b** of life. No one who
6:41 because he had said, "I am the **b** from heaven."
6:48 Yes, I am the **b** of life!
6:50 the **b** from heaven gives eternal life to everyone
6:51 I am the living **b** that came down out of heaven.
6:51 who eats this **b** will live forever; this **b** is my flesh,
6:58 I am the true **b** from heaven. Anyone who eats this
b will live forever and not
13:26 "It is the one to whom I give the **b** dipped in the
13:27 As soon as Judas had eaten the **b**, Satan entered
21: 9 and fish were frying over it, and there was **b**.
21:13 Then Jesus served them the **b** and the fish.
Ac 27:35 Then he took some **b**, gave thanks to God before
1Co 5: 8 not by eating the old **b** of wickedness and evil,
5: 8 but by eating the new **b** of purity and truth.
10:16 And when we break the loaf of **b**, aren't we
11:23 he was betrayed, the Lord Jesus took a loaf of **b**,
11:26 For every time you eat this **b** and drink this cup,
11:27 So if anyone eats this **b** or drinks this cup of the
11:28 you should examine yourself before eating the **b**
11:29 For if you eat the **b** or drink the cup unworthily,
2Co 9:10 one who gives seed to the farmer and then **b** to eat.
Heb 9: 2 a table, and loaves of holy **b** on the table.
Rev 6: 6 "A loaf of wheat **b** or three loaves of barley for a

BREADS (1) [BREAD]

1Ch 23:29 cakes cooked in olive oil, and the other mixed **b**.

BREAK (105) [BREAKERS, BREAKING, BREAKS, BROKE, BROKEN, BROKEN-DOWN, BROKENHEARTED, HEARTBROKEN]

Ge 38:29 "How did you **b** out first?" And ever after, he was
Ex 9: 9 causing boils to **b** out on people and animals
12:46 meat outside, and you may not **b** any of its bones.
23:24 conquer them and **b** down their shameful idols.
34:13 Instead, you must **b** down their pagan altars,
Lev 2: 6 **B** it into pieces and pour oil on it; it is a kind of
26:15 and if you **b** my covenant by rejecting my laws

26:19 I will **b** down your arrogant spirit by making the
Nu 9:12 and they must not **b** any of its bones.
9:20 Then at the LORD's command they would **b**
10:5 the tribes on the east side of the Tabernacle will **b**
11:33 and he caused a severe plague to **b** out among
30:2 or makes a pledge under oath must never **b** it.
Dt 1:7 It is time to **b** camp and move on. Go to the hill
4:23 So be careful not to **b** the covenant the LORD
4:23 You will **b** it if you make idols of any shape
7:5 you must **b** down their pagan altars and shatter
12:3 **B** down their altars and smash their sacred pillars.
21:4 through it. There they must **b** the cow's neck.
28:32 Your heart will **b** as you long for them, but nothing
31:16 and **b** the covenant I have made with them.
31:20 they will despise me and **b** my covenant.
Jos 23:16 If you **b** the covenant of the LORD your God by
Jdg 2:1 and I said I would never **b** my covenant with you.
1Ki 5:9 Then we will **b** the rafts apart and deliver the
15:19 **B** your treaty with King Baasha of Israel so that he
2Ki 3:26 **b** through the enemy lines near the king of Edom,
2Ch 16:3 **B** your treaty with King Baasha of Israel so that he
32:1 giving orders for his army to **b** through their walls.
Ne 6:9 imagining that they could **b** our resolve and stop
Job 19:2 How long will you try to **b** me with your words?
24:16 They **b** into houses at night and sleep in the
Ps 2:3 "Let us **b** their chains," they cry, / "and free
2:9 You will **b** them with an iron rod / and smash
10:15 **B** the arms of these wicked, evil people! / Go after
46:5 be destroyed. / God will protect it at the **b** of day.
58:6 **B** off their fangs, O God! / Smash the jaws of these
89:34 No, I will not **b** my covenant; / I will not take back
98:4 all the earth; / **b** out in praise and sing for joy!
110:4 LORD has taken an oath and will not **b** his vow:
Isa 2:15 He will **b** down every high tower and wall.
5:5 and let it be destroyed. / I will **b** down its walls
9:4 For God will **b** the chains that bind his people
10:27 He will **b** the yoke of slavery and lift it from their
14:25 I will **b** the Assyrians when they are in Israel;
44:23 **B** forth into song, O mountains and forests
52:9 Let the ruins of Jerusalem **b** into joyful song,
54:1 **B** forth into loud and joyful song, O Jerusalem,
Jer 2:34 You killed them even though they didn't **b** into
8:1 "the enemy will **b** open the graves of the kings
14:21 Do not **b** your covenant with us. Please don't
15:12 Can a man **b** a bar of iron from the north, or a bar
28:4 I will surely **b** the yoke that the king of Babylon
28:11 **b** the yoke of oppression from all the nations now
30:8 I will **b** the yoke from their necks and snap their
33:20 "If you can **b** my covenant with the day
43:13 He will **b** down the sacred pillars standing in the
50:26 **B** open her granaries. Crush her walls and houses
51:56 are captured, and their weapons **b** in their hands.
Eze 7:24 I will **b** down their proud fortresses and defile their
13:14 I will **b** down your wall right to the foundation,
17:15 Can Israel **b** her sworn treaties like that and get
26:12 and merchandise and **b** down your walls.
30:18 When I come to **b** the proud strength of Egypt,
30:22 I will **b** both of his arms—the good arm along with
30:24 But I will **b** the arms of Pharaoh, king of Egypt,
Da 4:27 **B** from your wicked past by being merciful to the
8:22 Empire will **b** into four sections with four kings,
Hos 10:2 The LORD will **b** down their foreign altars
10:11 Israel and Judah must now **b** up the hard ground;
Am 1:5 I will **b** down the gates of Damascus and slaughter
Mic 2:13 Your leader will **b** out and lead you out of exile.
3:3 cut away their skin, and **b** their bones.
5:5 invade our land and **b** through our defenses,
Na 1:13 Now I will **b** your chains and release you from
Mt 1:19 a just man, decided to **b** the engagement quietly,
5:19 So if you **b** the smallest commandment and teach
5:33 that the law of Moses says, 'Do not **b** your vows;
6:19 and get rusty, and where thieves **b** in and steal.
23:16 to swear 'by God's Temple'—you can **b** that oath.
23:36 will **b** upon the heads of this very generation.
24:6 And wars will **b** out near and far, but don't panic.
Mk 4:37 High waves began to **b** into the boat until it was
6:26 but he was embarrassed to **b** his oath in front of his
7:13 you **b** the law of God in order to protect your own
13:7 And wars will **b** out near and far, but don't panic.
Lk 1:78 the light from heaven is about to **b** upon us,
6:48 When the floodwaters rise and **b** against the house,
Jn 7:23 go ahead and do it, so as not to **b** the law of Moses.
19:33 that he was dead already, so they didn't **b** his legs.
Ac 23:3 What kind of judge are you to **b** the law yourself
27:41 by the force of the waves and began to **b** apart.
Ro 1:31 **b** their promises, and are heartless and unforgiving.
3:3 does that mean God will **b** his promises?
4:15 to avoid breaking the law is to have no law to **b**!)
5:13 And though there was no law to **b**, since it had not
1Co 10:16 And when we **b** the loaf of bread, aren't we
2Co 9:11 need them, they will **b** out in thanksgiving to God.
10:5 With these weapons we **b** down every proud
Gal 4:27 **B** forth into loud and joyful song,
Heb 2:14 and only by dying could he **b** the power of the
7:21 and will not **b** his vow: / 'You are a priest
Rev 5:2 "Who is worthy to **b** the seals on this scroll
5:5 is worthy to open the scroll and **b** its seven seals."
5:9 and **b** its seals and open it. / For you were killed,

BREAKERS (3) [BREAK]

Ps 93:4 of the seas, / mightier than the **b** on the shore—
Isa 17:13 But though they roar like **b** on a beach, God will
1Ti 1:10 and slave traders, for liars and oath **b**,

BREAKFAST (3)

Pr 31:15 She gets up before dawn to prepare **b** for her
Jn 21:12 "Now come and have some **b**!" Jesus said.
21:15 After **b** Jesus said to Simon Peter, "Simon son of

BREAKING (35) [BREAK]

Ge 19:9 they lunged at Lot and began **b** down the door.
31:7 **b** his wage agreement with me again and again.
Ex 13:13 the donkey must be killed by **b** its neck.
19:2 After **b** camp at Rephidim, they came to the base
22:2 "If a thief is caught in the act of **b** into a house
34:20 you must kill the donkey by **b** its neck.
Nu 10:2 to assemble and for signaling the **b** of camp.
24:8 nations that oppose him, / **b** their bones in pieces,
Jdg 11:35 "My daughter!" he cried out. "My heart is **b**!
21:22 And you are not guilty of **b** the vow since you did
Ezr 9:14 But now we are again **b** your commands
Ps 42:4 My heart is **b** / as I remember how it used to be:
La 3:51 My heart is **b** over the fate of all the women of
Eze 16:59 for you have taken your solemn vows lightly by **b**
17:19 I will punish him for **b** my covenant and despising
Da 8:7 at the ram and struck it, **b** off both its horns.
Hos 1:5 I will put an end to Israel's independence by **b** its
Joel 2:7 Straight forward they march, never **b** rank.
Mt 8:24 terrible storm came up, with waves **b** into the boat.
12:1 so they began **b** off heads of wheat and eating the
12:4 for the priests alone. That was **b** the law, too.
14:19 **B** the loaves into pieces, he gave some of the bread
Mk 2:23 his disciples began **b** off heads of wheat.
2:26 some to his companions. That was **b** the law, too."
6:41 **B** the loaves into pieces, he kept giving the bread
Lk 6:4 gave some to his friends. That was **b** the law, too."
9:16 **B** the loaves into pieces, he kept giving the bread
24:35 and how they had recognized him as he was **b** the
Jn 5:16 So the Jewish leaders began harassing Jesus for **b**
Ac 21:13 "Why all this weeping? You are **b** my heart!
Ro 2:23 of knowing the law, but you dishonor God by **b** it.
4:15 (The only way to avoid **b** the law is to have no law
Gal 3:17 the law to Moses. God would be **b** his promise.
1Ti 5:12 Then they would be guilty of **b** their previous
Jas 2:9 committing a sin, for you are guilty of **b** that law.

BREAKS (12) [BREAK]

Ex 1:10 If we don't and if war **b** out, they will join our
2Ki 18:21 you will find it to be a stick that **b** beneath your
Job 7:5 and scabs. My flesh **b** open, full of pus.
Ps 46:9 He **b** the bow and snaps the spear in two;
76:3 There he **b** the arrows of the enemy, / the shields
76:12 For he **b** the spirit of princes / and is feared by the
141:7 Even as a farmer **b** up the soil and brings up rocks,
Pr 17:14 so drop the matter before a dispute **b** out.
Isa 36:6 you will find it to be a stick that **b** beneath your
Eze 13:5 They have done nothing to strengthen the **b** in the
Am 4:3 You will leave by going straight through the **b** in
Jas 3:9 and sometimes it **b** out into curses against those

BREAST (13) [BREASTED, BREASTS]

Ex 29:26 Then take the **b** of Aaron's ordination ram, and lift
29:27 This includes the **b** and the thigh that were lifted
Lev 7:30 Bring the fat of the animal, together with the **b**,
7:31 but the **b** will belong to Aaron and his sons.
7:34 For I have designated the **b** and the right thigh for
8:29 Then Moses took the **b** and lifted it up in the
10:14 But the **b** and thigh that were lifted up may be
10:15 and **b** that are lifted up must be lifted up to the
Nu 6:20 along with the **b** and thigh pieces that were lifted
18:18 just like the **b** and right thigh that are presented by
Job 24:9 "The wicked snatch a widow's child from her **b**;
SS 8:1 were my brother, who nursed at my mother's **b**.
Eze 23:34 will smash it to pieces and beat your **b** in anguish.

BREASTED (1) [BREAST]

SS 8:10 "I am chaste, and I am now full **b**. And my lover

BREASTS (20) [BREAST]

Ge 49:25 earth beneath, / and blessings of the **b** and womb.
Lev 9:20 He placed these fat parts on top of the **b** of these
9:21 Aaron then lifted up the **b** and right thighs as an
Job 3:12 let me live? Why did she nurse me at her **b**?
Pr 5:19 a graceful deer. Let her **b** satisfy you always.
5:20 or embrace the **b** of an adulterous woman?
SS 1:13 lover is like a sachet of myrrh lying between my **b**.
4:5 Your **b** are like twin fawns of a gazelle,
7:3 Your **b** are like twin fawns of a gazelle.
7:7 palm tree, and your **b** are like its clusters of dates.
7:8 Now may your **b** be like grape clusters,
8:8 "We have a little sister too young for **b**. What will
Isa 32:12 Beat your **b** in sorrow for your bountiful farms that
66:11 even as an infant drinks at its mother's generous **b**.
66:12 Her children will be nursed at her **b**, carried in her
Eze 16:7 Your **b** became full, and your hair grew,
Hos 9:14 that don't give birth and **b** that give no milk.
Na 2:7 like doves; watch them beat their **b** in sorrow.
Lk 11:27 from which you came, and the **b** that nursed you!"
23:29 not borne a child and the **b** that have never nursed.'

BREATH (50) [BREATHE, BREATHED, BREATHES, BREATHING, BREATHLESS]

BREATH OF LIFE (2) Ge 2:7; Da 5:23

Ge 2:7 dust of the ground and breathed into it the **b** of life.
35:18 to die, but with her last **b** she named him Ben-oni;
Ex 15:8 At the blast of your **b**, the waters piled up!
15:10 But with a blast of your **b**, / the sea covered them.
2Sa 22:16 the command of the LORD, / at the blast of his **b**,
Job 4:9 They perish by a **b** from God. They vanish in a
7:7 O God, remember that my life is but a **b**, and I will
9:18 He will not let me catch my **b**, but fills me instead
12:10 thing is in his hand, and the **b** of all humanity.
15:30 and the **b** of God will destroy everything they
19:17 My **b** is repulsive to my wife. I am loathsome to
27:3 As long as I live, while I have **b** from God,
32:8 the **b** of the Almighty within them, that makes
33:4 made me, and the **b** of the Almighty gives me life.
34:14 were to take back his spirit and withdraw his **b**,
37:10 God's **b** sends the ice, freezing wide expanses of
41:21 Yes, its **b** would kindle coals, for flames shoot
Ps 18:15 your command, O LORD, / at the blast of your **b**,
39:5 a moment to you; / human existence is but a **b**."
39:11 Human existence is as frail as **b**. / *Interlude*
78:39 gone in a moment like a **b** of wind, never to return.
104:29 they panic. / When you take away their **b**, they die
104:33 long as I live. / I will praise my God to my last **b**!
116:2 and listens, / I will pray as long as I have **b**!
144:4 For we are like a **b** of air; / our days are like a
146:2 will sing praises to my God even with my dying **b**.
Pr 23:9 Don't waste your **b** on fools, for they will despise
SS 5:13 lips are like perfumed lilies. His **b** is like myrrh.
7:8 grape clusters, and the scent of your **b** like apples.
Isa 2:22 They are as frail as **b**. How can they be of help to
11:4 and destroy them with the **b** of his mouth.
30:33 The **b** of the LORD, like fire from a volcano,
33:11 Your own **b** will turn to fire and kill you.
40:7 and the flowers fade beneath the **b** of the LORD.
42:5 He gives **b** and life to everyone in all the world.
57:13 so helpless that a **b** of wind can knock them down!
59:19 For he will come like a flood tide driven by the **b**
Jer 2:25 But you say, 'Don't waste your **b**. I have fallen in
4:31 It is the cry of Jerusalem's people gasping for **b**,
15:9 The mother of seven grows faint and gasps for **b**;
18:12 But they replied, "Don't waste your **b**. We will
Eze 37:6 I will put **b** into you, and you will come to life.
37:8 cover their bodies, but they still had no **b** in them.
37:9 Come, O **b**, from the four winds! Breathe into
Da 5:23 not honored the God who gives you the **b** of life
Mt 11:7 him weak as a reed, moved by every **b** of wind?
Lk 7:24 him weak as a reed, moved by every **b** of wind?
Ac 9:1 Meanwhile, Saul was uttering threats with every **b**.
17:25 He himself gives life and **b** to everything, and he
2Th 2:8 whom the Lord Jesus will consume with the **b** of

BREATHE (7) [BREATH]

Job 14:10 They **b** their last, and then where are they?
Ps 27:12 I've never done / and **b** out violence against me.
Ecc 3:19 For humans and animals both **b** the same air,
Eze 37:5 I am going to **b** into you and make you live again!
37:9 **B** into these dead bodies so that they may live
37:10 the wind entered the bodies, and they began to **b**.
Da 10:17 my lord? My strength is gone, and I can hardly **b**."

BREATHED (7) [BREATH]

Ge 2:7 dust of the ground and **b** into it the breath of life.
7:22 Everything died that **b** and lived on dry land.
49:33 he lay back in the bed, **b** his last, and died.
Ps 33:6 He **b** the word, / and all the stars were born.
Mk 15:37 Then Jesus uttered another loud cry and **b** his last.
Lk 23:46 your hands!" And with those words he **b** his last.
Jn 20:22 Then he **b** on them and said to them,

BREATHES (1) [BREATH]

Pr 14:5 truthful witness does not lie; a false witness **b** lies.

BREATHING (2) [BREATH]

Ge 7:14 With them in the boat were pairs of every kind of **b**
Ps 146:4 When their **b** stops, they return to the earth,

BREATHLESS (2) [BREATH]

1Ki 10:5 she was **b**. She was also amazed at the food on his
2Ch 9:4 she was **b**. She was also amazed at the food on his

BRED (2) [BREED]

Est 8:10 who rode horses especially **b** for the king's service.
8:14 the messengers rode out swiftly on horses **b** for the

BREECHES [KJV] See UNDERCLOTHES, UNDERGARMENTS

BREED (3) [BRED, BREEDERS]

Ge 8:17 Release all the animals and birds so they can **b**
Lev 19:19 "Do not **b** your cattle with other kinds of animals.
Job 21:10 Their bulls never fail to **b**. Their cows bear calves

BREEDERS (3) [BREED]

Ge 46:32 'These men are shepherds and livestock **b**.
46:34 'We have been livestock **b** from our youth,
2Ki 3:4 King Mesha of Moab and his people were sheep **b**.

BREEZE (1)

Jer 4:11 It is not a gentle **b** useful for winnowing grain.

BRETHREN [KJV] See also BROTHERS, SISTERS

BREWED (1)

Rev 18:6 She **b** a cup of terror for others, so give her twice

BRIBE (11) [BRIBED, BRIBERY, BRIBES, BRIBING]
Ex 23: 8 for a **b** makes you ignore something that you
23: 8 A **b** always hurts the cause of the person who is in
Dt 16:19 Never accept a **b**, for bribes blind the eyes of the
1Sa 12: 3 Have I ever taken a **b**? Tell me and I will make
12: 4 and you have never taken even a single **b**."
Pr 6:35 is no compensation or **b** that will satisfy him.
17: 8 A **b** seems to work like magic for those who give
21:14 A secret gift calms anger; a secret **b** pacifies fury.
Mt 28:12 was called, and they decided to **b** the soldiers.
28:15 So the guards accepted the **b** and said what they
Ac 24:26 He also hoped that Paul would **b** him, so he sent

BRIBED (2) [BRIBE]
Ezr 4: 5 They **b** agents to work against them and to
Job 36:18 with wealth. Don't let yourself be **b** into sin.

BRIBERY (1) [BRIBE]
Job 15:34 Their homes, enriched through **b**, will be

BRIBES (20) [BRIBE]
Ex 18:21 honest men who fear God and hate **b**.
23: 8 "Take no **b**, for a bribe makes you ignore
Dt 10:17 who shows no partiality and takes no **b**.
16:19 for **b** blind the eyes of the wise and corrupt the
1Sa 8: 3 for money. They accepted **b** and perverted justice.
2Ch 19: 7 perverted justice, partiality, or the taking of **b**."
Ps 15: 5 and who refuse to accept **b** to testify against the
26:10 with wicked schemes, / and they constantly take **b**.
Pr 15:27 to the whole family, but those who hate **b** will live.
17:23 The wicked accept secret **b** to pervert justice.
28:16 will have a long reign if he hates dishonesty and **b**.
29: 4 to his nation, but one who demands **b** destroys it.
Ecc 7: 7 wise people into fools, and **b** corrupt the heart.
Isa 1:23 All of them take **b** and refuse to defend the
5:23 They take **b** to pervert justice. They let the wicked
33:15 a profit by fraud, who stay far away from **b**,
Am 5:12 You oppress good people by taking **b** and deprive
Mic 3:11 You rulers govern for the **b** you can get;
7: 3 Officials and judges alike demand **b**. The people
Hab 1: 4 and justice is perverted with **b** and trickery.

BRIBING (1) [BRIBE]
Eze 16:33 give gifts to your lovers, **b** them to come to you.

BRICK (4) [BRICKS]
Ge 11: 3 "let's make great piles of burnt **b** and collect
Ex 5: 8 don't reduce their production quotas by a single **b**.
2Sa 12:31 picks, and axes, and to work in the **b** kilns.
Eze 4: 1 take a large **b** and set it down in front of you.

BRICKKILN [KJV] See BRICK, KILNS, MOLDS

BRICKS (8) [BRICK]
Ex 1:14 forcing them to make **b** and mortar and to work
5: 7 the people with any more straw for making **b**.
5:11 But you must produce just as many **b** as before!"
5:13 "Meet your daily quota of **b**, just as you did
5:16 but we are still told to make as many **b** as before.
5:18 but you must still deliver the regular quota of **b**."
Isa 9:10 We will replace the broken **b** with cut stone,
Na 3:14 the defenses! Make **b** to repair the walls!

BRIDAL (2) [BRIDE]
Ge 29:27 "Wait until the **b** week is over, and you can have
Isa 49:18 be like jewels or **b** ornaments for you to display.

BRIDE (23) [BRIDAL, BRIDES, BRIDESMAIDS]
1Sa 18:23 afford the **b** price for the daughter of a king?"
18:25 "Tell David that all I want for the **b** price is one
2Sa 17: 3 and I will bring all the people back to you as a **b**
Ps 45:13 The **b**, a princess, waits within her chamber,
SS 4: 8 "Come with me from Lebanon, my **b**. Come down
4: 9 You have ravished my heart, my treasure, my **b**.
4:10 How sweet is your love, my treasure, my **b**!
4:11 Your lips, my **b**, are as sweet as honey. Yes,
4:12 "You are like a private garden, my treasure, my **b**!
5: 1 "I am here in my garden, my treasure, my **b**!
Isa 61:10 in his wedding suit or a **b** with her jewels.
62: 4 be the City of God's Delight and the **B** of God,
62: 5 O Jerusalem, just as a young man cares for his **b**.
62: 5 over you as a bridegroom rejoices over his **b**.
Jer 2: 2 you were to please me as a young **b** long ago,
2:32 her jewelry? Does a **b** hide her wedding dress? No!
Joel 2:16 from his quarters and the **b** from her private room.
Jn 3:29 The **b** will go where the bridegroom is.
2Co 11: 2 For I promised you as a pure **b** to one husband,
Rev 19: 7 feast of the Lamb, and his **b** has prepared herself.
21: 2 heaven like a beautiful **b** prepared for her husband.
21: 9 I will show you the **b**, the wife of the Lamb."
22:17 The Spirit and the **b** say, "Come." Let each one

BRIDECHAMBER [KJV] See BRIDEGROOM, WEDDING

BRIDEGROOM (12) [BRIDEGROOM'S, BRIDEGROOMS]
Ex 4:25 "What a blood-smeared **b** you are to me!"
4:26 (When she called Moses a "blood-smeared **b**,"
Ps 19: 5 It bursts forth like a radiant **b** / after his wedding.
Isa 61:10 I am like a **b** in his wedding suit or a bride with her
62: 5 Then God will rejoice over you as a **b** rejoices over
Joel 2:16 Call the **b** from his quarters and the bride from her
Mt 25: 1 who took their lamps and went to meet the **b**.
25: 5 When the **b** was delayed, they all lay down
25: 6 were roused by the shout, 'Look, the **b** is coming!
25:10 "But while they were gone to buy oil, the **b** came,
Jn 2: 9 of course, the servants knew), he called the **b** over.
3:29 The bride will go where the **b** is. A bridegroom's

BRIDEGROOM'S (2) [BRIDEGROOM]
Jn 3:29 A **b** friend rejoices with him. I am the **b** friend, and I am filled with joy at his

BRIDEGROOMS (4) [BRIDEGROOM]
Jer 7:34 The joyful voices of **b** and brides will no longer be
16: 9 The joyful voices of **b** and brides will no longer be
25:10 The joyful voices of **b** and brides will no longer be
33:11 The joyful voices of **b** and brides will be heard

BRIDES (5) [BRIDE]
Jer 7:34 and **b** will no longer be heard in the towns of
16: 9 of bridegrooms and **b** will no longer be heard.
25:10 of bridegrooms and **b** will no longer be heard.
33:11 voices of bridegrooms and **b** will be heard again,
Rev 18:23 There will be no happy voices of **b** and grooms.

BRIDESMAIDS (4) [BRIDE]
Ps 45:14 she is led to the king, / accompanied by her **b**.
Mt 25: 1 by the story of ten **b** who took their lamps
25: 7 "All the **b** got up and prepared their lamps.
25:11 Later, when the other five **b** returned, they stood

BRIDGE (1)
Job 11:16 It will all be gone like water under the **b**.

BRIDLE (6)
2Ki 19:28 and my **b** in your mouth. / I will make you return
Ps 32: 9 that needs a bit and **b** to keep it under control."
Pr 26: 3 Guide a horse with a whip, a donkey with a **b**,
Isa 30:28 He will **b** them and lead them off to their
37:29 and my **b** in your mouth. / I will make you return
Rev 14:20 about 180 miles long and as high as a horse's **b**.

BRIEF (10) [BRIEFLY]
Ezr 9: 8 "But now we have been given a **b** moment of
Ps 39: 4 remind me how **b** my time on earth will be.
Ecc 2: 3 most people find during their **b** life in this world.
Isa 54: 7 "For a **b** moment I abandoned you, but with great
Da 11:20 but after a very **b** reign, he will die, though neither
Jn 13:33 how **b** are these moments before I must go away
Heb 13:22 please listen carefully to what I have said in this **b**
3Jn 1: 9 I sent a **b** letter to the church about this,
Rev 17:10 the seventh is yet to come, but his reign will be **b**.
17:12 they will be appointed to their kingdoms for one **b**

BRIEFLY (4) [BRIEF]
Isa 63:18 How **b** your holy people possessed the holy place,
Mk 16: S Then they reported all these instructions **b** to Peter
Ac 24: 4 a moment as I **b** outline our case against this man.
Eph 3: 3 As I **b** mentioned earlier in this letter, God himself

BRIER (2) [BRIERS]
Isa 7:24 The entire land will be one vast **b** patch, a hunting
Mic 7: 4 Even the best of them is like a **b**; the straightest is

BRIERS (13) [BRIER]
Jdg 8: 7 flesh with the thorns and **b** of the wilderness."
8:16 them with thorns and **b** from the wilderness.
Isa 5: 6 I will let it be overgrown with **b** and thorns.
7:23 of silver, will become patches of **b** and thorns.
7:25 once grew, for **b** and thorns will cover them.
9:18 It burns not only **b** and thorns but the forests,
10:17 In a single night he will burn those thorns and **b**,
27: 4 If I find **b** and thorns bothering her, I will burn
32:13 For your land will be overgrown with thorns and **b**.
55:13 will grow. Where **b** grew, myrtles will sprout up.
Eze 2: 6 their threats are sharp as thorns and barbed like **b**,
28:24 neighbors prick and tear at her like thorns and **b**.
Hos 9: 6 **B** will take over your treasures of silver;

BRIGANDINE(S) [KJV] See ARMOR

BRIGHT (26) [BRIGHTEN, BRIGHTENED, BRIGHTER, BRIGHTEST, BRIGHTLY, BRIGHTNESS]
Ge 1:14 "Let **b** lights appear in the sky to separate the day
Lev 13:49 or the leather has turned **b** green or a reddish color,
14:37 If he finds **b** green or reddish streaks on the walls
Job 11:17 Any darkness will be as **b** as morning.
34:34 After all, **b** people will tell me, and wise people
Ps 139:12 To you the night shines as **b** as day. / Darkness
Pr 24:14 If you find it, you will have a **b** future, and your
SS 5:14 His body is like **b** ivory, aglow with sapphires.
6:10 like the dawn, as fair as the moon, as **b** as the sun,
Isa 30:26 The moon will be as **b** as the sun, and the sun will
42:16 I will make the darkness **b** before them
58:10 and the darkness around you will be as **b** as day.
Eze 1:13 The living beings looked like **b** coals of fire
27: 7 and purple awnings made **b** with dyes from the
Da 12: 3 Those who are wise will shine as **b** as the sky,
Mt 17: 5 But even as he said it, a **b** cloud came over them,
Ac 6:15 because his face became as **b** as an angel's.
12: 7 Suddenly, there was a **b** light in the cell, and an
22: 6 about noon a very **b** light from heaven suddenly
Rev 1:14 as snow. And his eyes were **b** like flames of fire.
1:15 His feet were as **b** as bronze refined in a furnace,
1:16 And his face was as **b** as the sun in all its
2:18 whose eyes are **b** like flames of fire, whose feet are
18: 1 and the earth grew **b** with his splendor.
19:12 His eyes were **b** like flames of fire, and on his head
22:16 the heir to his throne. I am the **b** morning star."

BRIGHTEN (2) [BRIGHT]
Job 11:15 Then your face will **b** in innocence. You will be
Jer 4:30 Why do you **b** your eyes with mascara?

BRIGHTENED (1) [BRIGHT]
Ezr 9: 8 Our God has **b** our eyes and granted us some relief

BRIGHTER (4) [BRIGHT]
Job 11:17 Your life will be **b** than the noonday. Any darkness
Pr 4:18 which shines ever **b** until the full light of day.
Isa 30:26 as the sun, and the sun will be seven times **b**—
Ac 26:13 a light from heaven **b** than the sun shone down on

BRIGHTEST (3) [BRIGHT]
SS 8: 6 Love flashes like fire, the **b** kind of flame.
Isa 59:10 Even at **b** noontime, we fall down as though it
Eze 32: 8 Even the **b** stars will become dark above you.

BRIGHTLY (6) [BRIGHT]
Job 37:21 for it shines **b** in the sky when the wind clears
Isa 31: 9 the LORD, whose flame burns **b** in Jerusalem.
Eze 10: 4 and the Temple courtyard glowed **b** with the glory
Jn 5:35 John shone **b** for a while, and you benefited
2Co 3:18 so that we can be mirrors that **b** reflect the glory of
Php 2:15 Let your lives shine **b** before them.

BRIGHTNESS (5) [BRIGHT]
2Sa 22:13 A great **b** shone before him, / and bolts of lightning
Isa 24:23 There will be such glory that the **b** of the sun
1Co 15:41 stars differ from each other in their beauty and **b**.
2Co 3: 7 even though the **b** was already fading away.
4: 6 has made us understand that this light is the **b** of

BRILLIANCE (3) [BRILLIANT]
Ps 18:12 The **b** of his presence broke through the clouds,
Hab 3:11 obscured by **b** from your arrows and the flashing
Rev 1:16 And his face was as bright as the sun in all its **b**.

BRILLIANT (15) [BRILLIANCE, BRILLIANTLY]
Ex 24:10 Under his feet there seemed to be a pavement of **b**
2Ch 2:13 craftsman named Huram-abi. He is a **b** man,
26:15 designed by **b** men to shoot arrows and hurl stones
Isa 29:14 and even the most **b** people lack understanding."
Eze 1: 4 that flashed with lightning and shone with **b** light.
1:13 beings looked like bright coals of fire or **b** torches,
Hab 3: 3 His **b** splendor fills the heavens, and the earth is
3: 4 Rays of **b** light flash from his hands. He rejoices in
Ac 9: 3 a **b** light from heaven suddenly beamed down upon
1Co 1:19 human wisdom / and discard their most **b** ideas."
1:20 the scholars, and the world's **b** debaters?
2: 1 lofty words and **b** ideas to tell you God's message.
1Ti 6:16 lives in light so **b** that no human can approach him.
2Pe 1:19 Christ appears and his **b** light shines in your hearts.
Rev 4: 3 The one sitting on the throne was as **b** as

BRILLIANTLY (1) [BRILLIANT]
Da 2:31 of a man, shining **b**, frightening and awesome.

BRIM (5)
2Ki 4: 6 Soon every container was full to the **b**! "Bring me
Jer 25:15 "Take from my hand this cup filled to the **b** with
Eze 27:25 Your island warehouse was filled to the **b**!
32: 6 way to the mountains, filling the ravines to the **b**.
Jn 2: 7 When the jars had been filled to the **b**,

BRIMSTONE [KJV] See also SULFUR

BRING (669) [BRINGING, BRINGS, BROUGHT]
Ge 1:24 "Let the earth **b** forth every kind of animal—
5:29 "He will **b** us relief from the painful labor of
6:19 **B** a pair of every kind of animal—a male and a
11: 4 This will **b** us together and keep us from scattering
15: 9 LORD told him, "**B** me a three-year-old heifer,
19: 5 **B** them out so we can have sex with them."
24:38 I was told to **b** back a young woman from here to
27: 4 so it's savory and good, and **b** it here for me to eat.
27: 9 out to the flocks and **b** me two fine young goats.
27:25 Then Isaac said, "Now, my son, **b** me the meat.
28:15 I will someday **b** you safely back to this land.
28:21 and if he will **b** me back safely to my father,
37:14 Jacob said. "Then come back and **b** me word."
37:22 and then he would **b** him back to his father.
38:24 "**B** her out and burn her!" Judah shouted.
42:20 But **b** your youngest brother back to me. In this
42:34 But **b** your youngest brother back to me. Then I
42:37 "You may kill my two sons if I don't **b** Benjamin
42:38 you would **b** my gray head down to the grave in

43: 7 have known he would say, '**B** me your brother'?"
43: 9 If I don't **b** him back to you, then let me bear the
43:31 under control. "**B** on the food!" he ordered.
44: 8 Didn't we **b** back the money we found in our
44:21 And you said to us, '**B** him here so I can see him.'
44:29 you would **b** my gray head down to the grave in
44:32 I told him, 'If I don't **b** him back to you, I will bear
45:13 you have seen, and **b** him to me quickly."
45:18 Tell them to **b** your father and all of their families,
45:19 and little ones and to **b** your father here.
46: 4 to Egypt, and I will **b** your descendants back again.
48: 9 And Jacob said, "**B** them over to me, and I will
48:21 will be with you and will **b** you again to Canaan,
50:24 He will **b** you back to the land he vowed to give to
Ex 6: 8 I will **b** you into the land I swore to give to
10:12 "Raise your hand over the land of Egypt to **b** on
12:42 This night had been reserved by the LORD to **b**
14:11 "Why did you **b** us out here to die in the
15:17 You will **b** them in and plant them on your own
17: 3 Why did you **b** us here? We, our children, and our
19:24 "Go down anyway and **b** Aaron back with you.
23:15 Everyone must **b** me a sacrifice at that time.
23:16 when you **b** me the first crops of your harvest.
23:19 **b** me a choice sample of the first day's harvest.
23:23 before you and **b** you into the land of the Amorites,
24: 1 up here to me, and **b** along Aaron, Nadab, Abihu,
25: 2 that everyone who wants to may **b** me an offering.
27:20 "Tell the people of Israel to **b** you pure olive oil
29:10 "Then **b** the young bull to the entrance of the
30:16 It will **b** you, the Israelites, to the LORD's
32: 2 off their gold earrings, and then **b** them to me."
32:14 and didn't **b** against his people the disaster he had
32:21 "How did they ever make you **b** such terrible sin
32:24 So I told them, '**B** me your gold earrings.'
34:26 You must **b** the best of the first of each year's crop
35: 5 Everyone is invited to **b** these offerings to the
36: 6 "**B** no more materials! You have already given
40: 4 Then **b** in the table, and arrange the utensils on it.
40: 4 And **b** in the lampstand, and set up the lamps.
40:12 "**B** Aaron and his sons to the entrance of the
40:14 Then **b** his sons and dress them in their tunics.
Lev 1: 2 you must **b** animals from your flocks and herds.
1: 3 **b** a bull with no physical defects to the entrance of
1:10 **b** a male sheep or goat with no physical defects.
1:14 "If you **b** a bird as a burnt offering to the LORD,
2: 1 "When you **b** a grain offering to the LORD,
2: 2 **B** this offering to one of Aaron's sons, and he will
2: 8 **b** it to the priests who will present it at the altar.
2:14 **b** kernels of new grain that have been roasted on a
3: 6 from the flock, you may **b** either a goat or a sheep.
3: 7 If you **b** a sheep as your gift, present it to the
3:12 "If you **b** a goat as your offering to the LORD,
4: 3 he must **b** to the LORD a young bull with no
4:14 the leaders of the community must **b** a young bull
4:16 The priest will **b** some of its blood into the
4:23 he must **b** as his offering a male goat with no
4:28 they must **b** as their offering a female goat with no
4:32 "If any of the people **b** a sheep as their sin
5: 6 and **b** to the LORD as their penalty a female from
5: 7 "If any of them cannot afford to **b** a sheep,
5: 7 they must **b** to the LORD two young turtledoves
5: 8 They must **b** them to the priest, who will offer one
5:11 "If any of the people cannot afford to **b** young
5:11 they must **b** two quarts of choice flour for their sin
5:15 they must **b** to the LORD a ram from the flock as
5:18 they must **b** to the priest a ram from the flock as a
6: 6 They must then **b** a guilt offering to the priest,
6:20 they must **b** to the LORD a grain offering of two
7:16 if you **b** an offering to fulfill a vow or as a freewill
7:29 **b** part of it as a special gift to the LORD.
7:30 **B** the fat of the animal, together with the breast,
7:38 **b** their offerings to the LORD in the wilderness of
8: 2 "Now **b** Aaron and his sons, along with their
12: 6 the woman must **b** a year-old lamb for a whole
12: 8 "If a woman cannot afford to **b** a sheep, she must **b**
two turtledoves or two young pigeons.
14:10 each person cured of the skin disease must **b** two
14:21 "But anyone who cannot afford two lambs must **b**
14:22 The person being cleansed must also **b** two
14:23 the person being cleansed must **b** the offerings to
14:32 but who cannot afford to **b** the sacrifices normally
15:14 On the eighth day he must **b** two turtledoves
15:29 she must **b** two turtledoves or two young pigeons
16: 3 He must first **b** a young bull for a sin offering
16: 5 then **b** him two male goats for a sin offering
16: 7 Then he must **b** the two male goats and present
16:15 the people and **b** its blood behind the inner curtain.
16:20 and the altar, he must **b** the living goat forward.
17: 4 and does not **b** it to the entrance of the Tabernacle
17: 5 It will cause them to **b** their sacrifices to the priest
17: 9 and do not **b** it to the entrance of the Tabernacle to
19:21 must **b** a ram as a guilt offering and present it to
22:16 The negligent priest would **b** guilt upon the people
22:20 Do not **b** an animal with physical defects,
22:21 "If you **b** a peace offering to the LORD from the
22:29 When you **b** a thanksgiving offering to the
23:10 **b** the priest some grain from the first portion of
23:16 and **b** an offering of new grain to the LORD.
23:17 **b** two loaves of bread to be lifted up before the
27:11 then you must **b** the animal to the priest.
Nu 2:31 They are to **b** up the rear whenever the Israelites
5: 9 All the sacred gifts that the Israelites **b** to a priest
5:15 the husband must **b** his wife to the priest with an
5:24 so it may **b** on the curse and cause bitter suffering
6:10 On the eighth day they must **b** two turtledoves
6:12 and each must **b** a one-year-old male lamb for a
7:11 "Let each leader **b** his gift on a different day for
8: 8 Have them **b** a young bull and a grain offering of
8:10 When you **b** the Levites before the LORD,
11:16 **B** them to the Tabernacle to stand there with you.
13:20 and **b** back samples of the crops you see."
14: 8 he will **b** us safely into that land and give it to us.
14:16 'The LORD was not able to **b** them into the land
14:24 to me, and I will **b** him into the land he explored.
14:31 Well, I will **b** them safely into the land, and they
15:27 the guilty person must **b** a one-year-old female
16:17 Aaron will also **b** his incense burner."
18: 2 "**B** your relatives of the tribe of Levi to assist you
18:19 offerings that the people of Israel **b** to the LORD.
19: 2 Tell the people of Israel to **b** you a red heifer that
20: 4 Did you **b** the LORD's people into this
20: 5 us leave Egypt and **b** us here to this terrible place?
20:10 "Must we **b** you water from this rock?"
Dt 1:17 **B** me any cases that are too difficult for you,
4:38 so he could **b** you in and give you their land as a
6:10 "The LORD your God will soon **b** you into the
7:15 in Egypt, but he will **b** them all on your enemies!
7:26 Do not **b** any detestable objects into your home,
9:28 because he wasn't able to **b** them to the land he
12: 6 There you will **b** to the LORD your burnt
12:11 you must **b** everything I command you—
14:23 **B** this tithe to the place the LORD your God
14:28 "At the end of every third year **b** the tithe of all
16:10 **B** him a freewill offering in proportion to the
16:16 and they must **b** a gift to the LORD.
18: 3 the oxen and sheep that the people **b** as offerings:
22: 8 That way you will not **b** the guilt of bloodshed on
22:15 and mother must **b** the proof of her virginity to the
23:18 Do not **b** to the house of the LORD your God any
24: 4 You must not **b** guilt upon the land the LORD
24:11 Stand outside and the owner will **b** it out to you.
24:19 and forget to **b** in a bundle of grain from your
26: 2 and **b** it to the place the LORD your God chooses
28:49 "The LORD will **b** a distant nation against you
28:60 He will **b** against you all the diseases of Egypt that
28:61 The LORD will **b** against you every sickness
30: 4 God will go and find you and **b** you back again.
30:12 and **b** it down so we can hear and obey it?'
30:13 'Who will cross the sea to **b** it to us so we can hear
31:20 For I will **b** them into the land I swore to give their
31:23 You must **b** the people of Israel into the land I
32:25 Outside, the sword will **b** death, / and inside,
32:41 out justice, / I will **b** vengeance on my enemies
33: 7 the cry of Judah / and **b** them again to their people.
Jos 2: 3 "**B** out the men who have come into your house.
6:18 and you will **b** trouble on all Israel.
6:22 Go to the prostitute's house and **b** her out,
7: 7 why did you **b** us across the Jordan River if you
7:25 The LORD will now **b** trouble on you." And all
10:22 opening of the cave and **b** the five kings to me."
23:15 he will also **b** disaster on you if you disobey him.
Jdg 6:18 away until I come back and **b** my offering to you."
6:30 "**B** out your son," they shouted to Joash.
7: 4 **B** them down to the spring, and I will sort out who
16:25 "**B** out Samson so he can perform for us!"
19:22 "**B** out the man who is staying with you so we can
19:24 I will **b** them out to you, and you can do whatever
Ru 3:15 also said to her, "**B** your cloak and spread it out."
1Sa 4: 3 "Let's **b** the Ark of the Covenant of the LORD
4: 4 So they sent men to Shiloh to **b** back the Ark of the
9:23 then instructed the cook to **b** Saul the finest cut of
10:27 And they despised him and refused to **b** him gifts.
11:12 rule over us? **B** them here, and we will kill them!"
12: 8 them from Egypt and to **b** them into this land.
13: 9 "**B** me the burnt offering and the peace
14:18 Then Saul shouted to Ahijah, "**B** the ephod here!"
14:34 '**B** the cattle and sheep here to kill them and drain
15:32 Then Samuel said, "**B** King Agag to me."
16:17 me someone who plays well and **b** him here."
17:18 getting along, and **b** me back a letter from them."
19:15 "Then **b** him to me in his bed," Saul ordered,
20:21 Then I will send a boy to **b** the arrows back.
21:14 said to his men, "Must you **b** me a madman?
23: 9 and told Abiathar the priest to **b** the ephod
28:19 The LORD will **b** the entire army of Israel down
30: 7 he said to Abiathar the priest, "**B** me the ephod!"
2Sa 1:10 and one of his bracelets so I could **b** them to you,
3:13 "but I will not negotiate with you unless you **b**
6: 2 He led them to Baalah of Judah to **b** home the Ark
6: 9 "How can I ever **b** the Ark of the LORD back
12:23 Can I **b** him back again? I will go to him one day,
12:28 Now **b** the rest of the army and finish the job,
13:10 "Now **b** the food into my bedroom and feed it to
14:10 the king said. "If anyone objects, **b** them to me.
14:13 because you have refused to **b** home your own
14:14 That is why God tries to **b** us back when we have
14:21 go and **b** back the young man Absalom."
15: 4 Then people could **b** their problems to me, and I
15: 8 in Hebron if he would **b** me back to Jerusalem."
15:25 "he will **b** me back to see the Ark
17: 3 and I will **b** all the people back to you as a bride
17: 5 then Absalom said, "**B** in Hushai the Arkite.
17:14 so that he could **b** disaster upon Absalom!
17:17 **b** them the message they were to take to King
19:14 to us, and **b** back all those who are with you."
23: 4 like the refreshing rains that **b** tender grass from
23:17 of these men who risked their lives to **b** it to me."
1Ki 1:35 When you **b** him back here, he will sit on my
3:24 All right, **b** me a sword." So a sword was brought
5: 9 My servants will **b** the logs from the Lebanon
8: 1 They were to **b** the Ark of the LORD's covenant
13:18 '**B** him home with you, and give him food to eat
14:10 I will **b** disaster on your dynasty and kill all your
17: 4 from the brook and eat what the ravens **b** you,
17: 4 for I have commanded them to **b** you food."
17:10 "Would you please **b** me a cup of water?"
17:11 he called to her, "**B** me a bite of bread, too."
18:19 Now **b** all the people of Israel to Mount Carmel,
18:23 Now **b** two bulls. The prophets of Baal may
20:10 "May the gods **b** tragedy on me, and even worse
21:21 The LORD is going to **b** disaster to you
2Ki 2:20 Elisha said, "**B** me a new bowl with salt in it."
3:15 Now **b** me someone who can play the harp."
4: 6 "**B** me another jar," she said to one of her sons.
4:41 Elisha said, "**B** me some flour." Then he threw it
10: 6 **b** the heads of the king's sons to me at Jezreel at
14:10 Why stir up trouble that will **b** disaster on you
20:20 a pool and dug a tunnel to **b** water into the city,
21:12 I will **b** such disaster on Jerusalem and Judah that
22:20 You will not see the disaster I am going to **b** on
1Ch 11:19 of these men who risked their lives to **b** it to me."
13: 3 It is time to **b** back the Ark of our God, for we
13: 6 to **b** back the Ark of God, which bears the name of
13:12 "How can I ever **b** the Ark of God back into my
15: 3 **b** the Ark of the LORD to the place he had
15:12 so you can **b** the Ark of the LORD, the God of
15:14 and the Levites purified themselves in order to **b**
15:25 **b** the Ark of the LORD's covenant up to
16:29 **B** your offering and come to worship him.
21: 2 and **b** me the totals so I may know how many there
22:19 so that you can **b** the Ark of the LORD's
2Ch 5: 2 They were to **b** the Ark of the LORD's covenant
24: 9 telling the people to **b** to the LORD the tax that
24:19 The LORD sent prophets to **b** them back to him,
25:19 Why stir up trouble that will **b** disaster on you
28:13 "You must not **b** the prisoners here!"
29:31 Now **b** your sacrifices and thanksgiving offerings
31: 4 he required the people in Jerusalem to **b** the
34:28 You will not see the disaster I am going to **b** on
35: 5 and help the families assigned to you as they **b**
Ne 1: 9 I will **b** you back to the place I have chosen for my
4: 8 against Jerusalem and to **b** about confusion there.
8: 1 They asked Ezra the scribe to **b** out the Book of the
10:31 if the people of the land should **b** any merchandise
10:34 and the common people should **b** wood to God's
10:35 "We promise always to **b** the first part of every
10:37 We will **b** the best of our flour and other grain
10:37 And we promise to **b** to the Levites a tenth of
10:39 and the Levites must **b** these offerings of grain,
Est 1:11 to **b** Queen Vashti to him with the royal crown on
2: 3 Let the king appoint agents in each province to **b**
6: 1 so he ordered an attendant to **b** the historical
6: 5 is out there." "**B** him in," the king ordered.
6: 8 he should **b** out one of the king's own royal robes,
Job 9:33 If only there were a mediator who could **b** us
10:17 of anger upon me and **b** fresh armies against me.
10:18 then, did you **b** me out of my mother's womb?
13:26 against me and **b** up all the sins of my youth.
20:18 will not be rewarded. His wealth will **b** him no joy.
24: 1 the Almighty open the court and **b** judgment?
28:11 and **b** to light the hidden treasures.
35:14 He will **b** about justice if you will only wait.
37: 9 from its chamber, and the driving winds **b** the cold.
38:13 of the earth, to **b** an end to the night's wickedness?
Ps 5: 3 Each morning I **b** my requests to you and wait
7: 6 of my enemies! / Wake up, my God, and **b** justice!
10:18 You will **b** justice to the orphans
12: 3 May the LORD **b** their flattery to an end
17:13 Stand against them and **b** them to their knees!
38: T of David, to **b** us to the LORD's remembrance.
45:17 I will **b** honor to your name in every generation.
50: 5 "**B** my faithful people to me—/ those who made a
50: 8 or the burnt offerings you constantly **b** to my altar.
51:16 not be pleased with sacrifices, / or I would **b** them.
55: 3 and wicked threats. / They **b** trouble on me,
59:11 them with your power, and **b** them to their knees,
60: 9 But who will **b** me into the fortified city? / Who
will **b** me victory over Edom?
65: 4 What joy for those you choose to **b** near,
68:22 "I will **b** my enemies down from Bashan;
68:22 I will **b** them up from the depths of the sea.
70: T of David, to **b** us to the LORD's remembrance.
71:13 **B** disgrace and destruction on those who accuse
72:10 of Tarshish and the islands / will **b** him tribute.
72:10 eastern kings of Sheba and Seba / will **b** him gifts.
72:17 nations be blessed through him / and **b** him praise.
75: 2 have planned, / I will **b** justice against the wicked.
76:11 Let everyone **b** tribute to the Awesome One.
96: 8 **B** your offering and come to worship him.
108:10 But who will **b** me into the fortified city? / Who
will **b** me victory over Edom?
109: 6 to turn on him. / Send an accuser to **b** him to trial.
118:27 **B** forward the sacrifice and put it on the altar.
119:78 **B** disgrace upon the arrogant people who lied
142: 7 **B** me out of prison / so I can thank you.
143: 2 Don't **b** your servant to trial! / Compared to you,
143:11 In your righteousness, **b** me out of this distress.
Pr 3:22 they fill you with life and **b** you honor and respect.
4:22 for they **b** life and radiant health to anyone who
6:26 For a prostitute will **b** you to poverty, and sleeping
11:29 Those who **b** trouble on their families inherit only
12:18 but the words of the wise **b** healing.
15: 4 Gentle words **b** life and health; a deceitful tongue
15: 6 the godly, but the earnings of the wicked **b** trouble.
15:20 Sensible children **b** joy to their father;
15:22 for lack of advice; many counselors **b** success.
18:16 it may **b** you before important people!
18:20 the right words on a person's lips **b** satisfaction.
21:12 of the wicked; he will **b** the wicked to disaster.
22:21 and **b** an accurate report to those who sent you.
23:11 He himself will **b** their charges against you.

25:14 gift is like clouds and wind that don't **b** rain.
27:1 since you don't know what the day will **b**.
28:7 those who seek out worthless companions **b** shame
Ecc 3:22 No one will **b** them back from death to enjoy life
SS 1:4 let's run! **B** me into your bedroom, O my king."
8:2 I would **b** you to my childhood home, and there
Isa 1:11 "Don't **b** me any more burnt offerings!
1:13 The incense you **b** me is a stench in my nostrils!
7:17 "The LORD will **b** a terrible curse on you,
11:11 In that day the Lord will **b** back a remnant of his
14:1 He will **b** them back to settle once again in their
18:7 They will **b** the gifts to the LORD Almighty in
19:22 The LORD will strike Egypt in a way that will **b**
20:3 a symbol of the terrible troubles I will **b** upon
21:14 of Tema, **b** food and water to these weary refugees.
22:23 He will **b** honor to his family name, for I will drive
22:24 and he will **b** honor to even the lowliest members
27:12 He will **b** them to his great threshing floor—
28:19 This message will **b** terror to your people.
29:2 Yet I will **b** disaster upon you, and there will be
30:30 With angry indignation he will **b** down his mighty
32:17 And this righteousness will **b** peace. Quietness
34:11 For God will **b** chaos and destruction to that land.
41:1 **B** your strongest arguments. Come now and speak.
42:3 He will **b** full justice to all who have been
42:15 and hills / and **b** a blight on all their greenery.
43:6 I will **b** my sons and daughters back to Israel from
43:8 **B** out the people who have eyes but are blind,
44:20 Yet he cannot **b** himself to ask, "Is this thing,
49:3 are my servant, Israel, and you will **b** me glory."
49:5 who commissioned me to **b** his people of Israel
49:6 and you will **b** my salvation to the ends of the
49:22 they will **b** your daughters on their shoulders.
52:7 are the feet of those who **b** good news of peace
55:13 This miracle will **b** great honor to the LORD's
56:7 I will **b** them also to my holy mountain of
56:8 I will **b** others, too, besides my people Israel."
60:5 to you. They will **b** you the wealth of many lands.
60:6 From Sheba they will **b** gold and incense for the
60:9 reserved to **b** the people of Israel home. They will
b their wealth with them, and it will **b** great honor
to the LORD your God,
60:16 and mighty nations will **b** the best of their goods to
60:21 with my own hands in order to **b** myself glory.
60:22 the LORD, will **b** it all to pass at the right time."
61:1 because the LORD has appointed me to **b** good
66:3 they sacrifice a lamb or **b** an offering of grain,
66:9 Would I ever **b** this nation to the point of birth
66:15 He will **b** punishment with the fury of his anger
66:20 They will **b** the remnant of your people back from
66:20 They will **b** them to my holy mountain in
Jer 2:9 I will **b** my case against you and will keep on
3:14 I will **b** you again to the land of Israel—one from
5:15 O Israel, I will **b** a distant nation against you,"
6:19 all the earth! I will **b** disaster upon my people.
10:9 They **b** beaten sheets of silver from Tarshish
11:11 the LORD, I am going to **b** calamity upon them,
11:23 for I will **b** disaster upon them when their time of
12:1 you always give me justice when I **b** a case before
12:1 Now let me **b** you this complaint: Why are the
12:9 **B** on the wild beasts to pick their corpses clean!
12:15 I will **b** them home to their own lands again,
15:8 At noontime I will **b** a destroyer against the
15:16 They **b** me great joy and are my heart's delight,
16:15 For I will **b** them back to this land that I gave their
17:18 **B** shame and terror on all who persecute me,
17:18 me peace. Yes, **b** double destruction upon them!
17:26 They will **b** their grain offerings, incense,
17:27 and if on the Sabbath day you **b** loads of
19:3 I will **b** such a terrible disaster on this place that
19:15 I will **b** disaster upon this city and its surrounding
21:4 I will **b** your enemies right into the heart of this
21:10 For I have decided to **b** disaster and not good upon
22:7 who will **b** out their tools to dismantle you.
23:3 I will **b** them back into their own fold, and they
23:12 For I will **b** disaster upon them when their time of
24:6 are well treated, and I will **b** them back here again.
25:9 I will **b** them all against this land and its people
25:13 I will **b** upon them all the terrors I have promised
25:31 for the LORD will **b** his case against all the
27:13 which the LORD will **b** against every nation that
27:22 But someday I will **b** them back to Jerusalem
28:3 I will **b** back all the Temple treasures that King
28:4 And I will **b** back Jehoiachin son of Jehoiakim,
28:6 I hope he does **b** back from Babylon the treasures
29:10 I have promised, and I will **b** you home again.
29:14 sent you and **b** you home again to your own land."
30:3 I will **b** them home to this land that I gave to their
30:10 For I will **b** you home again from distant lands,
30:18 When I **b** you home again from your captivity
31:8 For I will **b** them from the north and from the
31:23 "When I **b** them back again, the people of Judah
32:37 I will surely **b** my people back again from all the
32:37 I will **b** them back to this very city and let them
33:9 Then this city will **b** me joy, glory, and honor
33:15 At that time I will **b** to the throne of David a
39:14 sent messengers to **b** Jeremiah out of the prison.
41:8 go by promising to **b** him their stores of wheat,
42:10 for all the punishment I have had to **b** upon you.
42:17 None of you will escape from the disaster I will **b**
43:10 I will surely **b** my servant Nebuchadnezzar, king of
43:11 He will **b** death to those destined for death; he will
b captivity to those destined for captivity; he will
b the sword against those destined for the
44:27 For I will watch over you to **b** you disaster and not
45:5 I will **b** great disaster upon all these people, but I
46:11 But your many medicines will **b** you no healing.
46:27 For I will **b** you home again from distant lands,
49:5 I will **b** terror upon you," says the Lord,
49:8 For when I **b** disaster on Edom, I will punish you,
49:16 I will **b** you crashing down," says the LORD.
49:32 I will **b** calamity upon them from every direction,"
49:36 I will **b** enemies from all directions, and I will
49:37 My fierce anger will **b** great disaster upon the
50:3 and **b** such destruction that no one will live in her
50:9 I will **b** them against Babylon to attack her,
50:19 And I will **b** Israel home again to her own land,
51:27 **B** out the armies of Ararat, Minni, and Ashkenaz.
51:27 Appoint a leader, and **b** a multitude of horses!
51:28 **B** against her the armies of the kings of the Medes
51:40 "I will **b** them like lambs to the slaughter,
51:64 because of the disasters I will **b** upon her.' " This
La 1:21 Oh, **b** the day you promised, when you will destroy
5:21 Restore us, O LORD, and **b** us back to you again!
Eze 5:17 and I will **b** the sword of the enemy against you.
6:3 I am about to **b** war upon you, and I will destroy
7:5 With one blow after another I will **b** total disaster!
7:24 I will **b** the most ruthless of nations to occupy their
7:27 I will **b** against them the evil they have done to
9:1 "**B** on the men appointed to punish the city! Tell
them to **b** their weapons with them!"
12:4 **B** your baggage outside during the day so they can
12:13 I will **b** him to Babylon, the land of the
14:17 "Or suppose I were to **b** war against the land,
17:20 I will **b** him to Babylon and deal with him there for
20:4 **b** judgment against them and condemn them.
20:6 I promised that I would **b** her and her descendants
20:15 I would not **b** them into the land I had given them,
20:34 and fury I will **b** you out from the lands where you
20:35 I will **b** you into the wilderness of the nations,
20:38 I will **b** them out of the countries where they are in
20:39 but then don't turn around and **b** gifts to me.
20:40 There I will require that you **b** me all your
20:41 When I **b** you home from exile, you will be as
22:19 I will **b** you to my crucible in Jerusalem.
23:46 **B** an army against them and hand them over to be
24:5 **B** the pot to a boil, and cook the bones along with
25:11 I will **b** my judgment down on the Moabites.
26:3 O Tyre, and I will **b** many nations against you,
26:7 I will **b** King Nebuchadnezzar of Babylon—
26:21 I will **b** you to a terrible end, and you will be no
28:7 I will **b** against you an enemy army, the terror of
28:8 They will **b** you down to the pit, and you will die
28:22 When I **b** judgment against you and reveal my
29:8 I will **b** an army against you, O Egypt, and destroy
29:13 At the end of the forty years I will **b** the Egyptians
29:14 and **b** its people back to the land of Pathros in
32:8 I will **b** darkness everywhere across your land.
32:9 "And when I **b** your shattered remains to distant
32:10 Yes, I will **b** terror to many lands, and their kings
33:2 When I **b** an army against a country, the people of
34:13 I will **b** them back home to their own land of Israel
34:16 strayed away, and I will **b** them safely home again.
35:11 And I will **b** honor to my name by what I do to
36:11 of Israel, I will **b** people to live on you once again.
36:24 all the nations and **b** you home again to your land.
36:33 I will **b** people to live in your cities, and the ruins
36:35 And when I **b** you back, people will say,
37:12 Then I will **b** you back to the land of Israel.
37:21 I will **b** them home to their own land from the
38:16 I will **b** you against my land as everyone watches,
38:17 in future days I would **b** you against my people.
39:27 When I **b** them home from the lands of their
45:15 will make atonement for the people who **b** them,
46:6 he will **b** one young bull, six lambs, and one ram,
46:7 With the young bull he must **b** a half bushel of
46:7 With the ram he must **b** another half bushel of
46:7 And with each lamb he is to **b** whatever amount of
Da 1:3 to **b** to the palace some of the young men of
5:2 he gave orders to **b** in the gold and silver cups that
9:24 to **b** an end to sin, to atone for guilt, to **b** in
everlasting righteousness,
11:26 Those of his own household will **b** his downfall.
Hos 3:1 **B** her back to you and love her, even though she
4:8 the people sin and **b** their sin offerings to them.
7:12 and **b** them down like a bird from the sky.
9:13 But now Israel will **b** out her children to be
11:11 And I will **b** them home again," says the LORD.
13:14 O death, **b** forth your terrors! O grave, **b** forth your
plagues! For I will not relent!
14:2 **B** your petitions, and return to the LORD. Say to
Joel 1:14 **B** the leaders and all the people into the Temple of
2:16 **B** everyone—the elders, the children, and even the
3:7 But I will **b** them back again from all these places
Am 4:4 each morning and **b** your tithes every three days!
4:12 I will **b** upon you all these further disasters I have
5:18 That day will not **b** light and prosperity,
6:3 but your actions only **b** the day of judgment closer.
6:14 I am about to **b** an enemy nation against you,"
7:9 and I will **b** the dynasty of King Jeroboam to a
9:2 climb up into the heavens, I will **b** them down.
9:4 I am determined to **b** disaster upon them and not to
9:14 I will **b** my exiled people of Israel back from
Ob 1:4 nest among the stars, I will **b** you crashing down.
Jnh 1:8 "What have you done to **b** this awful storm down
Mic 1:15 I will **b** a conqueror to capture your town.
2:12 I will **b** you together again like sheep in a fold,
2:13 He will **b** you through the gates of your cities of
6:6 What can we **b** to the LORD to make up for what
6:13 wound you! I will **b** you to ruin for all your sins.
7:9 The LORD will **b** me out of my darkness into the
Na 2:13 Never again will you **b** back plunder from
Hab 3:19 as a deer and **b** me safely over the mountains.
Zep 3:19 I will **b** together those who were chased away.
3:20 I will gather you together and **b** you home again.
Hag 1:8 the hills, **b** down timber, and rebuild my house.
2:9 And in this place I will **b** peace. I, the LORD
Zec 3:8 Soon I am going to **b** my servant, the Branch.
6:10 and Jedaiah will **b** gifts of silver and gold from the
8:8 I will **b** them home again to live safely in
9:10 Your king will **b** peace to the nations. His realm
10:10 I will **b** them back from Egypt and Assyria
13:9 I will **b** that group through the fire and make them
Mal 1:9 But when you **b** that kind of offering, why should
2:2 "or I will **b** a terrible curse against you.
2:5 of my covenant with the Levites was to **b** life
3:10 **B** all the tithes into the storehouse so there will be
Mt 6:34 for tomorrow will **b** its own worries.
9:18 "but you can **b** her back to life again if you just
10:34 "Don't imagine that I came to **b** peace to the earth!
No, I came to **b** a sword.
12:10 say yes, so they could **b** charges against him.)
14:18 "**B** them here," he said.
16:5 the disciples discovered they had forgotten to **b**
17:17 long must I put up with you? **B** the boy to me."
18:23 **b** his accounts up to date with servants who had
21:2 with its colt beside it. Untie them and **b** them here.
Mk 3:9 Jesus instructed his disciples to **b** around a boat
6:27 to the prison to cut off John's head and **b** it to him.
8:14 discovered they had forgotten to **b** any food,
9:19 long must I put up with you? **B** the boy to me."
11:2 that has never been ridden. Untie it and **b** it here.
Lk 1:19 It was he who sent me to **b** you this good news!
2:10 "I **b** you good news of great joy for everyone!
6:7 eager to find some legal charge to **b** against him.
9:41 I be with you and put up with you? **B** him here."
12:49 "I have come to **b** fire to the earth, and I wish that
12:51 Do you think I have come to **b** peace to the earth?
No, I have come to **b** strife and division!
15:22 **B** the finest robe in the house and put it on him.
19:27 **b** them in and execute them right here in my
19:30 that has never been ridden. Untie it and **b** it here.
Jn 7:45 and Pharisees. "Why didn't you **b** him in?"
10:16 I must **b** them also, and they will listen to my
12:28 Father, **b** glory to your name." Then a voice spoke
13:32 And God will **b** me into my glory very soon.
16:14 He will **b** me glory by revealing to you whatever
17:5 **b** me into the glory we shared before the world
18:37 that purpose. And I came to **b** truth to the world.
19:4 the people, "I am going to **b** him out to you now,
21:10 "**B** some of the fish you've just caught,"
Ac 9:2 He wanted to **b** them—both men and women—
12:4 Herod's intention was to **b** Peter out for public trial
13:32 and I are here to **b** you this Good News.
13:47 to **b** salvation to the farthest corners of the
14:15 We have come to **b** you the Good News that you
22:5 authorizing me to **b** the Christians from there to
23:10 away from them and **b** him back to the fortress.
23:15 commander to **b** Paul back to the council again,"
23:18 me over and asked me to **b** this young man to you
23:20 "Some Jews are going to ask you to **b** Paul before
23:30 I have told his accusers to **b** their charges before
24:19 and they ought to be here to **b** charges if they have
Ro 1:9 Day and night I **b** you and your needs in prayer to
3:19 and to **b** the entire world into judgment before
7:13 Sin used what was good to **b** about my
10:6 (to find Christ and **b** him down to help you).
10:7 place of the dead" (to **b** Christ back to life again).
10:15 "How beautiful are the feet of those who **b** good
15:16 I **b** you the Good News and offer you up as a
1Co 1:28 and used them to **b** to nothing what the world
3:17 God will **b** ruin upon anyone who ruins this
4:5 he will **b** our deepest secrets to light and will
9:5 Don't we have the right to **b** a Christian wife along
9:19 servant of everyone so that I can **b** them to Christ.
9:20 become one of them so that I can **b** them to Christ.
9:20 subject to the law, so that I can **b** them to Christ.
9:21 I gain their confidence and **b** them to Christ.
9:22 their oppression so that I might **b** them to Christ.
9:22 with everyone so that I might **b** them to Christ.
10:19 Am I saying that the idols to whom the pagans **b**
11:34 so you won't **b** judgment upon yourselves when
14:6 But if I **b** you some revelation or some special
2Co 3:1 Some people need to **b** letters of recommendation
5:13 it seems that we are crazy, it is to **b** glory to God.
8:23 They are splendid examples of those who **b** glory
Gal 4:23 to **b** about the fulfillment of God's promise.
5:10 I am trusting the Lord to **b** you back to believing as
Eph 1:10 At the right time he will **b** everything together
4:30 And do not **b** sorrow to God's Holy Spirit by the
6:4 **b** them up with the discipline and instruction
Php 1:11 for this will **b** much glory and praise to God.
1Th 2:19 you will **b** us much joy as we stand together before
4:14 God will **b** back with Jesus all the Christians who
2Th 3:5 May the Lord **b** you into an ever deeper
1Ti 6:7 we didn't **b** anything with us when we came into
2Ti 2:10 I am willing to endure anything if it will **b**
4:11 **B** Mark with you when you come, for he will be
4:13 be sure to **b** the coat I left with Carpus at Troas.
4:13 Also **b** my books, and especially my papers.
4:18 and will **b** me safely to his heavenly Kingdom.
Tit 1:1 I have been sent to **b** faith to those God has chosen
2:5 Then they will not **b** shame on the word of God.
Heb 2:10 was made—should **b** his many children into glory.
2:10 one fit to **b** them into their salvation.
6:6 It is impossible to **b** such people to repentance
9:9 cleanse the consciences of the people who **b** them.
9:28 This time he will **b** salvation to all those who are
11:19 God was able to **b** him back to life again.
13:23 comes here soon, I will **b** him with me to see you.
Jas 5:20 and **b** about the forgiveness of many sins.

1Pe 1: 7 it will **b** you much praise and glory and honor on
3:18 but he died for sinners that he might **b** us safely
Jude 1:10 tell them, and they **b** about their own destruction.
1:15 He will **b** the people of the world / to judgment.
1:24 and who will **b** you into his glorious presence
Rev 15: 1 which would **b** God's wrath to completion.
21:24 of the world will come and **b** their glory to it.
21:26 And all the nations will **b** their glory and honor

BRINGING (72) [BRING]

Ge 27:14 his mother's instructions, **b** her the two goats.
44:31 We will be responsible for **b** his gray head down to
Ex 18:19 before God, **b** him their questions to be decided.
36: 6 So the people stopped **b** their offerings.
Lev 4: 3 high priest sins, **b** guilt upon the entire community,
7:18 and you will receive no credit for **b** it as an
20:22 otherwise the land to which I am **b** you will vomit
Dt 1:27 **b** us here from Egypt to be slaughtered by these
8: 7 For the LORD your God is **b** you into a good land
24: 5 one year, **b** happiness to the wife he has married.
28:51 calves, or lambs, **b** about your destruction.
29:27 **b** down on it all the curses recorded in this book.
Jdg 2:15 against them, **b** them defeat, just as he promised.
1Sa 5:10 "They are **b** the Ark of the God of Israel here to
10: 3 One will be **b** three young goats, another will have
2Sa 3:22 returned from a raid, **b** much plunder with them.
4:10 'Saul is dead,' thinking he was **b** me good news.
17:11 **b** them from as far away as Dan and Beersheba.
19:43 we were the first to speak of **b** him back to be our
1Ch 10: 6 sons died there together, **b** his dynasty to an end.
13: 5 to join in **b** the Ark of God from Kiriath-jearim.
2Ch 31:10 "Since the people began **b** their gifts to the
Ezr 7:23 for why should we risk **b** God's anger against the
Ne 13:12 And once more all the people of Judah began **b**
13:15 They were also **b** in bundles of grain and loading
13:15 And on that day they were **b** their wine, grapes,
13:16 There were also some men from Tyre **b** in fish
13:18 Now you are **b** even more wrath upon the people
Job 10: 2 tell me the charge you are **b** against me.
33:13 So why are you **b** a charge against him? You say,
39:12 on it to return, **b** your grain to the threshing floor?
Ps 19: 8 of the LORD are right, / **b** joy to the heart.
23: 3 guides me along right paths, / **b** honor to his name.
68:29 The kings of the earth are **b** tribute / to your
74:12 my king from ages past, / **b** salvation to the earth.
147: 2 and **b** the exiles back to Israel.
Isa 2:12 will punish the proud, **b** them down to the dust.
9:11 The LORD will reply to their bragging by **b**
30:30 and huge hailstones, **b** their destruction.
34: 2 completely destroy them, **b** about their slaughter.
50: 3 out across the skies, **b** it to a state of mourning."
52: 8 for before their very eyes they see the LORD **b**
Jer 4: 6 For I am **b** terrible destruction upon you from the
25: 7 **b** on yourselves all the disasters you now suffer.
33:11 along with the joyous songs of people **b**
Eze 13:18 Do you think you can trap others without **b**
20:22 who had seen my power in **b** them out of Egypt.
20:36 in the wilderness after **b** them out of Egypt,
27:18 **b** wine from Helbon and white wool from Zahar.
36:22 I am **b** you back again but not because you deserve
39: 2 mountains of Israel, **b** you from the distant north.
39:28 away to exile and responsible for **b** them home.
45:16 All the people of Israel must join the prince in **b**
Hos 12: 2 Now the LORD is **b** a lawsuit against Judah.
Am 5:25 "Was it to me you were **b** sacrifices and offerings
Mic 6:16 make an example of you, **b** you to complete ruin.
Na 1:15 He is **b** a message of peace. Celebrate your
Mal 1:12 By **b** contemptible food, you are saying it's all
Mt 14:35 and soon people were **b** all their sick to be healed.
Mk 11:16 and he stopped everyone from **b** in merchandise.
Jn 19:39 **b** about seventy-five pounds of embalming
Ac 5:16 **b** their sick and those possessed by evil spirits,
7:42 it is written, / 'Was it to me you were **b** sacrifices
21:28 and he even defiles it by **b** Gentiles in!"
Ro 1: 5 will believe and obey him, **b** glory to his name.
15:31 will be willing to accept the donation I am **b** them.
Eph 1: 5 family by **b** us to himself through Jesus Christ.
1Th 3: 6 **b** the good news that your faith and love are as
2Th 1: 8 **b** judgment on those who don't know God and on
2Ti 4: 5 suffering for the Lord. Work at **b** others to Christ.
Tit 2:11 of God has been revealed, **b** salvation to all people.
Heb 11:22 confidently spoke of God's **b** the people of Israel

BRINGS (74) [BRING]

Ex 13: 5 You must celebrate this day when the LORD **b**
13:11 **b** you into the land he swore to give your ancestors
Lev 17:11 the blood, representing life, that **b** you atonement.
Nu 5:18 holding the jar of bitter water that **b** a curse to
5:22 Now may this water that **b** the curse enter your
5:27 the water that **b** the curse will cause bitter
15: 4 whoever **b** it must also give to the LORD a grain
16:17 Be sure that each of your 250 followers **b** an
Dt 7: 1 "When the LORD your God **b** you into the land
11:29 "When the LORD your God **b** you into the land
1Sa 2: 6 The LORD **b** both death and life; / he **b** some down
to the grave but raises others up.
2: 7 another rich; / he **b** one down and lifts another up.
1Ch 21:12 **b** devastation throughout the land of Israel.
Job 12:22 with light; he **b** light to the deepest gloom.
34:24 He **b** the mighty to ruin without asking anyone,
Ps 21: 5 Your victory **b** him great honor, / and you have
46: 4 A river **b** joy to the city of our God, / the sacred
46: 8 See how he **b** destruction upon the world
73:14 is trouble all day long; / every morning **b** me pain.
107:36 He **b** the hungry to settle there / and build their
141: 7 Even as a farmer breaks up the soil and **b** up rocks,
147: 6 but he **b** the wicked down into the dust.
Pr 10: 1 A wise child **b** joy to a father; a foolish child **b**
grief to a mother.
10: 5 a youth who sleeps away the hour of opportunity **b**
12: 3 Wickedness never **b** stability; only the godly have
13:17 into trouble, but a reliable messenger **b** healing.
14:23 Work **b** profit, but mere talk leads to poverty!
15:15 For the poor, every day **b** trouble; for the happy
15:21 Foolishness **b** joy to those who have no sense;
15:27 Dishonest money **b** grief to the whole family,
15:30 A cheerful look **b** joy to the heart; good news
17:25 A foolish child **b** grief to a father and bitterness to
25:23 As surely as a wind from the north **b** rain, so a
28:19 have plenty of food; playing around **b** poverty.
29: 3 The man who loves wisdom **b** joy to his father,
29:23 Pride ends in humiliation, while humility **b** honor.
31:14 is like a merchant's ship; she **b** her food from afar.
Ecc 5:10 How absurd to think that wealth **b** true happiness!
10:12 wise words, but the speech of fools **b** them to ruin.
SS 2: 4 He **b** me to the banquet hall, so everyone can see
5: 9 what is it about your loved one that **b** you to tell us
Isa 25: 9 we trusted. Let us rejoice in the salvation he **b**!"
26: 5 the proud / and **b** the arrogant city to the dust.
40:10 See, he **b** his reward with him as he comes.
40:23 people of the world and **b** them all to nothing.
40:26 He **b** them out one after another, calling each by its
56: 8 who **b** back the outcasts of Israel, says:
62:11 See, he **b** his reward with him as he comes.' "
Jer 13:16 Acknowledge him before he **b** darkness upon you,
La 3:32 Though he **b** grief, he also shows compassion
Eze 30:25 and he **b** it against the land of Egypt,
Mal 2:12 and yet **b** an offering to the LORD Almighty.
Mt 12:20 until he **b** full justice with his final victory.
13:52 **b** out of the storehouse the new teachings as well
Mk 4:14 The farmer I talked about is the one who **b** God's
Jn 2:10 doesn't care, he **b** out the less expensive wines.
6:65 can't come to me unless the Father **b** them to me."
14:13 because the work of the Son **b** glory to the Father.
15: 8 much fruit. This **b** great glory to my Father.
Ro 2:13 For it is not merely knowing the law that **b** God's
3: 7 highlights his truthfulness and **b** him more glory?"
4:15 But the law **b** punishment on those who try to obey
4:17 because Abraham believed in the God who **b** the
4:17 and who **b** into existence what didn't exist before.
1Co 7:14 For the Christian wife **b** holiness to her marriage,
7:14 and the Christian husband **b** holiness to his
2Co 3: 9 which **b** condemnation, was glorious,
4:15 And as God's grace **b** more and more people to
2Th 2: 3 is revealed—the one who **b** destruction.
Heb 10:29 and enraged the Holy Spirit who **b** God's mercy to
10:35 Remember the great reward it **b** you!
Jas 5:20 you can be sure that the one who **b** that person

BRINK (1)

Pr 5:14 I have come to the **b** of utter ruin, and now I must

BROAD (15) [BROADER]

Nu 25: 4 and execute them before the LORD in **b** daylight,
Dt 28:29 You will grope around in **b** daylight, just like a
Ne 3: 8 They left out a section of Jerusalem as far as the **B**
12:38 wall past the Tower of the Ovens to the **B** Wall,
Eze 12: 3 Make your preparations in **b** daylight so the people
12: 7 In **b** daylight I brought my pack outside, filled with
17: 3 A great eagle with **b** wings full of many-colored
17: 5 of its seedlings in fertile ground beside a **b** river,
17: 7 But then another great eagle with **b** wings and full
Hos 4: 5 you will stumble in **b** daylight, just as you might at
Jnh 4: 6 and soon it spread its **b** leaves over Jonah's head,
Mt 7:13 The highway to hell is **b**, and its gate is wide for
2Pe 2:13 They love to indulge in evil pleasures in **b**
Rev 20: 9 And I saw them as they went up on the **b** plain of
21:12 Its walls were **b** and high, with twelve gates

BROADCAST (2)

Pr 12:23 a show of their knowledge, but fools **b** their folly.
Jer 11: 6 "**B** this message in the streets of Jerusalem.

BROADER (1) [BROAD]

Job 11: 9 It is **b** than the earth and wider than the sea.

BROILED (1)

Lk 24:42 They gave him a piece of **b** fish,

BROKE (84) [BREAK]

Ge 6: 6 was sorry he had ever made them. It **b** his heart.
13: 7 So an argument **b** out between the herdsmen of
14: 1 About this time war **b** out in the region.
27:38 bless me, too!" Then Esau **b** down and wept.
45: 2 Then he **b** down and wept aloud. His sobs could be
50:17 Joseph received the message, he **b** down and wept.
Ex 9:10 and terrible boils **b** out on the people and animals
21: 8 since he is the one who **b** the contract with her.
Nu 9:21 the cloud lifted, the people **b** camp and followed.
9:22 But as soon as it lifted, they **b** camp and moved on.
Dt 29:25 because the people of the land **b** the covenant they
32:51 For both of you **b** faith with me among the
Jos 9:20 for God would be angry with us if we **b** our oath.
Jdg 7:19 Suddenly, they blew the horns and **b** their clay jars.
7:20 all three groups blew their horns and **b** their jars.
Ru 1: 9 them good-bye, and they all **b** down and wept.
1Sa 4:18 He **b** his neck and died, for he was old and very
6:14 So the people **b** up the wood of the cart for a fire
11: 4 the people about their plight, everyone **b** into tears.
14:15 Suddenly, panic **b** out in the Philistine army,
14:45 But the people **b** in and said to Saul,
19: 8 War **b** out shortly after that, and David led his
2Sa 23:16 So the Three **b** through the Philistine lines,
2Ki 10:27 They **b** down the sacred pillar of Baal and wrecked
18: 4 He **b** up the bronze serpent that Moses had made,
19:36 Then King Sennacherib of Assyria **b** camp
20: 3 in your sight." Then he **b** down and wept bitterly.
25:13 The Babylonians **b** up the bronze pillars,
1Ch 11:18 So the Three **b** through the Philistine lines,
20: 4 After this, war **b** out with the Philistines at Gezer.
27:24 because the anger of God **b** out against Israel.
2Ch 13: 2 Then war **b** out between Abijah and Jeroboam.
15:16 He cut down the pole, **b** it up, and burned it in the
21:17 They marched against Judah, **b** down its defenses,
26: 6 on the Philistines and **b** down the walls of Gath,
26:19 leprosy suddenly **b** out on his forehead.
28:24 from the Temple of God and **b** them into pieces.
36:19 **b** down the walls of Jerusalem, burned all the
Ezr 8:31 We **b** camp at the Ahava Canal on April 19
Job 16:12 "I was living quietly until he **b** me apart. He took
29:17 I **b** the jaws of godless oppressors and made them
Ps 18:12 The brilliance of his presence **b** through the clouds,
55:20 of mine, he betrayed me; / he **b** his promises.
106:29 all these things, / so a plague **b** out among them.
107:12 That is why he **b** them with hard labor; / they fell,
107:16 For he **b** down their prison gates of bronze;
Isa 37:37 Then King Sennacherib of Assyria **b** camp
38: 3 in your sight." Then he **b** down and wept bitterly.
43:27 sinned against me—all your leaders **b** my laws.
Jer 2:20 Long ago I **b** your yoke and tore away the chains
28:10 prophet took the yoke off Jeremiah's neck and **b** it.
31:32 They **b** that covenant, though I loved them as a
39: 2 on July 18, the Babylonians **b** through the wall,
52:17 The Babylonians **b** up the bronze pillars,
Eze 17:16 him in power and whose treaty he despised and **b**.
17:18 For the king of Israel **b** his treaty after swearing to
23:17 disgusted with them and **b** off their relationship.
Hos 6: 7 you **b** my covenant and rebelled against me.
Am 1: 9 They **b** their treaty of brotherhood with Israel,
Zec 11:14 Then I **b** my other staff, Union, to show that the
Mt 15:36 thanked God for them, **b** them into pieces,
26:26 Then he **b** it in pieces and gave it to the disciples,
Mk 8: 6 thanked God for them, **b** them into pieces,
14: 3 She **b** the seal and poured the perfume over his
14:22 Then he **b** it in pieces and gave it to the disciples,
14:72 deny me three times." And he **b** down and cried.
Lk 6: 1 his disciples **b** off heads of wheat, rubbed off the
8:29 he simply **b** them and rushed out into the
22:19 he **b** it in pieces and gave it to the disciples, saying,
24:30 God's blessing on it, **b** it, then gave it to them.
Jn 7:53 Then the meeting **b** up and everybody went home.
19:32 and **b** the legs of the two men crucified with Jesus.
Ac 27:35 to God before them all, and **b** off a piece and ate it.
Ro 3: 3 but just because they **b** their promises, does that
1Co 11:24 he **b** it and said, "This is my body, which is given
2Ti 1:10 who **b** the power of death and showed us the way
Rev 6: 1 the Lamb **b** the first of the seven seals on the
6: 3 When the Lamb **b** the second seal, I heard the
6: 5 When the Lamb **b** the third seal, I heard the third
6: 7 And when the Lamb **b** the fourth seal, I heard the
6: 9 And when the Lamb **b** the fifth seal, I saw under
6:12 I watched as the Lamb **b** the sixth seal, and there
8: 1 When the Lamb **b** the seventh seal, there was
16: 2 malignant sores **b** out on everyone who had the

BROKEN (125) [BREAK]

Ex 9:11 because the boils had **b** out on them, too.
Lev 6:21 and it must be well mixed and **b** into pieces.
6:28 pot is used to boil the sacrificial meat, it must be **b**.
13:12 that a rash has **b** out all over someone's skin,
13:20 It is a contagious skin disease that has **b** out in the
13:25 a contagious skin disease has **b** out in the burn.
15:12 touched by the man with the discharge must be **b**,
21:19 or has a **b** foot or hand,
Dt 21: 6 their hands over the young cow whose neck was **b**.
Jos 7:11 Israel has sinned and **b** my covenant! They have
7:15 for he has **b** the covenant of the LORD and has
1Sa 2:10 Those who fight against the LORD will be **b**.
5: 4 This time his head and hands had **b** off and were
2Sa 12:18 "He was so **b** up about the baby being sick,"
1Ki 19:10 But the people of Israel have **b** their covenant with
19:14 But the people of Israel have **b** their covenant with
2Ki 25: 4 Then a section of the city wall was **b** down, and all
2Ch 24: 7 the followers of wicked Athaliah had **b** into the
32: 5 by repairing the wall wherever it was **b** down
Ne 2:13 and over to the Dung Gate to inspect the **b** walls
Job 2: 8 Then Job scraped his skin with a piece of **b** pottery
4: 5 But now when trouble strikes, you faint and are **b**.
4:10 fierce young lions, they will all be **b** and destroyed.
5:16 poor have hope, and the fangs of the wicked are **b**.
17:11 hopes have disappeared. My heart's desires are **b**.
24:20 Wicked people are **b** like a tree in the storm.
30:16 "And now my heart is **b**. Depression haunts my
Ps 31:12 ignored as if I were dead, / as if I were a **b** pot.
34:20 from harm—/ not one of their bones will be **b**!
37:15 with their own swords, / and their bows will be **b**.
38: 3 body is sick; / my health is **b** because of my sins.
38: 7 raging fever burns within me, / and my health is **b**.
51: 8 give me back my joy again; / you have **b** me—
51:17 The sacrifice you want is a **b** spirit. / A **b** and
repentant heart, O God, / you will not
60: 1 You have rejected us, O God, and **b** our defenses.
66:12 You sent troops to ride across our **b** bodies.
69:20 Their insults have **b** my heart, / and I am in
80:12 But now, why have you **b** down our walls / so that
89:40 You have **b** down the walls protecting him

119:126 you to act, / for these evil people have **b** your law.
124: 7 a hunter's trap. / The trap is **b**, and we are free!
Pr 6:15 destroyed suddenly, **b** beyond all hope of healing.
15:13 makes a happy face; a **b** heart crushes the spirit.
17:22 but a **b** spirit saps a person's strength.
24:31 covered with weeds, and its walls were **b** down.
25:19 chewing with a toothache or walking on a **b** foot.
29: 1 accept criticism will suddenly be **b** beyond repair.
Ecc 4:12 even better, for a triple-braided cord is not easily **b**.
12: 6 silver cord of life snaps and the golden bowl is **b**.
12: 6 at the spring and the pulley is **b** at the well.
Isa 5:27 Not a belt will be loose, not a sandal thong **b**.
9:10 We will replace the **b** bricks with cut stone,
14: 5 crushed your wicked power and **b** your evil rule.
14: 8 sing out this joyous song: 'Your power is **b**!
14:29 For even though that whip is **b**, his son will be
21: 9 All the idols of Babylon lie **b** on the ground!"
22: 5 The walls of Jerusalem have been **b**, and cries of
22:18 your glorious chariots will remain, **b** and useless.
24: 5 violated his laws, and **b** his everlasting covenant.
24:19 The earth has **b** down and has utterly collapsed.
27:11 **b** off and used for kindling beneath the cooking
33: 8 The Assyrians have **b** their peace pact and care
33:23 The enemies' sails hang loose on **b** masts with
54:10 My covenant of blessing will never be **b**,"
Jer 4: 8 on clothes of mourning and weep with **b** hearts,
8:18 My grief is beyond healing; my heart is **b**.
11:10 and Judah have both **b** the covenant I made with
11:16 to burn them with fire, leaving them charred and **b**.
22:28 is this man Jehoiachin like a discarded, **b** dish?
23: 9 My heart is **b** because of the false prophets, and I
28:13 You have **b** a wooden yoke, but you have replaced
33:21 will my covenant with David, my servant, be **b**.
34:19 or common people—for you have **b** your oath.
48: 1 the fortress will be humiliated and **b** down.
48:17 See how the strong scepter is **b**, how the beautiful
48:25 and her arms have been **b**," says the LORD.
48:31 my heart is **b** for the men of Kir-hareseth.
48:39 How it is **b**! Hear the wailing! See the shame of
50: 5 with an eternal covenant that will never again be **b**.
50:23 hammer in all the earth, lies **b** and shattered.
51:30 have burned the houses and **b** down the city gates.
52: 7 Then a section of the city wall was **b** down, and all
La 1: 1 Like a widow **b** with grief, she sits alone in her
1:20 My heart is **b** and my soul despairs, for I have
2: 2 In his anger he has **b** down the fortress walls of
2: 6 He has **b** down his Temple as though it were
2:11 My heart is **b**, my spirit poured out, as I see what
3: 4 my skin and flesh grow old. He has **b** my bones.
Eze 21: 6 before them with bitter anguish and a **b** heart.
26: 2 the rich trade routes to the east has been **b**,
26:10 shake as the horses gallop through your **b** gates,
27:34 are a wrecked ship, / **b** at the bottom of the sea.
30:21 "Son of man, I have **b** the arm of Pharaoh,
30:22 of his arms—the good arm along with the **b** one—
32:28 Egypt, will lie crushed and **b** among the outcasts,
34: 4 have not tended the sick or bound up the **b** bones.
34:27 When I have **b** their chains of slavery and rescued
44: 7 other disgusting sins, you have **b** my covenant.
Da 8: 8 at the height of its power, its large horn was **b** off.
8:25 but he will be **b**, though not by human power.
11: 4 his kingdom will be **b** apart and divided into four
Hos 5:11 of Israel will be crushed and **b** by my judgment
8: 1 for they have **b** my covenant and revolted against
Am 3:12 in Samaria are rescued with only a **b** chair
Na 2: 2 land of Israel lies empty and **b** after your attacks,
Zec 11:14 the bond of unity between Judah and Israel was **b**.
Mt 21:44 Anyone who stumbles over that stone will be **b** to
23:18 you say that to take an oath 'by the altar' can be **b**,
24:43 stay alert and not permit the house to be **b** into.
Lk 12:39 coming would not permit the house to be **b** into.
20:18 All who stumble over that stone will be **b** to
21:26 because the stability of the very heavens will be **b**
Jn 19:31 hasten their deaths by ordering that their legs be **b**.
19:36 that say, "Not one of his bones will be **b**,"
Ac 27:44 to try for it on planks and debris from the **b** ship.
Ro 7: 9 I realized I had **b** the law and was a sinner,
11:17 Abraham's tree, some of the Jews, have been **b** off.
11:18 grafted in to replace the branches that were **b** off.
11:19 "those branches were **b** off to make room for
11:20 were **b** off because they didn't believe God,
2Co 4: 8 side by troubles, but we are not crushed and **b**.
Eph 2:14 He has **b** down the wall of hostility that used to
Jas 2:10 guilty as the person who has **b** all of God's laws.
2:11 if you murder someone, you have **b** the entire law,

BROKEN-DOWN (2) [BREAK]

Ps 62: 3 To them I'm just a **b** wall / or a tottering fence.
Pr 25:28 self-control is as defenseless as a city with **b** walls.

BROKENHEARTED (4) [BREAK, HEART]

Ps 34:18 The LORD is close to the **b**; / he rescues those
109:16 and needy, / and he hounded the **b** to death.
147: 3 He heals the **b**, / binding up their wounds.
Isa 61: 1 He has sent me to comfort the **b** and to announce

BRONZE (162)

Ge 4:22 with metal, forging instruments of **b** and iron.
Ex 25: 3 you may accept on my behalf: gold, silver, and **b**;
26:11 and fasten them together with fifty **b** clasps.
26:37 with gold. The posts will fit into five **b** bases.
27: 2 one piece. Overlay the altar and its horns with **b**.
27: 3 meat hooks, and firepans will all be made of **b**.
27: 4 Make a **b** grating, with a metal ring at each corner.
27: 6 poles from acacia wood, and overlay them with **b**.
27:10 They will be held up by twenty **b** posts that fit into twenty **b** bases.
27:11 curtains held up by twenty posts fitted into **b** bases,
27:17 The posts are to be set in solid **b** bases.
27:18 The bases supporting its walls will be made of **b**.
27:19 and the courtyard curtains, must be made of **b**.
30:18 "Make a large **b** washbasin with a **b** pedestal.
31: 4 to create beautiful objects from gold, silver, and **b**.
35: 5 these offerings to the LORD: gold, silver, and **b**;
35:16 the **b** grating of the altar and its carrying poles
35:24 and **b** objects as their offering to the LORD.
35:32 to create beautiful objects from gold, silver, and **b**.
36:18 They also made fifty small **b** clasps to couple the
36:38 with gold. The five bases were molded from **b**.
38: 2 piece with the rest. This altar was overlaid with **b**.
38: 3 Then he made all the **b** utensils to be used with the
38: 4 Next he made a **b** grating that rested on a ledge
38: 6 made of acacia wood and were overlaid with **b**.
38: 8 The **b** washbasin and its **b** pedestal were cast from **b** mirrors
38:10 There were twenty posts, each with its own **b** base,
38:11 with twenty **b** posts and bases and with silver
38:17 Each post had a **b** base, and all the hooks and rods
38:19 It was supported by four posts set into four **b**
38:20 in the Tabernacle and courtyard were made of **b**.
38:29 The people also brought 5,310 pounds of **b**,
38:30 and for the **b** altar with its **b** grating and altar
38:31 **B** was also used to make the bases for the posts
39:39 the **b** altar; the **b** grating; its poles and utensils;
Lev 6:28 If a **b** kettle is used, it must be scoured and rinsed
26:19 as iron and the earth beneath as hard as **b**.
Nu 16:39 So Eleazar the priest collected the 250 **b** incense
21: 9 So Moses made a snake out of **b** and attached it to
21: 9 Whenever those who were bitten looked at the **b**
31:22 made of gold, silver, **b**, iron, tin, or lead—
Dt 28:23 The skies above will be as unyielding as **b**,
33:25 May the bolts of your gates be of iron and **b**;
Jos 6:19 Everything made from silver, gold, **b**, or iron is
6:24 Only the things made from silver, gold, **b**, or iron
22: 8 your silver and gold, your **b** and iron, and your
Jdg 16:21 where he was bound with **b** chains and made to
1Sa 17: 5 He wore a **b** helmet and a coat of mail that
17: 6 He also wore **b** leggings, and he slung a **b** javelin
17:38 his own armor—a **b** helmet and a coat of mail.
2Sa 8: 8 along with a large amount of **b** from Hadadezer's
8:10 David with many gifts of silver, gold, and **b**.
21:16 his **b** spearhead weighed more than seven pounds,
22:35 for battle; / he strengthens me to draw a bow of **b**.
1Ki 4:13 sixty great fortified cities with gates barred with **b**.
7:14 for he was a craftsman skilled in **b** work. He was
7:15 Huram cast two **b** pillars, each 27 feet tall and 18
7:16 tops of the pillars he made capitals of molded **b**,
7:25 The Sea rested on a base of twelve **b** oxen,
7:27 Huram also made ten **b** water carts, each 6 feet
7:30 Each of these carts had four **b** wheels and **b** axles.
7:30 of the carts were supporting posts for the **b** basins;
7:33 rims, and hubs were all cast from molten **b**.
7:38 Huram also made ten **b** basins, one for each cart.
7:45 made for Solomon were made of burnished **b**.
7:47 the weight of the **b** could not be measured.
8:64 because the **b** altar in the LORD's presence was
14:27 Afterward Rehoboam made **b** shields as
2Ki 16:14 Then King Ahaz removed the old **b** altar from the
16:15 The old **b** altar will be only for my personal use."
16:17 He also removed the Sea from the backs of the **b**
18: 4 He broke up the **b** serpent that Moses had made,
18: 4 incense to it. The **b** serpent was called Nehushtan.
25: 7 bound him in **b** chains, and led him away to
25:13 The Babylonians broke up the **b** pillars, the **b** water carts, and the **b** Sea that were at the LORD's Temple, and they carried all the **b** away
25:14 and all the other **b** utensils used for making
25:16 The **b** from the two pillars, the water carts,
25:17 The **b** capital on top of each pillar was 7-1/2 feet
25:17 and was decorated with a network of **b**
1Ch 15:19 and Ethan were chosen to sound the **b** cymbals.
18: 8 along with a large amount of **b** from Hadadezer's
18: 8 Later Solomon melted the **b** and used it for the
18: 8 He molded it into the **b** Sea, the pillars,
18: 8 and the various **b** utensils used at the Temple.
18:10 David with many gifts of gold, silver, and **b**.
22: 3 and more **b** than they could ever weigh.
22:14 so much iron and **b** that it cannot be weighed.
22:16 and silversmiths and workers of **b** and iron.
29: 2 there is enough gold, silver, **b**, iron, and wood,
29: 7 about 375 tons of silver, about 675 tons of **b**,
2Ch 1: 5 But the **b** altar made by Bezalel son of Uri
1: 6 Solomon went up to the **b** altar in the LORD's
2: 7 who can work with gold, silver, **b**, and iron;
2:14 at making things from gold, silver, **b**, and iron.
4: 1 Solomon also made a **b** altar 30 feet long, 30 feet
4: 4 The Sea rested on a base of twelve **b** oxen,
4: 9 the courtyard entrances and overlaid them with **b**.
4:16 out of burnished **b** for the Temple of the LORD,
4:18 Such great quantities of **b** were used that its weight
6:13 He had made a **b** platform 7-1/2 feet long,
7: 7 because the **b** altar he had built could not handle
12:10 King Rehoboam later replaced them with **b** shields
24:12 articles of iron and **b** for the LORD's Temple.
33:11 bound him in **b** chains, and led him away to
Ezr 8:27 2 fine articles of polished **b**, as precious as gold.
Job 6:12 strength as hard as stone? Is my body made of **b**?
40:18 Its bones are tubes of **b**. Its limbs are bars of iron.
41:27 iron is nothing but straw, and **b** is rotten wood.
Ps 18:34 for battle; / he strengthens me to draw a bow of **b**.
107:16 For he broke down their prison gates of **b**; / he cut
Isa 45: 2 I will smash down gates of **b** and cut through bars
48: 4 as unbending as iron. You are as hardheaded as **b**.
60:17 I will exchange your **b** for gold, your iron for silver, your wood for **b**,
Jer 1:18 cannot be captured, like an iron pillar or a **b** wall.
6:28 They are as insolent as **b**, as hard and cruel as iron.
15:12 break a bar of iron from the north, or a bar of **b**?
27:19 says about the **b** pillars in front of the Temple, the **b** Sea in the Temple courtyard, the **b** water carts,
52:11 bound him in **b** chains, and led him away to
52:17 The Babylonians broke up the **b** pillars, the **b** water carts, and the **b** Sea that were at the LORD's Temple, and they carried all the **b** away
52:18 and all the other **b** utensils used for making
52:20 The **b** from the two pillars, the water carts,
52:22 The **b** capital on top of each pillar was 7-1/2 feet
52:22 and was decorated with a network of **b**
Eze 1: 7 split like calves' feet and shone like burnished **b**.
8:16 At the entrance, between the foyer and the **b** altar,
9: 2 the Temple courtyard and stood beside the **b** altar.
27:13 Tubal, and Meshech brought slaves and **b** dishes.
40: 3 I saw a man whose face shone like **b** standing
Da 2:32 arms were of silver, its belly and thighs were of **b**,
2:35 into a heap of iron, clay, **b**, silver, and gold.
2:39 represented by the **b** belly and thighs,
2:45 to dust the statue of iron, **b**, clay, silver, and gold.
4:15 bound with a band of iron and **b** and surrounded by
4:23 bound with a band of iron and **b** and surrounded by
5: 4 made of gold, silver, **b**, iron, wood, and stone.
5:23 gods of silver, gold, **b**, iron, wood, and stone—
7:19 and crushed its victims with iron teeth and **b** claws,
10: 6 His arms and feet shone like polished **b**, and his
Mic 4:13 "For I will give you iron horns and **b** hooves,
Zec 6: 1 and saw four chariots coming from between two **b**
Jn 3:14 And as Moses lifted up the **b** snake on a pole in the
Rev 1:15 His feet were as bright as **b** refined in a furnace,
2:18 like flames of fire, whose feet are like polished **b**:
9:20 idols made of gold, silver, **b**, stone, and wood—
18:12 made of expensive wood, **b**, iron, and marble.

BROOD (4)

Nu 32:14 But here you are, a **b** of sinners, doing exactly the
Mt 3: 7 "You **b** of snakes!" he exclaimed.
12:34 You **b** of snakes! How could evil men like you
Lk 3: 7 "You **b** of snakes! Who warned you to flee God's

BROOK (27) [BROOKS]

Nu 21:12 From there they traveled to the valley of Zered **B**
34: 5 From Azmon the boundary will turn toward the **b**
Dt 2:13 "Then the LORD told us to cross Zered **B**,
2:14 at Kadesh-barnea until we finally crossed Zered **B**!
Jos 15: 4 to Azmon, until it finally reached the **b** of Egypt,
15:47 as far as the **b** of Egypt and along the coast of the
19:11 and proceeding to the **b** east of Jokneam.
1Sa 30: 9 men set out, and they soon came to Besor **B**.
30:10 of the men were too exhausted to cross the **b**,
30:21 When they reached Besor **B** and met the two
2Sa 17:20 "They were here, but they crossed the **b**."
1Ki 8:65 in the north to the **b** of Egypt in the south.
17: 3 and hide by Kerith **B** at a place east of where it
17: 4 Drink from the **b** and eat what the ravens bring
17: 5 LORD had told him and camped beside Kerith **B**.
17: 6 and evening, and he drank from the **b**.
17: 7 But after a while the **b** dried up, for there was no
2Ki 24: 7 from the **b** of Egypt to the Euphrates River.
2Ch 7: 8 in the north, to the **b** of Egypt in the south.
32: 4 cutting off the **b** that ran through the fields.
Job 6:15 you have proved as unreliable as a seasonal **b** that
6:17 the water disappears. The **b** vanishes in the heat.
Pr 18: 4 of true wisdom are as refreshing as a bubbling **b**.
Isa 27:12 from the Euphrates River in the east to the **b** of
Jer 15:18 Your help seems as uncertain as a seasonal **b**.
Eze 47:19 then follow the course of the **b** of Egypt to the
48:28 then follows the **b** of Egypt to the Mediterranean.

BROOKS (3) [BROOK]

Dt 10: 7 and from there to Jotbathah, a land with **b** of water.
Ps 110: 7 But he himself will be refreshed from **b** along the
SS 5:12 His eyes are like doves beside **b** of water; they are

BROOKS [KJV] See also NAHALE-GAASH, RAVINE, RIVER, STREAMS, VALLEY

BROOM (3)

1Ki 19: 4 He sat down under a solitary **b** tree and prayed that
19: 5 Then he lay down and slept under the **b** tree.
Isa 14:23 I will sweep the land with the **b** of destruction.

BROTH (2)

Jdg 6:19 carrying the meat in a basket and the **b** in a pot,
6:20 bread on this rock, and pour the **b** over it."

BROTHELS (1)

Jer 5: 7 committing adultery and lining up at the city's **b**.

BROTHER (226) [BROTHER'S, BROTHER-IN-LAW, BROTHERHOOD, BROTHERS]

BROTHER...SISTER (6) Eze 44:25; Mt 12:50; Mk 3:35; 1Co 8:9; Jas 2:15; 1Jn 3:17

Ge 4: 8 Later Cain suggested to his **b**, Abel, "Let's go out
4: 8 were together there, Cain attacked and killed his **b**.
4: 9 the LORD asked Cain, "Where is your **b**?

10:21 were also born to Shem, the older **b** of Japheth.
11:29 and his **b** Nahor married Milcah, the daughter of their **b** Haran.
20: 5 my sister,' and she herself said, 'Yes, he is my **b**.'
20:16 "I am giving your '**b**' a thousand pieces of silver
22:20 his **b** Nahor's wife, had borne Nahor eight sons.
24:10 and went to the village where Abraham's **b** Nahor
24:15 who was the son of Abraham's **b** Nahor and his
24:29 Now Rebekah had a **b** named Laban.
24:53 also gave valuable presents to her mother and **b**.
24:55 to stay at least ten days," her **b** and mother said.
25:33 all his rights as the firstborn to his younger **b**.
27:35 But Isaac said, "Your **b** was here, and he tricked
27:40 You will serve your **b** for a time, but then you will
28: 5 his mother's **b**, the son of Bethuel the Aramean.
29:10 the daughter of his mother's **b**, and
32: 3 Jacob now sent messengers to his **b**, Esau,
32:11 O LORD, please rescue me from my **b**, Esau.
33: 3 As he approached his **b**, he bowed low seven times
33: 9 "**B**, I have plenty," Esau answered. "Keep what
35: 1 who appeared to you when you fled from your **b**,
36: 6 of Canaan—and moved away from his **b**, Jacob.
37:26 to the others, "What can we gain by killing our **b**?
37:27 be responsible for his death; after all, he is our **b**!"
38: 8 Then Judah said to Er's **b** Onan, "You must marry
38: 8 as our law requires of the **b** of a man who has died.
38: 9 her from having a baby who would belong to his **b**.
38:10 thing for Onan to deny a child to his dead **b**.
42: 4 Jacob wouldn't let Joseph's younger **b**, Benjamin,
42:13 Our youngest **b** is there with our father, and one of
42:15 leave Egypt unless your youngest **b** comes here.
42:16 One of you go and get your **b**! I'll keep the rest of
42:16 If it turns out that you don't have a younger **b**,
42:20 But bring your youngest **b** back to me. In this way,
42:32 one **b** has disappeared, and the youngest is with
42:34 But bring your youngest **b** back to me. Then I will
42:34 be what you say, then I will give you back your **b**,
42:38 not go down with you, for his **b** Joseph is dead,
43: 5 to come and see me unless your **b** is with you.' "
43: 6 "Why did you ever tell him you had another **b**?"
43: 7 and he asked us if we had another **b** so we told
43: 7 have known he would say, 'Bring me your **b**'?"
43:13 Then take your **b** and go back to the man.
43:29 Looking at his **b**, Benjamin, Joseph asked, "Is this your youngest **b**, the one
43:30 because he was overcome with emotion for his **b**
44:16 we and our **b** who had your cup in his sack."
44:19 "You asked us, my lord, if we had a father or a **b**.
44:20 His **b** is dead, and he alone is left of his mother's
44:23 'You may not see me again unless your youngest **b**
44:26 'We can't unless you let our youngest **b** go with
44:26 of the grain unless our youngest **b** is with us.'
44:29 If you take away his **b** from me, too, and any harm
45: 4 "I am Joseph, your **b** whom you sold into Egypt.
45:12 and so can my **b** Benjamin, that I really am Joseph!
48:19 but his younger **b** will become even greater.
Ex 4:14 he said. "What about your **b**, Aaron the Levite?
7: 1 Your **b**, Aaron, will be your prophet; he will speak
28: 1 "Your **b**, Aaron, and his sons, Nadab, Abihu,
Lev 16: 2 "Warn your **b** Aaron not to enter the Most Holy
18:14 And do not violate your uncle, your father's **b**,
18:16 with your brother's wife; this would violate your **b**.
20:21 He has violated his **b**, and the guilty couple will
21: 2 mother or father, son or daughter, **b**
Nu 6: 7 if their own father, mother, **b**, or sister has died.
27:13 you have seen it, you will die as Aaron your **b** did,
36: 2 inheritance of our **b** Zelophehad to his daughters.
Dt 13: 6 "Suppose your **b**, son, daughter, beloved wife,
25: 5 her husband's **b** must marry her and fulfill the
25: 6 to him will be counted as the son of the dead **b**,
25: 7 But if the dead man's **b** refuses to marry the
25: 7 'My husband's **b** refuses to preserve his brother's
25: 9 to a man who refuses to raise up a son for his **b**.'
28:54 among you will have no compassion for his own **b**,
32:50 just as Aaron, your **b**, died on Mount Hor
Jos 15:17 Othniel, the son of Caleb's **b** Kenaz, was the one
22:12 and prepared to go to war against their **b** tribes.
Jdg 1:13 Othniel, the son of Caleb's younger **b** Kenaz,
3: 9 was Othniel, the son of Caleb's younger **b**, Kenaz.
9: 5 But the youngest **b**, Jotham, escaped and hid.
9:21 in Beer because he was afraid of his **b** Abimelech.
1Sa 14: 3 Ahijah was the son of Ahitub, Ichabod's **b**.
17:28 But when David's oldest **b**, Eliab, heard David
20:29 His **b** demanded that he be there, so I told him he
26: 6 the Hittite and Abishai son of Zeruiah, Joab's **b**.
2Sa 1:26 How I weep for you, my **b** Jonathan! / Oh,
2:22 I will never be able to face your **b** Joab if I have to
3:27 and killed Abner in revenge for killing his **b**
3:30 So Joab and his **b** Abishai killed Abner
3:30 because Abner had killed their **b** Asahel at the
10:10 of the army under the command of his **b** Abishai,
10:11 then come over and help me," Joab told his **b**.
13: 1 And Amnon, her half **b**, fell desperately in love
13: 3 He was the son of David's **b** Shimea.
13:12 "No, my **b**!" she cried. "Don't be foolish!
13:20 Her **b** Absalom saw her and asked, "Is it true that
13:20 Since he's your **b** anyway, don't worry about it."
13:26 how about sending my **b** Amnon instead?"
13:32 the son of David's **b** Shimea, arrived and said,
14: 7 your son. We will execute him for murdering his **b**.
18: 2 one-third under Joab's **b** Abishai son of Zeruiah,
20:10 Joab and his **b** Abishai left him lying there
21:19 Elhanan son of Jair from Bethlehem killed the **b** of
21:21 killed by Jonathan, the son of David's **b** Shimea.
23:18 Abishai son of Zeruiah, the **b** of Joab,
23:24 of the Thirty included: / Asahel, Joab's **b**;
1Ki 1:10 or the king's bodyguard, or his **b** Solomon.
2: 7 for they took care of me when I fled from your **b**
2:15 were turned, and everything went to my **b** instead;
2:21 "Then let your **b** Adonijah marry Abishag, the girl
2:22 You know that he is my older **b**, and that he has
9:13 "What kind of towns are these, my **b**?" he asked.
13:30 in his own grave, crying out in grief, "Oh, my **b**!"
20:32 Israel responded, "Is he still alive? He is my **b**!"
20:33 and they replied, "Yes, your **b** Ben-hadad!"
2Ki 1:17 to succeed him, his **b** Joram became the next king.
1Ch 2:32 Shammai's **b**, Jada, had two sons named Jether
2:42 the **b** of Jerahmeel, was Mesha, the father of Ziph.
4:11 Kelub (the **b** of Shuhah) was the father of Mehir.
5: 1 his birthright was given to the sons of his **b** Joseph.
7:35 The sons of his **b** Helem were Zophah, Imna,
8:39 Azel's **b** Eshek had three sons: Ulam (the oldest),
11:20 Abishai, the **b** of Joab, was the leader of the Thirty.
11:26 Asahel, Joab's **b**; / Elhanan son of Dodo from
11:38 Joel, the **b** of Nathan; / Mibhar son of Hagri;
11:45 Jediael son of Shimri; / Joha, his **b**, from Tiz;
12: 3 from Gibeah; his **b** Joash was second-in-command.
19:11 of the army under the command of his **b** Abishai,
19:12 then come over and help me," Joab told his **b**.
20: 5 son of Jair killed Lahmi, the **b** of Goliath of Gath.
20: 7 killed by Jonathan, the son of David's **b** Shimea.
24:25 along with Isshiah, the **b** of Micah.
26:22 The sons of Jehiel, Zetham and his **b** Joel, were in
27: 7 Asahel, the **b** of Joab, was commander of the
27:18 Judah | Elihu (a **b** of David) / Issachar | Omri son
2Ch 31:12 Levite was put in charge, assisted by his **b** Shimei.
36: 4 the **b** of Jehoahaz, as the next king of Judah
Ne 7: 2 of governing Jerusalem to my **b** Hanani,
Job 6:15 My **b**, you have proved as unreliable as a seasonal
30:29 I am considered a **b** to jackals and a companion to
Ps 50:20 You sit around and slander a **b**—/ your own
Pr 17:17 and a **b** is born to help in time of need.
18:24 each other, but a real friend sticks closer than a **b**.
Ecc 4: 8 of a man who is all alone, without a child or a **b**,
SS 8: 1 "Oh, if only you were my **b**, who nursed at my
Isa 3: 6 In those days a man will say to his **b**, "Since you
19: 2 **b** against **b**, neighbor against neighbor,
Jer 9: 4 "Beware of your neighbor! Beware of your **b**!
Eze 44:25 is his father, mother, child, **b**, or unmarried sister.
Hos 12: 3 Before Jacob was born, he struggled with his **b**;
Mal 1: 2 your ancestor Jacob. Yet Esau was Jacob's **b**,
Mt 10: 2 (also called Peter), / then Andrew (Peter's **b**),
10: 2 James (son of Zebedee), / John (James's **b**),
10:21 "**B** will betray **b** to death, fathers will betray
12:50 who does the will of My Father in heaven is my **b**
14: 3 Herodias (the former wife of Herod's **b** Philip).
22:24 his **b** should marry the widow and have a child
22:25 so the second **b** married the widow.
22:26 This **b** also died without children, and the wife was married to the next **b**, and so on
Mk 1:16 he saw Simon and his **b**, Andrew, fishing with a
3:35 Anyone who does God's will is my **b** and sister
6: 3 the son of Mary and **b** of James, Joseph, Judas,
6:17 She had been his **b** Philip's wife, but Herod had
12:19 his **b** should marry the widow and have a child
12:21 So the second **b** married the widow, but soon he
12:21 Then the next **b** married her and died without
13:12 "**B** will betray **b** to death, fathers will betray
Lk 3: 1 his **b** Philip was ruler over Iturea and Traconitis;
6:14 (he also called him Peter), / Andrew (Peter's **b**),
12:13 please tell my **b** to divide our father's estate with
15:27 'Your **b** is back,' he was told, 'and your father has
15:28 "The older **b** was angry and wouldn't go in.
15:32 For your **b** was dead and has come back to life!
20:28 his **b** should marry the widow and have a child
20:30 His **b** married the widow, but he also died. Still no
Jn 1:40 Andrew, Simon Peter's **b**, was one of these men
1:41 The first thing Andrew did was to find his **b**,
6: 8 Then Andrew, Simon Peter's **b**, spoke up.
11: 2 them with her hair. Her **b**, Lazarus, was sick.
11:21 if you had been here, my **b** would not have died.
11:23 Jesus told her, "Your **b** will rise again."
11:32 if you had been here, my **b** would not have died."
Ac 7: 9 "These sons of Jacob were very jealous of their **b**
9:17 He laid his hands on him and said, "**B** Saul,
12: 2 He had the apostle James (John's **b**) killed with a
21:20 But then they said, "You know, dear **b**, how many
22:13 came to me and stood beside me and said, '**B** Saul,
Ro 16:22 for Paul, send my greetings, too, as a Christian **b**.
16:23 his greetings, and so does Quartus, a Christian **b**.
1Co 1: 1 apostle of Christ Jesus, and from our **b** Sosthenes.
8: 9 Do not cause a **b** or sister with a weaker
16:12 Now about our **b** Apollos—I urged him to visit you
2Co 1: 1 of Christ Jesus, and from our dear **b** Timothy.
2:13 because my dear **b** Titus hadn't yet arrived with a
8:18 We are also sending another **b** with Titus. He is
8:22 And we are also sending with them another **b** who
12:18 Titus to visit you and sent our other **b** with him,
Gal 1:19 apostle I met at that time was James, our Lord's **b**.
Eph 6:21 a much loved **b** and faithful helper in the Lord's
Php 2:25 He is a true **b**, a faithful worker, and a courageous
Col 1: 1 apostle of Christ Jesus, and from our **b** Timothy.
4: 7 Tychicus, a much loved **b**, will tell you how I am
4: 9 a faithful and much loved **b**, one of your own
1Th 3: 2 and our **b** in proclaiming the Good News of Christ.
Phm 1: 1 News about Christ Jesus, and from our **b** Timothy.
1: 7 my **b**, because your kindness has so often refreshed
1:16 just a slave; he is a beloved **b**, especially to me.
1:16 more to you, both as a slave and as a **b** in the Lord.
1:20 Yes, dear **b**, please do me this favor for the Lord's
Heb 13:23 I want you to know that our **b** Timothy is now out
Jas 2:15 Suppose you see a **b** or sister who needs food
1Pe 5:12 the help of Silas, whom I consider a faithful **b**.
2Pe 3:15 This is just as our beloved **b** Paul wrote to you
1Jn 3:12 who belonged to the evil one and killed his **b**.
3:12 was evil, and his **b** had been doing what was right.
3:17 and sees a **b** or sister in need and refuses to help—
Jude 1: 1 a slave of Jesus Christ and a **b** of James.
1:11 follow the evil example of Cain, who killed his **b**.
Rev 1: 9 I am John, your **b**. In Jesus we are partners in

BROTHER'S (21) [BROTHER]

Ge 4:10 your **b** blood cries out to me from the ground!
4:11 the ground you have defiled with your **b** blood.
4:21 His **b** name was Jubal, the first musician—
10:25 and dispersed. His **b** name was Joktan.
27:44 Stay there with him until your **b** fury is spent.
38: 8 Her first son from you will be your **b** heir."
42:25 but he also gave secret instructions to return each **b**
44: 2 silver cup at the top of the youngest **b** sack,
44:12 Joseph's servant began searching the oldest **b** sack,
Lev 18:16 Do not have intercourse with your **b** wife;
20:21 If a man marries his **b** wife, it is an act of impurity.
Dt 25: 7 'My husband's brother refuses to preserve his **b**
1Ch 1:19 and dispersed. His **b** name was Joktan.
7:16 His **b** name was Sheresh. The sons of Peresh were
Job 1:13 and daughters were dining at the oldest **b** house,
1:18 and daughters were feasting in their oldest **b** home.
Mt 22:24 and have a child who will be the **b** heir.'
Mk 6:18 "It is illegal for you to marry your **b** wife."
12:19 the widow and have a child who will be the **b** heir.
Lk 3:19 ruler of Galilee, for marrying Herodias, his **b** wife,
20:28 the widow and have a child who will be the **b** heir.

BROTHER-IN-LAW (3) [BROTHER]

Nu 10:29 One day Moses said to his **b**, Hobab son of Reuel
Dt 25: 5 brother must marry her and fulfill the duties of a **b**.
Jdg 4:11 the Kenite, a descendant of Moses' **b** Hobab,

BROTHERHOOD (1) [BROTHER]

Am 1: 9 They broke their treaty of **b** with Israel,

BROTHERS (279) [BROTHER]

BROTHERS...SISTERS (81) Jos 2:13; Job 1:4; 42:11; Ps 22:22; Hos 2:1; Mt 13:55; 18:35; 19:29; 23:8; 25:40,45; Mk 3:32; 10:29,30; Lk 14:26; Ro 8:29; 9:3; 16:17; 1Co 1:10,26; 2:1; 3:1; 4:6; 6:8; 7:24,29; 10:1; 11:33; 12:1; 14:6,20,26,39; 15:1,50,58; 16:15; Gal 4:28; 6:10; Php 4:1; Col 1:2; 4:15; 1Th 1:4; 2:1,9,14; 4:1,13; 5:4,12,14,25; 2Th 1:3; 2:1,13,15; 3:1,6,13; 2Ti 4:21; Heb 2:11,12,17; Jas 1:2,16; 2:1,5,14; 3:1,10; 4:11; 5:7,9,12,19; 1Pe 1:22; 2:11,17; 1Jn 3:13; 4:21; Rev 12:10

Ge 9:22 father was naked and went outside and told his **b**.
16:12 Yes, he will live at odds with the rest of his **b**."
19: 7 "Please, my **b**," he begged, "don't do such a
27:29 your servants. May you be the master of your **b**.
27:37 and have declared that all his **b** will be his
34:11 Then Shechem addressed Dinah's father and **b**.
34:13 But Dinah's **b** deceived Shechem and Hamor
34:25 two of Dinah's **b**, Simeon and Levi, took their
37: 2 he often tended his father's flocks with his half **b**,
37: 2 his father some of the bad things his **b** were doing.
37: 4 But his **b** hated Joseph because of their father's
37: 5 a dream and promptly reported the details to his **b**,
37: 8 are going to be our king, are you?" his **b** taunted.
37: 9 Joseph had another dream and told his **b** about it.
37:10 This time he told his father as well as his **b**, and his
37:10 your **b**, and I actually come and bow before you?"
37:11 But while his **b** were jealous of Joseph, his father
37:12 Joseph's **b** went to pasture their father's flocks at
37:13 "Your **b** are over at Shechem with the flocks.
37:14 "Go and see how your **b** and the flocks are getting
37:16 "For my **b** and their flocks," Joseph replied.
37:17 I heard your **b** say they were going to Dothan."
37:17 So Joseph followed his **b** to Dothan and found
37:18 When Joseph's **b** saw him coming,
37:27 after all, he is our brother!" And his **b** agreed.
37:28 his **b** pulled Joseph out of the pit and sold him for
37:30 Then he went back to his **b** and lamented,
37:31 Then Joseph's **b** killed a goat and dipped the robe
38:11 was afraid Shelah would also die, like his two **b**.)
42: 3 So Joseph's ten older **b** went down to Egypt to buy
42: 6 the sale of the grain, it was to him that his **b** came.
42: 8 Joseph's **b** didn't recognize him, but Joseph
42:11 We are all **b** and honest men, sir! We are not
42:13 "Sir," they said, "there are twelve of us **b**,
42:13 our father, and one of our **b** is no longer with us."
42:28 "Look!" he exclaimed to his **b**. "My money is
42:32 We are twelve **b**, sons of one father; one brother
42:33 Leave one of your **b** here with me, and take grain
43:19 As the **b** arrived at the entrance to the palace,
43:24 The **b** were then led into the palace and given
43:32 and his **b** were served at a separate table.
43:33 Joseph told each of his **b** where to sit, and to their
44: 1 When his **b** were ready to leave, Joseph gave these
44: 3 The **b** were up at dawn and set out on their journey
44: 7 "What are you talking about?" the **b** responded.
44:14 was still at home when Judah and his **b** arrived,
44:33 of the boy, and let the boy return with his **b**.
45: 1 He wanted to be alone with his **b** when he told
45: 3 "I am Joseph!" he said to his **b**. "Is my father still alive?" But his **b** were speechless!
45:15 Then Joseph kissed each of his **b** and wept over
45:16 soon reached Pharaoh: "Joseph's **b** have come!"
45:17 "Tell your **b** to load their pack animals and return
45:19 And tell your **b** to take wagons from Egypt to carry
45:24 So he sent his **b** off, and as they left, he called after
46:31 And Joseph said to his **b** and to all their

47: 1 "My father and my **b** are here from Canaan.
47: 2 Joseph took five of his **b** with him and presented
47:11 to his father and **b**, just as Pharaoh had
47:12 and **b** in amounts appropriate to the number of
48:22 extra portion beyond what I have given your **b**—
49: 8 "Judah, your **b** will praise you. / You will defeat
49:26 the head of Joseph, / who is a prince among his **b**.
50: 8 Joseph also took his **b** and the entire household of
50:14 Then Joseph returned to Egypt with his **b** and all
50:15 their father was dead, Joseph's **b** became afraid.
50:17 'Forgive your **b** for the great evil they did to you.'
50:18 Then his **b** came and bowed low before him.
50:22 So Joseph and his **b** and their families continued to
50:24 "Soon I will die," Joseph told his **b**, "but God
Ex 1: 6 In time, Joseph and each of his **b** died, ending that
32:27 killing even your **b**, friends, and neighbors."
32:29 even though it meant killing your own sons and **b**.
Nu 20: 3 we had died in the LORD's presence with our **b**!
27: 9 has no daughters, turn his inheritance over to his **b**.
27:10 If he has no **b**, give his inheritance to his father's **b**.
27:11 But if his father has no **b**, pass on his inheritance to
32: 6 you want to stay back here while your **b** go across
Dt 25: 5 "If two **b** are living together on the same property
33:16 crowning the brow of the prince among his **b**.
33:24 above other sons; / may he be esteemed by his **b**;
Jos 2:13 along with my father and mother, my **b** and sisters,
2:18 your father, mother, **b**, and all your relatives—
6:23 and brought out Rahab, her father, mother, **b**,
14: 8 but my **b** who went with me frightened the people
Jdg 8:19 "They were my **b**!" Gideon exclaimed.
9: 1 went to Shechem to visit his mother's **b**.
9: 5 on one stone, they killed all seventy of his half **b**.
9:26 Gaal son of Ebed moved to Shechem with his **b**
9:31 of Ebed and his **b** have come to live in Shechem,
9:41 and Zebul drove Gaal and his **b** out of Shechem.
9:56 done against his father by murdering his seventy **b**.
11: 2 and when these half **b** grew up, they chased
11: 3 So Jephthah fled from his **b** and lived in the land of
16:31 Later his **b** and other relatives went down to get his
19:23 "No, my **b**, don't do such an evil thing. For this
21:22 And when their fathers and **b** come to us in protest,
1Sa 14:51 Ner, and Saul's father, Kish, were **b**;
16:13 So as David stood there among his **b**, Samuel took
17:14 Since David's three oldest **b** were in the army,
17:17 and these ten loaves of bread to your **b**.
17:18 See how your **b** are getting along, and bring me
17:19 David's **b** were with Saul and the Israelite army at
17:22 and hurried out to the ranks to greet his **b**.
22: 1 Soon his **b** and other relatives joined him there.
30:23 But David said, "No, my **b**! Don't be selfish with
2Sa 2:26 call off your men from chasing their Israelite **b**?"
4: 2 Now there were two **b**, Baanah and Recab,
1Ki 1: 9 He invited all his **b**—the other sons of King
22: 4 You and I are **b**, and my troops are yours to
2Ki 3: 7 You and I are **b**, and my troops are yours to
1Ch 4: 9 who was more distinguished than any of his **b**.
4:27 six daughters, but none of his **b** had large families.
28: 2 addressed them as follows: "My **b** and my people!
2Ch 5:12 Asaph, Heman, Jeduthun, and all their sons and **b**
11:18 (Eliab was one of David's **b**, a son of Jesse.)
18: 3 You and I are **b**, and my troops are yours to
21: 2 Jehoram's **b**—the other sons of Jehoshaphat—
21: 4 he killed all his **b** and some of the other leaders of
21:13 And you have even killed your own **b**, men who
35: 9 Conaniah and his **b** Shemaiah and Nethanel,
Ezr 8:18 along with eighteen of his sons and **b**.
8:19 of Merari, and twenty of his sons and **b**,
10:18 the family of Jeshua son of Jehozadak and his **b**:
Ne 1: 2 Hanani, one of my **b**, came to visit me with some
5:10 I myself, as well as my **b** and my workers,
Job 1: 4 they invited their **b** and sisters to join them for a
42:11 Then all his **b**, sisters, and former friends came
42:15 father put them into his will along with their **b**.
Ps 22:22 I will declare the wonder of your name to my **b**
69: 8 Even my own **b** pretend they don't know me;
133: 1 how pleasant, / when **b** live together in harmony!
Pr 6:19 out lies, / a person who sows discord among **b**.
SS 1: 6 My **b** were angry with me and sent me out to tend
Jer 12: 6 Even your own **b**, members of your own family,
35: 3 grandson of Habazziniah and all his **b** and sons—
49:10 Its children, its **b**, and its neighbors—all will be
Hos 2: 1 In that day you will call your **b** Ammi—
13:15 Ephraim was the most fruitful of all his **b**,
Mic 7: 2 all murderers, even setting traps for their own **b**.
Mt 1: 2 of Jacob. / Jacob was the father of Judah and his **b**.
1:11 and his **b** (born at the time of the exile to Babylon).
4:18 the shore beside the Sea of Galilee, he saw two **b**—
4:21 A little farther up the shore he saw two other **b**,
12:46 his mother and **b** were outside, wanting to talk
12:47 told Jesus, "Your mother and your **b** are outside,
12:48 "Who is my mother? Who are my **b**?"
12:49 and said, "These are my mother and **b**.
13:55 and we know Mary, his mother, and his **b**—
17: 1 Six days later Jesus took Peter and the two **b**,
18:35 will do to you if you refuse to forgive your **b**
19:29 or **b** or sisters or father or mother or children
22:25 Well, there were seven **b**. The oldest married
23: 8 and all of you are on the same level as **b**
25:40 when you did it to one of the least of these my **b**
25:45 when you refused to help the least of these my **b**
28:10 Go tell my **b** to leave for Galilee, and they will see
Mk 3:31 and **b** arrived at the house where he was teaching.
3:32 "Your mother and your **b** and sisters are outside,
3:33 "Who is my mother? Who are my **b**?"
3:34 around him and said, "These are my mother and **b**.
10:29 or **b** or sisters or mother or father or children
10:30 houses, **b**, sisters, mothers, children, and property
12:20 Well, there were seven **b**. The oldest of them
12:22 This continued until all the **b** had married her
Lk 8:19 Once when Jesus' mother and **b** came to see him,
8:20 told Jesus, "Your mother and your **b** are outside,
8:21 and my **b** are all those who hear the message of
14:12 invite your friends, **b**, relatives, and rich neighbors.
14:26 and mother, wife and children, **b** and sisters—
16:28 For I have five **b**, and I want him to warn them
16:29 Your **b** can read their writings anytime they want
18:29 given up house or wife or **b** or parents or children,
20:29 Well, there were seven **b**. The oldest married
21:16 your parents, **b**, relatives, and friends—will betray
22:32 to me again, strengthen and build up your **b**."
Jn 2:12 few days with his mother, his **b**, and his disciples.
7: 3 and Jesus' **b** urged him to go to Judea for the
7: 5 For even his **b** didn't believe in him.
7:10 But after his **b** had left for the festival, Jesus also
20:17 But go find my **b** and tell them that I am ascending
Ac 1:14 of Jesus, several other women, and the **b** of Jesus.
1:16 "**B**, it was necessary for the Scriptures to be
2:29 "Dear **b**, think about this! David wasn't referring
2:37 to the other apostles, "**B**, what should we do?"
7: 2 "**B** and honorable fathers, listen to me.
7:13 they went, Joseph revealed his identity to his **b**,
7:25 Moses assumed his **b** would realize that God had
7:26 to be a peacemaker. 'Men,' he said, 'you are **b**.
11:12 These six **b** here accompanied me, and we soon
12:17 "Tell James and the other **b** what happened,"
13:15 "**B**, if you have any word of encouragement for us,
13:26 "**B**—you sons of Abraham, and also all of you
13:38 "**B**, listen! In this man Jesus there is forgiveness
15: 7 "**B**, you all know that God chose me from among
15:13 James stood and said, "**B**, listen to me.
15:23 from the apostles and elders, your **b** in Jerusalem.
22: 1 "**B** and esteemed fathers," Paul said, "listen to
22: 5 For I received letters from them to our Jewish **b** in
23: 1 "**B**, I have always lived before God in all good
23: 5 "I'm sorry, **b**. I didn't realize he was the high
23: 6 so he shouted, "**B**, I am a Pharisee, as were all my
28:17 He said to them, "**B**, I was arrested in Jerusalem
Ro 8:29 would be the firstborn, with many **b** and sisters.
9: 3 for my people, my Jewish **b** and sisters. I would be
16:17 I make one more appeal, my dear **b** and sisters.
1Co 1:10 Now, dear **b** and sisters, I appeal to you by the
1:26 Remember, dear **b** and sisters, that few of you
2: 1 Dear **b** and sisters, when I first came to you I
3: 1 Dear **b** and sisters, when I was with you I couldn't
4: 6 Dear **b** and sisters, I have used Apollos and myself
6: 8 and cheat even your own Christian **b** and sisters.
7:24 So, dear **b** and sisters, whatever situation you were
7:29 Now let me say this, dear **b** and sisters: The time
9: 5 the other disciples and the Lord's **b** and Peter do?
10: 1 I don't want you to forget, dear **b** and sisters,
11:33 So, dear **b** and sisters, when you gather for the
12: 1 And now, dear **b** and sisters, I will write about the
14: 6 Dear **b** and sisters, if I should come to you talking
14:20 Dear **b** and sisters, don't be childish in your
14:26 Well, my **b** and sisters, let's summarize what I am
14:39 So, dear **b** and sisters, be eager to prophesy,
15: 1 Now let me remind you, dear **b** and sisters,
15:50 dear **b** and sisters, is that flesh and blood cannot
15:58 So, my dear **b** and sisters, be strong and steady,
16:15 to other Christians. I urge you, dear **b** and sisters,
2Co 8:23 And these **b** are representatives of the churches.
9: 3 But I am sending these **b** just to be sure that you
9: 5 So I thought I should send these **b** ahead of me to
11: 9 For the **b** who came from Macedonia brought me
Gal 4:28 And you, dear **b** and sisters, are children of the
6:10 especially to our Christian **b** and sisters.
Php 4: 1 Dear **b** and sisters, I love you and long to see you,
4:21 The **b** who are with me here send you their
Col 1: 2 of Colosse, who are faithful **b** and sisters in Christ.
4:15 Please give my greetings to our Christian **b**
1Th 1: 4 We know that God loves you, dear **b** and sisters,
2: 1 You yourselves know, dear **b** and sisters, that our
2: 9 Don't you remember, dear **b** and sisters, how hard
2:14 And then, dear **b** and sisters, you suffered
4: 1 Finally, dear **b** and sisters, we urge you in the
4:13 And now, **b** and sisters, I want you to know what
5: 4 in the dark about these things, dear **b** and sisters,
5:12 Dear **b** and sisters, honor those who are your
5:14 **B** and sisters, we urge you to warn those who are
5:25 Dear **b** and sisters, pray for us.
2Th 1: 3 Dear **b** and sisters, we always thank God for you,
2: 1 And now, **b** and sisters, let us tell you about the
2:13 God for you, dear **b** and sisters loved by the Lord.
2:15 dear **b** and sisters, stand firm and keep a strong
3: 1 Finally, dear **b** and sisters, I ask you to pray for us.
3: 6 And now, dear **b** and sisters, we give you this
3:13 And I say to the rest of you, dear **b** and sisters,
1Ti 5: 1 to the younger men as you would to your own **b**.
2Ti 4:21 Linus, Claudia, and all the **b** and sisters.
Heb 2:11 That is why Jesus is not ashamed to call them his **b**
2:12 "I will declare the wonder of your name to my **b**
2:17 his **b** and sisters, so that he could be our merciful
Jas 1: 2 Dear **b** and sisters, whenever trouble comes your
1:16 So don't be misled, my dear **b** and sisters.
2: 1 My dear **b** and sisters, how can you claim that you
2: 5 Listen to me, dear **b** and sisters. Hasn't God
2:14 Dear **b** and sisters, what's the use of saying you
3: 1 Dear **b** and sisters, not many of you should become
3:10 Surely, my **b** and sisters, this is not right!
4:11 evil against each other, my dear **b** and sisters.
5: 7 Dear **b** and sisters, you must be patient as you wait
5: 9 my **b** and sisters, or God will judge you.
5:12 But most of all, dear **b** and sisters, never take an
5:19 My dear **b** and sisters, if anyone among you
1Pe 1:22 Now you can have sincere love for each other as **b**
2:11 Dear **b** and sisters, you are foreigners and aliens
2:17 Love your Christian **b** and sisters. Fear God.
1Jn 3:13 So don't be surprised, dear **b** and sisters,
4:21 love not only him but our Christian **b** and sisters,
3Jn 1: 3 Some of the **b** recently returned and made me very
Rev 12:10 the one who accused our **b** and sisters before our
22: 9 of God, just like you and your **b** the prophets,

BROUGHT (622) [BRING]

Ge 2:19 He **b** them to Adam to see what he would call
2:22 made a woman from the rib and **b** her to Adam.
3:12 "but it was the woman you gave me who **b** me the
4: 1 "With the LORD's help, I have **b** forth a man!"
4: 3 At harvest time Cain **b** to the LORD a gift of his
4: 4 while Abel **b** several choice lambs from the best of
9:10 and with the animals you **b** with you—all these
14:18 a priest of God Most High, **b** him bread and wine.
15: 5 Then the LORD **b** Abram outside beneath the
15: 7 "I am the LORD who **b** you out of Ur of the
20: 2 sent for her and had her **b** to him at his palace.
21: 6 And Sarah declared, "God has **b** me laughter!
24:50 "The LORD has obviously **b** you here,
24:53 Then he **b** out silver and gold jewelry and lovely
24:67 And Isaac **b** Rebekah into his mother's tent,
25:28 in particular because of the wild game he **b** home,
27:31 his father's favorite meat dish and **b** it to him.
29:13 Laban then **b** him home, and Jacob told him his
30:14 growing in a field and **b** the roots to his mother,
39:14 "My husband has **b** this Hebrew slave here to
40:20 and they were **b** to him from the prison.
41:14 at once, and he was **b** hastily from the dungeon.
43: 2 When the grain they had **b** from Egypt was almost
43:21 in our sacks. Here it is; we have **b** it back again.
43:23 Then he released Simeon and **b** him out to them.
46: 5 Jacob left Beersheba, and his sons **b** him to Egypt.
46: 6 They **b** their livestock, too, and all the belongings
46:32 They have **b** with them their flocks and herds
47: 7 Then Joseph **b** his father, Jacob, and presented him
47:14 and he **b** the money to Pharaoh's treasure-house.
48:10 So Joseph **b** the boys close to him, and Jacob
50:20 He **b** me to the high position I have today so I
Ex 2:10 the child's mother **b** him back to the princess,
3:12 When you have **b** the Israelites out of Egypt,
9:20 They immediately **b** their livestock and servants in
10: 8 So Moses and Aaron were **b** back to Pharaoh.
10:13 morning arrived, the east wind had **b** the locusts.
12:17 for it will remind you that I **b** your forces out of
12:39 from the yeastless dough they had **b** from Egypt.
13: 3 For the LORD has **b** you out by his mighty
13:14 'With mighty power the LORD **b** us out of Egypt
13:16 who **b** you out of Egypt with great power."
15:19 the LORD **b** the water crashing down on them.
16: 3 But now you have **b** us into this desert to starve us
16: 6 the LORD who **b** you out of the land of Egypt.
16:32 in the wilderness when he **b** you out of Egypt."
18: 1 He had heard about how the LORD had **b** them
18: 5 and he **b** Moses' wife and two sons with him.
18: 9 had done for Israel as he **b** them out of Egypt.
18:22 too important or too complicated can be **b** to you.
18:26 They **b** the hard cases to Moses, but they judged
19: 4 You know how I **b** you to myself and carried you
19: 8 So Moses **b** the people's answer back to the
29:46 I am the one who **b** them out of Egypt so that I
32: 1 who **b** us here from Egypt, has disappeared.
32: 3 obeyed Aaron and **b** him their gold earrings.
32: 4 these are the gods who **b** you out of Egypt!"
32: 7 The people you **b** from Egypt have defiled
32: 8 your gods, O Israel, who **b** you out of Egypt.' "
32:11 so angry with your own people whom you **b** from
32:24 When they **b** them to me, I threw them into the
33: 1 "Now that you have **b** these people out of Egypt,
35:21 they **b** to the LORD their offerings of materials
35:22 Some **b** to the LORD their offerings of gold—
35:23 Others **b** blue, purple, and scarlet yarn, fine linen,
35:24 Others **b** silver and bronze objects as their offering
35:24 the LORD. And those who had acacia wood **b** it.
35:25 and fine linen cloth, and they **b** them in.
35:27 The leaders **b** onyx stones and the other gemstones
35:28 They also **b** spices and olive oil for the light,
35:29 through Moses—**b** their offerings to the LORD.
36: 3 Additional gifts were **b** each morning.
38:24 The people **b** gifts of gold totaling about 2,200
38:29 The people also **b** 5,310 pounds of bronze,
39:33 And they **b** the entire Tabernacle to Moses:
40:21 Then he **b** the Ark of the Covenant into the
Lev 7:34 It is their regular share of the peace offerings **b** by
8:14 Then Moses **b** in the bull for the sin offering,
9: 5 So the people **b** all of these things to the entrance
9: 9 His sons **b** him the blood, and he dipped his finger
9:12 His sons **b** him the blood, and he sprinkled it
9:16 Then he **b** the whole burnt offering and presented
9:17 He also **b** the grain offering, burning a handful of
9:18 His sons **b** him the blood, and he sprinkled it
11:45 am the one who **b** you up from the land of Egypt to
13: 2 they must be **b** to Aaron the priest or to one of his
14: 2 Those who have been healed must be **b** to the
14:42 Other stones will be **b** in to replace the ones that
16:27 whose blood Aaron **b** into the Most Holy Place to
18: 9 whether she was **b** up in the same family
19:36 am your God, who **b** you out of the land of Egypt.
22:15 No one may defile the sacred offerings **b** to the
23:14 or fresh kernels on that day until after you have **b**
24:11 So the man was **b** to Moses for judgment.
25:38 who **b** you out of Egypt to give you the land of
25:42 whom I **b** out of the land of Egypt, so they must

25:55 my servants, whom I **b** out of the land of Egypt.
26:13 who **b** you from the land of Egypt so you would no
26:41 and have **b** them to the land of their enemies,
26:45 whom I **b** out of Egypt while all the nations
Nu 7:2 organized the census—came and **b** their offerings.
7:3 Together they **b** six carts and twelve oxen.
7:14 He also **b** a gold container weighing about four
7:15 He **b** a young bull, a ram, and a one-year-old male
7:17 This was the offering **b** by Nahshon son of
7:20 He also **b** a gold container weighing about four
7:21 He **b** a young bull, a ram, and a one-year-old male
7:23 This was the offering **b** by Nethanel son of Zuar.
7:26 He also **b** a gold container weighing about four
7:27 He **b** a young bull, a ram, and a one-year-old male
7:29 This was the offering **b** by Eliab son of Helon.
7:32 He also **b** a gold container weighing about four
7:33 He **b** a young bull, a ram, and a one-year-old male
7:35 This was the offering **b** by Elizur son of Shedeur.
7:38 He also **b** a gold container weighing about four
7:39 He **b** a young bull, a ram, and a one-year-old male
7:41 This was the offering **b** by Shelumiel son of
7:44 He also **b** a gold container weighing about four
7:45 He **b** a young bull, a ram, and a one-year-old male
7:47 This was the offering **b** by Eliasaph son of Deuel.
7:50 He also **b** a gold container weighing about four
7:51 He **b** a young bull, a ram, and a one-year-old male
7:53 This was the offering **b** by Elishama son of
7:56 He also **b** a gold container weighing about four
7:57 He **b** a young bull, a ram, and a one-year-old male
7:59 This was the offering **b** by Gamaliel son of
7:62 He also **b** a gold container weighing about four
7:63 He **b** a young bull, a ram, and a one-year-old male
7:65 This was the offering **b** by Abidan son of Gideoni.
7:68 He also **b** a gold container weighing about four
7:69 He **b** a young bull, a ram, and a one-year-old male
7:71 This was the offering **b** by Ahiezer son of
7:74 He also **b** a gold container weighing about four
7:75 He **b** a young bull, a ram, and a one-year-old male
7:77 This was the offering **b** by Pagiel son of Ocran.
7:80 He also **b** a gold container weighing about four
7:81 He **b** a young bull, a ram, and a one-year-old male
7:83 This was the offering **b** by Ahira son of Enan.
7:84 **b** by the leaders of Israel at the time it was
7:87 Twelve male goats were **b** for the sin offerings.
11:31 Now the LORD sent a wind that **b** quail from the
12:15 and the people waited until she was **b** back before
15:41 I am the LORD your God who **b** you out of the
16:13 Isn't it enough that you **b** us out of Egypt, a land
16:14 you haven't **b** us into the land flowing with milk
17:6 tribal leaders, including Aaron, **b** Moses a staff.
17:9 When Moses **b** all the staffs out from the LORD's
18:8 holy gifts that are **b** to me by the people of Israel.
18:12 "I also give you the harvest gifts **b** by the people
20:16 heard us and sent an angel who **b** us out of Egypt.
21:5 "Why have you **b** us out of Egypt to die here in
23:7 the king of Moab **b** me from the eastern hills.
23:11 I **b** you to curse my enemies. Instead, you have
23:22 God has **b** them out of Egypt; / he is like a strong
24:8 God **b** them up from Egypt, / drawing them along
25:6 then one of the Israelite men **b** a Midianite woman
27:5 So Moses **b** their case before the LORD.
28:2 See to it that they are **b** at the appointed times
31:12 they **b** them all to Moses and Eleazar the priest,
31:54 and **b** the gold to the Tabernacle as a reminder to
32:17 until we have **b** them safely to their inheritance.
Dt 1:25 They picked some of its fruit and **b** it back to us.
1:31 cares for his child. Now he has **b** you to this place.'
4:37 and personally **b** you out of Egypt with a great
5:15 and that the LORD your God **b** you out with
6:21 but the LORD **b** us out of Egypt with amazing
6:23 He **b** us out of Egypt so he could give us this land
7:19 and the amazing power he used when he **b** you out
9:28 he **b** them into the wilderness to slaughter them."
9:29 whom you **b** from Egypt by your mighty power
13:5 who **b** you out of slavery in the land of Egypt.
16:1 for that was when the LORD your God **b** you out
19:12 have the murderer **b** back from the city of refuge
20:1 who **b** you safely out of Egypt, is with you!
26:3 **b** me into the land he swore to give our ancestors.'
26:8 So the LORD **b** us out of Egypt with amazing
26:9 He **b** us to this place and gave us this land flowing
26:10 I have **b** you a token of the first crops you have
29:25 when he **b** them out of the land of Egypt.
Jos 6:19 to the LORD and must be **b** into his treasury."
6:23 The young men went in and **b** out Rahab,
7:16 Early the next morning Joshua **b** the tribes of Israel
7:18 Every member of Zimri's family was **b** forward
7:23 the tent and **b** them to Joshua and all the Israelites.
7:24 he had, and they **b** them to the valley of Achor.
7:25 said to Achan, "Why have you **b** trouble on us?
8:23 the king of Ai was taken alive and **b** to Joshua.
10:23 So they **b** the five kings out of the cave—the kings
24:5 and Aaron, and I **b** terrible plagues on Egypt;
24:5 and afterward I **b** you out as a free people.
24:7 I **b** the sea crashing down on the Egyptians,
24:8 I **b** you into the land of the Amorites on the east
24:12 It was not your swords or bows that **b** you victory.
24:32 which the Israelites had **b** along with them when
Jdg 2:1 "I **b** you out of Egypt into this land that I swore to
2:12 of their ancestors, who had **b** them out of Egypt.
3:17 He **b** the tax money to Eglon, who was very fat.
5:25 In a bowl fit for kings, / she **b** him yogurt.
6:8 of Israel, says: I **b** you up out of slavery in Egypt
6:13 they say, 'The LORD **b** us up out of Egypt'?
6:19 he **b** them out and presented them to the angel,
6:21 up from the rock and consumed all he had **b**.
7:25 Afterward the Israelites **b** the heads of Oreb

12:9 and **b** in thirty young women from outside his clan
16:8 So the Philistine leaders **b** Delilah seven new
16:18 leaders returned and **b** the money with them.
16:25 So he was **b** from the prison and made to stand at
18:3 took him aside and asked him, "Who **b** you here,
19:1 One day he **b** home a woman from Bethlehem in
20:26 They also **b** burnt offerings and peace offerings to
21:12 and they **b** them to the camp at Shiloh in the land
Ru 1:21 away full, but the LORD has **b** me home empty.
1Sa 1:24 They **b** along a three-year-old bull for the sacrifice
2:14 and demand that whatever it **b** up be given to Eli's
2:19 and **b** it to him when she came with her husband
6:9 we will know it was the LORD who **b** this great
8:8 Ever since I **b** them from Egypt they have
9:22 Then Samuel **b** Saul and his servant into the great
9:24 So the cook **b** it in and placed it before Saul.
10:18 "I **b** you from Egypt and rescued you from the
10:21 Then he **b** each family of the tribe of Benjamin
10:23 So they found him and **b** him out, and he stood
12:6 "He **b** your ancestors out of the land of Egypt.
14:34 in it.' " So that night all the troops **b** their animals
15:20 I **b** back King Agag, but I destroyed everyone else.
15:21 Then my troops **b** in the best of the sheep
16:13 Samuel took the olive oil he had **b** and poured it on
17:57 Abner **b** him to Saul with the Philistine's head still
19:5 and how the LORD **b** a great victory to Israel as a
25:27 And here is a present I have **b** to you and your
27:3 David **b** his two wives along with him—
28:25 She **b** the meal to Saul and his men, and they ate it.
30:7 "Bring me the ephod!" So Abiathar **b** it.
30:11 an Egyptian man in a field and **b** him to David.
30:19 else that had been taken. David **b** everything back.
31:12 They **b** them to Jabesh, where they burned the
2Sa 1:13 Then David said to the young man who had **b** the
3:26 him at the pool of Sirah and **b** him back with them.
6:3 and **b** it from the hillside home of Abinadab.
6:12 and **b** the Ark to the City of David with a great
6:15 and all Israel **b** up the Ark of the LORD with
7:1 his palace and the LORD had **b** peace to the land,
7:6 from the day I **b** the Israelites out of Egypt until
7:18 what is my family, that you have **b** me this far?
8:2 became David's servants and **b** him tribute money.
8:6 became David's subjects and **b** him tribute money.
8:7 David **b** the gold shields of Hadadezer's officers to
9:5 David sent for him and **b** him from Makir's home.
11:27 David sent for her and **b** her to the palace, and she
14:23 went to Geshur and **b** Absalom back to Jerusalem.
14:32 "Because I wanted you to ask the king why he **b**
15:2 When people **b** a case to the king for judgment,
17:28 They **b** sleeping mats, cooking pots, serving bowls,
21:13 So David **b** the bones of Saul and Jonathan, as well
23:12 So the LORD **b** about a great victory.
23:16 some water from the well, and **b** it back to David.
1Ki 1:3 found Abishag from Shunem and **b** her to the king.
1:53 and they **b** him down from the altar.
2:19 he ordered that a throne be **b** for his mother,
3:1 He **b** her to live in the City of David until he could
3:24 bring me a sword." So a sword was **b** to the king.
4:28 They also **b** the necessary barley and straw for the
7:51 Then Solomon **b** all the gifts his father, David,
8:16 'From the day I **b** my people Israel out of Egypt,
8:21 with our ancestors when he **b** them out of Egypt."
8:51 whom you **b** out of the iron-smelting furnace of
8:53 For when you **b** our ancestors out of Egypt,
9:9 who **b** their ancestors out of Egypt, and they
9:9 That is why the LORD has **b** all these disasters
9:28 and **b** back to Solomon some sixteen tons of gold.
10:1 which **b** honor to the name of the LORD,
10:10 so many spices **b** in as those the queen of Sheba
10:11 (When Hiram's ships **b** gold from Ophir, they also **b** rich cargoes of almug wood
10:25 everyone who came to visit **b** him gifts of silver
11:20 who was **b** up in Pharaoh's palace among
12:28 these are the gods who **b** you out of Egypt!"
15:15 He **b** into the Temple of the LORD the silver
17:6 The ravens **b** him bread and meat each morning
17:20 why have you **b** tragedy on this widow who has
17:23 Then Elijah **b** him down from the upper room
18:37 and that you have **b** them back to yourself."
18:45 A heavy wind **b** a terrific rainstorm, and Ahab left
20:39 I was in the battle, and a man **b** me a prisoner.
2Ki 2:20 me a new bowl with salt in it." So they **b** it to him.
3:10 "The LORD has **b** the three of us here to let the
4:5 Her sons **b** many jars to her, and she filled one
4:42 One day a man from Baal-shalishah **b** the man of
6:33 "It is the LORD who has **b** this trouble on us!
8:1 Elisha had told the woman whose son he had **b**
8:5 king about the time Elisha had **b** a boy back to life.
8:5 is her son—the very one Elisha **b** back to life!"
10:8 "They have **b** the heads of the king's sons."
11:9 off duty. They **b** them all to Jehoiada the priest,
11:12 Then Jehoiada **b** out Joash, the king's son,
12:4 "Collect all the money **b** as a sacred offering to
12:10 the money that had been **b** to the LORD's Temple
12:13 The money **b** to the Temple was not used for
12:16 and sin offerings was not **b** into the LORD's
14:20 They **b** him back to Jerusalem on a horse, and he
17:7 who had **b** them safely out of their slavery in
17:36 who **b** you out of Egypt with such mighty miracles
23:8 Josiah **b** back to Jerusalem all the priests of the
23:16 He ordered that the bones be **b** out, and he burned
25:6 They **b** him to the king of Babylon at Riblah,
1Ch 2:7 **b** disaster on Israel by taking plunder that had been
10:12 their warriors went out and **b** the bodies of Saul
11:18 some water from the well, and **b** it back to David.
12:40 and Naphtali **b** food on donkeys, camels, mules,
12:40 cattle, and sheep were **b** to the celebration.

15:28 So all Israel **b** up the Ark of the LORD's
16:1 So they **b** the Ark of God into the special tent
17:5 from the day I **b** the Israelites out of Egypt until
17:16 what is my family, that you have **b** me this far?
18:2 became David's subjects and **b** him tribute money.
18:6 became David's subjects and **b** him tribute money.
18:7 David **b** the gold shields of Hadadezer's officers to
22:4 and Sidon had **b** vast amounts of cedar to David.
29:21 The next day they **b** a thousand bulls, a thousand
29:21 They also **b** drink offerings and many other
2Ch 5:1 he **b** in the gifts dedicated by his father,
6:5 'From the day I **b** my people out of Egypt, I have
7:22 God of their ancestors, who **b** them out of Egypt,
7:22 That is why he **b** all these disasters upon them.' "
8:18 and **b** back to Solomon almost seventeen tons of
9:10 crews of Hiram and Solomon **b** gold from Ophir, they also **b** rich cargoes of almug wood
9:14 and the governors of the land also **b** gold and silver
9:24 everyone who came to visit **b** him gifts of silver
14:7 with these projects and **b** them to completion.
15:18 He **b** into the Temple of God the silver and gold
17:5 All the people of Judah **b** gifts to Jehoshaphat,
17:11 Some of the Philistines **b** him gifts and silver as
17:11 and the Arabs **b** seventy-seven hundred rams
19:2 "What you have done has **b** the LORD's anger
22:9 They **b** him to Jehu, who killed him. Ahaziah was
23:11 Then Jehoiada and his sons **b** out Joash, the king's
24:10 and they gladly **b** their money and filled the chest
24:14 they **b** the remaining money to the king
25:14 he **b** with him idols taken from the people of Seir.
25:23 at Beth-shemesh and **b** him back to Jerusalem.
25:28 They **b** him back to Jerusalem on a horse, and he
29:21 They **b** seven bulls, seven rams, seven lambs,
29:23 then **b** before the king and the assembly of people,
29:31 So the people **b** their sacrifices and thanksgiving
29:31 and those whose hearts were willing **b** burnt
29:32 The people **b** to the LORD seventy bulls,
29:33 They also **b** six hundred bulls and three thousand
30:15 and **b** burnt offerings to the Temple of the LORD.
30:16 The Levites **b** the sacrificial blood to the priests,
31:5 of their fields. They **b** a tithe of all they owned.
31:6 **b** in the tithes of their cattle and sheep and a tithe
31:7 The first of these tithes was **b** in late spring,
31:12 the gifts and tithes were faithfully **b** to the Temple.
32:18 The Assyrian officials who **b** the letters shouted
32:30 and **b** the water down through a tunnel to the west
34:9 The gifts were **b** by people from Manasseh,
35:13 and **b** them out quickly so the people could eat
35:15 for their meals were **b** to them by their fellow
35:24 Then they **b** him back to Jerusalem, where he died.
36:17 So the LORD **b** the king of Babylon against
Ezr 1:7 King Cyrus himself **b** out the valuable items which
3:7 The logs were **b** down from the Lebanon
4:2 ever since King Esarhaddon of Assyria **b** us here."
Ne 8:2 So on October 8 Ezra the priest **b** the scroll of the
9:7 chose Abram and **b** him from Ur of the Chaldeans
9:18 'This is your god who **b** you out of Egypt!'
9:23 and **b** them into the land you had promised to their
12:28 The singers were **b** together from Jerusalem
12:47 the people **b** a daily supply of food for the singers,
13:9 and I **b** back the utensils for God's Temple,
13:18 so that our God **b** the present troubles upon us
13:19 so that no merchandise could be **b** in on the
13:31 of wood for the altar was **b** at the proper times
Est 2:8 was **b** to the king's harem at the fortress of Susa
2:14 and the next morning she was **b** to the second
8:1 Then Mordecai was **b** before the king, for Esther
Job 18:14 and they are **b** down to the king of terrors.
22:29 If someone is **b** low and you say, 'Help him up,'
27:15 Those who survive will be **b** down to the grave by
42:11 because of all the trials the LORD had **b** against
42:11 And each of them **b** him a gift of money and a gold
Ps 18:28 LORD, you have **b** light to my life; / my God,
22:9 Yet you **b** me safely from my mother's womb
30:3 You **b** me up from the grave, O LORD.
37:33 or let the godly be condemned when they are **b**
41:12 you have **b** me into your presence forever.
51:16 or I would bring them. / If I **b** you a burnt offering,
66:12 But you **b** us to a place of great abundance.
78:54 He **b** them to the border of his holy land, / to this
79:8 meet our needs, / for we are **b** low to the dust.
80:8 You **b** us from Egypt as though we were a tender
105:37 But he **b** his people safely out of Egypt,
105:43 So he **b** his people out of Egypt with joy,
106:42 crushed them / and **b** them under their cruel power.
107:30 was that stillness / as he **b** them safely into harbor!
136:11 He **b** Israel out of Egypt. / His faithful love
Pr 21:27 especially when it is **b** with ulterior motives.
SS 3:4 I didn't let him go until I had **b** him to my
6:11 and out to the valley to see the new growth **b** on by
Isa 2:9 So now everyone will be humbled and **b** low.
2:11 The day is coming when your pride will be **b** low
2:17 The arrogance of all people will be **b** low.
3:9 for them! They have **b** about their own destruction.
5:15 In that day the arrogant will be **b** down to the dust;
13:4 The LORD Almighty has **b** them here to form an
14:15 you will be **b** down to the place of the dead,
22:5 has **b** upon the Valley of Vision!
23:3 They **b** you grain from Egypt and harvests from
23:8 Who has **b** this disaster on Tyre, empire builder
26:21 been murdered. They will be **b** out for all to see.
28:1 for that city—the pride of a people **b** low by wine.
43:23 You have not **b** me lambs for burnt offerings.
43:24 You have not **b** me fragrant incense or pleased me
54:17 And everyone who tells lies in court will be **b** to
60:7 and the rams of Nebaioth will be **b** for my altars.
63:11 "Where is the one who **b** Israel through the sea,

Jer 2: 6 'Where is the LORD who **b** us safely out of
2: 7 "And when I **b** you into a fruitful land to enjoy its
2:17 And you have **b** this on yourselves by rebelling
4:18 "Your own actions have **b** this upon you.
11: 4 For I said to your ancestors when I **b** them out of
11: 7 For I solemnly warned your ancestors when I **b**
11: 8 I **b** upon them all the curses described in our
16:15 who **b** the people of Israel back to their own land
19:10 Jeremiah, smash the jar you **b** with you.
23: 8 who **b** the people of Israel back to their own land
26:23 him prisoner and **b** him back to King Jehoiakim.
31:28 I overthrew it, destroyed it, and **b** disaster upon it.
31:32 by the hand and **b** them out of the land of Egypt.
32:21 "You **b** Israel out of Egypt with mighty signs
36:21 Jehudi **b** it from Elishama's room and read it to the
38:22 All the women left in your palace will be **b** out
40: 2 "The LORD your God has **b** this disaster on this
41: 5 and had **b** along grain offerings and incense.
50:25 and **b** out weapons to vent his fury against his
52: 9 They **b** him to the king of Babylon at Riblah,
La 1:12 which the LORD **b** on me in the day of his fierce
2: 2 He has **b** to dust the kingdom and all its rulers.
2: 5 He has **b** unending sorrow and tears to Jerusalem.
3: 2 He has **b** me into deep darkness, shutting out all
Eze 8: 7 Then he **b** me to the door of the Temple courtyard,
8:14 He **b** me to the north gate of the LORD's Temple,
8:16 Then he **b** me into the inner courtyard of the
11: 1 and **b** me over to the east gateway of the LORD's
12: 7 In broad daylight I **b** my pack outside, filled with
17:12 away her king and princes, and **b** them to Babylon.
19: 9 and **b** him before the king of Babylon. / They held
20:10 So I **b** my people out of Egypt and led them into
20:28 for when I **b** them into the land I had promised
20:28 They **b** their perfumes and incense and poured out
20:42 Then when I have **b** you home to the land I
21:26 the lowly are exalted, and the mighty are **b** low.
23:27 to the lewdness and prostitution you **b** from Egypt.
23:30 You **b** all this on yourself by prostituting yourself
24:17 or accept any food **b** to you by consoling friends."
24:22 or console yourselves by eating the food **b** to you
27: 6 pine wood, **b** from the southern coasts of Cyprus.
27:13 Tubal, and Meshech **b** slaves and bronze dishes.
27:15 they **b** payment in ivory tusks and ebony wood.
27:21 and the princes of Kedar **b** lambs and rams
27:24 They **b** choice fabrics to trade—blue cloth,
28:18 So I **b** fire from within you, and it consumed you.
31:18 will be **b** down to the pit with all these other
32:27 They **b** terror to everyone while they were still
33:16 None of their past sins will be **b** up again, for they
36:20 the nations, they **b** dishonor to my holy name.
40: 3 As he **b** me nearer, I saw a man whose face shone
40: 4 You have been **b** here so I can show you many
40:17 Then the man **b** me through the gateway into the
40:48 Then he **b** me to the foyer of the Temple.
41: 1 After that, the man **b** me into the Holy Place,
43: 1 the man **b** me back around to the east gateway.
43: 5 took me up and **b** me into the inner courtyard,
44: 1 Then the man **b** me back to the east gateway in the
44: 4 Then the man **b** me through the north gateway to
44: 7 You have **b** uncircumcised foreigners into my
44:11 and they may still slaughter the animals **b** for burnt
44:29 and sacrifices **b** to the Temple by the people—
44:30 and all the gifts **b** to the LORD will go to the
46:19 Then the man **b** me through the entrance beside the
46:21 Then he **b** me back to the outer courtyard and led
47: 1 Then the man **b** me back to the entrance of the
47: 2 The man **b** me outside the wall through the north
Da 1: 3 who had been **b** to Babylon as captives.
1:18 the chief official **b** all the young men to King
3:13 Meshach, and Abednego to be **b** before him. When
they were **b** in,
5: 3 So they **b** these gold cups taken from the Temple
5: 7 astrologers, and fortune-tellers to be **b** before him.
5:13 So Daniel was **b** in before the king. The king asked
5:20 he was **b** down from his royal throne and stripped
5:23 and have had these cups from his Temple **b** before
5:26 the days of your reign and has **b** it to an end.
6:17 A stone was **b** and placed over the mouth of the
9:14 The LORD has **b** against us the disaster he
9:15 you **b** lasting honor to your name by rescuing your
Hos 8: 4 and gold, they have **b** about their own destruction.
10: 1 The richer the harvests they **b** in, the more
14: 1 LORD your God, for your sins have **b** you down.
Am 4: 6 "I **b** hunger to every city and famine to every
9: 7 "I **b** you out of Egypt, but have I not done as much
9: 7 I **b** the Philistines from Crete and led the Arameans
Mic 6: 4 For I **b** you out of Egypt and redeemed you from
Hag 1: 9 And when you **b** your harvest home, I blew it
Mal 3: 4 the offerings **b** to him by the people of Judah
Mt 1:24 Lord commanded. He **b** Mary home to be his wife,
5:22 you are in danger of being **b** before the court.
8:16 many demon-possessed people were **b** to Jesus.
9: 2 Some people **b** to him a paralyzed man on a mat.
9:32 some people **b** to him a man who couldn't speak
11:23 you will be **b** down to the place of the dead.
12:22 was both blind and unable to talk, was **b** to Jesus.
14:11 and his head was **b** on a tray and given to the girl,
15:30 A vast crowd **b** him the lame, blind, crippled,
16: 7 was saying this because they hadn't **b** any bread.
17:16 So I **b** him to your disciples, but they couldn't heal
18:24 one of his debtors was **b** in who owed him millions
19:13 Some children were **b** to Jesus so he could lay his
21: 7 They **b** the animals to him and threw their
22:10 "So the servants **b** in everyone they could find,
26:36 Then Jesus **b** them to an olive grove called
Mk 1:32 and demon-possessed people were **b** to Jesus.
4:22 now hidden or secret will eventually be **b** to light.
6:28 **b** his head on a tray, and gave it to the girl,
7:32 A deaf man with a speech impediment was **b** to
8:16 was saying this because they hadn't **b** any bread.
8:22 some people **b** a blind man to Jesus, and they
9:17 "Teacher, I **b** my son for you to heal him.
9:20 So they **b** the boy. But when the evil spirit saw
10:10 disciples in the house, they **b** up the subject again.
10:13 One day some parents **b** their children to Jesus
11: 7 Then they **b** the colt to Jesus and threw their
15:22 And they **b** Jesus to a place called Golgotha (which
Lk 4:40 people throughout the village **b** sick family
5: 7 A shout for help **b** their partners in the other boat,
7:37 and **b** a beautiful jar filled with expensive perfume.
8:17 or secret will eventually be **b** to light and made
9:47 their thoughts, so he **b** a little child to his side.
10:15 you will be **b** down to the place of the dead."
12:11 "And when you are **b** to trial in the synagogues
18:15 One day some parents **b** their little children to
18:40 he stopped and ordered that the man be **b** to him.
19:20 "But the third servant **b** back only the original
19:35 So they **b** the colt to Jesus and threw their
22:49 "Lord, should we fight? We **b** the swords!"
23:14 "You **b** this man to me, accusing him of leading a
Jn 1:16 We have all benefited from the rich blessings he **b**
1:42 Then Andrew **b** Simon to meet Jesus.
4:33 "Who **b** it to him?" the disciples asked each other.
4:36 and the fruit they harvest is people **b** to eternal life.
8: 3 and Pharisees **b** a woman they had caught in the
12:28 saying, "I have already **b** it glory, and I will do it
16:21 because she has **b** a new person into the world.
17: 4 I **b** glory to you here on earth by doing everything
18:33 back inside and called for Jesus to be **b** to him.
18:35 own people and their leading priests **b** you here.
19:11 So the one who **b** me to you has the greater sin."
19:13 they said this, Pilate **b** Jesus out to them again.
Ac 3:13 the God of all our ancestors who has **b** glory to his
4: 7 They **b** in the two disciples and demanded,
4:35 and **b** the money to the apostles to give to others in
4:37 and **b** the money to the apostles for those in need.
5: 2 He **b** part of the money to the apostles, but he
5:14 more people believed and were **b** to the Lord—
5:15 sick people were **b** out into the streets on beds
5:19 opened the gates of the jail, and **b** them out.
5:21 Then they sent for the apostles to be **b** for trial.
5:27 Then they **b** the apostles in before the council.
6:12 and **b** him before the high council.
7: 4 Then God **b** him here to the land where you now
7:40 has become of this Moses, who **b** us out of Egypt.'
9:27 Then Barnabas **b** him to the apostles and told them
11:24 And large numbers of people were **b** to the Lord.
11:26 When he found him, he **b** him back to Antioch.
14:13 and the crowd **b** oxen and wreaths of flowers,
16:30 He **b** them out and asked, "Sirs, what must I do to
16:34 Then he **b** them into his house and set a meal
16:39 Then they **b** them out and begged them to leave the
18:12 and **b** him before the governor for judgment.
19:19 been practicing magic **b** their incantation books
19:37 You have **b** these men here, but they have stolen
22: 3 and I was **b** up and educated here in Jerusalem
22:24 The commander **b** Paul inside and ordered him
22:30 He had Paul **b** in before them to try to find out
25:17 the case the very next day and ordered Paul **b** in.
25:23 men of the city. Festus ordered that Paul be **b** in.
25:26 So I have **b** him before all of you, and especially
Ro 4:20 faith grew stronger, and in this he **b** glory to God.
4:24 in God, who **b** Jesus our Lord back from the dead.
5: 2 Christ has **b** us into this place of highest privilege
5:12 Adam's sin **b** death, so death spread to everyone,
5:15 one man, Adam, **b** death to many through his sin.
5:15 **b** forgiveness to many through God's bountiful
5:18 Adam's one sin **b** condemnation upon everyone,
5:21 as sin ruled over all people and **b** them to death,
15:18 I have **b** the Gentiles to God by my message
1Co 2: 6 rulers of this world, who are being **b** to nothing.
9:13 meals from the food **b** to the Temple as offerings?
10: 1 and he **b** them all safely through the waters of the
2Co 5:18 who **b** us back to himself through what Christ did.
7: 7 so was the news he **b** of the encouragement he
11: 9 For the brothers who came from Macedonia **b** me
Gal 4:13 Surely you remember that I was sick when I first **b**
Eph 2:13 now you have been **b** near to him because of the
2:17 He has **b** this Good News of peace to you Gentiles
Php 1:16 for they know the Lord **b** me here to defend the
4:15 me financial help when I **b** you the Good News
Col 1: 7 was the one who **b** you the Good News.
1:13 and he has **b** us into the Kingdom of his dear Son.
1:22 yet now he has **b** you back as his friends. He has
1:22 he has **b** you into the very presence of God,
1Th 1: 5 For when we **b** you the Good News, it was not
1: 6 Holy Spirit in spite of the severe suffering it **b** you.
1Ti 5:10 Has she **b** up her children well? Has she been kind
2Ti 4:16 The first time I was **b** before the judge, no one was
Heb 11: 4 It was by faith that Abel **b** a more acceptable
13:11 the high priest **b** the blood of animals into the Holy
13:20[-21] who **b** again from the dead our Lord Jesus,
Jas 5:19 wanders away from the truth and is **b** back again,
2Pe 3: 5 and he **b** the earth up from the water
1Jn 4:12 and his love has been **b** to full expression through

BROW (1)
Dt 33:16 crowning the **b** of the prince among his brothers.

BROWN (2)
Eze 47:12 The leaves of these trees will never turn **b** and fall,
Zec 1: 8 Behind him were red, **b**, and white horses,

BRUISE (3) [BRUISED, BRUISES]
Ex 21:25 burn for burn, wound for wound, **b** for **b**.
Jer 30:12 Yours is an incurable **b**, a terrible wound.

BRUISED (1) [BRUISE]
Ps 105:18 There in prison, they **b** his feet with fetters

BRUISES (2) [BRUISE]
Pr 23:29 Who has unnecessary **b**? Who has bloodshot eyes?
Isa 1: 6 covered with **b**, welts, and infected wounds—

BRUIT [KJV] See DESTRUCTION, TERRIFYING (NOISE)

BRUSH (1) [BRUSHED, BRUSHES, BRUSHFIRE, UNDERBRUSH]
Hag 2:12 and happens to **b** against some bread or stew,

BRUSHED (2) [BRUSH]
Ps 109:23 I am falling like a grasshopper that is **b** aside.
Eze 3:13 of the living beings as they **b** against each other

BRUSHES (1) [BRUSH]
Hag 2:13 and then **b** against any of the things mentioned,

BRUSHFIRE (1) [BRUSH, FIRE]
Isa 9:18 This wickedness is like a **b**. It burns not only briers

BRUTAL (4) [BRUTALLY]
Ex 1:11 their slaves and put **b** slave drivers over them,
5:13 The slave drivers were **b**. "Meet your daily quota
5:23 he has been even more **b** to your people.
Mt 2:17 Herod's **b** action fulfilled the prophecy of

BRUTALLY (1) [BRUTAL]
Lk 21:24 They will be **b** killed by the sword or sent away as

BUBASTIS (1)
Eze 30:17 young men of Heliopolis and **B** will die in battle,

BUBBLE (1) [BUBBLED, BUBBLING]
Jas 3:11 Does a spring of water **b** out with both fresh water

BUBBLED (1) [BUBBLE]
Pr 8:24 before the springs **b** forth their waters.

BUBBLING (1) [BUBBLE]
Pr 18: 4 words of true wisdom are as refreshing as a **b**

BUCKET (2) [BUCKETFUL, BUCKETS]
Isa 40:15 They are but a drop in the **b**, dust on the scales.
Jn 4:11 "But sir, you don't have a rope or a **b**," she said,

BUCKETFUL (1) [BUCKET]
Ps 80: 5 us with sorrow / and made us drink tears by the **b**.

BUCKETS (3) [BUCKET]
Ex 27: 3 The ash **b**, shovels, basins, meat hooks,
38: 3 the ash **b**, shovels, basins, meat hooks,
Nu 24: 7 Water will gush out in **b**; / their offspring are

BUCKLE (1)
Jer 46: 3 "**B** on your armor and advance into battle!

BUCKLER(S) [KJV] See also SHIELD(S)

BUD (3) [BUDDED, BUDDING, BUDS]
Ge 40:10 It had three branches that began to **b** and blossom,
Job 14: 9 at the scent of water it may **b** and sprout again like
Isa 27: 6 Israel will **b** and blossom and fill the whole earth

BUDDED (1) [BUD]
SS 7:12 Let us see whether the vines have **b**,

BUDDING (2) [BUD]
SS 2:13 The fig trees are **b**, and the grapevines are in
6:11 I wanted to see whether the grapevines were **b** yet,

BUDS (8) [BUD]
Ex 25:31 the base, center stem, lamp cups, **b**, and blossoms.
25:33 an almond blossom, complete with **b** and petals.
25:34 four almond blossoms, complete with **b** and petals.
37:17 lamp cups, blossoms, and **b** were all of one piece.
37:19 an almond blossom, complete with **b** and petals.
Nu 17: 5 **B** will sprout on the staff belonging to the man I
Mt 24:32 When its **b** become tender and its leaves begin to
Mk 13:28 When its **b** become tender and its leaves begin to

BUFFET [KJV] See HIT, TORMENT

BUGLE (1) [BUGLER]
Job 39:25 It snorts at the sound of the **b**. It senses the battle

BUGLER (1) [BUGLE]
1Co 14: 8 And if the **b** doesn't sound a clear call, how will

BUILD (141) [BUILDER, BUILDERS, BUILDING, BUILDINGS, BUILDS, BUILT, REBUILD, REBUILDING, REBUILT, WELL-BUILT]

Ge 11: 4 Let's **b** a great city with a tower that reaches to the
22: 3 Then he chopped wood to **b** a fire for a burnt
35: 1 **B** an altar there to worship me—the God who
35: 3 where I will **b** an altar to the God who answered
Ex 1: 11 They forced them to **b** the cities of Pithom
20: 24 **B** altars in the places where I remind you who I
20: 25 If you **b** altars from stone, use only uncut stones.
25: 8 "I want the people of Israel to **b** me a sacred
27: 8 Be careful to **b** it just as you were shown on the
Lev 1: 7 the sons of Aaron the priest will **b** a wood fire on
Nu 23: 1 said to King Balak, "**B** me seven altars here,
23: 29 "**B** me seven altars and prepare me seven young
32: 16 "We simply want to **b** sheepfolds for our flocks
32: 17 our families will stay in the fortified cities we **b**
32: 24 Go ahead and **b** towns for your families
Dt 6: 10 with large, prosperous cities that you did not **b**.
17: 16 The king must not **b** up a large stable of horses for
22: 8 "Every new house you **b** must have a barrier
27: 5 Then **b** an altar there to the LORD your God,
28: 30 You will **b** a house, but someone else will live in
Jos 4: 6 We will use these stones to **b** a memorial.
9: 27 wherever the LORD would choose to **b** it.
22: 16 the LORD and **b** an altar in rebellion against him?
22: 26 So we decided to **b** the altar, not for burnt
24: 13 worked for, and I gave you cities you did not **b**—
Jdg 6: 26 Then **b** an altar to the LORD your God here on
1Sa 6: 7 Now **b** a new cart, and find two cows that have just
2Sa 5: 11 with carpenters and stonemasons to **b** him a palace.
7: 5 Are you the one to **b** me a temple to live in?
7: 11 " 'And now the LORD declares that he will **b** a
7: 13 He is the one who will **b** a house—a temple—
7: 27 because you have revealed that you will **b** a house
24: 18 and **b** an altar to the LORD on the threshing floor
24: 21 and to **b** an altar to the LORD there,
24: 22 and ox yokes for wood to **b** a fire on the altar.
1Ki 2: 36 "**B** a house here in Jerusalem and live there.
5: 3 was not able to **b** a Temple to honor the name of
5: 3 He could not **b** until the LORD gave him victory
5: 5 So I am planning to **b** a Temple to honor the name
5: 5 your throne, will **b** the Temple to honor my name.'
5: 9 to the Mediterranean Sea and **b** them into rafts.
6: 38 his reign. So it took seven years to **b** the Temple.
8: 17 wanted to **b** this Temple to honor the name of the
8: 18 'It is right for you to want to **b** the Temple to
8: 19 the one to do it. One of your sons will **b** it instead.'
9: 15 Solomon conscripted to **b** the LORD's Temple,
19: 21 and used the wood from the plow to **b** a fire to
2Ki 6: 2 There we can **b** a new place for us to meet."
19: 32 their shields and **b** banks of earth against its walls.
1Ch 14: 1 with stonemasons and carpenters to **b** him a palace.
17: 4 You are not the one to **b** me a temple to live in.
17: 10 " 'And now I declare that the LORD will **b** a
17: 12 He is the one who will **b** a house—a temple—
17: 25 because you have revealed that you will **b** a house
21: 18 **b** an altar to the LORD at the threshing floor of
21: 22 Then I will **b** an altar to the LORD there, so that
21: 23 and you can use the threshing tools for wood to **b** a
22: 6 and instructed him to **b** a Temple for the LORD,
22: 7 "I wanted to **b** a Temple to honor the name of the
22: 8 you will not be the one to **b** a Temple to honor my
22: 10 He is the one who will **b** a Temple to honor my
22: 19 **B** the sanctuary of the LORD God so that you can
28: 2 It was my desire to **b** a temple where the Ark of
28: 3 'You must not **b** a temple to honor my name,
28: 6 'Your son Solomon will **b** my Temple and its
28: 10 The LORD has chosen you to **b** a Temple as his
29: 1 for the Temple he will **b** is not just another
29: 16 even these materials that we have gathered to **b** a
29: 19 decrees, and principles, and to **b** this Temple,
2Ch 2: 1 Solomon now decided that the time had come to **b**
2: 4 I am about to **b** a Temple to honor the name of the
2: 6 But who can really **b** him a worthy home?
2: 9 for the Temple I am going to **b** will be very large
2: 12 who will **b** a Temple for the LORD and a royal
3: 1 So Solomon began to **b** the Temple of the LORD
6: 7 wanted to **b** this Temple to honor the name of the
6: 8 'It is right for you to want to **b** the Temple to
6: 9 the one to do it. One of your sons will **b** it instead.'
14: 6 he was able to **b** up the fortified cities throughout
14: 7 "Let us **b** towns and fortify them with walls,
21: 19 His people did not **b** a great fire to honor him at his
32: 27 He had to **b** special treasury buildings for his
36: 23 He has appointed me to **b** him a Temple at
Ezr 1: 2 He has appointed me to **b** him a Temple at
4: 2 and the other leaders and said, "Let us **b** with you,
4: 3 We alone will **b** the Temple for the LORD,
Ne 4: 2 Do they think they can **b** the wall in a day if they
8: 16 and used them to **b** shelters on the roofs of their
Job 19: 12 His troops advance. They **b** up roads to attack me.
Ps 107: 36 brings the hungry to settle there / and **b** their cities.
132: 5 until I find a place to **b** a house for the LORD,
Isa 22: 11 you **b** a reservoir for water from the old pool.
28: 16 and precious cornerstone that is safe to **b** on.
29: 3 I will **b** siege towers around it and will destroy it.
37: 33 their shields and **b** banks of earth against its walls.
54: 2 "Enlarge your house; **b** an addition; spread out
65: 21 people will live in the houses they **b** and eat the
66: 1 Could you ever **b** me a temple as good as that?
Could you **b** a dwelling place for me?
Jer 1: 10 You are to **b** others up and plant them."
6: 6 **B** ramps against the walls of Jerusalem. This is the
7: 18 gather wood and the fathers **b** sacrificial fires.
18: 9 And if I announce that I will **b** up and plant a
22: 14 'I will **b** a magnificent palace with huge rooms
24: 6 I will **b** them up and not tear them down. I will
29: 5 "**B** homes, and plan to stay. Plant gardens, and eat
29: 28 He said we should **b** homes and plan to stay for
31: 28 But in the future I will plant it and **b** it up,"
35: 7 And do not **b** houses or plant crops or vineyards,
42: 10 If you do, I will **b** you up and not tear you down;
Eze 4: 2 **B** siege ramps against the city walls. Surround it
11: 3 to the people, 'Is it not a good time to **b** houses?
16: 31 You **b** your pagan shrines on every street corner
21: 22 and **b** ramps against the walls to reach the top.
28: 26 and **b** their homes and plant their vineyards.
Ob 1: 4 as high as eagles and **b** your nest among the stars,
Hab 2: 12 "How terrible it will be for you who **b** cities with
Zec 5: 11 "To the land of Babylonia where they will **b** a
6: 12 out where he is and **b** the Temple of the LORD.
6: 13 He will **b** the LORD's Temple, and he will
Mt 16: 18 are Peter, and upon this rock I will **b** my church,
23: 29 For you **b** tombs for the prophets your ancestors
27: 40 destroy the Temple and **b** it again in three days,
Mk 14: 58 and in three days I will **b** another, made without
Lk 11: 47 For you **b** tombs for the very prophets your
12: 18 I'll tear down my barns and **b** bigger ones.
19: 43 Before long your enemies will **b** ramparts against
22: 32 to me again, strengthen and **b** up your brothers."
Jn 2: 20 "It took forty-six years to **b** this Temple, and you
Ac 7: 49 Could you ever **b** me a temple as good as that?'
7: 49 the Lord. / 'Could you **b** a dwelling place for me?
20: 32 his message that is able to **b** you up and give you
Ro 14: 19 harmony in the church and try to **b** each other up.
15: 2 do what helps them, we will **b** them up in the Lord.
1Co 14: 26 must be useful to all and **b** them up in the Lord.
2Co 10: 8 But this authority is to **b** you up, not to tear you
13: 10 the authority the Lord has given me to **b** you up,
Eph 4: 12 God's people to do his work and **b** up the church,
1Th 5: 11 So encourage each other and **b** each other up,
Heb 8: 5 For when Moses was getting ready to **b** the
Jude 1: 20 must continue to **b** your lives on the foundation of

BUILDER (6) [BUILD]

Isa 23: 8 on Tyre, empire **b** and chief trader of the world?
1Co 3: 10 to me, I have laid the foundation like an expert **b**.
3: 13 day to see what kind of work each **b** has done.
3: 14 work survives the fire, that **b** will receive a reward.
3: 15 the work is burned up, the **b** will suffer great loss.
Heb 3: 4 For every house has a **b**, but God is the one who

BUILDERS (17) [BUILD]

1Ki 5: 18 and Hiram's **b** prepare the timber and stone for the
2Ki 12: 11 on the LORD's Temple—the carpenters, the **b**,
22: 6 They will need to hire carpenters, **b**, and masons.
Ezr 3: 10 When the **b** completed the foundation of the
Ne 4: 5 you to anger here in the presence of the **b**."
4: 18 All the **b** had a sword belted to their side.
Ps 118: 22 The stone rejected by the **b** / has now become the
127: 1 builds a house, / the work of the **b** is useless.
Jer 51: 58 The **b** from many lands have worked in vain,
Eze 27: 4 boundaries into the sea. Your **b** made you glorious!
27: 27 your ship **b**, merchants, and warriors.
Mt 21: 42 'The stone rejected by the **b** / has now become the
Mk 12: 10 'The stone rejected by the **b** / has now become the
Lk 20: 17 'The stone rejected by the **b** / has now become the
Ac 4: 11 where it says, / 'The stone that you **b** rejected
1Co 3: 15 The **b** themselves will be saved, but like someone
1Pe 2: 7 reject him, / "The stone that was rejected by the **b**

BUILDING (63) [BUILD]

Ge 11: 5 to see the city and the tower the people were **b**.
11: 8 all over the earth; and that ended the **b** of the city.
Ex 38: 21 Here is an inventory of the materials used in **b** the
Jos 22: 19 or draw us into your rebellion by **b** another altar
22: 29 or turn away from him by **b** our own altar for burnt
1Ki 3: 1 the City of David until he could finish **b** his palace
6: 5 all the way around the sides and rear of the **b**.
6: 7 of hammer, ax, or any other iron tool at the **b** site.
6: 10 was a complex of rooms on three sides of the **b**,
6: 12 "Concerning this Temple you are **b**, if you keep
6: 14 So Solomon finished **b** the Temple.
6: 38 The entire **b** was completed in every detail by
9: 1 So Solomon finished **b** the Temple of the LORD,
9: 25 And so he finished the work of **b** the Temple.
15: 22 help to carry away the **b** stones and timbers that
2Ki 10: 24 Now Jehu had surrounded the **b** with eighty of his
1Ch 22: 2 preparing blocks of stone for **b** the Temple of God.
22: 5 So David collected vast amounts of **b** materials
22: 11 in **b** the Temple of the LORD your God.
22: 14 "I have worked hard to provide materials for **b** the
28: 2 I made the necessary preparations for **b** it,
29: 1 for the Temple he will build is not just another **b**—
29: 2 I have gathered as much as I could for **b** the
29: 3 This is in addition to the **b** materials I have already
2Ch 2: 3 to my father, David, when he was **b** his palace.
2: 6 So who am I to consider **b** a Temple for him,
5: 1 the work related to **b** the Temple of the LORD,
7: 11 So Solomon finished the Temple of the LORD,
8: 1 and the great **b** projects of the LORD's Temple
8: 16 to **b** the Temple of the LORD was carried out,
16: 6 out all the men of Judah to carry away the **b** stones
Ezr 4: 23 hurried to Jerusalem and forced the Jews to stop **b**.
5: 5 the leaders of the Jews were not prevented from **b**
Ne 3: 1 **b** the wall as far as the Tower of the Hundred,
3: 17 who supervised the **b** of the wall on behalf of his
4: 17 who were **b** the wall. The common laborers carried
6: 6 to rebel and that is why you are **b** the wall.
Ps 78: 58 They made God angry by **b** altars to other gods;
Pr 24: 27 Develop your business first before **b** your house.
Ecc 2: 4 I also tried to find meaning by **b** huge homes for
Isa 22: 16 **b** a beautiful tomb for yourself in the rock?
Jer 51: 26 Even your stones will never again be used for **b**.
Eze 26: 8 Then he will attack you by **b** a siege wall,
40: 45 "The **b** beside the north inner gate is for the priests
40: 46 The **b** beside the south inner gate is for the priests
41: 12 A large **b** stood on the west, facing the Temple
41: 13 The courtyard around the **b**, including its walls,
41: 15 The **b** to the west, including its two walls, was also
42: 14 the parts of the **b** complex open to the public."
Am 5: 11 never live in the beautiful stone houses you are **b**.
Mic 3: 10 You are **b** Jerusalem on a foundation of murder
Hag 1: 9 while you are all busy **b** your own fine houses.
Zec 8: 9 **b** the Temple of the LORD Almighty ever since
Lk 14: 28 For who would begin construction of a **b** without
14: 30 'There's the person who started that **b** and ran out
17: 28 and drinking, buying and selling, farming and **b**—
Ac 4: 31 this prayer, the **b** where they were meeting shook,
7: 46 and asked for the privilege of **b** a permanent
1Co 3: 9 to God. You are God's field, God's **b**—not ours.
3: 10 like an expert builder. Now others are **b** on it.
3: 10 But whoever is **b** on this foundation must be very
1Pe 2: 5 And now God is **b** you, as living stones, into his
3: 20 God waited patiently while Noah was **b** his boat.

BUILDINGS (15) [BUILD]

1Ki 7: 2 One of Solomon's **b** was called the Palace of the
7: 9 All these **b** were built entirely from huge,
9: 11 gold he had furnished for the construction of the **b**.
2Ki 23: 19 Then Josiah demolished all the **b** at the pagan
25: 9 He destroyed all the important **b** in the city.
1Ch 15: 1 David now built several **b** for himself in the City
29: 4 silver to be used for overlaying the walls of the **b**
2Ch 32: 27 He had to build special treasury **b** for his silver,
Ps 28: 5 So he will tear them down like old **b**, / and they
Jer 52: 13 He destroyed all the important **b** in the city.
Eze 40: 44 there were two one-room **b** for the singers,
Mt 24: 1 disciples pointed out to him the various Temple **b**.
24: 2 But he told them, "Do you see all these **b**? I assure
Mk 13: 1 "Teacher, look at these tremendous **b**!
13: 2 "These magnificent **b** will be so completely

BUILDS (12) [BUILD]

Ps 84: 3 finds a home there, / and the swallow **b** her nest
127: 1 Unless the LORD **b** a house, / the work of the
Pr 14: 1 A wise woman **b** her house; a foolish woman tears
Jer 22: 13 for Jehoiakim, who **b** his palace with forced labor.
22: 13 he **b** injustice into its walls and oppression into its
Mt 7: 24 is wise, like a person who **b** a house on solid rock.
7: 26 it is foolish, like a person who **b** a house on sand.
Lk 6: 48 It is like a person who **b** a house on a strong
6: 49 and doesn't obey is like a person who **b** a house
1Co 3: 12 Now anyone who **b** on that foundation may use
8: 1 it is love that really **b** up the church.
Heb 3: 3 just as a person who **b** a fine house deserves more

BUILT (194) [BUILD]

Ge 8: 20 Then Noah **b** an altar to the LORD and sacrificed
10: 10 He **b** the foundation for his empire in the land of
10: 11 where he **b** Nineveh, Rehoboth-ir, Calah,
12: 7 And Abram **b** an altar there to commemorate the
12: 8 There he **b** an altar and worshiped the LORD.
13: 4 This was the place where Abram had **b** the altar,
13: 18 is at Hebron. There he **b** an altar to the LORD.
22: 9 to go, he **b** an altar and placed the wood on it.
26: 25 Then Isaac **b** an altar there and worshiped the
30: 40 This is how he **b** his flock from Laban's.
33: 17 There he **b** himself a house and made shelters for
33: 20 And there he **b** an altar and called it
35: 7 Jacob **b** an altar there and named it El-bethel,
Ex 17: 15 Moses **b** an altar there and called it "The LORD
24: 4 Early the next morning he **b** an altar at the foot of
27: 5 into the firebox, resting it on the ledge **b** there.
32: 5 he **b** an altar in front of the calf and announced,
Nu 8: 4 It was **b** according to the exact design the LORD
23: 14 He **b** seven altars there and offered a young bull
32: 34 The people of Gad **b** the towns of Dibon, Ataroth,
32: 37 The people of Reuben **b** the towns of Heshbon,
Dt 8: 12 and prosperous and have **b** fine homes to live in,
20: 5 'Has anyone just **b** a new house but not yet
Jos 2: 15 since Rahab's house was **b** into the city wall,
4: 9 Joshua also **b** another memorial of twelve stones in
8: 30 Then Joshua **b** an altar to the LORD, the God of
11: 13 Joshua did not burn any of the cities **b** on mounds
22: 10 and the half-tribe of Manasseh **b** a very large altar
22: 11 When the rest of Israel heard they had **b** the altar at
22: 22 We have not **b** the altar in rebellion against the
22: 23 that we have not **b** an altar for ourselves to turn
22: 23 If we have **b** it for this purpose, may the LORD
22: 24 "We have **b** this altar because we fear that in the
Jdg 1: 26 moved to the land of the Hittites, where he **b** a city.
6: 24 And Gideon **b** an altar to the LORD there
6: 28 In their place a new altar had been **b**, and it had the
21: 4 Early the next morning the people **b** an altar
1Sa 7: 17 And Samuel **b** an altar to the LORD at Ramah.
14: 35 And Saul **b** an altar to the LORD, the first one he
had ever **b**.
2Sa 5: 9 He **b** additional fortifications around the city,
7: 7 "Why haven't you **b** me a beautiful cedar
18: 18 Absalom had **b** a monument to himself in the
20: 15 and **b** a ramp against the city wall and began
24: 25 David **b** an altar there to the LORD and offered

1Ki 3:2 the name of the LORD had not yet been **b**.
6:2 The Temple that King Solomon **b** for the LORD
6:5 A complex of rooms was **b** against the outer walls
6:6 by beams resting on ledges **b** out from the wall.
6:7 so the entire structure was **b** without the sound of
6:36 The walls of the inner courtyard were **b** so that
7:1 Solomon also **b** a palace for himself, and it took
7:6 He also **b** the Hall of Pillars, which was 75 feet
7:8 behind this hall; they were **b** the same way.
7:8 He also **b** similar living quarters for Pharaoh's
7:9 All these buildings were **b** entirely from huge,
7:12 The walls of the great courtyard were **b** so that
8:13 But I have **b** a glorious Temple for you, where you
8:16 where a temple should be **b** to honor my name.
8:20 I have **b** this Temple to honor the name of the
8:27 contain you. How much less this Temple I have **b**!
8:43 will know that this Temple I have **b** bears your
8:44 and toward this Temple that I have **b** for your
8:48 and toward this Temple I have **b** to honor your
9:3 I have set apart this Temple you have **b** so that my
9:10 which Solomon **b** the Temple of the LORD
9:17 He also **b** up the towns of Lower Beth-horon,
9:19 He **b** towns as supply centers and constructed
9:19 He **b** to his heart's content in Jerusalem
9:24 from the City of David to the new palace he had **b**
9:25 offerings to the LORD on the altar he had **b**.
9:26 Later King Solomon **b** a fleet of ships at
10:4 and when she saw the palace he had **b**,
10:26 Solomon **b** up a huge force of chariots and horses.
11:7 east of Jerusalem, he even **b** a shrine for Chemosh,
11:8 Solomon **b** such shrines for all his foreign wives to
12:25 then **b** up the city of Shechem in the hill country of
12:25 Later he went and **b** up the town of Peniel.
12:31 Jeroboam **b** shrines at the pagan high places
14:23 They **b** pagan shrines and set up sacred pillars
15:23 and the names of the cities he **b** are recorded in
16:24 He **b** a city on it and called the city Samaria in
16:32 First he **b** a temple and an altar for Baal in
22:39 and the cities he **b** are recorded in *The Book of*
22:48 Jehoshaphat also **b** a fleet of trading ships to sail to
2Ki 16:11 Uriah **b** an altar just like it by following the king's
17:9 They **b** pagan shrines for themselves in all their
17:29 at the pagan shrines that the people of Israel had **b**.
20:20 the extent of his power and how he **b** a pool
21:4 He even **b** pagan altars in the Temple of the
21:5 He **b** these altars for all the forces of heaven in
23:12 **b** on the palace roof above the upper room of
23:12 The king destroyed the altars that Manasseh had **b**
23:13 where King Solomon of Israel had **b** shrines for
23:19 They had been **b** by the various kings of Israel
25:1 the city and **b** siege ramps against its walls.
1Ch 6:10 the high priest at the Temple **b** by Solomon in
6:32 **b** the Temple of the LORD in Jerusalem.
7:24 She **b** the towns of Lower and Upper Beth-horon
8:12 Shemed (who **b** Ono and Lod and their villages),
15:1 David now **b** several buildings for himself in the
17:6 "Why haven't you **b** me a beautiful cedar
21:26 David **b** an altar there to the LORD and sacrificed
22:19 and the holy vessels of God into the Temple **b** to
2Ch 1:14 Solomon **b** up a huge military force,
3:1 The Temple was **b** on the threshing floor of
4:8 He also **b** ten tables and placed them in the
4:9 Solomon also **b** a courtyard for the priests
6:2 But I have **b** a glorious Temple for you, where you
6:5 where a temple should be **b** to honor my name.
6:10 I have **b** this Temple to honor the name of the
6:18 contain you. How much less this Temple I have **b**!
6:33 will know that this Temple I have **b** bears your
6:34 and toward this Temple that I have **b** for your
6:38 and toward this Temple I have **b** to honor your
7:7 because the bronze altar he had **b** could not handle
8:4 and **b** towns in the region of Hamath as supply
8:6 He **b** to his heart's content in Jerusalem
8:11 from the City of David to the new palace he had **b**
8:12 altar he had **b** in front of the foyer of the Temple.
9:3 and when she saw the palace he had **b**,
11:6 He **b** up Bethlehem, Etam, Tekoa,
16:14 and at his funeral the people **b** a huge fire in his
17:12 became more and more powerful and **b** fortresses
20:8 people settled here and **b** this Temple for you.
20:36 Together they **b** a fleet of trading ships at the port
21:11 He had **b** pagan shrines in the hill country of Judah
26:6 Then he **b** new towns in the Ashdod area and in
26:9 Uzziah **b** fortified towers in Jerusalem at the
27:4 He **b** towns in the hill country of Judah
32:29 He **b** many towns and acquired vast flocks
33:4 He even **b** pagan altars in the Temple of the
33:14 around the hill of Ophel, where it was **b** very high.
33:15 He tore down all the altars he had **b** on the hill
33:19 a list of the locations where he **b** pagan shrines
Ezr 5:11 and we are rebuilding the Temple that was **b** here
Ne 3:3 The Fish Gate was **b** by the sons of Hassenaah.
12:29 for the singers had **b** their own villages around
Job 27:18 The houses **b** by the wicked are as fragile as a
Ps 24:2 on the seas / and **b** it on the ocean depths.
78:69 There he **b** his towering sanctuary, / as solid
Pr 9:1 Wisdom has **b** her spacious house with seven
24:3 A house is **b** by wisdom and becomes strong
Ecc 2:6 I **b** reservoirs to collect the water to irrigate my
SS 3:9 "King Solomon has **b** a carriage for himself from
Isa 5:2 choice vines. / In the middle he **b** a watchtower
5:8 Your homes are **b** on great estates so you can be
14:32 Tell them that the LORD has **b** Jerusalem,
17:8 Asherah poles or burn incense on the altars they **b**.
23:13 They have **b** siege ramps against its walls,
28:15 for we have **b** a strong refuge made of lies
28:17 to check the foundation wall you have **b**.
Jer 7:14 I will now destroy this Temple that was **b** to honor
7:31 They have **b** the pagan shrines of Topheth in the
19:5 They have **b** pagan shrines to Baal, and there they
32:24 "See how the siege ramps have been **b** against the
32:31 "From the time this city was **b** until now, it has
32:35 They have **b** pagan shrines to Baal in the valley of
35:9 We haven't **b** houses or owned vineyards or farms
45:4 I will destroy this nation that I **b**. I will uproot
52:4 the city and **b** siege ramps against its walls.
Eze 13:10 It's as if the people have **b** a flimsy wall, and these
16:24 you **b** a pagan shrine and put altars to idols in
27:5 You were like a great ship **b** of the finest cypress
40:7 There were guard alcoves on each side **b** into the
40:17 and thirty rooms were **b** against the walls,
41:6 These rooms were **b** in three levels, one above the
41:8 I noticed that the Temple was **b** on a terrace,
42:3 The two blocks were **b** three levels high and stood
43:12 The entire top of the hill where the Temple is **b** is
43:18 and the sprinkling of blood when the altar is **b**.
Da 4:30 have **b** this beautiful city as my royal residence
Hos 8:11 "Israel has **b** many altars to take away sin,
8:14 "Israel has **b** great palaces, and Judah has fortified
10:1 the more beautiful the statues and idols they **b**.
Am 7:7 beside a wall that had been **b** using a plumb line.
Zep 1:13 a chance to live in the new homes they have **b**.
Zec 9:3 Tyre has **b** a strong fortress and has piled up
Mt 7:25 it won't collapse, because it is **b** on rock.
21:33 landowner planted a vineyard, **b** a wall around it,
21:33 pressing out the grape juice, and **b** a lookout tower.
Mk 12:1 "A man planted a vineyard, **b** a wall around it,
12:1 pressing out the grape juice, and **b** a lookout tower.
Lk 4:29 him to the edge of the hill on which the city was **b**.
6:48 the house, it stands firm because it is well **b**.
7:5 he loves the Jews and even **b** a synagogue for us."
Ac 7:47 But it was Solomon who actually **b** it.
28:2 so they **b** a fire on the shore to welcome us
1Co 15:1 for your faith is **b** on this wonderful message.
Eph 2:20 **b** on the foundation of the apostles
Heb 8:2 the true place of worship that was **b** by the Lord
11:7 It was by faith that Noah **b** an ark to save his
11:10 eternal foundations, a city designed and **b** by God.
Rev 21:19 The wall of the city was **b** on foundation stones

BUKKI (5)

Nu 34:22 Dan | **B** son of Jogli
1Ch 6:5 Abishua was the father of **B**. / **B** was the father of Uzzi.
6:51 **B**, Uzzi, Zerahiah,
Ezr 7:4 son of Zerahiah, son of Uzzi, son of **B**,

BUKKIAH (2)

1Ch 25:4 Heman's sons were **B**, Mattaniah, Uzziel, Shubael,
25:13 The sixth lot fell to **B** and twelve of his sons

BULGING (1)

Isa 30:13 It will be like a **b** wall that bursts and falls. In an

BULL (101) [BULL'S, BULLS]

Ex 21:28 "If a **b** gores a man or woman to death, the **b** must be stoned,
21:29 that the owner knew the **b** had gored people in the past, yet the **b** was not kept under control. If this is true and if the **b** kills someone,
21:30 owner of the **b** to compensate for the loss of life.
21:31 "The same principle applies if the **b** gores a boy
21:32 But if the **b** gores a slave, either male or female,
21:32 silver coins in payment, and the **b** must be stoned.
21:35 "If someone's **b** injures a neighbor's **b** and the injured **b** dies, then the two owners must sell the live **b** and divide
21:35 Each will also own half of the dead **b**.
21:36 But if the **b** was known from past experience to
21:36 The owner of the living **b** must pay in full for the dead **b**
29:1 Take a young **b** and two rams with no physical
29:3 along with the young **b** and the two rams.
29:10 "Then bring the young **b** to the entrance of the
29:36 Each day you must sacrifice a young **b** as an
Lev 1:3 bring a **b** with no physical defects to the entrance
3:1 offering from the herd, use either a **b** or a cow.
4:3 he must bring to the LORD a young **b** with no
4:4 He must present the **b** to the LORD at the
4:10 just as is done with the **b** or cow sacrificed as a
4:11 But the rest of the **b**—its hide, meat, head, legs,
4:14 the leaders of the community must bring a young **b**
4:21 then take what is left of the **b** outside the camp
8:2 the **b** for the sin offering, the two rams,
8:14 Then Moses brought in the **b** for the sin offering,
8:17 The rest of the **b**, including its hide, meat,
9:2 "Take a young **b** for a sin offering and a ram for a
9:4 Also tell them to take a **b** and a ram for a peace
9:18 Then Aaron slaughtered the **b** and the ram for the
9:19 Then he took the fat of the **b** and the ram—the fat
16:3 He must first bring a young **b** for a sin offering
16:6 "Aaron will present the **b** as a sin offering,
16:11 "Then Aaron will present the young **b** as a sin
16:11 After he has slaughtered this **b** for the sin offering,
16:14 Then he must dip his finger into the blood of the **b**
16:18 LORD by smearing some of the blood from the **b**
16:27 "The **b** and goat given as sin offerings,
17:3 If any Israelite sacrifices a **b** or a lamb or a goat
22:19 It may be either a **b**, a ram, or a male goat.
22:23 If the **b** or lamb is deformed or stunted, it may still
22:27 "When a **b** or a ram or a male goat is born, it must
23:18 one **b**, and two rams as burnt offerings to the
Nu 7:15 He brought a young **b**, a ram, and a one-year-old
7:21 He brought a young **b**, a ram, and a one-year-old
7:27 He brought a young **b**, a ram, and a one-year-old
7:33 He brought a young **b**, a ram, and a one-year-old
7:39 He brought a young **b**, a ram, and a one-year-old
7:45 He brought a young **b**, a ram, and a one-year-old
7:51 He brought a young **b**, a ram, and a one-year-old
7:57 He brought a young **b**, a ram, and a one-year-old
7:63 He brought a young **b**, a ram, and a one-year-old
7:69 He brought a young **b**, a ram, and a one-year-old
7:75 He brought a young **b**, a ram, and a one-year-old
7:81 He brought a young **b**, a ram, and a one-year-old
8:8 Have them bring a young **b** and a grain offering of
8:8 along with a second young **b** for a sin offering.
15:8 "When you present a young **b** as a burnt offering
15:11 for what is to accompany each sacrificial **b**,
15:24 the whole community must present a young **b** for a
23:2 and the two of them sacrificed a young **b** and a ram
23:4 and have sacrificed a young **b** and a ram on each
23:14 and offered a young **b** and a ram on each altar.
23:30 and offered a young **b** and a ram on each altar.
28:12 five quarts with each **b**, three quarts with the ram,
28:14 two quarts of wine with each **b**, two and a half
28:20 five quarts with each **b**, three quarts with the ram,
28:28 five quarts with each **b**, three quarts with the ram,
29:2 It will consist of one young **b**, one ram, and seven
29:3 five quarts with the **b**, three quarts with the ram,
29:8 It will consist of one young **b**, one ram, and seven
29:9 five quarts of choice flour with the **b**, three quarts
29:36 It will consist of one young **b**, one ram, and seven
Dt 33:17 Joseph has the strength and majesty of a young **b**;
Jdg 6:25 "Take the second best **b** from your father's herd,
6:26 Sacrifice the **b** as a burnt offering on the altar,
1Sa 1:24 They brought along a three-year-old **b** for the
1:25 After sacrificing the **b**, they took the child to Eli.
1Ki 18:23 I will prepare the other **b** and lay it on the wood on
18:33 He piled wood on the altar, cut the **b** into pieces,
18:38 down from heaven and burned up the young **b**,
2Ch 13:9 Whoever comes to be dedicated with a young **b**
Ps 29:6 a calf / and Mount Hermon to leap like a young **b**
69:31 an ox / or presenting a **b** with its horns and hooves.
92:10 But you have made me as strong as a wild **b**.
Eze 43:19 are to be given a young **b** for a sin offering,
43:21 Then take the young **b** for the sin offering and burn
43:22 the altar again, just as you did with the young **b**.
43:23 offer another young **b** that has no defects and a
43:25 "Every day for seven days a male goat, a young **b**,
45:18 sacrifice a young **b** with no physical defects to
45:22 will provide a young **b** as a sin offering for himself
45:24 and a gallon of olive oil with each young **b**
46:6 he will bring one young **b**, six lambs, and one ram,
46:7 With the young **b** he must bring a half bushel of
46:11 will be a half bushel of flour with each young **b**,

BULL'S (5) [BULL]

Lev 4:4 lay his hand on the **b** head, and slaughter it there in
4:7 The rest of the **b** blood must be poured out at the
4:8 The priest must remove all the fat around the **b**
4:15 leaders must then lay their hands on the **b** head
16:15 front of the Ark, just as he did with the **b** blood.

BULLOCK [KJV] See also BULL, CALF, OX

BULLS (58) [BULL]

Ge 32:15 forty cows, ten **b**, twenty female donkeys, and ten
Ex 24:5 young men to sacrifice young **b** as burnt offerings
Nu 7:87 Twelve **b**, twelve rams, and twelve one-year-old
7:88 Twenty-four young **b**, sixty rams, sixty male goats,
8:12 will lay their hands on the heads of the young **b**
23:1 and prepare seven young **b** and seven rams for a
23:29 me seven altars and prepare me seven young **b**
28:11 extra burnt offering to the LORD of two young **b**,
28:19 as a burnt offering to the LORD two young **b**,
28:27 It will consist of two young **b**, one ram, and seven
29:13 It will consist of thirteen young **b**, two rams,
29:14 five quarts for each of the thirteen **b**, three quarts
29:17 sacrifice twelve young **b**, two rams, and fourteen
29:18 Each of these offerings of **b**, rams, and lambs must
29:20 of the festival, sacrifice eleven young **b**, two rams,
29:21 Each of these offerings of **b**, rams, and lambs must
29:23 day of the festival, sacrifice ten young **b**, two rams,
29:24 Each of these offerings of **b**, rams, and lambs must
29:26 of the festival, sacrifice nine young **b**, two rams,
29:27 Each of these offerings of **b**, rams, and lambs must
29:29 of the festival, sacrifice eight young **b**, two rams,
29:30 Each of these offerings of **b**, rams, and lambs must
29:32 of the festival, sacrifice seven young **b**, two rams,
29:33 Each of these offerings of **b**, rams, and lambs must
1Ki 18:23 Now bring two **b**. The prophets of Baal may
18:25 Choose one of the **b** and prepare it and call on the
18:26 So they prepared one of the **b** and placed it on the
1Ch 15:26 they sacrificed seven **b** and seven lambs.
29:21 The next day they brought a thousand **b**,
2Ch 29:21 They brought seven **b**, seven rams, seven lambs,
29:22 So they killed the **b**, and the priests took the blood
29:32 The people brought to the LORD seventy **b**,
29:33 They also brought six hundred **b** and three
30:24 King Hezekiah gave the people one thousand **b**
30:24 and the officials donated one thousand **b** and ten
35:7 people's Passover offerings, and three thousand **b**.
35:8 and three hundred **b** as Passover offerings.
35:9 and five hundred **b** to the Levites for their Passover
35:12 the Book of Moses. They did the same with the **b**.
Ezr 6:9 whatever is needed in the way of young **b**,
6:17 one hundred young **b**, two hundred rams, and four
7:17 are to be used specifically for the purchase of **b**,

Job 21:10 Their **b** never fail to breed. Their cows bear calves
42: 8 Now take seven young **b** and seven rams and go to
Ps 22:12 My enemies surround me like a herd of **b**; / fierce **b** of Bashan have hemmed me in!
50: 9 But I want no more **b** from your barns; / I want no
50:13 I don't need the **b** you sacrifice; / I don't need the
51:19 and **b** will again be sacrificed on your altar.
66:15 And I will sacrifice **b** and goats. / *Interlude*
68:30 the reeds, / this herd of **b** among the weaker calves.
Isa 1:11 want to see the blood from your offerings of **b**
Jer 52:20 and the Sea with the twelve **b** beneath it was too
Eze 39:18 lambs, goats, and fat young **b** of Bashan!
45:23 This daily offering will consist of seven young **b**
Hos 12:11 And in Gilgal, too, they sacrifice **b**; their altars are
Heb 9:13 the blood of goats and **b** and the ashes of a young
10: 4 For it is not possible for the blood of **b** and goats to

BULRUSHES (1)
Job 8:11 no marsh? Can **b** flourish where there is no water?

BULWARKS [KJV] See FORTIFIED, SURROUNDED

BUMP (1)
Na 3: 2 and chariots clatter as they **b** wildly through the

BUMPER (5)
Ge 41:47 for the next seven years there were **b** crops
Lev 25:19 Then the land will yield **b** crops, and you will eat
25:21 so the land will produce a **b** crop, enough to
Ps 107:37 plant their vineyards, / and harvest their **b** crops.
Eze 34:27 and fields of my people will yield **b** crops,

BUNAH (1)
1Ch 2:25 were Ram (the oldest), **B**, Oren, Ozem, and Ahijah.

BUNCH (3) [BUNCHES]
Ex 32:22 know these people and what a wicked **b** they are.
Lev 19:10 do not strip every last **b** of grapes from the vines,
Ne 4: 2 army officers, "What does this **b** of poor,

BUNCHES (1) [BUNCH]
2Sa 16: 1 one hundred **b** of summer fruit, and a skin of wine.

BUNDLE (4) [BUNDLED, BUNDLES]
Ge 37: 7 My **b** stood up, and then your bundles all gathered
Lev 23:15 the day the **b** of grain was lifted up as an offering,
Nu 4:10 and the **b** must be placed on a carrying frame.
Dt 24:19 and forget to bring in a **b** of grain from your field,

BUNDLED (1) [BUNDLE]
Jdg 15: 5 the grain still in piles and all that had been **b**.

BUNDLES (6) [BUNDLE]
Ge 37: 7 "We were out in the field tying up **b** of grain.
37: 7 and then your **b** all gathered around and bowed
Ru 2:16 And pull out some heads of barley from the **b**
Ne 13:15 They were also bringing in **b** of grain and loading
Jer 9:22 fields like dung, or like **b** of grain after the harvest.
Mic 4:12 and trampled like **b** of grain on a threshing floor.

BUNNI (3)
Ne 9: 4 Bani, Kadmiel, Shebaniah, **B**, Sherebiah, Bani,
10:15 **B**, Azgad, Bebai,
11:15 son of Azrikam, son of Hashabiah, son of **B**;

BURDEN (32) [BURDENED, BURDENING, BURDENS]
Ge 49:14 "Issachar is a strong beast of **b**, / resting among
Ex 2:23 But the Israelites still groaned beneath their **b** of
6: 9 discouraged by the increasing **b** of their slavery.
18:18 This job is too heavy a **b** for you to handle all by
Nu 11:11 What did I do to deserve the **b** of a people like
11:17 They will bear the **b** of the people along with you,
Dt 1: 9 'You are too great a **b** for me to carry all by
1Sa 25:31 conscience the staggering **b** of needless bloodshed
2Sa 13:25 all came, we would be too much of a **b** on you."
15:33 told him, "If you go with me, you will only be a **b**.
19:35 they play. I would only be a **b** to my lord the king.
Job 7:20 have you made me your target? Am I a **b** to you?
Ps 38: 4 guilt overwhelms me—/ it is a **b** too heavy to bear.
66:11 in your net / and laid the **b** of slavery on our backs.
81: 6 "Now I will relieve your shoulder of its **b**;
Isa 1: 4 They are loaded down with a **b** of guilt. They are
26:16 We were bowed beneath the **b** of your discipline.
Jer 23:33 You must reply, 'You are the **b**! The LORD says
28: 9 So a prophet who predicts peace must carry the **b**
Hos 8:10 Then they will writhe under the **b** of the great
Zec 12: 3 make Jerusalem a heavy stone, a **b** for the world.
Mt 11:30 yoke fits perfectly, and the **b** I give you is light."
23: 4 and never lift a finger to help ease the **b**.
Lk 11:46 and you never lift a finger to help ease the **b**.
12:50 and I am under a heavy **b** until it is accomplished.
Ac 15:28 and to us to lay no greater **b** on you than these
2Co 11:28 I have the daily **b** of how the churches are getting
12:13 do in the other churches, was to become a **b** to you.
12:14 you for the third time, and I will not be a **b** to you.
12:16 Some of you admit I was not a **b** to you. But they
1Th 2: 9 so that our expenses would not be a **b** to anyone
2Th 3: 8 so that we would not be a **b** to any of you.

BURDENED (7) [BURDEN]
Jdg 2:18 who were **b** by oppression and suffering.
Isa 43:23 though I have not **b** and wearied you with my
43:24 you have **b** me with your sins and wearied me with
47: 3 You will be naked and **b** with shame. I will take
Jer 23:33 'What prophecy has the LORD **b** you with now?'
Hos 9: 7 for the nation is **b** with sin and shows only hatred
2Ti 3: 6 vulnerable women who are **b** with the guilt of sin

BURDENING (1) [BURDEN]
Ac 15:10 Why are you now questioning God's way by **b** the

BURDENS (8) [BURDEN]
Ex 1:11 hoping to wear them down under heavy **b**.
1Ki 12: 9 want me to lighten the **b** imposed by my father?"
2Ch 10: 9 want me to lighten the **b** imposed by my father?"
Ne 5:15 governors who had laid heavy **b** on the people,
Ps 55:22 Give your **b** to the LORD, / and he will take care
146: 8 The LORD lifts the **b** of those bent beneath their
Isa 47: 6 You have forced even the elderly to carry heavy **b**.
Mt 11:28 all of you who are weary and carry heavy **b**,

BUREAUCRACY (1)
Ecc 5: 8 matters of justice only get lost in red tape and **b**.

BURGLAR (2)
Mt 24:43 A homeowner who knew exactly when a **b** was
Lk 12:39 A homeowner who knew exactly when a **b** was

BURIAL (22) [BURY]
Ge 23: 4 Please let me have a piece of land for a **b** plot."
23: 9 so I may have a permanent **b** place for my
23:20 to Abraham by the Hittites as a permanent **b** place.
49:30 from Ephron the Hittite for a permanent **b** place.
50: 5 of Canaan, and bury me in our family's **b** cave.'
50: 5 After his **b** is complete, I will return without
50:13 **b** place in the field of Ephron the Hittite,
2Sa 2: 5 so loyal to your king and giving him a decent **b**.
1Ki 14:13 member of your family who will have a proper **b**,
2Ch 22: 9 Ahaziah was given a decent **b** because the people
26:23 he was buried nearby in a **b** field belonging to the
Ps 141: 7 of the wicked will be scattered without a decent **b**.
Ecc 6: 3 in life and in the end does not even get a decent **b**,
Isa 14:20 You will not be given a proper **b**, for you have
Eze 39:11 who travel there will be blocked by this **b** ground,
39:15 be set up beside them so the **b** crews will see them
Mt 26:12 this perfume on me to prepare my body for **b**.
Mk 14: 8 and has anointed my body for **b** ahead of time.
16: 1 and purchased **b** spices to put on Jesus' body.
Jn 12: 7 her alone. She did it in preparation for my **b**.
19:40 cloth with the spices, as is the Jewish custom of **b**.
Ac 9:37 Her friends prepared her for **b** and laid her in an

BURIED (125) [BURY]
Ge 23:19 So Abraham **b** Sarah there in Canaan, in the cave
25: 9 and Ishmael **b** him in the cave of Machpelah,
25:10 from the Hittites, where he had **b** his wife Sarah.
35: 4 and he **b** them beneath the tree near Shechem.
35: 8 She was **b** beneath the oak tree in the valley below
35:19 and was **b** on the way to Ephrath (that is,
35:29 in death. Then his sons, Esau and Jacob, **b** him.
48: 7 So with great sorrow I **b** her there beside the road
49:31 Abraham and his wife Sarah are **b**. There Isaac and his wife, Rebekah, are **b**. And there I **b** Leah.
50:13 of Canaan and **b** it there in the cave of Machpelah.
Ex 2:12 Moses killed the Egyptian and **b** him in the sand.
Nu 11:34 because they **b** the people there who had craved
20: 1 While they were there, Miriam died and was **b**.
Dt 10: 6 traveled to Moserah, where Aaron died and was **b**.
34: 6 He was **b** in a valley near Beth-peor in Moab,
Jos 7:21 my tent, with the silver **b** deeper than the rest."
7:22 Achan had said, with the silver **b** beneath the rest.
24:30 They **b** him in the land he had inherited,
24:32 them when they left Egypt, were **b** at Shechem,
24:33 He was **b** in the hill country of Ephraim,
Jdg 2: 9 They **b** him in the land he had inherited,
8:32 and he was **b** in the grave of his father, Joash,
10: 2 When he died, he was **b** in Shamir.
10: 5 When Jair died, he was **b** in Kamon.
12: 7 he died, he was **b** in one of the towns of Gilead.
12:10 When he died, he was **b** at Bethlehem.
12:12 When he died, he was **b** at Aijalon in Zebulun.
12:15 Then he died and was **b** at Pirathon in Ephraim,
16:31 back home and **b** him between Zorah and Eshtaol, where his father, Manoah, was **b**.
Ru 1:17 I will die where you die and will be **b** there.
1Sa 25: 1 his funeral. They **b** him near his home at Ramah.
28: 3 He was **b** in Ramah, his hometown. And Saul had
31:13 and **b** them beneath the tamarisk tree at Jabesh,
2Sa 2: 4 heard that the men of Jabesh-gilead had **b** Saul,
2:32 to Bethlehem and **b** him there beside his father.
3:32 They **b** Abner in Hebron, and the king and all the
4:12 and **b** it in Abner's tomb in Hebron.
17:23 He died there and was **b** beside his father.
19:37 my own town, where my father and mother are **b**.
21:14 He **b** them all in the tomb of Kish, Saul's father,
1Ki 2:10 Then David died and was **b** in the City of David.
2:34 and Joab was **b** at his home in the wilderness.
11:43 he was **b** in the city of his father, David.
13:22 your body will not be **b** in the grave of your
13:31 bury me in the grave where the man of God is **b**.
14:18 When the people of Israel **b** him, they mourned for
14:31 he was **b** among his ancestors in the City of David.
15: 8 When Abijam died, he was **b** in the City of David.
15:24 he was **b** with his ancestors in the City of David.
16: 6 When Baasha died, he was **b** in Tirzah. Then his
16:28 When Omri died, he was **b** in Samaria. Then his
22:37 and his body was taken to Samaria and **b** there.
22:40 When Ahab died, he was **b** among his ancestors.
22:50 he was **b** with his ancestors in the City of David.
2Ki 8:24 he was **b** with his ancestors in the City of David.
9:28 where they **b** him with his ancestors in the City of
10:35 Jehu died, he was **b** with his ancestors in Samaria.
12:21 Joash was **b** with his ancestors in the City of
13: 9 he was **b** in Samaria with his ancestors.
13:13 he was **b** with his ancestors in Samaria.
13:20 Then Elisha died and was **b**. Groups of Moabite
14:16 he was **b** with his ancestors in Samaria.
14:20 and he was **b** with his ancestors in the City of
14:29 he was **b** with his ancestors, the kings of Israel.
15: 7 he was **b** near his ancestors in the City of David.
15:38 he was **b** with his ancestors in the City of David.
16:20 he was **b** with his ancestors in the City of David.
21:18 he was **b** in the palace garden, the garden of Uzza.
21:26 He was **b** in his tomb in the garden of Uzza.
22:20 city until after you have died and been **b** in peace.
23:30 Megiddo to Jerusalem and **b** him in his own tomb.
1Ch 10:12 Then they **b** their remains beneath the oak tree at
2Ch 9:31 he died, he was **b** in the city of his father, David.
12:16 Rehoboam died, he was **b** in the City of David.
14: 1 When Abijah died, he was **b** in the City of David.
16:14 He was **b** in the tomb he had carved out for himself
21: 1 he was **b** with his ancestors in the City of David.
21:20 He was **b** in the City of David, but not in the royal
24:16 He was **b** among the kings in the City of David,
24:25 Then he was **b** in the City of David, but not in the
25:28 and he was **b** with his ancestors in the City of
26:23 he was **b** nearby in a burial field belonging to the
27: 9 When he died, he was **b** in the City of David,
28:27 he was **b** in Jerusalem but not in the royal
32:33 he was **b** in the upper area of the royal cemetery,
33:20 When Manasseh died, he was **b** at his palace.
34:28 until after you have died and been **b** in peace.
35:24 He was **b** there in the royal cemetery. And all
Ne 2: 3 For the city where my ancestors are **b** is in ruins,
2: 5 to rebuild the city where my ancestors are **b**."
Job 3:16 Why was I not **b** like a stillborn child, like a baby
21:26 Both alike are **b** in the same dust, both eaten by the
Ps 106:17 and **b** Abiram and the other rebels.
Ecc 8:10 I have seen wicked people **b** with honor.
Isa 14:11 and power are gone; they were **b** with you.
29: 4 like a ghost from the earth where you will lie **b**.
53: 9 But he was **b** like a criminal; he was put in a rich
Jer 8: 2 Their bones will not be gathered up again or **b**
17:13 They will be **b** in a dry and dusty grave, for they
20: 6 There you will die and be **b**, you and all your
22:19 He will be **b** like a dead donkey—dragged out of
26:23 a sword and had him **b** in an unmarked grave.)
La 3: 6 He has **b** me in a dark place, like a person long
Eze 26:20 Your city will lie in ruins, **b** beneath the earth,
32:24 "Elam lies there **b** with its hordes who descended
32:27 They are not **b** in honor like the fallen heroes of
39:15 and take them to be **b** in the Valley of Gog's
Da 12: 2 of those whose bodies lie dead and **b** will rise up,
Jnh 2: 3 I was **b** beneath your wild and stormy waves.
Mt 14:12 John's disciples came for his body and **b** it.
Mk 6:29 they came for his body and **b** it in a tomb.
Lk 16:22 with Abraham. The rich man also died and was **b**,
Ac 2:29 for he died and was **b**, and his tomb is still here
5: 6 him in a sheet and took him out and **b** him.
5: 9 Just outside that door are the young men who **b**
5:10 they carried her out and **b** her beside her husband.
7:16 and **b** in the tomb Abraham had bought from the
8: 2 people came and **b** Stephen with loud weeping.)
13:36 of God, he died and was **b**, and his body decayed.
Ro 6: 4 For we died and were **b** with Christ by baptism.
1Co 15: 4 He was **b**, and he was raised from the dead on the
Col 2:12 For you were **b** with Christ when you were

BURN (125) [BURNED, BURNED-OUT, BURNER, BURNERS, BURNING, BURNS, BURNT, HALF-BURNED]
Ge 38:24 "Bring her out and **b** her!" Judah shouted.
Ex 3: 2 the bush was engulfed in flames, but it didn't **b** up.
21:25 **b** for **b**, wound for wound, bruise for bruise.
29:13 two kidneys with their fat, and **b** them on the altar.
29:14 outside the camp, and **b** it as a sin offering.
29:18 and **b** them all on the altar. This is a burnt offering
29:25 and **b** it on the altar as a burnt offering that will be
30: 7 the lamps, he must **b** fragrant incense on the altar.
30: 8 he must again **b** incense in the LORD's presence.
30:20 and before they approach the altar to **b** offerings to
Lev 1: 9 Then the priests will **b** the entire sacrifice on the
1:13 Then the priests will **b** the entire sacrifice on the
1:15 twist off its head, and **b** the head on the altar.
1:17 Then he will **b** it on top of the wood fire on the
2: 2 and **b** this token portion on the altar fire.
2: 9 and **b** it on the altar as an offering made by fire,
2:16 and **b** it as an offering given to the LORD by fire.
3: 5 The sons of Aaron will **b** these on the altar on top
3:11 The priest will **b** them on the altar as food,
3:16 The priest will **b** them on the altar as food,
4:10 Then he must **b** them on the altar of burnt
4:12 He will **b** it all on a wood fire in the ash heap.
4:19 remove all the animal's fat and **b** it on the altar,
4:21 is left of the bull outside the camp and **b** it there,
4:26 He must **b** all the goat's fat on the altar, just as is
4:31 Then the priest will **b** the fat on the altar, and it

4:35 Then the priest will **b** the fat on the altar on top of
5:12 He will **b** this flour on the altar just like any other
6:12 then **b** the fat of the peace offerings on top of this
6:15 He will **b** this token portion on the altar, and it will
7: 5 The priests will **b** these parts on the altar as an
7:31 Then the priest will **b** the fat on the altar,
13:24 "If anyone has suffered a **b** on the skin
13:25 a contagious skin disease has broken out in the **b**.
13:28 and has faded, it is simply a scar from the **b**.
13:52 The priest must **b** the linen or wool clothing
16:25 He must also **b** all the fat of the sin offering on the
17: 6 and **b** the fat on the LORD's altar at the entrance
Nu 5:26 a handful as a token portion and **b** it on the altar.
16: 7 and **b** incense in them tomorrow before the
16:40 should ever enter the LORD's presence to **b**
18:17 and **b** their fat as an offering given by fire,
31:23 that is, metals that do not **b**—must be passed
Dt 7: 4 Then the anger of the LORD will **b** against you,
7: 5 Cut down their Asherah poles and **b** their idols.
7:25 "You must **b** their idols in fire, and do not desire
11:17 If you do, the LORD's anger will **b** against you.
12: 3 **B** their Asherah poles and cut down their carved
13:16 all the plunder in the middle of the street and **b** it.
29:20 His anger and jealousy will **b** against them.
Jos 11: 6 be dead. Cripple their horses and **b** their chariots."
11:13 Joshua did not **b** any of the cities built on mounds
23:16 serving other gods, his anger will **b** against you,
Jdg 2:14 This made the LORD **b** with anger against Israel,
12: 1 We are going to **b** down your house with you in
14:15 or we will **b** down your father's house with you in
1Sa 2:28 to offer sacrifices on my altar, to **b** incense, and to
1Ki 12:33 for Israel, and he went up to the altar to **b** incense.
13: 2 the pagan shrines who come here to **b** incense,
14:10 I will **b** up your royal dynasty as one burns up
2Ki 8:12 You will **b** their fortified cities, kill their young
23:18 So they did not **b** his bones or those of the old
1Ch 14:12 idols there, so David gave orders to **b** them up.
21:26 fire from heaven to **b** up the offering on the altar.
2Ch 2: 4 It will be a place set apart to **b** incense and sweet
2: 6 for him, except as a place to **b** sacrifices to him?
4:20 and their lamps of pure gold to **b** in front of the
26:18 is not for you, Uzziah, to **b** incense to the LORD.
Job 15:30 The flame will **b** them up, and the breath of God
30: 4 and they **b** the roots of shrubs for heat.
30:30 skin has turned dark, and my bones **b** with fever.
Ps 39: 3 and began to **b**, / igniting a fire of words:
79: 5 Forever? / How long will your jealousy **b** like fire?
89:46 How long will your anger **b** like fire?
102: 3 like smoke, / and my bones **b** like red-hot coals.
Pr 31:18 for bargains; her lights **b** late into the night.
Isa 10:17 In a single night he will **b** those thorns and briers,
17: 8 Asherah poles or **b** incense on the altars they built.
27: 4 and thorns bothering her, I will **b** them up.
64: 2 As fire causes wood to **b** and water to boil,
65: 3 They **b** incense on the rooftops of their homes.
66: 3 When they **b** incense, it is as if they had blessed an
Jer 4: 4 or my anger will **b** like an unquenchable fire
5:14 I will give you messages that will **b** them up as if
11:16 But now I have sent the fury of their enemies to **b**
17: 4 my anger into a roaring fire that will **b** forever."
19: 4 The people **b** incense to foreign gods—idols never
19: 5 and there they **b** their sons as sacrifices to Baal.
21:12 or my anger will **b** like an unquenchable fire
21:14 I will light a fire in your forests that will **b** up
23:29 Does not my word **b** like fire?" asks the LORD.
32:29 They will **b** down all these houses,
34: 2 city over to the king of Babylon, and he will **b** it.
34: 5 They will **b** incense in your memory, just as they
34:22 will fight against this city and will capture and **b** it.
36:25 and Gemariah begged the king not to **b** the scroll,
37: 8 and capture this city and **b** it to the ground.
37:10 from their tents and **b** this city to the ground!"
38:18 the Babylonians, and they will **b** it to the ground."
43:13 and he will **b** down the temples of Egypt's
44:17 We will **b** incense to the Queen of Heaven
48:35 the pagan shrines and **b** incense to their false gods.
49:27 that will **b** up the palaces of Ben-hadad."
50:32 of Babylon that will **b** everything around them."
Eze 5: 2 After acting out the siege, **b** it there.
16:41 They will **b** your homes and punish you in front of
23:47 their sons and daughters and **b** their homes.
24:10 many spices. Then empty the pot and **b** the bones.
28:18 I let it **b** you to ashes on the ground in the sight of
43:21 and **b** it at the appointed place outside the Temple
Da 2:46 to offer sacrifices and **b** sweet incense before him.
Hos 4:13 They go up into the hills to **b** incense in the
8:14 down fire on their palaces and **b** their fortresses."
Hab 1:16 worship their nets and **b** incense in front of them.
Zec 12: 6 They will **b** up all the neighboring nations right
Mt 13:30 and **b** them and to put the wheat in the barn.' "
13:42 they will throw them into the furnace and **b** them.
22: 7 his army to destroy the murderers and **b** their city.
Lk 1: 9 the sanctuary and **b** incense in the Lord's presence.
9:54 should we order down fire from heaven to **b** them
1Co 7: 9 and marry. It's better to marry than to **b** with lust.
2Co 11:29 Who is led astray, and I do not **b** with anger?
Heb 6: 8 The farmer will condemn that field and **b** it.
Rev 17:16 eat her flesh, and **b** her remains with fire.

BURNED (162) [BURN]

Ex 12:10 Whatever is not eaten that night must be **b** before
29:34 or bread remains until the morning, it must be **b**.
40:27 On it he **b** the fragrant incense made from sweet
Lev 2:11 or honey may be **b** as an offering to the LORD by
2:12 but these must never be **b** on the altar as an
6:22 regular share, and it must be completely **b** up.
6:23 grain offerings of the priests must be entirely **b** up.
6:30 meat may be eaten. It must be completely **b** up.
7:17 over until the third day must be completely **b** up.
7:19 may not be eaten; it must be completely **b** up.
8:16 and their fat, and he **b** them all on the altar.
8:17 its hide, meat, and dung, was **b** outside the camp,
8:20 Next he cut the ram into pieces and **b** the head,
8:21 Moses **b** the entire ram on the altar as a whole
8:28 and **b** them on the altar on top of the burnt offering
8:32 or bread that is left over must then be **b** up.
9:10 Then he **b** on the altar the fat, the kidneys,
9:11 and the hide, however, he **b** outside the camp.
9:13 including the head, and he **b** each part on the altar.
9:14 and also **b** them on the altar as a whole burnt
9:20 of these animals and then **b** them on the altar.
10: 2 forth from the LORD's presence and **b** them up,
10:16 sin offering, he discovered that it had been **b** up.
13:24 a burn on the skin and the **b** area changes color,
13:55 It must be completely **b** up, whether it is
13:57 and the contaminated object must be **b** up.
16: 1 who died when they **b** a different kind of fire than
16:27 for Israel, will be carried outside the camp to be **b**.
19: 6 leftovers that remain until the third day must be **b**.
20:14 All three of them must be **b** to death to wipe out
21: 9 holiness as well as herself, she must be **b** to death.
24: 7 to be **b** in place of the bread as an offering given to
Nu 3: 4 **b** before the LORD a different kind of fire than
11: 3 because fire from the LORD had **b** among them
16:35 and **b** up the 250 men who were offering incense.
16:47 but Aaron **b** the incense and made atonement for
19: 5 As Eleazar watches, the heifer must be **b**—its hide,
21:28 the city of Sihon. / It **b** the city of Ar in Moab;
26:61 and Abihu died when they **b** before the LORD a
31:10 They **b** all the towns and villages where the
Dt 12:31 They have even **b** their sons and daughters as
29:27 That is why the LORD's anger **b** against this
Jos 6:24 Then the Israelites **b** the city and everything in it.
7:15 set apart for destruction will himself be **b** with fire,
7:25 stoned Achan and his family and **b** their bodies.
11: 9 Joshua crippled the horses and **b** all the chariots,
11:11 person was spared. And then Joshua **b** the city.
13:14 their inheritance came from the offerings **b** on the
Jdg 2:20 So the LORD **b** with anger against Israel.
3: 8 Then the LORD **b** with anger against Israel,
10: 7 So the LORD **b** with anger against Israel, and he
15: 5 He **b** all their grain to the ground,
15: 6 got the woman and her father and **b** them to death.
16: 9 as if they were string that had been **b** in a fire.
18:27 killed all the people and **b** the town to the ground.
20:48 They also **b** down every town they came to.
1Sa 2:15 before the animal's fat had been **b** on the altar.
2:16 as much as you want, but the fat must first be **b**."
30: 1 raid into the Negev and had **b** Ziklag to the ground.
30:14 and the land of Caleb, and we had just **b** Ziklag."
31:12 brought them to Jabesh, where they **b** the bodies.
2Sa 24: 1 Once again the anger of the LORD **b** against
1Ki 3: 3 offered sacrifices and **b** incense at the local altars.
9:25 He also **b** incense to the LORD. And so he
13: 2 burn incense, and human bones will be **b** on you."
15:13 cut down the pole and **b** it in the Kidron Valley.
16:18 and **b** it down over himself and died in the flames.
18:38 down from heaven and **b** up the young bull,
22:43 people still offered sacrifices and **b** incense there.
2Ki 12: 3 people still offered sacrifices and **b** incense there.
14: 4 where the people offered sacrifices and **b** incense.
15: 4 where the people offered sacrifices and **b** incense.
15:35 where the people offered sacrifices and **b** incense.
16: 4 and **b** incense at the pagan shrines and on the hills
17:11 They **b** incense at the shrines, just like the nations
17:31 And the people from Sepharvaim even **b** their own
19:18 the gods of these nations into the fire and **b** them.
23: 4 The king had all these things **b** outside Jerusalem
23: 5 for they had **b** incense at the pagan shrines
23: 6 Jerusalem to the Kidron Valley, where he **b** it.
23: 8 where they had **b** incense, from Geba to
23:11 The king also **b** the chariots dedicated to the sun.
23:15 crushed the stones to dust and **b** the Asherah pole.
23:16 and he **b** them on the altar at Bethel to desecrate it.
23:20 and he **b** human bones on the altars to desecrate
23:26 the LORD's anger **b** against Judah because of all
25: 9 He **b** down the Temple of the LORD, the royal
2Ch 7: 1 and **b** up the burnt offerings and sacrifices,
15:16 the pole, broke it up, and **b** it in the Kidron Valley.
24:18 Then the anger of God **b** against Judah
28: 4 and **b** incense at the pagan shrines and on the hills
34: 5 Then he **b** the bones of the pagan priests on their
36:19 down the walls of Jerusalem, **b** all the palaces,
Ne 1: 3 has been torn down, and the gates have been **b**."
2: 3 is in ruins, and the gates have been **b** down."
2:13 Dung Gate to inspect the broken walls and **b** gates.
2:17 It lies in ruins, and its gates are **b**. Let us rebuild
10:34 to be **b** on the altar of the LORD our God,
Est 1:12 This made the king furious, and he **b** with anger.
Job 1:16 and **b** up your sheep and all the shepherds.
Ps 74: 8 So they **b** down all the places where God was
78:21 The fire of his wrath **b** against Jacob. / Yes,
80:16 For we are chopped up and **b** by our enemies.
106:40 That is why the LORD's anger **b** against his
120: 4 with sharp arrows / and **b** with glowing coals.
Pr 6:27 Can a man scoop fire into his lap and not be **b**?
SS 1: 6 my complexion is so dark. The sun has **b** my skin.
Isa 1: 7 Your country lies in ruins, and your cities are **b**.
6:13 a remnant—survive, it will be invaded again and **b**.
9: 5 bloodstained by war. All such equipment will be **b**.
33:12 Your people will be **b** up completely, like thorns
37:19 the gods of these nations into the fire and **b** them.
42:25 They were set on fire and **b**, but they still refused
43: 2 the fire of oppression, you will not be **b** up;
44:19 I **b** half of it for heat and used it to bake my bread
64:11 where our ancestors praised you has been **b** down,
65: 7 "For they also **b** incense on the mountains
Jer 19:13 all the houses where you **b** incense on the rooftops
29:22 and Ahab, whom the king of Babylon **b** alive!'
36:23 section by section, until the whole scroll was **b** up.
36:27 After the king had **b** Jeremiah's scroll, the LORD
36:28 just as you did on the scroll King Jehoiakim **b**.
36:29 You **b** the scroll because it said the king of
36:32 been on the scroll King Jehoiakim had **b** in the fire.
38:17 your family will live, and the city will not be **b**.
38:23 by the king of Babylon, and this city will be **b**."
39: 8 Meanwhile, the Babylonians **b** Jerusalem,
44: 3 They **b** incense and worshiped other gods—
44:15 and all the men who knew that their wives had **b**
44:23 because you have **b** incense to idols and sinned
49: 2 and the neighboring towns will be **b**.
51:30 The invaders have **b** the houses and broken down
51:58 leveled to the ground, and her high gates will be **b**.
52:13 He **b** down the Temple of the LORD, the royal
La 4:11 He started a fire in Jerusalem that **b** the city to its
Eze 15: 6 they are useless, I have set them aside to be **b**!
20:31 and give your little children to be **b** as sacrifices,
20:47 set you on fire, O forest, and every tree will be **b**—
23:25 as captives, and everything that is left will be **b**.
30:14 and they will lie in ruins, **b** up by my anger.
Hos 2:13 when she **b** incense to her images of Baal, put on
Joel 1:19 has consumed the pastures and **b** up all the trees.
Am 2: 1 the tomb of Edom's king and **b** his bones to ashes.
7: 4 The fire had **b** up the depths of the sea and was
Mic 1: 7 to pieces. All her sacred treasures will be **b** up.
Na 1:10 like drunks, will be **b** like dry straw in a field.
3:13 be opened wide to the enemy and set on fire and **b**.
Zec 9: 4 Tyre will be set on fire and **b** to the ground.
Mal 3: 3 of silver, watching closely as the dross is **b** away.
4: 1 and the wicked will be **b** up like straw on that day.
Mt 13:40 "Just as the weeds are separated out and **b**, so it
Lk 1:10 While the incense was being **b**, a great crowd
Jn 15: 6 Such branches are gathered into a pile to be **b**.
Ac 19:19 incantation books and **b** them at a public bonfire.
Ro 1:27 with women, **b** with lust for each other.
1Co 3:15 But if the work is **b** up, the builder will suffer great
Heb 10: 6 you were not pleased with animals **b** on the altar
10: 8 or grain offerings or animals **b** on the altar or other
13:11 but the bodies of the animals were **b** outside the
Rev 8: 7 One-third of the trees were **b**, and all the grass
was **b**.
16: 9 Everyone was **b** by this blast of heat, and they

BURNED-OUT (1) [BURN]

Isa 7: 4 need to fear the fierce anger of those two **b** embers,

BURNER (9) [BURN]

Lev 16:12 he will fill an incense **b** with burning coals from
16:12 he will carry the **b** and incense behind the inner
Nu 16:17 followers brings an incense **b** with incense on it,
16:17 the LORD. Aaron will also bring his incense **b**."
16:46 take an incense **b** and place burning coals on it
2Ch 26:19 and refused to set down the incense **b** he was
Eze 8:11 Each of them held an incense **b**, so there was a
Rev 8: 3 Then another angel with a gold incense **b** came
8: 5 Then the angel filled the incense **b** with fire from

BURNERS (8) [BURN]

Lev 10: 1 and Abihu put coals of fire in their incense **b**
Nu 16: 6 all your followers must do this: Take incense **b**,
16:18 So these men came with their incense **b**,
16:37 the priest to pull all the incense **b** from the fire,
16:38 from the **b** of these men who have sinned at the
16:38 then hammer the metal of the incense **b** into a
16:38 for these **b** have become holy because they were
16:39 **b** that had been used by the men who died in the

BURNING (90) [BURN]

Ge 19:24 and **b** sulfur from the heavens on Sodom
Ex 3: 3 Moses said to himself. "Why isn't that bush **b** up?
3:16 Isaac, and Jacob—appeared to me in a **b** bush.
11: 8 Then, **b** with anger, Moses left Pharaoh's presence.
27:20 for the lampstand, so it can be kept **b** continually.
27:21 and his sons will keep the lamps **b** in the LORD's
30: 1 "Then make a small altar out of acacia wood for **b**
38: 1 The altar for **b** animal sacrifices also was
Lev 6: 9 and the altar fire must be kept **b** all night.
6:12 Meanwhile, the fire on the altar must be kept **b**;
6:13 the fire must be kept **b** on the altar at all times.
6:16 After **b** this handful, the rest of the flour will
9:17 grain offering, **b** a handful of the flour on the altar,
10: 1 they disobeyed the LORD by **b** before him a
16:12 he will fill an incense burner with **b** coals from the
16:13 he will put the incense on the **b** coals so that a
16:28 The man who does the **b** must wash his clothes
24: 2 for the lampstand, so it can be kept **b** continually.
26:16 with wasting diseases, and with **b** fevers,
Nu 11: 3 area was known as Taberah—"the place of **b**"—
16:18 placed **b** coals and incense on them,
16:37 are holy. Also tell him to scatter the **b** incense
16:46 and place **b** coals on it from the altar.
19: 6 and throw them into the fire where the heifer is **b**.
Dt 4:11 the mountain, while the mountain was **b** with fire.
4:20 the **b** furnace of Egypt to become his own people
32:24 them wasting famine, / **b** fever, and deadly disease.
33:16 and the favor of the one who appeared in the **b**
1Ki 9:16 killing the Canaanite population and **b** it down.
11: 8 for all his foreign wives to use for **b** incense

2Ki 18: 4 of Israel had begun to worship it by **b** incense to it.
22:13 The LORD's anger is **b** against us because our
22:17 My anger is **b** against this place, and it will not be
2Ch 26:16 and personally **b** incense on the altar.
29: 7 They stopped **b** incense and presenting burnt
Job 18:15 will disappear beneath a fiery barrage of **b** sulfur.
Ps 11: 6 punishing them with **b** sulfur and scorching winds.
18:12 through the clouds, / raining down hail and **b** coals.
69:24 fury on them; / consume them with your **b** anger.
74: 7 They set the sanctuary on fire, **b** it to the ground.
124: 3 us alive / because of their **b** anger against us.
140:10 Let **b** coals fall down on their heads, / or throw
Pr 25:22 You will heap **b** coals on their heads,
Isa 1:31 The strongest among you will disappear like **b**
5:24 Therefore, they will all disappear like **b** straw.
6: 6 and he picked up a **b** coal with a pair of tongs.
9:18 Its **b** sends up vast clouds of smoke.
13: 8 as the flames of the **b** city reflect on their faces.
30:27 **b** with anger, surrounded by a thick, rising smoke.
30:33 Topheth—the place of **b**—has long been ready for
34: 9 The streams of Edom will be filled with **b** pitch,
34:10 will never end; the smoke of its **b** will rise forever.
47:14 But they are as useless as dried grass **b** in a fire.
62: 1 the dawn, and her salvation blazes like a **b** torch.
Jer 4:11 "A **b** wind is blowing in from the desert.
11:13 of shame—altars for **b** incense to your god Baal—
43:12 **b** all their idols and carrying away the people as
44: 5 They kept right on **b** incense to these gods.
44: 8 Why arouse my anger by **b** incense to the idols you
44:18 But ever since we quit **b** incense to the Queen of
44:21 and all the people were **b** incense to idols in the
51:32 The fortifications are **b**, and the army is in panic.
Eze 1:27 he looked like a **b** flame, shining with splendor.
5: 4 hairs out and throw them into the fire, **b** them up.
8: 2 From the waist down he looked like a **b** flame.
10: 6 and take some **b** coals from between the wheels."
10: 7 and took some live coals from the fire **b** among
23:37 and murder by **b** their children as sacrifices on
38:22 send torrential rain, hailstones, fire, and **b** sulfur!
43:18 These will be the regulations for the **b** of offerings
Hos 11: 2 to the images of Baal and **b** incense to idols.
11: 9 I will not punish you as much as my **b** anger tells
Am 6:10 one who is responsible for **b** the dead—
Na 1: 6 Who can survive his **b** fury? His rage blazes forth
Zec 3: 2 This man is like a **b** stick that has been snatched
12: 6 or like a **b** torch among sheaves of grain.
Mal 4: 1 "The day of judgment is coming, **b** like a furnace.
Mt 3:12 in his barn but **b** the chaff with never-ending fire."
Mk 12:26 the writings of Moses, in the story of the **b** bush?
Lk 3:17 in his barn but **b** the chaff with never-ending fire."
17:29 Then fire and **b** sulfur rained down from heaven
20:37 even Moses proved this when he wrote about the **b**
Jn 21: 9 they saw that a charcoal fire was **b** and fish were
Ac 7:30 an angel appeared to Moses in the flame of a **b**
7:35 Through the angel who appeared to him in the **b**
Rev 4: 5 of the throne were seven lampstands with **b** flames.
8:10 great flaming star fell out of the sky, **b** like a torch.
9:17 and **b** sulfur billowed from their mouths.
9:18 and **b** sulfur that came from the mouths of the
14:10 and **b** sulfur in the presence of the holy angels

BURNISHED (3)

1Ki 7:45 Huram made for Solomon were made of **b** bronze.
2Ch 4:16 Huram-abi made all these things out of **b** bronze
Eze 1: 7 split like calves' feet and shone like **b** bronze.

BURNS (27) [BURN]

Ex 15: 7 flashed forth; / it consumed them as fire **b** straw.
Nu 19: 8 The man who **b** the animal must also wash his
31:23 But everything that **b** must be purified by the water
Dt 32:22 and **b** to the depths of the grave. / It devours the
1Ki 14:10 I will burn up your royal dynasty as one **b** up trash
Job 19:11 His fury **b** against me; he counts me as an enemy.
Ps 38: 7 A raging fever **b** within me, / and my health is
46: 9 snaps the spear in two; / he **b** the shields with fire.
69: 9 Passion for your house **b** within me, / so those who
97: 3 Fire goes forth before him / and **b** up all his foes.
Isa 4: 4 bloodstains by a spirit of judgment that **b** like fire.
5:25 That is why the anger of the LORD **b** against his
9:18 It **b** not only briers and thorns but the forests,
21: 3 My stomach aches and **b** with pain. Sharp pangs of
31: 9 the LORD, whose flame **b** brightly in Jerusalem.
44:16 He **b** part of the tree to roast his meat and to keep
66:24 and the fire that **b** them will never go out.
Jer 20: 9 in his name, his word **b** in my heart like a fire.
La 1:13 "He has sent fire from heaven that **b** in my bones.
Eze 15: 4 be used for fuel, and even as fuel, it **b** too quickly.
Hos 8: 5 this idol you have made. My fury **b** against you.
Joel 2: 3 Fire **b** in front of them and follows them in every
Zec 10: 3 "My anger **b** against your shepherds, and I will
Jn 2:17 "Passion for God's house **b** within me."
Rev 19:20 thrown alive into the lake of fire that **b** with sulfur.
20:10 was thrown into the lake of fire that **b** with sulfur,
21: 8 their doom is in the lake that **b** with fire and sulfur.

BURNT (264) [BURN]

BURNT OFFERING (139) Ge 22:2,3,6,13; Ex 18:12; 29:18,25,42; 30:28; 31:9; 35:16; 40:6,10,29,29; Lev 1:3,9,10, 13,14,17; 3:5; 5:7,10; 6:9,9,10,12,12; 7:8,37; 8:18,21,28; 9:2, 3,7,12,14,16,17,22,24; 10:19; 12:6,8; 14:19,22,31; 15:15,30; 16:3,5,24,24; 17:8; 22:18; 23:12; Nu 6:11,14,16; 7:15,21,27, 33,39,45,51,57,63,69,75,81; 8:12; 15:3,3,5,8,24; 23:15; 28:6, 10,10,11,13,14,15,19,27,31; 29:2,8,11,13,16,19,22,25,28,31, 34,36,38; Dt 13:16; 18:10; Jdg 6:26; 11:31; 13:16,23; 1Sa 6:14; 7:9,10; 13:9,9,10,12; 2Sa 24:22; 2Ki 3:27; 10:25; 16:13, 15,15; 1Ch 6:49; 21:24; 2Ch 29:18,24,27,27; Ezr 8:35; Job 1:5; 42:8; Ps 51:16; Eze 43:24; 45:23,25; 46:2,4,12,13

BURNT OFFERINGS (121) Ex 10:25; 20:24; 24:5; 30:9; 32:6; Lev 4:7,10,18,24,25,29,30,33,34; 6:25; 7:2; 14:13; 20:2; 23:18,18,37; Nu 7:87; 10:10; 23:3,6,17; 28:3,24,31; 29:6,39; Dt 12:6,11,13,14,27; 27:6; 33:10; Jos 8:31; 22:23,27,28,29; Jdg 20:26; 21:4; 1Sa 6:15; 10:8; 15:22; 2Sa 6:17; 24:24,25; 1Ki 3:4,15; 8:64; 9:25; 10:5; 2Ki 5:17; 10:24; 16:15; 1Ch 16:1,40; 21:23,26; 22:1; 23:31; 29:21; 2Ch 1:6; 2:4; 7:1,7,7; 8:12; 9:4; 13:11; 23:18; 24:14,14; 29:7,28,31,32,34,35; 30:15; 31:2,3; 35:12,14,16; Ezr 3:2,3,4,5,6; 6:9; 8:35; Ne 10:33; Ps 20:3; 40:6; 50:8; 51:19; 66:13,15; Isa 1:11; 43:23; 56:7; Jer 6:20; 7:21,22; 14:12; 17:26; 33:18; Eze 40:39,42; 43:27; 44:11; 45:15,17; Hos 6:6; Am 5:22; Mk 12:33

Ge 11: 3 "let's make great piles of **b** brick and collect
22: 2 Sacrifice him there as a **b** offering on one of the
22: 3 Then he chopped wood to build a fire for a **b**
22: 6 Abraham placed the wood for the **b** offering on
22:13 and sacrificed it as a **b** offering on the altar in place
Ex 10:25 and **b** offerings to the LORD our God.
18:12 Then Jethro presented a **b** offering and gave
20:24 your **b** offerings and peace offerings, your sheep
24: 5 young men to sacrifice young bulls as **b** offerings
29:18 This is a **b** offering to the LORD, which is very
29:25 and burn it on the altar as a **b** offering that will be
29:42 "This is to be a daily **b** offering given from
30: 9 or any **b** offerings, grain offerings, or drink
30:28 the altar of **b** offering with all its utensils,
31: 9 the altar of **b** offering with all its utensils;
32: 6 up early the next morning to sacrifice **b** offerings
35:16 the altar of **b** offering; the bronze grating of the
40: 6 Place the altar of **b** offering in front of the
40:10 Sprinkle the anointing oil on the altar of **b** offering
40:29 and he placed the altar of **b** offering near the
40:29 On it he offered a **b** offering and a grain offering,
Lev 1: 3 "If your sacrifice for a whole **b** offering is from
1: 9 It is a whole **b** offering made by fire, very pleasing
1:10 "If your sacrifice for a whole **b** offering is from
1:13 It is a whole **b** offering made by fire, very pleasing
1:14 "If you bring a bird as a **b** offering to the LORD,
1:17 It is a whole **b** offering made by fire, very pleasing
3: 5 the altar on top of the **b** offering on the wood fire.
4: 7 of **b** offerings at the entrance of the Tabernacle.
4:10 Then he must burn them on the altar of **b** offerings,
4:18 then be poured out at the base of the altar of **b**
4:24 at the place where **b** offerings are slaughtered.
4:25 put it on the horns of the altar of **b** offerings,
4:29 and slaughter it at the place where **b** offerings are
4:30 put the blood on the horns of the altar of **b**
4:33 and slaughter it at the place where the **b** offerings
4:34 put it on the horns of the altar of **b** offerings,
5: 7 be a sin offering, and the other will be a **b** offering.
5:10 The priest will offer the second bird as a whole **b**
6: 9 instructions regarding the whole **b** offering.
6: 9 The **b** offering must be left on the altar until the
6:10 the priest on duty must clean out the ashes of the **b**
6:12 and arrange the daily whole **b** offering on it.
6:12 offerings on top of this daily whole **b** offering.
6:25 at the place where the **b** offerings are slaughtered.
7: 2 slaughtered where the **b** offerings are slaughtered,
7: 8 In the case of the whole **b** offering, the hide of the
7:37 These are the instructions for the whole **b** offering,
8:18 the ram to the LORD for the whole **b** offering,
8:21 the entire ram on the altar as a whole **b** offering.
8:28 and burned them on the altar on top of the **b**
9: 2 for a sin offering and a ram for a whole **b** offering,
9: 3 and a year-old lamb for a whole **b** offering,
9: 7 and your whole **b** offering to make atonement for
9:12 Next Aaron slaughtered the animal for the whole **b**
9:14 and also burned them on the altar as a whole **b**
9:16 Then he brought the whole **b** offering
9:17 in addition to the regular morning **b** offering.
9:22 the whole **b** offering, and the peace offering,
9:24 and consumed the **b** offering and the fat on the
10:19 sin offering and their **b** offering to the LORD,"
12: 6 must bring a year-old lamb for a whole **b** offering
12: 8 One will be for the whole **b** offering and the other
14:13 sin offerings and **b** offerings are slaughtered.
14:19 the priest will slaughter the whole **b** offering
14:22 a sin offering and the other for a whole **b** offering.
14:31 a sin offering and the other for a whole **b** offering,
15:15 a sin offering and the other for a whole **b** offering.
15:30 a sin offering and the other for a whole **b** offering.
16: 3 for a sin offering and a ram for a whole **b** offering.
16: 5 for a sin offering and a ram for a whole **b** offering.
16:24 and go out to sacrifice his own whole **b** offering
16:24 and the whole **b** offering for the people.
17: 8 If you offer a whole **b** offering or a sacrifice
20: 2 If any among them devote their children as **b**
22:18 If you offer a whole **b** offering to the LORD,
23:12 defects as a whole **b** offering to the LORD.
23:18 and two rams as **b** offerings to the LORD.
23:18 These whole **b** offerings, together with the
23:37 whole **b** offerings and grain offerings,
Nu 6:11 for a sin offering and the other for a **b** offering.
6:14 a one-year-old male lamb without defect for a **b**
6:16 first the sin offering and the **b** offering;
7:15 and a one-year-old male lamb as a **b** offering;
7:21 and a one-year-old male lamb as a **b** offering;
7:27 and a one-year-old male lamb as a **b** offering;
7:33 and a one-year-old male lamb as a **b** offering;
7:39 and a one-year-old male lamb as a **b** offering;
7:45 and a one-year-old male lamb as a **b** offering;
7:51 and a one-year-old male lamb as a **b** offering;
7:57 and a one-year-old male lamb as a **b** offering;
7:63 and a one-year-old male lamb as a **b** offering;
7:69 and a one-year-old male lamb as a **b** offering;
7:75 and a one-year-old male lamb as a **b** offering;
7:81 and a one-year-old male lamb as a **b** offering;
7:87 male lambs were donated for the **b** offerings,
8:12 be for a sin offering and the other for a **b** offering,
10:10 of each month to rejoice over your **b** offerings
15: 3 and you want to please the LORD with a **b**
15: 3 When it is an ordinary **b** offering, a sacrifice to
15: 5 For each lamb offered as a whole **b** offering,
15: 8 "When you present a young bull as a **b** offering
15:24 must present a young bull for a **b** offering.
19:17 put some of the ashes from the **b** purification
23: 3 said to Balak, "Stand here by your **b** offerings,
23: 6 the king was standing beside his **b** offerings with
23:15 "Stand here by your **b** offering while I go to meet
23:17 of Moab were standing beside Balak's **b** offerings.
28: 3 When you present your daily whole **b** offerings to
28: 6 This is the regular **b** offering ordained at Mount
28:10 This is the whole **b** offering to be presented each
28:10 in addition to the regular daily **b** offering and its
28:11 present an extra **b** offering to the LORD of two
28:13 This **b** offering must be presented by fire, and it
28:14 Present this monthly **b** offering on the first day of
28:15 This is in addition to the regular daily **b** offering
28:19 You must present as a **b** offering to the LORD
28:24 offered in addition to the regular whole **b** offerings
28:27 A special whole **b** offering will be offered that day,
28:31 These special **b** offerings, along with their drink
28:31 are in addition to the regular daily **b** offering
29: 2 On that day you must present a **b** offering,
29: 6 to your regular monthly and daily **b** offerings,
29: 8 You must present a **b** offering, very pleasing to the
29:11 and the regular daily **b** offering with its grain
29:13 That day you must present a special whole **b**
29:16 in addition to the regular daily **b** offering with its
29:19 in addition to the regular daily **b** offering with its
29:22 in addition to the regular daily **b** offering with its
29:25 in addition to the regular daily **b** offering with its
29:28 in addition to the regular daily **b** offering with its
29:31 in addition to the regular daily **b** offering with its
29:34 in addition to the regular daily **b** offering with its
29:36 You must present a **b** offering, very pleasing to the
29:38 in addition to the regular daily **b** offering with its
29:39 **b** offerings, grain offerings, drink offerings,
Dt 12: 6 There you will bring to the LORD your **b**
12:11 your **b** offerings, your sacrifices, your tithes,
12:13 Be careful not to sacrifice your **b** offerings just
12:14 There you must offer your **b** offerings and do
12:27 and blood of your **b** offerings on the altar of the
13:16 Put the entire town to the torch as a **b** offering to
18:10 sacrifice your son or daughter as a **b** offering.
27: 6 On the altar you must offer **b** offerings to the
33:10 and offer whole **b** offerings on the altar.
Jos 8:31 Then on the altar they presented **b** offerings
22:23 Nor will we use it for our **b** offerings or grain
22:26 we decided to build the altar, not for **b** sacrifices,
22:27 the LORD at his sanctuary with our **b** offerings,
22:28 It is not for **b** offerings or sacrifices; it is a
22:29 from him by building our own altar for **b** offerings,
Jdg 6:26 Sacrifice the bull as a **b** offering on the altar,
11:31 in triumph. I will sacrifice it as a **b** offering."
13:16 you may prepare a **b** offering as a sacrifice to the
13:23 he wouldn't have accepted our **b** offering and grain
15:14 ropes on his arms as if they were **b** strands of flax,
20:26 They also brought **b** offerings and peace offerings
21: 4 and presented their **b** offerings and peace offerings
1Sa 6:14 and sacrificed them to the LORD as a **b** offering.
6:15 Many **b** offerings and sacrifices were offered to the
7: 9 and offered it to the LORD as a whole **b** offering.
7:10 Just as Samuel was sacrificing the **b** offering,
10: 8 I will join you there to sacrifice **b** offerings
13: 9 "Bring me the **b** offering and the peace
13: 9 And Saul sacrificed the **b** offering himself.
13:10 Just as Saul was finishing with the **b** offering,
13:12 So I felt obliged to offer the **b** offering myself
15:22 your **b** offerings and sacrifices or your obedience
2Sa 6:17 And David sacrificed **b** offerings and peace
24:22 "Here are oxen for the **b** offering, and you can use
24:24 for I cannot present **b** offerings to the LORD my
24:25 and offered **b** offerings and peace offerings.
1Ki 3: 4 went there and sacrificed one thousand **b** offerings.
3:15 where he sacrificed **b** offerings and peace
8:64 He offered **b** offerings, grain offerings, and the fat
9:25 Three times each year Solomon offered **b** offerings
10: 5 and the **b** offerings Solomon made at the Temple
2Ki 3:27 and sacrificed him as a **b** offering on the wall.
5:17 From now on I will never again offer any **b**
10:24 the temple to offer sacrifices and **b** offerings.
10:25 As soon as Jehu had finished sacrificing the **b**
16:13 The king presented a **b** offering and a grain
16:15 "Use the new altar for the morning sacrifices of **b**
16:15 the king's **b** offering and grain offering,
16:15 The blood from the **b** offerings and sacrifices
1Ch 6:49 They presented the offerings on the altar of **b**
16: 1 and they sacrificed **b** offerings and peace offerings
16:40 They sacrificed the regular **b** offerings to the
21:23 "Here are oxen for the **b** offerings, and you can
21:24 I will not offer a **b** offering that has cost me
21:26 and sacrificed **b** offerings and peace offerings.
22: 1 and the place of the altar for Israel's **b** offerings!"
23:31 They assisted with the **b** offerings that were
29:21 and a thousand male lambs as **b** offerings to the
2Ch 1: 6 and sacrificed a thousand **b** offerings on it.
2: 4 and to sacrifice **b** offerings each morning
7: 1 and burned up the **b** offerings and sacrifices,
7: 7 so they could present **b** offerings and the fat from
7: 7 he had built could not handle all the **b** offerings,

8:12 Then Solomon sacrificed **b** offerings to the
9: 4 and the **b** offerings Solomon made at the Temple
13:11 They present **b** offerings and fragrant incense to
23:18 He also commanded them to present **b** offerings to
24:14 utensils for worship services and for **b** offerings,
24:14 And the **b** offerings were sacrificed continually in
29: 7 and presenting **b** offerings at the sanctuary of the
29:18 the altar of **b** offering with all its utensils,
29:24 The king had specifically commanded that this **b**
29:27 Then Hezekiah ordered that the **b** offering be
29:27 As the **b** offering was presented, songs of praise to
29:28 until all the **b** offerings were finished.
29:31 and those whose hearts were willing brought **b**
29:32 and two hundred lambs for **b** offerings.
29:34 But there were too few priests to prepare all the **b**
29:35 There was an abundance of **b** offerings, along with
30:15 and brought **b** offerings to the Temple of the
31: 2 and Levites into divisions to offer the **b** offerings
31: 3 for the daily morning and evening **b** offerings,
35:12 They divided the **b** offerings among the people by
35:14 from morning till night offering the **b** offerings
35:16 All the **b** offerings were sacrificed on the altar of
Ezr 3: 2 of Israel so they could sacrifice **b** offerings on it,
3: 3 Then they immediately began to sacrifice **b**
3: 4 sacrificing the **b** offerings specified for each day of
3: 5 They also offered the regular **b** offerings
3: 6 the priests had begun to sacrifice **b** offerings to the
6: 9 and lambs for the **b** offerings presented to the God
8:35 captivity sacrificed **b** offerings to the God of Israel.
8:35 All this was given as a **b** offering to the LORD.
Ne 10:33 for the regular grain offerings and **b** offerings;
Job 1: 5 and offer a **b** offering for each of them.
42: 8 servant Job and offer a **b** offering for yourselves.
Ps 20: 3 and look favorably on your **b** offerings.
40: 6 you don't require **b** offerings or sin offerings.
50: 8 or the **b** offerings you constantly bring to my altar.
51:16 I would bring them. / If I brought you a **b** offering,
51:19 and with our whole **b** offerings; / and bulls will
66:13 Now I come to your Temple with **b** offerings
66:15 That is why I am sacrificing **b** offerings to you—
Isa 1:11 "Don't bring me any more **b** offerings!
43:23 You have not brought me lambs for **b** offerings.
56: 7 I will accept their **b** offerings and sacrifices,
Jer 6:20 I cannot accept your **b** offerings.
7:21 "Away with your **b** offerings and sacrifices!
7:22 it was not **b** offerings and sacrifices I wanted from
14:12 When they present their **b** offerings and grain
17:26 the people will come with their **b** offerings
33:18 will always be Levitical priests to offer **b** offerings
Eze 40:39 animals were slaughtered for the **b** offerings,
40:42 of hewn stone for preparation of the **b** offerings,
43:24 and offer them as a **b** offering to the LORD.
43:27 the priests will sacrifice on the altar the **b** offerings
44:11 still slaughter the animals brought for **b** offerings
45:15 These will be the grain offerings, **b** offerings,
45:17 **b** offerings, grain offerings, drink offerings,
45:23 feast he will prepare a **b** offering to the LORD.
45:25 the **b** offering, and the grain offering, along with
46: 2 the gatepost while the priest offers his **b** offering
46: 4 present to the LORD a **b** offering of six lambs
46:12 Whenever the prince offers a voluntary **b** offering
46:13 must be sacrificed as a **b** offering to the LORD.
Hos 6: 6 know God; that's more important than **b** offerings.
Am 5:22 I will not accept your **b** offerings and grain
Mk 12:33 This is more important than to offer all of the **b**

BURST (27) [BURSTING, BURSTS]

Ge 1:11 "Let the land **b** forth with every sort of grass
7:11 the underground waters **b** forth on the earth,
21:16 to watch the boy die," she said, as she **b** into tears.
2Sa 5:20 "He **b** through my enemies like a raging flood!"
18:33 up to his room over the gateway and **b** into tears.
1Ch 14:11 "He used me to **b** through my enemies like a
15:13 the anger of the LORD our God **b** out against us.
16:32 Let the fields and their crops **b** forth with joy!
Job 26: 8 and the clouds do not **b** with the weight.
32:19 cask without a vent. My words are ready to **b** out!
38: 8 "Who defined the boundaries of the sea as it **b**
Ps 28: 7 filled with joy. / I **b** out in songs of thanksgiving.
96:12 Let the fields and their crops **b** forth with joy!
104:32 the mountains **b** into flame at his touch.
119:171 Let my lips **b** forth with praise, / for you have
Pr 3:20 By his knowledge the deep fountains of the earth **b**
Isa 28: 2 they will **b** upon it and dash it to the ground.
49:13 Rejoice, O earth! **B** into song, O mountains!
55:12 The mountains and hills will **b** into song,
64: 1 that you would **b** from the heavens and come
Jer 15:17 hand was on me. I **b** with indignation at their sins.
Joel 3:18 and a fountain will **b** forth from the LORD's
Mt 9:17 The old skins would **b** from the pressure,
Mk 2:22 The wine would **b** the wineskins, spilling the wine
Lk 5:37 The new wine would **b** the old skins,
19:40 the stones along the road would **b** into cheers!"
Ac 1:18 and falling there, he **b** open, spilling out his

BURSTING (4) [BURST]

2Sa 23: 4 like the sunrise **b** forth in a cloudless sky,
Ps 39: 2 the turmoil within me grew to the **b** point.
112: 4 darkness overtakes the godly, light will come **b** in.
Isa 54: 3 For you will soon be **b** at the seams.

BURSTS (6) [BURST]

2Sa 5:20 (which means "the Lord who **b** through").
1Ch 14:11 (which means "the Lord who **b** through").
Ps 19: 5 It **b** forth like a radiant bridegroom / after his
Isa 30:13 It will be like a bulging wall that **b** and falls.
Jer 23:19 The LORD's anger **b** out like a storm,
30:23 The LORD's anger **b** out like a storm, a driving

BURY (37) [BURIAL, BURIED, BURYING]

Ge 23: 4 in a foreign land, with no place to **b** my wife.
23: 6 the finest of our tombs so you can **b** her there."
23:11 my people, I give it to you. Go and **b** your dead."
23:13 full price for the field so I can **b** my dead there."
23:15 that between friends? Go ahead and **b** your dead."
47:29 honor this, my last request: Do not **b** me in Egypt.
47:30 me out of Egypt and **b** me beside my ancestors."
49:29 **B** me with my father and grandfather in the cave in
50: 5 of Canaan, and **b** me in our family's burial cave.'
50: 5 Now I need to go and **b** my father. After his burial
50: 6 "Go and **b** your father, as you promised," he said.
Dt 21:23 You must **b** the body that same day, for anyone
1Ki 2:31 "Kill him there beside the altar and **b** him.
11:15 to **b** some Israelites who had died in battle.
13:29 it back to the city to mourn over him and **b** him.
13:31 **b** me in the grave where the man of God is buried.
14:13 All Israel will mourn for him and **b** him. He is the
2Ki 9:10 the plot of land in Jezreel, and no one will **b** her."
9:34 he said, "Someone go and **b** this cursed woman,
9:35 But when they went out to **b** her, they found only
Job 40:13 **B** them in the dust. Imprison them in the world of
Ps 79: 3 all around Jerusalem; / no one is left to **b** the dead.
Jer 7:32 They will **b** so many bodies in Topheth that there
9:22 after the harvest. No one will be left to **b** them."
14:16 and war. There will be no one left to **b** them.
16: 4 No one will mourn for them or **b** them, and they
16: 6 in this land. No one will **b** them or mourn for them.
19:11 They will **b** the bodies in Topheth until there is no
25:33 for them or gather up their bodies to **b** them.
43: 9 **b** large rocks between the pavement stones at the
Eze 39:14 to search the land for any skeletons and to **b** them,
Hos 9: 6 will be conquered by Egypt. Memphis will **b** you.
10: 8 They will beg the mountains to **b** them
Mt 8:21 "Lord, first let me return home and **b** my father."
Lk 9:59 "Lord, first let me return home and **b** my father."
23:30 mountains to fall on them and the hills to **b** them.
Rev 11: 9 at their bodies. No one will be allowed to **b** them.

BURYING (4) [BURY]

Nu 33: 4 the Egyptians were **b** all their firstborn sons,
2Ki 13:21 Once when some Israelites were **b** a man,
13:21 So they hastily threw the body they were **b** into the
Eze 39:12 people of Israel to cleanse the land by **b** the bodies.

BUSH (12) [BUSHES]

Ge 21:15 was gone, she left the boy in the shade of a **b**.
22:13 looked up and saw a ram caught by its horns in a **b**.
Ex 3: 2 LORD appeared to him as a blazing fire in a **b**.
3: 2 was amazed because the **b** was engulfed in flames,
3: 3 said to himself. "Why isn't that **b** burning up?
3: 4 God called to him from the **b**, "Moses!
3:16 Isaac, and Jacob—appeared to me in a burning **b**.
Dt 33:16 the favor of the one who appeared in the burning **b**.
Mk 12:26 writings of Moses, in the story of the burning **b**?
Lk 20:37 proved this when he wrote about the burning **b**.
Ac 7:30 appeared to Moses in the flame of a burning **b**.
7:35 the angel who appeared to him in the burning **b**,

BUSHEL (14) [BUSHELS, HALF-BUSHEL, TWENTY-BUSHEL]

Jdg 6:19 and with half a **b** of flour he baked some bread
Ru 2:17 the grain that evening, it came to about half a **b**.
1Sa 1:24 the sacrifice and half a **b** of flour and some wine.
25:18 five dressed sheep, nearly a **b** of roasted grain,
Eze 45:13 one **b** of wheat or barley for every sixty you
45:24 The prince will provide a half **b** of flour as a grain
46: 5 He will present a grain offering of a half **b** of flour
46: 5 He is to offer one gallon of olive oil for each half **b**
46: 7 With the young bull he must bring a half **b** of flour
46: 7 With the ram he must bring another half **b** of flour.
46: 7 With each half **b** of flour he must offer one gallon
46:11 the grain offering will be a half **b** of flour with
46:11 another half **b** of flour with each ram, and as much
46:11 One gallon of oil is to be given with each half **b** of

BUSHELS (13) [BUSHEL]

Lev 27:16 for an area that produces five **b** of barley seed.
Nu 11:32 next day, too. No one gathered less than fifty **b**!
1Ki 4:22 for Solomon's palace were 150 **b** of choice flour
and 300 **b** of meal,
5:11 payment of 100,000 **b** of wheat for his household
2Ch 2:10 I will pay your men 100,000 **b** of crushed wheat,
2:10 100,000 **b** of barley, 110,000 gallons of wine,
27: 5 50,000 **b** of wheat, and 50,000 **b** of barley.
Ezr 7:22 500 **b** of wheat, 550 gallons of wine, 550 gallons
Hos 3: 2 and about five **b** of barley and a measure of wine.
Lk 16: 7 'A thousand **b** of wheat,' was the reply. 'Here,'
16: 7 and replace it with one for only eight hundred **b**.'

BUSHES (4) [BUSH]

Job 30: 7 sound like animals as they howl among the **b**;
Jer 4:29 They hide in the **b** and run for the mountains.
Lk 6:44 grow on thornbushes or grapes on bramble **b**.
Heb 9:19 using branches of hyssop **b** and scarlet wool.

BUSHY [KJV] See WAVY

BUSILY (1) [BUSY]

Pr 31:13 She finds wool and flax and **b** spins it.

BUSINESS (27) [BUSINESSES]

Ge 25:34 Esau ate and drank and went on about his **b**,
39: 4 and entrusted him with all his **b** dealings.
40: 8 "Interpreting dreams is God's **b**," Joseph replied.
1Sa 21: 8 The king's **b** was so urgent that I didn't even have
Ne 5:10 and grain, but now let us stop this **b** of loans.
Ps 35:20 innocent people / who are minding their own **b**.
112: 5 who lend freely and conduct their **b** fairly.
Pr 9:15 out to men going by who are minding their own **b**.
16:11 The LORD demands fairness in every **b** deal;
24:27 Develop your **b** first before building your house.
Isa 47:15 those with whom you have done **b** since childhood,
Eze 7:13 should survive, they will never return to their **b**.
Hos 4:10 Though they do a big **b** as prostitutes, they will
Mt 22: 5 had invited ignored them and went about their **b**,
Lk 8: 3 Joanna, the wife of Chuza, Herod's **b** manager;
17:28 People went about their daily **b**—eating
17:30 it will be '**b** as usual' right up to the hour when the
19: 2 influential Jews in the Roman tax-collecting **b**,
Ac 6: 3 and wisdom. We will put them in charge of this **b**.
7:27 Moses aside and told him to mind his own **b**.
19:24 a silversmith who had a large **b** manufacturing
19:25 you know that our wealth comes from this **b**.
19:27 talking about the loss of public respect for our **b**.
1Th 4:11 minding your own **b** and working with your hands,
2Th 3:11 and wasting time meddling in other people's **b**.
1Ti 5:13 getting into other people's **b** and saying things they
Jas 4:13 a year. We will do **b** there and make a profit."

BUSINESSES (3) [BUSINESS]

Isa 23:18 But in the end her **b** will give their profits to the
Jer 14: 2 "Judah wilts; her **b** have ground to a halt.
25:10 Your **b** will fail, and all your homes will stand

BUSTLING (2)

La 1: 1 once **b** with people, are now silent.
Zec 7: 7 and the towns of Judah were **b** with people,

BUSY (10) [BUSILY]

1Ki 20:40 But while I was **b** doing something else,
1Ch 21:20 who was **b** threshing wheat at the time, turned
2Ch 35:14 because the priests had been **b** from morning till
Ps 39: 6 and all our **b** rushing ends in nothing.
Pr 31:19 Her hands are **b** spinning thread, her fingers
Ecc 5: 3 Just as being too **b** gives you nightmares, being a
11: 6 Be sure to stay **b** and plant a variety of crops,
Isa 32:14 city will be deserted, and **b** towns will be empty.
Hag 1: 9 while you are all **b** building your own fine houses.
Ac 19:24 goddess Artemis. He kept many craftsmen **b**.

BUT (4392) See Index of Articles, Etc.

BUTCHER (7) [BUTCHERED, BUTCHERING]

Ge 18: 7 chose a fat calf and told a servant to hurry and **b** it.
Dt 12:15 "But you may **b** animals for meat in any town,
12:21 you may **b** any of the cattle or sheep the LORD
Eze 23:47 They will **b** their sons and daughters and burn their
26:11 They will **b** your people, and your famous pillars
34: 3 the milk, wear the wool, and **b** the best animals,
35: 5 Israel led you to **b** them when they were helpless,

BUTCHERED (6) [BUTCHER]

Nu 11:22 Even if we **b** all our flocks and herds, would that
Dt 28:31 Your ox will be **b** before your eyes, but you won't
1Sa 14:32 they flew upon the battle plunder and **b** the sheep,
2Ch 18: 2 They **b** great numbers of sheep and oxen for the
Ps 78:62 He gave his people over to be **b** by the sword,
Jer 12: 3 these people away like helpless sheep to be **b**!

BUTCHERING (1) [BUTCHER]

Eze 40:42 On these tables were placed the **b** knives and other

BUTLER [KJV] See CHIEF CUP-BEARER

BUTT (3) [BUTTED]

2Sa 2:23 so Abner thrust the **b** end of his spear through
Ps 44:14 You have made us the **b** of their jokes; / we are
Eze 34:21 For you fat sheep push and **b** and crowd my sick

BUTTED (1) [BUTT]

Da 8: 4 The ram **b** everything out of its way to the west,

BUTTER (2)

2Sa 17:29 honey, **b**, sheep, and cheese for David and those
Pr 30:33 As the beating of cream yields **b**, and a blow to the

BUTTOCKS (3)

2Sa 10: 4 cut off their robes at the **b**, and sent them back to
1Ch 19: 4 and shaved their beards, cut off their robes at the **b**,
Isa 20: 4 both young and old, their **b** uncovered,

BUTTRESS (4)

Ne 3:19 section of wall opposite the armory by the **b**.
3:20 who repaired an additional section from the **b** to
3:24 section of the wall from Azariah's house to the **b**
3:25 carried on the work from a point opposite the **b**

BUY (72) [BOUGHT, BUYER, BUYERS, BUYING, BUYS]

Ge 23:13 listen to me," he insisted. "I will **b** it from you.
41:57 lands also came to Egypt to **b** grain from Joseph
42: 2 and **b** some for us before we all starve to death."
42: 3 ten older brothers went down to Egypt to **b** grain.
42: 5 sons arrived in Egypt along with others to **b** food,
42: 7 they replied. "We have come to **b** grain."
42:10 they exclaimed. "We have come to **b** food.
42:34 and you may come as often as you like to **b**
43: 2 said to his sons, "Go again and **b** us a little food."
43: 4 come with us, we will go down and **b** some food.
43:20 to him, "Sir, after our first trip to Egypt to **b** food,
43:22 We also have additional money to **b** more grain.
44:25 he said, 'Go back again and **b** us a little food,'
47:19 **B** us and our land in exchange for food; we will
47:22 The only land he didn't **b** was that belonging to the
Ex 21: 2 "If you **b** a Hebrew slave, he is to serve for only
Lev 25:14 you make an agreement with a neighbor to **b**
25:15 When you **b** land from your neighbor, the price of
25:25 a kinsman redeemer, may **b** it back for them.
25:26 sold it manages to get enough money to **b** it back,
25:29 that time, the seller retains the right to **b** it back.
Dt 14:26 arrive, use the money to **b** anything you want—
17:16 and he must never send his people to Egypt to **b**
28:68 enemies as slaves, but no one will want to **b** you."
Ru 4: 4 then **b** it here in the presence of these witnesses.
4: 8 his sandal as he said to Boaz, "You **b** the land."
2Sa 12: 3 but a little lamb he had worked hard to **b**.
24:21 "I have come to **b** your threshing floor and to
1Ki 21: 2 I would like to **b** it to use as a vegetable garden.
2Ki 12:12 They also used the money to **b** timber and cut
22: 6 Also have them **b** the timber and the cut stone
1Ch 21:22 "Let me **b** this threshing floor from you at its full
Ne 5: 2 so we can **b** the food we need to survive."
10:31 or on any other holy day, we will refuse to **b** it.
Job 41: 6 Will merchants try to **b** it? Will they sell it in their
SS 8: 7 If a man tried to **b** love with everything he owned,
Isa 5: 8 Destruction is certain for you who **b** up property
13:17 and no amount of silver or gold will **b** them off.
47:11 and you won't be able to **b** your way out.
59:20 "to **b** back those in Israel who have turned from
Jer 13: 1 "Go and **b** a linen belt and put it around your
19: 1 The LORD said to me, "Go and **b** a clay jar.
32: 7 will come and say to you, '**B** my field at Anathoth. By law you have the right to **b** it before it is
32: 8 "**B** my field at Anathoth in the land of Benjamin. By law you have the right to **b** it before it is offered to anyone else, so **b** it for yourself."
32:15 and will **b** and sell houses and vineyards
32:25 you have told me to **b** the field—
Eze 7:19 It won't **b** their deliverance in that day of the
27:16 "Aram sent merchants to **b** your wares.
Hab 2: 9 You believe your wealth will **b** security,
Zep 1:11 market area, for all who **b** and sell there will die.
Mt 13:44 he owned to get enough money to **b** the field—
14:15 can go to the villages and **b** food for themselves."
25: 9 all of us. Go to a shop and **b** some for yourselves.'
25:10 "But while they were gone to **b** oil,
27: 7 After some discussion they finally decided to **b** the
Mk 6:36 and villages and **b** themselves some food."
6:37 "It would take a small fortune to **b** food for all this
Lk 9:13 to go and **b** enough food for this whole crowd?"
22:36 don't have a sword, sell your clothes and **b** one!
Jn 4: 8 because his disciples had gone into the village to **b**
6: 5 where can we **b** bread to feed all these people?"
Ac 7:12 still grain in Egypt, so he sent his sons to **b** some.
8:18 people's heads, he offered money to **b** this power.
Gal 4: 5 God sent him to **b** freedom for us who were slaves
Rev 3:18 I advise you to **b** gold from me—gold that has
3:18 And also **b** white garments so you will not be
3:18 And **b** ointment for your eyes so you will be able
13:17 And no one could **b** or sell anything without that
18:11 for her, for there is no one left to **b** their goods.

BUYER (2) [BUY]

Lev 25:30 city will become the permanent property of the **b**.
Pr 20:14 The **b** haggles over the price, saying,

BUYERS (3) [BUY]

Isa 24: 2 **b** and sellers, lenders and borrowers, bankers
Eze 7:12 There is no reason for **b** to rejoice over the
Zec 11: 5 The **b** will slaughter their sheep without remorse.

BUYING (3) [BUY]

Lev 25:27 After **b** it back, the original owner may then return
2Sa 24:24 the king replied to Araunah, "No, I insist on **b** it,
Lk 17:28 drinking, **b** and selling, farming and building—

BUYS (2) [BUY]

Lev 22:11 if the priest **b** slaves with his own money,
Pr 31:16 She goes out to inspect a field and **b** it; with her

BUZ (3) [BUZITE]

Ge 22:21 The oldest was named Uz, the next oldest was **B**,
1Ch 5:14 son of Jeshishai, son of Jahdo, son of **B**.
Jer 25:23 I went to Dedan, Tema, and **B**, and to the people

BUZI (1)

Eze 1: 3 gave a message to me, Ezekiel son of **B**, a priest,

BUZITE (2) [BUZ]

Job 32: 2 Then Elihu son of Barakel the **B**, of the clan of
32: 6 Elihu son of Barakel the **B** said, "I am young

BUZZARD (2) [BUZZARDS]

Lev 11:14 the **b**, kites of all kinds,
Dt 14:13 the **b**, kites of all kinds,

BUZZARDS (1) [BUZZARD]

Rev 18: 2 of demons and evil spirits, a nest for filthy **b**,

BY (2544) See Index of Articles, Etc.

BYSTANDER (1) [BYSTANDERS]

Pr 26:10 or a **b** is like an archer who shoots recklessly.

BYSTANDERS (5) [BYSTANDER]

Mt 26:73 A little later some other **b** came over to him
27:47 Some of the **b** misunderstood and thought he was
Mk 11: 5 some **b** demanded, "What are you doing,
14:70 A little later some other **b** began saying to Peter,
15:35 Some of the **b** misunderstood and thought he was

C

CABBON (1)

Jos 15:40 **C**, Lahmam, Kitlish,

CABINS [KJV] See CELL

CABUL (2)

Jos 19:27 and Neiel. It then continued north to **C**,
1Ki 9:13 So Hiram called that area **C**—"worthless"—

CAESAR (14) [CAESAR'S]

Mt 22:21 then," he said, "give to **C** what belongs to him.
Mk 12:17 Jesus said, "give to **C** what belongs to him.
Lk 20:25 he said, "give to **C** what belongs to him.
Jn 19:12 "If you release this man, you are not a friend of **C**.
19:12 who declares himself a king is a rebel against **C**."
19:15 "We have no king but **C**," the leading priests
Ac 17: 7 They are all guilty of treason against **C**, for they
25:11 me over to these men to kill me. I appeal to **C**!"
25:12 You have appealed to **C**, and to **C** you shall go!"
25:21 to jail until I could arrange to send him to **C**."
26:32 "He could be set free if he hadn't appealed to **C**!"
27:24 Paul, for you will surely stand trial before **C**!
28:19 the decision, I felt it necessary to appeal to **C**,

CAESAR'S (5) [CAESAR]

Mt 22:21 "**C**," they replied. "Well, then," he said, "give to
Mk 12:16 and title are stamped on it?" "**C**," they replied.
Lk 20:24 and title are stamped on it?" "**C**," they replied.
Ac 18: 2 of Claudius **C** order to deport all Jews from Rome.
Php 4:22 too, especially those who work in **C** palace.

CAESAREA (17)

Mt 16:13 When Jesus came to the region of **C** Philippi,
Mk 8:27 and went up to the villages of **C** Philippi.
Ac 8:40 and in every city along the way until he came to **C**.
9:30 they took him to **C** and sent him on to his
10: 1 In **C** there lived a Roman army officer named
10:24 They arrived in **C** the following day.
11:11 then three men who had been sent from **C** arrived
12:19 Afterward Herod left Judea to stay in **C** for a
18:22 The next stop was at the port of **C**. From there he
21: 8 Then we went on to **C** and stayed at the home of
21:16 Some believers from **C** accompanied us, and they
23:23 "Get two hundred soldiers ready to leave for **C** at
23:32 while the horsemen took him on to **C**.
23:33 When they arrived in **C**, they presented Paul
25: 1 Three days after Festus arrived in **C** to take over
25: 4 But Festus replied that Paul was at **C** and he
25: 6 Eight or ten days later he returned to **C**, and on the

CAGE (3)

Jer 5:27 Like a **c** filled with birds, their homes are filled
Eze 13:20 setting my people free like birds set free from a **c**.
19: 9 With hooks, they dragged him into a **c**

CAIAPHAS (10)

Mt 26: 3 other leaders were meeting at the residence of **C**,
26:57 who had arrested Jesus led him to the home of **C**,
Lk 3: 2 Annas and **C** were the high priests. At this time a
Jn 11:49 And one of them, **C**, who was high priest that year,
11:51 nation came from **C** in his position as high priest.
18:13 the father-in-law of **C**, the high priest that year.
18:14 **C** was the one who had told the other Jewish
18:24 Then Annas bound Jesus and sent him to **C**,
18:28 Jesus' trial before **C** ended in the early hours of
Ac 4: 6 priest was there, along with **C**, John, Alexander,

CAIN (18) [CAIN'S]

Ge 4: 1 the time came, she gave birth to **C**, and she said,
4: 2 Abel became a shepherd, while **C** was a farmer.
4: 3 At harvest time **C** brought to the LORD a gift of
4: 5 This made **C** very angry and dejected.
4: 8 Later **C** suggested to his brother, Abel, "Let's go
4: 8 together there, **C** attacked and killed his brother.
4: 9 Afterward the LORD asked **C**, "Where is your
4: 9 Where is Abel?" "I don't know!" **C** retorted.
4:13 **C** replied to the LORD, "My punishment is too
4:15 Then the LORD put a mark on **C** to warn anyone
4:16 So **C** left the LORD's presence and settled in the
4:17 When **C** founded a city, he named it Enoch after
4:24 If anyone who kills **C** is to be punished seven
4:25 another son in place of Abel, the one **C** killed."
Heb 11: 4 a more acceptable offering to God than **C** did.
1Jn 3:12 We must not be like **C**, who belonged to the evil
3:12 Because **C** had been doing what was evil, and his
Jude 1:11 For they follow the evil example of **C**, who killed

CAIN'S (2) [CAIN]

Ge 4: 5 but he did not accept **C**. This made Cain very
4:17 Then **C** wife became pregnant and gave birth to a

CAINAN (2)

Lk 3:36 Shelah was the son of **C**. / **C** was the son of Arphaxad.

CAKE (10) [CAKES]

Ex 29:23 take one loaf of bread, one **c** mixed with olive oil,
Lev 8:26 a **c** of unleavened bread soaked with olive oil,
Nu 6:19 one **c** made without yeast, and one wafer made
15:20 Present a **c** from the first of the flour you grind
1Sa 30:12 They also gave him part of a fig **c** and two clusters
2Sa 6:19 a loaf of bread, a **c** of dates, and a **c** of raisins.
1Ch 16: 3 a loaf of bread, a **c** of dates, and a **c** of raisins.
Hos 7: 8 they have become as worthless as a half-baked **c**!

CAKES (15) [CAKE]

Ex 16:31 like coriander seed, and it tasted like honey **c**.
29: 2 make loaves of bread, thin **c** mixed with olive oil,
Lev 2: 4 It may be presented in the form of **c** mixed with
7:12 loaves, wafers, and **c**—all made without yeast
Nu 6:15 **c** of choice flour mixed with olive oil and wafers
11: 8 Then they boiled it in a pot and made it into flat **c**.
11: 8 These **c** tasted like they had been cooked in olive
1Sa 25:18 one hundred raisin **c**, and two hundred fig **c**.
1Ki 14: 3 of ten loaves of bread, some **c**, and a jar of honey,
1Ch 12:40 of flour, fig **c**, raisins, wine, olive oil, cattle,
23:29 the **c** cooked in olive oil, and the other mixed
Jer 7:18 and make **c** to offer to the Queen of Heaven.
44:19 and making **c** marked with her image, without our
Eze 4:12 day prepare your bread as you would barley **c**.

CALAH (2)

Ge 10:11 where he built Nineveh, Rehoboth-ir, **C**,
10:12 of the empire, located between Nineveh and **C**.

CALAMITIES (4) [CALAMITY]

Isa 47: 9 Yes, these **c** will come upon you, despite all your
Jer 32:42 Just as I have sent all these **c** upon them, so I will
2Co 6: 4 endure troubles and hardships and **c** of every kind.
12:10 and with insults, hardships, persecutions, and **c**.

CALAMITY (24) [CALAMITIES]

2Ki 7: 9 some terrible **c** will certainly fall upon us.
2Ch 20: 9 'Whenever we are faced with any **c** such as war,
Job 6:21 no help. You have seen my **c**, and you are afraid.
18:12 by hunger, and **c** waits for them to stumble.
21:30 Evil people are spared in times of **c** and are
30:13 and do everything they can to hasten my **c**,
31: 3 It is **c** for the wicked, misfortune for those who do
Ps 34:21 **C** will surely overtake the wicked, / and those who
Pr 1:27 when **c** overcomes you like a storm, when you are
10:15 is their fortress; the poverty of the poor is their **c**.
19:13 A foolish child is a **c** to a father; a nagging wife
24:16 But one **c** is enough to lay the wicked low.
Isa 30:13 **c** will come upon you suddenly. It will be like a
47:11 **C** will fall upon you, and you won't be able to buy
Jer 11:11 says the LORD, I am going to bring **c** upon them,
48:16 "**C** is coming fast to Moab; it threatens ominously.
49:32 I will bring **c** upon them from every direction,"
Eze 7:26 **C** will follow **c**; rumor will follow rumor.
Ob 1:13 the land of Israel when they were suffering such **c**.
Mt 24:22 In fact, unless that time of **c** is shortened, the entire
Mk 13:20 In fact, unless the Lord shortens that time of **c**,
Ro 2: 9 and **c** for everyone who keeps on sinning—
8:35 mean he no longer loves us if we have trouble or **c**,

CALAMUS (2)

SS 4:14 and saffron, **c** and cinnamon, myrrh and aloes,
Eze 27:19 cassia, and **c** were bartered for your wares.

CALCOL (2)

1Ki 4:31 Ethan the Ezrahite and Heman, **C**, and Darda—
1Ch 2: 6 Zerah were Zimri, Ethan, Heman, **C**, and Darda—

CALEB (37) [CALEB'S]

Nu 13: 6 Judah | **C** son of Jephunneh
13:30 But **C** tried to encourage the people as they stood

14: 6 Joshua son of Nun and C son of Jephunneh,
14:10 began to talk about stoning Joshua and C.
14:24 But my servant C is different from the others.
14:30 The only exceptions will be C son of Jephunneh
14:38 the land, only Joshua and C remained alive.
26:65 The only exceptions were C son of Jephunneh
32:12 The only exceptions are C son of Jephunneh the
34:19 of the leaders: / Judah | C son of Jephunneh
Dt 1:36 except C son of Jephunneh. He will see this land
Jos 14: 6 led by C son of Jephunneh the Kenizzite, came to
14: 6 C said to Joshua, "Remember what the LORD
14:13 So Joshua blessed C son of Jephunneh and gave
14:14 Hebron still belongs to the descendants of C son of
15:13 some of Judah's territory to C son of Jephunneh.
15:13 So C was given the city of Arba (that is, Hebron),
15:14 C drove out the three Anakites—Sheshai, Ahiman,
15:16 C said, "I will give my daughter Acsah in
15:18 down off her donkey, C asked her, "What is it?
15:19 So C gave her the upper and lower springs.
21:12 and the surrounding villages were given to C son
Jdg 1:12 Then C said, "I will give my daughter Acsah in
1:14 down off her donkey, C asked her, "What is it?
1:15 So C gave her the upper and lower springs.
1:20 The city of Hebron was given to C as Moses had
1:20 And C drove out the people living there, who were
1Sa 25: 3 a descendant of C, was mean and dishonest in all
30:14 the territory of Judah, and the land of C, and we
1Ch 2: 9 The sons of Hezron were Jerahmeel, Ram, and C.
2:18 Hezron's son C had two wives named Azubah
2:19 After Azubah died, C married Ephrathah, and they
2:42 The oldest son of C, the brother of Jerahmeel,
2:49 and Gibea). C also had a daughter named Acsah.
2:50 These were all descendants of C. The sons of Hur,
4:15 The sons of C son of Jephunneh were Iru, Elah,
6:56 and outlying areas were given to C son of

CALEB'S (7) [CALEB]

Jos 15:17 Othniel, the son of C brother Kenaz, was the one
Jdg 1:13 Othniel, the son of C younger brother Kenaz,
3: 9 was Othniel, the son of C younger brother, Kenaz.
1Ch 2:42 C second son was Mareshah, the father of Hebron.
2:46 C concubine Ephah gave birth to Haran, Moza,
2:48 Another of C concubines, Maacah, gave birth to
2:50 sons of Hur, the oldest son of C wife Ephrathah,

CALEB-EPHRATHAH (1) [EPHRATHAH]

1Ch 2:24 Soon after Hezron died in the town of C, his wife

CALENDAR (2)

Job 3: 6 Let that night be blotted off the c, never again to be
14:13 has passed. But mark your c to think of me again!

CALF (31) [CALVES, CALVES']

Ge 18: 7 and chose a fat c and told a servant to hurry
Ex 32: 4 and molded and tooled it into the shape of a c.
32: 5 he built an altar in front of the c and announced,
32: 8 They have made an idol shaped like a c, and they
32:19 near the camp, Moses saw the c and the dancing.
32:20 He took the c they had made and melted it in the
32:24 I threw them into the fire—and out came this c!"
32:35 because they had worshiped the c Aaron had made.
Lev 9: 3 and a year-old c and a year-old lamb for a whole
9: 8 and slaughtered the c as a sin offering for himself.
Dt 9:16 There below me I could see the gold c you had
9:21 I took your sin—the c you had made—and I melted
1Sa 28:24 The woman had been fattening a c, so she hurried
2Sa 6:13 so David could sacrifice an ox and a fattened c.
1Ki 12:29 He placed these c idols at the southern
2Ch 11:15 they worshiped the goat and c idols he had made.
Ne 9:18 even though they made an idol shaped like a c
Ps 29: 6 He makes Lebanon's mountains skip like a c
106:19 The people made a c at Mount Sinai; / they bowed
Jer 31:18 I was like a c that needed to be trained for the yoke
34:18 I will cut you apart just as you cut apart the c when
48:13 as Israel was ashamed of her gold c at Bethel.
50:11 You frisk about like a c in a meadow and neigh
Hos 8: 5 "O Samaria, I reject this c—this idol you have
8: 6 This c you worship was crafted by your own
10: 5 The people of Samaria tremble for their c idol at
13: 2 to these," they cry, "and kiss the c idols!"
Lk 15:23 And kill the c we have been fattening in the pen.
15:27 'and your father has killed the c we were fattening
15:30 you celebrate by killing the finest c we have.'
Ac 7:41 So they made an idol shaped like a c, and they

CALL (182) [CALLED, CALLING, CALLS, SO-CALLED]

Ge 2:19 He brought them to Adam to see what he would c
17:15 longer be Sarai; from now on you will c her Sarah.
24:57 "we'll c Rebekah and ask her what she thinks."
31:53 I c on the God of our ancestors—the God of your
Ex 3:16 "Now go and c together all the leaders of Israel.
17: 5 Then c some of the leaders of Israel and walk on
17: 9 commanded Joshua, "C the Israelites to arms,
32:34 But when I c the people to account, I will certainly
33:12 You c me by name and tell me I have found favor
33:19 and I will c out my name, 'the LORD,' to you.
Lev 8: 3 Then c the entire community of Israel to meet you
13:45 they must cover their mouth and c out, 'Unclean!
23:24 You will c the people to a sacred assembly—
Nu 3: 6 "C forward the tribe of Levi and present them to
10: 7 But when you c the people to an assembly,
28:18 On the first day of the festival you must c a sacred
28:25 On the seventh day of the festival you must c
28:26 you must c a holy assembly of the people.
29: 1 You must c a solemn assembly of all the people on
29: 7 you must c another holy assembly of all the
29:12 you must c yet another holy assembly of all the
29:35 c all the people to another holy assembly.
Dt 3: 9 Sirion by the Sidonians; the Amorites c it Senir.)
4: 7 our God is near to us whenever we c on him?
4:26 "Today I c heaven and earth as witnesses against
18:11 or psychics, or c forth the spirits of the dead.
30:19 I c on heaven and earth to witness the choice you
31:12 C them all together—men, women, children,
31:14 C Joshua and take him with you to the Tabernacle,
31:28 so that I can speak to them and c heaven
Jdg 3:27 hill country of Ephraim, Ehud sounded a c to arms.
6:34 He blew a ram's horn as a c to arms, and the men
12: 1 "Why didn't you c for us to help you fight against
Ru 1:20 "Don't c me Naomi," she told them. "Instead, c me
Mara, for the Almighty has made
1:21 Why should you c me Naomi when the LORD
1Sa 3: 5 What do you need?" "I didn't c you," Eli replied.
3: 6 "I didn't c you, my son," Eli said. "Go on back to
13: 3 so Saul sounded the c to arms throughout Israel.
28: 8 he said. "Will you c up his spirit for me?"
28:11 "Well, whose spirit do you want me to c up?" "C
up Samuel," Saul replied.
2Sa 2:26 When will you c off your men from chasing their
3:21 me go and c all the people of Israel to your side.
22: 4 I will c on the LORD, who is worthy of praise,
1Ki 1:28 "C Bathsheba," David said. So she came back in
1:32 "C Zadok the priest, Nathan the prophet,
8:33 and if they turn to you and c on your name
18:24 Then c on the name of your god, and I will c on
the name of the LORD.
18:25 and prepare it and c on the name of your god.
21: 9 "C the citizens together for fasting and prayer
2Ki 4:15 "C her back again," Elisha told him.
4:36 "C the child's mother!" he said. And when she
5:11 and c on the name of the LORD his God and heal
9: 2 C him into a back room away from his friends,
10:19 worshipers of Baal, and c together all his priests.
1Ch 22: 2 So David gave orders to c together the foreigners
2Ch 6:24 and if they turn to you and c on your name
Ne 7: 5 So my God gave me the idea to c together all the
Job 14:15 You would c and I would answer, and you would
17:14 And I might c the grave my father, and the worm
19:16 I c my servant, but he doesn't come; I even plead
27:10 in the Almighty? Can they c to God at any time?
34: 6 I am innocent, but they c me a liar. My suffering is
Ps 4: 1 Answer me when I c, / O God who declares me
4: 3 The LORD will answer when I c to him.
10:13 can they think, "God will never c us to account"?
18: 3 I will c on the LORD, who is worthy of praise,
22: 2 Every day I c to you, my God, but you do not
31:17 O LORD, / for I c out to you for help.
31:22 my cry for mercy / and answered my c for help.
34:17 The LORD hears his people when they c to him
52: 1 You c yourself a hero, do you? / Why boast about
55:16 But I will c on God, / and the LORD will rescue
56: 9 On the very day I c to you for help, / my enemies
79: 6 on kingdoms that do not c upon your name.
80:18 Revive us so we can c on your name once more.
86: 7 I will c to you whenever trouble strikes, / and you
89:15 Happy are those who hear the joyful c to worship,
91:15 When they c on me, I will answer; / I will be with
102: 2 your ear / and answer me quickly when I c to you,
116:17 of thanksgiving / and c on the name of the LORD.
130: 1 depths of despair, O LORD, / I c for your help.
145:18 The LORD is close to all who c on him, / yes, to all
who c on him sincerely.
Pr 8: 4 "I c to you, to all of you! I am raising my voice to
19: 7 The poor c after them, but they are gone.
Isa 7:14 will give birth to a son and will c him Immanuel—
8: 3 the LORD said, "C him Maher-shalal-hash-baz.
8:10 C your councils of war, develop your strategies,
19: 3 They will c on spirits, mediums, and psychics to
22:20 then I will c my servant Eliakim son of Hilkiah to
30: 7 are worthless! I c her the Harmless Dragon.
41:25 will come against the nations and c on my name,
46:11 I will c a swift bird of prey from the east—a leader
47:12 "C out the demon hordes you have worshiped all
48: 1 the name of the LORD and c on the God of Israel.
48: 2 even though you c yourself the holy city and talk
55: 6 you can find him. C on him now while he is near.
58: 5 yourselves with ashes. Is this what you c fasting?
58: 9 Then when you c, the LORD will answer. 'Yes,
59: 1 is not becoming deaf. He can hear you when you c.
60:14 They will c you the City of the LORD, and Zion
65:15 and c his true servants by another name.
65:24 I will answer them before they even c to me.
Jer 2:28 Why don't you c on these gods you have made?
9:17 what is going on! C for the mourners to come.
10:25 on nations that do not c upon your name.
20:10 They c me "The Man Who Lives in Terror."
22: 7 I will c for wreckers, who will bring out their tools
25:29 I will c for war against all the nations of the earth.
34:22 I will c the Babylonian armies back again.
35:17 Because you refuse to listen or answer when I c,
50:29 "Send out a c for archers to come to Babylon.
La 3:61 LORD, you have heard the vile names they c me.
Eze 7: 3 I will c you to account for all your disgusting
7:14 "The trumpets c Israel's army to mobilize, but no
21:21 He will c his magicians to use divination.
39:17 son of man, c all the birds and wild animals,
Da 5:12 C for Daniel, and he will tell you what the writing
Hos 2: 1 In that day you will c your brothers Ammi—
2: 1 And you will c your sisters Ruhamah—'The ones I
2: 2 "But now, c Israel to account, for she is no longer
2:16 "you will c me 'my husband' instead of 'my
8:13 I will c my people to account for their sins, and I
10:10 I will c out the armies of the nations to punish you
11: 7 They c me the Most High, but they don't truly
13:10 is your king? Why don't you c on him for help?
14: 3 Never again will we c the idols we have made 'our
Joel 1:14 c the people together for a solemn meeting.
2:15 c the people together for a solemn meeting.
2:16 C the bridegroom from his quarters and the bride
3: 9 "Get ready for war! C out your best warriors!
3:11 And now, O LORD, c out your warriors!
Am 5:16 C for the farmers to weep with you, and summon
Hab 1: 2 How long, O LORD, must I c for help? But you
Zec 13: 9 They will c on my name, and I will answer them.
Mal 3:12 "Then all nations will c you blessed, for your land
Mt 6: 2 and streets to c attention to their acts of charity!
9:13 For I have come to c sinners, not those who think
20: 8 "That evening he told the foreman to c the
22:43 the inspiration of the Holy Spirit, c him Lord?
23: 8 Don't ever let anyone c you 'Rabbi,' for you have
23:10 And don't let anyone c you 'Master,' for there is
Mk 2:17 I have come to c sinners, not those who think they
10:18 "Why do you c me good?" Jesus asked.
15:12 "what should I do with this man you c the King of
Lk 1:48 generation after generation / will c me blessed.
5:32 I have come to c sinners to turn from their sins,
6:46 "So why do you c me 'Lord,' when you won't
11: 7 He would c out from his bedroom, 'Don't bother
15: 6 you would c together your friends and neighbors to
15: 9 she will c in her friends and neighbors to rejoice
18:19 "Why do you c me good?" Jesus asked him.
Jn 9:11 "The man they c Jesus made mud and smoothed it
10:36 why do you c it blasphemy when the Holy One
12:17 Those in the crowd who had seen Jesus c Lazarus
13:13 You c me 'Teacher' and 'Lord,' and you are right,
15:15 I no longer c you servants, because a master
Ac 4:12 in all of heaven for people to c on to save them."
24:14 I admit that I follow the Way, which they c a sect.
24:25 it is more convenient, I'll c for you again."
Ro 9:25 who were not my people, / I will now c my people.
10:14 But how can they c on him to save them unless
11:29 For God's gifts and his c can never be withdrawn.
1Co 5: 4 You are to c a meeting of the church, and I will be
14: 8 And if the bugler doesn't sound a clear c, how will
2Co 1:23 Now I c upon God as my witness that I am telling
6: 8 praise us. We are honest, but they c us impostors.
Gal 1: 1 My c is from Jesus Christ himself and from God
1:15 God in his kindness to choose me and c me,
4: 6 and now you can c God your dear Father.
Col 4:11 Jesus (the one we c Justus) also sends his
1Th 4:16 with the c of the archangel, and with the trumpet c
of God.
2Ti 2:22 and enjoy the companionship of those who c on the
Heb 2:11 That is why Jesus is not ashamed to c them his
6:16 they c on someone greater than themselves to hold
11:14 looking forward to a country they can c their own.
Jas 5:14 They should c for the elders of the church and have
Rev 2:24 false teaching ('deeper truths,' as they c them—

CALLED (444) [CALL]

Ge 1: 5 God c the light "day" and the darkness "night."
1: 8 And God c the space "sky." This happened on the
2:23 She will be c 'woman,' because she was taken out
3: 9 The LORD God c to Adam, "Where are you?"
5: 2 and he blessed them and c them "human."
11: 9 That is why the city was c Babel, because it was
12:18 So Pharaoh c for Abram and accused him sharply.
14: 2 of Zeboiim, and the king of Bela (now c Zoar).
14: 7 Then they swung around to En-mishpat (now c
14: 8 Admah, Zeboiim, and Bela (now c Zoar)
14:14 he c together the men born into his household,
20: 1 while between Kadesh and Shur at a place c Gerar.
20: 8 and hastily c a meeting of all his servants.
20: 9 Then Abimelech c for Abraham. "What is this you
21:17 and the angel of God c to Hagar from the sky,
22: 1 "Abraham!" God c. "Yes," he replied. "Here I
22:15 Then the angel of the LORD c again to Abraham
23: 2 she died at Kiriath-arba (now c Hebron) in the land
24:58 So they c Rebekah. "Are you willing to go with
25:25 wearing a piece of clothing. So they c him Esau.
25:26 So they c him Jacob. Isaac was sixty years old
26: 9 Abimelech c for Isaac and exclaimed, "She is
26:22 So Isaac c it "Room Enough," for he said,
26:33 the town that grew up there has been c Beersheba
27: 1 he c for Esau, his older son, and said, "My son?"
28: 1 So Isaac c for Jacob, blessed him, and said,
31: 4 Jacob c Rachel and Leah out to the field where he
31:49 This place was also c Mizpah, for Laban said,
33:20 And there he built an altar and c it El-Elohe-Israel.
35: 6 Finally, they arrived at Luz (now c Bethel)
35: 8 the tree has been c the "Oak of Weeping."
35:10 is no longer Jacob; you will now be c Israel."
35:15 Jacob c the place Bethel—"house of God"—
35:18 the baby's father, however, c him Benjamin.
35:27 which is near Kiriath-arba (now c Hebron),
38:14 but they had not c her to come and marry him.
38:29 break out first?" And ever after, he was c Perez.
41: 8 So he c for all the magicians and wise men of
41:15 and that is why I have c for you."
45:24 his brothers off, and as they left, he c after them,
46: 2 "Jacob! Jacob!" he c. "Here I am," Jacob replied.
47:29 he c for his son Joseph and said to him, "If you are
49: 1 Then Jacob c together all his sons and said,
Ex 1:18 Then the king c for the midwives. "Why have you
2: 8 So the girl rushed home and c the baby's mother.
3: 4 God c to him from the bush, "Moses!

4:26 (When she **c** Moses a "blood-smeared
4:29 to Egypt and **c** the leaders of Israel to a meeting.
7:11 Then Pharaoh **c** in his wise men and magicians,
8:25 Pharaoh hastily **c** for Moses and Aaron. "All right!
10:24 Then Pharaoh **c** for Moses. "Go and worship the
12:21 Then Moses **c** for the leaders of Israel and said,
14: 6 So Pharaoh **c** out his troops and led the chase in his
15:23 (That is why the place was **c** Marah, which means
16: 6 and Aaron **c** a meeting of all the people of Israel
17:15 altar there and **c** it "The LORD Is My Banner."
19: 3 The LORD **c** out to him from the mountain
19: 7 and **c** together the leaders of the people
19:20 and **c** Moses to the top of the mountain.
24:16 On the seventh day the LORD **c** to Moses from
34: 5 down in a pillar of cloud and **c** out his own name,
34:31 But Moses **c** to them and asked Aaron
35: 1 Now Moses **c** a meeting of all the people and told
Lev 1: 1 The LORD **c** to Moses from the Tabernacle
5: 1 "If any of the people are **c** to testify about
9: 1 Moses **c** together Aaron and his sons
10: 4 Then Moses **c** for Mishael and Elzaphan,
Nu 1:18 **c** together the whole community of Israel on that
11:34 So that place was **c** Kibroth-hattaavah—
12: 4 So immediately the LORD **c** to Moses, Aaron,
12: 5 and Miriam!" he **c**, and they stepped forward.
21: 3 and the place has been **c** Hormah ever since.
24:10 and shouted, "I **c** you to curse my enemies!
Dt 2:10 and powerful race of giants **c** the Emites had once
2:11 as the Rephaites, but the Moabites **c** them Emites.
3: 9 (Mount Hermon is **c** Sirion by the Sidonians;
4:48 Gorge to Mount Sirion, also **c** Mount Hermon.
5: 1 Moses **c** all the people of Israel together and said,
31: 7 Then Moses **c** for Joshua, and as all Israel watched
Jos 1:12 Then Joshua **c** together the tribes of Reuben,
3:16 the water began piling up at a town upstream **c**
4: 4 So Joshua **c** together the twelve men
5: 9 So that place has been **c** Gilgal to this day.
6: 6 So Joshua **c** together the priests and said, "Take up
7:26 That is why the place has been **c** the Valley of
8:16 and all the men in the city were **c** out to chase after
9:22 But Joshua **c** together the Gibeonite leaders
14:15 (Previously Hebron had been **c** Kiriath-arba.
15:15 in the town of Debir (formerly **c** Kiriath-sepher).
22: 1 Then Joshua **c** together the tribes of Reuben,
22:10 altar near the Jordan River at a place **c** Geliloth.
23: 2 **c** together all the elders, leaders, judges,
Jdg 1:10 Canaanites in Hebron (formerly **c** Kiriath-arba),
1:11 in the town of Debir (formerly **c** Kiriath-sepher).
2: 5 So they **c** the place "Weeping," and they offered
4:10 Barak **c** together the tribes of Zebulun
4:13 he **c** for all nine hundred of his iron chariots
6:32 From then on Gideon was **c** Jerubbaal,
9: 6 and Beth-millo **c** a meeting under the oak beside
10: 4 land of Gilead, which are still **c** the Towns of Jair.
12: 4 So Jephthah **c** out his army and attacked the men
16:19 and she **c** in a man to shave off his hair, making his
18:12 in Judah, which is **c** Mahaneh-dan to this day.
18:23 Why have you **c** these men together and chased
18:29 Israel's son, but it had originally been **c** Laish.
Ru 2:14 At lunchtime Boaz **c** to her, "Come over here
4: 1 Boaz **c** out to him, "Come over here, friend.
4: 2 Then Boaz **c** ten leaders from the town and asked
1Sa 3: 4 Suddenly, the LORD **c** out, "Samuel! Samuel!"
3: 6 Then the LORD **c** out again, "Samuel!"
3: 8 So now the LORD **c** a third time, and once more
3:10 And the LORD came and **c** as before, "Samuel!
3:16 But Eli **c** out to him, "Samuel, my son." "Here I
5: 8 So they **c** together the rulers of the five Philistine
6: 2 Then the Philistines **c** in their priests and diviners
9: 9 and ask the seer," for prophets used to be **c** seers.)
9:26 the next morning, Samuel **c** up to Saul, "Get up!
10:17 Later Samuel **c** all the people of Israel to meet
10:20 So Samuel **c** the tribal leaders together before the
12:18 So Samuel **c** to the LORD, and the LORD sent
14: 4 down between two rocky cliffs that were **c** Bozez
14:46 Then Saul **c** back the army from chasing the
19: 7 Afterward Jonathan **c** David and told him what had
23:28 the place where David was camped has been **c** the
24:16 Saul **c** back, "Is that really you, my son David?"
26:17 Saul recognized David's voice and **c** out, "Is that
28:15 So I have **c** for you to tell me what to do."
2Sa 2:20 saw him coming, he **c** out, "Is that you, Asahel?"
5: 7 the fortress of Zion, now **c** the City of David.
5: 9 the fortress his home, and he **c** it the City of David.
6: 8 "outbreak against Uzzah"). It is still **c** that today.
13:13 And you would be **c** one of the greatest fools in
20:16 But a wise woman in the city **c** out to Joab,
20:22 the trumpet and **c** his troops back from the attack,
22: 7 out to the LORD; / yes, I **c** to my God for help.
22:42 They **c** for help, but no one came to rescue them.
1Ki 7: 2 One of Solomon's buildings was **c** the Palace of
7:23 15 feet across from rim to rim; it was **c** the Sea.
9:13 So Hiram **c** that area Cabul—"worthless"—
12:20 they **c** an assembly and made him king over all
14: 6 at the door, he **c** out, "Come in, wife of Jeroboam!
16:24 on it and **c** the city Samaria in honor of Shemer.
17:11 As she was going to get it, he **c** to her, "Bring me
18:26 Then they **c** on the name of Baal all morning,
18:30 Then Elijah **c** to the people, "Come over here!"
20:15 Then he **c** out the rest of his army of seven
20:26 The following spring he **c** up the Aramean army
20:39 the prophet **c** out to him, "Sir, I was in the battle,
21:12 They **c** for a fast and put Naboth at a prominent
22: 9 So the king of Israel **c** one of his officials and said,
2Ki 3:13 For it was the LORD who **c** us three kings here to
6:11 He **c** in his officers and demanded, "Which of you
6:26 a woman **c** to him, "Please help me, my lord the

8: 1 for the LORD has **c** for a famine on Israel that
9:18 The watchman **c** out to the king, "The rider has
10:18 Then Jehu **c** a meeting of all the people of the city
12: 7 So King Joash **c** for Jehoiada and the other priests
12:18 So Hazael **c** off his attack on Jerusalem.
14: 7 changed its name to Joktheel, as it is **c** to this day.
18: 4 incense to it. The bronze serpent was **c** Nehushtan.
1Ch 4:14 so **c** because many craftsmen lived there.
11: 4 went to Jerusalem (or Jebus, as it used to be **c**),
11: 5 the fortress of Zion, now **c** the City of David.
11: 7 his home, and that is why it is **c** the City of David.
13: 6 and all Israel went to Baalah of Judah (also **c**
13:11 "outbreak against Uzzah"). It is still **c** that today.
15: 4 are the priests and Levites who were **c** together:
21:17 said to God, "I am the one who **c** for the census!
2Ch 1: 2 He **c** together all Israel—the generals and captains
4: 2 15 feet across from rim to rim; it was **c** the Sea.
7:14 Then if my people who are **c** by my name will
15: 9 Then Asa **c** together all the people of Judah
16: 6 Then King Asa **c** out all the men of Judah to carry
18: 8 So the king of Israel **c** one of his officials and said,
20:26 It is still **c** the Valley of Blessing today.
24: 6 So the king **c** for Jehoiada the high priest
29: 4 There he **c** together the priests and Levites
29:15 These men **c** together their fellow Levites, and they
Ezr 10:23 Jozabad, Shimei, Kelaiah (also **c** Kelita),
Ne 4:14 I **c** together the leaders and the people and said to
5: 7 Then I **c** a public meeting to deal with the problem.
5:12 Then I **c** the priests and made the nobles
9: 5 Shebaniah, and Pethahiah—**c** out to the people:
13:11 Then I **c** all the Levites back again and restored
13:25 So I confronted them and **c** down curses on them.
Est 2: 7 young cousin, Hadassah, who was also **c** Esther.
3: 7 lots were cast (the lots were **c** *purim*)
3:12 On April 17 Haman **c** in the king's secretaries
4: 8 issued in Susa that **c** for the death of all Jews,
4:11 And the king has not **c** for me to come to him in
9:12 he **c** for Queen Esther and said, "The Jews have
9:24 by casting lots (the lots were **c** *purim*).
9:26 (That is why this celebration is **c** Purim, because it
Ps 18:41 They **c** for help, but no one came to rescue them.
83:18 until they learn that you alone are **c** the LORD,
99: 6 among his priests; / Samuel also **c** on his name.
105:16 He **c** for a famine on the land of Canaan,
109: 7 When his case is **c** for judgment, / let him be
116: 4 Then I **c** on the name of the LORD: / "Please,
Pr 1:24 "I **c** you so often, but you didn't come. I reached
SS 5: 6 him anywhere. I **c** to him, but there was no reply.
Isa 1:26 Then Jerusalem will again be **c** the Home of
4: 1 Only let us be **c** by your name so we won't be
13: 3 I am exalted. I have **c** them to satisfy my anger."
21: 8 Then the watchman **c** out, "Day after day I have
22:12 the LORD Almighty, **c** you to weep and mourn.
34:12 It will be **c** the Land of Nothing, and its princes
41: 9 I have **c** you back from the ends of the earth
42: 6 have **c** you to demonstrate my righteousness.
43: 1 I have **c** you by name; you are mine.
43:17 I **c** forth the mighty army of Egypt with all its
45: 4 "And why have I **c** you for this work? It is for the
45: 4 I **c** you by name when you did not know me.
48: 1 who are **c** by the name of Israel and born into the
49: 1 The LORD **c** me before my birth; from within the
womb he **c** me by name.
51: 2 you came. Abraham was alone when I **c** him.
54: 6 For the LORD has **c** you back from your grief—
56: 7 because my Temple will be **c** a house of prayer for
61: 6 You will be **c** priests of the LORD, ministers of
62: 4 Never again will you be **c** the Godforsaken City
62:12 They will be **c** the Holy People and the People
65:12 the executioner, for when I **c**, you did not answer.
66: 4 For when I **c**, they did not answer. When I spoke,
Jer 7:13 I **c** out to you, but you refused to answer.
7:32 "when that place will no longer be **c** Topheth
11:16 the LORD, once **c** them a thriving olive tree,
19: 6 when this place will no longer be **c** Topheth
20: 3 From now on you are to be **c** 'The Man Who Lives
30:17 "Now you are **c** an outcast—'Jerusalem for whom
38:12 Ebed-melech **c** down to Jeremiah, "Put these rags
38:27 and asked him why the king had **c** for him.
40: 2 The captain of the guard **c** for Jeremiah and said,
42: 8 So he **c** for Johanan son of Kareah and the army
La 2:15 "Is this the city **c** 'Most Beautiful in All the
3:55 But I **c** on your name, LORD, from deep within
Eze 9: 3 And the LORD **c** to the man dressed in linen who
20:29 (This idol shrine has been **c** Bamah—'high place'
38: 8 A long time from now you will be **c** into action.
Da 1: 7 Daniel was **c** Belteshazzar. / Hananiah was **c**
Shadrach. / Mishael was **c** Meshach. / Azariah was
c Abednego.
2: 2 He **c** in his magicians, enchanters, sorcerers,
4:31 a voice **c** down from heaven, "O King
6:20 When he got there, he **c** out in anguish, "Daniel,
Hos 2:23 I will show love to those I **c** 'Not loved.'
2:23 And to those I **c** 'Not my people,' I will say,
11: 1 I loved him as a son, and I **c** my son out of Egypt.
11: 2 But the more I **c** to him, the more he rebelled,
Joel 2:32 be among the survivors whom the LORD has **c**.
3:12 "Let the nations be **c** to arms. Let them march to
Am 7:15 But the LORD **c** me away from my flock and told
9:12 of Edom and all the nations I have **c** to be mine.
Jnh 2: 2 I **c** to you from the world of the dead, and LORD,
Mic 6: 1 and his hills be **c** to witness your complaints.
Hag 1:11 I have **c** for a drought on your fields and hills—
Zec 6:12 Here is the man **c** the Branch. He will branch out
7:13 "Since they refused to listen when I **c** to them,
7:13 I would not listen when they **c** to me,
8: 3 Then Jerusalem will be **c** the Faithful City;
8: 3 the mountain of the LORD Almighty will be **c** the

11:10 Then I took my staff **c** Favor and snapped it in two,
Mal 1: 4 and their people will be **c** 'The People with Whom
2: 5 This **c** for reverence from them, and they greatly
Mt 1:16 was the mother of Jesus, who is **c** the Messiah.
1:23 give birth to a son, / and he will be **c** Immanuel
2: 4 He **c** a meeting of the leading priests and teachers
2:15 through the prophet: "I **c** my Son out of Egypt."
2:23 So they went and lived in a town **c** Nazareth.
2:23 the Messiah: "He will be **c** a Nazarene."
4:18 Simon, also **c** Peter, and Andrew—fishing with a
4:19 Jesus **c** out to them, "Come, be my disciples,
4:21 mending their nets. And he **c** them to come, too.
5: 9 for peace, / for they will be **c** the children of God.
10: 1 Jesus **c** his twelve disciples to him and gave them
10: 2 first Simon (also **c** Peter), / then Andrew (Peter's
10:25 the household, have been **c** the prince of demons,
12:14 Then the Pharisees **c** a meeting and discussed plans
14:28 Then Peter **c** to him, "Lord, if it's really you,
15:10 Then Jesus **c** to the crowds and said, "Listen to
15:32 Then Jesus **c** his disciples to him and said, "I feel
18: 2 Jesus **c** a small child over to him and put the child
18:32 Then the king **c** in the man he had forgiven
20:25 But Jesus **c** them together and said, "You know
20:32 Jesus stopped in the road and **c**, "What do you
21:13 'My Temple will be **c** a place of prayer,'
22:14 For many are **c**, but few are chosen."
22:45 Since David **c** him Lord, how can he be his son at
23: 7 get on the streets, and they enjoy being **c** 'Rabbi.'
25:12 But he **c** back, 'I don't know you!'
25:14 He **c** together his servants and gave them money to
25:19 and **c** them to give an account of how they had
26:36 Then Jesus brought them to an olive grove **c**
27: 8 That is why the field is still **c** the Field of Blood.
27:17 Barabbas, or Jesus who is **c** the Messiah?"
27:22 "what should I do with Jesus who is **c** the
27:27 their headquarters and **c** out the entire battalion.
27:33 Then they went out to a place **c** Golgotha (which
27:46 Jesus **c** out with a loud voice, "*Eli, Eli,*
28:12 A meeting of all the religious leaders was **c**,
Mk 1:17 Jesus **c** out to them, "Come, be my disciples,
1:20 He **c** them, too, and immediately they left their
3:13 and **c** the ones he wanted to go with him.
3:23 Jesus **c** them over and said to them by way of
6: 7 And he **c** his twelve disciples together and sent
7:14 Then Jesus **c** to the crowd to come and hear.
8: 1 of food again. Jesus **c** his disciples and told them,
8:34 Then he **c** his disciples and the crowds to come
9:35 sat down and **c** the twelve disciples over to him.
10:42 So Jesus **c** them together and said, "You know that
10:49 So they **c** the blind man. "Cheer up," they said.
11:17 'My Temple will be **c** a place of prayer for all
12:37 Since David himself **c** him Lord, how can he be his
12:43 He **c** his disciples to him and said, "I assure you,
14:32 And they came to an olive grove **c** Gethsemane,
15:16 their headquarters and **c** out the entire battalion.
15:22 And they brought Jesus to a place **c** Golgotha
15:34 Then, at that time Jesus **c** out with a loud voice,
15:44 so he **c** for the Roman military officer in charge
Lk 1:32 very great and will be **c** the Son of the Most High.
1:35 you will be holy, and he will be **c** the Son of God.
1:76 little son, / will be **c** the prophet of the Most High,
6:13 At daybreak he **c** together all of his disciples
6:14 Simon (he also **c** him Peter), / Andrew (Peter's
7:18 Jesus was doing. So John **c** for two of his disciples,
8: 8 When he had said this, he **c** out, "Anyone who is
9: 1 One day Jesus **c** together his twelve apostles
9:38 A man in the crowd **c** out to him, "Teacher,
11:27 As he was speaking, a woman in the crowd **c** out,
12:13 Then someone **c** from the crowd, "Teacher,
13:12 Jesus saw her, he **c** her over and said, "Woman,
15:19 and I am no longer worthy of being **c** your son.
15:21 and I am no longer worthy of being **c** your son.'
16: 2 So his employer **c** him in and said, 'What's this I
18:16 Then Jesus **c** for the children and said to the
19: 5 he looked up at Zacchaeus and **c** him by name.
19:12 "A nobleman was **c** away to a distant empire to be
19:13 he **c** together ten servants and gave them ten
19:15 the king **c** in the servants to whom he had given the
20:44 Since David **c** him Lord, how can he be his son at
22:25 and yet they are **c** 'friends of the people.'
23:13 Then Pilate **c** together the leading priests and other
23:33 Finally, they came to a place **c** The Skull. All three
23:37 They **c** out to him, "If you are the King of the
Jn 1:42 but you will be **c** Cephas" (which means Peter).
2: 9 the servants knew), he **c** the bridegroom over.
4:25 the Messiah will come—the one who is **c** Christ.
6:20 but he **c** out to them, "I am here! Don't be afraid."
7:28 he **c** out, "Yes, you know me, and you know
9:18 believe he had been blind, so they **c** in his parents.
9:24 So for the second time they **c** in the man who had
10:35 who received God's message, were **c** 'gods,'
11:28 She **c** Mary aside from the mourners and told her,
11:47 and Pharisees **c** the high council together to discuss
18:33 back inside and **c** for Jesus to be brought to him.
19: 7 ought to die because he **c** himself the Son of God."
19:13 platform that is **c** the Stone Pavement (in Hebrew,
19:17 Jesus went to the place **c** Skull Hill (in Hebrew,
21: 5 He **c** out, "Friends, have you caught any fish?"
Ac 1:23 Joseph **c** Barsabbas (also known as Justus)
2:39 all who have been **c** by the Lord our God."
3: 2 the Temple gate, the one **c** the Beautiful Gate,
4:18 So they **c** the apostles back in and told them never
5:40 They **c** in the apostles and had them flogged.
6: 2 So the Twelve **c** a meeting of all the believers.
6: 9 as it was **c**, started to debate with him.
7:31 he went to see, the voice of the Lord **c** out to him,
9:41 Then he **c** in the widows and all the believers,

10: 7 Cornelius c two of his household servants and a
10:24 waiting for him and had c together his relatives
11:26 Antioch that the believers were first c Christians.)
13: 1 Simeon (c "the black man"), Lucius (from
14:10 So Paul c to him in a loud voice, "Stand up!"
14:27 they c the church together and reported about their
15:17 the Gentiles—/ all those I have c to be mine.
15:22 Judas (also c Barsabbas) and Silas.
15:30 where they c a general meeting of the Christians
16:29 the jailer c for lights and ran to the dungeon
19:25 He c the craftsmen together, along with others
21:32 He immediately c out his soldiers and officers
23:17 Paul c one of the officers and said, "Take this
23:18 c me over and asked me to bring this young man to
23:23 Then the commander c two of his officers
24: 2 When Paul was c in, Tertullus laid charges against
25:17 I c the case the very next day and ordered Paul
25:19 their religion and about someone c Jesus who died,
27:14 of typhoon strength (a "northeaster," they c it)
27:21 Finally, Paul c the crew together and said, "Men,
28:17 he c together the local Jewish leaders.
Ro 1: 6 You are among those who have been c to belong to
1: 7 and he has c you to be his very own people.
8:28 and are c according to his purpose for them.
8:30 having chosen them, he c them to come to him.
1Co 1: 2 you who have been c by God to be his own holy
1:24 But to those c by God to salvation, both Jews
1:26 or powerful, or wealthy when God c you.
7:17 and continue on as you were when God first c you.
7:20 You should continue on as you were when God c
7:22 if you were a slave when the Lord c you,
7:22 And if you were free when the Lord c you, you are
14: 8 how will the soldiers know they are being c to
15: 9 and I am not worthy to be c an apostle after the
Gal 1: 6 and mercy c you to share the eternal life he gives
5: 8 isn't God, for he is the one who c you to freedom.
5:13 dear friends, have been c to live in freedom—
Eph 1:18 the wonderful future he has promised to those he c.
2:11 You were c "the uncircumcised ones" by the
4: 1 of your calling, for you have been c by God.
4: 4 and we have all been c to the same glorious future.
Col 3:15 For as members of one body you are all c to live in
1Th 2:12 For he c you into his Kingdom to share his glory.
4: 7 God has c us to be holy, not to live impure lives.
2Th 1:11 will make you worthy of the life to which he c you.
2:14 He c you to salvation when we told you the Good
Heb 3:13 each other every day, as long as it is c "today,"
5: 4 He has to be c by God for this work, just as Aaron
9: 2 holy bread on the table. This was c the Holy Place.
9: 3 and behind the curtain was the second room c the
9: 4 and a wooden chest c the Ark of the Covenant,
11: 8 It was by faith that Abraham obeyed when God c
11:16 That is why God is not ashamed to be c their God,
Jas 2:23 He was even c "the friend of God."
1Pe 2: 9 for he c you out of the darkness into his wonderful
2:21 This suffering is all part of what God has c you to.
3: 6 her husband, Abraham, when she c him her master.
4:11 Are you c to be a speaker? Then speak as though
4:11 Are you c to help others? Do it with all the strength
4:16 Praise God for the privilege of being c by his
5:10 In his kindness God c you to his eternal glory by
2Pe 1: 3 He has c us to receive his own glory and goodness!
1:10 to prove that you really are among those God has c
1:17 majestic voice c down from heaven, "This is my
1Jn 3: 1 for he allows us to be c his children, and we really
Jude 1: 1 I am writing to all who are c to live in the love of
Rev 6: 1 Then one of the four living beings c out with a
6:10 They c loudly to the Lord and said, "O Sovereign
10: 4 about to write. But a voice from heaven c to me:
10: 8 Then the voice from heaven c to me again: "Go
11: 8 the city which is c "Sodom" and "Egypt,"
12: 9 the ancient serpent c the Devil, or Satan, the one
14:15 and c out in a loud voice to the one sitting on the
16:16 and their armies to a place c *Armageddon* in
17:14 and his people are the c and chosen and faithful
20: 8 corner of the earth, which are c Gog and Magog.

CALLING (34) [CALL]

Dt 3:14 c it the Towns of Jair, as it is still known today.)
1Sa 3: 8 Then Eli realized it was the LORD who was c the
28:15 "Why have you disturbed me by c me back?"
Ps 78:70 his servant David, / c him from the sheep pens.
86: 3 O Lord, / for I am c on you constantly.
141: 1 O LORD, I am c to you. Please hurry!
Isa 21:11 Someone from Edom keeps c to me, "Watchman,
40:26 them out one after another, c each by its name.
42:17 But those who trust in idols, / c them their gods—
48:15 I have said it: I am c Cyrus! I will send him on this
Jer 1:15 I am c the armies of the kingdoms of the north to
3: 1 Yet I am still c you to come back to me.
3:19 I looked forward to your c me 'Father,' and I
La 2:22 as though you were c them to a day of feasting.
Da 4: 6 So I issued an order c in all the wise men of
8:16 And I heard a human voice c out from the Ulai
Hos 7:11 witless doves, first c to Egypt, then flying to
Mic 4:11 c for your blood, eager to gloat over your
6: 9 His voice is c out to everyone in Jerusalem:
Mt 25:11 they stood outside, c, 'Sir, open the door for us!'
27:47 and thought he was c for the prophet Elijah.
Mk 3:14 to be his regular companions, c them apostles.
10:49 "Cheer up," they said. "Come on, he's c you!"
15:35 and thought he was c for the prophet Elijah.
Ac 9:10 The Lord spoke to him in a vision, c, "Ananias!"
16:10 for we could only conclude that God was c us to
22:16 sins washed away, c on the name of the Lord.'
Ro 8:15 into his family—c him "Father, dear Father."
Eph 4: 1 the Lord, beg you to lead a life worthy of your c,
Php 3:14 through Christ Jesus, is c us up to heaven.
1Jn 1:10 we are c God a liar and showing that his word has
5:10 Those who don't believe this are actually c God a
Rev 3:20 If you hear me c and open the door, I will come in,
18: 4 Then I heard another voice c from heaven,

CALLS (23) [CALL]

Ge 46:33 So when Pharaoh c for you and asks you about
1Sa 3: 9 and if someone c again, say, 'Yes, LORD,
Job 11:10 or if he c the court to order, who is going to stop
12: 4 I am a man who c on God and receives an answer.
Ps 147: 4 He counts the stars / and c them all by name.
Pr 1:21 She c out to the crowds along the main street,
8: 1 Listen as wisdom c out! Hear as understanding
9: 3 She c out from the heights overlooking the city.
9:15 She c out to men going by who are minding their
Ecc 3:15 in the past. For God c each event back in its turn.
Isa 45: 3 the God of Israel, the one who c you by name.
58: 6 the kind of fasting I want c you to free those who
64: 7 Yet no one c on your name or pleads with you for
Joel 2:32 And anyone who c on the name of the LORD will
Zep 1:16 trumpet c, and battle cries. Down go the walled
Lk 23:15 Nothing this man has done c for the death penalty.
Jn 10: 3 He c his own sheep by name and leads them out.
Ac 2:21 And anyone who c on the name of the Lord
Ro 10:13 For "Anyone who c on the name of the Lord will
1Co 1: 2 whoever c upon the name of Jesus Christ, our Lord
1Th 5:24 God, who c you, is faithful; he will do this.
Heb 1: 7 God c his angels / "messengers swift as the wind,
Rev 2:20 that Jezebel who c herself a prophet—to lead my

CALM (10) [CALMED, CALMS]

Job 26:12 By his power the sea grew c. By his skill he
Pr 12:16 but a wise person stays c when insulted.
29: 8 town agitated, but those who are wise will c anger.
Eze 16:42 I will be c and will not be angry with you anymore.
32:14 Then I will let the waters of Egypt become c again,
Jnh 1:12 the sea," Jonah said, "and it will become c again.
Zep 3:17 With his love, he will c all your fears.
Mt 8:26 the wind and waves, and suddenly all was c.
Mk 4:39 the wind stopped, and there was a great c.
Lk 8:24 the raging waves. The storm stopped and all was c!

CALMED (1) [CALM]

Ps 107:29 He c the storm to a whisper / and stilled the waves.

CALMS (1) [CALM]

Pr 21:14 A secret gift c anger; a secret bribe pacifies fury.

CALNEH (2) [CALNO]

Ge 10:10 with the cities of Babel, Erech, Akkad, and C.
Am 6: 2 Go over to C and see what happened there.

CALNO (1) [CALNEH]

Isa 10: 9 We will destroy C just as we did Carchemish.

CALVARY [KJV] See SKULL

CALVES (26) [CALF]

Dt 28:51 you no grain, new wine, olive oil, c, or lambs,
1Sa 6: 7 a new cart, and find two cows that have just had c.
6: 7 the cart, but shut their c away from them in a pen.
6:10 Two cows with newborn c were hitched to the cart,
and their c were shut up in a pen.
14:32 and butchered the sheep, cattle, and c,
15: 9 best of the sheep and cattle, the fat c and lambs—
1Ki 1: 9 where he sacrificed sheep, oxen, and fattened c.
1:19 has sacrificed many oxen, fattened c, and sheep,
1:25 he has sacrificed many oxen, fattened c, and sheep,
12:28 advice of his counselors, the king made two gold c.
12:32 he himself offered sacrifices to the c he had made.
14: 9 and have made me furious with your gold c.
2Ki 10:29 however, destroy the gold c at Bethel and Dan,
17:16 the LORD their God and made two c from metal.
2Ch 13: 8 but with you are those gold c that Jeroboam made
Job 21:10 to breed. Their cows bear c without miscarriage.
Ps 68:30 the reeds, / this herd of bulls among the weaker c.
Isa 11: 6 C and yearlings will be safe among lions, and a
11: 7 among bears. Cubs and c will lie down together.
Jer 46:21 famed mercenaries have become like fattened c.
Am 6: 4 eating the meat of tender lambs and choice c.
Mic 6: 6 we bow before God with offerings of yearling c?
Mal 4: 2 go free, leaping with joy like c let out to pasture.
Heb 9:12 Most Holy Place, but not the blood of goats and c.
9:19 he took the blood of c and goats, along with water,

CALVES' (1) [CALF]

Eze 1: 7 but their feet were split like c feet and shone like

CAME (861) [COME] See Index of Articles, Etc.

CAMEL (11) [CAMELS]

Ge 24:32 and provided water for the c drivers to wash their
31:34 and had stuffed them into her c saddle,
Lev 11: 4 The c may not be eaten, for though it chews the
Dt 14: 7 So you may not eat the c, the hare, or the rock
Jer 2:23 You are like a restless female c, desperate for a
Mt 3: 4 John's clothes were woven from c hair, and he
19:24 it is easier for a c to go through the eye of a needle
23:24 accidentally swallow a gnat, then you swallow a c!
Mk 1: 6 His clothes were woven from c hair, and he wore a
10:25 It is easier for a c to go through the eye of a needle
Lk 18:25 It is easier for a c to go through the eye of a needle

CAMELS (50) [CAMEL]

Ge 12:16 cattle, donkeys, male and female servants, and c.
24:10 He loaded ten of Abraham's c with gifts and set
24:11 There the servant made the c kneel down beside a
24:14 'Yes, certainly, and I will water your c, too!'—
24:19 she said, "I'll draw water for your c, too,
24:20 She kept carrying water to the c until they had
24:22 Then at last, when the c had finished drinking,
24:25 Yes, we have plenty of straw and food for the c,
24:30 where the man was still standing beside his c.
24:31 all ready for you and a place prepared for the c!"
24:32 and Laban unloaded the c, gave him straw to bed
24:35 and gold, and many servants and c and donkeys.
24:44 And I'll water your c, too!" LORD, let her be the
24:46 'Certainly, sir, and I will water your c, too!'
24:61 Then Rebekah and her servants mounted the c
24:63 meditating, he looked up and saw the c coming.
30:43 very wealthy, with many servants, c, and donkeys.
31:17 So Jacob put his wives and children on c.
32: 7 along with the flocks and herds and c, into two
32:15 thirty female c with their young, forty cows,
37:25 they noticed a caravan of c in the distance coming
Ex 9: 3 destroy your horses, donkeys, c, cattle, and sheep.
Jdg 6: 5 arrived on droves of c too numerous to count.
7:12 Their c were like grains of sand on the seashore—
8:21 took the royal ornaments from the necks of their c.
8:26 the kings, or the chains around the necks of their c.
1Sa 15: 3 men, women, children, babies, cattle, sheep, c,
27: 9 He took the sheep, cattle, donkeys, c, and clothing
30:17 except four hundred young men who fled on c.
1Ki 10: 2 and a great caravan of c loaded with spices,
2Ki 8: 9 So Hazael loaded down forty c with the finest
1Ch 5:21 plunder taken from the Hagrites included 50,000 c,
12:40 brought food on donkeys, c, mules, and oxen.
27:30 Obil the Ishmaelite was in charge of the c.
2Ch 9: 1 and a great caravan of c loaded with spices,
14:15 and c before finally returning to Jerusalem.
Ezr 2:67 435 c, and 6,720 donkeys.
Ne 7:69 435 c, and 6,720 donkeys.
Job 1: 3 three thousand c, five hundred teams of oxen,
1:17 bands of Chaldean raiders have stolen your c
42:12 six thousand c, one thousand teams of oxen,
Isa 21: 7 and warriors mounted on donkeys and c."
30: 6 and c loaded with treasure to pay for Egypt's aid.
60: 6 Vast caravans of c will converge on you, the c of
Midian and Ephah.
66:20 in chariots and wagons, and on mules and c,"
Jer 49:29 their household goods and c will be taken away.
49:32 Their c and cattle will all be yours. I will scatter to
Eze 25: 5 I will turn the city of Rabbah into a pasture for c,
Zec 14:15 plague will strike the horses, mules, c, donkeys,

CAMON [KJV] See KAMON

CAMP (169) [CAMPED, CAMPING, CAMPS, CAMPSITE, ENCAMPMENT]

Ge 12: 6 and set up c beside the oak at Moreh.
12: 8 and set up c in the hill country between Bethel on
13:18 Then Abram moved his c to the oak grove owned
26:25 He set up his c at that place, and his servants dug a
28:11 At sundown he arrived at a good place to set up c
31:25 of Gilead, he set up his c not far from Jacob's.
32: 2 Jacob saw them, he exclaimed, "This is God's c!"
32:21 sent on ahead, and Jacob spent that night in the c.
32:24 This left Jacob all alone in the c, and a man came
33:18 in Canaan, and they set up c just outside the town.
34:26 from Shechem's house and returned to their c.
Ex 14: 2 C there along the shore, opposite Baal-zephon.
14:20 turned into a pillar of fire, lighting the Israelite c.
16:13 vast numbers of quail arrived and covered the c.
16:13 The next morning the desert all around the c was
19: 2 After breaking c at Rephidim, they came to the
base of Mount Sinai and set up c there.
19:17 Moses led them out from the c to meet with God,
29:14 outside the c, and burn it as a sin offering.
32:17 to Moses, "It sounds as if there is a war in the c!"
32:19 When they came near the c, Moses saw the calf
32:26 he stood at the entrance to the c and shouted,
32:27 and forth from one end of the c to the other,
33: 7 known as the Tent of Meeting far outside the c.
33:11 Afterward Moses would return to the c,
36: 6 and this message was sent throughout the c:
Lev 4:12 away to a ceremonially clean place outside the c,
4:21 then take what is left of the bull outside the c
6:11 and carry the ashes outside the c to a place that is
8:17 its hide, meat, and dung, was burned outside the c,
9:11 and the hide, however, he burned outside the c.
10: 4 away from the sanctuary to a place outside the c."
10: 5 and carried them out of the c by their tunics as
13:46 and must live in isolation outside the c.
14: 3 who will examine them at a place outside the c.
14: 8 and may return to live inside the c.
16:26 and bathe in water. Then he may return to the c.
16:27 will be carried outside the c to be burned.
16:28 bathe himself in water before returning to the c.
17: 3 a lamb or a goat anywhere inside or outside the c
24:14 "Take the blasphemer outside the c, and tell all
24:23 they led the blasphemer outside the c and stoned
Nu 1:50 and they must care for it and c around it.
1:53 But the Levites will c around the Tabernacle of the
2: 2 "Each tribe will be assigned its own area in the c,
2: 2 and the various groups will c beneath their family

2: 3[-4] Zebulun are to c toward the sunrise on the east
2: 9 all the troops on Judah's side of the c is 186,400.
2: 10[-11] and Gad are to c on the south side of the
2: 16 all the troops on Reuben's side of the c is 151,450.
2: 17 out from the middle of the c with the Tabernacle.
2: 17 the tribes are to travel in the same order that they c,
2: 18[-19] and Benjamin are to c on the west side of the
2: 24 the troops on Ephraim's side of the c is 108,100,
2: 25[-26] and Naphtali are to c on the north side of the
2: 31 So the total of all the troops on Dan's side of the c
2: 34 Each clan and family set up c and marched under
3: 23 the area to the west of the Tabernacle for their c.
3: 29 the area south of the Tabernacle for their c.
3: 35 the area north of the Tabernacle for their c.
4: 5 When the c moves, Aaron and his sons must enter
5: 2 from the c who has a contagious skin disease
5: 3 Remove them so they will not defile the c, where I
5: 4 and removed such people from the c.
9: 20 at the LORD's command they would break c.
9: 21 the cloud lifted, the people broke c and followed.
9: 22 the people of Israel stayed in c and did not move
9: 22 But as soon as it lifted, they broke c and moved on.
10: 2 to assemble and for signaling the breaking of c.
10: 5 on the east side of the Tabernacle will break c
10: 21 When they arrived at the next c, the Tabernacle
10: 31 the places in the wilderness where we should c.
11: 1 among them and destroyed the outskirts of the c.
11: 9 The manna came down on the c with the dew
11: 26 were still in the c when the Spirit rested upon
11: 26 the Tabernacle, so they prophesied there in the c.
11: 27 "Eldad and Medad are prophesying in the c!"
11: 30 Then Moses returned to the c with the leaders of
11: 31 and let them fall into the c and all around it!
11: 31 For many miles in every direction from the c there
11: 32 They spread the quail out all over the c.
12: 14 Banish her from the c for seven days, and after that
12: 15 So Miriam was excluded from the c for seven
13: 3 of Israel, from their c in the wilderness of Paran.
14: 44 nor the Ark of the LORD's covenant left the c.
15: 35 whole community must stone him outside the c."
15: 36 the whole community took the man outside the c
19: 3 and it will be taken outside the c and slaughtered in
19: 7 Afterward he may return to the c, though he will
19: 9 and place them in a purified place outside the c.
21: 12 traveled to the valley of Zered Brook and set up c.
25: 6 men brought a Midianite woman into the c,
31: 13 of the people went to meet them outside the c.
31: 19 or touched a dead body must stay outside the c for
31: 24 and be purified. Then you may return to the c."
33: 5 leaving Rameses, the Israelites set up c at Succoth.
Dt 1: 7 It is time to break c and move on. Go to the hill
1: 33 goes before you looking for the best places to c,
23: 10 because of a nocturnal emission must leave the c
23: 11 bathe himself, and at sunset he may return to the c.
23: 12 "Mark off an area outside the c for a latrine.
23: 14 The c must be holy, for the LORD your God moves around in your c
Jos 1: 11 "Go through the c and tell the people to get their
2: 1 sent out two spies from the Israelite c at Acacia.
3: 2 days later, the Israelite leaders went through the c
4: 3 and pile them up at the place where you c
5: 8 they rested in the c until they were healed.
6: 11 then everyone returned to spend the night in the c.
6: 14 marched around the city once and returned to the c.
6: 23 whole family to a safe place near the c of Israel.
8: 9 But Joshua remained among the people in the c
9: 6 When they arrived at the c of Israel at Gilgal,
10: 15 and the Israelite army returned to their c at Gilgal.
10: 21 Then the Israelites returned safely to their c at
10: 43 and the Israelite army returned to their c at Gilgal.
11: 5 They established their c around the water near
18: 9 Then they returned to Joshua in the c at Shiloh.
Jdg 7: 8 Now the Midianite c was in the valley just below
7: 9 Go down into the Midianite c, for I have given you
7: 10 go down to the c with your servant Purah.
7: 11 and went down to the outposts of the enemy c.
7: 13 bread came tumbling down into the Midianite c.
7: 15 Then he returned to the Israelite c and shouted,
7: 17 When I come to the edge of the c, do just as I do.
7: 18 those of you on the other sides of the c blow your
7: 19 with him reached the outer edge of the Midianite c.
7: 21 Each man stood at his position around the c
7: 22 the LORD caused the warriors in the c to fight
15: 9 The Philistines retaliated by setting up c in Judah
21: 12 and they brought them to the c at Shiloh in the land
1Sa 4: 3 the army of Israel retreated to their c, and their
4: 5 of the Covenant of the LORD coming into the c,
4: 6 "What's all the shouting about in the Hebrew c?"
4: 7 "The gods have come into their c!" they cried.
13: 16 The Philistines set up their c at Micmash.
13: 17 Three raiding parties soon left the c of the
14: 3 one realized that Jonathan had left the Israelite c.
14: 15 both in the c and in the field, including even the
14: 19 and confusion in the Philistine c grew louder
17: 20 He arrived at the outskirts of the c just as the
17: 53 and plundered the deserted Philistine c.
26: 5 David slipped over to Saul's c one night to look
26: 7 So David and Abishai went right into Saul's c
26: 13 David climbed the hill opposite the c until he was
28: 4 The Philistines set up their c at Shunem, and Saul
2Sa 1: 3 "I escaped from the Israelite c," the man replied.
17: 26 and the Israelite army set up c in the land of
2Ki 3: 24 When they arrived at the Israelite c, the army of
7: 5 So that evening they went out to the c of the
7: 8 When the lepers arrived at the edge of the c,
7: 10 that they had gone out to the Aramean c and no
7: 12 so they have left their c and have hidden in the
7: 16 Samaria rushed out and plundered the Aramean c.
19: 35 the angel of the LORD went out to the Assyrian c
19: 36 Then King Sennacherib of Assyria broke c
1Ch 9: 19 had guarded the Tabernacle in the c of the LORD.
Ezr 8: 31 We broke c at the Ahava Canal on April 19
Job 19: 12 up roads to attack me. They c all around my tent.
Ps 78: 28 He caused the birds to fall within their c / and all
106: 16 The people in the c were jealous of Moses
118: 15 of joy and victory are sung in the c of the godly.
Isa 13: 20 Nomads will refuse to c there, and shepherds will
37: 36 the angel of the LORD went out to the Assyrian c
37: 37 Then King Sennacherib of Assyria broke c
Jer 6: 3 They will set up c around the city and divide your
Eze 34: 25 Then my people will be able to c safely in the
Heb 13: 11 bodies of the animals were burned outside the c.
13: 13 So let us go out to him outside the c and bear the

CAMPAIGN (3)

Jos 10: 42 In a single c Joshua conquered all these kings
22: 3 even though the c has lasted for such a long time.
1Sa 21: 5 my men to be with women when they are on a c.

CAMPED (100) [CAMP]

Ge 13: 3 between Bethel and Ai where they had c before.
14: 13 who was c at the oak grove belonging to Mamre
18: 1 he was c near the oak grove belonging to Mamre.
25: 16 listed according to the places they settled and c.
25: 18 The clans descended from Ishmael c close to one
31: 25 So when Laban caught up with Jacob as he was c
33: 19 Jacob bought the land he c on from the family of
35: 21 then traveled on and c beyond the tower of Eder.
Ex 13: 20 they c at Etham on the edge of the wilderness.
14: 4 So the Israelites c there as they were told.
14: 9 as they were c beside the shore near Pi-hahiroth,
15: 27 palm trees. They c there beside the springs.
18: 5 and the people were c near the mountain of God.
Nu 9: 17 wherever the cloud settled, the people of Israel c.
9: 23 So they c or traveled at the LORD's command,
10: 14 The tribes that c with Judah headed the march with
10: 18 Then the tribes that c with Reuben set out with
10: 22 Then the tribes that c with Ephraim set out with
10: 25 the tribes that c with Dan set out under their
12: 16 they left Hazeroth and c in the wilderness of Paran.
20: 1 arrived in the wilderness of Zin and c at Kadesh.
20: 16 Now we are c at Kadesh, a town on the border of
21: 10 The Israelites traveled next to Oboth and c there.
22: 1 the plains of Moab and c east of the Jordan River,
24: 2 where he saw the people of Israel c, tribe by tribe.
25: 1 While the Israelites were c at Acacia, some of the
26: 3 At that time the entire nation of Israel was c on the
31: 12 which was c on the plains of Moab beside the
33: 6 and c at Etham on the edge of the wilderness.
33: 7 opposite Baal-zephon, and c near Migdol.
33: 8 days into the Etham wilderness and c at Marah.
33: 9 They left Marah and c at Elim, where there are
33: 10 They left Elim and c beside the Red Sea.
33: 11 They left the Red Sea and c in the Sin Desert.
33: 12 They left the Sin Desert and c at Dophkah.
33: 13 They left Dophkah and c at Alush.
33: 14 They left Alush and c at Rephidim, where there
33: 15 left Rephidim and c in the wilderness of Sinai.
33: 16 the wilderness of Sinai and c at Kibroth-hattaavah.
33: 17 They left Kibroth-hattaavah and c at Hazeroth.
33: 18 They left Hazeroth and c at Rithmah.
33: 19 They left Rithmah and c at Rimmon-perez.
33: 20 They left Rimmon-perez and c at Libnah.
33: 21 They left Libnah and c at Rissah.
33: 22 They left Rissah and c at Kehelathah.
33: 23 They left Kehelathah and c at Mount Shepher.
33: 24 They left Mount Shepher and c at Haradah.
33: 25 They left Haradah and c at Makheloth.
33: 26 They left Makheloth and c at Tahath.
33: 27 They left Tahath and c at Terah.
33: 28 They left Terah and c at Mithcah.
33: 29 They left Mithcah and c at Hashmonah.
33: 30 They left Hashmonah and c at Moseroth.
33: 31 They left Moseroth and c at Bene-jaakan.
33: 32 They left Bene-jaakan and c at Hor-haggidgad.
33: 33 They left Hor-haggidgad and c at Jotbathah.
33: 34 They left Jotbathah and c at Abronah.
33: 35 They left Abronah and c at Ezion-geber.
33: 36 and c at Kadesh in the wilderness of Zin.
33: 37 They left Kadesh and c at Mount Hor, at the border
33: 41 the Israelites left Mount Hor and c at Zalmonah.
33: 42 Then they left Zalmonah and c at Punon.
33: 43 They left Punon and c at Oboth.
33: 44 and c at Iye-abarim on the border of Moab.
33: 45 They left Iye-abarim and c at Dibon-gad.
33: 46 They left Dibon-gad and c at Almon-diblathaim.
33: 47 and c in the mountains east of the river,
33: 48 and c on the plains of Moab beside the Jordan
33: 49 Along the Jordan River they c from
33: 50 While they were c near the Jordan River on the
35: 1 While Israel was c beside the Jordan on the plains
36: 13 c on the plains of Moab beside the Jordan River,
Dt 1: 1 They were c in the Jordan Valley near Suph,
4: 46 and as they c in the valley near Beth-peor east of
Jos 3: 1 of the Jordan River, where they c before crossing.
4: 8 They carried them to the place where they c for the
4: 19 from Egypt. They c at Gilgal, east of Jericho.
5: 10 While the Israelites were c at Gilgal on the plains
8: 11 They c on the north side of Ai, with a valley
Jdg 7: 1 The armies of Midian were c north of them in the
10: 17 had gathered for war and were c in Gilead,
11: 18 and c on the other side of the Arnon River.
18: 12 They c at a place west of Kiriath-jearim in Judah,
20: 19 left early the next morning and c near Gibeah.
1Sa 4: 1 The Israelite army was c near Ebenezer,
13: 5 They c at Micmash east of Beth-aven.
14: 2 and his six hundred men were c on the outskirts of
17: 1 and c between Socoh in Judah and Azekah at
23: 28 the place where David was c has been called the
26: 3 Saul c along the road beside the hill of Hakilah,
28: 4 and Saul and the armies of Israel c at Gilboa.
29: 1 and the Israelites c at the spring in Jezreel.
2Sa 23: 13 the Philistine army was c in the valley of Rephaim.
24: 5 First they crossed the Jordan and c at Aroer,
1Ki 17: 5 LORD had told him and c beside Kerith Brook.
20: 29 The two armies c opposite each other for seven
1Ch 11: 15 the Philistine army was c in the valley of Rephaim.
19: 7 These forces c at Medeba, where they were joined
Ezr 8: 15 and we c there for three days while I went over the
Ne 13: 20 and tradesmen with a variety of wares c outside

CAMPHIRE [KJV] See FLOWERS

CAMPING (5) [CAMP]

Nu 1: 52 Each tribe of Israel will have a designated c area
Jdg 6: 4 c in the land and destroying crops as far away as
6: 33 and crossed the Jordan, c in the valley of Jezreel.
2Sa 11: 11 and Joab and his officers are c in the open fields.
Ne 13: 21 "What are you doing out here, c around the wall?

CAMPS (10) [CAMP]

Ge 32: 7 with the flocks and herds and camels, into two c.
32: 10 a walking stick, and now my household fills two c!
Ex 14: 20 cloud settled between the Israelite and Egyptian c.
Nu 10: 25 They served as the rear guard for all the tribal c.
1Ch 9: 18 These men served as gatekeepers for the c of the
2Ch 14: 15 They also attacked the c of herdsmen and captured
Eze 4: 2 Surround it with enemy c and battering rams.
25: 4 They will set up their c among you and pitch their
Zep 2: 6 a place of shepherd c and enclosures for sheep.
Zec 14: 15 donkeys, and all the other animals in the enemy c.

CAMPSITE (2) [CAMP]

Nu 2: 9 the way whenever the Israelites travel to a new c.
2: 31 the rear whenever the Israelites move to a new c."

CAN (1177) [CAN'T, CANNOT] See Index of Articles, Etc.

CAN'T (114) [CAN, NOT] See Index of Articles, Etc.

CANA (5)

Jn 2: 1 wedding celebration in the village of C in Galilee.
2: 11 This miraculous sign at C in Galilee was Jesus'
4: 46 he arrived at the town of C, where he had turned
4: 47 and was traveling in Galilee, he went over to C.
21: 2 Nathanael from C in Galilee, the sons of Zebedee,

CANAAN (92) [CANAAN'S, CANAANITE, CANAANITES]

LAND OF CANAAN (48) Ge 11:31; 13:12; 16:3; 17:8; 23:2; 31:18; 36:5,6; 37:1; 42:7,13,29,32; 45:25; 46:6,12,31; 48:3,4,7; 50:5,13; Ex 6:4; 16:35; Lev 25:38; Nu 13:2; 26:19; 32:30; 33:40,51; 34:2,29; 35:10,14; Dt 32:49; Jos 14:7,9; 21:2; 22:9,11,32; 24:3; Jdg 21:12; 1Ch 16:18; Ps 105:11,16; Zep 2:5; Heb 4:8

Ge 9: 22 Ham, the father of C, saw that his father was naked
9: 25 Then he cursed the descendants of C, the son of
9: 26 the LORD my God; / and may C be his servant.
9: 27 the prosperity of Shem; / and let C be his servant."
10: 6 of Ham were Cush, Mizraim, Put, and C.
10: 15 C was also the ancestor of the Hittites,
10: 19 Eventually the territory of C spread from Sidon to
11: 31 and left Ur of the Chaldeans to go to the land of C.
12: 5 his household at Haran—and finally arrived in C.
12: 6 Traveling through C, they came to a place near
13: 12 So while Abram stayed in the land of C,
16: 3 years after Abram first arrived in the land of C.)
17: 8 I will give all this land of C to you and to your
23: 2 Kiriath-arba (now called Hebron) in the land of C.
23: 19 So Abraham buried Sarah there in C, in the cave of
31: 18 and set out on his journey to the land of C,
33: 18 Then they arrived safely at Shechem, in C,
35: 6 they arrived at Luz (now called Bethel) in C.
36: 2 Esau married two young women from C: Adah,
36: 5 All these sons were born to Esau in the land of C.
36: 6 all the wealth he had gained in the land of C—
37: 1 So Jacob settled again in the land of C, where his
42: 5 to buy food, for the famine had reached C as well.
42: 7 "From the land of C," they replied.
42: 13 of us brothers, and our father is in the land of C.
42: 29 in the land of C and told him all that had
42: 32 the youngest is with our father in the land of C.'
45: 17 and return quickly to their homes in C.
45: 25 and returned to their father, Jacob, in the land of C.
46: 6 the belongings they had acquired in the land of C.
46: 12 (But Er and Onan had died in the land of C.)
46: 31 you have all come from the land of C to join me.
47: 1 "My father and my brothers are here from C.
47: 4 in Egypt, for there is no pasture for our flocks in C.
47: 13 crops continued to fail throughout Egypt and C.
47: 14 the money in Egypt and C in exchange for grain,
47: 15 When the people of Egypt and C ran out of money,
48: 3 Almighty appeared to me at Luz in the land of C

48: 4 and I will give this land of C to you and your
48: 7 from Paddan, Rachel died in the land of C.
48:21 will be with you and will bring you again to C,
49:30 cave in the field of Machpelah, near Mamre in C,
50: 5 take my body back to the land of C, and bury me
50:13 They carried his body to the land of C and buried it
50:25 he said, "When God comes to lead us back to C,
Ex 6: 4 its terms, I swore to give them the land of C,
15:15 All the people of C will melt with fear;
16:35 for forty years until they arrived in the land of C,
Lev 14:34 "When you arrive in C, the land I am giving you
18: 3 or like the people of C, where I am taking you.
25:38 brought you out of Egypt to give you the land of C
Nu 13: 2 "Send men to explore the land of C, the land I am
14:40 next morning and set out for the hill country of C.
14:44 people pushed ahead toward the hill country of C,
26:19 Er and Onan, who had died in the land of C.
32:30 accept land with the rest of you in the land of C."
32:32 We will cross the Jordan into C fully armed to
33:40 of Arad, who lived in the Negev in the land of C,
33:51 you cross the Jordan River into the land of C,
34: 2 When you come into the land of C, which I am
34:29 dividing of the land of C among the Israelites."
35:10 'When you cross the Jordan into the land of C,
35:14 and three on the west in the land of C.
Dt 2:12 In a similar way the peoples in C were driven from
32:49 Look out across the land of C, the land I am giving
Jos 5:12 that time on the Israelites ate from the crops of C.
11: 3 the kings of C, both east and west; the kings of the
14: 1 The remaining tribes of Israel inherited land in C
14: 7 me from Kadesh-barnea to explore the land of C.
14: 9 'The land of C on which you were just walking
21: 2 They spoke to them at Shiloh in the land of C,
22: 9 left the rest of Israel at Shiloh in the land of C.
22:10 But while they were still in C, before they crossed
22:11 Geliloth west of the Jordan River, in the land of C,
22:32 and returned to the land of C to tell the Israelites
24: 3 the Euphrates and led him into the land of C.
Jdg 3: 1 who had not participated in the wars of C.
5:19 "The kings of C fought at Taanach near
21:12 them to the camp at Shiloh in the land of C.
1Ch 1: 8 of Ham were Cush, Mizraim, Put, and C.
1:13 C was also the ancestor of the Hittites,
16:18 "I will give you the land of C / as your special
16:19 few in number, / a tiny group of strangers in C.
Ps 105:11 "I will give you the land of C / as your special
105:12 few in number, / a tiny group of strangers in C.
105:16 He called for a famine on the land of C,
106:38 By sacrificing them to the idols of C,
135:11 Og king of Bashan, / and all the kings of C.
Zep 2: 5 who live along the coast and in the land of C,
Ac 7:11 "But a famine came upon Egypt and C. There was
13:19 Then he destroyed seven nations in C and gave
Heb 4: 8 This new place of rest was not the land of C,

CANAAN'S (2) [CANAAN]
Ge 10:15 C oldest son was Sidon, the ancestor of the
1Ch 1:13 C oldest son was Sidon, the ancestor of the

CANAANITE (16) [CANAAN]
Ge 24: 3 not let my son marry one of these local C women.
24:37 not let Isaac marry one of the local C women.
28: 1 and said, "Do not marry any of these C women.
28: 6 and that he had warned Jacob not to marry a C
28: 8 to Esau that his father despised the local C women.
38: 2 There he met a C woman, the daughter of Shua,
46:10 and Shaul. (Shaul's mother was a C woman.)
Ex 6:15 Jakin, Zohar, and Shaul (whose mother was a C).
Nu 21: 1 The C king of Arad, who lived in the Negev,
33:40 It was then that the C king of Arad, who lived in
Jos 5: 1 and all the C kings who lived along the
Jdg 4: 2 them over to King Jabin of Hazor, a C king.
4:23 that day Israel saw God subdue Jabin, the C king.
1Ki 9:16 killing the C population and burning it down.
1Ch 2: 3 had three sons through Bathshua, a C woman.
Eze 16: 3 You are nothing but a C! Your father was an

CANAANITES (56) [CANAAN]
Ge 9:18 with their father. (Ham is the ancestor of the C.)
9:25 of Canaan, the son of Ham: / "A curse on the C!
12: 6 At that time, the area was inhabited by C.
13: 7 At that time C and Perizzites were also living in
15:21 Amorites, C, Girgashites, and Jebusites."
34:30 of this land—among all the C and Perizzites.
50:11 The local residents, the C, renamed the place
Ex 3: 8 the land where the C, Hittites, Amorites,
3:17 I will lead you to the land now occupied by the C,
13: 5 the LORD brings you into the land of the C,
13:11 long ago, the land where the C are now living.
23:23 Hittites, Perizzites, C, Hivites, and Jebusites,
23:28 of you to drive out the Hivites, C, and Hittites.
33: 2 I will send an angel before you to drive out the C,
34:11 the Amorites, C, Hittites, Perizzites, Hivites,
Nu 13:29 The C live along the coast of the Mediterranean
14:25 toward the land where the Amalekites and C live.
14:43 When you face the Amalekites and C in battle,
14:45 and the C who lived in those hills came down
21: 3 their request and gave them victory over the C.
Dt 1: 7 Go to the land of the C and to Lebanon, and all the
7: 1 Girgashites, Amorites, C, Perizzites, Hivites,
11:30 in the land of the C who live in the Jordan Valley,
20:17 Amorites, C, Perizzites, Hivites, and Jebusites,
Jos 3:10 He will surely drive out the C, Hittites, Hivites,
7: 9 For when the C and all the other people living in
9: 1 Amorites, C, Perizzites, Hivites, and Jebusites,
12: 8 the Amorites, the C, the Perizzites, the Hivites,
13: 3 territory that belongs to the C. This land extends
13: 4 all the land of the C, including Mearah (which
16:10 They did not drive the C out of Gezer, however,
17:12 They could not drive out the C who continued to
17:13 strong enough, they forced the C to work as slaves.
17:16 and the C in the lowlands around Beth-shan
17:18 And I am sure you can drive out the C from the
24:11 the Perizzites, the C, the Hittites, the Girgashites,
Jdg 1: 1 "Which tribe should attack the C first?"
1: 3 "Join with us to fight against the C living in the
1: 4 the LORD gave them victory over the C
1: 5 and the C and Perizzites were defeated.
1: 9 Then they turned south to fight the C living in the
1:10 Judah marched against the C in Hebron (formerly
1:17 Simeon to fight against the C living in Zephath,
1:27 because the C were determined to stay in that
1:28 grew stronger, they forced the C to work as slaves,
1:29 The tribe of Ephraim also failed to drive out the C
1:29 so the C continued to live there among them.
1:30 The tribe of Zebulun also failed to drive out the C
1:32 the C dominated the land where the people of
1:33 the C dominated the land where they lived.
3: 3 the five Philistine rulers), all the C, the Sidonians,
3: 5 So Israel lived among the C, Hittites, Amorites,
2Sa 24: 7 of Tyre, and all the cities of the Hivites and C.
Ezr 9: 1 have taken up the detestable practices of the C,
Ne 9: 8 to give him and his descendants the land of the C,
9:24 Even the kings and the C, who inhabited the land,

CANAL (3) [CANALS]
Ezr 8:15 I assembled the exiles at the Ahava C, and we
8:21 And there by the Ahava C, I gave orders for all of
8:31 We broke camp at the Ahava C on April 19

CANALS (3) [CANAL]
Ex 7:19 of Egypt—all its rivers, c, marshes, and reservoirs.
8: 5 c, and marshes of Egypt so there will be frogs in
Isa 19: 6 The c of the Nile will dry up, and the streams of

CANCEL (7) [CANCELED, CANCELING, CANCELS]
Lev 26:44 I will not c my covenant with them by wiping them
Dt 15: 1 "At the end of every seventh year you must c your
15: 2 Creditors must c the loans they have made to their
Ne 10:31 and to c the debts owed to us by other Jews.
Isa 28:18 I will c the bargain you made to avoid death,
Jer 26:13 he will c this disaster that he has announced
Jnh 4: 2 I knew how easily you could c your plans for

CANCELED (3) [CANCEL]
Lk 7:43 "I suppose the one for whom he c the larger
Gal 3:17 c 430 years later when God gave the law to Moses.
Col 2:14 He c the record that contained the charges against

CANCELING (2) [CANCEL]
Da 8:11 armies by c the daily sacrifices offered to him
Lk 7:42 so he kindly forgave them both, c their debts.

CANCELS (1) [CANCEL]
Heb 10: 9 He c the first covenant in order to establish the

CANCER (1)
2Ti 2:17 This kind of talk spreads like c. Hymenaeus

CANDLE(S) [KJV] See LAMP, LANTERNS

CANDLESTICK(S) [KJV] See also LAMP(S), LAMPSTAND(S), LANTERNS, TORCH

CANDLEWICK (1) [WICK]
Isa 43:17 their lives snuffed out like a smoldering c.

CANE (3)
Ex 30:23 6-1/4 pounds each of cinnamon and of sweet c,
Isa 10:15 unless a hand is moving it? Can a c walk by itself?
Zec 8: 4 and women will walk Jerusalem's streets with a c

CANKER [KJV] See CANCER

CANKERWORM [KJV] See LOCUST(S)

CANNEH (1)
Eze 27:23 Haran, C, Eden, Sheba, Asshur, and Kilmad came

CANNOT (221) [CAN, NOT] See Index of Articles, Etc.

CANOPY (8)
1Ki 7: 6 covered by a c that was supported by pillars.
8: 7 forming a c over the Ark and its carrying poles.
2Ki 16:18 he also removed the c that had been constructed
2Ch 5: 8 forming a c over the Ark and its carrying poles.
SS 3:10 Its posts are of silver, its c is gold, and its seat is
Isa 4: 5 There will be a c of smoke and cloud throughout
Jer 43:10 have hidden. He will spread his royal c over them.
Eze 41:25 And there was a wooden c over the front of the

CAPABLE (13)
Ex 18:21 But find some c, honest men who fear God
18:25 He chose c men from all over Israel and made
1Ki 11:28 Jeroboam was a very c young man, and when
1Ch 26: 7 Elihu and Semakiah, were also very c men.
26: 8 were very c men, well qualified for their work.
26: 9 eighteen sons and relatives were also very c men.
26:30 and his relatives—seventeen hundred c men—
26:31 and c men from the clan of Hebron were found at
26:32 There were twenty-seven hundred c men among
2Ch 22: 9 of Ahaziah's family was c of ruling the kingdom.
Pr 31:10 Who can find a virtuous and c wife? She is worth
31:29 are many virtuous and c women in the world,
Da 6: 3 Daniel soon proved himself more c than all the

CAPE (1) [CAPES]
Ac 27: 7 to the leeward side of Crete, past the c of Salmone.

CAPERNAUM (19)
Mt 4:13 he went to C, beside the Sea of Galilee,
8: 5 When Jesus arrived in C, a Roman officer came
11:23 And you people of C, will you be exalted to
17:24 On their arrival in C, the tax collectors for the
Mk 1:21 Jesus and his companions went to the town of C,
1:33 And a huge crowd of people from all over C
2: 1 Several days later Jesus returned to C,
9:33 After they arrived at C, Jesus and his disciples
10: 1 Then Jesus left C and went southward to the region
Lk 4:23 here in your hometown like those you did in C?'
4:31 Then Jesus went to C, a town in Galilee,
7: 1 had finished saying all this, he went back to C.
10:15 And you people of C, will you be exalted to
Jn 2:12 After the wedding he went to C for a few days
4:46 There was a government official in the city of C
4:47 and begged him to come to C with him to heal his
6:17 the boat and headed out across the lake toward C.
6:24 into the boats and went across to C to look for him.
6:59 while he was teaching in the synagogue in C.

CAPES (1) [CAPE]
Isa 3:22 party clothes, gowns, c, and purses;

CAPHTORITES (3)
Ge 10:14 Pathrusites, Casluhites, and the C, from whom the
Dt 2:23 A similar thing happened when the C from Crete
1Ch 1:12 Pathrusites, Casluhites, and the C, from whom the

CAPITAL (35) [CAPITALS]
Lev 17: 4 that person will be guilty of a c offense.
20: 9 be put to death. They are guilty of a c offense.
20:11 woman must die, for they are guilty of a c offense.
20:12 contrary to nature and are guilty of a c offense.
20:13 a detestable act and are guilty of a c offense.
20:16 Both must die, for they are guilty of a c offense.
20:19 Both parties are guilty of a c offense.
20:20 and woman involved are guilty of a c offense
20:27 death by stoning. They are guilty of a c offense."
Nu 21:26 Heshbon had been the c of King Sihon of the
Jos 11:10 (Hazor had at one time been the c of the federation
2Sa 2:11 David made Hebron his c, and he ruled as king of
4: 4 When news of the battle reached the c, the child's
8: 6 the Aramean c, and the Arameans became David's
12:26 ending their siege of Rabbah, the c of Ammon.
1Ki 7:17 Each c was decorated with seven sets of
7:20 Each c on the two pillars had two hundred
12:25 in the hill country of Ephraim, and it became his c.
16:17 away from Gibbethon to attack Tirzah, Israel's c.
20: 1 They went to besiege Samaria, the Israelite c,
2Ki 8: 7 Now Elisha went to Damascus, the c of Aram,
16: 9 So the Assyrians attacked the Aramean c of
19:36 He went home to his c of Nineveh and stayed
25:17 The bronze c on top of each pillar was 7-1/2 feet
1Ch 13: 4 Then David moved the c to Jerusalem, where he
18: 6 the Aramean c, and the Arameans became David's
2Ch 3:15 each topped by a c extending upward another 7-1/2
Isa 7: 8 because Aram is no stronger than its c, Damascus.
7: 9 Israel is no stronger than its c, Samaria.
37:37 He went home to his c of Nineveh and stayed
Jer 52:22 The bronze c on top of each pillar was 7-1/2 feet
Eze 21:20 one road going to Ammon and its c, Rabbah,
Mic 1: 5 to blame for Israel's rebellion? Samaria, its c city!
1: 5 the center of idolatry in Judah? In Jerusalem, its c!
Zep 2:13 He will destroy Assyria and make its great c,

CAPITALS (12) [CAPITAL]
1Ki 7:16 For the tops of the pillars he made c of molded
7:18 the latticework to decorate the c over the pillars.
7:19 The c on the columns inside the foyer were shaped
7:22 The c on the pillars were shaped like lilies. And
7:41 two bowl-shaped c on top of the pillars,
7:41 two networks of chains that decorated the c,
7:42 c (two rows of pomegranates for each of the chain
7:42 that were hung around the c on top of the pillars),
2Ch 4:12 two bowl-shaped c on top of the pillars,
4:12 two networks of chains that decorated the c,
4:13 c (two rows of pomegranates for each of the chain
4:13 that were hung around the c on top of the pillars),

CAPPADOCIA (2)
Ac 2: 9 Judea, C, Pontus, the province of Asia,
1Pe 1: 1 Galatia, C, the province of Asia, and Bithynia.

CAPTAIN (44) [CAPTAIN'S, CAPTAINS]

Ge 37:36 king of Egypt. Potiphar was c of the palace guard.
39: 1 of Egypt. Potiphar was the c of the palace guard.
40: 3 in the palace of Potiphar, the c of the guard.
41:10 and you imprisoned us in the palace of the c of the
41:12 man who was a servant of the c of the guard.
1Sa 17:18 And give these ten cuts of cheese to their c.
22:14 he is the c of your bodyguard and a highly honored
2Sa 8:18 Benaiah son of Jehoiada was c of the king's
15:19 king turned to Ittai, the c of the Gittites, and asked,
2Ki 1: 9 Then he sent an army c with fifty soldiers to arrest
1: 9 The c said to him, "Man of God, the king has
1:10 But Elijah replied to the c, "If I am a man of God,
1:11 So the king sent another c with fifty men.
1:11 The c said to him, "Man of God, the king says that
1:13 Once more the king sent a c with fifty men.
1:13 But this time the c fell to his knees before Elijah.
25: 8 Nebuzaradan, c of the guard, an official of the
25:10 Then the c of the guard supervised the entire
25:11 Nebuzaradan, c of the guard, then took as exiles
25:12 But the c of the guard allowed some of the poorest
25:15 Nebuzaradan, c of the guard, also took the firepans
25:18 The c of the guard took with him as prisoners
1Ch 18:17 Benaiah son of Jehoiada was c of the king's
2Ch 12:10 and entrusted them to the care of the c of his
Jer 39: 9 Then Nebuzaradan, the c of the guard, sent to
39:13 So Nebuzaradan, the c of the guard,
40: 1 c of the guard, had released him at Ramah.
40: 2 The c of the guard called for Jeremiah and said,
41:10 care in Mizpah by Nebuzaradan, c of the guard.
43: 6 the c of the guard, had left with Gedaliah.
52:12 Nebuzaradan, c of the guard, an official of the
52:14 Then the c of the guard supervised the entire
52:15 Nebuzaradan, c of the guard, then took as exiles
52:19 Nebuzaradan, c of the guard, also took the small
52:24 The c of the guard took with him as prisoners
52:30 his c of the guard, who took 745 more—
Jnh 1: 6 So the c went down after him. "How can you sleep
Lk 23:47 When the c of the Roman soldiers handling the
Ac 4: 1 the leading priests, the c of the Temple guard,
5:24 When the c of the Temple guard and the leading
5:26 The c went with his Temple guards and arrested
10: 1 who was a c of the Italian Regiment.
27: 1 officer named Julius, a c of the Imperial Regiment.
27:11 of the prisoners listened more to the ship's c

CAPTAIN'S (1) [CAPTAIN]

Job 39:25 noise of battle and the shout of the c commands.

CAPTAINS (18) [CAPTAIN]

Jos 10:24 Joshua told the c of his army, "Come and put your
2Sa 4: 2 who were c of Ishbosheth's raiding parties.
18: 1 now appointed generals and c to lead his troops.
1Ch 13: 1 including the generals and c of his army.
26:26 and the generals and c and other officers of the
27: 1 This is the list of Israelite generals and c, and their
28: 1 the other generals and c, the overseers of the royal
29: 6 the tribes of Israel, the generals and c of the army,
2Ch 1: 2 the generals and c of the army, the judges, and all
Jer 51:23 and flocks, farmers and oxen, c and rulers.
51:57 wise men, rulers, c, and warriors," says the King,
Eze 23: 6 c and commanders dressed in handsome blue,
23:12 those c and commanders in handsome uniforms—
23:23 handsome young c, commanders, chariot officers,
Lk 22: 4 and c of the Temple guard to discuss the best way
22:52 to the leading priests and c of the Temple guard
Rev 18:17 And all the shipowners and c of the merchant ships
19:18 and eat the flesh of kings, c, and strong warriors;

CAPTIVATED (2) [CAPTURE]

Pr 5:19 you always. May you always be c by her love.
5:20 Why be c, my son, with an immoral woman,

CAPTIVE (20) [CAPTURE]

Ex 12:29 to the firstborn son of the c in the dungeon.
Nu 14:31 " 'You said your children would be taken c.
24:22 will be destroyed / when Assyria takes you c."
1Ki 8:46 and take them c to a foreign land far or near.
2Ki 24:15 Nebuchadnezzar led King Jehoiachin away as a c
2Ch 6:36 and take them c to a foreign land far or near.
Pr 5:22 An evil man is held c by his own sins; they are
SS 7: 5 A king is held c in your queenly tresses.
Isa 45:13 He will restore my city and free my c people—
52: 2 slave bands from your neck, O c daughter of Zion.
Jer 20: 4 He will take them c to Babylon or run them
22:10 Instead, weep for the c king being led away!
22:11 his father, King Josiah, and was taken away as a c:
29: 7 to the LORD for that city where you are held c,
48: 7 in your wealth and skill, you will be taken c.
La 1:18 and daughters have been taken c to distant lands.
Eze 27:15 Numerous coastlands were your c markets;
Ac 8:23 that you are full of bitterness and held c by sin."
Ro 7: 6 with Christ, and we are no longer c to its power.
2Ti 2:26 For they have been held c by him to do whatever

CAPTIVES (65) [CAPTURE]

Ge 14:16 his possessions, and all the women and other c.
Nu 21:29 and his daughters as c of Sihon, the Amorite king.
31:11 After they had gathered the plunder and c,
31:19 and your c on the third and seventh days.
31:28 But first give the LORD his share of the c,
31:30 Also take one of every fifty of the c, cattle,
Dt 21:10 your God hands them over to you and you take c.
21:11 And suppose you see among the c a beautiful
32:42 the blood of the slaughtered and the c,
Jdg 5:12 Barak! / Lead your c away, son of Abinoam!
2Ki 5: 2 and among their c was a young girl who had been
15:29 and he took the people to Assyria as c.
16: 9 of Damascus and led its population away as c,
24:14 King Nebuchadnezzar took ten thousand c from
1Ch 5:21 250,000 sheep, 2,000 donkeys, and 100,000 c.
5:26 Gad, and the half-tribe of Manasseh as c.
2Ch 28:11 Listen to me and return these c you have taken,
28:17 of Edom had again invaded Judah and taken c.
Ne 4: 4 and may they themselves become c in a foreign
Ps 68:18 you ascended to the heights, / you led a crowd of c.
Isa 8:21 My people will be led away as c, weary
31: 8 strong young Assyrians will be taken away as c.
42: 7 the eyes of the blind and free the c from prison.
49:24 Who can demand that a tyrant let his c go?
49:25 LORD says, "The c of warriors will be released,
50: 1 No, you went away as c because of your sins.
51:14 Soon all you c will be released! Imprisonment,
60:11 The kings of the world will be led as c in a victory
61: 1 and to announce that c will be released
Jer 1: 3 the people of Jerusalem were taken away as c.
13:19 The people of Judah will be taken away as c.
15:14 I will tell their enemies to take them as c to a
17: 4 and I will send you away as c to a foreign land.
20: 6 and all your household will go as c to Babylon.
22:22 All your friends have been taken away as c.
28: 4 and all the other c that were taken to Babylon.
29: 4 sends this message to all the c he has exiled to
29:20 from the LORD, all you c there in Babylon.
40: 1 bound in chains among the c of Jerusalem
41:10 Ishmael made c of the king's daughters
41:14 And all the c from Mizpah escaped and began to
43:12 all their idols and carrying away the people as c.
48:46 and daughters have been taken away as c.
50:16 Let the c escape the sword of the enemy and rush
52:28 The number of c taken to Babylon in the seventh
52:30 who took 745 more—a total of 4,600 c in all.
Eze 12: 4 just as c do when they begin a long march to
23:25 Your children will be taken away as c,
30:18 and its daughters will be led away as c.
Da 1: 3 who had been brought to Babylon as c.
2:25 "I have found one of the c from Judah who will
6:13 "That man Daniel, one of the c from Judah,
Hos 10: 6 away with them when they go as c to Assyria,
Am 6: 7 Therefore, you will be the first to be led away as c.
7:17 And the people of Israel will certainly become c in
Ob 1:20 The c from Jerusalem exiled in the north will
Mic 1:11 You people of Shaphir, go as c into exile—naked
Na 2:12 filled your city and your homes with c and plunder.
3:10 Thebes fell, and her people were led away as c.
Hab 1: 9 the desert, sweeping c ahead of them like sand.
2: 6 But the time is coming when all their c will taunt
Lk 4:18 that c will be released, / that the blind will see,
21:24 or sent away as c to all the nations of the world.
2Co 2:14 who made us his c and leads us along in Christ's
Eph 4: 8 he ascended to the heights, / he led a crowd of c

CAPTIVITY (44) [CAPTURE]

Dt 28:41 not keep them, for they will be led away into c.
1Ch 5: 6 taken into c by King Tiglath-pileser of Assyria.
6:15 and Jerusalem into c under Nebuchadnezzar.
2Ch 29: 9 and our sons and daughters and wives are in c.
Ezr 2: 1 provinces who returned from their c to Jerusalem
8:35 Then the exiles who had returned from c sacrificed
Ne 1: 2 asked them about the Jews who had survived the c
7: 6 provinces who returned from their c to Jerusalem
8:17 So everyone who had returned from c lived in
Isa 5:29 will seize my people and carry them off into c,
22:17 He is going to send you into c, you strong man!
46: 2 protect the gods. They go off into c together.
48:20 Yet even now, be free from your c! Leave Babylon
57:14 and stones so my people can return from c.' "
Jer 15: 2 those who are destined for c, to c.'
24: 6 I have sent them into c for their own good. I will
25:12 "Then, after the seventy years of c are over,
29:14 "I will end your c and restore your fortunes.
29:28 predicting that our c will be a long one.
30:18 When I bring you home again from your c
34: 3 will not escape his grasp but will be taken into c.
43:11 he will bring c to those destined for c;
La 1: 3 Judah has been led away into c, afflicted
1:14 wove my sins into ropes to hitch me to a yoke of c.
Eze 1: 2 during the fifth year of King Jehoiachin's c.
8: 1 during the sixth year of King Jehoiachin's c,
19: 9 They held him in c, / so his voice could never
20: 1 during the seventh year of King Jehoiachin's c,
24: 1 during the ninth year of King Jehoiachin's c,
26: 1 during the twelfth year of King Jehoiachin's c,
29: 1 during the tenth year of King Jehoiachin's c,
29:17 the twenty-seventh year of King Jehoiachin's c,
30:20 during the eleventh year of King Jehoiachin's c,
31: 1 during the eleventh year of King Jehoiachin's c,
32: 1 during the twelfth year of King Jehoiachin's c,
33:21 On January 8, during the twelfth year of our c,
39:25 I will end the c of my people; I will have mercy on
40: 1 On April 28, during the twenty-fifth year of our c
Hos 2:15 was young, when I freed her from her c in Egypt.
Mic 2:13 will bring you through the gates of your cities of c,
Zec 14: 2 Half the population will be taken away into c,
Ac 7:43 So I will send you into c / far away in Babylon.'

CAPTORS (6) [CAPTURE]

1Ki 8:50 sinned against you. Make their c merciful to them,
2Ch 30: 9 your children will be treated mercifully by their c,
Ps 106:46 He even caused their c / to treat them with
137: 3 For there our c demanded a song of us.
Jer 50:33 Their c hold them and refuse to let them go.
Eze 12:16 so they can confess to their c about how wicked

CAPTURE (36) [CAPTIVATED, CAPTIVE, CAPTIVES, CAPTIVITY, CAPTORS, CAPTURED, CAPTURES, CAPTURING, RECAPTURED]

Dt 1:22 route to take and decide which towns we should c.'
Jdg 15:10 Philistines replied, "We've come to c Samson.
16: 9 "Samson! The Philistines have come to c you!"
16:12 "Samson! The Philistines have come to c you!"
16:14 "Samson! The Philistines have come to c you!"
16:19 in a man to shave off his hair, making his c certain.
16:20 "Samson! The Philistines have come to c you!"
1Sa 19:20 he sent troops to c him. But when they arrived
2Sa 5:17 of Israel, they mobilized all their forces to c him.
15:35 Tell them the plans that are being made to c me,
20:13 the way, everyone went on with Joab to c Sheba.
2Ki 7:12 and then they will take us alive and c the city."
1Ch 14: 8 all Israel, they mobilized all their forces to c him.
2Ch 32:18 to terrify them so it would be easier to c the city.
Job 41: 9 "No, it is useless to try to c it. The hunter who
Ps 7: 5 then let my enemies c me. / Let them trample me
10: 9 Like hunters they c their victims / and drag them
21: 8 You will c all your enemies. / Your strong right
Pr 18:19 with an offended friend than to c a fortified city.
Jer 26:22 to Egypt along with several other men to c Uriah.
32:28 king of Babylon, and he will c it.
34:22 will fight against this city and will c and burn it.
37: 8 come back and c this city and burn it to the ground.
38: 3 to the army of the king of Babylon, who will c it."
Eze 12:13 I will spread out my net and c him in my snare.
14: 5 I will do this to c the minds and hearts of all my
17:20 will throw my net over him and c him in my snare.
21:23 of their rebellion. Then he will attack and c them.
38:12 I will c vast amounts of plunder and take many
Da 11:15 will come and lay siege to a fortified city and c it.
Am 9: 3 Mount Carmel, I will search them out and c them.
Mic 1:15 I will bring a conqueror to c your town.
Na 2: 7 been decreed, and all the servant girls mourn its c.
Hab 1:10 pile ramps of earth against their walls and c them!
Mt 26: 4 to discuss how to c Jesus secretly and put him to
Mk 14: 1 still looking for an opportunity to c Jesus secretly

CAPTURED (93) [CAPTURE]

Ge 14:12 They also c Lot—Abram's nephew who lived in
14:14 When Abram learned that Lot had been c,
14:21 told him, "Give back my people who were c.
Nu 21:25 So Israel c all the towns of the Amorites
21:32 they c all the towns in the region and drove out the
31: 9 Then the Israelite army c the Midianite women
31:50 So we are presenting the items of gold we c as an
32:41 c many of the towns in Gilead and changed the
32:42 a man named Nobah c the town of Kenath and its
Dt 1:39 You were afraid they would be c, but they will be
Jos 6:20 straight into the city from every side and c it.
8: 2 But this time you may keep the c goods
8:19 into the city. They quickly c it and set it on fire.
10: 1 heard that Joshua had c and completely destroyed
10:35 They c it in one day, and as at Lachish,
10:39 They c the city, its king, and all of its surrounding
11:10 Joshua then turned back and c Hazor and killed its
11:14 And the Israelites took all the c goods and cattle of
19:47 They c it, slaughtered its people, and settled there.
Jdg 1: 6 but the Israelites soon c him and cut off his thumbs
1: 8 The men of Judah attacked Jerusalem and c it,
1:18 Judah c the cities of Gaza, Ashkelon, and Ekron,
5:30 'They are dividing the c goods they found—
7:25 They c Oreb and Zeeb, the two Midianite generals,
8:12 Gideon chased them down and c all their warriors.
8:14 There he c a young man from Succoth
9:45 on all day before Abimelech finally c the city.
9:50 Abimelech attacked the city of Thebez and c it.
12: 5 Jephthah c the shallows of the Jordan,
16:21 So the Philistines c him and gouged out his eyes.
1Sa 4:11 The Ark of God was c, and Hophni and Phinehas,
4:17 were killed, too. And the Ark of God has been c."
4:19 When she heard that the Ark of God had been c
4:21 him this because the Ark of God had been c and
4:22 from Israel, for the Ark of God has been c."
5: 1 After the Philistines c the Ark of God, they took it
7:14 and Gath that the Philistines had c were restored to
15: 8 He c Agag, the Amalekite king, but completely
30: 5 widow of Nabal of Carmel, were among those c.
2Sa 5: 7 But David c the fortress of Zion, now called the
8: 4 David c seventeen hundred charioteers and twenty
12:27 have fought against Rabbah and c its water supply.
12:29 David led the rest of his army to Rabbah and c it.
17:21 told him how Ahithophel had advised that he be c
1Ki 9:16 (The king of Egypt had attacked and c Gezer,
2Ki 10:14 And they c all forty-two of them and killed them at
12:17 Hazael of Aram went to war against Gath and c it.
14:13 King Jehoash of Israel c King Amaziah of Judah at
15:29 and he c the towns of Ijon, Abel-beth-maacah,
19:10 that Jerusalem will not be c by the king of Assyria.
1Ch 2:23 (Later Geshur and Aram c the Towns of Jair
11: 5 But David c the fortress of Zion, now called the
18: 4 David c one thousand chariots, seven thousand
2Ch 13:19 Jeroboam's troops and c some of his towns,
14:15 attacked the camps of herdsmen and c many sheep
15: 8 and in the towns he had c in the hill country of
25:12 They c another ten thousand and took them to the
25:23 King Jehoash of Israel c King Amaziah of Judah at
28: 8 The armies of Israel c 200,000 women

28:18 They had already c Beth-shemesh, Aijalon,
36: 6 of Babylon came to Jerusalem and c it,
Ezr 9: 7 c, robbed, and disgraced, just as we are today.
Ne 9:25 Our ancestors c fortified cities and fertile land.
Job 15:12 What has c your reason? What has weakened your
Ps 59:12 that is on their lips, / let them be c by their pride,
66:11 You c us in your net / and laid the burden of
78:61 He allowed the Ark of his might to be c;
137: 7 on the day the armies of Babylon c Jerusalem.
Isa 8:15 and fall, never to rise again. Many will be c."
10:13 By my own strength I have c many lands,
13:15 Anyone who is c will be run through with a sword.
14: 2 Those who c Israel will be c, and Israel will
20: 1 In the year when King Sargon of Assyria c the
22: 3 The people try to slip away, but they are c, too.
28:13 They will be injured, trapped, and c.
37:10 that Jerusalem will not be c by the king of Assyria.
Jer 1:18 You are strong like a fortified city that cannot be c,
21:10 It will be c by the king of Babylon, and he will
31:40 The city will never again be c or destroyed."
32: 4 King Zedekiah will be c by the Babylonians
38:28 of the guard until the day Jerusalem was c.
41:13 The people Ishmael had c shouted for joy when
47: 1 of Gaza, before it was c by the Egyptian army.
48: 1 The city of Kiriathaim will be humiliated and c;
49:29 Their flocks and tents will be c, and their
50: 9 against Babylon to attack her, and she will be c.
51:56 Her mighty men are c, and their weapons break in
La 1: 5 Her children have been c and taken away to distant
Eze 19: 8 out their nets for him / and c him in their pit.
Ob 1:14 You shouldn't have c the survivors, handing them
Zec 14:14 wealth of all the neighboring nations will be c—
Rev 19:20 And the beast was c, and with him the false

CAPTURES (2) [CAPTURE]

Jos 15:16 to the one who attacks and c Kiriath-sepher."
Jdg 1:12 to the one who attacks and c Kiriath-sepher."

CAPTURING (1) [CAPTURE]

Jos 10:37 c it and all of its surrounding towns. And just as

CARAVAN (4) [CARAVANS]

Ge 37:25 they noticed a c of camels in the distance coming
Jdg 8:11 Gideon circled around by the c route east of Nobah
1Ki 10: 2 and a great c of camels loaded with spices,
2Ch 9: 1 and a great c of camels loaded with spices,

CARAVANS (5) [CARAVAN]

Job 6:18 The c turn aside to be refreshed, but there is
6:19 the c from Tema and from Sheba stop for water,
Isa 21:13 O c from Dedan, hide in the deserts of Arabia.
60: 6 Vast c of camels will converge on you, the camels
Eze 27:25 The ships of Tarshish were your ocean c.

CARBUNCLE(S) [KJV] See EMERALD, GEMS

CARCAS (1)

Est 1:10 Biztha, Harbona, Bigtha, Abagtha, Zethar, and C,

CARCASE(S) [KJV] See also CARCASS(ES), BODY, CORPSE(S)

CARCASS (13) [CARCASSES]

Ex 22:13 the c must be shown as evidence, and no payment
22:31 a wild animal. Throw its c out for the dogs to eat.
29:14 Then take the c (including the skin and the dung)
Lev 11:28 If you pick up and move its c, you must
11:39 that is permitted for eating dies and you touch its c,
11:40 If you eat any of its meat or carry away its c,
17:15 If you eat from the c of an animal that died a
Jdg 14: 8 he turned off the path to look at the c of the lion.
14: 8 a swarm of bees had made some honey in the c.
14: 9 them he had taken the honey from the c of the lion.
Job 39:30 for it feeds on the c of the slaughtered."
Mt 24:28 Just as the gathering of vultures shows there is a c
Lk 17:37 the gathering of vultures shows there is a c nearby,

CARCASSES (2) [CARCASS]

Ge 15:11 Some vultures came down to eat the c, but Abram
15:17 a flaming torch pass between the halves of the c.

CARCHEMISH (3)

2Ch 35:20 Egypt to do battle at C on the Euphrates River,
Isa 10: 9 We will destroy Calno just as we did C.
Jer 46: 2 on the occasion of the battle of C when Pharaoh

CARE (166) [CARED, CAREFREE, CAREFUL, CAREFULLY, CARELESS, CARELESSLY, CARES, CARETAKERS, CARING]

Ge 2:15 the man in the Garden of Eden to tend and c for it.
30:35 He placed them in the c of his sons,
39:23 after that, because Joseph took c of everything.
40: 4 and Potiphar assigned Joseph to take c of them.
44:32 I made a pledge to my father that I would take c of
45:11 I will take c of you there, for there are still five
50:21 I myself will take c of you and your families."
Ex 12: 6 "Take special c of these lambs until the evening of
17: 7 "Is the LORD going to take c of us or not?"
18:22 But they can take c of the smaller matters
22:10 "Now suppose someone asks a neighbor to c for a
30:16 Use this money for the c of the Tabernacle. It will
Lev 22: 2 gifts that the Israelites set apart for me with great c,
Nu 1:50 and they must c for it and camp around it.
3:25 These two clans were responsible to c for the tent
3:28 They were responsible for the c of the sanctuary.
3:31 These four clans were responsible for the c of the
3:36 These two clans were responsible for the c of the
18: 4 with you to fulfill their responsibilities for the c
Dt 28:39 You will plant vineyards and c for them, but you
Ru 4:15 restore your youth and c for you in your old age.
4:16 Naomi took c of the baby and cared for him as if
1Sa 17:28 those few sheep you're supposed to be taking c of?
17:34 "I have been taking c of my father's sheep,"
25:29 you are safe in the c of the LORD your God,
2Sa 6: 9 bring the Ark of the LORD back into my c?"
13: 6 "Please let Tamar come to take c of me and cook
19:33 king said to Barzillai. "I will take c of you there."
1Ki 1: 4 and she waited on the king and took c of him.
1:15 very old now, and Abishag was taking c of him.
2: 7 for they took c of me when I fled from your
9: 3 I will always watch over it and c for it.
14:27 and he entrusted them to the c of the palace guard
2Ki 4:13 she replied, "my family takes good c of me."
25:12 to stay behind in Judah to c for the vineyards
1Ch 9:28 Some of the gatekeepers were assigned to c for the
13:12 can I ever bring the Ark of God back into my c?"
23:28 They also took c of the courtyards and side rooms,
26:28 All the other dedicated items were in their c,
29: 8 of the house of the LORD under the c of Jehiel,
2Ch 12:10 and entrusted them to the c of the captain of his
19: 7 Fear the LORD and judge with c, for the LORD
25:24 of God that had been in the c of Obed-edom.
Ezr 8:23 and earnestly prayed that our God would take c of
Ne 10:32 so that there will be enough money to c for the
Est 2: 8 at the fortress of Susa and placed in Hegai's c.
2:14 There she would be under the c of Shaashgaz,
Job 4: 6 Shouldn't you believe that God will c for those
10:12 unfailing love. My life was preserved by your c.
21:21 they will not c what happens to their family.
29: 2 "I long for the years gone by when God took c of
33:20 and do not c for even the most delicious food.
34:13 Who put the world in his c? Who has set the whole
34:19 He doesn't c how great a person may be, and he
Ps 8: 4 of us, / mere humans that you should c for us?
28: 5 They c nothing for what the LORD has done
31: 7 and you c about the anguish of my soul.
36: 6 You c for people and animals alike, O LORD.
37:17 be shattered, / but the LORD takes c of the godly.
37:18 Day by day the LORD takes c of the innocent,
50:21 I remained silent, / and you thought I didn't c.
54: 3 to kill me. / They c nothing for God. / *Interlude*
55:22 burdens to the LORD, / and he will take c of you.
65: 9 You take c of the earth and water it, / making it
69:16 Turn and take c of me, / for your mercy is
78:22 did not believe God / or trust him to c for them.
80:14 and see our plight. / Watch over and c for this vine
88: 5 as dead. / I am forgotten, / cut off from your c.
94: 7 "and besides, the God of Israel doesn't c."
95: 7 the people he watches over, / the sheep under his c.
106:24 for they wouldn't believe his promise to c for
112: 7 they confidently trust the LORD to c for them.
119:158 because they c nothing for your word.
144: 3 notice us, / mere humans that you should c for us?
Pr 5: 6 For she does not c about the path to life.
21:29 put up a bold front, but the upright proceed with c.
29: 7 the rights of the poor; the wicked don't c to know.
SS 8:12 pieces of silver to those who c for its vines."
Isa 1: 3 know their owner and appreciate his c, but not my
8: 6 "The people of Judah have rejected my gentle c
32:10 a year—you careless ones will suddenly begin to c.
33: 8 and c nothing for the promises they made before
33:22 and our king. He will c for us and save us.
44:15 And after his c, he uses part of the wood to make a
46: 4 I made you, and I will c for you. I will carry you
47: 7 You did not c at all about my people or think about
49:23 will serve you. They will c for all your needs.
53: 3 he went by. He was despised, and we did not c.
57: 1 their time. And no one seems to c or wonder why.
62: 5 Your children will c for you with joy, O Jerusalem,
Jer 1: 8 the people, for I will be with you and take c of you.
1:19 For I am with you, and I will take c of you. I,
9: 3 They c nothing for me," says the LORD.
13:20 your beautiful flock—that he gave you to c for?
22:18 he dies. His subjects will not even c that he is dead.
23: 1 and scattered the very ones they were expected to c
23: 4 Then I will appoint responsible shepherds to c for
30:14 have left you and do not c about you anymore.
31: 2 I will c for the survivors as they travel through the
31: 9 their faces, and I will lead them home with great c.
39:10 and he assigned them fields and vineyards to c for.
39:14 They put him under the c of Gedaliah son of
41:10 left under Gedaliah's c in Mizpah by Nebuzaradan,
52:16 to stay behind in Judah to c for the vineyards
Eze 4:16 It will be weighed out with great c and eaten
20:14 I destroyed them because I couldn't take c of them.
34: 4 You have not taken c of the weak. You have not
34: 8 You took c of yourselves and left the sheep to
35:10 of them. What do we c that the LORD is there!'
Hos 11: 3 or even c that it was I who took c of him.
13: 5 I took c of you in the wilderness, in that dry
Am 7:14 I'm just a shepherd, and I take c of fig trees.
Zec 11: 4 and c for a flock that is intended for slaughter.
11:16 not c for the sheep that are threatened by death,
Mt 6: 1 "Take c! Don't do your good deeds publicly,
6:30 gone tomorrow, won't he more surely c for you?
8:22 Let those who are spiritually dead c for their own
27: 4 "What do we c?" they retorted. "That's your
27:55 Jesus to c for him were watching from a distance.
Mk 1:13 among the wild animals, and angels took c of him.
4:38 don't you even c that we are going to drown?"
Lk 9:60 "Let those who are spiritually dead c for their own
10:34 and took him to an inn, where he took c of him.
10:35 pieces of silver and told him to take c of the man.
12:28 gone tomorrow, won't he more surely c for you?
16: 4 then I'll have plenty of friends to take c of me
17: 7 comes in from plowing or taking c of sheep,
Jn 2:10 "Then, when everyone is full and doesn't c,
5:44 but you don't c about the honor that comes from
17:11 Holy Father, keep them and c for them—all those
21:16 love you." "Then take c of my sheep," Jesus said.
Ac 5:35 take c what you are planning to do to these men!
14:23 turning them over to the c of the Lord, in whom
18:15 and names and your Jewish laws, you take c of it.
20:31 my constant watch and c over you night and day,
24:23 his friends to visit him and take c of his needs.
Ro 2: 4 and patient God is with you? Or don't you c?
1Co 9: 7 What shepherd takes c of a flock of sheep and isn't
12:23 honorable are those we clothe with the greatest c.
12:24 while other parts do not require this special c.
12:24 and c are given to those parts that have less
12:25 so that all the members c for each other equally.
2Co 7:12 you could show how much you really do c for us.
Eph 4:19 They don't c anymore about right and wrong,
Php 2:21 All the others c only for themselves and not for
4:19 And this same God who takes c of me will supply
1Th 5:14 Take tender c of those who are weak. Be patient
1Ti 3: 5 how can he take c of God's church?
5: 3 The church should c for any widow who has no one else to c for her.
5: 4 and repay their parents by taking c of them.
5: 8 But those who won't c for their own relatives,
5:14 have children, and take c of their own homes.
5:16 she must take c of them and not put the
5:16 Then the church can c for widows who are truly
Tit 2: 5 and be pure, to take c of their homes, to do good,
Heb 1:14 They are spirits sent from God to c for those who
2: 6 and the son of man that you should c for him?
Jas 1:27 God our Father means that we must c for orphans
1Pe 5: 2 C for the flock of God entrusted to you.
5: 3 Don't lord it over the people assigned to your c,
3Jn 1: 5 c of the traveling teachers who are passing
Jude 1: 1 love of God the Father and the c of Jesus Christ.
1:12 They are shameless in the way they c only about
Rev 12: 6 where God had prepared a place to give her c for

CAREAH [KJV] See KAREAH

CARED (28) [CARE]

Ge 30:36 Meanwhile, Jacob stayed and c for Laban's flock.
31:38 and all that time I c for your sheep and goats
Dt 1:31 And you saw how the LORD your God c for you
11: 5 They didn't see how the LORD c for you in the
Ru 4:16 of the baby and c for him as if he were her own.
2Sa 20: 3 Their needs were to be c for, he said, but he would
2Ki 10: 6 Now the seventy sons of the king were being c for
1Ch 26:28 and his relatives also c for the items dedicated to
2Ch 26:10 He had many workers who c for his farms
Job 31:18 No, from childhood I have c for orphans, and all my life I have c for widows.
Ps 71: 6 from my mother's womb you have c for me.
78:72 He c for them with a true heart / and led them with
104:16 The trees of the LORD are well c for—
Isa 1: 2 children I raised and c for have turned against me.
46: 3 and have c for you since before you were born.
Jer 23:18 Has even one of them c enough to listen?
40: 4 you are welcome. I will see that you are well c for.
Eze 16: 4 When you were born, no one c about you.
16: 5 interest in you; no one pitied you or c for you.
Zec 11: 7 So I c for the flock intended for slaughter—
Mt 4:11 Devil went away, and angels came and c for Jesus.
25:36 I was sick, and you c for me. I was in prison,
Mk 15:41 of Jesus and had c for him while he was in Galilee.
Jn 12: 6 Not that he c for the poor—he was a thief who was
Ac 7:20 His parents c for him at home for three months.
Gal 4:14 and c for me as though I were an angel from God
Rev 12:14 where she would be c for and protected from the

CAREFREE (2) [CARE]

Jdg 18: 7 where they noticed the people living c lives,
18:10 get there, you will find the people living c lives.

CAREFUL (74) [CARE]

Ge 24: 6 "Be c never to take my son there.
31:24 "Be c about what you say to Jacob!" he was told.
31:29 and told me, 'Be c about what you say to Jacob!'
Ex 19:12 Warn them, 'Be c! Do not go up on the mountain
23:22 But if you are c to obey him, following all my
27: 8 Be c to build it just as you were shown on the
28:15 "Then, with the most c workmanship, make a
34:12 "Be very c never to make treaties with the people
Lev 18: 4 obey all my regulations and be c to keep my laws,
18:30 So be c to obey my laws, and do not practice any
19:37 You must be c to obey all of my laws
26: 3 keep my laws and are c to obey my commands,
Nu 18: 3 they must be c not to touch any of the sacred
18:32 But be c not to treat the holy gifts of the people of
20:17 We will be c not to go through your fields
Dt 2: 4 in Seir. The Edomites will feel threatened, so be c.
4: 9 Be very c never to forget what you have seen the
4:15 "But be c! You did not see the LORD's form on
4:23 So be c not to break the covenant the LORD your
6: 3 Israel, to everything I say. Be c to obey.
6:12 be c not to forget the LORD, who rescued you

8: 1 "Be c to obey all the commands I am giving you
8:11 "But that is the time to be c! Beware that in your
8:14 that is the time to be c. Do not become proud at
11: 8 be c to obey every command I am giving you
11:22 "Be c to obey all my commands I give you;
11:32 you must be c to obey all the laws and regulations I
12:13 Be c not to sacrifice your burnt offerings just
12:19 Be very c never to forget the Levites as long as you
12:28 Be c to obey all my commands so that all will go
16:12 slaves in Egypt, so be c to obey all these laws.
18: 9 be very c not to imitate the detestable customs of
23:23 made a vow, be c to do as you have said,
Jos 22: 3 You have been c to obey the commands of the
22: 5 But be very c to obey all the commands
23: 6 Be very c to follow all the instructions written in
23:11 So be very c to love the LORD your God.
Jdg 6:29 And after asking around and making a c search,
1Ki 12:26 Jeroboam thought to himself, "Unless I am c,
2Ki 17:37 Be c to obey all the laws, regulations, instructions,
1Ch 28: 8 Be c to obey all the commands of the LORD your
2Ch 27: 6 because he was c to live in obedience to the
29:15 They were c to follow all the LORD's
Ezr 7:23 Be c to provide whatever the God of heaven
Job 13: 9 Be c that he doesn't find out what you are doing!
Ps 101: 2 I will be c to live a blameless life—/ when will you
Ecc 9: 3 That is why people are not more c to be good.
Isa 56: 2 Blessed are those who are c to do this. Blessed are
La 2: 8 He made c plans for their destruction, then he went
Eze 44: 5 LORD said to me, "Son of man, take c notice;
44: 5 Take c note of who may be admitted to the Temple
Mt 23:23 For you are c to tithe even the tiniest part of your
23:25 You are so c to clean the outside of the cup
Lk 1: 3 I have decided to write a c summary for you,
1: 6 c to obey all of the Lord's commandments
11:39 so c to clean the outside of the cup and the dish,
11:42 For you are c to tithe even the tiniest part of your
Ac 13:40 Be c! Don't let the prophets' words apply to you.
Ro 11:18 But you must be c not to brag about being grafted
1Co 3:10 is building on this foundation must be very c.
4: 5 So be c not to jump to conclusions before the Lord
8: 9 But you must be c with this freedom of yours.
10:12 If you think you are standing strong, be c, for you
2Co 8:21 We are c to be honorable before the Lord, but we
Gal 6: 1 And be c not to fall into the same temptation
Eph 5:15 So be c how you live, not as fools but as those who
Php 2:12 so c to follow my instructions when I was with
2:12 And now that I am away you must be even more c
2Ti 4:15 Be c of him, for he fought against everything we
Tit 3: 8 so that everyone who trusts in God will be c to do
Heb 3:12 Be c then, dear friends. Make sure that your own
1Pe 2:12 Be c how you live among your unbelieving
5: 8 Be c! Watch out for attacks from the Devil,
Jude 1:23 but be c that you aren't contaminated by their sins.

CAREFULLY (57) [CARE]

Ex 8: 2 If you refuse, then listen c to this: I will send vast
15:26 "If you will listen c to the voice of the LORD
24: 4 Then Moses c wrote down all the LORD's
Lev 20:22 "You must c obey all my laws and regulations;
22: 9 Warn all the priests to follow these instructions c;
Nu 8:20 c following all the LORD's instructions to Moses.
Dt 4: 1 listen c to these laws and regulations that I am
4: 6 If you obey them c, you will display your wisdom
5: 1 "Listen c to all the laws and regulations I am
11:13 "If you c obey all the commands I am giving you
12:32 C obey all the commands I give you. Do not add to
13:14 In such cases, you must examine the facts c.
15: 5 You will receive this blessing if you c obey the
24: 8 "Watch all contagious skin diseases c and follow
28:13 of the LORD your God and c obey them,
31:12 your God and c obey all the terms of this law.
Jos 11:15 c obeying all of the LORD's instructions to
Jdg 6:26 your God here on this hill, laying the stones c.
2Sa 20:17 he replied. So she said, "Listen c to your servant."
2Ki 18: 6 and he c obeyed all the commands the LORD had
1Ch 22:13 For if you c obey the laws and regulations that the
23:24 of their family groups, registered c by name.
2Ch 19: 6 "Always think c before pronouncing judgment.
Ne 10:29 They solemnly promised to c follow all the
Job 32:11 all this time, listening very c to your arguments,
34:21 "For God c watches the way people live; he sees
37: 2 Listen c to the thunder of God's voice as it rolls
Ps 49: 4 I listen c to many proverbs / and solve riddles with
85: 8 I listen c to what God the LORD is saying,
119: 4 have charged us / to keep your commandments c.
Pr 4:20 Pay attention, my child, to what I say. Listen c.
5: 1 to my wisdom; listen c to my wise counsel.
14:15 they are told! The prudent c consider their steps.
20: 8 When a king judges, he c weighs all the evidence,
31:27 She c watches all that goes on in her household
Ecc 9: 1 This, too, I c explored: Even though the actions of
Isa 41: 7 C they join the parts together, then fasten the thing
59:13 we have been, c planning our deceitful lies.
Eze 2: 2 and set me on my feet. I listened c to his words.
3:10 your own heart first. Listen to them c for yourself.
20:37 I will count you c and hold you to the terms of the
Da 10:11 loved of God, listen c to what I have to say to you.
Hos 14: 9 Let those who are discerning listen c. The paths of
Hag 2:18 of the LORD's Temple was laid—c consider this:
Zec 6:15 All this will happen if you c obey the commands of
Mt 2: 8 "Go to Bethlehem and search c for the child.
Mk 11:11 He looked around c at everything, and then he left
Lk 1: 3 Having c investigated all of these accounts from
Ac 2:14 "Listen c, all of you, fellow Jews and residents of
3:22 own people. Listen c to everything he tells you.'
22: 3 to follow our Jewish laws and customs very c.
1Co 12:23 So we c protect from the eyes of others those parts
Eph 2:21 We who believe are c joined together, becoming a
Php 3: 6 so c that I was never accused of any fault.
2Ti 1:14 within us, c guard what has been entrusted to you.
Heb 2: 1 So we must listen very c to the truth we have
13:22 please listen c to what I have said in this brief

CARELESS (2) [CARE]

Isa 32:10 a year—you c ones will suddenly begin to care.
Lk 21:34 Don't let me find you living in c ease

CARELESSLY (1) [CARE]

Lk 6:25 What sorrows await you who laugh c, / for your

CARES (26) [CARE]

Dt 1:31 in the wilderness, just as a father c for his child.
11:12 a land that the LORD your God c for. He watches
2Sa 14:14 He does not sweep away the lives of those he c
Ps 9:12 For he who avenges murder c for the helpless.
138: 6 Though the LORD is great, he c for the humble,
142: 4 will help me; / no one c a bit what happens to me.
146: 9 He c for the orphans and widows, / but he
Isa 59: 4 No one c about being fair and honest.
62: 5 O Jerusalem, just as a young man c for his bride.
Jer 12:11 The whole land is desolate, and no one even c.
30:17 an outcast—'Jerusalem for whom nobody c.'
Hos 14: 8 I am the one who looks after you and c for you.
Mt 6:30 And if God c so wonderfully for flowers that are
13:22 the message is crowded out by the c of this life
Mk 4:19 the message is crowded out by the c of this life,
Lk 8:14 all too quickly the message is crowded out by the c
12:28 And if God c so wonderfully for flowers that are
1Co 6:13 for the Lord, and the Lord c about our bodies.
8: 3 who loves God is the one God knows and c for.
2Co 7:15 Now he c for you more than ever when he
Eph 5:29 No one hates his own body but lovingly c for it,
5:29 just as Christ c for his body, which is the church.
Php 2:20 like Timothy, who genuinely c about your welfare.
2:28 be glad to see him, and that will lighten all my c.
1Pe 5: 7 Give all your worries and c to God, for he c about what happens to you.

CARESSED (2) [CARESSES]

Eze 23: 3 they allowed themselves to be fondled and c.
23:21 you first allowed yourself to be fondled and c.

CARESSES (1) [CARESSED]

Pr 7:18 of love until morning. Let's enjoy each other's c,

CARETAKERS (1) [CARE]

Eze 44:14 They are to serve as the Temple c and are relegated

CARGO (4) [CARGOES]

Jnh 1: 5 and threw the c overboard to lighten the ship.
Ac 27:10 shipwreck, loss of c, injuries, and danger to our
27:18 the ship, the crew began throwing the c overboard.
27:38 ship further by throwing the c of wheat overboard.

CARGOES (2) [CARGO]

1Ki 10:11 they also brought rich c of almug wood
2Ch 9:10 they also brought rich c of almug wood

CARING (5) [CARE]

Pr 27:23 and put your heart into c for your herds,
Am 6: 6 c nothing at all that your nation is going to ruin.
Mt 15: 5 'You don't need to honor your parents by c for
1Th 2: 7 as a mother feeding and c for her own children.
Heb 6:10 and how you have shown your love to him by c for

CARITE (2)

2Ki 11: 4 summoned the commanders, the C mercenaries,
11:19 the commanders, the C mercenaries, the guards,

CARMEL (27) [CARMEL'S]

Jos 12:22 The king of Kedesh / The king of Jokneam in C
15:55 Besides these, there were Maon, C, Ziph, Juttah,
19:26 The boundary on the west went from C to
1Sa 15:12 "Saul went to C to set up a monument to himself;
25: 2 Maon who owned property near the village of C.
25: 5 he sent ten of his young men to C. He told them to
25: 7 While your shepherds stayed among us near C,
25:40 When the messengers arrived at C, they told
27: 3 Ahinoam of Jezreel and Abigail of C,
30: 5 of Jezreel and Abigail, the widow of Nabal of C,
2Sa 2: 2 and Abigail, the widow of Nabal from C.
3: 3 mother was Abigail, the widow of Nabal from C.
23:35 Hezro from C; / Paarai from Arba;
1Ki 18:19 Now bring all the people of Israel to Mount C,
18:20 all the people and the prophets to Mount C.
18:42 But Elijah climbed to the top of Mount C and fell
2Ki 2:25 From there Elisha went to Mount C and finally
4:25 As she approached the man of God at Mount C,
1Ch 3: 1 was Kileab, whose mother was Abigail from C.
11:37 Hezro from C; / Paarai son of Ezbai;
SS 7: 5 Your head is as majestic as Mount C.
Isa 33: 9 a wilderness. Bashan and C have been plundered.
Jer 46:18 is as tall as Mount Tabor or Mount C by the sea!
50:19 own land, to feed in the fields of C and Bashan,
Am 1: 2 All the grass on Mount C withers and dies."
9: 3 Even if they hide at the very top of Mount C,
Na 1: 4 dry up, the lush pastures of Bashan and C fade,

CARMEL'S (1) [CARMEL]

Isa 35: 2 as lovely as Mount C pastures and the plain of

CARMI (7) [CARMITE]

Ge 46: 9 of Reuben were Hanoch, Pallu, Hezron, and C.
Ex 6:14 oldest son, included Hanoch, Pallu, Hezron, and C.
Nu 26: 6 The Carmite clan, named after its ancestor C.
Jos 7: 1 Achan was the son of C, of the family of Zimri,
1Ch 2: 7 Achan son of C, one of Zerah's descendants,
4: 1 of Judah were Perez, Hezron, C, Hur, and Shobal.
5: 3 son of Israel, were Hanoch, Pallu, Hezron, and C.

CARMITE (1) [CARMI]

Nu 26: 6 The C clan, named after its ancestor Carmi.

CARNAL(LY) [KJV] See EXTERNAL, SEXUAL, SINFUL, WORLDLY

CARNELIAN (5)

Ex 28:17 The first row will contain a red c, a chrysolite,
39:10 In the first row were a red c, a chrysolite, and an
Eze 28:13 red c, chrysolite, white moonstone, beryl, onyx,
Rev 4: 3 throne was as brilliant as gemstones—jasper and c.
21:20 the fifth onyx, the sixth c, the seventh chrysolite,

CAROUSE (1) [CAROUSING]

Pr 23:20 Do not c with drunkards and gluttons,

CAROUSING (1) [CAROUSE]

Eze 23:42 From your room came the sound of many men c.

CARPENTER (1) [CARPENTER'S, CARPENTERS, CARPENTRY]

Mk 6: 3 He's just the c, the son of Mary and brother of

CARPENTER'S (1) [CARPENTER]

Mt 13:55 He's just a c son, and we know Mary, his mother,

CARPENTERS (8) [CARPENTER]

2Sa 5:11 along with c and stonemasons to build him a
2Ki 12:11 on the LORD's Temple—the c, the builders,
22: 6 They will need to hire c, builders, and masons.
1Ch 14: 1 with stonemasons and c to build him a palace.
22:15 You have many skilled stonemasons and c
2Ch 24:12 and c to restore the Temple of the LORD.
34:11 they hired c and masons and purchased cut stone
Ezr 3: 7 Then they hired masons and c and bought cedar

CARPENTRY (1) [CARPENTER]

2Ch 2:14 also knows all about stonework, c, and weaving.

CARPETED (1) [CARPETS]

Ps 65:13 flocks of sheep, / and the valleys are c with grain.

CARPETS (1) [CARPETED]

Eze 27:24 and many-colored c bound with cords and made

CARPUS (1)

2Ti 4:13 be sure to bring the coat I left with C at Troas.

CARRIAGE (6)

SS 3: 7 Look, it is Solomon's c, with sixty of Israel's
3: 9 "King Solomon has built a c for himself from
Ac 8:28 Seated in his c, he was reading aloud from the
8:29 to Philip, "Go over and walk along beside the c."
8:31 And he begged Philip to come up into the c and sit
8:38 He ordered the c to stop, and they went down into

CARRIED (113) [CARRY]

Ge 22: 6 while he himself c the knife and the fire.
27:18 Jacob c the platter of food to his father and said,
27:35 and he tricked me. He has c away your blessing."
45: 2 and the news was quickly c to Pharaoh's palace.
46: 5 They c their little ones and wives in the wagons
50:13 They c his body to the land of Canaan and buried it
Ex 4:20 the land of Egypt. In his hand he c the staff of God.
12:34 their spare clothing and c them on their shoulders.
19: 4 brought you to myself and c you on eagle's wings.
28:30 to be c over Aaron's heart when he goes into the
Lev 4:12 must be c away to a ceremonially clean place
10: 5 and c them out of the camp by their tunics as
14:45 and plaster must be c out of town to the place
16:27 for Israel, will be c outside the camp to be burned.
Nu 8:22 So they c out all the commands that the LORD
14: 3 Our wives and little ones will be c off as slaves!
16:40 the LORD's instructions to Moses were c out.
23:19 Has he ever promised and not c it through?
31: 6 They c along the holy objects of the sanctuary
Dt 31: 9 who c the Ark of the LORD's covenant,
31:25 he gave these instructions to the Levites who c the
32:11 to take them in / and c them aloft on his pinions.
33:21 were assembled, / they c out the LORD's justice
Jos 4: 8 They c them to the place where they camped for
4: 9 at the place where the priests who c the Ark of the
4:10 which Moses had given to Joshua, were c out.
6:11 So the Ark of the LORD was c around the city
6:12 and the priests again c the Ark of the LORD.
Jdg 3:18 Ehud sent home those who had c the tax money.
5:19 but they c off no treasures of battle.

16: 3 and **c** them all the way to the top of the hill across
21:23 and **c** them off to the land of their own inheritance.
Ru 2:18 She **c** it back into town and showed it to her
1Sa 5: 2 They **c** the Ark of God into the temple of Dagon
6:10 So these instructions were **c** out. Two cows with
14: 1 One day Jonathan said to the young man who **c** his
15:13 he said. "I have **c** out the LORD's command!"
15:20 Saul insisted. "I **c** out the mission he gave me.
30: 2 They had **c** off the women and children
1Ki 2:26 because you **c** the Ark of the Sovereign LORD
8: 4 all its sacred utensils, and **c** them up to the Temple.
8: 6 Then the priests **c** the Ark of the LORD's
17:19 **c** him up to the upper room, where he lived,
2Ki 2:11 and Elijah was **c** by a whirlwind into heaven.
4:21 She **c** him up to the bed of the man of God,
4:37 Then she picked up her son and **c** him downstairs.
14:14 He **c** off all the gold and silver and all the utensils
17:23 So Israel was **c** off to the land of Assyria,
20:17 up by your ancestors—will be **c** off to Babylon.
23: 4 Kidron Valley, and he **c** the ashes away to Bethel.
24:13 Nebuchadnezzar **c** away all the treasures from the
25:13 and they **c** all the bronze away to Babylon.
1Ch 6:32 Then they **c** on their work there, following all the
15:15 Then the Levites **c** the Ark of God on their
15:26 as they **c** the Ark of the LORD's covenant,
15:27 as were the Levites who **c** the Ark, the singers,
23:32 and faithfully **c** out their duties of service at the
24:19 Each group **c** out its duties in the house of the
2Ch 5: 5 The Levitical priests **c** them all up to the Temple.
5: 7 Then the priests **c** the Ark of the LORD's
8:16 to building the Temple of the LORD was **c** out,
14:13 and the army of Judah **c** off vast quantities of
21:17 and **c** away everything of value in the royal palace,
24:11 became full, the Levites **c** it to the king's officials.
25:24 He **c** off all the gold and silver and all the utensils
30: 6 and Judah. They **c** letters which said:
32: 1 After Hezekiah had faithfully **c** out this work,
Ne 3:25 Palal son of Uzai **c** on the work from a point
4:17 The common laborers **c** on their work with one
4:23 We **c** our weapons with us at all times, even when
Job 21:18 Are they **c** away by the storm? Not at all!
21:32 When they are **c** to the grave, an honor guard keeps
Ps 18:42 I ground them as fine as dust **c** by the wind.
Isa 10:13 destroyed their kings, and **c** off their treasures.
28:19 day and night, until you are **c** away."
39: 6 up by your ancestors—will be **c** off to Babylon.
49:21 were killed, and the rest were **c** away into exile.
53: 4 Yet it was our weaknesses he **c**; it was our sorrows
60: 4 distant lands; your little daughters will be **c** home.
63: 9 He lifted them up and **c** them through all the years.
66:12 at her breasts, **c** in her arms, and treated with love.
Jer 2:14 of slaves? Why has she been **c** away as plunder?
10: 5 and it needs to be **c** because it cannot walk.
13:19 away as captives. They will all be **c** into exile.
20: 5 and silver of your kings—will be **c** off to Babylon.
27:18 articles will not be **c** away with you to Babylon!
27:22 They will all be **c** away to Babylon and will stay
28: 3 that King Nebuchadnezzar **c** off to Babylon.
38:11 He **c** these to the cistern and lowered them to
43: 3 killed by the Babylonians or be **c** off into exile."
52:17 and they **c** all the bronze away to Babylon.
Eze 9: 2 in linen and **c** a writer's case strapped to his side.
9:11 who **c** the writer's case, reported back and said,
11:24 Afterward the Spirit of God **c** me back again to
16:16 for idols, where you **c** out your acts of prostitution.
17: 4 Then he **c** it away to a city filled with merchants,
23:14 "Then she **c** her prostitution even further. She fell
30: 4 Their wealth will be **c** away and their foundations
37: 1 and I was **c** away by the Spirit of the LORD to a
Hos 9: 3 You will be **c** off to Egypt and Assyria, where you
13:15 thing they have will be plundered and **c** away.
Joel 3: 5 and you have **c** them off to your pagan temples.
Am 8: 3 They will be **c** out of the city in silence. I,
Ob 1:11 to help when foreign invaders **c** off their wealth
Mic 1: 7 and they will now be **c** away to pay prostitutes
Lk 16:22 and was **c** by the angels to be with Abraham.
Ac 3: 2 the Temple, a man lame from birth was being **c** in.
5:10 they **c** her out and buried her beside her husband.
7:44 "Our ancestors **c** the Tabernacle with them
Eph 3:11 and it has now been **c** out through Christ Jesus our
1Pe 2:24 He personally **c** away our sins in his own body on
2Pe 3:17 and not be **c** away by the errors of these wicked
Rev 6: 2 Its rider **c** a bow, and a crown was placed on his

CARRIERS (1) [CARRY]

Jos 9:27 and water **c** for the people of Israel and for the altar

CARRIES (5) [CARRY]

Nu 11:12 like a nurse **c** a baby—to the land you swore to
Job 27:21 The east wind **c** them away, and they are gone.
Ps 68:19 For each day he **c** us in his arms. / *Interlude*
Isa 40:24 their work withers. The wind **c** them off like straw.
Lk 11:22 strips him of his weapons, and **c** off his belongings.

CARRION (2)

Lev 11:18 the white owl, the pelican, the **c** vulture,
Dt 14:17 the pelican, the **c** vulture, the cormorant,

CARRY (134) [CARRIED, CARRIERS, CARRIES, CARRYING]

Ge 44: 1 of their sacks with as much grain as they can **c**,
45:19 to take wagons from Egypt to **c** their wives
Ex 12:11 and **c** your walking sticks in your hands.
12:46 You must not **c** any of its meat outside, and you
18:22 They will help you **c** the load, making the task
25:14 poles into the rings at the sides of the Ark to **c** it.
25:27 These rings will support the poles used to **c** the
27: 7 To **c** it, put the poles into the rings at two sides of
28:12 Aaron will **c** these names before the LORD as a
28:29 Aaron will **c** the names of the tribes of Israel on the
28:30 Aaron will always **c** the objects used to determine
37: 5 poles into the rings at the sides of the Ark to **c** it.
Lev 6:11 and **c** the ashes outside the camp to a place that is
10: 4 and **c** the bodies of your relatives away from the
11:40 If you eat any of its meat or **c** away its carcass,
15:10 If you touch or **c** anything that was under him,
16:12 he will **c** the burner and incense behind the inner
16:22 the goat will **c** all the people's sins upon itself into
26:25 I will send armies against you to **c** out these
Nu 1:50 They must **c** the Tabernacle and its equipment as
3:10 and his sons to **c** out the duties of the priesthood.
4:15 and **c** these things to the next destination.
4:15 of the Tabernacle that the Kohathites must **c**.
4:25 They must **c** the curtains of the Tabernacle,
4:26 They are also to **c** the curtains for the courtyard
4:27 must assign the Gershonites the loads they are to **c**.
4:31 They will be required to **c** the frames of the
4:49 Each man was assigned his task and told what to **c**,
5:25 lift it up before the LORD, and **c** it to the altar.
7: 9 since they were required to **c** the sacred objects of
11:12 Is that why you have told me to **c** them in my
11:14 I can't **c** all these people by myself! The load is far
11:17 along with you, so you will not have to **c** it alone.
13:23 so large that it took two of them to **c** it on a pole
15:22 "But suppose some of you unintentionally fail to **c**
16:46 and **c** it quickly among the people to make
Dt 1: 9 'You are too great a burden for me to **c** all by
10: 8 of Levi to **c** the Ark of the LORD's covenant,
29:11 among you who chop your wood and **c** your water.
32:41 my flashing sword / and begin to **c** out justice,
Jos 4: 5 pick up one stone and **c** it out on your shoulder—
9:21 and **c** the water for the entire community."
9:23 chop wood and **c** water for the house of my God."
Jdg 5:14 from Zebulun came those who **c** the rod of
Ru 4: 5 she can have children who will **c** on her husband's
4:10 This way she can have a son to **c** on the family
1Sa 3:12 I am going to **c** out all my threats against Eli
4: 3 If we **c** it into battle with us, it will save us from
4: 4 helped **c** the Ark of God to where the battle was
11: 7 and sent the messengers to **c** them throughout
19:16 But when they came to **c** David out,
25:31 Then you won't have to **c** on your conscience the
2Sa 14:26 then only because it was too heavy to **c** around.
18:18 for he had said, "I have no son to **c** on my name."
1Ki 8:25 **c** out your further promise to your servant David,
14:28 the guards would **c** them along and then return
15:22 help to **c** away the building stones and timbers that
18:12 the Spirit of the LORD will **c** you away to who
2Ki 4:19 one of the servants, "**C** him home to his mother."
5: 5 "I will send a letter of introduction for you to **c** to
5:23 and sent two of his servants to **c** the gifts for
1Ch 15: 2 God this time, no one except the Levites may **c** it.
15: 2 The LORD has chosen them to **c** the Ark of the
15:13 Because you Levites did not **c** the Ark the first
23:26 Now the Levites will no longer need to **c** the
24: 2 and Ithamar were left to **c** on as priests.
2Ch 6:16 **c** out your further promise to your servant David,
12:11 the guards would **c** them along and then return
16: 6 Then King Asa called out all the men of Judah to **c**
20:25 and other valuables—more than they could **c**.
35: 3 and you do not need to **c** it back and forth on your
Est 6:10 Do not fail to **c** out everything you have
Job 6:11 I do not have a goal that encourages me to **c** on.
24:10 They are forced to **c** food while they themselves
39: 2 Do you know how many months they **c** their
Ps 28: 9 like a shepherd, / and **c** them forever in your arms.
49:17 For when they die, they **c** nothing with them.
89:50 I **c** in my heart the insults of so many people.
103:20 you mighty creatures who **c** out his plans,
Pr 4:13 **C** out my instructions; don't forsake them.
Isa 5:29 will seize my people and **c** them off into captivity,
8: 4 and Samaria and **c** away their riches."
13: 5 they **c** his anger with them and will destroy the
15: 7 refugees take only the possessions they can **c**
28: 7 They make stupid mistakes as they **c** out their
30:14 left that is big enough to **c** coals from a fireplace
40:11 He will **c** the lambs in his arms, holding them close
44:26 But I **c** out the predictions of my prophets!
45:20 What fools they are who **c** around their wooden
46: 4 I will care for you. I will **c** you along and save you.
46: 7 They **c** it around on their shoulders, and when they
47: 6 You have forced even the elderly to **c** heavy
49:22 They will **c** your little sons back to you in their
52:11 you who **c** home the vessels of the LORD.
Jer 1:12 and I will surely **c** out my threats of punishment."
17:24 and do not **c** on your trade or work on the Sabbath
28: 9 So a prophet who predicts peace must **c** the burden
44:25 Then go ahead and **c** out your promises and vows
Eze 11: 9 and hand you over to foreigners who will **c** out my
12: 3 Pack whatever you can **c** on your back and leave
12: 5 are watching and **c** your possessions out through it.
12: 7 filled with the things I might **c** into exile.
12:12 in the wall, taking only what he can **c** with him.
25:14 They will **c** out my furious vengeance, and Edom
29:19 He will **c** off their wealth, plundering everything
Da 11: 8 he will **c** back their idols with him, along with
11:10 and **c** the battle as far as the enemy's fortress.
Hos 5:14 I will **c** them off, and there will be no one left to
Am 6:10 goes into the house to **c** away a dead body, he will
Jnh 3:10 and didn't **c** out the destruction he had threatened.
Mic 2: 1 and hurry to **c** out any of the wicked schemes you
Na 1:14 "You will have no more children to **c** on your
Mt 5:33 you must **c** out the vows you have made to the
5:41 If a soldier demands that you **c** his gear for a mile,
c it two miles.
10:10 Don't **c** a traveler's bag with an extra coat
11:28 all of you who are weary and **c** heavy burdens,
27:32 and they forced him to **c** Jesus' cross.
Mk 15:21 just then, and they forced him to **c** Jesus' cross.
Lk 14:27 And you cannot be my disciple if you do not **c**
15: 5 then you would joyfully **c** it home on your
23:26 was forced to follow Jesus and **c** his cross.
Jn 5:10 on the Sabbath! It's illegal to **c** that sleeping mat!"
9: 4 All of us must quickly **c** out the tasks assigned us
10:37 Don't believe me unless I **c** out my Father's work.
13: 2 of Simon Iscariot, to **c** out his plan to betray Jesus.
Ac 5: 9 your husband, and they will **c** you out, too."
27:43 to spare Paul, so he didn't let them **c** out their plan.
Ro 9:28 For the Lord will **c** out his sentence upon the earth
2Co 8:11 Now you should **c** this project through to
Col 4:17 "Be sure to **c** out the work the Lord gave you."
1Ti 6: 7 and we certainly cannot **c** anything with us when
Heb 11:22 so sure of it that he commanded them to **c** his
Rev 17:17 into their minds, a plan that will **c** out his purposes.

CARRYING (67) [CARRY]

Ge 24:20 She kept **c** water to the camels until they had
38:18 your cord, and the walking stick you are **c**."
Ex 25:15 These **c** poles must never be taken from the rings;
30: 4 attach two gold rings to support the **c** poles.
34: 4 had told him, **c** the two stone tablets in his hands.
34:29 When Moses came down the mountain **c** the stone
35:13 the table, its **c** poles, and all of its utensils;
35:15 the incense altar and its **c** poles; the anointing oil
35:16 grating of the altar and its **c** poles and utensils;
37:14 These were made to hold the **c** poles in place.
37:15 He made the **c** poles of acacia wood and overlaid
37:27 beneath the molding, to hold the **c** poles.
37:28 The **c** poles were made of acacia wood and were
38: 5 for each side of the grating to support the **c** poles.
38: 6 The **c** poles themselves were made of acacia wood
39:35 the Ark of the Covenant and its **c** poles; the Ark's
40:20 and then he attached the Ark's **c** poles.
Nu 4: 6 they must put the **c** poles of the Ark in place.
4: 8 Then they must insert the **c** poles into the table.
4:10 and the bundle must be placed on a **c** frame.
4:11 Then they are to attach the **c** poles to the altar.
4:12 fine goatskin leather, and placed on the **c** frame.
4:14 Finally, the **c** poles must be put in place.
4:24 will be in the areas of general service and **c** loads.
4:31 "Their duties at the Tabernacle will consist of **c**
10:17 in the line of march, **c** the Tabernacle with them.
10:21 **c** the sacred objects from the Tabernacle.
Jos 3: 3 "When you see the Levitical priests **c** the Ark of
3: 8 Give these instructions to the priests who are **c** the
3:13 The priests will be **c** the Ark of the LORD,
3:14 the priests who were **c** the Ark of the Covenant
3:15 But as soon as the feet of the priests who were **c**
3:17 the priests who were **c** the Ark of the LORD's
4:10 The priests who were **c** the Ark stood in the middle
4:16 "Command the priests **c** the Ark of the Covenant
4:18 And as soon as the priests **c** the Ark of the
6: 4 will walk ahead of the Ark, each **c** a ram's horn.
6: 6 priests to walk in front of it, each **c** a ram's horn."
6: 8 And the priests **c** the Ark of the LORD's
8:33 and between them stood the Levitical priests **c** the
Jdg 6:19 **c** the meat in a basket and the broth in a pot,
18:18 When the priest saw the men **c** all the sacred
1Sa 10: 3 of bread, and the third will be **c** a skin of wine.
17: 7 An armor bearer walked ahead of him **c** a huge
25:33 the man and **c** out vengeance with my own hands.
2Sa 6:13 After the men who were **c** it had gone six steps,
1Ki 8: 7 forming a canopy over the Ark and its **c** poles.
2Ki 7: 8 and **c** out silver and gold and clothing and hiding
1Ch 15:15 the Ark of God on their shoulders with its **c** poles,
2Ch 5: 8 forming a canopy over the Ark and its **c** poles.
25:13 and **c** off great quantities of plunder.
Isa 46: 2 the idols and the ones **c** them are bowed down.
Jer 17:21 Stop **c** on your trade at Jerusalem's gates on the
43:12 all their idols and **c** away the people as captives.
Eze 9: 2 that faces north, each **c** a battle club in his hand.
9: 3 man dressed in linen who was **c** the writer's case.
9: 8 While they were **c** out their orders, I was all alone.
46:20 They will do it here to avoid **c** the sacrifices
Hag 2:12 If one of you is **c** a holy sacrifice in his robes
Mk 2: 3 Four men arrived **c** a paralyzed man on a mat.
6:55 and began **c** sick people to him on mats.
14:13 "a man **c** a pitcher of water will meet you.
Lk 5:18 Some men came **c** a paralyzed man on a sleeping
22:10 a man **c** a pitcher of water will meet you.
Jn 19:17 **C** the cross by himself, Jesus went to the place
Rev 7: 2 coming from the east, **c** the seal of the living God.
14: 6 **c** the everlasting Good News to preach to the

CARSHENA (1)

Est 1:14 The names of these men were **C**, Shethar,

CART (20) [CART'S, CARTED, CARTS]

Nu 7: 3 There was a **c** for every two leaders and an ox for
1Sa 6: 7 Now build a new **c**, and find two cows that have
6: 7 Make sure the cows have never been yoked to a **c**.
6: 7 Hitch the cows to the **c**, but shut their calves away
6: 8 Put the Ark of the LORD on the **c**, and beside it
6:10 cows with newborn calves were hitched to the **c**,
6:11 the gold rats and gold tumors were placed on the **c**.
6:14 The **c** came into the field of a man named Joshua

6:14 So the people broke up the wood of the **c** for a fire
6:15 and gold tumors from the **c** and placed them on the
2Sa 6: 3 They placed the Ark of God on a new **c**
6: 3 and Ahio, Abinadab's sons, were guiding the **c**
1Ki 7:31 The top of each **c** had a circular frame for the
7:32 to axles that had been cast as one unit with the **c**.
7:34 and these, too, were cast as one unit with the **c**.
7:35 Around the top of each **c** there was a rim 9 inches
7:35 and side panels were cast as one unit with the **c**.
7:38 also made ten bronze basins, one for each **c**.
1Ch 13: 7 of God from the house of Abinadab on a new **c**,
Isa 28:28 He threshes it under the wheels of a **c**, but he

CART'S (1) [CART]

1Ki 7:31 It projected 1-1/2 feet above the **c** top like a round

CARTED (2) [CART]

2Ch 29:16 From there the Levites **c** it all out to the Kidron
Hos 10: 6 so much will be **c** away with them when they go as

CARTS (22) [CART]

Nu 7: 3 Together they brought six **c** and twelve oxen.
7: 5 these oxen and **c** for the work of the Tabernacle.
7: 6 So Moses presented the **c** and oxen to the Levites.
7: 7 He gave two **c** and four oxen to the Gershonite
7: 8 and four **c** and eight oxen to the Merarite division
7: 9 But he gave none of the **c** or oxen to the Kohathite
1Ki 7:27 Huram also made ten bronze water **c**, each 6 feet
7:30 Each of these **c** had four bronze wheels and bronze
7:30 At each corner of the **c** were supporting posts for
7:31 The panels of the **c** were square, not round.
7:34 were supports at each of the four corners of the **c**,
7:37 All ten water **c** were the same size and were made
7:39 He arranged five water **c** on the south side of the
7:43 the ten water **c** holding the ten basins,
2Ki 16:17 side panels and basins from the portable water **c**.
25:13 broke up the bronze pillars, the bronze water **c**,
25:16 The bronze from the two pillars, the water **c**,
2Ch 4:14 the water **c** holding the basins,
Isa 46: 1 Bel and Nebo, are being hauled away on ox **c**.
Jer 27:19 the bronze water **c**, and all the other ceremonial
52:17 broke up the bronze pillars, the bronze water **c**,
52:20 The bronze from the two pillars, the water **c**,

CARVE (3) [CARVED, CARVER, CARVES, CARVING, CARVINGS, WOOD-CARVER]

Jer 10: 3 and foolish. They cut down a tree and **c** an idol.
Eze 37:16 "Son of man, take a stick and **c** on it these words:
37:16 Then take another stick and **c** these words on it:

CARVED (35) [CARVE]

Ex 30: 2 with horns at the corners **c** from the same piece of
34:13 pillars they worship, and cut down their **c** images.
Lev 26: 1 "Do not make idols or set up **c** images,
Nu 33:52 You must destroy all their **c** and molten images
Dt 12: 3 their Asherah poles and cut down their **c** idols.
Jdg 17: 3 my son, I will have an image **c** and an idol cast."
18:14 some household idols, a **c** image, and a cast idol.
18:17 five spies entered the shrine and took the **c** image,
18:20 sacred ephod, the household idols, and the **c** image.
18:30 Then they set up the **c** image, and they appointed
18:31 So Micah's **c** image was worshiped by the tribe of
1Ki 7:29 and the crossbars were decorated with **c** lions,
2Ch 3: 7 and figures of cherubim were **c** on the walls.
16:14 He was buried in the tomb he had **c** out for himself
33: 7 Manasseh even took a **c** idol he had made and set it
33:19 the Asherah poles, and the **c** idols and cast images.
34: 3 the Asherah poles, and the **c** idols and cast images.
34: 4 the **c** idols, and the cast images were smashed
Job 19:24 **c** with an iron chisel and filled with lead,
Ps 74: 6 and picks, / they smashed the **c** paneling.
144:12 be like graceful pillars, / **c** to beautify a palace.
Isa 5: 2 and **c** a winepress in the nearby rocks.
42: 8 anyone else. I will not share my praise with **c** idols.
44:17 he takes what's left and makes his god: a **c** idol!
Jer 2:27 To an image **c** from a piece of wood they say,
8:19 why have they angered me with their **c** idols
Eze 27: 6 They **c** oars for you from the oaks of Bashan.
40:16 dividing walls were decorated with **c** palm trees.
41:19 The figures were **c** all along the inside of the
41:25 the Holy Place were decorated with **c** cherubim
41:26 recessed windows decorated with **c** palm trees.
Mic 1: 7 All her **c** images will be smashed to pieces. All her
Mt 27:60 own new tomb, which had been **c** out of the rock.
Mk 15:46 and laid it in a tomb that had been **c** out of the
Lk 23:53 and laid it in a new tomb that had been **c** out of
2Co 3: 3 It is **c** not on stone, but on human hearts.

CARVER (1) [CARVE]

Isa 41: 7 The **c** hurries the goldsmith, and the molder helps

CARVES (2) [CARVE]

Dt 27:15 'Cursed is anyone who **c** or casts idols and secretly
Isa 44:13 of wood, takes the tool, and **c** the figure of a man.

CARVING (3) [CARVE]

Ex 31: 5 in cutting and setting gemstones and in **c** wood.
35:33 in cutting and setting gemstones and in **c** wood.
Eze 41:18 and there was a palm tree **c** between each of the

CARVINGS (10) [CARVE]

Jdg 3:19 But when Ehud reached the stone **c** near Gilgal,
1Ki 6:18 and the paneling was decorated with **c** of gourds
6:29 and the main room were decorated with **c** of
6:32 These doors were decorated with **c** of cherubim,
6:35 These doors were decorated with **c** of cherubim,
7:30 these supports were decorated with **c** of wreaths on
7:31 it was decorated on the outside with **c** of wreaths.
7:36 **C** of cherubim, lions, and palm trees decorated the
2Ch 3: 5 and decorated with **c** of palm trees and chains.
Eze 41:18 All the walls were decorated with **c** of cherubim,

CASCADES (1)

Dt 9:21 I threw the dust into the stream that **c** down the

CASE (75) [CASES]

Ex 18:16 an argument arises, I am the one who settles the **c**.
21:28 In such a **c**, however, the owner will not be held
Lev 7: 8 In the **c** of the whole burnt offering, the hide of the
15: 3 or is stopped up. In either **c** the man is unclean.
Nu 27: 5 So Moses brought their **c** before the LORD.
Dt 6:24 our own prosperity and well-being, as is now the **c**.
15:17 "In that **c**, take an awl and push it through his
17: 8 "Suppose a **c** arises in a local court that is too hard
17: 8 or a **c** involving different kinds of assault.
17: 9 and the judge on duty will hear the **c** and decide
19:12 In that **c**, the leaders of the murderer's hometown
19:15 The facts of the **c** must be established by the
22:26 This **c** is similar to that of someone who attacks
Jdg 6:31 are you defending Baal? Will you argue his **c**?
6:31 Whoever pleads his **c** will be put to death by
11:25 Did he try to make a **c** against Israel for disputed
1Sa 1:17 "In that **c**," Eli said, "cheer up! May the God of
2Sa 15: 2 When people brought a **c** to the king for judgment,
15: 3 would say, "You've really got a strong **c** here!
16: 4 "In that **c**," the king told Ziba, "I give you
2Ch 19: 6 render the verdict in each **c** that comes before you.
19:10 Whenever a **c** comes to you from fellow citizens in
19:10 whether a murder **c** or some other violation of
Job 2: 7 and he struck Job with a terrible **c** of boils from
5: 8 to you is this: Go to God and present your **c** to him.
13: 3 I want to argue my **c** with God himself.
13: 8 in his favor? Will you argue God's **c** for him?
13:15 I cannot wait. I am going to argue my **c** with him.
13:18 I have prepared my **c**; I will be proved innocent.
23: 4 I would lay out my **c** and present my arguments.
33: 5 if you can; make your **c** and take your stand.
Ps 35:23 my defense! / Take up my **c**, my God and my Lord.
109: 7 When his **c** is called for judgment, / let him be
119:154 Argue my **c**; take my side! / Protect my life as you
Ecc 4: 8 This is the **c** of a man who is all alone, without a
Isa 3:13 presenting his **c** against his people!
5: 3 you have heard the **c**; you be the judges.
40:27 How can you say God refuses to hear your **c**?
41: 1 and speak. The court is ready for your **c**.
43:26 and you can present your **c** if you have one.
45:21 Consult together, argue your **c**, and state your
Jer 2: 9 I will bring my **c** against you and will keep on
12: 1 you always give me justice when I bring a **c** before
25:31 for the LORD will bring his **c** against all the
51:36 "I will be your lawyer to plead your **c**, and I will
La 3:58 Lord, you are my lawyer! Plead my **c**! For you
Eze 9: 2 and carried a writer's **c** strapped to his side.
9: 3 dressed in linen who was carrying the writer's **c**.
9:11 who carried the writer's **c**, reported back and said,
Mic 6: 1 "Stand up and state your **c** against me.
6: 2 He has a **c** against his people Israel!
7: 9 he will take up my **c** and punish my enemies for all
Mt 18:17 still refuses to listen, take your **c** to the church.
Mk 3: 9 and to have it ready in **c** he was crowded off the
Lk 5:12 Jesus met a man with an advanced **c** of leprosy.
23: 2 They began at once to state their **c**: "This man has
Ac 18:14 if this were a **c** involving some wrongdoing or a
19:38 and the craftsmen have a **c** against them,
19:38 are in session and the judges can take the **c** at once.
23:15 "Pretend you want to examine his **c** more fully.
23:35 "I will hear your **c** myself when your accusers
24: 4 moment as I briefly outline our **c** against this man.
24:22 arrives. Then I will decide the **c**."
25:14 Festus discussed Paul's **c** with the king.
25:14 he told him, "whose **c** was left for me by Felix.
25:17 I called the **c** the very next day and ordered Paul
25:25 However, he appealed his **c** to the emperor, and I
Ro 3: 4 in what he says, and he will win his **c** in court."
4:14 And in that **c**, the promise is also meaningless.
11: 6 For in that **c**, God's wonderful kindness would not
1Co 15:18 In that **c**, all who have died believing in Christ
2Co 13: 1 "The facts of every **c** must be established by the
Gal 3:15 amend an irrevocable agreement, so it is in this **c**.
Heb 7: 8 In the **c** of Jewish priests, tithes are paid to men
1Pe 2:23 He left his **c** in the hands of God, who always

CASES (20) [CASE]

Ex 18:22 can serve the people, resolving all the ordinary **c**.
18:26 They brought the hard **c** to Moses, but they judged
Lev 13:11 In such **c**, the person need not be quarantined for
13:13 In such **c**, the priest must examine the infected
Nu 5:24 on the curse and cause bitter suffering in **c** of guilt.
35:21 In such **c**, the victim's nearest relative must
Dt 1:17 Bring me any **c** that are too difficult for you,
13:14 In such **c**, you must examine the facts carefully.
17: 8 Take such **c** to the place the LORD your God will
19: 5 In such **c**, the slayer could flee to one of the cities
21: 2 In such **c**, your leaders and judges must determine
21:19 In such **c**, the father and mother must take the son
22:21 In such **c**, the judges must take the girl to the door
1Sa 7:17 his home at Ramah, and he would hear **c** there, too.
2Ch 19: 8 for **c** concerning both the law of the LORD
19:11 will have final say in all **c** concerning the LORD.
19:11 the tribe of Judah, will have final say in all civil **c**.
Ecc 5: 6 In such **c**, your mouth is making you sin.
Eze 44:25 or unmarried sister. In such **c** it is permitted.
1Co 7:15 In such **c** the Christian husband or wife is not

CASIPHIA (1)

Ezr 8:17 the leader of the Levites at **C**, to ask him and his

CASK (1)

Job 32:19 I am like a wine **c** without a vent. My words are

CASLUHITES (2)

Ge 10:14 Pathrusites, **C**, and the Caphtorites, from whom the
1Ch 1:12 Pathrusites, **C**, and the Caphtorites, from whom the

CASSIA (3)

Ex 30:24 12-1/2 pounds of **c**, and one gallon of olive oil.
Ps 45: 8 Your robes are perfumed with myrrh, aloes, and **c**.
Eze 27:19 Wrought iron, **c**, and calamus were bartered for

CAST (77) [CASTING, CASTS]

Ex 25:12 **C** four rings of gold for it, and attach them to its
37:13 Then he **c** four rings of gold and attached them to
38: 5 Four rings were **c** for each side of the grating to
38: 8 and its bronze pedestal were **c** from bronze mirrors
Lev 16: 8 He is to **c** sacred lots to determine which goat will
Dt 9:12 and have **c** an idol for themselves from gold.'
18:11 or **c** spells, or function as mediums or psychics,
Jos 18: 6 Then I will **c** sacred lots in the presence of the
18:10 Joshua **c** sacred lots in the presence of the LORD
Jdg 17: 3 I will have an image carved and an idol **c**."
18:14 household idols, a carved image, and a **c** idol.
18:17 sacred ephod, the household idols, and the **c** idol.
1Ki 7:15 Huram **c** two bronze pillars, each 27 feet tall
7:23 Then Huram **c** a large round tank, 15 feet across
7:24 and they had been **c** as part of the tank.
7:32 to axles that had been **c** as one unit with the cart.
7:33 rims, and hubs were all **c** from molten bronze.
7:34 and these, too, were **c** as one unit with the cart.
7:35 and side panels were **c** as one unit with the cart.
7:37 made alike, for each was **c** from the same mold.
7:46 The king had them **c** in clay molds in the Jordan
2Ch 4: 2 Then he **c** a large round tank, 15 feet across from
4: 3 and they had been **c** as part of the tank.
4: 7 then **c** ten gold lampstands according to the
4:17 The king had them **c** in clay molds in the Jordan
28: 2 of Israel and **c** images for the worship of Baal.
34: 3 Asherah poles, and the carved idols and **c** images.
34: 4 and the **c** images were smashed and scattered over
Ne 10:34 "We have **c** sacred lots to determine when—
Est 3: 7 lots were **c** (the lots were called *purim*)
La 2: 1 The Lord in his anger has **c** a dark shadow over
Eze 21:21 They will **c** lots by shaking arrows from the quiver.
23:27 You will never again **c** longing eyes on those
30:21 His arm has not been put in a **c** so that it may heal.
31: 3 full of thick branches that **c** deep forest shade with
Joel 3: 3 They **c** lots to decide which of my people would be
Ob 1:11 off their wealth and **c** lots to divide up Jerusalem.
Jnh 1: 7 Then the crew **c** lots to see which of them had
Na 3:10 Soldiers **c** lots to see who would get the Egyptian
Mt 7:22 in your name and **c** out demons in your name
8:12 will be **c** into outer darkness, where there will be
8:31 so the demons begged, "If you **c** us out, send us
9:33 So Jesus **c** out the demon, and instantly the man
9:34 "He can **c** out demons because he is empowered
10: 1 and gave them authority to **c** out evil spirits and to
10: 8 cure those with leprosy, and **c** out demons.
12:24 they said, "No wonder he can **c** out demons.
12:27 They **c** out demons, too, so they will judge you for
17:19 "Why couldn't we **c** out that demon?"
Mk 3:15 and he gave them authority to **c** out demons.
3:22 That's where he gets the power to **c** out demons."
3:23 way of illustration, "How can Satan **c** out Satan?
6: 7 out two by two, with authority to **c** out evil spirits.
6:13 And they **c** out many demons and healed many
9:18 So I asked your disciples to **c** out the evil spirit,
9:28 "Why couldn't we **c** out that evil spirit?"
9:29 "This kind can be **c** out only by prayer."
9:38 we saw a man using your name to **c** out demons,
16: 9 the woman from whom he had **c** out seven
16:17 They will **c** out demons in my name, and they will
Lk 6:18 and to be healed, and Jesus **c** out many evil spirits.
7:21 and he **c** out evil spirits and restored sight to the
8: 2 and from whom he had **c** out evil spirits.
8: 2 from whom he had **c** out seven demons;
9: 1 gave them power and authority to **c** out demons
9:40 I begged your disciples to **c** the spirit out, but they
9:49 we saw someone using your name to **c** out demons.
11:14 One day Jesus **c** a demon out of a man who
11:15 but some said, "No wonder he can **c** out demons.
11:18 himself by empowering me to **c** out his demons,
11:19 They **c** out demons, too, so they will judge you for
Jn 12:31 when the prince of this world will be **c** out.
Ac 1:26 Then they **c** lots, and in this way Matthias was
8: 7 Many evil spirits were **c** out, screaming as they left
26:10 And I **c** my vote against them when they were
1Co 5: 5 Then you must **c** this man out of the church
Gal 3: 1 What magician has **c** an evil spell on you?

CASTANETS (1)

2Sa 6: 5 lyres, harps, tambourines, **c**, and cymbals.

CASTAWAY [KJV] See DISQUALIFIED

CASTING (14) [CAST]

Ex 38:30 which was used for c the bases for the posts at the
Jos 18: 8 and I will assign the land to the tribes by c sacred
19:51 c sacred lots in the presence of the LORD at the
21: 8 and pasturelands to the Levites by c sacred lots.
1Ch 24: 6 of Eleazar and Ithamar took turns c lots.
Est 9:24 and month determined by c lots (the lots were
9:26 because it is the ancient word for c lots.)
Pr 18:18 C lots can end arguments and settle disputes
Jer 31:37 so I will not consider c them away forever for their
Mt 12:26 And if Satan is c out Satan, he is fighting against
12:28 But if I am c out demons by the Spirit of God,
Lk 11:20 But if I am c out demons by the power of God,
13:32 "Go tell that fox that I will keep on c out demons
Ac 19:13 c out evil spirits tried to use the name of the Lord

CASTLE(S) [KJV] See CAMPED, FORTRESS, GATE, VILLAGES

CASTRATED (1)

Lev 22:24 If an animal has damaged testicles or is c, it may

CASTS (4) [CAST]

Dt 27:15 who carves or c idols and secretly sets them up.
Isa 9: 2 all who live in the land where death c its shadow.
Mt 4:16 And for those who lived in the land where death c
Jas 1:17 he never changes or c shifting shadows.

CASUALTIES (3)

2Sa 2:30 When Joab counted his c, he discovered that only
2Ch 13:17 there were 500,000 c among Israel's finest troops
28: 5 defeated Ahaz and inflicted many c on his army.

CATASTROPHE (1)

Isa 47:11 A c will arise so fast that you won't know what hit

CATCH (33) [CATCHES, CATCHING, CAUGHT]

Ge 19:19 Disaster would c up to me there, and I would soon
Ex 15: 9 chase them, / c up with them, and destroy them.
Jos 2: 5 If you hurry, you can probably c up with them."
Jdg 8: 6 C them first, and then we will feed your warriors."
8:15 C them first, and then we will feed your exhausted
1Sa 9:13 Hurry and c him before he goes up the hill to eat.
17:35 turns on me, I c it by the jaw and club it to death.
23:20 and we will c him and hand him over to you!"
24:14 Who is the king of Israel trying to c anyway?
30: 8 "Should I chase them? Will I c them?"
2Sa 3:26 left David and sent messengers to c up with Abner.
17: 2 I will c up to him while he is weary
Job 9:18 He will not let me c my breath, but fills me instead
40:24 No one can c it off guard or put a ring in its nose
41: 1 "Can you c a crocodile with a hook or put a noose
Ps 94: 8 you fools! / When will you finally c on?
140: 5 The proud have set a trap to c me; / they have
Pr 5:22 by his own sins; they are ropes that c and hold him.
12:27 Lazy people don't even cook the game they c,
30:28 Lizards—they are easy to c, / but they are found
SS 2:15 C all the little foxes before they ruin the vineyard
Jer 16:16 am sending for many fishermen who will c them,"
Eze 19: 3 He learned to c and devour prey, / and he became a
19: 6 He learned to c and devour prey, / and he, too,
32: 3 I will send many people to c you in my net
Hos 2: 7 her lovers, she won't be able to c up with them.
Am 3: 5 ever spring shut when there's nothing there to c?
Mt 17:27 Open the mouth of the first fish you c, and you will
Lk 5: 4 and let down your nets, and you will c many fish."
5: 5 "we worked hard all last night and didn't c a thing.
5: 9 For he was awestruck by the size of their c,
21:34 of this life. Don't let that day c you unaware,
2Co 11:32 King Aretas kept guards at the city gates to c me.

CATCHES (2) [CATCH]

Job 5:13 He c those who think they are wise in their own
1Co 3:19 "God c those who think they are wise

CATCHING (3) [CATCH]

Job 34:28 they cause the poor to cry out, c God's attention.
Da 8:25 of deception, defeating many by c them off guard.
Am 3: 4 Does a young lion growl in its den without first c

CATERPILLARS (3)

1Ki 8:37 or crop disease, or attacks of locusts or c,
2Ch 6:28 or crop disease, or attacks of locusts or c,
Ps 78:46 He gave their crops to c; / their harvest was

CATERPILLER(S) [KJV] See CATERPILLARS, LOCUST

CATS (1)

Ps 73: 7 These fat c have everything / their hearts could

CATTLE (84)

Ge 12:16 sheep, c, donkeys, male and female servants,
13: 5 also very wealthy with sheep, c, and many tents.
24:35 has given him flocks of sheep and herds of c,
26:14 large flocks of sheep and goats, great herds of c,
34: 5 but his sons were out in the fields herding c so he
36: 6 children, household servants, c, and flocks—
36: 7 them both because of all their c and livestock.
Ex 9: 3 your horses, donkeys, camels, c, and sheep.
20:24 peace offerings, your sheep and goats and your c.
22:30 "You must also give me the firstborn of your c
34:19 firstborn male belongs to me—of both c and sheep.
Lev 19:19 "Do not breed your c with other kinds of animals.
26:22 that will kill your children and destroy your c,
27:26 not dedicate to the LORD the firstborn of your c
Nu 15: 3 flocks of sheep and goats or from your herds of c.
18:17 you may not redeem the firstborn of c, sheep,
22:40 where the king sacrificed c and sheep. He sent
31: 9 and children and seized their c and flocks and all
31:28 c, donkeys, sheep, and goats that belong to the
31:30 of every fifty of the captives, c, donkeys, sheep,
31:33 72,000 c,
31:38 36,000 c, of which 72 were the LORD's share;
31:44 36,000 c,
32:26 flocks, and c will stay here in the towns of Gilead.
35: 3 surrounding lands will provide pasture for their c,
Dt 7:13 and olives, and great herds of c, sheep, and goats.
11:15 He will give you lush pastureland for your c to
12:21 you may butcher any of the c or sheep the LORD
Jos 1:14 and c may remain here on the east side of the
6:21 and women, young and old, c, sheep, donkeys—
7:24 his sons, daughters, c, donkeys, sheep, tent,
8: 2 keep the captured goods and the c for yourselves.
8:27 Only the c and the treasures of the city were not
11:14 and c of the ravaged cities for themselves,
21: 2 us towns to live in and pasturelands for our c."
22: 8 Share with them your large herds of c, your silver
Jdg 6: 5 coming with their c and tents as thick as locusts,
20:48 in all the towns—the people, the c—everything.
1Sa 8:16 and female slaves and demand the finest of your c
14:32 and butchered the sheep, c, and calves,
14:34 'Bring the c and sheep here to kill them and drain
15: 3 men, women, children, babies, c, sheep, camels,
15: 9 Agag's life and kept the best of the sheep and c,
15:14 all the bleating of sheep and lowing of c I hear?"
15:15 that the army spared the best of the sheep and c,"
15:21 my troops brought in the best of the sheep and c
22:19 and babies, and all the c, donkeys, and sheep.
27: 9 He took the sheep, c, donkeys, camels,
2Sa 12: 2 The rich man owned many sheep and c.
1Ki 4:23 twenty pasture-fed c, one hundred sheep or goats,
2Ki 3:17 and for your c and your other animals.
1Ch 5: 9 since they had so many c in the land of Gilead,
12:40 of flour, fig cakes, raisins, wine, olive oil, c,
27:29 Shitrai from Sharon was in charge of the c on the
27:29 Shaphat son of Adlai was responsible for the c in
2Ch 31: 6 brought in the tithes of their c and sheep and a tithe
32:28 and he made many stalls for his c and folds for his
Ne 9:37 of our sins. They have power over us and our c.
Job 18: 3 Do you think we are c? Do you think we have no
Ps 8: 7 the sheep and the c / and all the wild animals,
50:10 are mine, / and I own the c on a thousand hills.
78:48 He abandoned their c to the hail, / their livestock to
104:14 You cause grass to grow for the c. / You cause
107:38 large families there, / and their herds of c increase.
Isa 7:25 cover them. C, sheep, and goats will graze there.
11: 7 The c will graze among bears. Cubs and calves
27:10 C will graze there, chewing on twigs and branches.
30:23 and plenty of pastureland for your c.
63:14 As with c going down into a peaceful valley,
Jer 5:17 your flocks of sheep and your herds of c.
9:10 the lowing of c is heard no more; the birds
31:27 and multiply the number of c here in Israel
49:32 Their camels and c will all be yours. I will scatter
50:27 Even destroy her c—it will be terrible for them,
Eze 25:13 wipe out their people, c, and flocks with the sword.
38:12 many slaves, for the people are rich with c now,
38:13 Who are you to drive away their c and seize their
Joel 1:18 The c wander about confused because there is no
Hab 3:17 flocks die in the fields, and the c barns are empty,
Zep 2:14 so proud will become a pasture for sheep and c.
Hag 1:11 a drought to starve both you and your c and to ruin
Jn 2:14 In the Temple area he saw merchants selling c,
4:12 water than he and his sons and his c enjoyed?"
Rev 18:13 fine flour, wheat, c, sheep, horses, chariots,

CAUDA (1)

Ac 27:16 We sailed behind a small island named C,

CAUGHT (71) [CATCH]

Ge 14:14 He chased after Kedorlaomer's army until he c up
19:15 or you will be c in the destruction of the city."
22:13 looked up and saw a ram c by its horns in a bush.
27:27 And when Isaac c the smell of his clothes, he was
31:23 He c up with them seven days later in the hill
31:25 So when Laban c up with Jacob as he was camped
44: 6 So the man c up with them and spoke to them in
Ex 3: 4 When the LORD saw that he had c Moses'
14: 9 The Egyptians c up with the people of Israel as
21:16 whether they are c in possession of their victims
22: 2 "If a thief is c in the act of breaking into a house
22: 3 "A thief who is c must pay in full for everything
Nu 5:13 but there is no witness since she was not c in the
11:22 Even if we c all the fish in the sea, would that be
11:32 So the people went out and c quail all that day
15:32 they c a man gathering wood on the Sabbath day.
Dt 22:28 "If a man is c in the act of raping a young woman
Jos 8:22 So the men of Ai were c in a trap, and all of them
Jdg 8: 6 "You haven't c Zebah and Zalmunna yet.
8:15 saying, 'You haven't c Zebah and Zalmunna yet.
15: 4 Then he went out and c three hundred foxes.
18:23 They were shouting as they c up with them.
1Sa 31: 3 and the Philistine archers c up with him
2Sa 16: 1 the servant of Mephibosheth, c up with him.
18: 9 the thick branches of a great oak, his head got c.
23:20 and slippery ground, he c the lion and killed it.
1Ki 1:50 the sacred tent and c hold of the horns of the altar.
2:28 of the LORD and c hold of the horns of the altar.
2Ki 4:27 fell to the ground before him and c hold of his feet.
25: 5 after them and c the king on the plains of Jericho,
1Ch 10: 3 and the Philistine archers c up with him
11:22 and slippery ground, he c the lion and killed it.
Ps 5:10 Let them be c in their own traps. / Drive them
9:15 for others. / They have been c in their own trap.
10: 2 Let them be c in the evil they plan for others.
18:37 I chased my enemies and c them; / I did not stop
35: 8 Let them be c in the snare they set for me!
Pr 3:26 He will keep your foot from being c in a trap.
6: 2 by your agreement and are c by what you said—
6:31 But if he is c, he will be fined seven times as much
17:12 of her cubs than to confront a fool c in folly.
26:27 set a trap for others, you will get c in it yourself.
Ecc 7:26 escape from her, but sinners will be c in her snare.
9:12 in a snare, people are often c by sudden tragedy.
Isa 51:20 lie in the streets, helpless as antelopes c in a net.
Jer 2:26 a thief, Israel feels shame only when she gets c.
14: 7 "LORD, our wickedness has c up with us.
39: 5 chased the king and c him on the plains of Jericho.
41:12 They c up with him at the pool near Gibeon.
48:27 Was she c in the company of thieves that you
50:24 You are c, for you have fought against the LORD.
52: 8 and c King Zedekiah on the plains of Jericho,
La 4:20 the very life of our nation, was c in their snares.
Am 3: 5 Does a bird ever get c in a trap that has no bait?
Hab 1:14 Are we but fish to be c and killed? Are we
2: 6 'You thieves! At last justice has c up with you!
2:17 You terrified the wild animals you c in your traps.
Mk 3:11 And whenever those possessed by evil spirits c
Jn 8: 3 and Pharisees brought a woman they had c in the
8: 4 "this woman was c in the very act of adultery.
21: 3 went out in the boat, but they c nothing all night.
21: 5 He called out, "Friends, have you c any fish?"
21:10 "Bring some of the fish you've just c," Jesus said.
Ac 8:39 of the water, the Spirit of the Lord c Philip away.
27:14 they called it) c the ship and blew it out to sea.
2Co 12: 2 I was c up into the third heaven fourteen years ago.
12: 4 But I do know that I was c up into paradise
1Th 2:16 But the anger of God has c up with them at last.
4:17 and remain on the earth will be c up in the clouds
2Pe 2:12 of instinct, who are born to be c and killed.
Rev 12: 5 the dragon and was c up to God and to his throne.

CAUL(S) [KJV] See (LONG) LOBE

CAULKING (1)

Eze 27: 9 Wise old craftsmen from Gebal did all the c.

CAUSE (95) [CAUSED, CAUSES, CAUSING]

Ge 12: 2 I will c you to become the father of a great nation.
17:20 I will c him to multiply and become a great nation.
26: 4 I will c your descendants to become as numerous
Ex 7: 3 But I will c Pharaoh to be stubborn so I can
8:29 "I will ask the LORD to c the swarms of flies to
9:22 and c the hail to fall throughout Egypt,
21:12 "Anyone who hits a person hard enough to c death
23: 8 A bribe always hurts the c of the person who is in
34:16 Then they will c your sons to commit adultery
Lev 17: 5 It will c them to bring their sacrifices to the priest
Nu 5:24 on the curse and c bitter suffering in cases of guilt.
5:27 the water that brings the curse will c bitter
Dt 20:18 which would c you to sin deeply against the
28:25 "The LORD will c you to be defeated by your
28:65 And the LORD will c your heart to tremble,
33: 7 Give them strength to defend their c; / help them
1Sa 2:34 I will c your two sons, Hophni and Phinehas,
2Sa 12:11 will c your own household to rebel against you.
1Ki 8:45 hear their prayers from heaven and uphold their c.
8:49 from heaven where you live. Uphold their c
8:59 so that the LORD our God may uphold my c and
the c of his people Israel,
2Ki 2:21 It will no longer c death or infertility."
10:30 Because of this I will c your descendants to be the
1Ch 21: 3 all your servants? Why must you c Israel to sin?"
2Ch 6:35 hear their prayers from heaven and uphold their c.
6:39 Uphold their c and forgive your people who have
Ne 12:43 for God had given the people c for great joy.
Job 2: 3 though you persuaded me to harm him without c."
9:17 and he multiplies my wounds without c.
18: 4 in anger, but will that c the earth to be abandoned?
34:28 So they c the poor to cry out, catching God's
38:35 lightning appear and c it to strike as you direct it?
Ps 7: 4 a friend / or plundered my enemy without c,
10:14 But you do see the trouble and grief they c.
35:19 Don't let those who hate me without c / gloat over
37: 6 and the justice of your c will shine like the
43: 1 O God, take up my c! / Defend me against these
69: 4 Those who hate me without c / are more numerous
69: 4 are doing so without c. / They attack me with lies,
69: 6 Don't let me c them to be humiliated, / O God of
74:22 Arise, O God, and defend your c. / Remember how
104:14 You c grass to grow for the cattle. / You c plants to
grow for people to use.
119:74 May all who fear you find in me a c for joy,
119:86 me from those who hunt me down without c.
119:161 Powerful people harass me without c, / but my
140:11 C disaster to fall with great force on the violent.
Pr 10:10 People who wink at wrong c trouble, but a bold
14:35 are doing; he is angry with those who c trouble.
23:24 The father of godly children has c for joy. What a
Ecc 10: 1 Dead flies will c even a bottle of perfume to stink!

12: 1 Don't let the excitement of youth c you to forget
Isa 19: 14 They c the land of Egypt to stagger like a sick
38: 8 I will c the sun's shadow to move ten steps
44: 25 I c wise people to give bad advice, thus proving
52: 4 Now they have been oppressed without c by
55: 10 They c the grain to grow, producing seed for the
Jer 11: 20 against them, for I have committed my c to you.
15: 8 I will c anguish and terror to come upon them
19: 12 I will c this city to become defiled like Topheth.
20: 12 against them, for I have committed my c to you.
25: 14 in proportion to the suffering they c my people."
31: 22 For the LORD will c something new and different
Eze 4: 16 I will c food to be very scarce in Jerusalem.
14: 23 these things are not being done to Israel without c,
29: 21 "And the day will come when I will c the ancient
34: 15 tend my sheep and c them to lie down in peace,
34: 26 I will c my people and their homes around my holy
36: 12 I will c my people to walk on you once again,
36: 15 longer be shamed by them or c your nation to fall,
37: 12 open your graves of exile and c you to rise again.
44: 18 They must not wear anything that would c them to
Da 8: 24 He will c a shocking amount of destruction
11: 18 to his insolence and will c him to retreat in shame.
Hos 2: 17 O Israel, I will c you to forget your images of Baal;
Joel 2: 30 "I will c wonders in the heavens and on the earth—
Zec 12: 4 I will c every horse to panic and every rider to lose
Mt 10: 21 rise against their parents and c them to be killed.
Mk 13: 12 rise against their parents and c them to be killed.
Jn 15: 25 the Scriptures said: 'They hated me without c.'
Ac 2: 19 And I will c wonders in the heavens above
13: 28 They found no just c to execute him, but they
19: 40 since there is no c for all this commotion.
28: 18 for they found no c for the death sentence.
Ro 7: 13 Did the law, which is good, c my doom? Of course
11: 9 all is well. / Let their blessings c them to stumble.
14: 21 or do anything else if it might c another Christian
16: 17 Watch out for people who c divisions and upset
1Co 3: 5 is Paul, that we should be the c of such quarrels?
8: 9 Do not c a brother or sister with a weaker
2Co 2: 2 For if I c you pain and make you sad, who is going
1Ti 1: 4 For these things only c arguments; they don't help
6: 5 These people always c trouble. Their minds are
1Jn 2: 10 in the light and does not c anyone to stumble.

CAUSED (57) [CAUSE]

Ge 2: 21 So the LORD God c Adam to fall into a deep
20: 16 for any embarrassment I may have c you.
Ex 8: 7 They, too, c frogs to come up on the land.
8: 31 did as Moses asked and c the swarms to disappear.
10: 13 and the LORD c an east wind to blow all that day
11: 3 (Now the LORD had c the Egyptians to look
12: 36 The LORD c the Egyptians to look favorably on
Nu 11: 33 and he c a severe plague to break out among them.
22: 28 Then the LORD c the donkey to speak.
31: 16 and c the people of Israel to rebel against the
31: 16 They are the ones who c the plague to strike the
Dt 19: 6 to chase down and kill the person who c the death.
Jos 11: 20 and c them to fight the Israelites instead of asking
20: 4 the one who c the accidental death will appear
20: 6 But the person who c the death must stay in that
Jdg 7: 22 the LORD c the warriors in the camp to fight
15: 19 So God c water to gush out of a hollow in the
Ru 1: 13 because the LORD himself has c me to suffer."
1: 21 me Naomi when the LORD has c me to suffer
1Sa 22: 22 Now I have c the death of all your father's family.
2Sa 24: 1 and he c David to harm them by taking a census.
2Ki 7: 6 For the Lord had c the whole army of Aram to hear
20: 11 and he c the shadow to move ten steps backward
21: 16 This was in addition to the sin that he c the people
1Ch 5: 26 So the God of Israel c King Pul of Assyria (also
14: 17 and the LORD c all the nations to fear David.
21: 1 and c David to take a census of the Israelites.
2Ch 20: 22 the LORD c the armies of Ammon, Moab,
21: 19 the disease c his bowels to come out, and he died
Ezr 9: 9 he c the kings of Persia to treat us favorably.
Job 29: 13 And I c the widows' hearts to sing for joy.
38: 12 to appear and c the dawn to rise in the east?
Ps 44: 13 You have c all our neighbors to mock us. / We are
74: 15 You c the springs and streams to gush forth,
78: 28 He c the birds to fall within their camp / and all
88: 8 You have c my friends to loathe me; / you have
106: 46 He even c their captors / to treat them with
Pr 4: 16 They cannot rest unless they have c someone to
27: 3 but the resentment c by a fool is heavier than both.
Isa 47: 10 and 'knowledge' have c you to turn away from me
Jer 32: 29 where the people c my fury to rise by offering
La 2: 17 and c her enemies to rejoice over her and boast of
Eze 31: 15 in black and c the trees of the field to wilt.
32: 32 For I have c my terror to fall upon all the living.
Am 2: 12 "But you c the Nazirites to sin by making them
Jnh 1: 7 had offended the gods and c the terrible storm.
Mal 2: 8 Your 'guidance' has c many to stumble into sin.
Ac 3: 16 Faith in Jesus' name has c this healing before your
26: 10 I c many of the believers in Jerusalem to be sent to
Ro 5: 17 sin of this one man, Adam, c death to rule over us,
1Co 3: 5 only servants. Through us God c you to believe.
2Co 2: 5 c all the trouble hurt your entire church more than
7: 9 but because the pain c you to have remorse
2Pe 1: 4 the decadence all around you c by evil desires
Rev 5: 10 And you have c them to become God's kingdom
11: 18 And you will destroy all who have c destruction on
16: 14 These miracle-working demons c all the rulers of

CAUSES (38) [CAUSE]

Nu 5: 19 from the effects of this bitter water that c the curse.
2Ch 21: 15 disease until it c your bowels to come out."
Job 33: 17 He c them to change their minds; he keeps them
37: 13 He c things to happen on earth, either as a
37: 15 and c the lightning to flash forth from his clouds?
Ps 46: 9 and c wars to end throughout the earth. / He breaks
135: 7 He c the clouds to rise over the earth. / He sends
Pr 21: 15 a joy to the godly, but it c dismay among evildoers.
25: 23 north brings rain, so a gossiping tongue c anger!
26: 28 A lying tongue hates its victims, and flattery c ruin.
28: 25 Greed c fighting; trusting the LORD leads to
30: 33 a blow to the nose c bleeding, so anger c quarrels.
Isa 8: 14 and Judah he will be a stone that c people to
64: 2 As fire c wood to burn and water to boil,
Jer 10: 13 He c the clouds to rise over the earth.
51: 16 He c the clouds to rise over the earth.
Da 8: 13 How long will the rebellion that c desecration stop
9: 27 he will set up a sacrilegious object that c
11: 31 and setting up the sacrilegious object that c
12: 11 and the sacrilegious object that c desecration is set
Mt 5: 29 c you to lust, gouge it out and throw it away.
5: 30 c you to sin, cut it off and throw it away.
5: 32 she has been unfaithful, c her to commit adultery.
13: 41 remove from my Kingdom everything that c sin
18: 6 But if anyone c one of these little ones who trusts
18: 7 "How terrible it will be for anyone who c others to
18: 8 So if your hand or foot c you to sin, cut it off
18: 9 And if your eye c you to sin, gouge it out
24: 15 the sacrilegious object that c desecration standing
Mk 9: 42 "But if anyone c one of these little ones who trusts
9: 43 If your hand c you to sin, cut it off. It is better to
9: 45 If your foot c you to sin, cut it off. It is better to
9: 47 And if your eye c you to sin, gouge it out. It is
13: 14 c desecration standing where it should not be"—
Ro 8: 28 And we know that God c everything to work
9: 33 "I am placing a stone in Jerusalem that c people to
Php 1: 20 and hope that I will never do anything that c me

CAUSEWAY [KJV] See GATEWAY

CAUSING (27) [CAUSE]

Ge 37: 5 to his brothers, c them to hate him even more.
Ex 9: 9 c boils to break out on people and animals alike."
21: 18 the other with a stone or fist, c injury but not death.
Lev 26: 16 c your eyes to fail and your life to ebb away.
Nu 25: 3 c the LORD's anger to blaze against his people.
36: 4 c it to be lost forever to our ancestral tribe."
1Ki 13: 26 The LORD has fulfilled his word by c the lion to
16: 2 You have aroused my anger by c my people to sin.
17: 20 has opened her home to me, c her son to die?"
2Ki 19: 25 Long ago I planned what I am now c to happen,
Est 9: 25 he issued a decree c Haman's evil plot to backfire,
Ps 106: 32 angered the LORD, / c Moses serious trouble.
107: 40 c them to wander in trackless wastelands.
Isa 37: 26 Long ago I planned what I am now c to happen,
44: 25 c events to happen that are contrary to their
51: 15 your God, who stirs up the sea, c its waves to roar.
Jer 13: 16 c you to stumble and fall on the dark mountains.
32: 35 What an incredible evil, c Judah to sin so greatly!
50: 38 It will even strike her water supply, c it to dry up.
La 3: 33 he does not enjoy hurting people or c them sorrow.
Eze 44: 12 to worship other gods, c Israel to fall into deep sin.
Jnh 1: 4 c a violent storm that threatened to send them to
Lk 23: 5 "But he is c riots everywhere he goes, all over
1Co 10: 8 of them did, c 23,000 of them to die in one day.
Tit 3: 10 If anyone is c divisions among you, give a first
Jas 4: 1 What is c the quarrels and fights among you?
Rev 16: 8 on the sun, c it to scorch everyone with its fire.

CAUTIOUS (1) [PRECAUTIONS]

Pr 14: 16 The wise are c and avoid danger; fools plunge

CAVALRY (8)

Ge 50: 9 So a great number of chariots, c, and people
Isa 31: 1 trusting their c and chariots instead of looking to
Eze 26: 7 against Tyre with his c, chariots, and great army.
26: 10 The hooves of his c will choke the city with dust,
38: 4 and c and make you a vast and mighty horde,
38: 15 your homeland in the distant north with your vast c
Da 11: 40 out against him with chariots, c, and a vast navy.
Na 3: 3 and glittering spears in the upraised arms of the c!

CAVE (35) [CAVERNS, CAVES]

Ge 19: 30 and he went to live in a c in the mountains with his
23: 9 to let me have the c of Machpelah, down at the end
23: 11 listen to me. I will give you the c and the field.
23: 17 This included the field, the c that was in it, and all
23: 19 in the c of Machpelah, near Mamre, which is at
23: 20 and the c were sold to Abraham by the Hittites as a
25: 9 and Ishmael buried him in the c of Machpelah,
49: 29 and grandfather in the c in Ephron's field.
49: 30 This is the c in the field of Machpelah, near Mamre
49: 32 It is the c that my grandfather Abraham bought
50: 5 of Canaan, and bury me in our family's burial c.'
50: 13 and buried it there in the c of Machpelah.
50: 13 This is the c that Abraham had bought for a
Jos 10: 16 the five kings escaped and hid in a c at Makkedah.
10: 18 "Cover the opening of the c with large rocks
10: 22 "Remove the rocks covering the opening of the c
10: 23 So they brought the five kings out of the c—
10: 27 and thrown into the c where they had been hiding.
10: 27 Then they covered the opening of the c with a
Jdg 15: 8 Then he went to live in a c in the rock of Etam.
15: 11 down to get Samson at the c in the rock of Etam.
1Sa 22: 1 David left Gath and escaped to the c of Adullam.
24: 3 Saul went into a c to relieve himself.
24: 3 David and his men were hiding in that very c!
24: 7 After Saul had left the c and gone on his way,
24: 10 placed you at my mercy back there in the c,
2Sa 17: 9 He has probably already hidden in some pit or c.
23: 13 when David was at the c of Adullam,
1Ki 18: 4 He had put fifty prophets in each c and had
19: 9 There he came to a c, where he spent the night.
19: 13 and went out and stood at the entrance of the c.
1Ch 11: 15 Once when David was at the rock near the c of
Ps 57: T the time he fled from Saul and went into the c.
142: T psalm of David, regarding his experience in the c.
Jn 11: 38 It was a c with a stone rolled across its entrance.

CAVERNS (1) [CAVE]

Isa 2: 21 They will crawl into c and hide among the jagged

CAVES (16) [CAVE]

Jdg 6: 2 where they made hiding places for themselves in c
1Sa 13: 6 they lost their nerve entirely and tried to hide in c,
1Ki 18: 4 Obadiah had hidden one hundred of them in two c.
18: 13 I hid a hundred of them in two c and supplied them
Job 30: 6 frightening ravines and in c and among the rocks.
Isa 2: 10 Crawl into c in the rocks. Hide from the terror of
2: 19 They will hide in c in the rocks from the terror of
7: 19 also in the desolate valleys, c, and thorny places.
Jer 16: 16 who will search for them in the forests and c.
48: 28 Live in the c like doves that nest in the clefts of the
49: 8 and flee! Hide in deep c, you people of Dedan!
49: 30 "Hide yourselves in deep c, you people of Hazor,
Eze 33: 27 Those hiding in the forts and c will die of disease.
Heb 11: 38 and mountains, hiding in c and holes in the ground.
2Pe 2: 4 in gloomy c and darkness until the judgment day.
Rev 6: 15 all hid themselves in the c and among the rocks of

CEASE (3) [CEASED, CEASELESS]

Est 9: 28 These days would never c to be celebrated among
Job 3: 17 For in death the wicked c from troubling,
34: 15 all life would c, and humanity would turn again to

CEASED (5) [CEASE]

Ge 8: 2 The underground water sources c their gushing,
Ex 9: 33 the thunder and hail stopped, and the downpour c.
Isa 14: 11 All the pleasant music in your palace has c.
16: 4 When oppression and destruction have c
16: 10 The treading out of grapes in the winepresses has c

CEASELESS (2) [CEASE]

Job 33: 19 and pain, with c aching in their bones.
Ecc 8: 16 I discovered that there is c activity, day and night.

CEDAR (45) [CEDARS, CEDARWOOD]

2Sa 5: 11 a palace. Hiram also sent many c logs for lumber.
7: 2 "Here I am living in this beautiful c palace,
7: 7 "Why haven't you built me a beautiful c
1Ki 4: 33 from the great c of Lebanon to the tiny hyssop that
5: 8 I can supply you with both c and cypress.
5: 10 So Hiram produced for Solomon as much c
6: 9 put in a ceiling made of beams and planks of c.
6: 10 attached to the Temple walls by c timbers.
6: 15 He paneled the walls and ceilings with c, and he
6: 16 and was paneled with c from floor to ceiling.
6: 18 C paneling completely covered the stone walls
6: 20 pure gold. He also overlaid the altar made of c.
6: 36 so that there was one layer of c beams after every
7: 2 The great c ceiling beams rested on four rows of c
pillars.
7: 3 It had a c roof supported by forty-five rafters that
7: 7 It was paneled with c from floor to ceiling.
7: 11 also cut to measure, and c beams were also used.
7: 12 so that there was one layer of c beams after every
9: 11 to King Hiram of Tyre as payment for all the c
2Ki 14: 9 a thistle sent a message to a mighty c tree:
1Ch 14: 1 a palace. Hiram also sent many c logs for lumber.
17: 1 "Here I am living in this beautiful c palace,
17: 6 "Why haven't you built me a beautiful c
22: 4 He also provided innumerable c logs, for the men
22: 4 and Sidon had brought vast amounts of c to David.
2Ch 2: 3 "Send me c logs like the ones that were supplied
2: 8 Also send me c, cypress, and almug logs from
25: 18 a thistle sent a message to a mighty c tree:
Ezr 3: 7 and bought c logs from the people of Tyre
Job 40: 17 Its tail is as straight as a c. The sinews of its thighs
SS 1: 17 shaded by c trees and spreading firs."
Isa 41: 19 c, acacia, myrtle, olive, cypress, fir, and pine—
44: 14 he plants the c in the forest to be nourished by the
Jer 22: 7 They will tear out all your fine c beams and throw
22: 14 paneled throughout with fragrant c and painted a
Eze 17: 3 He took hold of the highest branch of a c tree
17: 22 I will take a tender shoot from the top of a tall c,
17: 23 It will become a noble c, sending forth its branches
27: 5 They took a c from Lebanon to make a mast for
31: 3 Assyria, too, was once like a c of Lebanon, full of
Hos 14: 6 olive trees, as fragrant as the c forests of Lebanon.
Am 2: 9 The Amorites were as tall as c trees and strong as
Zep 2: 14 and the c paneling will lie open to the wind
Zec 11: 1 so that fire may sweep through your c forests.

CEDARS (21) [CEDAR]

Nu 24: 6 planted by the LORD, / like c beside the waters.
Jdg 9: 15 come out from me and devour the c of Lebanon.'
1Ki 5: 6 Now please command that c from Lebanon be cut
2Ki 19: 23 I have cut down its tallest c / and its choicest
Ps 29: 5 The voice of the LORD splits the mighty c;
29: 5 the LORD shatters the c of Lebanon.

80:10 the mighty c were covered with our branches.
92:12 palm trees / and grow strong like the c of Lebanon.
104:16 well cared for—/ the c of Lebanon that he planted.
148: 9 mountains and all hills, / fruit trees and all c,
SS 4:11 is like that of the mountains and the c of Lebanon.
5:15 of the finest gold, strong as the c of Lebanon.
Isa 2:13 He will cut down the tall c of Lebanon
9:10 with cut stone, the fallen sycamore trees with c."
14: 8 the cypress trees and the c of Lebanon—sing out
37:24 I have cut down its tallest c / and its choicest
44:14 He cuts down c; he selects the cypress and the oak;
Jer 22:23 palace lined with lumber from the c of Lebanon,
Eze 31: 8 This tree became taller than any of the other c in
Hos 14: 5 it will send roots deep into the soil like the c in
Zec 11: 2 Weep, you cypress trees, for all the ruined c;

CEDARWOOD (8) [CEDAR]

Lev 14: 4 along with some c, a scarlet cloth, and a hyssop
14: 6 along with the c, the scarlet cloth, and the hyssop
14:49 some c, a scarlet cloth, and a hyssop branch.
14:51 Then he will dip the c, the hyssop branch,
Nu 19: 6 Eleazar the priest must then take c, a hyssop
1Ki 10:27 And valuable c was as common as the sycamore
2Ch 1:15 And valuable c was as common as the sycamore
9:27 And valuable c was as common as the sycamore

CEDRON [KJV] See KIDRON

CEILING (7) [CEILINGS]

1Ki 6: 9 Solomon put in a c made of beams and planks of
6:15 The entire inside, from floor to c, was paneled with
6:16 and was paneled with cedar from floor to c.
6:20 Solomon overlaid its walls and c with pure gold.
7: 2 The great cedar c beams rested on four rows of
7: 7 It was paneled with cedar from floor to c.
2Ch 3: 4 of the foyer and the c were overlaid with pure gold.

CEILINGS (3) [CEILING]

1Ki 6:15 He paneled the walls and c with cedar, and he used
Jer 22:13 its walls and oppression into its doorframes and c.
Hab 2:11 and the beams in the c echo the complaint.

CELEBRATE (68) [CELEBRATED, CELEBRATES, CELEBRATING, CELEBRATION, CELEBRATIONS]

Ge 21: 8 Abraham gave a big party to c the happy occasion.
29:22 neighborhood to c with Jacob at a wedding feast.
Ex 12:14 Each year you will c it as a special festival to the
12:17 "C this Festival of Unleavened Bread, for it will
12:25 to give you, you will continue to c this festival.
12:47 The whole community of Israel must c this festival
12:48 among you who want to c the LORD's Passover,
12:48 Then they may come and c the Passover with you.
13: 5 You must c this day when the LORD brings you
13: 6 seventh day, you will c a great feast to the LORD.
13:10 "So c this festival at the appointed time each year.
23:14 "Each year you must c three festivals in my honor.
23:16 You must also c the Festival of Harvest, when you
23:16 you are to c the Festival of the Final Harvest at the
34:18 "Be sure to c the Festival of Unleavened Bread for
34:22 And you must remember to c the Festival of
34:22 and c the Festival of the Final Harvest at the end of
Lev 23:24 early autumn, you are to c a day of complete rest.
23:37 C them by gathering in sacred assemblies to
23:39 you will begin to c this seven-day festival to the
Nu 9: 2 "Tell the Israelites to c the Passover at the proper
9: 4 So Moses told the people to c the Passover
9:10 they may still c the LORD's Passover.
9:13 yet still refuse to c the Passover at the regular time,
9:14 And if foreigners living among you want to c the
28:16 in early spring, you must c the LORD's Passover.
Dt 12:12 You must c there with your sons and daughters
14:26 the LORD your God and c with your household.
16: 1 always c the Passover at the proper time in early
16:10 Then you must c the Festival of Harvest to honor
16:11 It is a time to c before the LORD your God at
16:11 C with your whole family, all your servants,
16:15 For seven days c this festival to honor the LORD
16:16 "Each year every man in Israel must c these three
26:11 Afterward go and c because of all the good things
1Sa 18: 6 came out from all the towns along the way to c
20: 5 "Tomorrow we c the new moon festival.
20:18 "Tomorrow we c the new moon festival.
2Sa 13:24 and his servants please come to c the occasion with
2Ki 23:21 "You must c the Passover to the LORD your
2Ch 30: 1 at Jerusalem to c the Passover of the LORD,
30: 2 and all the community of Jerusalem decided to c
30: 5 inviting everyone to come to Jerusalem to c the
30:13 assembled at Jerusalem in midspring to c Passover
Ne 8:10 "Go and c with a feast of choice foods and sweet
8:12 and to c with great joy because they had heard
Est 2:18 To c the occasion, he gave a banquet in Esther's
9:19 rural Jews living in unwalled villages c an annual
9:21 encouraging them to c an annual festival on these
9:22 He told them to c these days with feasting
9:27 They declared they would never fail to c these two
Ps 21:13 With music and singing we c your mighty acts.
135: 3 is good; / c his wonderful name with music.
145:11 they will c examples of your power.
La 1: 4 no longer filled with crowds on their way to c the
Eze 45:21 day of the new year, you must c the Passover.
Hos 12: 9 as you do each year when you c the Festival of
Na 1:15 C your festivals, O people of Judah, and fulfill all
Zec 14:16 and to c the Festival of Shelters.
14:19 all be punished if they don't go to c the festival.
Mt 25:21 you many more responsibilities. Let's c together!'
25:23 you many more responsibilities. Let's c together!'
Lk 15:23 been fattening in the pen. We must c with a feast,
15:30 you c by killing the finest calf we have.'
15:32 We had to c this happy day. For your brother was
Jn 18:28 and they wouldn't be allowed to c the Passover
1Co 5: 8 So let us c the festival, not by eating the old bread
Rev 11:10 c the death of the two prophets who had tormented

CELEBRATED (25) [CELEBRATE]

Ex 12:42 It must be c every year, from generation to
32: 6 After this, they c with feasting and drinking,
Lev 23:27 "Remember that the Day of Atonement is to be c
Nu 9: 5 And they c the festival there, just as the LORD
29: 1 "The Festival of Trumpets will be c on the
Jos 5:10 they c Passover on the evening of the fourteenth
1Ki 8:65 and all Israel c the Festival of Shelters in the
2Ki 23:23 This Passover was c to the LORD in Jerusalem
2Ch 7: 8 For the next seven days they c the Festival of
7: 9 for they had c the dedication of the altar for seven
30: 3 Passover was normally c one month earlier,
30:21 c the Festival of Unleavened Bread for seven days
30:23 seven days, so they c joyfully for another week.
35: 1 c in Jerusalem on the appointed day in early
35:17 All the Israelites present in Jerusalem c Passover
Ezr 3: 4 They c the Festival of Shelters as prescribed in the
6:19 On April 21 the returned exiles c Passover.
6:22 and c the Festival of Unleavened Bread for seven
Ne 8:17 The Israelites had not c this way since the days of
Est 8:15 And the people of Susa c the new decree.
9:28 and c by every family throughout the provinces
9:28 These days would never cease to be c among the
Ps 102:21 And so the LORD's fame will be c in Zion,
Eze 23:21 you c your former days as a young girl in Egypt,
1Co 10: 7 "The people c with feasting and drinking,

CELEBRATES (1) [CELEBRATE]

Pr 11:10 The whole city c when the godly succeed;

CELEBRATING (15) [CELEBRATE]

Ex 13: 8 you must explain to your children why you are c.
Dt 12:18 c in the presence of the LORD your God in all
1Sa 25:36 had thrown a big party and was c like a king.
2Sa 6: 5 and all the people of Israel were c before the
1Ki 1:41 Adonijah and his guests heard the c and shouting
1:45 just returned, and the whole city is c and rejoicing.
1Ch 13: 8 and all Israel were c before God with all their
2Ch 30: 5 The people had not been c it in great numbers as
Est 9:17 c their victory with a day of feasting and gladness.
Mt 9:15 "Should the wedding guests mourn while c with
Mk 2:19 "Do wedding guests fast while c with the groom?
Lk 5:34 "Do wedding guests fast while c with the groom?
15:27 a great feast. We are c because of his safe return.'
Col 2:16 or for not c certain holy days or new-moon
Jude 1:12 When these people join you in fellowship meals c

CELEBRATION (54) [CELEBRATE]

Ex 12:27 will reply, 'It is the c of the LORD's Passover,
13: 8 'This is a c of what the LORD did for us when we
32:18 victory nor a cry of defeat. It is the sound of a c."
Lev 23: 6 Then the day after the Passover c, the Festival of
Nu 9: 3 all my laws and regulations concerning this c."
33: 3 morning after the first Passover c in early spring.
Dt 16:13 "Another c, the Festival of Shelters, must be
26:11 and the foreigners living among you in the c.
Jdg 14:12 solve my riddle during these seven days of the c,
14:17 was with him and kept it up for the rest of the c.
21:23 They kidnapped the women who took part in the c
1Sa 25: 8 be kind to us, since we have come at a time of c?
2Sa 6:12 brought the Ark to the City of David with a great c.
19:22 "This is not a day for execution but for c!
1Ki 1:25 and he has invited your sons to attend the c.
1:40 The c was so joyous and noisy that the earth shook
8:65 The c went on for fourteen days in all—seven days
2Ki 23:22 There had not been a Passover c like that since the
1Ch 12:40 olive oil, cattle, and sheep were brought to the c.
15:25 LORD's covenant up to Jerusalem with a great c.
2Ch 7:10 Then at the end of the c, Solomon sent the people
8:13 the Passover c, the Festival of Harvest,
23:13 instruments were leading the people in a great c.
30:22 So for seven days the c continued. Peace offerings
30:26 for Jerusalem had not seen a c like this one since
35:10 When everything was ready for the Passover c,
35:19 This Passover c took place in the eighteenth year
Ne 12:43 The women and children also participated in the c,
Est 1: 4 The c lasted six months—a tremendous display of
8:17 the Jews rejoiced and had a great c and declared a
9:26 (That is why this c is called Purim, because it is the
9:31 an annual c of these days at the appointed time,
Job 1: 4 their brothers and sisters to join them for a c.
Ps 42: 4 and giving thanks—/ it was the sound of a great c!
Isa 24: 8 the happy cries of c will be heard no more.
33:20 you will see Zion as a place of worship and c.
Jer 31:13 and the men—old and young—will join in the c.
La 2: 7 the LORD's Temple as though it were a day of c.
Zec 8:19 festivals of joy and c for the people of Judah.
Mt 26: 2 the Passover c begins in two days, and I,
27:15 to the crowd each year during the Passover c—
Mk 14: 1 It was now two days before the Passover c
Lk 2:43 After the c was over, they started home to
22: 1 which begins with the Passover c, was drawing
Jn 2: 1 at a wedding c in the village of Cana in Galilee.
2: 2 Jesus and his disciples were also invited to the c.
2:13 It was time for the annual Passover c, and Jesus
2:23 signs he did in Jerusalem at the Passover c,
4:45 for they had been in Jerusalem at the Passover c
6: 4 (It was nearly time for the annual Passover c.)
7: 3 Jesus' brothers urged him to go to Judea for the c.
11:55 It was now almost time for the c of Passover,
13: 1 Before the Passover c, Jesus knew that his hour
Ac 12: 3 he arrested Peter during the Passover c

CELEBRATIONS (13) [CELEBRATE]

1Ch 23:31 at new moon c, and at all the appointed festivals.
2Ch 2: 4 and evening, on the Sabbaths, at new moon c,
Ezr 3: 5 and the offerings required for the new moon c
Ne 10:33 the new moon c, and the annual festivals;
Job 1: 5 When these c ended—and sometimes they lasted
Isa 1:13 Your c of the new moon and the Sabbath day,
Eze 45:17 the new moon c, the Sabbath days, and all other
46: 1 open on Sabbath days and the days of new moon c.
46: 3 on Sabbath days and the days of new moon c.
46: 6 At the new moon c, he will bring one young bull,
Hos 2:11 her new moon c, and her Sabbath days—
Joel 1:16 There are no joyful c in the house of our God.
Am 8:10 I will turn your c into times of mourning, and your

CELIBATE (1)

1Co 7: 1 asked in your letter. Yes, it is good to live a c life.

CELL (4)

Jer 37:16 Jeremiah was put into a dungeon c, where he
38: 6 So the officials took Jeremiah from his c
Ac 12: 7 Suddenly, there was a bright light in the c, and an
12: 9 So Peter left the c, following the angel. But all the

CELLARS [KJV] See SUPPLIES

CEMETERY (13)

2Ki 23: 6 the pole to dust and threw the dust in the public c.
2Ch 21:20 buried in the City of David, but not in the royal c.
24:25 buried in the City of David, but not in the royal c.
28:27 he was buried in Jerusalem but not in the royal c.
32:33 he was buried in the upper area of the royal c,
35:24 He was buried there in the royal c. And all Judah
Ne 3:16 He rebuilt the wall to a place opposite the royal c
Job 21:33 A great funeral procession goes to the c. Many pay
Mt 8:28 They lived in a c and were so dangerous that no
27: 7 and they made it into a c for foreigners.
27:53 They left the c, went into the holy city of
Mk 5: 2 a man possessed by an evil spirit ran out from a c
Lk 8:27 and naked, he had lived in a c for a long time.

CENCHREA (2)

Ac 18:18 (Earlier, at C, Paul had shaved his head according
Ro 16: 1 Our sister Phoebe, a deacon in the church in C,

CENSERS (1)

Ezr 1: 9 Cyrus donated: / silver trays | 1,000 / silver c | 29

CENSUS (44)

Ex 30:12 "Whenever you take a c of the people of Israel,
38:26 collected from each of those registered in the c.
Nu 1: 2 "Take a c of the whole community of Israel by
1:49 "Exempt the tribe of Levi from the c; do not
2:33 The Levites were exempted from this c by the
3:15 "Take a c of the tribe of Levi by its families
4: 2 "Take a c of the clans and families of the
4:22 "Take a c of the clans and families of the
4:29 "Now take a c of the clans and families of the
4:49 And so the c was completed, just as the LORD
7: 2 the tribal leaders who had organized the c—came
14:29 years old or older and were counted in the c
26: 2 "Take a c of all the men of Israel who are twenty
26: 3 and Eleazar the priest issued these c instructions to
26: 4 This is the c record of all the descendants of Israel
26:51 Israelite men counted in the c numbered 601,730.
26:53 to their populations, as indicated by the c.
26:55 of each ancestral tribe by means of the c listings.
26:57 This is the c record for the Levites who were
26:62 But the Levites were not included in the total c
26:63 So these are the c figures of the people of Israel as
26:64 and Aaron counted in this c had been among those
26:64 in the previous c taken in the wilderness of Sinai.
2Sa 24: 1 and he caused David to harm them by taking a c.
24: 2 his army, "Take a c of all the people in the land—
24: 4 But the king insisted that they take the c, so Joab
24:10 But after he had taken the c, David's conscience
24:10 have sinned greatly and shouldn't have taken the c.
1Ch 21: 1 and caused David to take a c of the Israelites.
21: 2 "Take a c of all the people in the land—
21: 4 But the king insisted that Joab take the c, so Joab
21: 6 of Levi and Benjamin in the c because he was
21: 7 God was very displeased with the c, and he
21: 8 have sinned greatly and shouldn't have taken the c.
21:17 said to God, "I am the one who called for the c!
27:23 When David took his c, he did not count those who
27:24 Joab began the c but never finished it
2Ch 2:17 Solomon took a c of all foreigners in the land of
2:17 like the c his father had taken, and he counted
25: 5 Then he took a c and found that he had an army of
Lk 2: 1 decreed that a c should be taken throughout the
2: 2 (This was the first c taken when Quirinius was
2: 3 returned to their own towns to register for this c.
Ac 5:37 After him, at the time of the c, there was Judas of

CENTER (31) [CENTERED, CENTERS, CENTRAL]

Ge 2: 9 At the **c** of the garden he placed the tree of life
3: 3 "It's only the fruit from the tree at the **c** of the
Ex 25:31 the base, **c** stem, lamp cups, buds, and blossoms.
25:32 three branches going out from each side of the **c**
25:34 The **c** stem of the lampstand will be decorated with
25:35 of branches where they extend from the **c** stem.
37:17 Its base, **c** stem, lamp cups, blossoms, and buds
37:18 three going out from each side of the **c** stem.
37:20 The **c** stem of the lampstand was also decorated
37:21 of branches, where they extended from the **c** stem.
Nu 2: 2 The Tabernacle will be located at the **c** of these
35: 5 east, south, west, north—with the town at the **c**.
Jdg 16:25 the prison and made to stand at the **c** of the temple,
16:29 Then Samson put his hands on the **c** pillars of the
1Ki 6:27 while their inner wings touched at the **c** of the
2Ch 6:13 and had placed it at the **c** of the Temple's outer
Ps 62:10 wealth increases, / don't make it the **c** of your life.
Jer 51:13 a great **c** of commerce, but your end has come.
Eze 1: 5 From the **c** of the cloud came four living beings
5: 2 Place a third of it at the **c** of your map of
5: 5 to Jerusalem. I placed her at the **c** of the nations,
27: 3 gateway to the sea, the trading **c** of the world.
48: 8 as the tribal territories, with the Temple at the **c**.
48:10 miles wide, with the LORD's Temple at the **c**.
48:15 and common lands, with a city at the **c**.
Mic 1: 5 Where is the **c** of idolatry in Judah? In Jerusalem,
Mt 21: 9 He was in the **c** of the procession, and the crowds
Mk 11: 9 He was in the **c** of the procession, and the crowds
Lk 23:33 Jesus on the **c** cross, and the two criminals on
Rev 4: 6 In the **c** and around the throne were four living
22: 2 coursing down the **c** of the main street. On each

CENTERED (1) [CENTER]

Eph 1: 9 it is a plan **c** on Christ, designed long ago

CENTERS (4) [CENTER]

Ex 1:11 of Pithom and Rameses as supply **c** for the king.
1Ki 9:19 He built towns as supply **c** and constructed cities
2Ch 8: 4 built towns in the region of Hamath as supply **c**.
8: 6 also rebuilt Baalath and other supply **c** at this time

CENTRAL (2) [CENTER]

1Ki 8:64 That same day the king dedicated the **c** area of the
2Ch 7: 7 then dedicated the **c** area of the courtyard in front

CENTURIES (3)

Mt 23:36 all the accumulated judgment of the **c** will break
Ac 2:16 what you see this morning was predicted **c** ago by
Col 1:26 This message was kept secret for **c** and generations

CEPHAS (1) [PETER]

Jn 1:42 but you will be called **C**" (which means Peter).

CEREMONIAL (7) [CEREMONY]

1Sa 21: 7 was there that day for **c** purification.
Jer 27:19 the bronze water carts, and all the other **c** articles.
Mt 15: 2 "They ignore our tradition of **c** hand washing
Lk 11:38 the **c** washing required by Jewish custom.
Jn 2: 6 they were used for Jewish **c** purposes and held
3:25 argument with John's disciples over **c** cleansing.
Heb 13: 9 not from **c** rules about food, which don't help those

CEREMONIALLY (99) [CEREMONY]

Lev 4:12 must be carried away to a **c** clean place outside the
5: 2 "Or if they touch something that is **c** unclean,
5: 2 such as the dead body of an animal that is **c**
5: 2 they will be considered **c** unclean and guilty,
6:11 ashes outside the camp to a place that is **c** clean.
7:19 "Meat that touches anything **c** unclean may not be
7:19 it may only be eaten by people who are **c** clean.
7:20 Anyone who is **c** unclean but eats meat from a
10:10 is ordinary, what is **c** unclean and what is clean.
10:14 lifted up may be eaten in any place that is **c** clean.
11: 8 their dead bodies. They are **c** unclean for you.
11:24 "The following creatures make you **c** unclean.
11:32 After that, it will be **c** clean and may be used again.
12: 2 birth to a son, she will be **c** unclean for seven days,
12: 5 to a daughter, she will be **c** defiled for two weeks,
12: 7 Then she will be **c** clean again after her bleeding at
12: 8 atonement for her, and she will be **c** clean."
13: 3 and the priest must pronounce the person **c**
13: 6 the priest will pronounce the person **c** clean.
13: 8 then he must pronounce this person **c** unclean,
13:11 and the priest must pronounce that person **c**
13:13 he will pronounce the person **c** clean
13:14 the infected person will be pronounced **c** unclean.
13:17 then the priest will pronounce the person **c** clean.
13:20 then the priest must pronounce that person **c**
13:22 the priest must pronounce the person **c** unclean,
13:23 and the priest will pronounce that person **c** clean.
13:25 priest must then pronounce that person **c** unclean,
13:27 the priest must pronounce that person **c** unclean,
13:28 The priest must then pronounce the person **c** clean.
13:30 the priest must pronounce the infected person **c**
13:34 the priest must pronounce that person **c** clean.
13:36 he must pronounce the infected person **c** unclean,
13:37 then pronounce the infected person **c** clean.
13:39 is a harmless skin rash, and the person is **c** clean.
13:40 and his head becomes bald, he is still **c** clean.
13:44 The priest must pronounce him **c** unclean
13:46 they will be **c** unclean and must live in isolation
13:58 it must be washed again; then it will be **c** clean.
13:59 will determine whether these things are **c** clean
14: 7 and the priest will pronounce that person to be **c**
14: 8 Then they will be **c** clean and may return to live
14: 9 in water. Then they will be pronounced **c** clean.
14:20 and the healed person will be **c** clean.
14:40 an area outside the town designated as **c** unclean.
14:45 out of town to the place designated as **c** unclean.
14:46 closed will be considered **c** unclean until evening.
14:53 atonement for the house, and it will be **c** clean.
14:57 to determine when something is **c** clean
15: 2 Any man who has a genital discharge is **c** unclean
15: 5 and you will remain **c** defiled until evening.
15:13 bathe in fresh springwater. Then he will be **c** clean.
15:16 and he will remain **c** defiled until evening.
15:19 she will be **c** unclean for seven days.
15:25 the woman will be **c** unclean as long as the
15:28 of seven days. After that, she will be **c** clean.
17:15 Then you will remain **c** unclean until evening;
20:25 therefore make a distinction between **c** clean
21: 1 "Tell the priests to avoid making themselves **c**
22: 3 Remind them that if any of their descendants are **c**
22: 4 or any kind of discharge that makes them **c**
22: 5 or by touching someone who is **c** unclean for any
27:27 if it is the firstborn of a **c** unclean animal,
Nu 8: 6 rest of the people of Israel and make them **c** clean.
8: 7 and wash their clothing. Then they will be **c** clean.
9: 6 But some of the men had been **c** defiled by
9: 7 "We have become **c** unclean by touching a dead
9:10 or in future generations are **c** unclean at Passover
9:13 " 'But those who are **c** clean and not away on a
18:11 Any member of your family who is **c** clean, male
18:13 Any member of your family who is **c** clean may
19: 7 though he will remain **c** unclean until evening.
19: 9 Then someone who is **c** clean will gather up the
19:10 and he will remain **c** unclean until evening.
19:11 "All those who touch a dead human body will be **c**
19:14 death occurred, will be **c** unclean for seven days.
19:18 Then someone who is **c** clean must take a hyssop
19:19 and seventh days the **c** clean person must sprinkle
19:22 and anyone that a defiled person touches will be **c**
31:23 must be passed through fire in order to be made **c**
Dt 12:15 All of you, whether **c** clean or unclean, may eat
12:22 Anyone, whether **c** clean or unclean, may eat that
14: 3 "You must not eat animals that are **c** unclean.
14: 8 All these animals are **c** unclean for you. You may
14:10 both fins and scales. They are **c** unclean for you.
14:11 "You may eat any bird that is **c** clean.
14:19 "All flying insects are **c** unclean for you and may
14:20 But you may eat any winged creature that is **c**
15:22 Anyone may eat it, whether **c** clean or unclean,
23:10 "Any man who becomes **c** defiled because of a
26:14 I have not touched it while I was **c** unclean; and I
1Sa 20:26 "Something must have made David **c** unclean.
2Ch 23:19 to keep those who were **c** unclean from entering.
Ezr 6:20 Levites had purified themselves and were **c** clean.
Ecc 9: 2 good or bad, **c** clean or unclean, religious
Eze 22:26 my people the difference between what is **c** clean
44:23 and what is common, what is **c** clean and unclean.
Hos 9: 3 where you will live on food that is **c** unclean.
Hag 2:13 "But if someone becomes **c** unclean by touching a

CEREMONIES (10) [CEREMONY]

1Ch 23:28 side rooms, helped perform the **c** of purification,
Ne 12:24 who stood opposite them during the **c** of praise
12:27 were asked to come to Jerusalem to assist in the **c**.
Da 8:12 sacrilege was committed against the Temple **c**,
Zep 1: 9 punish those who participate in pagan worship **c**,
Mt 27:62 The next day—on the first day of the Passover **c**—
Jn 2: 8 "Dip some out and take it to the master of **c**."
2: 9 When the master of **c** tasted the water that was
12: 1 Six days before the Passover **c** began, Jesus arrived
Col 2:16 certain holy days or new-moon **c** or Sabbaths.

CEREMONY (40) [CEREMONIAL, CEREMONIALLY, CEREMONIES]

Ge 26:30 they ate and drank in preparation for the treaty **c**.
Ex 12:26 'What does all this mean? What is this **c** about?'
13:16 this **c** will be like a mark branded on your hands
29: 1 "This is the **c** for the dedication of Aaron and his
29:27 lifted up before the LORD in the ordination **c**.
29:31 "Take the ram used in the ordination **c**, and boil its
29:33 bread used for their atonement in the ordination **c**.
29:35 The ordination **c** will go on for seven days.
Lev 7: 7 belongs to the priest in charge of the atonement **c**.
8:33 is the time it will take to complete the ordination **c**.
9: 1 After the ordination **c**, on the eighth day,
14: 4 he will perform a purification **c**, using two wild
14: 7 At the end of the **c**, the priest will set the living
14: 8 complete the cleansing **c** by washing their clothes,
14:19 and again perform the atonement **c** for the person
14:23 **c** to be performed in the LORD's presence at the
14:32 normally required for the **c** of cleansing."
16:32 the atonement **c** will be performed by the anointed
Nu 6:20 After this **c** the Nazirites may again drink wine.
9:10 are on a journey and cannot be present at the **c**,
19: 9 of Israel to use in the water for the purification **c**.
19: 9 This **c** is performed for the removal of sin.
1Sa 7: 6 in a great **c**, drew water from a well and poured it
11:15 and in a solemn **c** before the LORD they crowned
1Ch 23: 2 with the priests and Levites, for the coronation **c**.
2Ch 7: 9 On the eighth day they had a closing **c**, for they
29:31 "The dedication **c** has come to an end.
30:19 though they are not properly cleansed for the **c**."
35:16 The entire **c** for the LORD's Passover was
Ezr 6:17 During the dedication **c** for the Temple of God,
Eze 43:23 When you have finished the cleansing **c**,
Mk 7: 4 such as their **c** of washing cups, pitchers,
7: 5 eat without first performing the hand-washing **c**."
Lk 1:59 and friends came for the circumcision **c**.
Jn 11:55 so they could go through the cleansing **c** before the
Ac 21:24 to the Temple and join them in the purification **c**,
Ro 2:25 The Jewish **c** of circumcision is worth something
2:28 because you have gone through the Jewish **c** of
3: 1 Is there any value in the Jewish **c** of circumcision?
4:11 The circumcision **c** was a sign that Abraham

CERTAIN (67) [CERTAINLY]

Lev 25:16 land is actually selling you a **c** number of harvests.
Nu 21:29 Your destruction is **c**, O people of Moab! / You are
35: 2 the Levites from their property **c** towns to live in,
Jos 23:13 then know for **c** that the LORD your God will no
Jdg 3: 1 The LORD left **c** nations in the land to test those
14: 1 was in Timnah, he noticed a **c** Philistine woman.
16:19 a man to shave off his hair, making his capture **c**.
2Sa 12: 1 "There were two men in a **c** town. One was rich,
Ne 13:30 and Levites, making **c** that each knew his work.
Est 2: 5 Now at the fortress of Susa there was a **c** Jew
3: 8 "There is a **c** race of people scattered through all
Job 15:23 saying, 'Where is it?' They know their ruin is **c**.
Ecc 7:14 That way you will realize that nothing is **c** in this
10:16 Destruction is **c** for the land whose king is a child
Isa 5: 8 Destruction is **c** for you who buy up property
5:11 Destruction is **c** for you who get up early to begin
5:18 Destruction is **c** for those who drag their sins
5:20 Destruction is **c** for those who say that evil is good
5:21 Destruction is **c** for those who think they are wise
5:22 Destruction is **c** for those who are heroes when it
10: 1 Destruction is **c** for the unjust judges, for those
10: 5 "Destruction is **c** for Assyria, the whip of my
18: 1 Destruction is **c** for the land of Ethiopia, which lies
28: 1 Destruction is **c** for the city of Samaria—the pride
28: 1 Destruction is **c** for that city—the pride of a people
29: 1 "Destruction is **c** for Ariel, the City of David.
29:15 Destruction is **c** for those who try to hide their
30: 1 "Destruction is **c** for my rebellious children,"
31: 1 Destruction is **c** for those who look to Egypt for
33: 1 Destruction is **c** for you Assyrians, who have
45: 9 "Destruction is **c** for those who argue with their
Jer 18: 7 If I announce that a **c** nation or kingdom is to be
18: 9 I will build up and plant a **c** nation or kingdom,
22:13 the LORD says, "Destruction is **c** for Jehoiakim,
48: 1 "Destruction is **c** for the city of Nebo; it will soon
Eze 13: 3 Destruction is **c** for the false prophets who are
13:18 Destruction is **c** for you women who are ensnaring
16:23 "Your destruction is **c**, says the Sovereign
18: 5 "Suppose a **c** man is just and does what is lawful
24: 6 Destruction is **c** for Jerusalem, the city of
24: 9 Destruction is **c** for Jerusalem, the city of
30: 9 upon them on that day of Egypt's **c** destruction.
34: 2 Destruction is **c** for you shepherds who feed
Da 2:45 The dream is true, and its meaning is **c**."
10: 1 It concerned events **c** to happen in the future—
Hos 5: 9 One thing is **c**, Israel: When your day of
Mic 2: 2 When you want a **c** piece of land, you find a way
Zec 9: 2 Doom is **c** for Hamath, near Damascus, and for the
11:17 Doom is **c** for this worthless shepherd who
Mt 21:33 A **c** landowner planted a vineyard, built a wall
26:18 into the city," he told them, "you will see a **c** man.
Lk 7:37 A **c** immoral woman heard he was there
16:19 "There was a **c** rich man who was splendidly
18: 2 "There was a judge in a **c** city," he said,
Jn 3:25 At that time a **c** Jew began an argument with
10:34 "It is written in your own law that God said to **c**
Ro 2:20 For you are **c** that in God's law you have complete
4:16 And we are **c** to receive it, whether or not we
12: 6 God has given each of us the ability to do **c** things
14: 3 And those who won't eat **c** foods must not
1Co 15:31 This is as **c** as my pride in what the Lord Jesus
Gal 4:10 or don't do on **c** days or months or seasons
Col 2:16 or for not celebrating **c** holy days or new-moon
1Ti 4: 3 it is wrong to be married and wrong to eat **c** foods.
2Ti 4:17 Gentiles to hear. And he saved me from **c** death.
Heb 6:11 in order to make **c** that what you hope for will
Jas 4:13 "Today or tomorrow we are going to a **c** town

CERTAINLY (62) [CERTAIN]

Ge 23: 6 "**C**, for you are an honored prince among us.
24:14 If she says, 'Yes, **c**, and I will water your camels,
24:18 "**C**, sir," she said, and she quickly lowered the jug
24:44 And she will reply, "**C**! And I'll water your
24:46 her shoulder so I could drink, and she said, '**C**, sir,
Ex 10:10 "The LORD will **c** need to be with you if you try
19: 8 "We will **c** do everything the LORD asks of us."
19:12 touch its boundaries. Those who do will **c** die!
32:34 to account, I will **c** punish them for their sins."
Nu 13:30 to take the land," he said. "We can **c** conquer it!"
22:33 I would **c** have killed you by now and spared the
Dt 5:25 we will **c** die and be consumed by this awesome
8:19 and bowing down to them, you will **c** be destroyed.
30:18 then I warn you now that you will **c** be destroyed.
Jos 2:24 "The LORD will **c** give us the whole land,"
1Sa 12:20 "You have **c** done wrong, but make sure now that
12:23 I will **c** not sin against the LORD by ending my
19: 5 You were **c** happy about it then. Why should you
22:15 This was **c** not the first time I had consulted God
23: 3 We **c** don't want to go to Keilah to fight the whole
24: 4 'I will **c** put Saul into your power, to do with as
2Sa 5:19 "Yes, go ahead. I will **c** give you the victory."
18:13 and the king would **c** find out who did it—

1Ki 3:22 “It **c** was your son, and the living child is mine.”
2Ki 5:13 So you should **c** obey him when he says simply to
7: 9 some terrible calamity will **c** fall upon us.
2Ch 1:12 I will **c** give you the wisdom and knowledge you
18: 3 yours to command. We will **c** join you in battle.”
34:24 I will **c** destroy this city and its people.
Ecc 8: 8 wickedness will **c** not rescue those who practice it.
Isa 29:16 He is the Potter, and he is **c** greater than you.
44:28 ‘He is my shepherd,’ he will **c** do as I say.
Jer 15:21 I will **c** keep you safe from these wicked men.
Eze 33:33 terrible things happen to them—as they **c** will—
Am 5: 6 Your gods in Bethel **c** won’t be able to quench the
7:14 I **c** never trained to be one. I’m just a shepherd,
7:17 And the people of Israel will **c** become captives in
Jnh 4: 8 “Death is **c** better than this!” he exclaimed.
Mic 7: 7 for God to save me, and my God will **c** hear me.
Lk 1:20 For my words will **c** come true at the proper time.”
4:25 “**C** there were many widows in Israel who needed
Jn 5:23 then you are **c** not honoring the Father who sent
11:47 “This man **c** performs many miraculous signs.
Ac 16:37 So now they want us to leave secretly? **C** not!
21:22 be done? For they will **c** hear that you have come.
22:19 ‘they **c** know that I imprisoned and beat those in
22:27 a Roman citizen?” “Yes, I **c** am,” Paul replied.
23:29 **c** nothing worthy of imprisonment or death.
24:13 These men **c** cannot prove the things they accuse
Ro 5: 9 of Christ, he will **c** save us from God’s judgment.
5:10 we will **c** be delivered from eternal punishment by
1Co 5:12 but it **c** is your job to judge those inside the church
9: 2 if others think I am not an apostle, I **c** am to you,
11:22 Do you want me to praise you? Well, I **c** do not!
2Co 12:12 I **c** gave you every proof that I am truly an apostle,
Gal 2:10 to help the poor, and I have **c** been eager to do that.
5: 8 It **c** isn’t God, for he is the one who called you to
1Th 2: 7 As apostles of Christ we **c** had a right to make
1Ti 6: 7 and we **c** cannot carry anything with us when we
Heb 3: 5 Moses was **c** faithful in God’s house, but only as a
6:14 “I will **c** bless you richly, / and I will multiply
13:17 with sorrow. That would **c** not be for your benefit.

CHAFF (10)

Ps 1: 4 They are like worthless **c**, scattered by the wind.
35: 5 Blow them away like **c** in the wind—/ a wind sent
83:13 away like whirling dust, / like **c** before the wind!
Isa 17:13 They will flee like **c** scattered by the wind or like
29: 5 your ruthless enemies will be driven away like **c**
30:24 its **c** having been blown away by the wind.
41:15 tear all your enemies apart, making **c** of mountains.
Jer 13:24 just as **c** is scattered by the winds blowing in from
23:28 There is a difference between **c** and wheat!
51: 2 will come and winnow her, blowing her away as **c**.
Da 2:35 The pieces were crushed as small as **c** on a
Hos 13: 3 like **c** blown by the wind, like smoke from a
Am 8: 6 And you mix the wheat you sell with **c** swept from
Zep 2: 2 and your opportunity is blown away like **c**.
Mt 3:12 He is ready to separate the **c** from the grain with
3:12 his barn but burning the **c** with never-ending fire.”
Lk 3:17 He is ready to separate the **c** from the grain with
3:17 his barn but burning the **c** with never-ending fire.”

CHAIN (9) [CHAINED, CHAINS]

Ge 41:42 and placed the royal gold **c** about his neck.
1Ki 7:42 **c** networks that were hung around the capitals on
2Ch 4:13 **c** networks that were hung around the capitals on
Da 5: 7 royal honor and will wear a gold **c** around his neck.
5:16 and you will wear a gold **c** around your neck.
5:29 in purple robes, a gold **c** was hung around his neck,
Mk 5: 3 and could not be restrained, even with a **c**.
Ac 28:20 so I could tell you that I am bound with this **c**
Rev 20: 1 key to the bottomless pit and a heavy **c** in his hand.

CHAINED (6) [CHAIN]

2Sa 3:34 Your hands were not bound; / your feet were not **c**.
Ac 12: 6 he was asleep, **c** between two soldiers, with others
2Ti 2: 9 I am suffering and have been **c** like a criminal. But
the word of God cannot be **c**.
Heb 11:36 cut open with whips. Others were **c** in dungeons.
Jude 1: 6 God has kept them **c** in prisons of darkness,

CHAINS (53) [CHAIN]

Jdg 8:26 or the **c** around the necks of their camels.
16:21 where he was bound with bronze **c** and made to
1Ki 6:21 and he made gold **c** to protect the entrance to the
7:17 with seven sets of latticework and interwoven **c**.
7:41 two networks of **c** that decorated the capitals,
7:42 four hundred pomegranates that hung from the **c**
2Ki 25: 7 bound him in bronze **c**, and led him away to
2Ch 3: 5 and decorated with carvings of palm trees and **c**.
3:16 He made a network of interwoven **c** and used them
3:16 and attached them to the **c**.
4:12 two networks of **c** that decorated the capitals,
4:13 four hundred pomegranates that hung from the **c**
33:11 bound him in bronze **c**, and led him away to
36: 6 and he bound Jehoiakim in **c** and led him away to
Ps 2: 3 “Let us break their **c**,” they cry, / “and free
107:10 and deepest gloom, / miserable prisoners in **c**.
107:14 and deepest gloom; / he snapped their **c**.
149: 8 kings with shackles / and their leaders with iron **c**,
Isa 3:20 ankle **c**, sashes, perfumes, and charms;
9: 4 For God will break the **c** that bind his people
14: 3 rest from sorrow and fear, from slavery and **c**,
40:19 overlaid with gold, and decorated with silver **c**?
45:14 be yours. They will follow you as prisoners in **c**.
Jer 2:20 your yoke and tore away the **c** of your slavery,
30: 8 break the yoke from their necks and snap their **c**.
39: 7 he gouged out Zedekiah’s eyes, bound him in **c**,
40: 1 He had found Jeremiah bound in **c** among the
40: 4 Now I am going to take off your **c** and let you go.
52:11 bound him in bronze **c**, and led him away to
La 3: 7 and I cannot escape. He has bound me in heavy **c**.
Eze 7:23 “Prepare **c** for my people, for the land is bloodied
19: 4 They led him away in **c** / to the land of Egypt.
34:27 When I have broken their **c** of slavery and rescued
Na 1:13 Now I will break your **c** and release you from
3:10 as servants. All their leaders were bound in **c**.
Mk 5: 4 Whenever he was put into **c** and shackles—as he
5: 4 he snapped the **c** from his wrists and smashed the
Lk 8:29 Even when he was shackled with **c**, he simply
Ac 9: 2 both men and women—back to Jerusalem in **c**.
9:21 and take them in **c** to the leading priests.”
12: 7 “Quick! Get up!” And the **c** fell off his wrists.
16:26 flew open, and the **c** of every prisoner fell off!
21:33 arrested him and ordered him bound with two **c**.
22: 5 from there to Jerusalem, in **c**, to be punished.
22:30 The next day the commander freed Paul from his **c**
26:29 become the same as I am, except for these **c**.”
Eph 6:20 I am in **c** now for preaching this message as God’s
Php 1:13 knows that I am in **c** because of Christ.
1:17 intending to make my **c** more painful to me.
Col 4: 3 is also for you Gentiles. That is why I am here in **c**.
4:18 in my own handwriting—PAUL. Remember my **c**.
Phm 1:13 I am in these **c** for preaching the Good News,
Rev 20: 2 Satan—and bound him in **c** for a thousand years.

CHAIR (2)

2Ki 4:10 and furnish it with a bed, a table, a **c**, and a lamp.
Am 3:12 in Samaria are rescued with only a broken **c**

CHALCOL [KJV] See CALCOL

CHALDEAN (2) [CHALDEANS]

Job 1:17 “Three bands of **C** raiders have stolen your camels
Isa 13:19 the flower of **C** culture, will be devastated like

CHALDEANS (6) [CHALDEAN]

Ge 11:28 he died in Ur of the **C**, the place of his birth.
11:31 and left Ur of the **C** to go to the land of Canaan.
15: 7 you out of Ur of the **C** to give you this land.”
Ne 9: 7 chose Abram and brought him from Ur of the **C**
Eze 23:23 For the Babylonians will come with all the **C** from
Ac 7: 4 So Abraham left the land of the **C** and lived in

CHALLENGE (9) [CHALLENGED, CHALLENGING]

Jdg 12: 5 to go back across, the men of Gilead would **c** him.
1Sa 17:23 shouting his **c** to the army of Israel.
17:25 were asking. “He comes out each day to **c** Israel.
2Ki 14: 8 One day Amaziah sent this **c** to Israel’s king
2Ch 25:17 King Amaziah of Judah sent this **c** to Israel’s king
Job 9:19 he has it. As for justice, who can **c** him?
Jer 49:19 For who is like me, and who can **c** me? What ruler
50:44 For who is like me, and who can **c** me? What ruler
Da 4:35 No one can stop him or **c** him, / saying, ‘What do

CHALLENGED (2) [CHALLENGE]

Job 9: 4 so mighty. Who has ever **c** him successfully?
Da 8:11 He even **c** the Commander of heaven’s armies by

CHALLENGING (2) [CHALLENGE]

2Ki 18:24 how can you think of **c** even the weakest
Isa 36: 9 how can you think of **c** even the weakest

CHAMBER (4)

Job 37: 9 The stormy wind comes from its **c**, and the driving
Ps 45:13 The bride, a princess, waits within her **c**,
Ac 4:15 So they sent Peter and John out of the council **c**
5:34 apostles be sent outside the council **c** for a while.

CHAMBERLAIN [KJV] See EUNUCH, ASSISTANT, TREASURER

CHAMELEON (1)

Lev 11:30 the common lizard, the sand lizard, and the **c**.

CHAMOIS [KJV] See SHEEP

CHAMPION (3)

1Sa 17: 4 Then Goliath, a Philistine **c** from Gath, came out of
17:23 with them, he saw Goliath, the **c** from Gath,
17:51 When the Philistines saw that their **c** was dead,

CHANAAN [KJV] See CANAAN

CHANCE (20) [CHANCES]

Ex 23:12 This will give your ox and your donkey a **c** to rest.
1Sa 18:21 “Here’s another **c** to see him killed by the
2Ch 16: 7 you missed your **c** to destroy the army of the king
Job 6:13 I am utterly helpless, without any **c** of success.
Ps 17:12 like young lions in hiding, waiting for their **c**.
Ecc 9:11 It is all decided by **c**, by being at the right place at
Isa 20: 6 ‘If this can happen to Egypt, what **c** do we have?
Jer 15: 6 I am tired of always giving you another **c**.
Eze 21:13 the Sovereign LORD asks: What **c** do they have?
Da 3:15 I will give you one more **c**. If you bow down
6: 5 “Our only **c** of finding grounds for accusing
Zep 1:13 They will never have a **c** to live in the new homes
Mt 17:25 But before he had a **c** to speak, Jesus asked him,
Mk 6:21 Herodias’ **c** finally came. It was Herod’s birthday,
Lk 10:31 “By **c** a Jewish priest came along; but when he
13: 8 “The gardener answered, ‘Give it one more **c**.
1Co 7:21 worry you—but if you get a **c** to be free, take it.
Php 4:10 but for a while you didn’t have the **c** to help me.
Jas 1: 3 faith is tested, your endurance has a **c** to grow.
1Pe 4:18 what **c** will the godless and sinners have?”

CHANCELLOR [KJV] See GOVERNOR

CHANCES (1) [CHANCE]

Ac 16:24 So he took no **c** but put them into the inner

CHANGE (47) [CHANGED, CHANGERS, CHANGERS’, CHANGES, CHANGING]

Ge 41:14 After a quick shave and **c** of clothes, he went in
Ex 8:29 don’t **c** your mind again and refuse to let the
13:17 they might **c** their minds and return to Egypt.”
32:12 **C** your mind about this terrible disaster you are
Lev 6:11 Then he must **c** back into his normal clothing
Nu 23:19 He is not a human, that he should **c** his mind.
Dt 21:13 and **c** all her clothes. Then she must remain in your
32:36 and he will **c** his mind about his servants,
Jdg 17:10 of silver a year, plus a **c** of clothes and your food.”
1Sa 15:29 Glory of Israel will not lie, nor will he **c** his mind,
15:29 for he is not human that he should **c** his mind!”
2Ch 12: 7 When the LORD saw their **c** of heart, he gave this
Job 33:17 He causes them to **c** their minds; he keeps them
Ps 55:19 *Interlude* / For my enemies refuse to **c** their ways;
102:26 You will **c** them like a garment, / and they will
119:152 from my earliest days / that your decrees never **c**.
Isa 14:27 Almighty has spoken—who can **c** his plans?
31: 2 will send great disaster; he will not **c** his mind.
Jer 4:28 I have made up my mind and will not **c** it.”
13:23 Can an Ethiopian **c** the color of his skin? Can a
33:25 I would no more reject my people than I would **c**
33:26 or **c** the plan that David’s descendants will rule the
Eze 24:14 and I won’t hold back; I will not **c** my mind.
39:11 and they will **c** the name of the place to the Valley
Da 2: 9 to tell me lies in hopes that something will **c**.
7:25 He will try to **c** their sacred festivals and laws,
Jnh 4: 1 This **c** of plans upset Jonah, and he became very
Zec 8:14 I did not **c** my mind when your ancestors angered
8:15 Neither will I **c** my decision to bless Jerusalem
Mal 3: 6 “I am the LORD, and I do not **c**. That is why you
Mt 3: 9 God can **c** these stones here into children of
4: 3 Son of God, **c** these stones into loaves of bread.”
Lk 1:17 and he will **c** disobedient minds to accept godly
3: 8 God can **c** these stones here into children of
4: 3 the Son of God, **c** this stone into a loaf of bread.”
Jn 19:21 “**C** it from ‘The King of the Jews’ to ‘He said,
Ac 6:14 and **c** the customs Moses handed down to us.”
Ro 2:29 the body but a **c** of heart produced by God’s Spirit.
2:29 Whoever has that kind of **c** seeks praise from God,
2Co 7: 9 pain caused you to have remorse and **c** your ways.
13:11 Rejoice. **C** your ways. Encourage each other.
Gal 1: 7 those who twist and **c** the truth concerning Christ.
Php 3:21 and **c** them into glorious bodies like his own,
2Ti 2:25 Perhaps God will **c** those people’s hearts, and they
Heb 6:17 be perfectly sure that he would never **c** his mind.
7:15 The **c** in God’s law is even more evident from the
1Pe 1: 4 and undefiled, beyond the reach of **c** and decay.

CHANGED (38) [CHANGE]

Ge 31: 8 And when he **c** his mind and said I could have the
38:14 So she **c** out of her widow’s clothing and covered
Ex 14: 5 three days, Pharaoh and his officials **c** their minds.
Lev 13: 5 If the affected area has not **c** or spread on the skin,
13:55 If he sees that the affected area has not **c**
Nu 9:16 at night the cloud **c** to the appearance of fire.
13:16 By this time Moses had **c** Hoshea’s name to
32:38 They **c** the names of some of the towns they
32:41 and **c** the name of that region to the Towns of Jair.
1Sa 10: 6 with them. You will be **c** into a different person.
10: 9 Saul turned and started to leave, God **c** his heart,
2Sa 12:20 washed himself, put on lotions, and **c** his clothes.
2Ki 14: 7 He also conquered Sela and **c** its name to Joktheel,
17:34 descendants of Jacob, whose name he **c** to Israel.
23:34 his father, and he **c** Eliakim’s name to Jehoiakim.
24:17 next king, and he **c** Mattaniah’s name to Zedekiah.
2Ch 36: 4 and he **c** Eliakim’s name to Jehoiakim.
Ezr 6:22 because the LORD had **c** the attitude of the king
Ps 77:10 that the blessings of the Most High have **c** to
93: 5 Your royal decrees cannot be **c**. / The nature of
Jer 20: 3 “Pashhur, the LORD has **c** your name.
34:11 but later they **c** their minds. They took back the
Eze 7:13 God has said applies to everyone—it will not be **c**!
Da 6: 8 Majesty issue and sign this law so it cannot be **c**,
6:15 the Persians, no law that the king signs can be **c**.”
Mt 17: 2 Jesus’ appearance **c** so that his face shone like the
21:29 but later he **c** his mind and went anyway.
Mk 9: 2 As the men watched, Jesus’ appearance **c**,
16:12 him at first because he had **c** his appearance.
Lk 9:29 as he was praying, the appearance of his face **c**,
Ac 26:20 and prove they have **c** by the good things they do.
27:14 But the weather **c** abruptly, and a wind of typhoon
28: 6 they **c** their minds and decided he was a god.
2Co 1:17 You may be asking why I **c** my plan. Hadn’t I
Gal 6:15 What counts is whether we really have been **c** into
Col 1: 6 just as it **c** yours that very first day you heard
Heb 7:12 And when the priesthood is **c**, the law must also be
c to permit it.

CHANGERS (3) [CHANGE]

Mt 21:12 He knocked over the tables of the money c
Mk 11:15 He knocked over the tables of the money c
Jn 2:14 and he saw money c behind their counters.

CHANGERS' (1) [CHANGE]

Jn 2:15 scattered the money c coins over the floor,

CHANGES (8) [CHANGE]

Ge 45:22 but to Benjamin he gave five c of clothes and three
Lev 13:24 a burn on the skin and the burned area c color,
Dt 22:13 after sleeping with her, c his mind about her
1Ch 29:18 obey you. See to it that their love for you never c.
Ps 107:33 He c rivers into deserts, / and springs of water into
Ecc 1:4 Generations come and go, but nothing really c.
Eze 21:26 The old order c—now the lowly are exalted,
Jas 1:17 Unlike them, he never c or casts shifting shadows.

CHANGING (6) [CHANGE]

Ge 17:5 What's more, I am c your name. It will no longer
Jdg 7:19 after the c of the guard, when Gideon and the one
Eze 33:8 and you fail to warn them about c their ways,
Ro 12:2 but let God transform you into a new person by c
Eph 4:14 forever c our minds about what we believe
Col 1:6 It is c lives everywhere, just as it changed yours

CHANNEL (1) [CHANNELS]

Job 38:25 "Who created a c for the torrents of rain?

CHANNELS (2) [CHANNEL]

Isa 8:8 This flood will overflow all its c and sweep into
Ac 19:38 take the case at once. Let them go through legal c.

CHANT (1) [CHANTED]

Jer 7:10 and stand before me in my Temple and c,

CHANTED (2) [CHANT]

2Ki 2:23 they c. "Go away, you baldhead!"
Ne 8:6 the great God, and all the people c, "Amen!

CHAOS (4)

Ex 8:24 The whole country was thrown into c by the flies.
Isa 24:10 The city writhes in c; every home is locked to keep
34:11 For God will bring c and destruction to that land.
45:18 world to be lived in, not to be a place of empty c.

CHAPEL [KJV] See SANCTUARY

CHAPITER(S) [KJV] See CAPITALS

CHARACTER (10)

Dt 8:2 humbling you and testing you to prove your c,
Ps 89:8 as you, LORD? / Faithfulness is your very c.
103:7 He revealed his c to Moses / and his deeds to the
105:19 to fulfill his word, / the LORD tested Joseph's c.
Jn 8:44 When he lies, it is consistent with his c; for he is a
Ro 5:4 And endurance develops strength of c in us,
5:4 and c strengthens our confident expectation of
1Co 15:33 such things, for "bad company corrupts good c."
1Ti 3:10 responsibilities in the church as a test of their c
Jas 1:4 you will be strong in c and ready for anything.

CHARASHIM [KJV] See (VALLEY OF) CRAFTSMEN

CHARCHEMISH [KJV] See CARCHEMISH

CHARCOAL (3)

Pr 26:21 person starts fights as easily as hot embers light c
Jn 18:18 were standing around a c fire they had made
21:9 they saw that a c fire was burning and fish were

CHARGE (128) [CHARGED, CHARGES, CHARGING]

Ge 24:2 One day Abraham said to the man in c of his
39:4 Potiphar soon put Joseph in c of his entire
39:5 From the day Joseph was put in c, the LORD
39:22 the jailer put Joseph in c of all the other prisoners
41:33 in Egypt and put him in c of a nationwide program.
41:41 "I hereby put you in c of the entire land of
41:43 So Joseph was put in c of all Egypt.
41:45 So Joseph took c of the entire land of Egypt.
42:6 of all Egypt and in c of the sale of the grain,
43:19 they went over to the man in c of Joseph's
44:1 Joseph gave these instructions to the man in c of
44:26 We won't be allowed to see the man in c of the
47:6 special skills, put them in c of my livestock, too."
49:33 Then when Jacob had finished this c to his sons,
Ex 5:14 Then they whipped the Israelite foremen in c of the
18:25 They were put in c of groups of one thousand,
38:22 of the tribe of Judah, was in c of the whole project,
Lev 7:7 to the priest in c of the atonement ceremony.
25:15 The seller will c you only for the crop years left
25:36 or c interest on the money you lend them.
25:37 do not c your relatives interest on anything you
Nu 1:50 You must put the Levites in c of the Tabernacle of
18:8 "I have put the priests in c of all the holy gifts that
31:6 the sanctuary and the trumpets for sounding the c.
31:30 Give this share to the Levites in c of maintaining
Dt 21:8 Do not c your people Israel with the guilt of
23:19 "Do not c interest on the loans you make to a
23:20 You may c interest to foreigners, but not to
26:3 Go to the priest in c at that time and say to him,
27:11 That same day Moses gave this c to the people:
Jos 6:5 and the people can c straight into the city."
Jdg 5:2 "When Israel's leaders take c, / and the people
9:29 If I were in c, I would get rid of Abimelech.
1Sa 7:1 and ordained Eleazar, his son, to be in c of it.
2Sa 20:24 Adoniram was in c of the labor force.
1Ki 2:1 he gave this c to his son Solomon:
4:6 Adoniram son of Abda was in c of the labor force.
5:14 at home. Adoniram was in c of this labor force.
11:28 he put him in c of the labor force from the tribes of
12:18 who was in c of the labor force, to restore order,
18:3 summoned Obadiah, who was in c of the palace.
2Ki 11:9 The commanders took c of the men reporting for
11:15 the commanders who were in c of the troops,
15:5 The king's son Jotham was put in c of the royal
25:19 who was in c of recruitment, and sixty other
1Ch 9:20 Phinehas son of Eleazar had been in c of the
9:32 c of preparing the bread to be set on the table each
23:29 They were in c of the sacred bread that was set out
26:15 and his sons were put in c of the storehouses.
26:20 were in c of the treasuries of the house of God
26:22 were in c of the treasuries of the house of the
26:26 and his relatives were in c of the treasuries that
26:30 were put in c of the Israelite lands west of the
26:32 and put them in c of the tribes of Reuben and Gad
27:3 and was in c of all the army officers for the first
27:25 Azmaveth son of Adiel was in c of the palace
27:25 Jonathan son of Uzziah was in c of the regional
27:26 Ezri son of Kelub was in c of the field workers
27:27 Shimei from Ramah was in c of the king's
27:28 Baal-hanan from Geder was in c of the king's olive
27:29 Shitrai from Sharon was in c of the cattle on the
27:30 Obil the Ishmaelite was in c of the camels.
27:30 Jehdeiah from Meronoth was in c of the donkeys.
27:31 Jaziz the Hagrite was in c of the king's sheep.
28:8 I give you this c for all Israel, the LORD's
2Ch 10:18 who was in c of the labor force, to restore order,
23:8 The commanders took c of the men reporting for
23:14 the commanders who were in c of the troops,
23:18 Jehoiada now put the Levitical priests in c of the
24:13 So the men in c of the renovation worked hard,
26:21 His son Jotham was put in c of the royal palace,
31:12 Conaniah the Levite was put in c, assisted by his
31:14 was put in c of distributing the freewill offerings of
34:13 were put in c of the laborers of the various trades.
Ezr 3:8 or older were put in c of rebuilding the LORD's
8:25 to be in c of transporting the silver, the gold,
Ne 11:16 who were in c of the work outside the Temple of
12:8 who with his associates was in c of the songs of
12:25 and Akkub were the gatekeepers in c of the
12:44 On that day men were appointed to be in c of the
13:13 one of the Levites, in c of the storerooms.
Est 2:3 Hegai, the eunuch in c, will see that they are all
2:15 the advice of Hegai, the eunuch in c of the harem.
8:2 And Esther appointed Mordecai to be in c of
Job 10:2 tell me the c you are bringing against me.
13:6 Listen to my c; pay attention to my arguments.
15:26 their strong shields, they defiantly c against him.
33:13 So why are you bringing a c against him? You say,
Ps 8:6 You put us in c of everything you made,
15:5 Those who do not c interest on the money they
105:21 Joseph was put in c of all the king's household;
Pr 28:12 When the wicked take c, people go into hiding.
28:28 When the wicked take c, people hide.
Isa 3:6 you be our leader! Take c of this heap of ruins!"
Jer 20:1 the priest in c of the Temple of the LORD,
29:26 as the priest in c of the house of the LORD.
52:25 who was in c of recruitment, and sixty other
Eze 16:33 Prostitutes c for their services—but not you!
40:46 south inner gate is for the priests in c of the altar—
44:8 for you have hired foreigners to take c of my
Da 1:3 who was in c of the palace officials,
2:49 and Abednego to be in c of all the affairs of the
3:12 whom you have put in c of the province of
Mt 9:38 So pray to the Lord who is in c of the harvest;
24:47 the master will put that servant in c of all he owns.
27:37 above Jesus' head, announcing the c against him.
Mk 15:26 above Jesus' head, announcing the c against him.
15:44 so he called for the Roman military officer in c
Lk 6:7 because they were eager to find some legal c to
10:2 Pray to the Lord who is in c of the harvest, and ask
12:44 the master will put that servant in c of all he owns.
13:14 But the leader in c of the synagogue was indignant
22:63 Now the guards in c of Jesus began mocking
Jn 12:6 he was a thief who was in c of the disciples' funds,
18:29 and asked, "What is your c against this man?"
Ac 6:3 We will put them in c of this business.
7:10 and put him in c of all the affairs of the palace.
7:60 shouting, "Lord, don't c them with this sin!"
13:15 those in c of the service sent them this message:
25:26 the emperor? For there is no real c against him.
27:11 But the officer in c of the prisoners listened more
1Co 4:1 have been put in c of explaining God's secrets.
4:2 a person who is put in c as a manager must be
9:15 die than lose my distinction of preaching without c.
Phm 1:18 any wrong or stolen anything from you, c me for it.
Heb 3:6 the faithful Son, was in c of the entire household.
Rev 21:6 will give the springs of the water of life without c!
22:17 them come and drink the water of life without c.

CHARGED (11) [CHARGE]

Dt 27:1 and the leaders of Israel c the people as follows:
33:4 Moses c us with the law, / the special possession of
Jos 6:20 and the Israelites c straight into the city from every
2Sa 19:42 We have c him nothing. And he hasn't fed us
Ne 5:11 Repay the interest you c on their money, grain,
Job 4:18 his own angels and has c some of them with folly,
Ps 119:4 You have c us / to keep your commandments
Da 8:7 The goat c furiously at the ram and struck it,
Lk 11:51 the sanctuary. Yes, it will surely be c against you.
Ac 19:40 I am afraid we are in danger of being c with rioting
Rev 14:5 No falsehood can be c against them; they are

CHARGER [KJV] See also PLATE(S), PLATTER(S)

CHARGES (22) [CHARGE]

1Sa 13:21 (The schedule of c was as follows: a quarter of an
Job 31:35 Let my accuser write out the c against me.
39:21 and rejoices in its strength. When it c to war,
Ps 50:7 Here are my c against you, O Israel: / I am God,
50:21 I will rebuke you, / listing all my c against you.
Pr 23:11 is strong. He himself will bring their c against you.
Mt 12:10 would say yes, so they could bring c against him.)
26:62 "Well, aren't you going to answer these c?
27:13 "Don't you hear their many c against you?"
Mk 14:60 "Well, aren't you going to answer these c?
15:4 What about all these c against you?"
Lk 21:14 So don't worry about how to answer the c against
Ac 23:30 I have told his accusers to bring their c before
24:1 and the lawyer Tertullus, to press c against Paul.
24:2 Tertullus laid c against Paul in the following
24:19 and they ought to be here to bring c if they have
25:8 Paul denied the c. "I am not guilty," he said.
25:15 and other Jewish leaders pressed c against him
25:20 be willing to stand trial on these c in Jerusalem.
25:27 the emperor without specifying the c against him!"
28:19 even though I had no desire to press c against my
Col 2:14 He canceled the record that contained the c against

CHARGING (5) [CHARGE]

Ex 22:25 in need, do not be like a money lender, c interest.
23:7 "Keep far away from falsely c anyone with evil.
Ne 5:7 "You are oppressing your own relatives by c them
Job 16:14 and again he smashed me, c at me like a warrior.
Pr 28:8 A person who makes money by c interest will lose

CHARIOT (49) [CHARIOTEER, CHARIOTEERS, CHARIOTS]

Ge 41:43 Pharaoh also gave Joseph the c of his
46:29 Joseph prepared his c and traveled to Goshen to
Ex 14:6 called out his troops and led the chase in his c.
14:25 Their c wheels began to come off, making their
Jdg 4:15 Then Sisera leaped down from his c and escaped
5:28 saying, / 'Why is his c so long in coming?
5:28 Why don't we hear the sound of c wheels?'
1Sa 8:12 others will make his weapons and c equipment.
2Sa 8:4 he crippled all but one hundred of the c horses.
15:1 After this, Absalom bought a c and horses, and he
1Ki 4:26 Solomon had four thousand stalls for his c horses
7:33 and were similar to c wheels. The axles, spokes,
10:26 He stationed many of them in the c cities,
12:18 he quickly jumped into his c and fled to Jerusalem.
18:44 and tell him, 'Climb into your c and go back home.
18:46 and ran ahead of Ahab's c all the way to the
20:33 Ben-hadad arrived, Ahab invited him up into his c!
22:34 out of here!" Ahab groaned to the driver of his c.
22:35 and Ahab was propped up in his c facing the
22:35 from his wound ran down to the floor of his c,
22:38 Then his c was washed beside the pool of Samaria,
2Ki 2:11 and talking, suddenly a c of fire appeared,
5:21 he climbed down from his c and went to meet him.
5:26 Naaman stepped down from his c to meet you?
9:16 Then Jehu got into a c and rode to Jezreel to find
9:21 "Quick! Get my c ready!" King Joram
9:23 Then King Joram reined the c horses around
9:24 pierced his heart, and he sank down dead in his c.
9:27 So they shot Ahaziah in his c at the Ascent of Gur,
9:28 His officials took him by c to Jerusalem,
10:15 put out his hand, and Jehu helped him into the c.
23:30 Josiah's officers took his body back in a c from
1Ch 18:4 he crippled all but one hundred of the c horses.
2Ch 1:14 He stationed many of them in the c cities,
9:25 Solomon had four thousand stalls for his c horses
9:25 He stationed many of them in the c cities,
10:18 he quickly jumped into his c and fled to Jerusalem.
18:33 out of here!" Ahab groaned to the driver of his c.
18:34 and Ahab propped himself up in his c facing the
35:24 So they lifted Josiah out of his c and placed him in another c.
Jer 51:21 destroying the horse and rider, the c and charioteer.
Eze 23:15 They were dressed like c officers from the land of
23:23 handsome young captains, commanders, c officers,
27:14 Togarmah came riding horses, c horses, and mules.
Zec 6:2 The first c was pulled by red horses, the second by
6:6 The c with black horses is going north, the c with white horses is going west, and the c with dappled-gray horses is going

CHARIOTEER (1) [CHARIOT]

Jer 51:21 destroying the horse and rider, the chariot and c.

CHARIOTEERS (24) [CHARIOT]

Ex 14:9 all his horses, chariots, and c—were used in the
14:17 expense of Pharaoh and his armies, chariots, and c.
14:23 all of Pharaoh's horses, chariots, and c—

14:26 will rush back over the Egyptian chariots and c."
14:28 The waters covered all the chariots and c—
15:19 chariots, and c rushed into the sea,
Jdg 4:15 the LORD threw Sisera and all his c and warriors
2Sa 8:4 David captured seventeen hundred c and twenty
10:18 This time David's forces killed seven hundred c
1Ki 9:22 in his army, commanders of his chariots, and c.
22:31 of Aram had issued these orders to his thirty-two c:
22:32 So when the Aramean c saw Jehoshaphat in his
22:33 the c realized he was not the king of Israel,
2Ki 2:12 My father! The chariots and c of Israel!"
8:21 The Edomites surrounded him and his c, but he
13:14 My father! The chariots and c of Israel!" he cried.
1Ch 18:4 seven thousand c, and twenty thousand foot
19:18 This time David's forces killed seven thousand c
2Ch 8:9 in his army, commanders of his chariots, and c.
18:30 the king of Aram had issued these orders to his c:
18:31 So when the Aramean c saw Jehoshaphat in his
18:32 As soon as the c realized he was not the king of
21:9 The Edomites surrounded him and his c, but he
Hag 2:22 I will overturn their chariots and c. The horses will

CHARIOTS (102) [CHARIOT]

Ge 50:9 So a great number of c, cavalry, and people
Ex 14:7 He took with him six hundred of Egypt's best c,
14:7 along with the rest of the c of Egypt, each with a
14:9 all his horses, c, and charioteers—were used in the
14:17 glory at the expense of Pharaoh and his armies, c,
14:23 all of Pharaoh's horses, c, and charioteers—
14:25 to come off, making their c impossible to drive.
14:26 Then the waters will rush back over the Egyptian c
14:28 The waters covered all the charioteers—
15:4 Pharaoh's c and armies, / he has thrown into the
15:19 When Pharaoh's horses, c, and charioteers rushed
Dt 11:4 to the armies of Egypt and to their horses and c—
20:1 and you face horses and c and an army greater than
Jos 11:4 along with a vast array of horses and c,
11:6 all be dead. Cripple their horses and burn their c."
11:9 Joshua crippled the horses and burned all the c,
17:16 and the valley of Jezreel have iron c—
17:18 even though they are strong and have iron c."
24:6 the Egyptians chased after you with c and horses.
Jdg 1:19 in the plains because the people there had iron c.
4:3 Sisera, who had nine hundred iron c,
4:7 along with his c and warriors, to the Kishon River.
4:13 he called for all nine hundred of his iron c and all
4:16 and their c all the way to Harosheth-haggoyim,
1Sa 8:11 sons into his army and make them run before his c.
13:5 mustered a mighty army of three thousand c,
2Sa 1:6 on his spear with the enemy c closing in on him.
1Ki 1:5 So he provided himself with c and horses
9:19 and constructed cities where his c and horses could
9:22 in his army, commanders of his c, and charioteers.
10:26 Solomon built up a huge force of c and horses.
10:26 He had fourteen hundred c and twelve thousand
10:29 Egyptian c delivered to Jerusalem could be
16:9 Then Zimri, who commanded half of the royal c,
20:1 supported by the c and horses of thirty-two allied
20:21 However, the other horses and c were destroyed,
20:25 Give us the same number of horses, c, and men,
2Ki 2:12 My father! The c and charioteers of Israel!"
5:9 So Naaman went with his horses and c and waited
6:14 the king of Aram sent a great army with many c
6:15 there were troops, horses, and c everywhere.
6:17 around Elisha was filled with horses and c of fire.
7:6 army of Aram to hear the clatter of speeding c
7:14 So two c with horses were prepared, and the king
8:21 So Jehoram went with all his c to attack the town
9:21 and King Ahaziah of Judah rode out in their c to
10:2 and you have at your disposal c, horses, a fortified
13:7 ten c, and ten thousand foot soldiers.
13:14 The c and charioteers of Israel!" he cried.
18:24 even with the help of Egypt's c and horsemen?
19:23 You have said, "With my many c / I have
23:11 The king also burned the c dedicated to the sun.
1Ch 18:4 David captured one thousand c, seven thousand
19:6 Ammonites sent thirty-eight tons of silver to hire c
19:7 They also hired thirty-two thousand c and secured
2Ch 1:14 which included fourteen hundred c and twelve
1:17 Egyptian c delivered to Jerusalem could be
8:6 and constructed cities where his c and horses could
8:9 in his army, commanders of his c, and charioteers.
12:3 He came with twelve hundred c, sixty thousand
14:9 with an army of a million men and three hundred c.
16:8 their vast army, with all of their c and horsemen?
21:9 to attack Edom with his full army and all his c.
Ps 68:17 Surrounded by unnumbered thousands of c,
76:6 O God of Jacob, / their horses and c stood still.
104:3 You make the clouds your c; / you ride upon the
Isa 2:7 treasures of silver and gold and many horses and c.
5:28 hooves as the wheels of their c spin like the wind.
21:7 Tell him to sound the alert when he sees c drawn
21:9 at last—look! Here come the c and warriors!"
22:6 Elamites are the archers; Arameans drive the c.
22:18 and there your glorious c will remain, broken
31:1 and c instead of looking to the LORD,
36:9 even with the help of Egypt's c and horsemen?
37:24 You have said, "With my many c / I have
43:17 called forth the mighty army of Egypt with all its c
66:15 and his swift c of destruction roar like a whirlwind.
66:20 in c and wagons, and on mules and camels,"
Jer 4:13 His c are like whirlwinds; his horses are swifter
17:25 will always ride among the people of Judah in c
22:4 The king will ride through the palace gates in c
46:9 you horses and c and mighty warriors of Egypt!
47:3 and the rumble of wheels as the c rush by.
50:37 When it strikes her horses and c, her allies from
Eze 23:24 will all come against you from the north with c,
26:7 against Tyre with his cavalry, c, and great army.
26:10 through your broken gates, pulling c behind them.
Da 11:40 king of the north will storm out against him with c,
Joel 2:5 like the rumbling of c, like the roar of a fire
Mic 1:13 Use your swiftest c and flee, you people of
5:10 will destroy all your weapons—your horses and c.
Na 2:3 Watch as their glittering c move into position,
2:4 The c race recklessly along the streets and through
2:13 "Your c will soon go up in smoke.
3:2 Hear the crack of the whips as the c rush forward
3:2 and c clatter as they bump wildly through the
Hab 3:8 No, you were sending your c of salvation!
Hag 2:22 I will overturn their c and charioteers. The horses
Zec 6:1 and saw four c coming from between two bronze
9:10 I will remove the battle c from Israel
Rev 9:9 and their wings roared like an army of c rushing
18:13 olive oil, fine flour, wheat, cattle, sheep, horses, c,

CHARITY (2)

Mt 6:2 and streets to call attention to their acts of c!
Ac 10:2 He gave generously to c and was a man who

CHARITY [KJV] See also LOVE

CHARM (4) [CHARMERS, CHARMS]

Pr 31:30 C is deceptive, and beauty does not last; but a
Ecc 10:11 It does no good to c a snake after it has bitten you.
Isa 47:11 you suddenly, and you won't be able to c it away.
Jer 8:17 among you like poisonous snakes you cannot c,"

CHARMERS (1) [CHARM]

Ps 58:5 ignoring the tunes of the snake c, / no matter how

CHARMS (4) [CHARM]

Isa 3:20 ankle chains, sashes, perfumes, and c;
Eze 13:18 You tie magic c on their wrists and furnish them
13:20 I am against all your magic c, which you use to
Na 3:4 and faithless city, mistress of deadly c,

CHARRAN [KJV] See HARAN

CHARRED (3)

Ne 4:2 Look at those c stones they are pulling out of the
Jer 11:16 to burn them with fire, leaving them c and broken.
Rev 18:9 as they see the smoke rising from her c remains.

CHART (1)

Ps 139:3 You c the path ahead of me / and tell me where to

CHASE (45) [CHASED, CHASES, CHASING]

Ge 44:4 household manager, "C after them and stop them.
Ex 2:17 often come and c the girls and their flocks away.
14:4 harden Pharaoh's heart, and he will c after you.
14:6 called out his troops and led the c in his chariot.
14:9 chariots, and charioteers—were used in the c.
15:9 "The enemy said, 'I will c them, / catch up with
Lev 26:7 you will c down all your enemies and slaughter
26:8 Five of you will c a hundred, and a hundred of you
will c ten thousand!
Dt 19:6 an enraged avenger might be able to c down
28:26 and no one will be there to c them away.
32:30 How could one person c a thousand of them,
Jos 8:6 We will let them c us until they have all left the
8:16 and all the men in the city were called out to c after
8:17 in Ai or Bethel who did not c after the Israelites,
Jdg 7:23 who joined in the c after the fleeing army of
7:25 of Zeeb. And they continued to c the Midianites.
8:4 were exhausted, they continued to c the enemy.
20:32 so that the men of Benjamin would c them along
20:45 They continued the c until they had killed another
1Sa 14:22 the men who were hiding in the hills joined the c
14:36 "Let's c the Philistines all night and destroy every
23:28 So Saul quit the c and returned to fight the
30:8 Then David asked the LORD, "Should I c them?
2Sa 20:6 and c after him before he gets into a fortified city
2Ki 5:20 I will c after him and get something from him."
1Ch 12:21 They helped David c down bands of raiders,
Job 13:25 by the wind? Would you c a dry stalk of grass?
Ps 16:4 Those who c after other gods will be filled with
83:15 c them with your fierce storms; / terrify them with
Pr 13:21 chases sinners, while blessings c the righteous!
19:26 or c away their mother are a public disgrace
Isa 17:2 There will be no one to c them away.
30:17 One of them will c a thousand of you. Five of them
Jer 9:16 Their enemies will c them with the sword until I
49:5 "Your neighbors will c you from your land,
49:19 I will c Edom from its land, and I will appoint the
49:37 "Their enemies will c them with the sword until I
50:44 I will c Babylon from its land, and I will appoint
La 3:66 C them down in your anger, destroying them from
Eze 5:12 a third to the winds and c them with my sword.
Da 4:14 C the animals from its shade and the birds from its
Hos 8:3 is good, and now their enemies will c after them.
12:1 on the wind; they c after the east wind all day long.
Ob 1:7 They will help to c you from your land. They will

CHASED (44) [CHASE]

Ge 14:14 He c after Kedorlaomer's army until he caught up
14:15 but Abram c them to Hobah, north of Damascus.
15:11 down to eat the carcasses, but Abram c them away.
31:36 You have c me as though I were a criminal.
Ex 14:8 and he c after the people of Israel who had escaped
14:28 Of all the Egyptians who had c the Israelites into
Lev 26:36 You will run as though c by a warrior with a
Nu 14:45 and attacked them and c them as far as Hormah.
Dt 1:44 They c and battered you all the way from Seir to
Jos 7:5 c the Israelites from the city gate as far as the
10:10 Then the Israelites c the enemy along the road to
11:8 The Israelites c them as far as Great Sidon
24:6 the Egyptians c after you with chariots and horses.
Jdg 2:12 They c after other gods, worshiping the gods of the
4:16 Barak c the enemy and their chariots all the way to
8:12 but Gideon c them down and captured all their
11:2 half brothers grew up, they c Jephthah off the land.
18:23 called these men together and c after us like this?"
20:42 but the Israelites c after them and killed them.
1Sa 7:11 The men of Israel c them from Mizpah to Beth-car,
14:31 they c and killed the Philistines all day from
25:29 "Even when you are c by those who seek your life,
2Sa 2:27 for we would have c you all night if necessary."
11:23 he said. "And as we c them back to the city gates,
19:9 but Absalom c him out of the country.
22:38 "I c my enemies and destroyed them; / I did not
23:20 Another time he c a lion down into a pit. Then,
1Ki 20:20 The Israelites c them, but King Ben-hadad and a
2Ki 3:24 The army of Israel c them into the land of Moab,
25:5 But the Babylonians c after them and caught the
1Ch 11:22 Another time he c a lion down into a pit. Then,
2Ch 13:9 And you have c away the priests of the LORD
Ps 18:37 I c my enemies and caught them; / I did not stop
143:3 My enemy has c me. / He has knocked me to the
Jer 23:12 They will be c down dark and treacherous trails,
39:5 But the Babylonians c the king and caught him on
52:8 But the Babylonians c after them and caught King
La 1:3 Her enemies have c her down, and she has
3:43 c us down, and slaughtered us without mercy.
3:52 whom I have never harmed, c me like a bird.
Am 1:11 They c down their relatives, the Israelites,
Zep 3:19 I will bring together those who were c away.
Lk 20:12 thing happened. He, too, was wounded and c away.
Jn 2:15 from some ropes and c them all out of the Temple.

CHASES (2) [CHASE]

Pr 13:21 Trouble c sinners, while blessings chase the
Isa 41:3 He c them away and goes on safely, though he is

CHASING (33) [CHASE]

Lev 26:17 and you will run even when no one is c you!
26:37 Yes, though no one is c you, you will stumble over
Dt 11:4 drowned them in the Red Sea as they were c you,
Jos 2:22 The men who were c them had searched
10:19 The rest of you continue c the enemy and cut them
Jdg 8:5 I am c Zebah and Zalmunna, the kings of Midian."
18:22 and some of his neighbors came c after them.
20:43 and were relentless in c them down,
1Sa 14:46 Then Saul called back the army from c the
17:52 c them as far as Gath and the gates of Ekron.
24:14 Should he spend his time c one who is as worthless
26:18 Why are you c me? What have I done? What is my
2Sa 2:19 and he began c Abner. He was relentless
2:21 But Asahel refused and kept right on c Abner.
2:26 When will you call off your men from c their
2:28 and his men stopped c the troops of Israel.
18:16 and his men returned from c the army of Israel.
1Ki 22:33 was not the king of Israel, they stopped c him.
2Ch 18:32 he was not the king of Israel, they stopped c him.
36:17 young men, even c after them into the Temple.
Pr 28:1 The wicked run away when no one is c them,
Ecc 1:14 under the sun is meaningless, like c the wind.
1:17 But now I realize that even this was like c the
2:11 it was all so meaningless. It was like c the wind.
2:17 Everything is meaningless, like c the wind.
2:26 however, is meaningless, like c the wind.
4:4 But this, too, is meaningless, like c the wind.
4:16 So again, it is all meaningless, like c the wind.
6:9 nice things is meaningless; it is like c the wind.
Isa 30:16 to see is the swiftness of your enemies c you!
Hos 6:10 My people have defiled themselves by c after other
Mt 23:34 in your synagogues, c them from city to city.
1Pe 4:2 And you won't spend the rest of your life c after

CHASM (1)

Lk 16:26 And besides, there is a great c separating us.

CHASTE (2)

SS 8:9 If she is c, we will strengthen and encourage her.
8:10 "I am c, and I am now full breasted. And my lover

CHASTE [KJV] See also PURE

CHASTENING (1)

Job 5:17 Do not despise the c of the Almighty when you sin.

CHASTISE [KJV] See HARSH, PUNISH, FLOG(GED)

CHATTERED (1)

Isa 38:14 Delirious, I c like a swallow or a crane, / and

CHEAP (1)

2Ti 2:20 and the c ones are for everyday use.

CHEAT (17) [CHEATED, CHEATERS, CHEATING]
Lev 19:11 “Do not steal. “Do not c one another. “Do not lie.
19:13 “Do not c or rob anyone. “Always pay your hired
Dt 25:16 Those who c with dishonest weights and measures
Isa 59: 6 They c and shortchange everyone. Nothing they do
Hos 12: 7 selling from dishonest scales—they love to c.
Mal 1:14 “Cursed is the c who promises to give a fine ram
2: 6 They did not lie or c; they walked with me,
3: 5 I will speak against those who c employees of their
3: 8 “Should people c God? Yet you have cheated me!
3: 8 ‘What do you mean? When did we ever c you?’
Mk 10:19 Do not c. Honor your father and mother.’ ”
12:40 But they shamelessly c widows out of their
Lk 16:10 If you c even a little, you won’t be honest with
18:11 For I never c, I don’t sin, I don’t commit adultery,
20:47 But they shamelessly c widows out of their
1Co 6: 8 and c even your own Christian brothers and sisters.
1Th 4: 6 Never c another Christian in this matter by taking

CHEATED (6) [CHEAT]
1Sa 12: 3 or donkey have I stolen? Have I ever c any of you?
12: 4 “you have never c or oppressed us in any way,
Mal 3: 8 Yet you have c me! “But you ask, ‘What do you
3: 8 “You have c me of the tithes and offerings due to
1Co 6: 7 and leave it at that? Why not let yourselves be c?
Jas 5: 4 of the field workers whom you have c of their pay.

CHEATERS (1) [CHEAT]
Isa 32: 5 Wealthy c will not be respected as outstanding

CHEATING (7) [CHEAT]
Ps 55:11 threats and c are rampant in the streets.
Pr 11: 1 The LORD hates c, but he delights in honesty.
Eze 45: 9 Quit robbing and c my people out of their land!
Hos 12: 8 No one can say I got it by c! My record is
Am 8: 5 to end so you can get back to c the helpless.
Mic 6:10 Will there be no end of your getting rich by c?
Mal 3: 9 a curse, for your whole nation has been c me.

CHECK (8) [CHECKED, CHECKING, CHECKS]
1Sa 23:22 and c again to be sure of where he is staying
1Ki 18: 5 “We must c every spring and valley to see if we
2Ki 7:13 “We had better send out scouts to c into this.
1Ch 23:29 They were also responsible to c all the weights
Isa 8:20 “C their predictions against my testimony,”
22:10 You c the houses and tear some down to get stone
28:17 and the plumb line of righteousness to c the
Ac 17:11 They searched the Scriptures day after day to c up

CHECKED (2) [CHECK]
1Sa 14:17 And when they c, they found that Jonathan and his
1Ch 9:28 They c them in and out to avoid any loss.

CHECKING (3) [CHECK]
Lev 13:36 even without c for yellow hair.
Am 7: 7 He was c it with a plumb line to see if it was
Lk 14:28 then c to see if there is enough money to pay the

CHECKS (1) [CHECK]
Jer 6: 9 as when a harvester c each vine a second time to

CHEEK (6) [CHEEKS]
1Sa 10: 1 He kissed Saul on the c and said, “I am doing this
Job 16:10 and laugh at me. They slap my c in contempt.
La 3:30 Let them turn the other c to those who strike them.
Mt 5:39 If you are slapped on the right c, turn the other,
Lk 6:29 If someone slaps you on one c, turn the other c.

CHEEKS (8) [CHEEK]
Dt 18: 3 as offerings: the shoulder, the c, and the stomach.
SS 1:10 How lovely are your c, with your earrings setting
4: 3 Your c behind your veil are like pomegranate
5:13 His c are like sweetly scented beds of spices.
6: 7 Your c behind your veil are like pomegranate
Isa 50: 6 beat me and my c to those who pull out my beard.
La 1: 2 sobs through the night; tears stream down her c.
1:16 all these things I weep; tears flow down my c.

CHEER (8) [CHEERED, CHEERFUL, CHEERFULLY, CHEERS]
1Sa 1:17 “In that case,” Eli said, “c up! May the God of
18: 6 along the way to celebrate and to c for King Saul,
Ps 94:19 your comfort gave me renewed hope and c.
Ecc 2: 3 much thought, I decided to c myself with wine.
Isa 13: 2 waving as the enemy attacks. C them on, O Israel!
Zep 3:16 announcement to Jerusalem will be, “C up, Zion!
Mk 10:49 “C up,” they said. “Come on, he’s calling you!”
Php 2:19 he can c me up by telling me how you are getting

CHEERED (1) [CHEER]
Eze 25: 6 and c with glee at the destruction of my people,

CHEERFUL (4) [CHEER]
Job 9:27 if I decided to end my sadness and be c,
Pr 15:30 A c look brings joy to the heart; good news makes
17:22 A c heart is good medicine, but a broken spirit saps
25:20 Singing c songs to a person whose heart is heavy is

CHEERFULLY (6) [CHEER]
1Sa 15:13 Samuel finally found him, Saul greeted him c.
Isa 64: 5 You welcome those who c do good, who follow
2Co 9: 7 to pressure. For God loves the person who gives c.
Col 3:23 Work hard and c at whatever you do, as though
Heb 12: 9 should we not all the more c submit to the
1Pe 4: 9 C share your home with those who need a meal

CHEERS (3) [CHEER]
Jdg 9:13 ‘Should I quit producing the wine that c both God
Pr 12:25 person down; an encouraging word c a person up.
Lk 19:40 the stones along the road would burst into c!”

CHEESE (3)
Ge 18: 8 he took some c curds and milk and the roasted
1Sa 17:18 And give these ten cuts of c to their captain.
2Sa 17:29 and c for David and those who were with him.

CHELLUH [KJV] See KELUHI

CHEMARIMS [KJV] See IDOLATROUS

CHEMOSH (9)
Nu 21:29 You are finished, O worshipers of C! / C has left his sons as refugees,
Jdg 11:24 You keep whatever your god C gives you, and we
1Ki 11: 7 east of Jerusalem, he even built a shrine for C,
11:33 C, the god of Moab; and Molech, the god of the
2Ki 23:13 and for C, the detestable god of the Moabites;
Jer 48: 7 Your god C, with his priests and princes, will be
48:13 At last Moab will be ashamed of her idol C,
48:46 The people of the god C are destroyed! Your sons

CHEPHAR-HAAMMONAI [KJV] See KEPHAR-AMMONI

CHERETHIMS [KJV] See KERETHITES

CHERISH (2) [CHERISHED]
Pr 19: 8 people who c understanding will prosper.
Isa 51: 7 right from wrong and c my law in your hearts.

CHERISHED (1) [CHERISH]
Lk 20:13 owner asked himself. ‘I know! I’ll send my c son.

CHERUBIM (62) [CHERUB]
Ex 25:18 Then use hammered gold to make two c, and place
25:19 Attach the c to each end of the atonement cover,
25:20 The c will face each other, looking down on the
25:22 the gold c that hover over the Ark of the Covenant.
26: 1 with figures of c skillfully embroidered into them.
26:31 with c skillfully embroidered into the cloth using
36: 8 embroidered blue, purple, and scarlet c into them.
36:35 and c were skillfully embroidered into it with blue,
37: 7 He made two figures of c out of hammered gold
37: 9 The c faced each other as they looked down on the
Nu 7:89 from between the two c above the Ark’s cover—
1Sa 4: 4 who is enthroned between the c.
2Sa 6: 2 who is enthroned between the c.
1Ki 6:23 Within the inner sanctuary Solomon placed two c
6:24 The wingspan of each of the c was 15 feet,
6:25 The two c were identical in shape and size;
6:28 He overlaid the two c with gold.
6:29 the main room were decorated with carvings of c,
6:32 These doors were decorated with carvings of c,
6:35 These doors were decorated with carvings of c,
7:29 were decorated with carved lions, oxen, and c.
7:36 Carvings of c, lions, and palm trees decorated the
8: 6 and placed it beneath the wings of the c.
8: 7 The c spread their wings over the Ark, forming a
2Ki 19:15 of Israel, you are enthroned between the mighty c!
1Ch 13: 6 of the LORD who is enthroned between the c.
28:18 gold for the altar of incense and for the gold c,
2Ch 3: 7 and figures of c were carved on the walls.
3:10 Solomon made two figures shaped like c
3:11 The total wingspan of the two c standing side by
3:13 So the wingspan of both c together was 30 feet.
3:14 scarlet yarn, with figures of c embroidered on it.
5: 7 and placed it beneath the wings of the c.
5: 8 The c spread their wings out over the Ark,
Ps 80: 1 O God, enthroned above the c, / display your
99: 1 He sits on his throne between the c.
Isa 37:16 of Israel, you are enthroned between the mighty c!
Eze 9: 3 of the God of Israel rose up from between the c,
10: 1 above the crystal surface over the heads of the c.
10: 2 “Go in between the whirling wheels beneath the c,
10: 3 The c were standing at the south end of the Temple
10: 4 the glory of the LORD rose up from above the c
10: 5 The moving wings of the c sounded like the voice
10: 6 “Go between the c and take some burning coals
10: 7 Then one of the c reached out his hand and took
10: 8 (All the c had what looked like human hands
10: 9 Each of the four c had a wheel beside him,
10:11 The c could move forward in any of the four
10:12 Both the c and the wheels were covered with eyes.
10:12 The c had eyes all over their bodies, including their
10:14 Each of the four c had four faces—the first was the
10:15 Then the c rose upward. These were the same
10:16 When the c moved, the wheels moved with them.
10:17 When the c stood still, the wheels also stopped,
10:18 the door of the Temple and hovered above the c.
10:19 the c flew with their wheels to the east gate of the
10:20 I was by the Kebar River. I knew they were c,
11:22 Then the c lifted their wings and rose into the air
41:18 All the walls were decorated with carvings of c,
41:18 was a palm tree carving between each of the c.
41:25 into the Holy Place were decorated with carved c
Heb 9: 5 The glorious c were above the Ark. Their wings

CHESNUT [KJV] See PLANE (TREE)

CHEST (19) [CHESTPIECE, CHESTS]
Ex 25:10 a sacred c 3-3/4 feet long, 2-1/4 feet wide,
Dt 10: 1 and make a sacred c of wood to keep them in.
10: 2 Then place the tablets in the sacred c—the Ark of
10: 3 “So I made a c of acacia wood and cut two stone
1Sa 6: 8 and beside it place a c containing the gold rats
6:11 of the LORD and the c containing the gold rats
6:15 and the c containing the gold rats and gold tumors
2Ki 12: 9 the priest bored a hole in the lid of a large c
12: 9 put all of the people’s contributions into the c.
12:10 Whenever the c became full, the court secretary
2Ch 24: 8 So now Joash gave instructions for a c to be made
24:10 gladly brought their money and filled the c with it.
24:11 Whenever the c became full, the Levites carried it
24:11 and took the c back to the Temple again.
Da 2:32 its c and arms were of silver, its belly and thighs
Zec 13: 6 ‘Then what are those scars on your c?’
Lk 18:13 Instead, he beat his c in sorrow, saying, ‘O God,
Heb 9: 4 and a wooden c called the Ark of the Covenant,
Rev 1:13 wearing a long robe with a gold sash across his c.

CHESTPIECE (23) [CHEST]
Ex 25: 7 and other stones to be set in the ephod and the c.
28: 4 They are to make a c, an ephod, a robe,
28:15 make a c that will be used to determine God’s will.
28:16 This c will be made of two folds of cloth,
28:22 “To attach the c to the ephod, make braided cords
28:23 and attach them to the top corners of the c.
28:24 two gold cords will go through the rings on the c,
28:26 two lower inside corners of the c next to the ephod.
28:28 Then attach the bottom rings of the c to the rings
28:28 This will hold the c securely to the ephod above
28:29 c over his heart when he goes into the presence of
28:30 Insert into the pocket of the c the Urim
29: 5 of the ephod, the ephod itself, the c, and the sash.
35: 9 and other stones to be set in the ephod and the c.
35:27 other gemstones to be used for the ephod and the c.
39: 8 The c was made in the same style as the ephod,
39:15 To attach the c to the ephod, they made braided
39:16 and attached them to the top corners of the c.
39:17 cords were put through the gold rings on the c,
39:19 the lower inside corners of the c next to the ephod.
39:21 the bottom rings of the c to the rings on the ephod.
39:21 the c was held securely to the ephod above the
Lev 8: 8 Then Moses placed the c on Aaron and put the

CHESTS (2) [CHEST]
Mt 2:11 Then they opened their treasure c and gave him
Rev 15: 6 spotless white linen with gold belts across their c.

CHEW (6) [CHEWING, CHEWS]
Lev 11: 3 that have completely divided hooves and c the cud.
11: 4 because they either have split hooves or c the cud,
11: 7 for though it has split hooves, it does not c the cud.
11:26 or that does not c the cud is unclean for you.
Dt 14: 7 They c the cud but do not have split hooves.
14: 8 for though it has split hooves, it does not c the cud.

CHEWING (2) [CHEW]
Pr 25:19 Putting confidence in an unreliable person is like c
Isa 27:10 Cattle will graze there, c on twigs and branches.

CHEWS (2) [CHEW]
Lev 11: 4 camel may not be eaten, for though it c the cud,
Dt 14: 6 that has split hooves and c the cud may be eaten,

CHICKENS [KJV] See CHICKS

CHICKS (3)
Dt 32:11 Like an eagle that rouses her c / and hovers over
Mt 23:37 together as a hen protects her c beneath her wings,
Lk 13:34 together as a hen protects her c beneath her wings,

CHIDE [KJV] See ACCUSE, ARGUED, ARGUING, GRUMBLE

CHIEF (47) [CHIEFS]
CHIEF BAKER (7) Ge 40:1,16,20,22; 41:10,11,13
CHIEF CUP-BEARER (4) Ge 40:1,13,20,21
CHIEF OFFICER (9) 1Ch 9:11; 26:24; 27:4,6; Ne 11:9,14,22; Jer 39:3,13
CHIEF PRIEST (2) 2Ki 25:18; Jer 52:24
Ge 39:21 and he granted Joseph favor with the c jailer.
39:23 The c jailer had no more worries after that,
40: 1 Pharaoh’s c cup-bearer and c baker offended him.
40:13 and return you to your position as his c cup-bearer.
40:16 When the c baker saw that the first dream had such
40:20 He sent for his c cup-bearer and c baker,
40:21 then restored the c cup-bearer to his former
40:22 but he sentenced the c baker to be impaled on a
41:10 time ago, you were angry with the c baker and me,
41:11 One night the c baker and I each had a dream,

41:13 and the **c** baker was executed and impaled on a
Nu 3:32 was the **c** administrator over all the Levites,
1Sa 21:7 Now Doeg the Edomite, Saul's **c** herdsman,
2Ki 18:17 the king of Assyria sent his commander in **c**,
25:18 took with him as prisoners Seraiah the **c** priest,
25:18 assistant Zephaniah, and the three **c** gatekeepers.
25:19 the army commander's **c** secretary, who was in
1Ch 9:11 Azariah was the **c** officer of the house of God.
9:17 and their relatives. Shallum was the **c** gatekeeper.
9:26 The four **c** gatekeepers, all Levites, were in an
18:17 David's sons served as the king's **c** assistants.
26:24 of Moses. He was the **c** officer of the treasuries.
27:4 in his division, and Mikloth was his **c** officer.
27:6 the Thirty. His son Ammizabad was his **c** officer.
2Ch 11:22 Rehoboam made Maacah's son Abijah **c** among
31:13 and Azariah, the **c** official in the Temple of God.
Ne 11:9 Their **c** officer was Joel son of Zicri, who was
11:14 Their **c** officer was Zabdiel son of Haggedolim.
11:22 The **c** officer of the Levites in Jerusalem was Uzzi
Job 29:25 they should do and presided over them as their **c**.
Isa 23:8 on Tyre, empire builder and **c** trader of the world?
Jer 39:3 and Nebo-sarsekim, a **c** officer,
39:13 and Nebushazban, a **c** officer, and Nergal-sharezer,
52:24 took with him as prisoners Seraiah the **c** priest,
52:24 assistant Zephaniah, and the three **c** gatekeepers.
52:25 the army commander's **c** secretary, who was in
Da 1:7 The **c** official renamed them with these Babylonian
1:8 He asked the **c** official for permission to eat other
1:9 Now God had given the **c** official great respect for
1:11 appointed by the **c** official to look after Daniel,
1:18 the **c** official brought all the young men to King
2:48 of Babylon, as well as **c** over all his wise men.
5:11 made him **c** over all the magicians, enchanters,
Ac 14:12 because he was the **c** speaker, was Hermes.
28:7 belonging to Publius, the **c** official of the island.

CHIEFS (1) [CHIEF]

Jos 13:21 and was killed by Moses along with the **c** of

CHILD (180) [CHILD'S, CHILDBEARING, CHILDBIRTH, CHILDHOOD, CHILDISH, CHILDLESS, CHILDLIKE, CHILDREN, CHILDREN'S, GRANDCHILDREN]

LITTLE CHILD (9) 1Ki 3:7; Isa 11:6,8; Mt 18:4,5; Mk 9:36,37; Lk 9:47,48

MY CHILD (20) Ge 38:25; Pr 1:8,10,15; 2:1; 3:1,11,21; 4:10,20; 6:1; 19:27; 23:15,19; 24:13,21; 27:11; Ecc 12:12; Lk 8:54; Heb 12:5

ONLY CHILD (3) Jdg 11:34; Pr 4:3; Lk 8:42

Ge 11:31 and his grandson Lot (his son Haran's **c**)
17:12 Every male **c** must be circumcised on the eighth
25:21 Isaac pleaded with the LORD to give Rebekah a **c**
29:31 Leah was unloved, the LORD let her have a **c**,
30:22 and answered her prayers by giving her a **c**.
38:9 But Onan was not willing to have a **c** who would
38:10 thing for Onan to deny a **c** to his dead brother.
38:25 and walking stick is the father of my **c**.
38:28 thread around the wrist of the **c** who appeared first,
44:20 have a father, an old man, and a **c** of his old age,
49:3 are my oldest son, / the **c** of my vigorous youth.
Ex 2:9 "Take this **c** home and nurse him for me,"
21:22 a pregnant woman so her **c** is born prematurely.
Dt 1:31 in the wilderness, just as a father cares for his **c**.
8:5 should realize that just as a parent disciplines a **c**,
Jdg 11:34 home to Mizpah, his daughter—his only **c**—
Ru 4:15 May this **c** restore your youth and care for you in
1Sa 1:24 When the **c** was weaned, Hannah took him to the
1:25 After sacrificing the bull, they took the **c** to Eli.
1:27 I asked the LORD to give me this **c**, and he has
4:21 She named the **c** Ichabod—"Where is the
2Sa 4:4 son named Mephibosheth, who was crippled as a **c**.
12:14 to despise and blaspheme him, so your **c** will die."
12:16 David begged God to spare the **c**. He went without
12:18 he do to himself when we tell him the **c** is dead?"
12:22 "I fasted and wept while the **c** was alive, for I said,
12:22 LORD will be gracious to me and let the **c** live.'
12:24 named him Solomon. The LORD loved the **c**
1Ki 3:7 but I am like a little **c** who doesn't know his way
3:20 She laid her dead **c** in my arms and took mine to
3:22 certainly was your son, and the living **c** is mine."
3:23 Both of you claim the living **c** is yours, and each
says that the dead **c** belongs to the other.
3:25 "Cut the living **c** in two and give half to each of
3:26 woman who really was the mother of the living **c**,
3:26 my lord! Give her the **c**—please do not kill him!"
11:17 had fled. (Hadad was a very small **c** at the time.)
13:2 A **c** named Josiah will be born into the dynasty of
14:12 and when you enter the city, the **c** will die.
14:13 for this **c** is the only good thing that the LORD,
14:17 and the **c** died just as she walked through the door
16:11 of Baasha, and he did not leave a single male **c**.
17:21 And he stretched himself out over the **c** three times
17:22 and the life of the **c** returned, and he came back to
2Ki 4:18 One day when her **c** was older, he went out to visit
4:26 with your husband, and with your **c**?' " "Yes,"
4:31 to meet Elisha and told him, "The **c** is still dead."
4:32 When Elisha arrived, the **c** was indeed dead,
4:35 Then he stretched himself out again on the **c**.
11:2 him from Athaliah, so the **c** was not murdered.
19:3 It is like when a **c** is ready to be born,
2Ch 22:11 hid the **c** so that Athaliah could not murder him.
Job 3:16 Why was I not buried like a stillborn **c**, like a baby
24:9 "The wicked snatch a widow's **c** from her breast;
Ps 58:8 like a stillborn **c** who will never see the sun.
105:36 Then he killed the oldest **c** in each Egyptian home,
131:2 just as a small **c** is quiet with its mother.
131:2 Yes, like a small **c** is my soul within me.
Pr 1:8 Listen, my **c**, to what your father teaches you.
1:10 My **c**, if sinners entice you, turn your back on
1:15 Don't go along with them, my **c**! Stay far away
2:1 My **c**, listen to me and treasure my instructions.
3:1 My **c**, never forget the things I have taught you.
3:11 My **c**, don't ignore it when the LORD disciplines
3:12 just as a father corrects a **c** in whom he delights.
3:21 My **c**, don't lose sight of good planning
4:3 tenderly loved by my mother as an only **c**.
4:10 My **c**, listen to me and do as I say, and you will
4:20 Pay attention, my **c**, to what I say. Listen carefully.
6:1 My **c**, if you co-sign a loan for a friend
10:1 A wise **c** brings joy to a father; a foolish **c** brings
grief to a mother.
13:1 A wise **c** accepts a parent's discipline; a young
17:25 A foolish **c** brings grief to a father and bitterness to
19:13 A foolish **c** is a calamity to a father; a nagging wife
19:27 If you stop listening to instruction, my **c**, you have
23:15 My **c**, how I will rejoice if you become wise.
23:19 My **c**, listen and be wise. Keep your heart on the
24:13 My **c**, eat honey, for it is good, and the honeycomb
24:21 My **c**, fear the LORD and the king, and don't
27:11 My **c**, how happy I will be if you turn out to be
29:15 To discipline and reprimand a **c** produces wisdom,
29:15 but a mother is disgraced by an undisciplined **c**.
Ecc 4:8 of a man who is all alone, without a **c** or a brother,
10:16 Destruction is certain for the land whose king is a **c**
12:12 But, my **c**, be warned: There is no end of opinions
Isa 7:14 Look! The virgin will conceive a **c**! She will give
7:15 By the time this **c** is old enough to eat curds
8:2 to testify that I had written it before the **c** was
8:4 before this **c** is old enough to say 'Papa'
9:6 For a **c** is born to us, a son is given to us.
10:19 will survive—so few that a **c** could count them!
11:6 safe among lions, and a little **c** will lead them all.
11:8 a little **c** will put its hand in a nest of deadly snakes
37:3 It is like when a **c** is ready to be born,
49:15 "Never! Can a mother forget her nursing **c**?
49:15 Can she feel no love for a **c** she has borne?
54:1 even though you never gave birth to a **c**.
66:13 I will comfort you there as a **c** is comforted by its
Jer 4:31 like that of a woman giving birth to her first **c**.
31:9 I am Israel's father, and Ephraim is my oldest **c**.
31:20 "Is not Israel still my son, my darling **c**?"
44:7 or **c** among you who has come here from Judah,
Eze 4:14 From the time I was a **c** until now I have never
18:19 'Doesn't the **c** pay for the parent's sins?' No!
18:19 For if the **c** does what is right and keeps my laws,
18:19 is right and keeps my laws, that **c** will surely live.
18:20 The **c** will not be punished for the parent's sins,
44:25 his father, mother, **c**, brother, or unmarried sister.
Hos 1:4 And the LORD said, "Name the **c** Jezreel,
11:1 "When Israel was a **c**, I loved him as a son, and I
13:13 but they are like a **c** who resists being born.
Mal 3:17 them as a father spares an obedient and dutiful **c**.
Mt 1:20 For the **c** within her has been conceived by the
1:23 "Look! The virgin will conceive a **c**! / She will
2:8 "Go to Bethlehem and search carefully for the **c**.
2:9 and stopped over the place where the **c** was.
2:11 They entered the house where the **c** and his
2:13 "Get up and flee to Egypt with the **c** and his
2:13 because Herod is going to try to kill the **c**."
2:14 That night Joseph left for Egypt with the **c**
2:20 "Get up and take the **c** and his mother back to the
2:20 because those who were trying to kill the **c** are
18:2 Jesus called a small **c** over to him and put the **c**
among them.
18:4 anyone who becomes as humble as this little **c** is
18:5 And anyone who welcomes a little **c** like this on
22:24 and have a **c** who will be the brother's heir.'
Mk 5:39 he asked. "The **c** isn't dead; she is only asleep."
7:26 She begged him to release her **c** from the demon's
9:20 it threw the **c** into a violent convulsion, and he fell
9:25 "I command you to come out of this **c** and never
9:36 Then he put a little **c** among them. Taking the **c** in
his arms, he said to them,
9:37 "Anyone who welcomes a little **c** like this on my
10:20 obeyed all these commandments since I was a **c**."
12:19 and have a **c** who will be the brother's heir.
Lk 1:20 you won't be able to speak until the **c** is born.
1:41 Mary's greeting, Elizabeth's **c** leaped within her,
1:42 God above all other women, and your **c** is blessed.
1:66 "I wonder what this **c** will turn out to be?
2:7 She gave birth to her first **c**, a son. She wrapped
2:17 and what the angel had said to them about this **c**.
2:20 and because they had seen the **c**, just as the angel
2:22 required by the law of Moses after the birth of a **c**;
2:23 of the Lord says, "If a woman's first **c** is a boy,
2:28 He took the **c** in his arms and praised God, saying,
2:34 "This **c** will be rejected by many in Israel,
2:40 There the **c** grew up healthy and strong. He was
8:42 His only **c** was dying, a little girl twelve years old.
8:54 the hand and said in a loud voice, "Get up, my **c**!"
9:47 their thoughts, so he brought a little **c** to his side.
9:48 "Anyone who welcomes a little **c** like this on my
18:21 obeyed all these commandments since I was a **c**."
20:28 and have a **c** who will be the brother's heir.
23:29 the wombs that have not borne a **c** and the breasts
Jn 16:21 When her **c** is born, her anguish gives place to joy
Ac 7:20 time Moses was born—a beautiful **c** in God's eyes.
1Co 4:17 he is my beloved and trustworthy **c** in the Lord.
13:11 When I was a **c**, I spoke and thought and reasoned
as a **c** does.
Gal 3:16 God gave the promise to Abraham and his **c**.
3:16 But the promise was to his **c**—and that, of course,
3:19 of the **c** to whom God's promise was made.
4:7 Now you are no longer a slave but God's own **c**.
4:7 And since you are his **c**, everything he has belongs
4:27 even though you never gave birth to a **c**.
4:29 just as Isaac, the **c** of promise, was persecuted by
1Th 5:3 birth pains begin when her **c** is about to be born.
1Ti 1:2 It is written to Timothy, my true **c** in the faith.
Tit 1:4 to Titus, my true **c** in the faith that we share.
Heb 11:11 Sarah together with Abraham was able to have a **c**,
11:23 They saw that God had given them an unusual **c**,
12:5 "My **c**, don't ignore it when the Lord disciplines
12:7 Whoever heard of a **c** who was never disciplined?
1Jn 5:1 who believes that Jesus is the Christ is a **c** of God.
5:4 For every **c** of God defeats this evil world by
Rev 12:4 the woman as she was about to give birth to her **c**,
12:5 And the **c** was snatched away from the dragon
12:13 pursued the woman who had given birth to the **c**.

CHILD'S (14) [CHILD]

Ex 2:10 the **c** mother brought him back to the princess,
2Sa 4:4 the capital, the **c** nurse grabbed him and fled.
1Ki 17:21 my God, please let this **c** life return to him."
2Ki 4:29 Go quickly and lay the staff on the **c** face."
4:31 hurried on ahead and laid the staff on the **c** face,
4:34 the **c** body, placing his mouth on the **c** mouth, his
eyes on the **c** eyes, and his hands on the **c** hands.
4:34 And the **c** body began to grow warm again!
4:36 "Call the **c** mother!" he said. And when she came
5:14 And his flesh became as healthy as a young **c**,
Job 33:25 Then his body will become as healthy as a **c**,
Eze 18:20 and the parent will not be punished for the **c** sins.

CHILDBEARING (1) [BEAR, CHILD]

1Ti 2:15 But women will be saved through **c** and by

CHILDBIRTH (7) [BEAR, CHILD]

Ge 35:16 But Rachel's pains of **c** began while they were still
Lev 12:4 her purification from the blood of **c** is completed.
12:5 sixty-six days to be purified from the blood of **c**.
12:7 be ceremonially clean again after her bleeding at **c**.
1Sa 4:20 She died in **c**, but before she passed away the
Ps 48:6 like a woman writhing in the pain of **c**
Ro 8:22 as in the pains of **c** right up to the present time.

CHILDHOOD (17) [CHILD]

Ge 8:21 and actions are bent toward evil from **c**.
24:59 The woman who had been Rebekah's **c** nurse went
31:30 must go, and you long intensely for your **c** home,
2Ki 10:6 of Samaria, where they had been raised since **c**.
Job 31:18 No, from **c** I have cared for orphans, and all my
Ps 71:5 are my hope. / I've trusted you, O LORD, from **c**.
71:17 O God, you have taught me from my earliest **c**,
Pr 29:21 A servant who is pampered from **c** will later
SS 3:4 I didn't let him go until I had brought him to my **c**
8:2 I would bring you to my **c** home, and there you
Isa 47:15 those with whom you have done business since **c**,
48:8 You have been rebels from your earliest **c**,
Jer 3:24 From **c** we have watched as everything our
22:21 Since **c** you have been that way—you simply will
Ac 13:1 Manaen (the **c** companion of King Herod Antipas),
26:4 training from my earliest **c** among my own people
2Ti 3:15 You have been taught the holy Scriptures from **c**,

CHILDISH (2) [CHILD]

1Co 13:11 But when I grew up, I put away **c** things.
14:20 don't be **c** in your understanding of these things.

CHILDLESS (14) [CHILD]

Ge 25:21 to give Rebekah a child because she was **c**.
29:31 LORD let her have a child, while Rachel was **c**.
Lev 20:20 are guilty of a capital offense and will die **c**.
20:21 his brother, and the guilty couple will remain **c**.
Dt 7:14 None of your men or women will be **c**, and all your
1Sa 15:33 of many mothers, now your mother will be **c**."
2Sa 6:23 daughter of Saul, remained **c** throughout her life.
Job 24:21 For they have taken advantage of the **c** who have
Isa 23:4 For the sea says, "Now I am **c**; I have no sons
54:1 "Sing, O **c** woman! Break forth into loud
Jer 15:9 She sits **c** now, disgraced and humiliated.
22:30 the record show that this man Jehoiachin was **c**,
Lk 23:29 'Fortunate indeed are the women who are **c**,
Gal 4:27 when he prophesied, / "Rejoice, O **c** woman!

CHILDLIKE (3) [CHILD]

Ps 116:6 The LORD protects those of **c** faith; / I was
Mt 11:25 so wise and clever, and for revealing it to the **c**.
Lk 10:21 so wise and clever, and for revealing it to the **c**.

CHILDREN (561) [CHILD]

CHILDREN OF GOD (10) Mt 5:9; Lk 20:36; Jn 1:12; 11:52; Ro 8:14; 9:8; Gal 3:26; Php 2:15; 1Jn 3:10; 5:19

CHILDREN'S CHILDREN (7) 2Ki 5:27; Ps 17:14; 102:28; 103:17; Isa 14:22; 59:21; Jer 2:9

LITTLE CHILDREN (13) Ge 50:8; Isa 13:16; 28:9; Jer 49:20; 50:45; La 2:11,20; Eze 9:6; 20:31; Mt 18:3; 21:15; Lk 18:15; 2Co 12:14

WOMEN AND CHILDREN (17) Ge 33:5; 34:29; Ex 12:37; Nu 31:9; Dt 2:34; 3:6; Jos 8:35; Jdg 21:10; 1Sa 30:2; 2Ch 28:8; Ezr 10:1; Ne 12:43; Est 3:13; Jer 43:6; Mt 14:21; 15:38; Ac 4:4

Ge 3:16 "You will bear **c** with intense pain and suffering.
6: 4 they gave birth to **c** who became the heroes
9: 7 Now you must have many **c** and repopulate the
10: 1 Many **c** were born to them after the Flood.
11:30 Now Sarai was not able to have any **c**.
15: 3 You have given me no **c**, so one of my servants
16: 1 But Sarai, Abram's wife, had no **c**. So Sarai took
16: 2 and gave her to Abram so she could bear his **c**.
16: 2 "The LORD has kept me from having any **c**,"
16: 2 Perhaps I can have **c** through her." And Abram
18:11 and Sarah was long past the age of having **c**,
19:31 And our father will soon be too old to have **c**.
20:17 women of the household, so they could have **c**.
21:23 you won't deceive me, my **c**, or my grandchildren.
22:24 Nahor had four other **c** from his concubine
25:22 But the two **c** struggled with each other in her
28: 3 God Almighty bless you and give you many **c**.
29:35 the LORD!" And then she stopped having **c**.
30: 1 When Rachel saw that she wasn't having any **c**,
30: 1 "Give me **c**, or I'll die!" she exclaimed to Jacob.
30: 2 he asked. "He is the only one able to give you **c**!"
30: 3 my servant, Bilhah, and she will bear **c** for me."
30:26 Let me take my wives and **c**, for I have earned
31:17 So Jacob put his wives and **c** on camels.
31:43 and these **c** are my grandchildren, and these flocks
32:11 is coming to kill me, along with my wives and **c**.
33: 2 with his two concubines and their **c** at the front,
33: 2 Leah and her **c** next, and Rachel and Joseph last.
33: 5 Then Esau looked at the women and **c** and asked,
33: 5 "These are the **c** God has graciously given to me,"
33: 6 Then the concubines came forward with their **c**
33: 7 Next Leah came with her **c**, and they bowed down.
33:13 my lord, that some of the **c** are very young,
34:29 took all the women and **c** and wealth of every kind.
36: 6 **c**, household servants, cattle, and flocks—
36:15 Esau's **c** and grandchildren became the leaders of
37: 3 Jacob loved Joseph more than any of his other **c**
42:36 Jacob exclaimed, "You have deprived me of my **c**!
42:38 is dead, and he alone is left of his mother's **c**.
44:20 is dead, and he alone is left of his mother's **c**,
45:10 so you can be near me with all your **c**
48: 6 But the **c** born to you in the future will be your
48:11 but now God has let me see your **c**, too."
50: 8 But they left their little **c** and flocks and herds in
50:23 son Ephraim and the **c** of Manasseh's son Makir,
Ex 1: 7 But their descendants had many **c**
2: 6 "He must be one of the Hebrew **c**," she said.
10: 2 You will be able to tell wonderful stories to your **c**
10:24 stay here. You can even take your **c** with you."
12:26 Then your **c** will ask, 'What does all this mean?
12:37 about 600,000 men, plus all the women and **c**.
13: 8 you must explain to your **c** why you are
13:14 "And in the future, your **c** will ask you,
17: 3 us here? We, our **c**, and our livestock will all die!"
20: 5 but I punish the **c** for the sins of their parents to the
21: 4 but his wife and **c** will still belong to his master.
21: 5 'I love my master, my wife, and my **c**.
22:24 and your **c** will become fatherless.
34: 7 but I punish the **c** for the sins of their parents to the
Lev 18:21 "Do not give any of your **c** as a sacrifice to
20: 2 If any among them devote their **c** as burnt offerings
20: 3 and profaned my holy name by giving their **c** to
20: 4 the community ignore this offering of **c** to Molech
22:11 And if his slaves have **c**, they also may share his
22:13 a widow or is divorced and has no **c** to support her,
25:41 and their **c** will no longer be obligated to you,
25:45 You may also purchase the **c** of such resident
25:46 passing them on to your **c** as a permanent
25:54 then they and their **c** must be set free at that time.
26:22 I will release wild animals that will kill your **c**
Nu 5:28 will be unharmed and will still be able to have **c**.
11:12 Are they my **c**? Am I their father? Is that why you
14:18 but he punishes the **c** for the sins of their parents to
14:31 " 'You said your **c** would be taken captive.
14:33 And your **c** will be like shepherds, wandering in
16:27 of their tents with their wives and **c** and little ones.
31: 9 and **c** and seized their cattle and flocks and all their
32:16 our flocks and fortified cities for our wives and **c**.
32:26 Our **c**, wives, flocks, and cattle will stay here in the
Dt 1:39 I will give the land to your innocent **c**. You were
2:34 destroyed everyone—men, women, and **c**.
3: 6 town we conquered—men, women, and **c** alike.
3:19 Your wives, **c**, and numerous livestock, however,
4: 9 And be sure to pass them on to your **c**
4:10 and they will be able to teach my laws to their **c**.'
4:25 when you have **c** and grandchildren and have lived
4:40 you today, all will be well with you and your **c**.
5: 9 but I punish the **c** for the sins of their parents to the
6: 2 and so you and your **c** and grandchildren might
6: 3 and you will have many **c** in the land flowing with
6: 7 Repeat them again and again to your **c**. Talk about
6:20 "In the future your **c** will ask you, 'What is the
7:13 He will give you many **c** and give fertility to your
11: 2 I am not talking now to your **c**, who have never
11:19 Teach them to your **c**. Talk about them when you
11:21 and your **c** may flourish in the land the LORD
12:18 Eat them there with your **c**, your servants,
12:25 then all will go well with you and your **c**,
12:28 so that all will go well with you and your **c**,
20:14 all the women, **c**, livestock, and other plunder.
24:16 must not be put to death for the sins of their **c**,
24:16 nor the **c** for the sins of their parents.
28: 4 You will be blessed with many **c** and productive
28:11 many **c**, numerous livestock, and abundant crops.
28:18 You will be cursed with few **c** and barren fields.
28:54 own brother, his beloved wife, and his surviving **c**.
28:55 he is devouring—the flesh of one of his own **c**—
28:59 both you and your **c** with indescribable plagues.
30: 2 and your **c** begin wholeheartedly to obey all the
30: 9 He will give you many **c** and numerous livestock,
31:12 men, women, **c**, and the foreigners living in your
31:13 so that your **c** who have not known these laws will
32: 5 when they act like that, are they really his **c**?
32:20 they are a twisted generation, / **c** without integrity.
32:46 Pass them on as a command to your **c** so they will
33: 9 loyal to you / than to their parents, relatives, and **c**.
Jos 1:14 Your wives, **c**, and cattle may remain here on the
4: 6 In the future, your **c** will ask, 'What do these
4:21 "In the future, your **c** will ask, 'What do these
8:35 including the women and **c** and the foreigners who
24: 4 while Jacob and his **c** went down into Egypt.
Jdg 11:38 the hills and wept because she would never have **c**.
13: 2 was unable to become pregnant, and they had no **c**.
13: 3 "Even though you have been unable to have **c**,
18:21 on their way again, placing their **c**, livestock,
21:10 to kill everyone there, including women and **c**.
Ru 4: 5 she can have **c** who will carry on her husband's
1Sa 1: 2 Peninnah had **c**, while Hannah did not.
1: 4 of the sacrifice to Peninnah and each of her **c**.
1: 5 even though the LORD had given her no **c**.
1: 8 Why be so sad just because you have no **c**?
1:21 and their **c** went on their annual trip to offer a
2: 5 are now full. / The barren woman now has seven **c**;
2: 5 but the woman with many **c** will have no more.
2:20 "May the LORD give you other **c** to take the
2:33 and grief, and their **c** will die a violent death.
15: 3 men, women, **c**, babies, cattle, sheep, camels,
20:42 and each other's **c** into the LORD's hands
22:19 men and women, **c** and babies, and all the cattle,
30: 2 and **c** and everyone else but without killing
30: 6 were very bitter about losing their wives and **c**,
30:22 Give them their wives and **c**, and tell them to be
2Sa 12: 3 He raised that little lamb, and it grew up with his **c**.
1Ki 20: 3 and so are the best of your wives and **c**!' "
20: 5 that you give me your silver, gold, wives, and **c**.
20: 7 I give him my wives and **c** and silver and gold."
2Ki 5:27 you and your **c** and your children's **c** will suffer
8:12 kill their young men, dash their **c** to the ground,
11: 2 him away from among the rest of the king's **c**,
14: 6 However, he did not kill the **c** of the assassins,
14: 6 must not be put to death for the sins of their **c**,
14: 6 nor the **c** for the sins of their parents.
17:31 burned their own **c** as sacrifices to Adrammelech
1Ch 2:30 were Seled and Appaim. Seled died without **c**,
2:32 named Jether and Jonathan. Jether died without **c**,
6: 3 The **c** of Amram were Aaron, Moses, and Miriam.
8: 8 and Baara, he had **c** in the land of Moab.
16:13 O **c** of Israel, God's servant, / O descendants of
28: 5 my sons—for the LORD has given me many **c**—
28: 8 and leave it to your **c** as a permanent inheritance.
2Ch 20:13 the LORD with their little ones, wives, and **c**,
21:14 your people, your **c**, your wives, and all that is
22:11 him away from among the rest of the king's **c**,
25: 4 However, he did not kill the **c** of the assassins,
25: 4 must not be put to death for the sins of their **c**,
25: 4 nor the **c** for the sins of their parents.
28: 8 and **c** from Judah and took tremendous amounts of
30: 9 and your **c** will be treated mercifully by their
Ezr 8:21 would give us a safe journey and protect us, our **c**,
9:12 and leave this prosperity to our **c** as an inheritance
10: 1 men, women, and **c**—gathered and wept bitterly
10: 3 pagan wives and to send them away with their **c**.
10:44 a pagan wife, and some even had **c** by these wives.
Ne 5: 5 to the same family, and our **c** are just like theirs.
5: 5 Yet we must sell our **c** into slavery just to get
8: 2 and women and all the **c** old enough to understand.
12:43 and **c** also participated in the celebration,
13:24 half their **c** spoke in the language of Ashdod
13:25 **c** intermarry with the pagan people of the land.
Est 3:13 young and old, including women and **c**—must be
5:11 to them about his great wealth and his many **c**.
8:11 who might attack them or their **c** and wives,
Job 1: 5 they lasted several days—Job would purify his **c**.
1: 5 "Perhaps my **c** have sinned and have cursed God
1:19 The house collapsed, and all your **c** are dead.
5: 4 Their **c** are abandoned far from help, with no one
5:25 Your **c** will be many; your descendants will be as
8: 4 Your **c** obviously sinned against him, so their
17: 5 own advantage, so let their **c** faint with hunger.
18:19 They will have neither **c** nor grandchildren,
19:18 Even young **c** despise me. When I stand to speak,
20:10 His **c** will beg from the poor, for he must give back
21: 8 They live to see their **c** grow to maturity, and they
21:11 Their **c** skip about like lambs in a flock of sheep.
21:19 you say, 'at least God will punish their **c**!'
21:19 God should punish the ones who sin, not their **c**!
24: 5 go into the desert to search for food for their **c**.
27:14 If they have a multitude of **c**, their **c** will die in war or starve to death.
29: 5 was still with me, and my **c** were around me.
42:16 living to see four generations of his **c**
Ps 8: 2 You have taught **c** and nursing infants / to give you
17:14 in full. / May their **c** inherit more of the same,
17:14 may the judgment continue to their children's **c**.
21:10 You will wipe their **c** from the face of the earth;
22:30 Our **c** will hear about the wonders of the Lord.
25:13 and their **c** will inherit the Promised Land.
34:11 Come, my **c**, and listen to me, / and I will teach
37:25 nor seen their **c** begging for bread.
37:26 loans to others, / and their **c** are a blessing.
37:28 safe forever, / but the **c** of the wicked will perish.
72: 4 to defend the poor, / to rescue the **c** of the needy,
78: 4 We will not hide these truths from our **c** / but will
78: 5 our ancestors / to teach them to their **c**,
78: 6 even the **c** not yet born—/ that they in turn might teach their **c**.
82: 6 I say, 'You are gods / and **c** of the Most High.
90:16 miracles again; / let our **c** see your glory at work.
102:28 The **c** of your people / will live in security. / Their children's **c**
103:13 The LORD is like a father to his **c**, / tender
103:17 His salvation extends to the children's **c**
105: 6 O **c** of Abraham, God's servant, / O descendants of
109: 9 May his **c** become fatherless, / and may his wife
109:10 May his **c** wander as beggars; / may they be
109:12 be kind to him; / let no one pity his fatherless **c**.
112: 2 Their **c** will be successful everywhere; / an entire
115:14 the LORD richly bless / both you and your **c**.
127: 3 **C** are a gift from the LORD; / they are a reward
127: 4 **C** born to a young man / are like sharp arrows in a
128: 3 within your home. / And look at all those **c**!
145: 4 Let each generation tell its **c** / of your mighty acts.
147:13 bars of your gates / and blessed your **c** within you.
148:12 young men and maidens, / old men and **c**.
Pr 4: 1 My **c**, listen to me. Listen to your father's
8:32 "And so, my **c**, listen to me, for happy are all who
11:21 be punished, but the **c** of the godly will go free.
12: 7 and are gone, but the **c** of the godly stand firm.
13:24 If you refuse to discipline your **c**, it proves you
13:24 if you love your **c**, you will be prompt to discipline
14:26 are secure; he will be a place of refuge for their **c**.
15:20 Sensible **c** bring joy to their father; foolish **c** despise their mother.
17: 6 glory of the aged; parents are the pride of their **c**.
19:18 Discipline your **c** while there is hope. If you don't,
19:26 **C** who mistreat their father or chase away their
20: 7 walk with integrity; blessed are their **c** after them.
20:11 Even **c** are known by the way they act,
22: 6 Teach your **c** to choose the right path, and when
23:13 Don't fail to correct your **c**. They won't die if you
23:24 The father of godly **c** has cause for joy. What a pleasure it is to have wise **c**.
29:17 Discipline your **c**, and they will give you happiness
31:28 Her **c** stand and bless her. Her husband praises her:
Ecc 5:14 the end, there is nothing left to pass on to one's **c**.
6: 3 A man might have a hundred **c** and live to be very
Isa 1: 2 "The **c** I raised and cared for have turned against
1: 4 and corrupt **c** who have turned away from the
3: 4 Then he will appoint **c** to rule over them,
3:12 **C** oppress my people, and women rule over them.
8:18 and the **c** the LORD has given me have names
9:20 In the end they will even eat their own **c**.
10: 2 of justice. Yes, they rob widows and fatherless **c**!
13:16 Their little **c** will be dashed to death right before
13:18 and will show no compassion for the **c**.
14:21 Kill the **c** of this sinner! Do not let them rise
14:22 I will destroy his **c** and his children's **c**,
28: 9 like this? Are we little **c**, barely old enough to talk?
29:23 For when they see their many **c** and material
30: 1 "Destruction is certain for my rebellious **c**,"
43: 5 I will gather you and your **c** from east and west
44: 3 will pour out my Spirit and my blessings on your **c**.
47: 8 to anyone! I will never be a widow or lose my **c**.'
47: 9 widowhood and the loss of your **c**. Yes,
49:18 and see, for all your **c** will come back to you.
49:21 For most of my **c** were killed, and the rest were
49:21 I was left here all alone. Who bore these **c**?
49:25 fight those who fight you, and I will save your **c**.
51:18 Not one of your **c** is left alive to help you or tell
51:20 For your **c** have fainted and lie in the streets,
53:10 for sin, he will have a multitude of **c**, many heirs.
54: 1 For the woman who could bear no **c** now has more
57: 3 come here, you witches' **c**, you offspring of
57: 4 out your tongues? You **c** of sinners and liars!
57: 5 You slaughter your **c** as human sacrifices down in
58:12 Your **c** will rebuild the deserted ruins of your
59:21 They will be on your lips and on the lips of your **c** and your children's **c** forever.
60:14 "The **c** of your tormentors will come and bow
62: 5 Your **c** will care for you with joy, O Jerusalem,
65:23 and their **c** will not be doomed to misfortune.
65:23 by the LORD, and their **c**, too, will be blessed.
66:12 Her **c** will be nursed at her breasts, carried in her
Jer 2: 3 Israel was holy to the LORD, the first of my **c**.
2: 9 even against your children's **c** in the years to come.
2:30 I have punished your **c**, but it did them no good.
3:14 "Return home, you wayward **c**," says the LORD,
3:19 to myself, 'I would love to treat you as my own **c**!'
3:22 "My wayward **c**," says the LORD, "come back
4:22 "They are senseless **c** who have no understanding.
5: 7 pardon you? For even your **c** have turned from me.
6:11 even on **c** playing in the streets, on gatherings of
7:18 Watch how the **c** gather wood and the fathers build
9:21 **C** no longer play in the streets, and young men no
10:20 My **c** have been taken away, and I will never see
13:14 the other, even parents against **c**, says the LORD.
16: 2 "Do not marry or have **c** in this place.
16: 3 For this is what the LORD says about the **c** born
17: 2 Even their **c** go to worship at their sacred altars
18:21 So let their **c** starve! Let the sword pour out their
18:21 Let their wives become widows without any **c**!
19: 4 have filled this place with the blood of innocent **c**.
22:28 Why are he and his **c** to be exiled to distant lands?
22:30 for none of his **c** will ever sit on the throne of
29: 6 Marry, and have **c**. Then find spouses for them,
30:10 and your **c** will return from their exile.
30:20 Their **c** will prosper as they did long ago. I will
31:15 Rachel weeps for her **c**, refusing to be comforted—for her **c** are dead."
31:16 Your **c** will come back to you from the distant land
31:17 "Your **c** will come again to their own land.

32:18 though c suffer for their parents' sins.
38:23 and c will be led out to the Babylonians,
41:16 warriors, women, c, and palace officials.
43:6 were men, women, and c, the king's daughters,
46:27 and your c will return from their exile.
47:3 without a backward glance at their helpless c.
49:10 Its c, its brothers, and its neighbors—all will be
49:20 Even the little c will be dragged off, and their
50:45 Even little c will be dragged off, and their homes
51:22 old people and c, young men and maidens.
La 1:5 Her c have been captured and taken away to distant
1:16 My c have no future, for the enemy has conquered
2:11 Little c and tiny babies are fainting and dying in
2:19 Plead for your c as they faint with hunger in the
2:20 Should mothers eat their little c, those they once
2:22 The enemy has killed all the c I bore and raised."
4:2 See how the precious c of Jerusalem, worth their
4:4 The c cry for bread, but no one has any to give
4:10 Tenderhearted women have cooked their own c
5:13 and the c stagger under heavy loads of wood.
Eze 5:10 Parents will eat their own c, and c will eat their parents.
5:17 animals will attack you, robbing you of your c.
9:6 old and young, girls and women and little c.
16:20 and daughters—the c you had borne to me—
16:21 Must you also slaughter my c by sacrificing them
16:36 because you have slaughtered your c as sacrifices
16:45 For your mother loathed her husband and her c,
16:45 for they despised their husbands and their c.
18:4 people are mine to judge—both parents and c alike.
20:18 "Then I warned their c and told them not to follow
20:21 "But their c, too, rebelled against me.
20:26 and I allowed them to give their firstborn c as
20:31 and give your little c to be burned as sacrifices,
23:10 and killed her and took away her c as their slaves.
23:25 Your c will be taken away as captives,
23:37 and murder by burning their c as sacrifices on their
23:39 On the very day that they murdered their c in front
36:12 You will never again devour their c.
37:25 They and their c and their grandchildren after them
Da 6:24 into the lions' den, along with their wives and c.
Hos 1:2 so some of her c will be born to you from other
1:10 it will be said, 'You are c of the living God.'
2:4 And I will not love her c as I would my own because they are not my c!
4:6 the laws of your God, I will forget to bless your c.
4:10 a big business as prostitutes, they will have no c,
5:7 the honor of the LORD, bearing c that aren't his.
9:11 for your c will die at birth or perish in the womb
9:12 Even if your c do survive to grow up, I will take
9:13 But now Israel will bring out her c to be
9:16 if they give birth, I will slaughter their beloved c."
10:14 Even mothers and c were dashed to death there.
Joel 1:3 Tell your c about it in the years to come.
2:16 the elders, the c, and even the babies.
Mic 1:16 for the c you love will be snatched away,
2:9 and stripped their c of all their God-given rights.
6:7 Should we sacrifice our firstborn c to pay for the
Na 1:14 "You will have no more c to carry on your name.
Zec 10:7 Their c, too, will see it all and be glad; their hearts
10:9 With their c, they will survive and come home
Mal 2:10 Are we not all c of the same Father? Are we not all
2:15 Godly c from your union. So guard yourself;
4:6 preaching will turn the hearts of parents to their c, and the hearts of c to their parents.
Mt 2:18 Rachel weeps for her c, / refusing to be
3:9 God can change these stones here into c of
5:9 for peace, / for they will be called the c of God.
5:45 you will be acting as true c of your Father in
7:9 if your c ask for a loaf of bread, do you give them
7:11 people know how to give good gifts to your c,
10:21 brother to death, fathers will betray their own c,
10:21 and c will rise against their parents and cause them
11:16 These people are like a group of c playing a game
14:21 five loaves, in addition to all the women and c!
15:26 "It isn't right to take food from the c and throw it
15:38 fed that day, in addition to all the women and c.
18:3 you turn from your sins and become as little c,
18:25 so the king ordered that he, his wife, his c,
19:13 Some c were brought to Jesus so he could lay his
19:14 But Jesus said, "Let the c come to me. Don't stop
19:29 or brothers or sisters or father or mother or c
21:15 and heard even the little c in the Temple shouting,
21:16 "Do you hear what these c are saying?"
21:16 'You have taught c and infants to give you
22:24 "Teacher, Moses said, 'If a man dies without c,
22:25 The oldest married and then died without c,
22:26 This brother also died without c, and the wife was
23:37 How often I have wanted to gather your c together
27:25 take responsibility for his death—we and our c!"
Mk 7:27 It isn't right to take food from the c and throw it to
10:13 One day some parents brought their c to Jesus
10:14 He said to them, "Let the c come to me.
10:16 Then he took the c into his arms and placed his
10:24 But Jesus said again, "Dear c, it is very hard to get
10:29 or brothers or sisters or mother or father or c
10:30 houses, brothers, sisters, mothers, c, and property
12:19 leaving a wife without c, his brother should marry
12:20 oldest of them married and then died without c.
12:21 the widow, but soon he too died and left no c.
12:21 the next brother married her and died without c.
12:22 had married her and died, and still there were no c.
13:12 brother to death, fathers will betray their own c,
13:12 and c will rise against their parents and cause them
Lk 1:7 They had no c because Elizabeth was barren,
1:17 He will turn the hearts of the fathers to their c,
1:25 "He has taken away my disgrace of having no c!"
1:55 he promised our ancestors—Abraham and his c—
3:8 God can change these stones here into c of
6:35 and you will truly be acting as c of the Most High,
7:32 They are like a group of c playing a game in the
11:11 if your c ask for a fish, do you give them a snake
11:13 people know how to give good gifts to your c,
13:34 How often I have wanted to gather your c together
14:26 and mother, wife and c, brothers and sisters—
18:15 One day some parents brought their little c to Jesus
18:16 Then Jesus called for the c and said to the disciples, "Let the c come to me.
18:29 given up house or wife or brothers or parents or c,
19:44 will crush you to the ground, and your c with you.
20:28 leaving a wife but no c, his brother should marry
20:29 The oldest married and then died without c.
20:30 married the widow, but he also died. Still no c.
20:31 the seven had married her and died, leaving no c.
20:36 They are c of God raised up to new life.
23:28 for me, but weep for yourselves and for your c.
Jn 1:12 he gave the right to become c of God.
8:39 Jesus replied, "for if you were c of Abraham,
8:44 For you are the c of your father the Devil, and you
8:47 Since you don't, it proves you aren't God's c."
11:52 but for the gathering together of all the c of God
12:36 is still time; then you will become c of the light."
13:33 Dear c, how brief are these moments before I must
Ac 2:39 This promise is to you and to your c, and even to
3:25 You are the c of those prophets, and you are
4:4 five thousand men, not counting women and c.
7:5 and his descendants—though he had no c yet.
21:5 the entire congregation, including wives and c,
21:21 say that you teach people not to circumcise their c
Ro 2:20 instruct the ignorant and teach c the ways of God.
4:19 that Sarah, his wife, had never been able to have c.
8:14 For all who are led by the Spirit of God are c of
8:15 You should behave instead like God's very own c,
8:16 deep in our hearts and tells us that we are God's c.
8:17 And since we are his c, we will share his
8:19 day when God will reveal who his c really are.
8:21 it will join God's c in glorious freedom from death
8:23 day when God will give us our full rights as his c,
9:4 the people of Israel, chosen to be God's special c.
9:7 of Abraham doesn't make them truly Abraham's c.
9:7 be counted," though Abraham had other c, too.
9:8 physical descendants are not necessarily c of God.
9:8 It is the c of the promise who are considered to be Abraham's c.
9:26 he will say, / 'You are c of the living God.' "
11:16 patriarchs were holy, their c will also be holy.
11:17 the blessing God has promised Abraham and his c,
12:13 When God's c are in need, be the one to help them
16:8 whom I love as one of the Lord's own c,
1Co 4:14 to shame you, but to warn you as my beloved c.
7:14 your c would not have a godly influence,
7:15 with them, for God wants his c to live in peace.)
2Co 6:13 I am talking now as I would to my own c.
12:14 little c don't pay for their parents' food.
12:14 other way around; parents supply food for their c.
Gal 3:7 The real c of Abraham, then, are all those who put
3:16 notice that it doesn't say the promise was to his c,
3:26 So you are all c of God through faith in Christ
3:29 belong to Christ, you are the true c of Abraham.
4:1 father dies and leaves great wealth for his young c,
4:1 those c are not much better off than slaves until
4:5 so that he could adopt us as his very own c.
4:6 And because you Gentiles have become his c,
4:19 But oh, my dear c! I feel as if I am going through
4:25 in Arabia, because she and her c live in slavery.
4:27 For the woman who could bear no c / now has
4:28 dear brothers and sisters, are c of the promise,
4:31 dear friends, we are not c of the slave woman,
4:31 We are c of the free woman, acceptable to God
Eph 3:6 with the Jews in all the riches inherited by God's c.
4:14 Then we will no longer be like c, forever changing
5:1 in everything you do, because you are his dear c.
6:1 C, obey your parents because you belong to the
6:4 Don't make your c angry by the way you treat
Php 2:15 innocent lives as c of God in a dark world full of
Col 3:20 You c must always obey your parents, for this is
3:21 Fathers, don't aggravate your c. If you do,
1Th 2:7 you as a mother feeding and caring for her own c.
2:11 we treated each of you as a father treats his own c.
5:5 For you are all c of the light and of the day;
1Ti 3:4 own family well, with c who respect and obey him.
3:12 and he must manage his c and household well.
5:4 But if she has c or grandchildren, their first
5:10 Has she brought up her c well? Has she been kind
5:14 have c, and take care of their own homes.
Tit 1:6 and his c must be believers who are not wild
2:4 younger women to love their husbands and their c,
Heb 2:10 was made—should bring his many c into glory.
2:13 I am—together with the c God has given me."
2:14 Because God's c are human beings—made of flesh
11:12 Abraham, who was too old to have any c—
12:5 the encouraging words God spoke to you, his c?
12:6 and he punishes those he accepts as his c."
12:7 remember that God is treating you as his own c.
12:8 God doesn't discipline you as he does all of his c,
12:8 are illegitimate and are not really his c after all.
12:23 have come to the assembly of God's firstborn c,
Jas 1:18 In his goodness he chose to make us his own c by
1Pe 1:4 God has reserved a priceless inheritance for his c.
1:14 Obey God because you are his c. Don't slip back
1:15 just as God—who chose you to be his c—is holy.
4:17 and it must begin first among God's own c.
1Jn 2:1 My dear c, I am writing this to you so that you will
2:12 I am writing to you, my dear c, because your sins
2:14 I have written to you, c, because you have known
2:18 Dear c, the last hour is here. You have heard that
2:28 And now, dear c, continue to live in fellowship
2:29 also know that all who do what is right are his c.
3:1 for he allows us to be called his c, and we really
3:1 so they don't understand that we are his c.
3:2 Yes, dear friends, we are already God's c, and we
3:7 Dear c, don't let anyone deceive you about this:
3:10 So now we can tell who are c of God and who are c of the Devil.
3:18 Dear c, let us stop just saying we love each other;
4:4 But you belong to God, my dear c. You have
5:1 And everyone who loves the Father loves his c,
5:2 We know we love God's c if we love God
5:19 We know that we are c of God and that the world
5:21 Dear c, keep away from anything that might take
2Jn 1:1 It is written to the chosen lady and to her c,
1:4 How happy I was to meet some of your c and find
1:13 Greetings from the c of your sister, chosen by God.
3Jn 1:4 I could have no greater joy than to hear that my c
1:11 those who do good prove that they are God's c,
Rev 2:23 I will strike her c dead. And all the churches will
12:17 and he declared war against the rest of her c—
21:7 and I will be their God, and they will be my c.

CHILDREN'S (13) [CHILD]

CHILDREN'S CHILDREN (7) 2Ki 5:27; Ps 17:14; 102:28; 103:17; Isa 14:22; 59:21; Jer 2:9

Ge 31:16 our father are legally ours and our c to begin with.
2Ki 5:27 and your c children will suffer from Naaman's
Ps 17:14 and may the judgment continue to their c children.
102:28 will live in security. / Their c children
103:17 fear him. / His salvation extends to the c children
Isa 14:22 I will destroy his children and his c children,
59:21 lips of your children and your c children forever.
Jer 2:9 even against your c children in the years to come.
5:17 They will eat your harvests and your c bread,
31:29 sour grapes, but their c mouths pucker at the taste.'
La 4:3 They ignore their c cries, like the ostriches of the
Eze 18:2 but their c mouths pucker at the taste'?
Mk 7:28 table are given some crumbs from the c plates."

CHIMED (1)

Ac 24:9 Then the other Jews c in, declaring that

CHIMNEY (1)

Hos 13:3 like chaff blown by the wind, like smoke from a c.

CHIN (2)

Lev 13:29 or woman, has an open sore on the head or c,
13:30 is a contagious skin disease of the head or c.

CHIP (2)

Ex 20:25 Do not c or shape the stones with a tool, for that
Hos 10:7 and its king will disappear like a c of wood on an

CHIRPING (1)

Ecc 12:4 Even the c of birds will wake you up. But you

CHISEL (2) [CHISELED]

Job 19:24 carved with an iron c and filled with lead,
Jer 17:1 or with an iron c on the corners of their altars.

CHISELED (1) [CHISEL]

Jer 2:27 To an idol c out of stone they say, 'You are my

CHISLEU [KJV] See AUTUMN, DECEMBER

CHITTIM [KJV] See KITTIM

CHIUN [KJV] See KAIWAN

CHLOE'S (1)

1Co 1:11 For some members of C household have told me

CHOICE (78) [CHOICES, CHOICEST, CHOOSE, CHOOSES, CHOOSING, CHOSE, CHOSEN]

Ge 4:4 while Abel brought several c lambs from the best
13:9 Take your c of any section of the land you want,
49:11 to a grapevine, / the colt of his donkey to a c vine.
Ex 23:19 bring me a c sample of the first day's harvest.
30:23 "Collect c spices—12-1/2 pounds of pure myrrh,
Lev 2:1 to the LORD, the offering must consist of c flour.
2:4 it must be made of c flour mixed with olive oil
2:5 it must be made of c flour and olive oil, and it must
2:7 it also must be made of c flour and olive oil.
5:11 they must bring two quarts of c flour for their sin
6:15 The priest on duty will take a handful of the c flour
6:20 LORD a grain offering of two quarts of c flour,
14:10 along with five quarts of c flour mixed with olive
14:21 along with two quarts of c flour mixed with olive
23:13 of three quarts of c flour mixed with olive oil.
23:17 These loaves must be baked from three quarts of c
24:5 "You must bake twelve loaves of bread from c
Nu 6:15 cakes of c flour mixed with olive oil and wafers
7:13 These were both filled with grain offerings of c
7:19 These were both filled with grain offerings of c
7:25 These were both filled with grain offerings of c
7:31 These were both filled with grain offerings of c

7:37 These were both filled with grain offerings of **c**
7:43 These were both filled with grain offerings of **c**
7:49 These were both filled with grain offerings of **c**
7:55 These were both filled with grain offerings of **c**
7:61 These were both filled with grain offerings of **c**
7:67 These were both filled with grain offerings of **c**
7:73 These were both filled with grain offerings of **c**
7:79 These were both filled with grain offerings of **c**
8:8 and a grain offering of **c** flour mixed with olive oil,
15:4 quarts of **c** flour mixed with one quart of olive oil.
15:6 give three quarts of **c** flour mixed with two and a
15:9 quarts of **c** flour mixed with two quarts of olive oil,
28:5 quarts of **c** flour mixed with one quart of olive oil.
28:9 of three quarts of **c** flour mixed with olive oil,
28:12 These will be accompanied by grain offerings of **c**
28:20 These will be accompanied by grain offerings of **c**
28:28 These will be accompanied by grain offerings of **c**
29:3 These must be accompanied by grain offerings of **c**
29:9 grain offerings of **c** flour mixed with olive oil—
29:9 five quarts of **c** flour with the bull, three quarts of **c** flour with the ram,
29:10 and two quarts of **c** flour with each of the seven
29:14 a grain offering of **c** flour mixed with olive oil—
Dt 11:26 "Today I am giving you the **c** between a blessing
30:15 Today I am giving you a **c** between prosperity
30:19 "Today I have given you the **c** between life
30:19 call on heaven and earth to witness the **c** you make.
32:14 He gave them **c** rams and goats from Bashan,
33:13 with the **c** gift of rain from the heavens, / and water
Jdg 4:9 But since you have made this **c**, you will receive
1Ki 4:22 for Solomon's palace were 150 bushels of **c** flour
4:23 as well as deer, gazelles, roebucks, and **c** fowl.
1Ch 9:29 and the supplies such as **c** flour, wine, olive oil,
23:29 the **c** flour for the grain offerings, the wafers made
Ezr 1:6 They gave them many **c** gifts in addition to all the
Ne 8:10 "Go and celebrate with a feast of **c** foods
Est 2:13 she was given her **c** of whatever clothing
Job 34:33 The **c** is yours, not mine. Go ahead, share your
Ps 80:17 Strengthen the man you love, / the son of your **c**.
119:113 about you, / but my **c** is clear—I love your law.
Isa 5:2 cleared its stones, / and planted it with **c** vines.
25:6 good food, with clear, well-aged wine and **c** beef.
55:1 Come, take your **c** of wine or milk—it's all free!
Jer 21:8 the LORD says: Take your **c** of life or death!
49:19 from its land, and I will appoint the leader of my **c**.
50:44 from its land, and I will appoint the leader of my **c**.
Eze 20:40 me all your offerings and **c** gifts and sacrifices.
24:4 Fill it with **c** meat—the rump and the shoulder
27:24 They brought **c** fabrics to trade—blue cloth,
Hos 3:1 have turned to other gods, offering them **c** gifts."
Am 5:22 I won't even notice all your **c** peace offerings.
6:4 eating the meat of tender lambs and **c** calves.
Mt 13:45 is like a pearl merchant on the lookout for **c** pearls.
22:4 has been prepared, and **c** meats have been cooked.
1Co 9:17 and given me this sacred trust, and I have no **c**.
Jas 1:18 out of all creation, became his **c** possession.

CHOICES (4) [CHOICE]

2Sa 24:12 is what the LORD says: I will give you three **c**.
1Ch 21:10 is what the LORD says: I will give you three **c**.
21:11 "These are the **c** the LORD has given you.
Gal 5:17 and your **c** are never free from this conflict.

CHOICEST (4) [CHOICE]

Dt 32:14 and goats from Bashan, / together with the **c** wheat.
2Ki 19:23 cut down its tallest cedars / and its **c** cypress trees.
SS 4:16 Let him come into his garden and eat its **c** fruits."
Isa 37:24 cut down its tallest cedars / and its **c** cypress trees.

CHOIR (62) [CHOIRS]

1Ch 15:16 leaders to appoint a **c** of Levites who were singers
15:22 was chosen as the **c** leader because of his skill.
Ne 12:38 The second **c** went northward around the other way
12:42 and clearly under the direction of Jezrahiah the **c**
12:46 The custom of having **c** directors to lead the choirs
Ps 4:T For the **c** director: A psalm of David, to be
5:T For the **c** director: A psalm of David, to be
6:T For the **c** director: A psalm of David, to be
8:T For the **c** director: A psalm of David, to be
9:T For the **c** director: A psalm of David, to be sung to
11:T For the **c** director: A psalm of David.
12:T For the **c** director: A psalm of David, to be
13:T For the **c** director: A psalm of David.
14:T For the **c** director: A psalm of David.
18:T For the **c** director: A psalm of David, the servant of
19:T For the **c** director: A psalm of David.
20:T For the **c** director: A psalm of David.
21:T For the **c** director: A psalm of David.
22:T For the **c** director: A psalm of David, to be sung to
31:T For the **c** director: A psalm of David.
36:T For the **c** director: A psalm of David, the servant of
39:T For Jeduthun, the **c** director: A psalm of David.
40:T For the **c** director: A psalm of David.
41:T For the **c** director: A psalm of David.
42:T For the **c** director: A psalm of the descendants of
44:T For the **c** director: A psalm of the descendants of
45:T For the **c** director: A psalm of the descendants of
46:T For the **c** director: A psalm of the descendants of
47:T For the **c** director: A psalm of the descendants of
49:T For the **c** director: A psalm of the descendants of
51:T For the **c** director: A psalm of David,
52:T For the **c** director: A psalm of David,
53:T For the **c** director: A meditation of David.
54:T For the **c** director: A meditation of David,
55:T For the **c** director: A psalm of David, to be
56:T For the **c** director: A psalm of David,
57:T For the **c** director: A psalm of David,
58:T For the **c** director: A psalm of David, to be sung to
59:T For the **c** director: A psalm of David,
60:T For the **c** director: A psalm of David useful for
61:T For the **c** director: A psalm of David, to be
62:T For Jeduthun, the **c** director: A psalm of David.
64:T For the **c** director: A psalm of David.
65:T For the **c** director: A psalm of David. A song.
66:T For the **c** director: A psalm. A song.
67:T For the **c** director: A psalm, to be accompanied by
68:T For the **c** director: A psalm of David. A song.
69:T For the **c** director: A psalm of David, to be sung to
70:T For the **c** director: A psalm of David, to bring us to
75:T For the **c** director: A psalm of Asaph, to be sung to
76:T For the **c** director: A psalm of Asaph, to be
77:T For Jeduthun, the **c** director: A psalm of Asaph.
80:T For the **c** director: A psalm of Asaph, to be sung to
81:T For the **c** director: A psalm of Asaph, to be
84:T For the **c** director: A psalm of the descendants of
85:T For the **c** director: A psalm of the descendants of
88:T For the **c** director: A psalm of the descendants of
109:T For the **c** director: A psalm of David.
139:T For the **c** director: A psalm of David.
140:T For the **c** director: A psalm of David.
Hab 3:19 me safely over the mountains. (For the **c** director:
Rev 14:3 This great **c** sang a wonderful new song in front of

CHOIRS (5) [CHOIR]

2Ch 35:25 and to this day **c** still sing these sad songs about his
Ne 12:31 the wall and organized two large **c** to give thanks.
12:31 One of the **c** proceeded southward along the top of
12:40 The two **c** that were giving thanks then proceeded
12:46 The custom of having choir directors to lead the **c**

CHOKE (1) [CHOKED]

Eze 26:10 The hooves of his cavalry will **c** the city with dust,

CHOKED (3) [CHOKE]

Mt 13:7 thorns that shot up and **c** out the tender blades.
Mk 4:7 and **c** out the tender blades so that it produced no
Lk 8:7 thorns that shot up and **c** out the tender blades.

CHOLER [KJV] See ANGER

CHOOSE (73) [CHOICE]

Ge 20:15 and **c** a place where you would like to live,"
23:6 It will be a privilege to have you **c** the finest of our
47:6 **c** any place you like for them to live. Give them
Ex 10:26 We will have to **c** our sacrifices for the LORD
12:3 tenth day of this month each family must **c** a lamb
33:19 I will show kindness to anyone I **c**, and I will show mercy to anyone I **c**.
Lev 1:14 **c** either a turtledove or a young pigeon.
Nu 14:4 "Let's **c** a leader and go back to Egypt!"
17:5 will sprout on the staff belonging to the man I **c**.
31:3 "**C** some men to fight the LORD's war of
Dt 1:13 **C** some men from each tribe who have wisdom,
7:7 "The LORD did not **c** you and lavish his love on
12:5 **c** from among all the tribes for his name to be
12:11 to the place the LORD your God will **c** for his
12:14 so only at the place the LORD will **c** within one
12:18 of the LORD your God at the place he will **c**.
16:6 your God will **c** for his name to be honored.
17:8 cases to the place the LORD your God will **c**,
23:16 Let them live among you in whatever town they **c**,
30:19 Oh, that you would **c** life, that you and your
30:20 **C** to love the LORD your God and to obey him
Jos 3:12 Now **c** twelve men, one from each tribe.
4:2 "Now **c** twelve men, one from each tribe.
9:27 wherever the LORD would **c** to build it.
24:15 the LORD, then **c** today whom you will serve.
1Sa 14:42 Saul said, "Now **c** between me and Jonathan."
17:8 **C** someone to fight for you, and I will represent the
2Sa 17:1 "Let me **c** twelve thousand men to start out after
24:12 **C** one of these punishments, and I will do it.' "
24:13 "Will you **c** three years of famine throughout the
1Ki 5:9 float them along the coast to whatever place you **c**.
13:33 He continued to **c** priests from the rank and file of
18:23 The prophets of Baal may **c** whichever one they
18:25 **C** one of the bulls and prepare it and call on the
2Ki 18:32 a land of plenty. **C** life instead of death!
1Ch 21:10 **C** one of these punishments, and I will do it.' "
21:12 You may **c** three years of famine, three months of
Est 1:19 and that you **c** another queen more worthy than
Ps 25:12 He will show them the path they should **c**.
38:14 I **c** to hear nothing, / and I make no reply.
65:4 What joy for those you **c** to bring near, / those who
78:67 he did not **c** the tribe of Ephraim.
Pr 8:10 "**C** my instruction rather than silver,
22:1 **C** a good reputation over great riches, for being
22:6 Teach your children to **c** the right path, and when
Ecc 9:3 Instead, they **c** their own mad course, for they have
SS 6:9 But I would still **c** my dove, my perfect one,
Isa 7:14 All right then, the Lord himself will **c** the sign.
7:15 he will know enough to **c** what is right and reject
56:4 who **c** to do what pleases me and commit their
65:9 Those I **c** will inherit it and serve me there.
66:3 But those who **c** their own ways, delighting in their
Jer 27:5 I can give these things of mine to anyone I **c**.
27:13 Why should you **c** war, famine, and disease,
38:20 "You won't be handed over to them if you **c** to
Eze 33:2 a country, the people of that land **c** a watchman.
44:22 They may **c** their wives only from among the
Zec 1:17 comfort Zion and **c** Jerusalem as his own.' "
2:12 and he will once again **c** Jerusalem to be his own
Mt 7:13 and its gate is wide for the many who **c** the easy
19:12 and some **c** not to marry for the sake of the
Jn 15:16 You didn't **c** me. I chose you. I appointed you to
Ac 1:21 "So now we must **c** someone else to take Judas's
Ro 6:16 Don't you realize that whatever you **c** to obey
6:16 You can **c** sin, which leads to death, or you can **c** to obey God and receive his approval.
6:19 Now you must **c** to be slaves of righteousness
9:15 said to Moses, / "I will show mercy to anyone I **c**,
9:15 and I will show compassion to anyone I **c**."
1Co 4:21 Which do you **c**? Should I come with punishment
16:3 messengers you **c** to deliver your gift to Jerusalem.
Gal 1:15 For it pleased God in his kindness to **c** me and call

CHOOSES (30) [CHOICE]

Lev 16:2 Holy Place behind the inner curtain whenever he **c**;
Nu 16:7 Then we will see whom the LORD **c** as his holy
Dt 12:21 **c** for his name to be honored is a long way from
12:26 to fulfill a vow to the place the LORD **c** to dwell.
14:23 Bring this tithe to the place the LORD your God **c**
14:24 Now the place the LORD your God **c** for his
14:25 the money to the place the LORD your God **c**.
15:20 the LORD your God each year at the place he **c**.
16:2 God at the place he **c** for his name to be honored.
16:7 and eat it in the place the LORD your God **c**.
16:11 God at the place he **c** for his name to be honored.
16:15 to honor the LORD your God at the place he **c**,
16:16 God at the place he **c** on each of these occasions,
17:10 The decision they make at the place the LORD **c**
17:15 you select as king the man the LORD your God **c**.
18:6 wherever he is living, to the place the LORD **c**.
26:2 and bring it to the place the LORD your God **c** for
31:11 before the LORD your God at the place he **c**.
Isa 41:24 Anyone who **c** you becomes filthy, just like you!
49:7 faithful LORD, the Holy One of Israel, **c** you."
Eze 46:5 and whatever amount of flour he **c** to go with each
46:11 and as much flour as the prince **c** to give with each
Da 4:17 of the world and gives them to anyone he **c**—
4:25 of the world and gives them to anyone he **c**.
4:32 of the world and gives them to anyone he **c**."
Mt 11:27 and those to whom the Son **c** to reveal him."
Lk 10:22 and those to whom the Son **c** to reveal him."
Ro 9:11 (This message proves that God **c** according to his
9:16 hard for it. God will show mercy to anyone he **c**.
9:18 and he **c** to make some people refuse to listen.

CHOOSING (2) [CHOICE]

Ro 9:16 We can't get it by **c** it or working hard for it.
11:5 saved as a result of God's kindness in **c** them.

CHOP (7) [CHOPPED, CHOPPING, CHOPS, WOODCHOPPERS]

Dt 29:11 and the foreigners living among you who **c** your
Jos 9:21 But we will make them **c** the wood and carry the
9:23 From now on you will **c** wood and carry water for
2Sa 23:7 One must be armed to **c** them down; / they will be
Ecc 10:9 When you **c** wood, there is danger with each stroke
Isa 10:33 LORD Almighty, will **c** down the mighty tree!
Mic 3:3 You **c** them up like meat for the cooking pot.

CHOPPED (7) [CHOP]

Ge 22:3 Then he **c** wood to build a fire for a burnt offering
Jdg 9:48 He took an ax and **c** some branches from a tree,
Ps 74:5 They **c** down the entrance / like woodcutters in a
80:16 For we are **c** up and burned by our enemies.
Mt 3:10 that does not produce good fruit will be **c** down
7:19 So every tree that does not produce good fruit is **c**
Lk 3:9 that does not produce good fruit will be **c** down

CHOPPING (1) [CHOP]

2Ki 6:5 But as one of them was **c**, his ax head fell into the

CHOPS (1) [CHOP]

Isa 5:14 The grave is licking its **c** in anticipation of

CHORASHAN [KJV] See BOR-ASHAN

CHORDS (1)

Isa 24:8 The melodious **c** of the harp will be silent.

CHORUS (5)

Nu 14:2 Their voices rose in a great **c** of complaint against
Isa 6:3 In a great **c** they sang, "Holy, holy, holy is the
42:11 Join in the **c**, you desert towns; / let the villages of
Hos 2:22 And the whole grand **c** will sing together,
Rev 5:12 And they sang in a mighty **c**: / "The Lamb is

CHOSE (78) [CHOICE]

Ge 2:19 would call them, and Adam **c** a name for each one.
13:11 Lot **c** that land for himself—the Jordan Valley to
18:7 and **c** a fat calf and told a servant to hurry
42:24 He then **c** Simeon from among them and had him
Ex 18:25 He **c** capable men from all over Israel and made
Nu 31:5 So they **c** one thousand men from each tribe of
Dt 1:23 so I **c** twelve scouts, one from each of your tribes.
4:37 he **c** to bless their descendants and personally
10:15 Yet the LORD **c** your ancestors as the objects of
10:15 And he **c** you, their descendants, above every other
18:5 For the LORD your God **c** the tribe of Levi out of
Jos 8:3 Joshua **c** thirty thousand fighting men and sent
19:50 He **c** Timnath-serah in the hill country of Ephraim.

Jdg 5: 8 When Israel **c** new gods, / war erupted at the city
18: 2 So the men of Dan **c** five warriors from among
1Sa 2:28 I **c** your ancestor Aaron from among all his
24: 2 So Saul **c** three thousand special troops from
2Sa 6:21 who **c** me above your father and his family!
7: 8 I **c** you to lead my people Israel when you were
10: 9 on two fronts, he **c** the best troops in his army.
1Ki 11:34 the one whom I **c** and who obeyed my commands
16:16 they **c** Omri, commander of the army, as their new
2Ki 17:21 they **c** Jeroboam son of Nebat as their king.
1Ch 17: 7 I **c** you to lead my people Israel when you were
17:22 You **c** Israel to be your people forever, and you,
19:10 on two fronts, he **c** the best troops in his army.
28: 4 the families of Judah, he **c** my father's family.
28: 5 he **c** Solomon to succeed me on the throne of his
2Ch 24: 3 Jehoiada **c** two wives for Joash, and he had sons
Ne 9: 7 who **c** Abram and brought him from Ur of the
Ps 47: 4 He **c** the Promised Land as our inheritance,
74: 2 Remember that we are the people you **c** in ancient
78:68 He **c** instead the tribe of Judah, / Mount Zion,
78:70 He **c** his servant David, / calling him from the
89:38 Why are you so angry with the one you **c** as king?
132:10 do not reject the king you **c** for your people.
Pr 1:29 hated knowledge and **c** not to fear the LORD.
Isa 65:12 very eyes—and **c** to do what you know I despise."
66: 4 very eyes—and **c** to do what they know I despise."
Jer 2:21 When I planted you, I **c** a vine of the purest stock
33:24 'The LORD **c** Judah and Israel and
Eze 1:12 They went in whatever direction the spirit **c**,
20: 5 When I **c** Israel and revealed myself to her in
Da 6: 2 The king also **c** Daniel and two others as
Am 2:11 I **c** some of your sons to be prophets and others to
3: 2 among all the families on the earth, I **c** you alone.
Mk 3:16 These are the names of the twelve he **c**:
Lk 6:13 of his disciples and **c** twelve of them to be apostles.
10: 1 The Lord now **c** seventy-two other disciples
Jn 6:70 Then Jesus said, "I **c** the twelve of you, but one is
13:18 to all of you; I know so well each one of you I **c**.
15:16 I **c** you. I appointed you to go and produce fruit
15:19 I **c** you to come out of the world, and so it hates
Ac 6: 5 pleased the whole group, and they **c** the following:
13:17 "The God of this nation of Israel **c** our ancestors
15: 7 you all know that God **c** me from among you some
15:22 and the whole church in Jerusalem **c** delegates,
15:40 Paul **c** Silas, and the believers sent them off,
Ro 1:25 truth about God, they deliberately **c** to believe lies.
8:29 in advance, and he **c** them to become like his Son,
11: 2 own people, whom he **c** from the very beginning.
1Co 1:27 God deliberately **c** things the world considers
1:27 And he **c** those who are powerless to shame those
1:28 God **c** things despised by the world, things counted
Eph 1: 4 God loved us and **c** us in Christ to be holy
1:11 from God, for he **c** us from the beginning,
Col 3:12 Since God **c** you to be the holy people whom he
1Th 1: 4 and sisters, and that he **c** you to be his own people.
2Th 2:13 We are thankful that God **c** you to be among the
2Ti 1: 9 It is God who saved us and **c** us to live a holy life.
1:11 And God **c** me to be a preacher, an apostle, and a
Heb 2: 4 gifts of the Holy Spirit whenever he **c** to do so.
11:25 He **c** to share the oppression of God's people
Jas 1:18 In his goodness he **c** to make us his own children
1Pe 1: 2 God the Father **c** you long ago, and the Spirit has
1:15 as God—who **c** you to be his children—is holy.
1:20 God **c** him for this purpose long before the world
2: 4 the people, but he is precious to God who **c** him.

CHOSEN (171) [CHOICE]

Ex 31: 2 "Look, I have **c** Bezalel son of Uri, grandson of
35:30 "The LORD has **c** Bezalel son of Uri,
Lev 16: 9 The goat **c** to be sacrificed to the LORD will be
16:10 The goat **c** to be the scapegoat will be presented to
16:21 into the wilderness, led by a man **c** for this task.
16:26 "The man **c** to send the goat out into the
Nu 1: 5 and the names of the leaders **c** for the task:
1:16 own families, were **c** from among all the people.
1:17 Now Moses and Aaron and the **c** leaders
3:12 "I have **c** the Levites from among the Israelites as
16: 5 The LORD will allow those who are **c** to enter his
16: 9 **c** you from among all the people of Israel to be
18: 6 I myself have **c** your fellow Levites from among
Dt 7: 6 the LORD your God has **c** you to be his own
14: 2 and he has **c** you to be his own special treasure
21: 5 for the LORD your God has **c** them to minister
Jos 24:22 "You have **c** to serve the LORD." "Yes,"
Jdg 9:18 And you have **c** his slave woman's son,
10:14 Go and cry out to the gods you have **c**! Let them
20:10 One tenth of the men from each tribe will be **c** to
1Sa 10:20 the LORD, and the tribe of Benjamin was **c**.
10:21 the LORD, and the family of the Matrites was **c**.
10:21 And finally Saul son of Kish was **c** from among
10:24 "This is the man the LORD has **c** as your king.
12:13 All right, here is the king you have **c**. Look him
12:22 The LORD will not abandon his **c** people, for that
13: 2 He took two thousand of the **c** men with him to
13:14 The LORD has already **c** him to be king over his
14:41 And Jonathan and Saul were **c** as the guilty ones,
16: 8 "This is not the one the LORD has **c**."
16: 9 "Neither is this the one the LORD has **c**."
16:10 to Jesse, "The LORD has not **c** any of these."
24: 6 anointed one, for the LORD himself has **c** him."
2Sa 2:15 So twelve men were **c** from each side to fight
3:18 'I have **c** David to save my people from the
16:18 because I work for the man who is **c** by the
23: 5 "It is my family God has **c**! / Yes, he has made an
1Ki 1:48 who today has **c** someone to sit on my throne
3: 8 And here I am among your own **c** people, a nation
8:16 I have never **c** a city among the tribes of Israel as
8:16 But now I have **c** David to be king over my
8:44 pray to the LORD toward this city that you have **c**
8:48 gave to their ancestors, toward this city you have **c**,
11:13 and for the sake of Jerusalem, my **c** city."
11:32 which I have **c** out of all the tribes of Israel.
11:36 the city I have **c** to be the place for my name.
14:21 the city the LORD had **c** from among all the
2Ki 21: 7 the city I have **c** from among all the other tribes of
23:27 my presence and reject my **c** city of Jerusalem
1Ch 15: 2 The LORD has **c** them to carry the Ark of the
15:18 The following men were **c** as their assistants:
15:19 and Ethan were **c** to sound the bronze cymbals.
15:20 Maaseiah, and Benaiah were **c** to play the lyres.
15:21 Jeiel, and Azaziah were **c** to play the harps.
15:22 was **c** as the choir leader because of his skill.
15:23 Berekiah and Elkanah were **c** to guard the Ark.
15:24 were **c** to blow the trumpets as they marched in
15:24 Obed-edom and Jehiah were **c** to guard the Ark.
16:13 O descendants of Jacob, God's **c** one.
16:22 "Do not touch these people I have **c**, / and do not
16:41 and the others **c** by name to give thanks to the
28: 4 has **c** me from among all my father's family to be
28: 4 For he has **c** the tribe of Judah to rule, and from
28: 6 and its courtyards, for I have **c** him as my son,
28:10 The LORD has **c** you to build a Temple as his
29: 1 whom God has **c** to be the next king of Israel,
2Ch 6: 5 I have never **c** a city among the tribes of Israel as
6: 5 Nor have I **c** a king to lead my people Israel.
6: 6 But now I have **c** Jerusalem as that city, and David
6:34 if they pray to you toward this city that you have **c**
6:38 gave to their ancestors, toward this city you have **c**,
7:12 and have **c** this Temple as the place for making
7:16 for I have **c** this Temple and set it apart to be my
12:13 the city the LORD had **c** from among all the
29:11 The LORD has **c** you to stand in his presence,
33: 7 the city I have **c** from among all the other tribes of
Ezr 6:12 May the God who has **c** the city of Jerusalem as
Ne 1: 9 I will bring you back to the place I have **c** for my
11: 1 and Benjamin were **c** by sacred lots to live there,
Est 2: 9 He also assigned her seven maids specially **c** from
8:12 The day **c** for this event throughout all the
Job 31: 2 What has God above **c** for us? What is our
Ps 2: 6 "I have placed my **c** king on the throne
33:12 the LORD, / whose people he has **c** for his own.
68:16 at Mount Zion, where God has **c** to live,
89: 3 a solemn agreement with David, my **c** servant.
105: 6 O descendants of Jacob, God's **c** one.
105:15 "Do not touch these people I have **c**, / and do not
105:26 his servant, / along with Aaron, whom he had **c**.
105:43 out of Egypt with joy, / his **c** ones with rejoicing.
106: 5 Let me share in the prosperity of your **c** ones.
106:23 But Moses, his **c** one, stepped between the LORD
119:30 I have **c** to be faithful; / I have determined to live
119:173 for I have **c** to follow your commandments.
132:13 For the LORD has **c** Jerusalem; / he has desired it
135: 4 For the LORD has **c** Jacob for himself, / Israel for
Pr 1:31 experience the full terror of the path they have **c**.
Isa 41: 8 as for you, Israel my servant, Jacob my **c** one,
41: 9 For I have **c** you and will not throw you away.
42: 1 He is my **c** one, and I am pleased with him.
42:19 Who is as blind as my **c** people, the servant of the
43:10 You have been **c** to know me, believe in me,
43:20 in the desert, so that my **c** people can be refreshed.
44: 1 listen to me, Jacob my servant, Israel my **c** one.
44: 2 do not be afraid. O Israel, my **c** one, do not fear.
45: 4 for the sake of Jacob my servant, Israel my **c** one.
47: 6 For I was angry with my **c** people and began their
48:12 "Listen to me, O family of Jacob, Israel my **c** one!
48:14 and listen: 'The LORD has **c** Cyrus as his ally.
49: 7 will bow low because the LORD has **c** you.
Jer 5:23 turned against me and have **c** to practice idolatry.
12: 8 My **c** people have roared at me like a lion of the
12: 9 My **c** people have become as disgusting to me as a
44:10 No one has **c** to follow my law and the decrees I
50:11 and are glad, you plunderers of my **c** people.
Da 1: 6 and Azariah were four of the young men **c**,
Hab 3:13 You went out to rescue your **c** people, to save your
Zep 1: 7 for a great slaughter and has **c** their executioners.
Hag 2:23 says the LORD, for I have specially **c** you.
Zec 3: 2 Yes, the LORD, who has **c** Jerusalem,
Mt 12:18 "Look at my Servant, / whom I have **c**. / He is my
20:23 has prepared those places for the ones he has **c**."
22:14 For many are called, but few are **c**."
24:22 But it will be shortened for the sake of God's **c**
24:24 so as to deceive, if possible, even God's **c** ones.
24:31 and they will gather together his **c** ones from the
Mk 10:40 has prepared those places for the ones he has **c**."
13:20 But for the sake of his **c** ones he has shortened
13:22 so as to deceive, if possible, even God's **c** ones.
13:27 gather together his **c** ones from all over the world
Lk 1: 9 he was **c** by lot to enter the sanctuary and burn
9:35 from the cloud said, "This is my Son, my **C** One.
18: 7 give justice to his **c** people who plead with him day
23:35 "let him save himself if he is really God's **C** One,
Ac 1: 2 **c** apostles further instructions from the Holy Spirit.
1:17 was one of us, **c** to share in the ministry with us."
1:22 Whoever is **c** will join us as a witness of Jesus'
1:24 Then they all prayed for the right man to be **c**.
1:24 Show us which of these men you have **c**
1:26 and in this way Matthias was **c** and became an
9:15 For Saul is my **c** instrument to take my message to
10:41 but to us whom God had **c** beforehand to be his
15:22 The men **c** were two of the church leaders—
21: 8 one of the seven men who had been **c** to distribute
22:14 'The God of our ancestors has **c** you to know his
Ro 1: 1 **c** by God to be an apostle and sent out to preach
8:30 And having **c** them, he called them to come to him.
8:33 Who dares accuse us whom God has **c** for his
9: 4 the people of Israel, **c** to be God's special children.
11: 7 A few have—the ones God has **c**—but the rest
11:28 Yet the Jews are still his **c** people because of his
1Co 1: 1 **c** by the will of God to be an apostle of Christ
9:17 But God has **c** me and given me this sacred trust,
Eph 1: 1 **c** by God to be an apostle of Christ Jesus.
3: 8 I was **c** for this special joy of telling the Gentiles
3: 9 I was **c** to explain to everyone this plan that God,
Col 1: 1 **c** by God to be an apostle of Christ Jesus,
1Ti 2: 7 And I have been **c**—this is the absolute truth—
3: 6 because he might be proud of being **c** so soon,
2Ti 2:10 eternal glory in Christ Jesus to those God has **c**.
Tit 1: 1 I have been sent to bring faith to those God has **c**
Heb 5: 1 Now a high priest is a man **c** to represent other
5: 5 No, he was **c** by God, who said to him, / "You are
Jas 2: 5 Hasn't God **c** the poor in this world to be rich in
1Pe 1: 1 I am writing to God's **c** people who are living as
2: 6 am placing a stone in Jerusalem, / a **c** cornerstone,
2: 9 But you are not like that, for you are a **c** people.
2Pe 1:10 you really are among those God has called and **c**.
2Jn 1: 1 It is written to the **c** lady and to her children,
1:13 from the children of your sister, **c** by God.
Rev 17:14 his people are the called and **c** and faithful ones."

CHOZEBA [KJV] See COZEBA

CHRIST (558) [CHRIST'S, CHRISTIAN, CHRISTIAN'S, CHRISTIANITY, CHRISTIANS, MESSIAH]

CHRIST JESUS (87) Ac 24:24; Ro 3:24; 6:3,11,23; 8:1,2,34,39; 15:5,16,17; 16:3; 1Co 1:2,4,30; 4:15,17; 16:24; 2Co 1:1; 4:5; Gal 2:4,16; 3:14,26,28; 4:14; 5:6,24; Eph 1:1,1; 2:6,7,10,13,20; 3:1,6,11,21; Php 1:1,1,6,8,26; 2:5; 3:3,8,12,14; 4:7,19; Col 1:1,4; 2:6; 4:12; 1Th 2:14; 5:18; 1Ti 1:1,1,2,12,14,15,16; 2:5; 3:13; 4:6; 5:21; 6:13; 2Ti 1:1,1,2,9,10,13; 2:1,3,10; 3:12,15; 4:1; Tit 1:4; Phm 1:1,9,23

IN CHRIST (52) Ac 24:24; Ro 8:39; 12:5; 16:9; 1Co 1:30; 4:15; 15:18,19; 16:24; 2Co 3:14; 5:19; Gal 2:4,16,16,17; 3:9,23,24,25,26,28; 5:6; Eph 1:4,12,13; 2:10; 3:8,21; Php 1:1,29; 4:7,19; Col 1:2,4,19; 2:5,9; 1Th 2:14; 1Ti 1:19; 3:13; 2Ti 1:1,13; 2:1,10; 3:12,15; Phm 1:20,23; Heb 3:6; 1Pe 5:14; 1Jn 2:8,27

JESUS CHRIST (135) Jn 1:17; 17:3; Ac 2:38; 3:6; 4:10; 8:12; 9:34; 10:36,48; 11:17; 15:26; 16:18; 28:31; Ro 1:4,6,7,8; 2:16; 3:22; 5:1,11,15,17,21; 7:25; 13:14; 15:6,30; 16:20,25,27; 1Co 1:2,3,7,8,9,10; 2:2; 3:11; 6:11; 8:6; 15:31,57; 2Co 1:2,3,19; 4:6; 8:9; 13:5,13; Gal 1:1,3,12; 2:16; 3:22; 6:14,18; Eph 1:2,3,5,17; 5:20; 6:23,24; Php 1:2,11,19; 2:11,21; 3:20; 4:23; Col 1:3; 1Th 1:1,3; 5:9,23,28; 2Th 1:1,2,12; 2:1,14,16; 3:6,12,18; 1Ti 6:3,14; 2Ti 2:8; Tit 1:1; 2:13; 3:6; Phm 1:3,25; Heb 10:10; 13:8,20; Jas 1:1; 2:1,7; 1Pe 1:1,2,3,3,7,13; 2:5; 4:11; 5:10; 2Pe 1:1,8,11,14,16; 2:20; 3:18; 1Jn 1:1,3; 2:1; 3:23; 4:2; 5:6,20; 2Jn 1:3,7; Jude 1:1,1,4,17,21,25; Rev 1:1,2,5

LORD JESUS CHRIST (59) Ac 11:17; 15:26; 28:31; Ro 1:7; 5:11; 13:14; 15:6,30; 16:20; 1Co 1:3,7,8,10; 6:11; 8:6; 15:31; 2Co 1:2,3; 8:9; 13:13; Gal 1:3; 6:14,18; Eph 1:3,17; 5:20; 6:23,24; Php 1:2; 3:20; 4:23; Col 1:3; 1Th 1:1,3; 5:9,23,28; 2Th 1:1,2,12; 2:1,14,16; 3:6,12,18; 1Ti 6:3,14; Phm 1:3,25; Jas 1:1; 2:1; 1Pe 1:3; 2Pe 1:8,14,16; Jude 1:4,17,21

Jn 1:17 and faithfulness came through Jesus **C**.
1:41 have found the Messiah" (which means the **C**).
4:25 the Messiah will come—the one who is called **C**.
17: 3 to know you, the only true God, and Jesus **C**,
Ac 2:38 and be baptized in the name of Jesus **C** for the
3: 6 In the name of Jesus **C** of Nazareth, get up
4:10 in the name and power of Jesus **C** from Nazareth,
8:12 the Kingdom of God and the name of Jesus **C**.
9:34 Peter said to him, "Aeneas, Jesus **C** heals you!
10:36 that there is peace with God through Jesus **C**,
10:48 for them to be baptized in the name of Jesus **C**.
11:17 he gave us when we believed in the Lord Jesus **C**,
15:26 risked their lives for the sake of our Lord Jesus **C**.
16:18 "I command you in the name of Jesus **C** to come
24:24 they listened as he told them about faith in **C** Jesus.
26:11 in the synagogues to try to get them to curse **C**.
28:31 all boldness and teaching about the Lord Jesus **C**.
Ro 1: 4 And Jesus **C** our Lord was shown to be the Son of
1: 5 Through **C**, God has given us the privilege
1: 6 those who have been called to belong to Jesus **C**,
1: 7 yours from God our Father and the Lord Jesus **C**.
1: 8 How I thank God through Jesus **C** for each one of
1:16 For I am not ashamed of this Good News about **C**.
2:16 by Jesus **C**, will judge everyone's secret life.
3:22 when we trust in Jesus **C** to take away our sins.
3:24 He has done this through **C** Jesus, who has freed us
5: 1 because of what Jesus **C** our Lord has done for us.
5: 2 **C** has brought us into this place of highest
5: 6 **C** came at just the right time and died for us
5: 8 But God showed his great love for us by sending **C**
5: 9 been made right in God's sight by the blood of **C**,
5:11 because of what our Lord Jesus **C** has done for us.
5:14 What a contrast between Adam and **C**, who was
5:15 But this other man, Jesus **C**, brought forgiveness to
5:17 over sin and death through this one man, Jesus **C**.
5:21 and resulting in eternal life through Jesus **C** our
6: 3 and were baptized to become one with **C** Jesus,
6: 4 For we died and were buried with **C** by baptism.
6: 4 And just as **C** was raised from the dead by the
6: 6 Our old sinful selves were crucified with **C** so that
6: 7 For when we died with **C** we were set free from

6: 8 And since we died with **C**, we know we will also
6: 9 We are sure of this because **C** rose from the dead,
6: 11 and able to live for the glory of God through **C**
6: 23 but the free gift of God is eternal life through **C**
7: 4 to its power when you died with **C** on the cross.
7: 6 for we died with **C**, and we are no longer captive
7: 25 Thank God! The answer is in Jesus **C** our Lord.
8: 1 no condemnation for those who belong to **C** Jesus.
8: 2 **C** Jesus from the power of sin that leads to death.
8: 9 Spirit of **C** living in them are not Christians at all.)
8: 10 Since **C** lives within you, even though your body
8: 11 And just as he raised **C** from the dead, he will give
8: 17 for everything God gives to his Son, **C**, is ours too.
8: 32 gave him up for us all, won't God, who gave us **C**,
8: 34 Will **C** Jesus? No, for he is the one who died for us
8: 37 overwhelming victory is ours through **C**,
8: 39 love of God that is revealed in **C** Jesus our Lord.
9: 1 In the presence of **C**, I speak with utter
9: 3 cut off from **C**!—if that would save them.
9: 5 and **C** himself was a Jew as far as his human
10: 4 For **C** has accomplished the whole purpose of the
10: 6 "You don't need to go to heaven" (to find **C**
10: 7 place of the dead" (to bring **C** back to life again).
10: 8 Salvation that comes from trusting **C**—which is the
10: 17 message of Good News—the Good News about **C**.
11: 25 until the complete number of Gentiles comes to **C**.
12: 5 And since we are all one body in **C**, we belong to
13: 14 But let the Lord Jesus **C** take control of you,
14: 9 **C** died and rose again for this very purpose,
14: 15 Don't let your eating ruin someone for whom **C**
14: 18 If you serve **C** with this attitude, you will please
15: 3 For even **C** didn't please himself. As the Scriptures
15: 5 each with the attitude of **C** Jesus toward the other.
15: 6 and glory to God, the Father of our Lord Jesus **C**.
15: 7 So accept each other just as **C** has accepted you;
15: 8 Remember that **C** came as a servant to the Jews to
15: 16 a special messenger from **C** Jesus to you Gentiles.
15: 17 So it is right for me to be enthusiastic about all **C**
15: 19 I have fully presented the Good News of **C** all the
15: 20 News where the name of **C** has never been heard,
15: 29 I come, **C** will give me a great blessing for you.
15: 30 I urge you in the name of our Lord Jesus **C** to join
16: 3 They have been co-workers in my ministry for **C**
16: 9 and Urbanus, our co-worker in **C**, and beloved
16: 10 to Apelles, a good man whom **C** approves.
16: 16 All the churches of **C** send you their greetings.
16: 18 Such people are not serving **C** our Lord; they are
16: 20 May the grace of our Lord Jesus **C** be with you.
16: 25 It is the message about Jesus **C** and his plan for
16: 26 so that they might believe and obey **C**.
16: 27 alone is wise, be the glory forever through Jesus **C**.
1Co 1: 1 chosen by the will of God to be an apostle of **C**
1: 2 He made you holy by means of **C** Jesus, just as he
1: 2 whoever calls upon the name of Jesus **C**, our Lord
1: 3 and the Lord Jesus **C** give you his grace and peace.
1: 4 he has given you, now that you belong to **C** Jesus.
1: 6 This shows that what I told you about **C** is true.
1: 7 eagerly wait for the return of our Lord Jesus **C**.
1: 8 on the great day when our Lord Jesus **C** returns.
1: 9 friendship with his Son, Jesus **C** our Lord.
1: 10 Lord Jesus **C** to stop arguing among yourselves.
1: 12 or "I follow Peter," or "I follow only **C**."
1: 13 Can **C** be divided into pieces? Was I, Paul,
1: 17 For **C** didn't send me to baptize, but to preach the
1: 17 for fear that the cross of **C** would lose its power.
1: 23 So when we preach that **C** was crucified, the Jews
1: 24 **C** is the mighty power of God and the wonderful
1: 30 God alone made it possible for you to be in **C**
1: 30 For our benefit God made **C** to be wisdom itself.
2: 2 For I decided to concentrate only on Jesus **C**
2: 16 these things, for we have the mind of **C**.
3: 11 foundation than the one we already have—Jesus **C**.
3: 23 and you belong to **C**, and **C** belongs to God.
4: 1 and me as mere servants of **C** who have been put
4: 10 Our dedication to **C** makes us look like fools,
4: 15 you had ten thousand others to teach you about **C**,
4: 15 For I became your father in **C** Jesus when I
4: 17 He will remind you of what I teach about **C** Jesus
5: 7 **C**, our Passover Lamb, has been sacrificed for us.
6: 11 right with God because of what the Lord Jesus **C**
6: 15 realize that your bodies are actually parts of **C**?
6: 15 which belongs to **C**, and join it to a prostitute?
7: 22 the Lord called you, you are now a slave of **C**.
8: 6 And there is only one Lord, Jesus **C**,
8: 11 a weak Christian, for whom **C** died, will be
8: 12 And you are sinning against **C** when you sin
9: 12 an obstacle in the way of the Good News about **C**.
9: 19 a servant of everyone so that I can bring them to **C**.
9: 20 become one of them so that I can bring them to **C**.
9: 20 subject to the law, so that I can bring them to **C**.
9: 21 I gain their confidence and bring them to **C**.
9: 21 do not discard the law of God; I obey the law of **C**.
9: 22 their oppression so that I might bring them to **C**.
9: 22 with everyone so that I might bring them to **C**.
10: 4 rock that traveled with them, and that rock was **C**.
10: 9 Nor should we put **C** to the test, as some of them
10: 16 aren't we sharing in the benefits of the blood of **C**?
10: 16 aren't we sharing in the benefits of the body of **C**?
11: 3 A man is responsible to **C**, a woman is responsible
to her husband, and **C** is responsible to God.
11: 4 A man dishonors **C** if he covers his head while
11: 29 not honoring the body of **C**, you are eating
12: 12 up only one body. So it is with the body of **C**.
12: 28 the members that God has placed in the body of **C**:
15: 3 that **C** died for our sins, just as the Scriptures said.
15: 12 since we preach that **C** rose from the dead, why are
15: 13 of the dead, then **C** has not been raised either.
15: 14 And if **C** was not raised, then all our preaching is
15: 15 for we have said that God raised **C** from the grave,
15: 16 of the dead, then **C** has not been raised.
15: 17 And if **C** has not been raised, then your faith is
15: 18 all who have died believing in **C** have perished!
15: 19 And if we have hope in **C** only for this life, we are
15: 20 But the fact is that **C** has been raised from the
15: 21 from the dead has begun through another man, **C**.
15: 22 But all who are related to **C**, the other man, will be
15: 23 **C** was raised first; then when **C** comes back,
15: 25 For **C** must reign until he humbles all his enemies
15: 27 include God himself, who gave **C** his authority.)
15: 31 pride in what the Lord Jesus **C** has done in you.
15: 45 But the last Adam—that is, **C**—is a life-giving
15: 47 while **C**, the second man, came from heaven.
15: 49 the man of the earth, so we will someday be like **C**,
15: 57 over sin and death through Jesus **C** our Lord!
16: 24 My love to all of you in **C** Jesus.
2Co 1: 1 appointed by God to be an apostle of **C** Jesus,
1: 2 and the Lord Jesus **C** give you his grace and peace.
1: 3 praise to the God and Father of our Lord Jesus **C**.
1: 5 You can be sure that the more we suffer for **C**,
1: 5 God will shower us with his comfort through **C**.
1: 19 because Jesus **C**, the Son of God, never wavers
1: 20 "Amen" when we give glory to God through **C**.
1: 21 along with you, the ability to stand firm for **C**.
2: 12 to the city of Troas to preach the Good News of **C**,
2: 15 Our lives are a fragrance presented by **C** to God.
3: 3 Clearly, you are a letter from **C** prepared by us.
3: 4 because of our great trust in God through **C**.
3: 14 this veil can be removed only by believing in **C**.
4: 4 the message we preach about the glory of **C**,
4: 5 about ourselves; we preach **C** Jesus, the Lord.
4: 6 the glory of God that is seen in the face of Jesus **C**.
4: 15 as God's grace brings more and more people to **C**,
5: 10 For we must all stand before **C** to be judged.
5: 14 Since we believe that **C** died for everyone, we also
5: 15 Instead, they will live to please **C**, who died
5: 16 Once I mistakenly thought of **C** that way,
5: 18 who brought us back to himself through what **C**
5: 19 For God was in **C**, reconciling the world to
5: 20 as though **C** himself were here pleading with you,
5: 21 For God made **C**, who never sinned, to be the
5: 21 that we could be made right with God through **C**.
6: 15 What harmony can there be between **C**
8: 9 full of love and kindness our Lord Jesus **C** was.
8: 23 splendid examples of those who bring glory to **C**.
9: 13 that you are obedient to the Good News of **C**.
10: 1 and kindness that **C** himself would use,
10: 5 rebellious ideas, and we teach them to obey **C**.
10: 7 You must recognize that we belong to **C** just as
10: 7 those who proudly declare that they belong to **C**.
10: 14 travel all the way to you with the Good News of **C**.
11: 2 I promised you as a pure bride to one husband, **C**.
11: 3 led away from your pure and simple devotion to **C**,
11: 10 As surely as the truth of **C** is in me, I will never
11: 13 you by disguising themselves as apostles of **C**.
11: 23 They say they serve **C**? I know I sound like a
12: 9 so that the power of **C** may work through me.
13: 3 I will give you all the proof you want that **C** speaks
13: 3 **C** is not weak in his dealings with you; he is a
13: 5 If you cannot tell that Jesus **C** is among you,
13: 13 May the grace of our Lord Jesus **C**, the love of
Gal 1: 1 My call is from Jesus **C** himself and from God the
1: 3 from God our Father and from the Lord Jesus **C**.
1: 6 you to share the eternal life he gives through **C**.
1: 7 those who twist and change the truth concerning **C**.
1: 12 came by a direct revelation from Jesus **C** himself.
2: 4 came to spy on us and see our freedom in **C** Jesus.
2: 16 what the law commands, but by faith in Jesus **C**.
2: 16 So we have believed in **C** Jesus, that we might be
2: 16 be accepted by God because of our faith in **C**—
2: 17 seek to be made right with God through faith in **C**
2: 17 still sinners? Has **C** led us into sin? Of course not!
2: 19 I might live for God. I have been crucified with **C**.
2: 20 I myself no longer live, but **C** lives in me. So I live
2: 21 the law, then there was no need for **C** to die.
3: 1 a signboard with a picture of **C** dying on the cross.
3: 2 after you believed the message you heard about **C**.
3: 5 you believe the message you heard about **C**.
3: 9 All who put their faith in **C** share the same
3: 13 But **C** has rescued us from the curse pronounced
3: 14 Through the work of **C** Jesus, God has blessed the
3: 16 was to his child—and that, of course, means **C**.
3: 22 to receive God's promise is to believe in Jesus **C**.
3: 23 Until faith in **C** was shown to us as the way of
3: 24 our guardian and teacher to lead us until **C** came.
3: 24 So now, through faith in **C**, we are made right with
3: 25 But now that faith in **C** has come, we no longer
3: 26 So you are all children of God through faith in **C**
3: 27 And all who have been united with **C** in baptism
3: 28 For you are all Christians—you are one in **C** Jesus.
3: 29 And now that you belong to **C**, you are the true
4: 3 And that's the way it was with us before **C** came.
4: 13 sick when I first brought you the Good News of **C**.
4: 14 I were an angel from God or even **C** Jesus himself.
4: 19 and they will continue until **C** is fully developed in
5: 1 So **C** has really set us free. Now make sure that
5: 2 make you right with God, then **C** cannot help you.
5: 4 by keeping the law, you have been cut off from **C**!
5: 6 For when we place our faith in **C** Jesus, it makes
5: 11 preaching salvation through the cross of **C** alone.
5: 24 Those who belong to **C** Jesus have nailed the
6: 2 and problems, and in this way obey the law of **C**.
6: 12 for teaching that the cross of **C** alone can save.
6: 14 anything except the cross of our Lord Jesus **C**.
6: 18 may the grace of our Lord Jesus **C** be with you all.
Eph 1: 1 chosen by God to be an apostle of **C** Jesus.
1: 1 in Ephesus, who are faithful followers of **C** Jesus.
1: 2 to you from God our Father and Jesus **C** our Lord.
1: 3 we praise God, the Father of our Lord Jesus **C**,
1: 3 in the heavenly realms because we belong to **C**.
1: 4 God loved us and chose us in **C** to be holy
1: 5 family by bringing us to himself through Jesus **C**.
1: 9 it is a plan centered on **C**, designed long ago
1: 10 everything together under the authority of **C**—
1: 11 Furthermore, because of **C**, we have received an
1: 12 first to trust in **C** should praise our glorious God.
1: 13 And when you believed in **C**, he identified you as
1: 17 the glorious Father of our Lord Jesus **C**,
1: 20 that raised **C** from the dead and seated him in the
1: 22 God has put all things under the authority of **C**,
1: 23 it is filled by **C**, who fills everything everywhere
2: 5 he gave us life when he raised **C** from the dead.
2: 6 For he raised us from the dead along with **C**,
2: 6 all because we are one with **C** Jesus.
2: 7 as shown in all he has done for us through **C** Jesus.
2: 10 He has created us anew in **C** Jesus, so that we can
2: 12 In those days you were living apart from **C**.
2: 13 But now you belong to **C** Jesus. Though you once
2: 13 brought near to him because of the blood of **C**.
2: 14 For **C** himself has made peace between us Jews
2: 16 **C** reconciled both groups to God by means of his
2: 18 Holy Spirit because of what **C** has done for us.
2: 20 And the cornerstone is **C** Jesus himself.
3: 1 am a prisoner of **C** Jesus because of my preaching
3: 4 what I know about this plan regarding **C**.
3: 6 together the promise of blessings through **C** Jesus.
3: 8 about the endless treasures available to them in **C**.
3: 11 and it has now been carried out through **C** Jesus
3: 12 Because of **C** and our faith in him, we can now
3: 17 And I pray that **C** will be more and more at home
3: 19 May you experience the love of **C**, though it is
3: 21 and in **C** Jesus forever and ever through endless
4: 7 us a special gift according to the generosity of **C**.
4: 9 This means that **C** first came down to the lowly
4: 12 his work and build up the church, the body of **C**,
4: 13 in the Lord, measuring up to the full stature of **C**.
4: 15 becoming more and more in every way like **C**,
4: 20 what you were taught when you learned about **C**.
4: 32 just as God through **C** has forgiven you.
5: 2 following the example of **C**, who loved you
5: 5 or greedy person will inherit the Kingdom of **C**
5: 14 rise up from the dead, / and **C** will give you light."
5: 20 to God the Father in the name of our Lord Jesus **C**.
5: 21 will submit to one another out of reverence for **C**.
5: 23 For a husband is the head of his wife as **C** is the
5: 24 As the church submits to **C**, so you wives must
5: 25 wives with the same love **C** showed the church.
5: 29 just as **C** cares for his body, which is the church.
5: 32 but it is an illustration of the way **C** and the church
6: 5 Serve them sincerely as you would serve **C**.
6: 6 As slaves of **C**, do the will of God with all your
6: 23 from God the Father and the Lord Jesus **C**.
6: 24 who love our Lord Jesus **C** with an undying love.
Php 1: 1 letter is from Paul and Timothy, slaves of **C** Jesus.
1: 1 who believe in **C** Jesus, and to the elders
1: 2 and the Lord Jesus **C** give you grace and peace.
1: 5 about **C** from the time you first heard it until now.
1: 6 on that day when **C** Jesus comes back again.
1: 8 and long for you with the tender compassion of **C**
1: 10 may live pure and blameless lives until **C** returns.
1: 11 things that are produced in your life by Jesus **C**—
1: 13 knows that I am in chains because of **C**.
1: 14 and become more bold in telling others about **C**.
1: 15 But others preach about **C** with pure motives.
1: 17 do not have pure motives as they preach about **C**.
1: 18 the fact remains that the message about **C** is being
1: 19 pray for me and as the Spirit of Jesus **C** helps me,
1: 20 but that I will always be bold for **C**, as I have been
1: 20 and that my life will always honor **C**, whether I
1: 21 For to me, living is for **C**, and dying is even better.
1: 22 Yet if I live, that means fruitful service for **C**.
1: 23 to live, and sometimes I long to go and be with **C**.
1: 26 to boast about what **C** Jesus has done for me.
1: 27 in a manner worthy of the Good News about **C**,
1: 29 been given not only the privilege of trusting in **C**
2: 1 Is there any encouragement from belonging to **C**?
2: 5 Your attitude should be the same that **C** Jesus had.
2: 11 and every tongue will confess that Jesus **C** is Lord,
2: 16 tightly to the word of life, so that when **C** returns,
2: 21 for themselves and not for what matters to Jesus **C**.
2: 30 For he risked his life for the work of **C**, and he was
3: 3 we boast about what **C** Jesus has done for us.
3: 7 them worthless because of what **C** has done.
3: 8 the priceless gain of knowing **C** Jesus my Lord.
3: 8 counting it all as garbage, so that I may have **C**
3: 9 ability to obey God's law, but I trust **C** to save me.
3: 10 I can really know **C** and experience the mighty
3: 12 when I will finally be all that **C** Jesus saved me for
3: 14 through **C** Jesus, is calling us up to heaven.
3: 18 shows they are really enemies of the cross of **C**.
3: 20 citizens of heaven, where the Lord Jesus **C** lives.
4: 7 guard your hearts and minds as you live in **C** Jesus.
4: 13 For I can do everything with the help of **C** who
4: 19 which have been given to us in **C** Jesus.
4: 23 May the grace of the Lord Jesus **C** be with your
Col 1: 1 chosen by God to be an apostle of **C** Jesus,
1: 2 who are faithful brothers and sisters in **C**.
1: 3 give thanks to God the Father of our Lord Jesus **C**,
1: 4 for we have heard that you trust in **C** Jesus and that
1: 15 **C** is the visible image of the invisible God.
1: 16 **C** is the one through whom God created everything
1: 18 **C** is the head of the church, which is his body.

1:19 For God in all his fullness was pleased to live in C,
1:27 that the riches and glory of C are for you Gentiles,
1:27 C lives in you, and this is your assurance that you
1:28 So everywhere we go, we tell everyone about C.
1:28 them to God, perfect in their relationship to C.
2: 2 of God's secret plan, which is C himself.
2: 5 you should and because of your strong faith in C.
2: 6 just as you accepted C Jesus as your Lord,
2: 8 from the evil powers of this world, and not from C.
2: 9 For in C the fullness of God lives in a human
2:10 and you are complete through your union with C.
2:11 When you came to C, you were "circumcised,"
2:12 For you were buried with C when you were
2:12 mighty power of God, who raised C from the dead.
2:13 Then God made you alive with C. He forgave all
2:15 by his victory over them on the cross of C.
2:17 were only shadows of the real thing, C himself.
2:19 But they are not connected to C, the head of the
2:20 You have died with C, and he has set you free
3: 1 Since you have been raised to new life with C,
3: 1 where C sits at God's right hand in the place of
3: 3 For you died when C died, and your real life is hidden with C in God.
3: 4 And when C, who is your real life, is revealed to
3:10 renewed as you learn more and more about C,
3:11 C is all that matters, and he lives in all of us.
3:15 And let the peace that comes from C rule in your
3:16 Let the words of C, in all their richness, live in
3:24 your reward, and the Master you are serving is C.
4: 3 his secret plan—that C is also for you Gentiles.
4:12 Epaphras, from your city, a servant of C Jesus,
1Th 1: 1 belong to God the Father and the Lord Jesus C.
1: 3 anticipation of the return of our Lord Jesus C.
2: 7 As apostles of C we certainly had a right to make
2:14 because of their belief in C Jesus, suffered from
3: 2 our brother in proclaiming the Good News of C.
3:13 a result, C will make your hearts strong, blameless,
5: 9 God decided to save us through our Lord Jesus C,
5:18 for this is God's will for you who belong to C
5:23 until that day when our Lord Jesus C comes again.
5:28 And may the grace of our Lord Jesus C be with all
2Th 1: 1 belong to God our Father and the Lord Jesus C.
1: 2 and the Lord Jesus C give you grace and peace.
1:12 undeserved favor of our God and Lord, Jesus C.
2: 1 you about the coming again of our Lord Jesus C
2:14 you can share in the glory of our Lord Jesus C.
2:16 May our Lord Jesus C and God our Father,
3: 5 love of God and the endurance that comes from C.
3: 6 command with the authority of our Lord Jesus C:
3:12 In the name of the Lord Jesus C we appeal to such
3:18 May the grace of our Lord Jesus C be with you all.
1Ti 1: 1 This letter is from Paul, an apostle of C Jesus,
1: 1 of God our Savior and by C Jesus our hope.
1: 2 our Father and C Jesus our Lord give you grace,
1:12 How thankful I am to C Jesus our Lord for
1:13 even though I used to scoff at the name of C.
1:14 me completely with faith and the love of C Jesus.
1:15 C Jesus came into the world to save sinners—
1:16 so that C Jesus could use me as a prime example of
1:19 Cling tightly to your faith in C, and always keep
2: 5 reconcile God and people. He is the man C Jesus.
3:13 have increased confidence in their faith in C Jesus.
3:16 great mystery of our faith: / C appeared in the flesh
4: 6 be doing your duty as a worthy servant of C Jesus,
5:11 physical desires will overpower their devotion to C
5:21 command you in the presence of God and C Jesus
6: 3 wholesome teachings of the Lord Jesus C,
6:13 who gives life to all, and before C Jesus,
6:14 with you from now until our Lord Jesus C returns.
6:15 For at the right time C will be revealed from
2Ti 1: 1 is from Paul, an apostle of C Jesus by God's will,
1: 1 the life he has promised through faith in C Jesus.
1: 2 our Father and C Jesus our Lord give you grace,
1: 8 of me, either, even though I'm in prison for C.
1: 9 show his love and kindness to us through C Jesus.
1:10 all of this plain to us by the coming of C Jesus,
1:13 live in the faith and love that you have in C Jesus.
2: 1 with the special favor God gives you in C Jesus.
2: 3 along with me, as a good soldier of C Jesus.
2: 8 Never forget that Jesus C was a man born into
2:10 and eternal glory in C Jesus to those God has
3:12 and everyone who wants to live a godly life in C
3:15 the salvation that comes by trusting in C Jesus.
4: 1 urge you before God and before C Jesus—
4: 5 for the Lord. Work at bringing others to C.
Tit 1: 1 a slave of God and an apostle of Jesus C.
1: 4 and C Jesus our Savior give you grace and peace.
2:13 the glory of our great God and Savior, Jesus C,
3: 6 upon us because of what Jesus C our Savior did.
Phm 1: 1 in prison for preaching the Good News about C
1: 3 and the Lord Jesus C give you grace and peace.
1: 6 of all the good things we can do for C.
1: 8 I could demand it in the name of C because it is
1: 9 an old man, now in prison for the sake of C Jesus.
1:20 the Lord's sake. Give me this encouragement in C.
1:23 Epaphras, my fellow prisoner in C Jesus,
1:25 The grace of the Lord Jesus C be with your spirit.
Heb 3: 6 But C, the faithful Son, was in charge of the entire
3: 6 our courage and remain confident in our hope in C.
3:14 we will share in all that belongs to C.
5: 5 That is why C did not exalt himself to become
7:17 the psalmist pointed this out when he said of C,
7:20 God took an oath that C would always be a priest,
9:11 So C has now become the High Priest over all the
9:14 Just think how much more the blood of C will
9:14 C offered himself to God as a perfect sacrifice for
9:15 For C died to set them free from the penalty of the
9:24 For C has entered into heaven itself to appear now
9:28 so also C died only once as a sacrifice to take away
10: 1 not the reality of the good things C has done for
10: 5 That is why C, when he came into the world,
10: 8 C said, "You did not want animal sacrifices
10:10 sacrifice of the body of Jesus C once for all time.
10:20 life-giving way that C has opened up for us
10:32 those early days when you first learned about C.
13: 8 Jesus C is the same yesterday, today, and forever.
13:20[-21] in you, through the power of Jesus C,
Jas 1: 1 a slave of God and of the Lord Jesus C.
2: 1 C if you favor some people more than others?
2: 7 Aren't they the ones who slander Jesus C,
1Pe 1: 1 This letter is from Peter, an apostle of Jesus C.
1: 2 you have obeyed Jesus C and are cleansed by his
1: 3 honor to the God and Father of our Lord Jesus C,
1: 3 because Jesus C rose again from the dead.
1: 7 and honor on the day when Jesus C is revealed to
1:11 They wondered what the Spirit of C within them
1:13 that will come to you at the return of Jesus C.
1:19 He paid for you with the precious lifeblood of C,
1:21 Through C you have come to trust in God. And because God raised C from the dead
2: 4 Come to C, who is the living cornerstone of God's
2: 5 sacrifices that please him because of Jesus C.
2:21 C, who suffered for you, is your example.
3:15 Instead, you must worship C as Lord of your life.
3:16 what a good life you live because you belong to C.
3:18 C also suffered when he died for our sins once for
3:22 Now C has gone to heaven. He is seated in the
4: 1 So then, since C suffered physical pain, you must
4: 1 For if you are willing to suffer for C, you have
4:11 will be given glory in everything through Jesus C.
4:13 because these trials will make you partners with C
5: 1 am an elder and a witness to the sufferings of C.
5:10 you to his eternal glory by means of Jesus C.
5:14 Christian love. Peace be to all of you who are in C.
2Pe 1: 1 from Simon Peter, a slave and apostle of Jesus C.
1: 1 faith given to us by Jesus C, our God and Savior,
1: 8 and useful in your knowledge of our Lord Jesus C.
1:11 eternal Kingdom of our Lord and Savior Jesus C.
1:14 But the Lord Jesus C has shown me that my days
1:16 we told you about the power of our Lord Jesus C
1:19 until the day C appears and his brilliant light
2: 2 of them, C and his true way will be slandered.
2:20 and Savior Jesus C and then get tangled up with
3:18 and knowledge of our Lord and Savior Jesus C.
1Jn 1: 1 our own hands. He is Jesus C, the Word of life.
1: 3 is with the Father and with his Son, Jesus C.
1: 7 just as C is, then we have fellowship with each
2: 1 He is Jesus C, the one who pleases God
2: 6 they live in God should live their lives as C did.
2: 8 This commandment is true in C and is true among
2:13 to you who are mature because you know C,
2:14 to you who are mature because you know C,
2:22 The one who says that Jesus is not the C.
2:27 what he has taught you, and continue to live in C.
2:28 continue to live in fellowship with C so that when
3: 2 even imagine what we will be like when C returns.
3: 3 this will keep themselves pure, just as C is pure.
3: 7 because they are righteous, even as C is righteous.
3:16 what real love is because C gave up his life for us.
3:23 Jesus C, and love one another, just as he
4: 2 If a prophet acknowledges that Jesus C became a
4:17 because we are like C here in this world.
5: 1 Everyone who believes that Jesus is the C is a
5: 4 this evil world by trusting C to give the victory.
5: 6 And Jesus C was revealed as God's Son by his
5:20 we are in God because we are in his Son, Jesus C.
2Jn 1: 3 from God our Father and from Jesus C his Son,
1: 7 They do not believe that Jesus C came to earth in a
1: 9 For if you wander beyond the teaching of C,
1: 9 But if you continue in the teaching of C, you will
1:10 your meeting and does not teach the truth about C,
Jude 1: 1 a slave of Jesus C and a brother of James.
1: 1 the love of God the Father and the care of Jesus C.
1: 4 turned against our only Master and Lord, Jesus C.
1:17 what the apostles of our Lord Jesus C told you,
1:21 our Lord Jesus C in his mercy is going to give you.
1:25 alone is God our Savior, through Jesus C our Lord.
Rev 1: 1 This is a revelation from Jesus C, which God gave
1: 2 the word of God and the testimony of Jesus C—
1: 5 and from Jesus C, who is the faithful witness to
11:15 become the kingdom of our Lord and of his C,
12:10 kingdom of our God, and the authority of his C!
20: 4 and they reigned with C for a thousand years.
20: 6 but they will be priests of God and of C and will

CHRIST'S (26) [CHRIST]

Ro 1: 1 This letter is from Paul, Jesus C slave, chosen by
5:18 but C one act of righteousness makes all people
8:35 Can anything ever separate us from C love?
12: 5 so it is with C body. We are all parts of his one
1Co 11: 1 you should follow my example, just as I follow C.
12:13 But we have all been baptized into C body by one
12:27 Now all of you together are C body, and each one
15:48 but our heavenly bodies will be just like C.
2Co 2:10 I do so with C authority for your benefit,
2:14 and leads us along in C triumphal procession.
2:17 message with sincerity and with C authority.
5:14 Whatever we do, it is because C love controls us.
5:20 We are C ambassadors, and God is using us to
12:10 Since I know it is all for C good, I am quite
12:19 We tell you this as C servants, and we know that
Gal 1:10 trying to please people, I would not be C servant.
3: 1 For you used to see the meaning of Jesus C death
Col 1: 7 He is C faithful servant, and he is helping us in
1:24 for I am completing what remains of C sufferings
1:29 as I depend on C mighty power that works within
2:14 He took it and destroyed it by nailing it to C cross.
2Ti 1:18 show him special kindness on the day of C return.
2: 4 And as C soldier, do not let yourself become tied
Heb 10:22 been sprinkled with C blood to make us clean,
1Pe 1:11 when he told them in advance about C suffering
3:21 which now saves you by the power of Jesus C

CHRISTIAN (63) [CHRIST]

Ac 6: 5 to the Jewish faith, who had now become a C).
13: 8 trying to turn the governor away from the C faith.
26:28 "Do you think you can make me a C so quickly?"
Ro 8:12 So, dear C friends, you have no obligation
12: 1 And so, dear C friends, I plead with you to give
12:14 If people persecute you because you are a C,
14:10 So why do you condemn another C? Why do you look down on another C?
14:15 And if another C is distressed by what you eat,
14:21 or do anything else if it might cause another C to
16: 5 He was the very first person to become a C in the
16:16 Greet each other in C love. All the churches of
16:22 for Paul, send my greetings, too, as a C brother.
16:23 his greetings, and so does Quartus, a C brother.
1Co 3: 1 or as though you were infants in the C life.
5:11 who claims to be a C yet indulges in sexual sin,
6: 1 When you have something against another C,
6: 6 But instead, one C sues another—right in front of
6: 8 and cheat even your own C brothers and sisters.
7:12 If a C man has a wife who is an unbeliever and she
7:13 And if a C woman has a husband who is an
7:14 For the C wife brings holiness to her marriage,
7:14 and the C husband brings holiness to his marriage.
7:15 or wife who isn't a C insists on leaving,
7:15 In such cases the C husband or wife is not required
8:11 a weak C, for whom Christ died, will be destroyed.
8:13 If what I eat is going to make another C sin,
8:13 for I don't want to make another C stumble.
9: 5 Don't we have the right to bring a C wife along
9:10 C workers should be paid by those they serve.
10:27 If someone who isn't a C asks you home for
11: 2 and you are following the C teaching I passed on
16:20 to greet you for them. Greet each other in C love.
2Co 13:12 Greet each other in C love. All the Christians here
Gal 3: 3 After starting your C lives in the Spirit, why are
6: 1 Dear friends, if a C is overcome by some sin,
6:10 especially to our C brothers and sisters.
6:18 My dear C friends, may the grace of our Lord
Eph 3: 8 and though I am the least deserving C there is,
Php 2:29 Welcome him with C love and with great joy,
Col 4:15 Please give my greetings to our C brothers
1Th 4: 6 Never cheat another C in this matter by taking his
4: 9 But I don't need to write to you about the C love
5:26 Greet each other in C love.
2Th 3: 6 Stay away from any C who lives in idleness
3:15 but speak to them as you would to a C who needs
1Ti 3: 6 An elder must not be a new C, because he might
3: 9 be committed to the revealed truths of the C faith
5:16 If a C woman has relatives who are widows,
6: 2 If your master is a C, that is no excuse for being
Heb 5:13 is living on milk isn't very far along in the C life
13: 1 Continue to love each other with true C love.
1Pe 2:17 Love your C brothers and sisters. Fear God.
3:15 And if you are asked about your C hope, always be
4:14 Be happy if you are insulted for being a C, for
4:16 But it is no shame to suffer for being a C.
5:14 Greet each other in C love. Peace be to all of you
1Jn 2: 9 the light" but rejects another C is still in darkness.
3:15 Anyone who hates another C is really a murderer
3:16 so we also ought to give up our lives for our C
4:20 someone says, "I love God," but hates another C,
4:21 love not only him but our C brothers and sisters,
5:16 If you see any C sinning in a way that does not

CHRISTIAN'S (1) [CHRIST]

Ro 14:13 that you will not put an obstacle in another C path.

CHRISTIANITY (1) [CHRIST]

Heb 6: 1 So let us stop going over the basics of C again

CHRISTIANS (92) [CHRIST]

Ac 8:15 they prayed for these new C to receive the Holy
11:26 at Antioch that the believers were first called C.)
15: 1 men from Judea arrived and began to teach the C:
15:30 where they called a general meeting of the C
15:32 spoke extensively to the C, encouraging
15:33 with the blessings of the C, to those who had sent
18:18 and then said good-bye to the C and sailed for the
18:27 and the C in Ephesus encouraged him in this.
21:21 Our Jewish C here at Jerusalem have been told that
21:25 "As for the Gentile C, all we ask of them is what
22: 5 authorizing me to bring the C from there to
28:22 for the only thing we know about these C is that
Ro 6: 3 Or have you forgotten that when we became C
8: 9 the Spirit of Christ living in them are not C at all.)
8:23 And even we C, although we have the Holy Spirit
14: 1 Accept C who are weak in faith, and don't argue
15:25 I must go down to Jerusalem to take a gift to the C
15:26 taken up an offering for the C in Jerusalem,
15:27 blessings of the Good News from the Jewish C,
15:31 Pray also that the C there will be willing to accept
16: 7 among the apostles and became C before I did.
16:11 Greet the C in the household of Narcissus.
16:14 Hermas, and the other C who are with them.

1Co 1: 2 of Christ Jesus, just as he did all **C** everywhere—
2: 6 Yet when I am among mature **C**, I do speak with
2: 14 But people who aren't **C** can't understand these
3: 1 you I couldn't talk to you as I would to mature **C**.
3: 4 aren't you acting like those who are not **C**?
3: 17 God's temple is holy, and you **C** are that temple.
6: 1 instead of taking it to other **C** to decide who is
6: 2 Don't you know that someday we **C** are going to
6: 3 Don't you realize that we **C** will judge angels?
8: 7 However, not all **C** realize this. Some are
8: 10 Weak **C** who think it is wrong to eat this food will
8: 12 **C** by encouraging them to do something they
10: 24 Think of other **C** and what is best for them.
15: 52 the **C** who have died will be raised with
16: 1 Now about the money being collected for the **C** in
16: 15 and his household were the first to become **C** in
16: 15 they are spending their lives in service to other **C**.
2Co 1: 1 in Corinth and to all the **C** throughout Greece.
5: 17 What this means is that those who become **C**
8: 4 of sharing in the gift for the **C** in Jerusalem.
9: 1 write to you about this gift for the **C** in Jerusalem.
9: 2 **C** in Greece were ready to send an offering a year
9: 4 if some Macedonian **C** came with me, only to find
9: 12 the needs of the **C** in Jerusalem will be met,
11: 26 I have faced danger from men who claim to be **C**
13: 12 All the **C** here send you their greetings.
Gal 1: 2 All the **C** here join me in sending greetings to the
1: 13 Jewish religion—how I violently persecuted the **C**.
1: 22 And still the **C** in the churches in Judea didn't
2: 4 have come up except for some so-called **C** there—
2: 12 When he first arrived, he ate with the Gentile **C**,
2: 13 Then the other Jewish **C** followed Peter's
2: 16 And yet we Jewish **C** know that we become right
3: 14 and we **C** receive the promised Holy Spirit through
3: 28 For you are all **C**—you are one in Christ Jesus.
Eph 1: 15 in the Lord Jesus and your love for **C** everywhere,
6: 18 and be persistent in your prayers for all **C**
Php 1: 14 many of the **C** here have gained confidence
3: 15 I hope all of you who are mature **C** will agree on
4: 21 Give my greetings to all the **C** there. The brothers
4: 22 And all the other **C** send their greetings, too,
Col 4: 5 Live wisely among those who are not **C**, and make
4: 11 These are the only Jewish **C** among my
4: 13 and also for the **C** in Laodicea and Hierapolis.
1Th 1: 7 you yourselves became an example to all the **C** in
3: 3 that such troubles are going to happen to us **C**.
4: 10 your love is already strong toward all the **C** in all
4: 12 people who are not **C** will respect the way you
4: 13 I want you to know what will happen to the **C** who
4: 14 God will bring back with Jesus all the **C** who have
4: 16 all the **C** who have died will rise from their graves.
5: 27 the name of the Lord to read this letter to all the **C**.
1Ti 1: 5 The purpose of my instruction is that all the **C**
5: 10 kind to strangers? Has she served other **C** humbly?
6: 1 **C** who are slaves should give their masters full
2Ti 1: 15 all the **C** who came here from the province of Asia
Heb 5: 12 You have been **C** a long time now, and you ought
6: 10 have shown your love to him by caring for other **C**,
13: 24 The **C** from Italy send you their greetings.
Jas 1: 1 It is written to Jewish **C** scattered among the
1: 9 **C** who are poor should be glad, for God has
1Pe 4: 17 And if even we **C** must be judged, what terrible
5: 9 Remember that **C** all over the world are going
2Pe 1: 7 Godliness leads to love for other **C**, and finally you
1Jn 2: 10 But anyone who loves other **C** is walking in the
2: 11 Those who reject other **C** are wandering in
3: 10 and does not love other **C** does not belong to God.
3: 14 If we love other **C**, it proves that we have passed
3Jn 1: 7 and accept nothing from those who are not **C**.

CHRYSOLITE (7)

Ex 28: 17 will contain a red carnelian, a **c**, and an emerald.
39: 10 first row were a red carnelian, a **c**, and an emerald.
SS 5: 14 His arms are like round bars of gold, set with **c**.
Eze 1: 16 The wheels sparkled as if made of **c**. All four
10: 9 a wheel beside him, and the wheels sparkled like **c**.
28: 13 red carnelian, **c**, white moonstone, beryl, onyx,
Rev 21: 20 the seventh **c**, the eighth beryl, the ninth topaz,

CHRYSOPRASE (1)

Rev 21: 20 the eighth beryl, the ninth topaz, the tenth **c**,

CHUB [KJV] See LIBYA

CHUN [KJV] See CUN

CHUNK (3)

Isa 44: 19 Should I bow down to worship a **c** of wood?"
Eze 24: 6 So take the meat out **c** by **c** in whatever order

CHURCH (108) [CHURCHES]

Mt 16: 18 you are Peter, and upon this rock I will build my **c**,
18: 17 still refuses to listen, take your case to the **c**.
18: 17 If the **c** decides you are right, but the other person
Ac 2: 41 what Peter said were baptized and added to the **c**—
5: 11 Great fear gripped the entire **c** and all others who
8: 1 began that day, sweeping over the **c** in Jerusalem,
8: 3 Saul was going everywhere to devastate the **c**.
9: 31 The **c** then had peace throughout Judea, Galilee,
11: 22 When the **c** at Jerusalem heard what had happened,
11: 26 Both of them stayed there with the **c** for a full year,
11: 30 and Saul to take to the elders of the **c** in Jerusalem.
12: 1 began to persecute some believers in the **c**.
12: 5 was in prison, the **c** prayed very earnestly for him.
13: 1 and teachers of the **c** at Antioch of Syria were
14: 23 and Barnabas also appointed elders in every **c**
14: 27 they called the **c** together and reported about their
15: 3 The **c** sent the delegates to Jerusalem, and they
15: 4 and Barnabas were welcomed by the whole **c**,
15: 6 and **c** elders got together to decide this question.
15: 22 and the whole **c** in Jerusalem chose delegates,
15: 22 The men chosen were two of the **c** leaders—
15: 31 And there was great joy throughout the **c** that day
18: 22 there he went up and visited the **c** at Jerusalem and
20: 17 he sent a message to the elders of the **c** at Ephesus,
20: 28 God's flock—his **c**, purchased with his blood—
21: 18 and all the elders of the Jerusalem **c** were present.
Ro 14: 19 let us aim for harmony in the **c** and try to build
15: 20 rather than where a **c** has already been started by
16: 1 Our sister Phoebe, a deacon in the **c** in Cenchrea,
16: 5 Please give my greetings to the **c** that meets in
16: 23 I am his guest, and the **c** meets here in his home.
1Co 1: 2 We are writing to the **c** of God in Corinth, you who
1: 5 He has enriched your **c** with the gifts of eloquence
1: 10 real harmony so there won't be divisions in the **c**.
5: 1 I am told that you have a man in your **c** who is
5: 4 You are to call a meeting of the **c**, and I will be
5: 5 Then you must cast this man out of the **c** and into
5: 12 those inside the **c** who are sinning in these ways.
6: 4 to outside judges who are not respected by the **c**?
6: 5 Isn't there anyone in all the **c** who is wise enough
8: 1 feel important, it is love that really builds up the **c**.
10: 32 give offense to Jews or Gentiles or the **c** of God.
11: 18 are divisions among you when you meet as a **c**,
11: 22 Or do you really want to disgrace the **c** of God
12: 5 There are different kinds of service in the **c**,
12: 7 to each of us as a means of helping the entire **c**.
14: 4 speaks a word of prophecy strengthens the entire **c**.
14: 5 so that the whole **c** can get some good out of it.
14: 12 for those that will be of real help to the whole **c**.
14: 19 But in a **c** meeting I would much rather speak five
14: 28 they must be silent in your **c** meeting and speak in
14: 34 Women should be silent during the **c** meetings.
14: 35 for it is improper for women to speak in **c**
15: 9 an apostle after the way I persecuted the **c** of God.
16: 19 and all the others who gather in their home for **c**
2Co 1: 1 We are writing to God's **c** in Corinth and to all the
2: 5 the trouble hurt your entire **c** more than he hurt me.
Gal 2: 2 there I talked privately with the leaders of the **c**.
2: 6 And the leaders of the **c** who were there had
2: 9 and John, who were known as pillars of the **c**,
Eph 1: 22 he gave him this authority for the benefit of the **c**.
1: 23 And the **c** is his body; it is filled by Christ,
3: 10 and Gentiles are joined together in his **c**.
3: 21 May he be given glory in the **c** and in Christ Jesus
4: 11 He is the one who gave these gifts to the **c**:
4: 12 God's people to do his work and build up the **c**,
4: 15 way like Christ, who is the head of his body, the **c**.
5: 23 of his wife as Christ is the head of his body, the **c**;
5: 24 As the **c** submits to Christ, so you wives must
5: 25 wives with the same love Christ showed the **c**.
5: 27 He did this to present her to himself as a glorious **c**
5: 29 just as Christ cares for his body, which is the **c**.
5: 32 an illustration of the way Christ and the **c** are one.
Php 3: 6 Yes, in fact I harshly persecuted the **c**.
4: 15 traveled on from Macedonia. No other **c** did this.
Col 1: 18 Christ is the head of the **c**, which is his body.
1: 24 remains of Christ's sufferings for his body, the **c**.
1: 25 **c** by proclaiming his message in all its fullness to
2: 1 I have agonized for you and for the **c** at Laodicea,
4: 16 pass it on to the **c** at Laodicea so they can read it,
1Th 1: 1 It is written to the **c** in Thessalonica, you who
2Th 1: 1 It is written to the **c** in Thessalonica, you who
1Ti 3: 5 own household, how can he take care of God's **c**?
3: 7 people outside the **c** must speak well of him
3: 10 they should be given other responsibilities in the **c**
3: 15 This is the **c** of the living God, which is the pillar
4: 13 I get there, focus on reading the Scriptures to the **c**,
4: 14 when the elders of the **c** laid their hands on you.
5: 3 The **c** should care for any widow who has no one
5: 7 Give these instructions to the **c** so that the widows
5: 16 care of them and not put the responsibility on the **c**.
5: 16 Then the **c** can care for widows who are truly
5: 20 who sins should be rebuked in front of the whole **c**
Phm 1: 2 I am also writing to the **c** that meets in your house.
Jas 3: 1 not many of you should become teachers in the **c**,
5: 14 They should call for the elders of the **c** and have
1Pe 5: 13 Your sister **c** here in Rome sends you greetings,
3Jn 1: 6 They have told the **c** here of your friendship
1: 9 I sent a brief letter to the **c** about this,
1: 10 And when they do help, he puts them out of the **c**.
Rev 1: 3 blesses the one who reads this prophecy to the **c**,
2: 1 "Write this letter to the angel of the **c** in Ephesus.
2: 8 "Write this letter to the angel of the **c** in Smyrna.
2: 12 "Write this letter to the angel of the **c** in
2: 18 "Write this letter to the angel of the **c** in Thyatira.
3: 1 "Write this letter to the angel of the **c** in Sardis.
3: 7 "Write this letter to the angel of the **c** in
3: 14 "Write this letter to the angel of the **c** in Laodicea.

CHURCHES (39) [CHURCH]

Ac 15: 41 and Cilicia to strengthen the **c** there.
16: 5 So the **c** were strengthened in their faith and grew
Ro 16: 4 who is thankful to them; so are all the Gentile **c**.
16: 16 All the **c** of Christ send you their greetings.
1Co 4: 17 teach about Christ Jesus in all the **c** wherever I go.
7: 17 God first called you. This is my rule for all the **c**.
11: 16 and all the **c** of God feel the same way about it.
14: 33 a God of disorder but of peace, as in all the other **c**.
16: 1 the same procedures I gave to the **c** in Galatia.
16: 19 The **c** here in the province of Asia greet you
2Co 8: 1 what God in his kindness has done for the **c** in
8: 8 do it, even though the other **c** are eager to do it.
8: 18 He is highly praised in all the **c** as a preacher of the
8: 19 He was appointed by the **c** to accompany us as we
8: 23 And these brothers are representatives of the **c**.
8: 24 and prove to all the **c** that our boasting about you is
11: 8 I "robbed" other **c** by accepting their
11: 28 I have the daily burden of how the **c** are getting
12: 13 only thing I didn't do, which I do in the other **c**,
Gal 1: 2 join me in sending greetings to the **c** of Galatia.
1: 22 And still the Christians in the **c** in Judea didn't
1Th 2: 14 you imitated the believers in God's **c** in Judea who,
2Th 1: 4 We proudly tell God's other **c** about your
1Pe 5: 1 And now, a word to you who are elders in the **c**.
1Jn 2: 19 These people left our **c** because they never really
Rev 1: 4 This letter is from John to the seven **c** in the
1: 11 down what you see, and send it to the seven **c**:
1: 20 The seven stars are the angels of the seven **c**,
1: 20 and the seven lampstands are the seven **c**.
2: 5 remove your lampstand from its place among the **c**.
2: 7 and understand what the Spirit is saying to the **c**.
2: 11 and understand what the Spirit is saying to the **c**.
2: 17 and understand what the Spirit is saying to the **c**.
2: 23 And all the **c** will know that I am the one who
2: 29 and understand what the Spirit is saying to the **c**.
3: 6 and understand what the Spirit is saying to the **c**.
3: 13 and understand what the Spirit is saying to the **c**.
3: 22 and understand what the Spirit is saying to the **c**."
22: 16 sent my angel to give you this message for the **c**.

CHURNING (2) [CHURNS]

Da 7: 2 saw a great storm **c** the surface of a great sea,
Jude 1: 13 **c** up the dirty foam of their shameful deeds.

CHURNS (2) [CHURNING]

Job 41: 31 the water boil with its commotion. It **c** the depths.
Isa 57: 20 It is never still but continually **c** up mire and dirt.

CHUSHAN-RISHATHAIM [KJV] See CUSHAN-RISHATHAIM

CHUZA (1)

Lk 8: 3 Joanna, the wife of **C**, Herod's business manager;

CIELED [KJV] See LUXURIOUS, PANELED

CILICIA (12)

1Ki 10: 28 horses were imported from Egypt and from **C**;
10: 28 the king's traders acquired them from **C** at the
2Ch 1: 16 horses were imported from Egypt and from **C**;
1: 16 the king's traders acquired them from **C** at the
Ac 6: 9 Alexandria, **C**, and the province of Asia.
15: 23 to the Gentile believers in Antioch, Syria, and **C**.
15: 41 and **C** to strengthen the churches there.
21: 39 Paul replied, "I am a Jew from Tarsus in **C**,
22: 3 "I am a Jew, born in Tarsus, a city in **C**, and I was
23: 34 what province he was from. "**C**," Paul answered.
27: 5 We passed along the coast of the provinces of **C**
Gal 1: 21 I went north into the provinces of Syria and **C**.

CINNAMON (4)

Ex 30: 23 6-1/4 pounds each of **c** and of sweet cane,
Pr 7: 17 I've perfumed my bed with myrrh, aloes, and **c**.
SS 4: 14 and saffron, calamus and **c**, myrrh and aloes,
Rev 18: 13 She also bought **c**, spice, incense, myrrh,

CINNEROTH [KJV] See KINNERETH

CIRCLE (3) [CIRCLED, CIRCLES, CIRCUIT, CIRCULAR, CIRCUMFERENCE, ENCIRCLE, ENCIRCLED]

2Sa 5: 23 **c** around behind them and attack them near the
1Ch 14: 14 **c** around behind them and attack them near the
Isa 40: 22 It is God who sits above the **c** of the earth.

CIRCLED (3) [CIRCLE]

Jos 15: 10 The border **c** west of Baalah to Mount Seir,
Jdg 8: 11 Gideon **c** around by the caravan route east of
Rev 4: 3 And the glow of an emerald **c** his throne like a

CIRCLES (1) [CIRCLE]

Ac 6: 7 God's message was preached in ever-widening **c**.

CIRCUIT (1) [CIRCLE]

Lk 9: 6 So they began their **c** of the villages,

CIRCULAR (1) [CIRCLE]

1Ki 7: 31 The top of each cart had a **c** frame for the basin.

CIRCULATING (1)

Lk 1: 2 They used as their source material the reports **c**

CIRCUMCISE (2) [CIRCUMCISED, CIRCUMCISING, CIRCUMCISION]

Jos 5: 4 Joshua had to **c** them because all the men who
Ac 21: 21 They say that you teach people not to **c** their

CIRCUMCISED (52) [CIRCUMCISE]

Ge 17: 10 must keep: Each male among you must be **c**;

17:12 Every male child must be **c** on the eighth day after
17:13 All must be **c**. Your bodies will thus bear the mark
17:14 Anyone who refuses to be **c** will be cut off from
17:23 and every other male in his household and **c** them,
17:26 Both were **c** the same day,
21: 4 was born, Abraham **c** him as God had commanded.
34:14 couldn't possibly allow this, because you aren't **c**.
34:15 If every man among you will be **c** like we are,
34:22 Every one of us men must be **c**, just as they are.
34:24 So all the men agreed and were **c**.
Ex 4:25 his wife, took a flint knife and **c** her son.
12:44 has been purchased may eat it if he has been **c**.
12:48 the LORD's Passover, let all the males be **c**.
Lev 12: 3 On the eighth day, the boy must be **c**.
Jos 5: 2 "Use knives of flint to make the Israelites a **c**
5: 3 and **c** the entire male population of Israel at
5: 5 Those who left Egypt had all been **c**, but none of
5: 5 during the years in the wilderness, had been **c**.
5: 7 So Joshua **c** their sons who had not been **c** on the
way to the Promised Land—
5: 8 After all the males had been **c**, they rested in the
Jer 9:25 "when I will punish all those who are **c** in body
Eze 44: 9 will enter my sanctuary if they have not been **c**
Lk 2:21 Eight days later, when the baby was **c**, he was
Ac 7: 8 Abraham's son, was **c** when he was eight days old.
15: 5 and declared that all Gentile converts must be **c**
16: 3 he arranged for Timothy to be **c** before they left,
Ro 2:27 will be much better off than you Jews who are **c**
4:10 he declared righteous only after he had been **c**, or
was it before he was **c**?
4:10 God accepted him first, and then he was **c** later!
4:11 him to be righteous—even before he was **c**.
4:11 father of those who have faith but have not been **c**,
4:12 also the spiritual father of those who have been **c**,
4:12 same kind of faith Abraham had before he was **c**.
1Co 7:18 a man who was **c** before he became a believer
should not be **c** now.
7:19 no difference whether or not a man has been **c**.
Gal 2: 3 not even demand that my companion Titus be **c**,
5: 3 If you are trying to find favor with God by being **c**,
5: 6 no difference to God whether we are **c** or not **c**.
5:11 if I were still preaching that you must be **c**—
6:12 Those who are trying to force you to be **c** are doing
6:13 They only want you to be **c** so they can brag about
6:15 make any difference now whether we have been **c**
Php 3: 2 those mutilators who say you must be **c** to be
3: 3 God in the Spirit are the only ones who are truly **c**.
3: 5 For I was **c** when I was eight days old, having been
Col 2:11 When you came to Christ, you were "**c**," but not
3:11 **c** or uncircumcised, barbaric, uncivilized, slave,

CIRCUMCISING (1) [CIRCUMCISE]

Jn 7:23 For if the correct time for **c** your son falls on the

CIRCUMCISION (17) [CIRCUMCISE]

Ex 4:26 she was referring to the **c**.)
Lk 1:59 the relatives and friends came for the **c** ceremony.
Jn 7:22 the Sabbath, too, when you obey Moses' law of **c**.
7:22 this tradition of **c** is older than the law of Moses;
Ac 7: 8 God also gave Abraham the covenant of **c** at that
15: 1 "Unless you keep the ancient Jewish custom of **c**
Ro 2:25 The Jewish ceremony of **c** is worth something only
2:28 you have gone through the Jewish ceremony of **c**.
2:29 And true **c** is not a cutting of the body but a change
3: 1 Is there any value in the Jewish ceremony of **c**?
4:11 The **c** ceremony was a sign that Abraham already
Gal 2:12 the Gentile Christians, who don't bother with **c**.
5: 2 If you are counting on **c** to make you right with
5:12 to mutilate you by **c** would mutilate themselves.
6:13 And even those who advocate **c** don't really keep
Eph 2:11 who were proud of their **c**, even though it affected
Tit 1:10 This is especially true of those who insist on **c** for

CIRCUMFERENCE (4) [CIRCLE]

1Ki 7:15 bronze pillars, each 27 feet tall and 18 feet in **c**.
7:23 It was 7-1/2 feet deep and about 45 feet in **c**.
2Ch 4: 2 It was 7-1/2 feet deep and about 45 feet in **c**.
Jer 52:21 Each of the pillars was 27 feet tall and 18 feet in **c**.

CIRCUMSPECT [KJV] See OBEY

CIRCUMSTANCE (1) [CIRCUMSTANCES]

1Co 13: 7 is always hopeful, and endures through every **c**.

CIRCUMSTANCES (2) [CIRCUMSTANCE]

Ge 24: 8 But under no **c** are you to take my son there."
Ps 112: 6 Such people will not be overcome by evil **c**.

CIS [KJV] See KISH

CISTERN (9) [CISTERNS]

Lev 11:36 body of such an animal falls into a spring or a **c**,
Jer 38: 6 and lowered him by ropes into an empty **c** in the
38: 6 There was no water in the **c**, but there was a thick
38: 7 palace official, heard that Jeremiah was in the **c**.
38: 9 thing in putting Jeremiah the prophet into the **c**.
38:10 and pull Jeremiah out of the **c** before he dies."
38:11 He carried these to the **c** and lowered them to
41: 7 but ten of them and threw their bodies into a **c**.
41: 9 The **c** where Ishmael dumped the bodies of the

CISTERNS (5) [CISTERN]

Dt 6:11 You will draw water from **c** you did not dig,
1Sa 13: 6 tried to hide in caves, holes, rocks, tombs, and **c**.
2Ch 26:10 forts in the wilderness and dug many water **c**,
Ne 9:25 with **c** already dug and vineyards and olive groves
Jer 2:13 And they have dug for themselves cracked **c** that

CITADEL (3) [CITADELS]

1Ki 16:18 he went into the **c** of the king's house and burned it
2Ki 15:25 and Arieh, in the **c** of the palace at Samaria.
Mic 4: 8 As for you, O Jerusalem, the **c** of God's people,

CITADELS (1) [CITADEL]

Ps 48:13 Take note of the fortified walls, / and tour all the **c**,

CITIES (217) [CITY]

CITIES OF JUDAH (7) 2Ki 18:13; 2Ch 11:10; 17:2; 33:14; Ps 97:8; Isa 36:1; Jer 34:7

CITIES OF REFUGE (12) Nu 35:6,11,13; Dt 4:41; 19:2,5,7,9,11; Jos 20:2,7,8

FORTIFIED CITIES (28) Nu 32:16,17,36; Dt 3:5; Jos 10:20; 19:35; 1Ki 4:13; 2Ki 8:12; 18:13; 19:25; 2Ch 11:10,23; 12:4; 14:6; 17:2,19; 19:5; 21:3; 32:1; 33:14; Ne 9:25; Isa 17:3; 27:10; 36:1; 37:26; Jer 4:5; 5:17; 8:14

Ge 10:10 with the **c** of Babel, Erech, Akkad, and Calneh.
13:12 to a place near Sodom, among the **c** of the plain.
19:25 along with the other **c** and villages of the plain,
19:28 as from a furnace, rising from the **c** there.
19:29 removing him from the disaster that engulfed the **c**
41:35 and store it away so there will be food in the **c**.
41:48 and stored them for the government in nearby **c**.
Ex 1:11 They forced them to build the **c** of Pithom
Lev 25:32 they have sold within the **c** belonging to them.
25:33 all houses within the Levitical **c**—must be returned
25:33 the **c** reserved for the Levites are the only property
25:34 around each of the Levitical **c** may never be sold.
26:25 If you flee to your **c**, I will send a plague to destroy
26:31 I will make your **c** desolate and destroy your places
26:33 will become desolate, and your **c** will lie in ruins.
Nu 13:28 and their **c** and towns are fortified and very large.
32:16 and fortified **c** for our wives and children.
32:17 our families will stay in the fortified **c** we build
32:36 These were all fortified **c** with sheepfolds for their
35: 6 "You must give the Levites six **c** of refuge,
35:11 designate **c** of refuge for people to flee to if they
35:12 These **c** will be places of protection from a dead
35:13 Designate six **c** of refuge for yourselves,
35:15 These **c** are for the protection of Israelites,
Dt 3: 5 These were all fortified **c** with high walls
3:10 We had now conquered all the **c** on the plateau,
4:41 Then Moses set apart three **c** of refuge east of the
4:43 These were the **c**: Bezer on the wilderness plateau
6:10 with large, prosperous **c** that you did not build.
9: 1 They live in **c** with walls that reach to the sky!
19: 2 Then you must set apart three **c** of refuge in the
19: 3 three districts, with one of these **c** in each district.
19: 3 Keep the roads to these **c** in good repair so that
19: 4 the slayer may flee to any of these **c** and be safe.
19: 5 the slayer could flee to one of the **c** of refuge
19: 7 am commanding you to set aside three **c** of refuge.
19: 9 you must designate three additional **c** of refuge.
19:11 and then escapes to one of the **c** of refuge.
28:52 They will lay siege to your **c** until all the fortified
Jos 10: 2 as large as the royal **c** and larger than Ai.
10:19 Don't let them get back to their **c**, for the LORD
10:20 remnant that managed to reach their fortified **c**.
11:13 Joshua did not burn any of the **c** built on mounds
11:14 and cattle of the ravaged **c** for themselves,
12:24 In all, thirty-one kings and their **c** were destroyed.
13: 4 and includes the five Philistine **c** of Gaza, Ashdod,
13:31 and King Og's royal **c** of Ashtaroth and Edrei.
14:12 found the Anakites living there in great, walled **c**.
19:35 The fortified **c** included in this territory were
19:38 nineteen **c** with their surrounding villages.
20: 2 "Now tell the Israelites to designate the **c** of
20: 3 person unintentionally can run to one of these **c**
20: 4 "Upon reaching one of these **c**, the one who
20: 7 The following **c** were designated as **c** of
20: 8 the following **c** were designated as **c** of refuge:
20: 9 These **c** were set apart for Israelites as well as the
20: 9 another person could take refuge in one of these **c**.
21: 7 The clan of Merari received twelve **c** from the
24:13 worked for, and I gave you **c** you did not
build—the **c** in which you are now living.
Jdg 1:18 Judah captured the **c** of Gaza, Ashkelon,
1Sa 5: 8 called together the rulers of the five Philistine **c**
6:18 The five gold rats represented the five Philistine **c**
2Sa 8: 8 amount of bronze from Hadadezer's **c** of Tebah
10:12 bravely to save our people and the **c** of our God.
12:31 he dealt with the people of all the Ammonite **c**.
24: 7 and all the **c** of the Hivites and Canaanites.
1Ki 4:13 including sixty great fortified **c** with gates barred
9:15 and the **c** of Hazor, Megiddo, and Gezer.
9:19 and constructed **c** where his chariots and horses
10:26 He stationed many of them in the chariot **c**,
15:23 and the names of the **c** he built are recorded in
22:39 and the **c** he built are recorded in *The Book of the*
2Ki 3:19 You will conquer the best of their **c**,
3:25 They destroyed the **c**, covered their good land with
8:12 You will burn their fortified **c**, kill their young
17: 6 River in Gozan, and among the **c** of the Medes.
18:11 River in Gozan, and among the **c** of the Medes.
18:13 of Assyria came to attack the fortified **c** of Judah
19:25 that you should crush fortified **c** into heaps of
1Ch 18: 8 amount of bronze from Hadadezer's **c** of Tebah
19:13 bravely to save our people and the **c** of our God.
20: 3 he dealt with the people of all the Ammonite **c**.
2Ch 1:14 He stationed many of them in the chariot **c**,
8: 5 He fortified the **c** of Upper Beth-horon and Lower
8: 6 and constructed **c** where his chariots and horses
9:25 He stationed many of them in the chariot **c**,
11: 5 and fortified various **c** for the defense of Judah.
11:10 These became the fortified **c** of Judah
11:23 and stationed them in the fortified **c** throughout the
12: 4 Shishak conquered Judah's fortified **c** and
14: 6 he was able to build up the fortified **c** throughout
16: 4 Abel-beth-maacah, and all the store **c** in Naphtali.
17: 2 He stationed troops in all the fortified **c** of Judah,
17:12 and built fortresses and store **c** throughout Judah.
17:19 stationed in the fortified **c** throughout Judah.
19: 5 judges throughout the nation in all the fortified **c**,
21: 3 also the ownership of some of Judah's fortified **c**.
32: 1 He laid siege to the fortified **c**, giving orders for his
33:14 military officers in all of the fortified **c** of Judah.
Ne 9:25 Our ancestors captured fortified **c** and fertile land.
Est 9: 2 The Jews gathered in their **c** throughout all the
9:28 throughout the provinces and **c** of the empire.
Job 15:28 but their **c** will be ruined. They will live in
Ps 9: 6 have met their doom; / their **c** are perpetual ruins.
9: 6 Even the memory of their uprooted **c** is lost.
97: 8 and rejoiced, / and all the **c** of Judah are glad
107:36 brings the hungry to settle there / and build their **c**.
Isa 1: 7 Your country lies in ruins, and your **c** are burned.
6:11 And he replied, "Until their **c** are destroyed,
14:17 the king who demolished the world's greatest **c**
14:21 conquer the land or rebuild the **c** of the world."
14:31 Weep, you Philistine **c**, for you are doomed!
15: 1 In one night your **c** of Ar and Kir will be
15: 4 The cries from the **c** of Heshbon and Elealeh will
17: 2 The **c** of Aroer will be deserted. Sheep will graze
17: 3 The fortified **c** of Israel will also be destroyed,
17: 9 Their largest **c** will be as deserted as overgrown
17: 9 They will become like the **c** the Amorites
19:18 In that day five of Egypt's **c** will follow the
25: 2 You turn mighty **c** into heaps of ruins. **C** with
strong walls are turned to rubble.
27:10 Israel's fortified **c** will be silent and empty,
32:13 Your joyful homes and happy **c** will be gone.
36: 1 of Assyria came to attack the fortified **c** of Judah
37:26 that you should crush fortified **c** into heaps of
54: 3 will take over other nations and live in their **c**.
58:12 children will rebuild the deserted ruins of your **c**.
58:12 known as the people who rebuild their walls and **c**.
60:10 "Foreigners will come to rebuild your **c**. Kings
61: 4 the ancient ruins, repairing **c** long ago destroyed.
64:10 Your holy **c** are destroyed; even Jerusalem is a
Jer 2:15 has been destroyed, and the **c** are now in ruins.
2:16 marching from their **c** of Memphis and Tahpanhes,
2:28 For you have as many gods as there are **c**
4: 5 'Run for your lives! Flee to the fortified **c**!'
4:26 The **c** lay in ruins, crushed by the LORD's fierce
4:29 the people flee in terror from the **c**.
4:29 All the **c** have been abandoned—not a person
5:17 And they will destroy your fortified **c**, which you
8:14 Come, let's go to the fortified **c** to die there.
8:16 the land and everything in it—**c** and people alike.'
11:13 you have as many gods as there are **c** and towns.
15: 7 I will winnow you like grain at the gates of your **c**
20:16 Let him be destroyed like the **c** of old that the
25:20 and the kings of the Philistine **c** of Ashkelon,
31:21 back again, my virgin Israel; return to your **c** here.
31:23 the people of Judah and its **c** will again say,
33: 7 the fortunes of Judah and Israel and rebuild their **c**.
34: 7 the only **c** of Judah with their walls still standing.
44: 1 living in northern Egypt in the **c** of Migdol,
46:14 Publish it in the **c** of Migdol, Memphis,
47: 2 the land and everything in it—**c** and people alike.
48: 9 so she could fly away, for her **c** will be left empty,
48:21 All the **c** of the plateau lie in ruins, too.
48:24 and Bozrah—all the **c** of Moab, far and near.
48:28 people of Moab, flee from your **c** and towns!
48:41 "Her **c** will fall; her strongholds will be seized.
50:32 For I will light a fire in the **c** of Babylon that will
51:14 "Your **c** will be filled with enemies, like fields
51:43 Her **c** now lie in ruins; she is a dry wilderness
La 2: 1 The fairest of Israel's **c** lies in the dust,
Eze 6:14 and make their **c** desolate from the wilderness in
12:20 The **c** will be destroyed and the farmland deserted.
19: 7 and destroyed their towns and **c**. / Their farms
23:45 But righteous people will judge these sister **c** for
25: 9 and wipe out their glorious frontier **c**—
27:28 "Your **c** by the sea tremble as your helmsmen cry
29:12 Its **c** will be empty and desolate for forty years,
surrounded by other desolate **c**.
30: 7 by desolate nations, and its **c** will be in ruins,
surrounded by other ruined **c**.
33:24 of Judah living among the ruined **c** keep saying,
35: 4 I will demolish your **c** and make you desolate,
35: 9 you desolate forever. Your **c** will never be rebuilt.
36: 4 and long-deserted **c** that have been destroyed
36:10 and the ruined **c** will be rebuilt and filled with
36:33 I will bring people to live in your **c**, and the ruins
36:35 The ruined **c** now have strong walls, and they are
36:38 The ruined **c** will be crowded with people once
38:12 I will go to those once-desolate **c** that are again
Da 11:18 he will turn his attention to the coastal **c**
Hos 8:14 built great palaces, and Judah has fortified its **c**.
11: 6 War will swirl through their **c**; their enemies will
Joel 3: 4 against me, Tyre and Sidon and you **c** of Philistia?
Am 4:11 "I destroyed some of your **c**, as I destroyed Sodom
5: 3 "When one of your **c** sends a thousand men to
9:14 and they will rebuild their ruined **c** and live in
Mic 2:13 He will bring you through the gates of your **c** of

5:11 your walls and demolish the defenses of your c.
5:14 and destroy the c where your idol temples stand.
7:11 In that day, Israel, your c will be rebuilt, and your
Hab 2:8 filled the countryside with violence and all the c,
2:12 "How terrible it will be for you who build c with
2:17 of your murder and violence in c everywhere!
Zep 1:16 Down go the walled c and strongest battlements!
2:4 these Philistine c, too, will be rooted out and left in
3:6 Their c are now deserted; their streets are in silent
Zec 8:20 and c around the world will travel to Jerusalem.
9:2 and for the c of Tyre and Sidon, too, though they
Mt 9:35 Jesus traveled through all the c and villages of that
10:15 the wicked c of Sodom and Gomorrah will be
11:20 Then Jesus began to denounce the c where he had
Mk 6:56 he went—in villages and c and out on the farms—
Lk 8:1 long afterward Jesus began a tour of the nearby c
19:17 so you will be governor of ten c as your reward.'
19:19 the king said. 'You can be governor over five c.'
Ac 12:20 because their c were dependent upon Herod's
14:6 to the c of Lystra and Derbe and the surrounding
26:11 I even hounded them in distant c of foreign lands.
2Co 11:26 I have faced danger in the c, in the deserts, and on
2Pe 2:6 he turned the c of Sodom and Gomorrah into heaps
Jude 1:7 And don't forget the c of Sodom and Gomorrah
1:7 Those c were destroyed by fire and are a warning
Rev 16:19 and c around the world fell into heaps of rubble.

CITIZEN (9) [CITIZENS]

Est 1:16 also every official and c throughout your empire.
Ps 87:5 of Jerusalem, / "Everyone has become a c here."
87:6 will say, "This one has become a c of Jerusalem."
Ac 22:25 "Is it legal for you to whip a Roman c who hasn't
22:26 "What are you doing? This man is a Roman c!"
22:27 and asked Paul, "Tell me, are you a Roman c?"
22:28 "and it cost me plenty!" "But I am a c by birth!"
22:29 withdrew when they heard he was a Roman c,
23:27 When I learned that he was a Roman c, I removed

CITIZENS (48) [CITIZEN]

Lev 4:27 "If any of the c of Israel do something forbidden
Dt 13:13 c astray by encouraging them to worship foreign
17:20 and acting as if he is above his fellow c.
Jos 8:33 foreigners and c alike—along with the leaders,
1Sa 5:3 But when the c of Ashdod went to see it the next
11:1 But the c of Jabesh asked for peace. "Make a
1Ki 21:9 "Call the c together for fasting and prayer and give
2Ki 15:16 because its c refused to surrender the town.
25:19 was in charge of recruitment, and sixty other c.
2Ch 19:10 Whenever a case comes to you from fellow c in an
Ezr 2:29 The c of Nebo | 52
2:30 The c of Magbish | 156
2:31 The c of Elam | 1,254
2:32 The c of Harim | 320
2:33 The c of Lod, Hadid, and Ono | 725
2:34 The c of Jericho | 345
2:35 The c of Senaah | 3,630
Ne 7:5 the city, along with the ordinary c, for registration.
7:34 The c of Elam | 1,254
7:35 The c of Harim | 320
7:36 The c of Jericho | 345
7:37 The c of Lod, Hadid, and Ono | 721
7:38 The c of Senaah | 3,930
Ps 87:4 They have all become c of Jerusalem!
Pr 11:11 Upright c bless a city and make it prosper,
Ecc 7:19 A wise person is stronger than the ten leading c of
Isa 3:3 army officers, honorable c, advisers,
10:31 And the c of Gebim are preparing to run.
32:5 cheaters will not be respected as outstanding c.
54:13 I will teach all your c, and their prosperity will be
56:3 let them think that I consider them second-class c.
Jer 19:3 you kings of Judah and c of Jerusalem!
44:24 the LORD, all you c of Judah who live in Egypt.
46:19 Get ready to leave for exile, you c of Egypt!
52:25 was in charge of recruitment, and sixty other c.
Hos 6:9 Its c are bands of robbers, lying in ambush for their
Mic 6:12 Your c are so used to lying that their tongues can
Mt 17:26 "Well, then," Jesus said, "the c are free!
Mk 6:21 army officers, and the leading c of Galilee.
Lk 10:20 because your names are registered as c of heaven."
16:8 And it is true that the c of this world are more
Ac 16:37 without trial and jailed us—and we are Roman c.
16:38 alarmed to learn that Paul and Silas were Roman c.
19:35 down enough to speak. "C of Ephesus," he said.
Eph 2:19 You are c along with all of God's holy people.
Php 1:27 of the Good News about Christ, as c of heaven.
3:20 But we are c of heaven, where the Lord Jesus
Rev 3:12 them, and they will be c in the city of my God—

CITRUS (1)

Lev 23:40 On the first day, gather fruit from c trees,

CITY (808) [CITIES, CITY'S]

CITY OF DAVID (43) 2Sa 5:7,9; 6:10,12,16; 1Ki 2:10; 3:1; 8:1; 9:24; 14:31; 15:8,24; 22:50; 2Ki 8:24; 9:28; 12:21; 14:20; 15:7,38; 16:20; 1Ch 11:5,7; 13:13; 15:1,29; 2Ch 5:2; 8:11; 12:16; 14:1; 16:14; 21:1,20; 24:16,25; 25:28; 27:9; 32:5,30; 33:14; Ne 3:15; 12:37; Isa 29:1; Lk 2:11

CITY OF HIS FATHER, DAVID (3) 1Ki 11:27,43; 2Ch 9:31

CITY OF REFUGE (13) Nu 35:25,26,28,32; Dt 19:6,12; Jos 21:13,21,27,32,38; 1Ch 6:57,67

FORTIFIED CITY (8) Jos 19:29; 2Sa 20:6; 2Ki 10:2; Ps 60:9; 108:10; Pr 18:19; Jer 1:18; Da 11:15

GREAT CITY (16) Ge 11:4; Jer 22:8; 51:47; Da 4:30; Am 6:2; Jnh 1:2; 3:2; 4:11; Rev 14:8; 16:19; 17:18; 18:2,10,16,19,21

HOLY CITY (11) Ne 11:1,18; Ps 2:6; Isa 48:2; 52:1; Da 9:24; Mt 27:53; Rev 11:2; 21:2,10; 22:19

Ge 4:17 When Cain founded a c, he named it Enoch after
10:12 the main c of the empire, located between Nineveh
11:4 Let's build a great c with a tower that reaches to
11:5 But the LORD came down to see the c
11:8 over the earth; and that ended the building of the c.
11:9 That is why the c was called Babel, because it was
18:24 you find fifty innocent people there within the c—
18:26 in Sodom, I will spare the entire c for their sake."
18:28 Will you destroy the c for lack of five?"
19:1 two angels came to the entrance of the c of Sodom,
19:2 "we'll just spend the night out here in the c
19:4 came from all over the c and surrounded the house.
19:12 "Do you have any other relatives here in the c?"
19:13 For we will destroy the c completely. The stench
19:14 tell his daughters' fiancés, "Quick, get out of the c!
19:15 or you will be caught in the destruction of the c."
19:16 and rushed them to safety outside the c,
23:18 in the presence of the Hittite elders at the c gate.
36:32 son of Beor, who ruled from his c of Dinhabah.
36:35 Bedad became king and ruled from the c of Avith.
36:36 Samlah from the c of Masrekah became king.
36:37 Shaul from the c of Rehoboth on the Euphrates
36:39 Hadad became king and ruled from the c of Pau.
44:4 But when they were barely out of the c,
44:13 loaded the donkeys again, and returned to the c.
Ex 9:29 "As soon as I leave the c, I will lift my hands
9:33 So Moses left Pharaoh and went out of the c.
Lev 25:29 "Anyone who sells a house inside a walled c has
25:30 then the house within the walled c will become the
Nu 13:22 seven years before the Egyptian c of Zoan.)
21:25 including the c of Heshbon and its surrounding
21:27 "Come to Heshbon, c of Sihon! / May it be
21:28 a blaze from the c of Sihon. / It burned the c of Ar in Moab;
33:3 They set out from the c of Rameses on the morning
35:25 and they must send the slayer back to live in a c of
35:26 " 'But if the slayer leaves the c of refuge,
35:27 nearest relative finds him outside the c limits
35:28 The slayer should have stayed inside the c of
35:32 from someone who has fled to a c of refuge,
Dt 3:11 It can still be seen in the Ammonite c of Rabbah.)
19:6 If the distance to the nearest c of refuge was too
19:12 the murderer brought back from the c of refuge
34:3 with Jericho—the c of palms—as far as Zoar.
Jos 2:5 They left the c at dusk, as the c gates were about to close,
2:7 as the king's men had left, the c gate was shut.
2:15 since Rahab's house was built into the c wall,
2:22 but they finally returned to the c without success.
3:16 Then all the people crossed over near the c of
5:13 As Joshua approached the c of Jericho, he looked
6:3 Your entire army is to march around the c once a
6:4 On the seventh day you are to march around the c
6:5 Then the walls of the c will collapse,
6:5 and the people can charge straight into the c."
6:7 "March around the c, and the armed men will lead
6:11 So the Ark of the LORD was carried around the c
6:14 On the second day they marched around the c once
6:15 and marched around the c as they had done before.
6:15 But this time they went around the c seven times.
6:16 "Shout! For the LORD has given you the c!
6:17 The c and everything in it must be completely
6:20 and the Israelites charged straight into the c from
6:24 Then the Israelites burned the c and everything in
6:26 who tries to rebuild the c of Jericho. / At the cost
7:2 of his men from Jericho to spy out the c of Ai,
7:5 chased the Israelites from the c gate as far as the
8:1 you the king of Ai, his people, his c, and his land.
8:2 cattle for yourselves. Set an ambush behind the c."
8:4 "Hide in ambush close behind the c and be ready
8:6 will let them chase us until they have all left the c.
8:7 up from your ambush and take possession of the c,
8:8 Set the c on fire, as the LORD has commanded.
8:11 side of Ai, with a valley between them and the c.
8:12 between Bethel and Ai, on the west side of the c.
8:13 So they stationed the main army north of the c and the ambush west of the c.
8:14 he didn't realize there was an ambush behind the c.
8:16 and all the men in the c were called out to chase
8:16 In this way, they were lured away from the c.
8:17 after the Israelites, and the c was left wide open.
8:18 your spear toward Ai, for I will give you the c."
8:19 men in ambush jumped up and poured into the c.
8:20 smoke from the c was filling the sky, and they had
8:21 and that smoke was rising from the c,
8:22 Then the Israelites who were inside the c came out
8:24 army finished killing all the men outside the c,
8:27 and the treasures of the c were not destroyed,
8:29 down the body and threw it in front of the c gate.
10:1 just as he had destroyed the c of Jericho and killed
10:2 they heard all this because Gibeon was a large c—
10:28 That same day Joshua completely destroyed the c
10:28 the king. Not one person in the c was left alive.
10:30 too, the LORD gave them the c and its king.
10:30 They slaughtered everyone in the c and left no
10:33 had arrived with his army to help defend the c.
10:35 they completely destroyed everyone in the c.
10:39 They captured the c, its king, and all of its
11:11 completely destroyed every living thing in the c.
11:11 person was spared. And then Joshua burned the c.
12:23 The king of Dor in the c of Naphoth-dor
15:8 the Jebusites, where the c of Jerusalem is located.
15:13 So Caleb was given the c of Arba (that is, Hebron),
15:62 Nibshan, the C of Salt, and En-gedi—six towns
15:63 out the Jebusites, who lived in the c of Jerusalem,
19:29 turned toward Ramah and the fortified c of Tyre
19:47 They renamed the c Dan after their ancestor.
20:4 death will appear before the leaders at the c gate
20:4 They must allow the accused to enter the c and live
20:6 the person who caused the death must stay in that c
20:6 c until the death of the high priest who was in
21:12 But the fields beyond the c and the surrounding
21:13 Hebron (a c of refuge for those who accidentally
21:21 Shechem (a c of refuge for those who accidentally
21:27 Golan in Bashan (a c of refuge) and Be-eshterah.
21:32 they received Kedesh in Galilee (a c of refuge),
21:38 they received Ramoth in Gilead (a c of refuge),
Jdg 1:8 killing all its people and setting the c on fire.
1:20 The c of Hebron was given to Caleb as Moses had
1:24 who confronted a man coming out of the c.
1:24 They said to him, "Show us a way into the c,
1:25 and they killed everyone in the c except for this
1:26 to the land of the Hittites, where he built a c.
1:26 He named the c Luz, and it is known by that name
5:8 Israel chose new gods, / war erupted at the c gates.
5:11 of the LORD / marched down to the c gates.
9:30 But when Zebul, the leader of the c, heard what
9:31 and now they are inciting the c to rebel against
9:33 the morning, as soon as it is daylight, storm the c.
9:35 Gaal was standing at the c gates when Abimelech
9:38 The men you mocked are right outside the c!
9:40 covered with dead bodies all the way to the c gate.
9:43 Abimelech saw the people coming out of the c,
9:44 and his group stormed the c gate to keep the men
9:45 on all day before Abimelech finally captured the c.
9:45 He killed the people, leveled the c, and scattered
9:50 Then Abimelech attacked the c of Thebez
9:51 But there was a strong tower inside the c,
16:1 One day Samson went to the Philistine c of Gaza
16:2 and waited all night at the c gates.
16:3 got up, took hold of the c gates with its two posts,
19:11 late to travel; let's stay in this Jebusite c tonight."
19:12 "we can't stay in this foreign c where there are no
1Sa 5:1 the battleground at Ebenezer to the c of Ashdod.
5:8 and replied, "Move it to the c of Gath."
5:10 So they sent the Ark of God to the c of Ekron,
5:11 and great fear was sweeping across the c.
11:1 his army against the Israelite c of Jabesh-gilead.
11:9 What joy there was throughout the c when that
15:5 Then Saul went to the c of Amalek and lay in wait
20:40 to the boy and told him to take them back to the c.
20:42 Then David left, and Jonathan returned to the c.
21:1 David went to the c of Nob to see Ahimelech the
22:19 Then he went to Nob, the c of the priests,
23:7 to me, for he has trapped himself in a walled c!"
27:5 the country towns instead of here in the royal c."
31:10 and they fastened his body to the wall of the c of
2Sa 5:7 the fortress of Zion, now called the C of David.
5:8 from the defenders of the c reached David,
5:8 "Go up through the water tunnel into the c
5:9 fortress his home, and he called it the C of David.
5:9 He built additional fortifications around the c,
6:10 move the Ark of the LORD into the C of David.
6:12 and brought the Ark to the C of David with a great
6:16 But as the Ark of the LORD entered the C of
8:1 the Philistines by conquering Gath, their largest c.
10:3 David has sent them to spy out the c so that they
10:8 up their battle lines at the entrance of the c gates,
10:14 they ran from Abishai and retreated into the c.
11:1 In the process they laid siege to the c of Rabbah.
11:2 As he looked out over the c, he noticed a woman
11:16 So Joab assigned Uriah to a spot close to the c wall
11:20 and ask, 'Why did the troops go so close to the c?
11:23 "And as we chased them back to the c gates,
11:25 Fight harder next time, and conquer the c!"
12:30 David took a vast amount of plunder from the c.
13:34 a great crowd coming toward the c from the west.
15:2 every morning and went out to the gate of the c.
15:14 If we get out of the c before he arrives, both we
15:14 and the c of Jerusalem will be spared from
15:17 out on foot, and they paused at the edge of the c
15:25 Zadok to take the Ark of God back into the c.
15:27 and Abiathar should return quietly to the c with
15:29 and Abiathar took the Ark of God back to the c
17:13 And if David has escaped into some c, you will
17:13 and drag the walls of the c into the nearest valley
17:17 so as not to be seen entering and leaving the c.
18:3 and it is better that you stay here in the c and send
18:4 So he stood at the gate of the c as all the divisions
18:24 While David was sitting at the c gate,
19:3 They crept back into the c as though they were
19:8 So the king went out and sat at the c gate, and as the news spread throughout the c that he
20:6 and chase after him before he gets into a fortified c
20:14 his own clan of Bicri at the c of Abel-beth-maacah.
20:15 and built a ramp against the c wall and began
20:16 But a wise woman in the c called out to Joab,
20:18 to settle an argument, ask advice at the c of Abel.'
20:19 faithful in Israel. But you are destroying a loyal c.
20:20 "Believe me, I don't want to destroy your c!
20:21 him over to me, we will leave the c in peace."
21:12 the public square of the Philistine c of Beth-shan.)
1Ki 1:41 going on? Why is the c in such an uproar?"
1:45 and the whole c is celebrating and rejoicing.
2:10 Then David died and was buried in the C of David.
2:36 But don't step outside the c to go anywhere else.
3:1 He brought her to live in the C of David until he
3:1 Temple of the LORD and the wall around the c.

5:18 Men from the c of Gebal helped Solomon's
8: 1 covenant from its location in the C of David,
8:16 I have never chosen a c among the tribes of Israel
8:44 and if they pray to the LORD toward this c that
8:48 to their ancestors, toward this c you have chosen,
9:16 He gave the c to his daughter as a wedding gift
9:17 So Solomon rebuilt the c of Gezer.) He also built
9:24 from the C of David to the new palace he had built
11:13 and for the sake of Jerusalem, my chosen c."
11:26 He came from the c of Zeredah in Ephraim, and his
11:27 and repairing the walls of the c of his father,
11:36 the c I have chosen to be the place for my name.
11:43 he was buried in the c of his father, David.
12:25 then built up the c of Shechem in the hill country
13:29 and took it back to the c to mourn over him
14:11 your family who die in the c will be eaten by dogs,
14:12 "Go on home, and when you enter the c, the child
14:21 the c the LORD had chosen from among all the
14:31 he was buried among his ancestors in the C of
15: 8 Abijam died, he was buried in the C of David.
15:24 he was buried with his ancestors in the C of David.
16: 4 Those of your family who die in the c will be eaten
16:18 When Zimri saw that the c had been taken, he went
16:24 He built a c on it and called the c Samaria in honor
17: 9 in the village of Zarephath, near the c of Sidon.
20: 2 Ben-hadad sent messengers into the c to relay this
20:12 his officers. So they prepared to attack the c.
20:17 the provincial commanders marched out of the c.
20:30 Ben-hadad fled into the c and hid in a secret room.
21: 8 and other leaders of the c where Naboth lived.
21:13 So he was dragged outside the c and stoned to
21:14 The c officials then sent word to Jezebel,
21:19 dogs will lick your blood outside the c just as they
21:23 eat the body of your wife, Jezebel, at the c wall.
21:24 The members of your family who die in the c will
22: 3 are still occupying our c of Ramoth-gilead?
22:26 the governor of the c, and to my son Joash.
22:50 he was buried with his ancestors in the C of David.
2Ki 6:14 with many chariots and horses to surround the c.
6:19 This isn't the right c! Follow me, and I will take
6:25 As a result there was a great famine in the c.
6:26 king of Israel was walking along the wall of the c,
7: 3 with leprosy sitting at the entrance of the c gates.
7: 4 and we will starve if we go back into the c.
7:10 So they went back to the c and told the gatekeepers
7:12 They are expecting us to leave the c, and then they will take us alive and capture the c."
8:24 he was buried with his ancestors in the C of David.
9:28 where they buried him with his ancestors in the C
10: 1 Now Ahab had seventy sons living in the c of
10: 1 and sent copies to Samaria, to the officials of the c,
10: 2 horses, a fortified c, and weapons.
10: 5 So the palace and c administrators, together with
10: 8 "Pile them in two heaps at the entrance of the c
10:18 Jehu called a meeting of all the people of the c
11:20 and the c was peaceful because Athaliah had been
12:21 Joash was buried with his ancestors in the C of
14:20 and he was buried with his ancestors in the C of
15: 7 he was buried near his ancestors in the C of David.
15:38 he was buried with his ancestors in the C of David.
16:20 he was buried with his ancestors in the C of David.
17: 9 from the smallest outpost to the largest walled c.
18: 8 their smallest outpost to their largest walled c.
18: 9 and began a siege on the c of Samaria.
18:27 you do not surrender, this c will be put under siege.
18:30 This c will never be handed over to the Assyrian
19:29 the LORD will protect this c from Assyria's king.
19:33 he came. He will not enter this c, says the LORD.
20: 6 will rescue you and this c from the king of Assyria.
20:20 a pool and dug a tunnel to bring water into the c,
21: 7 the c I have chosen from among all the other tribes
22:16 I will destroy this c and its people, just as I stated
22:19 LORD when you heard what I said against this c
22:20 I will not send the promised disaster against this c
23: 8 This gate was located to the left of the c gate as one enters the c.
23:27 my presence and reject my chosen c of Jerusalem
24:11 Nebuchadnezzar himself arrived at the c during the
25: 1 They surrounded the c and built siege ramps
25: 3 the famine in the c had become very severe,
25: 4 Then a section of the c wall was broken down,
25: 4 all the soldiers made plans to escape from the c.
25: 4 But since the c was surrounded by the
25: 9 He destroyed all the important buildings in the c.
25:11 then took as exiles those who remained in the c,
25:19 And of the people still hiding in the c, he took an
1Ch 1:43 son of Beor, who ruled from his c of Dinhabah.
1:46 Bedad became king and ruled from the c of Avith.
1:47 Samlah from the c of Masrekah became king.
1:48 Shaul from the c of Rehoboth on the Euphrates
1:50 Hadad became king and ruled from the c of Pau.
6:57 Hebron (a c of refuge), Libnah, Jattir, Eshtemoa,
6:67 Shechem (a c of refuge in the hill country of
11: 5 the fortress of Zion, now called the C of David.
11: 7 and that is why it is called the C of David.
11: 8 He extended the c from the Millo to the
13:13 So David decided not to move the Ark into the C
15: 1 several buildings for himself in the C of David.
15:29 of the LORD's covenant entered the C of David,
19: 9 troops drew up their battle lines at the gate of the c,
19:15 they ran from Abishai and retreated into the c.
20: 1 In the process they laid siege to the c of Rabbah
20: 2 David took a vast amount of plunder from the c.
2Ch 5: 2 covenant from its location in the C of David,
6: 5 I have never chosen a c among the tribes of Israel
6: 6 But now I have chosen Jerusalem as that c,
6:34 and if they pray to you toward this c that you have
6:38 to their ancestors, toward this c you have chosen,
8: 3 that Solomon fought against the c of
8:11 from the C of David to the new palace he had built
9:31 he died, he was buried in the c of his father, David.
12:13 the c the LORD had chosen from among all the
12:16 Rehoboam died, he was buried in the C of David.
14: 1 Abijah died, he was buried in the C of David.
14: 9 They advanced to the c of Mareshah,
15: 6 Nation fought against nation, and c against c,
16:14 he had carved out for himself in the C of David.
18:25 the governor of the c, and to my son Joash.
21: 1 he was buried with his ancestors in the C of David.
21:20 He was buried in the C of David, but not in the
22: 9 and they found him hiding in the c of Samaria.
23:21 and the c was peaceful because Athaliah had been
24:16 He was buried among the kings in the C of David,
24:25 Then he was buried in the C of David, but not in
25:28 and he was buried with his ancestors in the C of
27: 9 When he died, he was buried in the C of David,
28:15 back to their own land—to Jericho, the c of palms.
29:20 morning King Hezekiah gathered the c officials
30:26 There was great joy in the c, for Jerusalem had not
32: 3 to stop the flow of the springs outside the c.
32: 5 He also reinforced the Millo in the C of David
32: 6 to assemble before him in the square at the c gate.
32: 9 message for Hezekiah and all the people in the c:
32:18 to the people gathered on the walls of the c,
32:18 terrify them so it would be easier to capture the c.
32:30 through a tunnel to the west side of the C of David.
33: 7 the c I have chosen from among all the other tribes
33:14 Manasseh rebuilt the outer wall of the C of David,
33:15 in Jerusalem, and he dumped them outside the c.
34:24 I will certainly destroy this c and its people.
34:27 God when you heard what I said against this c
34:28 I will not send the promised disaster against this c
Ezr 4:12 Babylon are rebuilding this rebellious and evil c.
4:13 But we wish you to know that if this c is rebuilt
4:15 where you will discover what a rebellious c this
4:16 We declare that if this c is rebuilt and its walls are
4:21 That c must not be rebuilt except at my express
6:12 May the God who has chosen the c of Jerusalem as
10:14 time with the leaders and judges of his c,
Ne 2: 3 For the c where my ancestors are buried is in ruins,
2: 5 send me to Judah to rebuild the c where my
2: 8 for the c walls, and for a house for myself."
2:16 The c officials did not know I had been out there
2:17 to them, "You know full well the tragedy of our c.
3: 2 People from the c of Jericho worked next to them,
3: 6 The Old C Gate was repaired by Joiada son of
3:15 far as the stairs that descend from the C of David.
4: 6 to half its original height around the entire c,
4: 9 But we prayed to our God and guarded the c day
7: 4 At that time the c was large and spacious,
7: 4 only a few houses were scattered throughout the c.
7: 5 me the idea to call together all the leaders of the c,
11: 1 were living in Jerusalem, the holy c, at this time.
11: 9 son of Hassenuah, second-in-command over the c.
11:18 In all, there were 284 Levites in the holy c.
12:37 the ascent of the c wall toward the C of David.
12:39 then past the Ephraim Gate to the Old C Gate,
13:18 brought the present troubles upon us and our c?
13:19 then on the gates of the c should be shut as
Est 3:15 to drink, but the c of Susa fell into confusion.
4: 1 put on sackcloth and ashes, and went out into the c,
6: 9 and to lead him through the c square on the king's
6:11 and led him through the c square, shouting,
8:11 The king's decree gave the Jews in every c
8:17 In every c and province, wherever the king's
Job 19: 6 cannot defend myself, for I am like a c under siege.
24:12 The groans of the dying rise from the c,
29: 7 "Those were the days when I went to the c gate
29:10 The highest officials of the c stood quietly,
39: 7 It hates the noise of the c, and it has no driver to
Ps 2: 6 king on the throne / in Jerusalem, my holy c."
31:21 He kept me safe when my c was under attack.
46: 4 A river brings joy to the c of our God, / the sacred
46: 5 God himself lives in that c; it cannot be destroyed.
48: 1 in the c of our God, / which is on his holy
48: 2 the holy mountain, / is the c of the great King!
48: 4 earth joined forces / and advanced against the c.
48: 8 seen it ourselves—/ the c of the LORD Almighty.
48: 8 It is the c of our God; / he will make it safe
48:12 Go, inspect the c of Jerusalem. / Walk around
55: 9 their speech, / for I see violence and strife in the c.
55:10 but the real danger is wickedness within the c.
60: 9 But who will bring me into the fortified c?
74: 3 Walk through the awful ruins of the c; / see how
87: 1 On the holy mountain stands the c founded by the
87: 2 He loves the c of Jerusalem / more than any other c in Israel.
87: 3 O c of God, / what glorious things are said of you!
87: 5 And the Most High will personally bless this c.
101: 8 and free the c of the LORD from their grip.
107: 7 straight to safety, / to a c where they could live.
108:10 But who will bring me into the fortified c?
122: 3 Jerusalem is a well-built c, / knit together as a
122: 6 of Jerusalem. / May all who love this c prosper.
127: 1 is useless. / Unless the LORD protects a c,
127: 5 when he confronts his accusers at the c gates.
132:15 I will make this c prosperous / and satisfy its poor
Pr 1:21 the main street, and to those in front of c hall.
8: 3 At the entrance to the c, at the c gates, she cries
9: 3 She calls out from the heights overlooking the c.
9:14 in her doorway on the heights overlooking the c.
11:10 The whole c celebrates when the godly succeed;
11:11 Upright citizens bless a c and make it prosper,
16:32 it is better to have self-control than to conquer a c.
18:19 an offended friend than to capture a fortified c.
21:22 The wise conquer the c of the strong and level the
25:28 is as defenseless as a c with broken-down walls.
Ecc 8:10 and are praised in the very c where they committed
SS 1: 6 you fair c girls, just because my complexion is
3: 2 I said to myself, 'I will get up now and roam the c,
Isa 1: 8 harvest is over. It is as helpless as a c under siege.
1:26 be called the Home of Justice and the Faithful C."
3:25 The men of the c will die in battle.
3:26 The c will be like a ravaged woman, huddled on
7: 1 The c withstood the attack, however, and was not
10:29 Fear strikes the c of Ramah. All the people of
10:29 the c of Saul—are running for their lives.
13: 8 as the flames of the burning c reflect on their faces.
13:21 animals of the desert will move into the ruined c.
19: 2 c against c, province against province.
19:18 One of these will be Heliopolis, the C of the Sun.
20: 1 of Assyria captured the Philistine c of Ashdod,
21: 6 "Put a watchman on the c wall to shout out what
22: 2 The whole c is in a terrible uproar. What do I see in this reveling c? Bodies are lying
22:11 Between the c walls, you build a reservoir for
23: 4 are put to shame, c of Sidon, fortress on the sea.
23: 7 silent ruin be all that is left of your once joyous c?
23:10 Tyre like the flooding Nile, for the c is defenseless.
23:12 Once you were a lovely c, but you will never again
23:15 But then the c will come back to life and sing
24:10 The c writhes in chaos; every home is locked to
24:12 The c is left in ruins, with its gates battered down.
26: 1 of Judah will sing this song: / Our c is now strong!
26: 5 the proud / and brings the arrogant c to the dust.
28: 1 Destruction is certain for the c of Samaria—
28: 1 Destruction is certain for that c—the pride of a
28: 3 The proud c of Samaria—the pride and joy of the
29: 1 "Destruction is certain for Ariel, the C of David.
31: 5 He will defend and save the c; he will pass over it
32:14 The palace and the c will be deserted, and busy
32:19 the forest will be destroyed and the c torn down,
33:18 much plunder they would get from your fallen c.
33:20 You will see Jerusalem, a c quiet and secure.
34: 6 the LORD will offer a great sacrifice in the rich c
36:12 you do not surrender, this c will be put under siege.
36:15 This c will never be handed over to the Assyrian
37:30 the LORD will protect this c from Assyria's king.
37:34 he came. He will not enter this c, says the LORD.
38: 6 will rescue you and this c from the king of Assyria. Yes, I will defend this c.
45:13 He will restore my c and free my captive people—
48: 2 even though you call yourself the holy c and talk
52: 1 O holy c of Jerusalem, for unclean and godless
54:11 "O storm-battered c, troubled and desolate!
60:14 They will call you the C of the LORD, and Zion
60:18 Salvation will surround you like c walls, and praise
62: 4 Never again will you be called the Godforsaken C
62: 4 Your new name will be the C of God's Delight
62:12 Desirable Place and the C No Longer Forsaken.
63: 1 from the c of Bozrah, with his clothing stained
66: 6 What is all the commotion in the c? What is that
Jer 1:15 They will set their thrones at the gates of the c.
1:18 You are strong like a fortified c that cannot be
5: 1 "Look high and low; search throughout the c!
5: 1 who is just and honest, I will not destroy the c.
6: 3 They will set up camp around the c and divide
6: 6 This is the c to be punished, for she is wicked
14:18 If I walk the c streets, there I see people who have
16: 3 LORD says about the children born here in this c
17:25 and on horses, and this c will remain forever.
19: 9 I will see to it that your enemies lay siege to the c
19:12 I will cause this c to become defiled like Topheth.
19:15 I will bring disaster upon this c and its surrounding
20: 5 All the famed treasures of the c—the precious
20: 7 Now I am mocked by everyone in the c.
21: 4 bring your enemies right into the heart of this c.
21: 6 I will send a terrible plague upon this c, and both
21: 7 and everyone else in the c have survived war,
21:10 decided to bring disaster and not good upon this c,
21:13 I will fight against this c of Jerusalem that boasts,
22: 8 from many nations will pass by the ruins of this c
22: 8 'Why did the LORD destroy such a great c?'
23:39 along with this c that I gave to you and your
25:29 the c where my own name is honored.
26:11 traitor he is, for he has prophesied against this c."
26:12 me to prophesy against this Temple and this c,"
26:15 on you, on this c, and on every person living in it.
26:20 he predicted the same terrible disaster against the c
27:17 will live. Why should this c be destroyed?
29: 7 Pray to the LORD for that c where you are held
31:24 And c dwellers and farmers and shepherds alike
31:40 The c will never again be captured or destroyed."
32: 3 I am about to hand this c over to the king of
32:24 the siege ramps have been built against the c walls!
32:24 the c has been handed over to the Babylonians,
32:25 even though the c will soon belong to the
32:28 I will hand this c over to the Babylonians and to
32:29 outside the walls will come in and set fire to the c.
32:31 "From the time this c was built until now, it has
32:36 "Now I want to say something more about this c.
32:37 I will bring them back to this very c and let them
33: 4 Though you have torn down the houses of this c
33: 5 The men of this c are already as good as dead,
33: 9 Then this c will bring me joy, glory, and honor
34: 2 I am about to hand this c over to the king of
34:21 And though Babylon's king has left this c for a
34:22 They will fight against this c and will capture
37: 8 and capture this c and burn it to the ground.
37:10 from their tents and burn this c to the ground!"
37:12 Jeremiah started to leave the c on his way to the

37:21 every day as long as there was any left in the **c**.
38:3 The **c** of Jerusalem will surely be handed over to
38:9 for almost all the bread in the **c** is gone."
38:17 your family will live, and the **c** will not be burned.
38:18 This **c** will be handed over to the Babylonians,
38:23 by the king of Babylon, and this **c** will be burned."
39:2 Babylonians broke through the wall, and the **c** fell.
39:4 and his royal guard saw the Babylonians in the **c**
39:8 the palace, and tore down the walls of the **c**.
39:16 I will do to this **c** everything I have threatened.
43:7 went to Egypt, going as far as the **c** of Tahpanhes.
46:19 The **c** of Memphis will be destroyed, without a
47:5 The **c** of Gaza will be demolished; Ashkelon will
47:7 For the **c** of Ashkelon and the people living along
48:1 "Destruction is certain for the **c** of Nebo; it will
48:1 The **c** of Kiriathaim will be humiliated
48:2 The **c** of Madmen, too, will be silenced; the sword
49:2 the LORD, "by destroying your **c** of Rabbah.
49:25 That famous **c**, a **c** of joy, will be forsaken!
50:29 Surround the **c** so none can escape. Do to her as
50:39 "Soon this **c** of Babylon will be inhabited by
51:13 You are a **c** rich with water, a great center of
51:30 burned the houses and broken down the **c** gates.
51:47 is surely coming when I will punish this great **c**
51:55 against her; the noise of battle rings through the **c**.
52:4 They surrounded the **c** and built siege ramps
52:6 the famine in the **c** had become very severe,
52:7 Then a section of the **c** wall was broken down,
52:7 all the soldiers made plans to escape from the **c**.
52:7 But since the **c** was surrounded by the
52:13 He destroyed all the important buildings in the **c**.
52:15 of the people and those who remained in the **c**,
52:25 And of the people still hiding in the **c**, he took an
La 1:4 The **c** gates are silent, her priests groan, her young
1:15 The Lord has trampled his beloved **c** as grapes are
1:19 My priests and leaders starved to death in the **c**,
2:15 "Is this the **c** called 'Most Beautiful in All the
4:11 He started a fire in Jerusalem that burned the **c** to
4:13 who defiled the **c** by shedding innocent blood.
5:14 The old men no longer sit in the **c** gates; the young
Eze 4:1 Then draw a map of the **c** of Jerusalem on it.
4:2 Build siege ramps against the **c** walls. Surround it
4:3 an iron griddle and place it between you and the **c**.
5:12 A third of your people will die in the **c** from
5:12 be slaughtered by the enemy outside the **c** walls.
7:15 Any who leave the **c** walls will be killed by enemy
9:1 "Bring on the men appointed to punish the **c**!
9:5 "Follow him through the **c** and kill everyone
9:7 So they went throughout the **c** and did as they were
9:9 land is full of murder; the **c** is filled with injustice.
10:2 of glowing coals and scatter them over the **c**."
11:1 where I saw twenty-five prominent men of the **c**.
11:2 for the wicked counsel being given in this **c**.
11:3 Our **c** is like an iron pot. Inside it we will be like
11:7 This **c** is an iron pot, but the victims of your
11:7 are not safe, for I will soon drag you from the **c**.
11:11 No, this **c** will not be an iron pot for you, and you
11:23 Then the glory of the LORD went up from the **c**
17:4 Then he carried it away to a **c** filled with
17:21 and those remaining in the **c** will be scattered to
22:2 Are you ready to judge this **c** of murderers?
22:3 O **c** of murderers, doomed and damned—**c** of idols
22:5 O infamous **c**, filled with confusion, you will be
24:6 is certain for Jerusalem, the **c** of murderers!
24:9 is certain for Jerusalem, the **c** of murderers!
25:5 And I will turn the **c** of Rabbah into a pasture for
26:10 The hooves of his cavalry will choke the **c** with
26:11 His horsemen will trample every street in the **c**.
26:17 'O famous island **c**, / once ruler of the sea,
26:19 Your **c** will lie in ruins, buried beneath the earth,
27:32 funeral song: / 'Was there ever such a **c** as Tyre,
28:21 look toward the **c** of Sidon and prophesy against it.
33:21 came to me and said, "The **c** has fallen!"
40:2 From there I could see what appeared to be a **c**
45:6 This will be set aside to be a **c** where anyone in
45:7 border with the east side of the sacred lands and **c**,
48:15 and common lands, with a **c** at the center.
48:16 The **c** will measure 1-1/2 miles on each side.
48:17 Open lands will surround the **c** for 150 yards in
48:18 Outside the **c** there will be a farming area that
48:18 will produce food for the people working in the **c**.
48:19 the various tribes to work in the **c** may farm it.
48:20 entire area—including the sacred lands and the **c**—
48:21 and to the west of the sacred lands and the **c**,
48:22 the areas set aside for the sacred lands and the **c**.
48:30 "These will be the exits to the **c**: On the north
48:35 "The distance around the entire **c** will be six miles.
48:35 And from that day the name of the **c** will be 'The
Da 4:30 As he looked out across the **c**, he said, "Just look at
this great **c** of Babylon!
4:30 have built this beautiful **c** as my royal residence
9:16 please turn your furious anger away from your **c** of
9:18 See how your **c** lies in ruins—for everyone knows
9:19 for your people and your **c** bear your name."
9:24 your people and your holy **c** to put down rebellion,
9:26 a ruler will arise whose armies will destroy the **c**
11:15 and lay siege to a fortified **c** and capture it.
Hos 6:8 Gilead is a **c** of sinners, tracked with footprints of
Joel 2:7 like warriors and scale **c** walls like trained soldiers.
2:9 They swarm over the **c** and run along its walls.
Am 3:6 When disaster comes to a **c**, isn't it
4:6 "I brought hunger to every **c** and famine to every
6:2 Then go to the great **c** of Hamath and on down to
the Philistine **c** of Gath.
6:8 I will give this **c** and everything in it to their
7:17 your wife will become a prostitute in this **c**,
8:3 They will be carried out of the **c** in silence. I,
Jnh 1:2 "Get up and go to the great **c** of Nineveh!
3:2 "Get up and go to the great **c** of Nineveh,
3:3 a **c** so large that it took three days to see it all.
3:4 On the day Jonah entered the **c**, he shouted to the
3:7 and his nobles sent this decree throughout the **c**:
4:5 Then Jonah went out to the east side of the **c**
4:5 he waited to see if anything would happen to the **c**.
4:11 Shouldn't I feel sorry for such a great **c**?"
Mic 1:5 blame for Israel's rebellion? Samaria, its capital **c**!
1:6 will make the **c** of Samaria a heap of rubble.
1:10 Don't tell our enemies in the **c** of Gath; don't weep
1:11 because the very foundations of their **c** have been
1:13 You were the first **c** in Judah to follow Israel in the
4:10 for you must leave this **c** to live in the open fields.
Na 2:10 Soon the **c** is an empty shambles, stripped of its
2:12 You filled your **c** and your homes with captives
3:1 it will be for Nineveh, the **c** of murder and lies!
3:4 because Nineveh, the beautiful and faithless **c**,
3:16 as the stars, have filled your **c** with vast wealth.
Zep 1:10 throughout the newer Mishneh section of the **c**.
2:14 The **c** that once was so proud will become a
2:15 This is the fate of that boisterous **c**, once so secure.
2:15 "In all the world there is no **c** as great as I,"
3:1 polluted Jerusalem, the **c** of violence and crime.
3:5 But the LORD is still there in the **c**, and he does
Zec 2:4 Many will live outside the **c** walls, with all their
2:5 And I will be the glory inside the **c**!' "
2:12 will once again choose Jerusalem to be his own **c**.
8:3 Then Jerusalem will be called the Faithful **C**;
8:4 streets with a cane and sit together in the **c** squares.
8:5 And the streets of the **c** will be filled with boys
8:21 The people of one **c** will say to the people in
9:1 against the land of Aram and the **c** of Damascus,
9:5 The **c** of Ashkelon will see Tyre fall and will be
9:6 Foreigners will occupy the **c** of Ashdod. Thus,
14:2 The **c** will be taken, the houses plundered,
14:2 and half will be left among the ruins of the **c**.
Mt 5:14 like a **c** on a mountain, glowing in the night for all
5:35 for Jerusalem is the **c** of the great King.
8:33 The herdsmen fled to the nearby **c**,
10:11 Whenever you enter a **c** or village, search for a
12:25 A **c** or home divided against itself is doomed.
20:29 As Jesus and the disciples left the **c** of Jericho,
21:10 The entire **c** of Jerusalem was stirred as he entered.
22:7 his army to destroy the murderers and burn their **c**.
23:34 in your synagogues, chasing them from **c** to **c**.
23:37 the **c** that kills the prophets and stones God's
26:18 "As you go into the **c**," he told them, "you will
27:53 the cemetery, went into the holy **c** of Jerusalem,
28:11 As the women were on their way into the **c**,
Mk 5:14 The herdsmen fled to the nearby **c**
11:19 That evening Jesus and the disciples left the **c**.
14:13 "As you go into the **c**," he told them, "a man
14:16 So the two disciples went on ahead into the **c**
Lk 2:11 been born tonight in Bethlehem, the **c** of David!
4:29 and took him to the edge of the hill on which the **c**
8:34 they fled to the nearby **c** and the surrounding
8:39 So he went all through the **c** telling about the great
13:34 the **c** that kills the prophets and stones God's
14:21 the streets and alleys of the **c** and invite the poor,
18:2 "There was a judge in a certain **c**," he said,
18:3 A widow of that **c** came to him repeatedly,
19:41 closer to Jerusalem and Jesus saw the **c** ahead,
21:21 and those outside the **c** should not enter it for
22:13 They went off to the **c** and found everything just as
24:49 But stay here in the **c** until the Holy Spirit comes
Jn 4:46 There was a government official in the **c** of
5:2 Inside the **c**, near the Sheep Gate, was the pool of
12:12 was on the way to Jerusalem swept through the **c**.
19:20 place where Jesus was crucified was near the **c**;
Ac 4:27 "That is what has happened here in this **c**!
7:58 They dragged him out of the **c** and began to stone
8:5 went to the **c** of Samaria and told the people there
8:8 So there was great joy in that **c**.
8:40 Philip found himself farther north at the **c** of
8:40 and in every **c** along the way until he came to
9:6 Now get up and go into the **c**, and you will be told
9:24 and night at the **c** gate so they could murder him.
9:25 in a large basket through an opening in the **c** wall.
10:9 day as Cornelius' messengers were nearing the **c**,
13:44 The following week almost the entire **c** turned out
13:50 religious women and the leaders of the **c**,
13:51 feet against them and went to the **c** of Iconium.
14:4 But the people of the **c** were divided in their
14:13 of Zeus was located on the outskirts of the **c**.
14:13 prepared to sacrifice to the apostles at the **c** gates.
14:19 They stoned Paul and dragged him out of the **c**,
14:20 around him, he got up and went back into the **c**.
15:21 every **c** on every Sabbath for many generations."
15:36 "Let's return to each **c** where we previously
16:8 they went on through Mysia to the **c** of Troas.
16:12 a major **c** of the district of Macedonia and a
16:13 On the Sabbath we went a little way outside the **c**
16:20 "The whole **c** is in an uproar because of these
16:22 and the **c** officials ordered them stripped
16:35 The next morning the **c** officials sent the police to
16:38 the **c** officials were alarmed to learn that Paul
16:39 brought them out and begged them to leave the **c**.
17:4 and also many important women of the **c**.
17:6 and took them before the **c** council.
17:6 and now they are here disturbing our **c**,"
17:8 The people of the **c**, as well as the **c** officials,
17:16 by all the idols he saw everywhere in the **c**.
18:10 because many people here in this **c** belong to me."
19:17 A solemn fear descended on the **c**, and the name of
19:29 to gather, and soon the **c** was filled with confusion.
20:23 the Holy Spirit has told me in **c** after **c** that jail
21:29 (For earlier that day they had seen him in the **c**
21:30 The whole population of the **c** was rocked by these
21:39 from Tarsus in Cilicia, which is an important **c**.
22:3 "I am a Jew, born in Tarsus, a **c** in Cilicia, and I
24:12 a riot in any synagogue or on the streets of the **c**.
25:23 by military officers and prominent men of the **c**.
27:8 finally arrived at Fair Havens, near the **c** of Lasea.
Ro 16:23 Erastus, the **c** treasurer, sends you his greetings,
2Co 2:12 when I came to the **c** of Troas to preach the Good
11:32 King Aretas kept guards at the **c** gates to catch me.
11:33 in a basket through a window in the **c** wall,
Gal 1:17 and later returned to the **c** of Damascus.
Col 1:2 It is written to God's holy people in the **c** of
4:12 Epaphras, from your **c**, a servant of Christ Jesus,
Heb 7:1 This Melchizedek was king of the **c** of Salem
11:10 because he was confidently looking forward to a **c**
11:10 eternal foundations, a **c** designed and built by God.
11:16 for he has prepared a heavenly **c** for them.
11:31 all the others in her **c** who refused to obey God.
12:22 to the **c** of the living God, the heavenly Jerusalem,
13:12 and died outside the **c** gates in order to make his
13:14 we are looking forward to our **c** in heaven,
Rev 2:13 "I know that you live in the **c** where that great
3:12 and they will be citizens in the **c** of my God—
11:2 They will trample the holy **c** for 42 months.
11:8 the **c** which is called "Sodom" and "Egypt,"
11:8 the **c** where their Lord was crucified.
11:13 a terrible earthquake that destroyed a tenth of the **c**.
14:8 "Babylon is fallen—that great **c** is fallen—
14:20 grapes were trodden in the winepress outside the **c**,
16:19 The great **c** of Babylon split into three pieces,
17:9 the seven hills of the **c** where this woman rules.
17:18 the great **c** that rules over the kings of the earth."
18:2 "Babylon is fallen—that great **c** is fallen!
18:10 how terrible for Babylon, that great **c**!
18:16 "How terrible, how terrible for that great **c**!
18:17 And in one single moment all the wealth of the **c** is
18:18 "Where in all the world is there another **c** like
18:19 "How terrible, how terrible for the great **c**!
18:21 into the ocean and shouted, "Babylon, the great **c**,
19:3 The smoke from that **c** ascends forever
20:9 and surrounded God's people and the beloved **c**.
21:2 And I saw the holy **c**, the new Jerusalem,
21:10 and he showed me the holy **c**, Jerusalem,
21:14 The wall of the **c** had twelve foundation stones,
21:15 his hand a gold measuring stick to measure the **c**,
21:18 of jasper, and the **c** was pure gold, as clear as glass.
21:19 The wall of the **c** was built on foundation stones
21:22 No temple could be seen in the **c**, for the Lord God
21:23 And the **c** has no need of sun or moon, for the
glory of God illuminates the **c**,
21:26 nations will bring their glory and honor into the **c**.
22:14 so they can enter through the gates of the **c** and eat
22:15 Outside the **c** are the dogs—the sorcerers,
22:19 and in the holy **c** that are described in this book.

CITY'S (2) [CITY]

Ps 48:8 We had heard of the **c** glory, / but now we have
Jer 5:7 committing adultery and lining up at the **c** brothels.

CIVIC (1) [CIVIL, CIVILIZATION]

Pr 31:23 for he sits in the council meeting with the other **c**

CIVIL (2) [CIVIC]

2Ch 19:8 both the law of the LORD and **c** disputes.
19:11 the tribe of Judah, will have final say in all **c** cases.

CIVILIZATION (2) [CIVIC]

Job 30:5 They are driven from **c**, and people shout after
30:8 They are nameless fools, outcasts of **c**.

CLAIM (55) [CLAIMED, CLAIMING, CLAIMS, RECLAIM]

Ge 20:16 This will settle any **c** against me in this matter."
Nu 8:18 I **c** the Levites in place of all the firstborn sons of
Dt 18:3 "These are the parts the priests may **c** as their
24:10 do not enter your neighbor's house to **c** the
28:60 that you feared so much, and they will **c** you.
Jos 22:25 and your people. You have no **c** to the LORD.'
22:27 able to say to ours, 'You have no **c** to the LORD.'
1Ki 3:23 Both of you **c** the living child is yours, and each
18:10 the king of that nation to swear to the truth of his **c**.
21:16 immediately went down to the vineyard to **c** it.
Ne 2:20 But you have no stake or **c** in Jerusalem."
5:18 Yet I refused to **c** the governor's food allowance
Job 3:5 let the darkness and utter gloom **c** it for its own.
11:4 You **c**, 'My teaching is pure,' and 'I am clean in
24:25 "Can anyone **c** otherwise? Who can prove me
25:4 mortal stand before God and **c** to be righteous?
35:2 "Do you think it is right for you to **c**, 'I am
Ps 94:20 Can unjust leaders **c** that God is on their side—
Ecc 10:14 Foolish people **c** to know all about the future
Isa 43:7 All who **c** me as their God will come, for I have
44:5 Some will proudly **c**, 'I belong to the LORD.'
44:11 mere humans—who **c** they can make a god.
47:10 have caused you to turn away from me and **c**,
48:11 the pagan nations will not be able to **c** that their
62:4 LORD delights in you and will **c** you as his own.
Jer 2:35 you severely because you **c** you have not sinned.
23:21 not sent these prophets, yet they **c** to speak for me.
27:16 Do not listen to your prophets who **c** that soon the
29:15 You may **c** that the LORD has raised up prophets
Eze 13:7 Can your visions be anything but false if you **c**,
14:10 evil people who **c** to want my advice—

20:14 of Egypt wouldn't be able to c I destroyed them
28: 2 In your great pride you c, 'I am a god! I sit on a
Mic 3:11 Yet all of you c you are depending on the LORD.
Hab 1:16 are the gods who have made us rich!" they will c.
Zep 1: 5 They c to follow the LORD, but then they
Mk 12:35 "Why do the teachers of religious law c that the
Lk 22:70 "Then you c you are the Son of God?"
Jn 4:20 while we Samaritans c it is here at Mount Gerizim,
9:41 "But you remain guilty because you c you can see.
Ro 4:14 So if you c that God's promise is for those who
1Co 14:37 If you c to be a prophet or think you are very
2Co 10:14 We are not going too far when we c authority over
10:15 Nor do we c credit for the work someone else has
11:26 And I have faced danger from men who c to be
Gal 6:13 they can brag about it and c you as their disciples.
Col 2:18 These people c to be so humble, but their sinful
2Th 2: 2 Even if they c to have had a vision, a revelation,
1Ti 2:10 For women who c to be devoted to God should
2Ti 2:19 and "Those who c they belong to the Lord must
Tit 1:16 Such people c they know God, but they deny him
Jas 1:26 If you c to be religious but don't control your
2: 1 how can you c that you have faith in our glorious
1Jn 1:10 If we c we have not sinned, we are calling God a
Jude 1: 8 who c authority from their dreams, live immoral

CLAIMED (14) [CLAIM]

Ge 26:20 then the local shepherds came and c the spring.
38:22 and that the men of the village had c they didn't
Lev 6: 4 to them, or a lost object that they c as their own,
Nu 8:16 I have c them for myself in place of all the
14:17 prove that your power is as great as you have c it
17: 9 them to the people. Each man c his own staff.
Dt 28:10 will see that you are a people c by the LORD,
2Ki 24: 7 occupied the entire area formerly c by Egypt—
Eze 13:16 They were lying prophets who c peace would
27: 3 You c, O Tyre, to be perfect in beauty.
Am 5:14 will truly be your helper, just as you have c he is.
Jn 1:19 to ask John whether he c to be the Messiah.
8:25 Jesus replied, "I am the one I have always c to be.
Ac 5: 2 to the apostles, but he c it was the full amount.

CLAIMING (10) [CLAIM]

Dt 22:17 c that she was not a virgin when he married her.
Da 11:36 and c to be greater than every god there is,
11:39 C this foreign god's help, he will attack the
Mk 13: 6 many will come in my name, c to be the Messiah.
Lk 21: 8 c to be the Messiah and saying, 'The time has
23: 2 the Roman government and by c he is the Messiah,
Ac 4: 2 were very disturbed that Peter and John were c,
8: 9 there for many years, c to be someone great.
Ro 1:22 C to be wise, they became utter fools instead.
2Th 2: 4 in the temple of God, c that he himself is God.

CLAIMS (12) [CLAIM]

Dt 18:20 But any prophet who c to give a message from
18:20 or who falsely c to speak for me must die.'
Isa 41:21 "Can your idols make such c as these? Let them
Jer 29:26 You are responsible to put anyone who c to be a
Hos 2:12 and orchards, things she c her lovers gave her.
Mt 16: 1 and Sadducees came to test Jesus' c by asking him
Jn 8:13 "You are making false c about yourself!"
8:14 "These c are valid even though I make them about
1Co 5:11 who c to be a Christian yet indulges in sexual sin,
8: 2 Anyone who c to know all the answers doesn't
1Jn 4: 1 do not believe everyone who c to speak by the
Rev 2: 2 You have examined the c of those who say they

CLAMOR (1)

Ac 23: 9 So a great c arose. Some of the teachers of

CLAMPED (1) [CLAMPS]

Ac 16:24 the inner dungeon and c their feet in the stocks.

CLAMPS (1) [CLAMPED]

1Ch 22: 3 be needed for the doors in the gates and for the c,

CLAN (128) [CLANS, SUBCLAN, SUBCLANS]

Ge 36:30 The Horite clans are named after their c leaders,
36:43 each c giving its name to the area it occupied.
Ex 6:17 and Shimei, each of whom is the ancestor of a c.
Lev 21:14 She must be a virgin from his own c,
21:15 his descendants among the members of his c,
25:10 that belonged to your ancestors and rejoins your c.
25:41 and they will return to their c and ancestral
Nu 1:20[-21] each listed according to his own c and family:
2:34 Each c and family set up camp and marched under
25:15 the daughter of Zur, the leader of a Midianite c.
26: 5 The Hanochite c, named after its ancestor Hanoch.
26: 5 The Palluite c, named after its ancestor Pallu.
26: 6 The Hezronite c, named after its ancestor Hezron.
26: 6 The Carmite c, named after its ancestor Carmi.
26:12 The Nemuelite c, named after its ancestor Nemuel.
26:12 The Jaminite c, named after its ancestor Jamin.
26:12 The Jakinite c, named after its ancestor Jakin.
26:13 The Zerahite c, named after its ancestor Zerah.
26:13 The Shaulite c, named after its ancestor Shaul.
26:15 The Zephonite c, named after its ancestor Zephon.
26:15 The Haggite c, named after its ancestor Haggi.
26:15 The Shunite c, named after its ancestor Shuni.
26:16 The Oznite c, named after its ancestor Ozni.
26:16 The Erite c, named after its ancestor Eri.
26:17 The Arodite c, named after its ancestor Arodi.
26:17 The Arelite c, named after its ancestor Areli.
26:20 The Shelanite c, named after its ancestor Shelah.
26:20 The Perezite c, named after its ancestor Perez.
26:20 The Zerahite c, named after its ancestor Zerah.
26:23 The Tolaite c, named after its ancestor Tola.
26:23 The Puite c, named after its ancestor Puah.
26:24 The Jashubite c, named after its ancestor Jashub.
26:24 The Shimronite c, named after its ancestor
26:26 The Seredite c, named after its ancestor Sered.
26:26 The Elonite c, named after its ancestor Elon.
26:26 The Jahleelite c, named after its ancestor Jahleel.
26:29 The Makirite c, named after its ancestor Makir.
26:29 The Gileadite c, named after its ancestor Gilead,
26:35 The Shuthelahite c, named after its ancestor
26:35 The Bekerite c, named after its ancestor Beker.
26:35 The Tahanite c, named after its ancestor Tahan.
26:38 The Belaite c, named after its ancestor Bela.
26:38 The Ashbelite c, named after its ancestor Ashbel.
26:38 The Ahiramite c, named after its ancestor Ahiram.
26:39 The Shuphamite c, named after its ancestor
26:39 The Huphamite c, named after its ancestor
26:42 The Shuhamite c, named after its ancestor Shuham.
26:44 The Imnite c, named after its ancestor Imnah.
26:44 The Ishvite c, named after its ancestor Ishvi.
26:44 The Beriite c, named after its ancestor Beriah.
26:48 The Jahzeelite c, named after its ancestor Jahzeel.
26:48 The Gunite c, named after its ancestor Guni.
26:49 The Jezerite c, named after its ancestor Jezer.
26:49 The Shillemite c, named after its ancestor Shillem.
26:57 The Gershonite c, named after its ancestor
26:57 The Kohathite c, named after its ancestor Kohath.
26:57 The Merarite c, named after its ancestor Merari.
27:11 on his inheritance to the nearest relative in his c.
32:41 people of Jair, another c of the tribe of Manasseh,
36: 1 Then the heads of the c of Gilead—descendants of
Dt 3:15 I gave Gilead to the c of Makir.
Jos 7: 1 of the family of Zimri, of the c of Zerah, and of the
7:14 and the LORD will point out the guilty c.
7:14 That c will then come forward, and the LORD
7:17 came forward, and the c of Zerah was singled out.
21: 4 who were members of the Kohathite c within the
21: 5 The other families of the Kohathite c were allotted
21: 6 The c of Gershon received thirteen towns from the
21: 7 The c of Merari received twelve cities from the
21:10 who were members of the Kohathite c within the
21:20 The rest of the Kohathite c from the tribe of Levi
21:26 were given to the rest of the Kohathite c.
21:27 of Gershon, another c within the tribe of Levi,
21:33 and their pasturelands were allotted to the c of
21:34 The rest of the Levites—the Merari c—were given
21:40 So twelve towns were allotted to the c of Merari.
22:20 a member of the c of Zerah, sinned by stealing the
Jdg 6:11 which belonged to Joash of the c of Abiezer.
6:15 My c is the weakest in the whole tribe of
6:24 The altar remains in Ophrah in the land of the c of
6:34 and the men of the c of Abiezer came to him.
8: 2 than the entire crop of my little c of Abiezer?
8:32 Joash, at Ophrah in the land of the c of Abiezer.
12: 9 He married his daughters to men outside his c
12: 9 young women from outside his c to marry his sons.
1Sa 1: 1 from the family of Tohu and the c of Zuph.
9: 1 from the family of Becorath and the c of Aphiah.
2Sa 20:14 his own c of Bicri at the city of Abel-beth-maacah.
1Ch 1:51 The c leaders of Edom were Timna, Alvah,
1:54 and Iram. These were the c leaders of Edom.
6:33 Heman the musician was from the c of Kohath.
6:39 Heman's first assistant was Asaph from the c of
6:44 Heman's second assistant was Ethan from the c of
6:54 of Aaron who were from the c of Kohath.
7: 2 Each of them was the leader of an ancestral c.
7: 9 their descendants, in addition to their c leaders.
7:40 of Asher was the head of an ancestral c.
9: 5 Others returned from the Shilonite c,
9: 6 From the Zerahite c, Jeuel returned with his
9:19 a descendant of Abiasaph, from the c of Korah.
9:32 And some members of the c of Kohath were in
12:30 were 20,800 warriors, each famous in his own c.
15: 5 There were 120 from the c of Kohath, with Uriel as
15: 6 There were 220 from the c of Merari, with Asaiah
15: 7 There were 130 from the c of Gershon, with Joel as
15:17 and Ethan son of Kushaiah from the c of Merari to
25: 9 The first lot fell to Joseph of the Asaph c
26: 6 who earned positions of great authority in the c.
26:10 Hosah, of the Merari c, appointed Shimri as the
26:21 From the family of Libni in the c of Gershon,
26:24 From the c of Amram, Shebuel was a descendant
26:29 From the c of Izhar came Kenaniah. He and his
26:30 From the c of Hebron came Hashabiah. He and his
26:31 Also from the c of Hebron came Jeriah, who was
26:31 and capable men from the c of Hebron were found
2Ch 1: 2 the judges, and all the political and c leaders.
19: 8 and c leaders in Israel to serve as judges in
23: 2 and c leaders in Judah's towns to come to
25: 5 assigning leaders to each c from Judah
26:12 Twenty-six hundred c leaders commanded these
29:12 From the c of Kohath: Mahath son of Amasai
29:12 From the c of Merari: Kish son of Abdi
29:12 From the c of Gershon: Joah son of Zimmah
34:12 of Jahath and Obadiah, Levites of the Merarite c,
34:12 and Meshullam, Levites of the Kohathite c.
Job 32: 2 Barakel the Buzite, of the c of Ram, became angry.
Isa 60:22 The smallest family will multiply into a large c.
Zec 9: 7 our God and be adopted as a new c in Judah.

CLANGING (2)

Ps 150: 5 clash of cymbals; / praise him with loud c cymbals.
1Co 13: 1 meaningless noise like a loud gong or a c cymbal.

CLANS (113) [CLAN]

Ge 25:13 Here is a list, by their names and c, of Ishmael's
25:18 The c descended from Ishmael camped close to
36:15 grandchildren became the leaders of different c.
36:15 became the leaders of the c of Teman, Omar,
36:16 These c in the land of Edom were descended from
36:17 son Reuel became the leaders of the c of Nahath,
36:17 These c in the land of Edom were descended from
36:18 Oholibamah became the leaders of the c of Jeush,
36:18 These are the c descended from Esau's wife
36:19 These are all the c descended from Esau (also
36:21 These were the Horite c, the descendants of Seir,
36:29 So the leaders of the Horite c were Lotan, Shobal,
36:30 The Horite c are named after their clan leaders,
36:40 These are the leaders of the c of Esau, who lived in
36:43 These are the names of the c of Esau, the ancestor
Ex 6:14 These are the ancestors of c from some of Israel's
6:14 Their descendants became the c of Reuben.
6:15 Their descendants became the c of Simeon.
6:19 These are the c of the Levites, listed according to
6:24 Their descendants became the c of Korah.
6:25 These are the ancestors of the Levite c,
Nu 1: 2 census of the whole community of Israel by their c
1:18 registered according to their ancestry by their c
3:15 a census of the tribe of Levi by its families and c.
3:18 The c descended from Gershon were named for
3:19 The c descended from Kohath were named for four
3:20 The c descended from Merari were named for two
3:20 These were the Levite c, listed according to their
3:21 were composed of the c descended from Libni
3:22 one month old or older among these Gershonite c.
3:24 The leader of the Gershonite c was Eliasaph son of
3:25 These two c were responsible to care for the tent of
3:27 were composed of the c descended from Amram,
3:28 one month old or older among these Kohathite c.
3:30 The leader of the Kohathite c was Elizaphan son of
3:31 These four c were responsible for the care of the
3:33 The descendants of Merari were composed of the c
3:34 one month old or older among these Merarite c.
3:35 The leader of the Merarite c was Zuriel son of
3:36 These two c were responsible for the care of the
3:39 So among the Levite c counted by Moses
4: 2 "Take a census of the c and families of the
4:18 "Don't let the Kohathite c be destroyed from
4:22 "Take a census of the c and families of the
4:29 "Now take a census of the c and families of the
4:34 community counted the Kohathite division by its c
4:37 c who were eligible to serve at the Tabernacle.
4:38 The Gershonite division was also counted by its c
4:41 c who were eligible to serve at the Tabernacle.
4:42 The Merarite division was also counted by its c
4:45 from the Merarite c who were eligible for service.
4:46 leaders of Israel counted all the Levites by their c
26: 5 These were the c descended from Reuben,
26: 7 The men from all the c of Reuben numbered
26:12 These were the c descended from the sons of
26:14 The men from all the c of Simeon numbered
26:15 These were the c descended from the sons of Gad:
26:18 The men from all the c of Gad numbered 40,500.
26:20 But the following c descended from Judah's
26:22 The men from all the c of Judah numbered 76,500.
26:23 These were the c descended from the sons of
26:25 The men from all the c of Issachar numbered
26:26 These were the c descended from the sons of
26:27 The men from all the c of Zebulun numbered
26:28 Two c were descended from Joseph through
26:29 These were the c descended from Manasseh:
26:34 The men from all the c of Manasseh numbered
26:35 These were the c descended from the sons of
26:37 The men from all the c of Ephraim numbered
26:37 These c of Manasseh and Ephraim were all
26:38 These were the c descended from the sons of
26:41 The men from all the c of Benjamin numbered
26:42 These were the c descended from the sons of Dan:
26:43 All the c of Dan were Shuhamite c,
26:43 and the men from these c numbered 64,400.
26:44 These were the c descended from the sons of
26:47 The men from all the c of Asher numbered 53,400.
26:48 These were the c descended from the sons of
26:50 The men from all the c of Naphtali numbered
26:57 the Levites who were counted according to their c:
26:62 The men from the Levite c who were one month
33:54 You must distribute the land among the c by sacred
33:54 of land will be allotted to each of the larger c,
33:54 inheritance will be allotted to each of the smaller c.
36:12 They married into the c of Manasseh son of
Jos 7:14 That tribe must come forward with its c,
7:17 Then the c of Judah came forward, and the clan of
Jdg 18: 2 of Dan chose five warriors from among their c,
1Sa 10:19 yourselves before the LORD by tribes and c."
1Ch 4:38 of some of the leaders of Simeon's wealthy c,
5: 7 relatives are listed in their genealogy by their c:
5:13 the leaders of seven other c, were Michael,
5:15 of Abdiel, son of Guni, was the leader of their c.
5:24 These were the leaders of their c: Epher, Ishi,
6:19 The following were the Levite c, listed according
7: 3 and Isshiah. These five became the leaders of c.
7: 5 from all the c of the tribe of Issachar was 87,000.
7: 7 and Iri. These five warriors were the leaders of c.
7:11 They were the leaders of the c of Jediael, and their
8: 6 leaders of the c living at Geba, were driven out
8:10 These sons all became the leaders of c.
8:13 They were the leaders of the c living in Aijalon,
8:28 These were the leaders of the ancestral c, and they
9: 9 These men were all leaders of c, and they were
9:13 They were heads of c and very able men.

23: 6 after the **c** descended from the three sons of Levi—
23:24 These were the descendants of Levi by **c**,
26:19 divisions of the gatekeepers from the **c** of Korah
2Ch 17:14 His army was enrolled according to ancestral **c**.
20:19 Then the Levites from the **c** of Kohath and Korah
Zec 12: 5 And the **c** of Judah will say to themselves,
12: 6 "On that day I will make the **c** of Judah like a

CLAP (8) [CLAPPED]

Ps 47: 1 Come, everyone, and **c** your hands for joy!
98: 8 Let the rivers **c** their hands in glee! / Let the hills
Isa 55:12 and the trees of the field will **c** their hands!
Eze 6:11 **C** your hands in horror, and stamp your feet.
21:14 prophesy to them and **c** your hands vigorously.
21:17 I, too, will **c** my hands, and I will satisfy my fury.
22:13 "But now I **c** my hands in indignation over your
Na 3:19 All who hear of your destruction will **c** their hands

CLAPPED (3) [CLAP]

Nu 24:10 He angrily **c** his hands and shouted, "I called you
2Ki 11:12 and all the people **c** their hands and shouted,
Eze 25: 6 Because you **c** and stamped and cheered with glee

CLARITY (1) [CLEAR]

1Co 13:12 but then we will see everything with perfect **c**.

CLASH (2) [CLASHED]

Ps 150: 5 Praise him with a **c** of cymbals; / praise him with
Isa 24: 8 The **c** of tambourines will be stilled; the happy

CLASHED (1) [CLASH]

Ezr 3:10 of Asaph, **c** their cymbals to praise the LORD,

CLASPS (6)

Ex 26: 6 Then make fifty gold **c** to fasten the loops of the
26:11 and fasten them together with fifty bronze **c**.
35:11 the **c**, frames, crossbars, posts, and bases;
36:13 Then fifty gold **c** were made to connect the loops
36:18 They also made fifty small bronze **c** to couple the
39:33 the **c**, frames, crossbars, posts, and bases;

CLASSIFIED (1)

Ecc 12: 9 he knew. He collected proverbs and **c** them.

CLATTER (4)

2Ki 7: 6 army of Aram to hear the **c** of speeding chariots
Jer 47: 3 Hear the **c** of hooves and the rumble of wheels as
Eze 30:22 and I will make his sword **c** to the ground.
Na 3: 2 and chariots **c** as they bump wildly through the

CLAUDA [KJV] See CAUDA

CLAUDIA (1)

2Ti 4:21 and so do Pudens, Linus, **C**, and all the brothers

CLAUDIUS (3)

Ac 11:28 (This was fulfilled during the reign of **C**.)
18: 2 They had been expelled from Italy as a result of **C**
23:26 "From **C** Lysias, to his Excellency,

CLAVE [KJV] See also CLUNG, CUT, DRAWN, FOLLOWED, JOINED, SPLIT

CLAWS (4)

1Sa 17:37 The LORD who saved me from the **c** of the lion
La 3:11 He dragged me off the path and tore me with his **c**,
Da 4:33 as eagles' feathers and his nails were like birds' **c**.
7:19 crushed its victims with iron teeth and bronze **c**,

CLAY (41)

Lev 6:28 If a **c** pot is used to boil the sacrificial meat,
11:33 "If such an animal dies and falls into a **c** pot,
11:35 If it is a **c** oven or cooking pot, it must be smashed
14: 5 over a **c** pot that is filled with fresh springwater.
14:50 He will slaughter one of the birds over a **c** pot that
15:12 Any **c** pot touched by the man with the discharge
Nu 5:17 He must take some holy water in a **c** jar and mix it
Jdg 7:16 man a ram's horn and a **c** jar with a torch in it.
7:19 they blew the horns and broke their **c** jars.
1Ki 7:46 The king had them cast in **c** molds in the Jordan
2Ch 4:17 The king had them cast in **c** molds in the Jordan
Job 4:19 how much less will he trust those made of **c**!
13:12 as ashes. Your defense is as fragile as a **c** pot.
33: 6 the same before God. I, too, was formed from **c**.
Ps 2: 9 with an iron rod / and smash them like **c** pots.' "
22:15 My strength has dried up like sunbaked **c**.
Pr 26:23 just as a pretty glaze covers a common **c** pot.
Isa 41:25 He will trample them as a potter treads on **c**.
45: 9 Does a **c** pot ever argue with its maker?
45: 9 Does the **c** dispute with the one who shapes it,
64: 8 our Father. We are the **c**, and you are the potter.
Jer 18: 2 "Go down to the shop where **c** pots and jars are
18: 4 so the potter squashed the jar into a lump of **c**
18: 6 can I not do to you as this potter has done to his **c**?
18: 6 As the **c** is in the potter's hand, so you are in my
19: 1 The LORD said to me, "Go and buy a **c** jar.
La 4: 2 their weight in gold, are now treated like pots of **c**.
Da 2:33 and its feet were a combination of iron and **c**.
2:34 It struck the feet of iron and **c**, smashing them to
2:35 into a heap of iron, **c**, bronze, silver, and gold.
2:41 and **c** show that this kingdom will be divided.
2:42 it will be as strong as iron, and others as weak as **c**.
2:43 and **c** also shows that these kingdoms will try to
2:43 this will not succeed, just as iron and **c** do not mix.
2:45 dust the statue of iron, bronze, **c**, silver, and gold.
Na 3:14 Go into the pits to trample **c**, and pack it into
Mk 2: 4 so they dug through the **c** roof above his head.
Ro 9:21 When a potter makes jars out of **c**, doesn't he have a right to use the same lump of **c**
2Ti 2:20 and silver, and some are made of wood and **c**.
Rev 2:27 with an iron rod and smash them like **c** pots.

CLEAN (96) [CLEANSE, CLEANSED, CLEANSES, CLEANSING]

Ge 35: 2 your idols, wash yourselves, and put on **c** clothing.
Lev 4:12 must be carried away to a ceremonially **c** place
6:10 the priest on duty must **c** out the ashes of the burnt
6:11 outside the camp to a place that is ceremonially **c**.
7:19 only be eaten by people who are ceremonially **c**.
10:10 what is ceremonially unclean and what is **c**.
10:14 may be eaten in any place that is ceremonially **c**.
11:32 it will be ceremonially **c** and may be used again.
11:36 into a spring or a cistern, the water will still be **c**.
11:37 in the field, the seed will still be considered **c**.
11:47 may not be eaten and what is **c** and may be eaten."
12: 7 Then she will be ceremonially **c** again after her
12: 8 for her, and she will be ceremonially **c**."
13: 6 priest will pronounce the person ceremonially **c**.
13:13 he will pronounce the person ceremonially **c**
13:17 priest will pronounce the person ceremonially **c**.
13:23 priest will pronounce that person ceremonially **c**.
13:28 then pronounce the person ceremonially **c**.
13:34 priest must pronounce that person ceremonially **c**.
13:34 After washing clothes, that person will be **c**.
13:35 begins to spread after the person is pronounced **c**,
13:37 then pronounce the infected person ceremonially **c**.
13:39 skin rash, and the person is ceremonially **c**.
13:40 his head becomes bald, he is still ceremonially **c**.
13:41 he simply has a bald forehead; he is still **c**.
13:58 be washed again; then it will be ceremonially **c**.
13:59 determine whether these things are ceremonially **c**
14: 7 will pronounce that person to be ceremonially **c**.
14: 8 Then they will be ceremonially **c** and may return to
14: 9 Then they will be pronounced ceremonially **c**.
14:20 and the healed person will be ceremonially **c**.
14:48 then he will pronounce the house **c**
14:53 for the house, and it will be ceremonially **c**.
14:57 to determine when something is ceremonially **c**
15:13 fresh springwater. Then he will be ceremonially **c**.
15:28 seven days. After that, she will be ceremonially **c**.
17:15 until evening; after that, you will be considered **c**.
20:25 make a distinction between ceremonially **c**
20:25 unclean animals, and between **c** and unclean birds.
22: 4 offerings until they have been pronounced **c**.
22: 7 they will be **c** again and may eat the sacred
27: 9 "If your vow involves giving a **c** animal—one that
Nu 8: 6 the people of Israel and make them ceremonially **c**.
8: 7 their clothing. Then they will be ceremonially **c**.
9:13 " 'But those who are ceremonially **c** and not away
18:11 Any member of your family who is ceremonially **c**,
18:13 Any member of your family who is ceremonially **c**
19: 9 Then someone who is ceremonially **c** will gather
19:18 Then someone who is ceremonially **c** must take a
19:19 and seventh days the ceremonially **c** person must
Dt 12:15 All of you, whether ceremonially **c** or unclean,
12:22 Anyone, whether ceremonially **c** or unclean,
14:11 "You may eat any bird that is ceremonially **c**.
14:20 may eat any winged creature that is ceremonially **c**.
15:22 may eat it, whether ceremonially **c** or unclean,
1Sa 21: 5 And since they stay **c** even on ordinary trips,
Ezr 6:20 had purified themselves and were ceremonially **c**.
Job 9:30 my hands with lye to make them absolutely **c**,
11: 4 teaching is pure,' and 'I am **c** in the sight of God.'
22:23 If you return to the Almighty and **c** up your life,
Ps 51: 2 Wash me **c** from my guilt. / Purify me from my
51: 7 Purify me from my sins, and I will be **c**; / wash me,
51:10 Create in me a **c** heart, O God. / Renew a right
Pr 14: 4 An empty stable stays **c**, but no income comes
Ecc 9: 2 good or bad, ceremonially **c** or unclean, religious
Isa 1:16 Wash yourselves and be **c**! Let me no longer see
1:18 I can make you as **c** as freshly fallen snow.
Jer 2:22 No amount of soap or lye can make you **c**. You are
12: 9 Bring on the wild beasts to pick their corpses **c**!
43:12 He will pick **c** the land of Egypt as a shepherd
La 4: 7 they were as **c** as snow and as elegant as jewels.
Eze 21: 4 I will make a **c** sweep throughout the land from
22:26 the difference between what is ceremonially **c**
36:25 "Then I will sprinkle **c** water on you, and you will be **c**.
39:14 and to bury them, so the land will be made **c** again.
44:23 is common, what is ceremonially **c** and unclean.
Zec 3: 5 could he also have a **c** turban on his head?"
3: 5 So they put a **c** priestly turban on his head
Mt 3:12 Then he will **c** up the threshing area,
12:44 and finds its former home empty, swept, and **c**.
23:25 You are so careful to **c** the outside of the cup
23:26 of the cup, and then the outside will become **c**, too.
Lk 3:17 Then he will **c** up the threshing area,
11:25 and finds that its former home is all swept and **c**.
11:39 so careful to **c** the outside of the cup and the dish,
11:41 you greedily possess, and you will be **c** all over.
Jn 13:10 need to wash, except for the feet, to be entirely **c**.
13:10 And you are **c**, but that isn't true of everyone
13:11 he meant when he said, "Not all of you are **c**."
Eph 5:26 to make her holy and **c**, washed by baptism
Php 2:15 You are to live **c**, innocent lives as children of God
2Ti 2:21 Your life will be **c**, and you will be ready for the
Heb 10:22 been sprinkled with Christ's blood to make us **c**,
12:14 with everyone, and seek to live a **c** and holy life,
1Pe 3:21 it is an appeal to God from a **c** conscience.

CLEANSE (34) [CLEAN]

Ex 29:36 Afterward make an offering to **c** the altar.
Lev 11:34 If the water used to **c** an unclean object touches
16:19 he will **c** it from Israel's defilement and return it to
Dt 10:16 **c** your sinful hearts and stop being stubborn.
19:19 In this way, you will **c** such evil from among you.
21: 9 you will **c** the guilt of murder from your
21:21 In this way, you will **c** this evil from among you,
22:24 man's wife. In this way, you will **c** the land of evil.
24: 7 must die. You must **c** the evil from among you.
30: 6 "The LORD your God will **c** your heart
32:43 on his enemies / and **c** his land and his people."
2Ch 29:16 the sanctuary of the Temple of the LORD to **c** it,
Job 9:30 and **c** my hands with lye to make them absolutely
Ps 19:12 in my heart? / **C** me from these hidden faults.
Isa 4: 4 He will **c** Jerusalem of its bloodstains by a spirit of
Jer 4: 4 **C** your minds and hearts before the LORD,
4:14 O Jerusalem, **c** your hearts that you may be saved.
6:29 But it will never purify and **c** them because there is
33: 8 I will **c** away their sins against me, and I will
Eze 24:13 And now, because I tried to **c** you but you refused,
36:29 I will **c** you of your filthy behavior. I will give you
36:33 When I **c** you from your sins, I will bring people to
37:23 I will **c** them. Then they will truly be my people,
39:12 people of Israel to **c** the land by burying the bodies.
43:20 This will **c** and make atonement for the altar.
43:22 Then **c** and make atonement for the altar again,
43:26 Do this each day for seven days to **c** and make
Zec 13: 1 a fountain to **c** them from all their sins
2Co 7: 1 let us **c** ourselves from everything that can defile
Tit 2:14 to **c** us, and to make us his very own people,
Heb 1: 3 After he died to **c** us from the stain of sin, he sat
9: 9 and sacrifices that the priests offer are not able to **c**
9:13 and the ashes of a young cow could **c** people's
1Jn 1: 9 just to forgive us and to **c** us from every wrong.

CLEANSED (25) [CLEAN]

Lev 14:18 before the LORD for the person being **c**.
14:20 priest will make atonement for the person being **c**,
14:21 thus making atonement for the person being **c**.
14:22 The person being **c** must also bring two turtledoves
14:23 the person being **c** must bring the offerings to the
14:29 priest will make atonement for the person being **c**.
14:31 before the LORD for the person being **c**.
16:30 and you will be **c** from all your sins in the
Nu 6: 9 Then they will be **c** from their defilement.
19:19 Then on the seventh day the people being **c** must
19:19 and that evening they will be **c** of their defilement.
Dt 22:21 Such evil must be **c** from among you.
22:22 be killed. In this way, the evil will be **c** from Israel.
Jos 22:17 We are not yet fully **c** of it, even after the plague
2Ch 30:19 even though they are not properly **c** for the
Pr 20: 9 Who can say, "I have **c** my heart; I am pure
Eze 39:16 means 'horde.') And so the land will finally be **c**.
44:26 return to his Temple duties after being ritually **c**
Da 11:35 they will be refined and **c** and made pure until the
12:10 Many will be purified, **c**, and refined by these
Ac 3:19 and turn to God, so you can be **c** of your sins.
15: 9 and them, for he also **c** their hearts through faith.
1Pe 1: 2 have obeyed Jesus Christ and are **c** by his blood.
1:22 because you were **c** from your sins when you
2Pe 1: 9 They have already forgotten that God has **c** them

CLEANSES (2) [CLEAN]

Pr 20:30 Physical punishment **c** away evil; such discipline
1Jn 1: 7 the blood of Jesus, his Son, **c** us from every sin.

CLEANSING (10) [CLEAN]

Lev 14: 8 "The people being purified must complete the **c**
14:11 the officiating priest will present that person for **c**,
14:23 **c** ceremony to be performed in the LORD's
14:32 These are the instructions for **c** those who have
14:32 normally required for the ceremony of **c**."
Eze 43:23 When you have finished the **c** ceremony,
Jn 3:25 argument with John's disciples over ceremonial **c**.
11:55 so they could go through the **c** ceremony before the
Heb 10: 1 but they were never able to provide perfect **c** for
10: 2 If they could have provided perfect **c**, the sacrifices

CLEAR (50) [CLARITY, CLEAR-EYED, CLEARED, CLEARER, CLEARLY, CLEARS]

Ge 21:22 "It is **c** that God helps you in everything you do,"
28: 8 It was now very **c** to Esau that his father despised
Ex 8:23 I will make a **c** distinction between your people
24:10 pavement of brilliant sapphire, as **c** as the heavens.
Lev 13:11 because it is **c** that the skin is defiled by the
24:12 the LORD's will in the matter should become **c**.
Dt 7: 1 he will **c** away many nations ahead of you:
7:22 You will not **c** them away all at once, for if you
34: 7 yet his eyesight was **c**, and he was as strong as
Jos 3: 4 keeping a **c** distance between you and the Ark.
17:15 **c** out land for yourselves in the forest where the
17:18 **C** as much of the land as you wish and live there.
1Sa 16:15 "It is **c** that a spirit from God is tormenting you,"
2Sa 19: 6 You have made it **c** today that we mean nothing to
2Ch 11:22 making it **c** that he would be the next king.
Job 27: 6 My conscience is **c** for as long as I live.
Ps 19: 8 The commands of the LORD are **c**,
37: 6 He will make your innocence as **c** as the dawn,

119:113 about you, / but my choice is c—I love your law.
Pr 8: 9 with understanding, c to those who want to learn.
Isa 25: 6 good food, with c, well-aged wine and choice beef.
57:14 C away the rocks and stones so my people can
Jer 48:34 can be heard from Heshbon c across to Elealeh
Hab 2: 2 c letters on a tablet, so that a runner can read it
Ac 21:14 When it was c that we couldn't persuade him,
24:16 I always try to maintain a c conscience before God
Ro 4:13 It is c, then, that God's promise to give the whole
13: 5 from being punished and to keep a c conscience.
15:19 all the way from Jerusalem c over into Illyricum.
1Co 4: 4 My conscience is c, but that isn't what matters.
14: 8 And if the bugler doesn't sound a c call, how will
2Co 1:12 and a c conscience that we have been honest
7:11 such concern to c yourselves, such indignation,
Gal 3:11 it is c that no one can ever be right with God by
Eph 5:13 on them, it becomes c how evil these things are.
1Th 4: 3 to be holy, so you should keep c of all sexual sin.
1Ti 1: 5 from a pure heart, a c conscience, and sincere faith.
1:19 faith in Christ, and always keep your conscience c.
3: 9 Christian faith and must live with a c conscience.
2Ti 1: 3 He is the God I serve with a c conscience, just as
4: 5 But you should keep a c mind in every situation.
Heb 13:18 for our conscience is c and we want to live
1Pe 3:16 and respectful way. Keep your conscience c.
2Pe 1:15 So I will work hard to make these things c to you.
1Jn 3:21 Dear friends, if our conscience is c, we can come
Rev 19:10 For the essence of prophecy is to give a c witness
21:11 sparkled like a precious gem, crystal c like jasper.
21:18 of jasper, and the city was pure gold, as c as glass.
21:21 And the main street was pure gold, as c as glass.
22: 1 c as crystal, flowing from the throne of God

CLEAR-EYED (1) [CLEAR, EYE]
Ecc 2: 9 I remained c so that I could evaluate all these

CLEARED (3) [CLEAR]
Ps 32: 2 for those / whose record the LORD has c of sin,
80: 9 You c the ground for us, / and we took root
Isa 5: 2 He plowed the land, c its stones, / and planted it

CLEARER (1) [CLEAR]
Ro 3:20 the c it becomes that we aren't obeying it.

CLEARLY (41) [CLEAR]
Ex 4:15 I will help both of you to speak c, and I will tell
23: 8 for a bribe makes you ignore something that you c
Lev 13:11 it is c a contagious skin disease, and the priest must
13:25 for it is c a contagious skin disease.
13:27 for it is c a contagious skin disease.
13:51 the material is c contaminated by an infectious
13:57 at a later time, however, the mildew is c spreading,
14:44 the walls are c contaminated with an infectious
14:48 because the infectious mildew is c gone.
Nu 24: 3 the prophecy of the man whose eyes see c,
24:15 the prophecy of the man whose eyes see c,
Dt 27: 8 you must c write all the terms of this law."
1Ki 11: 2 The LORD had c instructed his people not to
1Ch 15:26 because God was c helping the Levites as they
Ne 8: 8 and c explained the meaning of what was being
12:42 and c under the direction of Jezrahiah the choir
Ps 5: 8 enemies will conquer me. / Tell me c what to do,
Pr 5:21 For the LORD sees c what a man does,
Isa 8: 1 a large signboard and c write this name on it:
Jer 23:20 days to come, you will understand all this very c.
Eze 10: 5 and could be heard c in the outer courtyard.
11: 4 son of man, prophesy against them loudly and c."
18:18 doing what was c wrong among his people.
Mk 8:24 he said, "I see people, but I can't see them very c.
8:25 completely restored, and he could see everything c.
Lk 24:26 Wasn't it c predicted by the prophets that the
Jn 7:42 For the Scriptures c state that the Messiah will be
19: 4 but understand c that I find him not guilty."
Ac 2:36 So let it be c known by everyone in Israel that God
4:10 Let me c state to you and to all the people of Israel
10:34 "I see very c that God doesn't show partiality.
Ro 1:20 They can c see his invisible qualities—his eternal
16:19 I want you to see c what is right and to stay
1Co 6:18 No other sin so c affects the body as this one does.
14: 7 recognize the melody unless the notes are played c.
2Co 3: 3 C, you are a letter from Christ prepared by us.
Gal 3: 1 c as though I had shown you a signboard with a
Col 4: 4 Pray that I will proclaim this message as c as I
1Th 5: 8 But let us who live in the light think c,
1Ti 4: 1 Now the Holy Spirit tells us c that in the last times
1Pe 1:13 So think c and exercise self-control. Look forward

CLEARS (1) [CLEAR]
Job 37:21 for it shines brightly in the sky when the wind c

CLEAVE(D), CLEAVETH [KJV] See CLING, CLUNG, CUT, DIVIDED, FAITHFUL, FASTENED, HOLD, JOIN, REMAIN, SHRIVELED, SLASHED, SPLITS, STICK, STUCK, TEAR, UNITED

CLEFT (1) [CLEFTS]
Ex 33:22 I will put you in the c of the rock and cover you

CLEFTS (1) [CLEFT]
Jer 48:28 Live in the caves like doves that nest in the c of the

CLEMENCY [KJV] See ATTENTION

CLEMENT (1)
Php 4: 3 And they worked with C and the rest of my

CLENCH (1) [CLENCHED, CLENCHES]
Ps 138: 7 You will c your fist against my angry enemies!

CLENCHED (2) [CLENCH]
Job 15:25 For they have c their fists against God,
Jer 15: 6 "Therefore, I will raise my c fists to destroy you.

CLENCHES (1) [CLENCH]
Isa 31: 3 When the LORD c his fist against them, they will

CLEOPAS (1)
Lk 24:18 Then one of them, C, replied, "You must be the

CLEOPHAS [KJV] See CLOPAS

CLEVER (10) [CLEVERLY, CLEVERNESS]
Job 15: 5 what to say. Your words are based on c deception.
Pr 1: 4 These proverbs will make the simpleminded c.
Isa 5:21 they are wise and consider themselves to be c.
Jer 4:22 They are c enough at doing wrong, but they have
Zec 9: 2 cities of Tyre and Sidon, too, though they are so c.
Mt 11:25 from those who think themselves so wise and c,
Lk 10:21 from those who think themselves so wise and c,
1Co 1:17 and not with c speeches and high-sounding ideas,
2Pe 1:16 For we were not making up c stories when we told
2: 3 In their greed they will make up c lies to get hold

CLEVERLY (2) [CLEVER]
Eph 4:14 or because someone has c lied to us and made the
2Pe 2: 1 They will c teach their destructive heresies about

CLEVERNESS (2) [CLEVER]
Job 5:13 those who think they are wise in their own c,
1Co 3:19 those who think they are wise / in their own c."

CLIENT (1)
Jer 3: 2 sit like a prostitute beside the road waiting for a c.

CLIFF (10) [CLIFFS]
Nu 23: 9 I see them from the c tops; / I watch them from the
1Sa 14: 5 The c on the north was in front of Micmash,
2Ch 25:12 and took them to the top of a c and threw them off,
Job 14:18 and crumble and as rocks fall from a c,
18: 4 to be abandoned? Will it make rocks fall from a c?
Ps 73: 2 But as for me, I came so close to the edge of the c!
73:18 and send them sliding over the c to destruction.
141: 6 When their leaders are thrown down from a c,
SS 2:14 behind some rocks, behind an outcrop on the c.
Lk 4:29 was built. They intended to push him over the c,

CLIFFS (6) [CLIFF]
Dt 32:13 He nourished them with honey from the c,
1Sa 14: 4 Jonathan had to go down between two rocky c that
Job 39:28 It lives on the c, making its home on a distant,
Pr 30:26 but they make their homes among the rocky c.
Isa 2:21 and hide among the jagged rocks at the tops of c.
Eze 38:20 c will crumble; walls will fall to the earth.

CLIFT [KJV] See CLEFT

CLIMAX (3)
Eze 7:10 people's wickedness and pride have reached a c.
Da 9:27 Then as a c to all his terrible deeds, he will set up a
Jn 7:37 the c of the festival, Jesus stood and shouted to the

CLIMB (15) [CLIMBED, CLIMBING]
Ex 24: 2 none of the other people are allowed to c on the
Nu 27:12 "C to the top of the mountains east of the river,
Dt 5: 5 were afraid of the fire and did not c the mountain.
32:49 and c Mount Nebo, which is across from Jericho.
1Sa 9:14 Samuel was coming out toward them to c the hill.
14:12 "Come on, c right behind me," Jonathan said to
19:12 So she helped him c out through a window, and he
1Ki 18:44 tell him, 'C into your chariot and go back home.
Ps 24: 3 Who may c the mountain of the LORD?
SS 7: 8 'I will c up into the palm tree and take hold of its
Isa 14:14 I will c to the highest heavens and be like the Most
15: 5 Weeping, they c the road to Luhith.
Jer 48: 5 Her refugees will c the hills of Luhith,
Am 9: 2 Even if they c up into the heavens, I will bring
Hab 2: 1 I will c up into my watchtower now and wait to see

CLIMBED (25) [CLIMB]
Ex 19: 3 Then Moses c the mountain to appear before God.
19:20 the top of the mountain. So Moses c the mountain.
24:13 and his assistant Joshua c up the mountain of God.
24:18 Then Moses disappeared into the cloud as he c
34: 4 Early in the morning he c Mount Sinai as the
Dt 34: 1 Nebo from the plains of Moab and c Pisgah Peak,
Jdg 3:23 and locked the doors and c down the latrine
9: 7 he c to the top of Mount Gerizim and shouted,
9:51 themselves in and c up to the roof of the tower.
1Sa 10:13 had finished prophesying, he c the hill to the altar.
14:13 So they c up using both hands and feet,
26:13 David c the hill opposite the camp until he was at a
2Sa 15:30 their heads and wept as they c the mountain.
18:24 the watchman c to the roof of the gateway by the
1Ki 18:42 But Elijah c to the top of Mount Carmel and fell to
2Ki 5:21 he c down from his chariot and went to meet him.
Isa 57: 8 You have c right into bed with these detestable
Eze 40: 6 He c the steps and measured the threshold of the
Mt 9: 1 Jesus c into a boat and went back across the lake to
14:32 And when they c back into the boat, the wind
15:29 to the Sea of Galilee and c a hill and sat down.
Mk 6:51 Then he c into the boat, and the wind stopped.
6:54 and c out. The people standing there recognized
Lk 19: 4 he ran ahead and c a sycamore tree beside the road,
19: 6 Zacchaeus quickly c down and took Jesus to his

CLIMBING (5) [CLIMB]
1Sa 9:11 As they were c a hill toward the town, they met
Joel 2: 9 all the houses, c like thieves through the windows.
Mk 5: 2 Just as Jesus was c from the boat, a man possessed
Lk 8:27 As Jesus was c out of the boat, a man who was
Jn 6: 5 Jesus soon saw a great crowd of people c the hill,

CLING (13) [CLINGING, CLINGS, CLUNG]
Dt 10:20 LORD your God and worship him and c to him.
13: 4 his commands, listen to his voice, and c to him.
Job 8:15 They c to their home for security, but it won't last.
Ps 109:19 may his curses return and c to him like clothing;
119:31 I c to your decrees. / LORD, don't let me be put
119:83 But I c to your principles and obey them.
Jer 13:11 so I created Judah and Israel to c to me,"
Mt 10:39 If you c to your life, you will lose it; but if you
Lk 8:15 c to it, and steadily produce a huge harvest.
Jn 20:17 "Don't c to me," Jesus said, "for I haven't yet
Php 2: 6 he did not demand and c to his rights as God.
1Ti 1:19 C tightly to your faith in Christ, and always keep
Heb 4:14 Let us c to him and never stop trusting him.

CLINGING (3) [CLING]
Dt 11:22 your God by walking in his ways and c to him.
Pr 23:34 like a sailor tossed at sea, c to a swaying mast.
Ro 10: 3 they are c to their own way of getting right with

CLINGS (2) [CLING]
Jer 13:11 As a belt c to a person's waist, so I created Judah
Lk 17:33 Whoever c to this life will lose it, and whoever

CLIP (1)
Lev 19:27 hair on your temples or c the edges of your beards.

CLOAK (21) [CLOAKED, CLOAKS]
Ex 22:26 If you take your neighbor's c as a pledge of
Dt 24:12 is poor and has only a c to give as security, do not keep the c overnight.
24:13 Return the c to its owner by sunset so your
Jdg 8:25 They spread out a c, and each one threw in a gold
Ru 3:15 also said to her, "Bring your c and spread it out."
3:15 He measured out six scoops of barley into the c
2Sa 20:12 off the road into a field and threw a c over him.
1Ki 11:29 from Shiloh met him on the road, wearing a new c.
11:30 and Ahijah took the new c he was wearing and tore
18:46 He tucked his c into his belt and ran ahead of
19:13 he wrapped his face in his c and went out
19:19 over to him and threw his c across his shoulders
2Ki 2: 8 Then Elijah folded his c together and struck the
2:13 Then Elisha picked up Elijah's c and returned to
2:14 He struck the water with the c and cried out,
Est 8:15 and he wore an outer c of fine linen and purple.
Pr 30: 4 in his fists? Who wraps up the oceans in his c?
Isa 3: 6 "Since you have a c, you be our leader!
Jer 43:12 land of Egypt as a shepherd picks fleas from his c.
Eze 16: 8 So I wrapped my c around you to cover your

CLOAKED (1) [CLOAK]
Ge 1: 2 earth was empty, a formless mass c in darkness.

CLOAKS (2) [CLOAK]
Dt 22:12 must put tassels on the four corners of your c.
2Ki 9:13 They quickly spread out their c on the bare steps

CLOCK (1)
Isa 60:11 Your gates will stay open around the c to receive

CLODS (1)
Ps 65:10 with rain, / melting the c and leveling the ridges.

CLOPAS (1)
Jn 19:25 Mary (the wife of C), and Mary Magdalene.

CLOSE (75) [CLOSED, CLOSELY, CLOSER, CLOSES, CLOSEST, CLOSING, ENCLOSE, ENCLOSED, ENCLOSURE, ENCLOSURES]
Ge 5:22 Enoch lived another 300 years in c fellowship with
5:24 He enjoyed a c relationship with God throughout
6: 9 God's will and enjoyed a c relationship with him.
13: 6 with all their flocks and herds living so c together.
13: 8 got to stop," he said. "After all, we are c relatives!
25:18 The clans descended from Ishmael camped c to
48:10 So Joseph brought the boys c to him, and Jacob
Ex 7: 1 the LORD said to Moses, "Pay c attention to this.
24: 2 The others must not come too c. And remember,
25:27 c to the rim around the top. These rings will

Lev 18: 6 "You must never have sexual intercourse with a c
18:12 because she is your father's c relative.
18:13 because she is your mother's c relative.
18:17 They are c relatives, and to do this would be a
20:19 or his father's sister, he has violated a c relative.
21: 2 unless it is a c relative—mother or father, son
25:25 then a c relative, a kinsman redeemer, may buy it
25:48 They may be bought back by a c relative—
Nu 17:13 Everyone who even comes c to the Tabernacle of
Dt 15: 9 a loan because the year of release is c at hand.
30:14 The message is very c at hand; it is on your lips
Jos 2: 5 the city at dusk, as the city gates were about to c,
8: 4 "Hide in ambush c behind the city and be ready
Ru 3: 2 Boaz is a c relative of ours, and he's been very
1Sa 19: 1 because of his c friendship with David,
23:26 Just as Saul and his men began to c in on David
2Sa 11:16 So Joab assigned Uriah to a spot c to the city wall
11:20 and ask, 'Why did the troops go so c to the city?
Ne 8: 3 All the people paid c attention to the Book of the
Job 19:14 My neighbors and my c friends are all gone.
19:19 My c friends abhor me. Those I loved have turned
41:16 They are c together so no air can get between
Ps 23: 4 I will not be afraid, / for you are c beside me.
27:10 mother abandon me, / the LORD will hold me c.
34:18 The LORD is c to the brokenhearted; / he rescues
55:13 it is you—my equal, / my companion and c friend.
63: 8 I follow c behind you; / your strong right hand
73: 2 But as for me, I came so c to the edge of the cliff!
88:15 I have been sickly and c to death since my youth.
132: 4 not let my eyes sleep / nor c my eyelids in slumber
145:18 The LORD is c to all who call on him, / yes,
148:14 the people of Israel who are c to him.
Pr 17: 9 telling about them separates c friends.
28:27 But a curse will come upon those who c their eyes
Isa 6:10 C their ears, and shut their eyes. That way,
22:22 he will c doors, and no one will be able to open
40:11 the lambs in his arms, holding them c to his heart.
65: 5 'Don't come too c or you will defile me!
66: 5 "Your c relatives hate you and throw you out for
Jer 13:19 The towns of the Negev will c their gates, and no
42:16 and famine you fear will follow c behind you,
Eze 18:18 for being cruel and robbing c relatives, doing what
31: 8 No tree in the garden of God came c to it in beauty.
40: 4 Pay c attention to everything I show you.
Da 3:26 Then Nebuchadnezzar came as c as he could to the
Am 6:10 And when a c relative—one who is responsible for
Ob 1:10 Because of the violence you did to your c relatives
Mic 3: 6 Now the night will c around you, cutting off all
Hab 3: 5 marches before him; plague follows c behind.
Lk 15:31 said to him, 'Look, dear son, you and I are very c,
19:43 your walls and encircle you and c in on you.
Jn 19:42 the Passover and since the tomb was c at hand,
Ac 10:24 together his relatives and c friends to meet Peter.
23: 2 those c to Paul to slap him on the mouth.
27:13 they pulled up anchor and sailed along c to shore.
Ro 10: 8 the Scriptures say, "The message is c at hand;
1Co 10:11 live at the time when this age is drawing to a c.
2Co 6: 9 We live c to death, but here we are, still alive.
13:11 Dear friends, I c my letter with these last words:
Php 4: 8 let me say one more thing as I c this letter.
1Ti 4:16 Keep a c watch on yourself and on your teaching.
Jas 4: 8 Draw c to God, and God will draw c to you.
2Pe 1:19 Pay c attention to what they wrote, for their words
Rev 21:25 Its gates never c at the end of day because there is

CLOSED (28) [CLOSE]

Ge 2:21 and c up the place from which he had taken it.
Lev 14:46 Anyone who enters the house while it is c will be
Nu 16:33 The earth c over them, and they all vanished.
Jdg 3:23 Then Ehud c and locked the doors and climbed
1Sa 1: 6 of Hannah because the LORD had c her womb.
31: 2 The Philistines c in on Saul and his sons, and they
1Ch 10: 2 The Philistines c in on Saul and his sons, and they
2Ch 29:19 Ahaz when he was unfaithful and c the Temple.
Job 17: 4 You have c their minds to understanding, but do
Ps 78:53 not afraid; / but the sea c in upon their enemies.
Ecc 12: 4 are gone, keep your lips tightly c when you eat!
Isa 8:12 Do not be afraid that some plan conceived behind c
29:10 He has c the eyes of your prophets and visionaries.
44:18 Their eyes are c, and they cannot see.
57: 8 Behind c doors, you have set up your idols
Jer 6:10 I speak? Their ears are c, and they cannot hear.
Eze 44: 1 to the east gateway in the outer wall, but it was c.
44: 2 the LORD said to me, "This gate must remain c;
46: 1 The east gateway of the inner wall will be c during
46: 2 he came. The gateway will not be c until evening.
Jnh 2: 5 The waters c in around me, and seaweed wrapped
Zec 5: 8 her back into the basket and c the heavy lid again.
Mt 13:15 ears cannot hear, / and they have c their eyes—
Lk 12: 3 and what you have whispered behind c doors will
Ac 21:30 and immediately the gates were c behind him.
28:27 ears cannot hear, / and they have c their eyes—
Ro 11: 8 do not see, / and c their ears so they do not hear."
Eph 4:18 Their c minds are full of darkness; they are far

CLOSELY (18) [CLOSE]

Lev 25:49 a nephew, or anyone else who is c related.
Nu 16:25 and Abiram, followed c by the Israelite leaders.
Dt 6: 3 Listen c, Israel, to everything I say. Be careful to
19:18 They must be c questioned, and if the accuser is
Ru 3:12 there is another man who is more c related to you
1Ki 3:21 But when I looked more c in the morning light,
Job 13:17 "Listen c to what I am about to say. Hear me out.
21: 2 "Listen c to what I am saying. You can console
Ps 11: 4 He watches everything c, / examining everyone on
86: 6 Listen c to my prayer, O LORD; / hear my urgent
119:67 disciplined me; / but now I c follow your word.
Jer 16:17 I am watching them c, and I see every sin.
Zec 9: 8 invading armies. I am c watching their movements.
Mal 3: 3 of silver, watching c as the dross is burned away.
Mk 3: 2 it was the Sabbath, Jesus' enemies watched him c.
14:67 She looked at him c and then said, "You were one
Lk 6: 7 and the Pharisees watched c to see whether Jesus
14: 1 of the Pharisees. The people were watching him c,

CLOSER (9) [CLOSE]

Ge 45: 4 "Come over here," he said. So they came c.
Ex 3: 5 "Do not come any c," God told him. "Take off
Jos 3: 4 and the Ark. Make sure you don't come any c."
1Sa 17:48 As Goliath moved c to attack, David quickly ran
2Sa 18:25 is alone, he has news." As the messenger came c,
Pr 18:24 each other, but a real friend sticks c than a brother.
Isa 48:16 Come c and listen. I have always told you plainly
Am 6: 3 but your actions only bring the day of judgment c.
Lk 19:41 But as they came c to Jerusalem and Jesus saw the

CLOSES (2) [CLOSE]

Job 12:14 When he c in on someone, there is no escape.
Ps 22:16 me like a pack of dogs; / an evil gang c in on me.

CLOSEST (4) [CLOSE]

Dt 13: 6 or c friend comes to you secretly and says,
Ru 2:20 That man is one of our c relatives, one of our
Est 1:14 They were his c associates and held the highest
Lk 21:16 Even those c to you—your parents, brothers,

CLOSET (1)

Job 31:33 sins as people normally do, hiding my guilt in a c?

CLOSET [KJV] See also ROOM

CLOSING (5) [CLOSE]

Lev 23:36 This will be a solemn c assembly, and no regular
23:39 and c eighth day of the festival will be days of total
2Sa 1: 6 on his spear with the enemy chariots c in on him.
2Ch 7: 9 On the eighth day they had a c ceremony, for they
Gal 6:11 Notice what large letters I use as I write these c

CLOTH (72) [CLOTHS, HEADCLOTH, SACKCLOTH]

Ex 25: 4 purple, and scarlet yarn; fine linen; goat hair for c;
26: 7 "Make heavy sheets of c from goat hair to cover
26:31 with cherubim skillfully embroidered into the c
28: 5 These items must be made of fine linen c
28: 6 "The ephod must be made of fine linen c
28: 8 fine linen c embroidered with gold thread and blue,
28:15 fine linen c embroidered with gold thread and blue,
28:16 This chestpiece will be made of two folds of c,
28:31 "Make the robe of the ephod entirely of blue c,
28:39 "Weave Aaron's patterned tunic from fine linen c.
35: 6 purple, and scarlet yarn; fine linen; goat hair for c;
35:23 and scarlet yarn, fine linen, or goat hair for c.
35:25 purple, and scarlet yarn, and fine linen c, and they
35:26 their skills to spin and weave the goat hair into c.
35:35 in blue, purple, and scarlet yarn on fine linen c.
36:14 a roof covering was made from eleven sheets of c
36:35 The inner curtain was made of fine linen c,
36:37 It was made of fine linen c and embroidered with
38:18 entrance to the courtyard was made of fine linen c
38:23 purple, and scarlet yarn on fine linen c.
39: 1 beautiful garments of blue, purple, and scarlet c—
39: 1 This same c was used for Aaron's sacred garments,
39: 2 The ephod was made from fine linen c
39: 5 fine linen c; blue, purple, and scarlet yarn;
39: 8 crafted from fine linen c and embroidered with
39:27 made for Aaron and his sons from fine linen c.
39:29 The sashes were made of fine linen c
Lev 11:32 the object is made of wood, c, leather, or sackcloth.
14: 4 some cedarwood, a scarlet c, and a hyssop branch.
14: 6 the scarlet c, and the hyssop branch,
14:49 some cedarwood, a scarlet c, and a hyssop branch.
14:51 the cedarwood, the hyssop branch, the scarlet c,
Nu 4: 6 and the goatskin leather with a dark blue c.
4: 7 "Next they must spread a blue c over the table,
4: 7 spoons, bowls, cups, and the special bread on the c.
4: 8 They must spread a scarlet c over that, and finally
4: 8 of fine goatskin leather on top of the scarlet c.
4: 9 they must cover the lampstand with a dark blue c,
4:11 and his sons must also spread a dark blue c over
4:11 and cover this c with a covering of fine goatskin
4:12 of the sanctuary must be wrapped in a dark blue c,
4:13 and the altar must then be covered with a purple c.
4:14 are to be placed on the c, and a covering of fine
Dt 22:17 Then they must spread the c before the judges.
1Sa 21: 9 "It is wrapped in a c behind the ephod.
2Sa 17:19 The man's wife put a c over the top of the well
2Ki 18:17 near the road leading to the field where c is
2Ch 2: 7 who is expert at dyeing purple, scarlet, and blue c;
2:14 blue, and scarlet c and in working with linen.
Pr 31:22 She dresses like royalty in gowns of finest c.
SS 3:10 is gold, and its seat is upholstered in purple c.
Isa 7: 3 near the road leading to the field where c is
36: 2 near the road leading to the field where c is
38:12 cut short, / as when a weaver cuts c from a loom.
Eze 27:24 blue c, embroidery, and many-colored carpets
Mt 9:16 who would patch an old garment with unshrunk c?
9:16 the patch shrinks and pulls away from the old c,
27:59 took the body and wrapped it in a long linen c.
Mk 2:21 who would patch an old garment with unshrunk c?
2:21 new patch shrinks and pulls away from the old c,
15:46 Joseph bought a long sheet of linen c, and taking
15:46 he wrapped it in the c and laid it in a tomb that had
Lk 2: 7 She wrapped him snugly in strips of c and laid him
2:12 lying in a manger, wrapped snugly in strips of c!"
5:36 "No one tears a piece of c from a new garment
23:53 from the cross and wrapped it in a long linen c
Jn 19:40 Jesus' body in a long linen c with the spices,
20: 5 and looked in and saw the linen c lying there,
20: 7 while the c that had covered Jesus' head was
Ac 16:14 from Thyatira, a merchant of expensive purple c.
Rev 6:12 The sun became as dark as black c, and the moon
18:12 jewels, pearls, fine linen, purple dye, silk, scarlet c,

CLOTHE (9) [CLOTHED, CLOTHES, CLOTHING, GRAVECLOTHES, UNDERCLOTHES]

Ex 28:41 C Aaron and his sons with these garments, and
40:13 C Aaron with the holy garments and anoint him,
Ps 109:29 obvious to all; / c my accusers with disgrace.
132:18 I will c his enemies with shame, / but he will be a
Pr 1: 9 will crown you with grace and c you with honor.
Isa 52: 1 wake up, O Zion! C yourselves with strength.
Ro 13:12 C yourselves with the armor of right living,
1Co 12:23 honorable are those we c with the greatest care.
Col 3:12 you must c yourselves with tenderhearted mercy,

CLOTHED (38) [CLOTHE]

Lev 8: 7 He c Aaron with the embroidered tunic and tied the
8:13 and c them in their embroidered tunics,
2Ch 6:41 your priests, O LORD God, be c with salvation,
Job 8:22 Those who hate you will be c with shame,
10:11 You c me with skin and flesh, and you knit my
37:22 the mountain of God. He is c in dazzling splendor.
38: 9 and as I c it with clouds and thick darkness?
39:19 its strength or c its neck with a flowing mane?
Ps 21: 5 and you have c him with splendor and majesty.
30:11 away my clothes of mourning and c me with joy,
65:13 The meadows are c with flocks of sheep,
104: 6 You c the earth with floods of water, / water that
Pr 14:18 The simpleton is c with folly, but the wise person
31:25 She is c with strength and dignity, and she laughs
Isa 11: 5 He will be c with fairness and truth.
59:17 He c himself with the robes of vengeance
La 2:10 sit on the ground in silence, c in sackcloth.
Eze 31:15 I c Lebanon in black and caused the trees of the
Da 3:21 them up and threw them into the furnace, fully c.
5:16 you will be c in purple robes of royal honor,
Mt 11:21 c in sackcloth and throwing ashes on their heads to
Mk 5:15 for he was sitting there fully c and perfectly sane.
14:51 along behind, c only in a linen nightshirt.
16: 5 and there on the right sat a young man c in a white
Lk 8:35 demons sitting quietly at Jesus' feet, c and sane.
10:13 c in sackcloth and throwing ashes on their heads to
16:19 was a certain rich man who was splendidly c
24: 4 two men appeared to them, c in dazzling robes.
Col 3:10 In its place you have c yourselves with a
Rev 3: 5 All who are victorious will be c in white. I will
4: 4 They were all c in white and had gold crowns on
7: 9 They were c in white and held palm branches in
7:13 asked me, "Who are these who are c in white?
11: 3 and they will be c in sackcloth and will prophesy
12: 1 I saw a woman c with the sun, with the moon
15: 6 c in spotless white linen with gold belts across
18:16 like a woman c in finest purple and scarlet linens,
19:13 He was c with a robe dipped in blood, and his title

CLOTHES (137) [CLOTHE]

Ge 27:15 Then she took Esau's best c, which were there in
27:27 And when Isaac caught the smell of his c, he was
37:29 he tore his c in anguish and frustration.
37:34 Then Jacob tore his c and put on sackcloth.
41:14 After a quick shave and change of c, he went in
45:22 And he gave each of them new c—but to
Benjamin he gave five changes of c
49:11 He washes his c in wine / because his harvest is
Ex 12:11 "Wear your traveling c as you eat this meal,
29:21 Sprinkle it on Aaron and his sons and on their c.
29:30 c for seven days before beginning to minister in the
Lev 10: 6 letting your hair hang loose or by tearing your c.
11:25 you must immediately wash your c, and you will
11:28 its carcass, you must immediately wash your c,
11:40 or carry away its carcass, you must wash your c.
13: 6 So after washing the c, the person will be
13:34 After washing c, that person will be clean.
14: 8 the cleansing ceremony by washing their c,
14: 9 and wash their c and bathe themselves in water.
15: 5 you will be required to wash your c and bathe in
15: 6 you will be required to wash your c and bathe in
15:10 you will be required to wash your c and bathe in
15:11 then you will be required to wash your c and bathe
15:13 he must wash his c and bathe in fresh springwater.
15:21 her bed, you must wash your c and bathe in water,
15:27 You will be required to wash your c and bathe in
16:26 into the wilderness as a scapegoat must wash his c
16:28 The man who does the burning must wash his c
17:15 you must wash your c and bathe yourselves in
17:16 But if you do not wash your c and bathe, you will
Nu 8:21 Levites purified themselves and washed their c,
19: 7 "Then the priest must wash his c and bathe
19: 8 man who burns the animal must also wash his c
19:10 up the ashes of the heifer must also wash his c,
19:19 day the people being cleansed must wash their c
19:21 water of purification must afterward wash their c,
31:24 On the seventh day you must wash your c and be

Dt 8: 4 For all these forty years your c didn't wear out,
21: 13 and change all her c. Then she must remain in your
29: 5 yet your c and sandals did not wear out.
Jos 9: 5 They put on ragged c and worn-out,
Jdg 11: 35 When he saw her, he tore his c in anguish.
17: 10 of silver a year, plus a change of c and your food."
Ru 3: 3 and put on perfume and dress in your nicest c.
1Sa 4: 12 He had torn his c and put dust on his head to show
19: 24 He tore off his c and lay on the ground all day
2Sa 1: 2 He had torn his c and put dirt on his head to show
1: 11 and his men tore their c in sorrow when they heard
3: 31 were with him, "Tear your c and put on sackcloth.
12: 20 washed himself, put on lotions, and changed his c.
13: 31 His advisers also tore their c in horror and sorrow.
14: 2 wear mourning c and don't bathe or wear any
19: 24 or c nor trimmed his beard since the day the king
2Ki 5: 7 of Israel read it, he tore his c in dismay and said,
6: 30 When the king heard this, he tore his c in despair.
11: 14 she tore her c in despair and shouted, "Treason!
18: 37 They tore their c in despair, and they went in to see
19: 1 he tore his c and put on sackcloth and went into the
22: 11 in the Book of the Law, he tore his c in despair.
25: 29 He supplied Jehoiachin with new c to replace his
2Ch 23: 13 she tore her c in despair and shouted, "Treason!
28: 15 and distributed c from the plunder to the prisoners
34: 19 was written in the law, he tore his c in despair.
Ezr 9: 5 from where I had sat in mourning with my c torn.
Ne 4: 23 the guards who were with me—ever took off our c.
9: 21 Their c did not wear out, and their feet did not
Est 4: 1 he tore his c, put on sackcloth and ashes, and went
4: 2 for no one was allowed to enter while wearing c of
Job 31: 19 I saw someone who was homeless and without c,
37: 17 When you are sweltering in your c and the south
Ps 22: 18 They divide my c among themselves / and throw
30: 11 You have taken away my c of mourning
Pr 23: 21 to poverty. Too much sleep c a person with rags.
31: 21 her household because all of them have warm c.
Ecc 9: 8 Wear fine c, with a dash of cologne!
Isa 3: 7 "I can't help. I don't have any extra food or c.
3: 22 party c, gowns, capes, and purses;
20: 2 "Take off all your c, including your sandals."
22: 12 and to wear c of sackcloth to show your remorse.
32: 11 Strip off your pretty c, and wear sackcloth in your
36: 22 They tore their c in despair, and they went in to see
37: 1 he tore his c and put on sackcloth and went into the
50: 9 All my enemies will be destroyed like old c that
52: 1 Put on your beautiful c, O holy city of Jerusalem,
58: 7 Give c to those who need them, and do not hide
63: 2 Why are your c so red, as if you have been
63: 3 my foes. It is their blood that has stained my c.
Jer 4: 8 So put on c of mourning and weep with broken
41: 5 off their beards, torn their c, and cut themselves,
48: 37 slash their hands and put on c made of sackcloth.
49: 3 Put on your c of mourning. Weep and wail,
52: 33 He supplied Jehoiachin with new c to replace his
Eze 16: 13 Your c were made of fine linen and were
16: 18 You used the beautifully embroidered c I gave you
18: 7 to the hungry and provides c for people in need.
18: 16 this son feeds the hungry, provides c for the needy,
23: 26 They will strip you of your beautiful c and jewels.
42: 14 They must first take off the c they wore while ministering because these c are holy.
42: 14 They must put on other c before entering the parts
44: 19 they must take off the c they wear while
44: 19 leave them in the sacred rooms and put on other c
Am 8: 10 You will wear funeral c and shave your heads as
Zec 3: 4 the others standing there, "Take off his filthy c."
3: 4 and now I am giving you these fine new c."
3: 5 and dressed him in new c while the angel of the
13: 4 No one will wear prophet's c to try to fool the
Mal 3: 2 refines metal or like a strong soap that whitens c.
Mt 3: 4 John's c were woven from camel hair, and he wore
6: 25 whether you have enough food, drink, and c.
6: 28 "And why worry about your c? Look at the lilies
11: 8 you expecting to see a man dressed in expensive c?
22: 11 he noticed a man who wasn't wearing the proper c
22: 12 'how is it that you are here without wedding c?'
27: 31 took off the robe and put his own c on him again.
27: 35 the soldiers gambled for his c by throwing dice.
Mk 1: 6 His c were woven from camel hair, and he wore a
5: 30 in the crowd and asked, "Who touched my c?"
14: 52 they tore off his c, but he escaped and ran away
15: 20 off the purple robe and put his own c on him again.
15: 24 They gambled for his c, throwing dice to decide
Lk 7: 25 you expecting to see a man dressed in expensive c?
7: 25 people who wear beautiful c and live in luxury are
10: 30 They stripped him of his c and money, beat him
12: 22 whether you have enough food to eat or c to wear.
22: 36 if you don't have a sword, sell your c and buy one!
23: 34 And the soldiers gambled for his c by throwing
Jn 19: 23 they divided his c among the four of them.
19: 24 "They divided my c among themselves and threw
Ac 10: 30 a man in dazzling c was standing in front of me.
Ro 13: 12 Get rid of your evil deeds. Shed them like dirty c.
1Co 4: 11 and thirsty, without enough c to keep us warm.
1Ti 2: 9 or by wearing gold or pearls or expensive c.
Jas 2: 2 comes into your meeting dressed in fancy c
2: 2 comes in who is poor and dressed in shabby c.
5: 2 rotting away, and your fine c are moth-eaten rags.
1Pe 3: 3 fancy hairstyles, expensive jewelry, or beautiful c.

CLOTHING (150) [CLOTHE]

Ge 3: 21 And the LORD God made c from animal skins
24: 53 and gold jewelry and lovely c for Rebekah.
25: 25 that one would think he was wearing a piece of c.
28: 20 protect me on this journey and give me food and c,
35: 2 your idols, wash yourselves, and put on clean c.
38: 14 So she changed out of her widow's c and covered
38: 19 off her veil, and put on her widow's c as usual.
41: 42 He dressed him in beautiful c and placed the royal
44: 13 At this, they tore their c in despair,
Ex 3: 22 and fine c from their Egyptian neighbors
3: 22 With this c, you will dress your sons
12: 34 They wrapped their kneading bowls in their spare c
12: 35 and asked the Egyptians for c and articles of silver
19: 10 and tomorrow, and have them wash their c.
19: 14 them for worship and had them wash their c.
20: 26 someone might look up under the skirts of your c
21: 10 he may not reduce her food or c or fail to sleep
22: 9 donkey, sheep, article of c, or anything else.
28: 2 Make special c for Aaron to show his separation to
29: 21 and their c will be set apart as holy to the LORD.
35: 19 the beautifully stitched c for the priests to wear
39: 1 c to be worn while ministering in the Holy Place.
Lev 6: 10 after dressing in his special linen c
6: 11 Then he must change back into his normal c
6: 27 and if the sacrificial blood splatters anyone's c,
8: 2 and his sons, along with their special c,
8: 30 and his c and on his sons and their clothing.
8: 30 and his clothing and on his sons and their c.
8: 30 he made Aaron and his sons and their c holy.
13: 45 from any contagious skin disease must tear their c
13: 47 mildew contaminates some woolen or linen c,
13: 49 If the affected area in the c, the animal hide,
13: 52 burn the linen or wool c or the piece of leather
13: 53 and the affected spot has not spread in the c,
13: 56 he is to cut the spot from the c, the fabric,
13: 59 infectious mildew in woolen or linen c or fabric,
14: 47 who sleep or eat in the house must wash their c.
14: 55 whether in c, in a house,
15: 17 Any c or leather that comes in contact with the
19: 19 Do not wear c woven from two different kinds of
21: 10 must never let his hair hang loose or tear his c.
Nu 8: 7 have them shave their entire body and wash their c.
14: 6 of Nun and Caleb son of Jephunneh, tore their c.
15: 38 come you must make tassels for the hems of your c
31: 20 purify all your c and everything made of leather,
Dt 10: 18 living among you and gives them food and c.
22: 3 c, or anything else your neighbor loses.
22: 5 "A woman must not wear men's c, and a man must not wear women's c.
22: 11 "Do not wear c made of wool and linen woven
Jos 7: 6 and the leaders of Israel tore their c in dismay,
9: 13 And our c and sandals are worn out from our long,
22: 8 and gold, your bronze and iron, and your c."
Jdg 3: 16 it to his right thigh, keeping it hidden under his c.
8: 26 the crescents and pendants, the royal c of the kings,
14: 19 and gave their c to the men who had answered his
1Sa 27: 9 and c before returning home to see King Achish.
28: 8 So Saul disguised himself by wearing ordinary c
2Sa 1: 24 for he dressed you in fine c and gold ornaments.
15: 32 Hushai had torn his c and put dirt on his head as a
1Ki 10: 5 organization of his officials and their splendid c,
10: 25 to visit brought him gifts of silver and gold, c,
21: 27 he tore his c, dressed in sackcloth, and fasted.
2Ki 5: 5 of silver, 150 pounds of gold, and ten sets of c.
5: 22 of silver and two sets of c to give to them."
5: 23 He gave him two sets of c, tied up the money in
5: 26 and c and olive groves and vineyards and sheep
7: 8 carrying out silver and gold and c and hiding it.
7: 15 following a trail of c and equipment that the
22: 19 You tore your c in despair and wept before me in
2Ch 9: 4 organization of his officials and their splendid c,
9: 24 to visit brought him gifts of silver and gold, c,
20: 25 amounts of equipment, c, and other valuables—
28: 15 They provided c and sandals to wear, gave them
34: 27 You humbled yourself and tore your c in despair
Ezr 9: 3 When I heard this, I tore my c, pulled hair from my
Est 2: 13 she was given her choice of whatever c or jewelry
4: 4 She sent c to him to replace the sackcloth, but he
Job 9: 31 and I would be so filthy my own c would hate me.
22: 6 and then kept the c he gave you as a pledge.
24: 7 they lie naked in the cold, without c or covering.
24: 10 The poor must go about naked, without any c.
27: 16 the world, and they may store away mounds of c.
27: 17 But the righteous will wear that c, and the innocent
31: 20 did they not praise me for providing wool c to keep
Ps 73: 6 jeweled necklace, / and their c is woven of cruelty.
102: 26 you remain forever; / they will wear out like old c.
109: 18 Cursing is as much a part of him as his c, / or as
109: 19 Now may his curses return and cling to him like c;
Pr 27: 26 your sheep will provide wool for c, and your goats
SS 4: 11 The scent of your c is like that of the mountains
Isa 4: 1 marry you! We will provide our own food and c.
23: 18 good food and fine c for the LORD's priests.
51: 6 and the earth will wear out like a piece of c.
51: 8 For the moth will destroy them as it destroys c.
61: 10 For he has dressed me with the c of salvation
63: 1 from the city of Bozrah, with his c stained red?
Jer 2: 34 Your c is stained with the blood of the innocent
4: 30 Why do you dress up in your most beautiful c
38: 11 where he found some old rags and discarded c.
Eze 9: 11 Then the man in linen c, who carried the writer's
10: 2 Then the LORD spoke to the man in linen c
10: 6 The LORD said to the man in linen c,
10: 7 put the coals into the hands of the man in linen c,
16: 4 rubbed with salt, and dressed in warm c.
16: 10 I gave you expensive c of linen and silk,
26: 16 and take off their royal robes and beautiful c.
28: 13 Your c was adorned with every precious stone—
44: 17 to the inner courtyard, they must wear only linen c.
44: 19 by transmitting holiness to them through this c.
Da 3: 27 heads was singed, and their c was not scorched.
7: 9 His c was as white as snow, his hair like whitest
10: 5 I looked up and saw a man dressed in linen c,
Hos 2: 2 and suggestive c and to stop playing the prostitute.
2: 5 to them for food and drink, for c of wool and linen,
2: 9 and wool c I gave her to cover her nakedness.
Joel 2: 13 Don't tear your c in your grief; instead, tear your
Am 2: 8 they lounge around in c stolen from their debtors.
Hag 1: 6 You have c to wear, but not enough to keep you
Zec 3: 3 Jeshua's c was filthy as he stood there before the
14: 14 great quantities of gold and silver and fine c.
Mt 6: 25 Doesn't life consist of more than food and c?
6: 28 how they grow. They don't work or make their c,
6: 31 worry about having enough food or drink or c.
17: 2 like the sun, and his c became dazzling white.
25: 36 I was naked, and you gave me c. I was sick,
25: 38 show you hospitality? Or naked and give you c?
25: 43 I was naked, and you gave me no c. I was sick
26: 65 Then the high priest tore his c to show his horror,
28: 3 like lightning, and his c was as white as snow.
Mk 5: 28 "If I can just touch his c, I will be healed."
9: 3 and his c became dazzling white, far whiter than
14: 63 Then the high priest tore his c to show his horror
Lk 9: 29 his face changed, and his c became dazzling white.
12: 23 For life consists of far more than food and c.
12: 27 They don't work or make their c, yet Solomon in
22: 35 a traveler's bag, or extra c, did you lack
Ac 14: 14 they tore their c in dismay and ran out among the
20: 33 "I have never coveted anyone's money or fine c.
1Co 9: 11 it too much to ask, in return, for mere food and c?
2Co 5: 2 we will put on our heavenly bodies like new c.
11: 27 with cold, without enough c to keep me warm.
Col 3: 14 And the most important piece of c you must wear
1Ti 2: 9 They should wear decent and appropriate c and not
6: 8 So if we have enough food and c, let us be content.
Heb 1: 11 you remain forever. / They will wear out like old c.
1: 12 They will fade away like old c. / But you are
Jas 2: 15 you see a brother or sister who needs food or c,
2: 16 then you don't give that person any food or c.
Rev 17: 4 The woman wore purple and scarlet c and beautiful

CLOTHS (1) [CLOTH]

Ac 19: 12 or c that had touched his skin were placed on sick

CLOUD (91) [CLOUDBURSTS, CLOUDLESS, CLOUDS, CLOUDY, THUNDERCLOUD]

PILLAR OF CLOUD (14) Ex 13:21,22; 14:19,20; 33:9; 34:5; Nu 12:5; 14:14,14; Dt 1:33; 31:15; Ne 9:12,19; Ps 99:7

Ex 13: 21 The LORD guided them by a pillar of c during
13: 22 And the LORD did not remove the pillar of c
14: 19 and the pillar of c also moved around behind them.
14: 20 The c settled between the Israelite and Egyptian
14: 20 the pillar of c turned into a pillar of fire,
14: 20 But the c became darkness to the Egyptians,
14: 24 on the Egyptian army from the pillar of fire and c,
16: 10 Within the guiding c, they could see the awesome
19: 9 "I am going to come to you in a thick c
19: 16 and a dense c came down upon the mountain.
24: 15 Moses went up the mountain, and the c covered it.
24: 16 Mount Sinai, and the c covered it for six days.
24: 16 day the LORD called to Moses from the c.
24: 18 Then Moses disappeared into the c as he climbed
33: 9 the pillar of c would come down and hover at the
34: 5 Then the LORD came down in a pillar of c
40: 34 Then the c covered the Tabernacle,
40: 35 because the c had settled down over it,
40: 36 Now whenever the c lifted from the Tabernacle
40: 37 But if the c stayed, they would stay until it moved
40: 38 The c of the LORD rested on the Tabernacle
40: 38 and at night there was fire in the c so all the people
Lev 16: 2 and I myself am present in the c over the
16: 13 so that a c of incense will rise over the Ark's
Nu 9: 15 was set up, and on that day the c covered it.
9: 15 Then from evening until morning the c over the
9: 16 at night the c changed to the appearance of fire.
9: 17 When the c lifted from over the sacred tent,
9: 17 And wherever the c settled, the people of Israel
9: 18 were as long as the c stayed over the Tabernacle.
9: 19 If the c remained over the Tabernacle for a long
9: 20 Sometimes the c would stay over the Tabernacle
9: 21 Sometimes the c stayed only overnight and moved
9: 21 But day or night, when the c lifted, the people
9: 22 Whether the c stayed above the Tabernacle for two
10: 11 the c lifted from the Tabernacle of the Covenant.
10: 12 and traveled on in stages until the c stopped in the
10: 34 each day, the c of the LORD hovered over them.
11: 25 And the LORD came down in the c and spoke to
12: 5 Then the LORD descended in the pillar of c
12: 10 As the c moved from above the Tabernacle,
14: 14 your people in the pillar of c that hovers over them.
14: 14 that you go before them in the pillar of c by day
16: 42 the Tabernacle and saw that the c had covered it,
Dt 1: 33 by a pillar of fire at night and a pillar of c by day.
31: 15 And the LORD appeared to them in a pillar of c
Jdg 20: 38 They sent up a large c of smoke from the town,
1Ki 8: 10 a c filled the Temple of the LORD.
18: 44 "I saw a little c about the size of a hand rising
2Ch 5: 13 At that moment a c filled the Temple of the
Ne 9: 12 You led our ancestors by a pillar of c during the
9: 19 The pillar of c still led them forward by day,
Job 3: 5 Let a black c overshadow it, and let the darkness
7: 9 Just as a c dissipates and vanishes, those who die
14: 2 Like the shadow of a passing c, we quickly
30: 15 and my prosperity has vanished as a c before a
Ps 78: 14 In the daytime he led them by a c, / and at night by
99: 7 He spoke to them from the pillar of c, / and they

105:39 The LORD spread out a **c** above them as a
Ecc 5:17 Throughout their lives, they live under a **c**—
SS 3:6 "Who is this sweeping in from the deserts like a **c**
Isa 4:5 and **c** throughout the day and clouds of fire at
5:30 A **c** of darkness and sorrow will hover over Israel.
19:1 is advancing against Egypt, riding on a swift **c**.
25:5 You cool the land with the shade of a **c**.
25:7 In that day he will remove the **c** of gloom,
La 3:44 You have hidden yourself in a **c** so our prayers
Eze 1:4 driving before it a huge **c** that flashed with
1:4 The fire inside the **c** glowed like gleaming amber.
1:5 From the center of the **c** came four living beings
8:11 so there was a thick **c** of incense above their heads.
10:3 and the **c** of glory filled the inner courtyard.
10:4 The Temple was filled with this **c** of glory,
30:18 A dark **c** will cover Tahpanhes, and its daughters
32:7 I will cover the sun with a **c**, and the moon will not
38:9 on them like a storm and cover the land like a **c**.
38:16 and you will cover the land like a **c**. This will
Mt 17:5 But even as he said it, a bright **c** came over them,
17:5 and a voice from the **c** said, "This is my beloved
Mk 9:7 Then a **c** came over them, and a voice from the **c** said, "This is my beloved
Lk 9:34 even as he was saying this, a **c** came over them;
9:35 Then a voice from the **c** said, "This is my Son,
Ac 1:9 they were watching, and he disappeared into a **c**.
1Co 10:1 God guided all of them by sending a **c** that moved
10:2 they were all baptized in the **c** and the sea.
Rev 10:1 surrounded by a **c**, with a rainbow over his head.
11:12 And they rose to heaven in a **c** as their enemies
14:14 Then I saw the Son of Man sitting on a white **c**.
14:15 out in a loud voice to the one sitting on the **c**,
14:16 So the one sitting on the **c** swung his sickle over

CLOUDBURSTS (1) [CLOUD]

Isa 30:30 with **c**, thunderstorms, and huge hailstones,

CLOUDLESS (1) [CLOUD]

2Sa 23:4 like the sunrise bursting forth in a **c** sky,

CLOUDS (74) [CLOUD]

Ge 9:13 I have placed my rainbow in the **c**. It is the sign of
9:14 When I send **c** over the earth, the rainbow will be seen in the **c**,
9:16 When I see the rainbow in the **c**, I will remember
Dt 4:11 the sky, shrouded in black **c** and deep darkness.
5:22 of the fire, surrounded by **c** and deep darkness.
2Sa 22:10 came down; / dark storm **c** were beneath his feet.
22:12 veiling his approach with dense rain **c**.
1Ki 18:45 And sure enough, the sky was soon black with **c**.
Job 20:6 to the heavens and though his head touches the **c**,
22:14 For thick **c** swirl about him, and he cannot see us.
26:8 He wraps the rain in his thick **c**, and the **c** do not burst with the weight.
26:9 He shrouds his throne with his **c**.
35:5 Look up into the sky and see the **c** high above you.
36:28 The rain pours down from the **c**, and everyone
36:29 anyone really understand the spreading of the **c**
37:11 He loads the **c** with moisture, and they flash with
37:12 The **c** turn around and around under his direction.
37:15 and causes the lightning to flash forth from his **c**?
37:16 Do you understand how he balances the **c** with
37:21 in the sky when the wind clears away the **c**.
38:9 and as I clothed it with **c** and thick darkness?
38:34 "Can you shout to the **c** and make it rain?
38:37 Who is wise enough to count all the **c**? Who can
Ps 18:9 came down; / dark storm **c** were beneath his feet.
18:11 veiling his approach with dense rain **c**.
18:12 The brilliance of his presence broke through the **c**,
36:5 your faithfulness reaches beyond the **c**.
57:10 as the heavens. / Your faithfulness reaches to the **c**.
68:4 Sing loud praises to him who rides the **c**.
77:17 The **c** poured down their rain; / the thunder rolled
97:2 **C** and darkness surround him. / Righteousness
104:3 you lay out the rafters of your home in the rain **c**.
104:3 You make the **c** your chariots; / you ride upon the
108:4 the heavens. / Your faithfulness reaches to the **c**.
135:7 He causes the **c** to rise over the earth. / He sends
147:8 He covers the heavens with **c**, / provides rain for
148:4 skies above! / Praise him, vapors high above the **c**!
Pr 3:20 the earth burst forth, and the **c** poured down rain.
8:28 I was there when he set the **c** above, when he
25:14 A person who doesn't give a promised gift is like **c**
Ecc 11:3 When the **c** are heavy, the rains come down.
12:2 and there is no silver lining left among the **c**.
Isa 4:5 and cloud throughout the day and **c** of fire at night,
5:6 with briers and thorns. / I will command the **c**
5:30 will hover over Israel. The **c** will blot out the light.
9:18 too. Its burning sends up vast **c** of smoke.
44:22 I have scattered your offenses like the **c**. Oh,
60:8 "And what do I see flying like **c** to Israel,
Jer 10:13 He causes the **c** to rise over the earth.
51:16 He causes the **c** to rise over the earth.
Eze 1:28 glowing halo, like a rainbow shining through the **c**.
30:3 It is a day of **c** and gloom, a day of despair for the
31:3 deep forest shade with its top high among the **c**.
31:10 so high above the others, reaching to the **c**,
31:14 though it be higher than the **c**, for all are doomed.
Da 7:13 looked like a man coming with the **c** of heaven.
Hos 2:21 "I will answer the pleading of the sky for **c**,
Joel 2:2 and gloom, a day of thick **c** and deep blackness.
Na 1:3 The billowing **c** are the dust beneath his feet.
Zep 1:15 a day of darkness and gloom, of **c**, blackness,
Zec 10:1 It is the LORD who makes storm **c** that drop
Mt 24:30 And they will see the Son of Man arrive on the **c** of
26:64 of power and coming back on the **c** of heaven."
Mk 13:26 the Son of Man arrive on the **c** with great power
14:62 of power and coming back on the **c** of heaven."
Lk 12:54 "When you see **c** beginning to form in the west,
21:27 will see the Son of Man arrive on the **c** with power
Ac 2:19 the earth below—/ blood and fire and **c** of smoke.
1Th 4:17 and remain on the earth will be caught up in the **c**
2Pe 2:17 springs of water or as **c** blown away by the wind—
Jude 1:12 They are like **c** blowing over dry land without
Rev 1:7 Look! He comes with the **c** of heaven.

CLOUDY (2) [CLOUD]

Jdg 5:4 earth trembled / and the **c** skies poured down rain.
Eze 34:12 which they were scattered on that dark and **c** day.

CLOVEN [KJV] See SPLIT

CLUB (6) [CLUBS]

1Sa 17:35 I go after it with a **c** and take the lamb from its
17:35 turns on me, I catch it by the jaw and **c** it to death.
2Sa 23:21 Another time, armed only with a **c**, he killed a
1Ch 11:23 Another time, armed with only a **c**, he killed an
Isa 10:5 of my anger. Its military power is a **c** in my hand.
Eze 9:2 faces north, each carrying a battle **c** in his hand.

CLUBS (6) [CLUB]

Job 41:29 **C** do no good, and it laughs at the swish of the
Mt 26:47 with a mob that was armed with swords and **c**.
26:55 have come armed with swords and **c** to arrest me?
Mk 14:43 with a mob that was armed with swords and **c**.
14:48 you come armed with swords and **c** to arrest me?
Lk 22:52 have come armed with swords and **c** to arrest me?

CLUMPS (1)

Job 38:38 turning the dry dust to **c** of mud?

CLUMSY (2)

Ex 4:10 after you have spoken to me. I'm **c** with words."
Isa 45:9 Does the pot exclaim, 'How **c** can you be!'?

CLUNG (1) [CLING]

Mk 7:4 This is but one of many traditions they have **c** to—

CLUSTER (6) [CLUSTERS]

Ex 12:22 Then take a **c** of hyssop branches and dip it into the
Nu 13:23 they cut down a **c** of grapes so large that it took
13:24 "**c**"—because of the cluster of grapes they had cut
13:24 because of the **c** of grapes they had cut there.
Isa 65:8 "For just as good grapes are found among a **c** of
Mic 7:1 Not a **c** of grapes or a single fig can be found to

CLUSTERS (7) [CLUSTER]

Ge 40:10 and blossom, and soon there were **c** of ripe grapes.
Dt 32:32 Their grapes are poison, / and their **c** are bitter.
1Sa 30:12 gave him part of a fig cake and two **c** of raisins
2Sa 16:1 one hundred **c** of raisins, one hundred bunches of
SS 7:7 a palm tree, and your breasts are like its **c** of dates.
7:8 Now may your breasts be like grape **c**,
Rev 14:18 "Use your sickle now to gather the **c** of grapes

CLUTCH (1) [CLUTCHED, CLUTCHES]

Zec 8:23 and languages around the world will **c** at the hem

CLUTCHED (1) [CLUTCH]

Ecc 2:3 While still seeking wisdom, I **c** at foolishness.

CLUTCHES (4) [CLUTCH]

Job 5:15 He saves them from the **c** of the powerful.
Ps 71:4 of the wicked, / from the **c** of cruel oppressors.
Zec 11:6 "I will let them fall into each other's **c**, as well as into the **c** of their king.

CNIDUS (1)

Ac 27:7 and after great difficulty we finally neared **C**.

CO-SIGN (3) [SIGN]

Pr 6:1 if you **c** a loan for a friend or guarantee the debt of
17:18 It is poor judgment to **c** a friend's note, to become
22:26 Do not **c** another person's note or put up a

CO-WORKER (4) [WORK]

Ro 16:9 and Urbanus, our **c** in Christ, and beloved Stachys.
Col 1:7 Epaphras, our much loved **c**, was the one who
1Th 3:2 He is our **c** for God and our brother in proclaiming
Phm 1:1 It is written to Philemon, our much loved **c**,

CO-WORKERS (5) [WORK]

Ro 16:3 They have been **c** in my ministry for Christ Jesus.
Gal 2:9 and they accepted Barnabas and me as their **c**.
Php 4:3 they worked with Clement and the rest of my **c**,
Col 4:11 These are the only Jewish Christians among my **c**;
Phm 1:24 So do Mark, Aristarchus, Demas, and Luke, my **c**.

COAL (2) [COALS]

Isa 6:6 and he picked up a burning **c** with a pair of tongs.
6:7 and said, "See, this **c** has touched your lips.

COALITION (1)

Jer 49:14 "Form a **c** against Edom, and prepare for battle!"

COALS (23) [COAL]

Lev 10:1 and Abihu put **c** of fire in their incense burners
16:12 he will fill an incense burner with burning **c** from
16:13 he will put the incense on the burning **c** so that a
Nu 16:18 placed burning **c** and incense on them,
16:46 and place burning **c** on it from the altar.
2Sa 22:9 his mouth; / glowing **c** flamed forth from him.
Job 41:21 Yes, its breath would kindle **c**, for flames shoot
Ps 11:6 He rains down blazing **c** on the wicked,
18:8 his mouth; / glowing **c** flamed forth from him.
18:12 the clouds, / raining down hail and burning **c**.
102:3 like smoke, / and my bones burn like red-hot **c**.
120:4 with sharp arrows / and burned with glowing **c**.
140:10 Let burning **c** fall down on their heads, / or throw
Pr 6:28 Can he walk on hot **c** and not blister his feet?
25:22 You will heap burning **c** on their heads,
Isa 30:14 left that is big enough to carry **c** from a fireplace
54:16 I have created the blacksmith who fans the **c**
Eze 1:13 The living beings looked like bright **c** of fire
10:2 and take a handful of glowing **c** and scatter them
10:6 and take some burning **c** from between the
10:7 and took some live **c** from the fire burning among
10:7 He put the **c** into the hands of the man in linen
24:11 Now set the empty pot on the **c** to scorch away the

COARSE (2)

Job 30:4 They eat **c** leaves, and they burn the roots of shrubs
Eph 5:4 Obscene stories, foolish talk, and **c** jokes—

COAST (18) [COASTLANDS, COASTLINE, COASTS, SEACOAST, SEACOASTS]

Nu 13:29 The Canaanites live along the **c** of the
Jos 5:1 **c** heard how the LORD had dried up the Jordan
9:1 and along the **c** of the Mediterranean Sea as far
15:47 of Egypt and along the **c** of the Mediterranean Sea.
1Ki 5:9 We will float them along the **c** to whatever place
2Ch 2:16 and will float the logs in rafts down the **c** of the
Ezr 3:7 and floated along the **c** of the Mediterranean Sea to
Isa 23:2 you people of the **c** and you merchants of Sidon.
Ob 1:20 and occupy the Phoenician **c** as far north as
Zep 2:5 it will be for you Philistines who live along the **c**
Ac 17:14 sending Paul on to the **c**, while Silas and Timothy
18:18 to the Christians and sailed for the **c** of Syria,
27:2 stops at ports along the **c** of the province of Asia.
27:5 We passed along the **c** of the provinces of Cilicia
27:8 We struggled along the **c** with great difficulty
27:12 farther up the **c** of Crete, and spend the winter
27:17 across to the sandbars of Syrtis off the African **c**,
28:13 so the following day we sailed up the **c** to Puteoli.

COASTAL (3)

Dt 1:7 the western foothills, the Negev, and the **c** plain.
Da 11:18 he will turn his attention to the **c** cities and conquer
Zep 2:6 The **c** area will become a pasture, a place of

COASTLANDS (10) [COAST]

Est 10:1 tribute throughout his empire, even to the distant **c**.
Isa 11:11 Elam, Babylonia, Hamath, and all the distant **c**.
24:15 In the **c** of the sea, praise the name of the LORD,
42:10 who sail the seas, / all you who live in distant **c**.
42:12 Let the **c** glorify the LORD; / let them sing his
Jer 31:10 you nations of the world; proclaim it in distant **c**:
Eze 26:18 Now the **c** tremble at your fall. / The islands are
27:15 Numerous **c** were your captive markets;
27:35 All who live along the **c** / are appalled at your
Da 11:30 For warships from western **c** will scare him off,

COASTLINE (3) [COAST]

Nu 34:6 "Your western boundary will be the **c** of the
Eze 26:15 The whole **c** will tremble at the sound of your fall,
Ac 27:39 morning dawned, they didn't recognize the **c**,

COASTS (4) [COAST]

Nu 24:24 Ships will come from the **c** of Cyprus; / they will
Eze 27:6 pine wood, brought from the southern **c** of Cyprus.
27:7 made bright with dyes from the **c** of Elishah.
39:6 and on all your allies who live safely on the **c**.

COAT (18) [COATED, COATS]

Dt 27:2 set up some large stones and **c** them with plaster.
27:4 stones at Mount Ebal and **c** them with plaster,
1Sa 2:19 Each year his mother made a small **c** for him
17:5 and a **c** of mail that weighed 125 pounds.
17:38 his own armor—a bronze helmet and a **c** of mail.
Job 13:28 waste away like rotting wood, like a moth-eaten **c**.
Mal 2:16 as cruel as putting on a victim's bloodstained **c**,"
Mt 5:40 and your shirt is taken from you, give your **c**, too.
10:10 Don't carry a traveler's bag with an extra **c**
24:18 person in the field must not return even to get a **c**.
Mk 6:9 to wear sandals but not to take even an extra **c**.
10:50 Bartimaeus threw aside his **c**, jumped up, and came
13:16 person in the field must not return even to get a **c**.
Lk 6:29 If someone demands your **c**, offer your shirt also.
9:3 nor food, nor money. Not even an extra **c**.
Ac 12:8 "Now put on your **c** and follow me," the angel
2Ti 4:13 be sure to bring the **c** I left with Carpus at Troas.
Heb 1:12 You will roll them up like an old **c**. / They will

COAT OF MANY COLOURS [KJV] See ROBE

COATED (1) [COAT]
Dt 27: 8 On the stones **c** with plaster, you must clearly write

COATS (10) [COAT]
2Ch 26:14 spears, helmets, **c** of mail, bows, and sling stones.
Ne 4:16 guard with spears, shields, bows, and **c** of mail.
Mt 21: 8 Most of the crowd spread their **c** on the road ahead
Mk 11: 8 Many in the crowd spread their **c** on the road ahead
Lk 3:11 John replied, "If you have two **c**, give one to the
19:36 Then the crowds spread out their **c** on the road
Ac 7:58 The official witnesses took off their **c** and laid
9:39 and showing him the **c** and other garments Dorcas
22:20 I kept the **c** they laid aside as they stoned him.'
22:23 They yelled, threw off their **c**, and tossed handfuls

COBRAS (1)
Ps 58: 4 deadly snakes; / they are like **c** that refuse to listen,

COCKATRICE [KJV] See SNAKE, VIPER

COCKCROWING [KJV] See DAWN

COCKLE [KJV] See WEEDS

COFFER [KJV] See CHEST

COFFIN (2)
Ge 50:26 and his body was placed in a **c** in Egypt.
Lk 7:14 Then he walked over to the **c** and touched it,

COGNITIONS [KJV] See also THOUGHTS

COILED (1) [COILING]
Job 18:10 hidden in the ground. A rope lies **c** on their path.

COILING (1) [COILED]
Isa 27: 1 the **c**, writhing serpent, the dragon of the sea.

COIN (7) [COINS]
Mt 17:27 of the first fish you catch, and you will find a **c**. Take the **c** and pay the tax for both of us."
22:19 Here, show me the Roman **c** used for the tax." When they handed him the **c**,
Mk 12:15 Show me a Roman **c**, and I'll tell you."
Lk 15: 9 rejoice with her because she has found her lost **c**.
20:24 "Show me a Roman **c**. Whose picture and title are

COINCIDENCE (1)
1Sa 6: 9 we will know that the plague was simply a **c**

COINS (14) [COIN]
Ex 21:32 the slave's owner is to be given thirty silver **c** in
Jos 7:21 two hundred silver **c**, and a bar of gold weighing
Jdg 9: 4 They gave him seventy silver **c** from the temple of
17: 3 "I now dedicate these silver **c** to the LORD.
17: 4 So his mother took two hundred of the silver **c** to a
1Ch 29: 7 10,000 gold **c**, about 375 tons of silver, about 675
Ezr 2:69 The total of their gifts came to 61,000 gold **c**,
8:27 20 gold bowls, equal in value to 1,000 gold **c**,
Ne 7:70 The governor gave to the treasury 1,000 gold **c**,
7:71 leaders gave to the treasury a total of 20,000 gold **c**
7:72 The rest of the people gave 20,000 gold **c**,
Zec 11:13 So I took the thirty **c** and threw them to the potters
Lk 15: 8 "Or suppose a woman has ten valuable silver **c**
Jn 2:15 scattered the money changers' **c** over the floor,

COL-HOZEH (2)
Ne 3:15 Shallum son of **C**, the leader of the Mizpah district,
11: 5 son of **C**, son of Hazaiah, son of Adaiah, son of

COLD (17)
Ge 8:22 **c** and heat, winter and summer, day and night."
31:40 heat of the day and through **c** and sleepless nights.
Job 24: 7 All night they lie naked in the **c**, without clothing
37: 9 its chamber, and the driving winds bring the **c**.
Ps 147:17 like stones. / Who can stand against his freezing **c**?
Pr 25:20 is as bad as stealing someone's jacket in **c** weather
25:25 Good news from far away is like **c** water to the
Ecc 4:11 And on a **c** night, two under the same blanket can
Jer 18:14 Do the **c**, flowing streams from the crags of Mount
Na 3:17 crowding together in the hedges to survive the **c**.
Mt 10:42 And if you give even a cup of **c** water to one of the
24:12 and the love of many will grow **c**.
Jn 18:18 a charcoal fire they had made because it was **c**.
Ac 28: 2 It was **c** and rainy, so they built a fire on the shore
Ro 8:35 or are hungry or **c** or in danger or threatened with
2Co 11:27 Often I have shivered with **c**, without enough
Rev 3:15 all the things you do, that you are neither hot nor **c**.

COLLAPSE (13) [COLLAPSED, COLLAPSES]
Jos 6: 5 Then the walls of the city will **c**, and the people
Ne 4: 3 "That stone wall would **c** if even a fox walked
Job 8:14 Everything they count on will **c**. They are leaning
Ps 10:10 The helpless are overwhelmed and **c**; / they fall
20: 8 Those nations will fall down and **c**, / but we will
38:17 I am on the verge of **c**, / facing constant pain.
44:25 We **c** in the dust, / lying face down in the dirt.
Isa 30:13 In an instant it will **c** and come crashing down.
Jer 6:21 over them. Neighbors and friends will **c** together."
La 2:12 they cry, and then **c** in their mothers' arms.
Na 2: 6 The enemy has entered! The palace is about to **c**!
Mt 7:25 that house, it won't **c**, because it is built on rock.
Mk 3:24 A kingdom at war with itself will **c**.

COLLAPSED (7) [COLLAPSE]
Jos 6:20 Suddenly, the walls of Jericho **c**, and the Israelites
Jdg 19:26 She **c** at the door of the house and lay there until it
Job 1:19 The house **c**, and all your children are dead.
Ps 11: 3 The foundations of law and order have **c**.
Isa 24:19 The earth has broken down and has utterly **c**.
Eze 29: 6 for you **c** like a reed when Israel looked to you for
Da 2:35 The whole statue **c** into a heap of iron, clay,

COLLAPSES (2) [COLLAPSE]
Job 4:21 Their tent **c**; they die in ignorance.
Ps 60: 2 it open. / Seal the cracks before it completely **c**.

COLLAR (4)
Ex 28:32 The opening will be reinforced by a woven **c**
39:23 of this opening was reinforced with a woven **c**,
Job 30:18 my garment. He grips me by the **c** of my tunic.
Ps 105:18 feet with fetters / and placed his neck in an iron **c**.

COLLATERAL (3)
Job 24: 3 A poor widow must surrender her valuable ox as **c**
Pr 20:16 Be sure to get **c** from anyone who guarantees the
27:13 Be sure to get **c** from anyone who guarantees the

COLLEAGUES (9)
Ezr 4: 9 They greeted the king for all their **c**—the judges
4:17 and their **c** living in Samaria and throughout the
4:23 Shimshai, and their **c**, they hurried to Jerusalem
5: 3 and their **c** soon arrived in Jerusalem and asked,
6: 6 and to your **c** and other officials west of the
6:13 and their **c** complied at once with the command of
7:18 way you and your **c** feel is the will of your God.
Ne 12:36 And finally came Zechariah's **c** Shemaiah, Azarel,
Ac 5:35 Then he addressed his **c** as follows: "Men of

COLLECT (25) [COLLECTED, COLLECTION, COLLECTOR, COLLECTORS, TAX-COLLECTING, TAX-COLLECTION]
Ge 11: 3 burnt brick and **c** natural asphalt to use as mortar.
41:34 and let them **c** one-fifth of all the crops during the
Ex 29:20 **C** the blood and place some of it on the tip of the
30:23 "**C** choice spices—12-1/2 pounds of pure myrrh,
Lev 23:40 and **c** palm fronds and other leafy branches
Nu 3:47 **c** five pieces of silver for each person, each piece
2Sa 23:10 did not return until it was time to **c** the plunder!
2Ki 3:23 and killed each other! Let's go and **c** the plunder!"
12: 4 "**C** all the money brought as a sacred offering to
12: 8 So the priests agreed not to **c** any more money
2Ch 20:25 plunder that it took them three days just to **c** it all!
24: 5 towns of Judah and **c** the required annual offerings,
24: 6 and **c** the Temple taxes from the towns of Judah
Ne 10:37 for it is the Levites who **c** the tithes in all our rural
12:44 They were responsible to **c** these from the fields as
Ps 84: 6 where pools of blessing **c** after the rains!
Ecc 2: 6 I built reservoirs to **c** the water to irrigate my many
Mt 21:34 he sent his servants to **c** his share of the crop.
21:36 sent a larger group of his servants to **c** for him,
Mk 12: 2 sent one of his servants to **c** his share of the crop.
Lk 3:13 "Make sure you **c** no more taxes than the Roman
20:10 he sent one of his servants to **c** his share of the
1Co 16: 2 wait until I get there and then try to **c** it all at once.
Heb 7: 5 are commanded in the law of Moses to **c** a tithe
7: 9 that Levi's descendants, the ones who **c** the tithe,

COLLECTED (32) [COLLECT]
Ge 43:23 have put it there. We **c** your money all right."
47:14 Joseph **c** all the money in Egypt and Canaan in
Ex 29:16 Its blood will be **c** and sprinkled on the sides of the
38:26 silver **c** from each of those registered in the census.
Nu 3:49 So Moses **c** redemption money for the firstborn
3:50 The silver **c** on behalf of these firstborn sons of
16:39 So Eleazar the priest **c** the 250 bronze incense
Jdg 7: 8 So Gideon **c** the provisions and rams' horns of the
8:24 of the treasures you **c** from your fallen enemies."
2Ki 12:18 King Joash **c** all the sacred objects that
22: 4 have **c** from the people at the LORD's Temple.
22: 9 "Your officials have given the money **c** at the
23:35 Jehoiakim **c** a tax from the people of Judah,
1Ch 22: 5 So David **c** vast amounts of building materials
29: 3 materials I have already **c** for his holy Temple.
2Ch 24:11 day after day, and a large amount of money was **c**.
34: 9 **c** by the Levites who served as gatekeepers at the
34:14 recording the money **c** at the LORD's Temple,
34:17 The money that was **c** at the Temple of the LORD
Ezr 6: 8 without delay from my taxes **c** in your province
Ne 10:38 And a tenth of all that is **c** as tithes will be
13:31 and that the first part of the harvest was **c** for the
Ps 56: 8 You have **c** all my tears in your bottle.
Pr 25: 1 **c** by the advisers of King Hezekiah of Judah.
Ecc 2: 8 I **c** great sums of silver and gold, the treasure of
12: 9 he knew. He **c** proverbs and classified them.
12:11 The **c** sayings of the wise are like guidance from a
Hos 13:12 "The sins of Ephraim have been **c** and stored away
1Co 16: 1 Now about the money being **c** for the Christians in
2Co 9: 3 I told them you would be, with your money all **c**.
Heb 7: 6 not even related to Levi, **c** a tenth from Abraham.
7:10 loins when Melchizedek **c** the tithe from him.

COLLECTION (2) [COLLECT]
Mk 12:41 Jesus went over to the **c** box in the Temple and sat
Lk 21: 1 the rich people putting their gifts into the **c** box.

COLLECTOR (7) [COLLECT]
Da 11:20 who sent a tax **c** to maintain the royal splendor,
Mt 10: 3 Bartholomew, / Thomas, / Matthew (the tax **c**),
18:17 treat that person as a pagan or a corrupt tax **c**.
Lk 5:27 he saw a tax **c** named Levi sitting at his
18:10 was a Pharisee, and the other was a dishonest tax **c**.
18:11 everyone else, especially like that tax **c** over there!
18:13 "But the tax **c** stood at a distance and dared not

COLLECTORS (10) [COLLECT]
Mt 5:46 good is that? Even corrupt tax **c** do that much.
9:10 along with his fellow tax **c** and many other
17:24 the tax **c** for the Temple tax came to Peter
21:31 corrupt tax **c** and prostitutes will get into the
21:32 didn't believe him, while tax **c** and prostitutes did.
Mk 2:15 along with his fellow tax **c** and many other
Lk 3:12 Even corrupt tax **c** came to be baptized and asked,
5:29 Many of Levi's fellow tax **c** and other guests were
7:29 all the people, including the unjust tax **c**,
15: 1 Tax **c** and other notorious sinners often came to

COLOGNE (2)
Ecc 9: 8 Wear fine clothes, with a dash of **c**!
SS 1: 3 How fragrant your **c**, and how pleasing your name!

COLONIES (2) [COLONY]
2Ki 17: 6 They were settled in **c** in Halah, along the banks of
18:11 the Israelites to Assyria and put them in **c** in Halah,

COLONISTS (2) [COLONY]
Isa 23: 7 Think of all the **c** you sent to distant lands.
Jer 47: 4 is destroying the Philistines, those **c** from Crete.

COLONNADE (3) [COLUMN]
Jn 10:23 through the section known as Solomon's **C**.
Ac 3:11 They all rushed out to Solomon's **C**, where he was
5:12 at the Temple in the area known as Solomon's **C**.

COLONY (2) [COLONIES, COLONISTS]
Eze 3:15 Then I came to the **c** of Judean exiles in Tel-abib,
Ac 16:12 city of the district of Macedonia and a Roman **c**;

COLOR (5) [COLORED, COLORFUL, DARK-COLORED, MANY-COLORED]
Lev 13:24 a burn on the skin and the burned area changes **c**,
13:49 the leather has turned bright green or a reddish **c**,
Nu 11: 7 looked like small coriander seeds, pale yellow in **c**.
Jer 13:23 Can an Ethiopian change the **c** of his skin? Can a
Rev 6: 8 and saw a horse whose **c** was pale green like a

COLORED (1) [COLOR]
Pr 7:16 My bed is spread with **c** sheets of finest linen

COLORFUL (1) [COLOR]
Jdg 5:30 and **c**, beautifully embroidered robes for me.'

COLOSSE (1)
Col 1: 2 It is written to God's holy people in the city of **C**,

COLT (14)
Ge 49:11 a grapevine, / the **c** of his donkey to a choice vine.
Zec 9: 9 riding on a donkey—even on a donkey's **c**.
Mt 21: 2 will see a donkey tied there, with its **c** beside it.
21: 5 riding on a donkey—/ even on a donkey's **c**.' "
21: 7 to him and threw their garments over the **c**,
Mk 11: 2 you will see a **c** tied there that has never been
11: 4 disciples left and found the **c** standing in the street,
11: 5 "What are you doing, untying that **c**?"
11: 7 Then they brought the **c** to Jesus and threw their
Lk 19:30 you will see a **c** tied there that has never been
19:32 So they went and found the **c**, just as Jesus had
19:33 asked them, "Why are you untying our **c**?"
19:35 So they brought the **c** to Jesus and threw their
Jn 12:15 your King is coming, / sitting on a donkey's **c**."

COLUMN (2) [COLONNADE, COLUMNS]
Ge 33: 2 Jacob now arranged his family into a **c**, with his
Eze 40:49 ten steps leading up to it, with a **c** on each side.

COLUMNS (14) [COLUMN]
Ge 19:28 and Gomorrah and saw **c** of smoke and fumes,
1Ki 7:19 The capitals on the **c** inside the foyer were shaped
Jer 36:23 Whenever Jehudi finished reading three or four **c**,
Eze 40: 9 be 14 feet deep, with supporting **c** 3-1/2 feet thick.
40:31 It had palm tree decorations on its **c**, and there
40:34 It had palm tree decorations on its **c**, and there
40:37 and it had palm tree decorations on the **c**.
40:48 He measured its supporting **c** and found them to be
41: 1 and he measured the **c** that framed its doorway.
41: 3 He measured the **c** at the entrance and found them
41:21 There were square **c** at the entrance to the Holy
42: 6 and they did not have supporting **c** as in the
Am 9: 1 "Strike the tops of the Temple **c** so hard that the
9: 1 Smash the **c** so the roof will crash down on the

COMB (2)

Ps 19:10 than honey, / even honey dripping from the **c**.
Mt 6:17 But when you fast, **c** your hair and wash your face.

COMBAT (5)

1Sa 17:8 We will settle this dispute in single **c**!
2Sa 2:14 warriors put on an exhibition of hand-to-hand **c**."
1Ch 5:18 They were all skilled in **c** and armed with shields,
Eze 38:21 Your men will turn against each other in mortal **c**.
Zec 14:13 will fight against each other in hand-to-hand **c**;

COMBINATION (2) [COMBINED]

Da 2:33 were of iron, and its feet were a **c** of iron and clay.
2:41 The feet and toes you saw that were a **c** of iron

COMBINED (3) [COMBINATION]

Jos 9:2 These kings quickly **c** their armies to fight against
10:5 So these five Amorite kings **c** their armies for a
11:4 Their **c** armies, along with a vast array of horses

COME (1275) [CAME, COMES, COMING, COMINGS] See Index of Articles, Etc.

AGE TO COME (2) Lk 20:35; Heb 6:5
DAYS TO COME (5) Ge 49:1; Dt 31:29; Ecc 2:16; Jer 23:20; 30:24
THINGS TO COME (2) Zec 3:8; Heb 10:1
TIME TO COME (1) Mt 22:3

COMES (219) [COME] See Index of Articles, Etc.

COMFORT (47) [COMFORTED, COMFORTERS, COMFORTING, COMFORTLESS, COMFORTS]

Ge 21:18 Go to him and **c** him, for I will make a great nation
24:67 and she was a special **c** to him after the death of his
37:35 His family all tried to **c** him, but it was no use.
1Ch 7:22 them a long time, and his relatives came to **c** him.
Job 2:11 got together and traveled from their homes to **c**
6:10 At least I can take **c** in this: Despite the pain,
7:13 If I think, 'My bed will **c** me, and I will try to
10:20 me alone—that I may have a little moment of **c**
15:11 "Is God's **c** too little for you? Is his gentle word
21:34 "How can you **c** me? All your explanations are
Ps 10:17 Surely you will listen to their cries and **c** them.
23:4 Your rod and your staff / protect and **c** me.
69:20 show some pity; / if only one would turn and **c** me.
71:21 me to even greater honor / and **c** me once again.
86:17 put to shame, / for you, O LORD, help and **c** me.
94:19 your **c** gave me renewed hope and cheer.
119:52 on your age-old laws; / O LORD, they **c** me.
119:76 Now let your unfailing love **c** me, / just as you
119:82 your promises come true. / When will you **c** me?
Ecc 4:1 the tears of the oppressed, with no one to **c** them.
Isa 22:4 Leave me alone to weep; do not try to **c** me.
40:1 "**C**, **c** my people," says your God.
51:3 The LORD will **c** Israel again and make her
51:19 who is left to sympathize? Who is left to **c** you?
57:18 I will lead them and **c** those who mourn.
61:1 He has sent me to **c** the brokenhearted and to
66:13 I will **c** you there as a child is comforted by its
Jer 16:7 No one will offer a meal to **c** those who mourn for
31:13 I will **c** them and exchange their sorrow for
La 1:16 No one is here to **c** me; any who might encourage
1:21 heard my groans, but no one turned to **c** me.
2:13 O virgin daughter of Zion, how can I **c** you?
Da 4:4 was living in my palace in **c** and prosperity.
Zec 1:17 and the LORD will again **c** Zion and choose
Ac 9:31 the fear of the Lord and in the **c** of the Holy Spirit.
2Co 1:4 us in all our troubles so that we can **c** others.
1:4 we will be able to give them the same **c** God has
1:5 the more God will shower us with his **c** through
1:7 you share in suffering, you will also share God's **c**.
2:7 Now it is time to forgive him and **c** him.
Php 2:1 Any **c** from his love? Any fellowship together in
Col 4:11 Kingdom of God. And what a **c** they have been!
1Th 4:18 So **c** and encourage each other with these words.
2Th 2:16 and in his special favor gave us everlasting **c**
2:17 **c** your hearts and give you strength in every good
Phm 1:7 have gained much joy and **c** from your love,

COMFORTED (11) [COMFORT]

Ru 2:13 "You have **c** me by speaking so kindly to me,
2Sa 12:24 Then David **c** Bathsheba, his wife, and slept with
Job 42:11 And they consoled him and **c** him because of all
Isa 49:13 For the LORD has **c** his people and will have
52:9 into joyful song, for the LORD has **c** his people.
66:13 I will comfort you there as a child is **c** by its
Jer 31:15 Rachel weeps for her children, refusing to be **c**—
Mt 2:18 refusing to be **c**—for they are dead."
5:4 God blesses those who mourn, / for they will be **c**.
Lk 16:25 So now he is here being **c**, and you are in anguish.
1Th 3:7 So we have been greatly **c**, dear friends, in all of

COMFORTER [KJV] See COMFORT, ONE TO LIFT OUT, COUNSELOR

COMFORTERS (1) [COMFORT]

Job 16:2 heard all this before. What miserable **c** you are!

COMFORTING (2) [COMFORT]

Zec 1:13 and **c** words to the angel who talked with me.
1Co 14:3 others grow in the Lord, encouraging and **c** them.

COMFORTLESS (1) [COMFORT]

Zec 10:2 and interpreters of dreams pronounce **c** falsehoods.

COMFORTS (8) [COMFORT]

Job 29:25 his troops and as one who **c** those who mourn.
Ps 119:50 promise revives me; / it **c** me in all my troubles.
Isa 12:1 He was angry with me, / but now he **c** me.
51:12 "I, even I, am the one who **c** you. So why are you
La 1:17 Jerusalem pleads for help, but no one **c** her.
2Co 1:3 is the source of every mercy and the God who **c** us.
1:4 He **c** us in all our troubles so that we can comfort
1:6 For when God **c** us, it is so that we, in turn, can be

COMING (259) [COME] See Index of Articles, Etc.

TIME IS...COMING (28) 2Ki 20:17; Isa 27:6; 39:6; Jer 4:11; 7:32; 9:25; 10:15; 16:14; 19:6; 23:5; 30:3; 31:38; 48:12; 51:18,52; Hab 2:6; Zep 3:8; Mt 10:26; Lk 12:2; 17:22; 21:6; Jn 4:21,23; 5:25,28; 16:2,32; 2Ti 4:3

COMINGS (2) [COME]

2Ki 19:27 you well—/ your **c** and goings and all you do.
Isa 37:28 you well—/ your **c** and goings and all you do.

COMMAND (172) [COMMANDED, COMMANDER, COMMANDER'S, COMMANDERS, COMMANDING, COMMANDMENT, COMMANDMENTS, COMMANDS, SECOND-IN-COMMAND]

Ge 41:43 and wherever he went the **c** was shouted,
Ex 16:32 Then Moses gave them this **c** from the LORD:
17:1 At the LORD's **c**, the people of Israel left the Sin
36:6 So Moses gave the **c**, and this message was sent
Lev 17:8 "Give them this **c** as well, which applies both to
17:13 "And this **c** applies both to Israelites and to the
17:15 "And this **c** also applies both to Israelites
24:2 "**C** the people of Israel to provide you with pure
Nu 2:33 from this census by the LORD's **c** to Moses.
3:39 counted by Moses and Aaron at the LORD's **c**,
5:2 "**C** the people of Israel to remove anyone from the
9:18 they traveled at the LORD's **c** and stopped
9:20 Then at the LORD's **c** they would break camp.
9:23 So they camped or traveled at the LORD's **c**,
20:8 **c** the rock over there to pour out its water.
23:20 I received a **c** to bless; / he has blessed, and I
25:4 The LORD issued the following **c** to Moses:
31:49 for all the men who went out to battle under our **c**;
36:5 So Moses gave the Israelites this **c** from the
Dt 1:26 "But you rebelled against the **c** of the LORD
1:43 you again rebelled against the LORD's **c**
3:18 "At that time I gave this **c** to the tribes that will
9:23 the LORD sent you out with this **c**:
9:23 But you rebelled against the **c** of the LORD your
11:8 be careful to obey every **c** I am giving you today,
12:11 you must bring everything I **c** you—your burnt
12:14 your burnt offerings and do everything I **c** you.
15:15 redeemed you! That is why I am giving you this **c**.
18:18 and he will tell the people everything I **c** him.
24:18 redeemed you. That is why I have given you this **c**.
24:22 land of Egypt. That is why I am giving you this **c**.
25:2 the judge will **c** him to lie down and be beaten in
30:11 "This **c** I am giving you today is not too difficult
31:10 Then Moses gave them this **c**: "At the end of
32:46 Pass them on as a **c** to your children so they will
Jos 1:9 I **c** you—be strong and courageous! Do not be
1:16 answered Joshua, "We will do whatever you **c** us,
1:18 and does not obey your every **c** will be put to
4:16 "**C** the priests carrying the Ark of the Covenant to
4:17 So Joshua gave the **c**.
5:14 "I am at your **c**," Joshua said. "What do you want
7:13 **C** the people to purify themselves in preparation
8:35 Every **c** Moses had ever given was read to the
10:18 he issued this **c**: "Cover the opening of the cave
14:2 in accordance with the LORD's **c** through Moses.
21:3 So by the **c** of the LORD the Levites were given
21:8 So the Israelites obeyed the LORD's **c** to Moses
22:9 them according to the LORD's **c** through Moses.
Jdg 2:2 their altars. Why, then, have you disobeyed my **c**?
1Sa 13:13 "You have disobeyed the **c** of the LORD your
13:14 for you have not obeyed the LORD's **c**."
14:27 But Jonathan had not heard his father's **c**, and he
14:29 Jonathan exclaimed. "A **c** like that only hurts us.
15:13 he said. "I have carried out the LORD's **c**!"
15:24 disobeyed your instructions and the LORD's **c**,
15:26 Since you have rejected the LORD's **c**, he has
28:21 "Sir, I obeyed your **c** at the risk of my life.
2Sa 10:9 He placed them under his personal **c** and led them
10:10 He left the rest of the army under the **c** of his
10:16 These troops arrived at Helam under the **c** of
13:28 I'm the one who has given the **c**. Take courage
17:13 will have the entire army of Israel there at your **c**.
18:5 And the king gave this **c** to Joab, Abishai, and Ittai:
22:16 Then at the **c** of the LORD, / at the blast of his
1Ki 2:35 Then the king appointed Benaiah to **c** the army in
2:43 kept your oath to the LORD and obeyed my **c**?"
2:46 Then, at the king's **c**, Benaiah son of Jehoiada took
5:6 Now please **c** that cedars from Lebanon be cut for
5:17 At the king's **c**, the stonecutters quarried
8:44 "If your people go out at your **c** to fight their
11:10 but Solomon did not listen to the LORD's **c**.
13:1 At the LORD's **c**, a man of God from Judah went
13:2 Then at the LORD's **c**, he shouted, "O altar,
13:9 For the LORD gave me this **c**: 'You must not eat
13:17 For the LORD gave me this **c**: 'You must not eat
13:21 and have disobeyed the **c** the LORD your God
13:26 is the man of God who disobeyed the LORD's **c**.
18:36 Prove that I have done all this at your **c**.
22:4 and I are brothers, and my troops are yours to **c**.
2Ki 3:7 and I are brothers, and my troops are yours to **c**.
9:12 and that at the LORD's **c** he had been anointed
14:6 for he obeyed the **c** of the LORD written in the
17:15 disobeying the LORD's **c** not to imitate them.
24:3 happened to Judah according to the LORD's **c**.
1Ch 10:13 He failed to obey the LORD's **c**, and he even
12:27 of the family of Aaron, who had 3,700 under his **c**.
19:10 He placed them under his personal **c** and led them
19:11 He left the rest of the army under the **c** of his
19:16 These troops arrived under the **c** of Shobach,
28:21 and the leaders and the entire nation are at your **c**."
29:2 Using every resource at my **c**, I have gathered as
2Ch 6:34 "If your people go out at your **c** to fight their
7:13 rain falls, or I might **c** locusts to devour your crops,
17:14 in units of one thousand, under the **c** of Adnah.
17:15 Next in **c** was Jehohanan, who commanded
17:16 LORD's service, with 200,000 troops under his **c**.
17:17 They were under the **c** of Eliada, a veteran soldier.
17:18 Next in **c** was Jehozabad, who commanded
18:3 and I are brothers, and my troops are yours to **c**.
25:4 for he obeyed the **c** of the LORD written in the
30:6 At the king's **c**, messengers were sent throughout
Ezr 4:21 city must not be rebuilt except at my express **c**.
6:12 or nation that violates this **c** and destroys this
6:13 and their colleagues complied at once with the **c** of
Ne 10:32 we promise to obey the **c** to pay the annual Temple
Est 3:3 "Why are you disobeying the king's **c**?"
3:15 At the king's **c**, the decree went out by the swiftest
8:14 So urged on by the king's **c**, the messengers rode
9:32 So the **c** of Esther confirmed the practices of
Job 39:27 Is it at your **c** that the eagle rises to the heights to
Ps 18:15 Then at your **c**, O LORD, / at the blast of your
33:9 he spoke, the world began! / It appeared at his **c**.
44:4 and my God. / You **c** victories for your people.
147:18 Then, at his **c**, it all melts. / He sends his winds,
148:5 for he issued his **c**, and they came into being.
Ecc 8:4 The king's **c** is backed by great power. No one can
Isa 5:6 with briers and thorns. / I will **c** the clouds
30:31 At the LORD's **c**, the Assyrians will be shattered.
44:28 He will **c** that Jerusalem be rebuilt and that the
45:12 the heavens. All the millions of stars are at my **c**.
55:5 You also will **c** the nations, and they will come
Jer 7:31 it never even crossed my mind to **c** such a thing!
11:4 "If you obey me and do whatever I **c** you,
17:22 make it a holy day. I gave this **c** to your ancestors,
19:5 it never even crossed my mind to **c** such a thing!
32:35 it never even crossed my mind to **c** such a thing.
34:10 and all the people had obeyed the king's **c**,
34:15 and did what was right, following my **c**.
35:6 son of Recab, our ancestor, gave us this **c**:
43:4 and all the people refused to obey the LORD's **c**
La 1:15 At his **c** a great army has come to crush my young
Eze 36:27 so you will obey my laws and do whatever I **c**.
38:7 armies around you mobilized, and take **c** of them.
Da 3:4 and nations and languages, listen to the king's **c**!
3:28 They defied the king's **c** and were willing to die
5:29 Then at Belshazzar's **c**, Daniel was dressed in
9:23 The moment you began praying, a **c** was given.
9:25 **c** is given to rebuild Jerusalem until the Anointed
Am 6:11 When the LORD gives the **c**, homes both great
9:4 into exile, I will **c** the sword to kill them there.
Jnh 3:3 This time Jonah obeyed the LORD's **c** and went
Na 1:4 At his **c** the oceans and rivers dry up, the lush
Mal 2:1 "Listen, you priests; this **c** is for you!
Mk 9:25 "I **c** you to come out of this child and never enter
11:23 throw you into the sea,' and your **c** will be obeyed.
Lk 4:36 Even evil spirits obey him and flee at his **c**!"
4:41 and the demons came out at his **c**, shouting,
Jn 10:18 take it again. For my Father has given me this **c**."
15:12 I **c** you to love each other in the same way that I
15:17 I **c** you to love each other.
Ac 16:18 "I **c** you in the name of Jesus Christ to come out of
19:13 "I **c** you by Jesus, whom Paul preaches, to come
1Co 7:10 for those who are married I have a **c** that comes not
7:12 though I do not have a direct **c** from the Lord.
7:25 I do not have a **c** from the Lord for them.
14:37 you should recognize that what I am saying is a **c**
Gal 5:14 For the whole law can be summed up in this one **c**:
1Th 5:27 I **c** you in the name of the Lord to read this letter to
2Th 3:6 we give you this **c** with the authority of our Lord
3:12 Christ we appeal to such people—no, we **c** them:
1Ti 1:1 appointed by the **c** of God our Savior and by Christ
5:21 I solemnly **c** you in the presence of God and Christ
6:13 And I **c** you before God, who gives life to all,
2Ti 2:14 and **c** them in God's name to stop fighting over
Tit 1:3 It is by the **c** of God our Savior that I have been
Heb 1:3 sustains the universe by the mighty power of his **c**.
11:3 that the entire universe was formed at God's **c**,
12:20 They staggered back under God's **c**: "If even an
Jas 2:8 it is good when you truly obey our Lord's royal **c**
2Pe 3:5 that God made the heavens by the word of his **c**,
Rev 3:10 "Because you have obeyed my **c** to persevere,
12:7 and the angels under his **c** fought the dragon

COMMANDED (228) [COMMAND]

Ge 3:11 "Have you eaten the fruit I **c** you not to eat?"

6:22 So Noah did everything exactly as God had **c** him.
7: 5 So Noah did exactly as the LORD had **c** him.
7: 9 in pairs, male and female, just as God had **c** Noah.
7:16 male and female, just as God had **c**.
21: 4 was born, Abraham circumcised him as God had **c**.
45:21 Joseph gave them wagons, as Pharaoh had **c**,
47:11 to his father and brothers, just as Pharaoh had **c**.
50:12 So Jacob's sons did as he had **c** them.
Ex 4:23 I **c** you to let him go, so he could worship me.
4:28 then told Aaron everything the LORD had **c** them
7: 6 and Aaron did just as the LORD had **c** them.
7:20 and Aaron did just as the LORD had **c** them.
8:17 and Aaron did just as the LORD had **c** them.
8:27 to the LORD our God, just as he has **c** us."
9: 1 "Go back to Pharaoh," the LORD **c** Moses.
12:28 Israel did just as the LORD had **c** through Moses
16:34 Aaron did this, just as the LORD had **c** Moses.
17: 9 Moses **c** Joshua, "Call the Israelites to arms,
17:10 So Joshua did what Moses had **c**. He led his men
23:15 bread made without yeast, just as I **c** you before.
24: 7 "We will do everything the LORD has **c**.
32: 8 They have already turned from the way I **c** them to
35: 4 to all the people, "This is what the LORD has **c**.
35:10 Construct everything that the LORD has **c**:
36: 1 furnish the Tabernacle, just as the LORD has **c**."
38:22 the whole project, just as the LORD had **c** Moses.
39: 1 sacred garments, just as the LORD had **c** Moses.
39: 5 and gold thread, just as the LORD had **c** Moses.
39: 7 All this was done just as the LORD had **c** Moses.
39:21 All this was done just as the LORD had **c** Moses.
39:26 to the LORD, just as the LORD had **c** Moses.
39:29 and scarlet yarn, just as the LORD had **c** Moses.
39:31 with a blue cord, just as the LORD had **c** Moses.
39:32 done everything just as the LORD had **c** Moses.
39:43 because it had been done as the LORD had **c** him.
40:16 to do everything as the LORD had **c** him.
40:19 on the roof layers, just as the LORD had **c** him.
40:21 to shield it from view, just as the LORD had **c**.
40:23 before the LORD, just as the LORD had **c**.
40:25 the LORD's presence, just as the LORD had **c**.
40:27 made from sweet spices, just as the LORD had **c**.
40:29 and a grain offering, just as the LORD had **c**.
40:32 to stop and wash, just as the LORD had **c** Moses.
Lev 7:36 The LORD **c** that the Israelites were to give these
7:38 **c** the Israelites to bring their offerings to the
8: 5 "The LORD has **c** what I am now going to do!"
8: 9 at its front, just as the LORD had **c** him.
8:13 and their turbans, just as the LORD had **c** him.
8:17 outside the camp, just as the LORD had **c** Moses.
8:21 All this was done just as the LORD had **c** Moses.
8:29 ram of ordination, just as the LORD had **c** him.
8:31 the basket of ordination offerings, just as I **c** you.
8:34 What has been done today was **c** by the LORD in
8:36 and his sons did everything the LORD had **c**
9: 5 just as Moses had **c**, and the whole community
9: 7 for the people, just as the LORD has **c**."
9:10 the sin offering, just as the LORD had **c** Moses.
9:21 as an offering to the LORD, just as Moses had **c**.
10: 1 before him a different kind of fire than he had **c**.
10: 5 out of the camp by their tunics as Moses had **c**.
10: 7 the LORD is upon you." So they did as Moses **c**.
10:15 descendants forever, just as the LORD has **c**."
16: 1 a different kind of fire than the LORD had **c**.
24:23 him to death, just as the LORD had **c** Moses.
Nu 1:19 just as the LORD had **c** Moses. So Moses counted
1:54 did everything just as the LORD had **c** Moses.
2:34 did everything just as the LORD had **c** Moses.
3: 4 the LORD a different kind of fire than he had **c**.
3:16 So Moses counted them, just as the LORD had **c**.
3:42 of the people of Israel, just as the LORD had **c**.
3:51 money to Aaron and his sons as the LORD had **c**.
4:37 just as the LORD had **c** through Moses.
4:41 and Aaron counted them, just as the LORD had **c**.
4:45 just as the LORD had **c** through Moses.
4:49 to carry, just as the LORD had **c** through Moses.
4:49 was completed, just as the LORD had **c** Moses.
5: 4 So the Israelites did just as the LORD had **c**
8: 3 light forward, just as the LORD had **c** Moses.
9: 5 the festival there, just as the LORD had **c** Moses.
9:19 stayed for a long time, just as the LORD had **c**.
13: 3 So Moses did as the LORD **c** him. He sent out
15:23 to do everything the LORD has **c** through Moses.
15:36 him to death, just as the LORD had **c** Moses.
17:11 So Moses did as the LORD **c** him.
20:27 So Moses did as the LORD **c**. The three of them
26: 4 years old and older, just as the LORD **c** Moses."
26:61 the LORD a different kind of fire than he had **c**.
27:11 legal requirement, just as the LORD **c** Moses.' "
27:22 So Moses did as the LORD **c** and presented
27:23 just as the LORD had **c** through Moses.
29:40 the people of Israel, just as the LORD had **c** him.
30: 1 and told them, "This is what the LORD has **c**:
31: 7 They attacked Midian just as the LORD had **c**
31:31 and Eleazar the priest did as the LORD **c** Moses.
31:47 All this was done just as the LORD had **c** Moses.
32:31 said again, "Sir, we will do as the LORD has **c**!
36:10 The daughters of Zelophehad did as the LORD **c**
Dt 1: 3 telling them everything the LORD had **c** him to
2:37 all the places the LORD our God had **c** us to
4: 5 gave them to me and **c** me to pass them on to you.
4:13 proclaimed his covenant, which he **c** you to keep—
4:14 It was at that time that the LORD **c** me to issue
5:12 it holy, as the LORD your God has **c** you.
5:15 That is why the LORD your God has **c** you to
5:16 and mother, as the LORD your God **c** you.
5:33 Stay on the path that the LORD your God has **c**
6:24 And the LORD our God **c** us to obey all these
9:12 They have already turned from the way I **c** them to
9:16 from the path the LORD had **c** you to follow!
10: 5 which I had made, just as the LORD **c** me.
12:21 and you may eat the meat at your home as I have **c**
20:17 just as the LORD your God has **c** you.
26:13 foreigners, orphans, and widows, just as you **c** me.
26:14 my God and have done everything you **c** me.
26:16 "Today the LORD your God has **c** you to obey
29: 1 These are the terms of the covenant the LORD **c**
30:16 I have **c** you today to love the LORD your God
31: 5 and you will deal with them as I have **c** you.
31:29 and will turn from the path I have **c** you to follow.
34: 9 and did everything just as the LORD had **c**
Jos 1:10 Joshua then **c** the leaders of Israel,
1:13 what Moses, the servant of the LORD, **c** you:
4: 8 for each tribe, just as the LORD had **c** Joshua.
6:10 "Do not shout; do not even talk," Joshua **c**.
6:16 blast on their horns, Joshua **c** the people, "Shout!
7:11 They have stolen the things that I **c** to be set apart
8: 8 Set the city on fire, as the LORD has **c**. You have
8:18 I will give you the city." Joshua did as he was **c**.
8:27 these for themselves, as the LORD had **c** Joshua.
10:40 just as the LORD, the God of Israel, had **c**.
11:12 just as Moses, the servant of the LORD, had **c**.
11:15 LORD had **c** his servant Moses, so Moses **c** Joshua.
11:20 mercilessly destroyed, as the LORD had **c** Moses.
13: 6 Israel as a special possession, just as I have **c** you.
17: 4 "The LORD **c** Moses to give us an inheritance
17: 4 along with their uncles, as the LORD had **c**.
18: 8 Joshua **c** them, "Go and survey the land.
22: 2 done as Moses, the servant of the LORD, **c** you,
Jdg 3:19 So the king **c** his servants to be silent and sent
6:27 ten of his servants and did as the LORD had **c**.
2Sa 1:18 Later he **c** that it be taught to all the people of
5:25 So David did what the LORD **c**, and he struck
9:11 "Yes, my lord; I will do all that you have **c**."
14:30 So they set his field on fire, as Absalom had **c**.
24:19 So David went to do what the LORD had **c** him.
1Ki 12:24 the LORD and went home, as the LORD had **c**.
16: 9 Then Zimri, who **c** half of the royal chariots,
17: 4 bring you, for I have **c** them to bring you food."
18:40 Then Elijah **c**, "Seize all the prophets of Baal.
20:12 "Prepare to attack!" Ben-hadad **c** his officers.
20:18 "Take them alive," Ben-hadad **c**, "whether they
21: 9 In her letters she **c**: "Call the citizens together for
2Ki 1: 9 of God, the king has **c** you to come along with us."
6:13 The king **c**, "Go and find out where Elisha is,
9:21 "Quick! Get my chariot ready!" King Joram **c**.
10:25 he **c** his guards and officers, "Go in and kill all of
13:17 Then he **c**, "Open that eastern window," and he
17:13 which are contained in the whole law that I **c** your
17:27 The king of Assyria then **c**, "Send one of the
17:35 with the descendants of Jacob and **c** them:
1Ch 12:20 Each **c** a thousand troops from the tribe of
14:16 So David did what God **c**, and he struck down the
27: 6 This was the Benaiah who **c** David's elite military
2Ch 2: 4 our God. He has **c** Israel to do these things forever.
8:18 Hiram sent him ships **c** by his own officers
14: 4 He **c** the people of Judah to seek the LORD,
17:15 command was Jehohanan, who **c** 280,000 troops.
17:18 was Jehozabad, who **c** 180,000 armed men.
23:18 He also **c** them to present burnt offerings to the
26:12 Twenty-six hundred clan leaders **c** these regiments
29:15 the Temple of the LORD, just as the king had **c**.
29:21 The king **c** the priests, who were descendants of
29:24 The king had specifically **c** that this burnt offering
32:12 He **c** Judah and Jerusalem to worship at only the
Ezr 4: 3 God of Israel, just as King Cyrus of Persia **c** us."
6:14 as had been **c** by the God of Israel and decreed by
Ne 8:14 they discovered that the LORD had **c** through
9:14 And you **c** them, through Moses your servant,
9:15 You **c** them to go and take possession of the land
12:24 to the other, just as **c** by David, the man of God.
13:19 So I **c** that from then on the gates of the city should
13:22 Then I **c** the Levites to purify themselves and to
Est 1: 7 an abundance of royal wine, just as the king had **c**.
3: 2 whenever he passed by, for so the king had **c**.
Job 38:12 "Have you ever **c** the morning to appear
42: 9 and Zophar the Naamathite did as the LORD **c**
Ps 78: 5 he gave his law to Israel. / He **c** our ancestors
78:23 But he **c** the skies to open—/ he opened the doors
106: 9 He **c** the Red Sea to divide, and a dry path
Isa 48: 5 My wooden image and metal god **c** it to happen!'
Jer 7:31 I have never **c** such a horrible deed; it never even
19: 5 I have never **c** such a horrible deed; it never even
32:35 I have never **c** such a horrible deed; it never even
36:26 Then the king **c** his son Jerahmeel, Seraiah son of
37:21 So King Zedekiah **c** that Jeremiah not be returned
37:21 The king also **c** that Jeremiah be given a loaf of
50:21 destroy them, as I have **c** you," says the LORD.
Eze 9: 7 "Defile the Temple!" the LORD **c**. "Fill its
37:10 So I spoke as he **c** me, and the wind entered the
Da 2:46 and he **c** his people to offer sacrifices and burn
3:19 He **c** that the furnace be heated seven times hotter
4:17 decreed by the messengers; it is **c** by the holy ones.
Am 9: 9 "For I have **c** that Israel be persecuted by the other
Mt 1:24 woke up, he did what the angel of the Lord **c**.
8:16 All the spirits fled when he **c** them to leave; and he
8:32 "All right, go!" Jesus **c** them. So the demons
17: 9 As they descended the mountain, Jesus **c** them,
Mk 5:43 Jesus **c** them not to tell anyone what had happened,
7:34 up to heaven, he sighed and **c**, "Be opened!"
Lk 8:29 For Jesus had already **c** the evil spirit to come out
Ac 13:47 For this is as the Lord **c** us when he said, / 'I have
23: 2 Instantly Ananias the high priest **c** those close to
Ro 16:26 the prophets foretold and as the eternal God has **c**,
1Th 4:11 working with your hands, just as we **c** you before.
2Th 3: 4 Lord that you are practicing the things we **c** you,
Heb 7: 5 are **c** in the law of Moses to collect a tithe from all
11:22 so sure of it that he **c** them to carry his bones with
11:28 It was by faith that Moses **c** the people of Israel to
2Pe 3: 2 what our Lord and Savior **c** through your apostles.
3: 7 And God has also **c** that the heavens and the earth
1Jn 3:23 Jesus Christ, and love one another, just as he **c** us.
4:21 And God himself has **c** that we must love not only
2Jn 1: 4 in the truth, just as we have been **c** by the Father.
1: 6 Love means doing what God has **c** us, and he has **c**
us to love one another,
Rev 13:15 Then the statue **c** that anyone refusing to worship it

COMMANDER (89) [COMMAND]

Ge 21:22 came with Phicol, his army **c**, to visit Abraham.
21:32 Abimelech left with Phicol, the **c** of his army,
26:26 his adviser, Ahuzzath, and also Phicol, his army **c**.
Ex 14: 7 the rest of the chariots of Egypt, each with a **c**.
Jos 5:14 "I am **c** of the LORD's army." At this,
5:15 The **c** of the LORD's army replied, "Take off
Jdg 4: 2 The **c** of his army was Sisera, who lived in
4: 7 I will lure Sisera, **c** of Jabin's army, along with his
11: 6 "Come and be our **c**! Help us fight the
11:11 and he became their ruler and **c** of the army.
1Sa 14:50 The **c** of Saul's army was his cousin Abner,
18: 5 So Saul made him a **c** in his army, an appointment
18:13 and appointed him **c** over only a thousand men,
2Sa 2: 8 But Abner son of Ner, the **c** of Saul's army,
8:16 Joab son of Zeruiah was **c** of the army.
10:16 of Shobach, the **c** of all Hadadezer's forces.
10:18 including Shobach, the **c** of their army.
17:25 Absalom had appointed Amasa as **c** of his army,
17:25 replacing Joab, who had been **c** under David.
19:13 not appoint you as **c** of my army in place of Joab."
20:23 Joab once again became the **c** of David's army.
20:23 Benaiah son of Jehoiada was **c** of the king's
23: 8 the Hacmonite, who was **c** of the Three—
23:19 was the most famous of the Thirty and was their **c**,
23:23 And David made him **c** of his bodyguard.
24: 2 So the king said to Joab, the **c** of his army,
1Ki 1:19 and Abiathar the priest and Joab, the **c** of the army.
1:25 He also invited Joab, the **c** of the army,
2:32 **c** of the army of Israel, and Amasa son of Jether, **c**
of the army of Judah.
4: 4 Benaiah son of Jehoiada was **c** of the army.
11:15 David had gone to Edom with Joab, his army **c**,
11:21 in Egypt that David and his **c** Joab were both dead,
16:16 they chose Omri, **c** of the army, as their new king.
2Ki 4:13 word for her to the king or to the **c** of the army?"
5: 1 had high admiration for Naaman, the **c** of his army,
9: 5 "I have a message for you, **C**," he said.
9: 5 one of us?" Jehu asked. "For you, **C**," he replied.
15:25 the **c** of Pekahiah's army, conspired against him.
18:17 the king of Assyria sent his **c** in chief, his field **c**,
25:20 Nebuzaradan the **c** took them all to the king of
1Ch 11: 6 the Jebusites will become the **c** of my armies!"
11: 6 the attack, so he became the **c** of David's armies.
11:11 the Hacmonite, who was **c** of the Three—
11:21 was the most famous of the Thirty and was their **c**,
11:25 And David made him **c** of his bodyguard.
18:15 Joab son of Zeruiah was **c** of the army.
19:16 of Shobach, the **c** of all Hadadezer's forces.
19:18 including Shobach, the **c** of their army.
27: 2 Jashobeam son of Zabdiel was **c** of the first
27: 4 descendant of Ahoah, was **c** of the second division,
27: 5 Benaiah son of Jehoiada the priest was **c** of the
27: 7 the brother of Joab, was **c** of the fourth division,
27: 8 Shammah the Izrahite was **c** of the fifth division,
27: 9 Ira son of Ikkesh from Tekoa was **c** of the sixth
27:10 Ephraim from Pelon, was **c** of the seventh division,
27:11 Zerah from Hushah, was **c** of the eighth division,
27:12 territory of Benjamin was **c** of the ninth division,
27:13 Zerah from Netophah, was **c** of the tenth division,
27:14 Benaiah from Pirathon in Ephraim was **c** of the
27:15 from Netophah, was **c** of the twelfth division,
27:34 and by Abiathar. Joab was **c** of the Israelite army.
2Ch 28: 7 Azrikam, the king's palace **c**; and Elkanah,
Ne 7: 2 along with Hananiah, the **c** of the fortress, for he
Jer 52:26 Nebuzaradan the **c** took them all to the king of
Da 2:14 When Arioch, the **c** of the king's guard, came to
8:11 He even challenged the **C** of heaven's armies by
11:18 But a **c** from another land will put an end to his
Ac 21:31 word reached the **c** of the Roman regiment that all
21:32 When the mob saw the **c** and the troops coming,
21:33 The **c** arrested him and ordered him bound with
21:37 he said to the **c**, "May I have a word with you?"
21:37 "Do you know Greek?" the **c** asked, surprised.
21:40 The **c** agreed, so Paul stood on the stairs
22:24 The **c** brought Paul inside and ordered him lashed
22:26 The officer went to the **c** and asked, "What are
22:27 So the **c** went over and asked Paul, "Tell me,
22:28 "I am too," the **c** muttered, "and it cost me
22:29 and the **c** was frightened because he had ordered
22:30 The next day the **c** freed Paul from his chains
23:10 Finally, the **c**, fearing they would tear him apart,
23:15 and the high council should tell the **c** to bring Paul
23:17 and said, "Take this young man to the **c**.
23:19 The **c** took him by the arm, led him aside,
23:22 the **c** warned the young man as he sent him away.
23:23 Then the **c** called two of his officers and ordered,
24:22 "Wait until Lysias, the garrison **c**, arrives.
Rev 1: 5 the dead, and the **c** of all the rulers of the world.

COMMANDER'S (2) [COMMAND]

2Ki 25:19 the army **c** chief secretary, who was in charge of
Jer 52:25 the army **c** chief secretary, who was in charge of

COMMANDERS (46) [COMMAND]

Nu 31:14 But Moses was furious with all the military **c** who
31:48 Then all the military **c** came to Moses
31:51 the priest received the gold from all the military **c**,
31:52 the gold that the **c** presented as a gift to the
31:54 the priest accepted the gifts from the military **c**
Dt 20:9 they will announce the names of the unit **c**.
Jdg 5:14 followed you. / From Makir the **c** marched down;
1Sa 8:12 Some will be **c** of his troops, while others will be
14:38 I want all my army **c** to come here.
22:7 Has he promised to make you **c** in his army?
29:3 But the Philistine **c** demanded, "What are these
29:4 But the Philistine **c** were angry. "Send him back!"
29:9 But my **c** are afraid to have you with them in the
2Sa 18:5 the troops heard the king give this order to his **c**.
1Ki 2:5 that Joab son of Zeruiah murdered my two army **c**,
9:22 in his army, **c** of his chariots, and charioteers.
20:14 The troops of the provincial **c** will do it."
20:15 Ahab mustered the troops of the 232 provincial **c**.
20:17 the troops of the provincial **c** marched out of the
20:19 But by now Ahab's provincial **c** had led the army
20:24 Only this time replace the kings with field **c**!
2Ki 11:4 Jehoiada the priest summoned the **c**, the Carite
11:9 So the **c** did everything just as Jehoiada the priest
11:9 The **c** took charge of the men reporting for duty
11:15 Then Jehoiada the priest ordered the **c** who were in
11:19 Then the **c**, the Carite mercenaries, the guards,
25:23 When all the army **c** and their men learned that the
25:26 as well as the army **c**, fled in panic to Egypt,
1Ch 12:14 These warriors from Gad were army **c**.
12:21 and able warriors who became **c** in his army.
21:2 David gave these orders to Joab and his **c**: "Take a
25:1 David and the army **c** then appointed men from the
28:1 the **c** of the twelve army divisions, the other
29:24 All the royal officials, the army **c**, and the sons of
2Ch 8:9 in his army, **c** of his chariots, and charioteers.
11:11 their defenses and stationed **c** in them.
23:1 up his courage and made a pact with five army **c**:
23:8 The **c** took charge of the men reporting for duty
23:9 Then Jehoiada supplied the **c** with the spears
23:14 Then Jehoiada the priest ordered the **c** who were in
23:20 Then the **c**, nobles, rulers, and all the people
32:21 who destroyed the Assyrian army with all its **c**
Est 9:3 And all the **c** of the provinces, the princes,
Eze 23:6 captains and **c** dressed in handsome blue,
23:12 those captains and **c** in handsome uniforms—
23:23 handsome young captains, **c**, chariot officers,

COMMANDING (8) [COMMAND]

Dt 15:11 That is why I am **c** you to share your resources
19:7 That is why I am **c** you to set aside three cities of
27:4 and coat them with plaster, as I am **c** you today.
Hab 3:9 You were **c** your weapons of power! You split
Jn 18:12 So the soldiers, their **c** officer, and the Temple
Ac 27:31 But Paul said to the **c** officer and the soldiers,
27:43 But the **c** officer wanted to spare Paul, so he didn't
1Th 4:16 will come down from heaven with a **c** shout,

COMMANDMENT (16) [COMMAND]

Mt 5:19 So if you break the smallest **c** and teach others to
15:6 your own tradition, you nullify the direct **c** of God.
22:36 which is the most important **c** in the law of
22:38 This is the first and greatest **c**.
Mk 12:29 Jesus replied, "The most important **c** is this:
12:31 as yourself.' No other **c** is greater than these."
Jn 13:34 So now I am giving you a new **c**: Love each other.
Ro 5:14 even though they did not disobey an explicit **c** of
7:13 It uses God's good **c** for its own evil purposes.
13:9 and stealing and coveting—and any other **c**—
13:9 are all summed up in this one **c**:
1Jn 2:7 Dear friends, I am not writing a new **c**, for it is an
2:7 This **c**—to love one another—is the same message
2:8 This **c** is true in Christ and is true among you,
3:23 And this is his **c**: We must believe in the name of
2Jn 1:5 This is not a new **c**, but one we had from the

COMMANDMENTS (53) [COMMAND]

Ex 34:28 of the covenant—the Ten **C**—on the stone tablets.
Dt 4:13 which he commanded you to keep—the Ten **C**—
10:4 the Ten **C**—on them and gave them to me.
Ps 19:8 The **c** of the LORD are right, / bringing joy to the
103:18 faithful to his covenant, / of those who obey his **c**!
111:7 is just and good, / and all his **c** are trustworthy.
119:4 You have charged us / to keep your **c** carefully.
119:15 I will study your **c** / and reflect on your ways.
119:27 Help me understand the meaning of your **c**,
119:40 I long to obey your **c**! / Renew my life with your
119:45 in freedom, / for I have devoted myself to your **c**.
119:56 This is my happy way of life: / obeying your **c**.
119:63 you is my friend—/ anyone who obeys your **c**.
119:69 but in truth I obey your **c** with all my heart.
119:78 meanwhile, I will concentrate on your **c**.
119:87 finished me off, / but I refused to abandon your **c**.
119:93 I will never forget your **c**, / for you have used them
119:94 For I have applied myself to obey your **c**.
119:100 even wiser than my elders, / for I have kept your **c**.
119:104 Your **c** give me understanding; / no wonder I hate
119:110 along your path, / but I will not turn from your **c**.
119:128 Truly, each of your **c** is right. / That is why I hate
119:134 oppression of evil people; / then I can obey your **c**.
119:141 and despised, / but I don't forget your **c**.
119:159 See how I love your **c**, LORD. / Give back my
119:168 Yes, I obey your **c** and decrees, / because you
119:173 to help me, / for I have chosen to follow your **c**.
Pr 19:16 Keep the **c** and keep your life; despising them

Mt 15:3 by your traditions, violate the direct **c** of God?
19:17 you can receive eternal life if you keep the **c**."
19:20 "I've obeyed all these **c**," the young man replied.
22:40 All the other **c** and all the demands of the prophets
are based on these two **c**."
Mk 10:19 But as for your question, you know the **c**: 'Do not
10:20 "I've obeyed all these **c** since I was a child."
12:28 so he asked, "Of all the **c**, which is the most
Lk 1:6 careful to obey all of the Lord's **c** and regulations.
18:20 But as for your question, you know the **c**: 'Do not
18:21 "I've obeyed all these **c** since I was a child."
Jn 14:15 "If you love me, obey my **c**.
14:21 Those who obey my **c** are the ones who love me.
Ac 16:4 explaining the decision regarding the **c** that were to
Ro 13:9 For the **c** against adultery and murder and stealing
1Co 7:19 The important thing is to keep God's **c**.
Eph 6:2 This is the first of the Ten **C** that ends with a
Heb 9:4 of the covenant with the Ten **C** written on them.
2Pe 2:21 then reject the holy **c** that were given to them.
1Jn 2:3 be sure that we belong to him? By obeying his **c**.
2:4 but doesn't obey God's **c**, that person is a liar
3:24 Those who obey God's **c** live in fellowship with
5:2 love God's children if we love God and obey his **c**.
5:3 Loving God means keeping his **c**, and really,
Rev 12:17 all who keep God's **c** and confess that they belong

COMMANDS (192) [COMMAND]

Ge 26:5 all my requirements, **c**, regulations, and laws."
Ex 15:26 what is right in his sight, obeying his **c** and laws,
16:28 "How long will these people refuse to obey my **c**
20:6 my love on those who love me and obey my **c**,
24:12 that I have inscribed with my instructions and **c**.
25:22 From there I will give you my **c** for the people of
34:11 Your responsibility is to obey all the **c** I am giving
Lev 4:2 by doing anything forbidden by the LORD's **c**.
10:13 LORD by fire. These are the **c** I have been given.
17:2 and all the Israelites these **c** from the LORD:
22:31 "You must faithfully keep all my **c** by obeying
26:3 you keep my laws and are careful to obey my **c**,
26:14 if you do not listen to me or obey my **c**,
27:34 These are the **c** that the LORD gave to the
Nu 8:22 So they carried out all the **c** that the LORD gave
15:22 **c** that the LORD has given you through Moses.
15:31 with contempt and deliberately disobeyed his **c**,
15:39 The tassels will remind you of the **c** of the LORD,
15:39 and that you are to obey his **c** instead of following
15:40 help you remember that you must obey all my **c**
34:13 The LORD **c** that the land be divided up among
36:6 This is what the LORD **c** concerning the
36:13 These are the **c** and regulations that the LORD
Dt 4:2 or subtract from these **c** I am giving you from the
4:40 obey all the laws and **c** that I will give you today,
5:10 my love on those who love me and obey my **c**,
5:29 that they might fear me and obey all my **c**!
5:31 you stay here with me so I can give you all my **c**,
5:32 "You must obey all the **c** of the LORD your God,
6:1 "These are all the **c**, laws, and regulations that the
6:2 If you obey all his laws and **c**, you will enjoy a
6:6 wholeheartedly to these **c** I am giving you today.
6:17 You must diligently obey the **c** of the LORD your
6:25 For we are righteous when we obey all the **c** the
7:9 loves those who love him and obey his **c**.
7:11 Therefore, obey all these **c**, laws, and regulations I
8:1 "Be careful to obey all the **c** I am giving you
8:2 out whether or not you would really obey his **c**.
8:6 "So obey the **c** of the LORD your God by
8:11 not forget the LORD your God and disobey his **c**,
10:13 and to obey the LORD's **c** and laws that I am
11:1 obey all his requirements, laws, regulations, and **c**.
11:13 "If you carefully obey all the **c** I am giving you
11:22 "Be careful to obey all the **c** I give you; show love
11:27 You will be blessed if you obey the **c** of the
11:28 You will receive a curse if you reject the **c** of the
12:28 Be careful to obey all my **c** so that all will go well
12:32 Carefully obey all the **c** I give you. Do not add to
13:4 Obey his **c**, listen to his voice, and cling to him.
13:18 obey him and keep all the **c** I am giving you today,
15:5 **c** of the LORD your God that I am giving you
17:20 turning away from these **c** in the smallest way.
19:9 (He will give you this land if you obey all the **c** I
24:8 the Levitical priests; obey the **c** I have given them.
26:13 I have not violated or forgotten any of your **c**.
26:17 You have promised to obey his laws, **c**,
26:18 as he promised, and that you must obey all his **c**.
27:1 "Keep all these **c** that I am giving you today.
27:10 obey the LORD your God by keeping all these **c**
28:1 God by keeping all the **c** I am giving you today,
28:9 "If you obey the **c** of the LORD your God
28:13 If you listen to these **c** of the LORD your God
28:14 You must not turn away from any of the **c** I am
28:15 and do not obey all the **c** and laws I am giving you
28:45 and to obey the **c** and laws he has given you,
30:2 to obey all the **c** I have given you today,
30:8 and keep all the **c** I am giving you today.
30:10 and keep the **c** and laws written in this Book of the
30:16 to love the LORD your God and to keep his **c**,
Jos 22:3 You have been careful to obey the **c** of the LORD
22:5 But be very careful to obey all the **c** and the law
22:5 walk in all his ways, obey his **c**, be faithful to him,
Jdg 2:17 who had walked in obedience to the LORD's **c**.
2:20 I made with their ancestors and have ignored my **c**,
3:4 to see whether they would obey the **c** the LORD
4:6 is what the LORD, the God of Israel, **c** you:
1Sa 12:14 and if you do not rebel against the LORD's **c**,
12:15 But if you rebel against the LORD's **c** and refuse
1Ki 2:3 Keep each of the laws, **c**, regulations,
2:38 is fair; I will do whatever my lord the king **c**."
3:14 if you follow me and obey my **c** as your father,
6:12 all my laws and regulations and obey all my **c**,
8:58 to do his will in everything and to obey all the **c**,
8:61 May you always obey his laws and **c**, just as you
9:4 always obeying my **c** and keeping my laws
9:6 abandon me and disobey my **c** and laws,
11:34 one whom I chose and who obeyed my **c** and laws,
11:38 and if you obey my laws and **c**, as my servant
14:8 who obeyed my **c** and followed me with all his
15:5 and had obeyed the LORD's **c** throughout his life,
18:18 for you have refused to obey the **c** of the LORD
2Ki 17:13 Obey my **c** and laws, which are contained in the
17:16 They defied all the **c** of the LORD their God
17:19 But even the people of Judah refused to obey the **c**
17:34 and **c** he gave the descendants of Jacob,
17:37 instructions, and **c** that he wrote for you.
18:6 and he carefully obeyed all the **c** the LORD had
21:8 If the Israelites will obey my **c**—the whole law that
23:3 pledged to obey the LORD by keeping all his **c**,
1Ch 6:49 for Israel by following all the **c** that Moses,
24:19 Aaron in obedience to the **c** of the LORD,
28:7 And if he continues to obey my **c** and regulations
28:8 Be careful to obey all the **c** of the LORD your
29:19 the wholehearted desire to obey all your **c**,
2Ch 7:17 David, did and obey all my **c**, laws,
7:19 and disobey the laws and **c** I have given you,
8:13 day to day according to the **c** Moses had given.
8:14 following the **c** of David, the man of God.
8:15 in any way from David's **c** concerning the priests
14:4 of their ancestors, and to obey his law and his **c**.
17:4 and obeyed his **c** instead of following the practices
19:10 of God's instructions, **c**, laws, or regulations,
24:20 Why do you disobey the LORD's **c** so that you
29:25 He obeyed all the **c** that the LORD had given to
31:21 and in his efforts to follow the law and the **c**,
33:8 If the Israelites will obey my **c**—
34:31 pledged to obey the LORD by keeping all his **c**,
Ezr 7:11 the priest and scribe who studied and taught the **c**
9:10 all of this? For once again we have ignored your **c**!
9:14 But now we are again breaking your **c**
10:3 and by the others who respect the **c** of our God.
Ne 1:5 love with those who love him and obey his **c**,
1:7 We have sinned terribly by not obeying the **c**,
1:9 But if you return to me and obey my **c**, even if you
9:13 that were just, and laws and **c** that were true.
9:14 to obey all your **c**, laws, and instructions.
9:16 and stubborn lot, and they refused to obey your **c**.
9:29 became proud and obstinate and disobeyed your **c**.
9:34 your law or listen to your **c** and solemn warnings.
10:29 solemnly promised to carefully follow all the **c**,
Job 9:7 If he **c** it, the sun won't rise and the stars won't
23:12 I have not departed from his **c** but have treasured
37:12 They do whatever he **c** throughout the earth.
39:25 the noise of battle and the shout of the captain's **c**.
Ps 17:4 I have followed your **c**, / which have kept me from
19:8 The **c** of the LORD are clear, / giving insight to
78:7 his glorious miracles / and obeying his **c**.
89:31 do not obey my decrees / and fail to keep my **c**,
103:20 carry out his plans, / listening for each of his **c**.
105:28 for they had defied his **c** to let his people go.
112:1 happy are those who delight in doing what he **c**.
119:6 be disgraced / when I compare my life with your **c**.
119:10 to find you—/ don't let me wander from your **c**.
119:19 here on earth; / I need the guidance of your **c**.
119:21 those cursed proud ones / who wander from your **c**.
119:32 If you will help me, / I will run to follow your **c**.
119:35 Make me walk along the path of your **c**, / for that is
119:47 How I delight in your **c**! / How I love them!
119:48 I honor and love your **c**. / I meditate on your
119:60 I will hurry, without lingering, / to obey your **c**.
119:66 I believe in your **c**; / now teach me good judgment
119:73 Now give me the sense to follow your **c**.
119:86 All your **c** are trustworthy. / Protect me from those
119:96 perfection has its limits, / but your **c** have no limit.
119:98 Your **c** make me wiser than my enemies, / for your
c are my constant guide.
119:115 for I intend to obey the **c** of my God.
119:127 Truly, I love your **c** / more than gold,
119:131 panting expectantly, / longing for your **c**.
119:143 and stress bear down on me, / I find joy in your **c**.
119:151 you are near, O LORD, / and all your **c** are true.
119:166 your salvation, LORD, / so I have obeyed your **c**.
119:172 sing about your word, / for all your **c** are right.
119:176 and find me, / for I have not forgotten your **c**.
Pr 3:1 things I have taught you. Store my **c** in your heart,
6:20 My son, obey your father's **c**, and don't neglect
6:23 For these **c** and this teaching are a lamp to light the
6:24 These **c** and this teaching will keep you from the
7:1 Follow my advice, my son; always treasure my **c**.
Ecc 12:13 Fear God and obey his **c**, for this is the duty of
Isa 48:18 Oh, that you had listened to my **c**! Then you would
Jer 35:7 If you follow these **c**, you will live long, good lives
35:10 and have fully obeyed all the **c** of Jehonadab,
Eze 22:12 They never even think of me and my **c**,
Da 9:4 love to those who love you and keep your **c**.
9:5 against you and scorned your **c** and regulations.
Zec 6:15 All this will happen if you carefully obey the **c** of
Mal 1:13 and you turn up your noses at his **c**,"
3:14 What have we gained by obeying his **c** or by trying
Mt 15:9 for they replace God's **c** with their own man-made
28:20 Teach these new disciples to obey all the **c** I have
Mk 7:7 for they replace God's **c** with their own man-made
Ac 17:30 but now he **c** everyone everywhere to turn away
Ro 3:20 made right in God's sight by doing what his law **c**.
10:5 right with God requires obedience to all of its **c**.
Gal 2:16 not by doing what the law **c**, but by faith in Jesus

3:10 and obey all these **c** that are written in God's Book
3:12 by obeying the law, you must obey all of its **c**."
1Ti 6:14 that you obey his **c** with all purity. Then no one
Tit 1:14 and the **c** of people who have turned their backs on
1Jn 3:10 Anyone who does not obey God's **c** and does not
Rev 14:12 to the end, obeying his **c** and trusting in Jesus."

COMMEMORATE (2)

Ge 12:7 And Abram built an altar there to **c** the LORD's
Est 9:22 This would **c** a time when the Jews gained relief

COMMENDATIONS (1) [COMMENDS]

2Co 12:11 You ought to be writing **c** for me, for I am not at

COMMENDED (1) [COMMENDS]

Ne 11:2 And the people **c** everyone who volunteered to

COMMENDS (1) [COMMENDATIONS, COMMENDED]

2Co 10:18 But when the Lord **c** someone, that's different!

COMMENTARY (2) [COMMENTS]

2Ch 13:22 are recorded in *The **C** of Iddo the Prophet.*
24:27 ***C** on the Book of the Kings.* When Joash died,

COMMENTS (3) [COMMENTARY]

1Sa 21:12 David heard these **c** and was afraid of what King
Mk 5:36 But Jesus ignored their **c** and said to Jairus,
2Pe 3:16 Some of his **c** are hard to understand, and those

COMMERCE (1) [COMMERCIAL]

Jer 51:13 a great center of **c**, but your end has come.

COMMERCIAL (2) [COMMERCE]

Mt 4:18 fishing with a net, for they were **c** fishermen.
Mk 1:16 fishing with a net, for they were **c** fishermen.

COMMISSION (5) [COMMISSIONED]

Nu 27:19 and publicly **c** him with the responsibility of
Dt 3:28 But **c** Joshua and encourage him, for he will lead
31:14 you to the Tabernacle, and I will **c** him there."
Ezr 7:15 We also **c** you to take with you some silver
Ac 26:12 with the authority and **c** of the leading priests.

COMMISSIONED (4) [COMMISSION]

Nu 27:23 his hands on him and **c** him to his responsibilities,
Dt 31:23 Then the LORD **c** Joshua son of Nun with these
Isa 49:5 who **c** me to bring his people of Israel back to him.
2Co 1:21 the ability to stand firm for Christ. He has **c** us,

COMMIT (64) [COMMITMENT, COMMITMENTS, COMMITS, COMMITTED, COMMITTING]

Ex 20:14 "Do not **c** adultery.
34:16 Then they will cause your sons to **c** adultery
Lev 6:3 while under oath, or they **c** any other similar sin.
20:5 along with all those who **c** prostitution by
Dt 5:18 " 'Do not **c** adultery.
6:6 And you must **c** yourselves wholeheartedly to
11:18 So **c** yourselves completely to these words of mine.
26:16 You must **c** yourself to them without reservation.
30:20 your God and to obey him and **c** yourself to him,
1Ki 15:26 sins of idolatry that Jeroboam had led Israel to **c**.
15:30 had committed and the sins he had led Israel to **c**.
15:34 sins of idolatry that Jeroboam had led Israel to **c**.
16:13 and because of all the sins they led Israel to **c**,
16:19 sins of idolatry that Jeroboam had led Israel to **c**.
16:26 sins of idolatry that Jeroboam had led Israel to **c**.
2Ki 3:3 son of Nebat had led the people of Israel to **c**.
10:29 sin that Jeroboam son of Nebat had led Israel to **c**.
10:31 sins of idolatry that Jeroboam had led Israel to **c**.
13:2 that Jeroboam son of Nebat had led Israel to **c**.
13:11 that Jeroboam son of Nebat had led Israel to **c**.
14:24 that Jeroboam son of Nebat had led Israel to **c**.
15:9 that Jeroboam son of Nebat had led Israel to **c**.
15:18 that Jeroboam son of Nebat had led Israel to **c**.
15:24 that Jeroboam son of Nebat had led Israel to **c**.
15:28 that Jeroboam son of Nebat had led Israel to **c**.
17:21 following the LORD and made them **c** a great sin.
21:16 to the sin that he caused the people of Judah to **c**,
Ps 37:5 **C** everything you do to the LORD. / Trust him,
Pr 1:16 They rush to **c** crimes. They hurry to **c** murder.
16:3 **C** your work to the LORD, and then your plans
23:12 **C** yourself to instruction; attune your ears to hear
Isa 56:3 too, when they **c** themselves to the LORD.
56:4 to do what pleases me and **c** their lives to me:
56:6 "I will also bless the Gentiles who **c** themselves to
59:7 Their feet run to do evil, and they rush to **c** murder.
Jer 7:9 murder, **c** adultery, lie, and worship Baal and all
23:14 They **c** adultery, and they love dishonesty.
Eze 8:17 "Is it nothing to the people of Judah that they **c**
16:51 "Even Samaria did not **c** half your sins. You have
18:6 And suppose he does not **c** adultery or have
18:15 idols on the mountains, does not **c** adultery,
22:11 Within your walls live men who **c** adultery with
Hos 4:2 You curse and lie and kill and steal and **c** adultery.
4:13 and your daughters-in-law **c** adultery.
Mt 5:21 If you **c** murder, you are subject to judgment.'
5:27 that the law of Moses says, 'Do not **c** adultery.'
5:32 she has been unfaithful, causes her to **c** adultery.
19:18 " 'Do not murder. Do not **c** adultery. Do not steal.
Mk 10:19 'Do not murder. Do not **c** adultery. Do not steal.
Lk 18:11 For I never cheat, I don't sin, I don't **c** adultery,
18:20 'Do not **c** adultery. Do not murder. Do not steal.
Jn 8:22 Jewish leaders asked, "Is he planning to **c** suicide?
Ro 2:22 You say it is wrong to **c** adultery, but do you do it?
3:15 "They are quick to **c** murder.
7:3 and does not **c** adultery when she remarries.
Heb 13:4 people who are immoral and those who **c** adultery.
Jas 2:11 "Do not **c** adultery," also said, "Do not murder."
2:11 the entire law, even if you do not **c** adultery.
2Pe 2:14 They **c** adultery with their eyes, and their lust is
1Jn 5:16 I am not saying you should pray for those who **c** it.
Rev 2:15 who follow the same teaching and **c** the same sins.
2:20 eat food offered to idols, and **c** sexual sin.
2:22 and she will suffer greatly with all who **c** adultery

COMMITMENT (3) [COMMIT]

1Ch 16:15 the **c** he made to a thousand generations.
Ps 105:8 the **c** he made to a thousand generations.
Isa 9:7 The passionate **c** of the LORD Almighty will

COMMITMENTS (1) [COMMIT]

Nu 30:8 he nullifies her **c**, and the LORD will forgive her.

COMMITS (10) [COMMIT]

Lev 20:10 "If a man **c** adultery with another man's wife,
Pr 6:32 But the man who **c** adultery is an utter fool, for he
Jer 3:6 Like a wife who **c** adultery, Israel has worshiped
Eze 18:11 worships idols on the mountains, **c** adultery,
Mt 5:32 And anyone who marries a divorced woman **c**
19:9 divorces his wife and marries another **c** adultery—
Mk 10:11 and marries someone else **c** adultery against her.
10:12 her husband and remarries, she **c** adultery."
Lk 16:18 his wife and marries someone else **c** adultery,
16:18 and anyone who marries a divorced woman **c**

COMMITTED (55) [COMMIT]

Ex 32:30 said to the people, "You have **c** a terrible sin,
32:31 and said, "Alas, these people have **c** a terrible sin.
Lev 19:20 slave girl who is **c** to become someone else's wife,
20:13 They have **c** a detestable act and are guilty of a
Nu 12:11 don't punish us for this sin we have so foolishly **c**.
15:27 "If the unintentional sin is **c** by an individual,
Dt 12:31 These nations have **c** many detestable acts that the
21:1 giving you, and you don't know who **c** the murder.
21:22 "If someone has **c** a crime worthy of death and is
22:21 She has **c** a disgraceful crime in Israel by being
22:26 young woman; she has **c** no crime worthy of death.
31:18 all the sins they have **c** by worshiping other gods.
Jdg 19:30 "Such a horrible crime has not been **c** since Israel
20:6 for these men have **c** this terrible and shameful
1Sa 14:38 come here. We must find out what sin was **c** today.
1Ki 15:3 He **c** the same sins as his father before him, and his
15:30 by the sins he had **c** and the sins he had led Israel
2Ki 21:17 and all his deeds, including the sins he **c**,
2Ch 15:17 Asa remained fully **c** to the LORD throughout his
16:9 to strengthen those whose hearts are fully **c** to him.
17:6 He was **c** to the ways of the LORD. He knocked
19:3 the land, and you have **c** yourself to seeking God."
20:33 and the people never fully **c** themselves to
Ne 9:18 of Egypt!' They sinned and **c** terrible blasphemies.
9:26 to return to you, and they **c** terrible blasphemies.
Ps 51:T to him after David had **c** adultery with Bathsheba.
Ecc 8:10 and are praised in the very city where they **c** their
Isa 1:29 You will blush when you think of all the sins you **c**
57:7 You have **c** adultery on the mountaintops by
Jer 3:13 and **c** adultery against him by worshiping idols
11:20 against them, for I have **c** my cause to you.
20:12 against them, for I have **c** my cause to you.
29:23 They have **c** adultery with their neighbors' wives
37:18 Jeremiah asked the king, "What crime have I **c**?
44:9 sins you and your wives **c** in Judah and Jerusalem?
Eze 18:18 But the father will die for the many sins he **c**—
23:17 So they came and **c** adultery with her, defiling her
23:37 They have **c** both adultery and murder—
44:13 must bear the shame of all the sins they have **c**.
Da 8:12 sacrilege was **c** against the Temple ceremonies,
Hos 1:4 dynasty to avenge the murders he **c** at Jezreel.
Am 1:13 they **c** cruel crimes, ripping open pregnant women
Hab 2:10 But by the murders you **c**, you have shamed your
Mt 5:28 his eye has already **c** adultery with her in his heart.
27:23 Pilate demanded. "What crime has he **c**?"
Mk 15:14 Pilate demanded. "What crime has he **c**?"
Lk 23:22 time he demanded, "Why? What crime has he **c**?
Ac 14:26 and where they had been **c** to the grace of God for
25:8 "I have **c** no crime against the Jewish laws
1Ti 3:9 They must be **c** to the revealed truths of the
Tit 2:14 very own people, totally **c** to doing what is right.
Heb 9:7 and the sins the people have **c** in ignorance.
9:15 of the sins they had **c** under that first covenant.
Jas 5:15 And anyone who has **c** sins will be forgiven.
Rev 18:3 The rulers of the world have **c** adultery with her,

COMMITTING (11) [COMMIT]

Ex 34:15 **c** adultery against me by sacrificing to their gods.
Dt 22:22 "If a man is discovered **c** adultery, both he
Jos 24:25 **c** them to a permanent and binding contract
Ne 13:27 How could you even think of **c** this sinful deed
Pr 28:24 wrong with that?" is as serious as **c** murder.
Jer 3:9 she thought nothing of **c** adultery by worshiping
5:7 But they thanked me by **c** adultery and lining up at
Hos 1:2 openly **c** adultery against the LORD by
Ro 7:3 she would be **c** adultery if she married another
Jas 2:9 you are **c** a sin, for you are guilty of breaking that
Rev 2:14 by eating food offered to idols and by **c** sexual sin.

COMMON (39)

Ge 11:6 just begun to take advantage of their **c** language
Ex 28:1 and Ithamar, will be set apart from the **c** people.
Lev 11:30 the monitor lizard, the **c** lizard, the sand lizard,
22:32 Do not treat my holy name as **c** and ordinary.
Nu 18:32 gifts of the people of Israel as though they were **c**.
Dt 8:9 It is a land where iron is as **c** as stone, and copper
1Ki 5:15 Solomon also enlisted seventy thousand **c** laborers,
10:27 And valuable cedarwood was as **c** as the sycamore
14:7 'I promoted you from the ranks of the **c** people
1Ch 9:2 their property in their former towns were **c** people.
2Ch 1:15 And valuable cedarwood was as **c** as the sycamore
2:2 He enlisted a force of seventy thousand **c** laborers,
2:18 He enlisted 70,000 of them as **c** laborers, 80,000 as
9:27 And valuable cedarwood was as **c** as the sycamore
Ezr 2:70 and some of the **c** people settled in villages near
4:3 have no part in this work, for we have nothing in **c**.
Ne 4:17 The **c** laborers carried on their work with one hand
10:34 and the **c** people should bring wood to God's
Ps 89:19 I have selected him from the **c** people to be king.
Pr 7:7 and saw a simpleminded young man who lacked **c**
8:5 Let me give you **c** sense. O foolish ones, let me
10:21 but fools are destroyed by their lack of **c** sense.
21:16 The person who strays from **c** sense will end up in
22:2 The rich and the poor have this in **c**: The LORD
26:23 just as a pretty glaze covers a **c** clay pot.
29:13 The poor and the oppressor have this in **c**—
30:2 I am too ignorant to be human, and I lack **c** sense.
Isa 5:13 them will starve, and the **c** people will die of thirst.
Jer 8:1 the graves of the priests, prophets, and **c** people.
13:13 and the prophets, right on down to the **c** people.
34:19 or Jerusalem, court officials, priests, or **c** people—
Eze 22:29 Even **c** people oppress the poor, rob the needy,
42:20 all around it to separate the holy places from the **c**.
44:23 the difference between what is holy and what is **c**,
46:3 The **c** people will worship the LORD in front of
48:15 homes, pasturelands, and **c** lands, with a city at the
Zec 9:3 and gold that it is as **c** as dust in the streets!
1Co 9:22 I try to find **c** ground with everyone so that I might
Heb 10:29 treated the blood of the covenant as if it were **c**

COMMOTION (8)

2Sa 18:29 "When Joab told me to come, there was a lot of **c**.
Ezr 3:13 and weeping mingled together in a loud **c** that
Job 41:31 "The crocodile makes the water boil with its **c**.
Isa 66:6 What is all the **c** in the city? What is that terrible
Mk 5:38 Jesus saw the **c** and the weeping and wailing.
5:39 "Why all this weeping and **c**?" he asked.
Ac 12:18 there was a great **c** among the soldiers about what
19:40 since there is no cause for all this **c**.

COMMUNICATE (2) [COMMUNICATING]

Nu 12:6 I the LORD **c** by visions and dreams.
12:7 But that is not how I **c** with my servant Moses.

COMMUNICATING (1) [COMMUNICATE]

Lk 1:62 the baby's father, **c** to him by making gestures.

COMMUNION [KJV] See SHARING, FELLOWSHIP

COMMUNITY (96) [COMMUNITY'S]

Ex 12:3 Announce to the whole **c** that on the tenth day of
12:6 Then each family in the **c** must slaughter its lamb.
12:15 of the festival will be cut off from the **c** of Israel.
12:19 this week will be cut off from the **c** of Israel.
12:47 The whole **c** of Israel must celebrate this festival at
16:2 the whole **c** of Israel spoke bitterly against Moses
16:9 said to Aaron, "Say this to the entire **c** of Israel:
30:33 who is not a priest will be cut off from the **c**.' "
30:38 their own enjoyment will be cut off from the **c**."
31:14 who works on that day will be cut off from the **c**.
34:31 and asked Aaron and the **c** leaders to come over
Lev 4:3 high priest sins, bringing guilt upon the entire **c**,
4:13 "If the entire Israelite **c** does something forbidden
4:14 the leaders of the **c** must bring a young bull for a
4:21 This is a sin offering for the entire **c** of Israel.
7:20 to the LORD must be cut off from the **c**.
7:21 that person must be cut off from the **c**.
7:25 to the LORD by fire must be cut off from the **c**.
7:27 who eats blood must be cut off from the **c**."
8:3 Then call the entire **c** of Israel to meet you there."
9:5 and the whole **c** came and stood there in the
9:23 presence of the LORD appeared to the whole **c**.
10:6 and the LORD will be angry with the whole **c** of
10:17 It was given to you for removing the guilt of the **c**
16:33 the altar, the priests, and the entire **c**.
17:4 has shed blood and must be cut off from the **c**.
17:9 it to the LORD, you will be cut off from the **c**.
17:10 in any form. I will cut off such a person from the **c**,
18:29 things will be cut off from the **c** of Israel.
19:2 "Say this to the entire **c** of Israel: You must be
19:8 holy to the LORD and must be cut off from the **c**.
20:2 they must be stoned to death by people of the **c**.
20:3 will turn against them and cut them off from the **c**,
20:4 And if the people of the **c** ignore this offering of
20:5 will turn against them and cut them off from the **c**,
20:6 will turn against them and cut them off from the **c**.
20:17 Both of them must be publicly cut off from the **c**.
20:18 both of them must be cut off from the **c**,
23:29 that day in humility will be cut off from the **c**.

24: 14 his head. Then let the entire **c** stone him to death.
24: 16 must be stoned to death by the whole **c** of Israel.
Nu 1: 2 "Take a census of the whole **c** of Israel by their
1: 18 called together the whole **c** of Israel on that very
3: 7 They will serve Aaron and the whole **c**,
4: 34 and the other leaders of the **c** counted the
8: 9 Then assemble the whole **c** of Israel and present
8: 20 and the whole **c** of Israel dedicated the Levites,
9: 13 will be cut off from the **c** of Israel for failing to
13: 26 They reported to the whole **c** what they had seen
14: 7 They said to the **c** of Israel, "The land we explored
14: 10 But the whole **c** began to talk about stoning Joshua
14: 35 I will do these things to every member of the **c**
15: 24 done unintentionally, and the **c** was unaware of it,
15: 24 the whole **c** must present a young bull for a burnt
15: 25 will make atonement for the whole **c** of Israel,
15: 26 The whole **c** of Israel will be forgiven,
15: 30 the LORD, and they must be cut off from the **c**.
15: 33 taken before Moses, Aaron, and the rest of the **c**.
15: 35 The whole **c** must stone him outside the camp."
15: 36 So the whole **c** took the man outside the camp
16: 19 Korah had stirred up the entire **c** against Moses
16: 19 presence of the LORD appeared to the whole **c**,
16: 41 But the very next morning the whole **c** began
19: 13 and will be cut off from the **c** of Israel.
19: 20 do not purify themselves will be cut off from the **c**,
20: 8 must take the staff and assemble the entire **c**.
20: 22 The whole **c** of Israel left Kadesh as a group
20: 27 up Mount Hor together as the whole **c** watched.
26: 9 and Abiram are the same **c** leaders who conspired
27: 2 and the entire **c** at the entrance of the Tabernacle.
27: 16 living things, please appoint a new leader for the **c**.
27: 19 him to Eleazar the priest before the whole **c**,
27: 20 to him so the whole **c** of Israel will obey him.
27: 21 and the rest of the **c** of Israel will discover what
27: 22 Joshua to Eleazar the priest and the whole **c**.
31: 12 and Eleazar the priest, and to the whole **c** of Israel,
35: 12 must not be killed before being tried by the **c**.
Dt 14: 27 And do not forget the Levites in your **c**, for they
21: 9 you will cleanse the guilt of murder from your **c**.
Jos 9: 21 the wood and carry the water for the entire **c**."
20: 6 that city and be tried by the **c** and found innocent.
20: 9 in revenge prior to standing trial before the **c**.
22: 16 "The whole **c** of the LORD demands to know
Jdg 20: 7 the entire **c** of Israel must decide what should be
1Ki 8: 5 and the entire **c** of Israel sacrificed sheep
8: 14 Then the king turned around to the entire **c** of
8: 22 of the LORD in front of the entire **c** of Israel.
8: 55 and shouted this blessing over the entire **c** of Israel:
2Ch 5: 6 and the entire **c** of Israel sacrificed sheep
6: 3 Then the king turned around to the entire **c** of
6: 12 of the LORD in front of the entire **c** of Israel.
24: 6 levied this tax on the **c** of Israel in order to
30: 2 and all the **c** of Jerusalem decided to celebrate
Eze 13: 9 and they will be banished from the **c** of Israel.
14: 9 such prophets and cut them off from the **c** of Israel.
Jn 21: 23 So the rumor spread among the **c** of believers that

COMMUNITY'S (1) [COMMUNITY]
Lev 4: 13 by the LORD and the matter escapes the **c** notice,

COMPANION (7) [COMPANIONS, COMPANIONSHIP]
Ge 2: 18 to be alone. I will make a **c** who will help him."
2: 20 But still there was no **c** suitable for him.
Job 30: 29 considered a brother to jackals and a **c** to ostriches.
Ps 55: 13 it is you—my equal, / my **c** and close friend.
Mal 2: 14 though she remained your faithful **c**, the wife of
Ac 13: 1 Manaen (the childhood **c** of King Herod Antipas),
Gal 2: 3 They did not even demand that my **c** Titus be

COMPANIONS (20) [COMPANION]
Jdg 14: 11 young men from the town were invited to be his **c**.
1Sa 10: 26 hearts God had touched became his constant **c**.
Job 17: 5 They denounce their **c** for their own advantage,
Ps 88: 18 You have taken away my **c** and loved ones;
Pr 16: 29 Violent people deceive their **c**, leading them down
28: 7 those who seek out worthless **c** bring shame to
SS 1: 7 like a prostitute among the flocks of your **c**?"
8: 13 how wonderful that your **c** can listen to your voice.
Isa 1: 23 Your leaders are rebels, the **c** of thieves. All of
Mt 12: 3 King David did when he and his **c** were hungry?
Mk 1: 21 Jesus and his **c** went to the town of Capernaum,
2: 25 King David did when he and his **c** were hungry?
2: 26 for the priests alone, and then gave some to his **c**.
3: 14 he selected twelve of them to be his regular **c**,
16: S all these instructions briefly to Peter and his **c**.
Lk 6: 3 King David did when he and his **c** were hungry?
Ac 9: 9 So his **c** led him by the hand to Damascus.
19: 29 who were Paul's traveling **c** from Macedonia.
22: 11 and had to be led into Damascus by my **c**.
26: 13 brighter than the sun shone down on me and my **c**.

COMPANIONSHIP (2) [COMPANION]
Job 34: 8 He seeks the **c** of evil people. He spends his time
2Ti 2: 22 and enjoy the **c** of those who call on the Lord with

COMPANY (10)
Ge 13: 11 and servants and parted **c** with his uncle Abram.
2Ki 9: 17 tower of Jezreel saw Jehu and his **c** approaching,
9: 17 he shouted to Joram, "I see a **c** of troops coming!"
Pr 21: 16 common sense will end up in the **c** of the dead.
24: 1 Don't envy evil people; don't desire their **c**.
Jer 31: 8 women about to give birth. A great **c** will return!
48: 27 Was she caught in the **c** of thieves that you should
Eze 32: 18 For I will send them down to the world below in **c**
Ro 12: 16 act important, but enjoy the **c** of ordinary people.
1Co 15: 33 such things, for "bad **c** corrupts good character."

COMPARE (17) [COMPARED, COMPARING, COMPARISON]
Ne 13: 26 "There was no king from any nation who could **c**
Ps 35: 10 "LORD, who can **c** with you? / Who else rescues
71: 19 wonderful things. / Who can **c** with you, O God?
89: 6 For who in all of heaven can **c** with the LORD?
119: 6 when I **c** my life with your commands.
Pr 3: 15 than rubies; nothing you desire can **c** with her.
Ecc 2: 12 So I decided to **c** wisdom and folly, and anyone
Isa 40: 18 To whom, then, can we **c** God? What image might
40: 25 "To whom will you **c** me? Who is my equal?"
46: 5 "To whom will you **c** me? Who is my equal?
La 2: 13 of Jerusalem, to what can I **c** your anguish?
Eze 15: 2 "Son of man, how does a grapevine **c** to a tree?
31: 2 his people: To whom would you **c** your greatness?
31: 8 branches equal to it; no plane tree had boughs to **c**.
31: 18 to which of the trees of Eden will you **c** your
Lk 7: 31 Jesus asked. "With what will I **c** them?
Gal 6: 4 and you won't need to **c** yourself to anyone else.

COMPARED (28) [COMPARE]
Jdg 8: 2 But Gideon replied, "What have I done **c** to you?
8: 3 the Midianite army. What have I done **c** to that?"
1Ki 3: 13 No other king in all the world will be **c** to you for
10: 20 No other throne in all the world could be **c** with it!
2Ki 10: 18 "Ahab hardly worshiped Baal at all **c** to the way I
2Ch 9: 19 No other throne in all the world could be **c** with it!
Job 25: 5 even the moon and stars scarcely shine **c** to him.
Ps 113: 5 Who can be **c** with the LORD our God, / who is
143: 2 your servant to trial! / **C** to you, no one is perfect.
Pr 8: 11 than rubies. Nothing you desire can be **c** with it.
SS 2: 2 "Yes, **c** to other women, my beloved is like a lily
2: 3 "And **c** to other youths, my lover is like the finest
Isa 40: 19 Can he be **c** to an idol formed in a mold,
40: 20 Can God be **c** to an idol that must be placed on a
43: 18 all that—it is nothing **c** to what I am going to do.
59: 10 No wonder we are like corpses when **c** to vigorous
Jer 10: 14 **C** to him, all people are foolish / and have no
42: 2 we are only a tiny remnant **c** to what we were
51: 17 **C** to him, all people are foolish / and have no
Eze 16: 51 sisters ever did. They seem righteous **c** to you!
Da 1: 10 and thin **c** to the other youths your age,
1: 13 see how we look **c** to the other young men who are
4: 35 All the people of the earth / are nothing **c** to him.
Mt 18: 23 the Kingdom of Heaven can be **c** to a king who
Mk 13: 34 "The coming of the Son of Man can be **c** with that
Ro 8: 18 Yet what we suffer now is nothing **c** to the glory he
2Co 3: 10 that first glory was not glorious at all **c** with the
Php 3: 8 everything else is worthless when **c** with the

COMPARING (1) [COMPARE]
2Co 10: 12 But they are only **c** themselves with each other,

COMPARISON (6) [COMPARE]
1Ki 20: 27 **c** to the vast Aramean forces that filled the
Job 11: 8 the underworld—what can you know in **c** to him?
Isa 40: 15 for all the nations of the world are nothing in **c**
Eze 16: 52 In **c**, you make your sisters seem innocent!
16: 54 have done, for your sins make them feel good in **c**.
Hag 2: 3 it was before? In **c**, how does it look to you now?

COMPASS [KJV] See AROUND, CIRCLE, SURROUND

COMPASSION (30) [COMPASSIONATE]
Dt 13: 17 He will have **c** on you and make you a great
28: 54 man among you will have no **c** for his own brother,
2Ch 36: 15 for he had **c** on his people and his Temple.
Ne 13: 22 Have **c** on me according to your great
Ps 6: 2 Have **c** on me, LORD, for I am weak. / Heal me,
25: 6 Remember, O LORD, your unfailing love and **c**,
51: 1 Because of your great **c**, / blot out the stain of my
77: 9 Has he slammed the door on his **c**? / *Interlude*
135: 14 vindicate his people / and have **c** on his servants.
145: 9 to everyone. / He showers **c** on all his creation.
Isa 13: 18 helpless babies and will show no **c** for the children.
30: 18 to come to him so he can show you his love and **c**.
49: 13 his people and will have **c** on them in their sorrow.
54: 7 but with great **c** I will take you back.
54: 8 But with everlasting love I will have **c** on you,"
63: 15 on our behalf? Where are your mercy and **c** now?
Jer 12: 15 afterward I will return and have **c** on all of them.
13: 14 or mercy or **c** keep me from destroying them.' "
21: 7 will slaughter them all without mercy, pity, or **c**.'
La 3: 32 he also shows **c** according to the greatness of his
Hos 2: 19 you righteousness and justice, unfailing love and **c**.
11: 8 My heart is torn within me, and my **c** overflows.
Mic 7: 19 Once again you will have **c** on us. You will
Zec 11: 5 now rich!' Even the shepherds have no **c** for them.
Mt 14: 14 and he had **c** on them and healed their sick.
Mk 6: 34 and he had **c** on them because they were like sheep
Lk 7: 13 the Lord saw her, his heart overflowed with **c**.
15: 20 Filled with love and **c**, he ran to his son,
Ro 9: 15 I choose, / and I will show **c** to anyone I choose."
Php 1: 8 and long for you with the tender **c** of Christ Jesus.

COMPASSIONATE (5) [COMPASSION]
Ps 103: 13 his children, / tender and **c** to those who fear him.
112: 4 bursting in. / They are generous, **c**, and righteous.
Jnh 4: 2 I knew that you were a gracious and **c** God, slow to
Lk 6: 36 You must be **c**, just as your Father is **c**.

COMPELLED (3)
Est 1: 8 no one should be **c** to take more than he wanted.
Mk 1: 12 Immediately the Holy Spirit **c** Jesus to go into the
1Co 9: 16 I am **c** by God to do it. How terrible for me if I

COMPENSATE (3) [COMPENSATION]
Ge 20: 16 to **c** for any embarrassment I may have caused you.
Ex 21: 30 from the owner of the bull to **c** for the loss of life.
Eze 29: 18 and his army won no plunder to **c** them for all their

COMPENSATED (2) [COMPENSATION]
2Sa 22: 21 for doing right; / he **c** me because of my innocence.
Ps 18: 20 for doing right; / he **c** me because of my innocence.

COMPENSATION (4) [COMPENSATE, COMPENSATED]
Lev 19: 20 to become someone else's wife, **c** must be paid.
22: 16 guilt upon the people and require them to pay **c**.
Nu 18: 31 for it is your **c** for serving in the Tabernacle.
Pr 6: 35 There is no **c** or bribe that will satisfy him.

COMPETENT (1)
Pr 22: 29 Do you see any truly **c** workers? They will serve

COMPILE (1) [COMPILED]
Ex 38: 21 Moses directed the Levites to **c** the figures,

COMPILED (1) [COMPILE]
Ne 12: 22 a list was **c** of the family leaders of the Levites

COMPLACENCY (1) [COMPLACENT]
Pr 1: 32 They are fools, and their own **c** will destroy them.

COMPLACENT (1) [COMPLACENCY]
Eze 30: 9 messengers in ships to terrify the **c** Ethiopians.

COMPLAIN (17) [COMPLAINED, COMPLAINERS, COMPLAINING, COMPLAINT, COMPLAINTS]
Ex 17: 3 But tormented by thirst, they continued to **c**,
Nu 11: 1 The people soon began to **c** to the LORD about
11: 4 of Egypt, and the people of Israel also began to **c**.
14: 27 "How long will this wicked nation **c** about me?
2Sa 14: 10 to me. I can assure you they will never **c** again!"
19: 28 those who eat at your own table! So how can I **c**?"
Ne 4: 10 Then the people of Judah began to **c** that the
Job 6: 5 Don't I have a right to **c**? Wild donkeys bray when
6: 6 People **c** when there is no salt in their food.
7: 11 express my anguish. I must **c** in my bitterness.
10: 1 "I am disgusted with my life. Let me **c** freely.
Isa 29: 24 and those who constantly **c** will accept instruction.
La 3: 39 **c** when we are punished for our sins?
Mt 11: 16 game in the public square. They **c** to their friends,
Lk 7: 32 They **c** to their friends, 'We played wedding songs
15: 2 and teachers of religious law **c** that he was
Jn 6: 43 But Jesus replied, "Don't **c** about what I said.

COMPLAINED (19) [COMPLAIN]
Ge 21: 25 Then Abraham **c** to Abimelech about a well that
Ex 14: 11 Then they turned against Moses and **c**, "Why did
17: 2 So once more the people grumbled and **c** to Moses.
Nu 11: 20 who is here among you, and you have **c** to him,
14: 29 Because you **c** against me, none of you who are
21: 5 they **c**. "There is nothing to eat here and nothing to
Dt 1: 27 You murmured and **c** in your tents and said,
6: 16 your God as you did when you **c** at Massah.
1Sa 10: 27 But there were some wicked men who **c**,
2Sa 7: 7 And I have never once **c** to Israel's leaders,
19: 41 But the men of Israel **c** to the king that the men of
2Ki 4: 19 Suddenly he **c**, "My head hurts! My head hurts!"
1Ch 17: 6 And I never once **c** to Israel's leaders,
Ps 81: 7 at Meribah, / when you **c** that there was no water.
Jnh 4: 2 So he **c** to the LORD about it: "Didn't I say
Lk 5: 30 and their teachers of religious law **c** bitterly to
5: 33 The religious leaders **c** that Jesus' disciples were
Ac 6: 1 Those who spoke Greek **c** against those who spoke
Ro 11: 2 Elijah the prophet **c** to God about the people of

COMPLAINERS (3) [COMPLAIN]
1Ki 12: 10 men replied, "This is what you should tell those **c**:
2Ch 10: 10 men replied, "This is what you should tell those **c**:
Jude 1: 16 These people are grumblers and **c**, doing whatever

COMPLAINING (8) [COMPLAIN]
Nu 11: 13 They keep **c** and saying, 'Give us meat!'
16: 11 And who is Aaron that you are **c** about him?"
17: 5 put an end to this murmuring and **c** against you."
Dt 1: 34 "When the LORD heard your **c**, he became very
Pr 21: 19 live alone in the desert than with a crabby, **c** wife.
23: 29 Who is always fighting? Who is always **c**?
Jn 6: 61 knew within himself that his disciples were **c**,
Php 2: 14 everything you do, stay away from **c** and arguing,

COMPLAINT (12) [COMPLAIN]
Nu 14: 2 Their voices rose in a great chorus of **c** against

Job 21: 4 “My **c** is with God, not with people. No wonder
23: 2 “My **c** today is still a bitter one, and I try hard not
Ps 50: 8 I have no **c** about your sacrifices / or the burnt
64: 1 O God, listen to my **c**. / Do not let my enemies'
Jer 12: 1 Now let me bring you this **c**: Why are the wicked
Hos 4: 4 the blame! Look, you priests, my **c** is with you!
Mic 6: 2 “And now, O mountains, listen to the LORD's **c**!
Hab 2: 1 will say to me and how he will answer my **c**.
2:11 and the beams in the ceilings echo the **c**.
Rev 2: 4 But I have this **c** against you. You don't love me
2:20 But I have this **c** against you. You are permitting

COMPLAINTS (18) [COMPLAIN]

Ex 16: 7 He has heard your **c**, which are against the LORD
16: 8 for he has heard all your **c** against him.
16: 8 Yes, your **c** are against the LORD, not against
16: 9 and hear his reply to your **c**.’ ”
16:12 “I have heard the people's **c**. Now tell them,
18:13 Moses sat as usual to hear the people's **c** against
Nu 11:18 ‘The LORD has heard your whining and **c**:
17:10 This should put an end to their **c** against me
Ne 5: 6 When I heard their **c**, I was very angry.
Job 9:27 If I decided to forget my **c**, if I decided to end my
31:13 or female servants, if I have refused to hear their **c**,
33:13 You say, ‘He does not respond to people's **c**.’
Ps 142: 2 I pour out my **c** before him / and tell him all my
Pr 27:16 Trying to stop her **c** is like trying to stop the wind
Mic 6: 1 the mountains and hills be called to witness your **c**.
Ac 19:39 And if there are **c** about other matters, they can be
1Ti 5:19 Do not listen to **c** against an elder unless there are
Rev 2:14 And yet I have a few **c** against you. You tolerate

COMPLETE (56) [COMPLETED, COMPLETELY, COMPLETING, COMPLETION]

Ge 19: 3 **c** with fresh bread made without yeast.
20: 5 ‘Yes, he is my brother.’ I acted in **c** innocence!”
39: 6 So Potiphar gave Joseph **c** administrative
50: 5 After his burial is **c**, I will return without delay.”
Ex 25:33 like an almond blossom, **c** with buds and petals.
25:34 with four almond blossoms, **c** with buds and petals.
26:14 fine goatskin leather. This will **c** the roof covering.
36: 5 now to **c** the job the LORD has given us to do!”
36: 7 Their contributions were more than enough to **c** the
37:19 like an almond blossom, **c** with buds and petals.
Lev 8:33 for that is the time it will take to **c** the ordination
14: 8 “The people being purified must **c** the cleansing
23: 3 but on the seventh day all work must come to a **c**
23: 3 It is the LORD's Sabbath day of **c** rest, a holy day
23:24 early autumn, you are to celebrate a day of **c** rest.
Dt 7:23 He will throw them into **c** confusion until they are
Ru 2:11 and your own land to live here among **c** strangers.
2Sa 10: 2 “I am going to show **c** loyalty to Hanun
11:22 went to Jerusalem and gave a **c** report to David.
1Ki 7: 1 and it took him thirteen years to **c** the construction.
1Ch 19: 2 “I am going to show **c** loyalty to Hanun
2Ch 24:27 The **c** story about the sons of Joash, the prophecies
Ezr 4:12 the foundation for its walls and will soon **c** them.
Job 1: 1 He was blameless, a man of **c** integrity. He feared
1: 8 finest man in all the earth—a man of **c** integrity.
2: 3 finest man in all the earth—a man of **c** integrity.
8: 6 if you are pure and live with **c** integrity, he will
Ps 32: 2 cleared of sin, / whose lives are lived in **c** honesty!
139:22 Yes, I hate them with **c** hatred, / for your enemies
Pr 4:19 But the way of the wicked is like **c** darkness.
Isa 43:28 and assigned Israel a future of **c** destruction
Jer 4:20 roll over the land, until it lies in **c** desolation.
7:34 towns of Judah. The land will lie in **c** desolation.
La 3:22 By his mercies we have been kept from **c**
Eze 7: 8 Soon I will pour out my fury to **c** your punishment
Mic 6:16 make an example of you, bringing you to **c** ruin.
Zec 4: 9 laid the foundation of this Temple, and he will **c** it.
Mt 28:18 “I have been given **c** authority in heaven and on
Lk 14:29 you might **c** only the foundation before running out
Ro 2:20 For you are certain that in God's law you have **c**
11:25 but this will last only until the **c** number of
15: 5 help you live in **c** harmony with each other—
2Co 7: 1 And let us work toward **c** purity because we fear
7:16 happy now because I have **c** confidence in you.
8: 6 and encourage you to **c** your share in this ministry
Php 2:17 to **c** the sacrifice of your faithful service (that is,
Col 1: 9 We ask God to give you a **c** understanding of what
2: 2 because they have **c** understanding of God's secret
2:10 and you are **c** through your union with Christ.
1Ti 4:15 Give your **c** attention to these matters.
2Ti 4: 5 others to Christ. **C** the ministry God has given you.
Tit 1: 5 the island of Crete so you could **c** our work there
Jas 2:22 His faith was made **c** by what he did—by his
1Jn 1: 4 are writing these things so that our joy will be **c**.
2Jn 1:12 talk with you face to face. Then our joy will be **c**.
Rev 11: 7 When they **c** their testimony, the beast that comes

COMPLETED (32) [COMPLETE]

Ge 2: 1 and the earth and everything in them was **c**.
Lev 12: 4 of her purification from the blood of childbirth is **c**.
12: 6 “When the time of purification is **c** for either a son
Nu 4:49 And so the census was **c**, just as the LORD had
6:12 The days of their vow that were **c** before their
Jos 19:51 at Shiloh. So the division of the land was **c**.
Ru 2:21 with his harvesters until the entire harvest is **c**.”
2Sa 11: 4 (She had just **c** the purification rites after having
24: 8 they **c** their task in nine months and twenty days
1Ki 6:38 The entire building was **c** in every detail by
7:40 So at last Huram **c** everything King Solomon had
9: 1 royal palace. He **c** everything he had planned to do.
16:34 And when he finally **c** it by setting up the gates,
2Ch 4:11 So at last Huram-abi **c** everything King Solomon
7:11 royal palace. He **c** everything he had planned to do.
8: 1 LORD's Temple and his own royal palace were **c**.
29:17 eight days. So the entire task was **c** in sixteen days.
35:16 for the LORD's Passover was **c** that day.
Ezr 3:10 When the builders **c** the foundation of the
4:13 know that if this city is rebuilt and its walls are **c**,
4:16 declare that if this city is rebuilt and its walls are **c**,
5:16 working on it ever since, though it is not yet **c**.’
6:15 The Temple was **c** on March 12, during the sixth
Ne 4: 6 At last the wall was **c** to half its original height
Jer 48: 2 In Heshbon plans have been **c** to destroy her.
Eze 4: 8 to side until the days of your siege have been **c**.
Da 1:18 training period ordered by the king was **c**,
11:36 He will succeed—until the time of wrath is **c**.
Lk 12:49 the earth, and I wish that my task were already **c**!
Ac 14:26 to the grace of God for the work they had now **c**.
Ro 15:28 this money and **c** this good deed of theirs,
Rev 15: 8 seven angels had **c** pouring out the seven plagues.

COMPLETELY (156) [COMPLETE]

Ge 6: 7 “I will **c** wipe out this human race that I have
19:13 For we will destroy the city **c**. The stench of the
Ex 32:25 that Aaron had let the people get **c** out of control—
Lev 1:17 the priest will tear the bird apart, though not **c**.
6:22 regular share, and it must be **c** burned up.
6:30 meat may be eaten. It must be **c** burned up.
7:17 But anything left over until the third day must be **c**
7:19 unclean may not be eaten; it must be **c** burned up.
11: 3 include those that have **c** divided hooves and chew
13:13 because the skin has turned **c** white.
13:17 the affected areas have indeed turned **c** white,
13:52 infectious mildew. It must be **c** destroyed by fire.
13:55 It must be **c** burned up, whether it is contaminated
26:26 I will **c** destroy your food supply, so the bread
Nu 15:31 they must be **c** cut off and suffer the consequences
21: 2 these people, we will **c** destroy all their towns.”
21: 3 The Israelites **c** destroyed them and their towns,
21:30 We have **c** wiped them out / as far away as Nophah
32:11 Isaac, and Jacob, for they have not obeyed me **c**.
Dt 1:36 this land because he has followed the LORD **c**.
2:34 conquered all his towns and **c** destroyed everyone
3: 6 We **c** destroyed the kingdom of Bashan, just as we
7: 2 and you conquer them, you must **c** destroy them.
11:18 So commit yourselves **c** to these words of mine.
13:15 attack that town and **c** destroy all its inhabitants,
20:17 You must **c** destroy the Hittites, Amorites,
28:20 until at last you are **c** destroyed for doing evil
Jos 2:10 of the Jordan River, whose people you **c** destroyed.
6:17 and everything in it must be **c** destroyed as an
6:18 or you yourselves will be **c** destroyed, and you will
6:21 They **c** destroyed everything in it—men
8:26 everyone who had lived in Ai was **c** destroyed.
10: 1 and **c** destroyed Ai and killed its king,
10:28 That same day Joshua **c** destroyed the city of
10:35 at Lachish, they **c** destroyed everyone in the city.
10:37 at Eglon, they **c** destroyed the entire population.
10:39 They **c** destroyed Debir just as they had destroyed
10:40 He **c** destroyed everyone in the land, leaving no
11:11 The Israelites **c** destroyed every living thing in the
11:12 and their people, **c** destroying them, just as Moses,
11:20 So they were **c** and mercilessly destroyed,
11:21 He killed them all and **c** destroyed their towns.
14: 8 For my part, I followed the LORD my God **c**.
23:15 He will **c** wipe you out from this good land he has
Jdg 1:17 living in Zephath, and they **c** destroyed the town.
16:27 The temple was **c** filled with people.
21:11 “**C** destroy all the males and every woman who is
1Sa 14: 7 “I'm with you **c**, whatever you decide.”
15: 3 and **c** destroy the entire Amalekite nation—
15: 8 the Amalekite king, but **c** destroyed everyone else.
15:18 and told you, ‘Go and **c** destroy the sinners,
2Sa 10: 2 his father, Nahash, was always **c** loyal to me.”
1Ki 6:18 Cedar paneling **c** covered the stone walls
9:21 of the nations that Israel had not **c** destroyed.
11: 6 he refused to follow the LORD **c**, as his father,
15:14 Although the pagan shrines were not **c** removed,
18:21 then follow him!” But the people were **c** silent.
21:25 so **c** sold himself to what was evil in the LORD's
2Ki 13:17 for you will **c** conquer the Arameans at Aphek.
13:23 And to this day he still has not **c** destroyed them
14:27 had not said he would blot out the name of Israel **c**,
18:21 your hand. The pharaoh of Egypt is **c** unreliable!
1Ch 4:41 and **c** destroyed the homes of the descendants of
12:33 and prepared for battle and **c** loyal to David.
19: 2 his father, Nahash, was always **c** loyal to me.”
2Ch 8: 8 of the nations that Israel had not **c** destroyed.
12: 7 I will not **c** destroy them and will soon give them
12:12 was turned aside, and he did not destroy him **c**.
15:17 Although the pagan shrines were not **c** removed
36:19 the palaces, and **c** destroyed everything of value.
Ne 9:22 They **c** took over the land of King Sihon of
9:31 you did not destroy them **c** or abandon them
Est 6:12 Haman hurried home dejected and **c** humiliated.
Job 10: 8 you made me, and yet you **c** destroy me.
Ps 38: 8 I am exhausted and **c** crushed. / My groans come
41: 9 Even my best friend, the one I trusted **c**, / the one
59:13 Destroy them in your anger! / Wipe them out **c**!
60: 2 split it open. / Seal the cracks before it **c** collapses.
78:59 he was very angry, / and he rejected Israel **c**.
88:17 all day long. / They have encircled me **c**.
119:25 I lie in the dust, **c** discouraged; / revive me by your
Pr 28: 5 but those who follow the LORD understand **c**.
Isa 1: 9 we would have been wiped out as **c** as Sodom
1:28 But all sinners will be **c** destroyed, for they refuse
7: 8 sixty-five years it will be crushed and **c** destroyed.
10:18 The LORD will **c** destroy Assyria's warriors,
16: 9 But now the enemy has **c** destroyed that vine.
24: 3 The earth will be **c** emptied and looted.
30:14 so **c** that there won't be a piece left that is big
33:12 Your people will be burned up **c**, like thorns cut
34: 2 He will **c** destroy them, bringing about their
34: 5 will fall upon Edom, the nation I have **c** destroyed.
36: 6 your hand. The Pharaoh of Egypt is **c** unreliable!
55: 8 “My thoughts are **c** different from yours,”
Jer 3: 3 For you are a prostitute and are **c** unashamed.
3:23 orgies on the hills and mountains are **c** false.
4:27 land will be ruined, but I will not destroy it **c**.
5:18 “Yet even in those days I will not blot you out **c**,”
9:12 so **c** that no one even dares to travel through it?
9:16 with the sword until I have destroyed them **c**.”
10:21 Therefore, they fail **c**, and their flocks are
14:19 LORD, have you **c** rejected Judah? Do you really
23:39 I will forget you **c**. I will expel you from my
25: 9 I will **c** destroy you and make you an object of
30:11 I will **c** destroy the nations where I have scattered
34:22 towns of Judah are destroyed and left **c** empty.”
35:16 families of Recab have obeyed their ancestor **c**,
49:37 them with the sword until I have destroyed them **c**.
50:21 Pursue, kill, and **c** destroy them, as I have
50:26 heaps of rubble. Destroy her **c**, and leave nothing!
51: 3 Young and old alike will be **c** destroyed.
51:26 You will be **c** wiped out,” says the LORD.
La 1:10 The enemy has plundered her **c**, taking everything
Eze 2: 7 But they won't listen, for they are **c** rebellious!
5:11 says the Sovereign LORD, I will cut you off **c**.
16:39 beautiful jewels, leaving you **c** naked and ashamed.
17:10 it will wither away **c** when the east wind blows
25: 7 cut you off from being a nation and destroy you **c**.
29:11 people nor animals. It will be **c** uninhabited.
35: 3 I will raise my fist against you to destroy you **c**.
40: 5 I could see a wall **c** surrounding the Temple area.
44:20 let their hair grow too long nor shave it off **c**.
Da 7:26 all his power will be taken away and **c** destroyed.
Hos 10:15 the king of Israel will be **c** destroyed.
11: 9 I will not **c** destroy Israel, for I am God and not a
Am 5: 6 will roar through Israel like a fire, devouring you **c**.
9: 8 Yet I have promised that I will never **c** destroy the
Ob 1: 5 for the poor. But your enemies will wipe you out **c**!
1:10 Now you will be destroyed **c** and filled with shame
Mic 2: 4 “We are finished, / **c** ruined! / God has confiscated
2:10 for you have filled it with sin and ruined it **c**.
Na 1:15 your land again. They have been **c** destroyed!
Zep 2: 9 and Ammon will be destroyed as **c** as Sodom
Zec 5: 4 And my curse will remain in that house until it is **c**
9: 5 its king killed, and Ashkelon will be **c** deserted.
11:17 will become useless, and his right eye **c** blind!”
Mal 3: 6 descendants of Jacob are not already **c** destroyed.
Mt 24: 2 so **c** demolished that not one stone will be left on
Mk 7:37 for they were **c** amazed. Again and again they said,
8:25 As the man stared intently, his sight was **c** restored,
12:17 must be given to God.” This reply **c** amazed them.
13: 2 so **c** demolished that not one stone will be left on
Lk 7:10 to his house, they found the slave **c** healed.
8:29 into the wilderness, **c** under the demon's power.
11:21 For when Satan, who is **c** armed, guards his palace,
11:42 but you **c** forget about justice and the love of God.
21: 6 so **c** demolished that not one stone will be left on
Jn 7:23 for making a man **c** well on the Sabbath?
Ro 6:13 give yourselves **c** to God since you have been
9:29 been wiped out / as **c** as Sodom and Gomorrah.”
1Co 7: 5 so they can give themselves more **c** to prayer.
13:12 and incomplete, but then I will know everything **c**,
2Co 1: 8 We were crushed and **c** overwhelmed, and we
1Ti 1:14 He filled me **c** with faith and the love of Christ
1Jn 2: 1 He is Jesus Christ, the one who pleases God **c**.
Rev 17: 6 were witnesses for Jesus. I stared at her **c** amazed.

COMPLETING (3) [COMPLETE]

1Ki 6: 9 After **c** the Temple structure, Solomon put in a
Ac 24:18 My accusers saw me in the Temple as I was **c** a
Col 1:24 for I am **c** what remains of Christ's sufferings for

COMPLETION (5) [COMPLETE]

Ex 36: 3 donated by the people for the **c** of the sanctuary.
2Ch 8:16 the day its foundation was laid to the day of its **c**.
14: 7 ahead with these projects and brought them to **c**.
2Co 8:11 Now you should carry this project through to **c** just
Rev 15: 1 last plagues, which would bring God's wrath to **c**.

COMPLEX (9)

1Ki 6: 5 A **c** of rooms was built against the outer walls of
6: 6 The **c** was three stories high, the bottom floor
6:10 there was a **c** of rooms on three sides of the
6:10 Each story of the **c** was 7-1/2 feet high.
Ps 139:14 Thank you for making me so wonderfully **c**!
Eze 42: 4 It extended the entire 175 feet of the **c**, and all the
42:11 just like the **c** on the north side of the Temple.
42:11 This **c** of rooms was the same length and width as
42:14 the parts of the building **c** open to the public.”

COMPLEXION (1)

SS 1: 6 you fair city girls, just because my **c** is so dark.

COMPLICATED (1)

Ex 18:22 is too important or too **c** can be brought to you.

COMPLIED (1) [COMPLY]

Ezr 6:13 and their colleagues **c** at once with the command of

COMPLY (1) [COMPLIED]
Est 3: 4 after day, but still he refused to **c** with the order.

COMPOSED (7)
Nu 3:21 The descendants of Gershon were **c** of the clans
3:27 The descendants of Kohath were **c** of the clans
3:33 The descendants of Merari were **c** of the clans
2Sa 1:17 Then David **c** a funeral song for Saul and Jonathan.
1Ki 4:32 He **c** some 3,000 proverbs and wrote 1,005 songs.
2Ch 14: 8 Both armies were **c** of courageous fighting men.
35:25 The prophet Jeremiah **c** funeral songs for Josiah,

COMPOUNDS (1)
Nu 2: 2 will be located at the center of these tribal **c**.

COMPREHEND (2) [COMPREHENSION]
Job 37: 5 We cannot **c** the greatness of his power.
Ps 90:11 Who can **c** the power of your anger? / Your wrath

COMPREHENSION (1) [COMPREHEND]
Ps 147: 5 power is absolute! / His understanding is beyond **c**!

COMPROMISE (2)
Ps 119: 3 They do not **c** with evil, / and they walk only in his
Pr 25:26 If the godly **c** with the wicked, it is like polluting a

CONANIAH (2)
2Ch 31:12 **C** the Levite was put in charge, assisted by his
35: 9 **C** and his brothers Shemaiah and Nethanel,

CONCEAL (7) [CONCEALED]
Job 16:18 "O earth, do not **c** my blood. Let it cry out on my
27:11 I will not **c** anything that concerns the Almighty.
Ps 27: 5 For he will **c** me there when troubles come;
Pr 14:13 Laughter can **c** a heavy heart; when the laughter
25: 2 It is God's privilege to **c** things and the king's
Mk 4:11 But I am using these stories to **c** everything about
Lk 8:10 But I am using these stories to **c** everything about

CONCEALED (1) [CONCEAL]
Pr 26:26 While their hatred may be **c** by trickery, it will

CONCEDE (1) [CONCESSION]
Job 27: 5 I will never **c** that you are right; until I die, I will

CONCEIT (3) [CONCEITED]
Ps 36: 2 In their blind **c**, / they cannot see how wicked they
101: 5 their neighbors. / I will not endure **c** and pride.
2Co 12:20 of anger, selfishness, backstabbing, gossip, **c**,

CONCEITED (2) [CONCEIT]
Gal 5:26 Let us not become **c**, or irritate one another,
1Ti 6: 4 Anyone who teaches anything different is both **c**

CONCEIVE (4) [CONCEIVED, CONCEPTION]
Job 15:35 They **c** trouble and evil, and their hearts give birth
Ps 7:14 The wicked **c** evil; / they are pregnant with trouble
Isa 7:14 Look! The virgin will **c** a child! She will give birth
Mt 1:23 "Look! The virgin will **c** a child! / She will give

CONCEIVED (9) [CONCEIVE]
Job 3: 3 of my birth, and cursed be the night when I was **c**.
Ps 51: 5 a sinner—/ yes, from the moment my mother **c** me.
SS 3: 4 into my mother's bedroom, where I had been **c**.
Isa 8: 2 testify that I had written it before the child was **c**.
8:12 Do not be afraid that some plan **c** behind closed
Hos 2: 4 they are not my children! They were **c** in adultery.
9:11 at birth or perish in the womb or never even be **c**.
Mt 1:20 For the child within her has been **c** by the Holy
Lk 2:21 name given him by the angel even before he was **c**.

CONCENTRATE (3)
Ps 119:78 meanwhile, I will **c** on your commandments.
Pr 2: 2 Tune your ears to wisdom, and **c** on understanding.
1Co 2: 2 For I decided to **c** only on Jesus Christ and his

CONCEPTION (1) [CONCEIVE]
Job 10:10 You guided my **c** and formed me in the womb.

CONCERN (12) [CONCERNED, CONCERNING, CONCERNS]
Ex 2:25 on the Israelites and felt deep **c** for their welfare.
2Ki 4:13 "Tell her that we appreciate the kind **c** she has
Job 19: 4 And even if I have sinned, that is my **c**, not yours.
Ps 17:14 from those whose only **c** is earthly gain.
131: 1 I don't **c** myself with matters too great
Mt 6:33 and make the Kingdom of God your primary **c**.
Lk 12:31 if you make the Kingdom of God your primary **c**.
Jn 2: 4 "How does that **c** you and me?" Jesus asked.
10:13 he is merely hired and has no real **c** for the sheep.
1Co 7:29 husbands should not let marriage be their major **c**.
2Co 7:11 such **c** to clear yourselves, such indignation,
7:15 and welcomed him with such respect and deep **c**.

CONCERNED (26) [CONCERN]
Ge 41: 8 Pharaoh became very **c** as to what the dreams
50:20 As far as I am **c**, God turned into good what you
Ex 4:31 had seen their misery and was deeply **c** for them,
Jdg 3:25 out after a long delay, they became **c** and got a key.
1Sa 23:21 Saul said. "At last someone is **c** about me!
29: 9 But Achish insisted, "As far as I'm **c**, you're as
Job 35:13 say God doesn't listen, to say the Almighty isn't **c**.
Pr 12:10 The godly are **c** for the welfare of their animals,
Eze 36: 9 See, I am **c** for you, and I will come to help you.
36:21 Then I was **c** for my holy name, which had been
Da 10: 1 It **c** events certain to happen in the future—times of
Mic 1: 1 The messages **c** both Samaria and Jerusalem,
Mt 6:32 the pagans who are so deeply **c** about these things?
Lk 6:35 to them! And don't be **c** that they might not repay.
10:42 There is really only one thing worth being **c** about.
24:17 he said. "What are you so **c** about?"
Jn 6:27 shouldn't be so **c** about perishable things like food.
Ac 19:27 I'm also **c** that the temple of the great goddess
Ro 6:20 of sin, you weren't **c** with doing what was right.
7:18 and through so far as my old sinful nature is **c**.
9: 5 himself was a Jew as far as his human nature is **c**.
1Co 7:34 while the married woman must be **c** about her
11:20 It's not the Lord's Supper you are **c** about when
Php 4:10 and how I praise the Lord that you are **c** about me
4:10 I know you have always been **c** for me, but for a
1Pe 3: 3 Don't be **c** about the outward beauty that depends

CONCERNING (89) [CONCERN]
Ex 30:34 These were the LORD's instructions to Moses **c**
39: 7 These stones served as reminders to the LORD **c**
Nu 8:22 that the LORD gave Moses **c** the Levites.
9: 3 all my laws and regulations **c** this celebration."
9:12 They must follow all the normal regulations **c** the
20:24 against my instructions **c** the waters of Meribah.
30:16 LORD gave Moses **c** relationships between a man
36: 6 This is what the LORD commands **c** the
Jos 7: 1 But Israel was unfaithful **c** the things set apart for
1Sa 28:18 because you did not obey his instructions **c** the
2Sa 7:25 do as you have promised **c** me and my family.
1Ki 2:27 had made at Shiloh **c** the descendants of Eli.
5: 8 and I will do as you have asked **c** the timber.
6:12 "**C** this Temple you are building, if you keep all
8:38 and if your people offer a prayer **c** their troubles
15: 5 his life, except in the affair **c** Uriah the Hittite.
15:29 just as the LORD had promised **c** Jeroboam by
16:34 LORD **c** Jericho spoken by Joshua son of Nun.
2Ki 10:10 that was spoken **c** Ahab's family will not fail.
22:18 of Israel, says **c** the message you have just heard:
1Ch 11:10 just as the LORD had promised **c** Israel.
17:23 do as you have promised **c** me and my family.
28:13 The king also gave Solomon the instructions **c** the
2Ch 6:29 and if your people offer a prayer **c** their troubles
8:15 in any way from David's commands **c** the priests
9:29 and also in *The Visions of Iddo the Seer,* **c**
19: 8 Jerusalem for cases **c** both the law of the LORD
19:11 priest will have final say in all cases **c** the LORD.
34:26 of Israel, says **c** the message you have just heard:
Ezr 6: 3 a decree was sent out **c** the Temple of God at
10:14 God may be turned away from us **c** this affair."
Ne 9:14 You instructed them **c** the laws of your holy
Job 23:13 Nevertheless, his mind **c** me remains unchanged,
Ps 7: T which he sang to the LORD **c** Cush of the tribe of
Isa 1: 1 These visions **c** Judah and Jerusalem came to
2: 1 another vision that Isaiah son of Amoz saw **c** Judah
13: 1 Isaiah son of Amoz received this message **c** the
15: 1 This message came to me **c** Moab: In one night
17: 1 This message came to me **c** Damascus: "Look,
19: 1 This message came to me **c** Egypt: Look!
21: 1 This message came to me **c** the land of Babylonia:
21:11 This message came to me **c** Edom: Someone from
21:13 This message came to me **c** Arabia: O caravans
22: 1 This message came to me **c** Jerusalem: What is
23: 1 This message came to me **c** Tyre: Weep, O ships of
29:15 who try to keep him in the dark **c** what they do!
30: 8 Now go and write down these words **c** Egypt.
37:21 This is my answer to your prayer **c** King
Jer 22: 6 Now this is what the LORD says **c** the royal
23:15 this is what the LORD Almighty says **c** the
29:31 'This is what the LORD says **c** Shemaiah the
30: 4 This is the message the LORD gave **c** Israel
44: 1 This is the message Jeremiah received **c** the
46: 1 the prophet from the LORD **c** foreign nations.
46: 2 This message **c** Egypt was given in the fourth year
47: 1 to the prophet Jeremiah **c** the Philistines of Gaza,
48: 1 This message was given **c** Moab. This is what the
48:47 This is the end of Jeremiah's prophecy **c** Moab.
49: 1 This message was given **c** the Ammonites. This is
49: 7 This message was given **c** Edom. This is what the
49:23 This message was given **c** Damascus. This is what
49:28 This message was given **c** Kedar and the kingdoms
49:34 This message **c** Elam came to the prophet Jeremiah
50: 1 gave Jeremiah the prophet this message **c** Babylon
Eze 12:19 from the Sovereign LORD **c** those living in Israel
21:28 prophesy **c** the Ammonites and their mockery.
44: 5 you about the regulations **c** the LORD's Temple.
44: 8 You have not kept the laws I gave you **c** these
Ob 1: 1 LORD revealed to Obadiah **c** the land of Edom.
Na 1: 1 This message **c** Nineveh came as a vision to
1:14 And this is what the LORD says **c** the Assyrians
Zec 12: 1 This message **c** the fate of Israel came from the
Mt 2:23 This fulfilled what was spoken by the prophets **c**
12:17 This fulfilled the prophecy of Isaiah **c** him:
18:19 If two of you agree down here on earth **c** anything
Lk 8: 1 and villages to announce the Good News **c** the
18:31 all the predictions of the ancient prophets **c** the Son
Ac 1:16 it was necessary for the Scriptures to be fulfilled **c**
8:12 message of Good News **c** the Kingdom of God
13:29 "When they had fulfilled all the prophecies **c** his
13:33 second psalm is talking about when it says **c** Jesus,
15:27 and Silas to tell you what we have decided **c** your
19:23 serious trouble developed in Ephesus **c** the Way.
Ro 4: 1 What were his experiences **c** this question of being
9:25 **C** the Gentiles, God says in the prophecy of Hosea,
9:27 **C** Israel, Isaiah the prophet cried out,
1Co 5: 3 **C** the one who has done this, I have already
Gal 1: 7 by those who twist and change the truth **c** Christ.
Rev 1: 1 which God gave him **c** the events that will happen

CONCERNS (3) [CONCERN]
Job 27:11 I will not conceal anything that **c** the Almighty.
Da 10:14 in the future, for this vision **c** a time yet to come."
1Co 7:32 you do, I want you to be free from the **c** of this life.

CONCERTED (1)
Ac 18:12 some Jews rose in **c** action against Paul and brought

CONCESSION (2) [CONCEDE]
Mt 19: 8 "Moses permitted divorce as a **c** to your
Mk 10: 5 "He wrote those instructions only as a **c** to your

CONCISION [KJV] See MUTILATORS

CONCLUDE (1) [CONCLUDED, CONCLUSION, CONCLUSIONS]
Ac 16:10 for we could only **c** that God was calling us to

CONCLUDED (4) [CONCLUDE]
Nu 24:23 Balaam **c** his prophecies by saying: / "Alas,
Ecc 3:12 So I **c** that there is nothing better for people than to
4: 2 So I **c** that the dead are better off than the living.
Da 6: 5 So they **c**, "Our only chance of finding grounds

CONCLUSION (4) [CONCLUDE]
Nu 6:13 At the **c** of their time of separation as Nazirites,
Ecc 7:27 "This is my **c**," says the Teacher. "I came to this
12:13 Here is my final **c**: Fear God and obey his
Lk 23:15 Herod came to the same **c** and sent him back to us.

CONCLUSIONS (3) [CONCLUDE]
Ecc 2:12 and anyone else would come to the same **c** I did.
10:13 foolish premises, their **c** will be wicked madness.
1Co 4: 5 So be careful not to jump to **c** before the Lord

CONCORD [KJV] See PARTNER

CONCOURSE [KJV] COMMOTION, CROWDS

CONCUBINE (16) [CONCUBINE'S, CONCUBINES]
Ge 22:24 Nahor had four other children from his **c** Reumah.
35:22 was there, Reuben slept with Bilhah, his father's **c**,
36:12 another son named Amalek, born to Timna, his **c**.
Jdg 8:31 He also had a **c** in Shechem, who bore him a son
19: 1 a woman from Bethlehem in Judah to be his **c**.
19: 9 as he and his **c** and servant were preparing to leave,
19:10 So he took his two saddled donkeys and his **c**
19:24 Here, take my virgin daughter and this man's **c**.
19:25 Then the Levite took his **c** and pushed her out the
20: 4 said, "My **c** and I came to Gibeah, a town in the
20: 5 to kill me, and they raped my **c** until she was dead.
2Sa 21:11 David learned what Rizpah, Saul's **c**, had done,
1Ch 1:32 Abraham's **c**, were Zimran, Jokshan, Medan,
1:33 All these were sons of Abraham by his **c** Keturah.
2:46 Caleb's **c** Ephah gave birth to Haran, Moza,
7:14 born to his Aramean **c**, were Asriel and Makir.

CONCUBINE'S (1) [CONCUBINE]
Jdg 19:29 took a knife and cut his **c** body into twelve pieces.

CONCUBINES (25) [CONCUBINE]
Ge 25: 6 he gave gifts to the sons of his **c** and sent them off
31:33 and then he searched the tents of the two **c**,
32:22 night Jacob got up and sent his two wives, two **c**,
33: 2 with his two **c** and their children at the front,
33: 6 Then the **c** came forward with their children
2Sa 3: 7 Abner of sleeping with one of his father's **c**,
5:13 David married more wives and **c**, and he had many
15:16 He left no one behind except ten of his **c** to keep
16:21 told him, "Go and sleep with your father's **c**,
16:22 went into the tent to sleep with his father's **c**.
19: 5 your sons, your daughters, and your wives and **c**.
20: 3 he instructed that the ten **c** he had left to keep
1Ki 11: 3 He had seven hundred wives and three hundred **c**.
1Ch 2:48 Another of Caleb's **c**, Maacah, gave birth to
3: 9 the sons of David, not including the sons of his **c**.
5: 1 his father by sleeping with one of his father's **c**,
2Ch 11:21 Maacah more than any of his other wives and **c**.
11:21 In all, he had eighteen wives and sixty **c**, and they
Ps 45: 9 Kings' daughters are among your **c**. / At your right
Ecc 2: 8 both men and women, and had many beautiful **c**.
SS 6: 8 and eighty **c** and unnumbered virgins available to
6: 9 they see her; even queens and **c** sing her praises!
Da 5: 2 his wives, and his **c** might drink from them.
5: 3 his nobles, his wives, and his **c** drank from them.
5:23 and **c** have been drinking wine from them while

CONCUPISCENCE [KJV] See DESIRES, PASSION

CONDEMN (36) [CONDEMNATION, CONDEMNED, CONDEMNING, CONDEMNS, SELF-CONDEMNED]

Nu 23: 8 those whom God has not cursed? / How can I **c**
Job 10: 2 I will say to God, 'Don't simply **c** me—tell me the
15: 6 But why should I **c** you? Your own mouth does!
34: 17 Are you going to **c** the almighty Judge?
40: 8 my justice and **c** me so you can say you are right?
Ps 26: 9 fate of sinners. / Don't **c** me along with murderers.
94: 21 attack the righteous / and **c** the innocent to death.
109: 31 ready to save them from those who **c** them.
Pr 17: 15 those who acquit the guilty and **c** the innocent.
18: 5 for a judge to favor the guilty or **c** the innocent.
Eze 20: 4 of man, bring judgment against them and **c** them.
Mt 12: 41 against this generation on judgment day and **c** it,
12: 42 against this generation on judgment day and **c** it,
Mk 3: 2 on the Sabbath? If he did, they planned to **c** him.
Lk 11: 31 against this generation on judgment day and **c** it,
11: 32 against this generation on judgment day and **c** it,
Jn 3: 17 God did not send his Son into the world to **c** it,
8: 10 your accusers? Didn't even one of them **c** you?"
8: 26 I have much to say about you and much to **c**,
Ro 2: 3 that God will judge and **c** others for doing them
2: 22 You **c** idolatry, but do you steal from pagan
3: 7 and **c** me as a sinner if my dishonesty highlights
8: 34 Who then will **c** us? Will Christ Jesus? No, for he
14: 3 And those who won't eat certain foods must not **c**
14: 4 Who are you to **c** God's servants? They are
14: 10 So why do you **c** another Christian? Why do you
14: 13 So don't **c** each other anymore. Decide instead to
14: 22 Blessed are those who do not **c** themselves by
2Co 7: 3 I'm not saying this to **c** you, for I said before that
Col 2: 16 So don't let anyone **c** you for what you eat
2: 18 Don't let anyone **c** you by insisting on self-denial.
Tit 3: 11 the truth. They are sinning, and they **c** themselves.
Heb 6: 8 is useless. The farmer will **c** that field and burn it.
Jas 4: 11 If you criticize each other and **c** each other,
4: 12 So what right do you have to **c** your neighbor?
1Jn 3: 20 even if our hearts **c** us. For God is greater than our

CONDEMNATION (7) [CONDEMN]

Ezr 10: 10 Now we are even more deeply under **c** than we
Ro 5: 16 For Adam's sin led to **c**, but we have the free gift
5: 18 Yes, Adam's one sin brought **c** upon everyone,
7: 13 Sin used what was good to bring about my **c**.
8: 1 So now there is no **c** for those who belong to Christ
1Co 15: 17 is useless, and you are still under **c** for your sins.
2Co 3: 9 If the old covenant, which brings **c**, was glorious,

CONDEMNED (29) [CONDEMN]

Nu 23: 8 I condemn / those whom the LORD has not **c**?
Job 32: 3 because they had **c** God by their inability to answer
Ps 1: 5 They will be **c** at the time of judgment.
37: 33 or let the godly be **c** when they are brought before
79: 11 Demonstrate your great power by saving those **c** to
102: 20 groans of the prisoners, / to release those **c** to die.
Isa 24: 22 and put in prison until they are tried and **c**.
Da 2: 9 If you don't tell me the dream, you will be **c**.
Mt 12: 7 But you would not have **c** those who aren't guilty
12: 37 you will be justified by them or you will be **c**."
27: 3 betrayed him, realized that Jesus had been **c** to die,
Mk 14: 64 is your verdict?" And they all **c** him to death.
16: 16 But anyone who refuses to believe will be **c**.
Lk 24: 20 arrested him and handed him over to be **c** to death,
Jn 5: 24 They will never be **c** for their sins, but they have
7: 23 So why should I be **c** for making a man completely
Ac 26: 10 And I cast my vote against them when they were **c**
Ro 3: 8 Those who say such things deserve to be **c**,
14: 16 Then you will not be **c** for doing something you
14: 23 They would be **c** for not acting in faith before God.
1Co 4: 9 of war at the end of a victor's parade, **c** to die.
10: 30 and enjoy it, why should I be **c** for eating it?
11: 32 by the Lord, we will not be **c** with the world.
14: 24 of sin, and they will be **c** by what you say.
2Th 2: 12 Then they will be **c** for not believing the truth
Heb 11: 7 By his faith he **c** the rest of the world and was
Jas 5: 6 You have **c** and killed good people who had no
5: 12 or no, so that you will not sin and be **c** for it.
2Pe 2: 3 But God **c** them long ago, and their destruction is

CONDEMNING (3) [CONDEMN]

Ac 13: 27 and their leaders fulfilled prophecy by **c** Jesus to
Ro 2: 1 and should be punished, you are **c** yourself,
Jas 4: 11 then you are criticizing and **c** God's law.

CONDEMNS (1) [CONDEMN]

Pr 12: 2 who are good, but he **c** those who plan wickedness.

CONDESCENSION (2)

2Ki 19: 22 At whom did you look in such proud **c**? / It was the
Isa 37: 23 At whom did you look in such proud **c**? / It was the

CONDITION (6) [CONDITIONS]

Ge 34: 22 But they will consider staying here only on one **c**.
1Sa 11: 2 "All right," Nahash said, "but only on one **c**.
2Ki 12: 7 all be spent on getting the Temple into good **c**."
Ezr 9: 15 though in such a **c** none of us can stand in your
Jer 6: 18 all you nations. Take note of my people's **c**.
Eze 29: 16 Egypt's shattered **c** will remind Israel of how

CONDITIONS (4) [CONDITION]

Ex 15: 25 the following **c** to test their faithfulness to him:
1Ki 20: 34 Then Ahab said, "I will let you go under these **c**."
Ecc 11: 4 If you wait for perfect **c**, you will never get
Jer 32: 11 which contained the terms and **c** of the purchase,

CONDUCT (18)

Ex 18: 20 and show them how to **c** their lives.
2Sa 19: 31 from Rogelim to **c** the king across the Jordan.
Ezr 7: 14 and my Council of Seven hereby instruct you to **c**
Ne 13: 10 and the singers who were to **c** the worship services
Est 3: 4 about this to see if he would tolerate Mordecai's **c**,
Ps 112: 5 who lend freely and **c** their business fairly.
Pr 1: 3 good **c**, and doing what is right, just, and fair.
10: 23 for a fool, while wise **c** is a pleasure to the wise.
18: 1 snarling at every sound principle of **c**.
20: 11 the way they act, whether their **c** is pure and right.
Jer 32: 19 You are very aware of the **c** of all people, and you
Eze 16: 27 and even they were shocked by your lewd **c**!
36: 17 To me their **c** was as filthy as a bloody rag.
Ac 25: 20 I was perplexed as to how to **c** an investigation of
Gal 6: 5 For we are each responsible for our own **c**.
Php 3: 18 that there are many whose **c** shows they are really
1Ti 3: 15 you will know how people must **c** themselves in
Tit 2: 12 with self-control, right **c**, and devotion to God,

CONFECTION [KJV] See INCENSE

CONFECTIONARIES [KJV] See PERFUMES

CONFEDERACY [KJV] See ALLIES

CONFER (1) [CONFERENCE, CONFERRED]

2Ki 6: 8 he would **c** with his officers and say, "We will

CONFERENCE (2) [CONFER]

Jer 40: 15 Later Johanan had a private **c** with Gedaliah
Da 11: 27 these kings will plot against each other at the **c**

CONFERRED (2) [CONFER]

Ac 4: 15 of the council chamber and **c** among themselves.
25: 12 Festus **c** with his advisers and then replied,

CONFESS (26) [CONFESSED, CONFESSES, CONFESSING, CONFESSION]

Ex 10: 16 "I **c** my sin against the LORD your God
Lev 5: 5 guilt in any of these ways, they must **c** their sin
16: 21 and **c** over it all the sins and rebellion of the
26: 40 "But at last my people will **c** their sins and the sins
Nu 5: 7 They must **c** their sin and make full restitution for
1Ki 8: 35 and **c** your name and turn from their sins
2Ch 6: 26 and **c** your name and turn from their sins
Ezr 10: 2 "We **c** that we have been unfaithful to our God,
10: 11 **C** your sin to the LORD, the God of your
Ne 1: 6 I **c** that we have sinned against you. Yes, even my
Ps 32: 3 When I refused to **c** my sin, / I was weak
32: 5 to myself, "I will **c** my rebellion to the LORD."
32: 6 let all the godly **c** their rebellion to you while there
38: 18 But I **c** my sins; / I am deeply sorry for what I have
Pr 28: 13 But if they **c** and forsake them, they will receive
Isa 45: 23 and every tongue will **c** allegiance to my name."
Jer 3: 13 **C** that you refused to follow me. I, the LORD,
14: 20 we **c** our wickedness and that of our ancestors,
Eze 12: 16 so they can **c** to their captors about how wicked
Ac 22: 24 and ordered him lashed with whips to make him **c**
Ro 10: 9 For if you **c** with your mouth that Jesus is Lord
14: 11 and every tongue will **c** allegiance to God.' "
Php 2: 11 and every tongue will **c** that Jesus Christ is Lord,
Jas 5: 16 **C** your sins to each other and pray for each other
1Jn 1: 9 But if we **c** our sins to him, he is faithful and just
Rev 12: 17 and **c** that they belong to Jesus.

CONFESSED (18) [CONFESS]

Ex 9: 27 and Aaron. "I finally admit my fault," he **c**.
Nu 22: 34 Then Balaam **c** to the angel of the LORD,
Dt 1: 41 "Then you **c**, 'We have sinned against the
Jdg 16: 17 "My hair has never been cut," he **c**, "for I was
1Sa 7: 6 and **c** that they had sinned against the LORD.
12: 10 "Then they cried to the LORD again and **c**,
26: 21 Then Saul **c**, "I have sinned. Come back home,
2Sa 1: 16 "for you yourself **c** that you killed the LORD's
12: 13 Then David **c** to Nathan, "I have sinned against
2Ch 30: 22 and the people **c** their sins to the LORD, the God
Ne 9: 2 from all foreigners as they **c** their own sins
Ps 32: 5 Finally, I **c** all my sins to you / and stopped trying
66: 18 If I had not **c** the sin in my heart, / my Lord would
Da 9: 4 I prayed to the LORD my God and **c**: "O Lord,
Mt 3: 6 And when they **c** their sins, he baptized them in the
Mk 1: 5 And when they **c** their sins, he baptized them in the
Ac 19: 18 Many who became believers **c** their sinful
1Ti 6: 12 which you have **c** so well before many witnesses.

CONFESSES (2) [CONFESS]

Mt 18: 15 If the other person listens and **c** it, you have won
1Jn 2: 23 But anyone who **c** the Son has the Father also.

CONFESSING (3) [CONFESS]

Ne 9: 3 Then for three more hours they took turns **c** their
Da 9: 20 I went on praying and **c** my sin and the sins of my
Ro 10: 10 and it is by **c** with your mouth that you are saved.

CONFESSION (2) [CONFESS]

Jos 7: 19 Make your **c** and tell me what you have done.
Ezr 10: 1 While Ezra prayed and made this **c**, weeping

CONFIDE (2)

Jdg 16: 15 "How can you say you love me when you don't **c**
Jn 15: 15 because a master doesn't **c** in his servants.

CONFIDENCE (40) [CONFIDENT, CONFIDENTLY, SELF-CONFIDENCE]

Ex 19: 9 Then they will always have **c** in you." Moses told
Jdg 9: 26 and gained the **c** of the people of Shechem.
1Ki 1: 7 son of Zeruiah and Abiathar the priest into his **c**,
Job 4: 6 Does your reverence for God give you no **c**?
Ps 40: 4 trust the LORD, / who have no **c** in the proud,
118: 8 better to trust the LORD / than to put **c** in people.
118: 9 better to trust the LORD / than to put **c** in princes.
146: 3 Don't put your **c** in powerful people; / there is no
Pr 11: 13 but those who are trustworthy can keep a **c**.
14: 16 and avoid danger; fools plunge ahead with great **c**.
25: 19 Putting **c** in an unreliable person is like chewing
Isa 30: 15 In quietness and **c** is your strength. But you would
32: 17 Quietness and **c** will fill the land forever.
Jer 17: 7 and have made the LORD their hope and **c**.
Eze 38: 11 and destroy these people who live in such **c**!
Ac 24: 10 and this gives me **c** as I make my defense.
1Co 9: 21 In this way, I gain their **c** and bring them to Christ.
2Co 1: 12 We can say with **c** and a clear conscience that we
3: 12 Since this new covenant gives us such **c**, we can be
7: 4 I have the highest **c** in you, and my pride in you is
7: 16 very happy now because I have complete **c** in you.
8: 22 because of his increased **c** in you.
Php 1: 14 many of the Christians here have gained **c**
2: 24 And I have **c** from the Lord that I myself will come
3: 3 We put no **c** in human effort. Instead, we boast
3: 4 Yet I could have **c** in myself if anyone could.
3: 4 If others have reason for **c** in their own efforts,
Col 2: 2 I want them to have full **c** because they have
1Th 5: 8 and wearing as our helmet the **c** of our salvation.
1Ti 1: 18 May they give you the **c** to fight well in the Lord's
3: 13 and will have increased **c** in their faith in Christ
2Ti 3: 6 and win the **c** of vulnerable women who are
Tit 1: 2 This truth gives them the **c** of eternal life,
Heb 6: 18 for we can hold on to his promise with **c**.
6: 19 This **c** is like a strong and trustworthy anchor for
11: 20 He had **c** in what God was going to do in the
13: 6 That is why we can say with **c**, / "The Lord is my
2Pe 1: 19 we have even greater **c** in the message proclaimed
1Jn 3: 21 is clear, we can come to God with bold **c**.
4: 17 but we can face him with **c** because we are like

CONFIDENT (25) [CONFIDENCE]

2Ki 18: 19 What are you trusting in that makes you so **c**?
Job 18: 7 The **c** stride of the wicked will be shortened.
Ps 27: 3 no fear. / Even if they attack me, / I remain **c**.
27: 13 Yet I am **c** that I will see the LORD's goodness
57: 7 My heart is **c** in you, O God; / no wonder I can
108: 1 My heart is **c** in you, O God; / no wonder I can
112: 8 They are **c** and fearless / and can face their foes
Isa 36: 4 What are you trusting in that makes you so **c**?
Hos 12: 6 and always live in **c** dependence on your God.
Ro 5: 4 and character strengthens our **c** expectation of
2Co 1: 7 We are **c** that as you share in suffering, you will
1: 10 And we are **c** that he will continue to deliver us.
3: 4 We are **c** of all this because of our great trust in
5: 6 So we are always **c**, even though we know that as
5: 8 Yes, we are fully **c**, and we would rather be away
Col 4: 12 and perfect, fully **c** of the whole will of God.
2Th 3: 4 And we are **c** in the Lord that you are practicing
1Ti 1: 7 they are talking about, even though they seem so **c**.
Phm 1: 21 I am **c** as I write this letter that you will do what I
Heb 3: 6 up our courage and remain **c** in our hope in Christ.
6: 9 We are **c** that you are meant for better things,
10: 35 Do not throw away this **c** trust in the Lord,
11: 1 It is the **c** assurance that what we hope for is going
1Jn 3: 19 so we will be **c** when we stand before the Lord,
5: 14 And we can be **c** that he will listen to us whenever

CONFIDENTIALLY (1)

1Sa 18: 22 Then Saul told his men to say **c** to David,

CONFIDENTLY (7) [CONFIDENCE]

Ps 112: 7 they **c** trust the LORD to care for them.
Mic 7: 7 I wait **c** for God to save me, and my God will
Ro 5: 2 and we **c** and joyfully look forward to sharing
8: 25 we don't have yet, we must wait patiently and **c**.
Heb 11: 10 because he was **c** looking forward to a city with
11: 22 **c** spoke of God's bringing the people of Israel out
1Pe 1: 21 your faith and hope can be placed **c** in God.

CONFINED (2)

Ne 6: 10 grandson of Mehetabel, who was **c** to his home.
Jer 33: 1 While Jeremiah was still **c** in the courtyard of the

CONFIRM (8) [CONFIRMATION, CONFIRMED, CONFIRMING, CONFIRMS]

Ge 17: 19 and I will **c** my everlasting covenant with him
Nu 30: 13 So her husband may either **c** or nullify any vows
Dt 29: 13 He wants to **c** you today as his people and to **c** that
2Sa 7: 25 my family. **C** it as a promise that will last forever.
1Ki 1: 14 I will come and **c** everything you have said."

Da 9:24 to c the prophetic vision, and to anoint the Most
Ro 9:1 and the Holy Spirit c that what I am saying is true.

CONFIRMATION (2) [CONFIRM]

Ge 21:30 "They are my gift to you as a public c that I dug
Isa 42:6 for I have given you to my people as the personal c

CONFIRMED (11) [CONFIRM]

1Sa 3:20 that Samuel was c as a prophet of the LORD.
1Ki 2:24 The LORD has c me and placed me on the throne
2Ki 23:3 he c all the terms of the covenant that were written
1Ch 16:17 He c it to Jacob as a decree, / to the people of
Est 9:32 So the command of Esther c the practices of
Job 15:18 And it is c by the experience of wise men who
Ps 105:10 He c it to Jacob as a decree, / to the people of
Mt 18:16 so that everything you say may be c by two
Mk 15:45 The officer c the fact, and Pilate told Joseph he
Ac 15:8 c that he accepts Gentiles by giving them the Holy
2Ti 2:2 things that have been c by many reliable witnesses.

CONFIRMING (2) [CONFIRM]

Est 3:10 c his decision by removing his signet ring from his
Mk 16:20 c what they said by many miraculous signs.

CONFIRMS (2) [CONFIRM]

Ex 24:8 "This blood c the covenant the LORD has made
Heb 9:20 "This blood c the covenant God has made with

CONFISCATED (3) [CONFISCATION]

2Sa 5:21 their idols there, so David and his troops c them.
Isa 65:22 when invaders took the houses and c the vineyards.
Mic 2:4 God has c our land, / taking it from us.

CONFISCATES (1) [CONFISCATION]

Job 12:21 upon princes and c weapons from the strong.

CONFISCATION (1) [CONFISCATED, CONFISCATES]

Ezr 7:26 banishment, c of goods, or imprisonment."

CONFLICT (5)

Da 11:20 he will die, though neither in battle nor open c.
2Co 7:5 Outside there was c from every direction,
Gal 3:21 is there a c between God's law and God's
5:17 and your choices are never free from this c.
5:23 and self-control. Here there is no c with the law.

CONFRONT (8) [CONFRONTED, CONFRONTS]

Lev 19:17 "C your neighbors directly so you will not be held
2Ki 18:17 with a huge army to c King Hezekiah in Jerusalem.
Job 41:11 Who will c me and remain safe? Everything under
Pr 17:12 robbed of her cubs than to c a fool caught in folly.
Isa 22:15 the LORD Almighty, told me to c Shebna,
36:2 from Lachish to c King Hezekiah in Jerusalem.
Eze 16:2 "Son of man, c Jerusalem with her loathsome sins.
Mk 7:1 of religious law arrived from Jerusalem to c Jesus.

CONFRONTED (7) [CONFRONT]

Ex 4:24 the LORD c Moses and was about to kill him.
Jdg 1:24 who c a man coming out of the city. They said to
2Ch 26:18 They c King Uzziah and said, "It is not for you,
28:12 with this and c the men returning from battle.
Ne 13:11 I immediately c the leaders and demanded,
13:17 So I c the leaders of Judah, "Why are you
13:25 So I c them and called down curses on them.

CONFRONTS (1) [CONFRONT]

Ps 127:5 He will not be put to shame when he c his accusers

CONFUSE (3) [CONFUSED, CONFUSING, CONFUSION]

Ps 55:9 Destroy them, Lord, and c their speech, / for I see
144:6 your enemies! / Release your arrows and c them!
Isa 19:3 Egyptians will lose heart, and I will c their plans.

CONFUSED (15) [CONFUSE]

Ge 11:9 because it was there that the LORD c the people
Ex 14:3 Then Pharaoh will think, 'Those Israelites are c.
2Sa 22:15 his lightning flashed, and they were c.
Job 37:20 that I want to speak? Can we speak when we are c?
Ps 18:14 his lightning flashed, and they were greatly c.
73:10 And so the people are dismayed and c,
Isa 24:19 Everything is lost, abandoned, and c.
41:11 all your angry enemies lie there, c and ashamed.
Jer 13:13 in this land so c that they will seem drunk—
14:3 c and desperate, covering their heads in grief.
14:9 Are you also c? Are you helpless to save us?
Joel 1:18 The cattle wander about c because there is no
Lk 1:29 C and disturbed, Mary tried to think what the angel
Ro 1:21 The result was that their minds became dark and c.
Eph 4:17 longer as the ungodly do, for they are hopelessly c.

CONFUSING (1) [CONFUSE]

Gal 5:10 whoever it is, who has been troubling and c you.

CONFUSION (15) [CONFUSE]

Ex 14:24 pillar of fire and cloud, and he threw them into c.
Dt 7:23 He will throw them into complete c until they are
28:20 c, and disillusionment in everything you do,
1Sa 7:10 and the Philistines were thrown into such c that the
14:19 and c in the Philistine camp grew louder
14:20 each other. There was terrible c everywhere.
Ne 4:8 fight against Jerusalem and to bring about c there.
Est 3:15 sat down to drink, but the city of Susa fell into c.
Job 10:22 a land of utter gloom where c reigns and the light
Ps 35:4 those trying to kill me; / turn them back in c.
Isa 22:5 What a day of c and terror the Lord, the LORD
Eze 22:5 O infamous city, filled with c, you will be mocked
Ac 19:29 to gather, and soon the city was filled with c.
19:32 Everything was in c. In fact, most of them didn't
21:34 couldn't find out the truth in all the uproar and c,

CONGRATULATE (4) [CONGRATULATED]

2Sa 8:10 he sent his son Joram to c David on his success.
19:7 Now go out there and c the troops, for I swear by
1Ki 5:1 king of Israel, Hiram sent ambassadors to c him.
1Ch 18:10 he sent his son Joram to c David on his success.

CONGRATULATED (1) [CONGRATULATE]

1Ki 1:47 the royal officials went to King David and c him,

CONGREGATION (4)

Ps 35:18 Then I will thank you in front of the entire c.
107:32 Let them exalt him publicly before the c
118:2 Let the c of Israel repeat: / "His faithful love
Ac 21:5 the entire c, including wives and children,

CONIES [KJV] See (ROCK) BADGERS

CONNECT (1) [CONNECTED, CONNECTION]

Ex 36:13 Then fifty gold clasps were made to c the loops on

CONNECTED (10) [CONNECT]

Ex 26:24 These corner frames will be c at the bottom
27:17 All the posts around the courtyard must be c by
28:38 thus bearing the guilt c with any errors regarding
36:29 These corner frames were c at the bottom
36:38 This curtain was c by five hooks to five posts.
Nu 18:1 be held liable for violations c with the priesthood.
1Ki 6:6 The rooms were c to the walls of the Temple by
7:32 Under the panels were four wheels that were c to
Isa 19:23 that day Egypt and Assyria will be c by a highway.
Col 2:19 But they are not c to Christ, the head of the body.

CONNECTION (4) [CONNECT]

Nu 29:39 and offerings you present in c with vows,
Ecc 3:10 I have thought about this in c with the various
Da 6:5 will be in c with the requirements of his religion."
Heb 7:14 and Moses never mentioned Judah in c with the

CONONIAH [KJV] See CONANIAH

CONQUER (59) [CONQUERED, CONQUERING, CONQUEROR, CONQUEST, CONQUESTS]

Ge 14:20 Most High, / who has helped you c your enemies."
22:17 sand on the seashore. They will c their enemies,
Ex 23:24 you must utterly c them and break down their
34:24 and c your land when you go to appear before the
Nu 13:30 to take the land," he said. "We can certainly c it!"
21:2 "If you will help us c these people, we will
22:6 Then perhaps I will be able to c them and drive
22:11 Perhaps then I will be able to c them and drive
Dt 1:41 thinking it would be easy to c the hill country.
2:31 over to you. Begin now to c and occupy his land.'
2:36 "The LORD our God helped us c Aroer on the
7:2 hands these nations over to you and you c them,
7:17 'How can we ever c these nations that are so much
9:3 so that you will quickly c them and drive them out,
17:14 is giving you, and you will c it and settle there.
28:7 "The LORD will c your enemies when they
Jos 1:14 across the Jordan to help them c their territory.
9:24 instructed his servant Moses to c this entire land
21:44 for the LORD helped them c all their enemies.
Jdg 1:3 Then we will help you c your territory."
2:23 drive the nations out or allow Joshua to c them all.
1Sa 17:46 Today the LORD will c you, and I will kill you
23:4 to Keilah, for I will help you c the Philistines."
2Sa 10:3 spy out the city so that they can come in and c it!"
11:25 as another! Fight harder next time, and c the city!"
1Ki 8:46 angry with them and let their enemies c them
2Ki 3:19 You will c the best of their cities, even the fortified
13:17 for you will completely c the Arameans at Aphek.
16:5 on Ahaz. They besieged Jerusalem but did not c it.
1Ch 19:3 spy out the land so that they can come in and c it!"
2Ch 6:36 angry with them and let their enemies c them
24:24 the LORD helped them c the much larger army of
Ne 9:22 "Then you helped our ancestors c great kingdoms
9:28 and once more you let their enemies c them.
9:30 the pagan inhabitants of the land to c them.
Ps 5:8 right path, O LORD, / or my enemies will c me.
44:3 They did not c the land with their swords; / it was
91:10 no evil will c you; / no plague will come near your
Pr 16:32 it is better to have self-control than to c a city.
21:22 The wise c the city of the strong and level the
Ecc 4:12 but two can stand back-to-back and c.
Isa 10:7 my people as part of his plan to c the world.
14:21 Do not let them rise and c the land or rebuild the
Jer 15:20 They will not c you, for I will protect and deliver
27:7 But then many nations and great kings will c
27:9 who say, "The king of Babylon will not c you."
27:14 telling you, 'The king of Babylon will not c you.'
32:24 been handed over to the Babylonians, who will c it.
Da 2:44 that will never be destroyed; no one will ever c it.
11:18 turn his attention to the coastal cities and c many.
11:42 He will c many countries, and Egypt will not
Joel 3:17 and foreign armies will never c her again.
Mic 6:14 save a little, but I will give it to those who c you.
Hab 1:6 nation who will march across the world and c it.
Mt 16:18 my church, and all the powers of hell will not c it.
Ro 12:21 evil get the best of you, but c evil by doing good.
2Co 10:5 With these weapons we c their rebellious ideas,
Php 3:21 using the same mighty power that he will use to c
Rev 11:7 war against them. He will c them and kill them.

CONQUERED (63) [CONQUER]

Ge 14:5 They c the Rephaites in Ashteroth-karnaim,
Lev 26:25 you there, and you will be c by your enemies.
Nu 21:26 He had c a former Moabite king and seized all his
24:18 will be taken over, / and Seir, its enemy, will be c,
32:4 the LORD has c this whole area for the people of
32:29 then when the land is c, you must give them the
32:38 changed the names of some of the towns they c
32:39 of the tribe of Manasseh went to Gilead and c it,
Dt 2:34 We c all his towns and completely destroyed
3:4 We c all sixty of his towns, the entire Argob region
3:6 We destroyed all the people in every town we c—
3:10 We had now c all the cities on the plateau, and all
4:47 Israel c his land and that of King Og of Bashan—
4:48 So Israel c all the area from Aroer at the edge of
26:1 and you have c it and settled there,
Jos 2:13 when Jericho is c, you will let me live, along with
10:40 So Joshua c the whole region—the kings
10:42 In a single campaign Joshua c all these kings
11:16 So Joshua c the entire region—the hill country,
13:1 are growing old, and much land remains to be c.
13:4 of the Avvites in the south also remains to be c.
13:4 In the north, this area has not yet been c:
15:17 was the one who c it, so Acsah became Othniel's
21:43 give their ancestors, and they c it and settled there.
23:4 as well as the land of those we have already c—
Jdg 1:13 was the one who c it, so Acsah became Othniel's
3:30 So Moab was c by Israel that day, and the land was
1Sa 12:9 so he let them be c by Sisera, the general of
14:48 He did great deeds and c the Amalekites,
2Sa 8:2 David also c the land of Moab. He made the people
22:38 destroyed them; / I did not stop until they were c.
1Ki 4:21 The c peoples of those lands sent tribute money to
11:24 After David c Hadadezer, Rezon and his men fled
15:20 They c the towns of Ijon, Dan, Abel-beth-maacah,
2Ki 10:32 King Hazael c several sections of the country
10:33 He c the area from the town of Aroer by the Arnon
14:7 He also c Sela and changed its name to Joktheel,
15:29 He also c the regions of Gilead, Galilee,
18:8 He also c the Philistines as far distant as Gaza
18:13 to attack the fortified cities of Judah and c them.
19:23 I have c the highest mountains—/ yes, the remotest
1Ch 18:2 David also c the land of Moab, and the Moabites
2Ch 8:3 fought against the city of Hamath-zobah and c it.
12:4 Shishak c Judah's fortified cities and
16:4 They c the towns of Ijon, Dan, Abel-beth-maacah,
17:2 to the towns of Ephraim that his father, Asa, had c.
27:5 waged war against the Ammonites and c them.
Ps 18:37 and caught them; / I did not stop until they were c.
79:1 O God, pagan nations have c your land,
Isa 10:8 of my princes will soon be a king, ruling a c land.
36:1 to attack the fortified cities of Judah and c them.
37:24 I have c the highest mountains—/ yes, the remotest
48:11 will not be able to claim that their gods have c me.
Jer 27:8 and disease upon that nation until Babylon has c it.
32:23 Our ancestors came and c it and lived in it,
La 1:16 children have no future, for the enemy has c us."
Hos 9:6 destruction from Assyria, you will be c by Egypt.
Na 2:13 Never again will you bring back plunder from c
Zec 9:5 Gaza will be c and its king killed, and Ashkelon
Mt 17:25 their own people or the foreigners they have c?"
Lk 21:24 And Jerusalem will be c and trampled down by the
1Co 15:28 Then, when he has c all things, the Son will
Rev 5:5 the tribe of Judah, the heir to David's throne, has c.

CONQUERING (3) [CONQUER]

2Sa 8:1 and humbled the Philistines by c Gath,
1Ch 18:1 and humbled the Philistines by c Gath
Col 2:23 But they have no effect when it comes to c a

CONQUEROR (2) [CONQUER]

1Sa 26:25 You will do heroic deeds and be a great c."
Mic 1:15 of Mareshah, I will bring a c to capture your town.

CONQUEST (4) [CONQUER]

2Ch 25:19 You may be very proud of your c of Edom, but my
30:6 us who have survived the c of the Assyrian kings.
Isa 29:8 your enemies will dream of a victorious c over
Am 6:13 And just as stupid is this bragging about your c of

CONQUESTS (3) [CONQUER]

Isa 18:2 are feared far and wide for their c and destruction.
18:7 are feared far and wide for their c and destruction.
Hab 1:17 Will they succeed forever in their heartless c?

CONSCIENCE (30) [CONSCIENCES, CONSCIENTIOUS]

Ge 37:26 our brother? That would just give us a guilty c.

1Sa 24: 5 But then David's **c** began bothering him
25:31 Then you won't have to carry on your **c** the
2Sa 24:10 taken the census, David's **c** began to bother him.
Job 27: 6 My **c** is clear for as long as I live.
Pr 28:14 Blessed are those who have a tender **c**,
28:17 A murderer's tormented **c** will drive him into the
Ac 23: 1 I have always lived before God in all good **c**!"
24:16 I always try to maintain a clear **c** before God
Ro 7:16 and my bad **c** shows that I agree that the law is
9: 1 and my **c** and the Holy Spirit confirm that what I
13: 5 to keep from being punished and to keep a clear **c**.
14: 2 But another believer who has a sensitive **c** will eat
1Co 4: 4 My **c** is clear, but that isn't what matters. It is the
8: 9 a brother or sister with a weaker **c** to stumble.
8:10 but they will be encouraged to violate their **c** by
10:25 offered to idols, and then your **c** won't be bothered.
10:27 about it. Your **c** should not be bothered by this.
10:28 out of consideration for the **c** of the one who told
10:29 It might not be a matter of **c** for you, but it is for
2Co 1:12 and a clear **c** that we have been honest
1Ti 1: 5 from a pure heart, a clear **c**, and sincere faith.
1:19 your faith in Christ, and always keep your **c** clear.
3: 9 of the Christian faith and must live with a clear **c**.
2Ti 1: 3 He is the God I serve with a clear **c**, just as my
Heb 13:18 for our **c** is clear and we want to live honorably in
1Pe 2:19 is pleased with you when, for the sake of your **c**,
3:16 in a gentle and respectful way. Keep your **c** clear.
3:21 your body; it is an appeal to God from a clean **c**.
1Jn 3:21 Dear friends, if our **c** is clear, we can come to God

CONSCIENCES (7) [CONSCIENCE]

Ro 2:15 for their own **c** either accuse them or tell them they
1Co 8: 7 worship of real gods, and their weak **c** are violated.
1Ti 1:19 For some people have deliberately violated their **c**;
4: 2 They pretend to be religious, but their **c** are dead.
Tit 1:15 because their minds and **c** are defiled.
Heb 9: 9 able to cleanse the **c** of the people who bring them.
10:22 For our evil **c** have been sprinkled with Christ's

CONSCIENTIOUS (1) [CONSCIENCE]

2Ch 29:34 For the Levites had been more **c** about purifying

CONSCRIPT (2) [CONSCRIPTED]

1Ki 9:22 But Solomon did not **c** any of the Israelites for
2Ch 8: 9 But Solomon did not **c** any of the Israelites for

CONSCRIPTED (3) [CONSCRIPT]

1Ki 9:15 that Solomon **c** to build the LORD's Temple,
9:21 So Solomon **c** them for his labor force, and they
2Ch 8: 8 So Solomon **c** them for his labor force, and they

CONSENT (3) [CONSENTED]

Job 39: 9 "Will the wild ox **c** to being tamed? Will it stay in
Hos 8: 4 appointed kings and princes, but not with my **c**.
Phm 1:14 But I didn't want to do anything without your **c**.

CONSENTED (1) [CONSENT]

1Sa 17:37 Saul finally **c**. "All right, go ahead," he said.

CONSEQUENCES (19) [CONSEQUENTLY]

Lev 20:17 with his sister, he will suffer the **c** of his guilt.
24:15 Those who blaspheme God will suffer the **c** of
Nu 9:13 proper time. They will suffer the **c** of their guilt.
14:34 a year for each day, suffering the **c** of your sins.
15:31 completely cut off and suffer the **c** of their guilt."
30:15 a vow or pledge, he will suffer the **c** of her guilt."
Job 13:13 me alone. Let me speak—and I will face the **c**.
Pr 18:21 Those who love to talk will experience the **c**,
22: 3 the simpleton goes blindly on and suffers the **c**.
27:12 The simpleton goes blindly on and suffers the **c**.
31:27 and does not have to bear the **c** of laziness.
Isa 47: 7 my people or think about the **c** of your actions.
Eze 3:20 If you did not warn them of the **c**, then they will
23:35 you must bear the **c** of all your lewdness
44:10 idols must bear the **c** of their unfaithfulness.
44:12 and taken an oath that they must bear the **c** for their
Hos 13:16 The people of Samaria must bear the **c** of their
Mt 22:16 teach about the way of God regardless of the **c**.
Gal 6: 8 their own sinful desires will harvest the **c** of decay

CONSEQUENTLY (1) [CONSEQUENCES]

Gal 3:11 **C**, it is clear that no one can ever be right with God

CONSIDER (43) [CONSIDERABLE, CONSIDERATE, CONSIDERATION, CONSIDERED, CONSIDERING, CONSIDERS]

Ge 7: 1 people of the earth, I **c** you alone to be righteous.
30:13 The other women will **c** me happy indeed!"
34:22 But they will **c** staying here only on one condition.
Lev 11:20 "You are to **c** detestable all swarming insects that
11:23 But you are to **c** detestable all other swarming
11:41 "**C** detestable any animal that scurries along the
19:23 for the first three years and **c** it forbidden.
21: 8 You must **c** them holy because I, the LORD,
Nu 18:27 The LORD will **c** this to be your harvest offering,
Dt 15:18 "Do not **c** it a hardship when you release your
29:19 the warnings of this curse **c** themselves immune,
1Ki 11:38 follow my ways and do whatever I **c** to be right,
19:20 "Go on back! But **c** what I have done to you."
20: 6 They will take away everything you **c**
2Ch 2: 6 So who am I to **c** building a Temple for him,
Job 5:17 "But **c** the joy of those corrected by God! Do not
13:24 away from me? Why do you **c** me your enemy?
19:15 The servant girls **c** me a stranger. I am like a
37:14 Job; stop and **c** the wonderful miracles of God!
Ps 49:18 In this life they **c** themselves fortunate,
89:50 **C**, Lord, how your servants are disgraced! / I carry
Pr 14:15 they are told! The prudent carefully **c** their steps.
26:16 Lazy people **c** themselves smarter than seven wise
Isa 5:21 think they are wise and **c** themselves to be clever.
51: 1 **C** the quarry from which you were mined, the rock
56: 3 Do not let them think that I **c** them second-class
57:12 I will expose your so-called good deeds that you **c**
Jer 31:37 so I will not **c** casting them away forever for their
Eze 12: 3 for perhaps they will even yet **c** what this means,
34:10 I now **c** these shepherds my enemies, and I will
Hag 1: 5 Almighty says: **C** how things are going for you!
1: 7 Almighty says: **C** how things are going for you!
2:15 **c** how things were going for you before you began
2:18 of the LORD's Temple was laid—carefully **c** this:
Ro 6:11 So you should **c** yourselves dead to sin and able to
Php 3: 7 but now I **c** them worthless because of what Christ
1Th 2:12 live your lives in a way that God would **c** worthy.
1Ti 1: 9 who **c** nothing sacred and defile what is holy,
2Ti 3: 2 and ungrateful. They will **c** nothing sacred.
Phm 1:17 So if you **c** me your partner, give him the same
Heb 7: 4 **C** then how great this Melchizedek was.
Jas 5: 7 **C** the farmers who eagerly look for the rains in the
1Pe 5:12 with the help of Silas, whom I **c** a faithful brother.

CONSIDERABLE (2) [CONSIDER]

Ge 31: 2 And Jacob began to notice a **c** cooling in Laban's
Ac 13: 7 a man of **c** insight and understanding.

CONSIDERATE (2) [CONSIDER]

Ro 15: 1 We must be **c** of the doubts and fears of those who
Php 4: 5 Let everyone see that you are **c** in all you do.

CONSIDERATION (1) [CONSIDER]

1Co 10:28 out of **c** for the conscience of the one who told

CONSIDERED (32) [CONSIDER]

Ge 38:10 But the LORD **c** it a wicked thing for Onan to
Ex 11: 3 and Moses was **c** a very great man in the land of
Lev 2: 3 It will be **c** a most holy part of the offerings given
2:10 It will be **c** a most holy part of the offerings given
5: 2 they will be **c** ceremonially unclean and guilty,
5: 3 they will be **c** guilty as soon as they become aware
5: 4 they will be **c** guilty even if they were not fully
11:37 be planted in the field, the seed will still be **c** clean.
11:42 many feet. All such animals are to be **c** detestable.
13: 6 the clothes, the person will be **c** free of disease.
14:46 will be **c** ceremonially unclean until evening.
17:15 until evening; after that, you will be **c** clean.
27: 9 then your gift to the LORD will be **c** holy.
27:10 original animal and the substitute will be **c** holy.
27:33 and the substituted one will be **c** holy and cannot
Nu 18:30 it will be **c** as though it came from your own
18:32 You will not be **c** guilty for accepting the
35:27 city limits and kills him, it will not be **c** murder.
Dt 2:20 too, was once **c** the land of the Rephaites,
15: 9 cries out to the LORD, you will be **c** guilty of sin.
1Ki 10:21 because silver was **c** of little value in Solomon's
1Ch 7:17 All these were **c** Gileadites, descendants of Makir
2Ch 9:20 because silver was **c** of little value in Solomon's
Job 30:29 I am **c** a brother to jackals and a companion to
Isa 65:20 No longer will people be **c** old at one hundred!
Jer 2: 3 All who harmed my people were **c** guilty,
34:17 You will be **c** a disgrace by all the nations of the
Mt 1:20 As he **c** this, he fell asleep, and an angel of the
19:30 and those who are **c** least here will be the greatest
21:46 to try because the crowds **c** Jesus to be a prophet.
Mk 10:31 and those who are **c** least here will be the greatest
Ro 9: 8 It is the children of the promise who are **c** to be

CONSIDERING (2) [CONSIDER]

Ecc 6: 8 **C** this, do wise people really have any advantage
1Ti 1:12 How thankful I am to Christ Jesus our Lord for **c**

CONSIDERS (4) [CONSIDER]

Ex 31:15 Because the LORD **c** it a holy day, anyone who
Job 33:10 a quarrel with me, and he **c** me to be his enemy.
1Co 1:27 God deliberately chose things the world **c** foolish
1:28 and used them to bring to nothing what the world **c**

CONSIST (11) [CONSISTED, CONSISTING, CONSISTS]

Ex 26:15 "The framework of the Tabernacle will **c** of
28: 7 It will **c** of two pieces, front and back, joined at the
Lev 2: 1 to the LORD, the offering must **c** of choice flour.
Nu 4:31 "Their duties at the Tabernacle will **c** of carrying
28:27 It will **c** of two young bulls, one ram, and seven
29: 2 It will **c** of one young bull, one ram, and seven
29: 8 It will **c** of one young bull, one ram, and seven
29:13 It will **c** of thirteen young bulls, two rams,
29:36 It will **c** of one young bull, one ram, and seven
Eze 45:23 This daily offering will **c** of seven young bulls
Mt 6:25 Doesn't life **c** of more than food and clothing?

CONSISTED (15) [CONSIST]

Ex 38: 9 150 feet long. It **c** of curtains made of fine linen.
Nu 7:13 The offering **c** of a silver platter weighing about
7:19 The offering **c** of a silver platter weighing about
7:25 The offering **c** of a silver platter weighing about
7:31 The offering **c** of a silver platter weighing about
7:37 The offering **c** of a silver platter weighing about
7:43 The offering **c** of a silver platter weighing about
7:49 The offering **c** of a silver platter weighing about
7:55 The offering **c** of a silver platter weighing about
7:61 The offering **c** of a silver platter weighing about
7:67 The offering **c** of a silver platter weighing about
7:73 The offering **c** of a silver platter weighing about
7:79 The offering **c** of a silver platter weighing about
2Ch 26:13 The army **c** of 307,500 men, all elite troops.
Ezr 2:60 This group **c** of the families of Delaiah, Tobiah,

CONSISTENT (1) [CONSISTENTLY]

Jn 8:44 When he lies, it is **c** with his character; for he is a

CONSISTENTLY (3) [CONSISTENT]

Ge 6: 5 and he saw that all their thoughts were **c**
6: 9 He **c** followed God's will and enjoyed a close
Ps 119: 5 Oh, that my actions would **c** / reflect your

CONSISTING (2) [CONSIST]

Lev 23:13 A grain offering must accompany it **c** of three
Nu 28: 7 **c** of one quart of fermented drink with each lamb,

CONSISTS (2) [CONSIST]

Eze 45:12 One shekel **c** of twenty gerahs, and sixty shekels
Lk 12:23 For life **c** of far more than food and clothing.

CONSOLE (6) [CONSOLED, CONSOLING]

Job 2:11 traveled from their homes to comfort and **c** him.
21: 2 what I am saying. You can **c** me by listening to me.
Jer 16: 7 a father. No one will send a cup of wine to **c** them.
Eze 24:22 or **c** yourselves by eating the food brought to you
Jn 11:19 their respects and **c** Martha and Mary on their loss.
11:31 When the people who were at the house trying to **c**

CONSOLED (1) [CONSOLE]

Job 42:11 And they **c** him and comforted him because of all

CONSOLING (1) [CONSOLE]

Eze 24:17 or accept any food brought to you by **c** friends."

CONSPIRACIES (1) [CONSPIRE]

Eze 22:25 Your princes plot **c** just as lions stalk their prey.

CONSPIRACY (8) [CONSPIRE]

2Sa 15:12 also joined Absalom, and the **c** gained momentum.
15:13 "All Israel has joined Absalom in a **c** against
1Ki 16:20 and his **c** are recorded in *The Book of the History*
2Ki 9:14 and grandson of Nimshi formed a **c** against King
14:19 There was a **c** against Amaziah's life in Jerusalem,
15:15 of the events in Shallum's reign, including his **c**,
2Ch 25:27 there was a **c** against his life in Jerusalem, and he
Jer 11: 9 "I have discovered a **c** against me among the

CONSPIRATORS (1) [CONSPIRE]

1Sa 22:17 the LORD, for they are allies and **c** with David!

CONSPIRE (2) [CONSPIRACIES, CONSPIRACY, CONSPIRATORS, CONSPIRED, CONSPIRING]

Ps 31:13 My enemies **c** against me, / plotting to take my
31:20 safe from those who **c** against them.

CONSPIRED (13) [CONSPIRE]

Nu 14:35 member of the community who has **c** against me.
16: 1 **c** with Dathan and Abiram, the sons of Eliab,
26: 9 and Abiram are the same community leaders who **c**
1Sa 22: 8 Is that why you have **c** against me? For not one of
22:13 "Why have you and David **c** against me?"
2Ki 10: 9 "I am the one who **c** against my master and killed
15:10 Then Shallum son of Jabesh **c** against Zechariah,
15:25 the commander of Pekahiah's army, **c** against him.
15:30 Then Hoshea son of Elah **c** against Pekah
17: 4 Then Hoshea **c** against the king of Assyria by
21:24 land killed all those who had **c** against King Amon,
2Ch 33:25 land killed all those who had **c** against King Amon,
Da 2: 9 You have **c** to tell me lies in hopes that something

CONSPIRING (1) [CONSPIRE]

Ac 5: 9 like this—**c** together to test the Spirit of the Lord?

CONSTANT (30) [CONSTANTLY]

Ex 28:12 these names before the LORD as a **c** reminder.
Lev 26:36 You will live there in such **c** fear that the sound of
Dt 28:33 You will suffer under **c** oppression and harsh
Jdg 2: 3 and their gods will be a **c** temptation to you."
1Sa 10:26 hearts God had touched became his **c** companions.
2Sa 12:10 time on, the sword will be a **c** threat to your family,
1Ki 14:30 There was **c** war between Rehoboam
15: 7 *Kings of Judah*. There was **c** war between Abijam
15:16 There was **c** war between King Asa of Judah
15:32 There was **c** war between Asa and King Baasha of
Ps 38:17 I am on the verge of collapse, / facing **c** pain.
44:15 We can't escape the **c** humiliation; / shame is
119:98 my enemies, / for your commands are my **c** guide.
141: 5 But I am in **c** prayer / against the wicked and their
Pr 6:12 of worthless and wicked people: They are **c** liars,

6:33 Wounds and **c** disgrace are his lot. His shame will
8:30 I was his **c** delight, rejoicing always in his
18:6 Fools get into **c** quarrels; they are asking for a
19:13 a father; a nagging wife annoys like a **c** dripping.
27:15 A nagging wife is as annoying as the **c** dripping on
Isa 51:13 Will you remain in **c** dread of human oppression?
64:5 We are **c** sinners, so your anger is heavy on us.
Eze 30:16 will be torn apart; Memphis will live in **c** terror.
Lk 18:1 disciples a story to illustrate their need for **c** prayer
18:5 because she is wearing me out with her **c**
21:36 Keep a **c** watch. And pray that, if possible,
Ac 20:31 my **c** watch and care over you night and day,
20:35 And I have been a **c** example of how you can help
2Co 4:11 we live under **c** danger of death because we serve
Rev 2:19 And I can see your **c** improvement in all these

CONSTANTLY (35) [CONSTANT]

Ge 4:12 on the earth, **c** wandering from place to place."
28:15 I will be with you **c** until I have finished giving
Ex 18:26 These men were **c** available to administer justice.
Dt 7:9 and **c** loves those who love him and obey his
9:7 Egypt until now, you have **c** rebelled against him.
1Sa 14:52 The Israelites fought **c** with the Philistines
15:35 to meet with Saul again, but he mourned **c** for him.
2Sa 22:23 For all his laws are **c** before me; / I have never
23:5 He will **c** look after my safety and success.
1Ki 8:59 in the presence of the LORD be before him **c**,
Job 29:20 New honors are **c** bestowed on me, and my
Ps 18:22 For all his laws are **c** before me; / I have never
26:3 For I am **c** aware of your unfailing love, / and I
26:10 with wicked schemes, / and they **c** take bribes.
34:1 the LORD at all times. / I will **c** speak his praises.
44:8 all day long / and **c** praise your name. / *Interlude*
50:8 or the burnt offerings you **c** bring to my altar.
56:2 My slanderers hound me **c**, / and many are boldly
71:17 and I have **c** told others about the wonderful things
74:21 Don't let the downtrodden be **c** disgraced!
77:12 They are **c** in my thoughts. / I cannot stop thinking
86:3 Be merciful, O Lord, / for I am calling on you **c**.
103:9 He will not **c** accuse us, / nor remain angry forever.
119:109 My life **c** hangs in the balance, / but I will not stop
Pr 6:14 perverted hearts plot evil. They stir up trouble **c**.
Isa 29:24 and those who **c** complain will accept instruction.
La 3:63 their activities, they **c** mock me with their songs.
Ac 2:44 And all the believers met together **c** and shared
9:28 and after that he was **c** with them in Jerusalem,
24:5 a man who is **c** inciting the Jews throughout the
2Co 4:10 these bodies of ours **c** share in the death of Jesus
Gal 5:17 These two forces are **c** fighting each other,
Eph 1:16 stopped thanking God for you. I pray for you **c**,
1Th 1:2 always thank God for all of you and pray for you **c**.
2Ti 1:3 Night and day I **c** remember you in my prayers.

CONSTELLATION (1) [CONSTELLATIONS]

Job 38:32 or guide the **c** of the Bear with her cubs across the

CONSTELLATIONS (2) [CONSTELLATION]

2Ki 23:5 and to the sun, the moon, the **c**, and to all the
Job 9:9 Orion, the Pleiades, and the **c** of the southern sky.

CONSTRAIN [KJV] See FORCE

CONSTRUCT (6) [CONSTRUCTED, CONSTRUCTING, CONSTRUCTION, CONSTRUCTIVE]

Ge 6:14 Then **c** decks and stalls throughout its interior.
6:16 **C** an opening all the way around the boat,
Ex 35:10 **C** everything that the LORD has commanded:
36:1 and intelligence will **c** and furnish the Tabernacle,
1Ki 10:12 and to **c** harps and lyres for the musicians.
2Ch 9:11 and to **c** harps and lyres for the musicians.

CONSTRUCTED (15) [CONSTRUCT]

Ex 38:1 The altar for burning animal sacrifices also was **c**
38:9 Then he **c** the courtyard. The south wall was 150
Jos 4:8 camped for the night and **c** the memorial there.
1Ki 7:28 They were **c** with side panels braced with
9:19 and **c** cities where his chariots and horses could be
9:24 the new palace he had built for her, he **c** the Millo.
2Ki 16:18 he also removed the canopy that had been **c** inside
21:3 He **c** altars for Baal and set up an Asherah pole,
2Ch 1:3 the LORD's servant, had **c** in the wilderness.
8:6 and **c** cities where his chariots and horses could be
26:10 He also **c** forts in the wilderness and dug many
27:4 and **c** fortresses and towers in the wooded areas.
32:28 He also **c** many storehouses for his grain,
33:3 He **c** altars for the images of Baal and set up
Ac 7:44 It was **c** in exact accordance with the plan shown

CONSTRUCTING (2) [CONSTRUCT]

2Ch 32:5 and **c** a second wall outside the first.
Eze 26:8 **c** a ramp, and raising a roof of shields against you.

CONSTRUCTION (19) [CONSTRUCT]

Ge 11:3 They began to talk about **c** projects. "Come,"
1Ki 6:1 that he began the **c** of the Temple of the LORD.
6:7 The stones used in the **c** of the Temple were
7:1 and it took him thirteen years to complete the **c**.
9:11 and gold he had furnished for the **c** of the
2Ki 12:11 Then they gave the money to the **c** supervisors,
12:15 No accounting was required from the **c**
22:7 But there will be no need for the **c** supervisors to
1Ch 29:3 private treasures of gold and silver to help in the **c**.
29:7 For the **c** of the Temple of God, they gave almost
2Ch 3:2 The **c** began in midspring, during the fourth year of
24:12 and Jehoiada gave the money to the **c** supervisors,
Ezr 3:8 The **c** of the Temple of God began in midspring,
5:8 We wish to inform you that we went to the **c** site of
6:7 Do not disturb the **c** of the Temple of God. Let it
6:8 You must pay the full **c** costs without delay from
Job 3:14 prime ministers, famous for their great **c** projects.
Eze 43:11 describe to them all the specifications of its **c**—
Lk 14:28 For who would begin **c** of a building without first

CONSTRUCTIVE (1) [CONSTRUCT]

Pr 15:31 If you listen to **c** criticism, you will be at home

CONSULT (17) [CONSULTED, CONSULTING]

Ex 24:14 **c** with Aaron and Hur, who are here with you."
33:7 Everyone who wanted to **c** with the LORD would
Dt 18:14 The people you are about to displace **c** with
Jos 9:14 their bread, but they did not **c** the LORD.
21:1 Then the leaders of the tribe of Levi came to **c** with
2Ki 3:12 of Israel, Judah, and Edom went to **c** with Elisha.
19:8 left Jerusalem and went to **c** his king,
22:14 section of Jerusalem to **c** with the prophet Huldah.
2Ch 1:5 and the people gathered in front of it to **c** the
34:22 section of Jerusalem to **c** with the prophet Huldah.
Ezr 2:63 **c** the LORD about the matter by means of sacred
Ne 7:65 **c** the LORD about the matter by means of sacred
Isa 37:8 left Jerusalem and went to **c** his king,
45:21 **C** together, argue your case, and state your proofs
Mic 5:12 there will be no more fortune-tellers to **c**.
Gal 1:16 to me, I did not rush out to **c** with anyone else;
1:17 nor did I go up to Jerusalem to **c** with those who

CONSULTED (10) [CONSULT]

1Sa 22:10 Ahimelech **c** the LORD to find out what David
22:15 This was certainly not the first time I had **c** God for
2Sa 3:17 Meanwhile, Abner had **c** with the leaders of Israel.
2Ki 17:17 They **c** fortune-tellers and used sorcery and sold
21:6 and he **c** with mediums and psychics.
1Ch 10:13 the LORD's command, and he even **c** a medium
13:1 David **c** with all his officials,
2Ch 32:3 he **c** with his officials and military advisers,
33:6 and he **c** with mediums and psychics.
Est 1:13 He immediately **c** with his advisers, who knew all

CONSULTING (6) [CONSULT]

Lev 20:6 "If any among the people are unfaithful by **c**
2Ch 20:21 After **c** the leaders of the people, the king
25:17 After **c** with his advisers, King Amaziah of Judah
Isa 8:19 So why are you trying to find out the future by **c**
30:2 For without **c** me, you have gone down to Egypt to
Jn 5:30 But I do nothing without **c** the Father. I judge as I

CONSUME (16) [CONSUMED, CONSUMES, CONSUMING]

Job 24:19 consumes sinners just as drought and heat **c** snow.
Ps 21:9 you appear. / The LORD will **c** them in his anger;
69:24 fury on them; / **c** them with your burning anger.
78:45 He sent vast swarms of flies to **c** them / and hordes
Isa 10:23 LORD Almighty, has already decided to **c** them.
26:11 will be ashamed. / Let your fire **c** your enemies.
30:27 His lips are filled with fury; his words **c** like fire.
40:16 fuel to **c** a sacrifice large enough to honor him.
43:2 will not be burned up; the flames will not **c** you.
Jer 15:14 my anger blazes forth like fire, and it will **c** them."
44:12 on coming here to Egypt, and I will **c** them.
Eze 20:13 and I made plans to utterly **c** them in the desert.
Na 3:15 The enemy will **c** you like locusts,
Ac 21:25 nor **c** blood, nor eat meat from strangled animals,
2Th 2:8 whom the Lord Jesus will **c** with the breath of his
Heb 10:27 and the raging fire that will **c** his enemies.

CONSUMED (21) [CONSUME]

Ex 15:7 anger flashed forth; / it **c** them as fire burns straw.
Lev 9:24 and **c** the burnt offering and the fat on the altar.
Dt 5:25 we will certainly die and be **c** by this awesome fire.
Jdg 6:21 flamed up from the rock and **c** all he had brought.
2Sa 22:39 I **c** them; I struck them down so they could not get
23:7 chop them down; / they will be utterly **c** with fire."
Job 15:34 enriched through bribery, will be **c** by fire.
22:20 The last of them have been **c** in the fire.'
Ps 78:46 to caterpillars; / their harvest was **c** by locusts.
106:18 fell upon their followers; / a flame **c** the wicked.
Jer 7:20 and crops will be **c** by the unquenchable fire of my
Eze 28:18 So I brought fire from within you, and it **c** you.
43:8 name by such wickedness, so I **c** them in my anger.
Joel 1:19 The fire has **c** the pastures and burned up all the
1:20 streams have dried up, and fire has **c** the pastures.
Zec 8:2 and strong; I am **c** with passion for Jerusalem!
Mal 4:1 that day. They will be **c** like a tree—roots and all.
Ac 12:23 glory to God. So he was **c** with worms and died.
2Pe 3:7 and the earth will be **c** by fire on the day of
Rev 18:8 She will be utterly **c** by fire, for the Lord God who
20:9 came down on the attacking armies and **c** them.

CONSUMES (6) [CONSUME]

Job 24:19 Death **c** sinners just as drought and heat consume
Pr 5:11 will groan in anguish when disease **c** your body,
Isa 24:6 Therefore, a curse **c** the earth and its people.
La 2:3 He **c** the whole land of Israel like a raging fire.
Hos 5:12 I will destroy Israel as a moth **c** wool. I will sap
Rev 11:5 the mouths of the prophets and **c** their enemies.

CONSUMING (6) [CONSUME]

Job 20:26 A wildfire will devour his goods, **c** all he has left.
Isa 29:6 great noise, with whirlwind and storm and **c** fire.
Eze 22:31 my fury on them, **c** them in the fire of my anger.
Ac 15:20 and from **c** blood or eating the meat of strangled
15:29 from **c** blood or eating the meat of strangled
Heb 12:29 For our God is a **c** fire.

CONSUMMATION [KJV] See CLIMAX

CONSUMPTION [KJV] See CONSUME, DESTROY, DISEASE(S)

CONTACT (4)

Lev 5:3 "Or if they come into **c** with any source of human
15:17 or leather that comes in **c** with the semen must be
Mk 7:19 Food doesn't come in **c** with your heart, but only
1Co 7:31 Those in frequent **c** with the things of the world

CONTAGIOUS (22)

Lev 13:2 or a shiny patch on their skin that develops into a **c**
13:3 be more than skin-deep, then it is a **c** skin disease,
13:8 ceremonially unclean, for it is a **c** skin disease.
13:9 "Anyone who develops a **c** skin disease must go to
13:11 it is clearly a **c** skin disease, and the priest must
13:15 because open sores indicate the presence of a **c**
13:20 It is a **c** skin disease that has broken out in the boil.
13:22 because it is a **c** skin disease.
13:25 a **c** skin disease has broken out in the burn.
13:25 for it is clearly a **c** skin disease.
13:27 for it is clearly a **c** skin disease.
13:30 The infection is a **c** skin disease of the head
13:42 or the back of his head, this is a **c** skin disease.
13:44 the man is infected with a **c** skin disease and is
13:45 "Those who suffer from any **c** skin disease must
14:2 by those seeking purification from a **c** skin disease.
14:32 those who have recovered from a **c** skin disease
14:54 for dealing with the various kinds of **c** skin disease
14:57 be followed when dealing with any **c** skin disease
22:4 "If any of the priests have a **c** skin disease or any
Nu 5:2 anyone from the camp who has a **c** skin disease
Dt 24:8 "Watch all **c** skin diseases carefully and follow the

CONTAIN (11) [CONTAINED, CONTAINER, CONTAINERS, CONTAINING, CONTAINS]

Ex 28:17 The first row will **c** a red carnelian, a chrysolite,
28:18 The second row will **c** a turquoise, a sapphire,
28:19 The third row will **c** a jacinth, an agate, and an
28:20 The fourth row will **c** a beryl, an onyx, and a
Lev 2:5 of choice flour and olive oil, and it must **c** no yeast.
1Ki 8:27 Why, even the highest heavens cannot **c** you.
2Ch 2:6 Not even the highest heavens can **c** him!
6:18 Why, even the highest heavens cannot **c** you.
Isa 40:16 All Lebanon's forests do not **c** sufficient fuel to
Eze 12:10 These actions **c** a message for Zedekiah in
Jn 21:25 the whole world could not **c** the books.

CONTAINED (4) [CONTAIN]

2Ki 17:13 which are **c** in the whole law that I commanded
Jer 32:11 which **c** the terms and conditions of the purchase,
Ac 11:10 the sheet and all it **c** was pulled back up to heaven.
Col 2:14 He canceled the record that **c** the charges against

CONTAINER (19) [CONTAIN]

Ge 21:14 and strapped a **c** of water to Hagar's shoulders.
21:19 She immediately filled her water **c** and gave the
Ex 16:33 "Get a **c** and put two quarts of manna into it.
16:36 (The **c** used to measure the manna was an omer,
Lev 11:34 And any beverage that is in such an unclean **c** will
Nu 7:14 He also brought a gold **c** weighing about four
7:20 He also brought a gold **c** weighing about four
7:26 He also brought a gold **c** weighing about four
7:32 He also brought a gold **c** weighing about four
7:38 He also brought a gold **c** weighing about four
7:44 He also brought a gold **c** weighing about four
7:50 He also brought a gold **c** weighing about four
7:56 He also brought a gold **c** weighing about four
7:62 He also brought a gold **c** weighing about four
7:68 He also brought a gold **c** weighing about four
7:74 He also brought a gold **c** weighing about four
7:80 He also brought a gold **c** weighing about four
19:15 Any **c** in the tent that was not covered with a lid is
2Ki 4:6 Soon every **c** was full to the brim! "Bring me

CONTAINERS (8) [CONTAIN]

Lev 19:36 Your **c** for measuring dry goods or liquids must be
Nu 4:14 the firepans, hooks, shovels, basins, and all the **c**—
7:84 twelve silver basins, and twelve gold incense **c**.
7:86 about four ounces for each of the gold **c** that were
1Ki 17:14 and oil left in your **c** until the time when the
17:16 they used, there was always enough left in the **c**,
Ne 10:39 and place them in the sacred **c** near the ministering
2Co 4:7 is held in perishable **c**, that is, in our weak bodies.

CONTAINING (10) [CONTAIN]

1Sa 6:8 and beside it place a chest **c** the gold rats and gold
6:11 the Ark of the LORD and the chest **c** the gold rats
6:15 and the chest **c** the gold rats and gold tumors from
1Ki 10:16 each **c** over fifteen pounds of gold.
10:17 hammered gold, each **c** nearly four pounds of gold.
2Ch 9:15 of hammered gold, each **c** over 15 pounds of gold.
9:16 each **c** about 7-1/2 pounds of gold.

Lk 4:17 The scroll **c** the messages of Isaiah the prophet was
Heb 9:4 Inside the Ark were a gold jar **c** some manna,
Rev 21:9 held the seven bowls **c** the seven last plagues came

CONTAINS (4) [CONTAIN]

Lev 23:17 from three quarts of choice flour that **c** yeast.
1Ki 8:21 which **c** the covenant that the LORD made with
Zec 5:3 "This scroll **c** the curse that is going out over the
1Co 7:31 to them, for this world and all it **c** will pass away.

CONTAMINATE (1) [CONTAMINATED, CONTAMINATES, CONTAMINATION]

Lev 14:34 I may **c** some of your houses with an infectious

CONTAMINATED (11) [CONTAMINATE]

Lev 7:18 By then, the meat will be **c**; if you eat it, you will
13:49 it is **c** with an infectious mildew and must be taken
13:51 the material is clearly **c** by an infectious mildew
13:52 because it has been **c** by an infectious mildew.
13:54 the priest will order the **c** object to be washed
13:55 burned up, whether it is **c** on the inside or outside.
13:57 and the **c** object must be burned up.
14:40 The **c** material will then be thrown into an area
14:44 the walls are clearly **c** with an infectious mildew,
19:7 the third day, it will be **c**, and I will not accept it.
Jude 1:23 but be careful that you aren't **c** by their sins.

CONTAMINATES (1) [CONTAMINATE]

Lev 13:47 "Now suppose an infectious mildew **c** some

CONTAMINATION (1) [CONTAMINATE]

Lev 14:37 and the **c** appears to go deeper than the wall's

CONTEMN [KJV] See CURSING

CONTEMPT (34) [CONTEMPTIBLE, CONTEMPTUOUS, CONTEMPTUOUSLY]

Ge 16:4 she began to treat her mistress Sarai with **c**.
Lev 26:15 my laws and treating my regulations with **c**,
Nu 14:23 None of those who have treated me with **c** will
15:31 Since they have treated the LORD's word with **c**
1Sa 2:17 for they treated the LORD's offerings with **c**.
17:42 sneering in **c** at this ruddy-faced boy.
2Sa 6:16 before the LORD, she was filled with **c** for him.
19:43 Why did you treat us with such **c**? Remember,
1Ch 15:29 and leaping for joy, she was filled with **c** for him.
2Ch 7:20 I will make it a spectacle of **c** among the nations.
Est 1:18 There will be no end to the **c** and anger throughout
Job 16:10 and laugh at me. They slap my cheek in **c**.
30:15 They hold me in **c**, and my prosperity has vanished
31:34 Have I feared the crowd and its **c**, so that I refused
Ps 107:40 the LORD pours **c** on their princes,
119:51 The proud hold me in utter **c**, / but I do not turn
123:3 have mercy, / for we have had our fill of **c**.
123:4 scoffing of the proud / and the **c** of the arrogant.
Pr 18:3 When the wicked arrive, **c**, shame, and disgrace are
Isa 23:9 your pride and show his **c** for all human greatness.
Jer 25:9 you an object of horror and **c** and a ruin forever.
25:18 a desolate ruin, an object of horror, **c**, and cursing.
29:18 an object of damnation, horror, **c**, and mockery.
51:37 It will be an object of horror and **c**, without a
La 1:15 "The Lord has treated my mighty men with **c**.
5:12 their thumbs, and the old men are treated with **c**.
Eze 16:56 In your proud days you held Sodom in **c**.
25:15 against Judah out of revenge and long-standing **c**.
28:26 the neighboring nations that treated them with **c**,
36:5 because they have shown utter **c** for me by
Da 12:2 and some to shame and everlasting **c**.
Mic 6:16 You will be treated with **c**, mocked by all who see
Mk 9:12 of Man must suffer and be treated with utter **c**?
Lk 18:2 "who was a godless man with great **c** for

CONTEMPTIBLE (1) [CONTEMPT]

Mal 1:12 By bringing **c** food, you are saying it's all right to

CONTEMPTUOUS (1) [CONTEMPT]

Eze 35:12 have heard every **c** word you spoke against the

CONTEMPTUOUSLY (2) [CONTEMPT]

Ne 2:19 Geshem the Arab heard of our plan, they scoffed **c**.
Eze 22:7 Fathers and mothers are **c** ignored.

CONTENDED (1) [CONTENTIOUS]

Dt 33:8 and **c** with them at the waters of Meribah.

CONTENT (12) [CONTENTED, CONTENTMENT]

Jos 7:7 If only we had been **c** to stay on the other side!
2Sa 19:30 "I am **c** just to have you back again, my lord!"
1Ki 9:19 He built to his heart's **c** in Jerusalem and Lebanon
2Ki 14:10 about it. Be **c** with your victory and stay at home!
2Ch 8:6 He built to his heart's **c** in Jerusalem and Lebanon
Ps 12:4 They say, "We will lie to our hearts' **c**. / Our lips
Pr 13:25 The godly eat to their hearts' **c**, but the belly of the
Ecc 1:8 No matter how much we hear, we are not **c**.
SS 8:10 I am now full breasted. And my lover is **c** with me.
Lk 3:14 know they didn't do. And be **c** with your pay."
2Co 12:10 I am quite **c** with my weaknesses and with insults,
1Ti 6:8 if we have enough food and clothing, let us be **c**.

CONTENTED (2) [CONTENT]

1Ki 4:20 They were very **c**, with plenty to eat and drink.
Zep 1:12 to find and punish those who sit **c** in their sins,

CONTENTIOUS (2) [CONTENDED]

Pr 21:9 of an attic than with a **c** wife in a lovely home.
25:24 of an attic than with a **c** wife in a lovely home.

CONTENTMENT (2) [CONTENT]

Ecc 6:6 live a thousand years twice over but not find **c**.
1Ti 6:6 Yet true religion with **c** is great wealth.

CONTEXT (1)

Heb 2:13 And in the same **c** he said, "Here I am—

CONTINGENT (3)

1Sa 13:23 been secured by a **c** of the Philistine army.
2Ki 18:24 even the weakest **c** of my master's troops,
Isa 36:9 even the weakest **c** of my master's troops,

CONTINUAL (5) [CONTINUE]

Ge 17:9 and all your descendants have this **c** responsibility.
Lev 24:8 behalf of the Israelites as a **c** part of the covenant.
Pr 15:15 brings trouble; for the happy heart, life is a **c** feast.
Eze 35:5 Your **c** hatred for the people of Israel led you to
1Th 1:3 and your **c** anticipation of the return of our Lord

CONTINUALLY (31) [CONTINUE]

Ex 27:20 oil for the lampstand, so it can be kept burning **c**.
28:29 the LORD will be reminded of his people **c**.
Lev 24:2 oil for the lampstand, so it can be kept burning **c**.
24:3 and must arrange to have the lamps tended **c**,
24:4 must be tended **c** in the LORD's presence.
Dt 28:29 You will be oppressed and robbed **c**, and no one
Jos 1:8 Study this Book of the Law **c**. Meditate on it day
6:9 the Ark, with the priests **c** blowing the horns.
1Sa 3:13 I have warned him **c** that judgment is coming for
8:8 Ever since I brought them from Egypt they have **c**
2Ch 12:15 and Jeroboam were **c** at war with each other.
24:14 And the burnt offerings were sacrificed **c** in the
Job 29:20 bestowed on me, and my strength is **c** renewed.'
Ps 35:15 I don't even know; / they hurl slander at me **c**.
35:27 Let them **c** say, "Great is the LORD,
42:3 for food, / while my enemies **c** taunt me, saying,
119:20 I am overwhelmed **c** / with a desire for your laws.
119:117 then I will meditate on your principles **c**.
128:5 May the LORD **c** bless you from Zion. / May you
Isa 57:20 It is never still but **c** churns up mire and dirt.
58:11 The LORD will guide you **c**, watering your life
59:8 They **c** do wrong, and those who follow them
Jer 5:26 in a blind. They are **c** setting traps for other people.
Da 6:16 your God, whom you worship **c**, rescue you."
6:20 Was your God, whom you worship **c**, able to
Ac 1:14 They all met together **c** for prayer, along with
1Co 15:30 And why should we ourselves be **c** risking our
Col 1:10 and please the Lord, and you will **c** do good,
3:10 nature that is **c** being renewed as you learn more
Heb 13:15 let us **c** offer our sacrifice of praise to God by
Jas 5:13 And those who have reason to be thankful should **c**

CONTINUE (96) [CONTINUAL, CONTINUALLY, CONTINUED, CONTINUES, CONTINUING, CONTINUOUS, CONTINUOUSLY]

Ge 17:7 "I will **c** this everlasting covenant between us,
17:7 It will **c** between me and your offspring forever.
18:31 I have dared to speak to the Lord, let me **c**—
Ex 9:2 If you **c** to oppress them and refuse to let them go,
10:1 so I can **c** to display my power by performing
12:25 to give you, you will **c** to celebrate this festival.
18:19 You should **c** to be the people's representative
Lev 26:23 a lesson from this and **c** your hostility toward me,
Nu 19:12 they will **c** to be unclean even after the seventh
Jos 10:19 The rest of you **c** chasing the enemy and cut them
13:13 so they **c** to live among the Israelites to this day.
20:6 because the death was accidental must **c** to live in
Ru 2:13 "I hope I **c** to please you, sir," she replied.
1Sa 2:30 says: The terrible things you are doing cannot **c**!
12:23 And I will **c** to teach you what is good and right.
12:25 But if you **c** to sin, you and your king will be
2Sa 7:16 and your kingdom will **c** for all time before me,
7:29 so that our dynasty may **c** forever before you.
1Ki 8:11 The priests could not **c** their work
11:36 so that the descendants of David my servant will **c**
15:4 the LORD his God allowed his dynasty to **c**,
2Ki 8:19 and promised that his descendants would **c** to rule
18:31 Then I will allow each of you to **c** eating from your
1Ch 17:27 so that our dynasty will **c** forever before you.
2Ch 5:14 The priests could not **c** their work
21:7 and promised that his descendants would **c** to rule
30:9 to him, he will not **c** to turn his face from you."
30:23 then decided to **c** the festival another seven days,
Ne 6:9 the work. So I prayed for strength to **c** the work.
Est 6:13 against him. It will be fatal to **c** to oppose him."
Job 15:29 They will not **c** to be rich. Their wealth will not
22:15 "Will you **c** on the old paths where evil people
32:16 Should I **c** to wait, now that you are silent? Must I
33:2 Now that I have begun to speak, let me **c**.
Ps 17:14 and may the judgment **c** to their children's
19:2 Day after day they **c** to speak; / night after night
72:17 endure forever; / may it **c** as long as the sun shines.
84:7 They will **c** to grow stronger, / and each of them
92:8 in the heavens. / You, O LORD, **c** forever.
119:88 spare my life; / then I can **c** to obey your decrees.
Pr 23:17 envy sinners, but always **c** to fear the LORD.
Ecc 3:18 Then I realized that God allows people to **c** in their
Isa 1:5 Why do you **c** to invite punishment? Must you
36:16 Then I will allow each of you to **c** eating from your
51:8 My salvation will **c** from generation to
51:13 Will you **c** to fear the anger of your enemies from
64:12 to help us? Will you **c** to be silent and punish us?
Jer 14:18 The prophets and priests **c** with their work,
15:18 Why then does my suffering **c**? Why is my wound
15:19 to me, I will restore you so you can **c** to serve me.
17:25 then this nation will **c** forever. There will always
18:12 We will **c** to live as we want to, following our own
La 5:20 Why do you **c** to forget us? Why have you
Eze 4:7 **c** your demonstration of the siege of Jerusalem.
13:22 them life, even though they **c** in their sins.
20:31 you **c** to pollute yourselves to this day.
Da 1:13 decide whether or not to let us **c** eating our diet."
4:27 to the poor. Perhaps then you will **c** to prosper."
12:10 But the wicked will **c** in their wickedness,
Zep 3:7 they **c** their evil practices from dawn till dusk
Zec 7:3 "Should we **c** to mourn and fast each summer on
Mal 2:4 so that my covenant with the Levites may **c**,"
Ac 14:22 They encouraged them to **c** in the faith,
Ro 6:2 we have died to sin, how can we **c** to live in it?
11:22 but kind to you as you **c** to trust in his kindness.
1Co 7:12 and she is willing to **c** living with him,
7:13 and he is willing to **c** living with her, she must not
7:17 and **c** on as you were when God first called you.
7:20 You should **c** on as you were when God called
2Co 1:10 And we are confident that he will **c** to deliver us.
4:13 But we **c** to preach because we have the same kind
11:12 But I will **c** doing this to cut the ground out from
Gal 4:19 and they will **c** until Christ is fully developed in
Php 1:6 will **c** his work until it is finally finished on that
1:18 being preached, so I rejoice. And I will **c** to rejoice.
1:25 so I will **c** with you so that you will grow
Col 1:23 But you must **c** to believe this truth and stand in it
2:6 your Lord, you must **c** to live in obedience to him.
1Th 2:16 be saved. By doing this, they **c** to pile up their sins.
Heb 10:26 if we deliberately **c** sinning after we have received
10:36 what you need now, so you will **c** to do God's will.
13:1 **C** to love each other with true Christian love.
1Pe 4:8 of all, **c** to show deep love for each other,
1Jn 2:24 you will **c** to live in fellowship with the Son
2:27 So **c** in what he has taught you, and **c** to live in Christ.
2:28 **c** to live in fellowship with Christ so that when he
3:6 So if we **c** to live in him, we won't sin either.
4:7 Dear friends, let us **c** to love one another, for love
2Jn 1:9 But if you **c** in the teaching of Christ, you will
Jude 1:20 must **c** to build your lives on the foundation of
1:20 And **c** to pray as you are directed by the Holy
Rev 22:11 Let the one who is doing wrong **c** to do wrong; the one who is vile, **c** to be vile; the one who is good, **c** to do good; and the one who is holy, **c** in holiness.

CONTINUED (97) [CONTINUE]

Ge 7:12 The rain **c** to fall for forty days and forty nights.
8:5 and a half months later, as the waters **c** to go down,
13:3 Then they **c** traveling by stages toward Bethel,
26:13 became a rich man, and his wealth only **c** to grow.
33:11 Jacob **c** to insist, so Esau finally accepted them.
47:13 and the crops **c** to fail throughout Egypt
50:22 his brothers and their families **c** to live in Egypt.
Ex 1:20 and the Israelites **c** to multiply, growing more
6:2 And God **c**, "I am the LORD.
14:8 The LORD **c** to strengthen Pharaoh's resolve,
17:3 But tormented by thirst, they **c** to complain,
33:21 The LORD **c**, "Stand here on this rock beside
40:38 could see it. This **c** throughout all their journeys.
Dt 2:13 Moses **c**, "Then the LORD told us to cross Zered
2:24 Moses **c**, "Then the LORD said, 'Now cross the
Jos 10:11 terrible hailstorm that **c** until they reached Azekah.
10:20 So Joshua and the Israelite army **c** the slaughter
17:12 They could not drive out the Canaanites who **c** to
18:16 where the Jebusites lived, and **c** down to En-rogel.
19:13 Then it **c** east to Gath-hepher, Eth-kazin,
19:27 to Beth-emek and Neiel. It then **c** north to Cabul,
Jdg 1:29 so the Canaanites **c** to live there among them.
1:30 in Kitron and Nahalol, who **c** to live among them.
1:36 Scorpion Pass to Sela and **c** upward from there.
7:25 of Zeeb. And they **c** to chase the Midianites.
8:4 they were exhausted, they **c** to chase the enemy.
18:30 This family **c** as priests for the tribe of Dan until
20:45 They **c** the chase until they had killed another two
Ru 1:19 So the two of them **c** on their journey. When they
1Sa 2:26 he also **c** to gain favor with the LORD and with
3:21 The LORD **c** to appear at Shiloh and gave
7:15 Samuel **c** as Israel's judge for the rest of his life.
12:6 who appointed Moses and Aaron," Samuel **c**.
14:23 and the battle **c** to rage even out beyond Beth-aven.
18:14 David **c** to succeed in everything he did,
30:10 so David **c** the pursuit with his four hundred
2Sa 16:13 So David and his men **c** on, and Shimei kept pace
18:22 But Ahimaaz **c** to plead with Joab,
19:43 The argument **c** back and forth, and the men of
20:10 Abishai left him lying there and **c** after Sheba.
20:18 Then she **c**, "There used to be a saying, 'If you
1Ki 3:6 And you have **c** this great kindness to him today by
4:21 and **c** to serve him throughout his lifetime.
11:25 hated Israel intensely and **c** to reign in Aram.
12:17 But Rehoboam **c** to rule over the Israelites who
13:33 He **c** to choose priests from the rank and file of the
17:15 and her son **c** to eat from her supply of flour

22:19 Then Micaiah c, "Listen to what the LORD says!
22:46 who still c their practices from the days of his
2Ki 3: 3 Nevertheless he c in the sins of idolatry that
13: 6 But they c to sin, following the evil example of
17:29 But these various groups of foreigners also c to
17:33 they c to follow the religious customs of the
17:40 would not listen and c to follow their old ways.
1Ch 16:39 where they c to minister before the LORD.
28:20 Then David c, "Be strong and courageous, and do
2Ch 10:17 But Rehoboam c to rule over the Israelites who
12:13 established himself in Jerusalem and c to rule.
18:18 Then Micaiah c, "Listen to what the LORD says!
27: 2 Nevertheless, the people c in their corrupt ways.
30:22 So for seven days the celebration c.
31: 7 and the heaps c to grow until early autumn.
Ezr 6:14 So the Jewish leaders c their work, and they were
Ne 3:31 Then he c as far as the upper room at the corner.
8:10 And Nehemiah c, "Go and celebrate with a feast
9: 5 Then they c, "Praise his glorious name! It is far
11: 3 and descendants of Solomon's servants c to live in
12:39 Then we c on to the Sheep Gate and stopped at the
Est 2:20 Esther c to keep her nationality and family
9:18 But the Jews at Susa c killing their enemies on the
Job 27: 1 Job c speaking:
29: 1 Job c speaking:
36: 1 Elihu c speaking:
Ps 78:56 he did all this for them, / they c to test his patience.
106:43 he delivered them, / but they c to rebel against him,
Jer 1: 3 He c to give messages throughout the reign of
7:25 Egypt until now, I have c to send my prophets—
32: 3 put him there because he c to give this prophecy:
32:20 And you have c to do great miracles in Israel
Eze 20:27 Your ancestors c to blaspheme and betray me,
44:15 the Levitical priests of the family of Zadok c to
Da 7:11 I c to watch because I could hear the little horn's
7:13 As my vision c that night, I saw someone who
Mk 12:22 This c until all the brothers had married her
Lk 4:44 So he c to travel around, preaching in synagogues
10:38 and the disciples c on their way to Jerusalem,
17:11 As Jesus c on toward Jerusalem, he reached the
Jn 5:29 and those who have c in evil will rise to judgment.
Ac 1:20 Peter c, "This was predicted in the book of
2:40 Then Peter c preaching for a long time,
5:42 they c to teach and preach this message:
12:16 Meanwhile, Peter c knocking. When they finally
20:11 And Paul c talking to them until dawn; then he left.
27:18 next day, as gale-force winds c to batter the ship,
Gal 2: 9 the Gentiles, while they c their work with the Jews.
Col 1: 9 So we have c praying for you ever since we first
Rev 9:20 They c to worship demons and idols made of gold,

CONTINUES (15) [CONTINUE]
Ex 7:14 and he c to refuse to let the people go.
Lev 13: 7 But if the rash c to spread after this examination
15: 3 This defilement applies whether the discharge c
15:25 "If the menstrual flow of blood c for many days
15:25 be ceremonially unclean as long as the discharge c.
23: 6 This festival to the LORD c for seven days,
Nu 19:13 was not sprinkled on them, their defilement c.
24:18 will be conquered, / while Israel c on in triumph.
Jos 9:27 choose to build it. That arrangement c to this day.
1Ch 28: 7 And if he c to obey my commands and regulations
Ps 72: 5 the sun shines, / as long as the moon c in the skies.
100: 5 the LORD is good. / His unfailing love c forever,
100: 5 and his faithfulness c to each generation.
La 5:19 Your throne c from generation to generation.
1Th 2:13 And this word c to work in you who believe.

CONTINUING (10) [CONTINUE]
Ge 18: 5 Please stay awhile before c on your journey."
1Ki 15:26 c the sins of idolatry that Jeroboam had led Israel
15:34 c the sins of idolatry that Jeroboam had led Israel
16:19 c the sins of idolatry that Jeroboam had led Israel
16:26 c the sins of idolatry that Jeroboam had led Israel
2Ki 13: 2 c the sins of idolatry that Jeroboam son of Nebat
2Ch 33:14 and c around the hill of Ophel, where it was built
Eze 26:15 as the screams of the wounded echo in the c
Da 11:28 doing much damage before c his journey.
1Ti 2:15 through childbearing and by c to live in faith,

CONTINUOUS (2) [CONTINUE]
Ex 9:24 like that, with such severe hail and c lightning.
Zec 14: 7 yet there will be c day! Only the LORD knows

CONTINUOUSLY (2) [CONTINUE]
Dt 33:12 live in safety beside him. / He surrounds them c
Zec 14: 8 flowing c both in summer and in winter.

CONTRACT (3)
Ge 29:21 "I have fulfilled my c," Jacob said to Laban.
Ex 21: 8 since he is the one who broke the c with her.
Jos 24:25 and binding c between themselves

CONTRADICTED (1) [CONTRADICTS]
Mk 14:56 witnesses spoke against him, but they c each other.

CONTRADICTS (1) [CONTRADICTED]
1Ti 1:10 and for those who do anything else that c the right

CONTRARY (6)
Lev 20:12 They have acted c to nature and are guilty of a
2Ch 30:18 even though this was c to God's laws.
Isa 30: 1 "You make plans that are c to my will.
44:25 events to happen that are c to their predictions.
Ac 18:13 to worship God in ways that are c to the law."
Ro 16:17 things that are c to what you have been taught.

CONTRAST (3)
2Ch 13:21 By c, Abijah of Judah grew more and more
Ne 5:15 This was quite a c to the former governors who
Ro 5:14 What a c between Adam and Christ, who was yet

CONTRIBUTE (1) [CONTRIBUTED, CONTRIBUTING, CONTRIBUTION, CONTRIBUTIONS]
Ezr 1: 4 c toward their expenses by supplying them with

CONTRIBUTED (3) [CONTRIBUTE]
2Ki 12:16 the money that was c for guilt offerings and sin
1Ch 29: 8 They also c numerous precious stones, which were
2Ch 35: 7 Then Josiah c from his personal property thirty

CONTRIBUTING (1) [CONTRIBUTE]
Lk 8: 3 and many others who were c from their own

CONTRIBUTION (1) [CONTRIBUTE]
2Ch 31: 3 The king also made a personal c of animals for the

CONTRIBUTIONS (4) [CONTRIBUTE]
Ex 36: 7 Their c were more than enough to complete the
2Ki 12: 9 the entrance put all of the people's c into the chest.
2Ch 35: 8 The king's officials also made willing c to the
2Co 11: 8 I "robbed" other churches by accepting their c

CONTRITE (2)
Isa 57:15 and holy place with those whose spirits are c
66: 2 "I will bless those who have humble and c hearts,

CONTROL (53) [CONTROLLED, CONTROLLING, CONTROLS, SELF-CONTROL]
Ge 43:31 his face and came out, keeping himself under c.
Ex 21:29 in the past, yet the bull was not kept under c.
21:36 yet its owner failed to keep it under c, the money
22: 6 "If a fire gets out of c and goes into another
23:29 and the wild animals would become too many to c.
32:25 Aaron had let the people get completely out of c—
Jos 11:23 So Joshua took c of the entire land, just as the
18: 1 Now that the land was under Israelite c, the entire
Jdg 3:12 so the LORD gave King Eglon of Moab c over
3:28 And the Israelites took c of the shallows of the
11:21 So Israel took c of all the land of the Amorites,
14: 6 the Spirit of the LORD powerfully took c of him,
14:19 Then the Spirit of the LORD powerfully took c of
15:14 But the Spirit of the LORD powerfully took c of
2Sa 3:39 Joab and Abishai—are too strong for me to c.
8: 3 when Hadadezer marched out to strengthen his c
2Ki 7:17 The king appointed his officer to c the traffic at the
1Ch 4:31 These towns were under their c until the time of
18: 3 when Hadadezer marched out to strengthen his c
2Ch 1: 1 of King David, now took firm c of the kingdom,
11:12 So only Judah and Benjamin remained under his c.
17: 5 So the LORD established Jehoshaphat's c over
Ezr 4:15 the kings and countries who attempted to c it.
4:22 we must not permit the situation to get out of c."
Ps 4: 4 Don't sin by letting anger gain c over you.
19:13 Don't let them c me. / Then I will be free of guilt
32: 9 that needs a bit and bridle to keep it under c."
141: 3 Take c of what I say, O LORD, / and keep my
Pr 13: 3 Those who c their tongue will have a long life;
14:29 Those who c their anger have great understanding;
Ecc 2:19 And yet they will c everything I have gained by
Jer 27: 6 put everything, even the wild animals, under his c.
28:14 even the wild animals, under his c.' "
Da 2:38 has put even the animals and birds under your c.
7:25 and they will be placed under his c for a time,
11:43 He will gain c over the gold, silver, and treasures
Mk 5: 4 the shackles. No one was strong enough to c him.
7:26 him to release her child from the demon's c.
Lk 8:29 This spirit had often taken c of the man.
Ro 6:12 Do not let sin c the way you live; do not give in to
8: 3 God destroyed sin's c over us by giving his Son as
8: 8 That's why those who are still under the c of their
13:14 But let the Lord Jesus Christ take c of you,
1Co 7: 9 But if they can't c themselves, they should go
7:37 and there is no urgency and he can c his passion,
14:32 Remember that people who prophesy are in c of
Eph 4:26 And "don't sin by letting anger gain c over you."
5:18 your life. Instead, let the Holy Spirit fill and c you.
1Th 4: 4 Then each of you will c your body and live in
Jas 1:26 you claim to be religious but don't c your tongue,
3: 2 but those who c their tongues can also c
1Jn 5:19 around us is under the power and c of the evil one.

CONTROLLED (11) [CONTROL]
Jos 12: 3 Sihon also c the Jordan Valley as far north as the
1Sa 6:18 which were c by the five rulers.
Eze 26: 2 She who c the rich trade routes to the east has been
Ro 7: 5 When we were c by our old nature, sinful desires
8: 5 but those who are c by the Holy Spirit think about
8: 9 But you are not c by your sinful nature. You are c
by the Spirit if you have the Spirit of
1Co 3: 3 for you are still c by your own sinful desires.
3: 3 Doesn't that prove you are c by your own desires?
2Ti 3: 6 with the guilt of sin and c by many desires.
Heb 2: 5 the future world we are talking about will not be c

CONTROLLING (1) [CONTROL]
1Co 7:36 because he has trouble c his passions and time is

CONTROLS (8) [CONTROL]
Job 23:14 will do for me all he has planned. He c my destiny.
37:15 Do you know how God c the storm and causes the
Da 5:23 gives you the breath of life and c your destiny!
Ro 8: 6 If your sinful nature c your mind, there is death.
8: 6 But if the Holy Spirit c your mind, there is life
2Co 5:14 Whatever we do, it is because Christ's love c us.
Gal 5:22 But when the Holy Spirit c our lives, he will
2Pe 2:19 For you are a slave to whatever c you.

CONTROVERSIES (1) [CONTROVERSY]
Ac 26: 3 I know you are an expert on Jewish customs and c.

CONTROVERSY (1) [CONTROVERSIES]
1Ti 2: 8 holy hands lifted up to God, free from anger and c.

CONVENED (1)
Ac 5:21 and his officials arrived, they c the high council,

CONVENIENT (2)
1Ki 21: 2 "Since your vineyard is so c to the palace,
Ac 24:25 "When it is more c, I'll call for you again."

CONVERGE (1)
Isa 60: 6 Vast caravans of camels will c on you, the camels

CONVERSATION (8) [CONVERSATIONS]
Ge 17:22 That ended the c, and God left Abraham.
18:10 Now Sarah was listening to this c from the tent
18:33 his way when he had finished his c with Abraham,
27: 5 But Rebekah overheard the c. So when Esau left to
29: 9 As this c was going on, Rachel arrived with her
Ne 2:18 had been on me, and about my c with the king.
Jer 38:27 No one had overheard the c between Jeremiah
Col 4: 6 Let your c be gracious and effective so that you

CONVERSATIONS (1) [CONVERSATION]
Jer 8: 6 I listen to their c, and what do I hear? Is anyone

CONVERSION (2) [CONVERT]
Ac 15: 5 who had been Pharisees before their c stood up
15:15 And this c of Gentiles agrees with what the

CONVERT (2) [CONVERSION, CONVERTED, CONVERTING, CONVERTS]
Mt 23:15 For you cross land and sea to make one c, and
Ac 6: 5 and Nicolas of Antioch (a Gentile c to the Jewish

CONVERTED (6) [CONVERT]
Ne 13: 5 had c a large storage room and placed it at
Jer 37:15 Jonathan's house had been c into a prison.
Ac 6: 7 and many of the Jewish priests were c, too.
15: 3 that the Gentiles, too, were being c.
1Co 7:16 must remember that your husbands might be c
7:16 must remember that your wives might be c

CONVERTING (1) [CONVERT]
2Ki 10:27 wrecked the temple of Baal, c it into a public toilet.

CONVERTS (4) [CONVERT]
Ac 2:10 visitors from Rome (both Jews and c to Judaism),
13:43 and godly c to Judaism who worshiped at the
15: 5 and declared that all Gentile c must be circumcised
17: 4 Some who listened were persuaded and became c,

CONVEY (1) [CONVEYED]
Pr 26: 6 Trusting a fool to c a message is as foolish as

CONVEY [KJV] See also BRING, TRAVEL

CONVEYED (1) [CONVEY]
Est 1:12 But when they c the king's order to Queen Vashti,

CONVICT (5) [CONVICTED, CONVICTION]
Dt 19:15 "Never c anyone of a crime on the testimony of
Pr 24:25 But blessings are showered on those who c the
Jn 7:51 "Is it legal to c a man before he is given a
Ac 25:16 that Roman law does not c people without a trial.
Jude 1:15 He will c the ungodly of all the evil things

CONVICTED (4) [CONVICT]
2Sa 14:13 You have c yourself in making this decision,
Mk 15: 7 c along with others for murder during an
Ac 2:37 Peter's words c them deeply, and they said to him
1Co 14:24 they will be c of sin, and they will be condemned

CONVICTION (1) [CONVICT]
Ro 14: 5 Each person should have a personal c about this

CONVINCE (3) [CONVINCED, CONVINCING]

Job 32:13 'He is too wise for us. Only God can **c** him.'
Jn 16: 8 And when he comes, he will **c** the world of its sin,
Ac 18: 4 trying to **c** the Jews and Greeks alike.

CONVINCED (12) [CONVINCE]

Ge 3: 6 The woman was **c**. The fruit looked so fresh
27:27 he was finally **c**, and he blessed his son.
Ex 4:31 The leaders were soon **c** that the LORD had sent
2Sa 19:14 Then Amasa **c** all the leaders of Judah, and they
Jer 43: 3 Baruch son of Neriah has **c** you to say this, so we
Lk 20: 6 stone us, because they are **c** he was a prophet."
Jn 2:23 many people were **c** that he was indeed the
Ro 2:19 You are **c** that you are a guide for the blind and a
4:21 He was absolutely **c** that God was able to do
8:38 And I am **c** that nothing can ever separate us from
15:14 I am fully **c**, dear friends, that you are full of
Php 1:25 I am **c** of this, so I will continue with you so that

CONVINCING (1) [CONVINCE]

Job 6:26 Do you think your words are **c** when you disregard

CONVULSION (4) [CONVULSIONS]

Mk 1:26 the evil spirit screamed and threw the man into a **c**,
9:20 it threw the child into a violent **c**, and he fell to the
9:26 and threw the boy into another violent **c** and left
Lk 9:42 him to the ground and threw him into a violent **c**.

CONVULSIONS (1) [CONVULSION]

Lk 9:39 It throws him into **c** so that he foams at the mouth.

COOING (1)

SS 2:12 singing birds has come, even the **c** of turtledoves.

COOK (12) [COOKED, COOKING]

Ex 23:19 "You must not **c** a young goat in its mother's milk.
34:26 "You must not **c** a young goat in its mother's
1Sa 8:13 and force them to **c** and bake and make perfumes
9:23 then instructed the **c** to bring Saul the finest cut of
9:24 So the **c** brought it in and placed it before Saul.
2Sa 13: 6 to take care of me and **c** something for me to eat."
1Ki 17:12 I was just gathering a few sticks to **c** this last meal,
17:13 Go ahead and **c** that 'last meal,' but bake me a
Pr 12:27 Lazy people don't even **c** the game they catch,
Eze 24: 5 pot to a boil, and **c** the bones along with the meat.
24:10 **C** the meat well with many spices. Then empty the
46:20 "This is where the priests will **c** the meat from the

COOKED (11) [COOK]

Ge 27:14 She took them and **c** a delicious meat dish,
27:19 Here is the wild game, **c** the way you like it.
Lev 2: 5 If your grain offering is **c** on a griddle, it must be
6:21 It must be **c** on a griddle with olive oil, and it must
7: 9 or **c** on a griddle belongs to the priest who presents
Nu 11: 8 These cakes tasted like they had been **c** in olive oil.
Jdg 6:19 He **c** a young goat, and with half a bushel of flour
2Ki 6:29 So we **c** my son and ate him. Then the next day I
1Ch 23:29 the cakes **c** in olive oil, and the other mixed breads.
La 4:10 Tenderhearted women have **c** their own children
Mt 22: 4 has been prepared, and choice meats have been **c**.

COOKING (8) [COOK]

Ge 25:29 One day when Jacob was **c** some stew,
Lev 11:35 If it is a clay oven or **c** pot, it must be smashed to
2Sa 17:28 **c** pots, serving bowls, wheat and barley flour,
1Ki 17:12 in the jar and a little **c** oil in the bottom of the jug.
Isa 27:11 and used for kindling beneath the **c** pots.
Mic 3: 3 You chop them up like meat for the **c** pot.
Zec 14:20 And the **c** pots in the Temple of the LORD will
14:21 every **c** pot in Jerusalem and Judah will be set

COOL (5) [COOL-TEMPERED, COOLED, COOLING]

Jdg 3:20 Eglon as he was sitting alone in a **c** upstairs room
Isa 25: 5 You **c** the land with the shade of a cloud.
32: 2 and as the **c** shadow of a large rock in a hot
49:10 in his mercy will lead them beside **c** waters.
Lk 16:24 dip the tip of his finger in water and **c** my tongue,

COOL-TEMPERED (1) [COOL, TEMPER]

Pr 15:18 hothead starts fights; a **c** person tries to stop them.

COOLED (2) [COOL]

Ex 32:20 And when the metal had **c**, he ground it into
Est 2: 1 But after Xerxes' anger had **c**, he began thinking

COOLING (1) [COOL]

Ge 31: 2 And Jacob began to notice a considerable **c** in

COOPERATE (2) [COOPERATED, COOPERATION]

Ex 23: 1 Do not **c** with evil people by telling lies on the
Ezr 10: 4 in setting things straight, and we will **c** fully."

COOPERATED (1) [COOPERATE]

Ezr 8:36 who then **c** by supporting the people

COOPERATION (1) [COOPERATE]

Ac 9: 2 asking their **c** in the arrest of any followers of the

COOS [KJV] See COS

COPIED (2) [COPY]

Jos 8:32 Joshua **c** the law of Moses onto the stones of the
Eze 11:12 you have **c** the sins of the nations around you."

COPIES (4) [COPY]

2Ki 10: 1 So Jehu wrote a letter and sent **c** to Samaria,
2Ch 17: 9 They took **c** of the Book of the Law of the LORD
Jer 29:25 and you sent **c** to the other priests and people in
Heb 9:23 in it—which were **c** of things in heaven—

COPPER (4) [COPPERSMITH]

Dt 8: 9 as common as stone, and **c** is abundant in the hills.
Job 28: 2 to dig iron from the earth and smelt **c** from stone.
Eze 22:18 a useless mixture of **c**, tin, iron, and lead.
22:20 just as **c**, tin, iron, and lead are melted down in a

COPPERSMITH (1) [COPPER, SMITHS]

2Ti 4:14 Alexander the **c** has done me much harm,

COPULATION [KJV] See EMISSION

COPY (16) [COPIED, COPIES]

Dt 17:18 he must **c** these laws on a scroll for himself in the
17:19 He must always keep this **c** of the law with him
Jos 22:28 'Look at this **c** of the LORD's altar that our
2Ki 11:12 He presented Joash with a **c** of God's covenant
2Ch 23:11 They presented Joash with a **c** of God's laws
Ezr 4:11 This is a **c** of the letter they sent him:
7:11 King Artaxerxes had presented a **c** of this letter to
Est 3:14 A **c** of this decree was to be issued in every
4: 8 Mordecai gave Hathach a **c** of the decree issued in
8:13 A **c** of this decree was to be recognized as law in
Pr 3:31 Do not envy violent people; don't **c** their ways.
Jer 32:11 took the sealed deed and an unsealed **c** of the deed,
32:14 Take both this sealed deed and the unsealed **c**,
Ro 12: 2 Don't **c** the behavior and customs of this world,
Heb 8: 5 They serve in a place of worship that is only a **c**,
9:24 for that was merely a **c** of the real Temple in

CORAL (2)

Job 28:18 **C** and valuable rock crystal are worthless in trying
Eze 27:16 embroidery, fine linen, and jewelry of **c** and rubies.

CORD (7) [CORDS]

Ge 38:18 "I want your identification seal, your **c**,
Ex 28:37 to the front of Aaron's turban by means of a blue **c**.
39:31 This medallion was tied to the turban with a blue **c**,
Nu 15:38 and attach the tassels at each corner with a blue **c**.
Ecc 4:12 for a triple-braided **c** is not easily broken.
12: 6 before the silver **c** of life snaps and the golden
Eze 16: 4 Your umbilical **c** was left uncut, and you were

CORDIALLY (1)

Ac 21:17 All the believers in Jerusalem welcomed us **c**.

CORDS (19) [CORD]

Ex 28:14 and two **c** made of pure gold will be attached to the
28:22 to the ephod, make braided **c** of pure gold.
28:24 The two gold **c** will go through the rings on the
28:25 and the ends of the **c** will be tied to the gold
28:28 chestpiece to the rings on the ephod with blue **c**.
35:18 pegs of the Tabernacle and courtyard and their **c**;
39:15 to the ephod, they made braided **c** of pure gold.
39:17 The two gold **c** were put through the gold rings on
39:18 and the ends of the **c** were tied to the gold settings
39:21 Blue **c** were used to attach the bottom rings of the
39:40 at the courtyard entrance; the **c** and tent pegs;
Nu 3:26 the curtain at the courtyard entrance, the **c**,
3:37 of the courtyard and all their bases, pegs, and **c**.
4:26 the necessary **c**, and all the altar's accessories.
4:32 pegs, **c**, accessories, and everything else related to
Job 30:11 For God has cut the **c** of my tent. He has humbled
Ps 129: 4 he has cut the **c** used by the ungodly to bind me.
Isa 5:18 their sins behind them, tied with **c** of falsehood.
Eze 27:24 and many-colored carpets bound with **c** and made

CORE (2)

Ps 82: 5 in darkness, / the whole world is shaken to the **c**.
La 2:14 have said so many foolish things, false to the **c**.

CORIANDER (2)

Ex 16:31 It was white like **c** seed, and it tasted like honey
Nu 11: 7 The manna looked like small **c** seeds, pale yellow

CORINTH (8) [CORINTHIAN, CORINTHIANS]

Ac 18: 1 Then Paul left Athens and went to **C**.
18: 8 Many others in **C** also became believers and were
18:18 Paul stayed in **C** for some time after that and
19: 1 While Apollos was in **C**, Paul traveled through the
1Co 1: 2 We are writing to the church of God in **C**, you who
2Co 1: 1 We are writing to God's church in **C** and to all the
1:23 The reason I didn't return to **C** was to spare you
2Ti 4:20 Erastus stayed at **C**, and I left Trophimus sick at

CORINTHIAN (1) [CORINTH]

2Co 6:11 Oh, dear **C** friends! We have spoken honestly with

CORINTHIANS (1) [CORINTH]

1Co 14:36 of God's word begins and ends with you **C**?

CORMORANT (2)

Lev 11:17 the little owl, the **c**, the great owl,
Dt 14:17 the pelican, the carrion vulture, the **c**,

CORN (1)

Isa 47: 2 Take heavy millstones and grind the **c**.

CORN [KJV] See also GRAIN

CORNELIUS (12) [CORNELIUS']

Ac 10: 1 there lived a Roman army officer named **C**,
10: 3 of God coming toward him. "**C**!" the angel said.
10: 4 **C** stared at him in terror. "What is it, sir?"
10: 7 **C** called two of his household servants and a
10:17 Just then the men sent by **C** found the house
10:22 They said, "We were sent by **C**, a Roman officer.
10:24 **C** was waiting for him and had called together his
10:25 his home, **C** fell to the floor before him in worship.
10:27 So **C** got up, and they talked together and went
10:30 **C** replied, "Four days ago I was praying in my
10:31 He told me, '**C**, your prayers have been heard,
10:48 Afterward **C** asked him to stay with them for

CORNELIUS' (1) [CORNELIUS]

Ac 10: 9 The next day as **C** messengers were nearing the

CORNER (35) [CORNERED, CORNERS, CORNERSTONE]

Ex 8: 5 so there will be frogs in every **c** of the land."
26:23 along with an extra frame at each **c**.
26:24 These **c** frames will be connected at the bottom
26:24 Both of these **c** frames will be made the same way.
27: 4 Make a bronze grating, with a metal ring at each **c**.
36:28 plus an extra frame at each **c**.
36:29 These **c** frames were connected at the bottom
36:29 They made two of these, one for each rear **c**.
37:25 with its **c** horns made from the same piece of wood
Nu 15:38 and attach the tassels at each **c** with a blue cord.
Ru 3: 9 "Spread the **c** of your covering over me, for you
1Ki 7:30 At each **c** of the carts were supporting posts for the
7:39 The Sea was placed at the southeast **c** of the
2Ki 14:13 from the Ephraim Gate to the **C** Gate.
2Ch 4:10 The Sea was placed near the southeast **c** of the
25:23 from the Ephraim Gate to the **C** Gate.
26: 9 Uzziah built fortified towers in Jerusalem at the **C**
28:24 then set up altars to pagan gods in every **c** of
Ne 3:24 from Azariah's house to the buttress and the **c**.
3:25 and the **c** to the upper tower that projects from the
3:31 he continued as far as the upper room at the **c**.
3:32 and merchants repaired the wall from that **c** to the
9:22 and you placed your people in every **c** of the land.
Pr 7:12 in the streets and markets, soliciting at every **c**.
21: 9 It is better to live alone in the **c** of an attic than
25:24 It is better to live alone in the **c** of an attic than
Isa 45:19 I do not whisper obscurities in some dark **c** so no
Jer 31:38 for me, from the Tower of Hananel to the **C** Gate.
Eze 16:25 On every street **c** you defiled your beauty,
16:31 You build your pagan shrines on every street **c**
46:21 of its four corners. In each **c** I saw an enclosure.
Zec 14:10 then to the **C** Gate, and from the Tower of Hananel
Lk 15: 8 and look in every **c** of the house and sweep every
Ac 26:26 all familiar to him, for they were not done in a **c**!
Rev 20: 8 He will go out to deceive the nations from every **c**

CORNERED (1) [CORNER]

2Sa 21:16 He had **c** David and was about to kill him.

CORNERS (33) [CORNER]

Ex 25:26 and put the rings at the four **c** by the four legs,
27: 2 Make a horn at each of the four **c** of the altar
28:23 and attach them to the top **c** of the chestpiece.
28:26 and attach them to the two lower inside **c** of the
30: 2 with horns at the **c** carved from the same piece of
38: 2 There were four horns, one at each of the four **c**,
39: 4 which were attached to its **c** so it could be tied
39:16 and attached them to the top **c** of the chestpiece.
39:19 lower inside **c** of the chestpiece next to the ephod.
Dt 22:12 "You must put tassels on the four **c** of your cloaks.
1Ki 7:34 There were supports at each of the four **c** of the
2Ki 19:23 cypress trees. / I have reached its farthest **c**
2Ch 26:15 hurl stones from the towers and the **c** of the wall.
Isa 37:24 cypress trees. / I have reached its farthest **c**
43: 6 and daughters back to Israel from the distant **c** of
Jer 17: 1 or with an iron chisel on the **c** of their altars.
25:32 fury is rising from the most distant **c** of the earth!"
31: 8 from the north and from the distant **c** of the earth.
Eze 41: 3 extended 12-1/4 feet to the **c** of the inner room.
41:22 Its **c**, base, and sides were all made of wood.
43:15 with a horn rising up from each of the four **c**.
43:20 the four **c** of the upper ledge, and the curb that runs
45:19 the four **c** of the upper ledge on the altar,
46:21 the outer courtyard and led me to each of its four **c**.
Zep 1:12 with lanterns in Jerusalem's darkest **c** to find
Zec 9:15 a bowl, drenched with blood like the **c** of the altar.
Mt 6: 5 the hypocrites who love to pray publicly on street **c**
22: 9 Now go out to the street **c** and invite everyone you

Lk 11:36 If you are filled with light, with no dark **c**,
Ac 10:11 like a large sheet was let down by its four **c**.
11: 5 large sheet was let down by its four **c** from the sky.
13:47 to bring salvation to the farthest **c** of the earth.' "
Rev 7: 1 Then I saw four angels standing at the four **c** of the

CORNERSTONE (12) [CORNER, STONE]

Job 38: 6 What supports its foundations, and who laid its **c**
Ps 118:22 rejected by the builders / has now become the **c**.
Isa 28:16 a tested and precious **c** that is safe to build on.
Zec 10: 4 From Judah will come the **c**, the tent peg, the battle
Mt 21:42 has now become the **c**. / This is the Lord's doing,
Mk 12:10 rejected by the builders / has now become the **c**.
Lk 20:17 rejected by the builders / has now become the **c**.'
Ac 4:11 that you builders rejected / has now become the **c**.'
Eph 2:20 and the prophets. And the **c** is Christ Jesus himself.
1Pe 2: 4 to Christ, who is the living **c** of God's temple.
2: 6 "I am placing a stone in Jerusalem, / a chosen **c**,
2: 7 rejected by the builders / has now become the **c**."

CORNET(S) [KJV] See CASTANETS, HORNS

CORNFLOOR [KJV] See THRESHING (FLOOR)

CORONATION (2)

2Ki 11:14 by the pillar, as was the custom at times of **c**.
1Ch 23: 2 with the priests and Levites, for the **c** ceremony.

CORPSE (5) [CORPSES]

Lev 22: 4 any of the priests become unclean by touching a **c**,
Nu 19:16 And if someone outdoors touches the **c** of someone
Isa 14:19 Like a **c** trampled underfoot, you will be dumped
Rev 6: 8 saw a horse whose color was pale green like a **c**.
16: 3 on the sea, and it became like the blood of a **c**.

CORPSES (12) [CORPSE]

Lev 26:30 I will leave your **c** piled up beside your lifeless
2Ki 19:35 up the next morning, they found **c** everywhere.
Ps 83:10 at Endor, / and their decaying **c** fertilized the soil.
Isa 18: 6 to eat. The vultures will tear at **c** all summer.
37:36 up the next morning, they found **c** everywhere.
59:10 No wonder we are like **c** when compared to
Jer 7:33 The **c** of my people will be food for the vultures
12: 9 Bring on the wild beasts to pick their **c** clean!
41: 9 of Israel. Ishmael son of Nethaniah filled it with **c**.
Eze 6: 5 I will lay your **c** in front of your idols and scatter
6: 7 Then when the place is littered with **c**, you will
Zec 14:12 Their people will become like walking **c**,

CORRECT (10) [CORRECTED, CORRECTING, CORRECTION, CORRECTLY, CORRECTS]

Pr 23:13 Don't fail to **c** your children. They won't die if you
Jer 10:24 So **c** me, LORD, but please be gentle. Do not **c** me
in anger, for I would die.
Hab 1:12 to punish and **c** us for our terrible sins.
Lk 19:11 he told a story to **c** the impression that the
Jn 7:23 For if the **c** time for circumcising your son falls on
8:16 my judgment would be **c** in every respect because I
1Co 12: 1 for I must **c** your misunderstandings about them.
2Ti 4: 2 Patiently **c**, rebuke, and encourage your people
Tit 2: 8 Let your teaching be so **c** that it can't be criticized.

CORRECTED (6) [CORRECT]

Nu 15:25 and they have **c** it with their offering given to the
Job 5:17 "But consider the joy of those **c** by God! Do not
Pr 1:30 my advice and paid no attention when I **c** them.
Isa 57:11 because I have not **c** you that you have no fear of
Mt 16:22 But Peter took him aside and **c** him.
Heb 9:10 are in effect only until their limitations can be **c**.

CORRECTING (1) [CORRECT]

Tit 2:15 your people to do them, **c** them when necessary.

CORRECTION (8) [CORRECT]

Pr 1:25 ignored my advice and rejected the **c** I offered.
6:23 ahead of you. The **c** of discipline is the way to life.
10:17 People who accept **c** are on the pathway to life,
12: 1 you must love discipline; it is stupid to hate **c**.
15: 5 parent's discipline; whoever learns from **c** is wise.
15:10 be severely punished; whoever hates **c** will die.
15:32 but if you listen to **c**, you grow in understanding.
Zep 3: 2 No one can tell it anything; it refuses all **c**. It does

CORRECTLY (5) [CORRECT]

Ge 4: 7 But if you refuse to respond **c**, then watch out!
Jdg 12: 6 from Ephraim cannot pronounce the word **c**.
2Ki 17:26 because they have not worshiped him **c**."
1Ch 28:20 related to the Temple of the LORD is finished **c**.
2Ti 2:15 be ashamed and who **c** explains the word of truth.

CORRECTS (5) [CORRECT]

Pr 3:11 and don't be discouraged when he **c** you.
3:12 For the LORD **c** those he loves, just as a father **c** a
child in whom he delights.
Heb 12: 5 and don't be discouraged when he **c** you.
Rev 3:19 I am the one who **c** and disciplines everyone I love.

CORRESPONDING (2)

2Ch 3: 8 **c** to the width of the Temple, and it was also thirty
Eze 41: 7 **c** to the narrowing of the Temple wall as it rose

CORRUPT (32) [CORRUPTED, CORRUPTING, CORRUPTION, CORRUPTLY, CORRUPTS]

Ge 6:11 Now the earth had become **c** in God's sight,
Dt 4:16 So do not **c** yourselves by making a physical image
4:25 do not **c** yourselves by making idols of any kind.
9:12 the people you led out of Egypt have become **c**.
16:19 eyes of the wise and **c** the decisions of the godly.
31:29 know that after my death you will become utterly **c**
Jdg 2:19 the judge died, the people returned to their **c** ways,
2Ch 27: 2 Nevertheless, the people continued in their **c** ways.
Job 15:16 How much less pure is a **c** and sinful person with a
Ps 14: 1 They are **c**, and their actions are evil; / no one does
14: 3 have turned away from God; / all have become **c**.
53: 1 They are **c**, and their actions are evil; / no one does
53: 3 have turned away from God; / all have become **c**.
Pr 2:12 from evil people, from those whose speech is **c**.
4:24 Avoid all perverse talk; stay far from **c** speech.
10:32 are helpful, but the wicked speak only what is **c**.
19:28 A **c** witness makes a mockery of justice; the mouth
Ecc 3:16 in the courtroom. Yes, even the courts of law are **c**!
7: 7 turns wise people into fools, and bribes **c** the heart.
Isa 1: 4 and **c** children who have turned away from the
Jer 2:21 very best. How did you grow into this **c** wild vine?
3: 1 her back again, for that would surely **c** the land.
Eze 7:22 as these robbers invade my treasured land and **c** it.
21:25 "O you **c** and wicked prince of Israel, your final
Mt 5:46 good is that? Even **c** tax collectors do that much.
18:17 treat that person as a pagan or a **c** tax collector.
21:31 **c** tax collectors and prostitutes will get into the
Lk 3:12 Even **c** tax collectors came to be baptized
1Ti 6: 5 Their minds are **c**, and they don't tell the truth.
Tit 1:15 But nothing is pure to those who are **c**
Jas 1:27 in their troubles, and refuse to let the world **c** us.
Rev 21: 8 and unbelievers, and the **c**, and murderers,

CORRUPTED (5) [CORRUPT]

Jer 2: 7 my land and **c** the inheritance I had promised you.
Eze 28:17 You **c** your wisdom for the sake of your splendor.
Mal 2: 8 You have **c** the covenant I made with the Levites,"
Heb 12:15 whenever it springs up, many are **c** by its poison.
Rev 19: 2 He has punished the great prostitute who **c** the

CORRUPTING (1) [CORRUPT]

Am 2: 7 son sleep with the same woman, **c** my holy name.

CORRUPTION (14) [CORRUPT]

Ge 6:12 God observed all this **c** in the world, and he saw
2Ki 23:13 east of Jerusalem and south of the Mount of **C**,
Ezr 9:11 From one end to the other, the land is filled with **c**.
Pr 8:13 I hate pride, arrogance, **c**, and perverted speech.
Isa 59: 3 is full of lies, and your lips are tainted with **c**.
Jer 6:28 and cruel as iron. All of them lead others into **c**.
Eze 24: 6 the city of murderers! She is a pot filled with **c**.
24:11 pot on the coals to scorch away the filth and **c**.
24:12 But it's hopeless; the **c** remains. So throw it into
24:13 It is the filth and **c** of your lewdness and idolatry.
Mic 3:10 Jerusalem on a foundation of murder and **c**.
Hab 2:12 build cities with money gained by murder and **c**!
Lk 11:44 People walk over them without knowing the **c** they
2Pe 2:19 but they themselves are slaves to sin and **c**.

CORRUPTLY (1) [CORRUPT]

Dt 32: 5 "But they have acted **c** toward him; / when they

CORRUPTS (1) [CORRUPT]

1Co 15:33 such things, for "bad company **c** good character."

COS (1)

Ac 21: 1 we sailed straight to the island of **C**.

COSAM (2)

Lk 3:28 Addi was the son of **C**. / **C** was the son of
Elmadam.

COST (19) [COSTLY, COSTS]

Lev 19:16 "Do not try to get ahead at the **c** of your
25:50 whatever it would **c** to hire a servant for that
Nu 16:38 these men who have sinned at the **c** of their lives.
Jos 6:26 At the **c** of his firstborn son, / he will lay its
6:26 At the **c** of his youngest son, / he will set up its
2Sa 24:24 to the LORD my God that have **c** me nothing."
2Ki 6:25 and a cup of dove's dung **c** about two ounces of
7: 1 five quarts of fine flour will **c** only half an ounce of
7: 1 and ten quarts of barley grain will **c** only half an
7:18 five quarts of fine flour will **c** half an ounce of
7:18 and ten quarts of barley grain will **c** half an ounce
1Ch 12:19 "It will **c** us our lives if David switches loyalties to
21:24 I will not offer a burnt offering that has **c** me
Pr 6:26 and sleeping with another man's wife may **c** you
7:23 into a snare, little knowing it would **c** him his life.
20:25 make a rash promise to God before counting the **c**.
Lk 14:28 "But don't begin until you count the **c**. For who
Ac 22:28 the commander muttered, "and it **c** me plenty!"
2Co 11: 8 their contributions so I could serve you at no **c**.

COSTLY (7) [COST]

1Ki 5:17 and shaped **c** blocks of stone for the foundation of
7: 9 **c** blocks of stone, cut and trimmed to exact
7:11 The **c** blocks of stone used in the walls were also
1Ch 29: 2 other precious stones, **c** jewels, and all kinds of
2Ch 21: 3 gold, and **c** items, and also the ownership of some
Est 1: 6 marble, mother-of-pearl, and other **c** stones.
Da 11:38 on him gold, silver, precious stones, and **c** gifts.

COSTS (2) [COST]

Ezr 6: 8 You must pay the full construction **c** without delay
Pr 23: 7 They are always thinking about how much it **c**.

COTES [KJV] See FOLDS

COTTON (1)

Isa 19: 9 The weavers will have no flax or **c**, for the crops

COUCH (4) [COUCHES]

1Sa 28:23 and got up from the ground and sat on the **c**.
Est 7: 8 In despair he fell on the **c** where Queen Esther was
SS 1:12 "The king is lying on his **c**, enchanted by the
Eze 23:41 You sat with them on a beautifully embroidered **c**

COUCHES (2) [COUCH]

Est 1: 6 and silver **c** stood on a mosaic pavement of
Hos 7:14 Instead, they sit on their **c** and wail. They cut

COULD (449) [COULDN'T] See Index of Articles, Etc.

COULDN'T (72) [COULD, NOT] See Index of Articles, Etc.

COUNCIL (42) [COUNCILS]

Jdg 21: 5 our **c** in the presence of the LORD at Mizpah?"
Ezr 7:14 and my **C** of Seven hereby instruct you to conduct
7:28 before the king, his **c**, and all his mighty princes!
8:25 and the other items that the king, his **c**, his leaders,
Job 15: 8 Were you listening at God's secret **c**? Do you have
Pr 31:23 for he sits in the **c** meeting with the other civic
Mt 26:59 and the entire high **c** were trying to find witnesses
Mk 14:55 and the entire high **c** were trying to find witnesses
15: 1 the entire high **c**—met to discuss their next step.
15:43 an honored member of the high **c**, Joseph from
Lk 22:66 of religious law. Jesus was led before this high **c**,
23: 1 Then the entire **c** took Jesus over to Pilate,
23:50 He was a member of the Jewish high **c**,
Jn 11:47 and Pharisees called the high **c** together to discuss
Ac 4: 5 The next day the **c** of all the rulers and elders
4:13 The members of the **c** were amazed when they saw
4:14 right there among them, the **c** had nothing to say.
4:15 So they sent Peter and John out of the **c** chamber
4:21 The **c** then threatened them further, but they finally
5:21 and his officials arrived, they convened the high **c**,
5:22 were gone. So they returned to the **c** and reported,
5:27 Then they brought the apostles in before the **c**.
5:33 the high **c** was furious and decided to kill them.
5:34 and ordered that the apostles be sent outside the **c**
5:40 The **c** accepted his advice. They called in the
5:41 The apostles left the high **c** rejoicing that God had
6:12 and brought him before the high **c**.
6:15 At this point everyone in the **c** stared at Stephen
17: 6 believers instead and took them before the city **c**.
17:19 Then they took him to the **C** of Philosophers.
17:22 So Paul, standing before the **C**, addressed them as
17:34 a member of the **C**, a woman named Damaris,
22: 5 and the whole **c** of leaders can testify that this is
22:30 leading priests into session with the Jewish high **c**.
23: 1 Gazing intently at the high **c**, Paul began:
23: 6 Paul realized that some members of the high **c**
23: 7 This divided the **c**—the Pharisees against the
23:15 and the high **c** should tell the commander to bring
Paul back to the **c** again,"
23:20 to bring Paul before the Jewish high **c** tomorrow,
23:28 Then I took him to their high **c** to try to find out
24:20 what wrongdoing the Jewish high **c** found in me,

COUNCILS (1) [COUNCIL]

Isa 8:10 Call your **c** of war, develop your strategies,

COUNSEL (28) [COUNSELED, COUNSELOR, COUNSELORS]

2Sa 17:14 For the LORD had arranged to defeat the **c** of
1Ki 1:12 and the life of your son Solomon, follow my **c**.
12:14 and followed the **c** of his younger advisers. He told
2Ch 10:14 and followed the **c** of his younger advisers. He told
25:16 you have done this and have not accepted my **c**."
Est 1:21 made good sense, so he followed Memucan's **c**.
Job 5:27 is true. Listen to my **c**, and apply it to yourself."
12:13 power are with God; **c** and understanding are his.
29:22 they had nothing to add, for my **c** satisfied them.
Ps 37:30 The godly offer good **c**; / they know what is right
73:24 You will keep on guiding me with your **c**,
106:13 what he had done! / They wouldn't wait for his **c**!
107:11 words of God, / scorning the **c** of the Most High.
Pr 5: 1 to my wisdom; listen carefully to my wise **c**.
6:22 Wherever you walk, their **c** can lead you.
8:33 Listen to my **c** and be wise. Don't ignore it.
20:18 Plans succeed through good **c**; don't go to war
27: 9 The heartfelt **c** of a friend is as sweet as perfume

Isa 11: 2 and understanding, the Spirit of **c** and might,
19: 11 Their best **c** to the king of Egypt is stupid
19: 13 of Egypt have ruined the land with their foolish **c**.
Jer 49: 7 men of Teman? Is there no one left to give wise **c**?
Eze 7: 26 teaching from the priests and no **c** from the leaders.
11: 2 for the wicked **c** being given in this city.
Mic 4: 9 He is dead! Have you no wise people to **c** you?
1Co 2: 16 Who can give him **c**?" But we can understand
7: 40 and I think I am giving you **c** from God's Spirit
Col 3: 16 Use his words to teach and **c** each other.

COUNSELED (2) [COUNSEL]

1Ki 12: 6 the matter with the older men who had **c** his father,
2Ch 10: 6 the matter with the older men who had **c** his father,

COUNSELOR (10) [COUNSEL]

Ge 45: 8 And he has made me a **c** to Pharaoh—manager of
1Ch 27: 32 Jonathan, David's uncle, was a wise **c** to the king,
Isa 9: 6 Wonderful **C**, Mighty God, Everlasting Father,
40: 13 Who knows enough to be his teacher or **c**?
Jn 14: 16 will ask the Father, and he will give you another **C**,
14: 26 But when the Father sends the **C** as my
14: 26 and by the **C** I mean the Holy Spirit—he will teach
15: 26 "But I will send you the **C**—the Spirit of truth.
16: 7 I go away, because if I don't, the **C** won't come.
Ro 11: 34 Lord is thinking? Who knows enough to be his **c**?

COUNSELORS (18) [COUNSEL]

Ge 50: 7 with a great number of Pharaoh's **c** and advisers—
2Sa 15: 12 one of David's **c** who lived in Giloh.
1Ki 12: 7 The older **c** replied, "If you are willing to serve the
12: 13 to them, for he rejected the advice of the older **c**
12: 28 So on the advice of his **c**, the king made two gold
2Ch 10: 7 The older **c** replied, "If you are good to the people
10: 13 to them, for he rejected the advice of the older **c**
Job 12: 17 He leads **c** away stripped of good judgment;
Pr 11: 14 a nation falls; with many **c**, there is safety.
15: 22 go wrong for lack of advice; many **c** bring success.
24: 6 wise guidance; victory depends on having many **c**.
26: 16 consider themselves smarter than seven wise **c**.
Isa 1: 26 and wise **c** like the ones you used to have.
19: 11 What fools are the **c** of Zoan! Their best counsel to
19: 12 What has happened to your wise **c**, Pharaoh?
Jer 50: 36 And when it strikes her wise **c**, they will become
Da 3: 2 prefects, governors, advisers, **c**, judges,
Lk 14: 31 going to war without first sitting down with his **c**

COUNT (59) [COUNTED, COUNTING, COUNTLESS, COUNTS]

Ge 15: 5 up into the heavens and **c** the stars if you can.
15: 5 descendants will be like that—too many to **c**!"
16: 10 will give you more descendants than you can **c**."
31: 39 to you and ask you to reduce the **c** of your flock?
32: 12 as the sands along the seashore—too many to **c**."
Ex 30: 12 be no plagues among the people as you **c** them.
Lev 15: 13 he must **c** off a period of seven days.
15: 28 she must **c** off a period of seven days.
23: 15 was lifted up as an offering, **c** off seven weeks.
25: 8 "In addition, you must **c** off seven Sabbath years,
Nu 1: 49 do not include them when you **c** the rest of the
3: 15 **C** every male who is one month old or older."
3: 40 "Now **c** all the firstborn sons in Israel who are one
4: 3 **C** all the men between the ages of thirty and fifty
4: 23 **C** all the men between the ages of thirty and fifty
4: 30 **C** all the men between the ages of thirty and fifty
4: 35 The **c** included all the men between thirty and fifty
4: 39 The **c** included all the men between thirty and fifty
4: 43 The **c** included all the men between thirty and fifty
6: 12 completed before their defilement no longer **c**.
23: 10 Who can **c** Jacob's descendants, as numerous as
23: 10 Who can **c** even a fourth of Israel's people?
26: 4 "**C** all the men of Israel twenty years old
Dt 16: 9 "**C** off seven weeks from the beginning of your
24: 13 And the LORD your God will **c** it as a righteous
Jdg 6: 5 arrived on droves of camels too numerous to **c**.
7: 12 like grains of sand on the seashore—too many to **c**!
2Sa 24: 1 "Go and **c** the people of Israel and Judah,"
24: 4 and his officers went out to **c** the people of Israel.
1Ki 3: 8 a nation so great they are too numerous to **c**!
8: 5 the Ark in such numbers that no one could keep **c**!
2Ki 22: 4 and have him **c** the money the gatekeepers have
1Ch 21: 4 so Joab traveled throughout Israel to **c** the people.
27: 23 he did not **c** those who were younger than twenty
2Ch 5: 6 the Ark in such numbers that no one could keep **c**!
Ezr 1: 8 to **c** these items and present them to Sheshbazzar,
Job 8: 14 Everything they **c** on will collapse. They are
14: 16 For then you would **c** my steps, instead of
25: 3 Who is able to **c** his heavenly army? Does his light
38: 37 Who is wise enough to **c** all the clouds? Who can
Ps 22: 17 I can **c** every bone in my body. / My enemies stare
33: 17 Don't **c** on your warhorse to give you victory—
40: 12 For troubles surround me—/ too many to **c**!
44: 6 trust my bow; / I do not **c** on my sword to save me.
48: 12 Walk around and **c** the many towers.
109: 7 him be pronounced guilty. / **C** his prayers as sins.
139: 18 I can't even **c** them; / they outnumber the grains of
Isa 10: 19 will survive—so few that a child could **c** them!
48: 19 as the sands along the seashore—too many to **c**!
Eze 20: 37 I will **c** you carefully and hold you to the terms of
Hos 1: 10 be like the sands of the seashore—too many to **c**!
Joel 1: 6 It is a terrible army, too numerous to **c**! Its teeth
Lk 14: 28 "But don't begin until you **c** the cost. For who
Jn 8: 54 I am merely boasting about myself, it doesn't **c**.
2Co 10: 18 boast about themselves, it doesn't **c** for much.
Php 3: 9 I no longer **c** on my own goodness or my ability to
Heb 11: 12 the sand on the seashore, there is no way to **c** them.
Rev 7: 9 too great to **c**, from every nation and tribe
11: 1 and the altar, and **c** the number of worshipers.

COUNTED (54) [COUNT]

Ge 13: 16 many descendants that, like dust, they cannot be **c**!
21: 12 the son through whom your descendants will be **c**.
Ex 30: 12 each man who is **c** must pay a ransom for himself
Lev 27: 32 The LORD also owns every tenth animal **c** off
Nu 1: 19 So Moses **c** the people there in the wilderness of
1: 44 These were the men **c** by Moses and Aaron
1: 45 They were **c** by families—all the men of Israel who
3: 16 So Moses **c** them, just as the LORD had
3: 39 So among the Levite clans **c** by Moses and Aaron
3: 42 So Moses **c** the firstborn sons of the people of
4: 34 and the other leaders of the community **c** the
4: 37 Moses and Aaron **c** them, just as the LORD had
4: 38 The Gershonite division was also **c** by its clans
4: 41 Moses and Aaron **c** them, just as the LORD had
4: 42 The Merarite division was also **c** by its clans
4: 45 Moses and Aaron **c** them, just as the LORD had
4: 46 and the leaders of Israel **c** all the Levites by their
14: 29 twenty years old or older and were **c** in the census
26: 51 So the total number of Israelite men **c** in the census
26: 57 for the Levites who were **c** according to their clans:
26: 64 and Aaron **c** in this census had been among those
26: 64 **c** in the previous census taken in the wilderness of
Dt 24: 15 against you, and it would be **c** against you as sin.
25: 6 The first son she bears to him will be **c** as the son
Jdg 21: 9 For after they **c** all the people, no one from
1Sa 13: 15 When Saul **c** the men who were still with him,
2Sa 2: 30 When Joab **c** his casualties, he discovered that only
2Ki 12: 10 and the high priest **c** the money that had been
1Ch 23: 3 Levites who were thirty years old or older were **c**,
23: 11 Jeush and Beriah were **c** as a single family
2Ch 2: 17 the census his father had taken, and he **c** 153,600.
24: 11 and an officer of the high priest **c** the money
Job 3: 6 never again to be **c** among the days of the year,
15: 32 the prime of life, and all they **c** on will disappear.
Ps 69: 28 of Life; / don't let them be **c** among the righteous.
Pr 27: 14 too early in the morning, it will be **c** as a curse!
Isa 20: 5 who **c** on the power of Ethiopia and boasted of
20: 6 For we **c** on Egypt to protect us from the king of
33: 18 Assyrian officers outside your walls **c** your towers
53: 11 will make it possible for many to be **c** righteous,
53: 12 He was **c** among those who were sinners. He bore
Jer 18: 15 These can be **c** on, but not my people! For they
33: 22 And as the stars cannot be **c** and the sand on the
33: 24 and saying that Israel is not worthy to be **c** as a
Eze 25: 10 the Ammonites will no longer be **c** among the
Zec 11: 12 So they **c** out for my wages thirty pieces of silver.
Lk 22: 37 'He was **c** among those who were rebels.' Yes,
Jn 15: 24 no one else could do, they would not be **c** guilty.
Ac 5: 41 **c** them worthy to suffer dishonor for the name of
Ro 4: 8 whose sin is no longer **c** against them by the
9: 7 son through whom your descendants will be **c**,"
1Co 1: 28 despised by the world, things **c** as nothing at all,
2Ti 4: 16 abandoned me. I hope it will not be **c** against them.
Heb 11: 18 son through whom your descendants will be **c**."

COUNTER (1) [COUNTERED, COUNTERS]

2Sa 15: 34 Then you can frustrate and **c** Ahithophel's advice.

COUNTERED (1) [COUNTER]

1Sa 17: 2 Saul **c** by gathering his troops near the valley of

COUNTERFEIT (2)

2Th 2: 9 will come to do the work of Satan with **c** power
2Ti 3: 8 Their minds are depraved, and their faith is **c**.

COUNTERS (1) [COUNTER]

Jn 2: 14 and he saw money changers behind their **c**.

COUNTING (12) [COUNT]

Ge 46: 26 him to Egypt, not **c** his sons' wives, was sixty-six.
Lev 23: 16 Keep **c** until the day after the seventh Sabbath,
Dt 24: 15 before sunset because they are poor and are **c** on it.
Jdg 20: 17 armed with swords, not **c** Benjamin's warriors.
Ps 130: 5 I am **c** on the LORD; / yes, I am **c** on him.
Pr 20: 25 to make a rash promise to God before **c** the cost.
Ac 4: 4 five thousand men, not **c** women and children.
2Co 5: 19 to himself, no longer **c** people's sins against them.
Gal 5: 2 If you are **c** on circumcision to make you right
Php 3: 8 **c** it all as garbage, so that I may have Christ
Jas 5: 3 The very wealth you were **c** on will eat away your

COUNTLESS (4) [COUNT]

Ge 22: 17 I will multiply your descendants into **c** millions,
Nu 10: 36 "Return, O LORD, to the **c** thousands of Israel!"
2Ch 12: 3 and a **c** army of foot soldiers, including Libyans,
Heb 6: 14 and I will multiply your descendants into **c**

COUNTRIES (16) [COUNTRY]

Ge 41: 54 There were crop failures in all the surrounding **c**,
2Ch 9: 28 were imported from Egypt and many other **c**.
Ezr 4: 15 against the kings and **c** who attempted to control it.
Isa 13: 5 They came from **c** far away. They are the
Jer 16: 15 and from all the **c** to which he had exiled them.'
23: 8 and from all the **c** to which he had exiled them.'
25: 26 And I went to the kings of the northern **c**, far
27: 6 Now I will give your **c** to King Nebuchadnezzar of
32: 37 from all the **c** where I will scatter them in my fury.
40: 11 and the other nearby **c** heard that the king of
43: 5 returned from the nearby **c** to which they had fled.
49: 36 They will be exiled to **c** around the world.
51: 28 their generals, and the armies of all the **c** they rule.
Eze 11: 16 Although I have scattered you in the **c** of the
20: 38 I will bring them out of the **c** where they are in
Da 11: 42 He will conquer many **c**, and Egypt will not

COUNTRY (168) [COUNTRIES, COUNTRYMEN, COUNTRYSIDE]

HILL COUNTRY (88) Ge 12:8; 31:23,25; 36:8,9; Nu 13:17,29; 14:40,44; Dt 1:7,7,19,41,43; 2:3,5,37; 3:12,25; Jos 2:16,22,23; 9:1; 10:6,40; 11:2,3,16,21,21; 12:8; 13:6; 14:12; 15:48; 16:1; 17:15,16,18; 18:12; 19:50; 20:7,7,7; 21:11; 24:4,30,33; Jdg 1:9,19,34; 2:9; 3:3,27; 4:5; 7:24; 10:1; 12:15; 17:1; 18:2,13; 19:1,16,18; 1Sa 1:1; 9:4; 13:2; 23:14; 2Sa 20:21; 1Ki 4:8; 5:15; 12:25; 2Ki 5:22; 1Ch 6:67; 2Ch 2:18; 13:4; 15:8; 19:4; 21:11; 27:4; Jer 4:15; 17:26; 31:6; 32:44; 33:13; 50:19; Mal 1:3; Lk 1:39

HILL COUNTRY OF EPHRAIM (29) Jos 17:15; 19:50; 20:7; 24:30,33; Jdg 2:9; 3:27; 4:5; 7:24; 10:1; 17:1; 18:2,13; 19:1,16,18; 1Sa 1:1; 9:4; 2Sa 20:21; 1Ki 4:8; 12:25; 2Ki 5:22; 1Ch 6:67; 2Ch 13:4; 15:8; 19:4; Jer 4:15; 31:6; 50:19

Ge 12: 1 "Leave your **c**, your relatives, and your father's
12: 8 and set up camp in the hill **c** between Bethel on the
12: 20 then sent them out of the **c** under armed escort—
21: 23 loyal to me and to this **c** in which you are living."
21: 34 And Abraham lived in Philistine **c** for a long time.
25: 18 Ishmael's descendants were scattered across the **c**
26: 16 And Abimelech asked Isaac to leave the **c**.
27: 3 and a quiver full of arrows out into the open **c**,
31: 13 Now leave this **c** and return to the land you came
31: 23 with them seven days later in the hill **c** of Gilead.
31: 25 Jacob as he was camped in the hill **c** of Gilead,
36: 8 (also known as Edom) settled in the hill **c** of Seir.
36: 9 the Edomites, who live in the hill **c** of Seir.
Ex 1: 10 against us. Then they will escape from the **c**."
8: 24 The whole **c** was thrown into chaos by the flies.
10: 4 For tomorrow I will cover the whole **c** with
10: 15 For the locusts covered the surface of the whole **c**,
11: 1 you that he will practically force you to leave the **c**.
11: 10 so he wouldn't let the Israelites leave the **c**.
Nu 13: 17 "Go northward through the Negev into the hill **c**.
13: 27 sent us to see, and it is indeed a magnificent **c**—
13: 29 Jebusites, and Amorites live in the hill **c**.
14: 3 "Why is the LORD taking us to this **c** only to
14: 40 next morning and set out for the hill **c** of Canaan.
14: 44 But the people pushed ahead toward the hill **c** of
20: 17 Please let us pass through your **c**. We will be
20: 19 We only want to pass through your **c** and nothing
20: 21 refused to allow Israel to pass through their **c**,
34: 3 The southern portion of your **c** will extend from
Dt 1: 7 Go to the hill **c** of the Amorites and to all the
1: 7 the Jordan Valley, the hill **c**, the western foothills,
1: 19 and headed toward the hill **c** of the Amorites.
1: 41 thinking it would be easy to conquer the hill **c**.
1: 43 and arrogantly went into the hill **c** to fight.
2: 3 'You have been wandering around in this hill **c**
2: 4 "You will be passing through the **c** belonging to
2: 5 for I have given them all the hill **c** around Mount
2: 29 at Mount Seir allowed us to go through their **c**,
2: 37 the Jabbok River and the towns in the hill **c**—
3: 12 plus half of the hill **c** of Gilead with its towns,
3: 25 the beautiful hill **c** and the Lebanon mountains.'
22: 25 if the man meets the engaged woman out in the **c**,
22: 27 Since the man raped her out in the **c**, it must be
28: 3 You will be blessed in your towns and in the **c**.
28: 16 You will be cursed in your towns and in the **c**.
29: 2 to Pharaoh and all his servants and his whole **c**—
Jos 2: 16 "Escape to the hill **c**," she told them. "Hide there
2: 22 The spies went up into the hill **c** and stayed there
2: 23 Then the two spies came down from the hill **c**,
9: 1 Hivites, and Jebusites, who lived in the hill **c**,
9: 9 They answered, "We are from a very distant **c**.
10: 6 For all the Amorite kings who live in the hill **c**
10: 40 the kings and people of the hill **c**, the Negev,
11: 2 all the kings of the northern hill **c**; the kings in the
11: 3 of the Perizzites; the kings in the Jebusite hill **c**;
11: 16 the hill **c**, the Negev, the land of Goshen,
11: 21 who lived in the hill **c** of Hebron, Debir, Anab, and
the entire hill **c** of Judah and Israel.
12: 8 including the hill **c**, the western foothills,
13: 6 and all the hill **c** from Lebanon to
14: 12 So I'm asking you to give me the hill **c** that the
15: 48 also received the following towns in the hill **c**:
16: 1 through the wilderness and into the hill **c** of Bethel.
17: 15 "If the hill **c** of Ephraim is not large enough for
17: 16 They said, "The hill **c** is not enough for us,
17: 18 The forests of the hill **c** will be yours as well.
18: 12 then west through the hill **c** and the wilderness of
19: 50 He chose Timnath-serah in the hill **c** of Ephraim.
20: 7 Kedesh of Galilee, in the hill **c** of Naphtali;
20: 7 Shechem, in the hill **c** of Ephraim; and Kiriath-arba
20: 7 (that is, Hebron), in the hill **c** of Judah.
21: 11 (that is, Hebron), in the hill **c** of Judah,
24: 4 To Esau I gave the hill **c** of Seir, while Jacob
24: 30 at Timnath-serah in the hill **c** of Ephraim, north of
24: 33 He was buried in the hill **c** of Ephraim, in the town
Jdg 1: 9 south to fight the Canaanites living in the hill **c**,
1: 19 of Judah, and they took possession of the hill **c**.
1: 34 the Amorites forced them into the hill **c** and would
2: 9 at Timnath-serah in the hill **c** of Ephraim, north of
3: 3 and the Hivites living in the hill **c** of Lebanon from
3: 27 When he arrived in the hill **c** of Ephraim,
4: 5 and Bethel in the hill **c** of Ephraim,

7:24 Gideon also sent messengers throughout the hill c
10: 1 but lived in the town of Shamir in the hill c of
12:15 in Ephraim, in the hill c of the Amalekites.
17: 1 A man named Micah lived in the hill c of Ephraim.
18: 2 When these warriors arrived in the hill c of
18:13 Then they went up into the hill c of Ephraim
19: 1 living in a remote area of the hill c of Ephraim.
19:16 He was from the hill c of Ephraim, but he was
19:18 home to a remote area in the hill c of Ephraim,
Ru 1: 1 a man from Bethlehem in Judah left the c
1: 1 and two sons and went to live in the c of Moab.
1Sa 1: 1 who lived in Ramah in the hill c of Ephraim.
5:11 send the Ark of the God of Israel back to its own c,
9: 4 and traveled all through the hill c of Ephraim,
13: 2 men with him to Micmash and the hill c of Bethel.
23:14 of the wilderness and in the hill c of Ziph.
27: 5 we would rather live in one of the c towns instead
2Sa 19: 9 but Absalom chased him out of the c.
20:21 Sheba son of Bicri from the hill c of Ephraim,
1Ki 1: 3 So they searched throughout the c for a beautiful
4: 8 Ben-hur, in the hill c of Ephraim.
5:15 eighty thousand stonecutters in the hill c,
10: 6 "Everything I heard in my c about your
11:21 he said to Pharaoh, "Let me return to my own c."
12:25 then built up the city of Shechem in the hill c of
2Ki 5:22 from the hill c of Ephraim have just arrived.
10:32 King Hazael conquered several sections of the c
18:32 a c with bountiful harvests of grain and wine,
19:33 The king will return to his own c by the road on
1Ch 6:67 Shechem (a city of refuge in the hill c of Ephraim),
13: 5 people of Israel, from one end of the c to the other,
2Ch 2: 2 eighty thousand stonecutters in the hill c,
2:18 80,000 as stonecutters in the hill c, and 3,600 as
9: 5 "Everything I heard in my c about your
13: 4 When the army of Judah arrived in the hill c of
15: 8 and in the towns he had captured in the hill c of
19: 4 traveling from Beersheba to the hill c of Ephraim,
21:11 He had built pagan shrines in the hill c of Judah
27: 4 He built towns in the hill c of Judah
Job 18:19 nor any survivor in their home c.
Isa 1: 7 Your c lies in ruins, and your cities are burned.
6:11 are deserted and the whole c is an utter wasteland.
36:17 a c with bountiful harvests of grain and wine,
37:34 The king will return to his own c by the road on
66: 8 Has a c ever come forth in a mere moment?
Jer 4:15 From Dan and the hill c of Ephraim,
17:26 the western foothills and the hill c and the Negev,
22:12 in a distant land and never again see his own c."
22:26 from this land, and you will die in a foreign c.
25:12 I will make the c of the Babylonians an everlasting
27:11 to stay in their own c to farm the land as usual.
31: 6 watchmen will shout from the hill c of Ephraim,
32:44 in the towns of Judah and in the hill c,
33:13 their flocks will prosper in the towns of the hill c,
35:11 King Nebuchadnezzar of Babylon arrived in this c,
46:10 will receive a sacrifice today in the north c beside
50:19 and to be satisfied once more on the hill c of
51:34 with our riches. He has thrown us out of our own c.
Eze 14:13 suppose the people of a c were to sin against me,
21:30 No, I will destroy you in your own c, the land of
25: 4 nomads from the eastern deserts to overrun your c.
33: 2 When I bring an army against a c, the people of
Jnh 1: 8 What is your line of work? What c are you from?
Mal 1: 3 and I rejected Esau and devastated his hill c.
1: 4 Their c will be known as 'The Land of
Mt 11: 1 and preaching in towns throughout the c.
13:53 telling these stories, he left that part of the c.
21:33 vineyard to tenant farmers and moved to another c.
Mk 6: 1 Jesus left that part of the c and returned with his
12: 1 vineyard to tenant farmers and moved to another c.
15:21 from Cyrene, was coming in from the c just then,
16:12 two who were walking from Jerusalem into the c,
Lk 1:39 A few days later Mary hurried to the hill c of
4:14 became well known throughout the surrounding c.
14:23 'Go out into the c lanes and behind the hedges
20: 9 and moved to another c to live for several years.
23:26 of Cyrene, who was coming in from the c just then,
Jn 4:44 is honored everywhere except in his own c."
7:35 "Maybe he is thinking of leaving the c and going
11:55 and many people from the c arrived in Jerusalem
Ac 7: 5 that eventually the whole c would belong to
7: 6 c where they would be mistreated as slaves for four
7:29 he fled the c and lived as a foreigner in the land of
12:20 because their cities were dependent upon Herod's c
Heb 11:14 are looking forward to a c they can call their own.
11:15 If they had meant the c they came from,

COUNTRYMEN (4) [COUNTRY, MAN]

Ne 3:18 Next down the line were his c led by Binnui son of
Jer 34:17 Since you have not obeyed me by setting your c
Mic 5: 3 Then at last his fellow c will return from exile to
1Th 2:14 you suffered persecution from your own c.

COUNTRYSIDE (13) [COUNTRY]

Ge 37:15 a man noticed him wandering around the c.
49:15 When he sees how good the c is, / how pleasant the
1Sa 23:13 of them now—left Keilah and began roaming the c.
2Sa 18: 8 The battle raged all across the c, and more men
1Ki 20:27 to the vast Aramean forces that filled the c!
2Ki 15:16 and all the surrounding c as far as Tirzah,
Ps 132: 6 then we found it in the distant c of Jaar.
Jer 40: 7 The leaders of the Judean guerrilla bands in the c
40:12 then went out into the Judean c to gather a great
Hab 2: 8 You have filled the c with violence and all the
Mt 9:26 report of this miracle swept through the entire c.
Mk 5:14 fled to the nearby city and the surrounding c,
Lk 8:34 they fled to the nearby city and the surrounding c,

COUNTS (4) [COUNT]

Job 19:11 His fury burns against me; he c me as an enemy.
Ps 147: 4 He c the stars / and calls them all by name.
Isa 40:26 And he c them to see that none are lost or have
Gal 6:15 What c is whether we really have been changed

COUPLE (6)

Ex 21:21 If the slave recovers after a c of days, however,
36:18 They also made fifty small bronze clasps to c the
Lev 19:20 freed at the time, the c will not be put to death.
20:21 his brother, and the guilty c will remain childless.
Isa 8: 4 This name prophesies that within a c of years,
Lk 12: 6 is the price of five sparrows? A c of pennies?

COURAGE (37) [COURAGEOUS]

Jos 2:11 No one has the c to fight after hearing such things.
7: 5 fear at this turn of events, and their c melted away.
Jdg 5:21 the Kishon. / March on, my soul, with c!
20:22 But the Israelites took c and assembled at the same
2Sa 4: 1 he lost all c, and his people were paralyzed with
13:28 who has given the command. Take c and do it!"
22:46 They all lose their c / and come trembling from
1Ki 2: 2 on earth must someday go. Take c and be a man.
2Ch 15: 8 he took c and removed all the idols in the land of
19:11 Take c as you fulfill your duties, and may the
23: 1 He got up his c and made a pact with five army
25:11 Then Amaziah summoned his c and led his army to
Ezr 10: 4 Take c, for it is your duty to tell us how to proceed
Job 11:18 You will have c because you will have hope.
Ps 18:45 They all lose their c / and come trembling from
31:24 So be strong and take c, / all you who put your
40:12 than the hairs on my head. / I have lost all my c.
106:30 But Phinehas had the c to step in, / and the plague
Isa 28: 6 He will give great c to their warriors who stand at
57:15 and give new c to those with repentant hearts.
Jer 51:30 They stay in their barracks. Their c is gone.
Da 11:25 "Then he will stir up his c and raise a great army
Hag 2: 4 But now take c, Zerubbabel, says the LORD.
2: 4 Take c, Jeshua son of Jehozadak, the high priest.
2: 4 Take c, all you people still left in the land,
2: 4 Take c and work, for I am with you,
Mk 15:43 gathered his c and went to Pilate to ask for Jesus'
Lk 21:26 The c of many people will falter because of the
Jn 7:13 But no one had the c to speak favorably about him
Ac 27:22 But take c! None of you will lose your lives,
27:25 So take c! For I believe God. It will be just as he
28:15 When Paul saw them, he thanked God and took c.
1Th 2: 2 Yet our God gave us the c to declare his Good
Heb 3: 6 if we keep up our c and remain confident in our
6:18 we who have fled to him for refuge can take new c,
Jas 5: 8 And take c, for the coming of the Lord is near.
1Jn 2:28 you will be full of c and not shrink back from him

COURAGEOUS (23) [COURAGE]

Dt 31: 6 Be strong and c! Do not be afraid of them!
31: 7 Israel watched he said to him, "Be strong and c!
31:23 son of Nun with these words: "Be strong and c!
Jos 1: 6 "Be strong and c, for you will lead my people to
1: 7 Be strong and very c. Obey all the laws Moses
1: 9 I command you—be strong and c! Do not be afraid
1:18 will be put to death. So be strong and c!"
10:25 "Be strong and c, for the LORD is going to do
2Sa 10:12 Be c! Let us fight bravely to save our people
17:10 man your father is and how c his warriors are.
1Ch 19:13 Be c! Let us fight bravely to save our people
22:13 Be strong and c; do not be afraid or lose heart!
28:20 "Be strong and c, and do the work.
2Ch 13: 3 while Jeroboam mustered 800,000 c men from
14: 8 Both armies were composed of c fighting men.
15: 7 And now, you men of Judah, be strong and c,
32: 7 "Be strong and c! Don't be afraid of the king of
Ps 27:14 Be brave and c. / Yes, wait patiently for the
Isa 21:17 Only a few of its c archers will survive. I,
Eze 22:14 and c will you be in my day of reckoning?
Am 2:16 the most c of your fighting men will drop their
1Co 16:13 Stand true to what you believe. Be c. Be strong.
Php 2:25 is a true brother, a faithful worker, and a c soldier.

COURSE (83) [COURSING]

Ge 3: 2 "Of c we may eat it," the woman told him.
15:16 when the sin of the Amorites has run its c."
23: 9 I want to pay the full price, of c, whatever is
27:24 son Esau?" he asked. "Yes, of c," Jacob replied.
27:32 "Why, it's me, of c!" he replied. "It's Esau,
38:12 In the c of time Judah's wife died. After the time
42:23 Of c, they didn't know that Joseph understood
Ex 16:20 But, of c, some of them didn't listen and kept some
Jdg 11:25 for disputed land? Did he go to war? No, of c not.
Ru 1:13 marry someone else? No, of c not, my daughters!
4: 5 Then Boaz told him, "Of c, your purchase of the
1Sa 20:39 He, of c, didn't understand what Jonathan meant;
1Ki 22: 4 Jehoshaphat replied to King Ahab, "Why, of c!
2Ki 2: 3 "Quiet!" Elisha answered. "Of c I know it."
2: 5 "Quiet!" he answered again. "Of c I know it."
3: 7 And Jehoshaphat replied, "Why, of c! You and I
6:22 "Of c not!" Elisha told him. "Do we kill
19:18 But of c the Assyrians could destroy them!
1Ch 12:32 of the times and knew the best c for Israel to take.
2Ch 18: 3 And Jehoshaphat replied, "Why, of c! You and I
21:19 In the c of time, at the end of two years, the disease
Ezr 10:15 and Jahzeiah son of Tikvah opposed this c of
Job 38:21 But of c you know all this! For you were born
Ps 19: 6 and follows its c to the other end. / Nothing can
36: 4 sinful plots. / Their c of action is never good.
Pr 2: 9 and you will know how to find the right c of action
23:19 listen and be wise. Keep your heart on the right c.
Ecc 7:18 So try to walk a middle c—but those who fear God
9: 3 Instead, they choose their own mad c, for they
Isa 35: 9 Lions will not lurk along its c, and there will be no
37:19 But of c the Assyrians could destroy them!
Jer 10:23 is not his own. No one is able to plan his own c.
13:12 And they will reply, 'Of c, you don't need to tell us
44:19 husbands knowing it and helping us? Of c not!"
Eze 18:23 that I like to see wicked people die? Of c not!
18:24 should they be allowed to live? No, of c not!
47:19 then follow the c of the brook of Egypt to the
Da 2:21 He determines the c of world events; / he removes
Mt 6:27 worries add a single moment to your life? Of c not.
7:10 ask for a fish, do you give them a snake? Of c not!
12:10 (They were, of c, hoping he would say yes, so they
12:11 you get to work and pull it out? Of c you would.
17:25 "Of c he does," Peter replied. Then he went into
21:31 They replied, "The first, of c." Then Jesus
Mk 2:19 Of c not. They can't fast while they are with the
4:21 Of c not! A lamp is placed on a stand, where its
Lk 11:12 for an egg, do you give them a scorpion? Of c not!
12:25 worries add a single moment to your life? Of c not!
Jn 2: 9 of c, the servants knew), he called the bridegroom
4:46 In the c of his journey through Galilee, he arrived
Ac 19:27 Of c, I'm not just talking about the loss of public
25:16 Of c, I quickly pointed out to them that Roman law
27: 4 that made it difficult to keep the ship on c,
Ro 3: 4 Of c not! Though everyone else in the world is a
3: 6 Of c not! If God is not just, how is he qualified to
3:29 Isn't he also the God of the Gentiles? Of c he is.
3:31 Of c not! In fact, only when we have faith do we
6: 2 Of c not! Since we have died to sin, how can we
6:15 does this mean we can go on sinning? Of c not!
7: 7 Of c not! The law is not sinful, but it was the law
7:13 the law, which is good, cause my doom? Of c not!
9:14 can we say? Was God being unfair? Of c not!
11: 1 has God rejected his people, the Jews? Of c not!
11:11 and fall beyond recovery? Of c not!
13: 4 of c you should be afraid, for you will be punished.
1Co 9:10 Wasn't he also speaking to us? Of c he was.
11:19 But, of c, there must be divisions among you
12:29 Of c not. Is everyone a prophet? No. Are all
12:30 Does everyone have the gift of healing? Of c not.
15: 2 unless, of c, you believed something that was
15:27 (Of c, when it says "authority over all things,"
2Co 8:13 Of c, I don't mean you should give so much that
12:18 did Titus take advantage of you? No, of c not!
Gal 2:17 still sinners? Has Christ led us into sin? Of c not!
3: 2 Of c not, for the Holy Spirit came upon you only
3: 5 Of c not! It is because you believe the message you
3:16 was to his child—and that, of c, means Christ.
1Th 2:13 said as the very word of God—which, of c, it was.
3: 3 But, of c, you know that such troubles are going to
Jas 3: 6 It can turn the entire c of your life into a blazing
1Pe 2:20 Of c, you get no credit for being patient if you are
4: 4 Of c, your former friends are very surprised when
2Pe 2:16 But Balaam was stopped from his mad c when his

COURSING (1) [COURSE]

Rev 22: 2 c down the center of the main street. On each side

COURT (67) [COURTED, COURTROOM, COURTS, COURTYARD, COURTYARDS]

Ex 5:20 As they left Pharaoh's c, they met Moses
7:10 threw down his staff before Pharaoh and his c,
10: 7 The c officials now came to Pharaoh and appealed
Dt 17: 8 "Suppose a case arises in a local c that is too hard
25: 1 "Suppose two people take a dispute to c,
Jdg 4: 5 She would hold c under the Palm of Deborah,
1Sa 7:16 setting up his c first at Bethel, then at Gilgal,
8: 2 and Abijah, his oldest sons, held c in Beersheba.
2Sa 8:17 were the priests. Seraiah was the c secretary.
20:25 Sheva was the c secretary. Zadok and Abiathar
1Ki 4: 3 and Ahijah, the sons of Shisha, were c secretaries.
4:27 provided food for King Solomon and his c,
2Ki 12:10 the c secretary and the high priest counted the
18:18 Shebna the c secretary, and Joah son of Asaph,
18:37 Shebna the c secretary, and Joah son of Asaph,
19: 2 Shebna the c secretary, and the leading priests,
22: 3 and grandson of Meshullam, the c secretary,
22: 8 Hilkiah the high priest said to Shaphan the c
22:12 Acbor son of Micaiah, Shaphan the c secretary,
23:11 of Nathan-melech the eunuch, an officer of the c.
1Ch 18:16 were the priests. Seraiah was the c secretary.
2Ch 24:11 Then the c secretary and an officer of the high
34:15 Hilkiah said to Shaphan the c secretary, "I have
34:20 Acbor son of Micaiah, Shaphan the c secretary,
Ezr 4: 8 and Shimshai the c secretary wrote the letter,
4:17 Rehum the governor, Shimshai the c secretary,
Ne 3:25 from the king's house beside the c of the guard.
Est 4:11 c without being invited is doomed to die unless the
5: 1 royal robes and entered the inner c of the palace,
5: 2 he saw Queen Esther standing there in the inner c,
6: 4 "Who is that in the outer c?" the king inquired.
6: 4 Haman had just arrived in the outer c of the palace
10: 3 and was a friend at the royal c for all of them.
Job 9: 3 If someone wanted to take God to c, would it be
11:10 or if he calls the c to order, who is going to stop
24: 1 "Why doesn't the Almighty open the c and bring
Ps 82: 1 God presides over heaven's c; / he pronounces
Pr 22:22 because they are poor or exploit the needy in c.
25: 5 Remove the wicked from the king's c, and his

25: 8 don't be in a hurry to go to **c**. You might go down
29: 9 If a wise person takes a fool to **c**, there will be
Isa 3:13 The LORD takes his place in **c**. He is the great
7: 2 The news had come to the royal **c**: "Aram is allied
22:22 of David—the highest position in the royal **c**.
36: 3 Shebna the **c** secretary, and Joah son of Asaph,
36:22 Shebna the **c** secretary, and Joah son of Asaph,
37: 2 Shebna the **c** secretary, and the leading priests,
41: 1 Come now and speak. The **c** is ready for your case.
54:17 And everyone who tells lies in **c** will be brought to
Jer 26:10 sat down at the New Gate of the Temple to hold **c**.
26:24 and persuaded the **c** not to turn him over to the
29: 2 the queen mother, the **c** officials, the leaders of
34:19 officials of Judah or Jerusalem, **c** officials, priests,
38: 7 At that time the king was holding **c** at the
Da 1: 5 of them would be made his advisers in the royal **c**.
2:49 of Babylon, while Daniel remained in the king's **c**.
7:10 Then the **c** began its session, and the books were
7:26 "But then the **c** will pass judgment, and all his
Mt 5:22 you are in danger of being brought before the **c**.
5:25 before it is too late and you are dragged into **c**,
5:40 If you are ordered to **c** and your shirt is taken from
Lk 12:58 If you are on the way to **c** and you meet your
Ac 25: 7 On Paul's arrival in **c**, the Jewish leaders from
25:10 This is the official Roman **c**, so I ought to be tried
Ro 3: 4 in what he says, and he will win his case in **c**."
1Co 6: 1 a lawsuit and ask a secular **c** to decide the matter,
Jas 2: 6 it the rich who oppress you and drag you into **c**?

COURTED (1) [COURT]

Ps 95: 9 they **c** my wrath though they had seen my many

COURTEOUS [KJV] See HUMBLE

COURTEOUSLY (1) [COURTESY]

Ac 28: 7 He welcomed us **c** and fed us for three days.

COURTESY (1) [COURTEOUSLY]

Lk 7:46 You neglected the **c** of olive oil to anoint my head,

COURTROOM (3) [COURT]

Ecc 3:16 that throughout the world there is evil in the **c**.
Ac 18:16 And he drove them out of the **c**.
18:17 and had beaten him right there in the **c**.

COURTS (18) [COURT]

Ps 65: 4 to bring near, / those who live in your holy **c**.
84: 2 I faint with longing / to enter the **c** of the LORD.
84:10 A single day in your **c** / is better than a thousand
92:13 own house. / They flourish in the **c** of our God.
100: 4 gates with thanksgiving; / go into his **c** with praise.
135: 2 of the LORD, / in the **c** of the house of our God.
Ecc 3:16 the courtroom. Yes, even the **c** of law are corrupt!
Isa 1:12 Why do you keep parading through my **c** with your
32: 7 all the lies they use to oppress the poor in the **c**.
59:14 Our **c** oppose people who are righteous, and justice
La 3:36 They perverted justice in the **c**. Do they think the
Am 5:12 and deprive the poor of justice in the **c**.
5:15 is good; remodel your **c** into true halls of justice.
Hab 1: 4 and useless, and there is no justice given in the **c**.
Zec 8:16 Render verdicts in your **c** that are just and that lead
Mt 10:17 For you will be handed over to the **c** and beaten in
Mk 13: 9 You will be handed over to the **c** and beaten in the
Ac 19:38 the **c** are in session and the judges can take the case

COURTYARD (118) [COURT]

Ex 27: 9 "Then make a **c** for the Tabernacle, enclosed with
27:11 It will be the same on the north side of the **c**—
27:12 The curtains on the west end of the **c** will be 75
27:14 The **c** entrance will be on the east end, flanked by
27:16 "For the entrance to the **c**, make a curtain that is
27:17 All the posts around the **c** must be connected by
27:18 So the entire **c** will be 150 feet long and 75 feet
27:19 used to support the Tabernacle and the **c** curtains,
35:17 the curtains for the walls of the **c**; the posts
35:17 their bases; the curtain for the entrance to the **c**;
35:18 tent pegs of the Tabernacle and **c** and their cords;
38: 9 Then he constructed the **c**. The south wall was 150
38:14 The **c** entrance was on the east side, flanked by two
38:16 All the curtains used in the **c** walls were made of
38:18 The curtain that covered the entrance to the **c** was
38:18 7-1/2 feet high, just like the curtains of the **c** walls.
38:20 used in the Tabernacle and **c** were made of bronze.
38:31 the posts that supported the curtains around the **c**,
38:31 the bases for the curtain at the entrance of the **c**,
38:31 tent pegs used to hold the curtains of the **c** in place.
39:40 the curtains for the walls of the **c** and the posts
39:40 the curtain at the **c** entrance; the cords and tent
40: 8 Then set up the **c** around the outside of the tent,
and hang the curtain for the **c** entrance.
40:33 Then he hung the curtains forming the **c** around the
40:33 And he set up the curtain at the entrance of the **c**.
Lev 6:16 and eaten in a sacred place within the **c** of the
6:26 in a sacred place within the **c** of the Tabernacle.
Nu 3:26 the curtains of the **c** that surrounded the Tabernacle
3:26 and altar, the curtain at the **c** entrance,
3:37 They were also responsible for the posts of the **c**
4:26 They are also to carry the curtains for the **c** walls
4:26 and altar, the curtain across the **c** entrance,
4:32 the posts for the **c** walls with their bases, pegs,
2Sa 17:18 where a man hid them inside a well in his **c**.
1Ki 6:36 The walls of the inner **c** were built so that there
7: 8 Solomon's living quarters surrounded a **c** behind
7:12 The walls of the great **c** were built so that there
7:12 just like the walls of the inner **c** of the LORD's
8:64 area of the **c** in front of the LORD's Temple.
2Ki 20: 4 But before Isaiah had left the middle **c**,
1Ch 26:18 leading up to the Temple, and two to the **c**.
2Ch 4: 9 Solomon also built a **c** for the priests and the large
outer **c**.
4: 9 He made doors for the **c** entrances and overlaid
6:13 had placed it at the center of the Temple's outer **c**.
7: 7 then dedicated the central area of the **c** in front of
20: 5 and Jerusalem in front of the new **c** at the Temple
24:21 they stoned him to death in the **c** of the LORD's
29: 4 and Levites to meet him at the **c** east of the
29:16 and they took out to the Temple **c** all the defiled
Est 1: 5 and was held at Susa in the **c** of the palace garden.
1: 6 The **c** was decorated with beautifully woven white
2:11 Every day Mordecai would take a walk near the **c**
7: 9 that stands seventy-five feet tall in his own **c**.
Jer 27:19 the bronze Sea in the Temple **c**, the bronze water
32: 2 and Jeremiah was imprisoned in the **c** of the guard
33: 1 While Jeremiah was still confined in the **c** of the
36:10 This room was just off the upper **c** of the Temple,
37:21 he was imprisoned in the **c** of the guard in the royal
38:13 So Jeremiah was returned to the **c** of the guard—
38:28 And Jeremiah remained a prisoner in the **c** of the
Eze 8: 3 I was taken to the north gate of the inner **c** of the
8: 7 Then he brought me to the door of the Temple **c**,
8:16 Then he brought me into the inner **c** of the
9: 2 They all went into the Temple **c** and stood beside
10: 3 went in, and the cloud of glory filled the inner **c**.
10: 4 and the Temple **c** glowed brightly with the glory of
10: 5 and could be heard clearly in the outer **c**.
40:17 through the gateway into the outer **c** of the Temple.
40:17 A stone pavement ran along the walls of the **c**,
40:18 and extended out from the walls into the **c** the
40:19 across the Temple's outer **c** between the outer
40:23 inner **c** directly opposite this outer gateway.
40:25 where the gateway passage opened into the outer **c**.
40:27 was another gateway that led into the inner **c**.
40:28 me to the south gateway leading into the inner **c**.
40:30 leading into the inner **c** were 8-3/4 feet deep
40:31 foyer of the south gateway faced into the outer **c**.
40:32 took me to the east gateway leading to the inner **c**.
40:34 Its foyer faced into the outer **c**. It had palm tree
40:35 around to the north gateway leading to the inner **c**.
40:37 Its foyer faced into the outer **c**, and it had palm tree
40:44 Inside the inner **c** there were two one-room
40:47 Then the man measured the inner **c** and found it to
40:47 The altar stood there in the **c** in front of the
41:10 row of rooms along the outer wall of the inner **c**.
41:12 building stood on the west, facing the Temple **c**.
41:13 The **c** around the building, including its walls,
41:14 The inner **c** to the east of the Temple was also 175
42: 1 Then the man led me out of the Temple **c** by way
42: 1 We entered the outer **c** and came to a group of
42: 1 of rooms against the north wall of the inner **c**.
42: 3 rooms overlooked the 35-foot width of the inner **c**.
42: 3 rooms looked out onto the pavement of the outer **c**.
42: 7 wall that separated the rooms from the outer **c**;
42: 9 There was an entrance from the outer **c** to these
42:10 rooms just south of the inner **c** between the
Temple and the outer **c**.
42:14 they must not go directly to the outer **c**.
43: 5 Spirit took me up and brought me into the inner **c**,
44:17 When they enter the gateway to the inner **c**,
44:17 must wear no wool while on duty in the inner **c**
44:19 When they return to the outer **c** where the people
44:21 must never drink wine before entering the inner **c**.
44:27 to work and enters the inner **c** and the sanctuary,
45:19 and the gateposts at the entrance to the inner **c**.
46:12 the east gateway to the inner **c** will be opened for
46:20 to avoid carrying the sacrifices through the outer **c**
46:21 Then he brought me back to the outer **c** and led me
Mt 26:58 and eventually came to the **c** of the high priest's
26:69 Meanwhile, as Peter was sitting outside in the **c**,
Mk 14:54 then slipped inside the gates of the high priest's **c**.
14:66 Meanwhile, Peter was below in the **c**. One of the
Lk 22:55 The guards lit a fire in the **c** and sat around it,
22:62 And Peter left the **c**, crying bitterly.
Jn 18:15 so he was allowed to enter the **c** with Jesus.
Rev 11: 2 But do not measure the outer **c**, for it has been

COURTYARDS (15) [COURT]

Ex 8:13 frogs in the houses, the **c**, and the fields all died.
2Ki 21: 5 of heaven in both **c** of the LORD's Temple.
23:12 had built in the two **c** of the LORD's Temple.
1Ch 23:28 They also took care of the **c** and side rooms,
28: 6 son Solomon will build my Temple and its **c**,
28:12 he had in mind for the **c** of the LORD's Temple,
2Ch 23: 5 Everyone else should stay in the **c** of the LORD's
33: 5 He put these altars for the stars of heaven in both **c**
Ne 8:16 in their **c**, in the **c** of God's Temple,
13: 7 that he had provided Tobiah with a room in the **c**
Isa 62: 9 Within the **c** of the Temple, you yourselves will
Eze 9: 7 "Fill its **c** with the bodies of those you kill! Go!"
42: 6 they did not have supporting columns as in the **c**,
Zec 3: 7 will be given authority over my Temple and its **c**.

COUSIN (13) [COUSINS]

Ge 29:10 And because she was his **c**, the daughter of his
29:12 He explained that he was her **c** on her father's side,
36: 3 He also married his **c** Basemath, who was the
1Sa 14:50 The commander of Saul's army was his **c** Abner,
2Sa 13: 3 Amnon had a very crafty friend—his **c** Jonadab.
17:25 (Amasa was Joab's **c**. His father was Jether,
20: 9 "How are you, my **c**?" Joab said and took him by
2Ch 11:18 Rehoboam married his **c** Mahalath, the daughter of
11:20 Later Rehoboam married another **c**, Maacah,
Est 2: 7 This man had a beautiful and lovely young **c**,
Jer 32: 7 "Your **c** Hanamel son of Shallum will come
32:12 I did all this in the presence of my **c** Hanamel,
Col 4:10 you his greetings, and so does Mark, Barnabas's **c**.

COUSINS (3) [COUSIN]

Lev 10: 4 Moses called for Mishael and Elzaphan, Aaron's **c**,
Nu 36:11 and Noah all married **c** on their father's side.
1Ch 23:22 His daughters married their **c**, the sons of Kish.

COVENANT (312) [COVENANTS]

ARK OF...COVENANT (62) Ex 16:34; 25:22; 26:33,34; 30:6,26,36; 31:7; 39:35; 40:3,5,21; Lev 16:13; Nu 4:5; 7:89; 10:33; 14:44; 17:4,10; Dt 10:2,5,8; 31:9,25,26; Jos 3:3,6,8,11,14,17; 4:7,9,16,18; 6:6,8; 8:33; Jdg 20:27; 1Sa 4:3,4,5; 2Sa 15:24; 1Ki 3:15; 6:19; 8:1,6; 1Ch 15:25,26,28,29; 16:6,37; 17:1; 22:19; 28:2,18; 2Ch 5:2,7; Jer 3:16; Heb 9:4; Rev 11:19

BOOK OF THE COVENANT (4) Ex 24:7; 2Ki 23:2,21; 2Ch 34:30

COVENANT OF THE LORD* (7) Dt 31:26; Jos 3:3; 7:15; 23:16; 1Sa 4:3,4,5

HIS COVENANT (20) Ex 2:24; Nu 10:10; Dt 4:13; 7:9,12; 2Ki 13:23; 18:12; 1Ch 16:15; Ne 1:5; 9:32; Ps 25:10,14; 78:37; 103:18; 105:8; 106:45; 111:5,9; Isa 56:6; Rev 11:19

MY COVENANT (36) Ge 9:15,17; 17:4,21; Ex 6:5; 19:5; 31:17; 34:27; Lev 26:9,15,42,44; Dt 31:20; Jos 7:11; Jdg 2:1; 1Ki 11:11; Ps 89:28,34; 132:12; Isa 42:6; 54:10; 59:21; Jer 11:3; 33:20,21,21; Eze 16:62; 17:19; 44:7; Hos 6:7; 8:1; Zec 11:11; Mal 2:4,5; Ro 11:27; Heb 8:9

NEW COVENANT (15) Jer 31:31,33; Lk 22:20; 1Co 11:25; 2Co 3:6,9,10,11,12; Heb 8:8,10,13; 9:15; 10:16; 12:24

YOUR COVENANT (7) Ex 32:13; Dt 33:9; Ps 44:17; 74:20; 89:39; Jer 14:21; Eze 16:59

Ge 9: 9 "I am making a **c** with you and your descendants,
9:12 you a sign as evidence of my eternal **c** with you
9:15 and I will remember my **c** with you and with
9:16 I will remember the eternal **c** between God
9:17 this is the sign of my **c** with all the creatures of the
15:18 So the LORD made a **c** with Abram that day
17: 2 I will make a **c** with you, by which I will guarantee
17: 4 "This is my **c** with you: I will make you the father
17: 7 "I will continue this everlasting **c** between us,
17: 9 God told Abraham, "is to obey the terms of the **c**.
17:10 This is the **c** that you and your descendants must
17:11 be a sign that you and they have accepted this **c**.
17:13 bodies will thus bear the mark of my everlasting **c**.
17:14 off from the **c** family for violating the **c**."
17:19 and I will confirm my everlasting **c** with him
17:21 But my **c** is with Isaac, who will be born to you
21:32 After making their **c**, Abimelech left with Phicol,
26:28 decided we should have a treaty, a **c** between us.
Ex 2:24 and remembered his **c** promise to Abraham,
6: 4 And I entered into a solemn **c** with them. Under its
6: 5 the Egyptians. I have remembered my **c** with them.
16:34 placed it for safekeeping in the Ark of the **C**.
19: 5 Now if you will obey me and keep my **c**, you will
24: 7 Then he took the Book of the **C** and read it to the
24: 8 "This blood confirms the **c** the LORD has made
25:16 the stone tablets inscribed with the terms of the **c**,
25:21 the stone tablets inscribed with the terms of the **c**,
25:22 gold cherubim that hover over the Ark of the **C**.
26:33 curtain is in place, put the Ark of the **C** behind it.
26:34 on top of the Ark of the **C** inside the Most Holy
30: 6 place of atonement—that rests on the Ark of the **C**.
30:26 oil to anoint the Tabernacle, the Ark of the **C**,
30:36 and put some of it in front of the Ark of the **C**,
31: 7 the Ark of the **C**; the Ark's cover—
31:13 for the Sabbath is a sign of the **c** between me
31:17 It is a permanent sign of my **c** with them. For in six
31:18 two stone tablets inscribed with the terms of the **c**,
32:13 Remember your **c** with your servants—Abraham,
32:15 two stone tablets inscribed with the terms of the **c**.
34:10 This is the **c** I am going to make with you.
34:27 for they represent the terms of my **c** with you
34:28 At that time he wrote the terms of the **c**—the Ten
34:29 the stone tablets inscribed with the terms of the **c**,
38:21 materials used in building the Tabernacle of the **C**.
39:35 the Ark of the **C** and its carrying poles; the Ark's
40: 3 Place the Ark of the **C** inside, and install the inner
40: 5 the inner curtain, opposite the Ark of the **C**.
40:20 the stone tablets inscribed with the terms of the **c**,
40:21 Then he brought the Ark of the **C** into the
Lev 2:13 grain offerings with salt, to remind you of God's **c**.
16:13 place of atonement—that rests on the Ark of the **C**.
24: 8 behalf of the Israelites as a continual part of the **c**.
26: 9 and multiply your people and fulfill my **c** with you.
26:15 and if you break my **c** by rejecting my laws
26:25 I will send armies against you to carry out these **c**
26:42 Then I will remember my **c** with Jacob, with Isaac,
26:44 I will not cancel my **c** with them by wiping them
26:45 I will remember my ancient **c** with their ancestors,
Nu 1:50 the Levites in charge of the Tabernacle of the **C**,
1:53 **C** to offer the people of Israel protection from the
4: 5 inner curtain and cover the Ark of the **C** with it.
7:89 place of atonement—that rests on the Ark of the **C**.
10:10 remind the LORD your God of his **c** with you.
10:11 the cloud lifted from the Tabernacle of the **C**.
10:33 with the Ark of the LORD's **c** moving ahead of
14:44 nor the Ark of the LORD's **c** left the camp.
17: 4 in the Tabernacle in front of the Ark of the **C**,

17: 7 the LORD's presence in the Tabernacle of the **C**.
17: 8 When he went into the Tabernacle of the **C** the
17: 10 before the Ark of the **C** as a warning to rebels.
18: 2 sacred duties in front of the Tabernacle of the **C**.
18: 19 This is an unbreakable **c** between the LORD
25: 12 So tell him that I am making my special **c** of peace
25: 13 In this **c**, he and his descendants will be priests for
Dt 4: 13 He proclaimed his **c**, which he commanded you to
4: 23 So be careful not to break the **c** the LORD your
4: 31 or forget the solemn **c** he made with your
5: 2 the LORD our God made a **c** with us.
5: 3 The LORD did not make this **c** long ago with our
7: 9 He is the faithful God who keeps his **c** for a
7: 12 the LORD your God will keep his **c** of unfailing
8: 18 and he does it to fulfill the **c** he made with your
9: 9 with the **c** that the LORD had made with you.
9: 10 The LORD gave me the **c**, the tablets on which
9: 11 the two stone tablets with the **c** inscribed on them.
9: 15 holding in my hands the two stone tablets of the **c**.
10: 2 the tablets in the sacred chest—the Ark of the **C**.'
10: 4 The LORD again wrote the terms of the **c**—
10: 5 and placed the tablets in the Ark of the **C**,
10: 8 tribe of Levi to carry the Ark of the LORD's **c**,
17: 2 of the LORD your God and has violated the **c**
29: 1 These are the terms of the **c** the LORD
29: 1 in addition to the **c** he had made with them at
29: 9 obey the terms of this **c** so that you will prosper in
29: 12 You are standing here today to enter into a **c** with
29: 12 The LORD is making this **c** with you today,
29: 14 the LORD is making this **c** with its obligations.
29: 15 The LORD your God is making this **c** with you
29: 18 The LORD made this **c** with you so that no man,
29: 21 to pour out on them all the **c** curses recorded in this
29: 25 because the people of the land broke the **c** they
31: 9 the priests, who carried the Ark of the LORD's **c**,
31: 16 and break the **c** I have made with them.
31: 20 other gods; they will despise me and break my **c**.
31: 25 the Levites who carried the Ark of the LORD's **c**:
31: 26 and place it beside the Ark of the **C** of the LORD
33: 9 and guarded your **c**. / They were more loyal to you
Jos 3: 3 carrying the Ark of the **C** of the LORD your God,
3: 6 "Lift up the Ark of the **C** and lead the people
3: 8 to the priests who are carrying the Ark of the **C**:
3: 11 The Ark of the **C**, which belongs to the Lord of the
3: 14 the priests who were carrying the Ark of the **C**
3: 17 **c** stood on dry ground in the middle of the riverbed
4: 7 when the Ark of the LORD's **c** went across.'
4: 9 priests who carried the Ark of the **C** were standing.
4: 16 "Command the priests carrying the Ark of the **C** to
4: 18 Ark of the LORD's **c** came up out of the riverbed,
6: 6 the priests and said, "Take up the Ark of the **C**,
6: 8 And the priests carrying the Ark of the LORD's **c**
7: 11 Israel has sinned and broken my **c**! They have
7: 15 for he has broken the **c** of the LORD and has
8: 33 priests carrying the Ark of the LORD's **c**.
23: 16 If you break the **c** of the LORD your God by
24: 25 So Joshua made a **c** with the people that day at
Jdg 2: 1 and I said I would never break my **c** with you.
2: 20 "Because these people have violated the **c** I made
20: 27 (In those days the Ark of the **C** of God was in
1Sa 4: 3 "Let's bring the Ark of the **C** of the LORD from
4: 4 back the Ark of the **C** of the LORD Almighty,
4: 5 When the Israelites saw the Ark of the **C** of the
20: 8 for we made a **c** together before the LORD—
20: 16 So Jonathan made a **c** with David, saying,
23: 18 So the two of them renewed their **c** of friendship
2Sa 3: 21 They will make a **c** with you to make you their
5: 3 David made a **c** with the leaders of Israel before
15: 24 and the Levites took the Ark of the **C** of God
23: 5 Yes, he has made an everlasting **c** with me.
1Ki 3: 15 and stood before the Ark of the Lord's **c**,
6: 19 where the Ark of the LORD's **c** would be placed.
8: 1 They were to bring the Ark of the LORD's **c** from
8: 6 Then the priests carried the Ark of the LORD's **c**
8: 9 where the LORD made a **c** with the people of
8: 21 which contains the **c** that the LORD made with
11: 11 "Since you have not kept my **c** and have
19: 10 But the people of Israel have broken their **c** with
19: 14 But the people of Israel have broken their **c** with
2Ki 8: 19 for he had made a **c** with David and promised that
11: 12 He presented Joash with a copy of God's **c**
11: 17 Then Jehoiada made a **c** between the LORD
11: 17 He also made a **c** between the king and the people.
13: 23 He pitied them because of his **c** with Abraham,
17: 15 and the **c** he had made with their ancestors,
17: 35 For the LORD had made a **c** with the descendants
17: 38 Do not forget the **c** I made with you, and do not
18: 12 Instead, they had violated his **c**—all the laws the
23: 2 **C** that had been found in the LORD's Temple.
23: 3 and renewed the **c** in the LORD's presence.
23: 3 he confirmed all the terms of the **c** that were
23: 3 and all the people pledged themselves to the **c**.
23: 21 your God, as it is written in the Book of the **C**."
1Ch 5: 25 and violated their **c** with the God of their ancestors.
11: 3 So there at Hebron David made a **c** with the
15: 25 **c** up to Jerusalem with a great celebration.
15: 26 Levites as they carried the Ark of the LORD's **c**,
15: 28 So all Israel brought up the Ark of the LORD's **c**
15: 29 But as the Ark of the LORD's **c** entered the City
16: 6 the trumpets regularly before the Ark of God's **c**.
16: 15 He always stands by his **c**—/ the commitment he
16: 16 This is the **c** he made with Abraham / and the oath
16: 37 regularly before the Ark of the LORD's **c**,
17: 1 but the Ark of the LORD's **c** is out in a tent!"
22: 19 so that you can bring the Ark of the LORD's **c**
28: 2 to build a temple where the Ark of the LORD's **c**,
28: 18 were stretched out over the Ark of the LORD's **c**.
2Ch 5: 2 They were to bring the Ark of the LORD's **c** from
5: 7 Then the priests carried the Ark of the LORD's **c**
5: 10 when the LORD made a **c** with the people of
6: 11 and in the Ark is the **c** that the LORD made with
13: 5 made an unbreakable **c** with David, giving him
15: 12 Then they entered into a **c** to seek the LORD,
15: 15 All were happy about this **c**, for they had entered
21: 7 for he had made a **c** with David and promised that
23: 3 where they made a **c** with Joash, the young king.
23: 16 Then Jehoiada made a **c** between himself
24: 6 in order to maintain the Tabernacle of the **C**."
29: 10 But now I will make a **c** with the LORD, the God
34: 30 **C** that had been found in the LORD's Temple.
34: 31 and renewed the **c** in the LORD's presence.
34: 31 He promised to obey all the terms of the **c** that
34: 32 they renewed their **c** with God, the God of their
Ezr 10: 3 Let us now make a **c** with our God to divorce our
Ne 1: 5 and awesome God who keeps his **c** of unfailing
9: 8 you made a **c** with him to give him and his
9: 32 awesome God, who keeps his **c** of unfailing love,
Job 31: 1 "I made a **c** with my eyes not to look with lust
Ps 25: 10 all those who keep his **c** and obey his decrees.
25: 14 fear him. / With them he shares the secrets of his **c**.
44: 17 our loyalty to you. / We have not violated your **c**.
50: 5 those who made a **c** with me by giving sacrifices."
74: 20 Remember your **c** promises, / for the land is full of
78: 10 They did not keep God's **c**, / and they refused to
78: 37 were not loyal to him. / They did not keep his **c**.
80: T of Asaph, to be sung to the tune "Lilies of the **C**."
89: 28 to him forever; / my **c** with him will never end.
89: 34 No, I will not break my **c**; / I will not take back a
89: 39 You have renounced your **c** with him, / for you
103: 18 of those who are faithful to his **c**, / of those who
105: 8 He always stands by his **c**—/ the commitment he
105: 9 This is the **c** he made with Abraham / and the oath
106: 45 He remembered his **c** with them / and relented
111: 5 those who trust him; / he always remembers his **c**.
111: 9 He has guaranteed his **c** with them forever.
132: 12 If your descendants obey the terms of my **c**
Pr 2: 17 and ignores the **c** she made before God.
Isa 24: 5 violated his laws, and broken his everlasting **c**.
42: 6 as the personal confirmation of my **c** with them.
54: 10 My **c** of blessing will never be broken,"
55: 3 I am ready to make an everlasting **c** with you.
56: 6 Sabbath day of rest, and who have accepted his **c**.
59: 21 And this is my **c** with them," says the LORD.
61: 8 and make an everlasting **c** with them.
Jer 3: 16 when you possessed the Ark of the LORD's **c**.
11: 2 and Jerusalem about the terms of their **c** with me.
11: 3 is anyone who does not obey the terms of my **c**!
11: 6 and say, 'Remember the **c** your ancestors made,
11: 8 upon them all the curses described in our **c**.' "
11: 10 and Judah have both broken the **c** I made with their
14: 21 Do not break your **c** with us. Please don't forget
22: 9 'Because they violated their **c** with the LORD
31: 31 "when I will make a new **c** with the people of
31: 32 This **c** will not be like the one I made with their
31: 32 They broke that **c**, though I loved them as a
31: 33 "But this is the new **c** I will make with the people
32: 40 "And I will make an everlasting **c** with them,
33: 20 "If you can break my **c** with the day and the night
33: 21 only then will my **c** with David, my servant,
33: 21 The same is true for my **c** with the Levitical priests
34: 8 after King Zedekiah made a **c** with the people,
34: 13 I made a **c** with your ancestors long ago when I
34: 15 and made a solemn **c** with me in my Temple.
34: 18 Because you have refused the terms of our **c**,
50: 5 with an eternal **c** that will never again be broken.
Eze 16: 8 I made a **c** with you, says the Sovereign LORD,
16: 59 your solemn vows lightly by breaking your **c**.
16: 60 Yet I will keep the **c** I made with you when you
16: 60 and I will establish an everlasting **c** with you.
16: 61 even though they are not part of our **c**.
16: 62 And I will reaffirm my **c** with you, and you will
17: 19 I will punish him for breaking my **c** and despising
20: 37 you carefully and hold you to the terms of the **c**.
34: 25 "I will make a **c** of peace with them and drive
37: 26 And I will make a **c** of peace with them, an
everlasting **c**.
44: 7 your other disgusting sins, you have broken my **c**.
Da 11: 22 armies will be swept away, including a **c** prince.
11: 28 he will set himself against the people of the holy **c**,
11: 30 will vent his anger against the people of the holy **c**
and reward those who forsake the **c**.
11: 32 He will flatter those who have violated the **c**
Hos 2: 18 At that time I will make a **c** with all the wild
6: 7 you broke my **c** and rebelled against me.
8: 1 for they have broken my **c** and revolted against my
Zec 9: 11 Because of the **c** I made with you, sealed with
11: 10 showing that I had revoked the **c** I had made with
11: 11 That was the end of my **c** with them. Those who
Mal 2: 4 so that my **c** with the Levites may continue,"
2: 5 "The purpose of my **c** with the Levites was to
2: 8 You have corrupted the **c** I made with the
2: 10 to each other, violating the **c** of our ancestors?
3: 1 The messenger of the **c**, whom you look for
Mt 26: 28 which seals the **c** between God and his people.
Mk 14: 24 sealing the **c** between God and his people.
Lk 1: 72 by remembering his sacred **c** with them,
1: 73 the **c** he gave to our ancestor Abraham.
22: 20 "This wine is the token of God's new **c** to save
Ac 3: 25 and you are included in the **c** God promised to
7: 8 God also gave Abraham the **c** of circumcision at
Ro 11: 27 And then I will keep my **c** with them / and take
1Co 11: 25 "This cup is the new **c** between God and you,
2Co 3: 6 the one who has enabled us to represent his new **c**.
3: 6 This is a **c**, not of written laws, but of the Spirit.
3: 9 If the old **c**, which brings condemnation,
3: 9 how much more glorious is the new **c**,
3: 10 with the overwhelming glory of the new **c**.
3: 11 So if the old **c**, which has been set aside, was full
of glory, then the new **c**,
3: 12 Since this new **c** gives us such confidence, we can
3: 14 and even to this day whenever the old **c** is being
Heb 7: 22 who guarantees the effectiveness of this better **c**.
8: 6 for he is the one who guarantees for us a better **c**
8: 7 If the first **c** had been faultless, there would have
been no need for a second **c** to
8: 8 says the Lord, / when I will make a new **c**
8: 9 This **c** will not be like the one / I made with their
8: 9 They did not remain faithful to my **c**, / so I turned
8: 10 But this is the new **c** I will make / with the people
8: 13 When God speaks of a new **c**, it means he has
9: 1 Now in that first **c** between God and Israel,
9: 4 and a wooden chest called the Ark of the **C**,
9: 4 and the stone tablets of the **c** with the Ten
9: 15 That is why he is the one who mediates the new **c**
9: 15 of the sins they had committed under that first **c**.
9: 18 That is why blood was required under the first **c** as
9: 20 "This blood confirms the **c** God has made with
10: 9 He cancels the first **c** in order to establish the
10: 11 Under the old **c**, the priest stands before the altar
10: 16 "This is the new **c** I will make / with my people on
10: 29 and have treated the blood of the **c** as if it were
12: 24 the one who mediates the new **c** between God
13: 20[-21] Shepherd of the sheep by an everlasting **c**,
Rev 11: 19 and the Ark of his **C** could be seen inside the

COVENANTS (3) [COVENANT]

Jdg 2: 2 you were not to make any **c** with the people living
Ro 9: 4 He made **c** with them and gave his law to them.
Gal 4: 24 two women serve as an illustration of God's two **c**.

COVER (97) [COVERED, COVERING, COVERINGS, COVERS]

Ge 3: 7 leaves together around their hips to **c** themselves.
6: 17 I am about to **c** the earth with a flood that will
8: 13 the flood began, Noah lifted back the **c** to look.
28: 14 They will **c** the land from east to west and from
Ex 10: 4 For tomorrow I will **c** the whole country with
10: 12 Let them **c** the land and eat all the crops still left
21: 33 someone digs or uncovers a well and fails to **c** it,
25: 17 "Then make the Ark's **c**—the place of atonement
25: 18 and place them at the two ends of the atonement **c**.
25: 19 the cherubim to each end of the atonement **c**,
25: 20 looking down on the atonement **c** with their wings
25: 21 Then put the atonement **c** on top of the Ark.
25: 22 and talk to you from above the atonement **c**
26: 7 "Make heavy sheets of cloth from goat hair to **c**
26: 34 "Then put the Ark's **c**—the place of atonement—
30: 6 outside the inner curtain, opposite the Ark's **c**—
31: 7 the Covenant; the Ark's **c**—the place of atonement;
33: 22 and **c** you with my hand until I have passed.
35: 12 the Ark and its poles; the Ark's **c**—the place of
37: 6 Then, from pure gold, he made the Ark's **c**—
37: 7 placed them at the two ends of the atonement **c**.
37: 8 so they were actually a part of the atonement **c**—
37: 9 other as they looked down on the atonement **c**,
37: 9 stretched out above the atonement **c** to protect it.
39: 35 the Covenant and its carrying poles; the Ark's **c**—
40: 20 He also set the Ark's **c**—the place of atonement—
Lev 13: 45 they must **c** their mouth and call out, 'Unclean!
16: 2 For the Ark's **c**—the place of atonement—is there,
16: 2 am present in the cloud over the atonement **c**.
16: 13 that a cloud of incense will rise over the Ark's **c**—
16: 14 and sprinkle it on the front of the atonement **c**
16: 15 he will sprinkle the blood on the atonement **c**
17: 13 you must drain out the blood and **c** it with earth.
Nu 4: 5 inner curtain and **c** the Ark of the Covenant with it.
4: 6 Then they must **c** the inner curtain with fine
4: 9 "Next they must **c** the lampstand with a dark blue
4: 11 and **c** this cloth with a covering of fine goatskin
7: 89 between the two cherubim above the Ark's **c**—
16: 39 hammered out into a sheet of metal to **c** the altar.
22: 5 They **c** the face of the earth and are threatening me.
Dt 23: 13 dig a hole with the spade and **c** the excrement.
28: 35 The LORD will **c** you from head to foot with
Jos 10: 18 "**C** the opening of the cave with large rocks
2Ki 8: 21 but he escaped at night under **c** of darkness.
25: 30 to **c** his living expenses until the day of his death.
1Ch 28: 11 and the inner sanctuary where the Ark's **c**—
2Ch 21: 9 but he escaped at night under **c** of darkness.
Job 14: 17 in a pouch, and you would **c** over my iniquity.
22: 11 see in the darkness, and waves of water **c** you.
26: 6 There is no **c** for the place of destruction.
36: 20 Do not long for the **c** of night, for that is when
Ps 71: 13 May humiliation and shame **c** / those who want to
104: 9 the seas, / so they would never again **c** the earth.
Pr 10: 6 evil people **c** up their harmful intentions.
10: 11 to life; evil people **c** up their harmful intentions.
16: 6 Unfailing love and faithfulness **c** sin; evil is
28: 13 People who **c** over their sins will not prosper.
30: 32 about it—**c** your mouth with your hand in shame.
Isa 1: 29 Shame will **c** you when you think of the times you
7: 25 once grew, for briers and thorns will **c** them.
28: 20 to lie on. The blankets are too narrow to **c** you.
34: 15 will hatch her young and **c** them with her wings.
54: 9 that I would never again let a flood **c** the earth
58: 5 dress in sackcloth and **c** yourselves with ashes.
60: 2 Darkness as black as night will **c** all the nations of
Jer 14: 4 The farmers are afraid; they, too, **c** their heads.
46: 8 boasting that it will **c** the earth like a flood,

52:34 to **c** his living expenses until the day of his death.
Eze 7:18 in sackcloth; horror and shame will **c** them.
12:6 into the night. **C** your face and don't look around.
12:12 He will **c** his face, and his eyes will never see his
16:8 So I wrapped my cloak around you to **c** your
16:18 embroidered clothes I gave you to **c** your idols.
16:38 I will **c** you with blood in my jealous fury.
16:63 remember your sins and **c** your mouth in silence
24:7 the rocks for all to see. She doesn't even try to **c** it!
30:4 and those who are slaughtered will **c** the ground.
30:11 Egypt until slaughtered Egyptians **c** the ground.
30:18 A dark cloud will **c** Tahpanhes, and its daughters
32:5 I will **c** the hills with your flesh and fill the valleys
32:7 I will **c** the sun with a cloud, and the moon will not
37:6 put flesh and muscles on you and **c** you with skin.
37:8 Then skin formed to **c** their bodies, but they still
38:9 on them like a storm and **c** the land like a cloud.
38:16 and you will **c** the land like a cloud. This will
Hos 2:9 and wool clothing I gave her to **c** her nakedness.
Mic 3:6 Darkness will **c** you, making it impossible for you
3:7 Then you seers will **c** your faces in shame, and you
Na 3:6 I will **c** you with filth and show the world how vile
Zec 5:7 When the heavy lead **c** was lifted off the basket,
Mal 2:13 You **c** the LORD's altar with tears, weeping
Mk 12:40 and then, to **c** up the kind of people they really are,
Lk 8:16 light a lamp and then **c** it up or put it under a bed.
20:47 and then, to **c** up the kind of people they really are,
Heb 9:5 Their wings were stretched out over the Ark's **c**,
9:7 which he offers to God to **c** his own sins
10:26 there is no other sacrifice that will **c** these sins.

COVERED (86) [COVER]

Ge 7:10 One week later, the flood came and **c** the earth.
7:19 the water **c** even the highest mountains on the
7:24 And the water **c** the earth for 150 days.
9:23 into the tent, and **c** their father's naked body.
24:65 my master." So Rebekah **c** her face with her veil.
25:25 He was **c** with so much hair that one would think
29:2 But a heavy stone **c** the mouth of the well.
38:14 and **c** herself with a veil to disguise herself.
Ex 8:6 Aaron did so, and frogs **c** the whole land of Egypt!
8:18 And the gnats **c** all the people and animals.
8:21 with them, and the ground will be **c** with them.
10:15 For the locusts **c** the surface of the whole country,
14:28 The waters **c** all the chariots and charioteers—
15:5 The deep waters have **c** them; / they sank to the
15:10 But with a blast of your breath, / the sea **c** them.
16:13 vast numbers of quail arrived and **c** the camp.
16:14 thin flakes, white like frost, **c** the ground.
19:18 All Mount Sinai was **c** with smoke
22:15 because this loss was **c** by the rental fee.
24:15 Moses went up the mountain, and the cloud **c** it.
24:16 upon Mount Sinai, and the cloud **c** it for six days.
38:18 The curtain that **c** the entrance to the courtyard was
40:34 Then the cloud **c** the Tabernacle, and the glorious
Nu 4:10 utensils must then be **c** with fine goatskin leather,
4:12 **c** with fine goatskin leather, and placed on the
4:13 and the altar must then be **c** with a purple cloth.
9:15 was set up, and on that day the cloud **c** it.
16:42 the Tabernacle and saw that the cloud had **c** it,
19:15 Any container in the tent that was not **c** with a lid
Jos 10:27 Then they **c** the opening of the cave with a large
11:4 **c** the landscape like the sand on the seashore.
Jdg 4:18 he went into her tent, and she **c** him with a blanket.
4:19 she gave him some milk to drink and **c** him again.
6:40 dry in the morning, but the ground was **c** with dew.
9:40 and the ground was **c** with dead bodies all the way
1Sa 19:13 took an idol and put it in his bed, **c** it with blankets,
2Sa 15:30 His head was **c** and his feet were bare as a sign of
15:30 And the people who were with him **c** their heads
19:4 The king **c** his face with his hands and kept on
1Ki 1:1 and no matter how many blankets **c** him, he could
6:18 Cedar paneling completely **c** the stone walls
7:6 **c** by a canopy that was supported by pillars.
2Ki 3:25 **c** their good land with stones, stopped up the
Est 7:8 his attendants **c** Haman's face, signaling his doom.
Job 29:14 Righteousness **c** me like a robe, and I wore justice
41:30 Its belly is **c** with scales as sharp as glass.
Ps 35:26 triumph over me / be **c** with shame and dishonor.
44:19 You have **c** us with darkness and death.
68:13 now they are **c** with silver and gold, / as a dove is **c** by its wings.
80:10 The mountains were **c** with our shade; / the mighty cedars were **c** with our branches.
85:2 of your people—/ yes, you have **c** all their sins.
104:6 floods of water, / water that **c** even the mountains.
106:11 Then the water returned and **c** their enemies;
129:3 My back is **c** with cuts, / as if a farmer had plowed
Pr 24:31 It was **c** with weeds, and its walls were broken
Isa 1:6 **c** with bruises, welts, and infected wounds—
1:15 For your hands are **c** with the blood of your
6:2 With two wings they **c** their faces, with two they **c** their feet, and with the remaining
27:10 the houses abandoned, the streets **c** with grass.
28:8 Their tables are **c** with vomit; filth is everywhere.
29:2 as her name Ariel means—an altar **c** with blood.
34:6 It is **c** with fat as though it had been used for
34:9 burning pitch, and the ground will be **c** with fire.
50:2 I can turn rivers into deserts **c** with dying fish.
Jer 51:42 sea has risen over Babylon; she is **c** by its waves.
Eze 1:11 on either side of it, and the other pair **c** its body.
1:18 and they were **c** with eyes all around the edges.
2:10 and I saw that both sides were **c** with funeral
10:12 the cherubim and the wheels were **c** with eyes.
13:15 and those who **c** it with whitewash will be
24:23 Your heads must remain **c**, and your sandals must
37:2 among the old, dry bones that **c** the valley floor.
47:10 The shores will be **c** with nets drying in the sun.
Da 2:35 became a great mountain that **c** the whole earth.
9:7 but our faces are **c** with shame, just as you see us
9:8 and ancestors are **c** with shame because we have
Lk 9:34 over them; and terror gripped them as it **c** them.
Jn 5:2 was the pool of Bethesda, with five **c** porches.
20:7 while the cloth that had **c** Jesus' head was folded
2Co 3:15 their hearts are **c** with that veil, and they do not
Heb 9:4 the Covenant, which was **c** with gold on all sides.
Rev 4:6 living beings, each **c** with eyes, front and back.
4:8 and their wings were **c** with eyes, inside and out.

COVERING (32) [COVER]

Ge 7:17 **c** the ground and lifting the boat high above the
Ex 8:17 the entire land, **c** the Egyptians and their animals.
26:12 An extra half sheet of this roof **c** will be left to
26:13 and the **c** will hang down an extra eighteen inches
26:14 fine goatskin leather. This will complete the roof **c**.
36:14 a roof **c** was made from eleven sheets of cloth
36:18 the roof **c** was joined together in one piece.
36:19 Then they made two more layers for the roof **c**.
Lev 13:12 over someone's skin, **c** the body from head to foot.
Nu 4:8 and finally a **c** of fine goatskin leather on top of the
4:11 and cover this cloth with a **c** of fine goatskin
4:14 and a **c** of fine goatskin leather must be spread
4:15 and his sons have finished **c** the sanctuary
4:25 its coverings, the outer **c** of fine goatskin leather,
16:38 the incense burners into a sheet as a **c** for the altar,
16:38 The altar **c** will then serve as a warning to the
Jos 10:22 "Remove the rocks **c** the opening of the cave
Ru 3:9 "Spread the corner of your **c** over me, for you are
Job 24:7 they lie naked in the cold, without clothing or **c**.
Ps 105:39 The LORD spread out a cloud above them as a **c**
Isa 4:5 and clouds of fire at night, **c** the glorious land.
Jer 14:3 confused and desperate, **c** their heads in grief.
Eze 1:23 others' wings, and each had two wings **c** its body.
13:10 trying to hold it together by **c** it with whitewash!
32:27 their shields **c** their bodies, and their swords
Lk 24:2 They found that the stone **c** the entrance had been
1Co 11:5 if she prays or prophesies without a **c** on her head,
11:6 Yes, if she refuses to wear a head **c**, she should cut
11:6 or her head shaved, then she should wear a **c**.
11:10 So a woman should wear a **c** on her head as a sign
11:13 to pray to God in public without **c** her head?
11:15 and joy? For it has been given to her as a **c**.

COVERINGS (6) [COVER]

Ex 26:14 On top of these **c** place a layer of tanned ram skins,
35:11 including the sacred tent and its **c**, the clasps,
40:19 Then he spread the **c** over the Tabernacle
Nu 3:25 for the tent of the Tabernacle with its layers of **c**,
4:25 the Tabernacle itself with its **c**, the outer covering
2Ki 23:7 where the women wove **c** for the Asherah pole.

COVERS (10) [COVER]

Ex 29:13 Take all the fat that **c** the internal organs,
29:22 the fat tail and the fat that **c** the internal organs.
Lev 13:13 person to see if the disease **c** the entire body.
Job 16:16 eyes are red with weeping; darkness **c** my eyes.
Ps 147:8 He **c** the heavens with clouds, / provides rain for
Pr 10:12 Hatred stirs up quarrels, but love **c** all offenses.
26:23 just as a pretty glaze **c** a common clay pot.
1Co 11:4 A man dishonors Christ if he **c** his head while
2Co 3:14 a veil **c** their minds so they cannot understand the
1Pe 4:8 love for each other, for love **c** a multitude of sins.

COVET (5) [COVETED, COVETING]

Ex 20:17 "Do not **c** your neighbor's house. Do not **c** your neighbor's wife,
Dt 5:21 " 'Do not **c** your neighbor's wife. Do not **c** your neighbor's house or land,
Ro 7:7 is wrong if the law had not said, "Do not **c**."

COVETED (1) [COVET]

Ac 20:33 "I have never **c** anyone's money or fine clothing.

COVETOUSNESS [KJV] BRIBES, LOVE FOR/OF MONEY, GREED, GREEDY

COVETING (2) [COVET]

Ro 7:7 I would never have known that **c** is wrong if the
13:9 against adultery and murder and stealing and **c**—

COW (13) [COW'S, COWS]

Lev 3:1 offering from the herd, use either a bull or a **c**.
4:10 with the bull or **c** sacrificed as a peace offering.
Dt 21:3 Then the leaders of that town must select a young **c**
21:6 hands over the young **c** whose neck was broken.
Isa 7:21 a farmer will be fortunate to have a **c** and two
Jer 46:20 Egypt is as sleek as a young **c**, but a gadfly from
Eze 4:15 "You may bake your bread with **c** dung instead of
Da 4:25 You will eat grass like a **c**, and you will be
4:32 the wild animals, and you will eat grass like a **c**.
4:33 He ate grass like a **c**, and he was drenched with the
5:21 He ate grass like a **c**, and he was drenched with the
Lk 14:5 If your son or your **c** falls into a pit, don't you
Heb 9:13 and the ashes of a young **c** could cleanse people's

COW'S (1)

Dt 21:4 through it. There they must break the **c** neck.

COWARDS (1) [COWER]

Rev 21:8 But **c** who turn away from me, and unbelievers,

COWER (1) [COWARDS, COWERING]

Isa 19:16 They will **c** in fear beneath the upraised fist of the

COWERING (1) [COWER]

Ro 8:15 So you should not be like **c**, fearful slaves.

COWS (21) [COW]

Ge 32:15 forty **c**, ten bulls, twenty female donkeys, and ten
41:2 healthy-looking **c** suddenly came up out of the
41:3 Then seven other **c** came up from the river,
41:3 These **c** went over and stood beside the fat **c**.
41:4 Then the thin, ugly **c** ate the fat ones! At this point
41:18 healthy-looking **c** came up out of the river
41:19 But then seven other **c** came up from the river.
41:20 ugly **c** ate up the seven fat ones that had come out
41:26 The seven fat **c** and the seven plump heads of grain
41:27 ugly **c** and the seven withered heads of grain
1Sa 6:7 new cart, and find two **c** that have just had calves.
6:7 Make sure the **c** have never been yoked to a cart.
6:7 Hitch the **c** to the cart, but shut their calves away
6:8 gold tumors. Then let the **c** go wherever they want.
6:10 Two **c** with newborn calves were hitched to the
6:12 the **c** went straight along the road toward
6:14 up the wood of the cart for a fire and killed the **c**
Job 21:10 to breed. Their **c** bear calves without miscarriage.
29:6 In those days my **c** produced milk in abundance,
Am 4:1 Listen to me, you "fat **c**" of Samaria, you women

COYNESS (1)

Pr 6:25 lust for her beauty. Don't let her **c** seduce you.

COZ [KJV] See KOZ

COZBI (2)

Nu 25:15 The woman's name was **C**; she was the daughter
25:18 and because of **C**, the daughter of a Midianite

COZEBA (1)

1Ch 4:22 Jokim, the people of **C**, Joash, and Saraph,

CRABBY (1)

Pr 21:19 It is better to live alone in the desert than with a **c**,

CRACK (2) [CRACKED, CRACKING, CRACKS]

1Ki 13:5 At the same time a wide **c** appeared in the altar,
Na 3:2 Hear the **c** of the whips as the chariots rush

CRACKED (6) [CRACK]

Jos 9:13 when we filled them, but now they are old and **c**.
Jer 2:13 And they have dug for themselves **c** cisterns that
14:4 The ground is parched and **c** for lack of rain.
50:17 Then King Nebuchadnezzar of Babylon **c** their
Eze 22:28 word to them. They repair **c** walls with whitewash!
29:7 but like a **c** staff, you splintered and stabbed her in

CRACKING (1) [CRACK]

Nu 24:17 **c** the skulls of the people of Sheth.

CRACKLED (1) [CRACKLING]

Ps 77:17 their rain; / the thunder rolled and **c** in the sky.

CRACKLING (1) [CRACKLED]

Ecc 7:6 laughter is quickly gone, like thorns **c** in a fire.

CRACKNELS [KJV] See CAKES

CRACKS (2) [CRACK]

1Ki 4:33 to the tiny hyssop that grows from **c** in a wall.
Ps 60:2 it open. / Seal the **c** before it completely collapses.

CRAFT (1) [CRAFTED, CRAFTS, CRAFTSMAN, CRAFTSMANSHIP, CRAFTSMEN, CRAFTY]

Ex 31:5 in carving wood. Yes, he is a master at every **c**!

CRAFTED (6) [CRAFT]

Ex 39:8 **c** from fine linen cloth and embroidered with gold
39:24 These were finely **c** of blue, purple, and scarlet
39:41 the beautifully **c** garments to be worn while
Nu 31:51 all kinds of jewelry and **c** objects.
Eze 28:13 all beautifully **c** for you and set in the finest gold.
Hos 8:6 This calf you worship was **c** by your own hands!

CRAFTS (3) [CRAFT]

Ex 31:3 intelligence, and skill in all kinds of **c**.
35:31 intelligence, and skill in all kinds of **c**.
35:35 They excel in all the **c** needed for the work.

CRAFTSMAN (7) [CRAFT]

Ex 38:23 the tribe of Dan, a **c** expert at engraving, designing,
39:3 A skilled **c** made gold thread by beating gold into
1Ki 7:14 for he was a **c** skilled in bronze work. He was half
2Ch 2:7 "So send me a master **c** who can work with gold,
2:13 "I am sending you a master **c** named Huram-abi.

SS 7: 1 thighs are like jewels, the work of a skilled c.
Isa 46: 6 and gold and hire a c to make a god from it.

CRAFTSMANSHIP (1) [CRAFT]

Ps 19: 1 glory of God. / The skies display his marvelous c.

CRAFTSMEN (28) [CRAFT]

Ex 31: 6 given special skill to all the naturally talented c
35:10 "Come, all of you who are gifted c.
36: 1 and the other c whom the LORD has gifted with
36: 4 But finally the c left their work to meet with
36: 8 One of the c then embroidered blue, purple,
36:16 The c joined five of these sheets together to make
39: 1 the c made beautiful garments of blue, purple,
Dt 27:15 These idols, the work of c, are detestable to the
2Ki 24:14 and the best of the soldiers, c, and smiths.
24:16 of the best troops and one thousand c and smiths,
1Ch 4:14 the founder of the Valley of C, so called because many c lived there.
22:15 and c of every kind available to you.
29: 5 the other gold and silver work to be done by the c.
2Ch 2: 7 and a skilled engraver who can work with the c of
2:14 He will work with your c and those appointed by
Ne 11:35 Lod, Ono, and the Valley of C.
Isa 41: 7 The c rush to make new idols. The carver hurries
44:11 the LORD in shame, along with all these c—
Jer 10: 9 and they give these materials to skillful c who
24: 1 with the princes of Judah and all the skilled c,
29: 2 and all the c had been deported from Jerusalem.
52:15 along with the rest of the c and the troops who had
Eze 27: 9 Wise old c from Gebal did all the caulking.
Ac 17:29 we shouldn't think of God as an idol designed by c
19:24 the Greek goddess Artemis. He kept many c busy.
19:25 He called the c together, along with others
19:38 If Demetrius and the c have a case against them,

CRAFTY (5) [CRAFT]

1Sa 23:22 has seen him there, for I know that he is very c.
2Sa 13: 3 Now Amnon had a very c friend—his cousin
Job 5:12 He frustrates the plans of the c, so their efforts will
Ps 83: 3 They devise c schemes against your people,
Hos 12: 7 the people are like c merchants selling from

CRAG (1) [CRAGS]

Job 39:28 on the cliffs, making its home on a distant, rocky c.

CRAGS (1) [CRAG]

Jer 18:14 flowing streams from the c of Mount Hermon ever

CRAMMED (1)

Na 3: 1 and lies! She is c with wealth to be plundered.

CRANE (2)

Isa 38:14 Delirious, I chattered like a swallow or a c,
Jer 8: 7 as do the turtledove, the swallow, and the c.

CRANNY (2)

Ob 1: 6 and c of Edom will be searched and looted.
Lk 15: 8 and sweep every nook and c until she finds it?

CRASH (4) [CRASHED, CRASHING]

Hos 11: 6 their enemies will c through their gates and destroy
Am 9: 1 so the roof will c down on the people below.
Mt 7:27 against that house, it will fall with a mighty c."
Rev 19: 6 of mighty ocean waves, or the c of loud thunder:

CRASHED (4) [CRASH]

Jdg 16:30 And the temple c down on the Philistine leaders
Rev 8: 5 and thunder c, lightning flashed, and there was a
11:19 Lightning flashed, thunder c and roared; there was
16:18 Then the thunder c and rolled, and lightning

CRASHING (11) [CRASH]

Ex 15:19 the LORD brought the water c down on them.
Jos 24: 7 I brought the sea c down on the Egyptians,
1Ch 15:28 blowing of horns and trumpets, the c of cymbals,
Isa 26: 5 arrogant city to the dust. / Its walls come c down!
30:13 In an instant it will collapse and come c down.
Jer 49:16 I will bring you c down," says the LORD.
Eze 1:24 As they flew their wings roared like waves c
26: 3 like the waves of the sea c against your shoreline.
Ob 1: 4 your nest among the stars, I will bring you c down.
Zep 1:10 And a great c sound will come from the
Heb 11:30 Jericho seven days, and the walls came c down.

CRATES (1)

Mt 13:48 sit down, sort the good fish into c, and throw the

CRAVE (5) [CRAVED, CRAVES, CRAVING]

Nu 11: 4 the Israelites began to c the good things of Egypt,
Pr 13: 2 but those who are treacherous c violence.
31: 4 to guzzle wine. Rulers should not c liquor.
1Co 10: 6 so that we would not c evil things as they did
1Pe 2: 2 You must c pure spiritual milk so that you can

CRAVED (3) [CRAVE]

Nu 11:34 because they buried the people there who had c
Ps 78:18 God in their hearts, / demanding the foods they c.
78:30 before they finished eating this food they had c,

CRAVES (2) [CRAVE]

Gal 5:16 you won't be doing what your sinful nature c.
1Jn 2:17 world is fading away, along with everything it c.

CRAVING (3) [CRAVE]

Nu 11:34 was called Kibroth-hattaavah—"the graves of c"—
Pr 10: 3 but he refuses to satisfy the c of the wicked.
1Ti 6:10 And some people, c money, have wandered from

CRAWL (5) [CRAWLED, CRAWLING]

Lev 11:23 all other swarming insects that walk or c.
Isa 2:10 C into caves in the rocks. Hide from the terror of
2:19 his enemies will c with fear into holes in the
2:21 They will c into caverns and hide among the
11: 8 Babies will c safely among poisonous snakes.

CRAWLED (1) [CRAWL]

2Sa 17:21 Then the two men c out of the well and hurried on

CRAWLING (3) [CRAWL]

Ge 3:14 the dust as long as you live, c along on your belly.
1Sa 14:11 "Look! The Hebrews are c out of their holes!"
Mic 7:17 Like snakes c from their holes, they will come out

CRAZED (1) [CRAZY]

Jer 25:16 c by the warfare I will send against them."

CRAZY (8) [CRAZED]

2Ki 9:11 of them asked him, "What did that c fellow want?
Pr 23:33 will see hallucinations, and you will say c things.
Hos 9: 7 "The prophets are c!" the people shout.
Lk 18: 5 'but this woman is driving me c. I'm going to see
Jn 10:20 Some of them said, "He has a demon, or he's c.
Ac 26:24 you are insane. Too much study has made you c!"
1Co 14:23 in an unknown language, they will think you are c.
2Co 5:13 If it seems that we are c, it is to bring glory to God.

CREAM (3)

Ps 55:21 His words are as smooth as c, / but in his heart is
Pr 30:33 As the beating of c yields butter, and a blow to the
SS 4:11 as honey. Yes, honey and c are under your tongue.

CREATE (6) [CREATED, CREATES, CREATING, CREATION, CREATOR]

Ex 31: 4 He is able to c beautiful objects from gold, silver,
35:32 He is able to c beautiful objects from gold, silver,
Job 14: 4 Who can c purity in one born impure? No one!
Ps 51:10 C in me a clean heart, O God. / Renew a right
Isa 43:19 come home. I will c rivers for them in the desert!
65:18 I will c Jerusalem as a place of happiness.

CREATED (70) [CREATE]

Ge 1: 1 In the beginning God c the heavens and the earth.
1:21 So God c great sea creatures and every sort of fish
1:27 So God c people in his own image; / God patterned them after himself; / male and female he c them.
2: 8 in the east, and there he placed the man he had c.
5: 1 When God c people, he made them in the likeness
5: 2 He c them male and female, and he blessed them
6: 7 completely wipe out this human race that I have c.
7: 4 wipe from the earth all the living things I have c."
Dt 4:32 from the time God c people on the earth until now.
32: 6 Isn't he your Father who c you? / Has he not made
2Ki 19:15 of the earth. You alone c the heavens and the earth.
Job 26:10 He c the horizon when he separated the waters;
31:15 For God c both me and my servants. He c us both.
38:21 For you were born before it was all c, and you are
38:25 "Who c a channel for the torrents of rain?
Ps 33: 6 LORD merely spoke, / and the heavens were c.
89:11 everything in the world is yours—you c it all.
89:12 You c north and south. / Mount Tabor and Mount
90: 2 Before the mountains were c, / before you made
102:18 so that a nation yet to be c will praise the LORD.
103:22 Praise the LORD, everything he has c,
119:73 You made me; you c me. / Now give me the sense
119:90 every generation, / as enduring as the earth you c.
148: 5 Let every c thing give praise to the LORD,
Pr 8:22 me from the beginning, before he c anything else.
8:24 I was born before the oceans were c,
8:31 And how happy I was with what he c—his wide
21: 6 Wealth c by lying is a vanishing mist and a deadly
30: 4 Who has c the whole wide world? What is his
Ecc 7:29 I discovered that God c people to be upright,
8:17 can discover everything God has c in our world,
Isa 29:16 Should the thing that was c say to the one who
37:16 of the earth. You alone c the heavens and the earth.
40:26 Look up into the heavens. Who c all the stars?
42: 5 the LORD, c the heavens and stretched them out.
42: 5 He c the earth and everything in it. He gives breath
43: 1 But now, O Israel, the LORD who c you says:
43: 7 made them for my glory. It was I who c them."
45: 8 can sprout up together. I, the LORD, c them.
45:12 one who made the earth and c people to live on it.
45:18 and he c the heavens and earth and put everything
46: 3 I c you and have cared for you since before you
54:16 I have c the blacksmith who fans the coals beneath
54:16 And I have c the armies that destroy.
Jer 13:11 so I c Judah and Israel to cling to me,"
Eze 28:13 They were given to you on the day you were c.
28:15 day you were c until the day evil was found in you.
Am 5: 8 It is the LORD who c the stars, the Pleiades
Mal 2:10 Are we not all c by the same God? Then why are
Mk 13:19 horror than at any time since God c the world.
Jn 1: 3 He c everything there is. Nothing exists that he
Ac 17:26 From one man he c all the nations throughout the
Ro 1:20 From the time the world was c, people have seen
9:20 Should the thing that was c say to the one who
1Co 8: 6 the Father, who c everything, and we exist for him.
Eph 2:10 He has c us anew in Christ Jesus, so that we can do
4:24 you are a new person, c in God's likeness—
Col 1:16 Christ is the one through whom God c everything
1:16 Everything has been c through him and for him.
3:10 about Christ, who c this new nature within you.
1Ti 4: 3 But God c those foods to be eaten with
4: 4 Since everything God c is good, we should not
Heb 9:11 made by human hands and not part of this c world.
Jas 1:17 to us from God above, who c all heaven's lights.
2Pe 3: 4 exactly the same since the world was first c."
Rev 4:11 For you c everything, it is for your pleasure that they exist and were c."
10: 6 who c heaven and everything in it, the earth

CREATES (1) [CREATE]

Isa 45: 7 I am the one who c the light and makes the

CREATING (5) [CREATE]

Jdg 14: 4 c an opportunity to disrupt the Philistines,
Isa 65:17 I am c new heavens and a new earth—
Eph 2:15 and Gentiles by c in himself one new person from
Heb 4:10 their labors, just as God rested after c the world.
Jude 1:19 and they are the ones who are c divisions among

CREATION (18) [CREATE]

Ge 2: 1 So the c of the heavens and the earth
2: 3 it was the day when he rested from his work of c.
2: 4 This is the account of the c of the heavens
Ps 145: 9 to everyone. / He showers compassion on all his c.
Isa 65:18 Be glad; rejoice forever in my c! And look! I will
Mt 13:35 I will explain mysteries hidden since the c of the
Mk 10: 6 But God's plan was seen from the beginning of c,
Lk 11:50 of all God's prophets from the c of the world—
Ro 8:19 For all c is waiting eagerly for that future day
8:21 All c anticipates the day when it will join God's
8:22 For we know that all c has been groaning as in the
8:39 nothing in all c will ever be able to separate us
10:18 "The message of God's c has gone out to
Col 1:15 God made anything at all and is supreme over all c.
1:17 everything else began, and he holds all c together.
Heb 4:13 Nothing in all c can hide from him. Everything is
Jas 1:18 And we, out of all c, became his choice possession.
Rev 3:14 the faithful and true witness, the ruler of God's c:

CREATOR (24) [CREATE]

Ge 14:19 by God Most High, / C of heaven and earth.
14:22 God Most High, C of heaven and earth,
Job 4:17 before God? Can a person be pure before the C?'
32:22 And if I tried, my C would soon do away with me.
35:10 Yet they don't ask, 'Where is God my C, the one
36: 3 many illustrations of the righteousness of my C.
40:19 amazing handiwork. Only its C can threaten it.
Ecc 12: 1 excitement of youth cause you to forget your C.
12: 6 remember your C now while you are young,
Isa 17: 7 Then at last the people will think of their C
40:28 is the everlasting God, the C of all the earth?
43:15 the LORD, your Holy One, Israel's C and King.
44:24 The LORD, your Redeemer and C, says: "I am
45: 9 is certain for those who argue with their C.
45:11 the LORD, the C and Holy One of Israel, says:
51:13 your C, the one who put the stars in the sky
54: 5 for your C will be your husband. The LORD
Jer 10:16 He is the C of everything that exists,
38:16 "As surely as the LORD our C lives, I will not
51:19 He is the C of everything that exists,
Ac 4:24 Sovereign Lord, C of heaven and earth, the sea,
Ro 1:25 the things God made but not the C himself,
Eph 3: 9 the C of all things, had kept secret from the
3:15 the C of everything in heaven and on earth.

CREATURE (10) [CREATURES]

Ge 7: 3 that every kind of living c will survive the flood.
9:16 between God and every living c on earth."
Lev 17:11 for the life of any c is in its blood. I have given you
17:14 The life of every c is in the blood. That is why I
20:25 or bird or creeping c that I have forbidden.
22: 5 or by touching a creeping c that is unclean, or by
Dt 4:18 a creeping c or a fish.
14:20 But you may eat any winged c that is ceremonially
Job 14: 3 Must you keep an eye on such a frail c and demand
Rev 5:13 And then I heard every c in heaven and on earth

CREATURES (17) [CREATURE]

Ge 1:21 So God created great sea c and every sort of fish
3: 1 Now the serpent was the shrewdest of all the c the
6:13 to Noah, "I have decided to destroy all living c,
9:11 never to send another flood to kill all living c
9:12 of my eternal covenant with you and all living c.
9:17 this is the sign of my covenant with all the c of the
Lev 11:24 "The following c make you ceremonially unclean.
Job 41:34 Of all the c, it is the proudest. It is the king of
Ps 103:20 of his, / you mighty c who carry out his plans,
104:24 have made them all. / The earth is full of your c.
148: 7 from the earth, / you c of the ocean depths,
Isa 13:21 The houses will be haunted by howling c.
34:14 the ruins, and night c will come there to rest.
34:17 and divided the land and deeded it over to those c.

Eze 8:10 with all kinds of snakes, lizards, and hideous c.
Mic 7:17 They will come to realize what lowly c they really
2Pe 2:12 c of instinct, who are born to be caught and killed.

CREDIT (9) [CREDITOR, CREDITORS]

Lev 7:18 and you will receive no c for bringing it as an
1Sa 18:8 "They c David with ten thousands and me with
2Sa 12:28 so you will get c for the victory instead of me."
Est 2:22 king about it and gave Mordecai c for the report.
Jer 12:2 but in their hearts they give you no c at all.
Lk 6:32 "Do you think you deserve c merely for loving
2Co 10:15 Nor do we claim c for the work someone else has
Eph 2:8 And you can't take c for this; it is a gift from God.
1Pe 2:20 you get no c for being patient if you are beaten for

CREDITOR (3) [CREDIT]

2Ki 4:1 But now a c has come, threatening to take my two
Eze 18:7 Suppose he is a merciful c, not keeping the items
Mt 18:30 But his c wouldn't wait. He had the man arrested

CREDITORS (3) [CREDIT]

Dt 15:2 C must cancel the loans they have made to their
Ps 109:11 May c seize his entire estate, / and strangers take
Isa 50:1 LORD asks, "Did I sell you as slaves to my c?

CREEP (1) [CREEPING, CREPT]

Lev 11:29 the small animals that scurry or c on the ground,

CREEPING (4) [CREEP]

Lev 20:25 or bird or c creature that I have forbidden.
22:5 or by touching a c creature that is unclean, or by
Dt 4:18 a c creature or a fish.
Hab 1:14 but c things that have no leader to defend them

CREPT (5) [CREEP]

Jdg 4:21 Jael quietly c up to him with a hammer and tent
7:13 Gideon c up just as a man was telling his friend
1Sa 24:4 to do with as you wish.' " Then David c forward
2Sa 19:3 They c back into the city as though they were
Jer 9:21 For death has c in through our windows and has

CRESCENS (1)

2Ti 4:10 C has gone to Galatia, and Titus has gone to

CRESCENT (1) [CRESCENTS]

Isa 3:18 their ornaments, headbands, and c necklaces;

CRESCENTS (1) [CRESCENT]

Jdg 8:26 not including the c and pendants, the royal clothing

CRETANS (1) [CRETE]

Ac 2:11 C, and Arabians. And we all hear these people

CRETE (8) [CRETANS]

Dt 2:23 happened when the Caphtorites from C invaded
Jer 47:4 destroying the Philistines, those colonists from C.
Am 9:7 I brought the Philistines from C and led the
Ac 27:7 so we sailed down to the leeward side of C,
27:12 farther up the coast of C, and spend the winter
Tit 1:5 I left you on the island of C so you could complete
1:12 own men, a prophet from C, has said about them, "The people of C are all liars;

CRETES, CRETIANS [KJV] See CRETANS, PEOPLE OF CRETE

CREW (7) [CREWS]

2Ch 32:4 They organized a huge work c to stop the flow of
Eze 27:34 All your merchandise and your c / have passed
Jnh 1:7 Then the c cast lots to see which of them had
Ac 27:12 most of the c wanted to go to Phoenix, farther up
27:18 the ship, the c began throwing the cargo overboard.
27:21 Finally, Paul called the c together and said, "Men,
27:38 the c lightened the ship further by throwing the

CREWS (7) [CREW]

Ex 5:14 the Israelite foremen in charge of the work c.
1Ki 9:27 Hiram sent experienced c of sailors to sail the ships
2Ch 8:18 and manned by experienced c of sailors.
9:10 (When the c of Hiram and Solomon brought gold
Eze 39:14 special c will be appointed to search the land for
39:15 be set up beside them so the burial c will see them
Rev 18:17 merchant ships and their c will stand at a distance.

CRICKETS (1)

Lev 11:22 of all varieties, c, bald locusts, and grasshoppers.

CRIED (104) [CRY]

Ge 45:1 "Out, all of you!" he c out to his attendants.
Ex 2:23 They c out for help, and their pleas for deliverance
12:31 he c. "Go away, all of you! Go and serve the
14:10 to panic, and they c out to the LORD for help.
15:25 So Moses c out to the LORD for help,
Nu 12:11 he c out to Moses, "Oh, my lord! Please don't
12:13 So Moses c out to the LORD, "Heal her, O God,
14:1 people began weeping aloud, and they c all night.
20:16 But when we c out to the LORD, he heard us
21:7 Then the people came to Moses and c out,
Dt 26:7 we c out to the LORD, the God of our ancestors.
Jos 7:7 Then Joshua c out, "Sovereign LORD, why did
24:7 When you c out to the LORD, I put darkness
Jdg 3:9 But when Israel c out to the LORD for help,
3:15 But when Israel c out to the LORD for help,
4:3 Then the Israelites c out to the LORD for help.
6:6 Then the Israelites c out to the LORD for help.
6:7 When they c out to the LORD because of Midian,
6:22 he c out, "Sovereign LORD, I have seen the
10:10 Finally, they c out to the LORD, saying,
10:12 oppressed you, you c out to me, and I rescued you.
11:35 "My daughter!" he c out. "My heart is breaking!
14:17 So she c whenever she was with him and kept it up
15:18 was very thirsty, and he c out to the LORD,
15:19 that place "The Spring of the One Who C Out,"
16:9 the rooms of her house, and she c out, "Samson!
16:12 room as before, and again Delilah c out, "Samson!
16:14 with the loom shuttle. Again she c out, "Samson!
16:20 Then she c out, "Samson! The Philistines have
21:3 "O LORD, God of Israel," they c out, "why has
1Sa 4:7 come into their camp!" they c. "This is a disaster!
5:7 people realized what was happening, they c out,
5:10 but when the people of Ekron saw it coming they c
6:20 of the LORD, this holy God?" they c out.
12:8 Israelites were in Egypt and c out to the LORD,
12:10 "Then they c to the LORD again and confessed,
12:19 God for us, or we will die!" they c out to Samuel.
15:11 so deeply moved when he heard this that he c out
2Sa 1:7 and saw me, he c out for me to come to him.
13:12 "No, my brother!" she c. "Don't be foolish!
13:16 "No, no!" Tamar c. "To reject me now is a
14:4 face down to the floor in front of him and c out,
18:28 Then Ahimaaz c out to the king, "All is well!"
18:33 And as he went, he c, "O my son Absalom!
22:7 But in my distress I c out to the LORD; / yes,
22:42 They c to the LORD, but he refused to answer
1Ki 3:26 who loved him very much, c out, "Oh no, my lord!
13:6 The king c out to the man of God, "Please ask the
13:21 He c out to the man of God from Judah, "This is
17:20 Then Elijah c out to the LORD, "O LORD my
17:21 over the child three times and c out to the LORD,
18:39 they fell on their faces and c out, "The LORD is
22:32 they shouted. But when Jehoshaphat c out,
2Ki 2:12 Elisha saw it and c out, "My father! My father!
2:14 He struck the water with the cloak and c out,
3:10 "What should we do?" the king of Israel c out.
4:1 fellow prophets came to Elisha and c out to him,
4:40 after the men had eaten a bite or two they c out,
6:5 "Ah, my lord!" he c. "It was a borrowed ax!"
6:15 my lord, what will we do now?" he c out to Elisha.
7:6 and Egyptians to attack us!" they c out.
13:14 The chariots and charioteers of Israel!" he c.
1Ch 5:20 They c out to God during the battle, and he
2Ch 13:14 and the rear, they c out to the LORD for help.
14:11 Then Asa c out to the LORD his God,
18:31 But Jehoshaphat c out to the LORD to save him,
32:20 and the prophet Isaiah son of Amoz c out in prayer
33:12 and c out humbly to the God of his ancestors.
35:23 He c out to his men, "Take me from the battle,
Ne 9:27 But in their time of trouble they c to you, and you
9:28 Yet whenever your people c to you again for help,
Ps 3:4 I c out to the LORD, / and he answered me from
18:6 But in my distress I c out to the LORD; / yes,
18:41 They c to the LORD, but he refused to answer
30:2 O LORD my God, I c out to you for help,
30:8 I c out to you, O LORD. / I begged the Lord for
31:22 In sudden fear I had c out, / "I have been cut off
34:6 I c out to the LORD in my suffering, and he heard
66:17 For I c out to him for help, / praising him as I
81:7 You c to me in trouble, and I saved you;
88:1 my salvation, / I have c out to you day and night.
94:18 I c out, "I'm slipping!" / and your unfailing love,
99:6 They c to the LORD for help, / and he answered
102:24 But I c to him, "My God, who lives forever,
107:6 "LORD, help!" they c in their trouble, / and he
107:13 "LORD, help!" they c in their trouble, / and he
107:19 "LORD, help!" they c in their trouble, / and he
107:28 "LORD, help!" they c in their trouble, / and he
116:11 In my anxiety I c out to you, / "These people are
120:1 I c out to him, and he answered my prayer.
Isa 63:11 They c out, "Where is the one who brought Israel
La 2:11 I have c until the tears no longer come. My heart is
3:54 above my head, and I c out, "This is the end!"
Eze 9:8 I fell face down in the dust and c out,
11:13 Then I fell face down in the dust and c out,
Jnh 1:14 Then they c out to the LORD, Jonah's God.
2:2 "I c out to the LORD in my great trouble,
Hab 3:10 The mighty deep c out, lifting its hands to the
Mk 14:72 deny me three times." And he broke down and c.
Ro 9:27 Concerning Israel, Isaiah the prophet c out,
2Co 2:4 Heartbroken, I c over it. I didn't want to hurt you,
Rev 6:16 And they c to the mountains and the rocks,
12:2 and she c out in the pain of labor as she awaited
19:4 on the throne. They c out, "Amen! Hallelujah!"

CRIES (54) [CRY]

Ge 4:10 your brother's blood c out to me from the ground!
21:17 Then God heard the boy's c, and the angel of God
21:17 God has heard the boy's c from the place where
39:15 When he heard my loud c, he ran and left his shirt
Ex 2:6 the baby boy. His helpless c touched her heart.
2:24 God heard their c and remembered his covenant
3:7 I have heard their c for deliverance from their
3:9 The c of the people of Israel have reached me,
22:27 return it and your neighbor c out to me for help,
Dt 15:9 the loan and the needy person c out to the LORD,
33:27 enemy before you; / it is he who c, 'Destroy them!'
1Sa 17:20 leaving for the battlefield with shouts and battle c.
Ne 9:9 and you heard their c from beside the Red Sea.
Job 34:28 God's attention. Yes, he hears the c of the needy.
Ps 10:17 Surely you will listen to their c and comfort them.
22:1 so distant? / Why do you ignore my c for help?
22:5 You heard their c for help and saved them.
22:24 walked away. / He has listened to their c for help.
34:15 who do right; / his ears are open to their c for help.
39:12 my prayer, O LORD! / Listen to my c for help!
69:33 For the LORD hears the c of his needy ones;
74:4 your enemies shouted their victorious battle c;
106:44 pitied them in their distress / and listened to their c.
140:6 my God!" / Listen, O LORD, to my c for mercy!
144:14 no forced exile, / no c of distress in our squares.
145:19 he hears their c for help and rescues them.
Pr 1:20 shouts in the streets. She c out in the public square.
1:22 "You simpletons!" she c. "How long will you go
8:3 entrance to the city, at the city gates, she c aloud,
21:13 Those who shut their ears to the c of the poor will
Isa 5:7 but instead he heard c of oppression.
15:4 The c from the cities of Heshbon and Elealeh will
22:5 and c of death echo from the mountainsides.
24:8 the happy c of celebration will be heard no more.
30:19 He will respond instantly to the sound of your c.
Jer 4:19 of enemy trumpets and the roar of their battle c.
11:11 they beg for mercy, I will not listen to their c.
25:36 Listen to the frantic c of the shepherds,
46:12 The earth is filled with your c of despair.
48:5 while c of terror rise from Horonaim below.
48:34 their awful c of terror can be heard from Heshbon
La 1:9 "LORD, see my deep misery," she c.
2:20 "O LORD, think about this!" Jerusalem c.
4:3 They ignore their children's c, like the ostriches of
Eze 21:24 Again and again your guilt c out against you,
Hos 2:21 down water on the earth in answer to its c for rain.
2:22 Then the earth will answer the thirsty c of the
7:7 one after another, and no one c out to me for help.
Zep 1:16 trumpet calls, and battle c. Down go the walled
Zec 10:6 I am the LORD their God, who will hear their c.
Ac 7:34 I have heard their c. So I have come to rescue
Jas 5:4 Hear the c of the field workers whom you have
5:4 The c of the reapers have reached the ears of the
1Pe 2:2 Cry out for this nourishment as a baby c for milk,

CRIME (27) [CRIMES, CRIMINAL, CRIMINAL'S, CRIMINALS]

Ge 31:36 he demanded of Laban. "What is my c?
Dt 19:15 "Never convict anyone of a c on the testimony of
19:16 comes forward and accuses someone of a c,
21:22 "If someone has committed a c worthy of death
22:21 She has committed a disgraceful c in Israel by
22:26 she has committed no c worthy of death.
25:2 with the number of lashes appropriate to the c.
Jdg 19:30 "Such a horrible c has not been committed since
20:3 then asked how this terrible c had happened.
20:6 men have committed this terrible and shameful c.
1Sa 20:1 have I done?" he exclaimed. "What is my c?
26:18 you chasing me? What have I done? What is my c?
2Sa 3:28 and my people are innocent of this c against
13:12 You know what a serious c it is to do such a thing
Job 31:11 lust is a shameful sin, a c that should be punished.
Ps 52:1 a hero, do you? / Why boast about this c of yours,
Pr 29:24 You will be punished if you report the c, but you
Ecc 8:11 When a c is not punished, people feel it is safe to
Jer 37:18 asked the king, "What c have I committed?
Zep 3:1 polluted Jerusalem, the city of violence and c.
Mt 27:23 Pilate demanded. "What c has he committed?"
Mk 15:14 Pilate demanded. "What c has he committed?"
Lk 23:22 he demanded, "Why? What c has he committed?
Jn 18:38 and told them, "He is not guilty of any c.
Ac 18:14 a case involving some wrongdoing or a serious c,
22:24 him lashed with whips to make him confess his c.
25:8 "I have committed no c against the Jewish laws

CRIMES (14) [CRIME]

Lev 19:17 so you will not be held guilty for their c.
Dt 24:16 worthy of death must be executed for their own c.
2Ki 14:6 of death must be executed for their own c."
2Ch 25:4 of death must be executed for their own c."
Ps 64:6 As they plot their c, they say, / "We have devised
Pr 1:16 They rush to commit c. They hurry to commit
Ecc 8:10 in the very city where they committed their c!
Jer 18:23 Don't forgive their c and blot out their sins.
Eze 7:23 my people, for the land is bloodied by terrible c.
Hos 4:5 As a sentence for your c, you will stumble in broad
Joel 3:21 I will pardon my people's c, which I have not yet
Am 1:13 they committed cruel c, ripping open pregnant
3:9 witness the scandalous spectacle of all Israel's c."
Mk 15:3 Then the leading priests accused him of many c,

CRIMINAL (10) [CRIME]

Ge 31:36 You have chased me as though I were a c.
Isa 53:9 But he was buried like a c; he was put in a rich
Mt 26:55 Jesus said to the crowd, "Am I some dangerous c,
27:16 This year there was a notorious c in prison, a man
Mk 14:48 Jesus asked them, "Am I some dangerous c,
Lk 22:52 "Am I some dangerous c," he asked, "that you
23:40 But the other c protested, "Don't you fear God
Jn 18:30 have handed him over to you if he weren't a c!"
18:40 Not this man, but Barabbas!" (Barabbas was a c.)
2Ti 2:9 I am suffering and have been chained like a c.

CRIMINAL'S (1) [CRIME]

Php 2:8 himself even further by dying a c death on a cross.

CRIMINALS (10) [CRIME]
1Ki 1:21 and I will be treated as **c** as soon as you are dead."
Ps 59:2 Rescue me from these **c**; / save me from these
101:8 My daily task will be to ferret out **c** / and free the
Mt 27:38 Two **c** were crucified with him, their crosses on
27:44 And the **c** who were crucified with him also
Mk 15:27 Two **c** were crucified with him, their crosses on
15:32 Even the two **c** who were being crucified with
Lk 23:32 Two others, both **c**, were led out to be executed
23:33 on the center cross, and the two **c** on either side.
23:39 One of the **c** hanging beside him scoffed,

CRIMSON (1)
Isa 1:18 Even if you are stained as red as **c**, I can make you

CRINGE (4) [CRINGED]
2Sa 22:45 Foreigners **c** before me; / as soon as they hear of
Ps 18:44 hear of me, they submit; / foreigners **c** before me.
66:3 Your enemies **c** before your mighty power.
81:15 Those who hate the LORD would **c** before him;

CRINGED (1) [CRINGE]
Ps 107:26 sank again to the depths; / the sailors **c** in terror.

CRIPPLE (1) [CRIPPLED]
Jos 11:6 be dead. **C** their horses and burn their chariots."

CRIPPLED (19) [CRIPPLE]
Ge 49:6 murdered men, / and they **c** oxen just for sport.
Jos 11:9 Then Joshua **c** the horses and burned all the
2Sa 4:4 a son named Mephibosheth, who was **c** as a child.
4:4 as she was running, and he became **c** as a result.)
8:4 Then he **c** all but one hundred of the chariot horses.
9:3 one of Jonathan's sons is still alive, but he is **c**."
9:13 And Mephibosheth, who was **c** in both feet,
19:26 I can go with the king.' For as you know I am **c**.
1Ch 18:4 Then he **c** all but one hundred of the chariot horses.
Mal 1:8 And isn't it wrong to offer animals that are **c**
1:13 Animals that are stolen and mutilated, **c** and sick—
Mt 15:30 A vast crowd brought him the lame, blind, **c**, mute,
15:31 the **c** were made well, the lame were walking
18:8 It is better to enter heaven **c** or lame than to be
Lk 13:11 he saw a woman who had been **c** by an evil spirit.
14:13 invite the poor, the **c**, the lame, and the blind.
14:21 and invite the poor, the **c**, the lame, and the blind.'
Ac 4:9 because we've done a good deed for a **c** man?
14:8 Paul and Barnabas came upon a man with **c** feet.

CRISIS (1)
1Co 7:26 Because of the present **c**, I think it is best to remain

CRISPUS (2)
Ac 18:8 **C**, the leader of the synagogue, and all his
1Co 1:14 God that I did not baptize any of you except **C**

CRITIC (1) [CRITICISM]
Job 40:2 You are God's **c**, but do you have the answers?"

CRITICISM (6) [CRITIC, CRITICISMS, CRITICIZE, CRITICIZED, CRITICIZING, CRITICS]
Pr 13:18 If you ignore **c**, you will end in poverty
13:18 and disgrace; if you accept **c**, you will be honored.
15:31 If you listen to constructive **c**, you will be at home
15:32 If you reject **c**, you only harm yourself; but if you
25:12 Valid **c** is as treasured by the one who heeds it as
29:1 Whoever stubbornly refuses to accept **c** will

CRITICISMS (2) [CRITICISM]
Job 6:25 words are painful, but what do your **c** amount to?
16:4 I could spout off my **c** against you and shake my

CRITICIZE (5) [CRITICISM]
Nu 12:8 as he is. Should you not be afraid to **c** him?"
SS 8:1 matter who was watching, and no one would **c** me.
Da 6:4 his affairs, but they couldn't find anything to **c**.
Ro 9:20 Who are you, a mere human being, to **c** God?
Jas 4:11 If you **c** each other and condemn each other,

CRITICIZED (7) [CRITICISM]
Nu 12:1 Miriam and Aaron **c** Moses because he had
2Sa 14:9 "And I'll take the responsibility if you are **c** for
Ecc 7:5 It is better to be **c** by a wise person than to be
Lk 3:19 John also publicly **c** Herod Antipas, ruler of
Ac 11:2 in Jerusalem, some of the Jewish believers **c** him.
1Ti 5:7 so that the widows you support will not be **c**.
Tit 2:8 Let your teaching be so correct that it can't be **c**.

CRITICIZING (2) [CRITICISM]
Lk 6:37 Stop **c** others, or it will all come back on you.
Jas 4:11 then you are **c** and condemning God's law.

CRITICS (3) [CRITICISM]
Pr 27:11 out to be wise! Then I will be able to answer my **c**.
Mk 3:4 Then he turned to his **c** and asked, "Is it legal to do
Lk 6:9 Then Jesus said to his **c**, "I have a question for

CROCODILE (4) [CROCODILE'S]
Job 41:1 "Can you catch a **c** with a hook or put a noose
41:10 And since no one dares to disturb the **c**, who would
41:27 To the **c**, iron is nothing but straw, and bronze is
41:31 "The **c** makes the water boil with its commotion.

CROCODILE'S (1) [CROCODILE]
Job 41:12 emphasize the tremendous strength in the **c** limbs

CROOKED (19)
Jdg 5:6 main roads, / and travelers stayed on **c** side paths.
Ps 36:3 Everything they say is **c** and deceitful.
58:2 No, all your dealings are **c**; / you hand out violence
78:57 had been. / They were as useless as a **c** bow.
101:3 anything vile and vulgar. / I hate all **c** dealings;
125:5 But banish those who turn to **c** ways, O LORD.
Pr 2:15 What they do is **c**, and their ways are wrong.
5:6 She staggers down a **c** trail and doesn't even
8:8 and good. There is nothing **c** or twisted in it.
10:9 but those who follow **c** paths will slip and fall.
17:20 The **c** heart will not prosper; the twisted tongue
21:8 The guilty walk a **c** path; the innocent travel a
28:6 It is better to be poor and honest than rich and **c**.
28:18 from harm, but those who are **c** will be destroyed.
Ecc 7:13 for who can straighten out what he has made **c**?
Hos 7:16 They are like a **c** bow that always misses its target.
Mic 7:4 the straightest is more **c** than a hedge of thorns.
Hab 2:4 They trust in themselves, and their lives are **c**;
Php 2:15 lives as children of God in a dark world full of **c**

CROP (45) [CROPS]
Ge 41:54 There were **c** failures in all the surrounding
47:24 harvest it, a fifth of your **c** will belong to Pharaoh.
47:24 and use it to plant the next year's **c** and to feed
Ex 23:11 you harvest any volunteer **c** that may come up.
34:22 of Harvest with the first **c** of the wheat harvest,
34:26 You must bring the best of the first of each year's **c**
Lev 1:16 The priest must remove the **c** and the feathers
19:10 It is the same with your grape **c**—do not strip every
19:24 In the fourth year the entire **c** will be devoted to the
25:15 The seller will charge you only for the **c** years left
25:21 so the land will produce a bumper **c**, enough to
25:22 you will eat from the old **c** until the new harvest
Dt 22:9 "Do not plant any other **c** between the rows of
22:9 from the vineyard or the produce of the other **c**.
Jdg 8:2 better than the entire **c** of my little clan of Abiezer?
1Ki 8:37 or plagues, or **c** disease, or attacks of locusts
2Ch 6:28 or plagues, or **c** disease, or attacks of locusts
Ne 10:35 whether it be a **c** from the soil or from our fruit
Pr 27:25 After the hay is harvested, the new **c** appears,
Isa 5:7 He expected them to yield a **c** of justice,
32:10 For your fruit **c** will fail, and the harvest will never
Jer 12:13 They will harvest a **c** of shame, for the fierce anger
Eze 47:12 There will be a new **c** every month, without fail!
Hos 2:23 "At that time I will plant a **c** of Israelites and raise
10:12 and you will harvest a **c** of my love.
10:13 and raised a thriving **c** of sins.
Am 7:1 from the fields and as the main **c** was coming up.
Hab 3:17 even though the olive **c** fails, and the fields lie
Hag 2:16 When you hoped for a twenty-bushel **c**,
Mt 13:8 fell on fertile soil and produced a **c** that was thirty,
13:22 this life and the lure of wealth, so no **c** is produced.
13:26 When the **c** began to grow and produce grain,
21:34 he sent his servants to collect his share of the **c**.
21:41 will give him his share of the **c** after each harvest."
Mk 4:8 fell on fertile soil and produced a **c** that was thirty,
4:19 and the desire for nice things, so no **c** is produced.
12:2 sent one of his servants to collect his share of the **c**.
Lk 8:8 and produced a **c** one hundred times as much as
20:10 sent one of his servants to collect his share of the **c**.
1Co 9:7 have you ever heard of a farmer who harvests his **c**
2Co 9:6 who plants only a few seeds will get a small **c**.
9:6 one who plants generously will get a generous **c**.
Heb 6:7 that falls on it and bears a good **c** for the farmer,
Rev 14:15 come for you to harvest; the **c** is ripe on the earth."
22:2 twelve crops of fruit, with a fresh **c** each month.

CROPS (119) [CROP]
Ge 4:12 No longer will it yield abundant **c** for you,
26:12 That year Isaac's **c** were tremendous! He harvested
27:28 God always give you plenty of dew for healthy **c**
39:5 to run smoothly, and his **c** and livestock flourished.
41:34 and let them collect one-fifth of all the **c** during the
41:47 for the next seven years there were bumper **c**
41:48 Joseph took a portion of all the **c** grown in Egypt
47:13 and the **c** continued to fail throughout Egypt
47:26 that Pharaoh should receive one-fifth of all the **c**
Ex 9:22 on the people, the animals, and the **c**."
9:25 fields was destroyed—people, animals, and **c** alike.
10:12 and eat all the **c** still left after the hailstorm."
16:35 in the land of Canaan, where there were **c** to eat.
22:6 the one who started the fire must pay for the lost **c**.
22:29 back when you give me the tithe of your **c**
23:10 "Plant and harvest your **c** for six years,
23:16 when you bring me the first **c** of your harvest.
23:19 "As you harvest each of your **c**, bring me a choice
Lev 19:9 "When you harvest your **c**, do not harvest the
23:10 land I am giving you and you harvest your first **c**,
23:17 an offering to the LORD from the first of your **c**.
23:20 the loaves representing the first of your later **c**.
23:22 "When you harvest the **c** of your land, do not
25:3 and prune your vineyards and harvest your **c**,
25:4 Do not plant your **c** or prune your vineyards during
25:5 And don't store away the **c** that grow naturally
25:11 or store away any of the **c** that grow naturally,
25:19 Then the land will yield bumper **c**, and you will eat
25:20 we are not allowed to plant or harvest **c** that year?'
26:4 The land will then yield its **c**, and the trees will
26:10 You will have such a surplus of **c** that you will
26:16 You will plant your **c** in vain because your enemies
26:20 for your land will yield no **c**, and your trees will
Nu 13:20 and bring back samples of the **c** you see."
15:19 you will eat from the **c** that grow there. But you
Dt 7:13 you will have large **c** of grain, grapes, and olives,
11:14 their proper seasons so you can harvest **c** of grain,
14:22 "You must set aside a tithe of your **c**—
14:22 one-tenth of all the **c** you harvest each year.
14:25 you may sell the tithe portion of your **c** and herds
14:28 end of every third year bring the tithe of all your **c**
24:19 "When you are harvesting your **c** and forget to
26:10 I have brought you a token of the first **c** you have
26:12 third year you must offer a special tithe of your **c**.
28:11 numerous livestock, and abundant **c**.
28:33 have never heard about will eat the **c** you worked
28:38 but harvest little, for locusts will eat your **c**.
28:42 Swarms of insects will destroy your trees and **c**.
28:51 Its armies will devour your livestock and **c**,
32:13 he let them feast on the **c** of the fields.
32:22 of the grave. / It devours the earth and all its **c**
33:15 with the finest **c** of the ancient mountains,
Jos 5:12 So from that time on the Israelites ate from the **c** of
Jdg 6:3 Whenever the Israelites planted their **c**,
6:4 in the land and destroying **c** as far away as Gaza.
Ru 1:6 his people in Judah by giving them good **c** again.
1Sa 8:12 be forced to plow in his fields and harvest his **c**,
1Ki 17:14 the LORD sends rain and the **c** grow again!"
2Ki 8:6 including the value of any **c** that had been
19:29 But in the third year you will plant **c** and harvest
1Ch 16:32 Let the fields and their **c** burst forth with joy!
2Ch 7:13 or I might command locusts to devour your **c**,
31:5 and generously with the first of their **c** and grain,
Job 31:8 then let someone else harvest the **c** I have planted,
31:39 or if I have stolen its **c** or murdered its owners,
Ps 65:10 the earth with showers / and bless its abundant **c**.
72:16 May there be abundant **c** throughout the land,
78:46 He gave their **c** to caterpillars; / their harvest was
85:12 his blessings. / Our land will yield its bountiful **c**.
96:12 Let the fields and their **c** burst forth with joy!
105:35 everything green in the land, / destroying all the **c**.
105:44 and they harvested **c** that others had planted.
107:37 plant their vineyards, / and harvest their bumper **c**.
144:13 May our farms be filled / with **c** of every kind.
Pr 28:3 the poor is like a pounding rain that destroys the **c**.
Ecc 11:6 Be sure to stay busy and plant a variety of **c**,
Isa 7:20 off everything: your land, your **c**, and your people.
19:7 All the **c** will dry up, and everything will die.
19:9 will have no flax or cotton, for the **c** will fail.
24:4 The earth dries up, the **c** wither, the skies refuse to
28:27 He doesn't thresh all his **c** the same way. A heavy
32:20 they plant seed, bountiful **c** will spring up.
37:30 But in the third year you will plant **c** and harvest
Jer 7:20 and **c** will be consumed by the unquenchable fire
31:12 the good **c** of wheat, wine, and oil, and the healthy
35:7 And do not build houses or plant **c** or vineyards,
35:9 or owned vineyards or farms or planted **c**.
40:12 to gather a great harvest of grapes and other **c**.
50:16 Lead from Babylon all those who plant **c**; send all
Eze 19:7 farms were desolated, / and their **c** were destroyed.
34:27 and fields of my people will yield bumper **c**,
34:29 "And I will give them a land famous for its **c**,
36:8 But the mountains of Israel will produce heavy **c** of
36:9 Your ground will be tilled and your **c** planted.
36:29 I will give you good **c**, and I will abolish famine in
36:36 the ruins and planted lush **c** in the wilderness.
Hos 7:14 begging foreign gods for **c** and prosperity.
Joel 1:4 After the cutting locusts finished eating the **c**,
1:10 The fields are ruined and empty of **c**. The grain,
1:11 and barley—yes, all the field **c**—are ruined.
1:17 die in the parched ground, and the grain **c** fail.
Am 4:7 when you needed it the most, ruining all your **c**.
9:14 they will eat their **c** and drink their wine.
Mic 6:15 You will plant **c** but not harvest them. You will
Hag 1:10 withheld the dew and the earth has withheld its **c**.
1:11 and grapes and olives and all your other **c**,
2:19 and the olive tree have produced their **c**.
Zec 8:12 The earth will produce its **c**, and the sky will
Mal 3:11 Your **c** will be abundant, for I will guard them
Mt 25:24 harvesting **c** you didn't plant and gathering **c** you didn't cultivate.
25:26 harvesting **c** I didn't plant and gathering **c** I didn't cultivate?
Mk 4:28 because the earth produces **c** on its own. First a
Lk 12:16 rich man had a fertile farm that produced fine **c**.
19:21 what isn't yours and harvesting **c** you didn't plant.'
Ac 14:17 and good **c** and giving you food and joyful
Jas 5:18 grass turned green, and the **c** began to grow again.
Rev 22:2 bearing twelve **c** of fruit, with a fresh crop each

CROSS (104) [ACROSS, CROSSED, CROSSES, CROSSING, CROSSINGS]
Ge 31:52 I will not **c** this line to harm you, and you will not **c** it to harm me.
Ex 19:13 or animals that **c** the boundary must be stoned to
19:21 and warn the people not to **c** the boundaries.
19:24 or the people **c** the boundaries to come up here.
Nu 21:23 But King Sihon refused to let them **c** his land.
32:21 and if your troops **c** the Jordan until the LORD
32:27 all who are able to bear arms will **c** over to fight
32:29 to fight the LORD's battles **c** the Jordan with you,
32:30 But if they refuse to **c** over and march ahead of

32:32 We will **c** the Jordan into Canaan fully armed to
33:51 'When you **c** the Jordan River into the land of
35:10 'When you **c** the Jordan into the land of Canaan,
Dt 2:13 "Then the LORD told us to **c** Zered Brook,
2:18 'Today you will **c** the border of Moab at Ar
2:24 "Then the LORD said, 'Now **c** the Arnon Gorge!
2:29 Let us pass through until we **c** the Jordan into the
3:18 all your fighting men must **c** the Jordan, armed
3:25 Please let me **c** the Jordan to see the wonderful
3:27 but you may not **c** the Jordan River.
4:21 He vowed that I would never **c** the Jordan River
4:22 Though you will **c** the Jordan to occupy the land,
9:1 Today you are about to **c** the Jordan River to
9:3 But the LORD your God will **c** over ahead of you
11:31 For you are about to **c** the Jordan to occupy the
12:10 You will soon **c** the Jordan River and live in the
27:2 When you **c** the Jordan River and enter the land the
27:3 you will soon **c** the river to enter the land the
27:4 When you **c** the Jordan, set up these stones at
27:12 "When you **c** the Jordan River, the tribes of
30:13 'Who will **c** the sea to bring it to us so we can hear
31:2 The LORD has told me that I will not **c** the
31:3 But the LORD your God himself will **c** over
Jos 1:11 In three days you will **c** the Jordan River and take
3:14 When the people set out to **c** the Jordan, the priests
5:1 up the Jordan River so the people of Israel could **c**,
Jdg 11:19 asking for permission to **c** through his land to get
1Sa 6:9 If they **c** the border of our land and go to
14:8 told him. "We will **c** over and let them see us.
30:10 of the men were too exhausted to **c** the brook,
2Sa 17:21 "Quick!" they told him, "**c** the Jordan tonight!"
19:18 As the king was about to **c** the river, Shimei fell
19:41 to do most of the work in helping him **c** the Jordan.
1Ki 2:37 On the day you **c** the Kidron Valley, you will
Isa 33:21 like a wide river of protection that no enemy can **c**.
Jer 5:22 an everlasting boundary that the waters cannot **c**.
Eze 47:5 and the river was too deep to **c** without swimming.
Mt 8:18 he instructed his disciples to **c** to the other side of
10:38 If you refuse to take up your **c** and follow me,
14:22 and **c** to the other side of the lake while he sent the
16:24 selfish ambition, shoulder your **c**, and follow me.
23:15 For you **c** land and sea to make one convert,
27:32 and they forced him to carry Jesus' **c**.
27:35 After they had nailed him to the **c**, the soldiers
27:37 A signboard was fastened to the **c** above Jesus'
27:40 of God, save yourself and come down from the **c**!"
27:42 Let him come down from the **c**, and we will
Mk 4:35 "Let's **c** to the other side of the lake."
8:34 selfish ambition, shoulder your **c**, and follow me.
15:21 just then, and they forced him to carry Jesus' **c**.
15:24 Then they nailed him to the **c**. They gambled for
15:26 A signboard was fastened to the **c** above Jesus'
15:30 save yourself and come down from the **c**!"
15:32 come down from the **c** so we can see it and believe
15:46 and taking Jesus' body down from the **c**,
Lk 8:22 "Let's **c** over to the other side of the lake."
9:23 shoulder your **c** daily, and follow me.
14:27 be my disciple if you do not carry your own **c**
16:26 Anyone who wanted to **c** over to you from here is
16:26 at its edge, and no one there can **c** over to us.'
23:26 was forced to follow Jesus and carry his **c**.
23:33 Jesus on the center **c**, and the two criminals on
23:38 A signboard was nailed to the **c** above him with
23:53 Then he took the body down from the **c**
Jn 8:28 you have lifted up the Son of Man on the **c**,
12:32 And when I am lifted up on the **c**, I will draw
19:17 Carrying the **c** by himself, Jesus went to the place
19:25 Standing near the **c** were Jesus' mother, and his
Ac 2:23 you nailed him to the **c** and murdered him.
13:29 they took him down from the **c** and placed him in a
Ro 7:4 to its power when you died with Christ on the **c**.
1Co 1:17 for fear that the **c** of Christ would lose its power.
1:18 I know very well how foolish the message of the **c**
2:2 only on Jesus Christ and his death on the **c**.
2Co 13:4 Although he died on the **c** in weakness, he now
Gal 3:1 a signboard with a picture of Christ dying on the **c**.
3:13 When he was hung on the **c**, he took upon himself
5:11 preaching salvation through the **c** of Christ alone.
5:24 and desires of their sinful nature to his **c**
6:12 for teaching that the **c** of Christ alone can save.
6:14 anything except the **c** of our Lord Jesus Christ.
6:14 Because of that **c**, my interest in this world died
Php 2:8 even further by dying a criminal's death on a **c**.
3:18 shows they are really enemies of the **c** of Christ.
Col 1:20 and on earth by means of his blood on the **c**.
1:22 He has done this through his death on the **c** in his
2:14 took it and destroyed it by nailing it to Christ's **c**.
2:15 by his victory over them on the **c** of Christ.
Phm 1:2 and to Archippus, a fellow soldier of the **c**.
Heb 6:6 because they are nailing the Son of God to the **c**
7:27 once for all when he sacrificed himself on the **c**.
12:2 He was willing to die a shameful death on the **c**
1Pe 2:24 carried away our sins in his own body on the **c**
1Jn 5:6 in water and by shedding his blood on the **c**—

CROSS-EXAMINE (1) [EXAMINE]

Ps 26:2 Put me on trial, LORD, and **c** me. / Test my

CROSSBAR (2) [CROSSBARS]

Ex 26:28 The middle **c**, halfway up the frames, will run all
36:33 The middle **c** of the five was halfway up the

CROSSBARS (15) [CROSSBAR]

Ex 26:26 "Make **c** of acacia wood to run across the frames,
26:26 five **c** for the north side of the Tabernacle
26:27 Also make five **c** for the rear of the Tabernacle,
26:29 with gold and make gold rings to support the **c**.
Overlay the **c** with gold as well.
35:11 the clasps, frames, **c**, posts, and bases;
36:31 Then they made five **c** from acacia wood to tie the
36:34 The frames and **c** were all overlaid with gold.
36:34 The rings used to hold the **c** were made of pure
39:33 the clasps, frames, **c**, posts, and bases;
40:18 and attaching the **c** and raising the posts.
Nu 3:36 the **c**, the pillars, the bases, and all the equipment
4:31 the Tabernacle, the **c**, the pillars with their bases,
1Ki 7:28 were constructed with side panels braced with **c**.
7:29 and the **c** were decorated with carved lions,

CROSSED (48) [CROSS]

Ge 31:21 possessions with him and **c** the Euphrates River,
48:14 But Jacob **c** his arms as he reached out to lay his
Nu 20:17 and never leave it until we have **c** the opposite
21:22 We will stay on the king's road until we have **c**
33:8 and **c** the Red Sea into the wilderness beyond.
Dt 1:24 They **c** into the hills and came to the valley of
2:14 at Kadesh-barnea until we finally **c** Zered Brook!
Jos 2:23 down from the hill country, **c** the Jordan River,
3:16 Then all the people **c** over near the city of Jericho.
3:17 They waited there until everyone had **c** the Jordan
4:11 the priests **c** over with the Ark of the LORD.
4:13 and they **c** over to the plains of Jericho in the
4:19 The people **c** the Jordan on the tenth day of the
4:22 'This is where the Israelites **c** the Jordan on dry
4:23 Sea when he dried it up until we had all **c** over.
15:6 **c** to Beth-hoglah, then proceeded north of
22:10 before they **c** the Jordan River, Reuben, Gad,
22:13 They **c** the river to talk with the tribes of Reuben,
24:11 "When you **c** the Jordan River and came to
Jdg 6:33 formed an alliance against Israel and **c** the Jordan,
8:4 then **c** the Jordan River with his three hundred
10:9 The Ammonites also **c** to the west side of the
11:18 But they never once **c** the Arnon River into Moab.
12:1 Ephraim mobilized its army and **c** over to Zaphon.
1Sa 13:7 Some of them **c** the Jordan River and escaped into
2Sa 2:29 They **c** the Jordan River, traveling all through the
10:17 he mobilized all Israel, **c** the Jordan River, and led
15:23 They **c** the Kidron Valley and then went out
17:20 "They were here, but they **c** the brook."
19:18 They all **c** the ford and worked hard ferrying the
19:39 So all the people **c** the Jordan with the king.
24:5 First they **c** the Jordan and camped at Aroer,
1Ch 12:15 They **c** the Jordan River during its seasonal
19:17 he mobilized all Israel, **c** the Jordan River,
Isa 11:15 to divide it into seven streams that can easily be **c**.
23:2 you merchants of Sidon. Your traders **c** the sea,
Jer 7:31 it never even **c** my mind to command such a thing!
19:5 it never even **c** my mind to command such a thing!
32:35 it never even **c** my mind to command such a thing.
Mt 14:34 After they had **c** the lake, they landed at
15:39 into a boat and **c** over to the region of Magadan.
16:5 Later, after they **c** to the other side of the lake,
Mk 8:10 and **c** over to the region of Dalmanutha.
8:13 and left them, and he **c** to the other side of the lake.
Lk 10:31 he **c** to the other side of the road and passed him
Jn 6:1 After this, Jesus **c** over the Sea of Galilee,
18:1 Jesus **c** the Kidron Valley with his disciples
Ac 20:15 The following day, we **c** to the island of Samos.

CROSSES (2) [CROSS]

Mt 27:38 crucified with him, their **c** on either side of his.
Mk 15:27 crucified with him, their **c** on either side of his.

CROSSING (15) [CROSS]

Dt 4:26 you will quickly disappear from the land you are **c**
30:18 good life in the land you are **c** the Jordan to
31:13 Do this as long as you live in the land you are **c** the
32:47 in the land you are **c** the Jordan River to occupy."
Jos 2:7 leading to the shallow **c** places of the Jordan River.
3:1 of the Jordan River, where they camped before **c**.
18:16 **c** south of the slope where the Jebusites lived,
Jdg 3:28 across from Moab, preventing anyone from **c**.
11:16 on their journey from Egypt after **c** the Red Sea,
Job 33:18 from the grave, from **c** over the river of death.
Pr 7:8 He was **c** the street near the house of an immoral
Isa 10:29 They are **c** the pass and are staying overnight at
Da 8:5 **c** the land so swiftly that it didn't even touch the
Mk 8:15 As they were **c** the lake, Jesus warned them,
Lk 8:37 and left, **c** back to the other side of the lake.

CROSSINGS (1) [CROSS]

Isa 16:2 homeless birds at the shallow **c** of the Arnon River.

CROSSROADS (2) [ROAD]

Pr 8:2 She stands on the hilltop and at the **c**.
Ob 1:14 You shouldn't have stood at the **c**, killing those

CROSSWISE (2)

Eze 1:16 each wheel had a second wheel turning **c** within it.
10:10 each wheel had a second wheel turning **c** within it.

CROUCH (3) [CROUCHES]

Job 38:40 as they lie in their dens or **c** in the thicket?
39:3 They **c** down to give birth to their young
Ps 10:9 Like lions they **c** silently, / waiting to pounce on

CROUCHES (2) [CROUCH]

Ge 49:9 Like a lion he **c** and lies down; / like a lioness—
Nu 24:9 Like a lion, Israel **c** and lies down; / like a lioness,

CROW (1) [CROWED, CROWS]

Lk 22:34 The rooster will not **c** tomorrow morning until you

CROWD (144) [CROWDED, CROWDING, CROWDS]

Ge 20:8 what had happened, great fear swept through the **c**.
Ex 23:2 "Do not join a **c** that intends to do evil. When you
Ru 4:9 said to the leaders and to the **c** standing around,
2Sa 13:34 a great **c** coming toward the city from the west.
13:34 "I see a **c** of people coming from the Horonaim
20:12 and Joab's officer saw that a **c** was gathering
1Ki 8:65 A large **c** had gathered from as far away as
2Ki 10:9 and spoke to the **c** that had gathered around them.
2Ch 30:13 so a huge **c** assembled at Jerusalem in midspring to
Ezr 10:1 Temple of God, a large **c** of people from Israel—
Job 31:34 Have I feared the **c** and its contempt, so that I
Ps 68:18 ascended to the heights, / you led a **c** of captives.
142:7 so I can thank you. / The godly will **c** around me,
Isa 22:7 fill your beautiful valleys and **c** against your gates.
Jer 28:11 And Hananiah said again to the **c** that had
43:6 In the **c** were men, women, and children, the king's
44:15 a great **c** of all the Judeans living in Pathros,
Eze 34:21 For you fat sheep push and butt and **c** my sick
Mt 8:10 Turning to the **c**, he said, "I tell you the truth,
8:18 When Jesus noticed how large the **c** was growing,
9:8 Fear swept through the **c** as they saw this happen
9:24 she's only asleep." But the **c** laughed at him.
9:25 When the **c** was finally outside, Jesus went in
12:23 The **c** was amazed. "Could it be that Jesus is the
12:46 As Jesus was speaking to the **c**, his mother
13:2 where an immense **c** soon gathered. He got into a
14:14 A vast **c** was there as he stepped from the boat,
15:30 A vast **c** brought him the lame, blind, crippled,
15:31 The **c** was amazed! Those who hadn't been able to
15:36 to the disciples, who distributed the food to the **c**.
17:14 of the mountain, a huge **c** was waiting for them.
20:29 left the city of Jericho, a huge **c** followed behind.
20:31 The **c** told them to be quiet, but they only shouted
21:8 Most of the **c** spread their coats on the road ahead
26:55 Then Jesus said to the **c**, "Am I some dangerous
27:15 to the **c** each year during the Passover celebration
27:21 the **c** shouted back their reply: "Barabbas!"
27:23 But the **c** only roared the louder, "Crucify him!"
27:24 a bowl of water and washed his hands before the **c**,
Mk 1:33 And a huge **c** of people from all over Capernaum
2:4 They couldn't get to Jesus through the **c**, so they
3:7 followed by a huge **c** from all over Galilee, Judea,
3:32 There was a **c** around Jesus, and someone said,
4:1 There was such a large **c** along the shore that he
5:15 A **c** soon gathered around Jesus, but they were
5:17 and the **c** began pleading with Jesus to go away
5:21 a large **c** gathered around him on the shore.
5:24 Jesus went with him, and the **c** thronged behind.
5:25 And there was a woman in the **c** who had had a
5:27 so she came up behind him through the **c**
5:30 so he turned around in the **c** and asked,
5:31 said to him, "All this **c** is pressing around you.
5:37 Then Jesus stopped the **c** and wouldn't let anyone
5:40 The **c** laughed at him, but he told them all to go
6:34 A vast **c** was there as he stepped from the boat,
6:37 take a small fortune to buy food for all this **c**!"
6:39 Then Jesus told the **c** to sit down in groups on the
7:14 Then Jesus called to the **c** to come and hear.
7:33 Jesus led him to a private place away from the **c**.
7:36 Jesus told the **c** not to tell anyone, but the more he
8:1 About this time another great **c** had gathered,
8:6 to his disciples, who distributed the bread to the **c**.
8:9 There were about four thousand people in the **c**
9:14 At the foot of the mountain they found a great **c**
9:15 The **c** watched Jesus in awe as he came toward
9:17 One of the men in the **c** spoke up and said,
9:25 When Jesus saw that the **c** of onlookers was
9:26 A murmur ran through the **c**, "He's dead."
10:46 and his disciples left town, a great **c** was following.
11:8 Many in the **c** spread their coats on the road ahead
12:37 And the **c** listened to him with great interest.
15:8 The mob began to **c** in toward Pilate, asking him to
15:14 But the **c** only roared the louder, "Crucify him!"
15:15 So Pilate, anxious to please the **c**,
Lk 1:10 was being burned, a great **c** stood outside, praying.
3:10 The **c** asked, "What should we do?"
4:30 but he slipped away through the **c** and left them.
4:35 The demon threw the man to the floor as the **c**
5:18 They tried to push through the **c** to Jesus,
5:19 and lowered the sick man down into the **c**, still on
7:9 Turning to the **c**, he said, "I tell you, I haven't
7:11 the village of Nain, with a great **c** following him.
7:16 Great fear swept the **c**, and they praised God,
7:24 After they left, Jesus talked to the **c** about John.
8:4 One day Jesus told this story to a large **c** that had
8:35 A **c** soon gathered around Jesus, for they wanted to
8:35 clothed and sane. And the whole **c** was afraid.
8:43 And there was a woman in the **c** who had had a
8:45 "Master, this whole **c** is pressing up against you."
8:47 The whole **c** heard her explain why she had
8:53 But the **c** laughed at him because they all knew she
9:13 us to go and buy enough food for this whole **c**?"
9:23 Then he said to the **c**, "If any of you wants to be
9:37 had come down the mountain, a huge **c** met Jesus.
9:38 A man in the **c** called out to him, "Teacher,
11:14 man's voice returned to him. The **c** was amazed,
11:27 As he was speaking, a woman in the **c** called out,
11:29 As the **c** pressed in on Jesus, he said, "These are

12:13 Then someone called from the c, "Teacher,
12:54 Then Jesus turned to the c and said, "When you
13:14 six days of the week for working," he said to the c.
18:36 When he heard the noise of a c going past,
19:11 The c was listening to everything Jesus said.
19:39 But some of the Pharisees among the c said,
23:4 turned to the leading priests and to the c and said,
23:18 Then a mighty roar rose from the c, and with one
23:23 But the c shouted louder and louder for Jesus'
23:35 The c watched, and the leaders laughed
23:48 And when the c that came to see the crucifixion
Jn 1:26 but right here in the c is someone you do not know,
5:13 didn't know, for Jesus had disappeared into the c.
6:2 And a huge c kept following him wherever he
6:5 Jesus soon saw a great c of people climbing the
6:9 two fish. But what good is that with this huge c?"
6:24 When the c saw that Jesus wasn't there, nor his
7:20 The c replied, "You're demon possessed!
7:43 So the c was divided in their opinion about him.
8:2 A c soon gathered, and he sat down and taught
8:3 the act of adultery. They put her in front of the c.
8:9 until only Jesus was left in the middle of the c with
12:12 through the city. A huge c of Passover visitors
12:17 Those in the c who had seen Jesus call Lazarus
12:29 When the c heard the voice, some thought it was
12:34 "Die?" asked the c. "We understood from
Ac 2:13 But others in the c were mocking. "They're drunk,
2:14 with the eleven other apostles and shouted to the c,
3:12 Peter saw his opportunity and addressed the c.
14:11 When the listening c saw what Paul had done,
14:13 and the c brought oxen and wreaths of flowers,
17:5 and Silas so they could drag them out to the c.
19:29 A c began to gather, and soon the city was filled
19:34 But when the c realized he was a Jew, they started
21:32 and officers and ran down among the c.
21:33 Then he asked the c who he was and what he had
21:36 And the c followed behind shouting, "Kill him,
21:40 Soon a deep silence enveloped the c, and he
22:22 The c listened until Paul came to that word,
22:24 He wanted to find out why the c had become
24:18 There was no c around me and no rioting.
Eph 4:8 he ascended to the heights, / he led a c of captives
Heb 12:1 since we are surrounded by such a huge c of
Rev 7:9 After this I saw a vast c, too great to count,
19:1 I heard the sound of a vast c in heaven shouting,
19:6 again what sounded like the shout of a huge c,

CROWDED (9) [CROWD]

1Ki 18:30 They all c around him as he repaired the altar of
Isa 49:19 abandoned land will soon be c with your people.
49:20 and say, 'We need more room! It's c here!'
Eze 36:38 The ruined cities will be c with people once more,
Da 3:27 and advisers c around them and saw that the fire
Mt 13:22 but all too quickly the message is c out by the cares
Mk 3:9 and to have it ready in case he was c off the beach.
4:19 but all too quickly the message is c out by the cares
Lk 8:14 but all too quickly the message is c out by the cares

CROWDING (2) [CROWD]

Na 3:17 c together in the hedges to survive the cold.
Mk 3:10 As a result, many sick people were c around him,

CROWDS (81) [CROWD]

2Ch 7:8 with huge c gathered from all the tribes of Israel.
Ps 42:4 it used to be: / I walked among the c of worshipers,
Pr 1:21 She calls out to the c along the main street, and to
Isa 3:16 Their eyes rove among the c, flirting with the men.
5:14 lowly will be swallowed up, with all her drunken c.
La 1:4 no longer filled with c on their way to celebrate the
Jnh 3:4 the day Jonah entered the city, he shouted to the c:
Mic 2:12 Yes, your land will again be filled with noisy c!
Mt 4:25 Large c followed him wherever he went—
5:1 One day as the c were gathering, Jesus went up the
7:28 the c were amazed at his teaching,
8:1 Large c followed Jesus as he came down the
9:23 he noticed the noisy c and heard the funeral music.
9:33 and instantly the man could talk. The c marveled.
9:36 He felt great pity for the c that came, because their
11:7 had gone, Jesus began talking about him to the c.
13:34 and illustrations like these when speaking to the c.
13:36 Then, leaving the c outside, Jesus went into the
14:13 But the c heard where he was headed and followed
14:15 Send the c away so they can go to the villages
15:10 Then Jesus called to the c and said, "Listen to
19:2 Vast c followed him there, and he healed their sick.
21:9 and the c all around him were shouting,
21:11 And the c replied, "It's Jesus, the prophet from
21:46 because the c considered Jesus to be a prophet.
22:33 When the c heard him, they were impressed with
23:1 Then Jesus said to the c and to his disciples,
27:17 As the c gathered before Pilate's house that
27:20 and other leaders persuaded the c to ask for
Mk 1:45 such c soon surrounded Jesus that he couldn't enter
2:13 and taught the c that gathered around him.
2:15 (There were many people of this kind among the c
3:20 the c began to gather again, and soon he and his
4:36 leaving the c behind (although other boats
6:31 "Let's get away from the c for a while and rest."
6:36 Send the c away so they can go to the nearby farms
7:17 Jesus went into a house to get away from the c,
8:34 his disciples and the c to come over and listen.
10:1 As always there were the c, and as usual he taught
11:9 and the c all around him were shouting,
12:12 But they were afraid to touch him because of the c.
12:41 and watched as the c dropped in their money.
Lk 3:7 Here is a sample of John's preaching to the c that
3:21 One day when the c were being baptized,
4:42 The c searched everywhere for him, and when they
5:1 great c pressed in on him to listen to the word of
5:3 So he sat in the boat and taught the c from there.
5:15 and vast c came to hear him preach and to be
6:17 surrounded by many of his followers and by the c.
6:26 What sorrows await you who are praised by the c,
8:19 see him, they couldn't get to him because of the c.
8:40 On the other side of the lake the c received Jesus
8:42 Jesus went with him, he was surrounded by the c.
9:11 But the c found out where he was going, and they
9:12 "Send the c away to the nearby villages and farms,
12:1 the c grew until thousands were milling about
14:25 Great c were following Jesus. He turned around
18:39 The c ahead of Jesus tried to hush the man, but he
19:3 at Jesus, but he was too short to see over the c.
19:7 But the c were displeased. "He has gone to be the
19:36 Then the c spread out their coats on the road ahead
20:45 Then, with the c listening, he turned to his
21:38 The c gathered early each morning to hear him.
22:6 so they could arrest him quietly when the c weren't
23:27 Great c trailed along behind, including many
Jn 1:15 He shouted to the c, "This is the one I was talking
5:3 C of sick people—blind, lame, or paralyzed—
6:22 c began gathering on the shore, waiting to see
7:12 was a lot of discussion about him among the c.
7:31 Many among the c at the Temple believed in him.
7:32 When the Pharisees heard that the c were
7:37 Jesus stood and shouted to the c, "If you are
7:40 When the c heard him say this, some of them
7:49 These ignorant c do, but what do they know about
12:44 Jesus shouted to the c, "If you trust me, you are
Ac 5:14 brought to the Lord—c of both men and women.
5:16 C came in from the villages around Jerusalem,
6:12 Naturally, this roused the c, the elders,
8:6 C listened intently to what he had to say
13:45 But when the Jewish leaders saw the c, they were
14:19 and turned the c into a murderous mob.

CROWED (6) [CROW]

Ob 1:12 You shouldn't have c over them as they suffered
Mt 26:74 know the man." And immediately the rooster c.
Mk 14:68 went out into the entryway. Just then, a rooster c.
14:72 And immediately the rooster c the second time.
Lk 22:60 And as soon as he said these words, the rooster c.
Jn 18:27 Peter denied it. And immediately a rooster c.

CROWN (41) [CROWNED, CROWNING, CROWNS]

2Sa 1:10 Then I took his c and one of his bracelets so I
12:30 David removed the c from the king's head, and it
12:30 The c was made of gold and set with gems, and it
2Ki 11:12 the king's son, and placed the c on his head.
1Ch 20:2 at Rabbah, he removed the c from the king's head,
20:2 The c was made of gold and set with gems, and it
2Ch 23:11 the king's son, and placed the c on his head.
Est 1:11 to bring Queen Vashti to him with the royal c on
2:17 so delighted with her that he set the royal c on her
8:15 robe of blue and white and the great c of gold,
Job 19:9 me of my honor and removed the c from my head.
31:36 the accusation proudly. I would treasure it like a c.
Ps 21:3 You placed a c of finest gold on his head.
65:11 You c the year with a bountiful harvest;
89:39 with him, / for you have thrown his c in the dust.
Pr 1:9 What you learn from them will c you with grace
4:9 she will present you with a beautiful c."
12:4 A worthy wife is her husband's joy and c;
14:24 Wealth is a c for the wise; the effort of fools yields
16:31 Gray hair is a c of glory; it is gained by living a
27:24 and the c might not be secure for the next
SS 3:11 See the c with which his mother crowned him on
Isa 62:3 for all to see—a splendid c in the hands of God.
Eze 16:12 earrings for your ears, and a lovely c for your head.
21:26 Take off your jeweled c, says the Sovereign
Zec 6:11 their gifts and make a c from the silver and gold.
6:11 Then put the c on the head of Jeshua son of
6:14 "The c will be a memorial in the Temple of the
9:16 They will sparkle in his land like jewels in a c.
Mt 27:29 They made a c of long, sharp thorns and put it on
Mk 15:17 dressed him in a purple robe and made a c of long,
Jn 19:2 The soldiers made a c of long, sharp thorns and put
19:5 Then Jesus came out wearing the c of thorns
1Th 2:19 and joy, and what is our proud reward and c?
2Ti 4:8 the c of righteousness that the Lord, the righteous
Jas 1:12 Afterward they will receive the c of life that God
Rev 2:10 when facing death, and I will give you the c of life.
3:11 you have, so that no one will take away your c.
6:2 carried a bow, and a c was placed on his head.
12:1 her feet, and a c of twelve stars on her head.
14:14 He had a gold c on his head and a sharp sickle in

CROWNED (18) [CROWN]

Dt 28:36 and the king you c to a nation unknown to you
1Sa 11:15 ceremony before the LORD they c him king.
2Sa 2:4 to David and c him king over the tribe of Judah.
15:10 "you will know that Absalom has been c king in
2Ki 8:20 revolted against Judah and c their own king.
11:14 And she saw the newly c king standing in his place
14:21 of Judah then c Amaziah's sixteen-year-old son,
1Ch 29:22 And again they c David's son Solomon as their
2Ch 21:8 revolted against Judah and c their own king.
23:13 And she saw the newly c king standing in his place
26:1 of Judah then c Amaziah's sixteen-year-old son,
Ps 8:5 than God, / and you c us with glory and honor.
Pr 14:18 but the wise person is c with knowledge.
SS 3:11 See the crown with which his mother c him on his
Eze 23:15 their waists, and flowing turbans c their heads.
Lk 19:12 was called away to a distant empire to be c king
Heb 2:7 the angels, / and you c him with glory and honor.
2:9 and now is "c with glory and honor" because he

CROWNING (3) [CROWN]

Dt 33:16 c the brow of the prince among his brothers.
Pr 17:6 Grandchildren are the c glory of the aged;
Isa 28:5 LORD Almighty will himself be Israel's c glory.

CROWNS (9) [CROWN]

Ps 149:4 in his people; / he c the humble with salvation.
Jer 13:18 for your glorious c will soon be snatched from
Eze 23:42 on your wrists and beautiful c on your heads.
Rev 4:4 all clothed in white and had gold c on their heads.
4:10 And they lay their c before the throne and say,
9:7 They had gold c on their heads, and they had
12:3 and ten horns, with seven c on his heads.
13:1 seven heads and ten horns, with ten c on its horns.
19:12 like flames of fire, and on his head were many c.

CROWS (6) [CROW]

Mt 26:34 "the truth is, this very night, before the rooster c,
26:75 "Before the rooster c, you will deny me three
Mk 14:30 truth is, this very night, before the rooster c twice,
14:72 "Before the rooster c twice, you will deny me
Lk 22:61 "Before the rooster c tomorrow morning, you will
Jn 13:38 No, before the rooster c tomorrow morning,

CRUCIBLE (3)

Ps 66:10 you have purified us like silver melted in a c.
Jer 9:7 I will melt them in a c and test them like metal.
Eze 22:19 I will bring you to my c in Jerusalem.

CRUCIFIED (28) [CRUCIFY]

Mt 20:19 over to the Romans to be mocked, whipped, and c.
26:2 and I, the Son of Man, will be betrayed and c."
27:31 on him again. Then they led him away to be c.
27:38 Two criminals were c with him, their crosses on
27:44 And the criminals who were c with him also
28:5 "I know you are looking for Jesus, who was c.
Mk 15:20 on him again. Then they led him away to be c.
15:27 Two criminals were c with him, their crosses on
15:32 Even the two criminals who were being c with
16:6 are looking for Jesus, the Nazarene, who was c.
Lk 23:33 All three were c there—Jesus on the center cross,
24:7 be betrayed into the hands of sinful men and be c,
24:20 over to be condemned to death, and they c him.
Jn 19:16 Then Pilate gave Jesus to them to be c. / So they
19:18 There they c him. There were two others c with
19:20 The place where Jesus was c was near the city;
19:23 When the soldiers had c Jesus, they divided his
19:32 and broke the legs of the two men c with Jesus.
Ac 2:36 has made this Jesus whom you c to be both Lord
4:10 the man you c, but whom God raised from the
Ro 6:6 Our old sinful selves were c with Christ so that sin
1Co 1:13 be divided into pieces? Was I, Paul, c for you?
1:23 So when we preach that Christ was c, the Jews are
2:8 they would never have c our glorious Lord.
Gal 2:19 that I might live for God. I have been c with Christ.
5:24 of their sinful nature to his cross and c them there.
Rev 11:8 and "Egypt," the city where their Lord was c.

CRUCIFIXION (6) [CRUCIFY]

Mt 23:34 You will kill some by c and whip others in your
27:54 and the other soldiers at the c were terrified by the
Mk 15:25 It was nine o'clock in the morning when the c took
Lk 23:48 And when the crowd that came to see the c saw all
Jn 19:41 The place of c was near a garden, where there was
Ac 1:3 During the forty days after his c, he appeared to the

CRUCIFY (14) [CRUCIFIED, CRUCIFIXION, CRUCIFYING]

Mt 27:22 the Messiah?" And they all shouted, "C him!"
27:23 But the crowd only roared the louder, "C him!"
27:26 then turned him over to the Roman soldiers to c
Mk 15:13 They shouted back, "C him!"
15:14 But the crowd only roared the louder, "C him!"
15:15 then turned him over to the Roman soldiers to c
Lk 23:21 But they shouted, "C him! C him!"
Jn 19:6 shouting, "C! C!" "You c him," Pilate said.
19:10 that I have the power to release you or to c you?"
19:15 they yelled. "Away with him—c him!" "What? C your king?" Pilate asked.

CRUCIFYING (2) [CRUCIFY]

Ac 5:30 Jesus from the dead after you killed him by c him.
10:39 and in Jerusalem. They put him to death by c him,

CRUEL (23) [CRUELLY, CRUELTY]

Ge 49:7 for it is fierce; / cursed be their wrath, for it is c.
Ex 18:11 have escaped from the proud and c Egyptians."
Dt 28:56 will be c to the husband she loves and to her own
Jdg 6:2 so c that the Israelites fled to the mountains,
Job 30:21 You have become c toward me. You persecute me
Ps 17:4 which have kept me from going along with c
71:4 of the wicked, / from the clutches of c oppressors.
106:42 and brought them under their c power.
Pr 11:17 are kind, but you destroy yourself when you are c.
12:10 but even the kindness of the wicked is c.

27: 4 Anger is c, and wrath is like a flood, but who can
Isa 19: 4 c master, to a fierce king," says the Lord,
Jer 6:23 They are c and show no mercy. As they ride
6:28 are as insolent as bronze, as hard and c as iron.
15:21 wicked men. I will rescue you from their c hands."
50:42 They are c and show no mercy. As they ride
Eze 18:18 for being c and robbing close relatives, doing what
21:31 I will hand you over to c men who are skilled in
Am 1:13 they committed c crimes, ripping open pregnant
Hab 1: 6 They are a c and violent nation who will march
Mal 2:16 "It is as c as putting on a victim's bloodstained
2Ti 3: 3 they will be c and have no interest in what is good.
Tit 1:12 are all liars; they are c animals and lazy gluttons."

CRUELLY (1) [CRUEL]

Jer 30:14 I have wounded you c, as though I were your

CRUELTY (6) [CRUEL]

Ge 31:42 But God has seen your c and my hard work.
43: 6 "Why did you have to treat me with such c?"
Ps 73: 6 and their clothing is woven of c.
Eze 34: 4 Instead, you have ruled them with force and c.
Na 3:19 be found who has not suffered from your c?
Hab 1: 7 They are notorious for their c. They do as they

CRUMB (1) [CRUMBS]

Eze 5:16 and more severe until every c of food is gone.

CRUMBLE (7)

Job 14:18 "But as mountains fall and c and as rocks fall from
Ps 46: 2 and the mountains c into the sea.
46: 6 The nations are in an uproar, / and kingdoms c!
Eze 38:20 cliffs will c; walls will fall to the earth.
Hos 10: 8 shrines of Aven, the place of Israel's sin, will c.
Na 1: 6 and the mountains c to dust in his presence.
Lk 6:49 against that house, it will c into a heap of ruins."

CRUMBS (2) [CRUMB]

Mt 15:27 "but even dogs are permitted to eat c that fall
Mk 7:28 but even the dogs under the table are given some c

CRUMPLE (1)

Isa 22:18 He will c you up into a ball and toss you away into

CRUSE [KJV] See BOWL, CONTAINERS, JAR

CRUSH (45) [CRUSHED, CRUSHES, CRUSHING]

Ge 3:15 He will c your head, and you will strike his heel."
34:30 We are so few that they will come and c us.
Ex 7: 4 So I will c Egypt with a series of disasters,
17:13 and his troops were able to c the army of Amalek.
Nu 24:17 It will c the foreheads of Moab's people,
Dt 33:11 C the loins of their enemies; / strike down their
2Sa 22:30 In your strength I can c an army; / with my God I
2Ki 19:25 that you should c fortified cities into heaps of
Est 9:24 had plotted to c and destroy them on the day
Job 6: 9 I wish he would c me. I wish he would reach out
39:15 She doesn't worry that a foot might c them or that
Ps 18:29 In your strength I can c an army; / with my God I
72: 4 children of the needy, / and to c their oppressors.
73: 8 only evil; / in their pride they seek to c others.
91:13 you will c fierce lions and serpents under your
Pr 25:15 a prince, and soft speech can c strong opposition.
26:27 boulder down on others, it will roll back and c you.
Ecc 10: 9 you work in a quarry, stones might fall and c you!
Isa 5:25 That is why he has raised his fist to c them.
7:11 to prove that I will c your enemies as I have
13:11 I will c the arrogance of the proud
28:22 has plainly told me that he is determined to c you.
31: 2 who are wicked, and he will c their allies, too.
37:26 that you should c fortified cities into heaps of
42: 3 He will not c those who are weak or quench the
42:13 battle cry, / and he will c all his enemies.
53:10 But it was the LORD's good plan to c him and fill
Jer 25:30 like the harvesters do as they c juice from the
50:26 C her walls and houses into heaps of rubble.
La 1:15 At his command a great army has come to c my
Eze 6:14 I will c them and make their cities desolate from
13:14 to the foundation, and when it falls, it will c you.
14:13 and I lifted my fist to c them, cutting off their food
Da 2:40 kingdom will smash and c all previous empires,
Am 4: 1 you women who oppress the poor and c the needy
Zep 1: 4 "I will c Judah and Jerusalem with my fist
Zec 2: 9 I will raise my fist to c them, and their own slaves
Mt 12:20 He will not c those who are weak, / or quench the
21:44 to pieces, and it will c anyone on whom it falls."
23: 4 They c you with impossible religious demands
Lk 10:19 can walk among snakes and scorpions and c them.
11:46 For you c people beneath impossible religious
19:44 They will c you to the ground, and your children
20:18 to pieces, and it will c anyone on whom it falls."
Ro 16:20 The God of peace will soon c Satan under your

CRUSHED (54) [CRUSH]

Nu 14:42 You will only be c by your enemies
22:25 to squeeze by and c Balaam's foot against the wall.
Dt 1:42 If they do, they will be c by their enemies.'
2:33 to us, and we c him, his sons, and all his people.
23: 1 "If a man's testicles are c or his penis is cut off,
Jdg 9:53 that landed on Abimelech's head and c his skull.
1Sa 20:34 for he was c by his father's shameful behavior
2Ki 19:11 They have c everyone who stood in their way!
23:15 Josiah c the stones to dust and burned the Asherah
2Ch 2:10 I will pay your men 100,000 bushels of c wheat,
34: 7 and the Asherah poles, and he c the idols into dust.
Job 4:19 is dust, and they are c as easily as moths.
9:13 The mightiest forces against him are c beneath his
17: 1 "My spirit is c, and I am near death. The grave is
22: 9 helping them and c the strength of orphans.
26:12 grew calm. By his skill he c the great sea monster.
31:16 or c the hopes of widows who looked to me for
Ps 9:18 the hopes of the poor will not always be c.
34:18 he rescues those who are c in spirit.
38: 8 I am exhausted and completely c. / My groans
39:11 their lives can be c like the life of a moth.
44: 2 all the land to our ancestors; / you c their enemies,
44:19 Yet you have c us in the desert. / You have
74:14 You c the heads of Leviathan / and let the desert
89:10 You are the one who c the great sea monster.
106:42 Their enemies c them / and brought them under
119:116 that I may live! / Do not let my hope be c.
Pr 14:32 The wicked are c by their sins, but the godly have
18:14 a sick body, but who can bear it if the spirit is c?
Isa 7: 8 within sixty-five years it will be c and completely
14: 5 For the LORD has c your wicked power
25:10 Moab will be c like trampled straw and left to rot.
27: 9 has finished, all the pagan altars will be c to dust.
28:28 Bread grain is easily c, so he doesn't keep on
37:11 They have c everyone who stood in their way!
53: 5 But he was wounded and c for our sins. He was
63: 6 I c the nations in my anger and made them stagger
Jer 4:20 tent is destroyed; in a moment, every shelter is c.
4:26 cities lay in ruins, c by the LORD's fierce anger.
5: 3 You c them, but they refused to turn from sin.
51:34 has eaten and c us and emptied out our strength.
Eze 32:28 Egypt, will lie c and broken among the outcasts,
Da 2:35 The pieces were c as small as chaff on a threshing
3:29 and their houses will be c into heaps of rubble.
7: 7 It devoured and c its victims with huge iron teeth
7:19 It devoured and c its victims with iron teeth
Hos 5:11 The people of Israel will be c and broken by my
Na 2:12 You c your enemies to feed your cubs and your
Hab 3:13 You c the heads of the wicked and laid bare their
Zec 10:11 The pride of Assyria will be c, and the rule of
Mt 26:38 "My soul is c with grief to the point of death.
Mk 14:34 "My soul is c with grief to the point of death.
2Co 1: 8 We were c and completely overwhelmed, and we
4: 8 side by troubles, but we are not c and broken.

CRUSHES (3) [CRUSH]

Pr 15: 4 bring life and health; a deceitful tongue c the spirit.
15:13 makes a happy face; a broken heart c the spirit.
Da 2:40 just as iron smashes and c everything it strikes.

CRUSHING (11) [CRUSH]

Jdg 5:26 She hit Sisera, c his head. / She pounded the tent
2Ki 14: 9 animal came by and stepped on the thistle, c it!
2Ch 25:18 animal came by and stepped on the thistle, c it!
Ps 38: 2 have struck deep, / and your blows are c me.
68:21 c the skulls of those who love their guilty ways.
Pr 20:26 out like wheat, then runs the c wheel over them.
Isa 22: 5 Oh, what a day of c trouble! What a day of
Da 2:45 c to dust the statue of iron, bronze, clay, silver,
Am 5: 9 power he destroys the strong, c all their defenses.
Lk 12: 1 thousands were milling about and c each other.
1Th 3: 7 in all of our own c troubles and suffering,

CRUST (1)

Pr 17: 1 A dry c eaten in peace is better than a great feast

CRUTCH (1) [CRUTCHES]

Ex 21:19 even with a c, the assailant will be innocent.

CRUTCHES (1) [CRUTCH]

2Sa 3:29 or leprosy or who walks on c or who dies by the

CRY (132) [CRIED, CRIES, CRYING, OUTCRY]

Ge 27:34 Esau understood, he let out a loud and bitter c.
43:30 with emotion for his brother and wanted to c.
Ex 22:23 If you do and they c out to me, then I will surely
32:18 it's neither a c of victory nor a c of defeat.
Nu 10:35 Ark set out, Moses would c, "Arise, O LORD,
Dt 24:15 Otherwise they might c out to the LORD against
33: 7 "O LORD, hear the c of Judah / and bring them
Jdg 10:14 Go and c out to the gods you have chosen!
1Sa 9:16 on my people in mercy and have heard their c."
24:16 really you, my son David?" Then he began to c.
2Sa 22: 7 me from his sanctuary; / my c reached his ears.
1Ki 8:28 Hear the c and the prayer that your servant is
8:52 and answer them whenever they c out to you.
22:36 as the sun was setting, the c ran through his troops:
1Ch 16:35 C out, "Save us, O God of our salvation! / Gather
2Ch 6:19 Hear the c and the prayer that your servant is
13:15 At the sound of their battle c, God defeated
20: 9 We can c out to you to save us, and you will hear
Ne 5: 1 and their wives raised a c of protest against their
Job 5: 1 "You may c for help, but no one listens. You may
6:26 when you disregard my c of desperation?
16:18 do not conceal my blood. Let it c out on my behalf.
19: 7 "I c out for help, but no one hears me. I protest,
24:12 rise from the city, and the wounded c for help,
27: 9 Will God listen to their c when trouble comes upon
30:20 "I c to you, O God, but you don't answer me.
30:24 would turn against the needy when they c for help.
30:28 I stand in the public square and c for help.
34:28 So they cause the poor to c out, catching God's
35: 9 "The oppressed c out beneath the wrongs that are
35:12 "And if they do c out and God does not answer,
35:15 But do you c out against him because he does not
36:13 punishes them, they refuse to c out to him for help.
38:41 c out to God as they wander about in hunger?
Ps 2: 3 "Let us break their chains," they c, / "and free
5: 2 Listen to my c for help, my King and my God,
9:12 He does not ignore those who c to him for help.
17: 1 hear my plea for justice. / Listen to my c for help.
18: 6 me from his sanctuary; / my c reached his ears.
20: 1 of trouble, may the LORD respond to your c.
20: 9 our king, O LORD! / Respond to our c for help.
28: 2 to my prayer for mercy / as I c out to you for help,
28: 6 the LORD! / For he has heard my c for mercy.
31:22 But you heard my c for mercy / and answered my
40: 1 to help me, / and he turned to me and heard my c.
42: 9 "O God my rock," I c, / "Why have you forsaken
55: 1 my prayer, O God. / Do not ignore my c for help!
57: 2 I c out to God Most High, / to God who will fulfill
61: 1 O God, listen to my c! / Hear my prayer!
61: 2 the ends of the earth, / I will c to you for help,
72:12 He will rescue the poor when they c to him;
77: 1 I c out to God without holding back. / Oh, that God
86: 6 to my prayer, O LORD; / hear my urgent c.
88: 2 Now hear my prayer; / listen to my c.
88:13 O LORD, I c out to you. / I will keep on pleading
119:146 I c out to you; save me, / that I may obey your
119:147 I c out for help and put my hope in your words.
119:149 In your faithful love, O LORD, hear my c;
119:169 O LORD, listen to my c; / give me the discerning
130: 2 Hear my c, O Lord. / Pay attention to my prayer.
141: 1 Please hurry! / Listen when I c to you for help!
142: 1 I c out to the LORD; / I plead for the LORD's
142: 6 Hear my c, / for I am very low. / Rescue me from
147: 9 and the young ravens c to him for food.
Pr 1:28 "I will not answer when they c for help.
2: 3 C out for insight and understanding.
30:15 The leech has two suckers that c out, "More,
Ecc 3: 4 A time to c and a time to laugh. / A time to grieve
Isa 8: 9 "The Assyrians will c, 'Do your best to defend
14:10 With one voice they all c out, 'Now you are as
15: 4 The bravest warriors of Moab will c out in utter
16: 3 "Help us," they c. "Defend us against our
16:12 They will c to the gods in their temples, but no one
19:20 When the people c to the LORD for help against
22: 4 Let me c for my people as I watch them being
33:14 "Which one of us," they c, "can live here in the
42:13 full of fury. / He will shout his thundering battle c,
57:13 do anything for you when you c to them for help.
65:14 You will c in sorrow and despair, while my
Jer 2:27 but in times of trouble they c out for me to save
4:16 raising a battle c against the towns of Judah.
4:31 I hear a great c, like that of a woman giving birth
4:31 It is the c of Jerusalem's people gasping for breath,
8:20 is gone," the people c, "yet we are not saved!"
11:14 for I will not listen to them when they c out to me
12: 6 They have plotted, raising a c against you. Do not
12:11 made it an empty wasteland; I hear its mournful c.
14: 2 in mourning, and a great c rises from Jerusalem.
22:23 but soon you will c and groan in anguish—
25:31 His c of judgment will reach the ends of the earth,
31:15 "A c of anguish is heard in Ramah—mourning
48: 4 Moab is being destroyed. Her little ones will c out.
48:17 "You friends of Moab, weep for her and c!
49: 3 "C out, O Heshbon, for the town of Ai is
49:21 and its c of despair will be heard all the way to the
50:22 "Let the battle c be heard in the land, a shout of
50:46 and her c of despair will be heard around the
51:27 Sound the battle c! Bring out the armies of Ararat,
51:54 Hear the c of Babylon, the sound of great
La 2:12 they c, and then collapse in their mothers' arms.
2:18 C aloud before the Lord, O walls of Jerusalem!
2:19 Rise during the night and c out. Pour out your
3: 8 And though I c and shout, he shuts out my prayers.
3:18 I c out, "My splendor is gone! Everything I had
3:57 Yes, you came at my despairing c and told me,
4: 4 The children c for bread, but no one has any to
Eze 6:11 in horror, and stamp your feet. C out, 'Alas!'
13:12 And when the wall falls, the people will c out,
21:12 "Son of man, c out and wail; pound your thighs in
27:28 the sea tremble as your helmsmen c out in terror.
Hos 5: 8 Raise the battle c in Beth-aven! Lead on into
7:14 They do not c out to me with sincere hearts.
13: 2 "Sacrifice to these," they c, "and kiss the calf
Joel 1:14 of the LORD your God, and c out to him there.
1:20 Even the wild animals c out to you because they
Hab 1: 2 "Violence!" I c, but you do not come to save.
2:11 The very stones in the walls of your houses c out
Zep 1:10 "a c of alarm will come from the Fish Gate
1:14 it comes—a day when strong men will c bitterly.
Mal 2:14 You c out, "Why has the LORD abandoned us?"
Mt 2:18 "A c of anguish is heard in Ramah—/ weeping
Mk 15:37 Then Jesus uttered another loud c and breathed his
Lk 1:42 Elizabeth gave a glad c and exclaimed to Mary,
7:13 overflowed with compassion. "Don't c!" he said.
19:41 and Jesus saw the city ahead, he began to c.
Heb 5: 7 and pleadings, with a loud c and tears,
Jas 5: 4 The wages you held back c out against you.
1Pe 2: 2 C out for this nourishment as a baby cries for milk,
Rev 18:10 They will c out, "How terrible, how terrible for
18:14 fancy things you loved so much are gone," they c.
18:15 by her great torment. They will weep and c.

CRYING (28) [CRY]

Ge 47:15 of money, they came to Joseph c again for food.

Ex 14:15 LORD said to Moses, "Why are you **c** out to me?
1Sa 1:10 **c** bitterly as she prayed to the LORD.
11: 5 "What's the matter? Why is everyone **c**?"
2Sa 13:19 with her face in her hands, she went away **c**.
1Ki 13:30 in his own grave, **c** out in grief, "Oh, my brother!"
Ne 9: 4 on the stairs, **c** out to the LORD their God.
Est 4: 1 went out into the city, **c** with a loud and bitter wail.
Ps 6: 8 you who do evil, / for the LORD has heard my **c**.
69: 3 I am exhausted from **c** for help; / my throat is
Isa 15: 5 Their **c** can be heard all along the road to
24:11 Mobs gather in the streets, **c** out for wine. Joy has
26:17 about to give birth, / writhing and **c** out in pain.
65:19 the sound of weeping and **c** will be heard no more.
Jer 9:19 Hear the people of Jerusalem **c** in despair, 'We are
30: 5 I have heard the people **c**; there is only fear
48:38 **C** and sorrow will be in every Moabite home
La 1: 4 her priests groan, her young women are **c**—
Am 5:16 "There will be **c** in all the public squares and in
Mt 26:75 me three times." And he went away, **c** bitterly.
Lk 17:13 **c** out, "Jesus, Master, have mercy on us!"
22:62 And Peter left the courtyard, **c** bitterly.
Jn 20:11 Mary was standing outside the tomb **c**, and as she
20:13 "Why are you **c**?" the angels asked her.
20:15 "Why are you **c**?" Jesus asked her. "Who are you
Heb 12:24 which graciously forgives instead of **c** out for
Rev 8:13 And I heard a single eagle **c** loudly as it flew
21: 4 there will be no more death or sorrow or **c** or pain.

CRYSTAL (9)

Job 28:17 Wisdom is far more valuable than gold and **c**.
28:18 and valuable rock **c** are worthless in trying to get it.
Eze 1:22 out above them like the sky. It sparkled like **c**.
1:25 a voice spoke from beyond the **c** surface above
10: 1 above the **c** surface over the heads of the cherubim.
Rev 4: 6 throne was a shiny sea of glass, sparkling like **c**.
15: 2 I saw before me what seemed to be a **c** sea mixed
21:11 sparkled like a precious gem, **c** clear like jasper.
22: 1 clear as **c**, flowing from the throne of God and of

CUB (1) [CUBS]

Dt 33:22 "Dan is a lion's **c**, / leaping out from Bashan."

CUBE (1)

Rev 21:16 In fact, it was in the form of a **c**, for its length

CUBS (10) [CUB]

2Sa 17: 8 as a mother bear who has been robbed of her **c**.
Job 4:11 and the **c** of the lioness will be scattered.
38:32 or guide the constellation of the Bear with her **c**
Pr 17:12 It is safer to meet a bear robbed of her **c** than to
Isa 11: 7 among bears. **C** and calves will lie down together.
Eze 19: 2 lay down among the young lions / and reared her **c**.
19: 3 She raised one of her **c** / to become a strong young
19: 5 for him were gone, / she took another of her **c**
Hos 13: 8 I will rip you to pieces like a bear whose **c** have
Na 2:12 You crushed your enemies to feed your **c** and your

CUCUMBERS (1)

Nu 11: 5 And we had all the **c**, melons, leeks, onions,

CUD (8)

Lev 11: 3 have completely divided hooves and chew the **c**.
11: 4 they either have split hooves or chew the **c**,
11: 4 camel may not be eaten, for though it chews the **c**,
11: 7 though it has split hooves, it does not chew the **c**.
11:26 or that does not chew the **c** is unclean for you.
Dt 14: 6 that has split hooves and chews the **c** may be eaten,
14: 7 They chew the **c** but do not have split hooves.
14: 8 though it has split hooves, it does not chew the **c**.

CUDDLED (1)

2Sa 12: 3 his cup. He **c** it in his arms like a baby daughter.

CULTIVATE (6) [CULTIVATED, CULTIVATING]

Ge 2: 5 sent any rain. And no one was there to **c** the soil.
3:23 and he sent Adam out to **c** the ground from which
Job 4: 8 who plant trouble and **c** evil will harvest the same.
Isa 5: 4 What more could I have done / to **c** a rich harvest?
Mt 25:24 you didn't plant and gathering crops you didn't **c**.
25:26 crops I didn't plant and gathering crops I didn't **c**?

CULTIVATED (1) [CULTIVATE]

Hos 10:13 "But you have **c** wickedness and raised a thriving

CULTIVATING (1) [CULTIVATE]

Isa 28:24 Is he forever **c** the soil and never planting it?

CULTURE (2) [CULTURES]

Isa 13:19 the flower of Chaldean **c**, will be devastated like
Ro 1:14 I have a great sense of obligation to people in our **c**

CULTURES (1) [CULTURE]

Ro 1:14 to people in our culture and to people in other **c**,

CUMBERED [KJV] See WORRYING

CUMMIN (2)

Isa 28:25 **c**, wheat, barley, and spelt, each in its own section
28:27 A threshing wheel is never rolled on **c**; instead,

CUN (1) [BEROTHAI]

1Ch 18: 8 of bronze from Hadadezer's cities of Tebah and **C**.

CUNNING (2)

Job 5:13 so that their **c** schemes are thwarted.
Ps 64: 6 Yes, the human heart and mind are **c**.

CUP (72) [CUP-BEARER, CUP-BEARERS, CUPPED, CUPS]

Ge 40:11 I was holding Pharaoh's wine **c** in my hand,
40:11 into it. Then I placed the **c** in Pharaoh's hand."
44: 2 Then put my personal silver **c** at the top of the
44: 5 by stealing my master's personal silver drinking **c**,
44: 9 If you find his **c** with any one of us, let that one
44:12 the youngest. The **c** was found in Benjamin's sack!
44:16 and our brother who had your **c** in his sack."
44:17 "Only the man who stole the **c** will be my slave.
Ex 25:33 Each of the six branches will hold a **c** shaped like
37:19 Each of the six branches held a **c** shaped like an
Jdg 7: 5 In one group put all those who **c** water in their
2Sa 12: 3 ate from the man's own plate and drank from his **c**.
1Ki 7:26 and its rim flared out like a **c** and resembled a lily
17:10 "Would you please bring me a **c** of water?"
2Ki 6:25 and a **c** of dove's dung cost about two ounces of
2Ch 4: 5 and its rim flared out like a **c** and resembled a lily
Ps 16: 5 you alone are my inheritance, my **c** of blessing.
23: 5 my head with oil. / My **c** overflows with blessings.
75: 8 For the LORD holds a **c** in his hand; / it is full of
116:13 I will lift up a **c** symbolizing his salvation; / I will
Isa 51:17 You have drunk enough from the **c** of the
51:17 You have drunk the **c** of terror, tipping out its last
51:22 "See, I am taking the terrible **c** from your hands.
51:23 But I will put that **c** into the hands of those who
Jer 8:14 and has given us a **c** of poison to drink because we
16: 7 No one will send a **c** of wine to console them.
25:15 "Take from my hand this **c** filled to the brim with
25:17 So I took the **c** of anger from the LORD
25:18 and their kings and officials drank from the **c**.
25:19 his people. They, too, drank from that terrible **c**,
25:26 the king of Babylon himself drank from the **c** of
25:27 God of Israel, says: Drink from this **c** of my anger.
25:28 And if they refuse to accept the **c**, tell them,
49:12 go unpunished! You must drink this **c** of judgment!
51: 7 Babylon has been like a golden **c** in the LORD's
51: 7 a **c** from which he made the whole earth drink
La 3:15 He has given me a **c** of deep sorrow to drink.
4:21 must drink from the **c** of the LORD's anger.
Eze 23:32 You will drink from the same **c** of terror as your sister—a **c** that is large and deep.
23:34 In deep anguish you will drain that **c** of terror to
Hab 2:15 You force your **c** on them so that you can gloat
2:16 Drink from the **c** of the LORD's judgment,
Mt 10:42 And if you give even a **c** of cold water to one of
20:22 Are you able to drink from the bitter **c** of sorrow I
23:25 You are so careful to clean the outside of the **c**
23:26 First wash the inside of the **c**, and then the outside
26:27 And he took a **c** of wine and gave thanks to God
26:39 let this **c** of suffering be taken away from me.
26:42 If this **c** cannot be taken away until I drink it,
Mk 9:41 If anyone gives you even a **c** of water because you
10:38 Are you able to drink from the bitter **c** of sorrow I
10:39 "You will indeed drink from my **c** and be baptized
14:23 And he took a **c** of wine and gave thanks to God
14:36 Please take this **c** of suffering away from me.
Lk 11:39 so careful to clean the outside of the **c** and the dish,
22:17 Then he took a **c** of wine, and when he had given
22:20 After supper he took another **c** of wine and said,
22:42 please take this **c** of suffering away from me.
Jn 18:11 Shall I not drink from the **c** the Father has given
1Co 10:16 When we bless the **c** at the Lord's Table, aren't we
10:21 You cannot drink from the **c** of the Lord and from the **c** of demons,
11:25 he took the **c** of wine after supper, saying, "This **c** is the new covenant between God and you,
11:26 For every time you eat this bread and drink this **c**,
11:27 this bread or drinks this **c** of the Lord unworthily,
11:28 before eating the bread and drinking from the **c**.
11:29 For if you eat the bread or drink the **c** unworthily,
Rev 14:10 It is poured out undiluted into God's **c** of wrath.
16:19 and he made her drink the **c** that was filled with the
18: 6 She brewed a **c** of terror for others, so give her

CUP-BEARER (10) [BEAR, CUP]

Ge 40: 1 Pharaoh's chief **c** and chief baker offended him.
40: 5 One night the **c** and the baker each had a dream,
40: 9 The **c** told his dream first. "In my dream," he said,
40:13 and return you to your position as his chief **c**.
40:20 He sent for his chief **c** and chief baker, and they
40:21 then restored the chief **c** to his former position,
40:23 Pharaoh's **c**, however, promptly forgot all about
41: 9 Then the king's **c** spoke up. "Today I have been
41:13 I was restored to my position as **c**, and the chief
Ne 1:11 to be kind to me." In those days I was the king's **c**.

CUP-BEARERS (2) [BEAR, CUP]

1Ki 10: 5 and their splendid clothing, the **c** and their robes,
2Ch 9: 4 and their splendid clothing, the **c** and their robes,

CUPPED (1) [CUP]

Mk 7: 3 do not eat until they have poured water over their **c**

CUPS (14) [CUP]

Ex 25:31 the base, center stem, lamp **c**, buds, and blossoms.
35:14 its accessories; the lamp **c** and the oil for lighting;
37:17 Its base, center stem, lamp **c**, blossoms, and buds
39:37 its accessories; the lamp **c** and the oil for lighting;
Nu 4: 7 and place the dishes, spoons, bowls, **c**,
1Ki 7:50 the **c**, lamp snuffers, basins, dishes, and firepans,
10:21 All of King Solomon's drinking **c** were solid gold,
2Ki 12:13 to the Temple was not used for making silver **c**,
2Ch 9:20 All of King Solomon's drinking **c** were solid gold,
Jer 35: 5 I set **c** and jugs of wine before them and invited
Da 5: 2 bring in the gold and silver **c** that his predecessor,
5: 3 So they brought these gold **c** taken from the
5:23 and have had these **c** from his Temple brought
Mk 7: 4 such as their ceremony of washing **c**, pitchers,

CURB (5)

Ps 39: 1 and not sin in what I say. / I will **c** my tongue
Eze 40:12 front of each of the guard alcoves was a 21-inch **c**.
43:13 with a **c** 9 inches wide around its edge.
43:17 and a 10-1/2-inch **c** all around the edge.
43:20 upper ledge, and the **c** that runs around that ledge.

CURDS (4)

Ge 18: 8 he took some cheese **c** and milk and the roasted
Dt 32:14 He fed them **c** from the herd and milk from the
Isa 7:15 By the time this child is old enough to eat **c**
7:22 The few people still left in the land will live on **c**

CURE (5) [CURED, CURING]

Isa 30:26 to heal his people and **c** the wounds he gave them.
Jer 30:15 your punishment—this wound that has no **c**?
Hos 5:13 king there, but he could neither help nor **c** them.
Mt 10: 8 Heal the sick, raise the dead, **c** those with leprosy,
Lk 8:43 she had on doctors and still could find no **c**.

CURED (10) [CURE]

Lev 14:10 each person **c** of the skin disease must bring two
14:19 ceremony for the person **c** of the skin disease.
Dt 28:27 scurvy, and the itch, from which you cannot be **c**.
2Ki 5:13 when he says simply to go and wash and be **c**!"
Mt 11: 5 the lame walk, the lepers are **c**, the deaf hear,
Lk 6:19 power went out from him, and they were all **c**.
7:21 he **c** many people of their various diseases,
7:22 the lame walk, the lepers are **c**, the deaf hear,
Jn 5:10 They said to the man who was **c**, "You can't work
Ac 28: 9 other sick people on the island came and were **c**.

CURING (1) [CURE]

Lk 9:11 the Kingdom of God and **c** those who were ill.

CURIOUS (1)

Eze 28:17 to the earth and exposed you to the **c** gaze of kings.

CURRENTS (2)

Ex 14:27 swept the terrified Egyptians into the surging **c**.
Ps 8: 8 in the sea, / and everything that swims the ocean **c**.

CURSE (106) [CURSED, CURSES, CURSING]

Ge 3:17 told you not to eat, I have placed a **c** on the ground.
8:21 and said to himself, "I will never again **c** the earth,
9:25 the son of Ham: / "A **c** on the Canaanites!
12: 3 those who bless you and **c** those who **c** you.
27:12 and then he'll **c** me instead of blessing me."
27:13 "Let the **c** fall on me, dear son," said Rebekah.
27:29 All who **c** you are cursed, and all who bless you
Ex 22:28 blaspheme God or **c** anyone who rules over you.
Lev 20: 9 "All who **c** their father or mother must be put to
Nu 5:18 holding the jar of bitter water that brings a **c** to
5:19 the effects of this bitter water that causes the **c**.
5:21 "then may the people see that the LORD's **c** is
5:22 Now may this water that brings the **c** enter your
5:24 so it may bring on the **c** and cause bitter suffering
5:27 the water that brings the **c** will cause bitter
5:27 and her name will become a **c** word among her
22: 6 Please come and **c** them for me because they are
22: 6 I also know that the people you **c** are doomed."
22: 7 and took money with them to pay Balaam to **c**
22:11 Come at once to **c** them. Perhaps then I will be
22:12 "You are not to **c** these people, for I have blessed
22:17 ask of me. Just come and **c** these people for me!"
23: 7 'Come,' he said, '**c** Jacob for me! / Come
23: 8 But how can I **c** / those whom God has not cursed?
23:11 I brought you to **c** my enemies. Instead, you have
23:13 of the nation of Israel. **C** at least that many!"
23:23 No **c** can touch Jacob; / no sorcery has any power
23:25 "If you aren't going to **c** them, at least don't bless
23:27 Perhaps it will please God to let you **c** them from
24:10 and shouted, "I called you to **c** my enemies!
Dt 11:26 giving you the choice between a blessing and a **c**!
11:28 You will receive a **c** if you reject the commands of
11:29 from Mount Gerizim and a **c** from Mount Ebal.
23: 4 of Beor from Pethor in Aram-naharaim to **c** you.
23: 5 He turned the intended **c** into a blessing
27:13 must stand on Mount Ebal to proclaim a **c**.
29:19 Let none of those who hear the warnings of this **c**
Jos 6:26 At that time Joshua invoked this **c**:
6:26 "May the **c** of the LORD fall on anyone
24: 9 He asked Balaam son of Beor to **c** you,
Jdg 9:57 So the **c** of Jotham son of Gideon came true.
17: 2 "I heard you **c** the thief who stole eleven hundred
21:18 anyone who does this will fall under God's **c**."
1Sa 14:24 "Let a **c** fall on anyone who eats before evening—
2Sa 16: 9 "Why should this dead dog **c** my lord the king?"
16:10 If the LORD has told him to **c** me, who am I to

16: 11 Leave him alone and let him **c**, for the LORD has
1Ki 2: 8 He cursed me with a terrible **c** as I was fleeing to
Ne 10: 29 They vowed to accept the **c** of God if they failed to
13: 2 Instead, they hired Balaam to **c** them, though our God turned the **c** into a blessing.
Job 1: 11 he has, and he will surely **c** you to your face!"
2: 5 his health, and he will surely **c** you to your face!"
2: 9 trying to maintain your integrity? **C** God and die."
3: 8 are ready to rouse the sea monster—**c** that day.
3: 10 **C** it for its failure to shut my mother's womb,
3: 18 are at ease in death, with no guards to **c** them.
Ps 10: 3 they praise the greedy and **c** the LORD.
62: 4 friendly to my face, / but they **c** me in their hearts.
102: 8 taunt me day after day. / They mock and **c** me.
109: 17 He loved to **c** others; / now you **c** him.
109: 28 Then let them **c** me if they like, / but you will bless
Pr 3: 33 The **c** of the LORD is on the house of the wicked,
11: 26 People **c** those who hold their grain for higher
20: 20 If you **c** your father or mother, the lamp of your
26: 2 an unfair **c** will not land on its intended victim.
27: 14 too early in the morning, it will be counted as a **c**!
28: 27 But a **c** will come upon those who close their eyes
30: 10 If you do, the person will **c** you, and you will pay
30: 11 Some people **c** their father and do not thank their
Isa 7: 17 "The LORD will bring a terrible **c** on you,
8: 21 their fists at heaven and **c** their king and their God.
24: 6 Therefore, a **c** consumes the earth and its people.
65: 15 Your name will be a **c** word among my people,
Jer 15: 10 a borrower who refuses to pay—yet they all **c** me."
20: 14 Yet I **c** the day I was born! May the day of my
20: 15 I **c** the messenger who told my father,
23: 10 For the land is full of adultery, and it lies under a **c**.
29: 22 so that whenever the Judean exiles want to **c**
La 3: 65 stubborn hearts, and then let your **c** fall upon them!
Da 9: 13 Every **c** written against us in the law of Moses has
Hos 4: 2 You **c** and lie and kill and steal and commit
Joel 2: 14 sending you a blessing instead of this terrible **c**.
Zec 5: 3 "This scroll contains the **c** that is going out over
5: 4 I am sending this **c** into the house of every thief
5: 4 And my **c** will remain in that house until it is
Mal 2: 2 "or I will bring a terrible **c** against you.
2: 2 I will **c** even the blessings you receive. Indeed,
3: 9 You are under a **c**, for your whole nation has been
4: 6 I will come and strike the land with a **c**."
Mt 5: 22 And if you **c** someone, you are in danger of the
Lk 6: 28 Pray for the happiness of those who **c** you. Pray for
Jn 7: 49 do they know about it? A **c** on them anyway!"
Ac 26: 11 in the synagogues to try to get them to **c** Christ.
Ro 8: 20 everything on earth was subjected to God's **c**.
12: 14 because you are a Christian, don't **c** them;
1Co 4: 12 We bless those who **c** us. We are patient with those
12: 3 No one speaking by the Spirit of God can **c** Jesus,
Gal 1: 8 Let God's **c** fall on anyone, including myself,
1: 9 you welcomed, let God's **c** fall upon that person.
3: 10 law to make them right with God are under his **c**,
3: 13 But Christ has rescued us from the **c** pronounced
3: 13 he took upon himself the **c** for our wrongdoing.
Jude 1: 10 and **c** the things they do not understand.

CURSED (75) [CURSE]

Ge 3: 14 and wild animals of the whole earth to be **c**.
5: 29 of farming this ground that the LORD has **c**."
9: 25 Then he **c** the descendants of Canaan, the son of
27: 29 All who curse you are **c**, and all who bless you are
49: 7 **C** be their anger, for it is fierce; / **c** be their wrath,
Nu 23: 8 But how can I curse / those whom God has not **c**?
24: 9 O Israel, / and **c** is everyone who curses you."
Dt 21: 23 for anyone hanging on a tree is **c** of God.
27: 15 '**C** is anyone who carves or casts idols and secretly
27: 16 '**C** is anyone who despises father or mother.'
27: 17 '**C** is anyone who steals property from a neighbor
27: 18 '**C** is anyone who leads a blind person astray on
27: 19 '**C** is anyone who is unjust to foreigners, orphans,
27: 20 '**C** is anyone who has sexual intercourse with his
27: 21 '**C** is anyone who has sexual intercourse with an
27: 22 '**C** is anyone who has sexual intercourse with his
27: 23 '**C** is anyone who has sexual intercourse with his
27: 24 '**C** is anyone who kills another person in secret.'
27: 25 '**C** is anyone who accepts payment to kill an
27: 26 '**C** is anyone who does not affirm the terms of this
28: 16 You will be **c** in your towns and in the country.
28: 17 You will be **c** with baskets empty of fruit, and with
28: 18 You will be **c** with few children and barren fields.
28: 18 You will be **c** with infertile herds and flocks.
28: 19 You will be **c** wherever you go, both in coming
Jos 9: 23 May you be **c**! From now on you will chop wood
Jdg 5: 23 'Let the people of Meroz be **c**,' said the angel of the LORD. / 'Let them be utterly **c**
1Sa 14: 28 oath that anyone who eats food today will be **c**.
17: 43 And he **c** David by the names of his gods.
25: 26 own hands, let all your enemies be as **c** as Nabal is.
26: 19 then may those involved be **c** by the LORD.
2Sa 3: 29 May his family in every generation be **c** with a
19: 21 should die, for he **c** the LORD's anointed king!"
1Ki 2: 8 He **c** me with a terrible curse as I was fleeing to
2Ki 2: 24 at them, and he **c** them in the name of the LORD.
9: 34 he said, "Someone go and bury this **c** woman,
22: 19 that this land would be **c** and become desolate.
Job 1: 5 have sinned and have **c** God in their hearts."
3: 1 At last Job spoke, and he **c** the day of his birth.
3: 3 "**C** be the day of my birth, and **c** be the night when
24: 18 Everything they own is **c**, so that no one enters
31: 30 No, I have never **c** anyone or asked for revenge.
Ps 37: 22 will inherit the land, / but those **c** by him will die.
119: 21 You rebuke those **c** proud ones / who wander from
Pr 24: 24 will be **c** by many people and denounced by the
29: 24 you report the crime, but you will be **c** if you don't.
Isa 66: 3 their own ways, delighting in their sins, are **c**.
Jer 11: 3 **C** is anyone who does not obey the terms of my
17: 5 "**C** are those who put their trust in mere humans
24: 9 They will be disgraced and mocked, taunted and **c**,
48: 10 **C** be those who refuse to do the work the LORD
49: 13 and a heap of rubble; it will be mocked and **c**.
Mic 6: 5 how King Balak of Moab tried to have you **c**
Zec 8: 13 had become symbols of what it means to be **c**.
14: 11 safe at last, never again to be **c** and destroyed.
Mal 1: 14 "**C** is the cheat who promises to give a fine ram
2: 2 Indeed, I have already **c** them, because you have
Mt 25: 41 on the left and say, 'Away with you, you **c** ones,
Mk 11: 20 morning as they passed by the fig tree he had **c**,
11: 21 "Look, Teacher! The fig tree you **c** has withered!"
Lk 6: 22 you who are hated and excluded and mocked and **c**
Jn 9: 28 Then they **c** him and said, "You are his disciple,
Ro 9: 3 I would be willing to be forever **c**—cut off from
1Co 16: 22 If anyone does not love the Lord, that person is **c**.
Gal 1: 8 preaches any other message, let him be forever **c**.
3: 10 "**C** is everyone who does not observe and obey all
3: 13 "**C** is everyone who is hung on a tree."
2Pe 2: 14 themselves to be greedy; they are doomed and **c**.
Rev 16: 9 and they **c** the name of God, who sent all of these
16: 11 and they **c** the God of heaven for their pains
16: 21 They **c** God because of the hailstorm, which was a
22: 3 No longer will anything be **c**. For the throne of

CURSES (22) [CURSE]

Ex 21: 17 "Anyone who **c** father or mother must be put to
Nu 5: 23 Then the priest will write these **c** on a piece of
24: 9 O Israel, / and cursed is everyone who **c** you."
Dt 28: 15 all these **c** will come and overwhelm you:
28: 20 "The LORD himself will send against you **c**,
28: 45 all these **c** will pursue and overtake you until you
29: 20 All the **c** written in this book will come down on
29: 21 to pour out on them all the covenant **c** recorded in
29: 27 bringing down on it all the **c** recorded in this book.
30: 1 to you—the blessings and the **c** I have listed—
30: 7 The LORD your God will inflict all these **c** on
30: 19 between life and death, between blessings and **c**.
Jos 8: 34 and **c** Moses had written in the Book of the Law.
2Sa 16: 12 and will bless me because of these **c**."
2Ch 34: 24 All the **c** written in the scroll you have read will
Ne 13: 25 So I confronted them and called down **c** on them.
Ps 59: 12 be captured by their pride, / their **c**, and their lies.
109: 19 Now may his **c** return and cling to him like
109: 20 May those **c** become the LORD's punishment for
Jer 11: 8 I brought upon them all the **c** described in our
Da 9: 11 "So now the solemn **c** and judgments written in
Jas 3: 9 and sometimes it breaks out into **c** against those

CURSING (17) [CURSE]

Jdg 9: 27 flowed freely, and everyone began **c** Abimelech.
2Sa 16: 5 a man came out of the village **c** them.
16: 13 **c** as he went and throwing stones at David
1Ki 21: 10 Find two scoundrels who will accuse him of **c** God
21: 13 accused him before all the people of **c** God
Job 3: 8 Let those who are experts at **c**—those who are
Ps 10: 7 Their mouths are full of **c**, lies, and threats.
10: 13 Why do the wicked get away with **c** God?
109: 18 **C** is as much a part of him as his clothing, / or as
Jer 25: 18 desolate ruin, an object of horror, contempt, and **c**.
26: 6 And I will make Jerusalem an object of **c** in every
42: 18 an object of damnation, horror, **c**, and mockery.
44: 8 and make yourselves an object of **c**
44: 12 be an object of damnation, horror, **c**, and mockery.
44: 22 were doing that he made your land an object of **c**—
Ro 3: 14 "Their mouths are full of **c** and bitterness."
Jas 3: 10 and **c** come pouring out of the same mouth.

CURTAIN (60) [CURTAINS]

Ex 26: 31 the Tabernacle hang a special **c** made of fine linen,
26: 32 Hang this inner **c** on gold hooks set into four posts
26: 33 When the inner **c** is in place, put the Ark of the
26: 33 This **c** will separate the Holy Place from the Most
26: 35 the room from each other outside the inner **c**.
26: 36 "Make another **c** from fine linen for the entrance
26: 37 Hang this **c** on gold hooks set into five posts made
27: 14 The **c** on the right side will be 22-1/2 feet long,
27: 15 The **c** on the left side will also be 22-1/2 feet long,
27: 16 to the courtyard, make a **c** that is 30 feet long.
27: 18 and 75 feet wide, with **c** walls 7-1/2 feet high,
27: 21 The lampstand will be placed outside the inner **c** of
30: 6 Place the incense altar just outside the inner **c**,
35: 12 the inner **c** to enclose the Ark in the Most Holy
35: 15 the **c** for the entrance of the Tabernacle;
35: 17 their bases; the **c** for the entrance to the courtyard;
36: 35 The inner **c** was made of fine linen cloth,
36: 36 The **c** was then attached to four gold hooks set
36: 37 Then they made another **c** for the entrance to the
36: 38 This **c** was connected by five hooks to five posts.
38: 14 The **c** on the right side was 22-1/2 feet long
38: 15 The **c** on the left side was also 22-1/2 feet long
38: 18 The **c** that covered the entrance to the courtyard
38: 27 and for the posts supporting the inner **c** required
38: 31 the bases for the **c** at the entrance of the courtyard,
39: 34 the inner **c** that enclosed the Most Holy Place;
39: 38 the **c** for the entrance of the sacred tent;
39: 40 the **c** at the courtyard entrance; the cords and tent
40: 3 and install the inner **c** to enclose the Ark within the
40: 5 "Place the incense altar just outside the inner **c**,
40: 5 Set up the **c** made for the entrance of the
40: 8 the tent, and hang the **c** for the courtyard entrance.
40: 21 and set up the inner **c** to shield it from view,
40: 22 side of the Holy Place, just outside the inner **c**.
40: 26 in the Holy Place in front of the inner **c**.
40: 28 He attached the **c** at the entrance of the Tabernacle,
40: 33 And he set up the **c** at the entrance of the
Lev 4: 6 in front of the inner **c** of the Most Holy Place.
4: 17 times before the LORD in front of the inner **c**.
16: 2 Place behind the inner **c** whenever he chooses;
16: 12 carry the burner and incense behind the inner **c**.
16: 15 the people and bring its blood behind the inner **c**.
21: 23 he must never go behind the inner **c** or come near
24: 3 Aaron will set it up outside the inner **c** of the Most
Nu 3: 26 and altar, the **c** at the courtyard entrance,
3: 31 the inner **c**, and all the equipment related to their
4: 5 enter the Tabernacle first to take down the inner **c**
4: 6 Then they must cover the inner **c** with fine
4: 25 and the **c** for the Tabernacle entrance.
4: 26 and altar, the **c** across the courtyard entrance,
18: 7 with the altar and everything within the inner **c**.
2Ch 3: 14 Solomon hung a **c** made of fine linen and blue,
Ps 104: 2 You stretch out the starry **c** of the heavens;
Isa 40: 22 He is the one who spreads out the heavens like a **c**
Mt 27: 51 At that moment the **c** in the Temple was torn in
Mk 15: 38 And the **c** in the Temple was torn in two, from top
Heb 6: 19 It leads us through the **c** of heaven into God's inner
9: 3 Then there was a **c**, and behind the **c** was the second room called the
10: 20 Christ has opened up for us through the sacred **c**,

CURTAINS (23) [CURTAIN]

Ex 27: 9 enclosed with **c** made from fine linen.
27: 9 On the south side the **c** will stretch for 150 feet.
27: 10 The **c** will be held up with silver hooks attached to
27: 11 150 feet of **c** held up by twenty posts fitted into
27: 12 The **c** on the west end of the courtyard will be 75
27: 14 entrance will be on the east end, flanked by two **c**.
27: 19 used to support the Tabernacle and the courtyard **c**,
35: 17 the **c** for the walls of the courtyard; the posts
38: 9 150 feet long. It consisted of **c** made of fine linen.
38: 10 there were silver hooks and rods to hold up the **c**.
38: 12 The walls were made from **c** supported by ten
38: 14 entrance was on the east side, flanked by two **c**.
38: 16 All the **c** used in the courtyard walls were made of
38: 17 and the rods to hold up the **c** were solid silver.
38: 18 feet high, just like the **c** of the courtyard walls.
38: 31 the posts that supported the **c** around the courtyard,
38: 31 and all the tent pegs used to hold the **c** of the
39: 40 the **c** for the walls of the courtyard and the posts
40: 33 Then he hung the **c** forming the courtyard around
Nu 3: 25 Tabernacle with its layers of coverings, its entry **c**,
3: 26 the **c** of the courtyard that surrounded the
4: 25 They must carry the **c** of the Tabernacle,
4: 26 They are also to carry the **c** for the courtyard walls

CURVED (1) [CURVES]

Jos 16: 6 then **c** eastward past Taanath-shiloh to the east of

CURVES (2) [CURVED]

Isa 40: 4 Straighten out the **c** and smooth off the rough
Lk 3: 5 level the mountains and hills! / Straighten the **c**,

CUSH (10) [CUSH'S, CUSHITE]

Ge 2: 13 which flows around the entire land of **C**.
10: 6 The descendants of Ham were **C**, Mizraim, Put,
10: 7 The descendants of **C** were Seba, Havilah, Sabtah,
2Sa 18: 21 Then Joab said to a man from **C**, "Go tell the king
18: 23 and got to Mahanaim ahead of the man from **C**.
18: 31 Then the man from **C** arrived and said, "I have
1Ch 1: 8 The descendants of Ham were **C**, Mizraim, Put,
1: 9 The descendants of **C** were Seba, Havilah, Sabtah,
1: 10 **C** was also the ancestor of Nimrod, who was
Ps 7: T which he sang to the LORD concerning **C** of the

CUSH'S (1) [CUSH]

Ge 10: 8 One of **C** descendants was Nimrod, who became a

CUSHAN (1)

Hab 3: 7 I see the peoples of **C** and Midian trembling in

CUSHAN-RISHATHAIM (3)

Jdg 3: 8 and he handed them over to King **C** of
3: 8 And the Israelites were subject to **C** for eight
3: 10 He went to war against King **C** of Aram,

CUSHI (2)

Jer 36: 14 and great-grandson of **C**, to ask Baruch to come
Zep 1: 1 Zephaniah was the son of **C**, son of Gedaliah,

CUSHION (3)

1Sa 19: 13 with blankets, and put a **c** of goat's hair at its head.
19: 16 an idol in the bed with a **c** of goat's hair at its head.
Mk 4: 38 at the back of the boat with his head on a **c**.

CUSHITE (2) [CUSH]

Nu 12: 1 because he had married a **C** woman.
2Sa 18: 32 And the **C** replied, "May all of your enemies,

CUSTODY (5)

Lev 24: 12 They put the man in **c** until the LORD's will in
Nu 15: 34 They held him in **c** because they did not know
Ac 24: 23 He ordered an officer to keep Paul in **c** but to give
27: 1 and several other prisoners were placed in the **c** of
Gal 3: 23 We were kept in protective **c**, so to speak, until we

CUSTOM (21) [ACCUSTOMED, CUSTOMARY, CUSTOMS]

Ge 29: 3 It was the **c** there to wait for all the flocks to arrive
29:26 "It's not our **c** to marry off a younger daughter
Ex 33: 7 It was Moses' **c** to set up the tent known as the
Jdg 11:39 she died a virgin. So it has become a **c** in Israel
14:10 threw a party at Timnah, as was the **c** of the day.
Ru 4: 7 In those days it was the **c** in Israel for anyone
2Sa 13:18 as was the **c** in those days for the king's virgin
1Ki 18:28 they shouted louder, and following their normal **c**,
2Ki 11:14 by the pillar, as was the **c** at times of coronation.
Ne 12:46 The **c** of having choir directors to lead the choirs in
Est 9:23 Mordecai's suggestion and began this annual **c**.
Mt 27:15 Now it was the governor's **c** to release one prisoner
Mk 15: 6 Now it was the governor's **c** to release one prisoner
Lk 1: 9 As was the **c** of the priests, he was chosen by lot to
11:38 the ceremonial washing required by Jewish **c**.
Jn 18:39 But you have a **c** of asking me to release someone
19:40 cloth with the spices, as is the Jewish **c** of burial.
Ac 15: 1 "Unless you keep the ancient Jewish **c** of
17: 2 As was Paul's **c**, he went to the synagogue service,
18:18 Paul had shaved his head according to Jewish **c**,
1Co 11:16 all I can say is that we have no other **c** than this,

CUSTOMARY (6) [CUSTOM]

Ex 22:16 he must pay the **c** dowry and accept her as his
Dt 21:17 He must give the **c** double portion to his oldest son,
34: 8 of Moab, until the **c** period of mourning was over.
1Sa 1: 9 Eli the priest was sitting at his **c** place beside the
1Ki 10:13 besides all the other **c** gifts he had so generously
18:36 At the **c** time for offering the evening sacrifice,

CUSTOMERS (2)

Mt 21:12 and began to drive out the merchants and their **c**.
Mk 11:15 and began to drive out the merchants and their **c**.

CUSTOMS (21) [CUSTOM]

Lev 20:23 Do not live by the **c** of the people whom I will
Dt 18: 9 be very careful not to imitate the detestable **c** of the
20:18 you their detestable **c** in the worship of their gods,
2Ki 17:27 Let him teach the new residents the religious **c** of
17:33 they continued to follow the religious **c** of the
Ezr 4:13 then refuse to pay their tribute, **c**, and tolls to you.
4:20 and have received vast tribute, **c**, and tolls.
6:21 from their immoral **c** to worship the LORD,
Est 1:13 who knew all the Persian laws and **c**, for he always
Ps 106:35 among the pagans / and adopted their evil **c**.
Eze 20:25 I gave them over to worthless **c** and laws that
Zep 1: 8 princes of Judah and all those following pagan **c**.
Mk 7: 5 "Why don't your disciples follow our age-old **c**?
Ac 6:14 and change the **c** Moses handed down to us."
16:21 the people to do things that are against Roman **c**."
21:21 circumcise their children or follow other Jewish **c**.
22: 3 to follow our Jewish laws and **c** very carefully.
26: 3 for I know you are an expert on Jewish **c**
28:17 against our people or the **c** of our ancestors.
Ro 4:16 to receive it, whether or not we follow Jewish **c**,
12: 2 Don't copy the behavior and **c** of this world,

CUT (207) [CUTS, CUTTING, GEMCUTTER, STONECUTTERS, WOODCUTTERS]

Ge 15:10 He **c** each one down the middle and laid the halves
17:11 the flesh of his foreskin must be **c** off. This will be
17:14 Anyone who refuses to be circumcised will be **c**
40:19 Three days from now Pharaoh will **c** off your head
Ex 12:15 festival will be **c** off from the community of Israel.
12:19 week will be **c** off from the community of Israel.
29:17 **C** up the ram and wash off the internal organs
30:33 not a priest will be **c** off from the community.' "
30:38 enjoyment will be **c** off from the community."
31:14 anyone who works on that day will be **c** off from
34: 4 So Moses **c** two tablets of stone like the first ones.
34:13 they worship, and **c** down their carved images.
Lev 1: 6 the animal has been skinned and **c** into pieces,
1:12 Then you must **c** the animal in pieces,
3: 9 This includes the fat of the entire tail **c** off near the
7:20 to the LORD must be **c** off from the community.
7:21 that person must be **c** off from the community."
7:25 LORD by fire must be **c** off from the community.
7:27 Anyone who eats blood must be **c** off from the
8:20 Next he **c** the ram into pieces and burned the head,
13:56 he is to **c** the spot from the clothing, the fabric,
17: 4 shed blood and must be **c** off from the community.
17: 9 the LORD, you will be **c** off from the community.
17:10 I will **c** off such a person from the community,
17:14 So whoever eats or drinks blood must be **c** off.
18:29 things will be **c** off from the community of Israel.
19: 8 and must be **c** off from the community.
19:28 "Never **c** your bodies in mourning for the dead
20: 3 against them and **c** them off from the community,
20: 5 against them and **c** them off from the community,
20: 6 against them and **c** them off from the community.
20:17 Both of them must be publicly **c** off from the
20:18 both of them must be **c** off from the community,
21: 5 trim the edges of their beards, or **c** their bodies.
22: 3 the Israelites, they must be **c** off from my presence.
23:29 day in humility will be **c** off from the community.
26:30 your pagan shrines and **c** down your incense altars.
Nu 6: 5 "They must never **c** their hair throughout the time
9:13 will be **c** off from the community of Israel for
13:23 they **c** down a cluster of grapes so large that it took
13:24 because of the cluster of grapes they had **c** there.
15:30 and they must be **c** off from the community.
15:31 they must be completely **c** off and suffer the
19:13 and will be **c** off from the community of Israel.
19:20 and do not purify themselves will be **c** off from the
Dt 7: 5 **C** down their Asherah poles and burn their idols.
10: 3 and **c** two stone tablets like the first two,
12: 3 their Asherah poles and **c** down their carved idols.
14: 1 never **c** yourselves or shave the hair above your
19: 5 goes into the forest with a neighbor to **c** wood.
20:19 the trees. Eat the fruit, but do not **c** down the trees.
20:20 But you may **c** down trees that you know are not
21:12 where she must shave her head, **c** her fingernails,
23: 1 a man's testicles are crushed or his penis is **c** off,
25:12 her hand must be **c** off without pity.
Jos 3:13 the water, the flow of water will be **c** off upstream,
10:19 chasing the enemy and **c** them down from the rear.
Jdg 1: 6 captured him and **c** off his thumbs and big toes.
1: 7 had seventy kings with thumbs and big toes **c** off,
6:25 and **c** down the Asherah pole standing beside it.
6:26 using as fuel the wood of the Asherah pole you **c**
7:24 **C** them off at the shallows of the Jordan River at
9:44 while Abimelech's other two groups **c** them down
9:49 So each of them **c** down some branches,
13: 5 give birth to a son, and his hair must never be **c**.
16:17 "My hair has never been **c**," he confessed, "for I
19:29 and **c** his concubine's body into twelve pieces.
20: 6 So I **c** her body into twelve pieces and sent the
1Sa 1:11 dedicated to the LORD, his hair will never be **c**."
9:23 then instructed the cook to bring Saul the finest **c**
11: 7 He took two oxen and **c** them into pieces and sent
15:33 And Samuel **c** Agag to pieces before the LORD at
17:46 and I will kill you and **c** off your head.
17:51 David used it to kill the giant and **c** off his head.
24: 4 crept forward and **c** off a piece of Saul's robe.
24: 5 began bothering him because he had **c** Saul's robe.
24:11 a piece of your robe! I **c** it off, but I didn't kill you.
31: 9 So they **c** off Saul's head and stripped off his
2Sa 4: 7 they **c** off his head as he lay there on his bed.
4:12 They **c** off their hands and feet and hung their
10: 4 **c** off their robes at the buttocks, and sent them
14:16 and rescue us from those who would **c** us off from
14:26 He **c** his hair only once a year, and then only
16: 9 "Let me go over and **c** off his head!"
20:22 and they **c** off Sheba's head and threw it out to
1Ki 3:25 "**C** the living child in two and give half to each of
5: 6 command that cedars from Lebanon be **c** for me.
5: 6 there is no one among us who can **c** timber like
7: 9 **c** and trimmed to exact measure on all sides.
7:11 of stone used in the walls were also **c** to measure,
15:13 He **c** down the pole and burned it in the Kidron
18:23 and **c** it into pieces and lay it on the wood of their
18:28 they **c** themselves with knives and swords until the
18:33 He piled wood on the altar, **c** the bull into pieces,
2Ki 3:19 You will **c** down all their trees, stop up all their
3:25 stopped up the springs, and **c** down the good trees.
6: 6 Elisha **c** a stick and threw it into the water.
12:12 and **c** stone for repairing the LORD's Temple,
19:23 I have **c** down its tallest cedars / and its choicest
22: 6 and the **c** stone needed to repair the Temple.
23:14 the sacred pillars and **c** down the Asherah poles.
24:13 They **c** apart all the gold vessels that King
1Ch 10: 9 they stripped off Saul's armor and **c** off his head.
19: 4 their beards, **c** off their robes at the buttocks,
2Ch 2:16 We will **c** whatever timber you need from the
14: 3 the sacred pillars and **c** down the Asherah poles.
15:16 He **c** down the pole, broke it up, and burned it in
31: 1 **c** down the Asherah poles, and removed the pagan
34: 7 He **c** down the incense altars throughout the land
34:11 and masons and purchased **c** stone for the walls
Ne 8:16 So the people went out and **c** branches and used
Job 8:12 not ready to be **c**, they begin to wither.
14: 7 "If a tree is **c** down, there is hope that it will sprout
15:32 They will be **c** down in the prime of life, and all
28:10 They **c** tunnels in the rocks and uncover precious
30:11 For God has **c** the cords of my tent. He has
Ps 31:22 cried out, / "I have been **c** off from the LORD!"
57: 4 and arrows, / and whose tongues **c** like swords.
75:10 God says, "I will **c** off the strength of the wicked,
88: 5 as dead. / I am forgotten, / **c** off from your care.
88:16 has overwhelmed me. / Your terrors have **c** me off.
102:23 He has **c** me down in midlife, / shortening my
107:16 gates of bronze; / he **c** apart their bars of iron.
109:15 but may his name be **c** off from human memory.
129: 4 he has **c** the cords used by the ungodly to bind me.
143:12 In your unfailing love, **c** off all my enemies
Pr 10:27 one's life, but the years of the wicked are **c** short.
10:31 but the tongue that deceives will be **c** off.
21:28 A false witness will be **c** off, but an attentive
24:14 a bright future, and your hopes will not be **c** short.
Isa 2:13 He will **c** down the tall cedars of Lebanon
3: 1 will **c** off the supplies of food and water from
6:13 will remain a stump, like a tree that is **c** down,
9:10 We will replace the broken bricks with **c** stone,
10:34 The Mighty One will **c** down the enemy as an ax
14: 8 is broken! No one will come to **c** us down now!'
15: 2 shave their heads in sorrow and **c** off their beards.
18: 5 the LORD will **c** you off as though with pruning
33:12 like thorns **c** down and tossed in a fire.
37:24 I have **c** down its tallest cedars / and its choicest
38:12 a shepherd's tent in a storm. / It has been **c** short,
45: 2 down gates of bronze and **c** through bars of iron.
51: 1 you were mined, the rock from which you were **c**!
59: 2 is a problem—your sins have **c** you off from God.
Jer 6: 6 "**C** down the trees for battering rams.
10: 3 and foolish. They **c** down a tree and carve an idol.
16: 6 Their friends will not **c** themselves or shave their
34:18 I will **c** you apart just as you **c** apart the calf
34:19 Yes, I will **c** you apart, whether you are officials of
36:23 took his knife and **c** off that section of the scroll.
41: 5 their beards, torn their clothes, and **c** themselves,
46:23 They will **c** down her people like trees,"
48: 2 they say, 'we will **c** her off from being a nation.'
48:25 Her horns have been **c** off, and her arms have been
49:15 "I will **c** you down to size among the nations,
51:13 but your end has come. The thread of your life is **c**.
Eze 5:11 the Sovereign LORD, I will **c** you off completely.
14: 9 and **c** them off from the community of Israel.
17: 9 I will **c** off its fruit and let its leaves wither and die.
23:25 They will **c** off your nose and ears, and any
25: 7 I will **c** you off from being a nation and destroy
31:12 **c** it down and left it fallen on the ground.
39:10 They won't need to **c** wood from the fields
40:41 where the sacrifices were **c** up and prepared.
Da 2:34 a rock was **c** from a mountain by supernatural
2:45 That is the meaning of the rock **c** from the
4:14 The messenger shouted, "**C** down the tree; lop off
4:23 and saying, '**C** down the tree and destroy it.
Hos 6: 5 I sent my prophets to **c** you to pieces. I have
7:14 They **c** themselves, begging foreign gods for crops
10: 7 Samaria will be **c** off, and its king will disappear
12: 1 with Assyria and **c** deals with the Egyptians.
Am 3:14 The horns of the altar will be **c** off and fall to the
Ob 1: 2 "I will **c** you down to size among the nations,
1: 9 and everyone on the mountains of Edom will be **c**
Mic 3: 3 **c** away their skin, and break their bones.
Na 3:15 fire will devour you; the sword will **c** you down.
Hab 2:17 You **c** down the forests of Lebanon. Now you will be **c** down!
Zec 11:17 The sword will **c** his arm and pierce his right eye!
13: 8 Two-thirds of the people in the land will be **c** off
Mal 2:12 May the LORD **c** off from the nation of Israel
Mt 5:30 causes you to sin, **c** it off and throw it away.
18: 8 foot causes you to sin, **c** it off and throw it away.
21: 8 and others **c** branches from the trees and spread
Mk 1:25 Jesus **c** him short. "Be silent! Come out of the
6:27 So he sent an executioner to the prison to **c** off
9:43 If your hand causes you to sin, **c** it off. It is better
9:45 If your foot causes you to sin, **c** it off. It is better to
11: 8 and others **c** leafy branches in the fields and spread
Lk 4:35 Jesus **c** him short. "Be silent!" he told the demon.
13: 7 and there hasn't been a single fig! **C** it down.
13: 9 figs next year, fine. If not, you can **c** it down.' "
22:50 at the high priest's servant and **c** off his right ear.
Jn 18:26 a relative of the man whose ear Peter had **c** off,
Ac 3:23 to that Prophet will be **c** off from God's people
27:32 So the soldiers **c** the ropes and let the boat fall off.
27:40 So they **c** off the anchors and left them in the sea.
Ro 9: 3 **c** off from Christ!—if that would save them.
11:22 But if you stop trusting, you also will be **c** off.
1Co 11: 6 wear a head covering, she should **c** off all her hair.
11: 6 since it is shameful for a woman to have her hair **c**
2Co 11:12 But I will continue doing this to **c** the ground out
Gal 5: 4 keeping the law, you have been **c** off from Christ!
Col 2:13 because your sinful nature was not yet **c** away.
Heb 11:36 and their backs were **c** open with whips.

CUTHAH (2)

2Ki 17:24 **C**, Avva, Hamath, and Sepharvaim and resettled
17:30 Those from **C** worshiped their god Nergal.

CUTS (10) [CUT]

1Sa 17:18 And give these ten **c** of cheese to their captain.
Job 27: 8 For what hope do the godless have when God **c**
Ps 52: 2 Your tongue **c** like a sharp razor; / you're an expert
129: 3 My back is covered with **c**, / as if a farmer had
Isa 10:34 enemy as an ax **c** down the forest trees in Lebanon.
38:12 cut short, / as when a weaver **c** cloth from a loom.
44:14 He **c** down cedars; he selects the cypress
Eze 17:24 who **c** down the tall tree and helps the short tree to
24: 4 and the shoulder and all the most tender **c**.
Jn 15: 2 He **c** off every branch that doesn't produce fruit,

CUTTING (20) [CUT]

Ge 17:23 and circumcised them, **c** off their foreskins,
Ex 31: 5 He is skilled in **c** and setting gemstones and in
35:33 He is skilled in **c** and setting gemstones and in
39: 3 gold into thin sheets and **c** it into fine strips.
Jdg 6:30 altar of Baal and for **c** down the Asherah pole."
2Ki 6: 4 they arrived at the Jordan, they began **c** down trees.
2Ch 2: 8 for I know that your men are without equal at **c**
32: 4 **c** off the brook that ran through the fields.
Job 5:15 He rescues the poor from the **c** words of the strong.
Ps 105:16 on the land of Canaan, / **c** off its food supply.
Pr 12:18 Some people make **c** remarks, but the words of the
26: 6 convey a message is as foolish as **c** off one's feet
Isa 1: 4 Holy One of Israel, **c** themselves off from his help.
Eze 14:13 **c** off their food supply and sending a famine to
Joel 1: 4 After the **c** locusts finished eating the crops,
2:25 the **c** locusts, the swarming locusts,
Mic 3: 6 night will close around you, **c** off all your visions.
Ro 2:29 And true circumcision is not a **c** of the body
Col 2:11 the **c** away of your sinful nature.
Heb 4:12 **c** deep into our innermost thoughts and desires.

CYCLONE (1)

Pr 10:25 Disaster strikes like a **c**, whirling the wicked away,

CYMBAL (1) [CYMBALS]

1Co 13: 1 meaningless noise like a loud gong or a clanging **c**.

CYMBALS (17) [CYMBAL]

1Sa 18: 6 and danced for joy with tamboutines and **c**.

2Sa 6: 5 lyres, harps, tambourines, castanets, and **c**.
1Ch 13: 8 lyres, harps, tambourines, **c**, and trumpets.
15:16 songs to the accompaniment of lyres, harps, and **c**.
15:19 and Ethan were chosen to sound the bronze **c**.
15:28 blowing of horns and trumpets, the crashing of **c**,
16: 5 Asaph, the leader of this group, sounded the **c**.
16:42 They used their trumpets, **c**, and other instruments
25: 1 to the accompaniment of harps, lyres, and **c**.
25: 6 Their responsibilities included the playing of **c**,
2Ch 5:12 and stood at the east side of the altar playing **c**,
5:13 **c**, and other instruments, they raised their voices
29:25 the Levites at the Temple of the LORD with **c**,
Ezr 3:10 of Asaph, clashed their **c** to praise the LORD,
Ne 12:27 songs of thanksgiving and with the music of **c**,
Ps 150: 5 with a clash of **c**; / praise him with loud clanging **c**.

CYPRESS (17)

1Ki 5: 8 the timber. I can supply you with both cedar and **c**.
5:10 Solomon as much cedar and **c** timber as he desired.
6:15 ceilings with cedar, and he used **c** for the floors.
6:34 There were two folding doors of **c** wood, and each
9:11 and **c** lumber and gold he had furnished for the
2Ki 19:23 cut down its tallest cedars / and its choicest **c** trees.
2Ch 2: 8 Also send me cedar, **c**, and almug logs from
3: 5 The main room of the Temple was paneled with **c**
Isa 14: 8 the **c** trees and the cedars of Lebanon—sing out
37:24 cut down its tallest cedars / and its choicest **c** trees.
41:19 cedar, acacia, myrtle, olive, **c**, fir, and pine—
44:14 He cuts down cedars; he selects the **c** and the oak;
55:13 Where once there were thorns, **c** trees will grow.
60:13 the forests of **c**, fir, and pine—to beautify my
Eze 27: 5 You were like a great ship built of the finest **c** from
31: 8 No **c** had branches equal to it; no plane tree had
Zec 11: 2 Weep, you **c** trees, for all the ruined cedars;

CYPRUS (13)

Nu 24:24 Ships will come from the coasts of **C**; / they will
Isa 23: 1 it is gone! The rumors you heard in **C** are all true.
23:12 Even if you flee to **C**, you will find no rest."
Jer 2:10 "Go west to the land of **C**; go east to the land of
Eze 27: 6 pine wood, brought from the southern coasts of **C**.
Ac 4:36 the tribe of Levi and came from the island of **C**.
11:19 as far as Phoenicia, **C**, and Antioch of Syria.
11:20 some of the believers who went to Antioch from **C**
13: 4 of Seleucia and then sailed for the island of **C**.
15:39 took John Mark with him and sailed for **C**.
21: 3 We sighted the island of **C**, passed it on our left,
21:16 a man originally from **C** and one of the early
27: 4 so we sailed north of **C** between the island

CYRENE (7)

Mt 27:32 across a man named Simon, who was from **C**,
Mk 15:21 A man named Simon, who was from **C**,
Lk 23:26 As they led Jesus away, Simon of **C**, who was
Ac 2:10 Egypt, and the areas of Libya toward **C**,
6: 9 They were Jews from **C**, Alexandria, Cilicia,
11:20 and **C** began preaching to Gentiles about the Lord
13: 1 (called "the black man"), Lucius (from **C**),

CYRUS (25) [CYRUS'S]

2Ch 36:22 In the first year of King **C** of Persia, the LORD
36:22 the heart of **C** to put this proclamation into writing
36:23 "This is what King **C** of Persia says: The LORD,
Ezr 1: 1 In the first year of King **C** of Persia, the LORD
1: 1 the heart of **C** to put this proclamation into writing
1: 2 "This is what King **C** of Persia says: The LORD,
1: 7 King **C** himself brought out the valuable items
1: 8 **C** directed Mithredath, the treasurer of Persia,
1: 9 These were the items **C** donated: / silver trays
3: 7 to Joppa, for King **C** had given permission for this.
4: 3 of Israel, just as King **C** of Persia commanded us."
4: 5 This went on during the entire reign of King **C** of
5:13 However, King **C** of Babylon, during the first year
5:14 King **C** returned the gold and silver utensils that
5:14 whom King **C** appointed as governor of Judah.
5:17 **C** ever issued a decree to rebuild God's Temple in
6:14 by the God of Israel and decreed by **C**,
Isa 44:28 When I say of **C**, 'He is my shepherd,' he will
45: 1 This is what the LORD says to **C**, his anointed
45: 2 "I will go before you, **C**, and level the mountains.
45:13 I will raise up **C** to fulfill my righteous purpose,
48:14 and listen: 'The LORD has chosen **C** as his ally.
48:15 I have said it: I am calling **C**! I will send him on
Da 6:28 the reign of Darius and the reign of **C** the Persian.
10: 1 In the third year of the reign of King **C** of Persia,

CYRUS'S (2) [CYRUS]

Ezr 6: 3 "In the first year of King **C** reign, a decree was
Da 1:21 remained there until the first year of King **C**

D

DABBESHETH (1)

Jos 19:11 there it went west, going past Maralah, touching **D**,

DABERATH (3)

Jos 19:12 and from there to **D** and up to Japhia.
21:28 the tribe of Issachar they received Kishion, **D**,
1Ch 6:72 territory of Issachar, they were given Kedesh, **D**,

DAGGER (8) [DAGGERS]

Jdg 3:16 So Ehud made himself a double-edged **d** that was
3:21 pulled out the **d** strapped to his right thigh,
3:22 The **d** went so deep that the handle disappeared
3:22 So Ehud left the **d** in, and the king's bowels
2Sa 3:27 But then he drew his **d** and killed Abner in revenge
20: 8 Joab was wearing his uniform with a **d** strapped to
20: 8 he secretly slipped the **d** from its sheath.
20:10 Amasa didn't notice the **d** in his left hand,

DAGGERS (2) [DAGGER]

2Sa 18:14 Then he took three **d** and plunged them into
Ps 55:21 are as soothing as lotion, / but underneath are **d**!

DAGON (8) [BETH-DAGON]

Jdg 16:23 offering sacrifices and praising their god, **D**.
1Sa 5: 2 They carried the Ark of God into the temple of **D**
and placed it beside the idol of **D**.
5: 3 **D** had fallen with his face to the ground in front of
5: 5 That is why to this day neither the priests of **D** nor
5: 5 enters the temple of **D** will step on its threshold.
5: 7 We will all be destroyed along with our god **D**."
1Ch 10:10 fastened his head to the wall in the temple of **D**.

DAILY (50) [DAY]

Ex 5:13 "Meet your **d** quota of bricks, just as you did
16:23 On this day we will rest from our normal **d** tasks.
20: 9 Six days a week are set apart for your **d** duties
29:42 "This is to be a **d** burnt offering given from
Lev 6:12 and arrange the **d** whole burnt offering on it.
6:12 offerings on top of this **d** whole burnt offering.
Nu 4:16 the fragrant incense, the **d** grain offering,
28: 3 When you present your **d** whole burnt offerings to
28:10 in addition to the regular **d** burnt offering and its
28:15 This is in addition to the regular **d** burnt offering
28:31 are in addition to the regular **d** burnt offering
29: 6 to your regular monthly and **d** burnt offerings,
29:11 and the regular **d** burnt offering with its grain
29:16 in addition to the regular **d** burnt offering with its
29:19 in addition to the regular **d** burnt offering with its
29:22 in addition to the regular **d** burnt offering with its
29:25 in addition to the regular **d** burnt offering with its
29:28 in addition to the regular **d** burnt offering with its
29:31 in addition to the regular **d** burnt offering with its
29:34 in addition to the regular **d** burnt offering with its
29:38 in addition to the regular **d** burnt offering with its
Dt 5:13 Six days a week are set apart for your **d** duties
17:19 the law with him and read it **d** as long as he lives.
1Ki 4:22 The **d** food requirements for Solomon's palace
8:59 cause of his people Israel, fulfilling our **d** needs.
2Ch 8:14 in praise and to assist the priests in their **d** duties.
31: 3 personal contribution of animals for the **d** morning
31:16 who came **d** to the LORD's Temple to perform
Ne 5:15 demanding a **d** ration of food and wine, besides a
11:23 royal orders, which determined their **d** activities.
12:47 the people brought a **d** supply of food for the
Ps 101: 8 My **d** task will be to ferret out criminals / and free
Pr 8:34 watching for me **d** at my gates, waiting for me
Eze 45:23 This **d** offering will consist of seven young bulls
46:15 and the olive oil must be given as a **d** sacrifice
Da 1: 5 The king assigned them a **d** ration of the best food
8:11 armies by canceling the **d** sacrifices offered to him
8:13 that causes desecration stop the **d** sacrifices?
11:31 the sanctuary, putting a stop to the **d** sacrifices,
12:11 "From the time the **d** sacrifice is taken away
Mt 20: 2 He agreed to pay the normal **d** wage and sent them
Lk 9:23 shoulder your cross **d**, and follow me.
17:28 People went about their **d** business—eating
19:47 After that, he taught **d** in the Temple,
Ac 6: 1 discriminated against in the **d** distribution of food.
16: 5 strengthened in their faith and grew **d** in numbers.
17:17 and he spoke **d** in the public square to all who
19: 9 Then he began preaching **d** at the lecture hall of
1Co 15:31 For I swear, dear friends, I face death **d**. This is as
2Co 11:28 I have the **d** burden of how the churches are

DAINTY (2)

Pr 18: 8 What **d** morsels rumors are—but they sink deep
26:22 What **d** morsels rumors are—but they sink deep

DAINTY [KJV] See also DELICACIES, DELICIOUS, LUXURIES

DALAIAH [KJV] See DELAIAH

DALE [KJV] See VALLEY

DALMANUTHA (1)

Mk 8:10 his disciples and crossed over to the region of **D**.

DALMATIA (1)

2Ti 4:10 has gone to Galatia, and Titus has gone to **D**.

DALPHON (1)

Est 9: 7 They also killed Parshandatha, **D**, Aspatha,

DAM (1)

Job 28:11 They **d** up the trickling streams and bring to light

DAMAGE (3) [DAMAGED, DAMAGES, DAMAGING]

Jer 33: 6 the time will come when I will heal Jerusalem's **d**
Da 11:28 doing much **d** before continuing his journey.
Jas 3: 5 is a small thing, but what enormous **d** it can do.

DAMAGED (3) [DAMAGE]

Lev 21:20 oozing sores or scabs on his skin, or has **d** testicles.
22:24 If an animal has **d** testicles or is castrated, it may
Lk 11: 8 you what you want so his reputation won't be **d**.

DAMAGES (2) [DAMAGE]

Ex 21:22 then the person responsible must pay **d** in the
22: 5 then the animal's owner must pay **d** in the form of

DAMAGING (1) [DAMAGE]

Pr 26:18 Just as **d** as a mad man shooting a lethal weapon

DAMARIS (1)

Ac 17:34 of the Council, a woman named **D**, and others.

DAMASCUS (60)

Ge 14:15 but Abram chased them to Hobah, north of **D**.
15: 2 Since I don't have a son, Eliezer of **D**, a servant in
2Sa 8: 5 When Arameans from **D** arrived to help
8: 6 Then he placed several army garrisons in **D**,
1Ki 11:24 Rezon and his men fled to **D**, where he became
15:18 of Hezion, the king of Aram, who was ruling in **D**,
19:15 way you came, and travel to the wilderness of **D**.
20:34 and you may establish places of trade in **D**, as my
2Ki 5:12 and Pharpar River of **D** better than all the rivers of
8: 7 Now Elisha went to **D**, the capital of Aram,
8: 9 with the finest products of **D** as a gift for Elisha.
14:28 and how he recovered for Israel both **D**
16: 9 the Assyrians attacked the Aramean capital of **D**
16:10 then went to **D** to meet with King Tiglath-pileser
16:11 it was ready for the king when he returned from **D**.
1Ch 18: 5 When Arameans from **D** arrived to help
18: 6 Then he placed several army garrisons in **D**,
2Ch 16: 2 who was ruling in **D**, along with this message:
24:23 they sent all the plunder back to their king in **D**.
28: 5 and to exile large numbers of his people to **D**.
28:23 He offered sacrifices to the gods of **D** who had
SS 7: 4 is as fine as the tower of Lebanon overlooking **D**.
Isa 7: 8 because Aram is no stronger than its capital, **D**.
7: 8 And **D** is no stronger than its king, Rezin.
8: 4 the king of Assyria will invade both **D** and Samaria
10: 9 And we will destroy Samaria just as we did **D**.
17: 1 This message came to me concerning **D**: "Look, **D**
will disappear! It will become a heap of
17: 3 also be destroyed, and the power of **D** will end.
Jer 49:23 This message was given concerning **D**. This is
49:24 **D** has become feeble, and all her people turn to
49:27 "And I will start a fire at the edge of **D** that will
Eze 27:18 **D** traded for your rich variety of goods,
47:16 which are on the border between **D** and Hamath,
47:17 between Hamath to the north and **D** to the south.
47:18 border starts at a point between Hauran and **D**
48: 1 then runs on to Hazar-enan on the border of **D**,
Am 1: 3 "The people of **D** have sinned again and again,
1: 5 I will break down the gates of **D** and slaughter its
5:27 into exile, to a land east of **D**," says the LORD,
Zec 9: 1 LORD against the land of Aram and the city of **D**,
9: 2 near **D**, and for the cities of Tyre and Sidon,
Ac 9: 2 requested letters addressed to the synagogues in **D**,
9: 3 As he was nearing **D** on this mission, a brilliant
9: 9 So his companions led him by the hand to **D**.
9:10 Now there was a believer in **D** named Ananias.
9:14 the leading priests to arrest every believer in **D**."
9:19 Saul stayed with the believers in **D** for a few days.
9:22 and the Jews in **D** couldn't refute his proofs that
9:27 them how Saul had seen the Lord on the way to **D**.
9:27 how he boldly preached in the name of Jesus in **D**.
22: 5 letters from them to our Jewish brothers in **D**,
22: 6 "As I was on the road, nearing **D**, about noon a
22:10 And the Lord told me, 'Get up and go into **D**,
22:11 and had to be led into **D** by my companions.
22:12 and he was well thought of by all the Jews of **D**.
26:12 "One day I was on such a mission to **D**,
26:20 I preached first to those in **D**, then in Jerusalem
2Co 11:32 When I was in **D**, the governor under King Aretas
Gal 1:17 into Arabia and later returned to the city of **D**.

DAMNATION (4) [DAMNED]

Jer 29:18 I will make them an object of **d**, horror, contempt,
42:18 You will become an object of **d**, horror, cursing,
44:12 They will be an object of **d**, horror, cursing,
Ac 20:26 been faithful. No one's **d** can be blamed on me,

DAMNATION [KJV] See also CONDEMNED, GUILTY, JUDGMENT, (ETERNAL) SIN, PUNISHMENT

DAMNED (1) [DAMNATION]

Eze 22: 3 O city of murderers, doomed and **d**—city of idols,

DAMSEL [KJV] See CHILD, GIRL, MAID, VIRGIN, WOMAN

DAN (68) [DAN'S, DAN-JAAN, MAHANEH-DAN]

Ge 14:14 army until he caught up with them in **D**.
30: 6 Rachel named him **D**, for she said, "God has
35:25 of Bilhah, Rachel's servant, were **D** and Naphtali.
46:23 The son of **D** was Hushim.
49:16 "**D** will govern his people / like any other tribe in
Ex 1: 4 **D**, Naphtali, Gad, and Asher.
31: 6 of Ahisamach, of the tribe of **D**, to be his assistant.
35:34 and Oholiab son of Ahisamach, of the tribe of **D**,
38:23 of the tribe of **D**, a craftsman expert at engraving,
Lev 24:11 She was the daughter of Dibri of the tribe of **D**.
Nu 1:12 **D** I Ahiezer son of Ammishaddai
1:38[-39] **D** I 62,700
2:25[-26] "The divisions of **D**, Asher, and Naphtali are
2:25[-26] **D** I Ahiezer son of Ammishaddai I 62,700
7:66 leader of the tribe of **D**, presented his offering.
10:25 the tribes that camped with **D** set out under their
10:25 The tribe of **D** headed this group,
13:12 **D** I Ammiel son of Gemalli
26:42 were the clans descended from the sons of **D**:
26:43 All the clans of **D** were Shuhamite clans,
34:22 **D** I Bukki son of Jogli
Dt 27:13 And the tribes of Reuben, Gad, Asher, Zebulun, **D**,
33:22 Moses said this about the tribe of **D**: / **D** is a lion's cub, / leaping out from Bashan."
34: 1 him the whole land, from Gilead as far as **D**;
Jos 19:40 of land went to the families of the tribe of **D**.
19:47 But the tribe of **D** had trouble taking possession of
19:47 They renamed the city **D** after their ancestor.
19:48 the inheritance of the families of the tribe of **D**—
21: 5 of Ephraim, **D**, and the half-tribe of Manasseh.
21:23 were allotted to the priests from the tribe of **D**:
Jdg 1:34 As for the tribe of **D**, the Amorites forced them
5:17 And **D**, why did he stay home? / Asher sat
13: 2 a man named Manoah from the tribe of **D** lived in
18: 1 And the tribe of **D** was trying to find a place to
18: 2 So the men of **D** chose five warriors from among
18:11 So six hundred warriors from the tribe of **D** set out
18:16 As the six hundred warriors from the tribe of **D**
18:22 When the people from the tribe of **D** were quite a
18:23 The men of **D** turned around and said, "What do
18:25 The men of **D** said, "Watch what you say!
18:26 So the men of **D** went on their way. When Micah
18:27 his priest, the men of **D** came to the town of Laish,
18:28 Then the people of the tribe of **D** rebuilt the town
18:29 They renamed the town **D** after their ancestor,
18:30 This family continued as priests for the tribe of **D**
18:31 **D** as long as the Tabernacle of God remained at
20: 1 from **D** to Beersheba and from the land of Gilead,
2Sa 3:10 Israel as well as Judah, from **D** to Beersheba."
17:11 bringing them from as far away as **D**
24: 2 from **D** in the north to Beersheba in the south—
1Ki 4:25 And from **D** to Beersheba, each family had its own
12:29 and northern ends of Israel—in Bethel and in **D**.
12:30 people worshiped them, traveling even as far as **D**.
15:20 **D**, Abel-beth-maacah, and all Kinnereth, with all
2Ki 10:29 however, destroy the gold calves at Bethel and **D**,
1Ch 2: 2 **D**, Joseph, Benjamin, Naphtali, Gad, and Asher.
12:35 From the tribe of **D**, there were 28,600 warriors,
21: 2 from Beersheba in the south to **D** in the north—
27:22 **D** I Azarel son of Jeroham These were the leaders
2Ch 2:14 the son of a woman from **D** in Israel; his father is
16: 4 **D**, Abel-beth-maacah, and all the store cities in
30: 5 from Beersheba in the south to **D** in the north,
Jer 4:15 From **D** and the hill country of Ephraim,
8:16 heard all the way from the land of **D** in the north!
Eze 48: 1 The territory of **D** is in the extreme north.
48:32 gates will be named for Joseph, Benjamin, and **D**.
Am 8:14 **D**, and Beersheba will fall down, never to rise

DAN'S (4) [DAN]

Nu 2:31 So the total of all the troops on **D** side of the camp
Jos 19:41 The towns within **D** inheritance included Zorah,
Eze 48: 1 **D** territory extends all the way across the land of
48: 2 Asher's territory lies south of **D** and also extends

DAN-JAAN (1) [DAN]

2Sa 24: 6 of Tahtim-hodshi and to **D** and around to Sidon.

DANCE (9) [DANCED, DANCERS, DANCES, DANCING]

Ex 15:20 and led all the women in rhythm and **d**.
Ecc 3: 4 a time to laugh. / A time to grieve and a time to **d**.
Isa 13:21 the ruins, and wild goats will come there to **d**.
22:13 But instead, you **d** and play; you slaughter
Jer 31: 4 again be happy and **d** merrily with tambourines.
31:13 The young women will **d** for joy, and the men—
La 5:14 the city gates; the young men no longer **d** and sing.
Mt 14: 6 Herodias' daughter performed a **d** that greatly
Mk 6:22 and performed a **d** that greatly pleased them all.

DANCED (3) [DANCE]

1Sa 18: 6 and **d** for joy with tambourines and cymbals.
2Sa 6:14 And David **d** before the LORD with all his might,
1Ki 18:26 Then they **d** wildly around the altar they had made.

DANCERS (1) [DANCE]

SS 6:13 she moves so gracefully between two lines of **d**?"

DANCES (3) [DANCE]

Jdg 21:21 When the women of Shiloh come out for their **d**,
1Sa 21:11 "Isn't he the one the people honor with **d**, singing,
29: 5 about whom the women of Israel sing in their **d**,

DANCING (11) [DANCE]

Ex 32:19 came near the camp, Moses saw the calf and the **d**.
Jdg 11:34 meet him, playing on a tambourine and **d** for joy.
1Sa 30:16 eating and drinking and **d** with joy because of the
2Sa 6:16 saw King David leaping and **d** before the LORD,
6:21 retorted to Michal, "I was **d** before the LORD,
1Ch 15:29 When she saw King David **d** and leaping for joy,
Ps 30:11 You have turned my mourning into joyful **d**.
149: 3 Praise his name with **d**, / accompanied by
150: 4 Praise him with the tambourine and **d**; / praise him
La 5:15 hearts has ended; our **d** has turned to mourning.
Lk 15:25 returned home, he heard music and **d** in the house,

DANGER (32) [DANGEROUS, DANGERS, ENDANGER]

1Ki 1:29 LORD lives, who has rescued me from every **d**,
Ne 6:11 someone in my position run away from **d**?
Job 19:29 you yourselves are in **d** of punishment for your
36:16 "God has led you away from **d**, giving you
Ps 27: 1 The LORD protects me from **d**— / so why should
28: 7 LORD is my strength, my shield from every **d**.
55:10 but the real **d** is wickedness within the city.
Pr 11: 8 God rescues the godly from **d**, but he lets the
14:16 The wise are cautious and avoid **d**; fools plunge
22: 3 A prudent person foresees the **d** ahead and takes
27:12 A prudent person foresees the **d** ahead and takes
Ecc 10: 9 chop wood, there is **d** with each stroke of your ax!
Isa 56:10 his shepherds—are blind to every **d**.
56:10 watchdogs that give no warning when **d** comes.
Jer 2:28 When **d** comes, let them save you if they can!
La 4:18 We couldn't go into the streets without **d** to our
Am 2:15 warriors on horses won't be able to outrun the **d**.
Hab 2: 9 putting your families beyond the reach of **d**.
Mt 5:22 you are in **d** of being brought before the court.
5:22 curse someone, you are in **d** of the fires of hell.
Lk 8:23 threatened to swamp them, and they were in real **d**.
Jn 11:10 Only at night is there **d** of stumbling because there
Ac 19:40 I am afraid we are in **d** of being charged with
27:10 loss of cargo, injuries, and **d** to our lives."
Ro 8:35 or are hungry or cold or in **d** or threatened with
2Co 1:10 And he did deliver us from mortal **d**. And we are
4:11 we live under constant **d** of death because we serve
11:26 I have faced **d** from flooded rivers and from
11:26 I have faced **d** from my own people, the Jews,
11:26 I have faced **d** in the cities, in the deserts, and on
11:26 And I have faced **d** from men who claim to be
Heb 12:25 how terrible our **d** if we reject the One who speaks

DANGEROUS (15) [DANGER]

Nu 35:20 or throws a **d** object and the person dies,
Pr 11:15 Guaranteeing a loan for a stranger is **d**; it is better
20:25 It is **d** to make a rash promise to God before
26: 9 A proverb in a fool's mouth is as **d** as a thornbush
28:15 A wicked ruler is as **d** to the poor as a lion or bear
29:25 Fearing people is a **d** trap, but to trust the LORD
Eze 14:15 "Or suppose I were to send an invasion of **d** wild
34:25 and drive away the **d** animals from the land.
Mt 8:28 so **d** that no one could go through that area.
16:23 away from me, Satan! You are a **d** trap to me.
26:55 Jesus said to the crowd, "Am I some **d** criminal,
Mk 14:48 Jesus asked them, "Am I some **d** criminal,
Lk 22:52 "Am I some **d** criminal," he asked, "that you
Ac 27: 9 The weather was becoming **d** for long voyages by
Jude 1:12 they are like **d** reefs that can shipwreck you.

DANGERS (2) [DANGER]

Ps 91: 5 the terrors of the night, / nor fear the **d** of the day,
Isa 35: 9 lurk along its course, and there will be no other **d**.

DANGLED (1) [DANGLING]

2Sa 18:14 and plunged them into Absalom's heart as he **d**

DANGLING (2) [DANGLED]

2Sa 18: 9 His mule kept going and left him **d** in the air.
18:10 and told Joab, "I saw Absalom **d** in a tree."

DANIEL (76) [BELTESHAZZAR, DANIEL'S]

Ezr 8: 2 Gershom. / From the family of Ithamar: **D**.
Ne 10: 6 **D**, Ginnethon, Baruch,
Eze 14:14 Even if Noah, **D**, and Job were there,
14:20 Even if Noah, **D**, and Job were living there,
28: 3 You regard yourself as wiser than **D** and think no
Da 1: 6 **D**, Hananiah, Mishael, and Azariah were four of
1: 7 **D** was called Belteshazzar. / Hananiah was called
1: 8 But **D** made up his mind not to defile himself by
1: 9 had given the chief official great respect for **D**.
1:11 **D** talked it over with the attendant who had been
1:11 been appointed by the chief official to look after **D**,
1:12 days on a diet of vegetables and water," **D** said.
1:15 **D** and his three friends looked healthier and better
1:17 And God gave **D** special ability in understanding
1:19 and none of them impressed him as much as **D**,
1:21 **D** remained there until the first year of King
2:13 men were sent to find and kill **D** and his friends.
2:14 **D** handled the situation with wisdom
2:16 **D** went at once to see the king and requested more
2:17 Then **D** went home and told his friends Hananiah,
2:19 That night the secret was revealed to **D** in a vision. Then **D** praised the God of heaven,
2:24 Then **D** went in to see Arioch, who had been
2:24 **D** said to him, "Don't kill the wise men. Take me
2:25 Then Arioch quickly took **D** to the king and said,
2:26 The king said to **D** (also known as Belteshazzar),
2:27 **D** replied, "There are no wise men, enchanters,
2:46 Nebuchadnezzar bowed to the ground before **D**
2:47 The king said to **D**, "Truly, your God is the God of
2:48 Then the king appointed **D** to a high position
2:48 He made **D** ruler over the whole province of
2:49 of Babylon, while **D** remained in the king's court.
4: 8 At last **D** came in before me, and I told him the
4:19 Upon hearing this, **D** (also known as Belteshazzar)
5:12 This man **D**, whom the king named Belteshazzar,
5:12 Call for **D**, and he will tell you what the writing
5:13 So **D** was brought in before the king. The king asked him, "Are you **D**, who was exiled
5:17 **D** answered the king, "Keep your gifts or give
5:29 **D** was dressed in purple robes,
6: 2 The king also chose **D** and two others as
6: 3 **D** soon proved himself more capable than all the
6: 4 some fault in the way **D** was handling his affairs,
6: 5 **D** will be in connection with the requirements of
6:10 But when **D** learned that the law had been signed,
6:13 Then they told the king, "That man **D**, one of the
6:14 the law, and he tried to find a way to save **D**.
6:14 looking for a way to get **D** out of this predicament.
6:16 So at last the king gave orders for **D** to be arrested
6:17 so that no one could rescue **D** from the lions.
6:20 When he got there, he called out in anguish, "**D**,
6:21 **D** answered, "Long live the king!
6:23 and ordered that **D** be lifted from the den.
6:24 to arrest the men who had maliciously accused **D**.
6:26 should tremble with fear before the God of **D**.
6:27 in the heavens and on earth. / He has rescued **D**
6:28 So **D** prospered during the reign of Darius
7: 1 **D** had a dream and saw visions as he lay in his bed.
7: 2 In my vision that night, I, **D**, saw a great storm
7:15 I, **D**, was troubled by all I had seen, and my visions
7:28 I, **D**, was terrified by my thoughts and my face was
8: 1 King Belshazzar's reign, I, **D**, saw another vision,
8:15 As I, **D**, was trying to understand the meaning of
8:27 Then I, **D**, was overcome and lay sick for several
9: 2 During the first year of his reign, I, **D**,
9:22 He explained to me, "**D**, I have come here to give
10: 1 Cyrus of Persia, **D** (also known as Belteshazzar)
10: 1 and **D** understood what the vision meant.
10: 2 When this vision came to me, I, **D**, had been in
10: 7 I, **D**, am the only one who saw this vision.
10:11 the man said to me, "O **D**, greatly loved of God,
10:12 Then he said, "Don't be afraid, **D**. Since the first
12: 4 But you, **D**, keep this prophecy a secret; seal up the
12: 5 **D**, looked and saw two others standing on opposite
12: 9 But he said, "Go now, **D**, for what I have said is
Mt 24:15 "The time will come when you will see what **D**

DANIEL'S (4) [DANIEL]

Da 1:10 But he was alarmed by **D** suggestion. "My lord the
1:14 So the attendant agreed to **D** suggestion and tested
2:49 At **D** request, the king appointed Shadrach,
6:11 The officials went together to **D** house and found

DANNAH (1)

Jos 15:49 **D**, Kiriath-sannah (that is, Debir),

DAPPLED-GRAY (2)

Zec 6: 3 third by white horses, and the fourth by **d** horses.
6: 6 and the chariot with **d** horses is going south."

DARDA (2)

1Ki 4:31 Ethan the Ezrahite and Heman, Calcol, and **D**—
1Ch 2: 6 Zerah were Zimri, Ethan, Heman, Calcol, and **D**—

DARE (24) [DARED, DARES, DARING]

Ge 49: 9 like a lioness—who will **d** to rouse him?
2Sa 3:11 Ishbosheth didn't **d** say another word because he
Est 7: 5 Xerxes demanded. "Who would **d** touch you?"
Job 15:22 They **d** not go out into the darkness for fear they
19:28 "How **d** you go on persecuting me, saying,
32: 6 I held back and did not **d** to tell you what I think.
41:10 the crocodile, who would **d** to stand up to me?
Isa 3:15 How **d** you grind my people into the dust like
19:11 Will they **d** tell Pharaoh about their long line of
50: 8 Who will **d** to oppose me now? Where are my
Jer 5: 6 their towns, tearing apart any who **d** to venture out.
30:21 for who would **d** to come unless invited?
La 3:21 Yet I still **d** to hope when I remember this:
Eze 20: 3 How **d** you come to ask for my help? As surely as
Am 3: 8 I **d** not refuse to proclaim his message!
Mic 1:11 The people of Zaanan **d** not come outside their
Mal 3:15 and those who **d** God to punish them go free of
Mk 11:32 But do we **d** say it was merely human?" For they
Ro 15:18 I **d** not boast of anything else. I have brought the
1Co 10:22 Do you **d** to rouse the Lord's jealousy as Israel
2Co 10:12 I wouldn't **d** say that I am as wonderful as these
11:21 But whatever they **d** to boast about—I'm talking
Eph 3:20 infinitely more than we would ever **d** to ask
Jude 1: 9 did not **d** accuse Satan of blasphemy, but simply

DARED (12) [DARE]

Ge 18:31 "Since I have **d** to speak to the Lord, let me
Ex 17:16 "They have **d** to raise their fist against the
Jos 10:21 After that, no one **d** to speak a word against Israel.

2Sa 18:28 who has handed over the rebels who **d** to stand
La 4:14 so defiled by blood that no one **d** to touch them.
Mt 22:46 after that, no one **d** to ask him any more questions.
Mk 12:34 after that, no one **d** to ask him any more questions.
Lk 18:13 and **d** not even lift his eyes to heaven as he prayed.
20:40 ended their questions; no one **d** to ask any more.
Jn 21:12 And no one **d** ask him if he really was the Lord
Ac 5:13 No one else **d** to join them, though everyone had
7:32 Moses shook with terror and **d** not look.

DARES (6) [DARE]

Nu 24: 9 lies down; / like a lioness, who **d** to arouse her?
Job 9:12 Who **d** to ask him, 'What are you doing?'
41:10 And since no one **d** to disturb the crocodile,
Jer 9:12 so completely that no one even **d** to travel through
Na 1:11 Who is this king of yours who **d** to plot evil against
Ro 8:33 Who **d** accuse us whom God has chosen for his

DARING (1) [DARE]

2Pe 2:10 **d** even to scoff at the glorious ones without

DARIUS (19) [DARIUS'S]

Ezr 4: 5 and lasted until King **D** of Persia took the throne.
4:24 the second year of the reign of King **D** of Persia.
5: 5 from building until a report was sent to **D**
5: 6 west of the Euphrates River sent to King **D**:
5: 7 "Greetings to King **D**.
6: 1 So King **D** issued orders that a search be made in
6: 6 So King **D** sent this message: / "To Tattenai,
6:12 destroys this Temple. I, **D**, have issued this decree.
6:13 complied at once with the command of King **D**.
6:14 by Cyrus, **D**, and Artaxerxes, the kings of Persia.
Ne 12:22 During the reign of **D** II of Persia, a list was
Da 5:31 And **D** the Mede took over the kingdom at the age
6: 1 **D** the Mede decided to divide the kingdom into
6: 6 went to the king and said, "Long live King **D**!
6: 9 So King **D** signed the law.
6:25 Then King **D** sent this message to the people of
6:28 So Daniel prospered during the reign of **D**
9: 1 It was the first year of the reign of **D** the Mede,
11: 1 and defense since the first year of the reign of **D**

DARIUS'S (7) [DARIUS]

Ezr 6:15 March 12, during the sixth year of King **D** reign.
Hag 1: 1 On August 29 of the second year of King **D** reign,
1:15 September 21 of the second year of King **D** reign.
2:10 On December 18 of the second year of King **D**
Zec 1: 1 In midautumn of the second year of King **D** reign,
1: 7 Then on February 15 of the second year of King **D**
7: 1 On December 7 of the fourth year of King **D** reign,

DARK (62) [DARK-COLORED, DARKEN, DARKENED, DARKER, DARKEST, DARKNESS]

Ge 15:17 As the sun went down and it became **d**, Abram saw
29:23 That night, when it was **d**, Laban took Leah to
Nu 4: 6 and the goatskin leather with a **d** blue cloth.
4: 9 "Next they must cover the lampstand with a **d** blue
4:11 and his sons must also spread a **d** blue cloth over
4:12 of the sanctuary must be wrapped in a **d** blue cloth,
2Sa 22:10 came down; / **d** storm clouds were beneath his feet.
2Ch 15: 5 During those **d** times, it was not safe to travel.
Job 3: 9 Let its morning stars remain **d**. Let it hope for
10:22 It is a land as **d** as midnight, a land of utter gloom
10:22 and the light is as **d** as midnight.' "
15:24 That **d** day terrifies them. They live in distress
18: 6 The light in their tent will grow **d**. The lamp
30:30 My skin has turned **d**, and my bones burn with
Ps 10: 8 They lurk in **d** alleys, / murdering the innocent
18: 9 came down; / **d** storm clouds were beneath his feet.
23: 4 through the **d** valley of death, / I will not be afraid,
35: 6 Make their path **d** and slippery, / with the angel of
139:15 as I was woven together in the **d** of the womb.
Pr 2:13 These people turn from right ways to walk down **d**
7: 9 as the day was fading, as the **d** of night set in.
Ecc 8: 8 There is no escaping that obligation, that **d** battle.
11: 8 But let them also remember that the **d** days will be
SS 1: 5 "I am **d** and beautiful, O women of Jerusalem,
tanned as the **d** tents of Kedar.
1: 6 fair city girls, just because my complexion is so **d**.
5:10 "My lover is **d** and dazzling, better than ten
Isa 5:20 and good is evil; that **d** is light and light is **d**;
8:22 there will be trouble and anguish and **d** despair.
29:15 who try to keep him in the **d** concerning what they
42: 7 You will release those who sit in **d** dungeons.
45:19 I do not whisper obscurities in some **d** corner
59:10 we fall down as though it were **d**.
Jer 13:16 you to stumble and fall on the **d** mountains.
23:12 "Therefore, their paths will be **d** and slippery.
23:12 They will be chased down **d** and treacherous trails,
25:10 and all your homes will stand silent and **d**.
La 2: 1 The Lord in his anger has cast a **d** shadow over
3: 6 He has buried me in a **d** place, like a person long
Eze 2: 6 Do not be dismayed by their **d** scowls.
8:12 of Israel are doing with their idols in **d** rooms?
30:18 of Egypt, it will be a **d** day for Tahpanhes, too.
30:18 A **d** cloud will cover Tahpanhes, and its daughters
32: 8 Even the brightest stars will become **d** above you.
34:12 the places to which they were scattered on that **d**
Joel 2:10 The sun and moon grow **d**, and the stars no longer
3:15 The sun and moon will grow **d**, and the stars will
Am 5:20 the day of the LORD will be a **d** and hopeless
Lk 11:36 If you are filled with light, with no **d** corners,
12: 3 Whatever you have said in the **d** will be heard in
Jn 3: 1 After **d** one evening, a Jewish religious leader
12:46 I have come as a light to shine in this **d** world,
20: 1 Early Sunday morning, while it was still **d**,
Ro 1:21 The result was that their minds became **d**
Php 2:15 innocent lives as children of God in a **d** world full
1Th 5: 4 But you aren't in the **d** about these things,
2Pe 1:19 for their words are like a light shining in a **d**
Rev 6:12 The sun became as **d** as black cloth, and the moon
8:12 and one-third of the stars, and they became **d**.
8:12 And one-third of the day was **d** and one-third of
18:23 Her nights will be **d**, without a single lamp.

DARK-COLORED (3) [DARK, COLORED]

Ge 30:32 are speckled or spotted, along with all the **d** sheep.
30:35 spotted with any white patches, and all the **d** sheep.
30:40 toward the streaked and **d** rams in Laban's flock.

DARKEN (3) [DARK]

Ps 34: 5 with joy; / no shadow of shame will **d** their faces.
Eze 32: 7 blot you out, I will veil the heavens and **d** the stars.
Am 8: 9 down at noon and **d** the earth while it is still day.

DARKENED (3) [DARK]

Mt 24:29 after those horrible days end, / the sun will be **d**,
Mk 13:24 after those horrible days end, / the sun will be **d**,
Rev 9: 2 and the sunlight and air were **d** by the smoke.

DARKER (1) [DARK]

Ge 49:12 His eyes are **d** than wine, / and his teeth are whiter

DARKEST (3) [DARK]

Job 28: 3 **d** regions of the earth as they search for ore.
Ps 88: 6 me down to the lowest pit, / into the **d** depths.
Zep 1:12 "I will search with lanterns in Jerusalem's **d**

DARKNESS (158) [DARK]

Ge 1: 2 earth was empty, a formless mass cloaked in **d**.
1: 4 was good. Then he separated the light from the **d**.
1: 5 God called the light "day" and the **d** "night."
1:18 and the night, and to separate the light from the **d**.
15:12 He saw a terrifying vision of **d** and horror.
Ex 10:21 and terrifying **d** will descend on the land of
10:22 and there was deep **d** over the entire land for three
14:20 But the cloud became **d** to the Egyptians, and they
20:21 Moses entered into the deep **d** where God was.
Dt 4:11 into the sky, shrouded in black clouds and deep **d**.
5:22 heart of the fire, surrounded by clouds and deep **d**.
5:23 But when you heard the voice from the **d**,
28:29 just like a blind person groping in the **d**,
Jos 24: 7 I put **d** between you and the Egyptians.
1Sa 2: 9 his godly ones, / but the wicked will perish in **d**.
2Sa 22:12 He shrouded himself in **d**, / veiling his approach
22:29 are my light; / yes, LORD, you light up my **d**.
1Ki 8:12 you have said that you would live in thick **d**.
2Ki 8:21 but he escaped at night under cover of **d**.
2Ch 6: 1 you have said that you would live in thick **d**.
21: 9 but he escaped at night under cover of **d**.
Ne 13:19 then on the gates of the city should be shut as **d** fell
Job 3: 4 Let that day be turned to **d**. Let it be lost even to
God on high, and let it be shrouded in **d**.
3: 5 let the **d** and utter gloom claim it for its own.
3: 5 a black cloud overshadow it, and let the **d** terrify it.
10:21 before I leave for the land of **d** and utter gloom.
11:17 the noonday. Any **d** will be as bright as morning.
12:22 "He floods the **d** with light; he brings light to the
12:25 They grope in the **d** without a light. He makes
15:22 They dare not go out into the **d** for fear they will
15:30 "They will not escape the **d**. The flame will burn
16:16 My eyes are red with weeping; **d** covers my eyes.
17:13 I might go to the grave and make my bed in **d**.
18:18 They will be thrust from light into **d**, driven from
19: 8 has blocked my way and plunged my path into **d**.
20:26 "His treasures will be lost in deepest **d**. A wildfire
22:11 That is why you cannot see in the **d**, and waves of
22:13 I am doing! How can he judge through the thick **d**?
23:17 **D** is all around me; thick, impenetrable **d** is
everywhere.
24:17 They ally themselves with the terrors of the **d**.
28: 3 They know how to put light into **d** and explore the
29: 3 way before me and I walked safely through the **d**.
30:26 evil came instead. I waited for the light, but **d** fell.
34:22 No **d** is thick enough to hide the wicked from his
38: 9 and as I clothed it with clouds and thick **d**?
38:19 the light come from, and where does the **d** go?
Ps 18:11 He shrouded himself in **d**, / veiling his approach
18:28 light to my life; / my God, you light up my **d**.
42: 9 Why must I wander in **d**, / oppressed by my
43: 2 Why must I wander around in **d**, / oppressed by my
44:19 the desert. / You have covered us with **d** and death.
74:20 for the land is full of **d** and violence!
82: 5 they are so ignorant! / And because they are in **d**,
88:12 Can the **d** speak of your miracles? / Can anyone in
88:18 my companions and loved ones; / only **d** remains.
91: 6 nor dread the plague that stalks in **d**,
97: 2 Clouds and **d** surround him. / Righteousness
104:20 You send the **d**, and it becomes night, / when all
105:28 The LORD blanketed Egypt in **d**, / for they had
105:39 and gave them a great fire to light the **d**.
107:10 Some sat in **d** and deepest gloom,
107:14 He led them from the **d** and deepest gloom;
112: 4 When **d** overtakes the godly, light will come
139:11 I could ask the **d** to hide me / and the light around
139:12 but even in **d** I cannot hide from you. / To you the
139:12 as bright as day. / **D** and light are both alike to you.
143: 3 He forces me to live in **d** like those in the grave.
Pr 4:19 But the way of the wicked is like complete **d**.
Ecc 2:13 value than foolishness, just as light is better than **d**.
6: 4 birth would have been meaningless and ended in **d**.
Isa 5:30 A cloud of **d** and sorrow will hover over Israel.
8:22 dark despair. They will be thrown out into the **d**."
9: 1 that time of **d** and despair will not go on forever.
9: 2 The people who walk in **d** will see a great light—
29:18 and blind people will see through the gloom and **d**.
42:16 I will make the **d** bright before them
45: 3 And I will give you treasures hidden in the **d**—
45: 7 I am the one who creates the light and makes the **d**.
47: 5 daughter of Babylonia, sit now in **d** and silence.
49: 9 Through you I am saying to the prisoners of **d**,
50: 3 I am the one who sends **d** out across the skies,
50:10 If you are walking in **d**, without a ray of light,
58:10 Then your light will shine out from the **d**,
58:10 and the **d** around you will be as bright as day.
59: 9 No wonder we are in **d** when we expected light.
60: 2 **D** as black as night will cover all the nations of the
Jer 2:31 Have I been to them a land of **d**? Why then do my
13:16 Acknowledge him before he brings **d** upon you,
13:16 you look for light, you will find only terrible **d**.
39: 4 city gate, so they fled when the **d** of night arrived.
La 3: 2 He has brought me into deep **d**, shutting out all
Eze 12: 7 and went out into the **d** with my pack on my
32: 8 Yes, I will bring **d** everywhere across your land.
Da 2:22 and knows what lies hidden in **d**,
Joel 2: 2 It is a day of **d** and gloom, a day of thick clouds
2:31 The sun will be turned into **d**, and the moon will
Am 4:13 He turns the light of dawn into **d** and treads the
5: 8 It is he who turns **d** into morning and day into
5:18 not bring light and prosperity, but **d** and disaster.
Jnh 4:11 has more than 120,000 people living in spiritual **d**,
Mic 3: 6 **D** will cover you, making it impossible for you to
7: 8 Though I sit in **d**, the LORD himself will be my
7: 9 The LORD will bring me out of my **d** into the
Na 1: 8 He pursues his foes into the **d** of night.
Zep 1:15 a day of **d** and gloom, of clouds, blackness,
Mt 4:16 the people who sat in **d** / have seen a great light.
6:23 evil eye shuts out the light and plunges you into **d**.
6:23 If the light you think you have is really **d**, how
deep that **d** will be!
8:12 will be cast into outer **d**, where there will be
10:27 What I tell you now in the **d**, shout abroad when
22:13 and foot and throw him out into the outer **d**,
25:30 Now throw this useless servant into outer **d**,
27:45 **d** fell across the whole land until three o'clock.
Mk 15:33 **d** fell across the whole land until three o'clock.
Lk 1:79 to give light to those who sit in **d** and in the
11:34 evil eye shuts out the light and plunges you into **d**.
11:35 that the light you think you have is not really **d**.
22:53 the time when the power of **d** reigns."
23:44 and **d** fell across the whole land until three o'clock.
Jn 1: 5 The light shines through the **d**, and the **d** can never
extinguish it.
3:19 but they loved the **d** more than the light, for their
3:20 hate the light because they want to sin in the **d**.
6:17 But as **d** fell and Jesus still hadn't come back,
8:12 follow me, you won't be stumbling through the **d**,
12:35 you can, so you will not stumble when the **d** falls.
12:35 If you walk in the **d**, you cannot see where you are
12:46 put their trust in me will no longer remain in the **d**.
Ac 2:20 The sun will be turned into **d**, / and the moon will
13:11 Instantly mist and **d** fell upon him, and he began
26:18 to open their eyes so they may turn from **d** to light,
27:33 As the **d** gave way to the early morning light,
Ro 2:19 and a beacon light for people who are lost in **d**
13:12 So don't live in **d**. Get rid of your evil deeds.
2Co 4: 6 For God, who said, "Let there be light in the **d**,"
6:14 with wickedness? How can light live with **d**?
Eph 4:18 Their closed minds are full of **d**; they are far away
5: 8 For though your hearts were once full of **d**,
5:11 Take no part in the worthless deeds of evil and **d**;
6:12 against those mighty powers of **d** who rule this
Col 1:13 us from the one who rules in the kingdom of **d**,
1Th 5: 5 and of the day; we don't belong to **d** and night.
Heb 12:18 to a place of flaming fire, **d**, gloom, and whirlwind,
1Pe 2: 9 for he called you out of the **d** into his wonderful
2Pe 2: 4 in gloomy caves and **d** until the judgment day.
2:17 delivering nothing. They are doomed to blackest **d**.
1Jn 1: 5 to you: God is light and there is no **d** in him at all.
1: 6 fellowship with God but go on living in spiritual **d**.
2: 8 because the **d** is disappearing and the true light is
2: 9 the light" but rejects another Christian is still in **d**.
2:11 reject other Christians are wandering in spiritual **d**
2:11 they are going, for the **d** has made them blind.
Jude 1: 6 God has kept them chained in prisons of **d**,
1:13 heading for everlasting gloom and **d**.
Rev 16:10 of the beast, and his kingdom was plunged into **d**.

DARKON (2)

Ezr 2:56 Jaalah, **D**, Giddel,
Ne 7:58 Jaalah, **D**, Giddel,

DARLING (3)

2Sa 13:11 "Come to bed with me, my **d** sister."
SS 5: 2 'Open to me, my **d**, my treasure, my lovely dove,'
Jer 31:20 "Is not Israel still my son, my **d** child?"

DART (1) [DARTED, DARTING, DARTS]

Job 41:26 can stop it, nor spear nor **d** nor pointed shaft.

DARTED (1) [DART]

Eze 1:14 And the living beings **d** to and fro like flashes of

DARTING (1) [DART]
Pr 26: 2 Like a fluttering sparrow or a **d** swallow, an unfair

DARTS (1) [DART]
Job 41: 7 Will its hide be hurt by **d**, or its head by a

DARTS [KJV] See also ARROWS, SPEARS, WEAPONS

DASH (5) [DASHED, DASHES, DASHING]
2Ki 8:12 their young men, **d** their children to the ground,
25: 4 They made a **d** across the fields, in the direction of
Ecc 9: 8 Wear fine clothes, with a **d** of cologne!
Isa 28: 2 they will burst upon it and **d** it to the ground.
Jer 52: 7 They made a **d** across the fields, in the direction of

DASHED (8) [DASH]
Dt 9:17 I raised the stone tablets and **d** them to the ground.
Job 6:20 but finding none, their hopes are **d**.
16:12 He took me by the neck and **d** me to pieces.
Isa 13:16 Their little children will be **d** to death right before
Hos 10:14 Even mothers and children were **d** to death there.
13:16 their little ones **d** to death against the ground,
Na 3:10 Her babies were **d** to death against the stones of
Zec 9: 5 and so will Ekron, for their hopes will be **d**.

DASHES (1) [DASH]
Ex 15: 6 right hand, O LORD, / **d** the enemy to pieces.

DASHING (2) [DASH]
2Ch 25:12 them off, **d** them to pieces on the rocks below.
Eze 23: 6 dressed in handsome blue, **d** about on their horses.

DATE (5) [DATES]
Ne 2: 6 So the king agreed, and I set a **d** for my departure.
Eze 24: 2 "Son of man, write down today's **d**, because on
Mt 18:23 **d** with servants who had borrowed money from
Ac 21:26 Then he publicly announced the **d** when their vows
Heb 8:13 It is now out of **d** and ready to be put aside.

DATES (4) [DATE]
2Sa 6:19 a loaf of bread, a cake of **d**, and a cake of raisins.
1Ch 16: 3 a loaf of bread, a cake of **d**, and a cake of raisins.
SS 7: 7 and your breasts are like its clusters of **d**.
Ac 1: 7 "The Father sets those **d**," he replied, "and they

DATHAN (10)
Nu 16: 1 conspired with **D** and Abiram, the sons of Eliab,
16:12 Then Moses summoned **D** and Abiram, the sons of
16:24 away from the tents of Korah, **D**, and Abiram."
16:25 and rushed over to the tents of **D** and Abiram,
16:27 back from the tents of Korah, **D**, and Abiram.
16:27 Then **D** and Abiram came out and stood at the
26: 9 Eliab was the father of Nemuel, **D**, and Abiram.
26: 9 This **D** and Abiram are the same community
Dt 11: 6 They weren't there to see what he did to **D**
Ps 106:17 of this, the earth opened up; / it swallowed **D**

DAUB [KJV] See WHITEWASHERS

DAUGHTER (180) [DAUGHTER'S, DAUGHTER-IN-LAW, DAUGHTERS, DAUGHTERS', DAUGHTERS-IN-LAW, GRANDDAUGHTER, GRANDDAUGHTERS]
DAUGHTER OF BABYLONIA (2) Isa 47:1,5
DAUGHTER OF JERUSALEM (4) 2Ki 19:21; Isa 37:22; La 2:13; Zep 3:14
DAUGHTER OF ZION (5) 2Ki 19:21; Isa 37:22; 52:2; La 2:13; Zep 3:14
PHARAOH'S DAUGHTER (6) 1Ki 7:8; 9:24; 11:1; 2Ch 8:11; Ac 7:21; Heb 11:24

Ge 11:29 married Milcah, the **d** of their brother Haran.
19:31 One day the older **d** said to her sister, "There isn't
19:33 and the older **d** went in and slept with her father.
19:34 The next morning the older **d** said to her younger
19:35 and the younger **d** went in and slept with him.
19:37 When the older **d** gave birth to a son, she named
19:38 When the younger **d** gave birth to a son, she named
24:23 "Whose **d** are you?" he asked. "Would your
24:47 When I asked her whose **d** she was, she told me,
25:20 the **d** of Bethuel the Aramean from Paddan-aram
26:34 woman named Judith, the **d** of Beeri the Hittite.
26:34 also married Basemath, the **d** of Elon the Hittite.
28: 9 was the sister of Nebaioth and the **d** of Ishmael,
29: 6 Look, here comes his **d** Rachel with the sheep."
29:10 the **d** of his mother's brother, and
29:18 give me Rachel, your younger **d**, as my wife."
29:26 "It's not our custom to marry off a younger **d**
30:21 Later she gave birth to a **d** and named her Dinah.
34: 1 One day Dinah, Leah's **d**, went to visit some of the
34: 5 Word soon reached Jacob that his **d** had been
34: 8 "My son Shechem is truly in love with your **d**,
36: 2 Adah, the **d** of Elon the Hittite; and Oholibamah,
36: 2 the **d** of Anah and granddaughter of Zibeon the
36: 3 who was the **d** of Ishmael and the sister of
36:14 the **d** of Anah and granddaughter of Zibeon.
36:18 from Esau's wife Oholibamah, the **d** of Anah.
36:25 of Anah was Dishon, and Oholibamah was his **d**.
36:39 the **d** of Matred and granddaughter of Mezahab.
38: 2 the **d** of Shua, and he married her.
41:45 the **d** of Potiphera, priest of Heliopolis.
41:50 and his wife, Asenath, the **d** of Potiphera,
46:20 was Asenath, **d** of Potiphera, priest of Heliopolis.
Ex 6:23 the **d** of Amminadab and sister of Nahshon,
21: 7 "When a man sells his **d** as a slave, she will not be
21: 9 her as a slave girl, but he must treat her as his **d**.
Lev 12: 5 If a woman gives birth to a **d**, she will be
12: 6 of purification is completed for either a son or a **d**,
12: 7 to be followed after the birth of a son or a **d**.
18: 9 whether she is your father's **d** or your mother's **d**,
18:10 whether your son's **d** or your daughter's **d**;
18:11 Do not have sexual intercourse with the **d** of any of
18:17 and her **d** or marry both a woman and her
18:17 whether her son's **d** or her daughter's **d**.
19:29 "Do not defile your **d** by making her a prostitute,
20:17 the **d** of either his father or his mother, it is a
21: 2 close relative—mother or father, son or **d**, brother
21: 9 If a priest's **d** becomes a prostitute, defiling her
22:12 If a priest's **d** marries someone outside the priestly
24:11 She was the **d** of Dibri of the tribe of Dan.
Nu 25:15 she was the **d** of Zur, the leader of a Midianite
25:18 because of Cozbi, the **d** of a Midianite leader,
26:46 Asher also had a **d** named Serah.
30:16 a father and a young **d** who still lives at home.
Dt 13: 6 "Suppose your brother, son, **d**, beloved wife,
18:10 never sacrifice your son or **d** as a burnt offering.
22:16 tell them, 'I gave my **d** to this man to be his wife,
27:22 whether she is the **d** of his father or his mother.'
28:56 to the husband she loves and to her own son or **d**.
Jos 15:16 "I will give my **d** Acsah in marriage to the one
Jdg 1:12 "I will give my **d** Acsah in marriage to the one
11:34 When Jephthah returned home to Mizpah, his **d**—
11:35 "My **d**!" he cried out. "My heart is breaking!
11:40 days each year to lament the fate of Jephthah's **d**.
19:24 Here, take my virgin **d** and this man's concubine.
Ru 2: 2 And Naomi said, "All right, my **d**, go ahead."
2: 8 Boaz went over and said to Ruth, "Listen, my **d**.
3: 1 One day Naomi said to Ruth, "My **d**, it's time that
3:10 "The LORD bless you, my **d**!" Boaz exclaimed.
3:11 Now don't worry about a thing, my **d**. I will do
3:16 Naomi asked, "What happened, my **d**?"
3:18 Then Naomi said to her, "Just be patient, my **d**,
1Sa 14:50 Saul's wife was Ahinoam, the **d** of Ahimaaz.
18:17 "I am ready to give you my older **d**, Merab,
18:20 Saul's **d** Michal had fallen in love with David,
18:23 family afford the bride price for the **d** of a king?"
25:44 Saul, meanwhile, had given his **d** Michal,
30:19 small or great, son or **d**, or anything else that had
2Sa 3: 3 was Maacah, the **d** of Talmai, king of Geshur.
3:13 back my wife Michal, Saul's **d**, when you come."
6:16 Michal, the **d** of Saul, looked down from her
6:23 So Michal, the **d** of Saul, remained childless
11: 3 the **d** of Eliam and the wife of Uriah the Hittite."
12: 3 his cup. He cuddled it in his arms like a baby **d**.
14:27 He had three sons and one **d**. His daughter's name
17:25 His mother, Abigail **d** of Nahash, was the sister of
21: 8 whose mother was Rizpah **d** of Aiah.
21: 8 He also gave them the five sons of Saul's **d** Merab,
1Ki 7: 8 also built similar living quarters for Pharaoh's **d**,
9:16 He gave the city to his **d** as a wedding gift when
9:24 After Solomon moved his wife, Pharaoh's **d**,
11: 1 Besides Pharaoh's **d**, he married women from
15: 2 His mother was Maacah, the **d** of Absalom.
15:10 His grandmother was Maacah, the **d** of Absalom.
16:31 the **d** of King Ethbaal of the Sidonians,
22:42 His mother was Azubah, the **d** of Shilhi.
2Ki 9:34 this cursed woman, for she is the **d** of a king."
11: 2 the **d** of King Jehoram, took Ahaziah's infant son,
14: 9 'Give your **d** in marriage to my son.' But just
15:33 His mother was Jerusha, the **d** of Zadok.
18: 2 His mother was Abijah, the **d** of Zechariah.
19:21 'The virgin **d** of Zion / despises you and laughs at
19:21 The **d** of Jerusalem / scoffs and shakes her head as
21:19 was Meshullemeth, the **d** of Haruz from Jotbah.
22: 1 was Jedidah, the **d** of Adaiah from Bozkath.
23:10 a son or **d** in the fire as an offering to Molech.
23:31 was Hamutal, the **d** of Jeremiah from Libnah.
23:36 was Zebidah, the **d** of Pedaiah from Rumah.
24: 8 was Nehushta, the **d** of Elnathan from Jerusalem.
24:18 was Hamutal, the **d** of Jeremiah from Libnah.
1Ch 1:50 the **d** of Matred and granddaughter of Me-zahab.
2:21 he married Gilead's sister, the **d** of Makir.
2:49 and Gibea). Caleb also had a **d** named Acsah.
3: 2 was Maacah, the **d** of Talmai, king of Geshur.
3: 5 Bathsheba, the **d** of Ammiel, was the mother of
3: 9 his concubines. David also had a **d** named Tamar.
3:19 and Hananiah. He also had a **d** named Shelomith.
4: 3 were Jezreel, Ishma, Idbash, Hazzelelponi (his **d**),
7:24 Ephraim had a **d** named Sheerah. She built the
15:29 Michal, the **d** of Saul, looked down from her
2Ch 8:11 Solomon moved his wife, Pharaoh's **d**,
11:18 the **d** of David's son Jerimoth and of Abihail, the **d** of Eliab.
11:20 another cousin, Maacah, the **d** of Absalom.
13: 2 His mother was Maacah, a **d** of Uriel from Gibeah.
18: 1 and he arranged for his son to marry the **d** of King
20:31 His mother was Azubah, the **d** of Shilhi.
22:11 the **d** of King Jehoram, took Ahaziah's infant son,
25:18 'Give your **d** in marriage to my son.' But just
27: 1 His mother was Jerusha, the **d** of Zadok.
29: 1 His mother was Abijah, the **d** of Zechariah.
Ne 6:18 because his son Jehohanan was married to the **d** of
13:28 priest had married a **d** of Sanballat the Horonite,
Est 2: 7 her into his family and raised her as his own **d**.
9:29 Then Queen Esther, the **d** of Abihail, along with
Job 42:14 He named his first **d** Jemimah, the second Keziah,
Ps 45:10 Listen to me, O royal **d**; take to heart what I say.
SS 6: 9 my perfect one, the only beloved **d** of her mother!
Isa 23:12 "Never again will you rejoice, O **d** of Sidon.
37:22 'The virgin **d** of Zion / despises you and laughs at
37:22 The **d** of Jerusalem / scoffs and shakes her head as
47: 1 O **d** of Babylonia, never again will you be the
47: 5 "O **d** of Babylonia, sit now in darkness
52: 2 slave bands from your neck, O captive **d** of Zion.
Jer 6: 2 O Jerusalem, you are my beautiful and delicate **d**—
14:17 I cannot stop weeping, for my virgin **d**—
31:22 How long will you wander, my wayward **d**?
46:11 up to Gilead to get ointment, O virgin **d** of Egypt!
49: 4 You rebellious **d**, you trusted in your wealth
52: 1 was Hamutal, the **d** of Jeremiah from Libnah.
La 2:13 O **d** of Jerusalem, to what can I compare your
2:13 O virgin **d** of Zion, how can I comfort you?
Eze 16:44 up proverbs will say of you, 'Like mother, like **d**.'
Da 11: 6 The **d** of the king of the south will be given in
11:17 He will give him a **d** in marriage in order to
Hos 1: 3 the **d** of Diblaim, and she became pregnant
1: 6 became pregnant again and gave birth to a **d**.
1: 6 said to Hosea, "Name your **d** Lo-ruhamah—
Mic 7: 6 son despises his father. The **d** defies her mother.
Zep 3:14 Sing, O **d** of Zion; shout aloud, O Israel! Be glad
3:14 and rejoice with all your heart, O **d** of Jerusalem!
Mt 9:18 "My **d** has just died," he said, "but you can bring
9:22 Jesus turned around and said to her, "**D**,
10:35 man against his father, and a **d** against her mother,
10:37 or if you love your son or **d** more than me, you are
14: 6 Herodias' **d** performed a dance that greatly
15:22 For my **d** has a demon in her, and it is severely
15:28 is granted." And her **d** was instantly healed.
Mk 5:23 pleading with him to heal his little **d**. "She is about
5:34 And he said to her, "**D**, your faith has made you
5:35 Jairus' home with the message, "Your **d** is dead.
6:22 Then his **d**, also named Herodias, came in
7:29 you have answered so well, I have healed your **d**."
Lk 2:36 She was the **d** of Phanuel, of the tribe of Asher,
8:48 "**D**," he said to her, "your faith has made you
12:53 a division between father and son, mother and **d**,
Ac 7:21 Pharaoh's **d** found him and raised him as her own
Heb 11:24 refused to be treated as the son of Pharaoh's **d**.

DAUGHTER'S (4) [DAUGHTER]
Lev 18:10 whether your son's daughter or your **d** daughter;
18:17 whether her son's daughter or her **d** daughter.
Dt 22:17 But here is the proof of my **d** virginity.' Then they
2Sa 14:27 His **d** name was Tamar, and she was very

DAUGHTER-IN-LAW (14) [DAUGHTER]
Ge 11:31 Terah took his son Abram, his **d** Sarai, and his
38:11 Then Judah told Tamar, his **d**, not to marry again
38:16 with him, not realizing that she was his own **d**.
38:24 word reached Judah that Tamar, his **d**,
Lev 18:15 Do not have sexual intercourse with your **d**;
20:12 If a man has intercourse with his **d**, both must be
Ru 1:22 accompanied by her **d** Ruth, the young Moabite
2:20 "May the LORD bless him!" Naomi told her **d**.
4:15 For he is the son of your **d** who loves you so much
1Sa 4:19 Eli's **d**, the wife of Phinehas, was pregnant
1Ch 2: 4 had twin sons through Tamar, his widowed **d**.
Mic 7: 6 defies her mother. The **d** defies her mother-in-law.
Mt 10:35 her mother, and a **d** against her mother-in-law.
Lk 12:53 mother and daughter, mother-in-law and **d**."

DAUGHTERS (161) [DAUGHTER]
DAUGHTERS OF JERUSALEM (1) Lk 23:28
SONS AND DAUGHTERS (61) Ge 5:4,7,10,13,16,19,22,26,30; 11:11,13,15,17,19,21,23,25; 46:7; Ex 3:22; 10:9; 20:10; 32:2; Lev 10:14; 26:29; Nu 18:19; Dt 5:14; 7:3; 12:12,31; 28:32,41,53; 32:19; 2Sa 5:13; 2Ki 17:17; 1Ch 14:3; 2Ch 24:3; 29:9; 31:18; Job 1:13,18; Ps 106:38; Isa 43:6; 56:5; Jer 3:24; 7:31; 14:16; 19:9; 32:35; 48:46; La 1:18; Eze 16:20; 23:4,47; 24:21,25; Joel 2:28; 3:8; Am 7:17; Ac 2:17; 2Co 6:18

Ge 5: 4 another 800 years, and he had other sons and **d**.
5: 7 another 807 years, and he had other sons and **d**.
5:10 another 815 years, and he had other sons and **d**.
5:13 another 840 years, and he had other sons and **d**.
5:16 lived 830 years, and he had other sons and **d**.
5:19 another 800 years, and he had other sons and **d**.
5:22 fellowship with God, and he had other sons and **d**.
5:26 another 782 years, and he had other sons and **d**.
5:30 lived 595 years, and he had other sons and **d**.
11:11 lived another 500 years and had other sons and **d**.
11:13 lived another 403 years and had other sons and **d**.
11:15 lived another 403 years and had other sons and **d**.
11:17 lived another 430 years and had other sons and **d**.
11:19 lived another 209 years and had other sons and **d**.
11:21 lived another 207 years and had other sons and **d**.
11:23 lived another 200 years and had other sons and **d**.
11:25 lived another 119 years and had other sons and **d**.
19: 8 Look—I have two virgin **d**. Do with them as you
19:12 of this place—sons-in-law, sons, **d**, or anyone else.
19:15 "Take your wife and your two **d** who are here.
19:16 his hand and the hands of his wife and two **d**
19:30 to live in a cave in the mountains with his two **d**.
19:36 So both of Lot's **d** became pregnant by their father.
28: 2 and marry one of your uncle Laban's **d**.
28: 9 Ishmael's family and married one of Ishmael's **d**,
29:16 Now Laban had two **d**: Leah, who was the oldest,
31:26 "Are my **d** prisoners, the plunder of war, that you
31:28 Why didn't you let me kiss my **d**

31:31 said to myself, 'He'll take his **d** from me by force.'
31:41 fourteen of them earning your two **d**, and six years
31:43 Laban replied to Jacob, "These women are my **d**,
31:43 But what can I do now to my own **d**
31:50 I won't know about it if you are harsh to my **d**
31:55 and he kissed his **d** and grandchildren and blessed
34: 9 We invite you to let your **d** marry our sons, and we will give our **d** as wives for your young
46: 7 sons and **d**, grandsons and granddaughters—
Ex 2: 5 one of Pharaoh's **d** came down to bathe in the
2:16 **d** who came regularly to this well to draw water
2:21 In time, Reuel gave Moses one of his **d**, Zipporah,
3:22 With this clothing, you will dress your sons and **d**.
6:25 Eleazar son of Aaron married one of the **d** of
10: 9 will take our sons and **d** and our flocks and herds.
20:10 your sons and **d**, your male and female servants,
21: 4 and they had sons or **d**, then the man will be free in
32: 2 and sons and **d** to take off their gold earrings,
34:16 And you will accept their **d**, who worship other
Lev 10:14 and **d** as your regular share of the peace offerings
26:29 You will eat the flesh of your own sons and **d**.
Nu 18:19 They are for you and your sons and **d**, to be eaten
21:29 and his **d** as captives of Sihon, the Amorite king.
27: 1 One day a petition was presented by the **d** of
27: 7 "The **d** of Zelophehad are right. You must give
27: 8 and has no sons, then give his inheritance to his **d**.
27: 9 And if he has no **d**, turn his inheritance over to his
36: 2 the inheritance of our brother Zelophehad to his **d**.
36: 6 commands concerning the **d** of Zelophehad:
36: 8 The **d** throughout the tribes of Israel who are in
36:10 The **d** of Zelophehad did as the LORD
Dt 5:14 your sons and **d**, your male and female servants,
7: 3 don't let your **d** and sons marry their sons and **d**.
12:12 You must celebrate there with your sons and **d**
12:31 burned their sons and **d** as sacrifices to their gods.
28:32 watch as your sons and **d** are taken away as slaves.
28:41 You will have sons and **d**, but you will not keep
28:53 that you will eat the flesh of your own sons and **d**,
32:19 He was provoked to anger by his own sons and **d**.
Jos 7:24 of gold, his sons, **d**, cattle, donkeys, sheep, tent,
17: 3 and Gilead, had no sons. Instead, he had five **d**.
Jdg 3: 6 Israelite sons married their **d**, and Israelite **d** were given in marriage to their
12: 9 and he had thirty sons and thirty **d**. He married his **d** to men outside his clan
21: 1 **d** in marriage to a man from the tribe of Benjamin.
21: 7 the LORD not to give them our **d** in marriage?"
21:18 But we cannot give them our own **d** in marriage
21:22 Let them have your **d**, for we didn't find enough
21:22 you did not give your **d** in marriage to them.' "
Ru 1:12 No, my **d**, return to your parents' homes, for I am
1:13 to marry someone else? No, of course not, my **d**!
1Sa 2:21 the LORD gave Hannah three sons and two **d**.
8:13 The king will take your **d** from you and force them
14:49 He also had two **d**: Merab, who was older,
17:25 The king will give him one of his **d** for a wife,
2Sa 5:13 and concubines, and he had many sons and **d**.
13:18 the custom in those days for the king's virgin **d**.
19: 5 your sons, your **d**, and your wives and concubines.
1Ki 3: 1 the king of Egypt, and married one of his **d**.
4:11 (He was married to Taphath, one of Solomon's **d**.)
4:15 married to Basemath, another of Solomon's **d**.)
2Ki 8:18 as King Ahab, for he had married one of Ahab's **d**.
17:17 even sacrificed their own sons and **d** in the fire.
1Ch 2:34 Sheshan had no sons, though he did have **d**.
2:35 Sheshan gave one of his **d** to be the wife of Jarha,
4:27 Shimei had sixteen sons and six **d**, but none of his
7:15 his descendants was Zelophehad, who had only **d**.
14: 3 wives in Jerusalem, and they had many sons and **d**.
23:22 Eleazar died with no sons, only **d**. His **d** married their cousins, the sons of Kish.
25: 5 had honored him with fourteen sons and three **d**.
2Ch 11:21 they gave birth to twenty-eight sons and sixty **d**.
13:21 and had twenty-two sons and sixteen **d**.
21: 6 as King Ahab, for he had married one of Ahab's **d**.
24: 3 chose two wives for Joash, and he had sons and **d**.
29: 9 and our sons and **d** and wives are in captivity.
31:18 the little babies, the wives, and the sons and **d**.
Ezr 2:61 (This Barzillai had married one of the **d** of
9:12 You told us not to let our **d** marry their sons,
9:12 and not to let our sons marry their **d**, and not to
Ne 3:12 of Hallohesh and his **d** repaired the next section.
5: 5 We have already sold some of our **d**, and we are
7:63 (This Barzillai had married one of the **d** of
10:30 "We promise not to let our **d** marry the pagan
10:30 of the land, nor to let our sons marry their **d**.
Job 1: 2 He had seven sons and three **d**.
1:13 and **d** were dining at the oldest brother's house,
1:18 and **d** were feasting in their oldest brother's home.
42:13 also gave Job seven more sons and three more **d**.
42:15 were no other women as lovely as the **d** of Job.
Ps 45: 9 Kings' **d** are among your concubines. / At your
106:37 sacrificed their sons / and their **d** to the demons.
106:38 innocent blood, / the blood of their sons and **d**.
144:12 May our **d** be like graceful pillars,
Isa 23: 4 "Now I am childless; I have no sons or **d**."
43: 6 and **d** back to Israel from the distant corners of the
49:22 they will bring your **d** on their shoulders.
56: 5 they would have received by having sons and **d**.
60: 4 distant lands; your little **d** will be carried home.
Jer 3:24 their flocks and herds, their sons and **d**—
7:31 they sacrifice their little sons and **d** in the fire.
9:20 Teach your **d** to wail; teach one another how to
14:16 Husbands, wives, sons, and **d**—all will be gone.
19: 9 will have to eat their own sons and **d** and friends.
32:35 and there they sacrifice their sons and **d** to Molech.
35: 8 since then, nor have our wives, our sons, or our **d**.
41:10 Ishmael made captives of the king's **d**
43: 6 were men, women, and children, the king's **d**,
48:46 Your sons and **d** have been taken away as captives.
La 1:18 and **d** have been taken captive to distant lands.
Eze 16:20 "Then you took your sons and **d**—the children you
16:46 was Samaria, who lived with her **d** in the north.
16:46 was Sodom, who lived with her **d** in the south.
16:48 Sodom and her **d** were never as wicked as you and your **d**.
16:61 your sisters, Samaria and Sodom, to be your **d**,
23: 2 once there were two sisters who were **d** of the
23: 4 I married them, and they bore me sons and **d**.
23:47 will butcher their sons and **d** and burn their homes.
24:21 and **d** in Judea will be slaughtered by the sword.
24:25 I will also take away their sons and **d**.
30:18 and its **d** will be led away as captives.
Hos 4:13 "That is why your **d** turn to prostitution, and your
Joel 2:28 Your sons and **d** will prophesy. Your old men will
3: 8 I will sell your sons and **d** to the people of Judah,
Am 7:17 in this city, and your sons and **d** will be killed.
Lk 23:28 Jesus turned and said to them, "**D** of Jerusalem,
Ac 2:17 Your sons and **d** will prophesy, / your young men
21: 9 He had four unmarried **d** who had the gift of
2Co 6:18 be your Father, / and you will be my sons and **d**,
1Pe 3: 6 You are her **d** when you do what is right without

DAUGHTERS-IN-LAW (5) [DAUGHTER]

Ru 1: 6 and her **d** got ready to leave Moab to return to her
1: 7 With her two **d** she set out from the place where
1: 8 But on the way, Naomi said to her two **d**,
Eze 22:11 who defile their **d** or who rape their own sisters.
Hos 4:13 turn to prostitution, and your **d** commit adultery.

DAUGHTERS' (2) [DAUGHTER]

Ge 19:14 So Lot rushed out to tell his **d** fiancés, "Quick,
Nu 26:33 but his **d** names were Mahlah, Noah, Hoglah,

DAVID (1002) [DAVID'S]

CITY OF DAVID (43) 2Sa 5:7,9; 6:10,12,16; 1Ki 2:10; 3:1; 8:1; 9:24; 14:31; 15:8,24; 22:50; 2Ki 8:24; 9:28; 12:21; 14:20; 15:7,38; 16:20; 1Ch 11:5,7; 13:13; 15:1,29; 2Ch 5:2; 8:11; 12:16; 14:1; 16:14; 21:1,20; 24:16,25; 25:28; 27:9; 32:5,30; 33:14; Ne 3:15; 12:37; Isa 29:1; Lk 2:11

CITY OF HIS FATHER, DAVID (3) 1Ki 11:27,43; 2Ch 9:31

FAMILY OF DAVID (6) 1Ki 12:20; 14:8; Ezr 8:3; Isa 7:13; Zec 12:10,12

FATHER, DAVID (29) 1Ki 2:12,24; 3:3,6,7,14; 5:3; 6:12; 7:51; 8:15,17; 9:5; 11:4,6,12,27,33,43; 1Ch 29:23; 2Ch 1:8,9; 2:3,7; 6:4,7; 7:17,18; 8:14; 9:31

HOUSE OF DAVID (2) Ne 12:37; Isa 22:22

KING DAVID (60) 2Sa 3:31,38; 6:12,16; 7:18; 8:11; 13:21; 15:13; 17:17,21; 19:11,16; 20:21; 21:2; 1Ki 1:1,6,9,13,31,32,43,47; 2:44; 2Ki 11:10; 1Ch 4:31; 7:2; 15:29; 17:16; 18:11; 24:31; 26:26,32; 29:1,9,24; 2Ch 1:1; 3:1; 5:1; 7:6; 23:9; 29:25; 35:4; Ezr 3:10; 8:20; Am 6:5; Zec 12:8; Mt 1:1,6,17; 12:3; Mk 2:25; Lk 1:27; 2:4; 6:3; Jn 7:42; Ac 1:16; 2:25; 4:25; 7:45; Ro 4:6

PSALM OF DAVID (68) Ps 3:T; 4:T; 5:T; 6:T; 7:T; 8:T; 9:T; 11:T; 12:T; 13:T; 14:T; 15:T; 16:T; 18:T; 19:T; 20:T; 21:T; 22:T; 23:T; 24:T; 25:T; 26:T; 27:T; 28:T; 29:T; 30:T; 31:T; 32:T; 34:T; 35:T; 36:T; 37:T; 38:T; 39:T; 40:T; 41:T; 51:T; 52:T; 55:T; 56:T; 57:T; 58:T; 59:T; 60:T; 61:T; 62:T; 63:T; 64:T; 65:T; 68:T; 69:T; 70:T; 101:T; 103:T; 108:T; 109:T; 110:T; 122:T; 124:T; 131:T; 133:T; 138:T; 139:T; 140:T; 141:T; 142:T; 143:T; 144:T

SERVANT DAVID (31) 2Sa 7:5,8,26; 1Ki 8:24,25,26,66; 11:13,32,34,38; 14:8; 2Ki 19:34; 20:6; 1Ch 17:4,7,24; 2Ch 6:15,16,17,42; Ps 78:70; 89:20; 132:10; 144:10; Isa 37:35; Eze 34:23,24; 37:24,25; Lk 1:69

SON OF DAVID (16) Mt 1:20; 9:27; 12:23; 15:22; 20:30,31; 21:9,15; 22:42; Mk 10:47,48; 12:35; Lk 3:31; 18:38,39; 20:41

Ru 4:17 the father of Jesse and the grandfather of **D**.
4:22 was the father of Jesse. / Jesse was the father of **D**.
1Sa 16:13 So as **D** stood there among his brothers,
16:19 Jesse to say, "Send me your son **D**, the shepherd."
16:20 Jesse responded by sending **D** to Saul, along with a
16:21 **D** went to Saul and served him. Saul liked **D** very much, and **D** became one of Saul's armor bearers.
16:22 "Please let **D** join my staff, for I am very pleased
16:23 from God troubled Saul, **D** would play the harp.
17:12 Now **D** was the son of a man named Jesse,
17:14 **D** was the youngest of Jesse's sons. Since David's
17:15 But **D** went back and forth between working for
17:17 One day Jesse said to **D**, "Take this half-bushel of
17:20 So **D** left the sheep with another shepherd and set
17:22 **D** left his things with the keeper of supplies
17:26 **D** talked to some others standing there to verify the
17:27 And **D** received the same reply as before:
17:28 Eliab, heard **D** talking to the men, he was angry.
17:29 "What have I done now?" **D** replied. "I was only
17:32 "Don't worry about a thing," **D** told Saul. "I'll go
17:34 But **D** persisted. "I have been taking care of my
17:38 Then Saul gave **D** his own armor—a bronze helmet
17:39 **D** put it on, strapped the sword over it, and took a
17:41 Goliath walked out toward **D** with his shield bearer
17:43 "Am I a dog," he roared at **D**, "that you come
17:43 And he cursed **D** by the names of his gods.
17:45 **D** shouted in reply, "You come to me with sword,
17:48 closer to attack, **D** quickly ran out to meet him.
17:50 So **D** triumphed over the Philistine giant with only
17:51 **D** used it to kill the giant and cut off his head.
17:54 (**D** took Goliath's head to Jerusalem, but he stored
17:55 As Saul watched **D** go out to fight Goliath,
17:57 After **D** had killed Goliath, Abner brought him to
17:58 And **D** replied, "His name is Jesse, and we live in
18: 1 After **D** had finished talking with Saul, he met
18: 2 From that day on Saul kept **D** with him at the
18: 5 Whatever Saul asked **D** to do, **D** did it successfully.
18: 6 was returning home after **D** had killed Goliath.
18: 7 killed his thousands, / and **D** his ten thousands!"
18: 8 "They credit **D** with ten thousands and me with
18: 9 So from that time on Saul kept a jealous eye on **D**.
18:10 **D** began to play the harp, as he did whenever this
18:11 suddenly hurled it at **D**, intending to pin him to the
18:11 But **D** jumped aside and escaped. This happened
18:12 the LORD had left him and was now with **D**.
18:13 but **D** faithfully led his troops into battle.
18:14 **D** continued to succeed in everything he did,
18:16 But all Israel and Judah loved **D** because he was
18:17 One day Saul said to **D**, "I am ready to give you
18:18 **D** exclaimed. "My father's family is nothing!"
18:20 Saul's daughter Michal had fallen in love with **D**,
18:21 But to **D** he said, "I have a way for you to become
18:22 Then Saul told his men to say confidentially to **D**,
18:23 When Saul's men said these things to **D**,
18:25 "Tell **D** that all I want for the bride price is one
18:25 But what Saul had in mind was that **D** would be
18:26 **D** was delighted to accept the offer. So before the
18:27 the king. So Saul gave Michal to **D** to be his wife.
18:28 king realized how much the LORD was with **D**
18:30 **D** was more successful against them than all the
19: 1 his servants and his son Jonathan to assassinate **D**.
19: 1 because of his close friendship with **D**,
19: 4 morning Jonathan spoke with his father about **D**,
19: 4 "Please don't sin against **D**," Jonathan pleaded.
19: 5 Why should you murder an innocent man like **D**?
19: 6 surely as the LORD lives, **D** will not be killed."
19: 7 Afterward Jonathan called **D** and told him what
19: 7 Then he took **D** to see Saul, and everything was as
19: 8 and **D** led his troops against the Philistines.
19: 9 upon him again. As **D** played his harp for the king,
19:10 Saul hurled his spear at **D** in an attempt to kill him.
19:10 But **D** dodged out of the way and escaped into the
19:11 They were told to kill **D** when he came out the next
19:14 When the troops came to arrest **D**, she told them he
19:16 But when they came to carry **D** out,
19:18 So **D** got away and went to Ramah to see Samuel,
19:18 Then Samuel took **D** with him to live at Naioth.
19:19 When the report reached Saul that **D** was at Naioth
19:22 "Where are Samuel and **D**?" he demanded.
20: 1 **D** now fled from Naioth in Ramah and found
20: 3 Then **D** took an oath before Jonathan and said,
20: 5 **D** replied, "Tomorrow we celebrate the new moon
20:10 Then **D** asked, "How will I know whether or not
20:12 Then Jonathan told **D**, "I promise by the LORD,
20:16 So Jonathan made a covenant with **D**, saying,
20:17 And Jonathan made **D** reaffirm his vow of
20:17 for Jonathan loved **D** as much as he loved himself.
20:24 So **D** hid himself in the field, and when the new
20:26 "Something must have made **D** ceremonially
20:28 "**D** earnestly asked me if he could go to
20:30 "Do you think I don't know that you want **D** to be
20:33 that his father was really determined to kill **D**.
20:34 by his father's shameful behavior toward **D**.
20:39 what Jonathan meant; only Jonathan and **D** knew.
20:41 **D** came out from where he had been hiding near
20:41 Then **D** bowed to Jonathan with his face to the
20:41 each other and said good-bye, especially **D**.
20:42 At last Jonathan said to **D**, "Go in peace, for we
20:42 Then **D** left, and Jonathan returned to the city.
21: 1 **D** went to the city of Nob to see Ahimelech the
21: 2 king has sent me on a private matter," **D** said.
21: 5 "Don't worry," **D** replied. "I never allow my men
21: 8 **D** asked Ahimelech, "Do you have a spear
21: 9 is nothing like it!" **D** replied. "Give it to me!"
21:10 So **D** escaped from Saul and went to King Achish
21:11 "Isn't this **D**, the king of the land?" they asked.
21:11 killed his thousands, and **D** his ten thousands'?"
21:12 **D** heard these comments and was afraid of what
22: 1 So **D** left Gath and escaped to the cave of Adullam.
22: 2 until **D** was the leader of about four hundred men.
22: 3 Later **D** went to Mizpeh in Moab, where he asked
22: 4 and David's parents stayed in Moab while **D** was
22: 5 One day the prophet Gad told **D**,
22: 5 land of Judah." So **D** went to the forest of Hereth.
22: 7 "Has **D** promised you fields and vineyards?
22: 8 My own son—encouraging **D** to try and kill me!"
22: 9 he said, "I saw **D** talking to Ahimelech the priest.
22:10 the LORD to find out what **D** should do.
22:10 Then he gave **D** food and the sword of Goliath the
22:13 "Why have you and **D** conspired against me?"
22:14 among all your servants who is as faithful as **D**,
22:17 for they are allies and conspirators with **D**!
22:20 of the sons of Ahimelech, escaped and fled to **D**.
22:21 When he told **D** that Saul had killed the priests of
22:22 **D** exclaimed, "I knew it! When I saw Doeg there
23: 1 One day news came to **D** that the Philistines were
23: 2 **D** asked the LORD, "Should I go and attack
23: 4 So **D** asked the LORD again, and again the
23: 5 So **D** and his men went to Keilah.
23: 6 Abiathar the priest went to Keilah with **D**,
23: 6 taking the ephod with him to get answers for **D**
23: 7 Saul soon learned that **D** was at Keilah. "Good!"
23: 8 army to march to Keilah and attack **D** and his men.
23: 9 But **D** learned of Saul's plan and told Abiathar the
23:10 And **D** prayed, "O LORD, God of Israel, I have
23:12 Again **D** asked, "Will these men of Keilah really

23:13 So **D** and his men—about six hundred of them
23:13 Word soon reached Saul that **D** had escaped,
23:14 **D** now stayed in the strongholds of the wilderness
23:15 **D** received the news that Saul was on the way to
23:16 Jonathan went to find **D** and encouraged him to
23:18 Jonathan returned home, while **D** stayed at Horesh.
23:19 went to Saul in Gibeah and betrayed **D** to him. "We know where **D** is hiding," they said.
23:24 **D** and his men had moved into the wilderness of
23:25 When **D** heard that Saul and his men were
23:26 and **D** were now on opposite sides of a mountain.
23:26 Just as Saul and his men began to close in on **D**
23:28 the place where **D** was camped has been called the
23:29 **D** then went to live in the strongholds of En-gedi.
24:1 he was told that **D** had gone into the wilderness of
24:2 and went to search for **D** and his men near the
24:3 **D** and his men were hiding in that very cave!
24:4 to do with as you wish.' " Then **D** crept forward
24:7 So **D** sharply rebuked his men and did not let them
24:8 **D** came out and shouted after him, "My lord the
24:8 Saul looked around, **D** bowed low before him.
24:16 Saul called back, "Is that really you, my son **D**?"
24:17 And he said to **D**, "You are a better man than I
24:22 So **D** promised, and Saul went home. But **D** and his men went back to their stronghold.
25:1 Then **D** moved down to the wilderness of Maon.
25:4 When **D** heard that Nabal was shearing his sheep,
25:10 "Who is this fellow **D**?" Nabal sneered.
25:13 Four hundred men started off with **D**, and two
25:14 "**D** sent men from the wilderness to talk to our
25:20 she saw **D** and his men coming toward her.
25:21 **D** had just been saying, "A lot of good it did to
25:23 When Abigail saw **D**, she quickly got off her
25:32 **D** replied to Abigail, "Praise the LORD, the God
25:35 Then **D** accepted her gifts and told her,
25:36 about her meeting with **D** until the next morning.
25:39 When **D** heard that Nabal was dead, he said,
25:39 Then **D** wasted no time in sending messengers to
25:40 "**D** has sent us to ask if you will marry him."
25:43 **D** also married Ahinoam from Jezreel,
26:1 "**D** is hiding on the hill of Hakilah,
26:3 of Hakilah, near Jeshimon, where **D** was hiding. But **D** knew of Saul's arrival,
26:5 **D** slipped over to Saul's camp one night to look
26:6 **D** asked Ahimelech the Hittite and Abishai son of
26:7 So **D** and Abishai went right into Saul's camp
26:8 Abishai whispered to **D**. "Let me thrust that spear
26:9 "No!" **D** said. "Don't kill him. For who can
26:12 So **D** took the spear and jug of water that were near
26:13 **D** climbed the hill opposite the camp until he was
26:15 you're a great man, aren't you?" **D** taunted.
26:17 and called out, "Is that you, my son **D**?"
26:17 And **D** replied, "Yes, my lord the king.
26:22 "Here is your spear, O king," **D** replied. "Let one
26:25 Saul said to **D**, "Blessings on you, my son **D**.
26:25 Then **D** went away, and Saul returned home.
27:1 But **D** kept thinking to himself, "Someday Saul is
27:2 So **D** took his six hundred men and their families
27:3 **D** brought his two wives along with him—
27:4 Word soon reached Saul that **D** had fled to Gath,
27:5 One day **D** said to Achish, "If it is all right with
27:8 **D** and his men spent their time raiding the
27:9 **D** didn't leave one person alive in the villages he
27:10 And **D** would reply, "Against the south of Judah,
27:12 Achish believed **D** and thought to himself,
28:1 King Achish told **D**, "You and your men will be
28:2 "Very well!" **D** agreed. "Now you will see for
28:2 Then Achish told **D**, "I will make you my personal
28:17 kingdom from you and given it to your rival, **D**.
29:2 **D** and his men marched at the rear with King
29:3 And Achish told them, "This is **D**, the man who
29:5 Isn't this the same **D** about whom the women of
29:5 killed his thousands, and **D** his ten thousands'?"
29:6 So Achish finally summoned **D** and his men.
29:8 **D** demanded. "Why can't I fight the enemies of
29:11 So **D** headed back into the land of the Philistines,
30:1 when **D** and his men arrived home at their town of
30:3 When **D** and his men saw the ruins and realized
30:6 **D** was now in serious trouble because his men
30:6 But **D** found strength in the LORD his God.
30:8 Then **D** asked the LORD, "Should I chase them?
30:9 So **D** and his six hundred men set out, and they
30:10 so **D** continued the pursuit with his four hundred
30:11 an Egyptian man in a field and brought him to **D**.
30:13 **D** asked him. "I am an Egyptian—the slave of an
30:15 **D** asked. The young man replied, "If you swear by
30:16 When **D** and his men arrived, the Amalekites were
30:17 **D** and his men rushed in among them
30:18 **D** got back everything the Amalekites had taken,
30:19 that had been taken. **D** brought everything back.
30:20 "These all belong to **D** as his reward!" they said.
30:21 too tired to go with them, **D** greeted them joyfully.
30:23 But **D** said, "No, my brothers! Don't be selfish
30:25 From then on **D** made this a law for all of Israel,
30:26 **D** sent part of the plunder to the leaders of Judah,
30:27 sent to the leaders of the following towns where **D**
2Sa 1:1 **D** returned from his victory over the Amalekites
1:2 He fell to the ground before **D** in deep respect.
1:3 "Where have you come from?" **D** asked.
1:4 "What happened?" **D** demanded. "Tell me how
1:5 that Saul and Jonathan are dead?" **D** demanded.
1:10 "So I killed him," the Amalekite told **D**, "for I
1:11 **D** and his men tore their clothes in sorrow when
1:13 Then **D** said to the young man who had brought
1:14 to kill the LORD's anointed one?" **D** asked.
1:15 Then **D** said to one of his men, "Kill him!"
1:16 "You die self-condemned," **D** said, "for you
1:17 Then **D** composed a funeral song for Saul
2:1 After this, **D** asked the LORD, "Should I move
2:1 Then **D** asked, "Which town should I go to?"
2:2 widow of Nabal from Carmel. So **D** and his wives
2:4 Then Judah's leaders came to **D** and crowned him
2:4 When **D** heard that the men of Jabesh-gilead had
2:10 Meanwhile, the tribe of Judah remained loyal to **D**.
2:11 **D** made Hebron his capital, and he ruled as king of
2:17 men of Israel had been defeated by the forces of **D**.
3:1 been loyal to Saul and those who were loyal to **D**.
3:1 As time passed **D** became stronger and stronger,
3:2 These were the sons who were born to **D** in
3:5 These sons were all born to **D** in Hebron.
3:8 for you and your father by not betraying you to **D**,
3:9 May God deal harshly with me if I don't help **D**
3:10 go ahead and give **D** the rest of Saul's kingdom.
3:12 Then Abner sent messengers to **D**, saying,
3:13 "All right," **D** replied, "but I will not negotiate
3:14 **D** then sent this message to Ishbosheth, Saul's son:
3:17 told them, "you have wanted to make **D** your king.
3:18 'I have chosen **D** to save my people from the
3:19 Then he went to Hebron to tell **D** that all the
3:20 twenty men, **D** entertained them with a great feast.
3:21 Then Abner said to **D**, "Let me go and call all the
3:21 heart desires." So **D** sent Abner safely on his way.
3:26 Joab then left **D** and sent messengers to catch up
3:26 him back with them. But **D** knew nothing about it.
3:28 When **D** heard about it, he declared, "I vow by the
3:31 Then **D** said to Joab and all those who were with
3:31 And King **D** himself walked behind the procession
3:35 **D** had refused to eat anything the day of the
3:35 But **D** had made a vow, saying, "May God kill me
3:37 and Israel knew that **D** was not responsible for
3:38 Then King **D** said to the people, "Do you not
4:8 at Hebron and presented Ishbosheth's head to **D**.
4:9 But **D** said to Recab and Baanah, "As surely as the
4:12 So **D** ordered his young men to kill them, and they
5:1 Then all the tribes of Israel went to **D** at Hebron
5:3 **D** made a covenant with the leaders of Israel
5:4 **D** was thirty years old when he began to reign,
5:6 **D** then led his troops to Jerusalem to fight against
5:7 But **D** captured the fortress of Zion, now called the City of **D**.
5:8 message from the defenders of the city reached **D**,
5:9 So **D** made the fortress his home, and he called it the City of **D**.
5:10 And **D** became more and more powerful,
5:11 Then King Hiram of Tyre sent messengers to **D**,
5:12 And **D** realized that the LORD had made him
5:13 **D** married more wives and concubines, and he had
5:17 When the Philistines heard that **D** had been
5:17 But **D** was told they were coming and went into
5:19 So **D** asked the LORD, "Should I go out to fight
5:20 So **D** went to Baal-perazim and defeated the
5:20 "The LORD has done it!" **D** exclaimed.
5:20 So **D** named that place Baal-perazim (which means
5:21 idols there, so **D** and his troops confiscated them.
5:23 And once again **D** asked the LORD what to do.
5:25 So **D** did what the LORD commanded, and he
6:1 Then **D** mobilized thirty thousand special troops.
6:5 **D** and all the people of Israel were celebrating
6:8 **D** was angry because the LORD's anger had
6:9 **D** was now afraid of the LORD and asked,
6:10 So **D** decided not to move the Ark of the LORD into the City of **D**.
6:12 Then King **D** was told, "The LORD has blessed
6:12 **D** went there and brought the Ark to the City of **D**
6:13 they stopped and waited so **D** could sacrifice an ox
6:14 And **D** danced before the LORD with all his
6:15 So **D** and all Israel brought up the Ark of the
6:16 as the Ark of the LORD entered the City of **D**,
6:16 When she saw King **D** leaping and dancing before
6:17 inside the special tent that **D** had prepared for it.
6:17 And **D** sacrificed burnt offerings and peace
6:18 **D** blessed the people in the name of the LORD
6:20 When **D** returned home to bless his family,
6:21 **D** retorted to Michal, "I was dancing before the
7:2 **D** summoned Nathan the prophet. "Look!" **D** said.
7:5 "Go and tell my servant **D**, 'This is what the
7:8 "Now go and say to my servant **D**, 'This is what
7:17 So Nathan went back to **D** and told him everything
7:18 Then King **D** went in and sat before the LORD
7:26 And may the dynasty of your servant **D** be
8:1 **D** subdued and humbled the Philistines by
8:2 **D** also conquered the land of Moab. He made the
8:3 **D** also destroyed the forces of Hadadezer son of
8:4 **D** captured seventeen hundred charioteers
8:5 **D** killed twenty-two thousand of them.
8:6 So the LORD gave **D** victory wherever he went.
8:7 **D** brought the gold shields of Hadadezer's officers
8:9 When King Toi of Hamath heard that **D** had
8:10 he sent his son Joram to congratulate **D** on his
8:10 Joram presented **D** with many gifts of silver,
8:11 King **D** dedicated all these gifts to the LORD,
8:13 So **D** became very famous. After his return he
8:14 the LORD made **D** victorious wherever he went.
8:15 **D** reigned over all Israel and was fair to everyone.
9:1 One day **D** began wondering if anyone in Saul's
9:5 So **D** sent for him and brought him from Makir's
9:6 When he came to **D**, he bowed low in great fear
9:7 But **D** said, "Don't be afraid! I've asked you to
9:11 that time on, Mephibosheth ate regularly with **D**,
10:2 **D** said, "I am going to show complete loyalty to
10:2 So **D** sent ambassadors to express sympathy to
10:3 **D** has sent them to spy out the city so that they can
10:4 at the buttocks, and sent them back to **D** in shame.
10:5 When **D** heard what had happened, he sent
10:6 realized how seriously they had angered **D**,
10:7 When **D** heard about this, he sent Joab
10:17 When **D** heard what was happening, he mobilized
10:17 there in battle formation and then attacked **D**.
11:1 **D** sent Joab and the Israelite army to destroy the
11:1 city of Rabbah. But **D** stayed behind in Jerusalem.
11:2 Late one afternoon **D** got out of bed after taking a
11:4 Then **D** sent for her; and when she came to the
11:5 she was pregnant, she sent a message to inform **D**.
11:6 So **D** sent word to Joab: "Send me Uriah the
11:7 **D** asked him how Joab and the army were getting
11:8 **D** even sent a gift to Uriah after he had left the
11:10 When **D** heard what Uriah had done, he summoned
11:12 "Well, stay here tonight," **D** told him,
11:13 Then **D** invited him to dinner and got him drunk.
11:14 So the next morning **D** wrote a letter to Joab
11:18 Then Joab sent a battle report to **D**.
11:22 went to Jerusalem and gave a complete report to **D**.
11:25 "Well, tell Joab not to be discouraged," **D** said.
11:27 **D** sent for her and brought her to the palace,
11:27 But the LORD was very displeased with what **D**
12:1 So the LORD sent Nathan the prophet to tell **D**
12:5 **D** was furious. "As surely as the LORD lives,"
12:7 Then Nathan said to **D**, "You are that man!
12:13 Then **D** confessed to Nathan, "I have sinned
12:16 **D** begged God to spare the child. He went without
12:19 But when **D** saw them whispering, he realized
12:20 Then **D** got up from the ground, washed himself,
12:22 **D** replied, "I fasted and wept while the child was
12:24 Then **D** comforted Bathsheba, his wife, and slept
12:27 Joab sent messengers to tell **D**, "I have fought
12:29 So **D** led the rest of his army to Rabbah
12:30 **D** removed the crown from the king's head,
12:30 **D** took a vast amount of plunder from the city.
12:31 Then **D** and his army returned to Jerusalem.
13:7 So **D** agreed and sent Tamar to Amnon's house to
13:21 When King **D** heard what had happened, he was
13:30 the way back to Jerusalem, this report reached **D**:
13:37 And **D** mourned many days for his son Amnon.
13:39 And **D**, now reconciled to Amnon's death,
14:33 Then at last **D** summoned his estranged son,
14:33 and bowed low before the king, and **D** kissed him.
15:13 soon arrived in Jerusalem to tell King **D**,
15:14 or it will be too late!" **D** urged his men. "Hurry!
15:18 hundred Gittites who had come with **D** from Gath,
15:22 **D** replied, "All right, come with us." So Ittai
15:25 **D** instructed Zadok to take the Ark of God back
15:25 "If the LORD sees fit," **D** said, "he will bring
15:30 **D** walked up the road that led to the Mount of
15:31 When someone told **D** that his adviser Ahithophel
15:31 **D** prayed, "O LORD, let Ahithophel give
15:32 **D** found Hushai the Arkite waiting for him.
15:33 But **D** told him, "If you go with me, you will only
16:1 **D** was just past the top of the hill when Ziba,
16:5 As **D** and his party passed Bahurim, a man came
16:7 you murderer, you scoundrel!" he shouted at **D**.
16:11 Then **D** said to Abishai and the other officers,
16:13 So **D** and his men continued on, and Shimei kept
16:13 cursing as he went and throwing stones at **D**
16:17 "Is this the way you treat your friend **D**?"
16:23 followed Ahithophel's advice, just as **D** had done.
17:1 twelve thousand men to start out after **D** tonight.
17:12 When we find **D**, we can descend on him like the
17:13 And if **D** has escaped into some city, you will have
17:16 "Find **D** and urge him not to stay at the shallows
17:17 them the message they were to take to King **D**.
17:18 But a boy saw them leaving En-rogel to go to **D**,
17:21 crawled out of the well and hurried on to King **D**.
17:22 So **D** and all the people with him went across the
17:24 **D** soon arrived at Mahanaim. By now,
17:25 replacing Joab, who had been commander under **D**.
17:27 When **D** arrived at Mahanaim, he was warmly
17:29 and cheese for **D** and those who were with him.
18:1 **D** now appointed generals and captains to lead his
18:24 While **D** was sitting at the city gate, the watchman
18:25 He shouted the news down to **D**, and the king
19:10 Let's ask **D** to come back and be our king again."
19:11 Then King **D** sent Zadok and Abiathar, the priests,
19:13 And **D** told them to tell Amasa, "Since you are my
19:16 across with the men of Judah to welcome King **D**.
19:22 **D** exclaimed. "This is not a day for execution
19:23 Then, turning to Shimei, **D** vowed, "Your life will
19:29 "All right," **D** replied. "My decision is that you
19:39 After **D** had blessed and embraced him,
20:1 and shouted, "We have nothing to do with **D**.
20:2 So the men of Israel deserted **D** and followed
20:6 Then **D** said to Abishai, "That troublemaker Sheba
20:11 "If you are for Joab and **D**, come and follow
20:21 of Ephraim, who has revolted against King **D**.
21:1 for three years, so **D** asked the LORD about it.
21:2 So King **D** summoned the Gibeonites. They were
21:3 **D** asked them, "What can I do for you to make
21:4 **D** asked. "Just tell me and I will do it for you."
21:7 **D** spared Jonathan's son Mephibosheth, who was
21:7 because of the oath **D** and Jonathan had sworn
21:11 When **D** learned what Rizpah, Saul's concubine,
21:13 So **D** brought the bones of Saul and Jonathan,
21:15 And when **D** and his men were in the thick of battle, **D** became weak and exhausted.
21:16 He had cornered **D** and was about to kill him.
21:22 but they were killed by **D** and his warriors.
22:1 **D** sang this song to the LORD after the LORD
22:51 to **D** and all his descendants forever."
23:1 These are the last words of **D**: / "**D**, the son of Jesse, speaks— / **D**, the man to whom God gave
23:1 **D**, the man anointed by the God of Jacob, / **D**, the sweet psalmist of Israel.

23: 9 and **D** stood together against the Philistines when
23: 13 when **D** was at the cave of Adullam,
23: 14 **D** was staying in the stronghold at the time, and a
23: 15 **D** remarked longingly to his men, "Oh, how I
23: 16 water from the well, and brought it back to **D**.
23: 17 So **D** did not drink it. This is an example of the
23: 23 And **D** made him commander of his bodyguard.
24: 1 and he caused **D** to harm them by taking a census.
24: 12 "Go and say to **D**, 'This is what the LORD says:
24: 13 So Gad came to **D** and asked him, "Will you
24: 14 "This is a desperate situation!" **D** replied to Gad.
24: 17 When **D** saw the angel, he said to the LORD,
24: 18 That day Gad came to **D** and said to him, "Go
24: 19 So **D** went to do what the LORD had commanded
24: 21 And **D** replied, "I have come to buy your
24: 22 and use it as you wish," Araunah said to **D**.
24: 24 So **D** paid him fifty pieces of silver for the
24: 25 **D** built an altar there to the LORD and offered
1Ki 1: 1 Now King **D** was very old, and no matter how
1: 6 Now his father, King **D**, had never disciplined him
1: 8 But among those who remained loyal to **D**
1: 9 invited all his brothers—the other sons of King **D**
1: 11 and that our lord **D** doesn't even know about it?
1: 13 Go at once to King **D** and say to him, 'My lord,
1: 28 "Call Bathsheba," **D** said. So she came back in
1: 31 "May my lord King **D** live forever!"
1: 32 Then King **D** ordered, "Call Zadok the priest,
1: 43 "Our lord King **D** has just declared Solomon king!
1: 47 All the royal officials went to King **D**
2: 10 Then **D** died and was buried in the City of **D**.
2: 12 succeeded him as king, replacing his father, **D**,
2: 24 and placed me on the throne of my father, **D**;
2: 33 and may the LORD grant peace to **D** and his
2: 44 all the wicked things you did to my father, King **D**.
3: 1 He brought her to live in the City of **D** until he
3: 3 **D**, except that Solomon, too, offered sacrifices
3: 6 **D**, because he was honest and true and faithful to
3: 7 you have made me king instead of my father, **D**,
3: 14 as your father, **D**, did, I will give you a long life."
5: 1 Hiram of Tyre had always been a loyal friend of **D**,
5: 3 "You know that my father, **D**, was not able to
5: 7 "Praise the LORD for giving **D** a wise son to be
6: 12 through you the promise I made to your father, **D**.
7: 51 brought all the gifts his father, **D**, had dedicated—
8: 1 covenant from its location in the City of **D**,
8: 15 who has kept the promise he made to my father, **D**.
8: 16 But now I have chosen **D** to be king over my
8: 17 Then Solomon said, "My father, **D**, wanted to
8: 24 You have kept your promise to your servant **D**,
8: 25 carry out your further promise to your servant **D**,
8: 26 fulfill this promise to your servant **D**, my father.
8: 66 the LORD had been good to his servant **D**
9: 4 with integrity and godliness, as **D** your father did,
9: 5 For I made this promise to your father, **D**:
9: 24 from the City of **D** to the new palace he had built
11: 4 in the LORD his God, as his father, **D**, had done.
11: 6 the LORD completely, as his father, **D**, had done.
11: 12 But for the sake of your father, **D**, I will not do this
11: 13 for the sake of my servant **D** and for the sake of
11: 15 Years before, **D** had gone to Edom with Joab,
11: 21 When the news reached Hadad in Egypt that **D**
11: 24 After **D** conquered Hadadezer, Rezon and his men
11: 27 and repairing the walls of the city of his father, **D**.
11: 32 leave him one tribe for the sake of my servant **D**
11: 33 my laws and regulations as his father, **D**, did.
11: 34 For the sake of my servant **D**, the one whom I
11: 36 so that the descendants of **D** my servant will
11: 38 obey my laws and commands, as my servant **D** did,
11: 38 an enduring dynasty for you as I did for **D**,
11: 39 But I will punish the descendants of **D** because of
11: 43 he was buried in the city of his father, **D**.
12: 16 they shouted, "Down with **D** and his dynasty!
12: 16 Israel! Look out for your own house, O **D**!"
12: 19 to be ruled by a descendant of **D** to this day.
12: 20 tribe of Judah remained loyal to the family of **D**.
12: 26 the kingdom will return to the dynasty of **D**.
13: 2 named Josiah will be born into the dynasty of **D**.
14: 8 I ripped the kingdom away from the family of **D**
14: 8 But you have not been like my servant **D**,
14: 31 was buried among his ancestors in the City of **D**.
15: 3 his God, as the heart of his ancestor **D** had been.
15: 5 For **D** had done what was pleasing in the LORD's
15: 8 When Abijam died, he was buried in the City of **D**.
15: 11 in the LORD's sight, as his ancestor **D** had done.
15: 24 he was buried with his ancestors in the City of **D**.
22: 50 he was buried with his ancestors in the City of **D**.
2Ki 8: 19 for he had made a covenant with **D** and promised
8: 24 he was buried with his ancestors in the City of **D**.
9: 28 they buried him with his ancestors in the City of **D**.
11: 10 and shields that had once belonged to King **D**
12: 21 was buried with his ancestors in the City of **D**.
14: 3 in the LORD's sight, but not like his ancestor **D**.
14: 20 he was buried with his ancestors in the City of **D**.
15: 7 he was buried near his ancestors in the City of **D**.
15: 38 he was buried with his ancestors in the City of **D**.
16: 2 the LORD his God, as his ancestor **D** had done.
16: 20 he was buried with his ancestors in the City of **D**.
17: 21 LORD tore Israel away from the kingdom of **D**,
18: 3 LORD's sight, just as his ancestor **D** had done.
19: 34 my own honor and for the sake of my servant **D**,
20: 5 the LORD, the God of your ancestor **D**, says:
20: 6 my honor and for the sake of my servant **D**.' "
21: 7 the very place where the LORD had told **D**
22: 2 and followed the example of his ancestor **D**.
1Ch 2: 15 his sixth was Ozem, and his seventh was **D**.
3: 1 These were the sons who were born to **D** in
3: 4 These six sons were born to **D** in Hebron, where he
3: 4 Then **D** moved the capital to Jerusalem, where he
3: 5 The sons born to **D** in Jerusalem included Shimea,
3: 6 **D** also had nine other sons: Ibhar, Elishua, Elpelet,
3: 9 These were the sons of **D**, not including the sons of
3: 9 **D** also had a daughter named Tamar.
4: 31 were under their control until the time of King **D**.
6: 31 **D** assigned the following men to lead the music at
7: 2 At the time of King **D**, the total number of men
9: 22 **D** and Samuel the seer had appointed their
10: 14 and turned his kingdom over to **D** son of Jesse.
11: 1 Then all Israel went to **D** at Hebron and told him,
11: 3 So there at Hebron **D** made a covenant with the
11: 4 Then **D** and all Israel went to Jerusalem (or Jebus,
11: 5 The people of Jebus said to **D**, "You will never get
11: 5 But **D** captured the fortress of Zion, now called the City of **D**.
11: 6 **D** had said to his troops, "Whoever leads the
11: 7 **D** made the fortress his home, and that is why it is called the City of **D**.
11: 9 And **D** became more and more powerful,
11: 10 all Israel, they determined to make **D** their king,
11: 13 He was with **D** in the battle against the Philistines
11: 14 and **D** held their ground in the middle of the field
11: 15 Once when **D** was at the rock near the cave of
11: 16 **D** was staying in the stronghold at the time, and a
11: 17 **D** remarked longingly to his men, "Oh, how I
11: 18 water from the well, and brought it back to **D**.
11: 18 But **D** refused to drink it. Instead, he poured it out
11: 19 So **D** did not drink it. This is an example of the
11: 25 And **D** made him commander of his bodyguard.
12: 1 The following men joined **D** at Ziklag while he
12: 1 among the warriors who fought beside **D** in battle.
12: 8 **D** while he was at the stronghold in the wilderness.
12: 16 and Judah came to **D** at the stronghold.
12: 17 **D** went out to meet them and said, "If you have
12: 18 among the Thirty, and he said, / "We are yours, **D**!
12: 18 So **D** let them join him, and he made them officers
12: 19 and joined **D** when he went with the Philistines to
12: 19 the Philistine leaders refused to let **D** and his men
12: 19 "It will cost us our lives if **D** switches loyalties to
12: 20 who defected to **D** as he was returning to Ziklag:
12: 21 They helped **D** chase down bands of raiders,
12: 22 Day after day more men joined **D** until he had a
12: 23 of armed warriors who joined **D** at Hebron.
12: 23 They were all eager to see **D** become king instead
12: 31 for the express purpose of helping **D** become king.
12: 33 and prepared for battle and completely loyal to **D**.
12: 38 the single purpose of making **D** the king of Israel.
12: 38 all Israel agreed that **D** should be their king.
12: 39 They feasted and drank with **D** for three days,
13: 1 **D** consulted with all his officials,
13: 5 So **D** summoned all the people of Israel, from one
13: 6 Then **D** and all Israel went to Baalah of Judah (also
13: 8 **D** and all Israel were celebrating before God with
13: 11 **D** was angry because the LORD's anger had
13: 12 **D** was now afraid of God and asked, "How can I
13: 13 **D** decided not to move the Ark into the City of **D**.
14: 1 Now King Hiram of Tyre sent messengers to **D**,
14: 2 And **D** realized that the LORD had made him
14: 3 Then **D** married more wives in Jerusalem, and they
14: 8 When the Philistines heard that **D** had been
14: 8 But **D** was told they were coming, so he and his
14: 10 So **D** asked God, "Should I go out to fight the
14: 11 So **D** and his troops went to Baal-perazim
14: 11 Philistines there. "God has done it!" **D** exclaimed.
14: 12 their idols there, so **D** gave orders to burn them up.
14: 14 And once again **D** asked God what to do. "Do not
14: 16 So **D** did what God commanded, and he struck
14: 17 and the LORD caused all the nations to fear **D**.
15: 1 **D** now built several buildings for himself in the City of **D**.
15: 3 Then **D** summoned all the Israelites to Jerusalem to
15: 11 Then **D** summoned the priests, Zadok
15: 16 **D** also ordered the Levite leaders to appoint a choir
15: 25 Then **D** and the leaders of Israel and the generals
15: 27 **D** was dressed in a robe of fine linen, as were the
15: 27 song leader. **D** was also wearing a priestly tunic.
15: 29 of the LORD's covenant entered the City of **D**,
15: 29 When she saw King **D** dancing and leaping for joy,
16: 1 of God into the special tent **D** had prepared for it,
16: 2 **D** blessed the people in the name of the LORD.
16: 4 **D** appointed the following Levites to lead the
16: 7 That day **D** gave to Asaph and his fellow Levites
16: 37 **D** arranged for Asaph and his fellow Levites to
16: 39 **D** stationed Zadok the priest and his fellow priests
16: 41 **D** also appointed Heman, Jeduthun, and the others
16: 43 and **D** returned home to bless his family.
17: 1 Now when **D** was settled in his palace, he said to
17: 4 "Go and tell my servant **D**, 'This is what the
17: 7 "Now go and say to my servant **D**, 'This is what
17: 15 So Nathan went back to **D** and told him everything
17: 16 Then King **D** went in and sat before the LORD
17: 24 And may the dynasty of your servant **D** be
18: 1 **D** subdued and humbled the Philistines by
18: 2 **D** also conquered the land of Moab,
18: 3 Then **D** destroyed the forces of King Hadadezer of
18: 4 **D** captured one thousand chariots, seven thousand
18: 5 **D** killed twenty-two thousand of them.
18: 6 So the LORD gave **D** victory wherever he went.
18: 7 **D** brought the gold shields of Hadadezer's officers
18: 9 When King Toi of Hamath heard that **D** had
18: 10 he sent his son Joram to congratulate **D** on his
18: 10 Joram presented **D** with many gifts of gold, silver,
18: 11 King **D** dedicated all these gifts to the LORD,
18: 13 the LORD made **D** victorious wherever he went.
18: 14 **D** reigned over all Israel and was fair to everyone.
19: 2 **D** said, "I am going to show complete loyalty to
19: 2 So **D** sent ambassadors to express sympathy to
19: 3 **D** has sent them to spy out the land so that they can
19: 4 at the buttocks, and sent them back to **D** in shame.
19: 5 When **D** heard what had happened, he sent
19: 6 realized how seriously they had angered **D**,
19: 8 When **D** heard about this, he sent Joab and all his
19: 17 When **D** heard what was happening, he mobilized
19: 19 they surrendered to **D** and became his subjects.
20: 1 But **D** had stayed behind in Jerusalem.
20: 2 When **D** arrived at Rabbah, he removed the crown
20: 2 **D** took a vast amount of plunder from the city.
20: 3 Then **D** and his army returned to Jerusalem.
20: 8 but they were killed by **D** and his warriors.
21: 1 and caused **D** to take a census of the Israelites.
21: 2 **D** gave these orders to Joab and his commanders:
21: 5 and reported the number of people to **D**.
21: 8 Then **D** said to God, "I have sinned greatly
21: 10 "Go and say to **D**, 'This is what the LORD says:
21: 11 So Gad came to **D** and said, "These are the
21: 13 "This is a desperate situation!" **D** replied to Gad.
21: 16 **D** looked up and saw the angel of the LORD
21: 16 So **D** and the leaders of Israel put on sackcloth to
21: 17 And **D** said to God, "I am the one who called for
21: 18 **D** to build an altar to the LORD at the threshing
21: 19 So **D** obeyed the instructions the LORD had
21: 21 threshing floor and bowed to the ground before **D**.
21: 22 **D** said to Araunah, "Let me buy this threshing
21: 23 and use it as you wish," Araunah said to **D**.
21: 25 So **D** gave Araunah six hundred pieces of gold in
21: 26 **D** built an altar there to the LORD and sacrificed
21: 26 And when **D** prayed, the LORD answered him by
21: 28 When **D** saw that the LORD had answered his
21: 30 But **D** was not able to go there to inquire of God,
22: 1 Then **D** said, "This will be the location for the
22: 2 So **D** gave orders to call together the foreigners
22: 3 **D** provided large amounts of iron for the nails that
22: 4 and Sidon had brought vast amounts of cedar to **D**.
22: 5 **D** said, "My son Solomon is still young
22: 5 So **D** collected vast amounts of building materials
22: 6 Then **D** sent for his son Solomon and instructed
22: 7 the name of the LORD my God," **D** told him.
22: 17 Then **D** ordered all the leaders of Israel to assist
23: 1 When **D** was an old man, he appointed his son
23: 2 **D** summoned all the political leaders of Israel,
23: 4 Then **D** said, "Twenty-four thousand of them will
23: 6 Then **D** divided the Levites into divisions named
23: 25 For **D** said, "The LORD, the God of Israel,
24: 3 **D** divided Aaron's descendants into groups
24: 31 It was done in the presence of King **D**, Zadok,
25: 1 **D** and the army commanders then appointed men
26: 26 all the things dedicated to the LORD by King **D**,
26: 32 King **D** sent them to the east side of the Jordan
27: 18 Judah | Elihu (a brother of **D**) / Issachar | Omri
27: 23 When **D** took his census, he did not count those
28: 1 **D** summoned all his officials to Jerusalem—
28: 2 **D** rose and stood before them and addressed them
28: 11 Then **D** gave Solomon the plans for the Temple
28: 12 **D** also gave Solomon all the plans he had in mind
28: 14 **D** gave instructions regarding how much gold
28: 17 **D** also designated the amount of gold for the solid
28: 19 "Every part of this plan," **D** told Solomon,
28: 20 Then **D** continued, "Be strong and courageous,
29: 1 Then King **D** turned to the entire assembly
29: 9 to the LORD, and King **D** was filled with joy.
29: 10 Then **D** praised the LORD in the presence of the
29: 20 Then **D** said to the whole assembly, "Give praise
29: 23 **D**, and he prospered greatly, and all Israel obeyed
29: 24 and the sons of King **D** pledged their loyalty to
29: 26 So **D** son of Jesse reigned over all Israel.
2Ch 1: 1 Solomon, the son of King **D**, now took firm control
1: 4 **D** had already moved the Ark of God from
1: 8 have been so faithful and kind to my father, **D**,
1: 9 please keep your promise to **D** my father,
2: 3 to my father, **D**, when he was building his palace.
2: 7 and Jerusalem who were selected by my father, **D**.
2: 12 He has given **D** a wise son, gifted with skill
2: 14 your craftsmen and those appointed by my lord **D**,
3: 1 had appeared to Solomon's father, King **D**.
3: 1 Araunah the Jebusite, the site that **D** had selected.
5: 1 King **D**, including all the silver and gold and all the
5: 2 covenant from its location in the City of **D**,
6: 4 who has kept the promise he made to my father, **D**.
6: 6 Jerusalem as that city, and **D** as that king.' "
6: 7 Then Solomon said, "My father, **D**, wanted to
6: 15 You have kept your promise to your servant **D**,
6: 16 carry out your further promise to your servant **D**,
6: 17 of Israel, fulfill this promise to your servant **D**.
6: 42 your unfailing love for your servant **D**."
7: 6 King **D** had made for praising the LORD.
7: 10 so good to **D** and Solomon and to his people Israel.
7: 17 **D**, did and obey all my commands, laws,
7: 18 same promise I gave your father, **D**, when I said,
8: 11 from the City of **D** to the new palace he had built
8: 14 Solomon followed the regulations of his father, **D**.
8: 14 following the commands of **D**, the man of God.
9: 31 he died, he was buried in the city of his father, **D**.
10: 16 they shouted, "Down with **D** and his dynasty!
10: 16 Israel! Look out for your own house, O **D**!"
10: 19 to be ruled by a descendant of **D** to this day.
11: 17 LORD as they had done during the reigns of **D**
12: 16 Rehoboam died, he was buried in the City of **D**.
13: 5 made an unbreakable covenant with **D**, giving him
13: 8 of the LORD that is led by the descendants of **D**?
14: 1 When Abijah died, he was buried in the City of **D**.
16: 14 he had carved out for himself in the City of **D**.
21: 1 he was buried with his ancestors in the City of **D**.
21: 7 for he had made a covenant with **D** and promised

21:12 the LORD, the God of your ancestor **D**, says:
21:20 He was buried in the City of **D**, but not in the royal
23: 3 The LORD has promised that a descendant of **D**
23: 9 and shields that had once belonged to King **D**
23:18 following all the instructions given by **D**.
23:18 and to sing and rejoice as **D** had instructed.
24:16 He was buried among the kings in the City of **D**,
24:25 Then he was buried in the City of **D**, but not in the
25:28 he was buried with his ancestors in the City of **D**.
27: 9 When he died, he was buried in the City of **D**,
28: 1 sight of the LORD, as his ancestor **D** had done.
29: 2 LORD's sight, just as his ancestor **D** had done.
29:25 that the LORD had given to King **D** through Gad,
29:26 around the Temple with the instruments of **D**,
29:27 by the trumpets and other instruments of **D**,
29:30 Levites to praise the LORD with the psalms of **D**
32: 5 He also reinforced the Millo in the City of **D**
32:30 through a tunnel to the west side of the City of **D**.
33: 7 the very place where God had told **D** and his son
33:14 Manasseh rebuilt the outer wall of the City of **D**,
34: 2 and followed the example of his ancestor **D**.
34: 3 Josiah began to seek the God of his ancestor **D**.
35: 4 following the written instructions of King **D** of
35:15 following the orders given by **D**, Asaph, Heman,
Ezr 3:10 praise the LORD, just as King **D** had prescribed.
8: 3 From the family of **D**: Hattush son of Shecaniah.
8:20 of Temple workers first instituted by King **D**.
Ne 3:15 as far as the stairs that descend from the City of **D**.
12:24 just as commanded by **D**, the man of God.
12:36 used the musical instruments prescribed by **D**,
12:37 on the ascent of the city wall toward the City of **D**.
12:37 They passed the house of **D** and then proceeded to
12:45 as required by the laws of **D** and his son Solomon,
12:46 and thanks to God began long ago in the days of **D**
Ps 3: T A psalm of **D**, regarding the time **D** fled from his son Absalom.
4: T A psalm of **D**, to be accompanied by stringed
5: T A psalm of **D**, to be accompanied by the flute.
6: T A psalm of **D**, to be accompanied by an
7: T A psalm of **D**, which he sang to the LORD
8: T A psalm of **D**, to be accompanied by a stringed
9: T A psalm of **D**, to be sung to the tune "Death of the
11: T For the choir director: A psalm of **D**.
12: T A psalm of **D**, to be accompanied by an
13: T For the choir director: A psalm of **D**.
14: T For the choir director: A psalm of **D**.
15: T A psalm of **D**.
16: T A psalm of **D**.
17: T A prayer of **D**.
18: T A psalm of **D**, the servant of the LORD.
18:50 to **D** and all his descendants forever.
19: T For the choir director: A psalm of **D**.
20: T For the choir director: A psalm of **D**.
21: T For the choir director: A psalm of **D**.
22: T A psalm of **D**, to be sung to the tune "Doe of the
23: T A psalm of **D**.
24: T A psalm of **D**.
25: T A psalm of **D**.
26: T A psalm of **D**.
27: T A psalm of **D**.
28: T A psalm of **D**.
29: T A psalm of **D**.
30: T A psalm of **D**, sung at the dedication of the
31: T For the choir director: A psalm of **D**.
32: T A psalm of **D**.
34: T A psalm of **D**, regarding the time he pretended to
35: T A psalm of **D**.
36: T A psalm of **D**, the servant of the LORD.
37: T A psalm of **D**.
38: T A psalm of **D**, to bring us to the LORD's
39: T For Jeduthun, the choir director: A psalm of **D**.
40: T For the choir director: A psalm of **D**.
41: T For the choir director: A psalm of **D**.
51: T A psalm of **D**, regarding the time Nathan the
51: T after **D** had committed adultery with Bathsheba.
52: T A psalm of **D**, regarding the time Doeg the
52: T told Saul that Ahimelech had given refuge to **D**.
53: T For the choir director: A meditation of **D**.
54: T A meditation of **D**, regarding the time the Ziphites
54: T and said to Saul, "We know where **D** is hiding."
55: T A psalm of **D**, to be accompanied by stringed
56: T A psalm of **D**, regarding the time the Philistines
57: T A psalm of **D**, regarding the time he fled from Saul
58: T A psalm of **D**, to be sung to the tune "Do Not
59: T A psalm of **D**, regarding the time Saul sent soldiers
60: T A psalm of **D** useful for teaching,
60: T regarding the time **D** fought Aram-naharaim
61: T A psalm of **D**, to be accompanied by stringed
62: T For Jeduthun, the choir director: A psalm of **D**.
63: T A psalm of **D**, regarding a time when **D** was in the wilderness of
64: T For the choir director: A psalm of **D**.
65: T For the choir director: A psalm of **D**. A song.
68: T For the choir director: A psalm of **D**. A song.
69: T A psalm of **D**, to be sung to the tune "Lilies."
70: T A psalm of **D**, to bring us to the LORD's
72:20 (This ends the prayers of **D** son of Jesse.)
78:70 He chose his servant **D**, / calling him from the
78:71 He took **D** from tending the ewes and lambs
86: T A prayer of **D**.
89: 3 "I have made a solemn agreement with **D**,
89:20 I have found my servant **D**. / I have anointed him
89:35 I have sworn an oath to **D**, / and in my holiness I
89:49 You promised it to **D** with a faithful pledge.
101: T A psalm of **D**.
103: T A psalm of **D**.
108: T A psalm of **D**. A song.
109: T For the choir director: A psalm of **D**.
110: T A psalm of **D**.
122: T A song for the ascent to Jerusalem. A psalm of **D**.
122: 5 is given, / the thrones of the dynasty of **D**.
124: T A song for the ascent to Jerusalem. A psalm of **D**.
131: T A song for the ascent to Jerusalem. A psalm of **D**.
132: 1 LORD, remember **D** / and all that he suffered.
132:10 For the sake of your servant **D**, / do not reject the
132:11 The LORD swore to **D** / a promise he will never
132:17 Here I will increase the power of **D**; / my anointed
133: T A song for the ascent to Jerusalem. A psalm of **D**.
138: T A psalm of **D**.
139: T For the choir director: A psalm of **D**.
140: T For the choir director: A psalm of **D**.
141: T A psalm of **D**.
142: T A psalm of **D**, regarding his experience in the cave.
143: T A psalm of **D**.
144: T A psalm of **D**.
144:10 You are the one who rescued your servant **D**.
145: T A psalm of praise of **D**.
SS 4: 4 Your neck is as stately as the tower of **D**,
Isa 7:13 Isaiah said, "Listen well, you royal family of **D**!
9: 7 and justice from the throne of his ancestor **D**.
22:22 I will give him the key to the house of **D**—
29: 1 "Destruction is certain for Ariel, the City of **D**.
37:35 my own honor and for the sake of my servant **D**,
38: 5 the LORD, the God of your ancestor **D**, says:
55: 3 and unfailing love that I promised to **D**.
Jer 17:25 There will always be a descendant of **D** sitting on
21:12 This is what the LORD says to the dynasty of **D**:
22: 4 there will always be a descendant of **D** sitting on
22:30 will ever sit on the throne of **D** to rule in Judah.
30: 9 will serve the LORD their God and **D** their king,
33:15 At that time I will bring to the throne of **D** a
33:17 **D** will forever have a descendant sitting on the
33:21 only then will my covenant with **D**, my servant,
33:22 so I will multiply the descendants of **D**,
33:26 will never abandon the descendants of Jacob or **D**,
36:30 He will have no heirs to sit on the throne of **D**.
Eze 34:23 set one shepherd over them, even my servant **D**.
34:24 and my servant **D** will be a prince among my
37:24 "My servant **D** will be their king, and they will
37:25 And my servant **D** will be their prince forever.
Am 6: 5 yourselves to be great musicians, as King **D** was.
9:11 "In that day I will restore the fallen kingdom of **D**.
Zec 12: 7 and the royal line of **D** will not have greater honor
12: 8 weakest among them will be as mighty as King **D**!
12:10 and prayer on the family of **D** and on all the people
12:12 The family of **D** will mourn, along with the family
13: 1 day a fountain will be opened for the dynasty of **D**
Mt 1: 1 a descendant of King **D** and of Abraham:
1: 6 Jesse was the father of King **D**. / **D** was the father of Solomon (his mother was
1:17 fourteen generations from Abraham to King **D**,
1:20 "Joseph, son of **D**," the angel said, "do not be
9:27 shouting, "Son of **D**, have mercy on us!"
12: 3 read in the Scriptures what King **D** did when he
12:23 "Could it be that Jesus is the Son of **D**,
15:22 pleading, "Have mercy on me, O Lord, Son of **D**!
20:30 "Lord, Son of **D**, have mercy on us!"
20:31 "Lord, Son of **D**, have mercy on us!"
21: 9 were shouting, / "Praise God for the Son of **D**!
21:15 Temple shouting, "Praise God for the Son of **D**."
22:42 son is he?" They replied, "He is the son of **D**."
22:43 Jesus responded, "Then why does **D**,
22:43 of the Holy Spirit, call him Lord? For **D** said,
22:45 Since **D** called him Lord, how can he be his son at
Mk 2:25 read in the Scriptures what King **D** did when he
10:47 shout out, "Jesus, Son of **D**, have mercy on me!"
10:48 shouted louder, "Son of **D**, have mercy on me!"
11:10 Bless the coming kingdom of our ancestor **D**!
12:35 law claim that the Messiah will be the son of **D**?
12:36 For **D** himself, speaking under the inspiration of
12:37 Since **D** himself called him Lord, how can he be
Lk 1:27 to a man named Joseph, a descendant of King **D**.
1:32 God will give him the throne of his ancestor **D**.
1:69 from the royal line of his servant **D**,
2: 4 because Joseph was a descendant of King **D**,
2:11 has been born tonight in Bethlehem, the city of **D**!
3:31 was the son of Nathan. / Nathan was the son of **D**.
3:32 **D** was the son of Jesse. / Jesse was the son of
6: 3 read in the Scriptures what King **D** did when he
18:38 "Jesus, Son of **D**, have mercy on me!"
18:39 shouted louder, "Son of **D**, have mercy on me!"
20:41 "that the Messiah is said to be the son of **D**?
20:42 For **D** himself wrote in the book of Psalms:
20:44 Since **D** called him Lord, how can he be his son at
Jn 7:42 that the Messiah will be born of the royal line of **D**,
7:42 the village where King **D** was born."
Ac 1:16 ago by the Holy Spirit, speaking through King **D**.
2:25 King **D** said this about him: / 'I know the Lord is
2:29 **D** wasn't referring to himself when he spoke these
2:31 **D** was looking into the future and predicting the
2:34 For **D** himself never ascended into heaven, yet he
4:25 by the Holy Spirit through our ancestor King **D**,
7:45 And it was used there until the time of King **D**.
7:46 "**D** found favor with God and asked for the
13:22 him from the kingship and replaced him with **D**,
13:22 '**D** son of Jesse is a man after my own heart,
13:34 give you the sacred blessings I promised to **D**.'
13:36 Now this is not a reference to **D**, for after **D** had served his generation according to
15:16 and I will restore the fallen kingdom of **D**.
Ro 4: 6 King **D** spoke of this, describing the happiness of
11: 9 **D** spoke of this same thing when he said,
Heb 4: 7 God announced this through **D** a long time later in
11:32 Barak, Samson, Jephthah, **D**, Samuel, and all the
Rev 3: 7 and true. He is the one who has the key of **D**.
22:16 I am both the source of **D** and the heir to his

DAVID'S (127) [DAVID]

1Sa 16:13 olive oil he had brought and poured it on **D** head.
17:14 Since **D** three oldest brothers were in the army,
17:19 **D** brothers were with Saul and the Israelite army at
17:28 But when **D** oldest brother, Eliab, heard David
17:31 Then **D** question was reported to King Saul,
18: 3 And Jonathan made a special vow to be **D** friend,
18:29 and he remained **D** enemy for the rest of his life.
18:30 So **D** name became very famous throughout the
19:11 Then Saul sent troops to watch **D** house.
19:11 But Michal, **D** wife, warned him, "If you don't get
19:15 he lies there!" And he sent them back to **D** house.
20:25 and Abner beside him. But **D** place was empty.
20:27 But when **D** place was empty again the next day,
22: 4 and **D** parents stayed in Moab while David was
22: 8 you has ever told me that my own son is on **D** side.
23: 3 But **D** men said, "We're afraid even here in Judah.
24: 4 your opportunity!" **D** men whispered to him.
24: 5 But then **D** conscience began bothering him
25: 9 **D** young men gave this message to Nabal
25:12 So **D** messengers returned and told him what
25:13 was **D** reply as he strapped on his own.
25:15 But **D** men were very good to us, and we never
25:41 I am even willing to become a slave to **D**
25:42 mounted her donkey, and went with **D** messengers.
25:44 meanwhile, had given his daughter Michal, **D** wife,
26:17 Saul recognized **D** voice and called out, "Is that
30: 5 **D** two wives, Ahinoam of Jezreel and Abigail,
30:11 Some of **D** troops found an Egyptian man in a field
30:22 But some troublemakers among **D** men said,
2Sa 1: 2 On the third day after **D** return, a man arrived from
2: 2 **D** wives were Ahinoam from Jezreel and Abigail,
2:13 Joab son of Zeruiah led **D** troops from Hebron,
2:18 sons of Zeruiah, were among **D** forces that day.
3: 5 was Ithream, whose mother was **D** wife Eglah.
3:22 Joab and some of **D** troops returned from a raid,
5:14 These are the names of **D** sons who were born in
8: 2 The Moabites who were spared became **D** servants
8: 6 and the Arameans became **D** subjects and brought
8:14 and all the Edomites became **D** subjects.
8:18 **D** sons served as priestly leaders.
10: 2 But when **D** ambassadors arrived in the land of
10: 4 So Hanun seized **D** ambassadors and shaved off
10:18 This time **D** forces killed seven hundred
12:18 **D** advisers were afraid to tell him. "He was
12:30 the king's head, and it was placed on **D** own head.
13: 1 **D** son Absalom had a beautiful sister named
13: 3 He was the son of **D** brother Shimea.
13:32 the son of **D** brother Shimea, arrived and said,
15:12 one of **D** counselors who lived in Giloh.
15:18 to let **D** troops move past to lead the way.
15:37 So **D** friend Hushai returned to Jerusalem,
16:16 When **D** friend Hushai the Arkite arrived, he went
18: 7 and the Israelite troops were beaten back by **D**
18: 9 Absalom came unexpectedly upon some of **D** men.
18:10 One of **D** men saw what had happened and told
20:23 Joab once again became the commander of **D**
20:26 Ira the Jairite was **D** personal priest.
21: 1 There was a famine during **D** reign that lasted for
21:17 After that, **D** men declared, "You are not going
21:21 killed by Jonathan, the son of **D** brother Shimea.
23: 8 These are the names of **D** mightiest men. The first
23: 8 the three greatest warriors among **D** men.
23:13 an elite group among **D** fighting men) went down
24:10 the census, **D** conscience began to bother him.
24:11 LORD came to the prophet Gad, who was **D** seer.
1Ki 1: 5 About that time **D** son Adonijah, whose mother
1: 8 Shimei, Rei, and **D** personal bodyguard.
1:38 and Solomon rode on King **D** personal mule.
2: 1 As the time of King **D** death approached, he gave
2:45 and may one of **D** descendants always sit on this
5: 1 so when he learned that **D** son Solomon was the
15: 4 But for **D** sake, the LORD his God allowed his
1Ch 11: 6 And Joab, the son of **D** sister Zeruiah,
11: 6 so he became the commander of **D** armies.
11:10 These are the leaders of **D** mighty men.
11:11 Here is the record of **D** mightiest men: The first
11:11 the three greatest warriors among **D** men.
11:15 an elite group among **D** fighting men) went down
11:26 These were also included among **D** mighty men:
14: 4 These are the names of **D** sons who were born in
14:17 So **D** fame spread everywhere, and the LORD
18: 2 and the Moabites became **D** subjects and brought
18: 6 and the Arameans became **D** subjects and brought
18:13 and all the Edomites became **D** subjects.
18:17 **D** sons served as the king's chief assistants.
19: 2 But when **D** ambassadors arrived in the land of
19: 4 So Hanun seized **D** ambassadors and shaved their
19:18 This time **D** forces killed seven thousand
20: 2 the king's head, and it was placed on **D** own head.
20: 7 killed by Jonathan, the son of **D** brother Shimea.
21: 9 Then the LORD spoke to Gad, **D** seer. This was
23:27 It was according to **D** final instructions that all the
26:31 (In the fortieth year of **D** reign, a search was made
27: 6 This was the Benaiah who commanded **D** elite
27:24 The final total was never recorded in King **D**
27:31 All these officials were overseers of King **D**
27:32 Jonathan, **D** uncle, was a wise counselor to the
29:22 And again they crowned **D** son Solomon as their
29:29 All the events of King **D** reign, from beginning to
2Ch 8:11 He said, "My wife must not live in King **D** palace,
8:15 Solomon did not deviate in any way from **D**
11:18 the daughter of **D** son Jerimoth and of Abihail,

11:18 (Eliab was one of **D** brothers, a son of Jesse.)
13: 6 who was a mere servant of **D** son Solomon,
21: 7 But the LORD was not willing to destroy **D**
30:26 this one since the days of Solomon, King **D** son.
Ps 59: T regarding the time Saul sent soldiers to watch **D**
Pr 1: 1 are the proverbs of Solomon, **D** son, king of Israel.
Ecc 1: 1 the Teacher, King **D** son, who ruled in Jerusalem.
Isa 11: 1 Out of the stump of **D** family will grow a shoot—
11:10 In that day the heir to **D** throne will be a banner of
16: 5 then **D** throne will be established by love.
Jer 13:13 from the king sitting on **D** throne and from the
22: 2 you king of Judah, sitting on **D** throne.
23: 5 "when I will place a righteous Branch on King **D**
29:16 LORD says about the king who sits on **D** throne
33:26 or change the plan that **D** descendants will rule the
Hos 3: 5 to the LORD their God and to **D** descendant,
Mt 1:17 and fourteen from **D** time to the Babylonian exile,
Lk 2: 4 had to go to Bethlehem in Judea, **D** ancient home.
Ac 2:30 **D** own descendants would sit on **D** throne as the Messiah.
13:23 "And it is one of King **D** descendants, Jesus,
Ro 1: 3 came as a man, born into King **D** royal family line.
15:12 Isaiah said, / "The heir to **D** throne will come,
2Ti 2: 8 Jesus Christ was a man born into King **D** family
Rev 5: 5 tribe of Judah, the heir to **D** throne, has conquered.

DAWN (41) [DAWNED, DAWNING, DAWNS]

Ge 19:15 At **d** the next morning the angels became insistent.
32:24 and a man came and wrestled with him until **d**.
32:26 Then the man said, "Let me go, for it is **d**."
44: 3 The brothers were up at **d** and set out on their
Jos 6:15 On the seventh day the Israelites got up at **d**
Jdg 19:25 her until morning. Finally, at **d**, they let her go.
1Sa 11:11 But before **d** the next morning, Saul arrived,
2Sa 17:22 and they were all on the other bank before **d**.
Job 7: 4 But the night drags on, and I toss till **d**.
24:14 The murderer rises in the early **d** to kill the poor
38:12 to appear and caused the **d** to rise in the east?
38:14 as the light approaches, and the **d** is robed in red.
41:18 it flashes light! Its eyes are like the red of **d**.
Ps 22: T of David, to be sung to the tune "Doe of the **D**."
37: 6 He will make your innocence as clear as the **d**,
57: 8 and lyre! / I will waken the **d** with my song.
104:22 At **d** they slink back / into their dens to rest.
108: 2 and lyre! / I will waken the **d** with my song.
130: 6 more than sentries long for the **d**, / yes, more than sentries long for the **d**.
Pr 4:18 way of the righteous is like the first gleam of **d**,
31:15 She gets up before **d** to prepare breakfast for her
SS 2:17 Before the **d** comes and the shadows flee away,
4: 6 Before the **d** comes and the shadows flee away,
6:10 'Who is this,' they ask, 'arising like the **d**, as fair
Isa 17:14 Israel waits in terror, but by **d** its enemies are dead.
58: 8 these things, your salvation will come like the **d**.
62: 1 for her until her righteousness shines like the **d**,
Hos 6: 3 he will respond to us as surely as the arrival of **d**
Joel 2: 2 Suddenly, like **d** spreading across the mountains,
Am 4:13 He turns the light of **d** into darkness and treads the
Jnh 4: 7 The next morning at **d** the worm ate through the
Mic 2: 1 You rise at **d** and hurry to carry out any of the
Zep 3: 3 who by **d** have left no trace of their prey.
3: 7 they continue their evil practices from **d** till dusk and dusk till **d**."
Mk 13:35 at evening, midnight, early **d**, or late daybreak.
Lk 12:38 come in the middle of the night or just before **d**.
Jn 21: 4 At **d** the disciples saw Jesus standing on the beach,
Ac 12:18 At **d**, there was a great commotion among the
20:11 And Paul continued talking to them until **d**; then he

DAWNED (2) [DAWN]

Dt 33: 2 and **d** upon us from Mount Seir; / he shone forth
Ac 27:39 When morning **d**, they didn't recognize the

DAWNING (2) [DAWN]

Eze 7: 7 O people of Israel, the day of your destruction is **d**.
Mt 28: 1 as the new day was **d**, Mary Magdalene

DAWNS (1) [DAWN]

Hos 10:15 When the day of judgment **d**, the king of Israel will

DAY (1275) [DAILY, DAY'S, DAYBREAK, DAYLIGHT, DAYS, DAYS', DAYTIME, EVERYDAY, MIDDAY, SEVEN-DAY, SOMEDAY, THREE-DAY, WORKDAYS]

DAY AFTER DAY (20) Ge 39:10; Nu 11:6; Dt 11:12; Jdg 16:16; 1Sa 23:14; 1Ki 10:8; 1Ch 12:22; 2Ch 9:7; 24:11; Est 3:4; Ps 19:2; 61:8; 102:8; Isa 21:8; Jer 32:33; Ac 16:18; 17:11; Heb 10:11; 2Pe 2:8; Rev 4:8

DAY BY DAY (4) Ps 37:18; 88:13; Zep 3:5; Lk 11:3

DAY OF...DEATH (5) Jdg 13:7; 2Ki 15:5; 25:30; Ecc 8:8; Jer 52:34

DAY OF JUDGMENT (15) Ps 37:13; Pr 11:4; Eze 7:10; 39:8; Hos 10:15; Am 6:3; Zep 1:8; Mal 4:1; Jn 12:48; Ro 2:5; Jas 5:3; 2Pe 2:9; 3:7; 1Jn 4:17; Jude 1:6

DAY OF THE LORD* (13) Isa 13:9; Eze 13:5; 30:3; Joel 1:15; 2:1,11,31; 3:14; Am 5:18,20; Zep 1:14; Zec 14:1; Mal 4:5

DAY OF THE LORD (6) Jer 46:10; Ac 2:20; 1Th 5:2,4; 2Th 2:2; 2Pe 3:10

DAY OF TROUBLE (5) 2Ki 19:3; Isa 37:3; Jer 16:19; 51:2; Eze 7:7

EACH DAY (33) Ex 16:4; 29:36,38; Nu 10:34; 14:34; Dt 24:15; 1Sa 17:25; 1Ch 16:23,37; 26:17,18; 2Ch 30:21; Ezr 3:4; 6:9; Ne 5:18; Ps 42:8; 68:19; 88:9; 96:2; 110:3; Isa 27:3; 33:2; La 3:23; Eze 4:10,11,12; 43:26,27; 45:23; Lk 16:19; Ac 2:46,47; 3:2

EVERY DAY (27) Ge 27:2; Ex 29:37; Est 2:11; Ps 7:11; 13:2; 22:2; 44:22; 139:16; 145:2; Pr 15:15; Ecc 11:8; Isa 38:20; 58:2; Jer 37:21; Eze 43:25; Mt 26:55; Mk 14:49; Lk 21:37; 22:53; Jn 6:34; 11:9; Ac 5:42; Ro 8:36; 14:5; 2Co 4:16; Heb 3:13; 7:27

FIRST DAY (24) Ex 12:15,16; 40:2,17; Lev 23:7,35,39,39,40; Nu 7:12; 28:11,14,15,18,26; Eze 44:27; 45:18; Da 10:12; Mt 26:17; 27:62; Mk 14:12; Jn 20:19; Ac 20:7; Col 1:6

LAST DAY (7) Ex 12:41; Jn 6:39,40,44,54; 7:37; 1Pe 1:5

ON THAT DAY (72) Ex 16:26,29; 20:10; 31:14; 35:2,3; Lev 23:14,24,25,27,30,32; Nu 9:15; 28:18,25,26; 29:1,2,7,12,35; Dt 5:14; 16:8; Jdg 4:23; 5:1; 2Ch 15:11; Ne 12:44; 13:15; Est 8:13; 9:1; Isa 58:13; Jer 31:33; 36:6,9; Eze 24:26; 27:27; 30:9; 38:19; 39:13; Am 2:16; Zep 1:8,10,18; 2:3; 3:9,16,20; Zec 2:11; 3:10; 12:3,4,6,8,11; 13:1,2; 14:2,4,6,8,9,13,20,21; Mal 4:1; Lk 17:31; Ac 28:23; Php 1:6; 1Th 3:13; 2Th 1:10; Heb 8:10; 10:16

ONE DAY (119) Ge 1:5; 4:23; 9:21; 18:1; 19:31; 24:2; 25:29; 26:26; 27:45; 30:14; 34:1; 37:3; 39:11; 48:1; Ex 3:1; Lev 24:10; Nu 1:1; 10:11,29; 15:32; 16:1; 27:1,12; Jos 10:35; Jdg 4:6; 9:1; 14:1; 16:1; 17:2,7; 19:1; Ru 2:2; 3:1; 1Sa 2:27; 9:3; 14:1; 15:1; 17:17; 18:17; 19:9; 22:5; 23:1,15; 27:5; 2Sa 2:12; 3:7; 4:5; 9:1; 12:4,23; 13:4; 1Ki 2:13; 11:29; 16:9; 20:29; 21:2; 2Ki 1:2; 4:1,8,11,18,38,42; 5:3; 6:1,26,28; 12:4; 14:8; 19:37; Est 2:21; Job 1:6,13; 2:1; Ps 73:17; Pr 7:6; Isa 37:38; Jer 28:1; 38:14; Eze 4:5,6; Mt 4:18; 5:1; 9:14; 12:38; 16:1; 17:22; Mk 1:9,16; 2:18; 7:1; 10:13; Lk 1:8; 3:21; 5:1,17; 6:12; 8:4,22; 9:1,18; 10:25; 11:14; 17:1,5,20; 18:1,15; 20:1; Ac 6:9; 7:23; 11:5; 13:2; 16:16; 21:7; 22:17; 26:12; Ro 14:5; 1Co 10:8

SEVENTH DAY (39) Ge 2:2,3; Ex 12:16; 13:6; 16:26,29,30; 20:10,11; 24:16; 31:15,17; 35:2; Lev 13:5,6,34,51; 14:9,39; 23:3,8; Nu 7:48; 19:12,19; 28:25; 29:32; 31:24; Dt 5:14; 16:8; Jos 6:4,15; Jdg 14:17,18; 2Sa 12:18; 1Ki 20:29; Est 1:10; Eze 45:20; Heb 4:4,4

THIRD DAY (24) Ge 1:13; 22:4; 42:18; Ex 19:11,16; Lev 7:17,18; 19:6,7,8; Nu 7:24; 29:20; Jdg 20:30; 1Sa 20:5; 2Sa 1:2; Est 9:18; Mt 16:21; 20:19; 27:64; Lk 13:32; 18:33; 24:7,46; 1Co 15:4

Ge 1: 5 God called the light "**d**" and the darkness "night." Together these made up one **d**.
1: 8 the space "sky." This happened on the second **d**.
1:13 This all happened on the third **d**.
1:14 appear in the sky to separate the **d** from the night.
1:16 The greater one, the sun, presides during the **d**;
1:18 to govern the **d** and the night, and to separate the
1:19 This all happened on the fourth **d**.
1:23 This all happened on the fifth **d**.
1:31 in every way. This all happened on the sixth **d**.
2: 2 On the seventh **d**, having finished his task,
2: 3 And God blessed the seventh **d** and declared it
2: 3 because it was the **d** when he rested from his work
3:19 you will sweat to produce food, until your dying **d**.
4:23 One **d** Lamech said to Adah and Zillah, "Listen to
7: 1 the **d** came when the LORD said to Noah,
7:11 on the seventeenth **d** of the second month,
7:13 But Noah had gone into the boat that very **d** with
8:22 and heat, winter and summer, **d** and night."
9:21 One **d** he became drunk on some wine he had
15:18 So the LORD made a covenant with Abram that **d**
17:12 must be circumcised on the eighth **d** after his birth.
17:23 On that very **d** Abraham took his son Ishmael
17:26 Both were circumcised the same **d**,
18: 1 One **d** about noon, as Abraham was sitting at the
19:31 One **d** the older daughter said to her sister,
22: 4 On the third **d** of the journey, Abraham saw the
24: 2 One **d** Abraham said to the man in charge of his
25:29 One **d** when Jacob was cooking some stew,
26:26 One **d** Isaac had visitors from Gerar.
26:32 That very **d** Isaac's servants came and told him
27: 2 Isaac said, "and I expect every **d** to be my last.
27:45 for you. Why should I lose both of you in one **d**?"
29: 7 "They'll be hungry if you stop so early in the **d**."
30:14 One **d** during the wheat harvest, Reuben found
30:35 But that very **d** Laban went out and removed all
31:40 worked for you through the scorching heat of the **d**
33:16 So Esau started back to Seir that same **d**.
34: 1 One **d** Dinah, Leah's daughter, went to visit some
35:20 over her grave, and it can be seen there to this **d**.
37: 3 So one **d** he gave Joseph a special gift—a beautiful
39: 5 From the **d** Joseph was put in charge, the LORD
39:10 She kept putting pressure on him **d** after **d**,
39:11 One **d**, however, no one else was around when he
42:18 On the third **d** Joseph said to them, "I am a
48: 1 One **d** not long after this, word came to Joseph that
48:20 So Jacob blessed the boys that **d** with this blessing:
Ex 2:13 The next **d**, as Moses was out visiting his people
3: 1 One **d** Moses was tending the flock of his
5: 6 That same **d** Pharaoh sent this order to the slave
9: 5 that he would send the plague the very next **d**,
9:26 The only spot in all Egypt without hail that **d** was
10:13 the LORD caused an east wind to blow all that **d**
10:28 let me see you again! The **d** you do, you will die!"
12: 3 **d** of this month each family must choose a lamb
12: 6 the evening of the fourteenth **d** of this first month.
12:10 Do not leave any of it until the next **d**. Whatever is
12:14 "You must remember this **d** forever. Each year
12:15 On the very first **d** you must remove every trace of
12:16 On the first **d** of the festival, and again on the seventh **d**,
12:17 your forces out of the land of Egypt on this very **d**.
12:18 **d** of the month until the evening of the twenty-first **d** of the month.
12:41 it was on the last **d** of the 430th year that all the
12:51 And that very **d** the LORD began to lead the
13: 3 to the people, "This is a **d** to remember forever—
13: 3 the **d** you left Egypt, the place of your slavery.
13: 4 This **d** in early spring will be the anniversary of
13: 5 You must celebrate this **d** when the LORD brings
13: 6 Then on the seventh **d**, you will celebrate a great
13:21 guided them by a pillar of cloud during the **d**
13:21 That way they could travel whether it was **d**
14:30 LORD rescued Israel from the Egyptians that **d**.
16: 4 The people can go out each **d** and pick up as much food as they need for that **d**.
16: 5 as much as usual on the sixth **d** of each week."
16:22 On the sixth **d**, there was twice as much as usual
16:23 "The LORD has appointed tomorrow as a **d** of
16:23 On this **d** we will rest from our normal daily tasks.
16:26 food for six days, but the seventh **d** is a Sabbath.
16:26 will be no food on the ground for you on that **d**."
16:27 to gather food, even though it was the Sabbath **d**.
16:29 not realize that I have given them the seventh **d**, the Sabbath, as a **d** of rest?
16:29 why I give you twice as much food on the sixth **d**,
16:29 On the Sabbath **d** you must stay in your places.
16:29 Do not pick up food from the ground on that **d**."
16:30 So the people rested on the seventh **d**.
18:13 The next **d**, Moses sat as usual to hear the people's
18:14 The people have been standing here all **d** to get
19:11 Be sure they are ready on the third **d**, for I will
19:16 On the morning of the third **d**, there was a
20: 8 "Remember to observe the Sabbath **d** by keeping
20:10 but the seventh **d** is a **d** of rest dedicated to the
20:10 On that **d** no one in your household may do any
20:11 in them; then he rested on the seventh **d**.
20:11 That is why the LORD blessed the Sabbath **d**
22:30 for seven days; then give it to me on the eighth **d**.
24:16 On the seventh **d** the LORD called to Moses from
27:21 the lamps burning in the LORD's presence **d**
29:36 Each **d** you must sacrifice a young bull as an
29:37 Make atonement for the altar every **d** for seven
29:38 on the altar. Offer two one-year-old lambs each **d**,
31:13 "Tell the people of Israel to keep my Sabbath **d**,
31:14 Yes, keep the Sabbath **d**, for it is holy.
31:14 anyone who works on that **d** will be cut off from
31:15 but the seventh **d** must be a **d** of total rest.
31:15 Because the LORD considers it a holy **d**,
31:16 The people of Israel must keep the Sabbath **d**
31:17 but he rested on the seventh **d** and was refreshed."
32:28 and about three thousand people died that **d**.
32:30 The next **d** Moses said to the people, "You have
34:21 aside for work, but on the Sabbath **d** you must rest,
35: 2 The seventh **d** is a **d** of total rest, a holy **d** that belongs to the LORD. Anyone who works on that **d** will die.
35: 3 Do not even light fires in your homes on that **d**."
40: 2 "Set up the Tabernacle on the first **d** of the new
40:17 So the Tabernacle was set up on the first **d** of the
40:38 the LORD rested on the Tabernacle during the **d**,
Lev 6:20 "On the **d** Aaron and his sons are anointed,
6:22 this same sacrifice on the **d** they are anointed.
7:15 The animal's meat must be eaten on the same **d** it
7:16 the meat may be eaten on that same **d**,
7:16 whatever is left over may be eaten on the second **d**.
7:17 But anything left over until the third **d** must be
7:18 from this peace offering is eaten on the third **d**,
8:35 you must stay at the entrance of the Tabernacle **d**
9: 1 on the eighth **d**, Moses called together Aaron
12: 3 On the eighth **d**, the boy must be circumcised.
13: 5 On the seventh **d** the priest will make another
13: 6 priest will examine the skin again on the seventh **d**.
13:34 will examine the infection again on the seventh **d**.
13:51 On the seventh **d** the priest must inspect it again.
14: 9 On the seventh **d**, they must again shave off all
14:10 "On the next **d**, the eighth **d**, each person cured
14:23 On the eighth **d**, the person being cleansed must
14:39 On the seventh **d** the priest must return for another
15:14 On the eighth **d** he must bring two turtledoves
15:29 On the eighth **d**, she must bring two turtledoves
16:29 "On the appointed **d** in early autumn, you must spend the **d** fasting and not do any work.
16:30 On this **d**, atonement will be made for you,
16:31 It will be a Sabbath **d** of total rest, and you will spend the **d** in fasting.
19: 6 You must eat it on the same **d** you offer it or on the next **d** at the latest.
19: 6 Any leftovers that remain until the third **d** must be
19: 7 If any of the offering is eaten on the third **d**,
19: 8 If you eat it on the third **d**, you will answer for the
22:27 From the eighth **d** on, it will be acceptable as an
22:28 a mother animal and her offspring on the same **d**,
22:30 Eat the entire sacrificial animal on the **d** it is
22:30 Don't leave any of it until the second **d**. I am the
23: 3 but on the seventh **d** all work must come to a
23: 3 It is the LORD's Sabbath **d** of complete rest, a holy **d** to assemble for worship.
23: 5 which begins at twilight on its appointed **d** in early
23: 6 Then the **d** after the Passover celebration,
23: 7 On the first **d** of the festival, all the people must
23: 8 On the seventh **d**, the people must again stop all
23:11 On the **d** after the Sabbath, the priest will lift it up

23:12 That same **d** you must sacrifice a year-old male
23:14 or fresh kernels on that **d** until after you have
23:15 "From the **d** after the Sabbath, the **d** the bundle of grain was lifted up as an
23:16 Keep counting until the **d** after the seventh
23:21 That same **d**, you must stop all your regular work
23:24 "On the appointed **d** in early autumn, you are to celebrate a **d** of complete rest. All your work must stop on that **d**.
23:25 You must do no regular work on that **d**. Instead,
23:27 "Remember that the **D** of Atonement is to be
23:27 on the ninth **d** after the Festival of Trumpets.
23:27 On that **d** you must humble yourselves, gather for
23:28 Do no work during that entire **d** because it is the **D** of Atonement,
23:29 Anyone who does not spend that **d** in humility will
23:30 among you who does any kind of work on that **d**.
23:32 This will be a Sabbath **d** of total rest for you,
23:32 and on that **d** you must humble yourselves.
23:32 and fasting will begin the evening before the **D** of
23:32 of Atonement and extend until evening of that **d**."
23:34 Shelters on the fifth **d** after the **D** of Atonement.
23:35 It will begin with a sacred assembly on the first **d**,
23:36 On the eighth **d**, you must gather again for a sacred
23:36 and no regular work may be done that **d**.
23:37 and drink offerings—each on its proper **d**.
23:39 "Now, on the first **d** of the Festival of Shelters,
23:39 Remember that the first **d** and closing eighth **d** of the festival will be days of
23:40 On the first **d**, gather fruit from citrus trees,
24: 8 Every Sabbath **d** this bread must be laid out before
24:10 One **d** a man who had an Israelite mother and an
25: 9 Then on the **D** of Atonement of the fiftieth year,
Nu 1: 1 One **d** in midspring, during the second year after
1:18 the whole community of Israel on that very **d**.
3:13 From the **d** I killed all the firstborn sons of the
6:10 On the eighth **d** they must bring two turtledoves
6:11 Then they must renew their vow that **d** and let their
7: 1 On the **d** Moses set up the Tabernacle, he anointed
7:11 "Let each leader bring his gift on a different **d** for
7:12 On the first **d** Nahshon son of Amminadab,
7:18 On the second **d** Nethanel son of Zuar, leader of
7:24 On the third **d** Eliab son of Helon, leader of the
7:30 On the fourth **d** Elizur son of Shedeur, leader of
7:36 On the fifth **d** Shelumiel son of Zurishaddai,
7:42 On the sixth **d** Eliasaph son of Deuel, leader of the
7:48 On the seventh **d** Elishama son of Ammihud,
7:54 On the eighth **d** Gamaliel son of Pedahzur,
7:60 On the ninth **d** Abidan son of Gideoni, leader of
7:66 On the tenth **d** Ahiezer son of Ammishaddai,
7:72 On the eleventh **d** Pagiel son of Ocran, leader of
7:78 On the twelfth **d** Ahira son of Enan, leader of the
9: 3 at twilight on the appointed **d** in early spring.
9: 5 of Sinai as twilight fell on the appointed **d**.
9: 6 so they could not offer their Passover lambs that **d**. So they came to Moses and Aaron that **d**
9:11 one month later, at twilight on the appointed **d**.
9:15 was set up, and on that **d** the cloud covered it.
9:21 But **d** or night, when the cloud lifted, the people
10:11 One **d** in midspring, during the second year after
10:29 One **d** Moses said to his brother-in-law, Hobab son
10:34 As they moved on each **d**, the cloud of the LORD
11: 6 and **d** after **d** we have nothing to eat but this
11:19 And it won't be for just a **d** or two, or for five
11:32 So the people went out and caught quail all that **d**
11:32 and throughout the night and all the next **d**,
14:14 that you go before them in the pillar of cloud by **d**
14:34 a year for each **d**, suffering the consequences of
15:32 One **d** while the people of Israel were in the
15:32 caught a man gathering wood on the Sabbath **d**.
16: 1 One **d** Korah son of Izhar, a descendant of Kohath
17: 8 into the Tabernacle of the Covenant the next **d**,
19:12 continue to be unclean even after the seventh **d**.
19:19 Then on the seventh **d** the people being cleansed
25:18 who was killed on the **d** of the plague at Peor."
26:10 and 250 of their followers were destroyed that **d** by
26:11 However, the sons of Korah did not die that **d**.
27: 1 One **d** a petition was presented by the daughters of
27:12 One **d** the LORD said to Moses, "Climb to the
28: 9 "On the Sabbath **d**, sacrifice two one-year-old
28:10 burnt offering to be presented each Sabbath **d**,
28:11 "On the first **d** of each month, present an extra
28:14 Present this monthly burnt offering on the first **d** of
28:15 on the first **d** of each month you must offer one
28:16 "On the appointed **d** in early spring, you must
28:17 On the following **d** a joyous, seven-day festival
28:18 On the first **d** of the festival you must call a sacred
28:18 None of your regular work may be done on that **d**.
28:25 On the seventh **d** of the festival you must call
28:25 None of your regular work may be done on that **d**.
28:26 "On the first **d** of the Festival of Harvest,
28:26 None of your regular work may be done on that **d**.
28:27 special whole burnt offering will be offered that **d**,
29: 1 on the appointed **d** in early autumn each year.
29: 1 call a solemn assembly of all the people on that **d**,
29: 2 On that **d** you must present a burnt offering,
29: 7 On that **d**, the **D** of Atonement, the people must
29:12 and on that **d** no regular work may be done.
29:13 That **d** you must present a special whole burnt
29:17 "On the second **d** of this seven-day festival,
29:20 "On the third **d** of the festival, sacrifice eleven
29:23 "On the fourth **d** of the festival, sacrifice ten
29:26 "On the fifth **d** of the festival, sacrifice nine young
29:29 "On the sixth **d** of the festival, sacrifice eight
29:32 "On the seventh **d** of the festival, sacrifice seven
29:35 "On the eighth **d** of the festival, call all the people
29:35 You must do no regular work on that **d**.
30: 5 her fulfill the vow or pledge on the **d** he hears of it,
30: 7 and raises no objections on the **d** he hears of it,
30: 8 or impulsive pledge on the **d** he hears of it,
30:12 But if her husband refuses to accept it on the **d** he
30:14 But if he says nothing on the **d** he hears of it,
30:15 If he waits more than a **d** and then tries to nullify a
31:24 On the seventh **d** you must wash your clothes
33:38 This happened on a **d** in midsummer,
Dt 1: 3 on a **d** in midwinter, Moses gave these speeches to
1:33 a pillar of fire at night and a pillar of cloud by **d**.
2:22 The descendants of Esau live there to this **d**.
4:10 Tell them especially about the **d** when you stood
4:15 You did not see the LORD's form on the **d** he
5:12 " 'Observe the Sabbath **d** by keeping it holy,
5:14 but the seventh **d** is a **d** of rest dedicated to the
5:14 On that **d** no one in your household may do any
5:15 God has commanded you to observe the Sabbath **d**.
9: 7 From the **d** you left Egypt until now, you have
11: 4 how he has kept them devastated to this very **d**!
11:12 He watches over it **d** after **d** throughout the year!
16: 3 so that you will remember the **d** you departed from
16: 8 On the seventh **d** the people must assemble before
16: 8 your God, and no work may be done on that **d**.
21:23 You must bury the body that same **d**, for anyone
23:10 emission must leave the camp and stay away all **d**.
24:15 Pay them their wages each **d** before sunset
27:11 That same **d** Moses gave this charge to the people:
28:66 You will live night and **d** in fear, with no reason to
29: 4 But to this **d** the LORD has not given you minds
31:22 So that very **d** Moses wrote down the words of the
32:35 their feet will slip. / Their **d** of disaster will arrive,
32:48 That same **d** the LORD said to Moses,
34: 6 but to this **d** no one knows the exact place.
Jos 1: 8 Meditate on it **d** and night so you may be sure to
4: 9 The memorial remains there to this **d**.
4:14 That **d** the LORD made Joshua great in the eyes
4:19 The people crossed the Jordan on the tenth **d** of the
5: 9 So that place has been called Gilgal to this **d**.
5:10 the evening of the fourteenth **d** of the first month—
5:11 The very next **d** they began to eat unleavened
5:12 No manna appeared that **d**, and it was never seen
6: 3 is to march around the city once a **d** for six days.
6: 4 On the seventh **d** you are to march around the city
6:11 LORD was carried around the city once that **d**,
6:14 On the second **d** they marched around the city once
6:15 On the seventh **d** the Israelites got up at dawn
6:25 And she lives among the Israelites to this **d**.
7:26 of stones over Achan, which remains to this **d**.
8:25 the entire population of Ai was wiped out that **d**—
8:28 permanent mound of ruins, desolate to this very **d**.
9:27 But that **d** he made the Gibeonites the
9:27 to build it. That arrangement continues to this **d**.
10:12 On the **d** the LORD gave the Israelites victory
10:13 of the sky, and it did not set as on a normal **d**.
10:14 The LORD fought for Israel that **d**. Never before
10:14 or since has there been a **d** like that one,
10:27 a large pile of stones, which remains to this very **d**.
10:28 That same **d** Joshua completely destroyed the city
10:32 And the LORD gave it to them on the second **d**.
10:35 They captured it in one **d**, and as at Lachish,
13:13 they continue to live among the Israelites to this **d**.
14: 9 So that **d** Moses promised me, 'The land of
15:63 live there among the people of Judah to this **d**.
16:10 as slaves among the people of Ephraim to this **d**.
22: 3 of the LORD your God up to the present **d**.
22:22 If we have done so, do not spare our lives this **d**.
24:25 So Joshua made a covenant with the people that **d**
Jdg 1:21 So to this **d** the Jebusites live in Jerusalem among
1:26 city Luz, and it is known by that name to this **d**.
3:30 So Moab was conquered by Israel that **d**,
4: 6 One **d** she sent for Barak son of Abinoam,
4:23 So on that **d** Israel saw God subdue Jabin,
5: 1 On that **d** Deborah and Barak son of Abinoam sang
6:24 Ophrah in the land of the clan of Abiezer to this **d**.
9: 1 One **d** Gideon's son Abimelech went to Shechem
9:42 The next **d** the people of Shechem went out into
9:45 The battle went on all **d** before Abimelech finally
13: 7 moment of his birth until the **d** of his death.' "
13:10 "The man who appeared to me the other **d** is here
13:11 you the man who talked to my wife the other **d**?"
14: 1 One **d** when Samson was in Timnah, he noticed a
14:10 a party at Timnah, as was the custom of the **d**.
14:15 On the fourth **d** they said to Samson's wife,
14:17 At last, on the seventh **d**, he told her the answer
14:18 So before sunset of the seventh **d**, the men of the
15:19 Who Cried Out," and it is still in Lehi to this **d**.
16: 1 One **d** Samson went to the Philistine city of Gaza
16:16 So **d** after **d** she nagged him until he couldn't
17: 2 One **d** he said to his mother, "I heard you curse
17: 7 One **d** a young Levite from Bethlehem in Judah
18:12 in Judah, which is called Mahaneh-dan to this **d**.
19: 1 One **d** he brought home a woman from Bethlehem
19: 5 On the fourth **d** the man was up early, ready to
19: 8 On the morning of the fifth **d** he was up early
19: 8 this afternoon." So they had another **d** of feasting.
19:11 It was late in the **d** when they reached Jebus,
20:21 twenty-two thousand Israelites in the field that **d**.
20:22 at the same place they had fought the previous **d**.
20:30 They went out on the third **d** and assembled at the
20:35 and that **d** the Israelites killed 25,100 of
20:46 lost twenty-five thousand brave warriors that **d**,
Ru 2: 2 One **d** Ruth said to Naomi, "Let me go out into the
2:17 So Ruth gathered barley there all **d**, and when she
3: 1 One **d** Naomi said to Ruth, "My daughter,
1Sa 1: 4 On the **d** Elkanah presented his sacrifice, he would
2:27 One **d** a prophet came to Eli and gave him this
2:34 Hophni and Phinehas, to die on the same **d**!
4:10 was great; thirty thousand Israelite men died that **d**.
4:12 and arrived at Shiloh later that same **d**.
4:16 from the battlefront—I was there this very **d**."
5: 5 That is why to this **d** neither the priests of Dagon
6:15 and sacrifices were offered to the LORD that **d** by
6:16 all this and then returned to Ekron that same **d**.
7: 6 They also went without food all **d** and confessed
8:18 When that **d** comes, you will beg for relief from
9: 3 One **d** Kish's donkeys strayed away, and he told
9:15 Now the LORD had told Samuel the previous **d**,
10: 9 and all Samuel's signs were fulfilled that **d**.
14: 1 One **d** Jonathan said to the young man who carried
14:23 So the LORD saved Israel that **d**, and the battle
14:24 Now the men of Israel were worn out that **d**,
14:24 on my enemies." So no one ate a thing all **d**,
14:31 and killed the Philistines all **d** from Micmash to
14:37 us defeat them?" But God made no reply that **d**.
15: 1 One **d** Samuel said to Saul, "I anointed you king
16:13 LORD came mightily upon him from that **d** on.
17:16 For forty days, twice a **d**, morning and evening,
17:17 One **d** Jesse said to David, "Take this half-bushel
17:25 "He comes out each **d** to challenge Israel.
18: 2 From that **d** on Saul kept David with him at the
18:10 The very next **d**, in fact, a tormenting spirit from
18:17 One **d** Saul said to David, "I am ready to give you
19: 9 But one **d** as Saul was sitting at home,
19:24 and lay on the ground all **d** and all night,
20: 5 and stay there until the evening of the third **d**.
20:12 or the next **d** at the latest, I will talk to my father
20:19 The **d** after tomorrow, toward evening, go to the
20:26 Saul didn't say anything about it that **d**, for he said
20:27 when David's place was empty again the next **d**,
20:34 table in fierce anger and refused to eat all that **d**,
21: 6 It had just been replaced that **d** with fresh bread.
21: 7 was there that **d** for ceremonial purification.
22: 5 One **d** the prophet Gad told David,
22:22 When I saw Doeg there that **d**, I knew he would
23: 1 One **d** news came to David that the Philistines
23:14 Saul hunted him **d** after **d**, but God didn't let him
23:15 One **d** near Horesh, David received the news that
24: 4 "Today is the **d** the LORD was talking about
24:10 This very **d** you can see with your own eyes it isn't
25:16 **d** and night they were like a wall of protection to
27: 5 One **d** David said to Achish, "If it is all right with
27: 6 (which still belongs to the kings of Judah to this **d**),
28:20 for he had eaten nothing all **d** and all night.
30:17 that night and the entire next **d** until evening.
31: 6 and his troops all died together that same **d**.
31: 8 The next **d**, when the Philistines went out to strip
2Sa 1: 2 On the third **d** after David's return, a man arrived
1:12 They mourned and wept and fasted all **d** for Saul
1:12 nation of Israel, because so many had died that **d**.
2:12 One **d** Abner led some of Ishbosheth's troops from
2:17 and by the end of the **d** Abner and the men of
2:18 sons of Zeruiah, were among David's forces that **d**.
3: 7 One **d** Ishbosheth, Saul's son, accused Abner of
3:35 David had refused to eat anything the **d** of the
4: 5 One **d** Recab and Baanah, the sons of Rimmon
7: 6 from the **d** I brought the Israelites out of Egypt
9: 1 One **d** David began wondering if anyone in Saul's
11:12 So Uriah stayed in Jerusalem that **d** and the next.
12: 4 One **d** a guest arrived at the home of the rich man.
12:18 Then on the seventh **d** the baby died.
12:23 I will go to him one **d**, but he cannot return to
13: 4 One **d** Jonadab said to Amnon,
18: 7 twenty thousand men laid down their lives that **d**.
18:18 and it is known as Absalom's Monument to this **d**.
19:22 "This is not a **d** for execution but for celebration!
19:24 or clothes nor trimmed his beard since the **d** the
21:10 vultures from tearing at their bodies during the **d**
23:10 and the LORD gave him a great victory that **d**.
24:18 That **d** Gad came to David and said to him, "Go
1Ki 2:13 One **d** Adonijah, whose mother was Haggith,
2:24 the LORD lives, Adonijah will die this very **d**!"
2:37 On the **d** you cross the Kidron Valley, you will
8: 8 not from outside it. They are still there to this **d**.
8:16 'From the **d** I brought my people Israel out of
8:29 May you watch over this Temple both **d** and night,
8:59 **d** and night, so that the LORD our God may
8:64 That same **d** the king dedicated the central area of
9:21 and they serve in the labor force to this **d**.
10: 8 What a privilege for your officials to stand here **d** after **d**,
10:21 was considered of little value in Solomon's **d**!
11:29 One **d** as Jeroboam was leaving Jerusalem,
12:19 to be ruled by a descendant of David to this **d**.
12:32 held on a **d** in midautumn, similar to the annual
12:33 So on the appointed **d** in midautumn, a **d** that he himself had designated,
13: 3 That same **d** the man of God gave a sign to prove
13:11 what the man of God had done in Bethel that **d**.
16: 9 One **d** in Tirzah, Elah was getting drunk at the
19: 4 he went on alone into the desert, traveling all **d**.
20:29 seven days, and on the seventh **d** the battle began.
20:29 killed 100,000 Aramean foot soldiers in one **d**.
21: 2 One **d** Ahab said to Naboth, "Since your vineyard
22:35 The battle raged all that **d**, and Ahab was propped
2Ki 1: 2 One **d** Israel's new king, Ahaziah, fell through the
3:20 the next **d** at about the time when the morning
4: 1 One **d** the widow of one of Elisha's fellow
4: 8 One **d** Elisha went to the town of Shunem.
4:11 One **d** Elisha returned to Shunem, and he went up
4:18 One **d** when her child was older, he went out to
4:38 One **d** as the group of prophets was seated before
4:42 One **d** a man from Baal-shalishah brought the man
5: 3 One **d** the girl said to her mistress, "I wish my
6: 1 One **d** the group of prophets came to Elisha

6:26 One **d** as the king of Israel was walking along the
6:28 "This woman proposed that we eat my son one **d**
6:29 Then the next **d** I said, 'Kill your son so we can eat
6:31 I don't execute Elisha son of Shaphat this very **d**,"
7:16 flour were sold that **d** for half an ounce of silver,
8:15 But the next **d** Hazael took a blanket, soaked it in
8:22 Edom has been independent from Judah to this **d**.
10:27 a public toilet. That is what it is used for to this **d**.
12:4 One **d** King Joash said to the priests, "Collect all
13:23 And to this **d** he still has not completely destroyed
14:7 its name to Joktheel, as it is called to this **d**.
14:8 One **d** Amaziah sent this challenge to Israel's king
15:5 with leprosy, which lasted until the **d** of his death;
16:6 sent Edomites to live there, as they do to this **d**.
16:18 inside the palace for use on the Sabbath **d**,
17:23 to the land of Assyria, where they remain to this **d**.
17:41 And to this **d** their descendants do the same.
19:3 This is a **d** of trouble, insult, and disgrace.
19:37 One **d** while he was worshiping in the temple of
25:30 cover his living expenses until the **d** of his death.
1Ch 5:26 and the Gozan River, where they remain to this **d**.
9:32 the bread to be set on the table each Sabbath **d**.
10:8 The next **d** when the Philistines went out to strip
12:22 **D** after **d** more men joined David until he had a
16:7 That **d** David gave to Asaph and his fellow Levites
16:23 Each **d** proclaim the good news that he saves.
16:37 doing whatever needed to be done each **d**.
17:5 from the **d** I brought the Israelites out of Egypt
26:17 Six Levites were assigned each **d** to the east gate,
26:18 Six were assigned each **d** to the west gate, four to
29:21 The next **d** they brought a thousand bulls,
29:22 in the LORD's presence with great joy that **d**.
2Ch 5:9 not from outside it. They are still there to this **d**.
5:11 whether or not they were on duty that **d**.
6:5 'From the **d** I brought my people out of Egypt,
6:20 May you watch over this Temple both **d** and night,
7:9 On the eighth **d** they had a closing ceremony,
8:8 and they serve in the labor force to this **d**.
8:13 The number of sacrifices varied from **d** to **d**
8:16 from the **d** its foundation was laid to the **d** of its
9:7 What a privilege for your officials to stand here **d** after **d**,
9:20 was considered of little value in Solomon's **d**!
10:19 to be ruled by a descendant of David to this **d**.
13:17 casualties among Israel's finest troops that **d**.
15:11 On that **d** they sacrificed to the LORD some of
18:34 The battle raged all that **d**, and Ahab propped
20:26 On the fourth **d** they gathered in the Valley of
20:26 which got its name that **d** because the people
21:10 Edom has been independent from Judah to this **d**.
24:11 This went on **d** after **d**, and a large amount of
26:21 So King Uzziah had leprosy until the **d** he died.
28:6 In a single **d** Pekah son of Remaliah, Israel's king,
29:17 The work began on a **d** in early spring, and in eight
30:15 On the appointed **d** in midspring, the people
30:21 Each **d** the Levites and priests sang to the LORD,
35:1 in Jerusalem on the appointed **d** in early spring.
35:1 lambs were slaughtered at twilight of that **d**.
35:16 for the LORD's Passover was completed that **d**.
35:25 and to this **d** choirs still sing these sad songs about
Ezr 3:4 sacrificing the burnt offerings specified for each **d**
6:9 salt, wine, and olive oil that they need each **d**.
8:33 On the fourth **d** after our arrival, the silver, gold,
10:13 "This isn't something that can be done in a **d**
Ne 1:6 see me praying night and **d** for your people Israel.
4:2 Do they think they can build the wall in a **d** if they
4:9 But we prayed to our God and guarded the city **d**
4:22 guard duty at night as well as work during the **d**.
5:11 olive groves, and homes to them this very **d**.
5:18 The provisions required at my expense for each **d**
7:3 the gates open during the hottest part of the **d**.
8:9 said to them, "Don't weep on such a **d** as this!
8:9 For today is a sacred **d** before the LORD your
8:10 This is a sacred **d** before our Lord. Don't be
8:11 "Hush! Don't weep! For this is a sacred **d**."
9:12 led our ancestors by a pillar of cloud during the **d**
9:19 The pillar of cloud still led them forward by **d**,
10:31 to be sold on the Sabbath or on any other holy **d**,
12:43 Many sacrifices were offered on that joyous **d**,
12:44 On that **d** men were appointed to be in charge of
13:1 On that same **d**, as the Book of Moses was being
13:15 One Sabbath **d** I saw some men of Judah treading
13:15 And on that **d** they were bringing their wine,
13:19 merchandise could be brought in on the Sabbath **d**.
Est 1:10 On the seventh **d** of the feast, when King Xerxes
1:18 Before this **d** is out, the wife of every one of us,
2:11 Every **d** Mordecai would take a walk near the
2:21 One **d** as Mordecai was on duty at the palace,
3:4 They spoke to him **d** after **d**, but still he refused
3:7 to determine the best **d** and month to take action.
3:7 And the **d** selected was March 7, nearly a year
3:13 slaughtered, and annihilated on a single **d**.
3:14 would be ready to do their duty on the appointed **d**.
4:16 Do not eat or drink for three days, night or **d**.
7:2 And while they were drinking wine that **d**, the king
8:1 On that same **d** King Xerxes gave the estate of
8:12 The **d** chosen for this event throughout all the
8:13 That way the Jews would be ready on that **d** to take
9:1 On that **d**, the enemies of the Jews had hoped to
9:5 But the Jews went ahead on the appointed **d**
9:17 Then on the following **d** they rested,
9:17 celebrating their victory with a **d** of feasting
9:18 killing their enemies on the second **d** also,
9:18 and then rested on the third **d**, making that their
9:18 making that their **d** of feasting and gladness.
9:19 So to this **d**, rural Jews living in unwalled villages
9:24 had plotted to crush and destroy them on the **d**

Job 1:6 One **d** the angels came to present themselves
1:13 One **d** when Job's sons and daughters were dining
2:1 One **d** the angels came again to present themselves
3:1 At last Job spoke, and he cursed the **d** of his birth.
3:3 "Cursed be the **d** of my birth, and cursed be the
3:4 Let that **d** be turned to darkness. Let it be lost even
3:8 are ready to rouse the sea monster—curse that **d**.
7:2 like a worker who longs for the **d** to end, like a
15:24 That dark **d** terrifies them. They live in distress
17:12 They say that night is **d** and **d** is night; how they
26:10 the waters; he set the boundaries for **d** and night.
38:23 for the time of trouble, for the **d** of battle and war.
Ps 1:2 **d** and night they think about his law.
7:11 He is angry with the wicked every **d**.
13:2 in my soul, / with sorrow in my heart every **d**?
18:T He sang this song to the LORD on the **d** the
19:2 **D** after **d** they continue to speak; / night after
22:2 Every **d** I call to you, my God, but you do not
25:5 who saves me. / All **d** long I put my hope in you.
32:3 and miserable, / and I groaned all **d** long.
32:4 **D** and night your hand of discipline was heavy on
35:28 and goodness, / and I will praise you all **d** long.
37:13 for he sees their **d** of judgment coming.
37:18 **D** by **d** the LORD takes care of the innocent,
38:12 They think up treacherous deeds all **d** long.
42:3 **D** and night, I have only tears for food, / while my
42:8 Through each **d** the LORD pours his unfailing
44:8 O God, we give glory to you all **d** long
44:22 For your sake we are killed every **d**; / we are being
46:5 be destroyed. / God will protect it at the break of **d**.
49:19 before them / and never again see the light of **d**.
51:3 my shameful deeds— / they haunt me **d** and night.
52:2 All **d** long you plot destruction. / Your tongue cuts
55:10 Its walls are patrolled **d** and night against invaders,
56:1 press in on me. / My foes attack me all **d** long.
56:9 On the very **d** I call to you for help, / my enemies
59:16 my refuge, / a place of safety in the **d** of distress.
61:8 to your name / as I fulfill my vows **d** after **d**.
68:19 For each **d** he carries us in his arms. / *Interlude*
71:8 stop praising you; / I declare your glory all **d** long.
71:15 All **d** long I will proclaim your saving power,
71:24 all **d** long, / for everyone who tried to hurt me
72:15 always pray for him / and bless him all **d** long.
73:14 All I get is trouble all **d** long; / every morning
73:17 Then one **d** I went into your sanctuary, O God,
74:16 Both **d** and night belong to you; / you made the
74:22 Remember how these fools insult you all **d** long.
78:9 their backs and fled when the **d** of battle came.
84:10 A single **d** in your courts / is better than a thousand
88:1 my salvation, / I have cried out to you **d** and night.
88:9 my tears. / Each **d** I beg for your help, O LORD;
88:13 I cry out to you. / I will keep on pleading **d** by **d**.
88:17 They swirl around me like floodwaters all **d** long.
89:16 They rejoice all **d** long in your wonderful
91:5 terrors of the night, / nor fear the dangers of the **d**,
92:T A psalm to be sung on the LORD's **D**. A song.
96:2 Each **d** proclaim the good news that he saves.
102:8 My enemies taunt me **d** after **d**. / They mock
110:3 In that **d** of battle, / your people will serve you
110:3 your vigor will be renewed each **d** like the morning
110:5 He will strike down many kings in the **d** of his
118:24 This is the **d** the LORD has made. / We will
119:97 how I love your law! / I think about it all **d** long.
119:164 I will praise you seven times a **d** / because all your
121:6 The sun will not hurt you by **d**, / nor the moon at
136:8 the sun to rule the **d**, / His faithful love endures
137:7 on the **d** the armies of Babylon captured Jerusalem.
139:12 To you the night shines as bright as **d**. / Darkness
139:16 Every **d** of my life was recorded in your book.
139:16 was laid out / before a single **d** had passed.
140:2 evil in their hearts / and stir up trouble all **d** long.
140:7 strong savior, / you protected me on the **d** of battle.
145:2 I will bless you every **d**, / and I will praise you
Pr 4:16 sleep until they have done their evil deed for the **d**.
4:18 which shines ever brighter until the full light of **d**.
6:34 and he will have no mercy in his **d** of vengeance.
7:6 I was looking out the window of my house one **d**
7:9 at twilight, as the **d** was fading, as the dark of night
11:4 Riches won't help on the **d** of judgment, but right
15:15 For the poor, every **d** brings trouble; for the happy
27:1 since you don't know what the **d** will bring.
27:15 as annoying as the constant dripping on a rainy **d**.
Ecc 5:15 and empty-handed as on the **d** they were born.
7:1 the **d** you die is better than the **d** you are born.
8:8 None of us has the power to prevent the **d** of our
8:16 that there is ceaseless activity, **d** and night.
11:8 to be very old, let them rejoice in every **d** of life.
SS 3:11 which his mother crowned him on his wedding **d**, the **d** of his gladness."
Isa 1:13 celebrations of the new moon and the Sabbath **d**,
2:11 The **d** is coming when your pride will be brought
2:12 In that **d** the LORD Almighty will punish the
4:1 In that **d** few men will be left alive. Seven women
4:5 and cloud throughout the **d** and clouds of fire at
5:15 In that **d** the arrogant will be brought down to the
7:18 In that **d** the LORD will whistle for the army of
7:20 In that **d** the Lord will take this "razor"—
7:23 In that **d** the lush vineyards, now worth as much as
9:5 In that **d** of peace, battle gear will no longer be
9:14 Therefore, in a single **d**, the LORD will destroy
10:27 In that **d** the LORD will end the bondage of his
10:32 But the enemy stops at Nob for the rest of that **d**.
11:6 In that **d** the wolf and the lamb will live together;
11:10 In that **d** the heir to David's throne will be a banner
11:11 In that **d** the Lord will bring back a remnant of his
12:1 In that **d** you will sing: / "Praise the LORD!
12:4 In that wonderful **d** you will sing:

13:9 For see, the **d** of the LORD is coming—
13:9 the terrible **d** of his fury and fierce anger.
14:3 In that wonderful **d** when the LORD gives his
17:4 "In that **d** the glory of Israel will be very dim,
18:4 as quietly as the heat rises on a summer **d**, or as the
19:16 In that **d** the Egyptians will be as weak as women.
19:18 In that **d** five of Egypt's cities will follow the
19:19 In that **d** there will be an altar to the LORD in the
19:21 In that **d** the LORD will make himself known to
19:23 In that **d** Egypt and Assyria will be connected by a
21:8 "**D** after **d** I have stood on the watchtower,
22:5 Oh, what a **d** of crushing trouble! What a **d** of confusion and terror the Lord,
22:14 sin will never be forgiven you until the **d** you die.
24:21 In that **d** the LORD will punish the fallen angels
25:7 In that **d** he will remove the cloud of gloom,
25:9 In that **d** the people will proclaim, "This is our
26:1 In that **d**, everyone in the land of Judah will sing
27:1 In that **d** the LORD will take his terrible,
27:2 "In that **d** we will sing of the pleasant vineyard.
27:3 Each **d** I will water them; **d** and night I will watch to keep enemies away.
27:13 In that **d** the great trumpet will sound. Many who
28:19 morning after morning, **d** and night, until you are
29:18 In that **d** deaf people will hear words read from a
30:25 In that **d**, when your enemies are slaughtered,
31:7 I know the glorious **d** will come when every one of
32:5 In that **d** ungodly fools will not be heroes.
33:2 Be our strength each **d** and our salvation in times
33:6 In that **d** he will be your sure foundation,
34:8 For it is the **d** of the LORD's vengeance, the year
37:3 This is a **d** of trouble, insult, and disgrace.
37:38 One **d** while he was worshiping in the temple of
38:20 every **d** of my life / in the Temple of the LORD.
43:9 Can any of them predict something even a single **d**
49:8 to you. On the **d** of salvation, I will help you.
52:5 My name is being blasphemed all **d** long.
54:17 But in that coming **d**, no weapon turned against
56:6 and do not desecrate the Sabbath **d** of rest,
58:2 They come to the Temple every **d** and seem
58:10 and the darkness around you will be as bright as **d**.
58:13 "Keep the Sabbath **d** holy. Don't pursue your own interests on that **d**,
58:13 speak of it with delight as the LORD's holy **d**.
60:7 In that **d** I will make my Temple glorious.
61:2 with it, the **d** of God's anger against their enemies.
62:6 they will pray to the LORD **d** and night for the
65:2 "I opened my arms to my own people all **d** long,
65:3 All **d** long they insult me to my face by worshiping
66:8 as this? Has a nation ever been born in a single **d**?
Jer 3:17 In that **d** Jerusalem will be known as The Throne
4:9 "In that **d**," says the LORD, "the king
6:4 But now the **d** is fading, and the evening shadows
7:25 From the **d** your ancestors left Egypt until now,
7:25 continued to send my prophets—**d** in and **d** out.
8:1 "In that **d**," says the LORD, "the enemy will
9:1 I would sob **d** and night for all my people who
11:7 of Egypt, repeating over and over again to this **d**:
14:17 to them: 'Night and **d** my eyes overflow with tears.
15:9 for breath; her sun has gone down while it is yet **d**.
16:19 and fortress, my refuge in the **d** of trouble!
17:17 You alone are my hope in the **d** of disaster.
17:21 your trade at Jerusalem's gates on the Sabbath **d**.
17:22 do your work on the Sabbath, but make it a holy **d**.
17:24 not carry on your trade or work on the Sabbath **d**,
17:27 and if on the Sabbath **d** you bring loads of
20:3 The next **d**, when Pashhur finally released him,
20:14 Yet I curse the **d** I was born! May the **d** of my birth not be blessed.
20:16 Terrify him all **d** long with battle shouts,
23:6 In that **d** Judah will be saved, and Israel will live in
23:7 "In that **d**," says the LORD, "when people are
25:18 From that **d** until this, they have been a desolate
25:33 In that **d** those the LORD has slaughtered will fill
28:1 One **d** in late summer of that same year—
30:8 "For in that **d**, says the LORD Almighty, I will
30:16 "But in that coming **d**, all who destroy you will be
31:1 "In that **d**," says the LORD, "I will be the God
31:6 The **d** will come when watchmen will shout from
31:31 "The **d** will come," says the LORD, "when I
31:33 I will make with the people of Israel on that **d**,"
31:35 is the LORD who provides the sun to light the **d**
32:20 land of Egypt—things still remembered to this **d**!
32:33 **D** after **d**, year after year, I taught them right
33:14 "The **d** will come, says the LORD, when I will
33:16 In that **d** Judah will be saved, and Jerusalem will
33:20 "If you can break my covenant with the **d**
33:25 than I would change my laws of night and **d**,
36:6 So you go to the Temple on the next **d** of fasting,
36:6 On that **d** people will be there from all over Judah.
36:9 This happened on the **d** of sacred fasting held in
36:9 came to attend the services at the Temple on that **d**.
37:21 every **d** as long as there was any left in the city.
38:14 One **d** King Zedekiah sent for Jeremiah to meet
38:28 of the guard until the **d** Jerusalem was captured.
41:4 The next **d**, before anyone had heard about
46:10 For this is the **d** of the Lord, the LORD Almighty,
46:10 a **d** of vengeance on his enemies.
46:21 and run, for it is a **d** of great disaster for Egypt,
50:31 "Your **d** of reckoning has arrived.
51:2 every side to rise against her in her **d** of trouble.
52:34 cover his living expenses until the **d** of his death.
La 1:12 which the LORD brought on me in the **d** of his
1:13 made me desolate, racked with sickness all **d** long.
1:21 Oh, bring the **d** you promised, when you will
2:1 In his **d** of awesome fury, the Lord has shown no
2:7 Temple as though it were a **d** of celebration.

2:16 Long have we awaited this **d**, and it is finally
2:18 Give yourselves no rest from weeping **d** or night.
2:22 as though you were calling them to a **d** of feasting.
2:22 In the **d** of the LORD's anger, no one has escaped
3: 3 **D** and night his hand is heavy upon me.
3:14 at me. All **d** long they sing their mocking songs.
3:23 is his faithfulness; his mercies begin afresh each **d**.
3:62 enemies whisper and mutter against me all **d** long.
Eze 2: 3 and they are still in revolt to this very **d**.
4: 5 sins for 390 days—one **d** for each year of their sin.
4: 6 for 40 days—one **d** for each year of Judah's sin.
4:10 eight ounces of food for each **d**, and eat it at set
4:11 Then measure out a jar of water for each **d**,
4:12 Each **d** prepare your bread as you would barley
7: 7 of Israel, the **d** of your destruction is dawning.
7: 7 The time has come; the **d** of trouble is near. It will
7:10 "The **d** of judgment is here; your destruction
7:12 Yes, the time has come; the **d** is here! There is no
7:19 It won't buy their deliverance in that **d** of the
12: 4 Bring your baggage outside during the **d** so they
13: 5 it to stand firm in battle on the **d** of the LORD.
16: 5 On the **d** you were born, you were dumped in a
20:31 you continue to pollute yourselves to this **d**.
21:25 prince of Israel, your final **d** of reckoning is here!
21:29 for whom the **d** of final reckoning has come.
22: 4 and idolatry. Your **d** of destruction has come!
22:14 and courageous will you be in my **d** of reckoning?
22:24 In the **d** of my indignation, you will become like
23:38 defiled my Temple and violated my Sabbath **d**!
23:39 On the very **d** that they murdered their children in
24: 2 because on this very **d** the king of Babylon is
24:25 of man, on the **d** I take away their stronghold—
24:26 And on that **d** a refugee from Jerusalem will come
27:27 On that **d** of vast ruin, everyone on board sinks
28:13 They were given to you on the **d** you were created.
28:15 "You were blameless in all you did from the **d** you were created until the **d** evil was found in you.
29:21 "And the **d** will come when I will cause the
30: 3 the terrible **d** is almost here—the **d** of the LORD!
30: 3 It is a **d** of clouds and gloom, a **d** of despair for the nations!
30: 9 Great panic will come upon them on that **d** of
30:18 of Egypt, it will be a dark **d** for Tahpanhes, too.
32:10 my sword before them on the **d** of your fall.
34:12 they were scattered on that dark and cloudy **d**.
38:19 a mighty shaking in the land of Israel on that **d**.
39: 8 That **d** of judgment will come, says the Sovereign
39:13 for Israel when I demonstrate my glory on that **d**,
43:22 "On the second **d**, sacrifice as a sin offering a
43:25 "Every **d** for seven days a male goat, a young bull,
43:26 Do this each **d** for seven days to cleanse and make
43:27 On the eighth **d**, and on each **d** afterward,
44:24 see to it that the Sabbath is set apart as a holy **d**.
44:27 The first **d** he returns to work and enters the inner
45:18 In early spring, on the first **d** of each new year,
45:20 Do this also on the seventh **d** of the new year for
45:21 "On the fourteenth **d** of the new year, you must
45:22 On the **d** of Passover the prince will provide a
45:23 A male goat will also be given each **d** for a sin
46: 4 "Each Sabbath **d** the prince will present to the
48:35 And from that **d** the name of the city will be 'The
Da 6:10 He prayed three times a **d**, just as he had always
6:13 He still prays to his God three times a **d**."
6:14 He spent the rest of the **d** looking for a way to get
10:12 Since the first **d** you began to pray for
Hos 1:10 In that **d** its people will be like the sands of the
1:11 What a **d** that will be—the **d** of Jezreel—
2: 1 In that **d** you will call your brothers Ammi—
2: 3 I will strip her as naked as she was on the **d** she
2:16 "In that coming **d**," says the LORD, "you will
2:21 "In that **d**," says the LORD, "I will answer the
5: 9 When your **d** of punishment comes, you will
6: 5 My judgment will strike you as surely as **d** follows
9: 7 has come; the **d** of payment is almost here.
9:12 It will be a terrible **d** when I turn away and leave
10:15 When the **d** of judgment dawns, the king of Israel
12: 1 the wind; they chase after the east wind all **d** long.
Joel 1:15 The **d** of the LORD is on the way, the **d** when destruction comes from the Almighty. How terrible that **d** will be!
2: 1 in fear because the **d** of the LORD is upon us.
2: 2 It is a **d** of darkness and gloom, a **d** of thick clouds and deep blackness.
2:11 The **d** of the LORD is an awesome, terrible thing.
2:31 that great and terrible **d** of the LORD arrives.
3:14 It is there that the **d** of the LORD will soon
3:18 In that **d** the mountains will drip with sweet wine,
Am 2:16 On that **d**, the most courageous of your fighting
3:14 "On the very **d** I punish Israel for its sins, I will
5: 8 who turns darkness into morning and **d** into night.
5:18 who say, "If only the **d** of the LORD were here!
5:18 That **d** will not bring light and prosperity,
5:19 In that **d** you will be like a man who runs from a
5:20 the **d** of the LORD will be a dark and hopeless **d**,
6: 3 but your actions only bring the **d** of judgment
8: 3 In that **d** the riotous sounds of singing in the
8: 5 You can't wait for the Sabbath **d** to be over
8: 9 at noon and darken the earth while it is still **d**.
8:10 only son had died. How very bitter that **d** will be!
9:11 "In that **d** I will restore the fallen kingdom of
Ob 1:15 "The **d** is near when I, the LORD, will judge the
Jnh 3: 4 On the **d** Jonah entered the city, he shouted to the
Mic 2: 4 In that **d** your enemies will make fun of you by
3: 6 for you prophets, and your **d** will come to an end.
4: 6 "In that coming **d**," says the LORD, "I will
7: 4 But your judgment **d** is coming swiftly now.
7:11 In that **d**, Israel, your cities will be rebuilt,
Hab 1: 5 For I am doing something in your own **d**,
3:16 I will wait quietly for the coming **d** when disaster
Zep 1: 7 for the awesome **d** of the LORD's judgment has
1: 8 "On that **d** of judgment," says the LORD,
1:10 "On that **d**," says the LORD, "a cry of alarm
1:14 "That terrible **d** of the LORD is near. Swiftly it comes—a **d** when strong men will cry bitterly.
1:15 It is a **d** when the LORD's anger will be poured
1:15 It is a **d** of terrible distress and anguish, a **d** of ruin and desolation,
1:15 a **d** of darkness and gloom, of clouds, blackness,
1:18 and gold will be of no use to you on that **d** of the
2: 2 and the terrible **d** of the LORD's anger begins.
2: 3 protect you from his anger on that **d** of destruction.
3: 5 **D** by **d** his justice is more evident, but no one
3: 9 "On that **d** I will purify the lips of all people,
3:16 On that **d** the announcement to Jerusalem will be,
3:20 On that **d** I will gather you together and bring you
Hag 2:18 "On this eighteenth **d** of December—the **d** when the foundation of the LORD's Temple
2:19 their crops. From this **d** onward I will bless you."
Zec 2:11 will join themselves to the LORD on that **d**,
3: 9 and I will remove the sins of this land in a single **d**.
3:10 And on that **d**, says the LORD Almighty, each of
9:12 I promise this very **d** that I will repay you two
9:16 When that **d** arrives, the LORD their God will
12: 3 On that **d** I will make Jerusalem a heavy stone,
12: 4 "On that **d**, says the LORD, I will cause every
12: 6 "On that **d** I will make the clans of Judah like a
12: 8 On that **d** the LORD will defend the people of
12:11 and mourning in Jerusalem on that **d** will be like
13: 1 "On that **d** a fountain will be opened for the
13: 2 "And on that **d**, says the LORD Almighty,
14: 1 for the **d** of the LORD is coming when your
14: 2 On that **d** I will gather all the nations to fight
14: 4 On that **d** his feet will stand on the Mount of
14: 6 On that **d** the sources of light will no longer shine,
14: 7 yet there will be continuous **d**! Only the LORD
14: 7 There will be no normal **d** and night, for at evening
14: 8 On that **d** life-giving waters will flow out from
14: 9 On that **d** there will be one LORD—his name
14:13 On that **d** they will be terrified, stricken by the
14:20 On that **d** even the harness bells of the horses will
14:21 And on that **d** there will no longer be traders in the
Mal 2:14 other on your wedding **d** when you were young.
3:17 "On the **d** when I act, they will be my own special
4: 1 "The **d** of judgment is coming, burning like a
4: 1 the wicked will be burned up like straw on that **d**.
4: 3 On the **d** when I act, you will tread upon the
4: 5 the great and dreadful **d** of the LORD arrives.
Mt 4:18 One **d** as Jesus was walking along the shore beside
5: 1 One **d** as the crowds were gathering, Jesus went up
6:33 and he will give you all you need from **d** to **d** if
7:22 On judgment **d** many will tell me, 'Lord, Lord,
9:14 One **d** the disciples of John the Baptist came to
10:15 and Gomorrah will be better off on the judgment **d**
11:22 and Sidon will be better off on the judgment **d** than
11:24 Sodom will be better off on the judgment **d** than
12:10 "Is it legal to work by healing on the Sabbath **d**?"
12:36 that you must give an account on judgment **d** of
12:38 One **d** some teachers of religious law
12:41 will rise up against this generation on judgment **d**
12:42 also rise up against this generation on judgment **d**
13: 1 Later that same **d**, Jesus left the house and went
15:38 were four thousand men who were fed that **d**,
16: 1 One **d** the Pharisees and Sadducees came to test
16: 3 red sky in the morning means foul weather all **d**.'
16:21 be killed, and he would be raised on the third **d**.
17:22 One **d** after they had returned to Galilee, Jesus told
20: 4 pay them whatever was right at the end of the **d**.
20:12 paid us who worked all **d** in the scorching heat.'
20:13 Didn't you agree to work all **d** for the usual wage?
20:19 But on the third **d** he will be raised from the
22:23 That same **d** some Sadducees stepped forward—
24:36 no one knows the **d** or the hour when these things
24:37 of Man returns, it will be like it was in Noah's **d**.
24:42 because you don't know what **d** your Lord is
25:13 because you do not know the **d** or hour of my
26:17 On the first **d** of the Festival of Unleavened Bread,
26:29 I will not drink wine again until the **d** I drink it
26:55 me in the Temple? I was there teaching every **d**.
27:62 The next **d**—on the first **d** of the Passover ceremonies—
27:64 we request that you seal the tomb until the third **d**.
28: 1 as the new **d** was dawning, Mary Magdalene
Mk 1: 9 One **d** Jesus came from Nazareth in Galilee,
1:16 One **d** as Jesus was walking along the shores of the
1:21 and every Sabbath **d** he went into the synagogue
2:18 One **d** some people came to Jesus and asked,
2:23 One Sabbath **d** as Jesus was walking through some
3: 4 deeds on the Sabbath, or is it a **d** for doing harm?
3: 4 Is this a **d** to save life or to destroy it?"
3:10 There had been many healings that **d**. As a result,
5: 5 All **d** long and throughout the night he would
7: 1 One **d** some Pharisees and teachers of religious
8: 9 about four thousand people in the crowd that **d**,
10:13 One **d** some parents brought their children to Jesus
11:21 what Jesus had said to the tree on the previous **d**
13: 1 As Jesus was leaving the Temple that **d**, one of his
13:32 no one knows the **d** or hour when these things will
14:12 On the first **d** of the Festival of Unleavened Bread (the **d** the Passover lambs were sacrificed),
14:25 **d** when I drink it new in the Kingdom of God."
14:49 me in the Temple? I was there teaching every **d**.
15:42 the **d** of preparation, the **d** before the Sabbath.
Lk 1: 8 One **d** Zechariah was serving God in the Temple,
2:27 That **d** the Spirit led him to the Temple. So when
2:37 never left the Temple but stayed there **d** and night,
3:21 One **d** when the crowds were being baptized,
4:31 and taught there in the synagogue every Sabbath **d**.
4:38 After leaving the synagogue that **d**, Jesus went to
5: 1 One **d** as Jesus was preaching on the shore of the
5:17 One **d** while Jesus was teaching, some Pharisees
6: 1 One Sabbath **d** as Jesus was walking through some
6: 6 On another Sabbath **d**, a man with a deformed
6: 9 deeds on the Sabbath, or is it a **d** for doing harm?
6: 9 Is this a **d** to save life or to destroy it?"
6:12 One **d** soon afterward Jesus went to a mountain to
7:17 The report of what Jesus had done that **d** spread all
8: 4 One **d** Jesus told this story to a large crowd that
8:22 One **d** Jesus said to his disciples, "Let's cross over
9: 1 One **d** Jesus called together his twelve apostles
9:18 One **d** as Jesus was alone, praying, he came over to
9:37 The next **d**, after they had come down the
10:12 be better off than such a town on the judgment **d**.
10:14 and Sidon will be better off on the judgment **d** than
10:25 One **d** an expert in religious law stood up to test
10:35 The next **d** he handed the innkeeper two pieces of
11: 3 Give us our food **d** by **d**.
11:14 One **d** Jesus cast a demon out of a man who
11:31 will rise up against this generation on judgment **d**
11:32 will rise up against this generation on judgment **d**
12:31 He will give you all you need from **d** to **d** if you
13:10 One Sabbath **d** as Jesus was teaching in a
13:14 that Jesus had healed her on the Sabbath **d**.
13:15 "You hypocrite! You work on the Sabbath **d**!
13:16 Wasn't it necessary for me, even on the Sabbath **d**,
13:32 and the third **d** I will accomplish my purpose.
13:33 and the next **d** I must proceed on my way.
14: 1 One Sabbath **d** Jesus was in the home of a leader
14: 3 in the law to heal people on the Sabbath **d**,
15:32 We had to celebrate this happy **d**. For your brother
16:19 splendidly clothed and who lived each **d** in luxury.
17: 1 One **d** Jesus said to his disciples, "There will
17: 4 Even if he wrongs you seven times a **d** and each
17: 5 One **d** the apostles said to the Lord, "We need
17:20 One **d** the Pharisees asked Jesus, "When will the
17:26 the world will be like the people were in Noah's **d**.
17:31 On that **d** a person outside the house must not go
18: 1 One **d** Jesus told his disciples a story to illustrate
18: 7 justice to his chosen people who plead with him **d**
18:15 One **d** some parents brought their little children to
18:33 and kill him, but on the third **d** he will rise again."
20: 1 One **d** as Jesus was teaching and preaching the
21:34 of this life. Don't let that **d** catch you unaware,
21:35 For that **d** will come upon everyone living on the
21:37 Every **d** Jesus went to the Temple to teach,
22:53 I was there every **d**. But this is your moment,
23:12 had been enemies before, became friends that **d**.
23:54 the **d** of preparation for the Sabbath.
23:56 so they rested all that **d** as required by the law.
24: 7 and that he would rise again the third **d**?"
24:13 That same **d** two of Jesus' followers were walking
24:46 and die and rise again from the dead on the third **d**.
Jn 1:29 The next **d** John saw Jesus coming toward him
1:35 The following **d**, John was again standing with two
1:39 to the place, and they stayed there the rest of the **d**.
1:43 The next **d** Jesus decided to go to Galilee.
2: 1 The next **d** Jesus' mother was a guest at a wedding
5: 9 But this miracle happened on the Sabbath **d**.
6:34 "give us that bread every **d** of our lives."
6:39 that I should raise them to eternal life at the last **d**.
6:40 eternal life—that I should raise them at the last **d**."
6:44 and at the last **d** I will raise them from the dead.
6:54 have eternal life, and I will raise them at the last **d**.
7:37 On the last **d**, the climax of the festival,
11: 9 "There are twelve hours of daylight every **d**.
11:24 "when everyone else rises, on resurrection **d**."
12:12 The next **d**, the news that Jesus was on the way to
12:48 and my message will be judged at the **d** of
19:14 It was now about noon of the **d** of preparation for
19:31 didn't want the victims hanging there the next **d**,
19:42 because it was the **d** of preparation before the
20:19 That evening, on the first **d** of the week,
Ac 1: 2 until the **d** he ascended to heaven after giving his
1:15 on a **d** when about 120 believers were present,
1:22 from the time he was baptized by John until the **d**
2: 1 On the **d** of Pentecost, seven weeks after Jesus'
2:20 before that great and glorious **d** of the Lord arrives.
2:46 They worshiped together at the Temple each **d**,
2:47 And each **d** the Lord added to their group those
3: 2 Each **d** he was put beside the Temple gate, the one
4: 5 The next **d** the council of all the rulers and elders
5:42 And every **d**, in the Temple and in their homes,
6: 9 But one **d** some men from the Synagogue of Freed
7:23 "One **d** when he was forty years old, he decided to
7:26 "The next **d** he visited them again and saw two
8: 1 A great wave of persecution began that **d**,
9:24 and that they were watching for him **d** and night at
10: 9 The next **d** as Cornelius' messengers were nearing
10:23 The next **d** he went with them, accompanied by
10:24 They arrived in Caesarea the following **d**.
11: 5 "One **d** in Joppa," he said, "while I was praying,
12:21 When the **d** arrived, Herod put on his royal robes,
13: 2 One **d** as these men were worshiping the Lord
13:41 For I am doing something in your own **d**,
13:42 As Paul and Barnabas left the synagogue that **d**,
14:20 The next **d** he left with Barnabas for Derbe.
15:31 that **d** as they read this encouraging message.
16:11 and the next **d** we landed at Neapolis.
16:16 One **d** as we were going down to the place of
16:18 This went on **d** after **d** until Paul got
17:11 They searched the Scriptures **d** after **d** to check
17:31 For he has set a **d** for judging the world with

20: 7 On the first **d** of the week, we gathered to observe
20: 7 and since he was leaving the next **d**, he talked until
20: 15 The next **d** we passed the island of Kios.
20: 15 The following **d**, we crossed to the island of
20: 15 of Samos. And a **d** later we arrived at Miletus.
20: 18 "You know that from the **d** I set foot in the
20: 31 my constant watch and care over you night and **d**,
21: 1 The next **d** we reached Rhodes and then went to
21: 7 we greeted the believers but stayed only one **d**.
21: 18 The next **d** Paul went in with us to meet with
21: 26 and the next **d** he went through the purification
21: 29 (For earlier that **d** they had seen him in the city
22: 17 "One **d** after I returned to Jerusalem, I was
22: 30 The next **d** the commander freed Paul from his
25: 6 and on the following **d** Paul's trial began.
25: 17 I called the case the very next **d** and ordered Paul
25: 23 So the next **d** Agrippa and Bernice arrived at the
26: 7 twelve tribes of Israel worship God night and **d**,
26: 12 "One **d** I was on such a mission to Damascus,
27: 3 The next **d** when we docked at Sidon, Julius was
27: 18 The next **d**, as gale-force winds continued to batter
27: 19 The following **d** they even threw out the ship's
28: 13 A **d** later a south wind began blowing,
28: 13 so the following **d** we sailed up the coast to
28: 23 and on that **d** a large number of people came to
Ro 1: 9 **D** and night I bring you and your needs in prayer to
2: 5 For there is going to come a **d** of judgment when
2: 16 The **d** will surely come when God, by Jesus Christ,
8: 19 For all creation is waiting eagerly for that future **d**
8: 21 All creation anticipates the **d** when it will join
8: 23 wait anxiously for that **d** when God will give us
8: 36 "For your sake we are killed every **d**;
10: 21 God said, / "All **d** long I opened my arms to them,
11: 8 To this very **d** he has shut their eyes so they do not
13: 12 almost gone; the **d** of salvation will soon be here.
14: 5 some think one **d** is more holy than another **d**,
while others think every **d** is alike.
14: 6 Those who have a special **d** for worshiping the
1Co 1: 8 on the great **d** when our Lord Jesus Christ returns.
3: 13 **d** to see what kind of work each builder has done.
10: 8 them did, causing 23,000 of them to die in one **d**.
15: 4 and he was raised from the dead on the third **d**,
16: 2 On every Lord's **D**, each of you should put aside
2Co 1: 14 Then on the **d** when our Lord Jesus comes back
3: 14 and even to this **d** whenever the old covenant is
4: 16 are dying, our spirits are being renewed every **d**.
5: 2 and we long for the **d** when we will put on our
6: 2 On the **d** of salvation, I helped you." Indeed,
6: 2 to help you right now. Today is the **d** of salvation.
11: 25 Once I spent a whole night and a **d** adrift at sea.
Eph 4: 30 guaranteeing that you will be saved on the **d** of
Php 1: 6 on that **d** when Christ Jesus comes back again.
3: 12 But I keep working toward that **d** when I will
Col 1: 6 just as it changed yours that very first **d** you heard
1Th 2: 9 Night and **d** we toiled to earn a living so that our
3: 10 Night and **d** we pray earnestly for you, asking God
3: 13 **d** when our Lord Jesus comes with all those who
5: 2 for you know quite well that the **d** of the Lord will
5: 4 and you won't be surprised when the **d** of the Lord
5: 5 For you are all children of the light and of the **d**;
5: 23 and body be kept blameless until that **d** when our
2Th 1: 10 you will be among those praising him on that **d**,
2: 2 and troubled by those who say that the **d** of the
2: 3 For that **d** will not come until there is a great
3: 8 We worked hard **d** and night so that we would not
1Ti 5: 5 Night and **d** she asks God for help and spends
2Ti 1: 3 and **d** I constantly remember you in my prayers.
1: 12 I have entrusted to him until the **d** of his return.
1: 18 May the Lord show him special kindness on the **d**
4: 8 will give me on that great **d** of his return.
Heb 3: 13 You must warn each other every **d**, as long as it is
4: 4 because the Scriptures mention the seventh **d**,
4: 4 "On the seventh **d** God rested from all his work."
4: 8 God would not have spoken later about another **d**
7: 27 He does not need to offer sacrifices every **d** like
8: 8 "The **d** will come, says the Lord, / when I will
8: 10 with the people of Israel on that **d**, says the Lord:
10: 11 the priest stands before the altar **d** after **d**,
10: 16 with my people on that **d**, says the Lord: / I will
10: 25 especially now that the **d** of his coming back again
Jas 5: 3 as evidence against you on the last **d** of judgment.
1Pe 1: 5 It will be revealed on the last **d** for all to see.
1: 7 and honor on the **d** when Jesus Christ is revealed
2Pe 1: 19 until the **d** Christ appears and his brilliant light
2: 4 gloomy caves and darkness until the judgment **d**.
2: 8 by the wickedness he saw and heard **d** after **d**.
2: 9 the wicked right up until the **d** of judgment.
3: 7 and the earth will be consumed by fire on the **d** of
3: 8 that a **d** is like a thousand years to the Lord, and a
thousand years is like a **d**.
3: 10 But the **d** of the Lord will come as unexpectedly as
3: 12 You should look forward to that **d** and hurry it
3: 12 the **d** when God will set the heavens on fire
1Jn 4: 17 So we will not be afraid on the **d** of judgment,
Jude 1: 6 prisons of darkness, waiting for the **d** of judgment.
Rev 1: 10 It was the Lord's **D**, and I was worshiping in the
4: 8 **D** after **d** and night after night they keep on
6: 17 For the great **d** of their wrath has come, and who
7: 15 of God, serving him **d** and night in his Temple.
8: 12 And one-third of the **d** was dark and one-third of
9: 15 had been prepared for this hour and **d** and month
12: 10 and sisters before our God **d** and night.
14: 11 and ever, and they will have no relief **d** or night,
16: 14 Lord on that great judgment **d** of God Almighty.
18: 8 and famine will overtake her in a single **d**.
20: 10 There they will be tormented **d** and night forever
21: 25 Its gates never close at the end of **d** because there

DAY'S (7) [DAY]

Ex 23: 19 bring me a choice sample of the first **d** harvest.
Jdg 20: 44 Benjamin's greatest warriors died in that **d** battle.
2Sa 19: 2 the joy of that **d** victory was turned into deep
Pr 31: 15 and plan the **d** work for her servant girls.
Mt 20: 9 o'clock were paid, each received a full **d** wage.
20: 10 receive more. But they, too, were paid a **d** wage.
Rev 6: 6 wheat bread or three loaves of barley for a **d** pay.

DAYBREAK (9) [DAY]

Jdg 19: 26 At **d** the woman returned to the house where her
1Sa 9: 26 At **d** the next morning, Samuel called up to Saul,
2Sa 2: 32 they traveled all night and reached Hebron at **d**.
Mt 10: 27 now in the darkness, shout abroad when **d** comes.
Mk 1: 35 The next morning Jesus awoke long before **d**
13: 35 at evening, midnight, early dawn, or late **d**.
Lk 6: 13 At **d** he called together all of his disciples
22: 66 At **d** all the leaders of the people assembled,
Ac 5: 21 So the apostles entered the Temple about **d**

DAYLIGHT (12) [DAY, LIGHT]

Ex 22: 3 But if it happens in **d**, the one who killed the thief
Nu 25: 4 and execute them before the LORD in broad **d**,
Dt 28: 29 You will grope around in broad **d**, just like a blind
Jdg 9: 33 In the morning, as soon as it is **d**, storm the city.
Job 5: 14 They grope in the **d** as though they were blind;
38: 13 Have you ever told the **d** to spread to the ends of
Eze 12: 3 Make your preparations in broad **d** so the people
12: 7 In broad **d** I brought my pack outside, filled with
Hos 4: 5 you will stumble in broad **d**, just as you might at
Jn 11: 9 "There are twelve hours of **d** every day.
Ac 27: 29 out four anchors from the stern and prayed for **d**.
2Pe 2: 13 They love to indulge in evil pleasures in broad **d**.

DAYS (511) [DAY]

ALL THE DAYS (2) Ps 23:6; 27:4

DAYS OF...LIFE (3) Ps 21:4; 23:6; 27:4

DAYS OF OLD (4) Ps 143:5; Isa 51:9; 63:11; Heb 11:2

DAYS TO COME (5) Ge 49:1; Dt 31:29; Ecc 2:16; Jer 23:20; 30:24

FORTY DAYS (21) Ge 7:4,12,17; 8:6; 50:3; Ex 24:18; 34:28; Nu 13:25; 14:34; Dt 9:9,11,18,25; 10:10; 1Sa 17:16; 1Ki 19:8; Jnh 3:4; Mt 4:2; Mk 1:13; Lk 4:2; Ac 1:3

LAST DAYS (6) Isa 2:2; Hos 3:5; Mic 4:1; Ac 2:17; 2Ti 3:1; 2Pe 3:3

SEVEN DAYS (81) Ge 8:10; 31:23; Ex 12:15,15,19; 13:6,7; 22:30; 23:15; 29:30,35,37; 34:18; Lev 8:33,35; 12:2; 13:4,21,26,31,33,50; 14:8,38; 15:13,19,24,28; 22:27; 23:6,8,34,40; Nu 6:9; 12:14,14,15; 19:11,14,16; 28:24; 31:19; Dt 16:3,4,13,15; Jdg 14:12; 1Sa 10:8; 11:3; 13:8; 31:13; 1Ki 8:65,65; 16:15; 20:29; 2Ki 3:9; 1Ch 10:12; 2Ch 7:8,9,9; 30:21,22,23; 35:17; Ezr 6:22; Ne 8:17,18; Est 1:5; Job 2:13; Isa 30:26; Eze 3:15,16; 43:25,26; 44:26; 45:21,23,25; Ac 21:27; 28:14; Heb 11:30

SIX DAYS (18) Ex 16:26; 20:9,11; 23:12; 24:16; 31:15,17; 34:21; 35:2; Lev 23:3; Dt 5:13; 16:8; Jos 6:3,14; Mt 17:1; Mk 9:2; Lk 13:14; Jn 12:1

THREE DAYS (75) Ge 31:22; 34:25; 40:12,13,18,19,20; 42:17; Ex 10:22; 14:5; 15:22; Nu 10:33; 33:8; Jos 1:11; 2:16,22; 3:2; 9:16,17; Jdg 14:14; 19:4; 1Sa 9:20; 30:1,12,13; 2Sa 20:4,5; 24:13,15; 1Ki 3:18; 12:5,12; 2Ki 2:17; 20:5,8; 1Ch 12:39; 21:12; 2Ch 10:5,12; 20:25; Ezr 8:15,32; 10:8,9; Ne 2:11; Est 4:16; 5:1; Isa 38:22; Am 4:4; Jnh 1:17; 3:3; Mt 12:40,40; 15:32; 17:23; 26:61; 27:40,63; Mk 8:2,31; 9:31; 10:34; 14:58; 15:29; Lk 2:46; 9:22; 24:21; Jn 2:19,20; Ac 9:9; 10:40; 25:1; 28:7,12,17

Ge 1: 14 signs to mark off the seasons, the **d**, and the years.
6: 4 In those **d**, and even afterward, giants lived on the
7: 4 One week from today I will begin forty **d** and forty
7: 12 The rain continued to fall for forty **d** and forty
7: 17 For forty **d** the floods prevailed,
7: 24 And the water covered the earth for 150 **d**.
8: 3 the flood gradually began to recede. After 150 **d**,
8: 6 After another forty **d**, Noah opened the window he
8: 10 Seven **d** later, Noah released the dove again.
21: 4 Eight **d** after Isaac was born, Abraham circumcised
24: 55 "But we want Rebekah to stay at least ten **d**,"
29: 20 so strong that it seemed to him but a few **d**.
31: 22 Laban didn't learn of their flight for three **d**.
31: 23 He caught up with them seven **d** later in the hill
34: 25 But three **d** later, when their wounds were still
37: 34 He mourned deeply for his son for many **d**.
40: 12 Joseph said. "The three branches mean three **d**.
40: 13 Within three **d** Pharaoh will take you out of prison
40: 18 Joseph told him. "The three baskets mean three **d**.
40: 19 Three **d** from now Pharaoh will cut off your head
40: 20 Pharaoh's birthday came three **d** later, and he gave
42: 17 So he put them all in prison for three **d**.
49: 1 what is going to happen to you in the **d** to come.
50: 3 The embalming process took forty **d**, and there was
50: 3 was a period of national mourning for seventy **d**.
Ex 10: 22 was deep darkness over the entire land for three **d**.
12: 15 For seven **d**, you may eat only bread made without
12: 15 **d** of the festival will be cut off from the
12: 16 No work of any kind may be done on these **d**
12: 19 During those seven **d**, there must be no trace of
12: 20 during those **d** you must not eat anything made
13: 6 For seven **d** you will eat only bread without yeast.
13: 7 Eat only bread without yeast during those seven **d**.
13: 8 "During these festival **d** each year, you must
14: 5 were not planning to return to Egypt after three **d**,
15: 22 They traveled in this desert for three **d** without
16: 26 Gather the food for six **d**, but the seventh day is a
16: 29 on the sixth day, so there will be enough for two **d**.
19: 15 "Get ready for an important event two **d** from
20: 9 Six **d** a week are set apart for your daily duties
20: 11 For in six **d** the LORD made the heavens,
21: 21 If the slave recovers after a couple of **d**, however,
22: 30 the newborn animal with its mother for seven **d**;
23: 12 "Work for six **d**, and rest on the seventh. This will
23: 15 For seven **d** you are to eat bread made without
24: 16 Mount Sinai, and the cloud covered it for six **d**.
24: 18 He stayed on the mountain forty **d** and forty nights.
29: 30 **d** before beginning to minister in the Tabernacle
29: 35 The ordination ceremony will go on for seven **d**.
29: 37 atonement for the altar every day for seven **d**.
31: 15 Work six **d** only, but the seventh day must be a day
31: 17 For in six **d** the LORD made heaven and earth,
34: 18 the Festival of Unleavened Bread for seven **d**,
34: 21 "Six **d** are set aside for work, but on the Sabbath
34: 28 was up on the mountain with the LORD forty **d**
35: 2 Each week, work for six **d** only. The seventh day is
Lev 8: 33 Do not leave the Tabernacle entrance for seven **d**,
8: 35 of the Tabernacle day and night for seven **d**,
12: 2 she will be ceremonially unclean for seven **d**,
12: 4 Then the woman must wait for thirty-three **d** until
12: 5 then wait another sixty-six **d** to be purified from
13: 4 put the infected person in quarantine for seven **d**.
13: 5 will put the person in quarantine for seven more **d**.
13: 21 priest is to put the person in quarantine for seven **d**.
13: 26 put the infected person in quarantine for seven **d**.
13: 31 he must put the person in quarantine for seven **d**.
13: 33 put the person in quarantine for another seven **d**,
13: 50 the priest will put it away for seven **d**.
13: 54 to be washed and then isolated for seven more **d**.
14: 8 must still remain outside their tents for seven **d**.
14: 38 he will leave the house and lock it up for seven **d**.
15: 13 he must count off a period of seven **d**.
15: 19 she will be ceremonially unclean for seven **d**.
15: 24 He will remain defiled for seven **d**, and any bed on
15: 25 continues for many **d** beyond the normal period,
15: 28 she must count off a period of seven **d**.
19: 3 and you must always observe my Sabbath **d** of
19: 30 "Keep my Sabbath **d** of rest and show reverence
22: 27 is born, it must be left with its mother for seven **d**.
23: 2 the **d** when all of you will be summoned to
23: 3 You may work for six **d** each week, but on the
23: 6 This festival to the LORD continues for seven **d**,
23: 8 On each of the seven **d**, the people must
23: 16 fifty **d** later, and bring an offering of new grain to
23: 34 This festival to the LORD will last for seven **d**.
23: 36 On each of the seven festival **d**, you must present
23: 38 in addition to the LORD's regular Sabbath **d**.
23: 39 and closing eighth day of the festival will be **d** of
23: 40 rejoice before the LORD your God for seven **d**.
23: 42 During the seven festival **d**, all of you who are
26: 2 You must keep my Sabbath **d** of rest and show
Nu 6: 9 they must wait for seven **d** and then shave their
6: 12 The **d** of their vow that were completed before
9: 20 would stay over the Tabernacle for only a few **d**,
9: 20 so the people would stay for only a few **d**.
9: 22 the cloud stayed above the Tabernacle for two **d**,
10: 33 They marched for three **d** after leaving the
12: 14 wouldn't she have been defiled for seven **d**?
12: 14 Banish her from the camp for seven **d**, and after
12: 15 Miriam was excluded from the camp for seven **d**,
13: 25 After exploring the land for forty **d**, the men
14: 34 men who explored the land were there for forty **d**,
19: 11 body will be ceremonially unclean for seven **d**.
19: 12 and seventh **d** with the water of purification;
19: 12 if they do not do this on the third and seventh **d**,
19: 14 will be ceremonially unclean for seven **d**.
19: 16 or a grave, that person will be unclean for seven **d**.
19: 19 and seventh **d** the ceremonially clean person must
20: 29 had died, all Israel mourned for him thirty **d**.
28: 24 On each of the seven **d** of the festival, this is how
29: 7 "Ten **d** later, you must call another holy assembly
29: 12 "Five **d** later, you must call yet another holy
31: 19 dead body must stay outside the camp for seven **d**.
31: 19 and your captives on the third and seventh **d**.
33: 8 Then they traveled for three **d** into the Etham
Dt 1: 2 Normally it takes only eleven **d** to travel from
4: 30 "When those bitter **d** have come upon you far in
5: 13 Six **d** a week are set apart for your daily duties
9: 9 I was there for forty **d** and forty nights, and all that
9: 11 "At the end of the forty **d** and nights, the LORD
9: 18 Then for forty **d** and nights I lay prostrate before
9: 25 I fell down and lay before the LORD for forty **d**
10: 10 the mountain in the LORD's presence for forty **d**
16: 3 For seven **d** eat only bread made without yeast,
16: 4 in any house throughout your land for seven **d**.
16: 8 For the next six **d** you may not eat bread made
16: 13 must be observed for seven **d** at the end of the
16: 15 For seven **d** celebrate this festival to honor the
31: 29 In the **d** to come, disaster will come down on you,
32: 7 Remember the **d** of long ago; / think about the
33: 25 may your strength match the length of your **d**!"
34: 8 The people of Israel mourned thirty **d** for Moses on
Jos 1: 11 In three **d** you will cross the Jordan River and take
2: 16 "Hide there for three **d** until the men who are
2: 22 up into the hill country and stayed there three **d**.
3: 2 Three **d** later, the Israelite leaders went through
6: 3 is to march around the city once a day for six **d**.
6: 14 to the camp. They followed this pattern for six **d**.
9: 16 Three **d** later, the facts came out—these people of
9: 17 to investigate and reached their towns in three **d**.
Jdg 5: 6 "In the **d** of Shamgar son of Anath, and in the **d** of
Jael,

11:40 for young Israelite women to go away for four **d**
13: 2 In those **d**, a man named Manoah from the tribe of
14:12 If you solve my riddle during these seven **d** of the
14:14 Three **d** later they were still trying to figure it out.
17: 6 In those **d** Israel had no king, so the people did
18: 1 Now in those **d** Israel had no king. And the tribe of
19: 1 Now in those **d** Israel had no king. There was a
19: 4 so he stayed three **d**, eating, drinking, and sleeping
20:27 (In those **d** the Ark of the Covenant of God was in
21:25 In those **d** Israel had no king, so the people did
Ru 1: 1 In the **d** when the judges ruled in Israel, a man
4: 7 In those **d** it was the custom in Israel for anyone
1Sa 2:32 members of your family will ever live out their **d**.
3: 1 Now in those **d** messages from the LORD were
7:14 peace between Israel and the Amorites in those **d**.
9: 9 (In those **d** if people wanted a message from God,
9:20 about those donkeys that were lost three **d** ago,
10: 8 Gilgal ahead of me and wait for me there seven **d**.
11: 3 "Give us seven **d** to send messengers throughout
13: 8 Saul waited there seven **d** for Samuel, as Samuel
13:19 no blacksmiths in the land of Israel in those **d**.
17:16 For forty **d**, twice a day, morning and evening,
25:10 There are lots of servants these **d** who run away
25:38 About ten **d** later, the LORD struck him and he
30: 1 Three **d** later, when David and his men arrived
30:12 had anything to eat or drink for three **d** and nights.
30:13 "My master left me behind three **d** ago because I
31:13 tree at Jabesh, and they fasted for seven **d**.
2Sa 1: 1 over the Amalekites and spent two **d** in Ziklag.
13:18 as was the custom in those **d** for the king's virgin
13:37 And David mourned many **d** for his son Amnon.
20: 4 to mobilize the army of Judah within three **d**
20: 5 but it took him longer than the three **d** he had been
24: 8 and twenty **d** and then returned to Jerusalem.
24:13 or three **d** of severe plague throughout your land?
24:15 upon Israel that morning, and it lasted for three **d**.
1Ki 3:18 Three **d** later, she also had a baby. We were alone;
8:65 The celebration went on for fourteen **d** in all—
8:65 seven **d** for the dedication of the altar and seven **d**
for the Festival of Shelters.
12: 5 "Give me three **d** to think this over.
12:12 Three **d** later, Jeroboam and all the people returned
16:15 Asa's reign in Judah, but he reigned only seven **d**.
17:15 to eat from her supply of flour and oil for many **d**.
19: 8 the food gave him enough strength to travel forty **d**
20:29 armies camped opposite each other for seven **d**,
22:46 who still continued their practices from the **d** of his
2Ki 2:17 So fifty men searched for three **d** but did not find
3: 9 route through the wilderness for seven **d**.
13: 5 Israel lived in safety again as they had in former **d**.
15:37 In those **d** the LORD began to send King Rezin
20: 5 and three **d** from now you will get out of bed
20: 8 to the Temple of the LORD three **d** from now?"
25:16 the LORD's Temple in the **d** of King Solomon.
1Ch 5:17 records during the **d** of King Jotham of Judah
9:22 In all, there were 212 gatekeepers in those **d**,
10:12 the oak tree at Jabesh, and they fasted for seven **d**.
12:39 They feasted and drank with David for three **d**,
21:12 or three **d** of severe plague as the angel of the
23:31 that were presented to the LORD on Sabbath **d**,
29:15 Our **d** on earth are like a shadow, gone so soon
2Ch 7: 8 For the next seven **d** they celebrated the Festival of
7: 9 celebrated the dedication of the altar for seven **d**
and the Festival of Shelters for seven **d**.
10: 5 "Come back in three **d** for my answer."
10:12 Three **d** later, Jeroboam and all the people returned
13: 9 You let anyone become a priest these **d**!
20:25 so much plunder that it took them three **d** just to
26: 5 Uzziah sought God during the **d** of Zechariah,
29:17 and in eight **d** they had reached the foyer of the
29:17 of the LORD itself, which took another eight **d**.
29:17 So the entire task was completed in sixteen **d**.
30:21 of Unleavened Bread for seven **d** with great joy.
30:22 So for seven **d** the celebration continued.
30:23 decided to continue the festival another seven **d**,
30:26 a celebration like this one since the **d** of Solomon,
35:17 and the Festival of Unleavened Bread for seven **d**.
36: 9 reigned in Jerusalem only three months and ten **d**.
Ezr 3: 6 Fifteen **d** before the Festival of Shelters began,
6:22 the Festival of Unleavened Bread for seven **d**.
8:15 and we camped there for three **d** while I went over
8:32 safely in Jerusalem, where we rested for three **d**.
10: 8 Those who failed to come within three **d** would,
10: 9 Within three **d**, all the people of Judah
Ne 1: 4 In fact, for **d** I mourned, fasted, and prayed to the
1:11 to me." In those **d** I was the king's cup-bearer.
2:11 Three **d** after my arrival at Jerusalem,
5:18 And every ten **d** we needed a large supply of all
6:15 just fifty-two **d** after we had begun.
6:17 During those fifty-two **d**, many letters went back
8:17 in these shelters for the seven **d** of the festival,
8:17 this way since the **d** of Joshua son of Nun.
8:18 Law of God on each of the seven **d** of the festival.
9:32 and ancestors from the **d** when the kings of Assyria
12: 7 the priests and their associates in the **d** of Jeshua.
12:22 and the priests in the **d** of the following high
12:23 *The Book of History* down to the **d** of Johanan,
12:26 These all served in the **d** of Joiakim son of Jeshua,
12:26 and in the **d** of Nehemiah the governor and of Ezra
12:46 and thanks to God began long ago in the **d** of
12:47 So now, in the **d** of Zerubbabel and of Nehemiah,
Est 1: 1 This happened in the **d** of King Xerxes,
1: 5 It lasted for seven **d** and was held at Susa in the
4:16 Do not eat or drink for three **d**, night or day.
5: 1 Three **d** later, Esther put on her royal robes
9:21 them to celebrate an annual festival on these two **d**.
9:22 He told them to celebrate these **d** with feasting
9:27 two prescribed **d** at the appointed time each year.
9:28 These **d** would be remembered and kept from
9:28 These **d** would never cease to be celebrated among
9:31 an annual celebration of these **d** at the appointed
Job 1: 5 and sometimes they lasted several **d**—Job would
2:13 Then they sat on the ground with him for seven **d**
3: 6 never again to be counted among the **d** of the year,
7: 6 "My **d** are swifter than a weaver's shuttle flying
7:16 Oh, leave me alone for these few remaining **d**.
8: 9 Our **d** on earth are as transient as a shadow.
15:21 and even on good **d** they fear the attack of the
17:11 My **d** are over. My hopes have disappeared.
21:13 They spend their **d** in prosperity; then they go
29: 6 In those **d** my cows produced milk in abundance,
29: 7 "Those were the **d** when I went to the city gate
30:16 now my heart is broken. Depression haunts my **d**.
30:27 and restless. **D** of affliction have come upon me.
Ps 21: 4 his request. / The **d** of his life stretch on forever.
23: 6 unfailing love will pursue me / all the **d** of my life,
27: 4 is to live in the house of the LORD all the **d** of
38: 6 and racked with pain. / My **d** are filled with grief.
39: 4 Remind me that my **d** are numbered, / and that my
44: 1 of all you did in other **d**, / in **d** long ago:
56: 5 they spend their **d** plotting ways to harm me.
77: 5 I think of the good old **d**, long since ended,
89:29 his throne will be as endless as the **d** of heaven.
102: 3 for my **d** disappear like smoke, / and my bones
102:23 He has cut me down in midlife, / shortening my **d**.
103:15 Our **d** on earth are like grass; / like wildflowers,
119:152 I have known from my earliest **d** / that your
143: 5 I remember the **d** of old. / I ponder all your great
144: 4 a breath of air; / our **d** are like a passing shadow.
Pr 9:11 Wisdom will multiply your **d** and add years to your
24: 2 For they spend their **d** plotting violence, and their
Ecc 2:16 and the fool both die, and in the **d** to come,
2:23 Their **d** of labor are filled with pain and grief;
6:12 In the few **d** of our empty lives, who knows how
our **d** can best be spent?
7:10 Don't long for "the good old **d**," for you don't
8:13 Their **d** will never grow long like the evening
9: 9 **d** of life that God has given you in this world.
11: 8 But let them also remember that the dark **d** will be
Isa 1:13 the Sabbath day, and your special **d** for fasting—
2: 2 In the last **d**, the Temple of the LORD in
2: 3 For in those **d** the LORD's teaching and his word
3: 6 In those **d** a man will say to his brother,
5:17 In those **d** flocks will feed among the ruins; lambs
13:22 Babylon's **d** are numbered; its time of destruction
30:26 be seven times brighter—like the light of seven **d**!
35: 1 Even the wilderness will rejoice in those **d**.
38:22 to the Temple of the LORD three **d** from now?"
40: 2 Tell her that her sad **d** are gone and that her sins
41:23 If you are gods, tell what will occur in the **d** ahead.
44: 7 tell you what is going to happen in the **d** ahead?
47: 1 For your **d** of glory, pomp, and honor have ended.
51: 9 Rouse yourself as in the **d** of old when you slew
56: 2 Blessed are those who honor my Sabbath **d** of rest
56: 4 this to the eunuchs who keep my Sabbath **d** holy,
60:20 Your **d** of mourning will come to an end.
63:11 Then they remembered those **d** of old when Moses
65:16 put aside my anger and forget the evil of earlier **d**.
65:20 "No longer will babies die when only a few **d** old.
65:21 In those **d**, people will live in the houses they build
65:25 In those **d**, no one will be hurt or destroyed on my
Jer 2: 3 In those **d** Israel was holy to the LORD, the first
3: 4 you have been my guide since the **d** of my youth.
3:16 "you will no longer wish for 'the good old **d**'
3:16 Those **d** will not be missed or even thought about,
3:18 In those **d** the people of Judah and Israel will
5:18 "Yet even in those **d** I will not blot you out
17:27 through the gates of Jerusalem just as on other **d**,
23:20 In the **d** to come, you will understand all this very
26:18 "Think back to the **d** when Micah of Moresheth
29:12 In those **d** when you pray, I will listen.
30:24 In the **d** to come, you will understand all this.
31:19 thoroughly ashamed of all I did in my younger **d**.'
32:30 have done nothing but wrong since their earliest **d**.
36: 2 Begin with the first message back in the **d** of
36:30 lie unburied—exposed to hot **d** and frosty nights.
37:16 a dungeon cell, where he remained for many **d**.
42: 7 Ten **d** later, the LORD gave his reply to Jeremiah.
44:17 For in those **d** we had plenty to eat, and we were
48:47 But in the latter **d** I will restore the fortunes of
49:39 But in the latter **d** I will restore the fortunes of
50:20 In those **d**," says the LORD, "no sin will be
52:20 the LORD's Temple in the **d** of King Solomon.
La 2: 6 out all memory of the holy festivals and Sabbath **d**.
4:18 Our end was near; our **d** were numbered. We were
Eze 3:15 I sat there among them for seven **d**, overwhelmed.
3:16 At the end of the seven **d**, the LORD gave me a
4: 4 You are to bear their sins for the number of **d** you
4: 5 You will bear Israel's sins for 390 **d**—one day for
4: 6 turn over and lie on your right side for 40 **d**—
4: 8 side until the **d** of your siege have been completed.
4: 9 during the 390 **d** you will be lying on your side.
16:22 you have not once thought of the **d** long ago when
16:56 In your proud **d** you held Sodom in contempt.
20:12 And I gave them my Sabbath **d** of rest as a sign
20:13 And they also violated my Sabbath **d**. So I
20:16 my will for them, and violated my Sabbath **d**.
20:20 and keep my Sabbath **d** holy, for they are a sign to
20:21 them life. And they also violated my Sabbath **d**.
20:24 scorned my instructions by violating my Sabbath **d**
22: 8 my holy things and violate my Sabbath **d** of rest.
22:26 They disregard my Sabbath **d** so that my holy
23:21 you celebrated your former **d** as a young girl in
29:16 of how sinful she was to trust Egypt in earlier **d**.
38:17 in future **d** I would bring you against my people.
43:25 "Every day for seven **d** a male goat, a young bull,
43:26 Do this each day for seven **d** to cleanse and make
44:26 ritually cleansed and then waiting for seven **d**.
45:17 the new moon celebrations, the Sabbath **d**, and all
45:21 the Passover. This festival will last for seven **d**.
45:23 On each of the seven **d** of the feast he will prepare
45:25 "During the seven **d** of the Festival of Shelters,
46: 1 but it will be open on Sabbath **d** and the **d** of new
moon celebrations.
46: 3 the LORD in front of this gateway on Sabbath **d**
and the **d** of new moon celebrations.
46:12 offer his sacrifices just as he does on Sabbath **d**.
Da 1:12 "Test us for ten **d** on a diet of vegetables
1:13 "At the end of the ten **d**, see how we look
1:14 to Daniel's suggestion and tested them for ten **d**.
1:15 At the end of the ten **d**, Daniel and his three friends
5:26 God has numbered the **d** of your reign and has
6: 7 Give orders that for the next thirty **d** anyone who
6:12 "Did you not sign a law that for the next thirty **d**
8:27 Daniel, was overcome and lay sick for several **d**.
10:13 But for twenty-one **d** the spirit prince of the
12:11 is set up to be worshiped, there will be 1,290 **d**.
12:12 who wait and remain until the end of the 1,335 **d**!
12:13 You will rest, and then at the end of the **d**, you will
Hos 2:11 her new moon celebrations, and her Sabbath **d**—
3: 3 "You must live in my house for many **d** and stop
3: 5 and they will receive his good gifts in the last **d**.
9: 5 What then will you do on festival **d**? What will
you do on **d** of feasting in the LORD's
10:11 break up the hard ground; their **d** of ease are gone.
Joel 2:29 In those **d**, I will pour out my Spirit even on
Am 4: 4 each morning and bring your tithes every three **d**!
Jnh 1:17 And Jonah was inside the fish for three **d** and three
3: 3 a city so large that it took three **d** to see it all.
3: 4 "Forty **d** from now Nineveh will be destroyed!"
Mic 4: 1 In the last **d**, the Temple of the LORD in
4: 2 For in those **d** the LORD's teaching and his word
Zec 8:23 In those **d** ten people from nations and languages
14: 5 the earthquake in the **d** of King Uzziah of Judah.
Mal 3: 7 Ever since the **d** of your ancestors, you have
Mt 3: 1 In those **d** John the Baptist began preaching in the
4: 2 For forty **d** and forty nights he ate nothing
12:40 Jonah was in the belly of the great fish for three **d**
12:40 will be in the heart of the earth for three **d**
15:32 They have been here with me for three **d**, and they
17: 1 Six **d** later Jesus took Peter and the two brothers,
17:23 but three **d** later he will be raised from the dead."
24:19 and for mothers nursing their babies in those **d**.
24:29 "Immediately after those horrible **d** end, / the sun
24:38 In those **d** before the Flood, the people were
26: 2 the Passover celebration begins in two **d**, and I,
26:61 the Temple of God and rebuild it in three **d**.' "
27:40 destroy the Temple and build it again in three **d**,
27:63 'After three **d** I will be raised from the dead.'
Mk 1:13 He was there for forty **d**, being tempted by Satan.
2: 1 Several **d** later Jesus returned to Capernaum,
2:26 He went into the house of God (during the **d** when
4:27 As the **d** went by, the seeds sprouted and grew
8: 2 They have been here with me for three **d**, and they
8:31 be killed, and three **d** later he would rise again.
8:38 and my message in these adulterous and sinful **d**,
9: 2 Six **d** later Jesus took Peter, James, and John to the
9:31 but three **d** later he will rise from the dead."
10:34 and kill him, but after three **d** he will rise again."
13:17 and for mothers nursing their babies in those **d**.
13:19 For those will be **d** of greater horror than at any
13:20 sake of his chosen ones he has shortened those **d**.
13:24 "At that time, after those horrible **d** end, / the sun
14: 1 It was now two **d** before the Passover celebration
14:58 and in three **d** I will build another, made without
15:29 can destroy the Temple and rebuild it in three **d**,
Lk 1:39 A few **d** later Mary hurried to the hill country of
1:59 When the baby was eight **d** old, all the relatives
2:21 Eight **d** later, when the baby was circumcised,
2:46 Three **d** later they finally discovered him. He was
4: 2 where the Devil tempted him for forty **d**. He ate
9:22 but three **d** later I will be raised from the dead."
9:28 About eight **d** later Jesus took Peter, James,
13:14 "There are six **d** of the week for working,"
13:14 "Come on those **d** to be healed, not on the
15:13 "A few **d** later this younger son packed all his
17:22 you will long to share in the **d** of the Son of Man,
17:27 In those **d** before the flood, the people enjoyed
17:28 "And the world will be as it was in the **d** of Lot.
21:22 For those will be **d** of God's vengeance,
23:29 For the **d** are coming when they will say,
24:18 things that have happened there the last few **d**."
24:21 to rescue Israel. That all happened three **d** ago.
Jn 2:12 he went to Capernaum for a few **d** with his mother,
2:19 this temple, and in three **d** I will raise it up."
2:20 build this Temple, and you can do it in three **d**?"
4:40 him to stay at their village. So he stayed for two **d**,
5: 1 returned to Jerusalem for one of the Jewish holy **d**.
11: 6 he stayed where he was for the next two **d** and did
11: 7 Finally after two **d**, he said to his disciples,
11: 8 "only a few **d** ago the Jewish leaders in Judea
11:17 Lazarus had already been in his grave for four **d**.
11:39 be terrible because he has been dead for four **d**."
11:55 the country arrived in Jerusalem several **d** early
12: 1 Six **d** before the Passover ceremonies began,
20:26 Eight **d** later the disciples were together again,
Ac 1: 3 During the forty **d** after his crucifixion,
1: 5 but in just a few **d** you will be baptized with the
2:17 'In the last **d**, God said, / I will pour out my Spirit
2:18 In those **d** I will pour out my Spirit / upon all my
7: 8 was circumcised when he was eight **d** old.

9: 9 He remained there blind for three **d**. And all that
9: 19 stayed with the believers in Damascus for a few **d**.
10: 30 "Four **d** ago I was praying in my house at three
10: 40 but God raised him to life three **d** later. Then God
10: 48 asked him to stay with them for several **d**.
13: 31 And he appeared over a period of many **d** to those
14: 16 In earlier **d** he permitted all the nations to go their
16: 12 and a Roman colony; we stayed there several **d**.
20: 6 in Macedonia and five **d** later arrived in Troas,
21: 10 During our stay of several **d**, a man named
21: 27 The seven **d** were almost ended when some Jews
24: 1 Five **d** later Ananias, the high priest, arrived with
24: 11 **d** ago that I arrived in Jerusalem to worship at the
24: 24 A few **d** later Felix came with his wife, Drusilla,
25: 1 Three **d** after Festus arrived in Caesarea to take
25: 6 Eight or ten **d** later he returned to Caesarea, and on
25: 13 A few **d** later King Agrippa arrived with his sister,
25: 14 During their stay of several **d**, Festus discussed
27: 7 We had several **d** of rough sailing, and after great
27: 20 The terrible storm raged unabated for many **d**,
28: 7 welcomed us courteously and fed us for three **d**.
28: 12 first stop was Syracuse, where we stayed three **d**.
28: 14 who invited us to stay with them seven **d**.
28: 17 Three **d** after Paul's arrival, he called together the
Ro 6: 20 In those **d**, when you were slaves of sin,
Gal 1: 18 with Peter and stayed there with him for fifteen **d**.
4: 10 or don't do on certain **d** or months or seasons
4: 15 In those **d**, I know you would gladly have taken
Eph 2: 12 In those **d** you were living apart from Christ.
5: 16 of every opportunity for doing good in these evil **d**.
Php 3: 5 For I was circumcised when I was eight **d** old,
Col 2: 16 or for not celebrating certain holy **d** or new-moon
2Ti 3: 1 that in the last **d** there will be very difficult times.
Heb 1: 2 But now in these final **d**, he has spoken to us
10: 32 Don't ever forget those early **d** when you first
11: 2 God gave his approval to people in **d** of old
11: 30 people of Israel marched around Jericho seven **d**,
1Pe 1: 20 but now in these final **d**, he was sent to the earth
3: 10 "If you want a happy life and good **d**,
2Pe 1: 14 But the Lord Jesus Christ has shown me that my **d**
3: 3 I want to remind you that in the last **d** there will be
Rev 2: 10 you to the test. You will be persecuted for 'ten **d**.'
9: 6 In those **d** people will seek death but will not find
11: 3 and will prophesy during those 1,260 **d**."
11: 9 And for three and a half **d** all peoples, tribes,
11: 11 But after three and a half **d**, the spirit of life from
12: 6 had prepared a place to give her care for 1,260 **d**.

DAYS' (2) [DAY]

Ge 30: 36 and they took them three **d** distance from where
Jn 4: 43 At the end of the two **d** stay, Jesus went on into

DAYSMAN [KJV] See MEDIATOR

DAYSPRING [KJV] See DAWN, LIGHT

DAYTIME (4) [DAY]

Job 5: 14 they see no better in the **d** than at night.
24: 16 They break into houses at night and sleep in the **d**.
Ps 78: 14 In the **d** he led them by a cloud, / and at night by a
Isa 4: 6 It will be a shelter from **d** heat and a hiding place

DAZZLING (8)

Job 37: 22 the mountain of God. He is clothed in **d** splendor.
SS 5: 10 "My lover is dark and **d**, better than ten thousand
Da 10: 6 His body looked like a **d** gem. From his face came
Mt 17: 2 like the sun, and his clothing became **d** white.
Mk 9: 3 and his clothing became **d** white, far whiter than
Lk 9: 29 his face changed, and his clothing became **d** white.
24: 4 two men appeared to them, clothed in **d** robes.
Ac 10: 30 a man in **d** clothes was standing in front of me.

DEACON (2) [DEACONS]

Ro 16: 1 Our sister Phoebe, a **d** in the church in Cenchrea,
1Ti 3: 12 A **d** must be faithful to his wife, and he must

DEACONS (5) [DEACON]

Php 1: 1 believe in Christ Jesus, and to the elders and **d**.
1Ti 3: 8 **d** must be people who are respected and have
3: 10 Before they are appointed as **d**, they should be
3: 10 If they do well, then they may serve as **d**.
3: 13 Those who do well as **d** will be rewarded with

DEAD (403) [DIE]

DEAD SEA (25) Ge 14:3,8; Nu 34:3,12; Dt 3:17; 4:49; Jos 3:16; 12:3; 15:2,5,5; 18:19; 2Ki 14:25; 2Ch 20:2; Isa 16:8; Jer 48:32; Eze 39:11; 47:8,8,9,10,10,18; Joel 2:20; Zec 14:8

RAISED FROM THE DEAD (26) Mt 17:9,23; 20:19; 26:32; 27:52,63; 28:6,7; Mk 14:28; 16:6; Lk 9:22; 20:35; Jn 2:22; 12:1,9; 21:14; Ac 2:32; 4:10; Ro 4:25; 6:4; 7:4; 1Co 15:4,20; Eph 2:6; 1Th 1:10; 2Ti 2:8

RESURRECTION OF/FROM THE DEAD (15) Mt 22:31; Ac 4:2; 17:32; 23:6; 24:21; 1Co 15:12,13,15,16,21,32,42; Php 3:11; 2Ti 2:18; Heb 6:2

Ge 14: 3 in Siddim Valley (that is, the valley of the **D** Sea).
14: 8 prepared for battle in the valley of the **D** Sea
20: 3 in a dream and told him, "You are a **d** man,
23: 11 my people, I give it to you. Go and bury your **d**."
23: 13 full price for the field so I can bury my **d** there."
23: 15 that between friends? Go ahead and bury your **d**."
27: 41 to himself, "My father will soon be **d** and gone.
38: 10 thing for Onan to deny a child to his **d** brother.
42: 38 not go down with you, for his brother Joseph is **d**,
44: 20 His brother is **d**, and he alone is left of his
47: 30 When I am **d**, take me out of Egypt and bury me
50: 15 But now that their father was **d**, Joseph's brothers
Ex 4: 19 for all those who wanted to kill you are **d**."
9: 7 true that none of the Israelites' animals were **d**.
21: 30 the **d** person's relatives may accept payment from
21: 34 The owner of the well must pay in full for the **d**
21: 35 Each will also own half of the **d** bull.
21: 36 of the living bull must pay in full for the **d** bull
Lev 5: 2 such as the **d** body of an animal that is
7: 24 The fat of an animal found **d** or killed by a wild
11: 8 the meat of these animals or touch their **d** bodies.
11: 11 never eat their meat or even touch their **d** bodies.
11: 24 If you touch any of their **d** bodies, you will be
11: 25 If you move the **d** body of an unclean animal,
11: 26 If you touch the **d** body of such an animal, you will
11: 27 If you touch the **d** body of such an animal, you will
11: 31 If you touch the **d** body of such an animal, you will
11: 35 Any object on which the **d** body of such an animal
11: 36 if the **d** body of such an animal falls into a spring
11: 36 But anyone who removes the **d** body will be
11: 37 If the **d** body falls on seed grain to be planted in
11: 38 But if the seed is wet when the **d** body falls on it,
14: 7 The priest will also sprinkle the **d** bird's blood
19: 28 "Never cut your bodies in mourning for the **d**
21: 1 ceremonially unclean by touching a **d** relative
21: 11 He must never defile himself by going near a **d**
Nu 5: 2 or who has been defiled by touching a **d** person.
5: 8 But if the person who was wronged is **d**, and there
6: 6 And they may not go near a **d** body during the
6: 9 because someone suddenly falls **d** beside them,
6: 11 for the guilt they incurred from the **d** body.
9: 6 been ceremonially defiled by touching a **d** person,
9: 7 ceremonially unclean by touching a **d** person.
9: 10 at Passover time because of touching a **d** body,
14: 32 for you, your **d** bodies will fall in this wilderness.
14: 33 until the last of you lies **d** in the wilderness.
14: 37 were struck **d** with a plague before the LORD.
16: 48 the living and the **d** until the plague was stopped.
17: 12 of Israel said to Moses, "We are as good as **d**!
19: 11 "All those who touch a **d** human body will be
19: 13 All those who touch a **d** body and do not purify
31: 19 or touched a **d** body must stay outside the camp for
34: 3 boundary will begin on the east at the **D** Sea.
34: 12 and then along the Jordan River to the **D** Sea.
35: 12 These cities will be places of protection from a **d**
Dt 3: 17 all the way from the Sea of Galilee down to the **D**
4: 49 of the Jordan Valley as far south as the **D** Sea,
14: 1 the hair above your foreheads for the sake of the **d**.
14: 8 not eat or even touch the **d** bodies of such animals.
18: 11 or psychics, or call forth the spirits of the **d**.
19: 12 and handed over to the **d** person's avenger to be
25: 6 to him will be counted as the son of the **d** brother,
25: 7 But if the **d** man's brother refuses to marry the
26: 14 and I have not offered any of it to the **d**.
28: 26 Your **d** bodies will be food for the birds and wild
Jos 1: 2 "Now that my servant Moses is **d**, you must lead
3: 16 And the water below that point flowed on to the **D**
11: 6 By this time tomorrow they will all be **d**.
12: 3 of the Sea of Galilee and as far south as the **D** Sea,
15: 2 boundary began at the south bay of the **D** Sea,
15: 5 The eastern boundary extended along the **D** Sea to
15: 5 bay where the Jordan River empties into the **D** Sea,
18: 19 and ended at the north bay of the **D** Sea,
Jdg 3: 25 the door, they found their master **d** on the floor.
4: 22 her into the tent and found Sisera lying there **d**,
5: 27 He sank, he fell, / he lay **d** at her feet.
8: 33 As soon as Gideon was **d**, the Israelites prostituted
9: 40 and the ground was covered with **d** bodies all the
9: 55 When Abimelech's men saw that he was **d**,
20: 5 and they raped my concubine until she was **d**.
21: 16 since all the women of the tribe of Benjamin are **d**?
Ru 2: 20 his kindness to us as well as to your **d** husband.
4: 10 a son to carry on the family name of her **d** husband
1Sa 4: 17 "Thousands of Israelite troops are **d** on the
4: 19 and that her husband and father-in-law were **d**,
4: 21 because her husband and her father-in-law were **d**.
14: 44 May God strike me **d** if you are not executed for
15: 18 the sinners, the Amalekites, until they are all **d**.'
17: 46 then I will give the **d** bodies of your men to the
17: 51 the Philistines saw that their champion was **d**,
17: 52 The bodies of the **d** and wounded Philistines were
19: 11 get away tonight, you will be **d** by morning."
24: 14 his time chasing one who is as worthless as a **d** dog
25: 39 When David heard that Nabal was **d**, he said,
31: 5 When his armor bearer realized that Saul was **d**,
31: 7 had been routed and that Saul and his sons were **d**,
31: 8 when the Philistines went out to strip the **d**,
2Sa 1: 4 Many men are **d** and wounded on the battlefield,
1: 5 do you know that Saul and Jonathan are **d**?"
1: 19 Your pride and joy, O Israel, lies **d** on the hills!
1: 25 fallen in battle! / Jonathan lies **d** upon the hills.
1: 27 have fallen! / Stripped of their weapons, they lie **d**.
2: 7 And now that Saul is **d**, I ask you to be my strong
4: 10 Once before, someone told me, 'Saul is **d**,'
6: 7 and God struck him **d** beside the Ark of God.
9: 8 "Should the king show such kindness to a **d** dog
11: 26 When Bathsheba heard that her husband was **d**,
12: 18 he do to himself when we tell him the child is **d**?"
12: 19 "Is the baby **d**?" he asked. "Yes," they replied.
12: 21 But now that the baby is **d**, you have stopped your
12: 23 But why should I fast when he is **d**? Can I bring
13: 33 No, your sons aren't all **d**! It was only Amnon."
16: 9 "Why should this **d** dog curse my lord the king?"
18: 20 be good news to the king that his son is **d**.
19: 10 whom we anointed to rule over us, is **d**.
19: 13 may God strike me **d** if I do not appoint you as
1Ki 1: 21 will be treated as criminals as soon as you are **d**."
2: 23 "May God strike me **d** if Adonijah has not sealed
3: 20 She laid her **d** child in my arms and took mine to
3: 21 morning when I tried to nurse my son, he was **d**!
3: 22 "No," the first woman said, "the **d** one is yours,
3: 23 and each says that the **d** child belongs to the other.
11: 21 that David and his commander Joab were both **d**,
18: 14 Elijah is here'! Sir, if I do that, I'm as good as **d**!"
21: 15 sell you? Well, you can have it now! He's **d**!"
2Ki 4: 1 out to him, "My husband who served you is **d**,
4: 31 to meet Elisha and told him, "The child is still **d**."
4: 32 When Elisha arrived, the child was indeed **d**,
9: 24 his heart, and he sank down **d** in his chariot.
11: 1 King Ahaziah of Judah, learned that her son was **d**,
13: 21 the **d** man revived and jumped to his feet!
14: 25 of Israel between Lebo-hamath and the **D** Sea,
1Ch 10: 5 When his armor bearer realized that Saul was **d**,
10: 7 had been routed and that Saul and his sons were **d**,
10: 8 day when the Philistines went out to strip the **d**,
13: 10 and he struck him **d** because he had laid his hand
2Ch 20: 2 is marching against you from beyond the **D** Sea.
20: 24 there were **d** bodies lying on the ground for as far
22: 10 King Ahaziah of Judah, learned that her son was **d**,
Job 1: 19 The house collapsed, and all your children are **d**.
4: 20 but by evening they are **d**, gone forever without a
7: 8 for long. Your eyes will be on me, but I will be **d**.
14: 13 "I wish you would hide me with the **d** and forget
21: 21 For when they are **d**, they will not care what
26: 5 "The **d** tremble in their place beneath the waters.
40: 13 in the dust. Imprison them in the world of the **d**.
Ps 10: 4 to seek God. / They seem to think that God is **d**.
16: 10 For you will not leave my soul among the **d**
22: 15 You have laid me in the dust and left me for **d**.
31: 12 I have been ignored as if I were **d**, / as if I were a
79: 3 all around Jerusalem; / no one is left to bury the **d**.
88: 4 I have been dismissed as one who is **d**, / like a
88: 5 abandoned me to death, / and I am as good as **d**.
88: 10 Of what use to the **d** are your miracles?
88: 10 Do the **d** get up and praise you? / *Interlude*
106: 28 at Peor; / they even ate sacrifices offered to the **d**!
110: 6 and fill them with their **d**; / he will shatter heads
115: 17 The **d** cannot sing praises to the LORD, / for they
139: 8 if I go down to the place of the **d**, you are there.
Pr 21: 16 sense will end up in the company of the **d**.
Ecc 4: 2 So I concluded that the **d** are better off than the
6: 3 I say he would have been better off born **d**.
9: 4 "It is better to be a live dog than a **d** lion!"
9: 5 least know they will die, but the **d** know nothing.
10: 1 **D** flies will cause even a bottle of perfume to stink!
Isa 5: 9 homes will stand deserted, the owners **d** or gone.
7: 16 the kings of Israel and Aram—will both be **d**.
8: 19 Can the living find out the future from the **d**?
10: 4 will stumble along as prisoners or lie among the **d**.
14: 9 "In the place of the **d** there is excitement over
14: 9 and mighty kings long **d** are there to see you.
14: 15 you will be brought down to the place of the **d**,
14: 29 that the king who attacked you is **d**.
16: 8 Her shoots once reached as far as the **D** Sea.
17: 14 waits in terror, but by dawn its enemies are **d**.
18: 6 Your mighty army will be left **d** in the fields for
26: 14 Those we served before are **d** and gone.
26: 19 fall like dew / on his people in the place of the **d**!
27: 11 The people are like the **d** branches of a tree,
34: 3 Their **d** will be left unburied, and the stench of
38: 10 of my life, / must I now enter the place of the **d**?
38: 18 For the **d** cannot praise you; / they cannot raise
57: 9 You have traveled far, even into the world of the **d**,
59: 14 Truth falls **d** in the streets, and fairness has been
66: 24 they will see the **d** bodies of those who have
Jer 4: 10 the sword is even now poised to strike them **d**!"
11: 21 The men of Anathoth wanted me **d**. They said they
16: 7 a meal to comfort those who mourn for the **d**—
19: 7 The enemy will leave the **d** bodies as food for the
22: 10 Do not weep for the **d** king or mourn his loss.
22: 18 he dies. His subjects will not even care that he is **d**.
22: 19 He will be buried like a **d** donkey—dragged out of
31: 15 refusing to be comforted—for her children are **d**."
33: 5 The men of this city are already as good as **d**,
34: 5 will weep for you and say, "Alas, our king is **d**!"
36: 30 His **d** body will be thrown out to lie unburied—
38: 16 or hand you over to the men who want you **d**."
44: 27 will suffer war and famine until all of you are **d**.
48: 32 Your spreading vines once reached as far as the **D**
51: 4 They will fall **d** in the land of the Babylonians,
51: 47 will be disgraced, and her **d** will lie in the streets.
La 3: 6 has buried me in a dark place, like a person long **d**.
Eze 4: 14 any animal that died of sickness or that I found **d**.
6: 13 When their **d** lie scattered among their idols
11: 6 and filled your streets with the **d**.
17: 24 green tree wither and gives new life to the **d** tree.
26: 20 in the pit who have entered the world of the **d**.
32: 23 are now **d** at the hands of their enemies.
32: 24 of those who have gone to the world of the **d**.
32: 30 They lie there as outcasts with all the other **d** who
35: 8 I will fill your mountains with the **d**. Your hills,
37: 9 Breathe into these **d** bodies so that they may live
39: 11 in the Valley of the Travelers, east of the **D** Sea.
43: 7 or by raising monuments in honor of their **d** kings.
44: 25 in the presence of a **d** person unless it is his father,
47: 8 into the Jordan Valley, where it enters the **D** Sea.
47: 8 this stream will heal the salty waters of the **D** Sea
47: 9 Fish will abound in the **D** Sea, for its waters will
47: 10 Fishermen will stand along the shores of the **D**
47: 10 Fish of every kind will fill the **D** Sea, just as they
47: 18 past the **D** Sea and as far south as Tamar.
Da 12: 2 Many of those whose bodies lie **d** and buried will

Joel 2:20 Those in the rear will go into the **D** Sea; those at
Am 6:10 one who is responsible for burning the **d**—
6:10 goes into the house to carry away a **d** body, he will
8: 3 **D** bodies will be scattered everywhere. They will
9: 2 "Even if they dig down to the place of the **d**,
Jnh 2: 2 I called to you from the world of the **d**,
2: 6 out of life and imprisoned in the land of the **d**.
4: 3 I'd rather be **d** than alive because nothing I
Mic 4: 9 Have you no king to lead you? He is **d**! Have you
Na 3: 3 The **d** are lying in the streets—**d** bodies, heaps of bodies, everywhere.
3:18 O Assyrian king, your princes lie **d** in the dust.
Hag 2:13 ceremonially unclean by touching a **d** person
Zec 1: 5 and their prophets are now long **d**.
14: 8 half toward the **D** Sea and half toward the
Mt 2:18 refusing to be comforted—for they are **d**."
2:20 those who were trying to kill the child are **d**."
8:22 those who are spiritually **d** care for their own **d**."
9:24 He said, "Go away, for the girl isn't **d**; she's only
10: 8 Heal the sick, raise the **d**, cure those with leprosy,
11: 5 are cured, the deaf hear, the **d** are raised to life,
11:23 you will be brought down to the place of the **d**.
17: 9 the Son of Man, have been raised from the **d**."
17:23 but three days later he will be raised from the **d**."
20:19 But on the third day he will be raised from the **d**."
22:30 For when the **d** rise, they won't be married.
22:31 as to whether there will be a resurrection of the **d**
22:32 So he is the God of the living, not the **d**."
23:27 but filled on the inside with **d** people's bones
26:32 But after I have been raised from the **d**, I will go
27:52 and women who had died were raised from the **d**
27:63 'After three days I will be raised from the **d**.'
28: 4 when they saw him, and they fell into a **d** faint.
28: 6 He has been raised from the **d**, just as he said
28: 7 and tell his disciples he has been raised from the **d**,
Mk 5:35 home with the message, "Your daughter is **d**.
5:39 he asked. "The child isn't **d**; she is only asleep."
6:16 the man I beheaded, has come back from the **d**."
9: 9 until he, the Son of Man, had risen from the **d**.
9:10 each other what he meant by "rising from the **d**."
9:26 boy lay there motionless, and he appeared to be **d**.
9:26 A murmur ran through the crowd, "He's **d**."
9:31 but three days later he will rise from the **d**."
12:25 For when the **d** rise, they won't be married.
12:26 But now, as to whether the **d** will be raised—
12:27 So he is the God of the living, not the **d**. You have
14:28 But after I am raised from the **d**, I will go ahead of
15:44 Pilate couldn't believe that Jesus was already **d**,
16: 6 He has been raised from the **d**! Look, this is where
16: 9 on Sunday morning when Jesus rose from the **d**,
Lk 7:15 Then the **d** boy sat up and began to talk to those
7:22 are cured, the deaf hear, the **d** are raised to life,
8:49 home with the message, "Your little girl is **d**.
8:52 the weeping! She isn't **d**; she is only asleep."
9: 8 or some other ancient prophet risen from the **d**."
9:19 of the other ancient prophets risen from the **d**."
9:22 but three days later I will be raised from the **d**."
9:60 those who are spiritually **d** care for their own **d**.
10:15 you will be brought down to the place of the **d**."
10:30 beat him up, and left him half **d** beside the road.
15:24 for this son of mine was **d** and has now returned to
15:32 For your brother was **d** and has come back to life!
16:23 and his soul went to the place of the **d**. There,
16:30 But if someone is sent to them from the **d**,
16:31 won't listen even if someone rises from the **d**.' "
20:35 For those worthy of being raised from the **d** won't
20:37 But now, as to whether the **d** will be raised—
20:38 So he is the God of the living, not the **d**. They are
24: 6 He isn't here! He has risen from the **d**! Don't you
24:46 and die and rise again from the **d** on the third day.
Jn 2:22 After he was raised from the **d**, the disciples
5:21 He will even raise from the **d** anyone he wants to,
5:25 in fact it is here, when the **d** will hear my voice—
5:28 the time is coming when all the **d** in their graves
6:44 and at the last day I will raise them from the **d**.
11:14 Then he told them plainly, "Lazarus is **d**.
11:39 But Martha, the **d** man's sister, said, "Lord,
11:39 be terrible because he has been **d** for four days."
12: 1 of Lazarus—the man he had raised from the **d**.
12: 9 see Lazarus, the man Jesus had raised from the **d**.
19:33 they saw that he was **d** already, so they didn't
20: 9 that the Scriptures said he would rise from the **d**.
21:14 his disciples since he had been raised from the **d**.
Ac 2:27 For you will not leave my soul among the **d**
2:31 that the Messiah would not be left among the **d**
2:32 whom God raised from the **d**, and we all are
4: 2 of Jesus, that there is a resurrection of the **d**.
4:10 you crucified, but whom God raised from the **d**.
5:10 the young men came in and saw that she was **d**,
5:30 The God of our ancestors raised Jesus from the **d**
10:41 and drank with him after he rose from the **d**.
10:42 of God to be the judge of all—the living and the **d**.
13:30 But God raised him from the **d**!
13:34 For God had promised to raise him from the **d**,
14:19 and dragged him out of the city, apparently **d**.
17: 3 sufferings of the Messiah and his rising from the **d**.
17:31 everyone who this is by raising him from the **d**."
17:32 of the resurrection of a person who had been **d**,
23: 6 because my hope is in the resurrection of the **d**!"
24:21 because I believe in the resurrection of the **d**!' "
26: 8 incredible to any of you that God can raise the **d**?
26:23 and be the first to rise from the **d** as a light to Jews
28: 6 waited for him to swell up or suddenly drop **d**.
Ro 1: 4 raised him from the **d** by means of the Holy Spirit.
4:17 believed in the God who brings the **d** back to life
4:24 who brought Jesus our Lord back from the **d**.
4:25 and he was raised from the **d** to make us right with
6: 4 And just as Christ was raised from the **d** by the
6: 9 We are sure of this because Christ rose from the **d**,
6:11 So you should consider yourselves **d** to sin
7: 4 are united with the one who was raised from the **d**.
8:11 of God, who raised Jesus from the **d**, lives in you.
8:11 And just as he raised Christ from the **d**, he will
10: 7 "You don't need to go to the place of the **d**" (to
10: 9 in your heart that God raised him from the **d**,
11:15 will be. It will be life for those who were **d**!
1Co 6:14 And God will raise our bodies from the **d** by his
6:14 just as he raised our Lord from the **d**.
15: 4 and he was raised from the **d** on the third day,
15:12 since we preach that Christ rose from the **d**,
15:12 you saying there will be no resurrection of the **d**?
15:13 For if there is no resurrection of the **d**, then Christ
15:15 can't be true if there is no resurrection of the **d**.
15:16 If there is no resurrection of the **d**, then Christ has
15:20 the fact is that Christ has been raised from the **d**.
15:21 now the resurrection from the **d** has begun through
15:29 If the **d** will not be raised, then what point is there in people being baptized for those who are **d**?
15:29 Why do it unless the **d** will someday rise again?
15:32 if there will be no resurrection from the **d**?
15:35 But someone may ask, "How will the **d** be raised?
15:42 It is the same way for the resurrection of the **d**.
2Co 1: 9 rely on ourselves, but on God who can raise the **d**.
Gal 1: 1 from God the Father, who raised Jesus from the **d**.
6:14 and the world's interest in me is also long **d**.
Eph 1:20 that raised Christ from the **d** and seated him in the
2: 1 Once you were **d**, doomed forever because of your
2: 5 that even while we were **d** because of our sins,
2: 5 he gave us life when he raised Christ from the **d**.
2: 6 For he raised us from the **d** along with Christ,
5:14 is said, / "Awake, O sleeper, / rise up from the **d**,
Php 3:10 the mighty power that raised him from the **d**.
3:11 I can experience the resurrection from the **d**!
Col 1:18 He is the first of all who will rise from the **d**,
2:12 power of God, who raised Christ from the **d**.
2:13 You were **d** because of your sins and because your
1Th 1:10 from heaven—Jesus, whom God raised from the **d**.
5:10 whether we are **d** or alive at the time of his return.
1Ti 4: 2 pretend to be religious, but their consciences are **d**.
5: 6 widow who lives only for pleasure is spiritually **d**.
2Ti 2: 8 David's family and that he was raised from the **d**.
2:18 preaching the lie that the resurrection of the **d** has
4: 1 and the **d** when he appears to set up his Kingdom:
Heb 6: 2 the resurrection of the **d**, and eternal judgment.
9:16 it is proved that the person who wrote the will is **d**.
11: 4 And although Abel is long **d**, he still speaks to us
11:19 Abraham did receive his son back from the **d**.
13:20[-21] who brought again from the **d** our Lord Jesus,
Jas 2:17 by good deeds is no faith at all—it is **d** and useless.
2:26 Just as the body is **d** without a spirit, so also faith is **d** without good deeds.
1Pe 1: 3 because Jesus Christ rose again from the **d**.
1:21 And because God raised Christ from the **d**
2:24 so we can be **d** to sin and live for what is right.
4: 5 who will judge everyone, both the living and the **d**.
1Jn 3:14 But a person who doesn't love them is still **d**.
Jude 1:12 They are not only **d** but doubly **d**, for they have
Rev 1: 5 witness to these things, the first to rise from the **d**,
1:17 When I saw him, I fell at his feet as **d**. But he laid
2:23 I will strike her children **d**. And all the churches
3: 1 have a reputation for being alive—but you are **d**.
11:18 It is time to judge the **d** and reward your servants.
19:21 of the sky gorged themselves on the **d** bodies.
20: 5 (The rest of the **d** did not come back to life until
20:12 I saw the **d**, both great and small, standing before
20:12 And the **d** were judged according to the things
20:13 The sea gave up the **d** in it, and death and the grave gave up the **d** in them.

DEADLY (14) [DIE]

Ex 9: 3 the LORD will send a **d** plague to destroy your
Dt 32:24 wasting famine, / burning fever, and **d** disease.
32:33 is the venom of snakes, / the **d** poison of vipers.
Ps 7:13 He will prepare his **d** weapons / and ignite his
58: 4 They spit poison like **d** snakes; / they are like
Pr 16:14 The anger of the king is a **d** threat; the wise do
21: 6 created by lying is a vanishing mist and a **d** trap.
Isa 11: 8 a little child will put its hand in a nest of **d** snakes
59: 5 and energy spinning evil plans that end up in **d**
Jer 5:16 Their weapons are **d**; their warriors are mighty.
Eze 5:16 "I will shower you with the **d** arrows of famine to
Na 3: 4 and faithless city, mistress of **d** charms,
Ro 3:13 "The poison of a **d** snake drips from their lips."
Jas 3: 8 It is an uncontrollable evil, full of **d** poison.

DEAF (17) [DEAFNESS]

Lev 19:14 "Show your fear of God by treating the **d** with
Ps 38:13 But I am **d** to all their threats. / I am silent before
94: 9 Is the one who made your ears **d**? / Is the one who
Ecc 12: 4 But you yourself will be **d** and tuneless, with a
Isa 29:18 In that day **d** people will hear words read from a
35: 5 the eyes of the blind and unstop the ears of the **d**.
40:21 Are you **d** to the words of God—the words he gave
42:18 "Oh, how **d** and blind you are toward me!
42:19 my servant? Who is as **d** as my messengers?
43: 8 have eyes but are blind, who have ears but are **d**.
59: 1 too weak to save you, and he is not becoming **d**.
Mic 7:16 stand in silent awe, **d** to everything around them.
Mt 11: 5 the lame walk, the lepers are cured, the **d** hear,
Mk 7:32 A **d** man with a speech impediment was brought to
7:37 He even heals those who are **d** and mute."
Lk 7:22 the lame walk, the lepers are cured, the **d** hear,
Ac 7:51 You are heathen at heart and **d** to the truth.

DEAFNESS (1) [DEAF]

Mk 9:25 "Spirit of **d** and muteness," he said, "I command

DEAL (32) [DEALING, DEALINGS, DEALS, DEALT]

Ge 16: 6 your servant, you may **d** with her as you see fit."
Dt 18:19 I will personally **d** with anyone who will not listen
31: 5 and you will **d** with them as I have commanded
1Sa 25:22 May God **d** with me severely if even one man of
2Sa 3: 9 May God **d** harshly with me if I don't help David
7:19 Do you **d** with everyone this way, O Sovereign
18: 5 "For my sake, **d** gently with young Absalom."
2Ch 29:35 and a great **d** of fat from the many peace offerings.
Ne 5: 7 Then I called a public meeting to **d** with the
9:24 Your people could **d** with them as they pleased.
Ps 103:10 all our sins, / nor does he **d** with us as we deserve.
106: 3 Happy are those who **d** justly with others
109:21 But **d** well with me, O Sovereign LORD,
119:124 I am your servant; / **d** with me in unfailing love,
Pr 16:11 The LORD demands fairness in every business **d**;
Isa 28:15 avoid death and have made a **d** to dodge the grave.
28:18 and I will overturn your **d** to dodge the grave.
Jer 18:23 them die before you. **D** with them in your anger.
32: 5 Zedekiah to Babylon and will **d** with him there.
Eze 8:18 Therefore, I will **d** with them in fury. I will neither
17:20 and **d** with him there for this treason against me.
21:30 Should I return my sword to its sheath before I **d**
23:25 against you, and they will **d** furiously with you.
23:29 They will **d** with you in hatred and rob you of all
Zep 3:19 And I will **d** severely with all who have oppressed
Mt 7: 5 then perhaps you will see well enough to **d** with
Mk 5:26 She had suffered a great **d** from many doctors
Lk 6:42 then perhaps you will see well enough to **d** with
19:21 I was afraid because you are a hard man to **d** with,
2Co 13:10 hoping that I won't need to **d** harshly with you
Heb 5: 2 he is human, he is able to **d** gently with the people,
9:28 will come again but not to **d** with our sins again.

DEALING (13) [DEAL]

Lev 4: 2 **d** with those who sin unintentionally by doing
13:59 "These are the instructions for **d** with infectious
14:54 "These are the instructions for **d** with the various
14:57 These instructions must be followed when **d** with
15:32 These are the instructions for **d** with a man who
15:33 for **d** with a woman during her monthly menstrual
15:33 for **d** with anyone, man or woman, who has had a
15:33 and for **d** with a man who has had intercourse with
Nu 5:29 " 'This is the ritual law for **d** with jealousy.
Dt 6:22 **d** terrifying blows against Egypt and Pharaoh
Ezr 10:17 By March 27 of the next year they had finished **d**
Job 19: 3 You should be ashamed of **d** with me so harshly.
2Co 13: 4 God's power—the power we use in **d** with you.

DEALINGS (9) [DEAL]

Ge 39: 4 and entrusted him with all his business **d**.
1Sa 25: 3 of Caleb, was mean and dishonest in all his **d**.
2Ch 28:26 The rest of the events of Ahaz's reign and all his **d**,
Ps 58: 2 No, all your **d** are crooked; / you hand out violence
101: 3 anything vile and vulgar. / I hate all crooked **d**;
Jer 22:15 so long? Because he was just and right in all his **d**.
2Co 1:12 that we have been honest and sincere in all our **d**.
13: 3 Christ is not weak in his **d** with you; he is a mighty
Heb 5: 1 represent other human beings in their **d** with God.

DEALS (2) [DEAL]

Hos 12: 1 with Assyria and cut **d** with the Egyptians.
Heb 9:10 For that old system **d** only with food and drink

DEALT (4) [DEAL]

Lev 24:19 "Anyone who injures another person must be **d**
2Sa 12:31 That is how he **d** with the people of all the
1Ch 20: 3 That is how he **d** with the people of all the
Ecc 1:13 I soon discovered that God has **d** a tragic existence

DEAR (146) [DEAREST, DEARLY]

Ge 27:13 "Let the curse fall on me, **d** son," said Rebekah.
2Ch 29:11 My **d** Levites, do not neglect your duties any
Isa 43:22 "But, my **d** people, you refuse to ask for my help.
Jer 15: 7 your cities and take away everything you hold **d**.
Mk 10:24 But Jesus said again, "**D** children, it is very hard to
Lk 10:41 "My **d** Martha, you are so upset over all these
12: 4 "**D** friends, don't be afraid of those who want to
13:16 to free this **d** woman from the bondage in which
15:31 said to him, 'Look, **d** son, you and I are very close,
Jn 13:33 **D** children, how brief are these moments before I
Ac 1: 1 **D** Theophilus: In my first book I told you about
2:29 "**D** brothers, think about this! David wasn't
21:20 But then they said, "You know, **d** brother,
Ro 1: 7 **d** friends in Rome. God loves you dearly, and he
1:13 I want you to know, **d** friends, that I planned many
7: 1 Now, **d** friends—you who are familiar with the
7: 4 So then, **d** friends, the point is this: The law no
8:12 So, **d** Christian friends, you have no obligation
8:15 into his family—calling him "Father, **d** Father."
10: 1 **D** friends, the longing of my heart and my prayer
11:25 **d** friends, so that you will not feel proud and start
12: 1 And so, **d** Christian friends, I plead with you to
12:19 **D** friends, never avenge yourselves. Leave that to
15:14 I am fully convinced, **d** friends, that you are full of
15:30 **D** friends, I urge you in the name of our Lord Jesus
16: 5 meets in their home. Greet my **d** friend Epenetus.
16:12 and to **d** Persis, who has worked so hard for the
16:13 and also his **d** mother, who has been a mother to

16:17 I make one more appeal, my **d** brothers and sisters.
1Co 1:10 Now, **d** brothers and sisters, I appeal to you by the
1:11 have told me about your arguments, **d** friends.
1:26 Remember, **d** brothers and sisters, that few of you
2: 1 **D** brothers and sisters, when I first came to you I
3: 1 **D** brothers and sisters, when I was with you I
4: 6 **D** brothers and sisters, I have used Apollos
7:24 So, **d** brothers and sisters, whatever situation you
7:29 Now let me say this, **d** brothers and sisters:
10: 1 I don't want you to forget, **d** brothers and sisters,
10:14 So, my **d** friends, flee from the worship of idols.
11: 2 I am so glad, **d** friends, that you always keep me in
11:33 So, **d** brothers and sisters, when you gather for the
12: 1 And now, **d** brothers and sisters, I will write about
14: 6 **D** brothers and sisters, if I should come to you
14:20 **D** brothers and sisters, don't be childish in your
14:39 So, **d** brothers and sisters, be eager to prophesy,
15: 1 Now let me remind you, **d** brothers and sisters,
15:31 For I swear, **d** friends, I face death daily. This is as
15:50 **d** brothers and sisters, is that flesh and blood
15:58 So, my **d** brothers and sisters, be strong and steady,
16:15 other Christians. I urge you, **d** brothers and sisters,
2Co 1: 1 of Christ Jesus, and from our **d** brother Timothy.
1: 8 I think you ought to know, **d** friends,
2:13 because my **d** brother Titus hadn't yet arrived with
6:11 Oh, **d** Corinthian friends! We have spoken
7: 1 Because we have these promises, **d** friends, let us
8: 1 Now I want to tell you, **d** friends, what God in his
12:19 Everything we do, **d** friends, is for your benefit.
13:11 **D** friends, I close my letter with these last words:
Gal 1:11 **D** friends, I solemnly assure you that the Good
3:15 **D** friends, here's an example from everyday life.
4: 6 and now you can call God your **d** Father.
4:12 **D** friends, I plead with you to live as I do in
4:19 But oh, my **d** children! I feel as if I am going
4:28 And you, **d** brothers and sisters, are children of the
4:31 So, **d** friends, we are not children of the slave
5:11 **D** friends, if I were still preaching that you must be
5:13 For you, **d** friends, have been called to live in
6: 1 **D** friends, if a Christian is overcome by some sin,
6:18 My **d** Christian friends, may the grace of our Lord
Eph 5: 1 everything you do, because you are his **d** children.
6:23 **d** friends, and love with faith, from God the Father
Php 1:12 And I want you to know, **d** friends, that everything
3: 1 Whatever happens, **d** friends, may the Lord give
3:13 No, **d** friends, I am still not all I should be, but I
3:17 **D** friends, pattern your lives after mine, and learn
4: 1 **D** brothers and sisters, I love you and long to see
4: 1 So please stay true to the Lord, my **d** friends.
4: 8 And now, **d** friends, let me say one more thing as I
Col 1:13 and he has brought us into the Kingdom of his **d**
4:14 **D** Doctor Luke sends his greetings, and so does
1Th 1: 4 know that God loves you, **d** brothers and sisters,
2: 1 You yourselves know, **d** brothers and sisters,
2: 9 Don't you remember, **d** brothers and sisters,
2:14 And then, **d** brothers and sisters, you suffered
2:17 **D** friends, after we were separated from you for a
3: 7 **d** friends, in all of our own crushing troubles
4: 1 Finally, **d** brothers and sisters, we urge you in the
4:10 Even so, **d** friends, we beg you to love them more
5: 4 the dark about these things, **d** brothers and sisters,
5:12 **D** brothers and sisters, honor those who are your
5:25 **D** brothers and sisters, pray for us.
2Th 1: 3 **D** brothers and sisters, we always thank God for
2:13 for you, **d** brothers and sisters loved by the Lord.
2:15 **d** brothers and sisters, stand firm and keep a strong
3: 1 Finally, **d** brothers and sisters, I ask you to pray for
3: 6 And now, **d** brothers and sisters, we give you this
3:13 And I say to the rest of you, **d** brothers and sisters,
2Ti 1: 2 It is written to Timothy, my **d** son. May God our
2: 1 Timothy, my **d** son, be strong with the special
Phm 1:20 Yes, **d** brother, please do me this favor for the
Heb 3: 1 **d** friends who belong to God and are bound for
3:12 Be careful then, **d** friends. Make sure that your
6: 9 **D** friends, even though we are talking like this,
10:19 And so, **d** friends, we can boldly enter heaven's
10:26 **D** friends, if we deliberately continue sinning after
13:22 I urge you, **d** friends, please listen carefully to
Jas 1: 2 **D** brothers and sisters, whenever trouble comes
1:16 So don't be misled, my **d** brothers and sisters.
1:19 **D** friends, be quick to listen, slow to speak,
2: 1 My **d** brothers and sisters, how can you claim that
2: 5 Listen to me, **d** brothers and sisters. Hasn't God
2:14 **D** brothers and sisters, what's the use of saying
3: 1 **D** brothers and sisters, not many of you should
4:11 evil against each other, my **d** brothers and sisters.
5: 7 **D** brothers and sisters, you must be patient as you
5:12 But most of all, **d** brothers and sisters, never take
5:19 My **d** brothers and sisters, if anyone among you
1Pe 2:11 **D** brothers and sisters, you are foreigners
4:12 **D** friends, don't be surprised at the fiery trials you
2Pe 1:10 So, **d** friends, work hard to prove that you really
3: 1 This is my second letter to you, **d** friends, and in
3: 8 But you must not forget, **d** friends, that a day is
3:14 And so, **d** friends, while you are waiting for these
3:17 **d** friends, so that you can watch out and not be
1Jn 2: 1 My **d** children, I am writing this to you so that you
2: 7 **D** friends, I am not writing a new commandment,
2:12 I am writing to you, my **d** children, because your
2:18 **D** children, the last hour is here. You have heard
2:28 And now, **d** children, continue to live in fellowship
3: 2 Yes, **d** friends, we are already God's children,
3: 7 **D** children, don't let anyone deceive you about
3:13 So don't be surprised, **d** brothers and sisters,
3:18 **D** children, let us stop just saying we love each
3:21 **D** friends, if our conscience is clear, we can come
4: 1 **D** friends, do not believe everyone who claims to
4: 4 But you belong to God, my **d** children. You have
4: 7 **D** friends, let us continue to love one another,
4:11 **D** friends, since God loved us that much, we surely
5:21 **D** children, keep away from anything that might
2Jn 1: 5 And now I want to urge you, **d** lady, that we
3Jn 1: 1 It is written to Gaius, my **d** friend, whom I love in
1: 2 **D** friend, I am praying that all is well with you
1: 5 **D** friend, you are doing a good work for God when
1:11 **D** friend, don't let this bad example influence you.
Jude 1:17 But you, my **d** friends, must remember what the
1:20 But you, **d** friends, must continue to build your

DEAREST (4) [DEAR]

Jer 12: 7 I have surrendered my **d** ones to their enemies.
Eze 24:16 of man, I am going to take away your **d** treasure.
24:25 and glory, their heart's desire, their **d** treasure—
Php 2:12 **D** friends, you were always so careful to follow my

DEARLY (7) [DEAR]

Mk 12: 6 there was only one left—his son whom he loved **d**.
Lk 16:14 The Pharisees, who **d** loved their money,
Jn 16:27 for the Father himself loves you **d** because you
Ro 1: 7 God loves you **d**, and he has called you to be his
5: 5 For we know how **d** God loves us, because he has
Eph 1: 6 out on us because we belong to his **d** loved Son.
Jude 1: 3 **D** loved friends, I had been eagerly planning to

DEARTH [KJV] See FAMINE

DEATH (438) [DIE]

DAY OF...DEATH (5) Jdg 13:7; 2Ki 15:5; 25:30; Ecc 8:8; Jer 52:34

LIFE...DEATH (31) Lev 24:17; Dt 30:15,19; 1Sa 2:6; 2Sa 1:23; 15:21; 1Ki 3:11; 2Ki 18:32; 2Ch 1:11; Ps 22:20; 88:3; Pr 11:19; 12:28; 19:16; Ecc 3:22; Jer 21:8; Jn 5:24; Ac 2:24; Ro 6:22; 7:10; 8:38; 14:8; 1Co 3:22; 15:20; 2Co 4:10,12; 1Pe 1:23,23; 3:18; 1Jn 3:14; 5:16

Ge 24:67 and she was a special comfort to him after the **d** of
25: 8 he died at a ripe old age, joining his ancestors in **d**.
25:11 After Abraham's **d**, God poured out rich blessings
25:17 died at the age of 137 and joined his ancestors in **d**.
26:18 the Philistines had filled in after Abraham's **d**.
35:29 he died at a ripe old age, joining his ancestors in **d**.
37:27 Let's not be responsible for his **d**; after all, he is
42: 2 and buy some for us before we all starve to **d**."
47:29 As the time of his **d** drew near, he called for his
Ex 12:13 This plague of **d** will not touch you when I strike
16: 3 have brought us into this desert to starve us to **d**."
19:13 that cross the boundary must be stoned to **d**
21:12 hard enough to cause **d** must be put to **d**.
21:14 must be dragged even from my altar and put to **d**.
21:15 who strikes father or mother must be put to **d**.
21:17 who curses father or mother must be put to **d**.
21:18 other with a stone or fist, causing injury but not **d**.
21:23 If the result is **d**, the offender must be executed.
21:28 "If a bull gores a man or woman to **d**, the bull
23: 7 Never put an innocent or honest person to **d**.
31:15 who works on the Sabbath must be put to **d**.
Lev 10: 7 under penalty of **d**, for the anointing oil of the
16: 1 The LORD spoke to Moses after the **d** of Aaron's
16: 2 he chooses; the penalty for intrusion is **d**.
17:15 from the carcass of an animal that died a natural **d**
19:20 freed at the time, the couple will not be put to **d**.
20: 2 they must be stoned to **d** by people of the
20: 9 who curse their father or mother must be put to **d**.
20:10 both the man and the woman must be put to **d**.
20:12 with his daughter-in-law, both must be put to **d**.
20:13 "The penalty for homosexual acts is **d** to both
20:14 All three of them must be burned to **d** to wipe out
20:15 he must be put to **d**, and the animal must be killed.
20:16 with it, she and the animal must both be put to **d**.
20:27 or psychics must be put to **d** by stoning.
21: 9 as well as herself, she must be burned to **d**.
22: 8 may never eat an animal that has died a natural **d**
24:14 Then let the entire community stone him to **d**.
24:16 be stoned to **d** by the whole community of Israel.
24:17 who takes another person's life must be put to **d**.
24:21 but whoever kills another person must be put to **d**.
24:23 blasphemer outside the camp and stoned him to **d**,
27:29 be redeemed. Such a person must be put to **d**.
Nu 15:35 said to Moses, "The man must be put to **d**!
15:36 the man outside the camp and stoned him to **d**,
16:29 If these men die a natural **d**, then the LORD has
18: 7 comes too near the sanctuary will be put to **d**."
19:14 and those who were inside when the **d** occurred,
19:16 was killed with a sword or who died a natural **d**,
20:24 time has come for Aaron to join his ancestors in **d**.
35:12 dead person's relatives who want to avenge the **d**.
35:19 is responsible for putting the murderer to **d**.
35:25 live in a city of refuge until the **d** of the high priest.
35:28 the city of refuge until the **d** of the high priest.
35:28 But after the **d** of the high priest, the slayer may
35:30 No one may be put to **d** on the testimony of only
35:31 to execution; murderers must always be put to **d**.
35:32 to his property before the **d** of the high priest.
Dt 13: 5 who try to lead you astray must be put to **d**,
13: 9 You must put them to **d**! You must be the one to
13:10 Stone the guilty ones to **d** because they have tried
14:21 "Do not eat anything that has died a natural **d**.
17: 5 be taken to the gates of the town and stoned to **d**.
17: 6 But never put a person to **d** on the testimony of
17:12 represents the LORD your God must be put to **d**.
19: 6 chase down and kill the person who caused the **d**.
19: 6 even though there was no **d** sentence and the first
d had been an accident.
19:10 That way you will prevent the **d** of innocent people
21:21 Then all the men of the town must stone him to **d**.
21:22 "If someone has committed a crime worthy of **d**
22:21 and the men of the town will stone her to **d**.
22:24 them to the gates of the town and stone them to **d**.
22:26 she has committed no crime worthy of **d**.
24:16 "Parents must not be put to **d** for the sins of their
24:16 Those worthy of **d** must be executed for their own
28:51 your livestock and crops, and you will starve to **d**.
30:15 and disaster, between life and **d**.
30:19 I have given you the choice between life and **d**,
31:27 How much more rebellious will you be after my **d**!
31:29 I know that after my **d** you will become utterly
32:25 Outside, the sword will bring **d**, / and inside,
33: 1 of God, gave to the people of Israel before his **d**:
Jos 1: 1 After the **d** of Moses the LORD's servant,
1:18 not obey your every command will be put to **d**.
20: 4 the one who caused the accidental **d** will appear
20: 5 the accused to them, for the **d** was accidental.
20: 6 But the person who caused the **d** must stay in that
20: 6 because the **d** was accidental must continue to live
20: 6 **d** of the high priest who was in office at the time of
Jdg 4: 1 After Ehud's **d**, the Israelites again did what was
6:31 Whoever pleads his case will be put to **d** by
10: 1 After Abimelech's **d**, Tola, the son of Puah
13: 7 the moment of his birth until the day of his **d**.' "
15: 6 the woman and her father and burned them to **d**.
Ru 1:17 severely if I allow anything but **d** to separate us!"
2:11 your mother-in-law since the **d** of your husband.
1Sa 2: 6 The LORD brings both **d** and life; / he brings
2:25 the LORD was already planning to put them to **d**.
2:33 and grief, and their children will die a violent **d**.
14:43 bit on the end of a stick. Does that deserve **d**?"
14:45 people rescued Jonathan, and he was not put to **d**.
17:35 turns on me, I catch it by the jaw and club it to **d**.
20: 3 I swear to you that I am only a step away from **d**!
20:32 "Why should he be put to **d**?"
22:22 Now I have caused the **d** of all your father's
31: 9 Then they proclaimed the news of Saul's **d** in their
2Sa 1: 1 After the **d** of Saul, David returned from his
1:23 and Jonathan! / They were together in life and in **d**.
3:37 that David was not responsible for Abner's **d**.
4: 1 When Ishbosheth heard about Abner's **d** at
10: 2 to express sympathy to Hanun about his father's **d**.
13:39 And David, now reconciled to Amnon's **d**,
15:21 matter what happens—whether it means life or **d**."
19:28 my relatives and I could expect only **d** from you,
22: 5 "The waves of **d** surrounded me; / the floods of
22: 6 its ropes around me; / **d** itself stared me in the face.
24:16 But as the **d** angel was preparing to destroy
1Ki 2: 1 As the time of King David's **d** approached,
2: 9 and you will know how to arrange a bloody **d** for
2:25 to execute him, and Adonijah was put to **d**.
2:28 When Joab heard about Adonijah's **d**, he ran to the
3:11 or riches for yourself or the **d** of your enemies—
12: 2 Jeroboam son of Nebat heard of Solomon's **d**,
12:18 to restore order, but all Israel stoned him to **d**.
13:34 of Jeroboam's kingdom and the **d** of all his family.
18: 9 you are sending me to my **d** at the hands of Ahab?
21:10 the king. Then take him out and stone him to **d**."
21:13 So he was dragged outside the city and stoned to **d**.
21:14 word to Jezebel, "Naboth has been stoned to **d**."
22:11 these horns you will gore the Arameans to **d**!"
2Ki 1: 1 After King Ahab's **d**, the nation of Moab declared
2:21 It will no longer cause **d** or infertility."
3: 5 But after Ahab's **d**, the king of Moab rebelled
7:17 and trampled to **d** as the people rushed out.
7:20 for the people trampled him to **d** at the gate!
10:19 worshipers who fail to come will be put to **d**."
14: 6 "Parents must not be put to **d** for the sins of their
14: 6 Those worthy of **d** must be executed for their own
14:17 fifteen years after the **d** of King Jehoash of Israel.
14:22 After his father's **d**, Uzziah rebuilt the town of
15: 5 with leprosy, which lasted until the day of his **d**;
18:32 a land of plenty. Choose life instead of **d**!
25:21 the king of Babylon had them all put to **d**.
25:30 to cover his living expenses until the day of his **d**.
1Ch 10: 9 Then they proclaimed the news of Saul's **d** before
19: 2 to express sympathy to Hanun about his father's **d**.
21:15 the LORD relented and said to the **d** angel,
22: 5 vast amounts of building materials before his **d**.
2Ch 1:11 and honor or the **d** of your enemies or even a long
10: 2 Jeroboam son of Nebat heard of Solomon's **d**,
10:18 to restore order, but the Israelites stoned him to **d**.
15:13 the LORD, the God of Israel, would be put to **d**—
18:10 these horns you will gore the Arameans to **d**!"
22: 4 After the **d** of his father, members of Ahab's
24:17 But after Jehoiada's **d**, the leaders of Judah came
24:21 they stoned him to **d** in the courtyard of the
25: 4 "Parents must not be put to **d** for the sins of their
25: 4 Those worthy of **d** must be executed for their own
25:25 fifteen years after the **d** of King Jehoash of Israel.
26: 2 After his father's **d**, Uzziah rebuilt the town of
32:11 sentencing you to **d** by famine and thirst!
32:33 and all Judah and Jerusalem honored him at his **d**.
35:25 day choirs still sing these sad songs about his **d**.
Ezr 7:26 law of the king will be punished immediately by **d**,
Est 4: 8 issued in Susa that called for the **d** of all Jews,
Job 3:17 For in **d** the wicked cease from troubling,
3:18 Even prisoners are at ease in **d**, with no guards to
3:21 They long for **d**, and it won't come. They search
for **d** more eagerly than for hidden
5:20 He will save you from **d** in time of famine,
9:12 If he sends **d** to snatch someone away, who can
14:20 You disfigure them in **d** and send them away.

17: 1 "My spirit is crushed, and I am near d. The grave
18:13 Disease eats their skin; d devours their limbs.
19:20 and have escaped d by the skin of my teeth.
20:25 glistens with blood. The terrors of d are upon him.
24:19 D consumes sinners just as drought and heat
27:14 their children will die in war or starve to d.
28:22 But Destruction and D say, 'We have heard a
30:23 And I know that you are sending me to my d—
33:18 from the grave, from crossing over the river of d.
33:22 are at death's door; the angels of d wait for them.
38:17 Do you know where the gates of d are located?
Ps 6: 5 For in d, who remembers you? / Who can praise
9: T of David, to be sung to the tune "D of the Son."
9:13 who hate me. / Snatch me back from the jaws of d.
18: 4 The ropes of d surrounded me; / the floods of
18: 5 its ropes around me; / d itself stared me in the face.
22:20 Rescue me from a violent d; / spare my precious
23: 4 through the dark valley of d, / I will not be afraid,
30: 3 You kept me from falling into the pit of d.
33:19 He rescues them from d / and keeps them alive in
44:19 You have covered us with darkness and d.
49: 7 Yet they cannot redeem themselves from d
49:14 led to the grave, / where d will be their shepherd.
49:15 He will snatch me from the power of d.
55: 4 is in anguish. / The terror of d overpowers me.
55:15 Let d seize my enemies by surprise; / let the grave
56:13 For you have rescued me from d; / you have kept
68:20 The Sovereign LORD rescues us from d.
69:15 waters swallow me, / or the pit of d devour me.
76: 5 They lie before us in the sleep of d. / No warrior
82: 7 But in d you are mere men. / You will fall as any
86:13 You have rescued me from the depths of d!
88: 3 For my life is full of troubles, / and d draws near.
88: 5 They have abandoned me to d, / and I am as good
88:15 I have been sickly and close to d since my youth.
94:21 the righteous / and condemn the innocent to d.
103: 4 He ransoms me from d / and surrounds me with
107:18 Their appetites were gone, / and d was near.
107:20 they were healed— / snatched from the door of d.
109:16 and he hounded the brokenhearted to d.
116: 3 D had its hands around my throat; / the terrors of
116: 6 I was facing d, and then he saved me.
116: 8 He has saved me from d, / my eyes from tears,
118:18 me severely, / but he has not handed me over to d.
Pr 1:12 prime of life, they will go down into the pit of d.
1:32 they are simpletons who turn away from me—to d.
2:18 Entering her house leads to d; it is the road to hell.
5: 5 Her feet go down to d; her steps lead straight to the
7:27 the road to the grave. Her bedroom is the den of d.
8:36 have injured themselves. All who hate me love d."
10: 3 The LORD will not let the godly starve to d,
11: 4 but right living is a safeguard against d.
11:19 Godly people find life; evil people find d.
12:28 godly leads to life; their path does not lead to d.
13:14 those who accept it avoid the snares of d.
14:12 each person that seems right, but it ends in d.
14:27 it offers escape from the snares of d.
15:11 Even the depths of D and Destruction are known
16:25 each person that seems right, but it ends in d.
19:16 and keep your life; despising them leads to d.
23:14 Physical discipline may well save them from d.
24:11 Rescue those who are unjustly sentenced to d;
27:20 Just as D and Destruction are never satisfied,
Ecc 3:22 No one will bring them back from d to enjoy life in
7: 4 A wise person thinks much about d, while the fool
7:26 that a seductive woman is more bitter than d.
8: 8 of us has the power to prevent the day of our d.
8: 8 And in the face of d, wickedness will certainly not
9: 3 no hope. There is nothing ahead but d anyway.
SS 8: 6 For love is as strong as d, and its jealousy is as
Isa 9: 2 all who live in the land where d casts its shadow.
13:16 Their little children will be dashed to d right before
22: 5 and cries of d echo from the mountainsides.
25: 7 the shadow of d that hangs over the earth.
25: 8 He will swallow up d forever! The Sovereign
28:15 boast that you have struck a bargain to avoid d
28:18 I will cancel the bargain you made to avoid d,
38:17 this anguish, / for you have rescued me from d
51:14 starvation, and d will not be your fate!
53: 8 From prison and trial they led him away to his d.
53:12 and great, because he exposed himself to d.
Jer 2: 6 a land of deserts and pits, of drought and d,
4:21 How long must I be surrounded by war and d?
9:21 For d has crept in through our windows and has
15: 2 Those who are destined for d, to d; those who
16: 7 not even for the d of a mother or a father.
21: 8 the LORD says: Take your choice of life or d!
26:16 "This man does not deserve the d sentence,
43:11 He will bring d to those destined for d; he will
44:28 "Only a small number will escape d and return to
51: 4 land of the Babylonians, slashed to d in her streets.
52:27 the king of Babylon had them all put to d.
52:34 to cover his living expenses until the day of his d.
La 1:19 My priests and leaders starved to d in the city,
1:20 streets the sword kills, and at home there is only d.
Eze 3:18 saying, 'You are under the penalty of d,'
12:16 But I will spare a few of them from d by war,
22: 9 accuse others falsely and send them to their d.
33:11 I take no pleasure in the d of wicked people.
44:31 meat from any bird or animal that dies a natural d
Hos 6: 5 you with my words, threatening you with d.
10:14 Even mothers and children were dashed to d there.
12:14 so their Lord will now sentence them to d in
13:14 Should I redeem them from d? O d, bring forth
your terrors! O grave, bring forth
13:16 their little ones dashed to d against the ground,
Am 4:10 all your horses. The stench of d filled the air!
Jnh 1:14 And don't hold us responsible for his d, because it
2: 5 "I sank beneath the waves, and d was very near.
2: 6 have snatched me from the yawning jaws of d!
4: 8 "D is certainly better than this!" he exclaimed.
Na 3:10 Her babies were dashed to d against the stones of
Hab 2: 5 and wide, with their mouths opened as wide as d,
Zec 9:11 I will free your prisoners from d in a waterless
11:16 will not care for the sheep that are threatened by d,
Mt 2:15 and they stayed there until Herod's d. This fulfilled
4:16 And for those who lived in the land where d casts
10:21 "Brother will betray brother to d, fathers will
15: 4 speaks evil of father or mother must be put to d.'
21:41 "He will put the wicked men to a horrible d
22:23 of Jews who say there is no resurrection after d.
26: 4 how to capture Jesus secretly and put him to d.
26:38 "My soul is crushed with grief to the point of d.
26:59 would lie about Jesus, so they could put him to d.
27: 1 the Roman government to sentence Jesus to d.
27:20 to be released and for Jesus to be put to d.
27:25 "We will take responsibility for his d—
Mk 7:10 speaks evil of father or mother must be put to d.'
12:18 of Jews who say there is no resurrection after d.
13:12 "Brother will betray brother to d, fathers will
14: 1 to capture Jesus secretly and put him to d.
14:34 "My soul is crushed with grief to the point of d.
14:55 testify against Jesus, so they could put him to d.
14:64 your verdict?" And they all condemned him to d.
Lk 1:79 those who sit in darkness and in the shadow of d,
7: 2 slave of a Roman officer was sick and near d.
20:27 of Jews who say there is no resurrection after d.
23:15 Nothing this man has done calls for the d penalty.
23:22 I have found no reason to sentence him to d.
23:23 the crowd shouted louder and louder for Jesus' d,
24:20 and handed him over to be condemned to d,
Jn 5:24 but they have already passed from d into life.
7: 1 Judea where the Jewish leaders were plotting his d.
11: 4 it he said, "Lazarus's sickness will not end in d.
11:52 It was a prediction that Jesus' d would be not for
11:53 time on the Jewish leaders began to plot Jesus' d.
12:24 But its d will produce many new kernels—
21:19 Jesus said this to let him know what kind of d he
Ac 1:19 The news of his d spread rapidly among all the
2:24 God released him from the horrors of d and raised
2:24 to life again, for d could not keep him in its grip.
5:28 about Jesus, and you intend to blame us for his d!"
10:39 in Jerusalem. They put him to d by crucifying him,
11:19 after Stephen's d traveled as far as Phoenicia,
12:19 interrogated the guards and sentenced them to d.
13:27 fulfilled prophecy by condemning Jesus to d.
13:29 had fulfilled all the prophecies concerning his d,
20: 9 a deep sleep and fell three stories to his d below.
22: 4 hounding some to d, binding and delivering both
23:29 certainly nothing worthy of imprisonment or d.
25:11 If I have done something worthy of d, I don't
25:24 this is the man whose d is demanded both by the
25:25 in my opinion he has done nothing worthy of d.
26:10 vote against them when they were condemned to d.
26:31 "This man hasn't done anything worthy of d
28:18 for they found no cause for the d sentence.
Ro 1:32 They are fully aware of God's d penalty for those
5:10 the d of his Son while we were still his enemies,
5:12 Adam's sin brought d, so d spread to everyone, for
everyone sinned.
5:15 Adam, brought d to many through his sin.
5:17 of this one man, Adam, caused d to rule over us,
5:17 in triumph over sin and d through this one man,
5:21 as sin ruled over all people and brought them to d,
6: 5 Since we have been united with him in his d,
6: 9 die again. D no longer has any power over him.
6:16 You can choose sin, which leads to d, or you can
6:23 For the wages of sin is d, but the free gift of God is
7: 5 desires that produced sinful deeds, resulting in d.
7:10 me the way of life, instead gave me the d penalty.
7:11 the good law and used it to make me guilty of d.
8: 2 Christ Jesus from the power of sin that leads to d.
8: 6 If your sinful nature controls your mind, there is d.
8:21 join God's children in glorious freedom from d
8:35 or cold or in danger or threatened with d?
8:38 D can't, and life can't. The angels can't,
14: 8 So in life and in d, we belong to the Lord.
1Co 2: 2 only on Jesus Christ and his d on the cross.
3:22 and Peter; the whole world and life and d;
10:10 for that is why God sent his angel of d to destroy
11:26 you are announcing the Lord's d until he comes
15:21 just as d came into the world through a man,
15:26 And the last enemy to be destroyed is d.
15:30 risking our lives, facing d hour by hour?
15:31 For I swear, dear friends, I face d daily. This is as
15:54 will come true: / "D is swallowed up in victory.
15:55 O d, where is your victory? / O d, where is your
sting?"
15:56 For sin is the sting that results in d, and the law
15:57 over sin and d through Jesus Christ our Lord!
2Co 2:16 those who are perishing we are a fearful smell of d
3: 6 The old way ends in d; in the new way, the Holy
3: 7 That old system of law etched in stone led to d,
4:10 these bodies of ours constantly share in the d of
4:11 we live under constant danger of d because we
4:12 So we live in the face of d, but it has resulted in
6: 9 We live close to d, but here we are, still alive.
7:10 without repentance is the kind that results in d.
11:23 without number, and faced d again and again.
Gal 3: 1 d as clearly as though I had shown you a signboard
6: 8 will harvest the consequences of decay and d.
Eph 2:15 By his d he ended the whole system of Jewish law
2:16 reconciled both groups to God by means of his d,
2:16 and our hostility toward each other was put to d.
Php 2: 8 even further by dying a criminal's d on a cross.
2:30 and he was at the point of d while trying to do for
3:10 what it means to suffer with him, sharing in his d,
Col 1:22 He has done this through his d on the cross in his
3: 5 So put to d the sinful, earthly things lurking within
2Ti 1:10 who broke the power of d and showed us the way
4: 6 as an offering to God. The time of my d is near.
4:17 Gentiles to hear. And he saved me from certain d.
Heb 2: 9 and honor" because he suffered d for us.
2: 9 Jesus tasted d for everyone in all the world.
2:14 the power of the Devil, who had the power of d.
5: 7 to the one who could deliver him out of d.
9:14 will purify our hearts from deeds that lead to d
9:17 The will goes into effect only after the d of the
9:18 required under the first covenant as a proof of d.
9:26 the power of sin forever by his sacrificial d for us.
10:20 the sacred curtain, by means of his d for us.
10:28 put to d without mercy on the testimony of two
11:28 so that the angel of d would not kill their firstborn
11:34 of fire, and escaped d by the edge of the sword.
11:35 received their loved ones back again from d.
12: 2 He was willing to die a shameful d on the cross
12:20 touches the mountain, it must be stoned to d."
Jas 1:15 lead to evil actions, and evil actions lead to d.
5:20 brings that person back will save that sinner from d
1Pe 1:23 because the life they gave you will end in d.
3:18 He suffered physical d, but he was raised to life in
4: 6 so that although their bodies were punished with d,
1Jn 3:14 it proves that we have passed from d to eternal life.
5:16 Christian sinning in a way that does not lead to d,
5:16 But there is a sin that leads to d, and I am not
5:17 Every wrong is sin, but not all sin leads to d.
Rev 1:18 and ever! And I hold the keys of d and the grave.
2:10 Remain faithful even when facing d, and I will
2:11 is victorious will not be hurt by the second d.
3: 2 for even what is left is at the point of d.
6: 8 And D was the name of its rider, who was
9: 6 In those days people will seek d but will not find
it. They will long to die, but d will flee away!
11:10 the d of the two prophets who had tormented them.
13:10 Those who are destined for d will be killed.
18: 8 the sorrows of d and mourning and famine will
20: 6 For them the second d holds no power, but they
20:13 and d and the grave gave up the dead in them.
20:14 And d and the grave were thrown into the lake of
fire. This is the second d—the lake of fire.
21: 4 and there will be no more d or sorrow or crying
21: 8 burns with fire and sulfur. This is the second d."

DEATH'S (2) [DIE]

Job 33:22 They are at d door; the angels of death wait for
Ecc 12: 5 You will be standing at d door. And as you near

DEATH-WOUND (1) [DIE, WOUND]

Rev 13:12 worship the first beast, whose d had been healed.

DEATHBLOW (1) [BLOW, DIE]

Ps 74:11 Unleash your powerful fist and deliver a d.

DEATHLY (5) [DIE]

2Sa 12:15 the LORD made Bathsheba's baby d ill.
2Ki 20: 1 About that time Hezekiah became d ill,
2Ch 32:24 About that time, Hezekiah became d ill. He prayed
Isa 38: 1 About that time Hezekiah became d ill,
Da 10: 8 My strength left me, my face grew d pale, and I

DEATHS (7) [DIE]

Ge 43:14 And if I must bear the anguish of their d, then
Nu 17:10 complaints against me and prevent any further d."
1Ki 2:32 For my father was no party to the d of Abner son
Ps 78:64 and their widows could not mourn their d.
Eze 33: 6 to warn the people, he is responsible for their d.
33: 8 but I will hold you responsible for their d.
Jn 19:31 so they asked Pilate to hasten their d by ordering

DEBATE (5) [DEBATED, DEBATERS]

Ac 6: 9 as it was called, started to d with him.
17:17 He went to the synagogue to d with the Jews
17:18 He also had a d with some of the Epicurean
18:19 he went to the synagogue to d with the Jews.
18:28 all the Jews with powerful arguments in public d.

DEBATED (1) [DEBATE]

Ac 9:29 He d with some Greek-speaking Jews, but they

DEBATERS (1) [DEBATE]

1Co 1:20 the scholars, and the world's brilliant d?

DEBIR (11) [KIRIATH-SANNAH, KIRIATH-SEPHER]

Jos 10: 3 of Jarmuth, Japhia of Lachish, and D of Eglon.
10:38 Then they turned back and attacked D.
10:39 They completely destroyed D just as they had
11:21 D, Anab, and the entire hill country of Judah
12:13 The king of D / The king of Geder
15: 7 that point it went through the valley of Achor to D,
15:15 in the town of D (formerly called Kiriath-sepher).
15:49 Dannah, Kiriath-sannah (that is, D),
21:15 Holon, D,
Jdg 1:11 in the town of D (formerly called Kiriath-sepher).
1Ch 6:58 Holon, D,

DEBORAH (10)

Ge 35: 8 Soon after this, Rebekah's old nurse, **D**, died.
Jdg 4: 4 **D**, the wife of Lappidoth, was a prophet who had
4: 5 She would hold court under the Palm of **D**,
4: 9 of a woman." So **D** went with Barak to Kedesh.
4:10 marched up with him. **D** also marched with them.
4:14 Then **D** said to Barak, "Get ready!
5: 1 On that day **D** and Barak son of Abinoam sang this
5: 7 of Israel— / until **D** arose as a mother for Israel.
5:12 "Wake up, **D**, wake up! / Wake up, wake up,
5:15 The princes of Issachar were with **D** and Barak.

DEBRIS (1)

Ac 27:44 to try for it on planks and **d** from the broken ship.

DEBT (17) [DEBTORS, DEBTS]

Ex 22: 3 the thief must be sold as a slave to pay the **d**.
Dt 15: 3 This release from **d**, however, applies only to your
24:17 never accept a widow's garment in pledge of her **d**.
1Sa 22: 2 men who were in trouble or in **d** or who were just
Pr 6: 1 or guarantee the **d** of someone you hardly know—
20:16 from anyone who guarantees the **d** of a stranger.
20:16 Get a deposit if someone guarantees the **d** of a
27:13 from anyone who guarantees the **d** of a stranger.
27:13 Get a deposit if someone guarantees the **d** of an
Am 8: 6 Then you enslave poor people for a **d** of one piece
Mt 18:25 and everything he had be sold to pay the **d**.
18:27 for him, and he released him and forgave his **d**.
18:30 and jailed until the **d** could be paid in full.
18:32 I forgave you that tremendous **d** because you
Lk 7:43 the one for whom he canceled the larger **d**."
Ro 13: 8 Pay all your debts, except the **d** of love for others.
15:27 because they feel they owe a real **d** to them.

DEBTORS (7) [DEBT]

Isa 24: 2 sellers, lenders and borrowers, bankers and **d**—
Eze 18: 7 not keeping the items given in pledge by poor **d**,
18:12 steals from **d** by refusing to let them redeem what
18:16 but instead is fair to **d** and does not rob them.
Am 2: 8 they lounge around in clothing stolen from their **d**.
Hab 2: 7 Suddenly, your **d** will rise up in anger. They will
Mt 18:24 one of his **d** was brought in who owed him

DEBTS (6) [DEBT]

Dt 15: 1 end of every seventh year you must cancel your **d**.
2Ki 4: 7 said to her, "Now sell the olive oil and pay your **d**,
Ne 10:31 and to cancel the **d** owed to us by other Jews.
Pr 17:18 to become responsible for a neighbor's **d**.
Lk 7:42 so he kindly forgave them both, canceling their **d**.
Ro 13: 8 Pay all your **d**, except the debt of love for others.

DECADENCE (1)

2Pe 1: 4 He has promised that you will escape the **d** all

DECAY (6) [DECAYED, DECAYING, DECAYS]

Zec 14:12 and their tongues will **d** in their mouths.
Ac 13:37 whom God raised and whose body did not **d**.
Ro 8:21 children in glorious freedom from death and **d**.
1Co 15:42 Our earthly bodies, which die and **d**, will be
Gal 6: 8 sinful desires will harvest the consequences of **d**
1Pe 1: 4 and undefiled, beyond the reach of change and **d**.

DECAYED (3) [DECAY]

Nu 12:12 let her be like a stillborn baby, already **d** at birth."
Job 19:26 And after my body has **d**, yet in my body I will see
Ac 13:36 of God, he died and was buried, and his body **d**.

DECAYING (1) [DECAY]

Ps 83:10 at Endor, / and their **d** corpses fertilized the soil.

DECAYS (1) [DECAY]

Job 14: 8 roots have grown old in the earth and its stump **d**,

DECEASE(D) [KJV] See DEAD, DIED, DYING, GONE

DECEIT (8) [DECEIVE]

Nu 25:18 because they assaulted you with **d** by tricking you
Job 15:35 and evil, and their hearts give birth only to **d**."
Pr 12:20 **D** fills hearts that are plotting evil; joy fills hearts
Jer 23:26 If they are prophets, they are prophets of **d**,
Hos 11:12 Israel surrounds me with lies and **d**, but Judah still
Mk 7:22 adultery, greed, wickedness, **d**, eagerness for
1Th 2: 3 you can see that we were not preaching with any **d**
1Pe 2: 1 So get rid of all malicious behavior and **d**.

DECEITFUL (11) [DECEIVE]

Dt 32: 5 his children? / They are a **d** and twisted generation.
Ps 36: 3 Everything they say is crooked and **d**.
120: 2 O LORD, from liars / and from all **d** people.
Pr 15: 4 bring life and health; a **d** tongue crushes the spirit.
22: 5 The **d** walk a thorny, treacherous road;
22:12 but he ruins the plans of the **d**.
Isa 59:13 we have been, carefully planning our **d** lies.
Jer 17: 9 "The human heart is most **d** and desperately
42:20 For you were **d** when you sent me to pray to the
Da 11:23 By making **d** promises, he will make various
Hos 12: 2 He is about to punish Jacob for all his **d** ways.

DECEITFULNESS (1) [DECEIVE]

2Pe 2:13 They revel in **d** while they feast with you.

DECEIVE (20) [DECEIT, DECEITFUL, DECEITFULNESS, DECEIVED, DECEIVER, DECEIVERS, DECEIVES, DECEIVING, DECEPTION, DECEPTIVE]

Ge 21:23 "Swear to me in God's name that you won't **d** me,
2Ki 18:29 the king says: Don't let King Hezekiah **d** you.
19:10 Don't let this God you trust **d** you with promises
2Ch 32:15 Don't let him **d** you like this! I say it again—
Ps 25: 3 but disgrace comes to those who try to **d** others.
Pr 14: 8 to see what is coming, but fools **d** themselves.
16:29 Violent people **d** their companions, leading them
23:31 let the sparkle and smooth taste of wine **d** you.
Isa 36:14 the king says: Don't let King Hezekiah **d** you.
37:10 Don't let this God you trust **d** you with promises
Eze 13:10 "These evil prophets **d** my people by saying,
Da 11:27 at the conference table, attempting to **d** each other.
Mt 24:24 great miraculous signs and wonders so as to **d**,
Mk 13:22 perform miraculous signs and wonders so as to **d**,
Ro 16:18 and glowing words they **d** innocent people.
Col 2: 4 so that no one will be able to **d** you with persuasive
Tit 1:10 they engage in useless talk and **d** people.
1Jn 3: 7 Dear children, don't let anyone **d** you about this:
Rev 20: 3 so Satan could not **d** the nations anymore until the
20: 8 He will go out to **d** the nations from every corner

DECEIVED (20) [DECEIVE]

Ge 27:36 for he has **d** me twice, first taking my birthright
34:13 But Dinah's brothers **d** Shechem and Hamor
1Sa 28:12 saw Samuel, she screamed, "You've **d** me!
2Sa 19:26 "My lord the king, my servant Ziba **d** me.
Job 12:16 with him; deceivers and **d** are both in his power.
31: 5 "Have I lied to anyone or **d** anyone?
Isa 53: 9 He had done no wrong, and he never **d** anyone.
Jer 4:10 the people have been **d** by what you said,
Eze 14: 9 And if a prophet is **d** and gives a message anyway,
14: 9 it is because I, the LORD, have **d** that prophet.
Am 2: 4 They have been led astray by the same lies that **d**
Mic 1:14 The town of Aczib has **d** the kings of Israel,
2Co 11: 3 to Christ, just as Eve was **d** by the serpent.
1Ti 2:14 not Adam, who was **d** by Satan, and sin was the
2Ti 3:13 on deceiving others, and they themselves will be **d**.
Heb 3:13 so that none of you will be **d** by sin and hardened
1Pe 2:22 He never sinned, and he never **d** anyone.
Rev 13:14 he **d** all the people who belong to this world.
18:23 in the world, **d** the nations with her sorceries.
19:20 miracles that **d** all who had accepted the mark of

DECEIVER (2) [DECEIVE]

Mt 27:63 we remember what that **d** once said while he was
2Jn 1: 7 a real body. Such a person is a **d** and an antichrist.

DECEIVERS (4) [DECEIVE]

Job 12:16 are with him; **d** and deceived are both in his power.
Ps 5: 6 tell lies. / The LORD detests murderers and **d**.
101: 7 I will not allow **d** to serve me, / and liars will not
2Jn 1: 7 Many **d** have gone out into the world. They do not

DECEIVES (1) [DECEIVE]

Pr 10:31 wise advice, but the tongue that **d** will be cut off.

DECEIVING (4) [DECEIVE]

Zep 3:13 to each other, never telling lies or **d** one another.
Jn 7:12 "He's nothing but a fraud, **d** the people."
2Ti 3:13 They will go on **d** others, and they themselves will
Rev 12: 9 the Devil, or Satan, the one **d** the whole world—

DECEMBER (6)

Ezr 10: 9 This took place on **D** 19, and all the people were
10:16 On **D** 29, the leaders sat down to investigate the
Hag 2:10 On **D** 18 of the second year of King Darius's
2:18 "On this eighteenth day of **D**—the day when the
2:20 sent this second message to Haggai on **D** 18:
Zec 7: 1 On **D** 7 of the fourth year of King Darius's reign,

DECENT (6)

2Sa 2: 5 so loyal to your king and giving him a **d** burial.
2Ch 22: 9 Ahaziah was given a **d** burial because the people
Ps 141: 7 of the wicked will be scattered without a **d** burial.
Ecc 6: 3 in life and in the end does not even get a **d** burial,
Ro 13:13 We should be **d** and true in everything we do,
1Ti 2: 9 They should wear **d** and appropriate clothing

DECEPTION (13) [DECEIVE]

Jos 9: 4 they resorted to **d** to save themselves. They sent
Job 15: 5 what to say. Your words are based on clever **d**.
Pr 8: 7 for I speak the truth and hate every kind of **d**.
23: 3 don't desire all the delicacies—**d** may be involved.
Isa 28:15 we have built a strong refuge made of lies and **d**."
28:17 Since it is made of **d**, the enemy will come like a
Da 8:25 He will be a master of **d**, defeating many by
Ac 5: 2 was the full amount. His wife had agreed to this **d**.
Ro 1:29 sin, greed, hate, envy, murder, fighting, **d**,
Eph 4:22 is rotten through and through, full of lust and **d**.
2Th 2:10 He will use every kind of wicked **d** to fool those
2:11 So God will send great **d** upon them, and they will
1Jn 4: 6 if someone has the Spirit of truth or the spirit of **d**.

DECEPTIVE (2) [DECEIVE]

Ps 120: 3 O **d** tongue, what will God do to you? / How will
Pr 31:30 Charm is **d**, and beauty does not last; but a woman

DECIDE (39) [DECIDED, DECIDES, DECISION, DECISIONS, DECISIVE]

Ge 31:37 for all to see. Let them **d** who is the real owner!
39: 6 in the world, except to **d** what he wanted to eat!
Ex 13:13 But if you **d** not to make the exchange, the donkey
33: 5 and ornaments until I **d** what to do with you."
34:20 But if you **d** not to make the exchange, you must
Lev 27:19 If you **d** to redeem the dedicated field, you must
27:20 But if you **d** not to redeem the field, or if the field
Dt 1:22 to take and **d** which towns we should capture.'
17: 8 in a local court that is too hard for you to **d**—
17: 9 judge on duty will hear the case and **d** what to do.
21: 5 And they are to **d** all lawsuits and punishments.
21:14 if you marry her and then **d** you do not like her,
Jos 18: 6 to **d** which section will be assigned to each tribe.
Jdg 11:27 who is judge, **d** today which of us is right—
20: 7 the entire community of Israel must **d** what should
20: 9 we will draw lots to **d** who will attack Gibeah.
1Sa 14: 7 "I'm with you completely, whatever you **d**."
24:12 The LORD will **d** between us.
2Ch 30:19 who **d** to follow the LORD, the God of their
Est 1: 8 his staff to let everyone **d** this matter for himself.
Job 22:28 Whatever you **d** to do will be accomplished,
34:23 For it is not up to mortals to **d** when to come
Jer 40: 5 If you **d** to stay, then return to Gedaliah son of
Eze 21:22 Then they will **d** to turn toward Jerusalem!
Da 1:13 Then you can **d** whether or not to let us continue
Joel 3: 3 They cast lots to **d** which of my people would be
Mk 15:24 throwing dice to **d** who would get them.
Lk 12:14 who made me a judge over you to **d** such things as
12:57 "Why can't you **d** for yourselves what is right?
Ac 15: 6 and church elders got together to **d** this question.
24:22 arrives. Then I will **d** the case."
Ro 14:13 **D** instead to live in such a way that you will not
1Co 4: 4 It is the Lord himself who will examine me and **d**.
6: 1 a lawsuit and ask a secular court to **d** the matter,
6: 1 instead of taking it to other Christians to **d** who is
6: 2 can't you **d** these little things among yourselves?
6: 5 church who is wise enough to **d** these arguments?
10:15 **D** for yourselves if what I am about to say is true.
Jas 4:11 But you are not a judge who can **d** whether the law

DECIDED (81) [DECIDE]

Ge 6:13 to Noah, "I have **d** to destroy all living creatures,
26:28 So we **d** we should have a treaty, a covenant
Ex 1:13 and **d** to make their slavery more bitter still.
18:19 before God, bringing him their questions to be **d**.
Lev 27: 8 You will then pay the amount **d** by the priest.
Dt 32:26 I **d** to scatter them, / so even the memory of them
Jos 22:26 So we **d** to build the altar, not for burnt sacrifices,
Jdg 9: 3 they **d** in favor of Abimelech because he was their
9: 8 Once upon a time the trees **d** to elect a king.
1Sa 15: 2 'I have **d** to settle accounts with the nation of
2Sa 6:10 So David **d** not to move the Ark of the LORD
1Ki 1: 5 **d** to make himself king in place of his aged father.
1:24 have you **d** that Adonijah will be the next king
2Ki 19:25 It was I, the LORD, who **d** this long ago.
24: 3 He had **d** to remove Judah from his presence
1Ch 13:13 So David **d** not to move the Ark into the City of
26:13 or training, for it was all **d** by means of sacred lots.
2Ch 2: 1 Solomon now **d** that the time had come to build a
22: 7 a fatal mistake, for God had **d** to punish Ahaziah.
23: 1 of Athaliah's reign, Jehoiada the priest **d** to act.
24: 4 Joash **d** to repair and restore the Temple of the
24:18 They **d** to abandon the Temple of the LORD,
24:25 But his own officials **d** to kill him for murdering
30: 2 and all the community of Jerusalem **d** to celebrate
30:23 then **d** to continue the festival another seven days,
31:11 Hezekiah **d** to have storerooms prepared in the
32: 3 and they **d** to stop the flow of the springs outside
Ezr 10: 8 if the leaders and elders so **d**, forfeit all their
Est 3: 6 So he **d** it was not enough to lay hands on
3: 6 he **d** to destroy all the Jews throughout the entire
9:31 (The people **d** to observe this festival, just as they
had **d** for themselves and their
Job 9:27 If I **d** to forget my complaints, if I **d** to end my
sadness and be cheerful,
14: 5 You have **d** the length of our lives. You know how
Ecc 2: 3 After much thought, I **d** to cheer myself with wine.
2:12 So I **d** to compare wisdom and folly, and anyone
2:24 So I **d** there is nothing better than to enjoy food
6:10 Everything has already been **d**. It was known long
9:11 It is all **d** by chance, by being at the right place at
Isa 10:22 The LORD has rightly **d** to destroy his people.
10:23 LORD Almighty, has already **d** to consume them.
37:26 It was I, the LORD, who **d** this long ago.
Jer 21:10 For I have **d** to bring disaster and not good upon
35:11 Aramean armies. So we **d** to move to Jerusalem.
Eze 18:28 after thinking it over, they **d** to turn from their sins.
Da 6: 1 Darius the Mede **d** to divide the kingdom into 120
Jnh 3: 5 they **d** to go without food and wear sackcloth to
Mt 1:19 a just man, **d** to break the engagement quietly,
16: 7 They **d** he was saying this because they hadn't
18:23 **d** to bring his accounts up to date with servants
22:16 They **d** to send some of their disciples, along with
27: 7 After some discussion they finally **d** to buy the
28:12 leaders was called, and they **d** to bribe the soldiers.
Mk 8:16 They **d** he was saying this because they hadn't
Lk 1: 3 I have **d** to write a careful summary for you,
1:30 the angel told her, "for God has **d** to bless you!
Jn 1:43 The next day Jesus **d** to go to Galilee. He found

12:10 Then the leading priests **d** to kill Lazarus, too,
Ac 5:33 the high council was furious and **d** to kill them.
7:23 he **d** to visit his relatives, the people of Israel.
9:23 After a while the Jewish leaders **d** to kill him.
11:29 So the believers in Antioch **d** to send relief to the
12:15 When she insisted, they **d**, "It must be his angel."
14:5 with their leaders, **d** to attack and stone them.
14:12 They **d** that Barnabas was the Greek god Zeus
15:27 and Silas to tell you what we have **d** concerning
16:4 as **d** by the apostles and elders in Jerusalem.
16:10 So we **d** to leave for Macedonia at once, for we
17:26 He **d** beforehand which should rise and fall,
20:3 his life, so he **d** to return through Macedonia.
20:16 Paul had **d** against stopping at Ephesus this time
25:25 his case to the emperor, and I **d** to send him.
28:6 they changed their minds and **d** he was a god.
1Co 2:2 For I **d** to concentrate only on Jesus Christ and his
7:37 But if he has **d** firmly not to marry and there is no
Eph 1:11 and all things happen just as he **d** long ago.
1Th 3:1 no longer, we **d** that I should stay alone in Athens,
5:9 For God **d** to save us through our Lord Jesus
Tit 3:12 as you can, for I have **d** to stay there for the winter.
1Pe 4:1 to suffer for Christ, you have **d** to stop sinning.

DECIDES (5) [DECIDE]

Ps 75:7 who judges; / he **d** who will rise and who will fall.
Eze 18:14 father's wickedness but **d** against that kind of life.
46:7 to bring whatever amount of flour that he **d** to give.
Mt 18:17 If the church **d** you are right, but the other person
1Co 12:11 He alone **d** which gift each person should have.

DECISION (25) [DECIDE]

Ex 22:9 Both parties must come before God for a **d**,
Nu 33:54 The **d** of the sacred lot is final. In this way,
Dt 17:10 The **d** they make at the place the LORD chooses
Jos 24:22 "You are accountable for this **d**," Joshua said.
2Sa 14:13 You have convicted yourself in making this **d**,
19:29 "My **d** is that you and Ziba will divide your land
1Ki 1:20 all Israel is waiting for your **d** as to who will
3:28 Word of the king's **d** spread quickly throughout all
12:12 and all the people returned to hear Rehoboam's **d**,
2Ch 10:12 and all the people returned to hear Rehoboam's **d**,
Ezr 5:5 a report was sent to Darius and he returned his **d**.
5:17 then let the king send us his **d** in this matter."
Est 3:10 confirming his **d** by removing his signet ring from
Ps 83:5 This was their unanimous **d**. / They signed a treaty
Da 6:12 "Yes," the king replied, "that **d** stands; it is a law
Joel 3:14 upon thousands are waiting in the valley of **d**.
Zep 3:8 For it is my **d** to gather together the kingdoms of
Zec 8:15 Neither will I change my **d** to bless Jerusalem
Lk 18:7 Even he rendered a just **d** in the end, so don't you
23:51 but he had not agreed with the **d** and actions of the
Ac 3:13 before Pilate, despite Pilate's **d** to release him.
15:22 of Syria with Paul and Barnabas to report on this **d**.
15:25 good to us, having unanimously agreed on our **d**,
16:4 explaining the **d** regarding the commandments that
28:19 But when the Jewish leaders protested the **d**,

DECISIONS (12) [DECIDE]

Ex 18:16 I inform the people of God's **d** and teach them his
18:20 You should tell them God's **d**, teach them God's
Dt 1:17 When you make **d**, never favor those who are rich;
16:19 the eyes of the wise and corrupt the **d** of the godly.
1Sa 16:7 The LORD doesn't make **d** the way you do!
1Ki 3:28 God had given him to render **d** with justice.
Ps 82:2 "How long will you judges hand down unjust **d**?
119:75 I know, O LORD, that your **d** are fair;
119:137 O LORD, you are righteous, / and your **d** are fair.
Eze 44:24 Their **d** must be based on my regulations.
Ro 11:33 How impossible it is for us to understand his **d**
2Co 10:7 The trouble with you is that you make your **d** on

DECISIVE (1) [DECIDE]

Mt 7:21 The **d** issue is whether they obey my Father in

DECK (1) [DECKED, DECKS]

Eze 27:6 They made your **d** of pine wood, brought from the

DECKED (1) [DECK]

Rev 18:16 **d** out with gold and precious stones and pearls!

DECKEDST, DECKEST [KJV] See DRESS UP, PUT ON

DECKS (2) [DECK]

Ge 6:14 Then construct **d** and stalls throughout its interior.
6:16 Then put three **d** inside the boat—bottom, middle,

DECLARE (45) [DECLARED, DECLARES, DECLARING]

Ex 19:23 around the mountain and to **d** it off limits."
21:5 But the slave may plainly **d**, 'I love my master,
Dt 21:20 They must **d**: 'This son of ours is stubborn
25:1 and the judges **d** that one is right and the other is
26:13 Then you must **d** in the presence of the LORD
32:40 my hand to heaven / and **d**, "As surely as I live,
Jos 9:11 of Israel and **d** our people to be their servants,
1Ch 17:10 " 'And now I **d** that the LORD will build a
Ezr 4:16 We **d** that if this city is rebuilt and its walls are
Job 33:23 to intercede for a person, to **d** that he is upright,
33:27 He will **d** to his friends, 'I sinned, but it was not
Ps 5:10 O God, **d** them guilty. / Let them be caught in their
7:8 **D** me righteous, O LORD, / for I am innocent,
17:2 **D** me innocent, / for you know those who do right.
22:22 Then I will **d** the wonder of your name to my
26:1 **D** me innocent, O LORD, / for I have acted with
26:6 I wash my hands to **d** my innocence. / I come to
35:1 oppose me. / **D** war on those who are attacking me.
35:24 **D** me "not guilty," O LORD my God, for you
71:8 stop praising you; / I **d** your glory all day long.
88:11 Can those in the grave **d** your unfailing love?
91:2 This I **d** of the LORD: / He alone is my refuge,
92:15 They will **d**, "The LORD is just! / He is my rock!
97:6 The heavens **d** his righteousness; / every nation
Pr 31:31 she has done. Let her deeds publicly **d** her praise.
Isa 25:3 Therefore, strong nations will **d** your glory;
45:24 The people will **d**, "The LORD is the source of
50:9 LORD is on my side! Who will **d** me guilty?
66:19 There they will **d** my glory to the nations.
Jer 50:28 as they **d** in Jerusalem how the LORD our God
Mic 3:5 but you **d** war on anyone who refuses to pay you.
Mt 21:13 He said, "The Scriptures **d**, 'My Temple will be
Mk 11:17 He taught them, "The Scriptures **d**, 'My Temple
14:25 I solemnly **d** that I will not drink wine again until
Lk 19:46 He told them, "The Scriptures **d**, 'My Temple will
Jn 7:38 For the Scriptures **d** that rivers of living water will
13:18 The Scriptures **d**, 'The one who shares my food
Ro 4:24 assuring us that God will also **d** us to be righteous
2Co 10:7 as those who proudly **d** that they belong to Christ.
Gal 1:20 I am saying, for I **d** before God that I am not lying.
1Th 2:2 Yet our God gave us the courage to **d** his Good
Heb 2:12 "I will **d** the wonder of your name to my brothers
3:1 think about this Jesus whom we **d** to be God's
Rev 11:7 out of the bottomless pit will **d** war against them.
22:18 And I solemnly **d** to everyone who hears the

DECLARED (65) [DECLARE]

Ge 2:3 And God blessed the seventh day and **d** it holy,
15:6 and the LORD **d** him righteous because of his
21:6 And Sarah **d**, "God has brought me laughter!
27:37 and have **d** that all his brothers will be his servants.
Ex 5:3 God of the Hebrews has met with us," they **d**.
Dt 2:32 Then King Sihon **d** war on us and mobilized his
26:17 You have **d** today that the LORD is your God.
26:18 The LORD has **d** today that you are his people,
Jos 20:6 Then the one **d** innocent because the death was
1Sa 12:5 and his anointed one are my witnesses," Samuel **d**,
14:41 as the guilty ones, and the people were **d** innocent.
2Sa 3:28 When David heard about it, he **d**, "I vow by the
21:17 After that, David's men **d**, "You are not going out
1Ki 1:43 "Our lord King David has just **d** Solomon king!
2Ki 1:1 the nation of Moab **d** its independence from Israel.
10:10 The LORD **d** through his servant Elijah that this
16:5 of Aram and King Pekah of Israel **d** war on Ahaz.
25:11 and the troops who had **d** their allegiance to the
1Ch 22:18 "The LORD your God is with you," he **d**.
2Ch 17:10 so that none of them **d** war on Jehoshaphat.
20:1 and some of the Meunites **d** war on Jehoshaphat.
26:6 He **d** war on the Philistines and broke down the
28:13 they **d**. "We cannot afford to add to our sins
29:31 Then Hezekiah **d**, "The dedication ceremony has
Est 2:17 on her head and **d** her queen instead of Vashti.
8:17 and **d** a public festival and holiday.
9:27 They **d** they would never fail to celebrate these two
Job 9:2 But how can a person be **d** innocent in the eyes of
Ps 106:23 So he **d** he would destroy them. / But Moses,
Isa 43:12 I **d** what I would do, and then I did it—I saved you.
Jer 52:15 and the troops who had **d** their allegiance to the
Eze 16:8 to cover your nakedness and **d** my marriage vows.
39:8 Everything will happen just as I have **d** it.
Da 4:24 and what the Most High has **d** will happen to you.
Mt 26:24 Son of Man, must die, as the Scriptures **d** long ago.
26:33 Peter **d**, "Even if everyone else deserts you,
26:61 who **d**, "This man said, 'I am able to destroy the
27:4 "I have sinned," he **d**, "for I have betrayed an
Mk 14:21 Son of Man, must die, as the Scriptures **d** long ago.
Lk 5:33 they **d**, "and so do the disciples of the Pharisees.
Jn 1:36 walked by, John looked at him and then **d**, "Look!
7:40 some of them **d**, "This man surely is the Prophet."
8:39 "Our father is Abraham," they **d**. "No,"
12:29 while others **d** an angel had spoken to him.
Ac 3:18 But God was fulfilling what all the prophets had **d**
10:14 "Never, Lord," Peter **d**. "I have never in all my
13:39 him is freed from all guilt and **d** right with God—
13:46 Then Paul and Barnabas spoke out boldly and **d**,
15:5 and **d** that all Gentile converts must be circumcised
20:18 When they arrived he **d**, "You know that from the
Ro 2:13 Those who obey the law will be **d** right in God's
4:3 believed God, so God **d** him to be righteous."
4:5 But people are **d** righteous because of their faith,
4:6 of an undeserving sinner who is **d** to be righteous:
4:9 We have been saying he was **d** righteous by God
4:10 Was he **d** righteous only after he had been
4:11 already accepted him and **d** him to be righteous—
4:22 of Abraham's faith, God **d** him to be righteous.
4:23 wonderful truth—that God **d** him to be righteous—
Gal 3:6 so God **d** him righteous because of his faith."
3:22 But the Scriptures have **d** that we are all prisoners
Tit 3:7 He **d** us not guilty because of his great kindness.
Jas 2:21 that our ancestor Abraham was **d** right with God
2:23 believed God, so God **d** him to be righteous."
Rev 12:17 and he **d** war against the rest of her children—

DECLARES (11) [DECLARE]

Ex 22:9 and the person whom God **d** guilty must pay
2Sa 7:11 " 'And now the LORD **d** that he will build a
Ps 2:6 For the LORD **d**, "I have placed my chosen king
4:1 me when I call, / O God who **d** me innocent.
Eze 14:14 no one but themselves, **d** the Sovereign LORD.
Na 3:5 **d** the LORD Almighty. "And now I will lift your
Jn 19:12 Anyone who **d** himself a king is a rebel against
Ac 21:11 Then he said, "The Holy Spirit **d**, 'So shall the
Ro 3:5 **d** for people will see God's goodness when he **d** us
3:24 Yet now God in his gracious kindness **d** us not
3:26 and just in this present time when he **d** sinners to

DECLARING (4) [DECLARE]

Est 2:18 and **d** a public festival for the provinces.
Ac 20:27 for I didn't shrink from **d** all that God wants for
24:9 **d** that everything Tertullus said was true.
1Co 14:25 will fall down on their knees and worship God, **d**,

DECLINED (1)

Ac 18:20 They asked him to stay longer, but he **d**.

DECORATE (5) [DECORATED, DECORATION, DECORATIONS, DECORATIVE]

Ex 27:16 and **d** it with beautiful embroidery in blue, purple,
1Ki 7:18 the latticework to **d** the capitals over the pillars.
2Ch 3:16 and used them to **d** the tops of the pillars.
Jer 10:4 They **d** it with gold and silver and then fasten it
Mt 23:29 and **d** the graves of the godly people your

DECORATED (26) [DECORATE]

Ex 25:34 The center stem of the lampstand will be **d** with
26:1 These sheets are to be **d** with blue, purple,
36:38 The posts with their **d** tops and bands were
37:20 The center stem of the lampstand was also **d** with
1Ki 6:18 and the paneling was **d** with carvings of gourds
6:29 and the main room were **d** with carvings of
6:32 These doors were **d** with carvings of cherubim,
6:35 These doors were **d** with carvings of cherubim,
7:17 Each capital was **d** with seven sets of latticework
7:29 and the crossbars were **d** with carved lions,
7:30 these supports were **d** with carvings of wreaths on
7:31 it was **d** on the outside with carvings of wreaths.
7:36 and palm trees **d** the panels and supports wherever
7:41 two networks of chains that **d** the capitals,
2Ki 25:17 and was **d** with a network of bronze pomegranates
2Ch 3:5 and **d** with carvings of palm trees and chains.
3:6 The walls of the Temple were **d** with beautiful
4:12 two networks of chains that **d** the capitals,
Est 1:6 The courtyard was **d** with beautifully woven white
Ps 45:8 aloes, and cassia. / In palaces **d** with ivory,
Isa 40:19 overlaid with gold, and **d** with silver chains?
Jer 52:22 and was **d** with a network of bronze pomegranates
Eze 40:16 The surfaces of the dividing walls were **d** with
41:18 All the walls were **d** with carvings of cherubim,
41:25 The doors leading into the Holy Place were **d** with
41:26 were recessed windows **d** with carved palm trees.

DECORATION (1) [DECORATE]

Ro 9:21 to use the same lump of clay to make one jar for **d**

DECORATIONS (12) [DECORATE]

Ex 25:31 The entire lampstand and its **d** will be one piece—
25:36 The **d** and branches must all be one piece with the
37:22 The **d** and branches were all one piece with the
1Ki 7:29 and below the lions and oxen were wreath **d**.
7:49 in front of the Most Holy Place, the flower **d**,
2Ch 4:21 the flower **d**, lamps, and tongs, all of pure gold;
Eze 40:22 and the palm tree **d** were identical to those in the
40:26 and there were palm tree **d** along the dividing
40:31 It had palm tree **d** on its columns, and there were
40:34 It had palm tree **d** on its columns, and there were
40:37 and it had palm tree **d** on the columns.
Lk 21:5 of the Temple and the memorial **d** on the walls.

DECORATIVE (4) [DECORATE]

Lev 8:7 and attached the ephod with its **d** sash.
Nu 8:4 entire lampstand, from its base to its **d** blossoms,
1Ki 7:24 just below its rim by two rows of **d** gourds.
2Ch 3:16 He also made one hundred **d** pomegranates

DECREASE (1)

Ps 107:39 When they **d** in number and become impoverished

DECREE (47) [DECREED, DECREES]

1Ki 1:30 today I **d** that your son Solomon will be the next
1:36 the God of my lord the king, **d** it to be so.
2:27 thereby fulfilling the **d** the LORD had made at
1Ch 16:17 He confirmed it to Jacob as a **d**, / to the people of
Ezr 5:13 issued a **d** that the Temple of God should be
5:17 issued a **d** to rebuild God's Temple in Jerusalem.
6:3 a **d** was sent out concerning the Temple of God at
6:8 Moreover I hereby **d** that you are to help these
6:11 "Those who violate this **d** in any way will have a
6:12 destroys this Temple. I, Darius, have issued this **d**.
7:13 "I **d** that any of the people of Israel in my
7:21 hereby send this **d** to all the treasurers in the
7:24 I also **d** that no priest, Levite, singer, gatekeeper,
Est 1:19 we suggest that you issue a written **d**, a law of the
1:20 When this **d** is published throughout your vast
2:1 and what she had done and the **d** he had made.
2:8 As a result of the king's **d**, Esther, along with
3:9 Your Majesty, issue a **d** that they be destroyed,
3:14 A copy of this **d** was to be issued in every province
3:15 the **d** went out by the swiftest messengers,
4:3 And as news of the king's **d** reached all the

4: 8 Mordecai gave Hathach a copy of the **d** issued in
8: 5 send out a **d** reversing Haman's orders to destroy
8: 9 they wrote a **d** to the Jews and to the princes,
8: 9 The **d** was written in the scripts and languages of
8:11 The king's **d** gave the Jews in every city authority
8:13 A copy of this **d** was to be recognized as law in
8:14 The same **d** was also issued at the fortress of Susa.
8:15 And the people of Susa celebrated the new **d**.
8:17 and province, wherever the king's **d** arrived,
9:14 the king agreed, and the **d** was announced in Susa.
9:25 he issued a **d** causing Haman's evil plot to
Ps 2: 7 The king proclaims the LORD's **d**:
78: 5 For he issued his **d** to Jacob; / he gave his law to
81: 5 He made it a **d** for Israel / when he attacked Egypt
105:10 He confirmed it to Jacob as a **d**, / to the people of
Isa 65: 6 "Look, my **d** is written out in front of me: I will
Jer 4:28 in black, because of my **d** against my people.
22:18 this is the LORD's **d** of punishment against King
Da 2:13 And because of the king's **d**, men were sent to find
2:15 "Why has the king issued such a harsh **d**?"
3:10 You issued a **d** requiring all the people to bow
3:11 That **d** also states that those who refuse to obey
3:29 Therefore, I make this **d**: If any people,
4:17 The purpose of this **d** is that the whole world may
6:26 "I **d** that everyone throughout my kingdom should
Jnh 3: 7 and his nobles sent this **d** throughout the city:

DECREED (17) [DECREE]

Ge 41:32 it means that the matter has been **d** by God and that
Ezr 6:14 commanded by the God of Israel and **d** by Cyrus,
Ne 13: 5 Moses had **d** that these offerings belonged to the
Est 3:13 The letters **d** that all Jews—young and old,
9:31 **d** by both Mordecai the Jew and Queen Esther.
Job 20:29 awaits the wicked. It is the inheritance **d** by God."
Ps 104: 8 and valleys sank / to the levels you **d**.
Jer 8:14 For the LORD our God has **d** our destruction
16:10 'Why has the LORD **d** such terrible things
34: 5 king is dead!" This I have **d**, says the LORD.' "
Da 4:17 For this has been **d** by the messengers; it is
9:24 "A period of seventy sets of seven has been **d** for
9:26 and its miseries are **d** from that time to the very
9:27 until the end that has been **d** is poured out on this
Na 2: 7 Nineveh's exile has been **d**, and all the servant
Hab 1:12 you have **d** the rise of these Babylonians to punish
Lk 2: 1 **d** that a census should be taken throughout the

DECREES (33) [DECREE]

1Ch 29:19 **d**, and principles, and to build this Temple,
Ezr 8:36 The king's **d** were delivered to his lieutenants
Est 9: 1 So on March 7 the two **d** of the king were put into
Ps 19: 7 the soul. / The **d** of the LORD are trustworthy,
25:10 all those who keep his covenant and obey his **d**.
78:56 the Most High / and refused to follow his **d**.
89:31 if they do not obey my **d** / and fail to keep my
93: 5 Your royal **d** cannot be changed. / The nature of
99: 7 and they followed the **d** and principles he gave
119: 2 Happy are those who obey his **d** / and search for
119:14 I have rejoiced in your **d** / as much as in riches.
119:22 and insult me, / for I have obeyed your **d**.
119:24 Your **d** please me; / they give me wise advice.
119:31 I cling to your **d**. / LORD, don't let me be put to
119:36 Give me an eagerness for your **d**; / do not inflict
119:46 I will speak to kings about your **d**, / and I will not
119:79 with all who fear you and know your **d**.
119:88 spare my life; / then I can continue to obey your **d**.
119:95 to kill me, / I will quietly keep my mind on your **d**.
119:99 my teachers, / for I am always thinking of your **d**.
119:111 Your **d** are my treasure; / they are truly my heart's
119:119 you skim off; / no wonder I love to obey your **d**!
119:125 your servant; / then I will understand your **d**.
119:129 Your **d** are wonderful. / No wonder I obey them!
119:138 Your **d** are perfect; / they are entirely worthy of
119:144 Your **d** are always fair; / help me to understand
119:146 I cry out to you; save me, / that I may obey your **d**.
119:152 from my earliest days / that your **d** never change.
119:157 trouble me, / yet I have not swerved from your **d**.
119:167 I have obeyed your **d**, / and I love them very much.
119:168 Yes, I obey your commandments and **d**,
132:12 and follow the **d** that I teach them, / then your
Jer 44:10 and the **d** I gave to you and your ancestors before

DEDAN (11) [DEDAN'S]

Ge 10: 7 The descendants of Raamah were Sheba and **D**.
25: 3 Jokshan's two sons were Sheba and **D**.
1Ch 1: 9 The descendants of Raamah were Sheba and **D**.
1:32 The sons of Jokshan were Sheba and **D**.
Isa 21:13 O caravans from **D**, hide in the deserts of Arabia.
Jer 25:23 I went to **D**, Tema, and Buz, and to the people who
49: 8 and flee! Hide in deep caves, you people of **D**!
Eze 25:13 make a wasteland of everything from Teman to **D**.
27:15 Merchants came to you from **D**.
27:20 **D** traded their expensive saddle blankets with you.
38:13 But Sheba and **D** and the merchants of Tarshish

DEDAN'S (1) [DEDAN]

Ge 25: 3 **D** descendants were the Asshurites, Letushites,

DEDANIM [KJV] See DEDAN

DEDICATE (11) [DEDICATED, DEDICATING, DEDICATION, REDEDICATE]

Ex 13: 2 "**D** to me all the firstborn sons of Israel and every
Lev 27: 2 If you make a special vow to **d** someone to the
27:14 "If you **d** a house to the LORD, the priest must
27:16 "If you **d** to the LORD a piece of your ancestral
27:22 "If you **d** to the LORD a field that you have
27:26 "You may not **d** to the LORD the firstborn of
Dt 20: 5 the battle, and someone else would **d** your house!
Jdg 17: 3 "I now **d** these silver coins to the LORD.
1Ch 23:13 and his descendants were set apart to **d** the most
Ac 13: 2 "**D** Barnabas and Saul for the special work I have
2Co 8: 5 for their first action was to **d** themselves to the

DEDICATED (41) [DEDICATE]

Ex 20:10 but the seventh day is a day of rest **d** to the
Lev 27:17 If the field is **d** to the LORD in the Year of
27:18 But if the field is **d** after the Year of Jubilee,
27:19 If you decide to redeem the **d** field, you must pay
Nu 8:20 and the whole community of Israel **d** the Levites,
18: 6 They are **d** to the LORD for service in the
Dt 5:14 but the seventh day is a day of rest **d** to the
20: 5 'Has anyone just built a new house but not yet **d** it?
Jdg 13: 5 For he will be **d** to God as a Nazirite from birth.
13: 7 For your son will be **d** to God as a Nazirite from
16:17 "for I was **d** to God as a Nazirite from birth.
1Sa 1:11 and as a sign that he has been **d** to the LORD,
2Sa 8:11 King David **d** all these gifts to the LORD,
1Ki 7:51 brought all the gifts his father, David, had **d**—
8:63 the king and all Israel **d** the Temple of the LORD.
8:64 That same day the king **d** the central area of the
15:15 and the utensils that he and his father had **d**.
2Ki 12:18 and Ahaziah, the previous kings of Judah, had **d**, along with what he himself had **d**.
23:11 that the former kings of Judah had **d** to the sun.
23:11 The king also burned the chariots **d** to the sun.
1Ch 18:11 King David **d** all these gifts to the LORD,
26:26 held all the things **d** to the LORD by King David,
26:27 These men had **d** some of the plunder they had
26:28 and his relatives also cared for the items **d** to the
26:28 All the other **d** items were in their care, too.
28:12 of God's Temple, and the rooms for the **d** gifts.
2Ch 5: 1 he brought in the gifts **d** by his father, King David,
7: 5 the king and all the people **d** the Temple of God.
7: 7 then **d** the central area of the courtyard in front of
13: 9 Whoever comes to be **d** with a young bull
15:18 and the utensils that he and his father had **d**.
24: 7 and they had used all the **d** things from the Temple
31: 6 and a tithe of the things that had been **d** to the
31:14 and the things that had been **d** to the LORD.
Ezr 6:16 then **d** with great joy by the people of Israel,
Ne 3: 1 They **d** it and set up its doors, building the wall as
3: 1 which they **d**, and the Tower of Hananel.
12:30 The priests and Levites first **d** themselves,
Lk 2:23 first child is a boy, he must be **d** to the Lord."
1Co 8:10 by eating food that has been **d** to the idol.

DEDICATING (1) [DEDICATE]

Nu 8:11 of Israel, thus **d** them to the LORD's service.

DEDICATION (13) [DEDICATE]

Ex 29: 1 "This is the ceremony for the **d** of Aaron and his
Nu 7:10 The leaders also presented **d** gifts for the altar at
7:11 his gift on a different day for the **d** of the altar."
7:84 So this was the **d** offering for the altar, brought by
7:88 This was the **d** offering for the altar after it was
1Ki 8:65 seven days for the **d** of the altar and seven days for
2Ch 7: 9 for they had celebrated the **d** of the altar for seven
29:31 "The **d** ceremony has come to an end.
Ezr 6:17 During the **d** ceremony for the Temple of God,
Ne 12:27 During the **d** of the new wall of Jerusalem,
Ps 30: T A psalm of David, sung at the **d** of the Temple.
Da 3: 2 and all the provincial officials to come to the **d** of
1Co 4:10 Our **d** to Christ makes us look like fools, but you

DEED (19) [DEEDED, DEEDS]

2Sa 12: 9 the word of the LORD and done this horrible **d**?
Ne 13: 7 and learned the extent of this evil **d** of Eliashib—
13:14 Remember this good **d**, O my God, and do not
13:22 Remember this good **d** also, O my God!
13:27 could you even think of committing this sinful **d**
Pr 4:16 sleep until they have done their evil **d** for the day.
Jer 7:31 I have never commanded such a horrible **d**;
19: 5 I have never commanded such a horrible **d**;
26:15 The responsibility for such a **d** will lie on you,
32:10 and sealed the **d** of purchase before witnesses,
32:11 Then I took the sealed **d** and an unsealed copy of the **d**,
32:12 the witnesses who had signed the **d**, and all the
32:14 Take both this sealed **d** and the unsealed copy,
32:35 I have never commanded such a horrible **d**;
Mt 26:13 this woman's **d** will be talked about in her
Mk 14: 9 this woman's **d** will be talked about in her
Ac 4: 9 because we've done a good **d** for a crippled man?
Ro 15:28 this money and completed this good **d** of theirs,

DEEDED (1) [DEED]

Isa 34:17 divided the land and **d** it over to those creatures.

DEEDS (152) [DEED]

EVIL DEEDS (28) 1Sa 24:13; Ps 28:4; 106:39; Isa 1:16,31; 59:4,18; Jer 16:18; 22:3; 32:30; La 1:22; Eze 36:17; Ob 1:15; Mic 7:3; Lk 6:45; 23:41; Ro 2:8; 8:13; 13:12; Eph 5:14; Php 3:2; Heb 6:1; Rev 2:22; 3:4; 9:20; 16:11; 18:5,6

GOOD DEEDS (30) Job 35:8; Ps 112:3,9; Isa 57:12; Eze 3:20; 33:13; Mt 5:16; 6:1; Mk 3:4; Lk 6:9,45; Jn 10:32; Ro 3:27; 4:2; 7:4; 2Co 9:9; 1Ti 5:25; Tit 2:7; 3:8; Heb 10:24; Jas 2:17,18,18,18,20,26; 3:13,17; Rev 14:13; 19:8

MIGHTY DEEDS (6) Dt 5:15; 11:7; 1Ch 29:30; Ps 71:16; 145:12; Isa 41:4

RIGHTEOUS DEEDS (3) Ps 71:24; Isa 64:6; Rev 15:4

Dt 3:24 or on earth who can perform such great **d** as yours?
5:15 you out with amazing power and mighty **d**.
11: 7 But you have seen all the LORD's mighty **d** with
1Sa 2: 3 The LORD is a God who knows your **d**;
14:48 He did great **d** and conquered the Amalekites,
24:13 old proverb says, 'From evil people come evil **d**.'
26:25 You will do heroic **d** and be a great conqueror."
2Sa 3:39 repay these wicked men for their wicked **d**."
23:20 He did many heroic **d**, which included killing two
23:22 These are some of the **d** that made Benaiah almost
1Ki 14:29 and all his **d** are recorded in *The Book of the*
15: 7 and all his **d** are recorded in *The Book of the*
15:31 and all his **d** are recorded in *The Book of the*
16:14 and all his **d** are recorded in *The Book of the*
16:27 and all his **d** are recorded in *The Book of the*
2Ki 8:23 and all his **d** are recorded in *The Book of the*
10:34 The rest of the events in Jehu's reign and all his **d**
12:19 and all his **d** are recorded in *The Book of the*
13: 8 rest of the events in Jehoahaz's reign and all his **d**,
13:12 rest of the events in Jehoash's reign and all his **d**,
14:28 the events in the reign of Jeroboam II and all his **d**,
15: 6 and all his **d** are recorded in *The Book of the*
15:21 and all his **d** are recorded in *The Book of the*
15:26 and all his **d** are recorded in *The Book of the*
15:31 and all his **d** are recorded in *The Book of the*
15:36 and all his **d** are recorded in *The Book of the*
16:19 and his **d** are recorded in *The Book of the History*
21:17 rest of the events in Manasseh's reign and all his **d**,
21:25 and all his **d** are recorded in *The Book of the*
23:28 and all his **d** are recorded in *The Book of the*
24: 5 and all his **d** are recorded in *The Book of the*
1Ch 11:22 He did many heroic **d**, which included killing two
11:24 These are some of the **d** that made Benaiah as
16:24 Publish his glorious **d** among the nations.
29:30 These accounts include the mighty **d** of his reign
2Ch 13:22 of Abijah's reign, including his words and **d**,
Job 34:11 He repays people according to their **d**. He treats
35: 8 and your good **d** affect only other people.
Ps 9:11 Tell the world about his unforgettable **d**.
28: 4 Pay them back for all their evil **d**!
38:12 They think up treacherous **d** all day long.
40: 5 If I tried to recite all your wonderful **d**, / I would
45: 4 and justice. / Go forth to perform awe-inspiring **d**!
51: 3 For I recognize my shameful **d**— / they haunt me
65: 5 faithfully answer our prayers with awesome **d**,
66: 3 Say to God, "How awesome are your **d**!
71:16 I will praise your mighty **d**, O Sovereign LORD.
71:24 I will tell about your righteous **d** / all day long,
77:11 I remember your wonderful **d** of long ago.
78: 4 generation about the glorious **d** of the LORD.
96: 3 Publish his glorious **d** among the nations.
98: 1 song to the LORD, / for he has done wonderful **d**.
103: 7 to Moses / and his **d** to the people of Israel.
106:22 in that land, / such awesome **d** at the Red Sea.
106:39 They defiled themselves by their evil **d**, / and their
107: 8 his great love / and for all his wonderful **d** to them.
107:15 his great love / and for all his wonderful **d** to them.
107:21 his great love / and for all his wonderful **d** to them.
107:31 his great love / and for all his wonderful **d** to them.
111: 2 How amazing are the **d** of the LORD! / All who
112: 3 and their good **d** will never be forgotten.
112: 9 Their good **d** will never be forgotten. / They will
141: 5 in constant prayer / against the wicked and their **d**.
145: 6 Your awe-inspiring **d** will be on every tongue;
145:12 They will tell about your mighty **d** / and about the
Pr 31:31 she has done. Let her **d** publicly declare her praise.
Ecc 3:17 both good and bad, for all their **d**."
Isa 1:16 and be clean! Let me no longer see your evil **d**.
1:31 Your evil **d** are the spark that will set the straw on
41: 4 Who has done such mighty **d**, directing the affairs
55: 7 Let the people turn from their wicked **d**. Let them
57:12 "Now I will expose your so-called good **d** that you
59: 4 They spend their time plotting evil **d** and
59:18 He will repay his enemies for their evil **d**. His fury
64: 6 When we proudly display our righteous **d**, we find
Jer 5:28 and there is no limit to their wicked **d**.
7: 5 your wicked thoughts and **d** and are fair to others;
16:18 and filled my inheritance with their evil **d**."
22: 3 Quit your evil **d**! Do not mistreat foreigners,
32:19 and you reward them according to their **d**.
32:30 They have infuriated me with all their evil **d**,"
32:44 and sold—**d** signed and sealed and witnessed—
La 1:22 "Look at all their evil **d**, LORD. Punish them,
Eze 3:20 Their previous good **d** won't help them, and I will
18:26 for it. Yes, they will die because of their sinful **d**.
22: 2 of murderers? Denounce her terrible **d** in public,
23:36 accuse Oholah and Oholibah of all their awful **d**.
33:13 then none of their good **d** will be remembered.
33:20 But I will judge each of you according to your **d**."
35:11 I will pay back your angry **d** with mine.
36:17 in their own land, they defiled it by their evil **d**.
Da 9:27 Then as a climax to all his terrible **d**, he will set up
Hos 4: 9 both priests and people for all their wicked **d**.
5: 4 Your **d** won't let you return to your God. You are a
7: 2 Their sinful **d** are all around them; I see them all!
Am 8: 8 The earth will tremble for your **d**, and everyone
Ob 1:15 All your evil **d** will fall back on your own heads.
Mic 7: 3 They go about their evil **d** with both hands.
Mt 5:16 same way, let your good **d** shine out for all to see,
6: 1 Don't do your good **d** publicly, to be admired,
16:27 and will judge all people according to their **d**.
Mk 3: 4 "Is it legal to do good **d** on the Sabbath,
Lk 6: 9 Is it legal to do good **d** on the Sabbath, or is it a

6:45 A good person produces good **d** from a good heart,
6:45 and an evil person produces evil **d** from an evil
23:41 We deserve to die for our evil **d**, but this man
Jn 10:32 For which one of these good **d** are you killing
Ro 2:8 who refuse to obey the truth and practice evil **d**.
3:27 because our acquittal is not based on our good **d**.
4:2 because of his good **d** that God accepted him?
7:4 can produce good fruit, that is, good **d** for God.
7:5 aroused these evil desires that produced sinful **d**,
8:13 of the Holy Spirit you turn from it and its evil **d**,
13:12 So don't live in darkness. Get rid of your evil **d**.
2Co 9:9 the poor. / Their good **d** will never be forgotten."
11:15 get every bit of punishment their wicked **d** deserve.
Eph 5:11 Take no part in the worthless **d** of evil
5:14 where your light shines, it will expose their evil **d**.
Php 3:2 for those dogs, those wicked men and their evil **d**,
Col 3:9 off your old evil nature and all its wicked **d**.
1Th 1:3 we think of your faithful work, your loving **d**,
2Th 1:11 will fulfill all your good intentions and faithful **d**.
1Ti 5:25 but there are others whose good **d** won't be known
Tit 2:7 an example to them by doing good **d** of every kind.
3:8 in God will be careful to do good **d** all the time.
Heb 6:1 with the importance of turning away from evil **d**
9:14 will purify our hearts from **d** that lead to death
10:17 never again remember / their sins and lawless **d**."
10:24 one another to outbursts of love and good **d**.
Jas 2:17 Faith that doesn't show itself by good **d** is no faith
2:18 "Some people have faith; others have good **d**."
2:18 "I can't see your faith if you don't have good **d**,
2:18 but I will show you my faith through my good **d**."
2:20 that faith that does not result in good **d** is useless?
2:26 a spirit, so also faith is dead without good **d**.
3:13 so that only good **d** will pour forth.
3:17 It is full of mercy and good **d**. It shows no
3Jn 1:6 church here of your friendship and your loving **d**.
Jude 1:13 churning up the dirty foam of their shameful **d**.
Rev 2:6 You hate the **d** of the immoral Nicolaitans, just as I
2:22 unless they turn away from all their evil **d**.
3:2 Your **d** are far from right in the sight of God.
3:4 who have not soiled their garments with evil **d**.
9:20 these plagues still refused to turn from their evil **d**.
14:13 and trials; for their good **d** follow them!"
15:4 for your righteous **d** have been revealed."
16:11 But they refused to repent of all their evil **d**.
18:5 and God is ready to judge her for her evil **d**.
18:6 Give her a double penalty for all her evil **d**.
19:8 (Fine linen represents the good **d** done by the
20:13 in them. They were all judged according to their **d**.
22:12 reward is with me, to repay all according to their **d**.

DEEP (139) [DEEPENS, DEEPER, DEEPEST, DEEPLY, DEPTH, DEPTHS, SKIN-DEEP]

THE DEEP (6) Ex 15:5; 20:21; Ps 69:15; Pr 3:20; 8:28; Eze 31:15

DEEP SLEEP (7) Ge 2:21; 15:12; 1Sa 26:12; Job 33:15; Isa 29:10; Ac 20:9; Ro 11:8

Ge 2:21 So the LORD God caused Adam to fall into a **d**
15:12 the sun was going down, Abram fell into a **d** sleep.
37:20 let's kill him and throw him into a **d** pit.
42:38 my gray head down to the grave in **d** sorrow."
44:29 my gray head down to the grave in **d** sorrow.'
50:11 "This is a place of very **d** mourning for these
Ex 2:25 the Israelites and felt **d** concern for their welfare.
3:1 and he went **d** into the wilderness near Sinai,
10:21 and a **d** and terrifying darkness will descend on the
10:22 and there was **d** darkness over the entire land for
15:5 The **d** waters have covered them; / they sank to the
20:21 Moses entered into the **d** darkness where God was.
Dt 4:11 the sky, shrouded in black clouds and **d** darkness.
5:22 of the fire, surrounded by clouds and **d** darkness.
Jos 23:14 **D** in your hearts you know that every promise of
Jdg 3:22 so **d** that the handle disappeared beneath the king's
21:6 The Israelites felt **d** sadness for Benjamin and said,
1Sa 1:10 Hannah was in **d** anguish, crying bitterly as she
26:12 because the LORD had put Saul's men into a **d**
28:15 "Because I am in **d** trouble," Saul replied.
2Sa 1:2 He fell to the ground before David in **d** respect.
1:26 much I loved you! / And your love for me was **d**,
3:31 put on sackcloth. Go into **d** mourning for Abner."
14:2 Act like a woman who has been in **d** sorrow for a
15:23 There was **d** sadness throughout the land as the
18:17 They threw Absalom's body into a **d** pit in the
19:2 As the troops heard of the king's **d** grief for his
19:2 the joy of that day's victory was turned into **d**
22:17 and rescued me; / he drew me out of **d** waters.
1Ki 6:16 It was 30 feet **d** and was paneled with cedar from
7:23 It was 7-1/2 feet **d** and about 45 feet in
18:27 Perhaps he is **d** in thought, or he is relieving
21:27 slept in sackcloth and went about in **d** mourning.
2Ch 3:8 width of the Temple, and it was also thirty feet **d**.
4:2 It was 7-1/2 feet **d** and about 45 feet in
33:12 But while in **d** distress, Manasseh sought the
Ne 2:2 are you? You look like a man with **d** troubles."
Job 6:4 He has sent his poisoned arrows **d** within my spirit.
28:8 for they are **d** within the mines. No wild animal
33:15 in visions of the night when **d** sleep falls on people
Ps 7:9 For you look **d** within the mind and heart,
18:16 and rescued me; / he drew me out of **d** waters.
25:16 mercy on me, / for I am alone and in **d** distress.
36:1 Sin whispers to the wicked, **d** within their hearts.
38:2 Your arrows have struck **d**, / and your blows are
57:6 from distress. / They have dug a **d** pit in my path,
66:14 you heard me make / when I was in **d** trouble.
69:2 I am in **d** water, / and the floods overwhelm me.
69:14 who hate me, / and pull me from these **d** waters.
69:15 overwhelm me, / or the **d** waters swallow me,
69:17 answer me quickly, for I am in **d** trouble!
77:2 When I was in **d** trouble, / I searched for the Lord.
92:5 miracles you do! / And how **d** are your thoughts.
119:85 hate your law / have dug **d** pits for me to fall into.
140:10 or into **d** pits from which they can't escape.
144:7 and rescue me; / deliver me from **d** waters,
Pr 3:3 like a necklace; write them **d** within your heart.
3:20 By his knowledge the **d** fountains of the earth burst
4:21 my words. Let them penetrate **d** within your heart,
7:3 as a reminder. Write them **d** within your heart.
8:28 when he established the **d** fountains of the earth.
12:3 never brings stability; only the godly have **d** roots.
18:8 rumors are—but they sink **d** into one's heart.
20:5 Though good advice lies **d** within a person's heart,
22:14 The mouth of an immoral woman is a **d** pit;
22:18 For it is good to keep these sayings **d** within
23:27 A prostitute is a **d** pit; an adulterous woman is
26:22 rumors are—but they sink **d** into one's heart.
31:6 for the dying, and wine for those in **d** depression.
Isa 1:18 "No matter how **d** the stain of your sins, I can
19:17 Just to speak the name of Israel will strike **d** terror
23:3 sailing over **d** waters. They brought you grain from
29:10 For the LORD has poured out on you a spirit of **d**
43:2 When you go through **d** waters and great trouble,
Jer 17:8 a riverbank, with roots that reach **d** into the water.
49:8 and flee! Hide in **d** caves, you people of Dedan!
49:30 "Hide yourselves in **d** caves, you people of Hazor,
La 1:9 "LORD, see my **d** misery," she cries.
2:13 For your wound is as **d** as the sea. Who can heal
3:2 He has brought me into **d** darkness, shutting out all
3:13 He shot his arrows **d** into my heart.
3:15 He has given me a cup of **d** sorrow to drink.
3:55 on your name, LORD, from **d** within the well,
Eze 3:10 let all my words sink **d** into your own heart first.
23:32 of terror as your sister—a cup that is large and **d**.
23:34 In **d** anguish you will drain that cup of terror to the
27:31 weep for you with bitter anguish and **d** mourning.
31:3 full of thick branches that cast **d** forest shade with
31:4 **D** springs watered it and helped it to grow tall
31:7 for its roots went **d** into abundant water.
31:15 I made the **d** places mourn, and I restrained the
31:16 the ones whose roots went **d** into the water,
40:6 the threshold of the gateway; it was 10-1/2 feet **d**.
40:7 end of the gateway passage, was 10-1/2 feet **d**.
40:9 and found it to be 14 feet **d**, with supporting
40:30 leading into the inner courtyard were 8-3/4 feet **d**
43:13 all around the altar 21 inches wide and 21 inches **d**,
44:12 worship other gods, causing Israel to fall into **d** sin.
47:5 and the river was too **d** to cross without swimming.
Da 2:22 He reveals **d** and mysterious things / and knows
Hos 5:2 You have dug a **d** pit to trap them at Acacia.
14:5 it will send roots **d** into the soil like the cedars in
Joel 2:2 and gloom, a day of thick clouds and **d** blackness.
Mic 1:9 For my people's wound is far too **d** to heal. It has
Hab 3:2 In this time of our **d** need, begin again to help us,
3:10 The mighty **d** cried out, lifting its hands to the
Mt 6:23 is really darkness, how **d** that darkness will be!
11:21 their people would have sat in **d** repentance long
13:21 plants in such soil, their roots don't go very **d**.
24:30 and there will be **d** mourning among all the nations
26:37 he began to be filled with anguish and **d** distress.
Mk 4:17 plants in such soil, their roots don't go very **d**.
14:33 he began to be filled with horror and **d** distress.
Lk 2:46 discussing **d** questions with them.
8:13 plants in such soil, their roots don't go very **d**.
10:13 their people would have sat in **d** repentance long
10:33 and when he saw the man, he felt **d** pity.
22:15 "I have looked forward to this hour with **d**
23:48 all that had happened, they went home in **d** sorrow.
24:17 "You seem to be in a **d** discussion about
Jn 4:11 or a bucket," she said, "and this is a very **d** well.
9:16 So there was a **d** division of opinion among them.
Ac 2:43 A **d** sense of awe came over them all,
20:9 he sank into a **d** sleep and fell three stories to his
21:40 Soon a **d** silence enveloped the crowd, and he
27:28 and found the water was only 120 feet **d**.
Ro 8:16 For his Holy Spirit speaks to us **d** in our hearts
11:8 Scriptures say, / "God has put them into a **d** sleep.
1Co 2:10 out everything and shows us even God's **d** secrets.
2Co 7:15 welcomed him with such respect and **d** concern.
8:2 and **d** poverty have overflowed in rich generosity.
9:14 And they will pray for you with **d** affection
Eph 3:17 May your roots go down **d** into the soil of God's
3:18 how long, how high, and how **d** his love really is.
6:5 obey your earthly masters with **d** respect and fear.
Php 2:12 your lives, obeying God with **d** reverence and fear.
Heb 4:12 cutting **d** into our innermost thoughts and desires.
Jas 4:9 Let there be sorrow and **d** grief. Let there be
1Pe 4:8 of all, continue to show **d** love for each other,

DEEPENS (1) [DEEP]

Ps 143:7 LORD, and answer me, / for my depression **d**.

DEEPER (10) [DEEP]

Lev 14:37 and the contamination appears to go **d** than the
Jos 7:21 my tent, with the silver buried **d** than the rest."
2Sa 1:26 love for me was deep, / **d** than the love of women!
Job 11:8 It is **d** than the underworld—what can you know in
Ps 69:2 **D** and **d** I sink into the mire; / I can't find a
69:14 Pull me out of the mud; / don't let me sink any **d**!
Lk 5:4 "Now go out where it is **d** and let down your nets,
2Th 3:5 May the Lord bring you into an ever **d**
Rev 2:24 have not followed this false teaching ('**d** truths,'

DEEPEST (15) [DEEP]

2Ki 19:23 its farthest corners / and explored its **d** forests.
Est 5:7 Esther replied, "This is my request and **d** wish.
Job 12:22 darkness with light; he brings light to the **d** gloom.
20:26 "His treasures will be lost in **d** darkness.
Ps 5:7 with **d** awe I will worship at your Temple.
5:9 Their **d** desire is to destroy others. / Their talk is
107:10 Some sat in darkness and **d** gloom,
107:14 He led them from the darkness and **d** gloom;
107:24 in action, / his impressive works on the **d** seas.
Isa 37:24 its farthest corners / and explored its **d** forests.
Jer 11:20 and you examine the **d** thoughts of hearts
20:12 and you examine the **d** thoughts of hearts
Lk 2:35 the **d** thoughts of many hearts will be revealed.
Ro 8:39 we are high above the sky or in the **d** ocean,
1Co 4:5 he will bring our **d** secrets to light and will reveal

DEEPLY (34) [DEEP]

Ge 37:34 He mourned **d** for his son for many days.
Ex 4:31 seen their misery and was **d** concerned for them,
Dt 20:18 which would cause you to sin **d** against the
1Sa 15:11 so **d** moved when he heard this that he cried out to
17:11 heard this, they were terrified and **d** shaken.
2Sa 13:22 he hated Amnon **d** because of what he had done to
2Ki 4:27 Something is troubling her **d**, and the LORD has
Ezr 10:10 Now we are even more **d** under condemnation than
Est 4:4 and told her about Mordecai, she was **d** distressed.
Job 21:20 Let them drink **d** of the anger of the Almighty.
30:25 in trouble? Was I not **d** grieved for the needy?
Ps 38:18 my sins; / I am **d** sorry for what I have done.
42:6 my God! / Now I am **d** discouraged, / but I will
116:10 in you, so I prayed, / "I am **d** troubled, LORD."
Ecc 8:9 I have thought **d** about all that goes on here in the
SS 3:1 I yearned **d** for my lover, but he did not come.
5:1 eat and drink! Yes, drink **d** of this love!"
Isa 12:3 With joy you will drink **d** from the fountain of
66:11 Drink **d** of her glory even as an infant drinks at its
Eze 16:52 You should be **d** ashamed because your sins are
Da 10:19 be afraid," he said, "for you are **d** loved by God.
Hab 1:11 But they are **d** guilty, for their own strength is their
Mal 1:2 "I have loved you **d**," says the LORD. But you
Mt 2:3 Herod was **d** disturbed by their question, as was all
6:32 pagans who are so **d** concerned about these things?
13:57 And they were **d** offended and refused to believe in
Mk 3:5 because he was **d** disturbed by their hard hearts.
6:3 They were **d** offended and refused to believe in
8:12 When he heard this, he sighed **d** and said,
Jn 11:33 was moved with indignation and was **d** troubled.
11:38 And again Jesus was **d** troubled. Then they came
12:27 Now my soul is **d** troubled. Should I pray, 'Father,
Ac 2:37 Peter's words convicted them **d**, and they said to
17:16 he was **d** troubled by all the idols he saw

DEER (23)

Ge 49:21 "Naphtali is a **d** let loose, / producing magnificent
Dt 12:15 you want, just as you do now with gazelle and **d**.
12:22 that meat, just as you do now with gazelle and **d**.
14:5 the **d**, the gazelle, the roebuck, the wild goat,
15:22 or unclean, just as anyone may eat a gazelle or **d**.
2Sa 2:18 David's forces that day. Asahel could run like a **d**,
22:34 He makes me as surefooted as a **d**, / leading me
1Ki 4:23 one hundred sheep or goats, as well as **d**, gazelles,
1Ch 12:8 fierce as lions and as swift as **d** on the mountains.
Job 39:1 Have you watched as the wild **d** are born?
Ps 18:33 He makes me as surefooted as a **d**, / leading me
42:1 As the **d** pants for streams of water, / so I long for
Pr 5:19 She is a loving doe, a graceful **d**. Let her breasts
6:5 Save yourself like a **d** escaping from a hunter,
SS 2:7 by the swift gazelles and the **d** of the wild,
2:9 My lover is like a swift gazelle or a young **d**.
3:5 by the swift gazelles and the **d** of the wild,
8:14 or a young **d** on the mountains of spices."
Isa 13:14 rushing back to their own lands like hunted **d**,
35:6 The lame will leap like a **d**, and those who cannot
Jer 14:5 The **d** abandons her newborn fawn because there is
La 1:6 Her princes are like starving **d** searching for
Hab 3:19 He will make me as surefooted as a **d** and bring me

DEFEAT (36) [DEFEATED, DEFEATING, DEFEATS]

Ge 49:8 will praise you. / You will **d** your enemies.
Ex 23:31 I will help you **d** the people now living in the land,
32:18 "No, it's neither a cry of victory nor a cry of **d**.
Dt 2:24 Look, I will help you **d** Sihon the Amorite, king of
2:30 and defiant so he could help you **d** them,
23:14 in your camp to protect you and to **d** your enemies.
Jos 7:12 the Israelites are running from their enemies in **d**.
7:13 You will never **d** your enemies until you remove
23:9 for you, and no one has yet been able to **d** you.
Jdg 2:15 against them, bringing them **d**, just as he promised.
20:35 So the LORD helped Israel **d** Benjamin, and that
1Sa 14:10 be the LORD's sign that he will help us **d** them."
14:12 "for the LORD will help us **d** them!"
14:37 Will you help us **d** them?" But God made no reply
28:19 will bring the entire army of Israel down in **d**."
30:23 He has kept us safe and helped us **d** the enemy.
2Sa 17:14 For the LORD had arranged to **d** the counsel of
1Ki 20:23 After their **d**, Ben-hadad's officers said to him,
20:28 of the plains. So I will help you **d** this vast army.
2Ki 3:10 the three of us here to let the king of Moab **d** us."
13:3 and his son Ben-hadad to **d** them time after time.
2Ch 13:16 and God handed them over to Judah in **d**.
28:5 his God allowed the king of Aram to **d** Ahaz
28:9 was angry with Judah and let you **d** them.

Ps 25: 2 be disgraced, / or let my enemies rejoice in my **d**.
35: 19 let my treacherous enemies / rejoice over my **d**.
92: 11 with my own ears I have heard the **d** of my wicked
129: 5 who hate Jerusalem / be turned back in shameful **d**.
Pr 25: 8 go down before your neighbors in shameful **d**.
Jer 20: 11 They cannot **d** me. They will be shamed
Da 11: 7 the fortress of the king of the north and **d** him.
11: 11 by the king of the north and will **d** them.
Lk 14: 31 **d** the twenty thousand soldiers who are marching
Ro 6: 10 He died once to **d** sin, and now he lives for the
1Co 6: 7 To have such lawsuits at all is a real **d** for you.
Rev 17: 14 but the Lamb will **d** them because he is Lord over

DEFEATED (47) [DEFEAT]

Lev 26: 17 against you, and you will be **d** by all your enemies.
Nu 33: 4 The LORD had **d** the gods of Egypt that night
Dt 1: 4 This was after he had **d** King Sihon of the
28: 25 "The LORD will cause you to be **d** by your
29: 7 came out to fight against us, but we **d** them.
Jos 7: 4 warriors were sent, but they were soundly **d**.
10: 13 and moon stood still until the Israelites had **d** their
11: 19 the Hivites of Gibeon. All the others were **d**.
12: 2 of the Amorites, who lived in Heshbon, was **d**.
12: 7 and the Israelite armies **d** on the west side of the
12: 8 and the Jebusites.) These are the kings Israel **d**:
Jdg 1: 5 and the Canaanites and Perizzites were **d**.
9: 40 but he was **d** and ran away. Many of Shechem's
11: 33 He thoroughly **d** the Ammonites from Aroer to an
12: 4 and attacked the men of Ephraim and **d** them.
1Sa 4: 2 The Philistines attacked and **d** the army of Israel,
4: 3 "Why did the LORD allow us to be **d** by the
4: 10 fought desperately, and Israel was **d** again.
4: 17 "Israel has been **d**," the messenger replied.
7: 10 into such confusion that the Israelites **d** them.
13: 3 and **d** the garrison of Philistines at Geba.
2Sa 2: 17 and the men of Israel had been **d** by the forces of
5: 20 went to Baal-perazim and **d** the Philistines there.
10: 19 and his Aramean allies realized they had been **d** by
1Ki 8: 33 "If your people Israel are **d** by their enemies
16: 22 But Omri's supporters **d** the supporters of Tibni
2Ki 13: 25 Jehoash **d** Ben-hadad on three occasions, and
17: 3 of Assyria attacked and **d** King Hoshea,
1Ch 5: 10 of Saul, the Reubenites **d** the Hagrites in battle.
5: 20 in him. So the Hagrites and all their allies were **d**.
14: 11 went to Baal-perazim and **d** the Philistines there.
19: 19 of Hadadezer realized they had been **d** by Israel,
2Ch 6: 24 "If your people Israel are **d** by their enemies
13: 15 God **d** Jeroboam and the Israelite army and routed
13: 18 So Judah **d** Israel because they trusted in the
14: 12 So the LORD **d** the Ethiopians in the presence of
25: 8 you will be **d** no matter how well you fight.
28: 5 The armies of Israel also **d** Ahaz and inflicted
28: 23 sacrifices to the gods of Damascus who had **d** him,
Ps 13: 4 let my enemies gloat, saying, "We have **d** him!"
125: 1 they will not be **d** but will endure forever.
Ecc 4: 12 A person standing alone can be attacked and **d**,
Isa 10: 11 So when we have **d** Samaria and her gods, we will
54: 15 Your enemies will always be **d** because I am on
Jer 37: 17 "You will be **d** by the king of Babylon."
46: 2 and his army were **d** beside the Euphrates River by
Rev 12: 11 And they have **d** him because of the blood of the

DEFEATING (6) [DEFEAT]

Jdg 1: 10 **d** the forces of Sheshai, Ahiman, and Talmai.
20: 32 "We're **d** them as we did in the first battle!"
20: 39 "We're **d** them as we did in the first battle!"
2Ch 25: 14 When King Amaziah returned from **d** the
Da 7: 21 war against the holy people and was **d** them,
8: 25 of deception, **d** many by catching them off guard.

DEFEATS (1) [DEFEAT]

1Jn 5: 4 For every child of God **d** this evil world by trusting

DEFECT (6) [DEFECTED, DEFECTING, DEFECTIVE, DEFECTS]

Lev 21: 18 No one who has a **d** may come near to me,
21: 23 Yet because of his physical **d**, he must never go
Nu 6: 14 a one-year-old male lamb without **d** for a burnt
6: 14 a one-year-old female lamb without **d** for a sin
6: 14 a sin offering, a ram without **d** for a peace offering,
Dt 15: 21 But if this firstborn animal has any **d**, such as

DEFECTED (6) [DEFECT]

1Sa 29: 3 found a single fault in him since he **d** to me."
1Ch 12: 8 **d** to David while he was at the stronghold in the
12: 19 Some men from Manasseh **d** from the Israelite
12: 20 Here is a list of the men from Manasseh who **d** to
Jer 38: 19 hand me over to the Judeans who have **d** to them.
39: 9 the population as well as those who had **d** to him.

DEFECTING (1) [DEFECT]

Jer 37: 13 and said, "You are **d** to the Babylonians!"

DEFECTIVE (5) [DEFECT]

Lev 21: 20 or has a humped back or is a dwarf, or has a **d** eye,
22: 25 or **d** animals from foreigners to be offered as a
22: 25 be accepted on your behalf because they are **d**."
Dt 17: 1 "Never sacrifice a sick or **d** ox or sheep to the
Mal 1: 14 his flock but then sacrifices a **d** one to the Lord.

DEFECTS (47) [DEFECT]

Ex 12: 5 either a sheep or a goat, with no physical **d**.
29: 1 a young bull and two rams with no physical **d**.
Lev 1: 3 bring a bull with no physical **d** to the entrance of
1: 10 bring a male sheep or goat with no physical **d**.
3: 1 you offer to the LORD must have no physical **d**.
3: 6 or female, and it must have no physical **d**.
4: 3 to the LORD a young bull with no physical **d**.
4: 23 as his offering a male goat with no physical **d**.
4: 28 as their offering a female goat with no physical **d**.
4: 32 it must be a female with no physical **d**.
5: 15 The animal must have no physical **d**, and it must
5: 18 The animal must have no physical **d**, and it must
6: 6 This offering must be a ram with no physical **d**
9: 2 both with no physical **d**, and present them to the
9: 3 a whole burnt offering, each with no physical **d**.
14: 10 and one female year-old lamb with no physical **d**,
21: 17 his descendants who have physical **d** will not
21: 21 his physical **d** disqualify him from presenting
22: 19 only if it is a male animal with no physical **d**.
22: 20 Do not bring an animal with physical **d**, because it
22: 21 you must offer an animal that has no physical **d** of
23: 12 **d** as a whole burnt offering to the LORD.
23: 18 seven one-year-old lambs with no physical **d**,
Nu 19: 2 to bring you a red heifer that has no physical **d**
28: 3 two one-year-old male lambs with no physical **d**.
28: 9 two one-year-old male lambs with no physical **d**.
28: 11 one-year-old male lambs, all with no physical **d**.
28: 19 one-year-old male lambs, all with no physical **d**.
28: 31 all the animals you sacrifice have no physical **d**.
29: 2 one-year-old male lambs, all with no physical **d**.
29: 8 one-year-old male lambs, all with no physical **d**.
29: 13 one-year-old male lambs, all with no physical **d**.
29: 17 one-year-old male lambs, all with no physical **d**.
29: 20 one-year-old male lambs, all with no physical **d**.
29: 23 one-year-old male lambs, all with no physical **d**.
29: 26 one-year-old male lambs, all with no physical **d**.
29: 29 one-year-old male lambs, all with no physical **d**.
29: 32 one-year-old male lambs, all with no physical **d**.
29: 36 one-year-old male lambs, all with no physical **d**.
Eze 43: 22 offering a young male goat that has no physical **d**.
43: 23 offer another young bull that has no **d** and a perfect
43: 25 None of these animals may have physical **d** of any
45: 18 sacrifice a young bull with no physical **d** to purify
45: 23 seven young bulls and seven rams without any **d**.
46: 4 of six lambs and one ram, all with no physical **d**.
46: 6 six lambs, and one ram, all with no physical **d**.
46: 13 "Each morning a year-old lamb with no physical **d**

DEFEND (41) [DEFENDER, DEFENDERS, DEFENDING, DEFENDS, DEFENSE, DEFENSELESS, DEFENSES]

Dt 33: 7 Give them strength to **d** their cause; / help them
Jos 10: 33 Gezer had arrived with his army to help **d** the city.
Jdg 6: 31 let him **d** himself and destroy the one who knocked
6: 32 which means "Let Baal **d** himself,"
2Ki 19: 34 and for the sake of my servant David, I will **d** it."
20: 6 I will do this to **d** my honor and for the sake of my
Est 8: 11 in every city authority to unite to **d** their lives.
9: 2 **d** themselves against anyone who might try to
9: 16 provinces had gathered together to **d** their lives.
Job 5: 4 abandoned far from help, with no one to **d** them.
16: 6 as it is, my grief remains no matter how I **d** myself.
17: 3 "You must **d** my innocence, O God, since no one
19: 6 I cannot **d** myself, for I am like a city under siege.
27: 5 you are right; until I die, I will **d** my innocence.
Ps 43: 1 up my cause! / **D** me against these ungodly people.
54: 1 O God, and rescue me! / **D** me with your might.
72: 4 Help him to **d** the poor, / to rescue the children of
72: 12 help the oppressed, who have no one to **d** them.
74: 22 Arise, O God, and **d** your cause. / Remember how
106: 8 he saved them— / to **d** the honor of his name
Ecc 5: 6 And don't **d** yourself by telling the Temple
SS 3: 8 ready to **d** the king against an attack during the
Isa 1: 17 Seek justice. Help the oppressed. **D** the orphan.
1: 23 and refuse to **d** the orphans and the widows.
8: 9 Assyrians will cry, 'Do your best to **d** yourselves,
11: 4 He will **d** the poor and the exploited. He will rule
16: 3 "Help us," they cry. "**D** us against our enemies.
26: 11 Show them your eagerness to **d** your people.
31: 5 He will **d** and save the city; he will pass over it
37: 35 and for the sake of my servant David, I will **d** it."
38: 6 from the king of Assyria. Yes, I will **d** this city.
Jer 50: 34 He will **d** them and give them rest again in Israel.
Da 3: 16 we do not need to **d** ourselves before you.
Hab 1: 14 but creeping things that have no leader to **d** them
Zec 12: 8 On that day the LORD will **d** the people of
Ac 25: 16 They are given an opportunity to **d** themselves face
2Co 6: 7 as our weapon, both to attack and to **d** ourselves.
12: 19 Perhaps you think we are saying all this just to **d**
Php 1: 16 for they know the Lord brought me here to **d** the
Jas 5: 6 and killed good people who had no power to **d**
Jude 1: 3 urging you to **d** the truth of the Good News.

DEFENDER (5) [DEFEND]

Ps 10: 14 put their trust in you. / You are the **d** of orphans.
48: 3 Jerusalem's towers. / He reveals himself as her **d**.
68: 5 Father to the fatherless, **d** of widows— / this is
Pr 22: 23 For the LORD is their **d**. He will injure anyone
Isa 51: 22 the Sovereign LORD, your God and **D**, says:

DEFENDERS (1) [DEFEND]

2Sa 5: 8 When the insulting message from the **d** of the city

DEFENDING (8) [DEFEND]

Jdg 6: 31 Joash shouted to the mob, "Why are you **d** Baal?
20: 21 who were **d** the town, came out and killed
2Ki 9: 14 **d** Israel against the forces of King Hazael of Aram.
Job 13: 7 "Are you **d** God by means of lies and dishonest
36: 2 what I am saying. For I have not finished **d** God!
Ps 45: 4 ride out to victory, / **d** truth, humility, and justice.
89: 40 protecting him / and laid in ruins every fort **d** him.
Php 1: 7 **d** the truth and telling others the Good News.

DEFENDS (1) [DEFEND]

Pr 30: 5 He **d** all who come to him for protection.

DEFENSE (22) [DEFEND]

Ex 14: 14 for you. You won't have to lift a finger in your **d**!"
2Ch 11: 5 and fortified various cities for the **d** of Judah.
Ne 5: 8 And they had nothing to say in their **d**.
Job 9: 15 Even if I were innocent, I would have no **d**. I could
13: 12 value as ashes. Your **d** is as fragile as a clay pot.
31: 35 to see my side! Look, I will sign my name to my **d**.
Ps 35: 23 Wake up! Rise to my **d**! / Take up my case,
35: 27 who have stood with me in my **d**. / Let them
Pr 18: 11 The rich think of their wealth as an impregnable **d**;
Jer 26: 12 Then Jeremiah spoke in his own **d**. "The LORD
Da 11: 1 and **d** since the first year of the reign of Darius the
Mt 10: 19 don't worry about what to say in your **d**,
Mk 13: 11 don't worry about what to say in your **d**.
Lk 12: 11 don't worry about what to say in your **d**,
Ac 7: 24 So Moses came to his **d** and avenged him,
18: 14 But just as Paul started to make his **d**,
19: 33 He motioned for silence and tried to speak in **d**.
22: 1 Paul said, "listen to me as I offer my **d**."
24: 10 and this gives me confidence as I make my **d**.
26: 1 Agrippa said to Paul, "You may speak in your **d**."
26: 1 So Paul, with a gesture of his hand, started his **d**:
26: 2 that you are the one hearing my **d** against all these

DEFENSELESS (3) [DEFEND]

Pr 23: 10 Don't steal the land of **d** orphans by moving the
25: 28 A person without self-control is as **d** as a city with
Isa 23: 10 Tyre like the flooding Nile, for the city is **d**.

DEFENSES (14) [DEFEND]

2Ch 11: 11 Rehoboam strengthened their **d** and stationed
21: 17 They marched against Judah, broke down its **d**,
32: 5 Then Hezekiah further strengthened his **d** by
Ps 60: 1 You have rejected us, O God, and broken our **d**.
Isa 22: 8 Judah's **d** have been stripped away. You run to the
Da 9: 25 Jerusalem will be rebuilt with streets and strong **d**,
Am 3: 11 He will surround them and shatter their **d**.
5: 9 power he destroys the strong, crushing all their **d**.
Mic 5: 5 Assyrians invade our land and break through our **d**,
5: 11 down your walls and demolish the **d** of your cities.
Na 2: 1 Muster your **d**, and keep a sharp watch for the
2: 5 in their haste, rushing to the walls to set up their **d**.
3: 14 for the siege! Store up water! Strengthen the **d**!
Hab 1: 10 scoff at kings and princes and scorn all their **d**.

DEFERENCE (3) [DEFERRED]

Lev 19: 15 neither favoring the poor nor showing **d** to the rich.
2Ki 16: 18 In **d** to the king of Assyria, he also removed the
Ac 16: 3 In **d** to the Jews of the area, he arranged for

DEFERRED (1) [DEFERENCE]

Pr 13: 12 Hope **d** makes the heart sick, but when dreams

DEFIANCE (6) [DEFY]

2Ki 19: 16 Listen to Sennacherib's words of **d** against the
Ps 37: 12 plot against the godly; / they snarl at them in **d**.
66: 7 movement of the nations; / let no rebel rise in **d**.
75: 5 Don't lift your fists in **d** at the heavens / or speak
Isa 37: 17 Listen to Sennacherib's words of **d** against the
La 3: 35 of their God-given rights in **d** of the Most High.

DEFIANT (2) [DEFY]

Dt 2: 30 and **d** so he could help you defeat them,
Zep 2: 15 that way will laugh in derision or shake a **d** fist.

DEFIANTLY (3) [DEFY]

Ex 14: 8 after the people of Israel who had escaped so **d**.
Nu 33: 3 The people of Israel left **d**, in full view of all the
Job 15: 26 their strong shields, they **d** charge against him.

DEFIED (11) [DEFY]

1Sa 17: 36 too, for he has **d** the armies of the living God!
17: 45 the God of the armies of Israel, whom you have **d**.
2Sa 21: 21 **d** and taunted Israel. But he was killed by
1Ki 13: 21 You have **d** the LORD's message and have
2Ki 17: 16 They **d** all the commands of the LORD their God
1Ch 20: 7 **d** and taunted Israel. But he was killed by
Ps 105: 28 for they had **d** his commands to let his people go.
Jer 50: 29 for she has **d** the LORD, the Holy One of Israel.
Da 3: 12 They have **d** Your Majesty by refusing to serve
3: 28 They **d** the king's command and were willing to
5: 23 For you have **d** the Lord of heaven and have had

DEFIES (2) [DEFY]

Mic 7: 6 son despises his father. The daughter **d** her mother.
7: 6 The daughter-in-law **d** her mother-in-law.

DEFILE (40) [DEFILED, DEFILEMENT, DEFILER, DEFILES, DEFILING]

Lev 11: 43 Never **d** yourselves by touching such animals.
11: 44 So do not **d** yourselves by touching any of these

15:31 of Israel separate from things that will **d** them,
18:20 "Do not **d** yourself by having sexual intercourse
18:23 "A man must never **d** himself by having sexual
18:24 "Do not **d** yourselves in any of these ways,
18:30 Do not **d** yourselves by doing any of them, for I,
19:29 "Do not **d** your daughter by making her a
20:25 You must not **d** yourselves by eating any animal
21: 4 among his relatives, he must not **d** himself.
21:11 He must never **d** himself by going near a dead
22: 8 torn apart by wild animals, for this would **d** them.
22:15 No one may **d** the sacred offerings brought to the
Nu 5: 3 Remove them so they will not **d** the camp, where I
6: 7 They must not **d** the hair on their head, because it
19:13 and do not purify themselves in the proper way **d**
35:34 You must not **d** the land where you are going to
Dt 21:23 Do not **d** the land the LORD your God is giving
Isa 65: 5 'Don't come too close or you will **d** me!
Eze 7:21 from the most wicked of nations, and they will **d** it.
7:24 down their proud fortresses and **d** their sanctuaries.
9: 7 "**D** the Temple!" the LORD commanded.
20: 7 Do not **d** yourselves with the Egyptian gods,
22:11 who **d** their daughters-in-law or who rape their
28: 7 your marvelous wisdom and **d** your splendor!
43: 7 and their kings will not **d** my holy name any longer
44:25 A priest must never **d** himself by being in the
Da 1: 8 But Daniel made up his mind not to **d** himself by
Zep 3: 4 Its priests **d** the Temple by disobeying God's laws.
Mal 1: 7 "You **d** them by saying the altar of the LORD
1:12 you are saying it's all right to **d** the Lord's table.
Mt 15:18 from an evil heart and **d** the person who says them.
15:20 These are what **d** you. Eating with unwashed hands could never **d** you
Mk 7:18 "Can't you see that what you eat won't **d** you?
7:23 they are what **d** you and make you unacceptable to
Jn 18:28 didn't go in themselves because it would **d** them,
Ac 24: 6 Moreover he was trying to **d** the Temple when we
2Co 7: 1 let us cleanse ourselves from everything that can **d**
1Ti 1: 9 who consider nothing sacred and **d** what is holy,

DEFILED (121) [DEFILE]

Ge 4:11 the ground you have **d** with your brother's blood.
34: 5 soon reached Jacob that his daughter had been **d**,
34:27 the town because their sister had been **d** there.
Ex 32: 7 The people you brought from Egypt have **d**
Lev 5: 3 even if they don't realize they have been **d**,
5:16 holy things they have **d** by paying for the loss,
11:24 of their dead bodies, you will be **d** until evening.
11:25 your clothes, and you will remain **d** until evening.
11:26 of such an animal, you will be **d** until evening.
11:27 of such an animal, you will be **d** until evening.
11:28 your clothes, and you will remain **d** until evening.
11:31 of such an animal, you will be **d** until evening.
11:32 put into water, and it will remain **d** until evening.
11:33 falls into a clay pot, everything in the pot will be **d**,
11:34 object touches any food, all of that food will be **d**.
11:34 that is in such an unclean container will be **d**.
11:35 the dead body of such an animal falls will be **d**.
11:35 It has become **d**, and it will remain that way.
11:36 But anyone who removes the dead body will be **d**.
11:38 when the dead body falls on it, the seed will be **d**.
11:39 you touch its carcass, you will be **d** until evening.
11:40 Then you will remain **d** until evening.
12: 2 just as she is **d** during her menstrual period.
12: 5 she will be ceremonially **d** for two weeks,
12: 5 just as she is **d** during her menstrual period.
13:11 because it is clear that the skin is **d** by the disease.
13:55 even if it did not spread, the object is **d**.
14:44 with an infectious mildew, and the house is **d**.
15: 4 he lies and anything on which he sits will be **d**.
15: 5 and you will remain ceremonially **d** until evening.
15: 6 in water. You will then remain **d** until evening.
15: 9 Any blanket on which the man rides will be **d**.
15:10 in water, and you will remain **d** until evening.
15:11 in water, and you will remain **d** until evening.
15:16 and he will remain ceremonially **d** until evening.
15:17 must be washed, and it will remain **d** until evening.
15:18 must bathe, and they will remain **d** until evening.
15:19 her during that time, you will be **d** until evening.
15:20 on which she lies or sits during that time will be **d**.
15:21 in water, and you will remain **d** until evening.
15:24 He will remain **d** for seven days, and any bed on which he lies will be **d**.
15:26 on which she lies or sits during that time will be **d**,
15:27 or anything on which she sits, you will be **d**.
15:27 in water, and you will remain **d** until evening.
15:32 with a man who has been **d** by a genital discharge
18:24 from the Promised Land have **d** themselves.
18:25 As a result, the entire land has become **d**. That is
18:27 where I am taking you, and the land has become **d**.
19:31 and psychics, for you will be **d** by them.
20: 3 because they have **d** my sanctuary and profaned
21: 7 "The priests must not marry women **d** by
21:14 a divorced woman, or a woman **d** by prostitution.
22: 4 a corpse, or are **d** by an emission of semen,
22: 6 they will remain **d** until evening. They must not eat
Nu 5: 2 or who has been **d** by touching a dead person.
5:14 of his wife, even if she has not **d** herself,
5:19 and you have not **d** yourself by being unfaithful,
5:20 and **d** yourself by sleeping with another man"—
5:27 If she has **d** herself by being unfaithful to her
5:28 But if she has not **d** herself and is pure, she will be
6: 9 "If their hair is **d** because someone suddenly falls
9: 6 But some of the men had been ceremonially **d** by
12:14 her face, wouldn't she have been **d** for seven days?
19:15 in the tent that was not covered with a lid is also **d**.
19:20 "But those who become **d** and do not purify
19:20 for they have **d** the sanctuary of the LORD.
19:20 has not been sprinkled on them, they remain **d**.
19:21 water of purification will remain **d** until evening.
19:22 and anyone that a **d** person touches will be ceremonially **d** until evening."
25: 1 some of the men **d** themselves by sleeping with the
Dt 23:10 "Any man who becomes ceremonially **d**
24: 4 may not marry her again, for she has been **d**.
Jos 22:19 If you need the altar because your land is **d**,
2Sa 1:21 For there the shield of the mighty was **d**;
2Ki 23: 8 He also **d** all the pagan shrines, where they had
23:10 Then the king **d** the altar of Topheth in the valley
2Ch 29: 5 Remove all the **d** things from the sanctuary.
29:16 and they took out to the Temple courtyard all the **d**
Ezr 9:11 **d** by the detestable practices of the people living
Ne 13:29 for they have **d** the priesthood and the promises
Ps 74: 7 They utterly **d** the place that bears your holy name.
79: 1 They have **d** your holy Temple
106:39 They **d** themselves by their evil deeds, / and their
Jer 2: 7 you **d** my land and corrupted the inheritance I had
3: 2 where you have not been **d** by your adulteries?
3: 9 and stone. So now the land has been greatly **d**.
16:18 because they have **d** my land with lifeless images
19:12 I will cause this city to become **d** like Topheth.
34:16 and **d** my name by taking back the men
51:51 because the LORD's Temple has been **d** by
La 1: 9 She **d** herself with immorality with no thought of
4:13 who **d** the city by shedding innocent blood.
4:14 so **d** by blood that no one dared to touch them.
4:15 shouted at them. "You are **d**! Don't touch us!"
Eze 4:13 Israel will eat **d** bread in the Gentile lands, where I
4:14 must I be **d** by using human dung? For I have never been **d** before.
5:11 because you have **d** my Temple with idols and vile
16:25 On every street corner you **d** your beauty,
22:26 have violated my laws and **d** my holy things.
23:38 they **d** my Temple and violated my Sabbath day!
23:39 Temple to worship! They came in and **d** my house!
28:18 You **d** your sanctuaries with your many sins
36:17 in their own land, they **d** it by their evil deeds.
43: 8 They **d** my holy name by such wickedness, so I
Hos 5: 3 a prostitute leaves her husband; you are utterly **d**.
6:10 My people have **d** themselves by chasing after
9: 4 All who present such sacrifices will be **d**.
Hag 2:13 against any of the things mentioned, will it be **d**?"
2:14 Everything they do and everything they offer is **d**.
Mal 1: 7 "You have despised my name by offering **d**
1: 7 "Then you ask, 'How have we **d** the sacrifices?'
2:11 for the men of Judah have **d** the LORD's beloved
Mt 15:11 You are not **d** by what you eat; you are **d** by what
15:15 when you said people aren't **d** by what they eat."
Mk 7:15 You are not **d** by what you eat; you are **d** by what you say and do!"
Tit 1:15 because their minds and consciences are **d**.

DEFILEMENT (12) [DEFILE]

Lev 5: 2 and guilty, even if they are unaware of their **d**.
5: 3 come into contact with any source of human **d**,
7:21 whether it is human **d** or an unclean animal,
15: 3 This **d** applies whether the discharge continues
16:19 he will cleanse it from Israel's **d** and return it to its
Nu 6: 9 Then they will be cleansed from their **d**.
6:12 that were completed before their **d** no longer count.
19:13 was not sprinkled on them, their **d** continues.
19:17 "To remove the **d**, put some of the ashes from the
19:19 and that evening they will be cleansed of their **d**.
Zec 13: 1 a fountain to cleanse them from all their sins and **d**.
Heb 9:13 cow could cleanse people's bodies from ritual **d**.

DEFILER (1) [DEFILE]

Da 9:27 end that has been decreed is poured out on this **d**."

DEFILES (3) [DEFILE]

Nu 5:29 If a woman **d** herself by being unfaithful to her
Mk 7:20 then he added, "It is the thought-life that **d** you.
Ac 21:28 and he even **d** it by bringing Gentiles in!"

DEFILING (12) [DEFILE]

Lev 5:15 "If any of the people sin by unintentionally **d** the
15:31 so they will not die as a result of **d** my Tabernacle
16:16 because of the **d** sin and rebellion of the Israelites.
18:28 not give the land a reason to vomit you out for **d** it,
21: 9 **d** her father's holiness as well as herself, she must
Jer 7:30 abominable idols right in my own Temple, **d** it.
32:34 abominable idols right in my own Temple, **d** it.
Eze 20:18 parents' footsteps, **d** themselves with their idols.
23: 7 of Assyria, worshiping their idols and **d** herself.
23:13 she was going, **d** herself just like her older sister.
23:17 adultery with her, **d** her in the bed of love.
23:30 to other nations, **d** yourself with all their idols.

DEFINE (1) [DEFINED, DEFINES]

Nu 26:55 and **d** the inheritance of each ancestral tribe by

DEFINED (2) [DEFINE]

1Ch 23: 7 The Gershonite family units were **d** by their lines
Job 38: 8 "Who **d** the boundaries of the sea as it burst from

DEFINES (1) [DEFINE]

Jer 5:22 am the one who **d** the ocean's sandy shoreline,

DEFINITE (1) [DEFINITELY]

1Sa 23:23 hiding places, and come back with a more **d** report.

DEFINITELY (1) [DEFINITE]

Mk 14:69 telling the others, "That man is **d** one of them!"

DEFORMED (6) [FORM]

Lev 21:18 to me, whether he is blind or lame, stunted or **d**,
22:23 If the bull or lamb is **d** or stunted, it may still be
Mt 12:10 where he noticed a man with a **d** hand.
Mk 3: 1 synagogue again and noticed a man with a **d** hand.
Lk 6: 6 a man with a **d** right hand was in the synagogue
6: 8 He said to the man with the **d** hand, "Come

DEFRAUD (1) [FRAUD]

Jer 9: 5 They all fool and **d** each other; no one tells the

DEFY (6) [DEFIANCE, DEFIANT, DEFIANTLY, DEFIED, DEFIES, DEFYING]

1Sa 17:10 I **d** the armies of Israel! Send me a man who will
17:26 that he is allowed to **d** the armies of the living
Ps 9:19 O LORD! / Do not let mere mortals **d** you!
Da 7:25 He will **d** the Most High and wear down the holy
2Th 2: 4 He will exalt himself and **d** every god there is
Jude 1: 8 from their dreams, live immoral lives, **d** authority,

DEFYING (5) [DEFY]

Nu 26: 9 Korah against Moses and Aaron, **d** the LORD.
2Ki 19: 4 heard the Assyrian representative **d** the living God
2Ch 13: 7 **d** Solomon's son Rehoboam when he was young
Job 15:25 clenched their fists against God, **d** the Almighty.
Isa 37: 4 heard the Assyrian representative **d** the living God

DEGRADING (1)

Ro 1:24 they did vile and **d** things with each other's bodies.

DEGREE(S) [KJV] See ASCENT, ORDER, STANDING, STEPS

DEJECTED (6)

Ge 4: 5 accept Cain's. This made Cain very angry and **d**.
4: 6 the LORD asked him. "Why do you look so **d**?
40: 6 The next morning Joseph noticed the **d** look on
2Sa 13: 4 son of a king look so **d** morning after morning?"
Ne 8:10 Don't be **d** and sad, for the joy of the LORD is
Est 6:12 but Haman hurried home **d** and completely

DEKAR [KJV] See BEN-DEKER

DELAIAH (7)

1Ch 3:24 Eliashib, Pelaiah, Akkub, Johanan, **D**, and Anani—
24:18 The twenty-third lot fell to **D**. / The twenty-fourth
Ezr 2:60 This group consisted of the families of **D**, Tobiah,
Ne 6:10 Later I went to visit Shemaiah son of **D**
7:62 This group included the families of **D**, Tobiah,
Jer 36:12 along with **D** son of Shemaiah, Elnathan son of
36:25 Even when Elnathan, **D**, and Gemariah begged the

DELAY (16) [DELAYED, DELAYS]

Ge 43:10 by this time if you had let him come without **d**."
50: 5 his burial is complete, I will return without **d**."
Jdg 3:25 But when the king didn't come out after a long **d**,
2Ch 24: 5 Do not **d**!" But the Levites did not act right away.
Ezr 4:22 Do not **d**, for we must not permit the situation to
6: 8 You must pay the full construction costs without **d**
Ps 40:17 my helper and my savior. / Do not **d**, O my God.
70: 5 my helper and my savior; / O LORD, do not **d**!
90:13 come back to us! / How long will you **d**?
Ecc 5: 4 don't **d** in following through, for God takes no
Jer 4: 6 a signal toward Jerusalem: 'Flee now! Do not **d**!'
Eze 12:28 No more **d**! I will now do everything I have
Da 9:19 O my God, do not **d**, for your people and your city
Am 8: 2 I will not **d** their punishment again.
Ac 22:16 And now, why **d**? Get up and be baptized,
Heb 10:37 little while, / the Coming One will come and not **d**.

DELAYED (3) [DELAY]

Hab 2: 3 for it will surely take place. It will not be **d**.
Mt 25: 5 When the bridegroom was **d**, they all lay down
Ro 15:22 my visit to you has been **d** so long because I have

DELAYS (1) [DELAY]

Eze 12:25 There will be no more **d**, you rebels of Israel!

DELEGATES (2) [DELEGATION]

Ac 15: 3 The church sent the **d** to Jerusalem, and they
15:22 and the whole church in Jerusalem chose **d**,

DELEGATION (7) [DELEGATES]

Jos 14: 6 A **d** from the tribe of Judah, led by Caleb son of
22:13 they sent a **d** led by Phinehas son of Eleazar,
22:14 In this **d** were ten high officials of Israel, one from
Jdg 21:13 The Israelite assembly sent a peace **d** to the little
Lk 14:32 he will send a **d** to discuss terms of peace.
19:14 and sent a **d** after him to say they did not want him
Ac 12:20 So they sent a **d** to make peace with him

DELIBERATE (1) [DELIBERATELY]

Ps 19:13 Keep me from **d** sins! / Don't let them control me.

DELIBERATELY (12) [DELIBERATE]
Ex 21:14 if someone **d** attacks and kills another person,
Nu 15:31 with contempt and **d** disobeyed his commands,
Dt 19:11 and **d** ambushes and murders that neighbor and
Isa 65:12 You **d** sinned—before my very eyes—and chose to
66: 4 They **d** sinned—before my very eyes—and chose
Lk 8:46 But Jesus told him, "No, someone **d** touched me,
Ac 7:53 You **d** disobeyed God's law, though you received
Ro 1:25 the truth about God, they **d** chose to believe lies.
1Co 1:27 God **d** chose things the world considers foolish in
1Ti 1:19 For some people have **d** violated their consciences;
Heb 10:26 if we **d** continue sinning after we have received a
2Pe 3: 5 They **d** forget that God made the heavens by the

DELICACIES (4) [DELICATE]
Ps 141: 4 Don't let me share in the **d** / of those who do evil.
Pr 23: 3 and don't desire all the **d**—deception may be
23: 6 with people who are stingy; don't desire their **d**.
Isa 16: 7 people of Moab, mourn for the **d** of Kir-hareseth.

DELICATE (5) [DELICACIES]
Dt 28:56 The most tender and **d** woman among you—
28:56 so **d** she would not so much as touch her feet to the
Ps 139:13 You made all the **d**, inner parts of my body
Isa 47: 1 again will you be the lovely princess, tender and **d**.
Jer 6: 2 you are my beautiful and **d** daughter—

DELICIOUS (14)
Ge 2: 9 in the garden—beautiful trees that produced **d** fruit.
3: 6 The fruit looked so fresh and **d**, and it would make
27: 7 to prepare him a **d** meal of wild game. He wants to
27:14 She took them and cooked a **d** meat dish,
Job 33:20 and do not care for even the most **d** food.
Pr 23: 8 You will vomit up the **d** food they serve, and you
SS 2: 3 in his delightful shade, and his fruit is **d** to eat.
2:13 How **d** they smell! Yes, spring is here! Arise,
4: 3 veil are like pomegranate halves—lovely and **d**.
6: 7 veil are like pomegranate halves—lovely and **d**.
7: 2 Your navel is as **d** as a goblet filled with wine.
Isa 5:14 chops in anticipation of Jerusalem, this **d** morsel.
25: 6 It will be a **d** feast of good food, with clear,
Jer 17: 8 stay green, and they go right on producing **d** fruit.

DELIGHT (37) [DELIGHTED, DELIGHTFUL, DELIGHTING, DELIGHTS]
Dt 30: 9 for the LORD will **d** in being good to you as he
30:10 The LORD your God will **d** in you if you obey
1Sa 2: 1 for my enemies, / as I **d** in your deliverance.
Ne 1:11 Listen to the prayers of those of us who **d** in
Job 22:26 "Then you will **d** yourself in the Almighty
27:10 Can they take **d** in the Almighty? Can they call to
Ps 1: 2 But they **d** in doing everything the LORD wants;
36: 8 letting them drink from your rivers of **d**.
37: 4 Take **d** in the LORD, / and he will give you your
40: 6 You take no **d** in sacrifices or offerings. / Now that
40:14 to shame. / May those who take **d** in my trouble
62: 4 They **d** in telling lies about me. / They are friendly
68:30 tribute from us. / Scatter the nations that **d** in war.
70: 2 to shame. / May those who take **d** in my trouble
111: 2 All who **d** in him should ponder them.
112: 1 happy are those who **d** in doing what he
119:16 I will **d** in your principles / and not forget your
119:47 How I **d** in your commands! / How I love them!
119:70 hearts are dull and stupid, / but I **d** in your law.
119:77 so I may live, / for your law is my **d**.
119:111 are my treasure; / they are truly my heart's **d**.
119:174 longed for your salvation, / and your law is my **d**.
147:11 the LORD's **d** is in those who honor him,
Pr 8:30 I was his constant **d**, rejoicing always in his
23:26 May your eyes **d** in my ways of wisdom.
SS 7: 6 you are, my beloved; how pleasant for utter **d**!
Isa 11: 3 He will **d** in obeying the LORD. He will never
58:13 and speak of it with **d** as the LORD's holy day.
58:14 the LORD will be your **d**. I will give you great
62: 4 Your new name will be the City of God's **D**
65:19 I will rejoice in Jerusalem and **d** in my people.
66:11 **D** in Jerusalem! Drink deeply of her glory even as
Jer 9:24 love is unfailing, and that I **d** in these things.
15:16 They bring me great joy and are my heart's **d**,
Mic 7:18 people forever, because you **d** in showing mercy.
Mal 3:12 for your land will be such a **d**," says the LORD
Ro 12:10 and take **d** in honoring each other.

DELIGHTED (10) [DELIGHT]
Ex 18: 9 Jethro was **d** when he heard about all that the
1Sa 18:20 and Saul was **d** when he heard about it.
18:26 David was **d** to accept the offer. So before the time
Est 2:17 so **d** with her that he set the royal crown on her
SS 6: 9 The young women are **d** when they see her;
Isa 58: 2 the Temple every day and seem **d** to hear my laws.
Mk 14:11 The leading priests were **d** when they heard why
Lk 22: 5 They were **d** that he was ready to help them,
23: 8 Herod was **d** at the opportunity to see Jesus,
2Co 7:13 we were especially **d** to see how happy Titus was

DELIGHTFUL (4) [DELIGHT]
Ps 147: 1 to sing praises to our God! / How **d** and how right!
Pr 3:17 She will guide you down **d** paths; all her ways are
SS 2: 3 I am seated in his **d** shade, and his fruit is delicious
7: 6 "Oh, how **d** you are, my beloved; how pleasant for

DELIGHTING (2) [DELIGHT]
Ps 27: 4 the days of my life, / **d** in the LORD's perfections
Isa 66: 3 choose their own ways, **d** in their sins, are cursed.

DELIGHTS (14) [DELIGHT]
2Sa 22:20 of safety; / he rescued me because he **d** in me.
1Ki 10: 9 He **d** in you and has placed you on the throne of
2Ch 9: 8 He **d** in you and has placed you on the throne to
Ps 18:19 of safety; / he rescued me because he **d** in me.
37:23 by the LORD. / He **d** in every detail of their lives.
45:11 For your royal husband **d** in your beauty;
149: 4 For the LORD **d** in his people; / he crowns the
Pr 3:12 just as a father corrects a child in whom he **d**.
11: 1 The LORD hates cheating, but he **d** in honesty.
11:20 but he **d** in those who have integrity.
12:22 don't keep their word, but he **d** in those who do.
15: 8 the wicked, but he **d** in the prayers of the upright.
15:26 the thoughts of the wicked, but he **d** in pure words.
Isa 62: 4 for the LORD **d** in you and will claim you as his

DELILAH (11)
Jdg 16: 4 Later Samson fell in love with a woman named **D**,
16: 6 So **D** said to Samson, "Please tell me what makes
16: 8 So the Philistine leaders brought **D** seven new
16:10 Afterward **D** said to him, "You made fun of me
16:12 So **D** took new ropes and tied him up with them.
16:12 room as before, and again **D** cried out, "Samson!
16:13 Then **D** said, "You have been making fun of me
16:13 **D** wove the seven braids of his hair into the fabric
16:15 Then **D** pouted, "How can you say you love me
16:18 **D** realized he had finally told her the truth, so she
16:19 **D** lulled Samson to sleep with his head in her lap,

DELIRIOUS (1)
Isa 38:14 **D**, I chattered like a swallow or a crane, / and

DELIVER (27) [DELIVERANCE, DELIVERED, DELIVERER, DELIVERERS, DELIVERING, DELIVERS, DELIVERY]
Ex 5:18 but you must still **d** the regular quota of bricks."
Dt 31: 7 You are the one who will **d** it to them as their
Jdg 3:15 The Israelites sent Ehud to **d** their tax money to
1Sa 25: 5 men to Carmel. He told them to **d** this message:
2Sa 11:14 wrote a letter to Joab and gave it to Uriah to **d**.
1Ki 5: 9 will break the rafts apart and **d** the timber to you.
2Ki 1: 4 but you will surely die.' " So Elijah went to **d** the
19: 3 to be born, but the mother has no strength to **d** it.
Ezr 7:19 your God, **d** them in full to the God of Jerusalem.
Job 39: 3 to give birth to their young and **d** their offspring.
Ps 74:11 Unleash your powerful fist and **d** a deathblow.
82: 4 **d** them from the grasp of evil people.
144: 7 and rescue me; / **d** me from deep waters,
Isa 37: 3 to be born, but the mother has no strength to **d** it.
66: 9 this nation to the point of birth and then not **d** it?"
Jer 15:20 will not conquer you, for I will protect and **d** you.
Eze 3:18 but you fail to **d** the warning, they will die in their
20: 9 at Israel's God, who had promised to **d** his people.
Jnh 3: 2 and **d** the message of judgment I have given you."
Mt 6:13 us yield to temptation, / but **d** us from the evil one.
Lk 2:38 for the promised King to come and **d** Jerusalem.
1Co 16: 3 messengers you choose to **d** your gift to Jerusalem.
2Co 1:10 And he did **d** us from mortal danger. And we are confident that he will continue to **d** us.
2Ti 4:18 and the Lord will **d** me from every evil attack
Heb 2:15 Only in this way could he **d** those who have lived
5: 7 and tears, to the one who could **d** him out of death.

DELIVERANCE (11) [DELIVER]
Ex 2:23 out for help, and their pleas for **d** rose up to God.
3: 7 I have heard their cries for **d** from their harsh slave
12:42 to generation, to remember the LORD's **d**.
1Sa 2: 1 an answer for my enemies, / as I delight in your **d**.
Est 4:14 **d** for the Jews will arise from some other place,
Ps 119:123 My eyes strain to see your **d**, / to see the truth of
Isa 43:12 First I predicted your **d**; I declared what I would
51: 1 "Listen to me, all who hope for **d**—all who seek
59: 9 It is because of all this evil that **d** is far from us.
Eze 7:19 It won't buy their **d** in that day of the LORD's
Php 1:19 Christ helps me, this will all turn out for my **d**.

DELIVERED (34) [DELIVER]
Ex 18: 4 my helper; he **d** me from the sword of Pharaoh."
18: 8 and how the LORD had **d** his people from all
Nu 23: 7 This was the prophecy Balaam **d**:
23:18 This was the prophecy Balaam **d**: / "Rise up,
24: 3 and this is the prophecy he **d**: / "This is the
24:15 This is the prophecy Balaam **d**: / "This is the
24:20 over at the people of Amalek and **d** this prophecy:
Jdg 16:24 their god, saying, "Our god has **d** our enemy to us!
2Sa 22:18 He **d** me from my powerful enemies, / from those
1Ki 6: 1 were **d** from their slavery in the land of Egypt.
10:29 Egyptian chariots **d** to Jerusalem could be
16: 1 This message from the LORD was **d** to King
16: 7 It was **d** because Baasha had done what was evil in
2Ki 19: 5 After King Hezekiah's officials **d** the king's
2Ch 1:17 Egyptian chariots **d** to Jerusalem could be
Ezr 5:14 and **d** into the safekeeping of a man named
8:36 The king's decrees were **d** to his lieutenants
Ne 2: 9 the Euphrates River, I **d** the king's letters to them.
10:38 will be **d** by the Levites to the Temple of our God
Ps 18:17 He **d** me from my powerful enemies, / from those
106:43 Again and again he **d** them, / but they continued to
SS 8: 5 gave you birth, where in great pain she **d** you.
Isa 37: 5 After King Hezekiah's officials **d** the king's
Jer 19:14 from Topheth where he had **d** this message,
20:13 was poor and needy, he **d** me from my oppressors.
34: 6 So Jeremiah the prophet **d** the message to King
Hag 1:12 It had been **d** by the prophet Haggai,
Lk 23:25 But he **d** Jesus over to them to do as they wished.
Ac 7:10 and **d** him from his anguish. And God gave him
15:30 a general meeting of the Christians and **d** the letter.
Ro 5:10 we will certainly be **d** from eternal punishment by
15:28 As soon as I have **d** this money and completed this
2Ti 3:11 and Lystra—but the Lord **d** me from all of it.
Heb 2: 2 The message God **d** through angels has always

DELIVERER (3) [DELIVER]
2Ki 13: 5 So the LORD raised up a **d** to rescue the Israelites
Ps 144: 2 and my fortress, / my tower of safety, my **d**.
Ro 11:26 "A **D** will come from Jerusalem, / and he will turn

DELIVERERS (2) [DELIVER]
Ne 9:27 you sent them **d** who rescued them from their
Ob 1:21 **D** will go up to Mount Zion in Jerusalem to rule

DELIVERING (4) [DELIVER]
Jdg 3:18 After **d** the payment, Ehud sent home those who
Mt 27:43 trusted God—let God show his approval by **d** him!
Ac 22: 4 binding and **d** both men and women to prison.
2Pe 2:17 away by the wind—promising much and **d** nothing.

DELIVERS (1) [DELIVER]
Dt 32:39 who wounds and heals; / no one **d** from my power!

DELIVERY (5) [DELIVER]
Ge 35:17 After a very hard **d**, the midwife finally exclaimed,
38:27 In due season the time of Tamar's **d** arrived,
1Sa 4:19 of Phinehas, was pregnant and near her time of **d**.
Job 39: 2 their young? Are you aware of the time of their **d**?
Rev 12: 2 cried out in the pain of labor as she awaited her **d**.

DELUDED (2) [DELUSION]
Isa 19:13 Zoan are fools, and those from Memphis are **d**.
44:20 The poor, **d** fool feeds on ashes. He is trusting

DELUSION (1) [DELUDED]
Jer 3:24 their sons and daughters—was squandered on a **d**.

DEMAND (30) [DEMANDED, DEMANDING, DEMANDS]
Ge 34:12 No matter what dowry or gift you **d**, I will pay it—
Ex 6:13 and to **d** that he let the people of Israel leave
7: 2 He will **d** that the people of Israel be allowed to
7: 9 "Pharaoh will **d** that you show him a miracle to
7: 9 When he makes this **d**, say to Aaron, 'Throw down
Lev 25:36 Do not **d** an advance or charge interest on the
Dt 15: 2 They must not **d** payment from their neighbors
1Sa 2:14 and **d** that whatever it brought up be given to Eli's
2:15 He would **d** raw meat before it had been boiled
2:16 Then the servant would **d**, "No, give it to me now,
8:16 and female slaves and **d** the finest of your cattle
8:17 He will **d** a tenth of your flocks, and you will be
2Sa 4:11 his own bed? Should I not also **d** your very lives?"
1Ki 20: 9 but this last **d** of yours I simply cannot meet.' "
22:16 "How many times must I **d** that you speak only
2Ki 18:14 I will pay whatever tribute money you **d** if you will
2Ch 18:15 "How many times must I **d** that you speak only
Ne 5:12 and **d** nothing more from the people.
Job 14: 3 such a frail creature and **d** an accounting from me?
Ps 68:30 Humble those who **d** tribute from us.
Pr 25: 6 Don't **d** an audience with the king or push for a
Isa 49:24 Who can **d** that a tyrant let his captives go?
Mic 7: 3 Officials and judges alike **d** bribes. The people
Mt 26:63 "I **d** in the name of the living God that you tell us
Mk 15:11 mob to **d** the release of Barabbas instead of Jesus.
1Co 13: 5 or rude. Love does not **d** its own way. Love is not
Gal 2: 3 They did not even **d** that my companion Titus be
Php 2: 6 he did not **d** and cling to his rights as God.
3: 5 who **d** the strictest obedience to the Jewish law.
Phm 1: 8 I could **d** it in the name of Christ because it is the

DEMANDED (105) [DEMAND]
Ge 12:18 "What is this you have done to me?" he **d**.
20: 9 "What is this you have done to us?" he **d**.
21:10 So she turned to Abraham and **d**, "Get rid of that
31:26 Laban **d**. "Are my daughters prisoners, the plunder
31:36 did you find?" he **d** of Laban. "What is my crime?
34: 4 "Get this girl for me," he **d**. "I want to marry
42: 7 "Where are you from?" he **d** roughly.
44:15 "What were you trying to do?" Joseph **d**.
Ex 1:18 the midwives. "Why have you done this?" he **d**.
5:13 quota of bricks, just as you did before!" they **d**.
5:14 your quotas either yesterday or today?" they **d**.
15:24 "What are we going to drink?" they **d**.
17: 2 water to drink!" they **d**. "Quiet!" Moses replied.
21:30 of life. The owner will have to pay whatever is **d**.
32:21 to Aaron. "What did the people do to you?" he **d**.
Lev 10:16 When Moses **d** to know what had happened to the
10:17 he **d**. "It is a holy offering! It was given to you for
Nu 22:32 the angel of the LORD **d**. "I have come to block
23:11 Then King Balak **d** of Balaam, "What have you
31:15 "Why have you let all the women live?" he **d**.
Jos 9: 8 be your servants." "But who are you?" Joshua **d**.
Jdg 8:14 and **d** that he write down the names of all the

9:38 he **d**. “Wasn’t it you that said, ‘Who is Abimelech,
15: 6 the Philistines **d**. “Samson,” was the reply,
16:25 Half drunk by now, the people **d**, “Bring out
Ru 3: 9 “Who are you?” he **d**. “I am your servant Ruth,”
1Sa 1:14 here drunk?” he **d**. “Throw away your wine!”
4:16 there this very day.” “What happened?” Eli **d**.
13: 9 So he **d**, “Bring me the burnt offering
14:43 me what you have done,” Saul **d** of Jonathan.
15:14 of sheep and lowing of cattle I hear?” Samuel **d**.
15:24 for I was afraid of the people and did what they **d**.
17:28 “What are you doing around here anyway?” he **d**.
19:17 Saul **d** of Michal. “I had to,” Michal replied.
19:22 “Where are Samuel and David?” he **d**. “They are
20:29 His brother **d** that he be there, so I told him he
20:32 “But what has he done?” Jonathan **d**.
22:13 Saul **d**. “Why did you give him food and a sword?
26:14 “Wake up, Abner!” “Who is it?” Abner **d**.
28: 9 “Are you trying to get me killed?” the woman **d**.
29: 3 But the Philistine commanders **d**, “What are these
29: 4 “Send him back!” they **d**. “He can’t go into the
29: 8 David **d**. “Why can’t I fight the enemies of my
2Sa 1: 4 “What happened?” David **d**. “Tell me how the
1: 5 know that Saul and Jonathan are dead?” David **d**.
3:24 to see the king. “What have you done?” he **d**.
13:11 he grabbed her and **d**, “Come to bed with me,
13:17 He shouted for his servant and **d**, “Throw this
14:31 Then Joab came to Absalom and **d**, “Why did
16: 9 Abishai son of Zeruiah **d**. “Let me go over and cut
18:11 “What?” Joab **d**. “You saw him there and didn’t
18:29 the king **d**. “Is he all right?” Ahimaaz replied,
18:32 the king **d**. “Is he all right?” And the Cushite
1Ki 2:22 Solomon **d**. “You might as well be asking me to
2:42 So he sent for Shimei and **d**, “Didn’t I make you
20: 5 ‘I have already **d** that you give me your silver,
22:24 of the LORD leave me to speak to you?” he **d**.
2Ki 1: 7 “Who was this man?” the king **d**. “What did he
6:11 He called in his officers and **d**, “Which of you is
9:19 He rode up to them and **d**, “The king wants to
9:22 King Joram **d**, “Do you come in peace, Jehu?”
18:14 then **d** a settlement of more than eleven tons of
23:33 He also **d** that Judah pay 7,500 pounds of silver
23:35 the silver and gold **d** as tribute by Pharaoh Neco,
2Ch 18:23 of the LORD leave me to speak to you?” he **d**.
24: 6 “Why haven’t you **d** that the Levites go out
36: 3 who **d** a tribute from Judah of 7,500 pounds of
Ezr 5:10 And we **d** their names so that we could tell you
10: 5 and **d** that the leaders of the priests and the Levites
Ne 13: 9 Then I **d** that the rooms be purified, and I brought
13:11 I immediately confronted the leaders and **d**,
13:26 I **d**. “There was no king from any nation who
Est 1:15 must be done to Queen Vashti?” the king **d**.
7: 5 King Xerxes **d**. “Who would dare touch you?”
Ps 137: 3 For there our captors **d** a song of us.
Pr 5:12 I hated discipline! If only I had not **d** my own way!
Eze 16:31 so eager for sin that you have not even **d** payment
Da 2: 2 and he **d** that they tell him what he had dreamed.
2:23 asked of you / and revealed to us what the king **d**.”
3:22 in his anger, had **d** such a hot fire in the furnace,
Jnh 1: 8 they **d**. “Who are you? What is your line of work?
Mt 15: 2 disciples disobey our age-old traditions?” they **d**.
18:28 grabbed him by the throat and **d** instant payment.
21:23 They **d**, “By whose authority did you drive out the
27:13 hear their many charges against you?” Pilate **d**.
27:23 “Why?” Pilate **d**. “What crime has he
Mk 8:11 Testing him to see if he was from God, they **d**,
11: 5 some bystanders **d**, “What are you doing,
11:27 and the other leaders came up to him. They **d**,
15:14 “Why?” Pilate **d**. “What crime has he
Lk 20: 2 They **d**, “By whose authority did you drive out the
23:22 For the third time he **d**, “Why? What crime has he
23:24 So Pilate sentenced Jesus to die as they **d**.
Jn 2:18 the Jewish leaders **d**. “If you have this authority
5:12 “Who said such a thing as that?” they **d**.
7:45 “Why didn’t you bring him in?” they **d**.
8:25 “Tell us who you are,” they **d**. Jesus replied,
9:17 questioned the man who had been blind and **d**,
18:22 “Is that the way to answer the high priest?” he **d**.
19:10 “You won’t talk to me?” Pilate **d**. “Don’t you
Ac 3:14 and instead **d** the release of a murderer.
4: 7 They brought in the two disciples and **d**, “By what
5:28 the high priest **d**. “Instead, you have filled all
25:24 this is the man whose death is **d** both by the local
Ro 7: 9 felt fine when I did not understand what the law **d**.

DEMANDING (18) [DEMAND]

Ge 39:12 and grabbed him by his shirt, **d**, “Sleep with me!”
Nu 16:10 but now you are **d** the priesthood as well!
Jdg 11:12 **d** to know why Israel was being attacked.
1Sa 8:18 you will beg for relief from this king you are **d**,
2Sa 14: 7 Now the rest of the family is **d**, ‘Let us have your
1Ki 20: 7 I already agreed when he sent the message **d** that I
2Ki 15:20 **d** that each of them pay twenty ounces of silver in
Ne 5:15 **d** a daily ration of food and wine, besides a pound
Ps 69: 4 with lies, / **d** that I give back what I didn’t steal.
78:18 God in their hearts, / **d** the foods they craved.
Eze 3:18 I will hold you responsible, **d** your blood for theirs.
3:20 I will hold you responsible, **d** your blood for theirs.
Mk 8:12 “Why do you people keep **d** a miraculous sign?
Jn 8: 7 They kept **d** an answer, so he stood up again
Ac 7:35 same man his people had previously rejected by **d**,
1Co 9:18 to anyone, never **d** my rights as a preacher.
2Co 10:10 His letters are **d** and forceful, but in person he is
10:11 who say this must realize that we will be just as **d**

DEMANDS (26) [DEMAND]

Ex 5:16 slave drivers for making such unreasonable **d**.”
5:19 Since Pharaoh would not let up on his **d**,
7: 7 at the time they made their **d** to Pharaoh.
10: 1 “Return to Pharaoh and again make your **d**.
21:22 damages in the amount the woman’s husband **d**
Dt 23:21 For the LORD your God **d** that you promptly
Jos 22:16 “The whole community of the LORD **d** to know
1Ki 12: 4 “Lighten the harsh labor **d** and heavy taxes that
12:15 So the king paid no attention to the people’s **d**.
20: 8 “Don’t give in to any more **d**,” the leaders
2Ch 10: 4 “Lighten the harsh labor **d** and heavy taxes that
10:15 So the king paid no attention to the people’s **d**.
Ezr 7:23 whatever the God of heaven **d** for his Temple,
10:11 the God of your ancestors, and do what he **d**.
Job 34:33 “Must God tailor his justice to your **d**? But you
Pr 16:11 The LORD **d** fairness in every business deal;
29: 4 to his nation, but one who **d** bribes destroys it.
Isa 3:15 dust like that!” **d** the Lord, the LORD Almighty.
La 3:28 them sit alone in silence beneath the LORD’s **d**.
Mt 5:41 If a soldier **d** that you carry his gear for a mile,
22:40 and all the **d** of the prophets are based on these two
23: 4 They crush you with impossible religious **d**
Lk 6:29 If someone **d** your coat, offer your shirt also.
11:46 you crush people beneath impossible religious **d**,
Ac 19:40 And if Rome **d** an explanation, we won’t know
1Th 2: 7 we certainly had a right to make some **d** of you,

DEMAS (3)

Col 4:14 Doctor Luke sends his greetings, and so does **D**.
2Ti 4:10 **D** has deserted me because he loves the things of
Phm 1:24 So do Mark, Aristarchus, **D**, and Luke,

DEMETRIUS (3)

Ac 19:24 It began with **D**, a silversmith who had a large
19:38 If **D** and the craftsmen have a case against them,
3Jn 1:12 But everyone speaks highly of **D**, even truth itself.

DEMOLISH (10) [DEMOLISHED]

Nu 33:52 and molten images and **d** all their pagan shrines.
2Ki 14:13 Then Jehoash ordered his army to **d** six hundred
2Ch 25:23 Then Jehoash ordered his army to **d** six hundred
Ecc 10: 8 When you **d** an old wall, you could be bitten by a
Eze 26: 9 and **d** your towers with sledgehammers.
30:11 among the nations—have been sent to **d** the land.
33:28 I will destroy the land and **d** her pride.
35: 4 I will **d** your cities and make you desolate, and
Mic 5:11 down your walls and **d** the defenses of your cities.
Mal 1: 4 “They may try to rebuild, but I will **d** them again!

DEMOLISHED (13) [DEMOLISH]

2Ki 11:18 They **d** the altars and smashed the idols to pieces,
23:19 Then Josiah **d** all the buildings at the pagan shrines
2Ch 23:17 They **d** the altars and smashed the idols, and they
Job 19:10 He has **d** me on every side, and I am finished.
Isa 14:17 Is this the king who **d** the world’s greatest cities
25:12 The high walls of Moab will be **d** and ground to
Jer 47: 5 The city of Gaza will be **d**; Ashkelon will lie in
Eze 6: 4 All your altars will be **d**, and your incense altars
19: 7 He **d** fortresses in nearby nations / and destroyed
Da 2: 5 and your houses will be **d** into heaps of rubble!
Mt 24: 2 so completely **d** that not one stone will be left on
Mk 13: 2 so completely **d** that not one stone will be left on
Lk 21: 6 so completely **d** that not one stone will be left on

DEMON (25) [DEMON’S, DEMON-POSSESSED, DEMONIC, DEMONS]

Isa 47:12 “Call out the **d** hordes you have worshiped all
Mt 9:32 couldn’t speak because he was possessed by a **d**.
9:33 So Jesus cast out the **d**, and instantly the man could
11:18 he often fasted, and you say, ‘He’s **d** possessed.’
15:22 For my daughter has a **d** in her, and it is severely
17:18 Then Jesus rebuked the **d** in the boy, and it left
17:19 “Why couldn’t we cast out that **d**?”
Mk 5:15 when they saw the man who had been **d** possessed,
5:18 the man who had been **d** possessed begged to go,
7:30 girl was lying quietly in bed, and the **d** was gone.
Lk 4:33 a man possessed by a **d** began shouting at Jesus,
4:35 Jesus cut him short. “Be silent!” he told the **d**.
4:35 The **d** threw the man to the floor as the crowd
7:33 he often fasted, and you say, ‘He’s **d** possessed.’
8:38 The man who had been **d** possessed begged to go,
9:42 the **d** knocked him to the ground and threw him
11:14 One day Jesus cast a **d** out of a man who couldn’t
Jn 7:20 The crowd replied, “You’re **d** possessed!
8:48 we say all along that you were possessed by a **d**?”
8:49 “No,” Jesus said, “I have no **d** in me. For I honor
8:52 “Now we know you are possessed by a **d**.
10:20 Some of them said, “He has a **d**, or he’s crazy.
10:21 “This doesn’t sound like a man possessed by a **d**! Can a **d** open the eyes of the blind?”
Ac 16:18 that he turned and spoke to the **d** within her.

DEMON’S (2) [DEMON]

Mk 7:26 She begged him to release her child from the **d**
Lk 8:29 into the wilderness, completely under the **d** power.

DEMON-POSSESSED (6) [DEMON, POSSESS]

Mt 8:16 That evening many **d** people were brought to
8:33 telling everyone what happened to the **d** men.
12:22 Then a **d** man, who was both blind and unable to
Mk 1:32 many sick and **d** people were brought to Jesus.
Lk 8:36 told the others how the **d** man had been healed.
Ac 16:16 down to the place of prayer, we met a **d** slave girl.

DEMONIC (1) [DEMON]

Gal 5:20 idolatry, participation in **d** activities, hostility,

DEMONS (57) [DEMON]

Dt 32:17 They offered sacrifices to **d**, non-gods, / to gods
Ps 106:37 sacrificed their sons / and their daughters to the **d**.
Mt 4:24 and pain, or if they were possessed by **d**,
7:22 in your name and cast out **d** in your name
8:28 two men who were possessed by **d** met him.
8:31 so the **d** begged, “If you cast us out, send us into
8:32 So the **d** came out of the men and entered the pigs,
9:34 “He can cast out **d** because he is empowered by the prince of **d**.”
10: 8 the dead, cure those with leprosy, and cast out **d**.
10:25 of the household, have been called the prince of **d**,
12:24 they said, “No wonder he can cast out **d**.
12:24 He gets his power from Satan, the prince of **d**.”
12:27 And if I am empowered by the prince of **d**,
12:27 They cast out **d**, too, so they will judge you for
12:28 But if I am casting out **d** by the Spirit of God,
25:41 the eternal fire prepared for the Devil and his **d**!
Mk 1:34 and he ordered many **d** to come out of their
1:34 who he was, he refused to allow the **d** to speak.
1:39 the synagogues and expelling **d** from many people.
3:15 and he gave them authority to cast out **d**.
3:22 “He’s possessed by Satan, the prince of **d**.
3:22 That’s where he gets the power to cast out **d**.”
6:13 And they cast out many **d** and healed many sick
9:38 we saw a man using your name to cast out **d**,
16: 9 the woman from whom he had cast out seven **d**.
16:17 They will cast out **d** in my name, and they will
Lk 4:41 Some were possessed by **d**; and the **d** came out at his command, shouting,
8: 2 from whom he had cast out seven **d**;
8:27 a man who was possessed by **d** came out to meet
8:30 he replied—for the man was filled with many **d**.
8:31 The **d** kept begging Jesus not to send them into the
8:32 and the **d** pleaded with him to let them enter into
8:33 So the **d** came out of the man and entered the pigs,
8:35 been possessed by **d** sitting quietly at Jesus’ feet,
9: 1 and gave them power and authority to cast out **d**
9:49 we saw someone using your name to cast out **d**.
10:17 even the **d** obey us when we use your name!”
11:15 but some said, “No wonder he can cast out **d**.
11:15 He gets his power from Satan, the prince of **d**!”
11:18 You say I am empowered by the prince of **d**.
11:18 himself by empowering me to cast out his **d**,
11:19 And if I am empowered by the prince of **d**,
11:19 They cast out **d**, too, so they will judge you for
11:20 But if I am casting out **d** by the power of God,
13:32 “Go tell that fox that I will keep on casting out **d**
Ro 8:38 and life can’t. The angels can’t, and the **d** can’t.
1Co 10:20 I am saying is that these sacrifices are offered to **d**,
10:20 And I don’t want any of you to be partners with **d**.
10:21 from the cup of the Lord and from the cup of **d**,
10:21 cannot eat at the Lord’s Table and at the table of **d**,
1Ti 4: 1 lying spirits and teachings that come from **d**.
Jas 2:19 Well, even the **d** believe this, and they tremble in
Rev 9:20 They continued to worship **d** and idols made of
16:14 These miracle-working **d** caused all the rulers of
18: 2 She has become the hideout of **d** and evil spirits,

DEMONSTRATE (14) [DEMONSTRATED, DEMONSTRATING, DEMONSTRATION]

Nu 20:12 “Because you did not trust me enough to **d** my
27:14 you failed to **d** my holiness to them at the waters.”
Dt 32:51 You failed to **d** my holiness to the people of Israel
Job 2:12 and threw dust into the air over their heads to **d**
Ps 77:14 You **d** your awesome power among the nations.
79:11 **D** your great power by saving those condemned to
106: 8 the honor of his name / and to **d** his mighty power.
Isa 42: 6 have called you to **d** my righteousness.
52:10 The LORD will **d** his holy power before the eyes
Eze 4: 3 and **d** how the enemy will attack Jerusalem.
39:13 for it will be a glorious victory for Israel when I **d**
39:21 “Thus, I will **d** my glory among the nations.
Ac 19: 4 “John’s baptism was to **d** a desire to turn from sin
Ro 2:15 They **d** that God’s law is written within them,

DEMONSTRATED (3) [DEMONSTRATE]

Nu 20:13 and where he **d** his holiness among them.
Dt 34:12 And it was through Moses that the LORD **d** his
Eze 39:21 I have inflicted on them and the power I have **d**.

DEMONSTRATING (1) [DEMONSTRATE]

Ezr 7:28 And praise him for **d** such unfailing love to me by

DEMONSTRATION (3) [DEMONSTRATE]

Eze 4: 7 continue your **d** of the siege of Jerusalem.
12: 3 So now put on a **d** to show them what it will be
12:11 Then explain that your actions are a **d** of what will

DEMORALIZE (1) [DEMORALIZED]

Lev 26:36 I will **d** you in the land of your enemies far away.

DEMORALIZED (1) [DEMORALIZE]

Dt 1:28 we go on? Our scouts have **d** us with their report.

DEN (15) [DENS]

Pr 7:27 road to the grave. Her bedroom is the **d** of death.
Jer 4: 7 A lion stalks from its **d**, a destroyer of nations.
7:11 which honors my name, is a **d** of thieves?
25:38 He has left his **d** like a lion seeking its prey,
Da 6:16 to be arrested and thrown into the **d** of lions.
6:17 was brought and placed over the mouth of the **d**.
6:19 next morning, the king hurried out to the lions' **d**.
6:23 and ordered that Daniel be lifted from the **d**.
6:24 He had them thrown into the lions' **d**, along with
6:24 them apart before they even hit the floor of the **d**.
Am 3: 4 Does a young lion growl in its **d** without first
Mt 21:13 but you have turned it into a **d** of thieves!"
Mk 11:17 but you have turned it into a **d** of thieves."
Lk 19:46 but you have turned it into a **d** of thieves."
Rev 18: 2 for filthy buzzards, and a **d** for dreadful beasts.

DENIED (16) [DENY]

Ge 18:15 Sarah was afraid, so she **d** that she had laughed.
Jdg 11:17 But their request was **d**. Then they asked the king
Job 6:10 the pain, I have not **d** the words of the Holy One.
31:28 for it would mean I had **d** the God of heaven.
Mt 26:70 But Peter **d** it in front of everyone. "I don't know
26:72 Again Peter **d** it, this time with an oath. "I don't
Mk 14:68 Peter **d** it. "I don't know what you're talking
14:70 Peter **d** it again. A little later some other
Lk 8:45 Everyone **d** it, and Peter said, "Master, this whole
22:34 you have **d** three times that you even know me."
22:57 Peter **d** it. "Woman," he said, "I don't even know
Jn 1:20 He flatly **d** it. "I am not the Messiah," he said.
18:27 Again Peter **d** it. And immediately a rooster
Ac 25: 8 Paul **d** the charges. "I am not guilty," he said.
1Ti 5: 8 in the same household, have **d** what we believe.
1Jn 2:22 for they have **d** the Father and the Son.

DENIES (3) [DENY]

Mt 10:33 But if anyone **d** me here on earth, I will deny that
Lk 12: 9 But if anyone **d** me here on earth, I will deny that
1Jn 2:23 Anyone who **d** the Son doesn't have the Father

DENOUNCE (3) [DENOUNCED]

Job 17: 5 They **d** their companions for their own advantage,
Eze 22: 2 city of murderers? **D** her terrible deeds in public,
Mt 11:20 Then Jesus began to **d** the cities where he had done

DENOUNCED (3) [DENOUNCE]

Pr 24:24 be cursed by many people and **d** by the nations.
Mt 3: 7 and Sadducees coming to be baptized, he **d** them.
Ac 28:22 these Christians is that they are **d** everywhere."

DENS (8) [DEN]

Jdg 6: 2 made hiding places for themselves in caves and **d**.
Job 37: 8 The wild animals hide in the rocks or in their **d**.
38:40 as they lie in their **d** or crouch in the thicket?
Ps 104:22 At dawn they slink back / into their **d** to rest.
SS 4: 8 where lions have their **d** and panthers prowl.
Isa 13:22 and jackals will make their **d** in its palaces.
Mt 8:20 But Jesus said, "Foxes have **d** to live in, and birds
Lk 9:58 But Jesus replied, "Foxes have **d** to live in,

DENSE (3)

Ex 19:16 and a **d** cloud came down upon the mountain.
2Sa 22:12 veiling his approach with **d** rain clouds.
Ps 18:11 veiling his approach with **d** rain clouds.

DENY (26) [DENIED, DENIES, SELF-DENIAL]

Ge 38:10 thing for Onan to **d** a child to his dead brother.
Lev 6: 3 lie about it, or they **d** something while under oath,
Nu 30:13 nullify any vows or pledges she makes to **d** herself.
2Sa 14:19 woman replied, "My lord the king, how can I **d** it?
Pr 30: 9 For if I grow rich, I may **d** you and say, "Who is
Jer 5:28 justice to orphans and **d** the rights of the poor.
Am 2: 7 the dust and **d** justice to those who are oppressed.
2:11 Can you **d** this, my people of Israel?"
Mt 10:33 I will **d** that person before my Father in heaven.
26:34 the rooster crows, you will **d** me three times."
26:35 even if I have to die with you! I will never **d** you!"
26:75 the rooster crows, you will **d** me three times."
Mk 14:30 rooster crows twice, you will **d** me three times."
14:31 I will never **d** you!" And all the others vowed the
14:72 rooster crows twice, you will **d** me three times."
Lk 12: 9 on earth, I will **d** that person before God's angels.
22:61 tomorrow morning, you will **d** me three times."
Jn 13:38 you will **d** three times that you even know me.
Ac 4:16 "We can't **d** they have done a miraculous sign,
1Ti 6: 3 Some false teachers may **d** these things, but these
2Ti 2:12 reign with him. / If we **d** him, / he will **d** us.
2:13 he remains faithful, / for he cannot **d** himself.
Tit 1:16 know God, but they **d** him by the way they live.
Rev 2:13 And you refused to **d** me even when Antipas,
3: 8 yet you obeyed my word and did not **d** me.

DEPART (3) [DEPARTED, DEPARTING, DEPARTURE]

Ge 49:10 The scepter will not **d** from Judah, / nor the ruler's
Ecc 5:16 As people come into this world, so they **d**.
Isa 54:10 For the mountains may **d** and the hills disappear,

DEPARTED (7) [DEPART]

Ge 12: 4 So Abram **d** as the LORD had instructed him,
Nu 12: 9 The LORD was furious with them, and he **d**.
Dt 16: 3 so that you will remember the day you **d** from
Jdg 21:24 So the assembly of Israel **d** by tribes and families,
1Sa 4:22 Then she said, "The glory has **d** from Israel,
Job 23:12 I have not **d** from his commands but have treasured
Isa 17: 3 in Aram will share the fate of Israel's **d** glory,"

DEPARTING (2) [DEPART]

Ecc 8: 8 None of us can hold back our spirit from **d**.
Jn 17:11 Now I am **d** the world; I am leaving them behind

DEPARTURE (5) [DEPART]

Nu 1: 1 during the second year after Israel's **d** from Egypt,
9: 1 during the second year after Israel's **d** from Egypt,
10:11 during the second year after Israel's **d** from Egypt,
33:38 during the fortieth year after Israel's **d** from Egypt.
Ne 2: 6 So the king agreed, and I set a date for my **d**.

DEPEND (8) [DEPENDED, DEPENDENCE, DEPENDENT, DEPENDENTS, DEPENDING, DEPENDS]

Job 31:25 Does my happiness **d** on my wealth and all that I
Ps 33:20 We **d** on the LORD alone to save us. / Only he
Pr 3: 5 your heart; do not **d** on your own understanding.
Isa 10:20 They will no longer **d** on the Assyrians,
Jer 49:11 too, will be able to **d** on me for help."
Gal 3:10 But those who **d** on the law to make them right
Col 1:29 as I **d** on Christ's mighty power that works within
1Th 4:12 and you will not need to **d** on others to meet your

DEPENDED (1) [DEPEND]

2Co 1:12 We have **d** on God's grace, not on our own earthly

DEPENDENCE (2) [DEPEND]

Hos 12: 6 and always live in confident **d** on your God.
Jas 4:10 down before the Lord and admit your **d** on him,

DEPENDENT (3) [DEPEND]

Lev 21: 3 or virgin sister who was **d** because she had no
Ps 104:21 lions roar for their food, / but they are **d** on God.
Ac 12:20 because their cities were **d** upon Herod's country

DEPENDENTS (1) [DEPEND]

Ge 47:12 in amounts appropriate to the number of their **d**.

DEPENDING (4) [DEPEND]

1Ch 28:15 and lamps, **d** on how each would be used.
Isa 48: 2 the holy city and talk about **d** on the God of Israel,
Mic 3:11 Yet all of you claim you are **d** on the LORD.
Ro 9:32 the law and being good instead of by **d** on faith.

DEPENDS (9) [DEPEND]

Ex 12: 4 or not they share in this way **d** on the size of each
Ps 86: 4 Give me happiness, O Lord, / for my life **d** on you.
104:27 Every one of these **d** on you / to give them their
Pr 16:12 despises wrongdoing, for his rule **d** on his justice.
24: 6 victory **d** on having many counselors.
2Co 2: 3 Surely you know that my happiness **d** on your
Php 3: 9 For God's way of making us right with himself **d**
Heb 12: 2 on Jesus, on whom our faith **d** from start to finish.
1Pe 3: 3 the outward beauty that **d** on fancy hairstyles,

DEPLETED (2)

Job 18:12 Their vigor is **d** by hunger, and calamity waits for
Isa 23:11 spoken out against Phoenicia and **d** its strength.

DEPLOYED (1)

2Ch 14:10 so Asa **d** his armies for battle in the valley north of

DEPORT (1) [DEPORTED]

Ac 18: 2 Claudius Caesar's order to **d** all Jews from Rome.

DEPORTED (5) [DEPORT]

2Ki 18:11 At that time the king of Assyria **d** the Israelites to
Ezr 2: 1 They had been **d** to Babylon by King
4:10 and noble Ashurbanipal had **d** and relocated in
Ne 7: 6 They had been **d** to Babylon by King
Jer 29: 2 and all the craftsmen had been **d** from Jerusalem.

DEPOSED (4)

1Ki 2:27 So Solomon **d** Abiathar from his position as priest
15:13 He even **d** his grandmother Maacah from her
2Ch 15:16 King Asa even **d** his grandmother Maacah from
36: 3 Then he was **d** by Neco, the king of Egypt,

DEPOSIT (5) [DEPOSITED]

Lev 6: 2 have been dishonest with regard to a security **d**,
6: 4 taken by theft or extortion, whether a security **d**,
Pr 20:16 Get a **d** if someone guarantees the debt of a
27:13 Get a **d** if someone guarantees the debt of an
Lk 19:23 why didn't you **d** the money in the bank so I could

DEPOSITED (1) [DEPOSIT]

1Ch 29: 8 which were **d** in the treasury of the house of the

DEPRAVED (3) [DEPRAVITY]

Eze 23:11 And she was even more **d**, abandoning herself to
Hos 9: 9 The things my people do are as **d** as what they did
2Ti 3: 8 Their minds are **d**, and their faith is counterfeit.

DEPRAVITY (1) [DEPRAVED]

Ge 6:12 the world, and he saw violence and **d** everywhere.

DEPRESSING (1) [DEPRESSION]

Ecc 4: 8 pleasure now?" It is all so meaningless and **d**.

DEPRESSION (4) [DEPRESSING]

1Sa 16:14 sent a tormenting spirit that filled him with **d**
Job 30:16 "And now my heart is broken. **D** haunts my days.
Ps 143: 7 LORD, and answer me, / for my **d** deepens.
Pr 31: 6 is for the dying, and wine for those in deep **d**.

DEPRIVE (8) [DEPRIVED]

Isa 10: 2 They **d** the poor, the widows, and the orphans of
32: 6 they **d** the hungry of food and give no water to the
Eze 22:29 the poor, rob the needy, and **d** foreigners of justice.
Am 5:12 and **d** the poor of justice in the courts.
Mal 3: 5 or who **d** the foreigners living among you of
1Co 7: 3 The husband should not **d** his wife of sexual
7: 3 nor should the wife **d** her husband.
7: 5 So do not **d** each other of sexual relations.

DEPRIVED (4) [DEPRIVE]

Ge 42:36 Jacob exclaimed, "You have **d** me of my children!
Job 39:17 for God has **d** her of wisdom. He has given her no
Jer 5:25 Your wickedness has **d** you of these wonderful
La 3:35 They **d** people of their God-given rights in

DEPTH (3) [DEEP]

Pr 1: 6 by exploring the **d** of meaning in these proverbs,
25: 3 the **d** of the earth, or all that goes on in the king's
Eze 40:49 The **d** of the foyer was 35 feet and the width was

DEPTHS (27) [DEEP]

Dt 32:22 and burns to the **d** of the grave. / It devours the
Ne 9:11 then you hurled their enemies into the **d** of the sea.
Job 36:30 around him and how it lights up the **d** of the sea.
38:16 Have you walked about and explored their **d**?
41:31 the water boil with its commotion. It churns the **d**.
Ps 24: 2 foundation on the seas / and built it on the ocean **d**.
36: 6 mighty mountains, / your justice like the ocean **d**.
63: 9 to ruin. / They will go down into the **d** of the earth.
68:22 I will bring them up from the **d** of the sea.
71:20 life again / and lift me up from the **d** of the earth.
77:16 and trembled! / The sea quaked to its very **d**.
86:13 You have rescued me from the **d** of death!
88: 6 me down to the lowest pit, / into the darkest **d**.
95: 4 He owns the **d** of the earth, / and even the
107:26 and sank again to the **d**; / the sailors cringed in
130: 1 From the **d** of despair, O LORD, / I call for your
135: 6 and earth, / and on the seas and in their **d**.
148: 7 from the earth, / you creatures of the ocean **d**,
Pr 15:11 Even the **d** of Death and Destruction are known by
Isa 14:15 to the place of the dead, down to its lowest **d**.
40:28 No one can measure the **d** of his understanding.
Eze 27:27 everyone on board sinks into the **d** of the sea.
32:23 Their graves are in the **d** of the pit, and they are
Am 7: 4 The fire had burned up the **d** of the sea and was
Jnh 2: 3 You threw me into the ocean **d**, and I sank down to
Mic 7:19 your feet and throw them into the **d** of the ocean!
Rev 2:24 as they call them—**d** of Satan, really).

DEPUTY (2)

1Ki 22:47 There was no king in Edom at that time, only a **d**.
Jer 25: 9 of Babylon, whom I have appointed as my **d**.

DERBE (5)

Ac 14: 6 to the cities of Lystra and **D** and the surrounding
14:20 the city. The next day he left with Barnabas for **D**.
14:21 After preaching the Good News in **D** and making
16: 1 Paul and Silas went first to **D** and then on to
20: 4 Gaius, from **D**; Timothy; and Tychicus

DERIDE (1) [DERISION]

La 2:16 All your enemies **d** you. They scoff and grind their

DERIDED [KJV] See SCORN

DERISION (4) [DERIDE]

2Ch 30: 7 and became an object of **d**, as you yourselves can
Ps 44:13 an object of scorn and **d** to the nations around us.
79: 4 an object of scorn and **d** to those around us.
Zep 2:15 Everyone passing that way will laugh in **d** or shake

DESCEND (8) [DESCENDANT, DESCENDANTS, DESCENDED, DESCENDING, DESCENDS, DESCENT]

Ex 10:21 and terrifying darkness will **d** on the land of
2Sa 17:12 we can **d** on him like the dew that falls to the
Ne 3:15 and he rebuilt the wall as far as the stairs that **d**
Job 20:28 his house. God's anger will **d** on him in torrents.
28: 4 They **d** on ropes, swinging back and forth.
Isa 14:19 with those killed in battle. You will **d** to the pit.
30:30 It will **d** with devouring flames, with cloudbursts,
Eze 32:18 below in company with those who **d** to the pit.

DESCENDANT (56) [DESCEND]

Lev 21:21 Even though he is a **d** of Aaron, his physical
Nu 16: 1 a **d** of Kohath son of Levi, conspired with Dathan
16:40 no one who was not a **d** of Aaron—should ever

26:59 She also was a **d** of Levi, born among the Levites
Dt 11:6 and Abiram (the sons of Eliab, a **d** of Reuben)
Jos 17:3 who was a **d** of Manasseh, Makir, and Gilead,
Jdg 4:11 the Kenite, a **d** of Moses' brother-in-law Hobab,
9:28 Gaal shouted. "He's not a true **d** of Shechem!
10:1 Tola, the son of Puah and **d** of Dodo, came to
18:30 son of Gershom, a **d** of Moses, as their priest.
1Sa 25:3 a **d** of Caleb, was mean and dishonest in all his
2Sa 21:16 Ishbi-benob was a **d** of the giants; his bronze
21:18 from Hushah killed Saph, another **d** of the giants.
21:20 and six toes on each foot—a **d** of the giants—
23:9 the Three was Eleazar son of Dodai, a **d** of Ahoah.
1Ki 12:19 refused to be ruled by a **d** of David to this day.
1Ch 2:31 Ishi was Sheshan. Sheshan had a **d** named Ahlai.
9:4 son of Imri, son of Bani, a **d** of Perez son of Judah.
9:14 son of Azrikam, son of Hashabiah, a **d** of Merari;
9:19 of Kore, a **d** of Abiasaph, from the clan of Korah.
11:12 the Three was Eleazar son of Dodai, a **d** of Ahoah.
20:4 a **d** of the giants, and so the Philistines were
20:6 and six toes on each foot—a **d** of the giants—
24:3 who was a **d** of Eleazar, and of Ahimelech, who was a **d** of Ithamar,
26:24 Shebuel was a **d** of Gershom son of Moses.
27:3 He was a **d** of Perez and was in charge of all the
27:4 Dodai, a **d** of Ahoah, was commander of the
27:10 Helez, a **d** of Ephraim from Pelon,
27:11 Sibbecai, a **d** of Zerah from Hushah,
27:13 Maharai, a **d** of Zerah from Netophah,
27:15 Heled, a **d** of Othniel from Netophah,
29:8 LORD under the care of Jehiel, a **d** of Gershon.
2Ch 10:19 refused to be ruled by a **d** of David to this day.
20:14 son of Mattaniah, a Levite who was a **d** of Asaph.
23:3 The LORD has promised that a **d** of David will
Ezr 8:18 He was a very astute man and a **d** of Mahli, who was a **d** of Levi son of Israel.
10:2 Shecaniah son of Jehiel, a **d** of Elam, said to Ezra,
Ne 10:38 A priest—a **d** of Aaron—will be with the Levites
11:17 Mattaniah son of Mica, son of Zabdi, a **d** of Asaph,
11:22 son of Mattaniah, son of Mica, a **d** of Asaph,
11:24 son of Meshezabel, a **d** of Zerah son of Judah,
12:35 son of Micaiah, son of Zaccur, a **d** of Asaph.
Est 2:5 tribe of Benjamin and was a **d** of Kish and Shimei.
Isa 44:5 the LORD.' Others will say, 'I am a **d** of Jacob.'
Jer 17:25 There will always be a **d** of David sitting on the
22:4 there will always be a **d** of David sitting on the
33:15 I will bring to the throne of David a righteous **d**,
33:17 David will forever have a **d** sitting on the throne of
33:21 then will he no longer have a **d** to reign on his
Hos 3:5 return to the LORD their God and to David's **d**,
Mt 1:1 the Messiah, a **d** of King David and of Abraham:
Lk 1:27 to a man named Joseph, a **d** of King David.
2:4 And because Joseph was a **d** of King David,
Ro 11:1 a **d** of Abraham and a member of the tribe of

DESCENDANTS (441) [DESCEND]

DESCENDANTS OF AARON (14) Jos 21:4,10,13,19; 1Ch 6:50,54,57,60; 23:28; 24:31; 2Ch 13:10; 29:21; 31:19; Ne 12:47

DESCENDANTS OF ABRAHAM (10) Ge 25:4; 50:24; Jer 33:26; Mt 3:9; Lk 3:8; Jn 8:33,37; Ro 9:7; 2Co 11:22; Heb 2:16

DESCENDANTS OF ESAU (7) Ge 36:1; Dt 2:4,8,12, 22,22,29

HIS DESCENDANTS (43) Ge 17:19,20; 21:18; 46:7; 48:19; 49:10; Ex 28:43; 29:28,29; 30:21; Lev 7:35; 21:15,17; Nu 3:18,19,20; 14:24; 25:13; Dt 1:36; 17:20; Jdg 9:16,18,19; 1Sa 2:35,36; 2Sa 22:51; 1Ki 2:33,33; 21:29; 2Ki 8:19; 1Ch 6:49; 7:15; 23:13; 2Ch 13:5; 21:7; Ne 9:8; Ps 18:50; Jer 29:32; Eze 46:16; Ac 7:5,6; 8:33; Ro 4:13

THEIR DESCENDANTS (31) Ge 10:5; 49:7; Ex 1:7; 6:14,15,24; 33:1; Lev 22:3; Dt 1:8; 4:37; 5:29; 10:15; 11:9; 23:2,3; 31:21; 34:4; 2Ki 17:41; 1Ch 4:32; 7:4,7,9,11; 9:23; Ne 9:23; Est 9:27,28,31; Ps 106:27; Isa 61:9; Jer 32:39

YOUR DESCENDANTS (63) Ge 9:9; 15:5,13,16,18; 17:7,9,10; 21:12; 22:17,18; 24:60; 26:3,4,4; 28:3,4,13,14,14; 35:11,12; 46:4; 48:4; Ex 12:24; 32:13,13; Lev 3:17; 10:9,13, 15; Nu 15:23; 18:19; Dt 9:14; 28:46; 30:6,19; Jos 14:9; 22:24, 25,27,27; 1Sa 2:36; 2Sa 7:12; 1Ki 2:4; 8:25; 9:6; 2Ki 10:30; 15:12; 2Ch 6:16; Job 5:25; Ps 89:4; 132:11,12; Isa 49:17; 54:3; Jer 35:6; Mal 2:3; Ac 3:25; Ro 4:18; 9:7; Heb 6:14; 11:18

Ge 5:1 This is the history of the **d** of Adam. When God
9:9 "I am making a covenant with you and your **d**,
9:25 Then he cursed the **d** of Canaan, the son of Ham:
9:25 lowest of servants / to the **d** of Shem and Japheth."
10:2 The **d** of Japheth were Gomer, Magog, Madai,
10:3 The **d** of Gomer were Ashkenaz, Riphath,
10:4 The **d** of Javan were Elishah, Tarshish, Kittim,
10:5 Their **d** became the seafaring peoples in various
10:6 The **d** of Ham were Cush, Mizraim, Put,
10:7 The **d** of Cush were Seba, Havilah, Sabtah,
10:7 The **d** of Raamah were Sheba and Dedan.
10:8 One of Cush's **d** was Nimrod, who became a
10:20 These were the **d** of Ham, identified according to
10:21 Shem was the ancestor of all the **d** of Eber.
10:22 The **d** of Shem were Elam, Asshur, Arphaxad,
10:23 The **d** of Aram were Uz, Hul, Gether, and Mash.
10:30 The **d** of Joktan lived in the area extending from
10:31 These were the **d** of Shem, identified according to
13:16 And I am going to give you so many **d** that,
15:5 Your **d** will be like that—too many to count!"
15:13 "You can be sure that your **d** will be strangers in a
15:16 After four generations your **d** will return here to
15:18 and said, "I have given this land to your **d**,
16:10 "I will give you more **d** than you can count."
17:6 I will give you millions of **d** who will represent
17:7 be your God and the God of your **d** after you.
17:9 and all your **d** have this continual responsibility.
17:10 is the covenant that you and your **d** must keep:
17:16 of many nations. Kings will be among her **d**!"
17:19 my everlasting covenant with him and his **d**.
17:20 a great nation. Twelve princes will be among his **d**.
21:12 for Isaac is the son through whom your **d** will be
21:13 But I will make a nation of the **d** of Hagar's son
21:18 for I will make a great nation from his **d**."
22:17 I will multiply your **d** into countless millions,
22:18 and through your **d**, all the nations of the earth will
24:60 May your **d** overcome / all their enemies."
25:3 Dedan's **d** were the Asshurites, Letushites,
25:4 These were all **d** of Abraham through Keturah.
25:12 This is the history of the **d** of Ishmael, the son of
25:13 is a list, by their names and clans, of Ishmael's **d**:
25:18 Ishmael's **d** were scattered across the country from
25:23 the **d** of your older son will serve the **d**
26:3 I will give all this land to you and your **d**, just as I
26:4 I will cause your **d** to become as numerous as the
26:4 And through your **d** all the nations of the earth will
26:24 I will give you many **d**, and they will become a
28:3 And may your **d** become a great assembly of
28:4 and your **d** the blessings he promised to Abraham.
28:13 on belongs to you. I will give it to you and your **d**.
28:14 Your **d** will be as numerous as the dust of the
28:14 the earth will be blessed through you and your **d**.
32:12 and to multiply my **d** until they become as
35:11 even many nations. Kings will be among your **d**!
35:12 and Isaac. Yes, I will give it to you and your **d**."
36:1 This is the history of the **d** of Esau (also known as
36:9 This is a list of Esau's **d**, the Edomites, who live in
36:21 These were the Horite clans, the **d** of Seir,
46:4 down to Egypt, and I will bring your **d** back again.
46:7 grandsons and granddaughters—all his **d**.
46:8 the **d** of Jacob, who went with him to Egypt:
46:15 Jacob's **d** through Leah numbered thirty-three.
46:18 These sixteen were **d** of Jacob through Zilpah,
46:22 These fourteen were the **d** of Jacob and his wife
46:25 These seven were the **d** of Jacob through Bilhah,
46:26 So the total number of Jacob's direct **d** who went
48:4 to you and your **d** as an everlasting possession.'
48:19 His **d** will become a multitude of nations!"
49:7 for it is cruel. / Therefore, I will scatter their **d**
49:10 from Judah, / nor the ruler's staff from his **d**,
50:23 He lived to see three generations of **d** of his son
50:24 to the land he vowed to give to the **d** of Abraham,
Ex 1:5 down in Egypt. In all, Jacob had seventy direct **d**.
1:7 But their **d** had many children and grandchildren.
6:14 The **d** of Reuben, Israel's oldest son,
6:14 and Carmi. Their **d** became the clans of Reuben.
6:15 The **d** of Simeon included Jemuel, Jamin, Ohad,
6:15 a Canaanite). Their **d** became the clans of Simeon.
6:16 These are the **d** of Levi, listed according to their
6:17 The **d** of Gershon included Libni and Shimei,
6:18 The **d** of Kohath included Amram, Izhar, Hebron,
6:19 The **d** of Merari included Mahli and Mushi.
6:21 The **d** of Izhar included Korah, Nepheg, and Zicri.
6:22 The **d** of Uzziel included Mishael, Elzaphan,
6:24 The **d** of Korah included Assir, Elkanah,
6:24 and Abiasaph. Their **d** became the clans of Korah.
12:24 and must be observed by you and your **d** forever.
19:3 "Give these instructions to the **d** of Jacob,
28:43 This law is permanent for Aaron and his **d**.
29:28 parts will be the regular share of Aaron and his **d**.
29:29 must be preserved for his **d** who will succeed him,
30:21 This is a permanent law for Aaron and his **d**,
32:13 'I will make your **d** as numerous as the stars of
32:13 all of this land that I have promised to your **d**,
33:1 long ago that I would give this land to their **d**.
40:15 Aaron's **d** are set apart for the priesthood forever,
Lev 3:17 This is a permanent law for you and all your **d**,
6:18 Any of Aaron's male **d**, from generation to
7:35 and his **d** from the offerings given to the LORD
10:9 "You and your **d** must never drink wine or any
10:13 and your **d** as your regular share of the offerings
10:15 Then they will belong to you and your **d** forever,
21:15 that he may not dishonor his **d** among the members
21:17 his **d** who have physical defects will not qualify to
22:3 Remind them that if any of their **d** are
24:9 loaves of bread belong to Aaron and his male **d**,
Nu 3:18 from Gershon were named for two of his **d**,
3:19 from Kohath were named for four of his **d**,
3:20 from Merari were named for two of his **d**,
3:21 The **d** of Gershon were composed of the clans
3:27 The **d** of Kohath were composed of the clans
3:33 The **d** of Merari were composed of the clans
10:8 Only the priests, Aaron's **d**, are allowed to blow
13:22 Sheshai, and Talmai—all **d** of Anak—lived.
13:28 We also saw the **d** of Anak who are living there!
13:33 We even saw giants there, the **d** of Anak. We felt
14:24 His **d** will receive their full share of that land.
15:23 And suppose some of your **d** in the future fail to do
18:19 between the LORD and you and your **d**."
23:10 Who can count Jacob's **d**, as numerous as dust?
25:13 he and his **d** will be priests for all time,
26:4 This is the census record of all the **d** of Israel who
26:37 of Manasseh and Ephraim were all **d** of Joseph.
32:39 Then the **d** of Makir of the tribe of Manasseh went
32:40 the Makirites, **d** of Manasseh, and they lived there.
36:1 **d** of Makir, son of Manasseh, son of Joseph—
Dt 1:8 Isaac, and Jacob, and to all their **d**.'
1:28 They have even seen giants there—the **d** of Anak!'
1:36 and his **d** some of the land he walked over during
2:4 the Edomites, the **d** of Esau, who live in Seir.
2:8 past our relatives, the **d** of Esau, who live in Seir,
2:9 the **d** of Lot, or start a war with them.
2:12 were driven out and displaced by the **d** of Esau.
2:19 the **d** of Lot, or start a war with them.
2:22 He had similarly helped the **d** of Esau at Mount
2:22 in their place. The **d** of Esau live there to this day.
2:29 The **d** of Esau at Mount Seir allowed us to go
4:37 he chose to bless their **d** and personally brought
5:29 If they did, they and their **d** would prosper forever.
9:2 and tall—**d** of the famous Anakite giants.
9:14 Then I will make a mighty nation of your **d**,
10:15 And he chose you, their **d**, above every other
11:9 to give to your ancestors and to you, their **d**—
17:20 and his **d** will reign for many generations in Israel.
23:2 and their **d** for ten generations may not be included
23:3 or Moabites, or any of their **d** for ten generations,
28:46 and warning among you and your **d** forever.
29:22 both your own **d** and the foreigners who come
29:29 the revealed things belong to us and our **d** forever,
30:6 and the hearts of all your **d** so that you will love
30:19 would choose life, that you and your **d** might live!
31:21 for it will never be forgotten by their **d**.
34:4 and I told them I would give it to their **d**.
Jos 11:21 this period, Joshua destroyed all the **d** of Anak,
13:31 All this was given to the **d** of Makir, who was
14:9 your special possession and that of your **d** forever,
14:14 Hebron still belongs to the **d** of Caleb son of
15:14 Sheshai, Ahiman, and Talmai—**d** of Anak.
16:1 The allotment to the **d** of Joseph extended from the
17:1 half-tribe of Manasseh, the **d** of Joseph's older son.
17:6 because the female **d** of Manasseh received an inheritance along with the male **d**.
17:6 was given to the rest of the male **d** of Manasseh.)
17:12 But the **d** of Manasseh were unable to occupy
17:14 The **d** of Joseph came to Joshua and asked,
17:17 tribes of Ephraim and Manasseh, the **d** of Joseph,
21:4 The **d** of Aaron, who were members of the
21:10 to the **d** of Aaron, who were members of the
21:13 were given to the **d** of Aaron the priest:
21:19 towns were given to the priests, the **d** of Aaron.
21:27 The **d** of Gershon, another clan within the tribe of
22:24 because we fear that in the future your **d** will say to
22:25 And your **d** may make our **d** stop
22:27 It will remind our **d** and your **d** that we,
22:27 Then your **d** will not be able to say to ours,
22:28 If they say this, our **d** can reply, 'Look at this copy
24:3 I gave him many **d** through his son Isaac.
24:32 tribes of Ephraim and Manasseh, the **d** of Joseph.
Jdg 1:16 the Kenites, who were **d** of Moses' father-in-law,
1:20 living there, who were **d** of the three sons of Anak.
1:22 The **d** of Joseph attacked the town of Bethel,
1:35 but when the **d** of Joseph became stronger,
9:16 you have done right by Gideon and all of his **d**.
9:18 now you have revolted against my father and his **d**,
9:19 and in good faith toward Gideon and his **d**,
9:28 the men of Hamor, who are Shechem's true **d**.
Ru 4:12 And may the LORD give you **d** by this young
1Sa 2:35 I will bless his **d**, and his family will be priests to
2:36 Then all of your **d** will bow before his **d**,
24:21 will not kill my family and destroy my line of **d**!"
2Sa 7:12 For when you die, I will raise up one of your **d**,
22:51 to your anointed, / to David and all his **d** forever."
1Ki 2:4 'If your **d** live as they should and follow me
2:27 had made at Shiloh concerning the **d** of Eli.
2:33 and his **d** be forever guilty of these murders,
2:33 to David and his **d** and to his throne forever."
2:45 and may one of David's **d** always sit on this
8:25 'If your **d** guard their behavior as you have done,
9:6 "But if you or your **d** abandon me and disobey my
9:21 These were **d** of the nations that Israel had not
11:36 so that the **d** of David my servant will continue to
11:39 But I will punish the **d** of David because of
15:29 He immediately killed all the **d** of King Jeroboam,
16:3 just as I destroyed the **d** of Jeroboam son of Nebat.
21:21 He will not let a single one of your male **d**, slave
21:29 It will happen to his sons; I will destroy all his **d**."
2Ki 8:19 and promised that his **d** would continue to rule
10:30 Because of this I will cause your **d** to be the kings
15:12 "Your **d** will be kings of Israel down to the fourth
17:20 So the LORD rejected all the **d** of Israel.
17:34 and commands he gave the **d** of Jacob,
17:35 For the LORD had made a covenant with the **d** of
17:41 their idols. And to this day their **d** do the same.
20:18 Some of your own **d** will be taken away into exile.
1Ch 1:1 The **d** of Adam were Seth, Enosh,
1:5 The **d** of Japheth were Gomer, Magog, Madai,
1:6 The **d** of Gomer were Ashkenaz, Riphath,
1:7 The **d** of Javan were Elishah, Tarshish, Kittim,
1:8 The **d** of Ham were Cush, Mizraim, Put,
1:9 The **d** of Cush were Seba, Havilah, Sabtah,
1:9 The **d** of Raamah were Sheba and Dedan.
1:17 The **d** of Shem were Elam, Asshur, Arphaxad,
1:17 The **d** of Aram were Uz, Hul, Gether, and Mash.
1:23 Havilah, and Jobab. All these were **d** of Joktan.
2:7 Achan son of Carmi, one of Zerah's **d**,
2:23 All these were **d** of Makir, the father of Gilead.
2:33 and Zaza. These were all **d** of Jerahmeel.
2:50 These were all **d** of Caleb. The sons of Hur,
2:52 The **d** of Shobal (the father of Kiriath-jearim)
2:54 The **d** of Salma were Bethlehem,
3:10 The **d** of Solomon were Rehoboam, Abijah,
3:22 Shecaniah's **d** were Shemaiah and his sons,
4:1 Some of the **d** of Judah were Perez, Hezron,
4:3 The **d** of Etam were Jezreel, Ishma, Idbash,
4:4 These were the **d** of Hur (the firstborn of
4:12 the father of Ir-nahash. These were the **d** of Recah.
4:20 The **d** of Ishi were Zoheth and Ben-zoheth.

4:21 The **d** of Shelah were Er (the father of Lecah),
4:25 The **d** of Shaul were Shallum, Mibsam,
4:26 The **d** of Mishma were Hammuel, Zaccur,
4:32 Their **d** also lived in Etam, Ain, Rimmon, Token,
4:34 Other **d** of Simeon included Meshobab, Jamlech,
4:40 Some of Ham's **d** had been living in the region of
4:41 and completely destroyed the homes of the **d** of
5:2 It was the **d** of Judah that became the most
5:4 The **d** of Joel were Shemaiah, Gog, Shimei,
5:11 in the land of Bashan lived the **d** of Gad,
5:14 These were all **d** of Abihail son of Huri, son of
6:2 The **d** of Kohath were Amram, Izhar, Hebron,
6:17 The **d** of Gershon included Libni and Shimei.
6:18 The **d** of Kohath included Amram, Izhar, Hebron,
6:19 The **d** of Merari included Mahli and Mushi.
6:20 The **d** of Gershon were Libni, Jahath, Zimmah,
6:22 The **d** of Kohath were Amminadab, Korah, Assir,
6:25 The **d** of Elkanah were Amasai, Ahimoth,
6:29 The **d** of Merari were Mahli, Libni, Shimei,
6:49 Only Aaron and his **d** served as priests.
6:50 The **d** of Aaron were Eleazar, Phinehas, Abishua,
6:54 the **d** of Aaron who were from the clan of Kohath.
6:57 So the **d** of Aaron were given the following towns,
6:60 So a total of thirteen towns was given to the **d** of
6:61 The remaining **d** of Kohath received ten towns
6:62 The **d** of Gershon received by sacred lots thirteen
6:63 The **d** of Merari received by sacred lots twelve
6:66 The **d** of Kohath received from the territory of
6:70 The remaining **d** of Kohath were assigned these
6:71 The **d** of Gershon received from the territory of the
6:77 The remaining **d** of Merari received from the
7:4 for military service among their **d** was 36,000,
7:7 for military service among their **d** was 22,034.
7:9 men available for military service among their **d**,
7:11 and their **d** included 17,200 men available for
7:13 They were all **d** of Jacob's wife Bilhah.
7:15 One of his **d** was Zelophehad, who had only
7:17 **d** of Makir son of Manasseh.
7:20 The **d** of Ephraim were Shuthelah, Bered, Tahath,
7:28 The **d** of Ephraim lived in the territory that
7:29 The **d** of Joseph son of Israel lived in these towns.
7:40 Each of these **d** of Asher was the head of an
7:40 service among the **d** listed in their tribal genealogy.
8:40 150 in all. All these were **d** of Benjamin.
9:23 These gatekeepers and their **d**, by their divisions,
15:8 There were 200 **d** of Elizaphan, with Shemaiah as
15:9 There were 80 **d** of Hebron, with Eliel as their
15:10 There were 112 **d** of Uzziel, with Amminadab as
16:13 God's servant, / O **d** of Jacob, God's chosen one.
20:8 These Philistines were **d** of the giants of Gath,
23:8 Three of the **d** of Libni were Jehiel (the family
23:9 Three of the **d** of Shimei were Shelomoth, Haziel,
23:10 Four other **d** of Shimei were Jahath, Ziza, Jeush,
23:12 The **d** of Kohath included Amram, Izhar, Hebron,
23:13 and his **d** were set apart to dedicate the most holy
23:16 The **d** of Gershom included Shebuel, the family
23:17 the family leader. Rehabiah had numerous **d**.
23:18 The **d** of Izhar included Shelomith, the family
23:19 The **d** of Hebron included Jeriah (the family
23:20 The **d** of Uzziel included Micah (the family leader)
23:21 The **d** of Merari included Mahli and Mushi.
23:24 These were the **d** of Levi by clans, the leaders of
23:28 the **d** of Aaron, as they served at the house of the
24:1 This is how Aaron's **d**, the priests, were divided
24:3 David divided Aaron's **d** into groups according to
24:4 Eleazar's **d** were divided into sixteen groups
24:4 for there were more family leaders among the **d** of
24:5 in the sanctuary from among the **d** of both Eleazar
24:6 The **d** of Eleazar and Ithamar took turns casting
24:20 From the **d** of Amram, the leader was Shebuel.
24:20 From the **d** of Shebuel, the leader was Jehdeiah.
24:21 From the **d** of Rehabiah, the leader was Isshiah.
24:22 From the **d** of Izhar, the leader was Shelomith.
24:22 From the **d** of Shelomith, the leader was Jahath.
24:23 From the **d** of Hebron, Jeriah was the leader,
24:24 From the **d** of Uzziel, the leader was Micah.
24:24 From the **d** of Micah, the leader was Shamir,
24:25 From the **d** of Isshiah, the leader was Zechariah.
24:26 From the **d** of Merari, the leaders were Mahli
24:26 From the **d** of Jaaziah, the leader was Beno.
24:27 From the **d** of Merari through Jaaziah, the leaders
24:28 From the **d** of Mahli, the leader was Eleazar,
24:29 From the **d** of Kish, the leader was Jerahmeel.
24:30 From the **d** of Mushi, the leaders were Mahli,
24:30 These were the **d** of Levi in their various families.
24:31 Like the **d** of Aaron, they were assigned to their
26:8 All of these **d** of Obed-edom, including their sons
2Ch 6:16 'If your **d** guard their behavior and obey my law as
8:8 These were **d** of the nations that Israel had not
13:5 giving him and his **d** the throne of Israel forever?
13:8 of the LORD that is led by the **d** of David?
13:10 Only the **d** of Aaron serve the LORD as priests,
20:7 And did you not give this land forever to the **d** of
21:7 and promised that his **d** would continue to rule
29:21 king commanded the priests, who were **d** of Aaron,
31:19 As for the priests, the **d** of Aaron, who were living
35:15 The musicians, **d** of Asaph, were in their assigned
Ezr 2:6 The family of Pahath-moab (**d** of Jeshua and Joab)
2:16 The family of Ater (**d** of Hezekiah) | 98
2:40 families of Jeshua and Kadmiel (**d** of Hodaviah)
2:43 The **d** of the following Temple servants returned
2:55 The **d** of these servants of King Solomon returned
2:58 and the **d** of Solomon's servants numbered 392.
2:59 prove that they or their families were **d** of Israel.
3:9 and Kadmiel and his sons, all **d** of Hodaviah.
3:10 And the Levites, **d** of Asaph, clashed their cymbals
8:19 together with Jeshaiah from the **d** of Merari,
Ne 7:11 The family of Pahath-moab (**d** of Jeshua and Joab)
7:21 The family of Ater (**d** of Hezekiah) | 98
7:43 families of Jeshua and Kadmiel (**d** of Hodaviah)
7:46 "The **d** of the following Temple servants returned
7:57 "The **d** of these servants of King Solomon
7:60 and the **d** of Solomon's servants numbered 392.
7:61 prove that they or their families were **d** of Israel.
9:8 to give him and his **d** the land of the Canaanites,
9:23 You made their **d** as numerous as the stars in the
11:3 and **d** of Solomon's servants continued to live in
11:6 There were also 468 **d** of Perez who lived in
12:47 what they received to the priests, the **d** of Aaron.
Est 9:27 and to pass it on to their **d** and to all who became
9:28 of what happened ever die out among their **d**.
9:31 and their **d** to establish the times of fasting
Job 5:25 will be many; your **d** will be as plentiful as grass!
Ps 18:50 to your anointed, / to David and all his **d** forever.
21:10 from the face of the earth; / they will never have **d**.
22:23 Honor him, all you **d** of Jacob! / Show him reverence, all you **d** of Israel!
42:T For the choir director: A psalm of the **d** of Korah.
44:T For the choir director: A psalm of the **d** of Korah.
45:T A psalm of the **d** of Korah, to be sung to the tune
46:T A psalm of the **d** of Korah, to be sung by soprano
47:T For the choir director: A psalm of the **d** of Korah.
47:4 the proud possession of Jacob's **d**, whom he loves.
48:T A psalm of the **d** of Korah. A song.
49:T For the choir director: A psalm of the **d** of Korah.
69:36 The **d** of those who obey him will inherit the land,
77:15 the **d** of Jacob and Joseph by your might.
78:67 But he rejected Joseph's **d**; / he did not choose the
78:71 and made him the shepherd of Jacob's **d**—
83:8 joined them, too, / and is allied with the **d** of Lot.
84:T A psalm of the **d** of Korah, to be accompanied by a
85:T For the choir director: A psalm of the **d** of Korah.
87:T A psalm of the **d** of Korah. A song.
88:T A psalm of the **d** of Korah, to be sung to the tune
89:4 'I will establish your **d** as kings forever; / they will
105:6 God's servant, / O **d** of Jacob, God's chosen one.
106:27 that he would scatter their **d** among the nations,
118:3 Let Aaron's **d**, the priests, repeat: / "His faithful
132:11 take back: / "I will place your **d** on your throne.
132:12 If your **d** obey the terms of my covenant
Isa 14:1 But the LORD will have mercy on the **d** of Jacob.
39:7 Some of your own **d** will be taken away into exile.
49:17 Soon your **d** will come back, and all who are trying
49:21 think to yourself, 'Who has given me all these **d**?
54:3 Your **d** will take over other nations and live in
61:9 Their **d** will be known and honored among the
Jer 29:32 None of his **d** will see the good things I will do for
32:39 for their own good and for the good of all their **d**.
33:22 so I will multiply the **d** of David, my servant,
33:26 I will never abandon the **d** of Jacob or David,
33:26 or change the plan that David's **d** will rule the **d** of Abraham,
35:6 'You and your **d** must never drink wine.
35:19 Jehonadab son of Recab will always have **d** who
49:1 Are there no **d** of Israel to inherit the land of Gad?
Eze 20:6 and her **d** out of Egypt to a land I had discovered
40:46 the **d** of Zadok—for they alone of all the Levites
46:16 of his sons, it will belong to him and his **d** forever.
48:11 the **d** of Zadok who obeyed me and did not go
Da 11:4 It will not be ruled by the king's **d**, nor will the
Hos 12:13 Then the LORD led Jacob's **d**, the Israelites,
Zec 12:8 And the royal **d** will be like God, like the angel of
Mal 1:4 And Esau's **d** in Edom may say, "We have been
2:3 I will rebuke your **d** and splatter your faces with
3:6 That is why you **d** of Jacob are not already
Mt 3:9 just say, 'We're safe—we're the **d** of Abraham.'
23:31 you are accusing yourselves of being the **d** of those
Lk 3:8 just say, 'We're safe—we're the **d** of Abraham.'
Jn 8:33 "But we are **d** of Abraham," they said. "We have
8:37 Yes, I realize that you are **d** of Abraham. And yet
Ac 2:30 own **d** would sit on David's throne as the Messiah.
3:25 'Through your **d** all the families on earth will be
7:5 country would belong to Abraham and his **d**—
7:6 But God also told him that his **d** would live in a
8:33 and received no justice. / Who can speak of his **d**?
13:23 "And it is one of King David's **d**, Jesus, who is
Ro 4:13 and his **d** was not based on obedience to God's
4:18 "Your **d** will be as numerous as the stars,"
9:7 Just the fact that they are **d** of Abraham doesn't
9:7 "Isaac is the son through whom your **d** will be
9:8 This means that Abraham's physical **d** are not
9:12 "The **d** of your older son will serve the **d** of your younger son."
2Co 11:22 So am I. And they are **d** of Abraham? So am I.
Gal 3:16 promise was to his children, as if it meant many **d**.
Heb 2:16 We all know that Jesus came to help the **d** of
6:14 and I will multiply your **d** into countless
7:5 Now the priests, who are **d** of Levi,
7:9 In addition, we might even say that Levi's **d**,
11:18 "Isaac is the son through whom your **d** will be

DESCENDED (50) [DESCEND]

Ge 25:18 The clans **d** from Ishmael camped close to one
36:16 These clans in the land of Edom were **d** from
36:17 These clans in the land of Edom were **d** from
36:18 These are the clans **d** from Esau's wife
36:19 These are all the clans **d** from Esau (also known as
36:20 These are the names of the tribes that **d** from Seir
Ex 19:18 because the LORD had **d** on it in the form of fire.
Nu 3:18 The clans **d** from Gershon were named for two of
3:19 The clans **d** from Kohath were named for four of
3:20 The clans **d** from Merari were named for two of
3:21 Gershon were composed of the clans **d** from Libni
3:27 were composed of the clans **d** from Amram,
3:33 Merari were composed of the clans **d** from Mahli
12:5 Then the LORD **d** in the pillar of cloud and stood
26:5 These were the clans **d** from Reuben,
26:12 These were the clans **d** from the sons of Simeon:
26:15 These were the clans **d** from the sons of Gad:
26:20 But the following clans **d** from Judah's surviving
26:21 These were the subclans **d** from the Perezites:
26:23 These were the clans **d** from the sons of Issachar:
26:26 These were the clans **d** from the sons of Zebulun:
26:28 Two clans were **d** from Joseph through Manasseh
26:29 These were the clans **d** from Manasseh:
26:30 These were the subclans **d** from the Gileadites:
26:35 These were the clans **d** from the sons of Ephraim:
26:36 This was the subclan **d** from the Shuthelahites:
26:38 These were the clans **d** from the sons of Benjamin:
26:40 These were the subclans **d** from the Belaites:
26:42 These were the clans **d** from the sons of Dan:
26:44 These were the clans **d** from the sons of Asher:
26:45 These were the subclans **d** from the Beriites:
26:48 These were the clans **d** from the sons of Naphtali:
Jos 16:3 Then it **d** westward to the territory of the
Ru 4:11 and Leah, from whom all the nation of Israel **d**!
2Sa 21:22 These four Philistines were **d** from the giants of
1Ch 1:24 So this is the family line **d** from Shem: Arphaxad,
2:55 All these were Kenites who **d** from Hammath,
23:6 after the clans **d** from the three sons of Levi—
24:20 These were the other family leaders **d** from Levi:
26:23 These are the leaders that **d** from Amram, Izhar,
Ps 105:31 When he spoke, flies **d** on the Egyptians,
Isa 41:8 Jacob my chosen one, **d** from my friend Abraham,
Eze 26:20 the pit to lie there with those who **d** there long ago.
32:24 "Elam lies there buried with its hordes who **d** as
32:30 with all the other dead who have **d** to the pit.
Mt 17:9 As they **d** the mountain, Jesus commanded them,
Mk 9:9 As they **d** the mountainside, he told them not to tell
Lk 3:22 and the Holy Spirit **d** on him in the form of a dove.
Ac 19:17 A solemn fear **d** on the city, and the name of the
Rev 9:3 locusts came from the smoke and **d** on the earth,

DESCENDING (5) [DESCEND]

Mt 3:16 and he saw the Spirit of God **d** like a dove
Mk 1:10 split open and the Holy Spirit **d** like a dove on him.
Jn 1:32 "I saw the Holy Spirit **d** like a dove from heaven
1:33 'When you see the Holy Spirit **d** and resting upon
Rev 21:10 holy city, Jerusalem, **d** out of heaven from God.

DESCENDS (1) [DESCEND]

Hos 8:1 The enemy **d** like an eagle on the people of the

DESCENT (6) [DESCEND]

Ge 10:32 listed nation by nation according to their lines of **d**.
Nu 1:44 of Israel, all listed according to their ancestral **d**.
1Ch 6:19 Levite clans, listed according to their ancestral **d**:
7:25 Ephraim's line of **d** was Rephah, Resheph, Telah,
23:7 units were defined by their lines of **d** from Libni
Ne 9:2 Those of Israelite **d** separated themselves from all

DESCRIBE (9) [DESCRIBED, DESCRIBING, DESCRIPTION]

Job 13:1 "Look, I have seen many instances such as you **d**.
Ps 48:13 and tour all the citadels, / that you may **d** them
Eze 43:10 **d** to the people of Israel the Temple I have shown
43:11 **d** to them all the specifications of its construction—
Mt 11:16 "How shall I **d** this generation? These people are
26:54 how would the Scriptures be fulfilled that **d** what
Mk 4:30 Jesus asked, "How can I **d** the Kingdom of God?
10:32 Jesus once more began to **d** everything that was
Lk 7:31 "How shall I **d** this generation?" Jesus asked.

DESCRIBED (7) [DESCRIBE]

Ge 41:28 This will happen just as I have **d** it, for God has
Jer 11:8 I brought upon them all the curses **d** in our
Mt 24:33 when you see the events I've **d** beginning to
Mk 13:29 when you see the events I've **d** beginning to
Lk 21:31 when you see the events I've **d** taking place,
Rev 22:18 God will add to that person the plagues **d** in this
22:19 of life and in the holy city that are **d** in this book.

DESCRIBING (1) [DESCRIBE]

Ro 4:6 **d** the happiness of an undeserving sinner who is

DESCRIPTION (2) [DESCRIBE]

Pr 6:12 Here is a **d** of worthless and wicked people:
30:13 They are proud beyond **d** and disdainful.

DESECRATE (6) [DESECRATED, DESECRATES, DESECRATING, DESECRATION]

Lev 21:12 He must not **d** the sanctuary of his God by leaving
21:23 near the altar, for this would **d** my holy places.
2Ki 23:16 and he burned them on the altar at Bethel to **d** it.
23:20 and he burned human bones on the altars to **d**
Isa 56:6 worship him and do not **d** the Sabbath day of rest,
Eze 24:21 I will **d** my Temple, the source of your security

DESECRATED (7) [DESECRATE]

2Ki 23:13 The king also **d** the pagan shrines east of Jerusalem
23:14 Then he **d** these places by scattering human bones
Ne 13:18 by permitting the Sabbath to be **d** in this way!"

Jer 51:11 This is his vengeance against those who **d** his
Eze 25: 3 Because you scoffed when my Temple was **d**,
39: 7 I will not let it be **d** anymore. And the nations,
Am 2: 1 They **d** the tomb of Edom's king and burned his

DESECRATES (1) [DESECRATE]
Ex 31:14 Anyone who **d** it must die; anyone who works on

DESECRATING (1) [DESECRATE]
2Ch 36:14 **d** the Temple of the LORD in Jerusalem.

DESECRATION (7) [DESECRATE]
Eze 20:39 gifts to me. Such **d** of my holy name must stop!
Da 8:13 How long will the rebellion that causes **d** stop the
9:27 he will set up a sacrilegious object that causes **d**,
11:31 and setting up the sacrilegious object that causes **d**.
12:11 and the sacrilegious object that causes **d** is set up
Mt 24:15 the sacrilegious object that causes **d** standing in the
Mk 13:14 that causes **d** standing where it should not be"—

DESERT (94) [DESERTED, DESERTING, DESERTS, LONG-DESERTED]
Ge 16: 7 The angel of the LORD found Hagar beside a **d**
Ex 15:22 the Red Sea, and they moved out into the Shur **D**.
15:22 They traveled in this **d** for three days without
16: 1 Then they left Elim and journeyed into the Sin **D**,
16: 3 But now you have brought us into this **d** to starve
16:10 spoke to the people, they looked out toward the **d**.
16:13 The next morning the **d** all around the camp was
17: 1 the people of Israel left the Sin **D** and moved from
Nu 33:11 They left the Red Sea and camped in the Sin **D**.
33:12 They left the Sin **D** and camped at Dophkah.
Dt 2: 8 "Then as we traveled northward along the **d** route
32:10 "He found them in a **d** land, / in an empty,
Jos 1: 4 from the Negev **D** in the south to the Lebanon
1Ki 9:18 Baalath, and Tamar in the **d**, within his land.
19: 4 Then he went on alone into the **d**, traveling all day.
1Ch 5: 9 they spread eastward toward the edge of the **d** that
6:78 they received Bezer (a **d** town), Jahaz,
2Ch 8: 4 He rebuilt Tadmor in the **d** and built towns in the
Job 1:19 a powerful wind swept in from the **d** and hit the
6:18 nothing there to drink, and so they perish in the **d**.
12:15 If he holds back the rain, the earth becomes a **d**.
24: 5 Like the wild donkeys in the **d**, the poor must
24: 5 They go into the **d** to search for food for their
38:26 rain fall on barren land, in a **d** where no one lives?
Ps 29: 8 The voice of the LORD makes the **d** quake; / the
LORD shakes the **d** of Kadesh.
44:19 Yet you have crushed us in the **d**. / You have
72: 9 **D** nomads will bow before him; / his enemies will
73:27 But those who **d** him will perish, / for you destroy
74:14 heads of Leviathan / and let the **d** animals eat him.
78:17 their sin, / rebelling against the Most High in the **d**.
78:19 saying, / "God can't give us food in the **d**.
78:40 how often they rebelled against him in the **d**
102: 6 I am like an owl in the **d**, / like a lonely owl in a
106: 9 Israel across the sea bottom that was as dry as a **d**.
107: 4 Some wandered in the **d**, / lost and homeless.
126: 4 our fortunes, LORD, / as streams renew the **d**.
Pr 21:19 It is better to live alone in the **d** than with a crabby,
30:16 the grave, / the barren womb, / the thirsty **d**,
SS 8: 5 "Who is this coming up from the **d**, leaning on her
Isa 13:21 Wild animals of the **d** will move into the ruined
16: 8 spread out as far as Jazer and trailed out into the **d**.
21: 1 Disaster is roaring down on you from the **d**,
25: 5 or like the relentless heat of the **d**. But you silence
30: 6 moving slowly across the terrible **d** to Egypt—
32: 2 He will refresh her as a river in the **d** and as the
34:14 Wild animals of the **d** will mingle there with
35: 1 in those days. The **d** will blossom with flowers.
35: 6 in the wilderness, and streams will water the **d**.
35: 7 and rushes will flourish where **d** jackals once lived.
40: 3 a straight, smooth road through the **d** for our God.
42:11 Join in the chorus, you **d** towns; / let the villages of
43:19 come home. I will create rivers for them in the **d**!
43:20 Yes, I will make springs in the **d**, so that my
48:21 were not thirsty when he led them through the **d**.
49:10 and scorching **d** winds will not reach them
63:13 They were like fine stallions racing through the **d**,
Jer 2:31 of the LORD! Have I been like a **d** to Israel?
3: 2 You sit alone like a nomad in the **d**. You have
4:11 "A burning wind is blowing in from the **d**.
5: 6 a wolf from the **d** will pounce on them.
9: 2 and forget them and live in a shack in the **d**,
9:10 weep for the mountains and wail for the **d** pastures.
13:24 is scattered by the winds blowing in from the **d**.
17: 6 They are like stunted shrubs in the **d**, with no hope
17:17 LORD, do not **d** me now! You alone are my hope
25:24 of Arabia, the kings of the nomadic tribes of the **d**,
49:31 "They live alone in the **d** without walls or gates.
50:39 It will be a home for the wild animals of the **d**.
La 4: 3 their children's cries, like the ostriches of the **d**.
Eze 19:12 The **d** wind dried up its fruit / and tore off its
20:13 and I made plans to utterly consume them in the **d**.
22:24 like an uncleared wilderness or a **d** without rain.
29: 5 leave you and all your fish stranded in the **d** to die.
47: 8 "This river flows east through the **d** into the
Hos 2: 3 of thirst, as in a **d** or a dry and barren wilderness.
2:14 I will lead her out into the **d** and speak tenderly to
9:10 found you, it was like finding fresh grapes in the **d**!
11: 7 For my people are determined to **d** me. They call
13:15 a blast from the LORD—will arise in the **d**.
Am 2:10 and led you through the **d** for forty years
Hab 1: 9 Their hordes advance like a wind from the **d**,
Zep 2:13 Nineveh, a desolate wasteland, parched like a **d**.
Zec 7:14 The land that had been so pleasant became a **d**."
9:14 his enemies like a whirlwind from the southern **d**.
Mal 1: 3 I turned Esau's inheritance into a **d** for jackals."
Mt 12:43 it goes into the **d**, seeking rest but finding none.
24:26 'Look, the Messiah is out in the **d**,' don't bother to
26:31 "Tonight all of you will **d** me," Jesus told them.
Mk 14:27 "All of you will **d** me," Jesus told them.
Lk 11:24 a person, it goes into the **d**, searching for rest.
Ac 7:30 "Forty years later, in the **d** near Mount Sinai,
8:26 "Go south down the **d** road that runs from
21:38 members of the Assassins out into the **d**?"

DESERTED (42) [DESERT]
Lev 26:22 numbers will dwindle and your roads will be **d**.
26:43 land will enjoy its years of Sabbath rest as it lies **d**.
Jos 22: 3 You have not **d** the other tribes, even though the
1Sa 17:53 army returned and plundered the **d** Philistine camp.
2Sa 20: 2 So the men of Israel **d** David and followed Sheba.
2Ki 8:21 Jehoram's army, however, **d** him and fled.
Ps 44:18 Our hearts have not **d** you. / We have not strayed
69:25 their homes become desolate / and their tents be **d**.
Isa 5: 9 "Many beautiful homes will stand **d**, the owners
6:11 Until their houses are **d** and the whole country is
6:12 to distant lands and the entire land of Israel lies **d**.
17: 2 The cities of Aroer will be **d**. Sheep will graze in
17: 9 Their largest cities will be as **d** as overgrown
32:14 The palace and the city will be **d**, and busy towns
33: 8 Your roads are **d**; no one travels them anymore.
34:10 The land will lie **d** from generation to generation.
35: 8 And a main road will go through that once **d** land.
49:14 Yet Jerusalem says, "The LORD has **d** us;
58:12 Your children will rebuild the **d** ruins of your
Jer 18:15 For they have **d** me and turned to worthless idols.
22: 6 But I will destroy you and leave you **d**, with no
23: 2 you have **d** them and driven them to destruction.
50:13 Babylon will become a **d** wasteland.
Eze 8:12 LORD doesn't see us; he has **d** our land!' "
12:20 The cities will be destroyed and the farmland **d**.
Hos 2:13 I will punish her for all the times she **d** me,
4:10 for they have **d** the LORD to worship other gods.
7:13 "How terrible it will be for my people who have **d**
9:10 But then they **d** me for Baal-peor,
Ob 1:11 For you **d** your relatives in Israel during their time
Zep 3: 6 Their cities are now **d**; their streets are in silent
Zec 9: 5 its king killed, and Ashkelon will be completely **d**.
Mt 26:56 At that point, all the disciples **d** him and fled.
Mk 14:50 Meanwhile, all his disciples **d** him and ran away.
Lk 9:12 There is nothing to eat here in this **d** place."
Jn 6:66 point many of his disciples turned away and **d** him.
8:29 the one who sent me is with me—he has not **d** me.
12:11 because of him that many of the people had **d** them
Ac 1:25 for he has **d** us and gone where he belongs."
15:38 since John Mark had **d** them in Pamphylia and had
2Ti 1:15 came here from the province of Asia have **d** me;
4:10 Demas has **d** me because he loves the things of this

DESERTING (2) [DESERT]
Jer 1:16 all their evil—for **d** me and worshiping other gods.
Hos 4:12 the prostitute, serving other gods and **d** their God.

DESERTS (18) [DESERT]
Ex 23:31 and from the southern **d** to the Euphrates River.
Job 30: 3 with hunger and flee to the **d** and the wastelands,
Ps 107:33 He changes rivers into **d**, / and springs of water
107:35 But he also turns **d** into pools of water, / the dry
SS 3: 6 "Who is this sweeping in from the **d** like a cloud
Isa 21:13 O caravans from Dedan, hide in the **d** of Arabia.
35: 2 The **d** will become as green as the mountains of
41:18 In the **d** they will find pools of water. Rivers fed
50: 2 I can turn rivers into **d** covered with dying fish.
51: 3 will comfort Israel again and make her **d** blossom.
Jer 2: 6 a land of **d** and pits, of drought and death,
Eze 25: 4 I will allow nomads from the eastern **d** to overrun
25:10 will hand Moab over to nomads from the eastern **d**,
Hab 3: 3 moving across the **d** from Edom and Mount Paran.
Mt 26:33 "Even if everyone else **d** you, I never will."
Mk 14:29 "Even if everyone else **d** you, I never will."
2Co 11:26 in the cities, in the **d**, and on the stormy seas.
Heb 11:38 They wandered over **d** and mountains, hiding in

DESERVE (49) [DESERVED, DESERVES, DESERVING]
Ge 40:15 and now I'm here in jail, but I did nothing to **d** it."
Nu 11:11 What did I do to **d** the burden of a people like this?
Dt 32:35 I will take vengeance; I will repay those who **d** it.
1Sa 14:43 little bit on the end of a stick. Does that **d** death?"
26:16 by the LORD that you and your men **d** to die,
29: 8 "What have I done to **d** this treatment?"
2Sa 14: 7 He doesn't **d** to inherit his family's property.'
1Ki 2:26 You **d** to die, but I will not kill you now,
8:39 Give your people whatever they **d**, for you alone
2Ch 6:30 Give your people whatever they **d**, for you alone
Ezr 9:13 we have actually been punished far less than we **d**,
Job 11: 6 God is doubtless punishing you far less than you **d**!
34:36 you **d** the maximum penalty for the wicked way
42: 8 I will not treat you as you **d**, for you have not been
Ps 28: 4 Give them the punishment they so richly **d**!
90:11 Your wrath is as awesome as the fear you **d**.
94: 2 Sentence the proud to the penalties they **d**.
103:10 for all our sins, / nor does he deal with us as we **d**.
Pr 3:27 Do not withhold good from those who **d** it when
11:31 that the wicked and the sinner will get what they **d**!
14:14 Backsliders get what they **d**; good people receive
25:27 for people to think about all the honors they **d**.
Isa 3:11 destruction is sure. You, too, will get what you **d**.
Jer 15:15 Be merciful to me and give them what they **d**!
16:10 What have we done to **d** such treatment? What is
17:10 due rewards, according to what their actions **d**."
26:16 "This man does not **d** the death sentence,
Eze 7:27 they will receive the punishment they so richly **d**.
16:59 I will give you what you **d**, for you have taken
23:45 will sentence them to all the punishment they **d**.
36:22 bringing you back again but not because you **d** it.
36:32 I am not doing this because you **d** it.
Da 9:18 We do not ask because we **d** help, but because you
Na 1:14 because you are despicable and don't **d** to live!"
Hab 2: 6 Now you will get what you **d** for your oppression
Mal 1: 6 but where are the honor and respect I **d**?
Mt 10:10 because those who work **d** to be fed.
Lk 6:32 "Do you think you **d** credit merely for loving
10: 7 because those who work **d** their pay.
23:41 We **d** to die for our evil deeds, but this man hasn't
Ro 3: 8 Those who say such things **d** to be condemned,
12:19 will take vengeance; / I will repay those who **d** it,"
1Co 9:17 this of my own free will, then I would **d** payment.
2Co 5:10 We will each receive whatever we **d** for the good
11:15 get every bit of punishment their wicked deeds **d**.
Eph 3: 8 Though I did nothing to **d** it, and though I am the
1Ti 5:18 in another place, "Those who work **d** their pay!"
Heb 10:30 I will repay those who **d** it." He also said,
Rev 2:23 And I will give to each of you whatever you **d**.

DESERVED (9) [DESERVE]
Ne 9:33 sinned greatly, and you gave us only what we **d**.
Job 8: 4 against him, so their punishment was well **d**.
Jer 31:18 'You disciplined me severely, but I **d** it.
La 5: 7 We have suffered the punishment they **d**!
Eze 23:10 the land as a sinner who had received what she **d**.
31:11 mighty nation that destroyed it as its wickedness **d**.
Zec 1: 6 'We have received what we **d** from the LORD
Ro 1:27 within themselves the penalty they so richly **d**.
2Ti 1: 9 He did this not because we **d** it, but because that

DESERVES (12) [DESERVE]
Ge 20: 9 "What have I done to you that **d** treatment like
Nu 22:28 "What have I done to you that **d** your beating me
Jdg 9:16 Have you treated my father with the honor he **d**?
2Sa 12: 5 "any man who would do such a thing **d** to die!
1Ch 16:29 Give to the LORD the glory he **d**! / Bring your
Ps 48:10 As your name **d**, O God, / you will be praised to
96: 8 Give to the LORD the glory he **d**! / Bring your
Jer 51:56 and he is giving Babylon all she **d**.
Mal 1: 7 by saying the altar of the LORD **d** no respect.
Lk 7: 4 "If anyone **d** your help, it is he," they said,
Heb 3: 3 But Jesus **d** far more glory than Moses, just as a
person who builds a fine house **d** more

DESERVING (1) [DESERVE]
Eph 3: 8 and though I am the least **d** Christian there is,

DESIGN (6) [DESIGNED, DESIGNERS, DESIGNING, DESIGNS]
Ex 26:30 "Set up this Tabernacle according to the **d** you
Nu 8: 4 It was built according to the exact **d** the LORD
2Ki 16:10 to Uriah the priest, along with its **d** in full detail.
2Ch 2:14 an engraver and can follow any **d** given to him.
24:13 the Temple of God according to its original **d**
Heb 8: 5 to the **d** I have shown you here on the mountain."

DESIGNATE (5) [DESIGNATED, DESIGNATING]
Nu 6:27 and his sons will **d** the Israelites as my people,
35:11 **d** cities of refuge for people to flee to if they have
35:13 **D** six cities of refuge for yourselves,
Dt 19: 9 you must **d** three additional cities of refuge.
Jos 20: 2 "Now tell the Israelites to **d** the cities of refuge,

DESIGNATED (13) [DESIGNATE]
Lev 7:34 For I have **d** the breast and the right thigh for the
14:40 then be thrown into an area outside the town **d** as
14:45 out of town to the place **d** as ceremonially unclean.
Nu 1:52 Each tribe of Israel will have a **d** camping area
Dt 4:19 The LORD your God **d** these heavenly bodies for
29:26 to them, gods that the LORD had not **d** for them.
Jos 20: 7 The following cities were **d** as cities of refuge:
20: 8 the following cities were **d** as cities of refuge:
1Ki 12:33 day in midautumn, a day that he himself had **d**,
1Ch 28:16 He **d** the amount of gold for the table on which the
28:17 David also **d** the amount of gold for the solid gold
28:18 he **d** the amount of refined gold for the altar of
Heb 5:10 And God **d** him to be a High Priest in the line of

DESIGNATING (1) [DESIGNATE]
Ezr 10:16 **d** each of the representatives by name.

DESIGNED (4) [DESIGN]
2Ch 26:15 **d** by brilliant men to shoot arrows and hurl stones
Ac 17:29 we shouldn't think of God as an idol **d** by
Eph 1: 9 **d** long ago according to his good pleasure.
Heb 11:10 with eternal foundations, a city **d** and built by God.

DESIGNERS (1) [DESIGN]
Ex 35:35 **d**, weavers, and embroiderers in blue, purple,

DESIGNING (1) [DESIGN]

Ex 38:23 at engraving, **d**, and embroidering blue, purple,

DESIGNS (2) [DESIGN]

Ex 26:36 and embroider exquisite **d** into it, using blue,
Est 1: 7 Drinks were served in gold goblets of many **d**,

DESIRABLE (4) [DESIRE]

Ps 19:10 They are more **d** than gold, / even the finest gold.
Isa 62:12 And Jerusalem will be known as the **D** Place
Eze 23: 7 so she prostituted herself with the most **d** men of
23:12 in handsome uniforms—all of them **d**.

DESIRE (38) [DESIRABLE, DESIRED, DESIRES, DESIRING]

Ge 3:16 And though your **d** will be for your husband,
39: 7 Potiphar's wife began to **d** him and invited him to
Lev 27: 8 If you **d** to make such a vow but cannot afford to
Dt 7:25 and do not **d** the silver or gold with which they are
1Ki 8:58 May he give us the **d** to do his will in everything
1Ch 28: 2 It was my **d** to build a temple where the Ark of the
29:19 Give my son Solomon the wholehearted **d** to obey
2Ch 1:11 "Because your greatest **d** is to help your people,
30:12 giving them a strong **d** to unite in obeying the
Ps 5: 9 Their deepest **d** is to destroy others. / Their talk is
20: 4 May he grant your heart's **d** / and fulfill all your
21: 2 For you have given him his heart's **d**; / you have
51: 6 But you **d** honesty from the heart, / so you can
73:25 but you? / I **d** you more than anything on earth.
119:20 overwhelmed continually / with a **d** for your laws.
Pr 3:15 than rubies; nothing you **d** can compare with her.
8:11 Nothing you **d** can be compared with it.
23: 3 and don't **d** all the delicacies—deception may be
23: 6 people who are stingy; don't **d** their delicacies.
24: 1 Don't envy evil people; don't **d** their company.
27:20 are never satisfied, so human **d** is never satisfied.
Ecc 2: 8 I had everything a man could **d**!
12: 5 and withered, dragging along without any sexual **d**.
Isa 26: 8 your laws; / our heart's **d** is to glorify your name.
Jer 2:24 Those who **d** you do not even need to search,
22:27 You will never again return to the land of your **d**.
32:40 I will put a **d** in their hearts to worship me,
Eze 24:25 their joy and glory, their heart's **d**, their dearest
Mk 4:19 the lure of wealth, and the **d** for nice things,
Ac 19: 4 "John's baptism was to demonstrate a **d** to turn
28:19 even though I had no **d** to press charges against my
1Co 12:31 in any event, you should **d** the most helpful gifts.
14: 1 but also **d** the special abilities the Spirit gives,
Php 2:13 giving you the **d** to obey him and the power to do
1Ti 6: 4 Such a person has an unhealthy **d** to quibble over
Heb 6:11 Our great **d** is that you will keep right on loving
2Pe 2:18 With lustful **d** as their bait, they lure back into sin
3: 3 laugh at the truth and do every evil thing they **d**.

DESIRED (6) [DESIRE]

Ex 35:21 If their hearts were stirred and they **d** to do so,
1Ki 5:10 as much cedar and cypress timber as he **d**.
Ps 132:13 has chosen Jerusalem; / he has **d** it as his home.
132:14 he said. / "I will live here, for this is the place I **d**.
Eze 23: 9 over to her Assyrian lovers, whom she **d** so much.
Ro 1:24 and do whatever shameful things their hearts **d**.

DESIRES (57) [DESIRE]

Nu 15:39 his commands instead of following your own **d**
Dt 18: 6 so **d** may come from any town in Israel,
2Sa 3:21 will be able to rule over everything your heart **d**."
1Ki 11:37 and you will rule over all that your heart **d**.
2Ch 9: 8 so much and **d** this kingdom to last forever,
Job 17:11 hopes have disappeared. My heart's **d** are broken.
Ps 10: 3 For they brag about their evil **d**; / they praise the
37: 4 the LORD, / and he will give you your heart's **d**.
81:12 stubborn way, / living according to their own **d**.
106:14 In the wilderness, their **d** ran wild, / testing God's
140: 8 LORD, do not give in to their evil **d**. / Do not let
145:19 He fulfills the **d** of those who fear him; / he hears
Pr 21:25 The **d** of lazy people will be their ruin, for their
SS 7:10 "I am my lover's, the one he **d**.
Isa 58:13 you do, and don't follow your own **d** or talk idly.
Jer 3:17 will no longer stubbornly follow their own evil **d**.
7:24 following the stubborn **d** of their evil hearts.
9:14 they have stubbornly followed their own **d**
11: 8 Instead, they stubbornly followed their own evil **d**.
13:10 They stubbornly follow their own **d** and worship
16:12 You stubbornly follow your own evil **d** and refuse
18:12 to live as we want to, following our own evil **d**."
23:17 to those who stubbornly follow their own evil **d**,
Eze 36:26 I will give you a new heart with new and right **d**,
Da 5:21 and appoints anyone he **d** to rule over them.
Ro 1:26 is why God abandoned them to their shameful **d**.
6:12 the way you live; do not give in to its lustful **d**.
7: 5 by our old nature, sinful **d** were at work within us,
7: 5 and the law aroused these evil **d** that produced
7: 8 and aroused all kinds of forbidden **d** within me!
13:14 and don't think of ways to indulge your evil **d**.
1Co 3: 3 for you are still controlled by your own sinful **d**.
3: 3 that prove you are controlled by your own **d**?
Gal 5:17 And the Spirit gives us **d** that are opposite from what the sinful nature **d**.
5:19 When you follow the **d** of your sinful nature,
5:24 and **d** of their sinful nature to his cross
6: 8 Those who live only to satisfy their own sinful **d**
Eph 2: 3 following the passions and **d** of our evil nature.
Php 1:23 I'm torn between two **d**: Sometimes I want to live,
Col 2:23 to conquering a person's evil thoughts and **d**.
3: 5 do with sexual sin, impurity, lust, and shameful **d**.
1Ti 3: 1 to be an elder, he **d** an honorable responsibility.
5:11 because their physical **d** will overpower their
6: 9 and harmful **d** that plunge them into ruin
2Ti 3: 6 with the guilt of sin and controlled by many **d**.
4: 3 They will follow their own **d** and will look for
Tit 3: 3 and became slaves to many wicked **d** and evil
Heb 4:12 cutting deep into our innermost thoughts and **d**.
Jas 1:14 Temptation comes from the lure of our own evil **d**.
1:15 These evil **d** lead to evil actions, and evil actions
4: 1 Isn't it the whole army of evil **d** at war within you?
4: 6 and more strength to stand against such evil **d**.
1Pe 2:11 So I warn you to keep away from evil **d**
4: 2 spend the rest of your life chasing after evil **d**,
2Pe 1: 4 the decadence all around you caused by evil **d**
2:10 their own evil, lustful **d** and who despise authority.

DESIRING (1) [DESIRE]

Ecc 6: 9 Enjoy what you have rather than **d** what you don't

DESOLATE (64) [DESOLATED, DESOLATION, ONCE-DESOLATE]

Ge 47:19 and so the land will not become empty and **d**."
Lev 16:22 carry all the people's sins upon itself into a **d** land.
26:31 I will make your cities **d** and destroy your places
26:33 Your land will become **d**, and your cities will lie in
26:34 **d** during your years of exile in the land of your
Jos 8:28 a permanent mound of ruins, **d** to this very day.
2Sa 13:20 So Tamar lived as a **d** woman in Absalom's house.
2Ki 22:19 that this land would be cursed and become **d**.
2Ch 36:21 lying **d** for seventy years, just as the prophet had
Job 30: 3 to the deserts and the wastelands, **d** and gloomy.
Ps 69:25 May their homes become **d** / and their tents be
79: 7 people Israel, / making the land a **d** wilderness.
Isa 7:19 settle in the fertile areas and also in the **d** valleys,
14:23 I will make Babylon into a **d** land, a place of
24: 6 and its people. They are left **d**, destroyed by fire.
49:19 "Even the most **d** parts of your abandoned land
54:11 "O storm-battered city, troubled and **d**! I will
62: 4 you be called the Godforsaken City or the **D** Land.
64:10 are destroyed; even Jerusalem is a **d** wilderness.
Jer 9:10 For they are **d** and empty of life; the lowing of
10:25 your people Israel, making the land a **d** wilderness.
12:11 The whole land is **d**, and no one even cares.
18:16 Therefore, their land will become **d**, a monument
25:11 This entire land will become a **d** wasteland. Israel
25:18 they have been a **d** ruin, an object of horror,
25:38 and their land will be made **d** by the sword of the
33:12 though it is now **d** and the people and animals have
44: 6 the streets of Jerusalem, and now they are a **d** ruin.
44:22 a **d** ruin without a single inhabitant—as it is today.
49: 2 It will become a **d** heap, and the neighboring towns
49:13 All its towns and villages will be **d** forever."
49:33 be inhabited by jackals, and it will be **d** forever.
50:12 least of nations—a wilderness, a dry and **d** land.
50:23 and shattered. Babylon is **d** among the nations!
50:39 again will people live there; it will lie **d** forever.
51:26 You will be **d** forever. Even your stones will never
51:29 Babylon will be left **d** without a single inhabitant.
La 1:13 He has made me **d**, racked with sickness all day
3:11 tore me with his claws, leaving me helpless and **d**.
3:47 filled with fear, for we are trapped, **d**, and ruined."
5:18 For Jerusalem is empty and **d**, a place haunted by
Eze 6:14 and make their cities **d** from the wilderness in the
15: 8 And I will make the land **d** because my people
29: 9 The land of Egypt will become a **d** wasteland,
29:12 I will make Egypt **d**, and it will be surrounded by other **d** nations.
29:12 Its cities will be empty and **d** for forty years, surrounded by other **d** cities.
30: 7 Egypt will be **d**, surrounded by **d** nations,
35: 4 I will demolish your cities and make you **d**, and
35: 7 I will make Mount Seir utterly **d**, killing off all
35: 9 I will make you **d** forever. Your cities will never
35:14 The whole world will rejoice when I make you **d**.
36:34 The fields that used to lie empty and **d**—a shock to
Da 9: 2 that Jerusalem must lie **d** for seventy years.
9:17 own sake, Lord, smile again on your **d** sanctuary.
Mic 7:13 But the land will become empty and **d** because of
Zep 2:13 Nineveh, a **d** wasteland, parched like a desert.
Zec 7:14 so **d** that no one even traveled through it.
Mt 14:15 disciples came to him and said, "This is a **d** place,
23:38 now look, your house is left to you, empty and **d**.
Mk 6:35 disciples came to him and said, "This is a **d** place,
Ac 1:20 where it says, 'Let his home become **d**, with no

DESOLATED (1) [DESOLATE]

Eze 19: 7 their towns and cities. / Their farms were **d**,

DESOLATION (15) [DESOLATE]

Ps 81:15 cringe before him; / their **d** would last forever.
Isa 10: 3 What will you do when I send **d** upon you from a
51:19 **d** and destruction, famine and war. And who is left
60:18 your land; the **d** and destruction of war will end.
Jer 4:20 roll over the land, until it lies in complete **d**.
7:34 towns of Judah. The land will lie in complete **d**.
18:16 and shake their heads in amazement at its utter **d**.
Eze 6: 6 Wherever you live there will be **d**. I will destroy
23:32 all the world will mock and scorn you in your **d**.
25: 3 mocked Israel in her **d**, and laughed at Judah as she
35:15 You rejoiced at the **d** of Israel's inheritance.
Joel 2: 3 Behind them is nothing but **d**; not one thing
Zep 1:15 terrible distress and anguish, a day of ruin and **d**,
2: 4 too, will be rooted out and left in **d**.
2: 9 a place of stinging nettles, salt pits, and eternal **d**.

DESPAIR (38) [DESPAIRING, DESPAIRS]

Ge 44:13 At this, they tore their clothing in **d**,
Dt 28:65 your eyesight to fail, and your soul to **d**.
2Ki 6:30 When the king heard this, he tore his clothes in **d**.
11:14 she tore her clothes in **d** and shouted, "Treason!
18:37 They tore their clothes in **d**, and they went in to see
22:11 in the Book of the Law, he tore his clothes in **d**.
22:19 You tore your clothing in **d** and wept before me in
2Ch 23:13 she tore her clothes in **d** and shouted, "Treason!
34:19 was written in the law, he tore his clothes in **d**.
34:27 You humbled yourself and tore your clothing in **d**
Est 7: 8 In **d** he fell on the couch where Queen Esther was
Job 11:20 They have no escape. Their hope becomes **d**."
Ps 35:12 me with evil for the good I do. / I am sick with **d**.
40: 2 He lifted me out of the pit of **d**, / out of the mud
69:20 Their insults have broken my heart, / and I am in **d**.
130: 1 From the depths of **d**, O LORD, / I call for your
Ecc 2:20 So I turned in **d** from hard work. It was not the
Isa 8:22 there will be trouble and anguish and dark **d**.
9: 1 that time of darkness and **d** will not go on forever.
36:22 They tore their clothes in **d**, and they went in to see
61: 3 joy instead of mourning, praise instead of **d**.
65:14 You will cry in sorrow and **d**, while my servants
Jer 2:37 In **d**, you will be led into exile with your hands on
9:19 Hear the people of Jerusalem crying in **d**, 'We are
19: 9 and friends. They will be driven to utter **d**.'
25:36 to the leaders of the flock shouting in **d**,
46:12 The earth is filled with your cries of **d**.
49:21 and its cry of **d** will be heard all the way to the Red
50:46 and her cry of **d** will be heard around the world.
La 1:18 look upon my anguish and **d**, for my sons
2:10 They throw dust on their heads in sorrow and **d**.
Eze 7:27 and the prince will stand helpless, weeping in **d**,
12:19 and sip their tiny portions of water in utter **d**,
30: 3 of clouds and gloom, a day of **d** for the nations!
Joel 1:11 **D**, all you farmers! Wail, all you vine growers!
Mic 1:10 roll in the dust to show your anguish and **d**.
2: 4 by singing this song of **d** about your experience:
Eph 3:13 So please don't **d** because of what they are doing

DESPAIRING (1) [DESPAIR]

La 3:57 Yes, you came at my **d** cry and told me, "Do not

DESPAIRS (1) [DESPAIR]

La 1:20 My heart is broken and my soul **d**, for I have

DESPERATE (10) [DESPERATELY, DESPERATION]

2Sa 24:14 "This is a **d** situation!" David replied to Gad.
2Ki 3:26 he led seven hundred of his warriors in a **d** attempt
1Ch 21:13 "This is a **d** situation!" David replied to Gad.
Ps 88:15 I stand helpless and **d** before your terrors.
Isa 15: 7 The **d** refugees take only the possessions they can
Jer 2:23 You are like a restless female camel, **d** for a male!
10:19 My wound is **d**, and my grief is great. My sickness
14: 3 confused and **d**, covering their heads in grief.
Jnh 1: 5 the **d** sailors shouted to their gods for help
Lk 23: 5 Then they became **d**. "But he is causing riots

DESPERATELY (5) [DESPERATE]

Ge 34:19 in acting on this request, for he wanted Dinah **d**.
1Sa 4:10 So the Philistines fought **d**, and Israel was defeated
2Sa 13: 1 her half brother, fell **d** in love with her.
Jer 17: 9 "The human heart is most deceitful and **d** wicked.
22:25 seek to kill you, of whom you are so **d** afraid—

DESPERATION (2) [DESPERATE]

Job 6:26 are convincing when you disregard my cry of **d**?
Mk 5:23 "She is about to die," he said in **d**. "Please come

DESPICABLE (5)

Jer 23:11 I have seen their **d** acts right here in my own
Da 11:21 "The next to come to power will be a **d** man who
Na 1:14 because you are **d** and don't deserve to live!"
Lk 15: 2 that he was associating with such **d** people—
Tit 1:16 They are **d** and disobedient, worthless for doing

DESPISE (46) [DESPISED, DESPISES, DESPISING]

Ge 43:32 because Egyptians **d** Hebrews and refuse to eat
Lev 26:11 I will live among you, and I will not **d** you.
26:30 piled up beside your lifeless idols, and I will **d** you.
26:44 or **d** them while they are in exile in the land of
Dt 31:20 other gods; they will **d** me and break my covenant.
1Sa 2:30 who honor me, and I will **d** those who **d** me.
2Sa 12:14 the enemies of the LORD great opportunity to **d**
Est 1:17 Women everywhere will begin to **d** their husbands
Job 5:17 Do not **d** the chastening of the Almighty when you
9:21 but it makes no difference to me—I **d** my life.
19:18 Even young children **d** me. When I stand to speak,
30:10 They **d** me and won't come near me, except to spit
36: 5 "God is mighty, yet he does not **d** anyone! He is
Ps 15: 4 Those who **d** persistent sinners, / and honor the
51:17 and repentant heart, O God, / you will not **d**.
69:33 he does not **d** his people who are oppressed.
139:21 hate you? / Shouldn't I **d** those who resist you?
Pr 1: 7 of knowledge. Only fools **d** wisdom and discipline.
13:13 People who **d** advice will find themselves in
14: 2 the LORD; those who take the wrong path **d** him.

14:21 It is sin to **d** one's neighbors; blessed are those
15:20 joy to their father; foolish children **d** their mother.
19: 7 If the relatives of the poor **d** them, how much more
23: 9 breath on fools, for they will **d** the wisest advice.
23:22 and don't **d** your mother's experience when she is
29:27 The godly **d** the wicked; the wicked **d** the godly.
Isa 30:12 "Because you **d** what I tell you and trust instead in
65:12 very eyes—and chose to do what you know I **d**."
66: 4 very eyes—and chose to do what they know I **d**."
Jer 4:30 you no good! Your allies **d** you and will kill you.
23:17 They keep saying to these rebels who **d** my word,
48:27 of thieves that you should **d** her as you do?
La 1: 8 All who once honored her now **d** her, for they have
Eze 22: 8 Inside your walls you **d** my holy things and violate
Am 5:10 How you **d** people who tell the truth!
6: 8 "I **d** the pride and false glory of Israel, and I hate
Zec 4:10 Do not **d** these small beginnings, for the LORD
Mt 6:24 the other, or be devoted to one and **d** the other.
18:10 "Beware that you don't **d** a single one of these
Lk 16:13 the other, or be devoted to one and **d** the other.
Jn 12:25 Those who **d** their life in this world will keep it for
1Co 16:11 Don't let anyone **d** him. Send him on his way with
2Co 6: 8 We serve God whether people honor us or **d** us,
2Pe 2:10 their own evil, lustful desires and who **d** authority.

DESPISED (40) [DESPISE]

Ge 28: 8 It was now very clear to Esau that his father **d** the
46:34 for shepherds are **d** in the land of Egypt."
Lev 26:43 for they rejected my regulations and **d** my laws.
Nu 14:31 into the land, and they will enjoy what you have **d**.
16:30 then you will know that these men have **d** the
1Sa 10:27 And they **d** him and refused to bring him gifts.
2Sa 12: 9 have you **d** the word of the LORD and done this
12:10 because you have **d** me by taking Uriah's wife to
2Ki 17:15 with their ancestors, and they **d** all his warnings.
2Ch 36:16 these messengers of God and **d** their words.
Ps 22: 6 a worm and not a man. / I am scorned and **d** by all!
31:11 by all my enemies / and **d** by my neighbors—
119:141 I am insignificant and **d**, / but I don't forget your
129: 7 ignored by the harvester, / **d** by the binder.
Pr 12: 8 a person with good sense, but a warped mind is **d**.
14:20 The poor are **d** even by their neighbors,
28: 9 The prayers of a person who ignores the law are **d**.
Ecc 9:16 those who are wise will be **d** if they are poor.
SS 8: 7 he owned, his offer would be utterly **d**."
Isa 1: 4 They have **d** the Holy One of Israel,
5:24 They have **d** the word of the Holy One of Israel.
41:14 **D** though you are, O Israel, don't be afraid, for I
49: 7 says to the one who is **d** and rejected by a nation,
53: 3 He was **d** and rejected—a man of sorrows,
53: 3 when he went by. He was **d**, and we did not care.
60:14 before you. Those who **d** you will kiss your feet.
60:15 "Though you were once **d** and hated and rebuffed
Jer 49:15 among the nations, Edom. You will be **d** by all.
La 1:11 look," she mourns, "and see how I am **d**.
Eze 16:45 for they **d** their husbands and their children.
17:16 put him in power and whose treaty he **d** and broke.
Ob 1: 2 among the nations, Edom; you will be small and **d**.
Mal 1: 6 You have **d** my name! "But you ask, 'How have we ever **d** your name?'
1: 7 "You have **d** my name by offering defiled
2: 9 "So I have made you **d** and humiliated in the eyes
Lk 10:33 "Then a **d** Samaritan came along, and when he
13:30 Some who are **d** now will be greatly honored then;
13:30 and some who are greatly honored now will be **d**
1Co 1:28 God chose things **d** by the world, things counted as

DESPISES (16) [DESPISE]

Ge 16: 5 this servant of mine is pregnant, and she **d** me,
Dt 27:16 'Cursed is anyone who **d** father or mother.'
2Ki 19:21 **d** you and laughs at you. / The daughter of
Pr 15: 5 Only a fool **d** a parent's discipline; whoever learns
15: 9 The LORD **d** the way of the wicked, but he loves
15:26 The LORD **d** the thoughts of the wicked, but he
16: 5 The LORD **d** pride; be assured that the proud will
16:12 A king **d** wrongdoing, for his rule depends on his
17:15 The LORD **d** those who acquit the guilty
20:10 The LORD **d** double standards of every kind.
20:23 The LORD **d** double standards; he is not pleased
24: 9 schemes of a fool are sinful; everyone **d** a mocker.
30:17 and **d** a mother will be plucked out by ravens of
Isa 37:22 **d** you and laughs at you. / The daughter of
La 2: 7 has rejected his own altar; he **d** his own sanctuary.
Mic 7: 6 For the son **d** his father. The daughter defies her

DESPISING (2) [DESPISE]

Pr 19:16 and keep your life; **d** them leads to death.
Eze 17:19 and **d** the solemn oath he made in my name.

DESPITE (21)

Ge 31:35 So **d** his thorough search, Laban didn't find them.
Lev 26:44 "But **d** all this, I will not utterly reject or despise
Nu 14:44 **d** the fact that neither Moses nor the Ark of the
Jdg 8:35 Gideon), **d** all the good he had done for Israel.
2Sa 23:20 Then, **d** the snow and slippery ground, he caught
2Ki 17:12 **d** the LORD's specific and repeated warnings.
1Ch 11:22 Then, **d** the snow and slippery ground, he caught
Ne 9:26 "But **d** all this, they were disobedient and rebelled
Job 6:10 **D** the pain, I have not denied the words of the Holy
Ps 44:17 All this has happened **d** our loyalty to you.
49:12 They will not last long **d** their riches— / they will
59: 4 **D** my innocence, they prepare to kill me. / Rise up
73: 3 when I saw them prosper **d** their wickedness.
Isa 47: 9 come upon you, **d** all your witchcraft and magic.
Jer 2:37 you trust. You will not succeed **d** their help.
Da 9:25 and strong defenses, **d** the perilous times.
Lk 5:15 Yet **d** Jesus' instructions, the report of his power
Jn 12:37 But **d** all the miraculous signs he had done, most of
Ac 3:13 before Pilate, **d** Pilate's decision to release him.
Ro 8:37 No, **d** all these things, overwhelming victory is
2Co 7: 4 you have made me happy **d** all our troubles.

DESPITE [KJV] See also CONTEMPT, INSULTED

DESTINATION (5) [DESTINE]

Nu 4:15 will come and carry these things to the next **d**.
Jdg 11:19 to cross through his land to get to their **d**.
Job 30:23 are sending me to my death—the **d** of all who live.
Jn 6:21 him in, and immediately the boat arrived at their **d**!
1Co 16: 6 then you can send me on my way to the next **d**.

DESTINE (1) [DESTINATION, DESTINED, DESTINY, PREDESTINED]

Isa 65:12 I will '**d**' you to the sword. All of you will bow

DESTINED (11) [DESTINE]

Job 3:23 with no future, those **d** by God to live in distress?
Jer 15: 2 Those who are **d** for death, to death; those who are **d** for war, to war; those who are **d** for famine, to famine; those who are **d** for captivity, to captivity.'
43:11 He will bring death to those **d** for death; he will bring captivity to those **d** for captivity; he will bring the sword against those **d** for the
Heb 9:27 And just as it is **d** that each person dies only once
Rev 13:10 The people who are **d** for prison will be arrested
13:10 Those who are **d** for death will be killed.

DESTINY (9) [DESTINE]

Nu 24:20 the greatest of nations, / but its **d** is destruction!"
Dt 32:35 will arrive, / and their **d** will overtake them.'
Job 23:14 do for me all he has planned. He controls my **d**.
Ps 73:17 O God, / and I thought about the **d** of the wicked.
73:24 me with your counsel, / leading me to a glorious **d**.
Ecc 6:10 So there's no use arguing with God about your **d**.
9: 2 The same **d** ultimately awaits everyone,
Isa 65:11 his Temple and worship the gods of Fate and **D**,
Da 5:23 gives you the breath of life and controls your **d**!

DESTITUTE (3)

Job 20:19 For he oppressed the poor and left them **d**.
Ps 82: 3 uphold the rights of the oppressed and the **d**.
102:17 He will listen to the prayers of the **d**. / He will not

DESTROY (366) [ABADDON, DESTROYED, DESTROYER, DESTROYERS, DESTROYING, DESTROYS, DESTRUCTION, DESTRUCTIVE, DESTRUCTIVENESS, SELF-DESTRUCTIVE]

Ge 4: 7 Sin is waiting to attack and **d** you, and you must
6: 7 Yes, and I will **d** all the animals and birds, too.
6:13 to Noah, "I have decided to **d** all living creatures,
6:17 the earth with a flood that will **d** every living thing.
9:11 flood to kill all living creatures and **d** the earth."
9:15 Never again will there be a flood that will **d** all
18:23 "Will you **d** both innocent and guilty alike?
18:24 will you still **d** it, and not spare it for their sakes?
18:28 Will you **d** the city for lack of five?"
18:28 LORD said, "I will not **d** it if I find forty-five."
18:29 LORD replied, "I will not **d** it if there are forty."
18:30 "I will not **d** it if there are thirty."
18:31 "Then I will not **d** it for the sake of the twenty."
18:32 "Then, for the sake of the ten, I will not **d** it."
19:13 For we will **d** the city completely. The stench of the place has reached the LORD, and he has sent us to **d** it."
19:14 get out of the city! The LORD is going to **d** it."
19:21 grant your request. I will not **d** that little village.
31:29 I could **d** you, but the God of your father appeared
35: 2 "**D** your idols, wash yourselves, and put on clean
41:30 be forgotten and wiped out. Famine will **d** the land.
Ex 9: 3 the LORD will send a deadly plague to **d** your
12:27 and did not **d** us.' " Then all the people bowed
15: 9 will chase them, / catch up with them, and **d** them.
15: 9 will unsheath my sword; / my power will **d** them.'
19:22 LORD must purify themselves, or I will **d** them."
23:23 so you may live there. And I will **d** them.
24:11 Israel's leaders saw God, he did not **d** them.
32:10 so my anger can blaze against them and **d** them all.
33: 3 I would be tempted to **d** you along the way."
33: 5 among you for even a moment, I would **d** you.
Lev 23:30 And I will **d** anyone among you who does any kind
26:22 that will kill your children and **d** your cattle,
26:25 to your cities, I will send a plague to **d** you there,
26:26 I will completely **d** your food supply, so the bread
26:30 I will **d** your pagan shrines and cut down your
26:31 your cities desolate and **d** your places of worship,
Nu 14:12 I will disown them and **d** them with a plague.
16:21 from these people so that I may instantly **d** them!"
16:45 from these people so that I can instantly **d** them!"
21: 2 we will completely **d** all their towns."
24:19 will rise in Jacob / who will **d** the survivors of Ir."
25:17 "Attack the Midianites and **d** them,
33:52 You must **d** all their carved and molten images
Dt 4:31 he will not abandon you or **d** you or forget the
7: 2 you conquer them, you must completely **d** them.
7: 4 LORD will burn against you, and he will **d** you.
7:10 not hesitate to punish and **d** those who hate him.
7:16 "You must **d** all the nations the LORD your God
7:24 able to stand against you, and you will **d** them all.
9: 3 over ahead of you like a devouring fire to **d** them.
9: 8 at Mount Sinai, where he was ready to **d** you.
9:14 Leave me alone so I may **d** them and erase their
9:19 feared for you, for the LORD was ready to **d** you.
9:20 so angry with Aaron that he wanted to **d** him.
9:25 forty days and nights when he was ready to **d** you.
9:26 'O Sovereign LORD, do not **d** your own people.
9:28 If you **d** these people, the Egyptians will say,
10:10 the LORD yielded to my pleas and didn't **d** you.
12: 2 you must **d** all the places where they worship their
13:15 that town and completely **d** all its inhabitants,
19: 1 "The LORD your God will soon **d** the nations
20:16 a special possession, **d** every living thing in them.
20:17 You must completely **d** the Hittites, Amorites,
20:19 a town and the war drags on, do not **d** the trees.
25:19 you are to **d** the Amalekites and erase their
28:39 or eat the grapes, for worms will **d** the vines.
28:42 Swarms of insects will **d** your trees and crops.
31: 3 He will **d** the nations living there, and you will
31: 4 The LORD will **d** the nations living in the land,
33:27 enemy before you; / it is he who cries, '**D** them!'
Jos 7: 3 take more than two or three thousand of us to **d** it.
7:12 I will not remain with you any longer unless you **d**
8: 2 You will **d** them as you destroyed Jericho and its
9:24 this entire land and **d** all the people living in it.
10: 4 "Come and help me **d** Gibeon," he urged them,
24:20 other gods, he will turn against you and **d** you,
24:23 right then," Joshua said, "**d** the idols among you,
Jdg 2: 2 in this land; instead, you were to **d** their altars.
6:16 And you will **d** the Midianites as if you were
6:31 and **d** the one who knocked down his altar!"
21:11 "Completely **d** all the males and every woman
1Sa 14:36 Philistines all night and **d** every last one of them."
15: 3 and completely **d** the entire Amalekite nation—
15:18 and told you, 'Go and completely **d** the sinners,
20:16 saying, "May the LORD **d** all your enemies!"
23:10 planning to come and **d** Keilah because I am here.
24:21 not kill my family and **d** my line of descendants!"
2Sa 5: 8 the city and **d** those 'lame' and 'blind' Jebusites.
11: 1 and the Israelite army to **d** the Ammonites.
20:19 Why do you want to **d** what belongs to the
20:20 "Believe me, I don't want to **d** your city!
21: 5 they replied, "It was Saul who planned to **d** us,
24:16 But as the death angel was preparing to **d**
1Ki 14:14 over Israel who will **d** the family of Jeroboam.
16: 3 So now I will **d** you and your family, just as I
21:22 He is going to **d** your family as he did the family
21:29 happen to his sons; I will **d** all his descendants."
2Ki 1:10 down from heaven and **d** you and your fifty men!"
1:12 down from heaven and **d** you and your fifty men!"
8:19 But the LORD was not willing to **d** Judah, for he
9: 7 You are to **d** the family of Ahab, your master.
9: 9 I will **d** the family of Ahab as I destroyed the
10:19 But Jehu's plan was to **d** all the worshipers of
10:29 however, **d** the gold calves at Bethel and Dan,
10:30 following my instructions to **d** the family of Ahab.
11: 1 she set out to **d** the rest of the royal family.
12: 3 Yet even so, he did not **d** the pagan shrines,
14: 4 Amaziah did not **d** the pagan shrines,
15: 4 But he did not **d** the pagan shrines,
15:35 But he did not **d** the pagan shrines,
17:26 He has sent lions among them to **d** them
18:25 The LORD himself told us, 'Go and **d** it!' "
19:18 But of course the Assyrians could **d** them!
22:16 I will **d** this city and its people, just as I stated in
23:27 "I will **d** Judah just as I have destroyed Israel.
24: 2 and Ammonite raiders against Judah to **d** it,
1Ch 21:15 And God sent an angel to **d** Jerusalem. But just as the angel was preparing to **d** it,
21:17 and my family, but do not **d** your people."
2Ch 12: 7 I will not completely **d** them and will soon give
12:12 was turned aside, and he did not **d** him completely.
16: 7 you missed your chance to **d** the army of the king
20:10 so they went around them and did not **d** them.
20:37 King Ahaziah, the LORD will **d** your work."
21: 7 But the LORD was not willing to **d** David's
22:10 she set out to **d** the rest of Judah's royal family.
25:16 "I know that God has determined to **d** you
25:20 for God was arranging to **d** him for worshiping the
34:24 I will certainly **d** this city and its people.
35:21 with God, who is with me, or he will **d** you."
Ezr 6:12 as the place to honor his name **d** any king
9:14 Surely your anger will **d** us until even this little
Ne 9:31 you did not **d** them completely or abandon them
Est 3: 6 he decided to **d** all the Jews throughout the entire
8: 5 send out a decree reversing Haman's orders to **d**
8: 7 on the gallows because he tried to **d** the Jews.
9: 1 the enemies of the Jews had hoped to **d** them,
9:24 had plotted to crush and **d** them on the day
Job 10: 8 you made me, and yet you completely **d** me.
14:19 floods wash away the soil, so you **d** people's hope.
15:30 and the breath of God will **d** everything they have.
20:22 he will run into trouble, and disasters will **d** him.
30:22 me into the whirlwind and **d** me in the storm.
39:15 crush them or that wild animals might **d** them.
Ps 5: 6 You will **d** those who tell lies. / The LORD
5: 9 Their deepest desire is to **d** others. / Their talk is
21: 9 You will **d** them as in a flaming furnace
27: 2 When evil people come to **d** me, / when my
40:14 May those who try to **d** me / be humiliated and put
55: 9 **D** them, Lord, and confuse their speech, / for I see
57: T into the cave. To be sung to the tune "Do Not **D**!"
58: T of David, to be sung to the tune "Do Not **D**!"

59: T to kill him. To be sung to the tune "Do Not **D**!"
59: 1 Protect me from those who have come to **d** me.
59:13 **D** them in your anger! / Wipe them out
63: 9 But those plotting to **d** me will come to ruin.
69: 4 These enemies who seek to **d** me / are doing
70: 2 May those who try to **d** me / be humiliated and put
73:27 will perish, / for you **d** those who abandon you.
74: 8 Then they thought, "Let's **d** everything!"
74:19 Don't let these wild beasts **d** your doves.
75: T of Asaph, to be sung to the tune "Do Not **D**!"
78:38 and forgave their sins / and didn't **d** them all.
83: 4 We will **d** the very memory of its existence."
89:23 adversaries before him / and **d** those who hate him.
94:23 He will **d** them for their sins. / The LORD our God
will **d** them.
106:23 So he declared he would **d** them. / But Moses,
106:23 begged him to turn from his anger and not **d** them.
106:34 Israel failed to **d** the nations in the land,
109: 4 I love them, but they try to **d** me— / even as I am
137: 7 "**D** it!" they yelled. / "Level it to the ground!"
139:19 O God, if only you would **d** the wicked! / Get out
143:12 and **d** all my foes, / for I am your servant.
Pr 1:32 are fools, and their own complacency will **d** them.
11: 9 Evil words **d** one's friends; wise discernment
11:17 are kind, but you **d** yourself when you are cruel.
18:24 There are "friends" who **d** each other, but a real
30:14 They **d** the needy from the face of the earth.
Ecc 7:16 So don't be too good or too wise! Why **d** yourself?
9:18 of war, but one sinner can **d** much that is good.
Isa 1: 7 plunder your fields and **d** everything they see.
2:16 He will **d** the great trading ships and all the small
3: 2 He will **d** all the nation's leaders—the heroes,
9:14 the LORD will **d** both the head and the tail,
10: 9 We will **d** Calno just as we did Carchemish.
10: 9 And we will **d** Samaria just as we did Damascus.
10:11 and her gods, we will **d** Jerusalem with hers.' "
10:17 Holy One, will be a flaming fire that will **d** them.
10:18 The LORD will completely **d** Assyria's warriors,
10:20 depend on the Assyrians, who would **d** them.
10:22 The LORD has rightly decided to **d** his people.
10:25 and then my anger will rise up to **d** them."
10:33 He will **d** all that vast army of Assyria—officers
11: 4 and **d** them with the breath of his mouth.
11: 9 Nothing will hurt or **d** in all my holy mountain.
13: 2 Wave to them as they march against Babylon to **d**
13: 5 his anger with them and will **d** the whole land.
13: 6 time has arrived—the time for the Almighty to **d**.
14:22 I will **d** his children and his children's children,
14:29 snake will be born, a fiery serpent to **d** you!
14:30 you out with famine. I will **d** the few who remain.
17:14 of those who plunder and **d** the people of God.
23: 9 The LORD Almighty has done it to **d** your pride
24: 1 The LORD is about to **d** the earth and make it a
28:21 a strange, unusual thing: He will **d** his own people!
29: 3 I will build siege towers around it and will **d** it.
30:22 Then you will **d** all your silver idols and gold
34: 2 He will completely **d** them, bringing about their
35: 4 for your God is coming to **d** your enemies.
36:10 The LORD himself told us, 'Go and **d** it!' "
37:19 But of course the Assyrians could **d** them!
49:17 and all who are trying to **d** you will go away.
51: 8 For the moth will **d** them as it destroys clothing.
54: 9 again let a flood cover the earth and **d** its life,
54:16 And I have created the armies that **d**.
65: 8 "But I will not **d** them all," says the LORD.
65: 8 some good grapes there!'), so I will not **d** all Israel.
65:15 for the Sovereign LORD will **d** you and call his
Jer 1:10 and tear them down, to **d** and overthrow them.
4:27 land will be ruined, but I will not **d** it completely.
5: 1 person who is just and honest, I will not **d** the city.
5:10 "Go down the rows of the vineyards and **d** them,
5:17 And they will **d** your fortified cities, which you
6: 1 army is coming from the north to **d** this nation.
6: 2 and delicate daughter—but I will **d** you!
6: 5 So let us attack by night and **d** her palaces!' "
6:23 They are marching in battle formation to **d** you,
7:14 I will now **d** this Temple that was built to honor
11:19 "Let's **d** this man and all his words," they said.
15: 6 "Therefore, I will raise my clenched fists to **d** you.
15: 7 I will **d** my own people, because they refuse to turn
18: 8 its evil ways, I will not **d** it as I had planned.
22: 6 But I will **d** you and leave you deserted, with no
22: 8 'Why did the LORD **d** such a great city?'
25: 9 I will completely **d** you and make you an object of
26: 6 then I will **d** this Temple as I destroyed Shiloh,
30:11 I will completely **d** the nations where I have
scattered you, but I will not **d** you.
30:16 that coming day, all who **d** you will be destroyed,
33: 5 for I have determined to **d** them in my terrible
36:29 because it said the king of Babylon would **d** this
37:10 Even if you were to **d** the entire Babylonian army,
43:11 And when he comes, he will **d** the land of Egypt.
44: 8 You will only **d** yourselves and make yourselves
44:11 I have made up my mind to **d** every one of you!
45: 4 I will **d** this nation that I built. I will uproot what I
46:28 I will **d** the nations to which I have exiled you, but
I will not **d** you.
47: 2 It will **d** the land and everything in it—cities
48: 2 In Heshbon plans have been completed to **d** her.
48:18 for those who **d** Moab will shatter Dibon, too.
49:30 has plotted against you and is preparing to **d** you.
49:35 "I will **d** the archers of Elam—the best of their
49:38 the LORD, "and I will **d** its king and princes.
50:21 Pursue, kill, and completely **d** them, as I have
50:26 of rubble. **D** her completely, and leave nothing!
50:27 Even **d** her cattle—it will be terrible for them,
50:40 I will **d** it just as I destroyed Sodom and Gomorrah
50:42 They are marching in battle formation to **d** you.
51:11 of the Medes to march against Babylon and **d** her.
51:20 you I will shatter nations and **d** many kingdoms.
51:62 you have said that you will **d** Babylon so that
La 1:21 when you will **d** them as you have destroyed me.
2: 8 The LORD was determined to **d** the walls of
Eze 5: 4 then spread from this remnant and **d** all of Israel.
5:16 you with the deadly arrows of famine to **d** you.
6: 3 war upon you, and I will **d** your pagan shrines.
6: 6 I will **d** your pagan shrines, your altars, your idols,
6:12 War will **d** those who are nearby. And anyone who
14:13 and sending a famine to **d** both people and animals
14:17 and I told enemy armies to come and **d** everything.
16:39 these many nations—and they will **d** you.
18:30 Turn from your sins! Don't let them **d** you!
21: 3 and I am about to unsheath my sword to **d** your
21:27 Destruction! I will surely **d** the kingdom.
21:28 it is sharpened to **d**, flashing like lightning!
21:30 No, I will **d** you in your own country, the land of
22:27 They actually **d** people's lives for profit!
22:30 gap in the wall so I wouldn't have to **d** the land,
25: 7 you off from being a nation and **d** you completely.
25:16 and utterly **d** the people who live by the sea.
26: 4 They will **d** the walls of Tyre and tear down its
26: 8 First he will **d** your mainland villages. Then he
26:12 They will **d** your lovely homes and dump your
29: 8 O Egypt, and **d** both people and animals.
29:10 I will utterly **d** the land of Egypt, from Migdol to
30:10 of Babylon, I will **d** the hordes of Egypt.
30:12 I will **d** the land of Egypt and everything in it,
30:14 I will **d** Pathros, Zoan, and Thebes, and they will
32:12 I will **d** you with the swords of mighty warriors—
32:13 I will **d** all your flocks and herds that graze beside
32:15 And when I **d** Egypt and wipe out everything you
33:12 nor will the sins of evil people **d** them if they
33:13 will be remembered. I will **d** them for their sins.
33:28 I will **d** the land and demolish her pride.
34:16 But I will **d** those who are fat and powerful.
35: 3 and I will raise my fist against you to **d** you
38:11 and **d** these people who live in such confidence!
39:23 my back on them and let their enemies **d** them.
43: 3 and then when he came to **d** Jerusalem.
Da 4:23 and saying, 'Cut down the tree and **d** it.
8:24 He will **d** powerful leaders and devastate the holy
8:25 them off guard. Without warning he will **d** them.
9:26 and a ruler will arise whose armies will **d** the city
11:44 and he will set out in great anger to **d** many as he
Hos 2:12 I will **d** her vineyards and orchards, things she
4: 5 false prophets. And I will **d** your mother, Israel.
5:12 I will **d** Israel as a moth consumes wool. I will sap
11: 6 enemies will crash through their gates and **d** them,
11: 8 How can I **d** you like Admah and Zeboiim?
11: 9 I will not completely **d** Israel, for I am God and
not a mer mortal. I am the Holy One living among
you, and I will not come to **d**.
Am 1: 5 I will **d** the ruler in Beth-eden, and the people of
1: 8 the people of Ashdod and **d** the king of Ashkelon.
2: 3 And I will **d** their king and slaughter all their
3:14 for its sins, I will **d** the pagan altars at Bethel.
3:15 And I will **d** the beautiful homes of the wealthy—
5:17 for I will pass through and **d** them all.
9: 3 the great sea serpent after them to bite and **d** them.
9: 8 Yet I have promised that I will never completely **d**
Ob 1: 8 "For on the mountains of Edom I will **d** everyone
Mic 4:13 "Rise up and **d** the nations, O Jerusalem!"
5:10 says the LORD, "I will **d** all your weapons—
5:13 I will **d** all your idols and sacred pillars, so you
5:14 and **d** the cities where your idol temples stand.
Na 1: 9 He will **d** you with one blow; he won't need to
1:14 I will **d** all the idols in the temples of your gods.
Hab 1:13 Should you be silent while the wicked **d** people
Zep 1: 4 and **d** every last trace of their Baal worship.
1: 5 they worship Molech, too. So now I will **d** them!
1: 6 And I will **d** those who used to worship me
2: 5 The LORD will **d** you until not one of you is left.
2:13 He will **d** Assyria and make its great capital,
Hag 2:17 and hail to **d** all the produce of your labor.
Zec 1:21 They will throw them down and **d** them."
9: 6 Thus, I will **d** the pride of the Philistines.
9:10 and I will **d** all the weapons used in battle.
12: 9 For my plan is to **d** all the nations that come
Mt 10:28 only God, who can **d** both soul and body in hell.
22: 7 He sent out his army to **d** the murderers and burn
26:61 'I am able to **d** the Temple of God and rebuild it in
27:40 You can **d** the Temple and build it again in three
Mk 1:24 Jesus of Nazareth? Have you come to **d** us?
3: 4 doing harm? Is this a day to save life or to **d** it?"
14:58 'I will **d** this Temple made with human hands,
15:29 "You can **d** the Temple and rebuild it in three
Lk 4:34 Jesus of Nazareth? Have you come to **d** us?
6: 9 doing harm? Is this a day to save life or to **d** it?"
12:33 be safe—no thief can steal it and no moth can **d** it.
17:27 entered his boat and the flood came to **d** them all.
Jn 2:19 "**D** this temple, and in three days I will raise it
10:10 The thief's purpose is to steal and kill and **d**.
11:48 will come and **d** both our Temple and our nation."
Ac 6:14 say that this Jesus of Nazareth will **d** the Temple
9: 1 He was eager to **d** the Lord's followers, so he went
1Co 1:19 As the Scriptures say, / "I will **d** human wisdom
10:10 for that is why God sent his angel of death to **d**
Gal 1:23 us now preaches the very faith he tried to **d**!"
2Th 2: 8 of his mouth and **d** by the splendor of his coming.
Jas 4:12 among us. He alone has the power to save or to **d**.
2Pe 3: 6 Then he used the water to **d** the world with a
1Jn 3: 8 But the Son of God came to **d** these works of the
Rev 11:18 And you will **d** all who have caused destruction on
14:18 who has power to **d** the world with fire,

DESTROYED (340) [DESTROY]

Ge 7:23 They were all **d**, and only Noah was left alive,
13:10 (This was before the LORD had **d** Sodom
14: 7 and **d** the Amalekites, and also the Amorites living
19:25 He utterly **d** them, along with the other cities
36:35 He was the one who **d** the Midianite army in the
Ex 8:11 All the frogs will be **d**, except those in the river."
9:25 Everything left in the fields was **d**—people,
9:25 animals, and crops alike. Even all the trees were **d**.
9:31 All the flax and barley were **d** because the barley
9:32 But the wheat and the spelt were not **d**
22:20 to any god other than the LORD must be **d**.
Lev 10: 6 and Abihu, whom the LORD has **d** by fire.
13:52 infectious mildew. It must be completely **d** by fire.
Nu 4:18 "Don't let the Kohathite clans be **d** from among
11: 1 raged among them and **d** the outskirts of the camp.
16:26 to them. If you do, you will be **d** for their sins."
21: 3 The Israelites completely **d** them and their towns,
21:28 Ar in Moab; / it **d** the rulers of the Arnon heights.
21:30 We have utterly **d** them, / all the way from
24:22 But the Kenites will be **d** / when Assyria takes you
24:24 and Eber, / but they, too, will be utterly **d**."
26:10 and 250 of their followers were **d** that day by fire
Dt 2:21 But the LORD **d** them so the Ammonites could
2:22 for he **d** the Horites so they could settle there in
2:23 Caphtorites from Crete invaded and **d** the Avvites,
2:34 all his towns and completely **d** everyone—
3: 6 We completely **d** the kingdom of Bashan, just as
we had **d** King Sihon of Heshbon.
3: 6 We **d** all the people in every town we conquered—
4: 3 where the LORD your God **d** everyone who had
4:26 there only a short time; then you will be utterly **d**.
4:46 He and his people had been **d** by Moses
7:23 them into complete confusion until they are **d**.
8:19 and bowing down to them, you will certainly be **d**.
8:20 Just as the LORD has **d** other nations in your
8:20 you also will be **d** for not obeying the LORD
9:28 "The LORD **d** them because he wasn't able to
9:28 might say, "He **d** them because he hated them;
28:20 until at last you are completely **d** for doing evil
28:24 and it will pour down from the sky until you are **d**.
28:45 will pursue and overtake you until you are **d**.
28:48 They will oppress you harshly until you are **d**.
28:61 mentioned in this Book of the Law, until you are **d**.
29:23 and Zeboiim, which the LORD **d** in his anger.
30:18 then I warn you now that you will certainly be **d**.
31: 4 just as he **d** Sihon and Og, the kings of the
31:17 hiding my face from them, and they will be **d**.
Jos 2:10 the Jordan River, whose people you completely **d**.
6:17 and everything in it must be completely **d** as an
6:18 or you yourselves will be completely **d**, and you
6:21 They completely **d** everything in it—men
8: 2 You will destroy them as you **d** Jericho and its
8:26 everyone who had lived in Ai was completely **d**.
8:27 the cattle and the treasures of the city were not **d**,
10: 1 and completely **d** Ai and killed its king,
10: 1 just as he had **d** the city of Jericho and killed its
10:11 the LORD **d** them with a terrible hailstorm that
10:28 That same day Joshua completely **d** the city of
10:33 But Joshua's men killed him and **d** his entire army.
10:35 at Lachish, they completely **d** everyone in the city.
10:37 at Eglon, they completely **d** the entire population.
10:39 They completely **d** Debir just as they had **d** Libnah
10:40 He completely **d** everyone in the land, leaving no
11:11 The Israelites completely **d** every living thing in
11:20 So they were completely and mercilessly **d**,
11:21 this period, Joshua **d** all the descendants of Anak,
11:21 He killed them all and completely **d** their towns.
12: 6 and the Israelites had **d** the people of King Sihon
12:24 In all, thirty-one kings and their cities were **d**.
22:31 you have rescued Israel from being **d** by the
Jdg 1:17 living in Zephath, and they completely **d** the town.
4:24 against King Jabin, until they finally **d** him.
15: 5 He also **d** their grapevines and olive trees.
21:22 enough wives for them when we **d** Jabesh-gilead.
1Sa 4: 8 They are the same gods who **d** the Egyptians with
5: 7 We will all be **d** along with our god Dagon."
7: 4 So the Israelites **d** their images of Baal
12:25 you continue to sin, you and your king will be **d**."
13: 4 that the Philistine garrison at Geba had been **d**,
15: 8 Amalekite king, but completely **d** everyone else.
15: 9 They **d** only what was worthless or of poor quality.
15:15 LORD your God. We have **d** everything else."
15:20 I brought back King Agag, but I **d** everyone else.
2Sa 7: 9 you have gone, and I have **d** all your enemies.
8: 3 David also **d** the forces of Hadadezer son of
8: 9 When King Toi of Hamath heard that David had **d**
8:13 After his return he **d** eighteen thousand Edomites
22:38 "I chased my enemies and **d** them; / I did not stop
22:41 them turn and run; / I have **d** all who hated me.
1Ki 9:21 of the nations that Israel had not completely **d**.
16: 3 just as I **d** the descendants of Jeroboam son of
16: 7 because Baasha had **d** the family of Jeroboam.
16:11 male child. He even **d** distant relatives and friends.
16:12 So Zimri **d** the dynasty of Baasha as the LORD
20:21 However, the other horses and chariots were **d**,
20:42 Because you have spared the man I said must be **d**,
2Ki 1:14 See how the fire from heaven has **d** the first two
3:13 us three kings here to be **d** by the king of Moab!"
3:25 They **d** the cities, covered their good land with
9: 9 I will destroy the family of Ahab as I **d** the families
10:26 sacred pillar used in the worship of Baal and **d** it.
10:28 Jehu **d** every trace of Baal worship from Israel.
13:19 have beaten Aram until they were entirely **d**.
13:23 to the people of Israel, and they were not totally **d**.
13:23 And to this day he still has not completely **d** them

14:10 You have indeed **d** Edom and are very proud about
15:16 At that time Menahem **d** the town of Tappuah
17:20 them over to their attackers until they were **d**.
19:12 The former kings of Assyria **d** them all!
19:17 that the kings of Assyria have **d** all these nations,
21: 3 the pagan shrines his father, Hezekiah, had **d**.
21: 9 LORD had **d** when the Israelites entered the land.
23: 8 He **d** the shrines at the entrance to the gate of
23:12 The king **d** the altars that Manasseh had built in the
23:27 "I will destroy Judah just as I have **d** Israel.
25: 9 He **d** all the important buildings in the city.
1Ch 1:46 He was the one who **d** the Midianite army in the
4:41 and completely **d** the homes of the descendants of
4:43 They **d** the few Amalekites who had survived,
5:25 worshiped the gods of the nations that God had **d**.
17: 8 you have gone, and I have **d** all your enemies.
18: 3 Then David **d** the forces of King Hadadezer of
18: 9 When King Toi of Hamath heard that David had **d**
18:12 Abishai son of Zeruiah **d** eighteen thousand
20: 1 they laid siege to the city of Rabbah and **d** it.
2Ch 8: 8 of the nations that Israel had not completely **d**.
14:13 They were **d** by the LORD and his army,
17: 6 down the pagan shrines and **d** the Asherah poles.
32:12 is the very person who **d** all the LORD's shrines
32:21 And the LORD sent an angel who **d** the Assyrian
33: 3 rebuilt the pagan shrines his father Hezekiah had **d**.
33: 9 LORD had **d** when the Israelites entered the land.
34: 7 He **d** the pagan altars and the Asherah poles,
36:19 the palaces, and completely **d** everything of value.
Ezr 4:15 it was **d** because of its long history of sedition
5:12 who **d** this Temple and exiled the people to
Est 3: 9 please Your Majesty, issue a decree that they be **d**,
8: 6 see my people and my family slaughtered and **d**?"
Job 4: 7 When has the upright person been **d**?
4:10 fierce young lions, they will all be broken and **d**.
8:22 with shame, and the tent of the wicked will be **d**."
19:10 every side, and I am finished. He has **d** my hope.
22:19 the righteous will be happy to see the wicked **d**,
22:20 They will say, 'Surely our enemies have been **d**.
36:20 cover of night, for that is when people will be **d**.
Ps 2:12 and you will be **d** in the midst of your pursuits—
9: 3 in retreat; / they are overthrown and **d** before you.
9: 5 You have rebuked the nations and **d** the wicked;
10:15 evil people! / Go after them until the last one is **d**!
18:40 them turn and run; / I have **d** all who hated me.
37: 9 For the wicked will be **d**, / but those who trust in
37:34 giving you the land. / You will see the wicked **d**.
37:38 But the wicked will be **d**; / they have no future.
46: 5 God himself lives in that city; it cannot be **d**.
73:19 In an instant they are **d**, / swept away by terrors.
74: 3 the city; / see how the enemy has **d** your sanctuary.
78:47 He **d** their grapevines with hail / and shattered their
83:10 They were **d** at Endor, / and their decaying corpses
106:43 against him, / and they were finally **d** by their sin.
118:10 I **d** them all in the name of the LORD.
118:11 but I **d** them all in the name of the LORD.
118:12 But I **d** them all in the name of the LORD.
135: 8 He **d** the firstborn in each Egyptian home,
137: 8 O Babylon, you will be **d**. / Happy is the one who
140: 9 Let my enemies be **d** / by the very evil they have
Pr 2:22 from the land, and the treacherous will be **d**.
6:15 But they will be **d** suddenly, broken beyond all
10:21 but fools are **d** by their lack of common sense.
11: 3 treacherous people are **d** by their dishonesty.
13: 6 while the evil are **d** by their wickedness.
19: 9 will not go unpunished, and a liar will be **d**.
28:18 from harm, but those who are crooked will be **d**.
Isa 1:20 refusing to listen, you will be **d** by your enemies.
1:28 But all sinners will be completely **d**, for they
2:18 Idols will be utterly abolished and **d**.
5: 5 I will tear down its fences / and let it be **d**.
6:11 And he replied, "Until their cities are **d**, with no
7: 8 years it will be crushed and completely **d**.
9: 4 just as he did when he **d** the army of Midian with
10:13 **d** their kings, and carried off their treasures.
10:18 vast army is like a glorious forest, yet it will be **d**.
13: 9 The land will be **d** and all the sinners with it.
13:19 like Sodom and Gomorrah when God **d** them.
14: 4 You will say, "The mighty man has been **d**.
14:12 to the earth, you who **d** the nations of the world.
14:17 Is this the one who **d** the world and made it into a
14:20 for you have **d** your nation and slaughtered your
14:31 are doomed! Melt in fear, for everyone will be **d**.
15: 1 In one night your cities of Ar and Kir will be **d**.
16: 9 But now the enemy has completely **d** that vine.
16: 9 their summer fruits and harvests have all been **d**.
17: 3 The fortified cities of Israel will also be **d**,
21: 2 I see you plundered and **d**. Go ahead, you Elamites
22: 4 Let me cry for my people as I watch them being **d**.
23:14 O ships of Tarshish, for your home port is **d**!
24: 6 and its people. They are left desolate, **d** by fire.
26:14 You attacked them and **d** them, / and they are long
31: 8 "The Assyrians will be **d**, but not by the swords of
32:19 Even though the forest will be **d** and the city torn
33: 1 who have **d** everything around you but have never
33: 1 to them. Now you, too, will be betrayed and **d**!
33: 9 the land of Israel is in trouble. Lebanon has been **d**.
34: 5 fall upon Edom, the nation I have completely **d**.
37:12 The former kings of Assyria **d** them all!
37:18 that the kings of Assyria have **d** all these nations,
42:25 poured out such fury on them and **d** them in battle.
50: 9 All my enemies will be **d** like old clothes that have
60:10 For though I have **d** you in my anger, I will have
60:12 the nations that refuse to be your allies will be **d**.
61: 4 the ancient ruins, repairing cities long ago **d**.
63:18 the holy place, and now our enemies have **d** it.
64:10 Your holy cities are **d**; even Jerusalem is a desolate
64:11 burned down, and all the things of beauty are **d**.
65:25 no one will be hurt or **d** on my holy mountain.
Jer 2:15 The land has been **d**, and the cities are now in
2:16 have utterly **d** Israel's glory and power.
4:20 Suddenly, every tent is **d**; in a moment,
7:14 So just as I **d** Shiloh, I will now destroy this
9:16 with the sword until I have **d** them completely."
10:15 The time is coming when they will all be **d**.
10:22 The towns of Judah will be **d** and will become a
11:17 who planted this olive tree, have ordered it **d**.
12:17 who refuses to obey me will be uprooted and **d**.
13:22 you have been raped and **d** by invading armies.
18: 7 or kingdom is to be uprooted, torn down, and **d**,
20:16 Let him be **d** like the cities of old that the LORD
22:20 See, they are all **d**. Not one is left to help you.
23: 1 for they have **d** and scattered the very ones they
26: 6 then I will destroy this Temple as I **d** Shiloh,
26: 9 name that this Temple will be **d** like Shiloh?
26: 9 do you mean, saying that Jerusalem will be **d**?"
27:17 you will live. Why should this whole city be **d**?
30:16 in that coming day, all who destroy you will be **d**,
31:28 I overthrew it, **d** it, and brought disaster upon it.
31:40 The city will never again be captured or **d**."
34:17 I will set you free to be **d** by war, famine,
34:22 I will see to it that all the towns of Judah are **d**
46:19 The city of Memphis will be **d**, without a single
47: 4 "The time has come for the Philistines to be **d**,
47: 7 and the people living along the sea must be **d**."
48: 4 for all Moab is being **d**. Her little ones will cry out.
48: 8 "All the towns will be **d**, both on the plateaus
48:15 But now Moab and her towns will be **d**. Her most
48:20 the banks of the Arnon River: Moab has been **d**!'
48:46 The people of the god Chemosh are **d**! Your sons
49: 3 "Cry out, O Heshbon, for the town of Ai is **d**.
49:10 its brothers, and its neighbors—all will be **d**—
49:37 with the sword until I have **d** them completely.
50:28 taken vengeance against those who **d** his Temple.
50:40 I will destroy it just as I **d** Sodom and Gomorrah
51: 3 Young and old alike will be completely **d**.
51:18 The time is coming when they will all be **d**.
51:52 the time is coming when Babylon's idols will be **d**.
51:58 worked in vain, for their work will be **d** by fire!"
52:13 He **d** all the important buildings in the city.
La 1:21 when you will destroy them as you have **d** me.
2: 2 Without mercy the Lord has **d** every home in
2: 5 He has **d** her forts and palaces. He has brought
2: 9 All their locks and bars are **d**, for he has smashed
2:16 grind their teeth and say, "We have **d** her at last!
2:17 He has **d** Jerusalem without mercy and caused her
Eze 12:20 The cities will be **d** and the farmland deserted.
19: 7 and **d** their towns and cities. / Their farms were
desolated, / and their crops were **d**.
19:12 and tore off its branches. / Its stem was **d** by fire.
20:14 out of Egypt wouldn't be able to claim I **d** them
23:31 I will punish you with the same terrors that **d** her.
26: 2 Because she has been **d**, I will become wealthy!'
26: 6 and its mainland villages will be **d** by the sword.
26:17 once ruler of the sea, / how you have been **d**!
29:20 because he was working for me when he **d** Tyre.
30: 4 will be carried away and their foundations **d**.
30: 5 with all their other allies, will be **d** in that war.
30: 8 when I have set Egypt on fire and **d** all their allies.
31:11 I handed it over to a mighty nation that **d** it as its
31:17 Its allies, too, were all **d** and had passed away.
32:12 the pride of Egypt, and all its hordes will be **d**.
34:22 my flock, and they will no longer be abused and **d**.
35:12 For you said, 'They have been **d**; they have been
36: 4 and long-deserted cities that have been **d**
Da 2:44 heaven will set up a kingdom that will never be **d**;
6:26 will endure forever. / His kingdom will never be **d**,
7:11 fourth beast was killed and its body was **d** by fire.
7:14 it will never end. His kingdom will never be **d**.
7:20 came up afterward and **d** three of the other horns.
7:26 all his power will be taken away and completely **d**.
Hos 4: 6 My people are being **d** because they don't know
4:14 You will be **d**, for you refuse to understand.
10:14 just as they did when Shalman **d** Beth-arbel.
10:15 the king of Israel will be completely **d**.
13: 9 "You are about to be **d**, O Israel, though I am your
Joel 1: 7 They have **d** my grapevines and fig trees,
Am 1: 4 and the fortresses of King Ben-hadad will be **d**.
1: 7 the walls of Gaza, and all its fortresses will be **d**.
1:10 the walls of Tyre, and all its fortresses will be **d**."
1:12 on Teman, and the fortresses of Bozrah will be **d**."
1:14 the walls of Rabbah, and all its fortresses will be **d**.
2: 2 of Moab, and all the fortresses in Kerioth will be **d**.
2: 5 and all the fortresses of Jerusalem will be **d**."
2: 9 I **d** the Amorites before my people arrived in the
2: 9 as oaks, but I **d** their fruit and dug out their roots.
4:11 "I **d** some of your cities, as I **d** Sodom and
Gomorrah.
6: 2 better than they were, and look at how they were **d**.
7: 9 your ancestors and the temples of Israel will be **d**,
Ob 1:10 Now you will be **d** completely and filled with
Jnh 3: 4 "Forty days from now Nineveh will be **d**!"
Na 1: 5 melt away; the earth trembles, and its people are **d**.
1:12 have many allies, they will be **d** and disappear.
1:15 your land again. They have been completely **d**!
Hab 3:14 you **d** those who rushed out like a whirlwind,
Zep 2: 9 and Ammon will be **d** as completely as Sodom
Zec 5: 4 will remain in that house until it is completely **d**—
11: 3 for their thickets in the Jordan Valley have been **d**.
14:11 safe at last, never again to be cursed and **d**.
Mal 3: 6 descendants of Jacob are not already completely **d**.
Mt 23:29 the graves of the godly people your ancestors **d**.
24:22 is shortened, the entire human race will be **d**.
Mk 13:20 time of calamity, the entire human race will be **d**.
Lk 17:29 sulfur rained down from heaven and **d** them all.
Jn 11:50 Why should the whole nation be **d**? Let this one
Ac 3:23 will be cut off from God's people and utterly **d**.'
13:19 Then he **d** seven nations in Canaan and gave their
Ro 8: 3 God **d** sin's control over us by giving his Son as a
1Co 5: 5 so that his sinful nature will be **d** and he himself
8:11 a weak Christian, for whom Christ died, will be **d**.
10: 5 most of them, and he **d** them in the wilderness.
15:26 And the last enemy to be **d** is death.
2Co 10: 8 be put to shame by having my work among you **d**.
Php 1:28 will be a sign to them that they are going to be **d**,
Col 2:14 He took it and **d** it by nailing it to Christ's cross.
Heb 7:16 of Levi, but by the power of a life that cannot be **d**.
12:28 Since we are receiving a kingdom that cannot be **d**,
2Pe 2: 5 Then God **d** the whole world of ungodly people
2:12 so little about, and they will be **d** along with them.
Jude 1: 5 he later **d** every one of those who did not remain
1: 7 Those cities were **d** by fire and are a warning of
Rev 8: 9 And one-third of all the ships on the sea were **d**.
11:13 was a terrible earthquake that **d** a tenth of the city.

DESTROYER (8) [DESTROY]

Ex 12:23 He will not permit the **D** to enter and strike down
Job 15:21 even on good days they fear the attack of the **d**.
Jer 4: 7 A lion stalks from its den, a **d** of nations. And it is
15: 8 At noontime I will bring a **d** against the mothers of
48:32 as the Dead Sea, but the **d** has stripped you bare!
51: 1 "I will stir up a **d** against Babylon and the people
51:25 "Look, O mighty mountain, **d** of the earth! I am
Rev 9:11 is *Abaddon,* and in Greek, *Apollyon*—the **D**.

DESTROYERS (1) [DESTROY]

Jer 15: 3 "I will send four kinds of **d** against them,"

DESTROYING (40) [DESTROY]

Ge 8:21 **d** all living things, even though people's thoughts
18:25 do such a thing, **d** the innocent with the guilty.
Ex 22: 6 person's field, **d** the sheaves or the standing grain,
Nu 25:11 So I have stopped **d** all Israel as I had intended to
32:15 you will be responsible for **d** this entire nation!"
Dt 28:63 the LORD will find pleasure in **d** you,
Jos 11:12 and their people, completely **d** them, just as Moses,
Jdg 6: 4 in the land and **d** crops as far away as Gaza.
6:30 "He must die for **d** the altar of Baal and for cutting
2Sa 20:19 and faithful in Israel. But you are **d** a loyal city.
2Ki 3:24 into the land of Moab, **d** everything as they went.
2Ch 34: 3 and Jerusalem, **d** all the pagan shrines,
Job 34:25 and in the night he overturns them, **d** them.
Ps 64: 8 own words will be turned against them, **d** them.
78:49 He dispatched against them / a band of **d** angels.
105:35 up everything green in the land, / **d** all the crops.
Isa 48:14 the empire of Babylon, **d** the Babylonian armies.'
Jer 6:26 For suddenly, the **d** armies will be upon you!
12:12 **D** armies plunder the land. The sword of the
13:14 or mercy or compassion keep me from **d** them.' "
44: 7 of Israel, asks you: Why are you **d** yourselves?
46: 8 that it will cover the earth like a flood, **d** every foe.
47: 4 Yes, the LORD is **d** the Philistines,
49: 2 says the LORD, "by **d** your city of Rabbah.
51:21 **d** the horse and rider, the chariot and charioteer.
51:48 for out of the north will come **d** armies against
51:55 For the LORD is **d** Babylon. He will silence her.
51:56 **D** armies come against Babylon. Her mighty men
La 3:66 **d** them from beneath the LORD's heavens.
Eze 14: 8 and make a terrible example of them, **d** them.
14:21 beasts, and plague—**d** all her people and animals.
20:17 and held back from **d** them in the wilderness.
Da 8:11 sacrifices offered to him and by **d** his Temple.
8:12 But the army of heaven was restrained from **d** him
11:16 pause in the glorious land of Israel, intent on **d** it.
Joel 2:25 It was I who sent this great **d** army against you.
Jnh 3: 9 on us and hold back his fierce anger from **d** us."
4: 2 you could cancel your plans for **d** these people.
Hag 2:22 royal thrones, **d** the power of foreign kingdoms.
Gal 5:15 one another, watch out! Beware of **d** one another.

DESTROYS (21) [DESTROY]

Dt 12:29 "When the LORD your God **d** the nations
1Sa 20:15 even when the LORD **d** all your enemies."
Ezr 6:12 that violates this command and **d** this Temple.
Job 5: 2 Surely resentment **d** the fool, and jealousy kills the
9:22 I say, 'He **d** both the blameless and the wicked.'
12:14 What he **d** cannot be rebuilt. When he closes in on
12:23 He raises up nations, and he **d** them. He makes
31:12 It is a devastating fire that **d** to hell. It would wipe
Ps 145:20 all those who love him, / but he **d** the wicked.
Pr 6:32 adultery is an utter fool, for he **d** his own soul.
10:29 The LORD protects the upright but **d** the wicked.
15:25 The LORD **d** the house of the proud, but he
18: 9 A lazy person is as bad as someone who **d** things.
21: 7 is just, their violence boomerangs and **d** them.
28: 3 the poor is like a pounding rain that **d** the crops.
29: 4 to his nation, but one who demands bribes **d** it.
Isa 51: 8 For the moth will destroy them as it **d** clothing.
Eze 17:17 siege to Jerusalem again and **d** the lives of many.
Am 5: 9 With blinding speed and power he **d** the strong,
Na 1: 2 all who oppose him and furiously **d** his enemies!
Zep 2:11 The LORD will terrify them as he **d** all the gods

DESTRUCTION (161) [DESTROY]

Ge 19:15 or you will be caught in the **d** of the city."
Lev 26:32 occupy it will be utterly shocked at the **d** they see.
27:29 A person specially set apart by the LORD for **d**
Nu 21:29 Your **d** is certain, O people of Moab! / You are

24:20 was the greatest of nations, / but its destiny is **d**!"
Dt 7:26 then you will be set apart for **d** just like them.
7:26 detest such things, for they are set apart for **d**.
13:17 none of the plunder that has been set apart for **d**.
28:51 olive oil, calves, or lambs, bringing about your **d**.
Jos 6:18 Do not take any of the things set apart for **d**,
7:12 in defeat. For now Israel has been set apart for **d**.
7:12 the things among you that were set apart for **d**.
7:15 The one who has stolen what was set apart for **d**
2Sa 22:5 surrounded me; / the floods of **d** swept over me.
1Ki 13:34 and resulted in the **d** of Jeroboam's kingdom
1Ch 21:12 of famine, three months of **d** by your enemies,
Est 4:7 to pay into the royal treasury for the **d** of the Jews.
Job 5:21 and will have no fear of **d** when it comes.
5:22 You will laugh at **d** and famine; wild animals will
21:20 Let their own eyes see their **d**. Let them drink
26:6 There is no cover for the place of **d**.
28:22 But **D** and Death say, 'We have heard a rumor of
Ps 1:6 the godly, / but the path of the wicked leads to **d**.
18:4 surrounded me; / the floods of **d** swept over me.
35:8 Let them fall to **d** in the pit they dug for me.
46:8 the LORD: / See how he brings **d** upon the world
52:2 All day long you plot **d**. / Your tongue cuts like a
55:23 down to the pit of **d**. / Murderers and liars will die
71:13 Bring disgrace and **d** on those who accuse me.
73:18 and send them sliding over the cliff to **d**.
88:11 In the place of **d**, can they proclaim your
92:7 there is only eternal **d** ahead of them.
Pr 3:25 of disaster or the **d** that comes upon the wicked,
15:11 depths of Death and **D** are known by the LORD.
16:18 Pride goes before **d**, and haughtiness before a fall.
18:12 Haughtiness goes before **d**; humility precedes
27:20 Just as Death and **D** are never satisfied, so human
Ecc 10:16 **D** is certain for the land whose king is a child
Isa 3:9 be for them! They have brought about their own **d**.
3:11 But say to the wicked, "Your **d** is sure. You,
3:12 are leading you down a pretty garden path to **d**.
4:3 who have survived the **d** of Jerusalem, will be a
5:8 **D** is certain for you who buy up property so others
5:11 **D** is certain for you who get up early to begin long
5:18 **D** is certain for those who drag their sins behind
5:20 **D** is certain for those who say that evil is good
5:21 **D** is certain for those who think they are wise
5:22 **D** is certain for those who are heroes when it
6:5 Then I said, "My **d** is sealed, for I am a sinful man
9:16 of the people have led them down the path of **d**.
10:1 **D** is certain for the unjust judges, for those who
10:5 "**D** is certain for Assyria, the whip of my anger.
13:1 this message concerning the **d** of Babylon:
13:22 days are numbered; its time of **d** will soon arrive.
14:23 I will sweep the land with the broom of **d**. I,
16:4 When oppression and **d** have ceased and enemy
18:1 **D** is certain for the land of Ethiopia, which lies at
18:2 are feared far and wide for their conquests and **d**.
18:7 are feared far and wide for their conquests and **d**.
24:18 **D** falls on you from the heavens. The world is
28:1 **D** is certain for the city of Samaria—the pride
28:1 **D** is certain for that city—the pride of a people
29:1 "**D** is certain for Ariel, the City of David.
29:15 **D** is certain for those who try to hide their plans
30:1 "**D** is certain for my rebellious children,"
30:28 He will bridle them and lead them off to their **d**.
30:30 and huge hailstones, bringing their **d**.
31:1 **D** is certain for those who look to Egypt for help,
33:1 **D** is certain for you Assyrians, who have destroyed
33:1 around you but have never felt **d** yourselves.
34:11 For God will bring chaos and **d** to that land.
38:18 their voices in praise. / Those who go down to **d**
43:28 and assigned Israel a future of complete **d**
45:9 "**D** is certain for those who argue with their
48:19 There would have been no need for your **d**."
51:19 desolation and **d**, famine and war. And who is left
54:16 beneath the forge and makes the weapons of **d**.
59:7 Wherever they go, misery and **d** follow them.
60:18 your land; the desolation and **d** of war will end.
66:15 and his swift chariots of **d** roar like a whirlwind.
Jer 4:6 For I am bringing terrible **d** upon you from the
4:12 blast sent by me! Now I will pronounce your **d**!"
4:13 than eagles. How terrible it will be! Our **d** is sure!
4:15 country of Ephraim, your **d** has been announced.
4:20 Waves of **d** roll over the land, until it lies in
6:7 Her streets echo with the sounds of violence and **d**.
8:14 For the LORD our God has decreed our **d** and has
11:15 immoral things? Can their sacrifices avert their **d**?
13:27 and on the hills. Your **d** is sure, Jerusalem!
17:18 but give me peace. Yes, bring double **d** upon them!
19:8 be appalled and will gasp at the **d** they see there.
20:8 in a violent outburst. "Violence and **d**!" I shout.
22:13 And the LORD says, "**D** is certain for Jehoiakim,
23:2 you have deserted them and driven them to **d**.
39:16 send disaster, not prosperity. You will see its **d**,
46:14 for the sword of **d** will devour everyone around
48:1 "**D** is certain for the city of Nebo; it will soon lie
48:46 "O Moab, your **d** is sure! The people of the god
49:17 be appalled and will gasp at the **d** they see there.
49:18 It will be like the **d** of Sodom and Gomorrah
49:23 with fear, for they have heard the news of their **d**.
50:3 and bring such **d** that no one will live in her again.
50:13 be horrified and will gasp at the **d** they see there.
50:22 battle cry be heard in the land, a shout of great **d**.
50:35 "The sword of **d** will strike the Babylonians,"
51:54 the sound of great **d** from the land of the
La 2:8 He made careful plans for their **d**, then he went
3:22 his mercies we have been kept from complete **d**.
3:48 flow from my eyes because of the **d** of my people!
Eze 4:7 Lie there with your arm bared and prophesy her **d**.
6:8 "But I will let a few of my people escape **d**,
7:7 O people of Israel, the day of your **d** is dawning.
7:10 "The day of judgment is here; your **d** awaits!
12:25 I will fulfill my threat of **d** in your own lifetime,
13:3 **D** is certain for the false prophets who are
13:18 **D** is certain for you women who are ensnaring the
13:18 can trap others without bringing **d** on yourselves?
14:16 do no good—it wouldn't save the people from **d**.
16:23 "Your **d** is certain, says the Sovereign LORD.
21:27 **D**! **D**! I will surely destroy the kingdom.
21:31 hand you over to cruel men who are skilled in **d**.
22:4 both murder and idolatry. Your day of **d** has come!
24:6 **D** is certain for Jerusalem, the city of murderers!
24:9 **D** is certain for Jerusalem, the city of murderers!
25:6 and cheered with glee at the **d** of my people,
30:9 come upon them on that day of Egypt's certain **d**.
34:2 **D** is certain for you shepherds who feed yourselves
38:4 put hooks into your jaws to lead you out to your **d**.
Da 8:24 He will cause a shocking amount of **d** and succeed
Hos 8:4 and gold, they have brought about their own **d**.
9:6 Even if you escape **d** from Assyria, you will be
13:1 sinned by worshiping Baal and thus sealed their **d**.
Joel 1:15 the way, the day when **d** comes from the Almighty.
Ob 1:7 will promise you peace, while plotting your **d**.
1:13 You shouldn't have gloated over the **d** of your
Jnh 3:10 and didn't carry out the **d** he had threatened.
Mic 4:11 calling for your blood, eager to gloat over your **d**.
6:9 "The armies of **d** are coming; the LORD is
Na 3:7 Yet no one anywhere will regret your **d**."
3:19 All who hear of your **d** will clap their hands for
Hab 1:3 around me? Wherever I look, I see **d** and violence.
Zep 2:3 will protect you from his anger on that day of **d**.
Zec 7:3 each summer on the anniversary of the Temple's **d**,
Mal 1:5 When you see the **d** for yourselves, you will say,
Lk 21:20 then you will know that the time of its **d** has
Jn 17:12 that not one was lost, except the one headed for **d**,
Ro 3:16 Wherever they go, **d** and misery follow them.
9:22 the objects of his judgment and are fit only for **d**.
1Co 1:18 the cross sounds to those who are on the road to **d**.
Php 3:19 Their future is eternal **d**. Their god is their appetite,
2Th 1:9 They will be punished with everlasting **d**,
2:3 of lawlessness is revealed—the one who brings **d**.
2:10 deception to fool those who are on their way to **d**
1Ti 6:9 harmful desires that plunge them into ruin and **d**.
Jas 3:6 entire course of your life into a blazing flame of **d**,
2Pe 2:3 them long ago, and their **d** is on the way.
2:13 Their **d** is their reward for the harm they have
Jude 1:10 tell them, and they bring about their own **d**.
Rev 11:18 And you will destroy all who have caused **d** on the
17:8 up out of the bottomless pit and go to eternal **d**.

DESTRUCTIVE (3) [DESTROY]

Pr 16:27 hunt for scandal; their words are a **d** blaze.
17:4 listen to wicked talk; liars pay attention to **d** words.
2Pe 2:1 They will cleverly teach their **d** heresies about God

DESTRUCTIVENESS (1) [DESTROY]

Pr 27:4 like a flood, but who can survive the **d** of jealousy?

DETACHMENT (2) [DETACHMENTS]

2Sa 23:14 and a Philistine **d** had occupied the town of
1Ch 11:16 and a Philistine **d** had occupied the town of

DETACHMENTS (1) [DETACHMENT]

1Sa 11:11 Saul arrived, having divided his army into three **d**.

DETAIL (7) [DETAILED, DETAILS]

Dt 5:32 your God, following his instructions in every **d**.
1Ki 6:38 The entire building was completed in every **d** by
2Ki 16:10 to Uriah the priest, along with its design in full **d**.
Ne 8:13 met with Ezra to go over the law in greater **d**.
Ps 37:23 the LORD. / He delights in every **d** of their lives.
Isa 34:16 He will not miss a single **d**. Not one of these birds
Mt 5:18 even the smallest **d** of God's law will remain until

DETAILED (1) [DETAIL]

Ac 21:19 Paul gave a **d** account of the things God had

DETAILS (3) [DETAIL]

Ge 37:5 and promptly reported the **d** to his brothers,
Ecc 10:14 know all about the future and tell everyone the **d**!
Lk 10:41 dear Martha, you are so upset over all these **d**!

DETECT (1)

Mt 7:16 You can **d** them by the way they act, just as you

DETERMINATE [KJV] See PREARRANGED

DETERMINE (14) [DETERMINED, DETERMINES]

Ex 22:8 God will **d** whether or not it was the neighbor who
28:15 make a chestpiece that will be used to **d** God's
28:30 Aaron will always carry the objects used to **d** the
Lev 13:59 This is how the priest will **d** whether these things
14:57 to **d** when something is ceremonially clean
16:8 He is to cast sacred lots to **d** which goat will be
Nu 5:18 in her hands to **d** whether or not her husband's
27:21 who will **d** the LORD's will by means of sacred
Dt 21:2 and judges must **d** which town is nearest the body.
Jos 18:10 LORD to **d** which tribe should have each section.
1Sa 7:3 **D** to obey only the LORD; then he will rescue
Ne 10:34 "We have cast sacred lots to **d** when—at regular
Est 3:7 to **d** the best day and month to take action.
Jer 6:27 of metals, that you may **d** the quality of my people.

DETERMINED (35) [DETERMINE]

Jos 24:21 saying, "No, we are **d** to serve the LORD!"
Jdg 1:27 because the Canaanites were **d** to stay in that
1:35 The Amorites were **d** to stay in Mount Heres,
19:10 But this time the man was **d** to leave. So he took
1Sa 20:1 I offended your father that he is so **d** to kill me?"
20:33 realized that his father was really **d** to kill David.
1Ki 20:40 king replied. "You have **d** your own judgment."
22:23 For the LORD has **d** disaster for you."
1Ch 11:10 with all Israel, they **d** to make David their king,
2Ch 4:18 of bronze were used that its weight could not be **d**.
18:22 For the LORD has **d** disaster for you."
25:16 "I know that God has **d** to destroy you
Ezr 7:10 This was because Ezra had **d** to study and obey the
Ne 11:23 under royal orders, which **d** their daily activities.
Est 9:24 and month **d** by casting lots (the lots were called
Job 28:25 the winds blow and **d** how much rain should fall.
38:5 Do you know how its dimensions were **d** and who
Ps 17:3 nothing amiss, / for I am **d** not to sin in what I say.
119:30 to be faithful; / I have **d** to live by your laws.
119:112 I am **d** to keep your principles, / even forever,
Ecc 7:23 and actions. I said to myself, "I am **d** to be wise."
7:25 **d** to find wisdom and to understand the reason for
7:25 I was **d** to prove to myself that wickedness is
Isa 28:22 has plainly told me that he is **d** to crush you.
50:7 I have set my face like a stone, **d** to do his will.
Jer 5:3 They are **d**, with faces set like stone; they have
32:31 but anger me, so I am **d** to get rid of it.
33:5 for I have **d** to destroy them in my terrible anger.
La 2:8 The LORD was **d** to destroy the walls of
Da 11:36 For what has been **d** will surely take place.
Hos 5:11 my judgment because they are **d** to worship idols.
11:7 For my people are **d** to desert me. They call me the
Am 9:4 I am **d** to bring disaster upon them and not to help
Ac 17:26 should rise and fall, and he **d** their boundaries.
Jude 1:4 The fate of such people was **d** long ago, for they

DETERMINES (5) [DETERMINE]

Pr 16:9 can make our plans, but the LORD **d** our steps.
16:33 throw the dice, but the LORD **d** how they fall.
Da 2:21 He **d** the course of world events; / he removes
Mt 12:34 For whatever is in your heart **d** what you say.
Lk 6:45 Whatever is in your heart **d** what you say.

DETEST (5) [DETESTABLE, DETESTS]

Ex 8:26 The Egyptians would **d** the sacrifices that we offer
Lev 11:10 not have both fins and scales. You are to **d** them,
20:23 because they do these terrible things that I **d** them
Dt 7:26 You must utterly **d** such things, for they are set
23:7 "Do not **d** the Edomites or the Egyptians,

DETESTABLE (52) [DETEST]

Lev 11:13 you must never eat because they are **d** for you:
11:20 "You are to consider **d** all swarming insects that
11:23 But you are to consider **d** all other swarming
11:41 "Consider **d** any animal that scurries along the
11:42 many feet. All such animals are to be considered **d**.
18:22 "Do not practice homosexuality; it is a **d** sin.
18:26 and you must not do any of these **d** things.
18:27 "All these **d** activities are practiced by the people
18:29 Whoever does any of these **d** things will be cut off
18:30 and do not practice any of these **d** activities.
19:29 will be filled with promiscuity and **d** wickedness.
20:13 They have committed a **d** act and are guilty of a
Dt 7:25 a snare to you, for it is **d** to the LORD your God.
7:26 Do not bring any **d** objects into your home, for
12:31 These nations have committed many **d** acts that the
13:14 and can prove that such a **d** act has occurred
17:4 If it is true that this **d** thing has been done in Israel,
18:9 be very careful not to imitate the **d** customs of the
20:18 you their **d** customs in the worship of their gods,
23:18 a woman, for both are **d** to the LORD your God.
24:4 has been defiled. That would be **d** to the LORD.
25:16 and measures are **d** to the LORD your God.
27:15 the work of craftsmen, are **d** to the LORD.'
29:17 You have seen their **d** idols made of wood, stone,
32:16 foreign gods; / they provoked his fury with **d** acts.
1Ki 11:5 and Molech, the **d** god of the Ammonites.
11:7 the **d** god of Moab, and another for Molech, the **d** god of the Ammonites.
14:24 The people imitated the **d** practices of the pagan
2Ki 16:3 He imitated the **d** practices of the pagan nations the
21:2 imitating the **d** practices of the pagan nations
21:11 "King Manasseh of Judah has done many **d** things.
23:13 for Ashtoreth, the **d** goddess of the Sidonians;
23:13 and for Chemosh, the **d** god of the Moabites;
23:13 and for Molech, the **d** god of the Ammonites.
2Ch 28:3 He imitated the **d** practices of the pagan nations
33:2 imitating the **d** practices of the pagan nations
34:33 So Josiah removed all **d** idols from the entire land
Ezr 9:1 They have taken up the **d** practices of the
9:11 by the **d** practices of the people living there.
9:14 and intermarrying with people who do these **d**
Isa 57:8 You have climbed right into bed with these **d** gods.
Jer 4:1 "If you will throw away your **d** idols and go astray
16:18 defiled my land with lifeless images of their **d** gods
Eze 5:9 Because of your **d** idols, I will punish you more
7:9 I will repay you for all your **d** practices. Then you
7:20 gold jewelry and used it to make vile and **d** idols.
11:18 they will remove every trace of their **d** idol
14:5 who have turned from me to worship their **d** idols.
16:36 and because you have worshiped **d** idols, and
20:30 prostituting yourselves by worshiping **d** idols?

37:23 They will stop polluting themselves with their **d**

DETESTS (4) [DETEST]
Dt 17: 1 sheep to the LORD your God, for he **d** such gifts.
22: 5 The LORD your God **d** people who do this.
Ps 5: 6 tell lies. / The LORD **d** murderers and deceivers.
Pr 6:16 things the LORD hates—no, seven things he **d**:

DETOURS (1)
La 3: 9 He has twisted the road before me with many **d**.

DEUEL (5)
Nu 1:14 Gad | Eliasaph son of **D**
2:14[-15] Gad | Eliasaph son of **D** | 45,650
7:42 On the sixth day Eliasaph son of **D**, leader of the
7:47 was the offering brought by Eliasaph son of **D**.
10:20 The tribe of Gad was led by Eliasaph son of **D**.

DEVASTATE (5) [DEVASTATED, DEVASTATING, DEVASTATION, DEVASTATIONS]
Lev 26:32 Yes, I myself will **d** your land. Your enemies who
Eze 14:15 invasion of dangerous wild animals to **d** the land
20:26 so I might **d** them and show them that I alone am
Da 8:24 destroy powerful leaders and **d** the holy people.
Ac 8: 3 Saul was going everywhere to **d** the church.

DEVASTATED (7) [DEVASTATE]
Dt 11: 4 and how he has kept them **d** to this very day!
Job 16: 7 you have ground me down and **d** my family.
Isa 13:19 will be **d** like Sodom and Gomorrah when God
27: 7 punished her enemies? No, for he **d** her enemies,
Jer 50:27 For the time has come for Babylon to be **d**.
Eze 14:16 alone would be saved, but the land would be **d**.
Mal 1: 3 and I rejected Esau and **d** his hill country. I turned

DEVASTATING (2) [DEVASTATE]
Job 31:12 It is a **d** fire that destroys to hell. It would wipe out
Zep 3: 6 out many nations, **d** their fortress walls and towers.

DEVASTATION (3) [DEVASTATE]
Dt 29:22 will see the **d** of the land and the diseases the
1Ch 21:12 the LORD brings **d** throughout the land of Israel.
Ac 9:21 Jesus' followers with such **d** in Jerusalem?"

DEVASTATIONS (1) [DEVASTATE]
Dt 28:22 and mildew. These **d** will pursue you until you die.

DEVELOP (4) [DEVELOPED, DEVELOPING, DEVELOPS]
Pr 4: 5 Learn to be wise, and **d** good judgment.
24:27 **D** your business first before building your house.
Isa 8:10 Call your councils of war, **d** your strategies,
2Pe 1: 9 But those who fail to **d** these virtues are blind or,

DEVELOPED (5) [DEVELOP]
2Ch 16:12 year of his reign, Asa **d** a serious foot disease.
Lk 8:23 A fierce storm **d** that threatened to swamp them,
Ac 19:23 serious trouble **d** in Ephesus concerning the Way.
Gal 4:19 and they will continue until Christ is fully **d** in
Jas 1: 4 So let it grow, for when your endurance is fully **d**,

DEVELOPING (1) [DEVELOP]
Mt 27:24 he wasn't getting anywhere and that a riot was **d**.

DEVELOPS (3) [DEVELOP]
Lev 13: 2 or a shiny patch on their skin that **d** into a
13: 9 "Anyone who **d** a contagious skin disease must go
Ro 5: 4 And endurance **d** strength of character in us,

DEVIATE (2)
Jos 23: 6 the Law of Moses. Do not **d** from them in any way.
2Ch 8:15 Solomon did not **d** in any way from David's

DEVIL (36) [DEVIL'S]
Mt 4: 1 by the Holy Spirit to be tempted there by the **D**.
4: 3 Then the **D** came and said to him, "If you are the
4: 5 Then the **D** took him to Jerusalem, to the highest
4: 8 Next the **D** took him to the peak of a very high
4:11 Then the **D** went away, and angels came and cared
13:39 who planted the weeds among the wheat is the **D**.
25:41 into the eternal fire prepared for the **D** and his
Lk 4: 2 where the **D** tempted him for forty days. He ate
4: 3 Then the **D** said to him, "If you are the Son of
4: 5 Then the **D** took him up and revealed to him all the
4: 6 The **D** told him, "I will give you the glory of these
4: 9 Then the **D** took him to Jerusalem, to the highest
4:13 When the **D** had finished tempting Jesus, he left
8:12 but then the **D** comes and steals it away
Jn 6:70 "I chose the twelve of you, but one is a **d**."
8:44 For you are the children of your father the **D**,
8:48 The people retorted, "You Samaritan **d**! Didn't we
13: 2 and the **D** had already enticed Judas, son of Simon
Ac 10:38 and healing all who were oppressed by the **D**,
13:10 "You son of the **D**, full of every sort of trickery
2Co 6:15 harmony can there be between Christ and the **D**?
Eph 4:27 for anger gives a mighty foothold to the **D**.
6:11 stand firm against all strategies and tricks of the **D**.
1Ti 3: 6 and the **D** will use that pride to make him fall.
Heb 2:14 only by dying could he break the power of the **D**,
Jas 3:15 are earthly, unspiritual, and motivated by the **D**.
4: 7 Resist the **D**, and he will flee from you.
1Pe 5: 8 Watch out for attacks from the **D**, your great
1Jn 3: 8 keep on sinning, it shows they belong to the **D**,
3: 8 Son of God came to destroy these works of the **D**.
3:10 are children of God and who are children of the **D**.
Rev 2:10 The **D** will throw some of you into prison and put
12: 9 the ancient serpent called the **D**, or Satan, the one
12:12 For the **D** has come down to you in great anger,
20: 2 seized the dragon—that old serpent, the **D**, Satan—
20:10 Then the **D**, who betrayed them, was thrown into

DEVIL'S (3) [DEVIL]
2Co 10: 4 to knock down the **D** strongholds.
1Ti 3: 7 so that he will not fall into the **D** trap and be
2Ti 2:26 come to their senses and escape from the **D** trap.

DEVILS [KJV] See DEMONIC, DEMONS

DEVISE (2) [DEVISED]
Ps 83: 3 They **d** crafty schemes against your people,
Eze 38:10 to your mind, and you will **d** a wicked scheme.

DEVISED (1) [DEVISE]
Ps 64: 6 they say, / "We have **d** the perfect plan!"

DEVOTE (3) [DEVOTED, DEVOTION, DEVOUT]
Lev 20: 2 If any among them **d** their children as burnt
2Ch 31: 4 so they could **d** themselves fully to the law of the
Col 4: 2 **D** yourselves to prayer with an alert mind and a

DEVOTED (13) [DEVOTE]
Lev 19:24 In the fourth year the entire crop will be **d** to the
27:28 Anything **d** in this way has been set apart for the
1Ki 18: 3 (Now Obadiah was a **d** follower of the LORD.
2Ki 10:16 with me, and see how **d** I am to the LORD."
Ne 5:16 I **d** myself to working on the wall and refused to
Ps 86: 2 Protect me, for I am **d** to you. / Save me, for I
119:45 for I have **d** myself to your commandments.
Ecc 1:13 I **d** myself to search for understanding and to
Mt 6:24 love the other, or be **d** to one and despise the other.
Lk 16:13 love the other, or be **d** to one and despise the other.
Ac 2:42 and **d** themselves to the apostles' teaching
1Co 7:34 or has never been married can be more **d** to the
1Ti 2:10 For women who claim to be **d** to God should make

DEVOTION (10) [DEVOTE]
1Ch 29: 3 because of my **d** to the Temple of my God,
2Ch 32:32 and his acts of **d** are recorded in *The Vision of the*
35:26 and his acts of **d** done according to the written law
Jer 44:25 wives have said that you will never give up your **d**
Ac 22:12 He was a godly man in his **d** to the law, and he was
1Co 16:16 and others like them who serve with such real **d**.
2Co 11: 3 be led away from your pure and simple **d** to Christ,
Col 2:23 rules may seem wise because they require strong **d**,
1Ti 5:11 physical desires will overpower their **d** to Christ
Tit 2:12 with self-control, right conduct, and **d** to God,

DEVOUR (35) [DEVOURED, DEVOURING, DEVOURS]
Ex 10: 5 They will **d** everything that escaped the hailstorm,
Nu 22: 4 "This mob will **d** everything in sight, like an ox
Dt 28:51 Its armies will **d** your livestock and crops, and you
32:42 drunk with blood, / and my sword will **d** flesh—
Jdg 9:15 come out from me and **d** the cedars of Lebanon.'
9:20 and **d** the people of Shechem and Beth-millo;
9:20 of Shechem and Beth-millo and **d** Abimelech!"
2Ch 7:13 or I might command locusts to **d** your crops,
Job 20:26 A wildfire will **d** his goods, consuming all he has
Ps 21: 9 will consume them in his anger; / fire will **d** them.
57: 4 who greedily **d** human prey— / whose teeth pierce
69:15 deep waters swallow me, / or the pit of death **d** me.
Pr 30:14 They **d** the poor with teeth as sharp as swords
Isa 9:12 With bared fangs, they will **d** Israel. But even
9:21 will feed on Manasseh, and both will **d** Judah.
56: 9 wild animals of the forest! Come and **d** my people!
66:24 For the worms that **d** them will never die,
Jer 8:16 for it is coming to **d** the land and everything in it—
15: 3 to kill, the dogs to drag away, the vultures to **d**,
46:10 The sword will **d** until it is satisfied, yes,
46:14 for the sword of destruction will **d** everyone
48:45 to **d** the entire land with all its rebellious people.
Eze 19: 3 He learned to catch and **d** prey, / and he became a
19: 6 He learned to catch and **d** prey, / and he, too,
22:25 They **d** innocent people, seizing treasures
36:12 You will never again **d** their children.
36:14 But you will never again **d** your people or bereave
Da 7: 5 a voice saying to it, "Get up! **D** many people!"
7:23 It will **d** the whole world, trampling everything in
Hos 5: 7 Now their false religion will **d** them, along with
13: 8 I will tear you apart and **d** you like a hungry lion.
Na 3:15 middle of your preparations, the fire will **d** you;
Zec 11: 9 And those who remain will **d** each other!"
1Pe 5: 8 like a roaring lion, looking for some victim to **d**.
Rev 12: 4 ready to **d** the baby as soon as it was born.

DEVOURED (11) [DEVOUR]
Lev 26:38 and be **d** in the land of your enemies.
Ps 79: 7 For they have **d** your people Israel,
Jer 10:25 For they have utterly **d** your people Israel,
50: 7 All who found them **d** them. Their enemies said,
Eze 19:14 and **d** its fruit. / None of the remaining limbs
Da 7: 7 It **d** and crushed its victims with huge iron teeth
7:19 It **d** and crushed its victims with iron teeth
Am 4: 9 and mildew. Locusts **d** all your fig and olive trees.
Na 3:12 They will be **d** like the ripe figs that fall into the
Zep 1:18 For the whole land will be **d** by the fire of his
3: 8 All the earth will be **d** by the fire of my jealousy.

DEVOURING (10) [DEVOUR]
Ex 24:17 LORD on the mountaintop looked like a **d** fire.
Dt 4:24 The LORD your God is a **d** fire, a jealous God.
9: 3 over ahead of you like a **d** fire to destroy them.
28:55 refuse to give them a share of the flesh he is **d**—
Isa 30:30 It will descend with **d** flames, with cloudbursts,
Am 5: 6 roar through Israel like a fire, **d** you completely.
7: 4 up the depths of the sea and was **d** the entire land.
Ob 1:18 **d** everything and leaving no survivors in Edom.
Na 3:15 consume you like locusts, **d** everything they see.
Gal 5:15 you are always biting and **d** one another,

DEVOURS (8) [DEVOUR]
Ge 49:27 that prowls. / He **d** his enemies in the morning,
Nu 22: 4 devour everything in sight, like an ox **d** grass!"
24: 8 He **d** all the nations that oppose him,
Dt 32:22 depths of the grave. / It **d** the earth and all its crops
Job 18:13 Disease eats their skin; death **d** their limbs.
Ps 50: 3 Fire **d** everything in his way, / and a great storm
80:13 The boar from the forest **d** us, / and the wild
Eze 36:13 saying, 'Israel is a land that **d** her own people!'

DEVOUT (7) [DEVOTE]
Lk 2:25 He was a righteous man and very **d**. He was filled
Ac 10: 2 He was a **d** man who feared the God of Israel,
10: 7 two of his household servants and a **d** soldier,
10:22 He is a **d** man who fears the God of Israel and is
13:16 "and you **d** Gentiles who fear the God of Israel,
13:26 and also all of you **d** Gentiles who fear the God of
Tit 1: 8 and be fair. He must live a **d** and disciplined life.

DEW (31)
Ge 27:28 May God always give you plenty of **d** for healthy
Ex 16:13 the desert all around the camp was wet with **d**.
16:14 When the **d** disappeared later in the morning,
Nu 11: 9 The manna came down on the camp with the **d**
Dt 32: 2 fall on you like rain; / my speech will settle like **d**.
33:28 and wine, / while the heavens drop down **d**.
Jdg 6:37 If the fleece is wet with **d** in the morning
6:39 dry while the ground around it is wet with **d**."
6:40 in the morning, but the ground was covered with **d**.
2Sa 1:21 let there be no **d** or rain upon you or your slopes.
17:12 we can descend on him like the **d** that falls to the
1Ki 17: 1 there will be no **d** or rain during the next few years
Job 29:19 the water, whose branches are refreshed with the **d**.
38:28 the rain have a father? Where does **d** come from?
Ps 110: 3 vigor will be renewed each day like the morning **d**.
133: 3 Harmony is as refreshing as the **d** from Mount
Pr 19:12 a lion's roar, but his favor is like **d** on the grass.
SS 5: 2 My head is soaked with **d**, my hair with the
Isa 18: 4 or as the **d** forms on an autumn morning during the
26:19 sing for joy! / For God's light of life will fall like **d**
Da 4:15 Now let him be drenched with the **d** of heaven,
4:23 Let him be drenched with the **d** of heaven.
4:25 and you will be drenched with the **d** of heaven.
4:33 a cow, and he was drenched with the **d** of heaven.
5:21 a cow, and he was drenched with the **d** of heaven,
Hos 6: 4 morning mist and disappears like **d** in the sunlight.
13: 3 like **d** in the morning sun, like chaff blown by the
14: 5 I will be to Israel like a refreshing **d** from heaven.
Mic 5: 7 They will be like **d** sent by the LORD or like rain
Hag 1:10 That is why the heavens have withheld the **d**
Zec 8:12 produce its crops, and the sky will release the **d**.

DI-ZAHAB (1)
Dt 1: 1 and Tophel, Laban, Hazeroth, and **D** on the other.

DIALECT (1)
Ac 14:11 they shouted in their local **d**, "These men are gods

DIAMETER (1)
1Ki 7:32 unit with the cart. The wheels were 2-1/4 feet in **d**

DIAMOND (1)
Jer 17: 1 inscribed with a **d** point on their stony hearts,

DIAMOND [KJV] See also (WHITE) MOONSTONE

DIANA [KJV] See ARTEMIS

DIBLAIM (1)
Hos 1: 3 the daughter of **D**, and she became pregnant

DIBLATH [KJV] See RIBLAH

DIBON (12) [DIBON-GAD]
Nu 21:30 destroyed them, / all the way from Heshbon to **D**.
32: 3 **D**, Jazer, Nimrah, Heshbon, Elealeh, Sebam,
32:34 The people of Gad built the towns of **D**, Ataroth,
Jos 13: 9 the gorge) to the plain beyond Medeba, as far as **D**.
13:17 on the plain—**D**, Bamoth-baal, Beth-baal-meon,

Ne 11:25 **D** with its villages, and Jekabzeel with its villages.
Isa 15: 2 Your people in **D** will mourn at their temples
15: 9 The stream near **D** runs red with blood, but I am still not finished with **D**!
Jer 48:18 your glory and sit in the dust, you people of **D**,
48:18 for those who destroy Moab will shatter **D**, too.
48:22 and on **D** and Nebo and Beth-diblathaim,

DIBON-GAD (2) [DIBON, GAD]

Nu 33:45 They left Iye-abarim and camped at **D**.
33:46 They left **D** and camped at Almon-diblathaim.

DIBRI (1)

Lev 24:11 She was the daughter of **D** of the tribe of Dan.

DICE (7)

Ps 22:18 among themselves / and throw **d** for my garments.
Pr 16:33 We may throw the **d**, but the LORD determines
Mt 27:35 the soldiers gambled for his clothes by throwing **d**.
Mk 15:24 throwing **d** to decide who would get them.
Lk 23:34 the soldiers gambled for his clothes by throwing **d**.
Jn 19:24 "Let's not tear it but throw **d** to see who gets it."
19:24 among themselves and threw **d** for my robe."

DICTATED (6)

Est 3:12 in the king's secretaries and **d** letters to the princes,
8: 9 As Mordecai **d**, they wrote a decree to the Jews
Jer 36: 4 sent for Baruch son of Neriah, and as Jeremiah **d**,
36:18 "Jeremiah **d** them to me word by word,
36:32 another scroll and **d** again to his secretary Baruch.
45: 1 written down everything Jeremiah had **d** to him.

DID (889) [DO] See Index of Articles, Etc.

DIDN'T (251) [DO, NOT] See Index of Articles, Etc.

DIE (457) [DEAD, DEADLY, DEATH, DEATH'S, DEATH-WOUND, DEATHBLOW, DEATHLY, DEATHS, DIED, DIES, DYING]

Ge 2:17 and evil. If you eat of its fruit, you will surely **d**."
3: 3 we must not eat it or even touch it, or we will **d**."
3: 4 "You won't **d**!" the serpent hissed.
6:17 every living thing. Everything on earth will **d**!
9: 5 Animals that kill people must **d**, and any person
15:15 (But you will **d** in peace, at a ripe old age.)
19:17 Escape to the mountains, or you will **d**."
19:19 would catch up to me there, and I would soon **d**.
20: 7 be sure that you and your entire household will **d**."
21:16 "I don't want to watch the boy **d**," she said,
26:11 "Anyone who harms this man or his wife will **d**!"
27: 4 that belongs to you, my firstborn son, before I **d**."
27:46 I'd rather **d** than see Jacob marry one of them."
30: 1 "Give me children, or I'll **d**!" she exclaimed to
31:32 let the person who has taken them **d**!
33:13 too. If they are driven too hard, they may **d**.
35:18 Rachel was about to **d**, but with her last breath she
37:22 That way he will **d** without our having to touch
37:35 "I will **d** in mourning for my son," he would say,
38:11 do this because he was afraid Shelah would also **d**,
41:36 surely strike the land, and all the people will **d**."
42:22 And now we are going to **d** because we murdered
43: 8 Otherwise we will all **d** of starvation—and not only
44: 9 you find his cup with any one of us, let that one **d**.
44:22 boy cannot leave his father, for his father would **d**.'
44:31 sees that the boy is not with us, our father will **d**.
45:28 Joseph is alive! I will go and see him before I **d**."
46: 4 But you will **d** in Egypt with Joseph at your side."
46:30 Then Jacob said to Joseph, "Now let me **d**, for I
47:15 they said, "but give us bread. Why should we **d**?"
47:19 Why should we **d** before your very eyes? Buy us
48:21 "I am about to **d**, but God will be with you
49:29 Then Jacob told them, "Soon I will **d**. Bury me
50: 5 He said to me, 'I am about to **d**; take my body back
50:24 "Soon I will **d**," Joseph told his brothers,
Ex 5: 3 we will surely **d** by disease or the sword."
7:18 The fish in it will **d**, and the river will stink.
9: 4 Not a single one of Israel's livestock will **d**!' "
9: 6 all the livestock of the Egyptians began to **d**,
9:19 or animal left outside will **d** beneath the hail.' "
10:28 me see you again! The day you do, you will **d**!"
11: 5 All the firstborn sons will **d** in every family in
11: 5 Even the firstborn of the animals will **d**.
12:33 as possible, for they thought, "We will all **d**!"
14:11 "Why did you bring us out here to **d** in the
17: 3 We, our children, and our livestock will all **d**!"
19:12 its boundaries. Those who do will certainly **d**!
19:21 up here to see the LORD, for those who do will **d**.
20:19 God speak directly to us. If he does, we will **d**!"
28:35 LORD's presence. If he wears it, he will not **d**.
28:43 Thus they will not incur guilt and **d**. This law is
30:20 before ministering in these ways, or they will **d**.
31:14 Anyone who desecrates it must **d**; anyone who
35: 2 the LORD. Anyone who works on that day will **d**.
Lev 8:35 If you fail in this, you will **d**. This is what the
10: 6 If you do, you will **d**, and the LORD will be
10: 9 If you do, you will **d**. This is a permanent law for
15:31 so they will not **d** as a result of defiling my
16:13 If he follows these instructions, he will not **d**.
20:11 both the man and the woman must **d**, for they are
20:16 Both must **d**, for they are guilty of a capital
20:20 are guilty of a capital offense and will **d** childless.
22: 9 be subject to punishment and **d** for violating them.
24:16 who blasphemes the LORD's name will surely **d**.
26:38 You will **d** among the foreign nations and be
Nu 4:15 must not touch the sacred objects, or they will **d**.
4:19 and not **d** when they approach the most sacred
4:20 sacred objects for even a moment, or they will **d**."
14: 3 us to this country only to have us **d** in battle?
14:29 You will all **d** here in this wilderness! Because you
14:35 They will all **d** here in this wilderness!"
16:29 If these men **d** a natural death, then the LORD
18: 3 or the altar. If they do, both you and they will **d**.
18:22 come too near, they will be judged guilty and **d**.
18:32 they were common. If you do, you will **d**.' "
20: 4 the LORD's people into this wilderness to **d**,
20:26 his son. Aaron will **d** there and join his ancestors."
21: 5 "Why have you brought us out of Egypt to **d** here
23:10 Let me **d** like the righteous; / let my life end like
26:11 However, the sons of Korah did not **d** that day.
26:65 said of them, "They will all **d** in the wilderness."
27:13 have seen it, you will **d** as Aaron your brother did,
31: 2 After that, you will **d** and join your ancestors."
Dt 4:22 the land, I will **d** here on this side of the river.
5:25 But now, why should we **d**? If the LORD our
5:25 we will certainly **d** and be consumed by this
11:17 Then you will quickly **d** in that good land the
18:16 or see this blazing fire for fear you would **d**.
18:20 or who falsely claims to speak for me must **d**.'
19: 6 The slayer would **d**, even though there was no
20: 6 You might **d** in battle, and someone else would eat
20: 7 You might **d** in the battle, and someone else would
22:24 The man must **d** because he violated another man's
22:25 and he rapes her, then only the man should **d**.
24: 7 him as a slave or sells him, the kidnapper must **d**.
28:22 These devastations will pursue you until you **d**.
31:14 said to Moses, "The time has come for you to **d**.
31:16 "You are about to **d** and join your ancestors.
32:50 Then you must **d** there on the mountain and join
33: 6 "Let the tribe of Reuben live and not **d** out,
Jos 23:14 "Soon I will **d**, going the way of all the earth.
Jdg 5:31 "LORD, may all your enemies **d** as Sisera did!
6:23 "Do not be afraid. You will not **d**."
6:30 "He must **d** for destroying the altar of Baal and for
11:37 friends for two months, because I will **d** a virgin."
13:22 and he said to his wife, "We will **d**, for we have
15:18 Must I now **d** of thirst and fall into the hands of
16:30 "Let me **d** with the Philistines," he prayed.
21: 5 vowing that anyone who refused to come must **d**.
Ru 1:17 I will **d** where you **d** and will be buried there.
1Sa 2:31 All the members of your family will **d** before their
2:33 and grief, and their children will **d** a violent death.
2:34 Hophni and Phinehas, to **d** on the same day!
5:12 Those who didn't **d** were afflicted with tumors;
12:19 to the LORD your God for us, or we will **d**!"
14:39 who rescued Israel that the sinner will surely **d**,
14:44 "Yes, Jonathan," Saul said, "you must **d**!
14:45 "Should Jonathan, who saved Israel today, **d**?
15: 6 the Amalekites live or else you will **d** with them.
20:14 love of the LORD as long as I live. But if I **d**,
22:16 "You will surely **d**, Ahimelech, along with your
26:10 down someday, or he will **d** in battle or of old age.
26:16 by the LORD that you and your men deserve to **d**,
26:20 Must I **d** on foreign soil, far from the presence of
2Sa 1: 9 my misery, for I am in terrible pain and want to **d**.'
1:16 "You **d** self-condemned," David said, "for you
3:33 for Abner: / "Should Abner have died as fools **d**?
7:12 For when you **d**, I will raise up one of your
12: 5 man who would do such a thing deserves to **d**!
12:13 has forgiven you, and you won't **d** for this sin.
12:14 and blaspheme him, so your child will **d**."
14:14 All of us must **d** eventually. Our lives are like
17:16 Otherwise he will **d** and his entire army with
18: 3 we have to turn and run—and even if half of us **d**—
19:21 Abishai son of Zeruiah said, "Shimei should **d**,
19:37 Then let me return again to **d** in my own town,
1Ki 1:52 will not be harmed. But if he does not, he will **d**."
2: 6 what you think best, but don't let him **d** in peace.
2:24 the LORD lives, Adonijah will **d** this very day!"
2:26 You deserve to **d**, but I will not kill you now,
2:30 But Joab answered, "No, I will **d** here."
2:37 day you cross the Kidron Valley, you will surely **d**;
2:42 not to go anywhere else, or you would surely **d**?
13:31 Afterward the prophet said to his sons, "When I **d**,
14:11 vow that the members of your family who **d** in the
14:11 and those who **d** in the field will be eaten by
14:12 and when you enter the city, the child will **d**.
16: 4 Those of your family who **d** in the city will be
16: 4 and those who **d** in the field will be eaten by the
17:12 cook this last meal, and then my son and I will **d**."
17:20 opened her home to me, causing her son to **d**?"
19: 4 a solitary broom tree and prayed that he might **d**.
20:39 you will either **d** or pay a fine of seventy-five
20:42 now you must **d** in his place, and your people will **d** instead of his people."
21:24 The members of your family who **d** in the city will
21:24 and those who **d** in the field will be eaten by
2Ki 1: 4 but you will surely **d**.' " So Elijah went to deliver
1: 6 on which you are lying, but you will surely **d**.' "
1:16 on which you are lying, but you will surely **d**."
7: 3 "Why should we sit here waiting to **d**?"
7:13 than if they stay here and **d** with the rest of us."
8:10 the LORD has shown me that he will actually **d**!"
20: 1 Set your affairs in order, for you are going to **d**.
1Ch 17:11 For when you **d**, I will raise up one of your sons,
Ne 9:19 you did not abandon them to **d** in the wilderness.
Est 4:11 to **d** unless the king holds out his gold scepter.
4:14 some other place, but you and your relatives will **d**.
4:16 in to see the king. If I must **d**, I am willing to **d**."
9:28 nor would the memory of what happened ever **d**
Job 1:21 and I will be stripped of everything when I **d**.
2: 9 to maintain your integrity? Curse God and **d**."
3:11 "Why didn't I **d** at birth as I came from the
3:22 It is a blessed relief when they finally **d**, when they
4:21 Their tent collapses; they **d** in ignorance.
7: 9 and vanishes, those who **d** will not come back.
7:15 I would rather **d** of strangulation than go on
7:21 For soon I will lie down in the dust and **d**.
10:18 mother's womb? Why didn't you let me **d** at birth?
12: 2 And when you **d**, wisdom will **d** with you!
13:19 prove me wrong, I would remain silent until I **d**.
14:10 "But when people **d**, they lose all strength.
14:14 If mortals **d**, can they live again? This thought
27: 5 you are right; until I **d**, I will defend my innocence.
27:14 their children will **d** in war or starve to death.
29:18 'Surely I will **d** surrounded by my family after a
33:24 Do not make him **d**, for I have found a ransom for
34:20 In a moment they **d**. At midnight they all pass
36:12 perish in battle and **d** from lack of understanding.
36:14 They **d** young after wasting their lives in immoral
39:16 not her own. She is unconcerned though they **d**,
Ps 13: 3 my God! / Restore the light to my eyes, or I will **d**.
22:29 Let all mortals—those born to **d**—bow down in his
28: 1 if you are silent, / I might as well give up and **d**.
30: 9 "What will you gain if I **d**, / if I sink down into the
37:22 inherit the land, / but those cursed by him will **d**.
41: 5 "How soon will he **d** and be forgotten?" they ask.
48:14 and ever, / and he will be our guide until we **d**.
49:10 Those who are wise must finally **d**, / just like the
49:12 despite their riches— / they will **d** like the animals.
49:17 For when they **d**, they carry nothing with them.
49:19 But they will **d** like all others before them
49:20 don't understand / that they will **d** like the animals.
55:23 of destruction. / Murderers and liars will **d** young,
63:10 They will **d** by the sword / and become the food of
79:11 your great power by saving those condemned to **d**.
82: 7 You will fall as any prince, / for all must **d**.' "
83:11 Let their mighty nobles **d** as Oreb and Zeeb did.
83:11 Let all their princes **d** like Zebah and Zalmunna,
89:48 No one can live forever; all will **d**. / No one can
102:20 of the prisoners, / to release those condemned to **d**.
103:15 are like grass; / like wildflowers, we bloom and **d**.
104:29 When you take away their breath, they **d**
109:13 May all his offspring **d**. / May his family name be
116:15 are precious to him; / it grieves him when they **d**.
118:17 I will not **d**, but I will live / to tell what the
143: 7 Don't turn away from me, / or I will **d**.
Pr 5:23 He will **d** for lack of self-control; he will be lost
11: 7 When the wicked **d**, their hopes all perish, for they
11:10 they shout for joy when the godless **d**.
14:32 their sins, but the godly have a refuge when they **d**.
15:10 whoever hates correction will **d**.
23:13 your children. They won't **d** if you spank them.
24:11 to death; don't stand back and let them **d**.
30: 7 O God, I beg two favors from you before I **d**.
Ecc 2:15 Both of them **d**. Just as the fool will **d**, so will I.
2:16 For the wise person and the fool both **d**, and in the
3: 2 A time to be born and a time to **d**. / A time to plant
3:19 and animals both breathe the same air, and both **d**.
6: 2 They **d**, and others get it all! This is meaningless—
6: 6 And since he must **d** like everyone else—well,
7: 1 the day you **d** is better than the day you are born.
7: 2 For you are going to **d**, and you should think about
7:15 including the fact that some good people **d** young
7:17 be a fool! Why should you **d** before your time?
9: 5 The living at least know they will **d**, but the dead
Isa 3:25 The men of the city will **d** in battle.
5:13 will starve, and the common people will **d** of thirst.
8: 9 Prepare for battle—and **d**! Yes, **d**!
8:10 prepare your plans of attack—and then **d**!
19: 7 All the crops will dry up, and everything will **d**.
22:13 "What's the difference, for tomorrow we **d**."
22:14 sin will never be forgiven you until the day you **d**.
22:18 There you will **d**, and there your glorious chariots
31: 3 to help. They will all fall down and **d** together.
34: 7 The strongest will **d**—veterans and young men,
38: 1 Set your affairs in order, for you are going to **d**.
41:11 and ashamed. Anyone who opposes you will **d**.
51: 6 The people of the earth will **d** like flies, but my
57: 1 pass away; the godly often **d** before their time.
57: 2 For the godly who **d** will rest in peace.
65:20 "No longer will babies **d** when only a few days
65:20 No longer will adults **d** before they have lived a
65:20 old at one hundred! Only sinners will **d** that young!
66:24 For the worms that devour them will never **d**,
Jer 8: 3 wish to **d** rather than live where I will send them.
8:13 of figs and grapes. Their fruit trees will all **d**.
8:14 people will say, 'Why should we wait here to **d**?
8:14 Come, let's go to the fortified cities to **d** there.
8:17 what you do, they will bite you, and you will **d**."
10:24 Do not correct me in anger, for I would **d**.
11:22 Their young men will **d** in battle, and their little
14:15 but they themselves will **d** by war and famine!
16: 4 They will **d** from terrible diseases. No one will
16: 4 They will **d** from war and famine, and their bodies
16: 6 Both the great and the lowly will **d** in this land.
18:21 Let their old men **d** in a plague, and let their young
18:23 and blot out their sins. Let them **d** before you.
20: 6 There you will **d** and be buried, you and all your
21: 6 upon this city, and both people and animals will **d**.
21: 9 Everyone who stays in Jerusalem will **d** from war,
22:12 He will **d** in a distant land and never again see his
22:26 from this land, and you will **d** in a foreign country.
26:11 and the people. "This man should **d**!" they said.
27:10 you from your land and send you far away to **d**.
27:15 You will all **d**—you and all these prophets, too."

28:16 Therefore, the LORD says you must **d**. Your life
31:30 All people will **d** for their own sins—those who eat
34: 5 but will **d** peacefully among your people.
37:20 house of Jonathan the secretary, for I will **d** there."
38: 2 Everyone who stays in Jerusalem will **d** from war,
38: 4 went to the king and said, "Sir, this man must **d**!
38: 9 He will soon **d** of hunger, for almost all the bread
38:24 "Don't tell anyone you told me this, or you will **d**!
38:26 Jonathan's dungeon, for fear you would **d** there."
42:16 will follow close behind you, and you will **d** there.
42:17 Yes, you will **d** from war, famine, and disease.
42:22 So you can be sure that you will **d** from war,
44:12 All will **d**, from the least to the greatest.
49:26 Her young men will fall in the streets and **d**.
50:30 Her young men will fall in the streets and **d**.
La 2:20 and prophets **d** within the Lord's Temple?
4: 9 are far better off than those who **d** of hunger,
Eze 3:18 fail to deliver the warning, they will **d** in their sins.
3:19 and refuse to repent, they will **d** in their sins.
3:20 and don't listen to my warning, they will **d**.
3:20 of the consequences, then they will **d** in their sins.
5:12 A third of your people will **d** in the city from
6:11 Now they are going to **d** from war and famine
7:15 Those who stay inside will **d** of famine
12:13 though he will never see it, and he will **d** there.
13:19 to listen to lies, you kill those who should not **d**,
16: 5 you were dumped in a field and left to **d**,
17: 9 will cut off its fruit and let its leaves wither and **d**.
17:10 It will **d** in the same good soil where it had grown
17:16 the king of Israel will **d** in Babylon,
18:13 No! He must **d** and must take full blame.
18:17 Such a person will not **d** because of his father's
18:18 But the father will **d** for the many sins he
18:21 is just and right, they will surely live and not **d**.
18:23 that I like to see wicked people **d**?
18:24 will be forgotten, and they will **d** for their sins.
18:26 and start doing sinful things, they will **d** for it.
18:26 Yes, they will **d** because of their sinful deeds.
18:28 to turn from their sins. Such people will not **d**.
18:31 For why should you **d**, O people of Israel?
18:32 I don't want you to **d**, says the Sovereign LORD.
21:12 my people and their leaders—everyone will **d**!
24:16 Suddenly she will **d**. Yet you must not show any
28: 8 and you will **d** there on your island home in the
28:10 You will **d** like an outcast at the hands of
29: 5 and all your fish stranded in the desert to **d**.
30:17 men of Heliopolis and Bubastis will **d** in battle,
32: 4 I will leave you stranded on the land to **d**.
33: 4 to take action—well, it is their own fault if they **d**.
33: 6 They will **d** in their sins, but I will hold the
33: 8 I announce that some wicked people are sure to **d**
33: 8 then they will **d** in their sins, but I will hold you
33: 9 and they don't repent, they will **d** in their sins,
33:11 O people of Israel! Why should you **d**?
33:14 I tell some wicked people that they will surely **d**,
33:15 If they do this, then they will surely live and not **d**.
33:18 when righteous people turn to evil, they will **d**.
33:27 those living in the ruins will **d** by the sword.
33:27 hiding in the forts and caves will **d** of disease.
39: 4 and all your vast hordes will **d** on the mountains.
Da 3:28 and were willing to **d** rather than serve
11:20 but after a very brief reign, he will **d**,
11:33 But for a time many of these teachers will **d** by fire
Hos 2: 3 I will leave her to **d** of thirst, as in a desert or a dry
4:19 They will **d** in shame because they offer sacrifices
7:13 Let them **d**, for they have rebelled against me.
9:11 for your children will **d** at birth or perish in the
Joel 1:17 The seeds **d** in the parched ground, and the grain
2:20 into the parched wastelands, where they will **d**.
Am 6: 9 there are ten men left in one house, they will all **d**.
7:17 and you yourself will **d** in a foreign land.
9:10 But all the sinners will **d** by the sword—all those
Jnh 1:14 they pleaded, "don't make us **d** for this man's sin.
4: 8 on his head until he grew faint and wished to **d**.
4: 9 Jonah retorted, "even angry enough to **d**!"
Hab 3:17 even though the flocks **d** in the fields,
Zep 1: 3 the birds of the air and the fish in the sea will **d**.
1:11 market area, for all who buy and sell there will **d**.
Zec 11: 9 If you **d**, you **d**. If you are killed, you are killed.
13: 3 own father and mother will tell him, 'You must **d**,
13: 8 of the people in the land will be cut off and **d**,
Mt 16:28 here right now will not **d** before you see me,
20:18 of religious law. They will sentence him to **d**.
26:24 For I, the Son of Man, must **d**, as the Scriptures
26:35 Peter insisted. "Not even if I have to **d** with you!
26:66 "Guilty!" they shouted. "He must **d**!"
27: 3 realized that Jesus had been condemned to **d**,
Mk 5:23 "She is about to **d**," he said in desperation.
9: 1 **d** before you see the Kingdom of God arrive in
10:33 They will sentence him to **d** and hand him over to
14:21 For I, the Son of Man, must **d**, as the Scriptures
14:31 Peter insisted. "Not even if I have to **d** with you!
Lk 2:26 would not **d** until he had seen the Lord's Messiah.
2:29 "Lord, now I can **d** in peace! / As you promised
9:27 will not **d** before you see the Kingdom of God."
12:20 said to him, 'You fool! You will **d** this very night.
15:12 of your estate now, instead of waiting until you **d**.'
16:28 so they won't have to come here when they **d**.'
20:36 And they will never **d** again. In these respects they
22:22 Son of Man, must **d** since it is part of God's plan.
22:33 to go to prison with you, and even to **d** with you."
23:24 So Pilate sentenced Jesus to **d** as they demanded.
23:41 We deserve to **d** for our evil deeds, but this man
24:46 and **d** and rise again from the dead on the third
Jn 4:47 with him to heal his son, who was about to **d**.
6:58 will live forever and not **d** as your ancestors did,
8:21 You will search for me and **d** in your sin.
8:24 That is why I said that you will **d** in your sins;
8:24 that I am who I say I am, you will **d** in your sins."
8:51 anyone who obeys my teaching will never **d**!"
8:52 that those who obey your teaching will never **d**!
11:16 "Let's go, too—and **d** with Jesus."
11:25 even though they **d** like everyone else, will live
11:50 be destroyed? Let this one man **d** for the people."
11:51 This prophecy that Jesus should **d** for the entire
12:33 He said this to indicate how he was going to **d**.
12:34 "**D**?" asked the crowd. "We understood from
12:34 Why are you saying the Son of Man will **d**?
13:37 Lord?" he asked. "I am ready to **d** for you."
13:38 Jesus answered, "**D** for me? No, before the rooster
18:14 Jewish leaders, "Better that one should **d** for all."
18:32 Jesus' prediction about the way he would **d**.
19: 7 "By our laws he ought to **d** because he called
21:19 what kind of death he would **d** to glorify God.
21:23 of believers that that disciple wouldn't **d**.
Ac 7:19 to abandon their newborn babies so they would **d**.
13:34 to raise him from the dead, never again to **d**.
13:41 'Look you mockers, / be amazed and **d**! / For I am
21:13 but also to **d** for the sake of the Lord Jesus."
25:11 something worthy of death, I don't refuse to **d**.
27:31 "You will all **d** unless the sailors stay aboard."
Ro 4:25 He was handed over to **d** because of our sins,
5: 7 Now, no one is likely to **d** for a good person,
5: 7 though someone might be willing to **d** for a person
5: 8 Christ to **d** for us while we were still sinners.
6: 9 rose from the dead, and he will never **d** again.
7: 9 had broken the law and was a sinner, doomed to **d**.
8:10 even though your body will **d** because of sin,
14: 7 not our own masters when we live or when we **d**.
14: 8 And when we **d**, we go to be with the Lord. So in
1Co 4: 9 at the end of a victor's parade, condemned to **d**.
9:15 I would rather **d** than lose my distinction of
10: 8 them did, causing 23,000 of them to **d** in one day.
15:32 "Let's feast and get drunk, / for tomorrow we **d**!"
15:42 Our earthly bodies, which **d** and decay, will be
15:42 when they are resurrected, for they will never **d**.
15:51 Not all of us will **d**, but we will all be transformed.
15:52 living will be transformed so that we will never **d**.
15:53 transformed into heavenly bodies that will never **d**.
15:54 into heavenly bodies that will never **d**—
2Co 1: 9 In fact, we expected to **d**. But as a result,
5: 1 when we **d** and leave these bodies—we will have a
5: 4 but it's not that we want to **d** and have no bodies at
7: 3 our hearts forever. We live or **d** together with you.
Gal 2:21 the law, then there was no need for Christ to **d**.
Php 1:20 life will always honor Christ, whether I live or I **d**.
2:17 if I am to **d** for you), I will rejoice, and I want to
1Ti 6: 7 certainly cannot carry anything with us when we **d**.
6:16 He alone can never **d**, and he lives in light
2Ti 2:11 This is a true saying: / If we **d** with him, / we will
Heb 2:14 For only as a human being could he **d**, and only by
7: 8 Jewish priests, tithes are paid to men who will **d**.
9:26 he would have had to **d** again and again,
11:22 was by faith that Joseph, when he was about to **d**,
11:31 It was by faith that Rahab the prostitute did not **d**
11:35 preferring to **d** rather than turn from God and be
12: 2 He was willing to **d** a shameful death on the cross
2Pe 1:14 here on earth are numbered and I am soon to **d**.
Rev 9: 6 They will long to **d**, but death will flee away!
9:20 But the people who did not **d** in these plagues still
11: 5 This is how anyone who tries to harm them must **d**.
11:13 And everyone who did not **d** was terrified and gave
12:11 of their testimony. And they were not afraid to **d**.
13:15 that anyone refusing to worship it must **d**.
14:13 Blessed are those who **d** in the Lord from now on.

DIED (344) [DIE]

Ge 5: 5 He **d** at the age of 930.
5: 8 He **d** at the age of 912.
5:11 He **d** at the age of 905.
5:14 He **d** at the age of 910.
5:17 He **d** at the age of 895.
5:20 He **d** at the age of 962.
5:27 He **d** at the age of 969.
5:31 He **d** at the age of 777.
7:21 All the living things on earth **d**—birds,
7:22 Everything **d** that breathed and lived on dry land.
9:29 He was 950 years old when he **d**.
11:28 he **d** in Ur of the Chaldeans, the place of his birth.
11:32 lived for 205 years and **d** while still at Haran.
23: 2 she **d** at Kiriath-arba (now called Hebron)
25: 6 But before he **d**, he gave gifts to the sons of his
25: 8 and he **d** at a ripe old age, joining his ancestors in
25:17 Ishmael finally **d** at the age of 137 and joined his
35: 8 Soon after this, Rebekah's old nurse, Deborah, **d**.
35:19 So Rachel **d** and was buried on the way to Ephrath
35:29 and he **d** at a ripe old age, joining his ancestors in
36:33 When Bela **d**, Jobab son of Zerah from Bozrah
36:34 When Jobab **d**, Husham from the land of the
36:35 When Husham **d**, Hadad son of Bedad became
36:36 When Hadad **d**, Samlah from the city of Masrekah
36:37 When Samlah **d**, Shaul from the city of Rehoboth
36:38 When Shaul **d**, Baal-hanan son of Acbor became
36:39 When Baal-hanan **d**, Hadad became king and ruled
38: 8 our law requires of the brother of a man who has **d**.
38:12 In the course of time Judah's wife **d**. After the time
46:12 (But Er and Onan had **d** in the land of Canaan.)
47:28 in Egypt, so he was 147 years old when he **d**.
48: 7 from Paddan, Rachel **d** in the land of Canaan.
49:33 he lay back in the bed, breathed his last, and **d**.
50:16 to Joseph: "Before your father **d**, he instructed us
50:22 live in Egypt. Joseph was 110 years old when he **d**.
50:26 So Joseph **d** at the age of 110. They embalmed
Ex 1: 6 In time, Joseph and each of his brothers **d**,
2:23 Years passed, and the king of Egypt **d**.
7:21 The fish in the river **d**, and the water became
8:13 in the houses, the courtyards, and the fields all **d**.
12:30 was not a single house where someone had not **d**.
32:28 and about three thousand people **d** that day.
Lev 10: 2 them up, and they **d** there before the LORD.
16: 1 who **d** when they burned a different kind of fire
17:15 If you eat from the carcass of an animal that **d** a
22: 8 The priests may never eat an animal that has **d** a
Nu 3: 4 and Abihu **d** in the LORD's presence in the
6: 7 if their own father, mother, brother, or sister has **d**.
14: 2 "We wish we had **d** in Egypt, or even here in the
16:39 that had been used by the men who **d** in the fire,
16:49 But 14,700 people **d** in that plague, in addition to
those who had **d** in the incident
19:16 was killed with a sword or who **d** a natural death,
19:18 a person who was killed or who **d** naturally,
20: 1 While they were there, Miriam **d** and was buried.
20: 3 "We wish we had **d** in the LORD's presence with
20:28 Then Aaron **d** there on top of the mountain,
20:29 When the people realized that Aaron had **d**,
21: 6 among them, and many of them were bitten and **d**.
25: 9 but not before 24,000 people had **d**.
26:19 and Onan, who had **d** in the land of Canaan.
26:61 and Abihu **d** when they burned before the LORD
27: 3 "Our father **d** in the wilderness without leaving
27: 3 against the LORD. He **d** because of his own sin.
31: 8 Rekem, Zur, Hur, and Reba—**d** in the battle.
32:13 whole generation that sinned against him had **d**.
33:38 the LORD to go up the mountain, and there he **d**.
33:39 Aaron was 123 years old when he **d** there on
Dt 2:14 enough to fight in battle had **d** in the wilderness.
2:15 hand against them until all of them had finally **d**.
2:16 "When all the men of fighting age had **d**,
10: 6 to Moserah, where Aaron **d** and was buried.
14:21 "Do not eat anything that has **d** a natural death.
32:50 **d** on Mount Hor and joined his ancestors.
34: 5 of the LORD, **d** there in the land of Moab,
34: 7 Moses was 120 years old when he **d**, yet his
Jos 5: 4 arms when they left Egypt had **d** in the wilderness.
5: 6 enough to bear arms when they left Egypt had **d**.
8:22 men of Ai were caught in a trap, and all of them **d**.
22:20 He was not the only one who **d** because of that
24:29 the servant of the LORD, **d** at the age of 110.
24:33 Eleazar son of Aaron also **d**. He was buried in the
Jdg 1: 1 After Joshua **d**, the Israelites asked the LORD,
1: 7 They took him to Jerusalem, and he **d** there.
2: 8 the servant of the LORD, **d** at the age of 110.
2:10 After that generation **d**, another generation grew
2:19 But when the judge **d**, the people returned to their
2:21 nations that Joshua left unconquered when he **d**.
3:11 land for forty years. Then Othniel son of Kenaz **d**.
4:21 his temple and into the ground, and so he **d**.
8:32 Gideon **d** when he was very old, and he was buried
9:49 people who had lived in the tower of Shechem **d**,
9:54 young man stabbed him with his sword, and he **d**.
10: 2 When he **d**, he was buried in Shamir.
10: 3 After Tola **d**, a man from Gilead named Jair
10: 5 When Jair **d**, he was buried in Kamon.
11:39 her father kept his vow, and she **d** a virgin.
12: 7 When he **d**, he was buried in one of the towns of
12:10 When he **d**, he was buried at Bethlehem.
12:12 When he **d**, he was buried at Aijalon in Zebulun.
12:13 After Elon **d**, Abdon son of Hillel, from Pirathon,
12:15 Then he **d** and was buried at Pirathon in Ephraim,
16:30 So he killed more people when he **d** than he had
20:31 About thirty Israelites **d** in the open fields
20:44 Benjamin's greatest warriors **d** in that day's battle.
Ru 1: 3 Elimelech **d** and Naomi was left with her two sons.
1: 5 both Mahlon and Kilion **d**. This left Naomi alone,
1Sa 4:10 was great; thirty thousand Israelite men **d** that day.
4:18 He broke his neck and **d**, for he was old and very
4:20 She **d** in childbirth, but before she passed away the
25: 1 Now Samuel **d**, and all Israel gathered for his
25:38 ten days later, the LORD struck him and he **d**.
28: 3 Meanwhile, Samuel had **d**, and all Israel had
28: 8 "I have to talk to a man who has **d**," he said.
31: 5 he fell on his own sword and **d** beside the king.
31: 6 and his troops all **d** together that same day.
2Sa 1:12 nation of Israel, because so many had **d** that day.
2:16 his sword into the other's side so that all of them **d**.
2:23 his back. He stumbled to the ground and **d** there.
3:33 for Abner: / "Should Abner have **d** as fools die?
10: 1 time after this, King Nahash of the Ammonites **d**,
12:18 Then on the seventh day the baby **d**.
17:23 He **d** there and was buried beside his father.
18: 8 and more men **d** because of the forest than were
18:33 If only I could have **d** instead of you! O Absalom,
19: 6 If Absalom had lived and all of us had **d**,
20: 3 So each of them lived like a widow until she **d**.
20:10 did not need to strike again, and Amasa soon **d**.
21: 9 So all seven of them **d** together at the beginning of
21:12 and Jonathan had **d** in a battle with the Philistines,
24:15 Seventy thousand people **d** throughout the nation.
1Ki 2:10 Then David **d** and was buried in the City of David.
3:19 But her baby **d** during the night when she rolled
11:15 to bury some Israelites who had **d** in battle.
11:40 of Egypt and stayed there until Solomon **d**.
11:43 When Solomon **d**, he was buried in the city of his
14:17 and the child **d** just as she walked through the door
14:20 When Jeroboam **d**, his son Nadab became the next
14:31 When Rehoboam **d**, he was buried among his
15: 8 When Abijam **d**, he was buried in the City of
15:24 When Asa **d**, he was buried with his ancestors in
16: 6 When Baasha **d**, he was buried in Tirzah. Then his
16:18 burned it down over himself and **d** in the flames.

16:28 When Omri **d**, he was buried in Samaria. Then his
16:34 he laid the foundations, his oldest son, Abiram, **d**.
16:34 by setting up the gates, his youngest son, Segub, **d**.
17:17 He grew worse and worse, and finally he **d**.
22:35 floor of his chariot, and as evening arrived he **d**.
22:37 So the king **d**, and his body was taken to Samaria
22:40 When Ahab **d**, he was buried among his ancestors.
22:50 When Jehoshaphat **d**, he was buried with his
2Ki 1:17 So Ahaziah **d**, just as the LORD had promised
4:20 held him on her lap. But around noontime he **d**.
7: 4 But if they kill us, we would have **d** anyway."
8:15 in water, and held it over the king's face until he **d**.
8:24 When Jehoram **d**, he was buried with his ancestors
9:27 able to go on as far as Megiddo, but he **d** there.
10:35 When Jehu **d**, he was buried with his ancestors in
13: 9 When Jehoahaz **d**, he was buried in Samaria with
13:13 When Jehoash **d**, he was buried with his ancestors
13:20 Then Elisha **d** and was buried. Groups of Moabite
13:24 King Hazael of Aram **d**, and his son Ben-hadad
14:16 When Jehoash **d**, he was buried with his ancestors
14:29 When Jeroboam II **d**, he was buried with his
15: 7 When Uzziah **d**, he was buried near his ancestors
15:22 When Menahem **d**, his son Pekahiah became the
15:38 When Jotham **d**, he was buried with his ancestors
16:20 When Ahaz **d**, he was buried with his ancestors in
20:21 When Hezekiah **d**, his son Manasseh became the
21:18 When Manasseh **d**, he was buried in the palace
22:20 disaster against this city until after you have **d**
23:34 was taken to Egypt as a prisoner, where he **d**.
24: 6 When Jehoiakim **d**, his son Jehoiachin became the
1Ch 1:44 When Bela **d**, Jobab son of Zerah from Bozrah
1:45 When Jobab **d**, Husham from the land of the
1:46 When Husham **d**, Hadad son of Bedad became
1:47 When Hadad **d**, Samlah from the city of Masrekah
1:48 When Samlah **d**, Shaul from the city of Rehoboth
1:49 When Shaul **d**, Baal-hanan son of Acbor became
1:50 When Baal-hanan **d**, Hadad became king and ruled
1:51 Then Hadad **d**. The clan leaders of Edom were
2:19 After Azubah **d**, Caleb married Ephrathah,
2:24 Soon after Hezron **d** in the town of
2:30 were Seled and Appaim. Seled **d** without children,
2:32 and Jonathan. Jether **d** without children,
10: 5 that Saul was dead, he fell on his own sword and **d**.
10: 6 So Saul and his three sons **d** there together,
10:13 So Saul **d** because he was unfaithful to the
13:10 the Ark. So Uzzah **d** there in the presence of God.
19: 1 time after this, King Nahash of the Ammonites **d**,
21:14 and seventy thousand people **d** as a result.
23:22 Eleazar **d** with no sons, only daughters.
24: 2 But Nadab and Abihu **d** before their father did,
29:28 He **d** at a ripe old age, having enjoyed long life,
2Ch 9:31 When he **d**, he was buried in the city of his father,
12:16 When Rehoboam **d**, he was buried in the City of
13:20 and finally the LORD struck him down and he **d**.
14: 1 When Abijah **d**, he was buried in the City of
16:13 So he **d** in the forty-first year of his reign.
18:34 Then just as the sun was setting he **d**.
21: 1 When Jehoshaphat **d**, he was buried with his
21:19 caused his bowels to come out, and he **d** in agony.
21:20 No one was sorry when he **d**. He was buried in the
24:22 Zechariah's last words as he **d** were,
24:27 *on the Book of the Kings.* When Joash **d**,
26:21 So King Uzziah had leprosy until the day he **d**.
26:23 So Uzziah **d**, and since he had leprosy, he was
27: 9 When he **d**, he was buried in the City of David,
28:27 When King Ahaz **d**, he was buried in Jerusalem
32:33 When Hezekiah **d**, he was buried in the upper area
33:20 When Manasseh **d**, he was buried at his palace.
34:28 and its people until after you have **d** and been
35:24 they brought him back to Jerusalem, where he **d**.
Est 2: 7 When her father and mother had **d**,
Job 3:13 For if I had **d** at birth, I would be at peace now,
42:17 Then he **d**, an old man who had lived a long,
Ps 78:63 their young women **d** before singing their wedding
94:17 the LORD had helped me, / I would soon have **d**.
107: 5 Hungry and thirsty, / they nearly **d**.
119:92 me with joy, / I would have **d** in my misery.
Isa 6: 1 In the year King Uzziah **d**, I saw the Lord. He was
14:28 This message came to me the year King Ahaz **d**:
43: 4 Others **d** that you might live. I traded their lives for
Jer 14:18 there I see people who have **d** of starvation.
15:10 is mine, my mother. Oh, that I had **d** at birth!
20:17 Oh, that I had **d** in my mother's womb, that her
28:17 Two months later, Hananiah **d**.
La 5: 7 but they **d** before the hand of judgment fell.
Eze 4:14 I have never eaten any animal that **d** of sickness
11:13 still speaking, Pelatiah son of Benaiah suddenly **d**.
24:18 the next morning, and in the evening my wife **d**.
31:18 You will lie there among the outcasts who have **d**
32:20 The Egyptians will fall with the many who have **d**
32:32 there among the outcasts who have **d** by the sword.
Joel 1: 8 as a virgin weeps when her fiancé has **d**.
Am 8:10 heads as signs of sorrow, as if your only son had **d**.
Jnh 4: 7 of the plant, so that it soon **d** and withered away.
4: 9 it right for you to be angry because the plant **d**?"
Zec 12:10 bitterly for him as for a firstborn son who has **d**.
Mt 2:19 When Herod **d**, an angel of the Lord appeared in a
9:18 "My daughter has just **d**," he said, "but you can
13: 6 but they soon wilted beneath the hot sun and **d**
22:25 The oldest married and then **d** without children,
22:26 This brother also **d** without children, and the wife
22:27 And then she also **d**.
22:31 after Abraham, Isaac, and Jacob had **d**, God said,
27:52 and women who had **d** were raised from the dead
Mk 4: 6 but it soon wilted beneath the hot sun and **d**
12:20 of them married and then **d** without children.
12:21 the widow, but soon he too **d** and left no children.
12:21 next brother married her and **d** without children.
12:22 until all the brothers had married her and **d**,
12:22 were no children. Last of all, the woman **d**, too.
12:26 Isaac, and Jacob had **d**, God said to Moses,
15:39 officer who stood facing him saw how he had **d**,
16: 7 see him there, just as he told you before he **d**!"
Lk 2:36 for her husband had **d** when they had been married
7:12 The boy who had **d** was the only son of a widow,
8: 6 but soon it withered and **d** for lack of moisture.
8:53 laughed at him because they all knew she had **d**.
9:36 When the voice **d** away, Jesus was there alone.
13: 4 And what about the eighteen men who **d** when the
16:22 the beggar **d** and was carried by the angels to be
16:22 The rich man also **d** and was buried,
20:29 The oldest married and then **d** without children.
20:30 His brother married the widow, but he also **d**.
20:31 until each of the seven had married her and **d**,
20:32 Finally, the woman **d**, too.
20:37 Long after Abraham, Isaac, and Jacob had **d**,
Jn 6:49 ate manna in the wilderness, but they all **d**.
8:52 Even Abraham and the prophets **d**, but you say that
8:53 Are you greater than our father Abraham, who **d**?
8:53 Are you greater than the prophets, who **d**?
11:13 a good night's rest, but Jesus meant Lazarus had **d**.
11:21 if you had been here, my brother would not have **d**.
11:32 you had been here, my brother would not have **d**."
Ac 2:29 for he **d** and was buried, and his tomb is still here
5: 5 heard these words, he fell to the floor and **d**.
5:10 Instantly, she fell to the floor and **d**.
7: 4 the Chaldeans and lived in Haran until his father **d**.
7:15 went to Egypt. He **d** there, as did all his sons.
7:60 charge them with this sin!" And with that, he **d**.
9:37 About this time she became ill and **d**. Her friends
12:23 to God. So he was consumed with worms and **d**.
13:36 he **d** and was buried, and his body decayed.
25:19 and about someone called Jesus who **d**,
Ro 5: 6 came at just the right time and **d** for us sinners.
5:14 they all **d** anyway—even though they did not
6: 2 Since we have **d** to sin, how can we continue to
6: 3 to become one with Christ Jesus, we **d** with him?
6: 4 For we **d** and were buried with Christ by baptism.
6: 7 For when we **d** with Christ we were set free from
6: 8 And since we **d** with Christ, we know we will also
6:10 He **d** once to defeat sin, and now he lives for the
7: 4 because you **d** to its power when you **d** with
7: 6 for we **d** with Christ, and we are no longer captive
8:34 for he is the one who **d** for us and was raised to life
14: 9 Christ **d** and rose again for this very purpose,
14: 9 of those who are alive and of those who have **d**.
14:15 let your eating ruin someone for whom Christ **d**.
1Co 8:11 a weak Christian, for whom Christ **d**, will be
10: 9 as some of them did and then **d** from snakebites.
11:30 of you are weak and sick and some have even **d**.
15: 3 that Christ **d** for our sins, just as the Scriptures
15: 6 whom are still alive, though some have **d** by now.
15:18 all who have **d** believing in Christ have perished!
15:52 the Christians who have **d** will be raised with
2Co 5:14 Since we believe that Christ **d** for everyone,
5:14 we also believe that we have all **d** to the old life we
5:15 He **d** for everyone so that those who receive his
5:15 to please Christ, who **d** and was raised for them.
13: 4 Although he **d** on the cross in weakness, he now
Gal 1: 4 He **d** for our sins, just as God our Father planned,
2:19 So I **d** to the law so that I might live for God.
6:14 of that cross, my interest in this world **d** long ago,
Php 2:27 And he surely was ill; in fact, he almost **d**.
Col 2:20 You have **d** with Christ, and he has set you free
3: 3 For you **d** when Christ **d**, and your real life is
1Th 4:13 what will happen to the Christians who have **d**
4:14 For since we believe that Jesus **d** and was raised to
4:14 back with Jesus all the Christians who have **d**.
4:16 all the Christians who have **d** will rise from their
5:10 He **d** for us so that we can live with him forever,
Heb 1: 3 After he **d** to cleanse us from the stain of sin,
7:23 When one priest **d**, another had to take his place.
9:15 For Christ **d** to set them free from the penalty of
9:28 so also Christ **d** only once as a sacrifice to take
11:13 All these faithful ones **d** without receiving what
11:19 Abraham assumed that if Isaac **d**, God was able to
11:37 Some **d** by stoning, and some were sawed in half;
13:12 and **d** outside the city gates in order to make his
1Pe 3:18 Christ also suffered when he **d** for our sins once
3:18 but he **d** for sinners that he might bring us safely
4: 6 News was preached even to those who have **d**—
Rev 1:18 I am the living one who **d**. Look, I am alive forever
2: 8 who is the First and the Last, who **d** and is alive:
8: 9 And one-third of all things living in the sea **d**.
8:11 and many people **d** because the water was so bitter.
11:13 Seven thousand people **d** in that earthquake.
16: 3 the blood of a corpse. And everything in the sea **d**.
17: 8 at the reappearance of this beast who had **d**.
17:11 beast that was alive and then **d** is the eighth king.

DIES (45) [DIE]

Ge 27: 7 bless Esau in the LORD's presence before he **d**.
27:10 and bless you instead of Esau before he **d**."
Ex 21:20 "If a male or female slave is beaten and **d**,
21:35 injures a neighbor's bull and the injured bull **d**,
22:10 other animal, but it **d** or is injured or gets away,
Lev 11:32 If such an animal **d** and falls on something,
11:33 "If such an animal **d** and falls into a clay pot,
11:39 "If an animal that is permitted for eating **d**
18:18 But if your wife **d**, then it is all right to marry her
Nu 17:13 comes close to the Tabernacle of the LORD **d**.
19:14 ritual law that applies when someone **d** in a tent:
27: 8 'If a man **d** and has no sons, then give his
35:20 or throws a dangerous object and the person **d**,
35:21 hits another person with a fist and the person **d**,
35:23 though they were not enemies, and the person **d**.
Dt 24: 3 and the second husband also divorces her or **d**,
25: 5 the same property and one of them **d** without a son,
2Sa 3:29 or who **d** by the sword or who begs for food!"
Job 21:23 One person **d** in prosperity and security,
21:25 Another person **d** in bitter poverty, never having
37:17 and the south wind **d** down and everything is still,
Isa 40: 6 "Shout that people are like the grass that **d** away.
Jer 22:18 "His family will not weep for him when he **d**.
38:10 and pull Jeremiah out of the cistern before he **d**."
Eze 18: 4 The person who sins will be the one who **d**.
18:20 The one who sins is the one who **d**. The child will
44:31 meat from any bird or animal that **d** a natural death
44:31 or that **d** after being attacked by another animal.
Am 1: 2 All the grass on Mount Carmel withers and **d**."
Mt 22:24 Moses said, 'If a man **d** without children,
Mk 9:48 'where the worm never **d** and the fire never goes
12:19 "Teacher, Moses gave us a law that if a man **d**,
Lk 20:28 "Teacher, Moses gave us a law that if a man **d**,
Jn 4:49 "Lord, please come now before my little boy **d**."
12:24 the soil. Unless it **d** it will be alone—a single seed.
Ro 7: 2 But if he **d**, the laws of marriage no longer apply to
7: 3 But if her husband **d**, she is free from that law
1Co 7:39 If her husband **d**, she is free to marry whomever
15:22 Everyone **d** because all of us are related to Adam,
15:36 it doesn't grow into a plant unless it **d** first.
Gal 4: 1 If a father **d** and leaves great wealth for his young
1Ti 1:17 is the eternal King, the unseen one who never **d**;
Heb 9:16 Now when someone **d** and leaves a will, no one
9:27 And just as it is destined that each person **d** only
1Pe 1:24 prophet says, / "People are like grass that **d** away;

DIET (2)

Da 1:12 "Test us for ten days on a **d** of vegetables
1:13 or not to let us continue eating our **d**."

DIFFER (1) [DIFFERENCE, DIFFERENCES, DIFFERENT, DIFFERENTLY]

1Co 15:41 And even the stars **d** from each other in their

DIFFERENCE (26) [DIFFER]

2Sa 18: 3 of us die—it will make no **d** to Absalom's troops;
1Ki 3: 9 and know the **d** between right and wrong.
Job 6:30 Don't I know the **d** between right and wrong?
9:21 "I am innocent, but it makes no **d** to me—I despise
Ps 77: 6 I search my soul and think about the **d** now.
Isa 22:13 you say. "What's the **d**, for tomorrow we die."
Jer 23:28 every word. There is a **d** between chaff and wheat!
Eze 22:26 To them there is no **d** between what is holy
22:26 And they do not teach my people the **d** between
44:23 They will teach my people the **d** between what is
Da 11:27 But it will make no **d**, for an end will still come at
Hos 10: 3 we didn't fear the LORD. But what's the **d**?
Mal 3:18 Then you will again see the **d** between the
Lk 10:35 he said, 'I'll pay the **d** the next time I am here.'
Jn 7: 6 But you can go anytime, and it will make no **d**.
Ro 5:15 And what a **d** between our sin and God's generous
15: 1 We may know that these things make no **d**, but we
1Co 7:19 For it makes no **d** whether or not a man has been
15:11 So it makes no **d** whether I preach or they preach.
Gal 2: 6 their reputation as great leaders made no **d** to me,
3:19 And there is this further **d**. God gave his laws to
5: 6 it makes no **d** to God whether we are circumcised
6:15 It doesn't make any **d** now whether we have been
Heb 5:14 who have trained themselves to recognize the **d**
7:23 Another **d** is that there were many priests under the
1Jn 2:21 but because you know the **d** between truth

DIFFERENCES (1) [DIFFER]

2Sa 2:26 "Must we always solve our **d** with swords?

DIFFERENT (70) [DIFFER]

Ge 10:25 of the world were divided into **d** language groups
11: 7 Come, let's go down and give them **d** languages.
20:12 we both have the same father, though **d** mothers—
36:15 and grandchildren became the leaders of **d** clans.
Ex 8:22 But it will be very **d** in the land of Goshen,
Lev 7:11 "These are the instructions regarding the **d** kinds
10: 1 him a **d** kind of fire than he had commanded.
16: 1 who died when they burned a **d** kind of fire than
19:19 Do not wear clothing woven from two **d** kinds of
Nu 3: 4 LORD a **d** kind of fire than he had commanded.
7:11 "Let each leader bring his gift on a **d** day for the
10: 7 to an assembly, blow the trumpets using a **d** signal.
14:24 But my servant Caleb is **d** from the others. He has
26:61 LORD a **d** kind of fire than he had commanded.
33: 2 identified by the **d** places they stopped along the
Dt 17: 8 or a case involving **d** kinds of assault.
1Sa 10: 6 with them. You will be changed into a **d** person.
2Sa 14:20 He did it to place the matter before you in a **d** light.
2Ki 19:11 who stood in their way! Why should you be any **d**?
1Ch 1:19 of the world were divided into **d** language groups
Est 3: 8 Their laws are **d** from those of any other nation,
Isa 8:20 "If their predictions are **d** from mine, it is
14: 1 And people from many **d** nations will come
23:17 But she will be no **d** than she was before.
37:11 who stood in their way! Why should you be any **d**?
55: 8 "My thoughts are completely **d** from yours,"
Jer 31:22 will cause something new and **d** to happen—
51:39 their wine, I will prepare a **d** kind of feast for them.
Da 7: 3 came up out of the water, each **d** from the others.
7: 7 It was **d** from any of the other beasts, and it had ten

7:19 the one so **d** from the others and so terrifying.
7:23 It will be **d** from all the others. It will devour the
7:24 Then another king will arise, **d** from the other ten,
11:29 invade the south, but this time the result will be **d**.
Mt 5:47 to your friends, how are you **d** from anyone else?
20:26 But among you it should be quite **d**.
Mk 1:34 of sick people who had many **d** kinds of diseases,
10:43 But among you it should be quite **d**.
Ac 5:34 But one member had a **d** perspective. He was a
Ro 3:21 But now God has shown us a **d** way of being right
5:16 And the result of God's gracious gift is very **d**
8:3 But God put into effect a **d** plan to save us.
12:5 of his one body, and each of us has **d** work to do.
1Co 10:13 your life are no **d** from what others experience.
12:4 Now there are **d** kinds of spiritual gifts, but it is the
12:5 There are **d** kinds of service in the church, but it is
12:6 There are **d** ways God works in our lives, but it is
12:14 Yes, the body has many **d** parts, not just one part.
14:10 There are so many **d** languages in the world,
15:38 A **d** kind of plant grows from each kind of seed.
15:39 And just as there are **d** kinds of seeds and plants, so also there are **d** kinds of flesh—
15:40 The glory of the heavenly bodies is **d** from the
15:42 and decay, will be **d** when they are resurrected,
2Co 10:18 But when the Lord commends someone, that's **d**!
11:4 even if they preach about a **d** Jesus than the one we
11:4 or a **d** Spirit than the one you received, or a
11:4 or a **d** kind of gospel than the one you believed.
11:24 Five **d** times the Jews gave me thirty-nine lashes.
12:8 Three **d** times I begged the Lord to take it away.
Gal 1:6 through Christ. You are already following a **d** way
3:12 How **d** from this way of faith is the way of law,
6:15 really have been changed into new and **d** people.
Eph 4:14 because someone has told us something **d** or
1Ti 6:4 Anyone who teaches anything **d** is both conceited
Heb 7:11 why did God need to send a **d** priest from the line
7:13 For the one we are talking about belongs to a **d**
7:15 is even more evident from the fact that a **d** priest,
Jas 2:25 and sent them safely away by a **d** road.
2Pe 3:16 to mean something quite **d** from what he meant,

DIFFERENTLY (2) [DIFFER]

2Co 2:15 But this fragrance is perceived **d** by those being
5:16 a human being. How **d** I think about him now!

DIFFICULT (15) [DIFFICULTIES, DIFFICULTY]

Dt 1:17 Bring me any cases that are too **d** for you, and I
17:8 of murder or only of manslaughter, or a **d** lawsuit,
30:11 "This command I am giving you today is not too **d**
2Ki 2:10 "You have asked a **d** thing," Elijah replied.
Ne 5:18 because the people were already having a **d** time.
Ps 73:16 why the wicked prosper. / But what a **d** task it is!
Ecc 7:24 Wisdom is always distant and very **d** to find.
Isa 7:11 anything you like, and make it as **d** as you want."
Eze 3:6 sending you to people with strange and **d** speech.
Da 5:12 explain riddles, and solve **d** problems.
5:16 you can give interpretations and solve **d** problems.
Ac 27:4 we encountered headwinds that made it **d** to keep
2Ti 2:24 to teach effectively and be patient with **d** people.
3:1 that in the last days there will be very **d** times.
1Jn 5:3 his commandments, and really, that isn't **d**.

DIFFICULTIES (1) [DIFFICULT]

Mt 15:30 crippled, mute, and many others with physical **d**,

DIFFICULTY (5) [DIFFICULT]

Isa 43:2 When you go through rivers of **d**, you will not
Ac 27:7 and after great **d** we finally neared Cnidus.
27:8 We struggled along the coast with great **d**
27:16 where with great **d** we hoisted aboard the lifeboat
Php 4:14 have done well to share with me in my present **d**.

DIG (10) [DIGGING, DIGS, DUG]

Dt 6:11 You will draw water from cisterns you did not **d**,
23:13 you must **d** a hole with the spade and cover the
Job 28:2 They know how to **d** iron from the earth and smelt
Ps 7:15 They **d** a pit to trap others / and then fall into it
Ecc 10:8 When you **d** a well, you may fall in. When you
Jer 8:2 They will **d** out their bones and spread them out on
Eze 8:8 said to me, "Now, son of man, **d** into the wall."
12:5 **D** a hole through the wall while they are watching
Am 9:2 "Even if they **d** down to the place of the dead,
Lk 16:3 I don't have the strength to go out and **d** ditches,

DIGGING (1) [DIG]

Eze 13:4 these prophets of yours are like jackals **d** around in

DIGNITY (6)

Ex 28:2 beautiful garments that will lend **d** to his work.
28:40 and headdresses to give them **d** and respect.
Pr 31:25 She is clothed with strength and **d**, and she laughs
Ecc 10:6 people of proven worth their rightful place of **d**.
1Co 12:24 and care are given to those parts that have less **d**.
1Ti 2:2 can live in peace and quietness, in godliness and **d**.

DIGS (1) [DIG]

Ex 21:33 "Suppose someone **d** or uncovers a well and fails

DIKLAH (2)

Ge 10:27 Hadoram, Uzal, **D**,
1Ch 1:21 Hadoram, Uzal, **D**,

DILEAN (1)

Jos 15:38 **D**, Mizpeh, Joktheel,

DILIGENCE (1) [DILIGENT]

Ezr 6:12 issued this decree. Let it be obeyed with all **d**."

DILIGENT (3) [DILIGENCE, DILIGENTLY]

Pr 12:27 but the **d** make use of everything they find.
2Jn 1:8 Be **d** so that you will receive your full reward.
Rev 3:19 I love. Be **d** and turn from your indifference.

DILIGENTLY (1) [DILIGENT]

Dt 6:17 You must **d** obey the commands of the LORD

DILL (2)

Isa 28:25 Does he not finally plant his seeds for **d**, cummin,
28:27 A heavy sledge is never used on **d**; rather, it is

DIM (4)

Job 17:7 My eyes are **d** with weeping, and I am but a
Ecc 12:2 of the sun and moon and stars is **d** to your old eyes,
Isa 17:4 "In that day the glory of Israel will be very **d**,
La 5:17 are sick and weary, and our eyes grow **d** with tears.

DIMENSIONS (2)

Job 38:5 Do you know how its **d** were determined and who
Eze 42:11 and doors. The **d** of each were identical.

DIMINISH (2) [DIMINISHED]

Jer 23:20 The anger of the LORD will not **d** until it has
30:24 The fierce anger of the LORD will not **d** until it

DIMINISHED (1) [DIMINISH]

Hab 3:6 the eternal hills. But his power is not **d** in the least!

DIMNAH (1) [RIMMON, RIMMONO]

Jos 21:35 **D**, and Nahalal—four towns with their

DIMONAH (1)

Jos 15:22 Kinah, **D**, Adadah,

DINAH (6) [DINAH'S]

Ge 30:21 she gave birth to a daughter and named her **D**.
34:1 One day **D**, Leah's daughter, went to visit some of
34:3 But Shechem's love for **D** was strong, and he tried
34:19 acting on this request, for he wanted **D** desperately.
34:26 They rescued **D** from Shechem's house
46:15 to Leah in Paddan-aram, along with their sister, **D**.

DINAH'S (3) [DINAH]

Ge 34:11 Then Shechem addressed **D** father and brothers.
34:13 But **D** brothers deceived Shechem and Hamor
34:25 two of **D** brothers, Simeon and Levi, took their

DINAITES [KJV] See JUDGES

DINE (4) [DINING, DINNER]

2Sa 11:11 I go home to wine and **d** and sleep with my wife?
2Ki 25:29 and allowed him to **d** at the king's table for the rest
Est 5:12 And she has invited me to **d** with her and the king
Jer 52:33 and allowed him to **d** at the king's table for the rest

DINHABAH (2)

Ge 36:32 Bela son of Beor, who ruled from his city of **D**.
1Ch 1:43 Bela son of Beor, who ruled from his city of **D**.

DINING (2) [DINE]

Job 1:13 and daughters were **d** at the oldest brother's house,
Pr 23:1 When **d** with a ruler, pay attention to what is put

DINNER (11) [DINE]

1Sa 20:27 "Why hasn't the son of Jesse been here for **d**
2Sa 11:13 Then David invited him to **d** and got him drunk.
Jer 41:1 Gedaliah invited them to **d**. While they were
Mt 9:10 invited Jesus and his disciples to be his **d** guests,
Mk 2:15 invited Jesus and his disciples to be his **d** guests,
Lk 10:40 But Martha was worrying over the big **d** she was
14:7 When Jesus noticed that all who had come to the **d**
14:12 "When you put on a luncheon or a **d**," he said,
Jn 12:2 A **d** was prepared in Jesus' honor. Martha served,
Ro 12:13 get into the habit of inviting guests home for **d** or,
1Co 10:27 who isn't a Christian asks you home for **d**,

DIONYSIUS (1)

Ac 17:34 Among them were **D**, a member of the Council,

DIOTREPHES (1)

3Jn 1:9 but **D**, who loves to be the leader, does not

DIP (16) [DIPPED]

Ex 12:22 of hyssop branches and **d** it into the lamb's blood.
Lev 4:6 **d** his finger into the blood, and sprinkle it seven
4:17 **d** his finger into the blood, and sprinkle it seven
4:25 Then the priest will **d** his finger into the blood of
4:30 The priest will then **d** his finger into the blood,
4:34 The priest will then **d** his finger into the blood,
14:6 He will then **d** the living bird, along with the
14:16 He will **d** his right finger into the oil and sprinkle it
14:27 He will **d** his right finger into the oil and sprinkle
14:51 Then he will **d** the cedarwood, the hyssop branch,
16:14 Then he must **d** his finger into the blood of the bull
16:19 Then he must **d** his finger into the blood
Nu 19:18 must take a hyssop branch and **d** it into the water.
Ru 2:14 You can **d** your bread in the wine if you like."
Lk 16:24 Send Lazarus over here to **d** the tip of his finger in
Jn 2:8 "**D** some out and take it to the master of

DIPPED (7) [DIP]

Ge 37:31 brothers killed a goat and **d** the robe in its blood.
Lev 9:9 and he **d** his finger into it and put it on the horns of
1Sa 14:27 and he **d** a stick into a piece of honeycomb and ate
2Ki 5:14 to the Jordan River and **d** himself seven times,
Jn 13:26 "It is the one to whom I give the bread **d** in the
13:26 And when he had **d** it, he gave it to Judas, son of
Rev 19:13 He was clothed with a robe **d** in blood, and his title

DIRECT (15) [DIRECTED, DIRECTING, DIRECTION, DIRECTIONS, DIRECTLY, DIRECTOR, DIRECTORS, DIRECTS, MISDIRECTED]

Ge 18:19 I have singled him out so that he will **d** his sons
41:40 I hereby appoint you to **d** this project. You will
46:26 So the total number of Jacob's **d** descendants who
Ex 1:5 in Egypt. In all, Jacob had seventy **d** descendants.
Nu 1:3 to go to war. You and Aaron are to **d** the project,
4:27 and his sons will **d** the Gershonites regarding their
1Ch 15:17 from the clan of Merari to **d** the musicians.
Job 38:35 lightning appear and cause it to strike as you **d** it?
Ps 67:4 and **d** the actions of the whole world. / *Interlude*
Pr 3:6 his will in all you do, and he will **d** your paths.
Mt 15:3 violate the **d** commandments of God?
15:6 you nullify the **d** commandment of God.
Jn 21:18 and others will **d** you and take you where you
1Co 7:12 though I do not have a **d** command from the Lord.
Gal 1:12 For my message came by a **d** revelation from Jesus

DIRECTED (15) [DIRECT]

Ge 24:51 wife of your master's son, as the LORD has **d**."
Ex 38:21 Moses **d** the Levites to compile the figures,
Nu 31:41 to Eleazar the priest, just as the LORD had **d** him.
33:38 Aaron the priest was **d** by the LORD to go up the
Dt 1:19 "Then, just as the LORD our God **d** us, we left
Jos 4:12 Israelites across the Jordan, just as Moses had **d**.
2Ki 8:6 So he **d** one of his officials to see to it that
Ezr 1:8 Cyrus **d** Mithredath, the treasurer of Persia,
Ps 37:23 The steps of the godly are **d** by the LORD.
Pr 11:5 The godly are **d** by their honesty; the wicked fall
21:1 The king's heart is like a stream of water **d** by the
Jer 13:2 So I bought the belt as the LORD **d** me and put it
Mt 27:10 and purchased the potter's field, / as the Lord **d**."
Gal 5:18 But when you are **d** by the Holy Spirit, you are no
Jude 1:20 And continue to pray as you are **d** by the Holy

DIRECTING (1) [DIRECT]

Isa 41:4 **d** the affairs of the human race as each new

DIRECTION (49) [DIRECT]

Ge 13:10 fertile plains of the Jordan Valley in the **d** of Zoar.
13:14 to Abram, "Look as far as you can see in every **d**.
13:17 Take a walk in every **d** and explore the new
25:18 to Shur, which is east of Egypt in the **d** of Asshur.
Nu 11:31 For many miles in every **d** from the camp there
14:25 set out for the wilderness in the **d** of the Red Sea."
27:21 When **d** from the LORD is needed, Joshua will
33:2 At the LORD's **d**, Moses kept a written record of
34:4 then run south past Scorpion Pass in the **d** of Zin.
35:4 extend 1,500 feet from the town walls in every **d**.
35:5 off 3,000 feet outside the town walls in every **d**—
Dt 3:27 go to Pisgah Peak and view the land in every **d**,
28:7 They will attack you from one **d**, but they will
28:25 You will attack your enemies from one **d**, but you
Jos 8:20 For the Israelites who had fled in the **d** of the
19:12 In the other **d**, the boundary line went east from
Jdg 19:10 his concubine and headed in the **d** of Jebus (that is,
20:27 And the Israelites went up seeking **d** from the
1Sa 14:16 army of Philistines began to melt away in every **d**.
14:47 he fought against his enemies in every **d**—
2Sa 20:8 Amasa met them, coming from the opposite **d**.
24:5 south of the town in the valley, in the **d** of Gad.
2Ki 3:20 It was flowing from the **d** of Edom, and soon there
18:25 have invaded your land without the LORD's **d**?
25:4 across the fields, in the **d** of the Jordan Valley.
1Ch 25:2 They worked under the **d** of their father, Asaph,
25:3 They worked under the **d** of their father, Jeduthun,
25:6 All these men were under the **d** of their fathers as
2Ch 26:11 They were under the **d** of Hananiah, one of the
Ne 12:42 and clearly under the **d** of Jezrahiah the choir
Job 37:3 and his lightning flashes out in every **d**.
37:12 The clouds turn around and around under his **d**.
Ps 119:59 I pondered the **d** of my life, / and I turned to follow
Isa 36:10 have invaded your land without the LORD's **d**?
Jer 49:32 I will bring calamity upon them from every **d**,"
52:7 across the fields, in the **d** of the Jordan Valley.
Eze 1:9 The living beings were able to fly in any **d** without
1:12 They went in whatever **d** the spirit chose, and they
10:11 They went straight in the **d** in which their heads
19:8 attacked him, / surrounding him from every **d**.
28:23 The attack will come from every **d**, and your
48:17 will surround the city for 150 yards in every **d**.
Da 7:2 great sea, with strong winds blowing from every **d**.

Joel 2: 3 in front of them and follows them in every **d**!
Am 3: 3 people walk together without agreeing on the **d**?
Jnh 1: 3 and went in the opposite **d** in order to get away
Jn 10:32 "At my Father's **d** I have done many things to
2Co 7: 5 Outside there was conflict from every **d**, and inside
Eph 4:16 Under his **d**, the whole body is fitted together

DIRECTIONS (13) [DIRECT]

Ge 14:15 and attacked during the night from several **d**.
46:28 to meet Joseph and get **d** to the land of Goshen.
Ne 4:12 "They will come from all **d** and attack us!"
Job 30:14 They come at me from all **d**. They rush upon me
Jer 49:36 I will bring enemies from all **d**, and I will scatter
Eze 1:12 and they moved straight forward in all **d** without
1:17 move forward in any of the four **d** they faced,
10:11 move forward in any of the four **d** they faced,
36: 3 Your enemies have attacked you from all **d**,
43:11 down all these specifications and **d** as they watch
48:21 extending in opposite **d** to the eastern and western
Da 8: 8 prominent horns pointing in the four **d** of the earth.
2Co 8: 5 and to us for whatever **d** God might give them.

DIRECTLY (19) [DIRECT]

Ex 20:19 But don't let God speak **d** to us. If he does, we will
33:20 But you may not look **d** at my face, for no one may
Lev 19:17 "Confront your neighbors **d** so you will not be
Nu 4:28 They will be **d** responsible to Ithamar son of Aaron
4:33 They are **d** responsible to Ithamar son of Aaron the
12: 8 I speak to him face to face, **d** and not in riddles!
2Sa 16:23 as though it had come **d** from the mouth of God.
1Ch 25: 6 Jeduthun, and Heman reported **d** to the king.
Job 10:19 I would have gone **d** from the womb to the grave.
13: 3 Oh, how I long to speak **d** to the Almighty. I want
Jer 22: 1 to me, "Go over and speak **d** to the king of Judah.
35: 4 **d** above the room of Maaseiah son of Shallum,
36:17 these messages. Did they come **d** from Jeremiah?"
Eze 40:23 inner courtyard **d** opposite this outer gateway.
40:27 And here again, **d** opposite the outer gateway,
42:14 they must not go **d** to the outer courtyard.
Da 11:21 man who is not **d** in line for royal succession.
Jn 16:23 truth is, you can go **d** to the Father and ask him,
1Th 4:15 I can tell you this **d** from the Lord: We who are

DIRECTOR (57) [DIRECT]

Ne 12:42 clearly under the direction of Jezrahiah the choir **d**.
Ps 4: T For the choir **d**: A psalm of David, to be
5: T For the choir **d**: A psalm of David, to be
6: T For the choir **d**: A psalm of David, to be
8: T For the choir **d**: A psalm of David, to be
9: T For the choir **d**: A psalm of David, to be sung to
11: T For the choir **d**: A psalm of David.
12: T For the choir **d**: A psalm of David, to be
13: T For the choir **d**: A psalm of David.
14: T For the choir **d**: A psalm of David.
18: T For the choir **d**: A psalm of David, the servant of
19: T For the choir **d**: A psalm of David.
20: T For the choir **d**: A psalm of David.
21: T For the choir **d**: A psalm of David.
22: T For the choir **d**: A psalm of David, to be sung to
31: T For the choir **d**: A psalm of David.
36: T For the choir **d**: A psalm of David, the servant of
39: T For Jeduthun, the choir **d**: A psalm of David.
40: T For the choir **d**: A psalm of David.
41: T For the choir **d**: A psalm of David.
42: T For the choir **d**: A psalm of the descendants of
44: T For the choir **d**: A psalm of the descendants of
45: T For the choir **d**: A psalm of the descendants of
46: T For the choir **d**: A psalm of the descendants of
47: T For the choir **d**: A psalm of the descendants of
49: T For the choir **d**: A psalm of the descendants of
51: T For the choir **d**: A psalm of David,
52: T For the choir **d**: A psalm of David,
53: T For the choir **d**: A meditation of David.
54: T For the choir **d**: A meditation of David,
55: T For the choir **d**: A psalm of David, to be
56: T For the choir **d**: A psalm of David,
57: T For the choir **d**: A psalm of David,
58: T For the choir **d**: A psalm of David, to be sung to
59: T For the choir **d**: A psalm of David,
60: T For the choir **d**: A psalm of David useful for
61: T For the choir **d**: A psalm of David, to be
62: T For Jeduthun, the choir **d**: A psalm of David.
64: T For the choir **d**: A psalm of David.
65: T For the choir **d**: A psalm of David. A song.
66: T For the choir **d**: A psalm. A song.
67: T For the choir **d**: A psalm, to be accompanied by
68: T For the choir **d**: A psalm of David. A song.
69: T For the choir **d**: A psalm of David, to be sung to
70: T For the choir **d**: A psalm of David, to bring us to
75: T For the choir **d**: A psalm of Asaph, to be sung to
76: T For the choir **d**: A psalm of Asaph, to be
77: T For Jeduthun, the choir **d**: A psalm of Asaph.
80: T For the choir **d**: A psalm of Asaph, to be sung to
81: T For the choir **d**: A psalm of Asaph, to be
84: T For the choir **d**: A psalm of the descendants of
85: T For the choir **d**: A psalm of the descendants of
88: T For the choir **d**: A psalm of the descendants of
109: T For the choir **d**: A psalm of David.
139: T For the choir **d**: A psalm of David.
140: T For the choir **d**: A psalm of David.
Hab 3:19 me safely over the mountains. (For the choir **d**:

DIRECTORS (1) [DIRECT]

Ne 12:46 The custom of having choir **d** to lead the choirs in

DIRECTS (4) [DIRECT]

Ex 18:23 you follow this advice, and if God **d** you to do so,
Nu 22: 8 I will tell you whatever the LORD **d** me to say."
Job 37: 6 "He **d** the snow to fall on the earth and tells the
Pr 20:24 road we travel? It is the LORD who **d** our steps.

DIRT (9) [DIRTY]

2Sa 1: 2 and put **d** on his head to show that he was in
15:32 and put **d** on his head as a sign of mourning.
22:43 of the earth; / I swept them into the gutter like **d**.
Ps 18:42 by the wind. / I swept them into the gutter like **d**.
44:25 We collapse in the dust, / lying face down in the **d**.
113: 7 and he lifts the poor from the **d** / and the needy
Isa 10: 6 trampling them like **d** beneath its feet.
57:20 is never still but continually churns up mire and **d**.
1Pe 3:21 Baptism is not a removal of **d** from your body;

DIRTY (4) [DIRT]

Ps 26:10 Their hands are **d** with wicked schemes, / and they
Ro 13:12 rid of your evil deeds. Shed them like **d** clothes.
Col 3: 8 malicious behavior, slander, and **d** language.
Jude 1:13 churning up the **d** foam of their shameful deeds.

DISADVANTAGE (1)

Ezr 4:13 it will be much to your **d**, for the Jews will

DISAGREE (2) [DISAGREED, DISAGREEING, DISAGREEMENT, DISAGREEMENTS]

Gal 2: 2 I wanted to make sure they did not **d**, or my
Php 3:15 If you **d** on some point, I believe God will make it

DISAGREED (1) [DISAGREE]

Ac 15:38 But Paul **d** strongly, since John Mark had deserted

DISAGREEING (1) [DISAGREE]

Ac 15: 2 Paul and Barnabas, **d** with them, argued forcefully

DISAGREEMENT (3) [DISAGREE]

Jn 6:41 Then the people began to murmur in **d** because he
Ac 15:39 Their **d** over this was so sharp that they separated.
Php 4: 2 because you belong to the Lord, settle your **d**.

DISAGREEMENTS (2) [DISAGREE]

Eze 44:24 "They will serve as judges to resolve any **d** among
1Co 6: 3 So you should surely be able to resolve ordinary **d**

DISALLOW [KJV] See REFUSES

DISAPPEAR (60) [DISAPPEARED, DISAPPEARING, DISAPPEARS]

Ge 8: 1 blow across the waters, and the floods began to **d**.
Ex 8:29 LORD to cause the swarms of flies to **d** from you
8:31 did as Moses asked and caused the swarms to **d**.
Nu 27: 4 Why should the name of our father **d** just
Dt 4:26 you will quickly **d** from the land you are crossing
28:63 until you **d** from the land you are about to enter
32:26 so even the memory of them would **d**.
1Sa 25:29 But the lives of your enemies will **d** like stones
2Sa 14: 7 and family will **d** from the face of the earth."
15:28 Let me know what happens in Jerusalem before I **d**
Job 14: 2 Like the shadow of a passing cloud, we quickly **d**.
15:32 in the prime of life, and all they counted on will **d**.
18:15 The home of the wicked will **d** beneath a fiery
24:18 "But they **d** from the earth as quickly as foam is
Ps 37:10 In a little while, the wicked will **d**. / Though you
37:20 like flowers in a field— / they will **d** like smoke.
58: 7 May they **d** like water into thirsty ground.
90: 5 You sweep people away like dreams that **d**
90:10 and trouble; / soon they **d**, and we are gone.
102: 3 for my days **d** like smoke, / and my bones burn
104:35 the face of the earth; / let the wicked **d** forever.
Pr 22:10 and fighting, quarrels, and insults will **d**.
23: 5 For riches can **d** as though they had the wings of a
26:20 for lack of fuel, and quarrels **d** when gossip stops.
Isa 1:31 The strongest among you will **d** like burning straw.
5:24 Therefore, they will all **d** like burning straw.
17: 1 "Look, Damascus will **d**! It will become a heap of
25: 2 Beautiful palaces in distant lands **d** and will never
28: 1 rich valley, but its glorious beauty will suddenly **d**.
28: 4 but its glorious beauty will suddenly **d**.
29:21 the innocent guilty by their false testimony will **d**.
33:19 people with a strange, unknown language will **d**.
34: 4 above will melt away and **d** like a rolled-up scroll.
35:10 Sorrow and mourning will **d**, and they will be
47:15 will slip away and **d**, unable to help.
51: 6 For the skies will **d** like smoke, and the earth will
51:11 Sorrow and mourning will **d**, and they will be
51:12 of mere humans, who wither like the grass and **d**?
54:10 For the mountains may depart and the hills **d**,
56: 5 I give them is an everlasting one. It will never **d**!
60:18 Violence will **d** from your land; the desolation
66:22 with a name that will never **d**," says the LORD.
Eze 21: 7 heart will melt with fear; all strength will **d**.
Hos 4: 3 Even the animals, birds, and fish have begun to **d**.
10: 7 and its king will **d** like a chip of wood on an ocean
13: 3 Therefore, they will **d** like the morning mist,
13:15 All their flowing springs and wells will **d**.
Ob 1:16 nations will drink and stagger and **d** from history,
Na 1:12 have many allies, they will be destroyed and **d**.
3:17 to warm the earth, all of them will fly away and **d**.
Zep 1: 4 so that even the memory of them will **d**.
Hag 1: 6 Your wages **d** as though you were putting them in
Mt 5:18 I assure you, until heaven and earth **d**,
24:35 Heaven and earth will **d**, but my words will remain
Mk 13:31 Heaven and earth will **d**, but my words will remain
Lk 21:33 Heaven and earth will **d**, but my words will remain
1Co 13: 8 and special knowledge will all **d**.
13:10 when the end comes, these special gifts will all **d**.
2Pe 3:10 and everything in them will **d** in fire, and the earth
Rev 18:21 thrown away this stone, and she will **d** forever.

DISAPPEARED (36) [DISAPPEAR]

Ge 5:24 Then suddenly, he **d** because God took him.
31:15 He sold us, and what he received for us has **d**.
42:32 one brother has **d**, and the youngest is with our
42:36 Joseph has **d**, Simeon is gone, and now you want
Ex 16:14 When the dew **d** later in the morning, thin flakes,
16:21 the food they had not picked up melted and **d**.
24:18 Then Moses **d** into the cloud as he climbed higher
32: 1 who brought us here from Egypt, has **d**.
33: 8 They would all watch Moses until he **d** inside.
Jdg 3:22 so deep that the handle **d** beneath the king's fat.
6:21 all he had brought. And the angel of the LORD **d**.
1Sa 10:21 But when they looked for him, he had **d**!
1Ki 20:40 I was busy doing something else, the prisoner **d**!"
2Ki 2:12 And as they **d** from sight, Elisha tore his robe in
Job 17:11 My days are over. My hopes have **d**. My heart's
Isa 16: 4 destruction have ceased and enemy raiders have **d**,
Jer 12: 4 The wild animals and birds have **d** because of the
22:22 And now your allies have all **d** with a puff of wind.
32:43 a land where people and animals have all **d**.'
33:10 and the people and animals have all **d**.'
33:12 and the people and animals have all **d**—
48:36 and Kir-hareseth, for all their wealth has **d**.
Mic 7: 2 The godly people have all **d**; not one fair-minded
Mt 8: 3 he said. "Be healed!" And instantly the leprosy **d**.
Mk 1:42 Instantly the leprosy **d**—the man was healed.
Lk 5:13 he said. "Be healed!" And instantly the leprosy **d**.
17:14 to the priests." And as they went, their leprosy **d**.
24:31 they recognized him. And at that moment he **d**!
Jn 4:52 afternoon at one o'clock his fever suddenly **d**!"
5:13 man didn't know, for Jesus had **d** into the crowd.
Ac 1: 9 while they were watching, and he **d** into a cloud.
Heb 10: 2 all time, and their feelings of guilt would have **d**.
11: 5 "suddenly he **d** because God took him."
Rev 6:14 And all of the mountains and all of the islands **d**.
16:20 And every island **d**, and all the mountains were
21: 1 for the old heaven and the old earth had **d**.

DISAPPEARING (2) [DISAPPEAR]

Ps 12: 1 Help, O LORD, for the godly are fast **d**!
1Jn 2: 8 because the darkness is **d** and the true light is

DISAPPEARS (8) [DISAPPEAR]

Lev 13:58 But if the spot **d** after the object is washed, it must
Job 6: 7 My appetite **d** when I look at it; I gag at the
6:17 But when the hot weather arrives, the water **d**.
9:26 It **d** like a swift boat, like an eagle that swoops
14:11 evaporates from a lake and as a river **d** in drought,
Pr 13:11 Wealth from get-rich-quick schemes quickly **d**;
Hos 6: 4 the morning mist and **d** like dew in the sunlight.
Joel 1:16 We watch as our food **d** before our very eyes.

DISAPPOINT (3) [DISAPPOINTED, DISAPPOINTMENT]

Ro 5: 5 And this expectation will not **d** us. For we know
1Co 15:43 Our bodies now **d** us, but when they are raised,
2Co 7:14 how proud I was of you—and you didn't **d** me.

DISAPPOINTED (7) [DISAPPOINT]

1Ki 11:22 How have we **d** you that you want to go home?"
Ps 22: 5 They put their trust in you and were never **d**.
Pr 23:18 a future ahead of you; your hope will not be **d**.
Lk 13: 6 if there was any fruit on it, but he was always **d**.
Ro 9:33 But anyone who believes in him / will not be **d**."
10:11 "Anyone who believes in him will not be **d**."
1Pe 2: 6 anyone who believes in him / will never be **d**."

DISAPPOINTMENT (1) [DISAPPOINT]

Isa 33: 7 But now your ambassadors weep in bitter **d**,

DISAPPROVAL (1)

Jn 5:41 "Your approval or **d** means nothing to me,

DISARMED (1)

Col 2:15 In this way, God **d** the evil rulers and authorities.

DISASTER (93) [DISASTERS, DISASTROUS]

Ge 19:19 **D** would catch up to me there, and I would soon
19:29 removing him from the **d** that engulfed the cities
41:36 Otherwise **d** will surely strike the land, and all the
Ex 11: 1 "I will send just one more **d** on Pharaoh
32:12 Change your mind about this terrible **d** you are
32:14 and didn't bring against his people the **d** he had
Dt 30:15 I am giving you a choice between prosperity and **d**,
31:29 In the days to come, **d** will come down on you,
32:35 time their feet will slip. / Their day of **d** will arrive,
Jos 23:15 he will also bring **d** on you if you disobey him.
Jdg 20:34 that Benjamin didn't realize the impending **d**.
20:41 At this point Benjamin's warriors realized **d** was
1Sa 4: 7 come into their camp!" they cried. "This is a **d**!
6: 9 was the LORD who brought this great **d** upon us.
2Sa 15:14 and the city of Jerusalem will be spared from **d**."

17:14 so that he could bring **d** upon Absalom!
1Ki 14:10 I will bring **d** on your dynasty and kill all your
21:21 The LORD is going to bring **d** to you and sweep
22:23 For the LORD has determined **d** for you."
2Ki 14:10 Why stir up trouble that will bring **d** on you
17:7 This **d** came upon the nation of Israel
21:12 I will bring such **d** on Jerusalem and Judah that the
22:20 I will not send the promised **d** against this city
22:20 You will not see the **d** I am going to bring on this
1Ch 2:7 brought **d** on Israel by taking plunder that had been
2Ch 18:22 For the LORD has determined **d** for you."
20:37 So the ships met with **d** and never put out to sea.
25:19 Why stir up trouble that will bring **d** on you
34:28 I will not send the promised **d** against this city
34:28 You will not see the **d** I am going to bring on this
Job 5:3 for the moment, but then comes sudden **d**.
21:28 and wicked people who came to **d** because of their
Ps 91:6 in darkness, / nor the **d** that strikes at midday.
140:11 Cause **d** to fall with great force on the violent.
Pr 1:26 I will mock you when **d** overtakes you—
3:25 You need not be afraid of **d** or the destruction that
10:25 **D** strikes like a cyclone, whirling the wicked away,
17:19 loves sin; anyone who speaks boastfully invites **d**.
21:12 of the wicked; he will bring the wicked to **d**.
22:8 Those who plant seeds of injustice will harvest **d**,
24:22 For you will go down with them to sudden **d**.
28:28 When the wicked meet **d**, the godly multiply.
Isa 21:1 **D** is roaring down on you from the desert, like a
23:8 Who has brought this **d** on Tyre, empire builder
29:2 Yet I will bring **d** upon you, and there will be
31:2 In his wisdom, the LORD will send great **d**;
47:11 So **d** will overtake you suddenly, and you won't be
Jer 2:3 were considered guilty, and **d** fell upon them.
5:13 Their predictions of **d** will fall on themselves!' "
6:9 the LORD Almighty says: "**D** will fall upon you.
6:19 all the earth! I will bring **d** upon my people.
9:19 in despair, 'We are ruined! **D** has come upon us!
11:12 But the idols will not save them when **d** strikes!
11:23 for I will bring **d** upon them when their time of
17:16 I have not urged you to send **d**. It is your message I
17:17 me now! You alone are my hope in the day of **d**.
18:11 I am planning **d** against you instead of good.
19:3 I will bring such a terrible **d** on this place that the
19:15 I will bring **d** upon this city and its surrounding
21:10 For I have decided to bring **d** and not good upon
23:1 "I will send **d** upon the leaders of my people—
23:12 For I will bring **d** upon them when their time of
25:29 let you go unpunished? No, you will not escape **d**.
25:32 "Look! **D** will fall upon nation after nation!
26:3 Then I will be able to withhold the **d** I am ready to
26:13 he will cancel this **d** that he has announced against
26:19 Then the LORD held back the terrible **d** he had
26:20 And he predicted the same terrible **d** against the
29:11 "They are plans for good and not for **d**, to give
31:28 I overthrew it, destroyed it, and brought **d** upon it.
32:23 That is why you have sent this terrible **d** upon
39:16 I will send **d**, not prosperity. You will see its
40:2 "The LORD your God has brought this **d** on this
42:17 None of you will escape from the **d** I will bring
44:27 For I will watch over you to bring you **d** and not
45:5 I will bring great **d** upon all these people, but I will
46:21 and run, for it is a day of great **d** for Egypt,
49:8 For when I bring **d** on Edom, I will punish you,
49:37 My fierce anger will bring great **d** upon the people
La 2:17 He has fulfilled the promises of **d** he made long
4:6 where utter **d** struck in a moment with no one to
5:16 **D** has fallen upon us because we have sinned.
Eze 7:5 With one blow after another I will bring total **d**!
Da 9:12 Never in all history has there been a **d** like the one
9:14 The LORD has brought against us the **d** he
Am 3:6 When **d** comes to a city, isn't it
5:18 not bring light and prosperity, but darkness and **d**.
6:3 You push away every thought of coming **d**,
9:4 I am determined to bring **d** upon them and not to
Hab 3:16 I will wait quietly for the coming day when **d** will
Zep 3:15 troubles will be over, and you will fear **d** no more.
1Th 5:3 then **d** will fall upon them as suddenly as a
2Pe 3:16 parts of Scripture—and the result is **d** for them.

DISASTERS (19) [DISASTER]

Ex 7:4 So I will crush Egypt with a series of **d**,
10:7 to him. "How long will you let these **d** go on?
Lev 26:21 I will inflict you with seven more **d** for your sins.
Dt 31:17 'These **d** have come because God is no longer
31:21 Then great **d** will come down on them, and this
32:23 I will heap **d** upon them / and shoot them down
1Ki 9:9 That is why the LORD has brought all these **d**
2Ki 24:3 These **d** happened to Judah according to the
2Ch 7:22 That is why he brought all these **d** upon them.' "
Job 20:22 he will run into trouble, and **d** will destroy him.
Jer 5:12 No **d** will come upon us! There will be no war
25:7 bringing on yourselves all the **d** you now suffer.
35:17 and Jerusalem all the **d** I have threatened."
36:31 of Judah and Jerusalem all the **d** I have promised,
51:60 Jeremiah had recorded on a scroll all the terrible **d**
51:64 because of the **d** I will bring upon her.' " This is
Am 4:12 I will bring upon you all these further **d** I have
Ob 1:12 have crowed over them as they suffered these **d**.
Mic 2:6 like that. Such **d** will never come our way!"

DISASTROUS (1) [DISASTER]

Ex 23:33 sin of idol worship, and that would be **d** for you."

DISBANDED (1)

Jdg 9:55 he was dead, they **d** and returned to their homes.

DISBELIEF (1)

Ge 17:17 down to the ground, but he laughed to himself in **d**.

DISCARD (2) [DISCARDED, DISCARDING]

1Co 1:19 human wisdom / and **d** their most brilliant ideas."
9:21 But I do not **d** the law of God; I obey the law of

DISCARDED (7) [DISCARD]

Isa 14:19 but your body is thrown from the grave like a **d**
Jer 22:28 "Why is this man Jehoiachin like a **d**,
38:11 where he found some old rags and **d** clothing.
La 3:45 You have **d** us as refuse and garbage among the
Eze 31:11 it as its wickedness deserved. I myself **d** it.
Gal 2:14 have **d** the Jewish laws and are living like a
Php 3:8 I have **d** everything else, counting it all as garbage,

DISCARDING (1) [DISCARD]

Jer 6:30 because I, the LORD, am **d** them."

DISCERN (4) [DISCERNING, DISCERNMENT]

2Sa 14:17 are like an angel of God and can **d** good from evil.
Job 34:4 So let us **d** for ourselves what is right; let us learn
Ecc 11:5 God's ways are as hard to **d** as the pathways of the
1Co 12:3 So I want you to know how to **d** what is truly from

DISCERNING (2) [DISCERN]

Ps 119:169 to my cry; / give me the **d** mind you promised.
Hos 14:9 Let those who are **d** listen carefully. The paths of

DISCERNMENT (4) [DISCERN]

Ps 119:125 Give **d** to me, your servant; / then I will understand
Pr 8:12 I know where to discover knowledge and **d**.
11:9 destroy one's friends; wise **d** rescues the godly.
23:23 ever sell it; also get wisdom, discipline, and **d**.

DISCHARGE (14) [DISCHARGED, DISCHARGES]

Lev 15:2 Any man who has a genital **d** is ceremonially
15:3 This defilement applies whether the **d** continues
15:6 If you sit where the man with the **d** has sat,
15:7 apply if you touch the man who has the unclean **d**.
15:12 Any clay pot touched by the man with the **d** must
15:13 "When the man's **d** heals, he must count off a
15:15 for the man before the LORD for his **d**.
15:25 be ceremonially unclean as long as the **d** continues.
15:28 "When the woman's menstrual **d** stops, she must
15:30 for her before the LORD for her menstrual **d**.
15:32 with a man who has been defiled by a genital **d**
15:33 or woman, who has had a bodily **d** of any kind;
22:4 or any kind of **d** that makes them ceremonially
Nu 5:2 the camp who has a contagious skin disease or a **d**,

DISCHARGED (2) [DISCHARGE]

Nu 32:22 You will have **d** your duty to the LORD and to
2Ch 25:10 So Amaziah **d** the hired troops and sent them back

DISCHARGES (1) [DISCHARGE]

Lev 15:25 or if she **d** blood unrelated to her menstruation,

DISCIPLE (27) [DISCIPLES, DISCIPLES']

Mt 9:9 "Come, be my **d**," Jesus said to him. So Matthew
13:52 **d** in the Kingdom of Heaven is like a person who
14:19 he gave some of the bread and fish to each **d**,
Mk 2:14 "Come, be my **d**," Jesus said to him. So Levi got
Lk 5:27 "Come, be my **d**!" Jesus said to him.
9:59 He said to another person, "Come, be my **d**."
14:26 your own life. Otherwise, you cannot be my **d**.
14:27 And you cannot be my **d** if you do not carry your
14:33 So no one can become my **d** without giving up
Jn 1:43 found Philip and said to him, "Come, be my **d**."
9:28 Then they cursed him and said, "You are his **d**,
14:22 (not Judas Iscariot, but the other **d** with that name)
18:15 That other **d** was acquainted with the high priest,
18:16 Then the other **d** spoke to the woman watching at
19:26 his mother standing there beside the **d** he loved,
19:27 And he said to this **d**, "She is your mother."
19:27 And from then on this **d** took her into his home.
19:38 who had been a secret **d** of Jesus (because he
20:2 She ran and found Simon Peter and the other **d**,
20:3 Peter and the other **d** ran to the tomb to see.
20:4 The other **d** outran Peter and got there first.
20:8 Then the other **d** also went in, and he saw
21:7 Then the **d** whom Jesus loved said to Peter, "It is
21:20 and saw the **d** Jesus loved following them—
21:23 community of believers that that **d** wouldn't die.
21:24 This is that **d** who saw these events and recorded
Ac 16:1 a young **d** whose mother was a Jewish believer,

DISCIPLES (282) [DISCIPLE]

Isa 8:16 I will entrust it to my **d**, who will pass it down to
Mt 4:19 Jesus called out to them, "Come, be my **d**, and I
5:1 Jesus went up the mountainside with his **d** and sat
8:18 he instructed his **d** to cross to the other side of the
8:21 Another of his **d** said, "Lord, first let me return
8:23 into the boat and started across the lake with his **d**.
8:25 The **d** went to him and woke him up, shouting,
8:27 The **d** just sat there in awe. "Who is this?"
9:10 invited Jesus and his **d** to be his dinner guests,
9:11 teacher eat with such scum?" they asked his **d**.
9:14 One day the **d** of John the Baptist came to Jesus
9:14 and the Pharisees fast, but your **d** don't fast?"
9:19 and the **d** were going to the official's home,
9:37 He said to his **d**, "The harvest is so great,
10:1 Jesus called his twelve **d** to him and gave them
10:5 Jesus sent the twelve **d** out with these instructions:
11:1 finished giving these instructions to his twelve **d**,
11:2 Messiah was doing. So he sent his **d** to ask Jesus,
11:7 When John's **d** had gone, Jesus began talking
12:1 His **d** were hungry, so they began breaking off
12:2 and protested, "Your **d** shouldn't be doing that!
12:49 Then he pointed to his **d** and said, "These are my
13:10 His **d** came and asked him, "Why do you always
13:36 His **d** said, "Please explain the story of the weeds
14:12 John's **d** came for his body and buried it.
14:15 That evening the **d** came to him and said, "This is
14:19 to each disciple, and the **d** gave them to the people.
14:22 Jesus made his **d** get back into the boat and cross
14:24 the **d** were in trouble far away from land,
14:26 When the **d** saw him, they screamed in terror,
14:33 Then the **d** worshiped him. "You really are the
15:2 "Why do your **d** disobey our age-old traditions?"
15:12 Then the **d** came to him and asked, "Do you
15:23 a word. Then his **d** urged him to send her away.
15:32 Then Jesus called his **d** to him and said, "I feel
15:33 The **d** replied, "And where would we get enough
15:36 broke them into pieces, and gave them to the **d**,
16:5 the **d** discovered they had forgotten to bring any
16:13 he asked his **d**, "Who do people say that the Son
16:21 then on Jesus began to tell his **d** plainly that he had
16:24 Then Jesus said to the **d**, "If any of you wants to
17:6 The **d** were terrified and fell face down on the
17:10 His **d** asked, "Why do the teachers of religious
17:13 Then the **d** realized he had been speaking of John
17:16 So I brought him to your **d**, but they couldn't heal
17:19 Afterward the **d** asked Jesus privately,
18:1 About that time the **d** came to Jesus and asked,
19:10 Jesus' **d** then said to him, "Then it is better not to
19:13 pray for them. The **d** told them not to bother him.
19:23 Then Jesus said to his **d**, "I tell you the truth,
19:25 The **d** were astounded. "Then who in the world
20:17 he took the twelve **d** aside privately and told them
20:24 When the ten other **d** heard what James and John
20:29 As Jesus and the **d** left the city of Jericho, a huge
21:1 As Jesus and the **d** approached Jerusalem,
21:6 The two **d** did as Jesus said.
21:20 The **d** were amazed when they saw this and asked,
22:16 They decided to send some of their **d**, along with
23:1 Then Jesus said to the crowds and to his **d**,
24:1 his **d** pointed out to him the various Temple
24:3 His **d** came to him privately and asked,
26:1 had finished saying these things, he said to his **d**,
26:8 The **d** were indignant when they saw this. "What a
26:14 Then Judas Iscariot, one of the twelve **d**, went to
26:17 Unleavened Bread, the **d** came to Jesus and asked,
26:18 and I will eat the Passover meal with my **d** at your
26:19 So the **d** did as Jesus told them and prepared the
26:20 Jesus sat down at the table with the twelve **d**.
26:26 Then he broke it in pieces and gave it to the **d**,
26:35 deny you!" And all the other **d** vowed the same.
26:40 Then he returned to the **d** and found them asleep.
26:45 Then he came to the **d** and said, "Still sleeping?
26:47 even as he said this, Judas, one of the twelve **d**,
26:56 At that point, all the **d** deserted him and fled.
27:64 This will prevent his **d** from coming and stealing
28:7 and tell his **d** he has been raised from the dead,
28:8 and they rushed to find the **d** to give them the
28:13 'Jesus' **d** came during the night while we were
28:16 Then the eleven **d** left for Galilee, going to the
28:18 Jesus came and told his **d**, "I have been given
28:19 Therefore, go and make **d** of all the nations,
28:20 Teach these new **d** to obey all the commands I
Mk 1:17 Jesus called out to them, "Come, be my **d**, and I
1:29 After Jesus and his **d** left the synagogue, they went
2:15 Levi invited Jesus and his **d** to be his dinner guests,
2:16 they said to his **d**, "Why does he eat with such
2:18 John's **d** and the Pharisees sometimes fasted.
2:18 "Why do John's **d** and the Pharisees fast, but your **d** don't fast?"
2:23 his **d** began breaking off heads of wheat.
3:7 Jesus and his **d** went out to the lake, followed by a
3:9 Jesus instructed his **d** to bring around a boat
3:20 soon he and his **d** couldn't even find time to eat.
4:10 when Jesus was alone with the twelve **d** and with
4:34 but afterward when he was alone with his **d**,
4:35 As evening came, Jesus said to his **d**, "Let's cross
5:31 His **d** said to him, "All this crowd is pressing
5:40 and his three **d** into the room where the girl was
6:1 of the country and returned with his **d** to Nazareth,
6:7 And he called his twelve **d** together and sent them
6:12 So the **d** went out, telling all they met to turn from
6:29 When John's **d** heard what had happened,
6:35 Late in the afternoon his **d** came to him and said,
6:41 the bread and fish to the **d** to give to the people.
6:45 Jesus made his **d** get back into the boat and head
6:47 the **d** were in their boat out in the middle of the
7:2 They noticed that some of Jesus' **d** failed to follow
7:5 "Why don't your **d** follow our age-old customs?
7:17 and his **d** asked him what he meant by the
8:1 out of food again. Jesus called his **d** and told them,
8:4 for them here in the wilderness?" his **d** asked.
8:6 broke them into pieces, and gave them to his **d**,
8:7 also blessed these and told the **d** to pass them out.
8:10 he got into a boat with his **d** and crossed over to
8:14 But the **d** discovered they had forgotten to bring
8:27 Jesus and his **d** left Galilee and went up to the
8:32 As he talked about this openly with his **d**,
8:33 Jesus turned and looked at his **d** and then said to
8:34 Then he called his **d** and the crowds to come over

9:14 they found a great crowd surrounding the other **d**,
9:18 So I asked your **d** to cast out the evil spirit,
9:28 when Jesus was alone in the house with his **d**,
9:31 in order to spend more time with his **d** and teach
9:33 and his **d** settled in the house where they would be
9:35 He sat down and called the twelve **d** over to him.
10:10 Later, when he was alone with his **d** in the house,
10:13 bless them, but the **d** told them not to bother him.
10:14 was happening, he was very displeased with his **d**.
10:23 Jesus looked around and said to his **d**, "How hard
10:26 The **d** were astounded. "Then who in the world
10:28 mention all that he and the other **d** had left behind.
10:32 The **d** were filled with dread and the people
10:32 Taking the twelve **d** aside, Jesus once more began
10:41 When the ten other **d** discovered what James
10:46 Later, as Jesus and his **d** left town, a great crowd
11: 1 As Jesus and his **d** approached Jerusalem,
11: 4 The two **d** left and found the colt standing in the
11:11 Then he went out to Bethany with the twelve **d**.
11:14 eat your fruit again!" And the **d** heard him say it.
11:19 That evening Jesus and the **d** left the city.
11:20 the **d** noticed it was withered from the roots.
11:22 Then Jesus said to the **d**, "Have faith in God.
12:43 He called his **d** to him and said, "I assure you,
13: 1 one of his **d** said, "Teacher, look at these
14:10 Then Judas Iscariot, one of the twelve **d**, went to
14:12 Jesus' **d** asked him, "Where do you want us to go
14:14 where I can eat the Passover meal with my **d**?'
14:16 So the two **d** went on ahead into the city and found
14:17 In the evening Jesus arrived with the twelve **d**.
14:22 Then he broke it in pieces and gave it to the **d**,
14:37 Then he returned and found the **d** asleep.
14:43 as he said this, Judas, one of the twelve **d**,
14:50 Meanwhile, all his **d** deserted him and ran away.
16: 7 Now go and give this message to his **d**,
16:10 She went and found the **d**, who were grieving
16:14 Still later he appeared to the eleven **d** as they were
16:20 And the **d** went everywhere and preached,
Lk 1: 2 the reports circulating among us from the early **d**
5:30 of religious law complained bitterly to Jesus' **d**,
5:33 The religious leaders complained that Jesus' **d**
5:33 "John the Baptist's **d** always fast and pray,"
5:33 they declared, "and so do the **d** of the Pharisees.
6: 1 his **d** broke off heads of wheat, rubbed off the
6:13 At daybreak he called together all of his **d**
6:17 the **d** stood with Jesus on a large, level area,
6:20 Then Jesus turned to his **d** and said, / "God blesses
7:11 Soon afterward Jesus went with his **d** to the village
7:18 The **d** of John the Baptist told John about
7:18 Jesus was doing. So John called for two of his **d**,
7:20 John's two **d** found Jesus and said to him,
7:22 Then he told John's **d**, "Go back to John and tell
8: 1 Kingdom of God. He took his twelve **d** with him,
8: 3 their own resources to support Jesus and his **d**.
8: 9 His **d** asked him what the story meant.
8:22 One day Jesus said to his **d**, "Let's cross over to
8:24 The **d** woke him up, shouting, "Master, Master,
9:12 Late in the afternoon the twelve **d** came to him
9:16 the bread and fish to the **d** to give to the people.
9:18 praying, he came over to his **d** and asked them,
9:40 I begged your **d** to cast the spirit out, but they
9:43 wonderful things he was doing, Jesus said to his **d**,
10: 1 The Lord now chose seventy-two other **d** and sent
10:16 Then he said to the **d**, "Anyone who accepts your
10:17 When the seventy-two **d** returned, they joyfully
10:23 when they were alone, he turned to the **d** and said,
10:38 and the **d** continued on their way to Jerusalem,
11: 1 one of his **d** came to him as he finished and said,
11: 1 "Lord, teach us to pray, just as John taught his **d**."
12: 1 Jesus turned first to his **d** and warned them,
12:22 Then turning to his **d**, Jesus said, "So I tell you,
16: 1 Jesus told this story to his **d**: "A rich man hired a
17: 1 One day Jesus said to his **d**, "There will always be
17:22 Later he talked again about this with his **d**.
17:37 the **d** asked. Jesus replied, "Just as the gathering of
18: 1 One day Jesus told his **d** a story to illustrate their
18:15 bless them, but the **d** told them not to bother him.
18:16 Then Jesus called for the children and said to the **d**,
18:24 Jesus watched him go and then said to his **d**,
18:31 Gathering the twelve **d** around him, Jesus told
19:28 went on toward Jerusalem, walking ahead of his **d**.
19:29 on the Mount of Olives, he sent two **d** ahead.
19:34 And the **d** simply replied, "The Lord needs it."
20:45 the crowds listening, he turned to his **d** and said,
21: 5 Some of his **d** began talking about the beautiful
22: 3 into Judas Iscariot, who was one of the twelve **d**,
22:11 where I can eat the Passover meal with my **d**?'
22:19 he broke it in pieces and gave it to the **d**, saying,
22:23 Then the **d** began to ask each other which of them
22:39 Then, accompanied by the **d**, Jesus left the upstairs
22:45 At last he stood up again and returned to the **d**,
22:47 mob approached, led by Judas, one of his twelve **d**.
22:49 When the other **d** saw what was about to happen,
22:59 "This must be one of Jesus' **d** because he is a
24: 9 So they rushed back to tell his eleven **d**—
24:33 where the eleven **d** and the other followers of Jesus
Jn 1:35 John was again standing with two of his **d**.
1:37 Then John's two **d** turned and followed Jesus.
2: 2 and his **d** were also invited to the celebration.
2:11 display of his glory. And his **d** believed in him.
2:12 a few days with his mother, his brothers, and his **d**.
2:17 Then his **d** remembered this prophecy from the
2:22 the dead, the **d** remembered that he had said this.
3:22 Afterward Jesus and his **d** left Jerusalem, but they
3:25 argument with John's **d** over ceremonial cleansing.
3:26 John's **d** came to him and said, "Teacher, the man
4: 1 is baptizing and making more **d** than John"
4: 2 Jesus himself didn't baptize them—his **d** did).
4: 8 because his **d** had gone into the village to buy
4:27 Just then his **d** arrived. They were astonished to
4:31 Meanwhile, the **d** were urging Jesus to eat.
4:33 "Who brought it to him?" the **d** asked each other.
6: 3 into the hills and sat down with his **d** around him.
6:12 Jesus told his **d**, "so that nothing is wasted."
6:16 That evening his **d** went down to the shore to wait
6:22 knew that he and his **d** had come over together
6:22 and that the **d** had gone off in their boat,
6:24 nor his **d**, they got into the boats and went across
6:60 Even his **d** said, "This is very hard to understand.
6:61 Jesus knew within himself that his **d** were
6:66 At this point many of his **d** turned away
8:31 "You are truly my **d** if you keep obeying my
9: 2 "Teacher," his **d** asked him, "why was this man
9:27 hear it again? Do you want to become his **d**, too?"
9:28 "You are his disciple, but we are **d** of Moses.
11: 7 Finally after two days, he said to his **d**, "Let's go
11: 8 But his **d** objected. "Teacher," they said, "only a
11:12 The **d** said, "Lord, if he is sleeping, that means he
11:16 the Twin, said to his fellow **d**, "Let's go, too—
11:54 the village of Ephraim, and stayed there with his **d**.
12: 4 But Judas Iscariot, one of his **d**—the one who
12:16 His **d** didn't realize at the time that this was a
12:26 All those who want to be my **d** must come
13: 1 He now showed the **d** the full extent of his love.
13:22 The **d** looked at each other, wondering whom he
13:23 One of Jesus' **d**, the one Jesus loved, was sitting
13:35 will prove to the world that you are my **d**."
15: 8 My true **d** produce much fruit. This brings great
16:17 The **d** asked each other, "What does he mean
16:29 Then his **d** said, "At last you are speaking plainly
17:20 "I am praying not only for these **d** but also for all
17:25 know you, but I do; and these **d** know you sent me.
18: 1 Jesus crossed the Kidron Valley with his **d**
18: 2 Jesus had gone there many times with his **d**.
18:15 followed along behind, as did another of the **d**.
18:17 asked Peter, "Aren't you one of Jesus' **d**?"
18:25 they asked him again, "Aren't you one of his **d**?"
20:18 Mary Magdalene found the **d** and told them,
20:19 the **d** were meeting behind locked doors
20:24 One of the **d**, Thomas (nicknamed the Twin),
20:26 Eight days later the **d** were together again, and this
20:30 Jesus' **d** saw him do many other miraculous signs
21: 1 Later Jesus appeared again to the **d** beside the Sea
21: 2 Several of the **d** were there—Simon Peter,
21: 2 in Galilee, the sons of Zebedee, and two other **d**.
21: 4 At dawn the **d** saw Jesus standing on the beach,
21:14 This was the third time Jesus had appeared to his **d**
Ac 4: 7 They brought in the two **d** and demanded,
14:21 the Good News in Derbe and making many **d**,
21: 4 These **d** prophesied through the Holy Spirit that
21:16 man originally from Cyprus and one of the early **d**.
1Co 9: 5 bring a Christian wife along with us as the other **d**
Gal 6:13 so they can brag about it and claim you as their **d**.

DISCIPLES' (3) [DISCIPLE]

Mt 17:23 the dead." And the **d** hearts were filled with grief.
Jn 12: 6 he was a thief who was in charge of the **d** funds,
13: 5 Then he began to wash the **d** feet and to wipe them

DISCIPLINE (41) [DISCIPLINED, DISCIPLINES, SELF-DISCIPLINE]

Dt 11: 2 who have never experienced the **d** of the LORD
21:18 obey his father or mother, even though they **d** him.
Ps 6: 1 not rebuke me in your anger / or **d** me in your rage.
32: 4 Day and night your hand of **d** was heavy on me.
38: 1 me in your anger! / Don't **d** me in your rage!
39:11 When you **d** people for their sins, / their lives can
50:17 For you refuse my **d** / and treat my laws like trash.
94:12 Happy are those whom you **d**, LORD, / and those
Pr 1: 2 of these proverbs is to teach people wisdom and **d**,
1: 3 people will receive instruction in **d**, good conduct,
1: 7 of knowledge. Only fools despise wisdom and **d**.
5:12 and you will say, "How I hated **d**! If only I had not
6:23 ahead of you. The correction of **d** is the way to life.
12: 1 To learn, you must love **d**; it is stupid to hate
13: 1 A wise child accepts a parent's **d**; a young mocker
13:24 If you refuse to **d** your children, it proves you
13:24 love your children, you will be prompt to **d** them.
15: 5 Only a fool despises a parent's **d**; whoever learns
16:22 to those who possess it, but **d** is wasted on fools.
19:18 **D** your children while there is hope. If you don't,
20:30 cleanses away evil; such **d** purifies the heart.
22:15 is filled with foolishness, but **d** will drive it away.
23:14 Physical **d** may well save them from death.
23:23 ever sell it; also get wisdom, **d**, and discernment.
29:15 To **d** and reprimand a child produces wisdom,
29:17 **D** your children, and they will give you happiness
29:19 mere words are not enough—**d** is needed.
Isa 26:16 We were bowed beneath the burden of your **d**.
38:16 Lord, your **d** is good, / for it leads to life
Jer 17:23 to pay attention and would not respond to **d**.
30:11 But I must **d** you; I cannot let you go unpunished.
46:28 But I must **d** you; I cannot let you go unpunished."
La 3:27 good for the young to submit to the yoke of his **d**.
1Co 9:27 I **d** my body like an athlete, training it to do what it
Eph 6: 4 bring them up with the **d** and instruction approved
Col 2:23 strong devotion, humility, and severe bodily **d**.
Heb 12: 7 As you endure this divine **d**, remember that God is
12: 8 If God doesn't **d** you as he does all of his children,
12: 9 cheerfully submit to the **d** of our heavenly Father
12:10 But God's **d** is always right and good for us
12:11 No **d** is enjoyable while it is happening—it is

DISCIPLINED (11) [DISCIPLINE]

1Sa 3:13 sons are blaspheming God and he hasn't **d** them.
1Ki 1: 6 King David, had never **d** him at any time,
Ps 119:67 I used to wander off until you **d** me; / but now I
119:75 decisions are fair; / you **d** me because I needed it.
Jer 31:18 'You **d** me severely, but I deserved it.
1Co 11:32 But when we are judged and **d** by the Lord,
Tit 1: 8 and be fair. He must live a devout and **d** life.
Heb 12: 7 Whoever heard of a child who was never **d**?
12: 9 Since we respect our earthly fathers who **d** us,
12:10 For our earthly fathers **d** us for a few years,
1Pe 4: 7 Therefore, be earnest and **d** in your prayers.

DISCIPLINES (7) [DISCIPLINE]

Dt 8: 5 So you should realize that just as a parent **d** a child, the LORD your God **d** you to help you.
Job 33:19 Or God **d** people with sickness and pain,
Pr 3:11 My child, don't ignore it when the LORD **d** you,
Heb 12: 5 "My child, don't ignore it when the Lord **d** you,
12: 6 For the Lord **d** those he loves, / and he punishes
Rev 3:19 I am the one who corrects and **d** everyone I love.

DISCOMFITED, DISCOMFITURE [KJV]

See CRUSH, CHASED, PANIC

DISCOMFORT (2)

Ps 41: 3 when they are sick / and eases their pain and **d**.
Jnh 4: 6 This eased some of his **d**, and Jonah was very

DISCONTENT (1) [DISCONTENTED]

Ac 6: 1 rapidly multiplied, there were rumblings of **d**.

DISCONTENTED (1) [DISCONTENT]

1Sa 22: 2 who were in trouble or in debt or who were just **d**

DISCONTINUED (1)

Ezr 6: 8 in your province so that the work will not be **d**.

DISCORD (1)

Pr 6:19 out lies, / a person who sows **d** among brothers.

DISCOURAGE (2) [DISCOURAGED, DISCOURAGING]

Nu 32: 7 "Are you trying to **d** the rest of the people of Israel
Ezr 4: 4 Then the local residents tried to **d** and frighten the

DISCOURAGED (32) [DISCOURAGE]

Ex 6: 9 They had become too **d** by the increasing burden
Nu 32: 9 they **d** the people of Israel from entering the land
Dt 1:21 has promised you. Don't be afraid! Don't be **d**!'
31: 8 Do not be afraid or **d**, for the LORD is the one
Jos 1: 9 be strong and courageous! Do not be afraid or **d**.
8: 1 the LORD said to Joshua, "Do not be afraid or **d**.
10:25 "Don't ever be afraid or **d**," Joshua told his men.
14: 8 and **d** them from entering the Promised Land.
2Sa 11:25 "Well, tell Joab not to be **d**," David said.
17: 2 I will catch up to him while he is weary and **d**.
1Ch 28:20 Don't be afraid or **d** by the size of the task,
2Ch 20:15 Don't be **d** by this mighty army, for the battle is
20:17 of Judah and Jerusalem. Do not be afraid or **d**.
Job 29:24 When they were **d**, I smiled at them. My look of
Ps 34: 2 only in the LORD; / let all who are **d** take heart.
42: 5 Why am I **d**? / Why so sad? / I will put my hope in
42: 6 my God! / Now I am deeply **d**, / but I will
42:11 Why am I **d**? / Why so sad? / I will put my hope in
43: 5 Why am I **d**? / Why so sad? / I will put my hope in
119:25 I lie in the dust, completely **d**; / revive me by your
Pr 3:11 and don't be **d** when he corrects you.
Ecc 5:17 they live under a cloud—frustrated, **d**, and angry.
Isa 24:16 I am **d**, for evil still prevails, and treachery is
Jer 45: 5 things for yourself? Don't do it! But don't be **d**.
Eze 13:22 You have **d** the righteous with your lies, when I
Zec 8: 6 you now, a small and **d** remnant of God's people.
8:13 So don't be afraid or **d**, but instead get on with
2Co 2: 7 may become so **d** that he won't be able to recover.
7: 6 But God, who encourages those who are **d**,
Gal 6: 9 Don't get **d** and give up, for we will reap a harvest
Col 3:21 If you do, they will become **d** and quit trying.
Heb 12: 5 and don't be **d** when he corrects you.

DISCOURAGING (2) [DISCOURAGE]

Nu 13:32 So they spread **d** reports about the land among the
14:36 the LORD by spreading **d** reports about the land

DISCOVER (20) [DISCOVERED, DISCOVERS, DISCOVERY]

Ge 42:12 "You have come to **d** how vulnerable the famine
Lev 4:14 When they **d** their sin, the leaders of the
Nu 14:34 You will **d** what it is like to have me for an
27:21 and the rest of the community of Israel will **d** what
Jos 2: 3 They are spies sent here to **d** the best way to attack
1Sa 23:23 **D** his hiding places, and come back with a more
2Sa 3:25 to spy on you and to **d** everything you are doing!"
Ezr 4:15 where you will **d** what a rebellious city this has
5:17 **d** whether King Cyrus ever issued a decree to
Job 11: 7 Can you **d** everything there is to know about the
28:21 Even the sharp-eyed birds in the sky cannot **d** it.
Pr 8:12 I know where to **d** knowledge and discernment.
25: 2 conceal things and the king's privilege to **d** them.
25: 3 No one can **d** the height of heaven, the depth of the

Ecc 8:17 This reminded me that no one can **d** everything
Isa 9:9 and the people of Israel and Samaria will soon **d** it.
Jer 8:4 start down the wrong road and **d** their mistake,
Eze 29:6 "All the people of Egypt will **d** that I am the
Jn 3:33 Those who believe him **d** that God is true.
Ac 24:11 You can quickly **d** that it was no more than twelve

DISCOVERED (32) [DISCOVER]

Ge 36:24 This is the Anah who **d** the hot springs in the
37:29 When he **d** that Joseph was missing, he tore his
Lev 10:16 of the sin offering, he **d** that it had been burned up.
Dt 22:14 'I **d** she was not a virgin when I married her.'
22:22 "If a man is **d** committing adultery, both he
Jdg 6:28 someone **d** that the altar of Baal had been knocked
16:9 in a fire. So the secret of his strength was not **d**.
21:8 And they **d** that no one from Jabesh-gilead had
1Sa 19:16 they **d** that it was only an idol in the bed with a
2Sa 2:30 he **d** that only nineteen men were missing,
11:5 When Bathsheba **d** that she was pregnant, she sent
2Ki 6:20 LORD did, and they **d** that they were in Samaria.
17:4 When the king of Assyria **d** this treachery,
Ne 8:14 they **d** that the LORD had commanded through
13:10 I also **d** that the Levites had not been given what
Est 6:2 In those records he **d** an account of how Mordecai
Ecc 1:13 I soon **d** that God has dealt a tragic existence to the
7:26 I **d** that a seductive woman is more bitter than
7:29 I **d** that God created people to be upright, but they
8:16 I **d** that there is ceaseless activity, day and night.
Jer 11:9 "I have **d** a conspiracy against me among the
Eze 20:6 and her descendants out of Egypt to a land I had **d**
Mt 13:44 is like a treasure that a man **d** hidden in a field.
13:46 When he **d** a pearl of great value, he sold
16:5 the disciples **d** they had forgotten to bring any
Mk 8:14 But the disciples **d** they had forgotten to bring any
10:41 When the ten other disciples **d** what James
Lk 2:46 Three days later they finally **d** him. He was in the
10:42 Mary has **d** it—and I won't take it away from
Ac 20:3 He was preparing to sail back to Syria when he **d** a
23:29 I soon **d** it was something regarding their religious
Rev 2:2 are apostles but are not. You have **d** they are liars.

DISCOVERS (4) [DISCOVER]

Lev 13:12 "Now suppose the priest **d** after his examination
13:26 But if the priest **d** that there is no white hair in the
Dt 24:1 but later **d** something about her that is shameful.
Pr 4:22 and radiant health to anyone who **d** their meaning.

DISCOVERY (1) [DISCOVER]

Ps 145:3 most worthy of praise! / His greatness is beyond **d**!

DISCREDIT (2)

Ne 6:13 Then they would be able to accuse and **d** me.
Job 40:8 Are you going to **d** my justice and condemn me

DISCREET (1) [DISCRETION]

Pr 5:2 Then you will learn to be **d** and will store up

DISCRETION (4) [DISCREET]

1Ch 29:12 and it is at your **d** that people are made great
Pr 11:22 but lacks **d** is like a gold ring in a pig's snout.
16:22 **D** is a life-giving fountain to those who possess it,
Da 2:14 Daniel handled the situation with wisdom and **d**.

DISCRIMINATED (1) [DISCRIMINATION]

Ac 6:1 saying that their widows were being **d** against in

DISCRIMINATION (1) [DISCRIMINATED]

Jas 2:4 doesn't this **d** show that you are guided by wrong

DISCUSS (16) [DISCUSSED, DISCUSSING, DISCUSSION, DISCUSSIONS]

Ge 34:6 came out to **d** the matter with Jacob.
1Sa 8:4 the leaders of Israel met at Ramah to **d** the matter
1Ki 12:6 Then King Rehoboam went to **d** the matter with
2Ch 10:6 Then King Rehoboam went to **d** the matter with
Pr 25:9 So **d** the matter with them privately. Don't tell
Jer 40:12 They stopped at Mizpah to **d** their plans with
Mt 26:4 to **d** how to capture Jesus secretly and put him to
27:1 and other leaders met again to **d** how to persuade
Mk 1:27 and they began to **d** what had happened.
3:6 and met with the supporters of Herod to **d** plans for
15:1 the entire high council—met to **d** their next step.
Lk 6:11 wild with rage and began to **d** what to do with him.
14:32 he will send a delegation to **d** terms of peace.
16:5 money to his employer to come and **d** the situation.
22:4 and captains of the Temple guard to **d** the best way
Jn 11:47 and Pharisees called the high council together to **d**

DISCUSSED (4) [DISCUSS]

Ge 41:38 As they **d** who should be appointed for the job,
1Sa 5:8 The rulers **d** it and replied, "Move it to the city of
Mt 12:14 called a meeting and **d** plans for killing Jesus.
Ac 25:14 of several days, Festus **d** Paul's case with the king.

DISCUSSING (7) [DISCUSS]

Mk 2:8 Jesus knew what they were **d** among themselves,
9:33 asked them, "What were you **d** out on the road?"
16:3 On the way they were **d** who would roll the stone
Lk 2:46 the religious teachers, **d** deep questions with them.
14:31 and **d** whether his army of ten thousand is strong
Jn 4:27 him why he was doing it or what they had been **d**.
Ac 17:21 seemed to spend all their time **d** the latest ideas.)

DISCUSSION (9) [DISCUSS]

2Sa 19:9 throughout the tribes of Israel there was much **d**
1Ch 12:19 After much **d**, they sent them back, for they said,
Mt 27:7 After some **d** they finally decided to buy the
Mk 12:28 religious law was standing there listening to the **d**.
Lk 24:17 "You seem to be in a deep **d** about something,"
Jn 7:12 There was a lot of **d** about him among the crowds.
Ac 15:7 after a long **d**, Peter stood and addressed them as
15:12 There was no further **d**, and everyone listened as
17:33 That ended Paul's **d** with them,

DISCUSSIONS (3) [DISCUSS]

1Ti 6:20 foolish **d** with those who oppose you with their
2Ti 2:16 foolish **d** that lead to more and more ungodliness.
Tit 3:9 Do not get involved in foolish **d** about spiritual

DISDAINFUL (1)

Pr 30:13 They are proud beyond description and **d**.

DISEASE (75) [DISEASED, DISEASES]

Ex 5:3 If we don't, we will surely die by **d** or the sword."
Lev 13:2 their skin that develops into a contagious skin **d**,
13:3 more than skin-deep, then it is a contagious skin **d**,
13:6 the clothes, the person will be considered free of **d**.
13:8 ceremonially unclean, for it is a contagious skin **d**.
13:9 "Anyone who develops a contagious skin **d** must
13:11 it is clearly a contagious skin **d**, and the priest must
13:11 because it is clear that the skin is defiled by the **d**.
13:13 person to see if the **d** covers the entire body.
13:15 sores indicate the presence of a contagious skin **d**.
13:20 If the priest finds the **d** to be more than skin-deep,
13:20 It is a contagious skin **d** that has broken out in the
13:22 because it is a contagious skin **d**.
13:25 a contagious skin **d** has broken out in the burn.
13:25 for it is clearly a contagious skin **d**.
13:27 for it is clearly a contagious skin **d**.
13:30 The infection is a contagious skin **d** of the head
13:42 or the back of his head, this is a contagious skin **d**.
13:44 the man is infected with a contagious skin **d**
13:45 "Those who suffer from any contagious skin **d**
13:46 As long as the **d** lasts, they will be ceremonially
14:2 seeking purification from a contagious skin **d**.
14:3 finds that someone has been healed of the skin **d**,
14:10 each person cured of the skin **d** must bring two
14:19 ceremony for the person cured of the skin **d**.
14:32 who have recovered from a contagious skin **d**
14:35 'It looks like my house has some kind of **d**.'
14:54 dealing with the various kinds of contagious skin **d**
14:57 followed when dealing with any contagious skin **d**
22:4 "If any of the priests have a contagious skin **d**
Nu 5:2 anyone from the camp who has a contagious skin **d**
Dt 28:22 The LORD will strike you with wasting **d**,
32:24 wasting famine, / burning fever, and deadly **d**.
1Ki 8:37 or plagues, or crop **d**, or attacks of locusts
2Ch 6:28 or plagues, or crop **d**, or attacks of locusts
16:12 year of his reign, Asa developed a serious foot **d**.
16:12 Even when the **d** became life threatening, he did
20:9 faced with any calamity such as war, **d**, or famine,
21:15 **d** until it causes your bowels to come out."
21:18 struck Jehoram with the severe intestinal **d**.
21:19 the **d** caused his bowels to come out, and he died
Job 18:13 **D** eats their skin; death devours their limbs.
Ps 38:11 loved ones and friends stay away, fearing my **d**.
Pr 5:11 Afterward you will groan in anguish when **d**
Isa 22:2 are lying everywhere, killed by famine and **d**.
Jer 14:12 I will give them only war, famine, and **d**."
21:7 else in the city have survived war, famine, and **d**,
21:9 famine, or **d**, but those who go out and surrender to
24:10 and **d** until they have vanished from the land of
27:8 and **d** upon that nation until Babylon has
27:13 Why should you choose war, famine, and **d**,
28:8 always warning of war, famine, and **d**.
29:17 and **d** upon them and make them like rotting figs—
29:18 Yes, I will pursue them with war, famine, and **d**,
32:24 Because of war, famine, and **d**, the city has been
32:36 the king of Babylon through war, famine, and **d**.'
34:17 set you free to be destroyed by war, famine, and **d**.
38:2 stays in Jerusalem will die from war, famine, or **d**,
42:17 Yes, you will die from war, famine, and **d**. None of
42:22 famine, and **d** in Egypt, where you insist on
44:13 them in Jerusalem, by war, famine, and **d**.
Eze 5:12 your people will die in the city from famine and **d**.
5:17 **D** and war will stalk your land, and I will bring the
6:11 they are going to die from war and famine and **d**.
6:12 **D** will strike down those who are far away in exile.
7:15 Those who stay inside will die of famine and **d**.
12:16 a few of them from death by war, famine, or **d**,
14:19 my fury by sending an epidemic of **d** into the land,
33:27 Those hiding in the forts and caves will die of **d**.
38:22 punish you and your hordes with **d** and bloodshed;
Mal 3:11 for I will guard them from insects and **d**.
Mt 4:23 people who had every kind of sickness and **d**.
9:35 he healed people of every sort of **d** and illness.
10:1 evil spirits and to heal every kind of **d** and illness.
Rev 6:8 with the sword and famine and **d** and wild animals.

DISEASED (3) [DISEASE]

1Ki 15:23 *Kings of Judah.* In his old age his feet became **d**.
Mal 1:8 it wrong to offer animals that are crippled and **d**?
Lk 16:20 At his door lay a **d** beggar named Lazarus.

DISEASES (16) [DISEASE]

Ex 15:26 then I will not make you suffer the **d** I sent on the
Lev 26:16 with wasting **d**, and with burning fevers,
Dt 7:15 He will not let you suffer from the terrible **d** you
24:8 "Watch all contagious skin **d** carefully and follow
28:21 The LORD will send **d** among you until none of
28:60 He will bring against you all the **d** of Egypt that
29:22 the land and the **d** the LORD will send against it.
Ps 103:3 He forgives all my sins / and heals all my **d**.
Jer 16:4 They will die from terrible **d**. No one will mourn
Mt 8:17 "He took our sicknesses and removed our **d**."
Mk 1:34 of sick people who had many different kinds of **d**,
Lk 4:40 No matter what their **d** were, the touch of his hand
5:15 to hear him preach and to be healed of their **d**.
7:21 very time, he cured many people of their various **d**,
9:1 and authority to cast out demons and to heal all **d**.
Ac 19:12 they were healed of their **d**, and any evil spirits

DISFIGURE (1) [DISFIGURED]

Job 14:20 You **d** them in death and send them away.

DISFIGURED (1) [DISFIGURE]

Isa 52:14 so **d** one would scarcely know he was a person.

DISGRACE (39) [DISGRACED, DISGRACEFUL]

Ge 34:14 It would be a **d** for her to marry a man like you!
Lev 20:17 of either his father or his mother, it is a terrible **d**.
1Sa 11:2 right eye of every one of you as a **d** to all Israel!"
2Ki 19:3 This is a day of trouble, insult, and **d**.
2Ch 32:21 So Sennacherib returned home in **d** to his own
Ne 1:3 They are in great trouble and **d**. The wall of
2:17 the wall of Jerusalem and rid ourselves of this **d**!"
Job 12:21 He pours **d** upon princes and confiscates weapons
Ps 25:3 but **d** comes to those who try to deceive others.
35:4 Humiliate and **d** those trying to kill me; / turn them
40:14 take delight in my trouble / be turned back in **d**.
69:19 the insults I endure— / the humiliation and **d**.
70:2 take delight in my trouble / be turned back in **d**.
71:13 Bring **d** and destruction on those who accuse me.
83:16 Utterly **d** them / until they submit to your name,
109:29 obvious to all; / clothe my accusers with **d**.
119:78 Bring **d** upon the arrogant people who lied about
Pr 5:14 brink of utter ruin, and now I must face public **d**."
6:33 Wounds and constant **d** are his lot. His shame will
11:2 Pride leads to **d**, but with humility comes wisdom.
13:5 godly hate lies; the wicked come to shame and **d**.
13:18 ignore criticism, you will end in poverty and **d**;
14:34 exalts a nation, but sin is a **d** to any people.
18:3 contempt, shame, and **d** are sure to follow.
19:26 or chase away their mother are a public **d** and an
Isa 22:18 broken and useless. You are a **d** to your master.
37:3 This is a day of trouble, insult, and **d**.
Jer 10:14 They make idols, but the idols will **d** their makers,
14:21 Do not **d** yourself and the throne of your glory.
34:17 You will be considered a **d** by all the nations of the
50:12 homeland will be overwhelmed with shame and **d**.
51:17 They make idols, but the idols will **d** their makers,
Da 5:19 to honor and disgraced those he wanted to **d**.
Hos 4:7 They have exchanged the glory of God for the **d** of
Mt 1:19 the engagement quietly, so as not to **d** her publicly.
Lk 1:25 "He has taken away my **d** of having no children!"
1Co 11:22 Or do you really want to **d** the church of God
Heb 13:13 out to him outside the camp and bear the **d** he bore.
2Pe 2:13 They are a **d** and a stain among you. They revel in

DISGRACED (35) [DISGRACE]

2Sa 17:23 Ahithophel was publicly **d** when Absalom refused
Ezr 9:7 captured, robbed, and **d**, just as we are today.
Ps 6:10 May all my enemies be **d** and terrified. / May they
25:2 I trust in you, my God! / Do not let me be **d**,
25:3 No one who trusts in you will ever be **d**,
25:20 from them! / Do not let me be **d**, for I trust in you.
31:17 Don't let me be **d**, O LORD, / for I call out to you for help. / Let the wicked be **d**;
35:26 be humiliated and **d**. / May those who triumph
52:1 crime of yours, / you who have **d** God's people?
71:1 O LORD, you are my refuge; / never let me be **d**.
74:21 Don't let the downtrodden be constantly **d**!
89:45 before his time / and publicly **d** him. / *Interlude*
89:50 Consider, Lord, how your servants are **d**! / I carry
97:7 Those who worship idols are **d**— / all who brag
109:28 When they attack me, they will be **d**! / But I,
119:6 Then I will not be **d** / when I compare my life with
Pr 25:7 than to be sent to the end of the line, publicly **d**!
29:15 but a mother is **d** by an undisciplined child.
Isa 30:3 in trusting Pharaoh, you will be humiliated and **d**.
43:28 That is why I have **d** your priests and assigned
45:16 All who make idols will be humiliated and **d**.
45:17 be humiliated and **d** throughout everlasting ages.
Jer 15:9 She sits childless now, **d** and humiliated.
17:13 all who turn away from you will be **d** and shamed.
24:9 They will be **d** and mocked, taunted and cursed,
50:2 Her gods Bel and Marduk will be utterly **d**.
51:47 Her whole land will be **d**, and her dead will lie in
51:51 "We are insulted and **d** because the LORD's
Da 5:19 wanted to honor and **d** those he wanted to disgrace.
Joel 2:26 for you. Never again will my people be **d** like this.
2:27 My people will never again be **d** like this.
Mic 3:7 your faces in shame, and you diviners will be **d**.
Zep 3:18 for the appointed festivals; you will be **d** no more.
1Ti 3:7 that he will not fall into the Devil's trap and be **d**.

DISGRACEFUL (3) [DISGRACE]
Ge 34: 7 Shechem had done a **d** thing against Jacob's
Dt 22:21 She has committed a **d** crime in Israel by being
1Co 11:14 Isn't it obvious that it's **d** for a man to have long

DISGUISE (6) [DISGUISED, DISGUISING]
Ge 38:14 and covered herself with a veil to **d** herself.
1Ki 14: 2 "**D** yourself so that no one will recognize you as
20:38 having placed a bandage over his eyes to **d**
22:30 I will **d** myself so no one will recognize me,
2Ch 18:29 I will **d** myself so no one will recognize me,
2Co 11:14 Even Satan can **d** himself as an angel of light.

DISGUISED (4) [DISGUISE]
1Sa 28: 8 So Saul **d** himself by wearing ordinary clothing
1Ki 22:30 So Ahab **d** himself, and they went into battle.
2Ch 18:29 So Ahab **d** himself, and they went into battle.
Mt 7:15 "Beware of false prophets who come **d** as

DISGUISING (1) [DISGUISE]
2Co 11:13 They have fooled you by **d** themselves as apostles

DISGUST (3) [DISGUSTED, DISGUSTING]
Dt 18:12 things is an object of horror and **d** to the LORD.
2Sa 6:20 Michal came out to meet him and said in **d**,
Eze 23:22 very nations from which you turned away in **d**.

DISGUSTED (4) [DISGUST]
Job 10: 1 "I am **d** with my life. Let me complain freely.
Ecc 2:18 I am **d** that I must leave the fruits of my hard work
Eze 23:17 she became **d** with them and broke off their
23:18 "So I became **d** with Oholibah, just as I was with

DISGUSTING (11) [DISGUST]
Jer 6:15 Are they ashamed when they do these **d** things?
8:12 Are they ashamed when they do these **d** things?
12: 9 My chosen people have become as **d** to me as a
Eze 7: 3 I will call you to account for all your **d** behavior.
7: 8 complete your punishment for all your **d** behavior.
7:20 That is why I will make all their wealth **d** to them.
16:43 For to all your **d** sins, you have added these lewd
16:58 This is your punishment for all your **d** sins,
33:29 I have ruined the land because of their **d** sins,
44: 6 O people of Israel, enough of your **d** sins!
44: 7 Thus, in addition to all your other **d** sins, you have

DISH (9) [DISHES]
Ge 27: 9 I'll prepare your father's favorite **d** from them.
27:14 She took them and cooked a delicious meat **d**,
27:17 Then she gave him the meat **d**, with its rich aroma,
27:31 Esau prepared his father's favorite meat **d**
2Ki 21:13 away the people of Jerusalem as one wipes a **d**
1Ch 28:17 as well as the amount of silver for every **d**.
Jer 22:28 is this man Jehoiachin like a discarded, broken **d**?
Mt 23:25 so careful to clean the outside of the cup and the **d**,
Lk 11:39 so careful to clean the outside of the cup and the **d**,

DISHAN (5)
Ge 36:21 Dishon, Ezer, and **D**. These were the Horite clans,
36:28 The sons of **D** were Uz and Aran.
36:30 Dishon, Ezer, and **D**. The Horite clans are named
1Ch 1:38 Shobal, Zibeon, Anah, Dishon, Ezer, and **D**.
1:42 and Akan. The sons of **D** were Uz and Aran.

DISHES (11) [DISH]
Ex 25:29 And make gold plates and **d**, as well as pitchers
37:16 using pure gold, he made the plates, **d**, bowls,
Nu 4: 7 and place the **d**, spoons, bowls, cups,
1Ki 7:50 the cups, lamp snuffers, basins, **d**, and firepans,
2Ki 25:14 also took all the pots, shovels, lamp snuffers, **d**,
1Ch 28:17 sacrificial meat and for the basins, pitchers, and **d**,
2Ch 4:22 basins, **d**, and firepans, all of pure gold;
Jer 52:18 took all the pots, shovels, lamp snuffers, basins, **d**,
52:19 small bowls, firepans, basins, pots, lampstands, **d**,
Eze 27:13 Tubal, and Meshech brought slaves and bronze **d**.
Da 11: 8 with him, along with priceless gold and silver **d**.

DISHEVELED (1)
Mt 6:16 who try to look pale and **d** so people will admire

DISHON (7)
Ge 36:21 **D**, Ezer, and Dishan. These were the Horite clans,
36:25 The son of Anah was **D**, and Oholibamah was his
36:26 The sons of **D** were Hemdan, Eshban, Ithran,
36:30 **D**, Ezer, and Dishan. The Horite clans are named
1Ch 1:38 Shobal, Zibeon, Anah, **D**, Ezer, and Dishan.
1:41 The son of Anah was **D**. The sons of **D** were Hemdan, Eshban, Ithran,

DISHONEST (18) [DISHONESTLY, DISHONESTY]
Lev 6: 2 Or suppose they have been **d** with regard to a
19:35 "Do not use **d** standards when measuring length,
Dt 25:16 Those who cheat with **d** weights and measures are
1Sa 25: 3 of Caleb, was mean and **d** in all his dealings.
Job 13: 7 defending God by means of lies and **d** arguments?
Pr 15:27 **D** money brings grief to the whole family,
16: 8 It is better to be poor and godly than rich and **d**.
19: 1 to be poor and honest than to be a fool and **d**.
19:22 person attractive. And it is better to be poor than **d**.
20:23 double standards; he is not pleased by **d** scales.
Eze 22:13 I clap my hands in indignation over your **d** gain
28:18 sanctuaries with your many sins and your **d** trade.
Hos 12: 7 the people are like crafty merchants selling from **d**
Am 8: 5 in false measures and weigh it out on **d** scales.
Mic 6:11 can I tolerate all your merchants who use **d** scales
Lk 16: 1 went around that the manager was thoroughly **d**.
16: 8 "The rich man had to admire the **d** rascal for being
18:10 was a Pharisee, and the other was a **d** tax collector.

DISHONESTLY (1) [DISHONEST]
Mic 6:10 gained by **d** measuring out grain in short measures.

DISHONESTY (7) [DISHONEST]
1Sa 17:28 I know about your pride and **d**. You just want to
Pr 11: 3 treacherous people are destroyed by their **d**.
28:16 but a king will have a long reign if he hates **d**
Jer 22:17 "But you! You are full of selfish greed and **d**!
23:14 They commit adultery, and they love **d**.
Ro 3: 7 and condemn me as a sinner if my **d** highlights his
Rev 21:27 no one who practices shameful idolatry and **d**—

DISHONOR (14) [DISHONORED, DISHONORS]
Lev 21: 6 apart to God as holy and must never **d** his name.
21:15 that he may not **d** his descendants among the
1Sa 12:22 his chosen people, for that would **d** his great name.
Ps 35:26 triumph over me / be covered with shame and **d**.
44: 9 But now you have tossed us aside in **d**. / You no
74:10 Will you let them **d** your name forever?
Isa 61: 7 Instead of shame and **d**, you will inherit a double
Jer 3:25 Let us now lie down in shame and **d**, for we
20:11 Their **d** will never be forgotten.
Eze 36:20 the nations, they brought **d** to my holy name.
Mal 1:12 "But you **d** my name with your actions.
Jn 8:49 in me. For I honor my Father—and you **d** me.
Ac 5:41 them worthy to suffer **d** for the name of Jesus.
Ro 2:23 of knowing the law, but you **d** God by breaking it.

DISHONORED (9) [DISHONOR]
Ge 49: 4 with one of my wives; / you **d** me in my own bed.
1Ch 5: 1 But since he **d** his father by sleeping with one of
Ezr 4:14 and we do not want to see you **d** in this way,
Ps 74:18 LORD. / A foolish nation has **d** your name.
Eze 22:16 And when you have been **d** among the nations,
22:26 so that my holy name is greatly **d** among them.
36:21 which had been **d** by my people throughout the
36:22 which you **d** while you were scattered among the
36:23 great name is—the name you **d** among the nations.

DISHONORS (2) [DISHONOR]
1Co 11: 4 A man **d** Christ if he covers his head while praying
11: 5 But a woman **d** her husband if she prays

DISILLUSIONMENT (1)
Dt 28:20 you curses, confusion, and **d** in everything you do,

DISLOYAL (1) [DISLOYALTY]
Mal 2:14 But you have been **d** to her, though she remained

DISLOYALTY (1) [DISLOYAL]
Da 9: 7 you have driven us because of our **d** to you.

DISMANTLE (1)
Jer 22: 7 who will bring out their tools to **d** you.

DISMAY (7) [DISMAYED]
Jos 7: 6 and the leaders of Israel tore their clothing in **d**,
2Ki 5: 7 of Israel read it, he tore his clothes in **d** and said,
Pr 21:15 a joy to the godly, but it causes **d** among evildoers.
Isa 21: 3 I hear what God is planning; I am blinded with **d**.
Jer 2:12 at such a thing and shrink back in horror and **d**,
Eze 4:16 drop by drop, and the people will drink it with **d**.
Ac 14:14 they tore their clothing in **d** and ran out among the

DISMAYED (10) [DISMAY]
Ps 49:16 So don't be **d** when the wicked grow rich,
73:10 And so the people are **d** and confused, / drinking in
Isa 20: 5 How **d** will be the Philistines, who counted on the
41:10 for I am with you. Do not be **d**, for I am your God.
50: 7 the Sovereign LORD helps me, I will not be **d**.
Jer 30:10 my servant; do not be **d**, Israel, says the LORD.
46:27 be afraid, Jacob, my servant; do not be **d**, Israel.
Eze 2: 6 Do not be **d** by their dark scowls. For remember,
26:18 at your fall. / The islands are **d** as you pass away.'
Rev 13:10 But do not be **d**, for here is your opportunity to

DISMISSED (4)
1Ki 1:53 and Solomon **d** him, saying, "Go on home."
Ps 88: 4 I have been **d** as one who is dead, / like a strong
Lk 16: 2 report in order, because you are going to be **d**.'
Ac 19:41 Then he **d** them, and they dispersed.

DISMOUNTED (1)
Ge 24:64 Rebekah looked up and saw Isaac, she quickly **d**.

DISOBEDIENCE (5) [DISOBEY]
Ps 89:32 their sin with the rod, / and their **d** with beating.
Hos 10:10 I will attack you, too, for your rebellion and **d**.
Ro 4: 7 "Oh, what joy for those whose **d** is forgiven,
11:32 For God has imprisoned all people in their own **d**
Heb 2: 2 for every violation of the law and every act of **d**.

DISOBEDIENT (10) [DISOBEY]
Lev 26:41 then at last their **d** hearts will be humbled, and they
Ne 9:26 all this, they were **d** and rebelled against you.
Lk 1:17 and he will change **d** minds to accept godly
Ac 26:19 I was not **d** to that vision from heaven.
Ro 1:30 new ways of sinning and are **d** to their parents.
2Co 10: 6 And we will punish those who remained **d** after the
1Ti 1: 9 They are for people who are **d** and rebellious,
2Ti 3: 2 scoffing at God, **d** to their parents, and ungrateful.
Tit 1:16 They are despicable and **d**, worthless for doing
3: 3 Once we, too, were foolish and **d**. We were misled

DISOBEY (13) [DISOBEDIENCE, DISOBEDIENT, DISOBEYED, DISOBEYING, DISOBEYS]
Lev 26:18 "And if, in spite of this, you still **d** me, I will
Dt 4:26 If you **d** me, you will quickly disappear from the
8:11 forget the LORD your God and **d** his commands,
Jos 23:15 he will also bring disaster on you if you **d** him.
1Ki 9: 6 abandon me and **d** my commands and laws,
2Ch 7:19 "But if you abandon me and **d** the laws
24:20 Why do you **d** the LORD's commands so that
Ps 119:136 gush from my eyes / because people **d** your law.
Ecc 8: 3 For the king will punish those who **d** him.
Mt 15: 2 "Why do your disciples **d** our age-old traditions?"
Ac 21:28 and tells everybody to **d** the Jewish laws.
Ro 5:14 even though they did not **d** an explicit
Eph 5: 6 anger of God comes upon all those who **d** him.

DISOBEYED (18) [DISOBEY]
Lev 10: 1 they **d** the LORD by burning before him a
Nu 15:31 with contempt and deliberately **d** his commands,
Jos 5: 6 For they had **d** the LORD, and the LORD
Jdg 2: 2 their altars. Why, then, have you **d** my command?
1Sa 13:13 "You have **d** the command of the LORD your
15:24 I have **d** your instructions and the LORD's
1Ki 11:11 have not kept my covenant and have **d** my laws,
13:21 and have **d** the command the LORD your God
13:26 "It is the man of God who **d** the LORD's
Ne 9:29 and obstinate and **d** your commands.
Jer 40: 3 people have sinned against the LORD and **d** him.
Da 9:11 All Israel has **d** your law and turned away,
Ac 7:53 You deliberately **d** God's law, though you received
Ro 5:19 Because one person **d** God, many people became
11:22 He is severe to those who **d**, but kind to you as you
Heb 3:18 place of rest? He was speaking to those who **d** him.
4: 6 the Good News failed to enter because they **d** God.
1Pe 3:20 those who **d** God long ago when God waited

DISOBEYING (8) [DISOBEY]
Nu 14:41 "Why are you now **d** the LORD's orders to
2Ki 17:15 **d** the LORD's command not to imitate them.
Est 3: 3 "Why are you **d** the king's command?"
Am 4: 4 and Gilgal. Keep on **d**—your sins are mounting up!
Zep 3: 4 Its priests defile the Temple by **d** God's laws.
Jn 5:18 In addition to **d** the Sabbath rules, he had spoken
Ro 10:21 but they kept **d** me and arguing with me."
1Th 4: 8 Anyone who refuses to live by these rules is not **d**

DISOBEYS (1) [DISOBEY]
Heb 4:11 For anyone who **d** God, as the people of Israel did,

DISORDER (2) [DISORDERLY]
1Co 14:33 For God is not a God of **d** but of peace, as in all the
Jas 3:16 there you will find **d** and every kind of evil.

DISORDERLY (1) [DISORDER]
2Co 12:20 backstabbing, gossip, conceit, and **d** behavior.

DISOWN (2)
Nu 14:12 I will **d** them and destroy them with a plague.
Isa 63:16 Even if Abraham and Jacob would **d** us, LORD,

DISPATCHED (1)
Ps 78:49 all his fury, rage, and hostility. / He **d** against them

DISPENSATION [KJV] See RESPONSIBILITY, (SPECIAL) MINISTRY

DISPERSE (1) [DISPERSED]
Zep 3:15 of judgment and will **d** the armies of your enemy.

DISPERSED (3) [DISPERSE]
Ge 10:25 were divided into different language groups and **d**.
1Ch 1:19 were divided into different language groups and **d**.
Ac 19:41 Then he dismissed them, and they **d**.

DISPLACE (2) [DISPLACED]
Dt 18:14 The people you are about to **d** consult with
19: 1 and you will **d** them and settle in their towns

DISPLACED (1) [DISPLACE]
Dt 2:12 were driven out and **d** by the descendants of Esau.

DISPLAY (19) [DISPLAYED, DISPLAYING, DISPLAYS]

Ex 10: 1 so I can continue to **d** my power by performing
34:10 the awesome power I will **d** through you.
Dt 4: 6 you will **d** your wisdom and intelligence to the
4:37 brought you out of Egypt with a great **d** of power.
2Ch 2: 4 spices before him, to **d** the special sacrificial bread,
Est 1: 4 a tremendous **d** of the opulent wealth and glory of
Job 10:16 like a lion and **d** your awesome power against me.
Ps 19: 1 of God. / The skies **d** his marvelous craftsmanship.
68:28 **D** your power, O God, as you have in the past.
80: 1 above the cherubim, / **d** your radiant glory
Isa 35: 2 There the LORD will **d** his glory, the splendor of
49:18 be like jewels or bridal ornaments for you to **d**.
64: 6 When we proudly **d** our righteous deeds, we find
Eze 20:41 And I will **d** my holiness in you as all the nations
Da 9:15 your people from Egypt in a great **d** of power.
Lk 9:43 Awe gripped the people as they saw this **d** of
Jn 2:11 at Cana in Galilee was Jesus' first **d** of his glory.
1Co 4: 9 sometimes I think God has put us apostles on **d**,
Eph 4:24 You must **d** a new nature because you are a new

DISPLAYED (10) [DISPLAY]

Ex 14:31 that the LORD had **d** against the Egyptians,
Nu 4: 7 where the Bread of the Presence is **d**, and place the
14:13 "They know full well the power you **d** in rescuing
2Ch 30:22 for the skill they **d** as they served the LORD.
Ne 9:10 You **d** miraculous signs and wonders against
Isa 5:16 The holiness of God is **d** by his righteousness.
55: 4 He **d** my power by being my witness and a leader
Eze 38:16 and my holiness will be **d** by what happens to you.
39:27 their enemies, my holiness will be **d** to the nations.
1Pe 4:13 of sharing his glory when it is **d** to all the world.

DISPLAYING (2) [DISPLAY]

Nu 25:11 by **d** passionate zeal among them on my behalf.
Ro 9:17 "I have appointed you for the very purpose of **d**

DISPLAYS (2) [DISPLAY]

Isa 3: 9 on their faces gives them away and **d** their guilt.
Na 1: 3 He **d** his power in the whirlwind and the storm.

DISPLEASE (1) [DISPLEASED, DISPLEASURE]

1Th 2:15 driven us out. They **d** God and oppose everyone

DISPLEASED (7) [DISPLEASE]

2Sa 11:27 But the LORD was very **d** with what David had
1Ch 21: 7 God was very **d** with the census, and he punished
Pr 24:18 For the LORD will be **d** with you and will turn
Isa 59:15 and was **d** to find that there was no justice.
Hab 3: 8 Were you **d** with them? No, you were sending your
Mk 10:14 was happening, he was very **d** with his disciples.
Lk 19: 7 But the crowds were **d**. "He has gone to be the

DISPLEASURE (1) [DISPLEASE]

Pr 22:14 those living under the LORD's **d** will fall into it.

DISPOSAL (2)

2Ki 10: 2 and you have at your **d** chariots, horses, a fortified
Ne 13: 5 a large storage room and placed it at Tobiah's **d**.

DISPOSSESSED [KJV] See DROVE, TOOK (AWAY)

DISPUTE (6) [DISPUTED, DISPUTES]

Ex 22: 9 "Suppose there is a **d** between two people as to
Dt 25: 1 "Suppose two people take a **d** to court,
Jdg 12: 2 "I summoned you at the beginning of the **d**,
1Sa 17: 8 We will settle this **d** in single combat!
Pr 17:14 so drop the matter before a **d** breaks out.
Isa 45: 9 Does the clay **d** with the one who shapes it, saying,

DISPUTED (1) [DISPUTE]

Jdg 11:25 Did he try to make a case against Israel for **d** land?

DISPUTES (6) [DISPUTE]

Jdg 4: 5 and the Israelites came to her to settle their **d**.
2Ch 19: 8 concerning both the law of the LORD and civil **d**.
Pr 18:18 and settle **d** between powerful opponents.
Isa 2: 4 The LORD will settle international **d**.
Mic 4: 3 The LORD will settle international **d**.
1Co 6: 4 If you have legal **d** about such matters, why do you

DISQUALIFIED (2) [DISQUALIFY]

1Co 9:27 that after preaching to others I myself might be **d**.
2Ti 2: 5 either follows the rules or is **d** and wins no prize.

DISQUALIFY (1) [DISQUALIFIED]

Lev 21:21 his physical defects **d** him from presenting

DISREGARD (4) [DISREGARDED, DISREGARDING]

Job 6:26 are convincing when you **d** my cry of desperation?
Eze 22:26 They **d** my Sabbath days so that my holy name is
Mk 7:12 You let them **d** their needy parents.
Tit 2:15 so don't let anyone ignore you or **d** what you say.

DISREGARDED (1) [DISREGARD]

Ps 119:139 with rage, / for my enemies have **d** your words.

DISREGARDING (1) [DISREGARD]

Pr 17: 9 **D** another person's faults preserves love;

DISRESPECTFUL (1) [DISRESPECTFULLY]

1Ti 6: 2 master is a Christian, that is no excuse for being **d**.

DISRESPECTFULLY (1) [DISRESPECTFUL]

2Pe 2:11 never speak out **d** against the glorious ones.

DISRUPT (1)

Jdg 14: 4 creating an opportunity to **d** the Philistines,

DISSEMBLED, DISSIMULATION [KJV] See DECEITFUL, PRETEND, HYPOCRISY, LIED

DISSIPATES (1)

Job 7: 9 Just as a cloud **d** and vanishes, those who die will

DISSOLVE (1)

Ps 58: 8 May they be like snails that **d** into slime, / like a

DISTANCE (56) [DISTANT]

Ge 22: 4 of the journey, Abraham saw the place in the **d**.
29: 2 He saw in the **d** three flocks of sheep lying in an
30:36 and they took them three days' **d** from where
31:19 Laban was some **d** away, shearing his sheep.
32:16 of animals by itself, separated by a **d** in between.
33: 1 Then, in the **d**, Jacob saw Esau coming with his
35:16 began while they were still some **d** away.
37:18 they recognized him in the **d** and made plans to kill
37:25 they noticed a caravan of camels in the **d** coming
48: 7 just a short **d** from Ephrath (that is, Bethlehem).
Ex 2: 4 The baby's sister then stood at a **d**, watching to see
14:10 the people of Israel could see them in the **d**,
20:18 they stood at a **d**, trembling with fear.
20:21 As the people stood in the **d**, Moses entered into
24: 1 Israel's leaders. All of them must worship at a **d**.
Dt 19: 6 If the **d** to the nearest city of refuge was too far,
32:52 So you will see the land from a **d**, but you may not
Jos 3: 4 keeping a clear **d** between you and the Ark.
Jdg 18: 7 And they lived a great **d** from Sidon and had no
18:22 tribe of Dan were quite a **d** from Micah's home,
18:28 for they lived a great **d** from Sidon and had no
1Sa 26:13 the hill opposite the camp until he was at a safe **d**.
2Ki 2: 7 and watched from a **d** as Elijah and Elisha stopped
4:25 of God at Mount Carmel, Elisha saw her in the **d**.
Ezr 3:13 a loud commotion that could be heard far in the **d**.
Job 2:12 When they saw Job from a **d**, they scarcely
36:25 Everyone has seen these things, but only from a **d**.
39:25 It senses the battle even at a **d**. It quivers at the
Ps 38:11 my disease. / Even my own family stands at a **d**.
38:21 LORD. / Do not stand at a **d**, my God.
138: 6 the humble, / but he keeps his **d** from the proud.
Isa 33:17 and you will see a land that stretches into the **d**.
Eze 40: 7 with a **d** between them of 8-3/4 feet along the
40:13 measuring the **d** between the back walls of facing guard alcoves; this **d** was 43-3/4 feet.
40:14 up to the gateway's foyer; this **d** was 105 feet.
40:18 the courtyard the same **d** as the gateway entrance.
40:19 the outer and inner gateways; the **d** was 175 feet.
40:23 The **d** between the two gateways was 175 feet.
40:27 The **d** between the two gateways was 175 feet.
48:35 "The **d** around the entire city will be six miles.
Mt 8:30 A large herd of pigs was feeding in the **d**,
27:55 with Jesus to care for him were watching from a **d**.
Mk 5: 6 When Jesus was still some **d** away, the man saw
8: 3 the road. For some of them have come a long **d**."
15:40 Some women were there, watching from a **d**,
Lk 15:20 And while he was still a long **d** away, his father
16:23 he saw Lazarus in the far **d** with Abraham.
17:12 he entered a village there, ten lepers stood at a **d**,
18:13 "But the tax collector stood at a **d** and dared not
23:49 followed him from Galilee, stood at a **d** watching.
Gal 4:20 But at this **d** I frankly don't know what else to do.
Heb 11:13 but they saw it all from a **d** and welcomed the
Rev 18:10 They will stand at a **d**, terrified by her great
18:15 by selling her these things will stand at a **d**,
18:17 merchant ships and their crews will stand at a **d**.

DISTANT (88) [DISTANCE]

Nu 24:17 I perceive him, but far in the **d** future.
Dt 20:15 But these instructions apply only to **d** towns,
28:49 "The LORD will bring a **d** nation against you
29:22 and the foreigners who come from **d** lands,
30:12 It is not up in heaven, so **d** that you must ask,
33:17 He will gore **d** nations, / driving them to the ends
Jos 9: 6 "We have come from a **d** land to ask you to make
9: 9 They answered, "We are from a very **d** country.
9:22 Why did you say that you live in a **d** land when
1Ki 8:41 and come from **d** lands to worship your great
16:11 He even destroyed **d** relatives and friends.
2Ki 18: 8 He also conquered the Philistines as far **d** as Gaza
20:14 "They came from the **d** land of Babylon."
2Ch 6:32 and they come from **d** lands to worship your great
Est 10: 1 throughout his empire, even to the **d** coastlands.
Job 39:28 on the cliffs, making its home on a **d**, rocky crag.
Ps 22: 1 have you forsaken me? / Why do you remain so **d**?
56: T To be sung to the tune "Dove on **D** Oaks."
65: 5 everyone on earth, / even those who sail on **d** seas.
85: 5 Will you prolong your wrath to **d** generations?
87: 4 also Philistia and Tyre, and even **d** Ethiopia.
106:27 among the nations, / exiling them to **d** lands.
132: 6 then we found it in the **d** countryside of Jaar.
Ecc 7:24 Wisdom is always **d** and very difficult to find.
Isa 6:12 the LORD has sent everyone away to **d** lands
10: 3 do when I send desolation upon you from a **d** land?
11:11 Babylonia, Hamath, and all the **d** coastlands.
22:18 you up into a ball and toss you away into a **d**,
23: 1 O ships of Tarshish, returning home from **d** lands!
23: 7 Think of all the colonists you sent to **d** lands.
25: 2 Beautiful palaces in **d** lands disappear and will
30:17 You will be left like a lonely flagpole on a **d**
39: 3 "They came from the **d** land of Babylon."
42: 4 Even **d** lands beyond the sea will wait for his
42:10 sail the seas, / all you who live in **d** coastlands.
43: 6 and daughters back to Israel from the **d** corners of
46:11 a leader from a **d** land who will come and do my
46:13 set things right, not in the **d** future, but right now!
59:18 evil deeds. His fury will fall on his foes in **d** lands.
60: 4 Your sons are coming from **d** lands; your little
Jer 4:16 'The enemy is coming from a **d** land, raising a
5:15 O Israel, I will bring a **d** nation against you,"
9:16 the world, and they will be strangers in **d** lands.
9:26 Moabites, the people who live in **d** places, and yes,
22:12 He will die in a **d** land and never again see his own
22:28 are he and his children to be exiled to **d** lands?
25:23 and Buz, and to the people who live in **d** places.
25:32 A great whirlwind of fury is rising from the most **d**
30:10 For I will bring you home again from **d** lands,
31: 8 from the north and from the **d** corners of the earth.
31:10 nations of the world; proclaim it in **d** coastlands:
31:16 Your children will come back to you from the **d**
46:27 For I will bring you home again from **d** lands,
48: 7 his priests and princes, will be exiled to **d** lands!
49:32 to the winds these people who live in **d** places.
50:26 Yes, come against her from **d** lands. Break open
La 1: 5 have been captured and taken away to **d** lands.
1:18 and daughters have been taken captive to **d** lands.
2: 9 Her kings and princes have been exiled to **d** lands;
4:15 So they fled to **d** lands and wandered there among
Eze 12: 4 do when they begin a long march to **d** lands.
23:40 "You sisters sent messengers to **d** lands to get
27:10 Men from **d** Persia, Lydia, and Libya served in
28:25 For I will gather them from the **d** lands where I
29:12 I will scatter the Egyptians to **d** lands.
32: 9 "And when I bring your shattered remains to **d**
34:21 and hungry flock until they are scattered to **d**
38: 6 along with the armies of Beth-togarmah from the **d**
38: 8 In the **d** future you will swoop down on the land of
38:15 You will come from your homeland in the **d** north
38:16 land like a cloud. This will happen in the **d** future.
39: 2 mountains of Israel, bringing you from the **d** north.
Am 9:14 I will bring my exiled people of Israel back from **d**
Ob 1:12 gloated when they exiled your relatives to **d** lands.
Mic 1:16 for your little ones will be exiled to **d** lands.
4:10 You will soon be sent into exile in **d** Babylon.
5: 2 from you, one whose origins are from the **d** past.
7:12 and from many **d** seas and mountains.
Hab 1: 8 Their horsemen race forward from **d** places.
Zec 6:15 Many will come from **d** lands to rebuild the
7:14 I scattered them as with a whirlwind among the **d**
10: 9 the nations, still they will remember me in **d** lands.
Mt 12:42 because she came from a **d** land to hear the
Mk 5:10 and again not to send them to some **d** place.
Lk 11:31 because she came from a **d** land to hear the
15:13 all his belongings and took a trip to a **d** land,
19:12 "A nobleman was called away to a **d** empire to be
Ac 26:11 I even hounded them in **d** cities of foreign lands.

DISTASTE (1)

Eze 35: 6 Sovereign LORD, since you show no **d** for blood,

DISTILLS (1)

Job 36:27 draws up the water vapor and then **d** it into rain.

DISTINCT (1) [DISTINCTION]

Ex 33:16 and **d** from all other people on the earth?"

DISTINCTION (7) [DISTINCT]

Ex 8:23 I will make a clear **d** between your people and my
9: 4 But the LORD will again make a **d** between the
11: 7 Then you will know that the LORD makes a **d**
Lev 20:25 therefore make a **d** between ceremonially clean
Zep 3:20 a name of **d** among all the nations of the earth.
Ac 15: 9 He made no **d** between us and them, for he also
1Co 9:15 I would rather die than lose my **d** of preaching

DISTINGUISH (3) [DISTINGUISHED, DISTINGUISHING]

Lev 10:10 You are to **d** between what is holy and what is
11:47 so you can **d** between what is unclean and may not
Ecc 1:17 So I worked hard to **d** wisdom from foolishness.

DISTINGUISHED (2) [DISTINGUISH]

Nu 22:15 This time he sent a larger number of even more **d**
1Ch 4: 9 There was a man named Jabez who was more **d**

DISTINGUISHING (1) [DISTINGUISH]

Pr 20: 8 weighs all the evidence, **d** the bad from the good.

DISTORT (2) [DISTORTED]
Ac 20:30 Even some of you will **d** the truth in order to draw
2Co 4: 2 to trick anyone, and we do not **d** the word of God.

DISTORTED (1) [DISTORT]
Da 3:19 and Abednego that his face became **d** with rage.

DISTRACTING (1) [DISTRACTIONS]
Ex 5: 4 Pharaoh shouted, "**d** the people from their tasks?

DISTRACTIONS (1) [DISTRACTING]
1Co 7:35 you serve the Lord best, with as few **d** as possible.

DISTRAUGHT (1)
1Sa 28:21 When the woman saw how **d** he was, she said,

DISTRESS (43) [DISTRESSED]
Ge 35: 3 God who answered my prayers when I was in **d**.
Dt 28:57 and terrible **d** that your enemy will inflict on all
Jdg 10: 9 and Ephraim. The Israelites were in great **d**.
10:14 Let them rescue you in your hour of **d**!"
2Sa 22: 7 But in my **d** I cried out to the LORD; / yes,
1Ch 21:16 leaders of Israel put on sackcloth to show their **d**
2Ch 15: 4 But whenever you were in **d** and turned to the
33:12 But while in deep **d**, Manasseh sought the LORD
Job 3:23 with no future, those destined by God to live in **d**?
15:24 They live in **d** and anguish, like a king preparing
36:19 your wealth and mighty efforts keep you from **d**?
Ps 4: 1 Take away my **d**. / Have mercy on me and hear my
18: 6 But in my **d** I cried out to the LORD; / yes,
25:16 have mercy on me, / for I am alone and in deep **d**.
31: 9 Have mercy on me, LORD, for I am in **d**.
55:17 Morning, noon, and night / I plead aloud in my **d**,
57: 6 have set a trap for me. / I am weary from **d**.
59:16 been my refuge, / a place of safety in the day of **d**.
68: 6 But for rebels, there is only famine and **d**.
102: 2 from me / in my time of **d**. / Bend down your ear
106:44 Even so, he pitied them in their **d** / and listened to
107: 6 in their trouble, / and he rescued them from their **d**.
107:13 in their trouble, / and he saved them from their **d**.
107:19 in their trouble, / and he saved them from their **d**.
107:28 in their trouble, / and he saved them from their **d**.
107:41 But he rescues the poor from their **d**
118: 5 In my **d** I prayed to the LORD, / and the LORD
143:11 In your righteousness, bring me out of this **d**.
144:14 no forced exile, / no cries of **d** in our squares.
Pr 1:27 and when anguish and **d** overwhelm you.
Isa 25: 4 To the needy in **d**, you are a shelter from the rain
26:16 LORD, in **d** we searched for you. / We were
Jer 11:14 not listen to them when they cry out to me in **d**.
15:11 to plead on their behalf in times of trouble and **d**.
18:17 my back on them and refuse to notice their **d**."
La 3: 5 and surrounded me with anguish and **d**.
Eze 23:33 drunkard beneath the awful blows of sorrow and **d**,
Zep 1:15 It is a day of terrible **d** and anguish, a day of ruin
Zec 10:11 They will pass safely through the sea of **d**,
Mt 26:37 and he began to be filled with anguish and deep **d**.
Mk 14:33 and he began to be filled with horror and deep **d**.
Lk 21:23 For there will be great **d** in the land and wrath
Ro 8:26 And the Holy Spirit helps us in our **d**. For we don't

DISTRESSED (9) [DISTRESS]
Jdg 2:15 just as he promised. And the people were very **d**.
1Ch 21: 6 he was so **d** at what the king had made him do.
Est 4: 4 and told her about Mordecai, she was deeply **d**.
Ps 77: 4 You don't let me sleep. / I am too **d** even to pray!
Mt 26:22 Greatly **d**, one by one they began to ask him,
Mk 14:19 Greatly **d**, one by one they began to ask him,
Ro 14:15 And if another Christian is **d** by what you eat,
Php 2:26 and he was very **d** that you heard he was ill.
2Pe 2: 8 he was a righteous man who was **d** by the

DISTRIBUTE (8) [DISTRIBUTED, DISTRIBUTES, DISTRIBUTING, DISTRIBUTION, DISTRIBUTIONS]
Nu 7: 5 **D** them among the Levites according to the work
33:54 You must **d** the land among the clans by sacred lot
1Sa 8:15 and **d** it among his officers and attendants.
2Ch 31:19 men were appointed to **d** portions to every male
Pr 8:18 honor, wealth, and justice are mine to **d**.
Eze 47:22 **D** the land as an inheritance for yourselves and for
Da 11:24 **d** among his followers the plunder and wealth of
Ac 21: 8 one of the seven men who had been chosen to **d**

DISTRIBUTED (7) [DISTRIBUTE]
2Ch 28:15 and **d** clothes from the plunder to the prisoners
31:15 They **d** the gifts among the families of priests in
31:16 They also **d** the gifts to all males three years old
31:17 And they **d** gifts to the priests who were listed in
Eze 48:12 It will be their special portion when the land is **d**,
Mt 15:36 them to the disciples, who **d** the food to the crowd.
Mk 8: 6 to his disciples, who **d** the bread to the crowd.

DISTRIBUTES (2) [DISTRIBUTE]
Job 21:17 and God skips them when he **d** sorrows in his
1Co 12:11 It is the one and only Holy Spirit who **d** these gifts.

DISTRIBUTING (1) [DISTRIBUTE]
2Ch 31:14 was put in charge of **d** the freewill offerings of

DISTRIBUTION (3) [DISTRIBUTE]
Jos 14: 5 So the **d** of the land was in strict accordance with
2Ch 31:20 King Hezekiah handled the **d** throughout all Judah,
Ac 6: 1 being discriminated against in the daily **d** of food.

DISTRIBUTIONS (1) [DISTRIBUTE]
Ne 13:13 and it was their job to make honest **d** to their

DISTRICT (13) [DISTRICTS]
Dt 19: 3 three districts, with one of these cities in each **d**.
1Ki 4: 5 Azariah son of Nathan presided over the **d**
4: 7 Solomon also had twelve **d** governors who were
4:27 The **d** governors faithfully provided food for King
Ne 3: 9 son of Hur, the leader of half the **d** of Jerusalem,
3:12 He was the leader of the other half of the **d** of
3:14 son of Recab, the leader of the Beth-hakkerem **d**.
3:15 son of Col-hozeh, the leader of the Mizpah **d**,
3:16 son of Azbuk, the leader of half the **d** of Beth-zur.
3:17 came Hashabiah, the leader of half the **d** of Keilah,
3:17 the building of the wall on behalf of his own **d**.
3:18 the leader of the other half of the **d** of Keilah.
Ac 16:12 a major city of the **d** of Macedonia and a Roman

DISTRICTS (1) [DISTRICT]
Dt 19: 3 the LORD your God is giving you into three **d**,

DISTRUST (1)
Ac 14: 2 stirred up **d** among the Gentiles against Paul

DISTURB (5) [DISTURBED, DISTURBING, DISTURBS]
2Ki 23:18 "Leave it alone. Don't **d** his bones."
Ezr 6: 7 Do not **d** the construction of the Temple of God.
Job 41:10 And since no one dares to **d** the crocodile,
Eze 32: 9 that you have never seen, I will **d** many hearts.
32:13 or animals **d** those waters with their feet.

DISTURBED (18) [DISTURB]
1Sa 28:15 "Why have you **d** me by calling me back?"
2Sa 7:10 a secure place where they will never be **d**.
14:11 "not a hair on your son's head will be **d**!"
2Ki 19: 6 Do not be **d** by this blasphemous speech against
1Ch 17: 9 a secure place where they will never be **d**.
2Ch 28: 9 killing them without mercy, and all heaven is **d**.
Job 20: 2 "I must reply because I am greatly **d**.
40:23 It is not **d** by raging rivers, not even when the
Pr 10:30 The godly will never be **d**, but the wicked will be
Isa 37: 6 Do not be **d** by this blasphemous speech against
Da 2: 1 Nebuchadnezzar had a dream that **d** him so much
Mt 2: 3 Herod was deeply **d** by their question, as was all of
Mk 3: 5 because he was deeply **d** by their hard hearts.
6:20 Herod was **d** whenever he talked with John,
Lk 1:29 Confused and **d**, Mary tried to think what the angel
Ac 4: 2 They were very **d** that Peter and John were
19:36 you shouldn't be **d**, no matter what is said.
1Th 3: 3 and to keep you from becoming **d** by the troubles

DISTURBING (2) [DISTURB]
Est 7: 4 been a matter too trivial to warrant **d** the king."
Ac 17: 6 and now they are here **d** our city," they shouted.

DISTURBS (1) [DISTURB]
Job 38:15 The light **d** the haunts of the wicked, and it stops

DITCH (4) [DITCHES]
1Ki 18:38 the dust. It even licked up all the water in the **d**!
Job 9:31 you would plunge me into a muddy **d**, and I would
Mt 15:14 guides another, they will both fall into a **d**."
Lk 6:39 The first one will fall into a **d** and pull the other

DITCHES (2) [DITCH]
Dt 11:10 and dug out irrigation **d** with your foot as in a
Lk 16: 3 and I don't have the strength to go out and dig **d**,

DIVERS, DIVERSE [KJV] See DIFFERENT, KINDS, QUANTITIES

DIVIDE (28) [DIVIDED, DIVIDES, DIVIDING, DIVISION, DIVISIONS]
Ge 15:10 by side. He did not, however, **d** the birds in half.
Ex 15: 9 with them, and destroy them. / I will **d** the plunder,
21:35 sell the live bull and **d** the money between them.
Nu 26:53 "**D** the land among the tribes in proportion to their
31:27 Then **d** the plunder into two parts, and give half to
34:13 "This is the territory you are to **d** among
34:17 "These are the men who are to **d** the land among
36: 2 the LORD instructed you to **d** the land by sacred
Dt 19: 3 **D** the land the LORD your God is giving you into
Jos 13: 7 when you **d** the land among the nine tribes
Jdg 7: 5 the LORD told him, "**D** the men into two groups.
2Sa 19:29 and Ziba will **d** your land equally between you."
1Ki 3:26 be neither yours nor mine; **d** him between us!"
Job 27:17 and the innocent will **d** all that money.
Ps 22:18 They **d** my clothes among themselves / and throw
60: 6 by his holiness: / "I will **d** up Shechem with joy.
68:12 while the women of Israel **d** the plunder.
106: 9 He commanded the Red Sea to **d**, and a dry path
108: 7 by his holiness: / "I will **d** up Shechem with joy.
Ecc 11: 2 **D** your gifts among many, for you do not know
Isa 11:15 sending a mighty wind to **d** it into seven streams
Jer 6: 3 around the city and **d** your pastures for their flocks.
Eze 45: 1 "When you **d** the land among the tribes of Israel,
47:21 "**D** the land within these boundaries among the
Da 6: 1 Darius the Mede decided to **d** the kingdom into
Ob 1:11 off their wealth and cast lots to **d** up Jerusalem.
Lk 12:13 please tell my brother to **d** our father's estate with
15:12 So his father agreed to **d** his wealth between his

DIVIDED (54) [DIVIDE]
Ge 10:25 of the world were **d** into different language groups
14:15 There he **d** his men and attacked during the night
32: 7 He **d** his household, along with the flocks
Ex 21:36 to keep it under control, the money will not be **d**.
Lev 11: 3 include those that have completely **d** hooves
11:26 "Any animal that has **d** but unsplit hooves or that
Nu 26:62 of land when it was **d** among the Israelites.
33:54 the land will be **d** among your ancestral tribes.
34:13 The LORD commands that the land be **d** up
Dt 32: 8 to the nations, / when he **d** up the human race,
Jos 8:33 officers, and judges, were **d** into two groups.
19:49 After all the land was **d** among the tribes,
Jdg 7:16 He **d** the three hundred men into three groups
9:43 he **d** his men into three groups and set an ambush
1Sa 11:11 having **d** his army into three detachments.
1Ki 16:21 But now the people of Israel were **d** into two
18: 6 So they **d** the land between them. Ahab went one
2Ki 2: 8 The river **d**, and the two of them went across on
2:14 Then the river **d**, and Elisha went across.
1Ch 1:19 of the world were **d** into different language groups
23: 6 Then David **d** the Levites into divisions named
24: 1 the priests, were **d** into groups for service.
24: 3 David **d** Aaron's descendants into groups
24: 4 Eleazar's descendants were **d** into sixteen groups
26:16 up to the Temple. Guard duties were **d** evenly.
2Ch 35:12 They **d** the burnt offerings among the people by
Ezr 6:18 and Levites were **d** into their various divisions to
Ne 9:11 You **d** the sea for your people so they could walk
Ps 78:13 For he **d** the sea before them and led them through!
Isa 7:17 the years since Solomon's empire was **d** into Israel
18: 2 Take a message to your land **d** by rivers, to your
18: 7 will receive gifts from this land **d** by rivers,
33:23 Their treasure will be **d** by the people of God.
34:17 He has surveyed and **d** the land and deeded it over
48:21 He **d** the rock, and water gushed out for them to
63:12 Where is the one whose power **d** the sea before
Eze 37:22 them all; no longer will they be **d** into two nations.
Da 2:41 of iron and clay show that this kingdom will be **d**.
5:28 *Parsin* means '**d**'—your kingdom has been **d** and given to the Medes
11: 4 kingdom will be broken apart and **d** into four parts.
Am 7:17 Your land will be **d** up, and you yourself will die
Mic 2: 5 people will have no say in how the land is **d**.
Mt 12:25 A city or home **d** against itself is doomed.
Mk 3:25 A home **d** against itself is doomed.
Lk 11:17 with itself is doomed. A **d** home is also doomed.
Jn 7:43 So the crowd was **d** in their opinion about him.
10:19 the people were again **d** in their opinions about
19:23 they **d** his clothes among the four of them.
19:24 "They **d** my clothes among themselves and threw
Ac 14: 4 But the people of the city were **d** in their opinion
23: 7 This **d** the council—the Pharisees against the
1Co 1:13 Can Christ be **d** into pieces? Was I, Paul,
7:34 His interests are **d**. In the same way, a woman who

DIVIDES (2) [DIVIDE]
Ge 49:27 and in the evening he **d** the plunder."
Dt 21:16 When the man **d** the inheritance, he may not give

DIVIDING (19) [DIVIDE]
Ge 2:10 watering the garden and then **d** into four branches.
Nu 34:29 the **d** of the land of Canaan among the Israelites."
Jos 11:23 special possession, **d** the land among the tribes.
Jdg 5:30 'They are **d** the captured goods they found—
2Ch 31:15 **d** the gifts fairly among young and old alike.
Isa 9: 3 They will shout with joy like warriors **d** the
Eze 40:10 and the **d** walls separating them were also
40:14 He measured the **d** walls all along the inside of the
40:16 the walls of the guard alcoves and their **d** walls.
40:16 The surfaces of the **d** walls were decorated with
40:21 alcoves on each side, with **d** walls and a foyer.
40:26 and there were palm tree decorations along the **d**
40:29 Its guard alcoves, **d** walls, and foyer were the same
40:33 Its guard alcoves, **d** walls, and foyer were the same
40:36 The guard alcoves, **d** walls, and foyer of this
47:13 "Follow these instructions for **d** the land for the
Da 11:39 and **d** the land among them as their reward.
Joel 3: 2 among the nations, and for **d** up my land.
Mt 25:15 **d** it in proportion to their abilities—and then left on

DIVINATION (6) [DIVINE, DIVINERS, DIVINERS']
Ge 30:27 "for I have learned by **d** that the LORD has
Nu 24: 1 so he did not resort to **d** as he often did.
2Ki 21: 6 He practiced sorcery and **d**, and he consulted with
2Ch 33: 6 He practiced sorcery, **d**, and witchcraft, and he
Isa 2: 6 foreigners from the East who practice magic and **d**,
Eze 21:21 or Rabbah. He will call his magicians to use **d**.

DIVINE (13) [DIVINATION]
Pr 16:10 The king speaks with **d** wisdom; he must never
29:18 When people do not accept **d** guidance, they run
Jer 5:13 are windbags full of words with no **d** authority.
Eze 28: 2 a god! I sit on a **d** throne in the heart of the sea.'
Da 3:25 the flames! And the fourth looks like a **d** being!"

5:12 has a sharp mind and is filled with **d** knowledge
6:7 days anyone who prays to anyone, **d** or human—
6:12 days anyone who prays to anyone, **d** or human—
Ro 1:20 invisible qualities—his eternal power and **d** nature.
2Co 1:19 Silas, and I preached to you, and he is the **d** Yes—
Heb 12:7 As you endure this **d** discipline, remember that
2Pe 1:3 his **d** power gives us everything we need for living
1:4 evil desires and that you will share in his **d** nature.

DIVINERS (3) [DIVINATION]

1Sa 6:2 called in their priests and **d** and asked them,
Isa 3:2 the heroes, soldiers, judges, prophets, **d**, elders,
Mic 3:7 your faces in shame, and you **d** will be disgraced.

DIVINERS' (1) [DIVINATION]

Jdg 9:37 group is coming down the road past the **D** Oak."

DIVISION (47) [DIVIDE]

Ge 10:25 The first was named Peleg—"**d**"—for during his
Ex 6:26 of Israel out of the land of Egypt, **d** by **d**."
12:51 the people of Israel out of Egypt, **d** by **d**.
Nu 4:2 and families of the Kohathite **d** of the Levite tribe.
4:22 and families of the Gershonite **d** of the tribe of
4:29 and families of the Merarite **d** of the Levite tribe.
4:34 community counted the Kohathite **d** by its clans
4:38 The Gershonite **d** was also counted by its clans
4:42 The Merarite **d** was also counted by its clans
7:7 and four oxen to the Gershonite **d** for their work,
7:8 and eight oxen to the Merarite **d** for their work.
7:9 gave none of the carts or oxen to the Kohathite **d**,
10:21 Next came the Kohathite **d** of the Levites,
10:28 order in which the tribes marched, **d** by **d**.
Jos 19:51 at Shiloh. So the **d** of the land was completed.
1Ch 1:19 The first was named Peleg—"**d**"—for during his
27:1 Each **d** served for one month and had twenty-four
27:2 son of Zabdiel was commander of the first **d**,
27:2 There were twenty-four thousand troops in his **d**.
27:4 of Ahoah, was commander of the second **d**,
27:4 There were twenty-four thousand troops in his **d**,
27:5 Jehoiada the priest was commander of the third **d**,
27:5 There were twenty-four thousand troops in his **d**.
27:7 brother of Joab, was commander of the fourth **d**,
27:7 There were twenty-four thousand troops in his **d**.
27:8 the Izrahite was commander of the fifth **d**,
27:8 There were twenty-four thousand troops in his **d**.
27:9 Ikkesh from Tekoa was commander of the sixth **d**,
27:9 There were twenty-four thousand troops in his **d**.
27:10 from Pelon, was commander of the seventh **d**,
27:10 There were twenty-four thousand troops in his **d**.
27:11 from Hushah, was commander of the eighth **d**,
27:11 There were twenty-four thousand troops in his **d**.
27:12 of Benjamin was commander of the ninth **d**,
27:12 There were twenty-four thousand troops in his **d**.
27:13 from Netophah, was commander of the tenth **d**,
27:13 There were twenty-four thousand troops in his **d**.
27:14 in Ephraim was commander of the eleventh **d**,
27:14 There were twenty-four thousand troops in his **d**.
27:15 from Netophah, was commander of the twelfth **d**,
27:15 There were twenty-four thousand troops in his **d**.
Lk 12:51 to the earth? No, I have come to bring strife and **d**!
12:53 There will be a **d** between father and son, mother
Jn 9:16 So there was a deep **d** of opinion among them.

DIVISIONS (32) [DIVIDE]

Nu 2:3[-4] "The **d** of Judah, Issachar, and Zebulun are to
2:10[-11] "The **d** of Reuben, Simeon, and Gad are to
2:18[-19] "The **d** of Ephraim, Manasseh, and Benjamin
2:25[-26] "The **d** of Dan, Asher, and Naphtali are to
10:17 and Merarite **d** of the Levites were next in the line
Jos 18:4 report of their proposed **d** of the inheritance.
22:14 and each a leader within the family **d** of Israel.
2Sa 18:4 So he stood at the gate of the city as all the **d** of
1Ch 9:23 and their descendants, by their **d**,
23:6 Then David divided the Levites into **d** named after
26:1 These are the **d** of the gatekeepers:
26:12 These **d** of the gatekeepers were named for their
26:19 These were the **d** of the gatekeepers from the clans
27:1 who served the king by supervising the army **d** that
28:1 the commanders of the twelve army **d**, the other
28:13 concerning the work of the various **d** of priests
28:21 The various **d** of priests and Levites will serve in
2Ch 8:14 assigned the gatekeepers to their gates by their **d**,
31:2 and Levites into **d** to offer the burnt offerings
31:15 by their **d**, dividing the gifts fairly among young
31:16 Temple to perform their official duties, by their **d**.
31:17 who were listed according to their jobs and their **d**.
35:4 Report for duty according to the family **d** of your
35:10 organized by their **d**, according to the king's
Ezr 6:18 and Levites were divided into their various **d** to
Ro 16:17 Watch out for people who cause **d** and upset
1Co 1:10 be real harmony so there won't be **d** in the church.
11:18 I hear that there are **d** among you when you meet
11:19 there must be **d** among you so that those of you
Gal 5:20 jealousy, outbursts of anger, selfish ambition, **d**,
Tit 3:10 If anyone is causing **d** among you, give a first
Jude 1:19 and they are the ones who are creating **d** among

DIVORCE (14) [DIVORCED, DIVORCES]

Dt 22:19 remain the man's wife, and he may never **d** her.
22:29 violated her, and he will never be allowed to **d** her.
24:1 So he writes her a letter of **d**, gives it to her,
Ezr 10:3 Let us now make a covenant with our God to **d** our
10:19 They vowed to **d** their wives, and they each
Mal 2:16 "For I hate **d**!" says the LORD, the God of
Mt 5:31 'A man can **d** his wife by merely giving her a letter of **d**.'
19:3 "Should a man be allowed to **d** his wife for any
19:7 say a man could merely write an official letter of **d**
19:8 "Moses permitted **d** as a concession to your
Mk 10:2 "Should a man be allowed to **d** his wife?"
10:3 "What did Moses say about **d**?" Jesus asked them.
10:4 merely has to write his wife an official letter of **d**

DIVORCED (10) [DIVORCE]

Lev 21:7 defiled by prostitution or women who have been **d**,
21:14 He must not marry a widow, a **d** woman, or a
22:13 But if she becomes a widow or is **d** and has no
Nu 30:9 If, however, a woman is a widow or is **d**, she must
1Ch 8:8 After Shaharaim **d** his wives Hushim and Baara,
Isa 50:1 mother gone because I **d** her and sent her away?
Jer 3:8 She saw that I had **d** faithless Israel and sent her
Eze 44:22 They may not marry other widows or **d** women.
Mt 5:32 And anyone who marries a **d** woman commits
Lk 16:18 and anyone who marries a **d** woman commits

DIVORCES (7) [DIVORCE]

Dt 24:3 and the second husband also **d** her or dies,
Jer 3:1 "If a man **d** a woman and she marries someone
Mt 5:32 But I say that a man who **d** his wife, unless she has
19:9 a man who **d** his wife and marries another commits
Mk 10:11 "Whoever **d** his wife and marries someone else
10:12 And if a woman **d** her husband and remarries,
Lk 16:18 "Anyone who **d** his wife and marries someone

DO (2229) [DID, DIDN'T, DOES, DOESN'T, DOING, DONE, DON'T, OVERDO] See Index of Articles, Etc.

DOCKED (1)

Ac 27:3 The next day when we **d** at Sidon, Julius was very

DOCTOR (4) [DOCTORS]

Mt 9:12 Jesus replied, "Healthy people don't need a **d**—
Mk 2:17 he told them, "Healthy people don't need a **d**—
Lk 5:31 answered them, "Healthy people don't need a **d**—
Col 4:14 Dear **D** Luke sends his greetings, and so does

DOCTORS (3) [DOCTOR]

Job 13:4 me with lies. As **d**, you are worthless quacks.
Mk 5:26 She had suffered a great deal from many **d** through
Lk 8:43 She had spent everything she had on **d** and still

DOCTRINE (1)

1Ti 1:3 and stop those who are teaching wrong **d**.

DOCUMENT (2)

Ne 9:38 On this sealed **d** are the names of our princes
10:1 The **d** was ratified and sealed with the following

DODAI (3)

2Sa 23:9 in rank among the Three was Eleazar son of **D**,
1Ch 11:12 in rank among the Three was Eleazar son of **D**,
27:4 **D**, a descendant of Ahoah, was commander of the

DODAVAHU (1)

2Ch 20:37 Then Eliezer son of **D** from Mareshah prophesied

DODGE (2) [DODGED]

Isa 28:15 to avoid death and have made a deal to **d** the grave.
28:18 and I will overturn your deal to **d** the grave.

DODGED (1) [DODGE]

1Sa 19:10 But David **d** out of the way and escaped into the

DODO (3)

Jdg 10:1 Tola, the son of Puah and descendant of **D**,
2Sa 23:24 Elhanan son of **D** from Bethlehem;
1Ch 11:26 Elhanan son of **D** from Bethlehem;

DOE (2)

Ps 22:T of David, to be sung to the tune "**D** of the Dawn."
Pr 5:19 She is a loving **d**, a graceful deer. Let her breasts

DOEG (6)

1Sa 21:7 Now **D** the Edomite, Saul's chief herdsman,
22:9 Then **D** the Edomite, who was standing there with
22:18 Then the king said to **D**, "You do it." So **D** turned on them and killed them,
22:22 When I saw **D** there that day, I knew he would tell
Ps 52:T regarding the time **D** the Edomite told Saul that

DOES (289) [DO] See Index of Articles, Etc.

DOESN'T (99) [DO, NO] See Index of Articles, Etc.

DOG (10) [DOG'S, DOGS, SHEEPDOGS, WATCHDOGS]

Ex 11:7 it will be so peaceful that not even a **d** will bark.
1Sa 17:43 "Am I a **d**," he roared at David, "that you come
24:14 time chasing one who is as worthless as a dead **d**
2Sa 3:8 "Am I a Judean **d** to be kicked around like this?"
9:8 "Should the king show such kindness to a dead **d**
16:9 "Why should this dead **d** curse my lord the king?"
Pr 26:11 As a **d** returns to its vomit, so a fool repeats his
Ecc 9:4 "It is better to be a live **d** than a dead lion!"
Isa 66:3 it is as bad as putting a **d** or the blood of a pig on
2Pe 2:22 "A **d** returns to its vomit," and "A washed pig

DOG'S (1) [DOG]

Pr 26:17 Yanking a **d** ears is as foolish as interfering in

DOGS (24) [DOG]

Ex 22:31 wild animal. Throw its carcass out for the **d** to eat.
Jdg 7:5 their hands and lap it up with their tongues like **d**.
1Ki 14:11 your family who die in the city will be eaten by **d**,
16:4 your family who die in the city will be eaten by **d**,
21:19 **d** will lick your blood outside the city just as they
21:23 The LORD has also told me that the **d** of Jezreel
21:24 your family who die in the city will be eaten by **d**,
22:38 and **d** came and licked the king's blood,
2Ki 9:10 **D** will eat Ahab's wife, Jezebel, at the plot of land
9:36 plot of land in Jezreel, **d** will eat Jezebel's flesh.
Ps 22:16 My enemies surround me like a pack of **d**; / an evil
22:20 spare my precious life from these **d**.
59:6 They come at night, / snarling like vicious **d**
59:14 enemies come out at night, / snarling like vicious **d**
68:23 their blood, / and even your **d** will get their share!"
Isa 56:11 And they are as greedy as **d**, never satisfied.
Jer 15:3 to kill, the **d** to drag away, the vultures to devour,
Mt 15:26 take food from the children and throw it to the **d**,"
15:27 "but even **d** are permitted to eat crumbs that fall
Mk 7:27 take food from the children and throw it to the **d**."
7:28 but even the **d** under the table are given some
Lk 16:21 the **d** would come and lick his open sores.
Php 3:2 Watch out for those **d**, those wicked men and their
Rev 22:15 Outside the city are the **d**—the sorcerers,

DOING (261) [DO] See Index of Articles, Etc.

DOLEFUL [KJV] See HOWLING

DOLLARS (3)

Mt 18:24 was brought in who owed him millions of **d**.
18:28 a fellow servant who owed him a few thousand **d**.
Ac 19:19 The value of the books was several million **d**.

DOMESTIC (4) [DOMESTICATED]

Ge 3:14 You are singled out from all the **d** and wild
7:14 **d** and wild, large and small—along with birds
7:21 birds, **d** animals, wild animals, all kinds of small
Ne 5:18 six fat sheep, and a large number of **d** fowl.

DOMESTICATED (1) [DOMESTIC]

Lev 5:2 whether a wild animal, a **d** animal, or an animal

DOMINATE (1) [DOMINATED]

Lk 12:30 These things **d** the thoughts of most people,

DOMINATED (4) [DOMINATE]

Jdg 1:32 the Canaanites **d** the land where the people of
1:33 the Canaanites **d** the land where they lived.
Ro 7:24 Who will free me from this life that is **d** by sin?
8:5 Those who are **d** by the sinful nature think about

DOMINION (2)

1Ki 4:24 Solomon's **d** extended over all the kingdoms west
Ps 110:2 The LORD will extend your powerful **d** from

DON'T (1038) [DO, NO] See Index of Articles, Etc.

DONATED (7) [DONATION]

Ex 36:3 Moses gave them the materials **d** by the people for
38:8 **d** by the women who served at the entrance of the
Nu 7:86 The weight of the **d** gold came to about three
7:87 and twelve one-year-old male lambs were **d** for the
7:88 and sixty one-year-old male lambs were **d** for the
2Ch 30:24 and the officials **d** one thousand bulls and ten
Ezr 1:9 These were the items Cyrus **d**: / silver trays

DONATING (1) [DONATION]

1Ch 29:4 I am **d** more than 112 tons of gold from Ophir

DONATION (2) [DONATED, DONATING, DONATIONS]

Lev 27:23 value of the land as a sacred **d** to the LORD.
Ro 15:31 will be willing to accept the **d** I am bringing them.

DONATIONS (2) [DONATION]

Nu 5:10 Each priest may keep the sacred **d** that he
Ezr 7:17 These **d** are to be used specifically for the purchase

DONE (530) [DO] See Index of Articles, Etc.

DONKEY (77) [DONKEY'S, DONKEYS]

Ge 16:12 will be a wild one—free and untamed as a wild **d**!
22:3 He saddled his **d** and took two of his servants with
22:5 "Stay here with the **d**," Abraham told the young
49:11 to a grapevine, / the colt of his **d** to a choice vine.
Ex 4:20 So Moses took his wife and sons, put them on a **d**,

13:13 A firstborn male **d** may be redeemed from the
13:13 the **d** must be killed by breaking its neck.
20:17 neighbor's wife, male or female servant, ox or **d**,
21:33 fails to cover it, and then an ox or a **d** falls into it.
22: 4 If someone steals an ox or a **d** or a sheep and it is
22: 9 **d**, sheep, article of clothing, or anything else.
22:10 suppose someone asks a neighbor to care for a **d**,
23: 4 upon your enemy's ox or **d** that has strayed away,
23: 5 If you see the **d** of someone who hates you
23:12 This will give your ox and your **d** a chance to rest.
34:20 A firstborn male **d** may be redeemed from the
34:20 you must kill the **d** by breaking its neck.
Nu 16:15 I have not taken so much as a **d** from them, and I
22:21 So the next morning Balaam saddled his **d**
22:23 Balaam's **d** suddenly saw the angel of the LORD
22:23 The **d** bolted off the road into a field, but Balaam
22:25 When the **d** saw the angel of the LORD standing
22:25 foot against the wall. So Balaam beat the **d** again.
22:26 a place so narrow that the **d** could not get by at all.
22:27 This time when the **d** saw the angel, it lay down
22:28 Then the LORD caused the **d** to speak.
22:30 the same **d** you always ride on," the **d** answered.
22:32 "Why did you beat your **d** those three times?"
22:33 Three times the **d** saw me and shied away;
22:33 have killed you by now and spared the **d**."
Dt 5:21 or land, male or female servant, ox or **d**,
22: 3 Do the same if you find your neighbor's **d**,
22: 4 you see your neighbor's ox or **d** lying on the road,
22:10 not plow with an ox and a **d** harnessed together.
28:31 Your **d** will be driven away, never to be returned.
Jos 15:18 As she got down off her **d**, Caleb asked her,
Jdg 1:14 As she got down off her **d**, Caleb asked her,
15:16 And Samson said, / "With the jawbone of a **d**,
15:16 made heaps on heaps! / With the jawbone of a **d**,
19: 3 and an extra **d** to Bethlehem to persuade her to
19:28 So he put her body on his **d** and took her home.
1Sa 12: 3 his anointed one—whose ox or **d** have I stolen?
16:20 and a **d** loaded down with food and wine.
25:20 As she was riding her **d** into a mountain ravine,
25:23 she quickly got off her **d** and bowed low before
25:42 mounted her **d**, and went with David's messengers.
2Sa 17:23 So he saddled his **d**, went to his hometown, set his
19:26 'Saddle my **d** so that I can go with the king.'
1Ki 2:40 he saddled his **d** and went to Gath to search for
13:13 "Quick, saddle the **d**," the old man said.
13:13 And when they had saddled the **d** for him,
13:23 the prophet saddled his own **d** for him,
13:24 the road, with the **d** and the lion standing beside it.
13:27 "Saddle a **d** for me." So they saddled a **d**,
13:28 The **d** and lion were still standing there beside it,
13:28 the lion had not eaten the body nor attacked the **d**.
13:29 prophet laid the body of the man of God on the **d**
2Ki 4:22 "Send one of the servants and a **d** so that I can
4:24 So she saddled the **d** and said to the servant,
Ne 2:12 with us, except the **d** that I myself was riding.
2:14 but my **d** couldn't get through the rubble.
Job 11:12 any more than a wild **d** can bear human offspring!
39: 5 "Who makes the wild **d** wild?
Pr 26: 3 Guide a horse with a whip, a **d** with a bridle,
Isa 1: 3 the **d** and the ox—know their owner and appreciate
Jer 2:24 You are like a wild **d**, sniffing the wind at mating
22:19 He will be buried like a dead **d**—dragged out of
Hos 8: 9 Like a wild **d** looking for a mate, they have gone
Zec 9: 9 and victorious, yet he is humble, riding on a **d**—
Mt 21: 2 he said, "and you will see a **d** tied there, with its
21: 5 is coming to you. / He is humble, riding on a **d**—
Lk 10:34 Then he put the man on his own **d** and took him to
13:15 your ox or your **d** from their stalls on the Sabbath
Jn 12:14 Jesus found a young **d** and sat on it,
2Pe 2:16 when his **d** rebuked him with a human voice.

DONKEY'S (5) [DONKEY]

Jdg 15:15 Then he picked up a **d** jawbone that was lying on
2Ki 6:25 After a while even a **d** head sold for two pounds of
Zec 9: 9 is humble, riding on a donkey—even on a **d** colt.
Mt 21: 5 riding on a donkey— / even on a **d** colt.' "
Jn 12:15 Look, your King is coming, / sitting on a **d** colt."

DONKEYS (72) [DONKEY]

Ge 12:16 sheep, cattle, **d**, male and female servants,
24:35 and gold, and many servants and camels and **d**.
30:43 very wealthy, with many servants, camels, and **d**.
32: 5 **d**, sheep, goats, and many servants, both men
32:15 ten bulls, twenty female **d**, and ten male **d**.
34:28 They seized all the flocks and herds and **d**—
36:24 the wilderness while he was grazing his father's **d**.
42:26 So they loaded up their **d** with the grain and started
42:27 opened his sack to get some grain to feed the **d**,
43:18 Then he will seize us as slaves and take our **d**."
43:24 given water to wash their feet and food for their **d**.
44: 3 and set out on their journey with their loaded **d**.
44:11 quickly took their sacks from the backs of their **d**
44:13 loaded the **d** again, and returned to the city.
45:23 He sent his father ten **d** loaded with the good
45:23 and ten **d** loaded with grain and all kinds of other
47:17 and **d** of Egypt were in Pharaoh's possession.
Ex 9: 3 to destroy your horses, **d**, camels, cattle, and sheep.
Nu 31:28 cattle, **d**, sheep, and goats that belong to the army.
31:30 one of every fifty of the captives, cattle, **d**, sheep,
31:34 61,000 **d**,
31:39 30,500 **d**, of which 61 were the LORD's share;
31:45 30,500 **d**,
Dt 5:14 your oxen and **d** and other livestock,
Jos 6:21 and women, young and old, cattle, sheep, **d**—
7:24 of gold, his sons, daughters, cattle, **d**, sheep, tent,
9: 4 loading their **d** with weathered saddlebags and old
Jdg 5:10 "You who ride on fine **d** / and sit on fancy saddle
6: 4 nothing to eat, taking all the sheep, oxen, and **d**.
10: 4 His thirty sons rode around on thirty **d**, and they
12:14 and thirty grandsons, who rode on seventy **d**.
19:10 So he took his two saddled **d** and his concubine
19:19 We have straw and fodder for our **d** and plenty of
19:21 So he took them home with him and fed their **d**.
1Sa 8:16 the finest of your cattle and **d** for his own use.
9: 3 One day Kish's **d** strayed away, and he told Saul,
9: 4 but they couldn't find the **d** anywhere.
9: 5 will be more worried about us than about the **d**!"
9:20 And don't worry about those **d** that were lost three
10: 2 They will tell you that the **d** have been found
10:14 "We went to look for the **d**," Saul replied,
10:16 "He said the **d** had been found," Saul replied.
15: 3 children, babies, cattle, sheep, camels, and **d**.' "
22:19 and babies, and all the cattle, **d**, and sheep.
25:18 She packed them on **d** and said to her servants,
27: 9 He took the sheep, cattle, **d**, camels, and clothing
2Sa 16: 1 He was leading two **d** loaded with two hundred
16: 2 "The **d** are for your people to ride on,
2Ki 7: 7 their tents, horses, **d**, and everything else,
7:10 The horses and **d** were tethered and the tents were
1Ch 5:21 250,000 sheep, 2,000 **d**, and 100,000 captives.
12:40 and Naphtali brought food on **d**, camels, mules,
27:30 Jehdeiah from Meronoth was in charge of the **d**.
2Ch 28:15 They put those who were weak on **d** and took all
Ezr 2:67 435 camels, and 6,720 **d**.
Ne 7:69 435 camels, and 6,720 **d**.
13:15 in bundles of grain and loading them on their **d**.
Job 1: 3 hundred teams of oxen, and five hundred female **d**,
1:14 were plowing, with the **d** feeding beside them,
6: 5 Wild **d** bray when they find no green grass,
24: 3 and they even take **d** from the poor and fatherless.
24: 5 Like the wild **d** in the desert, the poor must spend
42:12 teams of oxen, and one thousand female **d**.
Ps 104:11 all the animals, / and the wild **d** quench their thirst.
Isa 21: 7 by horses and warriors mounted on **d** and camels."
30: 6 **d** and camels loaded with treasure to pay for
30:24 and **d** that till the ground will eat good grain,
32:14 Herds of **d** and goats will graze on the hills where
Jer 14: 6 The wild **d** stand on the bare hills panting like
Da 5:21 mind of an animal, and he lived among the wild **d**.
Zec 14:15 plague will strike the horses, mules, camels, **d**,

DOOM (14) [DOOMED]

Nu 23: 7 Jacob for me! / Come and announce Israel's **d**.'
Est 7: 8 attendants covered Haman's face, signaling his **d**.
Ps 9: 6 My enemies have met their **d**; / their cities are
Pr 14:28 is a king's glory; a dwindling nation is his **d**.
Eze 2:10 other words of sorrow, and pronouncements of **d**.
7: 6 It has finally arrived! Your final **d** is waiting!
Zec 9: 2 **D** is certain for Hamath, near Damascus, and for
11:17 **D** is certain for this worthless shepherd who
Lk 10:11 from our feet as a public announcement of your **d**.
Ro 6:21 things you used to do, things that end in eternal **d**.
7:13 Did the law, which is good, cause my **d**? Of course
2Co 2:16 are perishing we are a fearful smell of death and **d**.
Rev 17:11 is like the other seven, and he, too, will go to his **d**.
21: 8 their **d** is in the lake that burns with fire and sulfur.

DOOMED (21) [DOOM]

Nu 17:13 the Tabernacle of the LORD dies. We are all **d**!"
22: 6 I also know that the people you curse are **d**."
Est 4:11 **d** to die unless the king holds out his gold scepter.
7: 7 life with Queen Esther, for he knew that he was **d**.
Pr 2:19 The man who visits her is **d**. He will never reach
Isa 14:31 Weep, you Philistine cities, for you are **d**! Melt in
65:23 and their children will not be **d** to misfortune.
Jer 48:15 Her most promising youth are **d** to slaughter,"
La 4:18 was near; our days were numbered. We were **d**!
Eze 22: 3 O city of murderers, **d** and damned—city of idols,
31:14 though it be higher than the clouds, for all are **d**.
Hos 5: 1 These words of judgment are for you: You are **d**!
Mt 12:25 and replied, "Any kingdom at war with itself is **d**.
12:25 A city or home divided against itself is **d**.
Mk 3:25 A home divided against itself is **d**.
Lk 11:17 so he said, "Any kingdom at war with itself is **d**. A divided home is also **d**.
Ro 7: 9 I had broken the law and was a sinner, **d** to die.
Eph 2: 1 were dead, **d** forever because of your many sins.
2Pe 2:14 themselves to be greedy; they are **d** and cursed.
2:17 They are **d** to blackest darkness.

DOOR (76) [DOORFRAME, DOORFRAMES, DOORKEEPER, DOORPOSTS, DOORS, DOORSTEP, DOORWAY, DOORWAYS]

Ge 6:16 bottom, middle, and upper—and put a **d** in the side.
19: 6 outside to talk to them, shutting the **d** behind him.
19: 9 they lunged at Lot and began breaking down the **d**.
19:10 reached out and pulled Lot in and bolted the **d**.
Ex 21: 6 Then his master must take him to the **d**
Dt 15:17 an awl and push it through his earlobe into the **d**.
22:21 the judges must take the girl to the **d** of her father's
Jdg 3:25 And when they opened the **d**, they found their
4:20 "Stand at the **d** of the tent," he told her.
19:22 They began beating at the **d** and shouting to the old
19:25 took his concubine and pushed her out the **d**.
19:26 She collapsed at the **d** of the house and lay there
19:27 When her husband opened the **d** to leave, he found
2Sa 13:17 this woman out, and lock the **d** behind her!"
1Ki 6:34 and each **d** was hinged to fold back upon itself.
14: 6 So when Ahijah heard her footsteps at the **d**,
14:17 and the child died just as she walked through the **d**
2Ki 4: 4 house with your sons and shut the **d** behind you.
4:21 the man of God, then shut the **d** and left him there.
4:33 He went in alone and shut the **d** behind him
5: 9 and chariots and waited at the **d** of Elisha's house.
6:32 When he arrives, shut the **d** and keep him out.
9: 3 Then open the **d** and run for your life!"
9:10 Then the young prophet opened the **d** and ran.
Ne 3:20 to the **d** of the home of Eliashib the high priest.
3:21 the **d** of Eliashib's house to the side of the house.
Est 2:21 who were guards at the **d** of the king's private
6: 2 two of the eunuchs who guarded the **d** to the king's
Job 33:22 They are at death's **d**; the angels of death wait for
Ps 77: 9 Has he slammed the **d** on his compassion?
105:20 the ruler of the nation opened his prison **d**.
107:20 they were healed— / snatched from the **d** of death.
Pr 5: 8 Run from her! Don't go near the **d** of her house!
26:14 As a **d** turns back and forth on its hinges,
Ecc 12: 5 You will be standing at death's **d**. And as you near
SS 5: 2 He was knocking at my bedroom **d**. 'Open to me,
5: 4 "My lover tried to unlatch the **d**, and my heart
Eze 8: 7 Then he brought me to the **d** of the Temple
8: 8 into the wall and uncovered a **d** to a hidden room.
10: 4 the cherubim and went over to the **d** of the Temple.
10:18 Then the glory of the LORD moved from the **d** of
16:49 while the poor and needy suffered outside her **d**.
40:38 A **d** led from the foyer of the inner gateway on the
41:11 feet wide. One **d** faced north and the other south.
41:17 The space above the **d** leading into the Most Holy
Da 3:26 as close as he could to the **d** of the flaming furnace
Mt 6: 6 go away by yourself, shut the **d** behind you,
7: 7 Keep on knocking, and the **d** will be opened.
7: 8 And the **d** is opened to everyone who knocks.
24:33 you can know his return is very near, right at the **d**.
25:10 him to the marriage feast, and the **d** was locked.
25:11 they stood outside, calling, 'Sir, open the **d** for us!'
Mk 1:33 over Capernaum gathered outside the **d** to watch.
2: 2 room for one more person, not even outside the **d**.
13:29 be sure that his return is very near, right at the **d**.
Lk 11: 7 The **d** is locked for the night, and we are all in bed.
11: 9 Keep on knocking, and the **d** will be opened.
11:10 And the **d** is opened to everyone who knocks.
12:36 Then you will be ready to open the **d** and let him in
13:24 "The **d** to heaven is narrow. Work hard to get in,
13:25 but when the head of the house has locked the **d**,
13:25 and pleading, 'Lord, open the **d** for us!'
16:20 At his **d** lay a diseased beggar named Lazarus.
Ac 5: 9 Just outside that **d** are the young men who buried
12:13 He knocked at the **d** in the gate, and a servant girl
12:14 so overjoyed that, instead of opening the **d**,
12:14 and told everyone, "Peter is standing at the **d**!"
12:16 When they finally went out and opened the **d**,
14:27 and how he had opened the **d** of faith to the
18: 7 worshiped God and lived next **d** to the synagogue.
1Co 16: 9 for there is a wide-open **d** for a great work here,
Jas 5: 9 The great Judge is coming. He is standing at the **d**!
Rev 3: 8 and I have opened a **d** for you that no one can shut.
3:20 "Look! Here I stand at the **d** and knock. If you hear me calling and open the **d**, I will come
4: 1 as I looked, I saw a **d** standing open in heaven,

DOORFRAME (3) [DOOR, FRAME]

Ex 12: 7 and sides of the **d** of the house where the lamb will
12:22 Strike the hyssop against the top and sides of the **d**,
12:23 he sees the blood on the top and sides of the **d**,

DOORFRAMES (1) [DOOR, FRAME]

Jer 22:13 into its walls and oppression into its **d** and ceilings.

DOORKEEPER (2) [DOOR, KEEP]

2Sa 4: 6 The **d**, who had been sifting wheat,
4: 6 So Recab and Baanah slipped past the **d**, went into

DOORPOSTS (8) [DOOR, POST]

Ex 12:13 The blood you have smeared on your **d** will serve
Dt 6: 9 Write them on the **d** of your house and on your
11:20 Write them on the **d** of your house and on your
1Ki 6:31 double doors of olive wood with five-sided **d**.
6:33 Then he made four-sided **d** of olive wood for the
2Ki 18:16 and from the **d** he had overlaid with gold,
Eze 45:19 this sin offering and put it on the **d** of the Temple,
Heb 11:28 and to sprinkle blood on the **d** so that the angel of

DOORS (56) [DOOR]

Jdg 3:23 Then Ehud closed and locked the **d** and climbed
3:24 and found the **d** to the upstairs room locked.
1Sa 3:15 and opened the **d** of the Tabernacle as usual.
21:13 scratching on **d** and drooling down his beard.
1Ki 6:31 Solomon made double **d** of olive wood with
6:32 These **d** were decorated with carvings of cherubim,
6:32 open flowers, and the **d** were overlaid with gold.
6:34 There were two folding **d** of cypress wood,
6:35 These **d** were decorated with carvings of cherubim,
6:35 open flowers, and the **d** were overlaid with gold.
7:50 the **d** for the entrances to the Most Holy Place
2Ki 18:16 Hezekiah even stripped the gold from the **d** of the
1Ch 22: 3 nails that would be needed for the **d** in the gates
2Ch 3: 7 All the walls, beams, **d**, and thresholds throughout
4: 9 He made **d** for the courtyard entrances
4:22 the **d** for the entrances to the Most Holy Place
28:24 He shut the **d** of the LORD's Temple so that no
29: 3 Hezekiah reopened the **d** of the Temple of the
29: 7 They also shut the **d** to the Temple's foyer,
Ne 3: 1 They dedicated it and set up its **d**, building the wall
3: 3 laid the beams, hung the **d**, and put the bolts
3: 6 They laid the beams, set up the **d**, and installed the

3:13 hung its **d**, and installed the bolts and bars.
3:14 he hung the **d** and installed the bolts and bars.
3:15 He rebuilt it, roofed it, hung its **d**, and installed its
6: 1 though we had not yet hung the **d** in the gates—
6:10 inside the Temple of God and bolt the **d** shut.
7: 1 wall was finished and I had hung the **d** in the gates,
7: 3 are still on duty, have them shut and bar the **d**.
Job 31:32 a stranger but have opened my **d** to everyone.
Ps 24: 7 Open up, ancient gates! / Open up, ancient **d**.
24: 9 Open up, ancient gates! / Open up, ancient **d**,
78:23 the skies to open— / he opened the **d** of heaven—
SS 7:13 and the rarest fruits are at our **d**, the new as well as
Isa 8:12 conceived behind closed **d** will be the end of you.
22:22 He will open **d**, and no one will be able to shut
22:22 he will close **d**, and no one will be able to open
26:20 Go home, my people, and lock your **d**! Hide until
57: 8 Behind closed **d**, you have set up your idols
Eze 33:30 you in their houses and whisper about you at the **d**,
41:11 Two **d** opened from the side rooms into the terrace
41:24 each with two swinging **d**.
41:25 The **d** leading into the Holy Place were decorated
42: 4 the complex, and all the **d** faced toward the north.
42:11 the other one, and it had the same entrances and **d**.
42:12 So there was an entrance in the wall facing the **d** of
43:11 including its entrances and **d**—and everything else
Zec 11: 1 Open your **d**, Lebanon, so that fire may sweep
Mal 1:10 that someone among you would shut the Temple **d**
Lk 12: 3 and what you have whispered behind closed **d** will
Jn 20:19 the disciples were meeting behind locked **d**
20:26 The **d** were locked; but suddenly, as before,
Ac 16:26 All the **d** flew open, and the chains of every
16:27 The jailer woke up to see the prison **d** wide open.
Rev 3: 7 He opens **d**, and no one can shut them; he shuts **d**, and no one can open them.

DOORSTEP (1) [DOOR]
Am 7:10 a plot against you right here on your very **d**!

DOORWAY (5) [DOOR, WAY]
Ge 19:11 the men of Sodom so they couldn't find the **d**.
1Sa 5: 4 and hands had broken off and were lying in the **d**.
2Ki 4:15 Elisha said to her as she stood in the **d**,
Pr 9:14 She sits in her **d** on the heights overlooking the
Eze 41: 1 and he measured the columns that framed its **d**.

DOORWAYS (3) [DOOR, WAY]
1Ki 7: 5 All the **d** were rectangular in frame; they were in
Eze 41:23 Holy Place and the Most Holy Place had double **d**,
Zep 2:14 Rubble will block all the **d**, and the cedar paneling

DOPHKAH (2)
Nu 33:12 They left the Sin Desert and camped at **D**.
33:13 They left **D** and camped at Alush.

DOR (4) [HAMMOTH-DOR, NAPHOTH-DOR]
Jos 12:23 The king of **D** in the city of Naphoth-dor
17:11 Beth-shan, Ibleam, **D** (that is, Naphoth-dor),
Jdg 1:27 Taanach, **D**, Ibleam, Megiddo, and their
1Ch 7:29 Taanach, Megiddo, **D**, and their surrounding

DORCAS (2) [TABITHA]
Ac 9:36 in Joppa named Tabitha (which in Greek is **D**).
9:39 the coats and other garments **D** had made for them.

DOSE (1)
Jer 4:18 This punishment is a bitter **d** of your own

DOTED [KJV] See DESIRED, LUSTED

DOTHAN (3)
Ge 37:17 I heard your brothers say they were going to **D**."
37:17 So Joseph followed his brothers to **D** and found
2Ki 6:13 And the report came back: "Elisha is at **D**."

DOUBLE (17) [DOUBLE-EDGED, DOUBLED, DOUBLY]
Ge 43:12 Take **d** the money that you found in your sacks,
43:15 and the gifts and **d** the money and hurried to
Ex 22: 4 then the thief must pay **d** the value.
22: 7 is found, the fine is **d** the value of what was stolen.
22: 9 whom God declares guilty must pay **d** to the other.
Dt 15:18 the services worth **d** the wages of hired workers,
21:17 He must give the customary **d** portion to his oldest
1Ki 6:31 Solomon made **d** doors of olive wood with
Job 41:13 and who can penetrate its **d** layer of armor?
Pr 20:10 The LORD despises **d** standards of every kind.
20:23 The LORD despises **d** standards; he is not
Isa 61: 7 you will inherit a **d** portion of prosperity
Jer 17:18 me peace. Yes, bring **d** destruction upon them!
Eze 41:23 and the Most Holy Place had **d** doorways,
Lk 13:11 She had been bent **d** for eighteen years and was
2Co 1:15 and trust, I wanted to give you a **d** blessing.
Rev 18: 6 Give her a **d** penalty for all her evil deeds.

DOUBLE-EDGED (2) [DOUBLE, EDGE]
Jdg 3:16 So Ehud made himself a **d** dagger that was
Pr 5: 4 the result is as bitter as poison, sharp as a **d** sword.

DOUBLED (6) [DOUBLE]
Ex 26: 9 The sixth sheet of the second set is to be **d** over at
39: 9 It was **d** over to form a pouch, nine inches square.
Mt 25:16 immediately to invest the money and soon **d** it.
25:17 of gold also went right to work and **d** the money.
25:20 bags of gold to invest and I have **d** the amount.'
25:22 bags of gold to invest, and I have **d** the amount.'

DOUBLY (2) [DOUBLE]
Jer 16:18 I will punish them **d** for all their sins, because they
Jude 1:12 They are not only dead but **d** dead, for they have

DOUBT (12) [DOUBTED, DOUBTFUL, DOUBTING, DOUBTLESS, DOUBTS]
Dt 28:66 Your lives will hang in **d**. You will live night
1Ki 20:25 There's not a shadow of a **d** that we will beat
Mt 14:31 much faith," Jesus said. "Why did you **d** me?"
21:21 "I assure you, if you have faith and don't **d**,
Mk 9:24 "I do believe, but help me not to **d**!"
11:23 that you really believe and do not **d** in your heart.
Lk 17:24 Son of Man returns, you will know it beyond all **d**.
24:38 he asked. "Why do you **d** who I am?
Ac 10:38 And no **d** you know that God anointed Jesus of
10:46 And there could be no **d** about it, for they heard
28: 4 and said to each other, "A murderer, no **d**!
1Co 14:17 You will be giving thanks very nicely, no **d**,

DOUBTED (1) [DOUBT]
Mt 28:17 they worshiped him—but some of them still **d**!

DOUBTFUL (1) [DOUBT]
Jas 1: 6 for a **d** mind is as unsettled as a wave of the sea

DOUBTING (1) [DOUBT]
Lk 24:41 Still they stood there **d**, filled with joy and wonder.

DOUBTLESS (2) [DOUBT]
Ge 44:28 **d** torn to pieces by some wild animal.
Job 11: 6 God is **d** punishing you far less than you deserve!

DOUBTS (3) [DOUBT]
Ps 94:19 When **d** filled my mind, / your comfort gave me
Ro 14:23 But if people have **d** about whether they should eat
15: 1 We must be considerate of the **d** and fears of those

DOUGH (9)
Ex 12:34 The Israelites took with them their bread **d** made
12:39 they baked bread from the yeastless **d** they had
1Sa 28:24 She kneaded **d** and baked unleavened bread.
2Sa 13: 8 was lying down so he could watch her mix some **d**.
Jer 7:18 See how the women knead **d** and make cakes to
Hos 7: 4 hot even while the baker is still kneading the **d**.
Mt 13:33 of flour, the yeast permeated every part of the **d**."
Lk 13:21 of flour, the yeast permeated every part of the **d**."
Gal 5: 9 spreads quickly through the whole batch of **d**!

DOVE (16) [DOVE'S, DOVES, TURTLEDOVE, TURTLEDOVES]
Ge 8: 8 Then he sent out a **d** to see if it could find dry
8: 9 But the **d** found no place to land because the water
8: 9 Noah held out his hand and drew the **d** back inside.
8:10 Seven days later, Noah released the **d** again.
8:12 A week later, he released the **d** again, and this time
Ps 55: 6 Oh, how I wish I had wings like a **d**; / then I would
56: T To be sung to the tune "**D** on Distant Oaks."
68:13 and gold, / as a **d** is covered by its wings.
SS 2:14 "My **d** is hiding behind some rocks, behind an
5: 2 my darling, my treasure, my lovely **d**,' he said,
6: 9 But I would still choose my **d**, my perfect one,
Isa 38:14 or a crane, / and then I moaned like a mourning **d**.
Mt 3:16 and he saw the Spirit of God descending like a **d**
Mk 1:10 and the Holy Spirit descending like a **d** on him.
Lk 3:22 Holy Spirit descended on him in the form of a **d**.
Jn 1:32 "I saw the Holy Spirit descending like a **d** from

DOVE'S (1) [DOVE]
2Ki 6:25 and a cup of **d** dung cost about two ounces of

DOVES (16) [DOVE]
Ps 74:19 Don't let these wild beasts destroy your **d**.
SS 1:15 how beautiful! Your eyes are soft like **d**."
4: 1 Your eyes behind your veil are like **d**.
5:12 His eyes are like **d** beside brooks of water; they are
Isa 59:11 growl like hungry bears; we moan like mournful **d**.
60: 8 flying like clouds to Israel, like **d** to their nests?
Jer 48:28 Live in the caves like **d** that nest in the clefts of the
Eze 7:16 and escape to the mountains will moan like **d**,
Hos 7:11 witless **d**, first calling to Egypt, then flying to
11:11 Flying like **d**, they will return from Assyria.
Na 2: 7 Listen to them moan like **d**; watch them beat their
Mt 10:16 Be as wary as snakes and harmless as **d**.
21:12 money changers and the stalls of those selling **d**.
Mk 11:15 money changers and the stalls of those selling **d**,
Jn 2:14 selling cattle, sheep, and **d** for sacrifices;
2:16 Then, going over to the people who sold **d**, he told

DOWN (1034) [DOWNCAST, DOWNFALL, DOWNPOUR, DOWNSTAIRS, DOWNTRODDEN, DOWNWARD] See Index of Articles, Etc.

DOWN FROM HEAVEN (28) 2Sa 22:17; 1Ki 18:38; 2Ki 1:10,12; 2Ch 7:1; Ps 14:2; 18:16; 33:13; 53:2; 80:14; 85:11; 144:7; Isa 63:15; La 3:50; Da 4:13,23,31; Mt 28:2; Lk 17:29; Jn 6:33,38,42; 1Th 4:16; 2Pe 1:17; Rev 3:12; 10:1; 18:1; 20:1

DOWN TO EGYPT (7) Ge 12:10; 42:3; 46:3,4; Nu 20:15; Isa 30:2; Hos 8:13

DOWNCAST (1) [DOWN, CAST]
Job 22:29 and you say, 'Help him up,' God will save the **d**.

DOWNFALL (8) [DOWN, FALL]
2Ch 26:16 he also became proud, which led to his **d**.
Job 18: 7 be shortened. Their own schemes will be their **d**.
Ps 13: 4 defeated him!" / Don't let them rejoice at my **d**.
38:16 my enemies gloat over me / or rejoice at my **d**."
92:11 With my own eyes I have seen the **d** of my
106:36 They worshiped their idols, / and this led to their **d**.
Pr 29:16 But the godly will live to see the tyrant's **d**.
Da 11:26 Those of his own household will bring his **d**.

DOWNPOUR (1) [DOWN, POUR]
Ex 9:33 the thunder and hail stopped, and the **d** ceased.

DOWNSTAIRS (1) [DOWN, STAIRS]
2Ki 4:37 Then she picked up her son and carried him **d**.

DOWNTRODDEN (2) [DOWN, TREAD]
Ps 74:21 Don't let the **d** be constantly disgraced! / Instead,
Lk 4:18 that the **d** will be freed from their oppressors,

DOWNWARD (3) [DOWN]
1Sa 17:49 and Goliath stumbled and fell face **d** to the ground.
Ecc 3:21 and the spirit of animals goes **d** into the earth?
7:29 but they have each turned to follow their own **d**

DOWRY (3)
Ge 34:12 No matter what **d** or gift you demand, I will pay
Ex 22:16 he must pay the customary **d** and accept her as his
22:17 the man must still pay the money for her **d**.

DRAFT (1) [DRAFTED]
1Sa 8:11 "The king will **d** your sons into his army

DRAFTED (2) [DRAFT]
Dt 24: 5 "A newly married man must not be **d** into the
1Sa 14:52 who was brave and strong, he **d** him into his army.

DRAG (13) [DRAGGED, DRAGGING, DRAGS]
2Sa 17:13 and **d** the walls of the city into the nearest valley
Ps 10: 9 capture their victims / and **d** them away in nets.
28: 3 Don't **d** me away with the wicked— / with those
52: 5 and **d** you from the land of the living. / *Interlude*
119:61 Evil people try to **d** me into sin, / but I am firmly
Isa 5:18 Destruction is certain for those who **d** their sins
Jer 12: 3 **D** these people away like helpless sheep to be
15: 3 to kill, the dogs to **d** away, the vultures to devour,
Eze 11: 7 are not safe, for I will soon **d** you from the city.
29: 4 and **d** you out on the land with fish sticking to your
Mt 13:48 the net is full, they **d** it up onto the shore, sit down,
Ac 17: 5 and Silas so they could **d** them out to the crowd.
Jas 2: 6 it the rich who oppress you and **d** you into court?

DRAGGED (23) [DRAG]
Ex 21:14 then the slayer must be **d** even from my altar
1Ki 21:13 So he was **d** outside the city and stoned to death.
2Ki 10:25 and the guards and officers **d** their bodies outside.
10:26 They **d** out the sacred pillar used in the worship of
Jer 22:19 **d** out of Jerusalem and dumped outside the gate!
49:20 Even the little children will be **d** off, and their
50:45 Even little children will be **d** off, and their homes
La 3:11 He **d** me off the path and tore me with his claws,
Eze 19: 9 With hooks, they **d** him into a cage / and brought
32:20 Egypt will be **d** away to its judgment.
Am 4: 2 Every last one of you will be **d** away like a fish on
5: 5 For the people of Gilgal will be **d** off into exile,
Hab 1:15 and **d** out in their nets while they rejoice?
Mt 5:25 enemy before it is too late and you are **d** into court,
Lk 20:15 So they **d** him out of the vineyard and murdered
21:12 You will be **d** into synagogues and prisons,
Jn 21:11 Peter went aboard and **d** the net to the shore.
Ac 7:58 They **d** him out of the city and began to stone him.
14:19 They stoned Paul and **d** him out of the city,
16:19 and **d** them before the authorities at the
17: 6 they **d** out Jason and some of the other believers
21:30 Paul was **d** out of the Temple, and immediately the
Rev 12: 4 His tail **d** down one-third of the stars, which he

DRAGGING (3) [DRAG]
Ecc 12: 5 and withered, **d** along without any sexual desire.
Ac 8: 3 **d** out both men and women to throw them into jail.
19:29 the amphitheater, **d** along Gaius and Aristarchus,

DRAGON (18)
Isa 27: 1 the coiling, writhing serpent, the **d** of the sea.
30: 7 promises are worthless! I call her the Harmless **D**.
51: 9 of old when you slew Egypt, the **d** of the Nile.
Rev 12: 3 I saw a large red **d** with seven heads and ten horns,
12: 5 And the child was snatched away from the **d**

12: 7 and the angels under his command fought the **d**
12: 8 And the **d** lost the battle and was forced out of
12: 9 This great **d**—the ancient serpent called the Devil,
12:13 And when the **d** realized that he had been thrown
12:14 be cared for and protected from the **d** for a time,
12:15 Then the **d** tried to drown the woman with a flood
12:16 the river that gushed out from the mouth of the **d**.
12:17 Then the **d** became angry at the woman, and he
13: 2 And the **d** gave him his own power and throne
13: 4 They worshiped the **d** for giving the beast such
13:11 of a lamb, and he spoke with the voice of a **d**.
16:13 that looked like frogs leap from the mouth of the **d**,
20: 2 He seized the **d**—that old serpent, the Devil,

DRAGONS [KJV] See JACKALS, (SEA) MONSTERS, SNAKES

DRAGS (4) [DRAG]

Dt 20:19 "When you are besieging a town and the war **d** on,
Job 7: 4 But the night **d** on, and I toss till dawn.
24:22 "God, in his power, **d** away the rich. They may
41:30 They tear up the ground as it **d** through the mud.

DRAIN (5) [DRAINED, DRAINING]

Ex 12:22 **D** each lamb's blood into a basin. Then take a
Lev 1:15 then let its blood **d** out against the sides of the
17:13 you must **d** out the blood and cover it with earth.
1Sa 14:34 and sheep here to kill them and **d** the blood.
Eze 23:34 In deep anguish you will **d** that cup of terror to the

DRAINED (3) [DRAIN]

Lev 5: 9 and the rest will be **d** out at the base of the altar.
19:26 "Never eat meat that has not been **d** of its blood.
Ps 31:10 Misery has **d** my strength; / I am wasting away

DRAINING (2) [DRAIN]

1Sa 14:32 and calves, but they ate them without **d** the blood.
Ps 75: 8 and all the wicked must drink it, / **d** it to the dregs.

DRAMS [KJV] See COINS

DRANK (32) [DRINK]

Ge 25:34 Esau ate and **d** and went on about his business,
26:30 and **d** in preparation for the treaty ceremony.
27:25 ate it. He also **d** the wine that Jacob served him.
43:34 So they all feasted and **d** freely with him.
Ex 34:28 forty nights. In all that time he neither ate nor **d**.
Nu 20:11 So all the people and their livestock **d** their fill.
Dt 9: 9 and all that time I ate nothing and **d** no water.
32:14 You **d** the finest wine, / made from the juice of
32:38 and **d** the wine of their offerings? / Let those gods
Jdg 7: 6 Only three hundred of the men **d** from their hands.
7: 6 their knees and **d** with their mouths in the stream.
15:19 ground at Lehi, and Samson was revived as he **d**.
2Sa 12: 3 ate from the man's own plate and **d** from his cup.
1Ki 13:19 and **d** some water at the prophet's home.
13:22 and **d** water where he told you not to eat or drink.
17: 6 and evening, and he **d** from the brook.
19: 6 a jar of water! So he ate and **d** and lay down again.
19: 8 So he got up and ate and **d**, and the food gave him
2Ki 9:34 Then Jehu went into the palace and ate and **d**.
1Ch 12:39 They feasted and **d** with David for three days,
29:22 and **d** in the LORD's presence with great joy that
Jer 25:18 and their kings and officials **d** from the cup.
25:19 and his people. They, too, **d** from that terrible cup,
25:26 the king of Babylon himself **d** from the cup of the
Da 5: 1 for a thousand of his nobles and **d** wine with them.
5: 3 his wives, and his concubines **d** from them.
5: 4 They **d** toasts from them to honor their idols made
Mk 14:23 for it. He gave it to them, and they all **d** from it.
Lk 13:26 You will say, 'But we ate and **d** with you, and you
Ac 10:41 and **d** with him after he rose from the dead.
1Co 10: 4 and all of them **d** the same miraculous water.
10: 4 For they all **d** from the miraculous rock that

DRAPED (2)

Isa 61:10 of salvation and **d** me in a robe of righteousness.
Jer 4:28 earth will mourn, the heavens will be **d** in black,

DRAUGHT [KJV] See TOILET, CATCH

DRAW (32) [DRAWING, DRAWN, DRAWS, DREW]

Ge 24:11 and the women were coming out to **d** water.
24:13 women of the village are coming out to **d** water.
24:19 she said, "I'll **d** water for your camels, too,
24:43 I will say to some young woman who comes to **d**
Ex 2:16 who came regularly to this well to **d** water
2:17 Then he helped them **d** water for their flocks.
Dt 6:11 You will **d** water from cisterns you did not dig,
13:10 because they have tried to **d** you away from the
Jos 22:19 or **d** us into your rebellion by building another altar
Jdg 8:20 But Jether did not **d** his sword, for he was only a
9:54 young armor bearer, "**D** your sword and kill me!
20: 9 we will **d** lots to decide who will attack Gibeah.
1Sa 9:11 they met some young women coming out to **d**
2Sa 22:35 he strengthens me to **d** a bow of bronze.
Ps 18:34 he strengthens me to **d** a bow of bronze.
37:14 The wicked **d** their swords / and string their bows
Pr 20: 5 deep within a person's heart, the wise will **d** it out.
Jer 51: 3 let the archers put on their armor or **d** their bows.
Eze 4: 1 of you. Then **d** a map of the city of Jerusalem on it.
28: 7 They will suddenly **d** their swords against your
Zep 3: 2 It does not trust in the LORD or **d** near to its God.
Hag 2:16 When you expected to **d** fifty gallons from the
Jn 4: 7 Soon a Samaritan woman came to **d** water,
12:32 up on the cross, I will **d** everyone to myself."
21: 6 and they couldn't **d** in the net because there were
Ac 20:30 you will distort the truth in order to **d** a following.
Col 2: 7 down into him and **d** up nourishment from him,
1Ti 2: 9 and not **d** attention to themselves by the way they
Heb 7:19 taken its place. And that is how we **d** near to God.
Jas 3:12 and you can't **d** fresh water from a salty pool.
4: 8 **D** close to God, and God will **d** close to you.

DRAWING (4) [DRAW]

Nu 24: 8 them up from Egypt, / **d** them along like a wild ox.
Lk 22: 1 begins with the Passover celebration, was **d** near.
1Co 10:11 who live at the time when this age is **d** to a close.
Heb 10:25 that the day of his coming back again is **d** near.

DRAWN (16) [DRAW]

Nu 22:23 standing in the road with a **d** sword in his hand.
22:31 in the roadway with a **d** sword in his hand.
Dt 30:17 and if you are **d** away to serve and worship other
Jdg 20:31 out to attack, they were **d** away from the town.
20:32 them along the roads and be **d** away from the town.
Ru 2: 9 help yourself to the water they have **d** from the
2Ki 2:11 a chariot of fire appeared, **d** by horses of fire.
1Ch 21:16 between heaven and earth with his sword **d**,
21:30 because he was terrified by the **d** sword of the
Isa 21: 7 Tell him to sound the alert when he sees chariots **d**
21:15 They have fled from **d** swords and sharp arrows
Jer 31: 3 With unfailing love I have **d** you to myself.
Eze 21:28 My sword is **d** for your slaughter; it is sharpened to
32:20 died by the sword, for the sword is **d** against them.
Mic 5: 6 They will rule Assyria with **d** swords and enter the
Ac 20:22 **d** there irresistibly by the Holy Spirit, not knowing

DRAWS (5) [DRAW]

Job 36:27 He **d** up the water vapor and then distills it into
Ps 88: 3 For my life is full of troubles, / and death **d** near.
Am 5: 8 It is he who **d** up water from the oceans and pours
9: 6 He **d** up water from the oceans and pours it down
Jn 6:44 to me unless the Father who sent me **d** them to me,

DREAD (9) [DREADED, DREADFUL]

Ex 15:16 terror and **d** will overcome them. / Because of your
Dt 2:25 about you, they will tremble with **d** and fear.'
11:25 your God will send fear and **d** ahead of you,
2Ch 29: 8 He has made us an object of **d**, horror, and ridicule,
Job 9:28 I would **d** all the pain he would send. For I know
Ps 91: 6 nor **d** the plague that stalks in darkness,
105:38 they were gone, / for the **d** of them was great.
Isa 51:13 Will you remain in constant **d** of human
Mk 10:32 The disciples were filled with **d** and the people

DREADED (1) [DREAD]

Job 3:25 has happened to me. What I **d** has come to be.

DREADFUL (5) [DREAD]

1Sa 6: 6 go until God had ravaged them with **d** plagues.
Job 25: 2 "God is powerful and **d**. He enforces peace in the
Da 7: 7 I saw a fourth beast, terrifying, **d**, and very strong.
Mal 4: 5 before the great and **d** day of the LORD arrives.
Rev 18: 2 a nest for filthy buzzards, and a den for **d** beasts.

DREAM (81) [DREAMED, DREAMER, DREAMERS, DREAMING, DREAMS]

Ge 20: 3 But one night God came to Abimelech in a **d**
31:10 I had a **d** and saw that the male goats mating with
31:11 Then in my **d**, the angel of God said to me,
31:24 previous night God had appeared to Laban in a **d**.
37: 5 One night Joseph had a **d** and promptly reported
37: 6 "Listen to this **d**," he announced.
37: 8 And they hated him all the more for his **d** and what
37: 9 Then Joseph had another **d** and told his brothers
37: 9 "Listen to this **d**," he said. "The sun, moon,
40: 5 night the cup-bearer and the baker each had a **d**,
and each **d** had its own meaning.
40: 9 The cup-bearer told his **d** first. "In my **d**," he said,
"I saw a vine in front of me.
40:12 "I know what the **d** means," Joseph said.
40:16 When the chief baker saw that the first **d** had such
a good meaning, he told his **d** to Joseph, too.
40:16 "In my **d**," he said, "there were three baskets of
41: 2 In his **d**, seven fat, healthy-looking cows suddenly
41: 4 fat ones! At this point in the **d**, Pharaoh woke up.
41: 5 Soon he fell asleep again and had a second **d**.
41: 7 Pharaoh woke up again and realized it was a **d**.
41:11 One night the chief baker and I each had a **d**, and
each **d** had a meaning.
41:15 "I had a **d** last night," Pharaoh told him,
41:17 So Pharaoh told him the **d**. "I was standing on the
41:22 "A little later I had another **d**. This time there were
41:32 As for having the **d** twice, it means that the matter
Jdg 7:13 up just as a man was telling his friend about a **d**.
7:13 The man said, "I had this **d**, and in my **d** a loaf of
barley bread came tumbling
7:14 friend said, "Your **d** can mean only one thing—
7:15 When Gideon heard the **d** and its interpretation,
1Ki 3: 5 night the LORD appeared to Solomon in a **d**,
3:15 Solomon woke up and realized it had been a **d**.
2Ch 1: 7 That night God appeared to Solomon in a **d**.
Job 20: 8 He will fade like a **d** and not be found. He will
Ps 73:20 Their present life is only a **d** / that is gone when
126: 1 restored his exiles to Jerusalem, / it was like a **d**!
SS 5: 2 night as I was sleeping, my heart awakened in a **d**.
Isa 29: 7 fighting against Jerusalem will vanish like a **d**!
29: 8 your enemies will **d** of a victorious conquest over
Jer 23:25 'Listen to the **d** I had from God last night.'
Da 2: 1 Nebuchadnezzar had a **d** that disturbed him
2: 3 he said, "I have had a **d** that troubles me. Tell me
2: 4 Tell us the **d**, and we will tell you what it means."
2: 5 If you don't tell me what my **d** was and what it
2: 6 you tell me what I dreamed and what the **d** means,
2: 6 and honors. Just tell me the **d** and what it means!"
2: 7 Tell us the **d**, and we will tell you what it means."
2: 9 If you don't tell me the **d**, you will be condemned.
2: 9 But tell me the **d**, and then I will know that you
2:10 isn't a man alive who can tell Your Majesty his **d**!
2:11 No one except the gods can tell you your **d**,
2:16 so he could tell the king what the **d** meant.
2:24 the king, and I will tell him the meaning of his **d**."
2:25 will tell Your Majesty the meaning of your **d**!"
2:26 Can you tell me what my **d** was and what it
2:28 Now I will tell you your **d** and the visions you saw
2:30 any living person that I know the secret of your **d**,
2:36 "That was the **d**; now I will tell Your Majesty
2:45 The **d** is true, and its meaning is certain."
4: 5 But one night I had a **d** that greatly frightened me;
4: 6 so they could tell me what my **d** meant.
4: 7 and fortune-tellers came in, I told them the **d**,
4: 8 Daniel came in before me, and I told him the **d**.
4: 9 for you to solve. Now tell me what my **d** means.
4:18 " 'O Belteshazzar, that was the **d** that I,
4:19 for a time, aghast at the meaning of the **d**.
4:19 don't be alarmed by the **d** and what it means."
4:19 how I wish the events foreshadowed in this **d**
4:24 "This is what the **d** means, Your Majesty,
7: 1 Daniel had a **d** and saw visions as he lay in his bed.
7: 1 He wrote the **d** down, and this is what he saw.
Joel 2:28 will prophesy. Your old men will **d** dreams.
Mt 1:20 and an angel of the Lord appeared to him in a **d**.
2:12 because God had warned them in a **d** not to return
2:13 an angel of the Lord appeared to Joseph in a **d**.
2:19 an angel of the Lord appeared in a **d** to Joseph in
2:22 Then, in another **d**, he was warned to go to Galilee.
Lk 14:31 "Or what king would ever **d** of going to war
Ac 2:17 will see visions, / and your old men will **d** dreams.

DREAMED (9) [DREAM]

Ge 21: 7 For who would have **d** that I would ever have a
28:12 he **d** of a stairway that reached from earth to
41: 1 Pharaoh **d** that he was standing on the bank of the
Job 20:20 Of all the things he **d** about, nothing remains.
Da 2: 2 and he demanded that they tell him what he had **d**.
2: 3 Tell me what I **d**, for I must know what it means."
2: 6 But if you tell me what I **d** and what the dream
2:29 Majesty was sleeping, you **d** about coming events.
4:10 " 'While I was lying in my bed, this is what I **d**.

DREAMER (1) [DREAM]

Ge 37:19 "Here comes that **d**!" they exclaimed.

DREAMERS (1) [DREAM]

Dt 13: 5 or **d** who try to lead you astray must be put to

DREAMING (4) [DREAM]

Ecc 5: 7 **D** all the time instead of working is foolishness.
6: 9 Just **d** about nice things is meaningless; it is like
Isa 56:10 They love to lie around, sleeping and **d**.
Da 4:13 " 'Then as I lay there **d**, I saw a messenger,

DREAMS (36) [DREAM]

Ge 37:20 Then we'll see what becomes of all his **d**!"
40: 8 And they replied, "We both had **d** last night,
40: 8 "Interpreting **d** is God's business,"
41: 8 Pharaoh became very concerned as to what the **d**
41: 8 and wise men of Egypt and told them about his **d**,
41:12 We told the **d** to a young Hebrew man who was a
41:12 of the guard. He told us what each of our **d** meant,
41:15 But I have heard that you can interpret **d**, and that
41:24 I told these **d** to my magicians, but not one of them
41:25 "Both **d** mean the same thing," Joseph told
41:39 "Since God has revealed the meaning of the **d** to
42: 9 And he remembered the **d** he had had many years
Nu 12: 6 I the LORD communicate by visions and **d**.
Dt 13: 1 or those who have **d** about the future, and they
1Sa 28: 6 either by **d** or by sacred lots or by the prophets.
28:15 God has left me and won't reply by prophets or **d**.
Job 7:14 you shatter me with **d**. You terrify me with visions.
33:15 He speaks in **d**, in visions of the night when deep
Ps 90: 5 You sweep people away like **d** that disappear
Pr 3:24 can lie down without fear and enjoy pleasant **d**.
13:12 but when **d** come true, there is life and joy.
13:19 It is pleasant to see **d** come true, but fools will not
Isa 29: 8 A hungry person **d** of eating but is still hungry.
29: 8 A thirsty person **d** of drinking but is still faint from
Jer 23:27 By telling these false **d**, they are trying to get my
23:28 Let these false prophets tell their **d**, but let my true
23:32 Their imaginary **d** are flagrant lies that lead my
27: 9 fortune-tellers, interpreters of **d**, mediums,
29: 8 there in Babylon trick you. Do not listen to their **d**
44:14 Of those who fled to Egypt with **d** of returning
Da 1:17 in understanding the meanings of visions and **d**.
5:12 He can interpret **d**, explain riddles, and solve
Joel 2:28 will prophesy. Your old men will dream **d**.
Zec 10: 2 and interpreters of **d** pronounce comfortless

Ac 2:17 will see visions, / and your old men will dream **d**.
Jude 1:8 who claim authority from their **d**, live immoral

DREGS (1)

Ps 75:8 all the wicked must drink it, / draining it to the **d**.

DRENCH (3) [DRENCHED]

Ps 6:6 out from sobbing. / Every night tears **d** my bed;
65:10 You **d** the plowed ground with rain,
Eze 32:6 I will **d** the earth with your gushing blood all the

DRENCHED (7) [DRENCH]

Isa 34:6 The sword of the LORD is **d** with blood. It is
Da 4:15 Now let him be **d** with the dew of heaven, and let
4:23 tender grass. Let him be **d** with the dew of heaven.
4:25 a cow, and you will be **d** with the dew of heaven.
4:33 like a cow, and he was **d** with the dew of heaven.
5:21 like a cow, and he was **d** with the dew of heaven,
Zec 9:15 a bowl, **d** with blood like the corners of the altar.

DRESS (15) [DRESSED, DRESSES, DRESSING, HEADDRESSES]

Ex 3:22 this clothing, you will **d** your sons and daughters.
29:8 Next present his sons, and **d** them in their tunics
40:14 Then bring his sons and **d** them in their tunics.
Ru 3:3 and put on perfume and **d** in your nicest clothes.
Est 6:9 Instruct one of the king's most noble princes to **d**
Ps 69:11 When I **d** in sackcloth to show sorrow, / they make
Isa 58:5 You **d** in sackcloth and cover yourselves with
Jer 2:32 her jewelry? Does a bride hide her wedding **d**? No!
4:30 Why do you **d** up in your most beautiful clothing
6:26 Now my people, **d** yourselves in sackcloth, and sit
10:9 Then they **d** these gods in royal purple robes made
Eze 7:18 They will **d** themselves in sackcloth; horror
27:31 because of you and **d** themselves in sackcloth.
Joel 1:13 **D** yourselves in sackcloth, you priests! Wail,
Mt 11:8 Those who **d** like that live in palaces, not out in the

DRESSED (42) [DRESS]

Ge 27:15 were there in the house, and **d** Jacob with them.
41:42 He **d** him in beautiful clothing and placed the royal
Lev 8:7 He **d** him in the robe of the ephod, along with the
1Sa 25:18 two skins of wine, five **d** sheep, nearly a bushel of
2Sa 1:24 for he **d** you in fine clothing and gold ornaments.
1Ki 21:27 he tore his clothing, **d** in sackcloth, and fasted.
22:10 King Jehoshaphat of Judah, **d** in their royal robes,
2Ki 19:2 and the leading priests, all **d** in sackcloth,
1Ch 15:27 David was **d** in a robe of fine linen, as were the
2Ch 5:12 were **d** in fine linen robes and stood at the east side
18:9 King Jehoshaphat of Judah, **d** in their royal robes,
28:15 and drink, and **d** their wounds with olive oil.
Ne 9:1 This time they fasted and **d** in sackcloth
Ps 45:13 her chamber, / **d** in a gown woven with gold.
104:2 you are **d** in a robe of light. / You stretch out the
Pr 7:10 approached him, **d** seductively and sly of heart.
SS 5:3 Should I get **d** again? I have washed my feet.
Isa 37:2 and the leading priests, all **d** in sackcloth,
61:10 For he has **d** me with the clothing of salvation
Jer 1:17 "Get up and get **d**. Go out, and tell them whatever
Eze 9:2 One of them was **d** in linen and carried a writer's
9:3 And the LORD called to the man **d** in linen who
16:4 rubbed with salt, and **d** in warm clothing.
23:6 captains and commanders **d** in handsome blue,
23:15 They were **d** like chariot officers from the land of
Da 5:7 and tell me what it means will be **d** in purple robes
5:29 Daniel was **d** in purple robes,
10:5 I looked up and saw a man **d** in linen clothing,
12:6 One of them asked the man **d** in linen, who was
12:7 The man **d** in linen, who was standing above the
Jnh 3:6 He **d** himself in sackcloth and sat on a heap of
Zec 3:5 and **d** him in new clothes while the angel of the
Mt 6:29 yet Solomon in all his glory was not **d** as
11:8 Or were you expecting to see a man **d** in expensive
Mk 15:17 They **d** him in a purple robe and made a crown of
Lk 7:25 Or were you expecting to see a man **d** in expensive
12:27 yet Solomon in all his glory was not **d** as
12:35 "Be **d** for service and well prepared,
Ac 12:8 angel told him, "Get **d** and put on your sandals."
Jas 2:2 suppose someone comes into your meeting **d** in
2:2 comes in who is poor and **d** in shabby clothes.
Rev 19:14 The armies of heaven, **d** in pure white linen,

DRESSES (1) [DRESS]

Pr 31:22 She **d** like royalty in gowns of finest cloth.

DRESSING (2) [DRESS]

Lev 6:10 after **d** in his special linen clothing
1Ki 20:11 "A warrior still **d** for battle should not boast like a

DREW (28) [DRAW]

Ge 8:9 Noah held out his hand and **d** the dove back inside.
24:45 down to the spring and **d** water and filled the jug.
38:29 But then he **d** back his hand, and the other baby
47:29 As the time of his death **d** near, he called for his
Ex 2:10 for she said, "I **d** him out of the water."
2:19 "And then he **d** water for us and watered our
24:6 blood from these animals and **d** it off into basins.
Ru 4:8 So the other family redeemer **d** off his sandal as he
1Sa 7:6 **d** water from a well and poured it out before the
2Sa 3:27 But then he **d** his dagger and killed Abner in
10:8 The Ammonite troops **d** up their battle lines at the
22:17 and rescued me; / he **d** me out of deep waters.
23:16 **d** some water from the well, and brought it back to
2Ki 9:24 Then Jehu **d** his bow and shot Joram between the
14:11 The two armies **d** up their battle lines at
17:21 Then Jeroboam **d** Israel away from following the
1Ch 11:18 **d** some water from the well, and brought it back to
19:9 The Ammonite troops **d** up their battle lines at the
2Ch 25:21 The two armies **d** up their battle lines at
Ne 5:14 neither I nor my officials **d** on our official food
Ps 18:16 and rescued me; / he **d** me out of deep waters.
Pr 8:27 the heavens, when he **d** the horizon on the oceans.
Isa 43:17 I **d** them beneath the waves, and they drowned,
Jer 41:2 Ishmael and his ten men suddenly **d** their swords
Lk 9:51 As the time **d** near for his return to heaven,
Jn 18:10 Then Simon Peter **d** a sword and slashed off the
Ac 7:17 "As the time **d** near when God would fulfill his
16:27 had escaped, so he **d** his sword to kill himself.

DRIED (19) [DRY]

Jos 4:23 For the LORD your God **d** up the river right
4:23 just as he did at the Red Sea when he **d** it up until
5:1 heard how the LORD had **d** up the Jordan River
Jdg 16:7 seven new bowstrings that have not yet been **d**,
1Ki 17:7 But after a while the brook **d** up, for there was no
Ps 22:15 My strength has **d** up like sunbaked clay.
74:15 gush forth, / and you **d** up rivers that never run dry.
Isa 15:6 Even the waters of Nimrim are **d** up! The grassy
47:14 But they are as useless as **d** grass burning in a fire.
51:10 you not the same today, the one who **d** up the sea,
Jer 23:10 land itself is in mourning—its pastures are **d** up.
48:34 Even the waters of Nimrim are **d** up now.
Eze 4:12 bake it over a fire using **d** human dung as fuel
19:12 The desert wind **d** up its fruit / and tore off its
Hos 9:16 Their roots are **d** up; they will bear no more fruit.
Joel 1:12 and apple trees—yes, all the fruit trees—have **d** up. All joy has **d** up with them.
1:20 The streams have **d** up, and fire has consumed the
Rev 16:12 and it **d** up so that the kings from the east could

DRIED-UP (1) [DRY]

2Pe 2:17 These people are as useless as **d** springs of water

DRIES (2) [DRY]

Isa 24:4 The earth **d** up, the crops wither, the skies refuse to
Jas 1:11 The hot sun rises and **d** up the grass; the flower

DRIFT (2)

Col 1:23 Don't **d** away from the assurance you received
Heb 2:1 the truth we have heard, or we may **d** away from it.

DRINK (270) [DRANK, DRINKER, DRINKERS, DRINKING, DRINKS, DRUNK, DRUNKARD, DRUNKARDS, DRUNKEN, DRUNKENNESS, DRUNKS]

DRINK OFFERING (30) Ex 29:40; Lev 23:13; Nu 6:17; 15:5,7,10,24; 28:7,8,9,10,14,15; 29:16,18,19,21,22,24,25,27,28,30,31,33,34,37,38; 2Ki 16:13; Php 2:17

DRINK OFFERINGS (23) Ex 25:29; 30:9; 37:16; Lev 23:18,37; Nu 6:15; 28:24,31; 29:6,11,39; 2Ki 16:15; 1Ch 29:21; 2Ch 29:35; Ezr 7:17; Isa 57:6; Jer 7:18; 19:13; 32:29; 44:19; 52:19; Eze 20:28; 45:17

STRONG DRINK (2) Dt 29:6; Isa 24:9

Ge 21:19 filled her water container and gave the boy a **d**.
24:14 I will ask one of them for a **d**. If she says, 'Yes,
24:17 to her, the servant asked, "Please give me a **d**."
24:18 and she quickly lowered the jug for him to **d**.
24:43 to draw water, "Please give me a **d** of water!"
24:45 filled the jug. So I said to her, 'Please give me a **d**.'
24:46 lowered the jug from her shoulder so I could **d**,
30:38 Laban's flocks would see them as they came to **d**,
Ex 7:18 The Egyptians will not be able to **d** any water
7:21 so foul that the Egyptians couldn't **d** it.
7:24 drinking water, for they couldn't **d** from the river.
15:23 But the people couldn't **d** it because it was bitter.
15:24 "What are we going to **d**?" they demanded.
15:25 it into the water. This made the water good to **d**.
17:2 "Give us water to **d**!" they demanded. "Quiet!"
17:6 Then the people will be able to **d**." Moses did just
25:29 and bowls to be used in pouring out **d** offerings.
29:40 also, offer one quart of wine as a **d** offering.
30:9 any burnt offerings, grain offerings, or **d** offerings.
32:20 mixed it with water. Then he made the people **d** it.
37:16 These utensils were to be used in pouring out **d**
Lev 10:9 "You and your descendants must never **d** wine
10:9 or any other alcoholic **d** before going into the
17:12 who live among you must never eat or **d** blood.'
17:14 I have told the people of Israel never to eat or **d** it,
23:13 you must also offer one quart of wine as a **d**
23:18 the accompanying grain offerings and **d** offerings,
23:37 burnt offerings, grain offerings, sacrificial meals and **d** offerings—
Nu 5:24 He will then make the woman **d** the bitter water,
5:26 Then he will require the woman to **d** the water.
6:3 they must not **d** other fermented drinks or fresh
6:4 to eat or **d** anything that comes from a grapevine,
6:15 their prescribed grain offerings and **d** offerings.
6:17 make the prescribed grain offering and **d** offering.
6:20 After this ceremony the Nazirites may again **d**
15:5 you must also present one quart of wine for a **d**
15:7 give two and a half pints of wine for a **d** offering.
15:10 plus two quarts of wine for the **d** offering.
15:24 and **d** offering and with one male goat for a sin
20:2 There was no water for the people to **d** at that
20:5 or pomegranates. And there is no water to **d**!"
20:17 We won't even **d** water from your wells.
21:5 "There is nothing to eat here and nothing to **d**.
21:22 or touch your vineyards or **d** your well water."
28:7 Along with it you must present the proper **d**
28:7 consisting of one quart of fermented **d** with each
28:8 with the same grain offering and **d** offering.
28:9 choice flour mixed with olive oil, and a **d** offering.
28:10 burnt offering and its accompanying **d** offering.
28:14 You must also give a **d** offering with each
28:15 burnt offering and its accompanying **d** offering.
28:24 the regular whole burnt offerings and **d** offerings.
28:31 burnt offerings, along with their **d** offerings,
29:6 their prescribed grain offerings and **d** offerings.
29:11 grain offering, and their accompanying **d** offerings.
29:16 its accompanying grain offering and **d** offering.
29:18 by the prescribed grain offering and **d** offering.
29:19 its accompanying grain offering and **d** offering.
29:21 by the prescribed grain offering and **d** offering.
29:22 its accompanying grain offering and **d** offering.
29:24 by the prescribed grain offering and **d** offering.
29:25 its accompanying grain offering and **d** offering.
29:27 by the prescribed grain offering and **d** offering.
29:28 its accompanying grain offering and **d** offering.
29:30 by the prescribed grain offering and **d** offering.
29:31 its accompanying grain offering and **d** offering.
29:33 by the prescribed grain offering and **d** offering.
29:34 its accompanying grain offering and **d** offering.
29:37 by the prescribed grain offering and **d** offering.
29:38 its accompanying grain offering and **d** offering.
29:39 burnt offerings, grain offerings, **d** offerings,
33:14 where there was no water for the people to **d**.
Dt 2:28 every bite of food we eat and all the water we **d**.
28:39 but you will not **d** the wine or eat the grapes,
29:6 You had no bread or wine or other strong **d**,
Jdg 4:19 So she gave him some milk to **d** and covered him
7:5 and **d** with their mouths in the stream."
13:4 You must not **d** wine or any other alcoholic **d**
13:7 You must not **d** wine or any other alcoholic **d**
13:14 or raisins, **d** wine or any other alcoholic **d**,
19:6 sat down together and had something to eat and **d**.
1Sa 30:11 gave him some bread to eat and some water to **d**.
30:12 had anything to eat or **d** for three days and nights.
2Sa 23:16 But he refused to **d** it. Instead, he poured it out
23:17 "The LORD forbid that I should **d** this!"
23:17 So David did not **d** it. This is an example of the
1Ki 4:20 were very contented, with plenty to eat and **d**.
13:8 not eat any food or **d** any water in this place.
13:9 eat any food or **d** any water while you are there,
13:16 to eat any food or **d** any water here in this place.
13:17 eat any food or **d** any water while you are there,
13:18 and water to **d**.' " But the old man was lying to
13:22 and drank water where he told you not to eat or **d**.
17:4 **D** from the brook and eat what the ravens bring
2Ki 6:22 Give them food and **d** and send them home again
16:13 and a grain offering, poured a **d** offering over it,
16:15 offerings of the people, including their **d** offerings.
18:27 will eat their own dung and **d** their own urine."
1Ch 11:18 But David refused to **d** it. Instead, he poured it out
11:19 "God forbid that I should **d** this!" he exclaimed.
11:19 So David did not **d** it. This is an example of the
29:21 They also brought **d** offerings and many other
2Ch 28:15 and sandals to wear, gave them enough food and **d**,
29:35 of burnt offerings, along with the usual **d** offerings,
Ezr 7:17 and the appropriate grain offerings and **d** offerings,
10:6 the night there, but he did not eat any food or **d**.
Ne 8:12 people went away to eat and **d** at a festive meal,
Est 3:15 Then the king and Haman sat down to **d**,
4:16 Do not eat or **d** for three days, night or day.
Job 1:4 occasions they would get together to eat and **d**.
6:18 but there is nothing there to **d**, and so they perish
21:20 Let them **d** deeply of the anger of the Almighty.
Ps 36:8 letting them **d** from your rivers of delight.
60:3 hard on us, / making us **d** wine that sent us reeling.
75:8 out in judgment, / and all the wicked must **d** it,
78:44 into blood, / so no one could **d** from the streams.
80:5 with sorrow / and made us **d** tears by the bucketful.
102:9 instead of my food. / My tears run down into my **d**
Pr 4:17 They eat wickedness and **d** violence!
5:15 **D** water from your own well—share your love only
7:18 Come, let's **d** our fill of love until morning.
9:5 "Come, eat my food, and **d** the wine I have mixed.
20:1 Whoever is led astray by **d** cannot be wise.
23:7 "Eat and **d**," they say, but they don't mean it.
23:35 When will I wake up so I can have another **d**?"
25:21 to eat. If they are thirsty, give them water to **d**.
31:5 For if they **d**, they may forget their duties and be
31:7 Let them **d** to forget their poverty and remember
Ecc 2:24 enjoy food and **d** and to find satisfaction in work.
3:13 And people should eat and **d** and enjoy the fruits of
5:18 **d** a good glass of wine, and enjoy their work—
8:15 to do in this world than to eat, **d**, and enjoy life.
9:7 Eat your food and **d** your wine with a happy heart,
SS 4:12 You are like a spring that no one else can **d** from,
5:1 I **d** my wine with my milk." / "Oh, lover and beloved, eat and **d**! Yes, **d** deeply of this love!"
8:2 I would give you spiced wine to **d**, my sweet
Isa 12:3 With joy you will **d** deeply from the fountain of
22:13 sacrificial animals, feast on meat, and **d** wine. "Let's eat, **d**, and be merry," you say.
24:9 and song; strong **d** now turns bitter in the mouth.
30:20 gave you adversity for food and affliction for **d**,
36:12 will eat their own dung and **d** their own urine."
48:21 the rock, and water gushed out for them to **d**.
51:22 You will **d** no more of my fury. It is gone at last!
55:1 Come and **d**—even if you have no money! Come,
57:6 You worship them with **d** offerings and grain
62:9 you yourselves will **d** the wine that you have

65:13 You will be thirsty, but they will **d**. You will be
66:11 **D** deeply of her glory even as an infant drinks at its
Jer 7:18 And they give **d** offerings to their other idol gods!
8:14 and has given us a cup of poison to **d** because we
9:15 them with bitterness and give them poison to **d**.
16:8 and parties. Do not eat and **d** with them at all.
19:13 and where **d** offerings were poured out to your
23:15 them with bitterness and give them poison to **d**.
25:15 and make all the nations to whom I send you **d**
25:16 When they **d** from it, they will stagger, crazed by
25:17 the LORD and made all the nations **d** from it—
25:27 God of Israel, says: **D** from this cup of my anger.
25:28 You must **d** from it. You cannot escape!
32:29 and by pouring out **d** offerings to other gods.
35:5 of wine before them and invited them to have a **d**,
35:6 "We don't **d** wine, because Jehonadab son of
35:6 'You and your descendants must never **d** wine.
35:8 We have never had a **d** of wine since then,
35:14 The Recabites do not **d** wine because their ancestor
44:19 pouring out **d** offerings to her, and making cakes
49:12 go unpunished! You must **d** this cup of judgment!
51:7 a cup from which he made the whole earth **d**
51:39 I will make them **d** until they fall asleep,
52:19 lampstands, dishes, bowls used for **d** offerings,
La 3:15 He has given me a cup of deep sorrow to **d**.
4:21 must **d** from the cup of the LORD's anger.
5:4 We have to pay for water to **d**, and even firewood
Eze 4:11 out a jar of water for each day, and **d** it at set times.
4:16 drop by drop, and the people will **d** it with dismay.
12:18 **D** your water with fear, as if it were your last.
20:28 and poured out their **d** offerings to them!
23:32 You will **d** from the same cup of terror as your
34:3 You **d** the milk, wear the wool, and butcher the
34:19 All they have to **d** is water that you have fouled.
39:17 of Israel, and there eat the flesh and **d** the blood!
39:18 and **d** the blood of princes as though they were
39:19 until you are glutted; **d** blood until you are drunk.
44:21 The priests must never **d** wine before entering the
45:17 burnt offerings, grain offerings, **d** offerings,
Da 5:2 his wives, and his concubines might **d** from them.
Hos 2:5 other lovers and sell myself to them for food and **d**,
Joel 1:20 cry out to you because they have no water to **d**.
Am 2:12 the Nazirites to sin by making them **d** your wine,
4:1 are always asking your husbands for another **d**!
4:8 People staggered from one town to another for a **d**
5:11 You will never **d** wine from the lush vineyards you
6:6 You **d** wine by the bowlful, and you perfume
9:14 they will eat their crops and **d** their wine.
Ob 1:16 you nations will **d** and stagger and disappear from
Jnh 3:7 not even the animals, may eat or **d** anything at all.
Mic 2:11 "I'll preach to you the joys of wine and **d**!"
Hab 2:16 soon it will be your turn! Come, **d** and be exposed!
2:16 **D** from the cup of the LORD's judgment, and all
Zep 1:13 They will never **d** wine from the vineyards they
Hag 1:6 You have wine to **d**, but not enough to satisfy your
Zec 12:2 and Judah like an intoxicating **d** to all the nearby
Mt 6:25 whether you have enough food, **d**, and clothes.
6:31 worry about having enough food or **d** or clothing.
11:18 For John the Baptist didn't **d** wine and he often
11:19 feast and **d**, and you say, 'He's a glutton and a
20:22 Are you able to **d** from the bitter cup of sorrow I am about to **d**?"
20:23 "You will indeed **d** from it," he told them. "But I
25:35 you fed me. I was thirsty, and you gave me a **d**.
25:37 feed you? Or thirsty and give you something to **d**?
25:42 I was thirsty, and you didn't give me anything to **d**.
26:27 gave it to them and said, "Each of you **d** from it,
26:29 I will not **d** wine again until the day I **d** it new
26:42 If this cup cannot be taken away until I **d** it,
27:34 but when he had tasted it, he refused to **d** it.
27:48 holding it up to him on a stick so he could **d**.
Mk 10:38 Are you able to **d** from the bitter cup of sorrow I am about to **d**?"
10:39 "You will indeed **d** from my cup and be baptized
14:25 declare that I will not **d** wine again until that day when I **d** it new in the Kingdom of God."
15:36 holding it up to him on a stick so he could **d**.
16:18 and if they **d** anything poisonous, it won't hurt
Lk 5:30 "Why do you eat and **d** with such scum?"
7:33 For John the Baptist didn't **d** wine and he often
7:34 feast and **d**, and you say, 'He's a glutton and a
12:19 to come. Now take it easy! Eat, **d**, and be merry!'
12:29 And don't worry about food—what to eat and **d**.
22:18 For I will not **d** wine again until the Kingdom of
22:30 to eat and **d** at my table in that Kingdom. And you
23:36 mocked him, too, by offering him a **d** of sour wine.
Jn 4:7 and Jesus said to her, "Please give me a **d**."
4:9 Why are you asking me for a **d**?"
6:53 eat the flesh of the Son of Man and **d** his blood,
6:54 who eat my flesh and **d** my blood have eternal life,
6:55 flesh is the true food, and my blood is the true **d**.
6:56 who eat my flesh and **d** my blood remain in me,
7:38 If you believe in me, come and **d**!
18:11 Shall I not **d** from the cup the Father has given
Ac 23:12 oath to neither eat nor **d** until they had killed Paul.
23:14 oath to neither eat nor **d** until we have killed Paul.
23:21 have vowed not to eat or **d** until they kill him.
Ro 12:20 If they are thirsty, give them something to **d**,
14:17 of God is not a matter of what we eat or **d**,
14:21 Don't eat meat or **d** wine or do anything else if it
1Co 9:7 of sheep and isn't allowed to **d** some of the milk?
10:21 You cannot **d** from the cup of the Lord and from
10:31 Whatever you eat or **d** or whatever you do,
11:25 Do this in remembrance of me as often as you **d**
11:26 For every time you eat this bread and **d** this cup,
11:29 For if you eat the bread or **d** the cup unworthily,
Php 2:17 But even if my life is to be poured out like a **d**
Col 2:16 let anyone condemn you for what you eat or **d**,
1Ti 5:23 Don't **d** only water. You ought to **d** a little wine for the sake of your
Heb 5:12 You are like babies who **d** only milk and cannot
9:10 deals only with food and **d** and ritual washing—
Rev 14:8 and made them **d** the wine of her passionate
14:10 must **d** the wine of God's wrath. It is poured out
16:6 So you have given their murderers blood to **d**.
16:19 and he made her **d** the cup that was filled with the
22:17 them come and **d** the water of life without charge.

DRINKER (2) [DRINK]

1Ti 3:3 He must not be a heavy **d** or be violent. He must be
Tit 1:7 he must not be a heavy **d**, violent, or greedy for

DRINKERS (2) [DRINK]

1Ti 3:8 They must not be heavy **d** and must not be greedy
Tit 2:3 speaking evil of others and must not be heavy **d**.

DRINKING (38) [DRINK]

Ge 24:20 water to the camels until they had finished **d**.
24:22 Then at last, when the camels had finished **d**,
44:5 by stealing my master's personal silver **d** cup,
Ex 7:24 dug wells along the riverbank to get **d** water,
32:6 After this, they celebrated with feasting and **d**,
Nu 23:24 feasted on prey, / **d** the blood of the slaughtered!"
Dt 9:18 the LORD, neither eating bread nor **d** water.
Jdg 19:4 he stayed three days, eating, **d**, and sleeping there.
1Sa 1:13 but hearing no sound, he thought she had been **d**.
30:16 eating and **d** and dancing with joy because of the
1Ki 1:25 They are feasting and **d** with him and shouting,
10:21 All of King Solomon's **d** cups were solid gold,
13:23 after the man of God had finished eating and **d**,
20:12 and the other kings as they were **d** in their tents.
2Ki 7:8 eating, **d** wine, and carrying out silver and gold
18:31 from your own garden and **d** from your own well.
2Ch 9:20 All of King Solomon's **d** cups were solid gold,
Est 1:8 The only restriction on the **d** was that no one
5:6 And while they were **d** wine, the king said to
7:2 And while they were **d** wine that day, the king
Ps 73:10 are dismayed and confused, / **d** in all their words.
Pr 26:6 is as foolish as cutting off one's feet or **d** poison!
Isa 5:11 to begin long **d** bouts that last late into the night.
5:22 for those who are heroes when it comes to **d**,
21:5 Everyone is eating and **d**. Quick! Grab your shields
29:8 A thirsty person dreams of **d** but is still faint from
36:16 from your own garden and **d** from your own well.
51:21 sit in a drunken stupor, though not from **d** wine.
Da 5:2 While Belshazzar was **d**, he gave orders to bring in
5:23 and concubines have been **d** wine from them while
Hos 4:18 The men of Israel finish up their **d** bouts and off
Lk 10:7 in one place, eating and **d** what they provide you.
17:28 eating and **d**, buying and selling, farming
Jn 4:13 "People soon become thirsty again after **d** this
1Co 10:7 "The people celebrated with feasting and **d**,
11:22 Don't you have your own homes for eating and **d**?
11:28 before eating the bread and **d** from the cup.
11:29 are eating and **d** God's judgment upon yourself.

DRINKS (13) [DRINK]

Lev 17:10 among you, who eats or **d** blood in any form.
17:14 So whoever eats or **d** blood must be cut off.
Nu 6:3 they must give up wine and other alcoholic **d**.
6:3 they must not drink other fermented **d** or fresh
20:19 If any of our livestock **d** your water, we will pay
Ne 8:10 celebrate with a feast of choice foods and sweet **d**,
Est 1:7 **D** were served in gold goblets of many designs,
Ps 109:18 a part of him as his clothing, / or as the water he **d**,
Pr 23:30 spends long hours in the taverns, trying out new **d**.
Isa 66:11 Drink deeply of her glory even as an infant **d** at its
Hos 7:5 and **d** with those who are making fun of him.
Lk 5:39 But no one who **d** the old wine seems to want the
1Co 11:27 this bread or **d** this cup of the Lord unworthily,

DRIP (2) [DRIPPED, DRIPPING, DRIPS]

Joel 3:18 In that day the mountains will **d** with sweet wine,
Am 9:13 on the hills of Israel will **d** with sweet wine!

DRIPPED (1) [DRIP]

SS 5:5 My hands **d** with perfume, my fingers with lovely

DRIPPING (3) [DRIP]

Ps 19:10 sweeter than honey, / even honey **d** from the comb.
Pr 19:13 a father; a nagging wife annoys like a constant **d**.
27:15 A nagging wife is as annoying as the constant **d** on

DRIPS (2) [DRIP]

Ps 140:3 a snake; / the poison of a viper **d** from their lips.
Ro 3:13 "The poison of a deadly snake **d** from their lips."

DRIVE (68) [DRIVEN, DRIVER, DRIVERS, DRIVES, DRIVING, DROVE]

Ex 14:25 to come off, making their chariots impossible to **d**.
23:28 I will send hornets ahead of you to **d** out the
23:30 I will **d** them out a little at a time until your
23:31 in the land, and you will **d** them out ahead of you.
33:2 And I will send an angel before you to **d** out the
34:11 Then I will surely **d** out all those who stand in your
34:24 I will **d** out the nations that stand in your way
Nu 22:6 be able to conquer them and **d** them from the land.
22:11 to conquer them and **d** them from the land.' "
33:52 you must **d** out all the people living there.
33:55 But if you fail to **d** out the people who live in the
Dt 6:19 You will **d** out all the enemies living in your land,
7:20 then the LORD your God will send hornets to **d**
7:22 The LORD your God will **d** those nations out
9:3 that you will quickly conquer them and **d** them out,
9:5 The LORD your God will **d** these nations out
11:23 Then the LORD will **d** out all the nations in your
12:2 "When you **d** out the nations that live there,
12:29 and you **d** them out and occupy their land,
18:12 LORD your God will **d** them out ahead of you.
Jos 3:10 He will surely **d** out the Canaanites, Hittites,
13:6 "I will **d** these people out of the land for the
13:13 But the Israelites failed to **d** out the people of
14:12 I will **d** them out of the land, just as the LORD
15:63 But the tribe of Judah could not **d** out the Jebusites,
16:10 They did not **d** the Canaanites out of Gezer,
17:12 They could not **d** out the Canaanites who
17:13 as slaves. But they did not **d** them out of the land.
17:18 And I am sure you can **d** out the Canaanites from
23:5 for the LORD your God will **d** out all the people
23:13 God will no longer **d** them out from your land.
24:12 And I sent hornets ahead of you to **d** out the two
Jdg 1:19 But they failed to **d** out the people living in the
1:21 however, failed to **d** out the Jebusites,
1:27 The tribe of Manasseh failed to **d** out the people
1:28 but they never did **d** them out of the land.
1:29 The tribe of Ephraim also failed to **d** out the
1:30 The tribe of Zebulun also failed to **d** out the
1:31 The tribe of Asher also failed to **d** out the residents
1:32 In fact, because they did not **d** them out,
1:33 The tribe of Naphtali also failed to **d** out the
2:3 I will no longer **d** out the people living in your
2:21 I will no longer **d** out the nations that Joshua left
2:23 That is why the LORD did not quickly **d** the
2Ch 20:7 did you not **d** out those who lived in this land when
Ps 5:10 **D** them away because of their many sins,
68:2 **D** them off like smoke blown by the wind.
Pr 22:15 with foolishness, but discipline will **d** it away.
28:17 A murderer's tormented conscience will **d** him into
Isa 22:6 Elamites are the archers; Arameans **d** the chariots.
22:19 "Yes, I will **d** you out of office,"
22:23 For I will **d** him firmly in place like a tent stake.
Jer 27:10 and I will **d** you from your land and send you far
27:15 you lies in my name, so I will **d** you from this land.
Eze 8:6 of Israel are doing to **d** me from my Temple?
11:9 I will **d** you out of Jerusalem and hand you over to
34:25 and **d** away the dangerous animals from the land.
38:13 Who are you to **d** away their cattle and seize their
39:2 turn you and **d** you toward the mountains of Israel,
Hos 9:15 I will **d** them from my land because of their evil
10:11 I will **d** her in front of the plow. Israel and Judah
Joel 2:20 I will **d** them back into the parched wastelands,
Mt 21:12 and began to **d** out the merchants and their
21:23 "By whose authority did you **d** out the merchants
Mk 11:15 and began to **d** out the merchants and their
11:28 "By whose authority did you **d** out the merchants
Lk 19:45 and began to **d** out the merchants from their stalls.
20:2 "By whose authority did you **d** out the merchants

DRIVEN (43) [DRIVE]

Ge 33:13 too. If they are **d** too hard, they may die.
Lev 26:36 of a leaf **d** by the wind will send you fleeing.
Nu 32:21 the Jordan until the LORD has **d** out his enemies,
Dt 2:12 but they were **d** out and displaced by the
2:12 In a similar way the peoples in Canaan were **d**
28:31 Your donkey will be **d** away, never to be returned.
Jos 13:12 for Moses had attacked them and **d** them out.
23:9 "For the LORD has **d** out great and powerful
Jdg 18:1 for they had not yet **d** out the people who lived in
1Sa 26:19 For you have **d** me from my home, so I can no
1Ki 14:24 had **d** from the land ahead of the Israelites.
21:26 the people whom the LORD had **d** from the land
2Ki 16:3 had **d** from the land ahead of the Israelites.
17:8 the LORD had **d** from the land before them,
17:11 just like the nations the LORD had **d** from the
21:2 had **d** from the land ahead of the Israelites.
1Ch 8:6 at Geba, were **d** out and moved to Manahath.
2Ch 28:3 had **d** from the land ahead of the Israelites.
33:2 had **d** from the land ahead of the Israelites.
Job 18:18 thrust from light into darkness, **d** from the world.
21:18 Are they **d** before the wind like straw? Are they
30:5 They are **d** from civilization, and people shout
Isa 29:5 your ruthless enemies will be **d** away like chaff
59:19 For he will come like a flood tide **d** by the breath
Jer 19:9 and friends. They will be **d** to utter despair.'
23:2 you have deserted them and **d** them to destruction.
23:3 remnant of my flock from wherever I have **d** them.
46:15 because the LORD has **d** them away.
Eze 12:11 for they will be **d** from their homes and sent away
Da 4:25 You will be **d** from human society, and you will
4:32 You will be **d** from human society. You will live in
4:33 and Nebuchadnezzar was **d** from human society.
5:21 He was **d** from human society. He was given the
9:7 wherever you have **d** us because of our disloyalty
Am 9:4 Even if they are **d** into exile, I will command the
Jnh 2:4 'O LORD, you have **d** me from your presence.
Ac 27:17 The sailors were afraid of being **d** across to the
27:17 the sea anchor and were thus **d** before the wind.
27:27 as we were being **d** across the Sea of Adria,
27:29 At this rate they were afraid we would soon be **d**
28:3 a poisonous snake, **d** out by the heat, fastened itself
1Th 2:15 Now they have persecuted us and **d** us out.
Jas 1:6 mind is as unsettled as a wave of the sea that is **d**

DRIVER (3) [DRIVE]

1Ki 22:34 out of here!" Ahab groaned to the **d** of his chariot.

2Ch 18:33 out of here!" Ahab groaned to the **d** of his chariot.
Job 39: 7 the noise of the city, and it has no **d** to shout at it.

DRIVERS (7) [DRIVE]
Ge 24:32 and provided water for the camel **d** to wash their
Ex 1:11 their slaves and put brutal slave **d** over them,
3: 7 their cries for deliverance from their harsh slave **d**.
5: 6 same day Pharaoh sent this order to the slave **d**
5:10 So the slave **d** and foremen informed the people:
5:13 The slave **d** were brutal. "Meet your daily quota of
5:16 It is the fault of your slave **d** for making such

DRIVES (3) [DRIVE]
Job 12:17 of good judgment; he **d** judges to madness.
Pr 16:26 to have an appetite; an empty stomach **d** them on.
19: 4 makes many "friends"; poverty **d** them away.

DRIVING (6) [DRIVE]
Dt 33:17 distant nations, / **d** them to the ends of the earth.
2Ki 9:20 be Jehu son of Nimshi, for he is **d** so recklessly."
Job 37: 9 from its chamber, and the **d** winds bring the cold.
Jer 30:23 a **d** wind that swirls down on the heads of the
Eze 1: 4 **d** before it a huge cloud that flashed with lightning
Lk 18: 5 'but this woman is **d** me crazy. I'm going to see

DROMEDARIES, DROMEDARY [KJV] See CAMEL(S), HORSE

DROOLING (1)
1Sa 21:13 scratching on doors and **d** down his beard.

DROP (13) [DROPLETS, DROPPED, DROPS]
Lev 19: 9 and do not pick up what the harvesters **d**.
23:22 and do not pick up what the harvesters **d**.
Dt 28:40 for the trees will **d** the fruit before it is ripe.
33:28 and wine, / while the heavens **d** down dew.
Ru 2:16 from the bundles and **d** them on purpose for her.
Pr 17:14 so **d** the matter before a dispute breaks out.
Isa 5: 6 command the clouds / to **d** no more rain on it."
40:15 They are but a **d** in the bucket, dust on the scales.
Eze 4:16 The water will be portioned out **d** by **d**,
Am 2:16 the most courageous of your fighting men will **d**
Zec 10: 1 It is the LORD who makes storm clouds that **d**
Ac 28: 6 waited for him to swell up or suddenly **d** dead.

DROPLETS (1) [DROP]
Ex 30:34 resin **d**, mollusk scent, galbanum, and pure

DROPPED (6) [DROP]
2Sa 4: 4 But she fell and **d** him as she was running, and he
La 3:53 They threw me into a pit and **d** stones on me.
Mk 12:41 and watched as the crowds **d** in their money.
12:42 Then a poor widow came and **d** in two pennies.
15:19 spit on him, and **d** to their knees in mock worship.
Lk 21: 2 Then a poor widow came by and **d** in two pennies.

DROPS (3) [DROP]
Nu 35:23 or accidentally **d** a stone on someone, though they
Isa 51:17 have drunk the cup of terror, tipping out its last **d**.
Lk 22:44 his sweat fell to the ground like great **d** of blood.

DROSS (3)
Pr 25: 4 Remove the **d** from silver, and the sterling will be
Eze 22:18 They are the **d** that is left over—a useless mixture
Mal 3: 3 of silver, watching closely as the **d** is burned away.

DROUGHT (9)
Dt 28:22 with scorching heat and **d**, and with blight
1Ki 18: 1 in the third year of the **d**, the LORD said to
Job 14:11 from a lake and as a river disappears in **d**,
24:19 Death consumes sinners just as **d** and heat
Jer 2: 6 a land of deserts and pits, of **d** and death, where no
17: 8 by the heat or worried by long months of **d**.
Hag 1:11 I have called for a **d** on your fields and hills—
1:11 a **d** to wither the grain and grapes and olives
1:11 a **d** to starve both you and your cattle and to ruin

DROVE (24) [DRIVE, DROVES]
Ge 31:18 He **d** the flocks in front of him—all the livestock
Nu 21:32 the region and **d** out the Amorites who lived there.
32:39 and conquered it, and they **d** out the Amorites,
Dt 4:38 He **d** out nations far greater than you, so he could
Jos 15:14 Caleb **d** out the three Anakites—Sheshai, Ahiman,
24:18 It was the LORD who **d** out the Amorites
Jdg 1:20 And Caleb **d** out the people living there, who were
4:21 Then she **d** the tent peg through his temple
6: 9 I **d** out your enemies and gave you their land.
9:41 and Zebul **d** Gaal and his brothers out of Shechem.
11: 7 who hated me and **d** me from my father's house?
1Sa 30:20 up all the flocks and herds and **d** them on ahead.
2Sa 7:23 and **d** out the nations and gods that stood in their
2Ki 2:11 It **d** between them, separating them, and Elijah was
16: 6 He **d** out the people of Judah and sent Edomites to
1Ch 8:13 in Aijalon, and they **d** out the inhabitants of Gath.
12:15 and **d** out all the people living in the lowlands on
17:21 and **d** out the nations that stood in their way.
Ps 44: 2 You **d** out the pagan nations / and gave all the land
78:55 He **d** out the nations before them; / he gave them
80: 8 you **d** away the pagan nations and transplanted us
Jn 2:15 He **d** out the sheep and oxen, scattered the money
Ac 7:45 the Gentile nations that God **d** out of this land,
18:16 And he **d** them out of the courtroom.

DROVES (1) [DROVE]
Jdg 6: 5 arrived on **d** of camels too numerous to count.

DROWN (8) [DROWNED, DROWNING]
Ps 32: 6 that they may not **d** in the floodwaters of
SS 8: 7 waters cannot quench love; neither can rivers **d** it.
Isa 10:26 or when the LORD's staff was raised to **d** the
43: 2 you go through rivers of difficulty, you will not **d**!
Mt 8:25 shouting, "Lord, save us! We're going to **d**!"
Mk 4:38 don't you even care that we are going to **d**?"
Lk 8:24 shouting, "Master, Master, we're going to **d**!"
Rev 12:15 Then the dragon tried to **d** the woman with a flood

DROWNED (7) [DROWN]
Ex 15: 4 of Pharaoh's officers / have been **d** in the Red Sea.
Dt 11: 4 how he **d** them in the Red Sea as they were chasing
Isa 43:17 I drew them beneath the waves, and they **d**,
Mt 8:32 the steep hillside into the lake and **d** in the water.
Mk 5:13 down the steep hillside into the lake, where they **d**.
Lk 8:33 down the steep hillside into the lake, where they **d**.
Heb 11:29 But when the Egyptians followed, they were all **d**.

DROWNING (3) [DROWN]
Jos 24: 7 the sea crashing down on the Egyptians, **d** them.
Ac 7:57 and **d** out his voice with their shouts, they rushed
1Pe 3:20 Only eight people were saved from **d** in that

DROWSY (3)
2Sa 4: 6 had been sifting wheat, became **d** and fell asleep.
Lk 9:32 Peter and the others were very **d** and had fallen
Ac 20: 9 sitting on the windowsill, became very **d**.

DRUGGED (1)
Mk 15:23 They offered him wine **d** with myrrh, but he

DRUNK (45) [DRINK]
Ge 9:21 One day he became **d** on some wine he had made
19:32 let's get him **d** with wine, and then we will sleep
19:33 So that night they got him **d**, and the older
19:34 Let's get him **d** with wine again tonight, and you
19:35 So that night they got him **d** again, and the younger
Dt 32:42 I will make my arrows **d** with blood, / and my
Jdg 16:25 Half **d** by now, the people demanded, "Bring out
1Sa 1:14 "Must you come here **d**?" he demanded.
1:15 "Oh no, sir!" she replied, "I'm not **d**! But I am
25:36 He was very **d**, so she didn't tell him anything
2Sa 11:13 Then David invited him to dinner and got him **d**.
13:28 Absalom told his men, "Wait until Amnon gets **d**;
1Ki 16: 9 in Tirzah, Elah was getting **d** at the home of Arza,
20:16 allied kings were still in their tents getting **d**,
Est 1:10 when King Xerxes was half **d** with wine, he told
Ecc 10:17 only to gain strength for their work, not to get **d**.
Isa 16: 8 vineyards used to make the rulers of the nations **d**.
49:26 They will be **d** with rivers of their own blood.
51:17 You have **d** enough from the cup of the LORD's
51:17 You have **d** the cup of terror, tipping out its last
56:12 Let's all get **d**. Let this go on and on,
Jer 13:13 in this land so confused that they will seem **d**—
25:27 Get **d** and vomit, and you will fall to rise no more,
46:10 devour until it is satisfied, yes, **d** with your blood!
51:57 "I will make **d** her officials, wise men, rulers,
Eze 39:19 until you are glutted; drink blood until you are **d**.
Da 10: 3 I had eaten no rich food or meat, had **d** no wine,
Hos 7: 5 "On royal holidays, the princes get **d**. The king
Joel 3: 3 and little girls for enough wine to get **d**.
Hab 2:15 it will be for you who make your neighbors **d**!
Zec 9:15 They will shout in battle as though **d** with wine,
Mt 24:49 the other servants, partying, and getting **d**—
Lk 12:45 the other servants, partying, and getting **d**—
Ac 2:13 were mocking. "They're **d**, that's all!" they said.
2:15 Some of you are saying these people are **d**. It isn't
2:15 People don't get **d** by nine o'clock in the morning.
Ro 13:13 Don't participate in wild parties and getting **d**,
1Co 11:21 As a result, some go hungry while others get **d**.
15:32 If there is no resurrection, / "Let's feast and get **d**,
Eph 5:18 Don't be **d** with wine, because that will ruin your
1Th 5: 7 the time for sleep and the time when people get **d**.
Rev 17: 2 have been made **d** by the wine of her immorality."
17: 6 I could see that she was **d**—**d** with the blood of God's holy people who were
18: 3 For all the nations have **d** the wine of her

DRUNKARD (11) [DRINK]
Dt 21:20 and refuses to obey. He is a worthless **d**.'
Pr 26: 9 is as dangerous as a thornbush brandished by a **d**.
Isa 19:14 cause the land of Egypt to stagger like a sick **d**.
24:20 The earth staggers like a **d**. It trembles like a tent
Jer 23: 9 I stagger like a **d**, like someone overcome by wine,
48:26 "Let her stagger and fall like a **d**, for she has
Eze 23:33 You will reel like a **d** beneath the awful blows of
Na 3:11 And you, Nineveh, will also stagger like a **d**.
Mt 11:19 and drink, and you say, 'He's a glutton and a **d**,
Lk 7:34 and drink, and you say, 'He's a glutton and a **d**,
1Co 5:11 worships idols, or is abusive, or a **d**, or a swindler.

DRUNKARDS (9) [DRINK]
Job 12:25 without a light. He makes them stagger like **d**.
Ps 69:12 topic of town gossip, / and all the **d** sing about me.
107:27 They reeled and staggered like **d** / and were at their
Pr 23:20 Do not carouse with **d** and gluttons,
Isa 28: 1 of Samaria—the pride and joy of the **d** of Israel!
28: 3 of Samaria—the pride and joy of the **d** of Israel—
Eze 23:42 They were lustful men and **d** from the wilderness,
Joel 1: 5 Wake up, you **d**, and weep! All the grapes are
1Co 6:10 thieves, greedy people, **d**, abusers, and swindlers—

DRUNKEN (5) [DRINK]
Ge 9:24 When Noah woke up from his **d** stupor, he learned
Ps 78:65 like a mighty man aroused from a **d** stupor.
Isa 5:14 lowly will be swallowed up, with all her **d** crowds.
51:21 to this, you afflicted ones, who sit in a **d** stupor,
Jer 51:38 "In their **d** feasts, the people of Babylon roar like

DRUNKENNESS (4) [DRINK]
La 4:21 You, too, will be stripped naked in your **d**.
Lk 21:34 Don't let me find you living in careless ease and **d**,
Gal 5:21 envy, **d**, wild parties, and other kinds of sin.
1Pe 4: 3 and lust, their feasting and **d** and wild parties,

DRUNKS (2) [DRINK]
Isa 28: 7 Now, however, Israel is being led by **d**! The priests
Na 1:10 tangled up like thorns, staggering like **d**,

DRUSILLA (1)
Ac 24:24 later Felix came with his wife, **D**, who was Jewish.

DRY (92) [DRIED, DRIED-UP, DRIES, DRYING]
Ge 1: 9 gathered into one place so **d** ground may appear."
1:10 God named the **d** ground "land" and the water
7:22 Everything died that breathed and lived on **d** land.
8: 7 that flew back and forth until the earth was **d**.
8: 8 Then he sent out a dove to see if it could find **d**
8:14 more months went by, and at last the earth was **d**!
Ex 4: 9 the Nile River and pour it out on the **d** ground.
14:16 the people of Israel will walk through on **d** ground.
14:21 blew all that night, turning the seabed into **d** land.
14:22 So the people of Israel walked through the sea on **d**
14:29 walked through the middle of the sea on **d** land,
15:19 But the people of Israel had walked through on **d**
Lev 7:10 whether flour mixed with olive oil or **d** flour,
19:36 Your containers for measuring **d** goods or liquids
Dt 8:15 and scorpions, where it was so hot and **d**.
Jos 2:10 For we have heard how the LORD made a **d** path
3:16 flowed on to the Dead Sea until the riverbed was **d**.
3:17 **d** ground in the middle of the riverbed as the
3:17 until everyone had crossed the Jordan on **d** ground.
4:22 the Israelites crossed the Jordan on **d** ground.'
4:23 and he kept it **d** until you were all across,
9: 5 And they took along **d**, moldy bread for
9:12 we left. But now, as you can see, it is **d** and moldy.
Jdg 6:37 is wet with dew in the morning but the ground is **d**,
6:39 This time let the fleece remain **d** while the ground
6:40 The fleece was **d** in the morning, but the ground
2Sa 17:19 the top of the well with grain on it to **d** in the sun;
2Ki 2: 8 and the two of them went across on **d** ground!
3:16 This **d** valley will be filled with pools of water!
Ne 9:11 your people so they could walk through on **d** land!
Job 13:25 by the wind? Would you chase a **d** stalk of grass?
18:16 Their roots will **d** up, and their branches will
38:38 turning the **d** dust to clumps of mud?
41:20 like steam from a boiling pot on a fire of **d** rushes.
Ps 65: 9 and fertile. / The rivers of God will not run **d**;
66: 6 He made a **d** path through the Red Sea, / and his
69: 3 from crying for help; / my throat is parched and **d**.
74:15 and you dried up rivers that never run **d**.
90: 6 but by evening it is **d** and withered.
95: 5 for he made it. / His hands formed the **d** land, too.
105:41 to form a river through the **d** and barren land.
106: 9 the Red Sea to divide, and a **d** path appeared.
106: 9 He led Israel across the sea bottom that was as **d** as
106:14 ran wild, / testing God's patience in that **d** land.
107:33 into deserts, / and springs of water into **d** land.
107:35 pools of water, / the **d** land into flowing springs.
Pr 17: 1 A **d** crust eaten in peace is better than a great feast
Isa 11:15 The LORD will make a **d** path through the Red
19: 5 the fields. The riverbed will be parched and **d**.
19: 6 The canals of the Nile will **d** up, and the streams of
19: 7 All the crops will **d** up, and everything will die.
41:18 Rivers fed by springs will flow across the **d**,
42:15 I will turn the rivers into **d** land / and will **d** up all the pools.
43:16 the waters, making a **d** path through the sea.
44:27 When I speak to the rivers and say, 'Be **d**!' they will be **d**.
50: 2 For I can speak to the sea and make it **d**!
53: 2 sprouting from a root in **d** and sterile ground.
58:11 watering your life when you are **d** and keeping you
Jer 14: 3 send servants to get water, but all the wells are **d**.
15:18 seasonal brook. It is like a spring that has gone **d**."
17:13 They will be buried in a **d** and dusty grave,
18:14 from the crags of Mount Hermon ever run **d**?
50:12 of nations—a wilderness, a **d** and desolate land.
50:38 even strike her water supply, causing it to **d** up.
51:36 avenge you. I will **d** up her river, her water supply,
51:43 she is a **d** wilderness where no one lives or even
La 4: 8 sticks to their bones; it is as **d** and hard as wood.
Eze 19:13 in the wilderness, / where the ground is hard and **d**.
20:47 every tree will be burned—green and **d** trees alike.
30:12 I will **d** up the Nile River and hand the land over to
37: 2 the old, **d** bones that covered the valley floor.
37: 4 to me, "Speak to these bones and say, '**D** bones,
37:11 They are saying, 'We have become old, **d** bones—
45:10 and scales, honest **d** volume measures,
Hos 2: 3 as in a desert or a **d** and barren wilderness.

5:12 I will sap Judah's strength as **d** rot weakens wood.
13: 5 of you in the wilderness, in that **d** and thirsty land.
Joel 3:18 Water will fill the **d** streambeds of Judah, and a
Am 1: 2 Suddenly, the lush pastures of the shepherds **d** up.
5:24 a river of righteous living that will never run **d**.
Ob 1:18 be a raging fire, and Edom, a field of **d** stubble.
Na 1: 4 At his command the oceans and rivers **d** up,
1:10 like drunks, will be burned like **d** straw in a field.
Hag 2: 6 I will shake the oceans and the **d** land, too.
Zec 10:11 And the waters of the Nile will become **d**.
Lk 23:31 the tree is green, what will happen when it is **d**?"
1Co 10: 1 safely through the waters of the sea on **d** ground.
15:37 but only a **d** little seed of wheat or whatever it is
Heb 11:29 the Red Sea as though they were on **d** ground.
Jude 1:12 They are like clouds blowing over **d** land without

DRYING (3) [DRY]

Ge 8:13 lifted back the cover to look. The water was **d** up.
Eze 47:10 The shores will be covered with nets **d** in the sun.
Hos 13:15 against the people of Ephraim, **d** up their land.

DUE (11) [DULY]

Ge 38:27 In **d** season the time of Tamar's delivery arrived,
Lev 26:43 At last the people will receive the **d** punishment for
Dt 32:35 In **d** time their feet will slip. / Their day of disaster
1Sa 1:20 and in **d** time she gave birth to a son. She named
Ne 13:10 the Levites had not been given what was **d** them,
Ecc 3:17 "In **d** season God will judge everyone, both good
Jer 13:25 that which is **d** you," says the LORD.
17:10 I give all people their **d** rewards, according to what
Mal 3: 8 cheated me of the tithes and offerings **d** to me.
Ro 13: 7 and give respect and honor to all to whom it is **d**.
1Co 4: 5 God will give to everyone whatever praise is **d**.

DUG (35) [DIG]

Ge 21:30 to you as a public confirmation that I **d** this well."
26:15 These were the wells that had been **d** by the
26:18 He reopened the wells his father had **d**,
26:19 His shepherds also **d** in the Gerar Valley and found
26:21 Isaac's men then **d** another well, but again there
26:22 Abandoning that one, he **d** another well,
26:25 up his camp at that place, and his servants **d** a well.
26:32 and told him about a well they had **d**.
Ex 7:24 Then the Egyptians **d** wells along the riverbank to
Nu 21:18 Sing of this well, / which princes **d**, / which great
Dt 11:10 and **d** out irrigation ditches with your foot as in a
1Ki 18:32 Then he **d** a trench around the altar large enough to
2Ki 19:24 I have **d** wells in many a foreign land
20:20 a pool and **d** a tunnel to bring water into the city,
2Ch 26:10 forts in the wilderness and **d** many water cisterns,
Ne 9:25 with cisterns already **d** and vineyards and olive
Job 18: 8 They fall into a pit that's been **d** in the path.
Ps 9:15 The nations have fallen into the pit they **d** for
35: 7 I did them no wrong, / they **d** a pit for me.
35: 8 Let them fall to destruction in the pit they **d** for
57: 6 from distress. / They have **d** a deep pit in my path,
94:13 from troubled times / until a pit is **d** for the wicked.
119:85 hate your law / have **d** deep pits for me to fall into.
Isa 37:25 I have **d** wells in many a foreign land
Jer 2:13 And they have **d** for themselves cracked cisterns
13: 7 and **d** it out of the hole where I had hidden it.
18:22 For they have **d** a pit for me, and they have hidden
Eze 8: 8 So I **d** into the wall and uncovered a door to a
12: 7 I **d** through the wall with my hands and went out
Hos 5: 2 You have **d** a deep pit to trap them at Acacia.
Am 2: 9 but I destroyed their fruit and **d** out their roots.
Mt 21:33 around it, **d** a pit for pressing out the grape juice,
25:18 But the servant who received the one bag of gold **d**
Mk 2: 4 so they **d** through the clay roof above his head.
12: 1 around it, **d** a pit for pressing out the grape juice,

DUKE(S) [KJV] See CLAN LEADERS

DULCIMER [KJV] See PIPES

DULL (4)

Ps 119:70 Their hearts are **d** and stupid, / but I delight in your
Ecc 10:10 Since a **d** ax requires great strength,
La 4: 1 lost its luster! Even the finest gold has become **d**.
Heb 6:12 Then you will not become spiritually **d**

DULY (1) [DUE]

Est 2:23 This was all **d** recorded in *The Book of the*

DUMAH (3)

Ge 25:14 Mishma, **D**, Massa,
Jos 15:52 Also included were the towns of Arab, **D**, Eshan,
1Ch 1:30 Mishma, **D**, Massa, Hadad, Tema,

DUMB [KJV] See MUTE, SILENT, SPEECHLESS

DUMP (3) [DUMPED]

Ps 113: 7 from the dirt / and the needy from the garbage **d**.
Jer 31:40 including the graveyard and ash **d** in the valley,
Eze 26:12 and **d** your stones and timbers and even your dust

DUMPED (6) [DUMP]

Lev 14:41 and the scrapings **d** in the unclean place outside the
2Ch 33:15 were in Jerusalem, and he **d** them outside the city.
Isa 14:19 you will be **d** into a mass grave with those killed in
Jer 22:19 dragged out of Jerusalem and **d** outside the gate!
41: 9 The cistern where Ishmael **d** the bodies of the men
Eze 16: 5 you were **d** in a field and left to die, unwanted.

DUNG (24)

Ex 29:14 take the carcass (including the skin and the **d**)
Lev 4:11 its hide, meat, head, legs, internal organs, and **d**—
8:17 The rest of the bull, including its hide, meat, and **d**,
16:27 the animals' hides, the internal organs, and the **d**.
Nu 19: 5 must be burned—its hide, meat, blood, and **d**.
2Ki 6:25 and a cup of dove's **d** cost about two ounces of
9:37 Her body will be scattered like **d** on the field of
18:27 so hungry and thirsty that they will eat their own **d**
Ne 2:13 and over to the **D** Gate to inspect the broken walls
3:13 the fifteen hundred feet of wall to the **D** Gate.
3:14 The **D** Gate was repaired by Malkijah son of
12:31 southward along the top of the wall to the **D** Gate.
Job 20: 7 he will perish forever, thrown away like his own **d**.
Isa 36:12 so hungry and thirsty that they will eat their own **d**
Jer 8: 2 or buried but will be scattered on the ground like **d**.
9:22 "Bodies will be scattered across the fields like **d**,
16: 4 and they will lie scattered on the ground like **d**.
25:33 They will be scattered like **d** on the ground.
Eze 4:12 bake it over a fire using dried human **d** as fuel
4:14 must I be defiled by using human **d**?
4:15 bake your bread with cow **d** instead of human **d**."
Mal 2: 3 and splatter your faces with the **d** of your festival sacrifices, and I will add you to the **d** heap.

DUNGEON (9) [DUNGEONS]

Ge 41:14 at once, and he was brought hastily from the **d**.
Ex 12:29 to the firstborn son of the captive in the **d**.
Jer 37:16 Jeremiah was put into a **d** cell, where he remained
37:20 Don't send me back to the **d** in the house of
37:21 commanded that Jeremiah not be returned to the **d**.
38:26 begged me not to send you back to Jonathan's **d**,
Zec 9:11 free your prisoners from death in a waterless **d**.
Ac 16:24 he took no chances but put them into the inner **d**
16:29 the jailer called for lights and ran to the **d** and fell

DUNGEONS (2) [DUNGEON]

Isa 42: 7 You will release those who sit in dark **d**.
Heb 11:36 cut open with whips. Others were chained in **d**.

DUNGHILL [KJV] See DUMP, FERTILIZER, PILE, ROT, RUBBLE

DURA (1)

Da 3: 1 and set it up on the plain of **D** in the province of

DURING (253)

Ge 1:16 The greater one, the sun, presides **d** the day;
4:26 It was **d** his lifetime that people first began to
6:19 into the boat with you to keep them alive **d** the
10:25 for **d** his lifetime the people of the world were
14:15 and attacked **d** the night from several directions.
30:14 One day **d** the wheat harvest, Reuben found some
31:10 **D** the mating season, I had a dream and saw that
32:22 But **d** the night Jacob got up and sent his two
41:34 and let them collect one-fifth of all the crops **d** the
41:48 **D** those years, Joseph took a portion of all the
41:50 **D** this time, before the arrival of the first of the
45: 6 **d** which there will be neither plowing nor harvest.
46: 2 **D** the night God spoke to him in a vision. "Jacob!
Ex 2: 1 **D** this time, a man and woman from the tribe of
2:11 **D** his visit, he saw an Egyptian beating one of the
10:23 **D** all that time the people scarcely moved, for they
12:15 **d** the seven days of the festival will be cut off from
12:19 **D** those seven days, there must be no trace of yeast
12:19 Anyone who eats anything made with yeast **d** this
12:20 **d** those days you must not eat anything made with
12:30 and all the people of Egypt woke up **d** the night,
12:31 Pharaoh sent for Moses and Aaron **d** the night.
13: 7 Eat only bread without yeast **d** those seven days.
13: 7 or anywhere within the borders of your land **d** this
13: 8 "**D** these festival days each year, you must explain
13:21 The LORD guided them by a pillar of cloud **d** the
22:27 Your neighbor will need it to stay warm **d** the
23:11 let the land rest and lie fallow **d** the seventh year.
34:21 even **d** the seasons of plowing and harvest.
40:38 of the LORD rested on the Tabernacle **d** the day,
Lev 12: 2 just as she is defiled **d** her menstrual period.
12: 4 **D** this time of purification, she must not touch
12: 5 just as she is defiled **d** her menstrual period.
13:22 If **d** that time the affected area spreads on the skin,
15:13 **D** that time, he must wash his clothes and bathe in
15:19 If you touch her **d** that time, you will be defiled
15:20 on which she lies or sits **d** that time will be defiled.
15:24 If a man has sexual intercourse with her **d** this
15:26 on which she lies or sits **d** that time will be defiled,
15:26 just as it would be **d** her normal menstrual period.
15:33 for dealing with a woman **d** her monthly menstrual
15:33 has had intercourse with a woman **d** her period."
18:19 with her **d** her period of menstrual impurity.
23: 6 and **d** that time all the bread you eat must be made
23:28 Do no work **d** that entire day because it is the Day
23:42 **D** the seven festival days, all of you who are
24:11 **D** the fight, this son of an Israelite woman
25: 4 but **d** the seventh year the land will enjoy a
25: 4 or prune your vineyards **d** that entire year.
25: 6 produce that grows naturally **d** the Sabbath year.
25:11 **D** that year, do not plant any seeds or store away
25:20 might ask, 'What will we eat **d** the seventh year,
25:29 **D** that time, the seller retains the right to buy it
26:34 **d** your years of exile in the land of your enemies.
Nu 1: 1 **d** the second year after Israel's departure from
6: 6 And they may not go near a dead body **d** the entire
9: 1 **d** the second year after Israel's departure from
10:11 **d** the second year after Israel's departure from
11: 9 came down on the camp with the dew **d** the night.
33:38 **d** the fortieth year after Israel's departure from
Dt 1:36 of the land he walked over **d** his scouting mission.'
2: 7 **D** these forty years, the LORD your God has been
28:55 because he has nothing else to eat **d** the siege that
28:57 She will have nothing else to eat **d** the siege
31:10 the Year of Release, **d** the Festival of Shelters,
Jos 5: 5 **d** the years in the wilderness, had been
10:16 **D** the battle, the five kings escaped and hid in a
10:33 **D** the attack on Lachish, King Horam of Gezer had
11:21 **D** this period, Joshua destroyed all the descendants
23: 3 LORD your God has done for you **d** my lifetime.
Jdg 7: 9 **D** the night, the LORD said, "Get up! Go down
9:27 **D** the annual harvest festival at Shechem, held in
14:12 If you solve my riddle **d** these seven days of the
15: 1 Later on, **d** the wheat harvest, Samson took a
16: 2 They kept quiet **d** the night, saying to themselves,
16:30 when he died than he had **d** his entire lifetime.
Ru 1: 2 in the land of Judah. **D** their stay in Moab,
1Sa 7: 2 **D** that time, all Israel mourned because it seemed
12:17 rain at this time of the year **d** the wheat harvest.
2Sa 17:22 with him went across the Jordan River **d** the night,
18: 9 **D** the battle, Absalom came unexpectedly upon
18:18 **D** his lifetime, Absalom had built a monument to
19:32 He was the one who provided food for the king **d**
21: 1 There was a famine **d** David's reign that lasted for
21:10 vultures from tearing at their bodies **d** the day
23:13 Once **d** harvesttime, when David was at the cave
1Ki 3:19 But her baby died **d** the night when she rolled over
4:27 and his court, each **d** his assigned month.
6: 1 in midspring, **d** the fourth year of Solomon's reign,
9:10 Now at the end of the twenty years **d** which
14:22 **D** Rehoboam's reign, the people of Judah did what
16:34 It was **d** his reign that Hiel, a man from Bethel,
17: 1 or rain **d** the next few years unless I give the
21:29 I will not do what I promised **d** his lifetime.
22: 2 Then **d** the third year, King Jehoshaphat of Judah
22: 3 **D** the visit, Ahab said to his officials, "Do you
22:43 **D** his reign, however, he failed to remove all the
2Ki 8: 6 any crops that had been harvested **d** her absence.
8:20 **D** Jehoram's reign, the Edomites revolted against
13:22 King Hazael of Aram had oppressed Israel **d** the
15:18 **D** his entire reign, he refused to turn from the sins
15:29 **D** his reign, King Tiglath-pileser of Assyria
18: 9 **D** the fourth year of Hezekiah's reign, which was
18:10 **d** the sixth year of King Hezekiah's reign
20:19 there will be peace and security **d** my lifetime."
23:23 **d** the eighteenth year of King Josiah's reign.
24: 1 **D** Jehoiakim's reign, King Nebuchadnezzar of
24:10 **D** Jehoiachin's reign, the officers of King
24:11 Nebuchadnezzar himself arrived at the city **d** the
25: 1 January 15, **d** the ninth year of Zedekiah's reign,
1Ch 1:19 for **d** his lifetime the people of the world were
4:41 But **d** the reign of King Hezekiah of Judah,
5:10 **D** the reign of Saul, the Reubenites defeated the
5:17 records **d** the days of King Jotham of Judah
5:20 They cried out to God **d** the battle, and he
12:15 They crossed the Jordan River **d** its seasonal
13: 3 our God, for we neglected it **d** the reign of Saul."
20: 5 **D** another battle with the Philistines, Elhanan son
22: 9 and I will give peace and quiet to Israel **d** his reign.
27: 2 first division, which was on duty **d** the first month.
27: 4 which was on duty **d** the second month.
27: 5 which was on duty **d** the third month.
27: 7 which was on duty **d** the fourth month.
27: 8 fifth division, which was on duty **d** the fifth month.
27: 9 which was on duty **d** the sixth month.
27:10 which was on duty **d** the seventh month.
27:11 which was on duty **d** the eighth month.
27:12 which was on duty **d** the ninth month.
27:13 which was on duty **d** the tenth month.
27:14 which was on duty **d** the eleventh month.
27:15 which was on duty **d** the twelfth month.
2Ch 1:15 **D** Solomon's reign, silver and gold were as
3: 2 in midspring, **d** the fourth year of Solomon's reign.
11:17 the LORD as they had done **d** the reigns of David
13:20 So Jeroboam of Israel never regained his power **d**
14: 6 **D** those peaceful years, he was able to build up the
15: 5 **D** those dark times, it was not safe to travel.
15: 9 Many had moved to Judah **d** Asa's reign when
15:10 in late spring, **d** the fifteenth year of Asa's reign.
20:33 **D** his reign, however, he failed to remove all the
21: 8 **D** Jehoram's reign, the Edomites revolted against
22: 7 It was **d** this visit that Ahaziah went out with
24:14 of the LORD **d** the lifetime of Jehoiada the priest.
26: 5 Uzziah sought God **d** the days of Zechariah,
32:26 did not come against them **d** Hezekiah's lifetime.
34: 3 **D** the eighth year of his reign, while he was still
Ezr 3: 8 **d** the second year after they arrived in Jerusalem.
4: 5 This went on **d** the entire reign of King Cyrus of
4: 7 And even later **d** the reign of King Artaxerxes of
5:13 Cyrus of Babylon, **d** the first year of his reign,
6:15 March 12, **d** the sixth year of King Darius's reign.
6:17 **D** the dedication ceremony for the Temple of God,
7: 1 **d** the reign of King Artaxerxes of Persia,
8: 1 me from Babylon **d** the reign of King Artaxerxes:
Ne 2: 1 **d** the twentieth year of King Artaxerxes' reign,
2:12 I slipped out **d** the night, taking only a few others
4:22 on guard duty at night as well as work **d** the day.
4:23 **D** this time, none of us—not I, nor my relatives,
5: 3 vineyards, and homes to get food **d** the famine."
6:17 **D** those fifty-two days, many letters went back
7: 3 "Do not leave the gates open **d** the hottest part of

8:14 live in shelters **d** the festival to be held that month.
8:15 shelters in which they would live **d** the festival,
9:12 You led our ancestors by a pillar of cloud **d** the day
12:9 and Unni, stood opposite them **d** the service.
12:22 **D** the reign of Darius II of Persia, a list was
12:24 who stood opposite them **d** the ceremonies of
12:27 **D** the dedication of the new wall of Jerusalem,
Est 3:7 of April, **d** the twelfth year of King Xerxes' reign,
Ps 72:7 May all the godly flourish **d** his reign. / May there
Ecc 2:3 most people find **d** their brief life in this world.
SS 3:8 ready to defend the king against an attack **d** the
Isa 1:1 and Jerusalem came to Isaiah son of Amoz **d** the
7:1 **D** the reign of Ahaz son of Jotham and grandson of
18:4 or as the dew forms on an autumn morning **d** the
39:8 there will be peace and security **d** my lifetime."
Jer 1:2 The LORD first gave messages to Jeremiah **d** the
3:6 **D** the reign of King Josiah, the LORD said to me,
25:1 **d** the fourth year of Jehoiakim's reign over Judah.
26:18 prophesied **d** the reign of King Hezekiah of Judah.
36:1 **D** the fourth year that Jehoiakim son of Josiah was
36:9 **d** the fifth year of the reign of Jehoiakim son of
39:1 It was in January **d** the ninth year of King
51:59 This was **d** the fourth year of Zedekiah's reign.
52:4 January 15, **d** the ninth year of Zedekiah's reign,
La 2:19 Rise **d** the night and cry out. Pour out your hearts
Eze 1:2 This happened **d** the fifth year of King
4:9 Use this food to make bread for yourself **d** the 390
8:1 **d** the sixth year of King Jehoiachin's captivity,
11:16 I will be a sanctuary to you **d** your time in exile.
12:4 Bring your baggage outside **d** the day so they can
18:6 or have intercourse with a woman **d** her menstrual
20:1 **d** the seventh year of King Jehoiachin's captivity,
24:1 **d** the ninth year of King Jehoiachin's captivity,
26:1 **d** the twelfth year of King Jehoiachin's captivity,
29:1 **d** the tenth year of King Jehoiachin's captivity,
29:17 **d** the twenty-seventh year of King Jehoiachin's
30:20 **d** the eleventh year of King Jehoiachin's captivity,
31:1 **d** the eleventh year of King Jehoiachin's captivity,
32:1 **d** the twelfth year of King Jehoiachin's captivity,
32:17 On March 17, **d** the twelfth year, another message
33:21 On January 8, **d** the twelfth year of our captivity,
40:1 April 28, **d** the twenty-fifth year of our captivity—
45:21 Only bread without yeast may be eaten **d** that time.
45:25 "**D** the seven days of the Festival of Shelters,
46:1 The east gateway of the inner wall will be closed **d**
46:9 to worship the LORD **d** the religious festivals,
Da 1:1 **D** the third year of King Jehoiakim's reign in
2:1 One night **d** the second year of his reign,
2:44 "**D** the reigns of those kings, the God of heaven
5:11 **D** Nebuchadnezzar's reign, this man was found to
6:28 So Daniel prospered **d** the reign of Darius
7:1 **d** the first year of King Belshazzar's reign in
8:1 **D** the third year of King Belshazzar's reign,
9:2 **D** the first year of his reign, I, Daniel, was studying
Hos 1:1 to Hosea son of Beeri **d** the years when Uzziah,
3:3 **D** this time, you will not have sexual intercourse
Am 1:14 There will be wild shouts **d** the battle, swirling like
5:25 and offerings **d** the forty years in the wilderness,
Ob 1:11 For you deserted your relatives in Israel **d** their
Mic 1:1 to Micah of Moresheth **d** the years when Jotham,
Zec 1:8 In a vision **d** the night, I saw a man sitting on a red
7:5 '**D** those seventy years of exile, when you fasted
Mt 2:1 of Bethlehem in Judea, **d** the reign of King Herod.
26:5 "But not **d** the Passover," they agreed, "or there
26:7 **D** supper, a woman came in with a beautiful jar of
27:15 the crowd each year **d** the Passover celebration—
28:13 'Jesus' disciples came **d** the night while we were
Mk 2:26 He went into the house of God (**d** the days when
6:47 **D** the night, the disciples were in their boat out in
14:2 "But not **d** the Passover," they agreed, "or there
14:3 **D** supper, a woman came in with a beautiful jar of
15:7 convicted along with others for murder **d** an
Lk 16:25 remember that **d** your lifetime you had everything
Jn 2:3 The wine supply ran out **d** the festivities, so Jesus'
17:12 **D** my time here, I have kept them safe. I guarded
21:20 the one who had leaned over to Jesus **d** supper
Ac 1:3 **D** the forty days after his crucifixion, he appeared
1:15 **D** this time, on a day when about 120 believers
7:24 **D** this visit, he saw an Egyptian mistreating a man
7:42 **d** those forty years in the wilderness, Israel?
9:25 So **d** the night, some of the other believers let him
11:19 the believers who had fled from Jerusalem **d** the
11:27 **D** this time, some prophets traveled from
11:28 (This was fulfilled **d** the reign of Claudius.)
12:3 he arrested Peter **d** the Passover celebration
21:10 **D** our stay of several days, a man named Agabus,
25:14 **D** their stay of several days, Festus discussed
1Co 14:34 Women should be silent **d** the church meetings.
1Pe 1:12 that these things would not happen **d** their lifetime, but many years later, **d** yours.
1:17 So you must live in reverent fear of him **d** your
Rev 11:3 and will prophesy **d** those 1,260 days."

DURST [KJV] See DARE

DUSK (5)

Jos 2:5 They left the city at **d**, as the city gates were about
Ps 109:23 I am fading like a shadow at **d**; / I am falling like a
Hab 1:8 are a fierce people, more fierce than wolves at **d**.
Zep 3:7 evil practices from dawn till **d** and **d** till dawn."

DUST (121) [DUSTY]

DUST OF... (8) Ge 2:7; 28:14; 2Sa 22:43; 2Ch 1:9; Mt 10:14; Lk 10:11; Ac 13:51; 1Co 15:47

Ge 2:7 formed a man's body from the **d** of the ground
3:14 You will grovel in the **d** as long as you live,
3:19 For you were made from **d**, and to the **d** you will return."
13:16 descendants that, like **d**, they cannot be counted!
17:3 At this, Abram fell face down in the **d**. Then God
18:27 to my Lord, even though I am but **d** and ashes.
28:14 Your descendants will be as numerous as the **d** of
Ex 8:16 "Tell Aaron to strike the **d** with his staff.
8:16 The **d** will turn into swarms of gnats throughout
8:17 All the **d** in the land of Egypt turned into gnats.
9:9 It will spread like fine **d** over the whole land of
Nu 5:17 and mix it with **d** from the Tabernacle floor.
23:10 can count Jacob's descendants, as numerous as **d**?
Dt 9:21 and I melted it in the fire and ground it into fine **d**.
9:21 I threw the **d** into the stream that cascades down
28:24 The LORD will turn your rain into sand and **d**,
32:24 by poisonous snakes that glide in the **d**.
Jos 7:6 their clothing in dismay, threw **d** on their heads,
1Sa 2:8 He lifts the poor from the **d**— / yes, from a pile of
4:12 his clothes and put **d** on his head to show his grief.
2Sa 16:13 throwing stones at David and tossing **d** into the air.
22:43 I ground them as fine as the **d** of the earth;
1Ki 16:2 "I lifted you out of the **d** to make you ruler of my
18:38 up the young bull, the wood, the stones, and the **d**.
20:10 if there remains enough **d** from Samaria to provide
2Ki 13:7 killed the others like they were **d** under his feet.
23:6 Then he ground the pole to **d** and threw the **d** in the public cemetery.
23:15 Josiah crushed the stones to **d** and burned the
2Ch 1:9 over a people as numerous as the **d** of the earth!
34:7 the Asherah poles, and he crushed the idols into **d**.
Ne 9:1 in sackcloth and sprinkled **d** on their heads.
Job 2:12 and threw **d** into the air over their heads to
4:19 Their foundation is **d**, and they are crushed as
7:21 For soon I will lie down in the **d** and die.
10:9 Remember that I am made of **d**—will you turn me back to **d** so soon?
16:15 in sackcloth. I have surrendered, and I sit in the **d**.
17:16 me to the grave. We will rest together in the **d**!"
20:11 just a young man, but his bones will lie in the **d**.
21:26 Both alike are buried in the same **d**, both eaten by
28:6 "People know how to find sapphires and gold **d**—
30:19 me into the mud. I have become as **d** and ashes.
34:15 would cease, and humanity would turn again to **d**.
38:38 turning the dry **d** to clumps of mud?
39:14 top of the earth, letting them be warmed in the **d**.
40:13 Bury them in the **d**. Imprison them in the world of
42:6 and I sit in **d** and ashes to show my repentance."
Ps 7:5 Let my honor be left in the **d**. / *Interlude*
18:42 I ground them as fine as **d** carried by the wind.
22:15 You have laid me in the **d** and left me for dead.
30:9 the grave? / Can my **d** praise you from the grave?
44:25 We collapse in the **d**, / lying face down in the dirt.
72:9 his enemies will fall before him in the **d**.
78:27 He rained down meat as thick as **d**— / birds as
79:8 meet our needs, / for we are brought low to the **d**.
83:13 O my God, blow them away like whirling **d**,
89:39 with him, / for you have thrown his crown in the **d**.
90:3 You turn people back to **d**, saying, / "Return to **d**!"
102:14 and show favor even to the **d** in her streets.
103:14 how weak we are; / he knows we are only **d**.
104:29 away their breath, they die / and turn again to **d**.
119:25 I lie in the **d**, completely discouraged; / revive me
147:6 but he brings the wicked down into the **d**.
Ecc 3:20 the **d** from which they came and to which they
12:7 For then the **d** will return to the earth, and the spirit
Isa 2:12 punish the proud, bringing them down to the **d**.
2:17 Their pride will lie in the **d**. The LORD alone will
3:15 How dare you grind my people into the **d** like
5:15 day the arrogant will be brought down to the **d**;
17:13 by the wind or like **d** whirling before a storm.
25:12 walls of Moab will be demolished and ground to **d**.
26:5 the proud / and brings the arrogant city to the **d**.
27:9 all the pagan altars will be crushed to **d**.
40:15 They are but a drop in the bucket, **d** on the scales.
47:1 "Come, Babylon, unconquered one, sit in the **d**.
49:23 the earth before you and lick the **d** from your feet.
51:23 I will give it to those who trampled you into the **d**
52:2 Rise from the **d**, O Jerusalem. Remove the slave
Jer 13:18 "Come down from your thrones and sit in the **d**,
18:17 before their enemies as the east wind scatters **d**.
25:34 Roll in the **d**, you leaders of the flock!
48:18 Come down from your glory and sit in the **d**,
La 2:1 The fairest of Israel's cities lies in the **d**,
2:2 He has brought to **d** the kingdom and all its rulers.
2:10 They throw **d** on their heads in sorrow and despair.
3:16 my teeth on gravel. He has rolled me in the **d**.
3:29 Let them lie face down in the **d**; then at last there is
Eze 1:28 When I saw it, I fell face down in the **d**, and I
3:23 by the Kebar River. And I fell face down in the **d**.
9:8 I fell face down in the **d** and cried out,
11:13 Then I fell face down in the **d** and cried out,
26:10 hooves of his cavalry will choke the city with **d**,
26:12 and timbers and even your **d** into the sea.
27:30 They weep bitterly as they throw **d** on their heads
43:3 And I fell down before him with my face in the **d**.
44:4 and I fell to the ground with my face in the **d**.
Da 2:45 crushing to **d** the statue of iron, bronze, clay,
Am 2:7 They trample helpless people in the **d** and deny
Mic 1:10 roll in the **d** to show your anguish and despair.
Na 1:3 The billowing clouds are the **d** beneath his feet.
1:6 and the mountains crumble to **d** in his presence.
3:18 O Assyrian king, your princes lie dead in the **d**.
Zep 1:17 Your blood will be poured out into the **d**, and your
Zec 9:3 and gold that it is as common as **d** in the streets!
Mal 4:3 you will tread upon the wicked as if they were **d**
Mt 10:14 shake off the **d** of that place from your feet as you
Mk 6:11 to you, shake off its **d** from your feet as you leave.
Lk 5:12 he fell to the ground, face down in the **d**,
7:44 you didn't offer me water to wash the **d** from my
9:5 enter it, shake off its **d** from your feet as you leave.
10:11 'We wipe the **d** of your town from our feet as a
Jn 8:6 stooped down and wrote in the **d** with his finger.
8:8 Then he stooped down again and wrote in the **d**.
Ac 13:51 But they shook off the **d** of their feet against them
18:6 Paul shook the **d** from his robe and said,
22:23 their coats, and tossed handfuls of **d** into the air.
1Co 15:47 was made from the **d** of the earth, while Christ,
Rev 18:19 And they will throw **d** on their heads to show their

DUSTY (1) [DUST]

Jer 17:13 They will be buried in a dry and **d** grave, for they

DUTIES (40) [DUTY]

Ex 20:9 Six days a week are set apart for your daily **d**
28:43 the altar in the Holy Place to perform their **d**.
Nu 3:7 performing their sacred **d** in and around the
3:10 and his sons to carry out the **d** of the priesthood.
4:4 "The **d** of the Kohathites at the Tabernacle will
4:24 "The **d** of the Gershonites will be in the areas of
4:27 sons will direct the Gershonites regarding their **d**,
4:28 So these are the **d** assigned to the Gershonites at
4:31 "Their **d** at the Tabernacle will consist of carrying
4:33 So these are the **d** of the Merarites at the
8:22 went into the Tabernacle to perform their **d**,
8:26 This is how you will assign **d** to the Levites."
18:2 and your sons as you perform the sacred **d** in front
18:3 But as the Levites go about their **d** under your
18:5 "You yourselves must perform the sacred **d** within
Dt 5:13 Six days a week are set apart for your daily **d**
10:8 blessings in his name. These are still their **d**.
25:5 marry her and fulfill the **d** of a brother-in-law.
1Sa 2:13 or for their **d** as priests. Whenever anyone offered
10:25 the people what the rights and **d** of a king were.
1Ch 6:49 and they performed all the other **d** related to the
9:25 their relatives in the villages came to share their **d**
23:32 and faithfully carried out their **d** of service at the
24:3 into groups according to their various **d**.
24:19 Each group carried out its **d** in the house of the
24:31 they were assigned to their **d** by means of sacred
26:16 up to the Temple. Guard **d** were divided evenly.
2Ch 8:14 In assigning the priests to their **d**,
8:14 in praise and to assist the priests in their daily **d**.
19:11 Take courage as you fulfill your **d**, and may the
29:11 My dear Levites, do not neglect your **d** any longer!
31:16 to the LORD's Temple to perform their official **d**,
35:2 Josiah also assigned the priests to their **d**
Ne 13:11 back again and restored them to their proper **d**.
Pr 31:5 they may forget their **d** and be unable to give
Eze 44:26 But such a priest can only return to his Temple **d**
Da 1:10 king will have me beheaded for neglecting my **d**."
8:27 I got up and performed my **d** for the king,
Ro 13:7 Pay your taxes and import **d**, and give respect
Heb 9:6 room regularly as they performed their religious **d**.

DUTIFUL (1) [DUTY]

Mal 3:17 them as a father spares an obedient and **d** child.

DUTY (50) [DUTIES, DUTIFUL]

Ex 39:41 the priest and for his sons to wear while on **d**.
Lev 4:5 The priest on **d** will then take some of the animal's
6:10 the priest on **d** must clean out the ashes of the
6:15 The priest on **d** will take a handful of the choice
Nu 4:19 and assign a specific **d** or load to each person.
8:26 Levites by performing guard **d** at the Tabernacle,
32:22 You will have discharged your **d** to the LORD
Dt 17:9 and the judge on **d** will hear the case and decide
19:17 and judges who are on **d** before the LORD.
2Ki 11:5 A third of you who are on **d** on the Sabbath are to
11:7 The other two units who are off **d** on the Sabbath
11:9 charge of the men reporting for **d** that Sabbath,
11:9 as well as those who were going off **d**.
1Ch 9:27 the house of God, since it was their **d** to guard it.
9:33 there since they were on **d** at all hours.
26:13 They were assigned by families for guard **d** at the
27:1 divisions that were on **d** each month of the year.
27:2 which was on **d** during the first month.
27:4 which was on **d** during the second month.
27:5 which was on **d** during the third month.
27:7 which was on **d** during the fourth month.
27:8 which was on **d** during the fifth month.
27:9 which was on **d** during the sixth month.
27:10 which was on **d** during the seventh month.
27:11 which was on **d** during the eighth month.
27:12 which was on **d** during the ninth month.
27:13 which was on **d** during the tenth month.
27:14 which was on **d** during the eleventh month.
27:15 which was on **d** during the twelfth month.
2Ch 5:11 whether or not they were on **d** that day.
23:4 the priests and Levites come on **d** on the Sabbath,
23:6 and Levites on **d** may enter the Temple of the
23:8 charge of the men reporting for **d** that Sabbath,
23:8 as well as those who were going off **d**.
35:4 Report for **d** according to the family divisions of
35:15 the gates and did not need to leave their posts of **d**,
Ezr 10:4 for it is your **d** to tell us how to proceed in setting
Ne 4:22 and their servants could go on guard **d** at night as
7:3 And while the gatekeepers are still on **d**, have them
Est 2:21 One day as Mordecai was on **d** at the palace,
3:14 so that they would be ready to do their **d** on the
Ecc 8:3 Don't try to avoid doing your **d**, and don't take a
12:13 his commands, for this is the **d** of every person.

Eze 44:17 They must wear no wool while on d in the inner
Mt 12: 5 on d in the Temple may work on the Sabbath?
Lk 1: 8 in the Temple, for his order was on d that week.
9:60 Your d is to go and preach the coming of the
12:47 for though he knew his d, he refused to do it.
17:10 We are servants who have simply done our d.' "
1Ti 4: 6 you will be doing your d as a worthy servant of

DWARF (1)

Lev 21:20 or has a humped back or is a d, or has a defective

DWELL (4) [DWELLERS, DWELLING, DWELLS]

Dt 12:26 fulfill a vow to the place the LORD chooses to d.
Ps 101: 6 on the godly, / so they may d with me in safety.
139: 9 of the morning, / if I d by the farthest oceans,
Isa 33:16 These are the ones who will d on high. The rocks

DWELLERS (1) [DWELL]

Jer 31:24 And city d and farmers and shepherds alike will

DWELLING (15) [DWELL]

Dt 26:15 Look down from your holy d place in heaven
1Ch 16:27 surround him; / strength and beauty are in his d.
2Ch 30:27 and God heard them from his holy d in heaven.
Ps 68: 5 of widows— / this is God, whose d is holy.
78:60 Then he abandoned his d at Shiloh,
84: 1 How lovely is your d place, / O LORD Almighty.
91:10 conquer you; / no plague will come near your d.
132: 7 Let us go to the d place of the LORD; / let us bow
150: 1 Praise the LORD! / Praise God in his heavenly d;
Isa 18: 4 "I will watch quietly from my d place—as quietly
66: 1 as good as that? Could you build a d place for me?
Jer 25:30 against his own land from his holy d in heaven.
Zec 2:13 for he is springing into action from his holy d."
Ac 7:49 asks the Lord. / 'Could you build a d place for me?
Eph 2:22 as part of this d where God lives by his Spirit.

DWELLS (2) [DWELL]

Ex 15:13 your strength / to the place where your holiness d.
Isa 18: 7 in Jerusalem, the place where his name d.

DWINDLE (2) [DWINDLING]

Lev 26:22 so your numbers will d and your roads will be
Jer 29: 6 many grandchildren. Multiply! Do not d away!

DWINDLING (1) [DWINDLE]

Pr 14:28 is a king's glory; a d nation is his doom.

DYE (1) [DYEING, DYES]

Rev 18:12 silver, jewels, pearls, fine linen, purple d, silk,

DYEING (2) [DYE]

2Ch 2: 7 someone who is expert at d purple, scarlet,
2:14 He is an expert in d purple, blue, and scarlet cloth

DYES (2) [DYE]

Eze 27: 7 and purple awnings made bright with d from the
27:16 purple d, embroidery, fine linen, and jewelry of

DYING (31) [DIE]

Ge 3:19 you will sweat to produce food, until your d day.
25:32 "Look, I'm d of starvation!" said Esau.
Ex 14:12 Our Egyptian slavery was far better than d out here
2Ch 24:15 Jehoiada lived to a very old age, finally d at 130.
Job 24:12 The groans of the d rise from the city,
Ps 31:10 I am d from grief; / my years are shortened by
91: 7 your side, / though ten thousand are d around you,
146: 2 I will sing praises to my God even with my d
Pr 31: 6 Liquor is for the d, and wine for those in deep
Isa 27:13 Many who were d in exile in Assyria and Egypt
50: 2 I can turn rivers into deserts covered with d fish.
53: 8 But who among the people realized that he was d
Jer 27:13 "Why do you insist on d—you and your people?
La 2:11 and tiny babies are fainting and d in the streets.
Hos 4: 3 and all living things are becoming sick and d.
Lk 8:42 His only child was d, a little girl twelve years old.
9:31 was about to fulfill God's plan by d in Jerusalem.
15:17 food enough to spare, and here I am, d of hunger!
23:40 "Don't you fear God even when you are d?
Jn 11:37 Why couldn't he keep Lazarus from d?"
2Co 4:11 so that the life of Jesus will be obvious in our d
4:16 Though our bodies are d, our spirits are being
5: 4 Our d bodies make us groan and sigh, but it's not
5: 4 so that these d bodies will be swallowed up by
Gal 3: 1 a signboard with a picture of Christ d on the cross.
Php 1:21 For to me, living is for Christ, and d is even better.
2: 8 even further by d a criminal's death on a cross.
Heb 2:14 and only by d could he break the power of the
2:15 have lived all their lives as slaves to the fear of d.
11: 5 that Enoch was taken up to heaven without d—
11:21 It was by faith that Jacob, when he was old and d,

DYNASTY (37)

1Sa 13:14 But now your d must end, for the LORD has
25:28 LORD will surely reward you with a lasting d,
2Sa 3: 1 while Saul's d became weaker and weaker.
3: 6 leader among those who were loyal to Saul's d.
7:11 that he will build a house for you—a d of kings!
7:16 Your d and your kingdom will continue for all
7:19 you speak of giving me a lasting d!
7:26 And may the d of your servant David be
7:27 that you will build a house for me—an eternal d!
7:29 so that our d may continue forever before you.
1Ki 2:24 David; he has established my d as he promised.
9: 5 then I will establish the throne of your d over
11:38 I will establish an enduring d for you as I did for
12:16 they shouted, "Down with David and his d!
12:26 the kingdom will return to the d of David.
13: 2 A child named Josiah will be born into the d of
14:10 I will bring disaster on your d and kill all your
14:10 I will burn up your royal d as one burns up trash
15: 4 the LORD his God allowed his d to continue,
16:12 So Zimri destroyed the d of Baasha as the LORD
2Ki 10: 3 be your king, and prepare to fight for Ahab's d."
1Ch 10: 6 sons died there together, bringing his d to an end.
17:10 LORD will build a house for you—a d of kings!
17:14 I will establish him over my d and my kingdom for
17:17 you speak of giving me a lasting d!
17:24 And may the d of your servant David be
17:25 that you will build a house for me—an eternal d!
17:27 so that our d will continue forever before you.
2Ch 10:16 they shouted, "Down with David and his d!
21: 7 the LORD was not willing to destroy David's d,
22: 7 whom the LORD had appointed to end the d of
Ps 89:36 His d will go on forever; / his throne is as secure as
122: 5 judgment is given, / the thrones of the d of David.
Jer 21:12 This is what the LORD says to the d of David:
Hos 1: 4 for I am about to punish King Jehu's d to avenge
Am 7: 9 and I will bring the d of King Jeroboam to a
Zec 13: 1 "On that day a fountain will be opened for the d of

DYSENTERY (1)

Ac 28: 8 Publius's father was ill with fever and d.

E

EACH (810)

EACH DAY (33) Ex 16:4; 29:36,38; Nu 10:34; 14:34; Dt 24:15; 1Sa 17:25; 1Ch 16:23,37; 26:17,18; 2Ch 30:21; Ezr 3:4; 6:9; Ne 5:18; Ps 42:8; 68:19; 88:9; 96:2; 110:3; Isa 27:3; 33:2; La 3:23; Eze 4:10,11,12; 43:26,27; 45:23; Lk 16:19; Ac 2:46,47; 3:2

EACH OF THEM (22) Ge 45:22; Nu 6:19; Jdg 9:49; 2Sa 20:3; 1Ki 4:7; 2Ki 15:20; 1Ch 7:2; 25:7; 2Ch 11:11,23; 21:3; Job 1:5; 42:11; Ps 84:7; SS 8:11; Isa 4:1; Eze 8:11; Da 1:19; Mt 22:26; Ac 2:3; 21:26; Rev 6:11

EACH OF US (10) Jdg 16:5; Ro 1:12; 12:5,5,6; 14:10,12; 1Co 3:5; 12:1,7

EACH OF YOU (24) Lev 19:3; 25:10,13; Nu 15:12; Dt 23:13; Jos 4:5; Jdg 8:24; 21:21; 2Ki 18:31; Isa 36:16; Jer 18:11; Eze 18:30; 20:7; 33:20; Zec 3:10; Mt 26:27; Ac 2:38; 3:26; Ro 12:3; 1Co 16:2; 1Th 2:11; 4:4; 1Pe 4:10; Rev 2:23

EACH OTHER (165) Ge 11:7; 25:22; 42:28; 48:20; Ex 18:13; 25:20; 26:35; 36:18; 37:9; Lev 25:14,17; 26:37; Jdg 6:29; 7:22; 10:18; Ru 3:14; 1Sa 14:20; 17:3,21; 20:23,41,42; 2Sa 2:13,15,17,26; 1Ki 7:4,5; 20:29; 2Ki 3:23; 7:3,9; 10:15; 1Ch 8:32; 9:38; 2Ch 12:15; 20:23; Ne 4:19; Est 9:19,22; Ps 12:2; 64:5; Pr 18:24; Ecc 4:11; 8:9; Isa 3:5; 11:13; 19:2; 65:5; Jer 9:5; 23:30,35; 46:12,16; 51:46; Eze 3:13; 38:21; 42:3; Da 2:43; 8:13; 11:27,27; Joel 2:8; Zep 3:13; Hag 2:22; Zec 7:10; 8:10,16,17; 11:9; 14:13; Mal 2:10,14; 3:16; Mt 24:7,10; Mk 9:10,50; 13:8; 14:56; Lk 2:15; 5:21; 12:1; 20:14; 21:10; 22:23; 24:32; Jn 4:33; 5:44; 6:52; 9:8; 11:47,56; 12:19; 13:22,34,34; 15:12,17; 16:17; Ac 2:12; 4:16; 7:26; 28:4; Ro 1:26,27; 12:5,10,10,16; 14:13,19; 15:5,7,32; 16:16; 1Co 3:3; 7:5; 11:33; 12:25; 15:41; 16:20; 2Co 10:12; 13:11,12; Gal 5:17; Eph 2:16; 4:2,25,32; Php 1:9; 2:2; Col 3:9,16; 1Th 3:12; 4:18; 5:11,11,13,15,26; 2Th 1:3; Heb 3:13; 10:25; 12:15; 13:1; Jas 4:11,11,11; 5:9,16,16; 1Pe 1:22,22; 3:8; 4:8; 5:5,14; 1Jn 1:7; 3:18; 4:11,12,19; Rev 2:4; 11:10

Ge 1:25 e able to reproduce more of its own kind.
2:19 call them, and Adam chose a name for e one.
6:20 Pairs of e kind of bird and e kind of animal,
7: 2 Take along seven pairs of e animal that I have
7: 2 for sacrifice, and take one pair of e of the others.
7: 3 and a female in e pair to ensure that every kind of
10: 5 in various lands, e tribe with its own language.
11: 7 Then they won't be able to understand e other."
15:10 He cut e one down the middle and laid the halves
17:10 E male among you must be circumcised;
25:22 But the two children struggled with e other in her
26:31 they e took a solemn oath of nonaggression.
31:49 keep this treaty when we are out of e other's sight.
32:16 e group of animals by itself, separated by a
32:19 Jacob gave the same instructions to e of the
36:43 e clan giving its name to the area it occupied.
40: 5 night the cup-bearer and the baker e had a dream, and e dream had its own meaning.
41:11 One night the chief baker and I e had a dream, and e dream had a meaning.
41:12 the guard. He told us what e of our dreams meant,
42:25 but he also gave secret instructions to return e
42:28 They were filled with terror and said to e other,
42:35 there at the top of e one was the bag of money paid
43:33 Joseph told e of his brothers where to sit, and to
44: 1 "Fill e of their sacks with as much grain as they
44: 1 and put e man's money back into his sack.
45:15 Then Joseph kissed e of his brothers and wept over
45:22 And he gave e of them new clothes—but to
48:20 of Israel will use your names to bless e other.
49:28 E received a blessing that was appropriate to him.
Ex 1: 1 went with their father to Egypt, e with his family:
1: 6 In time, Joseph and e of his brothers died,
6:17 and Shimei, e of whom is the ancestor of a clan.
12: 3 day of this month e family must choose a lamb
12: 4 share in this way depends on the size of e family
12: 6 Then e family in the community must slaughter its
12:14 E year you will celebrate it as a special festival to
12:21 "Tell e of your families to slaughter the lamb they
12:22 Drain e lamb's blood into a basin. Then take a
13: 8 "During these festival days e year, you must
13:10 "So celebrate this festival at the appointed time e
14: 7 rest of the chariots of Egypt, e with a commander.
14:22 sea on dry ground, with walls of water on e side!
16: 4 The people can go out e day and pick up as much
16: 5 as much as usual on the sixth day of e week."
16:16 The LORD says that e household should gather as much as it needs. Pick up two quarts for e person."
16:18 By gathering two quarts for e person, everyone had
16:18 little had enough. E family had just what it needed.
16:21 by morning, e family according to its need.
16:22 four quarts for e person instead of two.
17:12 Then they stood on e side, holding up his hands
18: 7 They asked about e other's health and then went to
18:13 to hear the people's complaints against e other.
21:35 E will also own half of the dead bull.
22: 1 For oxen the fine is five oxen for e one stolen.
22: 1 For sheep the fine is four sheep for e one stolen.
23:14 "E year you must celebrate three festivals in my
23:17 At these three times e year, every man in Israel
23:19 "As you harvest e of your crops, bring me a choice
24: 4 the altar, one for e of the twelve tribes of Israel.
25:12 and attach them to its four feet, two rings on e side.
25:19 Attach the cherubim to e end of the atonement
25:20 The cherubim will face e other, looking down on
25:32 three branches going out from e side of the center
25:33 E of the six branches will hold a cup shaped like
25:35 One blossom will be set beneath e pair of branches
26: 2 E sheet must be forty-two feet long and six feet
26: 4 blue yarn along the edge of the last sheet in e set.
26: 8 e forty-five feet long and six feet wide. All eleven
26:10 Put fifty loops along the edge of the last sheet in e
26:13 will hang down an extra eighteen inches on e side.
26:16 E frame must be 15 feet high and 2-1/4 feet wide.
26:17 There will be two pegs on e frame so they can be
26:19 into forty silver bases—two bases under e frame.
26:21 with their forty silver bases, two bases for e frame.
26:23 along with an extra frame at e corner.
26:25 by sixteen silver bases—two bases under e frame.
26:35 and lampstand across the room from e other
27: 2 Make a horn at e of the four corners of the altar
27: 4 a bronze grating, with a metal ring at e corner.
28:10 Six names will be on e stone, naming all the tribes
28:21 E stone will represent one of the tribes of Israel,
29:36 E day you must sacrifice a young bull as an
29:38 on the altar. Offer two one-year-old lambs e day,
30: 8 And e evening when he tends to the lamps, he must
30:12 e man who is counted must pay a ransom for
30:23 6-1/4 pounds e of cinnamon and of sweet cane,
30:34 weighing out the same amounts of e.
34:18 at the appointed time e year in early spring,
34:23 Three times e year all the men of Israel must
34:24 the LORD your God those three times e year.
34:26 You must bring the best of the first of e year's crop
35: 2 E week, work for six days only. The seventh day is
36: 3 Additional gifts were brought e morning.
36: 9 E sheet was exactly the same size—forty-two feet
36:11 placed along the edge of the last sheet in e set.
36:13 made to connect the loops on the edge of e set.
36:15 E sheet was exactly the same size—forty-five feet
36:17 fifty loops along the edge of the last sheet in e set.
36:18 so the two sets of sheets were firmly attached to e
36:21 E frame was 15 feet high and 2-1/4 feet wide.
36:22 There were two pegs on e frame so they could be
36:24 along with forty silver bases, two for e frame.
36:26 along with forty silver bases, two for e frame.
36:28 plus an extra frame at e corner.
36:29 They made two of these, one for e rear corner.
36:30 along with sixteen silver bases, two for e frame.
36:33 along e side, running from one end to the other.
37: 3 were fastened to its four feet, two rings at e side.
37: 9 The cherubim faced e other as they looked down
37:18 three going out from e side of the center stem.
37:19 E of the six branches held a cup shaped like an
37:21 One blossom was set beneath e pair of branches,
38: 2 There were four horns, one at e of the four corners,
38: 5 Four rings were cast for e side of the grating to
38:10 were twenty posts, e with its own bronze base,
38:17 E post had a bronze base, and all the hooks
38:26 collected from e of those registered in the census.
38:27 7,500 pounds of silver, about 75 pounds for e base.
39:13 and a jasper. E of these gemstones was set in gold.
39:14 e with the name of one of the twelve tribes of
Lev 6:12 E morning the priest will add fresh wood to the
7:14 One of e kind of bread must be presented as a gift
9: 3 a whole burnt offering, e with no physical defects.
9:13 the head, and he burned e part on the altar.
14:10 e person cured of the skin disease must bring two
16:18 from the bull and the goat on e of the altar's horns.
16:34 to make atonement for the Israelites once e year."
19: 3 E of you must show respect for your mother

23: 3 You may work for six days **e** week, but on the
23: 4 occasions to be observed at the proper time **e** year.
23: 8 On **e** of the next seven days, the people must
23:36 On **e** of the seven festival days, you must present
23:37 and drink offerings—**e** on its proper day.
23:43 This will remind **e** new generation of Israelites that
24: 5 choice flour, using three quarts of flour for **e** loaf.
24: 6 arrange the loaves in two rows, with six in **e** row.
24: 7 Sprinkle some pure frankincense near **e** row.
25:10 when **e** of you returns to the lands that belonged to
25:13 In the Year of Jubilee **e** of you must return to the
25:14 you must never take advantage of **e** other.
25:17 fear of God by not taking advantage of **e** other.
25:34 The strip of pastureland around **e** of the Levitical
26:10 the previous year to make room for **e** new harvest.
26:37 you will stumble over **e** other in flight, as though
Nu 1: 4 assisted by one family leader from **e** tribe."
1:20[-21] **e** listed according to his own clan and family:
1:52 **E** tribe of Israel will have a designated camping
2: 2 "**E** tribe will be assigned its own area in the camp,
2:17 **e** in position under the appropriate family banner.
2:34 **E** clan and family set up camp and marched under
3:40 are one month old or older, and register **e** name.
3:47 collect five pieces of silver for **e** person, **e** piece
4:19 and assign a specific duty or load to **e** person.
4:32 You must assign the various loads to **e** man by
4:49 **E** man was assigned his task and told what to
5:10 **E** priest may keep the sacred donations that he
6:12 and **e** must bring a one-year-old male lamb for a
6:13 they must **e** go to the entrance of the Tabernacle
6:19 After **e** Nazirite's head has been shaved, the priest
will take for **e** of them the boiled
7: 3 a cart for every two leaders and an ox for **e** leader.
7:10 They **e** placed their gifts before the altar.
7:11 "Let **e** leader bring his gift on a different day for
7:85 about 3-1/4 pounds for **e** platter and 1-3/4 pounds
for **e** basin.
7:86 about four ounces for **e** of the gold containers that
10:10 and at the beginning of **e** month to rejoice over
10:34 As they moved on **e** day, the cloud of the LORD
13: 2 Send one leader from **e** of the twelve ancestral
14:34 a year for **e** day, suffering the consequences of
15: 5 For **e** lamb offered as a whole burnt offering,
15:11 for what is to accompany **e** sacrificial bull,
15:12 **E** of you must do this with **e** offering you
15:21 you are to present this offering to the LORD **e**
15:38 and attach the tassels at **e** corner with a blue cord.
16:17 Be sure that **e** of your 250 followers brings an
17: 2 one from **e** of Israel's ancestral tribes,
17: 2 and inscribe **e** tribal leader's name on his staff.
17: 3 for there must be one staff for the leader of **e**
17: 6 and **e** of the twelve tribal leaders, including Aaron,
17: 9 them to the people. **E** man claimed his own staff.
18:16 **e** piece weighing the same as the standard
23: 2 them sacrificed a young bull and a ram on **e** altar.
23: 4 have sacrificed a young bull and a ram on **e** altar."
23:14 and offered a young bull and a ram on **e** altar.
23:30 and offered a young bull and a ram on **e** altar.
26: 2 to find out how many of **e** family are of military
26:54 **e** group's inheritance reflecting the size of its
26:55 and define the inheritance of **e** ancestral tribe by
26:56 **E** inheritance must be assigned by lot among the
28: 5 With **e** lamb you must offer a grain offering of two
28: 7 consisting of one quart of fermented drink with **e**
28:10 This is the whole burnt offering to be presented **e**
28:11 "On the first day of **e** month, present an extra
28:12 five quarts with **e** bull, three quarts with the ram,
28:13 and two quarts with **e** lamb. This burnt offering
28:14 You must also give a drink offering with **e**
28:14 two quarts of wine with **e** bull, two and a half pints
28:14 a half pints for the ram, and one quart for **e** lamb.
28:14 on the first day of **e** month throughout the year.
28:15 on the first day of **e** month you must offer one
28:20 five quarts with **e** bull, three quarts with the ram,
28:21 and two quarts with **e** of the seven lambs.
28:24 On **e** of the seven days of the festival, this is how
28:28 five quarts with **e** bull, three quarts with the ram,
28:29 and two quarts with **e** of the seven lambs.
29: 1 on the appointed day in early autumn **e** year.
29: 4 and two quarts with **e** of the seven lambs.
29:10 and two quarts of choice flour with **e** of the seven
29:14 **E** of these offerings must be accompanied by a
29:14 for **e** of the thirteen bulls, three quarts for **e** of the
29:15 and two quarts for **e** of the fourteen lambs.
29:18 **E** of these offerings of bulls, rams, and lambs must
29:21 **E** of these offerings of bulls, rams, and lambs must
29:24 **E** of these offerings of bulls, rams, and lambs must
29:27 **E** of these offerings of bulls, rams, and lambs must
29:30 **E** of these offerings of bulls, rams, and lambs must
29:33 **E** of these offerings of bulls, rams, and lambs must
29:37 **E** of these offerings must be accompanied by the
31: 4 From **e** tribe of Israel, send one thousand men into
31: 5 So they chose one thousand men from **e** tribe of
31: 6 Moses sent them out, a thousand men from **e** tribe,
31:26 and the family leaders of **e** tribe are to make a list
33:54 A larger inheritance of land will be allotted to **e** of
33:54 and a smaller inheritance will be allotted to **e** of the
34:18 Also enlist one leader from **e** tribe to help them
35: 8 **E** tribe will give in proportion to its inheritance."
36: 9 **e** tribe of Israel must hold on to its allotted
Dt 1:13 Choose some men from **e** tribe who have wisdom,
1:23 so I chose twelve scouts, one from **e** of your tribes.
14:22 one-tenth of all the crops you harvest **e** year.
15:20 LORD your God **e** year at the place he chooses.
16:16 "**E** year every man in Israel must celebrate these
16:16 at the place he chooses on **e** of these occasions,
16:18 and officials for **e** of your tribes in all the towns the
19: 3 three districts, with one of these cities in **e** district.
23:13 **E** of you must have a spade as part of your
24:15 Pay them their wages **e** day before sunset
26: 2 put some of the first produce from **e** harvest into a
33:14 in the sun, / and the bounty produced **e** month;
Jos 3:12 Now choose twelve men, one from **e** tribe.
4: 2 "Now choose twelve men, one from **e** tribe.
4: 5 **E** of you must pick up one stone and carry it out on
4: 5 twelve stones in all, one for **e** of the twelve tribes.
4: 8 one for **e** tribe, just as the LORD had commanded
6: 4 walk ahead of the Ark, **e** carrying a ram's horn.
6: 6 to walk in front of it, **e** carrying a ram's horn."
7:14 **e** member of the guilty family must come one by
8:33 **E** group faced the other, and between them stood
10:26 Then Joshua killed **e** of the five kings and hung
18: 4 Select three men from **e** tribe, and I will send them
18: 6 to decide which section will be assigned to **e** tribe.
18: 9 into seven sections, listing the towns in **e** section.
18:10 to determine which tribe should have **e** section.
22:14 high officials of Israel, one from **e** of the ten tribes,
22:14 and **e** a leader within the family divisions of Israel.
23:10 **E** one of you will put to flight a thousand of the
24:28 sent the people away, **e** to his own inheritance.
Jdg 2: 6 **e** of the tribes left to take possession of the land
6:29 The people said to **e** other, "Who did this?"
7:16 and gave **e** man a ram's horn and a clay jar with a
7:21 **E** man stood at his position around the camp
7:22 the camp to fight against **e** other with their swords.
8:24 **E** of you can give me an earring out of the
8:25 and **e** one threw in a gold earring he had gathered.
9:49 So **e** of them cut down some branches,
10:18 The leaders of Gilead said to **e** other,
11:40 **e** year to lament the fate of Jephthah's daughter.
15: 4 in pairs, and he fastened a torch to **e** pair of tails.
16: 5 Then **e** of us will give you eleven hundred pieces
19:29 Then he sent one piece to **e** tribe of Israel.
20:10 One tenth of the men from **e** tribe will be chosen to
20:16 **e** of whom could sling a rock and hit a target
21:21 and **e** of you can take one of them home to be your
Ru 3:14 it was light enough for people to recognize **e** other.
1Sa 1: 3 **E** year Elkanah and his family would travel to
1: 4 of the sacrifice to Peninnah and **e** of her children.
2:19 **E** year his mother made a small coat for him
7:16 **E** year he traveled around, setting up his court first
7:16 He judged the people of Israel at **e** of these places.
10:21 Then he brought **e** family of the tribe of Benjamin
14:20 the battle and found the Philistines killing **e** other.
17: 3 and Israelites faced **e** other on opposite hills,
17:21 and Philistine forces stood facing **e** other,
17:25 "He comes out **e** day to challenge Israel.
20:23 the LORD make us keep our promises to **e** other,
20:41 Both of them were in tears as they embraced **e**
20:42 We have entrusted **e** other and **e** other's children
into the LORD's hands
2Sa 2:13 facing **e** other from opposite sides of the pool.
2:15 So twelve men were chosen from **e** side to fight
against **e** other.
2:16 **E** one grabbed his opponent by the hair and thrust
2:17 The two armies then began to fight **e** other, and by
2:26 thing we will gain is bitterness toward **e** other?
10: 4 and shaved off half of **e** man's beard,
20: 3 So **e** of them lived like a widow until she died.
21:20 a huge man with six fingers on **e** hand and six toes
on **e** foot—
1Ki 2: 3 Keep **e** of the laws, commands, regulations,
3:23 and **e** says that the dead child belongs to the other.
3:25 child in two and give half to **e** of these women!"
4: 7 **E** of them arranged provisions for one month of
4:25 **e** family had its own home and garden.
4:27 and his court, **e** during his assigned month.
5:14 so that **e** man would be one month in Lebanon
6:10 **E** story of the complex was 7-1/2 feet high.
6:23 two cherubim made of olive wood, **e** 15 feet tall.
6:24 wingspan of **e** of the cherubim was 15 feet, **e** wing
6:26 **e** was 15 feet tall.
6:34 and **e** door was hinged to fold back upon itself.
7: 3 that rested on three rows of pillars, fifteen in **e** row.
7: 4 On **e** of the side walls there were three rows of
windows facing **e** other.
7: 5 in frame; they were in sets of three, facing **e** other.
7:15 **e** 27 feet tall and 18 feet in circumference.
7:16 made capitals of molded bronze, **e** 7-1/2 feet tall.
7:17 **E** capital was decorated with seven sets of
7:20 **E** capital on the two pillars had two hundred
7:27 **e** 6 feet long, 6 feet wide, and 4-1/2 feet tall.
7:30 **E** of these carts had four bronze wheels and bronze
7:30 At **e** corner of the carts were supporting posts for
7:30 were decorated with carvings of wreaths on **e** side.
7:31 The top of **e** cart had a circular frame for the basin.
7:34 There were supports at **e** of the four corners of the
7:35 Around the top of **e** cart there was a rim 9 inches
7:37 made alike, for **e** was cast from the same mold.
7:38 Huram also made ten bronze basins, one for **e** cart.
7:38 **E** basin was 6 feet across and could hold 220
7:42 **e** of the chain networks that were hung around the
9:25 Three times **e** year Solomon offered burnt
10:14 **E** year Solomon received about twenty-five tons of
10:16 **e** containing over fifteen pounds of gold.
10:17 **e** containing nearly four pounds of gold.
10:19 with the figure of a lion standing on **e** side of the
10:20 one standing on **e** end of **e** of the six steps.
17: 6 him bread and meat **e** morning and evening,
18: 4 He had put fifty prophets in **e** cave and had
18:10 And **e** time when he was told, 'Elijah isn't here,'
18:31 one to represent **e** of the tribes of Israel,
20:10 provide more than a handful for **e** of my soldiers."
20:20 **E** Israelite soldier killed his Aramean opponent,
20:29 The two armies camped opposite **e** other for seven
2Ki 3:23 three armies have attacked and killed **e** other!
7: 3 we sit here waiting to die?" they asked **e** other.
7: 9 Finally, they said to **e** other, "This is not right.
10:15 After they had greeted **e** other, Jehu said to him,
13:20 of Moabite raiders used to invade the land **e** spring.
15:20 demanding that **e** of them pay twenty ounces of
18:31 Then I will allow **e** of you to continue eating from
25:17 **E** of the pillars was 27 feet tall. The bronze capital
on top of **e** pillar was 7-1/2 feet
1Ch 5:24 **E** of these men had a great reputation as a warrior
6:57 **e** with its surrounding pasturelands:
6:60 Alemeth, and Anathoth, **e** with its pasturelands.
6:66 these towns, **e** with its surrounding pasturelands:
6:70 Aner and Bileam, **e** with its pasturelands.
6:75 Hukok, and Rehob, **e** with its pasturelands.
6:76 Hammon, and Kiriathaim, **e** with its pasturelands.
6:77 Rimmono, and Tabor, **e** with its pasturelands.
6:79 Kedemoth, and Mephaath, **e** with its pasturelands.
6:81 Heshbon, and Jazer, **e** with its pasturelands.
7: 2 **E** of them was the leader of an ancestral clan.
7:40 **E** of these descendants of Asher was the head of an
8:32 All these families lived near **e** other in Jerusalem.
9:32 the bread to be set on the table **e** Sabbath day.
9:38 All these families lived near **e** other in Jerusalem.
12:20 **E** commanded a thousand troops from the tribe of
12:30 were 20,800 warriors, **e** famous in his own clan.
16:23 **E** day proclaim the good news that he saves.
16:37 doing whatever needed to be done **e** day.
16:40 regular burnt offerings to the LORD **e** morning
20: 6 a huge man with six fingers on **e** hand and six toes
on **e** foot—
23:24 **E** had to be twenty years old or older to qualify for
23:30 And **e** morning and evening they stood before the
24:19 **E** group carried out its duties in the house of the
25: 7 making music before the LORD, and **e** of them—
26:17 Six Levites were assigned **e** day to the east gate,
26:17 to the south gate, and two to **e** of the storehouses.
26:18 Six were assigned **e** day to the west gate, four to
27: 1 divisions that were on duty **e** month of the year.
27: 1 **E** division served for one month and had
28:15 and lamps, depending on how **e** would be used.
2Ch 2: 4 and to sacrifice burnt offerings **e** morning
3: 9 gold nails that weighed about twenty ounces **e**.
3:15 **e** topped by a capital extending upward another
4:13 **e** of the chain networks that were hung around the
9:13 **E** year Solomon received about 25 tons of gold.
9:15 **e** containing over 15 pounds of gold.
9:16 **e** containing about 7-1/2 pounds of gold.
9:18 with the figure of a lion standing on **e** side of the
9:19 one standing on **e** end of **e** of the six steps.
11:11 In **e** of them, he stored supplies of food, olive oil,
11:23 and arranged for **e** of them to have several wives.
12:15 and Jeroboam were continually at war with **e** other.
19: 6 render the verdict in **e** case that comes before you.
20:23 off the army of Seir, they turned on **e** other.
21: 3 Their father had given **e** of them valuable gifts of
25: 5 assigning leaders to **e** clan from Judah
30:21 **E** day the Levites and priests sang to the LORD,
Ezr 2:69 and **e** leader gave as much as he could. The total of
3: 3 the LORD. They did this **e** morning and evening.
3: 4 sacrificing the burnt offerings specified for **e** day
6: 9 salt, wine, and olive oil that they need **e** day.
10:16 designating **e** of the representatives by name.
10:19 and they **e** acknowledged their guilt by offering a
10:44 **E** of these men had a pagan wife, and some even
Ne 3:28 **e** one doing the section immediately opposite his
4:19 and we are widely separated from **e** other along the
5:18 The provisions required at my expense for **e** day
6: 4 same message, and **e** time I gave the same reply.
8: 8 helping the people understand **e** passage.
8:18 Ezra read from the Book of the Law of God on **e** of
10:34 at regular times **e** year—the families of the priests,
13:30 and Levites, making certain that **e** knew his work.
Est 1:22 to **e** province in its own script and language,
2: 3 Let the king appoint agents in **e** province to bring
2:12 Before **e** young woman was taken to the king's
3:12 and the local officials of **e** province in their own
9:19 when they rejoice and send gifts to **e** other.
9:22 and gladness and by giving gifts to **e** other and to
9:27 two prescribed days at the appointed time **e** year.
Job 1: 5 and offer a burnt offering for **e** of them.
36:32 hands with lightning bolts. He hurls **e** at its target.
42:11 And **e** of them brought him a gift of money and a
Ps 1: 3 the riverbank, / bearing fruit **e** season without fail.
5: 3 **E** morning I bring my requests to you and wait
12: 2 Neighbors lie to **e** other, / speaking with flattering
19: 9 The laws of the LORD are true; / **e** one is fair.
34:19 but the LORD rescues them from **e** and every
42: 8 Through **e** day the LORD pours his unfailing love
42: 8 upon me, / and through **e** night I sing his songs,
56: 8 You have recorded **e** one in your book.
59:16 I will shout with joy **e** morning because of your
64: 5 They encourage **e** other to do evil / and plan how
68:19 For **e** day he carries us in his arms. / *Interlude*
78: 7 So **e** generation can set its hope anew on God,
78:51 He killed the oldest son in **e** Egyptian family,
84: 7 and **e** of them will appear before God in Jerusalem.
86: 9 All the nations—and you made **e** one— / will come
88: 9 my tears. / **E** day I beg for your help, O LORD;
96: 2 **E** day proclaim the good news that he saves.
100: 5 and his faithfulness continues to **e** generation.
103:20 out his plans, / listening for **e** of his commands.
105:36 Then he killed the oldest child in **e** Egyptian home,
/ the pride and joy of **e** family.
110: 3 your vigor will be renewed **e** day like the morning
119:128 Truly, **e** of your commandments is right. / That is

135: 8 He destroyed the firstborn in **e** Egyptian home,
145: 4 Let **e** generation tell its children / of your mighty
Pr 7: 18 love until morning. Let's enjoy **e** other's caresses,
12: 12 Thieves are jealous of **e** other's loot,
14: 10 **E** heart knows its own bitterness, and no one else
14: 12 There is a path before **e** person that seems right,
16: 25 There is a path before **e** person that seems right,
18: 24 There are "friends" who destroy **e** other, but a real
24: 16 trip seven times, but **e** time they will rise again.
Ecc 3: 15 in the past. For God calls **e** event back in its turn.
4: 11 the same blanket can gain warmth from **e** other.
6: 10 It was known long ago what **e** person would be.
7: 29 but they have **e** turned to follow their own
8: 9 where people have the power to hurt **e** other.
10: 9 there is danger with **e** stroke of your ax!
SS 3: 8 **E** one wears a sword on his thigh, ready to defend
8: 11 **E** of them pays one thousand pieces of silver for its
Isa 3: 5 People will take advantage of **e** other—man against
4: 1 Seven women will fight over **e** of them and say,
6: 2 him were mighty seraphim, **e** with six wings.
10: 8 He will say, '**E** of my princes will soon be a king,
11: 13 They will not fight against **e** other anymore.
14: 31 the north. **E** soldier rushes forward ready to fight.
19: 2 "I will make the Egyptians fight against **e** other—
27: 3 **E** day I will water them; day and night I will watch
28: 25 barley, and spelt, **e** in its own section of his land?
33: 2 Be our strength **e** day and our salvation in times of
34: 15 And the vultures will come, **e** one with its mate.
36: 16 Then I will allow **e** of you to continue eating from
38: 19 **E** generation can make known your faithfulness to
40: 26 them out one after another, calling **e** by its name.
41: 4 directing the affairs of the human race as **e** new
65: 5 Yet they say to **e** other, 'Don't come too close
Jer 5: 8 lusty stallions, **e** neighing for his neighbor's wife.
5: 24 for he gives us rain **e** spring and fall, assuring us of
6: 9 as when a harvester checks **e** vine a second time to
8: 7 the crane. They all return at the proper time **e** year.
9: 5 They all fool and defraud **e** other; no one tells the
12: 15 own lands again, **e** nation to its own inheritance.
17: 19 the king goes out, and then at **e** of the other gates.
18: 11 your evil ways, **e** of you, and do what is right.' "
23: 30 prophets who get their messages from **e** other—
23: 35 You should keep asking **e** other, 'What is the
25: 5 **E** time the message was this: 'Turn from the evil
46: 12 Your mightiest warriors will stumble across **e** other
46: 16 They stumble and fall over **e** other and say among
51: 46 of violence as the leaders fight against **e** other.
52: 21 **E** of the pillars was 27 feet tall and 18 feet in
52: 22 The bronze capital on top of **e** pillar was 7-1/2 feet
La 3: 23 is his faithfulness; his mercies begin afresh **e** day.
Eze 1: 6 except that **e** had four faces and two pairs of wings.
1: 8 Beneath **e** of their wings I could see human hands.
1: 9 The wings of **e** living being touched the wings of
1: 10 **E** had a human face in the front, the face of a lion
1: 11 **E** had two pairs of outstretched wings—one pair
1: 15 ground beneath them, one wheel belonging to **e**.
1: 16 **e** wheel had a second wheel turning crosswise
1: 23 Beneath this surface the wings of **e** living being
1: 23 and **e** had two wings covering its body.
3: 13 of the living beings as they brushed against **e** other
4: 5 sins for 390 days—one day for **e** year of their sin.
4: 6 side for 40 days—one day for **e** year of Judah's sin.
4: 10 eight ounces of food for **e** day, and eat it at set
4: 11 Then measure out a jar of water for **e** day,
4: 12 **E** day prepare your bread as you would barley
8: 11 **E** of them held an incense burner, so there was a
9: 2 faces north, **e** carrying a battle club in his hand.
10: 9 **E** of the four cherubim had a wheel beside him,
10: 10 **e** wheel had a second wheel turning crosswise
10: 14 **E** of the four cherubim had four faces—the first
10: 21 for **e** had four faces and four wings and what
18: 30 "Therefore, I will judge **e** of you, O people of
20: 7 Then I said to them, '**E** of you, get rid of your
33: 20 But I will judge **e** of you according to your deeds."
37: 7 The bones of **e** body came together and attached
38: 21 Your men will turn against **e** other in mortal
40: 7 There were guard alcoves on **e** side built into the
40: 7 **E** of these alcoves was 10-1/2 feet square, with a
40: 10 There were three guard alcoves on **e** side of the
40: 10 **E** had the same measurements, and the dividing
40: 12 In front of **e** of the guard alcoves was a 21-inch
40: 21 too, there were three guard alcoves on **e** side,
40: 39 On **e** side of this foyer were two tables,
40: 40 on **e** side of the stairs going up to the north
40: 42 **e** 31-1/2 inches square and 21 inches high.
40: 43 There were hooks, **e** three inches long, fastened to
40: 49 ten steps leading up to it, with a column on **e** side.
41: 2 and the walls on **e** side were 8-3/4 feet wide.
41: 3 and the walls on **e** side of the entrance extended
41: 5 along the outside wall; **e** room was 7 feet wide.
41: 6 one above the other, with thirty rooms on **e** level.
41: 7 **E** level was wider than the one below it,
41: 18 with carvings of cherubim, **e** with two faces,
41: 18 and there was a palm tree carving between **e** of the
41: 24 **e** with two swinging doors.
42: 3 three levels high and stood across from **e** other.
42: 5 **E** of the two upper levels of rooms was narrower
42: 6 **e** of the upper levels was set back from the level
42: 11 and doors. The dimensions of **e** were identical.
42: 20 So the area was 875 feet on **e** side with a wall all
43: 15 with a horn rising up from **e** of the four corners.
43: 17 measuring 24-1/2 feet on **e** side, with a 21-inch
43: 26 Do this **e** day for seven days to cleanse and make
43: 27 On the eighth day, and on **e** day afterward,
44: 30 The first samples of **e** grain harvest and the first of
45: 8 land to the people, giving an allotment to **e** tribe.
45: 11 and the bath will **e** measure one-tenth of a homer.
45: 18 In early spring, on the first day of **e** new year,
45: 23 On **e** of the seven days of the feast he will prepare
45: 23 A male goat will also be given **e** day for a sin
45: 24 and a gallon of olive oil with **e** young bull and ram.
46: 1 will be closed during the six workdays **e** week,
46: 4 "**E** Sabbath day the prince will present to the
46: 5 amount of flour he chooses to go with **e** lamb.
46: 5 He is to offer one gallon of olive oil for **e** half
46: 7 And with **e** lamb he is to bring whatever amount of
46: 7 With **e** half bushel of flour he must offer one
46: 11 will be a half bushel of flour with **e** young bull,
46: 11 another half bushel of flour with **e** ram, and as
46: 11 flour as the prince chooses to give with **e** lamb.
46: 11 One gallon of oil is to be given with **e** half bushel
46: 13 "**E** morning a year-old lamb with no physical
46: 21 outer courtyard and led me to **e** of its four corners.
In **e** corner I saw an enclosure.
46: 22 **E** of these enclosures was 70 feet long and 52-1/2
47: 14 Otherwise **e** tribe will receive an equal share.
48: 1 the tribes of Israel and the territory **e** is to receive.
48: 16 The city will measure 1-1/2 miles on **e** side.
48: 20 is a square that measures 8-1/3 miles on **e** side.
48: 21 **E** of these areas will be 8-1/3 miles wide,
48: 29 These are the allotments that will be set aside for **e**
48: 31 be three gates, **e** one named after a tribe of Israel.
Da 1: 19 The king talked with **e** of them, and none of them
2: 43 alliances with **e** other through intermarriage.
6: 1 and he appointed a prince to rule over **e** province.
7: 3 up out of the water, **e** different from the others.
8: 13 Then I heard two of the holy ones talking to **e**
11: 27 Seeking nothing but **e** other's harm, these kings
will plot against **e** other at the conference table,
attempting to deceive **e** other.
Hos 2: 9 and ripened grain I generously provided **e** harvest
12: 9 as you do **e** year when you celebrate the Festival of
Joel 2: 8 They never jostle **e** other; **e** moves in exactly the
right place.
Am 4: 4 Offer sacrifices **e** morning and bring your tithes
Zep 2: 11 will worship the LORD, **e** in their own land.
3: 13 of Israel who survive will do no wrong to **e** other,
Hag 2: 22 horses will fall, and their riders will kill **e** other.
Zec 1: 8 brown, and white horses, **e** with its own rider.
3: 10 **e** of you will invite your neighbor into your home
4: 2 **e** one having seven spouts with wicks.
4: 3 I see two olive trees, one on **e** side of the bowl."
4: 11 "What are these two olive trees on **e** side of the
7: 3 and fast **e** summer on the anniversary of the
7: 10 And do not make evil plans to harm **e** other.
8: 10 on all sides. I had turned everyone against **e** other.
8: 16 this is what you must do: Tell the truth to **e** other.
8: 17 Do not make evil plots to harm **e** other. And stop
9: 12 I will repay you two mercies for **e** of your woes!
11: 6 "I will let them fall into **e** other's clutches, as well
11: 9 And those who remain will devour **e** other!"
12: 12 **e** family by itself, with the husbands and wives in
12: 14 **E** of the surviving families from Judah will mourn
14: 13 They will fight against **e** other in hand-to-hand
14: 16 will go up to Jerusalem **e** year to worship the King,
Mal 2: 10 Then why are we faithless to **e** other,
2: 14 and your wife made to **e** other on your wedding
3: 16 Then those who feared the LORD spoke with **e**
Mt 14: 19 he gave some of the bread and fish to **e** disciple,
20: 9 o'clock were paid, **e** received a full day's wage.
21: 41 will give him his share of the crop after **e** harvest."
22: 26 so on until she had been the wife of **e** of them.
24: 7 and kingdoms will proclaim war against **e** other,
24: 10 turn away from me and betray and hate **e** other.
26: 27 gave it to them and said, "**E** of you drink from it,
27: 15 the crowd **e** year during the Passover celebration—
Mk 6: 10 "When you enter **e** village, be a guest in only one
9: 10 but they often asked **e** other what he meant by
9: 50 among yourselves and live in peace with **e** other."
13: 8 and kingdoms will proclaim war against **e** other,
13: 34 He gave **e** of his employees instructions about the
14: 56 spoke against him, but they contradicted **e** other.
15: 6 to release one prisoner **e** year at Passover time—
Lk 2: 15 the shepherds said to **e** other, "Come on, let's go
5: 21 and teachers of religious law said to **e** other.
9: 4 When you enter **e** village, be a guest in only one
9: 14 sit down on the ground in groups of about fifty **e**,"
12: 1 thousands were milling about and crushing **e** other.
16: 5 "So he invited **e** person who owed money to his
16: 19 splendidly clothed and who lived **e** day in luxury.
17: 4 and **e** time turns again and asks forgiveness,
20: 14 they said to **e** other, 'Here comes the heir to this
20: 31 until **e** of the seven had married her and died,
21: 10 and kingdoms will proclaim war against **e** other.
21: 37 and **e** evening he returned to spend the night on the
21: 38 The crowds gathered early **e** morning to hear him.
22: 23 Then the disciples began to ask **e** other which of
24: 32 They said to **e** other, "Didn't our hearts feel
Jn 2: 6 and held twenty to thirty gallons **e**.
3: 27 "God in heaven appoints **e** person's work.
4: 33 brought it to him?" the disciples asked **e** other.
5: 44 For you gladly honor **e** other, but you don't care
6: 52 Then the people began arguing with **e** other about
9: 8 who knew him as a blind beggar asked **e** other,
11: 47 "What are we going to do?" they asked **e** other.
11: 56 they asked **e** other, "What do you think?
12: 19 Then the Pharisees said to **e** other, "We've lost.
13: 14 washed your feet, you ought to wash **e** other's feet.
13: 18 to all of you; I know so well **e** one of you I chose.
13: 22 The disciples looked at **e** other, wondering whom
13: 34 Love **e** other. Just as I have loved you, you should
love **e** other.
14: 21 And I will reveal myself to **e** one of them."
15: 12 I command you to love **e** other in the same way
15: 17 I command you to love **e** other.
16: 17 The disciples asked **e** other, "What does he mean
16: 32 **e** one going his own way, leaving me alone.
17: 2 He gives eternal life to **e** one you have given him.
18: 39 to release someone from prison **e** year at Passover.
Ac 2: 3 tongues of fire appeared and settled on **e** of them.
2: 12 "What can this mean?" they asked **e** other.
2: 38 "**E** of you must turn from your sins and turn to
2: 46 They worshiped together at the Temple **e** day,
2: 47 And **e** day the Lord added to their group those who
3: 2 **E** day he was put beside the Temple gate, the one
3: 26 to bless you by turning **e** of you back from your
4: 16 should we do with these men?" they asked **e** other.
7: 26 'you are brothers. Why are you hurting **e** other?'
12: 4 under the guard of four squads of four soldiers **e**.
15: 36 "Let's return to **e** city where we previously
18: 4 **E** Sabbath found Paul at the synagogue, trying to
21: 26 and sacrifices would be offered for **e** of them.
28: 4 the island saw it hanging there and said to **e** other,
Ro 1: 8 How I thank God through Jesus Christ for **e** one of
1: 12 In this way, **e** of us will be a blessing to the other.
1: 24 did vile and degrading things with **e** other's bodies.
1: 26 have sex and instead indulged in sex with **e** other.
1: 27 with women, burned with lust for **e** other.
12: 3 As God's messenger, I give **e** of you this warning:
12: 4 have many parts and **e** part has a special function,
12: 5 his one body, and **e** of us has different work to do.
12: 5 belong to **e** other, and **e** of us needs all the others.
12: 6 God has given **e** of us the ability to do certain
12: 10 Love **e** other with genuine affection, and take
delight in honoring **e** other.
12: 16 Live in harmony with **e** other. Don't try to act
14: 5 **E** person should have a personal conviction about
14: 10 **e** of us will stand personally before the judgment
14: 12 **e** of us will have to give a personal account to God.
14: 13 So don't condemn **e** other anymore. Decide instead
14: 19 harmony in the church and try to build **e** other up.
15: 5 help you live in complete harmony with **e** other—
15: 5 **e** with the attitude of Christ Jesus toward the other.
15: 7 So accept **e** other just as Christ has accepted you;
15: 32 and we will be an encouragement to **e** other.
16: 16 Greet **e** other in Christian love. All the churches of
1Co 3: 3 are jealous of one another and quarrel with **e** other.
3: 5 to believe. **E** of us did the work the Lord gave us.
3: 13 day to see what kind of work **e** builder has done.
7: 2 **e** man should have his own wife,
7: 2 and **e** woman should have her own husband.
7: 5 So do not deprive **e** other of sexual relations.
11: 33 you gather for the Lord's Supper, wait for **e** other.
12: 1 the special abilities the Holy Spirit gives to **e** of us,
12: 7 A spiritual gift is given to **e** of us as a means of
12: 11 He alone decides which gift **e** person should have.
12: 18 and he has put **e** part just where he wants it.
12: 25 so that all the members care for **e** other equally.
12: 27 and **e** one of you is a separate and necessary part of
15: 38 A different kind of plant grows from **e** kind of
15: 41 while the moon and stars **e** have another kind.
15: 41 And even the stars differ from **e** other in their
16: 2 **e** of you should put aside some amount of money
16: 20 greet you for them. Greet **e** other in Christian love.
2Co 5: 10 We will **e** receive whatever we deserve for the
9: 7 You must **e** make up your own mind as to how
10: 12 But they are only comparing themselves with **e**
12: 9 **E** time he said, "My gracious favor is all you
12: 18 have the same Spirit and walk in **e** other's steps,
13: 11 Encourage **e** other. Live in harmony and peace.
13: 12 Greet **e** other in Christian love. All the Christians
Gal 5: 17 These two forces are constantly fighting **e** other,
6: 2 Share **e** other's troubles and problems, and in this
6: 5 For we are **e** responsible for our own conduct.
Eph 2: 16 and our hostility toward **e** other was put to death.
4: 2 Be patient with **e** other, making allowance for **e**
other's faults because of
4: 7 he has given **e** one of us a special gift according to
4: 16 As **e** part does its own special work, it helps the
4: 25 neighbor the truth" because we belong to **e** other.
4: 32 Instead, be kind to **e** other, tenderhearted,
5: 33 **e** man must love his wife as he loves himself,
6: 8 Remember that the Lord will reward **e** one of us
Php 1: 9 I pray that your love for **e** other will overflow more
2: 2 happy by agreeing wholeheartedly with **e** other,
Col 3: 9 Don't lie to **e** other, for you have stripped off your
3: 13 You must make allowance for **e** other's faults
3: 16 Use his words to teach and counsel **e** other.
1Th 2: 11 And you know that we treated **e** of you as a father
3: 12 and overflow to **e** other and to everyone else,
4: 4 Then **e** of you will control your body and live in
4: 18 and encourage **e** other with these words.
5: 11 So encourage **e** other and build **e** other up,
5: 13 And remember to live peaceably with **e** other.
5: 15 but always try to do good to **e** other and to
5: 26 Greet **e** other in Christian love.
2Th 1: 3 and you are all growing in love for **e** other.
Tit 1: 5 and appoint elders in **e** town as I instructed you.
Heb 3: 13 You must warn **e** other every day, as long as it is
9: 27 And just as it is destined that **e** person dies only
10: 25 some people do, but encourage and warn **e** other,
11: 21 blessed **e** of Joseph's sons and bowed in worship
12: 15 Look after **e** other so that none of you will miss out
13: 1 Continue to love **e** other with true Christian love.
Jas 4: 11 Don't speak evil against **e** other, my dear brothers
4: 11 If you criticize **e** other and condemn **e** other,
5: 9 Don't grumble about **e** other, my brothers
5: 16 Confess your sins to **e** other and pray for **e** other so
that you may be healed.
1Pe 1: 22 Now you can have sincere love for **e** other as
1: 22 So see to it that you really do love **e** other intensely

3: 8 be of one mind, full of sympathy toward e other,
4: 8 of all, continue to show deep love for e other,
4: 10 God has given gifts to e of you from his great
5: 5 And all of you, serve e other in humility, for
5: 14 Greet e other in Christian love. Peace be to all of
1Jn 1: 7 as Christ is, then we have fellowship with e other,
3: 18 let us stop just saying we love e other;
4: 11 us that much, we surely ought to love e other.
4: 12 But if we love e other, God lives in us, and his love
4: 19 We love e other as a result of his loving us first.
3Jn 1: 15 Please give my personal greetings to e of our
Rev 2: 4 You don't love me or e other as you did at first!
2: 17 And I will give to e one a white stone, and on the
2: 23 And I will give to e of you whatever you deserve.
4: 6 living beings, e covered with eyes, front and back.
4: 8 E of these living beings had six wings, and their
5: 8 E one had a harp, and they held gold bowls filled
6: 11 Then a white robe was given to e of them.
11: 10 e other to celebrate the death of the two prophets
13: 1 And written on e head were names that
15: 7 And one of the four living beings handed e of the
21: 13 There were three gates on e side—east, north,
21: 16 its length and width and height were e 1,400 miles.
21: 21 were made of pearls—e gate from a single pearl!
22: 2 On e side of the river grew a tree of life,
22: 2 twelve crops of fruit, with a fresh crop e month.
22: 17 "Come." Let e one who hears them say, "Come."

EAGER (34) [EAGERLY, EAGERNESS]

Jdg 7: 11 Then you will be e to attack." So Gideon took
1Ki 8: 23 love to all who obey you and are e to do your will.
1Ch 12: 23 They were all e to see David become king instead
2Ch 6: 14 love to all who obey you and are e to do your will.
26: 20 And the king himself was e to get out
Ps 17: 12 They are like hungry lions, e to tear me apart—
19: 5 It rejoices like a great athlete / e to run the race.
56: 6 watching my every step, e to kill me.
Ecc 4: 15 Everyone is e to help such a youth, even to help
Jer 2: 2 I remember how e you were to please me as a
Eze 16: 31 so e for sin that you have not even demanded
Joel 2: 13 is filled with kindness and is e not to punish you.
Mic 4: 11 for your blood, e to gloat over your destruction.
Zec 6: 7 The powerful horses were e to be off, to patrol
Lk 3: 15 and they were e to know whether John might be
6: 7 because they were e to find some legal charge to
16: 16 and e multitudes are forcing their way in.
Jn 6: 21 Then they were e to let him in, and immediately
Ac 9: 1 He was e to destroy the Lord's followers, so he
Ro 1: 12 I'm e to encourage you in your faith, but I also
1: 15 So I am e to come to you in Rome, too, to preach
11: 24 he will be far more e to graft the Jews back into the
15: 23 all these long years of waiting, I am e to visit you.
1Co 14: 12 Since you are so e to have spiritual gifts, ask God
14: 39 So, dear brothers and sisters, be e to prophesy,
2Co 8: 8 even though the other churches are e to do it.
8: 12 If you are really e to give, it isn't important how
8: 17 In fact, he himself was e to go and see you.
9: 2 For I know how e you are to help, and I have been
Gal 2: 10 the poor, and I have certainly been e to do that.
4: 18 Now it's wonderful if you are e to do good,
Php 1: 20 For I live in e expectation and hope that I will
1Pe 3: 13 who will want to harm you if you are e to do good?
5: 2 get out of it, but because you are e to serve God.

EAGERLY (20) [EAGER]

Nu 23: 17 "What did the LORD say?" Balak asked e.
2Ch 15: 15 E they sought after God, and they found him.
Job 3: 21 They search for death more e than for hidden
14: 14 and through my struggle I would e wait for release.
29: 23 They waited e, for my words were as refreshing as
Mal 3: 1 whom you look for so e, is surely coming,"
Lk 2: 25 and he e expected the Messiah to come and rescue
Ac 3: 5 The lame man looked at them e, expecting a gift.
17: 11 and they listened e to Paul's message.
Ro 8: 19 For all creation is waiting e for that future day
8: 24 we are saved, we e look forward to this freedom.
15: 26 the believers in Greece have e taken up an offering
1Co 1: 7 you e wait for the return of our Lord Jesus Christ.
Gal 5: 5 But we who live by the Spirit e wait to receive
Php 3: 20 And we are e waiting for him to return as our
2Ti 4: 8 but for all who e look forward to his glorious
Heb 9: 28 salvation to all those who are e waiting for him.
Jas 5: 7 Consider the farmers who e look for the rains in
1Pe 1: 12 so wonderful that even the angels are e watching
Jude 1: 3 I had been e planning to write to you about the

EAGERNESS (6) [EAGER]

Ps 119: 36 Give me an e for your decrees; / do not inflict me
Isa 26: 11 Show them your e to defend your people.
Mk 7: 22 deceit, e for lustful pleasure, envy, slander, pride,
2Co 8: 19 that glorifies the Lord and shows our e to help.
12: 21 sexual immorality, and e for lustful pleasure.
Gal 5: 19 impure thoughts, e for lustful pleasure,

EAGLE (19) [EAGLE'S, EAGLES, EAGLES']

Lev 11: 13 detestable for you: the e, the vulture, the osprey,
Dt 14: 12 you may not eat: the e, the vulture, the osprey,
28: 49 the earth, and it will swoop down on you like an e.
32: 11 Like an e that rouses her chicks / and hovers over
Job 9: 26 swift boat, like an e that swoops down on its prey.
39: 27 Is it at your command that the e rises to the heights
Pr 30: 19 how an e glides through the sky, / how a snake
Jer 48: 40 "An e swoops down on the land of Moab,"
49: 22 The enemy will come as swiftly as an e, and he
Eze 1: 10 ox on the left side, and the face of an e at the back.
10: 14 face of a lion, and the fourth was the face of an e.
17: 3 A great e with broad wings full of many-colored
17: 6 Its branches turned up toward the e, and its roots
17: 7 But then another great e with broad wings and full
Hos 8: 1 The enemy descends like an e on the people of the
Mic 1: 16 Make yourselves as bald as an e, for your little
Rev 4: 7 and the fourth had the form of an e with wings
8: 13 And I heard a single e crying loudly as it flew
12: 14 she was given two wings like those of a great e.

EAGLE'S (2) [EAGLE]

Ex 19: 4 brought you to myself and carried you on e wings.
Ps 103: 5 with good things. / My youth is renewed like the e!

EAGLES (8) [EAGLE]

2Sa 1: 23 in life and in death. / They were swifter than e;
Isa 40: 31 They will fly high on wings like e. They will run
Jer 4: 13 are like whirlwinds; his horses are swifter than e.
49: 16 Though you live among the peaks with the e,
La 4: 19 Our enemies were swifter than the e. If we fled to
Eze 17: 12 you understand the meaning of this riddle of the e?
Ob 1: 4 Though you soar as high as e and build your nest
Hab 1: 8 Like e they swoop down to pounce on their prey.

EAGLES' (2) [EAGLE]

Da 4: 33 He lived this way until his hair was as long as e
7: 4 The first beast was like a lion with e wings. As I

EAR (24) [EARS, EARLOBE, EARLOBES]

Ex 21: 6 to the door and publicly pierce his e with an awl.
Lev 8: 23 its blood and put it on the lobe of Aaron's right e,
14: 14 and put it on the tip of the healed person's right e,
14: 17 left hand on the tip of the healed person's right e,
14: 25 some of its blood on the tip of the person's right e,
14: 28 from his hand on the lobe of the person's right e,
Job 4: 12 given me in secret, as though whispered in my e.
12: 11 tastes good food, so the e tests the words it hears.
33: 16 He whispers in their e and terrifies them with his
34: 3 tastes good food, the e tests the words it hears.'
Ps 71: 2 you are just. / Turn your e to listen and set me free.
102: 2 in my time of distress. / Bend down your e
Isa 64: 4 no e has heard and no eye has seen a God like you,
Am 3: 12 mouth will recover only two legs and a piece of e.
Mt 26: 51 and slashed off an e of the high priest's servant.
Mk 14: 47 and slashed off an e of the high priest's servant.
Lk 22: 50 at the high priest's servant and cut off his right e.
22: 51 And he touched the place where the man's e had
Jn 18: 10 a sword and slashed off the right e of Malchus,
18: 26 a relative of the man whose e Peter had cut off,
1Co 2: 9 when they say, / "No eye has seen, no e has heard,
12: 16 And if the e says, "I am not part of the body
12: 16 the body because I am only an e and not an eye,"
12: 17 Or if your whole body were just one big e,

EARED, EARING [KJV] See PLOWED, PLOWING

EARLIER (23) [EARLY]

Dt 2: 12 In e times the Horites had lived at Mount Seir,
Jos 2: 4 the two men, replied, "The men were here e,
1Sa 13: 8 as Samuel had instructed him e, but Samuel still
1Ki 2: 28 Although he had not followed Absalom e, Joab had
1Ch 9: 20 had been in charge of the gatekeepers in e times,
2Ch 30: 3 Passover was normally celebrated one month e,
34: 11 They restored what e kings of Judah had allowed
Isa 65: 16 put aside my anger and forget the evil of e days.
Eze 29: 16 of how sinful she was to trust Egypt in e days.
Da 7: 1 E, during the first year of King Belshazzar's reign
9: 21 Gabriel, whom I had seen in the e vision,
Zec 1: 4 would not listen when the e prophets said to them,
7: 12 had sent them by his Spirit through the e prophets.
Mt 2: 16 the star first appeared to them about two years e.
20: 10 When those hired e came to get their pay,
Jn 7: 50 Nicodemus, the leader who had met with Jesus e,
16: 4 I didn't tell you e because I was going to be with
Ac 14: 16 In e days he permitted all the nations to go their
18: 18 (E, at Cenchrea, Paul had shaved his head
21: 29 (For e that day they had seen him in the city with
2Co 12: 21 because many of you who sinned e have not
Eph 3: 3 As I briefly mentioned e in this letter, God himself
1Ti 1: 18 based on the prophetic words spoken about you e.

EARLIEST (9) [EARLY]

Ps 71: 17 O God, you have taught me from my e childhood,
119: 152 I have known from my e days / that your decrees
129: 1 From my e youth my enemies have persecuted
129: 2 from my e youth my enemies have persecuted me,
Isa 48: 8 You have been rebels from your e childhood,
Jer 32: 30 have done nothing but wrong since their e days.
48: 11 "From her e history, Moab has lived in peace.
Zec 13: 5 been my means of livelihood from my e youth.'
Ac 26: 4 I was given a thorough Jewish training from my e

EARLOBE (1) [EAR]

Dt 15: 17 take an awl and push it through his e into the door.

EARLOBES (1) [EAR]

Ex 29: 20 and place some of it on the tip of the right e of

EARLY (103) [EARLIER, EARLIEST]

Ge 19: 2 then get up in the morning as e as you like
19: 27 The next morning Abraham was up e and hurried
20: 8 Abimelech got up e the next morning and hastily
21: 14 So Abraham got up e the next morning,
22: 3 The next morning Abraham got up e. He saddled
24: 54 But e the next morning, he said, "Send me back to
26: 31 E the next morning, they each took a solemn oath
28: 18 The next morning he got up very e. He took the
29: 7 "They'll be hungry if you stop so e in the day."
31: 55 Laban got up e the next morning, and he kissed his
Ex 8: 20 "Get up e in the morning and meet Pharaoh as he
9: 13 LORD said to Moses, "Get up e in the morning.
13: 4 This day in e spring will be the anniversary of your
14: 24 But e in the morning, the LORD looked down on
23: 15 an annual event at the appointed time in e spring,
24: 4 E the next morning he built an altar at the foot of
32: 6 So the people got up e the next morning to
34: 4 E in the morning he climbed Mount Sinai as the
34: 18 at the appointed time each year in e spring,
Lev 16: 29 "On the appointed day in e autumn, you must
23: 5 which begins at twilight on its appointed day in e
23: 24 "On the appointed day in e autumn, you are to
Nu 9: 1 The LORD gave these instructions to Moses in e
9: 3 at twilight on the appointed day in e spring.
14: 40 So they got up e the next morning and set out for
20: 1 In e spring the people of Israel arrived in the
28: 16 "On the appointed day in e spring, you must
29: 1 on the appointed day in e autumn each year.
33: 3 after the first Passover celebration in e spring.
Dt 16: 1 the Passover at the proper time in e spring,
Jos 3: 1 E the next morning Joshua and all the Israelites left
6: 12 Joshua got up e the next morning, and the priests
7: 16 E the next morning Joshua brought the tribes of
8: 10 E the next morning Joshua roused his men
8: 14 and all his army hurriedly went out e the next
Jdg 6: 28 E the next morning, as the people of the town
7: 1 and his army got up e and went as far as the spring
19: 5 On the fourth day the man was up e, ready to
19: 8 On the morning of the fifth day he was up e again,
19: 9 Tomorrow you can get up e and be on your way."
20: 19 So the Israelites left e the next morning
21: 4 E the next morning the people built an altar
1Sa 1: 19 The entire family got up e the next morning
15: 12 E the next morning Samuel went to find Saul.
17: 20 and set out e the next morning with the gifts.
29: 10 Now get up e in the morning, and leave with your
2Sa 15: 2 He got up e every morning and went out to the gate
1Ki 8: 2 king at the annual Festival of Shelters in e autumn.
2Ki 6: 15 When the servant of the man of God got up e the
2Ch 5: 3 king at the annual Festival of Shelters in e autumn.
17: 3 because he followed the example of his father's e
20: 20 E the next morning the army of Judah went out
29: 17 The work began on a day in e spring, and in eight
29: 20 E the next morning King Hezekiah gathered the
30: 3 normally celebrated one month earlier, in e spring,
31: 7 and the heaps continued to grow until e autumn.
35: 1 in Jerusalem on the appointed day in e spring.
Ezr 3: 1 Now in e autumn, when the Israelites had settled in
Ne 2: 1 E the following spring, during the twentieth year
4: 21 We worked e and late, from sunrise to sunset.
8: 3 inside the Water Gate from e morning until noon
Est 2: 16 palace in e winter of the seventh year of his reign,
Job 1: 5 He would get up e in the morning and offer a burnt
24: 14 The murderer rises in the e dawn to kill the poor
29: 4 In my e years, the friendship of God was felt in my
Ps 119: 147 I rise e, before the sun is up; / I cry out for help
127: 2 so hard / from e morning until late at night,
Pr 20: 21 An inheritance obtained e in life is not a blessing
27: 14 greeting to your neighbor too e in the morning,
SS 7: 12 Let us get up e and go out to the vineyards. Let us
Isa 5: 11 Destruction is certain for you who get up e to
28: 4 as an e fig is hungrily picked and eaten.
61: 11 His righteousness will be like a garden in e spring,
Jer 26: 1 This message came to Jeremiah from the LORD e
27: 1 This message came to Jeremiah from the LORD e
Eze 27: 17 wheat from Minnith, e figs, honey, oil, and balm.
45: 18 In e spring, on the first day of each new year,
45: 25 of Shelters, which occurs every year in e autumn,
Da 6: 19 Very e the next morning, the king hurried out to
Hos 6: 3 arrival of dawn or the coming of rains in e spring."
Zec 7: 5 in the summer and at the festival in e autumn,
8: 19 and times of mourning you have kept in e summer,
Mt 20: 1 out e one morning to hire workers for his vineyard.
27: 1 Very e in the morning, the leading priests
28: 1 E on Sunday morning, as the new day was
Mk 11: 13 because it was too e in the season for fruit.
13: 35 at evening, midnight, e dawn, or late daybreak.
15: 1 Very e in the morning the leading priests,
16: 2 Very e on Sunday morning, just at sunrise,
16: 9 It was e on Sunday morning when Jesus rose from
Lk 1: 2 reports circulating among us from the e disciples
4: 42 E the next morning Jesus went out into the
21: 38 The crowds gathered e each morning to hear him.
24: 1 But very e on Sunday morning the women came to
24: 22 of his followers were at his tomb e this morning,
Jn 8: 2 but e the next morning he was back again at the
11: 55 the country arrived in Jerusalem several days e
18: 28 Jesus' trial before Caiaphas ended in the e hours of
20: 1 E Sunday morning, while it was still dark,
Ac 2: 15 are drunk. It isn't true! It's much too e for that.
21: 16 originally from Cyprus and one of the e disciples.
27: 33 As the darkness gave way to the e morning light,
Heb 10: 32 Don't ever forget those e days when you first

EARN (9) [EARNED, EARNINGS, WELL-EARNED]

Pr 19: 11 their anger; they e esteem by overlooking wrongs.
Ecc 2: 21 I gain to people who haven't worked to e it.

Isa 58: 6 Treat them fairly and give them what they **e**.
Ro 4: 4 wages are not a gift. Workers **e** what they receive.
1Co 4: 12 We have worked wearily with our own hands to **e**
Gal 2: 19 the law, I realized I could never **e** God's approval.
1Th 2: 9 Night and day we toiled to **e** a living so that our
2Th 3: 12 Settle down and get to work. **E** your own living.
2Pe 2: 15 of Beor, who loved to **e** money by doing wrong.

EARNED (8) [EARN, EARNING, EARNINGS]

Ge 30: 26 and children, for I have **e** them from you,
1Ch 26: 6 who **e** positions of great authority in the clan.
Ps 109: 11 his entire estate, / and strangers take all he has **e**.
Hos 12: 12 to the land of Aram and **e** a wife by tending sheep.
Mic 1: 7 These things were bought with the money **e** by her
Lk 19: 24 this servant, and give it to the one who **e** the most.'
Ac 16: 16 She was a fortune-teller who **e** a lot of money for
1Co 16: 2 amount of money in relation to what you have **e**

EARNEST (8) [EARNESTLY, EARNESTNESS]

1Ki 8: 30 May you hear the humble and **e** requests from me
2Ch 6: 21 May you hear the humble and **e** requests from me
Jer 29: 13 If you look for me in **e**, you will find me when you
Jnh 2: 7 And my **e** prayer went out to you in your holy
Hag 1: 12 and the people worshiped the LORD in **e**.
2Co 8: 22 and has shown how **e** he is on many occasions.
Jas 5: 16 The **e** prayer of a righteous person has great power
1Pe 4: 7 Therefore, be **e** and disciplined in your prayers.

EARNESTLY (12) [EARNEST]

1Sa 20: 28 "David **e** asked me if he could go to Bethlehem.
2Ch 11: 17 and **e** sought to obey the LORD as they had done
Ezr 8: 23 and **e** prayed that our God would take care of us,
Ps 63: 1 O God, you are my God; / I **e** search for you.
Isa 26: 9 All night long I search for you; / **e** I seek for God.
Jnh 3: 8 is required to wear sackcloth and pray **e** to God.
Lk 7: 4 So they **e** begged Jesus to come with them
Ac 12: 5 was in prison, the church prayed very **e** for him.
Ro 11: 7 found the favor of God they are looking for so **e**.
Col 4: 12 He always prays **e** for you, asking God to make
1Th 3: 10 Night and day we pray **e** for you, asking God to let
Jas 5: 17 and yet when he prayed **e** that no rain would fall,

EARNESTNESS (1) [EARNEST]

2Co 7: 11 Such **e**, such concern to clear yourselves,

EARNING (1) [EARN]

Ge 31: 41 fourteen of them **e** your two daughters, and six

EARNINGS (4) [EARN]

Dt 23: 18 your God any offering from the **e** of a prostitute,
Pr 10: 16 The **e** of the godly enhance their lives, but evil
15: 6 of the godly, but the **e** of the wicked bring trouble.
31: 16 and buys it; with her **e** she plants a vineyard.

EARRING (2) [EARRINGS, RING]

Jdg 8: 24 Each of you can give me an **e** out of the treasures
8: 25 and each one threw in a gold **e** he had gathered.

EARRINGS (13) [EARRING]

Ge 35: 4 So they gave Jacob all their idols and their **e**,
Ex 32: 2 and sons and daughters to take off their gold **e**,
32: 3 people obeyed Aaron and brought him their gold **e**.
32: 24 So I told them, 'Bring me your gold **e**.' When they
35: 22 medallions, **e**, rings from their fingers,
Nu 31: 50 armbands, bracelets, rings, **e**, and necklaces.
Jdg 8: 24 (The enemies, being Ishmaelites, all wore gold **e**.)
8: 26 The weight of the gold **e** was forty-three pounds,
SS 1: 10 are your cheeks, with your **e** setting them afire!
1: 11 We will make **e** of gold for you and beads of
Isa 3: 19 their **e**, bracelets, and veils of shimmering gauze.
Eze 16: 12 a ring for your nose and **e** for your ears, and a
Hos 2: 13 put on her **e** and jewels, and went out looking for

EARS (46) [EAR]

Lev 8: 24 put some of the blood on the lobe of their right **e**,
Dt 29: 4 that understand, nor eyes that see, nor **e** that hear!
2Sa 22: 7 me from his sanctuary; / my cry reached his **e**.
2Ki 21: 12 and Judah that the **e** of those who hear about it will
Ps 18: 6 me from his sanctuary; / my cry reached his **e**.
34: 15 who do right; / his **e** are open to their cries for help.
44: 1 O God, we have heard it with our own **e**—
78: 1 to my teaching. / Open your **e** to what I am saying,
92: 11 with my own **e** I have heard the defeat of my
94: 9 Is the one who made your **e** deaf? / Is the one who
115: 6 They cannot hear with their **e**, / or smell with their
135: 17 They cannot hear with their **e** / or smell with their
Pr 2: 2 Tune your **e** to wisdom, and concentrate on
20: 12 **E** to hear and eyes to see—both are gifts from the
21: 13 Those who shut their **e** to the cries of the poor will
23: 12 attune your **e** to hear words of knowledge.
26: 17 Yanking a dog's **e** is as foolish as interfering in
Ecc 5: 1 of God, keep your **e** open and your mouth shut!
Isa 5: 9 With my own **e** I heard him say, "Many beautiful
6: 10 Close their **e**, and shut their eyes. That way,
6: 10 hear with their **e**, understand with their hearts,
35: 5 the eyes of the blind and unstop the **e** of the deaf.
43: 8 have eyes but are blind, who have **e** but are deaf.
55: 3 "Come to me with your **e** wide open. Listen,
Jer 5: 21 but do not see, who have **e** but do not hear.
6: 10 I speak? Their **e** are closed, and they cannot hear.
9: 20 of the LORD; open your **e** to what he has to say.
19: 3 that the **e** of those who hear about it will ring!
26: 11 "You have heard with your own **e** what a traitor he
Eze 16: 12 a ring for your nose and earrings for your **e**, and a
23: 25 They will cut off your nose and **e**, and any
44: 5 of man, take careful notice; use your eyes and **e**.
Am 5: 23 They are only noise to my **e**. I will not listen to
Zec 7: 11 and put their fingers in their **e** to keep from
Mt 10: 27 What I whisper in your **e**, shout from the housetops
13: 15 people are hardened, / and their **e** cannot hear,
13: 15 so their eyes cannot see, / and their **e** cannot hear,
13: 16 because they see; and your **e**, because they hear.
Mk 7: 33 He put his fingers into the man's **e**. Then,
8: 18 can't you see? You have **e**—can't you hear?'
Ac 7: 57 Then they put their hands over their **e**,
28: 27 people are hardened, / and their **e** cannot hear,
28: 27 so their eyes cannot see, / and their **e** cannot hear,
Ro 11: 8 not see, / and closed their **e** so they do not hear."
Jas 5: 4 The cries of the reapers have reached the **e** of the
1Pe 3: 12 who do right, / and his **e** are open to their prayers.

EARTH (691) [EARTH'S, EARTHLY]

ALL THE EARTH (46) Ge 9:13; 18:25; Ex 9:14; 19:5; 34:10; Jos 3:13; 23:14; 1Sa 2:8; 1Ki 10:23; 1Ch 16:30; 2Ch 9:22; Job 1:8; 2:3; 25:3,4; Ps 19:4; 47:2,7; 57:5,11; 66:1; 83:18; 96:9; 97:5,9; 98:4; 108:5; 138:4; Ecc 7:20; Isa 40:28; 54:5; Jer 6:19; 50:23; La 2:15; 4:12; Mic 4:13; Na 3:5; Hab 2:14,20; Zep 3:8; Zec 4:14; 6:5; 14:9; Jn 17:2; Rev 11:4; 13:12

DUST OF THE EARTH (4) Ge 28:14; 2Sa 22:43; 2Ch 1:9; 1Co 15:47

END OF THE EARTH (2) Dt 28:49,64

ENDS OF EARTH (26) Dt 13:7; 30:4; 33:17; Ne 1:9; Job 38:13; Ps 2:8; 48:10; 61:2; 65:8; 72:8; Pr 17:24; Isa 5:26; 11:12; 24:16; 41:9; 42:10; 48:20; 49:6; 52:10; Jer 25:31; Eze 27:33; Da 4:22; Zec 9:10; Mt 24:31; Mk 13:27; Ac 1:8

FOUNDATIONS[S] OF THE EARTH (5) 2Sa 22:16; Job 38:4; Ps 18:15; Isa 48:13; Zec 12:1

HEAVEN...EARTH; EARTH...HEAVEN (97) Ge 14:19,22; 24:3; 28:12; Ex 31:17; Dt 3:24; 4:19,26,36,39; 30:19; 31:28; 1Sa 2:10; 1Ki 8:23,43; 1Ch 21:16; 2Ch 6:14,33; 20:6; 36:23; Ezr 1:2; 5:11; Ne 9:6; Ps 11:4; 50:4; 69:34; 73:25; 76:8; 85:11; 102:19; 115:15; 134:3; 135:6; 146:6; 148:13; Pr 25:3; Ecc 5:2; Isa 14:12; 26:21; 66:1,2; Jer 25:30; Da 4:22,35; Mic 1:3; Zec 6:5; Mt 5:18; 6:10; 10:32,33; 11:25; 16:19,19,19; 18:18,18,19; 23:9; 24:30,31,35; 28:18; Mk 13:27,31; Lk 2:14; 10:21; 16:17; 21:33; Jn 3:12,13,31; Ac 4:24; 7:49,50; 14:15; 17:24; 1Co 8:5; 13:1; 15:47,49; Eph 1:10; 3:15; Php 2:10; Col 1:16,20; 3:2; Jas 5:12; Rev 1:7; 5:3,13; 10:6; 13:13; 14:7; 18:1; 20:9; 21:1,1

HEAVENS AND...EARTH (9) 1Ch 29:11; Isa 45:18; 66:22; Jer 10:11; 23:24; 32:17; 33:2; 51:48; Da 6:27

KINGDOMS OF THE EARTH (12) Dt 28:25; 2Ki 19:15,19; 2Ch 20:6; 36:23; Ezr 1:2; Ps 68:32; Isa 23:11; 37:16,20; Jer 15:4; Zep 3:8

KINGS OF THE EARTH (11) Ps 2:2; 47:9; 48:4; 68:29; 76:12; 102:15; 148:11; Ac 4:26; Rev 6:15; 17:18; 19:19

WHOLE EARTH (25) Ge 3:14; Jos 3:11; 1Ch 16:23; 2Ch 16:9; Job 9:24; 28:24; Ps 22:27; 48:2; 72:19; 96:1; 98:3; 99:1; 110:6; Isa 6:3; 14:26; 27:6; Jer 10:10; 51:7; Eze 32:4; Da 2:35; Zec 1:11; Mt 5:5; Ac 17:26; Ro 4:13; Rev 14:16

Ge 1: 1 the beginning God created the heavens and the **e**.
1: 2 The **e** was empty, a formless mass cloaked in
1: 15 Let their light shine down upon the **e**." And
1: 16 the sun and the moon, to shine down upon the **e**.
1: 17 God set these lights in the heavens to light the **e**,
1: 22 the oceans. Let the birds increase and fill the **e**."
1: 24 "Let the **e** bring forth every kind of animal—
1: 28 told them, "Multiply and fill the **e** and subdue it.
1: 29 given you the seed-bearing plants throughout the **e**
2: 1 So the creation of the heavens and the **e**
2: 4 account of the creation of the heavens and the **e**.
2: 4 the LORD God made the heavens and the **e**,
2: 5 there were no plants or grain growing on the **e**,
3: 14 and wild animals of the whole **e** to be cursed.
4: 12 now on you will be a homeless fugitive on the **e**,
6: 1 human population began to grow rapidly on the **e**,
6: 4 and even afterward, giants lived on the **e**,
6: 9 the only blameless man living on **e** at the time.
6: 11 Now the **e** had become corrupt in God's sight,
6: 13 for the **e** is filled with violence because of them.
6: 13 Yes, I will wipe them all from the face of the **e**!
6: 17 I am about to cover the **e** with a flood that will
6: 17 every living thing. Everything on **e** will die!
7: 1 for among all the people of the **e**, I consider you
7: 4 And I will wipe from the **e** all the living things I
7: 10 One week later, the flood came and covered the **e**.
7: 11 the underground waters burst forth on the **e**,
7: 17 the ground and lifting the boat high above the **e**.
7: 19 water covered even the highest mountains on the **e**,
7: 21 All the living things on **e** died—birds,
7: 23 Every living thing on the **e** was wiped out—people,
7: 24 And the water covered the **e** for 150 days.
8: 7 raven that flew back and forth until the **e** was dry.
8: 14 more months went by, and at last the **e** was dry!
8: 21 and said to himself, "I will never again curse the **e**,
8: 22 As long as the **e** remains, there will be springtime
9: 1 his sons and told them, "Multiply and fill the **e**.
9: 7 you must have many children and repopulate the **e**.
Yes, multiply and fill the **e**!"
9: 11 flood to kill all living creatures and destroy the **e**."
9: 13 of my permanent promise to you and to all the **e**.
9: 14 When I send clouds over the **e**, the rainbow will be
9: 16 between God and every living creature on **e**."
9: 17 of my covenant with all the creatures of the **e**."
9: 19 came all the people now scattered across the **e**.
10: 32 The **e** was populated with the people of these
11: 8 that way, the LORD scattered them all over the **e**;
11: 9 many languages, thus scattering them across the **e**.
12: 3 All the families of the **e** will be blessed through
14: 19 by God Most High, / Creator of heaven and **e**.
14: 22 God Most High, Creator of heaven and **e**,
18: 18 and all the nations of the **e** will be blessed through
18: 25 Should not the Judge of all the **e** do what is right?"
22: 18 all the nations of the **e** will be blessed—
24: 3 "Swear by the LORD, the God of heaven and **e**,
26: 4 descendants all the nations of the **e** will be blessed.
26: 15 and they filled up all of Isaac's wells with **e**.
28: 12 he dreamed of a stairway that reached from **e** to
28: 14 will be as numerous as the dust of the **e**!
28: 14 All the families of the **e** will be blessed through
35: 11 "I am God Almighty. Multiply and fill the **e**!
49: 25 of the heavens above, / blessings of the **e** beneath,
Ex 9: 14 you that there is no other God like me in all the **e**.
9: 15 that would have wiped you from the face of the **e**.
9: 16 and that my fame might spread throughout the **e**.
9: 23 sent thunder and hail, and lightning struck the **e**.
9: 29 This will prove to you that the **e** belongs to the
15: 12 up your hand, / and the **e** swallowed our enemies.
19: 5 treasure from among all the nations of the **e**; for all
the **e** belongs to me.
20: 11 the heavens, the **e**, the sea, and everything in them;
20: 24 altars you make for me must be simple altars of **e**.
31: 17 For in six days the LORD made heaven and **e**,
32: 12 kill them and wipe them from the face of the **e**.'
33: 16 and distinct from all other people on the **e**?"
34: 10 have never been done before anywhere in all the **e**
Lev 11: 46 that move through the water or swarm over the **e**,
17: 13 you must drain out the blood and cover it with **e**.
26: 19 as iron and the **e** beneath as hard as bronze.
Nu 12: 3 was more humble than any other person on **e**.
14: 21 and as surely as the **e** is filled with the LORD's
16: 32 The **e** opened up and swallowed the men,
16: 33 The **e** closed over them, and they all vanished.
16: 34 fearing that the **e** would swallow them, too.
22: 5 They cover the face of the **e** and are threatening
26: 10 But the **e** opened up and swallowed them with
Dt 2: 25 make all people throughout the **e** terrified of you.
3: 24 or on **e** who can perform such great deeds as
4: 19 these heavenly bodies for all the peoples of the **e**.
4: 26 I call heaven and **e** as witnesses against you.
4: 32 from the time God created people on the **e** until
4: 36 He let you see his great fire here on **e** so he could
4: 39 The LORD is God both in heaven and on **e**,
6: 15 up against you and wipe you from the face of the **e**.
7: 6 Of all the people on **e**, the LORD your God has
7: 14 You will be blessed above all the nations of the **e**.
7: 24 you will erase their names from the face of the **e**.
10: 14 The highest heavens and the **e** and everything in it
11: 6 when the **e** opened up and swallowed them,
11: 21 so that as long as the sky remains above the **e**,
13: 7 live nearby or who come from the ends of the **e**.
14: 2 own special treasure from all the nations of the **e**.
28: 23 as bronze, and the **e** beneath will be as hard as iron.
28: 25 be an object of horror to all the kingdoms of the **e**.
28: 49 a distant nation against you from the end of the **e**,
28: 64 all the nations from one end of the **e** to the other.
30: 4 Though you are at the ends of the **e**, the LORD
30: 19 on heaven and **e** to witness the choice you make.
31: 28 and call heaven and **e** to witness against them.
32: 1 and I will speak! / Hear, O **e**, the words that I say!
32: 22 of the grave. / It devours the **e** and all its crops
33: 13 from the heavens, / and water from beneath the **e**;
33: 16 with the best gifts of the **e** and its fullness,
33: 17 distant nations, / driving them to the ends of the **e**.
Jos 2: 11 God of the heavens above and the **e** below.
3: 11 which belongs to the Lord of the whole **e**,
3: 13 the Ark of the LORD, the Lord of all the **e**.
4: 24 so that all the nations of the **e** might know the
7: 9 will surround us and wipe us off the face of the **e**.
23: 14 "Soon I will die, going the way of all the **e**.
Jdg 5: 4 across the fields of Edom, / the **e** trembled
1Sa 2: 8 in seats of honor. / "For all the **e** is the LORD's,
2: 10 the LORD judges throughout the **e**.
28: 13 "I see a god coming up out of the **e**," she said.
2Sa 7: 9 I will make your name famous throughout the **e**!
7: 23 What other nation on **e** is like Israel? What other
14: 7 and family will disappear from the face of the **e**."
22: 8 "Then the **e** quaked and trembled;
22: 16 and the foundations of the **e** were laid bare.
22: 43 I ground them as fine as the dust of the **e**; / I swept
23: 4 refreshing rains that bring tender grass from the **e**.'
1Ki 1: 40 and noisy that the **e** shook with the sound.
2: 2 "I am going where everyone on **e** must someday
8: 23 there is no God like you in all of heaven or **e**.
8: 27 "But will God really live on **e**? Why,
8: 43 Then all the people of the **e** will come to know
8: 53 of the **e** to be your own special possession."
8: 60 May people all over the **e** know that the LORD is
10: 23 and wiser than any other king in all the **e**.
18: 10 and kingdom on **e** from end to end to find you.
2Ki 5: 17 me to load two of my mules with **e** from this place,
19: 15 You alone are God of all the kingdoms of the **e**.
You alone created the heavens and the **e**.
19: 19 then all the kingdoms of the **e** will know that you
19: 32 their shields and build banks of **e** against its walls.
1Ch 1: 10 who was known across the **e** as a heroic warrior.
16: 23 Let the whole **e** sing to the LORD! / Each day
16: 30 Let all the **e** tremble before him. / The world is
16: 31 Let the heavens be glad, and let the **e** rejoice!
16: 33 the LORD! / For he is coming to judge the **e**.
17: 8 I will make your name famous throughout the **e**!
17: 21 What other nation on **e** is like Israel? What other

21:16 between heaven and **e** with his sword drawn,
29:11 Everything in the heavens and on **e** is yours,
29:15 Our days on **e** are like a shadow, gone so soon
2Ch 1:9 over a people as numerous as the dust of the **e**!
2:12 the God of Israel, who made the heavens and the **e**!
6:14 there is no God like you in all of heaven and **e**.
6:18 "But will God really live on **e** among people?
6:33 Then all the people of the **e** will come to know
9:22 and wiser than any other king in all the **e**.
16:9 The eyes of the LORD search the whole **e** in
20:6 You are ruler of all the kingdoms of the **e**. You are
32:13 before me have done to all the people of the **e**!
36:23 of heaven, has given me all the kingdoms of the **e**.
Ezr 1:2 of heaven, has given me all the kingdoms of the **e**.
5:11 'We are the servants of the God of heaven and **e**,
Ne 1:9 even if you are exiled to the ends of the **e**,
9:6 You made the **e** and the seas and everything in
Job 1:7 "I have been going back and forth across the **e**,
1:8 He is the finest man in all the **e**—a man of
2:2 "I have been going back and forth across the **e**,
2:3 He is the finest man in all the **e**—a man of
5:6 the soil, and trouble does not sprout from the **e**.
5:10 He gives rain for the **e**. He sends water for the
8:9 Our days on **e** are as transient as a shadow.
8:19 and others spring up from the **e** to replace it.
9:6 He shakes the **e** from its place, and its foundations
9:24 The whole **e** is in the hands of the wicked, and God
11:9 It is broader than the **e** and wider than the sea.
12:8 Speak to the **e**, and it will instruct you. Let the fish
12:15 If he holds back the rain, the **e** becomes a desert. If he releases the waters, they flood the **e**.
14:8 Though its roots have grown old in the **e** and its
16:18 "O **e**, do not conceal my blood. Let it cry out on
18:4 in anger, but will that cause the **e** to be abandoned?
18:17 memory of their existence will perish from the **e**.
19:25 and that he will stand upon the **e** at last.
20:4 that ever since people were first placed on the **e**,
20:27 his guilt, and the **e** will give testimony against him.
21:33 body is laid to rest and the **e** gives sweet repose.
24:18 "But they disappear from the **e** as quickly as foam
25:3 Does his light not shine on all the **e**?
25:4 and claim to be righteous? Who in all the **e** is pure?
26:7 sky over empty space and hangs the **e** on nothing.
28:2 They know how to dig iron from the **e** and smelt
28:3 darkest regions of the **e** as they search for ore.
28:4 They sink a mine shaft into the **e** far from where
28:5 Bread comes from the **e**, but below the surface the **e** is melted as by fire.
28:24 for he looks throughout the whole **e**, under all the
37:6 "He directs the snow to fall on the **e** and tells the
37:12 They do whatever he commands throughout the **e**.
37:13 He causes things to happen on **e**, either as a
38:4 were you when I laid the foundations of the **e**?
38:13 ever told the daylight to spread to the ends of the **e**,
38:14 For the features of the **e** take shape as the light
38:18 Do you realize the extent of the **e**? Tell me about it
38:33 the laws of the universe and how God rules the **e**?
39:14 She lays her eggs on top of the **e**, letting them be
39:21 It paws the **e** and rejoices in its strength. When it
41:33 There is nothing else so fearless anywhere on **e**.
Ps 2:2 The kings of the **e** prepare for battle; / the rulers
2:8 the ends of the **e** as your possession.
2:10 act wisely! / Be warned, you rulers of the **e**!
8:1 our Lord, the majesty of your name fills the **e**!
8:9 our Lord, the majesty of your name fills the **e**!
11:4 everything closely, / examining everyone on **e**.
12:1 The faithful have vanished from the **e**!
18:7 Then the **e** quaked and trembled; / the foundations
18:15 and the foundations of the **e** were laid bare.
19:4 yet their message has gone out to all the **e**,
21:10 You will wipe their children from the face of the **e**;
22:27 The whole **e** will acknowledge the LORD
22:29 Let the rich of the **e** feast and worship. / Let all
24:1 The **e** is the LORD's, and everything in it.
33:5 and good, / and his unfailing love fills the **e**.
33:14 From his throne he observes / all who live on the **e**.
34:16 do evil; / he will erase their memory from the **e**.
39:4 remind me how brief my time on **e** will be.
46:6 God thunders, / and the **e** melts!
46:9 and causes wars to end throughout the **e**.
47:2 is awesome. / He is the great King of all the **e**.
47:7 For God is the King over all the **e**. / Praise him
47:9 For all the kings of the **e** belong to God. / He is
48:2 in elevation— / the whole **e** rejoices to see it!
48:4 The kings of the **e** joined forces / and advanced
48:10 O God, / you will be praised to the ends of the **e**.
50:4 Heaven and **e** will be his witnesses / as he judges
57:5 May your glory shine over all the **e**.
57:11 May your glory shine over all the **e**.
58:11 surely there is a God who judges justly here on **e**."
61:2 From the ends of the **e**, / I will cry to you for help,
63:9 They will go down into the depths of the **e**.
65:5 our savior. / You are the hope of everyone on **e**,
65:8 Those who live at the ends of the **e** / stand in awe
65:9 You take care of the **e** and water it, / making it rich
65:10 leveling the ridges. / You soften the **e** with showers
66:1 Shout joyful praises to God, all the **e**!
66:4 Everything on **e** will worship you; / they will sing
67:2 May your ways be known throughout the **e**,
67:6 Then the **e** will yield its harvests, / and God,
68:8 the **e** trembled, and the heavens poured rain
68:29 The kings of the **e** are bringing tribute / to your
68:32 Sing to God, you kingdoms of the **e**. / Sing praises
69:34 Praise him, O heaven and **e**, / the seas and all that
71:20 life again / and lift me up from the depths of the **e**.
72:6 like the showers that water the **e**.
72:8 and from the Euphrates River to the ends of the **e**.
72:19 Let the whole **e** be filled with his glory. / Amen
73:9 and their words strut throughout the **e**.
73:25 but you? / I desire you more than anything on **e**.
74:2 And remember Jerusalem, your home here on **e**.
74:12 king from ages past, / bringing salvation to the **e**.
74:17 You set the boundaries of the **e**, / and you make
75:3 When the **e** quakes and its people live in turmoil,
75:6 For no one on **e**—from east or west, / or even from
76:8 the **e** trembled and stood silent before you.
76:9 O God, / and to rescue the oppressed of the **e**.
76:12 of princes / and is feared by the kings of the **e**.
77:18 lit up the world! / The **e** trembled and shook.
78:69 as solid and enduring as the **e** itself.
82:8 Rise up, O God, and judge the **e**, / for all the
83:18 alone are the Most High, supreme over all the **e**.
85:11 Truth springs up from the **e**, / and righteousness
89:11 The heavens are yours, and the **e** is yours;
89:27 him my firstborn son, / the mightiest king on **e**.
90:2 before you made the **e** and the world,
94:2 Arise, O judge of the **e**. / Sentence the proud to the
95:4 He owns the depths of the **e**, / and even the
96:1 the LORD! / Let the whole **e** sing to the LORD!
96:9 holy splendor. / Let all the **e** tremble before him.
96:11 Let the heavens be glad, and let the **e** rejoice!
96:13 LORD is coming! / He is coming to judge the **e**.
97:1 The LORD is king! Let the **e** rejoice!
97:4 out across the world. / The **e** sees and trembles.
97:5 before the LORD, / before the Lord of all the **e**.
97:9 For you, O LORD, are most high over all the **e**;
98:3 The whole **e** has seen the salvation of our God.
98:4 Shout to the LORD, all the **e**; / break out in praise
98:7 his praise! / Let the **e** and all living things join in.
98:9 For the LORD is coming to judge the **e**.
99:1 between the cherubim. / Let the whole **e** quake!
100:1 Shout with joy to the LORD, O **e**!
102:15 The kings of the **e** will tremble before his glory.
102:19 He looked to the **e** from heaven
102:25 In ages past you laid the foundation of the **e**,
103:11 is as great as the height of the heavens above the **e**.
103:15 Our days on **e** are like grass; / like wildflowers,
104:6 You clothed the **e** with floods of water, / water that
104:9 the seas, / so they would never again cover the **e**.
104:13 and you fill the **e** with the fruit of your labor.
104:14 You allow them to produce food from the **e**—
104:24 made them all. / The **e** is full of your creatures.
104:30 new life is born / to replenish all the living of the **e**.
104:32 The **e** trembles at his glance; / the mountains burst
104:35 Let all sinners vanish from the face of the **e**;
106:17 Because of this, the **e** opened up; / it swallowed
108:5 May your glory shine over all the **e**.
110:6 he will shatter heads / over the whole **e**.
113:6 Far below him are the heavens and the **e**.
114:7 Tremble, O **e**, at the presence of the Lord,
115:15 blessed by the LORD, / who made heaven and **e**.
115:16 but he has given the **e** to all humanity.
116:9 walk in the LORD's presence / as I live here on **e**!
117:1 you nations. / Praise him, all you people of the **e**.
119:19 I am but a foreigner here on **e**; / I need the
119:64 O LORD, the **e** is full of your unfailing love;
119:90 as enduring as the **e** you created.
119:119 All the wicked of the **e** are the scum you skim off;
121:2 the LORD, / who made the heavens and the **e**!
124:8 the LORD, / who made the heavens and the **e**.
134:3 May the LORD, who made heaven and **e**,
135:6 throughout all heaven and **e**, / and on the seas
135:7 He causes the clouds to rise over the **e**. / He sends
136:6 Give thanks to him who placed the **e** on the water.
138:4 Every king in all the **e** will give you thanks,
145:21 and everyone on **e** will bless his holy name
146:4 When their breathing stops, they return to the **e**,
146:6 He is the one who made heaven and **e**, / the sea,
147:8 the heavens with clouds, / provides rain for the **e**,
148:7 Praise the LORD from the **e**, / you creatures of
148:11 kings of the **e** and all people, / rulers and judges of the **e**,
148:13 his glory towers over the **e** and heaven!
Pr 3:19 By wisdom the LORD founded the **e**;
3:20 By his knowledge the deep fountains of the **e** burst
8:23 in ages past, at the very first, before the **e** began.
8:26 before he had made the **e** and fields and the first
8:28 when he established the deep fountains of the **e**.
11:31 If the righteous are rewarded here on **e**, how much
17:24 but a fool's eyes wander to the ends of the **e**.
25:3 the depth of the **e**, or all that goes on in the king's
30:14 They destroy the needy from the face of the **e**.
30:21 There are three things that make the **e** tremble—
30:24 There are four things on **e** that are small
30:29 There are three stately monarchs on the **e**—no,
Ecc 3:21 the spirit of animals goes downward into the **e**?
5:2 for he is in heaven, and you are only here on **e**.
7:20 There is not a single person in all the **e** who is
8:16 to observe everything that goes on all across the **e**.
9:6 They no longer have a part in anything here on **e**.
12:7 For then the dust will return to the **e**, and the spirit
Isa 1:2 Hear, O heavens! Listen, O **e**! This is what the
2:2 will become the most important place on **e**.
2:19 When the LORD rises to shake the **e**, his enemies
2:21 the glory of his majesty as he rises to shake the **e**.
5:26 He will whistle to those at the ends of the **e**,
6:3 The whole **e** is filled with his glory!"
11:9 so the **e** will be filled with people who know the
11:12 scattered people of Judah from the ends of the **e**.
13:13 the heavens, and the **e** will move from its place.
14:12 You have been thrown down to the **e**, you who
14:16 'Can this be the one who shook the **e**
14:26 I have a plan for the whole **e**, for my mighty power
23:11 He shakes the kingdoms of the **e**. He has spoken
24:1 The LORD is about to destroy the **e** and make it a
24:1 he is scattering the people over the face of the **e**.
24:3 The **e** will be completely emptied and looted.
24:4 The **e** dries up, the crops wither, the skies refuse to
24:5 The **e** suffers for the sins of its people, for they
24:6 Therefore, a curse consumes the **e** and its people.
24:13 Throughout the **e** the story is the same—
24:16 as they sing to the LORD from the ends of the **e**.
24:17 and snares will be your lot, you people of the **e**.
24:19 The **e** has broken down and has utterly collapsed.
24:20 The **e** staggers like a drunkard. It trembles like a
24:21 and the proud rulers of the nations on **e**.
25:7 the shadow of death that hangs over the **e**.
26:9 for God. / For only when you come to judge the **e**
26:18 the world; / no one has been born to populate the **e**.
26:19 Those who sleep in the **e** / will rise up and sing for
26:21 heaven to punish the people of the **e** for their sins.
26:21 The **e** will no longer hide those who have been
27:6 and blossom and fill the whole **e** with her fruit!
29:4 Your voice will whisper like a ghost from the **e**
34:1 Come here and listen, O nations of the **e**.
37:16 You alone are God of all the kingdoms of the **e**. You alone created the heavens and the **e**.
37:20 then all the kingdoms of the **e** will know that you
37:33 their shields and build banks of **e** against its walls.
40:12 Who else knows the weight of the **e** or has
40:22 It is God who sits above the circle of the **e**.
40:28 is the everlasting God, the Creator of all the **e**?
41:9 I have called you back from the ends of the **e**
42:4 and righteousness prevail throughout the **e**.
42:5 He created the **e** and everything in it. He gives
42:10 Sing his praises from the ends of the **e**! / Sing,
43:6 back to Israel from the distant corners of the **e**.
44:23 Shout, O **e**! Break forth into song, O mountains
44:24 By myself I made the **e** and everything in it.
45:8 Let the **e** open wide so salvation and righteousness
45:12 I am the one who made the **e** and created people to
45:18 and he created the heavens and **e** and put
48:13 It was my hand that laid the foundations of the **e**.
48:20 Shout to the ends of the **e** that the LORD has
49:6 you will bring my salvation to the ends of the **e**."
49:13 Sing for joy, O heavens! Rejoice, O **e**! Burst into
49:23 They will bow to the **e** before you and lick the dust
51:6 the skies above, and gaze down on the **e** beneath.
51:6 and the **e** will wear out like a piece of clothing.
51:6 The people of the **e** will die like flies, but my
51:13 who put the stars in the sky and established the **e**.
51:16 I set all the stars in space and established the **e**.
52:10 The ends of the **e** will see the salvation of our God.
54:5 the Holy One of Israel, the God of all the **e**.
54:9 that I would never again let a flood cover the **e**.
55:9 For just as the heavens are higher than the **e**,
55:10 the heavens and stay on the ground to water the **e**.
60:2 as black as night will cover all the nations of the **e**,
62:7 Jerusalem the object of praise throughout the **e**.
65:17 I am creating new heavens and a new **e**—
66:1 "Heaven is my throne, and the **e** is my footstool.
66:2 My hands have made both heaven and **e**, and they
66:22 "As surely as my new heavens and **e** will remain,
Jer 4:23 I looked at the **e**, and it was empty and formless.
4:28 The **e** will mourn, the heavens will be draped in
6:19 Listen, all the **e**! I will bring disaster upon my
10:7 Among all the wise people of the **e** and in all the
10:10 The whole **e** trembles at his anger.
10:11 who did not make the heavens and **e**, will vanish from the **e**."
10:12 But God made the **e** by his power, / and he
10:13 He causes the clouds to rise over the **e**.
15:4 an object of horror to all the kingdoms of the **e**.
19:8 I will wipe Jerusalem from the face of the **e**,
22:29 O **e**, **e**, **e**! Listen to this message from the
23:24 Am I not everywhere in all the heavens and **e**?"
24:9 an object of horror and evil to every nation on **e**.
25:29 I will call for war against all the nations of the **e**.
25:30 He will shout against everyone on the **e**,
25:31 His cry of judgment will reach the ends of the **e**,
25:31 He will judge all the people of the **e**,
25:32 is rising from the most distant corners of the **e**!"
25:33 will fill the **e** from one end to the other.
26:6 an object of cursing in every nation on **e**.' "
27:5 By my great power I have made the **e** and all its
31:8 the north and from the distant corners of the **e**.
31:37 and the foundation of the **e** cannot be explored,
32:17 have made the heavens and **e** by your great power.
33:2 "The LORD, the Maker of the heavens and **e**—
33:9 glory, and honor before all the nations of the **e**!
33:25 change my laws of night and day, of **e** and sky.
34:17 be considered a disgrace by all the nations of the **e**.
44:8 of cursing and mockery for all the nations of the **e**.
46:8 boasting that it will cover the **e** like a flood,
46:12 The **e** is filled with your cries of despair.
49:21 The **e** will shake with the noise of Edom's fall,
50:23 Babylon, the mightiest hammer in all the **e**,
50:46 The **e** will shake with the noise of Babylon's fall,
51:7 a cup from which he made the whole **e** drink
51:15 He made the **e** by his power, / and he preserves it
51:16 He causes the clouds to rise over the **e**.
51:25 "Look, O mighty mountain, destroyer of the **e**!
51:41 is fallen—great Babylon, praised throughout the **e**!
51:48 The heavens and **e** will rejoice, for out of the north
La 2:15 in All the World,' and 'Joy of All the **E**'?"
4:12 Not a king in all the **e**—no one in all the world—
4:20 we could hold our own against any nation on **e**!
Eze 5:10 the few who survive to the far reaches of the **e**.
20:15 with milk and honey, the most beautiful place on **e**.
26:20 Your city will lie in ruins, buried beneath the **e**,
27:33 Kings at the ends of the **e** / were enriched by your

28:17 So I threw you to the **e** and exposed you to the
32: 4 and the wild animals of the whole **e** will gorge
32: 6 I will drench the **e** with your gushing blood all the
34: 6 the mountains and hills, across the face of the **e**,
38:20 cliffs will crumble; walls will fall to the **e**.
Da 2:35 became a great mountain that covered the whole **e**.
4:10 I dreamed. I saw a large tree in the middle of the **e**.
4:22 up to heaven, and your rule to the ends of the **e**.
4:35 All the people of the **e** / are nothing compared to
4:35 and with those who live on **e**. / No one can stop
6:27 and wonders / in the heavens and on **e**.
7:17 represent four kingdoms that will arise from the **e**.
7:23 beast is the fourth world power that will rule the **e**.
8: 8 horns pointing in the four directions of the **e**.
Hos 2:21 which will pour down water on the **e** in answer to
2:22 Then the **e** will answer the thirsty cries of the
Joel 2:10 The **e** quakes as they advance, and the heavens
2:30 will cause wonders in the heavens and on the **e**—
3:16 and the **e** and heavens will begin to shake.
Am 3: 2 "From among all the families on the **e**, I chose you
8: 8 The **e** will tremble for your deeds, and everyone
8: 9 down at noon and darken the **e** while it is still day.
9: 6 are in the heavens, while its foundation is on the **e**.
9: 8 I will uproot it and scatter its people across the **e**.
Mic 1: 3 He leaves his throne in heaven and comes to **e**,
4: 1 will become the most important place on **e**.
4:13 acquired as offerings to me, the Lord of all the **e**."
7: 2 not one fair-minded person is left on the **e**.
Na 1: 5 the **e** trembles, and its people are destroyed.
3: 5 so all the **e** will see your nakedness and shame.
3:17 fly away when the sun comes up to warm the **e**,
Hab 1:10 They simply pile ramps of **e** against their walls
2:14 For the time will come when all the **e** will be filled,
2:20 holy Temple. Let all the **e** be silent before him."
3: 3 fills the heavens, and the **e** is filled with his praise!
3: 6 When he stops, the **e** shakes. When he looks,
3: 9 of power! You split open the **e** with flowing rivers!
Zep 1:18 will make a terrifying end of all the people on **e**.
3: 8 decision to gather together the kingdoms of the **e**
3: 8 All the **e** will be devoured by the fire of my
3:20 name of distinction among all the nations of the **e**.
Hag 1:10 withheld the dew and the **e** has withheld its crops.
2: 6 while I will again shake the heavens and the **e**.
2:21 that I am about to shake the heavens and the **e**.
Zec 1:10 the ones the LORD has sent out to patrol the **e**."
1:11 "We have patrolled the **e**, and the whole **e** is at peace."
4:14 anointed ones who assist the Lord of all the **e**."
6: 5 of heaven who stand before the Lord of all the **e**.
6: 7 to be off, to patrol back and forth across the **e**.
6: 7 And the LORD said, "Go and patrol the **e**!"
8:12 The **e** will produce its crops, and the sky will
9:10 and from the Euphrates River to the ends of the **e**.
12: 1 out the heavens, laid the foundations of the **e**,
14: 9 And the LORD will be king over all the **e**.
Mt 5: 5 and lowly, / for the whole **e** will belong to them.
5:13 "You are the salt of the **e**. But what good is salt if
5:18 I assure you, until heaven and **e** disappear,
5:35 And if you say, 'By the **e**!' it is a sacred vow because the **e** is his footstool.
6:10 May your will be done here on **e**, / just as it is in
6:19 "Don't store up treasures here on **e**, where they
9: 6 of Man, have the authority on **e** to forgive sins."
10:32 "If anyone acknowledges me publicly here on **e**,
10:33 But if anyone denies me here on **e**, I will deny that
10:34 imagine that I came to bring peace to the **e**!
11:25 "O Father, Lord of heaven and **e**, thank you for
12:40 will be in the heart of the **e** for three days and three
16:19 Whatever you lock on **e** will be locked in heaven,
16:19 and whatever you open on **e** will be opened in
18:18 Whatever you prohibit on **e** is prohibited in
18:18 and whatever you allow on **e** is allowed in heaven.
18:19 If two of you agree down here on **e** concerning
23: 9 And don't address anyone here on **e** as 'Father,'
24:30 be deep mourning among all the nations of the **e**.
24:31 his chosen ones from the farthest ends of the **e**
24:35 Heaven and **e** will disappear, but my words will
25:25 lose your money, so I hid it in the **e** and here it is.'
27:51 from top to bottom. The **e** shook, rocks split apart,
28:18 been given complete authority in heaven and on **e**.
Mk 2:10 of Man, have the authority on **e** to forgive sins."
4:28 because the **e** produces crops on its own. First a
13:27 from the farthest ends of the **e** and heaven.
13:31 Heaven and **e** will disappear, but my words will
Lk 2:14 and peace on **e** to all whom God favors."
5:24 of Man, have the authority on **e** to forgive sins."
10:21 and said, "O Father, Lord of heaven and **e**,
12: 8 If anyone acknowledges me publicly here on **e**,
12: 9 But if anyone denies me here on **e**, I will deny that
12:49 "I have come to bring fire to the **e**, and I wish that
12:51 Do you think I have come to bring peace to the **e**?
12:56 You know how to interpret the appearance of the **e**
16:17 is stronger and more permanent than heaven and **e**.
20:34 Jesus replied, "Marriage is for people here on **e**.
21:25 And down here on **e** the nations will be in turmoil,
21:26 of the fearful fate they see coming upon the **e**,
21:33 Heaven and **e** will disappear, but my words will
21:35 that day will come upon everyone living on the **e**.
Jn 1:14 became human and lived here on **e** among us.
3:12 when I tell you about things that happen here on **e**,
3:13 have come to **e** and will return to heaven again.
3:31 I am of the **e**, and my understanding is limited to the things of **e**,
8:33 "We have never been slaves to anyone on **e**.
16:33 Here on **e** you will have many trials and sorrows.
17: 2 given him authority over everyone in all the **e**.
17: 3 true God, and Jesus Christ, the one you sent to **e**.
17: 4 I brought glory to you here on **e** by doing
Ac 1: 8 in Samaria, and to the ends of the **e**."
2:19 and signs on the **e** below— / blood and fire
3:25 'Through your descendants all the families on **e**
4:24 Sovereign Lord, Creator of heaven and **e**, the sea,
4:26 The kings of the **e** prepared for battle; / the rulers
7:49 'Heaven is my throne, / and the **e** is my footstool.
7:50 Didn't I make everything in heaven and **e**?'
8:33 For his life was taken from the **e**."
13:47 bring salvation to the farthest corners of the **e**.' "
14:15 who made heaven and **e**, the sea, and everything in
17:24 Since he is Lord of heaven and **e**, he doesn't live in
17:26 he created all the nations throughout the whole **e**.
Ro 1:20 people have seen the **e** and sky and all that God
4:13 that God's promise to give the whole **e** to Abraham
8:20 everything on **e** was subjected to God's curse.
9:17 so that my fame might spread throughout the **e**."
9:28 For the Lord will carry out his sentence upon the **e**
15:11 praise him, all you people of the **e**."
1Co 6: 3 able to resolve ordinary disagreements here on **e**.
8: 5 and many lords, both in heaven and on **e**.
10:26 For "the **e** is the Lord's, and everything in it."
13: 1 language in heaven or on **e** but didn't love others,
15:40 bodies in the heavens, and there are bodies on **e**.
15:47 was made from the dust of the **e**, while Christ,
15:49 Just as we are now like Adam, the man of the **e**,
Eph 1:10 of Christ—everything in heaven and on **e**.
3:15 the Creator of everything in heaven and on **e**.
Php 2:10 will bow, in heaven and on **e** and under the **e**,
3:19 and all they think about is this life here on **e**.
Col 1:16 whom God created everything in heaven and **e**.
1:20 and on **e** by means of his blood on the cross.
3: 2 Do not think only about things down here on **e**.
1Th 4:17 and remain on the **e** will be caught up in the clouds
Heb 1:10 in the beginning you laid the foundation of the **e**,
5: 7 While Jesus was here on **e**, he offered prayers
8: 4 If he were here on **e**, he would not even be a priest,
9: 1 regulations for worship and a sacred tent here on **e**.
11:13 no more than foreigners and nomads here on **e**.
12:26 spoke from Mount Sinai his voice shook the **e**,
12:26 "Once again I will shake not only the **e**
12:27 This means that the things on **e** will be shaken,
13:10 the priests in the Temple on **e** have no right to eat.
Jas 5: 5 You have spent your years on **e** in luxury,
5:12 never take an oath, by heaven or **e** or anything else.
1Pe 1:17 of him during your time as foreigners here on **e**.
1:20 these final days, he was sent to the **e** for all to see.
2Pe 1:14 shown me that my days here on **e** are numbered
2: 6 of ashes and swept them off the face of the **e**.
3: 5 and he brought the **e** up from the water
3: 7 and the **e** will be consumed by fire on the day of
3:10 and the **e** and everything on it will be exposed to
3:13 to the new heavens and new **e** he has promised,
2Jn 1: 7 They do not believe that Jesus Christ came to **e** in a
Rev 1: 7 And all the nations of the **e** will weep because of
5: 3 But no one in heaven or on **e** or under the **e** was able to open the scroll
5: 6 of God that are sent out into every part of the **e**.
5:10 and his priests. / And they will reign on the **e**."
5:13 and on **e** and under the **e** and in the sea.
6: 4 and the authority to remove peace from the **e**.
6: 8 They were given authority over one-fourth of the **e**,
6:13 Then the stars of the sky fell to the **e** like green figs
6:15 Then the kings of the **e**, the rulers, the generals,
7: 1 four angels standing at the four corners of the **e**,
7: 1 back the four winds from blowing upon the **e**.
8: 5 fire from the altar and threw it down upon the **e**;
8: 7 mixed with blood were thrown down upon the **e**, and one-third of the **e** was set on fire.
9: 1 and I saw a star that had fallen to **e** from the sky,
9: 3 came from the smoke and descended on the **e**,
9:15 turned loose to kill one-third of all the people on **e**.
9:18 One-third of all the people on **e** were killed by
10: 6 the **e** and everything in it, and the sea
11: 4 lampstands that stand before the Lord of all the **e**.
11: 6 and to send every kind of plague upon the **e** as
11:18 destroy all who have caused destruction on the **e**."
12: 4 one-third of the stars, which he threw to the **e**.
12: 9 was thrown down to the **e** with all his angels.
12:10 For the Accuser has been thrown down to **e**—
12:12 rejoice! But terror will come on the **e** and the sea.
12:13 realized that he had been thrown down to the **e**,
12:16 But the **e** helped her by opening its mouth
13:11 Then I saw another beast come up out of the **e**.
13:12 And he required all the **e** and those who belong to
13:13 such as making fire flash down to **e** from heaven
14: 3 those 144,000 who had been redeemed from the **e**.
14: 4 the people on the **e** as a special offering to God
14: 7 Worship him who made heaven and **e**, the sea,
14:15 come for you to harvest; the crop is ripe on the **e**."
14:16 sitting on the cloud swung his sickle over the **e**, and the whole **e** was harvested.
14:18 the clusters of grapes from the vines of the **e**,
14:19 So the angel swung his sickle on the **e** and loaded
16: 1 out the seven bowls of God's wrath on the **e**."
16: 2 left the Temple and poured out his bowl over the **e**,
16: 6 and their blood was poured out on the **e**.
17:18 the great city that rules over the kings of the **e**."
18: 1 and the **e** grew bright with his splendor.
19: 2 prostitute who corrupted the **e** with her immorality,
19:19 Then I saw the beast gathering the kings of the **e**
20: 8 to deceive the nations from every corner of the **e**,
20: 9 them as they went up on the broad plain of the **e**
20:11 The **e** and sky fled from his presence, but they
21: 1 Then I saw a new heaven and a new **e**, for the old heaven and the old **e** had disappeared.
21:24 The nations of the **e** will walk in its light,

EARTH'S (2) [EARTH]

Ps 24: 2 For he laid the **e** foundation on the seas / and built
Pr 8:29 And when he marked off the **e** foundations,

EARTHLY (27) [EARTH]

2Ch 12: 8 better it is to serve me than to serve **e** rulers."
Ps 17:14 from those whose only concern is **e** gain.
Ecc 9: 9 God gives you is your reward for all your **e** toil.
Mk 9: 3 far whiter than any **e** process could ever make it.
Lk 12:21 a person is a fool to store up **e** wealth but not have
Jn 18:36 Then Jesus answered, "I am not an **e** king. If I
1Co 7:33 He has to think about his **e** responsibilities
7:34 must be concerned about her **e** responsibilities
15:40 bodies is different from the beauty of the **e** bodies.
15:42 Our **e** bodies, which die and decay, will be
15:48 Every human being has an **e** body just like
15:53 For our perishable **e** bodies must be transformed
15:54 when our perishable **e** bodies have been
2Co 1:12 on God's grace, not on our own **e** wisdom.
5: 1 For we know that when this **e** tent we live in is
Gal 2:20 So I live my life in this **e** body by trusting in the
Eph 6: 5 obey your **e** masters with deep respect and fear.
Col 3: 5 put to death the sinful, **e** things lurking within you.
3:22 You slaves must obey your **e** masters in everything
Heb 9:23 That is why the **e** tent and everything in it—
9:24 He did not go into the **e** place of worship, for that
9:25 like the **e** high priest who enters the Most Holy
12: 9 Since we respect our **e** fathers who disciplined us,
12:10 For our **e** fathers disciplined us for a few years,
12:25 the **e** messenger, how terrible our danger if we
Jas 3:15 Such things are **e**, unspiritual, and motivated by the
1Pe 1:23 Your new life did not come from your **e** parents

EARTHQUAKE (17) [QUAKE]

Ex 19:18 and the whole mountain shook with a violent **e**.
1Sa 14:15 And just then an **e** struck, and everyone was
1Ki 19:11 After the wind there was an **e**, but the LORD was not in the **e**.
19:12 And after the **e** there was a fire, but the LORD
Isa 29: 6 against them with thunder and **e** and great noise,
Am 1: 1 this message in visions two years before the **e**,
Zec 14: 5 you will flee as you did from the **e** in the days of
Mt 27:54 soldiers at the crucifixion were terrified by the **e**
28: 2 Suddenly there was a great **e**, because an angel of
Ac 16:26 Suddenly, there was a great **e**, and the prison was
Rev 6:12 Lamb broke the sixth seal, and there was a great **e**.
8: 5 lightning flashed, and there was a terrible **e**.
11:13 And in the same hour there was a terrible **e** that
11:13 Seven thousand people died in that **e**.
11:19 and the world was shaken by a mighty **e**.
16:18 And there was an **e** greater than ever before in

EARTHQUAKES (4) [QUAKE]

Ps 46: 2 So we will not fear, even if **e** come
Mt 24: 7 will be famines and **e** in many parts of the world.
Mk 13: 8 and there will be **e** in many parts of the world,
Lk 21:11 There will be great **e**, and there will be famines

EASE (12) [EASED, EASES, EASIER, EASILY, EASY]

Ge 41:16 will tell you what it means and will set you at **e**."
Job 3:18 Even prisoners are at **e** in death, with no guards to
12: 5 People who are at **e** mock those in trouble.
Ps 73:12 enjoying a life of **e** while their riches multiply.
Isa 32: 9 Listen, you women who lie around in lazy **e**.
32:11 Tremble, you women of **e**; throw off your
47: 8 living at **e** and feeling secure,
Hos 10:11 break up the hard ground; their days of **e** are gone.
Mt 23: 4 and never lift a finger to help **e** the burden.
Lk 11:46 and you never lift a finger to help **e** the burden.
21:34 Don't let me find you living in careless **e**
2Co 7:13 the way you welcomed him and set his mind at **e**.

EASED (1) [EASE]

Jnh 4: 6 This **e** some of his discomfort, and Jonah was very

EASES (1) [EASE]

Ps 41: 3 they are sick / and **e** their pain and discomfort.

EASIER (8) [EASE]

Ex 18:22 help you carry the load, making the task **e** for you.
2Ch 32:18 to terrify them so it would be **e** to capture the city.
Mt 9: 5 Is it **e** to say, 'Your sins are forgiven' or 'Get up
19:24 it is **e** for a camel to go through the eye of a needle
Mk 2: 9 Is it **e** to say to the paralyzed man, 'Your sins are
10:25 It is **e** for a camel to go through the eye of a needle
Lk 5:23 Is it **e** to say, 'Your sins are forgiven' or 'Get up
18:25 It is **e** for a camel to go through the eye of a needle

EASILY (21) [EASE]

Ge 27:11 Jacob replied. "He won't be fooled that **e**.
Jdg 14: 6 He did it as **e** as if it were a young goat. But he
1Ki 20:23 they won. But we can beat them **e** on the plains.
2Ki 19:26 as the grass, / as **e** trampled as tender green shoots.
19:26 sprouting on a housetop, / **e** scorched by the sun.
Job 4:19 is dust, and they are crushed as **e** as moths.
13: 9 Or do you think you can fool him as **e** as you fool
Ps 49: 8 Redemption does not come so **e**, / for no one can
Pr 14: 6 but knowledge comes **e** to those with
26:21 A quarrelsome person starts fights as **e** as hot
28: 2 moral rot within a nation, its government topples **e**.
Ecc 4:12 for a triple-braided cord is not **e** broken.

Isa 11:15 divide it into seven streams that can e be crossed.
28:28 Bread grain is e crushed, so he doesn't keep on
37:27 as the grass, / as e trampled as tender green shoots.
37:27 sprouting on a housetop, / e scorched by the sun.
Eze 17: 9 I will pull it out e enough—it won't take a strong
Joel 2:13 he is gracious and merciful. He is not e angered.
Jnh 4: 2 I knew how e you could cancel your plans for
2Th 2: 2 Please don't be so e shaken and troubled by those
Heb 12: 1 especially the sin that so e hinders our progress.

EAST (201) [EASTERN, EASTWARD, NORTHEAST, NORTHEASTER, SOUTHEAST]

EAST SIDE (27) Ex 38:14; Lev 1:16; Nu 2:3; 10:5; 32:19,22; 34:11,15; 35:14; Jos 1:14,15; 13:8; 14:3; 17:1; 18:7; 20:8; 22:4; 24:8; Jdg 21:19; 1Ch 9:18; 12:37; 26:32; 2Ch 5:12; Eze 42:16; 43:17; 45:7; Jnh 4:5

EAST WIND (14) Ge 41:6,23; Ex 10:13,13; 14:21; Job 27:21; 38:24; Ps 48:7; 78:26; Jer 18:17; Eze 17:10; Hos 12:1; 13:15; Jnh 4:8

OF THE EAST (10) Ge 29:1; Jdg 6:3,33; 7:12; 8:10; 1Ki 4:30; Ne 3:29; Job 38:24; Eze 40:21; 47:2

Ge 2: 8 in the e, and there he placed the man he had
2:14 is the Tigris, which flows to the e of Asshur.
3:24 stationed mighty angelic beings to the e of Eden.
4:16 and settled in the land of Nod, e of Eden.
12: 8 between Bethel on the west and Ai on the e.
13:11 for himself—the Jordan Valley to the e of them.
25: 6 sons of his concubines and sent them off to the e,
25:18 which is e of Egypt in the direction of Asshur.
28:14 They will cover the land from e to west and from
29: 1 hurried on, finally arriving in the land of the e.
41: 6 these were shriveled and withered by the e wind.
41:23 seven withered heads, shriveled by the e wind.
Ex 10:13 and the LORD caused an e wind to blow all that
10:13 the e wind had brought the locusts.
14:21 up a path through the water with a strong e wind.
27:13 The e end will also be 75 feet long.
27:14 The courtyard entrance will be on the e end,
38:13 The e end was also 75 feet wide.
38:14 The courtyard entrance was on the e side,
Lev 1:16 and throw them to the e side of the altar among the
Nu 2: 3[-4] the sunrise on the e side of the Tabernacle,
3:38 The area in front of the Tabernacle in the e toward
10: 5 the tribes on the e side of the Tabernacle will break
22: 1 plains of Moab and camped e of the Jordan River,
27:12 "Climb to the top of the mountains e of the river,
32:19 We would rather live here on the e side where we
32:22 And the land on the e side of the Jordan will be
33:47 and camped in the mountains e of the river,
33:48 They left the mountains e of the river and camped
34: 3 The southern boundary will begin on the e at the
34:11 then down to Riblah on the e side of Ain.
34:15 on the e side of the Jordan River, across from
35: 5 e, south, west, north—with the town at the center.
35:14 three on the e side of the Jordan River and three on
Dt 1: 1 they were in the wilderness e of the Jordan River.
1: 5 were in the land of Moab e of the Jordan River.
3: 8 of the two Amorite kings e of the Jordan River—
3:17 to the Dead Sea, with the slopes of Pisgah on the e.
3:18 to the tribes that will live e of the Jordan:
4:41 Then Moses set apart three cities of refuge e of the
4:46 and as they camped in the valley near Beth-peor e
4:47 of Bashan—the two Amorite kings e of the Jordan.
11:24 and from the Euphrates River in the e to the
32:49 "Go to Moab, to the mountains e of the river,
Jos 1: 4 from the Euphrates River on the e to the
1:14 and cattle may remain here on the e side of the
1:15 then may you settle here on the e side of the Jordan
2:10 the two Amorite kings e of the Jordan River,
4:19 from Egypt. They camped at Gilgal, e of Jericho.
7: 2 spy out the city of Ai, e of Bethel, near Beth-aven.
9:10 to the two Amorite kings e of the Jordan River—
11: 3 the kings of Canaan, both e and west; the kings of
12: 1 These are the kings e of the Jordan River who had
12: 1 and included all the land e of the Jordan Valley.
12: 5 Salecah in the north and to all of Bashan in the e,
13: 5 and all of the Lebanon mountain area to the e,
13: 8 their inheritance on the e side of the Jordan,
13:32 of Moab, across the Jordan River, e of Jericho.
14: 3 and a half tribes on the e side of the Jordan River.
16: 1 e of the waters of Jericho, through the wilderness
16: 6 began at the Mediterranean, ran e past Micmethath,
16: 6 then curved eastward past Taanath-shiloh to the e
17: 1 and Bashan on the e side of the Jordan had already
17: 7 of Asher to Micmethath, which is e of Shechem.
17:10 of Asher, and to the e was the territory of Issachar.
18: 7 gave them on the e side of the Jordan River."
19:11 and proceeding to the brook e of Jokneam.
19:12 the boundary line went e from Sarid to the border
19:13 Then it continued e to Gath-hepher, Eth-kazin,
19:27 turned e toward Beth-dagon, and ran as far as
19:34 Asher on the west, and the Jordan River on the e.
20: 8 On the e side of the Jordan River, across from
22: 4 gave you on the e side of the Jordan River.
22: 7 to the half-tribe of Manasseh e of the Jordan.
24: 8 land of the Amorites on the e side of the Jordan.
Jdg 5:17 Gilead remained e of the Jordan. / And Dan,
6: 3 and the people of the e would attack Israel,
6:33 and the people of the e formed an alliance against
7:12 and the people of the e had settled in the valley like
8:10 all that remained of the allied armies of the e—
8:11 Gideon circled around by the caravan route e of
10: 8 e of the Jordan River in the land of the Amorites
20:43 them down, finally overtaking them e of Gibeah.
21:19 along the e side of the road that goes from Bethel
1Sa 13: 5 They camped at Micmash e of Beth-aven.
15: 7 from Havilah all the way to Shur, e of Egypt.
1Ki 4:30 wisdom exceeded that of all the wise men of the E
7:25 faced west, three faced south, and three faced e.
11: 7 On the Mount of Olives, e of Jerusalem, he even
17: 3 "Go to the e and hide by Kerith Brook at a place e of where it
2Ki 10:33 e of the Jordan River, including all of Gilead,
23:13 The king also desecrated the pagan shrines e of
1Ch 4:39 in the e part of the valley, seeking pastureland for
5:11 of Gad, who were spread as far e as Salecah.
6:62 from the Bashan area of Manasseh, e of the Jordan.
6:78 of Reuben, e of the Jordan River opposite Jericho,
7:28 Naaran to the e, Gezer and its villages to the west,
9:18 they were responsible for the King's Gate on the e
9:24 on all four sides—e, west, north, and south.
12:15 all the people living in the lowlands on both the e
12:37 From the e side of the Jordan River—
26:14 The responsibility for the e gate went to
26:17 Six Levites were assigned each day to the e gate,
26:32 King David sent them to the e side of the Jordan
27:21 Manasseh (e) | Iddo son of Zechariah
2Ch 4: 4 faced west, three faced south, and three faced e.
5:12 and stood at the e side of the altar playing cymbals,
29: 4 and Levites to meet him at the courtyard e of the
31:14 the Levite, who was the gatekeeper at the E Gate,
Ne 3:26 the wall as far as the Water Gate toward the e
3:29 son of Shecaniah, the gatekeeper of the E Gate.
12:37 and then proceeded to the Water Gate on the e.
Job 18:20 appalled at their fate; people in the e are horrified.
23: 8 "I go e, but he is not there. I go west, but I cannot
27:21 The e wind carries them away, and they are gone.
38:12 to appear and caused the dawn to rise in the e?
38:24 origin of light? Where is the home of the e wind?
Ps 48: 7 of Tarshish / being shattered by a powerful e wind.
50: 1 he has summoned all humanity from e to west!
75: 6 For no one on earth—from e or west, / or even
78:26 He released the e wind in the heavens / and guided
80:11 our limbs e to the Euphrates River.
89:25 to the Tigris and Euphrates rivers in the e.
103:12 as far away from us as the e is from the west.
107: 3 from e and west, from north and south.
113: 3 Everywhere—from e to west— / praise the name
Isa 2: 6 with foreigners from the E who practice magic
9:12 along with Arameans from the e and Philistines
11:14 they will attack and plunder the nations to the e.
27: 8 land as though blown away in a storm from the e.
27:12 from the Euphrates River in the e to the brook of
41: 2 "Who has stirred up this king from the e,
41:25 I have stirred up a leader from the north and e.
43: 5 will gather you and your children from e and west
45: 6 so all the world from e to west will know there is
46:11 I will call a swift bird of prey from the e—a leader
Jer 2:10 to the land of Cyprus; go e to the land of Kedar.
18:17 before their enemies as the e wind scatters dust.
22:20 Search for them in the regions e of the river.
31:40 and all the fields out to the Kidron Valley on the e
49:28 against Kedar! Blot out the warriors from the E!
Eze 7: 2 Wherever you look—e, west, north, or south—
10:19 the cherubim flew with their wheels to the e gate
11: 1 and brought me over to the e gateway of the
11:23 the city and stopped above the mountain to the e.
17:10 it will wither away completely when the e wind
26: 2 She who controlled the rich trade routes to the e
39:11 in the Valley of the Travelers, e of the Dead Sea.
40:20 a gateway on the north just like the one on the e,
40:21 All the measurements matched those of the e
40:22 were identical to those in the e gateway.
40:23 Here on the north side, just as on the e, there was
40:32 Then he took me to the e gateway leading to the
41:14 The inner courtyard to the e of the Temple was
42: 9 from the outer courtyard to these rooms from the e.
42:12 and another on the e at the end of the interior
42:15 he led me out through the e gateway to measure
42:16 He measured the e side; it was 875 feet long.
43: 1 the man brought me back around to the e gateway.
43: 2 the glory of the God of Israel appeared from the e.
43: 4 came into the Temple through the e gateway.
43:17 There are steps going up the e side of the altar."
44: 1 Then the man brought me back to the e gateway in
45: 7 One section will share a border with the e side of
46: 1 The e gateway of the inner wall will be closed
46:12 the e gateway to the inner courtyard will be opened
47: 2 out through the south side of the e gateway.
47: 8 "This river flows e through the desert into the
48: 1 all the way across the land of Israel from e to west.
48: 2 south of Dan's and also extends from e to west.
48: 3 south of Asher's, also extending from e to west.
48: 4 and its territory also extends from e to west.
48: 7 all of whose boundaries extend from e to west.
48: 8 It will be 8-1/3 miles wide and will extend as far e
48:18 be a farming area that stretches 3-1/3 miles to the e
48:21 to the e and to the west of the sacred lands
48:23 across the entire land of Israel from e to west.
48:24 also extending across the land from e to west.
48:26 which also extends across the land from e to west.
48:27 south of Zebulun with the same borders to the e
48:32 On the e wall, also 1-1/2 miles long, the gates will
Da 8: 9 It extended toward the south and the e and toward
11:44 "But then news from the e and the north will
Hos 12: 1 the wind; they chase after the e wind all day long.
13:15 most fruitful of all his brothers, but the e wind—
Am 5:27 to a land e of Damascus," says the LORD,
Jnh 4: 5 Then Jonah went out to the e side of the city
4: 8 God sent a scorching e wind to blow on Jonah.
Zec 8: 7 can be sure that I will rescue my people from the e
14: 4 Mount of Olives, which faces Jerusalem on the e.
14: 4 making a wide valley running from e to west,
Mt 4:25 all over Judea, and from e of the Jordan River.
19: 1 of Judea and into the area e of the Jordan River.
Mk 3: 8 Jerusalem, Idumea, from e of the Jordan River,
10: 1 of Judea and into the area e of the Jordan River.
16: S Afterward Jesus himself sent them out from e to
Jn 1:28 a village e of the Jordan River, where John was
Rev 7: 2 And I saw another angel coming from the e,
16:12 so that the kings from the e could march their
21:13 three gates on each side—e, north, south, and west.

EASTER [KJV] See PASSOVER

EASTERN (28) [EAST]

Ge 10:30 extending from Mesha toward the e hills of Sephar.
Nu 21:11 in the wilderness on the e border of Moab.
23: 7 the king of Moab brought me from the e hills.
34:10 "The e boundary will start at Hazar-enan and run
34:11 From there the boundary will run down along the e
Dt 3:17 including the Jordan River and its e banks,
4:49 And they took the e bank of the Jordan Valley as
Jos 15: 5 The e boundary extended along the Dead Sea to
16: 5 The e boundary of their inheritance began at
18:20 The e boundary was the Jordan River. This was the
Jdg 11:18 They traveled along Moab's e border and camped
2Ki 13:17 "Open that e window," and he opened it.
1Ch 5:10 Hagrite settlements all along the e edge of Gilead.
Ps 72:10 The e kings of Sheba and Seba / will bring him
Isa 24:15 In e lands, give glory to the LORD.
Eze 25: 4 I will allow nomads from the e deserts to overrun
25: 9 I will open up their e flank and wipe out their
25:10 And I will hand Moab over to nomads from the e
27:26 Your mighty vessel flounders in the heavy e gale.
40: 6 over to the gateway that goes through the e wall.
45: 7 Then the far e and western borders of the prince's lands will line up with the e
47: 2 north gateway and led me around to the e entrance.
47:18 "The e border starts at a point between Hauran
47:18 as far south as Tamar. This will be the e border.
48:21 extending in opposite directions to the e
48:25 Next is the territory of Issachar with the same e
Mt 2: 1 About that time some wise men from e lands

EASTWARD (7) [EAST]

Ge 11: 2 As the people migrated e, they found a plain in the
Nu 34: 7 at the Mediterranean Sea and run e to Mount Hor,
Jos 11: 8 and e into the valley of Mizpah,
16: 6 then curved e past Taanath-shiloh to the east of
1Ch 5: 9 they spread e toward the edge of the desert that
Eze 8:16 They were facing e, worshiping the sun!
47: 1 There I saw a stream flowing e from beneath the

EASY (13) [EASE]

Ge 30:33 This will make it e for you to see whether or not I
Dt 1:41 thinking it would be e to conquer the hill country.
2Ki 19:26 so little power / and are such e prey for you.
Pr 15:19 trouble all through life; the path of the upright is e!
30:28 Lizards—they are e to catch, / but they are found
Isa 37:27 so little power / and are such e prey for you.
Eze 34: 5 a shepherd. They are e prey for any wild animal.
Hos 10:11 to treading out the grain—an e job that she loves.
Hab 3:14 like a whirlwind, thinking Israel would be e prey.
Mt 7:13 and its gate is wide for the many who choose the e
Lk 12:19 to come. Now take it e! Eat, drink, and be merry!'
Ro 6:19 of slaves and masters, because it is e to understand.
10: 8 the message we preach—is already within e reach.

EAT (465) [ATE, EATEN, EATER, EATING, EATS, GRASS-EATING, MAN-EATER, MOTH-EATEN]

MAY EAT (37) Ge 3:2; Ex 12:15,44; 29:33; Lev 6:18,26,29; 7:6; 11:9,21; 19:25; 21:22; 22:7,11,13; 25:6; Nu 18:10,11,13,31; Dt 12:15,15,20,21,22,27; 14:4,9,11,20; 15:22,22; 18:8; 23:24; Hos 9:4; Jnh 3:7; 1Co 10:25

MUST EAT (9) Ex 12:8,46; Lev 19:6; 24:9; Nu 9:11; 18:10; Dt 12:18; 15:20; Pr 1:31

NOT EAT (34) Ge 3:1,3; Ex 12:20,45; 22:31; 29:33; Lev 11:8; 22:4,6; 23:14; Nu 6:3; Dt 12:23,25; 14:3,7,8,12,21,21; 15:23; 16:8; Jdg 13:14,16; 1Ki 13:8,9,17; 2Ki 4:40; Ezr 10:6; Est 4:16; Jer 16:8; Mk 7:3; Jn 6:13; Ac 21:25; 2Th 3:10

SHOULD EAT (3) Ecc 3:13; Ro 14:23; 1Co 8:4

Ge 2:16 "You may freely e any fruit in the garden
2:17 and evil. If you e of its fruit, you will surely die."
3: 1 "Did God really say you must not e any of the
3: 2 "Of course we may e it," the woman told him.
3: 3 center of the garden that we are not allowed to e.
3: 3 God says we must not e it or even touch it, or we
3: 5 knows that your eyes will be opened when you e it.
3:11 you eaten the fruit I commanded you not to e?"
3:17 to your wife and ate the fruit I told you not to e,
3:18 and thistles for you, though you will e of its grains.
3:22 and evil. What if they e the fruit of the tree of life?
9: 4 But you must never e animals that still have their
15:11 Some vultures came down to e the carcasses,
24:33 "I don't want to e until I have told you why I have
27: 4 it's savory and good, and bring it here for me to e.
27:10 then he can e it and bless you instead of Esau
27:19 Sit up and e it so you can give me your blessing."
27:25 I will e it, and then I will give you my blessing."
27:31 Sit up and e it so you can give me your blessing."

32:32 That is why even today the people of Israel don't e
37:25 Then, just as they were sitting down to e,
39: 6 in the world, except to decide what he wanted to e!
41:36 That way there will be enough to e when the seven
43:16 "These men will e with me this noon.
43:32 despise Hebrews and refuse to e with them.
Ex 10:12 and e all the crops still left after the hailstorm."
12: 4 If a family is too small to e an entire lamb, let them
12: 4 the size of each family and how much they can e.
12: 8 That evening everyone must e roast lamb with
12:11 "Wear your traveling clothes as you e this meal,
12:11 E the food quickly, for this is the LORD's
12:15 you may e only bread made without yeast.
12:20 during those days you must not e anything made
12:20 you live, e only bread that has no yeast in it."
12:39 Whenever they stopped to e, they baked bread
12:43 No foreigners are allowed to e the Passover lamb.
12:44 But any slave who has been purchased may e it if
12:45 Hired servants and visiting foreigners may not e it.
12:46 All who e the lamb must e it together in one
12:48 But an uncircumcised male may never e of the
13: 6 For seven days you will e only bread without
13: 7 E only bread without yeast during those seven
16: 3 killed us there! At least there we had plenty to e.
16: 8 The LORD will give you meat to e in the evening
16:12 tell them, 'In the evening you will have meat to e,
16:35 in the land of Canaan, where there were crops to e.
22:31 do not e any animal that has been attacked
22:31 Throw its carcass out for the dogs to e.
23:11 Leave the rest for the animals to e. The same
23:15 For seven days you are to e bread made without
29:32 Aaron and his sons are to e this meat, along with
29:33 They alone may e the meat and bread used for their
29:33 The ordinary people may not e them, for these
Lev 3:17 "You must never e any fat or blood. This is a
6:18 to generation, may e of the grain offering,
6:26 The priest who offers the sacrifice may e his
6:29 Only males from a priest's family may e of this
7: 6 All males from a priest's family may e the meat,
7:18 if you e it, you will have to answer for your sin.
7:23 You must never e fat, whether from oxen or sheep
7:26 you must never e the blood of any bird or animal.
8:31 and e it along with the bread that is in the basket of
10:12 in it, and e it beside the altar, for it is most holy.
10:17 "Why didn't you e the sin offering in the
11: 4 e the animals named here because they either have
11: 8 You may not e the meat of these animals or touch
11: 9 you may e whatever has both fins and scales.
11:10 e marine animals that do not have both fins
11:11 You must never e their meat or even touch their
11:13 "These are the birds you must never e
11:21 there are some exceptions that you may e.
11:40 If you e any of its meat or carry away its carcass,
14:47 or e in the house must wash their clothing.
17:12 the foreigners who live among you must never e
17:14 is why I have told the people of Israel never to e
17:15 If you e from the carcass of an animal that died a
19: 6 You must e it on the same day you offer it or on
19: 8 If you e it on the third day, you will answer for the
19:25 Finally, in the fifth year you may e the fruit.
19:26 "Never e meat that has not been drained of its
21:22 However, he may e from the food offered to God,
22: 4 they may not e the sacred offerings until they have
22: 6 They must not e any of the sacred offerings until
22: 7 will be clean again and may e the sacred offerings.
22: 8 The priests may never e an animal that has died a
22:10 "No one outside a priest's family may ever e the
22:11 slaves with his own money, they may e of his food.
22:12 she may no longer e the sacred offerings.
22:13 father's home, she may e her father's food again.
22:13 families are allowed to e the sacred offerings.
22:16 by allowing unauthorized people to e them.
22:30 E the entire sacrificial animal on the day it is
23: 6 and during that time all the bread you e must be
23:14 Do not e any bread or roasted grain or fresh
24: 9 who must e them in a sacred place,
25: 6 and any foreigners who live with you may e the
25: 7 and the wild animals will also be allowed to e of
25:12 e the produce that grows naturally in the fields that
25:19 and you will e your fill and live securely in it.
25:20 'What will we e during the seventh year,
25:22 you will e from the old crop until the new harvest
26: 5 You will e your fill and live securely in your land.
26:16 crops in vain because your enemies will e them.
26:26 and even if you have food to e, you will not be
26:29 You will e the flesh of your own sons
Nu 6: 3 grape juice, and they must not e grapes or raisins.
6: 4 they are not allowed to e or drink anything that
9:11 They must e the lamb at that time with bitter herbs
11: 5 "We remember all the fish we used to e for free in
11: 6 and day after day we have nothing to e but this
11:18 for tomorrow they will have meat to e.
11:18 and complaints: "If only we had meat to e!
11:18 will give you meat, and you will have to e it.
11:20 You will e it for a whole month until you gag
15:19 you will e from the crops that grow there. But you
18:10 You must e it as a most holy offering.
18:10 All the males may e of it, and you must treat it as
18:11 male and female alike, may e of these offerings.
18:13 family who is ceremonially clean may e this food.
18:31 and your families may e this food anywhere you
21: 5 "There is nothing to e here and nothing to drink.
Dt 2:28 We will pay for every bite of food we e and all the
4:28 gods that neither see nor hear nor e nor smell.
6:11 and you will e from vineyards and olive trees you
11:15 graze in, and you yourselves will have plenty to e.
12:15 You may e as many animals as the LORD your
12:15 ceremonially clean or unclean, may e that meat.
12:16 The only restriction is that you are not to e the
12:18 You must e these in the presence of the LORD
12:18 E them there with your children, your servants,
12:20 has promised, you may e meat whenever you want.
12:21 and you may e the meat at your home as I have
12:22 ceremonially clean or unclean, may e that meat,
12:23 The only restriction is never to e the blood,
12:23 the life, and you must not e the life with the meat.
12:25 Do not e the blood; then all will go well with you
12:27 of the LORD your God, but you may e the meat.
14: 3 "You must not e animals that are ceremonially
14: 4 These are the animals you may e: the ox,
14: 7 So you may not e the camel, the hare, or the rock
14: 8 You may not e or even touch the dead bodies of
14: 9 you may e whatever has both fins and scales.
14:10 e marine animals that do not have both fins
14:11 "You may e any bird that is ceremonially clean.
14:12 These are the birds you may not e: the eagle,
14:20 But you may e any winged creature that is
14:21 "Do not e anything that has died a natural death.
14:21 But do not e it yourselves, for you are set apart as
14:23 name to be honored, and e it there in his presence.
14:29 in your towns, so they can e and be satisfied.
15:20 and your family must e these animals in the
15:22 Anyone may e it, whether ceremonially clean
15:22 or unclean, just as anyone may e a gazelle or deer.
15:23 But do not e the blood. You must pour it out on the
16: 3 E it with bread made without yeast. For seven days
e only bread made without yeast,
16: 3 E this bread—the bread of suffering—so that you
16: 7 and e it in the place the LORD your God chooses.
16: 8 For the next six days you may not e bread made
18: 1 and Levites will e from the offerings given to the
18: 8 He may e his share of the sacrifices and offerings,
20: 6 die in battle, and someone else would e from it!
20:19 the trees. E the fruit, but do not cut down the trees.
23:24 "You may e your fill of grapes from your
26:12 so that they will have enough to e in your towns.
28:33 A foreign nation you have never heard about will e
28:38 but harvest little, for locusts will e your crops.
28:39 but you will not drink the wine or e the grapes,
28:53 so severe that you will e the flesh of your own sons
28:55 because he has nothing else to e during the siege
28:57 has borne, so that she herself can secretly e them.
28:57 She will have nothing else to e during the siege
31:20 they will e all the food they want and become well
Jos 5:11 The very next day they began to e unleavened
Jdg 6: 4 They left the Israelites with nothing to e, taking all
13: 4 any other alcoholic drink or e any forbidden food.
13: 7 any other alcoholic drink or e any forbidden food.
13:14 She must not e grapes or raisins, drink wine
13:14 other alcoholic drink, or e any forbidden food."
13:15 until we can prepare a young goat for you to e."
13:16 of the LORD replied, "but I will not e anything.
14:14 "From the one who eats came something to e;
19: 5 father said, "Have something to e before you go."
19: 6 down together and had something to e and drink.
19: 8 the woman's father said, "Have something to e;
Ru 2:14 and Boaz gave her food—more than she could e.
1Sa 1: 7 finally be reduced to tears and would not even e.
1:18 Then she went back and began to e again, and she
2:36 among the priests so we will have enough to e.' "
9:13 and catch him before he goes up the hill to e.
9:19 to the place of sacrifice, and we'll e there together.
9:24 it before Saul. "Go ahead and e it," Samuel said.
14:30 If the men had been allowed to e freely from the
16:11 "We will not sit down to e until he arrives."
20:24 new moon festival began, the king sat down to e.
20:34 table in fierce anger and refused to e all that day,
21: 3 Now, what is there to e? Give me five loaves of
28:22 and let me give you something to e so you can
28:23 The men who were with him also urged him to e,
30:11 They gave him some bread to e and some water to
30:12 because he hadn't had anything to e or drink for
2Sa 3:35 David had refused to e anything the day of the
3:35 of the funeral, and now everyone begged him to e.
3:35 "May God kill me if I e anything before
12:17 nation pleaded with him to get up and e with them,
12:21 baby was still living, you wept and refused to e.
13: 6 take care of me and cook something for me to e."
13: 9 she set the serving tray before him, he refused to e.
16: 2 and summer fruit are for the young men to e.
19:28 honored me among those who e at your own table!
1Ki 4:20 were very contented, with plenty to e and drink.
13: 7 to the palace with me and have something to e,
13: 8 I would not e any food or drink any water in this
13: 9 'You must not e any food or drink any water while
13:15 of God, "Come home with me and e some food."
13:16 "I am not allowed to e any food or drink any water
13:17 'You must not e any food or drink any water while
13:18 and give him food to e and water to drink.' " But
13:22 and drank water where he told you not to e
17: 4 from the brook and e what the ravens bring you,
17:15 and her son continued to e from her supply of flour
19: 5 angel touched him and told him, "Get up and e!"
19: 7 touched him and said, "Get up and e some more,
21: 4 to bed with his face to the wall and refused to e!
21: 7 "Get up and e and don't worry about it.
21:23 the dogs of Jezreel will e the body of your wife,
2Ki 4: 8 lived there, and she invited him to e some food.
4: 8 he passed that way, he would stop there to e.
4:40 poison in this stew!" So they would not e it.
4:41 and said, "Now it's all right; go ahead and e."
4:42 "Give it to the group of prophets so they can e."
4:43 "Give it to the group of prophets so they can e,
6:28 "This woman proposed that we e my son one day
6:29 next day I said, 'Kill your son so we can e him,'
7: 2 it happen, but you won't be able to e any of it!"
7:19 it happen, but you won't be able to e any of it!"
9:10 Dogs will e Ahab's wife, Jezebel, at the plot of
9:36 plot of land in Jezreel, dogs will e Jezebel's flesh.
18:27 and thirsty that they will e their own dung
19:29 This year you will e only what grows up by itself,
19:29 and next year you will e what springs up from that.
19:29 you will tend vineyards and e their fruit.
23: 9 but they were allowed to e unleavened bread with
2Ch 30:18 and they were allowed to e the Passover meal
31:10 we have had enough to e and plenty to spare,
35:13 them out quickly so the people could e them.
Ezr 2:63 The governor would not even let them e the
10: 6 the night there, but he did not e any food or drink.
Ne 7:65 The governor would not even let them e the
8:12 So the people went away to e and drink at a festive
Est 4:16 Do not e or drink for three days, night or day.
Job 1: 4 On these occasions they would get together to e
3:24 I cannot e for sighing; my groans pour out like
24:20 Worms will find him sweet to e. No one will
30: 4 They e coarse leaves, and they burn the roots of
Ps 14: 4 evil never learn? / They e up my people like bread;
22:26 The poor will e and be satisfied. / All who seek the
35:25 what we wanted! / Now we will e him alive!"
53: 4 evil never learn? / They e up my people like bread;
74:14 of Leviathan / and let the desert animals e him.
78:24 and rained down manna for them to e. / He gave
102: 9 I e ashes instead of my food. / My tears run down
127: 2 late at night, / anxiously working for food to e;
Pr 1:31 That is why they must e the bitter fruit of living
4:17 They e wickedness and drink violence!
9: 5 "Come, e my food, and drink the wine I have
13:25 The godly e to their hearts' content, but the belly
20:13 Keep your eyes open, and there will be plenty to e!
23: 6 Don't e with people who are stingy; don't desire
23: 7 "E and drink," they say, but they don't mean it.
24:13 My child, e honey, for it is good,
25:16 Don't e too much of it, or it will make you sick!
25:21 If your enemies are hungry, give them food to e.
25:27 Just as it is not good to e too much honey, it is not
27:18 Workers who tend a fig tree are allowed to e its
Ecc 2:25 For who can e or enjoy anything apart from him?
3:13 And people should e and drink and enjoy the fruits
5:12 hard sleep well, whether they e little or much.
5:18 It is good for people to e well, drink a good glass
8:15 better for people to do in this world than to e,
9: 7 E your food and drink your wine with a happy
12: 4 are gone, keep your lips tightly closed when you e!
SS 2: 3 his delightful shade, and his fruit is delicious to e.
4:16 him come into his garden and e its choicest fruits."
5: 1 my spices and e my honeycomb with my honey.
5: 1 "Oh, lover and beloved, e and drink! Yes,
Isa 1:19 and let me help you, then you will have plenty to e.
7:15 By the time this child is old enough to e curds
9:20 In the end they will even e their own children.
11: 7 And lions will e grass as the livestock do.
18: 6 fields for the mountain birds and wild animals to e.
22:13 "Let's e, drink, and be merry," you say.
30:24 and donkeys that till the ground will e good grain,
36:12 and thirsty that they will e their own dung
37:30 This year you will e only what grows up by itself,
37:30 and next year you will e what springs up from that.
37:30 you will tend vineyards and e their fruit.
51: 8 The worm will e away at them as it eats wool.
65: 4 They also e pork and other forbidden foods.
65:13 "You will starve, but my servants will e. You will
65:21 they build and e the fruit of their own vineyards.
65:25 will feed together. The lion will e straw like the ox.
Jer 5:17 They will e your harvests and your children's
5:17 of cattle. Yes, they will e your grapes and figs.
7:21 burnt offerings and sacrifices! E them yourselves!
14: 6 They strain their eyes looking for grass to e,
16: 8 and parties. Do not e and drink with them at all.
19: 9 Then those trapped inside will have to e their own
24: 8 I will treat them like spoiled figs, too rotten to e.
29: 5 to stay. Plant gardens, and e the food you produce.
29:17 and make them like rotting figs—too bad to e.
29:28 because we will be here to e the fruit for many
31: 5 of Samaria and e from your own gardens there.
31:29 'The parents e sour grapes, but their children's
31:30 those who e the sour grapes will be the ones whose
44:17 For in those days we had plenty to e, and we were
La 2:20 Should mothers e their little children, those they
Eze 2: 8 a rebel. Open your mouth, and e what I give you."
3: 1 said to me, "Son of man, e what I am giving
you—e this scroll!
3: 3 "E it all," he said. And when I ate it, it tasted as
4:10 ounces of food for each day, and e it at set times.
4:12 dried human dung as fuel and then e the bread.
4:13 Israel will e defiled bread in the Gentile lands,
5:10 Parents will e their own children, and children will
e their parents.
12:18 "Son of man, tremble as you e your food.
12:19 They will e their food with trembling and sip their
33:25 You e meat with blood in it, you worship idols,
34:19 All that is left for my flock to e is what you have
35:12 they have been given to us as food to e!'
39:17 of Israel, and there e the flesh and drink the blood!
39:18 E the flesh of mighty men and drink the blood of
42:13 to the LORD will e the most holy offerings.
44:31 The priests may never e meat from any bird
Da 1: 8 He asked the chief official for permission to e
1:10 "My lord the king has ordered that you e this food
4:12 and it was loaded with fruit for all to e.
4:21 and it was loaded with fruit for all to e.
4:23 Let him e grass with the animals of the field for

4:25 You will **e** grass like a cow, and you will be
4:32 the wild animals, and you will **e** grass like a cow.
Hos 2:12 where only wild animals will **e** the fruit.
4:10 They will **e** and still be hungry. Though they do a
8:7 And if there is any grain, foreigners will **e** it.
9:4 They may **e** this food to feed themselves, but they
Am 9:14 they will **e** their crops and drink their wine.
Jnh 3:7 even the animals, may **e** or drink anything at all.
Mic 3:3 You **e** my people's flesh, cut away their skin,
6:14 You will **e** but never have enough. Your hunger
7:1 picker after the harvest who can find nothing to **e**.
Hag 1:6 You have food to **e**, but not enough to fill you up.
Zec 9:7 They will no longer **e** meat with blood in it or feed
11:16 this shepherd will **e** the meat of the fattest sheep
Mt 9:11 "Why does your teacher **e** with such scum?"
15:2 of ceremonial hand washing before they **e**."
15:11 You are not defiled by what you **e**; you are defiled
15:15 you said people aren't defiled by what they **e**."
15:17 "Anything you **e** passes through the stomach
15:27 "but even dogs are permitted to **e** crumbs that fall
15:32 me for three days, and they have nothing left to **e**.
15:33 out here in the wilderness for all of them to **e**?"
26:18 and I will **e** the Passover meal with my disciples at
26:26 saying, "Take it and **e** it, for this is my body."
Mk 2:16 his disciples, "Why does he **e** with such scum?"
3:20 and his disciples couldn't even find time to **e**.
5:43 and he told them to give her something to **e**.
6:31 and his apostles didn't even have time to **e**.
7:3 do not **e** until they have poured water over their
7:4 they **e** nothing bought from the market unless they
7:5 For they **e** without first performing the
7:15 You are not defiled by what you **e**; you are defiled
7:18 "Can't you see that what you **e** won't defile you?
8:2 me for three days, and they have nothing left to **e**.
11:14 to the tree, "May no one ever **e** your fruit again!"
14:14 Where is the guest room where I can **e** the
Lk 5:30 "Why do you **e** and drink with such scum?"
7:36 so Jesus accepted the invitation and sat down to **e**.
8:55 Then Jesus told them to give her something to **e**.
9:12 There is nothing to **e** here in this deserted place."
10:8 town welcomes you, **e** whatever is set before you
11:6 arrived for a visit, and I have nothing for him to **e**.'
11:38 His host was amazed to see that he sat down to **e**
12:19 Now take it easy! **E**, drink, and be merry!'
12:22 whether you have enough food to **e** or clothes to
12:29 And don't worry about food—what to **e** and drink.
12:37 put on an apron, and serve them as they sit and **e**!
17:7 care of sheep, he doesn't just sit down and **e**.
22:8 the Passover meal, so we can **e** it together."
22:11 Where is the guest room where I can **e** the
22:15 anxious to **e** this Passover meal with you before
22:16 For I tell you now that I won't **e** it again until it
22:30 to **e** and drink at my table in that Kingdom.
24:30 As they sat down to **e**, he took a small loaf of
24:41 he asked them, "Do you have anything here to **e**?"
Jn 4:31 Meanwhile, the disciples were urging Jesus to **e**.
6:13 filled with the pieces of bread the people did not **e**!
6:31 'Moses gave them bread from heaven to **e**.' "
6:52 "How can this man give us his flesh to **e**?"
6:53 unless you **e** the flesh of the Son of Man and drink
6:54 But those who **e** my flesh and drink my blood have
6:56 All who **e** my flesh and drink my blood remain in
Ac 10:13 said to him, "Get up, Peter; kill and **e** them."
11:6 reptiles, and birds that we are not allowed to **e**.
11:7 heard a voice say, 'Get up, Peter; kill and **e** them.'
21:25 They should not **e** food offered to idols,
21:25 consume blood, nor **e** meat from strangled animals,
23:12 and bound themselves with an oath to neither **e** nor
23:14 "We have bound ourselves under oath to neither **e**
23:21 They have vowed not to **e** or drink until they kill
27:33 the early morning light, Paul begged everyone to **e**.
27:34 "Please **e** something now for your own good.
Ro 14:2 one person believes it is all right to **e** anything.
14:2 has a sensitive conscience will **e** only vegetables.
14:3 Those who think it is all right to **e** anything must
14:3 And those who won't **e** certain foods must not
14:6 Those who **e** all kinds of food do so to honor the
14:6 And those who won't **e** everything also want to
14:14 Jesus that no food, in and of itself, is wrong to **e**.
14:15 if another Christian is distressed by what you **e**,
you are not acting in love if you **e** it.
14:17 the Kingdom of God is not a matter of what we **e**
14:20 Don't tear apart the work of God over what you **e**.
14:20 But it is wrong to **e** anything if it makes another
14:21 Don't **e** meat or drink wine or do anything else if it
14:23 doubts about whether they should **e** something,
they shouldn't **e** it.
1Co 5:11 or a swindler. Don't even **e** with such people.
8:4 Should we **e** meat that has been sacrificed to idols?
8:7 so when they **e** food that has been offered to idols,
8:8 that we can't win God's approval by what we **e**.
8:8 We don't miss out on anything if we don't **e** it,
8:10 Weak Christians who think it is wrong to **e** this
8:13 If what I **e** is going to make another Christian sin,
8:13 I will never **e** meat again as long as I live—
9:7 his crop and doesn't have the right to **e** some of it?
10:17 And we all **e** from one loaf, showing that we are
10:18 all who **e** the sacrifices are united by that act.
10:21 You cannot **e** at the Lord's Table and at the table
10:25 You may **e** any meat that is sold in the
10:27 **E** whatever is offered to you and don't ask any
10:28 Don't **e** it, out of consideration for the conscience
10:31 Whatever you **e** or drink or whatever you do,
11:21 For I am told that some of you hurry to **e** your own
11:26 For every time you **e** this bread and drink this cup,
11:29 For if you **e** the bread or drink the cup unworthily,
11:34 **e** at home so you won't bring judgment upon
2Co 9:10 who gives seed to the farmer and then bread to **e**.
Gal 2:12 Peter wouldn't **e** with the Gentiles anymore
Col 2:16 So don't let anyone condemn you for what you **e**
2:21 "Don't handle, don't **e**, don't touch."
2Th 3:10 this rule: "Whoever does not work should not **e**."
1Ti 4:3 wrong to be married and wrong to **e** certain foods.
Heb 5:12 who drink only milk and cannot **e** solid food.
13:10 priests in the Temple on earth have no right to **e**.
Jas 2:16 stay warm and **e** well"—but then you don't give
5:3 The very wealth you were counting on will **e** away
Rev 2:7 Everyone who is victorious will **e** from the tree of
2:17 Everyone who is victorious will **e** of the manna
2:20 **e** food offered to idols, and commit sexual sin.
10:9 "Yes, take it and **e** it," he said. "At first it will
17:16 They will strip her naked, **e** her flesh, and burn her
19:18 Come and **e** the flesh of kings, captains, and strong
22:14 gates of the city and **e** the fruit from the tree of life.

EATEN (91) [EAT]

Ge 3:11 "Have you **e** the fruit I commanded you not to
14:24 is what these young men of mine have already **e**.
27:33 I have already **e** it, and I blessed him with an
37:20 We can tell our father that a wild animal has **e** him.
37:33 son's robe. A wild animal has attacked and **e** him.
45:23 and all kinds of other food to be **e** on his journey.
Ex 12:7 doorframe of the house where the lamb will be **e**.
12:9 The meat must never be **e** raw or boiled; roast it
12:10 Whatever is not **e** that night must be burned before
12:18 Only bread without yeast may be **e** from the
21:28 the bull must be stoned, and its flesh may not be **e**.
29:34 it must be burned. It may not be **e**, for it is holy.
Lev 6:16 and **e** in a sacred place within the courtyard of the
6:23 entirely burned up. None of the flour may be **e**."
6:30 people's sins, none of that animal's meat may be **e**.
7:6 and it must be **e** in a sacred place, for it is most
7:15 The animal's meat must be **e** on the same day it is
7:16 the meat may be **e** on that same day,
7:16 and whatever is left over may be **e** on the second
7:18 If any of the meat from this peace offering is **e** on
7:19 anything ceremonially unclean may not be **e**;
7:19 And as for meat that may be **e**, it may only be **e** by
people who are ceremonially
7:24 or killed by a wild animal may never be **e**,
10:13 It must be **e** in a sacred place, for it has been given
10:14 and thigh that were lifted up may be **e** in any place
10:18 you should have **e** the meat in the sanctuary area as
10:19 Would the LORD have approved if I had **e** the sin
11:4 The camel may not be **e**, for though it chews the
11:6 and the hare, so they also may never be **e**.
11:7 And the pig may not be **e**, for though it has split
11:22 bald locusts, and grasshoppers. All these may be **e**.
11:41 along the ground; such animals may never be **e**.
11:47 and may not be **e** and what is clean and may be **e**."
19:7 If any of the offering is **e** on the third day, it will
22:14 realizing it must pay the priest for the amount **e**,
Nu 18:19 and daughters, to be **e** as your regular share.
28:17 will begin, but no bread made with yeast may be **e**.
Dt 6:11 not plant. When you have **e** your fill in this land,
8:10 When you have **e** your fill, praise the LORD your
12:17 "But your offerings must not be **e** at home—
14:6 that has split hooves and chews the cud may be **e**,
14:7 if the animal doesn't have both, it may not be **e**.
14:8 And the pig may not be **e**, for though it has split
14:19 are ceremonially unclean for you and may not be **e**.
16:5 "The Passover must not be **e** in the towns that the
20:6 planted a vineyard but not yet **e** any of its fruit?
26:14 I have not **e** any of it while in mourning; I have not
1Sa 14:27 the honey. After he had **e** it, he felt much better.
14:29 See how much better I feel now that I have **e** this
20:5 I've always **e** with your father on this occasion,
28:20 for he had **e** nothing all day and all night.
1Ki 13:28 for the lion had not **e** the body nor attacked the
14:11 your family who die in the city will be **e** by dogs,
14:11 and those who die in the field will be **e** by
16:4 Those of your family who die in the city will be **e**
16:4 and those who die in the field will be **e** by the
21:24 your family who die in the city will be **e** by dogs,
21:24 and those who die in the field will be **e** by
2Ki 4:40 But after the men had **e** a bite or two they cried
Ezr 6:21 The Passover meal was **e** by the people of Israel
Job 20:14 the food he has **e** turns sour within him,
21:26 buried in the same dust, both **e** by the same worms.
Pr 9:17 is refreshing; food **e** in secret tastes the best!"
17:1 A dry crust **e** in peace is better than a great feast
30:17 out by ravens of the valley and **e** by vultures.
Isa 28:4 as an early fig is hungrily picked and **e**.
50:9 like old clothes that have been **e** by moths!
Jer 24:2 with figs that were spoiled and could not be **e**.
51:34 "King Nebuchadnezzar of Babylon has **e**
La 4:10 and **e** them in order to survive the siege.
Eze 4:14 I have never **e** any animal that died of sickness
4:14 And I have never **e** any of the animals that our
4:16 will be weighed out with great care and **e** fearfully.
18:2 'The parents have **e** sour grapes, but their
33:27 Those living in the open fields will be **e** by wild
45:21 Only bread without yeast may be **e** during that
Da 10:3 All that time I had **e** no rich food or meat,
Hos 10:13 You have **e** the fruit of lies—trusting in your
13:6 But when you had **e** and were satisfied, then you
Mt 6:19 where they can be **e** by moths and get rusty,
14:21 About five thousand men had **e** from those five
Mk 6:44 Five thousand men had **e** from those five loaves!
8:9 that day, and he sent them home after they had **e**.
Jn 6:23 Lord had blessed the bread and the people had **e**.
13:27 As soon as Judas had **e** the bread, Satan entered
Ac 10:14 "I have never in all my life **e** anything forbidden
11:8 'I have never **e** anything forbidden by our Jewish
27:21 No one had **e** for a long time. Finally, Paul called
1Ti 4:3 But God created those foods to be **e** with

EATER (1) [EAT]

Pr 23:2 If you are a big **e**, put a knife to your throat,

EATING (73) [EAT]

Ge 7:2 pairs of each animal that I have approved for **e**
7:8 those approved for **e** and sacrifice and those that
43:25 They were told they would be **e** there, so they
49:9 Judah is a young lion / that has finished **e** its prey.
Lev 11:39 "If an animal that is permitted for **e** dies and you
17:13 and kill an animal or bird that is approved for **e**,
20:25 You must not defile yourselves by **e** any animal
25:22 you will still be **e** the produce of the previous year.
Nu 11:33 But while they were still **e** the meat, the anger of
Dt 9:18 the LORD, neither **e** bread nor drinking water.
25:4 "Do not keep an ox from **e** as it treads out the
Jdg 1:7 and big toes cut off, **e** scraps from under my table.
19:4 stayed three days, **e**, drinking, and sleeping there.
1Sa 1:8 "Why aren't you **e**? Why be so sad just
14:33 the men are sinning against the LORD by **e** meat
14:34 Do not sin against the LORD by **e** meat with the
30:16 **e** and drinking and dancing with joy because of the
2Sa 12:21 you have stopped your mourning and are **e** again."
21:10 and stopped wild animals from **e** them at night.
1Ki 13:23 Now after the man of God had finished **e**
21:5 "What has made you so upset that you are not **e**?"
2Ki 7:8 **e**, drinking wine, and carrying out silver and gold
18:31 Then I will allow each of you to continue **e** from
Job 6:7 when I look at it; I gag at the thought of **e** it!
Ps 78:30 But before they finished **e** this food they had
Isa 21:5 Everyone is **e** and drinking. Quick! Grab your
29:8 A hungry person dreams of **e** but is still hungry.
31:4 shepherd's shouts and noise. It just goes right on **e**.
36:16 Then I will allow each of you to continue **e** from
Jer 41:1 invited them to dinner. While they were **e**,
Eze 24:22 or console yourselves by **e** the food brought to you
Da 1:8 up his mind not to defile himself by **e** the food
1:13 other young men who are **e** the king's rich food.
1:13 or not to let us continue **e** our diet."
1:15 men who had been **e** the food assigned by the king.
Joel 1:4 After the cutting locusts finished **e** the crops,
Am 6:4 **e** the meat of tender lambs and choice calves.
Mt 12:1 began breaking off heads of wheat and **e** the grain.
15:20 **E** with unwashed hands could never defile you
26:21 While they were **e**, he said, "The truth is, one of
26:23 "One of you who is **e** with me now will betray me.
26:26 As they were **e**, Jesus took a loaf of bread
Mk 2:16 were Pharisees saw him **e** with people like that,
7:2 the usual Jewish ritual of hand washing before **e**.
14:18 As they were sitting around the table **e**, Jesus said,
14:18 will betray me, one of you who is here **e** with me."
14:20 is one of you twelve, one who is **e** with me now.
14:22 As they were **e**, Jesus took a loaf of bread
16:14 to the eleven disciples as they were **e** together.
Lk 10:7 in one place, **e** and drinking what they provide you.
15:2 with such despicable people—even **e** with them!
17:8 and serve him his supper before **e** his own.
17:28 **e** and drinking, buying and selling, farming
Ac 1:4 In one of these meetings as he was **e** a meal with
15:20 and tell them to abstain from **e** meat sacrificed to
15:20 or **e** the meat of strangled animals.
15:29 You must abstain from **e** food offered to idols,
15:29 or **e** the meat of strangled animals,
27:37 and all 276 of us began **e**—for that is the number
27:38 After **e**, the crew lightened the ship further by
Ro 14:6 the Lord, since they give thanks to God before **e**.
14:15 Don't let your **e** ruin someone for whom Christ
1Co 5:8 not by **e** the old bread of wickedness and evil, but
by **e** the new bread of purity and truth.
8:10 eat this food will see you **e** in the temple of an idol.
8:10 by **e** food that has been dedicated to the idol.
9:9 "Do not keep an ox from **e** as it treads out the
10:30 and enjoy it, why should I be condemned for **e** it?
11:22 Don't you have your own homes for **e**
11:28 That is why you should examine yourself before **e**
11:29 you are **e** and drinking God's judgment upon
1Ti 5:18 "Do not keep an ox from **e** as it treads out the
Rev 2:14 He taught them to worship idols by **e** food offered

EATS (20) [EAT]

Ex 12:15 Anyone who **e** bread made with yeast at any time
12:19 Anyone who **e** anything made with yeast during
Lev 7:20 but **e** meat from a peace offering that was
7:21 and then **e** meat from the LORD's sacrifices,
7:25 Anyone who **e** fat from an offering given to the
7:27 Anyone who **e** blood must be cut off from the
17:10 among you, who **e** or drinks blood in any form.
17:14 So whoever **e** or drinks blood must be cut off.
22:14 "Anyone who **e** the sacred offerings without
Jdg 14:14 "From the one who **e** came something to eat;
1Sa 14:24 "Let a curse fall on anyone who **e** before evening
14:28 oath that anyone who **e** food today will be cursed.
Job 18:13 Disease **e** their skin; death devours their limbs.
40:15 I made it, just as I made you. It **e** grass like an ox.
Ps 109:18 or as the water he drinks, / or the rich food he **e**.
Isa 51:8 The worm will eat away at them as it **e** wool.
Jn 6:50 heaven gives eternal life to everyone who **e** it.
6:51 Anyone who **e** this bread will live forever;
6:58 Anyone who **e** this bread will live forever and not
1Co 11:27 So if anyone **e** this bread or drinks this cup of the

EAVESDROP (1)
Ecc 7:21 Don't e on others—you may hear your servant

EBAL (7)
Ge 36:23 were Alvan, Manahath, E, Shepho, and Onam.
Dt 11:29 from Mount Gerizim and a curse from Mount E.
27: 4 set up these stones at Mount E and coat them with
27:13 and Naphtali must stand on Mount E to proclaim a
Jos 8:30 altar to the LORD, the God of Israel, on Mount E.
8:33 Mount Gerizim, the other at the foot of Mount E.
1Ch 1:40 were Alvan, Manahath, E, Shepho, and Onam.

EBB (3)
Lev 26:16 causing your eyes to fail and your life to e away.
Isa 24:11 crying out for wine. Joy has reached its lowest e.
La 2:12 Their lives e away like the life of a warrior

EBED (3)
Jdg 9:26 At that time Gaal son of E moved to Shechem with
9:31 "Gaal son of E and his brothers have come to live
Ezr 8: 6 of Adin: E son of Jonathan and 50 other men.

EBED-MELECH (6)
Jer 38: 7 But E the Ethiopian, an important palace official,
38: 8 so E rushed from the palace to speak with him.
38:10 So the king told E, "Take along thirty of my men,
38:11 So E took the men with him and went to a room in
38:12 E called down to Jeremiah, "Put these rags under
39:16 "Say to E the Ethiopian, 'The LORD Almighty,

EBENEZER (3)
1Sa 4: 1 The Israelite army was camped near E,
5: 1 they took it from the battleground at E to the city
7:12 He named it E—"the stone of help"—for he said,

EBER (17)
Ge 10:21 Shem was the ancestor of all the descendants of E.
10:24 father of Shelah, and Shelah was the father of E.
10:25 E had two sons. The first was named Peleg—
11:14 Shelah was 30 years old, his son E was born.
11:15 After the birth of E, Shelah lived another 403 years
11:16 When E was 34 years old, his son Peleg was born.
11:17 E lived another 430 years and had other sons
Nu 24:24 of Cyprus; / they will oppress both Assyria and E,
1Ch 1:18 the father of Shelah. Shelah was the father of E.
1:19 E had two sons. The first was named Peleg—
1:25 E, Peleg, Reu,
5:13 Meshullam, Sheba, Jorai, Jacan, Zia, and E.
8:12 The sons of Elpaal were E, Misham, Shemed (who
8:22 Ishpan, E, Eliel,
Ne 12:20 of Sallu. / E was leader of the family of Amok.
Lk 3:35 Peleg was the son of E. / E was the son of Shelah.

EBEZ (1)
Jos 19:20 Rabbith, Kishion, E,

EBONY (1)
Eze 27:15 they brought payment in ivory tusks and e wood.

EBRONAH [KJV] See ABRONAH

ECBATANA (1)
Ezr 6: 2 But it was at the fortress at E in the province of

ECHO (5) [ECHOES]
Isa 22: 5 and cries of death e from the mountainsides.
Jer 6: 7 Her streets e with the sounds of violence
Eze 26:15 as the screams of the wounded e in the continuing
Hab 2:11 and the beams in the ceilings e the complaint.
Zep 1:10 and e throughout the newer Mishneh section of the

ECHOES (1) [ECHO]
Ps 29: 3 The voice of the LORD e above the sea.

ED [KJV] See WITNESS

EDEN (17) [BETH-EDEN, EDEN'S]
Ge 2: 8 Then the LORD God planted a garden in E,
2:10 A river flowed from the land of E,
2:15 God placed the man in the Garden of E to tend
3:23 banished Adam and his wife from the Garden of E,
3:24 stationed mighty angelic beings to the east of E.
4:16 and settled in the land of Nod, east of E.
2Ki 19:12 and the people of E who were in Tel-assar?
2Ch 29:12 Joah son of Zimmah and E son of Joah.
31:15 His faithful assistants were E, Miniamin, Jeshua,
Isa 37:12 and the people of E who were in Tel-assar?
51: 3 barren wilderness will become as beautiful as E—
Eze 27:23 Haran, Canneh, E, Sheba, Asshur, and Kilmad
28:13 You were in E, the garden of God. Your clothing
31: 9 it was the envy of all the other trees of E,
31:16 And all the other proud trees of E, the most
31:18 to which of the trees of E will you compare your
Joel 2: 3 land lies as fair as the Garden of E in all its beauty.

EDEN'S (1) [EDEN]
Eze 36:35 'This godforsaken land is now like E garden!

EDER (5)
Ge 35:21 traveled on and camped beyond the tower of E.
Jos 15:21 Edom in the extreme south are Kabzeel, E, Jagur,
1Ch 8:15 Zebadiah, Arad, E,
23:23 three sons of Mushi were Mahli, E, and Jerimoth.
24:30 of Mushi, the leaders were Mahli, E, and Jerimoth.

EDGE (45) [DOUBLE-EDGED, EDGES, TWO-EDGED]
Ge 14: 6 as far as El-paran at the e of the wilderness.
Ex 2: 3 and laid it among the reeds along the e of the Nile
13:20 they camped at Etham on the e of the wilderness.
25:25 Put a rim about three inches wide around the top e,
26: 4 Put loops of blue yarn along the e of the last sheet
26: 5 The fifty loops along the e of one set are to match the fifty loops along the e of the other.
26:10 Put fifty loops along the e of the last sheet in each
36:11 Fifty blue loops were placed along the e of the last
36:12 The fifty loops along the e of the first set of sheets
36:12 matched the loops along the e of the second set.
36:13 made to connect the loops on the e of each set.
36:17 Then they made fifty loops along the e of the last
37:11 pure gold, with a gold molding all around the e.
37:26 pure gold and ran a gold molding around the e.
39:23 The e of this opening was reinforced with a woven
39:24 Pomegranates were attached to the bottom e of the
Nu 33: 6 and camped at Etham on the e of the wilderness.
34: 3 from the wilderness of Zin, along the e of Edom.
34:11 run down along the eastern e of the Sea of Galilee,
Dt 2:36 us conquer Aroer on the e of the Arnon Gorge,
4:48 So Israel conquered all the area from Aroer at the e
22: 8 must have a barrier around the e of its flat rooftop.
Jos 3:15 carrying the Ark touched the water at the river's e,
12: 2 included Aroer, on the e of the Arnon Gorge,
13: 9 Their territory extended from Aroer on the e of the
13:16 Their territory extended from Aroer on the e of the
18:14 then ran south along the western e of the hill facing
Jdg 7:17 When I come to the e of the camp, do just as I do.
7:19 him reached the outer e of the Midianite camp.
1Sa 9:27 When they reached the e of town, Samuel told Saul
2Sa 15:17 set out on foot, and they paused at the e of the city
2Ki 7: 8 When the lepers arrived at the e of the camp,
1Ch 5: 9 they spread eastward toward the e of the desert that
5:10 settlements all along the eastern e of Gilead.
Ps 73: 2 But as for me, I came so close to the e of the cliff!
Pr 10:26 in the eyes or vinegar that sets the teeth on e.
Jer 49:27 "And I will start a fire at the e of Damascus that
Eze 19:10 planted by the water's e. / It had lush, green foliage
43:13 with a curb 9 inches wide around its e.
43:17 and a 10-1/2-inch curb all around the e.
Lk 4:29 and took him to the e of the hill on which the city
5: 2 He noticed two empty boats at the water's e,
16:26 to cross over to you from here is stopped at its e,
Heb 11:34 of fire, and escaped death by the e of the sword.

EDGES (7) [EDGE]
Ex 37:12 3 inches wide was attached along the e of the table,
Lev 19: 9 do not harvest the grain along the e of your fields,
19:27 hair on your temples or clip the e of your beards.
21: 5 trim the e of their beards, or cut their bodies.
23:22 do not harvest the grain along the e of your fields,
Eze 1:18 and they were covered with eyes all around the e.
Hos 12:11 the heaps of stone along the e of a plowed field.

EDOM (106) [EDOM'S, EDOMITE, EDOMITES, ESAU]
Ge 25:30 (This was how Esau got his other name, E—
32: 3 to his brother, Esau, in E, the land of Seir.
36: 1 of the descendants of Esau (also known as E).
36: 8 So Esau (also known as E) settled in the hill
36:16 These clans in the land of E were descended from
36:17 These clans in the land of E were descended from
36:19 the clans descended from Esau (also known as E).
36:21 the descendants of Seir, who lived in the land of E.
36:31 These are the kings who ruled in E before there
Ex 15:15 The leaders of E will be terrified; / the nobles of
Nu 20:14 he sent ambassadors to the king of E with this
20:18 But the king of E said, "Stay out of my land
20:20 But the king of E replied, "Stay out! You may not
20:21 Because E refused to allow Israel to pass through
20:23 Aaron at Mount Hor on the border of the land of E,
21: 4 the road to the Red Sea to go around the land of E.
24:18 E will be taken over, / and Seir, its enemy, will be
33:37 and camped at Mount Hor, at the border of E.
34: 3 from the wilderness of Zin, along the edge of E.
Jos 15: 1 of Judah reached southward to the border of E,
15:21 The towns of Judah situated along the borders of E
Jdg 5: 4 and marched across the fields of E, / the earth
11:17 they sent messengers to the king of E asking for
11:18 they went around E and Moab through the
1Sa 14:47 against Moab, Ammon, E, the kings of Zobah,
2Sa 8:12 E, Moab, Ammon, Philistia, and Amalek—
8:14 He placed army garrisons throughout E, and all the
1Ki 9:26 a port near Elath in the land of E, along the shore
11: 1 Ammon, E, Sidon, and from among the Hittites.
11:15 Years before, David had gone to E with Joab,
11:15 Israelite army had killed nearly every male in E.
22:47 There was no king in E at that time, only a deputy.
2Ki 3: 8 "We will attack from the wilderness of E,"
3: 9 The king of E and his troops joined them, and all
3:12 of Israel, Judah, and E went to consult with Elisha.
3:20 It was flowing from the direction of E, and soon
3:26 break through the enemy lines near the king of E,
8:22 E has been independent from Judah to this day.
14:10 You have indeed destroyed E and are very proud
16: 6 At that time the king of E recovered the town of Elath for E.
1Ch 1:43 These are the kings who ruled in E before there
1:51 The clan leaders of E were Timna, Alvah, Jetheth,
1:54 and Iram. These were the clan leaders of E.
18:11 E, Moab, Ammon, Philistia, and Amalek.
18:13 He placed army garrisons throughout E, and all the
2Ch 8:17 to Ezion-geber and Elath, ports in the land of E,
20: 2 "A vast army from E is marching against you
21: 9 So Jehoram went to attack E with his full army
21:10 E has been independent from Judah to this day.
25:19 You may be very proud of your conquest of E,
25:20 to destroy him for worshiping the gods of E.
28:17 The armies of E had again invaded Judah
Ps 60: 8 my lowly servant, / and E will be my slave.
60: 9 fortified city? / Who will bring me victory over E?
108: 9 my lowly servant, / and E will be my slave.
108:10 fortified city? / Who will bring me victory over E?
Isa 11:14 They will occupy all the lands of E, Moab,
21:11 This message came to me concerning E:
21:11 Someone from E keeps calling to me, "Watchman,
34: 5 It will fall upon E, the nation I have completely
34: 6 of Bozrah. He will make a mighty slaughter in E.
34: 8 the year when E will be paid back for all it did to
34: 9 The streams of E will be filled with burning pitch,
34:10 This judgment on E will never end; the smoke of
63: 1 Who is this who comes from E, from the city of
Jer 25:21 Then I went to the nations of E, Moab,
27: 3 Then send messages to the kings of E, Moab,
40:11 When the Judeans in Moab, Ammon, E,
49: 7 This message was given concerning E. This is
49: 8 For when I bring disaster on E, I will punish you,
49:10 But I will strip bare the land of E, and there will be
49:10 all will be destroyed—and E itself will be no more.
49:14 "Form a coalition against E, and prepare for
49:15 "I will cut you down to size among the nations, E.
49:17 "E will be an object of horror. All who pass by
49:19 I will chase E from its land, and I will appoint the
49:20 Listen to the LORD's plans for E and the people
La 4:21 you rejoicing in the land of Uz, O people of E?
4:22 But E, your punishment is just beginning;
Eze 16:57 by E and all her neighbors and by Philistia.
25:12 The people of E have sinned greatly by avenging
25:13 I will raise my fist of judgment against E.
25:14 furious vengeance, and E will know it is from me.
32:29 "E is there with its kings and princes. Mighty as
35:15 you people of Mount Seir and all who live in E!
36: 5 anger is on fire against these nations, especially E,
Da 11:41 of Israel, and many nations will fall, but Moab, E,
Joel 3:19 Egypt will become a wasteland and E a wilderness,
Am 1: 6 my people into exile, selling them as slaves in E.
1: 9 with Israel, selling whole villages as slaves to E.
1:11 "The people of E have sinned again and again,
9:12 And Israel will possess what is left of E and all the
Ob 1: 1 revealed to Obadiah concerning the land of E.
1: 1 Let's assemble our armies and attack E!"
1: 2 "I will cut you down to size among the nations, E;
1: 6 and cranny of E will be searched and looted.
1: 8 wise person will be left in the whole land of E!"
1: 8 "For on the mountains of E I will destroy
1: 9 and everyone on the mountains of E will be cut
1:18 will be a raging fire, and E, a field of dry stubble.
1:18 and leaving no survivors in E.
1:19 in the Negev will occupy the mountains of E.
1:21 Zion in Jerusalem to rule over the mountains of E.
Hab 3: 3 moving across the deserts from E and Mount
Mal 1: 4 And Esau's descendants in E may say, "We have

EDOM'S (3) [EDOM]
1Ki 11:14 a member of E royal family, to be an enemy
Jer 49:21 The earth will shake with the noise of E fall,
Am 2: 1 They desecrated the tomb of E king and burned his

EDOMITE (5) [EDOM]
1Sa 21: 7 Now Doeg the E, Saul's chief herdsman, was there
22: 9 Then Doeg the E, who was standing there with
1Ki 11:14 Then the LORD raised up Hadad the E,
2Ch 25:11 where they killed ten thousand E troops from Seir.
Ps 52: T regarding the time Doeg the E told Saul that

EDOMITES (21) [EDOM]
Ge 36: 9 the E, who live in the hill country of Seir.
36:43 names of the clans of Esau, the ancestor of the E,
Dt 2: 4 the country belonging to your relatives the E,
2: 4 in Seir. The E will feel threatened, so be careful.
23: 7 "Do not detest the E or the Egyptians, because the E are your relatives,
2Sa 8:13 After his return he destroyed eighteen thousand E
8:14 and all the E became David's subjects.
2Ki 8:20 the E revolted against Judah and crowned their
8:21 The E surrounded him and his charioteers, but he
14: 7 It was Amaziah who killed ten thousand E in the
16: 6 out the people of Judah and sent E to live there,
1Ch 18:12 eighteen thousand E in the Valley of Salt.
18:13 and all the E became David's subjects.
2Ch 21: 8 the E revolted against Judah and crowned their
21: 9 The E surrounded him and his charioteers, but he
25:14 King Amaziah returned from defeating the E,
Ps 60: T and killed twelve thousand E in the Valley of Salt.
83: 6 these E and Ishmaelites, / Moabites and Hagrites,
137: 7 O LORD, remember what the E did / on the day
Jer 9:26 the Egyptians, E, Ammonites, Moabites,

EDREI (8)
Nu 21:33 of Bashan and all his people attacked them at E.
Dt 1: 4 Og of Bashan, who had ruled in Ashtaroth and E.
3: 1 where King Og and his army attacked us at E.
3:10 and Bashan as far as the towns of Salecah and E,
Jos 12: 4 the last of the Rephaites, lived at Ashtaroth and E.
13:12 of Bashan, who had reigned in Ashtaroth and E.
13:31 and King Og's royal cities of Ashtaroth and E.
19:37 Kedesh, E, En-hazor,

EDUCATE (1) [EDUCATED]
Pr 17:16 It is senseless to pay tuition to e a fool who has no

EDUCATED (3) [EDUCATE]
Ecc 9:11 And those who are e don't always lead successful
Ac 22: 3 and e here in Jerusalem under Gamaliel.
Ro 1:14 in other cultures, to the e and uneducated alike.

EFFECT (8) [EFFECTIVE, EFFECTIVELY, EFFECTIVENESS, EFFECTS]
Est 2: 4 to the king, so he put the plan into e immediately.
9: 1 7 the two decrees of the king were put into e.
Job 35: 6 sin again and again, what e will it have on him?
Ac 19:20 the Lord spread widely and had a powerful e.
Ro 8: 3 But God put into e a different plan to save us.
Col 2:23 But they have no e when it comes to conquering a
Heb 9:10 external regulations that are in e only until their
9:17 The will goes into e only after the death of the

EFFECTIVE (1) [EFFECT]
Col 4: 6 Let your conversation be gracious and e so that

EFFECTIVELY (1) [EFFECT]
2Ti 2:24 They must be able to teach e and be patient with

EFFECTIVENESS (1) [EFFECT]
Heb 7:22 it is Jesus who guarantees the e of this better

EFFECTS (2) [EFFECT]
Nu 5:19 may you be immune from the e of this bitter water
Jer 44:18 and have suffered the e of war and famine."

EFFEMINATE [KJV] See (MALE) PROSTITUTES

EFFORT (7) [EFFORTS]
Jdg 11:26 Why have you made no e to recover it before now?
Pr 14:24 crown for the wise; the e of fools yields only folly.
Jn 6:63 gives eternal life. Human e accomplishes nothing.
Gal 3: 3 trying to become perfect by your own human e?
Php 3: 3 We put no confidence in human e. Instead,
2Pe 1: 5 So make every e to apply the benefits of these
3:14 make every e to live a pure and blameless life.

EFFORTS (9) [EFFORT]
2Ch 31:21 and in his e to follow the law and the commands,
Job 5:12 the plans of the crafty, so their e will not succeed.
36:19 your wealth and mighty e keep you from distress?
Ps 90:17 and make our e successful. / Yes, make our e successful!
Isa 33:11 You Assyrians will gain nothing by all your e.
Mk 14:55 could put him to death. But their e were in vain.
Php 3: 4 If others have reason for confidence in their own e,
1Ti 6: 2 you are helping another believer by your e.

EGG (2) [EGGS]
Job 6: 6 And how tasteless is the uncooked white of an e!
Lk 11:12 Or if they ask for an e, do you give them a

EGGS (5) [EGG]
Dt 22: 6 or e in it with the mother sitting in the nest,
Job 39:14 She lays her e on top of the earth, letting them be
Isa 10:14 and gathered up kingdoms as a farmer gathers e.
34:15 There the owl will make her nest and lay her e.
Jer 17:11 Like a bird that hatches e she has not laid, so are

EGLAH (2)
2Sa 3: 5 was Ithream, whose mother was David's wife E.
1Ch 3: 3 The sixth was Ithream, whose mother was E.

EGLAIM (1) [EN-EGLAIM]
Isa 15: 8 from one end to the other—from E to Beer-elim.

EGLATH-SHELISHIYAH (2)
Isa 15: 5 Its people flee to Zoar and E. Weeping, they climb
Jer 48:34 from Zoar all the way to Horonaim and E.

EGLON (15)
Jos 10: 3 of Jarmuth, Japhia of Lachish, and Debir of E.
10:23 of Jerusalem, Hebron, Jarmuth, Lachish, and E.
10:34 Then Joshua and the Israelite army went to E
10:36 After leaving E, they attacked Hebron,
10:37 And just as they had done at E, they completely
12:12 The king of E / The king of Gezer
15:39 Lachish, Bozkath, E,
Jdg 3:12 so the LORD gave King E of Moab control over
3:13 E attacked Israel and took possession of Jericho.
3:14 And the Israelites were subject to E of Moab for
3:15 to deliver their tax money to King E of Moab.
3:17 He brought the tax money to E, who was very fat.
3:19 He came to E and said, "I have a secret message
3:20 Ehud walked over to E as he was sitting alone in a
3:20 for you from God!" As King E rose from his seat,

EGYPT (641) [EGYPT'S, EGYPTIAN, EGYPTIAN'S, EGYPTIANS, EGYPTIANS']

BROOK OF EGYPT (9) Nu 34:5; Jos 15:4,47; 1Ki 8:65; 2Ki 24:7; 2Ch 7:8; Isa 27:12; Eze 47:19; 48:28

DOWN TO EGYPT (7) Ge 12:10; 42:3; 46:3,4; Nu 20:15; Isa 30:2; Hos 8:13

KING OF EGYPT (27) Ge 37:36; 39:1; 41:46; Ex 1:15; 2:23; 3:18,19; 6:13; 14:5; 1Ki 3:1; 9:16; 2Ki 17:4; 23:29; 24:7; 2Ch 36:3,4; Isa 19:11; Jer 44:30; 46:2,17; Eze 29:3; 30:21,22,24; 31:2; 32:2; Ac 7:10

LAND OF EGYPT (98) Ge 13:10; 41:19,29,41,44,45,55; 45:9,18,20,26; 46:20,27,34; 47:6,11,20,26; 48:5; 50:24; Ex 4:20; 6:26,27; 7:3,21; 8:6,16,17; 9:9,23; 10:12,14,15,19,21; 11:1,3,6,9; 12:1,12,12,13,17,29,30,42; 13:15; 16:6; 22:21; 23:9; 32:11; Lev 11:45; 19:34,36; 23:43; 25:42,55; 26:13; Nu 15:41; 26:59; Dt 6:12; 7:18; 8:14; 10:19; 11:10; 13:5,10; 15:15; 24:22; 29:16,25; 34:11; Jos 24:17; 1Sa 12:6; 1Ki 6:1; 8:9; Ps 78:51; 81:10; Isa 19:14,20; Jer 16:14; 23:7; 31:32; 32:20; 43:11,12; 44:26; Eze 19:4; 29:9,10,19,20; 30:12,25; Na 3:9; Heb 8:9; 11:27

OUT OF EGYPT (75) Ge 47:30; Ex 3:8,10,11,12; 12:39,51; 13:14,16,19; 16:32; 17:3; 18:1,9; 29:46; 32:4,8,23; 33:1; Lev 25:38; 26:45; Nu 16:13; 20:16; 21:5; 23:22; 26:4; 33:1; Dt 4:37; 6:21,23; 7:19; 9:12; 16:1; 20:1; 23:4; 26:8; Jdg 2:1,12; 6:13; 11:13; 2Sa 7:6; 1Ki 8:16,21,53; 9:9; 12:28; 2Ki 17:36; 21:15; 1Ch 17:5; 2Ch 6:5; 7:22; Ne 9:18; Ps 105:37,43; 136:11; Isa 63:11; Jer 2:6; 7:22; 11:7; 32:21; Eze 20:6,10,14,22,36; Hos 11:1; 12:13; Am 9:7; Mic 6:4; Hag 2:5; Mt 2:15; Ac 7:36,40; Heb 3:16; 11:22

Ge 12:10 the land, so Abram went down to E to wait it out.
12:11 As he was approaching the borders of E,
12:14 And sure enough, when they arrived in E,
13: 1 So they left E and traveled north into the Negev—
13:10 garden of the LORD or the beautiful land of E.
15:18 all the way from the border of E to the great
21:21 a marriage for him with a young woman from E.
25:18 which is east of E in the direction of Asshur.
26: 2 appeared to him there and said, "Do not go to E.
37:25 taking spices, balm, and myrrh from Gilead to E.
37:28 and the Ishmaelite traders took him along to E.
37:36 Meanwhile, in E, the traders sold Joseph to
37:36 to Potiphar, an officer of Pharaoh, the king of E.
39: 1 Now when Joseph arrived in E with the Ishmaelite
39: 1 of the personal staff of Pharaoh, the king of E.
41: 8 and wise men of E and told them about his dreams,
41:19 never seen such ugly animals in all the land of E.
41:29 period of great prosperity throughout the land of E.
41:33 suggestion is that you find the wisest man in E
41:41 hereby put you in charge of the entire land of E."
41:43 So Joseph was put in charge of all E.
41:44 or a foot in the entire land of E without your
41:45 So Joseph took charge of the entire land of E.
41:46 he entered the service of Pharaoh, the king of E.
41:48 Joseph took a portion of all the crops grown in E
41:54 but in E there was plenty of grain in the
41:55 Throughout the land of E the people began to
41:57 And people from surrounding lands also came to E
42: 1 Jacob heard that there was grain available in E,
42: 2 I have heard there is grain in E. Go down and buy
42: 3 So Joseph's ten older brothers went down to E to
42: 5 So Jacob's sons arrived in E along with others to
42: 6 Since Joseph was governor of all E and in charge
42:15 leave E unless your youngest brother comes here.
43: 2 When the grain they had brought from E was
43:15 the gifts and double the money and hurried to E,
43:20 to him, "Sir, after our first trip to E to buy food,
45: 4 "I am Joseph, your brother whom you sold into E.
45: 8 of his entire household and ruler over all E.
45: 9 God has made me master over all the land of E.
45:13 Tell my father how I am honored here in E.
45:18 all of their families, and to come here to E to live.
45:18 to you the very best territory in the land of E.
45:19 And tell your brothers to take wagons from E to
45:20 for the best of all the land of E is yours."
45:23 ten donkeys loaded with the good things of E,
45:25 And they left E and returned to their father, Jacob,
45:26 told him. "And he is ruler over all the land of E!"
46: 1 So Jacob set out for E with all his possessions.
46: 3 Do not be afraid to go down to E, for I will see to
46: 4 I will go with you down to E, and I will bring your
46: 4 But you will die in E with Joseph at your side."
46: 5 left Beersheba, and his sons brought him to E.
46: 6 Jacob and his entire family arrived in E—
46: 8 the descendants of Jacob, who went with him to E:
46:20 Joseph's sons, born in the land of E,
46:26 direct descendants who went with him to E,
46:27 Joseph also had two sons who had been born in E.
46:27 members of Jacob's family in the land of E.
46:34 for shepherds are despised in the land of E."
47: 4 We have come to live here in E, for there is no
47: 6 Give them the best land of E—the land of Goshen
47:11 So Joseph assigned the best land of E—the land of
47:13 and the crops continued to fail throughout E
47:14 Joseph collected all the money in E and Canaan in
47:15 When the people of E and Canaan ran out of
47:17 and donkeys of E were in Pharaoh's possession.
47:20 So Joseph bought all the land of E for Pharaoh.
47:21 all the people of E became servants to Pharaoh.
47:26 then made it a law throughout the land of E—
47:27 people of Israel settled in the land of Goshen in E.
47:28 lived for seventeen years after his arrival in E,
47:29 honor this, my last request: Do not bury me in E.
47:30 take me out of E and bury me beside my
48: 5 who were born here in the land of E before I
48: 9 "these are the sons God has given me here in E."
50: 7 and advisers—all the senior officers of E.
50:14 Then Joseph returned to E with his brothers
50:22 and their families continued to live in E.
50:24 come for you, to lead you out of this land of E.
50:26 and his body was placed in a coffin in E.
Ex 1: 1 the sons of Jacob who went with their father to E,
1: 5 Joseph was already down in E. In all, Jacob had
1: 8 Then a new king came to the throne of E who
1:15 Then Pharaoh, the king of E, gave this order to the
2:23 Years passed, and the king of E died.
3: 7 be sure I have seen the misery of my people in E.
3: 8 and lead them out of E into their own good
3:10 You will lead my people, the Israelites, out of E."
3:11 can you expect me to lead the Israelites out of E?"
3:12 When you have brought the Israelites out of E,
3:16 and have seen what is happening to you in E.
3:18 Then all of you must go straight to the king of E
3:19 "But I know that the king of E will not let you go
3:20 and strike at the heart of E with all kinds of
4:18 "I would like to go back to E to visit my family.
4:19 said to him, "Do not be afraid to return to E,
4:20 on a donkey, and headed back to the land of E.
4:21 "When you arrive back in E, go to Pharaoh
4:29 So Moses and Aaron returned to E and called the
5: 5 Look, there are many people here in E, and you are
6: 6 and I will free you from your slavery in E.
6: 7 God who has rescued you from your slavery in E.
6:11 and tell him to let the people of Israel leave E."
6:13 and Aaron to return to Pharaoh, king of E,
6:13 to demand that he let the people of Israel leave E.
6:26 "Lead all the people of Israel out of the land of E,
6:27 permission to lead the people from the land of E.
7: 2 that the people of Israel be allowed to leave E.
7: 3 my miraculous signs and wonders in the land of E.
7: 4 So I will crush E with a series of disasters,
7:19 Aaron to point his staff toward the waters of E—
7:19 Everywhere in E the water will turn into blood,
7:21 was blood everywhere throughout the land of E.
7:22 But again the magicians of E used their secret arts,
8: 3 Every home in E will be filled with them.
8: 5 and marshes of E so there will be frogs in every
8: 6 did so, and frogs covered the whole land of E!
8:16 into swarms of gnats throughout the land of E."
8:17 All the dust in the land of E turned into gnats.
8:21 I will send swarms of flies throughout E.
8:24 flies in Pharaoh's palace and in every home in E.
9: 9 will spread like fine dust over the whole land of E,
9:10 broke out on the people and animals throughout E.
9:22 and cause the hail to fall throughout E,
9:23 a tremendous hailstorm against all the land of E.
9:24 Never in all the history of E had there been a storm
9:25 It left all of E in ruins. Everything left in the fields
9:26 The only spot in all E without hail that day was the
10: 6 the homes of your officials and all the houses of E.
10: 6 Never in the history of E has there been a plague
10: 7 their God! Don't you realize that E lies in ruins?"
10:12 "Raise your hand over the land of E to bring on
10:14 And the locusts swarmed over the land of E from
10:15 neither tree nor plant, throughout the land of E.
10:19 Not a single locust remained in all the land of E.
10:21 terrifying darkness will descend on the land of E."
11: 1 one more disaster on Pharaoh and the land of E.
11: 3 was considered a very great man in the land of E.
11: 4 About midnight I will pass through E.
11: 5 All the firstborn sons will die in every family in E,
11: 6 a loud wail will be heard throughout the land of E;
11: 8 All the officials of E will come running to me,
11: 9 to do even more mighty miracles in the land of E."
12: 1 and Aaron while they were still in the land of E:
12:12 On that night I will pass through the land of E
12:12 and firstborn male animals in the land of E.
12:12 I will execute judgment against all the gods of E,
12:13 will not touch you when I strike the land of E.
12:17 your forces out of the land of E on this very day.
12:27 for he passed over the homes of the Israelites in E.
12:29 killed all the firstborn sons in the land of E,
12:30 and all the people of E woke up during the night,
12:30 loud wailing was heard throughout the land of E.
12:39 from the yeastless dough they had brought from E.
12:39 because the people were rushed out of E
12:40 The people of Israel had lived in E for 430 years.
12:42 LORD to bring his people out from the land of E,
12:51 LORD began to lead the people of Israel out of E,
13: 3 the day you left E, the place of your slavery.
13: 8 of what the LORD did for us when we left E.'
13: 9 it was the LORD who rescued you from E with
13:14 the LORD brought us out of E from our slavery.
13:15 all the firstborn males throughout the land of E,
13:16 who brought you out of E with great power."
13:17 even though that was the shortest way from E to
13:17 they might change their minds and return to E."
13:18 and the Israelites left E like a marching army.
13:19 his bones with them when God led them out of E
14: 5 When word reached the king of E that the
14: 5 were not planning to return to E after three days,
14: 7 along with the rest of the chariots of E, each with a
14:11 Weren't there enough graves for us in E? Why did
14:12 tell you to leave us alone while we were still in E?
14:18 his army, all E will know that I am the LORD!"
16: 1 They arrived there a month after leaving E.

16: 3 "Oh, that we were back in **E**," they moaned.
16: 6 the LORD who brought you out of the land of **E**.
16:32 in the wilderness when he brought you out of **E**."
17: 3 to complain, "Why did you ever take us out of **E**?
18: 1 how the LORD had brought them safely out of **E**.
18: 9 had done for Israel as he brought them out of **E**.
18:10 He has rescued Israel from the power of **E**!
19: 1 of Sinai exactly two months after they left **E**.
20: 2 your God, who rescued you from slavery in **E**.
22:21 yourselves were once foreigners in the land of **E**.
23: 9 Remember your own experience in the land of **E**.
23:15 for that is the anniversary of your exodus from **E**.
29:46 I am the one who brought them out of **E** so that I
32: 1 who brought us here from **E**, has disappeared.
32: 4 these are the gods who brought you out of **E**!"
32: 7 The people you brought from **E** have defiled
32: 8 your gods, O Israel, who brought you out of **E**.' "
32:11 brought from the land of **E** with such great power
32:23 happened to this man Moses, who led us out of **E**.'
33: 1 that you have brought these people out of **E**,
34:18 year in early spring, for that was when you left **E**.
Lev 11:45 am the one who brought you up from the land of **E**
18: 3 So do not act like the people in **E**, where you used
19:34 that you were once foreigners in the land of **E**.
19:36 your God, who brought you out of the land of **E**.
22:33 It was I who rescued you from **E**, that I might be
23:43 in shelters when I rescued them from the land of **E**.
25:38 who brought you out of **E** to give you the land of
25:42 whom I brought out of the land of **E**, so they must
25:55 my servants, whom I brought out of the land of **E**.
26:13 who brought you from the land of **E** so you would
26:45 whom I brought out of **E** while all the nations
Nu 1: 1 the second year after Israel's departure from **E**,
9: 1 the second year after Israel's departure from **E**,
10:11 the second year after Israel's departure from **E**,
11: 4 the Israelites began to crave the good things of **E**,
11: 5 remember all the fish we used to eat for free in **E**.
11:18 had meat to eat! Surely we were better off in **E**!"
11:20 to him, "Why did we ever leave **E**?" ' "
11:34 the people there who had craved meat from **E**.
14: 2 "We wish we had died in **E**, or even here in the
14: 3 as slaves! Let's get out of here and return to **E**!"
14: 4 "Let's choose a leader and go back to **E**!"
14:13 you displayed in rescuing these people from **E**.
14:19 as you have forgiven them ever since they left **E**."
14:22 and the miraculous signs I performed both in **E**
15:41 you out of the land of **E** that I might be your God.
16:13 Isn't it enough that you brought us out of **E**,
20: 5 Why did you make us leave **E** and bring us here to
20:15 and that our ancestors went down to **E**. We lived
20:16 and sent an angel who brought us out of **E**.
21: 5 "Why have you brought us out of **E** to die here in
22: 5 "A vast horde of people has arrived from **E**.
22:11 'A vast horde of people has come from **E** and has
23:22 God has brought them out of **E**; / he is like a strong
24: 8 God brought them up from **E**, / drawing them
26: 4 of all the descendants of Israel who came out of **E**.
26:59 of Levi, born among the Levites in the land of **E**.
32:11 'Of all those I rescued from **E**, no one who is
33: 1 marched out of **E** under the leadership of Moses
33: 4 The LORD had defeated the gods of **E** that night
33:38 the fortieth year after Israel's departure from **E**.
34: 5 the boundary will turn toward the brook of **E**
Dt 1:27 bringing us here from **E** to be slaughtered by these
1:30 He will fight for you, just as you saw him do in **E**.
4:20 the burning furnace of **E** to become his own people
4:34 that is what the LORD your God did for you in **E**,
4:37 and personally brought you out of **E** with a great
4:45 gave to the people of Israel when they left **E**,
4:46 and the Israelites as they came up from **E**.
5: 6 your God, who rescued you from slavery in **E**.
5:15 Remember that you were once slaves in **E** and that
6:12 who rescued you from slavery in the land of **E**.
6:21 must tell them, 'We were Pharaoh's slaves in **E**,
6:21 but the LORD brought us out of **E** with amazing
6:22 dealing terrifying blows against **E** and Pharaoh
6:23 He brought us out of **E** so he could give us this
7: 8 power from your slavery under Pharaoh in **E**.
7:15 suffer from the terrible diseases you knew in **E**,
7:18 your God did to Pharaoh and to all the land of **E**.
7:19 power he used when he brought you out of **E**.
8:14 who rescued you from slavery in the land of **E**.
9: 7 From the day you left **E** until now, you have
9:12 because the people you led out of **E** have become
9:26 redeemed from **E** by your mighty power
9:29 whom you brought from **E** by your mighty power
10:19 yourselves were once foreigners in the land of **E**.
10:22 When your ancestors went down into **E**, there were
11: 3 and wonders he performed in **E** against Pharaoh
11: 4 didn't see what the LORD did to the armies of **E**
11:10 and occupy is not like the land of **E** from which
13: 5 who brought you out of slavery in the land of **E**.
13:10 who rescued you from the land of **E**, the place of
15:15 Remember that you were slaves in the land of **E**
16: 1 LORD your God brought you out of **E** by night.
16: 3 as you did when you escaped from **E** in such a
16: 3 the day you departed from **E** as long as you live.
16: 6 down on the anniversary of your exodus from **E**.
16:12 Remember that you were slaves in **E**, so be careful
17:16 and he must never send his people to **E** to buy
17:16 has told you, 'You must never return to **E**.'
20: 1 who brought you safely out of **E**, is with you!
23: 4 you with food and water when you came out of **E**.
23: 8 you from **E** may enter the assembly of the LORD.
24: 9 God did to Miriam as you were coming from **E**.
24:18 Always remember that you were slaves in **E**
24:22 Remember that you were slaves in the land of **E**.
25:17 the Amalekites did to you as you came from **E**.
26: 5 was a wandering Aramean who went to live in **E**.
26: 5 but in **E** they became a mighty and numerous
26: 8 So the LORD brought us out of **E** with amazing
28:27 "The LORD will afflict you with the boils of **E**
28:60 He will bring against you all the diseases of **E** that
28:68 Then the LORD will send you back to **E** in ships,
29: 2 eyes everything the LORD did in **E** to Pharaoh
29:16 you remember how we lived in the land of **E**
29:25 when he brought them out of the land of **E**.
34:11 and wonders in the land of **E** against Pharaoh,
Jos 2:10 path for you through the Red Sea when you left **E**.
4:19 the month that marked their exodus from **E**.
5: 4 arms when they left **E** had died in the wilderness.
5: 5 Those who left **E** had all been circumcised,
5: 6 old enough to bear arms when they left **E** had died.
5: 9 have rolled away the shame of your slavery in **E**."
5:10 the month that marked their exodus from **E**.
9: 9 of the LORD your God and of all he did in **E**.
13: 3 which is on the boundary of **E**, northward to the
15: 4 to Azmon, until it finally reached the brook of **E**,
15:47 as far as the brook of **E** and along the coast of the
24: 4 while Jacob and his children went down into **E**.
24: 5 and Aaron, and I brought terrible plagues on **E**;
24:14 they lived beyond the Euphrates River and in **E**.
24:17 and our ancestors from slavery in the land of **E**.
24:32 had brought along with them when they left **E**,
Jdg 2: 1 "I brought you out of **E** into this land that I swore
2:12 of their ancestors, who had brought them out of **E**.
6: 8 says: I brought you up out of slavery in **E**
6:13 they say, 'The LORD brought us up out of **E**'?
11:13 "When the Israelites came out of **E**,
11:16 on their journey from **E** after crossing the Red Sea,
19:30 crime has not been committed since Israel left **E**.
1Sa 2:27 when the people of Israel were slaves in **E**?
8: 8 Ever since I brought them from **E** they have
10:18 "I brought you from **E** and rescued you from the
12: 6 "He brought your ancestors out of the land of **E**.
12: 8 "When the Israelites were in **E** and cried out to the
12: 8 he sent Moses and Aaron to rescue them from **E**
15: 2 for opposing Israel when they came from **E**.
15: 6 the people of Israel when they came up from **E**."
15: 7 from Havilah all the way to Shur, east of **E**.
27: 8 near Shur, along the road to **E**, since ancient times.
2Sa 7: 6 from the day I brought the Israelites out of **E** until
7:23 for yourself when you rescued your people from **E**.
1Ki 3: 1 the king of **E**, and married one of his daughters.
4:21 of the Philistines, as far south as the border of **E**.
4:30 all the wise men of the East and the wise men of **E**.
6: 1 were delivered from their slavery in the land of **E**.
8: 9 people of Israel as they were leaving the land of **E**.
8:16 'From the day I brought my people Israel out of **E**,
8:21 our ancestors when he brought them out of **E**."
8:51 you brought out of the iron-smelting furnace of **E**.
8:53 For when you brought our ancestors out of **E**,
8:65 in the north to the brook of **E** in the south.
9: 9 who brought their ancestors out of **E**, and they
9:16 (The king of **E** had attacked and captured Gezer,
10:28 Solomon's horses were imported from **E** and from
11:18 Then they traveled to **E** and went to Pharaoh,
11:21 When the news reached Hadad in **E** that David
11:40 but he fled to King Shishak of **E** and stayed there
12: 2 he returned from **E**, for he had fled to **E** to escape
from King Solomon.
12:20 of Israel learned of Jeroboam's return from **E**,
12:28 these are the gods who brought you out of **E**!"
14:25 King Shishak of **E** came up and attacked
2Ki 17: 4 So of **E** to help him shake free of Assyria's power
17: 7 had brought them safely out of their slavery in **E**.
17:36 who brought you out of **E** with such mighty
18:21 Will **E**? If you lean on **E**, you will find it
18:21 The pharaoh of **E** is completely unreliable!
19:24 I even stopped up the rivers of **E** / so that my
21:15 me ever since their ancestors came out of **E**."
23:29 While Josiah was king, Pharaoh Neco, king of **E**,
23:34 Jehoahaz was taken to **E** as a prisoner, where he
24: 7 The king of **E** never returned after that,
24: 7 occupied the entire area formerly claimed by **E**—
24: 7 from the brook of **E** to the Euphrates River.
25:26 well as the army commanders, fled in panic to **E**,
1Ch 17: 5 from the day I brought the Israelites out of **E** until
17:21 for yourself when you rescued your people from **E**.
2Ch 1:16 Solomon's horses were imported from **E** and from
5:10 covenant with the people of Israel after they left **E**.
6: 5 'From the day I brought my people out of **E**,
7: 8 in the north, to the brook of **E** in the south.
7:22 God of their ancestors, who brought them out of **E**,
9:26 to the land of the Philistines and the border of **E**.
9:28 Solomon's horses were imported from **E** and many
10: 2 he returned from **E**, for he had fled to **E** to escape
from King Solomon.
12: 2 King Shishak of **E** attacked Jerusalem in the fifth
12: 9 So King Shishak of **E** came to Jerusalem and took
20:10 ancestors invade those nations when Israel left **E**,
26: 8 and his fame spread even to **E**, for he had become
35:20 King Neco of **E** led his army up from **E** to do
36: 3 Then he was deposed by Neco, the king of **E**,
36: 4 The king of **E** appointed Eliakim, the brother of
36: 4 Then Neco took Jehoahaz to **E** as a prisoner.
Ne 9: 9 the sufferings and sorrows of our ancestors in **E**,
9:17 a leader to take them back to their slavery in **E**!
9:18 'This is your god who brought you out of **E**!'
13: 2 not been friendly to the Israelites when they left **E**.
Ps 68: 7 O God, when you led your people from **E**,
68:31 Let **E** come with gifts of precious metals;
78:12 the miracles he did for their ancestors in **E**,
78:43 They forgot his miraculous signs in **E**,
78:51 the flower of youth throughout the land of **E**.
80: 8 You brought us from **E** as though we were a tender
81: 5 for Israel / when he attacked **E** to set us free.
81:10 your God, / who rescued you from the land of **E**.
87: 4 I will record **E** and Babylon among those who
105:17 Then he sent someone to **E** ahead of them—
105:23 Then Israel arrived in **E**; / Jacob lived as a
105:28 The LORD blanketed **E** in darkness, / for they
105:31 on the Egyptians, / and gnats swarmed across **E**.
105:37 But he brought his people safely out of **E**,
105:38 **E** was glad when they were gone, / for the dread of
105:43 So he brought his people out of **E** with joy,
106: 7 Our ancestors in **E** / were not impressed by the
106:21 who had done such great things in **E**—
114: 1 When the Israelites escaped from **E**—
135: 9 He performed miraculous signs and wonders in **E**;
136:10 Give thanks to him who killed the firstborn of **E**.
136:11 He brought Israel out of **E**. / His faithful love
Pr 7:16 colored sheets of finest linen imported from **E**.
Isa 7:18 the LORD will whistle for the army of Upper **E**
11:11 Lower **E**, Upper **E**, Ethiopia, Elam, Babylonia,
11:16 did for Israel long ago when they returned from **E**.
19: 1 This message came to me concerning **E**: Look!
19: 1 The LORD is advancing against **E**, riding on a
swift cloud. The idols of **E** tremble.
19: 4 I will hand **E** over to a hard, cruel master, to a
19: 6 and the streams of **E** will become foul with rotting
19:11 Their best counsel to the king of **E** is stupid
19:12 what the LORD Almighty is going to do to **E**.
19:13 The leaders of **E** have ruined the land with their
19:14 They cause the land of **E** to stagger like a sick
19:15 Nobody in **E**, whether rich or poor, important
19:19 will be an altar to the LORD in the heart of **E**,
19:20 a witness to the LORD Almighty in the land of **E**.
19:22 The LORD will strike **E** in a way that will bring
19:23 In that day **E** and Assyria will be connected by a
19:25 Almighty will say, "Blessed be **E**, my people.
20: 3 symbol of the terrible troubles I will bring upon **E**
20: 4 their buttocks uncovered, to the shame of **E**.
20: 5 power of Ethiopia and boasted of their allies in **E**!
20: 6 They will say, 'If this can happen to **E**,
20: 6 For we counted on **E** to protect us from the king
23: 3 They brought you grain from **E** and harvests from
23: 5 When **E** hears the news about Tyre, there will be
27:12 River in the east to the brook of **E** in the west.
27:13 and **E** will return to Jerusalem to worship the
30: 2 you have gone down to **E** to find help.
30: 6 moving slowly across the terrible desert to **E**—
30: 6 All this, and **E** will give you nothing in return.
30: 8 Now go and write down these words concerning **E**.
30:16 You said, 'No, we will get our help from **E**.
31: 1 Destruction is certain for those who look to **E** for
36: 6 Will **E**? If you lean on **E**, you will find it to be
36: 6 The Pharaoh of **E** is completely unreliable!
37:25 I even stopped up the rivers of **E** / so that my
43: 3 I gave **E**, Ethiopia, and Seba as a ransom for your
43:17 I called forth the mighty army of **E** with all its
49:12 to the north and west, and from as far south as **E**."
51: 9 yourself as in the days of old when you slew **E**,
52: 4 my people went to live as resident foreigners in **E**.
63:11 days of old when Moses led his people out of **E**.
Jer 2: 6 is the LORD who brought us safely out of **E**
2:18 "What have you gained by your alliances with **E**
2:36 But your new friends in **E** will let you down,
7:22 When I led your ancestors out of **E**, it was not
7:25 From the day your ancestors left **E** until now,
11: 4 ancestors when I brought them out of slavery in **E**,
11: 7 your ancestors when I brought them out of **E**,
16:14 rescued the people of Israel from the land of **E**.'
23: 7 rescued the people of Israel from the land of **E**.'
24: 8 people left in Jerusalem, and those who live in **E**.
25:19 I went to **E** and spoke to Pharaoh, his officials,
26:21 But Uriah heard about the plot and escaped to **E**.
26:22 to **E** along with several other men to capture Uriah.
31:32 by the hand and brought them out of the land of **E**.
32:20 miraculous signs and wonders in the land of **E**—
32:21 "You brought Israel out of **E** with mighty signs
34:13 ago when I rescued them from their slavery in **E**.
37: 5 At this time the army of Pharaoh Hophra of **E**
37: 7 that Pharaoh's army is about to return to **E**,
41:17 where they prepared to leave for **E**.
42:14 and if you insist on going to live in **E** where you
42:15 the God of Israel, says: 'If you insist on going to **E**,
42:17 every one of you who insists on going to live in **E**.
42:18 they will be poured out on you when you enter **E**.
42:19 The LORD has told you: 'Do not go to **E**!'
42:22 famine, and disease in **E**, where you insist on
43: 2 LORD our God hasn't forbidden us to go to **E**!
43: 7 people refused to obey the LORD and went to **E**,
43:10 king of Babylon, here to **E**.
43:11 And when he comes, he will destroy the land of **E**.
43:12 He will pick clean the land of **E** as a shepherd
43:13 pillars standing in the temple of the sun in **E**,
44: 1 living in northern **E** in the cities of Migdol,
44: 1 and Memphis, and throughout southern **E** as well:
44: 8 incense to the idols you have made here in **E**?
44:12 of Judah that insisted on coming here to **E**,
44:12 They will fall here in **E**, killed by war and famine.
44:13 I will punish them in **E** just as I punished them in
44:14 Of those who fled to **E** with dreams of returning
44:15 living in Pathros, the southern region of **E**—
44:24 all you citizens of Judah who live in **E**.
44:26 from the LORD, all you Judeans now living in **E**:
44:26 be spoken by any of the Judeans in the land of **E**.
44:28 will escape death and return to Judah from **E**.
44:28 Then all those who come to **E** will find out whose
44:30 I will turn Pharaoh Hophra, king of **E**, over to his

46: 2 This message concerning **E** was given in the fourth
46: 2 of Carchemish when Pharaoh Neco, king of **E**,
46: 9 you horses and chariots and mighty warriors of **E**!
46: 11 to Gilead to get ointment, O virgin daughter of **E**!
46: 13 about King Nebuchadnezzar's plans to attack **E**.
46: 14 "Shout it out in **E**! Publish it in the cities of
46: 17 There they will say, 'Pharaoh, the king of **E**,
46: 18 "one is coming against **E** who is as tall as Mount
46: 19 Get ready to leave for exile, you citizens of **E**!
46: 20 **E** is as sleek as a young cow, but a gadfly from the
46: 21 and run, for it is a day of great disaster for **E**,
46: 22 Silent as a serpent gliding away, **E** flees.
46: 24 **E** will be humiliated; she will be handed over to
46: 25 the god of Thebes, and all the other gods of **E**.
La 5: 6 We submitted to **E** and Assyria to get enough food
Eze 16: 26 Then you added lustful **E** to your lovers,
17: 15 sending ambassadors to **E** to request a great army
19: 4 They led him away in chains / to the land of **E**.
20: 5 I chose Israel and revealed myself to her in **E**,
20: 6 and her descendants out of **E** to a land I had
20: 8 not get rid of their idols or forsake the gods of **E**.
20: 8 them to satisfy my anger while they were still in **E**.
20: 10 So I brought my people out of **E** and led them into
20: 14 of **E** wouldn't be able to claim I destroyed them
20: 22 who had seen my power in bringing them out of **E**.
20: 36 in the wilderness after bringing them out of **E**,
23: 3 They became prostitutes in **E**. Even as young girls,
23: 8 For when she left **E**, she did not leave her spirit of
23: 19 her youth when she was a prostitute in **E**.
23: 21 celebrated your former days as a young girl in **E**,
23: 27 the lewdness and prostitution you brought from **E**.
23: 27 those things or fondly remember your time in **E**.
29: 2 turn toward **E** and prophesy against Pharaoh the king and all the people of **E**.
29: 3 I am your enemy, O Pharaoh, king of **E**—you great
29: 6 "All the people of **E** will discover that I am the
29: 8 O **E**, and destroy both people and animals.
29: 9 The land of **E** will become a desolate wasteland,
29: 10 I will utterly destroy the land of **E**, from Migdol to
29: 12 I will make **E** desolate, and it will be surrounded
29: 14 I will restore the prosperity of **E** and bring its
29: 14 of Pathros in southern **E** from which they came.
29: 14 But **E** will remain an unimportant, minor kingdom.
29: 16 will no longer be tempted to trust in **E** for help.
29: 16 of how sinful she was to trust **E** in earlier days.
29: 19 I will give the land of **E** to Nebuchadnezzar,
29: 20 I have given him the land of **E** as a reward for his
30: 4 A sword will come against **E**, and those who are
30: 7 **E** will be desolate, surrounded by desolate nations,
30: 8 And the people of **E** will know that I am the LORD when I have set **E** on fire
30: 10 of Babylon, I will destroy the hordes of **E**.
30: 11 They will make war against **E** until slaughtered
30: 12 I will destroy the land of **E** and everything in it,
30: 13 I will smash the idols of **E** and the images at
30: 13 There will be no rulers left in **E**; anarchy will
30: 15 my fury on Pelusium, the strongest fortress of **E**,
30: 16 Yes, I will set fire to all **E**! Pelusium will be
30: 18 When I come to break the proud strength of **E**,
30: 19 And so I will greatly punish **E**, and they will know
30: 21 I have broken the arm of Pharaoh, the king of **E**.
30: 22 I am the enemy of Pharaoh, the king of **E**! I will
30: 24 But I will break the arms of Pharaoh, king of **E**,
30: 25 and he brings it against the land of **E**, **E** will know that I am the LORD.
31: 2 message to Pharaoh, king of **E**, and all his people:
31: 18 "O **E**, to which of the trees of Eden will you
32: 2 "Son of man, mourn for Pharaoh, king of **E**,
32: 12 They will shatter the pride of **E**, and all its hordes
32: 14 Then I will let the waters of **E** become calm again,
32: 15 And when I destroy **E** and wipe out everything you
32: 16 Yes, this is the funeral song they will sing for **E**.
32: 16 Let all the nations mourn for **E** and its hordes.
32: 18 weep for the hordes of **E** and for the other mighty
32: 19 Say to them, 'O **E**, are you lovelier than the other
32: 20 **E** will be dragged away to its judgment.
32: 21 grave mighty leaders will mockingly welcome **E**
32: 28 "You too, **E**, will lie crushed and broken among
47: 19 then follow the course of the brook of **E** to the
48: 28 then follows the brook of **E** to the Mediterranean.
Da 9: 15 your people from **E** in a great display of power.
11: 8 When he returns again to **E**, he will carry back
11: 42 conquer many countries, and **E** will not escape.
11: 43 silver, and treasures of **E**, and the Libyans
Hos 2: 15 when I freed her from her captivity in **E**.
7: 11 witless doves, first calling to **E**, then flying to
7: 16 Then the people of **E** will laugh at them.
8: 13 I will punish them. They will go back down to **E**.
9: 3 You will be carried off to **E** and Assyria,
9: 6 from Assyria, you will be conquered by **E**.
11: 1 I loved him as a son, and I called my son out of **E**.
11: 5 they will go back to **E** and will be forced to serve
11: 11 Like a flock of birds, they will come from **E**.
12: 9 who rescued you from your slavery in **E**.
12: 13 out of **E** by a prophet, who guided and protected
13: 4 who rescued you from your slavery in **E**.
Joel 3: 19 **E** will become a wasteland and Edom a wilderness,
Am 2: 10 It was I who rescued you from **E** and led you
3: 1 and Judah—the entire family I rescued from **E**:
3: 9 Announce this to the leaders of Philistia and **E**:
4: 10 you like the plagues I sent against **E** long ago.
9: 7 "I brought you out of **E**, but have I not done as
Mic 6: 4 For I brought you out of **E** and redeemed you from
7: 12 from Assyria all the way to the towns of **E**,
7: 12 and from **E** all the way to the Euphrates River,
7: 15 those I did when I rescued you from slavery in **E**."
Na 3: 9 and the land of **E** were the source of her strength,
Hag 2: 5 just as I promised when you came out of **E**.
Zec 10: 10 I will bring them back from **E** and Assyria
10: 11 Assyria will be crushed, and the rule of **E** will end.
14: 18 And if the people of **E** refuse to attend the festival,
14: 19 **E** and the other nations will all be punished if they
Mt 2: 13 "Get up and flee to **E** with the child and his
2: 14 That night Joseph left for **E** with the child
2: 15 through the prophet: "I called my Son out of **E**."
2: 19 of the Lord appeared in a dream to Joseph in **E**
Ac 2: 10 Phrygia, Pamphylia, **E**, and the areas of Libya
7: 9 and they sold him to be a slave in **E**.
7: 10 God gave him favor before Pharaoh, king of **E**.
7: 10 that Pharaoh appointed him governor over all of **E**
7: 11 "But a famine came upon **E** and Canaan.
7: 12 Jacob heard that there was still grain in **E**, so he
7: 14 Jacob, and all his relatives to come to **E**,
7: 15 So Jacob went to **E**. He died there, as did all his
7: 17 the number of our people in **E** greatly increased.
7: 18 then a new king came to the throne of **E** who knew
7: 34 sure that I have seen the misery of my people in **E**.
7: 34 to rescue them. Now go, for I will send you to **E**.'
7: 36 and wonders he led them out of **E**,
7: 39 rejected Moses and wanted to return to **E**.
7: 40 become of this Moses, who brought us out of **E**.'
13: 17 chose our ancestors and made them prosper in **E**.
18: 24 had just arrived in Ephesus from Alexandria in **E**.
Heb 3: 16 Weren't they the ones Moses led out of **E**?
8: 9 by the hand / and led them out of the land of **E**.
11: 22 of God's bringing the people of Israel out of **E**.
11: 26 sake of the Messiah than to own the treasures of **E**,
11: 27 It was by faith that Moses left the land of **E**.
Jude 1: 5 the Lord rescued the whole nation of Israel from **E**,
Rev 11: 8 the city which is called "Sodom" and "**E**,"

EGYPT'S (14) [EGYPT]

Ex 9: 18 send a hailstorm worse than any in all of **E** history.
14: 7 He took with him six hundred of **E** best chariots,
2Ki 18: 24 even with the help of **E** chariots and horsemen?
Isa 19: 18 In that day five of **E** cities will follow the LORD
30: 6 and camels loaded with treasure to pay for **E** aid.
30: 7 **E** promises are worthless! I call her the Harmless
36: 9 even with the help of **E** chariots and horsemen?
Jer 43: 12 He will set fire to the temples of **E** gods,
43: 13 and he will burn down the temples of **E** gods.' "
46: 21 **E** famed mercenaries have become like fattened
Eze 27: 7 Your sails were made of **E** finest linen, and they
29: 16 **E** shattered condition will remind Israel of how
30: 6 All of **E** allies will fall, and the pride of their
30: 9 Great panic will come upon them on that day of **E**

EGYPTIAN (46) [EGYPT]

Ge 16: 1 Sarai took her servant, an **E** woman named Hagar,
16: 3 took Hagar the **E** servant and gave her to Abram as
21: 9 the son of Abraham and her **E** servant Hagar—
25: 12 son of Abraham through Hagar, Sarah's **E** servant.
39: 2 greatly as he served in the home of his **E** master.
Ex 1: 19 They are not slow in giving birth like **E** women."
2: 11 he saw an **E** beating one of the Hebrew slaves.
2: 12 Moses killed the **E** and buried him in the sand.
2: 14 Do you plan to kill me as you killed that **E**
2: 19 "An **E** rescued us from the shepherds," they told
3: 22 and fine clothing from their **E** neighbors
9: 14 to you and your officials and all the **E** people.
10: 14 It was the worst locust plague in **E** history,
11: 2 and women to ask their **E** neighbors for articles of
11: 3 by Pharaoh's officials and the **E** people alike.)
14: 12 Our **E** slavery was far better than dying out here in
14: 20 cloud settled between the Israelite and **E** camps.
14: 24 the LORD looked down on the **E** army from the
14: 26 Then the waters will rush back over the **E** chariots
Lev 24: 10 and an **E** father got into a fight with one of the
Nu 13: 22 founded seven years before the **E** city of Zoan.)
1Sa 30: 11 Some of David's troops found an **E** man in a field
30: 13 "I am an **E**—the slave of an Amalekite,"
30: 16 So the **E** led them to the Amalekite encampment.
2Sa 23: 21 he killed a great **E** warrior who was armed with a
1Ki 10: 29 **E** chariots delivered to Jerusalem could be
1Ch 2: 34 He also had an **E** servant named Jarha.
4: 17 Mered married an **E** woman, who became the
4: 18 Mered's **E** wife was named Bithiah, and she was an **E** princess.
11: 23 he killed an **E** warrior who was seven and a half
2Ch 1: 17 **E** chariots delivered to Jerusalem could be
Ps 78: 51 He killed the oldest son in each **E** family,
105: 36 Then he killed the oldest child in each **E** home,
135: 8 He destroyed the firstborn in each **E** home,
Isa 10: 26 staff was raised to drown the **E** army in the sea.
Jer 46: 5 But look! The **E** army flees in terror. The bravest
46: 8 It is the **E** army, boasting that it will cover the
47: 1 of Gaza, before it was captured by the **E** army.
Eze 20: 7 Do not defile yourselves with the **E** gods, for I am
Na 3: 10 Soldiers cast lots to see who would get the **E**
Ac 7: 24 this visit, he saw an **E** mistreating a man of Israel.
7: 24 to his defense and avenged him, killing the **E**.
7: 28 'Are you going to kill me as you killed that **E**
21: 38 "Aren't you the **E** who led a rebellion some time
27: 6 There the officer found an **E** ship from Alexandria

EGYPTIAN'S (2) [EGYPT]

2Sa 23: 21 Benaiah wrenched the spear from the **E** hand
1Ch 11: 23 Benaiah wrenched the spear from the **E** hand

EGYPTIANS (100) [EGYPT]

Ge 12: 12 When the **E** see you, they will say, 'This is his
12: 13 then the **E** will treat me well because of their
41: 56 opened up the storehouses and sold grain to the **E**.
43: 32 The **E** sat at their own table because **E** despise Hebrews and refuse to eat with
47: 20 All the **E** sold him their fields because the famine
50: 11 is a place of very deep mourning for these **E**."
Ex 1: 11 So the **E** made the Israelites their slaves and put
1: 12 But the more the **E** oppressed them, the more
1: 12 Israelites multiplied! The **E** soon became alarmed
3: 8 So I have come to rescue them from the **E** and lead
3: 9 and I have seen how the **E** have oppressed them
3: 17 to rescue you from the oppression of the **E**.
3: 21 And I will see to it that the **E** treat you well.
3: 22 In this way, you will plunder the **E**!"
6: 5 the people of Israel, who are now slaves to the **E**.
7: 5 When I show the **E** my power and force them to let
7: 18 The **E** will not be able to drink any water from the
7: 21 water became so foul that the **E** couldn't drink it.
7: 24 Then the **E** dug wells along the riverbank to get
8: 17 the entire land, covering the **E** and their animals.
8: 26 The **E** would detest the sacrifices that we offer to
9: 4 the property of the Israelites and that of the **E**.
9: 6 The next morning all the livestock of the **E** began
10: 2 among the **E** to prove that I am the LORD."
11: 3 (Now the LORD had caused the **E** to look
11: 7 that the LORD makes a distinction between the **E**
12: 23 will pass through the land and strike down the **E**.
12: 27 And though he killed the **E**, he spared our families
12: 33 All the **E** urged the people of Israel to get out of
12: 35 and asked the **E** for clothing and articles of silver
12: 36 The LORD caused the **E** to look favorably on the
12: 36 like a victorious army, they plundered the **E**!
14: 4 After this, the **E** will know that I am the LORD!"
14: 9 The **E** caught up with the people of Israel as they
14: 13 The **E** that you see today will never be seen again.
14: 17 Yet I will harden the hearts of the **E**, and they will
14: 20 But the cloud became darkness to the **E**, and they
14: 23 Then the **E**—all of Pharaoh's horses, chariots,
14: 25 to drive. "Let's get out of here!" the **E** shouted.
14: 27 and the LORD swept the terrified **E** into the
14: 28 Of all the **E** who had chased the Israelites into the
14: 30 the LORD rescued Israel from the **E** that day.
14: 30 And the Israelites could see the bodies of the **E**
14: 31 that the LORD had displayed against the **E**,
15: 26 not make you suffer the diseases I sent on the **E**;
18: 8 had done to rescue Israel from Pharaoh and the **E**.
18: 10 "for he has saved you from the **E** and from
18: 11 people have escaped from the proud and cruel **E**."
19: 4 'You have seen what I did to the **E**. You know
32: 12 The **E** will say, 'God tricked them into coming to
Nu 3: 13 the day I killed all the firstborn sons of the **E**,
8: 17 on the night I killed all the firstborn sons of the **E**.
14: 13 "But what will the **E** think when they hear about
20: 15 there a long time and suffered as slaves to the **E**.
33: 3 of Israel left defiantly, in full view of all the **E**.
33: 4 the **E** were burying all their firstborn sons,
Dt 9: 28 If you destroy these people, the **E** will say,
23: 7 "Do not detest the Edomites or the **E**,
23: 7 and you lived as foreigners among the **E**.
23: 8 The third generation of **E** who came with you from
26: 6 When the **E** mistreated and humiliated us by
Jos 24: 6 the **E** chased after you with chariots and horses.
24: 7 the LORD, I put darkness between you and the **E**.
24: 7 I brought the sea crashing down on the **E**,
Jdg 6: 9 and rescued you from the **E** and from all who
10: 11 "Did I not rescue you from the **E**, the Amorites,
1Sa 4: 8 They are the same gods who destroyed the **E** with
6: 6 and rebellious as Pharaoh and the **E** were.
10: 18 you from Egypt and rescued you from the **E**
2Ki 7: 6 of Israel has hired the Hittites and **E** to attack us!"
Ezr 9: 1 Perizzites, Jebusites, Ammonites, Moabites, **E**,
Ne 9: 10 for you knew how arrogantly the **E** were treating
Ps 105: 25 Then he turned the **E** against the Israelites,
105: 27 They performed miraculous signs among the **E**,
105: 31 When he spoke, flies descended on the **E**,
Isa 10: 24 when they oppress you just as the **E** did long ago.
19: 1 Egypt tremble. The hearts of the **E** melt with fear.
19: 2 "I will make the **E** fight against each other—
19: 3 The **E** will lose heart, and I will confuse their
19: 16 In that day the **E** will be as weak as women.
19: 21 day the LORD will make himself known to the **E**.
19: 22 For the **E** will turn to the LORD, and he will
19: 23 The **E** and Assyrians will move freely between
20: 4 For the king of Assyria will take away the **E**
31: 3 For these **E** are mere humans, not God!
45: 14 "The **E**, Ethiopians, and Sabeans will be subject to
Jer 2: 16 **E**, marching from their cities of Memphis
9: 26 the **E**, Edomites, Ammonites, Moabites, the people
Eze 23: 8 when the **E** satisfied their lusts with her and robbed
29: 9 and the **E** will know that I am the LORD.
29: 12 desolate cities. I will scatter the **E** to distant lands.
29: 13 At the end of the forty years I will bring the **E**
30: 11 Egypt until slaughtered **E** cover the ground.
30: 23 I will scatter the **E** to many lands throughout the
30: 26 I will scatter the **E** among the nations. Then they
32: 20 The **E** will fall with the many who have died by
Hos 12: 1 alliances with Assyria and cut deals with the **E**.
Ac 7: 22 Moses was taught all the wisdom of the **E**, and he
Heb 11: 29 But when the **E** followed, they were all drowned.

EGYPTIANS' (1) [EGYPT]

Ps 78: 50 anger against them; / he did not spare the **E** lives

EHI (1)

Ge 46: 21 Beker, Ashbel, Gera, Naaman, **E**, Rosh, Muppim,

EHUD (15) [EHUD'S]

Jdg 3:15 His name was **E** son of Gera, of the tribe of
3:15 The Israelites sent **E** to deliver their tax money to
3:16 So **E** made himself a double-edged dagger that was
3:18 **E** sent home those who had carried the tax money.
3:19 But when **E** reached the stone carvings near Gilgal,
3:20 **E** walked over to Eglon as he was sitting alone in a
3:21 **E** reached with his left hand, pulled out the dagger
3:22 So **E** left the dagger in, and the king's bowels
3:23 Then **E** closed and locked the doors and climbed
3:24 After **E** was gone, the king's servants returned
3:26 While the servants were waiting, **E** escaped,
3:27 hill country of Ephraim, **E** sounded a call to arms.
3:31 After **E**, Shamgar son of Anath rescued Israel.
1Ch 7:10 Benjamin, **E**, Kenaanah, Zethan, Tarshish,
8:6 The sons of **E**, leaders of the clans living at Geba,

EHUD'S (2) [EHUD]

Jdg 4:1 After **E** death, the Israelites again did what was
1Ch 8:7 **E** sons were Naaman, Ahijah, and Gera. Gera,

EIGHT (37) [EIGHT-STRINGED, EIGHTH, 8]

Ge 21:4 **E** days after Isaac was born, Abraham circumcised
22:20 his brother Nahor's wife, had borne Nahor **e** sons.
22:24 In addition to his **e** sons from Milcah, Nahor had
Ex 26:25 So there will be **e** frames on that end of the
36:30 So for the west side they made a total of **e** frames,
Nu 7:8 and **e** oxen to the Merarite division for their work.
29:29 of the festival, sacrifice **e** young bulls, two rams,
Jdg 3:8 were subject to Cushan-rishathaim for **e** years.
12:14 seventy donkeys. He was Israel's judge for **e** years.
1Sa 17:12 an old man at that time, and he had **e** sons in all.
2Sa 23:8 He once used his spear to kill **e** hundred enemy
2Ki 8:17 became king, and he reigned in Jerusalem **e** years.
22:1 Josiah was **e** years old when he became king,
1Ch 24:4 divided into sixteen groups and Ithamar's into **e**,
2Ch 21:5 became king, and he reigned in Jerusalem **e** years.
21:20 became king, and he reigned in Jerusalem **e** years.
29:17 and in **e** days they had reached the foyer of the
29:17 of the LORD itself, which took another **e** days.
34:1 Josiah was **e** years old when he became king,
Jer 41:15 and **e** of his men escaped from Johanan into the
Eze 4:10 **e** ounces of food for each day, and eat it at set
40:31 and there were **e** steps leading to its entrance.
40:34 and there were **e** steps leading to its entrance.
40:37 There were **e** steps leading to its entrance.
40:41 So there were **e** tables in all, four inside and four
Mic 5:5 seven rulers to watch over us, **e** princes to lead us.
Lk 1:59 When the baby was **e** days old, all the relatives
2:21 **E** days later, when the baby was circumcised,
9:28 About **e** days later Jesus took Peter, James,
16:6 'I owe him **e** hundred gallons of olive oil.'
16:7 and replace it with one for only **e** hundred
Jn 20:26 **E** days later the disciples were together again,
Ac 7:8 was circumcised when he was **e** days old.
9:33 who had been paralyzed and bedridden for **e** years.
25:6 **E** or ten days later he returned to Caesarea, and on
Php 3:5 For I was circumcised when I was **e** days old,
1Pe 3:20 Only **e** people were saved from drowning in that

EIGHT-STRINGED (2) [EIGHT, STRING]

Ps 6:T of David, to be accompanied by an **e** instrument.
12:T of David, to be accompanied by an **e** instrument.

EIGHTEEN (18) [EIGHTEENTH, 18]

Ex 26:13 and the covering will hang down an extra **e** inches
30:2 It must be **e** inches square and three feet high,
37:25 It was **e** inches square and three feet high, with its
Jdg 3:14 were subject to Eglon of Moab for **e** years.
3:16 a double-edged dagger that was **e** inches long,
10:8 For **e** years they oppressed all the Israelites east of
20:25 but the men of Benjamin killed another **e** thousand
20:44 **E** thousand of Benjamin's greatest warriors died in
2Sa 8:13 After his return he destroyed **e** thousand Edomites
2Ki 24:8 Jehoiachin was **e** years old when he became king,
1Ch 18:12 Abishai son of Zeruiah destroyed **e** thousand
26:9 Meshelemiah's **e** sons and relatives were also very
2Ch 11:21 In all, he had **e** wives and sixty concubines,
36:9 Jehoiachin was **e** years old when he became king,
Ezr 8:18 along with **e** of his sons and brothers.
Lk 13:4 And what about the **e** men who died when the
13:11 She had been bent double for **e** years and was
13:16 bondage in which Satan has held her for **e** years?"

EIGHTEENTH (12) [EIGHTEEN]

1Ki 15:1 Abijam began to rule over Judah in the **e** year of
2Ki 3:1 Ahab's son Joram began to rule over Israel in the **e**
22:3 In the **e** year of his reign, King Josiah sent Shaphan
23:23 Jerusalem during the **e** year of King Josiah's reign.
1Ch 24:15 lot fell to Hezir. / The **e** lot fell to Happizzez.
25:25 The **e** lot fell to Hanani and twelve of his sons
2Ch 13:1 Abijah began to rule over Judah in the **e** year of
34:8 In the **e** year of his reign, after he had purified the
35:19 This Passover celebration took place in the **e** year
Jer 32:1 This was also the **e** year of the reign of King
52:29 Then in Nebuchadnezzar's **e** year he took 832
Hag 2:18 "On this **e** day of December—the day when the

EIGHTH (29) [EIGHT]

Ge 17:12 Every male child must be circumcised on the **e** day
Ex 22:30 for seven days; then give it to me on the **e** day.
Lev 9:1 on the **e** day, Moses called together Aaron and his
12:3 On the **e** day, the boy must be circumcised.
14:10 "On the next day, the **e** day, each person cured of
14:23 On the **e** day, the person being cleansed must bring
15:14 On the **e** day he must bring two turtledoves or two
15:29 On the **e** day, she must bring two turtledoves
22:27 From the **e** day on, it will be acceptable as an
23:36 On the **e** day, you must gather again for a sacred
23:39 and closing **e** day of the festival will be days of
25:22 As you plant the seed in the **e** year, you will still be
Nu 6:10 On the **e** day they must bring two turtledoves
7:54 On the **e** day Gamaliel son of Pedahzur, leader of
29:35 "On the **e** day of the festival, call all the people to
1Sa 13:21 and an **e** of an ounce for sharpening an ax, a sickle,
2Ki 24:12 In the **e** year of Nebuchadnezzar's reign, he took
1Ch 12:12 Johanan was **e**. / Elzabad was ninth.
24:10 lot fell to Hakkoz. / The **e** lot fell to Abijah.
25:15 The **e** lot fell to Jeshaiah and twelve of his sons
26:5 Issachar (the seventh), and Peullethai (the **e**).
27:11 from Hushah, was commander of the **e** division,
27:11 which was on duty during the **e** month.
2Ch 7:9 On the **e** day they had a closing ceremony, for they
34:3 During the **e** year of his reign, while he was still
Ne 10:32 annual Temple tax of an **e** of an ounce of silver,
Eze 43:27 On the **e** day, and on each day afterward,
Rev 17:11 beast that was alive and then died is the **e** king.
21:20 the **e** beryl, the ninth topaz, the tenth chrysoprase,

EIGHTY (11) [EIGHTIETH, 80]

Ex 7:7 Moses was **e** years old, and Aaron was eighty-three
Jdg 3:30 that day, and the land was at peace for **e** years.
2Sa 19:32 He was very old, about **e**, and very wealthy.
19:35 I am **e** years old today, and I can no longer enjoy
1Ki 5:15 **e** thousand stonecutters in the hill country,
2Ki 10:24 Now Jehu had surrounded the building with **e** of
2Ch 2:2 **e** thousand stonecutters in the hill country,
26:17 Azariah the high priest went in after him with **e**
Ps 90:10 years are given to us! / Some may even reach **e**.
SS 6:8 and **e** concubines and unnumbered virgins
Jer 41:5 **e** men arrived from Shechem, Shiloh, and Samaria.

EIGHTY-FIVE (2)

Jos 14:10 in the wilderness. Today I am **e** years old.
1Sa 22:18 turned on them and killed them, **e** priests in all,

EIGHTY-FOUR (1)

Lk 2:37 She was now **e** years old. She never left the

EIGHTY-SIX (1)

Ge 16:16 Abram was **e** years old at that time.

EIGHTY-THREE (1)

Ex 7:7 and Aaron was **e** at the time they made their

EITHER (59)

Ge 31:53 to punish **e** one of us who harms the other."
Ex 5:14 "Why haven't you met your quotas **e** yesterday
12:5 **e** a sheep or a goat, with no physical defects.
21:32 But if the bull gores a slave, **e** male or female,
Lev 1:14 choose **e** a turtledove or a young pigeon.
3:1 peace offering from the herd, use **e** a bull or a cow.
3:6 from the flock, you may bring **e** a goat or a sheep.
3:6 It may be **e** male or female, and it must have no
5:6 a female from the flock, **e** a sheep or a goat.
11:4 because they **e** have split hooves or chew the cud,
12:6 "When the time of purification is completed for **e**
13:24 becoming **e** a shiny reddish white or white,
15:3 or is stopped up. In **e** case the man is unclean.
20:17 the daughter of **e** his father or his mother, it is a
22:19 It may be **e** a bull, a ram, or a male goat.
Nu 6:2 If some of the people, **e** men or women,
30:13 So her husband may **e** confirm or nullify any vows
Dt 2:27 and won't turn off into the fields on **e** side.
16:2 Your Passover sacrifice may be from **e** the flock
22:9 you are forbidden to use **e** the grapes from the
Jdg 11:17 but he wouldn't let them pass through **e**.
19:13 We will find a place to spend the night in **e** Gibeah
1Sa 20:27 the son of Jesse been here for dinner **e** yesterday
28:6 **e** by dreams or by sacred lots or by the prophets.
1Ki 20:39 you will **e** die or pay a fine of seventy-five pounds
2Ki 9:20 "The rider has met them, but he isn't returning **e**!
18:5 him in the land of Judah, **e** before or after his time.
Job 37:13 **e** as a punishment or as a sign of his unfailing love.
Pr 27:10 Never abandon a friend—**e** yours or your father's.
Ecc 7:17 On the other hand, don't be too wicked **e**—
7:18 but those who fear God will succeed **e** way.
10:20 And don't make fun of a rich man, **e**.
Jer 29:19 And you who are in exile have not listened **e**,"
Eze 1:11 touch the wings of the living beings on **e** side of it,
Am 7:6 "I won't do that **e**," said the Sovereign LORD.
Zec 8:10 were no jobs and no wages for **e** people or animals.
Mt 12:32 **e** in this world or in the world to come.
12:37 **e** you will be justified by them or you will be
21:27 "Then I won't answer your question **e**.
27:38 crucified with him, their crosses on **e** side of his.
Mk 7:18 "Don't you understand **e**?" he asked. "Can't you
11:33 "Then I won't answer your question **e**."
12:5 Others who were sent were **e** beaten or killed,
15:27 crucified with him, their crosses on **e** side of his.
Lk 2:24 "**e** a pair of turtledoves or two young pigeons."
20:8 "Then I won't answer your question **e**."
23:33 the center cross, and the two criminals on **e** side.
Jn 19:18 with him, one on **e** side, with Jesus between them.
Ac 20:20 telling you the truth, **e** publicly or in your homes.
Ro 2:15 for their own consciences **e** accuse them or tell
11:21 he put there in the first place, he won't spare you **e**.
1Co 15:13 of the dead, then Christ has not been raised **e**.
2Ti 1:8 And don't be ashamed of me, **e**, even though I'm
2:5 just as an athlete **e** follows the rules or is
Tit 3:12 I am planning to send **e** Artemas or Tychicus to
Jas 1:13 to do wrong, and he never tempts anyone else **e**.
1Jn 2:23 who denies the Son doesn't have the Father **e**.
3:6 So if we continue to live in him, we won't sin **e**.
Rev 13:17 which was **e** the name of the beast or the number

EKER (1)

1Ch 2:27 oldest son of Jerahmeel, were Maaz, Jamin, and **E**.

EKRON (23)

Jos 13:3 of Egypt, northward to the boundary of **E**,
13:4 cities of Gaza, Ashdod, Ashkelon, Gath, and **E**.
15:11 then proceeded to the slope of the hill north of **E**,
15:45 Judah also included all the towns and villages of **E**.
15:46 From **E** the boundary extended west and included
19:43 Elon, Timnah, **E**,
Jdg 1:18 captured the cities of Gaza, Ashkelon, and **E**,
1Sa 5:10 So they sent the Ark of God to the city of **E**,
5:10 but when the people of **E** saw it coming they cried
6:16 all this and then returned to **E** that same day.
6:17 rulers of Ashdod, Gaza, Ashkelon, Gath, and **E**.
7:14 The Israelite towns near **E** and Gath that the
17:52 chasing them as far as Gath and the gates of **E**.
17:52 the road from Shaaraim, as far as Gath and **E**.
2Ki 1:2 the god of **E**, to ask whether he would recover.
1:3 'Why are you going to Baal-zebub, the god of **E**,
1:6 'Why are you going to Baal-zebub, the god of **E**,
1:16 the god of **E**, to ask whether you will get well?
Jer 25:20 Gaza, **E**, and what remains of Ashdod.
Am 1:8 Then I will turn to attack **E**, and the few Philistines
Zep 2:4 Gaza, Ashkelon, Ashdod, **E**—these Philistine
Zec 9:5 Gaza will shake with terror, and so will **E**, for their
9:7 And the Philistines of **E** will join my people,

EL-BETHEL (1) [BETHEL]

Ge 35:7 Jacob built an altar there and named it **E**,

EL-ELOHE-ISRAEL (1) [ISRAEL]

Ge 33:20 And there he built an altar and called it **E**.

EL-PARAN (1) [PARAN]

Ge 14:6 as far as **E** at the edge of the wilderness.

ELA (1)

1Ki 4:18 Shimei son of **E**, in Benjamin.

ELABORATE (1)

Ex 39:5 They also made an **e** woven sash of the same

ELAH (14) [ELAH'S]

Ge 36:41 Oholibamah, **E**, Pinon,
1Sa 17:2 by gathering his troops near the valley of **E**.
17:19 with Saul and the Israelite army at the valley of **E**,
21:9 whom you killed in the valley of **E**," the priest
1Ki 16:6 in Tirzah. Then his son **E** became the next king.
16:8 **E** son of Baasha began to rule over Israel from
16:9 **E** was getting drunk at the home of Arza,
16:13 because of the sins of Baasha and his son **E** and
2Ki 15:30 Then Hoshea son of **E** conspired against Pekah
17:1 Hoshea son of **E** began to rule over Israel in the
1Ch 1:52 Oholibamah, **E**, Pinon,
4:15 of Caleb son of Jephunneh were Iru, **E**, and Naam.
The son of **E** was Kenaz.
9:8 son of Jeroham; **E** son of Uzzi, son of Micri;

ELAH'S (1) [ELAH]

1Ki 16:14 The rest of the events in **E** reign and all his deeds

ELAM (26) [ELAM'S, ELAMITES]

Ge 10:22 The descendants of Shem were **E**, Asshur,
14:1 King Arioch of Ellasar, King Kedorlaomer of **E**,
14:9 against King Kedorlaomer of **E** and the kings of
1Ch 1:17 The descendants of Shem were **E**, Asshur,
8:24 Hananiah, **E**, Anthothijah,
26:3 **E** (the fifth), Jehohanan (the sixth), and Eliehoenai
Ezr 2:7 The family of **E** | 1,254
2:31 The citizens of **E** | 1,254
4:9 and the people of Erech and Susa (that is, **E**).
8:7 From the family of **E**: Jeshaiah son of Athaliah
10:2 son of Jehiel, a descendant of **E**, said to Ezra,
10:26 From the family of **E**: Mattaniah, Zechariah,
Ne 7:12 The family of **E** | 1,254
7:34 The citizens of **E** | 1,254
10:14 signed were Parosh, Pahath-moab, **E**, Zattu, Bani,
12:42 Eleazar, Uzzi, Jehohanan, Malkijah, **E**, and Ezer.
Isa 11:11 Upper Egypt, Ethiopia, **E**, Babylonia, Hamath,
Jer 25:25 and to the kings of Zimri, **E**, and Media.
49:34 This message concerning **E** came to the prophet
49:35 "I will destroy the archers of **E**—the best of their
49:36 and I will scatter the people of **E** to the four winds.
49:37 will bring great disaster upon the people of **E**,"
49:38 I will set my throne in **E**," says the LORD,
49:39 in the latter days I will restore the fortunes of **E**,"
Eze 32:24 "**E** lies there buried with its hordes who descended
Da 8:2 in the province of **E**, standing beside the Ulai

ELAM'S (1) [ELAM]

Jer 49:37 I myself will go with **E** enemies to shatter it.

ELAMITES (3) [ELAM]

Isa 21: 2 Go ahead, you **E** and Medes, take part in the siege.
22: 6 **E** are the archers; Arameans drive the chariots.
Ac 2: 9 Parthians, Medes, **E**, people from Mesopotamia,

ELASAH (2)

Ezr 10:22 Maaseiah, Ishmael, Nethanel, Jozabad, and **E**.
Jer 29: 3 He sent the letter with **E** son of Shaphan

ELATH (6)

Dt 2: 8 through the Arabah Valley that comes up from **E**
1Ki 9:26 a port near **E** in the land of Edom, along the shore
2Ki 14:22 Uzziah rebuilt the town of **E** and restored it to
16: 6 king of Edom recovered the town of **E** for Edom.
2Ch 8:17 Later Solomon went to Ezion-geber and **E**, ports in
26: 2 Uzziah rebuilt the town of **E** and restored it to

ELDAAH (2)

Ge 25: 4 sons were Ephah, Epher, Hanoch, Abida, and **E**.
1Ch 1:33 Midian were Ephah, Epher, Hanoch, Abida, and **E**.

ELDAD (2)

Nu 11:26 Two men, **E** and Medad, were still in the camp
11:27 "**E** and Medad are prophesying in the camp!"

ELDER (11) [ELDERLY, ELDERS]

1Ti 3: 1 It is a true saying that if someone wants to be an **e**,
3: 2 For an **e** must be a man whose life cannot be
3: 6 An **e** must not be a new Christian, because he
5:19 Do not listen to complaints against an **e** unless
5:22 Never be in a hurry about appointing an **e**. Do not
Tit 1: 6 An **e** must be well thought of for his good life.
1: 7 An **e** must live a blameless life because he is God's
1Pe 5: 1 am an **e** and a witness to the sufferings of Christ.
5: 1 he returns. As a fellow **e**, this is my appeal to you:
2Jn 1: 1 This letter is from John, the **E**. It is written to the
3Jn 1: 1 This letter is from John, the **E**. It is written to

ELDERLY (2) [ELDER]

Lev 19:32 of God by standing up in the presence of **e** people
Isa 47: 6 You have forced even the **e** to carry heavy

ELDERS (53) [ELDER]

ELDERS OF THE CHURCH (4) Ac 11:30; 20:17; 1Ti 4:14; Jas 5:14

Ge 23: 3 leaving her body, he went to the Hittite **e** and said,
23:10 speaking publicly before all the **e** of the town.
23:18 in the presence of the Hittite **e** at the city gate.
Dt 32: 7 Inquire of your **e**, and they will tell you.
Jos 23: 2 called together all the **e**, leaders, judges,
24: 1 along with their **e**, leaders, judges, and officers.
1Ki 12: 8 But Rehoboam rejected the advice of the **e**
21: 8 and sent them to the **e** and other leaders of the city
21:11 So the **e** and other leaders followed the instructions
2Ch 10: 8 But Rehoboam rejected the advice of the **e**
Ezr 10: 8 if the leaders and **e** so decided, forfeit all their
Job 12:20 trusted adviser, and he removes the insight of the **e**.
32: 9 But sometimes the **e** are not wise.
Ps 119:100 I am even wiser than my **e**, / for I have kept your
Isa 3: 2 the heroes, soldiers, judges, prophets, diviners, **e**,
Jer 29: 1 Jeremiah wrote a letter from Jerusalem to the **e**,
Joel 2:16 the **e**, the children, and even the babies.
Ac 4: 5 The next day the council of all the rulers and **e**
4: 8 said to them, "Leaders and **e** of our nation,
4:23 told them what the leading priests and **e** had said.
5:21 the high council, along with all the **e** of Israel.
6:12 Naturally, this roused the crowds, the **e**,
11:30 and Saul to take to the **e** of the church in
14:23 and Barnabas also appointed **e** in every church
15: 2 to talk to the apostles and **e** about this question.
15: 4 by the whole church, including the apostles and **e**.
15: 6 and church **e** got together to decide this question.
15:22 Then the apostles and **e** and the whole church in
15:23 "This letter is from the apostles and **e**,
16: 4 as decided by the apostles and **e** in Jerusalem.
20:17 he sent a message to the **e** of the church at
20:28 over whom the Holy Spirit has appointed you as **e**.
21: 1 After saying farewell to the Ephesian **e**, we sailed
21:18 and all the **e** of the Jerusalem church were present.
Php 1: 1 believe in Christ Jesus, and to the **e** and deacons.
1Ti 4:14 when the **e** of the church laid their hands on you.
5:17 **E** who do their work well should be paid well,
Tit 1: 5 and appoint **e** in each town as I instructed you.
Jas 5:14 They should call for the **e** of the church and have
1Pe 5: 1 And now, a word to you who are **e** in the churches.
5: 5 You younger men, accept the authority of the **e**.
Rev 4: 4 surrounded him, and twenty-four **e** sat on them.
4:10 the twenty-four **e** fall down and worship the one
5: 5 But one of the twenty-four **e** said to me,
5: 6 four living beings and among the twenty-four **e**.
5: 8 and the twenty-four **e** fell down before the Lamb.
5:11 around the throne and the living beings and the **e**.
5:14 And the twenty-four **e** fell down and worshiped
7:11 and around the **e** and the four living beings.
7:13 Then one of the twenty-four **e** asked me, "Who are
11:16 And the twenty-four **e** sitting on their thrones
14: 3 before the four living beings and the twenty-four **e**.
19: 4 Then the twenty-four **e** and the four living beings

ELEAD (1)

1Ch 7:21 and **E** were killed trying to steal livestock from the

ELEADAH (1)

1Ch 7:20 were Shuthelah, Bered, Tahath, **E**, Tahath,

ELEALEH (5)

Nu 32: 3 Dibon, Jazer, Nimrah, Heshbon, **E**, Sebam, Nebo,
32:37 Reuben built the towns of Heshbon, **E**, Kiriathaim,
Isa 15: 4 the cities of Heshbon and **E** will be heard far away,
16: 9 My tears will flow for Heshbon and **E**, for their
Jer 48:34 terror can be heard from Heshbon clear across to **E**

ELEASAH (5) [ELEASAH'S]

1Ch 2:39 the father of Helez. / Helez was the father of **E**.
2:40 **E** was the father of Sismai. / Sismai was the father
8:37 Rephaiah was the father of **E**. / **E** was the father of Azel.
9:43 Rephaiah's son was **E**. / Eleasah's son was Azel.

ELEASAH'S (1) [ELEASAH]

1Ch 9:43 Rephaiah's son was Eleasah. / **E** son was Azel.

ELEAZAR (77) [ELEAZAR'S]

Ex 6:23 and she bore him Nadab, Abihu, **E**, and Ithamar.
6:25 **E** son of Aaron married one of the daughters of
28: 1 and his sons, Nadab, Abihu, **E**, and Ithamar,
Lev 10: 6 Moses said to Aaron and his sons **E** and Ithamar,
10:12 to Aaron and his remaining sons, **E** and Ithamar,
10:16 a result, he became very angry with **E** and Ithamar,
Nu 3: 2 were Nadab (the firstborn), Abihu, **E**, and Ithamar.
3: 4 this left only **E** and Ithamar to serve as priests with
3:32 **E** the priest, Aaron's son, was the chief
4:16 "**E** son of Aaron the priest will be responsible for
16:37 "Tell **E** son of Aaron the priest to pull all the
16:39 So **E** the priest collected the 250 bronze incense
19: 3 Give it to **E** the priest, and it will be taken outside
19: 4 **E** will take some of its blood on his finger
19: 5 As **E** watches, the heifer must be burned—its hide,
19: 6 **E** the priest must then take cedarwood, a hyssop
20:25 Now take Aaron and his son **E** up Mount Hor.
20:26 Aaron's priestly garments and put them on **E**,
20:28 priestly garments from Aaron and put them on **E**,
20:28 the mountain, and Moses and **E** went back down.
25: 7 When Phinehas son of **E** and grandson of Aaron
25:11 "Phinehas son of **E** and grandson of Aaron the
26: 1 the LORD said to Moses and to **E** son of Aaron,
26: 3 and **E** the priest issued these census instructions to
26:60 Aaron were born Nadab, Abihu, **E**, and Ithamar.
26:63 and **E** the priest on the plains of Moab beside the
27: 2 stood before Moses, **E** the priest, the tribal leaders,
27:19 Present him to **E** the priest before the whole
27:21 is needed, Joshua will stand before **E** the priest,
27:22 and presented Joshua to **E** the priest and the whole
31: 6 and Phinehas son of **E** the priest led them into
31:12 they brought them all to Moses and **E** the priest,
31:13 Moses, **E** the priest, and all the leaders of the
31:21 Then **E** the priest said to the men who were in the
31:26 "You and **E** the priest and the family leaders of
31:29 Give this share of their half to **E** the priest as an
31:31 and **E** the priest did as the LORD commanded
31:41 Moses gave all the LORD's share to **E** the priest,
31:51 and **E** the priest received the gold from all the
31:54 and **E** the priest accepted the gifts from the
32: 2 they came to Moses, **E** the priest, and the other
32:28 So Moses gave orders to **E**, Joshua, and the tribal
34:17 the people: **E** the priest and Joshua son of Nun.
Dt 10: 6 His son **E** became the high priest in his place.
Jos 14: 1 inherited land in Canaan as allotted by **E** the priest,
17: 4 These women came to **E** the priest, Joshua son of
19:51 These are the territories that **E** the priest,
21: 1 the tribe of Levi came to consult with **E** the priest,
22:13 they sent a delegation led by Phinehas son of **E**,
22:31 Phinehas son of **E**, the priest, replied to them,
22:32 Then Phinehas son of **E**, the priest, and the ten
24:33 **E** son of Aaron also died. He was buried in the hill
Jdg 20:28 and Phinehas son of **E** and grandson of Aaron was
1Sa 7: 1 it to the hillside home of Abinadab and ordained **E**,
2Sa 23: 9 Next in rank among the Three was **E** son of Dodai,
23: 9 Once **E** and David stood together against the
1Ch 6: 3 sons of Aaron were Nadab, Abihu, **E**, and Ithamar.
6: 4 **E** was the father of Phinehas. / Phinehas was the
6:50 The descendants of Aaron were **E**, Phinehas,
9:20 Phinehas son of **E** had been in charge of the
11:12 Next in rank among the Three was **E** son of Dodai,
11:14 But **E** and David held their ground in the middle of
23:21 and Mushi. The sons of Mahli were **E** and Kish.
23:22 **E** died with no sons, only daughters. His daughters
24: 1 sons of Aaron were Nadab, Abihu, **E**, and Ithamar.
24: 2 So only **E** and Ithamar were left to carry on as
24: 3 who was a descendant of **E**, and of Ahimelech,
24: 4 more family leaders among the descendants of **E**.
24: 5 sanctuary from among the descendants of both **E**
24: 6 The descendants of **E** and Ithamar took turns
24:28 of Mahli, the leader was **E**, though he had no sons.
Ezr 7: 5 son of Abishua, son of Phinehas, son of **E**, son of
8:33 son of Uriah the priest and to **E** son of Phinehas,
10:25 Ramiah, Izziah, Malkijah, Mijamin, **E**, Hashabiah,
Ne 12:42 Maaseiah, Shemaiah, **E**, Uzzi, Jehohanan,
Mt 1:15 Eliud was the father of **E**. / **E** was the father of Matthan.

ELEAZAR'S (2) [ELEAZAR]

Nu 4:16 and everything in it will be **E** responsibility."
1Ch 24: 4 **E** descendants were divided into sixteen groups

ELECT (1)

Jdg 9: 8 Once upon a time the trees decided to **e** a king.

ELEGANT (1)

La 4: 7 they were as clean as snow and as **e** as jewels.

ELEMENTS (1)

2Pe 3:12 on fire and the **e** will melt away in the flames.

ELEVATED (1) [ELEVATION]

Est 4:14 but that you have been **e** to the palace for just such

ELEVATION (1) [ELEVATED]

Ps 48: 2 It is magnificent in **e**— / the whole earth rejoices to

ELEVEN (23) [ELEVENTH]

Ge 32:22 and **e** sons across the Jabbok River.
37: 9 moon, and **e** stars bowed low before me!"
Ex 26: 7 the Tabernacle. There must be **e** of these sheets,
26: 8 All **e** of these sheets must be exactly the same size.
36:14 a roof covering was made from **e** sheets of cloth
Nu 29:20 of the festival, sacrifice **e** young bulls, two rams,
Dt 1: 2 Normally it takes only **e** days to travel from Mount
Jos 15:51 **e** towns with their surrounding villages.
Jdg 16: 5 Then each of us will give you **e** hundred pieces of
17: 2 "I heard you curse the thief who stole **e** hundred
1Ki 19:19 There were **e** teams of oxen ahead of him, and he
2Ki 18:14 then demanded a settlement of more than **e** tons of
23:36 became king, and he reigned in Jerusalem **e** years.
24:18 became king, and he reigned in Jerusalem **e** years.
2Ch 36: 5 became king, and he reigned in Jerusalem **e** years.
36:11 became king, and he reigned in Jerusalem **e** years.
Jer 52: 1 became king, and he reigned in Jerusalem **e** years.
Mt 28:16 Then the **e** disciples left for Galilee, going to the
Mk 16:14 Still later he appeared to the **e** disciples as they
Lk 24: 9 So they rushed back to tell his **e** disciples—
24:33 where the **e** disciples and the other followers of
Ac 1:26 and became an apostle with the other **e**.
2:14 Then Peter stepped forward with the **e** other

ELEVENTH (16) [ELEVEN]

Nu 7:72 On the **e** day Pagiel son of Ocran, leader of the
1Ki 6:38 detail by midautumn of the **e** year of his reign.
2Ki 9:29 Ahaziah's reign over Judah had begun in the **e** year
25: 2 Jerusalem was kept under siege until the **e** year of
25: 3 By July 18 of Zedekiah's **e** year, the famine in the
1Ch 12:13 Jeremiah was tenth. / Macbannai was **e**.
24:12 The **e** lot fell to Eliashib. / The twelfth lot fell to
25:18 The **e** lot fell to Uzziel and twelve of his sons
27:14 in Ephraim was commander of the **e** division,
27:14 which was on duty during the **e** month.
Jer 1: 3 until the **e** year of King Zedekiah's reign in Judah.
52: 5 Jerusalem was kept under siege until the **e** year of
52: 6 By July 18 of Zedekiah's **e** year, the famine in the
Eze 30:20 during the **e** year of King Jehoiachin's captivity,
31: 1 during the **e** year of King Jehoiachin's captivity,
Rev 21:20 the **e** jacinth, the twelfth amethyst.

ELHANAN (4)

2Sa 21:19 **E** son of Jair from Bethlehem killed the brother of
23:24 Joab's brother; / **E** son of Dodo from Bethlehem;
1Ch 11:26 Joab's brother; / **E** son of Dodo from Bethlehem;
20: 5 **E** son of Jair killed Lahmi, the brother of Goliath

ELI (37) [ELI'S]

1Sa 1: 3 the LORD at that time were the two sons of **E**—
1: 9 **E** the priest was sitting at his customary place
1:12 As she was praying to the LORD, **E** watched her.
1:17 "In that case," **E** said, "cheer up! May the God of
1:25 After sacrificing the bull, they took the child to **E**.
2:11 the LORD's helper, for he assisted **E** the priest.
2:12 Now the sons of **E** were scoundrels who had no
2:20 **E** would bless Elkanah and his wife and say,
2:22 Now **E** was very old, but he was aware of what his
2:23 **E** said to them, "I have been hearing reports from
2:27 One day a prophet came to **E** and gave him this
3: 1 Samuel was serving the LORD by assisting **E**.
3: 2 One night **E**, who was almost blind by now,
3: 5 He jumped up and ran to **E**. "Here I am. What do you need?" "I didn't call you," **E** replied.
3: 6 "Samuel!" Again Samuel jumped up and ran to **E**.
3: 6 "I didn't call you, my son," **E** said. "Go on back
3: 8 and once more Samuel jumped up and ran to **E**.
3: 8 Then **E** realized it was the LORD who was
3:12 I am going to carry out all my threats against **E**
3:14 So I have vowed that the sins of **E** and his sons
3:15 He was afraid to tell **E** what the LORD had said
3:16 But **E** called out to him, "Samuel, my son."
3:18 So Samuel told **E** everything; he didn't hold
3:18 "It is the LORD's will," **E** replied.
4: 4 Hophni and Phinehas, the sons of **E**, helped carry
4:11 and Phinehas, the two sons of **E**, were killed.
4:13 **E** was waiting beside the road to hear the news of
4:14 "What is all the noise about?" **E** asked. The messenger rushed over to **E**,
4:16 He said to **E**, "I have just come from the
4:16 this very day." "What happened?" **E** demanded.
4:18 **E** fell backward from his seat beside the gate.
14: 3 was the son of Phinehas and the grandson of **E**,
1Ki 2:27 made at Shiloh concerning the descendants of **E**.
Mt 27:46 Jesus called out with a loud voice, ***"E, E,***

ELI'S (4) [ELI]

1Sa 2:13 **E** sons would send over a servant with a
2:14 that whatever it brought up be given to **E** sons.
2:25 But **E** sons wouldn't listen to their father,
4:19 **E** daughter-in-law, the wife of Phinehas,

ELIAB (21)

Nu 1: 9 Zebulun | **E** son of Helon
2: 7[-8] Zebulun | **E** son of Helon | 57,400
7:24 On the third day **E** son of Helon, leader of the tribe
7:29 This was the offering brought by **E** son of Helon.
10:16 The tribe of Zebulun was led by **E** son of Helon.
16: 1 conspired with Dathan and Abiram, the sons of **E**,
16:12 summoned Dathan and Abiram, the sons of **E**,
26: 8 Pallu was the ancestor of **E**,
26: 9 and **E** was the father of Nemuel, Dathan,
Dt 11: 6 what he did to Dathan and Abiram (the sons of **E**,
1Sa 16: 6 Samuel took one look at **E** and thought,
17:13 three oldest sons—**E**, Abinadab, and Shammah—
17:28 **E**, heard David talking to the men, he was angry.
1Ch 2:13 Jesse's first son was **E**, his second was Abinadab,
6:27 **E**, Jeroham, Elkanah, and Samuel.
12: 9 their leader. / Obadiah was second. / **E** was third.
15:18 Jehiel, Unni, **E**, Benaiah, Maaseiah, Mattithiah,
15:20 Aziel, Shemiramoth, Jehiel, Unni, **E**, Maaseiah,
16: 5 Jehiel, Mattithiah, **E**, Benaiah, Obed-edom,
2Ch 11:18 son Jerimoth and of Abihail, the daughter of **E**.
11:18 (**E** was one of David's brothers, a son of Jesse.)

ELIADA (5)

2Sa 5:16 Elishama, **E**, and Eliphelet.
1Ki 11:23 God also raised up Rezon son of **E** to be an enemy
1Ch 3: 8 Elishama, **E**, and Eliphelet.
14: 7 Elishama, **E**, and Eliphelet.
2Ch 17:17 They were under the command of **E**, a veteran

ELIAH [KJV] See ELIJAH

ELIAHBA (2)

2Sa 23:32 **E** from Shaalbon; / the sons of Jashen;
1Ch 11:33 Azmaveth from Bahurim; / **E** from Shaalbon;

ELIAKIM (16) [ELIAKIM'S]

2Ki 18:18 **E** son of Hilkiah, the palace administrator,
18:26 Then **E** son of Hilkiah, Shebna, and Joah said to
18:37 Then **E** son of Hilkiah, the palace administrator,
19: 2 And he sent **E** the palace administrator,
23:34 Pharaoh Neco then installed **E**, another of Josiah's
2Ch 36: 4 The king of Egypt appointed **E**, the brother of
Ne 12:41 **E**, Maaseiah, Miniamin, Micaiah, Elioenai,
Isa 22:20 then I will call my servant **E** son of Hilkiah to
36: 3 **E** son of Hilkiah, the palace administrator,
36:11 Then **E**, Shebna, and Joah said to the king's
36:22 Then **E** son of Hilkiah, the palace administrator,
37: 2 And he sent **E** the palace administrator,
Mt 1:13 Abiud was the father of **E**. / **E** was the father of
Lk 3:30 was the son of Jonam. / Jonam was the son of **E**.
3:31 **E** was the son of Melea. / Melea was the son of

ELIAKIM'S (2) [ELIAKIM]

2Ki 23:34 of his father, and he changed **E** name to Jehoiakim.
2Ch 36: 4 and he changed **E** name to Jehoiakim.

ELIAM (2) [AMMIEL]

2Sa 11: 3 the daughter of **E** and the wife of Uriah the
23:34 from Maacah; / **E** son of Ahithophel from Giloh;

ELIAS [KJV] See ELIJAH

ELIASAPH (6)

Nu 1:14 Gad | **E** son of Deuel
2:14[-15] Gad | **E** son of Deuel | 45,650
3:24 The leader of the Gershonite clans was **E** son of
7:42 On the sixth day **E** son of Deuel, leader of the tribe
7:47 This was the offering brought by **E** son of Deuel.
10:20 The tribe of Gad was led by **E** son of Deuel.

ELIASHIB (15) [ELIASHIB'S]

1Ch 3:24 **E**, Pelaiah, Akkub, Johanan, Delaiah, and Anani—
24:12 The eleventh lot fell to **E**. / The twelfth lot fell to
Ezr 10: 6 and went to the room of Jehohanan son of **E**.
10:24 This is the singer who was guilty: **E**. These are the
10:27 Elioenai, **E**, Mattaniah, Jeremoth, Zabad,
10:36 Vaniah, Meremoth, **E**,
Ne 3: 1 Then **E** the high priest and the other priests started
3:20 to the door of the home of **E** the high priest.
12:10 Joiakim was the father of **E**. / **E** was the father of
12:22 high priests: **E**, Joiada, Johanan, and Jaddua.
12:23 down to the days of Johanan, the grandson of **E**.
13: 4 Before this had happened, **E** the priest, who had
13: 7 and learned the extent of this evil deed of **E**—
13:28 One of the sons of Joiada son of **E** the high priest

ELIASHIB'S (1) [ELIASHIB]

Ne 3:21 the door of **E** house to the side of the house.

ELIATHAH (2)

1Ch 25: 4 Shubael, Jerimoth, Hananiah, Hanani, **E**, Geddalti,
25:27 The twentieth lot fell to **E** and twelve of his sons

ELIDAD (1)

Nu 34:21 Benjamin | **E** son of Kislon

ELIEHOENAI (2)

1Ch 26: 3 Jehohanan (the sixth), and **E** (the seventh).
Ezr 8: 4 **E** son of Zerahiah and 200 other men.

ELIEL (10)

1Ch 5:24 Epher, Ishi, **E**, Azriel, Jeremiah, Hodaviah,
6:34 Elkanah, Jeroham, **E**, Toah,
8:20 Elienai, Zillethai, **E**,
8:22 Ishpan, Eber, **E**,
11:46 **E** from Mahavah; / Jeribai and Joshaviah, the sons
11:47 **E** and Obed; / Jaasiel from Zobah.
12:11 Attai was sixth. / **E** was seventh.
15: 9 80 descendants of Hebron, with **E** as their leader.
15:11 Uriel, Asaiah, Joel, Shemaiah, **E**, and Amminadab.
2Ch 31:13 Azaziah, Nahath, Asahel, Jerimoth, Jozabad, **E**,

ELIENAI (1)

1Ch 8:20 **E**, Zillethai, Eliel,

ELIEZER (15)

Ge 15: 2 Since I don't have a son, **E** of Damascus, a servant
Ex 18: 4 The name of his second son was **E**, for Moses had
1Ch 7: 8 Joash, **E**, Elioenai, Omri, Jeremoth, Abijah,
15:24 Nethanel, Amasai, Zechariah, Benaiah, and **E**—
23:15 The sons of Moses were Gershom and **E**.
23:17 **E** had only one son, Rehabiah, the family leader.
26:25 His relatives through **E** were Rehabiah, Jeshaiah,
27:16 and their leaders: / Reuben | **E** son of Zicri
2Ch 20:37 Then **E** son of Dodavahu from Mareshah
Ezr 8:16 So I sent for **E**, Ariel, Shemaiah, Elnathan, Jarib,
10:18 and his brothers: Maaseiah, **E**, Jarib, and Gedaliah.
10:23 (also called Kelita), Pethahiah, Judah, and **E**.
10:31 **E**, Ishijah, Malkijah, Shemaiah, Shimeon,
Lk 3:29 Joshua was the son of **E**. / **E** was the son of Jorim.

ELIGIBLE (9)

Nu 4:23 and fifty who are **e** to serve in the Tabernacle.
4:30 and fifty who are **e** to serve in the Tabernacle.
4:35 and fifty years of age who were **e** for service in the
4:37 clans who were **e** to serve at the Tabernacle.
4:39 and fifty years of age who were **e** for service in the
4:41 clans who were **e** to serve at the Tabernacle.
4:43 and fifty years of age who were **e** for service in the
4:45 from the Merarite clans who were **e** for service.
4:47 and fifty years of age who were **e** for service in the

ELIHOENAI [KJV] See ELIEHOENAI

ELIHOREPH (1)

1Ki 4: 3 **E** and Ahijah, the sons of Shisha, were court

ELIHU (10)

1Sa 1: 1 He was the son of Jeroham and grandson of **E**,
1Ch 12:20 Adnah, Jozabad, Jediael, Michael, Jozabad, **E**,
26: 7 Their relatives, **E** and Semakiah, were also very
27:18 Judah | **E** (a brother of David) / Issachar | Omri
Job 32: 2 Then **E** son of Barakel the Buzite, of the clan of
32: 4 **E** had waited for the others to speak because they
32: 6 **E** son of Barakel the Buzite said, "I am young
34: 1 Then **E** said:
35: 1 Then **E** said:
36: 1 **E** continued speaking:

ELIJAH (114) [ELIJAH'S]

1Ki 17: 1 Now **E**, who was from Tishbe in Gilead, told King
17: 2 Then the LORD said to **E**,
17: 5 So **E** did as the LORD had told him and camped
17: 8 Then the LORD said to **E**,
17:13 But **E** said to her, "Don't be afraid! Go ahead
17:15 So she did as **E** said, and she and **E** and her son continued to eat from
17:16 just as the LORD had promised through **E**.
17:18 She then said to **E**, "O man of God, what have you
17:19 But **E** replied, "Give me your son." And he took
17:20 Then **E** cried out to the LORD, "O LORD my
17:23 Then **E** brought him down from the upper room
17:24 Then the woman told **E**, "Now I know for sure
18: 1 the LORD said to **E**, "Go and present yourself to
18: 2 So **E** went to appear before Ahab. Meanwhile,
18: 7 was walking along, he saw **E** coming toward him.
18: 7 "Is it really you, my lord **E**?" he asked.
18: 8 "Yes, it is," **E** replied. "Now go and tell your
18:10 And each time when he was told, 'E isn't here,'
18:11 you say, 'Go and tell your master that **E** is here'!
18:14 you say, 'Go and tell your master that **E** is here'!
18:15 But **E** said, "I swear by the LORD Almighty,
18:16 So Obadiah went to tell Ahab that **E** had come,
18:18 "I have made no trouble for Israel," **E** replied.
18:21 Then **E** stood in front of them and said,
18:22 Then **E** said to them, "I am the only prophet of the
18:25 Then **E** said to the prophets of Baal, "You go first,
18:27 About noontime **E** began mocking them.
18:30 Then **E** called to the people, "Come over here!"
18:36 **E** the prophet walked up to the altar and prayed,
18:40 Then **E** commanded, "Seize all the prophets of
18:40 and **E** took them down to the Kishon Valley
18:41 Then **E** said to Ahab, "Go and enjoy a good meal!
18:42 But **E** climbed to the top of Mount Carmel and fell
18:43 and looked, but he returned to **E** and said,
18:43 Seven times **E** told him to go and look, and seven
18:44 Then **E** shouted, "Hurry to Ahab and tell him,
18:46 Now the LORD gave special strength to **E**.
19: 1 he told Jezebel what **E** had done and that he had
19: 2 So Jezebel sent this message to **E**: "May the gods
19: 3 **E** was afraid and fled for his life. He went to
19: 9 said to him, "What are you doing here, **E**?"
19:10 **E** replied, "I have zealously served the LORD
19:11 And as **E** stood there, the LORD passed by,
19:13 When **E** heard it, he wrapped his face in his cloak
19:13 And a voice said, "What are you doing here, **E**?"
19:19 So **E** went and found Elisha son of Shaphat
19:19 **E** went over to him and threw his cloak across his
19:20 ran after **E**, and said to him, "First let me go
19:20 then I will go with you!" **E** replied, "Go on back!
19:21 they all ate. Then he went with **E** as his assistant.
21:17 But the LORD said to **E**, who was from Tishbe,
21:20 Ahab exclaimed to **E**. "Yes," **E** answered, "I have
21:28 another message from the LORD came to **E**,
2Ki 1: 3 But the angel of the LORD told **E**, who was from
1: 4 but you will surely die.' " So **E** went to deliver
1: 8 "It was **E** from Tishbe!" the king exclaimed.
1:10 But **E** replied to the captain, "If I am a man of
1:12 **E** replied, "If I am a man of God, let fire come
1:13 But this time the captain fell to his knees before **E**.
1:15 Then the angel of the LORD said to **E**, "Don't be
1:15 Go with him." So **E** got up and went to the king.
1:16 And **E** said to the king, "This is what the LORD
1:17 just as the LORD had promised through **E**.
2: 1 When the LORD was about to take **E** up to
2: 1 **E** and Elisha were traveling from Gilgal.
2: 2 And **E** said to Elisha, "Stay here, for the LORD
2: 4 Then **E** said to Elisha, "Stay here, for the LORD
2: 6 Then **E** said to Elisha, "Stay here, for the LORD
2: 7 and watched from a distance as **E** and Elisha
2: 8 Then **E** folded his cloak together and struck the
2: 9 When they came to the other side, **E** said to Elisha,
2:10 "You have asked a difficult thing," **E** replied.
2:11 and **E** was carried by a whirlwind into heaven.
2:14 cried out, "Where is the LORD, the God of **E**?"
2:17 men searched for three days but did not find **E**.
9:36 which he spoke through his servant **E** from Tishbe:
10:10 The LORD declared through his servant **E** that
10:17 just as the LORD had promised through **E**.
1Ch 8:27 Jaareshiah, **E**, and Zicri were the sons of Jeroham.
2Ch 21:12 Then **E** the prophet wrote Jehoram this letter:
Ezr 10:21 Maaseiah, **E**, Shemaiah, Jehiel, and Uzziah.
10:26 Zechariah, Jehiel, Abdi, Jeremoth, and **E**.
Mal 4: 5 I am sending you the prophet **E** before the great
Mt 11:14 he is **E**, the one the prophets said would come.
16:14 some say **E**, and others say Jeremiah or one of the
17: 3 Moses and **E** appeared and began talking with
17: 4 one for you, one for Moses, and one for **E**."
17:10 "Why do the teachers of religious law insist that **E**
17:11 "**E** is indeed coming first to set everything in
27:47 and thought he was calling for the prophet **E**.
27:49 Let's see whether **E** will come and save him."
Mk 6:15 Others thought Jesus was the ancient prophet **E**.
8:28 "some say John the Baptist, some say **E**,
9: 4 Then **E** and Moses appeared and began talking
9: 5 one for you, one for Moses, and one for **E**."
9: 8 they looked around, and Moses and **E** were gone,
9:11 "Why do the teachers of religious law insist that **E**
9:12 "**E** is indeed coming first to set everything in
9:13 But I tell you, **E** has already come, and he was
15:35 and thought he was calling for the prophet **E**.
15:36 Let's see whether **E** will come and take him
Lk 1:17 He will be a man with the spirit and power of **E**,
4:26 Yet **E** was not sent to any of them. He was sent
9: 8 "It is **E** or some other ancient prophet risen from
9:19 "some say John the Baptist, some say **E**,
9:30 Moses and **E**, appeared and began talking with
9:33 As Moses and **E** were starting to leave, Peter,
9:33 one for you, one for Moses, and one for **E**."
Jn 1:21 they asked. "Are you **E**?" "No," he replied.
1:25 "If you aren't the Messiah or **E** or the Prophet,
Ro 11: 2 **E** the prophet complained to God about the people
Jas 5:17 **E** was as human as we are, and yet when he prayed

ELIJAH'S (5) [ELIJAH]

1Ki 17:22 The LORD heard **E** prayer, and the life of the
2Ki 2:13 Then Elisha picked up **E** cloak and returned to the
2:15 "Elisha has become **E** successor!"
3:11 is here. He used to be **E** personal assistant."
Lk 4:25 many widows in Israel who needed help in **E** time,

ELIKA (1)

2Sa 23:25 Shammah from Harod; / **E** from Harod;

ELIM (5)

Ex 15:27 After leaving Marah, they came to **E**, where there
16: 1 Then they left **E** and journeyed into the Sin Desert, between **E** and Mount Sinai.
Nu 33: 9 They left Marah and camped at **E**, where there are
33:10 They left **E** and camped beside the Red Sea.

ELIMELECH (6)

Ru 1: 2 The man's name was **E**, and his wife was Naomi.
1: 3 **E** died and Naomi was left with her two sons.
2: 1 who was a relative of Naomi's husband, **E**.
2: 3 to Boaz, the relative of her father-in-law, **E**.
4: 3 is selling the land that belonged to our relative **E**.
4: 9 I have bought from Naomi all the property of **E**,

ELIMINATING (1)
Ge 19:25 the other cities and villages of the plain, **e** all life—

ELIOENAI (7)
1Ch 3:23 The sons of Neariah were **E**, Hizkiah,
3:24 The sons of **E** were Hodaviah, Eliashib, Pelaiah,
4:36 **E**, Jaakobah, Jeshohaiah, Asaiah, Adiel, Jesimiel,
7: 8 Joash, Eliezer, **E**, Omri, Jeremoth, Abijah,
Ezr 10:22 **E**, Maaseiah, Ishmael, Nethanel, Jozabad,
10:27 **E**, Eliashib, Mattaniah, Jeremoth, Zabad,
Ne 12:41 Eliakim, Maaseiah, Miniamin, Micaiah, **E**,

ELIPHAL (1)
1Ch 11:35 Ahiam son of Sharar from Harar; / **E** son of Ur;

ELIPHAZ (14)
Ge 36: 4 Esau and Adah had a son named **E**. Esau
36:10 Among Esau's sons were **E**, the son of Esau's wife
36:11 The sons of **E** were Teman, Omar, Zepho, Gatam,
36:12 **E** had another son named Amalek, born to Timna,
36:15 The sons of Esau's oldest son, **E**,
36:16 clans in the land of Edom were descended from **E**,
1Ch 1:35 The sons of Esau were **E**, Reuel, Jeush, Jalam,
1:36 The sons of **E** were Teman, Omar, Zepho, Gatam,
Job 2:11 Three of Job's friends were **E** the Temanite,
4: 1 Then **E** the Temanite replied to Job:
15: 1 Then **E** the Temanite replied:
22: 1 Then **E** the Temanite replied:
42: 7 speaking to Job, he said to **E** the Temanite:
42: 9 So **E** the Temanite, Bildad the Shuhite, and Zophar

ELIPHELEHU (2)
1Ch 15:18 Benaiah, Maaseiah, Mattithiah, **E**, Mikneiah,
15:21 Mattithiah, **E**, Mikneiah, Obed-edom, Jeiel,

ELIPHELET (7)
2Sa 5:16 Elishama, Eliada, and **E**.
23:34 **E** son of Ahasbai from Maacah; / Eliam son of
1Ch 3: 8 Elishama, Eliada, and **E**.
8:39 (the oldest), Jeush (the second), and **E** (the third).
14: 7 Elishama, Eliada, and **E**.
Ezr 8:13 came later: **E**, Jeuel, Shemaiah, and 60 other men.
10:33 Mattenai, Mattattah, Zabad, **E**, Jeremai, Manasseh,

ELISABETH [KJV] See ELIZABETH

ELISEUS [KJV] See ELISHA

ELISHA (108) [ELISHA'S]
1Ki 19:16 and anoint **E** son of Shaphat from Abel-meholah to
19:17 and those who escape Jehu will be killed by **E**!
19:19 and found **E** son of Shaphat plowing a field with a
19:20 **E** left the oxen standing there, ran after Elijah,
19:21 **E** then returned to his oxen, killed them, and used
2Ki 2: 1 Elijah and **E** were traveling from Gilgal.
2: 2 And Elijah said to **E**, "Stay here, for the LORD
2: 2 But **E** replied, "As surely as the LORD lives
2: 3 The group of prophets from Bethel came to **E**
2: 3 "Quiet!" **E** answered. "Of course I know it."
2: 4 Then Elijah said to **E**, "Stay here, for the LORD
2: 4 But **E** replied again, "As surely as the LORD
2: 5 Then the group of prophets from Jericho came to **E**
2: 6 Then Elijah said to **E**, "Stay here, for the LORD
2: 6 But again **E** replied, "As surely as the LORD
2: 7 as Elijah and **E** stopped beside the Jordan River.
2: 9 When they came to the other side, Elijah said to **E**,
2: 9 And **E** replied, "Please let me become your
2:12 **E** saw it and cried out, "My father! My father!
2:12 they disappeared from sight, **E** tore his robe in two.
2:13 Then **E** picked up Elijah's cloak and returned to
2:14 Then the river divided, and **E** went across.
2:15 "**E** has become Elijah's successor!"
2:16 some valley." "No," **E** said, "don't send them."
2:18 **E** was still at Jericho when they returned.
2:19 Now the leaders of the town of Jericho visited **E**.
2:20 **E** said, "Bring me a new bowl with salt in it."
2:22 has remained wholesome ever since, just as **E** said.
2:23 **E** left Jericho and went up to Bethel. As he was
2:24 **E** turned around and looked at them, and he cursed
2:25 From there **E** went to Mount Carmel and finally
3:11 officers replied, "**E** son of Shaphat is here.
3:12 of Israel, Judah, and Edom went to consult with **E**.
3:13 want no part of you," **E** said to the king of Israel.
3:14 **E** replied, "As surely as the LORD Almighty
3:15 the power of the LORD came upon **E**,
4: 1 of one of Elisha's fellow prophets came to **E**
4: 2 **E** asked. "Tell me, what do you have in the
4: 3 And **E** said, "Borrow as many empty jars as you
4: 8 One day **E** went to the town of Shunem. A wealthy
4:11 One day **E** returned to Shunem, and he went up to
4:13 **E** said to Gehazi, "Tell her that we appreciate the
4:14 Later **E** asked Gehazi, "What do you think we can
4:15 "Call her back again," **E** told him.
4:15 **E** said to her as she stood in the doorway,
4:17 following year she had a son, just as **E** had said.
4:25 God at Mount Carmel, **E** saw her in the distance.
4:29 Then **E** said to Gehazi, "Get ready to travel;
4:30 unless you go with me." So **E** returned with her.
4:31 He returned to meet **E** and told him, "The child is
4:32 When **E** arrived, the child was indeed dead,
4:35 **E** got up and walked back and forth in the room a
4:36 Then **E** summoned Gehazi. "Call the child's
4:36 when she came in, **E** said, "Here, take your son!"
4:38 **E** now returned to Gilgal, but there was a famine in
4:41 **E** said, "Bring me some flour." Then he threw it
4:42 **E** said, "Give it to the group of prophets so they
4:43 But **E** repeated, "Give it to the group of prophets
5: 8 But when **E**, the man of God, heard about the
5:10 But **E** sent a messenger out to him with this
5:16 But **E** replied, "As surely as the LORD lives,
5:16 Naaman urged him to take the gifts, **E** refused.
5:19 "Go in peace," **E** said. So Naaman started home
5:25 **E** asked him, "Where have you been, Gehazi?"
5:26 But **E** asked him, "Don't you realize that I was
6: 1 One day the group of prophets came to **E** and told
6: 6 the place, **E** cut a stick and threw it into the water.
6: 7 "Grab it," **E** said to him. And the man reached out
6: 9 But immediately **E**, the man of God, would warn
6:12 "**E**, the prophet in Israel, tells the king of Israel
6:13 king commanded, "Go and find out where **E** is,
6:13 And the report came back: "**E** is at Dothan."
6:15 my lord, what will we do now?" he cried out to **E**.
6:16 "Don't be afraid!" **E** told him. "For there are
6:17 Then **E** prayed, "O LORD, open his eyes and let
6:17 he saw that the hillside around **E** was filled with
6:18 **E** prayed, "O LORD, please make them blind."
And the LORD did as **E** asked.
6:19 Then **E** went out and told them, "You have come
6:20 **E** prayed, "O LORD, now open their eyes
6:21 he shouted to **E**, "My father, should I kill them?"
6:22 "Of course not!" **E** told him. "Do we kill
6:31 "May God kill me if I don't execute **E** son of
6:32 **E** was sitting in his house at a meeting with the
6:32 before the messenger arrived, **E** said to the leaders,
6:33 While **E** was still saying this, the messenger
7: 1 **E** replied, "Hear this message from the LORD!
7: 2 But **E** replied, "You will see it happen, but you
8: 1 **E** had told the woman whose son he had brought
8: 4 "Tell me some stories about the great things **E** has
8: 5 And Gehazi was telling the king about the time **E**
8: 5 is her son—the very one **E** brought back to life!"
8: 7 Now **E** went to Damascus, the capital of Aram,
8: 9 the finest products of Damascus as a gift for **E**.
8:10 And **E** replied, "Go and tell him, 'You will
8:11 **E** stared at Hazael with a fixed gaze until Hazael
8:12 **E** replied, "I know the terrible things you will do
8:13 But **E** answered, "The LORD has shown me that
8:14 the king asked him, "What did **E** tell you?"
9: 1 **E** the prophet had summoned a member of the
13:14 When **E** was in his last illness, King Jehoash of
13:15 **E** told him, "Get a bow and some arrows."
13:16 Then **E** told the king of Israel to put his hand on
13:16 and **E** laid his own hands on the king's hands.
13:17 Then **E** proclaimed, "This is the LORD's arrow,
13:20 Then **E** died and was buried. Groups of Moabite
13:21 the body they were burying into the tomb of **E**.
Lk 4:27 Or think of the prophet **E**, who healed Naaman,

ELISHA'S (4) [ELISHA]
2Ki 4: 1 One day the widow of one of **E** fellow prophets
5: 9 and chariots and waited at the door of **E** house.
5:20 But Gehazi, **E** servant, said to himself,
13:21 But as soon as the body touched **E** bones, the dead

ELISHAH (3)
Ge 10: 4 The descendants of Javan were **E**, Tarshish,
1Ch 1: 7 The descendants of Javan were **E**, Tarshish,
Eze 27: 7 made bright with dyes from the coasts of **E**.

ELISHAMA (15) [ELISHAMA'S]
Nu 1:10 Ephraim son of Joseph | **E** son of Ammihud
2:18[-19] Ephraim | **E** son of Ammihud | 40,500
7:48 On the seventh day **E** son of Ammihud, leader of
7:53 This was the offering brought by **E** son of
10:22 under the leadership of **E** son of Ammihud.
2Sa 5:16 **E**, Eliada, and Eliphelet.
2Ki 25:25 Ishmael son of Nethaniah and grandson of **E**,
1Ch 2:41 father of Jekamiah. / Jekamiah was the father of **E**.
3: 8 **E**, Eliada, and Eliphelet.
7:26 Ladan, Ammihud, **E**,
14: 7 **E**, Eliada, and Eliphelet.
2Ch 17: 8 He also sent out the priests, **E** and Jehoram.
Jer 36:12 **E** the secretary was there, along with Delaiah son
36:20 for safekeeping in the room of **E** the secretary
41: 1 Ishmael son of Nethaniah and grandson of **E**,

ELISHAMA'S (1) [ELISHAMA]
Jer 36:21 Jehudi brought it from **E** room and read it to the

ELISHAPHAT (1)
2Ch 23: 1 Maaseiah son of Adaiah, and **E** son of Zicri.

ELISHEBA (1)
Ex 6:23 Aaron married **E**, the daughter of Amminadab

ELISHUA (3)
2Sa 5:15 Ibhar, **E**, Nepheg, Japhia,
1Ch 3: 6 David also had nine other sons: Ibhar, **E**, Elpelet,
14: 5 Ibhar, **E**, Elpelet,

ELITE (6)
2Sa 20: 7 and Joab set out after Sheba with an **e** guard from
23:13 an **e** group among David's fighting men)
2Ki 24:15 the queen mother, and all Jerusalem's **e**.
1Ch 11:15 an **e** group among David's fighting men)
27: 6 This was the Benaiah who commanded David's **e**
2Ch 26:13 The army consisted of 307,500 men, all **e** troops.

ELIUD (2)
Mt 1:14 the father of Akim. / Akim was the father of **E**.
1:15 **E** was the father of Eleazar. / Eleazar was the

ELIZABETH (11) [ELIZABETH'S]
Lk 1: 5 His wife, **E**, was also from the priestly line of
1: 6 Zechariah and **E** were righteous in God's eyes,
1: 7 They had no children because **E** was barren,
1:13 your prayer, and your wife, **E**, will bear you a son!
1:24 **E**, became pregnant and went into seclusion for
1:36 your relative **E** has become pregnant in her old
1:40 She entered the house and greeted **E**.
1:41 within her, and **E** was filled with the Holy Spirit.
1:42 **E** gave a glad cry and exclaimed to Mary,
1:56 Mary stayed with **E** about three months and
1:60 But **E** said, "No! His name is John!"

ELIZABETH'S (3) [ELIZABETH]
Lk 1:26 In the sixth month of **E** pregnancy, God sent the
1:41 of Mary's greeting, **E** child leaped within her,
1:57 Now it was time for **E** baby to be born, and it was

ELIZAPHAN (4)
Nu 3:30 The leader of the Kohathite clans was **E** son of
34:25 Zebulun | **E** son of Parnach
1Ch 15: 8 There were 200 descendants of **E**, with Shemaiah
2Ch 29:13 From the family of **E**: Shimri and Jeiel.

ELIZUR (5)
Nu 1: 5 chosen for the task: / Reuben | **E** son of Shedeur
2:10[-11] Reuben | **E** son of Shedeur | 46,500
7:30 On the fourth day **E** son of Shedeur, leader of the
7:35 This was the offering brought by **E** son of Shedeur.
10:18 under the leadership of **E** son of Shedeur.

ELKANAH (22)
Ex 6:24 of Korah included Assir, **E**, and Abiasaph.
1Sa 1: 1 There was a man named **E** who lived in Ramah in
1: 2 **E** had two wives, Hannah and Peninnah.
1: 3 Each year **E** and his family would travel to Shiloh
1: 4 On the day **E** presented his sacrifice, he would
1: 8 "What's the matter, Hannah?" **E** would ask.
1:19 When **E** slept with Hannah, the LORD
1:21 The next year **E**, Peninnah, and their children went
1:23 "Whatever you think is best," **E** agreed.
2:11 Then **E** and Hannah returned home to Ramah
2:20 Eli would bless **E** and his wife and say,
1Ch 6:23 **E**, Abiasaph, Assir,
6:25 The descendants of **E** were Amasai, Ahimoth,
6:26 **E**, Zophai, Nahath,
6:27 Eliab, Jeroham, **E**, and Samuel.
6:34 **E**, Jeroham, Eliel, Toah,
6:35 Zuph, **E**, Mahath, Amasai,
6:36 **E**, Joel, Azariah, Zephaniah,
9:16 and Berekiah son of Asa, son of **E**, who lived in
12: 6 **E**, Isshiah, Azarel, Joezer, and Jashobeam,
15:23 Berekiah and **E** were chosen to guard the Ark.
2Ch 28: 7 and **E**, the king's second-in-command.

ELKOSH (1)
Na 1: 1 came as a vision to Nahum, who lived in **E**.

ELLASAR (2)
Ge 14: 1 King Arioch of **E**, King Kedorlaomer of Elam,
14: 9 and the kings of Goiim, Babylonia, and **E**—

ELMADAM (2)
Lk 3:28 Cosam was the son of **E**. / **E** was the son of Er.

ELNAAM (1)
1Ch 11:46 Jeribai and Joshaviah, the sons of **E**;

ELNATHAN (7)
2Ki 24: 8 was Nehushta, the daughter of **E** from Jerusalem.
Ezr 8:16 Ariel, Shemaiah, **E**, Jarib, **E**, Nathan,
8:16 I also sent for Joiarib and **E**, who were very wise
Jer 26:22 Then King Jehoiakim sent **E** son of Acbor to Egypt
36:12 **E** son of Acbor, Gemariah son of Shaphan,
36:25 Even when **E**, Delaiah, and Gemariah begged the

ELOI (2)
Mk 15:34 *"E, E, lema sabachthani?"* which means,

ELON (7) [ELONITE]
Ge 26:34 married Basemath, the daughter of **E** the Hittite.
36: 2 Adah, the daughter of **E** the Hittite;
46:14 The sons of Zebulun were Sered, **E**, and Jahleel.
Nu 26:26 The Elonite clan, named after its ancestor **E**.
Jos 19:43 **E**, Timnah, Ekron,
Jdg 12:11 After him, **E** from Zebulun became Israel's judge.
12:13 After **E** died, Abdon son of Hillel, from Pirathon,

ELON-BETHHANAN (1)
1Ki 4: 9 in Makaz, Shaalbim, Beth-shemesh, and **E**.

ELONITE (1) [ELON]
Nu 26:26 The **E** clan, named after its ancestor Elon.

ELOQUENCE (1) [ELOQUENT]
1Co 1: 5 He has enriched your church with the gifts of **e**

ELOQUENT (2) [ELOQUENCE]
Pr 17: 7 **E** speech is not fitting for a fool; even less are lies
Ac 18:24 an **e** speaker who knew the Scriptures well,

ELPAAL (3)
1Ch 8:11 Hushim had already given birth to Abitub and **E**.
8:12 The sons of **E** were Eber, Misham, Shemed (who
8:18 Ishmerai, Izliah, and Jobab were the sons of **E**.

ELPELET (2)
1Ch 3: 6 David also had nine other sons: Ibhar, Elishua, **E**,
14: 5 Ibhar, Elishua, **E**,

ELSE (188) [ELSE'S, ELSEWHERE]
Ge 19:12 sons-in-law, sons, daughters, or anyone **e**.
26:16 "Go somewhere **e**," he said, "for you have
39:11 no one **e** was around when he was doing his work
Ex 4:13 again pleaded, "Lord, please! Send someone **e**."
15:11 "Who **e** among the gods is like you, O LORD?
20:17 or donkey, or anything **e** your neighbor owns."
22: 9 donkey, sheep, article of clothing, or anything **e**.
28: 3 that will set Aaron apart from everyone **e**,
33:16 How **e** will they know we are special and distinct
34: 3 No one **e** may come with you. In fact, no one is
Lev 16:17 No one **e** is allowed inside the Tabernacle while
18: 9 brought up in the same family or somewhere **e**.
19:34 They should be treated like everyone **e**, and you
25:49 a nephew, or anyone **e** who is closely related.
27:20 or if the field is sold to someone **e** by the priests,
27:27 the priest may sell it to someone **e** for its assessed
Nu 1:51 Anyone **e** who goes too near the Tabernacle will be
3:10 Anyone **e** who comes too near the sanctuary must
4:32 accessories, and everything **e** related to their use.
6:21 **e** beyond what is required by their normal Nazirite
16: 3 anyone **e** among all these people of the LORD?"
20:19 want to pass through your country and nothing **e**."
22:19 to see if the LORD has anything **e** to say to me."
Dt 5:21 or donkey, or anything **e** your neighbor owns.'
8:13 and gold have multiplied along with everything **e**,
15:21 or blind, or if anything **e** is wrong with it,
20: 5 and someone **e** would dedicate your house!
20: 6 die in battle, and someone **e** would eat from it!
20: 7 and someone **e** would marry your fiancée.'
20: 8 If you are, go home before you frighten anyone **e**.'
22: 3 clothing, or anything **e** your neighbor loses.
23:19 or anything **e** that may be loaned with interest.
28:30 will build a house, but someone **e** will live in it.
28:55 because he has nothing **e** to eat during the siege
28:57 She will have nothing **e** to eat during the siege
33:29 Who **e** is like you, a people saved by the LORD?
Jdg 16: 7 not yet been dried, I will be as weak as anyone **e**."
16:11 never been used, I will be as weak as anyone **e**."
16:13 the loom shuttle, I will be as weak as anyone **e**."
16:17 and I would become as weak as anyone **e**."
Ru 1:13 them to grow up and refuse to marry someone **e**?
1Sa 9: 2 and shoulders taller than anyone **e** in the land.
10:23 and he stood head and shoulders above anyone **e**.
15: 6 the Amalekites live or **e** you will die with them.
15: 8 but completely destroyed everyone **e**.
15:15 your God. We have destroyed everything **e**."
15:20 back King Agag, but I destroyed everyone **e**.
15:28 from you today and has given it to someone **e**—
21: 3 me five loaves of bread or anything **e** you have."
21: 9 that if you want it, for there is nothing **e** here."
24:19 Who **e** would let his enemy get away when he had
30: 2 and children and everyone **e** but without killing
30:19 or daughter, or anything **e** that had been taken.
2Sa 2:21 "Go fight someone **e**!" Abner warned. "Take on
7:19 Sovereign LORD, in addition to everything **e**,
1Ki 2: 5 "And there is something **e**. You know that Joab
2:36 But don't step outside the city to go anywhere **e**.
2:42 by the LORD and warn you not to go anywhere **e**,
3:12 and understanding mind such as no one **e** has ever
4:31 He was wiser than anyone **e**, including Ethan the
14: 5 wife will come here, pretending to be someone **e**.
14: 6 Why are you pretending to be someone **e**?"
20:40 But while I was busy doing something **e**,
21:25 No one **e** so completely sold himself to what was
2Ki 7: 7 their tents, horses, donkeys, and everything **e**,
1Ch 17:17 And now, O God, in addition to everything **e**,
2Ch 23: 5 Everyone **e** should stay in the courtyards of the
Ne 2:16 the officials, or anyone **e** in the administration.
Job 17: 3 O God, since no one **e** will stand up for me.
31: 8 then let someone **e** harvest the crops I have
41:33 There is nothing **e** so fearless anywhere on earth.
Ps 22:11 for trouble is near, / and no one **e** can help me.
35:10 Who **e** rescues the weak and helpless from the
35:10 Who **e** protects the poor and needy from those who
39: 6 We heap up wealth for someone **e** to spend.
45: 7 out the oil of joy on you more than on anyone **e**.
73: 5 or plagued with problems like everyone **e**.
84:10 your courts / is better than a thousand anywhere **e**!
109: 8 be few; / let his position be given to someone **e**.
Pr 4: 7 And whatever **e** you do, get good judgment.
4:15 their haunts. Turn away and go somewhere **e**,
4:23 Above all **e**, guard your heart, for it affects
5:10 and someone **e** will enjoy the fruit of your labor.
8:22 from the beginning, before he created anything **e**.
14:10 own bitterness, and no one **e** can fully share its joy.
25: 9 the matter with them privately. Don't tell anyone **e**,
Ecc 2:12 and anyone **e** would come to the same conclusions
6: 6 And since he must die like everyone **e**—well,
9:11 I have observed something **e** in this world of ours.
SS 4:12 You are like a spring that no one **e** can drink from,
Isa 8:11 "Do not think like everyone **e** does.
8:13 If you fear him, you need fear nothing **e**.
9:19 are fuel for the fire, and no one spares anyone **e**.
40:12 Who **e** has held the oceans in his hand? Who has
40:12 Who **e** knows the weight of the earth or has
41:26 Who **e** predicted this, making you admit that he
was right? No one **e** said a word!
42: 8 is my name! I will not give my glory to anyone **e**.
44: 7 Who **e** can tell you what is going to happen in the
46: 9 I alone! I am God, and there is no one **e** like me.
56: 3 the eunuchs. They are as much mine as anyone **e**.
Jer 3: 1 man divorces a woman and she marries someone **e**,
9: 7 test them like metal. What **e** can I do with them?
21: 7 and everyone **e** in the city have survived war,
23:34 If any prophet, priest, or anyone **e** says, 'I have a
32: 7 right to buy it before it is offered to anyone **e**.' "
32: 8 the right to buy it before it is offered to anyone **e**,
Eze 39:10 They will need nothing **e** for their fires.
43:11 its entrances and doors—and everything **e** about it.
Da 4:18 tell me what it means, for no one **e** can help me.
5:17 "Keep your gifts or give them to someone **e**,
Hos 4: 4 "Don't point your finger at someone **e** and try to
Am 6:10 the last survivor, "Is there anyone **e** with you?"
Hab 2: 2 so that a runner can read it and tell everyone **e**.
Mt 5:47 your friends, how are you different from anyone **e**?
11: 3 or should we keep looking for someone **e**?"
19:20 the young man replied. "What **e** must I do?"
26:33 "Even if everyone **e** deserts you, I never will."
Mk 9: 2 No one **e** was there. As the men watched,
9:35 take last place and be the servant of everyone **e**."
10:11 and marries someone **e** commits adultery against
14:29 "Even if everyone **e** deserts you, I never will."
Lk 7:19 or should we keep looking for someone **e**?"
7:20 or should we keep looking for someone **e**?' "
13: 7 It's taking up space we can use for something **e**.'
13:20 also asked, "What **e** is the Kingdom of God like?
16:18 his wife and marries someone **e** commits adultery,
18: 9 had great self-confidence and scorned everyone **e**:
18:11 God, that I am not a sinner like everyone **e**,
22:58 After a while someone **e** looked at him and said,
22:59 About an hour later someone **e** insisted,
24: 9 and everyone **e**—what had happened.
Jn 3:31 has come from above and is greater than anyone **e**.
4:37 'One person plants and someone **e** harvests.'
5: 7 get there, someone **e** always gets in ahead of me."
5:32 But someone **e** is also testifying about me, and I
10:29 to me, and he is more powerful than anyone **e**.
11:24 "Yes," Martha said, "when everyone **e** rises,
11:25 even though they die like everyone **e**, will live
15:24 signs among them that no one **e** could do,
Ac 1:20 'Let his position be given to someone **e**.'
1:21 "So now we must choose someone **e** to take
4:12 There is salvation in no one **e**! There is no other
5:13 No one **e** dared to join them, though everyone had
8:34 "Was Isaiah talking about himself or someone **e**?"
13:37 No, it was a reference to someone **e**—
24:16 a clear conscience before God and everyone **e**.
25:11 neither you nor anyone **e** has a right to turn me
27:19 and anything **e** they could lay their hands on.
Ro 3: 4 Though everyone **e** in the world is a liar, God is
8:32 who gave us Christ, also give us everything **e**?
14:21 or do anything **e** if it might cause another Christian
15:18 I dare not boast of anything **e**. I have brought the
15:20 a church has already been started by someone **e**.
1Co 1:16 I don't remember baptizing anyone **e**.)
2:11 No one can know what anyone **e** is really thinking
4: 3 it matters very little what you or anyone **e** thinks.
4: 7 What makes you better than anyone **e**? What do
7:11 let her remain single or **e** go back to him.
9: 1 Do I not have as much freedom as anyone **e**?
10:29 my freedom be limited by what someone **e** thinks?
12: 9 and to someone **e** he gives the power to heal the
12:10 He gives someone **e** the ability to know whether it
12:31 let me tell you about something **e** that is better than
2Co 8:21 but we also want everyone **e** to know we are
10:15 Nor do we claim credit for the work someone **e** has
10:16 are far beyond you, where no one **e** is working.
Gal 1:12 from Jesus Christ himself. No one **e** taught me.
1:16 to me, I did not rush out to consult with anyone **e**;
4:20 But at this distance I frankly don't know what **e** to
6: 4 you won't need to compare yourself to anyone **e**.
Eph 1:21 or power or leader or anything **e** in this world
2: 3 we were under God's anger just like everyone **e**.
Php 2:20 I have no one **e** like Timothy, who genuinely cares
3: 8 everything **e** is worthless when compared with the
3: 8 I have discarded everything **e**, counting it all as
Col 1:17 He existed before everything **e** began, and he holds
1Th 2: 6 we have never asked for it from you or anyone **e**.
3:12 and overflow to each other and to everyone **e**,
5:15 try to do good to each other and to everyone **e**.
1Ti 1:10 and for those who do anything **e** that contradicts
5: 3 for any widow who has no one **e** to care for her.
Heb 1: 9 out the oil of joy on you more than on anyone **e**."
Jas 1:13 to do wrong, and he never tempts anyone **e** either.
2: 3 "You can stand over there, or **e** sit on the floor"—
5:12 take an oath, by heaven or earth or anything **e**.
2Jn 1: 1 as does everyone **e** who knows God's truth—
Jude 1: 3 But now I find that I must write about something **e**,

ELSE'S (5) [ELSE]
Ex 22: 5 and the owner lets it stray into someone **e** field to
Lev 19:20 girl who is committed to become someone **e** wife,
Pr 22:26 or put up a guarantee for someone **e** loan.
26:17 is as foolish as interfering in someone **e** argument.
2Co 10:16 be no question about being in someone **e** territory.

ELSEWHERE (1) [ELSE, WHERE]
Mic 1: 7 will now be carried away to pay prostitutes **e**."

ELTEKEH (2)
Jos 19:44 **E**, Gibbethon, Baalath,
21:23 to the priests from the tribe of Dan: **E**, Gibbethon,

ELTEKON (1)
Jos 15:59 Maarath, Beth-anoth, and **E**—six towns with their

ELTOLAD (2)
Jos 15:30 **E**, Kesil, Hormah,
19: 4 **E**, Bethul, Hormah,

ELUZAI (1)
1Ch 12: 5 **E**, Jerimoth, Bealiah, Shemariah, and Shephatiah

ELYMAS (1)
Ac 13: 8 But **E**, the sorcerer (as his name means in Greek),

ELZABAD (2)
1Ch 12:12 Johanan was eighth. / **E** was ninth.
26: 7 Their names were Othni, Rephael, Obed, and **E**.

ELZAPHAN (2)
Ex 6:22 of Uzziel included Mishael, **E**, and Sithri.
Lev 10: 4 Then Moses called for Mishael and **E**,

EMBALM (2) [EMBALMED, EMBALMING]
Ge 50: 2 Then Joseph told his morticians to **e** the body.
Lk 23:56 and prepared spices and ointments to **e** him.

EMBALMED (1) [EMBALM]
Ge 50:26 They **e** him, and his body was placed in a coffin in

EMBALMING (2) [EMBALM]
Ge 50: 3 The **e** process took forty days, and there was a
Jn 19:39 bringing about seventy-five pounds of **e** ointment

EMBARRASSED (6) [EMBARRASSMENT]
2Sa 10: 5 grew out, for they were very **e** by their appearance.
2Ki 2:17 But they kept urging him until he was **e**, and he
1Ch 19: 5 grew out, for they were very **e** by their appearance.
Mic 7:16 They will be **e** that their power is so insignificant.
Mk 6:26 but he was **e** to break his oath in front of his guests.
Lk 14: 9 Then you will be **e** and will have to take whatever

EMBARRASSMENT (2) [EMBARRASSED]
Ge 20:16 to compensate for any **e** I may have caused you.
Pr 19:26 away their mother are a public disgrace and an **e**.

EMBEDDED (1)
Est 1: 6 fastened by purple ribbons to silver rings **e** in

EMBERS (2)
Pr 26:21 person starts fights as easily as hot **e** light charcoal
Isa 7: 4 to fear the fierce anger of those two burned-out **e**,

EMBITTERED (1) [BITTER]
Job 27: 2 my rights, by the Almighty who has **e** my soul.

EMBLEM (1)
Est 6: 8 as well as the king's own horse with a royal **e** on

EMBRACE (6) [EMBRACED, EMBRACES, EMBRACING]
Pr 3:18 Wisdom is a tree of life to those who **e** her;
4: 8 she will exalt you. **E** her and she will honor you.
5:20 or **e** the breasts of an adulterous woman?
Ecc 3: 5 A time to **e** and a time to turn away.
SS 8: 3 be under my head and your right hand would **e** me.
Jer 31:22 and different to happen—Israel will **e** her God."

EMBRACED (10) [EMBRACE]
Ge 33: 4 meet him and **e** him affectionately and kissed him.
45:14 Weeping with joy, he **e** Benjamin, and Benjamin
46:29 he **e** his father and wept on his shoulder for a long
48:10 boys close to him, and Jacob kissed and **e** them.
1Sa 20:41 Both of them were in tears as they **e** each other
2Sa 15: 5 Instead, he took them by the hand and **e** them.
19:39 After David had blessed and **e** him,
Eze 14: 3 They have **e** things that lead them into sin.
Lk 15:20 he ran to his son, **e** him, and kissed him.
Ac 20:37 They wept aloud as they **e** him in farewell,

EMBRACES (2) [EMBRACE]
Pr 6:29 man's wife. He who **e** her will not go unpunished.
SS 2: 6 hand is under my head, and his right hand **e** me.

EMBRACING (1) [EMBRACE]
Eze 16:29 You added to your lovers by **e** that great merchant

EMBROIDER (1) [EMBROIDERED, EMBROIDERERS, EMBROIDERING, EMBROIDERY]
Ex 26:36 and **e** exquisite designs into it, using blue, purple,

EMBROIDERED (25) [EMBROIDER]
Ex 26: 1 with figures of cherubim skillfully **e** into them.
26:31 with cherubim skillfully **e** into the cloth using blue,
28: 4 an ephod, a robe, an **e** tunic, a turban, and a sash.
28: 5 of fine linen cloth and **e** with gold thread and blue,
28: 6 and skillfully **e** with gold thread and blue,
28: 8 fine linen cloth **e** with gold thread and blue, purple,
28:15 fine linen cloth **e** with gold thread and blue, purple,
28:39 out of this linen as well. Also make him an **e** sash.
29: 5 along with the **e** robe of the ephod, the ephod
36: 8 One of the craftsmen then **e** blue, purple,
36:35 and cherubim were skillfully **e** into it with blue,
36:37 It was made of fine linen cloth and **e** with blue,
38:18 was made of fine linen cloth and **e** with blue,
39: 2 fine linen cloth and **e** with gold thread and blue,
39: 3 He then **e** it into the linen with the blue, purple,
39: 8 fine linen cloth and **e** with gold thread and blue,
39:29 were made of fine linen cloth and **e** with blue,
Lev 8: 7 He clothed Aaron with the **e** tunic and tied the sash
8:13 Aaron's sons and clothed them in their **e** tunics,
Jdg 5:30 and colorful, beautifully **e** robes for me.'
2Ch 3:14 and scarlet yarn, with figures of cherubim **e** on it.
Eze 16:10 expensive clothing of linen and silk, beautifully **e**,
16:13 were made of fine linen and were beautifully **e**.
16:18 You used the beautifully **e** clothes I gave you to
23:41 You sat with them on a beautifully **e** couch and put

EMBROIDERERS (1) [EMBROIDER]
Ex 35:35 designers, weavers, and **e** in blue, purple,

EMBROIDERING (1) [EMBROIDER]
Ex 38:23 expert at engraving, designing, and **e** blue, purple,

EMBROIDERY (3) [EMBROIDER]
Ex 27:16 and decorate it with beautiful **e** in blue, purple,
Eze 27:16 purple dyes, **e**, fine linen, and jewelry of coral
27:24 blue cloth, **e**, and many-colored carpets bound with

EMEK-KEZIZ (1)
Jos 18:21 of the tribe of Benjamin. / Jericho, Beth-hoglah, **E**,

EMERALD (5)
Ex 28:17 will contain a red carnelian, a chrysolite, and an **e**.
39:10 row were a red carnelian, a chrysolite, and an **e**.
Eze 28:13 beryl, onyx, jasper, sapphire, turquoise, and **e**—
Rev 4: 3 And the glow of an **e** circled his throne like a
21:19 the second sapphire, the third agate, the fourth **e**,

EMERGE (1)
Nu 24:17 will rise from Jacob; / a scepter will **e** from Israel.

EMERODS [KJV] See TUMORS

EMISSION (4)
Lev 15:16 "Whenever a man has an **e** of semen, he must
15:32 defiled by a genital discharge or an **e** of semen;
22: 4 touching a corpse, or are defiled by an **e** of semen,
Dt 23:10 because of a nocturnal **e** must leave the camp

EMITES (4)
Ge 14: 5 Zuzites in Ham, the **E** in the plain of Kiriathaim,
Dt 2:10 and powerful race of giants called the **E** had once
2:11 Both the **E** and the Anakites are often referred to
2:11 as the Rephaites, but the Moabites called them **E**.

EMMAUS (3)
Lk 24:13 Jesus' followers were walking to the village of **E**,
24:28 By this time they were nearing **E** and the end of
24:35 Then the two from **E** told their story of how Jesus

EMMOR [KJV] See HAMOR

EMOTION (2)
Ge 43:30 because he was overcome with **e** for his brother
2Sa 18:33 The king was overcome with **e**. He went up to his

EMPEROR (6) [EMPIRE]
Lk 2: 1 At that time the Roman **e**, Augustus, decreed that a
3: 1 year of the reign of Tiberius, the Roman **e**.
Ac 25:21 But Paul appealed to the **e**. So I ordered him back
25:25 However, he appealed his case to the **e**, and I
25:26 But what shall I write the **e**? For there is no real
25:27 the **e** without specifying the charges against him!"

EMPHASIZE (4)
Job 41:12 "I want to **e** the tremendous strength in the
Ecc 12:11 spur students to action and **e** important truths.
Ro 3:31 Well then, if we **e** faith, does this mean that we can
15:15 I have been bold enough to **e** some of these points,

EMPIRE (28) [EMPEROR, EMPIRES, IMPERIAL]
Ge 10:10 He built the foundation for his **e** in the land of
10:12 the main city of the **e**, located between Nineveh
Est 1: 2 At that time he ruled his **e** from his throne at the
1: 4 display of the opulent wealth and glory of his **e**.
1:14 and held the highest positions in the **e**.
1:16 also every official and citizen throughout your **e**.
1:18 of every one of us, your officials throughout the **e**,
1:20 this decree is published throughout your vast **e**,
1:22 He sent letters to all parts of the **e**, to each province
2: 2 "Let us search the **e** to find beautiful young virgins
3: 1 making him the most powerful official in the **e**
3: 6 all the Jews throughout the entire **e** of Xerxes.
3: 8 scattered through all the provinces of your **e**.
3:13 sent by messengers into all the provinces of the **e**.
8: 9 and languages of all the peoples of the **e**,
9:28 family throughout the provinces and cities of the **e**.
9:30 throughout the 127 provinces of the **e** of Xerxes.
10: 1 King Xerxes imposed tribute throughout his **e**,
Isa 7:17 the years since Solomon's **e** was divided into Israel
23: 8 on Tyre, **e** builder and chief trader of the world?
48:14 He will use him to put an end to the **e** of Babylon,
Da 6: 3 the king made plans to place him over the entire **e**.
7:24 Its ten horns are ten kings that will rule that **e**.
8:21 its eyes represents the first king of the Greek **E**.
8:22 **E** will break into four sections with four kings,
11: 4 For his **e** will be uprooted and given to others.
Lk 2: 1 a census should be taken throughout the Roman **E**.
19:12 "A nobleman was called away to a distant **e** to be

EMPIRES (1) [EMPIRE]
Da 2:40 That kingdom will smash and crush all previous **e**,

EMPLOYED (2) [EMPLOYEES, EMPLOYER, EMPLOYER'S]
Job 1: 3 hundred female donkeys, and he **e** many servants.
Ac 19:25 along with others **e** in related trades, and addressed

EMPLOYEES (2) [EMPLOYED]
Mal 3: 5 I will speak against those who cheat **e** of their
Mk 13:34 He gave each of his **e** instructions about the work

EMPLOYER (7) [EMPLOYED]
Pr 10:26 Lazy people are a pain to their **e**. They are like
25:13 heat of summer. They revive the spirit of their **e**.
26:10 An **e** who hires a fool or a bystander is like an
30:10 Never slander a person to his **e**. If you do,
Lk 16: 2 So his **e** called him in and said, 'What's this I hear
16: 5 each person who owed money to his **e** to come
16: 7 " 'And how much do you owe my **e**?' he asked

EMPLOYER'S (1) [EMPLOYED]
Pr 27:18 workers who protect their **e** interests will be

EMPOWER (1) [EMPOWERED, EMPOWERING]
Isa 45: 1 his anointed one, whose right hand he will **e**.

EMPOWERED (5) [EMPOWER]
Ex 4:21 and perform the miracles I have **e** you to do.
Mt 9:34 because he is **e** by the prince of demons."
12:27 And if I am **e** by the prince of demons, what about
Lk 11:18 You say I am **e** by the prince of demons. But if
11:19 And if I am **e** by the prince of demons, what about

EMPOWERING (1) [EMPOWER]
Lk 11:18 But if Satan is fighting against himself by **e** me to

EMPTIED (6) [EMPTY]
Ge 24:20 So she quickly **e** the jug into the watering trough
42:35 As they **e** out the sacks, there at the top of each one
Lev 14:36 he must have the house **e** so everything inside will
Jdg 3:22 Ehud left the dagger in, and the king's bowels **e**.
Isa 24: 3 The earth will be completely **e** and looted.
Jer 51:34 has eaten and crushed us and **e** out our strength.

EMPTIES (1) [EMPTY]
Jos 15: 5 bay where the Jordan River **e** into the Dead Sea,

EMPTINESS (3) [EMPTY]
Job 15:31 fooling themselves, for **e** will be their only reward.
Isa 40:17 eyes they are less than nothing—mere **e** and froth.
Mic 6:14 Your hunger pangs and **e** will still remain.

EMPTY (64) [EMPTIED, EMPTIES, EMPTINESS, EMPTY-HANDED, EMPTY-HEADED]
Ge 1: 2 The earth was **e**, a formless mass cloaked in
37:24 used to store water, but it was **e** at the time.
47:19 and so the land will not become **e** and desolate."
Dt 28:17 You will be cursed with baskets **e** of fruit, and with kneading bowls **e** of bread.
32:10 them in a desert land, / in an **e**, howling wasteland.
Ru 1:21 away full, but the LORD has brought me home **e**.
1Sa 20:18 will be missed when your place at the table is **e**.
20:25 and Abner beside him. But David's place was **e**.
20:27 But when David's place was **e** again the next day,
2Ki 4: 3 "Borrow as many **e** jars as you can from your
Job 15:31 Let them no longer trust in **e** riches. They are only
26: 7 God stretches the northern sky over **e** space
Ps 89:47 my life is, / how **e** and futile this human existence!
Pr 14: 4 An **e** stable stays clean, but no income comes from an **e** stable.
16:26 to have an appetite; an **e** stomach drives them on.
Ecc 5: 7 And there is ruin in a flood of **e** words. Fear God
6:12 In the few days of our **e** lives, who knows how our
Isa 27:10 Israel's fortified cities will be silent and **e**,
32:14 the city will be deserted, and busy towns will be **e**.
41:29 Your idols are all as **e** as the wind.
45:18 world to be lived in, not to be a place of **e** chaos.
50: 2 why the house is silent and **e** when I come home?
61: 4 though they have been **e** for many generations.
Jer 4: 7 Your towns will lie in ruins, **e** of people.
4:23 I looked at the earth, and it was **e** and formless.
6: 8 Jerusalem! If you do not listen, I will **e** the land."
9:10 For they are desolate and **e** of life; the lowing of
12:11 They have made it an **e** wasteland; I hear its
14: 3 The servants return with **e** pitchers, confused
33:10 Yet in the **e** streets of Jerusalem and Judah's other
34:22 of Judah are destroyed and left completely **e**."
38: 6 and lowered him by ropes into an **e** cistern in the
48: 9 so she could fly away, for her cities will be left **e**,
49:20 will be dragged off, and their homes will be **e**.
50:45 will be dragged off, and their homes will be **e**.
51:62 remain here. She will lie **e** and abandoned forever.'
La 5:18 For Jerusalem is **e** and desolate, a place haunted by
Eze 24:10 many spices. Then **e** the pot and burn the bones.
24:11 Now set the **e** pot on the coals to scorch away the
29:12 Its cities will be **e** and desolate for forty years,
36:34 The fields that used to lie **e** and desolate—a shock
45: 2 of land 87-1/2 feet wide is to be left **e** all around it.
Hos 10: 4 They spout **e** words and make promises they don't
Joel 1:10 The fields are ruined and **e** of crops. The grain,
1:17 The barns and granaries stand **e** and abandoned.
Mic 7:13 But the land will become **e** and desolate because of
Na 2: 2 For the land of Israel lies **e** and broken after your
2:10 Soon the city is an **e** shambles, stripped of its
Hab 3:17 the olive crop fails, and the fields lie **e** and barren;
3:17 flocks die in the fields, and the cattle barns are **e**,
Mt 12:44 So it returns and finds its former home **e**, swept,
23:38 now look, your house is left to you, **e** and desolate.
Lk 1:53 good things / and sent the rich away with **e** hands.
5: 2 He noticed two **e** boats at the water's edge,
13:35 And now look, your house is left to you **e**. And you
24:12 he peered in and saw the **e** linen wrappings;
1Co 14: 9 You might as well be talking to an **e** room.
Php 4:12 whether it is with a full stomach or **e**, with plenty
Col 2: 8 Don't let anyone lead you astray with **e** philosophy
1Pe 1:18 from the **e** life you inherited from your ancestors.
2Pe 2:18 They brag about themselves with **e**,
Rev 16: 1 and **e** out the seven bowls of God's wrath on the

EMPTY-HANDED (8) [EMPTY, HAND]
Ex 3:21 load you down with gifts so you will not leave **e**.
Dt 15:13 release a male servant, do not send him away **e**.
Ru 3:17 'Don't go back to your mother-in-law **e**.' "
2Sa 1:22 strongest foes; / they did not return from battle **e**.
Ecc 5:15 lives as naked and **e** as on the day they were born.
Mk 12: 3 the servant, beat him up, and sent him back **e**.
Lk 20:10 the servant, beat him up, and sent him back **e**.
20:11 and treated shamefully, and he went away **e**.

EMPTY-HEADED (1) [EMPTY, HEAD]
Job 11:12 An **e** person won't become wise any more than a

EN-EGLAIM (1) [EGLAIM]
Eze 47:10 Dead Sea, fishing all the way from En-gedi to **E**.

EN-GANNIM (3)
Jos 15:34 Zanoah, **E**, Tappuah, Enam,
19:21 Remeth, **E**, En-haddah, and Beth-pazzez.
21:29 Jarmuth, and **E**—four towns with their

EN-GEDI (6) [HAZAZON-TAMAR]
Jos 15:62 Nibshan, the City of Salt, and **E**—six towns with
1Sa 23:29 David then went to live in the strongholds of **E**.
24: 1 told that David had gone into the wilderness of **E**.
2Ch 20: 2 (This was another name for **E**.)
SS 1:14 is like a bouquet of flowers in the gardens of **E**."
Eze 47:10 Dead Sea, fishing all the way from **E** to En-eglaim.

EN-HADDAH (1)
Jos 19:21 Remeth, En-gannim, **E**, and Beth-pazzez.

EN-HAZOR (1)
Jos 19:37 Kedesh, Edrei, **E**,

EN-MISHPAT (1) [KADESH]
Ge 14: 7 Then they swung around to **E** (now called Kadesh)

EN-RIMMON (1) [RIMMON]
Ne 11:29 They were also in **E**, Zorah, Jarmuth,

EN-ROGEL (6)
Jos 15: 7 extended to the springs at En-shemesh and on to **E**.
18:16 the Jebusites lived, and continued down to **E**.
18:17 From **E** the boundary proceeded northeast to
2Sa 17:17 Jonathan and Ahimaaz had been staying at **E**
17:18 But a boy saw them leaving **E** to go to David,
1Ki 1: 9 went to the stone of Zoheleth near the spring of **E**,

EN-SHEMESH (2)
Jos 15: 7 From there the border extended to the springs at **E**
18:17 En-rogel the boundary proceeded northeast to **E**

ENABLED (3) [ABLE]
Ru 4:13 with her, the LORD **e** her to become pregnant,
2Co 3: 6 He is the one who has **e** us to represent his new
Col 1:12 who has **e** you to share the inheritance that belongs

ENACTED (1) [ACT]
Ac 24: 2 given peace to us Jews and have **e** reforms for us.

ENAIM (1)
Ge 38:14 beside the road at the entrance to the village of **E**,

ENAM (1)
Jos 15:34 Zanoah, En-gannim, Tappuah, **E**,

ENAN (5) [HAZAR ENAN]
Nu 1:15 Naphtali | Ahira son of **E**
2:29[-30] Naphtali | Ahira son of **E** | 53,400
7:78 On the twelfth day Ahira son of **E**, leader of the
7:83 This was the offering brought by Ahira son of **E**.
10:27 The tribe of Naphtali was led by Ahira son of **E**.

ENCAMPMENT (1) [CAMP]
1Sa 30:16 So the Egyptian led them to the Amalekite **e**.

ENCHANTED (1) [ENCHANTER, ENCHANTERS, ENCHANTING]
SS 1:12 on his couch, **e** by the fragrance of my perfume.

ENCHANTER (1) [ENCHANTED]
Da 2:10 such a thing of any magician, **e**, or astrologer!

ENCHANTERS (8) [ENCHANTED]
Isa 3: 3 advisers, skilled magicians, and expert **e**.
Da 1:20 of all the magicians and **e** in his entire kingdom.
2: 2 in his magicians, **e**, sorcerers, and astrologers,
2:27 "There are no wise men, **e**, magicians,
4: 7 When all the magicians, **e**, astrologers,
5: 7 The king shouted for the **e**, astrologers,
5:11 **e**, astrologers, and fortune-tellers of Babylon.
5:15 and **e** have tried to read this writing on the wall,

ENCHANTING (1) [ENCHANTED]
Na 3: 4 all to worship her false gods, **e** people everywhere.

ENCIRCLE (1) [CIRCLE]
Lk 19:43 against your walls and **e** you and close in on you.

ENCIRCLED (5) [CIRCLE]
1Ki 7:18 He also made two rows of pomegranates that **e** the
7:24 The Sea was **e** just below its rim by two rows of
2Ch 4: 3 The Sea was **e** just below its rim by two rows of
Ps 88:17 all day long. / They have **e** me completely.
Eze 23:15 Handsome belts **e** their waists, and flowing turbans

ENCLOSE (2) [CLOSE]
Ex 35:12 the inner curtain to **e** the Ark in the Most Holy
40: 3 and install the inner curtain to **e** the Ark within the

ENCLOSED (2) [CLOSE]
Ex 27: 9 **e** with curtains made from fine linen.
39:34 the inner curtain that **e** the Most Holy Place;

ENCLOSURE (2) [CLOSE]
Eze 25: 5 and all the land of the Ammonites into an **e** for
46:21 each of its four corners. In each corner I saw an **e**.

ENCLOSURES (2) [CLOSE]
Eze 46:22 Each of these **e** was 70 feet long and 52-1/2 feet
Zep 2: 6 a place of shepherd camps and **e** for sheep.

ENCOUNTERED (2)
Jdg 1: 5 While at Bezek they **e** King Adoni-bezek
Ac 27: 4 we **e** headwinds that made it difficult to keep the

ENCOURAGE (36) [ENCOURAGED, ENCOURAGEMENT, ENCOURAGES, ENCOURAGING]
Nu 13:30 But Caleb tried to **e** the people as they stood before
Dt 1:38 into the land. **E** him as he prepares to enter it.
3:28 But commission Joshua and **e** him, for he will lead
13: 5 for they **e** rebellion against the LORD your God,
1Sa 4:20 but before she passed away the midwives tried to **e**
22:13 Why did you **e** him to revolt against me and to
Ps 64: 5 They **e** each other to do evil / and plan how to set
119:28 I weep with grief; / **e** me by your word.
138: 3 you **e** me by giving me the strength I need.
SS 8: 9 If she is chaste, we will strengthen and **e** her.
Isa 35: 3 tired hands, and **e** those who have weak knees.
41: 6 They **e** one another with the words, "Be strong!"
Jer 23:14 They **e** those who are doing evil instead of turning
La 1:16 to comfort me; any who might **e** me are far away.
Ro 1:12 I'm eager to **e** you in your faith, but I also want to
1:32 And, worse yet, they **e** others to do them, too.
12: 8 If your gift is to **e** others, do it! If you have money,
2Co 8: 6 and **e** you to complete your share in this ministry
13:11 **E** each other. Live in harmony and peace.
Eph 6:22 will let you know how we are, and he will **e** you.
Col 4: 8 to let you know how we are doing and to **e** you.
1Th 3: 2 sent him to strengthen you, to **e** you in your faith,
4: 1 this already, and we **e** you to do so more and more.
4:18 So comfort and **e** each other with these words.
5:11 So **e** each other and build each other up, just as you
5:14 **E** those who are timid. Take tender care of those
1Ti 6: 2 Timothy, and **e** everyone to obey them.
2Ti 4: 2 rebuke, and **e** your people with good teaching.
Tit 1: 9 then he will be able to **e** others with right teaching
2: 6 **e** the young men to live wisely in all they do.
2:15 teach these things and **e** your people to do them,
Heb 10:24 Think of ways to **e** one another to outbursts of love
10:25 as some people do, but **e** and warn each other,
1Pe 5:12 My purpose in writing is to **e** you and assure you
2Jn 1:10 invite him into your house or **e** him in any way.
Rev 14:12 Let this **e** God's holy people to endure persecution

ENCOURAGED (37) [ENCOURAGE]
Jdg 7:11 Midianites are saying, and you will be greatly **e**.
1Sa 23:16 and **e** him to stay strong in his faith in God.
2Ch 22: 3 for his mother **e** him in doing wrong.
28:19 for he had **e** his people to sin and had been utterly
30:22 Hezekiah **e** the Levites for the skill they displayed
32: 6 city gate. Then Hezekiah **e** them with this address:
32: 8 battles for us!" These words greatly **e** the people.
33:16 He also **e** the people of Judah to worship the
35: 2 and **e** them in their work at the Temple of the
Ezr 6:14 and they were greatly **e** by the preaching of the
7:28 I felt **e** because the gracious hand of the LORD
Ne 9:26 they killed the prophets who **e** them to return to
Job 4: 3 "In the past you have **e** many a troubled soul to
Eze 13:22 And you have **e** the wicked by promising them life,
44:12 But they **e** my people to worship other gods,
Mt 9:22 turned around and said to her, "Daughter, be **e**!
Ac 11:23 and he **e** the believers to stay true to the Lord.
14:22 They **e** them to continue in the faith,
16:40 and **e** them once more before leaving town.
18:27 and the Christians in Ephesus **e** him in this.
19:33 of the Jews, who **e** him to explain the situation.
20: 1 all over, Paul sent for the believers and **e** them.
20: 2 he **e** the believers in all the towns he passed
23:11 the Lord appeared to Paul and said, "Be **e**, Paul.
27:36 Then everyone was **e**,
Ro 1:12 you in your faith, but I also want to be **e** by yours.
1Co 8:10 but they will be **e** to violate their conscience by
14:31 after the other, so that everyone will learn and be **e**.
2Co 7: 4 You have greatly **e** me; you have made me happy
7: 6 who are discouraged, **e** us by the arrival of Titus.
7:13 We have been **e** by this. In addition to our own
8: 6 who **e** your giving in the first place, to return to
Gal 2: 9 They **e** us to keep preaching to the Gentiles,
Eph 3:13 I am suffering, so you should feel honored and **e**.
Col 2: 2 My goal is that they will be **e** and knit together by
1Th 2:12 We pleaded with you, **e** you, and urged you to live
2Ti 1:16 all his family because he often visited and **e** me.

ENCOURAGEMENT (12) [ENCOURAGE]
Ac 4:36 nicknamed Barnabas (which means "Son of **E**").
13:15 if you have any word of **e** for us, come and give
Ro 15: 4 and **e** as we wait patiently for God's promises.
15: 5 May God, who gives this patience and **e**, help you
15:32 a happy heart, and we will be an **e** to each other.
1Co 16:18 They have been a wonderful **e** to me, as they have
2Co 1: 6 it is so that we, in turn, can be an **e** to you.
7: 7 so was the news he brought of the **e** he received
7:13 In addition to our own **e**, we were especially
Eph 4:29 so that your words will be an **e** to those who hear
Php 2: 1 Is there any **e** from belonging to Christ?
Phm 1:20 favor for the Lord's sake. Give me this **e** in Christ.

ENCOURAGES (3) [ENCOURAGE]
Job 6:11 I do not have a goal that **e** me to carry on.
2Co 7: 6 But God, who **e** those who are discouraged,
2Jn 1:11 Anyone who **e** him becomes a partner in his evil

ENCOURAGING (13) [ENCOURAGE]
Dt 13:13 citizens astray by **e** them to worship foreign gods.
1Sa 22: 8 of it! My own son—**e** David to try and kill me!"
2Ch 19: 4 **e** the people to return to the LORD, the God of
Est 9:21 **e** them to celebrate an annual festival on these two
Pr 12:25 a person down; an **e** word cheers a person up.
Ac 15:31 the church that day as they read this **e** message.
15:32 to the Christians, **e** and strengthening their faith.
18:23 **e** them and helping them to grow in the Lord.
1Co 8:12 by **e** them to do something they believe is wrong.
14: 3 others grow in the Lord, **e** and comforting them.
1Ti 4:13 to the church, **e** the believers, and teaching them.
Heb 12: 5 And have you entirely forgotten the **e** words God
Rev 2:20 She is **e** them to worship idols, eat food offered to

END (274) [ENDED, ENDING, ENDLESS, ENDLESSLY, ENDS, NEVER-ENDING]
END OF THE EARTH (2) Dt 28:49,64
PUT AN END TO (17) Ex 1:10; Nu 17:5,10; 1Sa 2:31; Ps 54:5; Isa 48:14; Jer 7:34; 16:9; 48:35; Eze 12:23; 23:48; Da 9:27; 11:18; Hos 1:5; 2:11; Mic 5:12; Zep 1:4

Ge 15:14 and in the **e** they will come away with great
23: 9 the cave of Machpelah, down at the **e** of his field.
41:53 At last the seven years of plenty came to an **e**.
Ex 1:10 We must find a way to put an **e** to this. If we don't
9:28 Please beg the LORD to **e** this terrifying thunder
21: 7 she will not be freed at the **e** of six years as the
23:16 of the Final Harvest at the **e** of the harvest season.
25:19 Attach the cherubim to each **e** of the atonement
26:25 So there will be eight frames on that **e** of the
26:28 will run all the way from one **e** of the Tabernacle
27:12 The curtains on the west **e** of the courtyard will be
27:13 The east **e** will also be 75 feet long.
27:14 The courtyard entrance will be on the east **e**,
32:27 and forth from one **e** of the camp to the other,
34:22 of the Final Harvest at the **e** of the harvest season.
36:20 they made frames of acacia wood standing on **e**.
36:33 along each side, running from one **e** to the other.
38:12 The west **e** was 75 feet wide. The walls were made
38:13 The east **e** was also 75 feet wide.
Lev 13:27 If at the **e** of that time the affected area has spread
13:32 If at the **e** of that time the affected area has not
14: 7 At the **e** of the ceremony, the priest will set the
Nu 17: 5 Then I will finally put an **e** to this murmuring
17:10 This should put an **e** to their complaints against me
23:10 die like the righteous; / let my life **e** like theirs."
34: 5 the brook of Egypt and **e** at the Mediterranean Sea.
Dt 4:32 Then search from one **e** of the heavens to the other.
9:11 "At the **e** of the forty days and nights, the LORD
14:28 "At the **e** of every third year bring the tithe of all
15: 1 "At the **e** of every seventh year you must cancel
16:13 must be observed for seven days at the **e** of the
28:49 a distant nation against you from the **e** of the earth,
28:64 all the nations from one **e** of the earth to the other.
31:10 "At the **e** of every seventh year, the Year of
32:20 'I will abandon them; / I will see to their **e**!
Jos 15: 8 and on up to the northern **e** of the valley of
18:16 at the northern **e** of the valley of Rephaim.
18:19 which is the southern **e** of the Jordan River.
Ru 2:23 and gathered grain with them until the **e** of the
1Sa 2:31 I will put an **e** to your family, so it will no longer
3:20 All the people of Israel from one **e** of the land to
13:14 But now your dynasty must **e**, for the LORD has
14:43 "It was only a little bit on the **e** of a stick.
17:26 and putting an **e** to his abuse of Israel?"
2Sa 2:17 and by the **e** of the day Abner and the men of Israel
2:23 so Abner thrust the butt **e** of his spear through
1Ki 6:16 the Most Holy Place—at the far **e** of the Temple.
9:10 Now at the **e** of the twenty years during which
10:20 one standing on each **e** of each of the six steps.
18:10 and kingdom on earth from **e** to **e** to find you.
2Ki 10:21 and filled the temple of Baal from one **e** to the
21:16 filled from one **e** to the other with innocent blood.
1Ch 10: 6 died there together, bringing his dynasty to an **e**.
13: 5 of Israel, from one **e** of the country to the other,
29:29 events of King David's reign, from beginning to **e**,
2Ch 7:10 Then at the **e** of the celebration, Solomon sent the
9:19 one standing on each **e** of each of the six steps.
9:29 events of Solomon's reign, from beginning to **e**,
12:15 events of Rehoboam's reign, from beginning to **e**,
16:11 of the events of Asa's reign, from beginning to **e**,
20:16 **e** of the valley that opens into the wilderness of
20:34 events of Jehoshaphat's reign, from beginning to **e**,
20:35 But near the **e** of his life, King Jehoshaphat of
21:19 In the course of time, at the **e** of two years,
22: 7 whom the LORD had appointed to **e** the dynasty
25:26 events of Amaziah's reign, from beginning to **e**,
26:22 the events of Uzziah's reign, from beginning to **e**,
28:26 and all his dealings, from beginning to **e**,
29:31 "The dedication ceremony has come to an **e**.
35:27 from beginning to **e**, are recorded in *The Book of*
Ezr 9:11 From one **e** to the other, the land is filled with
Ne 4:11 down on them and kill them and **e** their work."
Est 1:18 There will be no **e** to the contempt and anger
Job 7: 2 like a worker who longs for the day to **e**, like a
7: 6 shuttle flying back and forth. They **e** without hope.
8: 7 you started with little, you will **e** with much.
8:19 That is the **e** of its life, and others spring up from
9:27 if I decided to **e** my sadness and be cheerful,
38:13 the earth, to bring an **e** to the night's wickedness?
Ps 7: 9 **E** the wickedness of the ungodly, / but help all
12: 3 May the LORD bring their flattery to an **e**
19: 6 The sun rises at one **e** of the heavens / and follows its course to the other **e**.
40: 5 I would never come to the **e** of them.
46: 9 and causes wars to **e** throughout the earth.
54: 5 Do as you promised and put an **e** to them.
72: 7 May there be abundant prosperity until the **e** of
74: 9 are gone; / no one can tell us when it will **e**.
89:28 him forever; / my covenant with him will never **e**.
90: 2 the world, / you are God, without beginning or **e**.
90: 9 beneath your wrath. / We **e** our lives with a groan.
90:14 so we may sing for joy to the **e** of our lives.
102:27 But you are always the same; / your years never **e**.
107:27 like drunkards / and were at their wits' **e**.
119:112 keep your principles, / even forever, to the very **e**.
132:12 I teach them, / then your royal line will never **e**."
146: 4 and in a moment all their plans come to an **e**.
Pr 13:18 you will **e** in poverty and disgrace;
18:18 Casting lots can **e** arguments and settle disputes
20:13 If you love sleep, you will **e** in poverty. Keep your
20:21 obtained early in life is not a blessing in the **e**.
21:16 The person who strays from common sense will **e**
22: 8 harvest disaster, and their reign of terror will **e**.
22:16 or by showering gifts on the rich will **e** in poverty.
23:32 For in the **e** it bites like a poisonous serpent;
24:22 punishment from the LORD and the king will **e**?
25: 7 for an invitation than to be sent to the **e** of the line,
28: 8 It will **e** up in the hands of someone who is kind to
28:23 In the **e**, people appreciate frankness more than
Ecc 3:11 whole scope of God's work from beginning to **e**.
5:14 In the **e**, there is nothing left to pass on to one's
5:15 People who live only for wealth come to the **e** of
6: 3 and in the **e** does not even get a decent burial,
12:12 There is no **e** of opinions ready to be expressed.

Isa 2: 4 will stop, and military training will come to an **e**.
7: 3 You will find the king at the **e** of the aqueduct that
8: 8 It will submerge Immanuel's land from one **e** to
8: 12 conceived behind closed doors will be the **e** of you.
9: 7 ever expanding, peaceful government will never **e**.
9: 20 In the **e** they will even eat their own children.
10: 25 In a little while my anger against you will **e**,
10: 27 In that day the LORD will **e** the bondage of his
11: 13 at last the jealousy between Israel and Judah will **e**.
15: 8 is a land of weeping from one **e** to the other—
17: 3 be destroyed, and the power of Damascus will **e**.
21: 2 the groaning of all the nations she enslaved will **e**.
21: 16 the Lord, "all the glory of Kedar will come to an **e**.
23: 18 But in the **e** her businesses will give their profits to
25: 11 He will **e** their pride and all their works.
30: 8 then stand until the **e** of time as a witness to
34: 10 This judgment on Edom will never **e**; the smoke of
48: 14 He will use him to put an **e** to the empire of
51: 6 lasts forever. My righteous rule will never **e**!
59: 5 and energy spinning evil plans that **e** up in deadly
60: 18 the desolation and destruction of war will **e**.
60: 20 Your days of mourning will come to an **e**.
66: 17 will come to a terrible **e**," says the LORD.
Jer 2: 32 Yet for years on **e** my people have forgotten me.
5: 31 that way! But what will you do when the **e** comes?
7: 34 I will put an **e** to the happy singing and laughter in
12: 12 The sword of the LORD kills people from one **e**
16: 9 I will put an **e** to the happy singing and laughter in
17: 11 at the **e** of their lives, will become poor old fools.
25: 33 will fill the earth from one **e** to the other.
28: 16 Your life will **e** this very year because you have
29: 14 "I will **e** your captivity and restore your fortunes.
30: 7 my people Israel. Yet in the **e**, they will be saved!
48: 35 "I will put an **e** to Moab," says the LORD,
48: 47 This is the **e** of Jeremiah's prophecy concerning
51: 13 a great center of commerce, but your **e** has come.
51: 64 upon her.' " This is the **e** of Jeremiah's messages.
La 3: 54 above my head, and I cried out, "This is the **e**!"
4: 18 Our **e** was near; our days were numbered. We were
4: 22 O Jerusalem, your punishment will **e**; you will
Eze 3: 16 At the **e** of the seven days, the LORD gave me a
7: 2 The **e** is here! Wherever you look—east, west,
7: 6 The **e** has come! It has finally arrived! Your final
10: 3 The cherubim were standing at the south **e** of the
12: 23 I will put an **e** to this proverb, and you will soon
16: 41 and **e** your payments to your many lovers.
22: 4 has come! You have reached the **e** of your years.
23: 48 I will put an **e** to lewdness and idolatry in the land,
26: 21 I will bring you to a terrible **e**, and you will be no
27: 36 the sight of you, / for you have come to a horrible **e**
28: 19 You have come to a terrible **e**, and you are no
29: 13 At the **e** of the forty years I will bring the
30: 6 allies will fall, and the pride of their power will **e**.
33: 28 her pride. Her arrogant power will come to an **e**.
39: 14 At the **e** of the seven months, special crews will be
39: 25 I will **e** the captivity of my people; I will have
40: 7 which led to the foyer at the inner **e** of the gateway
40: 9 This foyer was at the inner **e** of the gateway
40: 15 passage was 87-1/2 feet from one **e** to the other.
40: 22 and the foyer was at the inner **e** of the gateway
41: 3 Then he went into the inner room at the **e** of the
42: 12 and another on the east at the **e** of the interior
46: 19 He showed me a place at the extreme west **e** of
Da 1: 13 "At the **e** of the ten days, see how we look
1: 15 At the **e** of the ten days, Daniel and his three
2: 39 "But after your kingdom comes to an **e**,
5: 26 the days of your reign and has brought it to an **e**.
6: 26 will never be destroyed, / and his rule will never **e**.
7: 14 obey him. His rule is eternal—it will never **e**.
7: 18 But in the **e**, the holy people of the Most High will
7: 28 That was the **e** of the vision. I, Daniel, was terrified
8: 17 seen in your vision relate to the time of the **e**."
8: 19 What you have seen pertains to the very **e** of time.
8: 23 "At the **e** of their rule, when their sin is at its
9: 24 to bring an **e** to sin, to atone for guilt, to bring in
9: 26 The **e** will come with a flood, and war and its
9: 26 miseries are decreed from that time to the very **e**.
9: 27 he will put an **e** to the sacrifices and offerings.
9: 27 until the **e** that has been decreed is poured out on
11: 18 But a commander from another land will put an **e**
11: 27 for an **e** will still come at the appointed time.
11: 35 and cleansed and made pure until the time of the **e**,
11: 40 "Then at the time of the **e**, the king of the south
12: 4 a secret; seal up the book until the time of the **e**.
12: 7 of the holy people has finally come to an **e**,
12: 8 So I asked, "How will all this finally **e**, my lord?"
12: 9 Daniel, for what I have said is for the time of the **e**.
12: 12 who wait and remain until the **e** of the 1,335 days!
12: 13 "As for you, go your way until the **e**. You will rest, and then at the **e** of the days,
Hos 1: 5 I will put an **e** to Israel's independence by breaking
2: 11 I will put an **e** to her annual festivals, her new
Am 6: 7 away as captives. Suddenly, all your revelry will **e**.
7: 9 the dynasty of King Jeroboam to a sudden **e**."
8: 5 and the religious festivals to **e** so you can get back
Mic 3: 6 for you prophets, and your day will come to an **e**.
4: 3 will stop, and military training will come to an **e**.
5: 12 I will put an **e** to all witchcraft; there will be no
6: 10 Will there be no **e** of your getting rich by cheating?
6: 14 save your money, it will come to nothing in the **e**.
Na 2: 9 There seems no **e** to Nineveh's many treasures—
Zep 1: 4 I will put an **e** to all the idolatrous priests, so that
1: 18 He will make a terrifying **e** of all the people on
Zec 10: 11 will be crushed, and the rule of Egypt will **e**.
11: 11 That was the **e** of my covenant with them.
14: 16 In the **e**, the enemies of Jerusalem who survive the
Mt 10: 22 But those who endure to the **e** will be saved.
13: 39 The harvest is the **e** of the world,
13: 40 and burned, so it will be at the **e** of the world.
13: 49 That is the way it will be at the **e** of the world.
20: 4 pay them whatever was right at the **e** of the day.
24: 3 time to signal your return and the **e** of the world?"
24: 6 must come, but the **e** won't follow immediately.
24: 13 But those who endure to the **e** will be saved.
24: 14 will hear it; and then, finally, the **e** will come.
24: 28 so these signs indicate that the **e** is near.
24: 29 "Immediately after those horrible days **e**, / the sun
28: 20 I am with you always, even to the **e** of the age."
Mk 13: 7 must come, but the **e** won't follow immediately.
13: 13 But those who endure to the **e** will be saved.
13: 24 "At that time, after those horrible days **e**, / the sun
Lk 1: 33 over Israel forever; his Kingdom will never **e**!"
17: 37 so these signs indicate that the **e** is near."
18: 7 Even he rendered a just decision in the **e**, so don't
21: 9 must come, but the **e** won't follow immediately."
21: 24 until the age of the Gentiles comes to an **e**.
24: 28 were nearing Emmaus and the **e** of their journey.
Jn 4: 43 At the **e** of the two days' stay, Jesus went on into
9: 4 before the night falls and all work comes to an **e**.
11: 4 it he said, "Lazarus's sickness will not **e** in death.
Ac 5: 24 were perplexed, wondering where it would all **e**.
7: 7 'and in the **e** they will come out and worship me in
21: 5 When we returned to the ship at the **e** of the week,
21: 26 announced the date when their vows would **e**
Ro 6: 21 you used to do, things that **e** in eternal doom.
1Co 1: 8 He will keep you strong right up to the **e**, and he
4: 9 like prisoners of war at the **e** of a victor's parade,
7: 27 If you have a wife, do not **e** the marriage. If you do
13: 10 But when the **e** comes, these special gifts will all
15: 24 After that the **e** will come, when he will turn the
2Co 11: 15 In the **e** they will get every bit of punishment their
Php 3: 14 I strain to reach the **e** of the race and receive the
2Th 3: 17 I do this at the **e** of all my letters to prove that they
Heb 3: 14 For if we are faithful to the **e**, trusting God just as
7: 3 any of his ancestors—no beginning or **e** to his life.
7: 24 a priest forever; his priesthood will never **e**.
9: 26 He came once for all time, at the **e** of the age,
11: 40 for they can't receive the prize at the **e** of the race
1Pe 1: 23 because the life they gave you will **e** in death.
4: 7 The **e** of the world is coming soon. Therefore,
2Pe 2: 1 bought them. Theirs will be a swift and terrible **e**.
1Jn 2: 18 From this we know that the **e** of the world has
Rev 1: 8 the beginning and the **e**," says the Lord God.
2: 26 all who are victorious, who obey me to the very **e**,
14: 12 persecution patiently and remain firm to the **e**,
20: 7 When the thousand years **e**, Satan will be let out of
21: 6 and the Omega—the Beginning and the **E**.
21: 25 Its gates never close at the **e** of day because there is
22: 13 the First and the Last, the Beginning and the **E**."

ENDANGER (2) [DANGER]

Ru 4: 6 "because this might **e** my own estate.
Pr 22: 25 or you will learn to be like them and **e** your soul.

ENDEAVOUR [KJV] See WORK

ENDED (36) [END]

Ge 11: 8 over the earth; and that **e** the building of the city.
17: 22 That **e** the conversation, and God left Abraham.
Nu 26: 1 After the plague had **e**, the LORD said to Moses
Jos 15: 11 It passed Jabneel and **e** at the Mediterranean Sea.
16: 7 touched Jericho, and **e** at the Jordan River.
18: 19 and **e** at the north bay of the Dead Sea,
19: 14 passed Hannathon and **e** at the valley of Iphtah-el.
2Sa 21: 14 After that, God **e** the famine in the land of Israel.
2Ki 8: 3 After the famine **e** she returned to the land of
2Ch 23: 8 priest did not let anyone go home after their shift **e**.
31: 1 Now when the festival **e**, the Israelites who
Ne 13: 19 not to be opened until the Sabbath **e**.
Job 1: 5 When these celebrations **e**—and sometimes they
31: 40 and weeds instead of barley." Job's words are **e**.
Ps 77: 5 I think of the good old days, long since **e**,
78: 33 So he **e** their lives in failure / and gave them years
85: 3 your fury. / You have **e** your blazing anger.
89: 44 You have **e** his splendor / and overturned his
Ecc 6: 4 would have been meaningless and **e** in darkness.
Isa 14: 4 man has been destroyed. Yes, your insolence is **e**.
16: 10 has ceased forever. I have **e** all their harvest joys.
16: 14 without fail, the glory of Moab will be **e**,
47: 1 For your days of glory, pomp, and honor have **e**.
Jer 48: 25 "The strength of Moab has **e**. Her horns have been
La 5: 15 The joy of our hearts has **e**; our dancing has turned
Eze 11: 24 And so **e** the vision of my visit to Jerusalem.
Zec 8: 19 midsummer, autumn, and winter are now **e**.
Mk 16: 1 when the Sabbath **e**, Mary Magdalene and Salome
Lk 20: 40 And that **e** their questions; no one dared to ask any
Jn 18: 28 Jesus' trial before Caiaphas **e** in the early hours of
Ac 17: 33 That **e** Paul's discussion with them,
20: 6 As soon as the Passover season **e**, we boarded a
21: 27 The seven days were almost **e** when some Jews
Eph 2: 15 By his death he **e** the whole system of Jewish law
Jas 5: 11 we see how the Lord's plan finally **e** in good,
Rev 20: 5 come back to life until the thousand years had **e**.)

ENDING (7) [END]

Ex 1: 6 and each of his brothers died, **e** that generation.
Jos 18: 14 **e** at the village of Kiriath-baal (that is,
19: 22 and Beth-shemesh, **e** at the Jordan River—
19: 33 and as far as Lakkum, **e** at the Jordan River.
1Sa 12: 23 I will certainly not sin against the LORD by **e** my
2Sa 12: 26 and the Israelite army were successfully **e** their
1Ti 6: 4 This stirs up arguments **e** in jealousy, fighting,

ENDLESS (5) [END]

Ps 89: 29 his throne will be as **e** as the days of heaven.
Eze 16: 25 offering your body to every passerby in an **e**
Eph 3: 8 about the **e** treasures available to them in Christ.
3: 21 in Christ Jesus forever and ever through **e** ages.
1Ti 1: 4 Don't let people waste time in **e** speculation over

ENDLESSLY (3) [END]

Job 16: 3 What have I said that makes you speak so **e**?
La 3: 49 My tears flow down **e**. They will not stop
Eze 11: 6 You have murdered **e** and filled your streets with

ENDOR (3)

Jos 17: 11 (that is, Naphoth-dor), **E**, Taanach, and Megiddo,
1Sa 28: 7 His advisers replied, "There is a medium at **E**."
Ps 83: 10 They were destroyed at **E**, / and their decaying

ENDORSED (1)

Ac 2: 22 God publicly **e** Jesus of Nazareth by doing

ENDOWED (1)

Ps 21: 6 You have **e** him with eternal blessings. / You have

ENDS (45) [END]

ENDS OF THE EARTH (26) Dt 13:7; 30:4; 33:17; Ne 1:9; Job 38:13; Ps 2:8; 48:10; 61:2; 65:8; 72:8; Pr 17:24; Isa 5:26; 11:12; 24:16; 41:9; 42:10; 48:20; 49:6; 52:10; Jer 25:31; Eze 27:33; Da 4:22; Zec 9:10; Mt 24:31; Mk 13:27; Ac 1:8

Ex 25: 18 and place them at the two **e** of the atonement
28: 25 and the **e** of the cords will be tied to the gold
37: 7 and placed them at the two **e** of the atonement
39: 18 and the **e** of the cords were tied to the gold settings
Dt 13: 7 live nearby or who come from the **e** of the earth.
30: 4 Though you are at the **e** of the earth, the LORD
33: 17 distant nations, / driving them to the **e** of the earth.
1Ki 8: 8 so long that their **e** could be seen from the front
12: 29 calf idols at the southern and northern **e** of Israel—
2Ch 5: 9 so long that their **e** could be seen from the front
Ne 1: 9 even if you are exiled to the **e** of the earth,
Job 38: 13 Have you ever told the daylight to spread to the **e**
Ps 2: 8 the **e** of the earth as your possession.
39: 6 and all our busy rushing **e** in nothing.
48: 10 O God, / you will be praised to the **e** of the earth.
61: 2 From the **e** of the earth, / I will cry to you for help,
65: 8 Those who live at the **e** of the earth / stand in awe
72: 8 and from the Euphrates River to the **e** of the earth.
72: 20 (This **e** the prayers of David son of Jesse.)
Pr 1: 19 are greedy for gain. It **e** up robbing them of life.
14: 12 each person that seems right, but it **e** in death.
14: 13 heavy heart; when the laughter **e**, the grief remains.
16: 25 each person that seems right, but it **e** in death.
17: 24 but a fool's eyes wander to the **e** of the earth.
29: 23 Pride **e** in humiliation, while humility brings
Isa 5: 26 He will whistle to those at the **e** of the earth,
11: 12 scattered people of Judah from the **e** of the earth.
24: 16 as they sing to the LORD from the **e** of the earth.
41: 9 I have called you back from the **e** of the earth
42: 10 Sing his praises from the **e** of the earth! / Sing,
48: 20 Shout to the **e** of the earth that the LORD has
49: 6 and you will bring my salvation to the **e** of the
52: 10 The **e** of the earth will see the salvation of our
Jer 25: 31 His cry of judgment will reach the **e** of the earth,
La 3: 22 The unfailing love of the LORD never **e**! By his
Eze 27: 33 Kings at the **e** of the earth / were enriched by your
Da 4: 22 up to heaven, and your rule to the **e** of the earth.
Zec 9: 10 and from the Euphrates River to the **e** of the earth.
Mt 24: 31 his chosen ones from the farthest **e** of the earth
Mk 13: 27 from the farthest **e** of the earth and heaven.
Jn 4: 35 begin until the summer **e** four months from now?
Ac 1: 8 in Samaria, and to the **e** of the earth."
1Co 14: 36 of God's word begins and **e** with you Corinthians?
2Co 3: 6 The old way **e** in death; in the new way, the Holy
Eph 6: 2 This is the first of the Ten Commandments that **e**

ENDURANCE (15) [ENDURE]

Ro 5: 4 And **e** develops strength of character in us,
Col 1: 11 that you will have all the patience and **e** you need.
2Th 1: 4 We proudly tell God's other churches about your **e**
3: 5 the love of God and the **e** that comes from Christ.
2Ti 3: 10 You know my love and my patient **e**.
Heb 10: 36 Patient **e** is what you need now, so you will
12: 1 And let us run with **e** the race that God has set
Jas 1: 3 your faith is tested, your **e** has a chance to grow.
1: 4 So let it grow, for when your **e** is fully developed,
2Pe 1: 6 Self-control leads to patient **e**, and patient **e** leads to godliness.
Rev 1: 9 in suffering and in the Kingdom and in patient **e**.
2: 2 I have seen your hard work and your patient **e**.
2: 19 your faith, your service, and your patient **e**.
13: 10 for here is your opportunity to have **e** and faith.

ENDURE (34) [ENDURANCE, ENDURED, ENDURES, ENDURING]

Ex 18: 23 to do so, then you will be able to **e** the pressures,
Est 8: 6 For how can I **e** to see my people and my family
Job 6: 11 But I do not have the strength to **e**. I do not have a
8: 15 won't last. They try to hold it fast, but it will not **e**.
15: 29 Their wealth will not **e**, and their possessions will
20: 3 I have had to **e** your insults, but now my spirit
20: 21 therefore, his prosperity will not **e**.
Ps 69: 19 You know the insults I **e**— / the humiliation
72: 17 May the king's name **e** forever; / may it continue

101: 5 their neighbors. / I will not **e** conceit and pride.
102:12 Your fame will **e** to every generation.
125: 1 they will not be defeated but will **e** forever.
Pr 18:14 The human spirit can **e** a sick body, but who can
30:21 that make the earth tremble—no, four it cannot **e**:
Da 6:26 For he is the living God, / and he will **e** forever.
Joel 2:11 is an awesome, terrible thing. Who can **e** it?
3:20 and Jerusalem will **e** through all future generations.
Mal 3: 2 "But who will be able to **e** it when he comes?
Mt 10:22 to me. But those who **e** to the end will be saved.
24:13 But those who **e** to the end will be saved.
Mk 13:13 to me. But those who **e** to the end will be saved.
Ro 5: 3 that they are good for us—they help us learn to **e**.
1Co 13:13 There are three things that will **e**—faith, hope,
2Co 1: 6 Then you can patiently **e** the same things we
6: 4 We patiently **e** troubles and hardships
2Ti 2: 3 **E** suffering along with me, as a good soldier of
2:10 I am willing to **e** anything if it will bring salvation
2:12 If we **e** hardship, / we will reign with him. / If we
Heb 12: 7 As you **e** this divine discipline, remember that God
Jas 1:12 God blesses the people who patiently **e** testing.
5:11 We give great honor to those who **e** under
1Pe 1: 6 even though it is necessary for you to **e** many trials
2:19 your conscience, you patiently **e** unfair treatment.
Rev 14:12 Let this encourage God's holy people to **e**

ENDURED (6) [ENDURE]

Ac 20:19 I have **e** the trials that came to me from the plots of
1Co 4:11 We have **e** many beatings, and we have no homes
2Co 6: 5 worked to exhaustion, **e** sleepless nights,
2Ti 3:11 how much persecution and suffering I have **e**.
Heb 12: 3 Think about all he **e** when sinful people did such
Jas 5:11 Job is an example of a man who **e** patiently.

ENDURES (47) [ENDURE]

FAITHFUL LOVE ENDURES FOREVER (40) 1Ch 16:34,41; 2Ch 5:13; 7:3,6; 20:21; Ps 106:1; 107:1; 118:1,2,3, 4,29; 136:1,2,3,4,5,6,7,8,9,10,11,12,13,14,15,16,17,18,19,20, 21,22,23,24,25,26; Jer 33:11

1Ch 16:34 for he is good! / His faithful love **e** forever.
16:41 to the LORD, "for his faithful love **e** forever."
2Ch 5:13 "He is so good! / His faithful love **e** forever!"
7: 3 "He is so good! / His faithful love **e** forever!"
7: 6 who were singing, "His faithful love **e** forever!"
20:21 to the LORD; / his faithful love **e** forever!"
Ezr 3:11 so good! / His faithful love for Israel **e** forever!"
Ps 45: 6 Your throne, O God, **e** forever and ever.
106: 1 for he is good! / His faithful love **e** forever.
107: 1 for he is good! / His faithful love **e** forever.
117: 2 the faithfulness of the LORD **e** forever.
118: 1 for he is good! / His faithful love **e** forever.
118: 2 of Israel repeat: / "His faithful love **e** forever."
118: 3 the priests, repeat: / "His faithful love **e** forever."
118: 4 the LORD repeat: / "His faithful love **e** forever."
118:29 for he is good! / His faithful love **e** forever.
135:13 Your name, O LORD, **e** forever; / your fame,
136: 1 for he is good! / His faithful love **e** forever.
136: 2 to the God of gods. / His faithful love **e** forever.
136: 3 to the Lord of lords. / His faithful love **e** forever.
136: 4 does mighty miracles. / His faithful love **e** forever.
136: 5 so skillfully. / His faithful love **e** forever.
136: 6 the earth on the water. / His faithful love **e** forever.
136: 7 the heavenly lights— / His faithful love **e** forever.
136: 8 the sun to rule the day, / His faithful love **e** forever.
136: 9 stars to rule the night. / His faithful love **e** forever.
136:10 the firstborn of Egypt. / His faithful love **e** forever.
136:11 Israel out of Egypt. / His faithful love **e** forever.
136:12 and powerful arm. / His faithful love **e** forever.
136:13 parted the Red Sea. / His faithful love **e** forever.
136:14 Israel safely through, / His faithful love **e** forever.
136:15 his army into the sea. / His faithful love **e** forever.
136:16 the wilderness. / His faithful love **e** forever.
136:17 down mighty kings. / His faithful love **e** forever.
136:18 powerful kings— / His faithful love **e** forever.
136:19 king of the Amorites, / His faithful love **e** forever.
136:20 Og king of Bashan. / His faithful love **e** forever.
136:21 as an inheritance— / His faithful love **e** forever.
136:22 to his servant Israel. / His faithful love **e** forever.
136:23 our utter weakness. / His faithful love **e** forever.
136:24 us from our enemies. / His faithful love **e** forever.
136:25 to every living thing. / His faithful love **e** forever.
136:26 to the God of heaven. / His faithful love **e** forever.
138: 8 for your faithful love, O LORD, **e** forever.
Jer 33:11 the LORD is good. / His faithful love **e** forever!'
1Co 13: 7 always hopeful, and **e** through every circumstance.
Heb 1: 8 "Your throne, O God, **e** forever and ever.

ENDURING (5) [ENDURE]

1Ki 11:38 I will establish an **e** dynasty for you as I did for
Ps 78:69 as solid and **e** as the earth itself.
89: 2 Your faithfulness is as **e** as the heavens.
119:90 to every generation, / as **e** as the earth you created.
SS 8: 6 as death, and its jealousy is as **e** as the grave.

ENEMIES (452) [ENEMY]

HIS ENEMIES (41) Ge 49:27; Nu 32:21; Dt 32:43; 1Sa 14:47; 2Sa 22:1,15; 1Ki 5:3; 2Ki 14:19; 1Ch 22:9; 2Ch 14:6; 25:27; 28:16; Ps 18:T,14; 68:21; 72:9; 78:66; 89:22,42; 132:18; Isa 2:19; 30:28,30; 42:13; 59:18; 66:6,14; Jer 44:30; 46:10; 50:25; Da 11:12; Na 1:2,8,10; Zec 9:14; Lk 13:17; Ro 5:10; 1Co 15:25; Col 1:21; Heb 10:13,27

MY ENEMIES (99) Nu 23:11; 24:10; Dt 32:41; 1Sa 2:1; 14:24; 18:25; 2Sa 4:9; 5:20; 22:4,38,40,49,49; 1Ch 12:17; 14:11; Job 6:23; 31:29; Ps 3:7; 5:8,9; 6:7,10; 7:5,6; 9:3,6; 13:4; 18:3,37,39,48,48; 22:12,16,17; 23:5; 25:2,15; 27:2,6,11; 30:1; 31:2,4,11,13; 35:3,24; 38:12,16,19; 41:5; 42:3,9; 43:2; 54:7; 55:3,15,19; 56:9; 57:6; 59:1,10,14; 61:3; 68:22; 69:18,19; 71:2,10; 92:11; 102:8; 119:98,121,139; 129:1,2; 138:7; 139:22; 140:9; 142:3; 143:9,12; 144:7,11; Isa 1:24; 50:8,9; 63:3; Jer 11:18; La 1:14,21; 3:52,60,62; Eze 34:10; Mic 7:8,9,10

OUR ENEMIES (36) Ex 1:10; 15:12; Dt 32:31; Jos 24:17; Jdg 10:15; 1Sa 4:3; 12:10; 14:30; 2Sa 19:9; 2Ch 14:7; Ne 4:11,15; 6:1,16; Job 22:20; Ps 44:5,7,10; 47:3; 60:11; 74:10; 76:5; 80:6,16; 108:12; 136:24; Isa 16:3,4; 63:18; La 3:46; 4:19; 5:11; Am 5:18; Mic 1:10; Lk 1:71,74

THEIR ENEMIES (80) Ge 22:17; 24:60; Ex 32:25; Lev 26:41,44; Dt 1:42; 33:7,11; Jos 7:12; 10:13; 11:8; 21:44,44; 23:1; Jdg 2:14,16,18; 8:34; 1Sa 11:10; 1Ki 8:33,44,46; 2Ki 21:14; 2Ch 6:24,34,36; 15:15; 20:27; Ne 9:11,27,27,28; Est 8:11,13; 9:5,5,16,18,22; Ps 10:5; 17:7; 41:2; 44:2; 78:42,53; 81:14; 105:24; 106:10,11,42; Pr 16:7; Isa 61:2; Jer 6:12; 9:16; 11:16; 12:7; 15:14; 18:17; 49:37; 50:7; La 1:17; 3:30; Eze 23:47; 32:23; 39:23,27; Hos 1:7; 7:16; 8:3; 11:6; Am 6:8; Ob 1:14; Mic 5:3,9; Hab 1:14; Zec 9:15,15; 10:5; Rev 11:5,12

YOUR ENEMIES (125) Ge 14:20; 49:8; Ex 23:22; Lev 26:6,7,8,16,17,25,32,34,36,37,38; Nu 10:9,9,35; 14:42; Dt 7:15; 12:10; 20:1,4,14; 21:10; 23:9,14; 25:19; 28:7,25,25,31,48,68; 30:7; 33:29; Jos 7:13; 10:25; 22:8; 23:3; Jdg 5:31; 6:9; 11:36; 1Sa 20:15,16; 25:26,29; 2Sa 7:9,11; 18:32; 24:13; 1Ki 3:11; 2Ki 17:39; 1Ch 17:8,10; 21:12; 2Ch 1:11; Ne 6:10; Ps 8:2; 21:8; 53:5; 66:3; 68:1; 74:4,23; 76:8; 83:2; 89:10,51; 92:9; 107:2; 110:1,2; 139:20,22; 144:6; Pr 24:17; 25:21; Isa 1:20; 7:11; 26:11,20; 29:8; 30:16,25; 35:4; 41:15; 49:19,26; 51:13; 54:14,15; 62:8; 64:2; Jer 15:11; 17:3; 19:9; 20:5; 21:4; 30:16; 34:20; La 2:16; Eze 16:27; 23:28; 36:2,3; Da 4:19; Ob 1:5; Mic 2:4; 4:10; 7:6; Na 1:15; 2:12; Mt 5:43; 10:36; 22:44; Mk 12:36; Lk 6:27,35; 19:43,44; 20:43; Ac 2:34; Ro 12:20; Php 1:28; Heb 1:13

Ge 3:15 From now on, you and the woman will be **e**,
3:15 and your offspring and her offspring will be **e**.
14:20 Most High, / who has helped you conquer your **e**."
22:17 the sand on the seashore. They will conquer their **e**,
24:60 May your descendants overcome / all their **e**."
49: 8 brothers will praise you. / You will defeat your **e**.
49:27 that prowls. / He devours his **e** in the morning,
Ex 1:10 breaks out, they will join our **e** and fight against us.
15:12 up your hand, / and the earth swallowed our **e**.
23:22 my instructions, then I will be an enemy to your **e**,
32:25 control—and much to the amusement of their **e**—
Lev 26: 6 from your land and protect you from your **e**.
26: 7 you will chase down all your **e** and slaughter them
26: 8 All your **e** will fall beneath the blows of your
26:16 your crops in vain because your **e** will eat them.
26:17 against you, and you will be defeated by all your **e**.
26:25 you there, and you will be conquered by your **e**.
26:32 Your **e** who come to occupy it will be utterly
26:34 during your years of exile in the land of your **e**.
26:36 I will demoralize you in the land of your **e** far
26:37 You will have no power to stand before your **e**.
26:38 and be devoured in the land of your **e**.
26:41 and have brought them to the land of their **e**,
26:44 them while they are in exile in the land of their **e**.
Nu 10: 9 in your own land and go to war against your **e**,
10: 9 will remember you and rescue you from your **e**.
10:35 "Arise, O LORD, and let your **e** be scattered!
14:42 You will only be crushed by your **e**
23:11 I brought you to curse my **e**. Instead, you have
24:10 and shouted, "I called you to curse my **e**!
32:21 the Jordan until the LORD has driven out his **e**,
35:23 though they were not **e**, and the person dies.
Dt 1:42 If they do, they will be crushed by their **e**.'
6:19 You will drive out all the **e** living in your land,
7:15 in Egypt, but he will bring them all on your **e**!
12:10 he gives you rest and security from all your **e**,
20: 1 "When you go out to fight your **e** and you face
20: 4 He will fight for you against your **e**, and he will
20:14 You may enjoy the spoils of your **e** that the
20:19 the trees. They are not **e** that need to be attacked!
21:10 "Suppose you go to war against your **e**
23: 9 "When you go to war against your **e**, stay away
23:14 in your camp to protect you and to defeat your **e**.
25:19 **e** in the land he is giving you as a special
28: 7 "The LORD will conquer your **e** when they
28:25 LORD will cause you to be defeated by your **e**.
28:25 You will attack your **e** from one direction, but you
28:31 Your sheep will be given to your **e**, and no one will
28:48 you will serve your **e** whom the LORD will send
28:68 There you will offer to sell yourselves to your **e** as
30: 7 your God will inflict all these curses on your **e**
32:31 But the rock of our **e** is not like our Rock, / as even
32:41 carry out justice, / I will bring vengeance on my **e**
32:43 He will take vengeance on his **e** / and cleanse his
33: 7 to defend their cause; / help them against their **e**!"
33:11 Crush the loins of their **e**; / strike down their foes
33:29 Your **e** will bow low before you,
Jos 7: 8 am I to say, now that Israel has fled from its **e**?
7:12 That is why the Israelites are running from their **e**
7:13 You will never defeat your **e** until you remove
10:13 stood still until the Israelites had defeated their **e**.
10:25 for the LORD is going to do this to all of your **e**."
11: 8 And the LORD gave them victory over their **e**.
21:44 None of their **e** could stand against them,
21:44 for the LORD helped them conquer all their **e**.
22: 8 home the great wealth you have taken from your **e**.
23: 1 had given the people of Israel rest from all their **e**.
23: 3 your God has fought for you against your **e**.
24:17 we traveled through the wilderness among our **e**,
Jdg 2:14 He sold them to their **e** all around, and they were
2:16 up judges to rescue the Israelites from their **e**.
2:18 and rescued the people from their **e** throughout the
5:31 "LORD, may all your **e** die as Sisera did!
6: 9 I drove out your **e** and gave you their land.
8:24 of the treasures you collected from your fallen **e**."
8:24 (The **e**, being Ishmaelites, all wore gold earrings.)
8:34 who had rescued them from all their **e** surrounding
10:15 us as you see fit, only rescue us today from our **e**."
11:36 LORD has given you a great victory over your **e**,
1Sa 2: 1 Now I have an answer for my **e**, / as I delight in
4: 3 it into battle with us, it will save us from our **e**."
11:10 The men of Jabesh then told their **e**,
12:10 and you alone if you will rescue us from our **e**.'
14:24 before I have full revenge on my **e**."
14:30 to eat freely from the food they found among our **e**,
14:47 he fought against his **e** in every direction—
18:25 Vengeance on my **e** is all I really want." But what
20:15 even when the LORD destroys all your **e**."
20:16 saying, "May the LORD destroy all your **e**!"
25:26 own hands, let all your **e** be as cursed as Nabal is.
25:29 But the lives of your **e** will disappear like stones
29: 8 "Why can't I fight the **e** of my lord, the king?"
30:26 for you, taken from the LORD's **e**," he said.
2Sa 3:18 from the Philistines and from all their other **e**.' "
4: 9 the one who saves me from my **e**, I will tell you the
5:20 "He burst through my **e** like a raging flood!"
7: 9 you have gone, and I have destroyed all your **e**.
7:11 And I will keep you safe from all your **e**.
8:10 Hadadezer and Toi had long been **e**, and there had
12:14 But you have given the **e** of the LORD great
18:32 "May all of your **e**, both now and in the future,
19: 9 "The king saved us from our **e**, the Philistines,
22: 1 after the LORD had rescued him from all his **e**
22: 4 is worthy of praise, / for he saves me from my **e**.
22:15 He shot his arrows and scattered his **e**;
22:18 He delivered me from my powerful **e**, / from those
22:38 "I chased my **e** and destroyed them; / I did not
22:40 the battle; / you have subdued my **e** under my feet.
22:49 and rescues me from my **e**. / You hold me safe
beyond the reach of my **e**;
24:13 three months of fleeing from your **e**, or three days
1Ki 3:11 or riches for yourself or the death of your **e**—
5: 3 until the LORD gave him victory over all his **e**.
5: 4 peace on every side, and I have no **e** and all is well.
8:33 "If your people Israel are defeated by their **e**
8:37 or if your people's **e** are in the land besieging their
8:44 people go out at your command to fight their **e**,
8:46 angry with them and let their **e** conquer them
2Ki 14:19 But his **e** sent assassins after him, and they killed
17:39 is the one who will rescue you from all your **e**."
21:14 and I will hand them over as plunder for their **e**.
1Ch 12:17 But if you have come to betray me to my **e** when I
14:11 "He used me to burst through my **e** like a raging
17: 8 you have gone, and I have destroyed all your **e**.
17:10 to rule my people. And I will subdue all your **e**.
18:10 Hadadezer and Toi had long been **e**, and there had
21:12 of famine, three months of destruction by your **e**,
22: 9 I will give him peace with his **e** in all the
2Ch 1:11 and honor or the death of your **e** or even a long
6:24 "If your people Israel are defeated by their **e**
6:28 or if your people's **e** are in the land besieging their
6:34 people go out at your command to fight their **e**,
6:36 angry with them and let their **e** conquer them
14: 6 for the LORD was giving him rest from his **e**.
14: 7 our God, and he has given us rest from our **e**."
15:15 And the LORD gave them rest from their **e** on
20:27 the LORD had given them victory over their **e**.
20:29 LORD himself had fought against the **e** of Israel,
25:27 But his **e** sent assassins after him, and they killed
28:16 asked the king of Assyria for help against his **e**.
Ezr 4: 1 The **e** of Judah and Benjamin heard that the exiles
4: 6 the **e** of Judah wrote him a letter of accusation
4: 7 the **e** of Judah, led by Bishlam, Mithredath,
8:22 accompany us and protect us from **e** along the way.
8:31 and saved us from **e** and bandits along the way.
Ne 4:11 Meanwhile, our **e** were saying, "Before they know
4:15 When our **e** heard that we knew of their plans
6: 1 and the rest of our **e** found out that I had finished
6:10 doors shut. Your **e** are coming to kill you tonight."
6:16 When our **e** and the surrounding nations heard
9:11 then you hurled their **e** into the depths of the sea.
9:27 So you handed them over to their **e**. But in their
9:27 them deliverers who rescued them from their **e**.
9:28 and once more you let their **e** conquer them.
Est 8:11 and wives, and to take the property of their **e**.
8:13 be ready on that day to take revenge on their **e**.
9: 1 the **e** of the Jews had hoped to destroy them,
9: 5 and struck down their **e** with the sword.
9: 5 They killed and annihilated their **e** and did as they
9:16 They gained relief from all their **e**,
9:18 But the Jews at Susa continued killing their **e** on
9:22 a time when the Jews gained relief from their **e**,
Job 6:23 Have I ever asked you to rescue me from my **e**?
22:20 They will say, 'Surely our **e** have been destroyed.
31:29 "Have I ever rejoiced when my **e** came to ruin
Ps 3: 1 O LORD, I have so many **e**; / so many are against
3: 6 I am not afraid of ten thousand **e** / who surround
3: 7 Rescue me, my God! / Slap all my **e** in the face!
5: 8 right path, O LORD, / or my **e** will conquer me.
5: 9 My **e** cannot speak one truthful word.
6: 7 my eyes are worn out because of all my **e**.
6:10 May all my **e** be disgraced and terrified. / May they
7: 5 then let my **e** capture me. / Let them trample me
7: 6 in anger! / Stand up against the fury of my **e**!
8: 2 to give you praise. / They silence your **e**
9: 3 My **e** turn away in retreat; / they are overthrown
9: 6 My **e** have met their doom; / their cities are

10: 5 awaiting them. / They pour scorn on all their **e**.
13: 4 Don't let my **e** gloat, saying, "We have defeated
17: 7 your strength / those who seek refuge from their **e**.
17: 9 attack me, / from murderous **e** who surround me.
18: T on the day the LORD rescued him from all his **e**
18: 3 is worthy of praise, / for he saves me from my **e**.
18:14 He shot his arrows and scattered his **e**;
18:17 He delivered me from my powerful **e**, / from those
18:37 I chased my **e** and caught them; / I did not stop
18:39 the battle; / you have subdued my **e** under my feet.
18:48 and rescues me from my **e**. / You hold me safe beyond the reach of my **e**;
21: 8 You will capture all your **e**. / Your strong right
22:12 My **e** surround me like a herd of bulls;
22:16 My **e** surround me like a pack of dogs; / an evil
22:17 bone in my body. / My **e** stare at me and gloat.
23: 5 prepare a feast for me / in the presence of my **e**.
25: 2 me be disgraced, / or let my **e** rejoice in my defeat.
25:15 for he alone can rescue me from the traps of my **e**.
25:19 See how many **e** I have, / and how viciously they
27: 2 to destroy me, / when my **e** and foes attack me,
27: 6 my head high, / above my **e** who surround me.
27:11 of honesty, / for my **e** are waiting for me to fall.
30: 1 You refused to let my **e** triumph over me.
31: 2 of safety, / a fortress where my **e** cannot reach me.
31: 4 Pull me from the trap my **e** set for me, / for I find
31:11 I am scorned by all my **e** / and despised by my
31:13 My **e** conspire against me, / plotting to take my
35: 3 your spear and javelin / and block the way of my **e**.
35:19 Don't let my treacherous **e** / rejoice over my
35:24 Don't let my **e** laugh about me in my troubles.
37:20 The LORD's **e** are like flowers in a field—
38:12 Meanwhile, my **e** lay traps for me; / they make
38:16 I prayed, "Don't let my **e** gloat over me
38:19 My **e** are many; / they hate me though I have done
41: 2 them prosperity / and rescues them from their **e**.
41: 5 But my **e** say nothing but evil about me.
42: 3 for food, / while my **e** continually taunt me, saying,
42: 9 must I wander in darkness, / oppressed by my **e**?"
43: 2 I wander around in darkness, / oppressed by my **e**?
44: 2 all the land to our ancestors; / you crushed their **e**,
44: 5 Only by your power can we push back our **e**;
44: 7 It is you who gives us victory over our **e**; / it is you
44:10 You make us retreat from our **e** / and allow them to
44:16 of our mockers. / All we see are our vengeful **e**.
47: 3 nations before us, / putting our **e** beneath our feet.
49: 5 of trouble come, / when **e** are surrounding me.
53: 5 God will scatter the bones of your **e**. / You will put
54: 7 my troubles / and help me to triumph over my **e**.
55: 3 My **e** shout at me, / making loud and wicked
55:15 Let death seize my **e** by surprise; / let the grave
55:19 *Interlude* / For my **e** refuse to change their ways;
56: 9 very day I call to you for help, / my **e** will retreat.
57: 6 My **e** have set a trap for me. / I am weary from
59: 1 Rescue me from my **e**, O God. / Protect me from
59: 3 an ambush for me. / Fierce **e** are out there waiting,
59:10 He will let me look down in triumph on all my **e**.
59:14 My **e** come out at night, / snarling like vicious dogs
60:11 Oh, please help us against our **e**, / for all human
61: 3 a fortress where my **e** cannot reach me.
62: 3 So many **e** against one man— / all of them trying
66: 3 Your **e** cringe before your mighty power.
68: 1 Arise, O God, and scatter your **e**. / Let those who
68:21 But God will smash the heads of his **e**,
68:22 Lord says, "I will bring my **e** down from Bashan;
69: 4 These **e** who seek to destroy me / are doing
69:18 Come and rescue me; / free me from all my **e**.
69:19 and disgrace. / You have seen all my **e**
71: 2 Rescue me! Save me from my **e**, for you are just.
71:10 For my **e** are whispering against me. / They are
72: 9 before him; / his **e** will fall before him in the dust.
74: 4 There your **e** shouted their victorious battle cries;
74:10 O God, will you allow our **e** to mock you?
74:18 See how these **e** scoff at you, LORD. / A foolish
74:23 Don't overlook these things your **e** have said.
76: 5 The mightiest of our **e** have been plundered.
76: 8 From heaven you sentenced your **e**; / the earth
78:42 his power / and how he rescued them from their **e**.
78:53 were not afraid; / but the sea closed in upon their **e**.
78:66 He routed his **e** / and sent them to eternal shame.
80: 6 of neighboring nations. / Our **e** treat us as a joke.
80:16 For we are chopped up and burned by our **e**;
81:14 How quickly I would then subdue their **e**!
83: 2 Don't you hear the tumult of your **e**? / Don't you see what your arrogant **e** are doing?
89:10 You scattered your **e** with your mighty arm.
89:22 His **e** will not get the best of him, / nor will the
89:42 You have strengthened his **e** against him
89:51 Your **e** have mocked me, O LORD; / they mock
92: 9 Your **e**, LORD, will surely perish; / all evildoers
92:11 my own eyes I have seen the downfall of my **e**;
102: 8 My **e** taunt me day after day. / They mock
105:24 of Israel / until they became too mighty for their **e**.
106:10 So he rescued them from their **e** / and redeemed
106:11 Then the water returned and covered their **e**;
106:42 Their **e** crushed them / and brought them under
107: 2 Tell others he has saved you from your **e**.
108:12 Oh, please help us against our **e**, / for all human
110: 1 in honor at my right hand / until I humble your **e**,
110: 2 from Jerusalem; / you will rule over your **e**.
119:98 Your commands make me wiser than my **e**,
119:121 Don't leave me to the mercy of my **e**, / for I have
119:139 with rage, / for my **e** have disregarded your words.
129: 1 From my earliest youth my **e** have persecuted me
129: 2 from my earliest youth my **e** have persecuted me,
132:18 I will clothe his **e** with shame, / but he will be a
136:24 He saved us from our **e**. / His faithful love endures
138: 7 you will preserve me against the anger of my **e**.
138: 7 You will clench your fist against my angry **e**!
139:20 blaspheme you; / your **e** take your name in vain.
139:22 with complete hatred, / for your **e** are my **e**.
140: 9 Let my **e** be destroyed / by the very evil they have
142: 3 Wherever I go, / my **e** have set traps for me.
143: 9 Save me from my **e**, LORD; / I run to you to hide
143:12 In your unfailing love, cut off all my **e**
144: 6 Release your lightning bolts and scatter your **e**!
144: 7 me from deep waters, / from the power of my **e**.
144:11 Rescue me from the power of my **e**. / Their mouths
Pr 16: 7 he makes even their **e** live at peace with them.
24:17 Do not rejoice when your **e** fall into trouble.
25:21 If your **e** are hungry, give them food to eat. If they
Isa 1:20 refusing to listen, you will be destroyed by your **e**.
1:24 says, "I will pour out my fury on you, my **e**!
2:19 his **e** will crawl with fear into holes in the ground.
7:11 to prove that I will crush your **e** as I have
9:11 will reply to their bragging by bringing Rezin's **e**,
14: 2 will be captured, and Israel will rule over its **e**.
16: 3 "Help us," they cry. "Defend us against our **e**.
16: 4 Hide them from our **e** until the terror is past."
17:14 Israel waits in terror, but by dawn its **e** are dead.
26:11 will be ashamed. / Let your fire consume your **e**.
26:20 Hide until the LORD's anger against your **e** has
27: 3 day and night I will watch to keep **e** away.
27: 5 These **e** will be spared only if they surrender
27: 7 Israel in the same way he has punished her **e**? No, for he devastated her **e**,
29: 5 your ruthless **e** will be driven away like chaff
29: 8 your **e** will dream of a victorious conquest over
30:16 going to see is the swiftness of your **e** chasing you!
30:25 In that day, when your **e** are slaughtered, there will
30:28 His anger pours out like a flood on his **e**,
30:30 he will bring down his mighty arm on his **e**.
35: 4 not fear, for your God is coming to destroy your **e**.
41:11 "See, all your angry **e** lie there, confused
41:15 You will tear all your **e** apart, making chaff of
42:13 thundering battle cry, / and he will crush all his **e**.
49:19 Your **e** who enslaved you will be far away.
49:26 I will feed your **e** with their own flesh. They will
50: 8 me now? Where are my **e**? Let them appear!
50: 9 All my **e** will be destroyed like old clothes that
51:13 Will you continue to fear the anger of your **e** from
54:14 Your **e** will stay far away; you will live in peace.
54:15 Your **e** will always be defeated because I am on
59:18 He will repay his **e** for their evil deeds. His fury
61: 2 and with it, the day of God's anger against their **e**.
62: 8 "I will never again hand you over to your **e**.
63: 3 In my anger I have trampled my **e** as if they were
63:18 the holy place, and now our **e** have destroyed it.
64: 2 Then your **e** would learn the reason for your fame!
66: 6 of the LORD taking vengeance against his **e**.
66:14 LORD on his people—and his anger against his **e**.
Jer 6:12 Their homes will be turned over to their **e**, and
9:16 Their **e** will chase them with the sword until I have
11:16 But now I have sent the fury of their **e** to burn
11:18 Then the LORD told me about the plots my **e**
12: 7 I have surrendered my dearest ones to their **e**.
15:11 Your **e** will ask you to plead on their behalf in
15:14 I will tell their **e** to take them as captives to a
17: 3 as plunder to your **e**, for sin runs rampant in your
18:17 I will scatter my people before their **e** as the east
19: 9 I will see to it that your **e** lay siege to the city until
20: 5 And I will let your **e** plunder Jerusalem.
21: 4 I will bring your **e** right into the heart of this city.
30:16 be destroyed, and all your **e** will be sent into exile.
34:20 I will give you to your **e**, and they will kill you.
44:30 king of Egypt, over to his **e** who want to kill him,
46:10 the LORD Almighty, a day of vengeance on his **e**.
49:36 I will bring **e** from all directions, and I will scatter
49:37 I myself will go with Elam's **e** to shatter it.
49:37 "Their **e** will chase them with the sword until I
50: 7 Their **e** said, 'We are allowed to attack them freely,
50:25 brought out weapons to vent his fury against his **e**.
51:14 "Your cities will be filled with **e**, like fields filled
51:53 I will send **e** to plunder her," says the LORD.
51:55 Waves of **e** pound against her; the noise of battle
La 1: 2 her friends have betrayed her; they are now her **e**.
1: 3 Her **e** have chased her down, and she has nowhere
1: 5 have become her masters, and her **e** prosper,
1:14 Lord sapped my strength and gave me to my **e**;
1:17 LORD has said, "Let their neighbors be their **e**!
1:21 When my **e** heard of my troubles, they were happy
2: 7 He has given Jerusalem's palaces to her **e**.
2:16 All your **e** deride you. They scoff and grind their
2:17 and caused her **e** to rejoice over her and boast of
3:30 strike them. Let them accept the insults of their **e**.
3:46 "All our **e** have spoken out against us.
3:52 My **e**, whom I have never harmed, chased me like
3:60 You have seen the plots my **e** have laid against me.
3:62 the plots my **e** whisper and mutter against me all
4:19 Our **e** were swifter than the eagles. If we fled to the
5:11 Our **e** rape the women and young girls in
Eze 16:27 I handed you over to your **e**, the Philistines,
23:28 I will surely hand you over to your **e**, to those you
23:47 For their **e** will stone them and kill them with
32:23 everywhere are now dead at the hands of their **e**.
34:10 I now consider these shepherds my **e**, and I will
36: 2 Your **e** have taunted you, saying, 'Aha!
36: 3 Your **e** have attacked you from all directions,
39:23 my back on them and let their **e** destroy them.
39:27 When I bring them home from the lands of their **e**,
Da 4:19 in this dream would happen to your **e**,
11:12 and will have many thousands of his **e** killed.
Hos 1: 7 I will personally free them from their **e** without any
7:16 Their leaders will be killed by their **e** because of
8: 3 is good, and now their **e** will chase after them.
11: 6 their **e** will crash through their gates and destroy
Am 5:18 then the LORD would rescue us from all our **e**."
6: 8 I will give this city and everything in it to their **e**."
Ob 1: 5 the poor. But your **e** will wipe you out completely!
1:11 You acted as though you were one of Israel's **e**.
1:14 handing them over to their **e** in that terrible time of
Mic 1:10 Don't tell our **e** in the city of Gath; don't weep at
2: 4 In that day your **e** will make fun of you by singing
4:10 he will redeem you from the grip of your **e**.
5: 3 The people of Israel will be abandoned to their **e**
5: 9 up to their foes, and all their **e** will be wiped out.
7: 6 Your **e** will be right in your own household.
7: 8 Do not gloat over me, my **e**! For though I fall,
7: 9 and punish my **e** for all the evil they have done to
7:10 Then my **e** will see that the LORD is on my side.
Na 1: 2 all who oppose him and furiously destroys his **e**!
1: 8 But he sweeps away his **e** in an overwhelming
1:10 His **e**, tangled up like thorns, staggering like
1:15 for your **e** from Nineveh will never invade your
2:12 You crushed your **e** to feed your cubs and your
Hab 1:14 that have no leader to defend them from their **e**?
Zec 8:10 safe from the enemy, for there were **e** on all sides.
9:14 he will go out against his **e** like a whirlwind from
9:15 and they will subdue their **e** with sling stones.
9:15 drunk with wine, shedding the blood of their **e**.
10: 5 trampling their **e** in the mud under their feet.
12: 4 of Judah, but I will blind the horses of her **e**.
14:16 the **e** of Jerusalem who survive the plague will go
Mt 5:44 But I say, love your **e**! Pray for those who
10:36 Your **e** will be right in your own household!
22:44 until I humble your **e** beneath your feet.'
Mk 3: 2 it was the Sabbath, Jesus' **e** watched him closely.
12:36 until I humble your **e** beneath your feet.'
Lk 1:71 Now we will be saved from our **e** / and from all
1:74 We have been rescued from our **e**, / so we can
6:11 the **e** of Jesus were wild with rage and began to
6:27 "But if you are willing to listen, I say, love your **e**.
6:35 "Love your **e**! Do good to them! Lend to them!
13:17 This shamed his **e**. And all the people rejoiced at
19:27 And now about these **e** of mine who didn't want
19:43 Before long your **e** will build ramparts against your
19:44 Your **e** will not leave a single stone in place,
20:43 until I humble your **e**, / making them a footstool
23:12 Herod and Pilate, who had been **e** before,
Ac 2:34 in honor at my right hand / until I humble your **e**,
Ro 5:10 by the death of his Son while we were still his **e**,
11:28 Many of the Jews are now **e** of the Good News.
12:20 "If your **e** are hungry, feed them. / If they are
1Co 15:24 the Father, having put down all **e** of every kind.
15:25 For Christ must reign until he humbles all his **e**
Php 1:28 Don't be intimidated by your **e**. This will be a sign
3:18 shows they are really **e** of the cross of Christ.
Col 1:21 You were his **e**, separated from him by your evil
2Th 3:15 Don't think of them as **e**, but speak to them as you
Heb 1:13 in honor at my right hand / until I humble your **e**,
10:13 There he waits until his **e** are humbled as a
10:27 and the raging fire that will consume his **e**.
Rev 11: 5 the mouths of the prophets and consumes their **e**.
11:12 And they rose to heaven in a cloud as their **e**

ENEMIES' (7) [ENEMY]

Ps 45: 5 Your arrows are sharp, / piercing your **e** hearts.
54: 5 May my **e** plans for evil be turned against them.
64: 1 Do not let my **e** threats overwhelm me.
Isa 28: 3 of Israel—will be trampled beneath its **e** feet.
33:23 The **e** sails hang loose on broken masts with
Jer 8:16 The snorting of the **e** warhorses can be heard all
50: 9 The **e** arrows will go straight to the mark; they will

ENEMY (181) [ENEMIES, ENEMIES', ENEMY'S]

MY ENEMY (9) 1Sa 19:17; 1Ki 21:20; Job 27:7; Ps 7:4; 13:2; 31:8; 41:11; 118:13; 143:3

THE ENEMY (85) Ex 15:6,9; Dt 32:27,42; 33:27; Jos 8:22; 10:10,11,19; 23:10; Jdg 4:16; 7:11; 8:4; 1Sa 30:23; 2Sa 1:6; 11:23; 2Ki 3:26; 1Ch 19:17; 2Ch 14:12; 20:24; 35:22,23; Ne 4:12,14; Est 3:10; 8:1; 9:10,24; Ps 56:1; 68:14; 74:3; 76:3; Isa 5:30; 10:32,34; 13:2; 14:32; 16:9; 28:17; 33:3; Jer 4:16; 6:24,25; 8:1; 14:18; 15:9,13; 19:7; 20:4; 25:38; 31:16; 33:4; 46:16; 49:22; 50:16,43; La 1:9,10,16; 2:3,21,22; Eze 4:3; 5:12,17; 29:10; 30:22; 33:3,6; Da 11:12; Hos 8:1; Mic 5:1; Na 2:1,6; 3:13,15; Zep 1:13; Zec 8:10; 10:5; 14:15; Mt 13:39; Lk 10:19; 14:32; Eph 6:13; 1Ti 5:14

YOUR ENEMY (25) Dt 28:55,57; Jdg 3:28; 1Sa 26:8; 28:16; 2Sa 4:8; Job 13:24; Isa 29:3; Jer 30:14; 50:31; 51:25; Eze 5:8; 21:3; 26:3; 28:22; 29:3; 35:3; 38:3; 39:1; Na 2:13; 3:5; Zep 3:15; Mt 5:25,44; Gal 4:16

Ex 15: 6 right hand, O LORD, / dashes the **e** to pieces.
15: 9 "The **e** said, 'I will chase them, / catch up with
23:22 then I will be an **e** to your enemies,
Lev 26:39 Those still left alive will rot away in **e** lands
Nu 14:34 will discover what it is like to have me for an **e**.'
24:18 be taken over, / and Seir, its **e**, will be conquered,
Dt 28:55 the siege that your **e** will inflict on all your towns.
28:57 and terrible distress that your **e** will inflict on all
29:16 and how we traveled through the lands of the **e** nations
32:27 But I feared the taunt of the **e**, / that their
32:42 the captives, / and the heads of the **e** leaders." '
33:27 He thrusts out the **e** before you; / it is he who cries,
Jos 8:22 came out and started killing the **e** from the rear.
10:10 Then the Israelites chased the **e** along the road to
10:11 The hail killed more of the **e** than the Israelites
10:19 The rest of you continue chasing the **e** and cut
11: 8 of Mizpah, until not one **e** warrior was left alive.
23:10 one of you will put to flight a thousand of the **e**,

Jdg 1: 4 and they killed ten thousand **e** warriors at the town
3: 28 LORD has given you victory over Moab your **e**."
4: 16 Barak chased the **e** and their chariots all the way to
6: 5 These **e** hordes, coming with their cattle and tents
7: 11 and went down to the outposts of the **e** camp.
8: 4 they were exhausted, they continued to chase the **e**.
16: 23 "Our god has given us victory over our **e**
16: 24 saying, "Our god has delivered our **e** to us!
1Sa 13: 6 When the men of Israel saw the vast number of **e**
18: 29 and he remained David's **e** for the rest of his life.
19: 17 "Why have you tricked me and let my **e** escape?"
24: 19 Who else would let his **e** get away when he had
26: 8 "God has surely handed your **e** over to you this
28: 16 if the LORD has left you and has become your **e**?
30: 23 He has kept us safe and helped us defeat the **e**.
2Sa 1: 6 I saw Saul there leaning on his spear with the **e**
4: 8 the son of your **e** Saul who tried to kill you.
11: 23 "The **e** came out against us," he said. "And as we
18: 19 the LORD has saved him from his **e** Absalom."
23: 8 He once used his spear to kill eight hundred **e**
23: 18 He once used his spear to kill three hundred **e**
1Ki 11: 14 Edom's royal family, to be an **e** against Solomon.
11: 23 God also raised up Rezon son of Eliada to be an **e**
11: 25 Rezon was Israel's bitter **e** for the rest of
20: 13 the LORD says: Do you see all these **e** forces?
21: 20 "So my **e** has found me!" Ahab exclaimed to
2Ki 3: 26 to break through the **e** lines near the king of Edom,
1Ch 11: 11 He once used his spear to kill three hundred **e**
11: 20 He once used his spear to kill three hundred **e**
19: 17 Then he engaged the **e** troops in battle, and they
2Ch 14: 12 of Asa and the army of Judah, and the **e** fled.
20: 24 could see. Not a single one of the **e** had escaped.
26: 13 were prepared to assist the king against any **e**.
35: 22 his royal robes so the **e** would not recognize him.
35: 23 But the **e** archers hit King Josiah with their arrows
Ne 4: 12 The Jews who lived near the **e** came and told us
4: 14 and said to them, "Don't be afraid of the **e**!
5: 9 God in order to avoid being mocked by **e** nations?
Est 3: 10 of Hammedatha the Agagite—the **e** of the Jews.
7: 6 Esther replied, "This wicked Haman is our **e**."
8: 1 of Haman, the **e** of the Jews, to Queen Esther.
9: 10 of Haman son of Hammedatha, the **e** of the Jews.
9: 24 the **e** of the Jews, had plotted to crush and destroy
Job 13: 24 away from me? Why do you consider me your **e**?
19: 11 His fury burns against me; he counts me as an **e**.
27: 7 "May my **e** be punished like the wicked,
33: 10 a quarrel with me, and he considers me to be his **e**.
Ps 7: 4 a friend / or plundered my **e** without cause,
13: 2 How long will my **e** have the upper hand?
31: 8 You have not handed me over to my **e** / but have
41: 11 for you have not let my **e** triumph over me.
55: 12 It is not an **e** who taunts me— / I could bear that.
56: 1 have mercy on me. / The **e** troops press in on me.
62: 7 He is my refuge, a rock where no **e** can reach me.
68: 12 **E** kings and their armies flee, / while the women of
68: 14 The Almighty scattered the **e** kings / like a blowing
68: 30 Rebuke these **e** nations— / these wild animals
74: 3 see how the **e** has destroyed your sanctuary.
76: 3 There he breaks the arrows of the **e**, / the shields
78: 61 he surrendered his glory into **e** hands.
118: 13 You did your best to kill me, O my **e**,
143: 3 My **e** has chased me. / He has knocked me to the
Pr 27: 6 a friend are better than many kisses from an **e**.
Isa 5: 30 The **e** nations will growl over their victims like the
10: 32 But the **e** stops at Nob for the rest of that day.
10: 34 The Mighty One will cut down the **e** as an ax cuts
13: 2 "See the flags waving as the **e** attacks. Cheer them
14: 32 What should we tell the **e** messengers? Tell them
16: 4 have ceased and **e** raiders have disappeared,
16: 9 But now the **e** has completely destroyed that vine.
28: 17 the **e** will come like a flood to sweep it away.
28: 18 When the terrible **e** floods in, you will be trampled
29: 3 I will be your **e**, surrounding Jerusalem
33: 3 The **e** runs at the sound of your voice. When you
33: 21 He will be like a wide river of protection that no **e**
63: 10 That is why he became their **e** and fought against
Jer 4: 13 Our **e** rushes down on us like a storm wind!
4: 16 'The **e** is coming from a distant land, raising a
4: 19 For I have heard the blast of **e** trumpets
6: 3 **E** shepherds will surround you. They will set up
6: 24 We have heard reports about the **e**, and we are
6: 25 The **e** is everywhere, and they are ready to kill.
8: 1 "the **e** will break open the graves of the kings
8: 17 "I will send these **e** troops among you like
14: 18 I see the bodies of people slaughtered by the **e**.
15: 9 I will hand over to the **e** to be killed,"
15: 13 over their wealth and treasures as plunder to the **e**.
19: 7 The **e** will leave the dead bodies as food for the
20: 4 as they are slaughtered by the swords of the **e**.
25: 38 land will be made desolate by the sword of the **e**
30: 14 wounded you cruelly, as though I were your **e**.
31: 16 come back to you from the distant land of the **e**.
33: 4 the walls against the siege weapons of the **e**,
46: 16 Let's get away from the sword of the **e**!'
49: 22 The **e** will come as swiftly as an eagle, and he will
50: 16 Let the captives escape the sword of the **e** and rush
50: 31 "See, I am your **e**, O proud people,"
50: 43 king of Babylon has received reports about the **e**,
51: 25 of the earth! I am your **e**," says the LORD.
La 1: 6 for pasture, too weak to run from the pursuing **e**.
1: 7 But then she fell to her **e**, and there was no one to
1: 7 Her **e** struck her down and laughed as she fell.
1: 9 deep misery," she cries. "The **e** has triumphed."
1: 10 The **e** has plundered her completely,
1: 16 have no future, for the **e** has conquered us."
2: 3 The Lord has withdrawn his protection as the **e**
2: 4 bow against his people as though he were their **e**.
2: 5 Yes, the Lord has vanquished Israel like an **e**.
2: 21 boys and girls, killed by the swords of the **e**.
2: 22 The **e** has killed all the children I bore and raised."
4: 12 would have believed an **e** could march through the
Eze 4: 2 Surround it with **e** camps and battering rams.
4: 3 and demonstrate how the **e** will attack Jerusalem.
5: 8 I myself, the Sovereign LORD, am now your **e**.
5: 12 A third of them will be slaughtered by the **e**
5: 17 and I will bring the sword of the **e** against you.
7: 15 Any who leave the city walls will be killed by **e**
14: 17 and I told **e** armies to come and destroy everything.
21: 3 I am your **e**, O Israel, and I am about to unsheath
26: 3 I am your **e**, O Tyre, and I will bring many nations
26: 19 You will sink beneath the terrible waves of **e**
28: 7 I will bring against you an **e** army, the terror of the
28: 22 I am your **e**, O Sidon, and I will reveal my glory by
29: 3 I am your **e**, O Pharaoh, king of Egypt—you great
29: 10 I am now the **e** of both you and your river. I will
30: 22 I am the **e** of Pharaoh, the king of Egypt! I will
33: 3 When the watchman sees the **e** coming, he blows
33: 6 But if the watchman sees the **e** coming and doesn't
35: 3 I am your **e**, O Mount Seir, and I will raise my fist
38: 3 from the Sovereign LORD: Gog, I am your **e**!
39: 1 I am your **e**, O Gog, ruler of the nations of
Da 11: 12 After the **e** army is swept away, the king of the
Hos 8: 1 The **e** descends like an eagle on the people of the
Am 3: 11 says the Sovereign LORD, "an **e** is coming!
6: 14 I am about to bring an **e** nation against you,"
Mic 5: 1 your troops! The **e** is laying siege to Jerusalem.
Na 2: 1 Nineveh, you are already surrounded by **e** armies!
2: 1 and keep a sharp watch for the **e** attack to begin!
2: 6 The river gates are open! The **e** has entered!
2: 13 "I am your **e**!" says the LORD Almighty.
3: 5 "No wonder I am your **e**!" declares the LORD
3: 11 You will hide for fear of the attacking **e**.
3: 13 The gates of your land will be opened wide to the **e**
3: 15 The **e** will consume you like locusts,
Zep 1: 13 ones whose property will be plundered by the **e**,
3: 15 of judgment and will disperse the armies of your **e**.
Zec 8: 10 No traveler was safe from the **e**, for there were
10: 5 they will overthrow even the horsemen of the **e**.
14: 15 donkeys, and all the other animals in the **e** camps.
Mt 5: 25 Come to terms quickly with your **e** before it is too
5: 43 Moses says, 'Love your neighbor' and hate your **e**.
13: 25 his **e** came and planted weeds among the wheat.
13: 28 " 'An **e** has done it!' the farmer exclaimed.
13: 39 The **e** who planted the weeds among the wheat is
Lk 10: 19 given you authority over all the power of the **e**,
14: 32 If he is not able, then while the **e** is still far away,
Ac 13: 10 sort of trickery and villainy, **e** of all that is good,
1Co 15: 26 And the last **e** to be destroyed is death.
Gal 4: 16 Have I now become your **e** because I am telling
Eph 6: 13 Use every piece of God's armor to resist the **e** in
1Ti 5: 14 Then the **e** will not be able to say anything against
Jas 4: 4 friendship with this world makes you an **e** of God?
1Pe 5: 8 Watch out for attacks from the Devil, your great **e**.

ENEMY'S (3) [ENEMY]

Ex 23: 4 "If you come upon your **e** ox or donkey that has
2Sa 11: 16 where he knew the **e** strongest men were fighting.
Da 11: 10 a flood and carry the battle as far as the **e** fortress.

ENERGETIC (1) [ENERGY]

Pr 31: 17 She is **e** and strong, a hard worker.

ENERGIES (1) [ENERGY]

Php 3: 13 but I am focusing all my **e** on this one thing:

ENERGY (6) [ENERGETIC, ENERGIES]

Dt 8: 17 your own strength and **e** that made you wealthy.
Ezr 5: 8 The work is going forward with great **e**
Isa 59: 5 and **e** spinning evil plans that end up in deadly
Jn 6: 27 Spend your **e** seeking the eternal life that I, the Son
1Ti 4: 7 and **e** in training yourself for spiritual fitness.
1Pe 4: 11 Do it with all the strength and **e** that God supplies.

ENFORCED (1) [ENFORCES]

Da 6: 7 Majesty should make a law that will be strictly **e**.

ENFORCES (1) [ENFORCED]

Job 25: 2 and dreadful. He **e** peace in the heavens.

ENGAGE (3) [ENGAGED, ENGAGEMENT, ENGAGES, ENGAGING]

Dt 18: 10 allow them to interpret omens, or **e** in witchcraft,
1Co 10: 8 And we must not **e** in sexual immorality as some
Tit 1: 10 they **e** in useless talk and deceive people.

ENGAGED (10) [ENGAGE]

Ex 22: 16 "If a man seduces a virgin who is not **e** to anyone
Dt 20: 7 Has anyone just become **e**? Well, go home and get
22: 23 a virgin who is **e** to be married, and he has sexual
22: 25 "But if the man meets the **e** woman out in the
22: 28 in the act of raping a young woman who is not **e**,
28: 30 "You will be **e** to a woman, but another man will
1Ki 16: 15 then **e** in attacking the Philistine town of
1Ch 19: 17 Then he **e** the enemy troops in battle, and they
Mt 1: 18 His mother, Mary, was **e** to be married to Joseph.
Lk 1: 27 She was **e** to be married to a man named Joseph,

ENGAGEMENT (1) [ENGAGE]

Mt 1: 19 being a just man, decided to break the **e** quietly,

ENGAGING (1) [ENGAGE]

Nu 21: 23 Israel in the wilderness, **e** them in battle at Jahaz.

ENGRAFTED [KJV] See PLANTED

ENGRAVE (3) [ENGRAVED, ENGRAVER, ENGRAVES, ENGRAVING]

Ex 28: 9 and **e** on them the names of the tribes of Israel.
28: 11 **E** these names in the same way a gemcutter
Zec 3: 9 I will **e** an inscription on it, says the LORD

ENGRAVED (7) [ENGRAVE]

Ex 28: 21 and the name of that tribe will be **e** on it as though
39: 6 The stones were **e** with the names of the tribes of Israel, just as initials are **e** on a seal.
39: 14 The stones were **e** like a seal, each with the name
Job 19: 24 and filled with lead, **e** forever in the rock.
Eze 8: 10 and saw the walls **e** with all kinds of snakes,
Rev 2: 17 and on the stone will be **e** a new name that no one

ENGRAVER (4) [ENGRAVE]

Ex 28: 36 Using the techniques of an **e**, inscribe it with these
39: 30 Using the techniques of an **e**, they inscribed it with
2Ch 2: 7 and a skilled **e** who can work with the craftsmen of
2: 14 He is also an **e** and can follow any design given to

ENGRAVES (1) [ENGRAVE]

Ex 28: 11 these names in the same way a gemcutter **e** a seal.

ENGRAVING (1) [ENGRAVE]

Ex 38: 23 the tribe of Dan, a craftsman expert at **e**, designing,

ENGULFED (5) [ENGULFS]

Ge 19: 29 removing him from the disaster that **e** the cities on
Ex 3: 2 was amazed because the bush was **e** in flames,
Ps 124: 4 The waters would have **e** us; / a torrent would have
Pr 1: 27 when you are **e** by trouble, and when anguish
La 3: 43 "You have **e** us with your anger, chased us down,

ENGULFS (1) [ENGULFED]

Ps 88: 7 anger lies heavy on me; / wave after wave **e** me.

ENHANCE (2) [ENHANCES]

Est 2: 13 or jewelry she wanted to **e** her beauty.
Pr 10: 16 The earnings of the godly **e** their lives, but evil

ENHANCES (1) [ENHANCE]

Ps 76: 10 Human opposition only **e** your glory, / for you use

ENJOIN(ED) [KJV] See also COMMAND, DIRECTED, ORDAINED, PRESCRIBED

ENJOY (64) [ENJOYABLE, ENJOYED, ENJOYING, ENJOYMENT, ENJOYS]

Ge 17: 18 "Yes, may Ishmael **e** your special blessing!"
Lev 25: 4 but during the seventh year the land will **e** a
26: 34 Then the land will finally rest and **e** its Sabbaths.
26: 43 And the land will **e** its years of Sabbath rest as it
Nu 14: 31 the land, and they will **e** what you have despised.
Dt 4: 40 Then you will **e** a long life in the land the LORD
6: 2 all his laws and commands, you will **e** a long life.
11: 9 you will **e** a long life in the land the LORD swore
20: 14 You may **e** the spoils of your enemies that the
22: 7 mother go, so you may prosper and **e** a long life.
25: 15 so that you will **e** a long life in the land the
28: 30 will plant a vineyard, but you will never **e** its fruit.
32: 47 By obeying them you will **e** a long life in the land
Jdg 19: 6 father said, "Please stay the night and **e** yourself."
19: 9 it's getting late. Stay the night and **e** yourself.
2Sa 19: 35 years old today, and I can no longer **e** anything.
1Ki 18: 41 Then Elijah said to Ahab, "Go and **e** a good meal!
Ezr 9: 12 You promised that we would **e** the good produce of
Job 20: 17 He will never again **e** abundant streams of olive oil
21: 8 grow to maturity, and they **e** their grandchildren.
Ps 128: 2 You will **e** the fruit of your labor. / How happy you
128: 6 May you live to **e** your grandchildren. / And may
Pr 2: 14 and they **e** evil as it turns things upside down.
3: 24 can lie down without fear and **e** pleasant dreams.
5: 10 and someone else will **e** the fruit of your labor.
7: 18 love until morning. Let's **e** each other's caresses,
13: 2 Good people **e** the positive results of their words,
Ecc 2: 24 So I decided there is nothing better than to **e** food
2: 25 For who can eat or **e** anything apart from him?
3: 12 be happy and to **e** themselves as long as they can.
3: 13 should eat and drink and **e** the fruits of their labor,
3: 22 No one will bring them back from death to **e** life in
5: 18 drink a good glass of wine, and **e** their work—
5: 19 wealth from God and the good health to **e** it.
5: 19 To **e** your work and accept your lot in life—that is
6: 2 but then he doesn't give them the health to **e** it.
6: 9 **E** what you have rather than desiring what you
7: 14 **E** prosperity while you can. But when hard times
8: 15 to do in this world than to eat, drink, and **e** life.
11: 9 it's wonderful to be young! **E** every minute of it.
12: 1 youth before you grow old and no longer **e** living.
Isa 53: 10 He will **e** a long life, and the LORD's plan will
58: 13 but **e** the Sabbath and speak of it with delight as
65: 22 and will have time to **e** their hard-won gains.
Jer 2: 7 "And when I brought you into a fruitful land to **e**
La 3: 33 For he does not **e** hurting people or causing them

Mic 7:14 Let them **e** the fertile pastures of Bashan
Zec 1:15 But I am very angry with the other nations that **e**
Mt 23:7 They **e** the attention they get on the streets, and they **e** being called 'Rabbi.'
Ro 12:16 but **e** the company of ordinary people.
1Co 9:23 the Good News, and in doing so I **e** its blessings.
10:30 If I can thank God for the food and **e** it,
2Co 11:19 who think you are so wise, **e** listening to fools!
Gal 6:4 then you will **e** the personal satisfaction of having
Eph 3:6 and **e** together the promise of blessings through
1Ti 3:2 He must **e** having guests in his home and must be
2Ti 2:6 Hardworking farmers are the first to **e** the fruit of
2:22 and **e** the companionship of those who call on the
Tit 1:8 He must **e** having guests in his home and must love
Jas 4:4 I say it again, that if your aim is to **e** this world,
1Pe 4:3 in the past of the evil things that godless people **e**—
1Jn 2:25 And in this fellowship we **e** the eternal life he
Jude 1:18 is to **e** themselves in every evil way imaginable.

ENJOYABLE (1) [ENJOY]

Heb 12:11 No discipline is **e** while it is happening—it is

ENJOYED (16) [ENJOY]

Ge 5:24 He **e** a close relationship with God throughout his
6:9 God's will and **e** a close relationship with him.
1Ch 29:28 ripe old age, having **e** long life, wealth, and honor.
2Ch 14:5 So Asa's kingdom **e** a period of peace.
18:1 Now Jehoshaphat **e** great riches and high esteem,
36:21 The land finally **e** its Sabbath rest, lying desolate
Ne 9:25 grew fat and **e** themselves in all your blessings.
Est 2:14 to the king again unless he had especially **e** her
Job 20:12 "He **e** the taste of his wickedness, letting it melt
Ps 55:14 What good fellowship we **e** / as we walked
Isa 21:4 The sleep I once **e** at night is now a faint memory.
54:17 These benefits are **e** by the servants of the LORD;
Lk 17:27 the people **e** banquets and parties and weddings
Jn 4:12 better water than he and his sons and his cattle **e**?"
Ro 15:24 And after I have **e** your fellowship for a little
Rev 18:9 and **e** her great luxury will mourn for her as they

ENJOYING (6) [ENJOY]

Jdg 19:22 While they were **e** themselves, some of the wicked
Ps 73:12 **e** a life of ease while their riches multiply.
Mt 24:38 the people were **e** banquets and parties
Ac 2:47 praising God and **e** the goodwill of all the people.
2Th 2:12 not believing the truth and for **e** the evil they do.
Heb 11:25 people instead of **e** the fleeting pleasures of sin.

ENJOYMENT (2) [ENJOY]

Ex 30:38 Those who make it for their own **e** will be cut off
1Ti 6:17 who richly gives us all we need for our **e**.

ENJOYS (2) [ENJOY]

Ps 35:27 is the LORD, / who **e** helping his servant."
Pr 15:23 Everyone **e** a fitting reply; it is wonderful to say

ENLARGE (3) [LARGE]

Ge 9:27 May God **e** the territory of Japheth, / and may he
Ex 34:24 that stand in your way and will **e** your boundaries.
Isa 54:2 "**E** your house; build an addition; spread out your

ENLARGED (1) [LARGE]

2Co 10:15 and that our work among you will be greatly **e**.

ENLARGES (3) [LARGE]

Dt 12:20 "When the LORD your God **e** your territory as
19:8 "If the LORD your God **e** your territory, as he
33:20 "Blessed is the one who **e** Gad's territory!

ENLIGHTENED (2) [LIGHT]

Job 26:3 How you have **e** my stupidity! What wise things
Heb 6:4 to restore to repentance those who were once **e**—

ENLIST (1) [ENLISTED]

Nu 34:18 Also **e** one leader from each tribe to help them

ENLISTED (5) [ENLIST]

1Ki 5:13 Then King Solomon **e** thirty thousand laborers
5:15 Solomon also **e** seventy thousand common
2Ch 2:2 He **e** a force of seventy thousand common laborers,
2:18 He **e** 70,000 of them as common laborers,
2Ti 2:4 then you cannot satisfy the one who has **e** you in

ENOCH (13)

Ge 4:17 and gave birth to a son, and they named him **E**.
4:17 Cain founded a city, he named it **E** after his son.
4:18 **E** was the father of Irad. / Irad was the father of
5:18 When Jared was 162 years old, his son **E** was born.
5:19 After the birth of **E**, Jared lived another 800 years,
5:21 When **E** was 65 years old, his son Methuselah was
5:22 **E** lived another 300 years in close fellowship with
5:23 **E** lived 365 years in all.
1Ch 1:3 **E**, Methuselah, Lamech,
Lk 3:37 Methuselah was the son of **E**. / **E** was the son of
Heb 11:5 It was by faith that **E** was taken up to heaven
Jude 1:14 Now **E**, who lived seven generations after Adam,

ENORMOUS (3) [ENORMOUSLY]

1Ch 29:1 The work ahead of him is **e**, for the Temple he will
Job 41:12 in the crocodile's limbs and throughout its **e** frame.
Jas 3:5 is a small thing, but what **e** damage it can do.

ENORMOUSLY (1) [ENORMOUS]

Ge 30:30 before I came, and your wealth has increased **e**.

ENOSH (8)

Ge 4:26 Seth grew up, he had a son and named him **E**.
5:6 When Seth was 105 years old, his son **E** was born.
5:7 After the birth of **E**, Seth lived another 807 years,
5:9 When **E** was 90 years old, his son Kenan was born.
5:10 **E** lived another 815 years, and he had other sons
1Ch 1:1 The descendants of Adam were Seth, **E**,
Lk 3:38 Kenan was the son of **E**. / **E** was the son of Seth.

ENOUGH (199)

Ge 6:21 take **e** food for your family and for all the
12:14 And sure **e**, when they arrived in Egypt,
24:19 water for your camels, too, until they have had **e**!"
26:22 So Isaac called it "Room **E**," for he said, "At last
30:15 "Wasn't it **e** that you stole my husband?
33:11 I have more than **e**." Jacob continued to insist,
34:21 For the land is large **e** to hold them, and we can
36:7 There was not **e** land to support them both
38:11 his youngest son, Shelah, was old **e** to marry her.
41:36 That way there will be **e** to eat when the seven
41:47 And sure **e**, for the next seven years there were
44:10 "Fair **e**," the man replied, "except that only the
Ex 2:15 And sure **e**, when Pharaoh heard about it, he gave
5:8 They obviously don't have **e** to do. If they did,
5:17 You obviously don't have **e** to do. If you did,
14:11 Weren't there **e** graves for us in Egypt? Why did
16:18 two quarts for each person, everyone had just **e**.
16:18 and those who gathered only a little had **e**.
16:29 on the sixth day, so there will be **e** for two days.
21:12 "Anyone who hits a person hard **e** to cause death
23:30 your population has increased **e** to fill the land.
36:5 "We have more than **e** materials on hand now to
36:6 You have already given more than **e**."
36:7 Their contributions were more than **e** to complete
Lev 25:21 a bumper crop, **e** to support you for three years.
25:26 but the person who sold it manages to get **e** money
Nu 11:22 we caught all the fish in the sea, would that be **e**?"
16:13 Isn't it **e** that you brought us out of Egypt, a land
20:8 You will get **e** water from the rock to satisfy all the
20:12 "Because you did not trust me **e** to demonstrate
Dt 1:6 to us, 'You have stayed at this mountain long **e**.
2:3 been wandering around in this hill country long **e**;
2:14 old **e** to fight in battle had died in the wilderness.
3:26 'That's **e**!' he ordered. 'Speak of it no more.
17:12 Anyone arrogant **e** to reject the verdict of the judge
26:12 so that they will have **e** to eat in your towns.
Jos 5:4 because all the men who were old **e** to bear arms
5:6 old **e** to bear arms when they left Egypt had died.
15:19 You have been kind **e** to give me land in the
17:13 however, when the Israelites became strong **e**,
17:15 "If the hill country of Ephraim is not large **e** for
17:16 They said, "The hill country is not **e** for us,
22:17 Was our sin at Peor not **e**? We are not yet fully
Jdg 1:15 You have been kind **e** to give me land in the
21:14 But there were not **e** women for all of them.
21:22 for we didn't find **e** wives for them when we
Ru 3:14 but she got up before it was light **e** for people to
1Sa 2:36 among the priests so we will have **e** to eat.' "
6:12 And sure **e**, the cows went straight along the road
16:1 to Samuel, "You have mourned long **e** for Saul.
21:15 We already have **e** of them around here!
2Sa 7:27 I have been bold **e** to pray this prayer because you
12:8 And if that had not been **e**, I would have given you
18:14 "**E** of this nonsense," Joab said. Then he took
24:16 and said to the angel, "Stop! That is **e**!"
1Ki 11:3 And sure **e**, they led his heart away from the
16:31 And as though it were not **e** to live like Jeroboam,
17:13 Afterward there will still be **e** food for you
17:16 they used, there was always **e** left in the containers,
18:5 and valley to see if we can find **e** grass to save at
18:32 Then he dug a trench around the altar large **e** to
18:45 And sure **e**, the sky was soon black with clouds.
19:4 "I have had **e**, LORD," he said. "Take my life,
19:8 and the food gave him **e** strength to travel forty
20:10 if there remains **e** dust from Samaria to provide
20:36 And sure **e**, when he had gone, a lion attacked
21:19 Isn't killing Naboth bad **e**? Must you rob him,
22:25 "You will find out soon **e** when you find yourself
2Ki 2:22 And sure **e**! The water has remained wholesome
3:20 And sure **e**, the next day at about the time when the
4:7 and there will be **e** money left over to support you
4:17 But sure **e**, the woman soon became pregnant.
4:44 And sure **e**, there was plenty for all and some left
1Ch 17:25 I have been bold **e** to pray this prayer because you
21:15 and said to the death angel, "Stop! That is **e**!"
29:2 Now there is **e** gold, silver, bronze, iron, and wood,
2Ch 18:24 And Micaiah replied, "You will find out soon **e**,
28:15 and sandals to wear, gave them **e** food and drink,
30:3 but not **e** priests could be purified by that time,
31:10 we have had **e** to eat and plenty to spare,
Ne 4:2 build the wall in a day if they offer **e** sacrifices?
5:5 children into slavery just to get **e** money to live.
8:2 and all the children old **e** to understand.
10:28 to serve God, and who were old **e** to understand—
10:32 so that there will be **e** money to care for the
13:18 Wasn't it **e** that your ancestors did this sort of
Est 3:6 So he decided it was not **e** to lay hands on
Job 15:11 comfort too little for you? Is his gentle word not **e**?
24:5 the poor must spend all their time just getting **e** to
34:22 No darkness is thick **e** to hide the wicked from his
38:37 Who is wise **e** to count all the clouds? Who can tilt
Ps 33:16 a king, / nor is great strength **e** to save a warrior.
37:19 even in famine they will have more than **e**.
49:8 not come so easily, / for no one can ever pay **e**
106:2 of the LORD? / Who can ever praise him half **e**?
Pr 24:16 But one calamity is **e** to lay the wicked low.
26:24 with hate in their hearts may sound pleasant **e**,
27:27 And you will have **e** goats' milk for you,
29:19 For a servant, mere words are not **e**—discipline is
30:8 nor riches! Give me just **e** to satisfy my needs.
Ecc 5:10 Those who love money will never have **e**.
6:7 scratching for food, but they never seem to have **e**.
Isa 7:15 By the time this child is old **e** to eat curds
7:15 he will know **e** to choose what is right and reject
8:4 before this child is old **e** to say 'Papa' or 'Mama,'
28:9 Are we little children, barely old **e** to talk?
30:11 We have heard more than **e** about your 'Holy One
30:14 left that is big **e** to carry coals from a fireplace
40:13 Who knows **e** to be his teacher or counselor?
40:16 fuel to consume a sacrifice large **e** to honor him.
47:13 You have more than **e** advisers, astrologers,
51:17 You have drunk **e** from the cup of the LORD's
Jer 4:22 They are clever **e** at doing wrong, but they have no
9:12 Who is wise **e** to understand all this? Who has
23:18 the LORD well **e** to hear what he is saying? Has even one of them cared **e** to listen?
38:27 Sure **e**, it wasn't long before the king's officials
45:3 with trouble! Haven't I had **e** pain already?
La 5:6 to Egypt and Assyria to get **e** food to survive.
Eze 16:8 and saw you again, you were old **e** to be married.
16:20 Was it not **e** that you should be a prostitute?
16:28 too. It seems you can never find **e** new lovers!
17:9 I will pull it out easily **e**—it won't take a strong
19:11 very strong, / strong **e** to be a ruler's scepter.
19:14 is strong **e** to be a ruler's scepter.' This is a funeral
29:15 never again great **e** to rise above its neighbors.
30:21 up with a splint to make it strong **e** to hold a sword.
31:4 so abundant that there was **e** for all the trees
34:18 Is it not **e** for you to keep the best of the pastures
34:18 Is it not **e** for you to take the best water for
39:9 for fuel. There will be **e** to last them seven years!
44:6 O people of Israel, **e** of your disgusting sins!
45:9 **E**, you princes of Israel! Stop all your violence
Joel 2:19 and wine and olive oil, **e** to satisfy your needs.
3:3 and little girls for **e** wine to get drunk.
Am 2:15 The swiftest soldiers won't be fast **e** to escape.
4:8 another for a drink of water, but there was never **e**.
Jnh 4:9 "Yes," Jonah retorted, "even angry **e** to die!"
Mic 6:14 You will eat but never have **e**. Your hunger pangs
6:15 your olives but not get **e** oil to anoint yourselves.
Hag 1:6 You have food to eat, but not **e** to fill you up.
1:6 have wine to drink, but not **e** to satisfy your thirst.
1:6 have clothing to wear, but not **e** to keep you warm.
Zec 2:4 so full of people that it won't have room **e** for
10:10 and Lebanon. There won't be **e** room for them all!
Mal 3:10 so there will be **e** food in my Temple.
3:10 so great you won't have **e** room to take it in!
Mt 5:37 'Yes, I will,' or 'No, I won't.' Your word is **e**.
6:25 whether you have **e** food, drink, and clothes.
6:31 "So don't worry about having **e** food or drink
6:34 its own worries. Today's trouble is **e** for today.
7:5 then perhaps you will see well **e** to deal with the
9:13 not those who think they are already good **e**."
13:44 and sold everything he owned to get **e** money to
15:33 "And where would we get **e** food out here in the
17:20 "You didn't have **e** faith," Jesus told them.
25:4 but the other five were wise **e** to take along extra
25:9 the others replied, 'We don't have **e** for all of us.
26:41 For though the spirit is willing **e**, the body is
Mk 2:17 not those who think they are already good **e**."
5:4 the shackles. No one was strong **e** to control him.
8:4 "How are we supposed to find **e** food for them
14:38 For though the spirit is willing **e**, the body is
14:41 third time he said, "Still sleeping? Still resting? **E**!
Lk 5:32 with those who think they are already good **e**."
6:42 then perhaps you will see well **e** to deal with the
9:13 us to go and buy **e** food for this whole crowd?"
11:8 if you keep knocking long **e**, he will get up
12:18 Then I'll have room **e** to store everything.
12:19 you have **e** stored away for years to come.
12:22 whether you have **e** food to eat or clothes to wear.
14:28 then checking to see if there is **e** money to pay the
14:31 **e** to defeat the twenty thousand soldiers who are
15:17 'At home even the hired men have food **e** to spare,
19:25 master,' they said, 'that servant has **e** already!'
19:33 And sure **e**, as they were untying it, the owners
22:38 have two swords among us." "That's **e**," he said.
24:24 and sure **e**, Jesus' body was gone, just as the
Jn 3:2 Your miraculous signs are proof **e** that God is with
4:41 long **e** for many of them to hear his message
9:21 He is old **e** to speak for himself. Ask him."
9:23 why they said, "He is old **e** to speak for himself.
Ac 19:35 At last the mayor was able to quiet them down **e** to
Ro 4:14 and think they are "good **e**" in God's sight,
11:34 is thinking? Who knows **e** to be his counselor?
15:15 I have been bold **e** to emphasize some of these
1Co 4:11 and thirsty, without **e** clothes to keep us warm.
6:5 Isn't there anyone in all the church who is wise **e**
2Co 2:6 He was punished **e** when most of you were united
8:15 and those who gathered only a little had **e**.
11:9 when I was with you and didn't have **e** to live on,
11:21 I'm ashamed to say that we were not strong **e** to do
11:27 with cold, without **e** clothing to keep me warm.
1Ti 6:8 So if we have **e** food and clothing, let us be
Jas 1:21 in your hearts, for it is strong **e** to save your souls.
2:17 So you see, it isn't **e** just to have faith. Faith that
2:19 Do you still think it's **e** just to believe that there is
1Pe 4:3 You have had **e** in the past of the evil things that
1Jn 3:17 But if one of you has money **e** to live well and sees

ENQUIRE(D), ENQUIREST, ENQUIRY [KJV] See also ASKED, ASKING, CALL, CONSULT, DISCUSSING, FIND OUT, INQUIRE, INQUIRY, INQUIRING, LOOK, QUESTIONED, SOUGHT

ENRAGED (5) [RAGE]

Dt 19: 6 an e avenger might be able to chase down and kill
2Sa 17: 8 Right now they are probably as e as a mother bear
Isa 34: 2 For the LORD is e against the nations. His fury is
Mk 6:19 Herodias was e and wanted John killed in revenge,
Heb 10:29 and e the Holy Spirit who brings God's mercy to

ENRICH (1) [RICH]

Pr 31:11 can trust her, and she will greatly e his life.

ENRICHED (6) [RICH]

Job 15:34 Their homes, e through bribery, will be consumed
Isa 34: 7 will be soaked with blood and the soil e with fat.
Eze 27:33 at the ends of the earth / were e by your trade.
Ro 11:12 Now if the Gentiles were e because the Jews
1Co 1: 5 He has e your church with the gifts of eloquence
2Co 9:11 you will be e so that you can give even more

ENROLLED (1)

2Ch 17:14 His army was e according to ancestral clans.

ENSAMPLE [KJV] See EXAMPLE

ENSHRINED (1) [SHRINE]

Pr 14:33 Wisdom is e in an understanding heart; wisdom is

ENSLAVE (3) [SLAVE]

Isa 10: 6 Assyria will e my people, who are a godless
Jer 25:14 and great kings will e the Babylonians,
Am 8: 6 Then you e poor people for a debt of one piece of

ENSLAVED (10) [SLAVE]

Job 36: 8 come upon them and they are e and afflicted,
Isa 21: 2 and the groaning of all the nations she e will end.
42:22 they have been robbed, e, imprisoned, and trapped.
49:19 Your enemies who e you will be far away.
52: 5 asks the LORD. "Why are my people e again?
Jer 25:14 enslave the Babylonians, just as they e my people.
La 1: 3 has been led away into captivity, afflicted and e.
Eze 34:27 and rescued them from those who e them,
1Co 7:23 you at a high price. Don't be e by the world.
Gal 4:24 Sinai where people first became e to the law.

ENSLAVES (3) [SLAVE]

Ge 15:14 But I will punish the nation that e them, and in the
Ac 7: 7 'But I will punish the nation that e them,' God told
Ro 6:14 no longer subject to the law, which e you to sin.

ENSNARE (1) [SNARE]

Eze 13:20 which you use to e my people like birds.

ENSNARING (1) [SNARE]

Eze 13:18 Destruction is certain for you women who are e the

ENSURE (6)

Ge 7: 3 and a female in each pair to e that every kind of
33: 8 "They are gifts, my lord, to e your goodwill."
Nu 35:33 This will e that the land where you live will not be
Dt 17:20 This will e that he and his descendants will reign
Job 38:32 Can you e the proper sequence of the seasons
Pr 31: 8 e justice for those who are perishing.

ENTANGLES (1) [TANGLED]

Isa 8:14 people of Jerusalem he will be a trap that e them.

ENTER (151) [ENTERED, ENTERING, ENTERS, ENTRANCE, ENTRANCES, ENTRY, ENTRYWAY]

Ex 12:23 He will not permit the Destroyer to e and strike
28:43 whenever Aaron and his sons e the Tabernacle
40:32 Whenever they walked past the altar to e the
40:35 Moses was no longer able to e the Tabernacle
Lev 16: 2 "Warn your brother Aaron not to e the Most Holy
16:17 No one may e until he comes out again after
19:23 "When you e the land and plant fruit trees,
Nu 4: 5 and his sons must e the Tabernacle first to take
5:22 Now may this water that brings the curse e your
13:20 E the land boldly, and bring back samples of the
14:22 not one of these people will ever e that land.
14:23 those who have treated me with contempt will e it.
14:30 will e the land I swore to give you. The only
14:40 but now we are ready to e the land the LORD has
16: 5 The LORD will allow those who are chosen to e
16:40 should ever e the LORD's presence to burn
19:14 Those who e that tent, and those who were inside
20:24 He will not e the land I am giving the people of
Dt 1:37 said to me, 'You will never e the Promised Land!
1:38 into the land. Encourage him as he prepares to e it.
2:19 and e the land of Ammon. But do not bother the
4: 1 so you may e and occupy the land the LORD,
4: 5 when you arrive in the land you are about to e
4:14 you must obey in the land you are about to e
5:33 and prosperous lives in the land you are about to e
6: 1 you may obey them in the land you are about to e
6:18 Then you will e and occupy the good land that the
7: 1 God brings you into the land you are about to e
8: 1 and you will e and occupy the land the LORD
11: 8 to go in and occupy the land you are about to e.
11:10 For the land you are about to e and occupy is not
23: 8 from Egypt may e the assembly of the LORD.
23:20 in everything you do in the land you are about to e
24:10 do not e your neighbor's house to claim the
27: 2 and e the land the LORD your God is giving you,
27: 3 you will soon cross the river to e the land the
28:21 none of you are left in the land you are about to e
28:63 you disappear from the land you are about to e
29:12 You are standing here today to e into a covenant
30:16 and the land you are about to e and occupy.
32:52 but you may not e the land I am giving to the
34: 4 allowed you to see it, but you will not e the land."
Jos 5: 6 and the LORD vowed he would not let them e the
20: 4 They must allow the accused to e the city and live
2Sa 5: 8 "The blind and the lame may not e the house."
1Ki 14:12 "Go on home, and when you e the city, the child
2Ki 11:16 and led her out to the gate where horses e the
19:32 His armies will not e Jerusalem to shoot their
19:33 he came. He will not e this city, says the LORD.
2Ch 6:41 arise and e this resting place of yours,
7: 2 The priests could not even e the Temple of the
23: 6 and Levites on duty may e the Temple of the
23:15 and led her out to the gate where horses e the
27: 2 Jotham did not e the Temple of the LORD.
Ne 6:11 Should someone in my position e the Temple to
13: 1 or Moabite should ever be permitted to e the
Est 4: 2 for no one was allowed to e while wearing clothes
Ps 5: 7 Because of your unfailing love, I can e your house;
15: 1 Who may e your presence on your holy hill?
24: 6 They alone may e God's presence / and worship
24: 7 ancient doors, / and let the King of glory e.
24: 9 ancient doors, / and let the King of glory e.
45:15 as they e the king's palace!
84: 2 I faint with longing / to e the courts of the LORD.
95:11 a vow: / 'They will never e my place of rest.' "
100: 4 E his gates with thanksgiving; / go into his courts
101: 7 and liars will not be allowed to e my presence.
106:24 The people refused to e the pleasant land, / for they
118:19 Open for me the gates where the righteous e,
118:20 presence of the LORD, / and the godly e there.
132: 8 Arise, O LORD, and e your sanctuary,
Pr 2:10 For wisdom will e your heart, and knowledge will
Ecc 5: 1 As you e the house of God, keep your ears open
Isa 26: 2 to all who are righteous; / allow the faithful to e.
37:33 His armies will not e Jerusalem to shoot their
37:34 he came. He will not e this city, says the LORD.
38:10 of my life, / must I now e the place of the dead?
52: 1 and godless people will no longer e your gates.
60:18 and praise will be on the lips of all who e there.
Jer 33: 5 the Babylonians will still e. The men of this city
42:18 so they will be poured out on you when you e
La 1:10 the place the LORD had forbidden them to e.
Eze 20:38 are in exile, but they will never e the land of Israel.
44: 9 will e my sanctuary if they have not been
44:16 They are the ones who will e my sanctuary
44:17 When they e the gateway to the inner courtyard,
46: 2 The prince will e the foyer of the gateway from the
46: 8 "The prince must e the gateway through the foyer,
46:10 The prince will e and leave with the people on
46:12 to the inner courtyard will be opened for him to e,
Da 11: 7 and e the fortress of the king of the north
11:24 Without warning he will e the richest areas of the
11:41 He will e the glorious land of Israel, and many
Joel 2: 9 They e all the houses, climbing like thieves
Mic 5: 6 and e the gates of the land of Nimrod.
Mt 5:20 you can't e the Kingdom of Heaven at all!
7:13 "You can e God's Kingdom only through the
7:21 but they still won't e the Kingdom of Heaven.
10:11 Whenever you e a city or village, search for a
12:29 You can't e a strong man's house and rob him
12:45 than itself, and they all e the person and live there.
18: 8 It is better to e heaven crippled or lame than to be
18: 9 It is better to e heaven half blind than to have two
19:24 than for a rich person to e the Kingdom of God!"
23:13 For you won't let others e the Kingdom of Heaven,
Mk 1:45 Jesus that he couldn't e a town anywhere publicly.
3:27 You can't e a strong man's house and rob him
6:10 "When you e each village, be a guest in only one
9:25 to come out of this child and never e him again!"
9:43 It is better to e heaven with only one hand than to
9:45 It is better to e heaven with only one foot than to
9:47 It is better to e the Kingdom of God half blind than
10:25 than for a rich person to e the Kingdom of God!"
11: 2 he told them, "and as soon as you e it,
Lk 1: 9 he was chosen by lot to e the sanctuary and burn
8:32 and the demons pleaded with him to let them e into
9: 4 When you e each village, be a guest in only one
9: 5 village won't receive your message when you e it,
10: 5 "Whenever you e a home, give it your blessing.
10: 7 When you e a town, don't move around from home
11:26 than itself, and they all e the person and live there.
11:33 it is put on a lampstand to give light to all who e
11:52 You don't e the Kingdom yourselves, and you
13:24 Work hard to get in, because many will try to e,
18:25 than for a rich person to e the Kingdom of God!"
19:30 village over there," he told them, "and as you e it,
21:21 and those outside the city should not e it for
22:10 He replied, "As soon as you e Jerusalem, a man
Jn 3: 5 no one can e the Kingdom of God without being
12:23 "The time has come for the Son of Man to e into
13:31 the Son of Man, to e into my glory, and God will
18:15 so he was allowed to e the courtyard with Jesus.
Ac 3: 3 When he saw Peter and John about to e, he asked
14:22 reminding them that they must enter into the Kingdom
Gal 3:20 Now a mediator is needed if two people e into an
Heb 3:11 a vow: / 'They will never e my place of rest.' "
3:18 he vowed that they would never e his place of rest?
3:19 So we see that they were not allowed to e his rest
4: 3 For only we who believe can e his place of rest.
4: 3 'They will never e my place of rest,' " even
4: 5 God said, "They will never e my place of rest."
4: 6 So God's rest is there for people to e. But those
4: 6 who formerly heard the Good News failed to e
4:10 For all who e into God's rest will find rest from
4:11 Let us do our best to e that place of rest.
9:25 Nor did he e heaven to offer himself again
10:19 we can boldly e heaven's Most Holy Place
2Pe 1:11 for you to e into the eternal Kingdom of our Lord
Rev 15: 8 No one could e the Temple until the seven angels
21:27 Nothing evil will be allowed to e—no one who
22:14 so they can e through the gates of the city and eat

ENTERED (57) [ENTER]

Ge 34:25 took their swords, e the town without opposition,
41:46 He was thirty years old when he e the service of
Ex 6: 4 And I e into a solemn covenant with them.
20:21 Moses e into the deep darkness where God was.
Lev 16:23 garments he wore when he e the Most Holy Place,
25: 2 When you have e the land I am giving you as an
Dt 31:21 even before they have e the land I swore to give
Jdg 18:17 the five spies e the shrine and took the carved
1Sa 9: 5 Finally, they e the region of Zuph, and Saul said to
9:14 So they e the town, and as they passed through the
2Sa 6:16 But as the Ark of the LORD e the City of David,
2Ki 6:20 As soon as they had e Samaria, Elisha prayed,
9:31 When Jehu e the gate of the palace, she shouted at
21: 9 had destroyed when the Israelites e the land.
1Ch 15:29 But as the Ark of the LORD's covenant e the City
2Ch 15:12 Then they e into a covenant to seek the LORD,
15:15 for they had e into it with all their hearts.
32:21 And when he e the temple of his god, some of his
33: 9 had destroyed when the Israelites e the land.
Ne 2:15 I turned back and e again at the Valley Gate.
Est 5: 1 her royal robes and e the inner court of the palace,
Jer 9:21 in through our windows and has e our mansions.
Eze 26:20 like those in the pit who have e the world of the
37:10 and the wind e the bodies, and they began to
42: 1 We e the outer courtyard and came to a group of
44: 2 for the LORD, the God of Israel, e here.
46: 9 And those who e through the south gateway must
46:12 Then he will turn and leave the way he e,
Jnh 3: 4 On the day Jonah e the city, he shouted to the
Na 2: 6 The river gates are open! The enemy has e!
Mt 2:11 They e the house where the child and his mother,
8:32 So the demons came out of the men and e the pigs,
21:10 The entire city of Jerusalem was stirred as he e.
21:12 Jesus e the Temple and began to drive out the
24:38 and weddings right up to the time Noah e his boat.
Mk 5:13 the evil spirits came out of the man and e the pigs,
11:15 Jesus e the Temple and began to drive out the
16: 5 So they e the tomb, and there on the right sat a
Lk 1:40 She e the house and greeted Elizabeth.
7:44 When I e your home, you didn't offer me water to
8:33 So the demons came out of the man and e the pigs,
17:12 As he e a village there, ten lepers stood at a
17:27 and weddings right up to the time Noah e his boat
19: 1 Jesus e Jericho and made his way through the
19:45 Then Jesus e the Temple and began to drive out the
22: 3 Then Satan e into Judas Iscariot, who was one of
Jn 7:39 because Jesus had not yet e into his glory.)
12:16 But after Jesus e into his glory, they remembered
13:27 as Judas had eaten the bread, Satan e into him.
18: 1 with his disciples and e a grove of olive trees.
Ac 5:21 So the apostles e the Temple about daybreak
10:25 As Peter e his home, Cornelius fell to the floor
11: 3 "You e the home of Gentiles and even ate with
Ro 5:12 When Adam sinned, sin e the entire human race.
Heb 9:11 He has e that great, perfect sanctuary in heaven,
9:24 For Christ has e into heaven itself to appear now
Rev 11:11 and a half days, the spirit of life from God e them,

ENTERING (16) [ENTER]

Nu 32: 9 they discouraged the people of Israel from e the
Jos 14: 8 and discouraged them from e the Promised Land.
2Sa 17:17 so as not to be seen e and leaving the city.
1Ki 15:17 fortified Ramah in order to prevent anyone from e
2Ch 16: 1 fortified Ramah in order to prevent anyone from e
23:19 keep those who were ceremonially unclean from e.
26:16 He sinned against the LORD his God by e the
Pr 2:18 E her house leads to death; it is the road to hell.
Eze 42:14 They must put on other clothes before e the parts
44:21 The priests must never drink wine before e the
Lk 8:16 where they can be seen by those e the house.
11:52 and you prevent others from e."
24:26 suffer all these things before e his time of glory?"
Ac 19:31 begging him not to risk his life by e the
Heb 4: 1 God's promise of e his place of rest still stands,
4: 7 So God set another time for e his place of rest,

ENTERS (15) [ENTER]

Ex 28:35 Aaron will wear this robe whenever he e the Holy
Lev 14:46 Anyone who e the house while it is closed will be
16: 3 "When Aaron e the sanctuary area, he must follow
16:23 "As Aaron e the Tabernacle, he must take off the
1Sa 5: 5 e the temple of Dagon will step on its threshold.
1Ki 17: 3 at a place east of where it e the Jordan River.

2Ki 23: 8 located to the left of the city gate as one **e** the city.
2Ch 23: 7 Any unauthorized person who **e** the Temple must
Job 24:18 they own is cursed, so that no one **e** their vineyard.
Eze 44:27 and **e** the inner courtyard and the sanctuary,
47: 8 into the Jordan Valley, where it **e** the Dead Sea.
Mk 14:14 At the house he **e**, say to the owner, 'The Teacher
Lk 22:10 will meet you. Follow him. At the house he **e**,
Jn 10: 2 For a shepherd **e** through the gate.
Heb 9:25 like the earthly high priest who **e** the Most Holy

ENTERTAINED (3) [ENTERTAINMENT]

2Sa 3:20 his twenty men, David **e** them with a great feast.
Ps 45: 8 with ivory, / you are **e** by the music of harps.
Heb 13: 2 for some who have done this have **e** angels without

ENTERTAINING (1) [ENTERTAINMENT]

Eze 33:32 You are very **e** to them, like someone who sings

ENTERTAINMENT (1) [ENTERTAINING, ENTERTAINED]

Da 6:18 He refused his usual **e** and couldn't sleep at all that

ENTHRONED (8) [THRONE]

1Sa 4: 4 LORD Almighty, who is **e** between the cherubim.
2Sa 6: 2 LORD Almighty, who is **e** between the cherubim.
2Ki 19:15 of Israel, you are **e** between the mighty cherubim!
1Ch 13: 6 which bears the name of the LORD who is **e**
Ps 80: 1 O God, **e** above the cherubim, / display your
113: 5 with the LORD our God, / who is **e** on high?
123: 1 I lift my eyes to you, / O God, **e** in heaven.
Isa 37:16 of Israel, you are **e** between the mighty cherubim!

ENTHUSIASM (8) [ENTHUSIASTIC, ENTHUSIASTICALLY]

Dt 28:47 and **e** for the abundant benefits you have received,
Hag 1:14 So the LORD sparked the **e** of Zerubbabel son of
Ac 18:25 and talked to others with great **e** and accuracy
Ro 10: 2 I know what **e** they have for God, but it is
2Co 8: 7 such gifted speakers, such knowledge, such **e**,
8:16 he has given Titus the same **e** for you that I have.
9: 2 it was your **e** that stirred up many of them to begin
Eph 6: 7 Work with **e**, as though you were working for the

ENTHUSIASTIC (5) [ENTHUSIASM]

Ps 45:15 What a joyful, **e** procession / as they enter the
Mk 11:18 the people were so **e** about Jesus' teaching.
Ro 15:17 So it is right for me to be **e** about all Christ Jesus
1Co 15:58 and steady, always **e** about the Lord's work,
2Co 8:22 He is now even more **e** because of his increased

ENTHUSIASTICALLY (2) [ENTHUSIASM]

Ro 12:11 Never be lazy in your work, but serve the Lord **e**.
2Co 8:11 through to completion just as **e** as you began it.

ENTICE (3) [ENTICED, ENTICEMENT]

1Ki 22:20 'Who can **e** Ahab to go into battle against
2Ch 18:19 'Who can **e** King Ahab of Israel to go into battle
Pr 1:10 My child, if sinners **e** you, turn your back on them!

ENTICED (5) [ENTICE]

2Ch 18: 2 Then Ahab **e** Jehoshaphat to join forces with him
Job 31:27 and been secretly **e** in my heart to worship them?
Pr 7:21 with her pretty speech. With her flattery she **e** him.
Na 3: 4 of deadly charms, **e** the nations with her beauty.
Jn 13: 2 and the Devil had already **e** Judas, son of Simon

ENTICEMENT (1) [ENTICE]

Isa 33:15 who shut their eyes to all **e** to do wrong.

ENTIRE (254) [ENTIRELY]

Ge 2:11 which flows around the **e** land of Havilah,
2:13 the Gihon, which flows around the **e** land of Cush.
18:26 in Sodom, I will spare the **e** city for their sake."
19:31 "There isn't a man anywhere in this **e** area for us
20: 7 be sure that you and your **e** household will die."
39: 4 Potiphar soon put Joseph in charge of his **e**
39: 8 "my master trusts me with everything in his **e**
41:41 "I hereby put you in charge of the **e** land of
41:44 or a foot in the **e** land of Egypt without your
41:45 So Joseph took charge of the **e** land of Egypt.
45: 8 manager of his **e** household and ruler over all
46: 6 Jacob and his **e** family arrived in Egypt—
50: 8 took his brothers and the **e** household of Jacob.
Ex 7:25 An **e** week passed from the time the LORD
8: 2 I will send vast hordes of frogs across your **e** land
8:17 Suddenly, gnats infested the **e** land,
10:22 and there was deep darkness over the **e** land for
12: 4 If a family is too small to eat an **e** lamb, let them
14:28 and charioteers—the **e** army of Pharaoh.
16: 9 to Aaron, "Say this to the **e** community of Israel:
25:31 The **e** lampstand and its decorations will be one
27:18 So the **e** courtyard will be 150 feet long and 75 feet
30: 3 and run a gold molding around the **e** altar.
35:11 the **e** Tabernacle, including the sacred tent and its
37:24 The **e** lampstand, along with its accessories,
39:33 And they brought the **e** Tabernacle to Moses:
Lev 1: 9 Then the priests will burn the **e** sacrifice on the
1:13 Then the priests will burn the **e** sacrifice on the
3: 9 This includes the fat of the **e** tail cut off near the
4: 3 priest sins, bringing guilt upon the **e** community,
4:13 "If the **e** Israelite community does something
4:21 This is a sin offering for the **e** community of Israel.
8: 3 Then call the **e** community of Israel to meet you
8:21 Moses burned the **e** ram on the altar as a whole
13:13 person to see if the disease covers the **e** body.
14:41 Next the inside walls of the **e** house must be
15:16 an emission of semen, he must wash his **e** body,
16: 4 Then he must wash his **e** body and put on his linen
16:16 and he will do the same for the **e** Tabernacle,
16:24 Then he must bathe his **e** body with water in a
16:33 the altar, the priests, and the **e** community.
18:25 As a result, the **e** land has become defiled. That is
19: 2 "Say this to the **e** community of Israel: You must
19:24 In the fourth year the **e** crop will be devoted to the
22:30 Eat the **e** sacrificial animal on the day it is
23:28 Do no work during that **e** day because it is the Day
24:14 Then let the **e** community stone him to death.
25: 4 or prune your vineyards during that **e** year.
27:17 Year of Jubilee, then the **e** assessment will apply.
Nu 4:16 the supervision of the **e** Tabernacle and everything
5:30 and the priest will apply this **e** ritual law to her.
6: 6 And they may not go near a dead body during the **e**
8: 4 The **e** lampstand, from its base to its decorative
8: 7 And have them shave their **e** body and wash their
12: 7 servant Moses. He is entrusted with my **e** house.
15:26 for the **e** population was involved in the sin.
16:19 Korah had stirred up the **e** community against
18:21 Tabernacle with the tithes from the **e** land of Israel.
20: 8 must take the staff and assemble the **e** community.
21:23 he mobilized his **e** army and attacked Israel in the
21:34 I have given you victory over Og and his **e** army,
26: 3 At that time the **e** nation of Israel was camped on
26:10 This served as a warning to the **e** nation of Israel.
27: 2 and the **e** community at the entrance of the
32:15 you will be responsible for destroying this **e**
Dt 1:35 'Not one of you from this **e** wicked generation will
3: 2 over Og and his army, giving you his **e** land.
3: 4 the **e** Argob region in his kingdom of Bashan.
13:16 Put the **e** town to the torch as a burnt offering to
31:24 When Moses had finished writing down this **e**
31:30 So Moses recited this **e** song to the assembly of
34:11 against Pharaoh, all his servants, and his **e** land.
Jos 5: 3 and circumcised the **e** male population of Israel at
6: 3 Your **e** army is to march around the city once a day
8: 1 Take the **e** army and attack Ai, for I have given to
8:25 So the **e** population of Ai was wiped out that day—
8:35 Moses had ever given was read to the **e** assembly,
9:21 and carry the water for the **e** community."
9:24 instructed his servant Moses to conquer this **e** land
10: 7 So Joshua and the **e** Israelite army left Gilgal
10:32 Here, too, the **e** population was slaughtered,
10:33 Joshua's men killed him and destroyed his **e** army.
10:37 they completely destroyed the **e** population.
11:16 So Joshua conquered the **e** region—the hill
11:21 Anab, and the **e** hill country of Judah and Israel.
11:23 So Joshua took control of the **e** land, just as the
13:21 the towns of the plain and the **e** kingdom of Sihon.
18: 1 the **e** Israelite assembly gathered at Shiloh and set
18: 9 and mapped the **e** territory into seven sections,
22:17 even after the plague that struck the **e** assembly of
Jdg 6:15 of Manasseh, and I am the least in my **e** family!"
8: 2 better than the **e** crop of my little clan of Abiezer?
9:51 inside the city, and the **e** population fled to it.
16:30 when he died than he had during his **e** lifetime.
18:19 Isn't it better to be a priest for an **e** tribe of Israel
20: 7 the **e** community of Israel must decide what should
21:17 so that an **e** tribe of Israel will not be lost forever.
Ru 1:19 the **e** town was stirred by their arrival.
2:21 and stay with his harvesters until the **e** harvest is
1Sa 1:11 He will be yours for his **e** lifetime, and as a sign
1:19 The **e** family got up early the next morning
9: 4 the Shaalim area, and the **e** land of Benjamin,
13: 4 So the **e** Israelite army mobilized again and met
15: 3 and completely destroy the **e** Amalekite nation—
22:16 surely die, Ahimelech, along with your **e** family!"
23: 8 So Saul mobilized his **e** army to march to Keilah
25:28 And you have not done wrong throughout your **e**
28:19 The LORD will bring the **e** army of Israel down
29: 1 The **e** Philistine army now mobilized at Aphek,
30:17 that night and the **e** next day until evening.
2Sa 1: 4 The man replied, "Our **e** army fled. Many men are
3:12 and I will help turn the **e** nation of Israel over to
4: 8 has given you revenge on Saul and his **e** family!"
6:11 and the LORD blessed him and his **e** household.
10: 7 he sent Joab and the **e** Israelite army to fight them.
17:11 "I suggest that you mobilize the **e** army of Israel,
17:13 you will have the **e** army of Israel there at your
17:16 Otherwise he will die and his **e** army with him."
17:24 Absalom had mobilized the **e** army of Israel
21:10 on a rock and stayed there the **e** harvest season.
23: 9 the Philistines when the **e** Israelite army had fled.
24: 8 Having gone through the **e** land, they completed
1Ki 4:24 And there was peace throughout the **e** land.
6: 3 running across the **e** width of the Temple.
6: 7 so the **e** structure was built without the sound of
6:15 The **e** inside, from floor to ceiling, was paneled
6:22 So he finished overlaying the **e** Temple with gold,
6:38 The **e** building was completed in every detail by
8: 5 and the **e** community of Israel sacrificed sheep
8:14 Then the king turned around to the **e** community of
8:22 the LORD in front of the **e** community of Israel.
8:55 and shouted this blessing over the **e** community of
9:19 and Lebanon and throughout the **e** realm.
11:34 " 'But I will not take the **e** kingdom from
14:13 the God of Israel, sees in the **e** family of Jeroboam.
16:11 Zimri immediately killed the **e** royal family of
20:20 and suddenly the **e** Aramean army panicked
2Ki 5:15 and his **e** party went back to find the man of God.
6:24 King Ben-hadad of Aram mobilized his **e** army
9: 8 The **e** family of Ahab must be wiped out—
13:22 Israel during the **e** reign of King Jehoahaz.
15:16 He killed the **e** population and ripped open the
15:18 During his **e** reign, he refused to turn from the sins
17: 5 Then the king of Assyria invaded the **e** land,
18:23 If you can find two thousand horsemen in your **e**
23: 2 There the king read to them the **e** Book of the
24: 7 for the king of Babylon occupied the **e** area
25: 1 King Nebuchadnezzar of Babylon led his **e** army
25:10 Then the captain of the guard supervised the **e**
1Ch 13: 2 Then he addressed the **e** assembly of Israel as
13:14 and the LORD blessed him and his **e** household.
28:21 the leaders and the **e** nation are at your command."
29: 1 Then King David turned to the **e** assembly
29:20 And the **e** assembly praised the LORD, the God
29:25 so the **e** nation of Israel stood in awe of him,
2Ch 1: 3 Then Solomon led the **e** assembly to the hill at
3: 4 running across the **e** width of the Temple.
5: 6 and the **e** community of Israel sacrificed sheep
6: 3 Then the king turned around to the **e** community of
6:12 the LORD in front of the **e** community of Israel.
6:13 He stood on the platform before the **e** assembly,
8: 6 and Lebanon and throughout the **e** realm.
26:14 Uzziah provided the **e** army with shields, spears,
29:17 So the **e** task was completed in sixteen days.
29:28 The **e** assembly worshiped the LORD as the
30:23 The **e** assembly then decided to continue the
30:25 The **e** assembly of Judah rejoiced,
34:30 There the king read to them the **e** Book of the
34:33 So Josiah removed all detestable idols from the **e**
35:16 The **e** ceremony for the LORD's Passover was
Ezr 4: 5 This went on during the **e** reign of King Cyrus of
4:20 and the **e** province west of the Euphrates River
Ne 4: 6 to half its original height around the **e** city,
5:14 I would like to mention that for the **e** twelve years
Est 3: 6 he decided to destroy all the Jews throughout the **e**
Job 1: 3 He was, in fact, the richest person in that **e** area.
Ps 14: 2 looks down from heaven / on the **e** human race;
35:18 Then I will thank you in front of the **e**
39: 5 An **e** lifetime is just a moment to you;
53: 2 looks down from heaven / on the **e** human race;
109:11 May creditors seize his **e** estate, / and strangers
112: 2 an **e** generation of godly people will be blessed.
Isa 6: 4 and the **e** sanctuary was filled with smoke.
6:12 distant lands and the **e** land of Israel lies deserted.
7:24 The **e** land will be one vast brier patch, a hunting
16: 7 The **e** land of Moab weeps. Yes, you people of
36: 8 If you can find two thousand horsemen in your **e**
41: 2 He puts **e** armies to the sword. He scatters them in
Jer 3: 2 Is there anywhere in the **e** land where you have not
20:18 My **e** life has been filled with trouble, sorrow,
23:34 I will punish that person along with his **e** family.
25:11 This **e** land will become a desolate wasteland.
26: 2 Give them my **e** message; include every word.
31:40 And the **e** area—including the graveyard and ash
37:10 Even if you were to destroy the **e** Babylonian
48:45 to devour the **e** land with all its rebellious people.
52: 4 King Nebuchadnezzar of Babylon led his **e** army
52:14 Then the captain of the guard supervised the **e**
Eze 9: 9 The **e** land is full of murder; the city is filled with
32:31 that he is not alone in having his **e** army killed,
33:24 and yet he gained possession of the **e** land!
40:13 Then he measured the **e** width of the gateway,
42: 4 It extended the **e** 175 feet of the complex, and all
42:15 the east gateway to measure the **e** Temple area.
43:12 The **e** top of the hill where the Temple is built is
45: 1 6-2/3 miles wide. The **e** area will be holy ground.
48:20 This **e** area—including the sacred lands
48:23 and it extends across the **e** land of Israel from east
48:35 "The distance around the **e** city will be six miles.
Da 1:20 all the magicians and enchanters in his **e** kingdom.
6: 3 the king made plans to place him over the **e**
11:17 He will make plans to come with the might of his **e**
Am 3: 1 and Judah—the **e** family I rescued from Egypt:
7: 4 the depths of the sea and was devouring the **e** land.
Zec 5: 3 contains the curse that is going out over the **e** land.
Mt 8:34 The **e** town came out to meet Jesus, but they
9:26 The report of this miracle swept through the **e**
21:10 The **e** city of Jerusalem was stirred as he entered.
24:22 is shortened, the **e** human race will be destroyed.
24:27 For as the lightning lights up the **e** sky, so it will be
26:59 and the **e** high council were trying to find
27:27 their headquarters and called out the **e** battalion.
Mk 1:28 done spread quickly through that **e** area of Galilee.
5:13 and the **e** herd of two thousand pigs plunged down
13:20 of calamity, the **e** human race will be destroyed.
14:55 and the **e** high council were trying to find
15: 1 the **e** high council—met to discuss their next step.
15:16 their headquarters and called out the **e** battalion.
Lk 23: 1 Then the **e** council took Jesus over to Pilate,
Jn 4:53 the officer and his **e** household believed in Jesus.
11:51 This prophecy that Jesus should die for the **e** nation
Ac 5:11 Great fear gripped the **e** church and all others who
10: 2 feared the God of Israel, as did his **e** household.
11:28 great famine was coming upon the **e** Roman world.
13: 6 the **e** island until finally they reached Paphos,
13:44 The following week almost the **e** city turned out to
16:31 you will be saved, along with your **e** household."
16:34 He and his **e** household rejoiced because they all
19:26 here in Ephesus but throughout the **e** province!
21: 5 the **e** congregation, including wives and children,
Ro 3:19 and to bring the **e** world into judgment before God.
5:12 When Adam sinned, sin entered the **e** human race.
1Co 4: 9 We have become a spectacle to the **e** world—
12: 7 to each of us as a means of helping the **e** church.
14: 4 a word of prophecy strengthens the **e** church.

2Co 2: 5 trouble hurt your **e** church more than he hurt me.
Eph 4: 10 so that his rule might fill the **e** universe.
Heb 3: 2 and was entrusted with God's **e** house.
3: 6 the faithful Son, was in charge of the **e** household.
9: 8 and the **e** system it represents were still in use.
11: 3 By faith we understand that the **e** universe was
Jas 2: 11 if you murder someone, you have broken the **e** law,
3: 6 It can turn the **e** course of your life into a blazing
Rev 19: 21 Their **e** army was killed by the sharp sword that

ENTIRELY (18) [ENTIRE]

Ex 28: 31 "Make the robe of the ephod **e** of blue cloth,
30: 29 Sanctify them to make them **e** holy. After this,
39: 22 The robe of the ephod was woven **e** of blue yarn,
Lev 6: 23 All such grain offerings of the priests must be **e**
1Sa 13: 6 they lost their nerve **e** and tried to hide in caves,
1Ki 7: 9 All these buildings were built **e** from huge,
2Ki 13: 19 have beaten Aram until they were **e** destroyed.
25: 3 very severe, with the last of the food **e** gone.
Ps 119: 138 decrees are perfect; / they are **e** worthy of our trust.
Isa 48: 8 "Yes, I will tell you of things that are **e** new,
Jer 52: 6 very severe, with the last of the food **e** gone.
Jn 13: 10 not need to wash, except for the feet, to be **e** clean.
17: 19 And I give myself **e** to you so they also might be
17: 19 entirely to you so they also might be **e** yours.
Ro 3: 25 God was being **e** fair and just when he did not
3: 26 And he is **e** fair and just in this present time when
Tit 2: 10 but they must show themselves to be **e** trustworthy
Heb 12: 5 And have you **e** forgotten the encouraging words

ENTRANCE (149) [ENTER]

Ge 18: 1 as Abraham was sitting at the **e** to his tent,
19: 1 That evening the two angels came to the **e** of the
38: 14 Then she sat beside the road at the **e** to the village
38: 21 was sitting beside the road at the **e** to the village?"
43: 19 As the brothers arrived at the **e** to the palace,
Ex 26: 9 set is to be doubled over at the **e** of the sacred tent.
26: 36 "Make another curtain from fine linen for the **e** of
27: 14 The courtyard **e** will be on the east end, flanked by
27: 16 "For the **e** to the courtyard, make a curtain that is
29: 3 and present them at the **e** of the Tabernacle,
29: 4 and his sons at the **e** of the Tabernacle,
29: 10 "Then bring the young bull to the **e** of the
29: 11 then slaughter it in the LORD's presence at the **e**
29: 32 with the bread in the basket, at the Tabernacle **e**.
29: 42 it in the LORD's presence at the Tabernacle **e**,
32: 26 he stood at the **e** to the camp and shouted, "All of
33: 9 and hover at the **e** while the LORD spoke with
35: 15 the curtain for the **e** of the Tabernacle;
35: 17 their bases; the curtain for the **e** to the courtyard;
36: 37 Then they made another curtain for the **e** to the
38: 8 the women who served at the **e** of the Tabernacle.
38: 14 The courtyard **e** was on the east side, flanked by
38: 18 The curtain that covered the **e** to the courtyard was
38: 30 the bases for the posts at the **e** to the Tabernacle,
38: 31 the bases for the curtain at the **e** of the courtyard,
39: 38 the curtain for the **e** of the sacred tent;
39: 40 the curtain at the courtyard **e**; the cords and tent
40: 5 Set up the curtain made for the **e** of the Tabernacle.
40: 6 altar of burnt offering in front of the Tabernacle **e**.
40: 8 the tent, and hang the curtain for the courtyard **e**.
40: 12 and his sons to the **e** of the Tabernacle,
40: 28 He attached the curtain at the **e** of the Tabernacle,
40: 29 the altar of burnt offering near the Tabernacle **e**.
40: 33 And he set up the curtain at the **e** of the courtyard.
Lev 1: 3 bring a bull with no physical defects to the **e** of the
3: 2 and slaughter it at the **e** of the Tabernacle.
3: 8 and slaughtering it at the **e** of the Tabernacle.
3: 13 its head, and slaughter it at the **e** of the Tabernacle.
4: 4 He must present the bull to the LORD at the **e** of
4: 7 altar of burnt offerings at the **e** of the Tabernacle.
4: 14 and present it at the **e** of the Tabernacle.
4: 18 altar of burnt offerings at the **e** of the Tabernacle.
8: 3 to the **e** of the Tabernacle. Then call the entire
8: 4 and all the people assembled at the Tabernacle **e**.
8: 31 "Boil the rest of the meat at the Tabernacle **e**,
8: 33 Do not leave the Tabernacle **e** for seven days,
8: 35 you must stay at the **e** of the Tabernacle day
9: 5 So the people brought all of these things to the **e** of
10: 7 But you are not to leave the **e** of the Tabernacle,
12: 6 She must take her offerings to the priest at the **e** of
14: 11 before the LORD at the **e** of the Tabernacle.
14: 23 in the LORD's presence at the Tabernacle **e**.
15: 14 and present himself to the LORD at the **e** of the
15: 29 and present them to the priest at the **e** of the
16: 7 and present them to the LORD at the **e** of the
17: 4 and does not bring it to the **e** of the Tabernacle to
17: 5 sacrifices to the priest at the **e** of the Tabernacle,
17: 6 and burn the fat on the LORD's altar at the **e** of
17: 9 and do not bring it to the **e** of the Tabernacle to
19: 21 and present it to the LORD at the **e** of the
Nu 3: 26 and altar, the curtain at the courtyard **e**,
4: 25 and the curtain for the Tabernacle **e**.
4: 26 and altar, the curtain across the courtyard **e**,
6: 10 or two young pigeons to the priest at the **e** of the
6: 13 they must each go to the **e** of the Tabernacle
6: 18 "Then the Nazirites will shave their hair at the **e** of
8: 9 and present the Levites at the **e** of the Tabernacle.
10: 3 are to gather before you at the **e** of the Tabernacle.
12: 5 pillar of cloud and stood at the **e** of the Tabernacle.
16: 18 and stood at the **e** of the Tabernacle with Moses
16: 19 and they all assembled at the Tabernacle **e**.
16: 43 Aaron came and stood at the **e** of the Tabernacle,
16: 50 Aaron returned to Moses at the **e** of the
20: 6 the people and went to the **e** of the Tabernacle,
25: 6 as they were weeping at the **e** of the Tabernacle.
27: 2 and the entire community at the **e** of the
Dt 31: 15 them in a pillar of cloud at the **e** to the sacred tent.
Jos 10: 18 and place guards at the **e** to keep the kings inside.
19: 51 of the LORD at the **e** of the Tabernacle at Shiloh.
Jdg 9: 52 the tower. But as he prepared to set fire to the **e**,
1Sa 1: 9 was sitting at his customary place beside the **e**.
2: 22 women who assisted at the **e** of the Tabernacle.
2Sa 10: 8 drew up their battle lines at the **e** of the city gates,
11: 9 He stayed that night at the palace **e** with some of
11: 13 go home to his wife. Again he slept at the palace **e**.
1Ki 6: 8 The **e** to the bottom floor was on the south side of
6: 21 and he made gold chains to protect the **e** to the
6: 31 For the **e** to the inner sanctuary, Solomon made
6: 33 doorposts of olive wood for the **e** to the Temple.
7: 12 courtyard of the LORD's Temple with its **e** foyer.
7: 21 Huram set the pillars at the **e** of the Temple,
8: 8 seen from the front **e** of the Temple's main room—
18: 46 of Ahab's chariot all the way to the **e** of Jezreel.
19: 13 and went out and stood at the **e** of the cave.
2Ki 7: 3 men with leprosy sitting at the **e** of the city gates.
10: 8 "Pile them in two heaps at the **e** of the city gate,
12: 9 and set it on the right-hand side of the altar at the **e**
12: 9 The priests guarding the **e** put all of the people's
16: 14 which had stood between the **e** and the new altar,
16: 18 as well as the king's outer **e** to the Temple of the
23: 8 He destroyed the shrines at the **e** to the gate of
23: 11 He removed from the **e** of the LORD's Temple
1Ch 9: 19 were responsible for guarding the **e** to the
9: 21 responsible for guarding the **e** to the Tabernacle.
9: 23 were responsible for guarding the **e** to the house of
2Ch 3: 14 Across the **e** of the Most Holy Place,
3: 17 Then he set up the two pillars at the **e** of the
3: 17 one to the south of the **e** and the other to the north.
5: 9 seen from the front **e** of the Temple's main room—
23: 13 his place of authority by the pillar at the Temple **e**.
Est 5: 1 king was sitting on his royal throne, facing the **e**.
Ps 74: 5 They chopped down the **e** / like woodcutters in a
Pr 8: 3 At the **e** to the city, at the city gates, she cries
Jer 7: 2 "Go to the **e** of the LORD's Temple, and give
19: 2 the son of Hinnom by the **e** to the Potsherd Gate,
36: 10 courtyard of the Temple, near the New Gate **e**.
38: 14 to meet him at the third **e** of the LORD's Temple.
43: 9 at the **e** of Pharaoh's palace here in Tahpanhes.
Eze 8: 5 to the north, beside the **e** to the gate of the altar,
8: 16 At the **e**, between the foyer and the bronze altar,
9: 3 it had rested, and moved to the **e** of the Temple.
40: 3 shone like bronze standing beside a gateway **e**.
40: 11 The man measured the gateway **e**, which was
40: 18 the courtyard the same distance as the gateway **e**.
40: 22 were seven steps leading up to the gateway **e**,
40: 31 and there were eight steps leading up to its **e**.
40: 34 and there were eight steps leading to its **e**.
40: 37 There were eight steps leading to its **e**.
40: 40 on each side of the stairs going up to the north **e**,
40: 48 The **e** was 24-1/2 feet wide with walls 5-1/4 feet
41: 2 The **e** was 17-1/2 feet wide, and the walls on each
41: 3 He measured the columns at the **e** and found them
41: 3 The **e** was 10-1/2 feet wide, and the walls on each
41: 3 and the walls on each side of the **e** extended 12-1/4
41: 21 There were square columns at the **e** to the Holy
41: 21 and the ones at the **e** of the Most Holy Place were
42: 2 whose **e** opened toward the north, was 175 feet
42: 9 There was an **e** from the outer courtyard to these
42: 12 So there was an **e** in the wall facing the doors of
45: 19 and the gateposts at the **e** to the inner courtyard.
46: 19 Then the man brought me through the **e** beside the
47: 1 Then the man brought me back to the **e** of the
47: 2 north gateway and led me around to the eastern **e**.
Mt 27: 60 Then he rolled a great stone across the **e** as he left.
Mk 15: 46 of the rock. Then he rolled a stone in front of the **e**.
16: 3 would roll the stone away from the **e** to the tomb.
Lk 24: 2 They found that the stone covering the **e** had been
Jn 11: 38 It was a cave with a stone rolled across its **e**.
20: 1 that the stone had been rolled away from the **e**.

ENTRANCES (8) [ENTER]

Ex 33: 8 the people would get up and stand in their tent **e**.
33: 10 the people would stand and bow low at their tent **e**.
Nu 16: 27 and stood at the **e** of their tents with their wives
1Ki 7: 50 the doors for the **e** to the Most Holy Place
2Ch 4: 9 He made doors for the courtyard **e** and overlaid
4: 22 the doors for the **e** to the Most Holy Place
Eze 42: 11 as the other one, and it had the same **e** and doors.
43: 11 including its **e** and doors—and everything else

ENTREAT (1)

Ps 45: 12 People of great wealth will **e** your favor.

ENTRIES, ENTRY [KJV] See also DOOR(S), ENTRANCE(S), GATEWAY(S)

ENTRUST (5) [TRUST]

2Ki 22: 5 **E** this money to the men assigned to supervise the
Ps 31: 5 I **e** my spirit into your hand. / Rescue me, LORD,
Isa 8: 16 I will **e** it to my disciples, who will pass it down to
Lk 23: 46 "Father, I **e** my spirit into your hands!"
Ac 20: 32 "And now I **e** you to God and the word of his

ENTRUSTED (20) [TRUST]

Ge 39: 4 and **e** him with all his business dealings.
Lev 6: 2 that an item **e** to their safekeeping has been lost
6: 4 whether a security deposit, or property **e** to them,
Nu 12: 7 my servant Moses. He is **e** with my entire house.
1Sa 20: 42 We have **e** each other and each other's children
1Ki 14: 27 and he **e** them to the care of the palace guard
1Ch 9: 31 was **e** with baking the bread used in the offerings.
2Ch 12: 10 and **e** them to the care of the captain of his
34: 10 He **e** the money to the men assigned to supervise
Ezr 8: 33 and **e** to Meremoth son of Uriah the priest and to
Mt 25: 20 The servant to whom he had **e** the five bags of gold
Lk 19: 17 You have been faithful with the little I **e** to you,
Ro 3: 2 the Jews were **e** with the whole revelation of God.
1Th 2: 4 approved by God to be **e** with the Good News.
1Ti 1: 11 that comes from the glorious Good News **e** to me
6: 20 Timothy, guard what God has **e** to you.
2Ti 1: 12 and I am sure that he is able to guard what I have **e**
1: 14 within us, carefully guard what has been **e** to you.
Heb 3: 2 and was **e** with God's entire house.
1Pe 5: 2 Care for the flock of God **e** to you. Watch over it

ENTRUSTING (3) [TRUST]

Ezr 7: 19 But as for the utensils we are **e** to you for the
Ac 11: 30 **e** their gifts to Barnabas and Saul to take to the
15: 40 believers sent them off, **e** them to the Lord's grace.

ENTRUSTS (1) [TRUST]

Ex 22: 7 "Suppose someone **e** money or goods to a

ENTRY (1) [ENTER]

Nu 3: 25 with its layers of coverings, its **e** curtains,

ENTRYWAY (1) [ENTER]

Mk 14: 68 talking about," he said, and he went out into the **e**.

ENVELOPED (1)

Ac 21: 40 Soon a deep silence **e** the crowd, and he addressed

ENVIED (1) [ENVY]

Ps 73: 3 For I **e** the proud / when I saw them prosper

ENVIOUS (1) [ENVY]

Ps 106: 16 and **e** of Aaron, the LORD's holy priest.

ENVOYS (2)

2Ki 20: 13 Hezekiah welcomed the Babylonian **e** and showed
Isa 39: 2 Hezekiah welcomed the Babylonian **e** and showed

ENVY (17) [ENVIED, ENVIOUS, ENVYING]

1Sa 2: 32 You will watch with **e** as I pour out prosperity on
Ps 37: 1 about the wicked. / Don't **e** those who do wrong.
37: 8 Do not **e** others— / it only leads to harm.
68: 16 Why do you look with **e**, O rugged mountains,
Pr 3: 31 Do not **e** violent people; don't copy their ways.
23: 17 Don't **e** sinners, but always continue to fear the
24: 1 Don't **e** evil people; don't desire their company.
24: 19 not fret because of evildoers; don't **e** the wicked.
Ecc 4: 4 motivated to success by their **e** of their neighbors.
Eze 31: 9 it was the **e** of all the other trees of Eden,
35: 11 punish you for all your acts of anger, **e**, and hatred.
Mt 27: 18 that the Jewish leaders had arrested Jesus out of **e**.)
Mk 7: 22 lustful pleasure, **e**, slander, pride, and foolishness.
15: 10 that the leading priests had arrested Jesus out of **e**.)
Ro 1: 29 sin, greed, hate, **e**, murder, fighting, deception,
Gal 5: 21 **e**, drunkenness, wild parties, and other kinds of sin.
Tit 3: 3 Our lives were full of evil and **e**. We hated others,

ENVYING (1) [ENVY]

Ecc 9: 6 their lifetime—loving, hating, **e**—is all long gone.

EPAPHRAS (3)

Col 1: 7 **E**, our much loved co-worker, was the one who
4: 12 **E**, from your city, a servant of Christ Jesus,
Phm 1: 23 **E**, my fellow prisoner in Christ Jesus, sends you

EPAPHRODITUS (2)

Php 2: 25 Meanwhile, I thought I should send **E** back to you.
4: 18 supplied with the gifts you sent me with **E**.

EPENETUS (1)

Ro 16: 5 that meets in their home. Greet my dear friend **E**.

EPHAH (6)

Ge 25: 4 Midian's sons were **E**, Epher, Hanoch, Abida,
1Ch 1: 33 The sons of Midian were **E**, Epher, Hanoch,
2: 46 Caleb's concubine **E** gave birth to Haran, Moza,
2: 47 Jotham, Geshan, Pelet, **E**, and Shaaph.
Isa 60: 6 will converge on you, the camels of Midian and **E**.
Eze 45: 11 The **e** and the bath will each measure one-tenth of

EPHAI (1)

Jer 40: 8 son of Tanhumeth, the sons of **E** the Netophathite,

EPHER (4)

Ge 25: 4 sons were Ephah, **E**, Hanoch, Abida, and Eldaah.
1Ch 1: 33 were Ephah, **E**, Hanoch, Abida, and Eldaah.
4: 17 sons of Ezrah were Jether, Mered, **E**, and Jalon.
5: 24 **E**, Ishi, Eliel, Azriel, Jeremiah, Hodaviah,

EPHES-DAMMIM (1) [PAS-DAMMIM]

1Sa 17: 1 camped between Socoh in Judah and Azekah at **E**.

EPHESIAN (1) [EPHESUS]
Ac 21: 1 After saying farewell to the E elders, we sailed

EPHESIANS (3) [EPHESUS]
Ac 19:28 they began shouting, "Great is Artemis of the E!"
19:34 it up for two hours: "Great is Artemis of the E! Great is Artemis of the E!"

EPHESUS (21) [EPHESIAN, EPHESIANS]
Ac 18:19 When they arrived at the port of E, Paul left the
18:21 back later, God willing." Then he set sail from E.
18:24 had just arrived in E from Alexandria in Egypt.
18:27 and the Christians in E encouraged him in this.
19: 1 Finally, he came to E, where he found several
19:17 of what happened spread quickly all through E,
19:23 serious trouble developed in E concerning the
19:26 And this is happening not only here in E
19:35 down enough to speak. "Citizens of E," he said.
19:35 "Everyone knows that E is the official guardian of
20:16 Paul had decided against stopping at E this time
20:17 he sent a message to the elders of the church at E,
21:29 a Gentile from E, and they assumed Paul had taken
1Co 15:32 those men of E—if there will be no resurrection
16: 8 I will be staying here at E until the Festival of
Eph 1: 1 It is written to God's holy people in E, who are
1Ti 1: 3 I urged you to stay there in E and stop those who
2Ti 1:18 And you know how much he helped me at E.
4:12 I sent Tychicus to E.
Rev 1:11 E, Smyrna, Pergamum, Thyatira, Sardis,
2: 1 "Write this letter to the angel of the church in E.

EPHLAL (2)
1Ch 2:37 Zabad was the father of E. / E was the father of Obed.

EPHOD (44)
Ex 25: 7 and other stones to be set in the e
28: 4 an e, a robe, an embroidered tunic, a turban,
28: 6 "The e must be made of fine linen cloth
28:12 of the e as memorial stones for the people of Israel.
28:14 attached to the settings on the shoulders of the e.
28:15 Use the same materials as you did for the e:
28:22 "To attach the chestpiece to the e, make braided
28:25 to the gold settings on the shoulder-pieces of the e.
28:26 lower inside corners of the chestpiece next to the e.
28:27 gold rings and attach them to the e near the sash.
28:28 the chestpiece to the rings on the e with blue cords.
28:28 This will hold the chestpiece securely to the e
28:31 "Make the robe of the e entirely of blue cloth,
29: 5 along with the embroidered robe of the e, the e itself, the chestpiece, and the sash.
35: 9 and other stones to be set in the e
35:27 and the other gemstones to be used for the e
39: 2 The e was made from fine linen cloth
39: 4 They made two shoulder-pieces for the e,
39: 6 attached to the shoulder-pieces of the e,
39: 8 chestpiece was made in the same style as the e,
39:15 To attach the chestpiece to the e, they made
39:18 to the gold settings on the shoulder-pieces of the e.
39:19 lower inside corners of the chestpiece next to the e.
39:20 Then two gold rings were attached to the e near the
39:21 bottom rings of the chestpiece to the rings on the e.
39:21 the chestpiece was held securely to the e above the
39:22 The robe of the e was woven entirely of blue yarn,
Lev 8: 7 He dressed him in the robe of the e, along with the e itself,
8: 7 and attached the e with its decorative sash.
Nu 34:23 Manasseh son of Joseph | Hanniel son of E
Jdg 8:27 Gideon made a sacred e from the gold and put it in
17: 5 and he made a sacred e and some household idols.
18:14 "There is a shrine here with a sacred e,
18:17 the sacred e, the household idols, and the cast idol.
18:20 so he took along the sacred e, the household idols,
1Sa 14: 3 Ahijah the priest, who was wearing the linen e.
14:18 Then Saul shouted to Ahijah, "Bring the e here!"
14:18 For at that time Ahijah was wearing the e in front
21: 9 "It is wrapped in a cloth behind the e.
23: 6 taking the e with him to get answers for David
23: 9 and told Abiathar the priest to bring the e
30: 7 he said to Abiathar the priest, "Bring me the e!"

EPHRAIM (130) [EPHRAIM'S, EPHRAIMITES]
HILL COUNTRY OF EPHRAIM (29) Jos 17:15; 19:50; 20:7; 24:30,33; Jdg 2:9; 3:27; 4:5; 7:24; 10:1; 17:1; 18:2,13; 19:1,16,18; 1Sa 1:1; 9:4; 2Sa 20:21; 1Ki 4:8; 12:25; 2Ki 5:22; 1Ch 6:67; 2Ch 13:4; 15:8; 19:4; Jer 4:15; 31:6; 50:19
TRIBE OF EPHRAIM (12) Nu 7:48; Jos 16:5,8; 17:8,9; 21:20; Jdg 1:29; 12:1,5; 1Ch 12:30; Ps 78:67; Hos 13:1
Ge 41:52 Joseph named his second son E, for he said,
46:20 born in the land of Egypt, were Manasseh and E.
48: 1 he took with him his two sons, Manasseh and E.
48: 5 E and Manasseh, who were born here in the land
48: 6 land they inherit will be within the territories of E
48:13 positioned the boys so E was at Jacob's left hand
48:14 So his right hand was on the head of E,
48:20 'May God make you as prosperous as E
48:20 In this way, Jacob put E ahead of Manasseh.
50:23 see three generations of descendants of his son E
Nu 1:10 E son of Joseph | Elishama son of Ammihud
1:32[-33] E son of Joseph | 40,500
2:18[-19] "The divisions of E, Manasseh,
2:18[-19] E | Elishama son of Ammihud | 40,500
7:48 leader of the tribe of E, presented his offering.
10:22 Then the tribes that camped with E set out with
13: 8 E | Hoshea son of Nun
26:28 descended from Joseph through Manasseh and E.
26:35 were the clans descended from the sons of E:
26:37 The men from all the clans of E numbered 32,500.
26:37 of Manasseh and E were all descendants of Joseph.
34:24 E son of Joseph | Kemuel son of Shiphtan
Dt 33:17 This is my blessing for the multitudes of E
34: 2 the land of E and Manasseh; all the land of Judah,
Jos 14: 4 had become two separate tribes—Manasseh and E.
16: 4 Manasseh and E, received their inheritance.
16: 5 to the families of the tribe of E as their inheritance.
16: 8 inheritance given to the families of the tribe of E.
16: 9 E was also given some towns with surrounding
16:10 live as slaves among the people of E to this day.
17: 8 Manasseh's territory, belonged to the tribe of E.)
17: 9 in Manasseh's territory belonged to the tribe of E.)
17:10 The land south of the ravine belonged to E,
17:15 "If the hill country of E is not large enough for
17:17 Then Joshua said to the tribes of E and Manasseh,
19:50 He chose Timnath-serah in the hill country of E.
20: 7 Shechem, in the hill country of E; and Kiriath-arba
21: 5 were allotted ten towns from the territories of E,
21:20 these towns and pasturelands from the tribe of E:
24:30 at Timnath-serah in the hill country of E, north of
24:32 located in the territory allotted to the tribes of E
24:33 He was buried in the hill country of E, in the town
Jdg 1:29 The tribe of E also failed to drive out the
2: 9 at Timnath-serah in the hill country of E, north of
3:27 When he arrived in the hill country of E,
4: 5 and Bethel in the hill country of E,
5:14 They came down from E—a land that once
7:24 sent messengers throughout the hill country of E,
7:24 And the men of E did as they were told.
8: 1 Then the people of E asked Gideon, "Why have
8: 3 When the men of E heard Gideon's answer,
10: 1 in the town of Shamir in the hill country of E.
10: 9 of the Jordan and attacked Judah, Benjamin, and E.
12: 1 Then the tribe of E mobilized its army and crossed
12: 4 The leaders of E responded, "The men of Gilead are nothing more than rejects from E
12: 4 and attacked the men of E and defeated them.
12: 5 and whenever a fugitive from E tried to go back
12: 5 "Are you a member of the tribe of E?"
12: 6 If he was from E, he would say "Sibboleth,"
12: 6 because people from E cannot pronounce the word
12:15 Then he died and was buried at Pirathon in E,
17: 1 A man named Micah lived in the hill country of E.
17: 8 arrived in that area of E, looking for a good place
18: 2 these warriors arrived in the hill country of E,
18:13 Then they went up into the hill country of E
19: 1 living in a remote area of the hill country of E.
19:16 He was from the hill country of E, but he was
19:18 way home to a remote area in the hill country of E,
1Sa 1: 1 who lived in Ramah in the hill country of E.
9: 4 and traveled all through the hill country of E,
2Sa 2: 9 Jezreel, E, Benjamin, the land of the Ashurites,
13:23 sheep were being sheared at Baal-hazor near E,
18: 6 So the battle began in the forest of E,
20:21 Sheba son of Bicri from the hill country of E,
1Ki 4: 8 Ben-hur, in the hill country of E.
11:26 He came from the city of Zeredah in E, and his
11:28 in charge of the labor force from the tribes of E
12:25 up the city of Shechem in the hill country of E,
2Ki 5:22 from the hill country of E have just arrived.
14:13 from the E Gate to the Corner Gate.
1Ch 6:66 received from the territory of E these towns,
6:67 Shechem (a city of refuge in the hill country of E),
7:20 The descendants of E were Shuthelah, Bered,
7:22 Their father, E, mourned for them a long time,
7:23 Afterward E slept with his wife, and she became
7:23 E named him Beriah because of the tragedy his
7:24 E had a daughter named Sheerah. She built the
7:28 The descendants of E lived in the territory that
9: 3 Benjamin, E, and Manasseh came and settled in
12:30 From the tribe of E, there were 20,800 warriors,
27:10 Helez, a descendant of E from Pelon,
27:14 Benaiah from Pirathon in E was commander of the
27:20 E | Hoshea son of Azaziah / Manasseh (west)
2Ch 13: 4 the army of Judah arrived in the hill country of E,
15: 8 the towns he had captured in the hill country of E.
15: 9 along with the people of E, Manasseh,
17: 2 land of Judah and to the towns of E that his father,
19: 4 traveling from Beersheba to the hill country of E,
25: 7 not with Israel. He will not help those people of E!
25:10 the hired troops and sent them back to E.
25:23 from the E Gate to the Corner Gate.
28: 7 Then Zicri, a warrior from E, killed Maaseiah,
30: 1 and he wrote letters of invitation to E
30:10 messengers went from town to town throughout E
30:18 Most of those who came from E, Manasseh,
31: 1 Benjamin, E, and Manasseh, and they smashed the
34: 6 E, and Simeon, even as far as Naphtali.
34: 9 E, and from all the remnant of Israel, as well as
Ne 8:16 squares just inside the Water Gate and the E Gate.
12:39 then past the E Gate to the Old City Gate,
Ps 60: 7 Manasseh is mine. / E will produce my warriors,
78: 9 The warriors of E, though fully armed,
78:67 he did not choose the tribe of E.
80: 2 to E, Benjamin, and Manasseh. / Show us your
108: 8 Manasseh is mine. / E will produce my warriors,
Isa 9:21 Manasseh will feed on E, E will feed on Manasseh, and both will devour
Jer 4:15 From Dan and the hill country of E,
31: 6 watchmen will shout from the hill country of E,
31: 9 For I am Israel's father, and E is my oldest child.
50:19 to be satisfied once more on the hill country of E
Eze 48: 5 South of Manasseh is E,
Hos 13: 1 In the past when the tribe of E spoke, the people
13: 1 But the people of E sinned by worshiping Baal
13:12 "The sins of E have been collected and stored
13:15 E was the most fruitful of all his brothers,
13:15 It will blow hard against the people of E, drying up
Ob 1:19 and take over the fields of E and Samaria.
Jn 11:54 to the village of E, and stayed there with his

EPHRAIM'S (5) [EPHRAIM]
Ge 48:17 that his father had laid his right hand on E head.
Nu 2:24 So the total of all the troops on E side of the camp
Jdg 8: 2 Aren't the last grapes of E harvest better than the
1Ch 7:21 E sons Ezer and Elead were killed trying to steal
7:25 E line of descent was Rephah, Resheph, Telah,

EPHRAIMITES (1) [EPHRAIM]
Jdg 12: 6 So forty-two thousand E were killed at that time.

EPHRAIN [KJV] See EPHRON

EPHRATH (4) [EPHRATHITE, EPHRATHITES]
Ge 35:16 they traveled on toward E (that is, Bethlehem).
35:19 and was buried on the way to E (that is,
48: 7 just a short distance from E (that is, Bethlehem).
48: 7 sorrow I buried her there beside the road to E."

EPHRATHAH (6) [BETHLEHEM, CALEB-EPHRATHAH]
Ru 4:11 May you be great in E and famous in Bethlehem.
1Ch 2:19 After Azubah died, Caleb married E, and they had
2:50 The sons of Hur, the oldest son of Caleb's wife E,
4: 4 were the descendants of Hur (the firstborn of E),
Ps 132: 6 We heard that the Ark was in E; / then we found it
Mic 5: 2 But you, O Bethlehem E, are only a small village

EPHRATHITE (1) [EPHRATH]
1Sa 17:12 an E from Bethlehem in the land of Judah.

EPHRATHITES (1) [EPHRATH]
Ru 1: 2 They were E from Bethlehem in the land of Judah.

EPHRON (11) [EPHRON'S]
Ge 23: 8 how you feel, be so kind as to ask E son of Zohar
23:10 E was sitting there among the others, and he
23:13 and he replied to E as everyone listened. "No,
23:14 "Well," E answered,
23:16 So Abraham paid E the amount he had suggested,
23:17 He bought the plot of land belonging to E at
25: 9 in the field of E son of Zohar the Hittite.
49:30 which Abraham bought from E the Hittite for a
50:13 permanent burial place in the field of E the Hittite,
Jos 15: 9 and from there to the towns on Mount E.
2Ch 13:19 of his towns, including Bethel, Jeshanah, and E,

EPHRON'S (1) [EPHRON]
Ge 49:29 my father and grandfather in the cave in E field.

EPICUREAN (1)
Ac 17:18 He also had a debate with some of the E and Stoic

EPIDEMIC (1) [EPIDEMICS]
Eze 14:19 my fury by sending an e of disease into the land,

EPIDEMICS (1) [EPIDEMIC]
Lk 21:11 and there will be famines and e in many lands,

EPILEPTICS (1)
Mt 4:24 by demons, or were e, or were paralyzed—

EPISTLE [KJV] See LETTER

EQUAL (13) [EQUALITY, EQUALLY, EQUIVALENT]
1Sa 10:24 No one in all Israel is his e!" And all the people
2Ch 2: 8 for I know that your men are without e at cutting
Ezr 8:27 20 gold bowls, e in value to 1,000 gold coins,
Ps 55:13 Instead, it is you—my e, / my companion and close
Isa 40:25 compare me? Who is my e?" asks the Holy One.
46: 5 "To whom will you compare me? Who is my e?
Eze 5: 1 Use a scale to weigh the hair into three e parts.
31: 8 No cypress had branches e to it; no plane tree had
45:12 twenty gerahs, and sixty shekels are e to one mina.
47:14 Otherwise each tribe will receive an e share.
Jn 5:18 as his Father, thereby making himself e with God.
Eph 3: 6 The Gentiles have an e share with the Jews in all
1Pe 3: 7 but she is your e partner in God's gift of new life.

EQUALITY (1) [EQUAL]
2Co 8:13 too little. I only mean that there should be some e.

EQUALLY (5) [EQUAL]
2Sa 19:29 and Ziba will divide your land e between you."
Pr 30:20 E amazing is how an adulterous woman can satisfy
Mt 22:39 A second is e important: 'Love your neighbor as
Mk 12:31 The second is e important: 'Love your neighbor as
1Co 12:25 so that all the members care for each other e.

EQUIP (2) [BEST-EQUIPED, EQUIPMENT, EQUIPPED]

Eph 4:12 Their responsibility is to **e** God's people to do his
Heb 13:20[-21] **e** you with all you need for doing his will.

EQUIPMENT (15) [EQUIP]

Nu 1:50 of the Covenant, along with its furnishings and **e**.
1:50 must carry the Tabernacle and its **e** as you travel,
3:26 the cords, and all the **e** related to their use.
3:31 the inner curtain, and all the **e** related to their use.
3:36 the bases, and all the **e** related to their use.
Dt 20:20 Use them to make the **e** you need to besiege the
23:13 Each of you must have a spade as part of your **e**.
1Sa 8:12 while others will make his weapons and chariot **e**.
25:13 and two hundred remained behind to guard their **e**.
30:24 those who go to battle and those who guard the **e**."
2Ki 7:15 and **e** that the Arameans had thrown away in their
2Ch 20:25 They found vast amounts of **e**, clothing, and other
Isa 9:5 be bloodstained by war. All such **e** will be burned.
10:28 They are storing some of their **e** at Micmash.
Ac 27:19 The following day they even threw out the ship's **e**

EQUIPPED (3) [EQUIP]

2Ch 17:17 there were 200,000 troops **e** with bows and shields.
Da 11:13 the king of the north will return with a fully **e** army
2Ti 3:17 fully **e** for every good thing God wants us to do.

EQUIVALENT (1) [EQUAL]

Lev 6:6 physical defects or the animal's **e** value in silver.

ER (11) [ER'S]

Ge 38:3 and had a son, and Judah named the boy **E**.
38:6 When his oldest son, **E**, grew up, Judah arranged
38:7 But **E** was a wicked man in the LORD's sight,
46:12 The sons of Judah were **E**, Onan, Shelah, Perez,
46:12 (But **E** and Onan had died in the land of Canaan.)
Nu 26:19 Judah had two sons, **E** and Onan, who had died in
1Ch 2:3 Their names were **E**, Onan, and Shelah.
2:3 But the oldest son, **E**, was a wicked man,
4:21 The descendants of Shelah were **E** (the father of
Lk 3:28 the son of Elmadam. / Elmadam was the son of **E**.
3:29 **E** was the son of Joshua. / Joshua was the son of

ER'S (1) [ER]

Ge 38:8 Then Judah said to **E** brother Onan, "You must

ERAN (1) [ERANITES]

Nu 26:36 The Eranites, named after their ancestor **E**.

ERANITES (1) [ERAN]

Nu 26:36 The **E**, named after their ancestor Eran.

ERASE (8) [ERASED]

Dt 7:24 and you will **e** their names from the face of the
9:14 destroy them and **e** their name from under heaven.
12:3 **E** the names of their gods from those places!
25:19 and **e** their memory from under heaven.
29:20 and the LORD will **e** their names from under
Ps 34:16 do evil; / he will **e** their memory from the earth.
69:28 **E** their names from the Book of Life; / don't let
Rev 3:5 I will never **e** their names from the Book of Life,

ERASED (4) [ERASE]

Ge 41:31 that even the memory of the good years will be **e**.
Ps 109:14 may his mother's sins never be **e** from the record.
Pr 6:3 your pride; go and beg to have your name **e**.
6:33 disgrace are his lot. His shame will never be **e**.

ERASTUS (3)

Ac 19:22 He sent his two assistants, Timothy and **E**,
Ro 16:23 **E**, the city treasurer, sends you his greetings,
2Ti 4:20 **E** stayed at Corinth, and I left Trophimus sick at

ERECH (2)

Ge 10:10 with the cities of Babel, **E**, Akkad, and Calneh.
Ezr 4:9 and the people of **E** and Susa (that is, Elam).

ERECTED (1)

Eze 43:9 and the sacred pillars **e** to honor their kings,

ERI (2) [ERITE]

Ge 46:16 Haggi, Shuni, Ezbon, **E**, Arodi, and Areli.
Nu 26:16 The Erite clan, named after its ancestor **E**.

ERITE (1) [ERI]

Nu 26:16 The **E** clan, named after its ancestor Eri.

ERRAND (2)

Isa 48:15 I will send him on this **e** and will help him
Jer 47:7 can it be still when the LORD has sent it on an **e**?

ERRAND [KJV] See also MESSAGE

ERROR (3) [ERRORS]

Isa 29:24 Those in **e** will then believe the truth, and those
Eze 45:20 the new year for anyone who has sinned through **e**
Mk 12:27 not the dead. You have made a serious **e**."

ERRORS (2) [ERROR]

Ex 28:38 thus bearing the guilt connected with any **e**
2Pe 3:17 and not be carried away by the **e** of these wicked

ERUPTED (1)

Jdg 5:8 Israel chose new gods, / war **e** at the city gates.

ESAIAS [KJV] See ISAIAH

ESARHADDON (3)

2Ki 19:37 and another son, **E**, became the next king of
Ezr 4:2 We have sacrificed to him ever since King **E** of
Isa 37:38 and another son, **E**, became the next king of

ESAU (87) [EDOM, ESAU'S]

Ge 25:25 wearing a piece of clothing. So they called him **E**.
25:27 As the boys grew up, **E** became a skillful hunter,
25:28 Isaac loved **E** in particular because of the wild
25:29 **E** arrived home exhausted and hungry from a hunt.
25:30 **E** said to Jacob, "I'm starved! Give me some of
25:30 (This was how **E** got his other name, Edom—
25:32 "Look, I'm dying of starvation!" said **E**.
25:33 So **E** swore an oath, thereby selling all his rights as
25:34 Then Jacob gave **E** some bread and lentil stew.
25:34 **E** ate and drank and went on about his business,
26:34 of forty, **E** married a young woman named Judith,
27:1 he called for **E**, his older son, and said, "My son?"
"Yes, Father?" **E** replied.
27:5 So when **E** left to hunt for the wild game,
27:6 her son Jacob, "I overheard your father asking **E**
27:7 He wants to bless **E** in the LORD's presence
27:10 eat it and bless you instead of **E** before he dies."
27:11 Think how hairy **E** is and how smooth my skin is!
27:18 my son," he answered. "Who is it—**E** or Jacob?"
27:19 Jacob replied, "It's **E**, your older son. I've done as
27:21 want to touch you to make sure you really are **E**."
27:24 "Are you really my son **E**?" he asked. "Yes,
27:30 had left his father, **E** returned from his hunting trip.
27:31 **E** prepared his father's favorite meat dish
27:32 of course!" he replied. "It's **E**, your older son."
27:34 When **E** understood, he let out a loud and bitter
27:36 **E** said bitterly, "No wonder his name is Jacob,
27:37 Isaac said to **E**, "I have made Jacob your master
27:38 **E** pleaded, "Not one blessing left for me? O my
27:38 bless me, too!" Then **E** broke down and wept.
27:41 **E** hated Jacob because he had stolen his blessing,
27:42 But someone got wind of what **E** was planning
27:42 and told him, "**E** is threatening to kill you.
28:6 **E** heard that his father had blessed Jacob and sent
28:8 It was now very clear to **E** that his father despised
32:3 to his brother, **E**, in Edom, the land of Seir.
32:4 He told them, "Give this message to my master **E**:
32:6 The messengers returned with the news that **E** was
32:8 He thought, "If **E** attacks one group,
32:11 O LORD, please rescue me from my brother, **E**.
32:13 he was for the night and prepared a present for **E**:
32:17 "When you meet **E**, he will ask, 'Where are you
32:18 They are a present for his master **E**! He is coming
32:19 "You are all to say the same thing to **E** when you
32:20 **E** with the presents before meeting him face to
33:1 Jacob saw **E** coming with his four hundred men.
33:4 Then **E** ran to meet him and embraced him
33:5 Then **E** looked at the women and children
33:8 **E** asked. Jacob replied, "They are gifts, my lord,
33:9 "Brother, I have plenty," **E** answered.
33:11 continued to insist, so **E** finally accepted them.
33:12 "Well, let's be going," **E** said. "I will stay with
33:15 "Well," **E** said, "at least let me leave some of my
33:16 So **E** started back to Seir that same day.
35:1 to you when you fled from your brother, **E**."
35:7 to him there at Bethel when he was fleeing from **E**.
35:29 in death. Then his sons, **E** and Jacob, buried him.
36:1 This is the history of the descendants of **E** (also
36:2 **E** married two young women from Canaan: Adah,
36:4 **E** and Adah had a son named Eliphaz. **E** and
Basemath had a son named Reuel.
36:5 **E** and Oholibamah had sons named Jeush, Jalam,
36:5 All these sons were born to **E** in the land of
36:6 Then **E** took his wives, children,
36:8 So **E** (also known as Edom) settled in the hill
36:14 **E** also had sons through Oholibamah, the daughter
36:16 descended from Eliphaz, the son of **E** and Adah.
36:17 descended from Reuel, the son of **E** and Basemath.
36:18 The sons of **E** and his wife Oholibamah became
36:19 These are all the clans descended from **E** (also
36:40 These are the leaders of the clans of **E**, who lived
36:43 These are the names of the clans of **E**, the ancestor
Dt 2:4 the descendants of **E**, who live in Seir.
2:8 the descendants of **E**, who live in Seir,
2:12 driven out and displaced by the descendants of **E**.
2:22 He had similarly helped the descendants of **E** at
2:22 The descendants of **E** live there to this day.
2:29 The descendants of **E** at Mount Seir allowed us to
Jos 24:4 To Isaac I gave Jacob and **E**. To **E** I gave the hill
country of Seir, while Jacob
1Ch 1:34 of Isaac. The sons of Isaac were **E** and Israel.
1:35 The sons of **E** were Eliphaz, Reuel, Jeush, Jalam,
Mal 1:2 your ancestor Jacob. Yet **E** was Jacob's brother,
1:3 and I rejected **E** and devastated his hill country.
Ro 9:13 the Scriptures, "I loved Jacob, but I rejected **E**."
Heb 11:20 faith that Isaac blessed his two sons, Jacob and **E**.
12:16 sure that no one is immoral or godless like **E**.

ESAU'S (17) [ESAU]

Ge 25:26 other twin was born with his hand grasping **E** heel.
26:35 But **E** wives made life miserable for Isaac
27:15 Then she took **E** best clothes, which were there in
27:22 but the hands are **E**," Isaac said to himself.
27:23 because Jacob's hands felt hairy just like **E**.
36:9 This is a list of **E** descendants, the Edomites,
36:10 Among **E** sons were Eliphaz, the son of **E** wife
Adah; and Reuel, the son of **E** wife Basemath.
36:12 These were all grandchildren of **E** wife Adah.
36:13 These were all grandchildren of **E** wife Basemath.
36:15 **E** children and grandchildren became the leaders
36:15 The sons of **E** oldest son, Eliphaz,
36:17 The sons of **E** son Reuel became the leaders of the
36:18 These are the clans descended from **E** wife
Mal 1:3 I turned **E** inheritance into a desert for jackals."
1:4 And **E** descendants in Edom may say, "We have

ESCAPE (92) [ESCAPED, ESCAPES, ESCAPING]

Ge 7:7 and he went aboard the boat to **e**—he and his wife
19:17 look back! **E** to the mountains, or you will die."
32:8 Esau attacks one group, perhaps the other can **e**."
37:22 Reuben was secretly planning to help Joseph **e**,
Ex 1:10 against us. Then they will **e** from the country."
Dt 4:9 Do not let these things **e** from your mind as long as
23:15 "If slaves should **e** from their masters and take
Jos 2:16 "**E** to the hill country," she told them.
20:9 they could **e** being killed in revenge prior to
1Sa 19:17 "Why have you tricked me and let my enemy **e**?"
20:13 kill me if I don't warn you so you can **e** and live.
23:28 David was camped has been called the Rock of **E**.
27:1 The best thing for me to do is **e** to the Philistines.
2Sa 18:9 He tried to **e** on his mule, but as he rode beneath
1Ki 12:2 for he had fled to Egypt to **e** from King Solomon.
18:40 Don't let a single one **e**!" So the people seized
19:17 and those who **e** Jehu will be killed by Elisha!
2Ki 3:26 lines near the king of Edom, but they failed to **e**.
7:15 Arameans had thrown away in their mad rush to **e**.
9:15 don't let anyone **e** to Jezreel to report what we
10:24 and had warned them, "If you let anyone **e**,
10:25 and kill all of them. Don't let a single one **e**!"
25:4 and all the soldiers made plans to **e** from the city.
2Ch 10:2 for he had fled to Egypt to **e** from King Solomon.
Est 4:13 "Don't think for a moment that you will **e** there in
Job 11:20 They have no **e**. Their hope becomes despair."
12:14 When he closes in on someone, there is no **e**.
15:30 "They will not **e** the darkness. The flame will burn
20:24 He will try to **e**, but God's arrow will pierce him.
21:30 spared in times of calamity and are allowed to **e**.
Ps 44:15 We can't **e** the constant humiliation; / shame is
55:8 How quickly I would **e**— / far away from this wild
88:8 them all away. / I am in a trap with no way of **e**.
89:48 No one can **e** the power of the grave. / *Interlude*
139:7 I can never **e** from your spirit! / I can never get
140:10 the fire, / or into deep pits from which they can't **e**.
141:10 the wicked fall into their own snares, / but let me **e**.
Pr 12:13 by their own words, but the godly **e** such trouble.
14:27 it offers **e** from the snares of death.
19:5 witness will not go unpunished, nor will a liar **e**.
29:6 by sin, but the righteous **e**, shouting for joy.
Ecc 7:26 Those who please God will **e** from her, but sinners
Isa 2:21 they will try to **e** the terror of the LORD
24:18 and those who **e** the trap will step into a snare.
51:10 making a path of **e** when you saved your people?
Jer 11:11 to bring calamity upon them, and they will not **e**.
12:12 one end of the nation to the other. No one will **e**!
25:28 You must drink from it. You cannot **e**!
25:29 let you go unpunished? No, you will not **e** disaster.
25:35 find no place to hide; there will be no way to **e**.
34:3 You will not **e** his grasp but will be taken into
38:18 But if you refuse to surrender, you will not **e**!
38:23 be led out to the Babylonians, and you will not **e**.
42:17 None of you will **e** from the disaster I will bring
44:14 of returning home to Judah, only a handful will **e**."
44:28 "Only a small number will **e** death and return to
46:6 cannot flee; the mightiest warriors cannot **e**.
48:44 and those who **e** the trap will step into a snare.
50:16 Let the captives **e** the sword of the enemy and rush
50:29 Surround the city so none can **e**. Do to her as she
51:32 All the **e** routes are blocked. The fortifications are
52:7 and all the soldiers made plans to **e** from the city.
La 3:7 He has walled me in, and I cannot **e**. He has bound
Eze 6:8 "But I will let a few of my people **e** destruction,
7:16 and **e** to the mountains will moan like doves,
15:7 And I will see to it that if they **e** from one fire,
17:18 after swearing to obey; therefore, he will not **e**.
35:7 killing off all who try to **e** and any who return.
Da 11:41 Edom, and the best part of Ammon will **e**.
11:42 will conquer many countries, and Egypt will not **e**.
Hos 9:6 Even if you **e** destruction from Assyria, you will be
Joel 2:32 will be people on Mount Zion in Jerusalem who **e**,
Am 2:15 The swiftest soldiers won't be fast enough to **e**.
9:1 survive will be slaughtered in battle. No one will **e**!
Ob 1:14 stood at the crossroads, killing those who tried to **e**.
1:17 Jerusalem will become a refuge for those who **e**;
Jnh 1:3 hoping that by going away to the west he could **e**
Mic 2:3 reward your evil with evil; you won't be able to **e**!
Na 3:15 There will be no **e**, even if you multiply like
Zec 2:7 **E** to Jerusalem, you who are exiled in Babylon!"
12:3 None of the nations who try to lift it will **e**
Mt 23:33 of vipers! How will you **e** the judgment of hell?
Lk 21:21 Let those in Jerusalem **e**, and those outside the city
21:36 you may **e** these horrors and stand before the Son
Ac 16:23 The jailer was ordered to make sure they didn't **e**.
27:42 to make sure they didn't swim ashore and **e**.
1Th 5:3 child is about to be born. And there will be no **e**.

2Ti 2:26 come to their senses and **e** from the Devil's trap.
Heb 2: 3 What makes us think that we can **e** if we are
12:25 For if the people of Israel did not **e** when they
2Pe 1: 4 He has promised that you will **e** the decadence all
2:20 And when people **e** from the wicked ways of the

ESCAPED (63) [ESCAPE]

Ge 14:10 into the tar pits, while the rest **e** into the mountains.
14:13 One of the men who **e** came and told Abram the
Ex 2:15 fled from Pharaoh and **e** to the land of Midian.
10: 5 They will devour everything that **e** the hailstorm,
14: 8 and he chased after the people of Israel who had **e**
18:11 because his people have **e** from the proud and cruel
Dt 16: 3 as you did when you **e** from Egypt in such a hurry.
Jos 8:22 all of them died. Not a single person survived or **e**.
10:16 the five kings **e** and hid in a cave at Makkedah.
Jdg 1: 6 Adoni-bezek **e**, but the Israelites soon captured
3:23 down the latrine and **e** through the sewage access.
3:26 While the servants were waiting, Ehud **e**,
3:29 and bravest warriors. Not one of them **e**.
4:15 Sisera leaped down from his chariot and **e** on foot.
9: 5 But the youngest brother, Jotham, **e** and hid.
9:21 Then Jotham **e** and lived in Beer because he was
20:47 leaving only six hundred men who **e** to the rock of
1Sa 13: 7 and **e** into the land of Gad and Gilead.
18:11 But David jumped aside and **e**. This happened
19:10 David dodged out of the way and **e** into the night,
19:12 helped him climb out through a window, and he **e**.
21:10 So David **e** from Saul and went to King Achish of
22: 1 So David left Gath and **e** to the cave of Adullam.
22:20 one of the sons of Ahimelech, **e** and fled to David.
23:13 Word soon reached Saul that David had **e**, so he
30:17 None of the Amalekites **e** except four hundred
2Sa 1: 3 "I **e** from the Israelite camp," the man replied.
4: 6 and stabbed him in the stomach. Then they **e**.
13:34 Meanwhile Absalom **e**. Then the watchman on the
17:13 And if David has **e** into some city, you will have
17:18 Meanwhile, they **e** to Bahurim, where a man hid
1Ki 2:39 two of Shimei's slaves **e** to King Achish of Gath.
11:18 They **e** from Midian and went to Paran,
20:20 but King Ben-hadad and a few others **e** on horses.
2Ki 8:21 but he **e** at night under cover of darkness.
10:14 them at the well of Beth-eked. None of them **e**.
19:30 left in Judah, who have **e** the ravages of the siege,
19:37 They then **e** to the land of Ararat, and another son,
2Ch 20:24 could see. Not a single one of the enemy had **e**.
21: 9 but he **e** at night under cover of darkness.
Ezr 9:15 before you in our guilt as nothing but an **e** remnant,
Job 1:15 I am the only one who **e** to tell you."
1:16 I am the only one who **e** to tell you."
1:17 I am the only one who **e** to tell you."
1:19 are dead. I am the only one who **e** to tell you."
19:20 and have **e** death by the skin of my teeth.
Ps 114: 1 When the Israelites **e** from Egypt—
124: 7 We **e** like a bird from a hunter's trap. / The trap is
Isa 37:31 left in Judah, who have **e** the ravages of the siege,
37:38 They then **e** to the land of Ararat, and another son,
Jer 26:21 But Uriah heard about the plot and **e** to Egypt.
41:14 And all the captives from Mizpah **e** and began to
41:15 and eight of his men **e** from Johanan into the land
50:28 Listen to the people who have **e** from Babylon,
51:50 Go, you who **e** the sword! Do not stand
La 2:22 of the LORD's anger, no one has **e** or survived.
Eze 33:21 a man who had **e** from Jerusalem came to me
Mk 14:52 tore off his clothes, but he **e** and ran away naked.
Ac 16:27 He assumed the prisoners had **e**, so he drew his
27:44 from the broken ship. So everyone **e** safely ashore!
28: 4 Though he **e** the sea, justice will not permit him to
Heb 11:34 of fire, and **e** death by the edge of the sword.
2Pe 2:18 they lure back into sin those who have just **e** from

ESCAPES (4) [ESCAPE]

Lev 4:13 and the matter **e** the community's notice,
Dt 19:11 and then **e** to one of the cities of refuge.
1Ki 19:17 Anyone who **e** from Hazael will be killed by Jehu,
Joel 2: 3 them is nothing but desolation; not one thing **e**.

ESCAPING (4) [ESCAPE]

Pr 6: 5 Save yourself like a deer **e** from a hunter, like a
Ecc 8: 8 There is no **e** that obligation, that dark battle.
Am 5:19 After **e** the bear, he leans his hand against a wall in
1Co 3:15 but like someone **e** through a wall of flames.

ESCHEW [KJV] See TURN AWAY

ESCORT (2) [ESCORTED, ESCORTING]

Ge 12:20 then sent them out of the country under armed **e**—
2Sa 19:15 to Gilgal to meet him and **e** him across the river.

ESCORTED (4) [ESCORT]

2Sa 19:40 and half the army of Israel **e** him across the river.
20: 2 and **e** him from the Jordan River to Jerusalem.
2Ki 11:19 and all the people of the land **e** the king from the
2Ch 23:20 and all the people **e** the king from the Temple of

ESCORTING (1) [ESCORT]

Ac 17:15 Those **e** Paul went with him to Athens, then they

ESHAN (1)

Jos 15:52 Also included were the towns of Arab, Dumah, **E**,

ESHBAAL (2)

1Ch 8:33 father of Jonathan, Malkishua, Abinadab, and **E**.
9:39 father of Jonathan, Malkishua, Abinadab, and **E**.

ESHBAN (2)

Ge 36:26 of Dishon were Hemdan, **E**, Ithran, and Keran.
1Ch 1:41 of Dishon were Hemdan, **E**, Ithran, and Keran.

ESHCOL (6)

Ge 14:13 Mamre and his relatives, **E** and Aner,
14:24 of the goods to my allies—Aner, **E**, and Mamre."
Nu 13:23 came to what is now known as the valley of **E**,
13:24 At that time the Israelites renamed the valley **E**—
32: 9 After they went up to the valley of **E** and scouted
Dt 1:24 and came to the valley of **E** and explored it.

ESHEK (1)

1Ch 8:39 Azel's brother **E** had three sons: Ulam (the oldest),

ESHKALONITES [KJV] See ASHKELON

ESHTAOL (8)

Jos 15:33 were also given to Judah: **E**, Zorah, Ashnah,
19:41 Dan's inheritance included Zorah, **E**, Ir-shemesh,
Jdg 13:25 is located between the towns of Zorah and **E**,
16:31 back home and buried him between Zorah and **E**,
18: 2 who lived in the towns of Zorah and **E**, to scout
18: 8 When the men returned to Zorah and **E**,
18:11 from the tribe of Dan set out from Zorah and **E**.
1Ch 2:53 from whom came the people of Zorah and **E**.

ESHTEMOA (5)

Jos 21:14 Jattir, **E**,
1Sa 30:28 Aroer, Siphmoth, **E**,
1Ch 4:17 of Miriam, Shammai, and Ishbah (the father of **E**).
4:19 and another was the father of **E** the Maacathite.
6:57 Hebron (a city of refuge), Libnah, Jattir, **E**,

ESHTEMOH (1)

Jos 15:50 Anab, **E**, Anim,

ESHTON (2)

1Ch 4:11 was the father of Mehir. Mehir was the father of **E**.
4:12 **E** was the father of Beth-rapha, Paseah,

ESLI (2)

Lk 3:25 Nahum was the son of **E**. / **E** was the son of

ESPECIALLY (32) [SPECIAL]

Dt 4:10 Tell them **e** about the day when you stood before
Jos 2: 1 other side of the Jordan River, **e** around Jericho."
1Sa 20:41 embraced each other and said good-bye, **e** David.
1Ki 21:26 He was **e** guilty because he worshiped idols just as
Ne 8:15 made throughout their towns and **e** in Jerusalem,
Est 2:14 never going to the king again unless he had **e**
8:10 who rode horses **e** bred for the king's service.
Pr 21:27 **e** when it is brought with ulterior motives.
Ecc 4: 6 **e** when in the long run everything is so futile.
Jer 13:25 "I have measured it out **e** for you, because you
Eze 36: 5 anger is on fire against these nations, **e** Edom,
Am 7:13 **e** not here where the royal sanctuary is!"
Mk 7: 3 (The Jews, **e** the Pharisees, do not eat until they
Lk 18:11 everyone else, **e** like that tax collector over there!
Ac 25:26 and **e** you, King Agrippa, so that after we examine
Ro 5: 7 might be willing to die for a person who is **e** good.
11:13 I am saying all of this **e** for you Gentiles. God has
1Co 14: 1 abilities the Spirit gives, **e** the gift of prophecy.
2Co 1:12 we have acted toward everyone, and **e** toward you.
7:13 we were **e** delighted to see how happy Titus was at
Gal 4:18 eager to do good, and **e** when I am not with you.
6:10 to everyone, **e** to our Christian brothers and sisters.
Php 4:22 too, **e** those who work in Caesar's palace.
1Ti 5: 8 **e** those living in the same household, have denied
5:17 **e** those who work hard at both preaching
2Ti 4:13 at Troas. Also bring my books, and **e** my papers.
Tit 1:10 This is **e** true of those who insist on circumcision
Phm 1:16 longer just a slave; he is a beloved brother, **e** to me.
Heb 10:25 **e** now that the day of his coming back again is
12: 1 **e** the sin that so easily hinders our progress.
13:19 I **e** need your prayers right now so that I can come
2Pe 2:10 He is **e** hard on those who follow their own evil,

ESPIED, ESPY [KJV] See DISCOVERED, EXPLORE(D), FOUND, WATCH

ESPOUSALS, ESPOUSED [KJV] See BOUGHT, ENGAGED, FIANCEE, PROMISED

ESROM [KJV] See HEZRON

ESSENCE (2)

Jn 12: 3 jar of expensive perfume made from **e** of nard,
Rev 19:10 For the **e** of prophecy is to give a clear witness for

ESTABLISH (14) [ESTABLISHED, ESTABLISHES, ESTABLISHING, REESTABLISH, REESTABLISHED]

Dt 28: 9 the LORD will **e** you as his holy people as he
2Sa 7:13 And I will **e** the throne of his kingdom forever.
1Ki 9: 5 then I will **e** the throne of your dynasty over Israel
11:38 I will **e** an enduring dynasty for you as I did for
20:34 and you may **e** places of trade in Damascus,
1Ch 17:12 a temple—for me. And I will **e** his throne forever.
17:14 I will **e** him over my dynasty and my kingdom for
22:10 And I will **e** the throne of his kingdom over Israel
Est 9:29 behind Mordecai's letter to **e** the Festival of Purim.
9:31 and their descendants to **e** the times of fasting
Ps 89: 4 'I will **e** your descendants as kings forever;
Jer 30:20 I will **e** them as a nation before me, and I will
Eze 16:60 and I will **e** an everlasting covenant with you.
Heb 10: 9 He cancels the first covenant in order to **e** the

ESTABLISHED (35) [ESTABLISH]

Lev 23: 4 addition to the Sabbath, the LORD has **e** festivals,
Dt 19:15 The facts of the case must be **e** by the testimony of
32: 6 created you? / Has he not made you and **e** you?
32: 8 human race, / he **e** the boundaries of the peoples
Jos 11: 5 They **e** their camp around the water near Merom to
1Sa 13:13 the LORD would have **e** your kingdom over
2Sa 7:26 And may the dynasty of your servant David be **e** in
1Ki 2:12 David, and he was firmly **e** on the throne.
2:24 David; he has **e** my dynasty as he promised.
2Ki 14: 5 When Amaziah was well **e** as king, he executed the
17:19 walked down the same evil paths that Israel had **e**.
1Ch 16:30 The world is firmly **e** and cannot be shaken.
17:24 And may your name be **e** and honored forever
17:24 And may the dynasty of your servant David be **e** in
24:19 **e** by their ancestor Aaron in obedience to the
2Ch 12: 1 But when Rehoboam was firmly **e** and strong,
12:13 King Rehoboam firmly **e** himself in Jerusalem
17: 5 So the LORD **e** Jehoshaphat's control over the
21: 4 But when Jehoram had become solidly **e** as king,
25: 3 When Amaziah was well **e** as king, he executed the
Est 9:31 These letters **e** the Festival of Purim—an annual
Job 28:27 measured it. He **e** it and examined it thoroughly.
Ps 93: 1 The world is firmly **e**; / it cannot be shaken.
93: 2 O LORD, has been **e** from time immemorial.
96:10 The world is firmly **e** and cannot be shaken.
99: 4 Mighty king, lover of justice, / you have **e** fairness.
148: 6 He **e** them forever and forever. / His orders will
Pr 3:19 the earth; by understanding he **e** the heavens.
8:27 "I was there when he **e** the heavens, when he drew
8:28 when he **e** the deep fountains of the earth.
Isa 16: 5 then David's throne will be **e** by love. From that
51:13 the one who put the stars in the sky and **e** the earth.
51:16 I set all the stars in space and **e** the earth. I am the
Ro 13: 4 The authorities are **e** by God for that very purpose,
2Co 13: 1 "The facts of every case must be **e** by the

ESTABLISHES (1) [ESTABLISH]

Job 36: 7 but he **e** and exalts them with kings forever.

ESTABLISHING (1) [ESTABLISH]

Isa 63:12 Moses lifted up his hand, **e** his reputation forever?

ESTATE (15) [ESTATES]

Ru 4: 6 "because this might endanger my own **e**.
Est 8: 1 On that same day King Xerxes gave the **e** of
8: 7 the Jew, "I have given Esther the **e** of Haman,
Ps 109:11 May creditors seize his entire **e**, / and strangers
Mt 20: 1 **e** who went out early one morning to hire workers
20: 7 "The owner of the **e** told them, 'Then go on out
21:38 said to one another, 'Here comes the heir to this **e**.
21:38 let's kill him and get the **e** for ourselves!'
Mk 12: 7 said to one another, 'Here comes the heir to this **e**.
12: 7 Let's kill him and get the **e** for ourselves!'
Lk 12:13 please tell my brother to divide our father's **e** with
15:12 son told his father, 'I want my share of your **e** now,
20:14 said to each other, 'Here comes the heir to this **e**.
20:14 Let's kill him and get the **e** for ourselves!'
Ac 28: 7 Near the shore where we landed was an **e**

ESTATES (3) [ESTATE]

Ps 49:11 They may name their **e** after themselves,
49:14 will rot in the grave, / far from their grand **e**.
Isa 5: 8 Your homes are built on great **e** so you can be

ESTEEM (5) [ESTEEMED]

2Ch 18: 1 Now Jehoshaphat enjoyed great riches and high **e**,
32:27 Hezekiah was very wealthy and held in high **e**.
Est 10: 3 great among the Jews, who held him in high **e**,
Pr 19:11 their anger; they earn **e** by overlooking wrongs.
22: 1 for being held in high **e** is better than having silver

ESTEEMED (3) [ESTEEM]

Dt 33:24 above other sons; / may he be **e** by his brothers;
2Ch 17: 5 so he became very wealthy and highly **e**.
Ac 22: 1 "Brothers and **e** fathers," Paul said, "listen to me

ESTHER (43) [ESTHER'S, HADASSAH]

Est 2: 7 young cousin, Hadassah, who was also called **E**.
2: 8 As a result of the king's decree, **E**, along with
2: 9 Hegai was very impressed with **E** and treated her
2:10 **E** had not told anyone of her nationality and family
2:11 near the courtyard of the harem to ask about **E**
2:16 When **E** was taken to King Xerxes at the royal
2:20 **E** continued to keep her nationality and family
2:22 the plot and passed the information on to Queen **E**.
4: 5 Then **E** sent for Hathach, one of the king's
4: 8 of all Jews, and he asked Hathach to show it to **E**.
4: 9 So Hathach returned to **E** with Mordecai's
4:10 Then **E** told Hathach to go back and relay this
4:13 Mordecai sent back this reply to **E**: "Don't think

4:15 Then **E** sent this reply to Mordecai:
4:17 So Mordecai went away and did as **E** told him.
5:1 **E** put on her royal robes and entered the inner
5:2 When he saw Queen **E** standing there in the inner
5:2 scepter to her. So **E** approached and touched its tip.
5:3 the king asked her, "What do you want, Queen **E**?
5:4 And **E** replied, "If it please Your Majesty,
5:5 to come quickly to a banquet, as **E** has requested."
5:6 while they were drinking wine, the king said to **E**,
5:7 **E** replied, "This is my request and deepest wish.
5:12 Queen **E** invited only me and the king himself to
6:14 to take Haman to the banquet **E** had prepared.
7:2 asked her, "Tell me what you want, Queen **E**.
7:3 And so Queen **E** replied, "If Your Majesty is
7:6 **E** replied, "This wicked Haman is our enemy."
7:7 stayed behind to plead for his life with Queen **E**,
7:8 In despair he fell on the couch where Queen **E** was
8:1 of Haman, the enemy of the Jews, to Queen **E**.
8:1 for **E** had told the king how they were related.
8:2 And **E** appointed Mordecai to be in charge of
8:3 Now once more **E** came before the king,
8:4 Again the king held out the gold scepter to **E**.
8:7 Then King Xerxes said to Queen **E** and Mordecai
8:7 the Jew, "I have given **E** the estate of Haman,
9:12 he called for Queen **E** and said, "The Jews have
9:13 And **E** said, "If it please Your Majesty,
9:25 But when **E** came before the king, he issued a
9:29 Then Queen **E**, the daughter of Abihail, along with
9:31 decreed by both Mordecai the Jew and Queen **E**.
9:32 So the command of **E** confirmed the practices of

ESTHER'S (6) [ESTHER]

Est 2:15 When it was **E** turn to go to the king, she accepted
2:18 he gave a banquet in **E** honor for all his princes
4:4 When Queen **E** maids and eunuchs came and told
4:12 So Hathach gave **E** message to Mordecai.
5:5 So the king and Haman went to **E** banquet.
7:1 So the king and Haman went to Queen **E** banquet.

ESTIMATE (1) [ESTIMATED, ESTIMATES, ESTIMATION]

Ro 12:3 Be honest in your **e** of yourselves, measuring your

ESTIMATED (1) [ESTIMATE]

Isa 33:18 and **e** how much plunder they would get from your

ESTIMATES (1) [ESTIMATE]

Lk 14:28 construction of a building without first getting **e**

ESTIMATION (1) [ESTIMATE]

Pr 26:5 or they will become wise in their own **e**.

ESTRANGED (1) [STRANGE]

2Sa 14:33 Then at last David summoned his **e** son,

ETAM (5)

Jdg 15:8 Then he went to live in a cave in the rock of **E**.
15:11 down to get Samson at the cave in the rock of **E**.
1Ch 4:3 The descendants of **E** were Jezreel, Ishma, Idbash,
4:32 Their descendants also lived in **E**, Ain, Rimmon,
2Ch 11:6 He built up Bethlehem, **E**, Tekoa,

ETCHED (1)

2Co 3:7 That old system of law **e** in stone led to death,

ETERNAL (110) [ETERNITY]

Ge 9:12 "I am giving you a sign as evidence of my **e**
9:16 I will remember the **e** covenant between God
21:33 he worshiped the LORD, the **E** God, at that place.
49:26 be greater than the blessings of the **e** mountains,
Dt 33:27 The **e** God is your refuge, / and his everlasting
2Sa 7:27 that you will build a house for me—an **e** dynasty!
7:29 O Sovereign LORD, it is an **e** blessing!"
23:5 His agreement is **e**, final, sealed. / He will
1Ki 10:9 Because the LORD loves Israel with an **e** love,
1Ch 17:25 that you will build a house for me—an **e** dynasty!
17:27 grant a blessing, O LORD, it is an **e** blessing!"
Ps 21:6 You have endowed him with **e** blessings.
41:13 God of Israel, / who lives forever from **e** ages past.
49:11 The grave is their **e** home, / where they will stay
78:66 He routed his enemies / and sent them to **e** shame.
89:37 as **e** as the moon, / my faithful witness in the sky!"
92:7 there is only **e** destruction ahead of them.
119:142 Your justice is **e**, / and your law is perfectly true.
Isa 26:4 for the LORD GOD is the **e** Rock.
45:17 will save the people of Israel with **e** salvation.
Jer 17:12 we worship at your throne—**e**, high, and glorious!
50:5 They will bind themselves to the LORD with an **e**
Da 4:34 His rule is everlasting, / and his kingdom is **e**.
7:14 would obey him. His rule is **e**—it will never end.
Hab 1:12 O LORD my God, my Holy One, you who are **e**—
3:6 the everlasting mountains and levels the **e** hills.
Zep 2:9 place of stinging nettles, salt pits, and **e** desolation.
Mt 19:16 what good things must I do to have **e** life?"
19:17 you can receive **e** life if you keep the
19:29 times as much in return and will have **e** life.
25:41 into the **e** fire prepared for the Devil and his
25:46 And they will go away into **e** punishment,
25:46 but the righteous will go into **e** life."
Mk 3:29 Holy Spirit will never be forgiven. It is an **e** sin."
10:17 "Good Teacher, what should I do to get **e** life?"
10:30 And in the world to come they will have **e** life.
16:S and unfailing message of salvation that gives **e** life.
Lk 10:25 "Teacher, what must I do to receive **e** life?"
18:18 "Good teacher, what should I do to get **e** life?"
18:30 as well as receiving **e** life in the world to come."
Jn 3:15 so that everyone who believes in me will have **e**
3:16 who believes in him will not perish but have **e** life.
3:36 And all who believe in God's Son have **e** life.
3:36 don't obey the Son will never experience **e** life,
4:14 perpetual spring within them, giving them **e** life."
4:36 and the fruit they harvest is people brought to **e**
5:24 and believe in God who sent me have **e** life.
5:29 Those who have done good will rise to **e** life,
5:39 because you believe they give you **e** life.
5:40 to come to me so that I can give you this **e** life.
6:27 Spend your energy seeking the **e** life that I, the Son
6:39 but that I should raise them to **e** life at the last day.
6:40 see his Son and believe in him should have **e** life—
6:47 anyone who believes in me already has **e** life.
6:50 the bread from heaven gives **e** life to everyone who
6:53 drink his blood, you cannot have **e** life within you.
6:54 who eat my flesh and drink my blood have **e** life,
6:63 It is the Spirit who gives **e** life. Human effort
6:68 we go? You alone have the words that give **e** life.
10:28 I give them **e** life, and they will never perish.
11:26 They are given **e** life for believing in me and will
12:25 their life in this world will keep it for **e** life.
12:50 And I know his instructions lead to **e** life; so I say
17:2 He gives **e** life to each one you have given him.
17:3 And this is the way to have **e** life—to know you,
Ac 4:28 everything they did occurred according to your **e**
11:18 privilege of turning from sin and receiving **e** life."
13:46 and judged yourselves unworthy of **e** life—
13:48 and all who were appointed to **e** life became
Ro 1:20 invisible qualities—his **e** power and divine nature.
2:7 He will give **e** life to those who persist in doing
5:10 we will certainly be delivered from **e** punishment
5:21 and resulting in **e** life through Jesus Christ our
6:21 things you used to do, things that end in **e** doom.
6:22 things that lead to holiness and result in **e** life.
6:23 but the free gift of God is **e** life through Christ
9:5 rules over everything and is worthy of **e** praise!
16:26 and as the **e** God has commanded,
1Co 9:25 that will fade away, but we do it for an **e** prize.
2Co 4:12 face of death, but it has resulted in **e** life for you.
5:1 an **e** body made for us by God himself and not by
Gal 1:6 and mercy called you to share the **e** life he gives
Php 3:19 Their future is **e** destruction. Their god is their
1Ti 1:16 that they, too, can believe in him and receive **e** life.
1:17 He is the **e** King, the unseen one who never dies;
6:12 Hold tightly to the **e** life that God has given you,
2Ti 2:10 and **e** glory in Christ Jesus to those God has
Tit 1:2 This truth gives them the confidence of **e** life,
3:7 And now we know that we will inherit **e** life.
Heb 5:9 and he became the source of **e** salvation for all
6:2 the resurrection of the dead, and **e** judgment.
6:20 He has become our **e** High Priest in the line of
9:14 For by the power of the **e** Spirit, Christ offered
9:15 so that all who are invited can receive the **e**
11:10 looking forward to a city with **e** foundations,
12:27 will be shaken, so that only **e** things will be left.
1Pe 1:23 life will last forever because it comes from the **e**,
5:10 In his kindness God called you to his **e** glory by
2Pe 1:11 for you to enter into the **e** Kingdom of our Lord
1Jn 1:2 and announce to you that he is the one who is **e**
2:25 And in this fellowship we enjoy the **e** life he
3:14 it proves that we have passed from death to **e** life.
3:15 And you know that murderers don't have **e** life
4:9 the world so that we might have **e** life through him.
5:11 He has given us **e** life, and this life is in his Son.
5:13 Son of God, so that you may know you have **e** life.
5:20 He is the only true God, and he is **e** life.
Jude 1:7 and are a warning of the **e** fire that will punish all
1:21 **e** life that our Lord Jesus Christ in his mercy is
Rev 17:8 up out of the bottomless pit and go to **e** destruction.

ETERNITY (8) [ETERNAL]

Ps 89:4 they will sit on your throne from now until **e**.' "
Ecc 3:11 He has planted **e** in the human heart, but even so,
Isa 43:13 "From **e** to **e** I am God. No one can oppose
57:15 The high and lofty one who inhabits **e**, the Holy
Gal 1:5 all glory belongs to God through all the ages of **e**.
Eph 3:11 This was his plan from all **e**, and it has now been
Heb 10:34 knew you had better things waiting for you in **e**.

ETH-KAZIN (1)

Jos 19:13 **E**, and Rimmon and turned toward Neah.

ETHAM (4)

Ex 13:20 they camped at **E** on the edge of the wilderness.
Nu 33:6 and camped at **E** on the edge of the wilderness.
33:7 They left **E** and turned back toward Pi-hahiroth,
33:8 Then they traveled for three days into the **E**

ETHAN (8) [ETHAN'S]

1Ki 4:31 including **E** the Ezrahite and Heman, Calcol,
1Ch 2:6 Zerah were Zimri, **E**, Heman, Calcol, and Darda—
2:8 The son of **E** was Azariah.
6:42 **E**, Zimmah, Shimei,
6:44 Heman's second assistant was **E** from the clan of
15:17 and **E** son of Kushaiah from the clan of Merari to
15:19 and **E** were chosen to sound the bronze cymbals.
Ps 89:T A psalm of **E** the Ezrahite.

ETHAN'S (1) [ETHAN]

1Ch 6:44 **E** genealogy was traced back through Kishi,

ETHBAAL (1)

1Ki 16:31 the daughter of King **E** of the Sidonians,

ETHER (2)

Jos 15:42 Besides these, there were Libnah, **E**, Ashan,
19:7 It also included Ain, Rimmon, **E**, and Ashan—

ETHIOPIA (21) [ETHIOPIAN, ETHIOPIANS]

2Ki 19:9 of **E** was leading an army to fight against him.
Est 1:1 over 127 provinces stretching from India to **E**.
8:9 of all the 127 provinces stretching from India to **E**.
Job 28:19 Topaz from **E** cannot be exchanged for it. Its value
Ps 68:31 precious metals; / let **E** bow in submission to God.
87:4 also Philistia and Tyre, and even distant **E**.
Isa 11:11 Upper Egypt, **E**, Elam, Babylonia, Hamath,
18:1 Destruction is certain for the land of **E**, which lies
20:3 the terrible troubles I will bring upon Egypt and **E**.
20:5 who counted on the power of **E** and boasted of
37:9 of **E** was leading an army to fight against him.
43:3 I gave Egypt, **E**, and Seba as a ransom for your
Jer 46:9 Come, all you allies from **E**, Libya, and Lydia who
Eze 29:10 Migdol to Aswan, as far south as the border of **E**.
30:4 The land of **E** will be ravished.
30:5 **E**, Libya, Lydia, and Arabia, with all their other
38:5 Persia, **E**, and Libya will join you, too, with all
Na 3:9 **E** and the land of Egypt were the source of her
Zep 3:10 the rivers of **E** will come to present their offerings.
Ac 8:27 So he did, and he met the treasurer of **E**, a eunuch of great authority under the queen of **E**.

ETHIOPIAN (4) [ETHIOPIA]

2Ch 14:9 Once an **E** named Zerah attacked Judah with an
Jer 13:23 Can an **E** change the color of his skin? Can a
38:7 But Ebed-melech the **E**, an important palace
39:16 "Say to Ebed-melech the **E**, 'The LORD

ETHIOPIANS (11) [ETHIOPIA]

2Ch 12:3 foot soldiers, including Libyans, Sukkites, and **E**.
14:12 So the LORD defeated the **E** in the presence of
14:13 so many **E** fell that they were unable to rally.
16:8 Don't you remember what happened to the **E**
21:16 the Philistines and the Arabs, who lived near the **E**,
Isa 20:4 will take away the Egyptians and **E** as prisoners.
45:14 "The Egyptians, **E**, and Sabeans will be subject to
Eze 30:9 messengers in ships to terrify the complacent **E**.
Da 11:43 and the Libyans and **E** will be his servants.
Am 9:7 think you are more important to me than the **E**?"
Zep 2:12 "You **E** will also be slaughtered by my sword,"

ETHNAN (1)

1Ch 4:7 Helah gave birth to Zereth, Izhar, **E**,

ETHNI (1)

1Ch 6:41 **E**, Zerah, Adaiah,

EUBULUS (1)

2Ti 4:21 **E** sends you greetings, and so do Pudens, Linus,

EUNICE (1)

2Ti 1:5 of your mother, **E**, and your grandmother, Lois.

EUNUCH (8) [EUNUCHS]

2Ki 23:11 were near the quarters of Nathan-melech the **e**,
Est 2:3 Hegai, the **e** in charge, will see that they are all
2:15 the advice of Hegai, the **e** in charge of the harem.
Ac 8:27 a **e** of great authority under the queen of Ethiopia.
8:27 The **e** had gone to Jerusalem to worship,
8:34 The **e** asked Philip, "Was Isaiah talking about
8:36 they came to some water, and the **e** said, "Look!
8:39 The **e** never saw him again but went on his way

EUNUCHS (15) [EUNUCH]

2Ki 9:32 my side?" And two or three **e** looked out at him.
20:18 They will become **e** who will serve in the palace of
Est 1:10 Zethar, and Carcas, the seven **e** who attended him,
1:15 the king's orders, properly sent through his **e**?"
2:14 the care of Shaashgaz, another of the king's **e**.
2:21 two of the king's **e**, Bigthana and Teresh—
4:4 When Queen Esther's maids and **e** came and told
4:5 one of the king's **e** who had been appointed as her
6:2 two of the **e** who guarded the door to the king's
6:14 the king's **e** arrived to take Haman to the banquet
7:9 Then Harbona, one of the king's **e**, said,
Isa 39:7 They will become **e** who will serve in the palace of
56:3 And my blessings are also for the **e**. They are as
56:4 For I say this to the **e** who keep my Sabbath days
Mt 19:12 Some are born as **e**, some have been made that way

EUODIA (1)

Php 4:2 to plead with those two women, **E** and Syntyche.

EUPHRATES (61)

Ge 2:14 to the east of Asshur. The fourth branch is the **E**.
15:18 all the way from the border of Egypt to the great **E**
31:21 his possessions with him and crossed the **E** River,
36:37 Shaul from the city of Rehoboth on the **E** River
Ex 23:31 and from the southern deserts to the **E** River.

Nu 22: 5 living in his native land of Pethor near the **E** River.
Dt 1: 7 to Lebanon, and all the way to the great **E** River.
11: 24 and from the **E** River in the east to the
Jos 1: 4 from the **E** River on the east to the Mediterranean
24: 2 of Abraham and Nahor, lived beyond the **E** River,
24: 3 ancestor Abraham from the land beyond the **E**
24: 14 worshiped when they lived beyond the **E** River
24: 15 the gods your ancestors served beyond the **E**?
2Sa 8: 3 out to strengthen his control along the **E** River.
10: 16 by Hadadezer from the other side of the **E** River.
1Ki 4: 21 King Solomon ruled all the kingdoms from the **E**
4: 24 over all the kingdoms west of the **E** River,
14: 15 and will scatter them beyond the **E** River,
2Ki 23: 29 went to the **E** River to help the king of Assyria.
24: 7 by Egypt—from the brook of Egypt to the **E** River.
1Ch 1: 48 Shaul from the city of Rehoboth on the **E** River
5: 9 the edge of the desert that stretches to the **E** River.
18: 3 out to strengthen his control along the **E** River.
19: 16 Aramean troops from the other side of the **E** River.
2Ch 9: 26 He ruled over all the kings from the **E** River to the
35: 20 Egypt to do battle at Carchemish on the **E** River,
Ezr 4: 10 lands of the province west of the **E** River.
4: 11 loyal subjects in the province west of the **E** River.
4: 16 the province west of the **E** River will be lost to
4: 17 and throughout the province west of the **E** River.
4: 20 and the entire province west of the **E** River
5: 3 governor of the province west of the **E**,
5: 6 province west of the **E** River sent to King Darius:
6: 6 governor of the province west of the **E** River,
6: 6 your colleagues and other officials west of the **E**:
6: 13 governor of the province west of the **E** River,
7: 21 the treasurers in the province west of the **E** River:
7: 25 all the people in the province west of the **E** River.
8: 36 and the governors of the province west of the **E**
Ne 2: 7 the governors of the province west of the **E** River,
2: 9 the governors of the province west of the **E** River,
3: 7 the governor of the province west of the **E** River.
Ps 72: 8 and from the **E** River to the ends of the earth.
80: 11 Mediterranean Sea, / our limbs east to the **E** River.
89: 25 in the west / to the Tigris and **E** rivers in the east.
Isa 8: 7 them with a mighty flood from the **E** River—
11: 15 He will wave his hand over the **E** River, sending a
27: 12 from the **E** River in the east to the brook of Egypt
Jer 2: 18 good to you are the waters of the Nile and the **E**?
13: 4 linen belt you are wearing, and go to the **E** River.
13: 5 and hid it at the **E** as the LORD had instructed
13: 6 "Go back to the **E** and get the linen belt that I told
13: 7 So I went to the **E** and dug it out of the hole where
46: 2 and his army were defeated beside the **E** River by
46: 6 By the **E** River to the north they stumble and fall.
46: 10 today in the north country beside the **E** River.
51: 63 tie it to a stone, and throw it into the **E** River.
Mic 7: 12 and from Egypt all the way to the **E** River,
Zec 9: 10 and from the **E** River to the ends of the earth.
Rev 9: 14 four angels who are bound at the great **E** River."
16: 12 angel poured out his bowl on the great **E** River,

EUROCLYDON [KJV] See NORTHEASTER

EUTYCHUS (1)
Ac 20: 9 As Paul spoke on and on, a young man named **E**,

EVALUATE (3) [EVALUATING]
Lev 27: 8 go to the priest and he will **e** your ability to pay.
Ecc 2: 9 so that I could **e** all these things.
1Co 14: 29 or three prophesy, and let the others **e** what is said.

EVALUATING (1) [EVALUATE]
2Co 5: 16 So we have stopped **e** others by what the world

EVANGELIST (1) [EVANGELISTS]
Ac 21: 8 to Caesarea and stayed at the home of Philip the **E**,

EVANGELISTS (1) [EVANGELIST]
Eph 4: 11 the apostles, the prophets, the **e**, and the pastors

EVAPORATED (1) [EVAPORATES]
Ps 32: 4 My strength **e** like water in the summer heat.

EVAPORATES (1) [EVAPORATED]
Job 14: 11 As water **e** from a lake and as a river disappears in

EVE (4)
Ge 3: 20 Then Adam named his wife **E**, because she would
4: 1 slept with his wife, **E**, and she became pregnant.
2Co 11: 3 to Christ, just as **E** was deceived by the serpent.
1Ti 2: 13 God made Adam first, and afterward he made **E**.

EVEN (1068) [EVENLY] See Index of Articles, Etc.

EVEN-TEMPERED (1) [TEMPER]
Pr 17: 27 uses few words; a person with understanding is **e**.

EVENING (129) [EVENINGS]

IN THE EVENING (17) Ge 49:27; Ex 16:6,8,12; 29:39,41; Lev 6:20; Nu 28:4,8; Dt 28:67; Ps 92:2; Isa 17:14; Eze 12:4,7; 24:18; Da 6:15; Mk 14:17

MORNING...EVENING; EVENING...MORNING (31) Ge 49:27; Ex 16:8,12,13; 18:13; 29:39,41; Lev 6:20; 24:3; Nu 9:15; 28:4; Dt 28:67,67; 1Sa 17:16; 1Ki 17:6; 2Ki 16:15; 1Ch 16:40; 23:30; 2Ch 2:4; 13:11; 31:3; Ezr 3:3; Est 2:14; Job 4:20; Ps 90:6; 92:2; Eze 24:18,18; 33:22; Ac 4:3; 28:23

UNTIL [THE] EVENING (44) Ex 12:6,18; Lev 11:24,25, 26,27,28,31,32,39,40; 14:46; 15:5,6,10,11,16,17,18,19,21,27; 17:15; 22:6; 23:32; Nu 19:7,8,10,21,22; Jos 7:6; 8:29; 10:26; Jdg 20:23,26; 21:2; 1Sa 20:5; 30:17; 1Ki 18:28,29; 2Ch 18:34; Ezr 9:4; Ps 104:23; Eze 46:2

Ge 3: 8 Toward **e** they heard the LORD God walking
8: 11 This time, toward **e**, the bird returned to him with a
15: 12 That **e**, as the sun was going down, Abram fell into
19: 1 That **e** the two angels came to the entrance of the
24: 11 It was **e**, and the women were coming out to draw
24: 63 One **e** as he was taking a walk out in the fields,
30: 16 So that **e**, as Jacob was coming home from the
49: 27 the morning, / and in the **e** he divides the plunder."
Ex 12: 6 "Take special care of these lambs until the **e** of the
12: 8 That **e** everyone must eat roast lamb with bitter
12: 18 Only bread without yeast may be eaten from the **e**
12: 18 until the **e** of the twenty-first day of the month.
16: 6 "In the **e** you will realize that it was the LORD
16: 8 The LORD will give you meat to eat in the **e**
16: 12 Now tell them, 'In the **e** you will have meat to eat,
16: 13 That **e** vast numbers of quail arrived and covered
18: 13 were lined up in front of him from morning till **e**.
29: 39 one in the morning and the other in the **e**.
29: 41 Offer the other lamb in the **e**, along with the same
30: 8 And each **e** when he tends to the lamps, he must
Lev 6: 20 in the morning and half to be offered in the **e**.
11: 24 of their dead bodies, you will be defiled until **e**.
11: 25 your clothes, and you will remain defiled until **e**.
11: 26 body of such an animal, you will be defiled until **e**.
11: 27 body of such an animal, you will be defiled until **e**.
11: 28 your clothes, and you will remain defiled until **e**.
11: 31 body of such an animal, you will be defiled until **e**.
11: 32 be put into water, and it will remain defiled until **e**.
11: 39 you touch its carcass, you will be defiled until **e**.
11: 40 your clothes. Then you will remain defiled until **e**.
14: 46 will be considered ceremonially unclean until **e**.
15: 5 and you will remain ceremonially defiled until **e**.
15: 6 in water. You will then remain defiled until **e**.
15: 10 bathe in water, and you will remain defiled until **e**.
15: 11 bathe in water, and you will remain defiled until **e**.
15: 16 and he will remain ceremonially defiled until **e**.
15: 17 must be washed, and it will remain defiled until **e**.
15: 18 must bathe, and they will remain defiled until **e**.
15: 19 her during that time, you will be defiled until **e**.
15: 21 bathe in water, and you will remain defiled until **e**.
15: 27 bathe in water, and you will remain defiled until **e**.
17: 15 Then you will remain ceremonially unclean until **e**;
22: 6 they will remain defiled until **e**. They must not eat
23: 32 and fasting will begin the **e** before the Day of
Atonement and extend until **e** of that day."
24: 3 from **e** until morning, before the LORD.
Nu 9: 15 Then from **e** until morning the cloud over the
19: 7 he will remain ceremonially unclean until **e**.
19: 8 in water, and he, too, will remain unclean until **e**.
19: 10 and he will remain ceremonially unclean until **e**.
19: 19 and that **e** they will be cleansed of their defilement.
19: 21 the water of purification will remain defiled until **e**.
19: 22 touches will be ceremonially defiled until **e**."
28: 4 be sacrificed in the morning and the other in the **e**.
28: 8 Offer the second lamb in the **e** with the same grain
Dt 23: 11 Toward **e** he must bathe himself, and at sunset he
28: 67 And in the **e** you will say, 'If only it were
Jos 5: 10 they celebrated Passover on the **e** of the fourteenth
7: 6 bowed down facing the Ark of the LORD until **e**.
8: 29 the king of Ai on a tree and left him there until **e**.
10: 26 the five kings and hung them on five trees until **e**.
Jdg 19: 16 That **e** an old man came home from his work in the
20: 23 and wept in the presence of the LORD until **e**.
20: 26 in the presence of the LORD and fasted until **e**.
21: 2 to Bethel and sat in the presence of God until **e**,
Ru 2: 17 and when she beat out the grain that **e**, it came to
1Sa 14: 24 "Let a curse fall on anyone who eats before **e**—
14: 32 That **e** they flew upon the battle plunder
17: 16 For forty days, twice a day, morning and **e**,
20: 5 the field and stay there until the **e** of the third day.
20: 19 The day after tomorrow, toward **e**, go to the place
30: 17 that night and the entire next day until **e**.
1Ki 17: 6 brought him bread and meat each morning and **e**,
18: 29 They raved all afternoon until the time of the **e**
18: 36 At the customary time for offering the **e** sacrifice,
22: 35 to the floor of his chariot, and as **e** arrived he died.
2Ki 7: 5 So that **e** they went out to the camp of the
16: 15 the **e** grain offering, the king's burnt offering
1Ch 16: 40 and **e** on the altar set aside for that purpose,
23: 30 and **e** they stood before the LORD to sing songs
2Ch 2: 4 to sacrifice burnt offerings each morning and **e**,
13: 11 incense to the LORD every morning and **e**.
13: 11 and they light the gold lampstand every **e**.
18: 34 up in his chariot facing the Arameans until **e**.
31: 3 for the daily morning and **e** burnt offerings,
Ezr 3: 3 to the LORD. They did this each morning and **e**.
9: 4 utterly appalled until the time of the **e** sacrifice.
Ne 13: 19 city should be shut as darkness fell every Friday **e**,
Est 2: 14 That **e** she was taken to the king's private rooms,
9: 11 That **e**, when the king was informed of the number
Job 4: 20 but by **e** they are dead, gone forever without a
Ps 90: 6 and flourishes, / but by **e** it is dry and withered.
92: 2 love in the morning, / your faithfulness in the **e**,
102: 11 My life passes as swiftly as the **e** shadows.
104: 23 they labor until the **e** shadows fall again.
141: 2 to you, / and my upraised hands as an **e** offering.
Ecc 8: 13 Their days will never grow long like the **e**
Isa 17: 14 In the **e** Israel waits in terror, but by dawn its
Jer 6: 4 the day is fading, and the **e** shadows are falling.
Eze 12: 4 as they are watching, leave your house in the **e**,
12: 7 Then in the **e** while the people looked on, I dug
24: 18 the next morning, and in the **e** my wife died.
33: 22 The previous **e** the LORD had taken hold of me
46: 2 he came. The gateway will not be closed until **e**.
Da 6: 15 In the **e** the men went together to the king and said,
9: 21 came swiftly to me at the time of the **e** sacrifice.
Zep 3: 3 Its judges are like ravenous wolves at **e** time,
Zec 14: 7 and night, for at **e** time it will still be light.
Mt 8: 16 That **e** many demon-possessed people were
14: 15 That **e** the disciples came to him and said, "This is
20: 6 At five o'clock that **e** he was in town again
20: 8 "That **e** he told the foreman to call the workers in
26: 20 When it was **e**, Jesus sat down at the table with the
27: 57 As **e** approached, Joseph, a rich man from
Mk 1: 32 That **e** at sunset, many sick and demon-possessed
4: 35 As **e** came, Jesus said to his disciples, "Let's cross
11: 19 That **e** Jesus and the disciples left the city.
13: 35 at **e**, midnight, early dawn, or late daybreak.
14: 17 In the **e** Jesus arrived with the twelve disciples.
15: 42 the day before the Sabbath. As **e** approached,
16: 1 The next **e**, when the Sabbath ended,
Lk 2: 44 But when he didn't show up that **e**, they started to
4: 40 As the sun went down that **e**, people throughout
21: 37 and each **e** he returned to spend the night on the
Jn 3: 1 After dark one **e**, a Jewish religious leader named
6: 16 That **e** his disciples went down to the shore to wait
20: 19 That **e**, on the first day of the week, the disciples
Ac 4: 3 They arrested them and, since it was already **e**,
28: 23 lecturing in the morning and went on into the **e**.

EVENINGS (2) [EVENING]
Da 8: 14 "It will take twenty-three hundred **e** and mornings;
8: 26 "This vision about the twenty-three hundred **e**

EVENLY (1) [EVEN]
1Ch 26: 16 up to the Temple. Guard duties were divided **e**.

EVENT (11) [EVENTS]
Ex 19: 15 "Get ready for an important **e** two days from now.
23: 15 This festival will be an annual **e** at the appointed
30: 10 a regular, annual **e** from generation to generation,
Jos 10: 13 Is this **e** not recorded in *The Book of Jashar*?
Est 8: 12 The day chosen for this **e** throughout all the
Ecc 3: 15 in the past. For God calls each **e** back in its turn.
1Co 12: 31 And in any **e**, you should desire the most helpful
Tit 2: 13 while we look forward to that wonderful **e** when
Rev 12: 1 Then I witnessed in heaven an **e** of great
12: 3 I witnessed in heaven another significant **e**.
15: 1 Then I saw in heaven another significant **e**, and it

EVENT [KJV] See also FATE

EVENTS (77) [EVENT]

THE REST OF THE EVENTS (47) 1Ki 11:41; 14:19,29; 15:7,23,31; 16:5,14,20,27; 22:39,45; 2Ki 1:18; 8:23; 10:34; 12:19; 13:8,12; 14:15,18,28; 15:6,11,15,21,26,31,36; 16:19; 20:20; 21:17,25; 23:28; 24:5; 2Ch 9:29; 12:15; 13:22; 16:11; 20:34; 25:26; 26:22; 27:7; 28:26; 32:32; 33:18; 35:26; 36:8

Ge 41: 32 by God and that he will make these **e** happen soon.
Jos 7: 5 Israelites were paralyzed with fear at this turn of **e**,
Jdg 9: 24 In the **e** that followed, God punished Abimelech
1Ki 11: 41 The rest of the **e** in Solomon's reign, including his
12: 15 This turn of **e** was the will of the LORD, for it
14: 19 The rest of the **e** of Jeroboam's reign, all his wars
14: 29 The rest of the **e** in Rehoboam's reign and all his
15: 7 The rest of the **e** in Abijam's reign and all his
15: 23 The rest of the **e** in Asa's reign, the extent of his
15: 31 The rest of the **e** in Nadab's reign and all his deeds
16: 5 The rest of the **e** in Baasha's reign and the extent
16: 14 The rest of the **e** in Elah's reign and all his deeds
16: 20 The rest of the **e** of Zimri's reign and his
16: 27 The rest of the **e** in Omri's reign, the extent of his
22: 39 The rest of the **e** in Ahab's reign and the story of
22: 45 The rest of the **e** in Jehoshaphat's reign, the extent
2Ki 1: 18 The rest of the **e** in Ahaziah's reign are recorded
8: 23 The rest of the **e** in Jehoram's reign and all his
10: 34 The rest of the **e** in Jehu's reign and all his deeds
12: 19 The rest of the **e** in Joash's reign and all his deeds
13: 8 The rest of the **e** in Jehoahaz's reign and all his
13: 12 The rest of the **e** in Jehoash's reign and all his
14: 15 The rest of the **e** in Jehoash's reign,
14: 18 The rest of the **e** in Amaziah's reign are recorded
14: 28 The rest of the **e** in the reign of Jeroboam II and all
15: 6 The rest of the **e** in Uzziah's reign and all his
15: 11 The rest of the **e** in Zechariah's reign are recorded
15: 15 The rest of the **e** in Shallum's reign, including his
15: 21 The rest of the **e** in Menahem's reign and all his
15: 26 The rest of the **e** in Pekahiah's reign and all his
15: 31 The rest of the **e** in Pekah's reign and all his deeds
15: 36 The rest of the **e** in Jotham's reign and all his
16: 19 The rest of the **e** in Ahaz's reign and his deeds are
20: 20 The rest of the **e** in Hezekiah's reign,
21: 17 The rest of the **e** in Manasseh's reign and all his
21: 25 The rest of the **e** in Amon's reign and all his deeds
23: 28 The rest of the **e** in Josiah's reign and all his deeds
24: 5 The rest of the **e** in Jehoiakim's reign and all his
1Ch 29: 29 All the **e** of King David's reign, from beginning to
2Ch 9: 29 The rest of the **e** of Solomon's reign,
10: 15 This turn of **e** was the will of God, for it fulfilled
12: 15 The rest of the **e** of Rehoboam's reign,
13: 22 The rest of the **e** of Abijah's reign, including his
16: 11 The rest of the **e** of Asa's reign, from beginning to

20:34 The rest of the e of Jehoshaphat's reign,
25:26 The rest of the e of Amaziah's reign,
26:22 The rest of the e of Uzziah's reign, from beginning
27: 7 The rest of the e of Jotham's reign, including his
28:26 The rest of the e of Ahaz's reign and all his
32:31 the remarkable e that had taken place in the land,
32:32 The rest of the e of Hezekiah's reign and his acts
33:18 The rest of the e of Manasseh's reign, his prayer to
35:26 The rest of the e of Josiah's reign and his acts of
36: 8 The rest of the e of Jehoiakim's reign, including all
Est 9:20 Mordecai recorded these e and sent letters to the
Isa 29:11 All these future e are a sealed book to them.
44:25 e to happen that are contrary to their predictions.
Da 2:21 He determines the course of world e; / he removes
2:29 was sleeping, you dreamed about coming e.
4:19 how I wish the e foreshadowed in this dream
8:13 them said, "How long will the e of this vision last?
8:17 "you must understand that the e you have seen in
10: 1 It concerned e certain to happen in the future—
12: 6 "How long will it be until these shocking e
Mt 24:33 when you see the e I've described beginning to
Mk 13:29 when you see the e I've described beginning to
13:30 from the scene until all these e have taken place.
Lk 1: 1 Many people have written accounts about the e
1:66 Everyone who heard about it reflected on these e
21:25 "And there will be strange e in the skies—signs in
21:31 when you see the e I've described taking place,
21:32 from the scene until all these e have taken place.
Jn 21:24 This is that disciple who saw these e and recorded
Ac 26:26 for I am sure these e are all familiar to him,
1Co 10: 6 These e happened as a warning to us, so that we
10:11 All these e happened to them as examples for us.
Rev 1: 1 which God gave him concerning the e that will

EVENTUALLY (10)

Ge 10:19 E the territory of Canaan spread from Sidon to
Ex 16:34 He e placed it for safekeeping in the Ark of the
17: 1 E they came to Rephidim, but there was no water
2Sa 14:14 All of us must die e. Our lives are like water
Mt 26:58 and e came to the courtyard of the high priest's
Mk 4:22 is now hidden or secret will e be brought to light.
Lk 8:17 or secret will e be brought to light and made plain
18: 4 ignored her for a while, but e she wore him out.
Jn 4: 5 E he came to the Samaritan village of Sychar,
Ac 7: 5 that e the whole country would belong to Abraham

EVER (258) [EVER-FLOWING, EVER-INCREASING, EVER-LIVING, EVER-WIDENING, EVERLASTING, EVERMORE, FOREVER, FOREVERMORE]

FOREVER AND EVER (31) Ex 15:18; 1Ch 29:10; Ps 10:16; 45:6,17; 48:14; 52:8; 79:13; 113:2; 145:1; Da 2:20; 7:18; Mic 4:5; Eph 3:21; Php 4:20; 1Ti 1:17; 2Ti 4:18; Heb 1:8; 13:20; 1Pe 4:11; 5:11; Rev 1:6,18; 4:9,10; 5:13; 10:6; 11:15; 14:11; 20:10; 22:5

Ge 6: 6 So the LORD was sorry he had e made them.
6: 7 and birds, too. I am sorry I e made them."
21: 7 For who would have dreamed that I would e have a
21:31 So e since, that place has been known as
24:16 and she was a virgin; no man had e slept with her.
35: 8 E since, the tree has been called the "Oak of
38:29 break out first?" And e after, he was called Perez.
39: 9 his wife. How could I e do such a wicked thing?
43: 6 "Why did you e tell him you had another
Ex 10:28 "Don't e let me see you again! The day you do,
15:18 The LORD will reign forever and e!"
17: 3 to complain, "Why did you e take us out of Egypt?
32:21 "How did they e make you bring such terrible sin
33:16 how will anyone e know that your people and I
Lev 22:10 "No one outside a priest's family may e eat the
Nu 11:20 to him, "Why did we e leave Egypt?" ' "
14:19 just as you have forgiven them e since they left
14:22 not one of these people will e enter that land.
16:40 should e enter the LORD's presence to burn
21: 3 and the place has been called Hormah e since.
22:30 "Have I e done anything like this before?" "No,"
23:19 Has he e spoken and failed to act? / Has he e promised and not carried it through?
32:11 or older will e see the land I solemnly promised to
Dt 4:32 See if anything as great as this has e happened
4:33 Has any nation e heard the voice of God speaking
7:17 'How can we e conquer these nations that are
8:19 If you e forget the LORD your God and follow
23:17 or woman may e become a temple prostitute.
25: 3 No more than forty lashes may e be given;
25:10 E afterward his family will be referred to as 'the
34: 7 his eyesight was clear, and he was as strong as e.
Jos 7:26 has been called the Valley of Trouble e since.
8:35 Every command Moses had e given was read to the
10:25 "Don't e be afraid or discouraged," Joshua told
Ru 2: 7 She has been hard at work e since, except for a few
3:10 "You are showing more family loyalty now than e
1Sa 2:32 But no members of your family will e live out their
8: 8 E since I brought them from Egypt they have
12: 3 Have I e cheated any of you? Have I e oppressed you? Have I e taken a bribe?
13: 4 the Philistines now hated the Israelites more than e.
14:35 an altar to the LORD, the first one he had e built.
15:11 "I am sorry that I e made Saul king, for he has not
15:35 And the LORD was sorry he had e made Saul
22: 8 For not one of you has e told me that my own son
23:28 E since that time, the place where David was
25: 7 harmed them, and nothing was e stolen from them.
29: 6 "you are some of the finest men I've e met.
2Sa 2:16 The place has been known e since as the Field of
6: 9 "How can I e bring the Ark of the LORD back
13: 2 and it seemed impossible that he could e fulfill his
13:32 Absalom has been plotting this e since Amnon
19: 7 Then you will be worse off than you have e been."
1Ki 3:12 and understanding mind such as no one else has e had or e will have!
2Ki 2:22 The water has remained wholesome e since,
8:13 "How could a nobody like me e accomplish such a
18:33 Have the gods of any other nations e saved their
18:35 What god of any nation has e been able to save its
21:15 and have angered me e since their ancestors came
23:10 so no one could e again use it to sacrifice a son
1Ch 4:43 had survived, and they have lived there e since.
13:12 "How can I e bring the Ark of God back into my
22: 3 and more bronze than they could e weigh.
29:10 ancestor Israel, may you be praised forever and e!
2Ch 1:12 and honor such as no other king has e had before you or will e have again!"
32:15 no god of any nation has e yet been able to rescue
35:18 None of the kings of Israel had e kept a Passover
Ezr 4: 2 We have sacrificed to him e since King
5:16 The people have been working on it e since,
5:17 e issued a decree to rebuild God's Temple in
Ne 4:23 guards who were with me—e took off our clothes.
13: 1 or Moabite should e be permitted to enter the
Est 6: 3 or recognition did we e give Mordecai for this?"
9:28 nor would the memory of what happened e die out
Job 6:22 But why? Have I e asked you for a gift? Have I
6:23 Have I e asked you to rescue me from my
9: 4 Who has e challenged him successfully?
15: 7 "Were you the first person e born? Were you born
16: 3 Won't you e stop your flow of foolish words?
20: 4 "Don't you realize that e since people were first
20: 9 Neither his friends nor his family will e see him
28: 8 No wild animal has e walked upon those treasures;
31:29 "Have I e rejoiced when my enemies came to ruin
34: 7 "Has there e been a man as arrogant as Job,
38:12 "Have you e commanded the morning to appear
38:13 Have you e told the daylight to spread to the ends
40: 4 "I am nothing—how could I e find the answers?
Ps 10: 6 to themselves, "Nothing bad will e happen to us!
10:16 The LORD is king forever and e! / Let those who
25: 3 No one who trusts in you will e be disgraced,
45: 6 Your throne, O God, endures forever and e.
45:17 the nations will praise you forever and e.
48:14 is what God is like. / He is our God forever and e,
49: 8 not come so easily, / for no one can e pay enough
49:16 and their homes become e more splendid.
52: 8 I trust in God's unfailing love / forever and e.
64: 5 to set their traps. / "Who will e notice?" they ask.
73: 7 cats have everything / their hearts could e wish for!
74:23 Their uproar of rebellion grows e louder.
79:13 of your pasture, / will thank you forever and e,
106: 2 the LORD? / Who can e praise him half enough?
106:31 regarded as a righteous man / e since that time.
113: 2 Blessed be the name of the LORD / forever and e.
130: 3 record of our sins, / who, O Lord, could e survive?
145: 1 and King, / and bless your name forever and e.
Pr 4:18 which shines e brighter until the full light of day.
23:23 Get the truth and don't e sell it; also get wisdom,
Ecc 6: 2 and gives them everything they could e want,
Isa 9: 7 His e expanding, peaceful government will never
14:29 his son will be worse than his father e was.
29:16 Does a jar e say, "The potter who made me is
36:18 Have the gods of any other nations e saved their
36:20 What god of any nation has e been able to save its
40:14 Has the LORD e needed anyone's advice?
43: 9 Which of their idols has e foretold such things?
43:12 I saved you. No foreign god has e done this before.
45: 9 Does a clay pot e argue with its maker?
45:21 What idol e told you they would happen? Was it
48:14 "Have any of your idols e told you this? Come,
49:16 E before me is a picture of Jerusalem's walls in
66: 1 Could you e build me a temple as good as that?
66: 8 Who has e seen or heard of anything as strange as this? Has a nation e been born in a single day? Has a country e come forth in a mere moment?
66: 9 Would I e bring this nation to the point of birth
Jer 2:10 See if anyone has e heard of anything as strange as
2:11 Has any nation e exchanged its gods for another
3:23 Only in the LORD our God will Israel e find
6: 7 Her sickness and sores are e before me.
18:13 LORD said, "Has anyone e heard of such a thing,
18:14 Does the snow e melt high up in the mountains of
18:14 from the crags of Mount Hermon e run dry?
20:18 Why was I e born? My entire life has been filled
22:30 for none of his children will e sit on the throne of
44: 3 nor you nor any of your ancestors have e known.
44:18 But e since we quit burning incense to the Queen
48: 2 No one will e brag about Moab again, for there is a
49: 4 your wealth and thought no one could e harm you.
La 2:13 In all the world has there e been such sorrow?
Eze 5: 9 than I have punished anyone before or e will again.
16:13 and olive oil—and became more beautiful than e.
16:16 Unbelievable! How could such a thing e happen?
16:51 far more loathsome things than your sisters e did.
20:29 has been called Bamah—'high place'—e since.)
27:32 funeral song: / 'Was there e such a city as Tyre,
44: 2 No man will e pass through it, for the LORD,
48:14 None of this special land will e be sold or traded
Da 2:10 has e asked such a thing of any magician,
2:20 saying, / "Praise the name of God forever and e,
2:44 will never be destroyed; no one will e conquer it.
7:18 the kingdom, and they will rule forever and e."
11:24 and do something that none of his predecessors e
Hos 10: 9 "O Israel, e since that awful night in Gibeah,
Joel 1: 2 has anything like this e happened before?
Am 3: 4 Does a lion e roar in a thicket without first finding
3: 5 Does a bird e get caught in a trap that has no bait?
3: 5 Does a trap e spring shut when there's nothing
Ob 1: 3 'Who can e reach us way up here?' you ask
Jnh 2: 4 How will I e again see your holy Temple?'
Mic 2: 3 none of you will e again walk proudly in the
4: 5 we will follow the LORD our God forever and e.
Zec 8: 9 LORD Almighty e since the foundation was laid.
9: 8 No foreign oppressor will e again overrun my
Mal 1: 6 you ask, 'How have we e despised your name?'
3: 7 E since the days of your ancestors, you have
3: 8 'What do you mean? When did we e cheat you?'
Mt 6: 2 they have received all the reward they will e get.
6: 5 I assure you, that is all the reward they will e get.
6:16 I assure you, that is the only reward they will e get.
7:14 and the road is narrow, and only a few e find it.
9:33 "Nothing like this has e happened in Israel!"
11:11 "I assure you, of all who have e lived, none is
12: 3 "Haven't you e read in the Scriptures what King
12: 5 And haven't you e read in the law of Moses that
16: 9 Won't you e understand? Don't you remember the
21:16 "Haven't you e read the Scriptures? For they say,
21:42 "Didn't you e read this in the Scriptures?
22:31 haven't you e read about this in the Scriptures?
23: 8 Don't e let anyone call you 'Rabbi,' for you have
24:21 greater horror than anything the world has e seen or will e see again.
25:37 when did we e see you hungry and feed you?
25:39 When did we e see you sick or in prison, and visit
25:44 when did we e see you hungry or thirsty or a
Mk 2:25 "Haven't you e read in the Scriptures what King
8:17 having no food? Won't you e learn or understand?
9: 3 far whiter than any earthly process could e make it.
11:14 to the tree, "May no one e eat your fruit again!"
12:10 Didn't you e read this in the Scriptures?
12:26 haven't you e read about this in the writings of
Lk 6: 3 "Haven't you e read in the Scriptures what King
7:28 I tell you, of all who have e lived, none is greater
9:39 and injuring him. It hardly e leaves him alone.
14:31 "Or what king would e dream of going to war
20:16 "But God forbid that such a thing should e
22:23 each other which of them would e do such a thing.
Jn 1:18 No one has e seen God. But his only Son, who is
4:29 and meet a man who told me everything I e did!
4:39 woman had said, "He told me everything I e did!"
6:35 No one who comes to me will e be hungry again.
6:46 (Not that anyone has e seen the Father; only I,
7:52 for yourself—no prophet e comes from Galilee!"
17:20 but also for all who will e believe in me because of
19: 8 Pilate heard this, he was more frightened than e.
Ac 7:49 Could you e build me a temple as good as that?'
20:25 I have preached the Kingdom will e see me again.
Ro 3:20 For no one can e be made right in God's sight by
8:31 as these? If God is for us, who can e be against us?
8:35 Can anything e separate us from Christ's love?
8:38 And I am convinced that nothing can e separate us
8:39 nothing in all creation will e be able to separate us
11:35 And who could e give him so much that he would
1Co 1:29 so that no one can e boast in the presence of God.
9: 7 And have you e heard of a farmer who harvests his
11:12 all men have been born from women e since,
15:58 for you know that nothing you do for the Lord is e
2Co 7:15 Now he cares for you more than e when he
Gal 2:16 For no one will e be saved by obeying the law."
3:11 it is clear that no one can e be right with God by
Eph 1:15 E since I first heard of your strong faith in the Lord
3:20 infinitely more than we would e dare to ask
3:21 in Christ Jesus forever and e through endless ages.
Php 3: 5 So I am a real Jew if there e was one!
4:11 Not that I was e in need, for I have learned how to
4:20 Now glory be to God our Father forever and e.
Col 1: 5 as you have been e since you first heard the truth
1: 9 So we have continued praying for you e since we
1Th 3: 6 news that your faith and love are as strong as e.
2Th 3: 5 May the Lord bring you into an e deeper
1Ti 1:17 Glory and honor to God forever and e. He is the
6:16 No one has e seen him, nor e will. To him be
2Ti 4:18 To God be the glory forever and e. Amen.
Heb 1: 8 "Your throne, O God, endures forever and e.
9:26 to die again and again, e since the world began.
10:32 Don't e forget those early days when you first
13:20[-21] To him be glory forever and e. Amen.
Jas 1:13 no one who wants to do wrong should e say,
2:20 When will you e learn that faith that does not result
1Pe 4:11 All glory and power belong to him forever and e.
5:11 All power is his forever and e. Amen.
2Pe 1:20 in Scripture e came from the prophets themselves
1Jn 4:12 No one has e seen God. But if we love each other,
Rev 1: 6 everlasting glory! He rules forever and e! Amen!
1:18 Look, I am alive forever and e! And I hold the
4: 9 on the throne, the one who lives forever and e,
4:10 and worship the one who lives forever and e.
5:13 on the throne / and to the Lamb forever and e."
10: 6 in the name of the one who lives forever and e,
11:15 and of his Christ, and he will reign forever and e."
14:11 The smoke of their torment rises forever and e,
16:18 And there was an earthquake greater than e before
20:10 they will be tormented day and night forever and e.
22: 5 shine on them. And they will reign forever and e.

EVER-FLOWING (1) [EVER, FLOW]

Isa 58:11 will be like a well-watered garden, like an e spring.

EVER-INCREASING (1) [EVER, INCREASE]

Job 10:17 You pour out an e volume of anger upon me

EVER-LIVING (1) [EVER, LIVE]

Ro 1:23 And instead of worshiping the glorious, e God,

EVER-WIDENING (1) [EVER, WIDE]

Ac 6: 7 God's message was preached in e circles.

EVERLASTING (55) [EVER]

Ge 17: 7 "I will continue this e covenant between us,
17:13 Your bodies will thus bear the mark of my e
17:19 and I will confirm my e covenant with him and his
48: 4 to you and your descendants as an e possession.'
49:26 reaching to the utmost bounds of the e hills.
Dt 33:15 and the abundance from the e hills;
33:27 God is your refuge, / and his e arms are under you.
2Sa 23: 5 Yes, he has made an e covenant with me.
1Ch 16:36 the God of Israel, / from e to e!
Ne 9: 5 your God, for he lives from e to e!"
Ps 22:26 praise him. / Their hearts will rejoice with e joy.
76: 4 and more majestic / than the e mountains.
93: 2 You yourself are from the e past.
106:48 the God of Israel, / from e to e!
139:24 offends you, / and lead me along the path of e life.
145:13 For your kingdom is an e kingdom. / You rule
Ecc 12: 5 And as you near your e home, the mourners will
Isa 9: 6 Mighty God, E Father, Prince of Peace.
24: 5 violated his laws, and broken his e covenant.
35:10 will return to Jerusalem, singing songs of e joy.
40:28 Don't you know that the LORD is the e God,
45:17 be humiliated and disgraced throughout e ages.
51:11 will return to Jerusalem, singing songs of e joy.
54: 8 But with e love I will have compassion on you,"
55: 3 I am ready to make an e covenant with you.
55:13 it will be an e sign of his power and love.
56: 5 For the name I give them is an e one.
60:19 for the LORD your God will be your e light,
60:20 not go down. For the LORD will be your e light.
61: 7 inherit a double portion of prosperity and e joy.
61: 8 their suffering and make an e covenant with them.
Jer 5:22 an e boundary that the waters cannot cross.
10:10 only true God, the living God. He is the e King!
25:12 I will make the country of the Babylonians an e
31: 3 "I have loved you, my people, with an e love.
32:40 "And I will make an e covenant with them,
Eze 16:60 and I will establish an e covenant with you.
37:26 a covenant of peace with them, an e covenant.
Da 4:34 His rule is e, / and his kingdom is eternal.
9:24 to atone for guilt, to bring in e righteousness,
12: 2 some to e life and some to shame and e contempt.
Hab 3: 6 He shatters the e mountains and levels the eternal
2Co 5: 4 these dying bodies will be swallowed up by e life.
Gal 6: 8 please the Spirit will harvest e life from the Spirit.
2Th 1: 9 They will be punished with e destruction,
2:16 loved us and in his special favor gave us e comfort
2Ti 1:10 and showed us the way to e life through the Good
Heb 13:20[-21] is the great Shepherd of the sheep by an e
Jude 1:13 wandering stars, heading for e gloom and darkness.
Rev 1: 6 Give to him e glory! He rules forever and ever!
14: 6 carrying the e Good News to preach to the people

EVERMORE (1) [EVER]

Ro 11:36 is intended for his glory. To him be glory e. Amen.

EVERY (535) [EVERYBODY, EVERYBODY'S, EVERYDAY, EVERYONE, EVERYONE'S, EVERYTHING, EVERYWHERE]

EVERY DAY (27) Ge 27:2; Ex 29:37; Est 2:11; Ps 7:11; 13:2; 22:2; 44:22; 139:16; 145:2; Pr 15:15; Ecc 11:8; Isa 38:20; 58:2; Jer 37:21; Eze 43:25; Mt 26:55; Mk 14:49; Lk 21:37; 22:53; Jn 6:34; 11:9; Ac 5:42; Ro 8:36; 14:5; 2Co 4:16; Heb 3:13; 7:27

EVERY GREEN TREE (12) Dt 12:2; 1Ki 14:23; 2Ki 16:4; 17:10; 2Ch 28:4; Isa 57:5; Jer 2:20; 3:6,13; 17:2; Eze 6:13; 20:28

EVERY KIND (40) Ge 1:20,21,24; 2:19; 6:19; 7:3,3,14,14; 34:29; Ex 34:7; 35:22; Nu 14:18; 1Ch 12:37; 22:15; 28:21; 2Ch 15:6; Ps 104:25; 130:8; 144:13; Pr 8:7; 20:10; Eze 47:10; Hos 6:9; Mt 4:23; 10:1; 13:47; Mk 7:19; Ro 1:29; 1Co 1:5; 15:24; 2Co 6:4; 1Th 5:22; 2Th 2:10; Tit 2:7,14; Jas 3:16; Jude 1:7; Rev 11:6; 18:12

EVERY MALE (5) Ge 17:12; Nu 3:15; 1Ki 11:15; 2Ki 9:8; 2Ch 31:19

EVERY MAN (12) Ge 34:15,25; Ex 23:17; 35:29; Dt 16:16; 20:13; Jdg 5:30; 2Sa 6:19; 2Ki 3:21; 1Ch 16:3; Est 1:22; Eze 16:15

EVERY MORNING (7) Ex 30:7; 2Sa 15:2; 1Ch 9:27; 2Ch 13:11; Job 7:18; Ps 73:14; Eze 46:15

EVERY NATION (19) 1Ki 4:34; 10:24; 18:10; 2Ch 9:23; Ps 22:27; 46:10; 97:6; 98:2; Isa 66:20; Jer 24:9; 25:17; 26:6; 27:13; 29:18; Mk 13:10; Ac 10:35; Rev 7:9; 14:6; 17:15

EVERY ONE (19) Ge 34:22; Jos 21:42; 1Sa 11:2; 2Sa 8:2; 1Ki 19:10,14; 2Ki 10:19; 2Ch 14:5; 20:23; Est 1:18; Ps 34:19; 104:27; 119:33; Isa 31:7; Jer 42:17; 44:11; Da 12:1; Lk 4:40; Jude 1:5

EVERY YEAR (5) Ex 12:42; Lev 23:41; Job 1:4; Eze 45:25; Lk 2:41

IN EVERY WAY (11) Ge 1:31; 24:1; 29:17; 2Sa 19:18; SS 5:16; Ro 16:2; Eph 4:15; 1Th 5:23; 1Ti 1:13; 2Ti 3:17; Tit 2:10

ON EVERY SIDE (8) Jos 21:44; 1Ki 5:4; 2Ch 15:15; 20:30; Job 19:10; Ps 3:6; Eze 23:24; 2Co 4:8

Ge 1:11 "Let the land burst forth with e sort of grass
1:20 Let the skies be filled with birds of e kind."
1:21 and e sort of fish and e kind of bird.
1:24 "Let the earth bring forth e kind of animal—
1:31 and he saw that it was excellent in e way.
2:19 So the LORD God formed from the soil e kind of
6:17 earth with a flood that will destroy e living thing.
6:19 Bring a pair of e kind of animal—a male and a
7: 3 Then select seven pairs of e kind of bird.
7: 3 and a female in each pair to ensure that e kind of
7:14 With them in the boat were pairs of e kind of
7:14 along with birds and flying insects of e kind.
7:23 E living thing on the earth was wiped out—people,
9:16 between God and e living creature on earth."
13:14 "Look as far as you can see in e direction.
13:17 Take a walk in e direction and explore the new
17:12 E male child must be circumcised on the eighth
17:23 and e other male in his household and circumcised
24: 1 and the LORD had blessed him in e way.
27: 2 Isaac said, "and I expect e day to be my last.
29:17 but Rachel was beautiful in e way, with a lovely
31:39 You made me pay for e animal stolen from the
34:15 If e man among you will be circumcised like we
34:22 E one of us men must be circumcised, just as they
34:25 without opposition, and slaughtered e man there,
34:29 all the women and children and wealth of e kind.
41: 5 on one stalk, with e kernel well formed and plump.
Ex 8: 3 E home in Egypt will be filled with them.
8: 5 so there will be frogs in e corner of the land."
8:24 flies in Pharaoh's palace and in e home in Egypt.
9:19 E person or animal left outside will die beneath
11: 5 All the firstborn sons will die in e family in Egypt,
12:15 On the very first day you must remove e trace of
12:42 It must be celebrated e year, from generation to
13: 2 firstborn sons of Israel and e firstborn male animal.
13:13 However, you must redeem e firstborn son.
17:14 I will blot out e trace of Amalek from under
23:17 e man in Israel must appear before the Sovereign
29:37 Make atonement for the altar e day for seven days.
30: 7 "E morning when Aaron trims the lamps, he must
31: 5 and in carving wood. Yes, he is a master at e craft!
34: 7 love to many thousands by forgiving e kind of sin
34:19 "E firstborn male belongs to me—of both cattle
34:20 However, you must redeem e firstborn son.
35:22 They presented gold objects of e kind to the
35:29 e man and woman who wanted to help in the work
35:33 in carving wood. In fact, he has e necessary skill.
Lev 15:12 and e wooden utensil he touches must be rinsed
17:14 The life of e creature is in the blood. That is why I
19:10 do not strip e last bunch of grapes from the vines,
23:41 this seven-day festival to the LORD e year.
24: 8 E Sabbath day this bread must be laid out before
25: 2 observe a Sabbath to the LORD e seventh year.
25:24 "With e sale of land there must be a stipulation
26:35 it will take the rest you never allowed it to take e
27:32 The LORD also owns e tenth animal counted off
Nu 3:15 Count e male who is one month old or older."
7: 3 There was a cart for e two leaders and an ox for
11:31 For many miles in e direction from the camp there
14:18 forgiving e kind of sin and rebellion.
14:35 I will do these things to e member of the
18:15 "The firstborn of e mother, whether human
31:28 Set apart one out of e five hundred as the
31:30 Also take one of e fifty of the captives, cattle,
31:47 Moses took one of e fifty prisoners and animals
35: 4 1,500 feet from the town walls in e direction.
35: 5 Measure off 3,000 feet outside the town walls in e
36: 7 for the inheritance of e tribe must remain fixed as
Dt 2: 7 and has watched your e step through this great
2: 7 and provided for your e need so that you lacked
2:28 We will pay for e bite of food we eat and all the
3: 6 We destroyed all the people in e town we
3:27 go to Pisgah Peak and view the land in e direction,
5:32 your God, following his instructions in e detail.
8: 3 real life comes by feeding on e word of the
10:15 chose you, their descendants, above e other nation,
11: 6 and tents and e living thing that belonged to them.
11: 8 be careful to obey e command I am giving you
12: 2 up on the hills, and under e green tree.
14:28 "At the end of e third year bring the tithe of all
15: 1 "At the end of e seventh year you must cancel
16:16 "Each year e man in Israel must celebrate these
20:13 God hands it over to you, kill e man in the town.
20:16 a special possession, destroy e living thing in them.
22: 8 "E new house you build must have a barrier
26:12 "E third year you must offer a special tithe of your
28:61 The LORD will bring against you e sickness
31:10 "At the end of e seventh year, the Year of Release,
32:46 your children so they will obey e word of this law.
33:12 and preserves them from e harm."
Jos 1:18 and does not obey your e command will be put to
6:20 Israelites charged straight into the city from e side
7:18 E member of Zimri's family was brought forward
8:35 E command Moses had ever given was read to the
11:11 The Israelites completely destroyed e living thing
21:42 E one of these towns had pasturelands surrounding
21:44 And the LORD gave them rest on e side, just as
22: 2 and you have obeyed e order I have given you.
23:14 Deep in your hearts you know that e promise of the
Jdg 2:15 E time Israel went out to battle, the LORD fought
5:30 goods they found— / a woman or two for e man.
20:40 and saw the smoke rising into the sky from e part
20:48 and slaughtered e living thing in all the towns—
20:48 They also burned down e town they came to.
21:11 all the males and e woman who is not a virgin."
1Sa 11: 2 I will gouge out the right eye of e one of you as a
14:16 of Philistines began to melt away in e direction.
14:36 all night and destroy e last one of them."
14:47 he fought against his enemies in e direction—
23:23 even if I have to search e hiding place in Judah!"
2Sa 3:29 May his family in e generation be cursed with a
6:19 Then he gave a gift of food to e man and woman in
8: 2 He measured off two groups to be executed for e
15: 2 He got up early e morning and went out to the gate
15:10 he sent secret messengers to e part of Israel to stir
16:23 For e word Ahithophel spoke seemed as wise as
17:13 into the nearest valley until e stone is torn down."
19:18 across the river, helping them in e way they could.
1Ki 1:29 LORD lives, who has rescued me from e danger,
4:34 And kings from e nation sent their ambassadors to
5: 4 the LORD my God has given me peace on e side,
5:14 them to Lebanon in shifts, ten thousand e month,
6:36 so that there was one layer of cedar beams after e
6:38 The entire building was completed in e detail by
7:12 so that there was one layer of cedar beams after e
10:22 Once e three years the ships returned, loaded down
10:24 People from e nation came to visit him and to hear
11:15 the Israelite army had killed nearly e male in
14:23 up sacred pillars and Asherah poles on e high hill
and under e green tree.
18: 5 "We must check e spring and valley to see if we
18:10 your God that the king has searched e nation
19:10 your altars, and killed e one of your prophets.
19:14 your altars, and killed e one of your prophets.
22:18 "He does it e time. He never prophesies anything
2Ki 3:21 they mobilized e man who could fight, young
4: 6 Soon e container was full to the brim! "Bring me
9: 8 wiped out—e male, slave and free alike, in Israel.
10:19 See to it that e one of them comes, for I am going
10:22 "Be sure that e worshiper of Baal wears one of
10:28 Jehu destroyed e trace of Baal worship from Israel.
16: 4 and on the hills and under e green tree.
17:10 sacred pillars and Asherah poles at the top of e hill
and under e green tree.
23:24 and e other kind of idol worship, both in Jerusalem
1Ch 9:27 It was also their job to open the gates e morning.
12:37 there were 120,000 troops armed with e kind of
16: 3 Then he gave a gift of food to e man and woman in
22:15 and craftsmen of e kind available to you.
28: 9 For the LORD sees e heart and understands and
knows e plan and thought.
28:17 as well as the amount of silver for e dish.
28:19 "E part of this plan," David told Solomon,
28:21 Others with skills of e kind will volunteer,
29: 2 Using e resource at my command, I have gathered
2Ch 7:15 I will listen to e prayer made in this place,
9:21 Once e three years the ships returned, loaded down
9:23 Kings from e nation came to visit him and to hear
13:11 and fragrant incense to the LORD e morning
13:11 and they light the gold lampstand e evening.
14: 5 as well as the incense altars from e one of Judah's
15: 5 to travel. Problems troubled the nation on e hand.
15: 6 for God was troubling you with e kind of problem.
15:15 gave them rest from their enemies on e side.
18:17 "He does it e time. He never prophesies anything
20:23 allies from Mount Seir and killed e one of them.
20:30 at peace, for his God had given him rest on e side.
28: 4 and on the hills and under e green tree.
28:24 then set up altars to pagan gods in e corner of
31:19 men were appointed to distribute portions to e
Ezr 6: 4 E three layers of specially prepared stones will be
Ne 5:18 And e ten days we needed a large supply of all
9:22 and you placed your people in e corner of the land.
9:33 E time you punished us you were being just.
10:31 And we promise not to do any work e seventh year
10:35 "We promise always to bring the first part of e
13:19 should be shut as darkness fell e Friday evening,
Est 1:16 but also e official and citizen throughout your
1:18 Before this day is out, the wife of e one of us,
1:22 proclaiming that e man should be the ruler of his
2:11 E day Mordecai would take a walk near the
3:14 A copy of this decree was to be issued in e
8:11 The king's decree gave the Jews in e city authority
8:13 decree was to be recognized as law in e province
8:17 In e city and province, wherever the king's decree
9:28 and celebrated by e family throughout the
Job 1: 4 E year when Job's sons had birthdays, they invited
7:18 you examine us e morning and test us e moment.
12:10 For the life of e living thing is in his hand,
18:11 surround the wicked and trouble them at e step.
19:10 He has demolished me on e side, and I am
21: 9 Their homes are safe from e fear, and God does not
31: 4 He sees everything I do and e step I take.
33:11 my feet in the stocks and watches e move I make.'
37: 3 and his lightning flashes out in e direction.
39: 8 where it searches for e blade of grass.
Ps 3: 6 ten thousand enemies / who surround me on e side.
6: 6 out from sobbing. / E night tears drench my bed;
7:11 perfectly fair. / He is angry with the wicked e day.
13: 2 in my soul, / with sorrow in my heart e day?
22: 2 E day I call to you, my God, but you do not
22: 2 E night you hear my voice, but I find no relief.
22:17 I can count e bone in my body. / My enemies stare
22:27 People from e nation will bow down before him.
28: 7 LORD is my strength, my shield from e danger.
34:19 but the LORD rescues them from each and e one.
37:23 the LORD. / He delights in e detail of their lives.
38: 9 know what I long for, Lord; / you hear my e sigh.
44:21 known it, / for he knows the secrets of e heart.
44:22 For your sake we are killed e day; / we are being
45:17 I will bring honor to your name in e generation.

46:10 that I am God! / I will be honored by **e** nation.
50:11 **E** bird of the mountains / and all the animals of the
56: 6 spy on me— / watching my **e** step, eager to kill me.
66: 7 He watches **e** movement of the nations; / let no
73:14 is trouble all day long; / **e** morning brings me pain.
89:40 and laid in ruins **e** fort defending him.
91: 3 For he will rescue you from **e** trap / and protect
97: 6 declare his righteousness; / **e** nation sees his glory.
97: 7 worthless gods— / for **e** god must bow to him.
98: 2 and has revealed his righteousness to **e** nation!
101: 4 reject perverse ideas / and stay away from **e** evil.
102:12 Your fame will endure to **e** generation.
102:14 For your people love **e** stone in her walls
104:25 vast and wide, / teeming with life of **e** kind,
104:27 **E** one of these depends on you / to give them their
119:33 O LORD, / to follow **e** one of your principles.
119:90 Your faithfulness extends to **e** generation,
119:104 no wonder I hate **e** false way of life.
119:128 is right. / That is why I hate **e** false way.
130: 8 He himself will free Israel / from **e** kind of sin.
135:13 your fame, O LORD, is known to **e** generation.
136:25 He gives food to **e** living thing. / His faithful love
138: 4 **E** king in all the earth will give you thanks,
139: 2 stand up. / You know my **e** thought when far away.
139: 3 and rest. / **E** moment you know where I am.
139:16 **E** day of my life was recorded in your book.
139:16 **E** moment was laid out / before a single day had
144:13 May our farms be filled / with crops of **e** kind.
145: 2 I will bless you **e** day, / and I will praise you
145: 6 Your awe-inspiring deeds will be on **e** tongue;
145:16 you satisfy the hunger and thirst of **e** living thing.
146: 6 He is the one who keeps **e** promise forever,
146:10 O Jerusalem, your God is King in **e** generation!
148: 5 Let **e** created thing give praise to the LORD,
Pr 2: 9 know how to find the right course of action **e** time.
5:21 what a man does, examining **e** path he takes.
7:12 in the streets and markets, soliciting at **e** corner.
8: 7 for I speak the truth and hate **e** kind of deception.
15:15 For the poor, **e** day brings trouble; for the happy
16:11 The LORD demands fairness in **e** business deal;
18: 1 snarling at **e** sound principle of conduct.
20:10 The LORD despises double standards of **e** kind.
20:27 the human spirit, exposing **e** hidden motive.
30: 5 **E** word of God proves true. He defends all who
Ecc 3: 1 a season for **e** activity under heaven.
5: 8 For **e** official is under orders from higher up,
7:27 after looking into the matter from **e** possible angle.
7:28 Just one out of **e** thousand men I interviewed can
11: 8 live to be very old, let them rejoice in **e** day of life.
11: 9 it's wonderful to be young! Enjoy **e** minute of it.
12:13 his commands, for this is the duty of **e** person.
12:14 including **e** secret thing, whether good or bad.
SS 3: 6 of myrrh and frankincense and **e** other spice?
4: 7 so beautiful, my beloved, so perfect in **e** part.
4:14 myrrh and aloes, perfume from **e** incense tree, and
e other lovely spice.
5:16 mouth is altogether sweet; he is lovely in **e** way.
Isa 2:15 He will break down **e** high tower and wall.
13: 7 **E** arm is paralyzed with fear. Even the strongest
15: 3 From **e** home will come the sound of weeping.
24:10 in chaos; **e** home is locked to keep out looters.
30:25 there will be streams of water flowing down **e**
31: 7 I know the glorious day will come when **e** one of
38:20 **e** day of my life / in the Temple of the LORD.
41: 2 king from the east, who meets victory at **e** step?
44:23 into song, O mountains and forests and **e** tree!
45:23 **E** knee will bow to me, and **e** tongue will confess
56:10 his shepherds—are blind to **e** danger.
57: 5 your idols with great passion beneath **e** green tree.
58: 2 They come to the Temple **e** day and seem
60:16 bring the best of their goods to satisfy your **e** need.
62:11 The LORD has sent this message to **e** land:
66:20 the remnant of your people back from **e** nation.
Jer 2:20 On **e** hill and under **e** green tree, you have
3: 6 Israel has worshiped other gods on **e** hill and under
e green tree.
3:13 against him by worshiping idols under **e** green tree.
4:20 Suddenly, **e** tent is destroyed; in a moment, **e**
shelter is crushed.
5: 1 "Run up and down **e** street in Jerusalem,"
6:25 they are ready to kill. We are terrorized at **e** turn!
11:13 to your god Baal—are along **e** street in Jerusalem.
16:17 I am watching them closely, and I see **e** sin.
17: 2 beneath **e** green tree and on **e** high hill.
23:28 my true messengers faithfully proclaim my **e** word.
24: 9 an object of horror and evil to **e** nation on earth.
25:17 drink from it—**e** nation the LORD sent me to.
26: 2 Give them my entire message; include **e** word.
26: 6 an object of cursing in **e** nation on earth.' "
26:12 "The LORD gave me **e** word that I have spoken.
26:15 lie on you, on this city, and on **e** person living in it.
26:15 LORD sent me to speak **e** word you have heard."
27: 5 made the earth and all its people and **e** animal.
27:13 which the LORD will bring against **e** nation that
29:18 In **e** nation where I send them, I will make them an
34:14 I told them that **e** Hebrew slave must be freed after
35:18 You have obeyed your ancestor Jehonadab in **e**
36: 2 and write down **e** message you have given, right up
37:21 **e** day as long as there was any left in the city.
42:17 That is the fate awaiting **e** one of you who insists
44:11 I have made up my mind to destroy **e** one of you!
46: 5 They are terrorized at **e** turn, says the LORD.
46: 8 it will cover the earth like a flood, destroying **e** foe.
48:38 sorrow will be in **e** Moabite home and on **e** street.
49:29 panic will be heard: 'We are terrorized at **e** turn!'
49:32 I will bring calamity upon them from **e** direction,"
50:15 Shout against her from **e** side. Look!
51: 2 They will come from **e** side to rise against her in
51:31 Messengers from **e** side come running to the king
La 2: 2 Without mercy the Lord has destroyed **e** home in
Eze 5:16 and more severe until **e** crumb of food is gone.
6:13 on **e** hill and mountain and under **e** green tree
11: 5 for I know **e** thought that comes into your minds.
11:18 they will remove **e** trace of their detestable idol
12:22 'Time passes, making a liar of **e** prophet'?
12:23 'The time has come for **e** prophecy to be fulfilled!'
16:15 You gave yourself as a prostitute to **e** man who
16:24 and put altars to idols in **e** town square.
16:25 On **e** street corner you defiled your beauty,
16:25 offering your body to **e** passerby in an endless
16:31 You build your pagan shrines on **e** street corner
and your altars to idols in **e** square.
17:23 Birds of **e** sort will nest in it, finding shelter
19: 8 attacked him, / surrounding him from **e** direction.
20:28 they offered sacrifices and incense on **e** high hill
and under **e** green tree they saw!
20:47 set you on fire, O forest, and **e** tree will be burned
21: 7 **E** spirit will faint; strong knees will tremble
21:15 melt with terror, for the sword glitters at **e** gate.
22: 6 "**E** leader in Israel who lives within your walls is
23:10 Her name was known to **e** woman in the land as a
23:24 They will take up positions on **e** side,
26:11 His horsemen will trample **e** street in the city.
27: 9 Ships came with goods from **e** land to barter for
28:13 Your clothing was adorned with **e** precious stone—
28:23 The attack will come from **e** direction, and your
34: 8 and left them to be attacked by **e** wild animal.
35:12 have heard **e** contemptuous word you spoke
43:25 "**E** day for seven days a male goat, a young bull,
45:13 bushel of wheat or barley for **e** sixty you harvest,
45:15 and one sheep for **e** two hundred in your flocks in
45:25 of Shelters, which occurs **e** year in early autumn,
46:15 be given as a daily sacrifice **e** morning without fail.
46:17 the Year of Jubilee, which comes **e** fiftieth year.
47:10 Fish of **e** kind will fill the Dead Sea, just as they
47:12 There will be a new crop **e** month, without fail!
48:17 will surround the city for 150 yards in **e** direction.
Da 1: 4 "Make sure they are well versed in **e** branch of
4: 1 sent this message to the people of **e** race
6:25 Darius sent this message to the people of **e** race
7: 2 with strong winds blowing from **e** direction.
7:14 so that people of **e** race and nation and language
9:13 **E** curse written against us in the law of Moses has
11:36 and claiming to be greater than **e** god there is,
12: 1 But at that time **e** one of your people whose name
Hos 6: 9 the road to Shechem and practice **e** kind of sin.
9: 1 offering sacrifices to other gods on **e** threshing
13:15 **E** precious thing they have will be plundered
Joel 2: 3 in front of them and follows them in **e** direction!
2: 6 grips all the people; **e** face grows pale with fright.
Am 4: 2 **E** last one of you will be dragged away like a fish
4: 4 each morning and bring your tithes **e** three days!
4: 6 "I brought hunger to **e** city and famine to **e** town.
4:13 stirs up the winds, and reveals his **e** thought.
5:16 be crying in all the public squares and in **e** street.
5:17 There will be wailing in **e** vineyard, for I will pass
6: 3 You push away **e** thought of coming disaster,
Ob 1: 6 **E** nook and cranny of Edom will be searched and
looted. **E** treasure will be found and taken.
Zep 1: 4 and destroy **e** last trace of their Baal worship.
Zec 5: 4 I am sending this curse into the house of **e** thief
10: 1 of rain so that **e** field becomes a lush pasture.
12: 4 cause **e** horse to panic and **e** rider to lose his nerve.
13: 2 I will get rid of **e** trace of idol worship throughout
14:21 **e** cooking pot in Jerusalem and Judah will be set
Mal 2:12 May the LORD cut off from the nation of Israel **e**
Mt 3: 5 People from Jerusalem and from **e** section of Judea
3:10 **e** tree that does not produce good fruit will be
4: 4 their life; / they must feed on **e** word of God.' "
4:23 And he healed people who had **e** kind of sickness
7:19 So **e** tree that does not produce good fruit is
9:35 he healed people of **e** sort of disease and illness.
10: 1 evil spirits and to heal **e** kind of disease and illness.
11: 7 him weak as a reed, moved by **e** breath of wind?
12:31 "**E** sin or blasphemy can be forgiven—
12:36 account on judgment day of **e** idle word you speak.
13:33 of flour, the yeast permeated **e** part of the dough."
13:47 is thrown into the water and gathers fish of **e** kind.
13:52 "**E** teacher of religious law who has become a
15:13 "**E** plant not planted by my heavenly Father will
18:34 sent the man to prison until he had paid **e** penny.
26:55 me in the Temple? I was there teaching **e** day.
Mk 1:21 and **e** Sabbath day he went into the synagogue
7:19 he showed that **e** kind of food is acceptable.)
13:10 And the Good News must first be preached to **e**
14:49 me in the Temple? I was there teaching **e** day.
Lk 2:41 **E** year Jesus' parents went to Jerusalem for the
3: 9 **e** tree that does not produce good fruit will be
4:31 and taught there in the synagogue **e** Sabbath day.
4:40 diseases were, the touch of his hand healed **e** one.
5:17 (It seemed that these men showed up from **e**
7:24 him weak as a reed, moved by **e** breath of wind?
13:21 of flour, the yeast permeated **e** part of the dough."
15: 8 and look in **e** corner of the house and sweep **e**
nook and cranny until she finds it?
19:48 because all the people hung on **e** word he said.
21:37 **E** day Jesus went to the Temple to teach, and each
22:53 I was there **e** day. But this is your moment,
Jn 6:34 they said, "give us that bread **e** day of our lives."
8:16 my judgment would be correct in **e** respect
11: 9 "There are twelve hours of daylight **e** day.
15: 2 He cuts off **e** branch that doesn't produce fruit,
Ac 1:24 "O Lord," they said, "you know **e** heart. Show us
3:24 **e** prophet spoke about what is happening today.
5:42 And **e** day, in the Temple and in their homes,
8:40 and in **e** city along the way until he came to
9: 1 Meanwhile, Saul was uttering threats with **e** breath.
9:14 leading priests to arrest **e** believer in Damascus."
10:35 In **e** nation he accepts those who fear him and do
13:10 of the Devil, full of **e** sort of trickery and villainy,
13:27 though they hear the prophets' words read **e**
14:23 and Barnabas also appointed elders in **e** church
15:21 in **e** city on **e** Sabbath for many generations."
16:26 flew open, and the chains of **e** prisoner fell off!
17:25 to everything, and he satisfies **e** need there is.
22:19 and beat those in **e** synagogue who believed on
Ro 1:29 Their lives became full of **e** kind of wickedness,
8:36 Scriptures say, "For your sake we are killed **e** day;
9:22 God has **e** right to exercise his judgment and his
14: 5 than another day, while others think **e** day is alike.
14:11 as I live,' says the Lord, / '**e** knee will bow to me /
and **e** tongue will confess allegiance to God.' "
16: 2 Help her in **e** way you can, for she has helped
1Co 1: 5 the gifts of eloquence and **e** kind of knowledge.
1: 7 Now you have **e** spiritual gift you need as you
9:26 So I run straight to the goal with purpose in **e** step.
11:26 For **e** time you eat this bread and drink this cup,
13: 7 and endures through **e** circumstance.
15:24 the Father, having put down all enemies of **e** kind.
15:48 **E** human being has an earthly body just like
16: 2 On **e** Lord's Day, each of you should put aside
2Co 1: 3 He is the source of **e** mercy and the God who
4: 8 We are pressed on **e** side by troubles, but we are
4:16 are dying, our spirits are being renewed **e** day.
6: 4 and hardships and calamities of **e** kind.
7: 5 Outside there was conflict from **e** direction,
10: 5 With these weapons we break down **e** proud
11:15 In the end they will get **e** bit of punishment their
12:12 I certainly gave you **e** proof that I am truly an
13: 1 "The facts of **e** case must be established by the
Gal 5:25 let us follow the Holy Spirit's leading in **e** part of
Eph 1: 3 who has blessed us with **e** spiritual blessing in the
4:15 becoming more and more in **e** way like Christ,
5:16 Make the most of **e** opportunity for doing good in
6:13 Use **e** piece of God's armor to resist the enemy in
6:16 In **e** battle you will need faith as your shield to stop
6:18 and on **e** occasion in the power of the Holy Spirit.
Php 1: 3 **E** time I think of you, I give thanks to my God.
2: 9 and gave him a name that is above **e** other name,
2:10 so that at the name of Jesus **e** knee will bow,
2:11 and **e** tongue will confess that Jesus Christ is Lord,
4:12 I have learned the secret of living in **e** situation,
Col 2:10 He is the Lord over **e** ruler and authority in the
4: 5 not Christians, and make the most of **e** opportunity.
1Th 5:22 Keep away from **e** kind of evil.
5:23 Now may the God of peace make you holy in **e**
2Th 2: 4 He will exalt himself and defy **e** god there is
2: 4 and tear down **e** object of adoration and worship.
2:10 He will use **e** kind of wicked deception to fool
2:17 and give you strength in **e** good thing you do
1Ti 1:13 down his people, harming them in **e** way I could.
2Ti 2:21 ready for the Master to use you for **e** good work.
3:17 It is God's way of preparing us in **e** way,
3:17 fully equipped for **e** good thing God wants us to
4: 5 But you should keep a clear mind in **e** situation.
4:18 and the Lord will deliver me from **e** evil attack
Tit 2: 7 an example to them by doing good deeds of **e** kind.
2:10 teaching about God our Savior attractive in **e** way.
2:14 He gave his life to free us from **e** kind of sin,
Heb 2: 2 and the people were punished for **e** violation of the
law and **e** act of disobedience.
2:17 it was necessary for Jesus to be in **e** respect like us,
3: 4 For **e** house has a builder, but God is the one who
3:13 You must warn each other **e** day, as long as it is
7:27 He does not need to offer sacrifices **e** day like the
8: 3 And since **e** high priest is required to offer gifts
12: 1 let us strip off **e** weight that slows us down,
Jas 3: 2 tongues can also control themselves in **e** other way.
3:16 there you will find disorder and **e** kind of evil.
5: 5 years on earth in luxury, satisfying your **e** whim.
2Pe 1: 5 So make **e** effort to apply the benefits of these
3: 3 laugh at the truth and do **e** evil thing they desire.
3:14 make **e** effort to live a pure and blameless life.
1Jn 1: 7 the blood of Jesus, his Son, cleanses us from **e** sin.
1: 9 just to forgive us and to cleanse us from **e** wrong.
5: 4 For **e** child of God defeats this evil world by
5:17 **E** wrong is sin, but not all sin leads to death.
Jude 1: 5 he later destroyed **e** one of those who did not
1: 7 sexual immorality and **e** kind of sexual perversion.
1:18 is to enjoy themselves in **e** evil way imaginable.
Rev 2:23 out the thoughts and intentions of **e** person.
5: 6 of God that are sent out into **e** part of the earth.
5: 9 from **e** tribe and language and people and nation.
5:13 And then I heard **e** creature in heaven and on earth
6:15 great power, and **e** slave and **e** free person—
7: 9 from **e** nation and tribe and people and language,
11: 6 and to send **e** kind of plague upon the earth as
13: 7 And he was given authority to rule over **e** tribe
14: 6 to **e** nation, tribe, language, and people.
16:20 And **e** island disappeared, and all the mountains
17:15 is sitting represent masses of people of **e** nation
18:12 **e** kind of perfumed wood, ivory goods,
20: 8 He will go out to deceive the nations from **e** corner

EVERYBODY (5) [BODY, EVERY]

Jn 3:26 And **e** is going over there instead of coming here to
7:53 Then the meeting broke up and **e** went home.
Ac 4:16 and **e** in Jerusalem knows about it.
21:28 our people and tells **e** to disobey the Jewish laws.
Tit 3:15 **E** here sends greetings. Please give my greetings to

EVERYBODY'S (1) [BODY, EVERY]

1Co 4:13 are treated like the world's garbage, like **e** trash—

EVERYDAY (4) [DAY, EVERY]

Mt 6:25 "So I tell you, don't worry about **e** life—
Lk 12:22 "So I tell you, don't worry about **e** life—
Gal 3:15 Dear friends, here's an example from **e** life. Just as
2Ti 2:20 special occasions, and the cheap ones are for **e** use.

EVERYONE (436) [EVERY, ONE]

Ge 12:14 when they arrived in Egypt, **e** spoke of her beauty.
16:12 He will be against **e**, and **e** will be against him.
23:13 and he replied to Ephron as **e** listened. "No,
29:22 So Laban invited **e** in the neighborhood to
31:54 a sacrifice to God and invited **e** to a feast.
35:2 So Jacob told **e** in his household, "Destroy your
Ex 2:14 because he realized that **e** knew what he had done.
12:8 That evening **e** must eat roast lamb with bitter
12:49 This law applies to **e**, whether a native-born
16:18 two quarts for each person, **e** had just enough.
23:15 **E** must bring me a sacrifice at that time.
25:2 "Tell the people of Israel that **e** who wants to may
28:3 the garments that will set Aaron apart from **e** else,
33:7 **E** who wanted to consult with the LORD would
35:5 **E** is invited to bring these offerings to the LORD:
Lev 19:34 They should be treated like **e** else, and you must
Nu 16:3 **E** in Israel has been set apart by the LORD,
17:13 **E** who even comes close to the Tabernacle of the
24:9 Blessed is **e** who blesses you, O Israel, / and
cursed is **e** who curses you."
25:5 So Moses ordered Israel's judges to execute **e** who
Dt 2:34 all his towns and completely destroyed **e**—
4:3 where the LORD your God destroyed **e** who had
17:13 Then **e** will hear about it and be afraid to act
Jos 2:9 "We are all afraid of you. **E** is living in terror.
3:17 They waited there until **e** had crossed the Jordan on
4:11 And when **e** was on the other side, the priests
6:11 then **e** returned to spend the night in the camp.
8:24 the city, they went back and finished off **e** inside.
8:26 For Joshua kept holding out his spear until **e** who
10:28 of Makkedah, killing **e** in it, including the king.
10:30 They slaughtered **e** in the city and left no
10:35 at Lachish, they completely destroyed **e** in the city.
10:39 And they killed **e** in it, leaving no survivors.
10:40 He completely destroyed **e** in the land, leaving no
Jdg 1:25 and they killed **e** in the city except for this man
9:25 on the hilltops and robbed **e** who passed that way.
9:27 flowed freely, and **e** began cursing Abimelech.
19:30 **E** who saw it said, "Such a horrible crime has not
20:37 rushed in from all sides and killed **e** in the town.
21:10 to Jabesh-gilead with orders to kill **e** there,
Ru 3:11 for **e** in town knows you are an honorable woman.
1Sa 11:4 the people about their plight, **e** broke into tears.
11:5 he asked, "What's the matter? Why is **e** crying?"
14:15 then an earthquake struck, and **e** was terrified.
14:28 will be cursed. That is why **e** is weary and faint."
15:8 Amalekite king, but completely destroyed **e** else.
15:20 I brought back King Agag, but I destroyed **e** else.
17:47 And **e** will know that the LORD does not need
30:2 and children and **e** else but without killing anyone.
2Sa 2:23 And **e** who came by that spot stopped and stood
3:35 day of the funeral, and now **e** begged him to eat.
3:37 So **e** in Judah and Israel knew that David was not
6:19 of dates, and a cake of raisins. Then **e** went home.
7:19 Do you deal with **e** this way, O Sovereign
8:15 David reigned over all Israel and was fair to **e**.
13:9 "**E** get out of here," Amnon told his servants.
15:24 Then they offered sacrifices there until **e** had
16:22 So they set up a tent on the palace roof where **e**
17:2 and his troops will panic, and **e** will run away.
17:9 and **e** will start shouting that your men are being
19:8 the city that he was there, **e** went to him.
20:13 of the way, **e** went on with Joab to capture Sheba.
1Ki 2:2 "I am going where **e** on earth must someday go.
2:15 was mine; **e** expected me to be the next king.
10:25 **e** who came to visit brought him gifts of silver
15:22 requiring that **e**, without exception, help to carry
2Ki 10:17 he killed **e** who was left there from Ahab's family,
14:26 For the LORD saw the bitter suffering of **e** in
18:22 and make **e** in Judah worship only at the altar here
18:27 "My master wants **e** in Jerusalem to hear this,
19:11 They have crushed **e** who stood in their way!
25:25 ten men and assassinated Gedaliah and **e** with him,
1Ch 4:41 They killed **e** who lived there and took the land for
16:9 yes, sing his praises. / Tell **e** about his miracles.
16:24 Tell **e** about the amazing things he does.
18:14 David reigned over all Israel and was fair to **e**.
2Ch 9:24 **e** who came to visit brought him gifts of silver
20:3 He also gave orders that **e** throughout Judah should
23:5 **E** else should stay in the courtyards of the
23:11 and **e** shouted, "Long live the king!"
29:29 the king and **e** with him bowed down in worship.
30:1 He asked **e** to come to the Temple of the LORD
30:5 inviting **e** to come to Jerusalem to celebrate the
34:32 And he required **e** in Jerusalem and the people of
34:33 and required **e** to worship the LORD their God.
Ezr 3:8 The work force was made up of **e** who had
10:14 **E** who has a pagan wife will come at the scheduled
Ne 4:22 I also told **e** living outside the walls to move into
7:3 of Jerusalem to act as guards, **e** on a regular watch.
8:3 and read aloud to **e** who could understand.
8:17 So **e** who had returned from captivity lived in these
8:17 days of the festival, and **e** was filled with great joy!
11:2 And the people commended **e** who volunteered to
Est 1:8 for the king had instructed his staff to let **e** decide
2:15 and she was admired by **e** who saw her.
2:18 giving generous gifts to **e** and declaring a public
9:2 a stand against them, for **e** was afraid of them.
Job 27:23 But **e** jeers at them and mocks them.
29:21 "**E** listened to me and valued my advice.
31:32 away a stranger but have opened my doors to **e**.
34:10 have understanding. **E** knows that God doesn't sin!
36:25 **E** has seen these things, but only from a distance.
36:28 pours down from the clouds, and **e** benefits from it.
37:7 **E** stops working at such a time so they can
Ps 11:4 watches everything closely, / examining **e** on earth.
11:5 and the wicked. / He hates **e** who loves violence.
22:7 **E** who sees me mocks me. / They sneer and shake
29:9 forests bare. / In his Temple **e** shouts, "Glory!"
33:8 Let **e** in the world fear the LORD, / and let **e** stand
in awe of him.
34:22 **E** who trusts in him will be freely pardoned.
35:28 Then I will tell **e** of your justice and goodness,
40:10 saving power. / I have told **e** in the great assembly
47:1 Come, **e**, and clap your hands for joy! / Shout to
49:1 all you people! / Pay attention, **e** in the world!
58:11 Then at last **e** will say, / "There truly is a reward
64:9 Then **e** will stand in awe, / proclaiming the mighty
65:5 O God our savior. / You are the hope of **e** on earth,
68:34 Tell **e** about God's power. / His majesty shines
71:15 I will tell **e** about your righteousness. / All day
71:16 I will tell **e** that you alone are just and good.
71:24 all day long, / for **e** who tried to hurt me / has been
73:5 other people / or plagued with problems like **e** else.
73:28 and I will tell **e** about the wonderful things you do.
76:11 Let **e** bring tribute to the Awesome One.
87:5 of Jerusalem, / "**E** has become a citizen here."
89:41 **E** who comes along has robbed him / while his
96:3 Tell **e** about the amazing things he does.
105:2 yes, sing his praises. / Tell **e** about his miracles.
109:30 repeated thanks to the LORD, / praising him to **e**.
145:7 **E** will share the story of your wonderful goodness;
145:9 The LORD is good to **e**. / He showers
145:21 and **e** on earth will bless his holy name
Pr 9:3 She has sent her servants to invite **e** to come.
12:8 **E** admires a person with good sense, but a warped
15:23 **E** enjoys a fitting reply; it is wonderful to say the
19:6 a prince; **e** is the friend of a person who gives gifts!
24:9 schemes of a fool are sinful; **e** despises a mocker.
28:12 When the godly succeed, **e** is glad.
Ecc 3:17 "In due season God will judge **e**, both good
4:15 **E** is eager to help such a youth, even to help him
6:6 And since he must die like **e** else—well,
9:2 The same destiny ultimately awaits **e**, whether they
10:14 to know all about the future and tell **e** the details!
SS 2:4 banquet hall, so **e** can see how much he loves me.
Isa 2:9 So now **e** will be humbled and brought low.
6:12 Do not stop until the LORD has sent **e** away to
8:11 the strongest terms: "Do not think like **e** else does.
13:14 **E** will run until exhausted, rushing back to their
14:16 **E** there will stare at you and ask, 'Can this be the
14:31 are doomed! Melt in fear, for **e** will be destroyed.
21:5 **E** is eating and drinking. Quick! Grab your shields
22:1 is happening? Why is **e** running to the rooftops?
25:6 spread a wonderful feast for **e** around the world.
26:1 that day, **e** in the land of Judah will sing this song:
32:3 Then **e** who can see will be looking for God,
32:6 **E** will recognize ungodly fools for what they are.
36:7 and make **e** in Judah worship only at the altar here
36:12 "My master wants **e** in Jerusalem to hear this,
37:11 They have crushed **e** who stood in their way!
41:20 **E** will see this miracle and understand that it is the
42:5 He gives breath and life to **e** in all the world.
54:17 And **e** who tells lies in court will be brought to
59:6 They cheat and shortchange **e**. Nothing they do is
60:4 "Look and see, for **e** is coming home! Your sons
61:9 **E** will realize that they are a people the LORD
61:11 **E** will praise him! His righteousness will be like a
66:14 **E** will see the good hand of the LORD on his
Jer 6:1 Warn **e** that a powerful army is coming from the
13:13 I will make **e** in this land so confused that they will
17:20 all you people of Judah and **e** living in Jerusalem.
20:7 Now I am mocked by **e** in the city.
21:7 and **e** else in the city have survived war, famine,
21:9 **E** who stays in Jerusalem will die from war,
25:30 He will shout against **e** on the earth,
31:34 For **e**, from the least to the greatest, will already
38:2 **E** who stays in Jerusalem will die from war,
40:7 in Judah, and that he hadn't exiled **e** to Babylon.
46:14 for the sword of destruction will devour **e** around
47:2 will scream in terror, and **e** in the land will weep.
50:2 a signal flag so **e** will know that Babylon will fall!
Eze 5:14 of the surrounding nations and to **e** who travels by.
7:13 For what God has said applies to **e**—it will not be
9:5 the city and kill **e** whose forehead is not marked.
9:8 Will your fury against Jerusalem wipe out **e** left in
11:13 are you going to kill **e** in Israel?"
16:44 **E** who makes up proverbs will say of you,
19:7 **E** in the land trembled in fear / when they heard
21:12 slaughter my people and their leaders—**e** will die!
27:27 **e** on board sinks into the depths of the sea.
28:22 **e** watching will know that I am the LORD.
28:23 Then **e** will know that I am the LORD.
32:27 They brought terror to **e** while they were still alive.
34:27 will yield bumper crops, and **e** will live in safety.
36:38 and **e** will know that I am the LORD."
38:16 I will bring you against my land as **e** watches,
39:13 **E** in Israel will help, for it will be a glorious
39:21 **E** will see the punishment I have inflicted on them
Da 6:26 "I decree that **e** throughout my kingdom should
9:18 your city lies in ruins—for **e** knows that it is yours.
11:2 he will stir up **e** to war against the kingdom of
Joel 1:2 **E** listen! In all your history, has anything like this
2:1 Let **e** tremble in fear because the day of the
2:16 Bring **e**—the elders, the children, and even the
Am 8:8 will tremble for your deeds, and **e** will mourn.
Ob 1:1 was sent to the nations to say, "Get ready, **e**!
1:8 "For on the mountains of Edom I will destroy **e**
1:9 and **e** on the mountains of Edom will be cut down
Jnh 3:8 **E** is required to wear sackcloth and pray earnestly
3:8 **E** must turn from their evil ways and stop all their
Mic 4:4 **E** will live quietly in their own homes in peace
6:9 are wise! His voice is calling out to **e** in Jerusalem:
Na 1:7 a strong refuge. And he knows **e** who trusts in him.
Hab 2:2 a tablet, so that a runner can read it and tell **e** else.
Zep 2:15 **E** passing that way will laugh in derision or shake
3:9 so that **e** will be able to worship the LORD
Zec 2:4 of people that it won't have room enough for **e**!
5:4 and into the house of **e** who swears falsely by my
5:6 and it is filled with the sins of **e** throughout the
8:10 on all sides. I had turned **e** against each other.
Mt 5:16 to see, so that **e** will praise your heavenly Father.
6:5 and in the synagogues where **e** can see them.
7:8 For **e** who asks, receives. **E** who seeks, finds. And
the door is opened to **e** who knocks.
8:4 of leprosy, so **e** will have proof of your healing."
8:33 telling **e** what happened to the demon-possessed
10:22 And **e** will hate you because of your allegiance to
13:25 But that night as **e** slept, his enemy came
13:54 **e** was astonished and said, "Where does he get his
19:11 "Not **e** can accept this statement," Jesus said.
19:29 And **e** who has given up houses or brothers
22:3 he sent his servants to notify **e** that it was time to
22:9 go out to the street corners and invite **e** you see.'
22:10 "So the servants brought in **e** they could find,
26:33 "Even if **e** else deserts you, I never will."
26:70 But Peter denied it in front of **e**. "I don't know
27:64 his body and then telling **e** he came back to life!
Mk 1:37 They said, "**E** is asking for you."
1:44 of leprosy, so **e** will have proof of your healing."
1:45 the news, telling **e** what had happened to him.
3:3 said to the man, "Come and stand in front of **e**."
5:14 as they ran. **E** rushed out to see for themselves.
5:16 happened to the man and to the pigs told **e** about it,
5:20 to tell **e** about the great things Jesus had done for
him; and **e** was amazed at what he told them.
9:35 must take last place and be the servant of **e** else."
9:49 "For **e** will be purified with fire.
10:29 "I assure you that **e** who has given up house
11:16 and he stopped **e** from bringing in merchandise.
11:32 start a riot, since **e** thought that John was a prophet.
12:38 and to have **e** bow to them as they walk in the
13:13 And **e** will hate you because of your allegiance to
13:26 Then **e** will see the Son of Man arrive on the
13:37 What I say to you I say to **e**: Watch for his
14:29 to him, "Even if **e** else deserts you, I never will."
16:15 into all the world and preach the Good News to **e**,
Lk 1:58 had been very kind to her, and **e** rejoiced with her.
1:66 **E** who heard about it reflected on these events
2:10 he said. "I bring you good news of great joy for **e**!
2:17 Then the shepherds told **e** what had happened
2:38 She talked about Jesus to **e** who had been waiting
3:15 **E** was expecting the Messiah to come soon,
4:15 taught in their synagogues and was praised by **e**.
4:20 **E** in the synagogue stared at him intently.
4:38 with a high fever. "Please heal her," **e** begged.
5:14 of leprosy, so **e** will have proof of your healing."
5:25 And immediately, as **e** watched, the man jumped to
5:26 **E** was gripped with great wonder and awe.
6:8 "Come and stand here where **e** can see."
6:19 **E** was trying to touch him, because healing power
8:45 **E** denied it, and Peter said, "Master, this whole
9:2 Then he sent them out to tell **e** about the coming of
9:43 While **e** was marveling over all the wonderful
11:10 For **e** who asks, receives. **E** who seeks, finds. And
the door is opened to **e** who knocks.
11:43 and the respectful greetings from **e** as you walk
12:41 "Lord, is this illustration just for us or for **e**?"
14:29 out of funds. And then how **e** would laugh at you!
18:2 was a godless man with great contempt for **e**.
18:9 who had great self-confidence and scorned **e** else:
18:11 'I thank you, God, that I am not a sinner like **e** else,
18:29 **e** who has given up house or wife or brothers
20:46 and to have **e** bow to them as they walk in the
21:17 And **e** will hate you because of your allegiance to
21:27 Then **e** will see the Son of Man arrive on the
21:35 For that day will come upon **e** living on the earth.
24:9 eleven disciples—and **e** else—what had happened.
Jn 1:4 Life itself was in him, and this life gives light to **e**.
1:7 to tell **e** about the light so that **e** might believe
because of his testimony.
1:9 The one who is the true light, who gives light to **e**,
2:10 "Then, when **e** is full and doesn't care, he brings
3:15 so that **e** who believes in me will have eternal life.
3:16 so that **e** who believes in him will not perish
3:21 so **e** can see that they are doing what God wants."
4:28 the well and went back to the village and told **e**,
5:23 so that **e** will honor the Son, just as they honor the
6:10 "Tell **e** to sit down," Jesus ordered. So all of
6:45 **E** who hears and learns from the Father comes to
6:50 the bread from heaven gives eternal life to **e** who
7:39 who would be given to **e** believing in him.
8:34 "I assure you that **e** who sins is a slave of sin.
11:24 "Yes," Martha said, "when **e** else rises,
11:25 even though they die like **e** else, will live again.
12:32 am lifted up on the cross, I will draw **e** to myself."
13:10 And you are clean, but that isn't true of **e** here."
17:2 For you have given him authority over **e** in all the
Ac 2:4 And **e** present was filled with the Holy Spirit

2:36 So let it be clearly known by **e** in Israel that God
3:11 **E** stood there in awe of the wonderful thing that
4:21 without starting a riot. For **e** was praising God
5:5 and died. **E** who heard about it was terrified.
5:13 to join them, though **e** had high regard for them.
6:15 At this point **e** in the council stared at Stephen
10:43 saying that **e** who believes in him will have their
11:29 believers in Judea, **e** giving as much as they could.
12:14 of opening the door, she ran back inside and told **e**,
13:24 John the Baptist preached the need for **e** in Israel to
13:39 **E** who believes in him is freed from all guilt
15:12 and **e** listened as Barnabas and Paul told about the
16:3 they left, for **e** knew that his father was a Greek.
16:33 and **e** in his household were immediately baptized.
17:30 but now he commands **e** everywhere to turn away
17:31 and he proved to **e** who this is by raising him from
19:29 **E** rushed to the amphitheater, dragging along
19:35 "**E** knows that Ephesus is the official guardian of
20:12 was taken home unhurt, and **e** was greatly relieved.
21:24 Then **e** will know that the rumors are all false
24:16 maintain a clear conscience before God and **e** else.
26:22 so that I am still alive today to tell these facts to **e**,
26:29 and **e** here in this audience might become the same
27:24 God in his goodness has granted safety to **e** sailing
27:33 to the early morning light, Paul begged **e** to eat.
27:36 Then **e** was encouraged,
27:44 from the broken ship. So **e** escaped safely ashore!
Ro 1:16 the power of God at work, saving **e** who believes—
2:9 and calamity for **e** who keeps on sinning—
3:4 Though **e** else in the world is a liar, God is true.
5:12 so death spread to **e**, for **e** sinned.
5:18 Adam's one sin brought condemnation upon **e**,
9:6 for not **e** born into a Jewish family is truly a Jew!
10:16 But not **e** welcomes the Good News, for Isaiah the
10:18 "The message of God's creation has gone out to **e**,
11:32 own disobedience so he could have mercy on **e**.
12:17 Do things in such a way that **e** can see you are
12:18 Do your part to live in peace with **e**, as much as
13:7 Give to **e** what you owe them: Pay your taxes
13:13 we do, so that **e** can approve of our behavior.
16:19 But **e** knows that you are obedient to the Lord.
1Co 4:5 then God will give to **e** whatever praise is due.
7:7 I wish **e** could get along without marrying, just as I
8:1 You think that **e** should agree with your perfect
9:19 yet I have become a servant of **e** so that I can bring
9:22 I try to find common ground with **e** so that I might
9:24 Remember that in a race **e** runs, but only one
10:33 I follow, too. I try to please **e** in everything I do.
12:29 Is **e** an apostle? Of course not. Is **e** a prophet? No.
12:29 Does **e** have the power to do miracles?
12:30 Does **e** have the gift of healing? Of course not.
12:30 Can **e** interpret unknown languages? No!
14:23 and hear **e** talking in an unknown language,
14:31 the other, so that **e** will learn and be encouraged.
15:22 **E** dies because all of us are related to Adam,
2Co 1:12 That is how we have acted toward **e**, and especially
3:2 and **e** can read it and recognize our good work
4:7 So **e** can see that our glorious power is from God
5:14 Since we believe that Christ died for **e**, we also
5:15 He died for **e** so that those who receive his new life
8:21 but we also want **e** else to know we are honorable.
Gal 3:10 "Cursed is **e** who does not observe and obey all
3:13 "Cursed is **e** who is hung on a tree."
5:20 the feeling that **e** is wrong except those in your
6:10 we should do good to **e**, especially to our Christian
Eph 2:3 and we were under God's anger just like **e** else.
3:9 I was chosen to explain to **e** this plan that God,
Php 1:13 For **e** here, including all the soldiers in the palace
4:5 Let **e** see that you are considerate in all you do.
Col 1:28 So everywhere we go, we tell **e** about Christ.
4:6 so that you will have the right answer for **e**.
1Th 2:15 driven us out. They displease God and oppose **e**
3:12 love grow and overflow to each other and to **e** else,
5:14 care of those who are weak. Be patient with **e**.
5:15 always try to do good to each other and to **e** else.
2Th 1:12 Then **e** will give honor to the name of our Lord
3:2 and evil people, for not **e** believes in the Lord.
1Ti 1:15 This is a true saying, and **e** should believe it:
2:4 for he wants **e** to be saved and to understand the
2:6 He gave his life to purchase freedom for **e**. This is
4:9 This is true, and **e** should accept it.
4:11 Teach these things and insist that **e** learn them.
4:15 into your tasks so that **e** will see your progress.
5:10 She must be well respected by **e** because of the
5:24 lead sinful lives, and **e** knows they will be judged.
5:25 **e** knows how much good some people do,
6:2 Timothy, and encourage **e** to obey them.
2Ti 2:14 Remind **e** of these things, and command them in
2:24 servants must not quarrel but must be kind to **e**.
3:9 Someday **e** will recognize what fools they are,
3:12 and **e** who wants to live a godly life in Christ Jesus
4:16 no one was with me. **E** had abandoned me.
Tit 1:3 revealed this Good News, and we announce it to **e**.
3:2 they should be gentle and show true humility to **e**.
3:8 so that **e** who trusts in God will be careful to do
3:8 These things are good and beneficial for **e**.
Heb 2:9 Jesus tasted death for **e** in all the world.
7:25 to save **e** who comes to God through him.
8:11 For **e**, from the least to the greatest, / will already
12:14 Try to live in peace with **e**, and seek to live a clean
1Pe 2:17 Show respect for **e**. Love your Christian brothers
4:5 who will judge **e**, both the living and the dead.
2Pe 1:7 finally you will grow to have genuine love for **e**.
3:9 to perish, so he is giving more time for **e** to repent.
3:13 has promised, a world where **e** is right with God.
1Jn 4:1 do not believe **e** who claims to speak by the Spirit.
5:1 **E** who believes that Jesus is the Christ is a child of
5:1 And **e** who loves the Father loves his children,
2Jn 1:1 the truth, as does **e** else who knows God's truth—
3Jn 1:12 But **e** speaks highly of Demetrius, even truth itself.
Rev 1:7 And **e** will see him—even those who pierced him.
2:7 **E** who is victorious will eat from the tree of life in
2:17 **E** who is victorious will eat of the manna that has
3:19 I am the one who corrects and disciplines **e** I love.
3:21 I will invite **e** who is victorious to sit with me on
11:13 And **e** who did not die was terrified and gave glory
13:13 down to earth from heaven while **e** was watching.
13:16 He required **e**—great and small, rich and poor,
16:2 malignant sores broke out on **e** who had the mark
16:8 bowl on the sun, causing it to scorch **e** with its fire.
16:9 **E** was burned by this blast of heat, and they cursed
22:18 And I solemnly declare to **e** who hears the

EVERYONE'S (6) [EVERY, ONE]

Eze 7:17 **E** hands will be feeble; their knees will be as weak
Lk 1:63 and to **e** surprise he wrote, "His name is John!"
Ac 15:3 They told them—much to **e** joy—that the Gentiles,
Ro 2:16 when God, by Jesus Christ, will judge **e** secret life.
1Co 3:13 **E** work will be put through the fire to see whether
2Co 8:14 when you need it. In this way, **e** needs will be met.

EVERYTHING (563) [EVERY, THING]

Ge 2:1 and the earth and **e** in them was completed.
3:5 just like God, knowing **e**, both good and evil."
3:22 become as we are, knowing **e**, both good and evil.
6:17 will destroy every living thing. **E** on earth will die!
6:22 So Noah did **e** exactly as God had commanded
7:22 **E** died that breathed and lived on dry land.
9:15 my covenant with you and with **e** that lives.
14:12 who lived in Sodom—and took **e** he owned.
14:16 Abram and his allies recovered **e**—the goods that
15:4 for you will have a son of your own to inherit **e** I
18:20 are extremely evil, and that **e** they do is wicked.
21:22 "It is clear that God helps you in **e** you do,"
24:10 taking with him the best of **e** his master owned.
24:36 and my master has given him **e** he owns.
25:5 Abraham left **e** he owned to his son Isaac.
28:15 I have finished giving you **e** I have promised."
28:22 and I will give God a tenth of **e** he gives me."
30:30 The LORD has blessed you from **e** I do! But now,
31:37 You have searched through **e** I own. Now show me
34:28 **e** they could lay their hands on, both inside the
39:3 was with Joseph, giving him success in **e** he did.
39:6 administrative responsibility over **e** he owned.
39:8 "my master trusts me with **e** in his entire
39:22 and over **e** that happened in the prison.
39:23 worries after that, because Joseph took care of **e**.
39:23 with him, making **e** run smoothly and successfully.
41:13 and **e** happened just as he said it would. I was
42:36 to take Benjamin, too. **E** is going against me!"
45:13 Tell him about **e** you have seen, and bring him to
46:32 with them their flocks and herds and **e** they own.'
Ex 4:28 then told Aaron **e** the LORD had commanded
4:30 Aaron told them **e** the LORD had told Moses,
7:2 Tell Aaron **e** I say to you and have him announce it
9:25 **E** left in the fields was destroyed—people,
10:5 They will devour **e** that escaped the hailstorm,
18:8 Moses told his father-in-law about **e** the LORD
19:8 "We will certainly do **e** the LORD asks of us."
20:11 made the heavens, the earth, the sea, and **e** in them;
22:3 "A thief who is caught must pay in full for **e** that
24:3 "We will do **e** the LORD has told us to do."
24:7 "We will do **e** the LORD has commanded.
25:40 "Be sure that you make **e** according to the pattern
33:14 I will give you rest—**e** will be fine for you."
35:10 Construct **e** that the LORD has commanded:
39:32 The Israelites had done **e** just as the LORD had
40:16 Moses proceeded to do **e** as the LORD had
Lev 8:10 and anointed the Tabernacle and **e** in it,
8:35 night for seven days, doing **e** the LORD requires.
8:36 and his sons did **e** the LORD had commanded
11:33 falls into a clay pot, **e** in the pot will be defiled,
14:36 so **e** inside will not be pronounced unclean.
Nu 1:54 So the Israelites did **e** just as the LORD had
2:34 So the people of Israel did **e** just as the LORD
4:16 and **e** in it will be Eleazar's responsibility."
4:32 cords, accessories, and **e** else related to their use.
14:27 I have heard **e** the Israelites have been saying.
15:23 do **e** the LORD has commanded through Moses.
16:32 who were standing with them, and **e** they owned.
18:7 with the altar and **e** within the inner curtain.
22:4 "This mob will devour **e** in sight, like an ox
31:20 purify all your clothing and **e** made of leather,
31:23 But **e** that burns must be purified by the water
32:24 for your flocks, but do **e** you have said."
Dt 1:3 telling them **e** the LORD had commanded him to
1:18 And at that time I gave you instructions about **e**
2:7 The LORD your God has blessed **e** you have
5:27 Then come and tell us **e** he tells you, and we will
6:3 Listen closely, Israel, to **e** I say. Be careful to obey.
8:13 and gold have multiplied along with **e** else,
10:14 and **e** in it all belong to the LORD your God.
12:11 you must bring **e** I command you—your burnt
12:14 your burnt offerings and do **e** I command you.
15:10 and the LORD your God will bless you in **e** you
18:18 and he will tell the people **e** I command him.
23:9 against your enemies, stay away from **e** impure.
23:20 so the LORD your God may bless you in **e** you do
26:14 my God and have done **e** you commanded me.
26:17 by walking in his ways and doing **e** he tells you.
28:8 "The LORD will bless **e** you do and will fill your
28:20 confusion, and disillusionment in **e** you do,
28:48 will be left hungry, thirsty, naked, and lacking in **e**.
29:2 "You have seen with your own eyes **e** the LORD
29:9 this covenant so that you will prosper in **e** you do.
30:9 your God will make you successful in **e** you do.
32:4 his work is perfect. / **E** he does is just and fair.
34:9 and did **e** just as the LORD had commanded
Jos 1:7 from them, and you will be successful in **e** you do.
6:17 and **e** in it must be completely destroyed as an
6:19 **E** made from silver, gold, bronze, or iron is sacred
6:21 They completely destroyed **e** in it—men
6:21 young and old, cattle, sheep, donkeys—**e**.
6:24 Then the Israelites burned the city and **e** in it.
7:15 along with **e** he has, for he has broken the covenant
7:24 cattle, donkeys, sheep, tent, and **e** he had,
23:3 You have seen **e** the LORD your God has done
24:27 "This stone has heard **e** the LORD said to us.
Jdg 15:3 "This time I cannot be blamed for **e** I am going to
16:18 one more time," she said, "for he has told me **e**."
19:19 even though we have **e** we need. We have straw
20:48 thing in all the towns—the people, the cattle—**e**.
Ru 3:5 "I will do **e** you say," Ruth replied.
3:16 Ruth told Naomi **e** Boaz had done for her,
1Sa 3:17 "What did the LORD say to you? Tell me **e**.
3:18 So Samuel told Eli **e**; he didn't hold anything back.
3:19 with him, and **e** Samuel said was wise and helpful.
9:6 by all the people because **e** he says comes true.
15:9 and lambs—**e**, in fact, that appealed to them.
15:15 the LORD your God. We have destroyed **e** else."
18:14 David continued to succeed in **e** he did,
19:3 him about you. Then I'll tell you **e** I can find out."
19:7 David to see Saul, and **e** was as it had been before.
20:2 for he always tells me **e** he's going to do,
25:6 and prosperity to you, your family, and **e** you own!
30:8 You will surely recover **e** that was taken from
30:18 David got back **e** the Amalekites had taken, and he
30:19 else that had been taken. David brought **e** back.
2Sa 3:21 Then you will be able to rule over **e** your heart
3:25 to spy on you and to discover **e** you are doing!"
3:36 very much. In fact, **e** the king did pleased them!
6:12 and **e** he has because of the Ark of God."
7:17 back to David and told him **e** the LORD had said.
7:19 And now, Sovereign LORD, in addition to **e** else,
9:9 "I have given your master's grandson **e** that
14:20 and you understand **e** that happens among us!"
16:4 told Ziba, "I give you **e** Mephibosheth owns."
1Ki 1:14 I will come and confirm **e** you have said."
2:15 were turned, and **e** went to my brother instead;
7:40 So at last Huram completed **e** King Solomon had
8:58 May he give us the desire to do his will in **e** and to
9:1 royal palace. He completed **e** he had planned to do.
10:2 they talked about **e** she had on her mind.
10:6 "**E** I heard in my country about your achievements
13:8 "Even if you gave me half of **e** you own, I would
14:26 of the LORD and the royal palace and stole **e**,
20:6 They will take away **e** you consider valuable!' "
20:9 'I will give you **e** you asked for the first time,
2Ki 3:24 into the land of Moab, destroying **e** as they went.
4:26 out to meet her and ask her, 'Is **e** all right with you,
4:26 the woman told Gehazi, "**e** is fine."
5:21 went to meet him. "Is **e** all right?" Naaman asked.
7:7 abandoning their tents, horses, donkeys, and **e** else,
7:17 So **e** happened exactly as the man of God had
8:6 So he directed one of his officials to see to it that **e**
9:11 "What did that crazy fellow want? Is **e** all right?"
11:9 So the commanders did **e** just as Jehoiada the priest
18:6 He remained faithful to the LORD in **e**, and he
18:7 with him, and Hezekiah was successful in **e** he did.
20:13 and showed them **e** in his treasure-houses—**e**!
20:15 Isaiah asked. "They saw **e**," Hezekiah replied.
20:15 "I showed them **e** I own—all my treasures."
20:17 The time is coming when **e** you have—
22:17 and I am very angry with them for **e** they have
1Ch 16:32 Let the sea and **e** in it shout his praise!
16:40 obeying **e** written in the law of the LORD,
17:15 back to David and told him **e** the LORD had said.
17:17 And now, O God, in addition to **e** else, you speak
29:11 **E** in the heavens and on earth is yours, O LORD,
29:12 honor come from you alone, for you rule over **e**.
29:14 **E** we have has come from you, and we give you
29:30 and **e** that happened to him and to Israel and to all
2Ch 4:11 So at last Huram-abi completed **e** King Solomon
7:11 royal palace. He completed **e** he had planned to do.
9:2 they talked about **e** she had on her mind.
9:5 "**E** I heard in my country about your achievements
21:17 and carried away **e** of value in the royal palace,
23:8 and the people did **e** just as Jehoiada the priest
29:36 for **e** had been accomplished so quickly.
32:30 the City of David. And so he succeeded in **e** he did.
34:16 "Your officials are doing **e** they were assigned to
34:25 and I am very angry with them for **e** they have
35:10 When **e** was ready for the Passover celebration,
36:8 all the evil things he did and **e** found against him,
36:19 the palaces, and completely destroyed **e** of value.
Ezr 7:6 and the king gave him **e** he asked for,
8:34 **E** was accounted for by number and weight,
Ne 5:12 "We will give back **e** and demand nothing more
6:19 man Tobiah was, and then they told him **e** I said.
9:6 You made the earth and the seas and **e** in them.
9:6 You preserve and give life to **e**, and all the angels
10:37 And we promise to bring to the Levites a tenth of **e**
13:30 So I purged out **e** foreign and assigned tasks to the
Est 6:10 Do not fail to carry out **e** you have suggested."
Job 1:7 forth across the earth, watching **e** that's going on."
1:10 You have made him prosperous in **e** he does.
1:11 But take away **e** he has, and he will surely curse
1:12 "Do whatever you want with **e** he possesses,
1:21 and I will be stripped of **e** when I die.
1:21 The LORD gave me **e** I had, / and the LORD

2: 2 forth across the earth, watching **e** that's going on."
2: 4 A man will give up **e** he has to save his life.
8:14 **E** they count on will collapse. They are leaning on
11: 7 Can you discover **e** there is to know about the
12: 2 "You really know **e**, don't you? And when you
15:30 and the breath of God will destroy **e** they have.
24:18 **E** they own is cursed, so that no one enters their
30:13 my road and do **e** they can to hasten my calamity,
31: 4 He sees **e** I do and every step I take.
31:12 fire that destroys to hell. It would wipe out **e** I own.
34:21 watches the way people live; he sees **e** they do.
37:17 and the south wind dies down and **e** is still,
41:11 and remain safe? **E** under heaven is mine.
42: 6 I take back **e** I said, and I sit in dust and ashes to
Ps 1: 2 But they delight in doing **e** the LORD wants;
8: 6 You put us in charge of **e** you made, / giving us
8: 8 in the sea, / and **e** that swims the ocean currents.
10: 5 Yet they succeed in **e** they do. / They do not see
11: 4 He watches **e** closely, / examining everyone on
22:31 yet unborn. / They will hear about **e** he has done.
23: 1 The LORD is my shepherd; / I have **e** I need.
24: 1 The earth is the LORD's, and **e** in it. / The world
33: 4 holds true, / and **e** he does is worthy of our trust.
33:15 made their hearts, / so he understands **e** they do.
36: 3 **E** they say is crooked and deceitful. / They refuse
37: 5 Commit **e** you do to the LORD. / Trust him,
50: 3 Fire devours **e** in his way, / and a great storm rages
50:12 it to you, / for all the world is mine and **e** in it.
66: 4 **E** on earth will worship you; / they will sing your
73: 7 These fat cats have **e** / their hearts could ever wish
74: 8 Then they thought, "Let's destroy **e**!" / So they
83:17 terrified forever. / Make them failures in **e** they do,
89:11 **e** in the world is yours—you created it all.
94:10 He knows **e**—doesn't he also know what you are
96:11 Let the sea and **e** in it shout his praise!
98: 7 Let the sea and **e** in it shout his praise!
103:19 the heavens his throne; / from there he rules over **e**.
103:22 Praise the LORD, **e** he has created,
105:35 They ate up **e** green in the land, / destroying all the
111: 3 **E** he does reveals his glory and majesty.
119:91 laws remain true today, / for **e** serves your plans.
119:168 and decrees, / because you know **e** I do.
139: 1 have examined my heart / and know **e** about me.
145:17 The LORD is righteous in **e** he does; / he is filled
146: 6 made heaven and earth, / the sea, and **e** in them.
150: 6 Let **e** that lives sing praises to the LORD!
Pr 3: 9 and with the best part of **e** your land produces.
4:23 all else, guard your heart, for it affects **e** you do.
5: 9 and hand over to merciless people **e** you have
6:31 even if it means selling **e** in his house to pay it
8: 6 I have excellent things to tell you. **E** I say is right,
11:24 more wealthy, but those who are stingy will lose **e**.
12:27 they catch, but the diligent make use of **e** they find.
13: 3 will have a long life; a quick retort can ruin **e**.
14:15 Only simpletons believe **e** they are told!
16: 4 The LORD has made **e** for his own purposes,
Ecc 1: 2 "**E** is meaningless," says the Teacher,
1: 8 **E** is so weary and tiresome! No matter how much
1:13 and to explore by wisdom **e** being done in the
1:14 **E** under the sun is meaningless, like chasing the
2: 8 beautiful concubines. I had **e** a man could desire!
2:11 But as I looked at **e** I had worked so hard to
2:17 because **e** done here under the sun is so irrational.
2:17 **E** is meaningless, like chasing the wind.
2:19 And yet they will control **e** I have gained by my
2:21 I must leave **e** I gain to people who haven't worked
3: 1 There is a time for **e**, / a season for every activity
3:11 God has made **e** beautiful for its own time. He has
4: 6 especially when in the long run **e** is so futile.
5: 6 and he might wipe out **e** you have achieved.
5:14 into risky investments that turn sour, and **e** is lost.
5:16 working for the wind, and **e** will be swept away.
6: 2 and gives them **e** they could ever want,
6:10 **E** has already been decided. It was known long ago
7:15 In this meaningless life, I have seen **e**,
8: 6 Yes, there is a time and a way for **e**, even as
8:16 I tried to observe **e** that goes on all across the earth.
8:17 This reminded me that no one can discover **e** God
8:17 Not even the wisest people know **e**, even if they
10:19 and wine gives happiness, and money gives **e**!
11: 8 days will be many. **E** still to come is meaningless.
11: 9 minute of it. Do **e** you want to do; take it all in.
11: 9 that you must give an account to God for **e** you do.
12: 9 Teacher was wise, he taught the people **e** he knew.
12:14 God will judge us for **e** we do, including every
SS 8: 7 If a man tried to buy love with **e** he owned,
Isa 1: 7 plunder your fields and destroy **e** they see.
7:20 hired to protect you—and use it to shave off **e**:
19: 7 All the crops will dry up, and **e** will die.
21:10 I have told you **e** the LORD Almighty,
22:25 **E** it supports will fall with it. I, the LORD,
24:19 **E** is lost, abandoned, and confused.
28:10 He tells us **e** over and over again, a line at a time,
33: 1 who have destroyed **e** around you but have never
34: 1 the earth. Let the world and **e** in it hear my words.
39: 2 and showed them **e** in his treasure-houses—**e**!
39: 4 asked Isaiah. "They saw **e**," Hezekiah replied.
39: 4 "I showed them **e** I own—all my treasures."
39: 6 The time is coming when **e** you have—
42: 5 He created the earth and **e** in it. He gives breath
42: 9 **E** I prophesied has come true, and now I will
44:24 the heavens. By myself I made the earth and **e** in it.
45:18 he created the heavens and earth and put **e** in place.
46:10 **E** I plan will come to pass, for I do whatever I
52:11 with **e** it represents, for it is unclean to you.
58:13 Honor the LORD in **e** you do, and don't follow
Jer 3:24 From childhood we have watched as **e** our
8:16 for it is coming to devour the land and **e** in it—
10:16 He is the Creator of **e** that exists, / including Israel,
11: 6 your ancestors made, and do **e** they promised.
15: 7 gates of your cities and take away **e** you hold dear.
20: 6 and all your friends to whom you promised that **e**
21:14 I will light a fire in your forests that will burn up **e**
22:16 to the poor and needy, and **e** went well for him.
23:16 with futile hopes. They are making up **e** they say.
23:26 they are prophets of deceit, inventing **e** they say.
26: 8 saying **e** the LORD had told him to say,
27: 6 I have put **e**, even the wild animals, under his
28: 6 come true! I hope the LORD does **e** you say.
28:14 I have put **e**, even the wild animals, under his
30: 2 Write down for the record **e** I have said to you,
32:24 **E** has happened just as you said it would.
36:28 and write **e** again just as you did on the scroll King
36:29 king of Babylon would destroy this land and **e** in it.
36:32 He wrote **e** that had been on the scroll King
39:16 says: I will do to this city **e** I have threatened.
42: 4 the LORD your God, and I will tell you **e** he says.
42: 6 For if we obey him, **e** will turn out well for us."
45: 1 after Baruch had written down **e** Jeremiah had
47: 2 It will destroy the land and **e** in it—cities
49: 9 thieves came at night, even they would not take **e**.
50: 3 **E** will be gone; both people and animals will flee.
50:32 cities of Babylon that will burn **e** around them."
51:10 let us announce in Jerusalem **e** the LORD our
51:19 He is the Creator of **e** that exists, / including his
51:29 for **e** the LORD has planned against her stands
51:61 you get to Babylon, read aloud **e** on this scroll.
La 1:10 her completely, taking **e** precious that she owns.
3:18 **E** I had hoped for from the LORD is lost!"
5: 1 LORD, remember **e** that has happened to us.
Eze 11:25 And I told the exiles **e** the LORD had shown me.
12:28 I will now do **e** I have threatened! I, the Sovereign
14:17 and I told enemy armies to come and destroy **e**.
16:54 Then you will be truly ashamed of **e** you have
20:47 they will scorch **e** from south to north.
23:25 away as captives, and **e** that is left will be burned.
24:18 The next morning I did **e** I had been told to do.
25:13 I will make a wasteland of **e** from Teman to
27:27 **E** is lost—your riches and wares, your sailors
29:19 plundering **e** they have to pay his army.
30:12 I will destroy the land of Egypt and **e** in it,
32:15 And when I destroy Egypt and wipe out **e** you have
37:14 You will see that I have done **e** just as I promised.
39: 8 **E** will happen just as I have declared it.
40: 4 and listen. Pay close attention to **e** I show you.
40: 4 people of Israel and tell them **e** you have seen."
43:11 its entrances and doors—and **e** else about it.
44: 5 Listen to **e** I tell you about the regulations
47: 9 **E** that touches the water of this river will live.
47: 9 be healed. Wherever this water flows, **e** will live.
48:22 So the prince's land will include **e** between the
Da 2:40 just as iron smashes and crushes **e** it strikes.
7:23 devour the whole world, trampling **e** in its path.
8: 4 The ram butted **e** out of its way to the west,
8:12 was overthrown. The horn succeeded in **e** it did.
8:24 amount of destruction and succeed in **e** he does.
9:14 and the LORD our God is just in **e** he does.
11: 3 a vast kingdom and accomplish **e** he sets out to do.
Hos 2: 8 She doesn't realize that it was I who gave her **e** she
Joel 3: 4 and pay you back for **e** you have done.
Am 6: 8 I will give this city and **e** in it to their enemies."
7: 2 In my vision the locusts ate **e** in sight that was
Ob 1: 5 at night and robbed you, they would not take **e**.
1:18 devouring **e** and leaving no survivors in Edom.
Mic 6: 5 did **e** I could to teach you about my faithfulness."
7:16 will stand in silent awe, deaf to **e** around them.
Na 3:15 consume you like locusts, devouring **e** they see.
Zep 1: 2 "I will sweep away **e** in all your land,"
3: 3 hunting for their victims—out for **e** they can get.
Hag 1:11 and your cattle and to ruin **e** you have worked
2:14 **E** they do and **e** they offer is defiled.
Mt 3:15 must be done, because we must do **e** that is right."
10:26 For the time is coming when **e** will be revealed;
11:27 "My Father has given me authority over **e**. No one
13:41 and they will remove from my Kingdom **e** that
13:44 and sold **e** he owned to get enough money to buy
13:46 of great value, he sold **e** he owned and bought it!
17:11 "Elijah is indeed coming first to set **e** in order.
18:16 so that **e** you say may be confirmed by two or three
18:25 his children, and **e** he had be sold to pay the debt.
19:26 it is impossible. But with God **e** is possible."
19:27 said to him, "We've given up **e** to follow you.
22: 4 meats have been cooked. **E** is ready. Hurry!'
22:21 But **e** that belongs to God must be given to God."
23: 5 "**E** they do is for show. On their arms they wear
23:20 'by the altar,' you are swearing by it and by **e** on it.
28:14 we'll stand up for you and **e** will be all right."
Mk 4:11 But I am using these stories to conceal **e** about it
4:22 "**E** that is now hidden or secret will eventually be
5:26 the years and had spent **e** she had to pay them,
7:37 and again they said, "**E** he does is wonderful.
8:25 completely restored, and he could see **e** clearly.
9:12 "Elijah is indeed coming first to set **e** in order.
10:27 But not with God. **E** is possible with God."
10:28 "We've given up **e** to follow you," he said.
10:32 Jesus once more began to describe **e** that was about
11:11 He looked around carefully at **e**, and then he left
12:17 But **e** that belongs to God must be given to God."
12:44 but she, poor as she is, has given **e** she has."
14:16 into the city and found **e** just as Jesus had said,
14:36 "Abba, Father," he said, "**e** is possible for you.
Lk 1:38 May **e** you have said come true." And
5:11 soon as they landed, they left **e** and followed Jesus.
5:28 So Levi got up, left **e**, and followed him.
7:18 The disciples of John the Baptist told John about **e**
8:10 But I am using these stories to conceal **e** about it
8:17 For **e** that is hidden or secret will eventually be
8:43 She had spent **e** she had on doctors and still could
9:10 apostles returned, they told Jesus **e** they had done.
10:22 "My Father has given me authority over **e**. No one
12: 2 The time is coming when **e** will be revealed;
12:18 bigger ones. Then I'll have room enough to store **e**.
14:33 become my disciple without giving up **e** for me.
15:31 you and I are very close, and **e** I have is yours.
16:25 remember that during your lifetime you had **e** you
19:11 The crowd was listening to **e** Jesus said. And
20:25 But **e** that belongs to God must be given to God."
21: 4 but she, poor as she is, has given **e** she has."
22:13 off to the city and found **e** just as Jesus had said,
22:37 **e** written about me by the prophets will come
24:14 As they walked along they were talking about **e**
24:44 I told you that **e** written about me by Moses
Jn 1: 3 He created **e** there is. Nothing exists that he didn't
3:35 his Son, and he has given him authority over **e**.
4:25 When he comes, he will explain **e** to us."
4:29 "Come and meet a man who told me **e** I ever did!
4:39 the woman had said, "He told me **e** I ever did!"
5:20 Father loves the Son and tells him **e** he is doing,
5:32 and I can assure you that **e** he says about me is
7:15 so much when he hasn't studied **e** we've studied?"
13: 3 that the Father had given him authority over **e**
14: 3 When **e** is ready, I will come and get you, so that
14:26 he will teach you **e** and will remind you of **e** I myself have told you.
15:15 since I have told you **e** the Father told me.
16:30 Now we understand that you know **e** and don't
17: 4 I brought glory to you here on earth by doing **e** you
17: 7 Now they know that **e** I have is a gift from you,
19:28 Jesus knew that **e** was now finished, and to fulfill
21:17 He said, "Lord, you know **e**. You know I love
Ac 1: 1 In my first book I told you about **e** Jesus began to
2:44 met together constantly and shared **e** they had.
3:22 own people. Listen carefully to **e** he tells you.'
4:24 of heaven and earth, the sea, and **e** in them—
4:28 **e** they did occurred according to your eternal will
4:32 owned was not their own; they shared **e** they had.
7:50 Didn't I make **e** in heaven and earth?'
13:22 after my own heart, for he will do **e** I want him to.'
14:15 who made heaven and earth, the sea, and **e** in them.
17:24 "He is the God who made the world and **e** in it.
17:25 He himself gives life and breath to **e**, and he
19:32 **E** was in confusion. In fact, most of them didn't
22: 3 I became very zealous to honor God in **e** I did,
24: 9 chimed in, declaring that **e** Tertullus said was true.
24:14 Jewish law and **e** written in the books of prophecy.
26: 9 "I used to believe that I ought to do **e** I could to
Ro 8:17 for **e** God gives to his Son, Christ, is ours too.
8:20 its will, **e** on earth was subjected to God's curse.
8:28 And we know that God causes **e** to work together
8:32 who gave us Christ, also give us **e** else?
9: 5 who rules over **e** and is worthy of eternal praise!
11:36 For **e** comes from him; **e** exists by his power and is
13:13 We should be decent and true in **e** we do, so that
14: 6 And those who won't eat **e** also want to please the
1Co 2:10 and his Spirit searches out **e** and shows us even
3:21 in following a particular leader. **E** belongs to you:
3:22 the present and the future. **E** belongs to you,
4: 8 You think you already have **e** you need! You are
6:12 But I reply, "Not **e** is good for you."
7:32 In **e** you do, I want you to be free from the
8: 6 the Father, who created **e**, and we exist for him.
8: 6 through whom God made **e** and through whom we
10:23 am allowed to do anything"—but not **e** is helpful.
10:23 allowed to do anything"—but not **e** is beneficial.
10:26 For "the earth is the Lord's, and **e** in it."
10:33 I follow, too. I try to please everyone in **e** I do.
11:12 from women ever since, and **e** comes from God.
13: 2 of the future and knew **e** about **e**,
13: 3 If I gave **e** I have to the poor and even sacrificed
13:12 but then we will see **e** with perfect clarity.
13:12 and incomplete, but then I will know **e** completely,
14:26 But **e** that is done must be useful to all and build
14:40 But be sure that **e** is done properly and in order.
15:28 will be utterly supreme over **e** everywhere.
16:14 And **e** you do must be done with love.
2Co 1:22 hearts as the first installment of **e** he will give us.
6: 4 In **e** we do we try to show that we are true
6:10 to others. We own nothing, and yet we have **e**.
7: 1 let us cleanse ourselves from **e** that can defile our
7:11 You showed that you have done **e** you could to
9: 8 Then you will always have **e** you need and plenty
11:20 take **e** you have, take advantage of you, put on airs,
12:19 **E** we do, dear friends, is for your benefit.
Gal 4: 1 even though they actually own **e** their father had.
4: 7 since you are his child, **e** he has belongs to you.
5: 5 **e** promised to us who are right with God through
Eph 1:10 At the right time he will bring **e** together under the
1:10 the authority of Christ—**e** in heaven and on earth.
1:14 The Spirit is God's guarantee that he will give us **e**
1:23 who fills **e** everywhere with his presence.
3:15 the Creator of **e** in heaven and on earth.
4:29 Let **e** you say be good and helpful, so that your
5: 1 Follow God's example in **e** you do, because you
5:20 And you will always give thanks for **e** to God the
5:24 so you wives must submit to your husbands in **e**.
Php 1:12 that **e** that has happened to me here has helped to
2:14 In **e** you do, stay away from complaining
3: 8 **e** else is worthless when compared with the
3: 8 I have discarded **e** else, counting it all as garbage,
3:21 same mighty power that he will use to conquer **e**,
4: 6 Don't worry about anything; instead, pray about **e**.

4:12 I know how to live on almost nothing or with **e**.
4:13 For I can do **e** with the help of Christ who gives
Col 1:16 Christ is the one through whom God created **e** in
1:16 **E** has been created through him and for him.
1:17 He existed before **e** else began, and he holds all
1:18 all who will rise from the dead, so he is first in **e**.
1:20 and by him God reconciled **e** to himself. He made
peace with **e** in heaven and on earth by
3:22 You slaves must obey your earthly masters in **e**
1Th 5: 3 **e** is peaceful and secure," then disaster will fall
5:21 but test **e** that is said. Hold on to what is good.
2Th 2:15 and keep a strong grip on **e** we taught you both in
1Ti 3:11 exercise self-control and be faithful in **e** they do.
4: 4 Since **e** God created is good, we should not reject
2Ti 4:15 Be careful of him, for he fought against **e** we said.
Tit 1:15 **E** is pure to those whose hearts are pure.
2: 7 Let **e** you do reflect the integrity and seriousness of
3:13 Do **e** you can to help Zenas the lawyer and Apollos
3:13 with their trip. See that they are given **e** they need.
Heb 1: 2 God promised **e** to the Son as an inheritance,
1: 2 through the Son he made the universe and **e** in it.
1: 3 and **e** about him represents God exactly.
2:10 who made **e** and for whom **e** was made—
3: 4 has a builder, but God is the one who made **e**.
4:13 from him. **E** is naked and exposed before his eyes.
8: 5 "Be sure that you make **e** according to the design I
9:21 blood on the sacred tent and on **e** used for worship.
9:22 nearly **e** was purified by sprinkling with blood.
9:23 That is why the earthly tent and **e** in it—
13:18 is clear and we want to live honorably in **e** we do.
Jas 1: 8 They waver back and forth in **e** they do.
1Pe 1:15 But now you must be holy in **e** you do, just as
4:11 Then God will be given glory in **e** through Jesus
2Pe 1: 3 his divine power gives us **e** we need for living a
3: 4 **e** has remained exactly the same since the world
3:10 and **e** in them will disappear in fire, and the earth
and **e** on it will be exposed to judgment.
3:11 Since **e** around us is going to melt away,
1Jn 2:16 the lust for **e** we see, and pride in our possessions.
2:17 this world is fading away, along with **e** it craves.
3:20 For God is greater than our hearts, and he knows **e**.
Rev 1: 2 and the testimony of Jesus Christ—**e** he saw.
3:17 You say, 'I am rich. I have **e** I want. I don't need a
4:11 and honor and power. / For you created **e**,
10: 6 who created heaven and **e** in it, the earth and **e** in
it, and the sea and **e** in it.
16: 3 like the blood of a corpse. And **e** in the sea died.

EVERYWHERE (91) [EVERY, WHERE]

Ge 3:20 because she would be the mother of all people **e**.
6:12 in the world, and he saw violence and depravity **e**.
13:10 The whole area was well watered **e**, like the garden
41:47 the next seven years there were bumper crops **e**.
41:56 So with severe famine **e** in the land, Joseph opened
Ex 7:19 **E** in Egypt the water will turn into blood,
7:21 There was blood **e** throughout the land of Egypt.
Jos 1: 3 '**E** you go, you will be on land I have given you—
2:22 The men who were chasing them had searched **e**
1Sa 5:12 afflicted with tumors; and there was weeping **e**.
14:20 killing each other. There was terrible confusion **e**.
2Ki 3:20 the direction of Edom, and soon there was water **e**.
6:15 there were troops, horses, and chariots **e**.
19:35 woke up the next morning, they found corpses **e**.
1Ch 14:17 So David's fame spread **e**, and the LORD caused
Ne 6: 6 "Geshem tells me that **e** he goes he hears that you
Est 1:17 Women **e** will begin to despise their husbands
1:20 husbands **e**, whatever their rank, will receive
8:16 filled with joy and gladness and were honored **e**.
Job 23:17 is all around me; thick, impenetrable darkness is **e**.
37:24 No wonder people **e** fear him. People who are truly
Ps 41: 6 and when they leave, they spread it **e**.
47: 9 the earth belong to God. / He is highly honored **e**.
55:11 Murder and robbery are **e** there; / threats
67: 2 the earth, / your saving power among people **e**.
75: 1 are near. / People **e** tell of your mighty miracles.
103:22 everything he has created, / **e** in his kingdom.
109:25 I am an object of mockery to people **e**; / when they
112: 2 Their children will be successful **e**; / an entire
113: 3 **E**—from east to west— / praise the name of the
Pr 15: 3 The LORD is watching **e**, keeping his eye on both
Ecc 7:25 I searched **e**, determined to find wisdom and to
Isa 22: 2 Bodies are lying **e**, killed by famine and disease.
24:16 for evil still prevails, and treachery is **e**.
28: 8 Their tables are covered with vomit; filth is **e**.
37:36 woke up the next morning, they found corpses **e**.
55:11 all I want it to, and it will prosper **e** I send it.
61:11 filled with young plants springing up **e**.
Jer 6:25 The enemy is **e**, and they are ready to kill.
15:10 Oh, that I had died at birth! I am hated **e** I go.
23:24 Am I not **e** in all the heavens and earth?"
49:29 be taken away. **E** shouts of panic will be heard:
La 1:18 Listen, people **e**; look upon my anguish
Eze 22:12 loan racketeers, and extortioners **e**!
32: 8 Yes, I will bring darkness **e** across your land.
32:23 **e** are now dead at the hands of their enemies.
36: 4 been destroyed and mocked by foreign nations **e**.
37: 2 They were scattered **e** across the ground.
Hos 4: 2 There is violence **e**, with one murder after another.
7:16 They look **e** except to heaven, to the Most High.
Joel 3:11 Come quickly, all you nations **e**! Gather together in
Am 4: 5 voluntary offerings so you can brag about it **e**!
8: 3 Dead bodies will be scattered **e**. They will be
8:12 People will stagger **e** from sea to sea, searching for
Na 3: 3 in the streets—dead bodies, heaps of bodies, **e**.
3: 4 all to worship her false gods, enchanting people **e**.
Hab 2:17 because of your murder and violence in cities **e**!
Mt 4:23 preaching **e** the Good News about the Kingdom.
13:57 "A prophet is honored **e** except in his own
24:12 Sin will be rampant **e**, and the love of many will
Mk 1:45 and people from **e** came to him there.
6: 4 "A prophet is honored **e** except in his own
6:14 because people **e** were talking about him.
16:15 and preach the Good News to everyone, **e**.
16:20 And the disciples went **e** and preached,
Lk 2:48 and I have been frantic, searching for you **e**."
4:42 The crowds searched **e** for him, and when they
23: 5 "But he is causing riots **e** he goes, all over Judea,
Jn 4:44 "A prophet is honored **e** except in his own
18:20 I have been heard by people **e**, and I teach nothing
Ac 1: 8 receive power and will tell people about me **e**—
8: 3 Saul was going **e** to devastate the church. He went
8: 4 But the believers who had fled Jerusalem went **e**
10:42 And he ordered us to preach **e** and to testify that
17:16 he was deeply troubled by all the idols he saw **e** in
17:30 but now he commands everyone **e** to turn away
22:15 You are to take his message **e**, telling the whole
28:22 these Christians is that they are denounced **e**."
Ro 1: 5 and authority to tell Gentiles **e** what God has done
16:26 this message is made known to all Gentiles **e**,
1Co 1: 2 of Christ Jesus, just as he did all Christians **e**—
15:28 will be utterly supreme over everything **e**.
Eph 1:15 in the Lord Jesus and your love for Christians **e**,
1:23 by Christ, who fills everything **e** with his presence.
6:18 be persistent in your prayers for all Christians **e**.
Php 3:21 power that he will use to conquer everything, **e**.
Col 1: 6 It is changing lives **e**, just as it changed yours that
1:28 So **e** we go, we tell everyone about Christ.
1Th 1: 8 of the Lord is ringing out from you to people **e**,
2Ti 1:17 he came to Rome, he searched **e** until he found me.
Rev 6: 4 from the earth. And there was war and slaughter **e**.

EVI (2)

Nu 31: 8 **E**, Rekem, Zur, Hur, and Reba—died in the battle.
Jos 13:21 **E**, Rekem, Zur, Hur, and Reba—princes living in

EVICTED (3)

Ps 109:10 may they be **e** from their ruined homes.
Eze 46:18 for I do not want any of my people unjustly **e** from
Mic 2: 9 You have **e** women from their homes and stripped

EVIDENCE (10) [EVIDENT]

Ge 9:12 "I am giving you a sign as **e** of my eternal
Ex 22:13 the carcass must be shown as **e**, and no payment
Dt 31:21 on them, and this song will stand as **e** against them,
Job 19: 5 overcome me, using my humiliation as **e** of my sin,
Ps 74: 9 as **e** that you will save us. / All the prophets are
Pr 20: 8 When a king judges, he carefully weighs all the **e**,
Isa 11: 3 will never judge by appearance, false **e**, or hearsay.
Jn 18:23 "If I said anything wrong, you must give **e** for it.
Heb 11: 1 to happen. It is the **e** of things we cannot yet see.
Jas 5: 3 This treasure you have accumulated will stand as **e**

EVIDENT (6) [EVIDENCE]

Dt 10:15 above every other nation, as is **e** today.
Pr 28:11 as wise, but their real poverty is **e** to the poor.
Eze 24: 7 for her wickedness is **e** to all. She murders boldly,
Zep 3: 5 Day by day his justice is more **e**, but no one takes
Lk 17:24 It will be as **e** as the lightning that flashes across
Heb 7:15 The change in God's law is even more **e** from the

EVIL (570) [EVILDOERS, EVIL-HEARTED, EVIL-MINDED, EVILS]

EVIL DEEDS (28) 1Sa 24:13; Ps 28:4; 106:39; Isa 1:16,31; 59:4,18; Jer 16:18; 22:3; 32:30; La 1:22; Eze 36:17; Ob 1:15; Mic 7:3; Lk 6:45; 23:41; Ro 2:8; 8:13; 13:12; Eph 5:14; Php 3:2; Heb 6:1; Rev 2:22; 3:4; 9:20; 16:11; 18:5,6

EVIL IN...SIGHT OF...LORD* (50) Dt 4:25; 17:2; 31:29; Jdg 2:11; 3:7,12; 4:1; 6:1; 10:6; 13:1; 1Ki 11:6; 14:22; 15:26,34; 16:7,19,25,30; 21:20,25; 22:52; 2Ki 3:2; 8:18,27; 13:2,11; 14:24; 15:9,18,24,28; 17:2; 21:2,6,16,20; 23:32,37; 24:9,19; 2Ch 21:6; 22:4; 29:6; 33:2,6,22; 36:5,9,12; Jer 52:2

EVIL SPIRIT (20) Mt 12:43; Mk 1:23,26; 3:30; 5:2,8; 7:25; 9:17,18,18,20,22,25,28; Lk 8:29; 9:39,42; 11:24; 13:11; Ac 19:15

EVIL SPIRITS (19) Lev 17:7; Isa 65:4; Mt 10:1; Mk 1:27; 3:11; 5:12,13; 6:7; Lk 4:36; 6:18; 7:21; 8:2; 10:20; Ac 5:16; 8:7; 19:12,13; Rev 16:13; 18:2

EVIL WAY (3) Ne 13:17; Eze 36:19; Jude 1:18

EVIL WAYS (19) Ex 34:12; 1Ki 13:33; 2Ki 17:13,22; Isa 23:17; Jer 7:3; 15:7; 17:1; 18:8,11; 23:22; 26:3; 36:7; Hos 7:8,12; Jnh 3:8,10; Zec 1:4; Lk 13:3

FROM EVIL (19) 1Sa 24:13; 2Sa 14:17; Job 1:1; 36:10,21; Ps 34:14; 36:4; 37:27; 140:1; Pr 2:12; 13:19; 16:17; Am 5:14; Mt 12:35; 15:18; Lk 6:45; Heb 6:1; 1Pe 2:11; 3:11

GOOD...EVIL; EVIL...GOOD (61) Ge 2:9,17; 3:5,22; 50:20; 1Sa 24:17; 25:21,21; 2Sa 14:17; Job 30:26; Ps 14:1; 34:14; 35:12; 36:4; 37:27; 38:20; 52:3; 53:1; 90:15; 109:5; Pr 11:27; 14:19,22; 15:3; 17:13; Isa 5:20,20; Jer 13:23; 18:11,20; Eze 33:12; Am 5:14,15; Mic 3:2; Mt 5:45; 12:34,35,35,35; 13:19,38; Lk 6:45,45,45; 16:15; Jn 5:29; Ro 7:13,13,13; 12:21; 2Co 4:4; 5:10; Eph 5:16; 1Th 5:15; 1Ti 6:11; Tit 2:3; 1Pe 3:10,11,16; 3Jn 1:11,11

THE EVIL ONE (8) Mt 6:13; 13:19,38; Jn 17:15; 2Th 3:3; 1Jn 3:12; 5:18,19

Ge 2: 9 and the tree of the knowledge of good and **e**.
2:17 fruit from the tree of the knowledge of good and **e**.
3: 5 like God, knowing everything, both good and **e**."
3:22 as we are, knowing everything, both good and **e**.
6: 5 all their thoughts were consistently and totally **e**.
8:21 and actions are bent toward **e** from childhood.
18:20 people of Sodom and Gomorrah are extremely **e**,
44: 4 have you repaid an act of kindness with such **e**?
50:15 "Now Joseph will pay us back for all the **e** we did
50:17 'Forgive your brothers for the great **e** they did to
50:20 God turned into good what you meant for **e**.
Ex 23: 1 Do not cooperate with **e** people by telling lies on
23: 2 "Do not join a crowd that intends to do **e**.
23: 7 far away from falsely charging anyone with **e**.
23:24 them in any way, and never follow their **e** example.
34:12 If you do, you soon will be following their **e** ways.
Lev 17: 7 by offering sacrifices to **e** spirits out in the fields.
Dt 4:25 This is **e** in the sight of the LORD your God
13: 5 you must execute them to remove the **e** from
17: 2 has done **e** in the sight of the LORD your God
17: 7 In this way, you will purge all **e** from among you.
17:12 be put to death. Such **e** must be purged from Israel.
19:19 this way, you will cleanse such **e** from among you.
19:20 about it will be afraid to do such an **e** thing again.
21:21 this way, you will cleanse this **e** from among you,
22:21 Such **e** must be cleansed from among you.
22:22 In this way, the **e** will be cleansed from Israel.
22:24 In this way, you will cleanse the land of **e**.
24: 7 must die. You must cleanse the **e** from among you.
28:20 at last you are completely destroyed for doing **e**
31:29 very angry by doing what is **e** in his sight."
Jdg 2:11 Then the Israelites did what was **e** in the LORD's
2:19 And they refused to give up their **e** practices
3: 7 The Israelites did what was **e** in the LORD's
3:12 Once again the Israelites did what was **e** in the
4: 1 the Israelites again did what was **e** in the LORD's
6: 1 Again the Israelites did what was **e** in the
9:56 God punished Abimelech for the **e** he had done
9:57 also punished the men of Shechem for all their **e**.
10: 6 Again the Israelites did **e** in the LORD's sight.
13: 1 Again the Israelites did what was **e** in the
19:23 "No, my brothers, don't do such an **e** thing.
20:13 Give up these **e** men from Gibeah so we can
execute them and purge Israel of this **e**."
1Sa 24:13 old proverb says, 'From **e** people come **e** deeds.'
24:17 man than I am, for you have repaid me good for **e**.
25:21 was lost or stolen. But he has repaid me **e** for good.
2Sa 14:17 like an angel of God and can discern good from **e**.
22:22 I have not turned from my God to follow **e**.
1Ki 8:47 in repentance and pray, 'We have sinned, done **e**,
11: 6 Solomon did what was **e** in the LORD's sight;
13:33 after this, Jeroboam did not turn from his **e** ways.
14: 9 You have done more **e** than all who lived before
14:22 the people of Judah did what was **e** in the
15:26 But he did what was **e** in the LORD's sight
15:34 But he did what was **e** in the LORD's sight
16: 2 but you have followed the **e** example of Jeroboam.
16: 7 because Baasha had done what was **e** in the
16:19 had done what was **e** in the LORD's sight
16:25 But Omri did what was **e** in the LORD's sight,
16:30 But Ahab did what was **e** in the LORD's sight,
21:20 because you have sold yourself to what is **e** in the
21:25 so completely sold himself to what was **e** in the
22:52 But he did what was **e** in the LORD's sight,
2Ki 3: 2 He did what was **e** in the LORD's sight, but he
8:18 So Jehoram did what was **e** in the LORD's sight.
8:27 Ahaziah followed the **e** example of King Ahab's
8:27 doing what was **e** in the LORD's sight,
13: 2 But he did what was **e** in the LORD's sight.
13: 6 to sin, following the **e** example of Jeroboam.
13:11 But he did what was **e** in the LORD's sight.
14:24 He did what was **e** in the LORD's sight.
15: 9 Zechariah did what was **e** in the LORD's sight,
15:18 But Menahem did what was **e** in the LORD's
15:24 But Pekahiah did what was **e** in the LORD's
15:28 But Pekah did what was **e** in the LORD's sight.
17: 2 He did what was **e** in the LORD's sight, but not
17:11 So the people of Israel had done many **e** things,
17:13 both Israel and Judah: "Turn from all your **e** ways.
17:17 and used sorcery and sold themselves to **e**,
17:19 They walked down the same **e** paths that Israel had
17:22 And the people of Israel persisted in all the **e** ways
21: 2 He did what was **e** in the LORD's sight,
21: 6 He did much that was **e** in the LORD's sight,
21: 9 and Manasseh led them to do even more **e** than the
21:15 For they have done great **e** in my sight and have
21:16 leading them to do **e** in the LORD's sight.
21:20 He did what was **e** in the LORD's sight, just as
23:32 He did what was **e** in the LORD's sight, just as
23:37 He did what was **e** in the LORD's sight, just as
24: 9 Jehoiachin did what was **e** in the LORD's sight,
24:19 But Zedekiah did what was **e** in the LORD's
2Ch 6:37 in repentance and pray, 'We have sinned, done **e**,
12:14 But he was an **e** king, for he did not seek the
21: 6 So Jehoram did what was **e** in the LORD's sight.
21:13 Instead, you have been as **e** as the kings of Israel.
22: 3 Ahaziah also followed the **e** example of King
22: 4 He did what was **e** in the LORD's sight, just as
22: 5 Following their **e** advice, Ahaziah made an alliance
29: 6 and did what was **e** in the sight of the LORD our
33: 2 He did what was **e** in the LORD's sight,
33: 6 He did much that was **e** in the LORD's sight,
33: 9 and Jerusalem to do even more **e** than the pagan
33:22 He did what was **e** in the LORD's sight, just as
36: 5 But he did what was **e** in the sight of the LORD
36: 8 including all the **e** things he did and everything
36: 9 Jehoiachin did what was **e** in the LORD's sight.
36:12 He did what was **e** in the sight of the LORD his
Ezr 4:12 Babylon are rebuilding this rebellious and **e** city.
Ne 6:14 all the **e** things that Tobiah and Sanballat have

13: 7 and learned the extent of this **e** deed of Eliashib—
13:17 "Why are you profaning the Sabbath in this **e**
Est 8: 3 and begging him with tears to stop Haman's **e** plot
9:25 he issued a decree causing Haman's **e** plot to
Job 1: 1 He feared God and stayed away from **e**.
1: 8 He fears God and will have nothing to do with **e**."
2: 3 He fears God and will have nothing to do with **e**.
4: 8 plant trouble and cultivate **e** will harvest the same.
5: 6 But **e** does not spring from the soil, and trouble
5:19 you again and again so that no **e** can touch you.
15:13 you turn against God and say all these **e** things?
15:35 They conceive trouble and **e**, and their hearts give
21:30 **E** people are spared in times of calamity and are
22:15 "Will you continue on the old paths where **e**
24: 2 **E** people steal land by moving the boundary
27: 4 my lips will speak no **e**, and my tongue will speak
27: 7 punished like the wicked, my adversary like **e** men.
27:16 "**E** people may have all the money in the world,
28:28 to forsake **e** is real understanding.' "
30:26 So I looked for good, but **e** came instead. I waited
31: 3 for the wicked, misfortune for those who do **e**.
34: 8 He seeks the companionship of **e** people.
34:32 Or 'I don't know what **e** I have done; tell me,
36:10 and says they must turn away from **e**.
36:21 Turn back from **e**, for it was to prevent you from
36:21 getting into a life of **e** that God sent this suffering.
Ps 5: 5 stand in your presence, / for you hate all who do **e**.
6: 8 Go away, all you who do **e**, / for the LORD has
7:14 The wicked conceive **e**; / they are pregnant with
10: 2 Let them be caught in the **e** they plan for others.
10: 3 For they brag about their **e** desires; / they praise the
10: 7 Trouble and **e** are on the tips of their tongues.
10:15 Break the arms of these wicked, **e** people!
12: 8 strut about, / and **e** is praised throughout the land.
14: 1 They are corrupt, and their actions are **e**; / no one
14: 4 Will those who do **e** never learn? / They eat up my
15: 3 harm their neighbors / or speak **e** of their friends.
17: 4 kept me from going along with cruel and **e** people.
18:21 I have not turned from my God to follow **e**.
21:11 against you, / their **e** schemes will never succeed.
22:16 like a pack of dogs; / an **e** gang closes in on me.
26: 5 I hate the gatherings of those who do **e**, / and I
27: 2 When **e** people come to destroy me, / when my
28: 3 away with the wicked— / with those who do **e**—
28: 3 to their neighbors / while planning **e** in their hearts.
28: 4 Pay them back for all their **e** deeds!
34:14 Turn away from **e** and do good. / Work hard at
34:16 the LORD turns his face against those who do **e**;
35:12 They repay me with **e** for the good I do. / I am sick
36: 4 never good. / They make no attempt to turn from **e**.
37: 7 to act. / Don't worry about **e** people who prosper
37:16 and have little / than to be **e** and possess much.
37:27 Turn from **e** and do good, / and you will live in the
37:32 Those who are **e** spy on the godly, / waiting for an
37:35 proud and **e** people thriving like mighty trees.
38:20 They repay me **e** for good / and oppose me
41: 5 But my enemies say nothing but **e** about me.
51: 4 have I sinned; / I have done what is **e** in your sight.
52: 3 You love **e** more than good / and lies more than
53: 1 They are corrupt, and their actions are **e**; / no one
53: 4 Will those who do **e** never learn? / They eat up my
54: 5 May my enemies' plans for **e** be turned against
55:15 them alive, / for **e** makes its home within them.
59:12 they say, / because of the **e** that is on their lips,
64: 2 the wicked, / from the scheming of those who do **e**.
64: 5 They encourage each other to do **e** / and plan how
73: 8 They scoff and speak only **e**; / in their pride they
76: 9 You stand up to judge those who do **e**, O God,
82: 4 deliver them from the grasp of **e** people.
90:15 former misery! / Replace the **e** years with good.
91:10 no **e** will conquer you; / no plague will come near
94:23 God will make the sins of **e** people fall back upon
97:10 You who love the LORD, hate **e**! / He protects
101: 4 reject perverse ideas / and stay away from every **e**.
106:35 among the pagans / and adopted their **e** customs.
106:39 They defiled themselves by their **e** deeds,
109: 5 They return **e** for good, / and hatred for my love.
109: 6 Arrange for an **e** person to turn on him. / Send an
112: 6 Such people will not be overcome by **e**
119: 3 They do not compromise with **e**, / and they walk
119:61 **E** people try to drag me into sin, / but I am firmly
119:101 I have refused to walk on any path of **e**, / that I
119:126 to act, / for these **e** people have broken your law.
119:133 by your word, / so I will not be overcome by any **e**.
119:134 Rescue me from the oppression of **e** people;
121: 7 The LORD keeps you from all **e** / and preserves
125: 5 O LORD. / Take them away with those who do **e**.
140: 1 O LORD, rescue me from **e** people. / Preserve me
140: 2 those who plot **e** in their hearts / and stir up trouble
140: 8 LORD, do not give in to their **e** desires. / Do not let
their **e** schemes succeed, O God.
140: 9 by the very **e** they have planned for me.
141: 4 Don't let me lust for **e** things; / don't let me share
in the delicacies / of those who do **e**.
141: 9 set for me, / out of the snares of those who do **e**.
Pr 2:12 Wisdom will save you from **e** people, from those
2:13 from right ways to walk down dark and **e** paths.
2:14 and they enjoy **e** as it turns things upside down.
3: 7 Instead, fear the LORD and turn your back on **e**.
4:16 for **e** people cannot sleep until they have done their
e deed for the day.
4:27 get sidetracked; keep your feet from following **e**.
5:22 An **e** man is held captive by his own sins; they are
6:14 Their perverted hearts plot **e**. They stir up trouble
6:18 a heart that plots **e**, / feet that race to do wrong,
8:13 All who fear the LORD will hate **e**. That is why I
10: 6 **e** people cover up their harmful intentions.
10:11 to life; **e** people cover up their harmful intentions.
10:16 but **e** people squander their money on sin.
11: 9 **E** words destroy one's friends; wise discernment
11:18 **E** people get rich for the moment, but the reward
11:19 Godly people find life; **e** people find death.
11:21 You can be sure that **e** people will be punished,
11:27 find favor; but if you search for **e**, it will find you!
12:20 Deceit fills hearts that are plotting **e**; joy fills hearts
13: 6 while the **e** are destroyed by their wickedness.
13:19 but fools will not turn from **e** to attain them.
14:19 **E** people will bow before good people; the wicked
14:22 If you plot **e**, you will be lost; but if you plan good,
15: 3 keeping his eye on both the **e** and the good.
15:28 think before speaking; the wicked spout **e** words.
16: 6 cover sin; **e** is avoided by fear of the LORD.
16:17 The path of the upright leads away from **e**;
16:30 With narrowed eyes, they plot **e**; without a word,
17:11 **E** people seek rebellion, but they will be severely
17:13 repay **e** for good, **e** will never leave your house.
19:28 of justice; the mouth of the wicked gulps down **e**.
20:30 Physical punishment cleanses away **e**;
21: 4 a proud heart, and **e** actions are all sin.
21:10 **E** people love to harm others; their neighbors get
21:27 God loathes the sacrifice of an **e** person,
24: 1 Don't envy **e** people; don't desire their company.
24: 8 A person who plans **e** will get a reputation as a
24:20 For the **e** have no future; their light will be snuffed
26:25 to be kind, their hearts are full of all kinds of **e**.
28: 5 **E** people don't understand justice, but those who
29: 6 **E** people are trapped by sin, but the righteous
30:32 you have been a fool by being proud or plotting **e**,
Ecc 3:16 I also noticed that throughout the world there is **e**
4: 3 For they have never seen all the **e** that is done in
5: 1 realize that mindless offerings to God are **e**.
8: 3 and don't take a stand with those who plot **e**.
10: 2 and the hearts of the foolish lead them to do **e**.
10: 5 There is another **e** I have seen as I have watched
Isa 1: 4 They are **e** and corrupt children who have turned
1:16 and be clean! Let me no longer see your **e** deeds.
1:31 Your **e** deeds are the spark that will set the straw
5:20 Destruction is certain for those who say that **e** is
good and good is **e**;
10:16 Because of all your **e** boasting, the Lord,
13:11 will punish the world for its **e** and the wicked for
14: 5 your wicked power and broken your **e** rule.
23:17 She will return again to all her **e** ways around the
24:16 I am discouraged, for **e** still prevails, and treachery
25:11 He will end their pride and all their **e** works.
29:20 be gone, and all those who plot **e** will be killed.
32: 7 The smooth tricks of **e** people will be exposed,
46:12 Listen to me, you stubborn, **e** people!
57: 1 that God is protecting them from the **e** to come.
59: 4 They spend their time plotting **e** deeds and
59: 5 and energy spinning **e** plans that end up in deadly
59: 7 Their feet run to do **e**, and they rush to commit
59: 9 because of all this **e** that deliverance is far from us.
59:18 He will repay his enemies for their **e** deeds.
65: 2 They follow their own **e** paths and thoughts.
65: 4 the graves and secret places to worship **e** spirits.
65:16 put aside my anger and forget the **e** of earlier days.
Jer 1:16 pronounce judgment on my people for all their **e**—
2:13 For my people have done two **e** things: They have
2:19 You will see what an **e**, bitter thing it is to forsake
3: 5 and keep right on doing all the **e** you can."
3:17 They will no longer stubbornly follow their own **e**
4:14 How long will you harbor your **e** thoughts?
5:27 filled with birds, their homes are filled with **e** plots.
6: 7 She spouts **e** like a fountain! Her streets echo with
7: 3 Even now, if you quit your **e** ways, I will let you
7:11 I see all the **e** going on there, says the LORD.
7:24 following the stubborn desires of their **e** hearts.
8: 3 And the people of this **e** nation who survive will
11: 8 they stubbornly followed their own **e** desires.
11:15 their destruction? They actually rejoice in doing **e**!
11:17 For the people of Israel and Judah have done **e**,
12: 1 so prosperous? Why are **e** people so happy?
12: 4 birds have disappeared because of the **e** in the land.
12:14 "As for all the **e** nations reaching out for the
13:23 can you start doing good, for you always do **e**.
15: 7 refuse to turn back to me from all their **e** ways.
16:12 You stubbornly follow your own **e** desires
16:18 and filled my inheritance with their **e** deeds."
17: 1 "My people act as though their **e** ways are laws to
18: 8 but then that nation renounces its **e** ways, I will not
18:10 but then that nation turns to **e** and refuses to obey
18:11 So turn from your **e** ways, each of you, and do
18:12 live as we want to, following our own **e** desires."
18:20 Should they repay **e** for good? They have set a trap
22: 3 Quit your **e** deeds! Do not mistreat foreigners,
22: 2 Now I will pour out judgment on you for the **e** you
23:10 For the prophets do **e** and abuse their power.
23:13 saw that the prophets of Samaria were terribly **e**,
23:14 They encourage those who are doing **e** instead of
23:17 And to those who stubbornly follow their own **e**
23:22 my words and turned my people from their **e** ways.
24: 9 an object of horror and **e** to every nation on earth.
25: 5 'Turn from the **e** road you are traveling and from
the **e** things you are doing.
25:34 Weep and moan, you **e** shepherds! Roll in the dust,
26: 3 Perhaps they will listen and turn from their **e** ways.
32:30 They have infuriated me with all their **e** deeds,"
32:35 What an incredible **e**, causing Judah to sin
36: 7 Perhaps even yet they will turn from their **e** ways
38: 9 "these men have done a very **e** thing in putting
44:22 because the LORD could no longer bear all the **e**
52: 2 But Zedekiah did what was **e** in the LORD's
La 1:22 "Look at all their **e** deeds, LORD. Punish them,
3:64 them back, LORD, for all the **e** they have done.
Eze 6:11 because of all the **e** that the people of Israel have
7: 4 show no pity, repaying you in full for all your **e**.
7:27 I will bring against them the **e** they have done to
13:10 "These **e** prophets deceive my people by saying,
14:10 **e** people who claim to want my advice—
16:43 but have angered me by doing all these **e** things,
16:61 Then you will remember with shame all the **e** you
18:11 And suppose that son does all the **e** things his
20:43 hate yourselves because of the **e** you have done.
24:23 You will mourn privately for all the **e** you have
28:15 you were created until the day **e** was found in you.
33:12 nor will the sins of **e** people destroy them if they
33:15 my life-giving laws, no longer doing what is **e**.
33:18 when righteous people turn to **e**, they will die.
36:17 in their own land, they defiled it by their **e** deeds.
36:19 lands to punish them for the **e** way they had lived.
36:31 and hate yourselves for all the **e** things you did.
38:10 At that time **e** thoughts will come to your mind,
Hos 7: 8 with godless foreigners, picking up their **e** ways.
7:12 the sky. I will punish them for all their **e** ways.
7:15 made them strong, yet now they plot **e** against me.
9:15 them from my land because of their **e** actions.
11: 6 destroy them, trapping them in their own **e** plans.
Am 5:13 who are wise will keep quiet, for it is an **e** time.
5:14 Do what is good and run from **e**—that you may
5:15 Hate **e** and love what is good; remodel your courts
Ob 1:15 All your **e** deeds will fall back on your own heads.
Jnh 3: 8 Everyone must turn from their **e** ways and stop all
3:10 When God saw that they had put a stop to their **e**
Mic 2: 1 you who lie awake at night, thinking up **e** plans.
2: 3 "I will reward your **e** with **e**; you won't be able
3: 2 you are the very ones who hate good and love **e**.
3: 4 After all the **e** you have done, he won't even look
6:16 "The only laws you keep are those of **e** King
7: 3 They go about their **e** deeds with both hands.
7: 9 and punish my enemies for all the **e** they have done
Na 1:11 Who is this king of yours who dares to plot **e**
Zep 3: 7 they continue their **e** practices from dawn till dusk
3: 8 when I will stand up and accuse these **e** nations.
Zec 1: 4 Turn from your **e** ways and stop all your **e** practices
7:10 And do not make **e** plans to harm each other.
8:17 Do not make **e** plots to harm each other. And stop
11: 8 I got rid of their three **e** shepherds in a single
Mal 3:15 For those who do **e** get rich, and those who dare
Mt 5:39 But I say, don't resist an **e** person! If you are
5:45 For he gives his sunlight to both the **e**
6:13 yield to temptation, / but deliver us from the **e** one.
6:23 But an **e** eye shuts out the light and plunges you
9: 4 "Why are you thinking such **e** thoughts?
10: 1 and gave them authority to cast out **e** spirits and to
12:34 How could **e** men like you speak what is good
12:35 and an **e** person produces **e** words from an **e** heart.
12:39 But Jesus replied, "Only an **e**, faithless generation
12:43 "When an **e** spirit leaves a person, it goes into the
12:45 Then the spirit finds seven other spirits more **e** than
12:45 That will be the experience of this **e** generation."
13:19 Then the **e** one comes and snatches the seed away
13:38 The weeds are the people who belong to the **e** one.
13:41 everything that causes sin and all who do **e**,
15: 4 and 'Anyone who speaks **e** of father or mother
15:18 But **e** words come from an **e** heart and defile the
15:19 For from the heart come **e** thoughts, murder,
16: 4 Only an **e**, faithless generation would ask for a
18:32 the man he had forgiven and said, 'You **e** servant!
22:18 But Jesus knew their **e** motives.
24:48 But if the servant is **e** and thinks, 'My master
Mk 1:23 A man possessed by an **e** spirit was in the
1:26 the **e** spirit screamed and threw the man into a
1:27 such authority! Even **e** spirits obey his orders!"
3:11 And whenever those possessed by **e** spirits caught
3:30 because they were saying he had an **e** spirit.
5: 2 a man possessed by an **e** spirit ran out from a
5: 8 to the spirit, "Come out of the man, you **e** spirit."
5:12 "Send us into those pigs," the **e** spirits begged.
5:13 So the **e** spirits came out of the man and entered
6: 7 out two by two, with authority to cast out **e** spirits.
7:10 and 'Anyone who speaks **e** of father or mother
7:21 come **e** thoughts, sexual immorality, theft, murder,
7:25 him whose little girl was possessed by an **e** spirit.
9:17 because he is possessed by an **e** spirit that won't let
9:18 And whenever this **e** spirit seizes him, it throws
9:18 So I asked your disciples to cast out the **e** spirit,
9:20 But when the **e** spirit saw Jesus, it threw the child
9:22 The **e** spirit often makes him fall into the fire
9:25 of onlookers was growing, he rebuked the **e** spirit.
9:28 "Why couldn't we cast out that **e** spirit?"
9:39 in my name will soon be able to speak **e** of me.
Lk 4:36 Even **e** spirits obey him and flee at his command!"
6:18 and to be healed, and Jesus cast out many **e** spirits.
6:45 and an **e** person produces **e** deeds from an **e** heart.
7:21 and he cast out **e** spirits and restored sight to the
8: 2 and from whom he had cast out **e** spirits.
8:29 For Jesus had already commanded the **e** spirit to
9:39 An **e** spirit keeps seizing him, making him scream.
9:42 But Jesus rebuked the **e** spirit and healed the boy.
10:20 But don't rejoice just because **e** spirits obey you;
11:24 "When an **e** spirit leaves a person, it goes into the
11:26 Then the spirit finds seven other spirits more **e** than
11:29 pressed in on Jesus, he said, "These are **e** times,
11:29 and this **e** generation keeps asking me to show
11:34 But an **e** eye shuts out the light and plunges you
13: 3 will also perish unless you turn from your **e** ways
13:11 he saw a woman who had been crippled by an **e**
13:27 I don't know you. Go away, all you who do **e**.'
16:15 look good in public, but God knows your **e** hearts.
18: 6 the Lord said, "Learn a lesson from this **e** judge.

23:41 We deserve to die for our **e** deeds, but this man
Jn 3:19 more than the light, for their actions were **e**.
5:29 and those who have continued in **e** will rise to
7: 7 but it does hate me because I accuse it of sin and **e**.
8:44 the Devil, and you love to do the **e** things he does.
17:15 of the world, but to keep them safe from the **e** one.
Ac 5:16 bringing their sick and those possessed by **e** spirits,
8: 7 Many **e** spirits were cast out, screaming as they left
8:22 the Lord. Perhaps he will forgive your **e** thoughts,
14: 2 saying all sorts of **e** things about them.
19:12 and any **e** spirits within them came out.
19:13 **e** spirits tried to use the name of the Lord Jesus.
19:15 But when they tried it on a man possessed by an **e**
23: 5 'Do not speak **e** of any one who rules over
Ro 1:28 he abandoned them to their **e** minds and let them
2: 8 who refuse to obey the truth and practice **e** deeds.
7: 5 and the law aroused these **e** desires that produced
7: 7 am I suggesting that the law of God is **e**?
7:13 It uses God's good commandment for its own **e**
7:17 it is sin inside me that makes me do these **e** things.
8:13 of the Holy Spirit you turn from it and its **e** deeds,
12:17 Never pay back **e** for **e** to anyone. Do things in
12:21 Don't let **e** get the best of you, but conquer **e** by doing good.
13:12 So don't live in darkness. Get rid of your **e** deeds.
13:14 and don't think of ways to indulge your **e** desires.
1Co 4:13 We respond gently when **e** things are said about us.
5: 1 something so **e** that even the pagans don't do it.
5: 8 not by eating the old bread of wickedness and **e**,
5:13 "You must remove the **e** person from among
10: 6 so that we would not crave **e** things as they did
14:20 Be innocent as babies when it comes to **e**, but be
2Co 2:11 For we are very familiar with his **e** schemes.
4: 4 Satan, the god of this **e** world, has blinded the
5:10 for the good or **e** we have done in our bodies.
Gal 1: 4 in order to rescue us from this **e** world in which we
3: 1 What magician has cast an **e** spell on you?
5:17 The old sinful nature loves to do **e**, which is just
5:19 your lives will produce these **e** results:
Eph 2: 3 following the passions and desires of our **e** nature.
2: 3 We were born with an **e** nature, and we were under
4:22 throw off your old **e** nature and your former way of
5:11 Take no part in the worthless deeds of **e**
5:13 on them, it becomes clear how **e** these things are.
5:14 your light shines, it will expose their **e** deeds.
5:16 every opportunity for doing good in these **e** days.
6:12 but against the **e** rulers and authorities of the
6:13 of God's armor to resist the enemy in the time of **e**,
Php 3: 2 those dogs, those wicked men and their **e** deeds,
Col 1:21 separated from him by your **e** thoughts and actions,
2: 8 and from the **e** powers of this world,
2:15 God disarmed the **e** rulers and authorities.
2:20 and he has set you free from the **e** powers of this
2:23 when it comes to conquering a person's **e** thoughts
3: 9 for you have stripped off your old **e** nature and all
3:25 For God has no favorites who can get away with **e**.
1Th 5:15 See that no one pays back **e** for **e**, but always try
5:22 Keep away from every kind of **e**.
2Th 2: 9 This **e** man will come to do the work of Satan with
2:12 believing the truth and for enjoying the **e** they do.
3: 2 that we will be saved from wicked and **e** people,
3: 3 make you strong and guard you from the **e** one.
1Ti 3:11 must be respected and must not speak **e** of others.
6: 4 in jealousy, fighting, slander, and **e** suspicions.
6:10 the love of money is at the root of all kinds of **e**.
6:11 so run from all these **e** things, and follow what is
2Ti 3:13 But **e** people and impostors will flourish. They will
4:18 and the Lord will deliver me from every **e** attack
Tit 2: 3 They must not go around speaking **e** of others
2:12 We should live in this **e** world with self-control,
3: 2 They must not speak **e** of anyone, and they must
3: 3 slaves to many wicked desires and **e** pleasures.
3: 3 Our lives were full of **e** and envy. We hated others,
Heb 3:12 Make sure that your own hearts are not **e**
6: 1 with the importance of turning away from **e** deeds
10:22 For our **e** consciences have been sprinkled with
Jas 1:14 Temptation comes from the lure of our own **e**
1:15 These **e** desires lead to **e** actions, and **e** actions lead to death.
1:21 So get rid of all the filth and **e** in your lives,
3: 8 It is an uncontrollable **e**, full of deadly poison.
3:16 there you will find disorder and every kind of **e**.
4: 1 Isn't it the whole army of **e** desires at war within
4: 6 and more strength to stand against such **e** desires.
4:11 Don't speak **e** against each other, my dear brothers
4:16 about your own plans, and all such boasting is **e**.
1Pe 1:14 Don't slip back into your old ways of doing **e**;
2:11 So I warn you to keep away from **e** desires
2:16 are free. But your freedom is not an excuse to do **e**.
3: 9 Don't repay **e** for **e**. Don't retaliate when people
3:10 good days, / keep your tongue from speaking **e**,
3:11 Turn away from **e** and do good. / Work hard at
3:12 the Lord turns his face / against those who do **e**."
3:16 Then if people speak **e** against you, they will be
4: 2 spend the rest of your life chasing after **e** desires,
4: 3 You have had enough in the past of the **e** things
4: 4 things they do, and they say **e** things about you.
2Pe 1: 4 the decadence all around you caused by **e** desires
2: 2 Many will follow their **e** teaching and shameful
2:10 is especially hard on those who follow their own **e**,
2:13 They love to indulge in **e** pleasures in broad
3: 3 laugh at the truth and do every **e** thing they desire.
1Jn 2:15 Stop loving this **e** world and all that it offers you,
2:16 not from the Father. They are from this **e** world.
3:12 who belonged to the **e** one and killed his brother.
3:12 Because Cain had been doing what was **e**, and his
5: 4 For every child of God defeats this **e** world by
5:18 and the **e** one cannot get his hands on them.
5:19 us is under the power and control of the **e** one.
2Jn 1:11 encourages him becomes a partner in his **e** work.
3Jn 1:11 and those who do **e** prove that they do not know
Jude 1: 7 of the eternal fire that will punish all who are **e**.
1:11 For they follow the **e** example of Cain, who killed
1:15 He will convict the ungodly of all the **e** things
1:16 and complainers, doing whatever **e** they feel like.
1:18 is to enjoy themselves in every **e** way imaginable.
Rev 2: 2 I know you don't tolerate **e** people.
2:22 unless they turn away from all their **e** deeds.
3: 4 who have not soiled their garments with **e** deeds.
9:20 plagues still refused to turn from their **e** deeds.
16:11 But they refused to repent of all their **e** deeds.
16:13 And I saw three **e** spirits that looked like frogs leap
18: 2 has become the hideout of demons and **e** spirits,
18: 5 and God is ready to judge her for her **e** deeds.
18: 6 Give her a double penalty for all her **e** deeds.
21:27 Nothing **e** will be allowed to enter—no one who

EVIL-HEARTED (1) [EVIL, HEART]

Isa 35: 8 of Holiness. **E** people will never travel on it.

EVIL-MERODACH (2)

2Ki 25:27 in Babylon, **E** ascended to the Babylonian throne.
Jer 52:31 in Babylon, **E** ascended to the Babylonian throne.

EVIL-MINDED (1) [EVIL, MIND]

Ps 119:115 Get out of my life, you **e** people, / for I intend to

EVILDOERS (9) [EVIL]

Job 8:20 a person of integrity, nor will he make **e** prosper.
Ps 92: 7 flourish like weeds, / and **e** blossom with success,
92: 9 LORD, will surely perish; / all **e** will be scattered.
94: 4 Hear their arrogance! / How these **e** boast!
94:16 the wicked? / Who will stand up for me against **e**?
Pr 4:14 Do not do as the wicked do or follow the path of **e**.
21:15 is a joy to the godly, but it causes dismay among **e**.
24:19 Do not fret because of **e**; don't envy the wicked.
Mal 2:17 LORD favors **e** since he does not punish them.

EVILS (4) [EVIL]

2Ki 23:26 because of all the great **e** of King Manasseh,
Ps 91: 7 are dying around you, / these **e** will not touch you.
Jer 7:10 only to go right back to all those **e** again?
Rev 21: 4 For the old world and its **e** are gone forever."

EWE (1) [EWES]

Ge 21:28 But when Abraham took seven additional **e** lambs

EWES (3) [EWE]

Ge 32:14 twenty male goats, two hundred **e**, twenty rams,
Ps 78:71 He took David from tending the **e** and lambs
SS 6: 6 Your teeth are white like freshly washed **e**,

EXACT (6) [EXACTLY]

Nu 8: 4 It was built according to the **e** design the LORD
Dt 34: 6 in Moab, but to this day no one knows the **e** place.
1Ki 7: 9 of stone, cut and trimmed to **e** measure on all sides.
Mt 2: 7 At this meeting he learned the **e** time when they
Ac 7:44 It was constructed in **e** accordance with the plan
2Co 4: 4 the glory of Christ, who is the **e** likeness of God.

EXACTLY (39) [EXACT]

Ge 6:22 So Noah did everything **e** as God had commanded
7: 5 So Noah did **e** as the LORD had commanded
8: 4 **e** five months from the time the flood began,
17:23 cutting off their foreskins, **e** as God had told him.
18:25 be treating the innocent and the guilty **e** the same!
21: 1 Then the LORD did **e** what he had promised.
27: 8 Now, my son, do **e** as I tell you.
Ex 19: 1 The Israelites arrived in the wilderness of Sinai **e**
25: 9 and its furnishings **e** according to the plans I will
26: 2 feet wide. All ten sheets must be **e** the same size.
26: 8 All eleven of these sheets must be **e** the same size.
31:11 They must follow **e** all the instructions I have
33:13 you more fully and do **e** what you want me to do.
36: 9 Each sheet was **e** the same size—forty-two feet
36:15 Each sheet was **e** the same size—forty-five feet
Nu 2:34 and marched under their banners **e** as the LORD
6:21 they must fulfill their special vow **e** as they have
30: 2 break it. He must do **e** what he said he would do.
32:14 you are, a brood of sinners, doing **e** the same thing!
32:25 your servants and will follow your instructions **e**.
Dt 17:10 will always stand. You must do **e** what they say.
1Sa 15:19 and do **e** what the LORD said not to do?"
2Ki 7:17 So everything happened **e** as the man of God had
Ne 13:26 "Wasn't this **e** what led King Solomon of Israel
Job 31:37 For I would tell him **e** what I have done. I would
Jer 42:21 And today I have told you **e** what he said, but you
Eze 16:45 And you are **e** like your sisters, for they despised
40:24 and he found they were **e** the same as in the others.
Da 9:12 You have done **e** what you warned you would do
Joel 2: 8 jostle each other; each moves in **e** the right place.
Mt 6: 8 because your Father knows **e** what you need even
24:43 A homeowner who knew **e** when a burglar was
Lk 12:39 A homeowner who knew **e** when a burglar was
Jn 12:38 This is **e** what Isaiah the prophet had predicted:
19:22 I have written, I have written. It stays **e** as it is."
Ac 11: 4 Then Peter told them **e** what had happened.
2Co 1:24 But that does not mean we want to tell you **e** how
Heb 1: 3 and everything about him represents God **e**.
2Pe 3: 4 everything has remained **e** the same since the

EXALT (11) [EXALTED, EXALTING, EXALTS]

Ex 15: 2 he is my father's God, and I will **e** him!
Dt 28: 1 the LORD your God will **e** you above all the
Ps 34: 3 LORD's greatness; / let us **e** his name together.
99: 5 **E** the LORD our God! / Bow low before his feet,
99: 9 **E** the LORD our God / and worship at his holy
107:32 Let them **e** him publicly before the congregation
118:28 praise you! / You are my God, and I will **e** you!
Pr 4: 8 If you prize wisdom, she will **e** you. Embrace her
Mt 23:12 But those who **e** themselves will be humbled,
2Th 2: 4 He will **e** himself and defy every god there is
Heb 5: 5 That is why Christ did not **e** himself to become

EXALTED (20) [EXALT]

Nu 24: 7 be greater than Agag; / their kingdom will be **e**.
2Sa 22:47 May God, the rock of my salvation, be **e**!
1Ch 29:25 And the LORD **e** Solomon so the entire nation of
Job 36:26 "Look, God is **e** beyond what we can understand.
Ps 18:46 be my rock! / May the God of my salvation be **e**!
57: 5 Be **e**, O God, above the highest heavens!
57:11 Be **e**, O God, above the highest heavens.
92: 8 But you are **e** in the heavens. / You, O LORD,
97: 9 over all the earth; / you are **e** far above all gods.
108: 5 Be **e**, O God, above the highest heavens.
Isa 2:11 be brought low and the LORD alone will be **e**.
2:17 will lie in the dust. The LORD alone will be **e**!
5:16 But the LORD Almighty is **e** by his justice.
13: 3 to these armies, and they will rejoice when I am **e**.
52:13 my servant will prosper; he will be highly **e**.
Eze 21:26 now the lowly are **e**, and the mighty are brought
Mt 11:23 people of Capernaum, will you be **e** to heaven?
23:12 and those who humble themselves will be **e**.
Lk 1:52 taken princes from their thrones / and **e** the lowly.
10:15 people of Capernaum, will you be **e** to heaven?

EXALTING (1) [EXALT]

Da 11:36 **e** himself and claiming to be greater than every god

EXALTS (2) [EXALT]

Job 36: 7 but he establishes and **e** them with kings forever.
Pr 14:34 Godliness **e** a nation, but sin is a disgrace to any

EXAMINATION (7) [EXAMINE]

Lev 13: 5 On the seventh day the priest will make another **e**.
13: 7 But if the rash continues to spread after this **e**
13: 9 skin disease must go to the priest for an **e**.
13:12 "Now suppose the priest discovers after his **e** that
13:17 If, after another **e**, the affected areas have indeed
13:31 if the priest's **e** reveals that the infection is only
13:36 the priest must do another **e**. If the infection has

EXAMINE (25) [CROSS-EXAMINE, EXAMINATION, EXAMINED, EXAMINES, EXAMINING]

Lev 13: 3 then **e** the affected area of a person's skin.
13: 6 The priest will **e** the skin again on the seventh day.
13:13 the priest must **e** the infected person to see if the
13:25 then the priest must **e** it. If the hair in the affected
13:30 the priest must **e** the infection. If it appears to be
13:34 and he will **e** the infection again on the seventh
13:39 the priest must **e** the affected area. If the patch is
13:43 The priest must **e** him, and if he finds swelling
14: 3 who will **e** them at a place outside the camp.
Dt 13:14 In such cases, you must **e** the facts carefully.
1Ch 29:17 that you **e** our hearts and rejoice when you find
Job 7:18 For you **e** us every morning and test us every
Jer 11:20 and you **e** the deepest thoughts of hearts
17:10 the LORD, search all hearts and **e** secret motives.
20:12 and you **e** the deepest thoughts of hearts
La 3:40 Instead, let us test and **e** our ways. Let us turn
Mt 8: 4 "Go right over to the priest and let him **e** you.
Mk 1:44 "Go right over to the priest and let him **e** you.
Lk 5:14 He said, "Go right to the priest and let him **e** you.
Ac 23:15 "Pretend you want to **e** his case more fully.
25:26 King Agrippa, so that after we **e** him,
1Co 4: 4 It is the Lord himself who will **e** me and decide.
11:28 That is why you should **e** yourself before eating the
11:31 But if we **e** ourselves, we will not be examined by
2Co 13: 5 **E** yourselves to see if your faith is really genuine.

EXAMINED (10) [EXAMINE]

Lev 13: 7 the infected person must return to be **e** again.
13:19 its place, that person must go to the priest to be **e**.
13:49 and must be taken to the priest to be **e**.
Jos 9:14 So the Israelite leaders **e** their bread, but they did
Job 28:27 measured it. He established it and **e** it thoroughly.
Ps 17: 3 tested my thoughts and **e** my heart in the night.
139: 1 O LORD, you have **e** my heart / and know
Lk 23:14 I have **e** him thoroughly on this point in your
1Co 11:31 we will not be **e** by God and judged in this way.
Rev 2: 2 You have **e** the claims of those who say they are

EXAMINES (6) [EXAMINE]

Lev 13:53 "But if the priest **e** it again and the affected spot
14:36 Before the priest **e** the house, he must have the
Ps 11: 5 The LORD **e** both the righteous and the wicked.
Pr 16: 2 in their own eyes, but the LORD **e** their motives.
21: 2 are doing what is right, but the LORD **e** the heart.
1Th 2: 4 He is the one who **e** the motives of our hearts.

EXAMINING (4) [EXAMINE]

Lev 13:50 After **e** the affected spot, the priest will put it away

Ps 11: 4 watches everything closely, / **e** everyone on earth.
Pr 5:21 clearly what a man does, **e** every path he takes.
Ac 24: 8 You can find out the truth of our accusations by **e**

EXAMPLE (71) [EXAMPLES]

Ex 23:24 them in any way, and never follow their evil **e**.
Dt 12:30 do not be trapped into following their **e** in
12:30 worship their gods? I want to follow their **e**.'
18:10 For **e**, never sacrifice your son or daughter as a
19: 5 For **e**, suppose someone goes into the forest with a
Jdg 9:49 cut down some branches, following Abimelech's **e**.
2Sa 8:14 This was another **e** of how the LORD made
23:17 drink it. This is an **e** of the exploits of the Three.
1Ki 15:26 LORD's sight and followed the **e** of his father,
15:34 LORD's sight and followed the **e** of Jeroboam,
16: 2 but you have followed the evil **e** of Jeroboam.
16:19 LORD's sight and followed the **e** of Jeroboam,
16:26 He followed the **e** of Jeroboam, continuing the sins
22:43 was a good king, following the **e** of his father, Asa.
22:52 following the **e** of his father and mother and the **e** of Jeroboam son of Nebat,
2Ki 8:18 But Jehoram followed the **e** of the kings of Israel
8:27 Ahaziah followed the evil **e** of King Ahab's
13: 2 He followed the **e** of Jeroboam son of Nebat,
13: 6 continued to sin, following the evil **e** of Jeroboam.
14: 3 Instead, he followed the **e** of his father, Joash.
16: 3 Instead, he followed the **e** of the kings of Israel,
17:15 They followed the **e** of the nations around them,
21:21 He followed the **e** of his father,
22: 2 and followed the **e** of his ancestor David.
1Ch 11:19 drink it. This is an **e** of the exploits of the Three.
18:13 This was another **e** of how the LORD made
29: 5 the craftsmen. Now then, who will follow my **e**?
2Ch 17: 3 because he followed the **e** of his father's early
21: 6 But Jehoram followed the **e** of the kings of Israel
21:12 You have not followed the good **e** of your father,
22: 3 Ahaziah also followed the evil **e** of King Ahab's
28: 2 he followed the **e** of the kings of Israel and cast
34: 2 and followed the **e** of his ancestor David.
Job 22: 6 "For **e**, you must have lent money to your friend
40:19 It is a prime **e** of God's amazing handiwork.
Ps 71: 7 My life is an **e** to many, / because you have been
Ecc 4: 7 I observed yet another **e** of meaninglessness in our
Jer 48:39 object of ridicule, an **e** of ruin to all her neighbors.
Eze 14: 8 against such people and make a terrible **e** of them,
23:48 be a warning to others not to follow their wicked **e**.
24:24 Ezekiel is an **e** for you to follow; you will do as he
Mic 6:16 the only **e** you follow is that of wicked King Ahab!
6:16 Therefore, I will make an **e** of you, bringing you to
Mt 23: 3 whatever they say to you, but don't follow their **e**.
Mk 7:13 And this is only one **e**. There are many,
Jn 8:39 children of Abraham, you would follow his good **e**.
13:15 I have given you an **e** to follow. Do as I have done
Ac 8: 5 Philip, for **e**, went to the city of Samaria and told
20:35 And I have been a constant **e** of how you can help
1Co 4:16 So I ask you to follow my **e** and do as I do.
11: 1 And you should follow my **e**, just as I follow
Gal 3:15 Dear friends, here's an **e** from everyday life.
Eph 5: 1 Follow God's **e** in everything you do, because you
5: 2 following the **e** of Christ, who loved you and gave
Php 3:17 after mine, and learn from those who follow our **e**.
1Th 1: 7 you yourselves became an **e** to all the Christians in
2Th 3: 7 For you know that you ought to follow our **e**.
3: 9 feed us, but we wanted to give you an **e** to follow.
1Ti 1:16 so that Christ Jesus could use me as a prime **e** of
4:12 Be an **e** to all believers in what you teach,
Tit 2: 7 And you yourself must be an **e** to them by doing
Heb 6:12 you will follow the **e** of those who are going to
6:13 For **e**, there was God's promise to Abraham.
Jas 2:25 Rahab the prostitute is another **e** of this. She was
5:11 Job is an **e** of a man who endured patiently.
1Pe 2:21 Christ, who suffered for you, is your **e**. Follow in
5: 3 to your care, but lead them by your good **e**.
2Pe 2: 6 He made them an **e** of what will happen to ungodly
3Jn 1:11 Dear friend, don't let this bad **e** influence you.
Jude 1:11 For they follow the evil **e** of Cain, who killed his

EXAMPLES (8) [EXAMPLE]

Ps 145:11 they will celebrate **e** of your power.
1Co 10:11 All these events happened to them as **e** for us.
14: 7 are **e** of the need for speaking in plain language.
2Co 8:23 They are splendid **e** of those who bring glory to
Eph 2: 7 so God can always point to us as **e** of the incredible
1Ti 1:20 Hymenaeus and Alexander are two **e** of this.
2Ti 2:17 like cancer. Hymenaeus and Philetus are **e** of this.
Jas 5:10 For **e** of patience in suffering, look at the prophets

EXASPERATED (1)

Ac 16:18 so **e** that he turned and spoke to the demon within

EXCEEDED (2) [EXCEEDINGLY]

Nu 3:49 sons of Israel who **e** the number of Levites.
1Ki 4:30 his wisdom **e** that of all the wise men of the East

EXCEEDINGLY (1) [EXCEEDED]

Ex 29:37 After that, the altar will be **e** holy, and whatever

EXCEL (3) [EXCELLENCE, EXCELLENCY, EXCELLENT]

Ex 35:35 They **e** in all the crafts needed for the work.
2Co 8: 7 Since you **e** in so many ways—you have so much
8: 7 now I want you to **e** also in this gracious ministry

EXCELLENCE (2) [EXCEL]

2Pe 1: 5 Then your faith will produce a life of moral **e**.
1: 5 A life of moral **e** leads to knowing God better.

EXCELLENCY (2) [EXCEL]

Ac 23:26 "From Claudius Lysias, to his **E**, Governor Felix.
24: 2 "Your **E**, you have given peace to us Jews

EXCELLENT (7) [EXCEL]

Ge 1:31 had made, and he saw that it was **e** in every way.
Ne 13:13 These men had an **e** reputation, and it was their job
Est 6:10 "**E**!" the king said to Haman. "Hurry and get the
Pr 8: 6 Listen to me! For I have **e** things to tell you.
Ac 26:25 But Paul replied, "I am not insane, Most **E** Festus.
1Co 14:10 and all are **e** for those who understand them,
Php 4: 8 Think about things that are **e** and worthy of praise.

EXCEPT (85) [EXCEPTION, EXCEPTIONALLY, EXCEPTIONS]

Ge 2:17 **e** fruit from the tree of the knowledge of good
31:42 In fact, **e** for the grace of God—the God of my
32:10 I left home, I owned nothing **e** a walking stick,
39: 6 in the world, **e** to decide what he wanted to eat!
39: 9 He has held back nothing from me **e** you,
44:10 "**e** that only the one who stole it will be a slave.
Ex 3:19 Egypt will not let you go **e** under heavy pressure.
8:11 the frogs will be destroyed, **e** those in the river."
12:16 No work of any kind may be done on these days **e**
13:15 **e** that the firstborn sons are always redeemed.'
Lev 13:33 the infected person must shave off all hair **e** the
Nu 23:12 "Can I say anything **e** what the LORD tells me?"
35:33 And no atonement can be made for murder **e** by
Dt 1:36 **e** Caleb son of Jephunneh. He will see this land
Jos 10:20 and wiped out the five armies **e** for a tiny remnant
11:13 not burn any of the cities built on mounds **e** Hazor.
11:19 peace with the Israelites **e** the Hivites of Gibeon.
Jdg 1:25 and they killed everyone in the city **e** for this man
Ru 2: 7 **e** for a few minutes' rest over there in the shelter."
1Sa 13:22 had a sword or spear, **e** for Saul and Jonathan.
30:17 None of the Amalekites escaped **e** four hundred
2Sa 15:16 He left no one behind **e** ten of his concubines to
22:32 For who is God **e** the LORD? / Who but our God
1Ki 3: 3 David, **e** that Solomon, too, offered sacrifices
8: 9 Nothing was in the Ark **e** the two stone tablets that
15: 5 his life, **e** in the affair concerning Uriah the Hittite.
2Ki 3:14 I would not bother with you **e** for my respect for
4: 2 "Nothing at all, **e** a flask of olive oil," she replied.
5:15 last that there is no God in all the world **e** in Israel.
5:17 or sacrifices to any other god **e** the LORD.
1Ch 15: 2 of God this time, no one **e** the Levites may carry it.
2Ch 2: 6 for him, **e** as a place to burn sacrifices to him?
5:10 Nothing was in the Ark **e** the two stone tablets that
Ezr 4:21 That city must not be rebuilt **e** at my express
Ne 2:12 with us, **e** the donkey that I myself was riding.
Est 2:15 She asked for nothing **e** what he suggested, and she
Job 30:10 and won't come near me, **e** to spit in my face.
Ps 18:31 For who is God **e** the LORD? / Who but our God
Ecc 5:11 **e** perhaps to watch it run through your fingers!
Isa 8:13 Do not fear anything **e** the LORD Almighty.
Eze 1: 6 **e** that each had four faces and two pairs of wings.
48:22 **e** for the areas set aside for the sacred lands
Da 2:11 No one **e** the gods can tell you your dream,
3:28 than serve or worship any god **e** their own God.
6: 7 to anyone, divine or human—**e** to Your Majesty—
6:12 to anyone, divine or human—**e** to Your Majesty—
10:21 to help me against these spirit princes **e** Michael,
Hos 7:16 They look everywhere **e** to heaven, to the Most
Mt 6:18 **e** your Father, who knows what you do in secret.
11:27 No one really knows the Son **e** the Father, and no one really knows the Father **e** the Son
12:31 **e** blasphemy against the Holy Spirit, which can
13:57 "A prophet is honored everywhere **e** in his own
Mk 5:37 and wouldn't let anyone go with him **e** Peter
6: 4 "A prophet is honored everywhere **e** in his own
6: 5 he couldn't do any mighty miracles among them **e**
6: 8 He told them to take nothing with them **e** a
Lk 8:51 Jesus wouldn't let anyone go in with him **e** Peter,
10:22 No one really knows the Son **e** the Father, and no one really knows the Father **e** the Son
13:33 do for a prophet of God to be killed **e** in Jerusalem!
Jn 4:44 "A prophet is honored everywhere **e** in his own
13:10 need to wash, **e** for the feet, to be entirely clean.
14: 6 No one can come to the Father **e** through me.
17:12 not one was lost, **e** the one headed for destruction,
Ac 8: 1 and all the believers **e** the apostles fled into Judea
15:20 **e** that we should write to them and tell them to
20:23 **e** that the Holy Spirit has told me in city after city
24:21 **e** for one thing I said when I shouted out, 'I am on
26:22 I teach nothing **e** what the prophets and Moses said
26:29 become the same as I am, **e** for these chains."
Ro 8: 3 in a human body like ours, **e** that ours are sinful.
13: 8 Pay all your debts, **e** the debt of love for others.
1Co 1:14 I thank God that I did not baptize any of you **e**
2:11 anyone else is really thinking **e** that person alone,
2:11 and no one can know God's thoughts **e** God's own
12: 3 able to say, "Jesus is Lord," **e** by the Holy Spirit.
Gal 2: 4 Even that question wouldn't have come up **e** for
5:20 the feeling that everyone is wrong **e** those in your
6:14 God forbid that I should boast about anything **e** the
Jas 2:10 And the person who keeps all of the laws **e** one is
2Pe 2: 5 ancient world—**e** for Noah and his family of seven.
Rev 2:17 name that no one knows **e** the one who receives it.
2:25 **e** that you hold tightly to what you have until I
14: 3 And no one could learn this song **e** those 144,000

EXCEPTION (2) [EXCEPT]

1Ki 15:22 requiring that everyone, without **e**, help to carry
1Co 7: 5 The only **e** to this rule would be the agreement of

EXCEPTIONALLY (1) [EXCEPT]

Ge 2:12 The gold of that land is **e** pure; aromatic resin

EXCEPTIONS (5) [EXCEPT]

Lev 11:21 However, there are some **e** that you may eat.
22:13 But other than these **e**, only members of the
Nu 14:30 The only **e** will be Caleb son of Jephunneh
26:65 The only **e** were Caleb son of Jephunneh
32:12 The only **e** are Caleb son of Jephunneh the

EXCESS (1)

Nu 3:46 of Israel who are in **e** of the number of Levites,

EXCHANGE (14) [EXCHANGED]

Ge 30:15 "I will let him sleep with you tonight in **e** for the
47:14 all the money in Egypt and Canaan in **e** for grain,
47:16 give me your livestock. I will give you food in **e**."
47:17 So they gave their livestock to Joseph in **e** for food.
47:19 Buy us and our land in **e** for food; we will
Ex 13:13 But if you decide not to make the **e**, the donkey
34:20 But if you decide not to make the **e**, you must kill
Lev 27:10 But if such an **e** is in fact made, then both the
27:33 If any **e** is in fact made, then both the original
1Ki 21: 2 I will give you a better vineyard in **e**, or if you
Isa 60:17 I will **e** your bronze for gold, your iron for silver,
Jer 31:13 will comfort them and **e** their sorrow for rejoicing.
Eze 27:12 trading your wares in **e** for silver, iron, tin,
27:22 of spices, jewels, and gold in **e** for your wares.

EXCHANGED (7) [EXCHANGE]

Lev 27:10 The animal should never be **e** or substituted for
Job 28:19 Topaz from Ethiopia cannot be **e** for it. Its value is
Jer 2:11 Has any nation ever **e** its gods for another god,
2:11 Yet my people have **e** their glorious God for
Eze 27:14 All these things were **e** for your manufactured
Hos 4: 7 They have **e** the glory of God for the disgrace of
Ac 21:19 After greetings were **e**, Paul gave a detailed

EXCITED (2) [EXCITEMENT]

Ex 32: 5 When Aaron saw how **e** the people were about it,
Job 31:29 to ruin or become **e** when harm came their way?

EXCITEDLY (1) [EXCITEMENT]

Mk 1:27 they asked **e**. "It has such authority! Even evil

EXCITEMENT (4) [EXCITED, EXCITEDLY, EXCITING]

Ecc 12: 1 Don't let the **e** of youth cause you to forget your
Isa 14: 9 "In the place of the dead there is **e** over your
Mt 13:44 In his **e**, he hid it again and sold everything he
Lk 19: 6 and took Jesus to his house in great **e** and joy.

EXCITING (1) [EXCITEMENT]

SS 7: 9 May your kisses be as **e** as the best wine, smooth

EXCLAIM (2) [EXCLAIMED]

Dt 4: 6 they will **e**, 'What other nation is as wise
Isa 45: 9 Does the pot **e**, 'How clumsy can you be!'?

EXCLAIMED (90) [EXCLAIM]

Ge 2:23 "At last!" Adam **e**. "She is part of my own flesh
26: 9 Abimelech called for Isaac and **e**, "She is
26:10 "How could you treat us this way!" Abimelech **e**.
29:14 my very own flesh and blood!" Laban **e**.
30: 1 "Give me children, or I'll die!" she **e** to Jacob.
32: 2 When Jacob saw them, he **e**, "This is God's
35:17 the midwife finally **e**, "Don't be afraid—
37:19 "Here comes that dreamer!" they **e**.
38:23 "Then let her keep the pledges!" Judah **e**.
38:29 "What!" the midwife **e**. "How did you break out
42:10 "No, my lord!" they **e**. "We have come to buy
42:28 "Look!" he **e** to his brothers. "My money is here
42:36 Jacob **e**, "You have deprived me of my children!
47:25 they **e**. "May it please you, sir, to let us be
Ex 8:19 is the finger of God!" the magicians **e** to Pharaoh.
18:17 "This is not good!" his father-in-law **e**.
32: 4 The people **e**, "O Israel, these are the gods who
32:11 he **e**. "Why are you so angry with your own
32:17 he **e** to Moses, "It sounds as if there is a war in the
36: 5 the job the LORD has given us to do!" they **e**.
Nu 11: 4 began to complain. "Oh, for some meat!" they **e**.
Jdg 8:19 "They were my brothers!" Gideon **e**. "As surely
Ru 2:19 "So much!" Naomi **e**. "Where did you gather all
2:22 "This is wonderful!" Naomi **e**. "Do as he said.
3:10 "The LORD bless you, my daughter!" Boaz **e**.
1Sa 1:18 "Oh, thank you, sir!" she **e**. Then she went back
10:11 When his friends heard about it, they **e**, "What?
11:12 Then the people **e** to Samuel, "Now where are
13:13 "How foolish!" Samuel **e**. "You have disobeyed
14:29 Jonathan **e**. "A command like that only hurts us.
18:18 David **e**. "My father's family is nothing!"
19:24 The people who were watching **e**, "What? Is Saul
20: 1 "What have I done?" he **e**. "What is my crime?
20: 4 "Tell me what I can do!" Jonathan **e**.
20: 9 "Never!" Jonathan **e**. "You know that if I had the
22:22 David **e**, "I knew it! When I saw Doeg there that
23: 7 "Good!" he **e**. "We've got him now! God has

2Sa 4: 8 "Look!" they e. "Here is the head of Ishbosheth,
5: 20 "The LORD has done it!" David e.
9: 8 show such kindness to a dead dog like me?" he e.
16: 16 "Long live the king!" he e. "Long live the king!"
19: 22 David e. "This is not a day for execution but for
23: 17 LORD forbid that I should drink this!" he e.
1Ki 1: 31 Bathsheba bowed low before him again and e,
10: 6 She e to the king, "Everything I heard in my
21: 20 Ahab e to Elijah. "Yes," Elijah answered, "I have
2Ki 1: 8 "It was Elijah from Tishbe!" the king e.
2: 15 they e, "Elisha has become Elijah's successor!"
3: 23 "It's blood!" the Moabites e. "The three armies
4: 43 "What?" his servant e. "Feed one hundred people
8: 5 "Look, my lord!" Gehazi e. "Here is the woman
9: 20 The watchman e, "The rider has met them, but he
13: 19 have struck the ground five or six times!" he e.
1Ch 11: 19 "God forbid that I should drink this!" he e.
14: 11 the Philistines there. "God has done it!" David e.
2Ch 9: 5 She e to the king, "Everything I heard in my
Da 3: 24 jumped up in amazement and e to his advisers,
Jnh 4: 8 to die. "Death is certainly better than this!" he e.
Mt 3: 7 he denounced them. "You brood of snakes!" he e.
9: 33 like this has ever happened in Israel!" they e.
13: 28 " 'An enemy has done it!' the farmer e.
14: 17 "Impossible!" they e. "We have only five loaves
14: 33 "You really are the Son of God!" they e.
26: 49 "Greetings, Teacher!" he e and gave him the kiss.
Mk 2: 12 never seen anything like this before!" they e.
9: 5 "Teacher, this is wonderful!" Peter e. "We will
11: 21 had said to the tree on the previous day and e,
14: 45 to Jesus. "Teacher!" he e, and gave him the kiss.
15: 39 had died, he e, "Truly, this was the Son of God!"
Lk 1: 25 "How kind the Lord is!" she e. "He has taken
1: 42 Elizabeth gave a glad cry and e to Mary, "You are
1: 61 "What?" they e. "There is no one in all your
4: 36 Amazed, the people e, "What authority and power
14: 15 Hearing this, a man sitting at the table with Jesus e,
19: 17 'Well done!' the king e. 'You are a trustworthy
22: 49 about to happen, they e, "Lord, should we fight?
Jn 1: 46 "Nazareth!" e Nathanael. "Can anything good
2: 20 "What!" they e. "It took forty-six years to build
3: 4 "What do you mean?" e Nicodemus. "How can
6: 14 people saw this miraculous sign, they e, "Surely,
9: 27 "Look!" the man e. "I told you once. Didn't you
13: 9 Simon Peter e, "Then wash my hands and head as
13: 21 and he e, "The truth is, one of you will betray
20: 16 She turned toward him and e, "Teacher!"
20: 28 "My Lord and my God!" Thomas e.
Ac 2: 7 "How can this be?" they e. "These people are all
8: 19 "Let me have this power, too," he e, "so that
8: 24 "Pray to the Lord for me," Simon e, "that these
9: 13 "But Lord," e Ananias, "I've heard about the
Rev 13: 4 they e. "Who is able to fight against him?"

EXCLUDED (7) [EXCLUDING]

Nu 9: 7 But why should we be e from presenting the
12: 15 So Miriam was e from the camp for seven days,
2Ch 26: 21 in isolation, e from the Temple of the LORD.
Eze 44: 5 admitted to the Temple and who is to be e from it.
Lk 6: 22 you who are hated and e and mocked and cursed
Eph 2: 12 You were e from God's people, Israel, and you did
2: 15 the whole system of Jewish law that e the Gentiles.

EXCLUDING (1) [EXCLUDED]

Jos 18: 5 e Judah's territory in the south and Joseph's

EXCREMENT (1)

Dt 23: 13 you must dig a hole with the spade and cover the e.

EXCUSE (9) [EXCUSED, EXCUSES]

Ex 5: 21 his officials. You have given them an e to kill us!"
2Ki 5: 7 He is only trying to find an e to invade us again."
Ps 37: 32 spy on the godly, / waiting for an e to kill them.
Jn 15: 22 to them. But now they have no e for their sin.
Ro 1: 20 So they have no e whatsoever for not knowing
2: 1 But you are just as bad, and you have no e!
Eph 5: 6 Don't be fooled by those who try to e these sins,
1Ti 6: 2 is a Christian, that is no e for being disrespectful.
1Pe 2: 16 are free. But your freedom is not an e to do evil.

EXCUSED (1) [EXCUSE]

Lk 14: 18 and wanted to inspect it, so he asked to be e.

EXCUSES (5) [EXCUSE]

Pr 6: 30 E might be found for a thief who steals because he
22: 13 The lazy person is full of e, saying, "If I go
26: 13 The lazy person is full of e, saying, "I can't go
Lk 14: 18 But they all began making e. One said he had just
Ro 3: 19 for its purpose is to keep people from having e

EXECUTE (23) [EXECUTED, EXECUTING, EXECUTION, EXECUTIONER, EXECUTIONERS, EXECUTIONS]

Ge 9: 6 you must e anyone who murders another person,
Ex 12: 12 I will e judgment against all the gods of Egypt,
Lev 20: 4 to Molech and refuse to e the guilty parents,
Nu 25: 4 and e them before the LORD in broad daylight,
25: 5 So Moses ordered Israel's judges to e everyone
35: 19 When they meet, the avenger must e the murderer.
35: 21 the victim's nearest relative must e the murderer
Dt 13: 5 you must e them to remove the evil from among
Jdg 20: 13 so we can e them and purge Israel of this evil."
2Sa 14: 7 your son. We will e him for murdering his brother.
14: 32 he finds me guilty of anything, then let him e me."
21: 6 and we will e them before the LORD at Gibeon,
1Ki 2: 25 ordered Benaiah son of Jehoiada to e him,
2: 29 he sent Benaiah son of Jehoiada to e him.
2Ki 6: 31 "May God kill me if I don't e Elisha son of
Ps 149: 7 to e vengeance on the nations / and punishment on
149: 9 to e the judgment written against them. / This is the
Eze 25: 17 I will e terrible vengeance against them to rebuke
Da 2: 12 and he sent out orders to e all the wise men of
2: 24 who had been ordered to e the wise men of
Lk 19: 27 them in and e them right here in my presence.' "
Jn 18: 31 "Only the Romans are permitted to e someone,"
Ac 13: 28 They found no just cause to e him, but they asked

EXECUTED (29) [EXECUTE]

Ge 41: 13 and the chief baker was e and impaled on a pole."
Ex 21: 23 If the result is death, the offender must be e.
22: 19 who has sexual relations with an animal must be e.
Nu 1: 51 else who goes too near the Tabernacle will be e.
3: 10 else who comes too near the sanctuary must be e!"
3: 38 who came too near the sanctuary was to be e.
35: 16 to be murder, and the murderer must be e.
35: 17 it is murder, and the murderer must be e.
35: 18 to be murder, and the murderer must be e.
35: 30 " 'All murderers must be e, but only if there is
Dt 17: 11 a verdict, the sentence they impose must be fully e;
21: 22 worthy of death and is e and then hanged on a tree,
24: 16 Those worthy of death must be e for their own
1Sa 11: 13 But Saul replied, "No one will be e today,
14: 44 May God strike me dead if you are not e for this."
2Sa 8: 2 He measured off two groups to be e for every one
21: 4 "And we don't want to see the Israelites e in
21: 9 The men of Gibeon e them on the mountain before
21: 13 well as the bones of the men the Gibeonites had e.
2Ki 14: 5 he e the men who had assassinated his father.
14: 6 Those worthy of death must be e for their own
23: 20 He e the priests of the pagan shrines on their own
2Ch 24: 24 their ancestors, so judgment was e against Joash.
25: 3 he e the men who had assassinated his father.
25: 4 Those worthy of death must be e for their own
Isa 63: 5 So I e vengeance alone; unaided, I passed down
Da 2: 18 so they would not be e along with the other wise
Mt 14: 5 Herod would have e John, but he was afraid of a
Lk 23: 32 both criminals, were led out to be e with him.

EXECUTING (2) [EXECUTE]

2Ch 22: 8 While Jehu was e judgment against the family of
Ps 9: 7 reigns forever, / e judgment from his throne.

EXECUTION (5) [EXECUTE]

Nu 35: 31 someone judged guilty of murder and subject to e;
35: 33 made for murder except by the e of the murderer.
Dt 13: 9 You must be the one to initiate the e; then all the
2Sa 19: 22 "This is not a day for e but for celebration!
Jer 29: 21 turn them over to Nebuchadnezzar for a public e.

EXECUTIONER (3) [EXECUTE]

Isa 65: 12 All of you will bow before the e, for when I called,
Eze 21: 11 and polished; it is being prepared for the e!
Mk 6: 27 So he sent an e to the prison to cut off John's head

EXECUTIONERS (1) [EXECUTE]

Zep 1: 7 people for a great slaughter and has chosen their e.

EXECUTIONS (1) [EXECUTE]

Lk 23: 47 soldiers handling the e saw what had happened,

EXEMPT (3) [EXEMPTED]

Ge 47: 26 the priests' land, they were e from this payment.
Nu 1: 49 "E the tribe of Levi from the census; do not
1Ch 9: 33 They were e from other responsibilities there since

EXEMPTED (2) [EXEMPT]

Nu 2: 33 The Levites were e from this census by the
1Sa 17: 25 and his whole family will be e from paying taxes!"

EXERCISE (7) [EXERCISED]

Lev 25: 43 never e your power over them in a ruthless way.
Ro 9: 22 God has every right to e his judgment and his
1Ti 3: 11 They must e self-control and be faithful in
4: 8 Physical e has some value, but spiritual e is much more important,
Tit 2: 2 Teach the older men to e self-control, to be worthy
1Pe 1: 13 So think clearly and e self-control. Look forward

EXERCISED (1) [EXERCISE]

Rev 13: 12 He e all the authority of the first beast. And he

EXHAUST (2) [EXHAUSTED, EXHAUSTING, EXHAUSTION]

Isa 7: 13 of David! You aren't satisfied to e my patience. You e the patience of God as well!

EXHAUSTED (16) [EXHAUST]

Ge 25: 29 Esau arrived home e and hungry from a hunt.
Dt 25: 18 They attacked you when you were e and weary,
Jdg 8: 4 and though they were e, they continued to chase
8: 15 and then we will feed your e warriors.' "
1Sa 30: 10 But two hundred of the men were too e to cross the
2Sa 21: 15 in the thick of battle, David became weak and e.
Ps 38: 8 I am e and completely crushed. / My groans come
39: 10 I am e by the blows from your hand.
69: 3 I am e from crying for help; / my throat is parched
119: 83 like a wineskin in the smoke, e with waiting.
Ecc 10: 15 so e by a little work that they have no strength for
Isa 1: 14 Everyone will run until e, rushing back to their
40: 30 Even youths will become e, and young men will
La 5: 5 us are at our heels; we are e but are given no rest.
Mic 6: 3 Tell me why your patience is e! Answer me!
Lk 22: 45 only to find them asleep, e from grief.

EXHAUSTING (1) [EXHAUST]

Ecc 12: 12 them can go on forever and become very e!

EXHAUSTION (2) [EXHAUST]

Jdg 4: 21 But when Sisera fell asleep from e, Jael quietly
2Co 6: 5 been put in jail, faced angry mobs, worked to e,

EXHIBIT (1) [EXHIBITION]

1Ti 3: 2 He must e self-control, live wisely, and have a

EXHIBITION (1) [EXHIBIT]

2Sa 2: 14 "Let's have a few of our warriors put on an e of

EXILE (89) [EXILED, EXILES, EXILING]

Lev 26: 34 during your years of e in the land of your enemies.
26: 44 or despise them while they are in e in the land of
Dt 28: 36 "The LORD will e you and the king you crowned
28: 36 Then in e you will worship gods of wood
Jdg 18: 30 continued as priests for the tribe of Dan until the E.
2Sa 15: 19 for you are a guest in Israel, a foreigner in e.
1Ki 8: 47 But in that land of e, they may turn to you again in
2Ki 20: 18 of your own descendants will be taken away into e.
21: 8 I will not send them into e from this land that I
24: 20 and Judah from his presence and sent them into e.
25: 21 So the people of Judah were sent into e from their
25: 27 In the thirty-seventh year of King Jehoiachin's e in
1Ch 5: 22 in their land until they were taken away into e.
6: 15 who went into e when the LORD sent the people
2Ch 6: 37 But in that land of e, they may turn to you again in
28: 5 and to e large numbers of his people to Damascus.
33: 8 I will not send them into e from this land that I
Ezr 2: 2 number of the men of Israel who returned from e:
2: 36 These are the priests who returned from e:
2: 40 These are the Levites who returned from e:
2: 43 of the following Temple servants returned from e:
2: 55 these servants of King Solomon returned from e:
3: 8 made up of everyone who had returned from e,
6: 16 and the rest of the people who had returned from e.
6: 21 by the people of Israel who had returned from e
Ne 7: 7 the number of men of Israel who returned from e:
7: 39 "These are the priests who returned from e:
7: 43 "These are the Levites who returned from e:
7: 46 of the following Temple servants returned from e:
7: 57 these servants of King Solomon returned from e:
Ps 144: 14 May there be no breached walls, no forced e,
Isa 5: 13 So I will send my people into e far away
27: 13 Many who were dying in e in Assyria and Egypt
39: 7 of your own descendants will be taken away into e.
49: 20 The generations born in e will return and say,
49: 21 were killed, and the rest were carried away into e.
52: 3 "When I sold you into e, I received no payment.
Jer 2: 37 you will be led into e with your hands on your
3: 18 and Israel will return together from e in the north.
7: 15 And I will send you into e, just as I did your
8: 9 These wise teachers will be shamed by e for their
13: 17 the LORD's flock will be led away into e.
13: 19 away as captives. They will all be carried into e.
29: 19 And you who are in e have not listened either,"
30: 10 and your children will return from their e.
30: 16 and all your enemies will be sent into e.
39: 7 him in chains, and sent him away to e in Babylon.
40: 1 and Judah who were being sent to e in Babylon.
43: 3 killed by the Babylonians or be carried off into e."
46: 19 Get ready to leave for e, you citizens of Egypt!
46: 27 and your children will return from their e.
52: 3 and Judah from his presence and sent them into e.
52: 27 So the people of Judah were sent into e from their
52: 31 In the thirty-seventh year of King Jehoiachin's e in
La 2: 14 They did not try to hold you back from e by
4: 22 punishment will end; you will soon return from e.
Eze 3: 11 Then go to your people in e and say to them,
6: 12 will strike down those who are far away in e.
11: 15 in Jerusalem are talking about their relatives in e,
11: 16 I will be a sanctuary to you during your time in e.
11: 24 back again to Babylonia, to the Judeans in e there.
12: 3 to show them what it will be like to go off into e.
12: 7 filled with the things I might carry into e.
12: 11 be driven from their homes and sent away into e.
20: 38 bring them out of the countries where they are in e,
20: 41 When I bring you home from e, you will be as
25: 3 and laughed at Judah as she went away into e,
37: 12 I will open your graves of e and cause you to rise
38: 12 people who have returned from e in many nations.
39: 23 then know why Israel was sent away into e—
39: 28 responsible for sending them away to e
Hos 1: 11 one leader, and they will return from e together.
Am 1: 6 They sent my people into e, selling them as slaves
1: 15 their king and his princes will go into e together.
5: 5 For the people of Gilgal will be dragged off into e,
5: 27 So I will send you into e, to a land east of
7: 11 the people of Israel will be sent away into e.' "
7: 17 of Israel will certainly become captives in e,
9: 4 Even if they are driven into e, I will command the
Mic 1: 11 You people of Shaphir, go as captives into e—

2:13 Your leader will break out and lead you out of e.
4:10 You will soon be sent into e in distant Babylon.
5: 3 countrymen will return from e to their own land.
Na 2: 7 Nineveh's e has been decreed, and all the servant
Zec 7: 5 'During those seventy years of e, when you fasted
Mt 1:11 and his brothers (born at the time of the e to
1:12 After the Babylonian e: / Jehoiachin was the father
1:17 fourteen from David's time to the Babylonian e,
and fourteen from the Babylonian e to the Messiah.

EXILED (38) [EXILE]

Dt 29:28 people from their land and e them to another land,
30: 1 nations to which the LORD your God has e you.
2Ki 17: 6 and the people of Israel were e to Assyria.
17:27 "Send one of the e priests from Samaria back to
17:28 So one of the priests who had been e from Samaria
25:28 treatment over all the other e kings in Babylon.
1Ch 5:26 The Assyrians e them to Halah, Habor, Hara,
9: 1 The people of Judah were e to Babylon
Ezr 5:12 this Temple and e the people to Babylonia.
Ne 1: 9 even if you are e to the ends of the earth,
Est 2: 6 He had been e from Jerusalem to Babylon by King
Isa 27: 8 He has e her from her land as though blown away
Jer 16:15 and from all the countries to which he had e them.'
22:28 are he and his children to be e to distant lands?
23: 8 and from all the countries to which he had e them.'
24: 1 After King Nebuchadnezzar of Babylon e
27:20 them here when he e Jehoiachin son of Jehoiakim,
29: 1 and all the people who had been e to Babylon by
29: 4 sends this message to all the captives he has e to
29:16 your relatives who were not e to Babylon.
34: 3 and sentenced. Then you will be e to Babylon.'
40: 7 in Judah, and that he hadn't e everyone to Babylon.
46:28 I will destroy the nations to which I have e you,
48: 7 his priests and princes, will be e to distant lands!
49: 3 for your god Molech will be e along with his
49:36 They will be e to countries around the world.
52:32 treatment over all the other e kings in Babylon.
La 2: 9 Her kings and princes have been e to distant lands;
Eze 6: 9 Then when they are e among the nations, they will
17:13 He also e Israel's most influential leaders,
Da 5:13 who was e from Judah by my predecessor,
Am 9:14 I will bring my e people of Israel back from distant
Ob 1:12 You shouldn't have gloated when they e your
1:20 The captives from Jerusalem e in the north will
Mic 1:16 for your little ones will be e to distant lands.
Zec 2: 7 Escape to Jerusalem, you who are e in Babylon!"
6:10 gifts of silver and gold from the Jews e in Babylon.
Rev 1: 9 I was e to the island of Patmos for preaching the

EXILES (29) [EXILE]

2Ki 25:11 then took as e those who remained in the city,
Ezr 1: 8 the leader of the e returning to Judah.
1:11 Jerusalem when the e returned there from Babylon.
2: 1 Here is the list of the Jewish e of the provinces
4: 1 and Benjamin heard that the e were rebuilding a
6:19 On April 21 the returned e celebrated Passover.
6:20 the Passover lamb for all the returned e,
8:15 I assembled the e at the Ahava Canal, and we
8:35 Then the e who had returned from captivity
10: 6 because of the unfaithfulness of the returned e.
10: 7 and Jerusalem that all the returned e should come
10: 8 and be expelled from the assembly of the e.
Ne 7: 6 "Here is the list of the Jewish e of the provinces
Ps 107: 3 For he has gathered the e from many lands,
126: 1 When the LORD restored his e to Jerusalem,
147: 2 and bringing the e back to Israel.
Jer 24: 5 The good figs represent the e I sent from Judah to
29:22 so that whenever the Judean e want to curse
29:31 "Send an open letter to all the e in Babylon.
49: 5 your land, and no one will help your e as they flee.
52:15 then took as e some of the poorest of the people
Eze 1: 1 while I was with the Judean e beside the Kebar
3:15 Then I came to the colony of Judean e in Tel-abib,
11:16 give the e this message from the Sovereign
11:25 And I told the e everything the LORD had shown
14:22 and they will come here to join you as e in
Ob 1:20 The e of Israel will return to their land and occupy
Mic 4: 6 who are lame, who have been e, filled with grief.
Zep 3:19 I will give glory and renown to my former e,

EXILING (1) [EXILE]

Ps 106:27 among the nations, / e them to distant lands.

EXIST (8) [EXISTED, EXISTENCE, EXISTS]

Ps 39:13 I can smile again / before I am gone and e no more.
Ecc 1:10 How do you know it didn't already e long ago?
3:15 and whatever will e in the future has already
Ac 17:28 For in him we live and move and e. As one of your
Ro 4:17 and who brings into existence what didn't e before.
1Co 8: 6 who created everything, and we e for him.
Gal 4: 8 were slaves to so-called gods that do not even e.
Rev 4:11 and it is for your pleasure that they e and were

EXISTED (11) [EXIST]

1Ki 15:19 "Let us renew the treaty that e between your father
2Ch 16: 3 "Let us renew the treaty that e between your father
Ecc 3:15 and whatever will exist in the future has already e
Ob 1:16 from history, as though you had never even e.
Jn 1: 1 In the beginning the Word already e. He was with
1:15 greater than I am, for he e long before I did.' "
1:30 is far greater than I am, for he e long before I did.'
8:58 truth is, I e before Abraham was even born!"
Col 1:15 He e before God made anything at all and is
1:17 He e before everything else began, and he holds all
1Jn 1: 1 The one who e from the beginning is the one we

EXISTENCE (10) [EXIST]

Job 10:19 Then I would have been spared this miserable e.
18:17 All memory of their e will perish from the earth.
Ps 39: 5 just a moment to you; / human e is but a breath."
39:11 Human e is as frail as breath. / *Interlude*
83: 4 We will destroy the very memory of its e."
89:47 my life is, / how empty and futile this human e!
Ecc 1:13 I soon discovered that God has dealt a tragic e to
6: 5 would never have seen the sun or known of its e.
Da 12: 1 greater than any since nations first came into e.
Ro 4:17 and who brings into e what didn't exist before.

EXISTS (5) [EXIST]

Ecc 3:15 Whatever e today and whatever will exist in the
Jer 10:16 He is the Creator of everything that e,
51:19 He is the Creator of everything that e,
Jn 1: 3 everything there is. Nothing e that he didn't make.
Ro 11:36 everything e by his power and is intended for his

EXIT (1) [EXITS]

Ge 43:30 Then Joseph made a hasty e because he was

EXITS (1) [EXIT]

Eze 48:30 "These will be the e to the city: On the north wall,

EXODUS (6)

Ex 13: 4 in early spring will be the anniversary of your e.
23:15 for that is the anniversary of your e from Egypt.
Dt 16: 6 down on the anniversary of your e from Egypt.
Jos 4:19 the month that marked their e from Egypt.
5: 5 but none of those born after the E, during the years
5:10 the month that marked their e from Egypt.

EXOTIC (1)

Am 6: 6 and you perfume yourselves with e fragrances,

EXPAND (1) [EXPANDING, EXPANSES]

Job 12:23 He makes nations e, and he abandons them.

EXPANDING (1) [EXPAND]

Isa 9: 7 His ever e, peaceful government will never end.

EXPANSES (1) [EXPAND]

Job 37:10 breath sends the ice, freezing wide e of water.

EXPECT (16) [EXPECTANT, EXPECTANTLY, EXPECTATION, EXPECTATIONS, EXPECTED, EXPECTING, EXPECTS]

Ge 27: 2 Isaac said, "and I e every day to be my last.
Ex 3:11 "How can you e me to lead the Israelites out of
6:12 How can I e Pharaoh to listen? I'm no orator!"
2Sa 19:28 All my relatives and I could e only death from you,
Pr 11:23 to happiness, while the wicked can e only wrath.
Isa 33: 1 You e others to respect their promises to you,
Jer 5: 4 "But what can we e from the poor and ignorant?
7:27 "Tell them all this, but do not e them to listen.
7:27 out your warnings, but do not e them to respond.
Eze 13: 6 And yet they e him to fulfill their prophecies!
Mic 3: 4 Do you really e him to listen? After all the evil you
Jn 7:31 "would you e the Messiah to do more miraculous
1Co 9:10 and thresh the grain e a share of the harvest,
2Co 3: 8 Shouldn't we e far greater glory when the Holy
Jas 1: 6 ask him, be sure that you really e him to answer,
1: 7 People like that should not e to receive anything

EXPECTANT (1) [EXPECT]

Jer 31: 8 the e mothers and women about to give birth.

EXPECTANTLY (2) [EXPECT]

Ps 5: 3 morning I bring my requests to you and wait e.
119:131 I open my mouth, panting e, / longing for your

EXPECTATION (5) [EXPECT]

Ro 5: 4 and character strengthens our confident e of
5: 5 And this e will not disappoint us. For we know
Php 1:20 For I live in eager e and hope that I will never do
Heb 10:27 forward to but the terrible e of God's judgment
1Pe 1: 3 Now we live with a wonderful e because Jesus

EXPECTATIONS (2) [EXPECT]

Pr 10:28 in happiness, but the e of the wicked are all in vain.
Isa 64: 3 you did awesome things beyond our highest e.

EXPECTED (15) [EXPECT]

1Sa 28: 1 and your men will be e to join me in battle."
1Ki 2:15 was mine; everyone e me to be the next king.
2Ki 5:11 "I e him to wave his hand over the leprosy and call
Isa 5: 4 give me wild grapes / when I e sweet ones?
5: 7 He e them to yield a crop of justice, / but instead
he found bloodshed. / He e to find righteousness,
59: 9 No wonder we are in darkness when we e light.
Jer 23: 1 and scattered the very ones they were e to care
Da 11:21 But he will slip in when least e and take over the
Hag 2:16 When you e to draw fifty gallons from the
Mt 24:44 For the Son of Man will come when least e.
Lk 2:25 and he eagerly e the Messiah to come and rescue
12:40 for the Son of Man will come when least e."
Ac 25:18 made against him weren't at all what I e.
2Co 1: 9 In fact, we e to die. But as a result, we learned not

EXPECTING (12) [EXPECT]

2Ki 7:12 They are e us to leave the city, and then they will
Eze 33:13 they sin, e their past righteousness to save them,
Mt 11: 8 Or were you e to see a man dressed in expensive
Lk 3:15 Everyone was e the Messiah to come soon,
7:19 to ask him, "Are you the Messiah we've been e,
7:20 sent us to ask, 'Are you the Messiah we've been e,
7:25 Or were you e to see a man dressed in expensive
9:13 Or are you e us to go and buy enough food for this
Jn 6:14 "Surely, he is the Prophet we have been e!"
Ac 3: 5 The lame man looked at them eagerly, e a gift.
23:21 They are ready, e you to agree to their request."
2Co 11: 7 Good News to you without e anything in return?

EXPECTS (1) [EXPECT]

Jer 5: 4 They don't understand what God e of them.

EXPEDIENT [KJV] See also ADVANTAGE, APPROPRIATE, BENEFICIAL, BETTER, GAINED

EXPEDITION (1) [EXPEDITIONS]

1Ki 22:49 "Let my men sail an e with your men."

EXPEDITIONS (1) [EXPEDITION]

Dt 33:18 "May the people of Zebulun prosper in their e

EXPEL (4) [EXPELLED, EXPELLING, EXPELS]

Lev 20:23 customs of the people whom I will e before you.
Jer 22:26 I will e you and your mother from this land,
23:39 I will e you from my presence, along with this city
Jn 12:42 because of their fear that the Pharisees would e

EXPELLED (7) [EXPEL]

1Sa 28: 9 "You know that Saul has e all the mediums
Ezr 10: 8 and be e from the assembly of the exiles.
Ne 13: 3 all those of mixed ancestry were immediately e
Eze 28:16 I e you, O mighty guardian, from your place
Jn 9:22 was the Messiah would be e from the synagogue.
16: 2 For you will be e from the synagogues,
Ac 18: 2 They had been e from Italy as a result of Claudius

EXPELLING (3) [EXPEL]

Lev 18:24 because this is how the people I am e from the
Eze 45: 9 out of their land! Stop e them from their homes!
Mk 1:39 the synagogues and e demons from many people.

EXPELS (1) [EXPEL]

1Jn 4:18 love has no fear because perfect love e all fear.

EXPENSE (8) [EXPENSES, EXPENSIVE]

Ge 31: 1 "All his wealth has been gained at our father's e."
31: 9 God has made me wealthy at your father's e.
Ex 14: 4 so I will receive great glory at the e of Pharaoh
14:17 Then I will receive great glory at the e of Pharaoh
Ne 5:18 The provisions required at my e for each day were
Ob 1:13 their homes and making yourselves rich at their e.
1Co 4: 6 you won't brag about one of your leaders at the e
9:18 preaching the Good News without e to anyone,

EXPENSES (8) [EXPENSE]

Ex 21:19 of the injury and must pay for the medical e.
2Ki 12:12 and they paid any other e related to the Temple's
25:30 to cover his living e until the day of his death.
Ezr 1: 4 toward their e by supplying them with silver
6: 4 of timber. All e will be paid by the royal treasury.
Jer 52:34 to cover his living e until the day of his death.
1Co 9: 7 What soldier has to pay his own e? And have you
1Th 2: 9 so that our e would not be a burden to anyone there

EXPENSIVE (20) [EXPENSE]

Ecc 7: 1 A good reputation is more valuable than the most e
Jer 6:20 Keep your e perfumes! I cannot accept your burnt
La 5: 4 to pay for water to drink, and even firewood is e.
Eze 16:10 I gave you e clothing of linen and silk,
27:20 Dedan traded their e saddle blankets with you.
Mt 11: 8 Or were you expecting to see a man dressed in e
26: 7 a woman came in with a beautiful jar of e perfume
Mk 14: 3 a woman came in with a beautiful jar of e perfume.
14: 4 "Why was this e perfume wasted?" they asked.
Lk 7:25 Or were you expecting to see a man dressed in e
7:37 and brought a beautiful jar filled with e perfume.
Jn 2:10 and doesn't care, he brings out the less e wines.
11: 2 This is the Mary who poured the e perfume on the
12: 3 Then Mary took a twelve-ounce jar of e perfume
Ac 16:14 Lydia from Thyatira, a merchant of e purple cloth.
1Ti 2: 9 their hair or by wearing gold or pearls or e clothes.
2Ti 2:20 The e utensils are used for special occasions,
Jas 2: 2 meeting dressed in fancy clothes and e jewelry,
1Pe 3: 3 on fancy hairstyles, e jewelry, or beautiful clothes.
Rev 18:12 objects made of e wood, bronze, iron, and marble.

EXPERIENCE (37) [EXPERIENCED, EXPERIENCES, EXPERIENCING]

Ex 21:36 But if the bull was known from past e to gore,
23: 9 Remember your own e in the land of Egypt.

Dt 28: 2 You will e all these blessings if you obey the
Jdg 3: 2 to generations of Israelites who had no e in battle.
1Ch 22: 9 But you will have a son who will e peace and rest.
Job 4: 8 My e shows that those who plant trouble
5: 3 From my e, I know that fools who turn from God
5: 27 "We have found from e that all this is true.
7: 7 but a breath, and I will never again e pleasure.
8: 8 Pay attention to the e of our ancestors.
15: 17 you will listen, I will answer you from my own e.
15: 18 And it is confirmed by the e of wise men who have
Ps 142: T A psalm of David, regarding his e in the cave.
Pr 1: 31 They must e the full terror of the path they have
18: 21 Those who love to talk will e the consequences,
20: 29 the gray hair of e is the splendor of the old.
23: 22 and don't despise your mother's e when she is old.
Ecc 2: 3 I hoped to e the only happiness most people find
8: 15 That way they will e some happiness along with all
Isa 7: 17 You will soon e greater terror than has been known
38: 9 was well again, he wrote this poem about his e:
59: 8 and those who follow them cannot e a moment's
Mic 2: 4 you by singing this song of despair about your e:
Mt 12: 45 That will be the e of this evil generation."
Jn 3: 36 Those who don't obey the Son will never e eternal
Ac 19: 3 "Then what baptism did you e?" he asked.
26: 16 You are to tell the world about this e and about
1Co 10: 13 into your life are no different from what others e.
2Co 12: 5 That e is something worth boasting about, but I am
Eph 3: 19 May you e the love of Christ, though it is so great
Php 1: 25 so that you will grow and e the joy of your faith.
3: 10 and e the mighty power that raised him from the
3: 11 somehow, I can e the resurrection from the dead!
4: 7 If you do this, you will e God's peace, which is far
2Th 2: 13 God chose you to be among the first to e salvation,
Jas 5: 11 From his e we see how the Lord's plan finally
Rev 18: 7 I am no helpless widow. I will not e sorrow.'

EXPERIENCED (15) [EXPERIENCE]

Dt 11: 2 who have never e the discipline of the LORD
Jos 24: 31 those who had personally e all that the LORD had
Jdg 20: 25 all of whom were e with a sword.
20: 35 all of whom were e with a sword.
2Sa 17: 8 And remember that your father is an e soldier.
1Ki 9: 27 Hiram sent e crews of sailors to sail the ships with
1Ch 12: 8 and e warriors from the tribe of Gad also defected
2Ch 8: 18 his own officers and manned by e crews of sailors.
25: 6 silver to hire 100,000 e fighting men from Israel.
Est 9: 26 Mordecai's letter and because of what they had e,
Job 38: 21 before it was all created, and you are so very e!
SS 3: 8 They are all skilled swordsmen and e warriors.
Isa 53: 11 And because of what he has e, my righteous
Jer 2: 33 The most e prostitute could learn from you!
Heb 6: 4 those who have e the good things of heaven

EXPERIENCES (1) [EXPERIENCE]

Ro 4: 1 What were his e concerning this question of being

EXPERIENCING (1) [EXPERIENCE]

Jn 16: 21 It will be like a woman e the pains of labor.

EXPERT (17) [EXPERTS]

Ge 21: 20 in the wilderness of Paran. He became an e archer,
Ex 38: 23 tribe of Dan, a craftsman e at engraving, designing,
1Ch 8: 40 of Ulam were all skilled warriors and e archers.
12: 2 All of them were e archers, and they could shoot
12: 8 They were e with both shield and spear, as fierce
22: 16 They are e goldsmiths and silversmiths
2Ch 2: 7 someone who is e at dyeing purple, scarlet,
2: 14 He is an e in dyeing purple, blue, and scarlet cloth
Ps 52: 2 cuts like a sharp razor; / you're an e at telling lies.
Isa 3: 3 advisers, skilled magicians, and e enchanters.
Jer 10: 9 these gods in royal purple robes made by e tailors.
Mt 22: 35 One of them, an e in religious law, tried to trap him
Lk 10: 25 One day an e in religious law stood up to test Jesus
11: 45 "Teacher," said an e in religious law, "you have
Ac 5: 34 who was an e on religious law and was very
26: 3 for I know you are an e on Jewish customs
1Co 3: 10 to me, I have laid the foundation like an e builder.

EXPERTS (5) [EXPERT]

Job 3: 8 Let those who are e at cursing—those who are
Lk 7: 30 and e in religious law had rejected God's plan for
11: 46 "how terrible it will be for you e in religious law!
11: 52 "How terrible it will be for you e in religious law!
14: 3 Jesus asked the Pharisees and e in religious law,

EXPIRED (1)

1Sa 18: 26 to accept the offer. So before the time limit e,

EXPIRED [KJV] See also COMPLETED, ENDED, FULFILLED, OVER, PASSED, SPRING

EXPLAIN (25) [EXPLAINED, EXPLAINING, EXPLAINS, EXPLANATION, EXPLANATIONS]

Ex 13: 8 you must e to your children why you are
Dt 1: 5 the Jordan River. He began to e the law as follows:
Jos 20: 4 the leaders at the city gate and e what happened.
1Ki 10: 3 nothing was too hard for the king to e to her.
2Ch 9: 2 nothing was too hard for him to e to her.
Est 4: 8 He also asked Hathach to e it to her and to urge her
5: 8 Then tomorrow I will e what this is all about."
Jer 9: 12 instructed by the LORD and can e it to others?
Eze 12: 11 Then e that your actions are a demonstration of
Da 5: 12 He can interpret dreams, e riddles, and solve
10: 14 Now I am here to e what will happen to your
Mt 13: 35 I will e mysteries hidden since the creation of the
13: 36 "Please e the story of the weeds in the field."
15: 15 "E what you meant when you said people aren't
Lk 8: 47 The whole crowd heard her e why she had touched
Jn 3: 8 so you can't e how people are born of the Spirit."
4: 25 When he comes, he will e everything to us."
Ac 19: 33 of the Jews, who encouraged him to e the situation.
1Co 2: 13 using the Spirit's words to e spiritual truths.
Eph 3: 9 I was chosen to e to everyone this plan that God,
6: 19 Ask God to give me the right words as I boldly e
1Ti 4: 6 If you e this to the others, you will be doing your
Heb 4: 13 This is the God to whom we must e all that we
9: 5 But we cannot e all of these things now.
1Pe 3: 15 about your Christian hope, always be ready to e it.

EXPLAINED (21) [EXPLAIN]

Ge 24: 34 "I am Abraham's servant," he e.
29: 12 He e that he was her cousin on her father's side,
31: 35 "Forgive my not getting up, Father," Rachel e.
Nu 22: 7 and urgently e to him what Balak wanted.
Jdg 15: 2 "I really thought you hated her," her father e,
Ne 4: 19 Then I e to the nobles and officials and all the
8: 8 and clearly e the meaning of what was being read,
Jer 36: 18 So Baruch e, "Jeremiah dictated them to me word
Eze 46: 20 He e, "This is where the priests will cook the meat
Da 7: 16 asked him what it all meant. He e it to me like this:
9: 22 He e to me, "Daniel, I have come here to give you
Zec 1: 10 So the man standing among the myrtle trees e,
Mt 13: 11 Then he e to them, "You have been permitted to
21: 31 "The first, of course." Then Jesus e his meaning:
Mk 4: 34 alone with his disciples, he e the meaning to them.
Lk 24: 32 with us on the road and e the Scriptures to us?"
Jn 4: 34 Then Jesus e: "My nourishment comes from doing
10: 7 so he e it to them. "I assure you, I am the gate for
Ac 17: 21 (It should be e that all the Athenians as well as the
18: 26 him aside and e the way of God more accurately.
18: 28 Using the Scriptures, he e to them, "The Messiah

EXPLAINING (6) [EXPLAIN]

Jer 14: 1 the LORD, e why he was holding back the rain:
Lk 24: 27 e what all the Scriptures said about himself.
Ac 16: 4 e the decision regarding the commandments that
17: 3 He was e and proving the prophecies about the
23: 18 e, "Paul, the prisoner, called me over and asked
1Co 4: 1 who have been put in charge of e God's secrets.

EXPLAINS (5) [EXPLAIN]

Ge 2: 24 This e why a man leaves his father and mother
Mt 19: 5 'This e why a man leaves his father and mother
Mk 10: 7 'This e why a man leaves his father and mother
Ac 13: 35 Another psalm e more fully, saying, 'You will not
2Ti 2: 15 be ashamed and who correctly e the word of truth.

EXPLANATION (2) [EXPLAIN]

Mt 13: 18 "Now here is the e of the story I told about the
Ac 19: 40 And if Rome demands an e, we won't know what

EXPLANATIONS (1) [EXPLAIN]

Job 21: 34 can you comfort me? All your e are wrong!"

EXPLICIT (1)

Ro 5: 14 even though they did not disobey an e

EXPLODES (1)

Ps 76: 7 Who can stand before you when your anger e?

EXPLOIT (4) [EXPLOITED, EXPLOITING, EXPLOITS]

Ex 22: 22 "Do not e widows or orphans.
Lev 19: 33 "Do not e the foreigners who live in your land.
Pr 22: 22 because they are poor or e the needy in court.
Eze 18: 16 and does not e the poor, but instead is fair to

EXPLOITED (1) [EXPLOIT]

Isa 11: 4 He will defend the poor and the e. He will rule

EXPLOITING (1) [EXPLOIT]

Jer 7: 6 and if you stop e foreigners, orphans, and widows;

EXPLOITS (2) [EXPLOIT]

2Sa 23: 17 drink it. This is an example of the e of the Three.
1Ch 11: 19 drink it. This is an example of the e of the Three.

EXPLORE (10) [EXPLORED, EXPLORING]

Ge 13: 17 and e the new possessions I am giving you."
Nu 13: 2 "Send men to e the land of Canaan, the land I am
13: 16 These are the names of the men Moses sent to e the
13: 17 these instructions as he sent them out to e the land:
21: 32 After Moses sent men to e the Jazer area,
32: 8 I sent them from Kadesh-barnea to e the land.
Dt 1: 22 'First, let's send out scouts to e the land for us.
Jos 14: 7 sent me from Kadesh-barnea to e the land of
Job 28: 3 how to put light into darkness and e the farthest,
Ecc 1: 13 and to e by wisdom everything being done in the

EXPLORED (16) [EXPLORE]

Nu 13: 21 and e the land from the wilderness of Zin as far as
13: 31 But the other men who had e the land with him
13: 32 "The land we e will swallow up any who go to
14: 6 Two of the men who had e the land, Joshua son of
14: 7 of Israel, "The land we e is a wonderful land!
14: 24 loyal to me, and I will bring him into the land he e.
14: 34 " 'Because the men who e the land were there for
14: 38 Of the twelve who had e the land, only Joshua
Dt 1: 24 the hills and came to the valley of Eshcol and e it.
2Ki 19: 23 its farthest corners / and e its deepest forests.
Job 38: 16 "Have you e the springs from which the seas
38: 16 Have you walked about and e their depths?
Ecc 9: 1 This, too, I carefully e: Even though the actions of
Isa 37: 24 its farthest corners / and e its deepest forests.
Jer 31: 37 and the foundation of the earth cannot be e,
Eze 20: 6 Egypt to a land I had discovered and e for them—

EXPLORING (2) [EXPLORE]

Nu 13: 25 After e the land for forty days, the men returned
Pr 1: 6 by e the depth of meaning in these proverbs,

EXPOSE (6) [EXPOSED, EXPOSES, EXPOSING, EXPOSURE]

Isa 47: 2 and strip off your robe. E yourself to public view.
57: 12 "Now I will e your so-called good deeds that you
Jer 13: 26 I myself will e you to shame.
Eze 11: 8 I will e you to the war you so greatly fear,
Eph 5: 11 of evil and darkness; instead, rebuke and e them.
5: 14 where your light shines, it will e their evil deeds.

EXPOSED (18) [EXPOSE]

Lev 20: 18 because he e the source of her flow, and she
2Sa 6: 20 He e himself to the servant girls like any indecent
Ne 4: 13 behind the lowest parts of the wall in the e areas.
Est 6: 2 of how Mordecai had e the plot of Bigthana
Pr 12: 19 Truth stands the test of time; lies are soon e.
Isa 32: 7 The smooth tricks of evil people will be e,
53: 12 is mighty and great, because he e himself to death.
Jer 36: 30 to lie unburied—e to hot days and frosty nights.
Eze 16: 36 Because you have e yourself in prostitution to all
16: 57 But now your greater wickedness has been e to all
23: 29 The shame of your prostitution will be e to all the
28: 17 to the earth and e you to the curious gaze of kings.
Hab 2: 16 soon it will be your turn! Come, drink and be e!
Jn 3: 20 stay away from the light for fear their sins will be e
Ac 27: 12 And since Fair Havens was an e harbor—a poor
Heb 4: 13 Everything is naked and e before his eyes.
10: 33 Sometimes you were e to public ridicule and were
2Pe 3: 10 and everything on it will be e to judgment.

EXPOSES (2) [EXPOSE]

Isa 44: 25 I am the one who e the false prophets as liars by
Heb 4: 12 and desires. It e us for what we really are.

EXPOSING (2) [EXPOSE]

Pr 20: 27 penetrates the human spirit, e every hidden motive.
Mic 1: 6 down into the valley below, e all her foundations.

EXPOSURE (1) [EXPOSE]

Ac 27: 12 harbor with only a southwest and northwest e.

EXPRESS (9) [EXPRESSED, EXPRESSING, EXPRESSION]

2Sa 10: 2 So David sent ambassadors to e sympathy to
1Ch 12: 31 18,000 men were sent for the e purpose of helping
19: 2 So David sent ambassadors to e sympathy to
Ezr 4: 21 That city must not be rebuilt except at my e
Job 7: 11 cannot keep from speaking. I must e my anguish.
32: 10 So listen to me and let me e my opinion.
Eze 33: 31 They e love with their mouths, but their hearts seek
2Co 9: 12 and they will joyfully e their thanksgiving to God.
1Pe 2: 6 As the Scriptures e it, / "I am placing a stone in

EXPRESSED (4) [EXPRESS]

Ps 45: 6 and ever. / Your royal power is e in justice.
Ecc 12: 12 There is no end of opinions ready to be e.
Ro 8: 26 for us with groanings that cannot be e in words.
Heb 1: 8 and ever. / Your royal power is e in righteousness.

EXPRESSING (1) [EXPRESS]

Gal 5: 6 What is important is faith e itself in love.

EXPRESSION (5) [EXPRESS]

Lev 26: 41 when I have given full e to my hostility and have
Eze 24: 8 So I will splash her blood on a rock as an open e of
Da 4: 30 royal residence and as an e of my royal splendor."
Joel 2: 23 For the rains he sends are an e of his grace.
1Jn 4: 12 and his love has been brought to full e through us.

EXQUISITE (1)

Ex 26: 36 and embroider e designs into it, using blue, purple,

EXTEND (15) [EXTENDED, EXTENDING, EXTENDS, EXTENSIVE, EXTENSIVELY, EXTENT]

Ge 49: 13 be a harbor for ships; / his borders will e to Sidon.
Ex 25: 35 pair of branches where they e from the center stem.
Lev 23: 32 of Atonement and e until evening of that day."

26: 5 Your threshing season will **e** until the grape harvest will **e** until it is time to
Nu 21:15 which **e** as far as the settlement of Ar on the border
34: 3 The southern portion of your country will **e** from
35: 4 **e** 1,500 feet from the town walls in every direction.
1Ch 4:10 "Oh, that you would bless me and **e** my lands!
Ps 89:25 I will **e** his rule from the Mediterranean Sea in the
110: 2 The LORD will **e** your powerful dominion from
Eze 41: 6 but the supports did not **e** into the wall.
48: 7 all of whose boundaries **e** from east to west.
48: 8 It will be 8-1/3 miles wide and will **e** as far east
Am 1:13 When they attacked Gilead to **e** their borders,

EXTENDED (29) [EXTEND]

Ge 10:11 From there he **e** his reign to Assyria, where he built
Ex 37:21 of branches, where they **e** from the center stem.
Jos 11:17 The Israelite territory now **e** all the way from
12: 1 Their territory **e** from the Arnon Gorge to Mount
12: 2 and **e** from the middle of the Arnon Gorge to the
13: 9 Their territory **e** from Aroer on the edge of the
13:10 in Heshbon, and **e** as far as the borders of Ammon.
13:16 Their territory **e** from Aroer on the edge of the
13:26 It **e** from Heshbon to Ramath-mizpeh
13:30 Their territory **e** from Mahanaim, including all of
15: 5 The eastern boundary **e** along the Dead Sea to the
15: 7 From there the border **e** to the springs at
15: 9 From there the border **e** from the top of the
15:46 From Ekron the boundary **e** west and included the
16: 1 The allotment to the descendants of Joseph **e** from
16: 8 From Tappuah the border **e** westward,
17: 7 The boundary of the tribe of Manasseh **e** from the
19:33 and **e** across to Adami-nekeb, Jabneel, and as far as
1Ki 4:24 Solomon's dominion **e** over all the kingdoms west
1Ch 11: 8 He **e** the city from the Millo to the surrounding
Isa 26:15 made our nation great; / you have **e** our borders!
Eze 27: 4 You **e** your boundaries into the sea. Your builders
40:18 and **e** out from the walls into the courtyard the
41: 3 and the walls on each side of the entrance **e** 12-1/4
42: 4 It **e** the entire 175 feet of the complex, and all the
42: 8 which **e** for only 87-1/2 feet, while the inner
42: 8 the rooms toward the Temple—**e** for 175 feet.
Da 8: 9 It **e** toward the south and the east and toward the
Mic 7:11 cities will be rebuilt, and your borders will be **e**.

EXTENDING (9) [EXTEND]

Ge 10:30 The descendants of Joktan lived in the area **e** from
Dt 3:16 and Gad I gave the area **e** from Gilead to the
34: 2 all the land of Judah, **e** to the Mediterranean Sea;
Jos 13:27 western border, **e** as far north as the Sea of Galilee.
2Ch 3:15 each topped by a capital **e** upward another 7-1/2
Ne 3:21 **e** from a point opposite the door of Eliashib's
Eze 48: 3 land lies south of Asher's, also **e** from east to west.
48:21 **e** in opposite directions to the eastern and western
48:24 of Simeon, also **e** across the land from east to west.

EXTENDS (10) [EXTEND]

Jos 13: 3 This land **e** from the stream of Shihor, which is on
Ps 103:17 His salvation **e** to the children's children
119:90 Your faithfulness **e** to every generation,
Pr 31:20 She **e** a helping hand to the poor and opens her
Isa 30: 4 For though his power **e** to Zoan and Hanes,
Eze 48: 1 Dan's territory **e** all the way across the land of
48: 2 lies south of Dan's and also **e** from east to west.
48: 4 and its territory also **e** from east to west.
48:23 and it **e** across the entire land of Israel from east to
48:26 which also **e** across the land from east to west.

EXTENSIVE (1) [EXTEND]

2Ch 27: 3 and also did **e** rebuilding on the wall at the hill of

EXTENSIVELY (1) [EXTEND]

Ac 15:32 spoke **e** to the Christians, encouraging

EXTENT (15) [EXTEND]

Ge 6: 5 Now the LORD observed the **e** of the people's
1Ki 15:23 rest of the events in Asa's reign, the **e** of his power,
16: 5 and the **e** of his power are recorded in *The Book*
16:27 of the events in Omri's reign, the **e** of his power,
22:45 events in Jehoshaphat's reign, the **e** of his power,
2Ki 13: 8 and all his deeds, including the **e** of his power,
13:12 including the **e** of his power and his war with King
14:15 including the **e** of his power and his war with King
14:28 his deeds, including the **e** of his power, his wars,
20:20 including the **e** of his power and how he built a
Ne 13: 7 and learned the **e** of this evil deed of Eliashib—
Job 38:18 Do you realize the **e** of the earth? Tell me about it
Mic 6: 2 He will prosecute them to the full **e** of the law.
Jn 13: 1 He now showed the disciples the full **e** of his love.
1Co 11:18 you meet as a church, and to some **e** I believe it.

EXTERMINATED (1)

2Ki 23:24 Josiah also **e** the mediums and psychics,

EXTERNAL (1)

Heb 9:10 **e** regulations that are in effect only until their

EXTINGUISH (1)

Jn 1: 5 the darkness, and the darkness can never **e** it.

EXTORT (1) [EXTORTED, EXTORTING, EXTORTION, EXTORTIONERS]

Lk 3:14 John replied, "Don't **e** money, and don't accuse

EXTORTED (2) [EXTORT]

2Ki 15:20 Menahem **e** the money from the rich of Israel,
Isa 3:14 filling your barns with grain **e** from helpless

EXTORTING (1) [EXTORT]

Eze 22:25 innocent people, seizing treasures and **e** wealth.

EXTORTION (6) [EXTORT]

Lev 6: 2 or they have taken something by theft or **e**.
6: 4 give back whatever they have taken by theft or **e**,
Ps 62:10 Don't try to get rich / by **e** or robbery. / And if
Ecc 7: 7 **E** turns wise people into fools, and bribes corrupt
Mic 6:12 rich among you have become wealthy through **e**
Hab 2: 6 get what you deserve for your oppression and **e**!'

EXTORTIONERS (1) [EXTORT]

Eze 22:12 loan racketeers, and **e** everywhere!

EXTRA (23)

Ge 48:22 And I give you an **e** portion beyond what I have
Ex 26:12 An **e** half sheet of this roof covering will be left to
26:13 and the covering will hang down an **e** eighteen
26:23 along with an **e** frame at each corner.
36:28 plus an **e** frame at each corner.
Nu 3:48 and his sons as the redemption price for the **e**
28:11 present an **e** burnt offering to the LORD of two
Jdg 19: 3 and an **e** donkey to Bethlehem to persuade her to
2Ch 8:13 **E** sacrifices were offered on the Sabbaths, on new
Pr 6:10 A little **e** sleep, a little more slumber, a little
24:33 A little **e** sleep, a little more slumber, a little
Isa 3: 7 "I can't help. I don't have any **e** food or clothes.
Am 4: 5 Then give your **e** voluntary offerings so you can
Mt 10:10 Don't carry a traveler's bag with an **e** coat
23: 5 On their arms they wear **e** wide prayer boxes with
23: 5 and they wear **e** long tassels on their robes.
25: 4 but the other five were wise enough to take along **e**
Mk 6: 9 to wear sandals but not to take even an **e** coat.
Lk 9: 3 nor food, nor money. Not even an **e** coat.
10: 4 or a traveler's bag, or even an **e** pair of sandals.
22:35 a traveler's bag, or **e** clothing, did you lack
1Co 7:28 I am trying to spare you the **e** problems that come
12:24 put the body together in such a way that **e** honor

EXTREME (3) [EXTREMELY]

Jos 15:21 the borders of Edom in the **e** south are Kabzeel,
Eze 46:19 He showed me a place at the **e** west end of these
48: 1 is to receive. The territory of Dan is in the **e** north.

EXTREMELY (4) [EXTREME]

Ge 18:20 that the people of Sodom and Gomorrah are **e** evil,
Nu 11:10 tents weeping, and the LORD became **e** angry.
Dt 9:13 been watching this people, and they are **e** stubborn.
Ezr 10:13 for many of us are involved in this **e** sinful affair.

EXULT (6) [EXULTATION]

1Ch 16:10 **E** in his holy name; / O worshipers of the LORD,
Ps 89:16 They **e** in your righteousness.
105: 3 **E** in his holy name; / O worshipers of the LORD,
149: 2 O people of Jerusalem, **e** in your King.
Eze 31:14 Let no other nation proudly **e** in its own prosperity,
Zep 3:17 He will **e** over you by singing a happy song."

EXULTATION (1) [EXULT]

Isa 52: 5 enslaved again? Those who rule them shout in **e**.

EYE (53) [EYEBROWS, EYELIDS, EYES, EYESIGHT, EYEWITNESS, EYEWITNESSES, SHARP-EYED]

Ex 21:24 If an **e** is injured, injure the **e** of the person who did it.
21:26 or female slave in the **e** and the **e** is blinded, then the slave may go free because of the **e**.
Lev 21:20 a humped back or is a dwarf, or has a defective **e**,
24:20 fracture for fracture, **e** for **e**, tooth for tooth.
Dt 19:21 **e** for **e**, tooth for tooth, hand for hand, foot for
1Sa 11: 2 I will gouge out the right **e** of every one of you as a
18: 9 So from that time on Saul kept a jealous **e** on
Job 14: 3 Must you keep an **e** on such a frail creature
28: 7 no bird of prey can see, no falcon's **e** observe—
Ps 17: 8 Guard me as the apple of your **e**. / Hide me in the
101: 6 I will keep a protective **e** on the godly, / so they
Pr 15: 3 keeping his **e** on both the evil and the good.
30:17 The **e** that mocks a father and despises a mother
Isa 64: 4 no ear has heard and no **e** has seen a God like you,
Zec 11:17 The sword will cut his arm and pierce his right **e**!
11:17 become useless, and his right **e** completely blind!"
Mt 5:28 **e** has already committed adultery with her in his
5:29 So if your **e**—even if it is your good **e**—
5:38 'If an **e** is injured, injure the **e** of the person who did it.
6:22 "Your **e** is a lamp for your body. A pure **e** lets sunshine into your soul.
6:23 But an evil **e** shuts out the light and plunges you
7: 3 And why worry about a speck in your friend's **e**
7: 4 let me help you get rid of that speck in your **e**,'
7: 4 when you can't see past the log in your own **e**?
7: 5 First get rid of the log from your own **e**,
7: 5 enough to deal with the speck in your friend's **e**.
18: 9 And if your **e** causes you to sin, gouge it out
19:24 it is easier for a camel to go through the **e** of a
Mk 9:47 And if your **e** causes you to sin, gouge it out.
10:25 It is easier for a camel to go through the **e** of a
Lk 6:41 "And why worry about a speck in your friend's **e**
6:42 let me help you get rid of that speck in your **e**,'
6:42 when you can't see past the log in your own **e**?
6:42 First get rid of the log from your own **e**;
6:42 enough to deal with the speck in your friend's **e**!
11:34 Your **e** is a lamp for your body. A pure **e** lets sunshine into your soul. But an evil **e** shuts out the light and plunges you
18:25 It is easier for a camel to go through the **e** of a
Ac 13: 9 Holy Spirit, looked the sorcerer in the **e** and said,
1Co 2: 9 when they say, / "No **e** has seen, no ear has heard,
12:16 the body because I am only an ear and not an **e**,"
12:17 Suppose the whole body were an **e**—then how
12:21 The **e** can never say to the hand, "I don't need
15:52 It will happen in a moment, in the blinking of an **e**,

EYEBROWS (1) [EYE]

Lev 14: 9 including the hair of the beard and **e**, and wash

EYELIDS (3) [EYE]

2Ki 9:30 she painted her **e** and fixed her hair and sat at a
Ps 132: 4 not let my eyes sleep / nor close my **e** in slumber
Eze 23:40 you bathed yourselves, painted your **e**,

EYES (244) [EYE]

Ge 3: 5 "God knows that your **e** will be opened when you
3: 7 At that moment, their **e** were opened, and they
21:19 Then God opened Hagar's **e**, and she saw a well.
29:11 Then Jacob kissed Rachel, and tears came to his **e**.
29:17 Leah had pretty **e**, but Rachel was beautiful in
42:24 and had him tied up right before their **e**.
46:30 for I have seen you with my own **e** and know you
47:19 Why should we die before your very **e**? Buy us
49:12 His **e** are darker than wine, / and his teeth are
Lev 26:16 causing your **e** to fail and your life to ebb away.
Nu 22:31 Then the LORD opened Balaam's **e**, and he saw
24: 3 the prophecy of the man whose **e** see clearly,
24: 4 the Almighty, / who falls down with **e** wide open:
24:15 the prophecy of the man whose **e** see clearly,
24:16 the Almighty, / who falls down with **e** wide open:
25: 6 right before the **e** of Moses and all the people,
33:55 those who remain will be like splinters in your **e**
Dt 4:34 God did for you in Egypt, right before your very **e**.
6:22 Before our **e** the LORD did miraculous signs
7:19 You saw it all with your own **e**! And remember the
9:17 to the ground. I smashed them before your very **e**.
11: 7 all the LORD's mighty deeds with your own **e**!
16:19 for bribes blind the **e** of the wise and corrupt the
28:31 Your ox will be butchered before your **e**, but you
29: 2 "You have seen with your own **e** everything the
29: 4 that understand, nor **e** that see, nor ears that hear!
Jos 3: 7 "Today I will begin to make you great in the **e** of
4:14 That day the LORD made Joshua great in the **e** of
4:23 your God dried up the river right before your **e**,
23:13 to you, a pain in your side and a thorn in your **e**,
24: 7 With your very own **e** you saw what I did.
24:17 He performed mighty miracles before our very **e**.
Jdg 7:17 Then he said to them, "Keep your **e** on me.
16:21 the Philistines captured him and gouged out his **e**.
16:28 may pay back the Philistines for the loss of my **e**."
17: 6 people did whatever seemed right in their own **e**.
21:25 people did whatever seemed right in their own **e**.
1Sa 16:12 He was ruddy and handsome, with pleasant **e**.
24:10 This very day you can see with your own **e** it isn't
2Sa 22:28 but your **e** are on the proud to humiliate them.
1Ki 8:52 "May your **e** be open to my requests and to the
10: 7 it until I arrived here and saw it with my own **e**.
20:38 having placed a bandage over his **e** to disguise
20:41 Then the prophet pulled the bandage from his **e**,
2Ki 4:34 his **e** on the child's **e**, and his hands on the
4:35 the boy sneezed seven times and opened his **e**!
6:17 "O LORD, open his **e** and let him see!"
6:17 The LORD opened his servant's **e**, and when he
6:20 "O LORD, now open their **e** and let them see."
19:16 and hear! Open your **e**, O LORD, and see!
25: 7 Then they gouged out Zedekiah's **e**, bound him in
2Ch 7:16 My **e** and my heart will always be here.
9: 6 it until I arrived here and saw it with my own **e**.
16: 9 The **e** of the LORD search the whole earth in
Ezr 9: 8 Our God has brightened our **e** and granted us some
Est 7: 8 queen right here in the palace, before my very **e**?"
Job 4:16 There was a form before my **e**, and a hushed voice
7: 8 for long. Your **e** will be on me, but I will be dead.
9: 2 But how can a person be declared innocent in the **e**
9:24 and God blinds the **e** of the judges and lets them be
10: 4 Are your **e** only those of a human? Do you see
16: 9 gnashes his teeth at me and pierces me with his **e**.
16:16 My **e** are red with weeping; darkness covers my **e**.
17: 7 My **e** are dim with weeping, and I am but a shadow
19:27 him for myself. Yes, I will see him with my own **e**.
21:20 Let their own **e** see their destruction. Let them
28:21 For it is hidden from the **e** of all humanity.
29:15 I served as **e** for the blind and feet for the lame.
31: 1 "I made a covenant with my **e** not to look with lust
31: 7 or if my heart has lusted for what my **e** have seen,
34:22 is thick enough to hide the wicked from his **e**.
36: 7 His **e** never leave the innocent, but he establishes
39:29 it hunts its prey, keeping watch with piercing **e**.
41:18 it flashes light! Its **e** are like the red of dawn.
42: 5 but now I have seen you with my own **e**.
Ps 6: 7 my **e** are worn out because of all my enemies.
13: 3 my God! / Restore the light to my **e**, or I will die.
25: 7 look instead through the **e** of your unfailing love,
25:15 My **e** are always looking to the LORD for help,

34:15 The e of the LORD watch over those who do
35:21 "Aha! / With our own e we saw him do it!"
69: 3 and dry. / My e are swollen with weeping,
69:23 Let their e go blind so they cannot see, / and let
88: 9 My e are blinded by my tears. / Each day I beg for
91: 8 But you will see it with your e; / you will see how
92:11 With my own e I have seen the downfall of my
94: 9 ears deaf? / Is the one who formed your e blind?
115: 5 they have mouths, / or see, though they have e!
116: 8 He has saved me from death, / my e from tears,
119:18 Open my e to see / the wonderful truths in your
119:37 Turn my e from worthless things, / and give me
119:82 My e are straining to see your promises come true.
119:123 My e strain to see your deliverance, / to see the
119:136 Rivers of tears gush from my e / because people
123: 1 I lift my e to you, / O God, enthroned in heaven.
123: 2 just as servants keep their e on their master,
131: 1 my heart is not proud; / my e are not haughty.
132: 4 I will not let my e sleep / nor close my eyelids in
135:16 they have mouths, / or see, though they have e!
145:15 All e look to you for help; / you give them their
146: 8 The LORD opens the e of the blind.
Pr 4:25 and fix your e on what lies before you.
6:13 to their friends by making signs with their e
6:17 haughty e, / a lying tongue, / hands that kill the
10:26 They are like smoke in the e or vinegar that sets
16: 2 People may be pure in their own e, but the LORD
16:30 With narrowed e, they plot evil; without a word,
17:24 Sensible people keep their e glued on wisdom,
17:24 but a fool's e wander to the ends of the earth.
20:12 Ears to hear and e to see—both are gifts from the
20:13 Keep your e open, and there will be plenty to eat!
21: 4 Haughty e, a proud heart, and evil actions are all
23:26 May your e delight in my ways of wisdom.
23:29 has unnecessary bruises? Who has bloodshot e?
28:27 But a curse will come upon those who close their e
29:13 the LORD gives light to the e of both.
Ecc 12: 2 of the sun and moon and stars is dim to your old e,
SS 1:15 how beautiful! Your e are soft like doves."
4: 1 Your e behind your veil are like doves.
4: 9 I am overcome by one glance of your e, by a single
5:12 His e are like doves beside brooks of water;
6: 5 Look away, for your e overcome me! Your hair,
7: 4 Your e are like the sparkling pools in Heshbon by
Isa 3:16 Their e rove among the crowds, flirting with the
6:10 Close their ears, and shut their e. That way, they
will not see with their e, hear with
13:16 will be dashed to death right before their e.
29:10 He has closed the e of your prophets
30:20 You will see your teacher with your own e,
33:15 who shut their e to all enticement to do wrong.
33:17 Your e will see the king in all his splendor,
35: 5 he will open the e of the blind and unstop the ears
37:17 and hear! Open your e, O LORD, and see!
38:14 My e grew tired of looking to heaven for help.
40:17 In his e they are less than nothing—
42: 7 You will open the e of the blind and free the
43: 8 Bring out the people who have e but are blind,
44:18 Their e are closed, and they cannot see.
52: 8 for before their very e they see the LORD
52:10 his holy power before the e of all the nations.
60: 5 Your e will shine, and your hearts will thrill with
65:12 You deliberately sinned—before my very e—
66: 4 They deliberately sinned—before my very e—
Jer 4:30 Why do you brighten your e with mascara?
5:21 who have e but do not see, who have ears but do
7:30 people of Judah have sinned before my very e,"
9: 1 Oh, that my e were a fountain of tears; I would
9:18 your weeping! Let the tears flow from your e.
13:17 My e will overflow with tears
14: 6 They strain their e looking for grass to eat,
14:17 to them: 'Night and day my e overflow with tears.
16: 9 In your own lifetime, before your very e, I will put
39: 7 Then he gouged out Zedekiah's e, bound him in
51:41 The world can scarcely believe its e at her fall!
52:11 Then they gouged out Zedekiah's e, bound him in
La 3:48 Streams of tears flow from my e because of the
5:17 are sick and weary, and our e grow dim with tears.
Eze 1:18 and they were covered with e all around the edges.
5:14 a mockery in the e of the surrounding nations
6: 9 and lustful e that long for other gods.
7: 4 I will turn my e away and show no pity,
7:22 I will hide my e as these robbers invade my
10:12 the cherubim and the wheels were covered with e.
10:12 The cherubim had e all over their bodies,
12:12 and his e will never see his homeland again.
14:22 You will see with your own e how wicked they
23:27 You will never again cast longing e on those things
36:23 reveal my holiness through you before their very e,
44: 5 of man, take careful notice; use your e and ears.
Da 7: 8 This little horn had e like human e and a mouth
7:20 and had human e and a mouth that was boasting
8: 5 which had one very large horn between its e,
8:21 and the large horn between its e represents the first
9:18 my request. Open your e and see our wretchedness.
10: 6 like lightning, and his e were like flaming torches.
Joel 1:16 watch as our food disappears before our very e.
Mic 7:10 With my own e I will see them trampled down like
Zep 3:20 you as I restore your fortunes before their very e.
Zec 4:10 For these seven lamps represent the e of the
9: 1 and the city of Damascus, for the e of all humanity,
14:12 Their e will shrivel in their sockets, and their
Mal 2: 9 and humiliated in the e of all the people.
Mt 9: 8 crowd as they saw this happen right before their e.
9:29 Then he touched their e and said, "Because of
13:15 they have closed their e— / so their e cannot see,
13:16 "But blessed are your e, because they see;
18: 9 better to enter heaven half blind than to have two e
20:34 Jesus felt sorry for them and touched their e.
26:43 for they just couldn't keep their e open.
Mk 8:18 'You have e—can't you see? You have ears—
8:23 Then, spitting on the man's e, he laid his hands on
8:25 Then Jesus placed his hands over the man's e
9:47 the Kingdom of God half blind than to have two e
14:40 for they just couldn't keep their e open.
Lk 1: 6 Zechariah and Elizabeth were righteous in God's e,
1:15 for he will be great in the e of the Lord. He must
4:21 Scripture has come true today before your very e!"
18:13 and dared not even lift his e to heaven as he
24:31 Suddenly, their e were opened, and they
Jn 9: 6 and smoothed the mud over the blind man's e.
9:11 made mud and smoothed it over my e and told me,
9:15 he told them, "He smoothed the mud over my e,
9:17 and demanded, "This man who opened your e—
9:30 "He healed my e, and yet you don't know
9:32 been able to open the e of someone born blind.
10:21 a demon! Can a demon open the e of the blind?"
12:16 that these Scriptures had come true before their e.
12:40 "The Lord has blinded their e / and hardened their
hearts— / so their e cannot see,
Ac 1:10 As they were straining their e to see him,
3:16 name has caused this healing before your very e.
7:20 Moses was born—a beautiful child in God's e.
9:18 Instantly something like scales fell from Saul's e,
9:40 he said, "Get up, Tabitha." And she opened her e!
26:18 to open their e so they may turn from darkness to
28:27 they have closed their e— / so their e cannot see,
Ro 11: 8 To this very day he has shut their e so they do not
11:10 Let their e go blind so they cannot see, / and let
1Co 1:26 that few of you were wise in the world's e,
9: 1 Haven't I seen Jesus our Lord with my own e?
12:23 So we carefully protect from the e of others those
Gal 4:15 know you would gladly have taken out your own e
Eph 1: 4 us in Christ to be holy and without fault in his e.
Php 3:18 often before, and I say it again with tears in my e,
Heb 4:13 Everything is naked and exposed before his e.
11:27 because he kept his e on the one who is invisible.
12: 2 We do this by keeping our e on Jesus, on whom
1Pe 3:12 The e of the Lord watch over those who do right,
2Pe 1:16 have seen his majestic splendor with our own e.
2:14 They commit adultery with their e, and their lust is
1Jn 1: 1 We saw him with our own e and touched him with
4:14 we have seen with our own e and now testify that
Rev 1:14 as snow. And his e were bright like flames of fire.
2:18 whose e are bright like flames of fire, whose feet
3:18 And buy ointment for your e so you will be able to
4: 6 living beings, each covered with e, front and back.
4: 8 and their wings were covered with e, inside
5: 6 He had seven horns and seven e, which are the
19:12 His e were bright like flames of fire, and on his

EYESIGHT (2) [EYE]
Dt 28:65 to tremble, your e to fail, and your soul to despair.
34: 7 yet his e was clear, and he was as strong as ever.

EYEWITNESS (2) [EYE, WITNESS]
Ex 22:10 and there is no e to report just what happened.
Jn 19:35 This report is from an e giving an accurate

EYEWITNESSES (1) [EYE, WITNESS]
Lk 1: 2 and other e of what God has done in fulfillment of

EZBAI (1)
1Ch 11:37 Hezro from Carmel; / Paarai son of E;

EZBON (2)
Ge 46:16 Haggi, Shuni, E, Eri, Arodi, and Areli.
1Ch 7: 7 The sons of Bela were E, Uzzi, Uzziel, Jerimoth,

EZEKIAS [KJV] See HEZEKIAH

EZEKIEL (3)
Eze 1: 3 gave a message to me, E son of Buzi, a priest,
24:22 Then you will do as E has done. You will not
24:24 E is an example for you to follow; you will do as

EZEM (3)
Jos 15:29 Baalah, Iim, E,
19: 3 Hazar-shual, Balah, E,
1Ch 4:29 Bilhah, E, Tolad,

EZER (10)
Ge 36:21 Dishon, E, and Dishan. These were the Horite
36:27 The sons of E were Bilhan, Zaavan, and Akan.
36:30 Dishon, E, and Dishan. The Horite clans are
1Ch 1:38 Shobal, Zibeon, Anah, Dishon, E, and Dishan.
1:42 The sons of E were Bilhan, Zaavan, and Akan.
4: 4 (the father of Gedor), and E (the father of Hushah).
7:21 Ephraim's sons E and Elead were killed trying to
12: 9 E was their leader. / Obadiah was second.
Ne 3:19 Next to them, E son of Jeshua, the leader of
12:42 Eleazar, Uzzi, Jehohanan, Malkijah, Elam, and E.

EZION-GEBER (7) [GEBER]
Nu 33:35 They left Abronah and camped at E.
33:36 They left E and camped at Kadesh in the
Dt 2: 8 the Arabah Valley that comes up from Elath and E.
1Ki 9:26 Later King Solomon built a fleet of ships at E,
22:48 ships never set sail, for they were wrecked at E.
2Ch 8:17 Later Solomon went to E and Elath, ports in the
20:36 they built a fleet of trading ships at the port of E.

EZRA (27)
Ezr 7: 1 Artaxerxes of Persia, there was a man named E.
7: 6 This E was a scribe, well versed in the law of
7: 8 E arrived in Jerusalem in August of that year.
7:10 This was because E had determined to study
7:11 Artaxerxes had presented a copy of this letter to E,
7:12 from Artaxerxes, the king of kings, to E the priest,
7:21 'You are to give E whatever he requests of you,
7:25 "And you, E, are to use the wisdom God has given
10: 1 While E prayed and made this confession, weeping
10: 2 son of Jehiel, a descendant of Elam, said to E,
10: 5 So E stood up and demanded that the leaders of the
10: 6 Then E left the front of the Temple of God
10:10 Then E the priest stood and said to them:
10:16 E selected leaders to represent their families,
Ne 8: 1 They asked E the scribe to bring out the Book of
8: 2 So on October 8 E the priest brought the scroll of
8: 4 E the scribe stood on a high wooden platform that
8: 5 E stood on the platform in full view of all the
8: 6 Then E praised the LORD, the great God, and all
8: 9 Nehemiah the governor, E the priest and scribe,
8:13 and Levites met with E to go over the law in
8:18 E read from the Book of the Law of God on each
12: 1 and Jeshua the high priest: / Seraiah, Jeremiah, E,
12:13 Meshullam was leader of the family of E.
12:26 the governor and of E the priest and scribe.
12:33 along with Azariah, E, Meshullam,
12:36 the man of God. E the scribe led this procession.

EZRAH (1) [EZRAHITE]
1Ch 4:17 The sons of E were Jether, Mered, Epher,

EZRAHITE (3) [EZRAH]
1Ki 4:31 including Ethan the E and Heman, Calcol,
Ps 88: T of Affliction." A psalm of Heman the E. A song.
89: T A psalm of Ethan the E.

EZRI (1)
1Ch 27:26 E son of Kelub was in charge of the field workers

F

FABLES [KJV] See MYTHS, TALES

FABRIC (9) [FABRICS]
Lev 13:48 some woolen or linen f, the hide of an animal,
13:49 affected area in the clothing, the animal hide, the f,
13:53 has not spread in the clothing, the f, or the leather,
13:56 cut the spot from the clothing, the f, or the leather.
13:59 infectious mildew in woolen or linen clothing or f,
19:19 wear clothing woven from two different kinds of f.
Jdg 16:13 the seven braids of my hair into the f on your loom
16:13 Delilah wove the seven braids of his hair into the f
16:14 and yanked his hair away from the loom and the f.

FABRICS (1) [FABRIC]
Eze 27:24 They brought choice f to trade—blue cloth,

FACE (213) [FACED, FACES, FACING, RUDDY-FACED]
FACE TO FACE (15) Ge 32:20,30; Ex 33:11; 34:29; Nu 12:8; Dt 5:4; 34:10; Jdg 6:22; Ps 17:15; Eze 20:35; Hos 12:4; Jn 5:37; Ac 25:16; 2Jn 1:12; 3Jn 1:14
FACE...HID/HIDDEN/HIDE/HIDES/HIDING (6) Ex 3:6; Dt 31:17,18; Job 34:29; La 1:8; Rev 6:16
FACE TO THE GROUND (9) Nu 16:4; Jos 5:14; 1Sa 5:3; 20:41; 2Sa 18:28; 24:20; 2Ch 20:18; Da 8:18; 10:9
Ge 6:13 Yes, I will wipe them all from the f of the earth!
17: 3 At this, Abram fell f down in the dust. Then God
24:65 So Rebekah covered her f with her veil.
29:17 in every way, with a lovely f and shapely figure.
32:20 with the presents before meeting him f to f.
32:30 "f of God"—for he said, "I have seen God f to f,
38:15 thought she was a prostitute, since her f was veiled.
43:31 Then he washed his f and came out,
Ex 3: 6 he hid his f in his hands because he was afraid to
9:15 that would have wiped you from the f of the earth.
25:20 The cherubim will f each other, looking down on
26:27 the rear of the Tabernacle, which will f westward.
32:12 kill them and wipe them from the f of the earth.'
33:11 the LORD would speak to Moses f to f,
33:20 But you may not look directly at my f, for no one
33:23 see me from behind. But my f will not be seen."
34:29 he wasn't aware that his f glowed because he had
spoken to the LORD f to f.
34:30 the people of Israel saw the radiance of Moses' f,
34:33 speaking with them, he put a veil over his f.
34:35 and the people would see his f aglow.
Lev 9:24 shouted with joy and fell f down on the ground.

Nu 12: 8 I speak to him f to f, directly and not in riddles!
12: 14 said to Moses, "If her father had spit in her f,
14: 5 and Aaron fell f down on the ground before the
14: 43 When you f the Amalekites and Canaanites in
16: 4 he threw himself down with his f to the ground.
16: 22 But Moses and Aaron fell f down on the ground.
16: 45 But Moses and Aaron fell f down on the ground.
20: 6 where they fell f down on the ground.
22: 5 They cover the f of the earth and are threatening
22: 31 Balaam fell f down on the ground before him.
Dt 5: 4 The LORD spoke to you f to f from the heart
6: 15 against you and wipe you from the f of the earth.
7: 24 and you will erase their names from the f of the
20: 1 and you f horses and chariots and an army greater
25: 9 pull his sandal from his foot, and spit in his f.
31: 17 I will abandon them, hiding my f from them,
31: 18 At that time I will hide my f from them on account
34: 10 like Moses, whom the LORD knew f to f.
Jos 5: 14 Joshua fell with his f to the ground in reverence.
7: 9 will surround us and wipe us off the f of the earth.
7: 10 "Get up! Why are you lying on your f like this?
Jdg 6: 22 I have seen the angel of the LORD f to f!"
19: 27 She was lying f down, with her hands on the
1Sa 4: 7 We have never had to f anything like this before!
5: 3 Dagon had fallen with his f to the ground in front
5: 4 the idol had fallen f down before the Ark of the
17: 4 came out of the Philistine ranks to f the forces of
17: 49 and fell f downward to the ground.
20: 41 Then David bowed to Jonathan with his f to the
2Sa 2: 22 I will never be able to f your brother Joab if I have
13: 19 And then, with her f in her hands, she went away
14: 4 she fell with her f down to the floor in front of him
14: 7 and family will disappear from the f of the earth."
18: 28 He bowed low with his f to the ground and said,
19: 4 The king covered his f with his hands and kept on
22: 6 ropes around me; / death itself stared me in the f.
24: 20 and bowed before the king with his f to the ground.
1Ki 19: 13 he wrapped his f in his cloak and went out
21: 4 The king went to bed with his f to the wall
22: 24 walked up to Micaiah and slapped him across the f.
2Ki 4: 29 Go quickly and lay the staff on the child's f."
4: 31 hurried on ahead and laid the staff on the child's f,
8: 15 in water, and held it over the king's f until he died.
20: 2 he turned his f to the wall and prayed to the
2Ch 7: 3 they fell f down on the ground and worshiped
7: 14 and pray and seek my f and turn from their wicked
18: 23 walked up to Micaiah and slapped him across the f.
20: 18 Then King Jehoshaphat bowed down with his f to
30: 9 he will not continue to turn his f from you."
Ezr 9: 6 I am utterly ashamed; I blush to lift up my f to you.
Est 7: 8 his attendants covered Haman's f, signaling his
Job 1: 11 he has, and he will surely curse you to your f!"
2: 5 his health, and he will surely curse you to your f!"
4: 15 A spirit swept past my f. Its wind sent shivers up
6: 28 Look at me! Would I lie to your f?
11: 15 Then your f will brighten in innocence. You will
13: 15 Let me speak—and I will f the consequences.
13: 20 two things I beg of you, and I will be able to f you.
17: 6 of me among the people; they spit in my f.
24: 15 me then.' He masks his f so no one will know him.
30: 10 and won't come near me, except to spit in my f.
30: 12 These outcasts oppose me to my f. They send me
31: 14 how could I f God? What could I say when he
31: 36 I would f the accusation proudly. I would treasure
34: 29 But when he hides his f, who can find him?
Ps 3: 7 my God! / Slap all my enemies in the f!
4: 6 Let the smile of your f shine on us, LORD.
11: 7 Those who do what is right will see his f.
17: 15 will be fully satisfied, / for I will see you f to f.
18: 5 ropes around me; / death itself stared me in the f.
21: 10 You will wipe their children from the f of the
34: 16 But the LORD turns his f against those who do
34: 19 The righteous f many troubles, / but the LORD
44: 25 We collapse in the dust, / lying f down in the dirt.
60: 4 honor you— / a rallying point in the f of attack.
62: 4 They are friendly to my f, / but they curse me in
67: 1 May his f shine with favor upon us. / *Interlude*
69: 7 for your sake; / humiliation is written all over my f.
80: 3 Make your f shine down upon us. / Only then will
80: 7 Make your f shine down upon us. / Only then will
80: 19 Make your f shine down upon us. / Only then will
88: 14 Why do you turn your f away from me?
104: 35 Let all sinners vanish from the f of the earth;
112: 8 and fearless / and can f their foes triumphantly.
Pr 5: 14 of utter ruin, and now I must f public disgrace."
15: 13 A glad heart makes a happy f; a broken heart
27: 19 As a f is reflected in water, so the heart reflects the
30: 14 They destroy the needy from the f of the earth.
Ecc 8: 1 Wisdom lights up a person's f, softening its
8: 8 And in the f of death, wickedness will certainly not
SS 6: 5 Your hair, as it falls across your f, is like a flock of
Isa 24: 1 See how he is scattering the people over the f of
38: 2 he turned his f to the wall and prayed to the
50: 6 from shame, for they mock me and spit in my f.
50: 7 Therefore, I have set my f like a stone,
54: 8 In a moment of anger I turned my f away for a
65: 3 All day long they insult me to my f by worshiping
Jer 2: 23 valley in the land! F the awful sins you have done.
19: 8 I will wipe Jerusalem from the f of the earth,
La 1: 8 All she can do is groan and hide her f.
3: 29 Let them lie f down in the dust; then at last there is
Eze 1: 10 Each had a human f in the front, the f of a lion on the right side, the f of an ox on the left side, and the f of an eagle at the back.
1: 28 When I saw it, I fell f down in the dust, and I heard
3: 23 by the Kebar River. And I fell f down in the dust.
9: 8 I fell f down in the dust and cried out,
10: 14 the first was the f of an ox, the second was a human f, the third was the f of a lion, and the fourth was the f of an eagle.
11: 13 Then I fell f down in the dust and cried out,
12: 6 into the night. Cover your f and don't look around.
12: 12 He will cover his f, and his eyes will never see his
20: 35 of the nations, and there I will judge you f to f.
21: 14 to symbolize the great massacre they will f!
34: 6 the mountains and hills, across the f of the earth,
39: 24 I turned my f away and punished them in
40: 3 I saw a man whose f shone like bronze standing
41: 19 One f—that of a man—looked toward the palm
41: 19 The other f—that of a young lion—looked toward
43: 3 And I fell down before him with my f in the dust.
44: 4 and I fell to the ground with my f in the dust.
Da 3: 19 and Abednego that his f became distorted with
5: 6 and his f turned pale with fear. Such terror gripped
5: 9 even more alarmed, and his f turned ashen white.
7: 28 by my thoughts and my f was pale with fear,
8: 18 I fainted and lay there with my f to the ground.
10: 6 From his f came flashes like lightning, and his eyes
10: 8 My strength left me, my f grew deathly pale,
10: 9 I fainted and lay there with my f to the ground.
11: 15 will not be able to stand in the f of the onslaught.
Hos 12: 4 There at Bethel he met God f to f, and God
Joel 2: 6 grips all the people; every f grows pale with fright.
Mic 5: 1 a rod they will strike the leader of Israel in the f.
Mal 3: 2 will be able to stand and f him when he appears?
Mt 6: 17 when you fast, comb your hair and wash your f.
17: 2 so that his f shone like the sun,
17: 6 were terrified and fell f down on the ground.
26: 39 on a little farther and fell f down on the ground,
26: 67 Then they spit in Jesus' f and hit him with their
28: 3 His f shone like lightning, and his clothing was as
Mk 10: 22 At this, the man's f fell, and he went sadly away
14: 35 on a little farther and fell f down on the ground.
14: 65 they blindfolded him and hit his f with their fists.
Lk 5: 12 he fell to the ground, f down in the dust, begging to
9: 29 As he was praying, the appearance of his f changed,
17: 2 f the punishment in store for harming one of these
17: 16 He fell f down on the ground at Jesus' feet,
Jn 5: 37 have never heard his voice or seen him f to f,
11: 44 in graveclothes, his f wrapped in a headcloth.
18: 22 Temple guards standing there struck Jesus on the f.
Ac 6: 15 because his f became as bright as an angel's.
25: 16 to defend themselves f to f with their accusers.
1Co 15: 31 For I swear, dear friends, I f death daily. This is as
2Co 3: 7 people of Israel could not bear to look at Moses' f.
3: 7 For his f shone with the glory of God, even though
3: 13 who put a veil over his f so the people of Israel
4: 6 glory of God that is seen in the f of Jesus Christ.
4: 12 So we live in the f of death, but it has resulted in
11: 20 advantage of you, put on airs, and slap you in the f.
Jas 1: 23 it is like looking at your f in a mirror but doing
1Pe 3: 12 But the Lord turns his f / against those who do
4: 5 But just remember that they will have to f God,
2Pe 2: 6 of ashes and swept them off the f of the earth.
1Jn 4: 17 but we can f him with confidence because we are
2Jn 1: 12 to visit you soon and to talk with you f to f.
3Jn 1: 14 to see you soon, and then we will talk f to f.
Rev 1: 16 And his f was as bright as the sun in all its
4: 7 second looked like an ox; the third had a human f;
6: 16 and hide us from the f of the one who sits on the
7: 11 And they fell f down before the throne
10: 1 His f shone like the sun, and his feet were like
22: 4 And they will see his f, and his name will be

FACED (31) [FACE]

Ex 13: 17 God said, "If the people are f with a battle,
18: 8 He also told him about the problems they had f
37: 9 The cherubim f each other as they looked down on
Jos 8: 33 Each group f the other, and between them stood
1Sa 17: 3 and Israelites f each other on opposite hills,
1Ki 7: 25 Three f north, three f west, three f south, and three f east.
2Ch 3: 13 and f out toward the main room of the Temple.
4: 4 Three f north, three f west, three f south, and three f east.
20: 9 'Whenever we are f with any calamity such as war,
Ne 8: 3 He f the square just inside the Water Gate from
Eze 1: 17 move forward in any of the four directions they f,
10: 11 move forward in any of the four directions they f,
40: 31 The foyer of the south gateway f into the outer
40: 34 Its foyer f into the outer courtyard. It had palm tree
40: 37 Its foyer f into the outer courtyard, and it had palm
41: 11 feet wide. One door f north and the other south.
42: 4 the complex, and all the doors f toward the north.
46: 19 assigned to the priests, which f toward the north.
2Co 6: 5 have been beaten, been put in jail, f angry mobs,
11: 23 times without number, and f death again and again.
11: 26 I have f danger from flooded rivers and from
11: 26 I have f danger from my own people, the Jews,
11: 26 I have f danger in the cities, in the deserts, and on
11: 26 And I have f danger from men who claim to be
Heb 4: 15 for he f all of the same temptations we do, yet he

FACES (34) [FACE]

Ge 40: 6 Joseph noticed the dejected look on their f.
42: 6 bowed low before him, with their f to the ground.
Jdg 13: 20 wife saw this, they fell with their f to the ground.
1Ki 18: 39 they fell on their f and cried out, "The LORD is
1Ch 21: 16 and fell down with their f to the ground.
Ne 8: 6 and worshiped the LORD with their f to the
Ps 34: 5 with joy; / no shadow of shame will darken their f.
44: 15 shame is written across our f.
Pr 10: 8 be instructed, but babbling fools fall flat on their f.
Ecc 11: 10 life before it, still f the threat of meaninglessness.
Isa 3: 9 The very look on their f gives them away
6: 2 With two wings they covered their f, with two they
13: 8 as the flames of the burning city reflect on their f.
57: 4 you mock, making f and sticking out your tongues?
Jer 5: 3 They are determined, with f set like stone;
31: 9 Tears of joy will stream down their f, and I will
La 4: 8 But now their f are blacker than soot. No one even
Eze 1: 6 except that each had four f and two pairs of wings.
9: 2 Six men soon appeared from the upper gate that f
10: 14 Each of the four cherubim had four f—the first was
10: 21 for each had four f and four wings and what looked
10: 22 Their f, too, were just like the f of the beings I had seen at the
27: 35 are filled with horror / and look on with twisted f.
41: 18 with carvings of cherubim, each with two f,
Da 9: 7 but our f are covered with shame, just as you see
Hos 9: 8 he goes. He f hostility even in the house of God.
Mic 3: 7 Then you seers will cover your f in shame, and you
Na 2: 10 The people stand aghast, their f pale and trembling.
Zec 14: 4 Mount of Olives, which f Jerusalem on the east.
Mal 2: 3 and splatter your f with the dung of your festival
Lk 24: 17 They stopped short, sadness written across their f.
Rev 9: 7 gold crowns on their heads, and they had human f.
11: 16 sitting on their thrones before God fell on their f

FACETS (1)

Zec 3: 9 have set before Jeshua, a single stone with seven f.

FACING (27) [FACE]

Jos 5: 13 and saw a man f him with sword in hand.
7: 6 and bowed down f the Ark of the LORD until
18: 14 then ran south along the western edge of the hill f
1Sa 17: 21 and Philistine forces stood f each other,
2Sa 2: 13 f each other from opposite sides of the pool.
1Ki 7: 4 there were three rows of windows f each other.
7: 5 in frame; they were in sets of three, f each other.
7: 25 on a base of twelve bronze oxen, all f outward.
22: 35 and Ahab was propped up in his chariot f the
2Ch 4: 4 on a base of twelve bronze oxen, all f outward.
18: 34 and Ahab propped himself up in his chariot f the
Est 5: 1 king was sitting on his royal throne, f the entrance.
Job 31: 23 That would be better than f the judgment sent by
Ps 38: 17 I am on the verge of collapse, / f constant pain.
116: 6 I was f death, and then he saved me.
Eze 8: 16 They were f eastward, worshiping the sun!
40: 9 end of the gateway structure, f toward the Temple.
40: 13 measuring the distance between the back walls of f
40: 21 and 43-3/4 feet wide between the back walls of f
40: 25 and 43-3/4 feet wide between the back walls of f
40: 44 one beside the north gateway, f south,
40: 44 and the other beside the south gateway, f north.
41: 12 building stood on the west, f the Temple courtyard.
42: 12 So there was an entrance in the wall f the doors of
Mk 15: 39 When the Roman officer who stood f him saw how
1Co 15: 30 continually risking our lives, f death hour by hour?
Rev 2: 10 Remain faithful even when f death, and I will give

FACT (76) [FACTS]

Ge 25: 34 indifferent to the f that he had given up his
31: 42 In f, except for the grace of God—the God of my
41: 19 in f, I've never seen such ugly animals in all the
Ex 1: 7 In f, they multiplied so quickly that they soon
6: 1 In f, he will be so anxious to get rid of them that he
11: 1 In f, he will be so anxious to get rid of you that he
12: 41 In f, it was on the last day of the 430th year that all
13: 7 In f, there must be no yeast in your homes
24: 11 In f, they shared a meal together in God's
34: 3 In f, no one is allowed anywhere on the mountain.
35: 33 in carving wood. In f, he has every necessary skill.
Lev 25: 22 In f, you will eat from the old crop until the new
26: 7 In f, you will chase down all your enemies
27: 10 But if such an exchange is in f made, then both the
27: 33 If any exchange is in f made, then both the original
Nu 4: 16 In f, the supervision of the entire Tabernacle
14: 44 despite the f that neither Moses nor the Ark of the
Jdg 1: 32 In f, because they did not drive them out,
1Sa 15: 9 and lambs—everything, in f, that appealed to them.
18: 10 The very next day, in f, a tormenting spirit from
25: 16 In f, day and night they were like a wall of
2Sa 3: 36 In f, everything the king did pleased them!
1Ki 2: 14 In f, I have a favor to ask of you." "What is it?"
4: 30 In f, his wisdom exceeded that of all the wise men
1Ch 12: 38 In f, all Israel agreed that David should be their
Ezr 4: 15 In f, it was destroyed because of its long history of
4: 19 In f, rebellion and sedition are normal there!
Ne 1: 4 In f, for days I mourned, fasted, and prayed to the
Job 1: 3 He was, in f, the richest person in that entire area.
42: 10 In f, the LORD gave him twice as much as
Pr 18: 15 always open to new ideas. In f, they look for them.
Ecc 7: 11 wise is as good as being rich; in f, it is better.
7: 15 including the f that some good people die young
Hos 1: 5 In f, I will put an end to Israel's independence by
Zec 14: 21 In f, every cooking pot in Jerusalem and Judah will
Mt 13: 34 In f, he never spoke to them without using such
24: 22 In f, unless that time of calamity is shortened,
Mk 4: 34 In f, in his public teaching he taught only with
5: 26 but she had gotten no better. In f, she was worse.
13: 20 In f, unless the Lord shortens that time of calamity,
15: 45 The officer confirmed the f, and Pilate told Joseph
Lk 12: 17 In f, his barns were full to overflowing.
Jn 3: 19 Their judgment is based on this f: The light from
5: 25 in f it is here, when the dead will hear my voice—
5: 33 In f, you sent messengers to listen to John the
7: 19 the law of Moses! In f, you are trying to kill me."

8:17 about something, their witness is accepted as **f**.
16:32 But the time is coming—in **f**, it is already here—
Ac 3:15 raised him to life. And we are witnesses of this **f**!
4:28 In **f**, everything they did occurred according to
19:32 In **f**, most of them didn't even know why they were
19:36 Since this is an indisputable **f**, you shouldn't be
26:7 In **f**, that is why the twelve tribes of Israel worship
Ro 2:27 In **f**, uncircumcised Gentiles who keep God's law
3:31 In **f**, only when we have faith do we truly fulfill the
4:20 In **f**, his faith grew stronger, and in this he brought
7:21 It seems to be a **f** of life that when I want to do
9:7 Just the **f** that they are descendants of Abraham
10:8 In **f**, the Scriptures say, "The message is close at
15:22 In **f**, my visit to you has been delayed so long
16:4 In **f**, they risked their lives for me. I am not the
1Co 9:15 In **f**, I would rather die than lose my distinction of
12:22 In **f**, some of the parts that seem weakest and least
15:20 But the **f** is that Christ has been raised from the
2Co 1:9 In **f**, we expected to die. But as a result, we learned
3:10 In **f**, that first glory was not glorious at all
8:17 In **f**, he himself was eager to go and see you.
9:2 In **f**, it was your enthusiasm that stirred up many of
Gal 2:9 In **f**, James, Peter, and John, who were known as
5:11 The **f** that I am still being persecuted proves that I
Php 1:18 the **f** remains that the message about Christ is
2:27 And he surely was ill; in **f**, he almost died.
3:6 Yes, in **f** I harshly persecuted the church.
Heb 7:15 even more evident from the **f** that a different priest,
9:22 In **f**, we can say that according to the law of
Rev 21:16 In **f**, it was in the form of a cube, for its length

FACTS (8) [FACT]

Dt 13:14 In such cases, you must examine the **f** carefully.
19:15 The **f** of the case must be established by the
Jos 9:16 Three days later, the **f** came out—these people of
1Ki 3:23 Then the king said, "Let's get the **f** straight.
Pr 1:22 How long will you fools fight the **f**?
18:13 what folly, to give advice before listening to the **f**!
Ac 26:22 so that I am still alive today to tell these **f** to
2Co 13:1 "The **f** of every case must be established by the

FADE (12) [FADED, FADES, FADING]

Job 20:8 He will **f** like a dream and not be found. He will
Ps 37:2 For like grass, they soon **f** away. / Like springtime
102:26 change them like a garment, / and they will **f** away.
Isa 24:23 of the sun and moon will seem to **f** away.
40:7 and the flowers **f** beneath the breath of the
40:8 The grass withers, and the flowers **f**, but the word
Na 1:4 dry up, the lush pastures of Bashan and Carmel **f**,
Hab 3:11 The lofty sun and moon began to **f**, obscured by
1Co 9:25 They do it to win a prize that will **f** away, but we
Heb 1:12 They will **f** away like old clothing. / But you are
Jas 1:10 They will **f** away like a flower in the field.
1:11 wealthy people will **f** away with all of their

FADED (5) [FADE]

Lev 13:6 If the affected area has **f** and not spread, the priest
13:21 appear to be more than skin-deep and has **f**,
13:26 appears to be no more than skin-deep and has **f**,
13:28 area has not moved or spread on the skin and has **f**,
13:56 But if the priest sees that the affected area has **f**

FADES (3) [FADE]

Isa 40:6 Their beauty **f** as quickly as the beauty of flowers
Jas 1:11 the grass; the flower withers, and its beauty **f** away.
1Pe 1:24 their beauty **f** as quickly as the beauty of

FADING (6) [FADE]

Ps 109:23 I am **f** like a shadow at dusk; / I am falling like a
Pr 7:9 at twilight, as the day was **f**, as the dark of night set
Jer 6:4 But now the day is **f**, and the evening shadows are
2Co 3:7 even though the brightness was already **f** away.
3:13 so the people of Israel would not see the glory **f**
1Jn 2:17 And this world is **f** away, along with everything it

FAIL (55) [FAILED, FAILING, FAILS, FAILURE, FAILURES]

Ge 47:13 and the crops continued to **f** throughout Egypt
Ex 21:10 or clothing or **f** to sleep with her as his wife.
Lev 8:35 If you **f** in this, you will die. This is what the
26:16 causing your eyes to **f** and your life to ebb away.
26:23 "And if you **f** to learn a lesson from this
Nu 15:22 "But suppose some of you unintentionally **f** to
15:23 **f** to do everything the LORD has commanded
32:23 But if you **f** to keep your word, then you will have
33:55 But if you **f** to drive out the people who live in the
Dt 11:17 and hold back the rain, and your harvests will **f**.
28:65 your eyesight to **f**, and your soul to despair.
31:6 of you. He will neither **f** you nor forsake you."
31:8 with you; he will neither **f** you nor forsake you."
Jos 1:5 I was with Moses. I will not **f** you or abandon you.
1Ki 9:5 'You will never **f** to have a successor on the throne
2Ki 10:10 was spoken concerning Ahab's family will not **f**.
10:19 Any of Baal's worshipers who **f** to come will be
1Ch 28:20 is with you. He will not **f** you or forsake you.
2Ch 7:18 'You will never **f** to have a successor who rules
32:17 my power, so the God of Hezekiah will also **f**."
Ezr 6:9 And without **f**, provide them with the wheat,
Ne 5:13 my robe and said, "If you **f** to keep your promise,
Est 6:10 Do not **f** to carry out everything you have
9:27 They declared they would never **f** to celebrate
Job 21:10 Their bulls never **f** to breed. Their cows bear
Ps 1:3 the riverbank, / bearing fruit each season without **f**.
73:26 My health may **f**, and my spirit may grow weak,
89:30 sons forsake my law / and **f** to walk in my ways,
89:31 not obey my decrees / and **f** to keep my commands,
89:33 stop loving him, / nor let my promise to him **f**.
137:6 if I **f** to remember you, / if I don't make Jerusalem
Pr 23:13 Don't **f** to correct your children. They won't die if
24:10 If you **f** under pressure, your strength is not very
Ecc 10:6 and if they **f** to give people of proven worth their
Isa 16:14 the LORD says, "Within three years, without **f**,
19:5 The waters of the Nile will **f** to rise and flood the
19:9 will have no flax or cotton, for the crops will **f**.
24:7 The grape harvest will **f**, and there will be no wine.
32:10 For your fruit crop will **f**, and the harvest will
Jer 1:19 They will try, but they will **f**. For I am with you,
10:21 Therefore, they **f** completely, and their flocks are
25:10 Your businesses will **f**, and all your homes will
Eze 3:18 but you **f** to deliver the warning, they will die in
17:17 and all his mighty army will **f** to help Israel when
33:8 and you **f** to warn them about changing their ways,
46:15 given as a daily sacrifice every morning without **f**.
47:12 There will be a new crop every month, without **f**!
Da 11:17 the kingdom from within, but his plan will **f**.
Joel 1:17 die in the parched ground, and the grain crops **f**.
Am 2:15 The archers will **f** to stand their ground.
Lk 22:32 prayer for you, Simon, that your faith should not **f**.
Heb 4:1 with fear that some of you might **f** to get there.
13:5 For God has said, / "I will never **f** you. / I will
1Pe 4:19 to the God who made you, for he will never **f** you.
2Pe 1:9 But those who **f** to develop these virtues are blind

FAILED (40) [FAIL]

Ex 8:18 thing with their secret arts, but this time they **f**.
21:36 yet its owner **f** to keep it under control, the money
32:1 When Moses **f** to come back down the mountain
Nu 23:19 Has he ever spoken and **f** to act? / Has he ever
27:14 you **f** to demonstrate my holiness to them at the
Dt 32:51 You **f** to demonstrate my holiness to the people of
Jos 13:13 But the Israelites **f** to drive out the people of
23:14 your God has come true. Not a single one has **f**!
Jdg 1:19 But they **f** to drive out the people living in the
1:21 of Benjamin, however, **f** to drive out the Jebusites,
1:27 The tribe of Manasseh **f** to drive out the people
1:29 The tribe of Ephraim also **f** to drive out the
1:30 The tribe of Zebulun also **f** to drive out the
1:31 The tribe of Asher also **f** to drive out the residents
1:33 The tribe of Naphtali also **f** to drive out the
12:2 "You **f** to help us in our struggle against Ammon.
1Sa 26:16 because you **f** to protect your master, the LORD's
1Ki 8:56 Not one word has **f** of all the wonderful promises
19:2 **f** to take your life like those whom you killed."
22:43 however, he **f** to remove all the pagan shrines,
2Ki 3:26 lines near the king of Edom, but they **f** to escape.
1Ch 10:13 He **f** to obey the LORD's command, and he even
15:13 We **f** to ask God how to move it in the proper
2Ch 20:33 however, he **f** to remove all the pagan shrines,
32:17 "Just as the gods of all the other nations **f** to rescue
Ezr 10:8 Those who **f** to come within three days would,
Ne 10:29 They vowed to accept the curse of God if they **f** to
Ps 77:8 gone forever? / Have his promises permanently **f**?
106:34 Israel **f** to destroy the nations in the land,
Jer 3:3 That is why even the spring rains have **f**. For you
Da 4:18 All the wisest men of my kingdom have **f** me.
5:27 been weighed on the balances and have **f** the test.
Mal 3:7 you have scorned my laws and **f** to obey them.
Mk 7:2 They noticed that some of Jesus' disciples **f** to
Lk 18:34 and they **f** to grasp what he was talking about.
20:26 So they **f** to trap him in the presence of the people.
Ro 9:6 has God **f** to fulfill his promise to the Jews?
2Co 13:5 Christ is among you, it means you have **f** the test.
13:7 to do right even if we ourselves seem to have **f**.
Heb 4:6 But those who formerly heard the Good News **f** to

FAILING (3) [FAIL]

Ge 48:1 word came to Joseph that his father was **f** rapidly.
Nu 9:13 will be cut off from the community of Israel for **f**
Ps 71:9 Don't abandon me when my strength is **f**.

FAILS (5) [FAIL]

Ex 21:11 If he **f** in any of these three ways, she may leave as
21:33 someone digs or uncovers a well and **f** to cover it,
Ps 38:10 My heart beats wildly, my strength **f**, / and I am
111:3 his glory and majesty. / His righteousness never **f**.
Hab 3:17 even though the olive crop **f**, and the fields lie

FAILURE (4) [FAIL]

Ge 41:9 "Today I have been reminded of my **f**," he said.
Job 3:10 Curse it for its **f** to shut my mother's womb,
Ps 78:33 So he ended their lives in **f** / and gave them years
1Th 2:1 and sisters, that our visit to you was not a **f**.

FAILURES (2) [FAIL]

Ge 41:54 There were crop **f** in all the surrounding countries,
Ps 83:17 Make them **f** in everything they do,

FAINT (24) [FAINTED, FAINTING, FAINTS]

1Sa 14:28 be cursed. That is why everyone is weary and **f**."
14:31 Micmash to Aijalon, growing more and more **f**.
28:20 He was also **f** with hunger, for he had eaten
2Sa 16:2 you into the wilderness for those who become **f**."
Job 4:5 now when trouble strikes, you **f** and are broken.
17:5 own advantage, so let their children **f** with hunger.
23:16 God has made my heart **f**; the Almighty has
Ps 84:2 I long, yes, I **f** with longing / to enter the courts of
119:81 I **f** with longing for your salvation; / but I have put
Isa 21:3 I grow **f** when I hear what God is planning; I am
21:4 The sleep I once enjoyed at night is now a **f**
29:8 but is still **f** from thirst when morning comes.
40:28 of all the earth? He never grows **f** or weary.
40:31 and not grow weary. They will walk and not **f**.
44:12 work makes him hungry and thirsty, weak and **f**.
Jer 15:9 The mother of seven grows **f** and gasps for breath;
La 1:22 my sins. My groans are many, and my heart is **f**."
2:19 Plead for your children as they **f** with hunger in the
Eze 21:7 Every spirit will **f**; strong knees will tremble
Am 8:13 and fine young men will grow **f** and weary,
Jnh 4:8 The sun beat down on his head until he grew **f**
Mt 15:32 them away hungry, or they will **f** along the road."
28:4 fear when they saw him, and they fell into a dead **f**.
Mk 8:3 without feeding them, they will **f** along the road.

FAINTED (3) [FAINT]

Isa 51:20 For your children have **f** and lie in the streets,
Da 8:18 I **f** and lay there with my face to the ground.
10:9 I **f** and lay there with my face to the ground.

FAINTING (2) [FAINT]

Job 6:14 "One should be kind to a **f** friend, but you have
La 2:11 Little children and tiny babies are **f** and dying in

FAIR (43) [FAIR-MINDED, FAIREST, FAIRLY, FAIRNESS]

Ge 44:10 "**F** enough," the man replied, "except that only
Dt 1:16 the judges, 'You must be perfectly **f** at all times,
1:17 those who are rich; be **f** to lowly and great alike.
4:8 and regulations as **f** as this body of laws that I am
32:4 work is perfect. / Everything he does is just and **f**.
2Sa 8:15 reigned over all Israel and was **f** to everyone.
1Ki 2:38 Shimei replied, "Your sentence is **f**; I will do
2:42 And you replied, 'The sentence is **f**; I will do as
1Ch 18:14 reigned over all Israel and was **f** to everyone.
Job 23:6 in his greatness? No, he would give me a **f** hearing.
23:7 **F** and honest people can reason with him, so I
29:16 and made sure that even strangers received a **f** trial.
Ps 7:11 God is a judge who is perfectly **f**. / He is angry
19:9 The laws of the LORD are true; / each one is **f**.
82:3 "Give **f** judgment to the poor and the orphan;
119:75 I know, O LORD, that your decisions are **f**;
119:137 you are righteous, / and your decisions are **f**.
119:144 Your decrees are always **f**; / help me to understand
Pr 1:3 good conduct, and doing what is right, just, and **f**.
2:9 Then you will understand what is right, just, and **f**,
29:14 A king who is **f** to the poor will have a long reign.
SS 1:6 you **f** city girls, just because my complexion is
2:10 'Rise up, my beloved, my **f** one, and come away.
2:13 Arise, my beloved, my **f** one, and come away.' "
6:10 the dawn, as **f** as the moon, as bright as the sun,
Isa 33:15 who can live here are those who are honest and **f**,
42:22 They are **f** game for all and have no one to protect
54:14 You will live under a government that is just and **f**.
56:1 "Be just and **f** to all," says the LORD. "Do what
59:4 No one cares about being **f** and honest.
Jer 7:5 wicked thoughts and deeds and are **f** to others;
Eze 18:8 from injustice, is honest and **f** when judging others,
18:16 but instead is **f** to debtors and does not rob them.
Joel 2:3 Ahead of them the land lies as **f** as the Garden of
Am 5:7 and **f** play are meaningless fictions to you.
Mt 16:2 'Red sky at night means **f** weather tomorrow,
Ac 27:8 great difficulty and finally arrived at **F** Havens,
27:12 And since **F** Havens was an exposed harbor—
27:21 to me in the first place and not left **F** Havens.
Ro 3:25 God was being entirely **f** and just when he did not
3:26 And he is entirely **f** and just in this present time
Col 4:1 You slave owners must be just and **f** to your slaves.
Tit 1:8 He must live wisely and be **f**. He must live a

FAIR-MINDED (2) [FAIR, MIND]

Jer 22:3 the LORD says: Be **f** and just. Do what is right!
Mic 7:2 not one **f** person is left on the earth.

FAIREST (1) [FAIR]

La 2:1 The **f** of Israel's cities lies in the dust,

FAIRLY (11) [FAIR]

Lev 19:15 "Always judge your neighbors **f**, neither favoring
Dt 16:18 They will judge the people **f** throughout the land.
2Ch 31:15 dividing the gifts **f** among young and old alike.
Ps 58:1 meaning of the word? / Do you judge the people **f**?
72:2 in the right way; / let the poor always be treated **f**.
96:10 and cannot be shaken. / He will judge all peoples **f**.
112:5 who lend freely and conduct their business **f**.
Isa 58:6 Treat them **f** and give them what they earn.
Zec 7:9 Judge **f** and honestly, and show mercy
1Pe 2:23 his case in the hands of God, who always judges **f**.
Rev 19:11 and True. For he judges **f** and then goes to war.

FAIRNESS (8) [FAIR]

Ps 9:4 from your throne, you have judged with **f**.
9:8 the world with justice / and rule the nations with **f**.
98:9 the world with justice, / and the nations with **f**.
99:4 lover of justice, / you have established **f**.
Pr 16:11 The LORD demands **f** in every business deal;
Isa 9:7 He will rule forever with **f** and justice from the
11:5 He will be clothed with **f** and truth.
59:14 falls dead in the streets, and **f** has been outlawed.

FAIRS [KJV] See WARES

FAITH (235) [FAITHFUL, FAITHFULLY, FAITHFULNESS, FAITHLESS, FAITHLESSNESS]

BY...FAITH (35) Hab 2:4; Ac 26:18; Ro 1:17; 3:30; 4:1,11,13; 5:1; 9:30,32; Gal 2:16; 1Ti 4:6; Heb 10:38; 11:3,4,5,7,7,8,9,11,17,20,21,22,23,24,27,28,29,30,31,33; Jas 2:24,24

IN...FAITH (25) Jdg 9:16,19,20; 1Sa 23:16; Ac 11:24; 14:22; 16:5; Ro 1:12; 14:1,23; 2Co 1:24; Eph 4:13; Col 2:7; 1Th 3:2,7,10; 1Ti 1:2; 2:15; 3:13; 2Ti 1:13; Tit 1:4,13; Jas 2:5; 5:15; 1Pe 5:9

LITTLE FAITH (4) Mt 6:30; 8:26; 16:8; Lk 12:28

THE FAITH (11) Ac 14:22; Ro 14:22; 1Ti 1:2; 6:10,21; 2Ti 1:5,13; 2:18; Tit 1:4,13; Heb 11:32

THROUGH...FAITH (11) Ac 15:9; Ro 1:17; 3:28; 10:6; Gal 2:17; 3:11,14,24,26; 5:5; 2Ti 1:1

Ge 15: 6 LORD declared him righteous because of his **f**.
22: 1 Later on God tested Abraham's **f** and obedience.
Ex 14:31 and put their **f** in him and his servant Moses.
Dt 32:51 For both of you broke **f** with me among the
Jdg 9:16 and in good **f** by making Abimelech your king,
9:19 and in good **f** toward Gideon and his descendants,
9:20 But if you have not acted in good **f**, then may fire
1Sa 23:16 and encouraged him to stay strong in his **f** in God.
Ps 81: 7 of the thundercloud. / I tested your **f** at Meribah,
116: 6 The LORD protects those of childlike **f**; / I was
Hab 2: 4 are crooked; but the righteous will live by their **f**.
Mt 6:30 he more surely care for you? You have so little **f**!
8:10 I haven't seen **f** like this in all the land of Israel!
8:26 You have so little **f**!" Then he stood up
9: 2 Seeing their **f**, Jesus said to the paralyzed man,
9:22 be encouraged! Your **f** has made you well."
9:29 he touched their eyes and said, "Because of your **f**,
14:31 "You don't have much **f**," Jesus said.
15:28 "Woman," Jesus said to her, "your **f** is great.
16: 8 were thinking, so he said, "You have so little **f**!
17:20 "You didn't have enough **f**," Jesus told them.
17:20 even if you had **f** as small as a mustard seed you
18: 6 one of these little ones who trusts in me to lose **f**,
21:21 "I assure you, if you have **f** and don't doubt,
23:23 important things of the law—justice, mercy, and **f**.
Mk 2: 5 Seeing their **f**, Jesus said to the paralyzed man,
4:40 are you so afraid? Do you still not have **f** in me?"
5:34 said to her, "Daughter, your **f** has made you well.
9:42 one of these little ones who trusts in me to lose **f**,
10:15 anyone who doesn't have their kind of **f** will never
10:52 to him, "Go your way. Your **f** has healed you."
11:22 Then Jesus said to the disciples, "Have **f** in God.
Lk 5:20 Seeing their **f**, Jesus said to the man, "Son,
7: 9 I haven't seen **f** like this in all the land of Israel!"
7:50 Jesus said to the woman, "Your **f** has saved you;
8:25 Then he asked them, "Where is your **f**?" And they
8:48 he said to her, "your **f** has made you well.
12:28 he more surely care for you? You have so little **f**!
17: 5 the apostles said to the Lord, "We need more **f**;
17: 6 "Even if you had **f** as small as a mustard seed,"
17:19 "Stand up and go. Your **f** has made you well."
18: 8 of Man, return, how many will I find who have **f**?"
18:17 anyone who doesn't have their kind of **f** will never
18:42 "All right, you can see! Your **f** has healed you."
22:32 prayer for you, Simon, that your **f** should not fail.
Ac 3:16 **F** in Jesus' name has caused this healing before
6: 5 Stephen (a man full of **f** and the Holy Spirit),
6: 5 of Antioch (a Gentile convert to the Jewish **f**,
11:24 a good man, full of the Holy Spirit and strong in **f**.
13: 8 to turn the governor away from the Christian **f**.
14: 9 noticed him and realized he had **f** to be healed.
14:22 They encouraged them to continue in the **f**,
14:27 and how he had opened the door of **f** to the
15: 9 for he also cleansed their hearts through **f**.
15:32 encouraging and strengthening their **f**.
16: 5 So the churches were strengthened in their **f**
20:21 and turning to God, and of **f** in our Lord Jesus.
24:24 they listened as he told them about **f** in Christ
26:18 among God's people, who are set apart by **f** in me.'
Ro 1: 8 Let me say first of all that your **f** in God is
1:12 I'm eager to encourage you in your **f**, but I also
1:17 This is accomplished from start to finish by **f**.
1:17 "It is through **f** that a righteous person has life."
3:27 is not based on our good deeds. It is based on our **f**.
3:28 So we are made right with God through **f** and not
3:30 He makes people right with himself only by **f**,
3:31 Well then, if we emphasize **f**, does this mean that
3:31 only when we have **f** do we truly fulfill the law.
4: 1 concerning this question of being saved by **f**?
4: 5 people are declared righteous because of their **f**,
4: 9 he was declared righteous by God because of his **f**.
4:10 But how did his **f** help him? Was he declared
4:11 ceremony was a sign that Abraham already had **f**
4:11 Abraham is the spiritual father of those who have **f**
4:11 They are made right with God by **f**.
4:12 but only if they have the same kind of **f** Abraham
4:13 on the new relationship with God that comes by **f**.
4:14 in God's sight, then you are saying that **f** is useless.
4:16 So that's why **f** is the key! God's promise is given
4:16 Jewish customs, if we have **f** like Abraham's.
4:19 And Abraham's **f** did not weaken, even though he
4:20 In fact, his **f** grew stronger, and in this he brought
4:22 And because of Abraham's **f**, God declared him to
5: 1 since we have been made right in God's sight by **f**,
5: 2 Because of our **f**, Christ has brought us into this
9:30 The Gentiles have been made right with God by **f**,
9:32 and being good instead of by depending on **f**.
10: 6 But the way of getting right with God through **f**
10:17 Yet **f** comes from listening to this message of
12: 3 measuring your value by how much **f** God has
12: 6 speak out when you have **f** that God is speaking
14: 1 Accept Christians who are weak in **f**, and don't
14:22 You may have the **f** to believe that there is nothing
14:23 They would be condemned for not acting in **f**
16:17 and upset people's **f** by teaching things that are
1Co 12: 9 The Spirit gives special **f** to another, and to
13: 2 And if I had the gift of **f** so that I could speak to a
13: 7 never gives up, never loses **f**, is always hopeful,
13:13 **f**, hope, and love—and the greatest of these is love.
15: 1 for your **f** is built on this wonderful message.
15:17 if Christ has not been raised, then your **f** is useless,
2Co 1:24 to tell you exactly how to put your **f** into practice.
1:24 you will be full of joy as you stand firm in your **f**.
4:13 because we have the same kind of **f** the psalmist
8: 7 you have so much **f**, such gifted speakers,
10:15 we hope that your **f** will grow and that our work
13: 5 Examine yourselves to see if your **f** is really
Gal 1:23 us now preaches the very **f** he tried to destroy!"
2:16 what the law commands, but by **f** in Jesus Christ.
2:16 be accepted by God because of our **f** in Christ—
2:17 seek to be made right with God through **f** in Christ
3: 6 so God declared him righteous because of his **f**."
3: 7 then, are all those who put their **f** in God.
3: 8 accept the Gentiles, too, on the basis of their **f**.
3: 9 All who put their **f** in Christ share the same
blessing Abraham received because of his **f**.
3:11 "It is through **f** that a righteous person has life."
3:12 How different from this way of **f** is the way of law,
3:14 receive the promised Holy Spirit through **f**.
3:23 Until **f** in Christ was shown to us as the way of
3:23 until we could put our **f** in the coming Savior.
3:24 So now, through **f** in Christ, we are made right
3:25 But now that **f** in Christ has come, we no longer
3:26 So you are all children of God through **f** in Christ
4:31 free woman, acceptable to God because of our **f**.
5: 5 promised to us who are right with God through **f**.
5: 6 For when we place our **f** in Christ Jesus, it makes
5: 6 What is important is **f** expressing itself in love.
Eph 1:15 Ever since I first heard of your strong **f** in the Lord
3:12 Because of Christ and our **f** in him, we can now
4: 5 There is only one Lord, one **f**, one baptism,
4:13 until we come to such unity in our **f**
6:16 In every battle you will need **f** as your shield to
6:23 dear friends, and love with **f**, from God the Father
Php 1:25 you will grow and experience the joy of your **f**.
3: 9 way of making us right with himself depends on **f**.
Col 2: 5 you should and because of your strong **f** in Christ.
2: 7 you will grow in **f**, strong and vigorous in the
1Th 1: 8 go we find people telling us about your **f** in God.
3: 2 him to strengthen you, to encourage you in your **f**,
3: 5 I sent Timothy to find out whether your **f** was still
3: 6 bringing the good news that your **f** and love are as
3: 7 because you have remained strong in your **f**.
3:10 fill up anything that may still be missing in your **f**.
5: 8 protected by the body armor of **f** and love,
2Th 1: 3 for we are thankful that your **f** is flourishing
1Ti 1: 2 It is written to Timothy, my true child in the **f**.
1: 4 they don't help people live a life of **f** in God.
1: 5 from a pure heart, a clear conscience, and sincere **f**.
1:14 He filled me completely with **f** and the love of
1:19 Cling tightly to your **f** in Christ, and always keep
1:19 as a result, their **f** has been shipwrecked.
2: 7 and apostle to teach the Gentiles about **f** and truth.
2:15 through childbearing and by continuing to live in **f**,
3: 9 committed to the revealed truths of the Christian **f**
3:13 and will have increased confidence in their **f** in
3:16 Without question, this is the great mystery of our **f**:
4: 6 one who is fed by the message of **f** and the true
4:12 way you live, in your love, your **f**, and your purity.
6:10 have wandered from the **f** and pierced themselves
6:11 along with **f**, love, perseverance, and gentleness.
6:21 Some people have wandered from the **f** by
2Ti 1: 1 the life he has promised through **f** in Christ Jesus.
1: 5 for you have the **f** of your mother, Eunice,
1:13 And remember to live in the **f** and love that you
2:18 and they have undermined the **f** of some.
2:22 Pursue **f** and love and peace, and enjoy the
3: 8 minds are depraved, and their **f** is counterfeit.
3:10 You know my **f** and how long I have suffered.
Tit 1: 1 I have been sent to bring **f** to those God has chosen
1: 4 to Titus, my true child in the **f** that we share.
1:13 sternly as necessary to make them strong in the **f**.
2: 2 They must have strong **f** and be filled with love
Phm 1: 6 You are generous because of your **f**. And I am
Heb 6: 1 away from evil deeds and placing our **f** in God.
6:12 God's promises because of their **f** and patience.
10:38 And a righteous person will live by **f**. / But I will
10:39 seal their fate. We have **f** that assures our salvation.
11: 1 What is **f**? It is the confident assurance that what
11: 2 approval to people in days of old because of their **f**.
11: 3 By **f** we understand that the entire universe was
11: 4 It was by **f** that Abel brought a more acceptable
11: 4 is long dead, he still speaks to us because of his **f**.
11: 5 It was by **f** that Enoch was taken up to heaven
11: 6 you see, it is impossible to please God without **f**.
11: 7 It was by **f** that Noah built an ark to save his family
11: 7 By his **f** he condemned the rest of the world
11: 8 It was by **f** that Abraham obeyed when God called
11: 9 the land God promised him, he lived there by **f**—
11:11 It was by **f** that Sarah together with Abraham was
11:17 It was by **f** that Abraham offered Isaac as a
11:20 It was by **f** that Isaac blessed his two sons, Jacob
11:21 It was by **f** that Jacob, when he was old and dying,
11:22 And it was by **f** that Joseph, when he was about to
11:23 It was by **f** that Moses' parents hid him for three
11:24 It was by **f** that Moses, when he grew up,
11:27 It was by **f** that Moses left the land of Egypt.
11:28 It was by **f** that Moses commanded the people of
11:29 It was by **f** that the people of Israel went right
11:30 It was by **f** that the people of Israel marched
11:31 It was by **f** that Rahab the prostitute did not die
11:32 It would take too long to recount the stories of the **f**
11:33 By **f** these people overthrew kingdoms, ruled with
11:39 received God's approval because of their **f**,
12: 1 by such a huge crowd of witnesses to the life of **f**,
12: 2 on whom our **f** depends from start to finish.
Jas 1: 3 For when your **f** is tested, your endurance has a
2: 1 how can you claim that you have **f** in our glorious
2: 5 God chosen the poor in this world to be rich in **f**?
2:14 what's the use of saying you have **f** if you don't
2:14 by your actions? That kind of **f** can't save anyone.
2:17 So you see, it isn't enough just to have **f**. **F** that
doesn't show itself by good deeds is no **f**
2:18 Now someone may argue, "Some people have **f**;
2:18 "I can't see your **f** if you don't have good deeds,
2:18 but I will show you my **f** through my good deeds."
2:20 When will you ever learn that **f** that does not result
2:22 His **f** was made complete by what he did—by his
2:24 right with God by what we do, not by **f** alone.
2:26 a spirit, so also **f** is dead without good deeds.
5:15 And their prayer offered in **f** will heal the sick,
1Pe 1: 7 These trials are only to test your **f**, to show that it is
1: 7 and your **f** is far more precious to God than mere
1: 7 So if your **f** remains strong after being tried by
1:21 your **f** and hope can be placed confidently in God.
5: 9 a firm stand against him, and be strong in your **f**.
2Pe 1: 1 all of you who share the same precious **f** we have,
1: 1 **f** given to us by Jesus Christ, our God and Savior,
1: 5 Then your **f** will produce a life of moral
Jude 1:20 build your lives on the foundation of your holy **f**.
1:22 Show mercy to those whose **f** is wavering.
Rev 2:19 your love, your **f**, your service, and your patient
13:10 here is your opportunity to have endurance and **f**.
19:10 and other believers who testify of their **f** in Jesus.

FAITHFUL (168) [FAITH]

Ge 24:27 "The LORD has been so kind and **f** to Abraham,
Dt 4: 4 But all of you who were **f** to the LORD your God
7: 9 He is the **f** God who keeps his covenant for a
32: 4 and fair. / He is a **f** God who does no wrong;
33: 8 the sacred lots / to your **f** servants the Levites.
Jos 22: 5 in all his ways, obey his commands, be **f** to him,
23: 8 But be **f** to the LORD your God as you have done
1Sa 2:35 "Then I will raise up a **f** priest who will serve me
20:14 And may you treat me with the **f** love of the
20:15 treat my family with this **f** love, even when the
22:14 among all your servants who is as **f** as David,
2Sa 20:19 I am one who is peace loving and **f** in Israel.
22:26 "To the **f** you show yourself **f**;
1Ki 3: 6 because he was honest and true and **f** to you.
8:61 his people, always be **f** to the LORD our God.
15:14 Asa remained **f** to the LORD throughout his life.
2Ki 12:15 because they were honest and **f** workers.
18: 6 He remained **f** to the LORD in everything,
20: 3 how I have always tried to be **f** to you and do what
1Ch 16:34 for he is good! / His **f** love endures forever.
16:41 to the LORD, "for his **f** love endures forever."
2Ch 1: 8 "You have been so **f** and kind to my father,
5:13 "He is so good! / His **f** love endures forever!"
7: 3 "He is so good! / His **f** love endures forever!"
7: 6 who were singing, "His **f** love endures forever!"
20:21 to the LORD; / his **f** love endures forever!"
31:15 His **f** assistants were Eden, Miniamin, Jeshua,
31:18 For they had all been **f** in purifying themselves.
Ezr 3:11 so good! / His **f** love for Israel endures forever!"
Ne 7: 2 for he was a **f** man who feared God more than
9: 8 When he had proved himself **f**, you made a
Ps 12: 1 The **f** have vanished from the earth!
15: 4 and honor the **f** followers of the LORD
18:25 To the **f** you show yourself **f**; / to those with
31: 5 Rescue me, LORD, for you are a **f** God.
31:23 Love the LORD, all you **f** ones! / For the LORD
50: 5 "Bring my **f** people to me— / those who made a
71:22 because you are **f** to your promises, O God.
85: 8 for he speaks peace to his people, his **f** ones.
89:37 as eternal as the moon, / my **f** witness in the sky!"
89:49 You promised it to David with a **f** pledge.
91: 4 His **f** promises are your armor and protection.
98: 3 remembered his promise to love and be **f** to Israel.
103:18 of those who are **f** to his covenant, / of those who
106: 1 for he is good! / His **f** love endures forever.
107: 1 for he is good! / His **f** love endures forever.
107:43 they will see in our history the **f** love of the
109:21 Rescue me because you are so **f** and good.
118: 1 for he is good! / His **f** love endures forever.
118: 2 of Israel repeat: / "His **f** love endures forever."
118: 3 the priests, repeat: / "His **f** love endures forever."
118: 4 the LORD repeat: / "His **f** love endures forever."
118:29 for he is good! / His **f** love endures forever.
119:30 I have chosen to be **f**; / I have determined to live
119:149 In your **f** love, O LORD, hear my cry; / in your
136: 1 for he is good! / His **f** love endures forever.
136: 2 to the God of gods. / His **f** love endures forever.
136: 3 to the Lord of lords. / His **f** love endures forever.
136: 4 does mighty miracles. / His **f** love endures forever.
136: 5 so skillfully. / His **f** love endures forever.
136: 6 the earth on the water. / His **f** love endures forever.
136: 7 the heavenly lights— / His **f** love endures forever.
136: 8 the sun to rule the day, / His **f** love endures forever.
136: 9 stars to rule the night. / His **f** love endures forever.

136:10 the firstborn of Egypt. / His **f** love endures forever.
136:11 Israel out of Egypt. / His **f** love endures forever.
136:12 and powerful arm. / His **f** love endures forever.
136:13 parted the Red Sea. / His **f** love endures forever.
136:14 Israel safely through, / His **f** love endures forever.
136:15 his army into the sea. / His **f** love endures forever.
136:16 the wilderness. / His **f** love endures forever.
136:17 down mighty kings. / His **f** love endures forever.
136:18 powerful kings— / His **f** love endures forever.
136:19 king of the Amorites, / His **f** love endures forever.
136:20 Og king of Bashan. / His **f** love endures forever.
136:21 as an inheritance— / His **f** love endures forever.
136:22 to his servant Israel. / His **f** love endures forever.
136:23 our utter weakness. / His **f** love endures forever.
136:24 us from our enemies. / His **f** love endures forever.
136:25 to every living thing. / His **f** love endures forever.
136:26 to the God of heaven. / His **f** love endures forever.
138:8 for your **f** love, O LORD, endures forever.
143:1 Answer me because you are **f** and righteous.
145:10 LORD, / and your **f** followers will bless you.
145:13 The LORD is **f** in all he says; / he is gracious in
149:1 Sing his praises in the assembly of the **f**.
149:5 Let the **f** rejoice in this honor. / Let them sing for
149:9 This is the glory of his **f** ones. / Praise the LORD!
Pr 2:8 of justice and protects those who are **f** to him.
20:6 loyal friends, but who can find one who is really **f**?
25:13 **F** messengers are as refreshing as snow in the heat
Isa 1:21 See how Jerusalem, once so **f**, has become a
1:26 be called the Home of Justice and the **F** City."
16:5 From that throne a **f** king will reign, one who
26:2 to all who are righteous; / allow the **f** to enter.
30:18 and compassion. For the LORD is a **f** God.
38:3 how I have always tried to be **f** to you and do what
49:7 He, the **f** LORD, the Holy One of Israel,
Jer 33:11 the LORD is good. / His **f** love endures forever!'
42:5 "May the LORD your God be a **f** witness against
Da 6:4 He was **f** and honest and always responsible.
9:16 In view of all your **f** mercies, Lord, please turn
Hos 2:20 I will be **f** to you and make you mine, and you will
11:12 still walks with God and is **f** to the Holy One.
Zec 8:3 Then Jerusalem will be called the **F** City;
8:8 and I will be **f** and just toward them as their God.
Mal 2:14 though she remained your **f** companion, the wife of
Mt 24:45 "Who is a **f**, sensible servant, to whom the master
25:21 full of praise. 'Well done, my good and **f** servant.
25:21 You have been **f** in handling this small amount,
25:23 master said, 'Well done, my good and **f** servant.
25:23 You have been **f** in handling this small amount,
Lk 12:42 And the Lord replied, "I'm talking to any **f**,
16:10 "Unless you are **f** in small matters, you won't be **f** in large ones.
16:12 And if you are not **f** with other people's money,
19:17 You have been **f** with the little I entrusted to you,
Ac 13:43 two men urged them, "By God's grace, remain **f**."
16:15 "If you agree that I am **f** to the Lord," she said,
20:26 Let me say plainly that I have been **f**. No one's
1Co 4:2 who is put in charge as a manager must be **f**.
4:3 Have I been **f**? Well, it matters very little what you
4:5 the Lord returns as to whether or not someone is **f**.
10:13 And God is **f**. He will keep the temptation from
Eph 1:1 in Ephesus, who are **f** followers of Christ Jesus.
6:21 loved brother and **f** helper in the Lord's work,
Php 2:17 to complete the sacrifice of your **f** service (that is,
2:25 He is a true brother, a **f** worker, and a courageous
Col 1:2 of Colosse, who are **f** brothers and sisters in Christ.
1:7 He is Christ's **f** servant, and he is helping us in
4:7 He is a **f** helper who serves the Lord with me.
4:9 a **f** and much loved brother, one of your own
1Th 1:3 we think of your **f** work, your loving deeds,
5:24 God, who calls you, is **f**; he will do this.
2Th 1:11 will fulfill all your good intentions and **f** deeds.
3:3 But the Lord is **f**; he will make you strong
1Ti 3:2 He must be **f** to his wife. He must exhibit
3:11 and be **f** in everything they do.
3:12 A deacon must be **f** to his wife, and he must
5:9 is at least sixty years old and was **f** to her husband.
2Ti 2:13 If we are unfaithful, / he remains **f**, / for he cannot
3:14 But you must remain **f** to the things you have been
4:7 I have finished the race, and I have remained **f**.
Tit 1:6 He must be **f** to his wife, and his children must be
Heb 2:17 be our merciful and **f** High Priest before God.
3:2 For he was **f** to God, who appointed him, just as
3:5 Moses was certainly **f** in God's house, but only as
3:6 But Christ, the **f** Son, was in charge of the entire
3:14 For if we are **f** to the end, trusting God just as
8:9 They did not remain **f** to my covenant, / so I turned
10:32 Remember how you remained **f** even though it
11:13 All these **f** ones died without receiving what God
13:4 and remain **f** to one another in marriage.
Jas 4:5 has placed within us, jealously longs for us to be **f**?
1Pe 5:12 with the help of Silas, whom I consider a **f** brother.
1Jn 1:9 he is **f** and just to forgive us and to cleanse us from
2:24 So you must remain **f** to what you have been
Jude 1:5 destroyed every one of those who did not remain **f**.
Rev 1:5 Jesus Christ, who is the **f** witness to these things,
2:10 Remain **f** even when facing death, and I will give
2:13 my **f** witness, was martyred among you by Satan's
3:14 the **f** and true witness, the ruler of God's creation:
6:9 the word of God and for being **f** in their witness.
17:14 his people are the called and chosen and **f** ones."
19:11 And the one sitting on the horse was named **F**
22:20 He who is the **f** witness to all these things says,

FAITHFULLY (23) [FAITH]

Ge 17:1 serve me **f** and live a blameless life.
30:29 "You know how **f** I've served you through these
Lev 22:31 "You must **f** keep all my commands by obeying
Dt 7:12 "If you listen to these regulations and obey them **f**,
1Sa 18:13 but David **f** led his troops into battle.
1Ki 2:4 and follow me **f** with all their heart and soul,
4:27 The district governors **f** provided food for King
1Ch 23:32 and **f** carried out their duties of service at the house
2Ch 31:12 the gifts and tithes were **f** brought to the Temple.
32:1 After Hezekiah had **f** carried out this work,
34:12 The workers served **f** under the leadership of
Ne 13:14 and do not forget all that I have **f** done for the
Ps 65:5 You **f** answer our prayers with awesome deeds,
111:8 are forever true, / to be obeyed **f** and with integrity.
Isa 61:8 I will **f** reward my people for their suffering
Jer 23:28 but let my true messengers **f** proclaim my every
25:3 I have **f** passed them on to you, but you have not
32:41 I will rejoice in doing good to them and will **f**
Eze 18:9 and **f** obeys my laws and regulations. Anyone who
44:15 **f** in the Temple when Israel abandoned me for
2Co 6:7 We have **f** preached the truth. God's power has
Heb 3:2 just as Moses served **f** and was entrusted with
Rev 1:2 John **f** reported the word of God and the testimony

FAITHFULNESS (40) [FAITH]

UNFAILING LOVE AND...FAITHFULNESS (14)

Ex 34:6; 2Sa 15:20; Ps 25:10; 40:10,11; 57:3; 61:7; 115:1; 138:2; Pr 14:22; 16:6; 20:28; Jn 1:14,17

Ge 32:10 I am not worthy of all the **f** and unfailing love you
Ex 15:25 them the following conditions to test their **f** to him:
34:6 I am slow to anger and rich in unfailing love and **f**.
2Sa 15:20 the LORD show you his unfailing love and **f**."
Ps 25:10 The LORD leads with unfailing love and **f**
30:9 from the grave? / Can it tell the world of your **f**?
36:5 as the heavens; / your **f** reaches beyond the clouds.
40:10 I have talked about your **f** and saving power.
40:10 in the great assembly / of your unfailing love and **f**.
40:11 My only hope is in your unfailing love and **f**.
57:3 My God will send forth his unfailing love and **f**.
57:10 high as the heavens. / Your **f** reaches to the clouds.
61:7 your unfailing love and **f** to watch over him.
88:11 the place of destruction, can they proclaim your **f**?
89:1 Young and old will hear of your **f**.
89:2 last forever. / Your **f** is as enduring as the heavens.
89:5 myriads of angels will praise you for your **f**.
89:8 mighty as you, LORD? / **F** is your very character.
89:24 My **f** and unfailing love will be with him, / and he
92:2 love in the morning, / your **f** in the evening,
100:5 and his **f** continues to each generation.
108:4 than the heavens. / Your **f** reaches to the clouds.
115:1 goes all the glory / for your unfailing love and **f**.
117:2 the **f** of the LORD endures forever.
119:90 Your **f** extends to every generation, / as enduring
138:2 thanks to your name / for your unfailing love and **f**,
Pr 14:22 plan good, you will be granted unfailing love and **f**.
16:6 Unfailing love and **f** cover sin; evil is avoided by
20:28 Unfailing love and **f** protect the king; his throne is
Isa 38:18 down to destruction / can no longer hope in your **f**.
38:19 Each generation can make known your **f** to the
La 3:23 Great is his **f**; his mercies begin afresh each day.
Hos 4:1 "There is no **f**, no kindness, no knowledge of God
Mic 6:5 did everything I could to teach you about my **f**."
7:20 You will show us your **f** and unfailing love as you
Jn 1:14 He was full of unfailing love and **f**. And we have
1:17 unfailing love and **f** came through Jesus Christ.
Gal 5:22 love, joy, peace, patience, kindness, goodness, **f**,
2Th 1:4 and **f** in all the persecutions and hardships you are
3Jn 1:3 made me very happy by telling me about your **f**

FAITHLESS (15) [FAITH]

Ps 78:57 and were as **f** as their parents had been.
Jer 3:7 come back. And though her **f** sister Judah saw this,
3:8 She saw that I had divorced **f** Israel and sent her
3:10 her **f** sister Judah has never sincerely returned to
3:11 "Even **f** Israel is less guilty than treacherous
3:12 O Israel, my **f** people, come home to me again,
3:20 You have been like a **f** wife who leaves her
Na 3:4 All this because Nineveh, the beautiful and **f** city,
Mal 2:10 Then why are we **f** to each other,
Mt 12:39 **f** generation would ask for a miraculous sign;
16:4 **f** generation would ask for a miraculous sign,
17:17 Jesus replied, "You stubborn, **f** people! How long
Mk 9:19 Jesus said to them, "You **f** people! How long must
Lk 9:41 "You stubborn, **f** people," Jesus said, "how long
Jn 20:27 in my side. Don't be **f** any longer. Believe!"

FAITHLESSNESS (2) [FAITH]

Nu 14:33 In this way, they will pay for your **f**, until the last
Hos 14:4 "Then I will heal you of your idolatry and **f**,

FALCON'S (1)

Job 28:7 that no bird of prey can see, no **f** eye observe—

FALL (207) [FALLEN, FALLING, FALLS, FELL, FELLED]

Ge 2:21 So the LORD God caused Adam to **f** into a deep
7:12 The rain continued to **f** for forty days and forty
27:13 "Let the curse **f** on me, dear son," said Rebekah.
49:26 These blessings will **f** on the head of Joseph,
Ex 9:22 and cause the hail to **f** throughout Egypt,
Lev 19:10 and do not pick up the grapes that **f** to the ground.
25:35 "If any of your Israelite relatives **f** into poverty
26:8 All your enemies will **f** beneath the blows of your
26:36 and you will **f** even when no one is pursuing you.
Nu 11:31 and let them **f** into the camp and all around it!
14:32 for you, your dead bodies will **f** in this wilderness.
22:6 I know that blessings **f** on the people you bless.
Dt 32:2 My teaching will **f** on you like rain; / my speech
32:2 My words will **f** like rain on tender grass,
Jos 6:26 "May the curse of the LORD **f** on anyone
Jdg 15:18 and **f** into the hands of these pagan people?"
21:18 anyone who does this will **f** under God's curse."
1Sa 14:24 "Let a curse **f** on anyone who eats before
2Sa 17:9 he comes out and attacks and a few of your men **f**,
24:14 "But let us **f** into the hands of the LORD,
24:14 mercy is great. Do not let me **f** into human hands."
24:17 Let your anger **f** against me and my family."
2Ki 6:6 "Where did it **f**?" the man of God asked. When he
7:9 some terrible calamity will certainly **f** upon us.
1Ch 21:13 "But let me **f** into the hands of the LORD,
21:13 is very great. Do not let me **f** into human hands."
21:17 let your anger **f** against me and my family,
2Ch 34:11 earlier kings of Judah had allowed to **f** into ruin.
Ne 4:4 May their scoffing **f** back on their own heads,
Job 14:18 "But as mountains **f** and crumble and as rocks **f** from a cliff,
18:4 to be abandoned? Will it make rocks **f** from a cliff?
18:8 They **f** into a pit that's been dug in the path.
28:25 and determined how much rain should **f**.
37:6 "He directs the snow to **f** on the earth and tells the
38:26 Who makes the rain **f** on barren land, in a desert
Ps 7:15 a pit to trap others / and then **f** into it themselves.
10:10 they **f** beneath the strength of the wicked.
20:8 Those nations will **f** down and collapse, / but we
27:2 and foes attack me, / they will stumble and **f**.
27:11 for my enemies are waiting for me to **f**.
27:12 Do not let me **f** into their hands. / For they accuse
35:8 Let them **f** to destruction in the pit they dug for me.
37:24 Though they stumble, they will not **f**,
45:5 The nations **f** before you, / lying down beneath
55:22 of you. / He will not permit the godly to slip and **f**.
72:9 his enemies will **f** before him in the dust.
75:7 he decides who will rise and who will **f**.
78:28 He caused the birds to **f** within their camp / and all
82:7 You will **f** as any prince, / for all must die.' "
91:7 Though a thousand **f** at your side, / though ten
94:23 God will make the sins of evil people **f** back upon
104:23 they labor until the evening shadows **f** again.
119:85 hate your law / have dug deep pits for me to **f** into.
121:3 He will not let you stumble and **f**; / the one who
140:10 Let burning coals **f** down on their heads, / or throw
140:11 Cause disaster to **f** with great force on the violent.
141:10 Let the wicked **f** into their own snares, / but let me
Pr 10:8 but babbling fools **f** flat on their faces.
10:9 but those who follow crooked paths will slip and **f**.
11:5 the wicked **f** beneath their load of sin.
11:8 from danger, but he lets the wicked **f** into trouble.
16:18 goes before destruction, and haughtiness before a **f**.
16:33 the dice, but the LORD determines how they **f**.
22:14 those living under the LORD's displeasure will **f**
24:17 Do not rejoice when your enemies **f** into trouble.
28:10 Those who lead the upright into sin will **f** into their
Ecc 4:10 But people who are alone when they **f** are in real
7:13 Notice the way God does things; then **f** into line.
10:8 When you dig a well, you may **f** in. When you
10:9 work in a quarry, stones might **f** and crush you!
Isa 3:24 ropes for sashes, and their well-set hair will **f** out.
8:14 people to stumble and a rock that makes them **f**.
8:15 Many of them will stumble and **f**, never to rise
10:9 Hamath will **f** before us as Arpad did.
21:2 Babylon will **f**, and the groaning of all the nations
22:25 so firm. It will come out and **f** to the ground.
22:25 Everything it supports will **f** with it. I, the LORD,
24:18 Those who flee in terror will **f** into a trap,
26:19 for joy! / For God's light of life will **f** like dew
31:3 and **f** among those they are trying to help. They will all **f** down and die together.
34:4 The stars will **f** from the sky, just as withered leaves and fruit **f** from a tree.
34:5 It will **f** upon Edom, the nation I have completely
40:20 that must be placed on a stand so it won't **f** down?
41:7 then fasten the thing in place so it won't **f** over.
45:14 They will **f** to their knees in front of you and say,
47:6 and began their punishment by letting them **f** into
47:11 Calamity will **f** upon you, and you won't be able to
59:10 we **f** down as though it were dark.
59:18 His fury will **f** on his foes in distant lands.
63:6 and made them stagger and **f** to the ground."
64:6 Like autumn leaves, we wither and **f**. And our sins,
Jer 5:13 Their predictions of disaster will **f** on
5:24 for he gives us rain each spring and **f**, assuring us
6:9 LORD Almighty says: "Disaster will **f** upon you.
6:21 Fathers and sons will both **f** over them. Neighbors
8:4 When people **f** down, don't they get up again?
10:4 securely with hammer and nails so it won't **f** over.
12:5 If you stumble and **f** on open ground, what will
13:16 you to stumble and **f** on the dark mountains.
14:22 Does it **f** from the sky by itself? No, it comes from
23:12 and treacherous trails, where they will **f**.
25:27 and vomit, and you will **f** to rise no more,
25:32 "Look! Disaster will **f** upon nation after nation!
25:34 you will **f** and shatter like fragile pottery.
32:36 'It will **f** to the king of Babylon through war,
44:12 They will **f** here in Egypt, killed by war
46:6 Euphrates River to the north they stumble and **f**.
46:12 will stumble across each other and **f** together."
46:16 They stumble and **f** over each other and say among
48:26 "Let her stagger and **f** like a drunkard, for she has
48:41 "Her cities will **f**; her strongholds will be seized.
48:44 "Those who flee in terror will **f** into a trap,
49:21 The earth will shake with the noise of Edom's **f**,
49:26 Her young men will **f** in the streets and die.
50:2 so everyone will know that Babylon will **f**!

50:30 Her young men will f in the streets and die.
50:32 O land of pride, you will stumble and f, and no one
50:46 The earth will shake with the noise of Babylon's f,
51: 4 They will f dead in the land of the Babylonians,
51:39 I will make them drink until they f asleep,
51:41 The world can scarcely believe its eyes at her f!
51:57 "They will f asleep and never wake up again!"
La 2: 6 Kings and priests f together before his anger.
3:65 and then let your curse f upon them!
Eze 7:11 Their violence will f back on them as punishment
7:12 for all of them will f under my terrible anger.
13:11 Tell these whitewashers that their wall will soon f
14: 4 so they f into sin and then come to a prophet
14: 7 and set up idols in their hearts so they f into sin,
14:21 of these fearsome punishments f upon Jerusalem—
15: 7 they escape from one fire, they will f into another.
21:29 And now it will f with even greater force on the
26: 2 Tyre has rejoiced over the f of Jerusalem, saying,
26:15 whole coastline will tremble at the sound of your f,
26:18 Now the coastlands tremble at your f. / The islands
30: 6 All of Egypt's allies will f, and the pride of their
30:25 while the arms of Pharaoh f useless to his sides.
31:16 the nations shake with fear at the sound of its f,
32:10 my sword before them on the day of your f.
32:20 The Egyptians will f with the many who have died
32:32 For I have caused my terror to f upon all the living.
36:15 be shamed by them or cause your nation to f,
38:20 cliffs will crumble; walls will f to the earth.
39: 5 You will f in the open fields, for I have spoken,
40: 1 fourteen years after the f of Jerusalem—
44:12 other gods, causing Israel to f into deep sin.
47:12 leaves of these trees will never turn brown and f,
Da 11:19 refuge in his own fortresses but will stumble and f,
11:35 And some who are wise will f victim to
11:41 and many nations will f, but Moab, Edom,
Hos 5: 5 under her load of guilt. Judah, too, will f with her.
10: 8 mountains to bury them and the hills to f on them.
10:14 All your fortifications will f, just as they did when
14: 9 in them. But sinners stumble and f along the way.
Am 2: 2 The people will f in the noise of battle,
3:14 of the altar will be cut off and f to the ground.
8:14 Dan, and Beersheba will f down, never to rise
Ob 1:15 All your evil deeds will f back on your own heads.
Mic 7: 8 my enemies! For though I f, I will rise again.
Na 3: 3 over them, scramble to their feet, and f again.
3:12 All your fortresses will f. They will be devoured like the ripe figs that f into
Hag 2:22 The horses will f, and their riders will kill each
Zec 9: 5 The city of Ashkelon will see Tyre f and will be
11: 6 "I will let them f into each other's clutches,
Mt 7:27 against that house, it will f with a mighty crash."
10:29 can f to the ground without your Father knowing it.
15:14 guides another, they will both f into a ditch."
15:27 "but even dogs are permitted to eat crumbs that f
24:29 will not give light, / the stars will f from the sky,
Mk 3:11 they would f down in front of him shrieking,
9:22 The evil spirit often makes him f into the fire
13:25 the stars will f from the sky, / and the powers of
Lk 6:39 The first one will f into a ditch and pull the other
23:30 People will beg the mountains to f on them
Jn 16: 1 told you these things so that you won't f away.
Ac 5:15 so that Peter's shadow might f across some of them
17:26 He decided beforehand which should rise and f,
27: 9 voyages by then because it was so late in the f,
27:32 So the soldiers cut the ropes and let the boat f off.
Ro 3:23 have sinned; all f short of God's glorious standard.
9:33 people to stumble, / and a rock that makes them f.
11:11 Did God's people stumble and f beyond recovery?
1Co 10:12 be careful, for you too may f into the same sin.
14:25 and they will f down on their knees and worship
Gal 1: 8 Let God's curse f on anyone, including myself,
1: 9 you welcomed, let God's curse f upon that person.
6: 1 And be careful not to f into the same temptation
Eph 3:14 God's plan, I f to my knees and pray to the Father,
1Th 5: 3 then disaster will f upon them as suddenly as a
1Ti 3: 6 and the Devil will use that pride to make him f.
3: 7 so that he will not f into the Devil's trap and be
6: 9 But people who long to be rich f into temptation
Heb 4:11 disobeys God, as the people of Israel did, will f.
10:31 It is a terrible thing to f into the hands of the living
12:13 will not stumble and f but will become strong.
Jas 5: 7 the farmers who eagerly look for the rains in the f
5:17 yet when he prayed earnestly that no rain would f,
1Pe 1:24 The grass withers, / and the flowers f away.
2: 8 people stumble, / the rock that will make them f."
2Pe 1:10 Doing this, you will never stumble or f away.
Rev 4:10 the twenty-four elders f down and worship the one
6:16 "F on us and hide us from the face of the one who
11: 6 so that no rain will f for as long as they prophesy.

FALLEN (50) [FALL]

Jdg 8:24 the treasures you collected from your f enemies."
1Sa 5: 3 Dagon had f with his face to the ground in front of
5: 4 the idol had f face down before the Ark of the
18:20 Saul's daughter Michal had f in love with David,
2Sa 1:19 dead on the hills! / How the mighty heroes have f!
1:25 How the mighty heroes have f in battle!
1:27 How the mighty heroes have f! / Stripped of their
3:38 a great leader and a great man has f today in Israel?
2Ch 29: 8 That is why the LORD's anger has f upon Judah
Job 1:16 "The fire of God has f from heaven and burned up
4: 4 Your words have strengthened the f; you steadied
Ps 9:15 The nations have f into the pit they dug for others.
36:12 Look! They have f! / They have been thrown
57: 6 pit in my path, / but they themselves have f into it.
145:14 The LORD helps the f / and lifts up those bent
Isa 1:18 I can make you as clean as freshly f snow.
9:10 with cut stone, the f sycamore trees with cedars."
14:12 "How you are f from heaven, O shining star,
21: 9 Then the watchman said, "Babylon is f!
24:21 In that day the LORD will punish the f angels in
33: 4 so Jerusalem will strip the f army of Assyria!
33:18 how much plunder they would get from your f city.
Jer 2:25 I have f in love with these foreign gods, and I can't
50:15 Look! She surrenders! Her walls have f.
51: 8 But now suddenly, Babylon, too, has f. Weep for
51:41 "How Babylon is f—great Babylon,
51:44 and worship him. The wall of Babylon has f.
La 2: 8 the ramparts and walls have f down before him.
5:16 The garlands have f from our heads. Disaster has f upon us because we have sinned.
Eze 21:10 Those far stronger than you have f beneath its
31:12 the nations—cut it down and left it f on the ground.
31:13 The birds roosted on its f trunk, and the wild
32:27 They are not buried in honor like the f heroes of
33:21 Jerusalem came to me and said, "The city has f!"
Da 2:39 After that kingdom has f, yet a third great
Am 5: 2 "The virgin Israel has f, / never to rise again!
9:11 "In that day I will restore the f kingdom of David.
Zec 11: 2 the tallest and most beautiful of them are f.
Lk 9:32 and the others were very drowsy and had f asleep.
Jn 11:11 Then he said, "Our friend Lazarus has f asleep,
Ac 15:16 and I will restore the f kingdom of David.
Gal 5: 4 from Christ! You have f away from God's grace.
Rev 2: 5 Look how far you have f from your first love!
9: 1 and I saw a star that had f to earth from the sky,
14: 8 shouting, "Babylon is f—that great city is f—
17:10 Five kings have already f, the sixth now reigns,
18: 2 He gave a mighty shout, "Babylon is f—that great city is f!

FALLING (11) [FALL]

Est 8: 3 f down at his feet and begging him with tears to
Ps 30: 3 You kept me from f into the pit of death.
109:23 I am f like a grasshopper that is brushed aside.
Ecc 12: 5 You will be afraid of heights and of f, white-haired
Jer 6: 4 the day is fading, and the evening shadows are f.
13: 7 But now it was mildewed and f apart. The belt was
Am 4: 7 "I kept the rain from f when you needed it the
Mic 5: 7 dew sent by the LORD or like rain f on the grass,
Lk 10:18 "I saw Satan f from heaven as a flash of lightning!
Ac 1:18 and f there, he burst open, spilling out his
Rev 6:13 green figs f from trees shaken by mighty winds.

FALLOW (1)

Ex 23:11 let the land rest and lie f during the seventh year.

FALLOWDEER [KJV] See ROEBUCKS

FALLS (39) [FALL]

Ex 21:33 to cover it, and then an ox or a donkey f into it.
Lev 11:32 If such an animal dies and f on something,
11:33 "If such an animal dies and f into a clay pot,
11:35 the dead body of such an animal f will be defiled.
11:36 if the dead body of such an animal f into a spring
11:37 If the dead body f on seed grain to be planted in
11:38 But if the seed is wet when the dead body f on it,
Nu 6: 9 because someone suddenly f dead beside them,
24: 4 the Almighty, / who f down with eyes wide open:
24:16 the Almighty, / who f down with eyes wide open:
Dt 20:20 equipment you need to besiege the town until it f.
22: 8 on your household if someone f from the roof.
2Sa 17:12 we can descend on him like the dew that f to the
2Ch 7:13 times I might shut up the heavens so that no rain f,
Job 33:15 in visions of the night when deep sleep f on people
Ps 7:16 violence for others, / but it f on their own heads.
133: 3 that f on the mountains of Zion. / And the LORD
Pr 11:14 Without wise leadership, a nation f; with many
Ecc 4:10 If one person f, the other can reach out and help.
11: 3 When a tree f, whether south or north, there it lies.
SS 4: 1 Your hair f in waves, like flocks of goats frisking
6: 5 Your hair, as it f across your face, is like a flock of
Isa 24:18 Destruction f on you from the heavens. The world
24:20 It f and will not rise again, for its sins are very
30:13 It will be like a bulging wall that bursts and f.
44:17 He f down in front of it, worshiping and praying to
59:14 Truth f dead in the streets, and fairness has been
Jer 50:25 The terror that f upon the Babylonians will be the
Eze 13:12 And when the wall f, the people will cry out,
13:14 to the foundation, and when it f, it will crush you.
Zep 2: 2 before the fierce fury of the LORD f
Mt 17:15 He often f into the fire or into the water.
21:44 to pieces, and it will crush anyone on whom it f."
Lk 14: 5 If your son or your cow f into a pit, don't you
20:18 to pieces, and it will crush anyone on whom it f."
Jn 7:23 For if the correct time for circumcising your son f
9: 4 because there is little time left before the night f
12:35 so you will not stumble when the darkness f.
Heb 6: 7 When the ground soaks up the rain that f on it

FALSE (83) [FALSEHOOD, FALSEHOODS, FALSELY]

FALSE GODS (4) Jer 13:25; 48:35; Jnh 2:8; Na 3:4

FALSE PROPHET(S) (28) Dt 13:5; Isa 44:25; Jer 23:9,28; 27:9,14; Eze 13:2,3; 14:10; 21:29; Hos 4:5; Mic 3:5; Zec 13:2; Mt 7:15; 24:11,24,24; Mk 13:22,22; Lk 6:26; Ac 13:6; 2Pe 2:1; 1Jn 4:1,4; Rev 16:13; 19:20,20; 20:10

FALSE TEACHER(S) (8) Ac 20:29; Gal 4:17; 1Ti 6:3; 2Pe 2:1,1,11,12; Jude 1:8

FALSE VISIONS (4) Eze 12:24; 13:8; 21:29; 22:28

FALSE WITNESS(ES) (9) Pr 6:19; 12:17; 14:5,25; 19:5,9; 21:28; Mt 26:60; Mk 14:56

Ex 23: 1 "Do not pass along f reports. Do not cooperate
Dt 13: 5 The f prophets or dreamers who try to lead you
Job 11:11 For he knows those who are f, and he takes note of
35:14 And it is even more f to say he doesn't see what is
Ps 81: 9 you must not bow down before a f god.
119:104 no wonder I hate every f way of life.
119:128 is right. / That is why I hate every f way.
Pr 6:19 a f witness who pours out lies, / a person who sows
12:17 honest witness tells the truth; a f witness tells lies.
14: 5 witness does not lie; a f witness breathes lies.
14:25 witness saves lives, but a f witness is a traitor.
19: 5 A f witness will not go unpunished, nor will a liar
19: 9 A f witness will not go unpunished, and a liar will
21:28 A f witness will be cut off, but an attentive witness
Isa 1:13 your most pious meetings—are all sinful and f.
11: 3 never judge by appearance, f evidence, or hearsay.
29:21 Those who make the innocent guilty by their f
44:25 I am the one who exposes the f prophets as liars by
58: 9 the helpless and stop making f accusations
63: 8 Surely they will not be f again." And he became
Jer 3:23 orgies on the hills and mountains are completely f.
5:31 the prophets give f prophecies, and the priests rule
13:25 you have forgotten me and put your trust in f gods.
23: 9 My heart is broken because of the f prophets,
23:27 By telling these f dreams, they are trying to get my
23:28 Let these f prophets tell their dreams, but let my
27: 9 " 'Do not listen to your f prophets, fortune-tellers,
27:14 Do not listen to the f prophets who keep telling
48:30 says the LORD, "but her boasts are f;
48:35 the pagan shrines and burn incense to their f gods.
La 2:14 have said so many foolish things, f to the core.
2:14 Instead, they painted f pictures, filling you with f hope.
Eze 12:24 "Then you will see what becomes of all the f
13: 2 speak against the f prophets of Israel who are
13: 3 Destruction is certain for the f prophets who are
13: 7 Can your visions be anything but f if you claim,
13: 8 Because what you say is f and your visions are a
14:10 F prophets and hypocrites—evil people who claim
21:29 and f prophets have given f visions
22:28 And your prophets announce f visions and speak f messages.
Hos 4: 5 as you might at night, and so will your f prophets.
5: 7 Now their f religion will devour them, along with
Am 6: 8 "I despise the pride and f glory of Israel, and I
8: 5 You measure out your grain in f measures
Jnh 2: 8 Those who worship f gods turn their backs on all
Mic 3: 5 This is what the LORD says to you f prophets:
Na 3: 4 She taught them all to worship her f gods,
Zec 8:17 And stop this habit of swearing to things that are f.
10: 2 Household gods give f advice,
13: 2 I will remove from the land all f prophets
Mt 7:15 "Beware of f prophets who come disguised as
16:12 or bread but about the f teaching of the Pharisees
24:11 And many f prophets will appear and will lead
24:24 For f messiahs and f prophets will rise up
26:60 they found many who agreed to give f witness,
Mk 13:22 For f messiahs and f prophets will rise up
14:56 Many f witnesses spoke against him, but they
Lk 6:26 for their ancestors also praised f prophets.
Jn 8:13 "You are making f claims about yourself!"
Ac 13: 6 a Jewish sorcerer, a f prophet named Bar-Jesus.
20:29 I know full well that f teachers, like vicious
21:24 Then everyone will know that the rumors are all f
2Co 11:13 These people are f apostles. They have fooled you
Gal 2: 4 f ones, really—who came to spy on us and see our
4:17 Those f teachers who are so anxious to win your
1Ti 6: 3 Some f teachers may deny these things, but these
2Pe 2: 1 But there were also f prophets in Israel, just as there will be f teachers among you.
2:11 greater in power and strength than these f teachers,
2:12 These f teachers are like unthinking animals,
1Jn 4: 1 For there are many f prophets in the world.
4: 4 You have already won your fight with these f
Jude 1: 8 Yet these f teachers, who claim authority from
Rev 2:24 have not followed this f teaching ('deeper truths,'
16:13 mouth of the dragon, the beast, and the f prophet.
19:20 and with him the f prophet who did mighty
19:20 and his f prophet were thrown alive into the lake of
20:10 with sulfur, joining the beast and the f prophet.

FALSEHOOD (6) [FALSE]

Lev 19:12 "Do not use my name to swear a f and so profane
Ps 119:163 I hate and abhor all f, / but I love your law.
Isa 5:18 drag their sins behind them, tied with cords of f.
Eph 4:25 So put away all f and "tell your neighbor the
1Jn 2:21 you know the difference between truth and f.
Rev 14: 5 No f can be charged against them; they are

FALSEHOODS (1) [FALSE]

Zec 10: 2 interpreters of dreams pronounce comfortless f.

FALSELY (14) [FALSE]

Ex 20:16 "Do not testify f against your neighbor.
23: 7 "Keep far away from f charging anyone with evil.
Lev 6: 2 f telling their neighbor that an item entrusted to
6: 5 or anything gained by swearing f. When they
Dt 5:20 " 'Do not testify f against your neighbor.
18:20 or who f claims to speak for me must die.'
22:14 and f accuses her of having slept with another man.
22:19 pieces of silver, for he f accused a virgin of Israel.
Eze 22: 9 People accuse others f and send them to their

Zec 5: 3 the other side says that those who swear **f** will be
5: 4 and into the house of everyone who swears **f** by
Mt 19: 18 not commit adultery. Do not steal. Do not testify **f**.
Mk 10: 19 Do not steal. Do not testify **f**. Do not cheat.
Lk 18: 20 Do not murder. Do not steal. Do not testify **f**.

FALTER (1)

Lk 21: 26 The courage of many people will **f** because of the

FAME (17) [FAMED, FAMOUS]

Ex 9: 16 and that my **f** might spread throughout the earth.
Nu 14: 15 the nations that have heard of your **f** will say,
1Ki 1: 47 'May your God make Solomon's **f** even greater
4: 31 His **f** spread throughout all the surrounding
1Ch 14: 17 So David's **f** spread everywhere, and the LORD
2Ch 26: 8 and his **f** spread even to Egypt, for he had become
26: 15 His **f** spread far and wide, for the LORD helped
Est 9: 4 and his **f** spread throughout all the provinces as he
Ps 102: 12 Your **f** will endure to every generation.
102: 21 so the LORD's **f** will be celebrated in Zion,
135: 13 your **f**, O LORD, is known to every generation.
Isa 64: 2 your enemies would learn the reason for your **f**!
66: 19 lands beyond the sea that have not heard of my **f**
Eze 16: 14 Your **f** soon spread throughout the world on
16: 15 so you trusted instead in your **f** and beauty.
Mt 9: 31 But instead, they spread his **f** all over the region.
Ro 9: 17 so that my **f** might spread throughout the earth."

FAMED (2) [FAME]

Jer 20: 5 All the **f** treasures of the city—the precious jewels
46: 21 Egypt's **f** mercenaries have become like fattened

FAMILIAR (5)

Ezr 7: 25 If the people are not **f** with those laws, you must
Ac 24: 22 Felix, who was quite **f** with the Way,
26: 26 for I am sure these events are all **f** to him,
Ro 7: 1 Now, dear friends—you who are **f** with the law—
2Co 2: 11 For we are very **f** with his evil schemes.

FAMILIES (133) [FAMILY]

Ge 10: 1 This is the history of the **f** of Shem, Ham,
10: 32 These are the **f** that came from Noah's sons,
12: 3 All the **f** of the earth will be blessed through you."
18: 19 and their **f** to keep the way of the LORD and do
28: 14 All the **f** of the earth will be blessed through you
36: 20 the Horite, one of the **f** native to the land of Seir:
42: 19 rest of you may go on home with grain for your **f**.
42: 33 with me, and take grain for your **f** and go on home.
45: 7 God has sent me here to keep you and your **f** alive
45: 18 Tell them to bring your father and all of their **f**,
50: 21 Indeed, I myself will take care of you and your **f**."
50: 22 his brothers and their **f** continued to live in Egypt.
Ex 1: 21 midwives feared God, he gave them **f** of their own.
12: 21 "Tell each of your **f** to slaughter the lamb they
12: 27 he spared our **f** and did not destroy us.' " Then all
Lev 22: 13 only members of the priests' **f** are allowed to eat
26: 26 one oven will have to be stretched to feed ten **f**.
Nu 1: 2 the whole community of Israel by their clans and **f**.
1: 16 These tribal leaders, heads of their own **f**,
1: 18 according to their ancestry by their clans and **f**.
1: 45 They were counted by **f**—all the men of Israel who
2: 32 the troops of Israel listed by their **f** totaled 603,550.
3: 15 "Take a census of the tribe of Levi by its **f**
4: 2 and **f** of the Kohathite division of the Levite tribe.
4: 22 and **f** of the Gershonite division of the tribe of
4: 29 and **f** of the Merarite division of the Levite tribe.
4: 34 counted the Kohathite division by its clans and **f**.
4: 38 division was also counted by its clans and **f**.
4: 42 division was also counted by its clans and **f**.
4: 46 Israel counted all the Levites by their clans and **f**.
11: 10 Moses heard all the **f** standing in front of their tents
18: 31 and your **f** may eat this food anywhere you wish,
32: 17 our **f** will stay in the fortified cities we build here,
32: 24 Go ahead and build towns for your **f**
34: 14 The **f** of the tribes of Reuben, Gad, and half the
Dt 12: 7 and your **f** will feast in the presence of the LORD
Jos 2: 13 my brothers and sisters, and all their **f**."
7: 17 Then the **f** of Zerah came before the LORD,
13: 15 Moses had assigned the following area to the **f** of
13: 23 as an inheritance to the **f** of the tribe of Reuben.
13: 24 Moses had assigned the following area to the **f** of
13: 28 given as an inheritance to the **f** of the tribe of Gad.
13: 29 Moses had assigned the following area to the **f** of
15: 1 The land assigned to the **f** of the tribe of Judah
15: 12 These are the boundaries for the **f** of the tribe of
15: 20 This was the inheritance given to the **f** of the tribe
16: 4 The **f** of Joseph's sons, Manasseh and Ephraim,
16: 5 The following territory was given to the **f** of the
16: 8 This is the inheritance given to the **f** of the tribe of
17: 2 to the remaining **f** within the tribe of Manasseh:
18: 11 The first allotment of land went to the **f** of the tribe
18: 20 This was the inheritance for the **f** of the tribe of
18: 21 These were the towns given to the **f** of the tribe of
18: 28 This was the inheritance given to the **f** of the tribe
19: 1 The second allotment of land went to the **f** of the
19: 8 This was the inheritance of the **f** of the tribe of
19: 10 The third allotment of land went to the **f** of the
19: 16 This was the inheritance of the **f** of the tribe of
19: 17 The fourth allotment of land went to the **f** of the
19: 23 This was the inheritance of the **f** of the tribe of
19: 24 The fifth allotment of land went to the **f** of the tribe
19: 31 This was the inheritance of the **f** of the tribe of
19: 32 The sixth allotment of land went to the **f** of the
19: 39 This was the inheritance of the **f** of the tribe of
19: 40 and last allotment of land went to the **f** of the tribe
19: 48 This was the inheritance of the **f** of the tribe of
21: 5 The other **f** of the Kohathite clan were allotted ten
Jdg 21: 24 So the assembly of Israel departed by tribes and **f**,
1Sa 9: 21 and my family is the least important of all the **f** of
22: 19 the city of the priests, and killed the priests' **f**—
27: 2 So David took his six hundred men and their **f**
30: 3 the ruins and realized what had happened to their **f**,
2Sa 2: 3 and his men and their **f** all moved to Judah,
15: 22 and his six hundred men and their **f** went along.
1Ki 8: 1 the tribes and **f** of Israel to assemble in Jerusalem.
2Ki 9: 9 as I destroyed the **f** of Jeroboam son of Nebat
1Ch 2: 53 and the **f** of Kiriath-jearim—the Ithrites, Puthites,
2: 55 and the **f** of scribes living at Jabez—the Tirathites,
4: 2 and Lahad. These were the **f** of the Zorathites.
4: 8 Zobebah, and all the **f** of Aharhel son of Harum.
4: 21 the **f** of linen workers at Beth-ashbea,
4: 27 six daughters, but none of his brothers had large **f**.
7: 2 for military service from these **f** was 22,600.
8: 32 All these **f** lived near each other in Jerusalem.
9: 6 In all, 690 **f** from the tribe of Judah returned.
9: 9 In all, 956 **f** from the tribe of Benjamin returned.
9: 34 They were the heads of Levite **f** and were listed as
9: 38 All these **f** lived near each other in Jerusalem.
15: 12 said to them, "You are the leaders of the Levite **f**.
24: 30 were the descendants of Levi in their various **f**.
25: 1 then appointed men from the **f** of Asaph,
25: 7 and their **f** were all trained in making music before
26: 13 They were assigned by **f** for guard duty at the
28: 4 and from among the **f** of Judah, he chose my
2Ch 5: 2 the tribes and **f** of Israel to assemble in Jerusalem.
31: 15 They distributed the gifts among the **f** of priests in
31: 17 who were listed in the genealogical records by **f**,
31: 18 Food allotments were also given to all the **f** listed
35: 5 and help the **f** assigned to you as they bring their
Ezr 2: 40 The **f** of Jeshua and Kadmiel (descendants of
2: 42 The gatekeepers of the **f** of Shallum, Ater, Talmon,
2: 59 that they or their **f** were descendants of Israel.
2: 60 This group consisted of the **f** of Delaiah, Tobiah,
2: 61 Three **f** of priests—Hobaiah, Hakkoz,
10: 16 Ezra selected leaders to represent their **f**,
Ne 4: 13 I stationed the people to stand guard by **f**,
4: 14 fight for your friends, your **f**, and your homes!"
5: 2 They were saying, "We have such large **f**.
7: 43 The **f** of Jeshua and Kadmiel (descendants of
7: 45 The gatekeepers of the **f** of Shallum, Ater, Talmon,
7: 61 that they or their **f** were descendants of Israel.
7: 62 This group included the **f** of Delaiah, Tobiah,
7: 63 "Three **f** of priests—Hobaiah, Hakkoz,
10: 34 the **f** of the priests, Levites, and the common
11: 13 242 of his associates, who were heads of their **f**.
12: 23 The heads of the Levite **f** were recorded in *The*
Ps 68: 6 God places the lonely in **f**; / he sets the prisoners
107: 38 How he blesses them! / They raise large **f** there,
107: 41 and increases their **f** like vast flocks of sheep.
Pr 11: 29 Those who bring trouble on their **f** inherit only the
Jer 2: 4 the LORD, people of Jacob—all you **f** of Israel!
31: 1 "I will be the God of all the **f** of Israel,
35: 2 "Go to the settlement where the **f** of the Recabites
35: 3 and sons—representing all the Recabite **f**.
35: 16 The **f** of Recab have obeyed their ancestor
Eze 47: 22 have joined you and are raising their **f** among you.
Da 1: 3 men of Judah's royal family and other noble **f**,
Am 3: 2 "From among all the **f** on the earth, I chose you
Hab 2: 9 putting your **f** beyond the reach of danger.
Zec 12: 14 Each of the surviving **f** from Judah will mourn
Lk 12: 52 From now on **f** will be split apart, three in favor of
Ac 3: 25 'Through your descendants all the **f** on earth will
Tit 1: 11 they have already turned whole **f** away from the

FAMILY (450) [FAMILIES, FAMILY'S]

Ge 6: 9 This is the history of Noah and his **f**. Noah was a
6: 21 take enough food for your **f** and for all the
7: 1 "Go into the boat with all your **f**, for among all the
11: 10 This is the history of Shem's **f**. When Shem was
11: 27 This is the history of Terah's **f**. Terah was the
17: 12 This applies not only to members of your **f**,
17: 14 from the covenant **f** for violating the covenant."
19: 32 That way we will preserve our **f** line through our
19: 34 with him. That way our **f** line will be preserved."
21: 10 He is not going to share the **f** inheritance with my
23: 9 so I may have a permanent burial place for my **f**."
24: 28 The young woman ran home to tell her **f** about all
24: 40 son from among my relatives, from my father's **f**.
24: 48 to find a wife from the **f** of my master's relatives.
25: 19 This is the history of the **f** of Isaac, the son of
28: 9 So he visited his uncle Ishmael's **f** and married one
29: 19 give her to you than to someone outside the **f**."
30: 30 about me? When should I provide for my own **f**?"
33: 2 Jacob now arranged his **f** into a column, with his
33: 19 Jacob bought the land he camped on from the **f** of
34: 7 had done a disgraceful thing against Jacob's **f**,
34: 19 Shechem was a highly respected member of his **f**,
37: 2 This is the history of Jacob's **f**. When Joseph was
37: 35 His **f** all tried to comfort him, but it was no use.
41: 51 me forget all my troubles and the **f** of my father."
43: 7 "But the man specifically asked us about our **f**,"
46: 6 of Canaan. Jacob and his entire **f** arrived in Egypt
46: 27 there were seventy members of Jacob's **f** in the
47: 5 to Joseph, "Now that your **f** has joined you here,
Ex 1: 1 went with their father to Egypt, each with his **f**:
4: 18 "I would like to go back to Egypt to visit my **f**.
4: 24 when Moses and his **f** had stopped for the night,
6: 16 of Levi, listed according to their **f** groups.
6: 25 the Levite clans, listed according to their **f** groups.
11: 5 All the firstborn sons will die in every **f** in Egypt,
12: 3 tenth day of this month each **f** must choose a lamb
12: 4 If a **f** is too small to eat an entire lamb, let them share the lamb with another **f** in the
12: 4 they share in this way depends on the size of each **f**
12: 6 Then each **f** in the community must slaughter its
16: 18 a little had enough. Each **f** had just what it needed.
16: 21 morning by morning, each **f** according to its need.
Lev 6: 29 Only males from a priest's **f** may eat of this
7: 6 All males from a priest's **f** may eat the meat,
16: 6 to make atonement for himself and his **f**.
16: 11 young bull as a sin offering for himself and his **f**.
16: 17 atonement for himself, his **f**, and all the Israelites.
18: 9 whether she was brought up in the same **f**
22: 10 "No one outside a priest's **f** may ever eat the
22: 12 daughter marries someone outside the priestly **f**,
Nu 1: 4 assisted by one **f** leader from each tribe."
1: 20[-21] each listed according to his own clan and **f**:
1: 52 a designated camping area with its own **f** banner.
2: 2 and the various groups will camp beneath their **f**
2: 3[-4] side of the Tabernacle, beneath their **f** banners.
2: 10[-11] of the Tabernacle, beneath their **f** banner.
2: 17 each in position under the appropriate **f** banner.
2: 18[-19] of the Tabernacle, beneath their **f** banners.
2: 25[-26] of the Tabernacle, beneath their **f** banners.
2: 34 Each clan and **f** set up camp and marched under
3: 1 This is the **f** line of Aaron and Moses as it was
3: 20 the Levite clans, listed according to their **f** groups.
10: 30 I will not go. I must return to my own land and **f**."
18: 11 Any member of your **f** who is ceremonially clean,
18: 13 Any member of your **f** who is ceremonially clean
25: 14 of Salu, the leader of a **f** from the tribe of Simeon.
26: 2 to find out how many of each **f** are of military
31: 26 and the **f** leaders of each tribe are to make a list of
36: 1 to Moses and the **f** leaders of Israel with a petition.
Dt 15: 16 not leave you,' because he loves you and your **f**,
15: 20 and your **f** must eat these animals in the presence
15: 22 Instead, use it for food for your **f** at home.
16: 11 Celebrate with your whole **f**, all your servants,
16: 14 will be a happy time of rejoicing with your **f**,
25: 5 a son, his widow must not marry outside the **f**.
25: 10 Ever afterward his **f** will be referred to as 'the **f** of the man whose sandal was pulled off'!
26: 5 His **f** was few in number, but in Egypt they became
29: 18 this covenant with you so that no man, woman, **f**,
Jos 2: 12 be kind to me and my **f** since I have helped you.
2: 18 And all your **f** members—your father, mother,
6: 22 and bring her out, along with all her **f**."
6: 23 They moved her whole **f** to a safe place near the
7: 1 of the **f** of Zimri, of the clan of Zerah, and of the
7: 14 and the LORD will point out the guilty **f**.
7: 14 each member of the guilty **f** must come one by one.
7: 17 the LORD, and the **f** of Zimri was singled out.
7: 18 Every member of Zimri's **f** was brought forward
7: 25 stoned Achan and his **f** and burned their bodies.
17: 1 the Jordan had already been given to the **f** of Makir
22: 14 and each a leader within the **f** divisions of Israel.
24: 15 But as for me and my **f**, we will serve the
Jdg 1: 25 everyone in the city except for this man and his **f**.
4: 17 because Heber's **f** was on friendly terms with King
6: 15 of Manasseh, and I am the least in my entire **f**!"
8: 27 and it became a trap for Gideon and his **f**.
8: 35 Nor did they show any loyalty to the **f** of Jerubbaal
9: 1 He said to them and to the rest of his mother's **f**,
18: 25 and they might get angry and kill you and your **f**."
18: 30 This **f** continued as priests for the tribe of Dan until
21: 6 "Today we have lost one of the tribes from our **f**;
Ru 2: 20 of our closest relatives, one of our **f** redeemers."
3: 9 covering over me, for you are my **f** redeemer."
3: 10 "You are showing more **f** loyalty now than ever by
3: 12 While it is true that I am one of your **f** redeemers,
4: 1 When the **f** redeemer he had mentioned came by,
4: 3 And Boaz said to the **f** redeemer, "You know
4: 5 on her husband's name and keep the land in the **f**."
4: 6 "Then I can't redeem it," the **f** redeemer replied,
4: 8 So the other **f** redeemer drew off his sandal as he
4: 10 This way she can have a son to carry on the **f** name
4: 10 and to inherit the **f** property here in his hometown.
4: 14 "Praise the LORD who has given you a **f**
4: 18 This is their **f** line beginning with their ancestor
1Sa 1: 1 of Elihu, from the **f** of Tohu and the clan of Zuph.
1: 3 and his **f** would travel to Shiloh to worship
1: 19 The entire **f** got up early the next morning
2: 31 I will put an end to your **f**, so it will no longer
2: 31 All the members of your **f** will die before their
2: 32 But no members of your **f** will ever live out their
2: 35 and his **f** will be priests to my anointed kings
3: 12 to carry out all my threats against Eli and his **f**.
3: 13 him continually that judgment is coming for his **f**,
9: 1 from the **f** of Becorath and the clan of Aphiah.
9: 20 and your **f** are the focus of all Israel's hopes."
9: 21 and my **f** is the least important of all the families of
10: 21 Then he brought each **f** of the tribe of Benjamin
10: 21 the LORD, and the **f** of the Matrites was chosen.
17: 25 and his whole **f** will be exempted from paying
18: 18 and what is my **f** in Israel that I should be the
18: 18 David exclaimed. "My father's **f** is nothing!"
18: 23 "How can a poor man from a humble **f** afford the
20: 6 to go home to Bethlehem for an annual **f** sacrifice.
20: 15 treat my **f** with this faithful love, even when the
20: 29 He wanted to take part in a **f** sacrifice. His brother
22: 11 Saul immediately sent for Ahimelech and all his **f**,
22: 15 Please don't accuse me and my **f** in this matter,
22: 16 surely die, Ahimelech, along with your entire **f**!"
22: 22 Now I have caused the death of all your father's **f**.
24: 21 that when that happens you will not kill my **f**
25: 6 "Peace and prosperity to you, your **f**,
25: 17 going to be trouble for our master and his whole **f**.

2Sa 3:29 Joab and his **f** are the guilty ones. May his **f** in
every generation be cursed with a man
4: 8 has given you revenge on Saul and his entire **f**!"
5: 1 and told him, "We are all members of your **f**.
6:11 The Ark of the LORD remained there with the **f**
6:20 When David returned home to bless his **f**,
6:21 who chose me above your father and his **f**!
7:18 am I, O Sovereign LORD, and what is my **f**,
7:25 do as you have promised concerning me and my **f**.
7:29 may it please you to bless me and my **f** so that our
9: 1 wondering if anyone in Saul's **f** was still alive,
9: 3 asked him, "Is anyone still alive from Saul's **f**?
9: 9 everything that belonged to Saul and his **f**.
9:10 to farm the land for him to produce food for his **f**.
12:10 the sword will be a constant threat to your **f**,
14: 7 Now the rest of the **f** is demanding, 'Let us have
14: 7 and **f** will disappear from the face of the earth."
16: 5 It was Shimei son of Gera, a member of Saul's **f**.
16: 8 is paying you back for murdering Saul and his **f**.
21: 1 and his **f** are guilty of murdering the Gibeonites."
23: 5 "It is my **f** God has chosen! / Yes, he has made an
24:17 Let your anger fall against me and my **f**."
1Ki 2:31 senseless murders from me and from my father's **f**.
4:25 to Beersheba, each **f** had its own home and garden.
11:14 a member of Edom's royal **f**, to be an enemy
12:20 So only the tribe of Judah remained loyal to the **f**
13:34 of Jeroboam's kingdom and the death of all his **f**.
14: 8 I ripped the kingdom away from the **f** of David
14:11 vow that the members of your **f** who die in the city
14:13 He is the only member of your **f** who will have a
14:13 the God of Israel, sees in the entire **f** of Jeroboam.
14:14 over Israel who will destroy the **f** of Jeroboam.
15:29 so that not one of the royal **f** was left,
16: 3 So now I will destroy you and your **f**, just as I
16: 4 Those of your **f** who die in the city will be eaten by
16: 7 and his **f** through the prophet Jehu son of Hanani.
16: 7 just like the **f** of Jeroboam, and also
16: 7 because Baasha had destroyed the **f** of Jeroboam.
16:11 Zimri immediately killed the entire royal **f** of
18:18 "You and your **f** are the troublemakers, for you
21:22 He is going to destroy your **f** as he did the **f**
21:22 son of Nebat and the **f** of Baasha son of Ahijah,
21:24 The members of your **f** who die in the city will be
2Ki 4:13 "No," she replied, "my **f** takes good care of me."
8: 1 "Take your **f** and move to some other place,
8: 2 She took her **f** and lived in the land of the
8:27 followed the evil example of King Ahab's **f**,
8:27 because he was related by marriage to the **f** of
9: 7 You are to destroy the **f** of Ahab, your master.
9: 8 The entire **f** of Ahab must be wiped out—
9: 9 I will destroy the **f** of Ahab as I destroyed the
10:10 that was spoken concerning Ahab's **f** will not fail.
10:17 killed everyone who was left there from Ahab's **f**,
10:30 following my instructions to destroy the **f** of Ahab.
11: 1 she set out to destroy the rest of the royal **f**.
21:13 and by the same measure I used for the **f** of Ahab.
25:25 and grandson of Elishama, who was of the royal **f**,
1Ch 1:24 So this is the **f** line descended from Shem:
2:55 from Hammath, the father of the **f** of Recab.
4:33 and these names are recorded in their **f** genealogy.
7: 7 All of them were listed in their **f** genealogy.
7: 9 According to their **f** genealogy, there were 20,200
7:23 because of the tragedy his **f** had suffered.
9: 4 One **f** that returned was that of Uthai son of
11: 1 and told him, "We are all members of your **f**.
12:27 This included Jehoiada, leader of the **f** of Aaron,
12:28 with twenty-two members of his **f** who were all
13:14 The Ark of God remained there with the **f** of
16:43 and David returned home to bless his **f**.
17:16 "Who am I, O LORD God, and what is my **f**,
17:23 do as you have promised concerning me and my **f**.
17:27 it has pleased you to bless me and my **f** so that our
21:17 my God, let your anger fall against me and my **f**,
23: 7 The Gershonite **f** units were defined by their lines
23: 8 the descendants of Libni were Jehiel (the **f** leader),
23: 9 These were the leaders of the **f** of Libni. Three of
23:11 Jahath was the **f** leader, and Ziza was next. Jeush
and Beriah were counted as a single **f**
23:16 of Gershom included Shebuel, the **f** leader.
23:17 Eliezer had only one son, Rehabiah, the **f** leader.
23:18 of Izhar included Shelomith, the **f** leader.
23:19 The descendants of Hebron included Jeriah (the **f**
23:20 The descendants of Uzziel included Micah (the **f**
23:24 the leaders of their **f** groups, registered carefully by
24: 4 for there were more **f** leaders among the
24: 6 and the **f** leaders of the priests and Levites.
24:20 These were the other **f** leaders descended from
24:31 and the **f** leaders of the priests and the Levites.
26: 1 was Meshelemiah son of Kore, of the **f** of Asaph.
26:12 of the gatekeepers were named for their **f** leaders,
26:21 From the **f** of Libni in the clan of Gershon,
26:26 the **f** leaders, and the generals and captains
28: 4 has chosen me from among all my father's **f** to be
28: 4 the families of Judah, he chose my father's **f**.
29: 6 Then the **f** leaders, the leaders of the tribes of
2Ch 22: 3 also followed the evil example of King Ahab's **f**,
22: 4 members of Ahab's **f** became his advisers,
22: 8 While Jehu was executing judgment against the **f**
22: 9 None of the surviving members of Ahaziah's **f** was
22:10 she set out to destroy the rest of Judah's royal **f**.
29:13 From the **f** of Elizaphan: Shimri and Jeiel. / From
the **f** of Asaph: Zechariah
29:14 From the **f** of Heman: Jehiel and Shimei.
29:14 From the **f** of Jeduthun: Shemaiah and Uzziel.
31:10 the high priest, from the **f** of Zadok, replied,
35: 4 Report for duty according to the **f** divisions of your
35:12 burnt offerings among the people by their **f** groups,
Ezr 2: 3 The **f** of Parosh | 2,172
2: 4 The **f** of Shephatiah | 372
2: 5 The **f** of Arah | 775
2: 6 The **f** of Pahath-moab (descendants of Jeshua
2: 7 The **f** of Elam | 1,254
2: 8 The **f** of Zattu | 945
2: 9 The **f** of Zaccai | 760
2:10 The **f** of Bani | 642
2:11 The **f** of Bebai | 623
2:12 The **f** of Azgad | 1,222
2:13 The **f** of Adonikam | 666
2:14 The **f** of Bigvai | 2,056
2:15 The **f** of Adin | 454
2:16 The **f** of Ater (descendants of Hezekiah) | 98
2:17 The **f** of Bezai | 323
2:18 The **f** of Jorah | 112
2:19 The **f** of Hashum | 223
2:20 The **f** of Gibbar | 95
2:36 The **f** of Jedaiah (through the line of Jeshua)
2:37 The **f** of Immer | 1,052
2:38 The **f** of Pashhur | 1,247
2:39 The **f** of Harim | 1,017
2:41 The singers of the **f** of Asaph | 128
2:61 of Barzillai from Gilead and had taken her **f** name.)
2:68 some of the **f** leaders gave generously toward the
3: 2 and Zerubbabel son of Shealtiel with his **f** began to
3: 9 in this task by the Levites of the **f** of Henadad.
8: 1 Here is a list of the **f** leaders and the genealogies of
8: 2 From the **f** of Phinehas: Gershom. / From the **f** of
Ithamar: Daniel.
8: 3 From the **f** of David: Hattush son of Shecaniah.
8: 3 From the **f** of Parosh: Zechariah and 150 other
8: 4 From the **f** of Pahath-moab: Eliehoenai son of
8: 5 From the **f** of Zattu: Shecaniah son of Jahaziel
8: 6 From the **f** of Adin: Ebed son of Jonathan and 50
8: 7 From the **f** of Elam: Jeshaiah son of Athaliah
8: 8 From the **f** of Shephatiah: Zebadiah son of Michael
8: 9 From the **f** of Joab: Obadiah son of Jehiel and 218
8:10 From the **f** of Bani: Shelomith son of Josiphiah
8:11 From the **f** of Bebai: Zechariah son of Bebai
8:12 From the **f** of Azgad: Johanan son of Hakkatan
8:13 From the **f** of Adonikam, who came later:
8:14 From the **f** of Bigvai: Uthai, Zaccur, and 70 other
10:18 From the **f** of Jeshua son of Jehozadak and his
10:20 From the **f** of Immer: Hanani and Zebadiah.
10:21 From the **f** of Harim: Maaseiah, Elijah, Shemaiah,
10:22 From the **f** of Pashhur: Elioenai, Maaseiah,
10:25 From the **f** of Parosh: Ramiah, Izziah, Malkijah,
10:26 From the **f** of Elam: Mattaniah, Zechariah, Jehiel,
10:27 From the **f** of Zattu: Elioenai, Eliashib, Mattaniah,
10:28 From the **f** of Bebai: Jehohanan, Hananiah, Zabbai,
10:29 From the **f** of Bani: Meshullam, Malluch, Adaiah,
10:30 From the **f** of Pahath-moab: Adna, Kelal, Benaiah,
10:31 From the **f** of Harim: Eliezer, Ishijah, Malkijah,
10:33 From the **f** of Hashum: Mattenai, Mattattah,
10:34 From the **f** of Bani: Maadai, Amram, Uel,
10:38 From the **f** of Binnui: Shimei,
10:43 From the **f** of Nebo: Jeiel, Mattithiah, Zabad,
Ne 1: 6 Yes, even my own **f** and I have sinned!
5: 5 We belong to the same **f**, and our children are just
7: 8 The **f** of Parosh | 2,172
7: 9 The **f** of Shephatiah | 372
7:10 The **f** of Arah | 652
7:11 The **f** of Pahath-moab (descendants of Jeshua
7:12 The **f** of Elam | 1,254
7:13 The **f** of Zattu | 845
7:14 The **f** of Zaccai | 760
7:15 The **f** of Bani | 648
7:16 The **f** of Bebai | 628
7:17 The **f** of Azgad | 2,322
7:18 The **f** of Adonikam | 667
7:19 The **f** of Bigvai | 2,067
7:20 The **f** of Adin | 655
7:21 The **f** of Ater (descendants of Hezekiah) | 98
7:22 The **f** of Hashum | 328
7:23 The **f** of Bezai | 324
7:24 The **f** of Jorah | 112
7:25 The **f** of Gibbar | 95
7:39 The **f** of Jedaiah (through the line of Jeshua)
7:40 The **f** of Immer | 1,052
7:41 The **f** of Pashhur | 1,247
7:42 The **f** of Harim | 1,017
7:44 The singers of the **f** of Asaph | 148
7:63 of Barzillai from Gilead and had taken her **f** name.)
7:70 "Some of the **f** leaders gave gifts for the work.
8:13 On October 9 the **f** leaders and the priests
10: 9 Binnui from the **f** of Henadad, Kadmiel,
11: 4 of Shephatiah, son of Mahalalel, of the **f** of Perez;
11: 5 son of Joiarib, son of Zechariah, of the **f** of Shelah.
11:20 and the rest of the Israelites lived wherever their **f**
11:22 whose **f** served as singers at God's Temple.
12:12 the **f** leaders of the priests were as follows:
12:12 Meraiah was leader of the **f** of Seraiah.
12:12 Hananiah was leader of the **f** of Jeremiah.
12:13 Meshullam was leader of the **f** of Ezra.
12:13 Jehohanan was leader of the **f** of Amariah.
12:14 Jonathan was leader of the **f** of Malluch.
12:14 Joseph was leader of the **f** of Shecaniah.
12:15 Adna was leader of the **f** of Harim.
12:15 Helkai was leader of the **f** of Meremoth.
12:16 Zechariah was leader of the **f** of Iddo.
12:16 Meshullam was leader of the **f** of Ginnethon.
12:17 Zicri was leader of the **f** of Abijah.
12:17 There was also a leader of the **f** of Miniamin.
12:17 Piltai was leader of the **f** of Moadiah.
12:18 Shammua was leader of the **f** of Bilgah.
12:18 Jehonathan was leader of the **f** of Shemaiah.
12:19 Mattenai was leader of the **f** of Joiarib.
12:19 Uzzi was leader of the **f** of Jedaiah.
12:20 Kallai was leader of the **f** of Sallu.
12:20 Eber was leader of the **f** of Amok.
12:21 Hashabiah was leader of the **f** of Hilkiah.
12:21 Nethanel was leader of the **f** of Jedaiah.
12:22 a list was compiled of the **f** leaders of the Levites
12:24 These were the **f** leaders of the Levites: Hashabiah,
Est 2: 7 Mordecai adopted her into his **f** and raised her as
2:10 told anyone of her nationality and **f** background,
2:20 to keep her nationality and **f** background a secret.
8: 6 my people and my **f** slaughtered and destroyed?"
9:28 and celebrated by every **f** throughout the provinces
Job 16: 7 you have ground me down and devastated my **f**.
19:17 repulsive to my wife. I am loathsome to my own **f**.
20: 9 Neither his friends nor his **f** will ever see him
21:21 are dead, they will not care what happens to their **f**.
29:18 'Surely I will die surrounded by my **f** after a long,
Ps 35:14 I was sad, as though they were my friends or **f**,
38:11 my disease. / Even my own **f** stands at a distance.
78:51 He killed the oldest son in each Egyptian **f**,
105:36 each Egyptian home, / the pride and joy of each **f**.
109:13 May his **f** name be blotted out in a single
114: 1 when the **f** of Jacob left that foreign land—
115:12 people of Israel / and the **f** of Aaron, the priests.
122: 8 For the sake of my **f** and friends, I will say,
Pr 7: 4 a sister; make insight a beloved member of your **f**.
8:31 he created—his wide world and all the human **f**!
15:27 Dishonest money brings grief to the whole **f**,
27:27 goats' milk for you, your **f**, and your servants.
Isa 7:13 Isaiah said, "Listen well, you royal **f** of David!
7:17 a terrible curse on you, your nation, and your **f**.
11: 1 Out of the stump of David's **f** will grow a shoot—
22:23 He will bring honor to his **f** name, for I will drive
22:24 honor to even the lowliest members of his **f**."
48: 1 "Listen to me, O **f** of Jacob, who are called by the
48: 1 by the name of Israel and born into the **f** of Judah.
48:12 "Listen to me, O **f** of Jacob, Israel my chosen one!
60:22 The smallest **f** will multiply into a large clan.
Jer 12: 6 members of your own **f**, have turned on you.
21:11 "Say to the royal **f** of Judah, 'Listen to this
22:18 "His **f** will not weep for him when he dies.
23:34 I will punish that person along with his entire **f**.
29:32 I will punish him and his **f**. None of his
31:34 nor will they need to teach their **f**, saying,
36:31 I will punish him and his **f** and his officials
38: 6 It belonged to Malkijah, a member of the royal **f**.
38:17 you surrender to Babylon, you and your **f** will live,
41: 1 of Elishama, who was a member of the royal **f**,
Eze 17:13 He made a treaty with a member of the royal **f**
17:15 this man of Israel's royal **f** rebelled against
43:19 At that time, the Levitical priests of the **f** of Zadok,
44:15 the Levitical priests of the **f** of Zadok continued to
Da 1: 3 palace some of the young men of Judah's royal **f**
Hos 5: 1 Israel's leaders! Listen, all you men of the royal **f**!
Am 3: 1 and Judah—the entire **f** I rescued from Egypt:
5: 4 Now this is what the LORD says to the **f** of Israel:
9: 8 I will never completely destroy the **f** of Israel,"
Mic 2: 2 No one's **f** or inheritance is safe with you around!
2: 7 Should you talk that way, O **f** of Israel?
Zec 12:10 and prayer on the **f** of David and on all the people
12:12 each **f** by itself, with the husbands and wives in
12:12 The **f** of David will mourn, along with the **f** of
Nathan,
12:13 the **f** of Levi, and the **f** of Shimei.
Mt 13:57 in his own hometown and among his own **f**."
24:45 of managing his household and feeding his **f**?
Mk 3:21 When his **f** heard what was happening, they tried
6: 4 and among his relatives and his own **f**."
7:27 told her, "First I should help my own **f**, the Jews.
Lk 1:61 "There is no one in all your **f** by that name."
4:40 people throughout the village brought sick **f**
8:39 go back to your **f** and tell them all the wonderful
9:61 follow you, but first let me say good-bye to my **f**."
12:42 of managing his household and feeding his **f**.
Jn 8:35 A slave is not a permanent member of the **f**, but a
son is part of the **f** forever.
Ro 1: 3 came as a man, born into King David's royal **f** line.
8:15 like God's very own children, adopted into his **f**—
9: 6 for not everyone born into a Jewish **f** is truly a
Gal 4:30 for the son of the slave woman will not share the **f**
Eph 1: 5 **f** by bringing us to himself through Jesus Christ.
2:19 God's holy people. You are members of God's **f**.
Php 3: 5 having been born into a pure-blooded Jewish **f** that
1Ti 3: 4 He must manage his own **f** well, with children who
2Ti 1:16 and all his **f** because he often visited
2: 8 Jesus Christ was a man born into King David's **f**
Heb 8:11 nor will they need to teach their **f**,
11: 7 It was by faith that Noah built an ark to save his **f**
2Pe 2: 5 ancient world—except for Noah and his **f** of seven.
1Jn 3: 9 Those who have been born into God's **f** do not sin,
5:18 part of God's **f** do not make a practice of sinning,

FAMILY'S (2) [FAMILY]

Ge 50: 5 land of Canaan, and bury me in our **f** burial cave.'
2Sa 14: 7 He doesn't deserve to inherit his **f** property.'

FAMINE (96) [FAMINES]

Ge 12:10 At that time there was a severe **f** in the land,
26: 1 Now a severe **f** struck the land, as had happened
41:27 withered heads of grain represent seven years of **f**.
41:30 But afterward there will be seven years of **f**
41:30 be forgotten and wiped out. **F** will destroy the land.
41:31 This **f** will be so terrible that even the memory of
41:36 be enough to eat when the seven years of **f** come.
41:50 before the arrival of the first of the **f** years,

41:54 Then the seven years of f began, just as Joseph had
41:56 So with severe f everywhere in the land,
41:57 because the f was severe throughout the world.
42: 5 to buy food, for the f had reached Canaan as well.
42:12 "You have come to discover how vulnerable the f
43: 1 But there was no relief from the terrible f
45: 6 These two years of f will grow to seven,
45:11 for there are still five years of f ahead of us.
47: 4 our flocks in Canaan. The f is very severe there.
47:13 Meanwhile, the f became worse and worse,
47:20 sold him their fields because the f was so severe,
Dt 32:24 I will send against them wasting f, / burning fever,
Ru 1: 1 in Judah left the country because of a severe f.
2Sa 21: 1 There was a f during David's reign that lasted for
21: 1 "The f has come because Saul and his family are
21:14 After that, God ended the f in the land of Israel.
24:13 "Will you choose three years of f throughout the
1Ki 8:37 "If there is a f in the land, or plagues, or crop
18: 2 the f had become very severe in Samaria.
2Ki 4:38 returned to Gilgal, but there was a f in the land.
6:25 As a result there was a great f in the city. After a
8: 1 for the LORD has called for a f on Israel that will
8: 3 After the f ended she returned to the land of Israel,
25: 3 the f in the city had become very severe,
1Ch 21:12 You may choose three years of f, three months of
2Ch 6:28 "If there is a f in the land, or plagues, or crop
20: 9 faced with any calamity such as war, disease, or f,
32:11 sentencing you to death by f and thirst!
Ne 5: 3 vineyards, and homes to get food during the f."
Job 5:20 He will save you from death in time of f,
5:22 You will laugh at destruction and f; wild animals
Ps 33:19 from death / and keeps them alive in times of f.
37:19 even in f they will have more than enough.
68: 6 But for rebels, there is only f and distress.
105:16 He called for a f on the land of Canaan,
Isa 14:30 in peace. But as for you, I will wipe you out with f.
22: 2 are lying everywhere, killed by f and disease.
51:19 desolation and destruction, f and war. And who is
Jer 5:12 will come upon us! There will be no war or f!
14:12 I will give them only war, f, and disease."
14:13 telling them, 'All is well—no war or f will come.
14:15 They say that no war or f will come, but they themselves will die by war and f!
14:16 into the streets of Jerusalem, victims of f and war.
15: 2 to war; those who are destined for f, to f;
16: 4 They will die from war and f, and their bodies will
21: 7 else in the city have survived war, f, and disease,
21: 9 f, or disease, but those who go out and surrender to
24:10 I will send war, f, and disease until they have
27: 8 I will send war, f, and disease upon that nation
27:13 Why should you choose war, f, and disease,
28: 8 always warning of war, f, and disease.
29:17 "I will send war, f, and disease upon them
29:18 Yes, I will pursue them with war, f, and disease,
32:24 Because of war, f, and disease, the city has been
32:36 the king of Babylon through war, f, and disease.'
34:17 set you free to be destroyed by war, f, and disease.
38: 2 stays in Jerusalem will die from war, f, or disease,
42:14 you think you will be free from war, f, and alarms,
42:16 and f you fear will follow close behind you,
42:17 Yes, you will die from war, f, and disease. None of
42:22 f, and disease in Egypt, where you insist on
44:12 They will fall here in Egypt, killed by war and f.
44:13 punished them in Jerusalem, by war, f, and disease.
44:18 and have suffered the effects of war and f."
44:27 You will suffer war and f until all of you are dead.
52: 6 the f in the city had become very severe,
La 5:10 Because of the f, our skin has been blackened as
Eze 5:12 A third of your people will die in the city from f
5:16 "I will shower you with the deadly arrows of f to
5:16 The f will become more and more severe until
5:17 And along with the f, wild animals will attack you,
6:11 they are going to die from war and f and disease.
6:12 And anyone who survives will be killed by f.
7:15 Those who stay inside will die of f and disease.
12:16 a few of them from death by war, f, or disease,
14:13 and sending a f to destroy both people and animals
14:21 war, f, beasts, and plague—destroying all her
36:29 you good crops, and I will abolish f in the land.
Am 4: 6 brought hunger to every city and f to every town.
8:11 "when I will send a f on the land—
8:11 not a f of bread or water but of hearing the words
Lk 15:14 a great f swept over the land, and he began to
Ac 7:11 "But a f came upon Egypt and Canaan. There was
11:28 a great f was coming upon the entire Roman world.
Rev 6: 8 with the sword and f and disease and wild animals.
18: 8 and f will overtake her in a single day.

FAMINES (4) [FAMINE]

Eze 36:30 nations be able to scoff at your land for its f.
Mt 24: 7 and there will be f and earthquakes in many parts
Mk 13: 8 be earthquakes in many parts of the world, and f.
Lk 21:11 and there will be f and epidemics in many lands,

FAMOUS (25) [FAME]

Ge 12: 2 I will bless you and make you f, and I will make
Dt 9: 2 and tall—descendants of the f Anakite giants.
Jos 6:27 and his name became f throughout the land.
Ru 4:11 May you be great in Ephrathah and f in Bethlehem.
4:14 a family redeemer today! May he be f in Israel.
1Sa 18:30 So David's name became very f throughout the
2Sa 7: 9 Now I will make your name f throughout the earth!
8:13 So David became very f. After his return he
23:18 It was by such feats that he became as f as the
23:19 Abishai was the most f of the Thirty and was their
23:22 deeds that made Benaiah almost as f as the Three.
1Ch 11:20 It was by such feats that he became as f as the
11:21 Abishai was the most f of the Thirty and was their
11:24 of the deeds that made Benaiah as f as the Three.
12: 4 a f warrior and leader among the Thirty;
12:30 there were 20,800 warriors, each f in his own clan.
17: 8 Now I will make your name f throughout the earth!
22: 5 f and glorious throughout the world.
Job 3:14 f for their great construction projects.
Isa 66:19 to the Libyans and Lydians (who are f as archers),
Jer 49:25 That f city, a city of joy, will be forsaken!
Eze 26:11 butcher your people, and your f pillars will topple.
26:17 'O f island city, / once ruler of the sea,
34:29 "And I will give them a land f for its crops,
Am 6: 1 You are f and popular in Israel, you to whom the

FAN (1) [FANNING, FANS]

2Ti 1: 6 This is why I remind you to f into flames the

FANCY (8)

Jdg 5:10 fine donkeys / and sit on f saddle blankets, listen!
14:12 give you thirty plain linen robes and thirty f robes.
14:13 must give me thirty linen robes and thirty f robes."
Am 6: 5 and you f yourselves to be great musicians,
1Co 4:20 For the Kingdom of God is not just f talk; it is
Jas 2: 2 comes into your meeting dressed in f clothes
1Pe 3: 3 the outward beauty that depends on f hairstyles,
Rev 18:14 "All the f things you loved so much are gone,"

FANGS (4) [FANG]

Dt 32:24 They will be troubled by the f of wild beasts,
Job 5:16 have hope, and the f of the wicked are broken.
Ps 58: 6 Break off their f, O God! / Smash the jaws of these
Isa 9:12 With bared f, they will devour Israel. But even

FANNING (1) [FAN]

Eze 16:26 f the flames of my anger with your increasing

FANS (1) [FAN]

Isa 54:16 I have created the blacksmith who f the coals

FAR (267) [AFAR, FAR-OFF, FARTHER, FARTHEST]

Ge 13:14 "Look as f as you can see in every direction.
14: 6 as f as El-paran at the edge of the wilderness.
19: 9 We'll treat you f worse than those other men!"
20:13 When God sent me to travel f from my father's
24: 5 a young woman who will travel so f from home?
31:25 of Gilead, he set up his camp not f from Jacob's.
50:20 As f as I am concerned, God turned into good what
Ex 8:28 But don't go too f away. Now hurry, and pray for
14:12 Our Egyptian slavery was f better than dying out
23: 7 "Keep f away from falsely charging anyone with
33: 7 known as the Tent of Meeting f outside the camp.
Lev 26:36 I will demoralize you in the land of your enemies f
Nu 11:14 all these people by myself! The load is f too heavy!
13:21 the land from the wilderness of Zin as f as Rehob,
14:12 Then I will make you into a nation f greater
14:45 attacked them and chased them as f as Hormah.
16: 3 and Aaron and said, "You have gone too f!
16: 7 You Levites are the ones who have gone too f!"
21:13 Then they moved to the f side of the Arnon River,
21:15 which extend as f as the settlement of Ar on the
21:24 They went only as f as the Ammonite border
21:26 and seized all his land as f as the Arnon River.
21:30 them out / as f away as Nophah and Medeba."
24:17 I perceive him, but f in the distant future.
33:49 as f as Abel-shittim on the plains of Moab.
Dt 2:36 in the gorge, and the whole area as f as Gilead.
3:10 and Bashan as f as the towns of Salecah and Edrei,
4:30 "When those bitter days have come upon you f in
4:38 He drove out nations f greater than you, so he
4:49 of the Jordan Valley as f south as the Dead Sea,
11:30 toward the west, not f from the oaks of Moreh.)
19: 6 the distance to the nearest city of refuge was too f,
30:13 is not beyond the sea, so f away that you must ask,
34: 1 him the whole land, from Gilead as f as Dan;
34: 3 with Jericho—the city of palms—as f as Zoar.
Jos 7: 5 chased the Israelites from the city gate as f as the
9: 1 and along the coast of the Mediterranean Sea as f
11: 8 The Israelites chased them as f as Great Sidon
12: 3 Sihon also controlled the Jordan Valley as f north
12: 3 the Sea of Galilee and as f south as the Dead Sea,
13: 9 to the plain beyond Medeba, as f as Dibon.
13:10 and extended as f as the borders of Ammon.
13:11 of Mount Hermon, all of Bashan as f as Salecah,
13:25 as f as the town of Aroer just west of Rabbah.
13:27 extending as f north as the Sea of Galilee.
15:47 as f as the brook of Egypt and along the coast of
16: 3 of the Japhletites as f as Lower Beth-horon,
19: 8 including all the villages as f south as Baalath-beer
19:27 and ran as f as Zebulun in the valley of Iphtah-el,
19:28 Hammon, Kanah, and as f as Greater Sidon.
19:33 Jabneel, and as f as Lakkum, ending at the Jordan
22:29 F be it from us to rebel against the LORD or turn
Jdg 6: 4 in the land and destroying crops as f away as Gaza.
7: 1 got up early and went as f as the spring of Harod.
7:22 Those who were not killed fled to places as f away
11:33 twenty towns—and as f away as Abel-keramim.
Ru 1:13 Things are f more bitter for me than for you,
1Sa 6:12 The Philistine rulers followed them as f as the
14:45 who saved Israel today, die? F from it!
15:22 to his voice? Obedience is f better than sacrifice.
17:52 chasing them as f as Gath and the gates of Ekron.
17:52 the road from Shaaraim, as f as Gath and Ekron.
26:20 on foreign soil, f from the presence of the LORD?
29: 9 But Achish insisted, "As f as I'm concerned,
2Sa 3:16 Palti followed along behind her as f as Bahurim,
7:18 is my family, that you have brought me this f?
17:11 bringing them from as f away as Dan
19:34 "No," he replied, "I am f too old for that.
24: 7 they went south to Judah as f as Beersheba.
1Ki 4:21 of the Philistines, as f south as the border of Egypt.
6:16 the Most Holy Place—at the f end of the Temple.
8:46 and take them captive to a foreign land f or near.
8:65 A large crowd had gathered from as f away as
10: 7 and prosperity are f greater than what I was told.
12:30 people worshiped them, traveling even as f as Dan.
2Ki 9:27 He was able to go on as f as Megiddo, but he died
10:33 Aroer by the Arnon Gorge to as f north as Gilead
15:16 and all the surrounding countryside as f as Tirzah,
18: 8 He also conquered the Philistines as f distant as
1Ch 4:33 and their surrounding villages as f away as
5:11 of Gad, who were spread as f east as Salecah.
7:28 and its surrounding villages to the north as f as
12:40 And people from as f away as Issachar, Zebulun,
17:16 is my family, that you have brought me this f?
18: 3 of King Hadadezer of Zobah, as f as Hamath,
2Ch 6:36 and take them captive to a foreign land f or near.
7: 8 They came from as f away as Lebo-hamath in the
9: 6 Your wisdom is f greater than what I was told.
14:13 Asa and his army pursued them as f as Gerar,
20:24 there were dead bodies lying on the ground for as f
26:15 His fame spread f and wide, for the LORD helped
28: 9 But you have gone too f, killing them without
30:10 and Manasseh and as f as the territory of Zebulun.
32: 7 for there is a power f greater on our side!
34: 6 Ephraim, and Simeon, even as f as Naphtali.
Ezr 3:13 commotion that could be heard f in the distance.
9:13 But we have actually been punished f less than we
Ne 3: 1 building the wall as f as the Tower of the Hundred,
3: 8 They left out a section of Jerusalem as f as the
3:15 and he rebuilt the wall as f as the stairs that
3:16 the royal cemetery as f as the water reservoir
3:26 who repaired the wall as f as the Water Gate
3:31 repaired the wall as f as the housing for the Temple
3:31 Then he continued as f as the upper room at the
9: 5 It is f greater than we can think or say.
12:43 of the people of Jerusalem could be heard f away.
Est 9:20 these events and sent letters to the Jews near and f,
Job 5: 4 Their children are abandoned f from help, with no
11: 6 God is doubtless punishing you f less than you
19:13 "My relatives stay f away, and my friends have
28: 4 They sink a mine shaft into the earth f from where
28:17 Wisdom is f more valuable than gold and crystal.
28:18 to get it. The price of wisdom is f above pearls.
38:11 I said, 'Thus f and no farther will you come.
42: 3 I did not understand, things f too wonderful for me.
Ps 10: 1 O LORD, why do you stand so f away? / Why do
22:11 Do not stay so f from me, / for trouble is near,
31:20 them in your presence, / f from accusing tongues.
45:10 Forget your people and your homeland f away.
49:14 will rot in the grave, / f from their grand estates.
55: 7 I would fly f away / to the quiet of the wilderness.
55: 8 f away from this wild storm of hatred.
89: 7 He is f more awesome than those who surround his
97: 9 all the earth; / you are exalted f above all gods.
103:12 as f away from us as the east is from the west.
113: 4 his glory is f greater than the heavens.
113: 6 F below him are the heavens and the earth.
119:150 near to attack me; / they live f from your law.
119:155 The wicked are f from salvation, / for they do not
139: 2 You know my every thought when f away.
Pr 1:15 with them, my child! Stay f away from their paths.
4:24 Avoid all perverse talk; stay f from corrupt speech.
8:11 For wisdom is f more valuable than rubies.
15:29 The LORD is f from the wicked, but he hears the
25:25 Good news from f away is like cold water to the
27:10 to a neighbor than to a relative who lives f away.
Isa 5:13 So I will send my people into exile f away
5:26 He will send a signal to the nations f away. He will
10:10 whose gods were f greater than those in Jerusalem
13: 5 They came from countries f away. They are the
14:13 I will preside on the mountain of the gods f away
15: 4 of Heshbon and Elealeh will be heard f away,
16: 8 Her tendrils spread out as f as Jazer and trailed out
16: 8 Her shoots once reached as f as the Dead Sea.
18: 2 who are feared f and wide for their conquests
18: 7 who are feared f and wide for their conquests
29:13 me with their lips, but their hearts are f away.
30:27 The LORD is coming from f away, burning with
33:13 Listen to what I have done, you nations f away!
33:15 a profit by fraud, who stay f away from bribes,
49:12 See, my people will return from f away, from lands
49:12 the north and west, and from as f south as Egypt."
49:19 Your enemies who enslaved you will be f away.
54:14 Your enemies will stay f away; you will live in
55: 8 "And my ways are f beyond anything you could
56: 5 and a name f greater than the honor they would
57: 9 You have traveled f, even into the world of the
57:19 May they have peace, both near and f, for I will
59: 9 because of all this evil that deliverance is f from
59:11 We look to be rescued, but it is f away from us.
Jer 2: 5 ancestors find in me that led them to stray so f?
3:21 LORD their God and wandered f from his ways.
14:10 "You love to wander f from me and do not follow
25:26 northern countries, f and near, one after the other—
27:10 you from your land and send you f away to die.
31:40 Kidron Valley on the east as f as the Horse Gate—
43: 7 went to Egypt, going as f as the city of Tahpanhes.
48:24 and Bozrah—all the cities of Moab, f and near.
48:32 Your spreading vines once reached as f as the

48:45 "The people flee as **f** as Heshbon but are unable to
La 1:16 any who might encourage me are **f** away.
4:9 Those killed by the sword are **f** better off than
Eze 5:10 the few who survive to the **f** reaches of the earth.
6:12 Disease will strike down those who are **f** away in
11:15 saying, 'They are **f** away from the LORD, so now
16:47 to you. In a very short time you **f** surpassed them!
16:51 You have done **f** more loathsome things than your
21:10 Those **f** stronger than you have fallen beneath its
22:5 you will be mocked by people both **f** and near.
29:10 to Aswan, as **f** south as the border of Ethiopia.
39:17 Come from **f** and near to the mountains of Israel,
45:7 Then the **f** eastern and western borders of the
47:18 past the Dead Sea and as **f** south as Tamar.
48:8 It will be 8-1/3 miles wide and will extend as **f** east
Da 9:7 and Jerusalem and all Israel, scattered near and **f**,
11:2 be succeeded by a fourth, **f** richer than the others.
11:10 and carry the battle as **f** as the enemy's fortress.
11:13 fully equipped army **f** greater than the one he lost.
Hos 7:1 wanted to heal Israel, but its sins were **f** too great.
9:4 There, **f** from home, you will not be allowed to
Joel 2:20 these armies from the north and send them **f** away.
3:6 the Greeks, who took them **f** from their homeland.
3:8 sell them to the peoples of Arabia, a nation **f** away.
3:9 Say to the nations **f** and wide: "Get ready for war!
Am 7:17 become captives in exile, **f** from their homeland."
Ob 1:20 and occupy the Phoenician coast as **f** north as
Mic 1:9 For my people's wound is **f** too deep to heal.
4:7 They are weak and **f** from home, but I will make
Hab 1:4 The wicked **f** outnumber the righteous, and justice
2:5 They range **f** and wide, with their mouths opened
Zec 1:15 but the nations punished them **f** beyond my
Mal 1:5 the LORD's great power reaches **f** beyond our
Mt 3:11 But someone is coming soon who is **f** greater than
4:24 News about him spread **f** beyond the borders of
4:24 soon coming to be healed from as **f** away as Syria.
6:26 And you are **f** more valuable to him than they are.
14:24 the disciples were in trouble **f** away from land,
15:8 me with their words, / but their hearts are **f** away.
24:6 And wars will break out near and **f**, but don't
26:24 **F** better for him if he had never been born!"
26:58 Peter was following **f** behind and eventually came
Mk 1:7 "Someone is coming soon who is **f** greater than I
3:8 and even from as **f** away as Tyre and Sidon.
3:8 The news about his miracles had spread **f**
7:7 me with their lips, / but their hearts are **f** away.
9:3 **f** whiter than any earthly process could ever make
12:34 "You are not **f** from the Kingdom of God."
13:7 And wars will break out near and **f**, but don't
14:21 **F** better for him if he had never been born!"
14:54 Peter followed **f** behind and then slipped inside the
Lk 6:17 and from as **f** north as the seacoasts of Tyre
12:23 For life consists of **f** more than food and clothing.
12:24 And you are **f** more valuable to him than any birds!
14:32 he is not able, then while the enemy is still **f** away,
16:23 he saw Lazarus in the **f** distance with Abraham.
22:54 and Peter was following **f** behind.
Jn 1:15 'Someone is coming who is **f** greater than I am,
1:30 'Soon a man is coming who is **f** greater than I am,
5:20 and the Son will do **f** greater things than healing
Ac 7:43 I will send you into captivity / **f** away in Babylon.'
11:19 after Stephen's death traveled as **f** as Phoenicia,
17:27 find him—though he is not **f** from any one of us.
22:21 for I will send you **f** away to the Gentiles!' "
23:31 as ordered, the soldiers took Paul as **f** as Antipatris.
Ro 7:18 so **f** as my old sinful nature is concerned.
9:5 and Christ himself was a Jew as **f** as his human
11:24 he will be **f** more eager to graft the Jews back into
1Co 1:25 This "foolish" plan of God is **f** wiser than the
1:25 and God's weakness is **f** stronger than the greatest
2Co 2:9 I wrote to you as I did to find out how **f** you would
3:8 Shouldn't we expect **f** greater glory when the Holy
3:11 which remains forever, has **f** greater glory.
8:3 gave not only what they could afford but **f** more.
10:14 We are not going too **f** when we claim authority
10:16 Good News in other places that are **f** beyond you,
11:23 like a madman, but I have served him **f** more!
Eph 1:21 Now he is **f** above any ruler or authority or power
2:13 Though you once were **f** away from God, now you
2:17 peace to you Gentiles who were **f** away from him,
4:18 they are **f** away from the life of God because they
Php 1:23 and be with Christ. That would be **f** better for me,
2:30 things you couldn't do because you were **f** away.
4:7 which is **f** more wonderful than the human mind
Col 1:21 includes you who were once so **f** away from God.
2:5 For though I am **f** away from you, my heart is with
Heb 1:4 This shows that God's Son is **f** greater than the
1:4 just as the name God gave him is **f** greater than
3:3 But Jesus deserves **f** more glory than Moses,
5:13 And a person who is living on milk isn't very **f**
8:6 **f** superior to the ministry of those who serve under
9:23 with **f** better sacrifices than the blood of animals.
11:40 For God had **f** better things in mind for us that
1Pe 1:7 and your faith is **f** more precious to God than mere
2Pe 2:11 even though they are **f** greater in power
3:4 Why, as **f** back as anyone can remember,
Rev 2:5 Look how **f** you have fallen from your first love!
3:2 Your deeds are **f** from right in the sight of God.

FAR-OFF (6) [FAR]

Ge 24:38 I was to come to his relatives here in this **f** land,
Ps 102:6 in the desert, / like a lonely owl in a **f** wilderness.
Isa 49:1 Listen to me, all of you in **f** lands! The LORD
Jer 6:22 A great nation is rising against you from **f** lands.
50:41 and many kings are rising against you from **f** lands.
51:50 the LORD, even though you are in a **f** land,

FARCE (2)

Mt 15:9 Their worship is a **f**, / for they replace God's
Mk 7:7 but their hearts are far away. / Their worship is a **f**,

FAREWELL (6) [FAREWELLS]

Ge 31:27 I would have given you a **f** party, with joyful
Dt 15:14 Give him a generous **f** gift from your flock,
Mic 1:14 Send a **f** gift to Moresheth-gath; there is no hope of
Ac 15:29 If you do this, you will do well. **F**."
20:37 They wept aloud as they embraced him in **f**,
21:1 After saying **f** to the Ephesian elders, we sailed

FAREWELLS (1) [FAREWELL]

Ac 21:6 and said our **f**. Then we went aboard, and they

FARM (8) [FARMED, FARMER, FARMER'S, FARMERS, FARMHANDS, FARMING, FARMLAND, FARMS]

Ge 4:3 Cain brought to the LORD a gift of his **f** produce,
2Sa 9:10 and servants are to **f** the land for him to produce
Pr 13:23 A poor person's **f** may produce much food,
Jer 27:11 to stay in their own country to **f** the land as usual.
Eze 48:19 from the various tribes to work in the city may **f** it.
Mt 22:5 their business, one to his **f**, another to his store.
Lk 12:16 "A rich man had a fertile **f** that produced fine
1Co 9:10 Just as **f** workers who plow fields and thresh the

FARMED (2) [FARM]

1Ch 27:26 charge of the field workers who **f** the king's lands.
Eze 36:34 a shock to all who passed by—will again be **f**.

FARMER (27) [FARM]

Ge 4:2 Abel became a shepherd, while Cain was a **f**.
9:20 Noah became a **f** and planted a vineyard.
Ps 129:3 with cuts, / as if a **f** had plowed long furrows.
141:7 Even as a **f** breaks up the soil and brings up rocks,
Isa 7:21 a **f** will be fortunate to have a cow and two sheep
10:14 and gathered up kingdoms as a **f** gathers eggs.
28:24 Does a **f** always plow and never sow? Is he forever
28:26 The **f** knows just what to do, for God has given
28:29 and he gives the **f** great wisdom.
55:10 producing seed for the **f** and bread for the hungry.
Zec 13:5 'No,' he will say. 'I'm not a prophet; I'm a **f**.
Mt 13:3 such as this one: "A **f** went out to plant some seed.
13:18 of the story I told about the **f** sowing grain:
13:24 "The Kingdom of Heaven is like a **f** who planted
13:28 " 'An enemy has done it!' the **f** exclaimed.
13:37 the Son of Man, am the **f** who plants the good seed.
Mk 4:3 "Listen! A **f** went out to plant some seed.
4:14 The **f** I talked about is the one who brings God's
4:26 of God is like: A **f** planted seeds in a field,
4:29 is ready, the **f** comes and harvests it with a sickle."
Lk 8:5 "A **f** went out to plant some seed. As he scattered
15:15 He persuaded a local **f** to hire him to feed his pigs.
1Co 9:7 And have you ever heard of a **f** who harvests his
2Co 9:6 a **f** who plants only a few seeds will get a small
9:10 For God is the one who gives seed to the **f** and
Heb 6:7 rain that falls on it and bears a good crop for the **f**,
6:8 The **f** will condemn that field and burn it.

FARMER'S (3) [FARM]

Hos 10:4 up among them like poisonous weeds in a **f** field.
Mt 13:27 The **f** servants came and told him, 'Sir, the field
Mk 4:27 the seeds sprouted and grew without the **f** help,

FARMERS (23) [FARM]

1Ch 7:21 trying to steal livestock from the local **f** near Gath.
SS 8:11 at Baal-hamon, which he rents to some **f** there.
Jer 14:4 The **f** are afraid; they, too, cover their heads.
31:24 And city dwellers and **f** and shepherds alike will
51:23 and flocks, **f** and oxen, captains and rulers.
Joel 1:11 Despair, all you **f**! Wail, all you vine growers!
Am 5:16 Call for the **f** to weep with you, and summon
Mt 21:33 Then he leased the vineyard to tenant **f** and moved
21:35 But the **f** grabbed his servants, beat one, killed one,
21:38 "But when the **f** saw his son coming, they said to
21:40 "what do you think he will do to those **f**?"
21:45 pointing at them—that they were the **f** in his story.
Mk 12:1 Then he leased the vineyard to tenant **f** and moved
12:3 But the **f** grabbed the servant, beat him up,
12:7 "But the **f** said to one another, 'Here comes the
12:12 at them—they were the wicked **f** in his story.
Lk 20:9 man planted a vineyard, leased it out to tenant **f**,
20:10 But the **f** attacked the servant, beat him up,
20:14 "But when the **f** saw his son, they said to each
20:15 the owner of the vineyard will do to those **f**?"
20:19 pointing at them—that they were the **f** in the story.
2Ti 2:6 Hardworking **f** are the first to enjoy the fruit of
Jas 5:7 Consider the **f** who eagerly look for the rains in the

FARMHANDS (1) [FARM]

Job 1:15 They stole all the animals and killed all the **f**.

FARMING (3) [FARM]

Ge 5:29 "He will bring us relief from the painful labor of **f**
Eze 48:18 Outside the city there will be a **f** area that stretches
Lk 17:28 and drinking, buying and selling, **f** and building—

FARMLAND (2) [FARM, LAND]

Eze 12:20 The cities will be destroyed and the **f** deserted.
48:18 This **f** will produce food for the people working in

FARMS (11) [FARM]

2Ch 26:10 He had many workers who cared for his **f**
Ps 144:13 May our **f** be filled / with crops of every kind.
Isa 16:8 Weep for the abandoned **f** of Heshbon
32:12 Beat your breasts in sorrow for your bountiful **f**
Jer 8:10 I will give their wives and their **f** to others.
35:9 or owned vineyards or **f** or planted crops.
Eze 19:7 their towns and cities. / Their **f** were desolated,
Am 4:9 "I struck your **f** and vineyards with blight
Mk 6:36 so they can go to the nearby **f** and villages
6:56 he went—in villages and cities and out on the **f**—
Lk 9:12 the crowds away to the nearby villages and **f**,

FARTHER (11) [FAR]

Ge 22:5 "The boy and I will travel a little **f**. We will
Nu 22:26 Then the angel of the LORD moved **f** down the
1Sa 20:22 But if I tell him, 'Go **f**—the arrows are still ahead
23:25 he went even **f** into the wilderness to the great
Job 38:11 I said, 'Thus far and no **f** will you come. Here your
Mt 4:21 A little **f** up the shore he saw two other brothers,
26:39 He went on a little **f** and fell face down on the
Mk 1:19 A little **f** up the shore Jesus saw Zebedee's sons,
14:35 He went on a little **f** and fell face down on the
Ac 8:40 Philip found himself **f** north at the city of Azotus!
27:12 **f** up the coast of Crete, and spend the winter there.

FARTHEST (9) [FAR]

2Ki 19:23 choicest cypress trees. / I have reached its **f** corners
Job 22:12 higher than the heavens, higher than the **f** stars.
28:3 how to put light into darkness and explore the **f**,
Ps 97:1 Let the earth rejoice! / Let the **f** islands be glad.
139:9 wings of the morning, / if I dwell by the **f** oceans,
Isa 37:24 choicest cypress trees. / I have reached its **f** corners
Mt 24:31 his chosen ones from the **f** ends of the earth
Mk 13:27 from the **f** ends of the earth and heaven.
Ac 13:47 to bring salvation to the **f** corners of the earth.' "

FARTHING [KJV] See PENNIES, PENNY

FASHION (2)

Ex 27:16 **F** it from fine linen, and decorate it with beautiful
28:39 **F** the turban out of this linen as well. Also make

FAST (32) [FASTED, FASTER, FASTEST, FASTING, FASTS]

1Sa 25:17 You'd better think **f**, for there is going to be
2Sa 12:23 But why should I **f** when he is dead? Can I bring
1Ki 21:12 They called for a **f** and put Naboth at a prominent
2Ch 20:3 that everyone throughout Judah should observe a **f**.
Ezr 8:21 I gave orders for all of us to **f** and humble
Est 4:16 gather together all the Jews of Susa and **f** for me.
Job 8:15 They try to hold it **f**, but it will not endure.
Ps 12:1 O LORD, for the godly are **f** disappearing!
69:10 When I weep and **f** before the LORD, / they scoff
Isa 18:2 and ambassadors are sent in **f** boats down the Nile.
47:11 will arise so **f** that you won't know what hit you.
Jer 14:12 When they **f** in my presence, I will pay no
48:16 "Calamity is coming **f** to Moab; it threatens
Joel 2:4 They look like tiny horses, and they run as **f**.
Am 2:15 The swiftest soldiers won't be **f** enough to escape.
Zec 7:3 and **f** each summer on the anniversary of the
Mt 6:16 "And when you **f**, don't make it obvious,
6:17 But when you **f**, comb your hair and wash your
9:14 and asked him, "Why do we and the Pharisees **f**, but your disciples don't **f**?"
9:15 he will be taken from them, and then they will **f**.
Mk 2:18 "Why do John's disciples and the Pharisees **f**, but your disciples don't **f**?"
2:19 "Do wedding guests **f** while celebrating with the
2:19 They can't **f** while they are with the groom.
2:20 will be taken away from them, and then they will **f**.
7:24 As usual, the news of his arrival spread **f**.
Lk 5:33 "John the Baptist's disciples always **f** and pray,"
5:34 "Do wedding guests **f** while celebrating with the
5:35 be taken away from them, and then they will **f**."
18:12 I **f** twice a week, and I give you a tenth of my
Ac 27:41 The bow of the ship stuck **f**, while the stern was

FASTED (16) [FAST]

Jdg 20:26 in the presence of the LORD and **f** until evening.
1Sa 31:13 tamarisk tree at Jabesh, and they **f** for seven days.
2Sa 1:12 They mourned and wept and **f** all day for Saul
12:22 "I **f** and wept while the child was alive, for I said,
1Ki 21:27 he tore his clothing, dressed in sackcloth, and **f**.
1Ch 10:12 the oak tree at Jabesh, and they **f** for seven days.
Ezr 8:23 So we **f** and earnestly prayed that our God would
Ne 1:4 In fact, for days I mourned, **f**, and prayed to the
9:1 This time they **f** and dressed in sackcloth
Est 4:3 They **f**, wept, and wailed, and many people lay in
Ps 35:13 I grieved for them. / I even **f** and prayed for them,
Isa 58:3 'We have **f** before you!' they say. 'Why aren't you
Zec 7:5 when you **f** and mourned in the summer and at the
Mt 11:18 John the Baptist didn't drink wine and he often **f**,
Mk 2:18 John's disciples and the Pharisees sometimes **f**.
Lk 7:33 John the Baptist didn't drink wine and he often **f**,

FASTEN (6) [FASTENED]

Ex 26:6 Then make fifty gold clasps to **f** the loops of the
26:11 and **f** them together with fifty bronze clasps.
28:12 **F** the two stones on the shoulder-pieces of the
Isa 41:7 then **f** the thing in place so it won't fall over.
Jer 10:4 and then **f** it securely with hammer and nails
27:2 a yoke, and **f** it on your neck with leather thongs.

FASTENED (10) [FASTEN]
Ge 27:16 and she **f** a strip of the goat's skin around his neck.
Ex 37: 3 Four gold rings were **f** to its four feet, two rings at
Jdg 15: 4 in pairs, and he **f** a torch to each pair of tails.
1Sa 31:10 and they **f** his body to the wall of the city of
1Ch 10:10 and they **f** his head to the wall in the temple of
Est 1: 6 **f** by purple ribbons to silver rings embedded in
Eze 40:43 **f** to the foyer walls and set on the tables where the
Mt 27:37 A signboard was **f** to the cross above Jesus' head,
Mk 15:26 A signboard was **f** to the cross above Jesus' head,
Ac 28: 3 driven out by the heat, **f** itself onto his hand.

FASTER (3) [FAST]
Ps 58: 9 and old, / **f** than a pot heats on an open flame.
Am 9:13 and grapes will grow **f** than they can be harvested.
Lk 5:15 the report of his power spread even **f**,

FASTEST (2) [FAST]
Ecc 9:11 The **f** runner doesn't always win the race,
Am 2:14 Your **f** runners will not get away. The strongest

FASTING (27) [FAST]
Lev 16:29 you must spend the day **f** and not do any work.
16:31 day of total rest, and you will spend the day in **f**.
23:32 and **f** will begin the evening before the Day of
1Ki 21: 9 "Call the citizens together for **f** and prayer
Est 9:31 and their descendants to establish the times of **f**
Ps 109:24 My knees are weak from **f**, / and I am skin
Isa 1:13 and the Sabbath day, and your special days for **f**—
58: 3 you are living for yourselves even while you are **f**.
58: 4 What good is **f** when you keep on fighting
58: 4 This kind of **f** will never get you anywhere with
58: 5 yourselves with ashes. Is this what you call **f**?
58: 6 the kind of **f** I want calls you to free those who are
Jer 36: 6 So you go to the Temple on the next day of **f**,
36: 9 This happened on the day of sacred **f** held in late
Da 6:18 king returned to his palace and spent the night **f**.
9: 3 Lord God and pleaded with him in prayer and **f**.
Joel 1:14 Announce a time of **f**; call the people together for a
2:12 your hearts. Come with **f**, weeping, and mourning.
2:15 Announce a time of **f**; call the people together for a
Zec 7: 5 early autumn, was it really for me that you were **f**?
Mt 6:16 so people will admire them for their **f**.
6:18 Then no one will suspect you are **f**, except your
Lk 2:37 and night, worshiping God with **f** and prayer.
5:33 that Jesus' disciples were feasting instead of **f**.
Ac 13: 2 day as these men were worshiping the Lord and **f**,
13: 3 So after more **f** and prayer, the men laid their
14:23 elders in every church and prayed for them with **f**,

FASTS (1) [FAST]
Zec 8:19 The traditional **f** and times of mourning you have

FAT (94) [FATTENED, FATTENING, FATTEST]
Ge 18: 7 and chose a **f** calf and told a servant to hurry
41: 2 In his dream, seven **f**, healthy-looking cows
41: 3 These cows went over and stood beside the **f** cows.
41: 4 Then the thin, ugly cows ate the **f** ones! At this
41:18 "Suddenly, seven **f**, healthy-looking cows came up
41:20 ugly cows ate up the seven **f** ones that had come
41:26 The seven **f** cows and the seven plump heads of
45:18 land of Egypt. You will live off the **f** of the land!'
Ex 23:18 And no sacrificial **f** may be left unoffered until the
29:13 Take all the **f** that covers the internal organs,
29:13 lobe of the liver and the two kidneys with their **f**,
29:22 of Aaron and his sons, take the **f** of the ram,
29:22 including the **f** tail and the **f** that covers the internal organs.
29:22 the two kidneys with their **f**, and the right thigh.
Lev 1: 8 including its head and **f**, on the wood fire.
1:12 including the head and **f**, on top of the wood fire
3: 3 This includes the **f** around the internal organs,
3: 4 the two kidneys with the **f** around them near the
3: 9 This includes the **f** of the entire tail cut off near the backbone, the **f** around the internal organs,
3:10 the two kidneys with the **f** around them near the
3:14 This part includes the **f** around the internal organs,
3:15 the two kidneys with the **f** around them near the
3:16 Remember, all the **f** belongs to the LORD.
3:17 "You must never eat any **f** or blood. This is a
4: 8 The priest must remove all the **f** around the bull's
4: 9 the two kidneys with the **f** around them near the
4:19 The priest must remove all the animal's **f** and burn
4:26 He must burn all the goat's **f** on the altar, just as is
4:31 Those who are guilty must remove all the goat's **f**,
4:31 Then the priest will burn the **f** on the altar, and it
4:35 who are guilty must remove all the sheep's **f**,
4:35 Then the priest will burn the **f** on the altar on top of
6:12 then burn the **f** of the peace offerings on top of this
7: 3 The priest will then offer all its **f** on the altar, including the **f** from the tail, the **f** around the internal organs,
7: 4 the two kidneys with the **f** around them near the
7:23 You must never eat **f**, whether from oxen or sheep
7:24 The **f** of an animal found dead or killed by a wild
7:25 Anyone who eats **f** from an offering given to the
7:30 Bring the **f** of the animal, together with the breast,
7:31 Then the priest will burn the **f** on the altar,
7:33 the blood and offers the **f** of the peace offering.
8:16 He took all the **f** around the internal organs,
8:16 lobe of the liver, and the two kidneys and their **f**,
8:20 the head, some of its pieces, and the **f** on the altar.
8:25 Next he took the **f**, including the **f** from the tail,
8:25 the **f** around the internal organs, lobe of the liver, and the two kidneys with their **f**,
9:10 Then he burned on the altar the **f**, the kidneys,
9:19 Then he took the **f** of the bull and the ram—the **f** from the tail and from around the internal
9:20 He placed these **f** parts on top of the breasts of
9:24 consumed the burnt offering and the **f** on the altar.
10:15 along with the **f** of the offerings given by fire.
16:25 He must also burn all the **f** of the sin offering on
17: 6 and burn the **f** on the LORD's altar at the
Nu 18:17 and burn their **f** as an offering given by fire,
Dt 32:14 the flock, / together with the **f** of lambs and goats.
32:15 But Israel soon became **f** and unruly; / the people
32:38 are those gods, / who ate the **f** of their sacrifices
Jdg 3:17 brought the tax money to Eglon, who was very **f**.
3:22 that the handle disappeared beneath the king's **f**.
1Sa 2:15 before the animal's **f** had been burned on the altar.
2:16 much as you want, but the **f** must first be burned."
2:29 and they have become **f** from the best offerings of
4:18 broke his neck and died, for he was old and very **f**.
15: 9 of the sheep and cattle, the **f** calves and lambs—
15:22 Listening to him is much better than offering the **f**
1Ki 8:64 grain offerings, and the **f** of peace offerings there,
2Ch 7: 7 and the **f** from peace offerings there.
7: 7 burnt offerings, grain offerings, and sacrificial **f**.
29:35 and a great deal of **f** from the many peace
35:14 offering the burnt offerings and the **f** portions.
Ne 5:18 six **f** sheep, and a large number of domestic fowl.
9:25 So they ate until they were full and grew **f**
Job 15:27 "These wicked people are **f** and rich,
41:23 Its flesh is hard and firm, not soft and **f**.
Ps 73: 7 These **f** cats have everything / their hearts could
Isa 1:11 I don't want the **f** from your rams or other animals.
34: 6 It is covered with **f** as though it had been used for
34: 7 be soaked with blood and the soil enriched with **f**.
43:24 or pleased me with the **f** from sacrifices.
Eze 34:16 But I will destroy those who are **f** and powerful.
34:20 I will surely judge between the **f** sheep
34:21 For you **f** sheep push and butt and crowd my sick
39:18 lambs, goats, and **f** young bulls of Bashan!
44: 7 offered me my food, the **f** and blood of sacrifices.
44:15 and offer the **f** and blood of the sacrifices,
Am 4: 1 Listen to me, you "**f** cows" of Samaria,
Jas 5: 5 Now your hearts are nice and **f**, ready for the

FATAL (9) [FATALLY]
2Ch 22: 7 But this turned out to be a **f** mistake, for God had
Est 6:13 It will be **f** to continue to oppose him."
Ps 41: 8 "Whatever he has, it is **f**," they say. / "He will
42:10 Their taunts pierce me like a **f** wound. / They scoff,
91: 3 every trap / and protect you from the **f** plague.
144:11 Save me from the **f** sword! / Rescue me from the
Jer 20:10 old friends are watching me, waiting for a **f** slip.
Na 3:19 is no healing for your wound; your injury is **f**.
Rev 13: 3 beyond recovery—but the **f** wound was healed!

FATALLY (1) [FATAL]
Rev 13:14 who was **f** wounded and then came back to life.

FATE (40)
Dt 32:29 understand this! / Oh, that they might know their **f**!
Jdg 11:40 each year to lament the **f** of Jephthah's daughter.
1Ki 2:23 if Adonijah has not sealed his **f** with this request.
Job 8:13 Such is the **f** of all who forget God. The hope of
18:20 People in the west are appalled at their **f**; people in
20:29 This is the **f** that awaits the wicked. It is the
Ps 9:17 This is the **f** of all the nations who ignore God.
26: 9 Don't let me suffer the **f** of sinners.
49:13 This is the **f** of fools, / though they will be
77:10 And I said, "This is my **f**, / that the blessings of
Pr 1:19 Such is the **f** of all who are greedy for gain. It ends
Ecc 2:14 I saw that wise and foolish people share the same **f**.
9: 3 It seems so tragic that one **f** comes to all. That is
Isa 5: 9 But the LORD Almighty has sealed your awful **f**.
10:30 army comes. Poor Anathoth, what a **f** is yours!
15: 2 weeping for the **f** of Nebo and Medeba.
17: 3 The few left in Aram will share the **f** of Israel's
51:14 starvation, and death will not be your **f**!
65:11 his Temple and worship the gods of **F** and Destiny,
Jer 29:22 Their terrible **f** will become proverbial, so that
38:22 your feet sank in the mud, they left you to your **f**!'
42:17 That is the **f** awaiting every one of you who insists
La 3:51 My heart is breaking over the **f** of all the women of
Eze 27:35 are appalled at your terrible **f**. / Their kings are
28:19 All who knew you are appalled at your **f**. You have
31:18 This will be the **f** of Pharaoh and all his teeming
Hos 10:15 You will share that **f**, Bethel, because of your great
Zep 2:15 This is the **f** of that boisterous city, once so secure.
Zec 12: 1 This message concerning the **f** of Israel came from
Mt 10:25 The student shares the teacher's **f**. The servant shares the master's **f**.
12:37 The words you say now reflect your **f** then;
Mk 6:11 sign that you have abandoned that village to its **f**."
Lk 9: 5 sign that you have abandoned that village to its **f**."
21:26 because of the fearful **f** they see coming upon the
Heb 10:39 those who turn their backs on God and seal their **f**.
1Pe 2: 8 so they meet the **f** that has been planned for them.
4:17 what terrible **f** awaits those who have never
Jude 1: 4 The **f** of such people was determined long ago,
Rev 18:20 But you, O heaven, rejoice over her **f**. And you

FATFLESHED [KJV] See HEALTHY-LOOKING

FATHER (951) [FATHER'S, FATHER-IN-LAW, FATHER-IN-LAW'S, FATHERED, FATHERLESS, FATHERS, FATHERS', FOREFATHERS, GRANDFATHER, GRANDFATHER'S]

BECAME THE FATHER OF (4) Ge 11:26; 22:23; Ru 4:17; Ac 7:8

FATHER ABRAHAM (5) Lk 16:24,27,30; Jn 8:39,53

FATHER AND MOTHER (38) Ge 2:24; Ex 20:12; Dt 5:16; 21:13,19; 22:15; Jos 2:13; Jdg 14:2,3,4,9,19; Ru 2:11; 1Sa 22:3; 2Sa 19:37; 1Ki 19:20; 22:52; 2Ki 3:2,13; Est 2:7; Ps 27:10; Isa 45:10; Zec 13:3,3; Mt 15:4; 19:5,19; Mk 5:40; 7:10; 10:7,19; Lk 8:51; 14:26; 18:20; Jn 6:42; Eph 5:31; 6:2,3

FATHER IN HEAVEN (11) Mt 5:45,48; 6:1,9; 7:21; 10:32,33; 12:50; 16:17; 18:19; Mk 11:25

GOD AND FATHER (4) 2Co 1:3; Eph 4:6; 1Th 1:3; 1Pe 1:3

GOD OUR FATHER (18) Ro 1:7; 1Co 1:3; 2Co 1:2; Gal 1:3,4; Eph 1:2; Php 1:2; 4:20; Col 1:2; 1Th 3:13; 2Th 1:1,2; 2:16; 1Ti 1:2; 2Ti 1:2; Phm 1:3; Jas 1:27; 2Jn 1:3

GOD THE FATHER (17) Jn 6:27; Ro 15:6; 1Co 8:6; 15:24; 2Co 11:31; Gal 1:1; Eph 1:3; 5:20; 6:23; Php 2:11; Col 1:3; 3:17; 1Th 1:1; Tit 1:4; 1Pe 1:2; 2Pe 1:17; Jude 1:1

HEAVENLY FATHER (12) Mt 5:16; 6:14,26,32; 7:11; 15:13; 18:10,35; Lk 11:13; Heb 12:9; 1Pe 1:17; 1Jn 3:1

WAS THE FATHER OF (148) Ge 4:18,18,18,18; 10:24,24; 11:27; Nu 26:9; Jos 17:1; Ru 4:18,19,19,20,20,21, 21,22,22; 1Ch 1:18,18,34; 2:10,10,11,11,12,12,20,20,22, 36,36,37,37,38,38,39,39,40,40,41,41,44,44,44,45,46; 4:2,2, 11,11,12,12,14,14,19,19; 6:4,4,5,5,6,6,7,7,8,8,9,9,10,11,11, 12,12,13,13,14,14; 7:14; 8:32,33,33,33,34,34,35,36,36,36, 37,37,37,37; 9:38,39,39,39,40,40,42,42,42,43; Ne 12:10,10, 10,11,11; Mt 1:2,2,2,3,3,3,4,4,4,5,5,5,6,6,7,7,7,8,8,8,9,9,9, 10,10,10,11,12,12,13,13,13,14,14,14,15,15,15,16; Ac 7:8

Ge 2:24 This explains why a man leaves his **f** and mother
4:18 Enoch was the **f** of Irad. / Irad was the **f** of Mehujael. / Mehujael was the **f** of Methushael. / Methushael was the **f** of Lamech.
5: 3 was born, and Seth was the very image of his **f**.
9:18 three sons of Noah, survived the Flood with their **f**.
9:22 Ham, the **f** of Canaan, saw that his **f** was naked and went outside and told
10:24 Arphaxad was the **f** of Shelah, and Shelah was the **f** of Eber.
11:26 he became the **f** of Abram, Nahor, and Haran.
11:27 Terah was the **f** of Abram, Nahor, and Haran;
11:28 place of his birth. He was survived by Terah, his **f**.
12: 2 I will cause you to become the **f** of a great nation.
17: 4 I will make you the **f** of not just one nation, but a
17: 5 as Abraham, for you will be the **f** of many nations.
17:17 "How could I become a **f** at the age of one
19:31 And our **f** will soon be too old to have children.
19:32 we will preserve our family line through our **f**."
19:33 and the older daughter went in and slept with her **f**.
19:34 to her younger sister, "I slept with our **f** last night.
19:36 both of Lot's daughters became pregnant by their **f**.
20:12 we both have the same **f**, though different
22: 7 Isaac said, "**F**?" "Yes, my son,"
22:21 was Buz, followed by Kemuel (the **f** of Aram),
22:23 Bethuel became the **f** of Rebekah.
24:15 Her **f** was Bethuel, who was the son of Abraham's
24:23 "Would your **f** have any room to put us up for the
24:24 "My **f** is Bethuel," she replied. "My grandparents
24:47 she told me, 'My **f** is Bethuel, the son of Nahor
26: 3 just as I solemnly promised Abraham, your **f**.
26:15 the wells that had been dug by the servants of his **f**,
26:18 He reopened the wells his **f** had dug,
26:24 "I am the God of your **f**, Abraham," he said.
27: 1 his older son, and said, "My son?" "Yes, **F**?"
27: 6 to her son Jacob, "I overheard your **f** asking Esau
27:10 Take the food to your **f**; then he can eat it and bless
27:12 What if my **f** touches me? He'll see that I'm trying
27:18 Jacob carried the platter of food to his **f** and said, "My **f**?"
27:22 So Jacob went over to his **f**, and Isaac touched him.
27:25 So Jacob took the food over to his **f**, and Isaac ate
27:30 and almost before Jacob had left his **f**,
27:31 Then he said, "I'm back, **F**, and I have the wild
27:34 bitter cry. "O my **f**, bless me, too!" he begged.
27:38 O my **f**, bless me, too!" Then Esau broke down
27:39 His **f**, Isaac, said to him, "You will live off the
27:41 said to himself, "My **f** will soon be dead and gone.
28: 6 Esau heard that his **f** had blessed Jacob and sent
28: 8 It was now very clear to Esau that his **f** despised
28:13 your grandfather Abraham and the God of your **f**,
28:21 and if he will bring me back safely to my **f**, then I
29:12 So Rachel quickly ran and told her **f**, Laban.
29:18 Since Jacob was in love with Rachel, he told her **f**,
31: 1 "Jacob has robbed our **f**!" they said. "All his
31: 3 "Return to the land of your **f** and grandfather
31: 5 "Your **f** has turned against me and is not treating
31: 5 told them. "But the God of my **f** has been with me.
31: 6 You know how hard I have worked for your **f**,
31:16 The riches God has given you from our **f** are
31:18 to the land of Canaan, where his **f**, Isaac, lived.
31:29 but the God of your **f** appeared to me last night
31:35 "Forgive my not getting up, **F**," Rachel explained.
31:42 the awe-inspiring God of my **f**, Isaac—
31:53 took an oath before the awesome God of his **f**,
32: 9 "O God of my grandfather Abraham and my **f**,
33:19 Shechem's **f**, for a hundred pieces of silver.
34: 4 He even spoke to his **f** about it. "Get this girl for
34: 6 Meanwhile, Hamor, Shechem's **f**, came out to
34:11 Then Shechem addressed Dinah's **f** and brothers.

34:20 and he appeared with his **f** before the town leaders
35:18 the baby's **f**, however, called him Benjamin.
35:27 So Jacob came home to his **f** Isaac in Mamre,
37: 1 again in the land of Canaan, where his **f** had lived.
37: 2 But Joseph reported to his **f** some of the bad things
37:10 This time he told his **f** as well as his brothers, and his **f** rebuked him.
37:10 his **f** asked. "Will your mother, your brothers,
37:11 his **f** gave it some thought and wondered what it all
37:20 We can tell our **f** that a wild animal has eaten him.
37:22 and then he would bring him back to his **f**.
37:32 They took the beautiful robe to their **f** and asked
37:33 Their **f** recognized it at once. "Yes," he said,
38:25 and walking stick is the **f** of my child.
41:51 me forget all my troubles and the family of my **f**."
42:13 of us brothers, and our **f** is in the land of Canaan.
42:13 Our youngest brother is there with our **f**, and one
42:29 So they came to their **f**, Jacob, in the land of
42:32 We are twelve brothers, sons of one **f**; one brother
42:32 and the youngest is with our **f** in the land of
42:35 for the grain. Terror gripped them, as it did their **f**.
42:37 Then Reuben said to his **f**, "You may kill my two
43: 7 "He wanted to know whether our **f** was still living,
43: 8 Judah said to his **f**, "Send the boy with me, and we
43:11 So their **f**, Jacob, finally said to them, "If it can't
43:27 getting along, and then he said, "How is your **f**—
44:17 my slave. The rest of you may go home to your **f**."
44:19 "You asked us, my lord, if we had a **f** or a brother.
44:20 We said, 'Yes, we have a **f**, an old man, and a child
44:20 mother's children, and his **f** loves him very much.'
44:22 said to you, 'My lord, the boy cannot leave his **f**, for his **f** would die.'
44:24 So we returned to our **f** and told him what you had
44:27 Then my **f** said to us, 'You know that my wife had
44:30 my lord, I cannot go back to my **f** without the boy.
44:31 he sees that the boy is not with us, our **f** will die.
44:32 I made a pledge to my **f** that I would take care of
44:34 For how can I return to my **f** if the boy is not with
45: 3 he said to his brothers. "Is my **f** still alive?"
45: 9 "Hurry, return to my **f** and tell him, 'This is what
45:13 Tell my **f** how I am honored here in Egypt.
45:18 Tell them to bring your **f** and all of their families,
45:19 their wives and little ones and to bring your **f** here.
45:23 He sent his **f** ten donkeys loaded with the good
45:25 And they left Egypt and returned to their **f**, Jacob,
46: 1 he offered sacrifices to the God of his **f**, Isaac.
46: 3 "I am God," the voice said, "the God of your **f**.
46:18 the servant given to Leah by her **f**, Laban.
46:25 the servant given to Rachel by her **f**, Laban.
46:29 his chariot and traveled to Goshen to meet his **f**.
46:29 he embraced his **f** and wept on his shoulder for a
47: 1 "My **f** and my brothers are here from Canaan.
47: 7 Then Joseph brought his **f**, Jacob, and presented
47:11 to his **f** and brothers, just as Pharaoh had
47:12 And Joseph furnished food to his **f** and brothers in
48: 1 word came to Joseph that his **f** was failing rapidly.
48:15 before whom my grandfather Abraham and my **f**,
48:16 the names of my grandfather Abraham and my **f**,
48:17 But Joseph was upset when he saw that his **f** had
48:18 "No, **F**," he said, "this one over here is older.
48:19 But his **f** refused. "I know what I'm doing,
49: 2 O sons of Jacob; / listen to Israel, your **f**.
49:29 Bury me with my **f** and grandfather in the cave in
50: 1 Joseph threw himself on his **f** and wept over him
50: 5 "Tell Pharaoh that my **f** made me swear an oath.
50: 5 Now I need to go and bury my **f**. After his burial is
50: 6 "Go and bury your **f**, as you promised," he said.
50:10 a seven-day period of mourning for Joseph's **f**.
50:15 But now that their **f** was dead, Joseph's brothers
50:16 to Joseph: "Before your **f** died, he instructed us
50:17 So we, the servants of the God of your **f**, beg you
Ex 1: 1 These are the sons of Jacob who went with their **f**
2:18 When the girls returned to Reuel, their **f**, he asked,
2:20 "Well, where is he then?" their **f** asked. "Did you
6:16 (Levi, their **f**, lived to be 137 years old.)
20:12 "Honor your **f** and mother. Then you will live a
21:15 "Anyone who strikes **f** or mother must be put to
21:17 "Anyone who curses **f** or mother must be put to
22:17 But if her **f** refuses to let her marry him, the man
40:15 Anoint them as you did their **f**, so they may serve
Lev 18: 7 Do not violate your **f** by having sexual intercourse
18: 8 your father's wives, for this would violate your **f**.
19: 3 of you must show respect for your mother and **f**,
20: 9 "All who curse their **f** or mother must be put to
20:17 the daughter of either his **f** or his mother, it is a
21: 2 mother or **f**, son or daughter, brother
21:11 near a dead person, even if it is his **f** or mother.
24:10 and an Egyptian **f** got into a fight with one of the
Nu 3: 4 and Ithamar to serve as priests with their **f**,
6: 7 even if their own **f**, mother, brother, or sister has
11:12 Are they my children? Am I their **f**? Is that why
12:14 said to Moses, "If her **f** had spit in her face,
26: 9 and Eliab was the **f** of Nemuel, Dathan,
27: 1 Their **f**, Zelophehad, was the son of Hepher,
27: 3 "Our **f** died in the wilderness without leaving any
27: 4 Why should the name of our **f** disappear just
27: 7 the property that would have been given to their **f**.
27:11 But if his **f** has no brothers, pass on his inheritance
30: 4 and her **f** hears of the vow or pledge but says
30: 5 But if her **f** refuses to let her fulfill the vow
30: 5 because her **f** would not let her fulfill them.
30:16 and between a **f** and a young daughter who still
Dt 1:31 in the wilderness, just as a **f** cares for his child.
5:16 " 'Honor your **f** and mother, as the LORD your
21:13 for a full month, mourning for her **f** and mother.
21:17 even though he is the son of the wife his **f** does not
21:18 rebellious son who will not obey his **f** or mother,
21:19 the **f** and mother must take the son before the
22:15 the woman's **f** and mother must bring the proof of
22:16 Her **f** must tell them, 'I gave my daughter to this
22:19 The payment will be made to the woman's **f**.
22:29 he must pay fifty pieces of silver to her **f**. Then he
22:30 with his father's wife, for this would violate his **f**.
27:16 'Cursed is anyone who despises **f** or mother.'
27:20 with his father's wife, for he has violated his **f**.'
27:22 whether she is the daughter of his **f** or his mother.'
32: 6 Isn't he your **F** who created you? / Has he not
32: 7 Ask your **f** and he will inform you. / Inquire of
Jos 2:13 along with my **f** and mother, my brothers
2:18 your **f**, mother, brothers, and all your relatives—
6:23 and brought out Rahab, her **f**, mother, brothers,
15:18 she urged him to ask her **f** for an additional field.
17: 1 Manasseh's oldest son and was the **f** of Gilead.)
24: 2 including Terah, the **f** of Abraham and Nahor,
Jdg 1:14 she urged him to ask her **f** for an additional field.
8:32 and he was buried in the grave of his **f**, Joash,
9:16 Have you treated my **f** with the honor he deserves?
9:18 But now you have revolted against my **f** and his
9:56 against his **f** by murdering his seventy brothers.
11:36 And she said, "**F**, you have made a promise to the
11:39 her **f** kept his vow, and she died a virgin.
14: 2 When he returned home, he told his **f** and mother,
14: 3 His **f** and mother objected strenuously, "Isn't there
14: 3 But Samson told his **f**, "Get her for me. She is the
14: 4 His **f** and mother didn't realize the LORD was at
14: 6 But he didn't tell his **f** or mother about it.
14: 9 He also gave some to his **f** and mother, and they
14:10 As his **f** was making final arrangements for the
14:16 "I haven't even given the answer to my **f**
14:19 and he went back home to live with his **f**
15: 1 to sleep with her, but her **f** wouldn't let him in.
15: 2 "I really thought you hated her," her **f** explained,
15: 6 the Philistines went and got the woman and her **f**
16:31 and Eshtaol, where his **f**, Manoah, was buried.
17:10 Micah said, "and you can be a **f** and priest to me.
18:19 with us," they said. "Be a **f** and priest to all of us.
19: 3 she took him inside, and her **f** welcomed him.
19: 4 Her **f** urged him to stay awhile, so he stayed three
19: 5 up early, ready to leave, but the woman's **f** said,
19: 6 Then the woman's **f** said, "Please stay the night
19: 8 ready to leave, and again the woman's **f** said,
Ru 2:11 I have heard how you left your **f** and mother
4:17 He became the **f** of Jesse and the grandfather of
4:18 their ancestor Perez: / Perez was the **f** of Hezron.
4:19 Hezron was the **f** of Ram. / Ram was the **f** of Amminadab.
4:20 Amminadab was the **f** of Nahshon. / Nahshon was the **f** of Salmon.
4:21 Salmon was the **f** of Boaz. / Boaz was the **f** of Obed.
4:22 Obed was the **f** of Jesse. / Jesse was the **f** of David.
1Sa 2:25 But Eli's sons wouldn't listen to their **f**,
8: 3 But they were not like their **f**, for they were greedy
9: 5 By now my **f** will be more worried about us than
10: 2 and that your **f** is worried about you and is asking,
10:12 "It doesn't matter who his **f** is;
14: 1 But Jonathan did not tell his **f** what he was doing.
14:28 "Your **f** made the army take a strict oath that
14:29 "My **f** has made trouble for us all!"
14:51 Abner's **f**, Ner, and Saul's **f**, Kish, were brothers;
17:15 and helping his **f** with the sheep in Bethlehem.
17:58 "Tell me about your **f**, my boy," Saul said.
19: 2 told him what his **f** was planning.
19: 3 I'll ask my **f** to go out there with me, and I'll talk
19: 4 The next morning Jonathan spoke with his **f** about
20: 1 How have I offended your **f** that he is
20: 3 "Your **f** knows perfectly well about our friendship,
20: 5 I've always eaten with your **f** on this occasion,
20: 6 If your **f** asks where I am, tell him I asked
20: 8 or kill me yourself if I have sinned against your **f**.
20: 9 "You know that if I had the slightest notion my **f**
20:10 will I know whether or not your **f** is angry?"
20:12 I will talk to my **f** and let you know at once how he
20:13 LORD be with you as he used to be with my **f**.
20:33 So at last Jonathan realized that his **f** was really
22: 3 "Would you let my **f** and mother live here under
23:17 reassured him. "My **f** will never find you!
23:17 and I will be next to you, as my **f** is well aware."
24:11 Look, my **f**, at what I have in my hand. It is a piece
2Sa 2:32 to Bethlehem and buried him there beside his **f**.
3: 8 for you and your **f** by not betraying you to David,
6:21 who chose me above your **f** and his family!
7:14 I will be his **f**, and he will be my son. If he sins,
9: 7 I can be kind to you because of my vow to your **f**,
10: 2 to show complete loyalty to Hanun because his **f**,
10: 3 think these men are coming here to honor your **f**?
13: 5 When your **f** comes to see you, ask him to let
16:19 I helped your **f**, and now I will help you!"
17: 8 You know your **f** and his men; they are mighty
17: 8 And remember that your **f** is an experienced
17:10 For all Israel knows what a mighty man your **f** is
17:23 He died there and was buried beside his **f**.
17:25 His **f** was Jether, an Ishmaelite. His mother,
19:37 my own town, where my **f** and mother are buried.
21:14 He buried them all in the tomb of Kish, Saul's **f**,
1Ki 1: 5 to make himself king in place of his aged **f**.
1: 6 Now his **f**, King David, had never disciplined him
2:12 succeeded him as king, replacing his **f**, David,
2:24 confirmed me and placed me on the throne of my **f**,
2:26 carried the Ark of the Sovereign LORD for my **f**,
2:32 For my **f** was no party to the deaths of Abner son
2:44 remember all the wicked things you did to my **f**,
3: 3 and followed all the instructions of his **f**,
3: 6 "You were wonderfully kind to my **f**, David,
3: 7 now you have made me king instead of my **f**,
3:14 you follow me and obey my commands as your **f**,
5: 3 "You know that my **f**, David, was not able to build
5: 5 my God, just as he instructed my **f** that I should do.
6:12 fulfill through you the promise I made to your **f**,
7:14 and his **f** had been a foundry worker from Tyre.
7:51 Then Solomon brought all the gifts his **f**, David,
8:15 who has kept the promise he made to my **f**, David.
8:16 For he told my **f**, 'From the day I brought my
8:17 Then Solomon said, "My **f**, David, wanted to build
8:24 kept your promise to your servant David, my **f**.
8:25 your further promise to your servant David, my **f**.
8:26 fulfill this promise to your servant David, my **f**.
9: 4 with integrity and godliness, as David your **f** did,
9: 5 For I made this promise to your **f**, David: 'You will
11: 4 in the LORD his God, as his **f**, David, had done.
11: 6 the LORD completely, as his **f**, David, had done.
11:12 But for the sake of your **f**, David, I will not do this
11:27 and repairing the walls of the city of his **f**.
11:33 has not obeyed my laws and regulations as his **f**,
11:43 he was buried in the city of his **f**, David.
12: 4 "Your **f** was a hard master," they said.
12: 4 and heavy taxes that your **f** imposed on us.
12: 6 matter with the older men who had counseled his **f**,
12: 9 want me to lighten the burdens imposed by my **f**?"
12:11 Yes, my **f** was harsh on you, but I'll be even
12:11 My **f** used whips on you, but I'll use
12:14 He told the people, "My **f** was harsh on you,
12:14 My **f** used whips on you, but I'll use scorpions!"
13:12 So they told their **f** which road the man of God had
15: 3 He committed the same sins as his **f** before him,
15:15 and the utensils that he and his **f** had dedicated.
15:19 the treaty that existed between your **f** and my **f**.
15:26 LORD's sight and followed the example of his **f**,
19:20 "First let me go and kiss my **f** and mother
20:34 "I will give back the towns my **f** took from your **f**,
20:34 of trade in Damascus, as my **f** did in Samaria."
22:43 a good king, following the example of his **f**, Asa.
22:46 continued their practices from the days of his **f**,
22:52 following the example of his **f** and mother
22:53 the God of Israel, just as his **f** had done.
2Ki 2:12 Elisha saw it and cried out, "My **f**! My **f**!
3: 2 but he was not as wicked as his **f** and mother.
3: 2 down the sacred pillar of Baal that his **f** had set up.
3:13 "Go to the pagan prophets of your **f** and mother!"
4:18 when her child was older, he went out to visit his **f**,
4:19 His **f** said to one of the servants, "Carry him home
6:21 he shouted to Elisha, "My **f**, should I kill them?"
9:25 when you and I were riding along behind his **f**,
13:14 "My **f**! My **f**! The chariots and charioteers of
13:25 the towns that Hazael had taken from Jehoash's **f**,
14: 3 Instead, he followed the example of his **f**, Joash.
14: 5 he executed the men who had assassinated his **f**.
15: 3 LORD's sight, just as his **f**, Amaziah, had done.
15:34 the LORD's sight, just as his **f** Uzziah had done.
21: 3 He rebuilt the pagan shrines his **f**, Hezekiah,
21:20 LORD's sight, just as his **f**, Manasseh, had done.
21:21 He followed the example of his **f**,
21:21 worshiping the same idols that his **f** had worshiped.
23:34 another of Josiah's sons, to reign in place of his **f**,
24: 9 evil in the LORD's sight, just as his **f** had done.
1Ch 1:18 Arphaxad was the **f** of Shelah. Shelah was the **f** of Eber.
1:34 Abraham was the **f** of Isaac. The sons of Isaac
2:10 Ram was the **f** of Amminadab. / Amminadab was the **f** of Nahshon,
2:11 Nahshon was the **f** of Salmon. / Salmon was the **f** of Boaz.
2:12 Boaz was the **f** of Obed. / Obed was the **f** of Jesse.
2:20 Hur was the **f** of Uri. Uri was the **f** of Bezalel.
2:22 Segub was the **f** of Jair, who ruled twenty-three
2:23 these were descendants of Makir, the **f** of Gilead.
2:24 gave birth to a son named Ashhur (the **f** of Tekoa).
2:36 Attai was the **f** of Nathan. / Nathan was the **f** of Zabad.
2:37 Zabad was the **f** of Ephlal. / Ephlal was the **f** of Obed.
2:38 Obed was the **f** of Jehu. / Jehu was the **f** of Azariah.
2:39 Azariah was the **f** of Helez. / Helez was the **f** of Eleasah.
2:40 Eleasah was the **f** of Sismai. / Sismai was the **f** of Shallum.
2:41 Shallum was the **f** of Jekamiah. / Jekamiah was the **f** of Elishama.
2:42 the brother of Jerahmeel, was Mesha, the **f** of Ziph.
2:42 second son was Mareshah, the **f** of Hebron.
2:44 Shema was the **f** of Raham. Raham was the **f** of Jorkeam. Rekem was the **f** of Shammai.
2:45 Shammai was Maon. Maon was the **f** of Beth-zur.
2:46 Moza, and Gazez. Haran was the **f** of Gazez.
2:49 She also gave birth to Shaaph (the **f** of
2:49 and Sheva (the **f** of Macbenah and Gibea).
2:50 were Shobal (the **f** of Kiriath-jearim),
2:51 Salma (the **f** of Bethlehem), and Hareph (the **f** of Beth-gader).
2:52 The descendants of Shobal (the **f** of Kiriath-jearim)
2:55 from Hammath, the **f** of the family of Recab.
4: 2 Shobal's son Reaiah was the **f** of Jahath.
4: 2 Jahath was the **f** of Ahumai and Lahad. These were
4: 4 Penuel (the **f** of Gedor), and Ezer (the **f** of Hushah).
4: 5 Ashhur (the **f** of Tekoa) had two wives,
4:11 Kelub (the brother of Shuhah) was the **f** of Mehir. Mehir was the **f** of Eshton.
4:12 Eshton was the **f** of Beth-rapha, Paseah,
4:12 and Tehinnah. Tehinnah was the **f** of Ir-nahash.
4:14 Meonothai was the **f** of Ophrah. Seraiah was the **f** of Joab, the founder of the Valley

4:17 Shammai, and Ishbah (the **f** of Eshtemoa).
4:18 who became the mother of Jered (the **f** of Gedor),
4:18 Heber (the **f** of Soco), and Jekuthiel (the **f** of Zanoah).
4:19 One of her sons was the **f** of Keilah the Garmite,
4:19 and another was the **f** of Eshtemoa the Maacathite.
4:21 The descendants of Shelah were Er (the **f** of
4:21 Laadah (the **f** of Mareshah), the families of linen
5:1 But since he dishonored his **f** by sleeping with one
6:4 Eleazar was the **f** of Phinehas. / Phinehas was the **f** of Abishua.
6:5 Abishua was the **f** of Bukki. / Bukki was the **f** of Uzzi.
6:6 Uzzi was the **f** of Zerahiah. / Zerahiah was the **f** of Meraioth.
6:7 Meraioth was the **f** of Amariah. / Amariah was the **f** of Ahitub.
6:8 Ahitub was the **f** of Zadok. / Zadok was the **f** of Ahimaaz.
6:9 Ahimaaz was the **f** of Azariah. / Azariah was the **f** of Johanan.
6:10 Johanan was the **f** of Azariah, the high priest at the
6:11 Azariah was the **f** of Amariah. / Amariah was the **f** of Ahitub.
6:12 Ahitub was the **f** of Zadok. / Zadok was the **f** of Shallum.
6:13 Shallum was the **f** of Hilkiah. / Hilkiah was the **f** of Azariah.
6:14 Azariah was the **f** of Seraiah. / Seraiah was the **f** of Jehozadak,
7:14 were Asriel and Makir. Makir was the **f** of Gilead.
7:22 Their **f**, Ephraim, mourned for them a long time,
7:31 Beriah were Heber and Malkiel (the **f** of Birzaith).
8:7 Gera, the **f** of Uzza and Ahihud, led them when
8:29 Jeiel (the **f** of Gibeon) lived in Gibeon. His wife's
8:32 and Mikloth, who was the **f** of Shimeam. All these
8:33 Ner was the **f** of Kish. Kish was the **f** of Saul.
8:33 Saul was the **f** of Jonathan, Malkishua, Abinadab,
8:34 Jonathan was the **f** of Meribbaal. Meribbaal was the **f** of Micah.
8:35 Micah was the **f** of Pithon, Melech, Tahrea,
8:36 Ahaz was the **f** of Jadah. / Jadah was the **f** of Alemeth, Azmaveth, and Zimri. / Zimri was the **f** of Moza.
8:37 Moza was the **f** of Binea. / Binea was the **f** of Rephaiah.
8:37 Rephaiah was the **f** of Eleasah. / Eleasah was the **f** of Azel.
9:35 Jeiel (the **f** of Gibeon) lived in Gibeon. His wife's
9:38 Mikloth was the **f** of Shimeam. All these families
9:39 Ner was the **f** of Kish. Kish was the **f** of Saul.
9:39 Saul was the **f** of Jonathan, Malkishua, Abinadab,
9:40 Jonathan was the **f** of Meribbaal. Meribbaal was the **f** of Micah.
9:42 Ahaz was the **f** of Jadah. / Jadah was the **f** of Alemeth, Azmaveth, and Zimri. / Zimri was the **f** of Moza.
9:43 Moza was the **f** of Binea. / Binea's son was
17:13 I will be his **f**, and he will be my son. I will not
19:2 to show complete loyalty to Hanun because his **f**,
19:3 think these men are coming here to honor your **f**?
22:10 my name. He will be my son, and I will be his **f**.
24:2 But Nadab and Abihu died before their **f** did,
25:2 They worked under the direction of their **f**, Asaph,
25:3 They worked under the direction of their **f**,
28:6 I have chosen him as my son, and I will be his **f**.
29:23 took the throne of the LORD in place of his **f**,
29:25 Solomon even greater wealth and honor than his **f**.
2Ch 1:8 "You have been so faithful and kind to my **f**,
1:9 please keep your promise to David my **f**,
2:3 cedar logs like the ones that were supplied to my **f**,
2:7 and Jerusalem who were selected by my **f**,
2:14 of a woman from Dan in Israel; his **f** is from Tyre.
2:14 and those appointed by my lord David, your **f**.
2:17 like the census his **f** had taken, and he counted
3:1 where the LORD had appeared to Solomon's **f**,
5:1 he brought in the gifts dedicated by his **f**,
6:4 who has kept the promise he made to my **f**, David. For he told my **f**,
6:7 Then Solomon said, "My **f**, David, wanted to build
6:15 kept your promise to your servant David, my **f**.
6:16 your further promise to your servant David, my **f**.
7:17 if you follow me as your **f**, David, did and obey all
7:18 This is the same promise I gave your **f**, David,
8:14 Solomon followed the regulations of his **f**, David.
9:31 he died, he was buried in the city of his **f**, David.
10:4 "Your **f** was a hard master," they said.
10:4 and heavy taxes that your **f** imposed on us.
10:6 matter with the older men who had counseled his **f**,
10:9 want me to lighten the burdens imposed by my **f**?"
10:11 Yes, my **f** was harsh on you, but I'll be even
10:11 My **f** used whips on you, but I'll use
10:14 He told the people, "My **f** was harsh on you,
10:14 My **f** used whips on you, but I'll use scorpions!"
15:18 and the utensils that he and his **f** had dedicated.
16:3 the treaty that existed between your **f** and my **f**.
17:2 of Judah and to the towns of Ephraim that his **f**,
20:32 was a good king, following the ways of his **f**, Asa.
21:3 Their **f** had given each of them valuable gifts of
21:12 You have not followed the good example of your **f**,
22:4 After the death of his **f**, members of Ahab's family
25:3 he executed the men who had assassinated his **f**.
26:4 LORD's sight, just as his **f**, Amaziah, had done.
27:2 the LORD's sight, just as his **f**, Uzziah, had done.
33:3 He rebuilt the pagan shrines his **f** Hezekiah had
33:22 LORD's sight, just as his **f** Manasseh had done.
33:22 and sacrificed to all the idols his **f** had made.
33:23 But unlike his **f**, he did not humble himself before
Ne 12:10 Jeshua the high priest was the **f** of Joiakim.
12:10 Joiakim was the **f** of Eliashib. / Eliashib was the **f** of Joiada.
12:11 Joiada was the **f** of Johanan. / Johanan was the **f** of Jaddua.
Est 2:7 When her **f** and mother had died,
Job 15:10 are aged, gray-haired men much older than your **f**!
17:14 And I might call the grave my **f**, and the worm my
29:16 I was a **f** to the poor and made sure that even
38:28 "Does the rain have a **f**? Where does dew come
42:15 And their **f** put them into his will along with their
Ps 2:7 'You are my son. / Today I have become your **F**.
27:10 Even if my **f** and mother abandon me,
45:16 Your sons will become kings like their **f**.
68:5 **F** to the fatherless, defender of widows— / this is
89:26 And he will say to me, 'You are my **F**, / my God,
103:13 The LORD is like a **f** to his children, / tender
Pr 1:8 Listen, my child, to what your **f** teaches you.
3:12 just as a **f** corrects a child in whom he delights.
4:4 My **f** told me, "Take my words to heart.
10:1 A wise child brings joy to a **f**; a foolish child
15:20 Sensible children bring joy to their **f**;
17:21 parent of a fool; there is no joy for the **f** of a rebel.
17:25 A foolish child brings grief to a **f** and bitterness to
19:13 A foolish child is a calamity to a **f**; a nagging wife
19:26 Children who mistreat their **f** or chase away their
20:20 If you curse your **f** or mother, the lamp of your life
23:22 Listen to your **f**, who gave you life, and don't
23:24 The **f** of godly children has cause for joy. What a
29:3 The man who loves wisdom brings joy to his **f**,
30:11 Some people curse their **f** and do not thank their
30:17 The eye that mocks a **f** and despises a mother will
Isa 9:6 Mighty God, Everlasting **F**, Prince of Peace.
14:29 his son will be worse than his **f** ever was.
22:21 And he will be a **f** to the people of Jerusalem
45:10 terrible it would be if a newborn baby said to its **f**
63:16 Surely you are still our **F**! Even if Abraham
63:16 disown us, LORD, you would still be our **F**.
64:8 And yet, LORD, you are our **F**. We are the clay,
Jer 2:27 from a piece of wood they say, 'You are my **f**.'
3:4 Yet you say to me, '**F**, you have been my guide
3:19 I looked forward to your calling me '**F**,' and I
16:7 the dead—not even for the death of a mother or a **f**.
20:15 I curse the messenger who told my **f**,
22:11 who succeeded his **f**, King Josiah, and was taken
22:15 Why did your **f**, Josiah, reign so long? Because he
22:18 who succeeded his **f**, Josiah, on the throne:
31:9 For I am Israel's **f**, and Ephraim is my oldest child.
Eze 16:3 Your **f** was an Amorite and your mother a Hittite!
16:45 must have been a Hittite and your **f** an Amorite.
18:11 And suppose that son does all the evil things his **f**
18:18 But the **f** will die for the many sins he committed
44:25 in the presence of a dead person unless it is his **f**,
Da 11:6 will lose her influence over him, and so will her **f**.
Am 2:7 Both **f** and son sleep with the same woman,
Mic 7:6 For the son despises his **f**. The daughter defies her
Zec 13:3 his own **f** and mother will tell him, 'You must die,
13:3 Then his own **f** and mother will stab him.
Mal 1:6 "A son honors his **f**, and a servant respects his
1:6 I am your **f** and master, but where are the honor
2:10 Are we not all children of the same **F**? Are we not
3:17 I will spare them as a **f** spares an obedient
Mt 1:2 Abraham was the **f** of Isaac. / Isaac was the **f** of Jacob. / Jacob was the **f** of Judah and his brothers.
1:3 Judah was the **f** of Perez and Zerah (their mother
1:3 Perez was the **f** of Hezron. / Hezron was the **f** of Ram.
1:4 Ram was the **f** of Amminadab. / Amminadab was the **f** of Nahshon. / Nahshon was the **f** of Salmon.
1:5 Salmon was the **f** of Boaz (his mother was Rahab).
1:5 Boaz was the **f** of Obed (his mother was Ruth). / Obed was the **f** of Jesse.
1:6 Jesse was the **f** of King David. / David was the **f** of Solomon (his mother was
1:7 Solomon was the **f** of Rehoboam. / Rehoboam was the **f** of Abijah. / Abijah was the **f** of Asaph.
1:8 Asaph was the **f** of Jehoshaphat. / Jehoshaphat was the **f** of Jehoram. / Jehoram was the **f** of Uzziah.
1:9 Uzziah was the **f** of Jotham. / Jotham was the **f** of Ahaz. / Ahaz was the **f** of Hezekiah.
1:10 Hezekiah was the **f** of Manasseh. / Manasseh was the **f** of Amos. / Amos was the **f** of Josiah.
1:11 Josiah was the **f** of Jehoiachin and his brothers
1:12 Jehoiachin was the **f** of Shealtiel. / Shealtiel was the **f** of Zerubbabel.
1:13 Zerubbabel was the **f** of Abiud. / Abiud was the **f** of Eliakim. / Eliakim was the **f** of Azor.
1:14 Azor was the **f** of Zadok. / Zadok was the **f** of Akim. / Akim was the **f** of Eliud.
1:15 Eliud was the **f** of Eleazar. / Eleazar was the **f** of Matthan. / Matthan was the **f** of Jacob.
1:16 Jacob was the **f** of Joseph, the husband of Mary.
4:21 and John, sitting in a boat with their **f**, Zebedee,
4:22 followed him, leaving the boat and their **f** behind.
5:16 so that everyone will praise your heavenly **F**.
5:45 you will be acting as true children of your **F** in
5:48 to be perfect, even as your **F** in heaven is perfect.
6:1 then you will lose the reward from your **F** in
6:4 and your **F**, who knows all secrets, will reward
6:6 the door behind you, and pray to your **F** secretly.
6:6 Then your **F**, who knows all secrets, will reward
6:8 because your **F** knows exactly what you need even
6:9 Pray like this: / Our **F** in heaven, / may your name
6:14 sin against you, your heavenly **F** will forgive you.
6:15 to forgive others, your **F** will not forgive your sins.
6:18 except your **F**, who knows what you do in secret.
6:18 And your **F**, who knows all secrets, will reward
6:26 food in barns because your heavenly **F** feeds them.
6:32 Your heavenly **F** already knows all your needs,
7:11 how much more will your heavenly **F** give good
7:21 The decisive issue is whether they obey my **F** in
8:21 "Lord, first let me return home and bury my **f**."
10:20 it will be the Spirit of your **F** speaking through
10:29 can fall to the ground without your **F** knowing it.
10:32 I will openly acknowledge that person before my **F**
10:33 I will deny that person before my **F** in heaven.
10:35 I have come to set a man against his **f**, and a
10:37 If you love your **f** or mother more than you love
10:40 and anyone who welcomes me is welcoming the **F**
11:25 "O **F**, Lord of heaven and earth, thank you for
11:26 Yes, **F**, it pleased you to do it this way!
11:27 "My **F** has given me authority over everything.
11:27 No one really knows the Son except the **F**, and no one really knows the **F** except the Son
12:50 Anyone who does the will of my **F** in heaven is my
15:4 For instance, God says, 'Honor your **f** and mother,'
15:4 and 'Anyone who speaks evil of **f** or mother must
15:13 "Every plant not planted by my heavenly **F** will be
16:17 because my **F** in heaven has revealed this to you.
16:27 will come in the glory of my **F** with his angels
18:10 are always in the presence of my heavenly **F**.
18:19 you ask, my **F** in heaven will do it for you.
18:35 "That's what my heavenly **F** will do to you if you
19:5 'This explains why a man leaves his **f** and mother
19:19 Honor your **f** and mother. Love your neighbor as
19:29 or brothers or sisters or **f** or mother or children
20:23 My **F** has prepared those places for the ones he has
21:30 Then the **f** told the other son, 'You go,' and he
21:31 Which of the two was obeying his **f**?"
23:9 And don't address anyone here on earth as '**F**,'
23:9 for only God in heaven is your spiritual **F**.
24:36 in heaven or the Son himself. Only the **F** knows.
25:34 on the right, 'Come, you who are blessed by my **F**,
26:39 and fell face down on the ground, praying, "My **F**!
26:42 Again he left them and prayed, "My **F**! If this cup
26:53 Don't you realize that I could ask my **F** for
28:19 baptizing them in the name of the **F** and the Son
Mk 1:20 too, and immediately they left their **f**, Zebedee,
5:40 Then he took the girl's **f** and mother and his three
7:10 'Honor your **f** and mother,' and 'Anyone who speaks evil of **f** or mother must
8:38 I return in the glory of my **F** with the holy angels."
9:21 Jesus asked the boy's **f**. He replied, "Since he was
9:24 The **f** instantly replied, "I do believe, but help me
9:37 and anyone who welcomes me welcomes my **F**
10:7 'This explains why a man leaves his **f** and mother
10:19 Do not cheat. Honor your **f** and mother.' "
10:29 or brothers or sisters or mother or **f** or children
11:25 so that your **F** in heaven will forgive your sins,
13:32 in heaven or the Son himself. Only the **F** knows.
14:36 "Abba, **F**," he said, "everything is possible for
15:21 (Simon is the **f** of Alexander and Rufus.)
Lk 1:59 They wanted to name him Zechariah, after his **f**.
1:62 So they asked the baby's **f**, communicating to him
1:67 Then his **f**, Zechariah, was filled with the Holy
2:48 Your **f** and I have been frantic, searching for you
6:36 be compassionate, just as your **F** is compassionate.
8:51 James, John, and the little girl's **f** and mother.
9:26 and in the glory of the **F** and the holy angels.
9:42 healed the boy. Then he gave him back to his **f**.
9:48 and anyone who welcomes me welcomes my **F**
9:59 "Lord, first let me return home and bury my **f**."
10:21 with the joy of the Holy Spirit and said, "O **F**,
10:21 Yes, **F**, it pleased you to do it this way.
10:22 "My **F** has given me authority over everything.
10:22 No one really knows the Son except the **F**, and no one really knows the **F** except the Son
11:2 you should pray: / "**F**, may your name be honored.
11:13 how much more will your heavenly **F** give the
12:30 most people, but your **F** already knows your needs.
12:32 For it gives your **F** great happiness to give you the
12:53 There will be a division between **f** and son, mother
14:26 follower you must love me more than your own **f**
15:12 The younger son told his **f**, 'I want my share of
15:12 So his **f** agreed to divide his wealth between his
15:18 I will go home to my **f** and say, "**F**, I have
15:20 "So he returned home to his **f**. And while he was
15:20 still a long distance away, his **f** saw him coming.
15:21 His son said to him, '**F**, I have sinned against both
15:22 "But his **f** said to the servants, 'Quick!
15:27 'and your **f** has killed the calf we were fattening
15:28 wouldn't go in. His **f** came out and begged him,
15:31 "His **f** said to him, 'Look, dear son, you and I are
16:24 rich man shouted, '**F** Abraham, have some pity!
16:27 "Then the rich man said, 'Please, **F** Abraham,
16:30 "The rich man replied, 'No, **F** Abraham! But if
18:20 not testify falsely. Honor your **f** and mother.' "
22:29 And just as my **F** has granted me a Kingdom,
22:42 "**F**, if you are willing, please take this cup of
23:34 Jesus said, "**F**, forgive these people, because they
23:46 Then Jesus shouted, "**F**, I entrust my spirit into
24:49 I will send the Holy Spirit, just as my **F** promised.
Jn 1:14 seen his glory, the glory of the only Son of the **F**.
3:35 The **F** loves his Son, and he has given him
4:21 no longer matter whether you worship the **F** here
4:23 when true worshipers will worship the **F** in spirit
4:23 The **F** is looking for anyone who will worship him
4:53 Then the **f** realized it was the same time that Jesus
5:17 But Jesus replied, "My **F** never stops working,
5:18 he had spoken of God as his **F**, thereby making
5:19 He does only what he sees the **F** doing.
5:19 Whatever the **F** does, the Son also does.
5:20 For the **F** loves the Son and tells him everything he

5:21 the dead anyone he wants to, just as the **F** does.
5:22 And the **F** leaves all judgment to his Son,
5:23 will honor the Son, just as they honor the **F**.
5:23 then you are certainly not honoring the **F** who sent
5:26 The **F** has life in himself, and he has granted his
5:30 But I do nothing without consulting the **F**. I judge
5:36 They have been assigned to me by the **F**, and they testify that the **F** has sent me.
5:37 And the **F** himself has also testified about me.
5:43 For I have come to you representing my **F**, and you
5:45 it is not I who will accuse you of this before the **F**.
6:27 For God the **F** has sent me for that very purpose."
6:32 didn't give them bread from heaven. My **F** did.
6:37 those the **F** has given me will come to me,
6:42 We know his **f** and mother. How can he say,
6:44 For people can't come to me unless the **F** who sent
6:45 who hears and learns from the **F** comes to me.
6:46 (Not that anyone has ever seen the **F**; only I,
6:57 I live by the power of the living **F** who sent me;
6:65 can't come to me unless the **F** brings them to me."
8:16 I am not alone—I have with me the **F** who sent me.
8:18 one witness, and my **F** who sent me is the other."
8:19 "Where is your **f**?" they asked. Jesus answered,
8:19 know who I am, you don't know who my **F** is.
8:19 If you knew me, then you would know my **F**, too."
8:27 understand that he was talking to them about his **F**.
8:28 on my own, but I speak what the **F** taught me.
8:38 I am telling you what I saw when I was with my **F**.
8:38 But you are following the advice of your **f**."
8:39 "Our **f** is Abraham," they declared. "No,"
8:41 you are obeying your real **f** when you act that
8:41 born out of wedlock! Our true **F** is God himself."
8:42 Jesus told them, "If God were your **F**, you would
8:44 For you are the children of your **f** the Devil,
8:44 with his character; for he is a liar and the **f** of lies.
8:47 Anyone whose **F** is God listens gladly to the words
8:49 in me. For I honor my **F**—and you dishonor me.
8:53 Are you greater than our **f** Abraham, who died?
8:54 But it is my **F** who says these glorious things about
10:15 just as my **F** knows me and I know the **F**.
10:17 "The **F** loves me because I lay down my life that I
10:18 it again. For my **F** has given me this command."
10:25 The proof is what I do in the name of my **F**.
10:29 for my **F** has given them to me, and he is more
10:30 The **F** and I are one."
10:36 One who was sent into the world by the **F** says,
10:38 will realize that the **F** is in me, and I am in the **F**."
11:41 Then Jesus looked up to heaven and said, "**F**,
12:26 And if they follow me, the **F** will honor them.
12:27 Should I pray, '**F**, save me from what lies ahead'?
12:28 **F**, bring glory to your name." Then a voice spoke
12:49 The **F** who sent me gave me his own instructions
12:50 so I say whatever the **F** tells me to say!"
13:1 had come to leave this world and return to his **F**.
13:3 Jesus knew that the **F** had given him authority over
13:20 and anyone who welcomes me is welcoming the **F**
14:6 No one can come to the **F** except through me.
14:7 I am, then you would have known who my **F** is.
14:8 "Lord, show us the **F** and we will be satisfied."
14:9 Anyone who has seen me has seen the **F**! So why
14:10 you believe that I am in the **F** and the **F** is in me?
14:10 but my **F** who lives in me does his work through
14:11 Just believe that I am in the **F** and the **F** is in me.
14:12 greater works, because I am going to be with the **F**.
14:13 because the work of the Son brings glory to the **F**.
14:16 And I will ask the **F**, and he will give you another
14:20 you will know that I am in my **F**, and you are in
14:21 my **F** will love them, and I will love them.
14:23 My **F** will love them, and we will come to them
14:24 my own. This message is from the **F** who sent me.
14:26 But when the **F** sends the Counselor as my
14:28 because now I can go to the **F**, who is greater than
14:31 but I will do what the **F** requires of me, so that the world will know that I love the **F**.
15:1 "I am the true vine, and my **F** is the gardener.
15:8 much fruit. This brings great glory to my **F**.
15:9 "I have loved you even as the **F** has loved me.
15:10 just as I obey my **F** and remain in his love.
15:15 since I have told you everything the **F** told me.
15:16 so that the **F** will give you whatever you ask for,
15:23 Anyone who hates me hates my **F**, too.
15:24 that I did and yet hated both of us—me and my **F**.
15:26 He will come to you from the **F** and will tell you
16:3 because they have never known the **F** or me.
16:10 Righteousness is available because I go to the **F**,
16:15 All that the **F** has is mine; this is what I mean
16:17 does he mean when he says, 'I am going to the **F**'?
16:23 truth is, you can go directly to the **F** and ask him,
16:25 and I will tell you plainly all about the **F**.
16:26 I'm not saying I will ask the **F** on your behalf,
16:27 for the **F** himself loves you dearly because you
16:28 Yes, I came from the **F** into the world, and I will leave the world and return to the **F**."
16:32 Yet I am not alone because the **F** is with me.
17:1 he looked up to heaven and said, "**F**, the time has
17:5 And now, **F**, bring me into the glory we shared
17:11 Holy **F**, keep them and care for them—all those
17:21 that they will be one, just as you and I are one, **F**—
17:24 **F**, I want these whom you've given me to be with
17:25 "O righteous **F**, the world doesn't know you,
18:11 Shall I not drink from the cup the **F** has given
20:17 Jesus said, "for I haven't yet ascended to the **F**.
20:17 tell them that I am ascending to my **F** and your **F**,
20:21 be with you. As the **F** has sent me, so I send you."
Ac 1:4 "Do not leave Jerusalem until the **F** sends you
1:7 "The **F** sets those dates," he replied, "and they
2:33 And the **F**, as he had promised, gave him the Holy
7:4 the Chaldeans and lived in Haran until his **f** died.
7:8 Isaac became the **f** of Jacob, and Jacob was the **f** of the twelve patriarchs of the
7:14 Then Joseph sent for his **f**, Jacob, and all his
13:33 'You are my Son. / Today I have become your **F**.'
16:1 was a Jewish believer, but whose **f** was a Greek.
16:3 they left, for everyone knew that his **f** was a Greek.
28:8 Publius's **f** was ill with fever and dysentery.
Ro 1:7 May grace and peace be yours from God our **F**
4:11 So Abraham is the spiritual **f** of those who have
4:12 And Abraham is also the spiritual **f** of those who
4:16 For Abraham is the **f** of all who believe.
4:17 "I have made you the **f** of many nations."
4:18 that he would become the **f** of many nations,
4:19 even though he knew that he was too old to be a **f**
6:4 from the dead by the glorious power of the **F**,
8:15 into his family—calling him "**F**, dear **F**."
8:27 And the **F** who knows all hearts knows what the
15:6 and glory to God, the **F** of our Lord Jesus Christ.
1Co 1:3 May God our **F** and the Lord Jesus Christ give you
4:15 you about Christ, you have only one spiritual **f**.
4:15 For I became your **f** in Christ Jesus when I
8:6 the **F**, who created everything, and we exist for
15:24 when he will turn the Kingdom over to God the **F**,
2Co 1:2 May God our **F** and the Lord Jesus Christ give you
1:3 praise to the God and **F** of our Lord Jesus Christ.
6:18 And I will be your **F**, / and you will be my sons
11:31 God, the **F** of our Lord Jesus, who is to be praised
Gal 1:1 is from Jesus Christ himself and from God the **F**,
1:3 May grace and peace be yours from God our **F**
1:4 He died for our sins, just as God our **F** planned,
4:1 If a **f** dies and leaves great wealth for his young
4:1 even though they actually own everything their **f**
4:2 guardians until they reach whatever age their **f** set.
4:6 and now you can call God your dear **F**.
Eph 1:2 sent to you from God our **F** and Jesus Christ our
1:3 we praise God, the **F** of our Lord Jesus Christ,
1:17 the glorious **F** of our Lord Jesus Christ,
2:18 may come to the **F** through the same Holy Spirit
3:14 of God's plan, I fall to my knees and pray to the **F**,
4:6 and there is only one God and **F**, who is over us all
5:20 to God the **F** in the name of our Lord Jesus Christ.
5:31 "A man leaves his **f** and mother and is joined to
6:2 "Honor your **f** and mother." This is the first of the
6:3 If you honor your **f** and mother, "you will live a
6:23 from God the **F** and the Lord Jesus Christ.
Php 1:2 May God our **F** and the Lord Jesus Christ give you
2:11 that Jesus Christ is Lord, to the glory of God the **F**.
2:22 Like a son with his **f**, he has helped me in
4:20 Now glory be to God our **F** forever and ever.
Col 1:2 May God our **F** give you grace and peace.
1:3 and we give thanks to God the **F** of our Lord Jesus
1:12 always thanking the **F**, who has enabled you to
3:17 the while giving thanks through him to God the **F**.
1Th 1:1 you who belong to God the **F** and the Lord Jesus
1:3 As we talk to our God and **F** about you, we think
2:11 And you know that we treated each of you as a **f**
3:11 May God himself, our **F**, and our Lord Jesus make
3:13 and holy when you stand before God our **F** on that
2Th 1:1 you who belong to God our **F** and the Lord Jesus
1:2 May God our **F** and the Lord Jesus Christ give you
2:16 May our Lord Jesus Christ and God our **F**,
1Ti 1:2 May God our **F** and Christ Jesus our Lord give you
1:9 who murder their **f** or mother or other people.
5:1 to him respectfully as though he were your own **f**.
2Ti 1:2 May God our **F** and Christ Jesus our Lord give you
Tit 1:4 May God the **F** and Christ Jesus our Savior give
Phm 1:3 May God our **F** and the Lord Jesus Christ give you
Heb 1:5 are my Son. / Today I have become your **F**."
1:5 And again God said, / "I will be his **F**, / and he
2:11 and the ones he makes holy have the same **F**.
5:5 are my Son. / Today I have become your **F**."
7:3 There is no record of his **f** or mother or any of his
12:9 submit to the discipline of our heavenly **F**
Jas 1:27 and lasting religion in the sight of God our **F**
3:9 Sometimes it praises our Lord and **F**,
1Pe 1:2 God the **F** chose you long ago, and the Spirit has
1:3 honor to the God and **F** of our Lord Jesus Christ,
1:17 And remember that the heavenly **F** to whom you
2Pe 1:17 and glory from God the **F** when God's glorious,
1Jn 1:2 He was with the **F**, and then he was shown to us.
1:3 And our fellowship is with the **F** and with his Son,
2:1 there is someone to plead for you before the **F**.
2:14 to you, children, because you have known the **F**.
2:15 you show that you do not have the love of the **F** in
2:16 pride in our possessions. These are not from the **F**.
2:22 for they have denied the **F** and the Son.
2:23 Anyone who denies the Son doesn't have the **F**
2:23 But anyone who confesses the Son has the **F** also.
2:24 to live in fellowship with the Son and with the **F**.
3:1 See how very much our heavenly **F** loves us,
4:14 and now testify that the **F** sent his Son to be the
5:1 And everyone who loves the **F** loves his children,
2Jn 1:3 which come from God our **F** and from Jesus Christ
1:4 just as we have been commanded by the **F**.
1:9 you will have fellowship with both the **F**
Jude 1:1 all who are called to live in the love of God the **F**
Rev 1:6 and his priests who serve before God his **F**.
2:28 will have the same authority I received from my **F**,
3:5 but I will announce before my **F** and his angels
3:21 I was victorious and sat with my **F** on his throne.

FATHER'S (99) [FATHER]

FATHER'S HOUSE (7) Ge 12:1; 24:7; Jdg 11:7; 14:15; 19:3; Lk 2:49; Jn 2:16

Ge 9:23 into the tent, and covered their **f** naked body.
12:1 your country, your relatives, and your **f** house,
20:13 When God sent me to travel far from my **f** home,
24:7 who took me from my **f** house and my native land,
24:38 his relatives here in this far-off land, to his **f** home.
24:40 son from among my relatives, from my **f** family.
27:9 I'll prepare your **f** favorite dish from them.
27:31 Esau prepared his **f** favorite meat dish and brought
29:9 Rachel arrived with her **f** sheep, for she was a
29:12 He explained that he was her cousin on her **f** side,
31:1 "All his wealth has been gained at our **f** expense."
31:9 God has made me wealthy at your **f** expense.
31:14 none of our **f** wealth will come to us anyway.
31:19 Rachel stole her **f** household gods and took them
35:22 Reuben slept with Bilhah, his **f** concubine,
36:24 the wilderness while he was grazing his **f** donkeys.
37:2 he often tended his **f** flocks with his half brothers,
37:2 the sons of his **f** wives Bilhah and Zilpah.
37:4 brothers hated Joseph because of their **f** partiality.
37:12 Joseph's brothers went to pasture their **f** flocks at
44:30 the boy. Our **f** life is bound up in the boy's life.
50:14 and all who had accompanied him to his **f** funeral.
Ex 2:16 and fill the water troughs for their **f** flocks.
6:20 Amram married his **f** sister Jochebed, and she bore
15:2 praise him; / he is my **f** God, and I will exalt him!
Lev 18:8 Do not have sexual intercourse with any of your **f**
18:9 whether she is your **f** daughter or your mother's
18:11 with the daughter of any of your **f** wives;
18:12 not have intercourse with your aunt, your **f** sister, because she is your **f** close relative.
18:14 And do not violate your uncle, your **f** brother,
20:11 If a man has intercourse with his **f** wife,
20:19 whether his mother's sister or his **f** sister, he has
21:9 defiling her **f** holiness as well as herself, she must
22:13 to live in her **f** home, she may eat her **f** food again.
Nu 27:7 an inheritance of land along with their **f** relatives.
27:10 no brothers, give his inheritance to his **f** brothers.
30:3 under oath while she is still living at her **f** home,
36:11 and Noah all married cousins on their **f** side.
Dt 21:17 who represents the strength of his **f** manhood
22:21 the judges must take the girl to the door of her **f**
22:30 "A man must not have intercourse with his **f** wife,
27:20 anyone who has sexual intercourse with his **f** wife,
Jdg 6:25 "Take the second best bull from your **f** herd,
6:25 Pull down your **f** altar to Baal, and cut down the
6:27 was afraid of the other members of his **f** household
9:5 He took the soldiers to his **f** home at Ophrah,
11:2 "You will not get any of our **f** inheritance,"
11:7 who hated me and drove me from my **f** house?
14:15 or we will burn down your **f** house with you in it.
19:2 to him and returned to her **f** home in Bethlehem.
19:3 When he arrived at her **f** house, she took him
1Sa 14:27 But Jonathan had not heard his **f** command, and he
17:34 "I have been taking care of my **f** sheep," he said.
18:18 David exclaimed. "My **f** family is nothing!"
20:34 for he was crushed by his **f** shameful behavior
22:22 Now I have caused the death of all your **f** family.
2Sa 3:7 accused Abner of sleeping with one of his **f**
10:2 to express sympathy to Hanun about his **f** death.
15:34 just as I was your **f** adviser in the past.'
16:21 told him, "Go and sleep with your **f** concubines,
16:22 and Absalom went into the tent to sleep with his **f**
1Ki 2:31 senseless murders from me and from my **f** family.
8:20 he promised, for I have become king in my **f** place.
11:17 and a few of his **f** royal officials had fled.
12:10 'My little finger is thicker than my **f** waist—
2Ki 14:22 After his **f** death, Uzziah rebuilt the town of Elath
1Ch 5:1 his father by sleeping with one of his **f** concubines,
19:2 to express sympathy to Hanun about his **f** death.
28:4 has chosen me from among all my **f** family to be
28:4 among the families of Judah, he chose my **f** family.
28:4 And from among my **f** sons, the LORD was
2Ch 6:10 he promised, for I have become king in my **f** place.
10:10 'My little finger is thicker than my **f** waist—
17:3 because he followed the example of his **f** early
17:4 He sought his **f** God and obeyed his commands
26:2 After his **f** death, Uzziah rebuilt the town of Elath
Pr 4:1 listen to me. Listen to your **f** instruction.
4:3 For I, too, was once my **f** son, tenderly loved by
6:20 My son, obey your **f** commands, and don't neglect
27:10 Never abandon a friend—either yours or your **f**.
Eze 18:14 has a son who sees his **f** wickedness but decides
18:17 Such a person will not die because of his **f** sins;
Mt 13:43 Then the godly will shine like the sun in their **F**
18:14 it is not my heavenly **F** will that even one of these
26:29 day I drink it new with you in my **F** Kingdom."
Lk 2:49 "You should have known that I would be in my **F**
12:13 please tell my brother to divide our **f** estate with
16:27 'Please, Father Abraham, send him to my **f** home.
Jn 1:18 who is himself God, is near to the **F** heart;
2:16 Don't turn my **F** house into a marketplace!"
6:40 For it is my **F** will that all who see his Son
10:32 "At my **F** direction I have done many things to
10:37 Don't believe me unless I carry out my **F** work.
14:2 There are many rooms in my **F** home, and I am
1Co 5:1 in your church who is living in sin with his **f** wife.
Heb 12:17 And afterward, when he wanted his **f** blessing,
Rev 14:1 and his **F** name written on their foreheads.

FATHER-IN-LAW (21) [FATHER]

Ge 38:13 Someone told Tamar that her **f** had left for the
38:25 her out to kill her, she sent this message to her **f**:
Ex 3:1 One day Moses was tending the flock of his **f**,
4:18 back home and talked it over with Jethro, his **f**.
18:1 reached Jethro, the priest of Midian and Moses' **f**,
18:2 and his two sons to live with Jethro, his **f**.
18:6 Moses was told, "Jethro, your **f**, has come to visit

18: 7 So Moses went out to meet his **f**. He bowed to him
18: 8 Moses told his **f** about everything the LORD had
18:14 When Moses' **f** saw all that Moses was doing for
18:17 "This is not good!" his **f** exclaimed.
18:27 Soon after this, Moses said good-bye to his **f**,
Jdg 1:16 the Kenites, who were descendants of Moses' **f**,
15: 6 "because his **f** from Timnah gave Samson's wife
19: 7 but his **f** kept urging him to stay, so he finally gave
19: 9 to leave, his **f** said, "Look, it's getting late.
Ru 2: 3 belonged to Boaz, the relative of her **f**, Elimelech.
1Sa 4:19 and that her husband and **f** were dead,
4:21 and because her husband and her **f** were dead.
Ne 6:18 because his **f** was Shecaniah son of Arah and
Jn 18:13 the **f** of Caiaphas, the high priest that year.

FATHER-IN-LAW'S (1) [FATHER]

Ex 18:24 Moses listened to his **f** advice and followed his

FATHERED (1) [FATHER]

Dt 32:18 You neglected the Rock who had **f** you;

FATHERLESS (7) [FATHER]

Ex 22:24 become widows, and your children will become **f**.
Job 24: 3 and they even take donkeys from the poor and **f**.
Ps 68: 5 Father to the **f**, defender of widows— / this is God,
109: 9 May his children become **f**, / and may his wife
109:12 one be kind to him; / let no one pity his **f** children.
Isa 10: 2 of justice. Yes, they rob widows and **f** children!
La 5: 3 We are orphaned and **f**. Our mothers are widowed.

FATHERS (22) [FATHER]

Ex 18: 4 said at his birth, "The God of my **f** was my helper;
Lev 6:22 As the sons of the priests replace their **f**, they will
Jdg 21:22 And when their **f** and brothers come to us in
1Ch 25: 6 All these men were under the direction of their **f** as
2Ch 29: 9 Our **f** have been killed in battle, and our sons
Job 15:18 men who have heard the same thing from their **f**,
30: 1 by young men whose **f** are not worthy to run with
Jer 6:21 **F** and sons will both fall over them. Neighbors
7:18 gather wood and the **f** build sacrificial fires.
16: 3 born here in this city and about their mothers and **f**:
47: 3 Terrified **f** run madly, without a backward glance
Eze 22: 7 **F** and mothers are contemptuously ignored.
Mt 10:21 brother to death, **f** will betray their own children,
Mk 13:12 brother to death, **f** will betray their own children,
Lk 1:17 He will turn the hearts of the **f** to their children,
11:11 "You **f**—if your children ask for a fish, do you
Ac 7: 2 "Brothers and honorable **f**, listen to me.
22: 1 "Brothers and esteemed **f**," Paul said, "listen to
Eph 6: 4 And now a word to you **f**. Don't make your
Col 3:21 **F**, don't aggravate your children. If you do,
Heb 12: 9 Since we respect our earthly **f** who disciplined us,
12:10 For our earthly **f** disciplined us for a few years,

FATHERS' (2) [FATHER]

Jos 5: 7 those who had grown up to take their **f** places.
Eze 22:10 Men sleep with their **f** wives and have intercourse

FATTENED (5) [FAT]

2Sa 6:13 so David could sacrifice an ox and a **f** calf.
1Ki 1: 9 where he sacrificed sheep, oxen, and **f** calves.
1:19 He has sacrificed many oxen, **f** calves, and sheep,
1:25 he has sacrificed many oxen, **f** calves, and sheep,
Jer 46:21 Egypt's famed mercenaries have become like **f**

FATTENING (4) [FAT]

1Sa 28:24 The woman had been **f** a calf, so she hurried out
1Ki 4:23 ten oxen from the **f** pens, twenty pasture-fed cattle,
Lk 15:23 And kill the calf we have been **f** in the pen.
15:27 'and your father has killed the calf we were **f**

FATTEST (1) [FAT]

Zec 11:16 this shepherd will eat the meat of the **f** sheep

FAULT (23) [FAULTLESS, FAULTS]

Ge 16: 5 Then Sarai said to Abram, "It's all your **f**!
31:39 from the flocks, whether the loss was my **f** or not.
Ex 5:16 We are beaten for something that isn't our **f**!
5:16 It is the **f** of your slave drivers for making such
9:27 and Aaron. "I finally admit my **f**," he confessed.
1Sa 29: 3 and I've never found a single **f** in him since he
2Sa 3: 8 that you find **f** with me about this woman?
1Ki 20:40 "Well, it's your own **f**," the king replied.
Job 19:28 you go on persecuting me, saying, 'It's his own **f**'?
Eze 33: 4 to take action—well, it is their own **f** if they die.
Da 6: 4 and princes began searching for some **f** in the way
Hos 4: 6 It is all your **f**, you priests, for you yourselves
Jnh 1:12 For I know that this terrible storm is all my **f**."
1:14 us responsible for his death, because it isn't our **f**.
Mt 18:15 sins against you, go privately and point out the **f**.
2Co 6: 3 we act, and so no one can find **f** with our ministry.
8:20 for we are anxious that no one should find **f** with
Eph 1: 4 us in Christ to be holy and without **f** in his eyes.
5:27 Instead, she will be holy and without **f**.
Php 3: 6 so carefully that I was never accused of any **f**.
Col 1:22 as you stand before him without a single **f**.
1Ti 6:14 Then no one can find **f** with you from now until
Heb 8: 8 But God himself found **f** with the old one when he

FAULTLESS (2) [FAULT]

1Th 2:10 and honest and **f** toward all of you believers.
Heb 8: 7 If the first covenant had been **f**, there would have

FAULTS (5) [FAULT]

Ps 19:12 in my heart? / Cleanse me from these hidden **f**.
Pr 17: 9 Disregarding another person's **f** preserves love;
Isa 43:24 me with your sins and wearied me with your **f**.
Eph 4: 2 making allowance for each other's **f** because of
Col 3:13 You must make allowance for each other's **f**

FAVOR (94) [FAVORABLE, FAVORABLY, FAVORED, FAVORING, FAVORITE, FAVORITES, FAVORITISM, FAVORS]

Ge 6: 8 But Noah found **f** with the LORD.
39:21 and he granted Joseph **f** with the chief jailer.
40:14 have some pity on me when you are back in his **f**.
Ex 23: 3 And do not slant your testimony in **f** of a person
33:12 me by name and tell me I have found **f** with you.
33:16 that your people and I have found **f** with you?
33:17 for you have found **f** with me, and you are my
34: 9 "If it is true that I have found **f** in your sight,
Nu 6:26 May the LORD show you his **f** / and give you his
32: 5 If we have found **f** with you, please let us have this
Dt 1:17 you make decisions, never **f** those who are rich;
33:16 and the **f** of the one who appeared in the burning
33:23 "O Naphtali, you are rich in **f** / and full of the
Jdg 9: 3 they decided in **f** of Abimelech because he was
1Sa 2:26 he also continued to gain **f** with the LORD
1Ki 2:14 In fact, I have a **f** to ask of you." "What is it?"
2:16 So now I have just one **f** to ask of you. Please don't
Ne 1:11 success now as I go to ask the king for a great **f**.
13:31 the priests. / Remember this in my **f**, O my God.
Job 8: 5 if you pray to God and seek the **f** of the Almighty,
13: 8 but will you slant your testimony in his **f**?
13:10 in your hearts you slant your testimony in his **f**.
Ps 9: 4 For you have judged in my **f**; / from your throne,
30: 5 lasts for a moment, / but his **f** lasts a lifetime!
30: 7 Your **f**, O LORD, made me as secure as a
31:16 Let your **f** shine on your servant. / In your
45:12 People of great wealth will entreat your **f**.
51:18 Look with **f** on Zion and help her;
60: 1 have been angry with us; now restore us to your **f**.
67: 1 May his face shine with **f** upon us. / *Interlude*
69:13 hoping this is the time you will show me **f**.
77: 7 me forever? / Will he never again show me **f**?
84: 9 O God, look with **f** upon the king, our protector!
86:17 Send me a sign of your **f**. / Then those who hate
89:17 glorious strength. / Our power is based on your **f**.
102:14 and show **f** even to the dust in her streets.
106: 4 too, LORD, when you show **f** to your people;
Pr 3: 4 Then you will find **f** with both God and people,
3:34 mocks at mockers, but he shows **f** to the humble.
11:27 If you search for good, you will find **f**; but if you
16:15 there is life; his **f** refreshes like a gentle rain.
18: 5 It is wrong for a judge to **f** the guilty or condemn
18:22 finds a treasure and receives **f** from the LORD.
19:12 like a lion's roar, but his **f** is like dew on the grass.
29:26 Many seek the ruler's **f**, but justice comes from the
Ecc 9: 1 or not God will show them **f** in this life.
Isa 61: 2 mourn that the time of the LORD's **f** has come,
Da 7:22 and judged in **f** of the holy people of the Most
Zec 7: 2 along with their men, to seek the LORD's **f**.
11: 7 and named one **F** and the other Union.
11:10 Then I took my staff called **F** and snapped it in
Mal 1: 9 of offering, why should he show you any **f** at all?"
Mt 14: 3 and imprisoned John as a **f** to his wife Herodias
20:20 with her sons. She knelt respectfully to ask a **f**.
Mk 6:17 to arrest and imprison John as a **f** to Herodias.
10:35 "Teacher," they said, "we want you to do us a **f**."
Lk 2:40 his years, and God placed his special **f** upon him.
4:19 and that the time of the Lord's **f** has come."
12:37 There will be special **f** for those who are ready
12:38 there will be special **f** for his servants who are
12:52 be split apart, three in **f** of me, and two against—
Ac 4:33 Lord Jesus, and God's great **f** was upon them all.
7:10 And God gave him **f** before Pharaoh, king of
7:46 "David found **f** with God and asked for the
11:23 When he arrived and saw this proof of God's **f**,
15:11 the same way, by the special **f** of the Lord Jesus."
24:27 because Felix wanted to gain **f** with the Jewish
25: 3 They asked Festus as a **f** to transfer Paul to
Ro 11: 7 Most of the Jews have not found the **f** of God they
1Co 3:10 Because of God's special **f** to me, I have laid the
15:10 because God poured out his special **f** on me—
2Co 12: 9 Each time he said, "My gracious **f** is all you need.
Gal 4:10 You are trying to find **f** with God by what you do
4:17 so anxious to win your **f** are not doing it for your
5: 3 If you are trying to find **f** with God by being
Eph 2: 5 (It is only by God's special **f** that you have been
2: 7 to us as examples of the incredible wealth of his **f**
2: 8 God saved you by his special **f** when you believed.
3: 2 ministry of announcing his **f** to you Gentiles.
3: 7 By God's special **f** and mighty power, I have been
2Th 1:12 because of the undeserved **f** of our God and Lord,
2:16 and in his special **f** gave us everlasting comfort
1Ti 5:21 taking sides or showing special **f** to anyone.
2Ti 2: 1 be strong with the special **f** God gives you in
Phm 1: 8 That is why I am boldly asking a **f** of you. I could
1:20 please do me this **f** for the Lord's sake.
Heb 12:15 so that none of you will miss out on the special **f** of
13: 9 spiritual strength comes from God's special **f**,
Jas 2: 1 Christ if you **f** some people more than others?
4: 6 against the proud, / but he shows **f** to the humble."
1Pe 1: 2 May you have more and more of God's special **f**
5: 5 against the proud, / but he shows **f** to the humble."
2Pe 1: 2 May God bless you with his special **f**
3:18 But grow in the special **f** and knowledge of our

FAVORABLE (2) [FAVOR]

1Ki 12: 7 to serve the people today and give them a **f** answer,
2Ti 4: 2 Be persistent, whether the time is **f** or not.

FAVORABLY (7) [FAVOR]

Ex 11: 3 the Egyptians to look **f** on the people of Israel,
12:36 The LORD caused the Egyptians to look **f** on the
Lev 26: 9 "I will look **f** upon you and multiply your people
1Sa 20:12 If he speaks **f** about you, I will let you know.
Ezr 9: 9 Instead, he caused the kings of Persia to treat us **f**.
Ps 20: 3 and look **f** on your burnt offerings. / *Interlude*
Jn 7:13 But no one had the courage to speak **f** about him in

FAVORED (3) [FAVOR]

Ge 25:28 wild game he brought home, but Rebekah **f** Jacob.
Ps 44: 3 it was because you **f** them and smiled on them.
Lk 1:28 appeared to her and said, "Greetings, **f** woman!

FAVORING (1) [FAVOR]

Lev 19:15 neither **f** the poor nor showing deference to the

FAVORITE (4) [FAVOR]

Ge 27: 9 I'll prepare your father's **f** dish from them.
27:31 Esau prepared his father's **f** meat dish and brought
39: 4 So Joseph naturally became quite a **f** with him.
Ps 69:12 I am the **f** topic of town gossip, / and all the

FAVORITES (7) [FAVOR]

Job 32:21 I won't play **f** or try to flatter anyone.
Mt 22:16 You are impartial and don't play **f**.
Mk 12:14 honest you are. You are impartial and don't play **f**.
Gal 2: 6 made no difference to me, for God has no **f**.)
Eph 6: 9 have the same Master in heaven, and he has no **f**.
Col 3:25 For God has no **f** who can get away with evil.
1Pe 1:17 Father to whom you pray has no **f** when he judges.

FAVORITISM (2) [FAVOR]

Pr 24:23 It is wrong to show **f** when passing judgment.
Ro 2:11 For God does not show **f**.

FAVORS (7) [FAVOR]

Ps 82: 2 How long will you shower special **f** on the wicked?
Pr 19: 6 Many beg **f** from a prince; everyone is the friend of
30: 7 O God, I beg two **f** from you before I die.
Jer 16:13 idols all you like—and I will grant you no **f**!
Mal 2:17 LORD **f** evildoers since he does not punish them.
Lk 2:14 and peace on earth to all whom God **f**."
Jude 1:16 and they flatter others to get **f** in return.

FAWN (1) [FAWNS]

Jer 14: 5 The deer abandons her newborn **f** because there is

FAWNED (1)

Eze 23:12 She **f** over her Assyrian neighbors, those handsome

FAWNS (3) [FAWN]

Ge 49:21 is a deer let loose, / producing magnificent **f**.
SS 4: 5 Your breasts are like twin **f** of a gazelle,
7: 3 Your breasts are like twin **f** of a gazelle.

FEAR (266) [AFRAID, FEARED, FEARFUL, FEARFULLY, FEARING, FEARLESS, FEARLESSLY, FEARS, FEARSOME, FRIGHT, FRIGHTEN, FRIGHTENED, FRIGHTENING, GOD-FEARING]

DO NOT FEAR (12) Ex 9:30; Dt 28:58; Ps 55:19; 112:7; Ecc 8:13; Isa 8:13; 35:4; 44:2; Jer 42:11; La 3:57; Eze 2:6; Mal 3:5

FEAR AND TREMBLING (2) Ps 55:5; Jer 30:5

FEAR GOD (14) Ge 22:12; Ex 18:21; Ps 55:19; 66:16; Ecc 5:7; 7:18; 8:12,13; 12:13; Lk 12:5; 23:40; 2Co 7:1; 1Pe 2:17; Rev 14:7

FEAR OF GOD (14) Lev 19:14,32; 25:17,36,43; Dt 25:18; 2Sa 23:3; 2Ch 20:29; 26:5; Ne 5:15; Job 15:4; Ps 36:1; Ro 3:18; 1Ti 5:20

FEAR OF THE LORD* (12) 2Ch 17:10; 19:9; Pr 1:7; 9:10; 10:27; 14:27; 15:33; 16:6; 19:23; 22:4; Isa 11:2; 33:6

FEAR OF THE LORD (4) Job 28:28; Ac 9:31; 2Co 5:11; Col 3:22

FEAR THE LORD* (30) Ex 9:30; Dt 6:2,13; 10:20; 14:23; 17:19; 31:12,13; Jos 4:24; 1Sa 12:24; 2Ch 19:7; Ps 25:12; 33:8; 34:11; 112:1; 115:11,13; 118:4; 128:1; 135:20; Pr 1:29; 2:5; 3:7; 8:13; 14:2,26; 23:17; 24:21; Hos 10:3; Mic 6:9

Ge 20: 8 had happened, great **f** swept through the crowd.
22:12 in any way, for now I know that you truly **f** God.
42: 4 however, for **f** some harm might come to him.
Ex 9:30 I know that you still do not **f** the LORD God as
15:15 All the people of Canaan will melt with **f**;
18:21 honest men who **f** God and hate bribes.
20:18 they stood at a distance, trembling with **f**.
20:20 now on, let your **f** of him keep you from sinning!"
Lev 19:14 "Show your **f** of God by treating the deaf with
19:32 "Show your **f** of God by standing up in the
25:17 Show your **f** of God by not taking advantage of
25:36 show your **f** of God by letting them live with you
25:43 Show your **f** of God by treating them well;
26: 6 in the land, and you will be able to sleep without **f**.

26:36 You will live there in such constant **f** that the
Dt 2:25 about you, they will tremble with dread and **f**.'
4:10 they will learn to **f** me as long as they live,
5:29 that they might **f** me and obey all my commands!
6: 2 and grandchildren might **f** the LORD your God as
6:13 You must **f** the LORD your God and serve him.
6:24 and to **f** him for our own prosperity
7:19 will use this same power against the people you **f**.
10:12 He requires you to **f** him, to live according to his
10:20 You must **f** the LORD your God and worship him
11:25 for the LORD your God will send **f** and dread
13: 4 Serve only the LORD your God and **f** him alone.
14:23 The purpose of tithing is to teach you always to **f**
17:19 That way he will learn to **f** the LORD his God by
18:16 or see this blazing fire for **f** you would die.
25:18 who were lagging behind. They had no **f** of God.
28:58 and if you do not **f** the glorious and awesome name
28:66 You will live night and day in **f**, with no reason to
31:12 may listen and learn to **f** the LORD your God
31:13 hear them and will learn to **f** the LORD your God.
Jos 2:11 No wonder our hearts have melted in **f**! No one has
4:24 and that you might **f** the LORD your God
5: 1 they lost heart and were paralyzed with **f**.
7: 5 The Israelites were paralyzed with **f** at this turn of
22:24 because we **f** that in the future your descendants
1Sa 5:11 and great **f** was sweeping across the city.
12:14 "Now if you will **f** and worship the LORD
12:24 But be sure to **f** the LORD and sincerely worship
13: 7 at Gilgal, and his men were trembling with **f**.
13:19 The Philistines wouldn't allow them for **f** they
16:14 spirit that filled him with depression and **f**.
28: 5 the vast Philistine army, he became frantic with **f**.
2Sa 4: 1 all courage, and his people were paralyzed with **f**.
9: 6 he bowed low in great **f** and said, "I am your
17:10 have the heart of a lion, will be paralyzed with **f**.
23: 3 who rules righteously, / who rules in the **f** of God,
1Ki 8:40 Then they will **f** you and walk in your ways as long
8:43 people of the earth will come to know and **f** you,
2Ki 10: 4 But they were paralyzed with **f** and said,
1Ch 14:17 and the LORD caused all the nations to **f** David.
2Ch 6:31 Then they will **f** you and walk in your ways as long
6:33 people of the earth will come to know and **f** you,
17:10 Then the **f** of the LORD fell over all the
19: 7 **F** the LORD and judge with care, for the LORD
19: 9 "You must always act in the **f** of the LORD,
20:29 the enemies of Israel, the **f** of God came over them.
26: 5 of Zechariah, who instructed him in the **f** of God.
Ne 5: 9 Should you not walk in the **f** of our God in order to
5:15 But because of my **f** of God, I did not act that way.
Est 9: 3 and the royal officials helped the Jews for **f** of
Job 4:14 **F** gripped me; I trembled and shook with terror.
5:21 and will have no **f** of destruction when it comes.
6:14 but you have accused me without the slightest **f** of
9:35 Then I could speak to him without **f**, but I cannot
11:15 in innocence. You will be strong and free of **f**.
13:11 into your heart? Does not your **f** of him seize you?
15: 4 Have you no **f** of God, no reverence for him?
15:21 and even on good days they **f** the attack of the
15:22 They dare not go out into the darkness for **f** they
21: 9 Their homes are safe from every **f**, and God does
28:28 'The **f** of the Lord is true wisdom; to forsake evil
37:24 No wonder people everywhere **f** him. People who
Ps 2:11 Serve the LORD with reverent **f**, / and rejoice
9:20 Make them tremble in **f**, O LORD. / Let them
22:23 Praise the LORD, all you who **f** him!
25:12 Who are those who **f** the LORD? / He will show
25:14 with the LORD is reserved for those who **f** him.
27: 3 army surrounds me, / my heart will know no **f**.
31:22 In sudden **f** I had cried out, / "I have been cut off
33: 8 Let everyone in the world **f** the LORD, / and let
33:18 But the LORD watches over those who **f** him,
34: 7 For the angel of the LORD guards all who **f** him,
34:11 listen to me, / and I will teach you to **f** the LORD.
36: 1 They have no **f** of God to restrain them.
46: 2 So we will not **f**, even if earthquakes come
49: 5 There is no need to **f** when times of trouble come,
55: 5 **F** and trembling overwhelm me. / I can't stop
55:19 refuse to change their ways; / they do not **f** God.
61: 5 an inheritance reserved for those who **f** your name.
66:16 Come and listen, all you who **f** God, / and I will
67: 7 bless us, / and people all over the world will **f** him.
90:11 Your wrath is as awesome as the **f** you deserve.
91: 5 terrors of the night, / nor **f** the dangers of the day,
103:11 For his unfailing love toward those who **f** him
103:13 tender and compassionate to those who **f** him.
103:17 LORD remains forever / with those who **f** him.
112: 1 Happy are those who **f** the LORD. / Yes,
112: 7 They do not **f** bad news; / they confidently trust the
115:11 All you who **f** the LORD, trust the LORD!
115:13 He will bless those who **f** the LORD, / both great
118: 4 Let all who **f** the LORD repeat: / "His faithful
119:74 May all who **f** you find in me a cause for joy,
119:79 with all who **f** you and know your decrees.
119:120 I tremble in **f** of you; / I **f** your judgments.
128: 1 How happy are those who **f** the LORD— / all who
128: 4 That is the LORD's reward / for those who **f** him.
130: 4 offer forgiveness, / that we might learn to **f** you.
135:20 All you who **f** the LORD, praise the LORD!
143: 4 I am losing all hope; / I am paralyzed with **f**.
145:19 He fulfills the desires of those who **f** him;
Pr 1: 7 **F** of the LORD is the beginning of knowledge.
1:29 hated knowledge and chose not to **f** the LORD.
2: 5 Then you will understand what it means to **f** the
3: 7 Instead, **f** the LORD and turn your back on evil.
3:24 You can lie down without **f** and enjoy pleasant
8:13 All who **f** the LORD will hate evil. That is why I
9:10 **F** of the LORD is the beginning of wisdom.
10:27 **F** of the LORD lengthens one's life, but the years
14: 2 Those who follow the right path **f** the LORD;
14:26 Those who **f** the LORD are secure; he will be a
14:27 **F** of the LORD is a life-giving fountain; it offers
15:16 It is better to have little with **f** for the LORD than
15:33 **F** of the LORD teaches a person to be wise;
16: 6 cover sin; evil is avoided by **f** of the LORD.
19:23 **F** of the LORD gives life, security, and protection
22: 4 True humility and **f** of the LORD lead to riches,
23:17 envy sinners, but always continue to **f** the LORD.
24:21 My child, **f** the LORD and the king, and don't
31:21 She has no **f** of winter for her household
31:25 and dignity, and she laughs with no **f** of the future.
Ecc 3:14 God's purpose in this is that people should **f** him.
5: 7 is ruin in a flood of empty words. **F** God instead.
7:18 but those who **f** God will succeed either way.
8:12 I know that those who **f** God will be better off.
8:13 never live long, good lives, for they do not **f** God.
12:13 **F** God and obey his commands, for this is the duty
Isa 2:19 his enemies will crawl with **f** into holes in the
7: 2 hearts of the king and his people trembled with **f**,
7: 4 Tell him he doesn't need to **f** the fierce anger of
7:16 right from wrong, the two kings you **f** so much—
8:13 Do not **f** anything except the LORD Almighty.
8:13 Holy One. If you **f** him, you need **f** nothing else.
10:29 **F** strikes the city of Ramah. All the people of
11: 2 the Spirit of knowledge and the **f** of the LORD.
13: 7 Every arm is paralyzed with **f**. Even the strongest
13: 8 **F** grips them with terrible pangs, like those of a
14: 3 LORD gives his people rest from sorrow and **f**,
14:31 Melt in **f**, for everyone will be destroyed.
19: 1 The hearts of the Egyptians melt with **f**.
19:16 They will cower in **f** beneath the upraised fist of
29:22 "My people will no longer pale with **f** or be
33: 6 The **f** of the LORD is the key to this treasure.
33:14 The sinners among my people shake with **f**.
35: 4 to those who are afraid, "Be strong, and do not **f**,
41: 5 The lands beyond the sea watch in **f**. Remote lands
41:23 miracle that will fill us with amazement and **f**.
44: 2 do not be afraid. O Israel, my chosen one, do not **f**.
45: 1 Before him, mighty kings will be paralyzed with **f**.
51:13 Will you continue to **f** the anger of your enemies
54: 4 "**F** not; you will no longer live in shame.
57:11 I have not corrected you that you have no **f** of me?
63:17 given us stubborn hearts so we no longer **f** you?
Jer 2:19 forsake the LORD your God, having no **f** of him.
4: 9 "the king and the officials will tremble in **f**.
6:24 **F** and pain have gripped us, like that of a woman
10: 7 Who would not **f** you, O King of nations? That title
30: 5 the people crying; there is only **f** and trembling.
36:24 the king nor his officials showed any signs of **f**
38:26 to Jonathan's dungeon, for **f** you would die there."
39:17 but I will rescue you from those you **f** so much.
42:11 Do not **f** the king of Babylon anymore,
42:16 and famine you **f** will follow close behind you,
46:28 **F** not, Jacob, my servant," says the LORD,
49:16 You are proud that you inspire **f** in others. And you
49:23 towns of Hamath and Arpad are struck with **f**,
49:24 **F**, anguish, and pain have gripped her as they do a
50:43 **F** and pain have gripped him, like that of a woman
La 3:47 We are filled with **f**, for we are trapped, desolate,
3:57 at my despairing cry and told me, "Do not **f**."
Eze 2: 6 "Son of man, do not **f** them. Don't be afraid even
3: 9 So don't be afraid of them or **f** their angry looks,
7:27 and the people's hands will tremble with **f**.
11: 8 I will expose you to the war you so greatly **f**,
12:18 Drink your water with **f**, as if it were your last.
19: 7 Everyone in the land trembled in **f** / when they
21: 7 it comes true, the boldest heart will melt with **f**;
26:17 naval power, / once spread **f** around the world.
31:16 I made the nations shake with **f** at the sound of its
32:10 They will shudder in **f** for their lives as I brandish
34:25 wildest places and sleep in the woods without **f**.
Da 5: 6 and his face turned pale with **f**. Such terror gripped
5:19 and languages trembled before him in **f**.
6:26 should tremble with **f** before the God of Daniel.
7:28 by my thoughts and my face was pale with **f**,
10:11 he said this to me, I stood up, still trembling with **f**.
Hos 10: 3 have no king because we didn't **f** the LORD.
13: 1 the people shook with **f** because the other Israelite
Joel 2: 1 Let everyone tremble in **f** because the day of the
2: 6 **F** grips all the people; every face grows pale with
Am 3: 8 The lion has roared—tremble in **f**! The Sovereign
Mic 4: 4 and prosperity, for there will be nothing to **f**.
6: 9 Listen! **F** the LORD if you are wise! His voice is
7:17 They will **f** him greatly, trembling in terror at his
Na 2:11 and the young and tender lived with nothing to **f**?
3:11 You will hide for **f** of the attacking enemy.
Hab 3:16 when I heard all this; my lips quivered with **f**.
Zep 3:15 will be over, and you will **f** disaster no more.
Zec 9: 5 will see Tyre fall and will be filled with **f**.
Mal 3: 5 for these people do not **f** me," says the LORD
4: 2 "But for you who **f** my name, the Sun of
Mt 9: 8 **F** swept through the crowd as they saw this happen
10:28 **F** only God, who can destroy both soul and body in
28: 4 The guards shook with **f** when they saw him,
Mk 10:32 people following behind were overwhelmed with **f**.
Lk 1:12 Zechariah was overwhelmed with **f**.
1:50 from generation to generation, / to all who **f** him.
1:74 from our enemies, / so we can serve God without **f**,
7:16 Great **f** swept the crowd, and they praised God,
8:37 them alone, for a great wave of **f** swept over them.
12: 5 But I'll tell you whom to **f**. **F** God, who has the
power to kill people and
18: 4 'I **f** neither God nor man,' he said to himself,
23:40 "Don't you **f** God even when you are dying?
Jn 3:20 They stay away from the light for **f** their sins will
12:42 because of their **f** that the Pharisees would expel
Ac 5:11 Great **f** gripped the entire church and all others
9:31 The believers were walking in the **f** of the Lord
10:35 In every nation he accepts those who **f** him and do
13:16 "and you devout Gentiles who **f** the God of Israel,
13:26 and also all of you devout Gentiles who **f** the God
16:29 Trembling with **f**, the jailer called for lights
19:17 A solemn **f** descended on the city, and the name of
Ro 3:18 "They have no **f** of God to restrain them."
11:20 think highly of yourself, but **f** what could happen.
1Co 1:17 for **f** that the cross of Christ would lose its power.
9:27 I **f** that after preaching to others I myself might be
2Co 5:11 because we know this solemn **f** of the Lord that we
7: 1 us work toward complete purity because we **f** God.
7: 5 from every direction, and inside there was **f**.
11: 3 But I **f** that somehow you will be led away from
Gal 4:11 I **f** for you. I am afraid that all my hard work for
Eph 6: 5 obey your earthly masters with deep respect and **f**.
Php 2:12 your lives, obeying God with deep reverence and **f**.
Col 3:22 because of your reverent **f** of the Lord.
1Th 2:16 News to the Gentiles, for **f** some might be saved.
1Ti 5:20 so that others will have a proper **f** of God.
2Ti 1: 7 For God has not given us a spirit of **f** and timidity,
Heb 2:15 have lived all their lives as slaves to the **f** of dying.
4: 1 so we ought to tremble with **f** that some of you
12:28 and please God by worshiping him with holy **f**
1Pe 1:17 So you must live in reverent **f** of him during your
2:17 Love your Christian brothers and sisters. **F** God.
3: 6 is right without **f** of what your husbands might do.
1Jn 4:18 Such love has no **f** because perfect love expels all **f**.
4:18 If we are afraid, it is for **f** of judgment, and this
Rev 11:18 all who **f** your name, from the least to the greatest.
14: 7 "**F** God," he shouted. "Give glory to him.
15: 4 Who will not **f**, O Lord, and glorify your name?
19: 5 from the least to the greatest, all who **f** him."

FEARED (27) [FEAR]

Ex 1:17 But because the midwives **f** God, they refused to
1:21 And because the midwives **f** God, he gave them
14:31 they **f** the LORD and put their faith in him and his
Dt 9:19 How I **f** for you, for the LORD was ready to
18:22 prophet has spoken on his own and need not be **f**.
28:60 against you all the diseases of Egypt that you **f**
32:17 to gods their ancestors had never **f**.
32:27 But I **f** the taunt of the enemy, / that their
Jos 9:24 So we **f** for our lives because of you. That is why
1Sa 14:26 because they all **f** the oath they had taken.
2Ki 4: 1 you is dead, and you know how he **f** the LORD.
Ne 7: 2 for he was a faithful man who **f** God more than
Est 8:17 for they **f** what the Jews might do to them.
Job 1: 1 He **f** God and stayed away from evil.
3:25 What I always **f** has happened to me. What I
31:34 Have I **f** the crowd and its contempt, so that I
Ps 76: 7 No wonder you are greatly **f**! / Who can stand
76:12 spirit of princes / and is **f** by the kings of the earth.
Isa 18: 2 who are **f** far and wide for their conquests
18: 7 who are **f** far and wide for their conquests
66: 4 great troubles against them—all the things they **f**.
Mal 1:14 "and my name is **f** among the nations!
3:16 Then those who **f** the LORD spoke with each
3:16 was written to record the names of those who **f** him
Lk 22: 2 without starting a riot, a possibility they greatly **f**.
Jn 19:38 disciple of Jesus (because he **f** the Jewish leaders),
Ac 10: 2 He was a devout man who **f** the God of Israel,

FEARFUL (5) [FEAR]

Ps 89: 9 When their waves rise in **f** storms, you subdue
Jer 51:30 courage is gone. They have become as **f** as women.
Lk 21:26 because of the **f** fate they see coming upon the
Ro 8:15 So you should not be like cowering, **f** slaves.
2Co 2:16 To those who are perishing we are a **f** smell of

FEARFULLY (1) [FEAR]

Eze 4:16 It will be weighed out with great care and eaten **f**.

FEARING (6) [FEAR]

Nu 16:34 **f** that the earth would swallow them, too.
Dt 8: 6 your God by walking in his ways and **f** him.
Ps 38:11 loved ones and friends stay away, **f** my disease.
Pr 29:25 **F** people is a dangerous trap, but to trust the
Jnh 1: 5 **F** for their lives, the desperate sailors shouted to
Ac 23:10 the commander, **f** they would tear him apart,

FEARLESS (2) [FEAR]

Job 41:33 There is nothing else so **f** anywhere on earth.
Ps 112: 8 They are confident and **f** / and can face their foes

FEARLESSLY (3) [FEAR]

Ps 64: 4 ambush at the innocent, / attacking suddenly and **f**.
Mic 3: 8 and might, **f** pointing out Israel's sin and rebellion.
Eph 3:12 in him, we can now come **f** into God's presence,

FEARS (14) [FEAR]

Job 1: 8 He **f** God and will have nothing to do with evil."
1: 9 Satan replied to the LORD, "Yes, Job **f** God,
2: 3 He **f** God and will have nothing to do with evil.
22:10 is why you are surrounded by traps and sudden **f**.
Ps 34: 4 and he answered me, / freeing me from all my **f**.
34: 6 and he heard me. / He set me free from all my **f**.
119:63 Anyone who **f** you is my friend— / anyone who
Pr 10:24 The **f** of the wicked will all come true; so will the
31:30 but a woman who **f** the LORD will be greatly
Isa 50:10 Who among you **f** the LORD and obeys his

Zep 3:17 With his love, he will calm all your f.
Ac 10:22 He is a devout man who f the God of Israel and is
Ro 8:38 Our f for today, our worries about tomorrow,
15: 1 and f of those who think these things are wrong.

FEARSOME (1) [FEAR]

Eze 14:21 How terrible it will be when all four of these f

FEAST (55) [FEASTED, FEASTING, FEASTS]

Ge 19: 3 He set a great f before them, complete with fresh
26:30 So Isaac prepared a great f for them, and they ate
29:22 to celebrate with Jacob at a wedding f.
31:54 a sacrifice to God and invited everyone to a f.
43:16 this noon. Take them inside and prepare a big f."
Ex 13: 6 you will celebrate a great f to the LORD.
Dt 12: 7 and your families will f in the presence of the
14:26 Then f there in the presence of the LORD your
27: 7 and f there with great joy before the LORD your
32:13 he let them f on the crops of the fields.
1Sa 9:25 After the f, when they had returned to the town,
2Sa 3:20 twenty men, David entertained them with a great f.
13:23 Absalom invited all the king's sons to come to a f.
1Ki 18:42 So Ahab prepared a f. But Elijah climbed to the top
2Ki 6:23 So the king made a great f for them and then sent
2Ch 18: 2 great numbers of sheep and oxen for the f.
Ne 8:10 "Go and celebrate with a f of choice foods
Est 1:10 On the seventh day of the f, when King Xerxes
Ps 22:29 Let the rich of the earth f and worship. / Let all
23: 5 You prepare a f for me / in the presence of my
81: 3 Sound the trumpet for a sacred f / when the moon
Pr 15:15 for the happy heart, life is a continual f.
17: 1 A dry crust eaten in peace is better than a great f
Ecc 10:16 king is a child and whose leaders f in the morning.
10:17 and whose leaders f only to gain strength for their
Isa 21: 5 Look! They are preparing a great f. They are
22:13 sacrificial animals, f on meat, and drink wine.
25: 6 the LORD Almighty will spread a wonderful f for
25: 6 It will be a delicious f of good food, with clear,
Jer 51:39 I will prepare a different kind of f for them.
Eze 39:17 to them: Gather together for my great sacrificial f.
39:19 This is the sacrificial f I have prepared for you.
39:20 F at my banquet table—f on horses, riders, and valiant warriors,
44: 3 inside this gateway to f in the LORD's presence.
45:23 On each of the seven days of the f he will prepare a
Da 5: 1 King Belshazzar gave a great f for a thousand of
Mt 8:11 and Jacob at the f in the Kingdom of Heaven.
11:19 f and drink, and you say, 'He's a glutton and a
22: 2 a king who prepared a great wedding f for his son.
22: 4 'The f has been prepared, and choice meats have
22: 8 he said to his servants, 'The wedding f is ready,
25:10 who were ready went in with him to the marriage f,
Lk 7:34 f and drink, and you say, 'He's a glutton and a
12:36 for your master to return from the wedding f.
14: 8 "If you are invited to a wedding f, don't always
14:16 "A man prepared a great f and sent out many
15:23 fattening in the pen. We must celebrate with a f,
15:27 calf we were fattening and has prepared a great f.
15:29 me even one young goat for a f with my friends.
Jn 18:28 wouldn't be allowed to celebrate the Passover f.
1Co 15:32 If there is no resurrection, / "Let's f and get drunk,
2Pe 2:13 They revel in deceitfulness while they f with you.
Rev 19: 7 For the time has come for the wedding f of the
19: 9 Blessed are those who are invited to the wedding f

FEASTED (6) [FEAST]

Ge 43:34 the others. So they all f and drank freely with him.
Nu 23:24 They refuse to rest / until they have f on prey,
1Ch 12:39 They f and drank with David for three days,
29:22 They f and drank in the LORD's presence with
Job 42:11 former friends came and f with him in his home.
Eze 18: 6 and he has not f in the mountains before Israel's

FEASTING (15) [FEAST]

Ex 32: 6 After this, they celebrated with f and drinking,
Nu 25: 2 and soon the Israelites were f with them
Jdg 19: 8 time this afternoon." So they had another day of f.
1Ki 1:25 They are f and drinking with him and shouting,
Est 9:17 celebrating their victory with a day of f
9:18 third day, making that their day of f and gladness.
9:22 He told them to celebrate these days with f
Job 1:18 and daughters were f in their oldest brother's
Isa 66:17 f on pork and rats and other forbidden meats,
La 2:22 as though you were calling them to a day of f.
Hos 9: 5 What will you do on days of f in the LORD's
Lk 5:33 that Jesus' disciples were f instead of fasting.
5:33 of the Pharisees. Why are yours always f?"
1Co 10: 7 "The people celebrated with f and drinking,
1Pe 4: 3 and lust, their f and drunkenness and wild parties,

FEASTS (4) [FEAST]

Jer 15:17 I never joined the people in their merry f. I sat
16: 8 "And do not go to their f and parties. Do not eat
51:38 "In their drunken f, the people of Babylon roar
Eze 46:11 "So at the special f and sacred festivals, the grain

FEAT (1) [FEATS]

2Ki 8:13 a nobody like me ever accomplish such a great f?"

FEATHERS (5)

Lev 1:16 The priest must remove the crop and the f
Job 39:13 but they are no match for the f of the stork.
Ps 91: 4 you with his wings. / He will shelter you with his f.
Eze 17: 3 wings full of many-colored f came to Lebanon.
Da 4:33 this way until his hair was as long as eagles' f

FEATS (2) [FEAT]

2Sa 23:18 It was by such f that he became as famous as the
1Ch 11:20 It was by such f that he became as famous as the

FEATURES (1)

Job 38:14 For the f of the earth take shape as the light

FEBRUARY (2)

Eze 26: 1 On F 3, during the twelfth year of King
Zec 1: 7 Then on F 15 of the second year of King Darius's

FED (26) [FEED]

Ge 24:32 gave him straw to bed them down, f them,
Dt 8:16 He f you with manna in the wilderness, a food
32:14 He f them curds from the herd and milk from the
Jdg 19:21 he took them home with him and f their donkeys.
1Sa 2: 5 Those who were well f are now starving;
2Sa 19:42 And he hasn't f us or even given us gifts!"
Ne 5:17 even though I regularly f 150 Jewish officials at
Ps 80: 5 You have f us with sorrow / and made us drink
Isa 41:18 Rivers f by springs will flow across the dry,
61: 6 You will be f with the treasures of the nations
Jer 5: 7 I f my people until they were fully satisfied.
5:28 They are well f and well groomed, and there is no
Eze 3: 2 So I opened my mouth, and he f me the scroll.
Da 1:16 the attendant f them only vegetables instead of the
4:12 in its branches. All the world was f from this tree.
Hos 4: 8 "The priests get f when the people sin and bring
Mt 10:10 because those who work deserve to be f.
15:38 There were four thousand men who were f that
16: 9 Don't you remember the five thousand I f with five
16:10 Don't you remember the four thousand I f with
25:35 For I was hungry, and you f me. I was thirsty,
Mk 8:19 What about the five thousand men I f with five
8:20 "And when I f the four thousand with seven
Jn 6:26 you want to be with me because I f you, not
Ac 28: 7 welcomed us courteously and f us for three days.
1Ti 4: 6 one who is f by the message of faith and the true

FEDERATION (1)

Jos 11:10 (Hazor had at one time been the capital of the f of

FEE (1)

Ex 22:15 because this loss was covered by the rental f.

FEEBLE (6)

Ne 4: 2 this bunch of poor, f Jews think they are doing?
Ps 105:37 there were no sick or f people among them.
Pr 11: 7 all perish, for they rely on their own f strength.
Jer 49:24 Damascus has become f, and all her people turn to
Eze 7:17 Everyone's hands will be f; their knees will be as
Na 2:11 where the old and f and the young and tender lived

FEED (64) [FED, FEEDING, FEEDS, PASTURE-FED, WELL-FED]

Ge 42:27 opened his sack to get some grain to f the donkeys,
47:24 it to plant the next year's crop and to f yourselves,
Lev 26:26 one oven will have to be stretched to f ten families.
Jdg 8: 6 them first, and then we will f your warriors."
8:15 and then we will f your exhausted warriors.' "
2Sa 13:10 the food into my bedroom and f it to me here."
1Ki 17: 9 of Sidon. There is a widow there who will f you.
22:27 and f him nothing but bread and water until I
2Ki 4:43 "F one hundred people with only this?"
2Ch 18:26 and f him nothing but bread and water until I
Ps 36: 8 You f them from the abundance of your own
80:13 forest devours us, / and the wild animals f on us.
81:16 But I would f you with the best of foods. / I would
104:28 You open your hand to f them, and they are
Pr 19:24 so lazy that they won't even lift a finger to f
22: 9 those who are generous, because they f the poor.
26:15 so lazy that they won't lift a finger to f themselves.
SS 1: 8 the shepherds' tents, and there f your young goats.
2: 5 Oh, f me with your love—your 'raisins' and your
Isa 5:17 In those days flocks will f among the ruins; lambs
9:21 Manasseh will f on Ephraim, Ephraim will f on Manasseh, and both will devour
14:30 I will f the poor in my pasture; the needy will lie
40:11 He will f his flock like a shepherd. He will carry
49:26 I will f your enemies with their own flesh.
58:10 F the hungry and help those in trouble. Then your
61: 5 They will f your flocks and plow your fields
65:25 The wolf and lamb will f together. The lion will eat
Jer 9:15 I will f them with bitterness and give them poison
23:15 "I will f them with bitterness and give them poison
50:19 own land, to f in the fields of Carmel and Bashan,
La 4: 3 Even the jackals f their young, but not my people
Eze 7:19 It will neither satisfy nor f them, for their love of
34: 2 Destruction is certain for you shepherds who f
34: 2 of your flocks. Shouldn't shepherds f their sheep?
34:10 I will take away their right to f the flock,
34:10 the flock, along with their right to f themselves.
34:13 I will f them on the mountains of Israel and by the
34:14 in pleasant places and f in lush mountain pastures.
34:16 I will f them, yes—f them justice!
34:23 He will f them and be a shepherd to them.
Hos 9: 2 So now your harvests will be too small to f you.
9: 4 They may eat this food to f themselves, but they
11: 4 yoke from his neck, and I myself stooped to f him.
12: 1 The people of Israel f on the wind; they chase after
Na 2:12 You crushed your enemies to f your cubs and your
Zec 9: 7 meat with blood in it or f on other forbidden foods.
11:16 the young, nor heal the injured, nor f the healthy.
Mt 4: 4 their life; / they must f on every word of God.' "
14:16 Jesus replied, "That isn't necessary—you f them."
25:37 when did we ever see you hungry and f you?
25:42 For I was hungry, and you didn't f me. I was
Mk 6:37 But Jesus said, "You f them." "With what?"
Lk 9:13 But Jesus said, "You f them." "Impossible!"
15:15 He persuaded a local farmer to hire him to f his
Jn 6: 5 where can we buy bread to f all these people?"
6: 7 "It would take a small fortune to f them!"
21:15 I love you." "Then f my lambs," Jesus told him.
21:17 know I love you." Jesus said, "Then f my sheep.
Ac 20:28 Be sure that you f and shepherd God's flock—
Ro 12:20 "If your enemies are hungry, f them. / If they are
1Co 3: 2 I had to f you with milk and not with solid food,
2Th 3: 9 that we didn't have the right to ask you to f us,

FEEDING (13) [FEED]

Dt 8: 3 letting you go hungry and then f you with manna,
8: 3 real life comes by f on every word of the LORD.
2Sa 13:11 But as she was f him, he grabbed her
Job 1:14 were plowing, with the donkeys f beside them,
SS 4: 5 are like twin fawns of a gazelle, f among the lilies.
Mt 8:30 A large herd of pigs was f in the distance,
24:45 of managing his household and f his family?
Mk 5:11 There happened to be a large herd of pigs f on the
8: 3 And if I send them home without f them, they will
Lk 8:32 A large herd of pigs was f on the hillside nearby,
12:42 of managing his household and f his family.
15:16 so hungry that even the pods he was f the pigs
1Th 2: 7 but we were as gentle among you as a mother f

FEEDS (12) [FEED]

2Sa 13: 5 for you. Tell him you'll feel better if she f you."
2Ki 18:17 The Assyrians stopped beside the aqueduct that f
Job 39:30 for it f on the carcass of the slaughtered."
Ps 147: 9 He f the wild animals, / and the young ravens cry
Pr 15:14 person is hungry for truth, while the fool f on trash.
SS 2:16 lover is mine, and I am his. He f among the lilies!
Isa 7: 3 of the aqueduct that f water into the upper pool,
36: 2 The Assyrians stopped beside the aqueduct that f
44:20 The poor, deluded fool f on ashes. He is trusting
Eze 18:16 And suppose this son f the hungry,
Mt 6:26 food in barns because your heavenly Father f them.
Lk 12:24 or harvest or put food in barns because God f them.

FEEL (43) [FEELING, FEELINGS, FEELS, FELT, HEARTFELT]

Ge 23: 8 "Since this is how you f, be so kind as to ask
29:34 "Surely now my husband will f affection for me,
31:30 I know you f you must go, and you long intensely
Dt 2: 4 The Edomites will f threatened, so be careful.
19:13 Do not f sorry for that murderer! Purge the guilt of
1Sa 14:29 See how much better I f now that I have eaten this
16:23 Then Saul would f better, and the tormenting spirit
2Sa 13: 5 for you. Tell him you'll f better if she feeds you."
19: 5 Yet you act like this, making us f ashamed,
Ezr 7:18 and your colleagues f is the will of your God.
Job 21:19 not their children! Let them f their own penalty.
Ps 25:18 F my pain and see my trouble. / Forgive all my
115: 7 or f with their hands, / or walk with their feet,
Pr 23:35 And you will say, "They hit me, but I didn't f it.
30:12 They f pure, but they are filthy and unwashed.
Ecc 4: 6 They f it is better to be lazy and barely survive
8:11 is not punished, people f it is safe to do wrong.
Isa 3:14 and the princes will be the first to f the LORD's
49:15 Can she f no love for a child she has borne?
Jer 10:18 troubles upon you. At last you will f my anger."
13:21 How will you f when the LORD sets your foreign
15: 5 "Who will f sorry for you, Jerusalem? Who will
Eze 14:22 then you will f better about what I have done to
16:54 for your sins make them f good in comparison.
Jnh 4:10 the LORD said, "You f sorry about the plant,
4:11 Shouldn't I f sorry for such a great city?"
Mic 7: 1 I f like the fruit picker after the harvest who can
Mt 15:32 to him and said, "I f sorry for these people.
Mk 5:29 and she could f that she had been healed!
8: 2 "I f sorry for these people. They have been here
Lk 24:32 "Didn't our hearts f strangely warm as he talked
Jn 4:52 He asked them when the boy had begun to f better,
Ac 17:27 and perhaps f their way toward him and find him—
Ro 11:25 so that you will not f proud and start bragging.
15:27 because they f they owe a real debt to them.
15:27 they f the least they can do in return is help them
1Co 8: 1 While knowledge may make us f important,
11:16 and all the churches of God f the same way about
Gal 4:19 I f as if I am going through labor pains for you
Eph 3:13 so you should f honored and encouraged.
Php 1: 7 It is right that I should f as I do about all of you,
Heb 13: 3 as though you f their pain in your own bodies.
Jude 1:16 and complainers, doing whatever evil they f like.

FEELING (3) [FEEL]

Isa 47: 8 living at ease and f secure,
2Co 11:29 Who is weak without my f that weakness? Who is
Gal 5:20 the f that everyone is wrong except those in your

FEELINGS (1) [FEEL]

Heb 10: 2 and their f of guilt would have disappeared.

FEELS (4) [FEEL]

Ex 6: 1 "When he f my powerful hand upon him, he will

1Sa 20:12 and let you know at once how he **f** about you.
Ps 72:13 He **f** pity for the weak and the needy, / and he will
Jer 2:26 a thief, Israel **f** shame only when she gets caught.

FEET (416) [FOOT]

Ge 6:15 Make it 450 **f** long, 75 **f** wide, and 45 **f** high.
7:20 standing more than twenty-two **f** above the highest
18:4 while my servants get some water to wash your **f**.
19:2 he said, "come to my home to wash your **f**,
24:32 water for the camel drivers to wash their **f**.
43:24 led into the palace and given water to wash their **f**
Ex 4:25 She threw the foreskin at Moses' **f** and said,
24:10 Under his **f** there seemed to be a pavement of
25:10 a sacred chest 3-3/4 **f** long, 2-1/4 **f** wide, and 2-1/4 **f** high.
25:12 and attach them to its four **f**, two rings on each
25:17 It must be 3-3/4 **f** long and 2-1/4 **f** wide.
25:23 3 **f** long, 1-1/2 **f** wide, and 2-1/4 **f** high.
26:2 Each sheet must be forty-two **f** long and six **f** wide.
26:8 each forty-five **f** long and six **f** wide. All eleven
26:16 Each frame must be 15 **f** high and 2-1/4 **f** wide.
27:1 make a square altar 7-1/2 **f** wide, 7-1/2 **f** long, and 4-1/2 **f** high.
27:9 On the south side the curtains will stretch for 150 **f**.
27:11 150 **f** of curtains held up by twenty posts fitted into
27:12 on the west end of the courtyard will be 75 **f** long,
27:13 The east end will also be 75 **f** long.
27:14 The curtain on the right side will be 22-1/2 **f** long,
27:15 The curtain on the left side will also be 22-1/2 **f**
27:16 to the courtyard, make a curtain that is 30 **f** long.
27:18 So the entire courtyard will be 150 **f** long and 75 **f** wide, with curtain walls 7-1/2 **f** high,
29:20 their right thumbs and the big toes of their right **f**.
30:2 It must be eighteen inches square and three **f** high,
30:19 and his sons will wash their hands and **f** there
36:9 the same size—forty-two **f** long and six **f** wide.
36:15 the same size—forty-five **f** long and six **f** wide.
36:21 Each frame was 15 **f** high and 2-1/4 **f** wide.
37:1 It was 3-3/4 **f** long, 2-1/4 **f** wide, and 2-1/4 **f** high.
37:3 Four gold rings were fastened to its four **f**,
37:6 It was 3-3/4 **f** long and 2-1/4 **f** wide.
37:10 3 **f** long, 1-1/2 **f** wide, and 2-1/4 **f** high.
37:25 It was eighteen inches square and three **f** high,
38:1 It was 7-1/2 **f** square at the top and 4-1/2 **f** high.
38:9 the courtyard. The south wall was 150 **f** long.
38:11 The north wall was also 150 **f** long, with twenty
38:12 The west end was 75 **f** wide. The walls were made
38:13 The east end was also 75 **f** wide.
38:14 The curtain on the right side was 22-1/2 **f** long
38:15 The curtain on the left side was also 22-1/2 **f** long
38:18 It was 30 **f** long and 7-1/2 **f** high, just like the
40:31 Aaron's sons washed their hands and **f** in the basin.
Lev 8:24 of their right hands, and the big toe of their right **f**.
11:42 well as those with four legs and those with many **f**.
Nu 11:31 were quail flying about three **f** above the ground.
35:4 1,500 **f** from the town walls in every direction.
35:5 Measure off 3,000 **f** outside the town walls in
Dt 3:11 bed was more than thirteen **f** long and six **f** wide.
8:4 didn't wear out, and your **f** didn't blister or swell.
11:24 Wherever you set your **f**, the land will be yours.
22:4 Go and help your neighbor get it to its **f**!
28:56 would not so much as touch her **f** to the ground—
32:35 In due time their **f** will slip. / Their day of disaster
33:24 by his brothers; / may he bathe his **f** in olive oil.
Jos 3:13 When their **f** touch the water, the flow of water
3:15 But as soon as the **f** of the priests who were
10:24 "Come and put your **f** on the kings' necks."
Jdg 5:27 He sank, he fell, / he lay dead at her **f**.
19:21 After they washed their **f**, they had supper
Ru 2:10 Ruth fell at his **f** and thanked him warmly.
3:4 then go and uncover his **f** and lie down there.
3:7 Ruth came quietly, uncovered his **f**, and lay down.
3:8 He was surprised to find a woman lying at his **f**!
3:14 So Ruth lay at Boaz's **f** until the morning, but she
1Sa 14:13 So they climbed up using both hands and **f**,
17:4 was a giant of a man, measuring over nine **f** tall!
25:24 She fell at his **f** and said, "I accept all blame in this
2Sa 3:34 hands were not bound; / your **f** were not chained.
4:12 They cut off their hands and **f** and hung their
5:24 When you hear a sound like marching **f** in the tops
9:13 And Mephibosheth, who was crippled in both **f**,
15:30 and his **f** were bare as a sign of mourning.
19:24 He had not washed his **f** or clothes nor trimmed his
22:10 dark storm clouds were beneath his **f**.
22:37 You have made a wide path for my **f** / to keep
22:39 so they could not get up; / they fell beneath my **f**.
22:40 you have subdued my enemies under my **f**.
1Ki 6:2 King Solomon built for the LORD was 90 **f** long, 30 **f** wide, and 45 **f** high.
6:3 The foyer at the front of the Temple was 30 **f** wide,
6:3 It projected outward 15 **f** from the front of the
6:6 the bottom floor being 7-1/2 **f** wide, the second floor 9 **f** wide, and the top floor 10-1/2 **f** wide.
6:10 Each story of the complex was 7-1/2 **f** high.
6:16 It was 30 **f** deep and was paneled with cedar from
6:17 outside the Most Holy Place, was 60 **f** long.
6:20 This inner sanctuary was 30 **f** long, 30 **f** wide, and 30 **f** high.
6:23 two cherubim made of olive wood, each 15 **f** tall.
6:24 The wingspan of each of the cherubim was 15 **f**, each wing being 7-1/2 **f** long.
6:26 each was 15 **f** tall.
7:2 It was 150 **f** long, 75 **f** wide, and 45 **f** high.
7:6 of Pillars, which was 75 **f** long and 45 **f** wide.
7:10 Some of the huge foundation stones were 15 **f** long, and some were 12 **f** long.
7:15 each 27 **f** tall and 18 **f** in circumference.
7:16 made capitals of molded bronze, each 7-1/2 **f** tall.
7:19 foyer were shaped like lilies, and they were 6 **f** tall.
7:23 a large round tank, 15 **f** across from rim to rim;
7:23 It was 7-1/2 **f** deep and about 45 **f** in circumference.
7:27 each 6 **f** long, 6 **f** wide, and 4-1/2 **f** tall.
7:31 It projected 1-1/2 **f** above the cart's top like a
7:31 round pedestal, and its opening was 2-1/4 **f** across;
7:32 with the cart. The wheels were 2-1/4 **f** in diameter
7:38 Each basin was 6 **f** across and could hold 220
15:23 *of Judah.* In his old age his **f** became diseased.
2Ki 4:27 to the ground before him and caught hold of his **f**.
4:37 She fell at his **f**, overwhelmed with gratitude.
9:35 they found only her skull, her **f**, and her hands.
13:7 killed the others like they were dust under his **f**.
13:21 the dead man revived and jumped to his **f**!
14:13 to demolish six hundred **f** of Jerusalem's wall,
25:17 Each of the pillars was 27 **f** tall. The bronze capital on top of each pillar was 7-1/2 **f**
1Ch 11:23 Egyptian warrior who was seven and a half **f** tall
14:15 When you hear a sound like marching **f** in the tops
2Ch 3:3 The foundation for the Temple of God was ninety **f** long and thirty **f** wide.
3:4 The foyer at the front of the Temple was thirty **f**
3:4 pure gold. The roof of the foyer was thirty **f** high.
3:8 The Most Holy Place was thirty **f** wide,
3:8 width of the Temple, and it was also thirty **f** deep.
3:11 of the two cherubim standing side by side was 30 **f**.
3:11 One wing of the first figure was 7-1/2 **f** long,
3:11 The other wing, also 7-1/2 **f** long, touched one of
3:12 the second figure had one wing 7-1/2 **f** long that
3:12 The other wing, also 7-1/2 **f** long, touched the wing
3:13 the wingspan of both cherubim together was 30 **f**.
3:15 Solomon made two pillars that were 27 **f** tall,
3:15 by a capital extending upward another 7-1/2 **f**.
4:1 a bronze altar 30 **f** long, 30 **f** wide, and 15 **f** high.
4:2 a large round tank, 15 **f** across from rim to rim;
4:2 It was 7-1/2 **f** deep and about 45 **f** in circumference.
6:13 He had made a bronze platform 7-1/2 **f** long, 7-1/2 **f** wide, and 4-1/2 **f** high and had placed it at the
25:23 to demolish six hundred **f** of Jerusalem's wall,
Ezr 6:3 Its height will be ninety **f**, and its width will be ninety **f**.
Ne 3:13 They also repaired the fifteen hundred **f** of wall to
8:5 they saw him open the book, they all rose to their **f**.
9:21 clothes did not wear out, and their **f** did not swell!
Est 5:14 "Set up a gallows that stands seventy-five **f** tall,
7:7 Then the king jumped to his **f** in a rage and went
7:9 that stands seventy-five **f** tall in his own courtyard.
8:3 falling down at his **f** and begging him with tears to
Job 9:13 forces against him are crushed beneath his **f**.
13:27 You put my **f** in stocks. You watch all my paths.
29:15 I served as eyes for the blind and **f** for the lame.
33:11 He puts my **f** in the stocks and watches every move
Ps 18:9 dark storm clouds were beneath his **f**.
18:36 You have made a wide path for my **f** / to keep
18:38 so they could not get up; / they fell beneath my **f**.
18:39 you have subdued my enemies under my **f**.
22:16 in on me. / They have pierced my hands and **f**.
40:2 and the mire. / He set my **f** on solid ground
45:5 fall before you, / lying down beneath your **f**.
47:3 before us, / putting our enemies beneath our **f**.
56:13 me from death; / you have kept my **f** from slipping.
58:10 They will wash their **f** in the blood of the wicked.
66:9 in his hands, / and he keeps our **f** from stumbling.
68:23 my people, will wash your **f** in their blood,
73:2 My **f** were slipping, and I was almost gone.
91:13 will crush fierce lions and serpents under your **f**!
99:5 our God! / Bow low before his **f**, for he is holy!
105:18 There in prison, they bruised his **f** with fetters
110:1 making them a footstool under your **f**."
115:7 or feel with their hands, / or walk with their **f**,
116:8 my eyes from tears, / my **f** from stumbling.
119:105 Your word is a lamp for my **f** / and a light for my
Pr 3:23 safe on your way and keep your **f** from stumbling.
4:26 Mark out a straight path for your **f**; then stick to the
4:27 get sidetracked; keep your **f** from following evil.
5:5 Her **f** go down to death; her steps lead straight to
6:13 by making signs with their eyes and **f** and fingers.
6:18 a heart that plots evil, / **f** that race to do wrong,
6:28 Can he walk on hot coals and not blister his **f**?
26:6 a message is as foolish as cutting off one's **f**
29:5 To flatter people is to lay a trap for their **f**.
SS 5:3 I have washed my **f**. Should I get them soiled?'
7:1 "How beautiful are your sandaled **f**, O queenly
Isa 6:2 with two they covered their **f**, and with the
10:6 trampling them like dirt beneath its **f**.
28:3 of Israel—will be trampled beneath its enemies' **f**.
49:23 the earth before you and lick the dust from your **f**.
52:7 How beautiful on the mountains are the **f** of those
59:7 Their **f** run to do evil, and they rush to commit
60:14 Those who despised you will kiss your **f**.
Jer 38:22 When your **f** sank in the mud, they left you to your
52:21 Each of the pillars was 27 **f** tall and 18 **f** in circumference.
52:22 The bronze capital on top of each pillar was 7-1/2 **f**
Eze 1:7 but their **f** were split like calves' **f** and shone
2:2 came into me as he spoke and set me on my **f**.
3:24 Then the Spirit came into me and set me on my **f**.
6:11 Clap your hands in horror, and stamp your **f**.
32:2 in your own rivers, stirring up mud with your **f**.
32:13 or animals disturb those waters with their **f**.
34:18 Must you also muddy the rest with your **f**?
37:10 They all came to life and stood up on their **f**—
40:5 The man took a measuring rod that was 10-1/2 **f**
40:5 and the wall was 10-1/2 **f** thick and 10-1/2 **f** high.
40:6 the threshold of the gateway; it was 10-1/2 **f** deep.
40:7 Each of these alcoves was 10-1/2 **f** square, with a distance between them of 8-3/4 **f** along the
40:7 end of the gateway passage, was 10-1/2 **f** deep.
40:9 and found it to be 14 **f** deep, with supporting columns 3-1/2 **f** thick.
40:11 which was 17-1/2 **f** wide at the opening and 22-3/4 **f** wide in the gateway passage.
40:12 The alcoves themselves were 10-1/2 **f** square.
40:13 of facing guard alcoves; this distance was 43-3/4 **f**.
40:14 up to the gateway's foyer; this distance was 105 **f**.
40:15 passage was 87-1/2 **f** from one end to the other.
40:19 and inner gateways; the distance was 175 **f**.
40:21 The gateway passage was 87-1/2 **f** long and 43-3/4 **f** wide between the back walls of facing
40:23 The distance between the two gateways was 175 **f**.
40:25 the gateway passage was 87-1/2 **f** long and 43-3/4 **f** wide between the back walls of facing
40:27 The distance between the two gateways was 175 **f**.
40:29 passage was 87-1/2 **f** long and 43-3/4 **f** wide.
40:30 leading into the inner courtyard were 8-3/4 **f** deep and 43-3/4 **f** wide.)
40:33 The gateway passage measured 87-1/2 **f** long and 43-3/4 **f** wide.
40:36 The gateway passage measured 87-1/2 **f** long and 43-3/4 **f** wide.
40:47 the inner courtyard and found it to be 175 **f** square.
40:48 and found them to be 8-3/4 **f** square.
40:48 entrance was 24-1/2 **f** wide with walls 5-1/4 **f** thick.
40:49 The depth of the foyer was 35 **f** and the width was 19-1/4 **f**.
41:1 framed its doorway. They were 10-1/2 **f** square.
41:2 The entrance was 17-1/2 **f** wide, and the walls on each side were 8-3/4 **f** wide.
41:2 The Holy Place itself was 70 **f** long and 35 **f** wide.
41:3 at the entrance and found them to be 3-1/2 **f** thick.
41:3 The entrance was 10-1/2 **f** wide, and the walls on
41:3 extended 12-1/4 **f** to the corners of the inner room.
41:4 The inner room was 35 **f** square. "This," he told
41:5 of the Temple and found that it was 10-1/2 **f** thick.
41:5 along the outside wall; each room was 7 **f** wide.
41:8 for the side rooms. This terrace was 10-1/2 **f** high.
41:9 wall of the Temple's side rooms was 8-3/4 **f** thick.
41:10 This open area measured 35 **f** in width, and it went
41:11 into the terrace yard, which was 8-3/4 **f** wide.
41:12 It was 122-1/2 **f** wide and 157-1/2 **f** long, and its walls were 8-3/4 **f** thick.
41:13 the Temple, and he found it to be 175 **f** long.
41:13 its walls, was an additional 175 **f** in length.
41:14 to the east of the Temple was also 175 **f** wide.
41:15 including its two walls, was also 175 **f** wide.
41:22 made of wood, 3-1/2 **f** square and 5-1/4 **f** high.
42:2 the north, was 175 **f** long and 87-1/2 **f** wide.
42:4 two blocks of rooms ran a walkway 17-1/2 **f** wide.
42:4 It extended the entire 175 **f** of the complex, and all
42:7 from the outer courtyard; it was 87-1/2 **f** long.
42:8 which extended for only 87-1/2 **f**, while the inner
42:8 the rooms toward the Temple—extended for 175 **f**.
42:16 He measured the east side; it was 875 **f** long.
42:20 So the area was 875 **f** on each side with a wall all
43:7 of my throne and the place where I will rest my **f**.
43:14 From the gutter the altar rises 3-1/2 **f** to a ledge
43:14 From the lower ledge the altar rises 7 **f** to the upper
43:15 top of the altar, the hearth, rises still 7 **f** higher,
43:16 of the altar is square, measuring 21 **f** by 21 **f**.
43:17 measuring 24-1/2 **f** on each side, with a 21-inch
45:2 A section of this land, measuring 875 **f** by 875 **f**,
45:2 An additional strip of land 87-1/2 **f** wide is to be
46:22 these enclosures was 70 **f** long and 52-1/2 **f** wide,
47:3 he led me along the stream for 1,750 **f** and told me
47:4 He measured off another 1,750 **f** and told me to go
47:4 After another 1,750 **f**, it was up to my waist.
47:5 Then he measured another 1,750 **f**, and the river
Da 2:33 and its **f** were a combination of iron and clay.
2:34 It struck the **f** of iron and clay, smashing them to
2:41 The **f** and toes you saw that were a combination of
3:1 made a gold statue ninety **f** tall and nine **f** wide
7:4 and it was left standing with its two hind **f** on the
7:7 iron teeth and trampled what was left beneath its **f**.
7:19 and it trampled what was left beneath its **f**.
8:18 roused me with a touch and helped me to my **f**.
10:6 His arms and **f** shone like polished bronze, and his
Am 4:13 into darkness and treads the mountains under his **f**.
Mic 1:4 They melt beneath his **f** and flow into the valleys
7:19 You will trample our sins under your **f** and throw
Na 1:3 The billowing clouds are the dust beneath his **f**.
3:3 over them, scramble to their **f**, and fall again.
Zec 5:2 to be about thirty **f** long and fifteen **f** wide."
10:5 trampling their enemies in the mud under their **f**.
14:4 On that day his **f** will stand on the Mount of
Mal 4:3 the wicked as if they were dust under your **f**,"
Mt 10:14 shake off the dust of that place from your **f** as you
18:8 unquenchable fire with both of your hands and **f**.
22:44 until I humble your enemies beneath your **f**.'
28:9 they ran to him, held his **f**, and worshiped him.
Mk 5:33 came and fell at his **f** and told him what she had
6:11 to you, shake off its dust from your **f** as you leave.
7:25 about Jesus, and now she came and fell at his **f**.
9:27 Jesus took him by the hand and helped him to his **f**,
9:45 one foot than to be thrown into hell with two **f**.
12:36 until I humble your enemies beneath your **f**.'
Lk 5:25 the man jumped to his **f**, picked up his mat,
7:38 Then she knelt behind him at his **f**, weeping.
7:38 Her tears fell on his **f**, and she wiped them off with
7:38 Then she kept kissing his **f** and putting perfume on
7:44 didn't offer me water to wash the dust from my **f**,
7:45 but she has kissed my **f** again and again from the
7:46 but she has anointed my **f** with rare perfume.

8:35 possessed by demons sitting quietly at Jesus' **f**,
8:41 local synagogue, came and fell down at Jesus' **f**,
9:5 enter it, shake off its dust from your **f** as you leave.
10:11 'We wipe the dust of your town from our **f** as a
10:39 Her sister, Mary, sat at the Lord's **f**, listening to
15:22 Get a ring for his finger, and sandals for his **f**.
17:16 He fell face down on the ground at Jesus' **f**,
20:43 making them a footstool under your **f**.'
24:39 Look at my hands. Look at my **f**. You can see that
24:40 hands for them to see, and he showed them his **f**.
Jn 11:2 who poured the expensive perfume on the Lord's **f**
11:32 saw Jesus, she fell down at his **f** and said, "Lord,
12:3 and she anointed Jesus' **f** with it and wiped his **f** with her hair.
13:5 Then he began to wash the disciples' **f** and to wipe
13:6 to him, "Lord, why are you going to wash my **f**?"
13:8 Peter protested, "you will never wash my **f**!"
13:9 my hands and head as well, Lord, not just my **f**!"
13:10 need to wash, except for the **f**, to be entirely clean.
13:12 After washing their **f**, he put on his robe again
13:14 washed your **f**, you ought to wash each other's **f**.
21:8 for they were only out about three hundred **f**.
Ac 2:35 making them a footstool under your **f**.'
3:7 the man's **f** and anklebones were healed
3:8 He jumped up, stood on his **f**, and began to walk!
7:58 and laid them at the **f** of a young man named Saul.
13:51 But they shook off the dust of their **f** against them
14:8 and Barnabas came upon a man with crippled **f**.
14:10 And the man jumped to his **f** and started walking.
16:24 inner dungeon and clamped their **f** in the stocks.
21:11 Paul's belt and bound his own **f** and hands with it.
22:3 At his **f** I learned to follow our Jewish laws
27:28 and found the water was only 120 **f** deep.
27:28 little later they sounded again and found only 90 **f**.
Ro 10:15 "How beautiful are the **f** of those who bring good
16:20 God of peace will soon crush Satan under your **f**.
1Co 12:21 The head can't say to the **f**, "I don't need you."
15:25 until he humbles all his enemies beneath his **f**.
2Co 11:12 **f** of those who boast that their work is just like
Heb 1:13 making them a footstool under your **f**."
10:13 his enemies are humbled as a footstool under his **f**.
12:13 Mark out a straight path for your **f**. Then those who
Rev 1:15 His **f** were as bright as bronze refined in a furnace,
1:17 When I saw him, I fell at his **f** as dead. But he laid
2:18 flames of fire, whose **f** are like polished bronze:
3:9 but are not—to come and bow down at your **f**.
10:1 like the sun, and his **f** were like pillars of fire.
12:1 clothed with the sun, with the moon beneath her **f**,
13:2 a leopard, but it had bear's **f** and a lion's mouth!
19:10 Then I fell down at his **f** to worship him, but he
21:17 and found them to be 216 **f** thick (the angel used a

FELIX (9)

Ac 23:24 Paul to ride, and get him safely to Governor **F**."
23:26 Claudius Lysias, to his Excellency, Governor **F**.
23:33 they presented Paul and the letter to Governor **F**.
24:22 **F**, who was quite familiar with the Way,
24:24 A few days later **F** came with his wife, Drusilla,
24:25 and the judgment to come, **F** was terrified.
24:27 this way; then **F** was succeeded by Porcius Festus.
24:27 because **F** wanted to gain favor with the Jewish
25:14 he told him, "whose case was left for me by **F**.

FELL (216) [FALL]

Ge 7:11 and the rain **f** in mighty torrents from the sky.
15:12 sun was going down, Abram **f** into a deep sleep.
17:3 At this, Abram **f** face down in the dust. Then God
24:26 The man **f** down to the ground and worshiped the
41:5 Soon he **f** asleep again and had a second dream.
44:14 and they **f** to the ground before him.
Ex 34:8 Moses immediately **f** to the ground and worshiped.
Lev 9:24 shouted with joy and **f** face down on the ground.
Nu 9:5 in the wilderness of Sinai as twilight **f** on the
14:5 and Aaron **f** face down on the ground before the
16:22 But Moses and Aaron **f** face down on the ground.
16:45 But Moses and Aaron **f** face down on the ground.
20:6 where they **f** face down on the ground.
22:31 Balaam **f** face down on the ground before him.
Dt 9:25 "That is why I **f** down and lay before the LORD
Jos 5:14 Joshua **f** with his face to the ground in reverence.
21:10 tribe of Levi, since the sacred lot **f** to them first:
Jdg 4:21 But when Sisera **f** asleep from exhaustion,
5:27 He sank, he **f**, / he lay dead at her feet.
13:20 wife saw this, they **f** with their faces to the ground.
15:14 burnt strands of flax, and they **f** from his wrists.
16:4 Later Samson **f** in love with a woman named
Ru 2:10 Ruth **f** at his feet and thanked him warmly.
1Sa 4:18 Eli **f** backward from his seat beside the gate.
14:13 and the Philistines **f** back as Jonathan and his
17:49 and **f** face downward to the ground.
25:24 She **f** at his feet and said, "I accept all blame in
28:14 it was Samuel, and he **f** to the ground before him.
28:20 Saul **f** full length on the ground, paralyzed with
31:4 not do it. So Saul took his own sword and **f** on it.
31:5 he **f** on his own sword and died beside the king.
2Sa 1:2 He **f** to the ground before David in deep respect.
4:4 But she **f** and dropped him as she was running,
4:6 been sifting wheat, became drowsy and **f** asleep.
9:8 Mephibosheth **f** to the ground before the king.
13:1 her half brother, **f** desperately in love with her.
13:31 tore his robe, and **f** prostrate on the ground.
14:4 she **f** with her face down to the floor in front of
14:22 Joab **f** to the ground before the king and blessed
19:18 about to cross the river, Shimei **f** down before him.
22:39 so they could not get up; / they **f** beneath my feet.
1Ki 18:7 him at once and **f** to the ground before him.
18:39 they **f** on their faces and cried out, "The LORD is
18:42 of Mount Carmel and **f** to the ground and prayed.
20:30 but the wall **f** on them and killed another 27,000.
2Ki 1:2 **f** through the latticework of an upper room at his
1:10 Then fire **f** from heaven and killed them all.
1:12 And again the fire of God **f** from heaven and killed
1:13 But this time the captain **f** to his knees before
4:27 she **f** to the ground before him and caught hold of
4:37 She **f** at his feet, overwhelmed with gratitude.
6:5 of them was chopping, his ax head **f** into the river.
17:6 the ninth year of King Hoshea's reign, Samaria **f**,
18:10 year of King Hoshea's reign in Israel, Samaria **f**.
1Ch 10:4 not do it. So Saul took his own sword and **f** on it.
10:5 Saul was dead, he **f** on his own sword and died.
21:16 and **f** down with their faces to the ground.
24:7 first lot **f** to Jehoiarib. / The second lot **f** to Jedaiah.
24:8 third lot **f** to Harim. / The fourth lot **f** to Seorim.
24:9 fifth lot **f** to Malkijah. / The sixth lot **f** to Mijamin.
24:10 lot **f** to Hakkoz. / The eighth lot **f** to Abijah.
24:11 ninth lot **f** to Jeshua. / The tenth lot **f** to Shecaniah.
24:12 lot **f** to Eliashib. / The twelfth lot **f** to Jakim.
24:13 lot **f** to Huppah. / The fourteenth lot **f** to Jeshebeab.
24:14 lot **f** to Bilgah. / The sixteenth lot **f** to Immer.
24:15 lot **f** to Hezir. / The eighteenth lot **f** to Happizzez.
24:16 lot **f** to Pethahiah. / The twentieth lot **f** to Jehezkel.
24:17 lot **f** to Jakin. / The twenty-second lot **f** to Gamul.
24:18 The twenty-third lot **f** to Delaiah. / The twenty-fourth lot **f** to Maaziah.
25:9 The first lot **f** to Joseph of the Asaph clan
25:9 The second lot **f** to Gedaliah and twelve of his sons
25:10 The third lot **f** to Zaccur and twelve of his sons
25:11 The fourth lot **f** to Zeri and twelve of his sons
25:12 The fifth lot **f** to Nethaniah and twelve of his sons
25:13 The sixth lot **f** to Bukkiah and twelve of his sons
25:14 The seventh lot **f** to Asarelah and twelve of his
25:15 The eighth lot **f** to Jeshaiah and twelve of his sons
25:16 The ninth lot **f** to Mattaniah and twelve of his sons
25:17 The tenth lot **f** to Shimei and twelve of his sons
25:18 The eleventh lot **f** to Uzziel and twelve of his sons
25:19 The twelfth lot **f** to Hashabiah and twelve of his
25:20 The thirteenth lot **f** to Shubael and twelve of his
25:21 The fourteenth lot **f** to Mattithiah and twelve of his
25:22 The fifteenth lot **f** to Jerimoth and twelve of his
25:23 The sixteenth lot **f** to Hananiah and twelve of his
25:24 The seventeenth lot **f** to Joshbekashah and twelve
25:25 The eighteenth lot **f** to Hanani and twelve of his
25:26 The nineteenth lot **f** to Mallothi and twelve of his
25:27 The twentieth lot **f** to Eliathah and twelve of his
25:28 The twenty-first lot **f** to Hothir and twelve of his
25:29 The twenty-second lot **f** to Geddalti and twelve of
25:30 The twenty-third lot **f** to Mahazioth and twelve of
25:31 The twenty-fourth lot **f** to Romamti-ezer
2Ch 7:3 they **f** face down on the ground and worshiped
14:13 so many Ethiopians **f** that they were unable to
17:10 Then the fear of the LORD **f** over all the
Ezr 9:5 I **f** to my knees, lifted my hands to the LORD my
Ne 13:19 should be shut as darkness **f** every Friday evening,
Est 5:15 to drink, but the city of Susa **f** into confusion.
7:8 In despair he **f** on the couch where Queen Esther
Job 1:20 he shaved his head and **f** to the ground before God.
30:26 came instead. I waited for the light, but darkness **f**.
Ps 18:38 so they could not get up; / they **f** beneath my feet.
106:18 Fire **f** upon their followers; / a flame consumed the
107:12 they **f**, and no one helped them rise again.
Jer 2:3 were considered guilty, and disaster **f** upon them.
39:2 Babylonians broke through the wall, and the city **f**.
44:6 boiled over and **f** like fire on the towns of Judah
La 1:7 But then she **f** to her enemy, and there was no one
1:7 Her enemy struck her down and laughed as she **f**.
5:7 but they died before the hand of judgment **f**.
Eze 1:28 When I saw it, I **f** face down in the dust, and I
3:23 by the Kebar River. And I **f** face down in the dust.
9:8 I **f** face down in the dust and cried out,
11:13 Then I **f** face down in the dust and cried out,
23:14 She **f** in love with pictures that were painted on a
43:3 And I **f** down before him with my face in the dust.
44:4 and I **f** to the ground with my face in the dust.
Da 3:23 securely tied, **f** down into the roaring flames.
8:17 I became so terrified that I **f** to the ground.
Am 4:7 Rain **f** on one field, while another field withered
Na 3:10 Yet Thebes **f**, and her people were led away as
Mt 1:20 As he considered this, he **f** asleep, and an angel of
2:11 and they **f** down before him and worshiped him.
12:11 had one sheep, and it **f** into a well on the Sabbath,
13:4 some seeds **f** on a footpath, and the birds came
13:5 Other seeds **f** on shallow soil with underlying rock.
13:7 Other seeds **f** among thorns that shot up
13:8 But some seeds **f** on fertile soil and produced a
13:19 The seed that **f** on the hard path represents those
14:23 himself to pray. Night **f** while he was there alone.
17:6 were terrified and **f** face down on the ground.
18:26 But the man **f** down before the king and begged
18:29 His fellow servant **f** down before him and begged
26:39 on a little farther and **f** face down on the ground,
27:45 darkness **f** across the whole land until three
28:4 when they saw him, and they **f** into a dead faint.
Mk 4:4 some seed **f** on a footpath, and the birds came
4:5 Other seed **f** on shallow soil with underlying rock.
4:7 Other seed **f** among thorns that shot up and choked
4:8 Still other seed **f** on fertile soil and produced a crop
4:15 The seed that **f** on the hard path represents those
5:6 He ran to meet Jesus and **f** down before him.
5:22 name was Jairus, came and **f** down before him,
5:33 came and **f** at his feet and told him what she had
7:25 about Jesus, and now she came and **f** at his feet.
9:20 and he **f** to the ground, writhing and foaming at the
10:22 At this, the man's face **f**, and he went sadly away
14:35 on a little farther and **f** face down on the ground.
15:33 darkness **f** across the whole land until three
Lk 1:65 Wonder **f** upon the whole neighborhood,
4:22 and were amazed by the gracious words that **f** from
5:8 he **f** to his knees before Jesus and said, "Oh,
5:12 he **f** to the ground, face down in the dust,
7:38 Her tears **f** on his feet, and she wiped them off with
8:5 some seed **f** on a footpath, where it was stepped
8:6 Other seed **f** on shallow soil with underlying rock.
8:7 Other seed **f** among thorns that shot up and choked
8:8 Still other seed **f** on fertile soil. This seed grew
8:12 The seed that **f** on the hard path represents those
8:28 he shrieked and **f** to the ground before him,
8:41 local synagogue, came and **f** down at Jesus' feet,
8:47 she began to tremble and **f** to her knees before him.
13:4 who died when the Tower of Siloam **f** on them?
17:16 He **f** face down on the ground at Jesus' feet,
22:44 and he was in such agony of spirit that his sweat **f**
23:44 and darkness **f** across the whole land until three
Jn 6:17 But as darkness **f** and Jesus still hadn't come back,
11:32 saw Jesus, she **f** down at his feet and said, "Lord,
18:6 "I am he," they all **f** backward to the ground!
Ac 5:5 heard these words, he **f** to the floor and died.
5:10 Instantly, she **f** to the floor and died.
7:60 And he **f** to his knees, shouting, "Lord,
9:4 He **f** to the ground and heard a voice saying to him,
9:18 Instantly something like scales **f** from Saul's eyes,
10:10 while lunch was being prepared, he **f** into a trance.
10:25 Cornelius **f** to the floor before him in worship.
10:44 the Holy Spirit **f** upon all who had heard the
11:15 as I was getting started, the Holy Spirit **f** on them, just as he **f** on us at the beginning.
12:7 "Quick! Get up!" And the chains **f** off his wrists.
13:11 Instantly mist and darkness **f** upon him, and he
16:26 flew open, and the chains of every prisoner **f** off!
16:29 to the dungeon and **f** down before Paul and Silas.
19:35 whose image **f** down to us from heaven.
20:9 a deep sleep and **f** three stories to his death below.
22:7 I **f** to the ground and heard a voice saying to me,
22:17 I was praying in the Temple, and I **f** into a trance.
26:14 We all **f** down, and I heard a voice saying to me in
Heb 3:17 who sinned, whose bodies **f** in the wilderness?
Jas 5:17 none **f** for the next three and a half years!
Rev 1:17 When I saw him, I **f** at his feet as dead. But he laid
5:8 and the twenty-four elders **f** down before the
5:14 And the twenty-four elders **f** down and worshiped
6:13 Then the stars of the sky **f** to the earth like green
7:11 And they **f** face down before the throne
8:10 and a great flaming star **f** out of the sky,
8:10 It **f** upon one-third of the rivers and on the springs
11:16 sitting on their thrones before God **f** on their faces
16:19 and cities around the world **f** into heaps of rubble.
16:21 and hailstones weighing seventy-five pounds **f**
19:4 and the four living beings **f** down and worshiped
19:10 Then I **f** down at his feet to worship him, but he
22:8 I **f** down to worship the angel who showed them to

FELLED (1) [FALL]

Zec 11:2 as you watch the thickest forests being **f**.

FELLOW (50) [FELLOWS, FELLOWSHIP]

Ex 22:25 "If you lend money to a **f** Hebrew in need, do not
Nu 8:26 After retirement they may assist their **f** Levites by
16:10 special ministry only to you and your **f** Levites,
18:6 I myself have chosen your **f** Levites from among
32:17 and lead our **f** Israelites into battle until we have
Dt 1:16 be perfectly fair at all times, not only to **f** Israelites,
13:13 **f** citizens astray by encouraging them to worship
15:2 the loans they have made to their **f** Israelites.
15:3 however, applies only to your **f** Israelites—
17:15 You must appoint a **f** Israelite, not a foreigner.
17:20 and acting as if he is above his **f** citizens.
18:7 just like his **f** Levites who are serving the LORD
18:15 a prophet like me from among your **f** Israelites,
18:18 up a prophet like you from among their **f** Israelites.
23:19 interest on the loans you make to a **f** Israelite,
24:7 "If anyone kidnaps a **f** Israelite and treats him as a
24:14 whether **f** Israelites or foreigners living in your
1Sa 25:10 "Who is this **f** David?" Nabal sneered.
25:21 been saying, "A lot of good it did to help this **f**.
2Ki 4:1 One day the widow of one of Elisha's **f** prophets
9:11 Jehu went back to his **f** officers, and one of them asked him, "What did that crazy **f** want?
1Ch 15:12 You must purify yourselves and all your **f** Levites,
16:7 and his **f** Levites this song of thanksgiving to the
16:37 and his **f** Levites to minister regularly before the
16:39 and his **f** priests at the Tabernacle of the LORD
2Ch 19:10 Whenever a case comes to you from **f** citizens in
29:15 These men called together their **f** Levites, and they
35:15 for their meals were brought to them by their **f**
Ezr 3:2 Then Jeshua son of Jehozadak with his **f** priests
3:8 Jeshua son of Jehozadak and his **f** priests, and all
Ne 5:1 wives raised a cry of protest against their **f** Jews.
10:10 and their **f** Levites: Shebaniah, Hodiah, Kelita,
13:13 job to make honest distributions to their **f** Levites.
Jer 34:9 No one was to keep a **f** Judean in bondage.
Mic 5:3 Then at last his **f** countrymen will return from exile
Mt 9:10 along with his **f** tax collectors and many other
18:28 he went to a **f** servant who owed him a few
18:29 His **f** servant fell down before him and begged for
18:33 Shouldn't you have mercy on your **f** servant,
Mk 2:15 along with his **f** tax collectors and many other
Lk 5:29 Many of Levi's **f** tax collectors and other guests
Jn 11:16 the Twin, said to his **f** disciples, "Let's go, too—
Ac 2:14 all of you, **f** Jews and residents of Jerusalem!
5:36 Some time ago there was that **f** Theudas,

22:22 with one voice they shouted, "Away with such a f!
Ro 16:21 Timothy, my f worker, and Lucius, Jason,
Phm 1: 2 and to Archippus, a f soldier of the cross.
1:23 Epaphras, my f prisoner in Christ Jesus, sends you
1Pe 5: 1 he returns. As a f elder, this is my appeal to you:

FELLOWCITIZENS [KJV] See CITIZENS

FELLOWLABOURER [KJV] See CO-WORKER

FELLOWPRISONER [KJV] See (FELLOW) PRISONER

FELLOWS (1) [FELLOW]

Ac 17: 5 so they gathered some worthless f from the streets

FELLOWSERVANT [KJV] See (FELLOW) SERVANT

FELLOWSHIP (18) [FELLOW]

Ge 5:22 Enoch lived another 300 years in close f with God,
Ps 55:14 What good f we enjoyed / as we walked together to
Ac 2:42 devoted themselves to the apostles' teaching and f,
Ro 15:24 And after I have enjoyed your f for a little while,
1Co 5: 2 why haven't you removed this man from your f?
2Co 13:13 of God, and the f of the Holy Spirit be with you all.
Php 2: 1 Any f together in the Spirit? Are your hearts tender
1Jn 1: 3 and heard, so that you may have f with us.
1: 3 And our f is with the Father and with his Son,
1: 6 So we are lying if we say we have f with God
1: 7 just as Christ is, then we have f with each other,
2:24 you will continue to live in f with the Son and with
2:25 And in this f we enjoy the eternal life he promised
2:28 continue to live in f with Christ so that when he
3:24 Those who obey God's commandments live in f
2Jn 1: 9 teaching of Christ, you will not have f with God.
1: 9 you will have f with both the Father and the Son.
Jude 1:12 When these people join you in f meals celebrating

FELLOWSOLDIER [KJV] See (FELLOW) SOLDIER

FELLOWWORKERS [KJV] See CO-WORKERS

FELT (31) [FEEL]

Ge 2:25 wife were both naked, neither of them f any shame.
3: 7 and they suddenly f shame at their nakedness.
27:23 because Jacob's hands f hairy just like Esau's.
Ex 2:25 the Israelites and f deep concern for their welfare.
Nu 13:33 We f like grasshoppers next to them, and that's
Jdg 21: 6 The Israelites f deep sadness for Benjamin
21:15 The people f sorry for Benjamin
Ru 4: 4 I f that I should speak to you about it so that you
1Sa 13:12 So I f obliged to offer the burnt offering myself
14:27 the honey. After he had eaten it, he f much better.
Ezr 7:28 I f encouraged because the gracious hand of the
Job 29: 4 the friendship of God was f in my home.
31:24 my trust in money or f secure because of my gold?
Isa 33: 1 but have never f destruction yourselves.
38:15 my years / because of this anguish I have f.
47:10 "You f secure in all your wickedness. 'No one
Eze 1: 3 and I f the hand of the LORD take hold of me.
Da 10: 8 my face grew deathly pale, and I f very weak.
10:18 touched me again, and I f my strength returning.
10:19 I suddenly f stronger and said to him, "Now you
Mt 9:36 He f great pity for the crowds that came,
20:34 Jesus f sorry for them and touched their eyes.
Mk 10:21 Jesus f genuine love for this man as he looked at
11:12 as they were leaving Bethany, Jesus f hungry.
Lk 8:46 for I f healing power go out from me."
10:33 and when he saw the man, he f deep pity.
Ac 4:32 and they f that what they owned was not their own;
19:21 Afterward Paul f impelled by the Holy Spirit to go
28:19 the decision, I f it necessary to appeal to Caesar,
Ro 7: 9 I f fine when I did not understand what the law
Gal 4:15 Where is that joyful spirit we f together then?

FEMALE (40) [FEMALES]

Ge 1:27 them after himself; / male and f he created them.
5: 2 He created them male and f, and he blessed them
6:19 a pair of every kind of animal—a male and a f—
7: 3 and a f in each pair to ensure that every kind of
7: 9 They came into the boat in pairs, male and f,
7:16 male and f, just as God had commanded.
12:16 sheep, cattle, donkeys, male and f servants,
15: 9 a three-year-old f goat, a three-year-old ram,
32:14 two hundred f goats, twenty male goats,
32:15 thirty f camels with their young, forty cows, ten bulls, twenty f donkeys, and ten
Ex 20:10 your sons and daughters, your male and f servants,
20:17 neighbor's wife, male or f servant, ox or donkey,
21:20 "If a male or f slave is beaten and dies, the owner
21:26 a male or f slave in the eye and the eye is blinded,
21:27 an owner knocks out the tooth of a male or f slave,
21:32 But if the bull gores a slave, either male or f,
Lev 3: 6 It may be either male or f, and it must have no
4:28 they must bring as their offering a f goat with no
4:32 sin offering, it must be a f with no physical defects.
5: 6 and bring to the LORD as their penalty a f from
14:10 and one f year-old lamb with no physical defects,
25: 6 But you, your male and f slaves, your hired
25:44 or f slaves from among the foreigners who live
Nu 6:14 a one-year-old f lamb without defect for a sin
15:27 the guilty person must bring a one-year-old f goat
18:11 male and f alike, may eat of these offerings.
Dt 5:14 your male and f servants, your oxen and donkeys
5:14 All your male and f servants must rest as you do.
5:21 or land, male or f servant, ox or donkey,
15:17 "You must do the same for your f servants.
Jos 17: 6 because the f descendants of Manasseh received an
1Sa 8:16 He will want your male and f slaves and demand
Job 1: 3 teams of oxen, and five hundred f donkeys,
31:13 "If I have been unfair to my male or f servants,
42:12 teams of oxen, and one thousand f donkeys.
Jer 2:23 You are like a restless f camel, desperate for a
Mt 19: 4 from the beginning 'God made them male and f.'
Mk 10: 6 of creation, for 'He made them male and f.'
Gal 3:28 no longer Jew or Gentile, slave or free, male or f.

FEMALES (3) [FEMALE]

Ge 30:35 the f that were speckled and spotted with any white
30:41 Whenever the stronger f were ready to mate,
31:12 and spotted males are mating with the f of your

FENCE (2) [FENCES]

Ps 62: 3 them I'm just a broken-down wall / or a tottering f.
Hos 2: 6 "But I will f her in with thornbushes. I will block

FENCED [KJV] See also FORTIFIED, FORTRESS, KNIT, WALLED

FENCES (1) [FENCE]

Isa 5: 5 I will tear down its f / and let it be destroyed.

FERMENTED (2)

Nu 6: 3 they must not drink other f drinks or fresh grape
28: 7 consisting of one quart of f drink with each lamb,

FERRET (1)

Ps 101: 8 My daily task will be to f out criminals / and free

FERRYING (1)

2Sa 19:18 and worked hard f the king's household across the

FERTILE (28) [FERTILITY, FERTILIZED, FERTILIZER]

Ge 13:10 Lot took a long look at the f plains of the Jordan
Nu 13:20 How is the soil? Is it f or poor? Are there many
Dt 28: 4 You will be blessed with f herds and flocks.
Jdg 18: 7 were also wealthy because their land was very f.
18:10 God has given us a spacious and f land, lacking in
2Ch 26:10 both on the hillsides and in the f valleys.
Ne 9:25 Our ancestors captured fortified cities and f land.
9:35 You gave them a large, f land, but they refused to
Ps 65: 9 of the earth and water it, / making it rich and f.
Isa 5: 1 My beloved has a vineyard / on a rich and f hill.
7:19 They will settle in the f areas and also in the
7:25 No one will go to the f hillsides where the gardens
28: 4 It sits in a f valley, but its glorious beauty will
29:17 the wilderness of Lebanon will be a f field once
29:17 And the f fields will become a lush and f forest.
32:15 Then the wilderness will become a f field,
32:15 and the f field will become a lush and f forest.
32:16 in the wilderness and righteousness in the f field.
Jer 4:26 I looked, and the f fields had become a wilderness.
49: 4 You are proud of your f valleys, but they will soon
Eze 17: 5 "Then he planted one of its seedlings in f ground
Mic 7:14 Let them enjoy the f pastures of Bashan and Gilead
Mt 13: 8 But some seeds fell on f soil and produced a crop
Mk 4: 8 Still other seed fell on f soil and produced a crop
Lk 8: 8 Still other seed fell on f soil. This seed grew
12:16 "A rich man had a f farm that produced fine crops.

FERTILITY (1) [FERTILE]

Dt 7:13 and give f to your land and your animals.

FERTILIZED (1) [FERTILE]

Ps 83:10 at Endor, / and their decaying corpses f the soil.

FERTILIZER (2) [FERTILE]

Lk 13: 8 and I'll give it special attention and plenty of f.
14:35 Flavorless salt is good neither for the soil nor for f.

FERVENTLY (1)

Lk 22:44 He prayed more f, and he was in such agony of

FESTER (1)

Ps 38: 5 My wounds f and stink / because of my foolish

FESTIVAL (125) [FESTIVALS, FESTIVE, FESTIVITIES]

FESTIVAL OF HARVEST (6) Ex 23:16; 34:22; Nu 28:26; Dt 16:10,16; 2Ch 8:13

FESTIVAL OF PENTECOST (2) Ac 20:16; 1Co 16:8

FESTIVAL OF SHELTERS (20) Lev 23:34,39; Nu 29:12; Dt 16:13,16; 31:10; 1Ki 8:2,65,65; 12:32; 2Ch 5:3; 7:8,9; 8:13; Ezr 3:4,6; Eze 45:25; Hos 12:9; Zec 14:16; Jn 7:2

FESTIVAL OF THE FINAL HARVEST (2) Ex 23:16; 34:22

FESTIVAL OF TRUMPETS (3) Lev 3:24,27; Nu 29:1

FESTIVAL OF UNLEAVENED BREAD (14) Ex 12:17; 23:15; 34:18; Lev 23:6; Dt 16:16; 2Ch 30:13,21; 35:17; Ezr 6:22; Mt 26:17; Mk 14:1,12; Lk 22:1,7

Ex 5: 1 wilderness to hold a religious f in my honor.' "
10: 9 We must all join together in a f to the LORD."
12:14 Each year you will celebrate it as a special f to the
12:15 the f will be cut off from the community of Israel.
12:16 On the first day of the f, and again on the seventh
12:17 "Celebrate this F of Unleavened Bread, for it will
12:17 This f will be a permanent regulation for you,
12:25 to give you, you will continue to celebrate this f.
12:43 "These are the regulations for the f of Passover.
12:47 of Israel must celebrate this f at the same time.
13: 8 "During these f days each year, you must explain
13: 9 This annual f will be a visible reminder to you,
13:10 "So celebrate this f at the appointed time each
23:15 The first is the F of Unleavened Bread. For seven
23:15 This f will be an annual event at the appointed time
23:16 You must also celebrate the F of Harvest,
23:16 you are to celebrate the F of the Final Harvest at
32: 5 "Tomorrow there will be a f to the LORD!"
34:18 "Be sure to celebrate the F of Unleavened Bread
34:22 And you must remember to celebrate the F of
34:22 and celebrate the F of the Final Harvest at the end
Lev 23: 6 the F of Unleavened Bread begins.
23: 6 This f to the LORD continues for seven days,
23: 7 On the first day of the f, all the people must stop
23:24 the F of Trumpets—with loud blasts from a
23:27 on the ninth day after the F of Trumpets.
23:34 "Tell the Israelites to begin the F of Shelters on
23:34 This f to the LORD will last for seven days.
23:36 On each of the seven f days, you must present
23:39 "Now, on the first day of the F of Shelters,
23:39 you will begin to celebrate this seven-day f to the
23:39 and closing eighth day of the f will be days of total
23:41 You must observe this seven-day f to the LORD
23:42 During the seven f days, all of you who are
Nu 9: 5 And they celebrated the f there, just as the LORD
28:17 the following day a joyous, seven-day f will begin,
28:18 On the first day of the f you must call a sacred
28:24 On each of the seven days of the f, this is how you
28:25 On the seventh day of the f you must call another
28:26 "On the first day of the F of Harvest, when you
29: 1 "The F of Trumpets will be celebrated on the
29:12 It is the beginning of the F of Shelters, a seven-day f to the LORD.
29:17 "On the second day of this seven-day f,
29:20 "On the third day of the f, sacrifice eleven young
29:23 "On the fourth day of the f, sacrifice ten young
29:26 "On the fifth day of the f, sacrifice nine young
29:29 "On the sixth day of the f, sacrifice eight young
29:32 "On the seventh day of the f, sacrifice seven
29:35 "On the eighth day of the f, call all the people to
Dt 16:10 Then you must celebrate the F of Harvest to honor
16:13 "Another celebration, the F of Shelters, must be
16:14 This f will be a happy time of rejoicing with your
16:15 For seven days celebrate this f to honor the
16:15 your work. This f will be a time of great joy for all.
16:16 the F of Unleavened Bread, the F of Harvest, and the F of Shelters.
31:10 the Year of Release, during the F of Shelters,
Jdg 9:27 During the annual harvest f at Shechem, held in the
16:23 The Philistine leaders held a great f,
21:19 Then they thought of the annual f of the LORD
1Sa 20: 5 "Tomorrow we celebrate the new moon f.
20:18 "Tomorrow we celebrate the new moon f.
20:24 and when the new moon f began, the king sat down
1Ki 8: 2 They all assembled before the king at the annual F
8:65 and all Israel celebrated the F of Shelters in the
8:65 of the altar and seven days for the F of Shelters.
8:66 After the f was over, Solomon sent the people
12:32 Jeroboam also instituted a religious f in Bethel,
12:32 similar to the annual F of Shelters in Judah.
12:33 He instituted a religious f for Israel, and he went
2Ki 4:23 "It is neither a new moon f nor a Sabbath."
23:16 of God as Jeroboam stood beside the altar at the f.
2Ch 5: 3 They all assembled before the king at the annual F
7: 8 For the next seven days they celebrated the F of
7: 9 seven days and the F of Shelters for seven days.
8:13 the Passover celebration, the F of Harvest, and the F of Shelters.
30:13 celebrate Passover and the F of Unleavened Bread.
30:21 F of Unleavened Bread for seven days with great
30:23 then decided to continue the f another seven days,
30:25 the foreigners who came to the f, and all those who
31: 1 Now when the f ended, the Israelites who attended
35:17 and the F of Unleavened Bread for seven days.
Ezr 3: 4 They celebrated the F of Shelters as prescribed in
3: 4 the burnt offerings specified for each day of the f.
3: 6 Fifteen days before the F of Shelters began,
6:22 and celebrated the F of Unleavened Bread for
Ne 8:14 live in shelters during the f to be held that month.
8:15 shelters in which they would live during the f,
8:17 lived in these shelters for the seven days of the f,
8:18 the Law of God on each of the seven days of the f.
Est 2:18 and declaring a public f for the provinces.
8:17 and declared a public f and holiday.
9:19 living in unwalled villages celebrate an annual f
9:21 encouraging them to celebrate an annual f on these
9:29 Mordecai's letter to establish the F of Purim.
9:31 These letters established the F of Purim—
9:31 (The people decided to observe this f, just as they
Eze 45:21 the Passover. This f will last for seven days.

45:25 "During the seven days of the F of Shelters,
Hos 9: 5 What then will you do on f days? What will you do
12: 9 as you do each year when you celebrate the F of
Zec 7: 5 in the summer and at the f in early autumn,
14:16 and to celebrate the F of Shelters.
14:18 And if the people of Egypt refuse to attend the f,
14:19 all be punished if they don't go to celebrate the f.
Mal 2: 3 and splatter your faces with the dung of your f
Mt 26:17 On the first day of the F of Unleavened Bread,
Mk 14: 1 and the F of Unleavened Bread.
14:12 On the first day of the F of Unleavened Bread (the
Lk 2:41 parents went to Jerusalem for the Passover f.
2:42 was twelve years old, they attended the f as usual.
22: 1 The F of Unleavened Bread, which begins with the
22: 7 Now the F of Unleavened Bread arrived,
Jn 7: 2 But soon it was time for the F of Shelters,
7: 8 I am not yet ready to go to this f, because my time
7:10 But after his brothers had left for the f, Jesus also
7:11 The Jewish leaders tried to find him at the f
7:14 Then, midway through the f, Jesus went up to the
7:37 the climax of the f, Jesus stood and shouted to the
Ac 20:16 get to Jerusalem, if possible, for the F of Pentecost.
1Co 5: 8 So let us celebrate the f, not by eating the old bread
16: 8 I will be staying here at Ephesus until the F of

FESTIVALS (40) [FESTIVAL]

APPOINTED FESTIVALS (5) Lev 23:2; 1Ch 23:31; 2Ch 2:4; Hos 2:11; Zep 3:18

Ex 23:14 "Each year you must celebrate three f in my
Lev 23: 2 instructions regarding the LORD's appointed f,
23: 4 to the Sabbath, the LORD has established f,
23:37 "These are the LORD's appointed annual f.
23:38 These f must be observed in addition to the
23:44 the annual f of the LORD to the Israelites.
Nu 10:10 sounding them at your annual f and at the
15: 3 or a special sacrifice at any of the annual f,
29:39 these offerings to the LORD at your annual f.
Dt 16:16 every man in Israel must celebrate these three f:
1Ch 23:31 new moon celebrations, and at all the appointed f.
2Ch 2: 4 and at the other appointed f of the LORD our
8:13 on new moon f, and at the three annual f—
31: 3 for the weekly Sabbath f and monthly new moon f,
31: 3 and for the other annual f as required in the law of
Ezr 3: 5 and the other annual f to the LORD.
Ne 10:33 the new moon celebrations, and the annual f;
Ps 87: 7 At all the f, the people will sing, / "The source of
Ecc 7: 2 It is better to spend your time at funerals than at f.
Isa 1:14 I hate all your f and sacrifices. I cannot stand the
30:29 will sing a song of joy, like the songs at the holy f.
La 1: 4 crowds on their way to celebrate the Temple f.
2: 6 LORD has blotted out all memory of the holy f
Eze 36:38 that fill Jerusalem's streets at the time of her f.
44:24 obey my instructions and laws at all the sacred f,
45:17 provide offerings that are given at the religious f,
46: 9 to worship the LORD during the religious f,
46:11 "So at the special feasts and sacred f, the grain
Da 7:25 He will try to change their sacred f and laws,
Hos 2:11 I will put an end to her annual f, her new moon
2:11 and her Sabbath days—all her appointed f.
Am 2: 8 At their religious f, they lounge around in clothing
5:21 the hypocrisy of your religious f and solemn
8: 5 and the religious f to end so you can get back to
Na 1:15 Celebrate your f, O people of Judah, and fulfill all
Zep 3:18 "I will gather you who mourn for the appointed f;
Zec 7: 6 And even now in your holy f, you don't think
8:19 They will become f of joy and celebration for the

FESTIVE (1) [FESTIVAL]

Ne 8:12 the people went away to eat and drink at a f meal,

FESTIVITIES (1) [FESTIVAL]

Jn 2: 3 The wine supply ran out during the f, so Jesus'

FESTUS (14) [PORCIUS]

Ac 24:27 this way; then Felix was succeeded by Porcius F.
25: 1 Three days after F arrived in Caesarea to take over
25: 3 They asked F as a favor to transfer Paul to
25: 4 But F replied that Paul was at Caesarea and he
25: 9 Then F, wanting to please the Jews, asked him,
25:12 F conferred with his advisers and then replied,
25:13 with his sister, Bernice, to pay their respects to F.
25:14 F discussed Paul's case with the king.
25:22 And F replied, "You shall—tomorrow!"
25:23 men of the city. F ordered that Paul be brought in.
25:24 Then F said, "King Agrippa and all present,
26:24 Suddenly, F shouted, "Paul, you are insane.
26:25 Paul replied, "I am not insane, Most Excellent F.
26:32 And Agrippa said to F, "He could be set free if he

FETCH(ED) [KJV] See also BRING, CHANGE, GET, GO, SEIZE, TAKE

FETTERS (1)

Ps 105:18 There in prison, they bruised his feet with f

FEVER (12) [FEVERISH, FEVERS]

Dt 28:22 f, and inflammation, with scorching heat
32:24 wasting famine, / burning f, and deadly disease.
Job 30:30 skin has turned dark, and my bones burn with f.
Ps 38: 7 A raging f burns within me, / and my health is
Mt 8:14 Peter's mother-in-law was in bed with a high f.
8:15 But when Jesus touched her hand, the f left her.
Mk 1:30 mother-in-law was sick in bed with a high f.
1:31 the f suddenly left, and she got up and prepared a
Lk 4:38 Simon's mother-in-law very sick with a high f.
4:39 at her bedside, he spoke to the f, rebuking it,
Jn 4:52 "Yesterday afternoon at one o'clock his f suddenly
Ac 28: 8 Publius's father was ill with f and dysentery.

FEVERISH (1) [FEVER]

Isa 22:11 But all your f plans are to no avail because you

FEVERS (1) [FEVER]

Lev 26:16 with wasting diseases, and with burning f,

FEW (112) [FEWER]

Ge 29:20 so strong that it seemed to him but a f days.
34:30 We are so f that they will come and crush us.
Lev 25:52 If only a f years remain until the Year of Jubilee,
Nu 9:20 would stay over the Tabernacle for only a f days,
9:20 so the people would stay for only a f days.
13:18 people living there are strong or weak, f or many.
Dt 4:27 the nations, where only a f of you will survive.
7:20 to drive out the f survivors still hiding from you!
23:25 And you may pluck a f heads of your neighbor's
26: 5 His family was f in number, but in Egypt they
28:18 You will be cursed with f children and barren
28:62 f of you will be left because you would not listen
Jos 3: 8 take a f steps into the river and stop.' "
Jdg 5: 7 There were f people left in the villages of Israel—
21: 7 How can we find wives for the f who remain,
21:16 "How can we find wives for the f who remain,
Ru 2: 7 except for a f minutes' rest over there in the
1Sa 14: 6 battle whether he has many warriors or only a f!"
17:28 "What about those f sheep you're supposed to be
2Sa 2:14 "Let's have a f of our warriors put on an
17: 9 he comes out and attacks and a f of your men fall,
1Ki 11:17 and a f of his father's royal officials had fled.
17: 1 or rain during the next f years unless I give the
17:12 I was just gathering a f sticks to cook this last
20:20 King Ben-hadad and a f others escaped on horses.
2Ki 4:35 and walked back and forth in the room a f times.
21:14 Then I will reject even those f of my people who
1Ch 4:43 They destroyed the f Amalekites who had
16:19 He said this when they were f in number, / a tiny
2Ch 18: 2 A f years later, he went to Samaria to visit Ahab,
29:34 But there were too f priests to prepare all the burnt
30: 6 so that he will return to the f of us who have
36:20 The f who survived were taken away to Babylon,
Ezr 9: 8 for the LORD our God has allowed a f of us to
Ne 2:12 during the night, taking only a f others with me.
7: 4 And only a f houses were scattered throughout the
Job 7:16 Oh, leave me alone for these f remaining days.
12: 3 Well, I know a f things myself—and you're no
Ps 90: 4 years are as yesterday! / They are like a f hours!
105:12 He said this when they were f in number, / a tiny
109: 8 Let his years be f; / let his position be given to
Pr 17:27 A truly wise person uses f words; a person with
Ecc 5: 2 you are only here on earth. So let your words be f.
6:12 In the f days of our empty lives, who knows how
9:14 There was a small town with only a f people living
12: 3 Your teeth will be too f to do their work, and you
Isa 1: 9 If the LORD Almighty had not spared a f of us,
4: 1 In that day f men will be left alive. Seven women
7:22 The f people still left in the land will live on curds
10:19 Only a f from all that mighty army will survive—so f that a child could count them!
10:22 only a f of them will return at that time.
13:12 F will be left alive when I have finished my work.
14:30 out with famine. I will destroy the f who remain.
16:14 be ended, and f of its people will be left alive."
17: 3 The f left in Aram will share the fate of Israel's
17: 6 Only a f of its people will be left, like the stray
21:17 Only a f of its courageous archers will survive.
24: 6 left desolate, destroyed by fire. F will be left alive.
24:13 or the f grapes left on the vine after harvest,
65:20 "No longer will babies die when only a f days old.
Jer 5:10 and destroy them, but leave a scattered f alive.
6: 9 Even the f who remain in Israel will be gleaned
38: 4 the morale of the f fighting men we have left,
39:10 But Nebuzaradan left a f of the poorest people in
40: 6 and lived in Judah with the f who were still left in
40:11 the king of Babylon had left a f people in Judah
40:15 Why should the f of us who are still left be
49: 9 Those who harvest grapes always leave a f for the
Eze 5: 4 Then take a f of these hairs out and throw them
5:10 And I will punish you by scattering the f who
6: 8 "But I will let a f of my people escape destruction,
7:16 The f who survive and escape to the mountains
12:16 But I will spare a f of them from death by war,
13:19 You turn my people away from me for a f handfuls
Da 11:13 "A f years later, the king of the north will return
Am 1: 8 and the f Philistines still left will be killed.
Ob 1: 5 Those who harvest grapes always leave a f for the
Mic 2:12 O Israel, I will gather the f of you who are left.
5: 7 Then the f left in Israel will go out among the
Zep 2: 7 The f survivors of the tribe of Judah will pasture
Zec 10: 8 From the f that are left, their population will grow
Mt 7:14 and the road is narrow, and only a f ever find it.
9:37 "The harvest is so great, but the workers are so f.
13:58 And so he did only a f miracles there because of
15:34 They replied, "Seven, and a f small fish."
18:28 he went to a fellow servant who owed him a f
22:14 For many are called, but f are chosen."
Mk 6: 5 them except to place his hands on a f sick people
8: 7 A f small fish were found, too, so Jesus also
Lk 1:39 A f days later Mary hurried to the hill country of
10: 2 "The harvest is so great, but the workers are so f.
13:23 asked him, "Lord, will only a f be saved?"
13:31 A f minutes later some Pharisees said to him,
15:13 "A f days later this younger son packed all his
24:18 things that have happened there the last f days."
Jn 2:12 After the wedding he went to Capernaum for a f
3:32 and heard, but how f believe what he tells them!
11: 8 "only a f days ago the Jewish leaders in Judea
11:18 Bethany was only a f miles down the road from
Ac 1: 5 but in just a f days you will be baptized with the
9:19 Saul stayed with the believers in Damascus for a f
24:24 A f days later Felix came with his wife, Drusilla,
25:13 A f days later King Agrippa arrived with his sister,
Ro 9:29 "If the Lord Almighty / had not spared a f of us,
11: 5 A f are being saved as a result of God's kindness in
11: 7 A f have—the ones God has chosen—but the rest
1Co 1:26 that f of you were wise in the world's eyes,
7:35 the Lord best, with as f distractions as possible.
2Co 9: 6 a farmer who plants only a f seeds will get a small
Heb 12:10 For our earthly fathers disciplined us for a f years,
Rev 2:14 And yet I have a f complaints against you.

FEWER (2)

Lev 25:16 the price; the f the years, the lower the price.
Nu 35: 8 to the Levites, while the smaller tribes will give f.

FIANCÉ (2) [FIANCÉE, FIANCÉS]

Joel 1: 8 with sorrow, as a virgin weeps when her f has died.
Mt 1:19 Joseph, her f, being a just man, decided to break

FIANCÉE (3) [FIANCÉ]

Dt 20: 7 the battle, and someone else would marry your f.'
Lk 2: 5 He took with him Mary, his f, who was obviously
1Co 7:36 But if a man thinks he ought to marry his f

FIANCÉS (1) [FIANCÉ]

Ge 19:14 So Lot rushed out to tell his daughters' f, "Quick,

FIBER (1)

Pr 31:19 are busy spinning thread, her fingers twisting f.

FICKLE (2)

Jer 3: 6 said to me, "Have you seen what f Israel does?
Hos 10: 2 The hearts of the people are f; they are guilty

FICTIONS (1)

Am 5: 7 and fair play are meaningless f to you.

FIELD (149) [BATTLEFIELD, FIELDED, FIELDS, GRAINFIELDS]

Ge 23: 9 the cave of Machpelah, down at the end of his f.
23:11 listen to me. I will give you the cave and the f.
23:13 Let me pay the full price for the f so I can bury my
23:17 This included the f, the cave that was in it, and all
23:20 The f and the cave were sold to Abraham by the
25: 9 in the f of Ephron son of Zohar the Hittite.
25:10 This was the f Abraham had purchased from the
29: 2 flocks of sheep lying in an open f beside a well,
30:14 Reuben found some mandrakes growing in a f
31: 4 and Leah out to the f where he was watching the
37: 7 "We were out in the f tying up bundles of grain.
37:32 "We found this in the f," they told him.
49:29 and grandfather in the cave in Ephron's f.
49:30 This is the cave in the f of Machpelah, near Mamre
50:13 burial place in the f of Ephron the Hittite,
Ex 22: 5 "If an animal is grazing in a f or vineyard
22: 5 and the owner lets it stray into someone else's f to
22: 6 out of control and goes into another person's f,
Lev 11:37 dead body falls on seed grain to be planted in the f,
19:19 Do not plant your f with two kinds of seed.
27:17 If the f is dedicated to the LORD in the Year of
27:18 But if the f is dedicated after the Year of Jubilee,
27:19 If you decide to redeem the dedicated f, you must
27:19 20 percent. Then the f will again belong to you.
27:20 But if you decide not to redeem the f, or if the f is sold to someone else by the priests,
27:21 When the f is released in the Year of Jubilee,
27:21 will be holy, a f specially set apart for the LORD.
27:22 "If you dedicate to the LORD a f that you have
27:24 In the Year of Jubilee the f will be released to the
27:28 whether a person, an animal, or an inherited f—
Nu 22:23 The donkey bolted off the road into a f, but Balaam
Dt 21: 1 "Suppose someone is found murdered in a f in the
24:19 forget to bring in a bundle of grain from your f,
Jos 15:18 she urged him to ask her father for an additional f.
Jdg 1:14 she urged him to ask her father for an additional f.
13: 9 once again to his wife as she was sitting in the f.
20:21 and killed twenty-two thousand Israelites in the f
Ru 2: 3 she found herself working in a f that belonged to
2: 8 Stay right behind the women working in my f.
2: 9 See which part of the f they are harvesting, and
2:19 about the man in whose f she had worked.
1Sa 6:14 The cart came into the f of a man named Joshua
6:18 still stands in the f of Joshua as a reminder of what
11: 5 Saul was plowing in the f, and when he returned to
14:15 both in the camp and in the f, including even the
20: 5 but tomorrow I'll hide in the f and stay there until
20:11 "Come out to the f with me," Jonathan replied.
20:24 So David hid himself in the f, and when the new
20:35 Jonathan went out into the f and took a young boy
30:11 of David's troops found an Egyptian man in a f
2Sa 2:16 The place has been known ever since as the F of
14: 6 "My two sons had a fight out in the f. And since
14:30 and set fire to Joab's barley f, the f next to mine."

14:30 So they set his **f** on fire, as Absalom had
14:31 "Why did your servants set my **f** on fire?"
20:12 So he pulled him off the road into a **f** and threw a
23:11 and attacked the Israelites in a **f** full of lentils.
23:12 Shammah held his ground in the middle of the **f**
1Ki 11:29 a new cloak. The two of them were alone in a **f**,
14:11 and those who die in the **f** will be eaten by
16:4 and those who die in the **f** will be eaten by the
19:19 and found Elisha son of Shaphat plowing a **f** with a
20:24 Only this time replace the kings with **f**
21:24 and those who die in the **f** will be eaten by
2Ki 4:39 One of the young men went out into the **f** to gather
9:21 They met him at the **f** that had belonged to Naboth
9:25 "Throw him into the **f** of Naboth of Jezreel.
9:26 So throw him out on Naboth's **f**, just as the
9:37 Her body will be scattered like dung on the **f** of
18:17 sent his commander in chief, his **f** commander,
18:17 near the road leading to the **f** where cloth is
1Ch 11:13 The battle took place in a **f** full of barley,
11:14 and David held their ground in the middle of the **f**
27:26 Ezri son of Kelub was in charge of the **f** workers
2Ch 26:23 he was buried nearby in a burial **f** belonging to the
Job 5:23 You will be at peace with the stones of the **f**,
24:6 They harvest a **f** they do not own, and they glean in
39:10 hitch a wild ox to a plow? Will it plow a **f** for you?
Ps 37:20 The LORD's enemies are like flowers in a **f**—
50:11 and all the animals of the **f** belong to me.
72:16 they do in Lebanon, / sprouting up like grass in a **f**.
Pr 24:30 I walked by the **f** of a lazy person, the vineyard of
27:26 and your goats will be sold for the price of a **f**.
31:16 She goes out to inspect a **f** and buys it; with her
Isa 1:8 shelter in a vineyard or **f** after the harvest is over.
7:3 near the road leading to the **f** where cloth is
29:17 the wilderness of Lebanon will be a fertile **f** once
32:15 Then the wilderness will become a fertile **f**,
32:15 and the fertile **f** will become a lush and fertile
32:16 in the wilderness and righteousness in the fertile **f**.
36:2 near the road leading to the **f** where cloth is
40:6 fades as quickly as the beauty of flowers in a **f**.
55:12 and the trees of the **f** will clap their hands!
56:9 Come, wild animals of the **f**! Come, wild animals
Jer 4:17 surround Jerusalem like watchmen surrounding a **f**,
26:18 Mount Zion will be plowed like an open **f**;
32:7 will come and say to you, 'Buy my **f** at Anathoth.
32:8 "Buy my **f** at Anathoth in the land of Benjamin.
32:9 So I bought the **f** at Anathoth, paying Hanamel
32:25 Sovereign LORD, you have told me to buy the **f**—
Eze 16:5 you were dumped in a **f** and left to die, unwanted.
16:7 And I helped you to thrive like a plant in the **f**.
16:22 of the days long ago when you lay naked in a **f**,
31:15 in black and caused the trees of the **f** to wilt.
Da 4:23 Let him eat grass with the animals of the **f** for
Hos 4:16 and unprotected, like a helpless lamb in an open **f**.
10:4 among them like poisonous weeds in a farmer's **f**.
12:11 the heaps of stone along the edges of a plowed **f**.
Joel 1:11 and barley—yes, all the **f** crops—are ruined.
2:5 like the roar of a fire sweeping across a **f**,
2:22 Don't be afraid, you animals of the **f**! The pastures
Am 4:7 Rain fell on one **f**, while another **f** withered away.
Ob 1:18 will be a raging fire, and Edom, a **f** of dry stubble.
1:18 The fire will roar across the **f**,
Mic 3:12 of you, Mount Zion will be plowed like an open **f**;
Na 1:10 like drunks, will be burned like dry straw in a **f**.
Zec 10:1 of rain so that every **f** becomes a lush pasture.
Mt 13:4 As he scattered it across his **f**, some seeds fell on a
13:24 is like a farmer who planted good seed in his **f**.
13:27 the **f** where you planted that good seed is full of
13:31 of Heaven is like a mustard seed planted in a **f**.
13:36 "Please explain the story of the weeds in the **f**."
13:38 The **f** is the world, and the good seed represents the
13:44 like a treasure that a man discovered hidden in a **f**.
13:44 he owned to get enough money to buy the **f**—
24:18 A person in the **f** must not return even to get a coat.
24:40 "Two men will be working together in the **f**;
27:7 they finally decided to buy the potter's **f**,
27:8 That is why the **f** is still called the **F** of Blood.
27:10 and purchased the potter's **f**, / as the Lord
Mk 4:4 As he scattered it across his **f**, some seed fell on a
4:26 of God is like: A farmer planted seeds in a **f**,
13:16 A person in the **f** must not return even to get a coat.
Lk 8:5 As he scattered it across his **f**, some seed fell on a
11:44 be for you. For you are like hidden graves in a **f**.
14:18 One said he had just bought a **f** and wanted to
17:31 to pack. A person in the **f** must not return to town.
Ac 1:18 (Judas bought a **f** with the money he received for
1:19 name *Akeldama,* which means "**F** of Blood.")
4:37 He sold a **f** he owned and brought the money to the
1Co 3:9 You are God's **f**, God's building—not ours.
Heb 6:8 But if a **f** bears thistles and thorns, it is useless.
6:8 The farmer will condemn that **f** and burn it.
Jas 1:10 They will fade away like a flower in the **f**.
5:4 Hear the cries of the **f** workers whom you have

FIELDED (1) [FIELD]

2Ch 13:3 led by King Abijah, **f** 400,000 seasoned warriors,

FIELDS (130) [FIELD]

Ge 4:8 to his brother, Abel, "Let's go out into the **f**."
24:63 One evening as he was taking a walk out in the **f**,
24:65 "Who is that man walking through the **f** to meet
25:27 Esau became a skillful hunter, a man of the open **f**,
27:27 smell of the open **f** that the LORD has blessed.
30:16 as Jacob was coming home from the **f**,
34:5 but his sons were out in the **f** herding cattle so he
34:7 just as Jacob's sons were coming in from the **f**.
34:28 hands on, both inside the town and outside in the **f**.
47:20 All the Egyptians sold him their **f**
47:23 I will provide you with seed, so you can plant the **f**.
Ex 1:14 and mortar and to work long hours in the **f**.
8:13 in the houses, the courtyards, and the **f** all died.
9:19 your livestock and servants to come in from the **f**.
9:20 brought their livestock and servants in from the **f**.
9:25 Everything left in the **f** was destroyed—people,
10:5 the hailstorm, including all the trees in the **f**.
Lev 14:7 living bird free so it can fly away into the open **f**.
14:53 he will release the living bird in the open **f** outside
17:5 Israelites from sacrificing animals in the open **f**.
17:7 by offering sacrifices to evil spirits out in the **f**.
19:9 do not harvest the grain along the edges of your **f**,
23:22 do not harvest the grain along the edges of your **f**,
25:3 For six years you may plant your **f** and prune your
25:12 eat the produce that grows naturally in the **f** that
25:31 will be treated like property in the open **f**.
Nu 16:14 and honey or given us an inheritance of **f**
20:17 We will be careful not to go through your **f**
21:22 We will not trample your **f** or touch your vineyards
Dt 2:27 and won't turn off into the **f** on either side.
15:19 not use the firstborn of your herds to work your **f**,
28:4 be blessed with many children and productive **f**.
28:18 You will be cursed with few children and barren **f**.
30:9 and your **f** will produce abundant harvests,
32:13 he let them feast on the crops of the **f**.
Jos 21:12 But the **f** beyond the city and the surrounding
Jdg 5:4 and marched across the **f** of Edom, / the earth
9:32 Come by night with an army and hide out in the **f**.
9:42 the people of Shechem went out into the **f** to battle.
9:43 men into three groups and set an ambush in the **f**.
9:44 other two groups cut them down in the **f**.
15:5 and let the foxes run through the **f** of the
19:16 an old man came home from his work in the **f**.
20:31 About thirty Israelites died in the open **f** and along
Ru 2:2 "Let me go out into the **f** to gather leftover grain
2:8 us when you gather grain; don't go to any other **f**.
2:22 You will be safe there, unlike in other **f**."
2:23 So Ruth worked alongside the women in Boaz's **f**
1Sa 8:12 Some will be forced to plow in his **f** and harvest
8:14 He will take away the best of your **f** and vineyards
16:11 "But he's out in the **f** watching the sheep."
19:2 "you must find a hiding place out in the **f**.
22:7 "Has David promised you **f** and vineyards?
30:16 the Amalekites were spread out across the **f**,
2Sa 10:8 positioned themselves to fight in the open **f**.
10:9 and led them out to fight the Arameans in the **f**.
11:11 and his officers are camping in the open **f**.
2Ki 7:12 they have left their camp and have hidden in the **f**.
25:4 They made a dash across the **f**, in the direction of
25:12 behind in Judah to care for the vineyards and **f**.
1Ch 6:56 but the **f** and outlying areas were given to Caleb
16:32 Let the **f** and their crops burst forth with joy!
19:9 kings positioned themselves to fight in the open **f**.
19:10 and led them out to fight the Arameans in the **f**.
2Ch 31:5 olive oil, honey, and all the produce of their **f**.
32:4 cutting off the brook that ran through the **f**.
Ne 5:3 Others said, "We have mortgaged our **f**, vineyards,
5:4 "We have already borrowed to the limit on our **f**
5:5 for our **f** and vineyards are already mortgaged to
5:11 You must restore their **f**, vineyards, olive groves,
11:30 They were also in Lachish and its nearby **f**
12:44 They were responsible to collect these from the **f**
13:10 worship services had all returned to work their **f**.
Job 5:10 gives rain for the earth. He sends water for the **f**.
39:4 Their young grow up in the open **f**, then leave their
Ps 96:12 Let the **f** and their crops burst forth with joy!
107:37 They sow their **f**, plant their vineyards,
144:13 May the flocks in our **f** multiply by the thousands,
Pr 8:26 made the earth and **f** and the first handfuls of soil.
SS 7:11 let us go out into the **f** and spend the night among
Isa 1:7 foreigners plunder your **f** and destroy everything
18:6 Your mighty army will be left dead in the **f** for the
19:5 waters of the Nile will fail to rise and flood the **f**.
29:17 And the fertile **f** will become a lush and fertile
33:4 Just as locusts strip the **f** and vines, so Jerusalem
43:20 The wild animals in the **f** will thank me, the jackals
44:3 quench your thirst and to moisten your parched **f**.
61:5 and plow your **f** and tend your vineyards.
Jer 4:26 I looked, and the fertile **f** had become a wilderness.
6:12 to their enemies, and so will their **f** and their wives.
6:25 Don't go out to the **f**! Don't travel the roads!
9:22 "Bodies will be scattered across the **f** like dung,
12:4 Even the grass in the **f** has withered. The wild
13:27 and your abominable idol worship out in the **f**
14:18 If I go out into the **f**, I see the bodies of people
31:40 and all the **f** out to the Kidron Valley on the east as
32:15 and will buy and sell houses and vineyards and **f**."
32:43 "**F** will again be bought and sold in this land about
32:44 Yes, **f** will once again be bought and sold—
39:10 and he assigned them **f** and vineyards to care for.
50:19 own land, to feed in the **f** of Carmel and Bashan,
51:14 be filled with enemies, like **f** filled with locusts,
52:7 They made a dash across the **f**, in the direction of
52:16 behind in Judah to care for the vineyards and **f**.
Eze 20:46 out against it; prophesy against the **f** of the Negev.
33:27 Those living in the open **f** will be eaten by wild
34:27 and **f** of my people will yield bumper crops,
36:30 give you great harvests from your fruit trees and **f**,
36:34 The **f** that used to lie empty and desolate—a shock
39:5 You will fall in the open **f**, for I have spoken,
39:10 They won't need to cut wood from the **f** or forests,
Da 4:15 him live like an animal among the plants of the **f**.
4:25 and you will live in the **f** with the wild animals.
4:32 You will live in the **f** with the wild animals,
Joel 1:10 The **f** are ruined and empty of crops. The grain,
Am 7:1 after the king's share had been harvested from the **f**
Ob 1:19 and take over the **f** of Ephraim and Samaria.
Mic 2:4 our land, / taking it from us. / He has given our **f**
4:10 for you must leave this city to live in the open **f**.
Hab 3:17 the olive crop fails, and the **f** lie empty and barren;
3:17 even though the flocks die in the **f**, and the cattle
Hag 1:11 I have called for a drought on your **f** and hills—
Mt 9:38 ask him to send out more workers for his **f**."
Mk 11:8 and others cut leafy branches in the **f** and spread
Lk 2:8 That night some shepherds were in the **f** outside
2:20 The shepherds went back to their **f** and flocks,
10:2 and ask him to send out more workers for his **f**.
15:25 "Meanwhile, the older son was in the **f** working.
Jn 4:35 Vast **f** are ripening all around us and are ready now
1Co 9:10 Just as farm workers who plow **f** and thresh the

FIERCE (55) [FIERCELY, FIERCEST]

Ge 49:7 Cursed be their anger, for it is **f**; / cursed be their
Ex 32:12 face of the earth.' Turn away from your **f** anger.
Nu 1:53 of Israel protection from the LORD's **f** anger.
25:4 so his **f** anger will turn away from the people of
Dt 13:17 Then the LORD will turn from his **f** anger and be
28:50 a **f** and heartless nation that shows no respect for
1Sa 20:34 Jonathan left the table in **f** anger and refused to eat
31:3 The fighting grew very **f** around Saul,
2Sa 22:9 from his nostrils; / **f** flames leaped from his mouth;
2Ki 23:26 and he did not hold back his **f** anger from them.
1Ch 10:3 The fighting grew very **f** around Saul,
12:8 as **f** as lions and as swift as deer on the mountains.
2Ch 28:11 because now the LORD's **f** anger has been turned
28:13 and the LORD's **f** anger is already turned against
29:10 of Israel, so that his **f** anger will turn away from us.
30:8 so that his **f** anger will turn away from you.
Ezr 8:22 but his **f** anger rages against those who abandon
10:14 so that the **f** anger of our God may be turned away
Job 4:10 Though they are **f** young lions, they will all be
4:11 The **f** lion will starve, and the cubs of the lioness
Ps 2:5 he rebukes them, / terrifying them with his **f** fury.
18:8 from his nostrils; / **f** flames leaped from his mouth;
22:12 of bulls; / **f** bulls of Bashan have hemmed me in!
35:17 and do nothing? / Rescue me from their **f** attacks.
57:4 I am surrounded by **f** lions / who greedily devour
59:3 ambush for me. / **F** enemies are out there waiting,
78:49 He loosed on them his **f** anger— / all his fury,
83:15 chase them with your **f** storms; / terrify them with
88:16 Your **f** anger has overwhelmed me. / Your terrors
91:13 you will crush **f** lions and serpents under your feet!
Isa 7:4 Tell him he doesn't need to fear the **f** anger of
13:9 is coming—the terrible day of his fury and **f** anger.
13:13 will show my fury and **f** anger."
19:4 cruel master, to a **f** king," says the Lord,
33:19 These **f**, violent people with a strange,
Jer 4:8 for the **f** anger of the LORD is still upon us.
4:26 lay in ruins, crushed by the LORD's **f** anger.
12:13 for the **f** anger of the LORD is upon them."
25:37 turned into a wasteland by the LORD's **f** anger.
25:38 the sword of the enemy and the LORD's **f** anger.
30:24 The **f** anger of the LORD will not diminish until
49:37 My **f** anger will bring great disaster upon the
51:45 Save yourselves! Run from the LORD's **f** anger.
La 1:12 LORD brought on me in the day of his **f** anger.
Eze 22:22 and you will melt like silver in **f** heat. Then you
Da 8:23 a **f** king, a master of intrigue, will rise to power.
Jnh 3:9 and hold back his **f** anger from destroying us."
Na 1:6 Who can stand before his **f** anger? Who can
Hab 1:8 They are a **f** people, more **f** than wolves at dusk.
Zep 2:2 before the **f** fury of the LORD falls
Mk 4:37 But soon a **f** storm arose. High waves began to
Lk 8:23 A **f** storm developed that threatened to swamp
Rev 16:19 the cup that was filled with the wine of his **f** wrath.
19:15 and he trod the winepress of the **f** wrath of

FIERCELY (2) [FIERCE]

Job 39:24 **F** it paws the ground and rushes forward into battle
Jer 6:29 The bellows blow **f**. The refining fire grows hotter.

FIERCEST (3) [FIERCE]

2Sa 11:15 Uriah on the front lines where the battle is **f**.
La 4:11 is satisfied. His **f** anger has now been poured out.
Zep 3:8 and pour out my **f** anger and fury on them.

FIERY (8) [FIRE]

Dt 9:15 "So I came down from the **f** mountain, holding in
Job 18:15 The home of the wicked will disappear beneath a **f**
Isa 14:29 snake will be born, a **f** serpent to destroy you!
Da 7:9 He sat on a **f** throne with wheels of blazing fire,
Eph 6:16 shield to stop the **f** arrows aimed at you by Satan.
1Pe 1:7 faith remains strong after being tried by **f** trials,
4:12 don't be surprised at the **f** trials you are going
Rev 9:17 The riders wore armor that was **f** red and sky blue

FIFTEEN (15) [FIFTEENTH, 15]

Lev 27:7 A man older than sixty is valued at **f** pieces of
1Sa 17:7 tipped with an iron spearhead that weighed **f**
2Sa 9:10 Ziba, who had **f** sons and twenty servants, replied,
19:17 of Saul, and Ziba's **f** sons and twenty servants.
1Ki 7:3 that rested on three rows of pillars, **f** in each row.
10:16 each containing over **f** pounds of gold.
2Ki 14:17 King Amaziah of Judah lived on for **f** years after
20:6 I will add **f** years to your life, and I will rescue you
2Ch 25:25 King Amaziah of Judah lived on for **f** years after
Ezr 3:6 **F** days before the Festival of Shelters began,
Ne 3:13 They also repaired the **f** hundred feet of wall to the
Isa 38:5 and seen your tears. I will add **f** years to your life,
Hos 3:2 So I bought her back for **f** pieces of silver

Zec 5: 2 to be about thirty feet long and **f** feet wide."
Gal 1:18 with Peter and stayed there with him for **f** days.

FIFTEENTH (5) [FIFTEEN]

2Ki 14:23 began to rule over Israel in the **f** year of King
1Ch 24:14 The **f** lot fell to Bilgah. / The sixteenth lot fell to
25:22 The **f** lot fell to Jerimoth and twelve of his sons
2Ch 15:10 in late spring, during the **f** year of Asa's reign.
Lk 3: 1 It was now the **f** year of the reign of Tiberius,

FIFTH (29) [FIVE, ONE-FIFTH]

Ge 1:23 This all happened on the **f** day.
30:17 became pregnant again and gave birth to her **f** son.
47:24 harvest it, a **f** of your crop will belong to Pharaoh.
Lev 19:25 Finally, in the **f** year you may eat the fruit. In this
23:34 Shelters on the **f** day after the Day of Atonement.
Nu 7:36 On the **f** day Shelumiel son of Zurishaddai,
29:26 "On the **f** day of the festival, sacrifice nine young
Jos 19:24 The **f** allotment of land went to the families of the
Jdg 19: 8 On the morning of the **f** day he was up early again,
2Sa 3: 4 The **f** was Shephatiah, whose mother was Abital.
1Ki 14:25 In the **f** year of King Rehoboam's reign,
2Ki 8:16 Judah in the **f** year of King Joram's reign in Israel.
1Ch 2:14 his fourth was Nethanel, his **f** was Raddai,
3: 3 The **f** was Shephatiah, whose mother was Abital.
12:10 Mishmannah was fourth. / Jeremiah was **f**.
24: 9 The **f** lot fell to Malkijah. / The sixth lot fell to
25:12 The **f** lot fell to Nethaniah and twelve of his sons
26: 3 Elam (the **f**), Jehohanan (the sixth), and Eliehoenai
26: 4 (the third), Sacar (the fourth), Nethanel (the **f**),
27: 8 Shammah the Izrahite was commander of the **f**
27: 8 which was on duty during the **f** month.
2Ch 12: 2 King Shishak of Egypt attacked Jerusalem in the **f**
Ne 6: 5 The **f** time, Sanballat's servant came with an open
Jer 36: 9 during the **f** year of the reign of Jehoiakim son of
Eze 1: 2 This happened during the **f** year of King
Rev 6: 9 And when the Lamb broke the **f** seal, I saw under
9: 1 Then the **f** angel blew his trumpet, and I saw a star
16:10 Then the **f** angel poured out his bowl on the throne
21:20 the **f** onyx, the sixth carnelian, the seventh

FIFTIETH (4) [FIFTY]

Lev 25: 9 Then on the Day of Atonement of the **f** year,
25:11 Yes, the **f** year will be a jubilee for you.
2Ki 15:23 Israel in the **f** year of King Uzziah's reign in Judah.
Eze 46:17 the Year of Jubilee, which comes every **f** year.

FIFTY (50) [FIFTIETH, 50]

Ge 18:24 Suppose you find **f** innocent people there within
18:26 "If I find **f** innocent people in Sodom,
Ex 18:21 groups of one thousand, one hundred, **f**, and ten.
18:25 of groups of one thousand, one hundred, **f**, and ten.
26: 5 The **f** loops along the edge of one set are to match
the **f** loops along the edge of the other.
26: 6 Then make **f** gold clasps to fasten the loops of the
26:10 Put **f** loops along the edge of the last sheet in each
26:11 and fasten them together with **f** bronze clasps.
36:11 **F** blue loops were placed along the edge of the last
36:12 The **f** loops along the edge of the first set of sheets
36:13 Then **f** gold clasps were made to connect the loops
36:17 Then they made **f** loops along the edge of the last
36:18 They also made **f** small bronze clasps to couple the
Lev 23:16 **f** days later, and bring an offering of new grain to
27: 3 of twenty and sixty is valued at **f** pieces of silver;
27:16 **f** pieces of silver for an area that produces five
Nu 4: 3 and **f** who qualify to work in the Tabernacle.
4:23 and **f** who are eligible to serve in the Tabernacle.
4:30 and **f** who are eligible to serve in the Tabernacle.
4:35 and **f** years of age who were eligible for service in
4:39 and **f** years of age who were eligible for service in
4:43 and **f** years of age who were eligible for service in
4:47 and **f** years of age who were eligible for service in
8:25 and they must retire at the age of **f**.
11:32 next day, too. No one gathered less than **f** bushels!
31:30 Also take one of every **f** of the captives, cattle,
31:47 Moses took one of every **f** prisoners and animals
Dt 1:15 some for a hundred, some for **f**, and some for ten.
22:29 he must pay **f** pieces of silver to her father.
2Sa 15: 1 and he hired **f** footmen to run ahead of him.
24:24 So David paid him **f** pieces of silver for the
1Ki 1: 5 and recruited **f** men to run in front of him.
18: 4 He had put **f** prophets in each cave and had
2Ki 1: 9 Then he sent an army captain with **f** soldiers to
1:10 from heaven and destroy you and your **f** men!"
1:11 So the king sent another captain with **f** men.
1:12 from heaven and destroy you and your **f** men!"
1:13 Once more the king sent a captain with **f** men.
1:13 my life and the lives of these, your **f** servants.
2: 7 **F** men from the group of prophets also went
2:16 and **f** of our strongest men will search the
2:17 So **f** men searched for three days but did not find
13: 7 Jehoahaz's army was reduced to **f** mounted troops,
15:25 With **f** men from Gilead, Pekah assassinated the
Hag 2:16 When you expected to draw **f** gallons from the
Mk 6:40 So they sat in groups of **f** or a hundred.
Lk 7:41 pieces of silver to one and **f** pieces to the other.
9:14 sit down on the ground in groups of about **f** each,"
Jn 8:57 The people said, "You aren't even **f** years old.

FIFTY-FIVE (2)

2Ki 21: 1 became king, and he reigned in Jerusalem **f** years.
2Ch 33: 1 became king, and he reigned in Jerusalem **f** years.

FIFTY-SECOND (1) [FIFTY-TWO]

2Ki 15:27 Israel in the **f** year of King Uzziah's reign in Judah.

FIFTY-TWO (4) [FIFTY-SECOND, 52]

2Ki 15: 2 became king, and he reigned in Jerusalem **f** years.
2Ch 26: 3 became king, and he reigned in Jerusalem **f** years.
Ne 6:15 finally finished—just **f** days after we had begun.
6:17 During those **f** days, many letters went back

FIG (34) [FIGS, SYCAMORE-FIG]

Ge 3: 7 So they strung **f** leaves together around their hips
Dt 8: 8 a land of wheat and barley, of grapevines, **f** trees,
Jdg 9:10 "Then they said to the **f** tree, 'You be our king!'
9:11 But the **f** tree also refused, saying, 'Should I quit
1Sa 25:18 one hundred raisin cakes, and two hundred **f** cakes.
30:12 They also gave him part of a **f** cake and two
1Ch 12:40 of flour, **f** cakes, raisins, wine, olive oil, cattle,
Ne 8:15 from olive, wild olive, myrtle, palm, and **f** trees.
Ps 105:33 He ruined their grapevines and **f** trees
Pr 27:18 Workers who tend a **f** tree are allowed to eat its
SS 2:13 The **f** trees are budding, and the grapevines are in
Isa 28: 4 as an early **f** is hungrily picked and eaten.
Joel 1: 7 They have destroyed my grapevines and **f** trees,
1:12 The grapevines and the **f** trees have all withered.
2:22 **f** trees and grapevines will flourish once more.
Am 4: 9 Locusts devoured all your **f** and olive trees.
7:14 I'm just a shepherd, and I take care of **f** trees.
Mic 7: 1 or a single **f** can be found to satisfy my hunger.
Hab 3:17 Even though the **f** trees have no blossoms,
Hag 2:19 before the grapevine, the **f** tree, the pomegranate,
Mt 21:19 and he noticed a **f** tree beside the road. He went
21:19 And immediately the **f** tree withered up.
21:20 "How did the **f** tree wither so quickly?"
24:32 "Now learn a lesson from the **f** tree. When its buds
Mk 11:13 He noticed a **f** tree a little way off that was in full
11:20 The next morning as they passed by the **f** tree he
11:21 Teacher! The **f** tree you cursed has withered!"
13:28 "Now, learn a lesson from the **f** tree. When its
Lk 13: 6 "A man planted a **f** tree in his garden and came
13: 7 waited three years, and there hasn't been a single **f**!
21:29 "Notice the **f** tree, or any other tree.
Jn 1:48 "I could see you under the **f** tree before Philip
1:50 because I told you I had seen you under the **f** tree?
Jas 3:12 Can you pick olives from a **f** tree or figs from a

FIGHT (150) [FIGHTING, FIGHTS, FOUGHT]

Ge 26:21 dug another well, but again there was a **f** over it.
Ex 1:10 they will join our enemies and **f** against us.
14:14 The LORD himself will **f** for you. You won't
17: 8 the warriors of Amalek came to **f** against them.
17: 9 the Israelites to arms, and **f** the army of Amalek.
17:10 He led his men out to **f** the army of Amalek.
Lev 24:10 and an Egyptian father got into a **f** with one of the
24:11 During the **f**, this son of an Israelite woman
Nu 31: 3 "Choose some men to **f** the LORD's war of
32:27 all who are able to bear arms will cross over to **f**
32:29 and Reuben who are able to **f** the LORD's battles
32:32 into Canaan fully armed to **f** for the LORD,
Dt 1:30 He will **f** for you, just as you saw him do in Egypt.
1:41 We will go into the land and **f** for it, as the LORD
1:43 and arrogantly went into the hill country to **f**.
2:14 old enough to **f** in battle had died in the wilderness.
3:22 for the LORD your God will **f** for you.'
20: 1 "When you go out to **f** your enemies and you face
20: 3 Do not be afraid as you go out to **f** today! Do not
20: 4 He will **f** for you against your enemies, and he will
20:12 But if they refuse to make peace and prepare to **f**,
29: 7 and King Og of Bashan came out to **f** against us,
Jos 2:11 No one has the courage to **f** after hearing such
8: 5 the men of Ai will come out to **f** as they did before,
9: 2 These kings quickly combined their armies to **f**
11: 4 their warriors and uniting to **f** against Israel.
11: 5 around the water near Merom to **f** against Israel.
11:20 and caused them to **f** the Israelites instead of
14:11 and I can still travel and **f** as well as I could then.
Jdg 1: 3 "Join with us to **f** against the Canaanites living in
1: 9 Then they turned south to **f** the Canaanites living in
1:17 Then Judah joined with Simeon to **f** against the
7: 2 If I let all of you **f** the Midianites, the Israelites will
7: 3 leaving only ten thousand who were willing to **f**.
7:22 the LORD caused the warriors in the camp to **f**
8: 1 us when you first went out to **f** the Midianites?"
9:29 'Get some more soldiers, and come out and **f**!' "
9:38 are right outside the city! Go out and **f** them!"
11: 6 be our commander! Help us **f** the Ammonites!"
12: 1 "Why didn't you call for us to help you **f** against
12: 3 the Ammonites. So why have you come to **f** me?"
20:14 and gathered at Gibeah to **f** the Israelites.
20:23 "Should we **f** against our relatives from Benjamin
20:23 the LORD said, "Go out and **f** against them.")
20:24 So they went out to **f** against the warriors of
20:28 "Should we **f** against our relatives from Benjamin
1Sa 2:10 Those who **f** against the LORD will be broken.
4: 9 **F** as you never have before, Philistines! If you
14:10 But if they say, 'Come on up and **f**,' then we will
17: 8 Choose someone to **f** for you, and I will represent
17:10 of Israel! Send me a man who will **f** with me!"
17:13 had already joined Saul's army to **f** the Philistines.
17:32 David told Saul. "I'll go **f** this Philistine!"
17:40 and sling, he started across to **f** Goliath.
17:55 As Saul watched David go out to **f** Goliath,
18:25 in mind was that David would be killed in the **f**.
23: 3 We certainly don't want to go to Keilah to **f** the
23:28 Saul quit the chase and returned to **f** the Philistines.
29: 8 "Why can't I **f** the enemies of my lord, the king?"
2Sa 2:15 So twelve men were chosen from each side to **f**
2:17 The two armies then began to **f** each other, and by
2:21 "Go **f** someone else!" Abner warned. "Take on
5: 6 then led his troops to Jerusalem to **f** against the
5:19 the LORD, "Should I go out to **f** the Philistines?
10: 7 he sent Joab and the entire Israelite army to **f** them.
10: 8 and Maacah positioned themselves to **f** in the open
10: 9 When Joab saw that he would have to **f** on two
10: 9 and led them out to **f** the Arameans in the fields.
10:12 Let us **f** bravely to save our people and the cities of
11:25 **F** harder next time, and conquer the city!"
14: 6 "My two sons had a **f** out in the field. And since
1Ki 8:44 "If your people go out at your command to **f** their
12:21 to **f** against the army of Israel and to restore the
12:24 Do not **f** against your relatives, the Israelites.
20:19 provincial commanders had led the army out to **f**.
20:25 and men, and we will **f** against them in the plains.
2Ki 3: 7 Will you help me **f** him?" And Jehoshaphat
3:21 they mobilized every man who could **f**, young
10: 3 your king, and prepare to **f** for Ahab's dynasty."
19: 9 of Ethiopia was leading an army to **f** against him.
23:29 King Josiah marched out with his army to **f** him,
1Ch 12:19 when he went with the Philistines to **f** against Saul.
14:10 asked God, "Should I go out to **f** the Philistines?
19: 8 he sent Joab and all his warriors to **f** them.
19: 9 while the other kings positioned themselves to **f** in
19:10 When Joab saw that he would have to **f** on two
19:10 and led them out to **f** the Arameans in the fields.
19:13 Let us **f** bravely to save our people and the cities of
2Ch 6:34 "If your people go out at your command to **f** their
11: 1 to **f** against the army of Israel and to restore the
11: 4 Do not **f** against your relatives. Go back home,
11: 4 of the LORD and did not **f** against Jeroboam.
13:12 O people of Israel, do not **f** against the LORD,
20:17 But you will not even need to **f**. Take your
22: 5 They went out to **f** King Hazael of Aram at
25: 8 you will be defeated no matter how well you **f**.
32: 8 our God to help us and to **f** our battles for us!"
35:20 and Josiah and his army marched out to **f** him.
35:21 I only want to **f** the nation with which I am at war.
Ne 4: 8 all made plans to come and **f** against Jerusalem
4:14 who is great and glorious, and **f** for your friends,
4:20 it is sounding. Then our God will **f** for us!"
Ps 109: 3 and they **f** against me for no reason.
Pr 1:22 How long will you fools **f** the facts?
20: 3 Avoiding a **f** is a mark of honor; only fools insist
28: 4 to praise the wicked; to obey the law is to **f** them.
Ecc 7:13 Don't **f** the ways of God, for who can straighten
Isa 1:17 Defend the orphan. **F** for the rights of widows.
4: 1 Seven women will **f** over each of them and say,
7: 6 Then we will **f** our way into Jerusalem and install
9:20 They **f** against their own neighbors to steal food,
11:13 They will not **f** against each other anymore.
14:31 the north. Each soldier rushes forward ready to **f**.
19: 2 "I will make the Egyptians **f** against each other—
31: 4 LORD Almighty will come and **f** on Mount Zion.
37: 9 of Ethiopia was leading an army to **f** against him.
49:25 For I will **f** those who **f** you, and I will save
54:15 If any nation comes to **f** you, it will not be
57:16 For I will not **f** against you forever; I will not
Jer 15:20 They will **f** against you like an attacking army,
21: 5 I myself will **f** against you with great power,
21:13 I will **f** against this city of Jerusalem that boasts,
32: 5 If you **f** against the Babylonians, you will never
34:22 They will **f** against this city and will capture
51:30 Her mightiest warriors no longer **f**. They stay in
51:46 time of violence as the leaders **f** against each other.
Da 10:20 Soon I must return to **f** against the spirit prince of
Na 2:11 full of **f** and boldness, where the old and feeble
Hab 1: 3 am surrounded by people who love to argue and **f**.
Zec 10: 5 Since the LORD is with them as they **f**, they will
14: 2 On that day I will gather all the nations to **f** against
14: 3 Then the LORD will go out to **f** against those
14:13 They will **f** against each other in hand-to-hand
Mt 12:19 He will not **f** or shout; / he will not raise his voice
Lk 22:49 to happen, they exclaimed, "Lord, should we **f**?
Ac 26:14 It is hard for you to **f** against my will.'
Ro 7:23 This law wins the **f** and makes me a slave to the sin
Php 1:30 We are in this **f** together. You have seen me suffer
1Ti 1:18 May they give you the confidence to **f** well in the
6:12 **F** the good **f** for what we believe. Hold tightly
2Ti 3: 8 And these teachers **f** the truth just as Jannes
4: 7 I have fought a good **f**, I have finished the race,
Jas 4: 2 so you **f** and quarrel to take it away from them.
1Pe 2:11 evil desires because they **f** against your very souls.
1Jn 4: 4 You have already won your **f** with these false
Rev 2:16 and **f** against them with the sword of my mouth.
13: 4 they exclaimed. "Who is able to **f** against him?"
19:19 and their armies in order to **f** against the one sitting

FIGHTING (60) [FIGHT]

Ex 2:13 his people again, he saw two Hebrew men **f**.
14:25 "The LORD is **f** for Israel against us!"
21:22 "Now suppose two people are **f**, and in the
Nu 31:32 The plunder remaining from the spoils that the **f**
31:36 So the half of the plunder given to the **f** men
31:42 had separated from the half belonging to the **f** men,
31:53 All the **f** men had taken some of the plunder for
32: 6 while your brothers go across and do all the **f**?"
Dt 2:16 "When all the men of **f** age had died,
3:18 all your **f** men must cross the Jordan, armed
25:11 "If two Israelite men are **f** and the wife of one tries
Jos 8: 3 Joshua chose thirty thousand **f** men and sent them
10:42 the LORD, the God of Israel, was **f** for his people.
Jdg 6:16 the Midianites as if you were **f** against one man."
20:34 The **f** was so heavy that Benjamin didn't realize

1Sa 17:19 army at the valley of Elah, **f** against the Philistines.
18:5 an appointment that was applauded by the **f** men
18:17 to be a real warrior by **f** the LORD's battles."
24:1 After Saul returned from **f** the Philistines, he was
25:28 lasting dynasty, for you are **f** the LORD's battles.
31:3 The **f** grew very fierce around Saul,
2Sa 11:16 where he knew the enemy's strongest men were **f**.
23:13 an elite group among David's **f** men) went down to
1Ki 9:22 Instead, he assigned them to serve as **f** men,
22:4 "Will you join me in **f** against Ramoth-gilead?"
2Ki 9:15 But Joram had been wounded in the **f** and had
1Ch 5:22 in the battle because God was **f** against them.
10:3 The **f** grew very fierce around Saul,
11:15 an elite group among David's **f** men) went down to
2Ch 8:9 Instead, he assigned them to serve as **f** men,
14:8 Both armies were composed of courageous **f** men.
18:3 "Will you join me in **f** against Ramoth-gilead?"
20:22 and Mount Seir to start **f** among themselves.
25:6 to hire 100,000 experienced **f** men from Israel.
26:11 This great army of **f** men had been mustered
Pr 22:10 Throw out the mocker, and **f**, quarrels, and insults
23:29 has anguish? Who has sorrow? Who is always **f**?
28:25 Greed causes **f**; trusting the LORD leads to
Isa 3:5 each other—man against man, neighbor **f** neighbor.
29:7 All the nations **f** against Jerusalem will vanish like
58:4 What good is fasting when you keep on **f**
Jer 38:4 the morale of the few **f** men we have left,
46:5 The bravest of its **f** men run without a backward
Joel 3:9 Let all your **f** men advance for the attack!
Am 2:16 the most courageous of your **f** men will drop their
Zec 14:14 Judah, too, will be **f** at Jerusalem. The wealth of all
Mt 12:26 Satan is casting out Satan, he is **f** against himself.
14:24 wind had risen, and they were **f** heavy waves.
Mk 3:26 And if Satan is **f** against himself, how can he
Lk 11:18 But if Satan is **f** against himself by empowering me
Ac 5:39 You may even find yourselves **f** against God."
7:26 he visited them again and saw two men of Israel **f**.
Ro 1:29 sin, greed, hate, envy, murder, **f**, deception,
13:13 and immoral living, or in **f** and jealousy.
1Co 15:32 And what value was there in **f** wild beasts—
Gal 5:17 These two forces are constantly **f** each other,
Eph 6:12 For we are not **f** against people made of flesh
Php 1:27 side by side, **f** together for the Good News.
1Ti 6:4 ending in jealousy, **f**, slander, and evil suspicions.
2Ti 2:14 and command them in God's name to stop **f** over

FIGHTS (7) [FIGHT]

Jos 23:10 for the LORD your God **f** for you, just as he has
Pr 15:18 A hothead starts **f**; a cool-tempered person tries to
26:21 A quarrelsome person starts **f** as easily as hot
29:22 A hot-tempered person starts **f** and gets into all
2Ti 2:23 in foolish, ignorant arguments that only start **f**.
Tit 3:9 in quarrels and **f** about obedience to Jewish laws.
Jas 4:1 What is causing the quarrels and **f** among you?

FIGS (25) [FIG]

Nu 13:23 They also took samples of the pomegranates and **f**.
20:5 This land has no grain, **f**, grapes, or pomegranates.
2Ki 20:7 "Make an ointment from **f** and spread it over the
Ne 13:15 grapes, **f**, and all sorts of produce to Jerusalem to
Isa 38:21 "Make an ointment from **f** and spread it over the
Jer 5:17 of cattle. Yes, they will eat your grapes and **f**.
8:13 I will take away their rich harvests of **f** and grapes.
24:1 I saw two baskets of **f** placed in front of the
24:2 One basket was filled with fresh, ripe **f**,
24:2 while the other was filled with **f** that were spoiled
24:3 I replied, "**F**, some very good and some very
24:5 The good **f** represent the exiles I sent from Judah
24:8 "But the rotten **f**," the LORD said,
24:8 I will treat them like spoiled **f**, too rotten to eat.
29:17 disease upon them and make them like rotting **f**—
Eze 27:17 wheat from Minnith, early **f**, honey, oil, and balm.
Hos 9:10 it was like seeing the first ripe **f** of the season!
Na 3:12 They will be devoured like the ripe **f** that fall into
Mt 7:16 pick grapes from thornbushes, or **f** from thistles.
21:19 He went over to see if there were any **f** on it,
Mk 11:13 so he went over to see if he could find any **f** on it.
Lk 6:44 **F** never grow on thornbushes or grapes on bramble
13:9 If we get **f** next year, fine. If not, you can cut it
Jas 3:12 pick olives from a fig tree or **f** from a grapevine?
Rev 6:13 green **f** falling from trees shaken by mighty winds.

FIGURE (13) [FIGURED, FIGURES]

Ge 29:17 in every way, with a lovely face and shapely **f**.
Nu 26:62 included in the total census **f** of the people of Israel
Jdg 14:14 Three days later they were still trying to **f** it out.
1Ki 10:19 with the **f** of a lion standing on each side of the
2Ch 3:11 One wing of the first **f** was 7-1/2 feet long, and it
3:11 feet long, touched one of the wings of the second **f**.
3:12 the second **f** had one wing 7-1/2 feet long that
3:12 also 7-1/2 feet long, touched the wing of the first **f**.
9:18 with the **f** of a lion standing on each side of the
Isa 44:13 of wood, takes the tool, and carves the **f** of a man.
Eze 1:26 And high above this throne was a **f** whose
8:2 I saw a **f** that appeared to be a man. From the waist
Jn 7:4 "You can't become a public **f** if you hide like this!

FIGURED (1) [FIGURE]

Ge 20:11 Abraham said, "I **f** this to be a godless place.

FIGUREHEAD (1) [HEAD]

Ac 28:11 an Alexandrian ship with the twin gods as its **f**.

FIGURES (11) [FIGURE]

Ex 26:1 with **f** of cherubim skillfully embroidered into
37:7 He made two **f** of cherubim out of hammered gold
38:21 Moses directed the Levites to compile the **f**,
Nu 26:63 So these are the census **f** of the people of Israel as
1Ki 10:20 Solomon made twelve other lion **f**, one standing on
2Ch 3:7 and **f** of cherubim were carved on the walls.
3:10 Solomon made two **f** shaped like cherubim
3:14 scarlet yarn, with **f** of cherubim embroidered on it.
4:3 its rim by two rows of **f** that resembled oxen.
9:19 Solomon made twelve other lion **f**, one standing on
Eze 41:19 The **f** were carved all along the inside of the

FILE (3) [FILED]

1Ki 12:31 ordained priests from the rank and **f** of the people—
13:33 to choose priests from the rank and **f** of the people.
1Co 6:1 why do you **f** a lawsuit and ask a secular court to

FILED (1) [FILE]

Hos 4:1 The LORD has **f** a lawsuit against you, saying:

FILIGREE (2)

Ex 28:13 The settings are to be made of gold **f**,
39:6 shoulder-pieces of the ephod, were set in gold **f**.

FILL (72) [FILLED, FILLING, FILLS, FULL, FULLNESS, FULLY]

Ge 1:22 saying, "Let the fish multiply and **f** the oceans. Let the birds increase and **f** the earth."
1:28 told them, "Multiply and **f** the earth and subdue it.
9:1 his sons and told them, "Multiply and **f** the earth.
9:7 the earth. Yes, multiply and **f** the earth!"
35:11 "I am God Almighty. Multiply and **f** the earth!
42:25 then ordered his servants to **f** the men's sacks with
43:11 **F** your bags with the best products of the land.
44:1 "**F** each of their sacks with as much grain as they
Ex 2:16 and **f** the water troughs for their father's flocks.
8:3 They will **f** even your ovens and your kneading
23:30 your population has increased enough to **f** the land.
30:18 the Tabernacle and the altar, and **f** it with water.
40:7 the Tabernacle and the altar and **f** it with water.
Lev 16:12 he will **f** an incense burner with burning coals from
25:19 and you will eat your **f** and live securely in it.
26:5 You will eat your **f** and live securely in your land.
Nu 20:11 So all the people and their livestock drank their **f**.
Dt 6:11 not plant. When you have eaten your **f** in this land,
8:10 When you have eaten your **f**, praise the LORD
23:24 "You may eat your **f** of grapes from your
28:8 you do and will **f** your storehouses with grain.
1Sa 16:1 Now **f** your horn with olive oil and go to
1Ki 18:33 Then he said, "**F** four large jars with water,
Job 8:21 He will yet **f** your mouth with laughter and your
Ps 37:31 They **f** their hearts with God's law, / so they will
78:29 The people ate their **f**. / He gave them what they
81:10 your mouth wide, and I will **f** it with good things.
104:13 and you **f** the earth with the fruit of your labor.
110:6 and **f** them with their dead; / he will shatter heads
123:3 have mercy, / for we have had our **f** of contempt.
123:4 We have had our **f** of the scoffing of the proud
Pr 1:13 We'll **f** our houses with all kinds of things!
2:10 your heart, and knowledge will **f** you with joy.
3:10 Then he will **f** your barns with grain, and your vats
3:22 for they **f** you with life and bring you honor
7:18 Come, let's drink our **f** of love until morning.
8:21 who love me inherit wealth, for I **f** their treasuries.
12:21 the godly, but the wicked have their **f** of trouble.
Isa 11:9 And as the waters **f** the sea, so the earth will be
22:7 They **f** your beautiful valleys and crowd against
27:6 and blossom and **f** the whole earth with her fruit!
32:17 Quietness and confidence will **f** the land forever.
34:3 and the stench of rotting bodies will **f** the land.
40:4 **F** the valleys and level the hills. Straighten out the
41:16 And the joy of the LORD will **f** you to
41:23 Or perform a mighty miracle that will **f** us with
51:3 Lovely songs of thanksgiving will **f** the air.
53:10 good plan to crush him and **f** him with grief.
56:7 and will **f** them with joy in my house of prayer.
60:9 Holy One of Israel, for he will **f** you with splendor.
Jer 25:33 In that day those the LORD has slaughtered will **f**
Eze 9:7 "**F** its courtyards with the bodies of those you kill!
24:4 **F** it with choice meat—the rump and the shoulder
32:5 with your flesh and **f** the valleys with your bones.
35:8 I will **f** your mountains with the dead. Your hills,
36:38 I will multiply them like the sacred flocks that **f**
47:10 Fish of every kind will **f** the Dead Sea, just as they **f** the Mediterranean!
Hos 9:6 treasures of silver; brambles will **f** your homes.
Joel 3:18 Water will **f** the dry streambeds of Judah, and a
Hab 2:14 as the waters **f** the sea, with an awareness of the
Zep 1:9 and kill to **f** their masters' homes with loot.
Hag 1:6 You have food to eat, but not enough to **f** you up.
2:7 I will **f** this place with glory, says the LORD
Lk 3:5 **F** in the valleys, / and level the mountains
Jn 2:7 Jesus told the servants, "**F** the jars with water."
Ro 5:5 because he has given us the Holy Spirit to **f** our
Eph 4:10 so that his rule might **f** the entire universe.
5:18 Instead, let the Holy Spirit **f** and control you.
Col 3:2 Let heaven **f** your thoughts. Do not think only
1Th 3:10 asking God to let us see you again to **f** up anything

FILLED (281) [FILL]

Ge 1:12 The land was **f** with seed-bearing plants and trees,
1:20 Let the skies be **f** with birds of every kind."
6:11 corrupt in God's sight, and it was **f** with violence.
6:13 for the earth is **f** with violence because of them.
14:10 As it happened, the valley was **f** with tar pits.
21:19 She immediately **f** her water container and gave
24:16 down to the spring, **f** her jug, and came up again.
24:45 down to the spring and drew water and **f** the jug.
26:15 and they **f** up all of Isaac's wells with earth.
26:18 which the Philistines had **f** in after Abraham's
41:38 For he is a man who is obviously **f** with the spirit
41:49 seven years, the granaries were **f** to overflowing.
42:28 They were **f** with terror and said to each other,
Ex 1:7 so quickly that they soon **f** the land.
8:3 Every home in Egypt will be **f** with them.
8:14 into great heaps, and a terrible stench **f** the land.
8:21 Your homes will be **f** with them, and the ground
16:12 and in the morning you will be **f** with bread.
31:3 I have **f** him with the Spirit of God, giving him
35:31 The LORD has **f** Bezalel with the Spirit of God,
40:30 He **f** it with water so the priests could use it to
40:34 and the glorious presence of the LORD **f** it.
40:35 and the Tabernacle was **f** with the awesome glory
Lev 14:5 over a clay pot that is **f** with fresh springwater.
14:50 over a clay pot that is **f** with fresh springwater.
19:29 or the land will be **f** with promiscuity
Nu 7:13 These were both **f** with grain offerings of choice
7:14 about four ounces, which was **f** with incense.
7:19 These were both **f** with grain offerings of choice
7:20 about four ounces, which was **f** with incense.
7:25 These were both **f** with grain offerings of choice
7:26 about four ounces, which was **f** with incense.
7:31 These were both **f** with grain offerings of choice
7:32 about four ounces, which was **f** with incense.
7:37 These were both **f** with grain offerings of choice
7:38 about four ounces, which was **f** with incense.
7:43 These were both **f** with grain offerings of choice
7:44 about four ounces, which was **f** with incense.
7:49 These were both **f** with grain offerings of choice
7:50 about four ounces, which was **f** with incense.
7:55 These were both **f** with grain offerings of choice
7:56 about four ounces, which was **f** with incense.
7:61 These were both **f** with grain offerings of choice
7:62 about four ounces, which was **f** with incense.
7:67 These were both **f** with grain offerings of choice
7:68 about four ounces, which was **f** with incense.
7:73 These were both **f** with grain offerings of choice
7:74 about four ounces, which was **f** with incense.
7:79 These were both **f** with grain offerings of choice
7:80 about four ounces, which was **f** with incense.
7:86 of the gold containers that were **f** with incense.
14:21 and as surely as the earth is **f** with the LORD's
22:18 "Even if Balak were to give me a palace **f** with
24:13 'Even if Balak were to give me a palace **f** with
Dt 6:10 It is a land **f** with large, prosperous cities that you
28:5 with fruit, and with kneading bowls **f** with bread.
32:19 "The LORD saw this and was **f** with loathing.
Jos 9:13 These wineskins were new when we **f** them,
Jdg 16:27 The temple was completely **f** with people.
1Sa 16:14 and the LORD sent a tormenting spirit that **f** him
2Sa 6:16 the LORD, she was **f** with contempt for him.
1Ki 8:10 a cloud **f** the Temple of the LORD.
8:11 because the glorious presence of the LORD **f** the
20:27 to the vast Aramean forces that **f** the countryside!
2Ki 3:16 This dry valley will be **f** with pools of water!
3:17 the LORD, but this valley will be **f** with water.
4:4 into the jars, setting the jars aside as they are **f**."
4:5 many jars to her, and she **f** one after another.
6:17 he saw that the hillside around Elisha was **f** with
10:21 and **f** the temple of Baal from one end to the other.
21:16 **f** from one end to the other with innocent blood.
24:4 He had **f** Jerusalem with innocent blood,
1Ch 15:29 leaping for joy, she was **f** with contempt for him.
29:9 to the LORD, and King David was **f** with joy.
2Ch 5:13 At that moment a cloud **f** the Temple of the
5:14 because the glorious presence of the LORD **f** the
7:1 and the glorious presence of the LORD **f** the
7:2 because the glorious presence of the LORD **f** it.
24:10 gladly brought their money and **f** the chest with it.
Ezr 9:11 one end to the other, the land is **f** with corruption.
Ne 8:17 of the festival, and everyone was **f** with great joy!
Est 3:5 or show him respect, he was **f** with rage.
8:16 The Jews were **f** with joy and gladness and were
Job 3:15 wealthy princes whose palaces were **f** with gold
7:5 My skin is **f** with worms and scabs. My flesh
9:25 swiftly than a runner. It flees away, **f** with tragedy.
10:15 I am **f** with shame and misery so that I can't hold
19:24 carved with an iron chisel and **f** with lead,
22:18 But they forgot that he had **f** their homes with good
30:17 My weary nights are **f** with pain as though
33:28 me from the grave, and now my life is **f** with light.'
Ps 5:9 an open grave. / Their speech is **f** with flattery.
5:11 so all who love your name may be **f** with joy.
9:2 I will be **f** with joy because of you. / I will sing
16:4 Those who chase after other gods will be **f** with
16:9 No wonder my heart is **f** with joy, / and my mouth
28:7 my heart. / He helps me, and my heart is **f** with joy.
38:6 and racked with pain. / My days are **f** with grief.
40:16 all who search for you / be **f** with joy and gladness.
48:10 the earth. / Your strong right hand is **f** with victory.
49:3 are wise, / and my thoughts are **f** with insight.
50:19 Your mouths are **f** with wickedness, / and your
65:3 Though our hearts are **f** with sins, / you forgive
68:3 be glad in God's presence. / Let them be **f** with joy.
70:4 all who search for you / be **f** with joy and gladness.
72:19 Let the whole earth be **f** with his glory. / Amen
77:6 when my nights were **f** with joyful songs. / I search
80:9 ground for us, / and we took root and **f** the land.

85: 9 who honor him; / our land will be **f** with his glory.
90: 10 But even the best of these years are **f** with pain
94: 19 When doubts **f** my mind, / your comfort gave me
126: 2 We were **f** with laughter, / and we sang for joy.
144: 13 May our farms be **f** / with crops of every kind.
145: 17 in everything he does; / he is **f** with kindness.
Pr 22: 15 A youngster's heart is **f** with foolishness,
22: 20 sayings for you, **f** with advice and knowledge.
24: 4 Through knowledge its rooms are **f** with all sorts of
Ecc 2: 23 Their days of labor are **f** with pain and grief;
SS 7: 2 Your navel is as delicious as a goblet **f** with wine.
Isa 1: 21 and righteousness, she is now **f** with murderers.
2: 8 The land is **f** with idols. The people bow down
6: 1 lofty throne, and the train of his robe **f** the Temple.
6: 3 The whole earth is **f** with his glory!"
6: 4 and the entire sanctuary was **f** with smoke.
9: 1 the Jordan and the sea, will be **f** with glory.
11: 9 so the earth will be **f** with people who know the
14: 23 a place of porcupines, **f** with swamps and marshes.
29: 19 The humble will be **f** with fresh joy from the
30: 27 His lips are **f** with fury; his words consume like
30: 29 You will be **f** with joy, as when a flutist leads a
34: 9 The streams of Edom will be **f** with burning pitch,
59: 6 they do is productive; all their activity is **f** with sin.
61: 11 **f** with young plants springing up everywhere.
65: 10 the plain of Sharon will again be **f** with flocks,
Jer 3: 16 "And when your land is once more **f** with
5: 27 Like a cage **f** with birds, their homes are **f** with evil
6: 11 So now I am **f** with the LORD's fury. Yes,
16: 18 and **f** my inheritance with their evil deeds."
19: 4 And they have **f** this place with the blood of
20: 18 My entire life has been **f** with trouble, sorrow,
24: 2 One basket was **f** with fresh, ripe figs,
24: 2 while the other was **f** with figs that were spoiled
25: 15 "Take from my hand this cup **f** to the brim with
41: 9 Ishmael son of Nethaniah **f** it with corpses.
46: 12 The earth is **f** with your cries of despair.
50: 38 Because the whole land is **f** with idols,
51: 5 even though their land was **f** with sin against the
51: 14 will be **f** with enemies, like fields **f** with locusts,
51: 34 like a great monster and **f** his belly with our riches.
La 1: 4 no longer **f** with crowds on their way to celebrate
3: 15 He has **f** me with bitterness. He has given me a cup
3: 47 We are **f** with fear, for we are trapped, desolate,
Eze 7: 23 by terrible crimes. Jerusalem is **f** with violence.
9: 9 land is full of murder; the city is **f** with injustice.
10: 3 and the cloud of glory **f** the inner courtyard.
10: 4 The Temple was **f** with this cloud of glory,
11: 6 and **f** your streets with the dead.
12: 7 **f** with the things I might carry into exile.
17: 4 Then he carried it away to a city **f** with merchants,
21: 24 whatever you do, all your actions are **f** with sin.
22: 5 O infamous city, **f** with confusion, you will be
22: 9 You are **f** with idol worshipers and people who
24: 6 city of murderers! She is a pot **f** with corruption.
27: 25 Your island warehouse was **f** to the brim!
27: 35 Their kings are **f** with horror / and look on with
28: 16 Your great wealth **f** you with violence, and you
28: 17 Your heart was **f** with pride because of all your
35: 8 and your streams will be **f** with people slaughtered
36: 10 the ruined cities will be rebuilt and **f** with people.
36: 35 now have strong walls, and they are **f** with people!'
37: 1 the Spirit of the LORD to a valley **f** with bones.
38: 11 'Israel is an unprotected land **f** with unwalled
38: 12 **f** with people who have returned from exile in
43: 5 and the glory of the LORD **f** the Temple.
44: 4 and saw that the glory of the LORD **f** the Temple
Da 5: 12 has a sharp mind and is **f** with divine knowledge
5: 14 the gods within you and that you are **f** with insight,
11: 12 the king of the south will be **f** with pride and will
Hos 4: 3 It is **f** with sadness, and all living things are
7: 1 Samaria is **f** with liars, thieves, and bandits!
12: 11 But Gilead is **f** with sinners who worship idols.
Joel 2: 13 He is **f** with kindness and is eager not to punish
2: 22 The trees will again be **f** with luscious fruit;
Am 3: 10 "Their fortresses are **f** with wealth taken by theft
3: 15 summer houses, too—all their palaces **f** with ivory.
4: 10 all your horses. The stench of death **f** the air!
8: 1 another vision. In it I saw a basket **f** with ripe fruit.
Ob 1: 10 be destroyed completely and **f** with shame forever.
Jnh 4: 2 slow to get angry and **f** with unfailing love.
Mic 2: 10 for you have **f** it with sin and ruined it completely.
2: 12 your land will again be **f** with noisy crowds!
3: 8 I am **f** with power and the Spirit of the LORD.
3: 8 I am **f** with justice and might, fearlessly pointing
4: 6 who are lame, who have been exiles, **f** with grief.
6: 10 The homes of the wicked are **f** with treasures
Na 1: 2 is a jealous God, **f** with vengeance and wrath.
2: 12 You **f** your city and your homes with captives
3: 16 as the stars, have **f** your city with vast wealth.
Hab 2: 8 You have **f** the countryside with violence and all
2: 14 For the time will come when all the earth will be **f**,
3: 2 and I am **f** with awe by the amazing things you
3: 3 fills the heavens, and the earth is **f** with his praise!
Hag 1: 6 you were putting them in pockets **f** with holes!
Zec 5: 6 and it is **f** with the sins of everyone throughout the
8: 5 And the streets of the city will be **f** with boys
9: 5 Ashkelon will see Tyre fall and will be **f** with fear.
9: 15 They will be **f** with blood like a bowl,
14: 11 And Jerusalem will be **f**, safe at last, never again to
Mt 2: 10 When they saw the star, they were **f** with joy!
17: 23 And the disciples' hearts were **f** with grief.
18: 27 Then the king was **f** with pity for him, and he
22: 10 bad alike, and the banquet hall was **f** with guests.
23: 27 but **f** on the inside with dead people's bones
23: 28 but inside your hearts are **f** with hypocrisy
26: 37 and he began to be **f** with anguish and deep
27: 3 had been condemned to die, he was **f** with remorse.
27: 48 One of them ran and **f** a sponge with sour wine,
28: 8 were very frightened but also **f** with great joy,
Mk 4: 41 And they were **f** with awe and said among
10: 32 The disciples were **f** with dread and the people
14: 33 and he began to be **f** with horror and deep distress.
15: 36 One of them ran and **f** a sponge with sour wine,
Lk 1: 15 hard liquor, and he will be **f** with the Holy Spirit,
1: 41 and Elizabeth was **f** with the Holy Spirit.
1: 67 was **f** with the Holy Spirit and gave this prophecy:
2: 25 He was **f** with the Holy Spirit, and he eagerly
2: 40 He was **f** with wisdom beyond his years, and God
4: 14 returned to Galilee, **f** with the Holy Spirit's power.
5: 7 and soon both boats were **f** with fish and on the
7: 37 and brought a beautiful jar **f** with expensive
8: 25 And they were **f** with awe and amazement.
8: 30 he replied—for the man was **f** with many demons.
8: 52 The house was **f** with people weeping and wailing,
10: 21 Then Jesus was **f** with the joy of the Holy Spirit
11: 36 If you are **f** with light, with no dark corners,
15: 20 **F** with love and compassion, he ran to his son,
21: 34 and drunkenness, and **f** with the worries of this life.
24: 41 they stood there doubting, **f** with joy and wonder.
24: 52 and then returned to Jerusalem **f** with great joy.
Jn 2: 7 with water." When the jars had been **f** to the brim,
3: 29 and I am **f** with joy at his success.
6: 13 but twelve baskets were **f** with the pieces of bread
12: 3 with her hair. And the house was **f** with fragrance.
15: 11 told you this so that you will be **f** with my joy.
17: 13 I was with them so they would be **f** with my joy.
20: 20 They were **f** with joy when they saw their Lord!
Ac 2: 2 and it **f** the house where they were meeting.
2: 4 And everyone present was **f** with the Holy Spirit
2: 26 No wonder my heart is **f** with joy, / and my mouth
4: 8 Then Peter, **f** with the Holy Spirit, said to them,
4: 31 and they were all **f** with the Holy Spirit.
5: 3 Peter said, "Ananias, why has Satan **f** your heart?
5: 28 you have **f** all Jerusalem with your teaching about
9: 17 get your sight back and be **f** with the Holy Spirit."
9: 39 The room was **f** with widows who were weeping
11: 23 saw this proof of God's favor, he was **f** with joy,
13: 9 also known as Paul, **f** with the Holy Spirit,
13: 52 And the believers were **f** with joy and with the
19: 29 to gather, and soon the city was **f** with confusion.
Ro 3: 13 from an open grave. / Their speech is **f** with lies."
9: 2 My heart is **f** with bitter sorrow and unending
2Co 7: 7 how loyal your love is for me, I was **f** with joy!
Eph 1: 23 it is **f** by Christ, who fills everything everywhere
3: 19 Then you will be **f** with the fullness of life
4: 19 Their lives are **f** with all kinds of impurity
5: 2 Live a life **f** with love for others,
Php 1: 11 May you always be **f** with the fruit of your
Col 1: 11 and endurance you need. May you be **f** with joy,
1Ti 1: 5 would be **f** with love that comes from a pure heart,
1: 14 He **f** me completely with faith and the love of
2Ti 1: 4 And I will be **f** with joy when we are together
Tit 2: 2 have strong faith and be **f** with love and patience.
Jude 1: 7 which were **f** with sexual immorality and every
Rev 5: 8 a harp, and they held gold bowls **f** with incense—
8: 5 Then the angel **f** the incense burner with fire from
15: 7 angels a gold bowl **f** with the terrible wrath of God,
15: 8 The Temple was **f** with smoke from God's glory
16: 19 and he made her drink the cup that was **f** with the
21: 11 It was **f** with the glory of God and sparkled like a

FILLET [KJV] See CIRCUMFERENCE

FILLING (9) [FILL]

Lev 16: 12 Then, after **f** both his hands with fragrant incense,
Jos 8: 20 smoke from the city was **f** the sky, and they had
2Ch 7: 3 and the glorious presence of the LORD **f** the
Ecc 2: 5 and parks, **f** them with all kinds of fruit trees.
Isa 3: 14 **f** your barns with grain extorted from helpless
34: 14 mingle there with hyenas, their howls **f** the night.
Jer 23: 16 they prophesy to you, **f** you with futile hopes.
La 2: 14 they painted false pictures, **f** you with false hope.
Eze 32: 6 the way to the mountains, **f** the ravines to the brim.

FILLS (14) [FILL]

Ge 32: 10 and now my household **f** two camps!
Job 9: 18 my breath, but **f** me instead with bitter sorrows.
36: 32 He **f** his hands with lightning bolts. He hurls each
Ps 8: 1 our Lord, the majesty of your name **f** the earth!
8: 9 our Lord, the majesty of your name **f** the earth!
33: 5 and good, / and his unfailing love **f** the earth.
103: 5 He **f** my life with good things. / My youth is
107: 9 the thirsty / and **f** the hungry with good things.
Pr 12: 20 Deceit **f** hearts that are plotting evil; joy **f** hearts that are planning peace!
Jer 23: 15 because of Jerusalem's prophets that wickedness **f**
Hab 3: 3 His brilliant splendor **f** the heavens, and the earth
Lk 24: 49 Spirit comes and **f** you with power from heaven."
Eph 1: 23 who **f** everything everywhere with his presence.

FILLY (1)

SS 1: 9 What a lovely **f** you are, my beloved one!

FILTH (8) [FILTHY]

Ps 59: 7 Listen to the **f** that comes from their mouths,
Isa 4: 4 The Lord will wash the moral **f** from the women of
28: 8 tables are covered with vomit; **f** is everywhere.
Eze 24: 11 set the empty pot on the coals to scorch away the **f**
24: 13 It is the **f** and corruption of your lewdness
36: 25 Your **f** will be washed away, and you will no
Na 3: 6 I will cover you with **f** and show the world how
Jas 1: 21 So get rid of all the **f** and evil in your lives,

FILTHY (18) [FILTH]

Job 9: 31 I would be so **f** my own clothing would hate me.
Pr 30: 12 They feel pure, but they are **f** and unwashed.
Isa 30: 22 You will throw them out like **f** rags. "Ugh!"
41: 24 Anyone who chooses you becomes **f**, just like you!
59: 3 hands of murderers, and your fingers are **f** with sin.
64: 6 our righteous deeds, we find they are but **f** rags.
La 1: 8 so she has been tossed away like a **f** rag.
1: 17 Let them be thrown away like a **f** rag!"
Eze 22: 3 doomed and damned—city of idols, **f** and foul—
24: 13 you will remain **f** until my fury against you has
36: 17 To me their conduct was as **f** as a bloody rag.
36: 29 I will cleanse you of your **f** behavior. I will give
Zec 3: 3 Jeshua's clothing was **f** as he stood there before the
3: 4 the others standing there, "Take off his **f** clothes."
Mt 23: 25 of the cup and the dish, but inside you are **f**—
Lk 11: 39 of the cup and the dish, but inside you are still **f**—
2Co 6: 17 says the Lord. / Don't touch their **f** things,
Rev 18: 2 of demons and evil spirits, a nest for **f** buzzards,

FINAL (26) [FINALITY, FINALLY]

Ex 23: 16 you are to celebrate the Festival of the **F** Harvest at
34: 22 and celebrate the Festival of the **F** Harvest at the
Lev 27: 12 will assess its value, and his assessment will be **f**.
27: 14 assess its value. The priest's assessment will be **f**.
Nu 3: 38 who had the **f** responsibility for the sanctuary on
33: 54 The decision of the sacred lot is **f**. In this way,
Jdg 14: 10 As his father was making **f** arrangements for the
2Sa 23: 5 His agreement is eternal, **f**, sealed. / He will
2Ki 11: 6 And the **f** third must stand guard behind the palace
1Ch 23: 27 It was according to David's **f** instructions that all
27: 24 The **f** total was never recorded in King David's
2Ch 19: 11 "Amariah the high priest will have **f** say in all
19: 11 the tribe of Judah, will have **f** say in all civil cases.
23: 5 and the **f** third will be at the Foundation Gate.
Ecc 3: 14 And I know that whatever God does is **f**.
12: 13 Here is my **f** conclusion: Fear God and obey his
Eze 7: 6 It has finally arrived! Your **f** doom is waiting!
21: 25 prince of Israel, your **f** day of reckoning is here!
21: 29 wicked for whom the day of **f** reckoning has come.
Zec 4: 7 Then Zerubbabel will set the **f** stone of the Temple
Mt 12: 20 until he brings full justice with his **f** victory.
Ac 3: 21 until the time for the **f** restoration of all things,
28: 25 they left with this **f** word from Paul:
Eph 6: 10 A **f** word: Be strong with the Lord's mighty power.
Heb 1: 2 But now in these **f** days, he has spoken to us
1Pe 1: 20 but now in these **f** days, he was sent to the earth for

FINALITY (1) [FINAL]

Ro 9: 28 his sentence upon the earth / quickly and with **f**."

FINALLY (168) [FINAL]

Ge 7: 1 **F**, the day came when the LORD said to Noah,
7: 19 **F**, the water covered even the highest mountains
8: 13 **F**, when Noah was 601 years old, ten and a half
12: 5 his household at Haran—and **f** arrived in Canaan.
18: 32 **F**, Abraham said, "Lord, please do not get angry;
25: 17 Ishmael **f** died at the age of 137 and joined his
26: 22 another well, and the local people **f** left him alone.
27: 27 he was **f** convinced, and he blessed his son.
29: 1 Jacob hurried on, **f** arriving in the land of the east.
29: 21 **F**, the time came for him to marry her. "I have
31: 33 didn't find the gods. **F**, he went into Rachel's tent.
33: 7 **F**, Rachel and Joseph came and made their bows.
33: 11 Jacob continued to insist, so Esau **f** accepted them.
35: 6 **F**, they arrived at Luz (now called Bethel)
35: 17 the midwife **f** exclaimed, "Don't be afraid—
43: 11 So their father, Jacob, **f** said to them, "If it can't be
Ex 9: 27 and Aaron. "I **f** admit my fault," he confessed.
13: 17 When Pharaoh **f** let the people go, God did not lead
15: 23 When they came to Marah, they **f** found water.
17: 12 Moses' arms **f** became too tired to hold up the staff
23: 16 **F**, you are to celebrate the Festival of the Final
36: 4 But **f** the craftsmen left their work to meet with
39: 30 **F**, they made the sacred medallion of pure gold to
Lev 19: 25 **F**, in the fifth year you may eat the fruit. In this
26: 34 Then the land will **f** rest and enjoy its Sabbaths.
26: 41 **F**, when I have given full expression to my
Nu 4: 6 **F**, they must put the carrying poles of the Ark in
4: 8 and **f** a covering of fine goatskin leather on top of
4: 14 **F**, the carrying poles must be put in place.
15: 2 "When you **f** settle in the land I am going to give
17: 5 Then I will **f** put an end to this murmuring
32: 22 then you may return when the land is **f** subdued
Dt 2: 14 at Kadesh-barnea until we **f** crossed Zered Brook!
2: 15 his hand against them until all of them had **f** died.
4: 30 you will **f** return to the LORD your God
Jos 2: 22 but they **f** returned to the city without success.
7: 14 **F**, each member of the guilty family must come
11: 23 among the tribes. So the land **f** had rest from war.
15: 4 to Azmon, until it **f** reached the brook of Egypt,
24: 8 "**F**, I brought you into the land of the Amorites on
Jdg 4: 24 against King Jabin, until they **f** destroyed him.
9: 14 "Then all the trees **f** turned to the thornbush
9: 45 The battle went on all day before Abimelech **f**
10: 10 **F**, they cried out to the LORD, saying, "We have
11: 18 "**F**, they went around Edom and Moab through the
13: 21 Manoah **f** realized it was the angel of the LORD,
16: 17 **F**, Samson told her his secret. "My hair has never
16: 18 Delilah realized he had **f** told her the truth, so she
19: 7 him to stay, so he **f** gave in and stayed the night.
19: 25 her until morning. **F**, at dawn, they let her go.
20: 43 them down, **f** overtaking them east of Gibeah.

1Sa 1: 7 Hannah would f be reduced to tears and would not
8: 4 F, the leaders of Israel met at Ramah to discuss the
9: 5 F, they entered the region of Zuph, and Saul said
10: 21 And f Saul son of Kish was chosen from among
15: 13 When Samuel f found him, Saul greeted him
15: 24 Then Saul f admitted, "Yes, I have sinned. I have
15: 31 So Samuel f agreed and went with him, and Saul
16: 1 F, the LORD said to Samuel, "You have
17: 37 Saul f consented. "All right, go ahead," he said.
18: 13 F, Saul banned him from his presence
19: 22 F, Saul himself went to Ramah and arrived at the
21: 14 F, King Achish said to his men, "Must you bring
27: 1 Saul will stop hunting for me, and I will f be safe."
28: 11 F, the woman said, "Well, whose spirit do you
28: 23 so he f yielded and got up from the ground and sat
29: 6 So Achish f summoned David and his men.
2Sa 13: 27 But Absalom kept on pressing the king until he f
18: 4 that's the best plan, I'll do it," the king f agreed.
18: 23 he begged. Joab f said, "All right, go ahead."
24: 7 F, they went south to Judah as far as Beersheba.
1Ki 16: 34 And when he f completed it by setting up the gates,
17: 17 He grew worse and worse, and f he died.
18: 44 F the seventh time, his servant told him, "I saw a
22: 21 until f a spirit approached the LORD and said,
2Ki 2: 17 and he f said, "All right, send them."
2: 25 went to Mount Carmel and f returned to Samaria.
3: 25 F, only Kir-hareseth was left, but even that came
7: 9 F, they said to each other, "This is not right.
13: 7 F, Jehoahaz's army was reduced to fifty mounted
17: 6 F, in the ninth year of King Hoshea's reign,
17: 23 until the LORD f swept them away, just as all his
23: 20 to desecrate them. F, he returned to Jerusalem.
24: 20 f banished the people of Jerusalem and Judah from
1Ch 28: 18 F, he designated the amount of refined gold for the
2Ch 13: 20 and f the LORD struck him down and he died.
14: 15 and camels before f returning to Jerusalem.
18: 20 until f a spirit approached the LORD and said,
24: 15 Jehoiada lived to a very old age, f dying at 130.
29: 22 the altar. And f, they did the same with the lambs.
33: 13 Manasseh had f realized that the LORD alone is
36: 21 The land f enjoyed its Sabbath rest, lying desolate
Ezr 6: 14 The Temple was f finished, as had been
Ne 6: 15 So on October 2 the wall was f finished—
12: 36 And f came Zechariah's colleagues Shemaiah,
Job 3: 22 It is a blessed relief when they f die, when they
Ps 32: 5 F, I confessed all my sins to you / and stopped
40: 6 that you have made me listen, I f understand—
49: 10 Those who are wise must f die, / just like the
68: 10 There your people f settled, / and with a bountiful
78: 34 God killed some of them, the rest f sought him.
94: 8 you fools! / When will you f catch on?
106: 12 his promises. / Then they f sang his praise.
106: 43 and they were f destroyed by their sin.
Pr 26: 26 by trickery, it will f come to light for all to see.
30: 23 a bitter woman who f gets a husband, / a servant
Isa 7: 21 When they f stop plundering, a farmer will be
14: 7 the land is at rest and is quiet. F it can sing again!
28: 25 Does he not f plant his seeds for dill, cummin,
Jer 20: 3 The next day, when Pashhur f released him,
25: 26 And f, the king of Babylon himself drank from the
52: 3 f banished the people of Jerusalem and Judah from
La 2: 16 Long have we awaited this day, and it is f here!"
Eze 7: 6 The end has come! It has f arrived! Your final
39: 16 means 'horde.') And so the land will f be cleansed.
47: 16 and Hamath, and f to Hazer-hatticon,
Da 4: 19 F, the king said to him, "Belteshazzar, don't be
12: 7 When the shattering of the holy people has f come
12: 8 So I asked, "How will all this f end, my lord?"
Hos 2: 20 you mine, and you will f know me as LORD.
Mt 9: 25 When the crowd was f outside, Jesus went in
21: 27 So they f replied, "We don't know." And Jesus
21: 37 "F, the owner sent his son, thinking, 'Surely they
24: 14 nations will hear it; and then, f, the end will come.
26: 60 testimony they could use. F, two men were found
27: 7 After some discussion they f decided to buy the
27: 31 When they were f tired of mocking him, they took
Mk 4: 28 heads of wheat are formed, and f the grain ripens.
6: 21 Herodias' chance f came. It was Herod's birthday,
11: 33 So they f replied, "We don't know." And Jesus
12: 6 The owner f sent him, thinking, 'Surely they will
14: 57 F, some men stood up to testify against him with
15: 20 When they were f tired of mocking him, they took
Lk 1: 22 When he f did come out, he couldn't speak to
2: 46 Three days later they f discovered him. He was in
4: 42 and when they f found him, they begged him not to
13: 7 F, he said to his gardener, 'I've waited three years,
15: 17 "When he f came to his senses, he said to himself,
16: 22 F, the beggar died and was carried by the angels to
20: 7 F they replied, "We don't know."
20: 32 F, the woman died, too.
22: 56 F she said, "This man was one of Jesus'
23: 33 F, they came to a place called The Skull. All three
Jn 11: 7 F after two days, he said to his disciples, "Let's go
16: 31 Jesus asked, "Do you f believe?
Ac 4: 21 but they f let them go because they didn't know
12: 11 Peter f realized what had happened. "It's really
12: 16 When they f went out and opened the door,
13: 6 across the entire island until f they reached Paphos,
14: 26 F, they returned by ship to Antioch of Syria,
15: 2 F, Paul and Barnabas were sent to Jerusalem,
19: 1 F, he came to Ephesus, where he found several
20: 9 F, he sank into a deep sleep and fell three stories to
23: 10 F, the commander, fearing they would tear him
27: 7 and after great difficulty we f neared Cnidus.
27: 8 with great difficulty and f arrived at Fair Havens,
27: 21 F, Paul called the crew together and said, "Men,
Ro 11: 12 the world will share when the Jews f accept it.
Gal 1: 18 It was not until three years later that I f went to
Php 1: 6 will continue his work until it is f finished on that
3: 12 But I keep working toward that day when I will f
1Th 3: 1 F, when we could stand it no longer, we decided
4: 1 F, dear brothers and sisters, we urge you in the
2Th 3: 1 F, dear brothers and sisters, I ask you to pray for
Heb 7: 11 And f, if the priesthood of Levi could have
Jas 5: 11 From his experience we see how the Lord's plan f
1Pe 3: 8 F, all of you should be of one mind, full of
2Pe 1: 7 and f you will grow to have genuine love for

FINANCIAL (2) [FINANCIALLY]

Php 4: 15 you Philippians were the only ones who gave me f
1Th 4: 12 not need to depend on others to meet your f needs.

FINANCIALLY (1) [FINANCIAL]

Ro 15: 27 feel the least they can do in return is help them f.

FIND (314) [FINDING, FINDS, FOUND]

Ge 8: 8 Then he sent out a dove to see if it could f dry
18: 24 Suppose you f fifty innocent people there within
18: 26 "If I f fifty innocent people in Sodom,
18: 28 "I will not destroy it if I f forty-five."
19: 11 the men of Sodom so they couldn't f the doorway.
24: 4 my relatives, and f a wife there for my son Isaac."
24: 5 "But suppose I can't f a young woman who will
24: 7 and he will see to it that you f a young woman
24: 39 " 'But suppose I can't f a young woman willing to
24: 48 because he had led me along the right path to f a
27: 20 "How were you able to f it so quickly, my son?"
28: 6 and sent him to Paddan-aram to f a wife,
30: 33 If you f in my flock any white sheep or goats that
31: 32 If you f anything that belongs to you, I swear
31: 33 of the two concubines, but he didn't f the gods.
31: 34 Laban searched all the tents, he couldn't f them.
31: 35 despite his thorough search, Laban didn't f them.
31: 36 "What did you f?" he demanded of Laban.
38: 20 pledges he had given her, but Hirah couldn't f her.
38: 21 "Where can I f the prostitute who was sitting
38: 22 and told him that he couldn't f her anywhere
41: 33 "My suggestion is that you f the wisest man in
42: 16 Then we'll f out whether or not your story is true.
42: 33 'This is the way I will f out if you are honest men.
44: 9 If you f his cup with any one of us, let that one die.
Ex 1: 10 We must f a way to put an end to this. If we don't
2: 7 and f one of the Hebrew women to nurse the baby
5: 11 and get it yourselves. F it wherever you can.
7: 17 "You are going to f out that I am the LORD."
14: 20 to the Egyptians, and they couldn't f the Israelites.
18: 21 But f some capable, honest men who fear God
Lev 6: 3 Or suppose they f a lost item and lie about it,
18: 5 and regulations, you will f life through them.
Nu 5: 15 an offering of inquiry to f out if she is guilty.
13: 18 and f out whether the people living there are strong
26: 2 to f out how many of each family are of military
32: 23 and you may be sure that your sin will f you out.
Dt 4: 29 him with all your heart and soul, you will f him.
8: 2 and to f out whether or not you would really obey
13: 14 If you f it is true and can prove that such a
22: 3 Do the same if you f your neighbor's donkey,
22: 6 "If you f a bird's nest on the ground or in a tree
28: 63 the LORD will f pleasure in destroying you,
28: 65 There among those nations you will f no place of
29: 23 They will f its soil turned into sulfur and salt,
30: 4 God will go and f you and bring you back again.
Jdg 9: 19 his descendants, then may you f joy in Abimelech,
and may he f joy in you.
14: 3 Why must you go to the pagan Philistines to f a
16: 5 "F out from Samson what makes him so strong
18: 1 And the tribe of Dan was trying to f a place to
18: 8 their relatives asked them, "What did you f?"
18: 10 you will f the people living carefree lives.
19: 13 We will f a place to spend the night in either
21: 7 How can we f wives for the few who remain,
21: 16 "How can we f wives for the few who remain,
21: 22 for we didn't f enough wives for them when we
Ru 3: 8 He was surprised to f a woman lying at his feet!
1Sa 6: 7 new cart, and f two cows that have just had calves.
9: 4 but they couldn't f the donkeys anywhere.
9: 6 everything he says comes true. Let's go f him.
10: 14 Saul replied, "but we couldn't f them.
14: 17 "F out who isn't here," Saul ordered. And when
14: 33 Saul said. "F a large stone and roll it over here.
14: 38 We must f out what sin was committed today.
15: 12 Early the next morning Samuel went to f Saul.
16: 1 F a man named Jesse who lives there, for I have
16: 16 "Let us f a good musician to play the harp for you
16: 17 "F me someone who plays well and bring him
17: 56 "Well, f out!" the king told him.
19: 2 "you must f a hiding place out in the fields.
19: 3 Then I'll tell you everything I can f out."
20: 36 "so you can f the arrows as I shoot them."
22: 10 Ahimelech consulted the LORD to f out what
23: 16 Jonathan went to f David and encouraged him to
23: 17 reassured him. "My father will never f you!
28: 7 "F a woman who is a medium, so I can go and ask
2Sa 3: 8 that you f fault with me about this woman?
11: 3 He sent someone to f out who she was, and he was
15: 36 and Jonathan to f me and tell me what is going
17: 12 When we f David, we can descend on him like the
17: 16 "F David and urge him not to stay at the shallows
18: 13 and the king would certainly f out who did it—
22: 3 my God is my rock, in whom I f protection.
1Ki 1: 2 "We will f a young virgin who will wait on you
18: 5 and valley to see if we can f enough grass to save
18: 10 and kingdom on earth from end to end to f you.
18: 12 When Ahab comes and cannot f you, he will kill
21: 10 F two scoundrels who will accuse him of cursing
22: 5 "But first let's f out what the LORD says."
22: 25 "You will f out soon enough when you f
2Ki 2: 17 men searched for three days but did not f Elijah.
5: 7 He is only trying to f an excuse to invade us
5: 15 and his entire party went back to f the man of God.
6: 13 king commanded, "Go and f out where Elisha is,
9: 2 and f Jehu son of Jehoshaphat and grandson of
9: 16 into a chariot and rode to Jezreel to f King Joram,
9: 17 "Send out a rider to f out if they are coming in
18: 21 you will f it to be a stick that breaks beneath your
18: 23 If you can f two thousand horsemen in your entire
1Ch 28: 9 and thought. If you seek him, you will f him.
29: 17 our hearts and rejoice when you f integrity there.
2Ch 15: 2 Whenever you seek him, you will f him. But if you
18: 4 "But first let's f out what the LORD says."
18: 24 Micaiah replied, "You will f out soon enough,
18: 24 when you f yourself hiding in some secret room!"
20: 16 You will f them coming up through the ascent of
32: 4 of Assyria come here and f plenty of water?"
Ne 9: 12 pillar of fire at night so that they could f their way.
9: 29 by which people will f life if only they obey.
Est 2: 2 "Let us search the empire to f beautiful young
2: 11 and to f out what was happening to her.
4: 5 and f out what was troubling him and why he was
Job 3: 22 relief when they finally die, when they f the grave.
6: 5 Wild donkeys bray when they f no green grass,
13: 9 Be careful that he doesn't f out what you are
17: 10 try again! But I will not f a wise man among you.
17: 15 But where then is my hope? Can anyone f it?
23: 3 If only I knew where to f God, I would go to his
23: 8 but he is not there. I go west, but I cannot f him.
23: 9 he is hidden. I turn to the south, but I cannot f him.
24: 20 Worms will f him sweet to eat. No one will
27: 19 but wake up to f that all their wealth is gone.
28: 6 "People know how to f sapphires and gold dust—
28: 12 "But do people know where to f wisdom? Where
can they f understanding?
28: 13 No one knows where to f it, for it is not found
28: 20 "But do people know where to f wisdom? Where
can they f understanding?
32: 20 I must speak to f relief, so let me give my answers.
34: 29 But when he hides his face, who can f him?
40: 4 "I am nothing—how could I ever f the answers?
Ps 2: 12 But what joy for all who f protection in him!
18: 2 my God is my rock, in whom I f protection.
22: 2 Every night you hear my voice, but I f no relief.
31: 4 set for me, / for I f protection in you alone.
37: 36 Though I searched for them, I could not f them!
37: 40 He saves them, / and they f shelter in him.
64: 10 and f shelter in him. / And those who do what is
69: 2 sink into the mire; / I can't f a foothold to stand on.
91: 1 will f rest in the shadow of the Almighty.
119: 10 I have tried my best to f you— / don't let me
119: 74 May all who fear you f in me a cause for joy,
119: 143 bear down on me, / I f joy in your commands.
119: 176 wandered away like a lost sheep; / come and f me,
132: 5 until I f a place to build a house for the LORD,
141: 6 they will listen to my words and f them pleasing.
Pr 1: 28 they anxiously search for me, they will not f me.
2: 9 and you will know how to f the right course of
3: 4 Then you will f favor with both God and people,
7: 15 looking for! I came out to f you, and here you are!
8: 17 Those who search for me will surely f me.
11: 19 Godly people f life; evil people f death.
11: 27 If you search for good, you will f favor; but if you
search for evil, it will f you!
12: 27 but the diligent make use of everything they f.
13: 13 People who despise advice will f themselves in
14: 7 away from fools, for you won't f knowledge there.
20: 6 but who can f one who is really faithful?
21: 21 pursues godliness and unfailing love will f life,
24: 14 If you f it, you will have a bright future, and your
31: 10 Who can f a virtuous and capable wife? She is
Ecc 2: 3 most people f during their brief life in this world.
2: 4 I also tried to f meaning by building huge homes
2: 24 enjoy food and drink and to f satisfaction in work.
6: 6 a thousand years twice over but not f contentment.
7: 24 Wisdom is always distant and very difficult to f.
7: 25 determined to f wisdom and to understand the
8: 5 Those who are wise will f a time and a way to do
SS 5: 6 I searched for him, but I couldn't f him anywhere.
5: 8 If you f my beloved one, tell him that I am sick
6: 1 has your lover gone? We will help you f him."
Isa 5: 7 found bloodshed. / He expected to f righteousness,
7: 3 You will f the king at the end of the aqueduct that
8: 19 So why are you trying to f out the future by
8: 19 Can the living f out the future from the dead?
14: 32 and that the poor of his people will f refuge in its
23: 12 Even if you flee to Cyprus, you will f no rest."
27: 4 If I f briers and thorns bothering her, I will burn
30: 2 you have gone down to Egypt to f help.
36: 6 you will f it to be a stick that breaks beneath your
36: 8 If you can f two thousand horsemen in your entire
40: 18 What image might we f to resemble him?
40: 31 But those who wait on the LORD will f new
41: 18 In the deserts they will f pools of water. Rivers fed
55: 6 Seek the LORD while you can f him. Call on him
57: 9 into the world of the dead, to f new gods to love.
59: 15 and was displeased to f that there was no justice.
64: 6 our righteous deeds, we f they are but filthy rags.
Jer 2: 5 "What sin did your ancestors f in me that led them
3: 23 Only in the LORD our God will Israel ever f
5: 1 If you can f even one person who is just
6: 16 Travel its path, and you will f rest for your souls.

13:16 you look for light, you will f only terrible darkness.
18:18 "Come on, let's f a way to stop Jeremiah.
25:35 You will f no place to hide; there will be no way to
29: 6 Then f spouses for them, and have many
29:13 for me in earnest, you will f me when you seek me.
39:11 King Nebuchadnezzar had told Nebuzaradan to f
44:28 Then all those who came to Egypt will f out whose
45: 3 I am weary of my own sighing and can f no rest.'
Eze 7:12 for buyers to rejoice over the bargains they f
7:25 They will look for peace but will not f it.
16:28 It seems you can never f enough new lovers!
31:16 were relieved to f it there with them in the pit.
32:31 he will be relieved to f that he is not alone in
34:11 LORD says: I myself will search and f my sheep.
34:12 I will f my sheep and rescue them from all the
Da 2:13 men were sent to f and kill Daniel and his friends.
6: 4 his affairs, but they couldn't f anything to criticize.
6:14 the law, and he tried to f a way to save Daniel.
Hos 2: 7 She will search for them but not f them. Then she
4:18 and off they go to f some prostitutes.
5: 6 They will not f him, because he has withdrawn
7:10 return to the LORD his God or even try to f him.
14: 3 No, in you alone do the orphans f mercy."
Am 8:12 running here and going there, but they will not f it.
Mic 2: 2 want a certain piece of land, you f a way to seize it.
2: 7 do what is right, you would f my words to be good.
7: 1 picker after the harvest who can f nothing to eat.
Zep 1:12 with lanterns in Jerusalem's darkest corners to f
Mt 2: 8 And when you f him, come back and tell me
7: 7 Keep on looking, and you will f. Keep on
7:14 and the road is narrow, and only a few ever f it.
10:39 lose it; but if you give it up for me, you will f it.
11: 7 Did you f him weak as a reed, moved by every
11:29 and gentle, and you will f rest for your souls.
13:32 birds can come and f shelter in its branches."
16:25 if you give up your life for me, you will f true life.
17:27 of the first fish you catch, and you will f a coin.
22:10 "So the servants brought in everyone they could f,
26:59 and the entire high council were trying to f
28: 8 and they rushed to f the disciples to give them the
Mk 1:36 Later Simon and the others went out to f him.
3:20 and his disciples couldn't even f time to eat.
4:32 branches where birds can come and f shelter."
6:38 he asked. "Go and f out." They came back
8: 4 "How are we supposed to f enough food for them
8:35 for the sake of the Good News, you will f true life.
11:13 so he went over to see if he could f any figs on it.
13:36 Don't let him f you sleeping when he arrives
14:55 and the entire high council were trying to f
Lk 1:77 You will tell his people how to f salvation
2:12 You will f a baby lying in a manger,
2:45 When they couldn't f him, they went back to
6: 7 because they were eager to f some legal charge to
7:24 Did you f him weak as a reed, moved by every
8:43 she had on doctors and still could f no cure.
9:12 so they can f food and lodging for the night.
9:24 if you give up your life for me, you will f true life.
11: 9 Keep on looking, and you will f. Keep on
13:19 the birds come and f shelter among its branches."
14:23 behind the hedges and urge anyone you f to come,
18: 8 return, how many will I f who have faith?"
19:15 He wanted to f out what they had done with the
19:42 "I wish that even today you would f the way of
21:34 Don't let me f you living in careless ease
22:45 only to f them asleep, exhausted from grief.
23: 4 and said, "I f nothing wrong with this man!"
23:14 on this point in your presence and f him innocent.
24: 3 but they couldn't f the body of the Lord Jesus.
24:25 You f it so hard to believe all that the prophets
Jn 1:41 The first thing Andrew did was to f his brother,
4:27 They were astonished to f him talking to a woman,
5:15 Then the man went to f the Jewish leaders and told
7:11 The Jewish leaders tried to f him at the festival
7:34 You will search for me but not f me. And you
7:36 he says, 'You will search for me but not f me,'
8:37 because my message does not f a place in your
10: 9 Wherever they go, they will f green pastures.
19: 4 but understand clearly that I f him not guilty."
19: 6 crucify him," Pilate said. "I f him not guilty."
20:17 But go f my brothers and tell them that I am
Ac 5:39 You may even f yourselves fighting against God."
10: 5 Now send some men down to Joppa to f a man
11:13 'Send messengers to Joppa to f Simon Peter.
11:25 Then Barnabas went on to Tarsus to f Saul.
15:17 so that the rest of humanity might f the Lord,
17:27 and perhaps feel their way toward him and f him—
21:34 He couldn't f out the truth in all the uproar
22:24 He wanted to f out why the crowd had become
22:30 He had Paul brought in before them to try to f out
23:28 Then I took him to their high council to try to f out
24: 8 You can f out the truth of our accusations by
Ro 10: 6 "You don't need to go to heaven" (to f Christ
11:14 for I want to f a way to make the Jews want what
1Co 1:21 world would never f him through human wisdom,
4:19 then I'll f out whether these arrogant people are
9:22 I try to f common ground with everyone so that I
2Co 2: 9 I wrote to you as I did to f out how far you would
2:13 said good-bye and went on to Macedonia to f him.
6: 3 we act, and so no one can f fault with our ministry.
8:20 for we are anxious that no one should f fault with
9: 4 only to f that you still weren't ready after all I had
12:20 that when I come to visit you I won't like what I f,
12:20 I am afraid that I will f quarreling, jealousy,
Gal 2:17 in Christ and then f out that we are still sinners?
3:12 "If you wish to f life by obeying the law,
4:10 You are trying to f favor with God by what you do
5: 3 If you are trying to f favor with God by being
Eph 5:10 Try to f out what is pleasing to the Lord.
Php 2:23 I hope to send him to you just as soon as I f out
1Th 1: 8 for wherever we go we f people telling us about
3: 5 I sent Timothy to f out whether your faith was still
1Ti 6:14 Then no one can f fault with you from now until
Heb 4:10 For all who enter into God's rest will f rest from
4:16 and we will f grace to help us when we need it.
Jas 3:16 there you will f disorder and every kind of evil.
1Jn 4: 2 This is the way to f out if they have the Spirit of
2Jn 1: 4 of your children and f them living in the truth,
Jude 1: 3 But now I f that I must write about something else,
Rev 9: 6 those days people will seek death but will not f it.

FINDING (9) [FIND]

Job 6:20 but f none, their hopes are dashed.
Jer 38:27 and they left without f out the truth.
Eze 17:23 sort will nest in it, f shelter beneath its branches.
Da 6: 5 "Our only chance of f grounds for accusing Daniel
Hos 9:10 found you, it was like f fresh grapes in the desert!
Am 3: 4 Does a lion ever roar in a thicket without first f a
Mt 12:43 it goes into the desert, seeking rest but f none.
Ac 17: 6 Not f them there, they dragged out Jason and some
2Co 6: 3 be hindered from f the Lord by the way we act,

FINDS (31) [FIND]

Lev 13:20 If the priest f the disease to be more than
13:43 and if he f swelling around the reddish white sore,
14: 3 If the priest f that someone has been healed of the
14:37 If he f bright green or reddish streaks on the walls
14:48 and f that the affected areas have not reappeared
Nu 35:27 and the victim's nearest relative f him outside the
2Sa 14:32 if he f me guilty of anything, then let him execute
Ps 36: 7 unfailing love, O God! / All humanity f shelter
84: 3 Even the sparrow f a home there, / and the swallow
119:162 in your word / like one who f a great treasure.
Pr 3:13 Happy is the person who f wisdom and gains
8:35 For whoever f me f life and wins approval
14: 6 A mocker seeks wisdom and never f it,
18:22 The man who f a wife f a treasure and receives
20:26 A wise king f the wicked, lays them out like wheat,
31:13 She f wool and flax and busily spins it.
Ecc 6: 3 But if he f no satisfaction in life and in the end
Mt 7: 8 who asks, receives. Everyone who seeks, f.
12:44 So it returns and f its former home empty, swept,
12:45 Then the spirit f seven other spirits more evil than
18:13 And if he f it, he will surely rejoice over it more
24:46 and f that the servant has done a good job,
Lk 11:10 who asks, receives. Everyone who seeks, f.
11:24 But when it f none, it says, 'I will return to the
11:25 and f that its former home is all swept and clean.
11:26 Then the spirit f seven other spirits more evil than
12:43 and f that the servant has done a good job,
15: 8 and sweep every nook and cranny until she f it?
15: 9 And when she f it, she will call in her friends

FINE (111) [FINE-LOOKING, FINED, FINELY, FINEST]

FINE GOLD (2) Job 28:17; Da 2:32

FINE LEATHER (1) Eze 16:10

FINE LINEN (37) Ex 25:4; 26:1,31,36; 27:9,16,18; 28:5,6,8,15,39; 35:6,23,25,35; 36:8,35,37; 38:9,16,18,23; 39:2,5,8,27,28,29; 1Ch 15:27; 2Ch 3:14; 5:12; Est 8:15; Eze 16:13; 27:16; Rev 18:12; 19:8

Ge 27: 9 out to the flocks and bring me two f young goats.
31:14 Rachel and Leah said, "That's f with us!
47: 6 best land of Egypt—the land of Goshen will be f.
Ex 3:22 and f clothing from their Egyptian neighbors
9: 9 It will spread like f dust over the whole land of
22: 1 "A f must be paid by anyone who steals an ox
22: 1 For oxen the f is five oxen for each one stolen.
22: 1 For sheep the f is four sheep for each one stolen.
22: 7 the f is double the value of what was stolen.
25: 4 blue, purple, and scarlet yarn; f linen; goat hair for
25: 5 tanned ram skins and f goatskin leather;
26: 1 "Make the Tabernacle from ten sheets of f linen.
26:14 and over them put a layer of f goatskin leather.
26:31 Tabernacle hang a special curtain made of f linen,
26:36 "Make another curtain from f linen for the
27: 9 enclosed with curtains made from f linen.
27:16 Fashion it from f linen, and decorate it with
27:18 curtain walls 7-1/2 feet high, made from f linen.
28: 5 These items must be made of f linen cloth
28: 6 "The ephod must be made of f linen cloth
28: 8 f linen cloth embroidered with gold thread
28:15 f linen cloth embroidered with gold thread
28:39 "Weave Aaron's patterned tunic from f linen
29: 2 Then using f wheat flour and no yeast,
29:40 offer two quarts of f flour mixed with one quart of
30:36 Beat some of it very f and put some of it in front of
33:14 I will give you rest—everything will be f for you."
35: 6 blue, purple, and scarlet yarn; f linen; goat hair for
35: 7 tanned ram skins and f goatskin leather;
35:23 brought blue, purple, and scarlet yarn, f linen,
35:23 Some gave tanned ram skins or f goatskin leather.
35:25 purple, and scarlet yarn, and f linen cloth, and they
35:35 in blue, purple, and scarlet yarn on f linen cloth.
36: 8 The skilled weavers first made ten sheets from f
36:19 and the second was made of f goatskin leather.
36:35 The inner curtain was made of f linen cloth,
36:37 It was made of f linen cloth and embroidered with
38: 9 feet long. It consisted of curtains made of f linen.
38:16 used in the courtyard walls were made of f linen.
38:18 entrance to the courtyard was made of f linen cloth
38:23 purple, and scarlet yarn on f linen cloth.
39: 2 The ephod was made from f linen cloth
39: 3 gold into thin sheets and cutting it into f strips.
39: 5 f linen cloth; blue, purple, and scarlet yarn;
39: 8 crafted from f linen cloth and embroidered with
39:27 made for Aaron and his sons from f linen cloth.
39:28 and the undercloths were all made of this f linen.
39:29 The sashes were made of f linen cloth
39:34 layers of tanned ram skins and f goatskin leather;
Lev 13:30 and f yellow hair is found in the affected area,
Nu 4: 6 Then they must cover the inner curtain with f
4: 8 and finally a covering of f goatskin leather on top
4:10 then be covered with f goatskin leather,
4:11 and cover this cloth with a covering of f goatskin
4:12 covered with f goatskin leather, and placed on the
4:14 and a covering of f goatskin leather must be spread
4:25 the outer covering of f goatskin leather,
Dt 8:12 and prosperous and have built f homes to live in,
9:21 and I melted it in the fire and ground it into f dust.
18:17 "Then the LORD said to me, 'F, I will do as they
22:19 They will f him one hundred pieces of silver,
Jdg 5:10 "You who ride on f donkeys / and sit on fancy
1Sa 20: 7 If he says, 'F!' then you will know all is well.
2Sa 1:24 for he dressed you in f clothing and gold
22:43 I ground them as f as the dust of the earth; / I swept
1Ki 20:39 or pay a f of seventy-five pounds of silver!'
2Ki 4:26 the woman told Gehazi, "everything is f."
7: 1 five quarts of f flour will cost only half an ounce of
7:16 So it was true that five quarts of f flour were sold
7:18 five quarts of f flour will cost half an ounce of
1Ch 15:27 David was dressed in a robe of f linen, as were the
29: 2 costly jewels, and all kinds of f stone and marble.
2Ch 3:14 Solomon hung a curtain made of f linen and blue,
5:12 were dressed in f linen robes and stood at the east
9: 9 Never before had there been spices as f as those
Ezr 8:27 2 f articles of polished bronze, as precious as gold.
Est 8:15 and he wore an outer cloak of f linen and purple.
Job 28:17 It cannot be purchased with jewels mounted in f
Ps 18:42 I ground them as f as dust carried by the wind.
Pr 17:26 It is wrong to f the godly for being good or to
Ecc 9: 8 Wear f clothes, with a dash of cologne!
SS 7: 4 Your nose is as f as the tower of Lebanon
Isa 23:18 good food and f clothing for the LORD's priests.
41: 7 "Good," they say. "It's coming along f."
63:13 They were like f stallions racing through the
Jer 22: 7 They will tear out all your f cedar beams and throw
38:22 will taunt you, saying, 'What f friends you have!
Eze 16:10 and sandals made of f leather.
16:13 Your clothes were made of f linen and were
16:13 ate the finest foods—f flour, honey, and olive oil—
16:19 You set before them as a lovely sacrifice the f flour
23:12 those handsome young men on f horses,
27:16 purple dyes, embroidery, f linen, and jewelry of
33:32 a beautiful voice or plays f music on an instrument.
Da 2:32 The head of the statue was made of f gold, its chest
Am 8:13 and f young men will grow faint and weary,
Hag 1: 9 while you are all busy building your own f houses.
Zec 3: 4 and now I am giving you these f new clothes."
14:14 great quantities of gold and silver and f clothing.
Mal 1:14 "Cursed is the cheat who promises to give a f ram
Mt 13:21 At first they get along f, but they wilt as soon as
Mk 4:17 At first they get along f, but they wilt as soon as
Lk 12:16 "A rich man had a fertile farm that produced f
13: 9 If we get figs next year, f. If not, you can cut it
Ac 20:33 have never coveted anyone's money or f clothing.
Ro 7: 9 I felt f when I did not understand what the law
Heb 3: 3 just as a person who builds a f house deserves
Jas 5: 2 and your f clothes are moth-eaten rags.
Rev 18:12 silver, jewels, pearls, f linen, purple dye, silk,
18:13 f flour, wheat, cattle, sheep, horses, chariots,
19: 8 (F linen represents the good deeds done by the

FINE-LOOKING (1) [FINE, LOOK]

1Sa 16:18 He is also a f young man, and the LORD is with

FINED (1) [FINE]

Pr 6:31 he will be f seven times as much as he stole,

FINELY (1) [FINE]

Ex 39:24 These were f crafted of blue, purple, and scarlet

FINER [KJV] See SILVERSMITH

FINEST (37) [FINE]

Ge 23: 6 It will be a privilege to have you choose the f of
Dt 32:14 You drank the f wine, / made from the juice of
33:15 with the f crops of the ancient mountains,
1Sa 8:16 and female slaves and demand the f of your cattle
9:23 then instructed the cook to bring Saul the f cut of
29: 6 "you are some of the f men I've ever met.
2Ki 8: 9 So Hazael loaded down forty camels with the f
2Ch 13:17 there were 500,000 casualties among Israel's f
Job 1: 8 He is the f man in all the earth—a man of complete
2: 3 He is the f man in all the earth—a man of complete
Ps 19:10 are more desirable than gold, / even the f gold.
21: 3 You placed a crown of f gold on his head.
45: 9 the queen, / wearing jewelry of f gold from Ophir!
78:31 he struck down the f of Israel's young men.
119:127 your commands / more than gold, even the f gold.
147:14 and satisfies you with plenty of the f wheat.
Pr 3:10 and your vats will overflow with the f wine.
7:16 My bed is spread with colored sheets of f linen
25:12 the one who heeds it as jewelry made from f gold.
31:22 She dresses like royalty in gowns of f cloth.
SS 2: 3 my lover is like the f apple tree in the orchard.
5:11 His head is the f gold, and his hair is wavy

5:15 like pillars of marble set in sockets of the f gold,
Isa 17:10 You may plant the f imported grapevines,
Jer 3:19 this beautiful land—the f inheritance in the world.
La 2:4 His strength is used against them to kill their f
4:1 has lost its luster! Even the f gold has become dull.
Eze 16:13 You ate the f foods—fine flour, honey, and olive
23:40 your eyelids, and put on your f jewels for them.
27:5 You were like a great ship built of the f cypress
27:7 Your sails were made of Egypt's f linen, and they
28:13 all beautifully crafted for you and set in the f gold.
Na 2:13 The f of your youth will be killed in battle.
Lk 15:22 Bring the f robe in the house and put it on him.
15:30 you celebrate by killing the f calf we have.'
Rev 18:16 like a woman clothed in f purple and scarlet linens,
19:8 She is permitted to wear the f white linen."

FINGER (31) [FINGERNAILS, FINGERS]

Ge 41:42 ring on Joseph's f as a symbol of his authority.
Ex 8:19 "This is the f of God!" the magicians exclaimed
14:14 You won't have to lift a f in your defense!"
29:12 of its blood on the horns of the altar with your f,
31:18 the terms of the covenant, written by the f of God.
Lev 4:6 dip his f into the blood, and sprinkle it seven times
4:17 dip his f into the blood, and sprinkle it seven times
4:25 Then the priest will dip his f into the blood of the
4:30 The priest will then dip his f into the blood,
4:34 The priest will then dip his f into the blood, put it
8:15 and with his f he put it on the four horns of the
9:9 and he dipped his f into it and put it on the horns of
14:16 He will dip his right f into the oil and sprinkle it
14:27 He will dip his right f into the oil and sprinkle
16:14 Then he must dip his f into the blood of the bull
16:19 Then he must dip his f into the blood and sprinkle
Nu 19:4 Eleazar will take some of its blood on his f
1Ki 12:10 'My little f is thicker than my father's waist—
2Ch 10:10 'My little f is thicker than my father's waist—
Est 3:10 his decision by removing his signet ring from his f
Pr 19:24 so lazy that they won't even lift a f to feed
26:15 so lazy that they won't lift a f to feed themselves.
Hos 4:4 "Don't point your f at someone else and try to
Ob 1:11 refusing to lift a f to help when foreign invaders
Hag 2:23 I will treat you like a signet ring on my f,
Mt 23:4 and never lift a f to help ease the burden.
Lk 11:46 and you never lift a f to help ease the burden.
15:22 Get a ring for his f, and sandals for his feet.
16:24 Send Lazarus over here to dip the tip of his f in
Jn 8:6 stooped down and wrote in the dust with his f.
20:27 to Thomas, "Put your f here and see my hands.

FINGERNAILS (1) [FINGER]

Dt 21:12 where she must shave her head, cut her f,

FINGERS (16) [FINGER]

Ex 35:22 medallions, earrings, rings from their f,
2Sa 21:20 a huge man with six f on each hand and six toes on
1Ch 20:6 a huge man with six f on each hand and six toes on
Ps 8:3 I look at the night sky and see the work of your f—
Pr 6:13 by making signs with their eyes and feet and f.
7:3 Tie them on your f as a reminder. Write them deep
31:19 are busy spinning thread, her f twisting fiber.
Ecc 5:11 except perhaps to watch it run through your f!
SS 5:5 my f with lovely myrrh, as I pulled back the bolt.
Isa 40:12 Who has measured off the heavens with his f?
59:3 hands of murderers, and your f are filthy with sin.
Da 5:5 At that very moment they saw the f of a human
Zec 7:11 and put their f in their ears to keep from hearing.
Mk 7:33 He put his f into the man's ears. Then, spitting onto his own f, he touched the man's
Jn 20:25 put my f into them, and place my hand into the

FINING POT [KJV] See FIRE

FINISH (13) [FINISHED, FINISHES, FINISHING, PREFINISHED]

2Sa 12:28 Now bring the rest of the army and f the job,
1Ki 3:1 City of David until he could f building his palace
Job 14:6 hired hands, so let us f the task you have given us.
Ps 129:2 but they have never been able to f me off.
Jer 15:3 to devour, and the wild animals to f up what is left.
Hos 4:18 The men of Israel f up their drinking bouts and off
Zec 8:9 LORD Almighty says: Take heart and f the task!
Mt 23:32 Go ahead. F what they started.
Ro 1:17 This is accomplished from start to f by faith.
13:8 You can never f paying that! If you love your
2Co 8:10 I suggest that you f what you started a year ago,
Heb 11:40 the prize at the end of the race until we f the race.
12:2 on whom our faith depends from start to f.

FINISHED (110) [FINISH]

Ge 2:2 On the seventh day, having f his task, God rested
18:33 The LORD went on his way when he had f his
24:19 When he had f, she said, "I'll draw water for your
24:20 water to the camels until they had f drinking.
24:22 Then at last, when the camels had f drinking,
24:45 "Before I had f praying these words, I saw
28:15 I will be with you constantly until I have f giving
49:9 Judah is a young lion / that has f eating its prey.
49:33 Then when Jacob had f this charge to his sons,
Ex 14:18 When I am f with Pharaoh and his army, all Egypt
25:16 When the Ark is f, place inside it the stone tablets
31:18 Then as the LORD f speaking with Moses on
34:33 When Moses had f speaking with them, he put a
39:32 And so at last the Tabernacle was f. The Israelites
40:33 of the courtyard. So at last Moses f the work.
Lev 16:20 "When Aaron has f making atonement for the
Nu 4:15 and his sons have f covering the sanctuary
16:31 He had hardly f speaking the words when the
21:29 of Moab! / You are f, O worshipers of Chemosh!
Dt 20:9 When the officers have f saying this to their troops,
31:1 When Moses had f saying these things to all the
31:24 When Moses had f writing down this entire body
32:45 When Moses had f reciting these words to Israel,
Jos 8:24 When the Israelite army f killing all the men
8:24 the city, they went back and f off everyone inside.
Jdg 2:4 When the angel of the LORD f speaking,
15:17 When he f speaking, he threw away the jawbone;
Ru 3:3 but don't let Boaz see you until he has f his meal.
3:7 After Boaz had f his meal and was in good spirits,
1Sa 10:13 When Saul had f prophesying, he climbed the hill
18:1 After David had f talking with Saul, he met
2Sa 6:18 When he had f, David blessed the people in the
1Ki 6:14 So Solomon f building the Temple.
6:22 So he f overlaying the entire Temple with gold,
7:22 like lilies. And so the work on the pillars was f.
7:51 So King Solomon f all his work on the Temple of
8:54 When Solomon f making these prayers
9:1 So Solomon f building the Temple of the LORD,
9:25 And so he f the work of building the Temple.
13:23 Now after the man of God had f eating
18:34 And when they were f, he said, "Now do it a third
2Ki 10:25 As soon as Jehu had f sacrificing the burnt
1Ch 16:2 When he had f, David blessed the people in the
27:24 Joab began the census but never f it
28:20 related to the Temple of the LORD is f correctly.
2Ch 5:1 When Solomon had f all the work related to
7:1 When Solomon f praying, fire flashed down from
7:11 So Solomon f building the Temple of the LORD,
20:23 After they had f off the army of Seir, they turned
24:14 When all the repairs were f, they brought the
29:28 trumpets blew, until all the burnt offerings were f.
29:34 the Levites helped them until the work was f
35:20 After Josiah had f restoring the Temple, King Neco
Ezr 6:14 The Temple was finally f, as had been commanded
10:17 By March 27 of the next year they had f dealing
Ne 6:1 and the rest of our enemies found out that I had f
6:15 So on October 2 the wall was finally f—
7:1 After the wall was f and I had hung the doors in
Job 19:10 He has demolished me on every side, and I am f.
36:2 what I am saying. For I have not f defending God!
42:7 After the LORD had f speaking to Job, he said to
Ps 78:30 But before they f eating this food they had craved,
119:87 They almost f me off, / but I refused to abandon
Pr 7:14 "I've offered my sacrifices and just f my vows.
Isa 10:10 we have f off many a kingdom whose gods were
13:12 Few will be left alive when I have f my work.
15:9 red with blood, but I am still not f with Dibon!
27:9 When he has f, all the pagan altars will be crushed
34:5 And when my sword has f its work in the heavens,
Jer 8:20 "The harvest is f, and the summer is gone,"
23:20 will not diminish until it has f all his plans.
26:8 But when Jeremiah had f his message,
30:24 will not diminish until it has f all his plans.
36:16 By the time Baruch had f reading, they were badly
36:23 Whenever Jehudi f reading three or four columns,
43:1 When Jeremiah had f giving this message from the
51:25 When I am f, you will be nothing but a heap of
51:63 Then, when you have f reading the scroll, tie it to a
Eze 7:2 east, west, north, or south—your land is f.
9:11 and said, "I have f the work you gave me to do."
21:5 and it will not return to its sheath until its work is f.
42:15 When the man had f taking these measurements,
43:23 When you have f the cleansing ceremony,
Joel 1:4 After the cutting locusts f eating the crops,
Mic 2:4 "We are f, / completely ruined! / God has
Mt 7:28 After Jesus f speaking, the crowds were amazed at
11:1 When Jesus had f giving these instructions to his
13:53 When Jesus had f telling these stories, he left that
19:1 After Jesus had f saying these things, he left
26:1 When Jesus had f saying these things, he said to
Mk 16:19 When the Lord Jesus had f talking with them,
Lk 4:13 When the Devil had f tempting Jesus, he left him
5:4 When he had f speaking, he said to Simon,
7:1 When Jesus had f saying all this, he went back to
11:1 one of his disciples came to him as he f and said,
11:53 As Jesus f speaking, the Pharisees and teachers of
14:30 that building and ran out of money before it was f!'
23:56 But by the time they were f it was the Sabbath,
Jn 17:1 When Jesus had f saying all these things, he looked
19:28 Jesus knew that everything was now f, and to
19:30 When Jesus had tasted it, he said, "It is f!"
Ac 12:25 and Saul had f their mission in Jerusalem,
15:13 When they had f, James stood and said, "Brothers,
20:36 When he had f speaking, he knelt and prayed with
Ro 15:23 But now I have f my work in these regions,
Php 1:6 will continue his work until it is finally f on that
2Ti 4:7 I have fought a good fight, I have f the race,
Rev 16:17 throne of the Temple in heaven, saying, "It is f!"
20:3 nations anymore until the thousand years were f.
21:6 And he also said, "It is f! I am the Alpha

FINISHES (1) [FINISH]

Job 20:21 Nothing is left after he f gorging himself;

FINISHING (5) [FINISH]

1Sa 13:10 Just as Saul was f with the burnt offering,
1Ki 1:41 and shouting just as they were f their banquet.
Ecc 7:8 F is better than starting. Patience is better than
Jn 4:34 the will of God, who sent me, and from f his work.
Ac 13:25 As John was f his ministry he asked, 'Do you think

FINS (5)

Lev 11:9 you may eat whatever has both f and scales,
11:10 eat marine animals that do not have both f
11:12 any marine animal that does not have both f
Dt 14:9 you may eat whatever has both f and scales.
14:10 eat marine animals that do not have both f

FIR (2) [FIRS]

Isa 41:19 cedar, acacia, myrtle, olive, cypress, f, and pine—
60:13 the forests of cypress, f, and pine—to beautify my

FIRE (415) [AFIRE, BONFIRE, BRUSHFIRE, FIERY, FIREBOX, FIRELIGHT, FIREPANS, FIREPLACE, FIREPLACES, FIREPOT, FIRES, FIREWOOD, WILDFIRE]

CONSUMING FIRE (2) Isa 29:6; Heb 12:29
DEVOURING FIRE (3) Ex 24:17; Dt 4:24; 9:3
ETERNAL FIRE (2) Mt 25:41; Jude 1:7
OFFERING MADE BY FIRE (14) Ex 29:41; Lev 1:9,13, 17; 2:2,9; 3:3,5,9,14,16; Nu 15:10; 28:6,8
PILLAR OF FIRE (10) Ex 13:21,22; 14:20,24; Nu 9:15; 14:14; Dt 1:33; Ne 9:12,19; Ps 78:14
UNQUENCHABLE FIRE (4) Jer 4:4; 7:20; 21:12; Mt 18:8

Ge 19:24 Then the LORD rained down f and burning sulfur
22:3 Then he chopped wood to build a f for a burnt
22:6 while he himself carried the knife and the f.
22:7 "We have the wood and the f," said the boy,
Ex 3:2 LORD appeared to him as a blazing f in a bush.
13:21 of cloud during the day and a pillar of f at night.
13:22 the pillar of cloud or pillar of f from their sight.
14:20 the pillar of cloud turned into a pillar of f,
14:24 down on the Egyptian army from the pillar of f
15:7 flashed forth; / it consumed them as f burns straw.
19:18 the LORD had descended on it in the form of f.
22:6 "If a f gets out of control and goes into another
22:6 then the one who started the f must pay for the lost
24:17 on the mountaintop looked like a devouring f.
29:41 offering to the LORD, an offering made by f.
32:20 took the calf they had made and melted it in the f.
32:24 they brought them to me, I threw them into the f—
40:38 and at night there was f in the cloud so all the
Lev 1:7 the sons of Aaron the priest will build a wood f on
1:8 including its head and fat, on the wood f.
1:9 It is a whole burnt offering made by f,
1:12 the head and fat, on top of the wood f on the altar.
1:13 It is a whole burnt offering made by f,
1:17 Then he will burn it on top of the wood f on the
1:17 It is a whole burnt offering made by f,
2:2 and burn this token portion on the altar f.
2:2 It is an offering made by f, very pleasing to the
2:3 holy part of the offerings given to the LORD by f.
2:9 and burn it on the altar as an offering made by f,
2:10 holy part of the offerings given to the LORD by f.
2:11 may be burned as an offering to the LORD by f.
2:14 kernels of new grain that have been roasted on a f.
2:16 burn it as an offering given to the LORD by f.
3:3 presented to the LORD as an offering made by f.
3:5 the altar on top of the burnt offering on the wood f.
3:5 It is an offering made by f, very pleasing to the
3:9 presented to the LORD as an offering made by f.
3:11 altar as food, an offering given to the LORD by f.
3:14 presented to the LORD as an offering made by f.
3:16 them on the altar as food, an offering made by f;
4:12 He will burn it all on a wood f in the ash heap.
4:35 on top of the offerings given to the LORD by f.
5:12 like any other offering given to the LORD by f.
6:9 and the altar f must be kept burning all night.
6:12 Meanwhile, the f on the altar must be kept burning;
6:12 morning the priest will add fresh wood to the f
6:13 the f must be kept burning on the altar at all times.
6:17 as their share of the offerings presented to me by f.
6:18 share of the offerings given to the LORD by f.
7:5 the altar as an offering to the LORD made by f.
7:25 LORD by f must be cut off from the community.
7:30 own hands as an offering given to the LORD by f.
7:35 f from the time they were appointed to serve the
8:21 It was an offering given to the LORD by f,
8:28 It was an offering given to the LORD by f,
9:24 F blazed forth from the LORD's presence
10:1 and Abihu put coals of f in their incense burners
10:1 him a different kind of f than he had commanded.
10:2 So f blazed forth from the LORD's presence
10:6 and Abihu, whom the LORD has destroyed by f.
10:12 the handful has been presented to the LORD by f.
10:13 share of the offerings given to the LORD by f.
10:15 along with the fat of the offerings given by f.
13:52 It must be completely destroyed by f.
16:1 who died when they burned a different kind of f
21:6 ones who present the offerings to the LORD by f,
21:21 him from presenting offerings to the LORD by f.
22:22 or a scab must never be offered to the LORD by f
22:27 acceptable as an offering given to the LORD by f.
23:8 must present an offering to the LORD by f.
23:13 It will be an offering given to the LORD by f,
23:18 will be given to the LORD by f and will be
23:25 you are to present offerings to the LORD by f."
23:27 and present offerings to the LORD by f.
23:36 you must present offerings to the LORD by f.
23:36 and present another offering to the LORD by f.
23:37 all the various offerings to the LORD by f—
24:7 the bread as an offering given to the LORD by f.

24: 9 portion of the offerings given to the LORD by f."
Nu 3: 4 a different kind of f than he had commanded.
6: 18 and put it on the f beneath the peace-offering
9: 15 over the Tabernacle appeared to be a pillar of f.
9: 16 at night the cloud changed to the appearance of f.
11: 1 F from the LORD raged among them
11: 2 and when he prayed to the LORD, the f stopped.
11: 3 because f from the LORD had burned among
14: 14 pillar of cloud by day and the pillar of f by night.
15: 3 a burnt offering or any other offering given by f,
15: 10 This will be an offering made by f, very pleasing to
15: 13 an offering by f that is pleasing to the LORD,
15: 14 living among you want to present an offering by f,
15: 25 it with their offering given to the LORD by f
16: 35 Then f blazed forth from the LORD and burned
16: 37 the priest to pull all the incense burners from the f,
16: 39 that had been used by the men who died in the f,
18: 9 of the most holy offerings that is kept from the f.
18: 17 and burn their fat as an offering given by f,
19: 6 and throw them into the f where the heifer is
21: 28 A f flamed forth from Heshbon, / a blaze from the
26: 10 were destroyed that day by f from the LORD.
26: 61 a different kind of f than he had commanded.
28: 2 The offerings you present to me by f on the altar
28: 6 an offering made by f, very pleasing to the
28: 8 It, too, is an offering made by f, very pleasing to
28: 13 This burnt offering must be presented by f, and it
28: 24 prepare the food offerings to be presented by f,
29: 6 These offerings are given to the LORD by f
29: 13 must present a special whole burnt offering by f,
31: 23 must be passed through f in order to be made
Dt 1: 33 guiding you by a pillar of f at night and a pillar of
4: 11 while the mountain was burning with f.
4: 12 And the LORD spoke to you from the f.
4: 15 the day he spoke to you from the f at Mount Sinai.
4: 24 The LORD your God is a devouring f, a jealous
4: 33 ever heard the voice of God speaking from f—
4: 36 He let you see his great f here on earth so he could
5: 4 to face from the heart of the f on the mountain.
5: 5 for you were afraid of the f and did not climb the
5: 22 a loud voice to all of you from the heart of the f,
5: 23 while the mountain was blazing with f, all your
5: 24 we have heard his voice from the heart of the f.
5: 25 certainly die and be consumed by this awesome f.
5: 26 the voice of the living God from the heart of the f
7: 25 "You must burn their idols in f, and do not desire
9: 3 ahead of you like a devouring f to destroy them.
9: 10 he had spoken to you from the f on the mountain.
9: 21 and I melted it in the f and ground it into fine dust.
10: 4 f on the mountain as you were assembled below.
18: 1 eat from the offerings given to the LORD by f,
18: 16 or see this blazing f for fear you would die.
32: 22 For my anger blazes forth like f / and burns to the
33: 2 with flaming f at his right hand.
Jos 7: 15 apart for destruction will himself be burned with f,
8: 8 Set the city on f, as the LORD has commanded.
8: 19 the city. They quickly captured it and set it on f.
Jdg 1: 8 killing all its people and setting the city on f.
6: 21 and f flamed up from the rock and consumed all he
9: 15 let f come out from me and devour the cedars of
9: 20 then may f come out from Abimelech and devour
9: 20 and may f come out from the people of Shechem
9: 49 against the walls of the temple and set them on f.
9: 52 But as he prepared to set f to the entrance,
13: 20 the sky, the angel of the LORD ascended in the f.
16: 9 as if they were string that had been burned in a f.
1Sa 6: 14 So the people broke up the wood of the cart for a f
2Sa 14: 30 "Go and set f to Joab's barley field, the field next
14: 30 So they set his field on f, as Absalom had
14: 31 "Why did your servants set my field on f?"
23: 7 they will be utterly consumed with f."
24: 22 and ox yokes for wood to build a f on the altar.
1Ki 18: 23 the wood of their altar, but without setting f to it.
18: 23 lay it on the wood on the altar, but not set f to it.
18: 24 The god who answers by setting f to the wood is
18: 25 name of your god. But do not set f to the wood."
18: 38 Immediately the f of the LORD flashed down
19: 12 And after the earthquake there was a f, but the
LORD was not in the f.
19: 12 And after the f there was the sound of a gentle
19: 21 and used the wood from the plow to build a f to
2Ki 1: 10 let f come down from heaven and destroy you
1: 10 Then f fell from heaven and killed them all.
1: 12 let f come down from heaven and destroy you
1: 12 And again the f of God fell from heaven and killed
1: 14 See how the f from heaven has destroyed the first
2: 11 and talking, suddenly a chariot of f appeared,
drawn by horses of f.
6: 17 Elisha was filled with horses and chariots of f.
16: 3 of Israel, even sacrificing his own son in the f.
17: 17 sacrificed their own sons and daughters in the f.
19: 18 have thrown the gods of these nations into the f
21: 6 Manasseh even sacrificed his own son in the f.
23: 10 or daughter in the f as an offering to Molech.
1Ch 21: 23 threshing tools for wood to build a f on the altar.
21: 26 the LORD answered him by sending f from
2Ch 7: 1 f flashed down from heaven and burned up the
7: 3 When all the people of Israel saw the f coming
16: 14 and at his funeral the people built a huge f in his
21: 19 His people did not build a great f to honor him at
28: 3 of Hinnom, even sacrificing his own sons in the f.
33: 6 Manasseh even sacrificed his own sons in the f in
36: 19 Then his army set f to the Temple of God,
Ne 9: 12 and a pillar of f at night so that they could find
9: 19 and the pillar of f showed them the way through
Job 1: 16 "The f of God has fallen from heaven and burned
5: 7 as predictably as sparks fly upward from a f.
15: 34 enriched through bribery, will be consumed by f.
18: 5 be snuffed out. The sparks of their f will not glow.
22: 20 The last of them have been consumed in the f.'
23: 10 And when he has tested me like gold in a f, he will
28: 5 but below the surface the earth is melted as by f.
31: 12 It is a devastating f that destroys to hell. It would
41: 19 F and sparks leap from its mouth.
41: 20 like steam from a boiling pot on a f of dry rushes.
Ps 21: 9 consume them in his anger; / f will devour them.
39: 3 and began to burn, / igniting a f of words:
46: 9 the spear in two; / he burns the shields with f.
50: 3 F devours everything in his way, / and a great
66: 12 our broken bodies. / We went through f and flood.
68: 2 Melt them like wax in f. / Let the wicked perish in
74: 7 They set the sanctuary on f, burning it to the
78: 14 led them by a cloud, / and at night by a pillar of f.
78: 21 The f of his wrath burned against Jacob. / Yes,
78: 63 Their young men were killed by f; / their young
79: 5 How long will your jealousy burn like f?
83: 14 As a f roars through a forest / and as a flame sets
89: 46 How long will your anger burn like f?
97: 3 F goes forth before him / and burns up all his foes.
104: 4 your messengers; / flames of f are your servants.
105: 39 and gave them a great f to light the darkness.
106: 18 F fell upon their followers; / a flame consumed the
140: 10 fall down on their heads, / or throw them into the f,
148: 8 f and hail, snow and storm, / wind and weather that
Pr 6: 27 Can a man scoop f into his lap and not be burned?
17: 3 F tests the purity of silver and gold,
26: 20 F goes out for lack of fuel, and quarrels disappear
26: 21 as hot embers light charcoal or f lights wood.
27: 21 F tests the purity of silver and gold, but a person is
30: 16 barren womb, / the thirsty desert, / the blazing f.
Ecc 7: 6 is quickly gone, like thorns crackling in a f.
SS 8: 6 Love flashes like f, the brightest kind of flame.
Isa 1: 31 evil deeds are the spark that will set the straw on f,
4: 4 by a spirit of judgment that burns like f.
4: 5 cloud throughout the day and clouds of f at night,
9: 19 The people are fuel for the f, and no one spares
10: 16 and a flaming f will ignite your glory.
10: 17 will be a flaming f that will destroy them.
24: 6 its people. They are left desolate, destroyed by f.
26: 11 be ashamed. / Let your f consume your enemies.
29: 6 with whirlwind and storm and consuming f.
30: 27 lips are filled with fury; his words consume like f.
30: 33 like f from a volcano, will set it ablaze.
33: 11 Your own breath will turn to f and kill you.
33: 12 like thorns cut down and tossed in a f.
33: 14 live here in the presence of this all-consuming f?"
34: 9 and the ground will be covered with f.
37: 19 have thrown the gods of these nations into the f
42: 25 They were set on f and burned, but they still
43: 2 When you walk through the f of oppression,
44: 15 he uses part of the wood to make a f to warm
47: 14 they are as useless as dried grass burning in a f.
64: 2 As f causes wood to burn and water to boil,
66: 15 See, the LORD is coming with f, and his swift
66: 15 of his anger and the flaming f of his hot rebuke.
66: 16 The LORD will punish the world by f and by his
66: 24 and the f that burns them will never go out.
Jer 4: 4 or my anger will burn like an unquenchable f
6: 29 The refining f grows hotter. But it will never purify
7: 20 and crops will be consumed by the unquenchable f
7: 31 sacrifice their little sons and daughters in the f.
11: 16 sent the fury of their enemies to burn them with f,
15: 14 For my anger blazes forth like f, and it will
17: 4 For you have kindled my anger into a roaring f that
17: 27 as on other days, then I will set f to these gates.
17: 27 The f will spread to the palaces, and no one will
20: 9 in his name, his word burns in my heart like a f.
20: 9 It's like a f in my bones! I am weary of holding it
21: 12 or my anger will burn like an unquenchable f
21: 14 I will light a f in your forests that will burn up
22: 7 all your fine cedar beams and throw them on the f.
23: 29 Does not my word burn like f?" asks the LORD.
32: 29 outside the walls will come in and set f to the city.
36: 22 of the palace, sitting in front of a f to keep warm.
36: 23 He then threw it into the f, section by section,
36: 32 on the scroll King Jehoiakim had burned in the f.
43: 12 He will set f to the temples of Egypt's gods,
44: 6 boiled over and fell like f on the towns of Judah
48: 45 For a f comes from Heshbon, King Sihon's
49: 27 "And I will start a f at the edge of Damascus that
50: 32 For I will light a f in the cities of Babylon that will
51: 58 in vain, for their work will be destroyed by f!"
La 1: 13 "He has sent f from heaven that burns in my
2: 3 consumes the whole land of Israel like a raging f.
2: 4 His fury is poured out like f on beautiful
4: 11 He started a f in Jerusalem that burned the city to
Eze 1: 4 The f inside the cloud glowed like gleaming
1: 13 The living beings looked like bright coals of f
1: 27 he looked like gleaming amber, flickering like a f.
4: 12 bake it over a f using dried human dung as fuel
5: 4 a few of these hairs out and throw them into the f,
5: 4 A f will then spread from this remnant and destroy
10: 7 and took some live coals from the f burning among
15: 5 useless both before and after being put into the f!
15: 7 And I will see to it that if they escape from one f,
19: 12 tore off its branches. / Its stem was destroyed by f.
19: 14 A f has come from its branches / and devoured its
20: 47 I will set you on f, O forest, and every tree will be
20: 48 world will see that I, the LORD, have set this f.
21: 31 on you and blow on you with the f of my anger.
21: 32 You are fuel for the f, and your blood will be
22: 21 you together and blow the f of my anger upon you,
22: 31 on them, consuming them in the f of my anger.
24: 3 Put a pot of water on the f to boil.
24: 5 the flock and heap fuel on the f beneath the pot.
24: 10 on the wood! Let the f roar to make the pot boil.
24: 12 the corruption remains. So throw it into the f!
28: 14 of God and walked among the stones of f.
28: 16 from your place among the stones of f.
28: 18 So I brought f from within you, and it consumed
30: 8 that I am the LORD when I have set Egypt on f
30: 16 Yes, I will set f to all Egypt! Pelusium will be
36: 5 My jealous anger is on f against these nations,
38: 22 torrential rain, hailstones, f, and burning sulfur!
39: 6 And I will rain down f on Magog and on all your
Da 3: 22 had demanded such a hot f in the furnace,
3: 25 "I see four men, unbound, walking around in the f.
3: 26 Meshach, and Abednego stepped out of the f.
3: 27 and saw that the f had not touched them.
7: 9 He sat on a fiery throne with wheels of blazing f,
7: 10 and a river of f flowed from his presence.
7: 11 beast was killed and its body was destroyed by f.
11: 33 But for a time many of these teachers will die by f
Hos 7: 6 and in the morning it flames forth like a raging f.
8: 14 I will send down f on their palaces and burn their
Joel 1: 19 The f has consumed the pastures and burned up all
1: 20 have dried up, and f has consumed the pastures.
2: 3 F burns in front of them and follows them in every
2: 5 like the roar of a f sweeping across a field,
2: 30 and on the earth—blood and f and pillars of smoke.
Am 1: 4 So I will send down f on King Hazael's palace,
1: 7 So I will send down f on the walls of Gaza, and all
1: 10 So I will send down f on the walls of Tyre, and all
1: 12 So I will send down f on Teman, and the fortresses
1: 14 So I will send down f on the walls of Rabbah,
2: 2 So I will send down f on the land of Moab, and all
2: 5 So I will send down f on Judah, and all the
4: 11 were like half-burned sticks snatched from a f.
5: 6 If you don't, he will roar through Israel like a f,
7: 4 him preparing to punish his people with a great f.
7: 4 The f had burned up the depths of the sea and was
Ob 1: 18 At that time Israel will be a raging f, and Edom,
1: 18 The f will roar across the field,
Mic 1: 4 his feet and flow into the valleys like wax in a f,
Na 1: 6 His rage blazes forth like f, and the mountains
3: 13 opened wide to the enemy and set on f and burned.
3: 15 middle of your preparations, the f will devour you;
Zep 1: 18 For the whole land will be devoured by the f of his
3: 8 All the earth will be devoured by the f of my
Zec 2: 5 myself, will be a wall of f around Jerusalem,
3: 2 a burning stick that has been snatched from a f."
9: 4 Tyre will be set on f and burned to the ground.
11: 1 so that f may sweep through your cedar forests.
13: 9 I will bring that group through the f and make
13: 9 just as gold and silver are refined and purified by f.
Mal 3: 2 For he will be like a blazing f that refines metal
Mt 3: 10 fruit will be chopped down and thrown into the f.
3: 11 will baptize you with the Holy Spirit and with f.
3: 12 but burning the chaff with never-ending f."
7: 19 good fruit is chopped down and thrown into the f.
13: 50 throwing the wicked into the f. There will be
17: 15 He often falls into the f or into the water.
18: 8 or lame than to be thrown into the unquenchable f
25: 41 into the eternal f prepared for the Devil and his
Mk 9: 22 The evil spirit often makes him fall into the f
9: 48 the worm never dies and the f never goes out.'
9: 49 "For everyone will be purified with f.
14: 54 he sat with the guards, warming himself by the f.
14: 67 noticed Peter warming himself at the f. She looked
Lk 3: 9 fruit will be chopped down and thrown into the f."
3: 16 will baptize you with the Holy Spirit and with f.
3: 17 but burning the chaff with never-ending f."
9: 54 should we order down f from heaven to burn them
12: 49 "I have come to bring f to the earth, and I wish
17: 29 Then f and burning sulfur rained down from
22: 55 The guards lit a f in the courtyard and sat around it,
Jn 18: 18 were standing around a charcoal f they had made
18: 25 Meanwhile, as Simon Peter was standing by the f,
21: 9 they saw that a charcoal f was burning and fish
Ac 2: 3 what looked like flames or tongues of f appeared
2: 19 earth below— / blood and f and clouds of smoke.
28: 2 so they built a f on the shore to welcome us
28: 3 an armful of sticks and was laying them on the f,
28: 5 But Paul shook off the snake into the f and was
1Co 3: 13 Everyone's work will be put through the f to see
3: 14 If the work survives the f, that builder will receive
2Th 1: 8 in flaming f, bringing judgment on those who don't
Heb 1: 7 as the wind, / and servants made of flaming f."
10: 27 and the raging f that will consume his enemies.
11: 34 quenched the flames of f, and escaped death by the
12: 18 to a place of flaming f, darkness, gloom,
12: 29 For our God is a consuming f.
Jas 3: 5 it can do. A tiny spark can set a great forest on f.
3: 6 And the tongue is a flame of f. It is full of
3: 6 flame of destruction, for it is set on f by hell itself.
1Pe 1: 7 It is being tested as f tests and purifies gold—
2Pe 3: 7 and the earth will be consumed by f on the day of
3: 10 and everything in them will disappear in f,
3: 12 the day when God will set the heavens on f
Jude 1: 7 Those cities were destroyed by f and are a warning
of the eternal f that will punish
Rev 1: 14 as snow. And his eyes were bright like flames of f.
2: 18 whose eyes are bright like flames of f, whose feet
3: 18 gold from me—gold that has been purified by f.
8: 5 Then the angel filled the incense burner with f
8: 7 and f mixed with blood were thrown down upon
the earth, and one-third of the earth was set on f.
8: 8 and a great mountain of f was thrown into the sea.
9: 17 and f and smoke and burning sulfur billowed from
9: 18 by the f and the smoke and burning sulfur that
10: 1 like the sun, and his feet were like pillars of f.

11: 5 **f** flashes from the mouths of the prophets
13:13 such as making **f** flash down to earth from heaven
14:10 And they will be tormented with **f** and burning
14:18 who has power to destroy the world with **f**,
15: 2 me what seemed to be a crystal sea mixed with **f**.
16: 8 on the sun, causing it to scorch everyone with its **f**.
17:16 eat her flesh, and burn her remains with **f**.
18: 8 She will be utterly consumed by **f**, for the Lord
19:12 His eyes were bright like flames of **f**, and on his
19:20 alive into the lake of **f** that burns with sulfur.
20: 9 But **f** from heaven came down on the attacking
20:10 was thrown into the lake of **f** that burns with sulfur,
20:14 and the grave were thrown into the lake of **f**. This is the second death—the lake of **f**.
20:15 in the Book of Life was thrown into the lake of **f**.
21: 8 their doom is in the lake that burns with **f**

FIREBOX (2) [BOX, FIRE]

Ex 27: 5 Fit the grating halfway down into the **f**, resting it
38: 4 rested on a ledge about halfway down into the **f**.

FIRELIGHT (1) [FIRE]

Lk 22:56 A servant girl noticed him in the **f** and began

FIREPANS (7) [FIRE]

Ex 27: 3 meat hooks, and **f** will all be made of bronze.
38: 3 the ash buckets, shovels, basins, meat hooks, and **f**.
Nu 4:14 the **f**, hooks, shovels, basins, and all the
1Ki 7:50 the cups, lamp snuffers, basins, dishes, and **f**,
2Ki 25:15 captain of the guard, also took the **f** and basins,
2Ch 4:22 basins, dishes, and **f**, all of pure gold;
Jer 52:19 the small bowls, **f**, basins, pots, lampstands, dishes,

FIREPLACE (1) [FIRE]

Isa 30:14 piece left that is big enough to carry coals from a **f**

FIREPLACES (1) [FIRE]

Eze 46:23 of stone with **f** under the ledge all the way around.

FIREPOT (1) [FIRE, POT]

Ge 15:17 Abram saw a smoking **f** and a flaming torch pass

FIRES (6) [FIRE]

Ex 35: 3 Do not even light **f** in your homes on that day."
Isa 50:11 own light and warm yourselves by your own **f**.
Jer 7:18 gather wood and the fathers build sacrificial **f**.
Eze 39:10 They will need nothing else for their **f**. They won't
Mt 5:22 curse someone, you are in danger of the **f** of hell.
Mk 9:43 go into the unquenchable **f** of hell with two hands.

FIREWOOD (1) [FIRE, WOOD]

La 5: 4 to pay for water to drink, and even **f** is expensive.

FIRKINS [KJV] See GALLONS

FIRM (30) [FIRMLY]

2Ch 1: 1 of King David, now took **f** control of the kingdom,
20:20 LORD your God, and you will be able to stand **f**.
Job 8:17 grow down through a pile of rocks to hold it **f**.
33:25 as healthy as a child's, **f** and youthful again.
41:23 Its flesh is hard and **f**, not soft and fat.
Ps 15: 5 the innocent. / Such people will stand **f** forever.
20: 8 and collapse, / but we will rise up and stand **f**.
33:11 But the LORD's plans stand **f** forever;
75: 3 I am the one who keeps its foundations **f**.
104: 9 Then you set a **f** boundary for the seas, / so they
119:89 O LORD, / your word stands **f** in heaven.
143:10 gracious Spirit lead me forward / on a **f** footing.
Pr 10: 9 People with integrity have **f** footing, but those who
12: 7 and are gone, but the children of the godly stand **f**.
Isa 22:25 I will pull out the stake that seemed so **f**.
28:16 It is **f**, a tested and precious cornerstone that is safe
Eze 13: 5 They have not helped it to stand **f** in battle on the
Lk 6:48 the house, it stands **f** because it is well built.
21:19 By standing **f**, you will win your souls.
2Co 1:21 along with you, the ability to stand **f** for Christ.
1:24 so you will be full of joy as you stand **f** in your
Eph 6:11 so that you will be able to stand **f** against all
6:13 so that after the battle you will still be standing **f**.
2Th 2:15 stand **f** and keep a strong grip on everything we
2Ti 2:19 But God's truth stands **f** like a foundation stone
Heb 12:12 your tired hands and stand **f** on your shaky legs.
1Pe 5: 9 Take a **f** stand against him, and be strong in your
5:10 and he will place you on a **f** foundation.
2Pe 1:12 already know them and are standing **f** in the truth.
Rev 14:12 persecution patiently and remain **f** to the end,

FIRMAMENT [KJV] See HEAVEN, SKIES, SPACE, SURFACE

FIRMLY (20) [FIRM]

Ex 26:24 and **f** attached at the top with a single ring,
36:18 so the two sets of sheets were **f** attached to each
36:29 and **f** attached at the top with a single ring,
Dt 4:39 So remember this and keep it **f** in mind:
1Ki 2:12 David, and he was **f** established on the throne.
2:46 So the kingdom was now **f** in Solomon's grip.
1Ch 16:30 The world is **f** established and cannot be shaken.
2Ch 12: 1 But when Rehoboam was **f** established and strong,
12:13 King Rehoboam **f** established himself in Jerusalem
Ps 93: 1 The world is **f** established; / it cannot be shaken.
96:10 The world is **f** established and cannot be shaken.
119:61 drag me into sin, / but I am **f** anchored to your law.
Isa 22:23 for I will drive him **f** in place like a tent stake.
Am 9:15 I will **f** plant them there in the land I have given
Ac 24:14 and I **f** believe the Jewish law and everything
1Co 7:37 But if he has decided **f** not to marry and there is no
15: 2 And it is this Good News that saves you if you **f**
Col 1:23 must continue to believe this truth and stand in it **f**.
Heb 3:14 trusting God just as **f** as when we first believed,
Rev 3: 3 believed at first; hold to it **f** and turn to me again.

FIRS (2) [FIR]

Ps 104:17 and the storks make their homes in the **f**.
SS 1:17 shaded by cedar trees and spreading **f**."

FIRST (389) [FIRSTBORN, FIRSTFRUITS]

FIRST DAY (24) Ex 12:15,16; 40:2,17; Lev 23:7,35, 39,39,40; Nu 7:12; 28:11,14,15,18,26; Eze 44:27; 45:18; Da 10:12; Mt 26:17; 27:62; Mk 14:12; Jn 20:19; Ac 20:7; Col 1:6

FIRST...LAST; LAST...FIRST (11) Isa 41:4; 44:6; 48:12; Mt 20:8,16,16; Mk 9:35; 1Co 15:45; Rev 1:17; 2:8; 22:13

FIRST MONTH (7) Ex 12:2,6; Jos 4:19; 5:10; 1Ch 27:2,3; 2Ch 29:3

FIRST YEAR (10) 2Ch 29:3; 36:22; Ezr 1:1; 5:13; 6:3; Da 1:21; 7:1; 9:1,2; 11:1

Ge 4:20 He became the **f** of the herdsmen who live in tents.
4:21 His brother's name was Jubal, the **f** musician—
4:22 He was the **f** to work with metal,
4:26 It was during his lifetime that people **f** began to
10:25 The **f** was named Peleg—"division"—for during
16: 3 (This happened ten years after Abram **f** arrived in
21:26 "This is the **f** I've heard of it," Abimelech said.
25:25 The **f** was very red at birth. He was covered with
27:36 **f** taking my birthright and now stealing my
31:33 Laban went **f** into Jacob's tent to search there,
32:17 He gave these instructions to the men leading the **f**
38: 8 Her **f** son from you will be your brother's heir."
38:28 around the wrist of the child who appeared **f**, saying, "This one came out **f**."
38:29 and the other baby was actually the **f** to be born.
38:29 "How did you break out **f**?" And ever after,
40: 9 The cup-bearer told his dream **f**. "In my dream,"
40:16 When the chief baker saw that the **f** dream had
41:20 the seven fat ones that had come out of the river **f**,
41:50 before the arrival of the **f** of the famine years,
43:20 to him, "Sir, after our **f** trip to Egypt to buy food,
49: 3 You are **f** on the list in rank and honor.
49: 4 the waves of the sea, / and you will be **f** no longer.
Ex 4: 8 "If they do not believe the **f** miraculous sign,
6:16 In the **f** generation were Gershon, Kohath,
12: 2 this month will be the **f** month of the year for you.
12: 6 the evening of the fourteenth day of this **f** month.
12:15 On the very **f** day you must remove every trace of
12:16 On the **f** day of the festival, and again on the
18: 3 The name of Moses' **f** son was Gershom,
23:15 The **f** is the Festival of Unleavened Bread.
23:16 when you bring me the **f** crops of your harvest.
23:19 bring me a choice sample of the **f** day's harvest.
28:17 The **f** row will contain a red carnelian, a chrysolite,
34: 1 "Prepare two stone tablets like the **f** ones.
34: 4 So Moses cut two tablets of stone like the **f** ones.
34:22 of Harvest with the **f** crop of the wheat harvest,
34:26 You must bring the best of the **f** of each year's
36: 8 The skilled weavers **f** made ten sheets from fine
36:12 The fifty loops along the edge of the **f** set of sheets
36:19 The **f** was made of tanned ram skins,
39:10 In the **f** row were a red carnelian, a chrysolite,
40: 2 "Set up the Tabernacle on the **f** day of the new
40:17 So the Tabernacle was set up on the **f** day of the
Lev 1: 9 and legs must **f** be washed with water.
1:13 and legs must **f** be washed with water.
2:14 to the LORD from the **f** portion of your harvest,
15:11 If the man touches you without **f** rinsing his hands,
16: 3 He must **f** bring a young bull for a sin offering
19:23 leave the fruit unharvested for the **f** three years
23: 5 "**F** comes the LORD's Passover, which begins at
23: 7 On the **f** day of the festival, all the people must
23:10 land I am giving you and you harvest your **f** crops,
23:10 bring the priest some grain from the **f** portion of
23:17 They will be an offering to the LORD from the **f**
23:20 together with the loaves representing the **f** of your
23:35 It will begin with a sacred assembly on the **f** day,
23:39 "Now, on the **f** day of the Festival of Shelters,
23:39 Remember that the **f** day and closing eighth day of
23:40 On the **f** day, gather fruit from citrus trees,
Nu 4: 5 and his sons must enter the Tabernacle **f** to take
6:16 **f** the sin offering and the burnt offering;
7:12 On the **f** day Nahshon son of Amminadab,
13:20 (It happened to be the season for harvesting the **f**
13:22 they passed **f** through the Negev and arrived at
15:20 Present a cake from the **f** of the flour you grind
15:20 as you do with the **f** grain from the threshing floor.
15:21 LORD each year from the **f** of your ground flour.
18:27 as though it were the **f** grain from your own
22:15 officials than those he had sent the **f** time.
24:14 But **f** let me tell you what the Israelites will do to
28:11 "On the **f** day of each month, present an extra
28:14 Present this monthly burnt offering on the **f** day of
28:15 on the **f** day of each month you must offer one
28:18 On the **f** day of the festival you must call a sacred
28:26 "On the **f** day of the Festival of Harvest, when you present the **f** of your new grain to the
31:28 But **f** give the LORD his share of the captives,
33: 3 after the **f** Passover celebration in early spring.
36: 7 every tribe must remain fixed as it was **f** allotted.
Dt 1:22 "But you responded, '**F**, let's send out scouts to
2:14 So thirty-eight years passed from the time we **f**
10: 1 to me, 'Prepare two stone tablets like the **f** ones,
10: 3 and cut two stone tablets like the **f** two,
10:10 for forty days and nights, as I had done the **f** time.
17: 7 The witnesses must throw the **f** stones, and then all
18: 4 You must also give to the priests the **f** share of the
19: 6 and the **f** death had been an accident.
20:10 town to attack it, **f** offer its people terms for peace.
25: 6 The **f** son she bears to him will be counted as the
26: 2 put some of the **f** produce from each harvest into a
26:10 I have brought you a token of the **f** crops you have
Jos 4:19 the Jordan on the tenth day of the **f** month—
5:10 the evening of the fourteenth day of the **f** month—
18:11 The **f** allotment of land went to the families of the
21:10 the tribe of Levi, since the sacred lot fell to them **f**:
22:13 **F**, however, they sent a delegation led by Phinehas
Jdg 1: 1 "Which tribe should attack the Canaanites **f**?"
8: 1 Why didn't you send for us when you **f** went out to
8: 6 Catch them **f**, and then we will feed your
8:15 Catch them **f**, and then we will feed your
9: 8 a king. **F** they said to the olive tree, 'Be our king!'
10:18 "Whoever attacks the Ammonites **f** will become
11:31 I will give to the LORD the **f** thing coming out of
11:37 But **f** let me go up and roam in the hills and weep
20:18 The LORD answered, "Judah is to go **f**."
20:32 "We're defeating them as we did in the **f** battle!"
20:39 "We're defeating them as we did in the **f** battle!"
1Sa 2:16 much as you want, but the fat must **f** be burned."
7:16 setting up his court **f** at Bethel, then at Gilgal,
14:35 an altar to the LORD, the **f** one he had ever built.
14:36 is best." But the priest said, "Let's ask God **f**."
18:17 But **f** you must prove yourself to be a real warrior
22:15 This was certainly not the **f** time I had consulted
2Sa 18:13 you yourself would be the **f** to abandon me."
18:27 "The **f** man runs like Ahimaaz son of Zadok,"
19:20 the very **f** person in all Israel to greet you."
19:43 we were the **f** to speak of bringing him back to be
23: 8 The **f** was Jashobeam the Hacmonite, who was
24: 5 **F** they crossed the Jordan and camped at Aroer,
1Ki 3:22 "No," the **f** woman said, "the dead one is yours,
16:32 **F** he built a temple and an altar for Baal in
17:13 that 'last meal,' but bake me a little loaf of bread **f**.
18:25 of Baal, "You go **f**, for there are many of you.
19:20 "**F** let me go and kiss my father and mother
20: 9 'I will give you everything you asked for the **f**
20:14 "Should we attack **f**?" Ahab asked. "Yes,"
22: 5 "But **f** let's find out what the LORD says."
2Ki 1:14 See how the fire from heaven has destroyed the **f**
4:42 and twenty loaves of barley bread made from the **f**
17:25 did not worship the LORD when they **f** arrived,
1Ch 1:19 The **f** was named Peleg—"division"—for during
2:13 Jesse's **f** son was Eliab, his second was Abinadab,
6:39 Heman's **f** assistant was Asaph from the clan of
9: 2 The **f** to return to their property in their former
11:11 The **f** was Jashobeam the Hacmonite, who was
15:13 Because you Levites did not carry the Ark the **f**
24: 7 The **f** lot fell to Jehoiarib. / The second lot fell to
25: 9 The **f** lot fell to Joseph of the Asaph clan
27: 2 Jashobeam son of Zabdiel was commander of the **f**
27: 2 which was on duty during the **f** month.
27: 3 and was in charge of all the army officers for the **f**
2Ch 3:11 One wing of the **f** figure was 7-1/2 feet long,
3:12 7-1/2 feet long, touched the wing of the **f** figure.
18: 4 "But **f** let's find out what the LORD says."
29: 3 In the very **f** month of the **f** year of his reign,
31: 5 and generously with the **f** of their crops and grain,
31: 7 The **f** of these tithes was brought in late spring,
32: 5 and constructing a second wall outside the **f**.
36:22 In the **f** year of King Cyrus of Persia, the LORD
Ezr 1: 1 In the **f** year of King Cyrus of Persia, the LORD
3:12 and other leaders remembered the **f** Temple,
5:13 Cyrus of Babylon, during the **f** year of his reign,
6: 3 "In the **f** year of King Cyrus's reign, a decree was
8:20 a group of Temple workers **f** instituted by King
Ne 7: 5 record of those who had **f** returned to Judah.
9:32 the kings of Assyria **f** triumphed over us until now.
10:35 "We promise always to bring the **f** part of every
12:30 The priests and Levites **f** dedicated themselves,
12:44 for the gifts, the **f** part of the harvest, and the tithes.
13:31 and that the **f** part of the harvest was collected for
Job 15: 7 "Were you the **f** person ever born? Were you born
20: 4 "Don't you realize that ever since people were **f**
42:14 He named his **f** daughter Jemimah, the second
Pr 4:18 The way of the righteous is like the **f** gleam of
8:23 in ages past, at the very **f**, before the earth began.
8:26 made the earth and fields and the **f** handfuls of soil.
24:27 Develop your business **f** before building your
30: 8 **F**, help me never to tell a lie. Second, give me
Isa 3:14 and the princes will be the **f** to feel the LORD's
41: 4 It is I, the LORD, the **F** and the Last. I alone am
41:27 I was the **f** to tell Jerusalem, 'Look! Help is on the
43:12 **F** I predicted your deliverance; I declared what I
44: 6 I am the **F** and the Last; there is no other God.
48:12 chosen one! I alone am God, the **F** and the Last.
Jer 1: 2 The LORD **f** gave messages to Jeremiah during
2: 3 was holy to the LORD, the **f** of my children.
2:36 "**F** here, then there—you flit from one ally to
4:31 like that of a woman giving birth to her **f** child.
17:19 **f** at the gate where the king goes out, and then at
36: 2 Begin with the **f** message back in the days of
36:17 "But **f**, tell us how you got these messages.
50:17 **F** the king of Assyria ate them up. Then King
51:46 But do not panic when you hear the **f** rumor of
Eze 3:10 let all my words sink deep into your own heart **f**.
3:23 just as I had seen it in my **f** vision by the Kebar

10:14 the **f** was the face of an ox, the second was a
16:43 But **f**, because you have not remembered your
23:21 when you **f** allowed yourself to be fondled
26: 8 **F** he will destroy your mainland villages. Then he
42:14 They must **f** take off the clothes they wore while
43: 3 **f** by the Kebar River and then when he came to
44:27 The **f** day he returns to work and enters the inner
44:30 The **f** of the ripe fruits and all the gifts brought to
44:30 The **f** samples of each grain harvest and the **f** of
your flour must also be given to the
45:18 In early spring, on the **f** day of each new year,
48:31 The **f** will be named for Reuben, the second for
Da 1:21 Daniel remained there until the **f** year of King
7: 1 during the **f** year of King Belshazzar's reign in
7: 4 The **f** beast was like a lion with eagles' wings.
7: 8 Three of the **f** horns were wrenched out, roots
8:21 and the large horn between its eyes represents the **f**
8:22 with four kings, none of them as great as the **f**.
9: 1 It was the **f** year of the reign of Darius the Mede,
9: 2 During the **f** year of his reign, I, Daniel,
10:12 Since the **f** day you began to pray for
11: 1 and defense since the **f** year of the reign of Darius
12: 1 than any since nations **f** came into existence.
Hos 1: 2 When the LORD **f** began speaking to Israel
7:11 witless doves, **f** calling to Egypt, then flying to
9:10 The LORD says, "O Israel, when I **f** found you,
9:10 it was like seeing the **f** ripe figs of the season!
Am 3: 4 Does a lion ever roar in a thicket without **f** finding
3: 4 Does a young lion growl in its den without **f**
3: 7 "But always, **f** of all, I warn you through my
6: 7 you will be the **f** to be led away as captives.
Mic 1:13 You were the **f** city in Judah to follow Israel in the
Zec 6: 2 The **f** chariot was pulled by red horses, the second
12: 7 The LORD will give victory to the rest of Judah **f**,
Mt 2: 7 he learned the exact time when they **f** saw the star.
2:16 because the wise men had told him the star **f**
7: 5 **F** get rid of the log from your own eye,
8:21 "Lord, **f** let me return home and bury my father."
10: 2 **f** Simon (also called Peter), / then Andrew (Peter's
12:29 man's house and rob him without **f** tying him up.
13:21 At **f** they get along fine, but they wilt as soon as
17:11 "Elijah is indeed coming **f** to set everything in
17:27 Open the mouth of the **f** fish you catch, and you
20: 8 and pay them, beginning with the last workers **f**.
20:16 so it is, that many who are **f** now will be last then;
20:16 and those who are last now will be **f** then."
20:27 and whoever wants to be **f** must become your
21:31 They replied, "The **f**, of course." Then Jesus
22:38 This is the **f** and greatest commandment.
23:26 **F** wash the inside of the cup, and then the outside
26:17 On the **f** day of the Festival of Unleavened Bread,
27:62 on the **f** day of the Passover ceremonies—
27:64 we'll be worse off than we were at **f**."
Mk 3:27 man's house and rob him without **f** tying him up.
4:17 At **f** they get along fine, but they wilt as soon as
4:28 **F** a leaf blade pushes through, then the heads of
7: 5 For they eat without **f** performing the
7:27 "**F** I should help my own family, the Jews.
9:12 "Elijah is indeed coming **f** to set everything in
9:35 "Anyone who wants to be the **f** must take last
10:44 and whoever wants to be **f** must be the slave of all.
11:25 **f** forgive anyone you are holding a grudge against,
13:10 And the Good News must **f** be preached to every
14:12 On the **f** day of the Festival of Unleavened Bread
16: 9 and the **f** person who saw him was Mary
16:12 but they didn't recognize him at **f** because he had
Lk 2: 2 (This was the **f** census taken when Quirinius was
2: 7 She gave birth to her **f** child, a son. She wrapped
2:23 of the Lord says, "If a woman's **f** child is a boy,
2:43 in Jerusalem. His parents didn't miss him at **f**,
6:39 The **f** one will fall into a ditch and pull the other
6:42 **F** get rid of the log from your own eye;
7:45 my feet again and again from the time I **f** came in.
9:59 "Lord, **f** let me return home and bury my father."
9:61 but **f** let me say good-bye to my family."
11:38 **f** performing the ceremonial washing required by
12: 1 Jesus turned **f** to his disciples and warned them,
14:24 For none of those I invited **f** will get even the
14:28 of a building without **f** getting estimates
14:31 to war without **f** sitting down with his counselors
16: 5 He asked the **f** one, 'How much do you owe him?'
17: 8 He must **f** prepare his master's meal and serve him
17:25 But **f** the Son of Man must suffer terribly and be
19:16 The **f** servant reported a tremendous gain—
20: 3 "Let me ask you a question **f**," he replied.
Jn 1:41 The **f** thing Andrew did was to find his brother,
2:10 "Usually a host serves the best wine **f**," he said.
2:11 Cana in Galilee was Jesus' **f** display of his glory.
8: 7 But let those who have never sinned throw the **f**
10:40 to stay near the place where John was **f** baptizing.
18:13 **F** they took him to Annas, the father-in-law of
20: 4 The other disciple outran Peter and got there **f**.
20:19 That evening, on the **f** day of the week,
Ac 1: 1 In my **f** book I told you about everything Jesus
3:26 his servant, he sent him **f** to you people of Israel,
11:26 (It was there at Antioch that the believers were **f**
12:10 They passed the **f** and second guard posts
13:46 this Good News from God be given **f** to you Jews.
15:14 Peter has told you about the time God **f** visited the
16: 1 Paul and Silas went **f** to Derbe and then on to
20: 7 On the **f** day of the week, we gathered to observe
26:20 I preached **f** to those in Damascus, then in
26:23 and be the **f** to rise from the dead as a light to Jews
27:21 you should have listened to me in the **f** place
27:43 he ordered all who could swim to jump overboard **f**
28:12 Our **f** stop was Syracuse, where we stayed three
Ro 1: 8 Let me say **f** of all that your faith in God is
1:16 everyone who believes—Jews **f** and also Gentiles.
2: 9 on sinning—for the Jew **f** and also for the Gentile.
2:10 do good—for the Jew **f** and also for the Gentile.
3: 2 **F** of all, the Jews were entrusted with the whole
4:10 The answer is that God accepted him **f**, and then he
11:21 not spare the branches he put there in the **f** place,
13:11 salvation is nearer now than when we **f** believed.
16: 5 He was the very **f** person to become a Christian in
1Co 2: 1 when I **f** came to you I didn't use lofty words
7:17 and continue on as you were when God **f** called
11: 8 For the **f** man didn't come from woman, but the **f**
woman came from man.
11:12 For although the **f** woman came from man, all men
11:18 **F** of all, I hear that there are divisions among you
12:28 **f** are apostles, / second are prophets, / third are
12:31 **F**, however, let me tell you about something else
15: 2 you believed something that was never true in the **f**
15:20 He has become the **f** of a great harvest of those
15:22 because all of us are related to Adam, the **f** man.
15:23 Christ was raised **f**; then when Christ comes back,
15:36 it doesn't grow into a plant unless it dies **f**.
15:45 The Scriptures tell us, "The **f** man, Adam,
15:46 What came **f** was the natural body,
15:47 Adam, the **f** man, was made from the dust of the
16:15 and his household were the **f** to become Christians
2Co 1:22 as the **f** installment of everything he will give us.
3:10 that **f** glory was not glorious at all compared with
8: 5 for their **f** action was to dedicate themselves to the
8: 6 who encouraged your giving in the **f** place,
8:10 a year ago, for you were the **f** to propose this idea,
8:10 and you were the **f** to begin doing something about
10:14 for we were the **f** to travel all the way to you with
Gal 2:12 When he **f** arrived, he ate with the Gentile
4:12 You did not mistreat me when I **f** preached to you.
4:13 Surely you remember that I was sick when I **f**
4:24 represents Mount Sinai where people **f** became
Eph 1:12 God's purpose was that we who were the **f** to trust
1:15 Ever since I **f** heard of your strong faith in the Lord
4: 9 This means that Christ **f** came down to the lowly
6: 2 This is the **f** of the Ten Commandments that ends
Php 1: 5 about Christ from the time you **f** heard it until now.
Col 1: 5 as you have been ever since you **f** heard the truth
1: 6 just as it changed yours that very **f** day you heard
1: 9 praying for you ever since we **f** heard about you.
1:18 He is the **f** of all who will rise from the dead, so he
is **f** in everything.
1Th 4:16 **F**, all the Christians who have died will rise from
2Th 2:13 you to be among the **f** to experience salvation,
3: 1 Pray **f** that the Lord's message will spread rapidly
1Ti 2: 1 I urge you, **f** of all, to pray for all people. As you
2:13 For God made Adam **f**, and afterward he made
5: 4 their **f** responsibility is to show godliness at home
2Ti 2: 6 Hardworking farmers are the **f** to enjoy the fruit of
4:16 The **f** time I was brought before the judge, no one
Tit 3:10 divisions among you, give a **f** and second warning.
Heb 3:14 trusting God just as firmly as when we **f** believed,
7:27 They did this for their own sins **f** and then for the
8: 7 If the **f** covenant had been faultless, there would
8:13 it means he has made the **f** one obsolete.
9: 1 Now in that **f** covenant between God and Israel,
9: 2 In the **f** room were a lampstand, a table, and loaves
9: 6 and out of the **f** room regularly as they performed
9: 8 was not open to the people as long as the **f** room
9:15 the sins they had committed under that **f** covenant.
9:18 That is why blood was required under the **f**
10: 9 He cancels the **f** covenant in order to establish the
10:15 Holy Spirit also testifies that this is so. **F** he says,
10:32 Don't ever forget those early days when you **f**
13: 7 Remember your leaders who **f** taught you the word
Jas 3:17 But the wisdom that comes from heaven is **f** of all
1Pe 4:17 and it must begin **f** among God's own children.
2Pe 3: 3 **F**, I want to remind you that in the last days there
3: 4 exactly the same since the world was **f** created."
1Jn 4:19 We love each other as a result of his loving us **f**.
Rev 1: 5 witness to these things, the **f** to rise from the dead,
1:17 "Don't be afraid! I am the **F** and the Last.
2: 4 You don't love me or each other as you did at **f**!
2: 5 Look how far you have fallen from your **f** love!
2: 5 Turn back to me again and work as you did at **f**.
2: 8 This is the message from the one who is the **F**
3: 3 Go back to what you heard and believed at **f**;
4: 7 The **f** of these living beings had the form of a lion;
6: 1 the Lamb broke the **f** of the seven seals on the
8: 7 The **f** angel blew his trumpet, and hail and fire
9:12 The **f** terror is past, but look, two more terrors are
10: 9 "At **f** it will taste like honey, but when you
13:12 He exercised all the authority of the **f** beast.
13:12 who belong to this world to worship the **f** beast,
13:14 he was allowed to perform on behalf of the **f** beast,
13:14 of the world to make a great statue of the **f** beast,
16: 2 So the **f** angel left the Temple and poured out his
20: 5 This is the **f** resurrection. (The rest of the dead did
20: 6 and holy are those who share in the **f** resurrection.
21:19 the **f** was jasper, the second sapphire, the third
22:13 the **F** and the Last, the Beginning and the End."

FIRSTBEGOTTEN [KJV] See FIRSTBORN

FIRSTBORN (78) [FIRST, BEAR]

ALL THE FIRSTBORN (16) Ex 11:5; 12:12,29; 13:2,15,15; Nu 3:12,13,13,13,40; 8:16,17,17,18; Dt 15:19

Ge 25:33 thereby selling all his rights as the **f** to his younger
27: 4 that belongs to you, my **f** son, before I die."
29:26 to marry off a younger daughter ahead of the **f**,"
Ex 4:22 'This is what the LORD says: Israel is my **f** son.
4:23 have refused, be warned! I will kill your **f** son!' "
11: 5 All the **f** sons will die in every family in Egypt,
11: 5 lowliest slave. Even the **f** of the animals will die.
12:12 and kill all the **f** sons and **f** male animals in the
land of Egypt.
12:23 the Destroyer to enter and strike down your **f**.
12:29 And at midnight the LORD killed all the **f** sons in
12:29 from the **f** son of Pharaoh, who sat on the throne,
12:29 to the **f** son of the captive in the dungeon.
12:29 Even the **f** of their livestock were killed.
13: 2 all the **f** sons of Israel and every **f** male animal.
13:12 All **f** sons and **f** male animals must be presented to
13:13 A **f** male donkey may be redeemed from the
13:13 its neck. However, you must redeem every **f** son.
13:15 so the LORD killed all the **f** males throughout the
13:15 That is why we now offer all the **f** males to the
13:15 except that the **f** sons are always redeemed.'
22:29 necessary payment for redemption of your **f** sons.
22:30 "You must also give me the **f** of your cattle
34:19 "Every **f** male belongs to me—of both cattle
34:20 A **f** male donkey may be redeemed from the
34:20 its neck. However, you must redeem every **f** son.
Lev 27:26 "You may not dedicate to the LORD the **f** of
27:26 because the **f** of these animals already belong to
27:27 if it is the **f** of a ceremonially unclean animal,
Nu 3: 2 Aaron's sons were Nadab (the **f**), Abihu, Eleazar,
3:12 substitutes for all the **f** sons of the people of Israel.
3:13 because all the **f** sons are mine. From the day I
killed all the **f** sons of the
3:13 I set apart for myself all the **f** in Israel of both men
3:40 "Now count all the **f** sons in Israel who are one
3:41 for me as substitutes for the **f** sons of Israel;
3:41 for the **f** livestock of the whole nation of Israel."
3:42 So Moses counted the **f** sons of the people of
3:43 The total number of **f** sons who were one month
3:45 "Take the Levites in place of the **f** sons of the
3:45 for the **f** livestock of the people of Israel.
3:46 To redeem the 273 **f** sons of Israel who are in
3:48 and his sons as the redemption price for the extra **f**
3:49 So Moses collected redemption money for the **f**
3:50 The silver collected on behalf of these **f** sons of
8:16 I have claimed them for myself in place of all the **f**
8:17 For all the **f** males among the people of Israel are
8:17 on the night I killed all the **f** sons of the Egyptians.
8:18 I claim the Levites in place of all the **f** sons of
18:15 "The **f** of every mother, whether human or animal,
18:15 But you must always redeem your **f** sons
18:15 and the **f** males of ritually unclean animals.
18:17 you may not redeem the **f** of cattle, sheep, or goats.
33: 4 the Egyptians were burying all their **f** sons,
Dt 12: 6 and your offerings of the **f** animals of your flocks
12:17 and olive oil, nor the **f** of your flocks and herds,
14:23 olive oil, and the **f** males of your flocks and herds.
15:19 LORD your God all the **f** males from your flocks
15:19 Do not use the **f** of your herds to work your fields,
and do not shear the **f** of your flocks.
15:21 But if this **f** animal has any defect, such as being
21:15 And suppose the **f** son is the son of the wife he
21:17 and who owns the rights of the **f** son,
Jos 6:26 At the cost of his **f** son, / he will lay its foundation.
1Ch 4: 4 These were the descendants of Hur (the **f** of
5: 1 Reuben is not listed in the genealogy as the **f** son.
Ne 10:36 oldest sons and the **f** of all our herds and flocks,
Ps 89:27 I will make him my **f** son, / the mightiest king on
135: 8 He destroyed the **f** in each Egyptian home,
136:10 Give thanks to him who killed the **f** of Egypt.
Eze 20:26 and I allowed them to give their **f** children as
Mic 6: 7 Should we sacrifice our **f** children to pay for the
Zec 12:10 They will grieve bitterly for him as for a **f** son who
Ro 8:29 so that his Son would be the **f**, with many brothers
Heb 11:28 so that the angel of death would not kill their **f**
12:23 You have come to the assembly of God's **f**

FIRSTFRUITS (1) [FIRST]

Nu 18:13 All the **f** of the land that the people present to the

FIRSTLING [KJV] See FIRSTBORN

FISH (73) [FISHERMEN, FISHING]

Ge 1:20 "Let the waters swarm with **f** and other life.
1:21 and every sort of **f** and every kind of bird.
1:22 saying, "Let the **f** multiply and fill the oceans.
1:26 the **f** in the sea, the birds in the sky, and all the
1:28 Be masters over the **f** and birds and all the
9: 2 and all the birds and **f** will be afraid of you.
Ex 7:18 The **f** in it will die, and the river will stink.
7:21 The **f** in the river died, and the water became
20: 4 whether in the shape of birds or animals or **f**.
Nu 11: 5 "We remember all the **f** we used to eat for free in
11:22 Even if we caught all the **f** in the sea, would that be
Dt 4:18 a creeping creature or a **f**.
5: 8 whether in the shape of birds or animals or **f**.
1Ki 4:33 also speak about animals, birds, reptiles, and **f**.
2Ch 33:14 Gihon Spring in the Kidron Valley to the **F** Gate,
Ne 3: 3 The **F** Gate was built by the sons of Hassenaah.
12:39 past the **F** Gate and the Tower of Hananel,
13:16 There were also some men from Tyre bringing in **f**
Job 12: 8 will instruct you. Let the **f** of the sea speak to you.
Ps 8: 8 the birds in the sky, the **f** in the sea,
105:29 the nation's water into blood, / poisoning all the **f**.
Ecc 9:12 Like **f** in a net or birds in a snare, people are often
Isa 19: 8 Those who **f** with hooks and those who use nets
50: 2 I can turn rivers into deserts covered with dying **f**.
Eze 29: 4 and drag you out on the land with **f** sticking to your
29: 5 and all your **f** stranded in the desert to die.
38:20 all the **f**, birds, animals, and people—
47: 9 **F** will abound in the Dead Sea, for its waters will

47:10 **F** of every kind will fill the Dead Sea, just as they
Hos 4: 3 the animals, birds, and **f** have begun to disappear.
Am 4: 2 Every last one of you will be dragged away like a **f**
Jnh 1:17 Now the LORD had arranged for a great **f** to
1:17 And Jonah was inside the **f** for three days and three
2: 1 prayed to the LORD his God from inside the **f**.
2:10 Then the LORD ordered the **f** to spit up Jonah on
Hab 1:14 Are we but **f** to be caught and killed? Are we
Zep 1: 3 the birds of the air and the **f** in the sea will die.
1:10 "a cry of alarm will come from the **F** Gate
Mt 4:19 and I will show you how to **f** for people!"
7:10 Or if they ask for a **f**, do you give them a snake?
12:40 For as Jonah was in the belly of the great **f** for
13:47 thrown into the water and gathers **f** of every kind.
13:48 sit down, sort the good **f** into crates, and throw the
14:17 "We have only five loaves of bread and two **f**!"
14:19 And he took the five loaves and two **f**, looked up
14:19 he gave some of the bread and **f** to each disciple,
15:34 They replied, "Seven, and a few small **f**."
15:36 Then he took the seven loaves and the **f**,
17:27 Open the mouth of the first **f** you catch, and you
Mk 1:17 and I will show you how to **f** for people!"
6:38 "We have five loaves of bread and two **f**."
6:41 Jesus took the five loaves and two **f**, looked up
6:41 and **f** to the disciples to give to the people.
6:43 picked up twelve baskets of leftover bread and **f**.
8: 7 A few small **f** were found, too, so Jesus also
Lk 5: 4 let down your nets, and you will catch many **f**."
5: 7 and soon both boats were filled with **f** and on the
9:13 "We have only five loaves of bread and two **f**.
9:16 Jesus took the five loaves and two **f**, looked up
9:16 and **f** to the disciples to give to the people.
11:11 if your children ask for a **f**, do you give them a
24:42 They gave him a piece of broiled **f**,
Jn 6: 9 a young boy here with five barley loaves and two **f**.
6:11 the people. Afterward he did the same with the **f**.
21: 5 He called out, "Friends, have you caught any **f**?"
21: 6 side of the boat, and you'll get plenty of **f**!"
21: 6 draw in the net because there were so many **f** in it.
21: 9 charcoal fire was burning and **f** were frying over it,
21:10 "Bring some of the **f** you've just caught,"
21:11 There were 153 large **f**, and yet the net hadn't torn.
21:13 Then Jesus served them the bread and the **f**.
1Co 15:39 of flesh—whether of humans, animals, birds, or **f**.
Jas 3: 7 all kinds of animals and birds and reptiles and **f**,

FISHERMEN (8) [FISH]

Isa 19: 8 The **f** will weep for lack of work. Those who fish
Jer 16:16 "But now I am sending for many **f** who will catch
Eze 26: 5 It will be a place for **f** to spread their nets, for I
26:14 island a bare rock, a place for **f** to spread their nets.
47:10 **F** will stand along the shores of the Dead Sea,
Mt 4:18 fishing with a net, for they were commercial **f**.
Mk 1:16 fishing with a net, for they were commercial **f**.
Lk 5: 2 for the **f** had left them and were washing their nets.

FISHING (6) [FISH]

Eze 47:10 Dead Sea, **f** all the way from En-gedi to En-eglaim.
Mt 4:18 **f** with a net, for they were commercial fishermen.
13:47 the Kingdom of Heaven is like a **f** net that is
Mk 1:16 saw Simon and his brother, Andrew, **f** with a net,
Lk 5:10 be afraid! From now on you'll be **f** for people!"
Jn 21: 3 Simon Peter said, "I'm going **f**." "We'll come,

FISHPOOL [KJV] See SPARKLING (POOLS)

FIST (28) [FISTS, TIGHTFISTED]

Ex 17:16 "They have dared to raise their **f** against the
21:18 and one hits the other with a stone or **f**,
Nu 35:21 Or if someone angrily hits another person with a **f**
Ps 74:11 Unleash your powerful **f** and deliver a deathblow.
138: 7 You will clench your **f** against my angry enemies!
Isa 5:25 That is why he has raised his **f** to crush them.
5:25 will not be satisfied. His **f** is still poised to strike!
9:12 will not be satisfied. His **f** is still poised to strike.
9:17 will not be satisfied. His **f** is still poised to strike.
9:21 will not be satisfied. His **f** is still poised to strike.
10: 4 will not be satisfied. His **f** is still poised to strike.
10:32 He shakes his **f** at Mount Zion in Jerusalem.
19:16 They will cower in fear beneath the upraised **f** of
26:11 you threaten. / They do not see your upraised **f**.
31: 3 When the LORD clenches his **f** against them,
Jer 51:25 "I will raise my **f** against you, to roll you down
Eze 13: 9 I will raise my **f** against all the lying prophets,
14:13 and I lifted my **f** to crush them, cutting off their
16:27 That is why I struck you with my **f** and reduced
20:33 I will rule you with an iron **f** in great anger
25: 7 I will lift up my **f** against you. I will give you as
25:13 I will raise my **f** of judgment against Edom.
25:16 I will raise my **f** of judgment against the land of the
35: 3 and I will raise my **f** against you to destroy you
Zep 1: 4 "I will crush Judah and Jerusalem with my **f**
2:13 LORD will strike the lands of the north with his **f**.
2:15 that way will laugh in derision or shake a defiant **f**.
Zec 2: 9 I will raise my **f** to crush them, and their own

FISTS (10) [FIST]

Job 15:25 For they have clenched their **f** against God,
Ps 75: 4 I told the wicked, 'Don't raise your **f**!
75: 5 Don't lift your **f** in defiance at the heavens
Pr 30: 4 comes back down? Who holds the wind in his **f**?
Isa 8:21 they will rage and shake their **f** at heaven and curse
Jer 15: 6 I will raise my clenched **f** to destroy you.
Mt 26:67 they spit in Jesus' face and hit him with their **f**.
Mk 14:65 they blindfolded him and hit his face with their **f**.
Jn 19: 3 they mocked, and they hit him with their **f**.
Ac 7:54 and they shook their **f** in rage.

FIT (19) [FITS, FITTED, FITTING]

Ge 16: 6 your servant, you may deal with her as you see **f**."
49:20 "Asher will produce rich foods, / food **f** for kings.
Ex 25:14 **F** the poles into the rings at the sides of the Ark to
26:19 They will **f** into forty silver bases—two bases
26:32 with gold. The posts will **f** into silver bases.
26:37 with gold. The posts will **f** into five bronze bases.
27: 5 **F** the grating halfway down into the firebox,
27:10 They will be held up by twenty bronze posts that **f**
27:16 It will be attached to four posts that **f** into four
Nu 22:27 In a **f** of rage Balaam beat it again with his staff.
Jdg 5:25 and Jael gave him milk. / In a bowl **f** for kings,
10:15 Punish us as you see **f**, only rescue us today from
2Sa 15:25 "If the LORD sees **f**," David said, "he will bring
2Ki 24:16 and smiths, all of whom were strong and **f** for war.
Lk 9:62 then looks back is not **f** for the Kingdom of God."
Ac 22:22 with such a fellow! Kill him! He isn't **f** to live!"
Ro 9:22 of his judgment and are **f** only for destruction.
1Co 9:21 the Jewish law, I **f** in with them as much as I can.
Heb 2:10 one **f** to bring them into their salvation.

FITCHES [KJV] See DILL, SPELT

FITNESS (1)

1Ti 4: 7 and energy in training yourself for spiritual **f**.

FITS (1) [FIT]

Mt 11:30 For my yoke **f** perfectly, and the burden I give you

FITTED (2) [FIT]

Ex 27:11 150 feet of curtains held up by twenty posts **f** into
Eph 4:16 the whole body is **f** together perfectly.

FITTING (5) [FIT]

Ps 33: 1 with joy to the LORD, / for it is **f** to praise him.
Pr 15:23 Everyone enjoys a **f** reply; it is wonderful to say
17: 7 Eloquent speech is not **f** for a fool; even less are
lies **f** for a ruler.
Col 3:18 as is **f** for those who belong to the Lord.

FIVE (198) [FIFTH, FIVE-SIDED, FOUR-FIFTHS, ONE-FIFTH, THREE-FIFTHS]

Ge 8: 4 exactly **f** months from the time the flood began,
14: 9 Babylonia, and Ellasar—four kings against **f**.
18:28 Will you destroy the city for lack of **f**?"
43:34 **f** times as much as to any of the others.
45:11 for there are still **f** years of famine ahead of us.
45:22 but to Benjamin he gave **f** changes of clothes
47: 2 Joseph took **f** of his brothers with him
Ex 22: 1 For oxen the fine is **f** oxen for each one stolen.
26: 3 Join **f** of these sheets together into one set;
26: 3 then join the other **f** sheets into a second set.
26: 9 Join **f** of these together into one set, and join the
26:26 **f** crossbars for the north side of the Tabernacle
26:27 and **f** for the south side. Also make **f** crossbars for
26:37 Hang this curtain on gold hooks set into **f** posts
26:37 with gold. The posts will fit into **f** bronze bases.
36:10 **F** of these sheets were joined together to make one
set, and a second set was made of the other **f**.
36:16 The craftsmen joined **f** of these sheets together to
36:31 Then they made **f** crossbars from acacia wood to
36:32 They made another **f** for the north side and **f** for
the west side.
36:33 The middle crossbar of the **f** was halfway up the
36:38 This curtain was connected by **f** hooks to **f**
36:38 with gold. The **f** bases were molded from bronze.
Lev 14:10 along with **f** quarts of choice flour mixed with
26: 8 **F** of you will chase a hundred, and a hundred of
27: 5 A boy between **f** and twenty is valued at twenty
27: 6 and **f** years is valued at **f** pieces of silver;
27:16 fifty pieces of silver for an area that produces **f**
Nu 3:47 collect **f** pieces of silver for each person,
7:17 and two oxen, **f** rams, **f** male goats, and **f**
one-year-old male lambs for a peace offering.
7:23 and two oxen, **f** rams, **f** male goats, and **f**
one-year-old male lambs for a peace offering.
7:29 and two oxen, **f** rams, **f** male goats, and **f**
one-year-old male lambs for a peace offering.
7:35 and two oxen, **f** rams, **f** male goats, and **f**
one-year-old male lambs for a peace offering.
7:41 and two oxen, **f** rams, **f** male goats, and **f**
one-year-old male lambs for a peace offering.
7:47 and two oxen, **f** rams, **f** male goats, and **f**
one-year-old male lambs for a peace offering.
7:53 and two oxen, **f** rams, **f** male goats, and **f**
one-year-old male lambs for a peace offering.
7:59 and two oxen, **f** rams, **f** male goats, and **f**
one-year-old male lambs for a peace offering.
7:65 and two oxen, **f** rams, **f** male goats, and **f**
one-year-old male lambs for a peace offering.
7:71 and two oxen, **f** rams, **f** male goats, and **f**
one-year-old male lambs for a peace offering.
7:77 and two oxen, **f** rams, **f** male goats, and **f**
one-year-old male lambs for a peace offering.
7:83 and two oxen, **f** rams, **f** male goats, and **f**
one-year-old male lambs for a peace offering.
11:19 for just a day or two, or for **f** or ten or even twenty.
15: 9 **f** quarts of choice flour mixed with two quarts of
18:16 The redemption price is **f** pieces of silver,
28:12 **f** quarts with each bull, three quarts with the ram,
28:20 **f** quarts with each bull, three quarts with the ram,
28:28 **f** quarts with each bull, three quarts with the ram,
29: 3 **f** quarts with the bull, three quarts with the ram,
29: 9 **f** quarts of choice flour with the bull, three quarts
29:12 "**F** days later, you must call yet another holy
29:14 **f** quarts for each of the thirteen bulls, three quarts
31: 8 All **f** of the Midianite kings—Evi, Rekem, Zur,
31:28 Set apart one out of every **f** hundred as the
Jos 8:12 That night Joshua sent **f** thousand men to lie in
10: 5 So these **f** Amorite kings combined their armies for
10:16 the **f** kings escaped and hid in a cave at Makkedah.
10:20 and wiped out the **f** armies except for a tiny
10:22 opening of the cave and bring the **f** kings to me."
10:23 So they brought the **f** kings out of the cave—
10:26 Then Joshua killed each of the **f** kings and hung
them on **f** trees until evening.
13: 4 and includes the **f** Philistine cities of Gaza,
17: 3 had no sons. Instead, he had **f** daughters.
Jdg 3: 3 the Philistines (those living under the **f** Philistine
18: 2 So the men of Dan chose **f** warriors from among
18: 7 So the **f** men went on to the town of Laish,
18:14 The **f** men who had scouted out the land around
18:15 So the **f** men went over to Micah's house,
18:17 the **f** spies entered the shrine and took the carved
20:45 but Israel killed **f** thousand of them along the road.
1Sa 5: 8 So they called together the rulers of the **f** Philistine
6: 4 the plague has struck both you and your **f** rulers,
make **f** gold tumors and **f** gold rats,
6:16 The **f** Philistine rulers watched all this and
6:17 The **f** gold tumors that were sent by the Philistines
6:18 The **f** gold rats represented the **f** Philistine cities
6:18 which were controlled by the **f** rulers.
17:40 He picked up **f** smooth stones from a stream
21: 3 Give me **f** loaves of bread or anything else you
25:18 two skins of wine, **f** dressed sheep, nearly a bushel
25:42 she took along **f** of her servant girls as attendants,
2Sa 4: 4 He was **f** years old when Saul and Jonathan were
14:26 When he weighed it out, it came to **f** pounds!
21: 8 He also gave them the **f** sons of Saul's daughter
1Ki 7:39 He arranged **f** water carts on the south side of the
Temple and **f** on the north side.
7:49 **f** on the south and **f** on the north,
2Ki 7: 1 **f** quarts of fine flour will cost only half an ounce of
7:13 Let them take **f** of the remaining horses.
7:16 So it was true that **f** quarts of fine flour were sold
7:18 **f** quarts of fine flour will cost half an ounce of
13:19 "You should have struck the ground **f** or six
25:19 the Judean army, **f** of the king's personal advisers,
1Ch 2: 4 were Perez and Zerah. So Judah had **f** sons in all.
2: 6 Ethan, Heman, Calcol, and Darda—**f** in all.
3:20 His **f** other sons were Hashubah, Ohel, Berekiah,
4:32 Ain, Rimmon, Token, and Ashan—**f** towns
4:42 **F** hundred of these invaders from the tribe of
7: 3 and Isshiah. These **f** became the leaders of clans.
7: 4 for all **f** of them had many wives and many sons.
7: 7 and Iri. These **f** warriors were the leaders of clans.
2Ch 4: 6 **f** to the south of the Sea and **f** to the north.
4: 7 **F** were placed against the south wall, and **f** were
placed against the north wall.
4: 8 **f** along the south wall and **f** along the north wall.
23: 1 and made a pact with **f** army commanders:
35: 9 gave **f** thousand lambs and young goats and **f**
hundred bulls to the Levites for their
Est 9: 6 They killed **f** hundred people in the fortress of
9:12 "The Jews have killed **f** hundred people in the
Job 1: 3 three thousand camels, **f** hundred teams of oxen,
and **f** hundred female donkeys.
Isa 17: 6 four or **f** out on the tips of the limbs.
19:18 In that day **f** of Egypt's cities will follow the
30:17 of you. **F** of them will make all of you flee.
Hos 3: 2 and about **f** bushels of barley and a measure of
Mt 14:17 "We have only **f** loaves of bread and two fish!"
14:19 And he took the **f** loaves and two fish, looked up
14:21 About **f** thousand men had eaten from those **f**
16: 9 Don't you remember the **f** thousand I fed with **f**
20: 6 At **f** o'clock that evening he was in town again
20: 9 When those hired at **f** o'clock were paid,
25: 2 **F** of them were foolish, and **f** were wise.
25: 3 The **f** who were foolish took no oil for their lamps,
25: 4 but the other **f** were wise enough to take along
25: 8 Then the **f** foolish ones asked the others,
25:11 Later, when the other **f** bridesmaids returned,
25:15 He gave **f** bags of gold to one, two bags of gold to
25:16 The servant who received the **f** bags of gold began
25:20 The servant to whom he had entrusted the **f** bags of
25:20 you gave me **f** bags of gold to invest and I have
Mk 6:38 "We have **f** loaves of bread and two fish."
6:41 Jesus took the **f** loaves and two fish, looked up
6:44 **F** thousand men had eaten from those **f** loaves!
8:19 What about the **f** thousand men I fed with **f**
Lk 1:24 and went into seclusion for **f** months.
7:41 **f** hundred pieces of silver to one and fifty pieces to
9:13 "We have only **f** loaves of bread and two fish.
9:14 For there were about **f** thousand men there.
9:16 Jesus took the **f** loaves and two fish, looked up
12: 6 "What is the price of **f** sparrows? A couple of
14:19 Another said he had just bought **f** pair of oxen
16:28 For I have **f** brothers, and I want him to warn them
19:18 reported a good gain—**f** times the original amount.
19:19 the king said. 'You can be governor over **f** cities.'
Jn 4:18 for you have had **f** husbands, and you aren't even
5: 2 was the pool of Bethesda, with **f** covered porches.
6: 9 "There's a young boy here with **f** barley loaves
6:10 all of them—the men alone numbered **f** thousand—
6:13 There were only **f** barley loaves to start with,
Ac 4: 4 so that the number of believers totaled about **f**
20: 6 in Macedonia and **f** days later arrived in Troas,

24: 1 **F** days later Ananias, the high priest, arrived with
28: 23 from the **f** books of Moses and the books of the
1Co 14: 19 **f** understandable words that will help others than
15: 6 he was seen by more than **f** hundred of his
2Co 11: 24 **F** different times the Jews gave me thirty-nine
Rev 9: 5 but to torture them for **f** months with agony like
9: 10 This power was given to them for **f** months.
17: 10 **F** kings have already fallen, the sixth now reigns,

FIVE-SIDED (1) [FIVE, SIDE]
1Ki 6: 31 Solomon made double doors of olive wood with **f**

FIX (5) [FIXED]
Ex 23: 31 And I will **f** your boundaries from the Red Sea to
Pr 4: 25 and **f** your eyes on what lies before you.
Isa 22: 10 and tear some down to get stone to **f** the walls.
Php 4: 8 **F** your thoughts on what is true and honorable
1Ti 2: 9 attention to themselves by the way they **f** their hair

FIXED (4) [FIX]
Nu 36: 7 for the inheritance of every tribe must remain **f** as
2Ki 8: 11 Elisha stared at Hazael with a **f** gaze until Hazael
9: 30 her eyelids and **f** her hair and sat at a window.
Isa 26: 3 all who trust in you, / whose thoughts are **f** on you!

FLAG (5) [FLAGPOLE, FLAGS]
Isa 11: 12 He will raise a **f** among the nations for Israel to
18: 3 When I raise my battle **f** on the mountain, let all
62: 10 out the boulders; raise a **f** for all the nations to see.
Jer 50: 2 Raise a signal **f** so everyone will know that
51: 12 Raise the battle **f** against Babylon!

FLAG [KJV] See also BULRUSHES

FLAGPOLE (1) [FLAG, POLE]
Isa 30: 17 You will be left like a lonely **f** on a distant

FLAGRANT (1)
Jer 23: 32 Their imaginary dreams are **f** lies that lead my

FLAGS (2) [FLAG]
Isa 13: 2 "See the **f** waving as the enemy attacks.
31: 9 with terror and flee when they see the battle **f**,"

FLAIL (1)
Isa 28: 27 on cummin; instead, it is beaten softly with a **f**.

FLAKES (1)
Ex 16: 14 thin **f**, white like frost, covered the ground.

FLAME (13) [AFLAME, FLAMED, FLAMES, FLAMING]
Job 15: 30 The **f** will burn them up, and the breath of God will
Ps 58: 9 and old, / faster than a pot heats on an open **f**.
83: 14 through a forest / and as a **f** sets mountains ablaze,
104: 32 his glance; / the mountains burst into **f** at his touch.
106: 18 upon their followers; / a **f** consumed the wicked.
118: 12 like bees; / they blazed against me like a roaring **f**.
SS 8: 6 Love flashes like fire, the brightest kind of **f**.
Isa 31: 9 the LORD, whose **f** burns brightly in Jerusalem.
Eze 1: 27 he looked like a burning **f**, shining with splendor.
8: 2 From the waist down he looked like a burning **f**.
Ac 7: 30 an angel appeared to Moses in the **f** of a burning
Jas 3: 6 And the tongue is a **f** of fire. It is full of
3: 6 course of your life into a blazing **f** of destruction,

FLAMED (4) [FLAME]
Nu 21: 28 A fire **f** forth from Heshbon, / a blaze from the city
Jdg 6: 21 and fire **f** up from the rock and consumed all he
2Sa 22: 9 from his mouth; / glowing coals **f** forth from him.
Ps 18: 8 from his mouth; / glowing coals **f** forth from him.

FLAMES (30) [FLAME]
Ex 3: 2 was amazed because the bush was engulfed in **f**,
Dt 4: 11 **F** shot into the sky, shrouded in black clouds
Jdg 13: 20 As the **f** from the altar shot up toward the sky,
2Sa 22: 9 from his nostrils; / fierce **f** leaped from his mouth;
1Ki 16: 18 and burned it down over himself and died in the **f**.
Job 41: 21 would kindle coals, for **f** shoot from its mouth.
Ps 18: 8 from his nostrils; / fierce **f** leaped from his mouth;
104: 4 are your messengers; / **f** of fire are your servants.
Isa 13: 8 They look helplessly at one another as the **f** of the
30: 30 It will descend with devouring **f**, with cloudbursts,
43: 2 will not be burned up; the **f** will not consume you.
Jer 17: 27 and no one will be able to put out the roaring **f**.' "
Eze 16: 26 fanning the **f** of my anger with your increasing
20: 47 The terrible **f** will not be quenched; they will
Da 3: 22 the **f** leaped out and killed the soldiers as they
3: 23 securely tied, fell down into the roaring **f**.
3: 25 around in the fire. They aren't even hurt by the **f**!
Hos 7: 6 and in the morning it **f** forth like a raging fire.
Am 5: 6 in Bethel certainly won't be able to quench the **f**!
Lk 16: 24 my tongue, because I am in anguish in these **f**.'
Ac 2: 3 what looked like **f** or tongues of fire appeared
1Co 3: 15 but like someone escaping through a wall of **f**.
2Ti 1: 6 This is why I remind you to fan into **f** the spiritual
Heb 11: 34 quenched the **f** of fire, and escaped death by the
2Pe 3: 12 on fire and the elements will melt away in the **f**.
Jude 1: 23 Rescue others by snatching them from the **f** of
Rev 1: 14 as snow. And his eyes were bright like **f** of fire.
2: 18 whose eyes are bright like **f** of fire, whose feet are
4: 5 the throne were seven lampstands with burning **f**.
19: 12 His eyes were bright like **f** of fire, and on his head

FLAMING (14) [FLAME]
Ge 3: 24 And a **f** sword flashed back and forth,
15: 17 and a **f** torch pass between the halves of the
Dt 33: 2 from Meribah-kadesh / with **f** fire at his right hand.
Ps 7: 13 his deadly weapons / and ignite his **f** arrows.
21: 9 You will destroy them as in a **f** furnace / when you
Isa 10: 16 proud troops, and a **f** fire will ignite your glory.
10: 17 Holy One, will be a **f** fire that will destroy them.
66: 15 fury of his anger and the **f** fire of his hot rebuke.
Da 3: 26 as close as he could to the door of the **f** furnace
10: 6 like lightning, and his eyes were like **f** torches.
2Th 1: 8 in **f** fire, bringing judgment on those who don't
Heb 1: 7 swift as the wind, / and servants made of **f** fire."
12: 18 to a place of **f** fire, darkness, gloom,
Rev 8: 10 and a great **f** star fell out of the sky, burning like a

FLANK (1) [FLANKED]
Eze 25: 9 I will open up their eastern **f** and wipe out their

FLANKED (3) [FLANK]
Ex 27: 14 entrance will be on the east end, **f** by two curtains.
38: 14 entrance was on the east side, **f** by two curtains.
Eze 40: 18 This pavement **f** the gates and extended out from

FLAP (1) [FLAPS]
Isa 10: 14 No one can even **f** a wing against me or utter a

FLAPS (1) [FLAP]
Job 39: 13 "The ostrich **f** her wings grandly, but they are no

FLARE (2) [FLARED]
Dt 6: 15 His anger will **f** up against you and wipe you from
Ps 2: 12 for his anger can **f** up in an instant.

FLARED (2) [FLARE]
1Ki 7: 26 and its rim **f** out like a cup and resembled a lily
2Ch 4: 5 and its rim **f** out like a cup and resembled a lily

FLASH (8) [FLASHED, FLASHES, FLASHING]
Job 37: 11 clouds with moisture, and they **f** with his lightning.
37: 15 and causes the lightning to **f** forth from his clouds?
39: 23 arrows rattle against it, and the spear and javelin **f**.
Eze 21: 10 for terrible slaughter; it will **f** like lightning!
Na 2: 3 Shields **f** red in the sunlight! The attack begins!
Hab 3: 4 Rays of brilliant light **f** from his hands. He rejoices
Lk 10: 18 "I saw Satan falling from heaven as a **f** of
Rev 13: 13 such as making fire **f** down to earth from heaven

FLASHED (13) [FLASH]
Ge 3: 24 And a flaming sword **f** back and forth,
Ex 15: 7 Your anger **f** forth; / it consumed them as fire
2Sa 22: 15 his lightning **f**, and they were confused.
1Ki 18: 38 Immediately the fire of the LORD **f** down from
2Ch 7: 1 fire **f** down from heaven and burned up the burnt
Ps 18: 14 his lightning **f**, and they were greatly confused.
77: 17 crackled in the sky. / Your arrows of lightning **f**.
Eze 1: 4 driving before it a huge cloud that **f** with lightning
Mt 26: 75 Suddenly, Jesus' words **f** through Peter's mind:
Mk 14: 72 Suddenly, Jesus' words **f** through Peter's mind:
Rev 8: 5 and thunder crashed, lightning **f**, and there was a
11: 19 Lightning **f**, thunder crashed and roared; there was
16: 18 the thunder crashed and rolled, and lightning **f**.

FLASHES (11) [FLASH]
Job 37: 3 and his lightning **f** out in every direction.
41: 18 "When it sneezes, it **f** light! Its eyes are like the
Ps 97: 4 His lightning **f** out across the world. / The earth
105: 32 and **f** of lightning overwhelmed the land.
SS 8: 6 Love **f** like fire, the brightest kind of flame.
Eze 1: 14 living beings darted to and fro like **f** of lightning.
21: 15 It **f** like lightning; it is polished for slaughter!
Da 10: 6 From his face came **f** like lightning, and his eyes
Lk 17: 24 It will be as evident as the lightning that **f** across
Rev 4: 5 And from the throne came **f** of lightning
11: 5 fire **f** from the mouths of the prophets

FLASHING (5) [FLASH]
Dt 32: 41 when I sharpen my **f** sword / and begin to carry out
Eze 1: 13 and it looked as though lightning was **f** back
21: 28 it is sharpened to destroy, **f** like lightning!
Na 3: 3 See the **f** swords and glittering spears in the
Hab 3: 11 from your arrows and the **f** of your glittering spear.

FLASK (6)
1Sa 10: 1 Then Samuel took a **f** of olive oil and poured it
1Ki 1: 39 There Zadok the priest took a **f** of olive oil from
2Ki 4: 2 at all, except a **f** of olive oil," she replied.
4: 4 Pour olive oil from your **f** into the jars,
Jer 48: 11 She has not been poured from **f** to **f**, and she is

FLAT (6) [FLATLY, FLATS, FLATTEN]
Nu 11: 8 they boiled it in a pot and made it into **f** cakes.
Dt 22: 8 have a barrier around the edge of its **f** rooftop.
Jdg 7: 13 It hit a tent, turned it over, and knocked it **f**!"
Pr 10: 8 but babbling fools fall **f** on their faces.
Da 4: 29 he was taking a walk on the **f** roof of the royal
Ac 10: 9 nearing the city, Peter went up to the **f** roof to pray.

FLATLY (1) [FLAT]
Jn 1: 20 He **f** denied it. "I am not the Messiah," he said.

FLATS (1) [FLAT]
Jer 17: 6 on the salty **f** where no one lives.

FLATTEN (1) [FLAT]
Zec 4: 7 stand in Zerubbabel's way; it will **f** out before him!

FLATTER (4) [FLATTERING, FLATTERY]
Job 32: 21 I won't play favorites or try to **f** anyone.
Pr 29: 5 To **f** people is to lay a trap for their feet.
Da 11: 32 He will **f** those who have violated the covenant
Jude 1: 16 and they **f** others to get favors in return.

FLATTERING (1) [FLATTER]
Ps 12: 2 speaking with **f** lips and insincere hearts.

FLATTERY (9) [FLATTER]
Ps 5: 9 from an open grave. / Their speech is filled with **f**.
12: 3 May the LORD bring their **f** to an end
Pr 2: 16 from the **f** of the adulterous woman.
7: 5 from listening to the **f** of an adulterous woman.
7: 21 with her pretty speech. With her **f** she enticed him.
26: 28 A lying tongue hates its victims, and **f** causes ruin.
28: 23 the end, people appreciate frankness more than **f**.
Da 11: 21 and take over the kingdom by **f** and intrigue.
1Th 2: 5 Never once did we try to win you with **f**, as you

FLAUNTED (1)
Eze 23: 18 because she **f** herself before them and gave herself

FLAVOR (3) [FLAVORLESS]
Mt 5: 13 the earth. But what good is salt if it has lost its **f**?
Mk 9: 50 But if it loses its **f**, how do you make it salty again?
Lk 14: 34 But if it loses its **f**, how do you make it salty again?

FLAVORLESS (1) [FLAVOR]
Lk 14: 35 **F** salt is good neither for the soil nor for fertilizer.

FLAX (6)
Ex 9: 31 All the **f** and barley were destroyed
9: 31 the barley was ripe and the **f** was in bloom.
Jos 2: 6 up to the roof and hidden them beneath piles of **f**.)
Jdg 15: 14 ropes on his arms as if they were burnt strands of **f**,
Pr 31: 13 She finds wool and **f** and busily spins it.
Isa 19: 9 The weavers will have no **f** or cotton, for the crops

FLAY [KJV] See CUT, PREPARE, SKINNED

FLEA (2) [FLEAS]
1Sa 24: 14 one who is as worthless as a dead dog or a **f**?
26: 20 the king of Israel come out to search for a single **f**?

FLEAS (1) [FLEA]
Jer 43: 12 land of Egypt as a shepherd picks **f** from his cloak.

FLED (95) [FLEE]
Ge 14: 10 the army of the kings of Sodom and Gomorrah **f**,
14: 15 Kedorlaomer's army **f**, but Abram chased them to
35: 1 the God who appeared to you when you **f** from
39: 13 she saw that she had his shirt and that he had **f**,
Ex 2: 15 But Moses **f** from Pharaoh and escaped to the land
Nu 16: 34 All of the people of Israel **f** as they heard their
35: 32 from someone who has **f** to a city of refuge,
Dt 32: 37 are their gods, / the rocks they **f** to for refuge?
Jos 7: 8 am I to say, now that Israel has **f** from its enemies?
8: 15 and the Israelite army **f** toward the wilderness as
8: 20 For the Israelites who had **f** in the direction of the
Jdg 6: 2 so cruel that the Israelites **f** to the mountains,
7: 22 Those who were not killed **f** to places as far away
8: 12 Zebah and Zalmunna, the two Midianite kings, **f**,
9: 51 inside the city, and the entire population **f** to it.
11: 3 So Jephthah **f** from his brothers and lived in the
20: 45 The survivors **f** into the wilderness toward the rock
1Sa 4: 10 that day. The survivors turned and **f** to their tents.
20: 1 David now **f** from Naioth in Ramah and found
22: 20 of the sons of Ahimelech, escaped and **f** to David.
27: 4 Word soon reached Saul that David had **f** to Gath,
30: 17 except four hundred young men who **f** on camels.
31: 7 sons were dead, they abandoned their towns and **f**.
2Sa 1: 4 The man replied, "Our entire army **f**. Many men
4: 3 because the original people of Beeroth **f** to Gittaim,
4: 4 the capital, the child's nurse grabbed him and **f**.
4: 7 they **f** across the Jordan Valley through the night.
10: 18 But again the Arameans **f** from the Israelites.
13: 29 other sons of the king jumped on their mules and **f**.
13: 37 Absalom **f** to his grandfather, Talmai son of
18: 17 over it. And the army of Israel **f** to their homes.
19: 8 the Israelites who supported Absalom had **f** to their
23: 9 the Philistines when the entire Israelite army had **f**.
23: 11 in a field full of lentils. The Israelite army **f**,
1Ki 2: 7 for they took care of me when I **f** from your
11: 17 and a few of his father's royal officials had **f**.
11: 23 Rezon had **f** from his master, King Hadadezer of
11: 24 Rezon and his men **f** to Damascus, where he
11: 40 but he **f** to King Shishak of Egypt and stayed there
12: 2 for he had **f** to Egypt to escape from King
12: 18 quickly jumped into his chariot and **f** to Jerusalem.
19: 3 Elijah was afraid and **f** for his life. He went to

20:20 suddenly the entire Aramean army panicked and **f**.
20:30 The rest **f** behind the walls of Aphek, but the wall
20:30 Ben-hadad **f** into the city and hid in a secret room.
2Ki 7:7 So they panicked and **f** into the night,
7:7 and everything else, and they **f** for their lives.
8:21 Jehoram's army, however, deserted him and **f**.
9:23 King Joram reined the chariot horses around and **f**,
9:27 he **f** along the road to Beth-haggan.
14:12 of Israel, and its army scattered and **f** for home.
14:19 Amaziah's life in Jerusalem, and he **f** to Lachish.
25:4 and **f** through the gate between the two walls
25:26 well as the army commanders, **f** in panic to Egypt,
1Ch 10:7 sons were dead, they abandoned their towns and **f**.
11:13 in a field full of barley, and the Israelite army **f**.
19:18 But again the Arameans **f** from the Israelites.
2Ch 10:2 for he had **f** to Egypt to escape from King
10:18 quickly jumped into his chariot and **f** to Jerusalem.
12:5 who had all **f** to Jerusalem because of Shishak.
13:16 The Israelite army **f** from Judah, and God handed
14:12 of Asa and the army of Judah, and the enemy **f**.
25:22 of Israel, and its army scattered and **f** for home.
25:27 against his life in Jerusalem, and he **f** to Lachish.
Ps 3:T regarding the time David **f** from his son Absalom.
57:T regarding the time he **f** from Saul and went into the
78:9 their backs and **f** when the day of battle came.
104:7 At the sound of your rebuke, the water **f**;
104:7 at the sound of your thunder, it **f** away.
Isa 21:15 They have **f** from drawn swords and sharp arrows
Jer 9:10 no more; the birds and wild animals all have **f**.
39:4 so they **f** when the darkness of night arrived.
40:12 to Judah from the places to which they had **f**.
43:5 from the nearby countries to which they had **f**.
44:14 Of those who **f** to Egypt with dreams of returning
46:15 Why have your warriors **f** in terror? They cannot
52:7 and **f** through the gate between the two walls
La 4:15 So they **f** to distant lands and wandered there
4:19 If we **f** to the mountains, they found us. If we hid
Hos 12:12 Jacob **f** to the land of Aram and earned a wife by
Mt 8:16 All the spirits **f** when he commanded them to
8:33 The herdsmen **f** to the nearby city, telling everyone
26:56 At that point, all the disciples deserted him and **f**.
Mk 5:14 The herdsmen **f** to the nearby city
16:8 The women **f** from the tomb, trembling
Lk 8:34 they **f** to the nearby city and the surrounding
Ac 7:29 he **f** the country and lived as a foreigner in the land
8:1 and all the believers except the apostles **f** into
8:4 But the believers who had **f** Jerusalem went
11:19 the believers who had **f** from Jerusalem during the
14:6 the apostles learned of it, they **f** for their lives.
19:16 and attacked them with such violence that they **f**
Heb 6:18 we who have **f** to him for refuge can take new
Rev 12:6 And the woman **f** into the wilderness, where God
20:11 The earth and sky **f** from his presence, but they

FLEE (67) [FLED, FLEEING, FLEES]

Ge 27:43 you should do. **F** to your uncle Laban in Haran.
Lev 26:25 If you **f** to your cities, I will send a plague to
Nu 10:35 enemies be scattered! Let them **f** before you!"
35:6 has accidentally killed someone can **f** for safety.
35:11 designate cities of refuge for people to **f** to if they
35:15 Anyone who accidentally kills someone may **f**
Dt 4:42 having any previous hostility could **f** for safety.
19:3 so that anyone who has killed someone can **f** there
19:4 the slayer may **f** to any of these cities and be safe.
19:5 the slayer could **f** to one of the cities of refuge
1Sa 31:1 attacked Israel, forcing the Israelites to **f**.
2Sa 15:14 "Then we must **f** at once, or it will be too late!"
2Ki 19:21 of Jerusalem / scoffs and shakes her head as you **f**.
1Ch 10:1 attacked Israel, forcing the Israelites to **f**.
Job 27:22 without mercy. They struggle to **f** from its power.
30:3 and **f** to the deserts and the wastelands,
41:28 Arrows cannot make it **f**. Stones shot from a sling
Ps 68:12 Enemy kings and their armies **f**, / while the women
SS 2:17 Before the dawn comes and the shadows **f** away,
4:6 Before the dawn comes and the shadows **f** away,
Isa 15:5 Its people **f** to Zoar and Eglath-shelishiyah.
15:7 they can carry and **f** across the Ravine of Willows.
17:13 They will **f** like chaff scattered by the wind or like
22:3 All your leaders **f**. They surrender without
23:6 **F** now to Tarshish! Wail, you people who live by
23:12 Even if you **f** to Cyprus, you will find no rest."
24:18 Those who **f** in terror will fall into a trap, and those
30:17 of you. Five of them will make all of you **f**.
31:8 of God will strike them, and they will panic and **f**.
31:9 with terror and **f** when they see the battle flags,"
33:3 of your voice. When you stand up, the nations **f**!
37:22 of Jerusalem / scoffs and shakes her head as you **f**.
43:14 And the Babylonians will be forced to **f** in those
Jer 4:5 'Run for your lives! **F** to the fortified cities!'
4:6 a signal toward Jerusalem: '**F** now! Do not delay!'
4:29 the people **f** in terror from the cities.
6:1 you people of Benjamin! **F** from Jerusalem!
46:6 The swiftest cannot **f**; the mightiest warriors
46:6 **F** for your lives! Hide in the wilderness!
48:19 They shout to those who **f** from Moab, 'What has
48:28 people of Moab, **f** from your cities and towns!
48:44 "Those who **f** in terror will fall into a trap,
48:45 "The people **f** as far as Heshbon but are unable to
49:5 and no one will help your exiles as they **f**.
49:8 Turn and **f**! Hide in deep caves, you people of
49:24 has become feeble, and all her people turn to **f**.
49:30 **F** for your lives," says the LORD.
50:3 will be gone; both people and animals will **f**.
50:8 "But now, **f** from Babylon! Leave the land of the
51:6 **F** from Babylon! Save yourselves! Don't get
51:45 "Listen, my people, **f** from Babylon.
51:50 Do not stand and watch—**f** while you can!
Mic 1:13 Use your swiftest chariots and **f**, you people of
Zec 2:6 **F** from the north, for I have scattered you to the
14:5 You will **f** through this valley, for it will reach
14:5 you will **f** as you did from the earthquake in the
Mt 2:13 "Get up and **f** to Egypt with the child and his
3:7 "Who warned you to **f** God's coming judgment?
10:23 you are persecuted in one town, **f** to the next.
24:16 "Then those in Judea must **f** to the hills.
Mk 13:14 "Then those in Judea must **f** to the hills.
Lk 3:7 Who warned you to **f** God's coming judgment?
4:36 Even evil spirits obey him and **f** at his command!"
21:21 Then those in Judea must **f** to the hills. Let those in
1Co 10:14 my dear friends, **f** from the worship of idols.
Jas 4:7 Resist the Devil, and he will **f** from you.
Rev 9:6 They will long to die, but death will **f** away!

FLEE(TH) [KJV] See FLIGHT, FLY, FUGITIVE, HURRIED, RUN(NING)

FLEECE (4)

Jdg 6:37 If the **f** is wet with dew in the morning
6:38 he squeezed the **f** and wrung out a whole bowlful
6:39 This time let the **f** remain dry while the ground
6:40 The **f** was dry in the morning, but the ground was

FLEEING (9) [FLEE]

Ge 35:7 to him there at Bethel when he was **f** from Esau.
Lev 26:36 sound of a leaf driven by the wind will send you **f**.
26:37 over each other in flight, as though **f** in battle.
Jdg 7:23 who joined in the chase after the **f** army of Midian.
2Sa 24:13 three months of **f** from your enemies, or three days
1Ki 2:8 He cursed me with a terrible curse as I was **f** to
Ps 39:4 my days are numbered, / and that my life is **f** away.
Pr 6:5 escaping from a hunter, like a bird **f** from a net.
Isa 10:31 There go the people of Madmenah, all **f**.

FLEES (3) [FLEE]

Job 9:25 swiftly than a runner. It **f** away, filled with tragedy.
Jer 46:5 But look! The Egyptian army **f** in terror.
46:22 Silent as a serpent gliding away, Egypt **f**.

FLEET (6) [FLEETING]

1Ki 9:26 Later King Solomon built a **f** of ships at
10:22 The king had a **f** of trading ships that sailed with Hiram's **f**.
22:48 Jehoshaphat also built a **f** of trading ships to sail to
2Ch 9:21 The king had a **f** of trading ships manned by the
20:36 Together they built a **f** of trading ships at the port

FLEETING (1) [FLEET]

Heb 11:25 people instead of enjoying the **f** pleasures of sin.

FLESH (51)

FLESH AND BLOOD (7) Ge 29:14; Jdg 9:2; 2Sa 19:12; 1Co 15:50; Eph 6:12; Heb 2:14,14

Ge 2:23 "She is part of my own **f** and bone!
6:3 for such a long time, for they are only mortal **f**.
17:11 the **f** of his foreskin must be cut off. This will be a
29:14 "Just think, my very own **f** and blood!"
40:19 Then birds will come and peck away at your **f**."
Ex 21:28 the bull must be stoned, and its **f** may not be eaten.
Lev 26:29 You will eat the **f** of your own sons and daughters.
Dt 28:53 so severe that you will eat the **f** of your own sons
28:55 He will refuse to give them a share of the **f** he is devouring—the **f** of one of his own children—
32:42 drunk with blood, / and my sword will devour **f**—
Jdg 8:7 I will return and tear your **f** with the thorns
9:2 And remember, I am your own **f** and blood!"
1Sa 17:44 and I'll give your **f** to the birds and wild animals!"
2Sa 19:12 my relatives, my own tribe, my own **f** and blood!
1Ki 19:21 wood from the plow to build a fire to roast their **f**.
2Ki 5:14 And his **f** became as healthy as a young child's,
9:36 the plot of land in Jezreel, dogs will eat Jezebel's **f**.
Job 7:5 and scabs. My **f** breaks open, full of pus.
10:11 You clothed me with skin and **f**, and you knit my
16:9 God hates me and tears angrily at my **f**. He gnashes
41:23 Its **f** is hard and firm, not soft and fat.
Ps 79:2 for the birds of heaven. / The **f** of your godly ones
Isa 31:3 Their horses are puny **f**, not mighty spirits!
49:26 I will feed your enemies with their own **f**.
La 3:4 He has made my skin and **f** grow old. He has
Eze 32:5 I will cover the hills with your **f** and fill the valleys
37:6 I will put **f** and muscles on you and cover you with
37:8 as I watched, muscles and **f** formed over the bones.
39:17 of Israel, and there eat the **f** and drink the blood!
39:18 Eat the **f** of mighty men and drink the blood of
39:19 Gorge yourselves with **f** until you are glutted;
Mic 3:2 skin my people alive and tear the **f** off their bones.
3:3 You eat my people's **f**, cut away their skin,
Zec 14:12 become like walking corpses, their **f** rotting away.
Jn 6:51 this bread is my **f**, offered so the world may live."
6:52 "How can this man give us his **f** to eat?"
6:53 unless you eat the **f** of the Son of Man and drink
6:54 But those who eat my **f** and drink my blood have
6:55 For my **f** is the true food, and my blood is the true
6:56 All who eat my **f** and drink my blood remain in
1Co 15:39 and plants, so also there are different kinds of **f**—
15:50 is that **f** and blood cannot inherit the Kingdom of
2Co 12:7 I was given a thorn in my **f**, a messenger from
Eph 6:12 For we are not fighting against people made of **f**
1Ti 3:16 mystery of our faith: / Christ appeared in the **f**
Heb 2:14 made of **f** and blood—Jesus also became **f** and blood by being born in
Jas 5:3 you were counting on will eat away your **f** in hell.
Rev 17:16 They will strip her naked, eat her **f**, and burn her
19:18 Come and eat the **f** of kings, captains, and strong

FLESHHOOK [KJV] See FORK

FLEW (19) [FLY]

Ge 8:7 and released a raven that **f** back and forth until the
30:2 Jacob **f** into a rage. "Am I God?" he asked.
Nu 24:10 King Balak **f** into a rage against Balaam.
1Sa 14:32 That evening they **f** upon the battle plunder
2Sa 22:11 Mounted on a mighty angel, he **f**, / soaring on the
Ne 4:1 the wall. He **f** into a rage and mocked the Jews,
Ps 18:10 Mounted on a mighty angel, he **f**, / soaring on the
Isa 6:2 their feet, and with the remaining two they **f**.
6:6 Then one of the seraphim **f** over to the altar,
Eze 1:19 When they **f** upward, the wheels went up, too.
1:21 When the living beings **f** into the air, the wheels
1:24 As they **f** their wings roared like waves crashing
10:16 stayed beside them, going with them as they **f**.
10:19 the cherubim **f** with their wheels to the east gate of
27:7 finest linen, and they **f** as a banner above you.
Da 3:13 Then Nebuchadnezzar **f** into a rage and ordered
Zec 5:9 they picked up the basket and **f** with it into the sky.
Ac 16:26 All the doors **f** open, and the chains of every
Rev 8:13 And I heard a single eagle crying loudly as it **f**

FLICKERING (3)

Eze 1:27 he looked like gleaming amber, **f** like a fire.
Na 2:4 the squares, swift as lightning, **f** like torches.
Ac 20:8 where we met was lighted with many **f** lamps.

FLIES (13) [FLY]

Ex 8:21 I will send swarms of **f** throughout Egypt.
8:22 where the Israelites live. No **f** will be found there.
8:24 There were terrible swarms of **f** in Pharaoh's
8:24 The whole country was thrown into chaos by the **f**.
8:29 "I will ask the LORD to cause the swarms of **f** to
8:30 and asked the LORD to remove all the **f**.
Dt 19:5 them swings an ax and the ax head **f** off the handle,
Ps 78:45 He sent vast swarms of **f** to consume them
105:31 When he spoke, **f** descended on the Egyptians,
147:15 his orders to the world— / how swiftly his word **f**!
Ecc 10:1 Dead **f** will cause even a bottle of perfume to stink!
Isa 7:18 They will swarm around you like **f**. Like bees,
51:6 The people of the earth will die like **f**, but my

FLIGHT (9) [FLY]

Ge 31:22 Laban didn't learn of their **f** for three days.
Lev 26:37 you will stumble over each other in **f**, as though
Dt 32:30 of them, / and two people put ten thousand to **f**,
Jos 23:10 Each one of you will put to **f** a thousand of the
1Ki 6:8 and another **f** of stairs between the second
Mt 24:20 And pray that your **f** will not be in winter or on the
Mk 13:18 And pray that your **f** will not be in winter.
Heb 11:34 became strong in battle and put whole armies to **f**.
Rev 4:7 of an eagle with wings spread out as though in **f**.

FLIMSY (2)

Job 27:18 as a spiderweb, as **f** as a shelter made of branches.
Eze 13:10 It's as if the people have built a **f** wall, and these

FLING (1)

Jer 10:18 I will **f** you from this land and pour great troubles

FLINT (3) [FLINTY]

Ex 4:25 his wife, took a **f** knife and circumcised her son.
Jos 5:2 "Use knives of **f** to make the Israelites a
5:3 So Joshua made **f** knives and circumcised the

FLINTY (1) [FLINT]

Job 28:9 People know how to tear apart **f** rocks and overturn

FLIRTING (1)

Isa 3:16 Their eyes rove among the crowds, **f** with the men.

FLIT (1)

Jer 2:36 you **f** from one ally to another asking for help.

FLOAT (2) [FLOATED]

1Ki 5:9 We will **f** them along the coast to whatever place
2Ch 2:16 and will **f** the logs in rafts down the coast of the

FLOATED (3) [FLOAT]

Ge 7:18 above the ground, the boat **f** safely on the surface.
2Ki 6:6 Then the ax head rose to the surface and **f**.
Ezr 3:7 and **f** along the coast of the Mediterranean Sea to

FLOCK (78) [FLOCKED, FLOCKS]

Ge 4:4 brought several choice lambs from the best of his **f**.
29:10 rolled away the stone and watered his uncle's **f**.
30:33 If you find in my **f** any white sheep or goats that
30:36 Meanwhile, Jacob stayed and cared for Laban's **f**.
30:40 Jacob added them to his own **f**, thus separating the lambs from Laban's **f**.
30:40 the streaked and dark-colored rams in Laban's **f**.
30:40 This is how he built his **f** from Laban's.
31:8 the whole **f** began to produce speckled lambs.
31:10 and saw that the male goats mating with the **f** were

31:12 males are mating with the females of your f.
31:39 to you and ask you to reduce the count of your f?
31:41 your two daughters, and six years to get the f.
38:17 "I'll send you a young goat from my f,"
Ex 3: 1 One day Moses was tending the f of his
Lev 1:10 sacrifice for a whole burnt offering is from the f,
3: 6 present a peace offering to the LORD from the f,
5: 6 to the LORD as their penalty a female from the f,
5:15 they must bring to the LORD a ram from the f as
5:18 they must bring to the priest a ram from the f as a
22:21 a peace offering to the LORD from the herd or f,
22:28 on the same day, whether from the herd or the f.
Dt 15:14 Give him a generous farewell gift from your f,
16: 2 Your Passover sacrifice may be from either the f
32:14 fed them curds from the herd and milk from the f,
1Sa 17:34 a lion or a bear comes to steal a lamb from the f,
Job 21:11 Their children skip about like lambs in a f of
Ps 77:20 You led your people along that road like a f of
78:52 But he led his own people like a f of sheep,
80: 1 O Shepherd of Israel, / you who lead Israel like a f.
SS 1: 7 O my love, where are you leading your f today?
1: 8 follow the trail of my f to the shepherds' tents,
6: 5 is like a f of goats frisking down the slopes of
Isa 40:11 He will feed his f like a shepherd. He will carry the
Jer 13:17 because the LORD's f will be led away into exile.
13:20 Where is your f—your beautiful f—that he
23: 2 "Instead of leading my f to safety, you have
23: 3 But I will gather together the remnant of my f from
25:34 Roll in the dust, you leaders of the f!
25:36 to the leaders of the f shouting in despair,
31:10 and watch over them as a shepherd does his f.
Eze 24: 5 Use only the best sheep from the f and heap fuel on
34: 8 you abandoned my f and left them to be attacked
34:10 them responsible for what has happened to my f.
34:10 I will take away their right to feed the f, along with
34:10 I will rescue my f from their mouths; the sheep
34:12 I will be like a shepherd looking for his scattered f.
34:17 "And as for you, my f, my people, this is what the
34:19 All that is left for my f to eat is what you have
34:21 and hungry f until they are scattered to distant
34:22 So I will rescue my f, and they will no longer be
34:31 You are my f, the sheep of my pasture. You are my
43:23 that has no defects and a perfect ram from the f.
43:25 and a ram from the f will be sacrificed as a sin
Hos 11:11 Like a f of birds, they will come from Egypt.
Am 7:15 But the LORD called me away from my f
Mic 2:12 again like sheep in a fold, like a f in its pasture.
5: 4 And he will stand to lead his f with the LORD's
7:14 and rule your people; lead your f in green pastures.
Zec 10: 3 Almighty has arrived to look after his f of Judah;
11: 4 and care for a f that is intended for slaughter.
11: 7 So I cared for the f intended for slaughter—the f
that was oppressed.
11:17 for this worthless shepherd who abandons the f!
Mal 1:14 cheat who promises to give a fine ram from his f
Mt 10:31 you are more valuable to him than a whole f of
26:31 and the sheep of the f will be scattered.'
Lk 12: 7 you are more valuable to him than a whole f of
12:32 "So don't be afraid, little f. For it gives your
Jn 10: 4 After he has gathered his own f, he walks ahead of
10:12 And so the wolf attacks them and scatters the f.
10:16 and there will be one f with one shepherd.
10:26 don't believe me because you are not part of my f.
Ac 20:28 Be sure that you feed and shepherd God's f—
20:29 come in among you after I leave, not sparing the f.
1Co 9: 7 What shepherd takes care of a f of sheep and isn't
1Pe 5: 2 Care for the f of God entrusted to you. Watch over

FLOCKED (1) [FLOCK]

Jn 12: 9 they f to see him and also to see Lazarus, the man

FLOCKS (113) [FLOCK]

Ge 13: 6 and Lot with all their f and herds living so close
13:11 He went there with his f and servants and parted
24:35 The LORD has given him f of sheep and herds of
26:14 He acquired large f of sheep and goats, great herds
27: 9 Go out to the f and bring me two fine young goats.
29: 2 He saw in the distance three f of sheep lying in an
29: 3 It was the custom there to wait for all the f to
29: 7 "Why don't you water the f so they can get back
29: 8 and begin the watering until all the f and shepherds
30:29 many years, and how your f and herds have grown.
30:32 Let me go out among your f today and remove all
30:38 so Laban's f would see them as they came to drink,
30:39 So when the f mated in front of the white-streaked
30:40 he turned the f toward the streaked
30:43 As a result, Jacob's f increased rapidly, and he
31: 4 Leah out to the field where he was watching the f,
31:18 He drove the f in front of him—all the livestock he
31:39 made me pay for every animal stolen from the f,
31:43 and these f and all that you have—
32: 7 along with the f and herds and camels, into two
33: 8 "And what were all the f and herds I met as I
33:13 and the f and herds have their young, too.
33:17 a house and made shelters for his f and herds.
34:23 all their f and possessions will become ours.
34:28 They seized all the f and herds and donkeys—
36: 6 children, household servants, cattle, and f—
37: 2 he often tended his father's f with his half brothers,
37:12 Joseph's brothers went to pasture their father's f at
37:13 "Your brothers are over at Shechem with the f.
37:14 see how your brothers and the f are getting along,"
37:16 "For my brothers and their f," Joseph replied.
45:10 your children and grandchildren, your f and herds,
46:32 They have brought with them their f and herds
47: 1 They came with all their f and herds
47: 4 for there is no pasture for our f in Canaan.
47:17 Soon all the horses, f, herds, and donkeys of Egypt
50: 8 But they left their little children and f and herds in
Ex 2:16 and fill the water troughs for their father's f.
2:17 often come and chase the girls and their f away.
2:17 Then he helped them draw water for their f.
2:18 "How did you get the f watered so quickly
2:19 then he drew water for us and watered our f."
9: 6 Israelites didn't lose a single animal from their f
10: 9 take our sons and daughters and our f and herds.
10:24 he said. "But let your f and herds stay here.
10:25 "we must take our f and herds for sacrifices
12:32 Take your f and herds, and be gone. Go, but give
12:38 went with them, along with the many f and herds.
34: 3 Do not even let the f or herds graze near the
Lev 1: 2 you must bring animals from your f and herds.
27:32 tenth animal counted off from your herds and f.
Nu 11:22 Even if we butchered all our f and herds,
15: 3 the sacrifice must be an animal from your f of
31: 9 and children and seized their cattle and f and all
32: 1 and Gilead were ideally suited for their f
32: 4 of Israel. It is ideally suited for all our f and herds.
32:16 "We simply want to build sheepfolds for our f
32:24 towns for your families and sheepfolds for your f,
32:26 Our children, wives, f, and cattle will stay here in
32:36 were all fortified cities with sheepfolds for their f.
35: 3 pasture for their cattle, f, and other livestock.
Dt 8:13 and when your f and herds have become very large
12: 6 your offerings of the firstborn animals of your f
12:17 and olive oil, nor the firstborn of your f and herds,
14:23 and the firstborn males of your f and herds.
15:19 your God all the firstborn males from your f
15:19 your fields, and do not shear the firstborn of your f.
28: 4 You will be blessed with fertile herds and f.
28:18 You will be cursed with infertile herds and f.
Jos 14: 4 and the surrounding pasturelands for their f
Jdg 5:16 to hear the shepherds whistle for their f?
1Sa 8:17 He will demand a tenth of your f, and you will be
25:21 We protected his f in the wilderness, and nothing
30:20 His troops rounded up all the f and herds and drove
2Sa 12: 4 But instead of killing a lamb from his own f for
1Ki 20:27 But the Israelite army looked like two little f of
1Ch 4:39 part of the valley, seeking pastureland for their f.
4:41 they wanted its good pastureland for their f.
2Ch 32:28 for his cattle and folds for his f of sheep and goats.
32:29 He built many towns and acquired vast f and herds,
Ne 10:36 oldest sons and the firstborn of all our herds and f,
Job 24: 2 the boundary markers. They steal f of sheep,
Ps 65:13 The meadows are clothed with f of sheep,
107:41 and increases their families like vast f of sheep.
144:13 May the f in our fields multiply by the thousands,
Pr 27:23 Know the state of your f, and put your heart into
Ecc 2: 7 I also owned great herds and f, more than any of
SS 1: 7 a prostitute among the f of your companions?"
4: 1 like f of goats frisking across the slopes of Gilead.
Isa 5:17 In those days f will feed among the ruins; lambs
32:20 Their f and herds will graze in green pastures.
60: 7 The f of Kedar will be given to you, and the rams
61: 5 They will feed your f and plow your fields
65:10 the plain of Sharon will again be filled with f,
Jer 3:24 their f and herds, their sons and daughters—
5:17 your f of sheep and your herds of cattle.
6: 3 around the city and divide your pastures for their f.
10:21 they fail completely, and their f are scattered.
31:12 wine, and oil, and the healthy f and herds.
33:13 Once again their f will prosper in the towns of the
49:29 Their f and tents will be captured, and their
51:23 With you I will shatter shepherds and f, farmers
Eze 25: 4 wipe out their people, cattle, and f with the sword.
32:13 I will destroy all your f and herds that graze beside
34: 2 shepherds who feed yourselves instead of your f.
34: 3 butcher the best animals, but you let your f starve.
36:11 but your f and herds will also greatly multiply.
36:38 I will multiply them like the sacred f that fill
45:15 and one sheep for every two hundred in your f in
Hos 5: 6 they will come with their f and herds to offer
Hab 3:17 even though the f die in the fields, and the cattle
Lk 2: 8 fields outside the village, guarding their f of sheep.
2:20 The shepherds went back to their fields and f,

FLOG (1) [FLOGGED]

Lk 23:22 to death. I will therefore f him and let him go."

FLOGGED (8) [FLOG]

Dt 25: 2 If the person in the wrong is sentenced to be f,
Ezr 6:11 Then they will be tied to it and f, and their house
Jer 37:15 They were furious with Jeremiah and had him f
Mt 27:26 He ordered Jesus f with a lead-tipped whip,
Mk 15:15 He ordered Jesus f with a lead-tipped whip,
Lk 23:16 So I will have him f, but then I will release him."
Jn 19: 1 Then Pilate had Jesus f with a lead-tipped whip.
Ac 5:40 They called in the apostles and had them f.

FLOOD (48) [FLOODED, FLOODGATES, FLOODING, FLOODS, FLOODTIME, FLOODWATERS]

Ge 6:17 I am about to cover the earth with a f that will
6:19 the boat with you to keep them alive during the f.
7: 3 that every kind of living creature will survive the f.
7: 6 He was 600 years old when the f came,
7:10 One week later, the f came and covered the earth.
8: 3 So the f gradually began to recede. After 150 days,
8: 4 exactly five months from the time the f began,
8:13 years old, ten and a half months after the f began,
9:11 I solemnly promise never to send another f to kill
9:15 Never again will there be a f that will destroy all
9:18 sons of Noah, survived the F with their father.
9:20 After the F, Noah became a farmer and planted a
9:28 Noah lived another 350 years after the F.
10: 1 Many children were born to them after the F.
10:32 with the people of these nations after the F.
11:10 was born. This happened two years after the F.
2Sa 5:20 "He burst through my enemies like a raging f!"
1Ch 14:11 me to burst through my enemies like a raging f!"
Job 12:15 a desert. If he releases the waters, they f the earth.
20:28 A f will sweep away his house. God's anger will
Ps 66:12 our broken bodies. / We went through fire and f.
Pr 27: 4 Anger is cruel, and wrath is like a f, but who can
Ecc 5: 7 And there is ruin in a f of empty words. Fear God
Isa 8: 7 the Lord will overwhelm them with a mighty f
8: 8 This f will overflow all its channels and sweep into
19: 5 waters of the Nile will fail to rise and f the fields.
28:17 the enemy will come like a f to sweep it away.
28:19 Again and again that f will come, morning after
30:28 His anger pours out like a f on his enemies,
54: 9 that I would never again let a f cover the earth
59:19 For he will come like a f tide driven by the breath
Jer 46: 8 boasting that it will cover the earth like a f,
47: 2 "A f is coming from the north to overflow the
Eze 13:13 with a great f of anger, and with hailstones of fury.
Da 9:26 The end will come with a f, and war and its
11:10 assemble a mighty army that will advance like a f
11:40 various lands and sweep through them like a f.
Am 5:24 Instead, I want to see a mighty f of justice, a river
Na 1: 8 he sweeps away his enemies in an overwhelming f.
Mt 24:38 In those days before the F, the people were
24:39 realize what was going to happen until the F came
Lk 17:27 In those days before the f, the people enjoyed
17:27 entered his boat and the f came to destroy them all.
Heb 11: 7 that Noah built an ark to save his family from the f.
1Pe 3:20 people were saved from drowning in that terrible f.
2Pe 2: 5 the whole world of ungodly people with a vast f.
3: 6 the water to destroy the world with a mighty f.
Rev 12:15 Then the dragon tried to drown the woman with a f

FLOODED (3) [FLOOD]

Jos 4:18 the riverbed, the Jordan River f its banks as before.
2Co 11:26 I have faced danger from f rivers and from robbers.
Eph 1:18 I pray that your hearts will be f with light so that

FLOODGATE (1) [FLOOD, GATE]

Pr 17:14 Beginning a quarrel is like opening a f, so drop the

FLOODING (2) [FLOOD]

1Ch 12:15 They crossed the Jordan River during its seasonal f
Isa 23:10 sweep over your mother Tyre like the f Nile,

FLOODLIGHT (1) [LIGHT]

Lk 11:36 will be radiant, as though a f is shining on you."

FLOODS (12) [FLOOD]

Ge 7:17 For forty days the f prevailed, covering the ground
8: 1 across the waters, and the f began to disappear.
2Sa 22: 5 the f of destruction swept over me.
Job 12:22 "He f the darkness with light; he brings light to the
14:19 wears away the stones and f wash away the soil,
Ps 18: 4 the f of destruction swept over me.
69: 2 I am in deep water, / and the f overwhelm me.
69:15 Don't let the f overwhelm me, / or the deep waters
104: 6 You clothed the earth with f of water, / water that
Isa 28:18 When the terrible enemy f in, you will be trampled
Mt 7:27 When the rains and f come and the winds beat
Lk 6:49 When the f sweep down against that house, it will

FLOODTIME (3) [FLOOD]

Jer 46: 7 "Who is this, rising like the Nile River at f,
Am 8: 8 The land will rise up like the Nile River at f,
9: 5 The ground rises like the Nile River at f, and

FLOODWATERS (6) [FLOOD]

Ps 29:10 The LORD rules over the f. / The LORD reigns
32: 6 that they may not drown in the f of judgment.
69: 1 Save me, O God, / for the f are up to my neck.
88:17 They swirl around me like f all day long.
Mt 7:25 Though the rain comes in torrents and the f rise
Lk 6:48 When the f rise and break against the house,

FLOOR (55) [FLOORS]

Ge 50:10 When they arrived at the threshing f of Atad,
Nu 5:17 clay jar and mix it with dust from the Tabernacle f.
15:20 as you do with the first grain from the threshing f.
18:27 it were the first grain from your own threshing f
18:30 as though it came from your own threshing f
Dt 15:14 your flock, your threshing f, and your winepress.
Jdg 3:25 the door, they found their master dead on the f.
6:37 I will put some wool on the threshing f tonight.
Ru 3: 2 he will be winnowing barley at the threshing f.
3: 3 Then go to the threshing f, but don't let Boaz see
3: 6 So she went down to the threshing f that night
3:14 know that a woman was here at the threshing f."
2Sa 6: 6 But when they arrived at the threshing f of Nacon,
14: 4 she fell with her face down to the f in front of him
24:16 was by the threshing f of Araunah the Jebusite.
24:18 and build an altar to the LORD on the threshing f
24:21 "I have come to buy your threshing f and to build
24:24 paid him fifty pieces of silver for the threshing f
1Ki 6: 6 the bottom f being 7-1/2 feet wide, the second f 9
feet wide, and the top f 10-1/2 feet wide.

6: 8 The entrance to the bottom **f** was on the south side
6: 8 There were winding stairs going up to the second **f**,
6: 15 The entire inside, from **f** to ceiling, was paneled
6: 16 and was paneled with cedar from **f** to ceiling.
6: 30 The **f** in both rooms was overlaid with gold.
7: 7 It was paneled with cedar from **f** to ceiling.
22: 10 were sitting on thrones at the threshing **f** near the
22: 35 The blood from his wound ran down to the **f** of his
1Ch 13: 9 But when they arrived at the threshing **f** of Nacon,
21: 15 by the threshing **f** of Araunah the Jebusite.
21: 18 LORD at the threshing **f** of Araunah the Jebusite.
21: 21 he left his threshing **f** and bowed to the ground
21: 22 "Let me buy this threshing **f** from you at its full
21: 25 pieces of gold in payment for the threshing **f**.
21: 28 he offered sacrifices there at Araunah's threshing **f**.
2Ch 3: 1 The Temple was built on the threshing **f** of
18: 9 were sitting on thrones at the threshing **f** near the
Job 39: 12 it to return, bringing your grain to the threshing **f**?
Isa 27: 12 He will bring them to his great threshing **f**—
Jer 51: 33 "Babylon is like wheat on a threshing **f**, about to
Eze 37: 2 among the old, dry bones that covered the valley **f**.
41: 20 from the **f** to the top of the walls,
Da 2: 35 were crushed as small as chaff on a threshing **f**,
6: 24 and tore them apart before they even hit the **f** of the
Hos 9: 1 sacrifices to other gods on every threshing **f**.
Am 8: 6 mix the wheat you sell with chaff swept from the **f**!
Mic 4: 12 and trampled like bundles of grain on a threshing **f**.
Mt 27: 5 Then Judas threw the money onto the **f** of the
Lk 4: 35 The demon threw the man to the **f** as the crowd
Jn 2: 15 scattered the money changers' coins over the **f**,
Ac 5: 5 heard these words, he fell to the **f** and died.
5: 10 Instantly, she fell to the **f** and died.
10: 25 Cornelius fell to the **f** before him in worship.
Jas 2: 3 "You can stand over there, or else sit on the **f**"—

FLOORS (4) [FLOOR]

1Sa 23: 1 were at Keilah stealing grain from the threshing **f**.
1Ki 6: 8 flight of stairs between the second and third **f**.
6: 15 ceilings with cedar, and he used cypress for the **f**.
Joel 2: 24 The threshing **f** will again be piled high with grain,

FLOUNDERS (1)

Eze 27: 26 Your mighty vessel **f** in the heavy eastern gale.

FLOUR (99)

Ge 18: 6 Get three measures of your best **f**, and bake some
Ex 29: 2 Then using fine wheat **f** and no yeast, make loaves
29: 40 offer two quarts of fine **f** mixed with one quart of
29: 41 along with the same offerings of **f** and wine as in
Lev 2: 1 the LORD, the offering must consist of choice **f**.
2: 2 and he will take a handful of the **f** mixed with olive
2: 3 The rest of the **f** will be given to Aaron and his
2: 4 it must be made of choice **f** mixed with olive oil
2: 5 it must be made of choice **f** and olive oil, and it
2: 7 it also must be made of choice **f** and olive oil.
5: 11 they must bring two quarts of choice **f** for their sin
5: 12 They must take the **f** to the priest, who will scoop
5: 12 He will burn this **f** on the altar just like any other
5: 13 The rest of the **f** will belong to the priest, just as
6: 15 of the choice **f** that has been mixed with olive oil
6: 16 the rest of the **f** will belong to Aaron and his sons
6: 17 this **f** may never be prepared with yeast.
6: 20 LORD a grain offering of two quarts of choice **f**,
6: 23 entirely burned up. None of the **f** may be eaten."
7: 10 whether **f** mixed with olive oil or dry **f**,
9: 4 and **f** mixed with olive oil for a grain offering.
9: 17 burning a handful of the **f** on the altar,
14: 10 along with five quarts of choice **f** mixed with olive
14: 21 along with two quarts of choice **f** mixed with olive
23: 13 of three quarts of choice **f** mixed with olive oil.
23: 17 from three quarts of choice **f** that contains yeast.
24: 5 must bake twelve loaves of bread from choice **f**,
using three quarts of **f** for each loaf.
Nu 5: 15 quarts of barley **f** to be presented on her behalf.
6: 15 cakes of choice **f** mixed with olive oil and wafers
7: 13 grain offerings of choice **f** mixed with olive oil.
7: 19 grain offerings of choice **f** mixed with olive oil.
7: 25 grain offerings of choice **f** mixed with olive oil.
7: 31 grain offerings of choice **f** mixed with olive oil.
7: 37 grain offerings of choice **f** mixed with olive oil.
7: 43 grain offerings of choice **f** mixed with olive oil.
7: 49 grain offerings of choice **f** mixed with olive oil.
7: 55 grain offerings of choice **f** mixed with olive oil.
7: 61 grain offerings of choice **f** mixed with olive oil.
7: 67 grain offerings of choice **f** mixed with olive oil.
7: 73 grain offerings of choice **f** mixed with olive oil.
7: 79 grain offerings of choice **f** mixed with olive oil.
8: 8 and a grain offering of choice **f** mixed with olive
11: 8 and made **f** by grinding it with hand mills
15: 4 of choice **f** mixed with one quart of olive oil.
15: 6 give three quarts of choice **f** mixed with two
15: 9 of choice **f** mixed with two quarts of olive oil,
15: 20 Present a cake from the first of the **f** you grind
15: 21 LORD each year from the first of your ground **f**.
28: 5 of choice **f** mixed with one quart of olive oil.
28: 9 of three quarts of choice **f** mixed with olive oil,
28: 12 grain offerings of choice **f** mixed with olive oil—
28: 20 grain offerings of choice **f** mixed with olive oil—
28: 28 grain offerings of choice **f** mixed with olive oil—
29: 3 grain offerings of choice **f** mixed with olive oil—
29: 9 grain offerings of choice **f** mixed with olive oil—
29: 9 five quarts of choice **f** with the bull, three quarts of
choice **f** with the ram,
29: 10 and two quarts of choice **f** with each of the seven
29: 14 a grain offering of choice **f** mixed with olive oil—
Jdg 6: 19 and with half a bushel of **f** he baked some bread
1Sa 1: 24 the sacrifice and half a bushel of **f** and some wine.
2Sa 17: 28 wheat and barley **f**, roasted grain, beans, lentils,
1Ki 4: 22 for Solomon's palace were 150 bushels of choice **f**
17: 12 And I have only a handful of **f** left in the jar
17: 14 There will always be plenty of **f** and oil left in your
17: 15 and her son continued to eat from her supply of **f**
2Ki 4: 41 Elisha said, "Bring me some **f**." Then he threw it
7: 1 five quarts of fine **f** will cost only half an ounce of
7: 16 So it was true that five quarts of fine **f** were sold
7: 18 five quarts of fine **f** will cost half an ounce of
1Ch 9: 29 and the supplies such as choice **f**, wine, olive oil,
12: 40 Vast supplies of **f**, fig cakes, raisins, wine,
23: 29 the choice **f** for the grain offerings, the wafers
Ne 10: 37 We will bring the best of our **f** and other grain
Eze 16: 13 ate the finest foods—fine **f**, honey, and olive oil—
16: 19 You set before them as a lovely sacrifice the fine **f**
44: 30 and the first of your **f** must also be given to the
45: 24 The prince will provide a half bushel of **f** as a grain
46: 5 offering of a half bushel of **f** to go with the ram
46: 5 and whatever amount of **f** he chooses to go with
46: 5 one gallon of olive oil for each half bushel of **f**.
46: 7 must bring a half bushel of **f** for a grain offering.
46: 7 the ram he must bring another half bushel of **f**.
46: 7 bring whatever amount of **f** that he decides to give.
46: 7 With each half bushel of **f** he must offer one gallon
46: 11 the grain offering will be a half bushel of **f** with
46: 11 another half bushel of **f** with each ram, and as
much **f** as the prince chooses to give with
46: 11 of oil is to be given with each half bushel of **f**.
46: 14 and a half quarts of **f** with a third of a gallon of
olive oil to moisten the **f**.
46: 20 and bake the **f** from the grain offerings into bread.
Mt 13: 33 Even though she used a large amount of **f**,
24: 41 Two women will be grinding **f** at the mill; one will
Lk 13: 21 Even though she used a large amount of **f**,
17: 35 Two women will be grinding **f** together at the mill;
Rev 18: 13 fine **f**, wheat, cattle, sheep, horses, chariots,

FLOURISH (17) [FLOURISHED, FLOURISHES, FLOURISHING]

Dt 11: 21 and your children may **f** in the land the LORD
1Sa 24: 20 going to be king, and Israel will **f** under your rule.
2Ki 19: 30 in your own soil, and you will **f** and multiply.
Job 8: 11 Can bulrushes **f** where there is no water?
Ps 72: 7 May all the godly **f** during his reign. / May there be
72: 16 May the fruit trees **f** as they do in Lebanon,
92: 7 Although the wicked **f** like weeds, / and evildoers
92: 12 But the godly will **f** like palm trees / and grow
92: 13 own house. / They **f** in the courts of our God.
144: 12 May our sons **f** in their youth / like well-nurtured
Pr 11: 28 down you go! But the godly **f** like leaves in spring.
14: 11 wicked will perish, but the tent of the godly will **f**.
Isa 35: 7 and rushes will **f** where desert jackals once lived.
37: 31 in your own soil, and you will **f** and multiply.
Hos 14: 7 They will **f** like grain and blossom like grapevines.
Joel 2: 22 fig trees and grapevines will **f** once more.
2Ti 3: 13 But evil people and impostors will **f**. They will go

FLOURISHED (1) [FLOURISH]

Ge 39: 5 to run smoothly, and his crops and livestock **f**.

FLOURISHES (1) [FLOURISH]

Ps 90: 6 In the morning it blooms and **f**, / but by evening it

FLOURISHING (4) [FLOURISH]

Ps 72: 16 throughout the land, / **f** even on the mountaintops.
128: 3 will be like a fruitful vine, / **f** within your home.
Ecc 2: 6 to collect the water to irrigate my many **f** groves.
2Th 1: 3 for we are thankful that your faith is **f** and you are

FLOW (23) [EVER-FLOWING, FLOWED, FLOWING, FLOWS]

Lev 15: 25 "If the menstrual **f** of blood continues for many
20: 18 because he exposed the source of her **f**, and she
Jos 3: 13 the water, the **f** of water will be cut off upstream,
2Ch 32: 3 and they decided to stop the **f** of the springs
32: 4 They organized a huge work crew to stop the **f** of
Job 16: 3 Won't you ever stop your **f** of foolish words?
Ps 78: 16 the rock, / making the waters **f** down like a river!
Pr 10: 19 for it fosters sin. Be sensible and turn off the **f**!
Isa 16: 9 My tears will **f** for Heshbon and Elealeh, for their
34: 3 fill the land. The mountains will **f** with their blood.
41: 18 Rivers fed by springs will **f** across the dry,
66: 12 "The wealth of the nations will **f** to her.
Jer 9: 18 your weeping! Let the tears **f** from your eyes.
La 1: 16 all these things I weep; tears **f** down my cheeks.
2: 18 O walls of Jerusalem! Let your tears **f** like a river.
3: 48 Streams of tears **f** from my eyes because of the
3: 49 My tears **f** down endlessly. They will not stop
Eze 32: 14 and they will **f** as smoothly as olive oil,
Joel 3: 18 drip with sweet wine, and the hills will **f** with milk.
Mic 1: 4 his feet and **f** into the valleys like wax in a fire,
Zec 14: 8 On that day life-giving waters will **f** out from
Jn 7: 38 that rivers of living water will **f** out from within."
1Pe 4: 10 so that God's generosity can **f** through you.

FLOWED (9) [FLOW]

Ge 2: 10 A river **f** from the land of Eden,
Jos 3: 16 And the water below that point **f** on to the Dead
Jdg 9: 27 in the temple of the local god, the wine **f** freely,
Ps 79: 3 Blood has **f** like water all around Jerusalem;
La 3: 54 The water **f** above my head, and I cried out,
Da 7: 10 and a river of fire **f** from his presence. Millions of
Jn 19: 34 his side with a spear, and blood and water **f** out.
Rev 12: 15 woman with a flood of water that **f** from its mouth.
14: 20 and blood **f** from the winepress in a stream about

FLOWER (9) [FLOWERING, FLOWERS, WILDFLOWERS]

1Ki 7: 49 in front of the Most Holy Place, the **f** decorations,
2Ch 4: 21 the **f** decorations, lamps, and tongs, all of pure
Job 14: 2 Like a **f**, we blossom for a moment and
Ps 78: 51 the **f** of youth throughout the land of Egypt.
SS 7: 12 and whether the pomegranates are in **f**.
Isa 13: 19 the **f** of Chaldean culture, will be devastated like
Jer 9: 21 our mansions. It has killed off the **f** of our youth:
Jas 1: 10 They will fade away like a **f** in the field.
1: 11 the grass; the **f** withers, and its beauty fades away.

FLOWERING (1) [FLOWER]

Job 8: 12 While they are still **f**, not ready to be cut,

FLOWERS (18) [FLOWER]

1Ki 6: 18 was decorated with carvings of gourds and open **f**.
6: 29 with carvings of cherubim, palm trees, and open **f**.
6: 32 palm trees, and open **f**, and the doors were overlaid
6: 35 palm trees, and open **f**, and the doors were overlaid
Ps 37: 2 fade away. / Like springtime **f**, they soon wither.
37: 20 The LORD's enemies are like **f** in a field—
SS 1: 14 He is like a bouquet of **f** in the gardens of
2: 12 The **f** are springing up, and the time of singing
Isa 5: 24 Their roots will rot and their **f** wither, for they have
35: 1 in those days. The desert will blossom with **f**.
35: 2 there will be an abundance of **f** and singing
40: 6 Their beauty fades as quickly as the beauty of **f** in
40: 7 and the **f** fade beneath the breath of the LORD.
40: 8 The grass withers, and the **f** fade, but the word of
Mt 6: 30 God cares so wonderfully for **f** that are here today
Lk 12: 28 God cares so wonderfully for **f** that are here today
Ac 14: 13 and the crowd brought oxen and wreaths of **f**,
1Pe 1: 24 The grass withers, / and the **f** fall away.

FLOWING (40) [FLOW]

LAND FLOWING WITH MILK AND HONEY (20)
Ex 3:8,17; 13:5; 33:3; Lev 20:24; Nu 13:27; 14:8; 16:13,14; Dt 6:3; 11:9; 26:9,15; 27:3; 31:20; Jos 5:6; Jer 11:5; 32:22; Eze 20:6,15

Ex 3: 8 It is a land **f** with milk and honey—the land where
3: 17 and Jebusites—a land **f** with milk and honey." '
13: 5 give your ancestors—a land **f** with milk and honey.
33: 3 Theirs is a land **f** with milk and honey. But I will
Lev 20: 24 inherit their land, a land **f** with milk and honey.
Nu 13: 27 a land **f** with milk and honey.
14: 8 It is a rich land **f** with milk and honey, and he will
16: 13 a land **f** with milk and honey, to kill us here in this
16: 14 you haven't brought us into the land **f** with milk
Dt 6: 3 and you will have many children in the land **f** with
8: 7 God is bringing you into a good land of **f** streams
11: 9 their descendants—a land **f** with milk and honey!
26: 9 and gave us this land **f** with milk and honey!
26: 15 have given us—a land **f** with milk and honey—
27: 3 a land **f** with milk and honey, just as the LORD,
31: 20 give their ancestors—a land **f** with milk and honey.
Jos 4: 7 'They remind us that the Jordan River stopped **f**
5: 6 sworn to give us—a land **f** with milk and honey.
2Ki 3: 20 It was **f** from the direction of Edom, and soon there
4: 6 he told her. And then the olive oil stopped **f**.
Job 39: 19 its strength or clothed its neck with a **f** mane?
Ps 107: 35 into pools of water, / the dry land into **f** springs.
SS 7: 9 smooth and sweet, **f** gently over lips and teeth."
Isa 30: 25 there will be streams of water **f** down every
48: 18 Then you would have had peace **f** like a gentle
Jer 11: 5 to your ancestors to give you a land **f** with milk
18: 14 **f** streams from the crags of Mount Hermon ever
32: 22 long before—a land **f** with milk and honey.
Eze 20: 6 a good land, a land **f** with milk and honey, the best
20: 15 a land **f** with milk and honey, the most beautiful
23: 15 their waists, and **f** turbans crowned their heads.
47: 1 There I saw a stream **f** eastward from beneath the
47: 2 There I could see the stream **f** out through the
47: 12 For they are watered by the river **f** from the
Hos 13: 15 All their **f** springs and wells will disappear.
Hab 3: 9 of power! You split open the earth with **f** rivers!
Zec 14: 8 **f** continuously both in summer and in winter.
Mk 12: 38 For they love to parade in **f** robes and to have
Lk 20: 46 For they love to parade in **f** robes and to have
Rev 22: 1 **f** from the throne of God and of the Lamb,

FLOWN (1) [FLY]

Jer 4: 25 were gone. All the birds of the sky had **f** away.

FLOWS (6) [FLOW]

Ge 2: 11 which **f** around the entire land of Havilah,
2: 13 the Gihon, which **f** around the entire land of Cush.
2: 14 branch is the Tigris, which **f** to the east of Asshur.
Ecc 1: 7 returns again to the rivers and **f** again to the sea.
Eze 47: 8 "This river **f** east through the desert into the
47: 9 Wherever this water **f**, everything will live.

FLUNG (1)

Jnh 1: 4 suddenly the LORD **f** a powerful wind over the

FLUTE (8) [FLUTES, FLUTIST]

Ge 4: 21 the first musician—the inventor of the harp and **f**.

1Sa 10: 5 be playing a harp, a tambourine, a **f**, and a lyre,
Job 21:12 and harp. They make merry to the sound of the **f**.
30:31 sad music, and my **f** accompanies those who weep.
Ps 5: T A psalm of David, to be accompanied by the **f**.
Jer 48:36 My heart moans like a **f** for Moab
Da 3: 5 **f**, zither, lyre, harp, pipes, and other instruments,
1Co 14: 7 Even musical instruments like the **f** or the harp,

FLUTES (4) [FLUTE]

1Ki 1:40 to Jerusalem, playing **f** and shouting for joy.
Ps 150: 4 praise him with stringed instruments and **f**!
Isa 5:12 the harps, lyres, tambourines, and **f** are superb!
Rev 18:22 heard there—no more harps, songs, **f**, or trumpets.

FLUTIST (1) [FLUTE]

Isa 30:29 as when a **f** leads a group of pilgrims to

FLUTTERING (1)

Pr 26: 2 Like a **f** sparrow or a darting swallow, an unfair

FLUX [KJV] See DYSENTERY

FLY (18) [FLEW, FLIES, FLIGHT, FLOWN, FLYING, GADFLY]

Ex 8:31 to disappear. Not a single **f** remained in the land!
Lev 14: 7 bird free so it can **f** away into the open fields.
Job 5: 7 as predictably as sparks **f** upward from a fire.
Ps 11: 1 do you say to me, / "**F** to the mountains for safety!
55: 6 wings like a dove; / then I would **f** away and rest!
55: 7 I would **f** far away / to the quiet of the wilderness.
59: 7 the piercing swords that **f** from their lips.
Isa 5:28 Sparks will **f** from their horses' hooves as the
40:31 They will **f** high on wings like eagles. They will
Jer 48: 9 Oh, that Moab had wings so she could **f** away,
Eze 1: 9 The living beings were able to **f** in any direction
Hos 7:12 But as they **f** about, I will throw my net over them
9:11 The glory of Israel will **f** away like a bird, for your
Na 3:16 of locusts, they strip the land and then **f** away.
3:17 But like locusts that **f** away when the sun comes up
3:17 the earth, all of them will **f** away and disappear.
Zec 9:14 above his people; his arrows will **f** like lightning!
Rev 12:14 This allowed her to **f** to a place prepared for her in

FLYING (14) [FLY]

Ge 7:14 along with birds and **f** insects of every kind.
Nu 11:31 were quail **f** about three feet above the ground.
Dt 14:19 "All **f** insects are ceremonially unclean for you
Job 7: 6 "My days are swifter than a weaver's shuttle **f**
Ps 20: 5 hear of your victory, / **f** banners to honor our God.
Pr 7:23 He was like a bird **f** into a snare, little knowing it
Isa 60: 8 "And what do I see **f** like clouds to Israel,
Hos 7:11 first calling to Egypt, then **f** to Assyria.
11:11 **F** like doves, they will return from Assyria.
Zec 5: 1 looked up again and saw a scroll **f** through the air.
5: 2 the angel asked. "I see a **f** scroll," I replied.
5: 9 Then I looked up and saw two women **f** toward us,
Rev 14: 6 And I saw another angel **f** through the heavens,
19:17 the sun, shouting to the vultures **f** high in the sky:

FOAL (1)

Ge 49:11 He ties his **f** to a grapevine, / the colt of his donkey

FOAM (4) [FOAMING, FOAMS]

Job 24:18 "But they disappear from the earth as quickly as **f**
Ps 46: 3 Let the oceans roar and **f**. / Let the mountains
Mk 9:18 and makes him **f** at the mouth and grind his teeth
Jude 1:13 churning up the dirty **f** of their shameful deeds.

FOAMING (2) [FOAM]

Ps 75: 8 in his hand; / it is full of **f** wine mixed with spices.
Mk 9:20 he fell to the ground, writhing and **f** at the mouth.

FOAMS (1) [FOAM]

Lk 9:39 him into convulsions so that he **f** at the mouth.

FOCUS (2) [FOCUSING]

1Sa 9:20 and your family are the **f** of all Israel's hopes."
1Ti 4:13 get there, **f** on reading the Scriptures to the church,

FOCUSING (1) [FOCUS]

Php 3:13 but I am **f** all my energies on this one thing:

FODDER (1)

Jdg 19:19 We have straw and **f** for our donkeys and plenty of

FOE (2) [FOES]

Jos 5:13 went up to him and asked, "Are you friend or **f**?"
Jer 46: 8 will cover the earth like a flood, destroying every **f**.

FOES (18) [FOE]

Dt 33:11 strike down their **f** so they never rise again."
2Sa 1:22 Both Saul and Jonathan killed their strongest **f**;
Ps 27: 2 to destroy me, / when my enemies and **f** attack me,
44: 5 only in your name can we trample our **f**.
55:12 It is not my **f** who so arrogantly insult me—
56: 1 press in on me. / My **f** attack me all day long.
60:12 do mighty things, / for he will trample down our **f**.
76: 3 the shields and swords and weapons of his **f**.
81:14 How soon my hands would be upon their **f**!
97: 3 Fire goes forth before him / and burns up all his **f**.
106:10 their enemies / and redeemed them from their **f**.
108:13 do mighty things, / for he will trample down our **f**.
112: 8 and fearless / and can face their **f** triumphantly.
143:12 and destroy all my **f**, / for I am your servant.
Isa 59:18 His fury will fall on his **f** in distant lands.
63: 3 In my fury I have trampled my **f**. It is their blood
Mic 5: 9 The people of Israel will stand up to their **f**, and all
Na 1: 8 He pursues his **f** into the darkness of night.

FOG (1)

Jas 4:14 For your life is like the morning **f**—it's here a little

FOLD (5) [FOLDED, FOLDING, FOLDS]

1Ki 6:34 and each door was hinged to **f** back upon itself.
Ne 5:13 I shook out the **f** of my robe and said, "If you fail
Jer 23: 3 I will bring them back into their own **f**, and they
50: 6 and cannot remember how to get back to the **f**.
Mic 2:12 I will bring you together again like sheep in a **f**,

FOLDED (2) [FOLD]

2Ki 2: 8 Then Elijah **f** his cloak together and struck the
Jn 20: 7 while the cloth that had covered Jesus' head was **f**

FOLDING (3) [FOLD]

1Ki 6:34 There were two **f** doors of cypress wood, and each
Pr 6:10 a little more slumber, a little **f** of the hands to rest
24:33 a little more slumber, a little **f** of the hands to rest

FOLDS (2) [FOLD]

Ex 28:16 This chestpiece will be made of two **f** of cloth,
2Ch 32:28 his cattle and **f** for his flocks of sheep and goats.

FOLIAGE (1)

Eze 19:10 planted by the water's edge. / It had lush, green **f**

FOLK [KJV] See MEN, PEOPLE, WORK

FOLLOW (229) [FOLLOWED, FOLLOWER, FOLLOWERS, FOLLOWING, FOLLOWS]

Ge 24: 9 So the servant took a solemn oath that he would **f**
33:14 We will **f** at our own pace and meet you at Seir."
Ex 14:17 and they will **f** the Israelites into the sea.
16: 4 I will test them in this to see whether they will **f**
18:23 If you **f** this advice, and if God directs you to do
23:24 them in any way, and never **f** their evil example.
31:11 They must **f** exactly all the instructions I have
Lev 16: 3 sanctuary area, he must **f** these instructions fully.
22: 9 Warn all the priests to **f** these instructions
Nu 2:24 and they will **f** the Levites in the line of march.
8:24 "This is the rule the Levites must **f**: They must
9: 3 Be sure to **f** all my laws and regulations concerning
9:12 They must **f** all the normal regulations concerning
9:14 they must **f** these same laws and regulations.
10: 6 signal a second time, the tribes on the south will **f**.
15:13 to the LORD, you must **f** all these instructions.
15:14 to the LORD, they must **f** the same procedures.
18: 5 If you **f** these instructions, the LORD's anger will
32:25 your servants and will **f** your instructions exactly.
35:24 the assembly must **f** these regulations in making a
Dt 5:33 the LORD your God has commanded you to **f**.
8:19 ever forget the LORD your God and **f** other gods,
9:16 the path the LORD had commanded you to **f**!
12:30 worship their gods? I want to **f** their example.'
24: 8 and **f** the instructions of the Levitical priests;
28:14 I am giving you today to **f** after other gods
31:29 will turn from the path I have commanded you to **f**.
33: 3 They **f** in your steps / and accept your instruction.
Jos 3: 3 of the Covenant of the LORD your God, **f** them.
23: 6 Be very careful to **f** all the instructions written in
Jdg 3:28 "**F** me," he said, "for the LORD has given you
5: 2 leaders take charge, / and the people gladly **f**—
9: 4 he used to hire some soldiers who agreed to **f** him.
Ru 2: 9 of the field they are harvesting, and then **f** them.
1Sa 11: 7 happen to the oxen of anyone who refuses to **f** Saul
12:14 and if you and your king **f** the LORD your God,
25:19 "Go on ahead. I will **f** you shortly." But she didn't
2Sa 17: 6 Should we **f** Ahithophel's advice? If not,
20:11 "If you are for Joab and David, come and **f** Joab."
22:22 I have not turned from my God to **f** evil.
1Ki 1:12 and the life of your son Solomon, **f** my counsel.
2: 3 of the LORD your God and **f** all his ways.
2: 4 and **f** me faithfully with all their heart and soul,
3:14 And if you **f** me and obey my commands as your
9: 4 if you will **f** me with integrity and godliness,
11: 6 he refused to **f** the LORD completely, as his
11:38 If you listen to what I tell you and **f** my ways
18:21 If the LORD is God, **f** him! But if Baal is God, then **f** him!"
2Ki 6:19 **F** me, and I will take you to the man you are
6:32 and keep him out. His master will soon **f** him."
17:33 they continued to **f** the religious customs of the
17:34 They **f** their former practices instead of truly
17:40 would not listen and continued to **f** their old ways.
21:22 and he refused to **f** the LORD's ways.
1Ch 22:11 and give you success as you **f** his instructions in
29: 5 the craftsmen. Now then, who will **f** my example?
2Ch 2:14 also an engraver and can **f** any design given to him.
7:17 if you **f** me as your father, David, did and obey all
29:15 They were careful to **f** all the LORD's
30:19 who decide to **f** the LORD, the God of their
31:21 and in his efforts to **f** the law and the commands,
35: 6 **F** all the instructions that the LORD gave through
Ezr 10: 3 We will **f** the advice given by you and by the
Ne 9:29 They did not **f** your regulations, by which people
10:29 They solemnly promised to carefully **f** all the
Ps 1: 1 of those / who do not **f** the advice of the wicked,
18:21 I have not turned from my God to **f** evil.
25: 4 O LORD; / point out the right road for me to **f**.
49:17 Their wealth will not **f** them into the grave.
63: 8 I **f** close behind you; / your strong right hand holds
78:56 the Most High / and refused to **f** his decrees.
81:12 So I let them **f** their blind and stubborn way,
81:13 Oh, that Israel would **f** me, walking in my paths!
105:45 All this happened so they would **f** his principles
119: 1 people of integrity, / who **f** the law of the LORD.
119:32 you will help me, / I will run to **f** your commands.
119:33 O LORD, / to **f** every one of your principles.
119:59 of my life, / and I turned to **f** your statutes.
119:67 disciplined me; / but now I closely **f** your word.
119:73 Now give me the sense to **f** your commands.
119:173 for I have chosen to **f** your commandments.
128: 1 those who fear the LORD— / all who **f** his ways!
132:12 and **f** the decrees that I teach them, / then your
139: 5 You both precede and **f** me. / You place your hand
Pr 2:20 **F** the steps of good men instead, and stay on the
4: 4 words to heart. **F** my instructions and you will live.
4:14 not do as the wicked do or **f** the path of evildoers.
4:19 Those who **f** it have no idea what they are
7: 1 **F** my advice, my son; always treasure my
8:32 listen to me, for happy are all who **f** my ways.
10: 9 but those who **f** crooked paths will slip and fall.
14: 2 Those who **f** the right path fear the LORD;
18: 3 contempt, shame, and disgrace are sure to **f**.
28: 5 but those who **f** the LORD understand
Ecc 5: 5 to promise something that you don't **f** through on.
7:29 but they have each turned to **f** their own downward
SS 1: 8 **f** the trail of my flock to the shepherds' tents,
Isa 19:18 In that day five of Egypt's cities will **f** the LORD
21:12 "Morning is coming, but night will soon **f**.
35: 9 be no other dangers. Only the redeemed will **f** it.
45:14 all be yours. They will **f** you as prisoners in chains.
48: 1 You don't **f** through on any of your promises,
48:17 is good and leads you along the paths you should **f**.
53: 6 We have left God's paths to **f** our own.
58:13 you do, and don't **f** your own desires or talk idly.
59: 7 Wherever they go, misery and destruction **f** them.
59: 8 and those who **f** them cannot experience a
64: 5 those who cheerfully do good, who **f** godly ways.
65: 2 They **f** their own evil paths and thoughts.
Jer 3:13 Confess that you refused to **f** me. I, the LORD,
3:17 They will no longer stubbornly **f** their own evil
10:21 They no longer **f** the LORD or ask what he wants
13:10 They stubbornly **f** their own desires and worship
14:10 to wander far from me and do not **f** in my paths.
16:12 You stubbornly **f** your own evil desires and refuse
19: 1 the leaders of the people and of the priests to **f** you.
23:17 And to those who stubbornly **f** their own evil
32:23 in it, but they refused to obey you or **f** your law.
35: 7 If you **f** these commands, you will live long,
42:16 and famine you fear will **f** close behind you,
44:10 No one has chosen to **f** my law and the decrees I
44:23 refusing to obey him and **f** his instructions, laws,
48: 2 too, will be silenced; the sword will **f** you there.
La 1: 9 with no thought of the punishment that would **f**.
Eze 5: 6 She has refused to obey the laws I gave her to **f**.
7:26 Calamity will **f** calamity; rumor will **f** rumor.
9: 5 "**F** him through the city and kill everyone whose
20:18 and told them not to **f** in their parents' footsteps,
20:19 '**F** my laws, pay attention to my instructions,
20:21 refused to keep my laws and **f** my instructions,
21:19 routes on it for the sword of Babylon's king to **f**.
23:48 a warning to others not to **f** their wicked example.
24:24 Ezekiel is an example for you to **f**; you will do as
47:13 "**F** these instructions for dividing the land for the
47:19 then **f** the course of the brook of Egypt to the
Hos 11:10 "For someday the people will **f** the LORD.
Joel 2:11 This is his mighty army, and they **f** his orders.
Mic 1:13 You were the first city in Judah to **f** Israel in the
4: 5 we will **f** the LORD our God forever and ever.
6:16 the only example you **f** is that of wicked King
Zep 1: 5 They claim to **f** the LORD, but then they worship
Zec 3: 7 If you **f** my ways and obey my requirements,
Mt 8:19 "Teacher, I will **f** you no matter where you go!"
8:22 But Jesus told him, "**F** me now! Let those who are
10:38 If you refuse to take up your cross and **f** me,
16:24 selfish ambition, shoulder your cross, and **f** me.
19:21 will have treasure in heaven. Then come, **f** me."
19:27 said to him, "We've given up everything to **f** you.
23: 3 they say to you, but don't **f** their example.
24: 6 must come, but the end won't **f** immediately.
Mk 7: 2 **f** the usual Jewish ritual of hand washing before
7: 5 "Why don't your disciples **f** our age-old customs?
8:34 selfish ambition, shoulder your cross, and **f** me.
10:21 will have treasure in heaven. Then come, **f** me."
10:28 "We've given up everything to **f** you," he said.
13: 7 must come, but the end won't **f** immediately.
14:13 carrying a pitcher of water will meet you. **F** him.
Lk 7:35 is shown to be right by the lives of those who **f** it."
9:23 shoulder your cross daily, and **f** me.
9:57 to Jesus, "I will **f** you no matter where you go."
9:61 Another said, "Yes, Lord, I will **f** you, but first let
14:27 if you do not carry your own cross and **f** me.
18:22 will have treasure in heaven. Then come, **f** me."
21: 9 must come, but the end won't **f** immediately."
22:10 water will meet you. **F** him. At the house he enters,
23:26 just then, was forced to **f** Jesus and carry his cross.
Jn 8:12 If you **f** me, you won't be stumbling through the
8:39 of Abraham, you would **f** his good example.
10: 4 and they **f** him because they recognize his voice.
10: 5 They won't **f** a stranger; they will run from him

10:27 recognize my voice; I know them, and they **f** me.
11:48 the whole nation will **f** him, and then the Roman
12:26 who want to be my disciples must come and **f** me,
12:26 And if they **f** me, the Father will honor them.
13:15 I have given you an example to **f**. Do as I have
13:36 can't go with me now, but you will **f** me later."
21:19 die to glorify God. Then Jesus told him, "**F** me."
21:22 alive until I return, what is that to you? You **f** me."
Ac 5:37 He got some people to **f** him, but he was killed,
12:8 "Now put on your coat and **f** me," the angel
15:5 and be required to **f** the law of Moses.
21:21 their children or **f** other Jewish customs.
22:3 At his feet I learned to **f** our Jewish laws
24:14 "But I admit that I **f** the Way, which they call a
Ro 2:14 written law, instinctively **f** what the law says,
3:8 If you **f** that kind of thinking, however, you might
3:16 Wherever they go, destruction and misery **f** them.
4:16 to receive it, whether or not we **f** Jewish customs,
8:4 no longer **f** our sinful nature but instead **f** the Spirit.
13:2 are refusing to obey God, and punishment will **f**.
1Co 1:12 "I **f** Apollos," or "I **f** Peter," or "I **f** only Christ."
4:16 So I ask you to **f** my example and do as I do.
9:20 When I am with those who **f** the Jewish laws,
10:33 That is the plan I **f**, too. I try to please everyone in
11:1 And you should **f** my example, just as I **f** Christ's.
16:1 You should **f** the same procedures I gave to the
Gal 1:14 and I tried as hard as possible to **f** all the old
2:4 force us, like slaves, to **f** their Jewish regulations.
5:19 When you **f** the desires of your sinful nature,
5:25 let us **f** the Holy Spirit's leading in every part of
Eph 5:1 **F** God's example in everything you do,
Php 2:12 so careful to **f** my instructions when I was with
3:17 and learn from those who **f** our example.
2Th 3:6 and doesn't **f** the tradition of hard work we gave
3:7 For you know that you ought to **f** our example.
3:9 but we wanted to give you an example to **f**.
1Ti 4:1 they will **f** lying spirits and teachings that come
5:15 of them have already gone astray and now **f** Satan.
6:11 all these evil things, and **f** what is right and good.
2Ti 2:5 **F** the Lord's rules for doing his work, just as an
2:22 **F** anything that makes you want to do right.
4:3 They will **f** their own desires and will look for
4:4 They will reject the truth and **f** strange myths.
Heb 6:12 you will **f** the example of those who are going to
12:13 Then those who **f** you, though they are weak
13:9 about food, which don't help those who **f** them.
1Pe 2:21 suffered for you, is your example. **F** in his steps.
2Pe 2:2 Many will **f** their evil teaching and shameful
2:10 He is especially hard on those who **f** their own evil,
3Jn 1:11 bad example influence you. **F** only what is good.
Jude 1:11 For they **f** the evil example of Cain, who killed his
Rev 2:15 people who **f** the same teaching and commit the
14:13 their toils and trials; for their good deeds **f** them!"

FOLLOWED (140) [FOLLOW]

Ge 6:9 He consistently **f** God's will and enjoyed a close
22:21 oldest was Buz, **f** by Kemuel (the father of Aram),
25:13 oldest was Nebaioth, **f** by Kedar, Abdeel, Mibsam,
27:14 So Jacob **f** his mother's instructions, bringing her
37:17 So Joseph **f** his brothers to Dothan and found them
Ex 12:50 So the people of Israel **f** all the LORD's
14:23 **f** them across the bottom of the sea.
18:24 to his father-in-law's advice and **f** his suggestions.
39:42 So the people of Israel **f** all of the LORD's
Lev 8:4 So Moses **f** the LORD's instructions, and all the
9:6 "When you have **f** these instructions from the
12:7 These are the instructions to be **f** after the birth of a
14:2 "The following instructions must be **f** by those
14:57 These instructions must be **f** when dealing with
16:34 Moses **f** all these instructions that the LORD had
Nu 9:17 from over the sacred tent, the people of Israel **f** it.
9:21 when the cloud lifted, the people broke camp and **f**.
10:8 This is a permanent law to be **f** from generation to
16:25 and Abiram, **f** closely by the Israelite leaders.
23:2 Balak **f** his instructions, and the two of them
31:16 "These are the very ones who **f** Balaam's advice
32:12 for they have wholeheartedly **f** the LORD.'
33:1 This is the itinerary the Israelites **f** as they marched
Dt 1:36 this land because he has **f** the LORD completely.
Jos 6:8 the Ark of the LORD's covenant **f** behind them.
6:14 to the camp. They **f** this pattern for six days.
8:31 He **f** the instructions that Moses the LORD's
14:8 For my part, I **f** the LORD my God completely.
14:9 because you wholeheartedly **f** the LORD my
14:14 because he wholeheartedly **f** the LORD,
15:4 of Egypt, which it **f** to the Mediterranean Sea.
17:9 the border of Manasseh **f** the northern side of the
Jdg 2:19 They **f** other gods, worshiping and bowing down to
3:28 victory over Moab your enemy." So they **f** him.
4:22 So he **f** her into the tent and found Sisera lying
5:9 out to Israel's leaders, / and to those who gladly **f**.
5:14 to the Amalekites, / and Benjamin also **f** you.
5:15 and Barak. / They **f** Barak, rushing into the valley.
9:24 In the events that **f**, God punished Abimelech
9:52 Abimelech **f** them to attack the tower. But as he
Ru 3:6 and **f** the instructions of her mother-in-law.
3:18 The man won't rest until he has **f** through on this.
1Sa 6:12 The Philistine rulers **f** them as far as the border of
8:8 have continually forsaken me and **f** other gods.
30:25 made this a law for all of Israel, and it is still **f**.
2Sa 3:16 Palti **f** along behind her as far as Bahurim,
16:23 Absalom **f** Ahithophel's advice, just as David had
20:2 So the men of Israel deserted David and **f** Sheba.
1Ki 2:28 Although he had not **f** Absalom earlier, Joab had
3:3 the LORD and **f** all the instructions of his father,
11:33 He has not **f** my ways and done what is pleasing in
12:14 and **f** the counsel of his younger advisers. He told
14:8 obeyed my commands and **f** me with all his heart
15:26 the LORD's sight and **f** the example of his father,
15:34 the LORD's sight and **f** the example of Jeroboam,
16:2 but you have **f** the evil example of Jeroboam.
16:19 the LORD's sight and **f** the example of Jeroboam,
16:26 He **f** the example of Jeroboam, continuing the sins
21:11 and other leaders **f** the instructions Jezebel had
2Ki 8:18 But Jehoram **f** the example of the kings of Israel
8:27 Ahaziah **f** the evil example of King Ahab's family,
13:2 He **f** the example of Jeroboam son of Nebat,
14:3 Instead, he **f** the example of his father, Joash.
16:3 Instead, he **f** the example of the kings of Israel,
17:15 They **f** the example of the nations around them,
21:21 He **f** the example of his father,
22:2 and **f** the example of his ancestor David.
2Ch 8:14 Solomon **f** the regulations of his father, David.
10:14 and **f** the counsel of his younger advisers. He told
11:16 the God of Israel, **f** the Levites to Jerusalem,
12:1 law of the LORD, and all Israel **f** him in this sin.
17:3 because he **f** the example of his father's early years
21:6 But Jehoram **f** the example of the kings of Israel
21:12 You have not **f** the good example of your father,
22:3 Ahaziah also **f** the evil example of King Ahab's
28:2 he **f** the example of the kings of Israel and cast
34:2 and **f** the example of his ancestor David.
36:14 They **f** the pagan practices of the surrounding
Ezr 10:16 So this was the plan that they **f**. Ezra selected
Ne 12:32 Hoshaiah and half the leaders of Judah **f** them,
12:38 I **f** them, with the other half of the people,
Est 1:21 this made good sense, so he **f** Memucan's counsel.
2:12 **f** by six months with special perfumes
Job 23:11 I have **f** his ways and not turned aside.
Ps 17:4 I have **f** your commands, / which have kept me
78:36 But they **f** him only with their words; / they lied to
99:7 and they **f** the decrees and principles he gave them.
Pr 7:22 He **f** her at once, like an ox going to the slaughter
Jer 2:2 and **f** me even through the barren wilderness.
9:14 they have stubbornly **f** their own desires
11:8 Instead, they stubbornly **f** their own evil desires.
38:27 But Jeremiah **f** the king's instructions, and they left
Eze 23:11 to Oholah, her sister, she **f** right in her footsteps.
23:31 Because you have **f** in your sister's footsteps,
Da 9:10 for we have not **f** the laws he gave us through his
Mt 4:22 They immediately **f** him, leaving the boat and their
4:25 Large crowds **f** him wherever he went—
8:1 Large crowds **f** Jesus as he came down the
9:9 Jesus said to him. So Matthew got up and **f** him.
9:27 two blind men **f** along behind him, shouting,
12:15 He left that area, and many people **f** him.
14:13 he was headed and **f** by land from many villages.
19:2 Vast crowds **f** him there, and he healed their sick.
20:29 left the city of Jericho, a huge crowd **f** behind.
20:34 Instantly they could see! Then they **f** him.
Mk 2:14 Jesus said to him. So Levi got up and **f** him.
2:15 people of this kind among the crowds that **f** Jesus.)
3:7 **f** by a huge crowd from all over Galilee, Judea,
4:36 leaving the crowds behind (although other boats **f**).
10:52 man could see! Then he **f** Jesus down the road.
14:54 Peter **f** far behind and then slipped inside the gates
Lk 5:11 as they landed, they left everything and **f** Jesus.
5:28 So Levi got up, left everything, and **f** him.
9:11 found out where he was going, and they **f** him.
18:28 Peter said, "We have left our homes and **f** you."
18:43 the man could see, and he **f** Jesus, praising God.
23:49 including the women who had **f** him from Galilee,
23:55 the women from Galilee **f** and saw the tomb where
Jn 1:37 Then John's two disciples turned and **f** Jesus.
1:40 who had heard what John said and then **f** Jesus.
2:8 master of ceremonies." So they **f** his instructions.
10:41 And many **f** him. "John didn't do miracles,"
11:31 to Lazarus's grave to weep. So they **f** her there.
18:15 Simon Peter **f** along behind, as did another of the
Ac 2:23 But you **f** God's prearranged plan. With the help of
13:43 to Judaism who worshiped at the synagogue **f** Paul
16:17 She **f** along behind us shouting, "These men are
21:30 was rocked by these accusations, and a great riot **f**.
21:36 And the crowd **f** behind shouting, "Kill him,
Gal 1:13 You know what I was like when I **f** the Jewish
2:13 Then the other Jewish Christians **f** Peter's
1Ti 4:6 message of faith and the true teaching you have **f**.
Heb 11:29 But when the Egyptians **f**, they were all drowned.
2Pe 2:15 right road and **f** the way of Balaam son of Beor,
Rev 2:24 who have not **f** this false teaching ('deeper truths,'
6:8 name of its rider, who was **f** around by the Grave.
13:3 marveled at this miracle and **f** the beast in awe.
14:8 Then another angel **f** him through the skies,
14:9 Then a third angel **f** them, shouting, "Anyone who
19:14 dressed in pure white linen, **f** him on white horses.

FOLLOWER (7) [FOLLOW]

1Ki 18:3 (Now Obadiah was a devoted **f** of the LORD.
Mt 16:24 to the disciples, "If any of you wants to be my **f**,
Mk 8:34 "If any of you wants to be my **f**," he told them,
Lk 9:23 said to the crowd, "If any of you wants to be my **f**,
14:26 "If you want to be my **f** you must love me more
1Co 1:12 Some of you are saying, "I am a **f** of Paul."
3:4 "I am a **f** of Paul," and another says, "I prefer

FOLLOWERS (47) [FOLLOW]

Ex 11:8 And take all your **f** with you.' Only then will I
Nu 16:5 Then he said to Korah and his **f**,
16:6 You, Korah, and all your **f** must do this:
16:16 present yourself before the LORD with all your **f**.
16:17 Be sure that each of your 250 **f** brings an incense
16:32 and the **f** who were standing with them,
16:40 happen to him as happened to Korah and his **f**.
26:10 and 250 of their **f** were destroyed that day by fire
27:3 "But he was not among Korah's **f**, who rebelled
2Sa 15:23 throughout the land as the king and his **f** passed by.
2Ch 24:7 the **f** of wicked Athaliah had broken into the
Ps 15:4 and honor the faithful **f** of the LORD
106:18 Fire fell upon their **f**; / a flame consumed the
145:10 LORD, / and your faithful **f** will bless you.
Da 11:23 With a mere handful of **f**, he will become strong.
11:24 distribute among his **f** the plunder and wealth of
Mt 5:11 and lied about because you are my **f**.
10:18 before governors and kings because you are my **f**.
10:42 a cup of cold water to one of the least of my **f**,
12:27 by the prince of demons, what about your own **f**?
19:28 you who have been my **f** will also sit on twelve
27:57 rich man from Arimathea who was one of Jesus' **f**,
Mk 13:9 accused before governors and kings of being my **f**.
15:41 They had been **f** of Jesus and had cared for him
Lk 6:17 surrounded by many of his **f** and by the crowds.
11:19 by the prince of demons, what about your own **f**?
19:37 all of his **f** began to shout and sing as they walked
19:39 rebuke your **f** for saying things like that!"
21:12 accused before kings and governors of being my **f**.
22:56 Finally she said, "This man was one of Jesus' **f**!"
24:13 That same day two of Jesus' **f** were walking to the
24:22 Then some women from our group of his **f** were at
24:33 and the other **f** of Jesus were gathered.
Jn 7:3 "Go where your **f** can see your miracles!"
18:19 the high priest began asking Jesus about his **f**
18:36 my **f** would have fought when I was arrested by the
Ac 5:36 he was killed, and his **f** went their various ways.
5:37 but he was killed, too, and all his **f** were scattered.
9:1 He was eager to destroy the Lord's **f**, so he went to
9:2 asking their cooperation in the arrest of any **f** of the
9:21 "Isn't this the same man who persecuted Jesus' **f**
22:4 And I persecuted the **f** of the Way, hounding some
26:9 I could to oppose the **f** of Jesus of Nazareth.
1Co 10:2 As **f** of Moses, they were all baptized in the cloud
15:6 he was seen by more than five hundred of his **f** at
Eph 1:1 in Ephesus, who are faithful **f** of Christ Jesus.
Rev 2:13 was martyred among you by Satan's **f**.

FOLLOWING (147) [FOLLOW]

Ge 19:26 But Lot's wife looked back as she was **f** along
Ex 12:1 Now the LORD gave the **f** instructions to Moses
15:25 the **f** conditions to test their faithfulness to him:
23:22 you are careful to obey him, **f** all my instructions,
34:12 If you do, you soon will be **f** their evil ways.
34:25 lamb may be kept over until the **f** morning.
40:36 people of Israel would set out on their journey, **f** it.
Lev 1:2 "Give the **f** instructions to the Israelites:
4:2 "Give the Israelites the **f** instructions for dealing
4:20 **f** the same procedure as with the sin offering for
5:10 **f** all the procedures that have been prescribed.
6:9 and his sons the **f** instructions regarding the whole
11:2 "Give the **f** instructions to the Israelites:
11:24 "The **f** creatures make you ceremonially unclean.
14:2 "The **f** instructions must be followed by those
20:6 by consulting and **f** mediums or psychics,
27:2 "Give the **f** instructions to the Israelites: If you
Nu 8:20 carefully **f** all the LORD's instructions to Moses.
15:18 "Give the people of Israel the **f** instructions:
15:39 and that you are to obey his commands instead of **f**
25:4 The LORD issued the **f** command to Moses:
26:20 But the **f** clans descended from Judah's surviving
28:17 On the **f** day a joyous, seven-day festival will
Dt 5:32 your God, **f** his instructions in every detail.
12:30 do not be trapped into **f** their example in
13:5 Since they try to keep you from **f** the LORD your
21:9 By **f** these instructions and doing what is right in
Jos 11:1 he sent urgent messages to the **f** kings:
12:7 The **f** is a list of the kings Joshua and the Israelite
13:15 Moses had assigned the **f** area to the families of the
13:24 Moses had assigned the **f** area to the families of the
13:29 Moses had assigned the **f** area to the families of the
15:33 The **f** towns situated in the western foothills were
15:48 Judah also received the **f** towns in the hill country:
16:5 The **f** territory was given to the families of the tribe
16:8 **f** the Kanah Ravine to the Mediterranean Sea.
17:11 The **f** towns within the territory of Issachar
19:18 Its boundaries included the **f** towns: Jezreel,
20:7 The **f** cities were designated as cities of refuge:
20:8 the **f** cities were designated as cities of refuge:
21:3 inheritance the **f** towns with their pasturelands.
21:9 The Israelites gave the **f** towns from the tribes of
21:13 The **f** towns with their pasturelands were given to
21:17 the **f** towns with their surrounding pasturelands:
21:23 The **f** towns and pasturelands were allotted to the
21:25 The half-tribe of Manasseh allotted the **f** towns
21:34 were given the **f** towns from the tribe of Zebulun:
22:18 And yet today you are turning away from **f** the
Jdg 9:49 cut down some branches, **f** Abimelech's example.
11:3 of Tob. Soon he had a large band of rebels **f** him.
1Sa 30:27 The gifts were sent to the leaders of the **f** towns
2Sa 11:1 The **f** spring, the time of year when kings go to
1Ki 18:28 So they shouted louder, and **f** their normal custom,
20:26 The **f** spring he called up the Aramean army
22:43 was a good king, **f** the example of his father, Asa.
22:52 **f** the example of his father and mother
2Ki 4:17 And at that time the **f** year she had a son, just as
7:15 **f** a trail of clothing and equipment that the
10:30 "You have done well in **f** my instructions to
13:6 continued to sin, **f** the evil example of Jeroboam.
16:11 Uriah built an altar just like it by **f** the king's
17:21 Then Jeroboam drew Israel away from **f** the
1Ch 6:19 The **f** were the Levite clans, listed according to

6:31 David assigned the **f** men to lead the music at the
6:32 **f** all the regulations handed down to them.
6:49 They made atonement for Israel by **f** all the
6:57 So the descendants of Aaron were given the **f**
12:1 The **f** men joined David at Ziklag while he was
15:18 The **f** men were chosen as their assistants:
16:4 David appointed the **f** Levites to lead the people in
20:1 The **f** spring, the time of year when kings go to
23:31 all times, **f** all the procedures they had been given.
27:16 The **f** were the tribes of Israel and their leaders:
2Ch 8:14 **f** the commands of David, the man of God.
13:11 We are **f** the instructions of the LORD our God,
17:4 and obeyed his commands instead of **f** the
20:32 was a good king, **f** the ways of his father, Asa.
20:33 themselves to **f** the God of their ancestors.
22:5 **F** their evil advice, Ahaziah made an alliance with
23:18 the LORD, **f** all the instructions given by David.
30:12 his officials, who were **f** the word of the LORD.
35:4 **f** the written instructions of King David of Israel
35:15 **f** the orders given by David, Asaph, Heman,
36:10 In the spring of the **f** year, Jehoiachin was
Ezr 2:43 The descendants of the **f** Temple servants returned
6:18 **f** all the instructions recorded in the Book of
Ne 2:1 Early the **f** spring, during the twentieth year of
6:13 intimidate me and make me sin by **f** his suggestion.
7:46 "The descendants of the **f** Temple servants
10:1 document was ratified and sealed with the **f** names:
12:22 and the priests in the days of the **f** high priests:
Est 2:20 She was still **f** Mordecai's orders, just as she did
9:17 Then on the **f** day they rested, celebrating their
Job 34:27 For they turned aside from **f** him. They have no
Ps 17:5 on your path; / I have not wavered from **f** you.
119:9 stay pure? / By obeying your word and **f** its rules.
Pr 4:27 Don't get sidetracked; keep your feet from **f** evil.
Ecc 5:4 don't delay in **f** through, for God takes no pleasure
Isa 56:11 They are stupid shepherds, all **f** their own path,
Jer 7:24 **f** the stubborn desires of their evil hearts.
18:12 to live as we want to, **f** our own evil desires."
32:1 The **f** message came to Jeremiah from the LORD
34:15 and did what was right, **f** my command.
35:18 Jehonadab in every respect, **f** all his instructions.
39:15 The LORD had given the **f** message to Jeremiah
46:1 The **f** messages were given to Jeremiah the prophet
Eze 13:3 the false prophets who are **f** their own imaginations
Da 2:40 **F** that kingdom, there will be a fourth great
8:1 **f** the one that had already appeared to me.
Zep 1:8 and princes of Judah and all those **f** pagan customs.
Mt 26:58 Peter was **f** far behind and eventually came to the
Mk 10:32 and the people **f** behind were overwhelmed with
10:46 and his disciples left town, a great crowd was **f**.
14:51 There was a young man **f** along behind,
Lk 6:39 Then Jesus gave the **f** illustration: "What good is it
7:11 to the village of Nain, with a great crowd **f** him.
14:25 Great crowds were **f** Jesus. He turned around
22:54 high priest's residence, and Peter was **f** far behind.
Jn 1:35 The **f** day, John was again standing with two of his
1:38 Jesus looked around and saw them **f**. "What do
6:2 And a huge crowd kept **f** him wherever he went,
8:38 But you are **f** the advice of your father."
21:20 and saw the disciple Jesus loved **f** them—
Ac 6:5 idea pleased the whole group, and they chose the **f**:
8:13 He began **f** Philip wherever he went, and he was
10:24 They arrived in Caesarea the **f** day. Cornelius was
12:9 So Peter left the cell, **f** the angel. But all the time
13:44 The **f** week almost the entire city turned out to hear
20:15 The **f** day, we crossed to the island of Samos.
20:30 of you will distort the truth in order to draw a **f**.
24:2 Tertullus laid charges against Paul in the **f** address
25:6 to Caesarea, and on the **f** day Paul's trial began.
27:19 The **f** day they even threw out the ship's equipment
28:13 so the **f** day we sailed up the coast to Puteoli.
Ro 8:13 For if you keep on **f** it, you will perish. But if
15:21 I have been **f** the plan spoken of in the Scriptures,
1Co 3:21 So don't take pride in **f** a particular leader.
11:2 and you are **f** the Christian teaching I passed on to
Gal 1:6 through Christ. You are already **f** a different way
2:14 When I saw that they were not **f** the truth of the
5:7 with you to hold you back from **f** the truth?
Eph 2:3 **f** the passions and desires of our evil nature.
5:2 **f** the example of Christ, who loved you and gave
Col 2:20 So why do you keep on **f** rules of the world,
1Ti 6:21 Some people have wandered from the faith by **f**
2Ti 3:7 Such women are forever **f** new teachings, but they
Rev 14:4 pure as virgins, **f** the Lamb wherever he goes.

FOLLOWS (25) [FOLLOW]

Ex 20:1 Then God instructed the people as **f**:
Lev 16:13 If he **f** these instructions, he will not die.
Dt 1:5 the Jordan River. He began to explain the law as **f**:
27:1 and the leaders of Israel charged the people as **f**:
27:9 and the Levitical priests addressed all Israel as **f**:
Jdg 13:13 "Be sure your wife **f** the instructions I gave her.
1Sa 13:21 (The schedule of charges was as **f**: a quarter of an
1Ch 13:2 he addressed the entire assembly of Israel as **f**:
28:2 and stood before them and addressed them as **f**:
Ezr 8:26 as I gave it to them and found the totals to be as **f**:
Ne 12:12 the family leaders of the priests were as **f**:
Job 41:8 a hand on it, you will never forget the battle that **f**,
Ps 19:6 and **f** its course to the other end. / Nothing can hide
Pr 16:17 leads away from evil; whoever **f** that path is safe.
Eze 48:1 Its boundary line **f** the Hethlon road to
48:28 then **f** the brook of Egypt to the Mediterranean.
Hos 6:5 My judgment will strike you as surely as day **f**
Joel 2:3 in front of them and **f** them in every direction!
Hab 3:5 marches before him; plague **f** close behind.
Ac 1:15 Peter stood up and addressed them as **f**:
5:35 Then he addressed his colleagues as **f**: "Men of
15:7 Peter stood and addressed them as **f**:
17:22 standing before the Council, addressed them as **f**:
19:25 in related trades, and addressed them as **f**:
2Ti 2:5 just as an athlete either **f** the rules or is disqualified

FOLLY (10) [FOOL]

Job 4:18 own angels and has charged some of them with **f**,
Pr 5:23 he will be lost because of his incredible **f**.
9:13 The woman named **F** is loud and brash. She is
12:23 of their knowledge, but fools broadcast their **f**.
14:18 The simpleton is clothed with **f**, but the wise
14:24 crown for the wise; the effort of fools yields only **f**.
17:12 of her cubs than to confront a fool caught in **f**.
18:13 What a shame, what **f**, to give advice before
26:11 a dog returns to its vomit, so a fool repeats his **f**.
Ecc 2:12 So I decided to compare wisdom and **f**, and anyone

FOND (1) [FONDLY]

1Ki 11:19 Pharaoh grew very **f** of Hadad, and he gave him a

FONDLED (2) [FONDLING]

Eze 23:3 they allowed themselves to be **f** and caressed.
23:21 when you first allowed yourself to be **f**

FONDLING (1) [FONDLED]

Ge 26:8 looked out a window and saw Isaac **f** Rebekah.

FONDLY (1) [FOND]

Eze 23:27 on those things or **f** remember your time in Egypt.

FOOD (372) [FOODS]

Ge 1:29 the earth and all the fruit trees for your **f**.
1:30 green plants to the animals and birds for their **f**."
3:19 All your life you will sweat to produce **f**, until your
6:21 take enough **f** for your family and for all the
9:3 I have given them to you for **f**, just as I have given
14:11 taking all the wealth and **f** with them.
18:5 Let me prepare some **f** to refresh you. Please stay
18:8 When the **f** was ready, he took some cheese curds
21:14 early the next morning, prepared **f** for the journey,
24:25 we have plenty of straw and **f** for the camels,
27:10 Take the **f** to your father; then he can eat it
27:18 Jacob carried the platter of **f** to his father and said,
27:25 So Jacob took the **f** over to his father, and Isaac ate
28:20 me on this journey and give me **f** and clothing,
31:38 years I never touched a single ram of yours for **f**.
41:35 Have them gather all the **f** and grain of these good
41:35 and store it away so there will be **f** in the cities.
41:55 They pleaded with Pharaoh for **f**, and he told them,
42:5 sons arrived in Egypt along with others to buy **f**,
42:10 they exclaimed. "We have come to buy **f**.
43:2 said to his sons, "Go again and buy us a little **f**."
43:4 come with us, we will go down and buy some **f**.
43:20 to him, "Sir, after our first trip to Egypt to buy **f**,
43:24 water to wash their feet and **f** for their donkeys.
43:31 under control. "Bring on the **f**!" he ordered.
43:34 Their **f** was served to them from Joseph's own
44:25 when he said, 'Go back again and buy us a little **f**,'
45:23 and all kinds of other **f** to be eaten on his journey.
45:27 and when he saw the wagons loaded with the **f** sent
47:12 And Joseph furnished **f** to his father and brothers in
47:15 of money, they came to Joseph crying again for **f**.
47:16 me your livestock. I will give you **f** in exchange."
47:17 gave their livestock to Joseph in exchange for **f**.
47:17 But at least they were able to purchase **f** for that
47:19 Buy us and our land in exchange for **f**; we will
47:22 for they were assigned **f** from Pharaoh and didn't
49:20 "Asher will produce rich foods, / **f** fit for kings.
Ex 12:11 Eat the **f** quickly, for this is the LORD's
12:16 done on these days except in the preparation of **f**.
16:4 I'm going to rain down **f** from heaven for you.
16:4 and pick up as much **f** as they need for that day.
16:15 told them, "It is the **f** the LORD has given you.
16:17 the people of Israel went out and gathered this **f**—
16:21 The people gathered the **f** morning by morning,
16:21 the **f** they had not picked up melted
16:24 The next morning the leftover **f** was wholesome
16:25 Moses said, "This is your **f** for today, for today is
16:25 There will be no **f** on the ground today.
16:26 Gather the **f** for six days, but the seventh day is a
16:26 There will be no **f** on the ground for you on that
16:27 Some of the people went out anyway to gather **f**,
16:29 That is why I give you twice as much **f** on the sixth
16:29 Do not pick up **f** from the ground on that day."
16:31 In time, the **f** became known as manna. It was
21:10 he may not reduce her **f** or clothing or fail to sleep
23:25 If you do, I will bless you with **f** and water, and I
Lev 2:10 will be given to Aaron and his sons as their **f**.
3:11 The priest will burn them on the altar as **f**,
3:16 The priest will burn them on the altar as **f**,
6:16 flour will belong to Aaron and his sons for their **f**.
6:18 or anything that touches this **f** will become holy."
11:2 to the Israelites: The animals you may use for **f**
11:34 used to cleanse an unclean object touches any **f**, all of that **f** will be defiled.
14:4 using two wild birds of a kind permitted for **f**,
21:6 providing God with his **f**, and they must remain
21:8 them as holy because they offer up **f** to your God.
21:17 defects will not qualify to offer **f** to their God.
21:21 he has a blemish, he may not offer **f** to his God.
21:22 However, he may eat from the **f** offered to God,
22:3 approach the sacred **f** presented by the Israelites,
22:7 After all, this **f** has been set aside for them.
22:11 slaves with his own money, they may eat of his **f**.
22:11 his slaves have children, they also may share his **f**.
22:13 her father's home, she may eat her father's **f** again.
25:37 on anything you lend them, whether money or **f**.
26:26 I will completely destroy your **f** supply,
26:26 They will ration your **f** by weight, and even if you have **f** to eat, you will not be
Nu 18:13 family who is ceremonially clean may eat this **f**.
18:31 and your families may eat this **f** anywhere you
28:2 you present to me by fire on the altar are my **f**,
28:24 this is how you will prepare the **f** offerings to be
29:7 Day of Atonement, the people must go without **f**,
Dt 2:6 Pay them for whatever **f** or water you use.
2:28 We will pay for every bite of **f** we eat and all the
8:3 a **f** previously unknown to you and your ancestors.
8:9 It is a land where **f** is plentiful and nothing is
8:16 in the wilderness, a **f** unknown to your ancestors.
10:18 living among you and gives them **f** and clothing.
15:22 Instead, use it for **f** for your family at home.
20:20 down trees that you know are not valuable for **f**.
23:4 These nations did not welcome you with **f**
23:19 whether it is money, **f**, or anything else that may be
28:26 Your dead bodies will be **f** for the birds and wild
29:6 but he gave you **f** so you would know that he is the
31:20 they will eat all the **f** they want and become well
Jos 24:13 I gave you vineyards and olive groves for **f**,
Jdg 8:5 "Will you please give my warriors some **f**?
8:8 there Gideon went up to Peniel and asked for **f**,
13:4 or any other alcoholic drink or eat any forbidden **f**.
13:7 or any other alcoholic drink or eat any forbidden **f**.
13:14 any other alcoholic drink, or eat any forbidden **f**."
17:10 silver a year, plus a change of clothes and your **f**."
20:10 tribe will be chosen to supply the warriors with **f**,
Ru 2:14 over here and help yourself to some of our **f**.
2:14 she sat with his harvesters, and Boaz gave her **f**—
2:18 Ruth also gave her the **f** that was left over from her
1Sa 2:36 before his descendants, begging for money and **f**.
7:6 They also went without **f** all day and confessed that
9:7 "Even our **f** is gone, and we don't have a thing to
9:13 guests won't start until he arrives to bless the **f**."
14:28 oath that anyone who eats **f** today will be cursed.
14:30 freely from the **f** they found among our enemies,
16:20 and a donkey loaded down with **f** and wine.
21:6 So, since there was no other **f** available, the priest
22:10 Then he gave David **f** and the sword of Goliath the
22:13 "Why did you give him **f** and a sword?
2Sa 3:29 or who dies by the sword or who begs for **f**!"
6:19 Then he gave a gift of **f** to every man and woman
9:10 farm the land for him to produce **f** for his family.
12:4 instead of killing a lamb from his own flocks for **f**,
12:16 He went without **f** and lay all night on the bare
13:5 him to let Tamar come and prepare some **f** for you.
13:7 to Amnon's house to prepare some **f** for him.
13:10 "Now bring the **f** into my bedroom and feed it to
19:32 He was the one who provided **f** for the king during
19:35 **F** and wine are no longer tasty, and I cannot hear
1Ki 4:7 They were responsible for providing **f** from the
4:22 The daily **f** requirements for Solomon's palace
4:27 The district governors faithfully provided **f** for
5:9 to you. You can pay me with **f** for my household."
10:5 She was also amazed at the **f** on his tables,
11:18 who gave them a home, **f**, and some land.
13:8 I would not eat any **f** or drink any water in this
13:9 'You must not eat any **f** or drink any water while
13:15 of God, "Come home with me and eat some **f**."
13:16 "I am not allowed to eat any **f** or drink any water
13:17 'You must not eat any **f** or drink any water while
13:18 and give him **f** to eat and water to drink.' " But
13:19 and the man of God ate some **f** and drank some
13:22 You came back to this place and ate **f** and drank
17:4 for I have commanded them to bring you **f**."
17:13 Afterward there will still be enough **f** for you
18:4 each cave and had supplied them with **f** and water.)
18:13 in two caves and supplied them with **f** and water.
19:8 and the **f** gave him enough strength to travel forty
2Ki 4:8 lived there, and she invited him to eat some **f**.
6:22 Give them **f** and drink and send them home again
6:27 "I have neither **f** nor wine to give you."
25:3 very severe, with the last of the **f** entirely gone.
1Ch 12:40 and Naphtali brought **f** on donkeys, camels, mules,
16:3 Then he gave a gift of **f** to every man and woman
2Ch 9:4 She was also amazed at the **f** on his tables,
11:11 he stored supplies of **f**, olive oil, and wine.
28:15 and sandals to wear, gave them enough **f** and drink,
31:18 **F** allotments were also given to all the families
Ezr 2:63 **f** from the sacrifices until there was a priest who
3:7 of Tyre and Sidon, paying them with **f**, wine,
10:6 the night there, but he did not eat any **f** or drink.
Ne 5:2 so we can buy the **f** we need to survive."
5:3 vineyards, and homes to get **f** during the famine."
5:14 neither I nor my officials drew on our official **f**
5:15 demanding a daily ration of **f** and wine, besides a
5:18 Yet I refused to claim the governor's **f** allowance
7:65 **f** from the sacrifices until there was a priest who
8:10 and share gifts of **f** with people who have nothing
8:12 and drink at a festive meal, to share gifts of **f**,
12:47 the people brought a daily supply of **f** for the
Job 6:5 no green grass, and oxen low when they have no **f**.
6:6 People complain when there is no salt in their **f**.
12:11 Just as the mouth tastes good **f**, so the ear tests the
20:14 the **f** he has eaten turns sour within him,
22:7 refused water for the thirsty and **f** for the hungry.
24:5 They go into the desert to search for **f** for their
24:10 They are forced to carry **f** while they themselves
31:17 Have I been stingy with my **f** and refused to share
33:20 and do not care for even the most delicious **f**.
34:3 'Just as the mouth tastes good **f**, the ear tests the

36:31 he governs the people, giving them **f** in abundance.
38:41 Who provides **f** for the ravens when their young
40:20 The mountains offer it their best **f**, where all the
Ps 41: 9 I trusted completely, / the one who shared my **f**,
42: 3 Day and night, I have only tears for **f**, / while my
59:15 They scavenge for **f** / but go to sleep unsatisfied.
63:10 will die by the sword / and become the **f** of jackals.
69:21 But instead, they give me poison for **f**; / they offer
78:19 saying, / "God can't give us **f** in the desert.
78:25 They ate the **f** of angels! / God gave them all they
78:30 But before they finished eating this **f** they had
79: 2 as **f** for the birds of heaven. / The flesh of your
79: 2 godly ones / has become **f** for the wild animals.
102: 9 I eat ashes instead of my **f**. / My tears run down
104:14 You allow them to produce **f** from the earth—
104:21 Then the young lions roar for their **f**, / but they are
104:27 on you / to give them their **f** as they need it.
105:16 on the land of Canaan, / cutting off its **f** supply.
109:18 or as the water he drinks, / or the rich **f** he eats.
111: 5 He gives **f** to those who trust him; / he always
127: 2 until late at night, / anxiously working for **f** to eat;
132:15 this city prosperous / and satisfy its poor with **f**.
136:25 He gives **f** to every living thing. / His faithful love
145:15 you for help; / you give them their **f** as they need it.
146: 7 and **f** to the hungry. / The LORD frees the
147: 9 and the young ravens cry to him for **f**.
Pr 6: 8 labor hard all summer, gathering **f** for the winter.
9: 5 "Come, eat my **f**, and drink the wine I have mixed.
9:17 is refreshing; **f** eaten in secret tastes the best!"
12: 9 a servant than to be self-important but have no **f**.
13:23 A poor person's farm may produce much **f**,
18:20 Words satisfy the soul as **f** satisfies the stomach;
20: 4 the right season, you will have no **f** at the harvest.
23: 8 You will vomit up the delicious **f** they serve,
25:21 If your enemies are hungry, give them **f** to eat.
27: 7 is full, but even bitter **f** tastes sweet to the hungry.
28:19 Hard workers have plenty of **f**; playing around
30:25 aren't strong, / but they store up **f** for the winter.
31:14 like a merchant's ship; she brings her **f** from afar.
Ecc 2:24 So I decided there is nothing better than to enjoy **f**
6: 7 All people spend their lives scratching for **f**,
9: 7 Eat your **f** and drink your wine with a happy heart,
Isa 3: 1 will cut off the supplies of **f** and water from
3: 7 "I can't help. I don't have any extra **f** or clothes.
4: 1 We will provide our own **f** and clothing.
9:20 They fight against their own neighbors to steal **f**,
21:14 bring **f** and water to these weary refugees.
23:18 not be hoarded but will be used to provide good **f**
25: 6 It will be a delicious feast of good **f**, with clear,
30:20 Though the Lord gave you adversity for **f**
32: 6 they deprive the hungry of **f** and give no water to
33:16 **F** will be supplied to them, and they will have
55: 2 Why spend your money on **f** that does not give you
55: 2 Why pay for **f** that does you no good? Listen,
55: 2 and I will tell you where to get **f** that is good for
58: 7 I want you to share your **f** with the hungry and to
Jer 7:33 The corpses of my people will be **f** for the vultures
16: 4 and their bodies will be **f** for the vultures and wild
19: 7 The enemy will leave the dead bodies as **f** for the
19: 9 enemies lay siege to the city until all the **f** is gone.
29: 5 to stay. Plant gardens, and eat the **f** you produce.
34:20 Your bodies will be **f** for the vultures and wild
40: 5 Then Nebuzaradan gave Jeremiah some **f**
52: 6 very severe, with the last of the **f** entirely gone.
La 1:11 They have sold their treasures for **f** to stay alive.
1:19 even as they searched for **f** to save their lives.
2:12 "Mama, we want **f**," they cry, and then collapse in
4: 5 lived in palaces now search the garbage pits for **f**.
4: 9 who die of hunger, wasting away for want of **f**.
5: 6 to Egypt and Assyria to get enough **f** to survive.
5: 9 We must hunt for **f** in the wilderness at the risk of
Eze 4: 9 Use this **f** to make bread for yourself during the
4:10 eight ounces of **f** for each day, and eat it at set
4:16 I will cause **f** to be very scarce in Jerusalem.
4:17 **F** and water will be so scarce that the people will
5:16 and more severe until every crumb of **f** is gone.
12:18 "Son of man, tremble as you eat your **f**.
12:19 They will eat their **f** with trembling and sip their
14:13 cutting off their **f** supply and sending a famine to
18: 7 not rob the poor but instead gives **f** to the hungry
24:17 or accept any **f** brought to you by consoling
24:22 or console yourselves by eating the **f** brought to
29: 5 for I have given you as **f** to the wild animals
35:12 they have been given to us as **f** to eat!'
39: 4 I will give you as **f** to the vultures and wild
44: 7 profaned my Temple even as you offered me my **f**,
44:29 Their **f** will come from the gifts and sacrifices
47:12 The fruit will be for **f** and the leaves for healing."
48:18 This farmland will produce **f** for the people
Da 1: 5 The king assigned them a daily ration of the best **f**
1: 8 up his mind not to defile himself by eating the **f**
1:10 "My lord the king has ordered that you eat this **f**
1:13 other young men who are eating the king's rich **f**.
1:15 who had been eating the **f** assigned by the king.
10: 3 All that time I had eaten no rich **f** or meat,
Hos 2: 5 and sell myself to them for **f** and drink,
9: 3 where you will live on **f** that is ceremonially
9: 4 just as **f** touched by a person in mourning is
9: 4 They may eat this **f** to feed themselves, but they
Joel 1:16 We watch as our **f** disappears before our very eyes.
2:26 Once again you will have all the **f** you want,
Jnh 3: 5 they decided to go without **f** and wear sackcloth to
Mic 3: 5 You promise peace for those who give you **f**,
Hag 1: 6 You have **f** to eat, but not enough to fill you up.
2:12 or stew, wine or oil, or any other kind of **f**,
Mal 1:12 By bringing contemptible **f**, you are saying it's all
3:10 so there will be enough **f** in my Temple.
Mt 3: 4 a leather belt; his **f** was locusts and wild honey.
6:11 Give us our **f** for today,
6:25 whether you have enough **f**, drink, and clothes.
6:25 Doesn't life consist of more than **f** and clothing?
6:26 don't need to plant or harvest or put **f** in barns
6:31 "So don't worry about having enough **f** or drink
14:15 can go to the villages and buy **f** for themselves."
14:19 toward heaven, and asked God's blessing on the **f**.
15:26 "It isn't right to take **f** from the children and throw
15:33 "And where would we get enough **f** out here in the
15:36 to the disciples, who distributed the **f** to the crowd.
15:37 there were seven large baskets of **f** left over!
16: 5 discovered they had forgotten to bring any **f**.
16: 8 Why are you worried about having no **f**?
16: 9 and the baskets of **f** that were left over?
16:10 I fed with seven loaves, with baskets of **f** left over?
16:11 How could you even think I was talking about **f**?
Mk 1: 6 a leather belt; his **f** was locusts and wild honey.
6: 8 a walking stick—no **f**, no traveler's bag, no money.
6:36 and villages and buy themselves some **f**."
6:37 "It would take a small fortune to buy **f** for all this
6:38 "How much **f** do you have?" he asked. "Go
6:41 toward heaven, and asked God's blessing on the **f**.
7:19 **F** doesn't come in contact with your heart, but only
7:19 he showed that every kind of **f** is acceptable.)
7:27 It isn't right to take **f** from the children and throw it
8: 1 had gathered, and the people ran out of **f** again.
8: 4 "How are we supposed to find enough **f** for them
8: 8 there were seven large baskets of **f** left over!
8:14 discovered they had forgotten to bring any **f**,
8:17 "Why are you so worried about having no **f**?
Lk 3:11 If you have **f**, share it with those who are hungry."
9: 3 "nor a traveler's bag, nor **f**, nor money.
9:12 so they can find **f** and lodging for the night.
9:13 us to go and buy enough **f** for this whole crowd?"
9:16 toward heaven, and asked God's blessing on the **f**.
11: 3 Give us our **f** day by day.
12:22 whether you have enough **f** to eat or clothes to
12:23 For life consists of far more than **f** and clothing.
12:24 don't need to plant or harvest or put **f** in barns
12:29 And don't worry about **f**—what to eat and drink.
15:17 'At home even the hired men have **f** enough to
Jn 4: 8 disciples had gone into the village to buy some **f**.
4:32 "No," he said, "I have **f** you don't know about."
6:27 so concerned about perishable things like **f**.
6:55 For my flesh is the true **f**, and my blood is the true
13:18 'The one who shares my **f** has turned against me,'
13:29 and pay for the **f** or to give some money to the
Ac 6: 1 discriminated against in the daily distribution of **f**.
6: 2 of God, not administering a **f** program," they said.
7:11 great misery for our ancestors, as they ran out of **f**.
9: 9 And all that time he went without **f** and water.
9:19 Afterward he ate some **f** and was strengthened.
12:20 were dependent upon Herod's country for their **f**.
14:17 and good crops and giving you **f** and joyful
15:29 You must abstain from eating **f** offered to idols,
21: 8 the seven men who had been chosen to distribute **f**.
21:25 They should not eat **f** offered to idols, nor consume
27:33 "You haven't touched **f** for two weeks," he said.
Ro 14: 6 Those who eat all kinds of **f** do so to honor the
14:14 sure on the authority of the Lord Jesus that no **f**,
1Co 3: 2 I had to feed you with milk and not with solid **f**,
6:13 "**F** is for the stomach, and the stomach is for **f**."
8: 1 Now let's talk about **f** that has been sacrificed to
8: 7 so when they eat **f** that has been offered to idols,
8:10 Weak Christians who think it is wrong to eat this **f**
8:10 by eating **f** that has been dedicated to the idol.
9:11 too much to ask, in return, for mere **f** and clothing?
9:13 from the **f** brought to the Temple as offerings?
10: 3 And all of them ate the same miraculous **f**,
10:30 If I can thank God for the **f** and enjoy it,
2Co 6: 5 endured sleepless nights, and gone without **f**.
11:27 been hungry and thirsty and have gone without **f**.
12:14 little children don't pay for their parents' **f**.
12:14 way around; parents supply **f** for their children.
2Th 3: 8 We never accepted **f** from anyone without paying
1Ti 6: 8 So if we have enough **f** and clothing, let us be
Heb 5:12 babies who drink only milk and cannot eat solid **f**.
5:14 Solid **f** is for those who are mature, who have
9:10 For that old system deals only with **f** and drink
13: 9 not from ceremonial rules about **f**, which don't
Jas 2:15 you see a brother or sister who needs **f** or clothing,
2:16 but then you don't give that person any **f**
Rev 2:14 He taught them to worship idols by eating **f** offered
2:20 eat **f** offered to idols, and commit sexual sin.

FOODS (13) [FOOD]

Ge 49:20 "Asher will produce rich **f**, / food fit for kings.
Ne 8:10 "Go and celebrate with a feast of choice **f**
Ps 63: 5 You satisfy me more than the richest of **f**. / I will
78:18 God in their hearts, / demanding the **f** they craved.
81:16 But I would feed you with the best of **f**. / I would
Isa 65: 4 They also eat pork and other forbidden **f**.
La 4: 5 The people who once ate only the richest **f** now
Eze 16:13 You ate the finest **f**—fine flour, honey, and olive
Da 1:16 fed them only vegetables instead of the rich **f**
Zec 9: 7 meat with blood in it or feed on other forbidden **f**.
Ro 14: 3 And those who won't eat certain **f** must not
1Ti 4: 3 is wrong to be married and wrong to eat certain **f**.
4: 3 But God created those **f** to be eaten with

FOOL (76) [FOLLY, FOOL'S, FOOLED, FOOLING, FOOLISH, FOOLISHLY, FOOLISHNESS, FOOLS]

Ge 39:17 you've had around here tried to make a **f** of me,"
Nu 16:14 of fields and vineyards. Are you trying to **f** us?
22:29 "Because you have made me look like a **f**!"
1Sa 25:25 to him. He is a **f**, just as his name suggests.
26:21 life today. I have been a **f** and very, very wrong."
2Sa 6:21 So I am willing to act like a **f** in order to show my
2Ki 18:30 Don't let him **f** you into trusting in the LORD by
2Ch 16: 9 What a **f** you have been! From now on, you will be
32:15 Don't let Hezekiah **f** you! Don't let him deceive
Job 5: 2 Surely resentment destroys the **f**, and jealousy kills
13: 9 Or do you think you can **f** him as easily as you **f**
35:16 have protested in vain. You have spoken like a **f**."
Ps 92: 6 not know this! / Only a **f** would not understand it.
Pr 6:32 But the man who commits adultery is an utter **f**,
10:14 but the babbling of a **f** invites trouble.
10:18 To hide hatred is to be a liar; to slander is to be a **f**.
10:20 are like sterling silver; the heart of a **f** is worthless.
10:23 Doing wrong is fun for a **f**, while wise conduct is a
11:29 only the wind. The **f** will be a servant to the wise.
12:16 A **f** is quick-tempered, but a wise person stays
15: 5 Only a **f** despises a parent's discipline;
15:14 is hungry for truth, while the **f** feeds on trash.
17: 7 Eloquent speech is not fitting for a **f**; even less are
17:10 than a hundred lashes on the back of a **f**.
17:12 of her cubs than to confront a **f** caught in folly.
17:16 It is senseless to pay tuition to educate a **f** who has
17:21 It is painful to be the parent of a **f**; there is no joy
19: 1 to be poor and honest than to be a **f** and dishonest.
19:10 It isn't right for a **f** to live in luxury or for a slave
24: 7 Wisdom is too much for a **f**. When the leaders gather, the **f** has nothing to say.
24: 9 The schemes of a **f** are sinful; everyone despises a
26: 3 with a bridle, and a **f** with a rod to his back!
26: 6 Trusting a **f** to convey a message is as foolish as
26: 7 In the mouth of a **f**, a proverb becomes as limp as a
26: 8 Honoring a **f** is as foolish as tying a stone to a
26:10 An employer who hires a **f** or a bystander is like an
26:11 a dog returns to its vomit, so a **f** repeats his folly.
27: 3 but the resentment caused by a **f** is heavier than
29: 9 If a wise person takes a **f** to court, there will be
29:11 A **f** gives full vent to anger, but a wise person
29:20 There is more hope for a **f** than for someone who
30:22 becomes a king, / an overbearing **f** who prospers,
30:32 If you have been a **f** by being proud or plotting
Ecc 2:14 For the wise person sees, while the **f** is blind.
2:15 Both of them die. Just as the **f** will die, so will I.
2:16 For the wise person and the **f** both die, and in the
5: 1 Don't be a **f** who doesn't realize that mindless
5: 3 being a **f** makes you a blabbermouth.
7: 4 while the **f** thinks only about having a good time
7: 5 by a wise person than to be praised by a **f**!
7:17 don't be too wicked either—don't be a **f**!
Isa 36:15 Don't let him **f** you into trusting in the LORD by
44:10 Who but a **f** would make his own god—an idol that
44:20 The poor, deluded **f** feeds on ashes. He is trusting
Jer 7: 8 is here you will never suffer? Don't **f** yourselves!
9: 5 They all **f** and defraud each other; no one tells the
37: 9 Do not **f** yourselves that the Babylonians are gone
49:16 hide high in the mountains. But don't **f** yourselves!
Hos 7: 5 The king makes a **f** of himself and drinks with
Ob 1: 3 up here?' you ask boastfully. Don't **f** yourselves!
Zec 13: 4 No one will wear prophet's clothes to try to **f** the
Mt 22:18 "Whom are you trying to **f** with your trick
Mk 12:15 "Who are you trying to **f** with your trick
Lk 12:20 "But God said to him, 'You **f**! You will die this
12:21 a person is a **f** to store up earthly wealth but not
1Co 3:18 you will have to become a **f** so you can become
6: 9 Don't **f** yourselves. Those who indulge in sexual
2Co 11: 1 will be patient with me as I keep on talking like a **f**.
11:17 something the Lord wants, but I am acting like a **f**.
11:21 I'm talking like a **f** again—I can boast about it,
12: 6 plenty to boast about and would be no **f** in doing it,
12:11 You have made me act like a **f**—boasting like this.
2Th 2:10 He will use every kind of wicked deception to **f**
Jas 2:20 **F**! When will you ever learn that faith that does not

FOOL'S (3) [FOOL]

Pr 17:24 but a **f** eyes wander to the ends of the earth.
26: 9 A proverb in a **f** mouth is as dangerous as a
Ecc 7: 6 Indeed, a **f** laughter is quickly gone, like thorns

FOOLED (8) [FOOL]

Ge 27:11 Jacob replied. "He won't be **f** that easily.
Jer 7: 4 But do not be **f** by those who repeatedly promise
Ro 7:11 Sin took advantage of the law and **f** me; it took the
1Co 15:33 Don't be **f** by those who say such things, for "bad
2Co 11:13 They have **f** you by disguising themselves as
Gal 1: 7 You are being **f** by those who twist and change the
Eph 5: 6 Don't be **f** by those who try to excuse these sins,
2Th 2: 3 Don't be **f** by what they say. For that day will not

FOOLING (7) [FOOL]

Job 15:31 They are only **f** themselves, for emptiness will be
Ps 119:118 from your principles. / They are only **f** themselves.
1Co 3:18 Stop **f** yourselves. If you think you are wise by this
Gal 6: 3 to help someone in need, you are only **f** yourself.
Jas 1:22 listen to. If you don't obey, you are only **f** yourself.
1:26 don't control your tongue, you are just **f** yourself,
1Jn 1: 8 we are only **f** ourselves and refusing to accept the

FOOLISH (91) [FOOL]

Dt 32: 6 repay the LORD, / you **f** and senseless people?
32:21 I will provoke their fury by blessing the **f** Gentiles.
32:28 the people are **f**, without understanding.
1Sa 13:13 "How **f**!" Samuel exclaimed. "You have
2Sa 6:22 and I am willing to look even more **f** than this,

13:12 "No, my brother!" she cried. "Don't be f!
15:31 let Ahithophel give Absalom f advice!"
24:10 Please forgive me, LORD, for doing this f thing."
1Ch 21: 8 Please forgive me for doing this f thing."
Job 15: 2 to be a wise man, and yet you give us all this f talk.
16: 3 Won't you ever stop your flow of f words?
Ps 38: 5 My wounds fester and stink / because of my f sins.
49:10 wise must finally die, / just like the f and senseless,
69: 5 O God, you know how f I am; / my sins cannot be
73:22 I was so f and ignorant— / I must have seemed like
74:18 LORD. / A f nation has dishonored your name.
85: 8 But let them not return to their f ways.
Pr 8: 5 O f ones, let me give you understanding.
9: 6 Leave your f ways behind, and begin to live;
10: 1 joy to a father; a f child brings grief to a mother.
11:12 It is f to belittle a neighbor; a person with good
14: 1 a f woman tears hers down with her own hands.
14:17 Those who are short-tempered do f things,
15:20 joy to their father; f children despise their mother.
17:25 A f child brings grief to a father and bitterness to a
19:13 A f child is a calamity to a father; a nagging wife
26: 4 arguing with fools, don't answer their f arguments,
26: 4 or you will become as f as they are.
26: 5 with fools, be sure to answer their f arguments,
26: 6 Trusting a fool to convey a message is as f as
26: 8 Honoring a fool is as f as tying a stone to a
26:17 Yanking a dog's ears is as f as interfering in
28:26 Trusting oneself is f, but those who walk in
Ecc 2:14 I saw that wise and f people share the same fate.
2:19 can tell whether my successors will be wise or f?
2:21 to earn it. This is not only f but highly unfair.
4: 5 F people refuse to work and almost starve.
4:13 than to be an old and f king who refuses all advice.
9:17 a wise person are better than the shouts of a f king.
10: 2 and the hearts of the f lead them to do evil.
10: 6 if they give f people great authority, and if they fail
10:13 Since fools base their thoughts on f premises,
10:14 F people claim to know all about the future and tell
Isa 19:13 of Egypt have ruined the land with their f counsel.
27:11 Israel is a f and stupid nation, for its people have
29:14 I will show that human wisdom is f and even the
41:29 See, they are all f, worthless things. Your idols are
44: 9 How f are those who manufacture idols to be their
Jer 1:17 of them, or I will make you look f in front of them.
2: 5 worshiped f idols, only to become f themselves.
4:22 "My people are f and do not know me,"
5:21 Listen, you f and senseless people—who have eyes
10: 3 Their ways are futile and f. They cut down a tree
10: 8 of people who worship idols are stupid and f.
10:14 Compared to him, all people are f / and have no
16:19 will come to you and say, "Our ancestors were f,
51:17 Compared to him, all people are f / and have no
La 2:14 Your "prophets" have said so many f things,
Hos 4:12 Longing after idols has made them f. They have
4:14 with whores and shrine prostitutes. O f people!
13:13 resists being born. How stubborn they are! How f!
Hab 2:18 How f to trust in something made by your own
Mt 7:26 anyone who hears my teaching and ignores it is f,
25: 2 Five of them were f, and five were wise.
25: 3 The five who were f took no oil for their lamps,
25: 8 Then the five f ones asked the others, 'Please give
Lk 24:25 Then Jesus said to them, "You are such f people!
Ro 1:21 And they began to think up f ideas of what God
10:19 I will make you angry by blessing the f Gentiles."
1Co 1:18 I know very well how f the message of the cross
1:20 God has made them all look f and has shown their
1:21 he has used our f preaching to save all who
1:22 God's way seems f to the Jews because they want
1:22 And it is f to the Greeks because they believe only
1:25 This "f" plan of God is far wiser than the wisest
1:27 God deliberately chose things the world considers f
2:14 It all sounds f to them because only those who
15:36 What a f question! When you put a seed into the
2Co 11:16 if you do, listen to me, as you would to a f person,
12: 1 This boasting is all so f, but let me go on. Let me
Gal 3: 1 Oh, f Galatians! What magician has cast an evil
Eph 5: 4 Obscene stories, f talk, and coarse jokes—these are
1Ti 6: 9 and are trapped by many f and harmful desires that
6:20 f discussions with those who oppose you with their
2Ti 2:16 f discussions that lead to more and more
2:23 Again I say, don't get involved in f,
Tit 3: 3 Once we, too, were f and disobedient. We were
3: 9 Do not get involved in f discussions about spiritual
1Pe 2:15 silence those who make f accusations against you.
2Pe 2:18 brag about themselves with empty, f boasting.

FOOLISHLY (5) [FOOL]

Ge 31:28 and tell them good-bye? You have acted very f!
Nu 12:11 punish us for this sin we have so f committed.
Job 15: 3 It isn't right to speak so f. What good do such
Ps 106:33 They made Moses angry, / and he spoke f.
La 4:20 We had f boasted that under his protection we

FOOLISHNESS (18) [FOOL]

Pr 15: 2 person makes learning a joy; fools spout only f.
15:21 F brings joy to those who have no sense; a sensible
19: 3 People ruin their lives by their own f and then are
22:15 A youngster's heart is filled with f, but discipline
27:22 You cannot separate fools from their f,
Ecc 1:17 So I worked hard to distinguish wisdom from f.
2: 3 While still seeking wisdom, I clutched at f. In this
2:13 Wisdom is of more value than f, just as light is
5: 7 Dreaming all the time instead of working is f.
7:25 that wickedness is stupid and that f is madness.
10: 1 an ounce of f can outweigh a pound of wisdom
Isa 19:14 The LORD has sent a spirit of f on them, so all
Jer 14:14 They speak f made up in their own lying hearts.
Mk 7:22 for lustful pleasure, envy, slander, pride, and f.
1Co 3:19 For the wisdom of this world is f to God.
2Co 10:12 and measuring themselves by themselves. What f!
1Ti 1: 6 and spend their time arguing and talking f.
6:21 have wandered from the faith by following such f.

FOOLS (73) [FOOL]

2Sa 3:33 for Abner: / "Should Abner have died as f die?
13:13 And you would be called one of the greatest f in
Job 5: 3 I know that f who turn from God may be
30: 8 They are nameless f, outcasts of civilization.
Ps 14: 1 Only f say in their hearts, / "There is no God."
39: 8 my rebellion, / for even f mock me when I rebel.
49:13 This is the fate of f, / though they will be
53: 1 Only f say in their hearts, / "There is no God."
74:22 Remember how these f insult you all day long.
94: 8 Think again, you f! / When will you finally catch
107:17 Some were f in their rebellion; / they suffered for
Pr 1: 7 Only f despise wisdom and discipline.
1:22 your mocking? How long will you f fight the facts?
1:32 They are f, and their own complacency will
3:35 The wise inherit honor, but f are put to shame!
10: 8 be instructed, but babbling f fall flat on their faces.
10:13 but f will be punished with a rod.
10:21 but f are destroyed by their lack of common sense.
12:11 work means prosperity; only f idle away their time.
12:15 F think they need no advice, but the wise listen to
12:23 of their knowledge, but f broadcast their folly.
13:16 before they act; f don't and even brag about it!
13:19 but f will not turn from evil to attain them.
13:20 whoever walks with f will suffer harm.
14: 3 The talk of f is a rod for their backs, but the words
14: 7 Stay away from f, for you won't find knowledge
14: 8 to see what is coming, but f deceive themselves.
14: 9 F make fun of guilt, but the godly acknowledge it
14:16 f plunge ahead with great confidence.
14:24 crown for the wise; the effort of f yields only folly.
14:33 understanding heart; wisdom is not found among f.
15: 2 makes learning a joy; f spout only foolishness.
15: 7 the wise can give good advice; f cannot do so.
16:22 those who possess it, but discipline is wasted on f.
17:28 Even f are thought to be wise when they keep
18: 2 F have no interest in understanding; they only
18: 6 F get into constant quarrels; they are asking for a
18: 7 The mouths of f are their ruin; their lips get them
19:29 will be punished, and the backs of f will be beaten.
20: 3 fight is a mark of honor; only f insist on quarreling.
21:20 and luxury, but f spend whatever they get.
23: 9 Don't waste your breath on f, for they will despise
26: 1 Honor doesn't go with f any more than snow with
26: 4 When arguing with f, don't answer their foolish
26: 5 When arguing with f, be sure to answer their
26:12 There is more hope for f than for people who think
27:22 You cannot separate f from their foolishness,
Ecc 5: 4 following through, for God takes no pleasure in f.
6: 8 do wise people really have any advantage over f?
7: 7 Extortion turns wise people into f, and bribes
7: 9 be quick-tempered, for anger is the friend of f.
10: 3 You can identify f just by the way they walk down
10:12 wise words, but the speech of f brings them to ruin.
10:13 Since f base their thoughts on foolish premises,
10:15 F are so exhausted by a little work that they have
Isa 3:12 O my people, can't you see what f your rulers are?
19:11 What f are the counselors of Zoan! Their best
19:13 The wise men from Zoan are f, and those from
32: 5 In that day ungodly f will not be heroes.
32: 6 Everyone will recognize ungodly f for what they
35: 8 who walk in God's ways; f will never walk there.
44:25 to give bad advice, thus proving them to be f.
45:20 What f they are who carry around their wooden
Jer 17:11 at the end of their lives, will become poor old f.
50:36 it strikes her wise counselors, they will become f!
Hab 2:18 own hands! What f you are to believe such lies!
Mt 23:17 Blind f! Which is greater, the gold, or the Temple
Lk 11:40 F! Didn't God make the inside as well as the
Ro 1:22 Claiming to be wise, they became utter f instead.
1Co 4:10 Our dedication to Christ makes us look like f,
2Co 11:19 who think you are so wise, enjoy listening to f!
Eph 5:15 how you live, not as f but as those who are wise.
2Ti 3: 9 Someday everyone will recognize what f they are,

FOOT (65) [BAREFOOT, FEET, FOOTHOLD, FOOTING, FOOTPATH, FOOTPRINTS, FOOTSTEPS, FOOTSTOOL, SUREFOOTED, UNDERFOOT]

Ge 41:44 or a f in the entire land of Egypt without your
Ex 12:37 and children. And they were all traveling on f.
19:13 Then they must gather at the f of the mountain."
19:17 with God, and they stood at the f of the mountain.
21:24 the payment must be hand for hand, f for f,
24: 4 Early the next morning he built an altar at the f of
24:17 The Israelites at the f of the mountain saw an
32:19 smashing them at the f of the mountain.
Lev 8:23 of his right hand, and the big toe of his right f.
13:12 someone's skin, covering the body from head to f.
14:14 of the right hand, and on the big toe of the right f.
14:17 of the right hand, and on the big toe of the right f.
14:25 of the right hand, and on the big toe of the right f.
14:28 of the right hand, and on the big toe of the right f.
21:19 or has a broken f or hand,
Nu 11:21 "There are 600,000 f soldiers here with me,
22:25 and crushed Balaam's f against the wall.
33:38 While they were at the f of Mount Hor,
Dt 4:11 You came near and stood at the f of the mountain,
11:10 and dug out irrigation ditches with your f as in a
19:21 for eye, tooth for tooth, hand for hand, f for f.
25: 9 pull his sandal from his f, and spit in his face.
28:35 The LORD will cover you from head to f with
Jos 8:33 One group stood at the f of Mount Gerizim, the other at the f of Mount Ebal.
11:17 to Baal-gad at the f of Mount Hermon in the valley
Jdg 4:15 leaped down from his chariot and escaped on f.
2Sa 8: 4 and twenty thousand f soldiers.
14:25 From head to f, he was the perfect specimen of a
15:17 The king and his people set out on f, and they
21:20 six fingers on each hand and six toes on each f—
1Ki 7:24 There were about six gourds per f all the way
20:29 The Israelites killed 100,000 Aramean f soldiers in
2Ki 13: 7 ten chariots, and ten thousand f soldiers.
1Ch 18: 4 and twenty thousand f soldiers.
19:18 thousand charioteers and forty thousand f soldiers,
20: 6 six fingers on each hand and six toes on each f—
2Ch 4: 3 There were about six oxen per f all the way
12: 3 and a countless army of f soldiers,
16:12 of his reign, Asa developed a serious f disease.
Job 2: 7 Job with a terrible case of boils from head to f.
39:15 She doesn't worry that a f might crush them
Ps 66: 6 the Red Sea, / and his people went across on f.
91:12 to keep you from striking your f on a stone.
Pr 3:26 He will keep your f from being caught in a trap.
25:19 with a toothache or walking on a broken f.
Isa 1: 6 You are sick from head to f—covered with bruises,
Mt 4: 6 to keep you from striking your f on a stone.' "
17:14 When they arrived at the f of the mountain, a huge
18: 8 So if your hand or f causes you to sin, cut it off
22:13 'Bind him hand and f and throw him out into the
Mk 9:14 At the f of the mountain they found a great crowd
9:45 If your f causes you to sin, cut it off. It is better to enter heaven with only one f than to
Lk 4:11 to keep you from striking your f on a stone.' "
14: 9 and will have to take whatever seat is left at the f
14:10 "Do this instead—sit at the f of the table.
Jn 20:12 and f of the place where the body of Jesus had
Ac 7: 5 no inheritance here, not even one square f of land.
20:18 "You know that from the day I set f in the
1Co 12:15 If the f says, "I am not a part of the body because I
Rev 10: 2 with his right f on the sea and his left f on the land.

FOOTHILLS (19) [HILL]

Dt 1: 7 the hill country, the western f, the Negev,
Jos 9: 1 who lived in the hill country, in the western f,
10:40 the Negev, the western f, and the mountain slopes.
11: 2 the kings in the western f; the kings of
11:16 the western f, the Jordan Valley, and the mountains
12: 8 the western f, the Jordan Valley, the mountain
15:33 The following towns situated in the western f were
Jdg 1: 9 in the hill country, the Negev, and the western f.
1Ki 10:27 as the sycamore wood that grows in the f of Judah.
1Ch 27:28 and sycamore-fig trees in the f of Judah.
2Ch 1:15 as the sycamore wood that grows in the f of Judah.
9:27 as the sycamore wood that grows in the f of Judah.
26:10 because he kept great herds of livestock in the f of
28:18 had raided towns located in the f of Judah
Jer 17:26 from the western f and the hill country
32:44 in the f of Judah and in the Negev, too.
33:13 the f of Judah, the Negev, the land of Benjamin,
Ob 1:19 Those living in the f of Judah will possess the
Zec 7: 7 and the f of Judah were populated areas?' "

FOOTHOLD (2) [FOOT]

Ps 69: 2 I sink into the mire; / I can't find a f to stand on.
Eph 4:27 for anger gives a mighty f to the Devil.

FOOTING (3) [FOOT]

Ps 143:10 your gracious Spirit lead me forward / on a firm f.
Pr 10: 9 People with integrity have firm f, but those who
2Pe 3:17 I don't want you to lose your own secure f.

FOOTMEN (1) [MAN]

2Sa 15: 1 and horses, and he hired fifty f to run ahead of him.

FOOTMEN [KJV] See also FOOT SOLDIERS

FOOTPATH (3) [FOOT, PATH]

Mt 13: 4 some seeds fell on a f, and the birds came and ate
Mk 4: 4 some seed fell on a f, and the birds came and ate it.
Lk 8: 5 some seed fell on a f, where it was stepped on,

FOOTPRINTS (2) [FOOT]

Job 13:27 You watch all my paths. You trace all my f.
Hos 6: 8 Gilead is a city of sinners, tracked with f of blood.

FOOTSTEPS (4) [FOOT, STEP]

1Ki 14: 6 So when Ahijah heard her f at the door, he called
Eze 20:18 and told them not to follow in their parents' f,
23:11 to Oholah, her sister, she followed right in her f.
23:31 Because you have followed in your sister's f,

FOOTSTOOL (10) [FOOT, STOOL]

1Ch 28: 2 God's f, could rest permanently.
2Ch 9:18 six steps, and there was a f of gold attached to it.
Ps 110: 1 your enemies, / making them a f under your feet."
Isa 66: 1 "Heaven is my throne, and the earth is my f.
Mt 5:35 it is a sacred vow because the earth is his f.
Lk 20:43 your enemies, / making them a f under your feet.'
Ac 2:35 making them a f under your feet.'
7:49 'Heaven is my throne, / and the earth is my f.

Heb 1:13 your enemies, / making them a f under your feet."
10:13 There he waits until his enemies are humbled as a f

FOR (8187) See Index of Articles, Etc.

FORBAD [KJV] See COMMANDED, REBUKED

FORBID (10) [FORBIDDEN, FORBIDS]

1Sa 26:11 But the LORD f that I should kill the one he has
2Sa 23:17 "The LORD f that I should drink this!"
1Ki 21:3 "The LORD f that I should give you the
1Ch 11:19 "God f that I should drink this!" he exclaimed.
Jer 40:16 said to Johanan, "I f you to do any such thing,
Eze 4:14 never eaten any of the animals that our laws f."
Mt 16:22 and corrected him. "Heaven f, Lord," he said.
Lk 20:16 "But God f that such a thing should ever happen,"
1Co 14:39 eager to prophesy, and don't f speaking in tongues.
Gal 6:14 God f that I should boast about anything except the

FORBIDDEN (24) [FORBID]

Ge 9:5 And murder is f. Animals that kill people must die,
Lev 4:2 by doing anything f by the LORD's commands.
4:13 community does something f by the LORD
4:22 "If one of Israel's leaders does something f by the
4:27 "If any of the citizens of Israel do something f by
5:17 "If any of them sin by doing something f by the
11:11 and they will always be f to you. You must never
11:12 not have both fins and scales is strictly f to you.
19:23 for the first three years and consider it f.
20:25 or bird or creeping creature that I have f.
Dt 4:23 for the LORD your God has absolutely f this.
17:3 any of the forces of heaven, which I have strictly f.
22:9 you are f to use either the grapes from the vineyard
Jdg 13:4 or any other alcoholic drink or eat any f food.
13:7 or any other alcoholic drink or eat any f food.
13:14 or any other alcoholic drink, or eat any f food."
Isa 65:4 evil spirits. They also eat pork and other f foods.
66:17 feasting on pork and rats and other f meats,
Jer 43:2 The LORD our God hasn't f us to go to Egypt!
La 1:10 the place the LORD had f them to enter.
Zec 9:7 eat meat with blood in it or feed on other f foods.
Ac 10:14 "I have never in all my life eaten anything f by our
11:8 'I have never eaten anything f by our Jewish laws.'
Ro 7:8 and aroused all kinds of f desires within me!

FORBIDS (1) [FORBID]

Dt 18:14 but the LORD your God f you to do such things.

FORCE (36) [FORCED, FORCEFUL, FORCEFULLY, FORCES, FORCING]

Ge 31:31 to myself, 'He'll take his daughters from me by f.'
Ex 6:1 so anxious to get rid of them that he will f them to
7:5 my power and f them to let the Israelites go,
11:1 that he will practically f you to leave the country.
Nu 20:20 and marched out to meet them with an imposing f.
Dt 23:15 and take refuge with you, do not f them to return.
1Sa 2:16 "No, give it to me now, or I'll take it by f."
8:13 and f them to cook and bake and make perfumes
2Sa 15:20 and now should I f you to wander with us?
20:24 Adoniram was in charge of the labor f.
1Ki 4:6 son of Abda was in charge of the labor f.
5:14 at home. Adoniram was in charge of this labor f.
9:21 So Solomon conscripted them for his labor f,
9:21 and they serve in the labor f to this day.
10:26 Solomon built up a huge f of chariots and horses.
11:28 he put him in charge of the labor f from the tribes
12:18 who was in charge of the labor f, to restore order,
2Ch 1:14 Solomon built up a huge military f, which included
2:2 He enlisted a f of seventy thousand common
8:8 So Solomon conscripted them for his labor f,
8:8 and they serve in the labor f to this day.
10:18 who was in charge of the labor f, to restore order,
Ezr 3:8 The work f was made up of everyone who had
Ps 140:11 Cause disaster to fall with great f on the violent.
Jer 21:2 Perhaps he will f Nebuchadnezzar to withdraw his
Eze 21:29 And now it will fall with even greater f on the
34:4 Instead, you have ruled them with f and cruelty.
46:18 the prince may never take anyone's property by f.
Hab 2:15 You f your cup on them so that you can gloat over
Zec 4:6 It is not by f nor by strength, but by my Spirit,
Lk 16:17 But that doesn't mean that the law has lost its f in
Jn 6:15 Jesus saw that they were ready to take him by f
Ac 27:41 while the stern was repeatedly smashed by the f of
Gal 2:4 They wanted to f us, like slaves, to follow their
6:12 Those who are trying to f you to be circumcised
Rev 3:9 I will f those who belong to Satan—those liars who

FORCED (35) [FORCE]

Ge 49:15 his shoulder to the task / and submit to f labor.
Ex 1:11 They f them to build the cities of Pithom
2:11 and he saw how hard they were f to work.
Lev 25:25 go bankrupt and are f to sell some inherited land,
Nu 20:21 through their country, Israel was f to turn around.
Dt 20:11 then all the people inside will serve you in f labor.
Jos 17:13 they f the Canaanites to work as slaves.
Jdg 1:28 they f the Canaanites to work as slaves,
1:30 among them. But they f them to work as slaves.
1:33 and Beth-anath were sometimes f to work as slaves
1:34 the Amorites f them into the hill country
1:35 they f the Amorites to work as slaves.
1Sa 8:12 Some will be f to plow in his fields and harvest his
2Sa 12:31 people of Rabbah and f them to labor with saws,
1Ki 9:15 This is the account of the f labor that Solomon
9:22 did not conscript any of the Israelites for f labor.
18:10 King Ahab f the king of that nation to swear to the
2Ki 17:3 so Israel was f to pay heavy annual tribute to
1Ch 20:3 people of Rabbah and f them to labor with saws,
2Ch 8:9 did not conscript any of the Israelites for f labor.
Ezr 4:23 to Jerusalem and f the Jews to stop building.
Job 24:10 They are f to carry food while they themselves are
Ps 125:3 for then the godly might be f to do wrong.
144:14 May there be no breached walls, no f exile,
Isa 43:14 And the Babylonians will be f to flee in those ships
47:6 You have f even the elderly to carry heavy
Jer 22:13 for Jehoiakim, who builds his palace with f labor.
Eze 22:7 Resident foreigners are f to pay for protection.
Hos 11:5 go back to Egypt and will be f to serve Assyria.
Mt 27:32 from Cyrene, and they f him to carry Jesus' cross.
Mk 15:21 just then, and they f him to carry Jesus' cross.
Lk 23:26 just then, was f to follow Jesus and carry his cross.
Ac 7:19 and f parents to abandon their newborn babies
Phm 1:14 because you were f to do it but because you
Rev 12:8 the dragon lost the battle and was f out of heaven.

FORCEFUL (2) [FORCE]

2Co 10:10 His letters are demanding and f, but in person he is
10:11 and f in person as we are in our letters.

FORCEFULLY (2) [FORCE]

Mt 11:12 the Kingdom of Heaven has been f advancing,
Ac 15:2 disagreeing with them, argued f and at length.

FORCES (41) [FORCE]

Ex 7:4 after which I will lead the f of Israel out with great
12:17 for it will remind you that I brought your f out of
12:41 the 430th year that all the LORD's f left the land.
14:9 All the f in Pharaoh's army—all his horses,
Dt 2:32 declared war on us and mobilized his f at Jahaz.
4:19 see the sun, moon, and stars—all the f of heaven—
17:3 the sun, the moon, or any of the f of heaven,
Jdg 1:10 defeating the f of Sheshai, Ahiman, and Talmai.
9:48 so he led his f to Mount Zalmon. He took an ax
1Sa 17:4 came out of the Philistine ranks to face the f of
17:14 in the army, they stayed with Saul's f all the time.
17:21 and Philistine f stood facing each other,
2Sa 2:17 and the men of Israel had been defeated by the f of
2:18 sons of Zeruiah, were among David's f that day.
5:17 of Israel, they mobilized all their f to capture him.
8:3 David also destroyed the f of Hadadezer son of
10:16 of Shobach, the commander of all Hadadezer's f.
10:18 This time David's f killed seven hundred
20:15 When Joab's f arrived, they attacked
1Ki 20:13 the LORD says: Do you see all these enemy f?
20:27 to the vast Aramean f that filled the countryside!
2Ki 6:8 "We will mobilize our f at such and such a place."
9:14 defending Israel against the f of King Hazael of
17:16 and worshiped Baal and all the f of heaven.
21:3 He also bowed before all the f of heaven
21:5 He built these altars for all the f of heaven in both
23:4 to worship Baal, Asherah, and all the f of heaven.
23:5 the constellations, and to all the f of heaven.
1Ch 14:8 all Israel, they mobilized all their f to capture him.
18:3 Then David destroyed the f of King Hadadezer of
19:7 These f camped at Medeba, where they were
19:16 of Shobach, the commander of all Hadadezer's f.
19:18 This time David's f killed seven thousand
2Ch 18:2 Then Ahab enticed Jehoshaphat to join f with him
Job 9:13 The mightiest f against him are crushed beneath
Ps 48:4 The kings of the earth joined f / and advanced
143:3 He f me to live in darkness like those in the grave.
Isa 11:14 They will join f to swoop down on Philistia to the
Jer 51:46 when you hear the first rumor of approaching f.
Da 11:11 will rally against the vast f assembled by the king
Gal 5:17 These two f are constantly fighting each other,

FORCING (5) [FORCE]

Ex 1:14 f them to make bricks and mortar and to work long
1Sa 31:1 Philistines attacked Israel, f the Israelites to flee.
1Ch 10:1 Philistines attacked Israel, f the Israelites to flee.
Jer 28:14 f them into slavery under King Nebuchadnezzar of
Lk 16:16 and eager multitudes are f their way in.

FORD (1)

2Sa 19:18 They all crossed the f and worked hard ferrying the

FORECAST [KJV] See PLOT

FORECLOSE (1) [FORECLOSED]

Jer 15:10 I am neither a lender who has threatened to f nor a

FORECLOSED (1) [FORECLOSE]

Job 20:19 and left them destitute. He f on their homes.

FOREFATHERS (1) [FATHER]

Jer 11:10 They have returned to the sins of their f. They have

FOREFRONT [KJV] See ENTRANCE, FRONT, HEAD

FOREHEAD (14) [FOREHEADS]

Ex 13:9 like a mark branded on your hands or your f.
13:16 be like a mark branded on your hands or your f.
28:38 Aaron will wear it on his f, thus bearing the guilt
Lev 13:41 And if he loses hair on his f, he simply has a bald f;
Dt 6:8 hands as a reminder, and wear them on your f.
11:18 hands as a reminder, and wear them on your f.
1Sa 17:49 it from his sling and hit the Philistine in the f.
2Ch 26:19 leprosy suddenly broke out on his f.
Eze 9:5 the city and kill everyone whose f is not marked.
Rev 13:16 to be given a mark on the right hand or on the f.
14:9 or who accepts his mark on the f or the hand
17:5 A mysterious name was written on her f:
20:4 nor accepted his mark on their f or their hands.

FOREHEADS (7) [FOREHEAD]

Nu 24:17 from Israel. / It will crush the f of Moab's people,
Dt 14:1 or shave the hair above your f for the sake of the
Eze 9:4 and put a mark on the f of all those who weep
Rev 7:3 placed the seal of God on the f of his servants."
9:4 people who did not have the seal of God on their f.
14:1 his name and his Father's name written on their f.
22:4 his face, and his name will be written on their f.

FOREIGN (71) [FOREIGN-BORN, FOREIGNER, FOREIGNERS]

Ge 15:13 that your descendants will be strangers in a f land,
23:4 "Here I am, a stranger in a f land, with no place to
31:15 He has reduced our rights to those of f women.
Ex 2:22 for he said, "I have been a stranger in a f land."
18:3 boy was born, "I have been a stranger in a f land."
Lev 26:38 You will die among the f nations and be devoured
Nu 11:4 Then the f rabble who were traveling with the
Dt 4:28 There, in a f land, you will worship idols made
11:28 and turn from his way by worshiping f gods.
13:2 'Come, let us worship the gods of f nations,'
13:13 astray by encouraging them to worship f gods.
28:33 A f nation you have never heard about will eat the
28:64 There you will worship f gods that neither you nor
29:26 and worship other gods that were f to them,
31:16 these people will begin worshiping f gods,
32:12 alone guided them; / they lived without any f gods.
32:16 They stirred up his jealousy by worshiping f gods;
Jdg 10:16 Then the Israelites put aside their f gods and served
19:12 "we can't stay in this f city where there are no
1Sa 7:3 get rid of your f gods and your images of
26:20 Must I die on f soil, far from the presence of the
1Ki 8:46 and take them captive to a f land far or near.
11:1 Now King Solomon loved many f women.
11:8 Solomon built such shrines for all his f wives to
2Ki 17:25 But since these f settlers did not worship the
19:24 I have dug wells in many a f land / and refreshed
2Ch 6:36 and take them captive to a f land far or near.
33:15 Manasseh also removed the f gods from the hills
Ne 4:4 and may they themselves become captives in a f
13:26 But even he was led into sin by his f wives.
13:27 and acting unfaithfully toward God by marrying f
13:30 So I purged out everything f and assigned tasks to
Ps 44:20 our God / or spread our hands in prayer to f gods,
81:9 You must never have a f god; / you must not bow
114:1 when the family of Jacob left that f land—
137:4 sing the songs of the LORD / while in a f land?
Isa 25:5 of the desert. But you silence the roar of f nations.
28:11 God will speak to them through f oppressors who
37:25 I have dug wells in many a f land / and refreshed
43:12 I saved you. No f god has ever done this before.
62:8 Never again will f warriors come and take away
Jer 2:25 I have fallen in love with these f gods, and I can't
5:19 and gave yourselves to f gods in your own land.
13:21 How will you feel when the LORD sets your f
14:22 Can any of the f gods send us rain? Does it fall
15:14 their enemies to take them as captives to a f land.
16:13 of this land and send you into a f land where you
17:4 and I will send you away as captives to a f land.
19:4 The people burn incense to f gods—idols never
22:26 from this land, and you will die in a f country.
46:1 the prophet from the LORD concerning f nations.
La 1:3 She lives among f nations and has no place of rest.
4:15 distant lands and wandered there among f nations,
Eze 3:5 I am not sending you to some f people whose
31:12 A f army—the terror of the nations—cut it down
34:29 go hungry or be shamed by the scorn of f nations.
36:4 and mocked by f nations everywhere.
36:15 I will not allow those f nations to sneer at you,
Da 11:39 Claiming this f god's help, he will attack the
Hos 7:9 Worshiping f gods has sapped their strength,
7:14 begging f gods for crops and prosperity.
10:1 the more they poured it on the altars of their f
10:2 The LORD will break down their f altars
Joel 3:17 and f armies will never conquer her again.
Am 7:17 be divided up, and you yourself will die in a f land.
Ob 1:11 refusing to lift a finger to help when f invaders
Hag 2:22 royal thrones, destroying the power of f kingdoms.
Zec 9:8 No f oppressor will ever again overrun my
Ac 7:6 f country where they would be mistreated as slaves
17:18 Others said, "He's pushing some f religion."
26:11 I even hounded them in distant cities of f lands.

FOREIGN-BORN (1) [FOREIGN]

Ge 17:12 and the f servants whom you have purchased.

FOREIGNER (24) [FOREIGN]

Ex 12:49 or a f who has settled among you."
23:9 among you. You know what it is like to be a f.
Lev 17:10 whether an Israelite or a f living among you,
24:16 or f among you who blasphemes the LORD's
25:35 support them as you would a resident f and allow
25:47 "If a resident f becomes rich, and if some of your
25:47 go bankrupt and sell themselves to such a f,

25:53 The f must treat them as servants hired on a yearly
25:53 You must not allow a resident f to treat any of your
Dt 14:21 to a f living among you, or you may sell it to a f.
17:15 You must appoint a fellow Israelite, not a f.
Ru 2:10 so kind to me?" she asked. "I am only a f."
2Sa 1:13 And he replied, "I am a f, an Amalekite, who lives
15:19 for you are a guest in Israel, a f in exile.
Job 19:15 girls consider me a stranger. I am like a f to them.
Ps 105:23 in Egypt; / Jacob lived as a f in the land of Ham.
119:19 I am but a f here on earth; / I need the guidance of
Pr 20:16 Get a deposit if someone guarantees the debt of a f.
Jer 30:21 have their own ruler again, and he will not be a f.
Lk 4:26 to a widow of Zarephath—a f in the land of Sidon.
17:18 Does only this f return to give glory to God?"
Ac 7:29 the country and lived as a f in the land of Midian,
Heb 11:9 there by faith—for he was like a f, living in a tent.

FOREIGNERS (121) [FOREIGN]

Ge 28:4 May you own this land where we now are f,
Ex 12:19 These same regulations apply to the f living with
12:43 No f are allowed to eat the Passover lamb.
12:45 Hired servants and visiting f may not eat it.
12:48 "If there are f living among you who want to
20:10 your livestock, and any f living among you.
21:8 But he is not allowed to sell her to f, since he is the
22:21 "Do not oppress f in any way. Remember,
22:21 you yourselves were once f in the land of Egypt.
23:9 "Do not oppress the f living among you.
Lev 16:29 by birth, as well as to the f living among you.
17:8 both to Israelites and to the f living among you.
17:12 and the f who live among you must never eat
17:13 both to Israelites and to the f living among you.
17:15 both to Israelites and the f living among you.
18:26 Israelites by birth and to the f living among you.
19:10 them for the poor and the f who live among you,
19:33 "Do not exploit the f who live in your land.
19:34 Remember that you were once f in the land of
20:2 by birth as well as to the f living among you.
22:18 by birth as well as to the f living among you.
22:25 or defective animals from f to be offered as a
23:22 Leave it for the poor and the f living among you.
24:22 to Israelites by birth and f who live among you.
25:6 and any f who live with you may eat the produce
25:23 to me. You are only f and tenants living with me.
25:40 as hired servants or as resident f who live with you,
25:44 or female slaves from among the f who live among
25:45 may also purchase the children of such resident f,
Nu 9:14 And if f living among you want to celebrate the
9:14 both to you and to the f living among you.' "
15:14 And if any f living among you want to present an
15:15 and f are the same before the LORD
15:16 apply both to you and to the f living among you."
15:26 including the f living among you, for the entire
15:29 to native Israelites and the f living among you.
15:30 whether native Israelites or f,
19:10 people of Israel and any f who live among them.
35:15 of Israelites, resident f, and traveling merchants.
Dt 1:16 but also to the f living among you.
5:14 and other livestock, and any f living among you.
10:18 He shows love to the f living among you and gives
10:19 You, too, must show love to f, for you yourselves were once f in the land of
14:29 as well as to the f living among you, the orphans,
15:3 fellow Israelites—not to the f living among you.
16:11 the Levites from your towns, and the f, orphans,
16:14 your servants, and with the Levites, f, orphans,
23:7 and you lived as f among the Egyptians.
23:20 You may charge interest to f, but not to Israelites,
24:14 whether fellow Israelites or f living in your towns.
24:17 "True justice must be given to f living among you
24:19 to get it. Leave it for the f, orphans, and widows.
24:20 Leave some of the olives for the f, orphans,
24:21 but leave any remaining grapes for the f, orphans,
26:11 and the f living among you in the celebration.
26:12 f, orphans, and widows so that they will have
26:13 f, orphans, and widows, just as you commanded
27:19 'Cursed is anyone who is unjust to f, orphans,
28:43 The f living among you will become stronger
29:11 and the f living among you who chop your wood
29:22 and the f who come from distant lands,
31:12 women, children, and the f living in your towns—
Jos 8:33 f and citizens alike—along with the leaders,
8:35 and the f who lived among the Israelites.
20:9 for Israelites as well as the f living among them.
2Sa 4:3 Beeroth fled to Gittaim, where they still live as f.
22:45 F cringe before me; / as soon as they hear of me,
1Ki 8:41 "And when f hear of you and come from distant
2Ki 17:29 But these various groups of f also continued to
1Ch 22:2 So David gave orders to call together the f living in
2Ch 2:17 Solomon took a census of all f in the land of Israel,
6:32 "And when f hear of you and your mighty
30:25 the f who came to the festival, and all those who
Ne 5:8 who have had to sell themselves to pagan f,
9:2 from all f as they confessed their own sins
Job 15:19 the land was given long before any f arrived.
Ps 18:44 they hear of me, they submit; / f cringe before me.
94:6 They kill widows and f / and murder orphans.
146:9 The LORD protects the f among us. / He cares for
Isa 1:7 f plunder your fields and destroy everything they
2:6 "because they have made alliances with f from the
52:4 "Long ago my people went to live as resident f in
60:10 "F will come to rebuild your cities. Kings
61:5 F will be your servants. They will feed your flocks
Jer 5:19 Now you will serve f in a land that is not your
7:6 and if you stop exploiting f, orphans, and widows;
22:3 Do not mistreat f, orphans, and widows.
25:20 along with all the f living in that land. So did all
30:8 snap their chains. F will no longer be their masters.
51:2 F will come and winnow her, blowing her away as
51:51 the LORD's Temple has been defiled by f."
La 1:10 She has seen f violate her sacred Temple, the place
5:2 has been turned over to strangers, our homes to f.
Eze 7:21 I will give it as plunder to f from the most wicked
11:9 and hand you over to f who will carry out my
14:7 both Israelites and f, who reject me and set up idols
22:7 Resident f are forced to pay for protection.
22:29 the poor, rob the needy, and deprive f of justice.
28:10 You will die like an outcast at the hands of f.
30:12 land of Egypt and everything in it, using f to do it.
44:7 You have brought uncircumcised f into my
44:8 for you have hired f to take charge of my
44:9 No f, including those who live among the people
47:22 and for the f who have joined you and are raising
Hos 7:8 "My people of Israel mingle with godless f,
8:7 no grain. And if there is any grain, f will eat it.
Joel 2:17 name become a proverb of unbelieving f who say,
Zec 7:10 not oppress widows, orphans, f, and poor people.
9:6 F will occupy the city of Ashdod. Thus, I will
Mal 3:5 or who deprive the f living among you of justice,
Mt 17:25 their own people or the f they have conquered?"
17:26 "They tax the f," Peter replied. "Well, then,"
27:7 and they made it into a cemetery for f.
Ac 17:21 f in Athens seemed to spend all their time
1Co 14:21 and through the lips of f. / But even then, they will
Eph 2:19 So now you Gentiles are no longer strangers and f.
Heb 11:13 They agreed that they were no more than f
1Pe 1:1 people who are living as f in the lands of Pontus,
1:17 fear of him during your time as f here on earth.
2:11 Dear brothers and sisters, you are f and aliens here.

FOREKNOW [KJV] See CHOSE

FOREMAN (3) [MAN]

Ru 2:5 Then Boaz asked his f, "Who is that girl over
2:6 And the f replied, "She is the young woman from
Mt 20:8 "That evening he told the f to call the workers in

FOREMEN (9) [MAN]

Ex 5:6 and f he had set over the people of Israel:
5:10 So the slave drivers and f informed the people:
5:14 Then they whipped the Israelite f in charge of the
5:15 So the Israelite f went to Pharaoh and pleaded with
5:19 the Israelite f could see that they were in serious
5:21 The f said to them, "May the LORD judge you
1Ki 5:16 and thirty-six hundred f to supervise the work.
2Ch 2:2 in the hill country, and thirty-six hundred f.
2:18 as stonecutters in the hill country, and 3,600 as f.

FOREORDAINED [KJV] See CHOSE

FOREPART [KJV] See BOW, FRONT, INNER, OPPOSITE

FORESAIL (1) [SAIL]

Ac 27:40 the rudders, raised the f, and headed toward shore.

FORESEES (2) [SEE]

Pr 22:3 A prudent person f the danger ahead and takes
27:12 A prudent person f the danger ahead and takes

FORESHADOWED (1)

Da 4:19 how I wish the events f in this dream would

FORESHIP [KJV] See PROW

FORESKIN (2) [FORESKINS]

Ge 17:11 the flesh of his f must be cut off. This will be a
Ex 4:25 She threw the f at Moses' feet and said, "What a

FORESKINS (3) [FORESKIN]

Ge 17:23 and circumcised them, cutting off their f,
1Sa 18:25 want for the bride price is one hundred Philistine f!
18:27 and presented all their f to the king.

FOREST (37) [FORESTS]

Dt 19:5 suppose someone goes into the f with a neighbor to
Jos 17:15 clear out land for yourselves in the f where the
1Sa 14:25 they found honeycomb on the ground in the f.
22:5 land of Judah." So David went to the f of Hereth.
2Sa 18:6 So the battle began in the f of Ephraim,
18:8 because of the f than were killed by the sword.
18:17 They threw Absalom's body into a deep pit in the f
1Ki 7:2 was called the Palace of the F of Lebanon.
10:17 The king placed these shields in the Palace of the F
10:21 as were all the utensils in the Palace of the F of
1Ch 16:33 Let the trees of the f rustle with praise before the
2Ch 9:16 The king placed these shields in the Palace of the F
9:20 as were all the utensils in the Palace of the F of
Ne 2:8 send a letter to Asaph, the manager of the king's f,
Ps 50:10 For all the animals of the f are mine, / and I own
74:5 down the entrance / like woodcutters in a f.
80:13 The boar from the f devours us, / and the wild
83:14 As a fire roars through a f / and as a flame sets
96:12 with joy! / Let the trees of the f rustle with praise
104:20 when all the f animals prowl about.
Isa 10:18 Assyria's vast army is like a glorious f, yet it will
10:34 enemy as an ax cuts down the f trees in Lebanon.
14:8 Even the trees of the f—the cypress trees
29:17 the fertile fields will become a lush and fertile f.
32:15 and the fertile field will become a lush and fertile f.
32:19 Even though the f will be destroyed and the city
44:14 he plants the cedar in the f to be nourished by the
56:9 Come, wild animals of the f! Come and devour my
Jer 5:6 So now a lion from the f will attack them; a wolf
12:8 people have roared at me like a lion of the f,
26:18 A great f will grow on the hilltop,
Eze 15:6 like grapevines growing among the trees of the f.
20:47 I will set you on fire, O f, and every tree will be
31:3 full of thick branches that cast deep f shade with its
Mic 3:12 A great f will grow on the hilltop,
Na 2:3 with a f of spears waving above them.
Jas 3:5 it can do. A tiny spark can set a great f on fire.

FORESTS (18) [FOREST]

Jos 17:18 The f of the hill country will be yours as well.
2Ki 19:23 its farthest corners / and explored its deepest f.
Ps 29:9 and strips the f bare. / In his Temple everyone
SS 3:9 for himself from wood imported from Lebanon's f.
Isa 9:18 It burns not only briers and thorns but the f, too.
37:24 its farthest corners / and explored its deepest f.
40:16 All Lebanon's f do not contain sufficient fuel to
44:23 forth into song, O mountains and f and every tree!
60:13 the f of cypress, fir, and pine—to beautify my
Jer 16:16 for hunters who will search for them in the f
21:14 I will light a fire in your f that will burn up
22:6 me as fruitful Gilead and the green f of Lebanon.
Eze 39:10 They won't need to cut wood from the fields or f,
Hos 14:6 olive trees, as fragrant as the cedar f of Lebanon.
Na 1:4 and Carmel fade, and the green f of Lebanon wilt.
Hab 2:17 You cut down the f of Lebanon. Now you will be
Zec 11:1 so that fire may sweep through your cedar f.
11:2 of Bashan, as you watch the thickest f being felled.

FORETASTE (1) [TASTE]

Ro 8:23 although we have the Holy Spirit within us as a f

FORETOLD (3)

Isa 43:9 Which of their idols has ever f such things?
Jn 17:12 the one headed for destruction, as the Scriptures f.
Ro 16:26 But now as the prophets f and as the eternal God

FOREVER (368) [EVER]

FAITHFUL LOVE ENDURES FOREVER (40) 1Ch 16:34,41; 2Ch 5:13; 7:3,6; 20:21; Ps 106:1; 107:1; 118:1,2,3, 4,29; 136:1,2,3,4,5,6,7,8,9,10,11,12,13,14,15,16,17,18,19,20, 21,22,23,24,25,26; Jer 33:11

FOREVER AND EVER (31) Ex 15:18; 1Ch 29:10; Ps 10:16; 45:6,17; 48:14; 52:8; 79:13; 113:2; 145:1; Da 2:20; 7:18; Mic 4:5; Eph 3:21; Php 4:20; 1Ti 1:17; 2Ti 4:18; Heb 1:8; 13:20; 1Pe 4:11; 5:11; Rev 1:6,18; 4:9,10; 5:13; 10:6; 11:15; 14:11; 20:10; 22:5

LIVE FOREVER (15) Ge 3:22; 1Ki 1:31; 8:13; 2Ch 6:2; Ps 49:9; 61:4; 68:16; 89:48; 132:14; Jn 6:51,58; 12:34; 1Co 15:50; Heb 12:9; 1Jn 2:17

NAME (BE)...FOREVER (19) Ex 3:15; Dt 18:5; 2Sa 7:26; 1Ki 9:3; 2Ki 21:7; 1Ch 17:24; 23:13; 2Ch 33:4,7; Ps 72:17,19; 74:10; 86:12; 111:10; 113:2; 145:1,21; Da 2:20; Rev 10:6

WHO LIVES FOREVER (8) Ps 41:13; 102:24; Da 4:34; 12:7; Rev 4:9,10; 10:6; 15:7

Ge 3:22 the fruit of the tree of life? Then they will live f!"
17:7 It will continue between me and your offspring f.
17:8 this land of Canaan to you and to your offspring f.
43:9 him back to you, then let me bear the blame f.
44:9 all the rest of us will be your master's slaves f."
44:32 bring him back to you, I will bear the blame f.'
Ex 3:15 This will be my name f; it has always been my
12:14 "You must remember this day f. Each year you
12:24 must be observed by you and your descendants f.
13:3 said to the people, "This is a day to remember f—
15:18 The LORD will reign f and ever!"
16:32 and keep it f as a treasured memorial of the
21:6 After that, the slave will belong to his master f.
29:9 They will then be priests f. In this way, you will
31:13 is a sign of the covenant between me and you f.
31:16 The people of Israel must keep the Sabbath day f.
32:13 to your descendants, and they will possess it f.' "
40:15 descendants are set apart for the priesthood f,
Lev 10:15 they will belong to you and your descendants f,
Nu 36:4 causing it to be lost f to our ancestral tribe."
Dt 5:29 they and their descendants would prosper f.
13:16 That town must remain a ruin f; it may never be
18:5 all your tribes to minister in the LORD's name f.
28:46 and warning among you and your descendants f.
29:29 revealed things belong to us and our descendants f,
Jos 4:24 and that you might fear the LORD your God f."
14:9 special possession and that of your descendants f,
24:14 Put away f the idols your ancestors worshiped
Jdg 21:17 so that an entire tribe of Israel will not be lost f.
1Sa 2:35 his family will be priests to my anointed kings f.
13:13 would have established your kingdom over Israel f.
20:42 each other's children into the LORD's hands f."
27:12 Now he will have to stay here and serve me f!"
2Sa 7:13 And I will establish the throne of his kingdom f.
7:16 before me, and your throne will be secure f.' "
7:24 You made Israel your people f, and you,
7:25 my family. Confirm it as a promise that will last f.
7:26 And may your name be honored f so that all the
7:29 so that our dynasty may continue f before you.
22:51 to David and all his descendants f."
1Ki 1:31 and exclaimed, "May my lord King David live f!"

2:33 and his descendants be **f** guilty of these murders,
2:33 to David and his descendants and to his throne **f**."
8:13 a glorious Temple for you, where you can live **f**!"
9:3 have built so that my name will be honored there **f**.
9:5 establish the throne of your dynasty over Israel **f**.
11:39 because of Solomon's sin—though not **f**.' "
2Ki 5:27 children will suffer from Naaman's leprosy **f**."
8:19 that his descendants would continue to rule **f**.
21:7 "My name will be honored here **f** in this Temple
1Ch 15:2 Ark of the LORD and to minister before him **f**."
16:34 for he is good! / His faithful love endures **f**.
16:41 to the LORD, "for his faithful love endures **f**."
17:12 a temple—for me. And I will establish his throne **f**.
17:14 for all time, and his throne will be secure **f**.' "
17:22 You chose Israel to be your people **f**, and you,
17:23 and my family. May it be a promise that will last **f**.
17:24 and honored **f** so that all the world will say,
17:27 so that our dynasty will continue **f** before you.
22:10 establish the throne of his kingdom over Israel **f**.'
23:13 and to pronounce blessings in his name **f**.
28:4 all my father's family to be king over Israel **f**.
28:7 as he does now, I will make his kingdom last **f**.'
28:9 But if you forsake him, he will reject you **f**.
29:10 our ancestor Israel, may you be praised **f** and ever!
2Ch 2:4 He has commanded Israel to do these things **f**.
5:13 "He is so good! / His faithful love endures **f**!"
6:2 a glorious Temple for you, where you can live **f**!"
7:3 "He is so good! / His faithful love endures **f**!"
7:6 who were singing, "His faithful love endures **f**!"
7:16 this Temple and set it apart to be my home **f**.
9:8 so much and desires this kingdom to last **f**,
13:5 and his descendants the throne of Israel **f**?
20:7 And did you not give this land **f** to the descendants
20:21 to the LORD; / his faithful love endures **f**!"
21:7 that his descendants would continue to rule **f**.
30:8 to his Temple which he has set apart as holy **f**.
33:4 the LORD had said his name should be honored **f**.
33:7 "My name will be honored here **f** in this Temple
Ezr 3:11 so good! / His faithful love for Israel endures **f**!"
9:12 this prosperity to our children as an inheritance **f**.
Ne 9:31 not destroy them completely or abandon them **f**.
Est 1:19 It should order that Queen Vashti be **f** banished
Job 4:20 by evening they are dead, gone **f** without a trace.
7:10 They are gone **f** from their home—never to be seen
19:24 and filled with lead, engraved **f** in the rock.
20:7 yet he will perish **f**, thrown away like his own
22:16 the foundations of their lives were washed away **f**.
36:7 but he establishes and exalts them with kings **f**.
Ps 5:11 in you rejoice; / let them sing joyful praises **f**.
9:5 the wicked; / you have wiped out their names **f**.
9:7 But the LORD reigns **f**, / executing judgment
9:18 For the needy will not be forgotten **f**; / the hopes of
10:6 ever happen to us! / We will be free of trouble **f**!"
10:16 The LORD is king **f** and ever! / Let those who
12:7 preserving them **f** from this lying generation,
13:1 O LORD, how long will you forget me? **F**?
15:5 the innocent. / Such people will stand firm **f**.
16:11 and the pleasures of living with you **f**.
18:50 your anointed, / to David and all his descendants **f**.
19:9 Reverence for the LORD is pure, / lasting **f**.
21:4 his request. / The days of his life stretch on **f**.
23:6 and I will live in the house of the LORD / **f**.
28:9 like a shepherd, / and carry them **f** in your arms.
29:10 the floodwaters. / The LORD reigns as king **f**.
30:12 O LORD my God, I will give you thanks **f**!
33:11 But the LORD's plans stand firm **f**;
37:18 and they will receive a reward that lasts **f**.
37:27 and do good, / and you will live in the land **f**.
37:28 abandon the godly. / He will keep them safe **f**,
37:29 godly will inherit the land / and will live there **f**.
41:12 you have brought me into your presence **f**.
41:13 God of Israel, / who lives **f** from eternal ages past.
44:23 Why do you sleep? / Get up! Do not reject us **f**.
45:2 from your lips. / God himself has blessed you **f**.
45:6 Your throne, O God, endures **f** and ever.
45:17 Therefore, the nations will praise you **f** and ever.
48:8 It is the city of our God; / he will make it safe **f**.
48:14 that is what God is like. / He is our God **f** and ever,
49:9 to live **f** / and never see the grave.
49:11 is their eternal home, / where they will stay **f**.
52:8 I trust in God's unfailing love / **f** and ever.
52:9 I will praise you **f**, O God, / for what you have
55:19 God, who is king **f**, / will hear me and will humble
61:4 Let me live **f** in your sanctuary, / safe beneath the
61:7 May he reign under God's protection **f**.
66:7 For by his great power he rules **f**. / He watches
68:16 to live, / where the LORD himself will live **f**?
72:5 as long as the moon continues in the skies. / Yes, **f**!
72:17 May the king's name endure **f**; / may it continue as
72:19 Bless his glorious name **f**! / Let the whole earth be
73:26 remains the strength of my heart; / he is mine **f**.
74:1 O God, why have you rejected us **f**? / Why is your
74:10 Will you let them dishonor your name **f**?
74:19 your doves. / Don't forget your afflicted people **f**.
77:7 Has the Lord rejected me **f**? / Will he never again
77:8 Is his unfailing love gone **f**? / Have his promises
79:5 how long will you be angry with us? **F**?
79:13 sheep of your pasture, / will thank you **f** and ever,
81:15 cringe before him; / their desolation would last **f**.
83:17 Let them be ashamed and terrified **f**. / Make them
86:12 O Lord my God. / I will give glory to your name **f**,
89:1 I will sing of the tender mercies of the LORD **f**!
89:2 Your unfailing love will last **f**. / Your faithfulness
89:4 'I will establish your descendants as kings **f**;
89:28 I will love him and be kind to him **f**; / my covenant
89:36 His dynasty will go on **f**; / his throne is as secure as
89:46 long will this go on? / Will you hide yourself **f**?
89:48 No one can live **f**; all will die. / No one can escape
89:52 Blessed be the LORD **f**! / Amen and amen!
92:8 in the heavens. / You, O LORD, continue **f**.
93:5 The nature of your reign, O LORD, is holiness **f**.
100:5 LORD is good. / His unfailing love continues **f**,
102:12 But you, O LORD, will rule **f**. / Your fame will
102:24 But I cried to him, "My God, who lives **f**,
102:26 Even they will perish, but you remain **f**; / they will
103:9 will not constantly accuse us, / nor remain angry **f**.
103:17 But the love of the LORD remains **f** / with those
104:31 May the glory of the LORD last **f**! / The LORD
104:35 the face of the earth; / let the wicked disappear **f**.
106:1 for he is good! / His faithful love endures **f**.
107:1 for he is good! / His faithful love endures **f**.
110:4 "You are a priest **f** in the line of Melchizedek."
111:8 They are **f** true, / to be obeyed faithfully and with
111:9 He has guaranteed his covenant with them **f**.
111:10 come to all who obey him. / Praise his name **f**!
113:2 Blessed be the name of the LORD / **f** and ever.
115:18 the LORD / both now and **f**! / Praise the LORD!
117:2 the faithfulness of the LORD endures **f**.
118:1 for he is good! / His faithful love endures **f**.
118:2 of Israel repeat: / "His faithful love endures **f**."
118:3 the priests, repeat: / "His faithful love endures **f**."
118:4 the LORD repeat: / "His faithful love endures **f**."
118:29 for he is good! / His faithful love endures **f**.
119:44 I will keep on obeying your law / **f** and **f**.
119:89 **F**, O LORD, / your word stands firm in heaven.
119:112 to keep your principles, / even **f**, to the very end.
119:160 words are true; / all your just laws will stand **f**.
121:8 over you as you come and go, / both now and **f**.
125:1 they will not be defeated but will endure **f**.
125:2 and protects his people, both now and **f**.
132:14 "This is my home where I will live **f**," he said.
135:13 Your name, O LORD, endures **f**; / your fame,
136:1 for he is good! / His faithful love endures **f**.
136:2 to the God of gods. / His faithful love endures **f**.
136:3 to the Lord of lords. / His faithful love endures **f**.
136:4 does mighty miracles. / His faithful love endures **f**.
136:5 so skillfully. / His faithful love endures **f**.
136:6 the earth on the water. / His faithful love endures **f**.
136:7 the heavenly lights— / His faithful love endures **f**.
136:8 sun to rule the day, / His faithful love endures **f**.
136:9 stars to rule the night. / His faithful love endures **f**.
136:10 the firstborn of Egypt. / His faithful love endures **f**.
136:11 Israel out of Egypt. / His faithful love endures **f**.
136:12 and powerful arm. / His faithful love endures **f**.
136:13 parted the Red Sea. / His faithful love endures **f**.
136:14 Israel safely through, / His faithful love endures **f**.
136:15 his army into the sea. / His faithful love endures **f**.
136:16 the wilderness. / His faithful love endures **f**.
136:17 down mighty kings. / His faithful love endures **f**.
136:18 powerful kings— / His faithful love endures **f**.
136:19 king of the Amorites, / His faithful love endures **f**.
136:20 Og king of Bashan. / His faithful love endures **f**.
136:21 as an inheritance— / His faithful love endures **f**.
136:22 to his servant Israel. / His faithful love endures **f**.
136:23 our utter weakness. / His faithful love endures **f**.
136:24 us from our enemies. / His faithful love endures **f**.
136:25 to every living thing. / His faithful love endures **f**.
136:26 to the God of heaven. / His faithful love endures **f**.
138:8 for your faithful love, O LORD, endures **f**.
145:1 and King, / and bless your name **f** and ever.
145:2 I will bless you every day, / and I will praise you **f**.
145:21 on earth will bless his holy name / **f** and **f**.
146:6 in them. / He is the one who keeps every promise **f**,
146:10 The LORD will reign **f**. / O Jerusalem, your God
148:6 He established them **f** and **f**. / His orders will
Pr 27:24 for riches don't last **f**, and the crown might not be
Ecc 12:12 Studying them can go on **f** and become very
Isa 1:5 Must you rebel **f**? Your head is injured, and your
9:1 that time of darkness and despair will not go on **f**.
9:7 He will rule **f** with fairness and justice from the
16:10 out of grapes in the winepresses has ceased **f**.
25:8 He will swallow up death **f**! The Sovereign
25:8 He will remove **f** all insults and mockery against
28:24 Is he **f** cultivating the soil and never planting it?
32:17 Quietness and confidence will fill the land **f**.
34:10 will never end; the smoke of its burning will rise **f**.
34:17 They will possess it **f**, from generation to
40:8 flowers fade, but the word of our God stands **f**."
47:7 You thought, 'I will reign **f** as queen of the world!'
51:6 the earth will die like flies, but my salvation lasts **f**.
51:8 as it eats wool. But my righteousness will last **f**.
57:16 For I will not fight against you **f**; I will not always
59:21 lips of your children and your children's children **f**.
60:15 and rebuffed by all, you will be beautiful **f**.
60:21 They will possess their land **f**, for I will plant them
63:12 lifted up his hand, establishing his reputation **f**?
64:9 with us, LORD. Please don't remember our sins **f**.
65:18 Be glad; rejoice **f** in my creation! And look!
Jer 3:12 for I am merciful. I will not be angry with you **f**.
3:18 the land I gave their ancestors as an inheritance **f**.
7:7 in this land that I gave to your ancestors to keep **f**.
9:1 my eyes were a fountain of tears; I would weep **f**!
11:19 "Let's kill him, so his name will be forgotten **f**."
17:4 my anger into a roaring fire that will burn **f**."
17:25 then this nation will continue **f**. There will always
17:25 and on horses, and this city will remain **f**.
25:5 that the LORD gave to you and your ancestors **f**.
25:9 you an object of horror and contempt and a ruin **f**.
31:37 so I will not consider casting them away **f** for their
32:39 will give them one heart and mind to worship me **f**,
33:11 the LORD is good. / His faithful love endures **f**!'
33:17 David will **f** have a descendant sitting on the
49:13 All its towns and villages will be desolate **f**."
49:33 be inhabited by jackals, and it will be desolate **f**.
50:39 again will people live there; it will lie desolate **f**.
51:26 You will be desolate **f**. Even your stones will never
51:62 remain here. She will lie empty and abandoned **f**.'
La 3:31 For the Lord does not abandon anyone **f**.
5:19 But LORD, you remain the same **f**! Your throne
Eze 35:9 I will make you desolate **f**. Your cities will never
37:25 and their grandchildren after them will live there **f**,
37:25 And my servant David will be their prince **f**.
37:26 and I will put my Temple among them **f**.
37:28 And since my Temple will remain among them **f**,
43:7 I will remain here **f**, living among the people of
43:9 to honor their kings, and I will live among them **f**.
46:16 it will belong to him and his descendants **f**.
Da 2:20 saying, / "Praise the name of God **f** and ever,
2:44 kingdoms into nothingness, but it will stand **f**.
4:3 powerful his wonders! / His kingdom will last **f**,
4:34 the Most High and honored the one who lives **f**.
6:26 For he is the living God, / and he will endure **f**.
7:18 given the kingdom, and they will rule **f** and ever."
7:27 They will rule **f**, and all rulers will serve and obey
12:3 turn many to righteousness will shine like stars **f**.
12:7 and took this solemn oath by the one who lives **f**:
Hos 2:19 I will make you my wife **f**, showing you
14:4 will know no bounds, for my anger will be gone **f**!
Joel 3:17 Jerusalem will be holy **f**, and foreign armies will
3:20 "But Judah will remain **f**, and Jerusalem will
Ob 1:10 be destroyed completely and filled with shame **f**.
Mic 4:5 we will follow the LORD our God **f** and ever.
4:7 will rule from Jerusalem as their king **f**."
7:18 You cannot stay angry with your people **f**,
Hab 1:3 Must I **f** see this sin and misery all around me?
1:17 Will you let them get away with this **f**? Will they
succeed **f** in their heartless conquests?
Mal 1:4 'The People with Whom the LORD Is **F** Angry.'
Mt 24:35 earth will disappear, but my words will remain **f**.
Mk 13:31 earth will disappear, but my words will remain **f**.
Lk 1:33 And he will reign over Israel **f**; his Kingdom will
1:55 and his children— / to be merciful to them **f**."
1:75 in holiness and righteousness **f**.
21:33 earth will disappear, but my words will remain **f**.
Jn 6:51 Anyone who eats this bread will live **f**; this bread
6:58 Anyone who eats this bread will live **f** and not die
8:35 of the family, but a son is part of the family **f**.
12:34 from Scripture that the Messiah would live **f**.
Ac 7:51 deaf to the truth. Must you **f** resist the Holy Spirit?
Ro 1:25 but not the Creator himself, who is to be praised **f**.
1:30 They are **f** inventing new ways of sinning and are
9:3 I would be willing to be **f** cursed—cut off from
16:27 alone is wise, be the glory **f** through Jesus Christ.
1Co 13:8 Love will last **f**, but prophecy and speaking in
15:50 perishable bodies of ours are not able to live **f**.
2Co 3:11 which remains **f**, has far greater glory.
4:17 for us an immeasurably great glory that will last **f**!
4:18 will soon be over, but the joys to come will last **f**.
7:3 for I said before that you are in our hearts **f**.
11:31 who is to be praised **f**, knows I tell the truth.
Gal 1:8 preaches any other message, let him be **f** cursed.
Eph 2:1 were dead, doomed **f** because of your many sins.
3:21 and in Christ Jesus **f** and ever through endless
4:14 **f** changing our minds about what we believe
Php 4:20 Now glory be to God our Father **f** and ever. Amen.
1Th 4:17 to meet the Lord in the air and remain with him **f**.
5:10 He died for us so that we can live with him **f**,
2Th 1:9 **f** separated from the Lord and from his glorious
1Ti 1:17 Glory and honor to God **f** and ever. He is the
6:16 nor ever will. To him be honor and power **f**. Amen.
2Ti 3:7 Such women are **f** following new teachings,
4:18 To God be the glory **f** and ever. Amen.
Phm 1:15 for a little while so you could have him back **f**.
Heb 1:8 "Your throne, O God, endures **f** and ever.
1:11 Even they will perish, but you remain **f**. / They will
5:6 passage God said to him, / "You are a priest **f**
7:3 He remains a priest **f**, resembling the Son of God.
7:17 out when he said of Christ, / "You are a priest **f**
7:21 will not break his vow: / 'You are a priest **f**.' "
7:24 But Jesus remains a priest **f**; his priesthood will
7:25 Therefore he is able, once and **f**, to save everyone
7:25 He lives **f** to plead with God on their behalf.
7:28 with an oath, and his Son has been made perfect **f**.
9:12 own blood, and with it he secured our salvation **f**.
9:26 to remove the power of sin **f** by his sacrificial
10:14 For by that one offering he perfected **f** all those
12:9 to the discipline of our heavenly Father and live **f**?
13:8 Jesus Christ is the same yesterday, today, and **f**.
13:20[-21] his blood. To him be glory **f** and ever. Amen.
1Pe 1:23 But this new life will last **f** because it comes from
1:25 But the word of the Lord will last **f**." And that
4:11 All glory and power belong to him **f** and ever.
5:11 All power is his **f** and ever. Amen.
1Jn 2:17 But if you do the will of God, you will live **f**.
2Jn 1:2 the truth that lives in us and will be in our hearts **f**.
Rev 1:6 him everlasting glory! He rules **f** and ever! Amen!
1:18 Look, I am alive **f** and ever! And I hold the keys of
4:9 sitting on the throne, the one who lives **f** and ever,
4:10 and worship the one who lives **f** and ever.
5:13 sitting on the throne / and to the Lamb **f** and ever."
7:12 belong to our God **f** and **f**. Amen!"
10:6 swore an oath in the name of the one who lives **f**
11:15 and of his Christ, and he will reign **f** and ever."
14:11 The smoke of their torment rises **f** and ever,
15:7 the terrible wrath of God, who lives **f** and **f**.
18:14 much will never be yours again. They are gone **f**."
18:21 thrown away this stone, and she will disappear **f**.
19:3 The smoke from that city ascends **f** and **f**!"
20:10 they will be tormented day and night **f** and ever.
21:4 or pain. For the old world and its evils are gone **f**."
22:5 will shine on them. And they will reign **f** and ever.

FOREVERMORE (3) [EVER]
Ps 133: 3 LORD has pronounced his blessing, / even life **f**.
2Pe 3:18 To him be all glory and honor, both now and **f**.
Jude 1:25 belong to him, in the beginning, now, and **f**.

FOREWARN(ED) [KJV] See I'LL TELL, WARNED

FORFEIT (2) [FORFEITED]
Ezr 10: 8 **f** all their property and be expelled from the
Lk 9:25 but lose or **f** your own soul in the process?

FORFEITED (1) [FORFEIT]
Hab 2:10 you have shamed your name and **f** your lives.

FORGAT [KJV] See FORGOT

FORGAVE (7) [FORGIVE]
Ps 32: 5 And you **f** me! All my guilt is gone. / *Interlude*
78:38 Yet he was merciful and **f** their sins / and didn't
Mt 18:27 pity for him, and he released him and **f** his debt.
18:32 I **f** you that tremendous debt because you pleaded
Lk 7:42 so he kindly **f** them both, canceling their debts.
Col 2:13 God made you alive with Christ. He **f** all our sins.
3:13 Remember, the Lord **f** you, so you must forgive

FORGE (2) [FORGING]
Isa 44:12 The blacksmith stands at his **f** to make a sharp tool,
54:16 the blacksmith who fans the coals beneath the **f**

FORGET (93) [FORGETFULNESS, FORGETS, FORGETTING, FORGOT, FORGOTTEN]
Ge 41:51 "God has made me **f** all my troubles
Ex 33:13 don't **f** that this nation is your very own people."
Lev 2:13 Never **f** to add salt to your grain offerings.
Dt 4: 9 Be very careful never to **f** what you have seen the
4:31 or **f** the solemn covenant he made with your
6:12 be careful not to **f** the LORD, who rescued you
8:11 Beware that in your plenty you do not **f** the
8:14 proud at that time and **f** the LORD your God,
8:15 Do not **f** that he led you through the great
8:19 If you ever **f** the LORD your God and follow
12:19 Be very careful never to **f** the Levites as long as
14:27 And do not **f** the Levites in your community,
24:19 and **f** to bring in a bundle of grain from your field,
25:17 "Never **f** what the Amalekites did to you as you
25:19 their memory from under heaven. Never **f** this!
2Sa 19:19 "**F** the terrible thing I did when you left Jerusalem.
2Ki 17:38 Do not **f** the covenant I made with you, and do not
Ne 13:14 and do not **f** all that I have faithfully done for the
Job 7:13 and I will try to **f** my misery with sleep,'
8:13 Such is the fate of all who **f** God. The hope of the
9:27 If I decided to **f** my complaints, if I decided to end
11:16 You will **f** your misery. It will all be gone like
14:13 and **f** me there until your anger has passed.
24:20 Even the sinner's own mother will **f** him.
41: 8 hand on it, you will never **f** the battle that follows,
Ps 10:12 Punish the wicked, O God! / Do not **f** the helpless!
13: 1 O LORD, how long will you **f** me? Forever?
45:10 **F** your people and your homeland far away.
59:11 Don't kill them, for my people soon **f** such lessons;
74:19 your doves. / Don't **f** your afflicted people forever.
103: 2 and never **f** the good things he does for me.
109:14 May the LORD never **f** the sins of his ancestors;
111: 4 Who can **f** the wonders he performs?
119:16 delight in your principles / and not **f** your word.
119:93 I will never **f** your commandments, / for you have
119:141 and despised, / but I don't **f** your commandments.
137: 5 If I **f** you, O Jerusalem, / let my right hand **f** its skill upon the harp.
Pr 3: 1 My child, never **f** the things I have taught you.
4: 5 Don't **f** or turn away from my words.
31: 5 they may **f** their duties and be unable to give
31: 7 Let them drink to **f** their poverty and remember
Ecc 12: 1 Don't let the excitement of youth cause you to **f**
Isa 30:11 **F** all this gloom. We have heard more than enough
43:18 "But **f** all that—it is nothing compared to what I
44:21 the LORD, made you, and I will not **f** to help you.
46: 8 "Do not **f** this, you guilty ones.
46: 9 And do not **f** the things I have done throughout
49:15 "Never! Can a mother **f** her nursing child? Can she
49:15 But even if that were possible, I would not **f** you!
65:16 put aside my anger and **f** the evil of earlier days.
Jer 2:32 Does a young woman **f** her jewelry? Does a bride
3: 5 Surely you can **f** it!' So you talk, and keep right on
9: 2 that I could go away and **f** them and live in a shack
14:21 not break your covenant with us. Please don't **f** us!
23:27 they are trying to get my people to **f** me,
23:39 I will **f** you completely. I will expel you from my
31: 8 I will not **f** the blind and lame, the expectant
42:19 Don't **f** this warning I have given you today.
La 3:20 I will never **f** this awful time, as I grieve over my
5:20 Why do you continue to **f** us? Why have you
Hos 2:17 O Israel, I will cause you to **f** your images of Baal;
4: 6 laws of your God, I will **f** to bless your children.
5: 2 But never **f**—I will settle with all of you for what
9: 9 God will not **f**. He will surely punish them for their
Am 1: 3 have sinned again and again, and I will not **f** it.
1: 6 have sinned again and again, and I will not **f** it.
1: 9 have sinned again and again, and I will not **f** it.
1:11 have sinned again and again, and I will not **f** it.
1:13 have sinned again and again, and I will not **f** it.
2: 1 have sinned again and again, and I will not **f** it.
2: 4 have sinned again and again, and I will not **f** it.
2: 6 have sinned again and again, and I will not **f** it.
8: 7 "I will never **f** the wicked things you have done!
Lk 10:11 And don't **f** the Kingdom of God is near!'
11:42 but you completely **f** about justice and the love of
12: 6 Yet God does not **f** a single one of them.
Ro 3:31 does this mean that we can **f** about the law?
1Co 10: 1 I don't want you to **f**, dear brothers and sisters,
Eph 2:11 Don't **f** that you Gentiles used to be outsiders by
Col 4: 3 Don't **f** to pray for us, too, that God will give us
2Ti 2: 8 Never **f** that Jesus Christ was a man born into King
Heb 3:15 But never **f** the warning: / "Today you must listen
6:10 He will not **f** how hard you have worked for him
10:32 Don't ever **f** those early days when you first
13: 2 Don't **f** to show hospitality to strangers, for some
13: 3 Don't **f** about those in prison. Suffer with them as
13:16 Don't **f** to do good and to share what you have
Jas 1:24 see yourself, walk away, and **f** what you look like.
1:25 if you do what it says and don't **f** what you heard,
2Pe 3: 5 They deliberately **f** that God made the heavens by
3: 8 But you must not **f**, dear friends, that a day is like a
Jude 1: 7 And don't **f** the cities of Sodom and Gomorrah

FORGETFULNESS (1) [FORGET]
Ps 88:12 Can anyone in the land of **f** talk about your

FORGETS (1) [FORGET]
Ge 27:45 When he **f** what you have done, I will send for you.

FORGETTING (1) [FORGET]
Php 3:13 **F** the past and looking forward to what lies ahead,

FORGING (1) [FORGE]
Ge 4:22 work with metal, **f** instruments of bronze and iron.

FORGIVE (80) [FORGAVE, FORGIVEN, FORGIVENESS, FORGIVES, FORGIVING]
Ge 31:35 "**F** my not getting up, Father," Rachel explained.
50:17 '**F** your brothers for the great evil they did to you.'
50:17 of the God of your father, beg you to **f** us."
Ex 10:17 "**F** my sin only this once, and plead with the
23:21 not rebel against him, for he will not **f** your sins.
32:32 But now, please **f** their sin—and if not, then blot
Nu 30: 5 The LORD will **f** her because her father would
30: 8 her commitments, and the LORD will **f** her.
30:12 pledge will be nullified, and the LORD will **f** her.
Dt 21: 8 **f** your people Israel whom you have redeemed.
Jos 24:19 jealous God. He will not **f** your rebellion and sins.
1Sa 15:25 **f** my sin now and go with me to worship the
25:28 Please **f** me if I have offended in any way.
2Sa 19:19 "My lord the king, please **f** me," he pleaded.
24:10 Please **f** me, LORD, for doing this foolish thing."
1Ki 8:30 from heaven where you live, and when you hear, **f**.
8:34 then hear from heaven and **f** their sins and return
8:36 hear from heaven and **f** the sins of your servants,
8:39 then hear from heaven where you live, and **f**.
8:50 and **f** your people who have sinned against you.
2Ki 24: 4 innocent blood, and the LORD would not **f** this.
1Ch 21: 8 Please **f** me for doing this foolish thing."
2Ch 6:21 from heaven where you live, and when you hear, **f**.
6:25 then hear from heaven and **f** their sins and return
6:27 hear from heaven and **f** the sins of your servants,
6:30 then hear from heaven where you live, and **f**.
6:39 and **f** your people who have sinned against you.
7:14 and will **f** their sins and heal their land.
Job 10:14 and if I sinned, you would not **f** my iniquity.
Ps 25: 7 **F** the rebellious sins of my youth; / look instead
25:11 of your name, O LORD, / **f** my many, many sins.
25:18 Feel my pain and see my trouble. / **F** all my sins.
51:14 **F** me for shedding blood, O God who saves;
65: 3 our hearts are filled with sins, / you **f** them all.
79: 9 Oh, save us and **f** our sins / for the sake of your
86: 5 O Lord, you are so good, so ready to **f**, / so full of
Isa 33:24 and helpless," for the LORD will **f** their sins.
Jer 18:23 Don't **f** their crimes and blot out their sins.
31:34 "And I will **f** their wickedness and will never
33: 8 against me, and I will **f** all their sins of rebellion.
36: 3 Then I will be able to **f** their sins
50:20 or in Judah, for I will **f** the remnant I preserve.
Eze 16:63 and shame when I **f** you of all that you have done,
Da 9:19 "O Lord, hear. O Lord, **f**. O Lord, listen and act!
Hos 1: 6 longer show love to the people of Israel or **f** them.
14: 2 to him, "**F** all our sins and graciously receive us,
Am 7: 2 "O Sovereign LORD, please **f** your people!
Mt 6:12 and **f** us our sins, / just as we have forgiven those
6:14 "If you **f** those who sin against you, your heavenly Father will **f** you.
6:15 But if you refuse to **f** others, your Father will not **f** your sins.
9: 6 Son of Man, have the authority on earth to **f** sins."
18:21 how often should I **f** someone who sins against
18:35 will do to you if you refuse to **f** your brothers
26:28 his people. It is poured out to **f** the sins of many.
Mk 2: 7 This is blasphemy! Who but God can **f** sins!"
2:10 Son of Man, have the authority on earth to **f** sins."
11:25 first **f** anyone you are holding a grudge against,
11:25 so that your Father in heaven will **f** your sins,
Lk 5:21 "This is blasphemy! Who but God can **f** sins?"
5:24 Son of Man, have the authority on earth to **f** sins."
6:37 back on you. If you **f** others, you will be forgiven.
11: 4 And **f** us our sins— / just as we **f** those who have sinned against us.
17: 3 believer sins, rebuke him; then if he repents, **f** him.
17: 4 time turns again and asks forgiveness, **f** him."
23:34 Jesus said, "Father, **f** these people, because they
Jn 20:23 If you **f** anyone's sins, they are forgiven. If you refuse to **f** them, they are unforgiven."
Ac 8:22 to the Lord. Perhaps he will **f** your evil thoughts,
2Co 2: 7 Now it is time to **f** him and comfort him.
2:10 When you **f** this man, I **f** him, too. And when I **f** him (for whatever is to be forgiven),
12:13 a burden to you. Please **f** me for this wrong!
Col 3:13 other's faults and **f** the person who offends you.
3:13 the Lord forgave you, so you must **f** others.
Heb 8:12 And I will **f** their wrongdoings, / and I will never
1Jn 1: 9 he is faithful and just to **f** us and to cleanse us from

FORGIVEN (56) [FORGIVE]
Lev 4:20 make atonement for the people, and they will be **f**.
4:26 atonement for the leader's sin, and he will be **f**.
4:31 will make atonement for them, and they will be **f**.
4:35 will make atonement for them, and they will be **f**.
5:10 for those who are guilty, and they will be **f**.
5:13 for those who are guilty, and they will be **f**.
5:16 sacrificed as a guilt offering, and they will be **f**.
5:18 for those who are guilty, and they will be **f**.
6: 7 for them before the LORD, and they will be **f**."
19:22 ram of the guilt offering, and the man will be **f**.
Nu 14:19 just as you have **f** them ever since they left
15:25 the whole community of Israel, and they will be **f**.
15:26 The whole community of Israel will be **f**,
15:28 before the LORD, and that person will be **f**.
1Sa 3:14 and his sons will never be **f** by sacrifices
2Sa 12:13 Nathan replied, "Yes, but the LORD has **f** you,
Ps 32: 1 Oh, what joy for those / whose rebellion is **f**,
85: 2 You have **f** the guilt of your people— / yes,
Isa 6: 7 Now your guilt is removed, and your sins are **f**."
22:14 this sin will never be **f** you until the day you die.
38:17 rescued me from death / and have **f** all my sins.
La 3:42 have sinned and rebelled, and you have not **f** us.
Mt 6:12 just as we have **f** those who have sinned against us.
9: 2 paralyzed man, "Take heart, son! Your sins are **f**."
9: 5 to say, 'Your sins are **f**' or 'Get up and walk'?
12:31 "Every sin or blasphemy can be **f**—
12:31 against the Holy Spirit, which can never be **f**.
12:32 blasphemes against me, the Son of Man, can be **f**,
12:32 blasphemy against the Holy Spirit will never be **f**,
18:32 Then the king called in the man he had **f** and said,
Mk 1: 4 turned from their sins and turned to God to be **f**.
2: 5 to the paralyzed man, "My son, your sins are **f**."
2: 9 'Your sins are **f**' or 'Get up, pick up your mat,
3:28 "I assure you that any sin can be **f**,
3:29 blasphemes against the Holy Spirit will never be **f**.
4:12 So they will not turn from their sins / and be **f**.'
Lk 3: 3 turned from their sins and turned to God to be **f**.
5:20 Jesus said to the man, "Son, your sins are **f**."
5:23 to say, 'Your sins are **f**' or 'Get up and walk'?
6:37 back on you. If you forgive others, you will be **f**.
7:47 have been **f**, so she has shown me much love.
7:47 But a person who is **f** little shows only little love."
7:48 Then Jesus said to the woman, "Your sins are **f**."
12:10 those who speak against the Son of Man may be **f**,
12:10 blasphemies against the Holy Spirit will never be **f**.
Jn 20:23 If you forgive anyone's sins, they are **f**. If you
Ac 5:31 their sins and turn to God so their sins would be **f**.
10:43 in him will have their sins **f** through his name."
Ro 4: 7 what joy for those whose disobedience is **f**,
2Co 2:10 And when I forgive him (for whatever is to be **f**),
Eph 1: 7 through the blood of his Son, and our sins are **f**.
4:32 one another, just as God through Christ has **f** you.
Col 1:14 our freedom with his blood and has **f** all our sins.
Heb 10:18 Now when sins have been **f**, there is no need to
Jas 5:15 And anyone who has committed sins will be **f**.
1Jn 2:12 because your sins have been **f** because of Jesus.

FORGIVENESS (17) [FORGIVE]
FORGIVENESS OF SINS (5) Lk 1:77; 24:47; Ac 2:38; Heb 9:22; Jas 5:20

Ex 32:30 Perhaps I will be able to obtain **f** for you."
Ne 9:17 But you are a God of **f**, gracious and merciful,
Ps 51:14 who saves; / then I will joyfully sing of your **f**.
130: 4 But you offer **f**, / that we might learn to fear you.
Jer 36: 7 and ask the LORD's **f** before it is too late.
Lk 1:77 how to find salvation / through **f** of their sins.
17: 4 times a day and each time turns again and asks **f**,
24:47 'There is **f** of sins for all who turn to me.'
Ac 2:38 in the name of Jesus Christ for the **f** of your sins.
13:38 listen! In this man Jesus there is **f** for your sins.
26:18 Then they will receive **f** for their sins and be given
Ro 5:15 between our sin and God's generous gift of **f**.
5:15 brought **f** to many through God's bountiful gift.
6: 1 God can show us more and more kindness and **f**?
Heb 9:22 the shedding of blood, there is no **f** of sins.
Jas 5:20 from death and bring about the **f** of many sins.
Jude 1: 4 saying that God's **f** allows us to live immoral lives.

FORGIVES (2) [FORGIVE]
Ps 103: 3 He **f** all my sins / and heals all my diseases.
Heb 12:24 which graciously **f** instead of crying out for

FORGIVING (6) [FORGIVE]
Ex 34: 7 I show this unfailing love to many thousands by **f**
Nu 14:18 in unfailing love, **f** every kind of sin and rebellion.
Ps 99: 8 our God, you answered them. / You were a **f** God,
Da 9: 9 But the Lord our God is merciful and **f**,
Lk 7:49 does this man think he is, going around **f** sins?"
Eph 4:32 be kind to each other, tenderhearted, **f** one another,

FORGOT (14) [FORGET]

Ge 40:23 however, promptly **f** all about Joseph,
Dt 32:18 you **f** the God who had given you birth.
Jdg 3: 7 They **f** about the LORD their God, and they
8:34 They **f** the LORD their God, who had rescued
1Sa 12: 9 But the people soon **f** about the LORD their God,
1Ki 9: 9 'Because his people **f** the LORD their God,
Job 22:18 But they **f** that he had filled their homes with good
Ps 78:11 They **f** what he had done—/ the wonderful
78:42 They **f** about his power / and how he rescued them
78:43 They **f** his miraculous signs in Egypt, / his wonders
106: 7 They soon **f** his many acts of kindness to them.
106:13 Yet how quickly they **f** what he had done!
106:21 They **f** God, their savior, / who had done such
Hos 13: 6 were satisfied, then you became proud and **f** me.

FORGOTTEN (41) [FORGET]

Ge 41:30 so great that all the prosperity will be **f** and wiped
Dt 25: 6 so that his name will not be **f** in Israel.
26:13 I have not violated or **f** any of your commands.
31:21 for it will never be **f** by their descendants.
1Sa 19: 5 Have you **f** about the time he risked his life to kill
Ne 9:10 have a glorious reputation that has never been **f**.
Job 19:15 The members of my household have **f** me.
Ps 9:18 For the needy will not be **f** forever; / the hopes of
41: 5 "How soon will he die and be **f**?" they ask.
77: 9 Has God **f** to be kind? / Has he slammed the door
88: 5 as good as dead. / I am **f**, / cut off from your care.
112: 3 be wealthy, / and their good deeds will never be **f**.
112: 9 Their good deeds will never be **f**. / They will have
119:153 and rescue me, / for I have not **f** your law.
119:176 and find me, / for I have not **f** your commands.
Ecc 2:16 both die, and in the days to come, both will be **f**.
Isa 23:15 the length of a king's life, Tyre will be **f**.
26:14 and destroyed them, / and they are long **f**.
49:14 "The LORD has deserted us; the Lord has **f** us."
51:13 Yet you have **f** the LORD, your Creator, the one
Jer 2:32 No! Yet for years on end my people have **f** me.
3:21 For they have **f** the LORD their God
11:19 "Let's kill him, so his name will be **f** forever."
13:25 because you have **f** me and put your trust in false
20:11 Their dishonor will never be **f**.
44: 9 Have you **f** the sins of your ancestors, the sins of
La 3:17 stripped away, and I have **f** what prosperity is.
Eze 18:22 All their past sins will be **f**, and they will live
18:24 All their previous goodness will be **f**, and they will
23:35 And because you have **f** me and turned your back
Hos 4: 6 Since you have **f** the laws of your God, I will
8:14 But they have both **f** their Maker. Therefore,
Am 3:10 "My people have **f** what it means to do right,"
Zec 13: 2 so that even the names of the idols will be **f**.
Mt 16: 5 the disciples discovered they had **f** to bring any
Mk 8:14 But the disciples discovered they had **f** to bring any
Lk 1:54 He has not **f** his promise to be merciful.
Ro 6: 3 Or have you **f** that when we became Christians
2Co 9: 9 to the poor. / Their good deeds will never be **f**."
Heb 12: 5 And have you entirely **f** the encouraging words
2Pe 1: 9 They have already **f** that God has cleansed them

FORK (5) [FORKS]

1Sa 2:13 would send over a servant with a three-pronged **f**.
2:14 the servant would stick the **f** into the pot
Eze 21:21 The king of Babylon now stands at the **f**,
Mt 3:12 the chaff from the grain with his winnowing **f**.
Lk 3:17 the chaff from the grain with his winnowing **f**.

FORKS (1) [FORK]

Eze 21:19 comes out of Babylon where the road **f** into two—

FORM (30) [DEFORMED, FORMATION, FORMED, FORMING, FORMLESS, FORMS, WELL-FORMED]

Ex 19:18 because the LORD had descended on it in the **f** of
22: 5 then the animal's owner must pay damages in the **f**
39: 9 It was doubled over to **f** a pouch, nine inches
Lev 2: 4 It may be presented in the **f** of cakes mixed with
17:10 among you, who eats or drinks blood in any **f**.
Dt 4:12 You heard his words but didn't see his **f**; there was
4:15 You did not see the LORD's **f** on the day he
4:16 yourselves by making a physical image in any **f**—
4:23 will break it if you make idols of any shape or **f**,
2Ki 11: 8 **F** a bodyguard for the king and keep your weapons
15:20 twenty ounces of silver in the **f** of a special tax.
2Ch 23: 7 **f** a bodyguard for the king and keep your weapons
Job 4:16 There was a **f** before my eyes, and a hushed voice
15:33 tree that sheds its blossoms so the fruit cannot **f**.
Ps 104:18 and the rocks **f** a refuge for rock badgers.
105:41 to **f** a river through the dry and barren land.
Isa 13: 4 The LORD Almighty has brought them here to **f**
Jer 49:14 "**F** a coalition against Edom, and prepare for
Da 11:17 and will **f** an alliance with the king of the south.
Mic 1: 1 and they came to Micah in the **f** of visions.
Hab 1:13 But will you, who cannot allow sin in any **f**,
Lk 3:22 and the Holy Spirit descended on him in the **f** of a
12:54 "When you see clouds beginning to **f** in the west,
Ac 17: 5 some worthless fellows from the streets to **f** a mob
Php 2: 7 position of a slave and appeared in human **f**.
2: 8 And in human **f** he obediently humbled himself
Heb 2:14 became flesh and blood by being born in human **f**.
Rev 4: 7 The first of these living beings had the **f** of a lion;
4: 7 and the fourth had the **f** of an eagle with wings
21:16 In fact, it was in the **f** of a cube, for its length

FORMAL (1) [FORMALLY]

1Ki 5:12 and Solomon made a **f** alliance of peace.

FORMALLY (1) [FORMAL]

Ne 5:12 and officials **f** vow to do what they had promised.

FORMATION (4) [FORM]

2Sa 10:17 Arameans positioned themselves there in battle **f**
1Ch 19:17 Jordan River, and positioned his troops in battle **f**.
Jer 6:23 They are marching in battle **f** to destroy you,
50:42 They are marching in battle **f** to destroy you,

FORMED (30) [FORM]

Ge 2: 7 And the LORD God **f** a man's body from the dust
2:19 So the LORD God **f** from the soil every kind of
14: 3 and Bela **f** an alliance and mobilized their armies
41: 5 on one stalk, with every kernel well **f** and plump.
Jdg 6:33 and the people of the east **f** an alliance against
1Sa 26: 5 were sleeping inside a ring **f** by the slumbering
2Ki 9:14 and grandson of Nimshi **f** a conspiracy against
11:11 They **f** a line from the south side of the Temple
2Ch 23:10 They **f** a line from the south side of the Temple
Job 10: 8 " 'You **f** me with your hands; you made me,
10:10 You guided my conception and **f** me in the womb.
33: 6 I are the same before God. I, too, was **f** from clay.
Ps 65: 6 You **f** the mountains by your power / and armed
94: 9 your ears deaf? / Is the one who **f** your eyes blind?
95: 5 for he made it. / His hands **f** the dry land, too.
139:15 You watched me as I was being **f** in utter
Pr 8:22 "The LORD **f** me from the beginning, before he
8:25 Before the mountains and the hills were **f**, I was
Ecc 11: 5 and as mysterious as a tiny baby being **f** in a
Isa 40:19 Can he be compared to an idol **f** in a mold,
49: 5 he who **f** me in my mother's womb to be his
64: 8 and you are the potter. We are all **f** by your hand.
Jer 1: 5 "I knew you before I **f** you in your mother's
Eze 37: 8 as I watched, muscles and flesh **f** over the bones.
37: 8 Then skin **f** to cover their bodies, but they still had
Da 11: 6 an alliance will be **f** between the king of the north
Zec 12: 1 of the earth, and **f** the spirit within humans.
Mk 4:28 then the heads of wheat are **f**, and finally the grain
Ac 16:22 A mob quickly **f** against Paul and Silas,
Heb 11: 3 that the entire universe was **f** at God's command,

FORMER (35) [FORMERLY]

Ge 40:21 then restored the chief cup-bearer to his **f** position,
Lev 16:19 Israel's defilement and return it to its **f** holiness.
Nu 21:26 He had conquered a **f** Moabite king and seized all
Dt 3:13 of Gilead and all of Bashan—Og's **f** kingdom—
24: 4 the **f** husband may not marry her again, for she has
Jos 13:30 all of Bashan, all the **f** kingdom of King Og,
2Ki 13: 5 Then Israel lived in safety again as they had in **f**
17:34 They follow their **f** practices instead of truly
19:12 The **f** kings of Assyria destroyed them all!
23:11 that the **f** kings of Judah had dedicated to the sun.
1Ch 9: 2 The first to return to their property in their **f** towns
Ezr 6: 7 Let it be rebuilt on its **f** site, and do not hinder the
Ne 5:15 This was quite a contrast to the **f** governors who
Job 8: 8 "Just ask the **f** generation. Pay attention to the
8:10 They will teach you from the wisdom of **f**
17: 7 with weeping, and I am but a shadow of my **f** self.
42:11 and **f** friends came and feasted with him in his
Ps 79: 8 Oh, do not hold us guilty for our **f** sins! / Let your
90:15 Give us gladness in proportion to our **f** misery!
Pr 9:18 But the men don't realize that her **f** guests are now
Ecc 1:11 We don't remember what happened in those **f**
Isa 37:12 The **f** kings of Assyria destroyed them all!
Eze 23:21 you celebrated your **f** days as a young girl in
Am 9:11 but I will rebuild its walls and restore its **f** glory.
Zep 3:19 I will give glory and renown to my **f** exiles,
Zec 10: 8 their population will grow again to its **f** size.
Mal 3: 4 of Judah and Jerusalem, as he did in **f** times.
Mt 12:44 So it returns and finds its **f** home empty, swept,
14: 3 Herodias (the **f** wife of Herod's brother Philip).
Lk 11:25 and finds that its **f** home is all swept and clean.
Ac 17:30 God overlooked people's **f** ignorance about these
Ro 3:25 he did not punish those who sinned in **f** times.
1Co 2: 7 wisdom of God, which was hidden in **f** times,
Eph 4:22 off your old evil nature and your **f** way of life,
1Pe 4: 4 your **f** friends are very surprised when you no

FORMERLY (8) [FORMER]

Dt 4:46 (This land was **f** occupied by the Amorites under
Jos 15:15 in the town of Debir (**f** called Kiriath-sepher).
Jdg 1:10 Judah marched against the Canaanites in Hebron (**f**
1:11 in the town of Debir (**f** called Kiriath-sepher).
1:23 They sent spies to Bethel (**f** known as Luz),
2Ki 24: 7 for the king of Babylon occupied the entire area **f**
1Ch 9:23 house of the LORD, the house that was **f** a tent.
Heb 4: 6 But those who **f** heard the Good News failed to

FORMING (8) [FORM]

Ex 26:24 at the top with a single ring, **f** a single unit.
28:16 of two folds of cloth, **f** a pouch nine inches square.
36:29 a single ring, **f** a single unit from top to bottom.
40:33 Then he hung the curtains **f** the courtyard around
Jos 17:10 with the Mediterranean Sea **f** Manasseh's western
1Ki 8: 7 **f** a canopy over the Ark and its carrying poles.
2Ch 5: 8 **f** a canopy over the Ark and its carrying poles.
Da 2:43 **f** alliances with each other through intermarriage.

FORMLESS (2) [FORM]

Ge 1: 2 The earth was empty, a **f** mass cloaked in darkness.
Jer 4:23 I looked at the earth, and it was empty and **f**.

FORMS (2) [FORM]

Isa 18: 4 or as the dew **f** on an autumn morning during the
Eze 43:17 The upper ledge also **f** a square, measuring 24-1/2

FORNICATION [KJV] See ADULTERY, PROSTITUTE, IMMORALITY

FORSAKE (19) [FORSAKEN, FORSAKING, GODFORSAKEN]

Dt 31: 6 ahead of you. He will neither fail you nor **f** you."
31: 8 be with you; he will neither fail you nor **f** you."
Jos 24:16 "We would never **f** the LORD and worship other
24:20 If you **f** the LORD and serve other gods, he will
1Ki 6:13 the people of Israel and never **f** my people."
8:57 us as he was with our ancestors; may he never **f** us.
1Ch 28: 9 But if you **f** him, he will reject you forever.
28:20 my God, is with you. He will not fail you or **f** you.
Job 28:28 is true wisdom; to **f** evil is real understanding.' "
Ps 80:18 Then we will never **f** you again. / Revive us
89:30 But if his sons **f** my law / and fail to walk in my
Pr 4:13 Carry out my instructions; don't **f** them.
28:13 But if they confess and **f** them, they will receive
Isa 41:17 I, the God of Israel, will never **f** them.
42:16 I will indeed do these things; / I will not **f** them.
Jer 2:19 bitter thing it is to **f** the LORD your God,
Eze 20: 8 did not get rid of their idols or **f** the gods of Egypt.
Da 11:30 and reward those who **f** the covenant.
Heb 13: 5 "I will never fail you. / I will never **f** you."

FORSAKEN (18) [FORSAKE]

1Sa 8: 8 them from Egypt they have continually **f** me
Ps 22: 1 My God, my God! Why have you **f** me? / Why do
37:25 now I am old. / Yet I have never seen the godly **f**,
42: 9 "O God my rock," I cry, / "Why have you **f** me?
Isa 62:12 as the Desirable Place and the City No Longer **F**.
65:11 "But because the rest of you have **f** the LORD
Jer 2:13 They have **f** me—the fountain of living water.
7:29 and **f** this generation that has provoked his fury.'
15: 6 You have **f** me and turned your back on me,"
17:13 and dusty grave, for they have **f** the LORD,
19: 4 " 'For Israel has **f** me and turned this valley into a
49:25 That famous city, a city of joy, will be **f**!
51: 5 For the LORD Almighty has not **f** Israel
La 5:20 to forget us? Why have you **f** us for so long?
Eze 9: 9 doesn't see it! The LORD has **f** the land!'
Am 5: 2 never to rise again! / She lies **f** on the ground,
Mt 27:46 "My God, my God, why have you **f** me?"
Mk 15:34 "My God, my God, why have you **f** me?"

FORSAKING (1) [FORSAKE]

Dt 28:20 are completely destroyed for doing evil and **f** me.

FORSWEAR [KJV] See BREAK (VOWS)

FORT (1) [FORTRESS]

Ps 89:40 and laid in ruins every **f** defending him.

FORT [KJV] See also FORTIFICATIONS, FORTRESS(ES), SIEGE, STRONGHOLD(S)

FORTH (75)

Ge 1:11 "Let the land burst **f** with every sort of grass
1:24 "Let the earth bring **f** every kind of animal—
3:24 And a flaming sword flashed back and **f**,
4: 1 the LORD's help, I have brought **f** a man!"
7:11 the underground waters burst **f** on the earth,
8: 7 a raven that flew back and **f** until the earth was dry.
Ex 15: 7 Your anger flashed **f**; / it consumed them as fire
22:24 My anger will blaze **f** against you, and I will kill
32:27 and **f** from one end of the camp to the other,
Lev 9:24 Fire blazed **f** from the LORD's presence
10: 2 So fire blazed **f** from the LORD's presence
Nu 16:35 Then fire blazed **f** from the LORD and burned up
21:28 A fire flamed **f** from Heshbon, / a blaze from the
Dt 8: 7 with springs that gush **f** in the valleys and hills.
18:11 or psychics, or call **f** the spirits of the dead.
31:17 Then my anger will blaze **f** against them. I will
32:22 For my anger blazes **f** like fire / and burns to the
33: 2 from Mount Seir; / he shone **f** from Mount Paran
Jdg 9: 9 and people, just to wave back and **f** over the trees?'
9:11 sweet fruit just to wave back and **f** over the trees?'
9:13 and people, just to wave back and **f** over the trees?'
1Sa 17:15 David went back and **f** between working for Saul
2Sa 19:43 The argument continued back and **f**, and the men
22: 9 his mouth; / glowing coals flamed **f** from him.
22:13 shone before him, / and bolts of lightning blazed **f**.
23: 4 like the sunrise bursting **f** in a cloudless sky,
1Ki 3:22 And so they argued back and **f** before the king.
2Ki 4:35 and walked back and **f** in the room a few times.
1Ch 16:20 They wandered back and **f** between nations,
16:32 Let the fields and their crops burst **f** with joy!
2Ch 35: 3 not need to carry it back and **f** on your shoulders,
Ne 6:17 many letters went back and **f** between Tobiah
Job 1: 7 "I have been going back and **f** across the earth,
2: 2 "I have been going back and **f** across the earth,
7: 6 swifter than a weaver's shuttle flying back and **f**.
28: 4 They descend on ropes, swinging back and **f**.
36:29 and the thunder that rolls **f** from heaven?
37:15 and causes the lightning to flash **f** from his clouds?
Ps 18: 8 his mouth; / glowing coals flamed **f** from him.

19: 5 It bursts f like a radiant bridegroom / after his
45: 4 and justice. / Go f to perform awe-inspiring deeds!
57: 3 My God will send f his unfailing love
74: 15 You caused the springs and streams to gush f,
96: 12 Let the fields and their crops burst f with joy!
97: 3 Fire goes f before him / and burns up all his foes.
105: 13 They wandered back and f between nations,
119: 171 Let my lips burst f with praise, / for you have
Pr 3: 20 knowledge the deep fountains of the earth burst f,
8: 24 before the springs bubbled f their waters.
26: 14 As a door turns back and f on its hinges,
Ecc 1: 6 and north, here and there, twisting back and f,
SS 7: 13 There the mandrakes give f their fragrance,
Isa 35: 6 Springs will gush f in the wilderness, and streams
42: 13 The LORD will march f like a mighty man;
43: 17 I called f the mighty army of Egypt with all its
44: 23 Break f into song, O mountains and forests
54: 1 Break f into loud and joyful song, O Jerusalem,
66: 8 Has a country ever come f in a mere moment?
66: 8 the baby will be born; the nation will come f.
Jer 15: 14 For my anger blazes f like fire, and it will consume
Eze 1: 13 lightning was flashing back and f among them.
17: 23 sending f its branches and producing seed.
Hos 7: 6 and in the morning it flames f like a raging fire.
13: 14 O death, bring f your terrors! O grave, bring f your plagues! For I will not relent!
Joel 3: 18 and a fountain will burst f from the LORD's
Na 1: 6 His rage blazes f like fire, and the mountains
Zec 6: 7 to be off, to patrol back and f across the earth.
Mt 24: 31 And he will send f his angels with the sound of a
Mk 13: 27 And he will send f his angels to gather together his
Ac 7: 36 and f through the wilderness for forty years.
28: 25 they had argued back and f among themselves,
Gal 4: 27 Break f into loud and joyful song,
Jas 1: 8 They waver back and f in everything they do.
3: 13 so that only good deeds will pour f.

FORTHWITH [KJV] See SUDDENLY, QUICKLY, RUSHED

FORTIETH (2) [FORTY]

Nu 33: 38 during the f year after Israel's departure from
1Ch 26: 31 (In the f year of David's reign, a search was made

FORTIFICATIONS (5) [FORTRESS]

2Sa 5: 9 He built additional f around the city, starting at the
2Ch 32: 5 and by adding to the f and constructing a second
Jer 51: 32 The f are burning, and the army is in panic.
Hos 10: 14 All your f will fall, just as they did when Shalman
Zec 9: 4 and hurl its f into the Mediterranean Sea.

FORTIFIED (52) [FORTRESS]

FORTIFIED CITIES (28) Nu 32:16,17,36; Dt 3:5; Jos 10:20; 19:35; 1Ki 4:13; 2Ki 8:12; 18:13; 19:25; 2Ch 11:10,23; 12:4; 14:6; 17:2,19; 19:5; 21:3; 32:1; 33:14; Ne 9:25; Isa 17:3; 27:10; 36:1; 37:26; Jer 4:5; 5:17; 8:14

FORTIFIED CITY (8) Jos 19:29; 2Sa 20:6; 2Ki 10:2; Ps 60:9; 108:10; Pr 18:19; Jer 1:18; Da 11:15

Lev 25: 31 house in a village—a settlement without f walls—
Nu 13: 28 and their cities and towns are f and very large.
21: 24 because the boundary of the Ammonites was f.
32: 16 our flocks and f cities for our wives and children.
32: 17 our families will stay in the f cities we build here,
32: 36 These were all f cities with sheepfolds for their
Dt 3: 5 These were all f cities with high walls and barred
28: 52 They will lay siege to your cities until all the f
Jos 10: 20 a tiny remnant that managed to reach their f cities.
19: 29 turned toward Ramah and the f city of Tyre
19: 35 The f cities included in this territory were Ziddim,
2Sa 20: 6 and chase after him before he gets into a f city
1Ki 4: 13 including sixty great f cities with gates barred with
15: 17 and f Ramah in order to prevent anyone from
2Ki 3: 19 conquer the best of their cities, even the f ones.
8: 12 You will burn their f cities, kill their young men,
10: 2 disposal chariots, horses, a f city, and weapons.
18: 13 King Sennacherib of Assyria came to attack the f
19: 25 that you should crush f cities into heaps of rubble.
2Ch 8: 5 He f the cities of Upper Beth-horon and Lower
11: 5 and f various cities for the defense of Judah.
11: 10 These became the f cities of Judah and Benjamin.
11: 23 and stationed them in the f cities throughout the
12: 4 Shishak conquered Judah's f cities and
14: 6 he was able to build up the f cities throughout
16: 1 and f Ramah in order to prevent anyone from
17: 2 He stationed troops in all the f cities of Judah,
17: 19 besides those Jehoshaphat stationed in the f cities
19: 5 judges throughout the nation in all the f cities,
21: 3 and also the ownership of some of Judah's f cities.
26: 9 Uzziah built f towers in Jerusalem at the Corner
32: 1 He laid siege to the f cities, giving orders for his
33: 14 And he stationed his military officers in all of the f
Ne 9: 25 Our ancestors captured f cities and fertile land.
Ps 48: 13 Take note of the f walls, / and tour all the citadels,
60: 9 But who will bring me into the f city? / Who will
108: 10 But who will bring me into the f city? / Who will
147: 13 For he has f the bars of your gates / and blessed
Pr 18: 19 with an offended friend than to capture a f city.
Isa 17: 3 The f cities of Israel will also be destroyed,
27: 10 Israel's f cities will be silent and empty, the houses
36: 1 King Sennacherib of Assyria came to attack the f
37: 26 that you should crush f cities into heaps of rubble.
Jer 1: 18 You are strong like a f city that cannot be captured,
4: 5 the land: 'Run for your lives! Flee to the f cities!'
5: 17 And they will destroy your f cities, which you
8: 14 to die? Come, let's go to the f cities to die there.
15: 20 but I will make you as secure as a f wall.
41: 9 f Mizpah to protect himself against King Baasha of
Eze 21: 20 Rabbah, and the other to Judah and f Jerusalem.
Da 11: 15 will come and lay siege to a f city and capture it.
Hos 8: 14 has built great palaces, and Judah has f its cities.

FORTIFY (5) [FORTRESS]

1Ki 15: 22 and timbers that Baasha had been using to f
15: 22 Asa used these materials to f the town of Geba in
2Ch 14: 7 "Let us build towns and f them with walls, towers,
16: 6 and timbers that Baasha had been using to f
16: 6 Asa used these materials to f the towns of Geba

FORTIFYING (2) [FORTRESS]

1Ki 15: 21 he abandoned his project of f Ramah and withdrew
2Ch 16: 5 he abandoned his project of f Ramah.

FORTRESS (54) [FORT, FORTIFICATIONS, FORTIFIED, FORTIFY, FORTIFYING, FORTRESSES, FORTS]

2Sa 5: 7 But David captured the f of Zion, now called the
5: 9 So David made the f his home, and he called it the
22: 2 "The LORD is my rock, my f, and my savior;
22: 33 God is my strong f; / he has made my way safe.
2Ki 10: 25 Then Jehu's men went into the f of the temple of
1Ch 11: 5 But David captured the f of Zion, now called the
11: 7 David made the f his home, and that is why it is
Ezr 6: 2 But it was at the f at Ecbatana in the province of
Ne 1: 1 of King Artaxerxes' reign, I was at the f of Susa.
2: 8 it to make beams for the gates of the Temple f,
7: 2 along with Hananiah, the commander of the f,
Est 1: 2 ruled his empire from his throne at the f of Susa.
2: 5 Now at the f of Susa there was a certain Jew
2: 8 was brought to the king's harem at the f of Susa
3: 15 and it was proclaimed in the f of Susa.
8: 14 The same decree was also issued at the f of Susa.
9: 6 They killed five hundred people in the f of Susa.
9: 11 of the number of people killed in the f of Susa,
9: 12 "The Jews have killed five hundred people in the f
Ps 18: 2 The LORD is my rock, my f, and my savior;
31: 2 of safety, / a f where my enemies cannot reach me.
31: 3 You are my rock and my f. / For the honor of your
37: 39 saves the godly; / he is their f in times of trouble.
46: 7 is here among us; / the God of Israel is our f.
46: 11 is here among us; / the God of Israel is our f.
61: 3 a f where my enemies cannot reach me.
62: 2 my salvation, / my f where I will never be shaken.
62: 6 my salvation, / my f where I will not be shaken.
71: 3 order to save me, / for you are my rock and my f.
94: 22 But the LORD is my f; / my God is a mighty rock
144: 2 He is my loving ally and my f, / my tower of
Pr 10: 15 The wealth of the rich is their f; the poverty of the
18: 10 The name of the LORD is a strong f; the godly
21: 22 of the strong and level the f in which they trust.
Isa 23: 4 you are put to shame, city of Sidon, f on the sea.
33: 16 The rocks of the mountains will be their f of safety.
45: 1 Their f gates will be opened, never again to shut
Jer 16: 19 LORD, you are my strength and f, my refuge in
48: 1 the f will be humiliated and broken down.
49: 16 And you are proud because you live in a rock f
La 2: 2 In his anger he has broken down the f walls of
Eze 30: 15 out my fury on Pelusium, the strongest f of Egypt,
Da 8: 2 This time I was at the f of Susa, in the province of
11: 7 and enter the f of the king of the north and defeat
11: 10 a flood and carry the battle as far as the enemy's f.
11: 31 His army will take over the Temple f,
Joel 3: 16 LORD will be a welcoming refuge and a strong f.
Ob 1: 3 You are proud because you live in a rock f
Zep 3: 6 many nations, devastating their f walls and towers.
Zec 9: 3 Tyre has built a strong f and has piled up so much
Ac 21: 34 so he ordered Paul to be taken to the f.
23: 10 him away from them and bring him back to the f.
23: 16 heard of their plan and went to the f and told Paul.
23: 32 They returned to the f the next morning,

FORTRESSES (21) [FORTRESS]

1Ch 27: 25 throughout the towns, villages, and f of Israel.
2Ch 17: 12 became more and more powerful and built f
27: 4 and constructed f and towers in the wooded areas.
Isa 13: 22 Hyenas will howl in its f, and jackals will make
Eze 7: 24 I will break down their proud f and defile their
19: 7 He demolished f in nearby nations / and destroyed
Da 11: 19 He will take refuge in his own f but will stumble
11: 38 Instead of these, he will worship the god of f—
11: 39 foreign god's help, he will attack the strongest f.
Hos 8: 14 send down fire on their palaces and burn their f."
Am 1: 4 and the f of King Ben-hadad will be destroyed.
1: 7 on the walls of Gaza, and all its f will be destroyed.
1: 10 the walls of Tyre, and all its f will be destroyed."
1: 12 on Teman, and the f of Bozrah will be destroyed."
1: 14 the walls of Rabbah, and all its f will be destroyed.
2: 2 of Moab, and all the f in Kerioth will be destroyed.
2: 5 and all the f of Jerusalem will be destroyed."
3: 10 "Their f are filled with wealth taken by theft
3: 11 their defenses. Then he will plunder all their f."
4: 3 breaks in the wall; you will be thrown from your f.
Na 3: 12 All your f will fall. They will be devoured like the

FORTS (4) [FORTRESS]

2Ch 26: 10 He also constructed f in the wilderness and dug
Isa 34: 13 will overrun its palaces; nettles will grow in its f.
La 2: 5 He has destroyed her f and palaces. He has brought
Eze 33: 27 Those hiding in the f and caves will die of disease.

FORTUNATE (6) [FORTUNE]

Ge 30: 11 Leah named him Gad, for she said, "How f I am!"
Ps 49: 18 In this life they consider themselves f,
Ecc 4: 3 And most f of all are those who were never born.
Isa 7: 21 a farmer will be f to have a cow and two sheep left.
Lk 23: 29 'F indeed are the women who are childless,
Ac 26: 2 "I am f, King Agrippa, that you are the one

FORTUNATUS (1)

1Co 16: 17 I am so glad that Stephanas, F, and Achaicus have

FORTUNE (6) [FORTUNATE, FORTUNE-TELLER, FORTUNE-TELLERS, FORTUNE-TELLING, FORTUNES]

Ge 24: 35 a f in silver and gold, and many servants
Mt 26: 9 "She could have sold it for a f and given the
Mk 6: 37 "It would take a small f to buy food for all this
14: 5 "She could have sold it for a small f and given the
Jn 6: 7 "It would take a small f to feed them!"
12: 5 "That perfume was worth a small f. It should have

FORTUNE-TELLER (1) [FORTUNE]

Ac 16: 16 She was a f who earned a lot of money for her

FORTUNE-TELLERS (9) [FORTUNE]

Dt 18: 14 are about to displace consult with sorcerers and f,
2Ki 17: 17 They consulted f and used sorcery and sold
Jer 27: 9 f, interpreters of dreams, mediums, and sorcerers
Da 2: 27 magicians, or f who can tell the king such things.
4: 7 enchanters, astrologers, and f came in, I told them
5: 7 astrologers, and f to be brought before him.
5: 11 enchanters, astrologers, and f of Babylon.
Mic 5: 12 to all witchcraft; there will be no more f to consult.
Zec 10: 2 gods give false advice, f predict only lies,

FORTUNE-TELLING (2) [FORTUNE]

Lev 19: 26 of its blood. "Do not practice f or witchcraft.
Dt 18: 10 And do not let your people practice f or sorcery,

FORTUNES (14) [FORTUNE]

Dt 30: 3 then the LORD your God will restore your f.
Job 42: 10 prayed for his friends, the LORD restored his f.
Ps 85: 1 on your land! / You have restored the f of Israel.
126: 4 Restore our f, LORD, / as streams renew the
Jer 29: 14 "I will end your captivity and restore your f.
30: 3 For the time is coming when I will restore the f of
30: 18 home again from your captivity and restore your f,
33: 7 I will restore the f of Judah and Israel and rebuild
48: 47 But in the latter days I will restore the f of Moab,"
49: 6 But afterward I will restore the f of the
49: 39 But in the latter days I will restore the f of Elam,"
Eze 16: 53 "But someday I will restore the f of Sodom
Hos 6: 11 I wanted so much to restore the f of my people!
Zep 3: 20 They will praise you as I restore your f before their

FORTY (88) [FORTIETH, 40]

FORTY DAYS (21) Ge 7:4,12,17; 8:6; 50:3; Ex 24:18; 34:28; Nu 13:25; 14:34; Dt 9:9,11,18,25; 10:10; 1Sa 17:16; 1Ki 19:8; Jnh 3:4; Mt 4:2; Mk 1:13; Lk 4:2; Ac 1:3

FORTY NIGHTS (7) Ge 7:4,12; Ex 24:18; 34:28; Dt 9:9; 1Ki 19:8; Mt 4:2

FORTY YEARS (41) Ge 25:20; Ex 16:35; Nu 14:33,34; 32:13; Dt 1:3; 2:7; 8:2,4; 29:5; Jos 5:6; 14:7; Jdg 3:11; 5:31; 8:28; 13:1; 1Sa 4:18; 2Sa 2:10; 5:4; 1Ki 2:11; 11:42; 2Ki 12:1; 1Ch 29:27; 2Ch 9:30; 24:1; Ne 9:21; Ps 95:10; Eze 29:11,12,13; Am 2:10; 5:25; Ac 4:22; 7:23,30,36,42; 13:18,21; Heb 3:9,17

Ge 7: 4 I will begin f days and f nights of rain.
7: 12 The rain continued to fall for f days and f nights.
7: 17 For f days the floods prevailed,
8: 6 After another f days, Noah opened the window he
18: 29 "Suppose there are only f?" And the LORD
18: 29 "I will not destroy it if there are f."
25: 20 When Isaac was f years old, he married Rebekah,
26: 34 At the age of f, Esau married a young woman
32: 15 f cows, ten bulls, twenty female donkeys, and ten
50: 3 The embalming process took f days, and there was
Ex 16: 35 So the people of Israel ate manna for f years until
24: 18 He stayed on the mountain f days and f nights.
26: 19 They will fit into f silver bases—two bases under
26: 21 with their f silver bases, two bases for each frame.
34: 28 on the mountain with the LORD f days and f nights.
36: 24 along with f silver bases, two for each frame.
36: 26 along with f silver bases, two for each frame.
Nu 13: 25 After exploring the land for f days, the men
14: 33 wandering in the wilderness f years.
14: 34 men who explored the land were there for f days,
14: 34 you must wander in the wilderness for f years—
32: 13 and made them wander in the wilderness for f
Dt 1: 3 But f years after the Israelites left Mount Sinai,
2: 7 During these f years, the LORD your God has
8: 2 God led you through the wilderness for f years,
8: 4 For all these f years your clothes didn't wear out,
9: 9 I was there for f days and f nights, and all that
9: 11 "At the end of the f days and nights, the LORD
9: 18 Then for f days and nights I lay prostrate before
9: 25 I fell down and lay before the LORD for f days
10: 10 the mountain in the LORD's presence for f days
25: 3 No more than f lashes may ever be given;
25: 3 more than f lashes would publicly humiliate your
29: 5 For f years I led you through the wilderness,

Jos 4:13 These warriors—about **f** thousand strong—
5:6 The Israelites wandered in the wilderness for **f**
14:7 I was **f** years old when Moses, the servant of the
Jdg 3:11 So there was peace in the land for **f** years.
5:8 be seen / among **f** thousand warriors in Israel!
5:31 Then there was peace in the land for **f** years.
8:28 about **f** years—the land was at peace.
12:14 He had **f** sons and thirty grandsons, who rode on
13:1 who kept them in subjection for **f** years.
1Sa 4:18 was old and very fat. He had led Israel for **f** years.
17:16 For **f** days, twice a day, morning and evening,
2Sa 2:10 Ishbosheth was **f** years old when he became king,
5:4 he began to reign, and he reigned **f** years in all.
10:18 hundred charioteers and **f** thousand horsemen,
1Ki 2:11 He had reigned over Israel for **f** years, seven of
11:42 Solomon ruled in Jerusalem over all Israel for **f**
19:8 and the food gave him enough strength to travel **f**
days and **f** nights to Mount Sinai,
2Ki 8:9 So Hazael loaded down **f** camels with the finest
12:1 He reigned in Jerusalem **f** years. His mother was
1Ch 19:18 thousand charioteers and **f** thousand foot soldiers,
22:14 nearly **f** thousand tons of silver, and so much iron
29:27 He ruled Israel for **f** years in all, seven years from
2Ch 9:30 Solomon ruled in Jerusalem over all Israel for **f**
24:1 became king, and he reigned in Jerusalem **f** years.
Ne 9:21 For **f** years you sustained them in the wilderness.
Ps 95:10 For **f** years I was angry with them, and I said,
Eze 29:11 For **f** years not a soul will pass that way,
29:12 Its cities will be empty and desolate for **f** years,
29:13 At the end of the **f** years I will bring the Egyptians
Am 2:10 and led you through the desert for **f** years
5:25 and offerings during the **f** years in the wilderness,
Jnh 3:4 "**F** days from now Nineveh will be destroyed!"
Mt 4:2 For **f** days and **f** nights he ate nothing
Mk 1:13 He was there for **f** days, being tempted by Satan.
Lk 4:2 where the Devil tempted him for **f** days. He ate
Ac 1:3 During the **f** days after his crucifixion, he appeared
4:22 of a man who had been lame for more than **f** years.
7:23 "One day when he was **f** years old, he decided to
7:30 "**F** years later, in the desert near Mount Sinai,
7:36 and forth through the wilderness for **f** years.
7:42 during those **f** years in the wilderness, Israel?
13:18 He put up with them through **f** years of wandering
13:21 of the tribe of Benjamin, who reigned for **f** years.
23:13 There were more than **f** of them.
23:21 There are more than **f** men hiding along the way
Heb 3:9 even though they saw my miracles for **f** years.
3:17 And who made God angry for **f** years? Wasn't it

FORTY-EIGHT (2)

Nu 35:7 **f** towns with the surrounding pastureland will be
Jos 21:41 Israelite territory given to the Levites came to **f**.

FORTY-FIRST (1)

2Ch 16:13 So he died in the **f** year of his reign.

FORTY-FIVE (6) [45]

Ge 18:28 Suppose there are only **f**? Will you destroy the city
18:28 the LORD said, "I will not destroy it if I find **f**."
Ex 26:8 each **f** feet long and six feet wide. All eleven of
36:15 the same size—**f** feet long and six feet wide.
Jos 14:10 and well as he promised for all these **f** years since
1Ki 7:3 It had a cedar roof supported by **f** rafters that rested

FORTY-NINE (1)

Lev 25:8 seven years times seven, adding up to **f** years in all.

FORTY-ONE (4)

1Ki 14:21 He was **f** years old when he became king, and he
15:10 He reigned in Jerusalem **f** years. His grandmother
2Ki 14:23 in Judah. Jeroboam reigned in Samaria **f** years.
2Ch 12:13 He was **f** years old when he became king, and he

FORTY-SIX (1)

Jn 2:20 "It took **f** years to build this Temple, and you can

FORTY-THREE (1)

Jdg 8:26 The weight of the gold earrings was **f** pounds,

FORTY-TWO (8) [42]

Ex 26:2 Each sheet must be **f** feet long and six feet wide.
36:9 the same size—**f** feet long and six feet wide.
Nu 35:6 for safety. In addition, give them **f** other towns.
Jdg 12:6 So **f** thousand Ephraimites were killed at that time.
1Sa 13:1 when he became king, and he reigned for **f** years.
2Ki 2:24 bears came out of the woods and mauled **f** of them.
10:14 And they captured all **f** of them and killed them at
Rev 13:5 given authority to do what he wanted for **f** months.

FORUM (1)

Ac 28:15 and they came to meet us at the **F** on the Appian

FORWARD (78) [STRAIGHTFORWARD]

Ge 33:6 Then the concubines came **f** with their children
44:18 Then Judah stepped **f** and said, "My lord, let me
Ex 25:37 and set them so they reflect their light **f**.
Lev 10:5 So they came **f** and carried them out of the camp
16:20 and the altar, he must bring the living goat **f**.
Nu 3:6 "Call **f** the tribe of Levi and present them to Aaron
8:2 he is to place them so their light shines **f**."
8:3 up the seven lamps so they reflected their light **f**,
10:5 side of the Tabernacle will break camp and move **f**.
12:5 and Miriam!" he called, and they stepped **f**.
Dt 19:16 If a malicious witness comes **f** and accuses
20:2 the priest will come **f** to speak with the troops.
Jos 7:14 That tribe must come **f** with its clans,
7:14 That clan will then come **f**, and the LORD will
7:17 Then the clans of Judah came **f**, and the clan of
7:18 Every member of Zimri's family was brought **f**
1Sa 16:8 Then Jesse told his son Abinadab to step **f**
24:4 to do with as you wish.' " Then David crept **f**
2Sa 20:8 As he stepped **f** to greet Amasa, he secretly slipped
24:20 he came **f** and bowed before the king with his face
2Ki 20:9 Would you like the shadow on the sundial to go **f**
20:10 "The shadow always moves **f**," Hezekiah replied.
2Ch 28:15 Then the four men mentioned by name came **f**
Ezr 5:8 The work is going **f** with great energy and success.
Ne 9:19 The pillar of cloud still led them **f** by day,
Job 17:9 The righteous will move onward and **f**, and those
39:20 Did you give it the ability to leap **f** like a locust?
39:24 and rushes **f** into battle when the trumpet blows.
Ps 118:27 Bring **f** the sacrifice and put it on the altar.
143:10 May your gracious Spirit lead me **f** / on a firm
Pr 11:23 The godly can look **f** to happiness,
Isa 14:31 of the north. Each soldier rushes **f** ready to fight.
17:12 The armies rush **f** like waves thundering toward
58:8 Your godliness will lead you **f**, and the glory of the
Jer 3:19 I looked **f** to your calling me 'Father,' and I
6:23 As they ride **f**, the noise of their army is like a
7:24 their evil hearts. They went backward instead of **f**.
50:42 As they ride **f**, the noise of their army is like a
Eze 1:12 and they moved straight **f** in all directions without
1:17 The beings could move **f** in any of the four
10:11 The cherubim could move **f** in any of the four
Joel 2:7 Straight **f** they march, never breaking rank.
Na 3:2 Hear the crack of the whips as the chariots rush **f**
Hab 1:8 at dusk. Their horsemen race **f** from distant places.
Zec 5:5 Then the angel who was talking with me came **f**
Mt 11:13 all the teachings of the Scriptures looked **f** to this
22:23 That same day some Sadducees stepped **f**—a group
Mk 12:18 Then the Sadducees stepped **f**—a group of Jews
Lk 6:8 here where everyone can see." So the man came **f**.
9:42 As the boy came **f**, the demon knocked him to the
20:27 Then some Sadducees stepped **f**—a group of Jews
22:15 "I have looked **f** to this hour with deep longing,
Jn 8:56 Your ancestor Abraham rejoiced as he looked **f** to
18:4 Stepping **f** to meet them, he asked, "Whom are
Ac 2:14 Then Peter stepped **f** with the eleven other apostles
19:33 Alexander was thrust **f** by some of the Jews,
26:6 because I am looking **f** to the fulfillment of God's
Ro 5:2 and joyfully look **f** to sharing God's glory.
8:24 we are saved, we eagerly look **f** to this freedom.
8:25 But if we look **f** to something we don't have yet,
1Co 16:11 I am looking **f** to seeing him soon, along with the
2Co 4:18 rather, we look **f** to what we have not yet seen.
7:7 When he told me how much you were looking **f** to
Gal 3:8 the Scriptures looked **f** to this time when God
Php 3:13 the past and looking **f** to what lies ahead,
Col 1:5 because you are looking **f** to the joys of heaven—
1Th 1:10 And they speak of how you are looking **f** to the
2Ti 4:8 but for all who eagerly look **f** to his glorious return.
Tit 2:13 while we look **f** to that wonderful event when the
Heb 6:3 we will move **f** to further understanding.
10:27 There will be nothing to look **f** to but the terrible
11:10 because he was confidently looking **f** to a city with
11:14 are looking **f** to a country they can call their own.
13:14 we are looking **f** to our city in heaven, which is yet
1Pe 1:13 Look **f** to the special blessings that will come to
2Pe 3:12 You should look **f** to that day and hurry it along—
3:13 But we are looking **f** to the new heavens and new
Rev 5:7 He stepped **f** and took the scroll from the right

FORWARDNESS [KJV] See EAGER

FOSTERS (1)

Pr 10:19 Don't talk too much, for it **f** sin. Be sensible

FOUGHT (42) [FIGHT]

Ge 14:2 **f** against King Bera of Sodom, King Birsha of
Nu 31:27 and give half to the men who **f** the battle and half
Jos 10:14 The LORD **f** for Israel that day. Never before
15:15 Then he **f** against the people living in the town of
19:47 of their land, so they **f** against the town of Laish.
23:3 The LORD your God has **f** for you against your
24:8 They **f** against you, but I gave you victory over
24:11 came to Jericho, the men of Jericho **f** against you.
24:11 There were also many others who **f** you,
Jdg 1:5 encountered King Adoni-bezek and **f** against him,
2:15 the LORD **f** against them, bringing them defeat,
5:19 "The kings of Canaan **f** at Taanach near
5:20 The stars **f** from heaven. / The stars in their orbits **f**
against Sisera.
9:17 For he **f** for you and risked his life when he
20:22 and assembled at the same place they had **f** the
1Sa 4:4 the Ark of God to where the battle was being **f**.
4:10 So the Philistines **f** desperately, and Israel was
14:47 he **f** against his enemies in every direction—
14:52 The Israelites **f** constantly with the Philistines
2Sa 12:27 "I have **f** against Rabbah and captured its water
21:18 As they **f**, Sibbecai from Hushah killed Saph,
1Ch 12:1 They were among the warriors who **f** beside David
19:17 the enemy troops in battle, and they **f** against him.
20:4 As they **f**, Sibbecai from Hushah killed Saph,
22:8 killed many men in the great battles you have **f**.
2Ch 8:3 that Solomon **f** against the city of Hamath-zobah
15:6 Nation **f** against nation, and city against city,
20:29 himself had **f** against the enemies of Israel,
Ps 60:T regarding the time David **f** Aram-naharaim
Isa 63:10 is why he became their enemy and **f** against them.
Jer 34:1 and he **f** against Jerusalem and the towns of Judah.
50:24 You are caught, for you have **f** against the LORD.
Eze 29:18 the army of King Nebuchadnezzar of Babylon **f**
Hos 12:3 when he became a man, he even **f** with God.
Zec 14:3 against those nations, as he has **f** in times past.
14:12 a plague on all the nations that **f** against Jerusalem.
Jn 18:36 my followers would have **f** when I was arrested by
2Ti 3:8 truth just as Jannes and Jambres **f** against Moses.
4:7 I have **f** a good fight, I have finished the race,
4:15 careful of him, for he **f** against everything we said.
Rev 12:7 and the angels under his command **f** the dragon

FOUL (7) [FOULED]

Ex 7:21 so **f** that the Egyptians couldn't drink it.
Ps 5:9 Their talk is **f**, like the stench from an open grave.
Isa 19:6 and the streams of Egypt will become **f** with
Eze 22:3 doomed and damned—city of idols, filthy and **f**—
Mt 16:3 red sky in the morning means **f** weather all day.'
Ro 3:13 "Their talk is **f**, like the stench from an open
Eph 4:29 Don't use **f** or abusive language. Let everything

FOUL [KJV] See also EVIL, MUDDY, RED

FOULED (1) [FOUL]

Eze 34:19 All they have to drink is water that you have **f**.

FOUND (262) [FIND]

Ge 2:11 around the entire land of Havilah, where gold is **f**.
2:12 aromatic resin and onyx stone are also **f** there.
6:8 But Noah **f** favor with the LORD.
8:9 But the dove **f** no place to land because the water
11:2 they **f** a plain in the land of Babylonia and settled
16:7 The angel of the LORD **f** Hagar beside a desert
16:14 and it can still be **f** between Kadesh and Bered.
18:30 "Let me speak—suppose only thirty are **f**?"
18:32 but once more! Suppose only ten are **f** there?"
26:19 dug in the Gerar Valley and **f** a gushing spring.
26:32 a well they had dug. "We've **f** water!" they said.
28:11 Jacob **f** a stone for a pillow and lay down to sleep.
30:14 Reuben **f** some mandrakes growing in a field
30:16 for you with some mandrake roots my son has **f**."
31:37 Now show me what you have **f** that belongs to
37:17 followed his brothers to Dothan and **f** them there.
37:32 "We **f** this in the field," they told him.
42:24 left the room and **f** a place where he could weep.
42:27 to feed the donkeys, he **f** his money in the sack.
43:12 Take double the money that you **f** in your sacks,
44:8 Didn't we bring back the money we **f** in our sacks?
44:12 to the youngest. The cup was **f** in Benjamin's sack!
Ex 2:6 As the princess opened it, she **f** the baby boy.
4:27 where he **f** Moses and greeted him warmly.
8:22 where the Israelites live. No flies will be **f** there.
9:7 But even after he **f** it to be true, his heart remained
15:23 When they came to Marah, they finally **f** water.
16:27 it was the Sabbath day. But there was none to be **f**.
17:1 to Rephidim, but there was no water to be **f** there.
17:12 So Aaron and Hur **f** a stone for him to sit on.
22:7 If the thief is **f**, the fine is double the value of what
22:8 But if the thief is not **f**, God will determine
33:12 me by name and tell me I have **f** favor with you.
33:16 know that your people and I have **f** favor with you?
33:17 for you have **f** favor with me, and you are my
34:9 "If it is true that I have **f** favor in your sight,
Lev 7:24 The fat of an animal **f** dead or killed by a wild
13:30 and fine yellow hair is **f** in the affected area,
Nu 17:8 he **f** that Aaron's staff, representing the tribe of
32:5 If we have **f** favor with you, please let us have this
Dt 16:4 Let no yeast be **f** in any house throughout your
19:18 and if the accuser is **f** to be lying,
21:1 "Suppose someone is **f** murdered in a field in the
28:63 "Just as the LORD has **f** great pleasure in helping
32:10 "He **f** them in a desert land, / in an empty,
Jos 7:22 ran to the tent and **f** the stolen goods hidden there,
10:17 When Joshua heard that they had been **f**,
14:12 You will remember that as scouts we **f** the
20:6 and be tried by the community and **f** innocent.
20:6 the one **f** innocent is free to return home."
Jdg 3:24 and **f** the doors to the upstairs room locked.
3:25 the door, they **f** their master dead on the floor.
4:22 her into the tent and **f** Sisera lying there dead,
5:30 'They are dividing the captured goods they **f**—
6:27 He knew what would happen if they **f** out who had
14:8 And he **f** that a swarm of bees had made some
14:18 you wouldn't have **f** the answer to my riddle!"
19:27 husband opened the door to leave, he **f** her there.
21:12 Among the residents of Jabesh-gilead they **f** four
Ru 2:3 she **f** herself working in a field that belonged to
3:1 it's time that I **f** a permanent home for you,
1Sa 9:20 that were lost three days ago, for they have been **f**.
10:2 They will tell you that the donkeys have been **f**
10:16 "He said the donkeys had been **f**," Saul replied.
10:23 So they **f** him and brought him out, and he stood
11:8 he **f** that there were 300,000 men of Israel,
13:15 who were still with him, he **f** only six hundred left!
14:17 they **f** that Jonathan and his armor bearer were
14:20 to the battle and **f** the Philistines killing each other.
14:25 even though they **f** honeycomb on the ground in
14:30 eat freely from the food they **f** among our enemies,
15:13 When Samuel finally **f** him, Saul greeted him
20:1 now fled from Naioth in Ramah and **f** Jonathan.
23:14 him day after day, but God didn't let him be **f**.
25:36 she **f** that Nabal had thrown a big party and was
26:7 went right into Saul's camp and **f** him asleep,
29:3 and I've never **f** a single fault in him since he

30: 1 they **f** that the Amalekites had made a raid into the
30: 6 But David **f** strength in the LORD his God.
30: 11 Some of David's troops **f** an Egyptian man in a
31: 8 they **f** the bodies of Saul and his three sons on
2Sa 2: 24 When Joab and Abishai **f** out what had happened,
3: 26 They **f** him at the pool of Sirah and brought him
15: 32 David **f** Hushai the Arkite waiting for him.
1Ki 1: 3 and they **f** Abishag from Shunem and brought her
2: 40 When he had **f** them, he took them back to
13: 14 the man of God and **f** him sitting under an oak tree.
13: 28 and he went out and **f** the body lying in the road.
19: 19 and **f** Elisha son of Shaphat plowing a field with a
21: 20 "So my enemy has **f** me!" Ahab exclaimed to
2Ki 1: 9 They **f** him sitting on top of a hill. The captain said
9: 5 he **f** Jehu sitting in a meeting with the other army
9: 35 they **f** only her skull, her feet, and her hands.
19: 35 up the next morning, they **f** corpses everywhere.
22: 8 "I have **f** the Book of the Law in the LORD's
22: 13 the words written in this scroll that has been **f**.
23: 2 Covenant that had been **f** in the LORD's Temple.
23: 24 Hilkiah the priest had **f** in the LORD's Temple.
1Ch 4: 40 They **f** lush pastures there, and the land was quiet
7: 15 Makir **f** wives for Huppim and Shuppim.
10: 8 they **f** the bodies of Saul and his sons on Mount
26: 31 and capable men from the clan of Hebron were **f** at
2Ch 15: 4 the God of Israel, and sought him out, you **f** him.
15: 15 Eagerly they sought after God, and they **f** him.
20: 25 They **f** vast amounts of equipment, clothing,
22: 9 and they **f** him hiding in the city of Samaria.
25: 5 and **f** that he had an army of 300,000 men twenty
29: 16 the Temple courtyard all the defiled things they **f**.
30: 16 according to the regulations **f** in the law of Moses,
34: 14 he **f** the Book of the Law of the LORD as it had
34: 15 "I have **f** the Book of the Law in the LORD's
34: 21 the words written in this scroll that has been **f**.
34: 30 Covenant that had been **f** in the LORD's Temple.
36: 8 the evil things he did and everything **f** against him,
Ezr 1: 4 **f** should contribute toward their expenses by
4: 19 and have indeed **f** that Jerusalem has in times past
6: 2 in the province of Media that a scroll was **f**.
8: 15 I **f** that not one Levite had volunteered to come
8: 26 I gave it to them and **f** the totals to be as follows:
Ne 6: 1 and the rest of our enemies **f** out that I had finished
7: 5 I had **f** the genealogical record of those who had
13: 1 the people **f** a statement which said that no
Est 2: 23 was made and Mordecai's story was **f** to be true,
Job 5: 27 "We have **f** from experience that all this is true.
9: 29 Whatever happens, I will be **f** guilty. So what's the
20: 8 He will fade like a dream and not be **f**. He will
28: 13 where to find it, for it is not **f** among the living.
28: 22 have heard a rumor of where wisdom can be **f**.'
28: 23 "God surely knows where it can be **f**,
33: 24 make him die, for I have **f** a ransom for his life.'
Ps 17: 3 You have scrutinized me and **f** nothing amiss,
89: 20 I have **f** my servant David. / I have anointed him
105: 30 they were **f** even in the king's private rooms.
119: 35 for that is where my happiness is **f**.
132: 6 then we **f** it in the distant countryside of Jaar.
Pr 6: 30 Excuses might be **f** for a thief who steals
14: 33 understanding heart; wisdom is not **f** among fools.
30: 6 or he may rebuke you, and you will be **f** a liar.
30: 28 to catch, / but they are **f** even in kings' palaces.
Ecc 2: 1 in life." But I **f** that this, too, was meaningless.
2: 10 I even **f** great pleasure in hard work, an additional
SS 3: 4 A little while later I **f** him and held him. I didn't let
5: 7 The watchmen **f** me as they were making their
6: 12 I **f** myself in my princely bed with my beloved
Isa 5: 7 yield a crop of justice, / but instead he **f** bloodshed.
37: 36 up the next morning, they **f** corpses everywhere.
51: 3 of the LORD. Joy and gladness will be **f** there.
59: 11 We look for justice, but it is nowhere to be **f**.
59: 14 who are righteous, and justice is nowhere to be **f**.
65: 1 I am being **f** by people who were not looking for
65: 8 "For just as good grapes are **f** among a cluster of
Jer 8: 15 We hoped for a time of healing, but **f** only terror.
14: 6 looking for grass to eat, but there is none to be **f**."
14: 19 We hoped for a time of healing but **f** only terror.
18: 3 as he told me and **f** the potter working at his wheel.
29: 14 I will be **f** by you," says the LORD. "I will end
38: 11 where he **f** some old rags and discarded clothing.
40: 1 He had **f** Jeremiah bound in chains among the
50: 7 All who **f** them devoured them. Their enemies
50: 20 the LORD, "no sin will be **f** in Israel or in Judah,
La 4: 19 If we fled to the mountains, they **f** us. If we hid in
Eze 4: 14 any animal that died of sickness or that I **f** dead.
22: 30 I wouldn't have to destroy the land, but I **f** no one.
26: 21 You will be looked for, but you will never be **f**.
28: 15 you were created until the day evil was **f** in you.
39: 15 Whenever some bones are **f**, a marker will be set
40: 9 and **f** it to be 14 feet deep, with supporting
40: 24 and he **f** they were exactly the same as in the
40: 28 and **f** that it had the same measurements as the
40: 32 and **f** that it had the same measurements as the
40: 35 and **f** that it had the same measurements as the
40: 47 the inner courtyard and **f** it to be 175 feet square.
40: 48 and **f** them to be 8-3/4 feet square.
41: 3 at the entrance and **f** them to be 3-1/2 feet thick.
41: 5 of the Temple and **f** that it was 10-1/2 feet thick.
41: 13 the Temple, and he **f** it to be 175 feet long.
Da 1: 20 the king **f** the advice of these young men to be ten
2: 25 "I have **f** one of the captives from Judah who will
5: 11 this man was **f** to have insight, understanding,
6: 11 and **f** him praying and asking for God's help.
6: 22 not hurt me, for I have been **f** innocent in his sight.
6: 23 Not a scratch was **f** on him because he had trusted
Hos 9: 10 The LORD says, "O Israel, when I first **f** you,
Ob 1: 6 and looted. Every treasure will be **f** and taken.
Jnh 1: 3 of Joppa, where he **f** a ship leaving for Tarshish.
Mic 7: 1 or a single fig can be **f** to satisfy my hunger.
Na 3: 19 Where can anyone be **f** who has not suffered from
Hag 2: 16 gallons from the winepress, you **f** only twenty.
Zec 12: 5 'The people of Jerusalem have **f** strength in the
Mt 26: 40 he returned to the disciples and **f** them asleep.
26: 43 He returned to them again and **f** them sleeping,
26: 60 But even though they **f** many who agreed to give
26: 60 testimony they could use. Finally, two men were **f**
Mk 8: 7 A few small fish were **f**, too, so Jesus also blessed
9: 14 At the foot of the mountain they **f** a great crowd
11: 4 disciples left and **f** the colt standing in the street,
14: 16 into the city and **f** everything just as Jesus had said,
14: 37 Then he returned and **f** the disciples asleep.
14: 40 Again he returned to them and **f** them sleeping,
16: 10 She went and **f** the disciples, who were grieving
Lk 2: 16 They ran to the village and **f** Mary and Joseph.
4: 38 where he **f** Simon's mother-in-law very sick with a
4: 42 and when they finally **f** him, they begged him not
7: 10 to his house, they **f** the slave completely healed.
7: 20 John's two disciples **f** Jesus and said to him,
7: 25 beautiful clothes and live in luxury are **f** in palaces,
9: 11 But the crowds **f** out where he was going, and they
15: 4 to go and search for the lost one until you **f** it?
15: 6 to rejoice with you because your lost sheep was **f**.
15: 9 to rejoice with her because she has **f** her lost coin.
15: 24 He was lost, but now he is **f**.' So the party began.
15: 32 back to life! He was lost, but now he is **f**!' "
19: 32 So they went and **f** the colt, just as Jesus had said.
22: 13 to the city and **f** everything just as Jesus had said,
23: 22 I have **f** no reason to sentence him to death. I will
24: 2 They **f** that the stone covering the entrance had
Jn 1: 41 "We have **f** the Messiah" (which means the
1: 43 He **f** Philip and said to him, "Come, be my
1: 45 "We have **f** the very person Moses
1: 48 "I could see you under the fig tree before Philip **f**
4: 47 He **f** Jesus and begged him to come to Capernaum
5: 14 But afterward Jesus **f** him in the Temple and told
6: 25 When they arrived and **f** him, they asked,
9: 35 he **f** the man and said, "Do you believe in the Son
12: 14 Jesus **f** a young donkey and sat on it,
20: 1 and **f** that the stone had been rolled away from the
20: 2 She ran and **f** Simon Peter and the other disciple,
20: 18 Mary Magdalene **f** the disciples and told them,
Ac 4: 23 Peter and John **f** the other believers and told them
7: 21 Pharaoh's daughter **f** him and raised him as her
7: 46 "David **f** favor with God and asked for the
8: 40 Philip **f** himself farther north at the city of Azotus!
9: 2 in the arrest of any followers of the Way he **f** there.
9: 8 himself up off the ground, he **f** that he was blind.
9: 17 So Ananias went and **f** Saul. He laid his hands on
10: 17 Just then the men sent by Cornelius **f** the house
11: 26 When he **f** him, he brought him back to Antioch.
12: 19 When he couldn't be **f**, Herod interrogated the
13: 28 They **f** no just cause to execute him, but they asked
18: 4 Each Sabbath **f** Paul at the synagogue, trying to
19: 1 he came to Ephesus, where he **f** several believers.
21: 4 We went ashore, **f** the local believers, and stayed
24: 5 For we have **f** him to be a troublemaker, a man
24: 20 what wrongdoing the Jewish high council **f** in me,
27: 6 There the officer **f** an Egyptian ship from
27: 28 and **f** the water was only 120 feet deep.
27: 28 A little later they sounded again and **f** only 90 feet.
28: 14 There we **f** some believers, who invited us to stay
28: 18 for they **f** no cause for the death sentence.
Ro 10: 20 "I was **f** by people / who were not looking for me.
11: 7 Most of the Jews have not **f** the favor of God they
Gal 4: 9 And now that you have **f** God (or should I say,
now that God has **f** you),
2Ti 1: 17 to Rome, he searched everywhere until he **f** me.
Heb 8: 8 But God himself **f** fault with the old one when he
11: 15 came from, they would have **f** a way to go back.
Jas 2: 8 our Lord's royal command **f** in the Scriptures:
Rev 5: 4 because no one could be **f** who was worthy to open
20: 11 fled from his presence, but they **f** no place to hide.
20: 15 And anyone whose name was not **f** recorded in the
21: 16 When he measured it, he **f** it was a square, as wide
21: 17 and **f** them to be 216 feet thick (the angel used a

FOUNDATION (51) [FOUNDATIONS, FOUNDED, FOUNDER, FOUNDERS]

Ge 10: 10 He built the **f** for his empire in the land of
Jos 6: 26 At the cost of his firstborn son, / he will lay its **f**.
1Ki 5: 17 and shaped costly blocks of stone for the **f** of the
6: 37 The **f** of the LORD's Temple was laid in
7: 10 Some of the huge **f** stones were 15 feet long,
2Ch 3: 3 The **f** for the Temple of God was ninety feet long
8: 16 from the day its **f** was laid to the day of its
23: 5 and the final third will be at the **F** Gate.
Ezr 3: 6 This was also before they had started to lay the **f** of
3: 10 When the builders completed the **f** of the LORD's
3: 11 because the **f** of the LORD's Temple had been
3: 12 wept aloud when they saw the new Temple's **f**.
4: 12 They have already laid the **f** for its walls and will
Job 4: 19 Their **f** is dust, and they are crushed as easily as
Ps 24: 2 For he laid the earth's **f** on the seas / and built it on
97: 2 Righteousness and justice are the **f** of his throne.
102: 25 In ages past you laid the **f** of the earth,
104: 5 You placed the world on its **f** / so it would never be
111: 10 Reverence for the LORD is the **f** of true wisdom.
Pr 10: 25 the wicked away, but the godly have a lasting **f**.
Isa 28: 16 "Look! I am placing a **f** stone in Jerusalem.
28: 17 and the plumb line of righteousness to check the **f**
33: 6 In that day he will be your sure **f**, providing a rich
54: 11 I will rebuild you on a **f** of sapphires and make the
Jer 31: 37 and the **f** of the earth cannot be explored,
Eze 13: 14 I will break down your wall right to the **f**,
41: 8 on a terrace, which provided a **f** for the side rooms.
Am 9: 1 the Temple columns so hard that the **f** will shake.
9: 6 home are in the heavens, while its **f** is on the earth.
Mic 3: 10 You are building Jerusalem on a **f** of murder
Hag 2: 15 you began to lay the **f** of the LORD's Temple.
2: 18 the day when the **f** of the LORD's Temple was
Zec 4: 9 "Zerubbabel is the one who laid the **f** of this
8: 9 of the LORD Almighty ever since the **f** was laid.
Mt 25: 34 inherit the Kingdom prepared for you from the **f** of
Lk 6: 48 It is like a person who builds a house on a strong **f**
6: 49 is like a person who builds a house without a **f**.
14: 29 you might complete only the **f** before running out
1Co 3: 10 favor to me, I have laid the **f** like an expert builder.
3: 10 But whoever is building on this **f** must be very
3: 11 For no one can lay any other **f** than the one we
3: 12 Now anyone who builds on that **f** may use gold,
Eph 2: 20 built on the **f** of the apostles and the prophets.
1Ti 6: 3 Jesus Christ, and they are the **f** for a godly life.
6: 19 storing up their treasure as a good **f** for the future
2Ti 2: 19 But God's truth stands firm like a **f** stone with this
Heb 1: 10 in the beginning you laid the **f** of the earth,
1Pe 5: 10 strengthen you, and he will place you on a firm **f**.
Jude 1: 20 must continue to build your lives on the **f** of your
Rev 21: 14 The wall of the city had twelve **f** stones, and on
21: 19 The wall of the city was built on **f** stones inlaid

FOUNDATIONS (25) [FOUNDATION]

Dt 32: 22 all its crops / and ignites the **f** of the mountains.
2Sa 22: 8 and trembled; / the **f** of the heavens shook;
22: 16 be seen, / and the **f** of the earth were laid bare.
1Ki 16: 34 When he laid the **f**, his oldest son, Abiram, died.
Ezr 5: 16 and laid the **f** of the Temple of God in Jerusalem.
6: 3 to offer their sacrifices, retaining the original **f**.
Job 9: 6 shakes the earth from its place, and its **f** tremble.
22: 16 and the **f** of their lives were washed away forever.
26: 11 The **f** of heaven tremble at his rebuke.
38: 4 "Where were you when I laid the **f** of the earth?
38: 6 What supports its **f**, and who laid its cornerstone
Ps 11: 3 The **f** of law and order have collapsed. / What can
18: 7 and trembled; / the **f** of the mountains shook;
18: 15 be seen, / and the **f** of the earth were laid bare.
75: 3 live in turmoil, / I am the one who keeps its **f** firm.
Pr 8: 29 And when he marked off the earth's **f**,
Isa 6: 4 The glorious singing shook the Temple to its **f**,
48: 13 It was my hand that laid the **f** of the earth.
La 4: 11 a fire in Jerusalem that burned the city to its **f**.
Eze 30: 4 wealth will be carried away and their **f** destroyed.
Mic 1: 6 down into the valley below, exposing all her **f**.
1: 11 because the very **f** of their city have been swept
Zec 12: 1 stretched out the heavens, laid the **f** of the earth,
Ac 16: 26 and the prison was shaken to its **f**.
Heb 11: 10 confidently looking forward to a city with eternal **f**,

FOUNDED (5) [FOUNDATION]

Ge 4: 17 When Cain **f** a city, he named it Enoch after his
Nu 13: 22 (The ancient town of Hebron was **f** seven years
Ps 87: 1 On the holy mountain stands the city **f** by the
89: 14 Your throne is **f** on two strong pillars—
Pr 3: 19 By wisdom the LORD **f** the earth;

FOUNDER (2) [FOUNDATION]

1Ch 4: 14 the **f** of the Valley of Craftsmen, so called
Ro 4: 1 humanly speaking, the **f** of our Jewish nation.

FOUNDERS (1) [FOUNDATION]

Ge 25: 16 These twelve sons of Ishmael became the **f** of

FOUNDRY (1)

1Ki 7: 14 and his father had been a **f** worker from Tyre.

FOUNTAIN (20) [FOUNTAINS]

Ge 49: 22 "Joseph is a fruitful tree, / a fruitful tree beside a **f**.
Ne 2: 14 Then I went to the **F** Gate and to the King's Pool,
3: 15 leader of the Mizpah district, repaired the **F** Gate.
12: 37 At the **F** Gate they went straight up the steps on the
Ps 36: 9 For you are the **f** of life, / the light by which we
Pr 5: 18 Let your wife be a **f** of blessing for you. Rejoice in
13: 14 The advice of the wise is like a life-giving **f**;
14: 27 Fear of the LORD is a life-giving **f**; it offers
16: 22 Discretion is a life-giving **f** to those who possess it,
25: 26 it is like polluting a **f** or muddying a spring.
SS 4: 12 that no one else can drink from, a **f** of my own.
4: 15 You are a garden **f**, a well of living water,
Isa 12: 3 With joy you will drink deeply from the **f** of
Jer 2: 13 They have forsaken me—the **f** of living water.
6: 7 She spouts evil like a **f**! Her streets echo with the
9: 1 Oh, that my eyes were a **f** of tears; I would weep
17: 13 have forsaken the LORD, the **f** of living water.
Joel 3: 18 and a **f** will burst forth from the LORD's Temple,
Zec 13: 1 "On that day a **f** will be opened for the dynasty of
13: 1 a **f** to cleanse them from all their sins

FOUNTAINS (3) [FOUNTAIN]

Pr 3: 20 By his knowledge the deep **f** of the earth burst
8: 28 when he established the deep **f** of the earth.
Isa 41: 18 I will give them **f** of water in the valleys.

FOUR (206) [FOUR-FIFTHS, FOUR-SIDED, FOURS, FOURTH, ONE-FOURTH, 4]

Ge 2: 10 the garden and then dividing into **f** branches.
14: 9 Babylonia, and Ellasar—**f** kings against five.
15: 13 and they will be oppressed as slaves for **f** hundred

15:16 After **f** generations your descendants will return
22:24 Nahor had **f** other children from his concubine
23:15 "the land is worth **f** hundred pieces of silver,
23:16 **f** hundred pieces of silver, as was publicly agreed.
32:6 to meet Jacob—with an army of **f** hundred men!
33:1 Jacob saw Esau coming with his **f** hundred men.
Ex 16:22 **f** quarts for each person instead of two.
22:1 For sheep the fine is **f** sheep for each one stolen.
25:12 Cast **f** rings of gold for it, and attach them to its **f** feet, two rings on each side.
25:26 Make **f** gold rings, and put the rings at the **f** corners by the **f** legs,
25:34 will be decorated with **f** almond blossoms,
26:32 Hang this inner curtain on gold hooks set into **f**
27:2 Make a horn at each of the **f** corners of the altar
27:16 It will be attached to **f** posts that fit into **f** bases.
28:17 **F** rows of gemstones will be attached to it.
36:36 then attached to **f** gold hooks set into **f** posts of
36:36 were overlaid with gold and set into **f** silver bases.
37:3 **F** gold rings were fastened to its **f** feet,
37:13 Then he cast **f** rings of gold and attached them to the **f** table legs
37:20 was also decorated with **f** almond blossoms,
38:2 There were **f** horns, one at each of the **f** corners,
38:5 **F** rings were cast for each side of the grating to
38:19 It was supported by **f** posts set into **f** bronze
39:10 **F** rows of gemstones were set across it. In the first
Lev 8:15 and with his finger he put it on the **f** horns of the
11:42 as well as those with **f** legs and those with many
Nu 3:19 from Kohath were named for **f** of his descendants,
3:31 These **f** clans were responsible for the care of the
7:7 and **f** oxen to the Gershonite division for their
7:8 and **f** carts and eight oxen to the Merarite division
7:14 He also brought a gold container weighing about **f**
7:20 He also brought a gold container weighing about **f**
7:26 He also brought a gold container weighing about **f**
7:32 He also brought a gold container weighing about **f**
7:38 He also brought a gold container weighing about **f**
7:44 He also brought a gold container weighing about **f**
7:50 He also brought a gold container weighing about **f**
7:56 He also brought a gold container weighing about **f**
7:62 He also brought a gold container weighing about **f**
7:68 He also brought a gold container weighing about **f**
7:74 He also brought a gold container weighing about **f**
7:80 He also brought a gold container weighing about **f**
7:86 about **f** ounces for each of the gold containers that
Dt 22:12 "You must put tassels on the **f** corners of your
Jos 19:7 Ether, and Ashan—**f** towns with their villages,
21:18 Anathoth, and Almon—**f** towns.
21:22 Kibzaim, and Beth-horon—**f** towns.
21:24 Aijalon, and Gath-rimmon—**f** towns.
21:29 and En-gannim—**f** towns with their pasturelands.
21:31 and Rehob—**f** towns and their pasturelands.
21:35 and Nahalal—**f** towns with their pasturelands.
21:37 and Mephaath—**f** towns with their pasturelands.
21:39 and Jazer—**f** towns with their pasturelands.
Jdg 9:34 and his men went by night and split into **f** groups,
11:40 for young Israelite women to go away for **f** days
19:2 father's home in Bethlehem. After about **f** months,
20:47 rock of Rimmon, where they lived for **f** months.
21:12 Among the residents of Jabesh-gilead they found **f**
21:14 and the **f** hundred women of Jabesh-gilead who
1Sa 4:2 defeated the army of Israel, killing **f** thousand men.
22:2 until David was the leader of about **f** hundred men.
25:13 **F** hundred men started off with David, and two
27:7 among the Philistines for a year and **f** months.
30:10 so David continued the pursuit with his **f** hundred
30:17 None of the Amalekites escaped except **f** hundred
2Sa 12:6 He must repay **f** lambs to the poor man for the one
15:7 After **f** years, Absalom said to the king, "Let me
21:22 These **f** Philistines were descended from the giants
1Ki 4:26 Solomon had **f** thousand stalls for his chariot
7:2 The great cedar ceiling beams rested on **f** rows of
7:30 Each of these carts had **f** bronze wheels and bronze
7:32 Under the panels were **f** wheels that were
7:34 There were supports at each of the **f** corners of the
7:42 **f** hundred pomegranates that hung from the chains
10:17 each containing nearly **f** pounds of gold.
18:33 Then he said, "Fill **f** large jars with water,
22:6 about **f** hundred of them, and asked them,
2Ki 7:3 Now there were **f** men with leprosy sitting at the
1Ch 7:1 The **f** sons of Issachar were Tola, Puah, Jashub,
9:24 The gatekeepers were stationed on all **f** sides—
9:26 The **f** chief gatekeepers, all Levites, were in an
21:20 His **f** sons, who were with him, ran away and hid.
22:14 nearly **f** thousand tons of gold, nearly forty
23:5 **F** thousand will work as gatekeepers, and another **f** thousand will praise the LORD with
23:10 **F** other descendants of Shimei were Jahath, Ziza,
26:17 **f** to the north gate, **f** to the south gate, and two
26:18 **f** to the gateway leading up to the Temple, and two
2Ch 4:13 **f** hundred pomegranates that hung from the chains
9:25 Solomon had **f** thousand stalls for his chariot
18:5 his prophets, **f** hundred of them, and asked them,
28:15 Then the **f** men mentioned by name came forward
Ezr 6:17 and **f** hundred lambs were sacrificed.
Ne 6:4 **F** times they sent the same message, and each time
Job 42:16 living to see **f** generations of his children
Pr 30:15 three other things—no, **f**!—that are never satisfied:
30:18 that amaze me—no, **f** things I do not understand:
30:21 make the earth tremble—no, **f** it cannot endure:
30:24 There are **f** things on earth that are small
30:29 are three stately monarchs on the earth—no, **f**:
Isa 17:6 **f** or five out on the tips of the limbs.
Jer 15:3 "I will send **f** kinds of destroyers against them,"
36:23 Jehudi finished reading three or **f** columns,
49:36 and I will scatter the people of Elam to the **f** winds.
Eze 1:5 From the center of the cloud came **f** living beings
1:6 except that each had **f** faces and two pairs of
1:15 I saw **f** wheels on the ground beneath them,
1:16 All **f** wheels looked the same; each wheel had a
1:17 The beings could move forward in any of the **f**
1:18 The rims of the **f** wheels were awesomely tall,
1:19 When the **f** living beings moved, the wheels moved
1:20 The spirit of the **f** living beings was in the wheels.
10:9 Each of the **f** cherubim had a wheel beside him,
10:10 All **f** wheels looked the same; each wheel had a
10:11 The cherubim could move forward in any of the **f**
10:14 Each of the **f** cherubim had **f** faces—the first
10:21 for each had **f** faces and **f** wings and what
12:14 I will scatter his servants and guards to the **f** winds
14:21 How terrible it will be when all **f** of these fearsome
17:21 in the city will be scattered to the **f** winds.
37:9 Come, O breath, from the **f** winds! Breathe into
40:41 **f** inside and **f** outside, where the sacrifices were
40:42 There were also **f** tables of hewn stone for
43:15 with a horn rising up from each of the **f** corners.
43:20 of its blood and smear it on the **f** horns of the altar,
43:20 the **f** corners of the upper ledge, and the curb that
45:19 the **f** corners of the upper ledge on the altar,
46:21 outer courtyard and led me to each of its **f** corners.
Da 1:6 and Azariah were **f** of the young men chosen,
1:17 God gave these **f** young men an unusual aptitude
3:25 "I see **f** men, unbound, walking around in the fire.
7:3 Then **f** huge beasts came up out of the water,
7:6 It had **f** wings like birds' wings on its back, and it had **f** heads.
7:17 "These **f** huge beasts represent **f** kingdoms that
8:8 In the large horn's place grew **f** prominent horns pointing in the **f** directions of the earth.
8:22 The **f** prominent horns that replaced the one large
8:22 Empire will break into **f** sections with **f** kings,
11:4 will be broken apart and divided into **f** parts.
Zec 1:18 Then I looked up and saw **f** animal horns.
1:20 Then the LORD showed me **f** blacksmiths.
1:21 "The blacksmiths have come to terrify the **f** horns
2:6 the north, for I have scattered you to the **f** winds.
6:1 and saw **f** chariots coming from between two
6:5 "These are the **f** spirits of heaven who stand before
Mt 15:38 There were **f** thousand men who were fed that day,
16:10 Don't you remember the **f** thousand I fed with
Mk 2:3 **F** men arrived carrying a paralyzed man on a mat.
8:9 There were about **f** thousand people in the crowd
8:20 "And when I fed the **f** thousand with seven loaves,
Lk 16:6 and write another one for **f** hundred gallons.'
19:8 I will give them back **f** times as much!"
Jn 1:39 It was about **f** o'clock in the afternoon when they
4:35 begin until the summer ends **f** months from now?
6:19 or **f** miles out when suddenly they saw Jesus
11:17 Lazarus had already been in his grave for **f** days.
11:39 be terrible because he has been dead for **f** days."
19:23 they divided his clothes among the **f** of them.
Ac 5:36 About **f** hundred others joined him, but he was
7:6 would be mistreated as slaves for **f** hundred years.
10:11 like a large sheet was let down by its **f** corners.
10:30 "**F** days ago I was praying in my house at three
11:5 Something like a large sheet was let down by its **f**
12:4 placing him under the guard of **f** squads of **f**
15:30 The **f** messengers went at once to Antioch,
21:9 He had **f** unmarried daughters who had the gift of
21:23 We have **f** men here who have taken a vow and are
21:38 and took **f** thousand members of the Assassins out
27:29 so they threw out **f** anchors from the stern
Rev 4:6 and around the throne were **f** living beings,
5:6 and the **f** living beings and among the twenty-four
5:8 the **f** living beings and the twenty-four elders fell
5:14 And the **f** living beings said, "Amen!"
6:1 Then one of the **f** living beings called out with a
6:6 And a voice from among the **f** living beings said,
7:1 Then I saw **f** angels standing at the **f** corners of
7:1 holding back the **f** winds from blowing upon the
7:2 And he shouted out to those **f** angels who had been
7:11 and around the elders and the **f** living beings.
9:13 and I heard a voice speaking from the **f** horns of
9:14 "Release the **f** angels who are bound at the great
9:15 And the **f** angels who had been prepared for this
14:3 and before the **f** living beings and the twenty-four
15:7 And one of the **f** living beings handed each of the
19:4 and the **f** living beings fell down and worshiped

FOUR-FIFTHS (1) [FIVE, FOUR]

Ge 47:24 Keep **f** for yourselves, and use it to plant the next

FOUR-SIDED (1) [FOUR, SIDE]

1Ki 6:33 Then he made **f** doorposts of olive wood for the

FOURFOLD [KJV] See FOUR

FOURS (1) [FOUR]

Lev 11:27 Of the animals that walk on all **f**, those that have

FOURSCORE [KJV] See EIGHTY (and its compounds)

FOURSQUARE [KJV] See SQUARE

FOURTEEN (24) [FOURTEENTH, 14]

Ge 31:41 **f** of them earning your two daughters, and six
46:22 These **f** were the descendants of Jacob and his wife
Nu 29:13 two rams, and **f** one-year-old male lambs, all with
29:15 and two quarts for each of the **f** lambs.
29:17 two rams, and **f** one-year-old male lambs,
29:20 two rams, and **f** one-year-old male lambs,
29:23 two rams, and **f** one-year-old male lambs,
29:26 two rams, and **f** one-year-old male lambs,
29:29 two rams, and **f** one-year-old male lambs,
29:32 two rams, and **f** one-year-old male lambs,
Jos 15:36 there were **f** towns with their surrounding villages.
18:28 and Kiriath-jearim—**f** towns with their villages.
1Ki 8:65 The celebration went on for **f** days in all—
10:26 He had **f** hundred chariots and twelve thousand
1Ch 25:5 for God had honored him with **f** sons and three
2Ch 1:14 which included **f** hundred chariots and twelve
13:21 He married **f** wives and had twenty-two sons
Job 42:12 For now he had **f** thousand sheep, six thousand
Eze 40:1 **f** years after the fall of Jerusalem—the LORD
Mt 1:17 All those listed above include **f** generations from
1:17 and **f** from David's time to the Babylonian exile,
1:17 and **f** from the Babylonian exile to the Messiah.
2Co 12:2 I was caught up into the third heaven **f** years ago.
Gal 2:1 Then **f** years later I went back to Jerusalem again,

FOURTEENTH (9) [FOURTEEN]

Ex 12:6 until the evening of the **f** day of this first month.
12:18 **f** day of the month until the evening of the
Jos 5:10 they celebrated Passover on the evening of the **f**
2Ki 18:13 In the **f** year of King Hezekiah's reign,
1Ch 24:13 lot fell to Huppah. / The **f** lot fell to Jeshebeab.
25:21 The **f** lot fell to Mattithiah and twelve of his sons
Isa 36:1 In the **f** year of King Hezekiah's reign,
Eze 45:21 "On the **f** day of the new year, you must celebrate
Ac 27:27 About midnight on the **f** night of the storm, as we

FOURTH (62) [FOUR, ONE-FOURTH]

Ge 1:19 This all happened on the **f** day.
2:14 the east of Asshur. The **f** branch is the Euphrates.
Ex 20:5 sins of their parents to the third and **f** generations.
28:20 The **f** row will contain a beryl, an onyx, and a
34:7 sins of their parents to the third and **f** generations."
39:13 In the **f** row were a beryl, an onyx, and a jasper.
Lev 19:24 In the **f** year the entire crop will be devoted to the
Nu 7:30 On the **f** day Elizur son of Shedeur, leader of the
14:18 sins of their parents to the third and **f** generations.'
23:10 Who can count even a **f** of Israel's people?
29:23 "On the **f** day of the festival, sacrifice ten young
Dt 5:9 sins of their parents to the third and **f** generations.
Jos 19:17 The **f** allotment of land went to the families of the
Jdg 14:15 On the **f** day they said to Samson's wife,
19:5 On the **f** day the man was up early, ready to leave,
2Sa 3:4 The **f** was Adonijah, whose mother was Haggith.
1Ki 6:1 in midspring, during the **f** year of Solomon's reign,
6:37 laid in midspring of the **f** year of Solomon's reign.
22:41 Judah in the **f** year of King Ahab's reign in Israel.
2Ki 10:30 to be the kings of Israel down to the **f** generation."
15:12 will be kings of Israel down to the **f** generation."
18:9 During the **f** year of Hezekiah's reign, which was
1Ch 2:14 his **f** was Nethanel, his fifth was Raddai,
3:2 The **f** was Adonijah, whose mother was Haggith.
3:15 Zedekiah (the third), and Jehoahaz (the **f**).
12:10 Mishmannah was **f**. / Jeremiah was fifth.
23:19 Jahaziel (the third), and Jekameam (the **f**).
24:8 third lot fell to Harim. / The **f** lot fell to Seorim.
24:23 Jahaziel was third, and Jekameam was **f**.
25:11 The **f** lot fell to Zeri and twelve of his sons
26:2 (the second), Zebadiah (the third), Jathniel (the **f**),
26:4 Joah (the third), Sacar (the **f**), Nethanel (the fifth),
26:11 Tebaliah (the third), and Zechariah (the **f**).
27:7 brother of Joab, was commander of the **f** division,
27:7 which was on duty during the **f** month.
2Ch 3:2 in midspring, during the **f** year of Solomon's reign.
20:26 On the **f** day they gathered in the Valley of
Ezr 8:33 On the **f** day after our arrival, the silver, gold,
Jer 25:1 during the **f** year of Jehoiakim's reign over Judah.
28:1 the **f** year of the reign of Zedekiah, king of Judah—
36:1 During the **f** year that Jehoiakim son of Josiah was
45:1 the **f** year of the reign of Jehoiakim son of Josiah,
46:2 This message concerning Egypt was given in the **f**
51:59 This was during the **f** year of Zedekiah's reign.
Eze 10:14 face of a lion, and the **f** was the face of an eagle.
Da 2:40 there will be a **f** great kingdom, as strong as iron.
3:25 the flames! And the **f** looks like a divine being!"
7:7 I saw a **f** beast, terrifying, dreadful, and very
7:11 I kept watching until the **f** beast was killed and its
7:19 Then I wanted to know the true meaning of the **f**
7:20 I also asked about the ten horns on the **f** beast's
7:23 "This **f** beast is the **f** world power that will
11:2 to be succeeded by a **f**, far richer than the others.
Zec 6:3 by white horses, and the **f** by dappled-gray horses.
7:1 On December 7 of the **f** year of King Darius's
Rev 4:7 and the **f** had the form of an eagle with wings
6:7 And when the Lamb broke the **f** seal, I heard the **f** living being say, "Come!"
8:12 Then the **f** angel blew his trumpet, and one-third of
16:8 Then the **f** angel poured out his bowl on the sun,
21:19 the second sapphire, the third agate, the **f** emerald,

FOWL (2)

1Ki 4:23 as well as deer, gazelles, roebucks, and choice **f**.
Ne 5:18 six fat sheep, and a large number of domestic **f**.

FOWLS [KJV] See BIRDS

FOX (2) [FOXES]

Ne 4:3 "That stone wall would collapse if even a **f** walked
Lk 13:32 "Go tell that **f** that I will keep on casting out

FOXES (5) [FOX]
Jdg 15: 4 Then he went out and caught three hundred f.
15: 5 and let the f run through the fields of the
SS 2: 15 Catch all the little f before they ruin the vineyard
Mt 8: 20 But Jesus said, "F have dens to live in, and birds
Lk 9: 58 But Jesus replied, "F have dens to live in,

FOYER (40) [FOYERS]
1Ki 6: 3 The f at the front of the Temple was 30 feet wide,
7: 12 of the LORD's Temple with its entrance f.
7: 19 The capitals on the columns inside the f were
2Ch 3: 4 The f at the front of the Temple was thirty feet
3: 4 The inner walls of the f and the ceiling were
3: 4 pure gold. The roof of the f was thirty feet high.
8: 12 altar he had built in front of the f of the Temple.
15: 8 which stood in front of the f of the LORD's
29: 7 They also shut the doors to the Temple's f,
29: 17 and in eight days they had reached the f of the
Eze 8: 16 At the entrance, between the f and the bronze altar,
40: 7 which led to the f at the inner end of the gateway
40: 8 He also measured the f of the gateway
40: 9 This f was at the inner end of the gateway
40: 14 the inside of the gateway up to the gateway's f;
40: 16 There were also windows in the f structure.
40: 21 alcoves on each side, with dividing walls and a f.
40: 22 The windows, the f, and the palm tree decorations
40: 22 and the f was at the inner end of the gateway
40: 25 and there was a f where the gateway passage
40: 29 and f were the same size as those in the others.
40: 29 had windows along its walls and in the f structure.
40: 31 The f of the south gateway faced into the outer
40: 33 and f were the same size as those of the others,
40: 33 windows along the walls and in the f structure.
40: 34 Its f faced into the outer courtyard. It had palm tree
40: 36 and f of this gateway had the same measurements
40: 37 Its f faced into the outer courtyard, and it had palm
40: 38 A door led from the f of the inner gateway on the
40: 39 On each side of this f were two tables,
40: 40 Outside the f, on each side of the stairs going up to
40: 43 fastened to the f walls and set on the tables where
40: 48 Then he brought me to the f of the Temple.
40: 49 The depth of the f was 35 feet and the width was
41: 15 and the f of the Temple were all paneled with
41: 25 a wooden canopy over the front of the Temple's f.
41: 26 On both sides of the f there were recessed windows
44: 3 may come and go only through the gateway's f."
46: 2 The prince will enter the f of the gateway from the
46: 8 "The prince must enter the gateway through the f,

FOYERS (1) [FOYER]
Eze 40: 30 (The f of the gateways leading into the inner

FRACTURE (2)
Lev 24: 20 f for f, eye for eye, tooth for tooth.

FRAGILE (3)
Job 13: 12 value as ashes. Your defense is as f as a clay pot.
27: 18 The houses built by the wicked are as f as a
Jer 25: 34 has arrived; you will fall and shatter like f pottery.

FRAGRANCE (6) [FRAGRANCES, FRAGRANT]
SS 1: 12 on his couch, enchanted by the f of my perfume.
7: 13 There the mandrakes give forth their f,
Jer 6: 20 Your sacrifices have no sweet f for me."
Jn 12: 3 feet with her hair. And the house was filled with f.
2Co 2: 15 Our lives are a f presented by Christ to God.
2: 15 But this f is perceived differently by those being

FRAGRANCES (1) [FRAGRANCE]
Am 6: 6 and you perfume yourselves with exotic f,

FRAGRANT (23) [FRAGRANCE]
Ex 25: 6 spices for the anointing oil and the f incense;
29: 41 It will be a f offering to the LORD, an offering
30: 7 the lamps, he must burn f incense on the altar.
35: 8 spices for the anointing oil and the f incense;
35: 15 its carrying poles; the anointing oil and f incense;
35: 28 oil for the light, the anointing oil, and the f incense.
37: 29 oil for anointing the priests and the f incense,
39: 38 the gold altar; the anointing oil; the f incense;
40: 27 On it he burned the f incense made from sweet
Lev 16: 12 Then, after filling both his hands with f incense,
Nu 4: 16 the f incense, the daily grain offering,
2Ch 13: 11 and f incense to the LORD every morning
Ps 133: 2 For harmony is as precious as the f anointing oil
SS 1: 3 How f your cologne, and how pleasing your name!
4: 10 Your perfume is more f than the richest of spices.
Isa 43: 24 You have not brought me f incense or pleased me
Jer 22: 14 paneled throughout with f cedar and painted a
48: 11 from flask to flask, and she is now f and smooth.
Eze 16: 9 off your blood, and I rubbed f oils into your skin.
Da 10: 3 or meat, had drunk no wine, and had used no f oils.
Hos 14: 6 olive trees, as f as the cedar forests of Lebanon.
14: 7 They will be as f as the wines of Lebanon.
Ro 15: 16 and offer you up as a f sacrifice to God so that you

FRAIL (4)
Job 14: 1 "How f is humanity! How short is life, and how
14: 3 Must you keep an eye on such a f creature
Ps 39: 11 Human existence is as f as breath. / *Interlude*
Isa 2: 22 They are as f as breath. How can they be of help to

FRAIL [KJV] See also FLEETING

FRAME (19) [FRAMED, FRAMES, FRAMEWORK]
Ex 26: 16 Each f must be 15 feet high and 2-1/4 feet wide.
26: 17 There will be two pegs on each f so they can be joined to the next f.
26: 19 fit into forty silver bases—two bases under each f.
26: 21 with their forty silver bases, two bases for each f.
26: 23 along with an extra f at each corner.
26: 25 by sixteen silver bases—two bases under each f.
36: 21 Each f was 15 feet high and 2-1/4 feet wide.
36: 22 There were two pegs on each f so they could be joined to the next f.
36: 24 along with forty silver bases, two for each f.
36: 26 along with forty silver bases, two for each f.
36: 28 plus an extra f at each corner.
36: 30 along with sixteen silver bases, two for each f.
Nu 4: 10 and the bundle must be placed on a carrying f.
4: 12 fine goatskin leather, and placed on the carrying f.
1Ki 7: 5 All the doorways were rectangular in f; they were
7: 31 The top of each cart had a circular f for the basin.
Job 41: 12 crocodile's limbs and throughout its enormous f.

FRAMED (1) [FRAME]
Eze 41: 1 and he measured the columns that f its doorway.

FRAMES (28) [FRAME]
Ex 26: 15 Tabernacle will consist of f made of acacia wood.
26: 17 to the next frame. All the f must be made this way.
26: 18 Twenty of these f will support the south side of the
26: 20 the north side there will also be twenty of these f,
26: 22 On the west side there will be six f,
26: 24 These corner f will be connected at the bottom
26: 24 Both of these corner f will be made the same way.
26: 25 So there will be eight f on that end of the
26: 26 crossbars of acacia wood to run across the f,
26: 28 The middle crossbar, halfway up the f, will run all
26: 29 Overlay the f with gold and make gold rings to
35: 11 the clasps, f, crossbars, posts, and bases;
36: 20 they made f of acacia wood standing on end.
36: 22 to the next frame. All the f were made this way.
36: 23 They made twenty f to support the south side,
36: 25 They also made twenty f for the north side of the
36: 27 which was its rear, was made from six f,
36: 29 These corner f were connected at the bottom
36: 30 So for the west side they made a total of eight f,
36: 31 acacia wood to tie the f on the south side together.
36: 33 middle crossbar of the five was halfway up the f,
36: 34 The f and crossbars were all overlaid with gold.
38: 27 The 100 bases for the f of the sanctuary walls
39: 33 the clasps, f, crossbars, posts, and bases;
40: 18 Moses put it together by setting its f into their
Nu 3: 36 for the care of the f supporting the Tabernacle,
4: 31 They will be required to carry the f of the
Eze 41: 16 as were the f of the recessed windows. The inner

FRAMEWORK (3) [FRAME]
Ex 26: 15 "The f of the Tabernacle will consist of frames
36: 20 For the f of the Tabernacle, they made frames of
40: 19 Then he spread the coverings over the Tabernacle f

FRANKINCENSE (9) [INCENSE]
Ex 30: 34 mollusk scent, galbanum, and pure f—
Lev 24: 7 Sprinkle some pure f near each row. It will serve as
Nu 5: 15 Do not mix it with olive oil or f, for it is a jealousy
Ne 13: 5 f, Temple utensils, and tithes of grain, new wine,
13: 9 for God's Temple, the grain offerings, and the f.
SS 3: 6 it that smells of myrrh and f and every other spice?
4: 6 go to the mountain of myrrh and to the hill of f.
Mt 2: 11 and gave him gifts of gold, f, and myrrh.
Rev 18: 13 spice, incense, myrrh, f, wine, olive oil, fine flour,

FRANKLY (2) [FRANKNESS]
Ac 26: 26 I speak f, for I am sure these events are all familiar
Gal 4: 20 But at this distance I f don't know what else to do.

FRANKNESS (1) [FRANKLY]
Pr 28: 23 In the end, people appreciate f more than flattery.

FRANTIC (3) [FRANTICALLY]
1Sa 28: 5 the vast Philistine army, he became f with fear.
Jer 25: 36 Listen to the f cries of the shepherds, to the leaders
Lk 2: 48 Your father and I have been f, searching for you

FRANTICALLY (1) [FRANTIC]
Mk 4: 38 F they woke him up, shouting, "Teacher,

FRAUD (3) [DEFRAUD, FRAUDS]
Isa 33: 15 and fair, who reject making a profit by f,
Mic 2: 2 someone's house, you take it by f and violence.
Jn 7: 12 while others said, "He's nothing but a f,

FRAUDS (2) [FRAUD]
Jer 10: 14 the idols will disgrace their makers, / for they are f.
51: 17 the idols will disgrace their makers, / for they are f.

FRECKLED [KJV] See (HARMLESS) RASH

FREE (125) [FREEBORN, FREED, FREEDOM, FREEING, FREELY, FREES, FREEWILL]
Ge 16: 12 be a wild one—f and untamed as a wild donkey!
24: 8 come back with you, then you are f from this oath.
24: 41 to let her come, you will be f from your oath.'
27: 40 then you will shake loose from him and be f."
34: 10 with us. You are f to acquire property among us."
44: 10 stole it will be a slave. The rest of you may go f."
Ex 6: 6 and I will f you from your slavery in Egypt.
21: 2 Set him f in the seventh year, and he will owe you
21: 3 only he will go f in the seventh year.
21: 4 then the man will be f in the seventh year, but his
21: 5 my wife, and my children. I would rather not go f.'
21: 11 she may leave as a f woman without making any
21: 26 then the slave may go f because of the eye.
23: 7 I will not allow anyone guilty of this to go f.
Lev 13: 6 the person will be considered f of disease.
14: 7 the priest will set the living bird f so it can fly
16: 22 After the man sets it f in the wilderness, the goat
25: 54 and their children must be set f at that time.
26: 13 so you can walk f with your heads held high.
Nu 11: 5 "We remember all the fish we used to eat for f in
Dt 15: 12 in the seventh year you must set that servant f.
21: 14 decide you do not like her, you must let her go f.
24: 5 He must be f to be at home for one year,
32: 36 their strength is gone / and no one is left, slave or f.
Jos 20: 6 the one found innocent is f to return home."
24: 5 and afterward I brought you out as a f people.
Jdg 16: 20 "I will do as before and shake myself f."
1Ki 14: 10 your dynasty and kill all your sons, slave or f alike.
20: 34 So they made a treaty, and Ben-hadad was set f.
21: 21 slave or f alike, survive in Israel!
2Ki 9: 8 wiped out—every male, slave and f alike, in Israel.
17: 4 So of Egypt to help him shake f of Assyria's power
Job 3: 19 are there alike, and the slave is f from his master.
11: 15 in innocence. You will be strong and f of fear.
33: 24 God will be gracious and say, 'Set him f. Do not
Ps 2: 3 they cry, / "and f ourselves from this slavery."
10: 6 happen to us! / We will be f of trouble forever!"
19: 13 Then I will be f of guilt / and innocent of great sin.
34: 6 and he heard me. / He set me f from all my fears.
44: 2 you crushed their enemies, / setting our ancestors f.
68: 6 he sets the prisoners f and gives them joy.
69: 18 Come and rescue me; / f me from all my enemies.
69: 27 Pile their sins up high, / and don't let them go f.
71: 2 you are just. / Turn your ear to listen and set me f.
81: 5 for Israel / when he attacked Egypt to set us f.
81: 6 I will f your hands from their heavy tasks.
101: 8 and f the city of the LORD from their grip.
105: 20 Then Pharaoh sent for him and set him f; / the ruler
124: 7 a hunter's trap. / The trap is broken, and we are f!
130: 8 He himself will f Israel / from every kind of sin.
Pr 11: 21 be punished, but the children of the godly will go f.
20: 9 cleansed my heart; I am pure and f from sin"?
Isa 5: 23 They let the wicked go f while punishing the
42: 7 the eyes of the blind and f the captives from prison.
44: 22 to me, for I have paid the price to set you f."
45: 13 He will restore my city and f my captive people—
48: 20 Yet even now, be f from your captivity!
55: 1 Come, take your choice of wine or milk—it's all f!
58: 6 the kind of fasting I want calls you to f those who
Jer 2: 31 then do my people say, 'At last we are f from God!
34: 9 He had ordered all the people to f their Hebrew
34: 17 have not obeyed me by setting your countrymen f,
34: 17 I will set you f to be destroyed by war, famine,
42: 14 in Egypt where you think you will be f from war,
Eze 13: 20 setting my people f like birds set f from a cage.
46: 17 At that time the servant will be set f, and the land
Hos 1: 7 I will personally f them from their enemies without
Zec 9: 11 I will f your prisoners from death in a waterless
14: 21 All who come to worship will be f to use any of
Mal 3: 15 and those who dare God to punish them go f of
4: 2 And you will go f, leaping with joy like calves let
Mt 5: 26 I assure you that you won't be f again until you
17: 26 "Well, then," Jesus said, "the citizens are f!
Lk 12: 59 you won't be f again until you have paid the last
13: 16 to f this dear woman from the bondage in which
Jn 8: 32 will know the truth, and the truth will set you f."
8: 33 to anyone on earth. What do you mean, 'set f'?"
8: 36 So if the Son sets you f, you will indeed be f.
Ac 1: 6 are you going to f Israel now and restore our
16: 36 the jailer told Paul, "You and Silas are f to leave.
26: 32 "He could be set f if he hadn't appealed to
Ro 4: 16 is the key! God's promise is given to us as a f gift.
5: 16 but we have the f gift of being accepted by God,
6: 7 For when we died with Christ we were set f from
6: 14 you to sin. Instead, you are f by God's grace.
6: 15 So since God's grace has set us f from the law,
6: 18 Now you are f from sin, your old master, and you
6: 22 But now you are f from the power of sin and have
6: 23 but the f gift of God is eternal life through Christ
7: 3 she is f from that law and does not commit
7: 24 Who will f me from this life that is dominated by
11: 6 would not be what it really is—f and undeserved.
1Co 1: 8 and he will keep you f from all blame on the great
7: 21 worry you—but if you get a chance to be f, take it.
7: 22 the Lord has now set you f from the awful power
7: 22 And if you were f when the Lord called you,
7: 32 I want you to be f from the concerns of this life.
7: 39 she is f to marry whomever she wishes,
9: 17 If I were doing this of my own f will, then I would
12: 13 some are Gentiles, some are slaves, and some are f.
2Co 8: 3 but far more. And they did it of their own f will.
Gal 3: 28 longer Jew or Gentile, slave or f, male or female.
4: 12 become like you Gentiles were—f from the law.
4: 26 But Sarah, the f woman, represents the heavenly

4:30 the family inheritance with the **f** woman's son."
4:31 We are children of the **f** woman, acceptable to God
5:1 So Christ has really set us **f**. Now make sure that you stay **f**, and don't get tied
5:17 and your choices are never **f** from this conflict.
Eph 6:8 us for the good we do, whether we are slaves or **f**.
Col 2:20 and he has set you **f** from the evil powers of this
3:11 or uncircumcised, barbaric, uncivilized, slave, or **f**.
1Ti 2:8 lifted up to God, **f** from anger and controversy.
Tit 2:14 He gave his life to **f** us from every kind of sin,
Heb 9:15 For Christ died to set them **f** from the penalty of
11:35 to die rather than turn from God and be **f**.
Jas 1:25 the law that sets you **f**—and if you do what it says
2:12 be judged by the law of love, the law that set you **f**.
1Pe 2:16 You are not slaves; you are **f**. But your freedom is
2:16 excuse to do evil. You are **f** to live as God's slaves.
Rev 6:15 great power, and every slave and every **f** person—
13:16 great and small, rich and poor, slave and **f**—
19:18 of all humanity, both **f** and slave, small and great."

FREEBORN (2) [BEAR, FREE]
Gal 4:22 one from his slave-wife and one from his **f** wife.
4:23 But the son of the **f** wife was born as God's own

FREED (18) [FREE]
Ex 21:3 he became a slave, then his wife will be **f** with him.
21:7 she will not be **f** at the end of six years as the men
Lev 19:20 But since she had not been **f** at the time, the couple
Ps 116:16 and you have **f** me from my bonds!
Isa 61:1 captives will be released and prisoners will be **f**.
Jer 34:11 They took back the people they had **f**,
34:14 I told them that every Hebrew slave must be **f** after
34:15 You **f** your slaves and made a solemn covenant
34:16 by taking back the men and women you had **f**,
Hos 2:15 when I **f** her from her captivity in Egypt.
Lk 4:18 that the downtrodden will be **f** from their
Ac 4:23 As soon as they were **f**, Peter and John found the
6:9 But one day some men from the Synagogue of **F**
13:39 Everyone who believes in him is **f** from all guilt
22:30 The next day the commander **f** Paul from his
Ro 3:24 Christ Jesus, who has **f** us by taking away our sins.
8:2 For the power of the life-giving Spirit has **f** you
Rev 1:5 and has **f** us from our sins by shedding his blood

FREEDOM (27) [FREE]
Ex 21:2 and he will owe you nothing for his **f**.
Lev 25:50 The price of their **f** will be based on the number of
Job 36:16 "God has led you away from danger, giving you **f**.
Ps 119:45 I will walk in **f**, / for I have devoted myself to your
Isa 43:3 Ethiopia, and Seba as a ransom for your **f**.
49:9 of darkness, 'Come out! I am giving you your **f**!'
Jer 34:8 with the people, proclaiming **f** for the slaves.
Ac 24:23 but to give him some **f** and allow his friends to
Ro 8:21 it will join God's children in glorious **f** from death
8:24 we are saved, we eagerly look forward to this **f**.
1Co 1:30 and holy, and he gave himself to purchase our **f**.
8:9 But you must be careful with this **f** of yours.
9:1 Do I not have as much **f** as anyone else? Am I not
10:29 why should my **f** be limited by what someone else
2Co 3:17 and wherever the Spirit of the Lord is, he gives **f**.
Gal 2:4 came to spy on us and see our **f** in Christ Jesus.
4:5 God sent him to buy **f** for us who were slaves to
4:12 I plead with you to live as I do in **f** from these
5:8 isn't God, for he is the one who called you to **f**.
5:13 called to live in **f**—not **f** to satisfy your sinful nature, but **f** to serve one another in love.
Eph 1:7 so rich in kindness that he purchased our **f** through
Col 1:14 God has purchased our **f** with his blood and has
1Ti 2:6 He gave his life to purchase **f** for everyone. This is
1Pe 2:16 you are free. But your **f** is not an excuse to do evil.
2Pe 2:19 They promise **f**, but they themselves are slaves to

FREEING (1) [FREE]
Ps 34:4 and he answered me, / **f** me from all my fears.

FREELY (17) [FREE]
Ge 2:16 "You may **f** eat any fruit in the garden
43:34 So they all feasted and drank **f** with him.
45:15 over them, and then they began talking **f** with him.
Dt 15:10 Give **f** without begrudging it, and the LORD your
15:11 you to share your resources **f** with the poor
Jdg 9:27 in the temple of the local god, the wine flowed **f**,
1Sa 14:30 If the men had been allowed to eat **f** from the food
1Ch 29:9 for they had given **f** and wholeheartedly to the
Ezr 7:15 which we are **f** presenting as an offering to the God
Job 10:1 "I am disgusted with my life. Let me complain **f**.
Ps 34:22 Everyone who trusts in him will be **f** pardoned.
112:5 who lend **f** and conduct their business fairly.
Pr 11:24 It is possible to give **f** and become more wealthy,
Isa 19:23 and Assyrians will move **f** between their lands,
Jer 50:7 enemies said, 'We are allowed to attack them **f**,
Mt 10:8 cast out demons. Give as **f** as you have received!
1Co 2:12 so we can know the wonderful things God has **f**

FREEMAN [KJV] See FREE

FREES (1) [FREE]
Ps 146:7 food to the hungry. / The LORD **f** the prisoners.

FREEWILL (16) [FREE, WILL]
FREEWILL OFFERING (8) Lev 7:16; 22:18,21,23; Nu 15:3; Dt 16:10; Ezr 1:4; 8:28

FREEWILL OFFERINGS (8) Lev 23:38; Nu 29:39; Dt 12:6,17; 2Ch 31:14; Ezr 1:6; 3:5; 7:16

Lev 7:16 bring an offering to fulfill a vow or as a **f** offering,
22:18 whether to fulfill a vow or as a **f** offering,
22:21 or flock, whether to fulfill a vow or as a **f** offering,
22:23 or stunted, it may still be offered as a **f** offering,
23:38 and any **f** offerings that you present to the LORD.
Nu 15:3 a sacrifice to fulfill a vow, a **f** offering,
29:39 or as **f** offerings, burnt offerings, grain offerings,
Dt 12:6 your offerings to fulfill a vow, your **f** offerings,
12:17 a vow, nor your **f** offerings, nor your special gifts.
16:10 Bring him a **f** offering in proportion to the
2Ch 31:14 was put in charge of distributing the **f** offerings of
Ezr 1:4 as well as a **f** offering for the Temple of God in
1:6 many choice gifts in addition to all the **f** offerings.
3:5 **F** offerings were also sacrificed to the LORD by
7:16 as well as the **f** offerings of the people
8:28 This silver and gold is a **f** offering to the LORD,

FREEWOMAN [KJV] See FREEBORN

FREEZES (1) [FREEZING]
Job 38:30 ice as hard as rock, and the surface of the water **f**.

FREEZING (2) [FREEZES]
Job 37:10 breath sends the ice, **f** wide expanses of water.
Ps 147:17 hail like stones. / Who can stand against his **f** cold?

FREQUENT (1) [FREQUENTED]
1Co 7:31 Those in **f** contact with the things of the world

FREQUENTED (1) [FREQUENT]
Ecc 8:10 How strange that they were the very ones who **f**

FRESH (28) [AFRESH, FRESHLY]
Ge 3:6 The fruit looked so **f** and delicious, and it would
8:11 the bird returned to him with a **f** olive leaf in its
19:3 complete with **f** bread made without yeast.
30:37 Now Jacob took **f** shoots from poplar, almond,
Lev 6:12 Each morning the priest will add **f** wood to the fire
11:9 whether taken from **f** water or salt water.
14:5 over a clay pot that is filled with **f** springwater.
14:48 areas have not reappeared after the **f** plastering,
14:50 over a clay pot that is filled with **f** springwater.
15:13 must wash his clothes and bathe in **f** springwater.
23:14 or **f** kernels on that day until after you have
Nu 6:3 not drink other fermented drinks or **f** grape juice,
19:17 offering in a jar and pour **f** water over them.
1Sa 21:6 It had just been replaced that day with **f** bread.
2Ki 4:42 brought the man of God a sack of **f** grain
Job 10:17 of anger upon me and bring **f** armies against me.
Isa 29:19 The humble will be filled with **f** joy from the
Jer 24:2 One basket was filled with **f**, ripe figs,
37:21 **f** bread every day as long as there was any left in
Eze 47:8 waters of the Dead Sea and make them **f** and pure.
Da 4:12 It had **f** green leaves, and it was loaded with fruit
4:21 It had **f** green leaves, and it was loaded with fruit
Hos 9:10 it was like finding **f** grapes in the desert!
Mt 22:34 they thought up a **f** question of their own to ask
Lk 5:39 no one who drinks the old wine seems to want the **f**
Jas 3:11 Does a spring of water bubble out with both **f**
3:12 and you can't draw **f** water from a salty pool.
Rev 22:2 twelve crops of fruit, with a **f** crop each month.

FRESHLY (3) [FRESH]
Ge 27:17 with its rich aroma, and some **f** baked bread.
SS 6:6 Your teeth are white like **f** washed ewes,
Isa 1:18 I can make you as clean as **f** fallen snow.

FRET (2)
Ps 37:7 who prosper / or **f** about their wicked schemes.
Pr 24:19 Do not **f** because of evildoers; don't envy the

FRIDAY (3)
Ne 13:19 should be shut as darkness fell every **F** evening,
Mk 15:42 This all happened on **F**, the day of preparation,
Lk 23:54 This was done late on **F** afternoon, the day of

FRIEND (69) [FRIEND'S, FRIENDLY, FRIENDS, FRIENDSHIP]
Ge 38:12 and his **f** Hirah the Adullamite went to Timnah to
38:20 Judah asked his **f** Hirah the Adullamite to take the
Ex 33:11 to Moses face to face, as a man speaks to his **f**.
33:17 you have found favor with me, and you are my **f**."
Dt 13:6 or closest **f** comes to you secretly and says,
Jos 5:13 went up to him and asked, "Are you **f** or foe?"
Jdg 7:13 Gideon crept up just as a man was telling his **f**
7:14 His **f** said, "Your dream can mean only one thing
Ru 4:1 Boaz called out to him, "Come over here, **f**.
1Sa 18:3 And Jonathan made a special vow to be David's **f**,
20:8 Show me this kindness as my sworn **f**—for we
2Sa 13:3 Now Amnon had a very crafty **f**—his cousin
15:37 So David's **f** Hushai returned to Jerusalem,
16:16 When David's **f** Hushai the Arkite arrived, he went
16:17 "Is this the way you treat your **f** David?"
1Ki 5:1 King Hiram of Tyre had always been a loyal **f** of
1Ch 27:33 royal adviser. Hushai the Arkite was the king's **f**.
2Ch 20:7 forever to the descendants of your **f** Abraham?
Est 10:3 and was a **f** at the royal court for all of them.
Job 6:14 "One should be kind to a fainting **f**, but you have
6:27 would even send an orphan into slavery or sell a **f**.
22:6 you must have lent money to your **f** and then kept
Ps 7:4 if I have betrayed a **f** / or plundered my enemy
41:9 Even my best **f**, the one I trusted completely,
55:13 it is you—my equal, / my companion and close **f**.
55:20 As for this **f** of mine, he betrayed me; / he broke
119:63 Anyone who fears you is my **f**— / anyone who
Pr 6:1 if you co-sign a loan for a **f** or guarantee the debt
17:17 A **f** is always loyal, and a brother is born to help in
18:19 It's harder to make amends with an offended **f** than
18:24 each other, but a real **f** sticks closer than a brother.
19:6 everyone is the **f** of a person who gives gifts!
22:11 a pure heart and gracious speech is the king's **f**.
26:19 is someone who lies to a **f** and then says, "I was
27:6 Wounds from a **f** are better than many kisses from
27:9 The heartfelt counsel of a **f** is as sweet as perfume
27:10 Never abandon a **f**—either yours or your father's.
27:17 As iron sharpens iron, a **f** sharpens a **f**.
Ecc 7:9 be quick-tempered, for anger is the **f** of fools.
SS 5:16 O women of Jerusalem, is my lover, my **f**."
Isa 41:8 my chosen one, descended from my **f** Abraham,
Mic 7:5 trust anyone—not your best **f** or even your wife!
Mt 5:22 If you say to your **f**, 'You idiot,' you are in danger
7:4 How can you think of saying, '**F**, let me help you
11:19 a drunkard, and a **f** of the worst sort of sinners!'
20:13 answered one of them, '**F**, I haven't been unfair!
22:12 '**F**,' he asked, 'how is it that you are here without
26:50 "My **f**, go ahead and do what you have come for."
Lk 6:42 How can you think of saying, '**F**, let me help you
7:34 a drunkard, and a **f** of the worst sort of sinners!'
11:6 'A **f** of mine has just arrived for a visit, and I have
11:8 though he won't do it as a **f**, if you keep knocking
12:14 Jesus replied, "**F**, who made me a judge over you
12:19 And I'll sit back and say to myself, My **f**, you have
14:10 when your host sees you, he will come and say, '**F**,
22:21 "But here at this table, sitting among us as a **f**,
Jn 3:29 A bridegroom's **f** rejoices with him. I am the bridegroom's **f**, and I am filled with joy at
11:11 Then he said, "Our **f** Lazarus has fallen asleep,
19:12 "If you release this man, you are not a **f** of Caesar.
Ro 16:5 meets in their home. Greet my dear **f** Epenetus.
Phm 1:9 So take this as a request from your **f** Paul, an old
Jas 2:23 be righteous." He was even called "the **f** of God."
4:4 aim is to enjoy this world, you can't be a **f** of God.
3Jn 1:1 It is written to Gaius, my dear **f**, whom I love in
1:2 Dear **f**, I am praying that all is well with you
1:5 Dear **f**, you are doing a good work for God when
1:11 Dear **f**, don't let this bad example influence you.

FRIEND'S (7) [FRIEND]
Pr 6:3 You have placed yourself at your **f** mercy.
17:18 It is poor judgment to co-sign a **f** note, to become
Mt 7:3 And why worry about a speck in your **f** eye when
7:5 well enough to deal with the speck in your **f** eye.
Lk 6:41 "And why worry about a speck in your **f** eye when
6:42 well enough to deal with the speck in your **f** eye!
11:5 "Suppose you went to a **f** house at midnight,

FRIENDLY (9) [FRIEND]
Ge 26:27 "This is obviously no **f** visit, since you sent me
32:5 of my coming, hoping that you will be **f** to us.' "
32:20 "Perhaps," Jacob hoped, "he will be **f** to us."
33:10 "for what a relief it is to see your **f** smile.
Jdg 4:17 because Heber's family was on **f** terms with King
Ne 13:2 For they had not been **f** to the Israelites when they
Ps 28:3 those who speak **f** words to their neighbors
62:4 They are **f** to my face, / but they curse me in their
Heb 11:31 For she had given a **f** welcome to the spies.

FRIENDS (181) [FRIEND]
Ge 23:15 pieces of silver, but what is that between **f**?
34:21 "Those men are our **f**," they said. "Let's invite
Ex 32:27 killing even your brothers, **f**, and neighbors."
Jdg 11:37 in the hills and weep with my **f** for two months,
11:38 She and her **f** went into the hills and wept
1Sa 11:13 When his **f** heard about it, they exclaimed, "What?
18:1 love between them, and they became the best of **f**.
30:26 the plunder to the leaders of Judah, who were his **f**.
1Ki 16:11 He even destroyed distant relatives and **f**.
2Ki 4:3 as many empty jars as you can from your **f**
9:2 Call him into a back room away from his **f**,
10:11 all his important officials, personal **f**, and priests.
1Ch 12:17 "If you have come in peace to help me, we are **f**.
Ne 4:2 saying in front of his **f** and the Samarian army
4:14 who is great and glorious, and fight for your **f**,
Est 5:10 Then he gathered together his **f** and Zeresh,
5:14 So Haman's wife, Zeresh, and all his **f** suggested,
6:13 Zeresh, and all his **f** what had happened, they said,
Job 2:11 Three of Job's **f** were Eliphaz the Temanite,
12:4 Yet my **f** laugh at me. I am a man who calls on
16:20 My **f** scorn me, but I pour out my tears to God.
16:21 and me, as a person mediates between **f**.
19:13 stay far away, and my **f** have turned against me.
19:14 My neighbors and my close **f** are all gone.
19:19 My close **f** abhor me. Those I loved have turned
19:21 "Have mercy on me, my **f**, have mercy,
20:9 Neither his **f** nor his family will ever see him
32:1 Job's three **f** refused to reply further to him
32:3 He was also angry with Job's three **f** because they
33:27 He will declare to his **f**, 'I sinned, but it was not
35:4 "I will answer you and all your **f**, too.
42:7 "I am angry with you and with your two **f**, for you
42:10 When Job prayed for his **f**, the LORD restored his
42:11 and former **f** came and feasted with him in his
Ps 15:3 or harm their neighbors / or speak evil of their **f**.
31:11 even my **f** are afraid to come near me.
35:14 I was sad, as though they were my **f** or family,

38:11 My loved ones and f stay away, fearing my
41: 6 They visit me as if they are my f, / but all the while
88: 8 You have caused my f to loathe me; / you have
122: 8 For the sake of my family and f, I will say,
Pr 6:13 signaling their true intentions to their f by making
11: 9 Evil words destroy one's f; wise discernment
12:26 The godly give good advice to their f; the wicked
14:20 by their neighbors, while the rich have many "f."
16:28 plants seeds of strife; gossip separates the best of f.
17: 9 telling about them separates close f.
18:19 Arguments separate f like a gate locked with iron
18:24 There are "f" who destroy each other, but a real
19: 4 Wealth makes many "f"; poverty drives them
19: 7 how much more will their f avoid them.
20: 6 Many will say they are loyal f, but who can find
Isa 38:11 the land of the living. / Never again will I see my f
47:15 And all your f, those with whom you have done
Jer 2:36 But your new f in Egypt will let you down, just as
6:21 Neighbors and f will collapse together."
16: 6 Their f will not cut themselves or shave their heads
19: 9 will have to eat their own sons and daughters and f.
20: 4 I will send terror upon you and all your f, and you
20: 6 and all your f to whom you promised that
20:10 Even my old f are watching me, waiting for a fatal
22:22 All your f have been taken away as captives.
38:22 will taunt you, saying, 'What fine f you have!
48:17 "You f of Moab, weep for her and cry! See how
La 1: 2 All her f have betrayed her; they are now her
Eze 24:17 or accept any food brought to you by consoling f."
24:22 by eating the food brought to you by sympathetic f.
Da 1:15 Daniel and his three f looked healthier and better
2:13 men were sent to find and kill Daniel and his f.
2:17 Then Daniel went home and told his f Hananiah,
Ob 1: 7 Your trusted f will set traps for you, and you won't
Zec 13: 6 he will say, 'I was wounded at the home of f!'
Mt 5:47 If you are kind only to your f, how are you
11:16 in the public square. They complain to their f,
Mk 5:19 But Jesus said, "No, go home to your f, and tell
Lk 1:59 and f came for the circumcision ceremony.
2:44 because they assumed he was with f among the
2:44 started to look for him among their relatives and f.
6: 4 for the priests alone, and then gave some to his f.
7: 6 at the house, the officer sent some f to say, "Lord,
7:10 And when the officer's f returned to his house,
7:32 They complain to their f, 'We played wedding
12: 4 "Dear f, don't be afraid of those who want to kill
14:12 he said, "don't invite your f, brothers, relatives,
15: 6 you would call together your f and neighbors to
15: 9 she will call in her f and neighbors to rejoice with
15:29 gave me even one young goat for a feast with my f.
16: 4 then I'll have plenty of f to take care of me when I
16: 9 worldly resources to benefit others and make f.
21:16 your parents, brothers, relatives, and f—will betray
22:25 and yet they are called 'f of the people.'
23:12 who had been enemies before, became f that day.
23:49 But Jesus' f, including the women who had
Jn 15:13 shown when people lay down their lives for their f.
15:14 You are my f if you obey me.
15:15 Now you are my f, since I have told you
21: 5 He called out, "F, have you caught any fish?"
Ac 3:17 "F, I realize that what you did to Jesus was done
5:17 The high priest and his f, who were Sadducees,
6: 3 "Now look around among yourselves, f, and select
9:37 Her f prepared her for burial and laid her in an
10:24 together his relatives and close f to meet Peter.
12:20 They made f with Blastus, Herod's personal
14:15 "F, why are you doing this? We are merely human
19:31 the province, f of Paul, also sent a message to him,
24:23 and allow his f to visit him and take care of his
27: 3 kind to Paul and let him go ashore to visit with f
Ro 1: 7 dear f in Rome. God loves you dearly, and he has
1:13 I want you to know, dear f, that I planned many
5:11 Jesus Christ has done for us in making us f of God.
7: 1 Now, dear f—you who are familiar with the law—
7: 4 So then, dear f, the point is this: The law no longer
8:12 So, dear Christian f, you have no obligation
10: 1 Dear f, the longing of my heart and my prayer to
11:25 dear f, so that you will not feel proud and start
12: 1 And so, dear Christian f, I plead with you to give
12:19 Dear f, never avenge yourselves. Leave that to
15:14 I am fully convinced, dear f, that you are full of
15:30 Dear f, I urge you in the name of our Lord Jesus
1Co 1:11 have told me about your arguments, dear f.
10:14 So, my dear f, flee from the worship of idols.
11: 2 I am so glad, dear f, that you always keep me in
15:31 For I swear, dear f, I face death daily. This is as
2Co 1: 8 I think you ought to know, dear f, about the trouble
6:11 Oh, dear Corinthian f! We have spoken honestly
7: 1 Because we have these promises, dear f, let us
8: 1 Now I want to tell you, dear f, what God in his
9: 2 and I have been boasting to our f in Macedonia
12:19 Everything we do, dear f, is for your benefit.
13:11 Dear f, I close my letter with these last words:
Gal 1:11 Dear f, I solemnly assure you that the Good News
2:12 But afterward, when some Jewish f of James came,
3:15 Dear f, here's an example from everyday life.
4:12 Dear f, I plead with you to live as I do in freedom
4:31 So, dear f, we are not children of the slave woman,
5:11 Dear f, if I were still preaching that you must be
5:13 For you, dear f, have been called to live in
6: 1 Dear f, if a Christian is overcome by some sin,
6:18 My dear Christian f, may the grace of our Lord
Eph 6:23 dear f, and love with faith, from God the Father
Php 1:12 And I want you to know, dear f, that everything
2:12 Dearest f, you were always so careful to follow my
3: 1 Whatever happens, dear f, may the Lord give you
3:13 No, dear f, I am still not all I should be, but I am
3:17 Dear f, pattern your lives after mine, and learn
4: 1 So please stay true to the Lord, my dear f.
4: 8 And now, dear f, let me say one more thing as I
Col 1:22 yet now he has brought you back as his f. He has
2: 1 and for many other f who have never known me
1Th 2: 5 that we were not just pretending to be your f
2:17 Dear f, after we were separated from you for a
3: 7 dear f, in all of our own crushing troubles
4:10 Even so, dear f, we beg you to love them more
2Ti 3: 4 They will betray their f, be reckless, be puffed up
Heb 3: 1 dear f who belong to God and are bound for
3:12 Be careful then, dear f. Make sure that your own
6: 9 Dear f, even though we are talking like this,
10:19 And so, dear f, we can boldly enter heaven's Most
10:26 Dear f, if we deliberately continue sinning after we
13:22 I urge you, dear f, please listen carefully to what I
Jas 1:19 Dear f, be quick to listen, slow to speak, and slow
1Pe 4: 4 your former f are very surprised when you no
4:12 Dear f, don't be surprised at the fiery trials you are
2Pe 1:10 So, dear f, work hard to prove that you really are
3: 1 This is my second letter to you, dear f, and in both
3: 8 But you must not forget, dear f, that a day is like a
3:14 And so, dear f, while you are waiting for these
3:17 dear f, so that you can watch out and not be carried
1Jn 2: 7 Dear f, I am not writing a new commandment,
3: 2 Yes, dear f, we are already God's children, and we
3:16 also ought to give up our lives for our Christian f.
3:21 Dear f, if our conscience is clear, we can come to
4: 1 Dear f, do not believe everyone who claims to
4: 7 Dear f, let us continue to love one another, for love
4:11 Dear f, since God loved us that much, we surely
3Jn 1:15 be with you. Your f here send you their greetings.
1:15 Please give my personal greetings to each of our f
Jude 1: 3 Dearly loved f, I had been eagerly planning to
1:17 But you, my dear f, must remember what the
1:20 But you, dear f, must continue to build your lives
Rev 3:20 I will come in, and we will share a meal as f.

FRIENDSHIP (11) [FRIEND]

1Sa 19: 1 But Jonathan, because of his close f with David,
20: 3 "Your father knows perfectly well about our f,
20:17 And Jonathan made David reaffirm his vow of f
23:18 So the two of them renewed their covenant of f
Job 29: 4 my early years, the f of God was felt in my home.
Ps 25:14 F with the LORD is reserved for those who fear
Pr 3:32 to the LORD, but he offers his f to the godly.
Ro 5:10 For since we were restored to f with God by the
1Co 1: 9 who invited you into this wonderful f with his Son,
Jas 4: 4 Don't you realize that f with this world makes you
3Jn 1: 6 They have told the church here of your f and your

FRIGHT (6) [FEAR]

1Sa 17:24 army saw him, they began to run away in f.
28:20 paralyzed with f because of Samuel's words.
Est 7: 6 Haman grew pale with f before the king and queen.
Jer 6:24 reports about the enemy, and we are weak with f.
50:43 reports about the enemy, and he is weak with f.
Joel 2: 6 grips all the people; every face grows pale with f.

FRIGHTEN (5) [FEAR]

Dt 20: 8 If you are, go home before you f anyone else.'
Ezr 4: 4 and f the people of Judah to keep them from their
Ro 13: 3 For the authorities do not f people who are doing right, but they f those who do wrong.
2Co 10: 9 Now this is not just an attempt to f you by my

FRIGHTENED (22) [FEAR]

Ge 43:18 They were badly f when they saw where they were
Ex 2:14 Moses was badly f because he realized that
Jos 14: 8 but my brothers who went with me f the people
1Sa 7: 7 The Israelites were badly f when they learned that
Ne 2: 2 a man with deep troubles." Then I was badly f,
6:16 nations heard about it, they were f and humiliated.
Isa 31: 4 and fight on Mount Zion. He will not be f away!
Jer 36:16 Baruch had finished reading, they were badly f.
48:41 Even the mightiest warriors will be as f as a
49:22 Even the mightiest warriors will be as f as a
Da 4: 5 But one night I had a dream that greatly f me;
Mt 28: 8 They were very f but also filled with great joy,
Mk 5:15 but they were f when they saw the man who had
5:33 Then the f woman, trembling at the realization of
16: 8 nothing to anyone because they were too f to talk.
Lk 1:30 "Don't be f, Mary," the angel told her, "for God
2: 9 glory surrounded them. They were terribly f,
24:37 But the whole group was terribly f, thinking they
24:38 "Why are you f?" he asked. "Why do you doubt
Jn 19: 8 When Pilate heard this, he was more f than ever.
Ac 22:29 and the commander was f because he had ordered
Heb 12:21 Moses himself was so f at the sight that he said,

FRIGHTENING (2) [FEAR]

Job 30: 6 So now they live in f ravines and in caves
Da 2:31 statue of a man, shining brilliantly, f and awesome.

FRINGE (5)

Mt 9:20 came up behind him. She touched the f of his robe,
14:36 The sick begged him to let them touch even the f
Mk 5:27 through the crowd and touched the f of his robe.
6:56 The sick begged him to let them at least touch the f
Lk 8:44 up behind Jesus and touched the f of his robe.

FRISK (1) [FRISKING]

Jer 50:11 You f about like a calf in a meadow and neigh like

FRISKING (2) [FRISK]

SS 4: 1 like flocks of goats f across the slopes of Gilead.
6: 5 is like a flock of goats f down the slopes of Gilead.

FRO (1)

Eze 1:14 beings darted to and f like flashes of lightning.

FROGS (15)

Ex 8: 2 I will send vast hordes of f across your entire land
8: 4 and your people will be overwhelmed by f!'"
8: 5 so there will be f in every corner of the land."
8: 6 did so, and f covered the whole land of Egypt!
8: 7 They, too, caused f to come up on the land.
8: 8 "Plead with the LORD to take the f away from
8: 9 pray that you and your houses will be rid of the f.
8: 9 Then only the f in the Nile River will remain
8:11 All the f will be destroyed, except those in the
8:12 and Moses pleaded with the LORD about the f he
8:13 The f in the houses, the courtyards, and the fields
8:15 But when Pharaoh saw that the f were gone,
Ps 78:45 to consume them / and hordes of f to ruin them.
105:30 Then f overran the land; / they were found even in
Rev 16:13 And I saw three evil spirits that looked like f leap

FROM (5218) See Index of Articles, Etc.

FRONDS (1)

Lev 23:40 and collect palm f and other leafy branches

FRONT (157) [FRONTS]

Ge 30:39 So when the flocks mated in f of the
30:41 Jacob set up the peeled branches in f of them.
31:18 He drove the flocks in f of him—all the livestock
31:37 Set it out here in f of us, before our relatives,
33: 2 with his two concubines and their children at the f,
40: 9 "In my dream," he said, "I saw a vine in f of me.
45: 3 realize that Joseph was standing there in f of them.
Ex 18:13 They were lined up in f of him from morning till
28: 7 It will consist of two pieces, f and back, joined at
28:37 This medallion will be attached to the f of Aaron's
30:36 and put some of it in f of the Ark of the Covenant,
32: 5 he built an altar in f of the calf and announced,
32:15 They were inscribed on both sides, f and back.
34: 6 He passed in f of Moses and said, "I am the
39:30 of pure gold to be worn on the f of the turban.
40: 6 Place the altar of burnt offering in f of the
40:26 in the Holy Place in f of the inner curtain.
Lev 1: 5 sides of the altar that stands in f of the Tabernacle.
4: 6 and sprinkle it seven times before the LORD in f
4:17 and sprinkle it seven times before the LORD in f
6:14 present this offering to the LORD in f of the altar.
8: 9 head the turban with the gold medallion at its f,
13:42 if a reddish white infection appears on the f
16:14 and sprinkle it on the f of the atonement cover
16:14 and then seven times against the f of the Ark.
16:15 the atonement cover and against the f of the Ark,
Nu 3:38 The area in f of the Tabernacle in the east toward
7: 3 They presented these to the LORD in f of the
8:13 Then have the Levites stand in f of Aaron and his
11:10 Moses heard all the families standing in f of their
17: 4 Put these staffs in the Tabernacle in f of the Ark of
18: 2 and your sons as you perform the sacred duties in f
19: 4 and sprinkle it seven times toward the f of the
Dt 1:21 He has placed it in f of you. Go and occupy it as
Jos 4: 5 in f of the Ark of the LORD your God.
6: 6 and assign seven priests to walk in f of it,
6: 7 and the armed men will lead the way in f of the
6: 9 Armed guards marched both in f of the priests
6:13 horns marched in f of the Ark of the LORD,
6:13 Armed guards marched both in f of the priests with
8:29 down the body and threw it in f of the city gate.
10:12 Joshua prayed to the LORD in f of all the people
22:29 f of the Tabernacle may be used for that purpose."
Jdg 18:21 livestock, and possessions in f of them.
1Sa 5: 3 Dagon had fallen with his face to the ground in f of
14: 5 The cliff on the north was in f of Micmash,
14: 5 and the one on the south was in f of Geba.
14:18 For at that time Ahijah was wearing the ephod in f
16: 8 Abinadab to step forward and walk in f of Samuel.
17:16 the Philistine giant strutted in f of the Israelite
2Sa 6: 4 with the Ark of God on it, with Ahio walking in f.
11:15 "Station Uriah on the f lines where the battle is
14: 4 she fell with her face down to the floor in f of him
1Ki 1: 5 and recruited fifty men to run in f of him.
6: 3 The foyer at the f of the Temple was 30 feet wide,
6: 3 It projected outward 15 feet from the f of the
7: 6 There was a porch at its f, covered by a canopy
7:49 in f of the Most Holy Place, the flower decorations,
8: 8 so long that their ends could be seen from the f
8:22 the LORD in f of the entire community of Israel.
8:31 and is required to take an oath of innocence in f of
8:54 he stood up in f of the altar of the LORD,
8:64 area of the courtyard in f of the LORD's Temple.
18:21 Then Elijah stood in f of them and said,
22:10 All of Ahab's prophets were prophesying there in f
2Ki 11:18 and they killed Mattan the priest of Baal in f of the
16:14 bronze altar from the f of the LORD's Temple,
1Ch 15:24 trumpets as they marched in f of the Ark of God.
2Ch 1: 5 and grandson of Hur was still at Gibeon in f of the
1: 5 and the people gathered in f of it to consult the
1: 6 There in f of the Tabernacle, Solomon went up to
3: 4 The foyer at the f of the Temple was thirty feet
3:15 For the f of the Temple, Solomon made two pillars
4:20 and their lamps of pure gold to burn in f of the

5: 9 so long that their ends could be seen from the **f**
6:12 the LORD in **f** of the entire community of Israel.
6:22 and is required to take an oath of innocence in **f** of
7: 7 then dedicated the central area of the courtyard in **f**
8:12 altar he had built in **f** of the foyer of the Temple.
13:14 realized that they were being attacked from the **f**
15: 8 which stood in **f** of the foyer of the LORD's
18: 9 All of Ahab's prophets were prophesying there in **f**
20: 5 and Jerusalem in **f** of the new courtyard at the
23:17 and they killed Mattan the priest of Baal in **f** of the
25:14 up as his own gods, bowed down in **f** of them,
29:19 They are now in **f** of the altar of the LORD,
Ezr 10: 1 and throwing himself to the ground in **f** of the
10: 6 Then Ezra left the **f** of the Temple of God and went
Ne 4: 2 saying in **f** of his friends and the Samarian army
7: 3 regular posts and some in **f** of their own homes."
Est 4: 6 So Hathach went out to Mordecai in the square in **f**
Ps 34: T regarding the time he pretended to be insane in **f** of
35:18 Then I will thank you in **f** of the entire
57: 9 I will thank you, Lord, in **f** of all the people.
68:25 Singers are in **f**, musicians are behind; / with them
108: 3 I will thank you, LORD, in **f** of all the people.
Pr 1:21 along the main street, and to those in **f** of city hall.
21:29 The wicked put up a bold **f**, but the upright proceed
Ecc 6: 8 being wise and knowing how to act in **f** of others?
Isa 44:17 He falls down in **f** of it, worshiping and praying to
45:14 They will fall to their knees in **f** of you and say,
65: 6 "Look, my decree is written out in **f** of me: I will
Jer 1:17 or I will make you look foolish in **f** of them.
19:14 and he stopped in **f** of the Temple of the LORD.
24: 1 I saw two baskets of figs placed in **f** of the
26: 2 "Stand out in **f** of the Temple of the LORD,
26: 7 Jeremiah as he spoke in **f** of the LORD's Temple.
26: 9 And all the people threatened him as he stood in **f**
27:19 says about the bronze pillars in **f** of the Temple,
28: 5 Jeremiah responded to Hananiah as they stood in **f**
36:22 of the palace, sitting in **f** of a fire to keep warm.
Eze 1:10 Each had a human face in the **f**, the face of a lion
4: 1 take a large brick and set it down in **f** of you.
6: 4 I will kill your people in **f** of your idols.
6: 5 I will lay your corpses in **f** of your idols and scatter
16:37 and I will strip you naked in **f** of them so they can
16:41 your homes and punish you in **f** of many women.
20: 1 They sat down in **f** of me to wait for his reply.
23:39 that they murdered their children in **f** of their idols,
40:12 In **f** of each of the guard alcoves was a 21-inch
40:47 The altar stood there in the courtyard in **f** of the
41:25 And there was a wooden canopy over the **f** of the
42: 5 had to allow space for walkways in **f** of them.
44: 4 through the north gateway to the **f** of the Temple.
46: 3 The common people will worship the LORD in **f**
Da 2:31 in your vision you saw in **f** of you a huge
8: 3 I saw in **f** of me a ram with two long horns
8:15 who looked like a man suddenly stood in **f** of me.
10:16 I said to the one standing in **f** of me, "I am
Hos 9: 8 yet traps are laid in **f** of him wherever he goes.
10:11 I will drive her in **f** of the plow. Israel and Judah
Joel 2: 3 Fire burns in **f** of them and follows them in every
2:20 those at the **f** will go into the Mediterranean.
Hab 1:16 worship their nets and burn incense in **f** of them.
Zec 14: 1 possessions will be plundered right in **f** of you!
Mt 14: 9 because he didn't want to back down in **f** of his
26:70 But Peter denied it in **f** of everyone. "I don't know
Mk 1:40 A man with leprosy came and knelt in **f** of Jesus,
2: 4 the sick man on his mat, right down in **f** of Jesus.
3: 3 to the man, "Come and stand in **f** of everyone."
3:11 they would fall down in **f** of him shrieking,
6:26 but he was embarrassed to break his oath in **f** of his
15:46 Then he rolled a stone in **f** of the entrance.
Lk 5:19 into the crowd, still on his mat, right in **f** of Jesus.
14:10 Then you will be honored in **f** of all the other
Jn 8: 3 the act of adultery. They put her in **f** of the crowd.
Ac 10:30 a man in dazzling clothes was standing in **f** of me.
1Co 6: 6 Christian sues another—right in **f** of unbelievers!
Gal 2:14 I said to Peter in **f** of all the others, "Since you,
1Ti 5:20 Anyone who sins should be rebuked in **f** of the
Rev 4: 5 And in **f** of the throne were seven lampstands with
4: 6 In **f** of the throne was a shiny sea of glass,
4: 6 living beings, each covered with eyes, **f** and back.
7: 9 standing in **f** of the throne and before the Lamb.
7:15 That is why they are standing in **f** of the throne of
7:17 For the Lamb who stands in **f** of the throne will be
14: 3 This great choir sang a wonderful new song in **f** of

FRONTIER (2) [FRONTIERS]

Dt 3:16 all the way to the Jabbok River on the Ammonite **f**.
Eze 25: 9 eastern flank and wipe out their glorious **f** cities—

FRONTIERS (1) [FRONTIER]

Dt 11:24 Your **f** will stretch from the wilderness in the south

FRONTS (3) [FRONT]

2Sa 10: 9 Joab saw that he would have to fight on two **f**,
1Ki 7:50 of the Temple, with their **f** overlaid with gold.
1Ch 19:10 Joab saw that he would have to fight on two **f**,

FROST (3) [FROSTY]

Ex 16:14 thin flakes, white like **f**, covered the ground.
Job 38:29 the ice? Who gives birth to the **f** from the heavens?
Ps 147:16 he scatters **f** upon the ground like ashes.

FROSTY (1) [FROST]

Jer 36:30 to lie unburied—exposed to hot days and **f** nights.

FROTH (1)

Isa 40:17 they are less than nothing—mere emptiness and **f**.

FROWARD [KJV] See also CROOKED, HARSH, PERVERSE, TWISTED

FROWN (1)

Ps 80:16 May they perish at the sight of your **f**.

FRUIT (130) [FIRSTFRUITS, FRUITFUL, FRUITFULNESS, FRUITS]

Ge 1:11 And let there be trees that grow seed-bearing **f**.
1:29 the earth and all the **f** trees for your food.
2: 9 beautiful trees that produced delicious **f**.
2:16 "You may freely eat any **f** in the garden
2:17 except **f** from the tree of the knowledge of good and evil. If you eat of its **f**, you will surely die."
3: 1 "Did God really say you must not eat any of the **f**
3: 3 "It's only the **f** from the tree at the center of the
3: 6 The **f** looked so fresh and delicious, and it would make her so wise! So she ate some of the **f**.
3:11 "Have you eaten the **f** I commanded you not to
3:12 the woman you gave me who brought me the **f**,
3:17 to your wife and ate the **f** I told you not to eat,
3:22 and evil. What if they eat the **f** of the tree of life?
Ex 10:15 and all the **f** on the trees that had survived the
Lev 19:23 "When you enter the land and plant **f** trees,
19:23 leave the **f** unharvested for the first three years
19:25 Finally, in the fifth year you may eat the **f**. In this
23:40 On the first day, gather **f** from citrus trees,
26: 4 yield its crops, and the trees will produce their **f**.
26:20 will yield no crops, and your trees will bear no **f**.
27:30 whether grain or **f**, belongs to the LORD
27:31 If you want to redeem the LORD's tenth of the **f**
Nu 13:26 and showed them the **f** they had taken from the
13:27 with milk and honey. Here is some of its **f** as proof.
Dt 1:25 They picked some of its **f** and brought it back to
20: 6 planted a vineyard but not yet eaten any of its **f**?
20:19 the trees. Eat the **f**, but do not cut down the trees.
28: 5 will be blessed with baskets overflowing with **f**,
28:17 You will be cursed with baskets empty of **f**,
28:30 will plant a vineyard, but you will never enjoy its **f**.
28:40 for the trees will drop the **f** before it is ripe.
29:18 root among you would bear bitter and poisonous **f**.
Jdg 9:11 'Should I quit producing my sweet **f** just to wave
2Sa 16: 1 one hundred bunches of summer **f**, and a skin of
16: 2 and summer **f** are for the young men to eat.
2Ki 19:29 you will tend vineyards and eat their **f**.
Ne 10:35 it be a crop from the soil or from our **f** trees.
10:37 and other grain offerings, the best of our **f**,
Job 15:33 tree that sheds its blossoms so the **f** cannot form.
Ps 1: 3 the riverbank, / bearing **f** each season without fail.
72:16 May the **f** trees flourish as they do in Lebanon,
80:12 our walls / so that all who pass may steal our **f**?
92:14 Even in old age they will still produce **f**; / they will
104:13 and you fill the earth with the **f** of your labor.
128: 2 You will enjoy the **f** of your labor. / How happy
148: 9 mountains and all hills, / **f** trees and all cedars,
Pr 1:31 That is why they must eat the bitter **f** of living their
5:10 and someone else will enjoy the **f** of your labor.
11:30 The godly are like trees that bear life-giving **f**,
12:12 each other's loot, while the godly bear their own **f**.
27:18 Workers who tend a fig tree are allowed to eat its **f**.
Ecc 2: 5 and parks, filling them with all kinds of **f** trees.
SS 2: 3 in his delightful shade, and his **f** is delicious to eat.
4:13 You are like a lovely orchard bearing precious **f**,
Isa 4: 2 and the **f** of the land will be the pride of its people.
11: 1 yes, a new Branch bearing **f** from the old root.
27: 6 and blossom and fill the whole earth with her **f**!
32:10 For your **f** crop will fail, and the harvest will never
34: 4 just as withered leaves and **f** fall from a tree.
37:30 you will tend vineyards and eat their **f**.
55:11 my word. I send it out, and it always produces **f**.
65:21 they build and eat the **f** of their own vineyards.
Jer 6:19 It is the **f** of their own sin because they refuse to
8:13 of figs and grapes. Their **f** trees will all die.
11:16 olive tree, beautiful to see and full of good **f**.
17: 8 and they go right on producing delicious **f**.
29:28 He said we should plant **f** trees, because we will be here to eat the **f** for many years
Eze 17: 8 and produce rich leaves and luscious **f**.
17: 9 I will cut off its **f** and let its leaves wither and die.
19:12 The desert wind dried up its **f** / and tore off its
19:14 and devoured its **f**. / None of the remaining limbs
25: 4 They will harvest all your **f** and steal your
36: 8 crops of **f** to prepare for my people's return—
36:30 I will give you great harvests from your **f** trees
47:12 All kinds of **f** trees will grow along both sides of
47:12 and there will always be **f** on their branches.
47:12 The **f** will be for food and the leaves for healing."
Da 4:12 green leaves, and it was loaded with **f** for all to eat.
4:14 its branches! Shake off its leaves, and scatter its **f**!
4:21 green leaves, and it was loaded with **f** for all to eat.
Hos 2:12 where only wild animals will eat the **f**.
9:16 Their roots are dried up; they will bear no more **f**.
10: 1 Israel is—a luxuriant vine loaded with **f**!
10:13 You have eaten the **f** of lies—trusting in your
14: 8 giving my **f** to you all through the year."
Joel 1:12 apple trees—yes, all the **f** trees—have dried up.
2:22 The trees will again be filled with luscious **f**;
Am 2: 9 but I destroyed their **f** and dug out their roots.
6:12 and make bitter the sweet **f** of righteousness.
8: 1 In it I saw a basket filled with ripe **f**.
8: 2 he asked. I replied, "A basket full of ripe **f**."
8: 2 "This **f** represents my people of Israel—
Mic 7: 1 I feel like the **f** picker after the harvest who can
Zec 8:12 among you. The grapevines will be heavy with **f**.
Mt 3:10 every tree that does not produce good **f** will be
7:16 way they act, just as you can identify a tree by its **f**.
7:17 A healthy tree produces good **f**, and an unhealthy tree produces bad **f**.
7:18 A good tree can't produce bad **f**, and a bad tree can't produce good **f**.
7:19 So every tree that does not produce good **f** is
7:20 or a person is by the kind of **f** that is produced.
12:33 identified by its **f**. Make a tree good, and its **f** will be good. Make a tree bad, and its **f** will be bad.
21:19 Then he said to it, "May you never bear **f** again!"
21:43 and given to a nation that will produce the proper **f**.
Mk 11:13 because it was too early in the season for **f**.
11:14 to the tree, "May no one ever eat your **f** again!"
Lk 3: 9 every tree that does not produce good **f** will be
6:43 "A good tree can't produce bad **f**, and a bad tree can't produce good **f**.
6:44 A tree is identified by the kind of **f** it produces.
13: 6 and again to see if there was any **f** on it,
Jn 4:36 and the **f** they harvest is people brought to eternal
15: 2 He cuts off every branch that doesn't produce **f**,
15: 2 and he prunes the branches that do bear **f** so they
15: 4 For a branch cannot produce **f** if it is severed from
15: 5 remain in me, and I in them, will produce much **f**.
15: 8 My true disciples produce much **f**. This brings
15:16 I appointed you to go and produce **f** that will last,
Ro 7: 4 As a result, you can produce good **f**, that is,
Gal 5:22 our lives, he will produce this kind of **f** in us:
Php 1:11 May you always be filled with the **f** of your
2Ti 2: 6 Hardworking farmers are the first to enjoy the **f** of
Jude 1:12 They are like trees without **f** at harvesttime.
Rev 22: 2 bearing twelve crops of **f**, with a fresh crop each
22:14 gates of the city and eat the **f** from the tree of life.

FRUITFUL (16) [FRUIT]

Ge 41:52 "God has made me **f** in this land of my suffering."
49:22 "Joseph is a **f** tree, / a **f** tree beside a fountain.
Nu 24: 6 groves of palms, / like **f** gardens by the riverside.
Ps 72: 3 yield prosperity for all, / and may the hills be **f**,
107:34 He turns the **f** land into salty wastelands,
128: 3 Your wife will be like a **f** vine, / flourishing within
Isa 27: 3 the LORD, will watch over it and tend its **f** vines.
32:12 soon be gone, and for those **f** vines of other years.
Jer 2: 7 "And when I brought you into a **f** land to enjoy its
22: 6 "You are as beloved to me as **f** Gilead
23: 3 and they will be **f** and increase in number.
48:33 Joy and gladness are gone from **f** Moab.
Hos 13:15 Ephraim was the most **f** of all his brothers,
Jn 15: 4 from the vine, and you cannot be **f** apart from me.
Php 1:22 Yet if I live, that means **f** service for Christ. I really

FRUITFULNESS (1) [FRUITFUL]

Jn 15: 3 You have already been pruned for greater **f** by the

FRUITS (8) [FRUIT]

Ecc 2:18 I am disgusted that I must leave the **f** of my hard
3:13 should eat and drink and enjoy the **f** of their labor,
SS 4:16 him come into his garden and eat its choicest **f**."
7:13 and the rarest **f** are at our doors, the new as well as
Isa 16: 9 for their summer **f** and harvests have all been
Jer 40:10 Harvest the grapes and summer **f** and olives,
48:32 He has harvested your grapes and summer **f**.
Eze 44:30 The first of the ripe **f** and all the gifts brought to

FRUSTRATE (4) [FRUSTRATED, FRUSTRATES, FRUSTRATION]

2Sa 15:34 Then you can **f** and counter Ahithophel's advice.
2Ch 25: 8 for he has the power to help or to **f**."
Ezr 4: 5 agents to work against them and to **f** their aims.
Ps 14: 6 The wicked **f** the plans of the oppressed,

FRUSTRATED (3) [FRUSTRATE]

Ne 4:15 we knew of their plans and that God had **f** them,
Ps 78:41 God's patience / and **f** the Holy One of Israel.
Ecc 5:17 they live under a cloud—**f**, discouraged, and angry.

FRUSTRATES (2) [FRUSTRATE]

Job 5:12 He **f** the plans of the crafty, so their efforts will not
Ps 146: 9 and widows, / but he **f** the plans of the wicked.

FRUSTRATION (1) [FRUSTRATE]

Ge 37:29 was missing, he tore his clothes in anguish and **f**.

FRYING (1)

Jn 21: 9 a charcoal fire was burning and fish were **f** over it,

FRYINGPAN [KJV] See PAN

FUEL (11)

Jdg 6:26 using as **f** the wood of the Asherah pole you cut
Pr 26:20 Fire goes out for lack of **f**, and quarrels disappear
Isa 9:19 The people are **f** for the fire, and no one spares
40:16 All Lebanon's forests do not contain sufficient **f** to
Eze 4:12 bake it over a fire using dried human dung as **f**
15: 4 be used for **f**, and even as **f**, it burns too quickly.
21:32 You are **f** for the fire, and your blood will be
24: 5 the flock and heap **f** on the fire beneath the pot.
24: 9 I myself will pile up the **f** beneath her.
39: 9 javelins and spears, and they will use them for **f**.

FUGITIVE (3) [FUGITIVES]

Ge 4:12 From now on you will be a homeless **f** on the
4:14 your presence; you have made me a wandering **f**.
Jdg 12: 5 and whenever a **f** from Ephraim tried to go back

FUGITIVES (1) [FUGITIVE]

Isa 45:20 and come, you **f** from surrounding nations.

FULFILL (59) [FULFILLED, FULFILLING, FULFILLMENT, FULFILLS]

Lev 7:16 if you bring an offering to **f** a vow or as a freewill
22:18 whether to **f** a vow or as a freewill offering,
22:21 whether to **f** a vow or as a freewill offering,
22:23 but it may not be offered to **f** a vow.
26: 9 multiply your people and **f** my covenant with you.
Nu 6:21 they must **f** their special vow exactly as they have
15: 3 a sacrifice to **f** a vow, a freewill offering,
18: 4 The Levites must join with you to **f** their
30: 5 But if her father refuses to let her **f** the vow
30: 5 because her father would not let her **f** them.
30: 9 she must **f** all her vows and pledges no matter
Dt 8:18 and he does it to **f** the covenant he made with your
9: 5 and to **f** the oath he had sworn to your ancestors
12: 6 your special gifts, your offerings to **f** a vow,
12:11 your special gifts, and your offerings to **f** a vow—
12:17 your flocks and herds, nor an offering to **f** a vow,
12:26 and your offerings given to **f** a vow to the place the
23:21 God demands that you promptly **f** all your vows.
25: 5 must marry her and **f** the duties of a brother-in-law.
2Sa 13: 2 and it seemed impossible that he could ever **f** his
15: 9 the king told him. "Go and **f** your vow."
1Ki 6:12 I will **f** through you the promise I made to your
8:26 **f** this promise to your servant David, my father.
2Ch 6:17 God of Israel, **f** this promise to your servant David.
19:11 Take courage as you **f** your duties, and may the
Job 22:27 he will hear you, and you will **f** your vows to him.
Ps 20: 4 he grant your heart's desire / and **f** all your plans.
22:25 I will **f** my vows in the presence of those who
50:14 I want you to **f** your vows to the Most High.
56:12 I will **f** my vows to you, O God, / and offer a
57: 2 Most High, / to God who will **f** his purpose for me.
61: 8 to your name / as I **f** my vows day after day.
65: 1 to you in Zion. / We will **f** our vows to you,
66:13 burnt offerings / to **f** the vows I made to you—
76:11 Make vows to the LORD your God, and **f** them.
105:19 Until the time came to **f** his word, / the LORD
Isa 45:13 I will raise up Cyrus to **f** my righteous purpose,
Jer 51:12 for the LORD will **f** all his plans against Babylon.
Eze 12:25 I will **f** my threat of destruction in your own
13: 6 And yet they expect him to **f** their prophecies!
44:16 They are the ones who will **f** all my requirements.
Da 9: 4 You always **f** your promises of unfailing love to
11:14 own people will join them in order to **f** the vision,
Am 7: 3 So the LORD relented and did not **f** the vision.
Jnh 2: 9 you with songs of praise, and I will **f** all my vows.
Na 1:15 O people of Judah, and **f** all your vows,
Mt 1:22 All of this happened to **f** the Lord's message
5:17 the writings of the prophets. No, I came to **f** them.
21: 4 This was done to **f** the prophecy,
26:56 But this is all happening to **f** the words of the
Mk 14:49 But these things are happening to **f** what the
Lk 9:31 And they were speaking of how he was about to **f**
Jn 18: 9 He did this to **f** his own statement: "I have not lost
19:28 and to **f** the Scriptures he said, "I am thirsty."
Ac 7:17 "As the time drew near when God would **f** his
Ro 3:31 only when we have faith do we truly **f** the law.
9: 6 has God failed to **f** his promise to the Jews?
13: 8 you will **f** all the requirements of God's law.
2Th 1:11 will **f** all your good intentions and faithful deeds.

FULFILLED (42) [FULFILL]

Ge 29:21 "I have **f** my contract," Jacob said to Laban.
1Sa 10: 9 his heart, and all Samuel's signs were **f** that day.
1Ki 8:24 and today you have **f** it with your own hands.
12:15 for it **f** the LORD's message to Jeroboam son of
13:26 The LORD has **f** his word by causing the lion to
2Ch 6:15 and today you have **f** it with your own hands.
10:15 for it **f** the prophecy of the LORD spoken to
36:21 of the LORD spoken through Jeremiah was **f**.
36:22 the LORD **f** Jeremiah's prophecy by stirring the
Ezr 1: 1 the LORD **f** Jeremiah's prophecy by stirring the
Ps 119:123 to see the truth of your promise **f**.
Pr 4:13 Guard them, for they will lead you to a **f** life.
Isa 48: 6 You have heard my predictions and seen them **f**,
La 2:17 He has **f** the promises of disaster he made long
Eze 12:23 'The time has come for every prophecy to be **f**!'
Da 4:33 That very same hour the prophecy was **f**,
Hab 2: 3 the time approaches when the vision will be **f**.
Mt 2:15 This **f** what the Lord had spoken through the
2:17 Herod's brutal action **f** the prophecy of Jeremiah:
2:23 This **f** what was spoken by the prophets concerning
4:14 This **f** Isaiah's prophecy:
8:17 This **f** the word of the Lord through Isaiah,
12:17 This **f** the prophecy of Isaiah concerning him:
13:35 This **f** the prophecy that said, / "I will speak to you
26:54 how would the Scriptures be **f** that describe what
27: 9 This **f** the prophecy of Jeremiah that says,
Mk 4:12 so that the Scriptures might be **f**: / 'They see what I
13: 4 ahead of time to show us when all this will be **f**?"
Lk 2:39 When Jesus' parents had **f** all the requirements of
8:10 it from outsiders, so that the Scriptures might be **f**:
21:22 and the prophetic words of the Scriptures will be **f**.
22:37 time has come for this prophecy about me to be **f**:
Jn 15:25 This has **f** what the Scriptures said: 'They hated me
18:32 This **f** Jesus' prediction about the way he would
19:24 This **f** the Scripture that says, "They divided my
Ac 1:16 it was necessary for the Scriptures to be **f**
11:28 (This was **f** during the reign of Claudius.)
13:27 and their leaders **f** prophecy by condemning Jesus
13:29 "When they had **f** all the prophecies concerning
2Co 1:20 For all of God's promises have been **f** in him.
Rev 10: 7 blows his trumpet, God's mysterious plan will be **f**.
17:17 the scarlet beast, and so the words of God will be **f**.

FULFILLING (4) [FULFILL]

1Ki 2:27 thereby **f** the decree the LORD had made at
8:59 the cause of his people Israel, **f** our daily needs.
Jn 12:14 and sat on it, **f** the prophecy that said:
Ac 3:18 But God was **f** what all the prophets had declared

FULFILLMENT (10) [FULFILL]

Nu 15: 8 or a sacrifice in **f** of a special vow or as a peace
2Sa 15: 7 to the LORD in **f** of a vow I made to him.
Isa 62: 6 the LORD day and night for the **f** of his promises.
Lk 1: 2 and other eyewitnesses of what God has done in **f**
22:16 again until it comes to **f** in the Kingdom of God."
Jn 12:16 realize at the time that this was a **f** of prophecy.
19:36 These things happened in **f** of the Scriptures that
Ac 26: 6 because I am looking forward to the **f** of God's
Gal 4:23 attempt to bring about the **f** of God's promise.
4:23 wife was born as God's own **f** of his promise.

FULFILLS (3) [FULFILL]

2Ki 9:36 he stated, "This **f** the message from the LORD,
Ps 145:19 He **f** the desires of those who fear him; / he hears
Mt 13:14 This **f** the prophecy of Isaiah, which says:

FULL (198) [FILL]

Ge 23: 9 I want to pay the **f** price, of course, whatever is
23:13 Let me pay the **f** price for the field so I can bury
27: 3 and a quiver **f** of arrows out into the open country,
41:22 one stalk, and all seven heads were plump and **f**.
Ex 16:20 By then it was **f** of maggots and had a terrible
20:12 **f** life in the land the LORD your God will give
21:34 The owner of the well must pay in **f** for the dead
21:36 The owner of the living bull must pay in **f** for the
22: 3 "A thief who is caught must pay in **f** for
23:26 your people, and I will give you long, **f** lives.
Lev 24:18 another person's animal must pay it back in **f**—
24:21 "Whoever kills an animal must make **f** restitution,
25:29 has the right to redeem it for a **f** year after its sale.
26:28 then I will give **f** vent to my hostility. I will punish
26:41 when I have given **f** expression to my hostility
Nu 5: 7 and make **f** restitution for what they have done,
6:12 to the LORD for the **f** term of their vow,
14:13 "They know **f** well the power you displayed in
14:14 that you have appeared in **f** view of your people in
14:24 His descendants will receive their **f** share of that
33: 3 Israel left defiantly, in **f** view of all the Egyptians.
Dt 5:16 **f** life in the land the LORD your God will give
8:12 For when you have become **f** and prosperous
21:13 Then she must remain in your home for a **f** month,
25:14 and you must use **f** and honest measures.
33:23 are rich in favor / and **f** of the LORD's blessings;
34: 9 Now Joshua son of Nun was **f** of the spirit of
Jdg 5:31 But may those who love you rise like the sun at **f**
Ru 1:21 I went away **f**, but the LORD has brought me
1Sa 2: 5 and those who were starving are now **f**.
14:24 before I have **f** revenge on my enemies."
15:32 Agag arrived **f** of smiles, for he thought,
28:20 Saul fell **f** length on the ground, paralyzed with
2Sa 23:11 and attacked the Israelites in a field **f** of lentils.
2Ki 4: 6 Soon every container was **f** to the brim! "Bring me
12:10 Whenever the chest became **f**, the court secretary
13:17 is the LORD's arrow, **f** of victory over Aram,
16:10 to Uriah the priest, along with its design in **f** detail.
1Ch 11:13 The battle took place in a field **f** of barley,
21:22 "Let me buy this threshing floor from you at its **f**
2Ch 20:27 **f** of joy that the LORD had given them victory
21: 9 So Jehoram went to attack Edom with his **f** army
24:11 Whenever the chest became **f**, the Levites carried it
Ezr 6: 8 You must pay the **f** construction costs without
7:19 deliver them in **f** to the God of Jerusalem.
Ne 2:17 to them, "You know **f** well the tragedy of our city.
8: 5 Ezra stood on the platform in **f** view of all the
9:17 become angry, and **f** of unfailing love and mercy.
9:25 They took over houses **f** of good things,
9:25 So they ate until they were **f** and grew fat
Est 9:29 wrote another letter putting the queen's **f** authority
10: 2 and the **f** account of the greatness of Mordecai,
Job 7: 5 and scabs. My flesh breaks open, **f** of pus.
14: 1 How short is life, and how **f** of trouble!
30:13 knowing **f** well that I have no one to help me.
32:18 For I am pent up and **f** of words, and the spirit
36:13 For the godless are **f** of resentment. Even when he
Ps 10: 7 Their mouths are **f** of cursing, lies, and threats.
17:14 May they have their punishment in **f**. / May their
29: 4 the voice of the LORD is **f** of majesty.
50:19 with wickedness, / and your tongues are **f** of lies.
74:20 for the land is **f** of darkness and violence!
75: 8 it is **f** of foaming wine mixed with spices.
81: 3 when the moon is new, / when the moon is **f**.
86: 5 so **f** of unfailing love for all who ask your aid.
86:15 slow to get angry, / **f** of unfailing love and truth.
88: 3 For my life is **f** of troubles, / and death draws near.
103: 8 he is slow to get angry and **f** of unfailing love.
104:24 made them all. / The earth is **f** of your creatures.
109:22 I am poor and needy, / and my heart is **f** of pain.
111: 9 He has paid a **f** ransom for his people. / He has
119:64 O LORD, the earth is **f** of your unfailing love;
127: 5 How happy is the man whose quiver is **f** of them!
144: 8 Their mouths are **f** of lies; / they swear to tell the
144:11 Their mouths are **f** of lies; / they swear to tell the
145: 8 slow to get angry, **f** of unfailing love.
Pr 1:31 They must experience the **f** terror of the path they
4:18 which shines ever brighter until the **f** light of day.
7:20 He has taken a wallet **f** of money with him, and he
13: 9 The life of the godly is **f** of light and joy,
22:13 The lazy person is **f** of excuses, saying, "If I go
26:13 The lazy person is **f** of excuses, saying, "I can't go
26:25 to be kind, their hearts are **f** of all kinds of evil.
27: 7 Honey seems tasteless to a person who is **f**,
29:11 A fool gives **f** vent to anger, but a wise person
Ecc 1: 7 The rivers run into the sea, but the sea is never **f**.
SS 8:10 "I am chaste, and I am now **f** breasted. And my
Isa 32: 4 Even the hotheads among them will be **f** of sense
40: 2 the LORD has punished her in **f** for all her sins."
42: 3 He will bring **f** justice to all who have been
42:13 he will come out like a warrior, **f** of fury.
42:14 But now I will give **f** vent to my fury; / I will gasp
58:14 and give you your **f** share of the inheritance I
59: 3 Your mouth is **f** of lies, and your lips are tainted
65: 6 I will not stand silent; I will repay them in **f**!
65: 7 insulted me on the hills. I will pay them back in **f**!
65:20 No longer will adults die before they have lived a **f**
Jer 5:11 of Israel and Judah are **f** of treachery against me,"
5:13 God's prophets are windbags **f** of words with no
6:28 Are they not the worst of rebels, **f** of slander?
10: 6 For you are great, and your name is **f** of power.
11:16 olive tree, beautiful to see and **f** of good fruit.
13:12 says: All your wineskins will be **f** of wine.'
22:17 You are **f** of selfish greed and dishonesty!
23:10 For the land is **f** of adultery, and it lies under a
51:35 "May the people of Babylonia be paid in **f** for all
Eze 7: 4 show no pity, repaying you in **f** for all your evil.
9: 9 The entire land is **f** of murder; the city is filled with
16: 7 Your breasts became **f**, and your hair grew,
17: 3 A great eagle with broad wings **f** of many-colored
17: 7 eagle with broad wings and **f** plumage came along.
18:13 No! He must die and must take **f** blame.
22:31 I will heap on them the **f** penalty for all their sins,
23:49 worship of idols. Yes, you will suffer the **f** penalty!
31: 3 **f** of thick branches that cast deep forest shade with
36: 6 I am **f** of fury because you have suffered shame
40:15 The **f** length of the gateway passage was 87-1/2
Da 9:15 But we have sinned and are **f** of wickedness.
Joel 3:13 is ripe. Come, tread the winepress because it is **f**.
Am 8: 2 he asked. I replied, "A basket **f** of ripe fruit."
Mic 2:11 Suppose a prophet **f** of lies were to say to you,
6: 2 He will prosecute them to the **f** extent of the law.
Na 2:11 **f** of fight and boldness, where the old and feeble
Zec 2: 4 so **f** of people that it won't have room enough for
Mt 5: 6 and thirsty for justice, / for they will receive it in **f**.
12:20 until he brings **f** justice with his final victory.
13:27 the field where you planted that good seed is **f** of
13:48 When the net is **f**, they drag it up onto the shore,
15:37 They all ate until they were **f**, and when the scraps
18:30 and jailed until the debt could be paid in **f**.
20: 9 o'clock were paid, each received a **f** day's wage.
23:25 you are filthy—**f** of greed and self-indulgence!
25:21 The master was **f** of praise. 'Well done, my good
Mk 4:37 to break into the boat until it was nearly **f** of water.
8: 8 They ate until they were **f**, and when the scraps
11:13 He noticed a fig tree a little way off that was in **f**
Lk 4: 1 Then Jesus, **f** of the Holy Spirit, left the Jordan
5: 6 this time their nets were so **f** they began to tear!
6:34 Even sinners will lend to their own kind for a **f**
6:38 Your gift will return to you in **f** measure,
11:39 you are still filthy—**f** of greed and wickedness!
12:17 In fact, his barns were **f** to overflowing.
14:23 you find to come, so that the house will be **f**.
Jn 1:14 He was **f** of unfailing love and faithfulness.
2:10 "Then, when everyone is **f** and doesn't care,
6:11 with the fish. And they all ate until they were **f**.
13: 1 He now showed the disciples the **f** extent of his
Ac 5: 2 to the apostles, but he claimed it was the **f** amount.
6: 3 and are **f** of the Holy Spirit and wisdom.
6: 5 Stephen (a man **f** of faith and the Holy Spirit),
6: 8 Stephen, a man **f** of God's grace and power,
7:55 But Stephen, **f** of the Holy Spirit, gazed steadily
8:23 for I can see that you are **f** of bitterness and held
11:24 a good man, **f** of the Holy Spirit and strong in faith.
11:26 Both of them stayed there with the church for a **f**
13:10 the Devil, **f** of every sort of trickery and villainy,
18: 5 Paul spent his **f** time preaching and testifying to the
20:29 I know **f** well that false teachers, like vicious
Ro 1:29 Their lives became **f** of every kind of wickedness,
3:14 "Their mouths are **f** of cursing and bitterness."
8:23 when God will give us our **f** rights as his children,
15:13 you happy and **f** of peace as you believe in him.
15:14 dear friends, that you are **f** of goodness.
1Co 15:43 but when they are raised, they will be **f** of glory.
15:43 but when they are raised, they will be **f** of power.
2Co 1:24 so you will be **f** of joy as you stand firm in your
3:11 was **f** of glory, then the new covenant,
8: 9 You know how **f** of love and kindness our Lord
Eph 2: 2 **f** of sin, obeying Satan, the mighty prince of the
4:13 that we will be mature and **f** grown in the Lord,
measuring up to the **f** stature of Christ.
4:16 whole body is healthy and growing and **f** of love.
4:18 Their closed minds are **f** of darkness; they are far
4:22 rotten through and through, **f** of lust and deception.
5: 8 For though your hearts were once **f** of darkness,
5: 8 now you are **f** of light from the Lord, and your
6: 3 "you will live a long life, **f** of blessing."
Php 1: 4 and I make my requests with a heart **f** of joy

2:15 innocent lives as children of God in a dark world **f**
4: 4 Always be **f** of joy in the Lord. I say it again—
4:12 whether it is with a **f** stomach or empty,
Col 2: 2 I want them to have **f** confidence because they
1Th 1: 5 for the Holy Spirit gave you **f** assurance that what
4:13 so you will not be **f** of sorrow like people who
1Ti 6: 1 who are slaves should give their masters **f** respect
Tit 3: 3 Our lives were **f** of evil and envy. We hated others,
Heb 4:12 For the word of God is **f** of living power. It is
10:26 after we have received a **f** knowledge of the truth,
Jas 3: 6 It is **f** of wickedness that can ruin your whole life.
3: 8 It is an uncontrollable evil, **f** of deadly poison.
3:17 It is **f** of mercy and good deeds. It shows no
5:11 ended in good, for he is **f** of tenderness and mercy.
1Pe 3: 8 be of one mind, **f** of sympathy toward each other,
1Jn 2:28 you will be **f** of courage and not shrink back from
4:12 and his love has been brought to **f** expression
2Jn 1: 8 Be diligent so that you will receive your **f** reward.
Rev 6:11 And they were told to rest a little longer until the **f**
17: 4 She held in her hand a gold goblet **f** of obscenities

FULLNESS (8) [FILL]

Dt 33:16 with the best gifts of the earth and its **f**,
Jn 10:10 and destroy. My purpose is to give life in all its **f**.
Eph 3:19 Then you will be filled with the **f** of life and power
Col 1:19 For God in all his **f** was pleased to live in Christ,
1:25 proclaiming his message in all its **f** to you Gentiles.
2: 9 For in Christ the **f** of God lives in a human body,
2Ti 4:17 that I might preach the Good News in all its **f** for
1Pe 2: 2 so that you can grow into the **f** of your salvation.

FULLY (58) [FILL]

Ge 30:26 You know I have **f** paid for them with my service
Ex 33:13 me your intentions so I will understand you more **f**
Lev 5: 4 not **f** aware of what they were doing at the time.
16: 3 sanctuary area, he must follow these instructions **f**.
Nu 32:32 We will cross the Jordan into Canaan **f** armed to
Dt 17:11 the sentence they impose must be **f** executed;
28: 1 "If you **f** obey the LORD your God by keeping
Jos 1:14 of the Jordan River, but your warriors, **f** armed,
22:17 We are not yet **f** cleansed of it, even after the
Ru 2:12 you have come to take refuge, reward you **f**."
1Ch 12:33 They were **f** armed and prepared for battle
2Ch 15:17 Asa remained **f** committed to the LORD
16: 9 those whose hearts are **f** committed to him.
20:33 and the people never **f** committed themselves to
31: 4 so they could devote themselves **f** to the law of the
Ezr 10: 4 in setting things straight, and we will cooperate **f**."
Ps 17:15 I will see you. / When I awake, I will be **f** satisfied,
78: 9 The warriors of Ephraim, though **f** armed,
Pr 14:10 own bitterness, and no one else can **f** share its joy.
Jer 5: 7 I fed my people until they were **f** satisfied.
6:23 They are **f** armed for slaughter. They are cruel
35:10 and have **f** obeyed all the commands of Jehonadab,
50:42 They are **f** armed for slaughter. They are cruel
51: 6 LORD's time for vengeance; he will **f** repay her.
Eze 9:10 I will **f** repay them for all they have done."
11:21 I will repay them **f** for their sins,
16:43 I will **f** repay you for all of your sins,
23:24 wagons, and a great army **f** prepared for attack.
23:49 You will be **f** repaid for all your prostitution—
38: 4 and make you a vast and mighty horde, all **f** armed.
Da 3:21 them up and threw them into the furnace, **f** clothed.
11:13 the king of the north will return with a **f** equipped
Mt 3:17 is my beloved Son, and I am **f** pleased with him."
17: 5 is my beloved Son, and I am **f** pleased with him.
Mk 1:11 are my beloved Son, and I am **f** pleased with you."
5:15 for he was sitting there **f** clothed and perfectly
Lk 3:22 are my beloved Son, and I am **f** pleased with you."
Jn 18: 4 Jesus **f** realized all that was going to happen to
Ac 13:35 Another psalm explains more **f**, saying, 'You will
23:15 "Pretend you want to examine his case more **f**.
Ro 1:32 They are **f** aware of God's death penalty for those
8: 4 so that the requirement of the law would be **f**
15:14 I am **f** convinced, dear friends, that you are full of
15:19 I have **f** presented the Good News of Christ all the
1Co 16:16 to respect them **f** and others like them who serve
2Co 1:13 I hope someday you will **f** understand us,
1:14 even if you don't **f** understand us now. Then on the
5: 8 Yes, we are **f** confident, and we would rather be
Gal 4:19 and they will continue until Christ is **f** developed in
Eph 3:19 though it is so great you will never **f** understand it.
6:15 the Good News, so that you will be **f** prepared.
Col 4:12 and perfect, **f** confident of the whole will of God.
2Ti 3:17 **f** equipped for every good thing God wants us to
Heb 10:22 presence of God, with true hearts **f** trusting him.
Jas 1: 4 it grow, for when your endurance is **f** developed,
2Pe 1:17 is my beloved Son; I am **f** pleased with him."
Rev 7:16 and they will be **f** protected from the scorching
14:18 of the earth, for they are **f** ripe for judgment."

FUMES (1)

Ge 19:28 and Gomorrah and saw columns of smoke and **f**,

FUN (16)

Ge 21: 9 her Egyptian servant Hagar—making **f** of Isaac.
Jdg 16:10 said to him, "You made **f** of me and told me a lie!
16:13 "You have been making **f** of me and telling me
16:15 You've made **f** of me three times now, and you
16:27 who were watching Samson and making **f** of him.
1Sa 1: 6 But Peninnah made **f** of Hannah
2Ki 2:23 the town began mocking and making **f** of him.
2Ch 30:10 just laughed at the messengers and made **f** of them.
Ps 69:11 in sackcloth to show sorrow, / they make **f** of me.
Pr 10:23 Doing wrong is **f** for a fool, while wise conduct is
14: 9 Fools make **f** of guilt, but the godly acknowledge it
Ecc 8:15 So I recommend having **f**, because there is nothing
10:20 And don't make **f** of a rich man, either.
Eze 33:30 at the doors, saying, 'Come on, let's have some **f**!
Hos 7: 5 and drinks with those who are making **f** of him.
Mic 2: 4 In that day your enemies will make **f** of you by

FUNCTION (2)

Dt 18:11 or cast spells, or **f** as mediums or psychics, or call
Ro 12: 4 have many parts and each part has a special **f**,

FUNDS (3)

Ezr 7:20 you may requisition **f** from the royal treasury.
Lk 14:29 only the foundation before running out of **f**.
Jn 12: 6 was a thief who was in charge of the disciples' **f**,

FUNERAL (25) [FUNERALS]

Ge 50:10 Jordan River, they held a very great and solemn **f**,
50:14 and all who had accompanied him to his father's **f**.
Lev 21:12 of his God by leaving it to attend his parents' **f**,
1Sa 25: 1 Now Samuel died, and all Israel gathered for his **f**.
2Sa 1:17 Then David composed a **f** song for Saul
3:33 Then the king sang this **f** song for Abner:
3:35 David had refused to eat anything the day of the **f**,
2Ch 16:14 and at his **f** the people built a huge fire in his
21:19 him at his **f** as they had done for his ancestors.
35:25 The prophet Jeremiah composed **f** songs for Josiah,
Job 21:33 A great **f** procession goes to the cemetery.
Eze 2:10 and I saw that both sides were covered with **f**
19: 1 "Sing this **f** song for the princes of Israel:
19:14 This is a **f** song, and it is now time for the **f**."
26:17 Then they will wail for you, singing this **f** song:
27: 2 "Son of man, sing a **f** song for Tyre,
27:32 As they wail and mourn, they sing this sad **f** song:
32:16 Yes, this is the **f** song they will sing for Egypt.
Am 5: 1 people of Israel! Listen to this **f** song I am singing:
8:10 You will wear **f** clothes and shave your heads as
Mt 9:23 he noticed the noisy crowds and heard the **f** music.
11:17 so we played **f** songs, but you weren't sad.'
Lk 7:12 A **f** procession was coming out as he approached
7:32 so we played **f** songs, but you weren't sad.'

FUNERALS (2) [FUNERAL]

Ecc 7: 2 It is better to spend your time at **f** than at festivals.
Jer 16: 5 "Do not go to their **f** to mourn and show sympathy

FURBISHED [KJV] See POLISHED, SHARPENED

FURIOUS (32) [FURY]

Ge 34: 7 were shocked and **f** that their sister had been raped.
39:19 After hearing his wife's story, Potiphar was **f**!
Nu 12: 9 The LORD was **f** with them, and he departed.
22:22 But God was **f** that Balaam was going, so he sent
31:14 But Moses was **f** with all the military commanders
32:10 Then the LORD was **f** with them, and he vowed,
32:13 "The LORD was **f** with Israel and made them
Jdg 9:30 of the city, heard what Gaal was saying, he was **f**.
14:19 But Samson was **f** about what had happened,
2Sa 3: 8 Abner became **f**. "Am I a Judean dog to be kicked
12: 5 David was **f**. "As surely as the LORD lives,"
1Ki 14: 9 and have made me **f** with your gold calves.
2Ch 26:19 Uzziah was **f** and refused to set down the incense
Ne 4: 7 in the wall were being repaired, they became **f**.
Est 1:12 This made the king **f**, and he burned with anger.
5: 9 or trembling nervously before him, he was **f**.
Ps 119:53 I am **f** with the wicked, / those who reject your
Pr 6:34 For the woman's husband will be **f** in his jealousy,
Jer 21: 5 for I am very angry. You have made me **f**!
25: 7 "You made me **f** by worshiping your idols,
37:15 They were **f** with Jeremiah and had him flogged
Eze 5:15 the LORD turns against a nation in **f** rebuke.
25:14 They will carry out my **f** vengeance, and Edom
Da 2:12 The king was **f** when he heard this, and he sent out
3:19 Nebuchadnezzar was so **f** with Shadrach, Meshach,
9:16 please turn your **f** anger away from your city of
Mt 2:16 Herod was **f** when he learned that the wise men
22: 7 "Then the king became **f**. He sent out his army to
Lk 4:28 they heard this, the people in the synagogue were **f**.
11:53 the Pharisees and teachers of religious law were **f**.
Ac 5:33 the high council was **f** and decided to kill them.
22:24 wanted to find out why the crowd had become so **f**.

FURIOUSLY (3) [FURY]

Eze 23:25 anger against you, and they will deal **f** with you.
Da 8: 7 The goat charged **f** at the ram and struck it,
Na 1: 2 on all who oppose him and **f** destroys his enemies!

FURLONGS [KJV] See MILES

FURNACE (25)

Ge 19:28 and saw columns of smoke and fumes, as from a **f**,
Ex 9: 8 said to Moses and Aaron, "Take soot from a **f**,
9:10 So they gathered soot from a **f** and went to see
19:18 smoke billowed into the sky like smoke from a **f**,
Dt 4:20 the burning **f** of Egypt to become his own people
1Ki 8:51 whom you brought out of the iron-smelting **f** of
Ps 12: 6 promises are pure, / like silver refined in a **f**,
21: 9 You will destroy them as in a flaming **f** / when you
Isa 48:10 Rather, I have refined you in the **f** of suffering.
Eze 22:20 tin, iron, and lead are melted down in a **f**.
Da 3: 6 obey will immediately be thrown into a blazing **f**."
3:11 refuse to obey must be thrown into a blazing **f**.
3:15 you will be thrown immediately into the blazing **f**.
3:17 If we are thrown into the blazing **f**, the God whom
3:19 He commanded that the **f** be heated seven times
3:20 and Abednego and throw them into the blazing **f**.
3:21 So they tied them up and threw them into the **f**,
3:22 in his anger, had demanded such a hot fire in the **f**,
3:24 we tie up three men and throw them into the **f**?"
3:26 as close as he could to the door of the flaming **f**
Hos 7: 6 Their hearts blaze like a **f** with intrigue. Their plot
Mal 4: 1 "The day of judgment is coming, burning like a **f**.
Mt 13:42 and they will throw them into the **f** and burn them.
Rev 1:15 His feet were as bright as bronze refined in a **f**,
9: 2 smoke poured out as though from a huge **f**,

FURNISH (4) [FURNISHED, FURNISHINGS, FURNITURE]

Ex 36: 1 intelligence will construct and **f** the Tabernacle,
2Ki 4:10 a little room for him on the roof and **f** it with a bed,
Isa 5:12 You **f** lovely music and wine at your grand parties;
Eze 13:18 charms on their wrists and **f** them with magic veils.

FURNISHED (2) [FURNISH]

Ge 47:12 And Joseph **f** food to his father and brothers in
1Ki 9:11 and gold he had **f** for the construction of the

FURNISHINGS (12) [FURNISH]

Ex 25: 9 and its **f** exactly according to the plans I will show
31: 7 the place of atonement; all the **f** of the Tabernacle;
35:21 the Tabernacle and its **f** and for the holy garments.
39:33 the sacred tent with all its **f**, the clasps, frames,
40: 9 the Tabernacle and on all its **f** to make them holy.
Nu 1:50 of the Covenant, along with its **f** and equipment.
3: 8 They will also maintain all the **f** of the sacred tent,
7: 1 along with all its **f** and the altar with its utensils.
19:18 on all the **f** in the tent, and on anyone who was in
1Ki 7:48 So Solomon made all the **f** of the Temple of the
1Ch 9:29 Others were responsible for the **f**, the items in the
2Ch 4:19 So Solomon made all the **f** for the Temple of God:

FURNITURE (1) [FURNISH]

Lev 15:23 whether it is her bedding or any piece of **f**.

FURNITURE [KJV] See also FURNISHINGS, THINGS, UTENSILS

FURROWS (2)

Job 31:38 "If my land accuses me and all its **f** weep together,
Ps 129: 3 with cuts, / as if a farmer had plowed long **f**.

FURTHER (44) [FURTHERMORE]

Ge 18:27 let me go on and speak **f** to my Lord, even though I
18:29 Then Abraham pressed his request **f**.
Ex 18: 7 and then went to Moses' tent to talk **f**.
21:22 If no **f** harm results, then the person responsible
31:12 then gave these **f** instructions to Moses:
Lev 6:25 and his sons these **f** instructions regarding the sin
7:29 "Give these **f** instructions to the Israelites:
13:11 the person need not be quarantined for **f**
15: 2 "Give these **f** instructions to the Israelites:
Nu 17:10 complaints against me and prevent any **f** deaths."
18: 8 The LORD gave these **f** instructions to Aaron:
31:23 then be **f** purified with the water of purification.
Jos 15:19 She said, "Give me a **f** blessing. You have been
Jdg 1:15 She said, "Give me a **f** blessing. You have been
1Sa 10: 8 When I arrive, I will give you **f** instructions."
1Ki 8:25 carry out your **f** promise to your servant David,
2Ch 6:16 carry out your **f** promise to your servant David,
11:12 and spears in these towns as a **f** safety measure.
32: 5 Then Hezekiah **f** strengthened his defenses by
32:16 And Sennacherib's officials **f** mocked the LORD
Ne 5: 9 Then I pressed **f**, "What you are doing is not right!
10:31 We **f** promise that if the people of the land should
Job 32: 1 Job's three friends refused to reply **f** to him
32: 5 But when he saw that they had no **f** reply, he spoke
32:15 You sit there baffled, with no **f** response.
Pr 24:23 Here are some **f** sayings of the wise: It is wrong to
Ecc 9: 5 They have no **f** reward, nor are they remembered.
Eze 23:14 "Then she carried her prostitution even **f**. She fell
28:11 Then this **f** message came to me from the LORD:
36:16 Then this **f** message came to me from the LORD:
Am 4:12 I will bring upon you all these **f** disasters I have
Lk 4:35 then it left him without hurting him **f**.
15:11 To illustrate the point **f**, Jesus told them this story:
Ac 1: 2 chosen apostles **f** instructions from the Holy Spirit.
4:21 The council then threatened them **f**, but they finally
15:12 There was no **f** discussion, and everyone listened
20:16 because he didn't want to spend **f** time in the
27:38 the crew lightened the ship **f** by throwing the cargo
Gal 3:19 And there is this **f** difference. God gave his laws to
Eph 5:21 And **f**, you will submit to one another out of
Php 2: 8 even **f** by dying a criminal's death on a cross.
1Th 1: 5 among you was **f** proof of the truth of our message.
Heb 6: 2 You don't need **f** instruction about baptisms,
6: 3 we will move forward to **f** understanding.

FURTHERMORE (4) [FURTHER]

Isa 22:15 **F**, the Lord, the LORD Almighty, told me to
Eph 1:11 **F**, because of Christ, we have received an
Heb 2: 5 And **f**, the future world we are talking about will
1Jn 4:14 **F**, we have seen with our own eyes and now testify

FURY (81) [FURIOUS, FURIOUSLY]

Ge 27:44 Stay there with him until your brother's **f** is spent.
Dt 29:28 and **f** the LORD uprooted his people from their
32:16 they provoked his **f** with detestable acts.
32:21 they have provoked my **f** with useless idols.
32:21 I will provoke their **f** by blessing the foolish
Jdg 15: 8 So he attacked the Philistines with great **f**
1Sa 19: 8 He attacked them with such **f** that they all ran
Job 19:11 His **f** burns against me; he counts me as an enemy.
Ps 2: 5 he rebukes them, / terrifying them with his fierce **f**.
7: 6 in anger! / Stand up against the **f** of my enemies!
69:24 Pour out your **f** on them; / consume them with your
78:38 he held back his anger / and did not unleash his **f**!
78:49 his fierce anger— / all his **f**, rage, and hostility.
85: 3 You have withdrawn your **f**. / You have ended
90: 7 your anger; / we are overwhelmed by your **f**.
124: 5 Yes, the raging waters of their **f** / would have
Pr 20: 2 The king's **f** is like a lion's roar; to rouse his anger
21:14 A secret gift calms anger; a secret bribe pacifies **f**.
Isa 1:24 says, "I will pour out my **f** on you, my enemies!
9:19 The land is blackened by the **f** of the LORD
13: 9 the terrible day of his **f** and fierce anger.
13:13 will show my **f** and fierce anger."
30:27 His lips are filled with **f**; his words consume like
34: 2 His **f** is against all their armies. He will completely
42:13 he will come out like a warrior, full of **f**.
42:14 But now I will give full vent to my **f**; / I will gasp
42:25 That is why he poured out such **f** on them
51:17 drunk enough from the cup of the LORD's **f**.
51:20 The LORD has poured out his **f**; God has rebuked
51:22 You will drink no more of my **f**. It is gone at last!
59:17 himself with the robes of vengeance and godly **f**.
59:18 His **f** will fall on his foes in distant lands.
63: 3 In my **f** I have trampled my foes. It is their blood
66:15 He will bring punishment with the **f** of his anger
Jer 6:11 So now I am filled with the LORD's **f**. Yes,
6:11 "I will pour out my **f** over Jerusalem, even on
7:20 "I will pour out my terrible **f** on this place.
7:29 forsaken this generation that has provoked his **f**.'
11:16 But now I have sent the **f** of their enemies to burn
25:32 A great whirlwind of **f** is rising from the most
32:29 where the people caused my **f** to rise by offering
32:37 all the countries where I will scatter them in my **f**.
42:18 and **f** were poured out on the people of Jerusalem,
44: 6 And so my **f** boiled over and fell like fire on the
50:25 and brought out weapons to vent his **f** against his
La 2: 1 In his day of awesome **f**, the Lord has shown no
2: 3 All the strength of Israel vanishes beneath his **f**.
2: 4 His **f** is poured out like fire on beautiful Jerusalem.
Eze 5:13 And when my **f** against them has subsided,
6:12 by famine. So at last I will spend my **f** on them.
7: 8 Soon I will pour out my **f** to complete your
7:14 but no one listens, for my **f** is against them all.
8:17 their noses at me, and rousing my **f** against them?
8:18 Therefore, I will deal with them in **f**. I will neither
9: 8 Will your **f** against Jerusalem wipe out everyone
13:13 a great flood of anger, and with hailstones of **f**.
14:19 "Or suppose I were to pour out my **f** by sending an
16:38 I will cover you with blood in my jealous **f**.
16:42 "Then at last my **f** against you will be spent,
19:12 But the vine was uprooted in **f** / and thrown down
20: 8 Then I threatened to pour out my **f** on them to
20:13 So I threatened to pour out my **f** on them, and I
20:21 So again I threatened to pour out my **f** on them in
20:28 They roused my **f** as they offered up sacrifices to
20:34 and **f** I will bring you out from the lands where you
21:17 too, will clap my hands, and I will satisfy my **f**.
21:31 I will pour out my **f** on you and blow on you with
22:20 I will melt you down in the heat of my **f**, just as
22:22 the LORD, have poured out my **f** on you."
22:31 So now I will pour out my **f** on them,
24:13 you will remain filthy until my **f** against you has
30:15 I will pour out my **f** on Pelusium, the strongest
36: 6 I am full of **f** because you have suffered shame
36:18 by worshiping idols, so I poured out my **f** on them.
38:18 says the Sovereign LORD, my **f** will rise!
Hos 8: 5 this idol you have made. My **f** burns against you.
13:11 I gave you kings, and in my **f** I took them away.
Na 1: 6 Who can survive his burning **f**? His rage blazes
Hab 3:12 awesome anger and trampled the nations in your **f**.
Zep 2: 2 before the fierce **f** of the LORD falls
3: 8 and pour out my fiercest anger and **f** on them.

FUTILE (6) [FUTILITY]

Ps 2: 1 Why do the people waste their time with **f** plans?
89:47 my life is, / how empty and **f** this human existence!
Ecc 4: 6 especially when in the long run everything is so **f**.
Jer 10: 3 Their ways are **f** and foolish. They cut down a tree
23:16 they prophesy to you, filling you with **f** hopes.
Ac 4:25 Why did the people waste their time with **f** plans?

FUTILITY (1) [FUTILE]

Job 7: 3 I, too, have been assigned months of **f**, long

FUTURE (84)

Ge 6: 3 In the **f**, they will live no more than 120 years."
44: 5 silver drinking cup, which he uses to predict the **f**?
48: 6 But the children born to you in the **f** will be your
Ex 13:14 "And in the **f**, your children will ask you,
16:33 a sacred place as a reminder for all **f** generations."
27:21 of Israel, and it must be kept by all **f** generations.
29:28 In the **f**, whenever the people of Israel offer up
Lev 10: 9 for you, and it must be kept by all **f** generations.
16:32 In **f** generations, the atonement ceremony will be
21:17 "Tell Aaron that in all **f** generations,
23:41 for you, and it must be kept by all **f** generations.
24: 3 for you, and it must be kept by all **f** generations at
Nu 9:10 or in **f** generations are ceremonially unclean at
15:23 And suppose some of your descendants in the **f** fail
24:14 what the Israelites will do to your people in the **f**."
24:17 I perceive him, but far in the distant **f**.
Dt 4:25 "In the **f**, when you have children
4:30 those bitter days have come upon you far in the **f**,
6:20 "In the **f** your children will ask you, 'What is the
13: 1 or those who have dreams about the **f**, and they
29:15 and also with all **f** generations of Israel.
Jos 4: 6 In the **f**, your children will ask, 'What do these
4:21 "In the **f**, your children will ask, 'What do these
22:24 because we fear that in the **f** your descendants will
2Sa 18:32 both now and in the **f**, be as that young man is!"
Job 3:23 Why is life given to those with no **f**, those destined
Ps 22:30 **F** generations will also serve him. / Our children
31:15 My **f** is in your hands. / Rescue me from those who
37:37 for a wonderful **f** lies before those who love peace.
37:38 But the wicked will be destroyed; / they have no **f**.
48:13 that you may describe them / to **f** generations.
102:18 Let this be recorded for **f** generations, / so that a
Pr 23:18 For surely you have a **f** ahead of you; your hope
24:14 If you find it, you will have a bright **f**, and your
24:20 For the evil have no **f**; their light will be snuffed
31:25 and dignity, and she laughs with no fear of the **f**.
Ecc 1:11 And in **f** generations, no one will remember what
3:15 and whatever will exist in the **f** has already existed
3:22 bring them back from death to enjoy life in the **f**.
6:12 And who can tell what will happen in the **f** after we
10:14 Foolish people claim to know all about the **f**
Isa 4: 2 But in the **f**, Israel—the branch of the LORD—
8:16 who will pass it down to **f** generations.
8:19 So why are you trying to find out the **f** by
8:19 Can the living find out the **f** from the dead?
9: 1 but there will be a time in the **f** when Galilee of the
29:11 All these **f** events are a sealed book to them.
41:22 tell us what happened long ago or what the **f** holds.
42: 9 I will tell you the **f** before it happens."
43:28 and assigned Israel a **f** of complete destruction
46:13 set things right, not in the distant **f**, but right now!
47:13 them stand up and save you from what the **f** holds.
48: 3 you about what was going to happen in the **f**.
Jer 10: 2 other nations who try to read their **f** in the stars.
17: 6 stunted shrubs in the desert, with no hope for the **f**.
29:11 and not for disaster, to give you a **f** and a hope.
31:17 There is hope for your **f**," says the LORD.
31:28 But in the **f** I will plant it and build it up,"
La 1:16 My children have no **f**, for the enemy has
Eze 38: 8 In the distant **f** you will swoop down on the land of
38:16 land like a cloud. This will happen in the distant **f**.
38:17 that in **f** days I would bring you against my people.
Da 2:28 King Nebuchadnezzar what will happen in the **f**.
2:45 has shown Your Majesty what will happen in the **f**.
10: 1 It concerned events certain to happen in the **f**—
10:14 to explain what will happen to your people in the **f**,
Hos 4:12 They think a stick can tell them the **f**!
Joel 3:20 and Jerusalem will endure through all **f**
Mic 3: 6 making it impossible for you to predict the **f**.
Hag 2: 9 The **f** glory of this Temple will be greater than its
Mt 26:64 And in the **f** you will see me, the Son of Man,
Jn 16:13 you what he has heard. He will tell you about the **f**.
Ac 2:31 David was looking into the **f** and predicting the
Ro 8:19 For all creation is waiting eagerly for that **f** day
8:23 the Holy Spirit within us as a foretaste of **f** glory,
1Co 3:22 and life and death; the present and the **f**.
13: 2 and if I knew all the mysteries of the **f** and knew
Eph 1:18 so that you can understand the wonderful **f** he has
4: 4 and we have all been called to the same glorious **f**.
Php 3:19 Their **f** is eternal destruction. Their god is their
1Ti 6:19 up their treasure as a good foundation for the **f**
Heb 2: 5 the **f** world we are talking about will not be
11:20 confidence in what God was going to do in the **f**.
Rev 22: 6 Lord God, who tells his prophets what the **f** holds,

G

GAAL (10)

Jdg 9:26 At that time **G** son of Ebed moved to Shechem
9:28 "Who is Abimelech?" **G** shouted. "He's not a
9:30 the city, heard what **G** was saying, he was furious.
9:31 "**G** son of Ebed and his brothers have come to live
9:33 When **G** and those who are with him come out
9:35 **G** was standing at the city gates when Abimelech
9:36 When **G** saw them, he said to Zebul, "Look,
9:37 But again **G** said, "No, people are coming down
9:39 **G** then led the men of Shechem into battle against
9:41 and Zebul drove **G** and his brothers out of

GAASH (2)

Jos 24:30 in the hill country of Ephraim, north of Mount **G**.
Jdg 2: 9 in the hill country of Ephraim, north of Mount **G**.

GABA [KJV] See GEBA

GABBAI (1)

Ne 11: 8 and after him there were **G** and Sallai, and a total

GABBATHA (1)

Jn 19:13 that is called the Stone Pavement (in Hebrew, ***G***).

GABRIEL (7)

Da 8:16 "**G**, tell this man the meaning of his vision."
8:17 As **G** approached the place where I was standing,
8:18 But **G** roused me with a touch and helped me to
9:21 As I was praying, **G**, whom I had seen in the
Lk 1:19 Then the angel said, "I am **G**! I stand in the very
1:26 God sent the angel **G** to Nazareth, a village in
1:28 **G** appeared to her and said, "Greetings,

GAD (80) [BAAL-GAD, DIBON-GAD, GAD'S, GADITES, MIGDAL-GAD]

Ge 30:11 Leah named him **G**, for she said, "How fortunate I
35:26 sons of Zilpah, Leah's servant, were **G** and Asher.
46:16 The sons of **G** were Zephon, Haggi, Shuni, Ezbon,
49:19 "**G** will be plundered by marauding bands,
Ex 1: 4 Dan, Naphtali, **G**, and Asher.
Nu 1:14 **G** | Eliasaph son of Deuel
1:24[-25] **G** | 45,650
2:10[-11] and **G** are to camp on the south side of the
2:14[-15] **G** | Eliasaph son of Deuel | 45,650
7:42 leader of the tribe of **G**, presented his offering.
10:20 The tribe of **G** was led by Eliasaph son of Deuel.
13:15 **G** | Geuel son of Maki
26:15 were the clans descended from the sons of **G**:
26:18 The men from all the clans of **G** numbered 40,500.
32: 1 of Reuben and **G** owned vast numbers of livestock.
32:25 Then the people of **G** and Reuben replied,
32:29 "If all the men of **G** and Reuben who are able to
32:31 The tribes of **G** and Reuben said again, "Sir,
32:33 So Moses assigned to the tribes of **G**, Reuben,
32:34 The people of **G** built the towns of Dibon, Ataroth,
34:14 The families of the tribes of Reuben, **G**, and half
Dt 3:12 with its towns, to the tribes of Reuben and **G**.
3:16 and **G** I gave the area extending from Gilead to the
4:43 Ramoth in Gilead for the tribe of **G**; Golan in
27:13 And the tribes of Reuben, **G**, Asher, Zebulun, Dan,
29: 8 their land and gave it to the tribes of Reuben and **G**
33:20 Moses said this about the tribe of **G**: / "Blessed is
33:20 **G** is poised there like a lion / to tear off an arm
33:21 The people of **G** took the best land for themselves;
Jos 1:12 of Reuben, **G**, and the half-tribe of Manasseh.
4:12 The armed warriors from the tribes of Reuben, **G**,
12: 6 of Reuben, **G**, and the half-tribe of Manasseh.
13: 8 and **G** had already received their inheritance on the
13:24 the following area to the families of the tribe of **G**.
13:28 as an inheritance to the families of the tribe of **G**.
18: 7 And the tribes of **G**, Reuben, and the half-tribe of
20: 8 Ramoth in Gilead, in the territory of the tribe of **G**;
21: 7 cities from the tribes of Reuben, **G**, and Zebulun.
21:38 From the tribe of **G** they received Ramoth in
22: 1 of Reuben, **G**, and the half-tribe of Manasseh.
22: 9 So the men of Reuben, **G**, and the half-tribe of
22:10 before they crossed the Jordan River, Reuben, **G**,
22:13 of Reuben, **G**, and the half-tribe of Manasseh.
22:15 of Reuben, **G**, and the half-tribe of Manasseh,
22:21 Then the people of Reuben, **G**, and the half-tribe of
22:30 **G**, and the half-tribe of Manasseh, they were
22:32 officials left the tribes of Reuben and **G** in Gilead
22:33 and spoke no more of war against Reuben and **G**.
22:34 of Reuben and **G** named the altar "Witness,"
1Sa 13: 7 and escaped into the land of **G** and Gilead.
22: 5 One day the prophet **G** told David,
2Sa 23:36 Igal son of Nathan from Zobah; / Bani from **G**;
24: 5 of the town in the valley, in the direction of **G**.
24:11 the word of the LORD came to the prophet **G**,
24:13 So **G** came to David and asked him, "Will you
24:14 is a desperate situation!" David replied to **G**.
24:18 That day **G** came to David and said to him, "Go
2Ki 10:33 including all of Gilead, **G**, Reuben, and Manasseh.
1Ch 2: 2 Dan, Joseph, Benjamin, Naphtali, **G**, and Asher.
5:11 in the land of Bashan lived the descendants of **G**,
5:18 of Reuben, **G**, and the half-tribe of Manasseh.
5:26 the land and lead away the people of Reuben, **G**,
6:63 from the territories of Reuben, **G**, and Zebulun.
6:80 And from the territory of **G**, they received Ramoth
12: 8 and experienced warriors from the tribe of **G** also
12:14 These warriors from **G** were army commanders.
12:37 where the tribes of Reuben and **G**
21: 9 Then the LORD spoke to **G**, David's seer.
21:11 So **G** came to David and said, "These are the
21:13 is a desperate situation!" David replied to **G**.
21:18 Then the angel of the LORD told **G** to instruct
21:19 instructions the LORD had given him through **G**.
26:32 of Reuben and **G** and the half-tribe of Manasseh.
29:29 *the Prophet,* and *The Record of **G** the Seer.*
2Ch 29:25 the LORD had given to King David through **G**,
Jer 49: 1 no descendants of Israel to inherit the land of **G**?
Eze 48:27 The territory of **G** is just south of Zebulun with the
48:28 The southern border of **G** runs from Tamar to the
48:34 the gates will be named for **G**, Asher,
Rev 7: 5 from Reuben | 12,000 / from **G** | 12,000

GAD'S (1) [GAD]

Dt 33:20 "Blessed is the one who enlarges **G** territory!

GADARENES (1)

Mt 8:28 on the other side of the lake in the land of the **G**,

GADDEST [KJV] See FLIT

GADDI (1)
Nu 13:11 Manasseh son of Joseph | G son of Susi

GADDIEL (1)
Nu 13:10 Zebulun | G son of Sodi

GADFLY (1) [FLY]
Jer 46:20 a young cow, but a g from the north is on its way!

GADI (2)
2Ki 15:14 Then Menahem son of G went to Samaria from
15:17 Menahem son of G began to rule over Israel in the

GADITES (2) [GAD]
Nu 32: 6 the fighting?" Moses asked the Reubenites and G.
1Ch 5:16 The G lived in the land of Gilead, in Bashan

GAG (2)
Nu 11:20 You will eat it for a whole month until you g
Job 6: 7 when I look at it; I g at the thought of eating it!

GAHAM (1)
Ge 22:24 Their names were Tebah, G, Tahash, and Maacah.

GAHAR (2)
Ezr 2:47 Giddel, G, Reaiah,
Ne 7:49 Hanan, Giddel, G,

GAIN (35) [GAINED, GAINS, REGAIN, REGAINED]
Ge 37:26 the others, "What can we g by killing our brother?
1Sa 2:26 he also continued to g favor with the LORD
2Sa 2:26 Don't you realize the only thing we will g is
2Ki 15:19 g his support in tightening his grip on royal power.
Job 10: 3 What do you g by oppressing me? Why do you
22: 3 Would it be any g to him if you were perfect?
Ps 4: 4 Don't sin by letting anger g control over you.
17:14 from those whose only concern is earthly g.
30: 9 "What will you g if I die, / if I sink down into the
Pr 1:19 Such is the fate of all who are greedy for g. It ends
2: 5 the LORD, and you will g knowledge of God.
3: 4 and people, and you will g a good reputation.
3: 8 Then you will g renewed health and vitality.
10: 2 Ill-gotten g has no lasting value, but right living
Ecc 2:21 I must leave everything I g to people who haven't
4: 8 yet who works hard to g as much wealth as he can.
4:11 two under the same blanket can g warmth from
6: 8 Do poor people g anything by being wise
10:17 and whose leaders feast only to g strength for their
Isa 33:11 You Assyrians will g nothing by all your efforts.
56:11 their own path, all of them intent on personal g.
Eze 22:13 clap my hands in indignation over your dishonest g
Da 11:43 He will g control over the gold, silver,
Zep 3: 4 Its prophets are arrogant liars seeking their own g.
Mt 16:26 And how do you benefit if you g the whole world
Mk 8:36 And how do you benefit if you g the whole world
Lk 9:25 And how do you benefit if you g the whole world
19:16 The first servant reported a tremendous g—
19:18 "The next servant also reported a good g—
Ac 24:27 because Felix wanted to g favor with the Jewish
1Co 8: 8 we don't eat it, and we don't g anything if we do.
9:21 I g their confidence and bring them to Christ.
Eph 4:26 And "don't sin by letting anger g control over
Php 3: 8 the priceless g of knowing Christ Jesus my Lord.
Rev 6: 2 He rode out to win many battles and g the victory.

GAINED (21) [GAIN]
Ge 31: 1 "All his wealth has been g at our father's
36: 6 all the wealth he had g in the land of Canaan—
Ex 17:11 his hands, the Amalekites g the upper hand.
Lev 6: 5 or anything g by swearing falsely. When they
Jdg 9:26 and g the confidence of the people of Shechem.
2Sa 14:22 "At last I know that I have g your approval,
15:12 joined Absalom, and the conspiracy g momentum.
1Ch 26:27 g in battle to maintain the house of the LORD.
Est 9:16 They g relief from all their enemies,
9:22 This would commemorate a time when the Jews g
Pr 16:31 is a crown of glory; it is g by living a godly life.
Ecc 2:19 And yet they will control everything I have g by
Isa 63:14 LORD, and g a magnificent reputation."
Jer 2:18 "What have you g by your alliances with Egypt
Eze 33:24 and yet he g possession of the entire land!
Mic 6:10 The homes of the wicked are filled with treasures g
Hab 2:12 for you who build cities with money g by murder
2:18 "What have you g by worshiping all your
Mal 3:14 What have we g by obeying his commands or by
Php 1:14 many of the Christians here have g confidence
Phm 1: 7 I myself have g much joy and comfort from your

GAINS (2) [GAIN]
Pr 3:13 the person who finds wisdom and g understanding.
Isa 65:22 and will have time to enjoy their hard-won g.

GAINSAY(ERS) [KJV] See OPPOSE

GAINSAYING [KJV] See ARGUING, REBELLION

GAIUS (5)
Ac 19:29 dragging along G and Aristarchus,
20: 4 G, from Derbe; Timothy; and Tychicus
Ro 16:23 G says hello to you. I am his guest, and the church
1Co 1:14 I did not baptize any of you except Crispus and G,
3Jn 1: 1 It is written to G, my dear friend, whom I love in

GALAL (3)
1Ch 9:15 Bakbakkar; Heresh; G; Mattaniah son of Mica,
9:16 son of Shemaiah, son of G, son of Jeduthun;
Ne 11:17 Abda son of Shammua, son of G, son of Jeduthun.

GALATIA (6) [GALATIANS]
Ac 16: 6 Silas traveled through the area of Phrygia and G,
18:23 Paul went back to G and Phrygia, visiting all the
1Co 16: 1 the same procedures I gave to the churches in G.
Gal 1: 2 join me in sending greetings to the churches of G.
2Ti 4:10 Crescens has gone to G, and Titus has gone to
1Pe 1: 1 G, Cappadocia, the province of Asia, and Bithynia.

GALATIANS (1) [GALATIA]
Gal 3: 1 Oh, foolish G! What magician has cast an evil

GALBANUM (1)
Ex 30:34 resin droplets, mollusk scent, g, and pure

GALE (3) [GALE-FORCE]
Eze 27:26 mighty vessel flounders in the heavy eastern g.
Jn 6:18 Soon a g swept down upon them as they rowed,
Ac 27:15 so they gave up and let it run before the g.

GALE-FORCE (1) [GALE]
Ac 27:18 next day, as g winds continued to batter the ship,

GALEED (1) [JEGAR-SAHADUTHA]
Ge 31:47 in Laban's language and G in Jacob's.

GALILEAN (4) [GALILEE]
Mt 26:69 "You were one of those with Jesus the G."
26:73 be one of them; we can tell by your G accent."
Lk 22:59 must be one of Jesus' disciples because he is a G,
23: 6 "Oh, is he a G?" Pilate asked.

GALILEANS (2) [GALILEE]
Lk 13: 2 "Do you think those G were worse sinners than
Jn 4:45 The G welcomed him, for they had been in

GALILEE (86) [GALILEAN, GALILEANS, TIBERIAS]
Nu 34:11 run down along the eastern edge of the Sea of G,
Dt 3:17 all the way from the Sea of G down to the Dead
Jos 11: 2 the kings in the Jordan Valley south of G;
12: 3 as far north as the western shores of the Sea of G
13:27 extending as far north as the Sea of G.
20: 7 Kedesh of G, in the hill country of Naphtali;
21:32 they received Kedesh in G (a city of refuge),
1Ki 9:11 Solomon gave twenty towns in the land of G to
2Ki 15:29 conquered the regions of Gilead, G, and Naphtali,
1Ch 6:76 they were given Kedesh in G, Hammon,
Isa 9: 1 but there will be a time in the future when G of the
Mt 2:22 in another dream, he was warned to go to G.
3:13 Then Jesus went from G to the Jordan River to be
4:12 had been arrested, he left Judea and returned to G.
4:13 He went to Capernaum, beside the Sea of G,
4:15 in G where so many Gentiles live—
4:18 was walking along the shore beside the Sea of G,
4:23 Jesus traveled throughout G teaching in the
4:24 about him spread far beyond the borders of G
4:25 people from G, the Ten Towns, Jerusalem, from all
15:21 Jesus then left G and went north to the region of
15:29 Jesus returned to the Sea of G and climbed a hill
17:22 One day after they had returned to G, Jesus told
19: 1 he left G and went southward to the region of
21:11 "It's Jesus, the prophet from Nazareth in G."
26:32 I will go ahead of you to G and meet you there."
27:55 And many women who had come from G with
28: 7 from the dead, and he is going ahead of you to G.
28:10 Go tell my brothers to leave for G, and they will
28:16 Then the eleven disciples left for G, going to the
Mk 1: 9 One day Jesus came from Nazareth in G, and he
1:14 Jesus went to G to preach God's Good News.
1:16 was walking along the shores of the Sea of G,
1:28 done spread quickly through that entire area of G.
1:39 So he traveled throughout the region of G,
3: 7 followed by a huge crowd from all over G, Judea,
6:21 army officers, and the leading citizens of G.
7:24 Then Jesus left G and went north to the region of
7:31 then back to the Sea of G and the region of the Ten
8:27 Jesus and his disciples left G and went up to the
9:30 Leaving that region, they traveled through G.
14:28 I will go ahead of you to G and meet you there."
14:70 must be one of them because you are from G."
15:41 of Jesus and had cared for him while he was in G.
16: 7 including Peter: Jesus is going ahead of you to G.
Lk 1:26 sent the angel Gabriel to Nazareth, a village in G,
2: 4 traveled there from the village of Nazareth in G.
2:39 of the Lord, they returned home to Nazareth in G.
3: 1 over Judea; Herod Antipas was ruler over G;
3:19 ruler of G, for marrying Herodias, his brother's
4:14 Then Jesus returned to G, filled with the Holy
4:31 Then Jesus went to Capernaum, a town in G,
5: 1 Jesus was preaching on the shore of the Sea of G.
5:17 these men showed up from every village in all G
8:26 the land of the Gerasenes, across the lake from G.
13: 1 G as they were sacrificing at the Temple in
13: 2 were worse sinners than other people from G?"
17:11 he reached the border between G and Samaria.
23: 5 he goes, all over Judea, from G to Jerusalem!"
23: 7 because G was under Herod's jurisdiction,
23:49 the women who had followed him from G,
23:55 the women from G followed and saw the tomb
24: 6 Don't you remember what he told you back in G,
Jn 1:43 The next day Jesus decided to go to G. He found
2: 1 a wedding celebration in the village of Cana in G.
2:11 This miraculous sign at Cana in G was Jesus' first
4: 3 So he left Judea to return to G.
4:43 end of the two days' stay, Jesus went on into G.
4:46 In the course of his journey through G, he arrived
4:47 Jesus had come from Judea and was traveling in G,
4:54 This was Jesus' second miraculous sign in G after
6: 1 After this, Jesus crossed over the Sea of G,
7: 1 After this, Jesus stayed in G, going from village to
7: 9 So Jesus remained in G.
7:41 "But he can't be! Will the Messiah come from G?
7:52 They replied, "Are you from G, too?
7:52 see for yourself—no prophet ever comes from G!"
12:21 a visit to Philip, who was from Bethsaida in G.
21: 1 again to the disciples beside the Sea of G.
21: 2 Nathanael from Cana in G, the sons of Zebedee,
Ac 1:11 They said, "Men of G, why are you standing here
2: 7 they exclaimed. "These people are all from G,
5:37 at the time of the census, there was Judas of G.
9:31 G, and Samaria, and it grew in strength
10:37 beginning in G after John the Baptist began
13:31 who had gone with him from G to Jerusalem—

GALL (1)
Mt 27:34 The soldiers gave him wine mixed with bitter g,

GALLIM (2)
1Sa 25:44 to a man from G named Palti son of Laish.
Isa 10:30 Well may you scream in terror, you people of G!

GALLIO (3)
Ac 18:12 But when G became governor of Achaia, some Jews
18:14 G turned to Paul's accusers and said, "Listen,
18:17 there in the courtroom. But G paid no attention.

GALLON (6) [GALLONS]
Ex 30:24 12-1/2 pounds of cassia, and one g of olive oil.
Eze 45:24 and a g of olive oil with each young bull and ram.
46: 5 He is to offer one g of olive oil for each half bushel
46: 7 With each half bushel of flour he must offer one g
46:11 One g of oil is to be given with each half bushel of
46:14 and a half quarts of flour with a third of a g of

GALLONS (14) [GALLON]
1Ki 5:11 wheat for his household and 110,000 g of olive oil.
7:26 lily blossom. It could hold about 11,000 g of water.
7:38 was 6 feet across and could hold 220 g of water.
18:32 around the altar large enough to hold about three g.
2Ch 2:10 100,000 bushels of barley, 110,000 g of wine, and 110,000 g of olive oil."
4: 5 lily blossom. It could hold about 16,500 g of water.
Ezr 7:22 500 bushels of wheat, 550 g of wine, 550 g of olive oil,
Isa 5:10 Ten acres of vineyard will not produce even six g
Hag 2:16 When you expected to draw fifty g from the
Lk 16: 6 'I owe him eight hundred g of olive oil.'
16: 6 that bill and write another one for four hundred g.'
Jn 2: 6 and held twenty to thirty g each.

GALLOP (2) [GALLOPING]
Eze 26:10 and your walls will shake as the horses g through
Am 6:12 Can horses g over rocks? Can oxen be used to

GALLOPING (3) [GALLOP]
Jdg 5:22 the g, g of Sisera's mighty steeds.
2Ki 7: 6 and the g of horses and the sounds of a great army

GALLOWS (10)
Est 2:23 found to be true, the two men were hanged on a g.
5:14 "Set up a g that stands seventy-five feet tall,
5:14 Haman immensely, and he ordered the g set up.
6: 4 king to hang Mordecai from the g he had prepared.
7: 9 "Haman has set up a g that stands seventy-five
7:10 So they hanged Haman on the g he had set up for
8: 7 and he has been hanged on the g because he tried
9:13 the bodies of Haman's ten sons hung from the g."
9:14 hung the bodies of Haman's ten sons from the g.
9:25 and Haman and his sons were hanged on the g.

GAMALIEL (7)
Nu 1:10 Manasseh son of Joseph | G son of Pedahzur
2:20[-21] Manasseh | G son of Pedahzur | 32,200
7:54 On the eighth day G son of Pedahzur, leader of the
7:59 This was the offering brought by G son of
10:23 The tribe of Manasseh was led by G son of
Ac 5:34 He was a Pharisee named G, who was an expert on
22: 3 and educated here in Jerusalem under G.

GAMBLED (3)
Mt 27:35 the soldiers **g** for his clothes by throwing dice.
Mk 15:24 They **g** for his clothes, throwing dice to decide
Lk 23:34 And the soldiers **g** for his clothes by throwing dice.

GAME (12)
Ge 25:28 because of the wild **g** he brought home,
27: 3 the open country, and hunt some wild **g** for me.
27: 5 So when Esau left to hunt for the wild **g**,
27: 7 to prepare him a delicious meal of wild **g**.
27:19 Here is the wild **g**, cooked the way you like it.
27:31 he said, "I'm back, Father, and I have the wild **g**.
27:33 "Then who was it that just served me wild **g**?
Pr 12:27 Lazy people don't even cook the **g** they catch,
Isa 42:22 They are fair **g** for all and have no one to protect
Mt 11:16 group of children playing a **g** in the public square.
Lk 7:32 They are like a group of children playing a **g** in the
2Pe 2:14 They make a **g** of luring unstable people into sin.

GAMMAD (1)
Eze 27:11 Your towers were manned by men from **G**.

GAMUL (1) [BETH-GAMUL]
1Ch 24:17 lot fell to Jakin. / The twenty-second lot fell to **G**.

GANG (3) [GANGS]
1Ki 11:24 and had become the leader of a **g** of rebels.
2Ch 13: 7 Then a whole **g** of scoundrels joined him,
Ps 22:16 me like a pack of dogs; / an evil **g** closes in on me.

GANGS (1) [GANG]
Hos 6: 9 **G** of priests murder travelers along the road to

GAP (2) [GAPS]
Jdg 21:15 because the LORD had left this **g** in the tribes of
Eze 22:30 I searched for someone to stand in the **g** in the wall

GAPING (1)
Zep 2:14 ruins of its palaces, hooting from the **g** windows.

GAPS (3) [GAP]
Ne 4: 7 and that the **g** in the wall were being repaired,
6: 1 rebuilding the wall and that no **g** remained—
Joel 2: 8 They lunge through the **g**, and no weapon can stop

GARB (2)
2Ki 25:29 Jehoiachin with new clothes to replace his prison **g**
Jer 52:33 Jehoiachin with new clothes to replace his prison **g**

GARBAGE (7)
Ps 113: 7 from the dirt / and the needy from the **g** dump.
Isa 5:25 and the rotting bodies of his people are thrown as **g**
La 3:45 discarded us as refuse and **g** among the nations.
4: 5 Those who once lived in palaces now search the **g**
Ro 9:21 one jar for decoration and another to throw **g** into?
1Co 4:13 Yet we are treated like the world's **g**,
Php 3: 8 counting it all as **g**, so that I may have Christ

GARDEN (52) [GARDENER, GARDENS]
Ge 2: 8 Then the LORD God planted a **g** in Eden,
2: 9 the LORD God planted all sorts of trees in the **g**—
2: 9 At the center of the **g** he placed the tree of life
2:10 watering the **g** and then dividing into four
2:15 The LORD God placed the man in the **G** of Eden
2:16 "You may freely eat any fruit in the **g**
3: 1 say you must not eat any of the fruit in the **g**?"
3: 3 at the center of the **g** that we are not allowed to eat.
3: 8 they heard the LORD God walking about in the **g**,
3:23 banished Adam and his wife from the **G** of Eden,
3:24 After banishing them from the **g**, the LORD God
13:10 like the **g** of the LORD or the beautiful land of
Dt 11:10 ditches with your foot as in a vegetable **g**.
1Ki 4:25 to Beersheba, each family had its own home and **g**.
21: 2 I would like to buy it to use as a vegetable **g**.
2Ki 18:31 each of you to continue eating from your own **g**
21:18 he was buried in the palace **g**, the **g** of Uzza.
21:26 He was buried in his tomb in the **g** of Uzza.
Ne 3:15 the wall of the pool of Siloam near the king's **g**,
Est 1: 5 was held at Susa in the courtyard of the palace **g**.
7: 7 to his feet in a rage and went out into the palace **g**.
7: 8 just as the king returned from the palace **g**.
Job 8:16 the sunshine, its branches spreading across the **g**.
SS 4:12 "You are like a private **g**, my treasure, my bride!
4:15 You are a **g** fountain, a well of living water,
4:16 Blow on my **g** and waft its lovely perfume to my
4:16 Let him come into his **g** and eat its choicest
5: 1 "I am here in my **g**, my treasure, my bride!
6: 2 "He has gone down to his **g**, to his spice beds,
Isa 1:30 will wither away like an oak or **g** without water.
3:12 They are leading you down a pretty **g** path to
5: 7 Israel and Judah are his pleasant **g**. / He expected
36:16 each of you to continue eating from your own **g**
51: 3 become as beautiful as Eden—the **g** of the LORD.
58:11 You will be like a well-watered **g**, like an
61:11 His righteousness will be like a **g** in early spring,
66:17 "Those who 'purify' themselves in a sacred **g**,
Jer 10: 5 stands their god like a helpless scarecrow in a **g**!
31:12 Their life will be like a watered **g**, and all their
39: 4 a gate between the two walls behind the king's **g**
La 2: 6 his Temple as though it were merely a **g** shelter.
Eze 28:13 You were in Eden, the **g** of God. Your clothing
31: 8 taller than any of the other cedars in the **g** of God.
31: 8 No tree in the **g** of God came close to it in beauty.
31: 9 envy of all the other trees of Eden, the **g** of God.
36:35 'This godforsaken land is now like Eden's **g**!
Joel 2: 3 Ahead of them the land lies as fair as the **G** of
Mt 13:32 but it becomes the largest of **g** plants and grows
Lk 13: 6 "A man planted a fig tree in his **g** and came again
13:19 It is like a tiny mustard seed planted in a **g**;
Jn 19:41 The place of crucifixion was near a **g**, where there

GARDENER (4) [GARDEN]
Lk 13: 7 Finally, he said to his **g**, 'I've waited three years,
13: 8 "The **g** answered, 'Give it one more chance.
Jn 15: 1 "I am the true vine, and my Father is the **g**.
20:15 She thought he was the **g**. "Sir," she said, "if you

GARDENS (12) [GARDEN]
Nu 24: 6 groves of palms, / like fruitful **g** by the riverside.
2Ki 25: 4 the gate between the two walls behind the king's **g**.
Ecc 2: 5 I made **g** and parks, filling them with all kinds of
SS 1:14 He is like a bouquet of flowers in the **g** of
8:13 "O my beloved, lingering in the **g**, how wonderful
Isa 1:29 of all the sins you committed in your sacred **g**.
7:25 No one will go to the fertile hillsides where the **g**
65: 3 to my face by worshiping idols in their sacred **g**.
Jer 29: 5 plan to stay. Plant **g**, and eat the food you produce.
31: 5 of Samaria and eat from your own **g** there.
52: 7 the gate between the two walls behind the king's **g**.
Am 9:14 They will plant vineyards and **g**; they will eat their

GAREB (3)
2Sa 23:38 Ira from Jattir; / **G** from Jattir;
1Ch 11:40 Ira from Jattir; / **G** from Jattir;
Jer 31:39 line will be stretched out over the hill of **G**

GARISH (1)
Hos 2: 2 Tell her to take off her **g** makeup and suggestive

GARLANDS (1)
La 5:16 The **g** have fallen from our heads. Disaster has

GARLIC (1)
Nu 11: 5 melons, leeks, onions, and **g** that we wanted.

GARMENT (9) [GARMENTS, UNDERGARMENTS]
Dt 24:17 and you must never accept a widow's **g** in pledge
Job 30:18 With a strong hand, God grabs my **g**. He grips me
Ps 102:26 You will change them like a **g**, / and they will fade
Mt 9:16 And who would patch an old **g** with unshrunk
Mk 2:21 And who would patch an old **g** with unshrunk
Lk 5:36 "No one tears a piece of cloth from a new **g** and uses it to patch an old **g**.
5:36 For then the new **g** would be torn, and the patch wouldn't even match the old **g**.

GARMENTS (33) [GARMENT]
Ex 28: 2 beautiful **g** that will lend dignity to his work.
28: 3 the **g** that will set Aaron apart from everyone else,
28: 4 They will also make special **g** for Aaron's sons to
28:41 Clothe Aaron and his sons with these **g**, and
29:29 "Aaron's sacred **g** must be preserved for his
31:10 the beautifully stitched, holy **g** for Aaron the priest,
31:10 and the **g** for his sons to wear as they minister as
35:19 the sacred **g** for Aaron and his sons to wear while
35:21 and its furnishings and for the holy **g**.
39: 1 the craftsmen made beautiful **g** of blue, purple,
39: 1 This same cloth was used for Aaron's sacred **g**,
39:41 the beautifully crafted **g** to be worn while
39:41 the holy **g** for Aaron the priest and for his sons to
40:13 Clothe Aaron with the holy **g** and anoint him,
Lev 16: 4 linen turban on his head. These are his sacred **g**.
16:23 he must take off the linen **g** he wore when he
16:23 Most Holy Place, and he must leave the **g** there.
16:24 put on his **g**, and go out to sacrifice his own whole
16:32 his ancestor Aaron. He will put on the holy linen **g**
21:10 has been ordained to wear the special priestly **g**,
Nu 20:26 There you will remove Aaron's priestly **g** and put
20:28 Moses removed the priestly **g** from Aaron and put
1Sa 2:28 and to wear the priestly **g** as he served me.
Ps 22:18 among themselves / and throw dice for my **g**.
110: 3 will serve you willingly. / Arrayed in holy **g**,
Pr 31:24 She makes belted linen **g** and sashes to sell to the
Isa 3:23 their mirrors, linen **g**, head ornaments, and shawls.
Mt 21: 7 the animals to him and threw their **g** over the colt,
Mk 11: 7 brought the colt to Jesus and threw their **g** over it,
Lk 19:35 to Jesus and threw their **g** over it for him to ride on.
Ac 9:39 the coats and other **g** Dorcas had made for them.
Rev 3: 4 some who have not soiled their **g** with evil deeds.
3:18 And also buy white **g** so you will not be shamed by

GARMITE (1)
1Ch 4:19 One of her sons was the father of Keilah the **G**,

GARNER(S) [KJV] See BARN(S), FARMS, GRANARIES

GARRISON (4) [GARRISONS]
1Sa 10: 5 of God, where the **g** of the Philistines is located,
13: 3 and defeated the **g** of Philistines at Geba.
13: 4 He announced that the Philistine **g** at Geba had
Ac 24:22 "Wait until Lysias, the **g** commander, arrives.

GARRISONS (5) [GARRISON]
2Sa 8: 6 Then he placed several army **g** in Damascus,
8:14 He placed army **g** throughout Edom, and all the
1Ch 18: 6 Then he placed several army **g** in Damascus,
18:13 He placed army **g** throughout Edom, and all the
2Ch 17: 2 and he assigned additional **g** to the land of Judah

GASP (4) [GASPING, GASPS]
Isa 42:14 I will **g** and pant like a woman giving birth.
Jer 19: 8 and will **g** at the destruction they see there.
49:17 and will **g** at the destruction they see there.
50:13 and will **g** at the destruction they see there.

GASPING (1) [GASP]
Jer 4:31 It is the cry of Jerusalem's people **g** for breath,

GASPS (1) [GASP]
Jer 15: 9 The mother of seven grows faint and **g** for breath;

GAT [KJV] See also GATHERED, GET, GOT AWAY, RETURNED, SET OUT, TRAVELED, WENT

GATAM (3)
Ge 36:11 Eliphaz were Teman, Omar, Zepho, **G**, and Kenaz.
36:16 Korah, **G**, and Amalek. These clans in the land of
1Ch 1:36 Omar, Zepho, **G**, Kenaz, and Amalek, who was

GATE (141) [FLOODGATE, GATEKEEPER, GATEKEEPERS, GATEMEN, GATEPOST, GATEPOSTS, GATES, GATEWAY, GATEWAY'S, GATEWAYS]
Ge 23:18 in the presence of the Hittite elders at the city **g**.
Dt 25: 7 she must go to the town **g** and say to the leaders
Jos 2: 7 as the king's men had left, the city **g** was shut.
7: 5 chased the Israelites from the city **g** as far as the
8:29 down the body and threw it in front of the city **g**.
20: 4 death will appear before the leaders at the city **g**
Jdg 9:40 covered with dead bodies all the way to the city **g**.
9:44 and his group stormed the city **g** to keep the men of
18:16 from the tribe of Dan stood just outside the **g**,
Ru 4: 1 So Boaz went to the town **g** and took a seat there.
1Sa 4:18 Eli fell backward from his seat beside the **g**.
2Sa 15: 2 every morning and went out to the **g** of the city.
18: 4 So he stood at the **g** of the city as all the divisions
18:24 While David was sitting at the city **g**,
19: 8 So the king went out and sat at the city **g**, and as
23:15 from the well in Bethlehem, the one by the **g**."
1Ki 22:10 at the threshing floor near the **g** of Samaria.
2Ki 7:17 appointed his officer to control the traffic at the **g**,
7:20 for the people trampled him to death at the **g**!
9:31 When Jehu entered the **g** of the palace, she shouted
10: 8 them in two heaps at the entrance of the city **g**,
11: 6 third of you are to stand guard at the Sur **G**.
11:16 and led her out to the **g** where horses enter the
11:19 They went through the **g** of the guards and into the
14:13 from the Ephraim **G** to the Corner **G**.
15:35 He was the one who rebuilt the upper **g** of the
23: 8 He destroyed the shrines at the entrance to the **g** of
23: 8 This **g** was located to the left of the city **g** as one
25: 4 and fled through the **g** between the two walls
1Ch 9:18 they were responsible for the King's **G** on the east
11:17 from the well in Bethlehem, the one by the **g**."
19: 9 troops drew up their battle lines at the **g** of the city,
26:14 The responsibility for the east **g** went to
26:14 The north **g** was assigned to his son Zechariah,
26:15 The south **g** went to Obed-edom, and his sons were
26:16 Shuppim and Hosah were assigned the west **g**
26:17 Six Levites were assigned each day to the east **g**,
26:17 four to the north **g**, four to the south **g**, and two
26:18 Six were assigned each day to the west **g**, four to
2Ch 18: 9 at the threshing floor near the **g** of Samaria.
23: 5 and the final third will be at the Foundation **G**.
23:15 and led her out to the **g** where horses enter the
23:20 They went through the Upper **G** and into the
24: 8 and set outside the **g** leading to the Temple of the
25:23 from the Ephraim **G** to the Corner **G**.
26: 9 built fortified towers in Jerusalem at the Corner **G**,
26: 9 at the Valley **G**, and at the angle in the wall.
27: 3 Jotham rebuilt the Upper **G** to the LORD's
31:14 the Levite, who was the gatekeeper at the East **G**,
32: 6 to assemble before him in the square at the city **g**.
33:14 Gihon Spring in the Kidron Valley to the Fish **G**,
Ne 2:13 I went out through the Valley **G**, past the Jackal's
2:13 and over to the Dung **G** to inspect the broken walls
2:14 Then I went to the Fountain **G** and to the King's
2:15 I turned back and entered again at the Valley **G**.
3: 1 the other priests started to rebuild at the Sheep **G**.
3: 3 The Fish **G** was built by the sons of Hassenaah.
3: 6 The Old City **G** was repaired by Joiada son of
3:13 led by Hanun, rebuilt the Valley **G**, hung its doors,
3:13 the fifteen hundred feet of wall to the Dung **G**.
3:14 The Dung **G** was repaired by Malkijah son of
3:15 of the Mizpah district, repaired the Fountain **G**.
3:26 who repaired the wall as far as the Water **G** toward
3:28 repaired the wall up the hill from the Horse **G**,
3:29 son of Shecaniah, the gatekeeper of the East **G**.
3:31 and merchants, opposite the Inspection **G**.
3:32 repaired the wall from that corner to the Sheep **G**.
8: 1 as one person at the square just inside the Water **G**.

8: 3 He faced the square just inside the Water **G** from
8:16 just inside the Water **G** and the Ephraim **G**.
12:31 southward along the top of the wall to the Dung **G**.
12:37 At the Fountain **G** they went straight up the steps
12:37 and then proceeded to the Water **G** on the east.
12:39 then past the Ephraim **G** to the Old City **G**,
12:39 past the Fish **G** and the Tower of Hananel,
12:39 on to the Sheep **G** and stopped at the Guard **G**.
Est 3: 3 Then the palace officials at the king's **g** asked
4: 2 He stood outside the **g** of the palace, for no one
4: 6 to Mordecai in the square in front of the palace **g**.
5: 9 But when he saw Mordecai sitting at the **g**,
5:13 the Jew just sitting there at the palace **g**."
6:10 Mordecai the Jew, who sits at the **g** of the palace.
6:12 Afterward Mordecai returned to the palace **g**,
Job 29: 7 "Those were the days when I went to the city **g**
Pr 18:19 Arguments separate friends like a **g** locked with
SS 7: 4 pools in Heshbon by the **g** of Bath-rabbim.
Jer 17:19 first at the **g** where the king goes out, and then at
19: 2 son of Hinnom by the entrance to the Potsherd **G**,
20: 2 and put in stocks at the Benjamin **G** of the
22:19 out of Jerusalem and dumped outside the **g**!
26:10 and sat down at the New **G** of the Temple to hold
31:38 from the Tower of Hananel to the Corner **G**.
31:40 Kidron Valley on the east as far as the Horse **G**—
36:10 courtyard of the Temple, near the New **G** entrance.
37:13 But as he was walking through the Benjamin **G**,
38: 7 time the king was holding court at the Benjamin **G**,
39: 3 army came in and sat in triumph at the Middle **G**:
39: 4 his royal guard saw the Babylonians in the city **g**,
39: 4 They went out through a **g** between the two walls
52: 7 and fled through the **g** between the two walls
Eze 8: 3 I was taken to the north **g** of the inner courtyard of
8: 5 the north, beside the entrance to the **g** of the altar,
8:14 He brought me to the north **g** of the LORD's
9: 2 Six men soon appeared from the upper **g** that faces
10:19 the cherubim flew with their wheels to the east **g** of
21:15 melt with terror, for the sword glitters at every **g**.
40:45 "The building beside the north inner **g** is for the
40:46 The building beside the south inner **g** is for the
44: 2 LORD said to me, "This **g** must remain closed;
Zep 1:10 "a cry of alarm will come from the Fish **G**
Zec 14:10 the Benjamin **G** over to the site of the old **g**,
14:10 then to the Corner **G**, and from the Tower of
Mt 7:13 enter God's Kingdom only through the narrow **g**.
7:13 and its **g** is wide for the many who choose the easy
26:71 Later, out by the **g**, another servant girl noticed
Lk 7:12 was coming out as he approached the village **g**.
Jn 5: 2 Inside the city, near the Sheep **G**, was the pool of
10: 1 rather than going through the **g**, must surely be a
10: 2 For a shepherd enters through the **g**.
10: 3 The gatekeeper opens the **g** for him, and the sheep
10: 7 "I assure you, I am the **g** for the sheep," he said.
10: 9 Yes, I am the **g**. Those who come in through me
18:16 Peter stood outside the **g**. Then the other disciple
spoke to the woman watching at the **g**,
Ac 3: 2 Each day he was put beside the Temple **g**, the one
called the Beautiful **G**,
3:10 beggar they had seen so often at the Beautiful **G**,
9:24 and night at the city **g** so they could murder him.
10:17 found the house and stood outside at the **g**.
12: 6 with others standing guard at the prison **g**.
12:10 guard posts and came to the iron **g** to the street,
12:13 He knocked at the door in the **g**, and a servant girl
Rev 21:21 were made of pearls—each **g** from a single pearl!

GATEKEEPER (8) [GATE, KEEP]

1Ch 9:17 and their relatives. Shallum was the chief **g**.
2Ch 31:14 Imnah the Levite, who was the **g** at the East Gate,
Ezr 7:24 that no priest, Levite, singer, **g**, Temple servant,
Ne 3:29 Shemaiah son of Shecaniah, the **g** of the East Gate.
Ps 84:10 I would rather be a **g** in the house of my God
Jer 35: 4 room of Maaseiah son of Shallum, the Temple **g**.
Mk 13:34 to do, and he told the **g** to watch for his return.
Jn 10: 3 The **g** opens the gate for him, and the sheep hear

GATEKEEPERS (44) [GATE, KEEP]

2Ki 7:10 back to the city and told the **g** what had
happened—
7:11 Then the **g** shouted the news to the people in the
22: 4 and have him count the money the **g** have collected
23: 4 and the Temple **g** to remove from the LORD's
25:18 his assistant Zephaniah, and the three chief **g**.
1Ch 9:17 The **g** who returned were Shallum, Akkub,
9:18 These men served as **g** for the camps of the
9:20 Eleazar had been in charge of the **g** in earlier times,
9:22 In all, there were 212 **g** in those days, and they
9:23 These **g** and their descendants, by their divisions,
9:24 The **g** were stationed on all four sides—east,
9:26 The four chief **g**, all Levites, were in an office of
9:28 Some of the **g** were assigned to care for the various
15:18 Mattithiah, Eliphelehu, Mikneiah, and the **g**,
16:38 Hosah, and sixty-eight other Levites as **g**.
16:42 And the sons of Jeduthun were appointed as **g**.
23: 5 Four thousand will work as **g**, and another four
26: 1 These are the divisions of the **g**:
26: 4 The sons of Obed-edom, also **g**, were Shemaiah
26:11 Hosah's sons and relatives, who served as **g**,
26:12 These divisions of the **g** were named for their
26:19 These were the divisions of the **g** from the clans of
2Ch 8:14 And he assigned the **g** to their gates by their
23: 4 on the Sabbath, a third of them will serve as **g**.
23:19 He stationed **g** at the gates of the LORD's Temple
34: 9 the Levites who served as **g** at the Temple of God.
34:13 Still others assisted as secretaries, officials, and **g**.
35:15 The **g** guarded the gates and did not need to leave
Ezr 2:42 The **g** of the families of Shallum, Ater, Talmon,
2:70 So the priests, the Levites, the singers, the **g**,
7: 7 Levites, singers, **g**, and Temple servants,
10:24 Eliashib. These are the **g** who were guilty:
Ne 7: 1 the **g**, singers, and Levites were appointed.
7: 3 And while the **g** are still on duty, have them shut
7:45 The **g** of the families of Shallum, Ater, Talmon,
7:73 "So the priests, the Levites, the **g**, the singers,
10:28 the priests, Levites, **g**, singers, Temple servants,
10:39 near the ministering priests, the **g**, and the singers.
11:19 From the **g**: Akkub, Talmon, and 172 of their
12:25 and Akkub were the **g** in charge of the storerooms
12:45 his son Solomon, and so did the singers and the **g**.
12:47 of food for the singers, the **g**, and the Levites.
13: 5 belonged to the Levites, the singers, and the **g**.
Jer 52:24 his assistant Zephaniah, and the three chief **g**.

GATEMEN (1) [GATE, MAN]

Eze 44:11 They may still be Temple guards and **g**, and they

GATEPOST (1) [GATE, POST]

Eze 46: 2 Then he will stand by the **g** while the priest offers

GATEPOSTS (1) [GATE, POST]

Eze 45:19 and the **g** at the entrance to the inner courtyard.

GATES (123) [GATE]

Dt 3: 5 all fortified cities with high walls and barred **g**.
6: 9 on the doorposts of your house and on your **g**.
11:20 on the doorposts of your house and on your **g**,
17: 5 or woman must be taken to the **g** of the town
20:11 If they accept your terms and open the **g** to you,
22:24 you must take both of them to the **g** of the town
33:25 May the bolts of your **g** be of iron and bronze;
Jos 2: 5 the city at dusk, as the city **g** were about to close,
6: 1 Now the **g** of Jericho were tightly shut
6:26 the cost of his youngest son, / he will set up its **g**."
Jdg 5: 8 Israel chose new gods, / war erupted at the city **g**.
5:11 of the LORD / marched down to the city **g**.
9:35 Gaal was standing at the city **g** when Abimelech
16: 2 gathered together and waited all night at the city **g**.
16: 3 got up, took hold of the city **g** with its two posts,
1Sa 9:12 "Stay right on this road. He is at the town **g**.
9:14 entered the town, and as they passed through the **g**,
17:52 chasing them as far as Gath and the **g** of Ekron.
2Sa 10: 8 up their battle lines at the entrance of the city **g**,
11:23 "And as we chased them back to the city **g**,
1Ki 4:13 including sixty great fortified cities with **g** barred
16:34 when he finally completed it by setting up the **g**,
17:10 As he arrived at the **g** of the village, he saw a
2Ki 7: 3 with leprosy sitting at the entrance of the city **g**.
18:31 Make peace with me—open the **g** and come out.
19:32 They will not march outside its **g** with their shields
1Ch 9:27 It was also their job to open the **g** every morning.
22: 3 nails that would be needed for the doors in the **g**
26:13 by families for guard duty at the various **g**,
2Ch 8: 5 rebuilding their walls and installing barred **g**.
8:14 And he assigned the gatekeepers to their **g** by their
14: 7 and fortify them with walls, towers, **g**, and bars.
23:19 He stationed gatekeepers at the **g** of the LORD's
31: 2 and praise to the LORD at the **g** of the Temple.
35:15 The gatekeepers guarded the **g** and did not need to
Ne 1: 3 has been torn down, and the **g** have been burned."
2: 3 is in ruins, and the **g** have been burned down."
2: 8 I will need it to make beams for the **g** of the
2:13 Gate to inspect the broken walls and burned **g**.
2:17 It lies in ruins, and its **g** are burned. Let us rebuild
6: 1 though we had not yet hung the doors in the **g**—
7: 1 was finished and I had hung the doors in the **g**,
7: 3 "Do not leave the **g** open during the hottest part of
11:19 and 172 of their associates, who guarded the **g**.
12:25 gatekeepers in charge of the storerooms at the **g**.
12:30 then the people, the **g**, and the wall.
13:19 then on the **g** of the city should be shut as darkness
13:19 I also sent some of my own servants to guard the **g**
13:22 and to guard the **g** in order to preserve the holiness
Job 38:10 For I locked it behind barred **g**, limiting its shores.
38:17 Do you know where the **g** of death are located?
Have you seen the **g** of utter gloom?
Ps 9:14 so I can praise you publicly at Jerusalem's **g**,
24: 7 Open up, ancient **g**! / Open up, ancient doors,
24: 9 Open up, ancient **g**! / Open up, ancient doors,
100: 4 Enter his **g** with thanksgiving; / go into his courts
107:16 For he broke down their prison **g** of bronze;
118:19 Open for me the **g** where the righteous enter,
118:20 Those **g** lead to the presence of the LORD,
122: 2 we are standing here / inside your **g**, O Jerusalem.
127: 5 shame when he confronts his accusers at the city **g**.
147:13 For he has fortified the bars of your **g** / and blessed
Pr 8: 3 entrance to the city, at the city **g**, she cries aloud,
8:34 watching for me daily at my **g**, waiting for me
14:19 the wicked will bow at the **g** of the godly.
Isa 3:26 The **g** of Jerusalem will weep and mourn. The city
22: 7 your beautiful valleys and crowd against your **g**.
24:12 The city is left in ruins, with its **g** battered down.
26: 2 Open the **g** to all who are righteous;
28: 6 great courage to their warriors who stand at the **g**.
36:16 Make peace with me—open the **g** and come out.
37:33 They will not march outside its **g** with their shields
45: 1 Their fortress **g** will be opened, never again to shut
45: 2 I will smash down **g** of bronze and cut through
52: 1 and godless people will no longer enter your **g**.
54:12 and your **g** and walls of shining gems.
60:11 Your **g** will stay open around the clock to receive
Jer 1:15 They will set their thrones at the **g** of the city.
13:19 The towns of the Negev will close their **g**, and no
15: 7 I will winnow you like grain at the **g** of your cities
17:19 said to me, "Go and stand in the **g** of Jerusalem,
17:19 the king goes out, and then at each of the other **g**.
17:21 Stop carrying on your trade at Jerusalem's **g** on the
17:27 through the **g** of Jerusalem just as on other days,
then I will set fire to these **g**.
22: 4 The king will ride through the palace **g** in chariots
49:31 "They live alone in the desert without walls or **g**.
51:30 burned the houses and broken down the city **g**.
51:58 to the ground, and her high **g** will be burned.
La 1: 4 The city **g** are silent, her priests groan, her young
2: 9 Jerusalem's **g** have sunk into the ground. All their
4:12 an enemy could march through the **g** of Jerusalem.
5:14 The old men no longer sit in the city **g**; the young
Eze 21:22 With battering rams they will go against the **g**,
26:10 shake as the horses gallop through your broken **g**,
40:18 This pavement flanked the **g** and extended out
48:31 there will be three **g**, each one named after a tribe
48:32 the **g** will be named for Joseph, Benjamin,
48:33 will have **g** named for Simeon, Issachar,
48:34 the **g** will be named for Gad, Asher, and Naphtali.
Hos 11: 6 their enemies will crash through their **g**
Am 1: 5 I will break down the **g** of Damascus and slaughter
Mic 1: 9 has reached into Judah, even to the **g** of Jerusalem.
1:12 judgment reaches even to the **g** of Jerusalem.
2:13 He will bring you through the **g** of your cities of
5: 6 and enter the **g** of the land of Nimrod.
Na 2: 6 But too late! The river **g** are open! The enemy has
3:13 The **g** of your land will be opened wide to the
Mk 14:54 then slipped inside the **g** of the high priest's
Ac 5:19 opened the **g** of the jail, and brought them out.
5:23 but when we opened the **g**, no one was there!"
14:13 prepared to sacrifice to the apostles at the city **g**.
21:30 and immediately the **g** were closed behind him.
2Co 11:32 King Aretas kept guards at the city **g** to catch me.
Heb 13:12 and died outside the city **g** in order to make his
2Pe 1:11 And God will open wide the **g** of heaven for you to
Rev 21:12 and high, with twelve **g** guarded by twelve angels.
21:12 of the twelve tribes of Israel were written on the **g**.
21:13 There were three **g** on each side—east, north,
21:15 stick to measure the city, its **g**, and its wall.
21:21 The twelve **g** were made of pearls—each gate from
21:25 Its **g** never close at the end of day because there is
22:14 so they can enter through the **g** of the city and eat

GATEWAY (76) [GATE, WAY]

Ge 28:17 other than the house of God—the **g** to heaven!"
1Sa 9:18 Just then Saul approached Samuel at the **g**
2Sa 3:27 Joab took him aside at the **g** as if to speak with him
18:24 the watchman climbed to the roof of the **g** by the
18:33 He went up to his room over the **g** and burst into
1Ch 26:16 the west gate and the **g** leading up to the Temple.
26:18 four to the **g** leading up to the Temple, and two to
Eze 11: 1 and brought me over to the east **g** of the LORD's
27: 3 that mighty **g** to the sea, the trading center of the
40: 3 shone like bronze standing beside a **g** entrance.
40: 6 Then he went over to the **g** that goes through the
40: 6 the steps and measured the threshold of the **g**;
40: 7 guard alcoves on each side built into the **g** passage.
40: 7 which led to the foyer at the inner end of the **g**
40: 8 He also measured the foyer of the **g**
40: 9 This foyer was at the inner end of the **g** structure,
40:10 three guard alcoves on each side of the **g** passage.
40:11 The man measured the **g** entrance, which was
40:11 the opening and 22-3/4 feet wide in the **g** passage.
40:13 Then he measured the entire width of the **g**,
40:14 along the inside of the **g** up to the gateway's foyer;
40:15 The full length of the **g** passage was 87-1/2 feet
40:17 Then the man brought me through the **g** into the
40:18 the courtyard the same distance as the **g** entrance.
40:20 There was a **g** on the north just like the one on the
40:21 All the measurements matched those of the east **g**.
40:21 The **g** passage was 87-1/2 feet long and 43-3/4 feet
40:22 decorations were identical to those in the east **g**.
40:22 There were seven steps leading up to the **g**
40:22 and the foyer was at the inner end of the **g** passage.
40:23 there was another **g** leading to the Temple's inner
courtyard directly opposite this outer **g**.
40:24 Then the man took me around to the south **g**
40:25 and there was a foyer where the **g** passage opened
40:25 the **g** passage was 87-1/2 feet long and 43-3/4 feet
40:26 This **g** also had a stairway of seven steps leading
40:27 And here again, directly opposite the outer **g**,
40:27 was another **g** that led into the inner courtyard.
40:28 Then the man took me to the south **g** leading into
40:29 the **g** passage was 87-1/2 feet long and 43-3/4 feet
40:31 The foyer of the south **g** faced into the outer
40:32 Then he took me to the east **g** leading to the inner
40:33 The **g** passage measured 87-1/2 feet long
40:35 Then he took me around to the north **g** leading to
40:36 and foyer of this **g** had the same measurements as
40:36 The **g** passage measured 87-1/2 feet long
40:38 A door led from the foyer of the inner **g** on the
40:44 one beside the north **g**, facing south, and the other
beside the south **g**, facing north.
42: 1 out of the Temple courtyard by way of the north **g**.
42:15 he led me out through the east **g** to measure the
43: 1 the man brought me back around to the east **g**.
43: 4 LORD came into the Temple through the east **g**.
44: 1 Then the man brought me back to the east **g** in the
44: 3 Only the prince himself may sit inside this **g** to
44: 4 Then the man brought me through the north **g** to
44:17 When they enter the **g** to the inner courtyard,
46: 1 The east **g** of the inner wall will be closed during
46: 2 The prince will enter the foyer of the **g** from the

46: 2 He will worship inside the **g** passage and then go
46: 2 he came. The **g** will not be closed until evening.
46: 3 the LORD in front of this **g** on Sabbath days
46: 8 "The prince must enter the **g** through the foyer,
46: 9 But when the people come in through the north **g**
46: 9 religious festivals, they must leave by the south **g**.
46: 9 And those who entered through the south **g** must leave by the north **g**.
46: 9 They must never leave by the same **g** they came in; they must always use the opposite **g**.
46:12 the east **g** to the inner courtyard will be opened for
46:12 way he entered, and the **g** will be shut behind him.
46:19 man brought me through the entrance beside the **g**
47: 2 brought me outside the wall through the north **g**
47: 2 flowing out through the south side of the east **g**.
Hos 2:15 and transform the Valley of Trouble into a **g** of
Mt 7:14 But the **g** to life is small, and the road is narrow,

GATEWAY'S (3) [GATE, WAY]

Eze 40: 7 The **g** inner threshold, which led to the foyer at the
40:14 along the inside of the gateway up to the **g** foyer;
44: 3 he may come and go only through the **g** foyer."

GATEWAYS (7) [GATE, WAY]

Eze 40:19 outer courtyard between the outer and inner **g**;
40:23 The distance between the two **g** was 175 feet.
40:27 The distance between the two **g** was 175 feet.
40:28 that it had the same measurements as the other **g**.
40:30 (The foyers of the **g** leading into the inner
40:32 that it had the same measurements as the other **g**.
40:35 that it had the same measurements as the other **g**.

GATH (39) [GATH-HEPHER, GATH-RIMMON, MORESHETH-GATH]

Jos 11:22 some still remained in Gaza, **G**, and Ashdod.
13: 4 cities of Gaza, Ashdod, Ashkelon, **G**, and Ekron.
1Sa 5: 8 and replied, "Move it to the city of **G**."
5: 8 So they moved the Ark of the God of Israel to **G**.
5: 9 But when the Ark arrived at **G**, the LORD began
6:17 rulers of Ashdod, Gaza, Ashkelon, **G**, and Ekron.
7:14 and **G** that the Philistines had captured were
17: 4 Then Goliath, a Philistine champion from **G**,
17:23 with them, he saw Goliath, the champion from **G**,
17:52 chasing them as far as **G** and the gates of Ekron.
17:52 the road from Shaaraim, as far as **G** and Ekron.
21:10 escaped from Saul and went to King Achish of **G**.
22: 1 So David left **G** and escaped to the cave of
27: 2 and went to live at **G** under the protection of King
27: 4 Word soon reached Saul that David had fled to **G**,
27:11 No one was left alive to come to **G** and tell where
2Sa 1:20 Don't announce the news in **G**, / or the Philistines
6:10 He took it instead to the home of Obed-edom of **G**.
8: 1 and humbled the Philistines by conquering **G**,
15:18 Gittites who had come with David from **G**,
21:19 from Bethlehem killed the brother of Goliath of **G**.
21:20 In another battle with the Philistines at **G**, a huge
21:22 Philistines were descended from the giants of **G**,
1Ki 2:39 of Shimei's slaves escaped to King Achish of **G**.
2:40 his donkey and went to **G** to search for them.
2:41 had left Jerusalem and had gone to **G** and returned.
2Ki 12:17 time King Hazael of Aram went to war against **G**
1Ch 7:21 to steal livestock from the local farmers near **G**.
8:13 in Aijalon, and they drove out the inhabitants of **G**.
13:13 He took it instead to the home of Obed-edom of **G**.
18: 1 and humbled the Philistines by conquering **G**
20: 5 of Jair killed Lahmi, the brother of Goliath of **G**.
20: 6 In another battle with the Philistines at **G**, a huge
20: 8 Philistines were descendants of the giants of **G**,
2Ch 11: 8 **G**, Mareshah, Ziph,
26: 6 on the Philistines and broke down the walls of **G**,
Ps 56: T regarding the time the Philistines seized him in **G**.
Am 6: 2 of Hamath and on down to the Philistine city of **G**.
Mic 1:10 Don't tell our enemies in the city of **G**; don't weep

GATH-HEPHER (2) [GATH, HEPHER]

Jos 19:13 Then it continued east to **G**, Eth-kazin,
2Ki 14:25 through Jonah son of Amittai, the prophet from **G**.

GATH-RIMMON (4) [GATH, RIMMON]

Jos 19:45 Jehud, Bene-berak, **G**,
21:24 Aijalon, and **G**—four towns.
21:25 to the priests: Taanach and **G**—two towns.
1Ch 6:69 Aijalon, and **G**.

GATHER (91) [GATHERED, GATHERING, GATHERINGS, GATHERS]

Ge 31:46 He also told his men to **g** stones and pile them up
41:35 Have them **g** all the food and grain of these good
49: 1 together all his sons and said, "**G** around me,
Ex 12:16 all the people must **g** for a time of special worship.
16:16 The LORD says that each household should **g** as
16:26 **G** the food for six days, but the seventh day is a
16:27 Some of the people went out anyway to **g** food,
19:13 Then they must **g** at the foot of the mountain."
30:34 "**G** sweet spices—resin droplets, mollusk scent,
Lev 23: 7 their regular work and **g** for a sacred assembly.
23:21 all your regular work and **g** for a sacred assembly.
23:27 must humble yourselves, **g** for a sacred assembly,
23:36 you must **g** again for a sacred assembly and present
23:40 On the first day, **g** fruit from citrus trees,
Nu 10: 3 the people will know that they are to **g** before you
19: 9 Then someone who is ceremonially clean will **g** up
20:10 summoned the people to come and **g** at the rock.
Dt 30: 3 and **g** you back from all the nations where he has
Ru 2: 2 "Let me go out into the fields to **g** leftover grain
2: 3 So Ruth went out to **g** grain behind the harvesters.
2: 7 She asked me this morning if she could **g** grain
2: 8 Stay right here with us when you **g** grain; don't go
2:15 "Let her **g** grain right among the sheaves without
2:19 "Where did you **g** all this grain today?
3: 2 and he's been very kind by letting you **g** grain with
1Sa 20:35 and took a young boy with him to **g** his arrows.
2Ki 4:39 One of the young men went out into the field to **g**
18:15 To **g** this amount, King Hezekiah used all the
1Ch 16:35 **G** and rescue us from among the nations,
2Ch 20:25 and his men went out to **g** the plunder.
Est 4:16 "Go and **g** together all the Jews of Susa and fast
Ps 7: 7 **G** the nations before you. / Sit on your throne high
41: 6 are my friends, / but all the while they **g** gossip,
102:22 when multitudes **g** together / and kingdoms come
104:28 When you supply it, they **g** it. / You open your
106:47 save us! / **G** us back from among the nations,
Pr 16: 1 We can **g** our thoughts, but the LORD gives the
24: 7 When the leaders **g**, the fool has nothing to say.
Ecc 3: 5 A time to scatter stones and a time to **g** stones.
SS 5: 1 I **g** my myrrh with my spices and eat my
6: 2 to his spice beds, to graze and to **g** the lilies.
Isa 11:12 He will **g** the scattered people of Judah from the
24:11 Mobs **g** in the streets, crying out for wine. Joy has
27:12 Yet the time will come when the LORD will **g**
43: 5 I will **g** you and your children from east and west
43: 9 **G** the nations together! Which of their idols has
45:20 "**G** together and come, you fugitives from
66:18 So I will **g** all nations and peoples together,
Jer 7:18 Watch how the children **g** wood and the fathers
9:21 and young men no longer **g** in the squares.
23: 3 But I will **g** together the remnant of my flock from
25: 9 I will **g** together all the armies of the north under
25:33 mourn for them or **g** up their bodies to bury them.
29:14 I will **g** you out of the nations where I sent you
31:10 will **g** them together and watch over them as a
40:12 then went out into the Judean countryside to **g** a
Eze 11:17 will **g** you back from the nations where you are
16:37 I will **g** together all your allies—these lovers of
22:21 I will **g** you together and blow the fire of my anger
28:25 For I will **g** them from the distant lands where I
36:24 For I will **g** you up from all the nations and bring
37:21 I will **g** the people of Israel from among the
39:17 to them: **G** together for my great sacrificial feast.
Hos 8:10 to many lands, I will now **g** them together.
9: 2 The grapes you **g** will not quench your thirst.
Joel 3: 2 "I will **g** the armies of the world into the valley of
3:11 **G** together in the valley." And now, O LORD,
Mic 2:12 O Israel, I will **g** the few of you who are left.
4: 6 "I will **g** together my people who are lame,
Na 3:18 There is no longer a shepherd to **g** them together.
Zep 2: 1 **G** together and pray, you shameless nation.
2: 2 **G** while there is still time, before judgment begins
3: 8 For it is my decision to **g** together the kingdoms of
3:18 "I will **g** you who mourn for the appointed
3:20 On that day I will **g** you together and bring you
Zec 14: 2 On that day I will **g** all the nations to fight against
Mt 18:20 For where two or three **g** together because they are
23:37 How often I have wanted to **g** your children
24:31 and they will **g** together his chosen ones from the
Mk 3:20 the crowds began to **g** again, and soon he and his
13:27 And he will send forth his angels to **g** together his
Lk 13:34 How often I have wanted to **g** your children
Jn 4:38 done the work, and you will **g** the harvest."
6:12 "Now **g** the leftovers," Jesus told his disciples,
Ac 19:29 A crowd began to **g**, and soon the city was filled
1Co 11:33 and sisters, when you **g** for the Lord's Supper,
16:19 and all the others who **g** in their home for church
Rev 14:18 "Use your sickle now to **g** the clusters of grapes
16:14 **g** for battle against the Lord on that great judgment
19:17 **G** together for the great banquet God has prepared.
20: 8 He will **g** them together for battle—a mighty host,

GATHERED (91) [GATHER]

Ge 1: 9 "Let the waters beneath the sky be **g** into one
31:23 he **g** a group of his relatives and set out in hot
37: 7 and then your bundles all **g** around and bowed low
48: 2 he **g** his strength and sat up in bed to greet him.
Ex 9:10 So they **g** soot from a furnace and went to see
16:17 So the people of Israel went out and **g** this food—
16:18 Those who **g** a lot had nothing left over, and those who **g** only a little had enough.
16:21 The people **g** the food morning by morning,
Nu 11: 8 The people **g** it from the ground and made flour by
11:24 Then he **g** the seventy leaders and stationed them
11:32 the next day, too. No one **g** less than fifty bushels!
16:42 As the people **g** to protest to Moses and Aaron,
31:11 After they had **g** the plunder and captives,
Dt 33: 5 people assembled, / when the tribes of Israel **g**."
Jos 18: 1 the entire Israelite assembly **g** at Shiloh and set up
22:12 the whole assembly **g** at Shiloh and prepared to go
Jdg 5:11 Listen to the village musicians **g** at the watering
8:25 and each one threw in a gold earring he had **g**.
9:47 that the people were **g** together in the temple,
10:17 At that time the armies of Ammon had **g** for war
16: 2 so the men of Gaza **g** together and waited all night
20:11 were united, and they **g** together to attack the town.
20:14 their towns and **g** at Gibeah to fight the Israelites.
Ru 2:17 So Ruth **g** barley there all day, and when she beat
2:23 and **g** grain with them until the end of the barley
1Sa 7: 6 So they **g** there and, in a great ceremony,
7: 7 rulers heard that all Israel had **g** at Mizpah,
20:38 So the boy quickly **g** up the arrows and ran back to
25: 1 Now Samuel died, and all Israel **g** for his funeral.
25:18 She quickly **g** two hundred loaves of bread,
2Sa 14:14 out on the ground, which cannot be **g** up again.
23:11 One time the Philistines **g** at Lehi and attacked the
1Ki 8:65 A large crowd had **g** from as far away as
12: 1 where all Israel had **g** to make him king.
2Ki 10: 9 and spoke to the crowd that had **g** around them.
1Ch 22:14 I have also **g** lumber and stone for the walls,
29: 2 I have **g** as much as I could for building the
29:16 even these materials that we have **g** to build a
2Ch 1: 5 and the people **g** in front of it to consult the
7: 8 with huge crowds **g** from all the tribes of Israel.
10: 1 where all Israel had **g** to make him king.
15:10 The people **g** at Jerusalem in late spring,
20:26 On the fourth day they **g** in the Valley of Blessing,
23: 3 They all **g** at the Temple of God, where they made
29:20 Early the next morning King Hezekiah **g** the city
32:18 language to the people **g** on the walls of the city,
Ezr 7:28 And I **g** some of the leaders of Israel to return with
10: 1 and children—**g** and wept bitterly with him.
10: 9 people of Judah and Benjamin had **g** in Jerusalem.
Est 5:10 Then he **g** together his friends and Zeresh, his wife,
9: 2 The Jews **g** in their cities throughout all the king's
9:15 Then the Jews at Susa **g** together on March 8
9:16 provinces had **g** together to defend their lives.
Ps 47: 9 The rulers of the world have **g** together. / They join
107: 3 For he has **g** the exiles from many lands,
Pr 27:25 crop appears, and the mountain grasses are **g** in,
Isa 10:14 and **g** up kingdoms as a farmer gathers eggs.
Jer 8: 2 Their bones will not be **g** up again or buried
28:11 And Hananiah said again to the crowd that had **g**,
Mic 4:11 True, many nations have **g** together against you,
Hab 2: 5 In their greed they have **g** up many nations
Mt 13: 2 where an immense crowd soon **g**. He got into a
25:32 All the nations will be **g** in his presence, and he
26:57 teachers of religious law and other leaders had **g**.
27:17 As the crowds **g** before Pilate's house that
Mk 1:33 all over Capernaum **g** outside the door to watch.
2:13 and taught the crowds that **g** around him.
4:10 and with the others who were **g** around,
5:15 A crowd soon **g** around Jesus, but they were
5:21 the lake, a large crowd **g** around him on the shore.
8: 1 About this time another great crowd had **g**,
14:53 other leaders, and teachers of religious law had **g**.
15:43 **g** his courage and went to Pilate to ask for Jesus'
Lk 8: 4 crowd that had **g** from many towns to hear him:
8:35 A crowd soon **g** around Jesus, for they wanted to
21:38 The crowds **g** early each morning to hear him.
24:33 and the other followers of Jesus were **g**.
Jn 8: 2 A crowd soon **g**, and he sat down and taught them.
10: 4 After he has **g** his own flock, he walks ahead of
15: 6 Such branches are **g** into a pile to be burned.
Ac 4:26 the earth prepared for battle; / the rulers **g** together
12:12 of John Mark, where many were **g** for prayer.
17: 5 so they **g** some worthless fellows from the streets
20: 7 of the week, we **g** to observe the Lord's Supper.
25: 7 the Jewish leaders from Jerusalem **g** around
28: 3 As Paul **g** an armful of sticks and was laying them
2Co 8:15 "Those who **g** a lot had nothing left over,
8:15 and those who **g** only a little had enough."
2Th 2: 1 and how we will be **g** together to meet him.
Rev 16:16 And they **g** all the rulers and their armies to a place

GATHERING (18) [GATHER]

Ex 16:18 By **g** two quarts for each person, everyone had just
Lev 23:37 Celebrate them by **g** in sacred assemblies to
Nu 15:32 they caught a man **g** wood on the Sabbath day.
1Sa 17: 2 Saul countered by **g** his troops near the valley of
2Sa 20:12 and Joab's officer saw that a crowd was **g** around
1Ki 17:10 he saw a widow **g** sticks, and he asked her,
17:12 I was just **g** a few sticks to cook this last meal,
Pr 6: 8 they labor hard all summer, **g** food for the winter.
Mic 4:12 These nations don't know that he is **g** them
Mt 5: 1 One day as the crowds were **g**, Jesus went up the
24:28 Just as the **g** of vultures shows there is a carcass
25:24 you didn't plant and **g** crops you didn't cultivate.
25:26 crops I didn't plant and **g** crops I didn't cultivate?
Lk 17:37 "Just as the **g** of vultures shows there is a carcass
18:31 **G** the twelve disciples around him, Jesus told
Jn 6:22 crowds began **g** on the shore, waiting to see Jesus.
11:52 but for the **g** together of all the children of God
Rev 19:19 Then I saw the beast **g** the kings of the earth

GATHERINGS (2) [GATHER]

Ps 26: 5 I hate the **g** of those who do evil, / and I refuse to
Jer 6:11 on **g** of young men, and on husbands and wives

GATHERS (4) [GATHER]

Nu 19:10 The man who **g** up the ashes of the heifer must also
Job 16:10 slap my cheek in contempt. A mob **g** against me.
Isa 10:14 and gathered up kingdoms as a farmer **g** eggs.
Mt 13:47 is thrown into the water and **g** fish of every kind.

GAUNT (4)

Ge 41: 3 up from the river, but these were very ugly and **g**.
41:19 They were very thin and **g**—in fact, I've never seen
41:21 afterward they were still as ugly and **g** as before!
Job 30: 3 They are **g** with hunger and flee to the deserts

GAUZE (1)

Isa 3:19 their earrings, bracelets, and veils of shimmering **g**.

GAVE (684) [GIVE] See Index of Articles, Etc.

GAY [KJV] See RICH

GAZA (23)
Ge 10:19 near **G**, and to Sodom, Gomorrah, Admah,
Dt 2:23 who had lived in villages in the area of **G**.)
Jos 10:41 Joshua slaughtered them from Kadesh-barnea to **G**
11:22 though some still remained in **G**, Gath,
13: 4 and includes the five Philistine cities of **G**,
15:47 and villages and **G** with its towns and villages,
Jdg 1:18 Judah captured the cities of **G**, Ashkelon,
6: 4 in the land and destroying crops as far away as **G**.
16: 1 One day Samson went to the Philistine city of **G**
16: 2 so the men of **G** gathered together and waited all
16:21 They took him to **G**, where he was bound with
1Sa 6:17 rulers of Ashdod, **G**, Ashkelon, Gath, and Ekron.
1Ki 4:24 west of the Euphrates River, from Tiphsah to **G**.
2Ki 18: 8 also conquered the Philistines as far distant as **G**
Jer 25:20 **G**, Ekron, and what remains of Ashdod.
47: 1 prophet Jeremiah concerning the Philistines of **G**,
47: 5 The city of **G** will be demolished; Ashkelon will
Am 1: 6 "The people of **G** have sinned again and again,
1: 7 So I will send down fire on the walls of **G**, and all
Zep 2: 4 **G**, Ashkelon, Ashdod, Ekron—these Philistine
Zec 9: 5 **G** will shake with terror, and so will Ekron,
9: 5 **G** will be conquered and its king killed,
Ac 8:26 the desert road that runs from Jerusalem to **G**."

GAZATHITES [KJV] See GAZA

GAZE (5) [GAZED, GAZING]
2Ki 8:11 Elisha stared at Hazael with a fixed **g** until Hazael
Est 1:11 He wanted all the men to **g** on her beauty, for she
SS 6:13 "Why do you **g** so intently at this young woman of
Isa 51: 6 the skies above, and **g** down on the earth beneath.
Eze 28:17 and exposed you to the curious **g** of kings.

GAZED (2) [GAZE]
Ps 63: 2 your sanctuary / and **g** upon your power and glory.
Ac 7:55 **g** steadily upward into heaven and saw the glory of

GAZELLE (9) [GAZELLES]
Dt 12:15 you want, just as you do now with **g** and deer.
12:22 eat that meat, just as you do now with **g** and deer.
14: 5 the deer, the **g**, the roebuck, the wild goat, the ibex,
15:22 or unclean, just as anyone may eat a **g** or deer.
SS 2: 9 My lover is like a swift **g** or a young deer. Look,
2:17 Run like a **g** or a young stag on the rugged
4: 5 Your breasts are like twin fawns of a **g**,
7: 3 Your breasts are like twin fawns of a **g**.
8:14 Move like a swift **g** or a young deer on the

GAZELLES (3) [GAZELLE]
1Ki 4:23 or goats, as well as deer, **g**, roebucks,
SS 2: 7 by the swift **g** and the deer of the wild,
3: 5 by the swift **g** and the deer of the wild,

GAZER [KJV] See GEZER

GAZEZ (2)
1Ch 2:46 Haran, Moza, and **G**. Haran was the father of **G**.

GAZING (2) [GAZE]
SS 2: 9 is looking in through the window, **g** into the room.
Ac 23: 1 **G** intently at the high council, Paul began:

GAZINGSTOCK [KJV] See SHOW, RIDICULE

GAZZAM (2)
Ezr 2:48 Rezin, Nekoda, **G**,
Ne 7:51 **G**, Uzza, Paseah,

GEAR (2)
Isa 9: 5 that day of peace, battle **g** will no longer be issued.
Mt 5:41 If a soldier demands that you carry his **g** for a mile,

GEBA (17)
Jos 18:24 Kephar-ammoni, Ophni, and **G**—twelve towns
21:17 with their surrounding pasturelands: Gibeon, **G**,
1Sa 13: 3 and defeated the garrison of Philistines at **G**.
13: 4 He announced that the Philistine garrison at **G** had
13:16 and the troops with them were staying at **G**,
14: 5 and the one on the south was in front of **G**.
1Ki 15:22 Asa used these materials to fortify the town of **G** in
2Ki 23: 8 they had burned incense, from **G** to Beersheba.
1Ch 6:60 **G**, Alemeth, and Anathoth, each with its
8: 6 leaders of the clans living at **G**, were driven out
2Ch 16: 6 Asa used these materials to fortify the towns of **G**
Ezr 2:26 The peoples of Ramah and **G** | 621
Ne 7:30 The peoples of Ramah and **G** | 621
11:31 Some of the people of Benjamin lived at **G**,
12:29 from Beth-gilgal and the area of **G** and Azmaveth,
Isa 10:29 crossing the pass and are staying overnight at **G**.
Zec 14:10 All the land from **G**, north of Judah, to Rimmon,

GEBAL (2) [GEBALITES]
1Ki 5:18 Men from the city of **G** helped Solomon's
Eze 27: 9 Wise old craftsmen from **G** did all the caulking.

GEBALITES (2) [GEBAL]
Jos 13: 5 the land of the **G** and all of the Lebanon mountain
Ps 83: 7 **G**, Ammonites, and Amalekites, / and people from

GEBER (1) [BEN-GEBER, EZION-GEBER]
1Ki 4:19 **G** son of Uri, in the land of Gilead,

GEBIM (1)
Isa 10:31 And the citizens of **G** are preparing to run.

GECKO (1)
Lev 11:30 the **g**, the monitor lizard, the common lizard,

GEDALIAH (27) [GEDALIAH'S]
2Ki 25:22 Then King Nebuchadnezzar appointed **G** son of
25:23 the king of Babylon had appointed **G** as governor,
25:24 **G** vowed to them that the Babylonian officials
25:25 and assassinated **G** and everyone with him,
1Ch 25: 3 **G**, Zeri, Jeshaiah, Shimei, Hashabiah,
25: 9 The second lot fell to **G** and twelve of his sons
Ezr 10:18 and his brothers: Maaseiah, Eliezer, Jarib, and **G**.
Jer 38: 1 **G** son of Pashhur, Jehucal son of Shelemiah,
39:14 They put him under the care of **G** son of Ahikam
40: 5 then return to **G** son of Ahikam and grandson of
40: 6 So Jeremiah returned to **G** son of Ahikam at
40: 7 **G** son of Ahikam as governor over the poor people
40: 8 So they came to see **G** at Mizpah. These are the
40: 9 **G** assured them that it would be safe for them to
40:11 a few people in Judah and that **G** was the governor,
40:12 stopped at Mizpah to discuss their plans with **G**
40:13 and the other guerrilla leaders came to **G** at
40:14 assassinate you?" But **G** refused to believe them.
40:15 Later Johanan had a private conference with **G**
40:16 But **G** said to Johanan, "I forbid you to do any
41: 1 **G** invited them to dinner. While they were eating,
41: 2 ten men suddenly drew their swords and killed **G**,
41: 3 and Babylonian soldiers who were with **G** at
41: 6 "Oh, come and see what has happened to **G**!"
41:18 do when they heard that Ishmael had killed **G**,
43: 6 the captain of the guard, had left with **G**.
Zep 1: 1 son of **G**, son of Amariah, son of Hezekiah.

GEDALIAH'S (2) [GEDALIAH]
Jer 41: 4 before anyone had heard about **G** murder,
41:10 and the other people who had been left under **G**

GEDDALTI (2)
1Ch 25: 4 Shubael, Jerimoth, Hananiah, Hanani, Eliathah, **G**,
25:29 The twenty-second lot fell to **G** and twelve of his

GEDEON [KJV] See GIDEON

GEDER (2)
Jos 12:13 The king of Debir / The king of **G**
1Ch 27:28 Baal-hanan from **G** was in charge of the king's

GEDERAH (3)
Jos 15:36 Shaaraim, Adithaim, **G**, and Gederothaim. In all,
1Ch 4:23 They were the potters who lived in Netaim and **G**.
12: 4 Jeremiah, Jahaziel, Johanan, and Jozabad from **G**;

GEDEROTH (2)
Jos 15:41 **G**, Beth-dagon, Naamah, and Makkedah—
2Ch 28:18 Aijalon, **G**, Soco with its villages, Timnah with its

GEDEROTHAIM (1)
Jos 15:36 Shaaraim, Adithaim, Gederah, and **G**. In all,

GEDOR (8)
Jos 15:58 In addition, there were Halhul, Beth-zur, **G**,
1Ch 4: 4 Penuel (the father of **G**), and Ezer (the father of
4:18 who became the mother of Jered (the father of **G**),
4:39 who traveled to the region of **G**, in the east part of
4:40 descendants had been living in the region of **G**.
8:31 **G**, Ahio, Zechariah,
9:37 **G**, Ahio, Zechariah, and Mikloth.
12: 7 Joelah and Zebadiah, sons of Jeroham from **G**.

GEHAZI (19)
2Ki 4:12 He said to his servant **G**, "Tell the woman I want
4:13 Elisha said to **G**, "Tell her that we appreciate the
4:14 Later Elisha asked **G**, "What do you think we can
4:25 He said to **G**, "Look, the woman from Shunem is
4:26 the woman told **G**, "everything is fine."
4:27 **G** began to push her away, but the man of God
4:29 Then Elisha said to **G**, "Get ready to travel;
4:31 **G** hurried on ahead and laid the staff on the child's
4:36 Then Elisha summoned **G**. "Call the child's
5:20 But **G**, Elisha's servant, said to himself,
5:21 So **G** set off after him. When Naaman saw him
5:22 "Yes," **G** said, "but my master has sent me to tell
5:23 sent two of his servants to carry the gifts for **G**.
5:24 **G** took the gifts from the servants and sent the men
5:25 Elisha asked him, "Where have you been, **G**?"
5:27 When **G** left the room, he was leprous; his skin
8: 4 As she came in, the king was talking with **G**,
8: 5 And **G** was telling the king about the time Elisha
8: 5 "Look, my lord!" **G** exclaimed. "Here is the

GELILOTH (3)
Jos 18:17 and on to **G** (which is across from the slopes of
22:10 altar near the Jordan River at a place called **G**.
22:11 had built the altar at **G** west of the Jordan River,

GEM (2) [GEMCUTTER, GEMS, GEMSTONES]
Da 10: 6 His body looked like a dazzling **g**. From his face
Rev 21:11 the glory of God and sparkled like a precious **g**,

GEMALLI (1)
Nu 13:12 Dan | Ammiel son of **G**

GEMARIAH (5)
Jer 29: 3 with Elasah son of Shaphan and **G** son of Hilkiah,
36:10 from the Temple room of **G** son of Shaphan.
36:11 When Micaiah son of **G** and grandson of Shaphan
36:12 Elnathan son of Acbor, **G** son of Shaphan,
36:25 and **G** begged the king not to burn the scroll,

GEMCUTTER (1) [CUT, GEM]
Ex 28:11 Engrave these names in the same way a **g** engraves

GEMS (5) [GEM]
2Sa 12:30 The crown was made of gold and set with **g**,
1Ch 20: 2 The crown was made of gold and set with **g**,
Isa 54:12 and your gates and walls of shining **g**.
Rev 17: 4 jewelry made of gold and precious **g** and pearls.
21:19 built on foundation stones inlaid with twelve **g**:

GEMSTONES (8) [GEM, STONE]
Ex 28:17 Four rows of **g** will be attached to it. The first row
31: 5 in cutting and setting **g** and in carving wood.
35:27 and the other **g** to be used for the ephod
35:33 in cutting and setting **g** and in carving wood.
39:10 Four rows of **g** were set across it. In the first row
39:13 and a jasper. Each of these **g** was set in gold.
La 4: 1 The sacred **g** lie scattered in the streets!
Rev 4: 3 The one sitting on the throne was as brilliant as **g**—

GENDER [KJV] See BREED, START

GENEALOGICAL (11) [GENEALOGY]
1Ch 5:17 All of these were listed in the **g** records during the
9: 1 All Israel was listed in the **g** record in *The Book*
26:31 leader of the Hebronites according to the **g** records.
2Ch 12:15 *of Iddo the Seer,* which are part of the **g** record.
31:16 or older, regardless of their place in the **g** records,
31:17 who were listed in the **g** records by families,
31:18 also given to all the families listed in the **g** records,
31:19 and to all the Levites listed in the **g** records.
Ezr 2:62 But they had lost their **g** records, so they were not
Ne 7: 5 I had found the **g** record of those who had first
7:64 But they had lost their **g** records, so they were not

GENEALOGIES (3) [GENEALOGY]
Ex 6:19 the clans of the Levites, listed according to their **g**.
1Ch 9:22 and they were listed by **g** in their villages.
Ezr 8: 1 and the **g** of those who came with me from

GENEALOGY (13) [GENEALOGICAL, GENEALOGIES]
1Ch 4:33 and these names are recorded in their family **g**.
5: 1 Reuben is not listed in the **g** as the firstborn son.
5: 7 Beerah's relatives are listed in their **g** by their
6:33 His **g** was traced back through Joel, Samuel,
6:39 Asaph's **g** was traced back through Berekiah,
6:44 Ethan's **g** was traced back through Kishi, Abdi,
7: 5 All of them were listed in their tribal **g**.
7: 7 All of them were listed in their family **g**.
7: 9 According to their family **g**, there were 20,200
7:40 among the descendants listed in their tribal **g**.
8:28 and they were listed in their tribal **g**.
9: 9 of clans, and they were listed in their tribal **g**.
9:34 were listed as prominent leaders in their tribal **g**.

GENERAL (9) [GENERALS]
Nu 4:24 of the Gershonites will be in the areas of **g** service
27:11 The Israelites must observe this as a **g** legal
1Sa 12: 9 the **g** of Hazor's army, and by the Philistines
17:55 he asked Abner, the **g** of his army, "Abner,
26: 5 Saul and his **g**, Abner son of Ner, were sleeping
Eze 44:14 and helping the people in a **g** way.
Da 11:14 At that time there will be a **g** uprising against the
Ac 10:41 not to the **g** public, but to us whom God had
15:30 where they called a **g** meeting of the Christians

GENERAL [KJV] See also COMMANDER

GENERALS (13) [GENERAL]
Jdg 7:25 They captured Oreb and Zeeb, the two Midianite **g**,
8: 3 over Oreb and Zeeb, the **g** of the Midianite army.
2Sa 18: 1 David now appointed **g** and captains to lead his
1Ch 13: 1 including the **g** and captains of his army.
15:25 and the **g** of the army went to the home of
26:26 and the **g** and captains and other officers of the
27: 1 This is the list of Israelite **g** and captains, and their
28: 1 the other **g** and captains, the overseers of the royal
29: 6 the tribes of Israel, the **g** and captains of the army,
2Ch 1: 2 the **g** and captains of the army, the judges, and all
Isa 31: 9 Even their **g** will quake with terror and flee when
Jer 51:28 the armies of the kings of the Medes and their **g**,
Rev 6:15 of the earth, the rulers, the **g**, the wealthy people,

GENERATION (103) [GENERATIONS]

FROM GENERATION TO GENERATION (18) Ex 12:17,42; 29:42; 30:8,10,21; 40:15; Lev 6:18; Nu 10:8; 35:29; Est 9:28; Ps 79:13; Isa 34:10,17; 51:8; La 5:19; Joel 1:3; Lk 1:50

Ge 17: 7 covenant between us, **g** after **g**.
Ex 1: 6 and each of his brothers died, ending that **g**.
6:16 In the first **g** were Gershon, Kohath, and Merari.
12:17 regulation for you, to be kept from **g** to **g**.
12:42 be celebrated every year, from **g** to **g**,
17:16 the LORD will be at war with Amalek **g** after **g**."
29:42 to be a daily burnt offering given from **g** to **g**.
30: 8 This must be done from **g** to **g**.
30:10 be a regular, annual event from **g** to **g**,
30:21 his descendants, to be kept from **g** to **g**."
40:15 for the priesthood forever, from **g** to **g**."
Lev 6:18 from **g** to **g**, may eat of the grain offering,
17: 7 law for them, to be kept **g** after **g**.
23:43 This will remind each new **g** of Israelites that their
Nu 10: 8 This is a permanent law to be followed from **g** to **g**.
32:13 until the whole **g** that sinned against him had died.
35:29 laws for you to observe from **g** to **g**,
Dt 1:35 'Not one of you from this entire wicked **g** will live
23: 8 The third **g** of Egyptians who came with you from
32: 5 his children? / They are a deceitful and twisted **g**.
32:20 I will see to their end! / For they are a twisted **g**,
Jdg 2:10 After that **g** died, another **g** grew up who did not acknowledge the
2Sa 3:29 May his family in every **g** be cursed with a man
2Ki 10:30 to be the kings of Israel down to the fourth **g**."
15:12 will be kings of Israel down to the fourth **g**."
Est 9:28 be remembered and kept from **g** to **g**
Job 8: 8 "Just ask the former **g**. Pay attention to the
Ps 12: 7 preserving them forever from this lying **g**,
45:17 I will bring honor to your name in every **g**.
71:18 Let me proclaim your power to this new **g**,
78: 4 but will tell the next **g** about the glorious deeds of
78: 6 so the next **g** might know them—
78: 7 So each **g** can set its hope anew on God,
79:13 praising your greatness from **g** to **g**.
100: 5 and his faithfulness continues to each **g**.
102:12 rule forever. / Your fame will endure to every **g**.
109:13 May his family name be blotted out in a single **g**.
112: 2 an entire **g** of godly people will be blessed.
119:90 Your faithfulness extends to every **g**, / as enduring
135:13 your fame, O LORD, is known to every **g**.
145: 4 Let each **g** tell its children / of your mighty acts.
145:13 You rule **g** after **g**. / The LORD is
146:10 O Jerusalem, your God is King in every **g**!
Pr 27:24 and the crown might not be secure for the next **g**.
Ecc 4:16 But then the next **g** grows up and rejects him!
Isa 13:20 **G** after **g** will come and go, but the land
34:10 The land will lie deserted from **g** to **g**.
34:17 They will possess it forever, from **g** to **g**.
38:19 Each **g** can make known your faithfulness to the
41: 4 of the human race as each new **g** marches by?
51: 8 My salvation will continue from **g** to **g**."
Jer 7:29 and forsaken this **g** that has provoked his fury.'
19: 4 idols never before worshiped by this **g**, by their
La 5:19 Your throne continues from **g** to **g**.
Eze 37:25 them will live there forever, **g** after **g**.
Joel 1: 3 Pass the awful story down from **g** to **g**.
Mt 11:16 "How shall I describe this **g**? These people are like
12:39 faithless **g** would ask for a miraculous sign;
12:41 The people of Nineveh will rise up against this **g**
12:42 The queen of Sheba will also rise up against this **g**
12:45 That will be the experience of this evil **g**."
16: 4 an evil, faithless **g** would ask for a miraculous sign,
23:36 centuries will break upon the heads of this very **g**.
24:34 this **g** will not pass from the scene before all these
Mk 8:12 I assure you, I will not give this **g** any such sign."
13:30 this **g** will not pass from the scene until all these
Lk 1:48 his lowly servant girl, / and now **g** after **g**
1:50 His mercy goes on from **g** to **g**, / to all
7:31 "How shall I describe this **g**?" Jesus asked.
11:29 and this evil **g** keeps asking me to show them a
11:31 "The queen of Sheba will rise up against this **g** on
11:32 will rise up against this **g** on judgment day
11:50 "And you of this **g** will be held responsible for the
17:25 Man must suffer terribly and be rejected by this **g**.
21:32 this **g** will not pass from the scene until all these
Ac 2:40 "Save yourselves from this **g** that has gone
13:36 for after David had served his **g** according to the

GENERATIONS (54) [GENERATION]

ALL...GENERATIONS (13) Ex 3:15; 16:33; 27:21; Lev 10:9; 21:17; 23:41; 24:3; Dt 29:15; Ps 90:1; Isa 45:25; 60:15; Da 4:3; Joel 3:20

Ge 15:16 After four **g** your descendants will return here to
46:34 our youth, as our ancestors have been for many **g**.'
50:23 He lived to see three **g** of descendants of his son
Ex 3:15 been my name, and it will be used throughout all **g**.
16:32 later **g** will be able to see the bread that the
16:33 it in a sacred place as a reminder for all future **g**."
20: 5 the sins of their parents to the third and fourth **g**.
20: 6 and obey my commands, even for a thousand **g**.
27:21 people of Israel, and it must be kept by all future **g**.
34: 7 the sins of their parents to the third and fourth **g**."
Lev 7:36 This regulation applies throughout the **g** to come."
10: 9 law for you, and it must be kept by all future **g**.
16:32 In future **g**, the atonement ceremony will be
21:17 "Tell Aaron that in all future **g**, his descendants
23:41 law for you, and it must be kept by all future **g**.
24: 3 law for you, and it must be kept by all future **g**.
Nu 9:10 or in future **g** are ceremonially unclean at Passover
14:18 the sins of their parents to the third and fourth **g**.'
15:21 Throughout the **g** to come, you are to present this
15:38 'Throughout the **g** to come you must make tassels
Dt 5: 9 the sins of their parents to the third and fourth **g**.
5:10 and obey my commands, even for a thousand **g**.
7: 9 God who keeps his covenant for a thousand **g**
17:20 and his descendants will reign for many **g** in Israel.
23: 2 and their descendants for ten **g** may not be
23: 3 or Moabites, or any of their descendants for ten **g**,
29:15 presence today and also with all future **g** of Israel.
29:22 "Then the **g** to come, both your own descendants
32: 7 the days of long ago; / think about the **g** past.
Jdg 3: 2 He did this to teach warfare to **g** of Israelites who
1Ch 16:15 the commitment he made to a thousand **g**.
Job 8:10 They will teach you from the wisdom of former **g**.
42:16 living to see four **g** of his children
Ps 22:30 Future **g** will also serve him. / Our children will
48:13 that you may describe them / to future **g**.
61: 6 to the life of the king! / May his years span the **g**!
85: 5 Will you prolong your wrath to distant **g**?
90: 1 Lord, through all the **g** / you have been our home!
102:18 Let this be recorded for future **g**, / so that a nation
105: 8 the commitment he made to a thousand **g**.
Ecc 1: 4 **G** come and go, but nothing really changes.
1:11 And in future **g**, no one will remember what we are
Isa 8:16 to my disciples, who will pass it down to future **g**.
45:25 In the LORD all the **g** of Israel will be justified,
49:20 The **g** born in exile will return and say, 'We need
60:15 You will be a joy to all **g**, for I will make you so.
61: 4 though they have been empty for many **g**.
Da 4: 3 kingdom will last forever, / his rule through all **g**.
Joel 3:20 and Jerusalem will endure through all future **g**.
Mt 1:17 All those listed above include fourteen **g** from
Ac 15:21 in every city on every Sabbath for many **g**."
Eph 3: 5 God did not reveal it to previous **g**, but now he has
Col 1:26 message was kept secret for centuries and **g** past,
Jude 1:14 Now Enoch, who lived seven **g** after Adam,

GENEROSITY (8) [GENEROUS]

Lk 16: 9 your **g** stores up a reward for you in heaven.
Ac 2:46 and shared their meals with great joy and **g**—
2Co 8: 2 and deep poverty have overflowed in rich **g**.
9:10 and he will produce a great harvest of **g** in you.
9:13 For your **g** to them will prove that you are obedient
Eph 4: 7 one of us a special gift according to the **g** of Christ.
Phm 1: 6 And I am praying that you will really put your **g** to
1Pe 4:10 them well so that God's **g** can flow through you.

GENEROUS (19) [GENEROSITY, GENEROUSLY]

Ge 33:11 take my gifts, for God has been very **g** to me.
Dt 15: 8 Instead, be **g** and lend them whatever they need.
15:14 Give him a **g** farewell gift from your flock,
2Ch 11:23 He provided them with **g** provisions and arranged
Est 2:18 giving **g** gifts to everyone and declaring a public
Ps 37:21 and never repay, / but the godly are **g** givers.
37:26 The godly always give **g** loans to others, / and their
112: 4 They are **g**, compassionate, and righteous.
112: 5 All goes well for those who are **g**, / who lend
Pr 11:25 The **g** prosper and are satisfied; those who refresh
22: 9 Blessed are those who are **g**, because they feed the
Isa 32: 8 But good people will be **g** to others and will be
66:11 even as an infant drinks at its mother's **g** breasts.
Ro 5:15 between our sin and God's **g** gift of forgiveness.
1Co 1: 4 I can never stop thanking God for all the **g** gifts he
2Co 8:20 find fault with the way we are handling this **g** gift.
9: 6 But the one who plants generously will get a **g**
9:13 You will be glorifying God through your **g** gifts.
Phm 1: 6 You are **g** because of your faith. And I am praying

GENEROUSLY (17) [GENEROUS]

1Ki 10:13 all the other customary gifts he had so **g** given.
2Ch 31: 5 and **g** with the first of their crops and grain,
Ezr 2:68 some of the family leaders gave **g** toward the
Ps 112: 9 They give **g** to those in need. / Their good deeds
Ecc 11: 1 Give **g**, for your gifts will return to you later.
Hos 2: 9 and ripened grain I **g** provided each harvest season.
Ac 10: 2 He gave **g** to charity and was a man who regularly
Ro 10:12 who **g** gives his riches to all who ask for them.
12: 8 do it! If you have money, share it **g**.
2Co 9: 6 But the one who plants **g** will get a generous crop.
9: 8 And God will **g** provide all you need. Then you
9: 9 Scriptures say, / "Godly people give **g** to the poor.
9:11 will be enriched so that you can give even more **g**.
Eph 4:28 for honest work, and then give **g** to others in need.
Php 4:18 I am **g** supplied with the gifts you sent me with
1Ti 6:18 in good works and should give **g** to those in need,
Tit 3: 6 He **g** poured out the Spirit upon us because of what

GENITAL (2)

Lev 15: 2 Any man who has a **g** discharge is ceremonially
15:32 with a man who has been defiled by a **g** discharge

GENNESARET (2)

Mt 14:34 After they had crossed the lake, they landed at **G**.
Mk 6:53 When they arrived at **G** on the other side of the

GENTILE (23) [GENTILES]

Eze 4:13 Israel will eat defiled bread in the **G** lands, where I
Mt 15:22 A **G** woman who lived there came to him,
Mk 7:26 Since she was a **G**, born in Syrian Phoenicia,
Ac 6: 5 and Nicolas of Antioch (a **G** convert to the Jewish
7:45 when Joshua led the battles against the **G** nations
10:28 laws for me to come into a **G** home like this.
15: 5 and declared that all **G** converts must be
15:10 **G** believers with a yoke that neither we nor our
15:23 It is written to the **G** believers in Antioch, Syria,
18: 7 a **G** who worshiped God and lived next door to the
21:21 **G** world to turn their backs on the laws of Moses.
21:25 "As for the **G** Christians, all we ask of them is
21:29 a **G** from Ephesus, and they assumed Paul had
Ro 2: 9 on sinning—for the Jew first and also for the **G**.
2:10 who do good—for the Jew first and also for the **G**.
2:25 you are no better off than an uncircumcised **G**.
10:12 Jew and **G** are the same in this respect. They all
16: 4 who is thankful to them; so are all the **G** churches.
Gal 2: 3 Titus be circumcised, though he was a **G**.
2:12 When he first arrived, he ate with the **G** Christians,
2:14 discarded the Jewish laws and are living like a **G**,
3:28 There is no longer Jew or **G**, slave or free, male
Col 3:11 it doesn't matter if you are a Jew or a **G**,

GENTILES (125) [GENTILE]

Dt 32:21 I will provoke their fury by blessing the foolish **G**.
Isa 9: 1 will be a time in the future when Galilee of the **G**,
49: 6 I will make you a light to the **G**, and you will bring
56: 3 "And my blessings are for **G**, too, when they
56: 6 "I will also bless the **G** who commit themselves to
Mt 4:15 Jordan River— / in Galilee where so many **G** live
8:11 that many **G** will come from all over the world
10: 5 "Don't go to the **G** or the Samaritans,
15:24 people of Israel—God's lost sheep—not the **G**."
Lk 21:24 and trampled down by the **G** until the age of the **G** comes to an end.
Jn 7:35 to the Jews in other lands, or maybe even to the **G**!
Ac 2:23 With the help of lawless **G**, you nailed him to the
2:39 is to you and to your children, and even to the **G**—
4:27 Herod Antipas, Pontius Pilate the governor, the **G**,
9:15 my chosen instrument to take my message to the **G**
10:45 of the Holy Spirit had been poured out upon the **G**,
11: 1 and other believers in Judea that the **G** had
11: 3 "You entered the home of **G** and even ate with
11:12 go with them and not to worry about their being **G**.
11:17 And since God gave these **G** the same gift he gave
11:18 "God has also given the **G** the privilege of turning
11:20 and Cyrene began preaching to **G** about the Lord
11:21 and large numbers of these **G** believed and turned
13:16 "and you devout **G** who fear the God of Israel,
13:26 and also all of you devout **G** who fear the God of
13:46 of eternal life—well, we will offer it to **G**.
13:47 when he said, / 'I have made you a light to the **G**,
13:48 When the **G** heard this, they were very glad
14: 1 that a great number of both Jews and **G** believed.
14: 2 stirred up distrust among the **G** against Paul
14: 5 A mob of **G** and Jews, along with their leaders,
14:27 and how he had opened the door of faith to the **G**,
15: 3 that the **G**, too, were being converted.
15: 7 from among you some time ago to preach to the **G**
15: 8 confirmed that he accepts **G** by giving them the
15:12 wonders God had done through them among the **G**.
15:14 the **G** to take from them a people for himself.
15:15 And this conversion of **G** agrees with what the
15:17 humanity might find the Lord, / including the **G**—
15:19 we should stop troubling the **G** who turn to God,
17:17 to debate with the Jews and the God-fearing **G**,
18: 6 I am innocent. From now on I will go to the **G**."
20:21 I have had one message for Jews and **G** alike—
21:19 accomplished among the **G** through his ministry.
21:28 and he even defiles it by bringing **G** in!"
22:21 for I will send you far away to the **G**!' "
26:17 protect you from both your own people and the **G**. Yes, I am going to send you to the **G**,
26:20 and throughout all Judea, and also to the **G**,
26:23 rise from the dead as a light to Jews and **G** alike."
28:28 this salvation from God is also available to the **G**,
Ro 1: 5 and authority to tell **G** everywhere what God has
1:13 good results, just as I have done among other **G**.
1:16 everyone who believes—Jews first and also **G**.
2:12 God will punish the **G** when they sin, even though
2:14 Even when **G**, who do not have God's written law,
2:26 And if the **G** obey God's law, won't God give
2:27 uncircumcised **G** who keep God's law will be
3: 9 whether Jews or **G**, are under the power of sin.
3:29 Jews only, is he? Isn't he also the God of the **G**?
3:30 himself only by faith, whether they are Jews or **G**.
4: 9 this blessing only for the Jews, or is it for **G**, too?
9:24 he selected, both from the Jews and from the **G**.
9:25 Concerning the **G**, God says in the prophecy of
9:30 The **G** have been made right with God by faith,
10:19 I will make you angry by blessing the foolish **G**."
11:11 was to make his salvation available to the **G**,
11:12 Now if the **G** were enriched because the Jews
11:13 I am saying all of this especially for you **G**.
11:13 God has appointed me as the apostle to the **G**.
11:14 a way to make the Jews want what you **G** have,
11:17 And you **G**, who were branches from a wild olive
11:25 until the complete number of **G** comes to Christ.
11:28 your benefit, for God has given his gifts to you **G**.
11:30 Once, you **G** were rebels against God, but when
15: 9 so the **G** might also give glory to God for his
15: 9 "I will praise you among the **G**; / I will sing
15:10 in another place it is written, / "Rejoice, O you **G**,
15:11 And yet again, / "Praise the Lord, all you **G**;
15:12 throne will come, / and he will rule over the **G**.
15:16 a special messenger from Christ Jesus to you **G**.
15:18 I have brought the **G** to God by my message
15:27 Since the **G** received the wonderful spiritual
16:25 message about Jesus Christ and his plan for you **G**,
16:26 this message is made known to all **G** everywhere,
1Co 1:23 Jews are offended, and the **G** say it's all nonsense.

1:24 both Jews and **G**, Christ is the mighty power of
9:21 When I am with the **G** who do not have the Jewish
10:32 give offense to Jews or **G** or the church of God.
12:13 some are **G**, some are slaves, and some are free.
2Co 11:26 my own people, the Jews, as well as from the **G**.
Gal 1:16 proclaim the Good News about Jesus to the **G**.
2:2 to understand what I had been preaching to the **G**.
2:7 of preaching the Good News to the **G**,
2:8 Jews worked through me for the benefit of the **G**.
2:9 They encouraged us to keep preaching to the **G**,
2:12 Peter wouldn't eat with the **G** anymore because he
2:14 why are you trying to make these **G** obey the
2:15 and I are Jews by birth, not 'sinners' like the **G**.
3:8 to this time when God would accept the **G**,
3:14 God has blessed the **G** with the same blessing he
4:6 And because you **G** have become his children,
4:8 Before you **G** knew God, you were slaves to
4:12 these things, for I have become like you **G** were—
Eph 2:11 Don't forget that you **G** used to be outsiders by
2:14 us Jews and you **G** by making us all one people.
2:15 whole system of Jewish law that excluded the **G**.
2:15 and **G** by creating in himself one new person from
2:17 He has brought this Good News of peace to you **G**
2:18 Now all of us, both Jews and **G**, may come to the
2:19 So now you **G** are no longer strangers
2:22 Through him you **G** are also joined together as part
3:1 of Christ Jesus because of my preaching to you **G**.
3:2 special ministry of announcing his favor to you **G**.
3:6 The **G** have an equal share with the Jews in all the
3:8 I was chosen for this special joy of telling the **G**
3:10 when Jews and **G** are joined together in his church.
6:19 God's secret plan that the Good News is for the **G**,
Col 1:25 his message in all its fullness to you **G**.
1:27 that the riches and glory of Christ are for you **G**,
4:3 about his secret plan—that Christ is also for you **G**.
1Th 2:16 keep us from preaching the Good News to the **G**,
1Ti 2:7 and apostle to teach the **G** about faith and truth.
2Ti 4:17 Good News in all its fullness for all the **G** to hear.

GENTLE (22) [GENTLEMEN, GENTLENESS, GENTLY]

Dt 32:2 on tender grass, / like **g** showers on young plants.
1Ki 19:12 And after the fire there was the sound of a **g**
Job 15:11 too little for you? Is his **g** word not enough?
Ps 37:11 Those who are **g** and lowly will possess the land;
Pr 15:1 A **g** answer turns away wrath, but harsh words stir
15:4 **G** words bring life and health; a deceitful tongue
16:15 there is life; his favor refreshes like a **g** rain.
Isa 8:6 "The people of Judah have rejected my **g** care
42:2 He will be **g**—he will not shout or raise his voice
48:18 Then you would have had peace flowing like a **g**
Jer 4:11 It is not a **g** breeze useful for winnowing grain.
10:24 So correct me, LORD, but please be **g**. Do not
Mt 5:5 God blesses those who are **g** and lowly,
11:29 Let me teach you, because I am humble and **g**,
Gal 4:20 you right now, so that I could be more **g** with you.
Eph 4:2 Be humble and **g**. Be patient with each other,
1Th 2:7 but we were as **g** among you as a mother feeding
1Ti 3:3 He must be **g**, peace loving, and not one who loves
Tit 3:2 they should be **g** and show true humility to
Jas 3:17 It is also peace loving, **g** at all times, and willing to
1Pe 3:4 the unfading beauty of a **g** and quiet spirit, which is
3:16 But you must do this in a **g** and respectful way.

GENTLEMEN (1) [GENTLENESS, GENTLY]

Ac 19:25 "**G**, you know that our wealth comes from this

GENTLENESS (6) [GENTLE]

Ps 18:35 hand supports me; / your **g** has made me great.
1Co 4:21 or should I come with quiet love and **g**?
2Co 10:1 I plead with the **g** and kindness that Christ himself
Gal 5:23 **g**, and self-control. Here there is no conflict with
Col 3:12 kindness, humility, **g**, and patience.
1Ti 6:11 along with faith, love, perseverance, and **g**.

GENTLY (7) [GENTLE]

2Sa 18:5 "For my sake, deal **g** with young Absalom."
SS 7:9 smooth and sweet, flowing **g** over lips and teeth."
Isa 40:11 He will **g** lead the mother sheep with their young.
1Co 4:13 We respond **g** when evil things are said about us.
Gal 6:1 you who are godly should **g** and humbly help that
2Ti 2:25 They should **g** teach those who oppose the truth.
Heb 5:2 he is human, he is able to deal **g** with the people,

GENUBATH (1)

1Ki 11:20 She bore him a son, **G**, who was brought up in

GENUINE (5) [GENUINELY]

Mk 10:21 Jesus felt **g** love for this man as he looked at him.
Jn 7:18 to honor the one who sent them are good and **g**.
Ro 12:10 Love each other with **g** affection, and take delight
2Co 13:5 Examine yourselves to see if your faith is really **g**.
2Pe 1:7 and finally you will grow to have **g** love for

GENUINELY (1) [GENUINE]

Php 2:20 else like Timothy, who **g** cares about your welfare.

GERA (9)

Ge 46:21 Beker, Ashbel, **G**, Naaman, Ehi, Rosh, Muppim,
Jdg 3:15 His name was Ehud son of **G**, of the tribe of
2Sa 16:5 It was Shimei son of **G**, a member of Saul's
19:16 Then Shimei son of **G** the Benjaminite, the man
1Ki 2:8 "And remember Shimei son of **G**, the Benjaminite
1Ch 8:3 The sons of Bela were Addar, **G**, Abihud,
8:5 **G**, Shephuphan, and Huram.
8:7 Ehud's sons were Naaman, Ahijah, and **G**. **G**, the father of Uzza and Ahihud, led them when

GERAHS (1)

Eze 45:12 One shekel consists of twenty **g**, and sixty shekels

GERAR (9)

Ge 10:19 the territory of Canaan spread from Sidon to **G**,
20:1 between Kadesh and Shur at a place called **G**.
26:1 So Isaac moved to **G**, where Abimelech, king of
26:6 So Isaac stayed in **G**.
26:17 So Isaac moved to the **G** Valley and lived there
26:19 His shepherds also dug in the **G** Valley and found
26:26 One day Isaac had visitors from **G**.
2Ch 14:13 Asa and his army pursued them as far as **G**, and
14:14 While they were at **G**, they attacked all the towns

GERASENES (2)

Mk 5:1 at the other side of the lake, in the land of the **G**.
Lk 8:26 So they arrived in the land of the **G**, across the lake

GERIZIM (5)

Dt 11:29 you must pronounce a blessing from Mount **G**
27:12 and Benjamin must stand on Mount **G** to proclaim
Jos 8:33 One group stood at the foot of Mount **G**, the other
Jdg 9:7 he climbed to the top of Mount **G** and shouted,
Jn 4:20 while we Samaritans claim it is here at Mount **G**,

GERSHOM (7)

Ex 2:22 a baby boy, and Moses named him **G**, for he said,
18:3 The name of Moses' first son was **G**, for Moses
Jdg 18:30 and they appointed Jonathan son of **G**,
1Ch 23:15 The sons of Moses were **G** and Eliezer.
23:16 The descendants of **G** included Shebuel, the family
26:24 Shebuel was a descendant of **G** son of Moses.
Ezr 8:2 **G**. / From the family of Ithamar: Daniel.

GERSHON (24) [GERSHONITE, GERSHONITES]

Ge 46:11 The sons of Levi were **G**, Kohath, and Merari.
Ex 6:16 In the first generation were **G**, Kohath, and Merari.
6:17 The descendants of **G** included Libni and Shimei,
Nu 3:17 who were named **G**, Kohath, and Merari.
3:18 The clans descended from **G** were named for two
3:21 The descendants of **G** were composed of the clans
26:57 The Gershonite clan, named after its ancestor **G**.
Jos 21:6 The clan of **G** received thirteen towns from the
21:27 The descendants of **G**, another clan within the tribe
21:33 their pasturelands were allotted to the clan of **G**.
1Ch 6:1 The sons of Levi were **G**, Kohath, and Merari.
6:16 The sons of Levi were **G**, Kohath, and Merari.
6:17 The descendants of **G** included Libni and Shimei.
6:20 The descendants of **G** were Libni, Jahath, Zimmah,
6:39 first assistant was Asaph from the clan of **G**.
6:43 Jahath, **G**, and Levi.
6:62 The descendants of **G** received by sacred lots
6:71 The descendants of **G** received from the territory
15:7 There were 130 from the clan of **G**, with Joel as
23:6 the three sons of Levi—**G**, Kohath, and Merari.
23:7 of descent from Libni and Shimei, the sons of **G**.
26:21 From the family of Libni in the clan of **G**,
29:8 under the care of Jehiel, a descendant of **G**.
2Ch 29:12 From the clan of **G**: Joah son of Zimmah and Eden

GERSHONITE (9) [GERSHON]

Nu 3:22 one month old or older among these **G** clans.
3:24 The leader of the **G** clans was Eliasaph son of
4:22 and families of the **G** division of the tribe of Levi.
4:38 The **G** division was also counted by its clans
4:41 So this was the total of all those from the **G** clans
7:7 and four oxen to the **G** division for their work,
10:17 and the **G** and Merarite divisions of the Levites
26:57 The **G** clan, named after its ancestor Gershon.
1Ch 23:7 The **G** family units were defined by their lines of

GERSHONITES (5) [GERSHON]

Nu 4:24 "The duties of the **G** will be in the areas of general
4:26 The **G** are responsible for transporting all these
4:27 and his sons will direct the **G** regarding their
4:27 They must assign the **G** the loads they are to carry.
4:28 So these are the duties assigned to the **G** at the

GERUTH-KIMHAM (1)

Jer 41:17 They took them all to the village of **G** near

GESHAN (1)

1Ch 2:47 Jotham, **G**, Pelet, Ephah, and Shaaph.

GESHEM (4)

Ne 2:19 Tobiah, and **G** the Arab heard of our plan,
6:1 When Sanballat, Tobiah, **G** the Arab, and the rest
6:2 and **G** sent me a message asking me to meet them
6:6 "**G** tells me that everywhere he goes he hears that

GESHUR (11) [GESHURITES]

Jos 12:5 westward to the boundaries of the kingdoms of **G**
13:11 the territory of the kingdoms of **G** and Maacah,
13:13 the Israelites failed to drive out the people of **G**
2Sa 3:3 was Maacah, the daughter of Talmai, king of **G**.
13:37 Talmai son of Ammihud, the king of **G**.
13:38 He stayed there in **G** for three years.
14:23 Then Joab went to **G** and brought Absalom back to
14:32 me back from **G** if he didn't intend to see me.
15:8 For while I was at **G**, I promised to sacrifice to him
1Ch 2:23 (Later **G** and Aram captured the Towns of Jair
3:2 was Maacah, the daughter of Talmai, king of **G**.

GESHURITES (3) [GESHUR]

Dt 3:14 in Bashan all the way to the borders of the **G**
Jos 13:2 to occupy the land of the Philistines and the **G**—
1Sa 27:8 David and his men spent their time raiding the **G**,

GESTURE (2) [GESTURES]

Nu 6:20 then lift the gifts up before the LORD in a **g** of
Ac 26:1 So Paul, with a **g** of his hand, started his defense:

GESTURES (2) [GESTURE]

Lk 1:22 Then they realized from his **g** that he must have
1:62 baby's father, communicating to him by making **g**.

GET (479) [GETS, GETTING, GOT, GOTTEN, ILL-GOTTEN]

Ge 18:4 Rest in the shade of this tree while my servants **g**
18:6 **G** three measures of your best flour, and bake
18:32 Abraham said, "Lord, please do not **g** angry;
19:2 then **g** up in the morning as early as you like
19:12 "**G** them out of this place—sons-in-law, sons,
19:14 his daughters' fiancés, "Quick, **g** out of the city!
19:15 **G** out of here right now, or you will be caught in
19:32 let's **g** him drunk with wine, and then we will sleep
19:34 Let's **g** him drunk with wine again tonight,
20:11 'They will want my wife and will kill me to **g** her.'
21:10 and demanded, "**G** rid of that servant and her son.
24:40 you must **g** a wife for my son from among my
26:7 He thought they would kill him to **g** her,
26:9 "Because I was afraid someone would kill me to **g**
27:13 "Just do what I tell you. Go out and **g** the goats."
29:7 water the flocks so they can **g** back to grazing?"
31:41 your two daughters, and six years to **g** the flock.
34:4 "**G** this girl for me," he demanded. "I want to
37:29 Reuben returned to **g** Joseph out of the pit.
42:16 One of you go and **g** your brother! I'll keep the rest
42:27 and one of them opened his sack to **g** some grain to
46:28 and **g** directions to the land of Goshen.
Ex 1:19 so quickly that we cannot **g** there in time!
2:5 she told one of her servant girls to **g** it for her.
2:18 "How did you **g** the flocks watered so quickly
5:4 the people from their tasks? **G** back to work!
5:7 straw for making bricks. Let them **g** it themselves!
5:11 Go and **g** it yourselves. Find it wherever you can.
5:18 Now, **g** back to work! No straw will be given to
6:1 so anxious to **g** rid of them that he will force them
7:24 dug wells along the riverbank to **g** drinking water,
8:20 "**G** up early in the morning and meet Pharaoh as
9:13 said to Moses, "**G** up early in the morning.
10:26 which sacrifices he will require until we **g** there."
10:28 "**G** out of here!" Pharaoh shouted at Moses.
11:1 so anxious to **g** rid of you that he will practically
12:33 All the Egyptians urged the people of Israel to **g**
14:5 have we done, letting all these slaves **g** away?"
14:15 you crying out to me? Tell the people to **g** moving!
14:25 "Let's **g** out of here!" the Egyptians shouted.
16:33 "**G** a container and put two quarts of manna into
18:14 The people have been standing here all day to **g**
19:15 "**G** ready for an important event two days from
32:22 "Don't **g** upset, sir," Aaron replied.
32:25 When Moses saw that Aaron had let the people **g**
33:8 all the people would **g** up and stand in their tent
Lev 19:16 "Do not try to **g** ahead at the cost of your
25:26 but the person who sold it manages to **g** enough
25:49 They may also redeem themselves if they can **g** the
26:10 **g** rid of the leftovers from the previous year to
Nu 11:13 Where am I supposed to **g** meat for all these
14:3 as slaves! Let's **g** out of here and return to Egypt!"
16:21 "**G** away from these people so that I may instantly
16:24 "Then tell all the people to **g** away from the tents
16:26 "**G** away from the tents of these wicked men,
16:45 "**G** away from these people so that I can instantly
20:8 You will **g** enough water from the rock to satisfy
22:20 men have come for you, **g** up and go with them.
22:26 so narrow that the donkey could not **g** by at all.
24:11 Now **g** out of here! Go back home! I had planned
Dt 10:11 '**G** up and lead the people into the land I swore to
20:7 Well, go home and **g** married! You might die in the
22:4 Go and help your neighbor **g** it to its feet!
24:19 of grain from your field, don't go back to **g** it.
28:31 but you won't **g** a single bite of the meat.
Jos 1:11 and tell the people to **g** their provisions ready.
7:10 But the LORD said to Joshua, "**G** up! Why are
7:13 "**G** up! Command the people to purify themselves
10:19 Don't let them **g** back to their cities,
Jdg 4:14 Then Deborah said to Barak, "**G** ready!
7:9 During the night, the LORD said, "**G** up!
7:15 returned to the Israelite camp and shouted, "**G** up!
9:29 If I were in charge, I would **g** rid of Abimelech.
9:29 '**G** some more soldiers, and come out
11:2 "You will not **g** any of our father's inheritance,"
11:19 asking for permission to cross through his land to **g**
14:3 But Samson told his father, "**G** her for me. She is
14:15 "**G** the answer to the riddle from your husband,
15:11 So three thousand men of Judah went down to **g**
16:31 and other relatives went down to **g** his body.
18:10 When you **g** there, you will find the people living

18:25 and they might **g** angry and kill you and your
19: 9 Tomorrow you can **g** up early and be on your
19:28 He said, "**G** up! Let's go!" But there was no
Ru 1:12 and I were to **g** married tonight and bear sons,
1Sa 6:21 Ark of the LORD. Please come here and **g** it!"
7: 1 So the men of Kiriath-jearim came to **g** the Ark of
7: 3 **g** rid of your foreign gods and your images of
9:26 next morning, Samuel called up to Saul, "**G** up!
10: 3 "When you **g** to the oak of Tabor, you will see
14:19 Saul said to Ahijah, "Never mind; let's **g** going!"
17:26 "What will a man **g** for killing this Philistine
19:11 warned him, "If you don't **g** away tonight,
19:14 told them he was sick and couldn't **g** out of bed.
20:31 be king. Now go and **g** him so I can kill him!"
23: 6 taking the ephod with him to **g** answers for David
24:19 Who else would let his enemy **g** away when he had
25:13 "**G** your swords!" was David's reply as he
26:11 and his jug of water and then **g** out of here!"
26:22 "Let one of your young men come over and **g** it.
27: 1 to himself, "Someday Saul is going to **g** me.
28: 9 "Are you trying to **g** me killed?" the woman
29:10 Now **g** up early in the morning, and leave with
2Sa 2:22 Again Abner shouted to him, "**G** away from here!
3: 9 David **g** all that the LORD has promised him!
3:24 "What do you mean by letting Abner **g** away?
5: 6 "You'll never **g** in here," the Jebusites taunted.
11:13 then he couldn't **g** Uriah to go home to his wife.
11:20 But he might **g** angry and ask, 'Why did the troops
12:17 The leaders of the nation pleaded with him to **g** up
12:28 so you will **g** credit for the victory instead of me."
13: 9 "Everyone **g** out of here," Amnon told his
13:15 had loved her. "**G** out of here!" he snarled at her.
15:14 If we **g** out of the city before he arrives, both we
16: 3 'Today I will **g** back the kingdom of my
16: 7 "**G** out of here, you murderer, you scoundrel!"
22:39 I struck them down so they could not **g** up;
1Ki 3:23 Then the king said, "Let's **g** the facts straight.
17:11 As she was going to **g** it, he called to her,
19: 5 angel touched him and told him, "**G** up and eat!"
19: 7 touched him and said, "**G** up and eat some more,
20:22 "**G** ready for another attack by the king of Aram
20:33 "Go and **g** him," the king of Israel told them.
21: 7 "**G** up and eat and don't worry about it. I'll **g** you
Naboth's vineyard!"
22: 9 "Quick! Go and **g** Micaiah son of Imlah."
22:13 the messenger who went to **g** Micaiah said to him,
22:34 "**G** me out of here!" Ahab groaned to the driver
2Ki 1: 3 god of Ekron, to ask whether the king will **g** well?
1: 6 god of Ekron, to ask whether the king will **g** well?
1:16 the god of Ekron, to ask whether you will **g** well?
2:10 I am taken from you, then you will **g** your request.
4:29 Then Elisha said to Gehazi, "**G** ready to travel;
5:20 "My master should not have let this Aramean **g**
5:20 I will chase after him and **g** something from him."
8: 8 Then tell him to ask the LORD if I will **g** well
9: 1 "**G** ready to go to Ramoth-gilead," he told him.
9:18 "What do you know about peace? **G** behind me!"
9:19 "What do you know about peace? **G** behind me!"
9:21 "Quick! **G** my chariot ready!" King Joram
13:15 Elisha told him, "**G** a bow and some arrows."
20: 5 and three days from now you will **g** out of bed
23:35 In order to **g** the silver and gold demanded as
1Ch 11: 5 Jebus said to David, "You will never **g** in here!"
28: 9 my son, **g** to know the God of your ancestors.
2Ch 18: 8 "Quick! Go and **g** Micaiah son of Imlah."
18:12 the messenger who went to **g** Micaiah said to him,
18:33 "**G** me out of here!" Ahab groaned to the driver
26:18 **G** out of the sanctuary, for you have sinned.
26:20 And the king himself was eager to **g** out
Ezr 4:22 for we must not permit the situation to **g** out of
Ne 2:14 but my donkey couldn't **g** through the rubble.
4:10 so much rubble to be moved that we could never **g**
5: 3 and homes to **g** food during the famine."
5: 5 Yet we must sell our children into slavery just to **g**
6: 7 "You can be very sure that this report will **g** back
8:15 telling the people to go to the hills to **g** branches
Est 6:10 "Hurry and **g** the robe and my horse, and do just
Job 1: 4 On these occasions they would **g** together to eat
1: 5 He would **g** up early in the morning and offer a
11:14 **G** rid of your sins and leave all iniquity behind
21:17 "Yet the wicked **g** away with it time and time
28:18 valuable rock crystal are worthless in trying to **g** it.
31:21 an orphan because I thought I could **g** away with it,
38:20 take it to its home? Do you know how to **g** there?
41:16 are close together so no air can **g** between them.
Ps 10:13 Why do the wicked **g** away with cursing God?
18:38 I struck them down so they could not **g** up;
41: 8 they say. / "He will never **g** out of that bed!"
44:23 Wake up, O Lord! Why do you sleep? / **G** up!
56: 7 Don't let them **g** away with their wickedness;
57: 3 rescuing me from those who are out to **g** me.
62:10 Don't try to **g** rich / by extortion or robbery.
68:23 and even your dogs will **g** their share!"
71:11 "God has abandoned him. / Let's go and **g** him,
73:14 All I **g** is trouble all day long; / every morning
86:15 are a merciful and gracious God, / slow to **g** angry,
88:10 Do the dead **g** up and praise you? / *Interlude*
89:22 His enemies will not **g** the best of him, / nor will
103: 8 he is slow to **g** angry and full of unfailing love.
119:115 **G** out of my life, you evil-minded people, / for I
139: 7 I can never **g** away from your presence!
139:19 the wicked! / **G** out of my life, you murderers!
145: 8 slow to **g** angry, full of unfailing love.
Pr 1:13 And the loot we'll **g**! We'll fill our houses with all
3: 3 Never let loyalty and kindness **g** away from you!
4: 7 And whatever else you do, **g** good judgment.
4:27 Don't **g** sidetracked; keep your feet from following
6: 3 quick, **g** out of it if you possibly can! You have
9: 7 Anyone who rebukes a mocker will **g** a smart
9: 7 Anyone who rebukes the wicked will **g** hurt.
10: 4 Lazy people are soon poor; hard workers **g** rich.
11:16 women obtain wealth, and violent men **g** rich.
11:18 Evil people **g** rich for the moment, but the reward
11:31 the wicked and the sinner will **g** what they deserve!
12:14 People can **g** many good things by the words they
13: 4 Lazy people want much but **g** little, but those who
13: 8 a ransom, but the poor won't even **g** threatened.
14:14 Backsliders **g** what they deserve; good people
16:16 How much better to **g** wisdom than gold,
18: 6 Fools **g** into constant quarrels; they are asking for a
18: 7 fools are their ruin; their lips **g** them into trouble.
19:20 **G** all the advice and instruction you can, and be
20:16 Be sure to **g** collateral from anyone who
20:16 **G** a deposit if someone guarantees the debt of a
20:22 Don't say, "I will **g** even for this wrong." Wait for
21:10 their neighbors **g** no mercy from them.
21:20 and luxury, but fools spend whatever they **g**.
23: 4 Don't weary yourself trying to **g** rich. Why waste
23:23 **G** the truth and don't ever sell it; also **g** wisdom,
discipline, and discernment.
24: 8 A person who plans evil will **g** a reputation as a
24:29 back for all their meanness to me! I'll **g** even!"
26:27 a trap for others, you will **g** caught in it yourself.
27:13 Be sure to **g** collateral from anyone who
27:13 **G** a deposit if someone guarantees the debt of an
28:20 The trustworthy will **g** a rich reward.
28:20 But the person who wants to **g** rich quick will only
g into trouble.
28:22 A greedy person tries to **g** rich quick, but it only
29: 8 Mockers can **g** a whole town agitated, but those
31: 9 the poor and helpless, and see that they **g** justice.
Ecc 1: 3 What do people **g** for all their hard work?
2:22 So what do people **g** for all their hard work?
3: 9 What do people really **g** for all their hard work?
4: 9 much as one; they **g** a better return for their labor.
5: 8 and matters of justice only **g** lost in red tape
5:12 and seldom **g** a good night's sleep.
6: 2 They die, and others **g** it all! This is meaningless—
6: 3 and in the end does not even **g** a decent burial,
7:12 Wisdom or money can **g** you almost anything,
10:17 only to gain strength for their work, not to **g** drunk.
11: 4 perfect conditions, you will never **g** anything done.
SS 3: 2 said to myself, 'I will **g** up now and roam the city,
5: 3 Should I **g** dressed again? I have washed my feet.
Should I **g** them soiled?'
7:12 Let us **g** up early and go out to the vineyards.
Isa 3: 7 or clothes. Don't ask me to **g** involved!"
3:11 is sure. You, too, will **g** what you deserve.
5:11 Destruction is certain for you who **g** up early to
5:27 They will not **g** tired or stumble. They will run
22:10 and tear some down to **g** stone to fix the walls.
30:16 You said, 'No, we will **g** our help from Egypt.
33:18 and estimated how much plunder they would **g**
40:24 They hardly **g** started, barely taking root, when he
46: 7 It has no power to **g** anyone out of trouble.
47:14 You will **g** no help from them at all.
55: 2 and I will tell you where to **g** food that is good for
56:12 they say. "We will **g** some wine and have a party.
56:12 Let's all **g** drunk. Let this go on and on,
58: 4 This kind of fasting will never **g** you anywhere
Jer 1:17 "**G** up and **g** dressed. Go out, and tell them
6:13 they trick others to **g** what does not belong to them.
8: 4 When people fall down, don't they **g** up again?
8:10 they trick others to **g** what does not belong to them.
13: 6 and **g** the linen belt that I told you to hide there."
14: 3 The nobles send servants to **g** water, but all the
15: 1 Away with them! **G** them out of my sight!
17:11 so are those who **g** their wealth by unjust means.
20:10 "and then we will **g** our revenge on him."
23:27 they are trying to **g** my people to forget me,
23:30 "I stand against these prophets who **g** their
25:27 **G** drunk and vomit, and you will fall to rise no
32:31 but anger me, so I am determined to **g** rid of it.
33: 4 and even the king's palace to **g** materials to
36: 2 "**G** a scroll, and write down all my messages
36:21 The king sent Jehudi to **g** the scroll. Jehudi brought
36:28 "**G** another scroll, and write everything again just
46:11 Go up to Gilead to **g** ointment, O virgin daughter
46:16 Let's **g** away from the sword of the enemy!'
46:19 **G** ready to leave for exile, you citizens of Egypt!
48:44 I will see to it that you do not **g** away, for the time
50: 6 and cannot remember how to **g** back to the fold.
51: 6 Don't **g** trapped in her punishment!
51:61 He said to Seraiah, "When you **g** to Babylon,
La 4: 5 now beg in the streets for anything they can **g**.
4:15 "**G** away!" the people shouted at them. "You are
5: 6 to Egypt and Assyria to **g** enough food to survive.
Eze 4: 9 "Now go and **g** some wheat, barley, beans, lentils,
16:15 "But you thought you could **g** along without me,
17:15 her sworn treaties like that and **g** away with it?
18:31 and **g** for yourselves a new heart and a new spirit.
20: 7 I said to them, 'Each of you, **g** rid of your idols.
20: 8 They did not **g** rid of their idols or forsake the gods
23:40 "You sisters sent messengers to distant lands to **g**
38: 7 "**G** ready; be prepared! Keep all the armies around
Da 6:14 He spent the rest of the day looking for a way to **g**
7: 5 And I heard a voice saying to it, "**G** up!
Hos 3: 1 LORD said to me, "Go and **g** your wife again.
4: 8 "The priests **g** fed when the people sin and bring
7: 5 "On royal holidays, the princes **g** drunk. The king
Joel 3: 3 and little girls for enough wine to **g** drunk.
3: 9 Say to the nations far and wide: "**G** ready for war!
Am 2:14 Your fastest runners will not **g** away. The strongest
3: 5 Does a bird ever **g** caught in a trap that has no bait?
7:12 "**G** out of here, you seer! Go on back to the land
8: 5 to end so you can **g** back to cheating the helpless.
Ob 1: 1 was sent to the nations to say, "**G** ready, everyone!
Jnh 1: 2 "**G** up and go to the great city of Nineveh!
1: 3 and went in the opposite direction in order to **g**
1: 6 he shouted. "**G** up and pray to your god!
3: 2 "**G** up and go to the great city of Nineveh,
4: 2 slow to **g** angry and filled with unfailing love.
Mic 3:11 You rulers govern for the bribes you can **g**;
6:15 but not **g** enough oil to anoint yourselves.
6:15 the grapes but **g** no juice to make your wine.
Na 1: 3 The LORD is slow to **g** angry, but his power is
3:10 Soldiers cast lots to see who would **g** the Egyptian
3:14 **G** ready for the siege! Store up water!
Hab 1:17 Will you let them **g** away with this forever?
2: 6 Now you will **g** what you deserve for your
2: 9 "How terrible it will be for you who **g** rich by
Zep 3: 3 for their victims—out for everything they can **g**.
Hag 1:11 to ruin everything you have worked so hard to **g**."
Zec 8:13 but instead **g** on with rebuilding the Temple!
13: 2 I will **g** rid of every trace of idol worship
Mal 3:15 For those who do evil **g** rich, and those who dare
Mt 2:13 "**G** up and flee to Egypt with the child and his
2:20 "**G** up and take the child and his mother back to
4:10 "**G** out of here, Satan," Jesus told him.
6: 2 they have received all the reward they will ever **g**.
6: 5 I assure you, that is all the reward they will ever **g**.
6:16 assure you, that is the only reward they will ever **g**.
6:19 where they can be eaten by moths and **g** rusty,
7: 4 let me help you **g** rid of that speck in your eye,'
7: 5 First **g** rid of the log from your own eye,
9: 5 'Your sins are forgiven' or '**G** up and walk'?
12:11 wouldn't you **g** to work and pull it out?
13:21 At first they **g** along fine, but they wilt as soon as
13:44 and sold everything he owned to **g** enough money
to buy the field—and to **g** the treasure, too!
13:54 "Where does he **g** his wisdom and his miracles?
14:22 Jesus made his disciples **g** back into the boat
15:33 "And where would we **g** enough food out here in
16:23 turned to Peter and said, "**G** away from me, Satan!
17: 7 touched them. "**G** up," he said, "don't be afraid."
18: 3 you will never **g** into the Kingdom of Heaven.
19:23 it is very hard for a rich person to **g** into the
19:27 to follow you. What will we **g** out of it?"
20:10 When those hired earlier came to **g** their pay,
20:18 "When we **g** to Jerusalem," he said, "the Son of
21:31 and prostitutes will **g** into the Kingdom of God
21:38 let's kill him and **g** the estate for ourselves!'
23: 7 They enjoy the attention they **g** on the streets,
24:18 A person in the field must not return even to **g** a
Mk 2: 4 They couldn't **g** to Jesus through the crowd,
2: 9 'Your sins are forgiven' or '**G** up, pick up your
4:17 At first they **g** along fine, but they wilt as soon as
5:41 her hand, he said to her, "**G** up, little girl!"
6: 2 "Where did he **g** all his wisdom and the power to
6:31 "Let's **g** away from the crowds for a while
6:45 Jesus made his disciples **g** back into the boat
7:17 Then Jesus went into a house to **g** away from the
8:33 to Peter very sternly, "**G** away from me, Satan!
10:15 of faith will never **g** into the Kingdom of God."
10:17 what should I do to **g** eternal life?"
10:23 "How hard it is for rich people to **g** into the
10:24 it is very hard to **g** into the Kingdom of God.
10:33 "When we **g** to Jerusalem," he told them,
12: 7 Let's kill him and **g** the estate for ourselves!'
13:16 A person in the field must not return even to **g** a
14:59 But even then they didn't **g** their stories straight!
15:24 throwing dice to decide who would **g** them.
Lk 5:23 'Your sins are forgiven' or '**G** up and walk'?
6:30 are taken away from you, don't try to **g** them back.
6:42 let me help you **g** rid of that speck in your eye,'
6:42 First **g** rid of the log from your own eye;
7:14 bearers stopped. "Young man," he said, "**g** up."
8:19 they couldn't **g** to him because of the crowds.
8:54 and said in a loud voice, "**G** up, my child!"
11: 8 he will **g** up and give you what you want so his
12:20 will die this very night. Then who will **g** it all?'
13: 9 If we **g** figs next year, fine. If not, you can cut it
13:24 Work hard to **g** in, because many will try to enter,
13:31 "**G** out of here if you want to live, because Herod
14: 5 a pit, don't you proceed at once to **g** him out?"
14:24 For none of those I invited first will **g** even the
15:22 **G** a ring for his finger, and sandals for his feet.
16: 2 **G** your report in order, because you are going to be
17: 5 "We need more faith; tell us how to **g** it."
18:17 of faith will never **g** into the Kingdom of God."
18:18 what should I do to **g** eternal life?"
18:24 "How hard it is for rich people to **g** into the
18:31 And when we **g** there, all the predictions of the
19: 3 He tried to **g** a look at Jesus, but he was too short
19:23 the bank so I could at least **g** some interest on it?'
20:14 Let's kill him and **g** the estate for ourselves!'
20:20 They tried to **g** Jesus to say something that could
22:46 he asked. "**G** up and pray. Otherwise,
Jn 2:16 he told them, "**G** these things out of here.
4:11 deep well. Where would you **g** this living water?
4:16 "Go and **g** your husband," Jesus told her.
5: 6 he asked him, "Would you like to **g** well?"
5: 7 While I am trying to **g** there, someone else always
6:25 they asked, "Teacher, how did you **g** here?"
14: 3 When everything is ready, I will come and **g** you,
14: 4 you know where I am going and how to **g** there."
20:15 where you have put him, and I will go and **g** him."
21: 6 side of the boat, and you'll **g** plenty of fish!"
Ac 2:15 People don't **g** drunk by nine o'clock in the
3: 6 name of Jesus Christ of Nazareth, **g** up and walk!"
9: 6 Now **g** up and go into the city, and you will be told

9:17 has sent me so that you may **g** your sight back
9:34 Jesus Christ heals you! **G** up and make your bed!"
9:40 Turning to the body he said, "**G** up, Tabitha."
10:13 Then a voice said to him, "**G** up, Peter; kill and eat
11:7 And I heard a voice say, '**G** up, Peter; kill and eat
12:7 the side to awaken him and said, "Quick! **G** up!"
12:8 told him, "**G** dressed and put on your sandals."
20:16 He was hurrying to **g** to Jerusalem, if possible,
22:10 the Lord told me, '**G** up and go into Damascus,
22:16 **G** up and be baptized, and have your sins washed
23:20 pretending they want to **g** some more information.
23:23 "**G** two hundred soldiers ready to leave for
23:24 Paul to ride, and **g** him safely to Governor Felix."
26:11 in the synagogues to try to **g** them to curse Christ.
27:39 and wondered if they could **g** between the rocks
and **g** the ship safely to shore.
28:20 to come here today so we could **g** acquainted and
Ro 9:16 We can't **g** it by choosing it or working hard for it.
9:31 so hard to **g** right with God by keeping the law,
9:32 Because they were trying to **g** right with God by
12:13 And **g** into the habit of inviting guests home for
12:21 Don't let evil **g** the best of you, but conquer evil by
13:3 So do what they say, and you will **g** along well.
13:12 So don't live in darkness. **G** rid of your evil deeds.
1Co 7:7 I wish everyone could **g** along without marrying,
7:21 but if you **g** a chance to be free, take it.
7:27 If you do not have a wife, do not **g** married.
7:28 But if you do **g** married, it is not a sin. And if a
9:13 **g** their meals from the food brought to the Temple
9:13 And those who serve at the altar **g** a share of the
9:18 It is the satisfaction I **g** from preaching the Good
11:21 As a result, some go hungry while others **g** drunk.
12:28 those who can **g** others to work together,
14:5 so that the whole church can **g** some good out of it.
15:32 there is no resurrection, / "Let's feast and **g** drunk,
16:2 Don't wait until I **g** there and then try to collect it
2Co 4:9 We **g** knocked down, but we **g** up again and keep
going.
9:6 a farmer who plants only a few seeds will **g** a small
9:6 But the one who plants generously will **g** a
11:15 In the end they will **g** every bit of punishment their
Gal 1:13 the Christians. I did my best to **g** rid of them.
4:30 "**G** rid of the slave and her son, for the son of the
5:1 and don't **g** tied up again in slavery to the law.
6:7 that you can't ignore God and **g** away with it.
6:9 So don't **g** tired of doing what is good. Don't **g**
discouraged and give up, for we will reap
Eph 4:31 **G** rid of all bitterness, rage, anger, harsh words,
Php 3:1 give you joy. I never **g** tired of telling you this.
4:11 for I have learned how to **g** along happily whether
Col 2:19 and we grow only as we **g** our nourishment
3:8 But now is the time to **g** rid of anger, rage,
3:25 For God has no favorites who can **g** away with
1Th 5:7 time for sleep and the time when people **g** drunk.
2Th 3:12 we command them: Settle down and **g** to work.
3:13 and sisters, never **g** tired of doing good.
1Ti 4:13 Until I **g** there, focus on reading the Scriptures to
6:5 the truth. To them religion is just a way to **g** rich.
2Ti 2:23 Again I say, don't **g** involved in foolish,
3:9 But they won't **g** away with this for long.
4:21 Hurry so you can **g** here before winter.
Tit 3:9 Do not **g** involved in foolish discussions about
Heb 4:1 with fear that some of you might fail to **g** there.
9:17 no one can use the will to **g** any of the things
Jas 1:19 quick to listen, slow to speak, and slow to **g** angry.
1:21 So **g** rid of all the filth and evil in your lives,
4:2 you don't have, so you scheme and kill to **g** it.
4:3 you don't **g** it because your whole motive is
1Pe 2:1 So **g** rid of all malicious behavior and deceit.
2:20 you **g** no credit for being patient if you are beaten
2:23 When he suffered, he did not threaten to **g** even.
5:2 not for what you will **g** out of it, but because you
2Pe 2:3 In their greed they will make up clever lies to **g**
2:20 Savior Jesus Christ and then **g** tangled up with sin
1Jn 5:18 and the evil one cannot **g** his hands on them.
Jude 1:16 and they flatter others to **g** favors in return.

GET-RICH-QUICK (1) [RICH]

Pr 13:11 Wealth from **g** schemes quickly disappears;

GETHER (2)

Ge 10:23 descendants of Aram were Uz, Hul, **G**, and Mash.
1Ch 1:17 descendants of Aram were Uz, Hul, **G**, and Mash.

GETHSEMANE (2)

Mt 26:36 Jesus brought them to an olive grove called **G**,
Mk 14:32 And they came to an olive grove called **G**,

GETS (27) [GET]

Ex 21:24 If a tooth **g** knocked out, knock out the tooth of the
21:34 pay in full for the dead animal but then **g** to keep it.
21:36 pay in full for the dead bull but then **g** to keep it.
22:6 "If a fire **g** out of control and goes into another
22:10 other animal, but it dies or is injured or **g** away,
1Sa 29:10 and leave with your men as soon as it **g** light."
2Sa 13:28 told his men, "Wait until Amnon **g** drunk;
20:6 and chase after him before he **g** into a fortified city
1Ki 20:39 if for any reason he **g** away, you will either die
Job 36:10 He **g** their attention and says they must turn away
36:15 For he **g** their attention through adversity.
Pr 22:16 A person who **g** ahead by oppressing the poor
29:22 person starts fights and **g** into all kinds of sin.
30:23 a bitter woman who finally **g** a husband, / a servant
31:15 She **g** up before dawn to prepare breakfast for her
Jer 2:26 a thief, Israel feels shame only when she **g** caught.
Mt 5:38 If a tooth **g** knocked out, knock out the tooth of the
10:41 you will receive the same reward a prophet **g**.
12:24 He **g** his power from Satan, the prince of demons."
Mk 3:22 That's where he **g** the power to cast out demons."
Lk 11:15 He **g** his power from Satan, the prince of
18:5 I'm going to see that she **g** justice, because she is
Jn 5:7 get there, someone else always **g** in ahead of me."
19:24 "Let's not tear it but throw dice to see who **g** it."
1Co 7:28 And if a young woman **g** married, it is not a sin.
9:24 everyone runs, but only one person **g** the prize.
Heb 9:16 no one **g** anything until it is proved that the person

GETTING (53) [GET]

Ge 19:33 He was unaware of her lying down or **g** up again.
19:35 he was unaware of her lying down or **g** up again.
30:9 Leah realized that she wasn't **g** pregnant anymore,
31:35 "Forgive my not **g** up, Father," Rachel explained.
37:14 see how your brothers and the flocks are **g** along,"
43:27 He asked them how they had been **g** along, and
Ex 5:21 "May the LORD judge you for **g** us into this
16:17 this food—some **g** more, and some **g** less.
Dt 6:7 you are lying down and when you are **g** up again.
11:19 you are lying down and when you are **g** up again.
Jdg 9:44 gate to keep the men of Shechem from **g** back in,
19:9 to leave, his father-in-law said, "Look, it's **g** late.
19:11 man's servant said to him, "It's **g** too late to travel;
1Sa 17:18 See how your brothers are **g** along, and bring me
25:42 Quickly **g** ready, she took along five of her servant
2Sa 11:7 asked him how Joab and the army were **g** along
14:28 Jerusalem for two years without **g** to see the king.
15:37 to Jerusalem, **g** there just as Absalom arrived.
1Ki 16:9 in Tirzah, Elah was **g** drunk at the home of Arza,
20:16 allied kings were still in their tents **g** drunk,
2Ki 8:3 and she went to see the king about **g** back her
12:7 it must all be spent on **g** the Temple into good
Job 24:5 the poor must spend all their time just **g** enough to
36:21 for it was to prevent you from **g** into a life of evil
Pr 4:7 **G** wisdom is the most important thing you can do!
20:14 "It's worthless," then brags about **g** a bargain!
Ecc 1:6 and there, twisting back and forth, **g** nowhere.
Jnh 1:11 And since the storm was **g** worse all the time,
Mic 6:10 Will there be no end of your **g** rich by cheating?
Mt 14:15 and said, "This is a desolate place, and it is **g** late.
24:49 the other servants, partying, and **g** drunk—
27:24 Pilate saw that he wasn't **g** anywhere and that a
Mk 6:35 and said, "This is a desolate place, and it is **g** late.
Lk 12:45 the other servants, partying, and **g** drunk—
14:28 construction of a building without first **g** estimates
24:29 him to stay the night with them, since it was **g** late.
Jn 7:13 for they were afraid of **g** in trouble with the Jewish
11:12 if he is sleeping, that means he is **g** better!"
Ac 11:15 but just as I was **g** started, the Holy Spirit fell on
15:36 to see how the new believers are **g** along."
Ro 10:3 they are clinging to their own way of **g** right with
10:6 But the way of **g** right with God through faith says,
13:13 Don't participate in wild parties and **g** drunk,
2Co 11:28 I have the daily burden of how the churches are **g**
12:7 But to keep me from **g** puffed up, I was given a
12:7 Satan to torment me and keep me from **g** proud.
Gal 5:7 You were **g** along so well. Who has interfered with
Eph 6:21 will tell you all about how I am **g** along.
Php 2:19 he can cheer me up by telling me how you are **g**
Col 4:7 loved brother, will tell you how I am **g** along.
1Ti 5:13 **g** into other people's business and saying things
Heb 8:5 For when Moses was **g** ready to build the

GEUEL (1)

Nu 13:15 Gad | **G** son of Maki

GEZER (15)

Jos 10:33 King Horam of **G** had arrived with his army to
12:12 The king of Eglon / The king of **G**
16:3 then to **G** and on over to the Mediterranean Sea.
16:10 They did not drive the Canaanites out of **G**,
16:10 so the people of **G** live as slaves among the people
21:21 for those who accidentally killed someone), **G**,
Jdg 1:29 also failed to drive out the Canaanites living in **G**,
2Sa 5:25 down the Philistines all the way from Gibeon to **G**.
1Ki 9:15 and the cities of Hazor, Megiddo, and **G**.
9:16 (The king of Egypt had attacked and captured **G**,
9:17 So Solomon rebuilt the city of **G**.) He also built up
1Ch 6:67 (a city of refuge in the hill country of Ephraim), **G**,
7:28 **G** and its villages to the west, and Shechem and its
14:16 the Philistine army all the way from Gibeon to **G**.
20:4 After this, war broke out with the Philistines at **G**.

GEZRITES [KJV] See GIRZITES

GHOST (6) [GHOSTS]

Isa 29:4 Your voice will whisper like a **g** from the earth
Jer 9:11 The towns of Judah will be **g** towns, with no one
Mt 14:26 they screamed in terror, thinking he was a **g**.
Mk 6:49 they screamed in terror, thinking he was a **g**.
Lk 24:37 terribly frightened, thinking they were seeing a **g**!
24:39 Touch me and make sure that I am not a **g**,

(GIVE UP THE) GHOST [KJV] See BREATHED HIS LAST, DIE, PERISHED

(HOLY) GHOST [KJV] See (HOLY) SPIRIT

GHOSTS (1) [GHOST]

Lk 24:39 because **g** don't have bodies, as you see that I do!"

GIAH (1)

2Sa 2:24 down as they arrived at the hill of Ammah near **G**,

GIANT (9) [GIANTS]

Dt 3:11 King Og of Bashan was the last of the **g** Rephaites.
1Sa 17:4 He was a **g** of a man, measuring over nine feet tall!
17:16 the Philistine **g** strutted in front of the Israelite
17:25 "Have you seen the **g**?" the men were asking.
17:27 is true. That is the reward for killing the **g**."
17:50 So David triumphed over the Philistine **g** with only
17:51 David used it to kill the **g** and cut off his head.
19:5 the time he risked his life to kill the Philistine **g**
Job 37:18 he makes the skies reflect the heat like a **g** mirror.

GIANTS (13) [GIANT]

Ge 6:4 and even afterward, **g** lived on the earth,
Nu 13:33 We even saw **g** there, the descendants of Anak.
Dt 1:28 They have even seen **g** there—the descendants of
2:10 and powerful race of **g** called the Emites had once
2:10 were as tall as the Anakites, another race of **g**.
9:2 and tall—descendants of the famous Anakite **g**.
2Sa 21:16 Ishbi-benob was a descendant of the **g**; his bronze
21:18 Hushah killed Saph, another descendant of the **g**.
21:20 and six toes on each foot—a descendant of the **g**—
21:22 These four Philistines were descended from the **g**
1Ch 20:4 a descendant of the **g**, and so the Philistines were
20:6 and six toes on each foot—a descendant of the **g**—
20:8 These Philistines were descendants of the **g** of

GIBBAR (2)

Ezr 2:20 The family of **G** | 95
Ne 7:25 The family of **G** | 95

GIBBETHON (5)

Jos 19:44 Eltekeh, **G**, Baalath,
21:23 to the priests from the tribe of Dan: Eltekeh, **G**,
1Ki 15:27 army were laying siege to the Philistine town of **G**.
16:15 then engaged in attacking the Philistine town of **G**,
16:17 So Omri led the army of Israel away from **G** to

GIBEA (1)

1Ch 2:49 and Sheva (the father of Macbenah and **G**).

GIBEAH (42)

Jos 15:57 Kain, **G**, and Timnah—ten towns with their
18:28 Zela, Haeleph, Jebus (that is, Jerusalem), **G**,
24:33 in the town of **G**, which had been given to his son
Jdg 19:12 where there are no Israelites. We will go on to **G**.
19:13 We will find a place to spend the night in either **G**
19:14 The sun was setting as they came to **G**, a town in
19:16 but he was living in **G** in the territory of Benjamin.
20:4 said, "My concubine and I came to **G**, a town in
20:5 That night some of the leaders of **G** surrounded the
20:9 we will draw lots to decide who will attack **G**.
20:10 and the rest of us will take revenge on **G** for this
20:13 Give up these evil men from **G** so we can execute
20:14 and gathered at **G** to fight the Israelites.
20:15 **G** to join the seven hundred warriors who lived
20:19 left early the next morning and camped near **G**.
20:20 Then they advanced toward **G** to attack the men of
20:29 So the Israelites set an ambush all around **G**.
20:31 and along the roads leading to Bethel and **G**.
20:33 Then the Israelites hiding in ambush west of **G**
20:43 them down, finally overtaking them east of **G**.
1Sa 10:5 "When you arrive at **G** of God, where the garrison
10:10 When Saul and his servant arrived at **G**, they saw
10:26 When Saul returned to his home at **G**, a band of
11:4 When the messengers came to **G**,
13:2 Saul's son Jonathan to **G** in the land of Benjamin.
13:15 They went up from Gilgal to **G** in the land of
13:16 staying at Geba, near **G**, in the land of Benjamin.
14:2 hundred men were camped on the outskirts of **G**,
14:16 Saul's lookouts in **G** saw a strange sight—the vast
15:34 to Ramah, and Saul returned to his house at **G**.
22:6 was sitting beneath a tamarisk tree on the hill at **G**,
23:19 But now the men of Ziph went to Saul in **G**
26:1 from Ziph came back to Saul at **G** to tell him,
2Sa 23:29 Ithai son of Ribai from **G** (from the tribe of
1Ch 11:31 Ithai son of Ribai from **G** (from the tribe of
12:3 Their leader was Ahiezer son of Shemaah from **G**;
2Ch 13:2 mother was Maacah, a daughter of Uriel from **G**.
Isa 10:29 All the people of **G**—the city of Saul—are running
Hos 5:8 "Blow the ram's horn in **G**! Sound the alarm in
9:9 do are as depraved as what they did in **G** long ago.
10:9 "O Israel, ever since that awful night in **G**,
10:9 Was it not right that the wicked men of **G** were

GIBEATH-HAARALOTH (1)

Jos 5:3 the entire male population of Israel at **G**.

GIBEON (41) [GIBEONITE, GIBEONITES]

Jos 9:3 But when the people of **G** heard what had
9:16 facts came out—these people of **G** lived nearby!
9:17 The names of these towns were **G**, Kephirah,
10:2 they heard all this because **G** was a large city—
10:4 "Come and help me destroy **G**," he urged them.
10:5 moved all their troops into place and attacked **G**.
10:6 The men of **G** quickly sent messengers to Joshua at
10:7 Israelite army left Gilgal and set out to rescue **G**.
10:10 Israelites slaughtered them in great numbers at **G**.
10:12 He said, / "Let the sun stand still over **G**,
10:41 Kadesh-barnea to Gaza and from Goshen to **G**.

11:19 peace with the Israelites except the Hivites of **G**.
18:25 Also **G**, Ramah, Beeroth,
21:17 with their surrounding pasturelands: **G**, Geba,
2Sa 2:12 some of Ishbosheth's troops from Mahanaim to **G**.
2:13 from Hebron, and they met Abner at the pool of **G**.
2:24 near Giah, along the road to the wilderness of **G**.
3:30 had killed their brother Asahel at the battle of **G**.
5:25 down the Philistines all the way from **G** to Gezer.
20:8 As they arrived at the great stone in **G**, Amasa met
21:6 and we will execute them before the LORD at **G**,
21:9 The men of **G** executed them on the mountain
1Ki 3:4 The most important of these altars was at **G**,
9:2 a second time, as he had done before at **G**.
1Ch 6:60 from the territory of Benjamin they were given **G**,
8:29 Jeiel (the father of **G**) lived in **G**. His wife's
9:35 Jeiel (the father of **G**) lived in **G**. His wife's
12:4 Ishmaiah from **G**, a famous warrior and leader
14:16 the Philistine army all the way from **G** to Gezer.
16:39 at the Tabernacle of the LORD on the hill of **G**,
21:29 in the wilderness were located at the hill of **G**.
2Ch 1:3 the hill at **G** where God's Tabernacle was located.
1:5 and grandson of Hur was still at **G** in front of the
1:13 to Jerusalem from the Tabernacle at the hill of **G**,
Ne 3:7 Next to them were Melatiah from **G**, Jadon from Meronoth, and people from **G** and Mizpah,
Isa 28:21 at Mount Perazim and against the Amorites at **G**.
Jer 28:1 Hananiah son of Azzur, a prophet from **G**,
41:12 They caught up with him at the pool near **G**.

GIBEONITE (2) [GIBEON]

Jos 9:22 But Joshua called together the **G** leaders and said,
10:2 than Ai. And the **G** men were mighty warriors.

GIBEONITES (7) [GIBEON]

Jos 9:21 So the Israelites kept their promise to the **G**.
9:27 But that day he made the **G** the woodchoppers
10:1 He also learned that the **G** had made peace with
2Sa 21:1 and his family are guilty of murdering the **G**."
21:2 So King David summoned the **G**. They were not
21:4 "Well, money won't do it," the **G** replied.
21:13 as well as the bones of the men the **G** had

GIBLITES [KJV] See GEBALITES

GIDDEL (4)

Ezr 2:47 **G**, Gahar, Reaiah,
2:56 Jaalah, Darkon, **G**,
Ne 7:49 Hanan, **G**, Gahar,
7:58 Jaalah, Darkon, **G**,

GIDEON (65) [GIDEON'S, JERUBBAAL]

Jdg 6:11 **G** son of Joash had been threshing wheat at the
6:13 "Sir," **G** replied, "if the LORD is with us,
6:15 "But Lord," **G** replied, "how can I rescue Israel?
6:17 **G** replied, "If you are truly going to help me,
6:19 **G** hurried home. He cooked a young goat, and with
6:20 pour the broth over it." And **G** did as he was told.
6:22 When **G** realized that it was the angel of the
6:24 And **G** built an altar to the LORD there
6:25 That night the LORD said to **G**,
6:27 So **G** took ten of his servants and did as the
6:29 they learned that it was **G**, the son of Joash.
6:32 From then on **G** was called Jerubbaal,
6:34 the Spirit of the LORD took possession of **G**.
6:36 Then **G** said to God, "If you are truly going to use
6:38 When **G** got up the next morning, he squeezed the
6:39 Then **G** said to God, "Please don't be angry with
6:40 So that night God did as **G** asked. The fleece was
7:1 So Jerubbaal (that is, **G**) and his army got up early
7:2 The LORD said to **G**, "You have too many
7:4 But the LORD told **G**, "There are still too many!
7:5 When **G** took his warriors down to the water,
7:7 The LORD told **G**, "With these three hundred
7:8 So **G** collected the provisions and rams' horns of
7:8 the Midianite camp was in the valley just below **G**.
7:11 So **G** took Purah and went down to the outposts of
7:13 **G** crept up just as a man was telling his friend
7:14 God has given **G** son of Joash, the Israelite,
7:15 When **G** heard the dream and its interpretation,
7:18 and shout, 'For the LORD and for **G**!' "
7:19 when **G** and the one hundred men with him
7:20 "A sword for the LORD and for **G**!"
7:23 Then **G** sent for the warriors of Naphtali, Asher,
7:24 **G** also sent messengers throughout the hill country
7:25 Israelites brought the heads of Oreb and Zeeb to **G**,
8:1 Then the people of Ephraim asked **G**, "Why have
8:1 And they argued heatedly with **G**.
8:2 But **G** replied, "What have I done compared to
8:4 **G** then crossed the Jordan River with his three
8:5 reached Succoth, **G** asked the leaders of the town,
8:7 So **G** said, "After the LORD gives me victory
8:8 From there **G** went up to Peniel and asked for
8:11 **G** circled around by the caravan route east of
8:12 but **G** chased them down and captured all their
8:13 After this, **G** returned by way of Heres Pass.
8:15 **G** then returned to Succoth and said to the leaders,
8:16 Then **G** took the leaders of the town and taught
8:18 Then **G** asked Zebah and Zalmunna, "The men
8:19 "They were my brothers!" **G** exclaimed.
8:21 Then Zebah and Zalmunna said to **G**, "Don't ask a
8:21 So **G** killed them both and took the royal
8:22 Then the Israelites said to **G**, "Be our ruler!
8:23 But **G** replied, "I will not rule over you, nor will
8:27 **G** made a sacred ephod from the gold and put it in
8:27 and it became a trap for **G** and his family.
8:29 Then **G** son of Joash returned home.
8:32 **G** died when he was very old, and he was buried in
8:33 As soon as **G** was dead, the Israelites prostituted
8:35 **G**), despite all the good he had done for Israel.
9:16 and that you have done right by **G** and all of his
9:19 and in good faith toward **G** and his descendants,
9:28 He's merely the son of **G**, and Zebul is his
9:57 So the curse of Jotham son of **G** came true.
1Sa 12:11 Then the LORD sent **G**, Barak, Jephthah,
Isa 10:26 as he did when **G** triumphed over the Midianites at
Heb 11:32 too long to recount the stories of the faith of **G**,

GIDEON'S (7) [GIDEON]

Jdg 8:3 When the men of Ephraim heard **G** answer,
8:28 Throughout the rest of **G** lifetime—about forty
9:1 One day **G** son Abimelech went to Shechem to
9:2 they want to be ruled by all seventy of **G** sons
9:24 and the men of Shechem for murdering **G** seventy
2Sa 11:21 Wasn't **G** son Abimelech killed at Thebez by a
Isa 9:4 destroyed the army of Midian with **G** little band.

GIDEONI (5)

Nu 1:11 Benjamin | Abidan son of **G**
2:22[-23] Benjamin | Abidan son of **G** | 35,400
7:60 On the ninth day Abidan son of **G**, leader of the
7:65 This was the offering brought by Abidan son of **G**.
10:24 The tribe of Benjamin was led by Abidan son of **G**.

GIDOM (1)

Jdg 20:45 until they had killed another two thousand near **G**.

GIER [KJV] See CARRION VULTURE

GIFT (114) [GIFTED, GIFTS]

Ge 4:3 At harvest time Cain brought to the LORD a **g** of
21:30 "They are my **g** to you as a public confirmation
34:12 No matter what dowry or **g** you demand, I will pay
37:3 So one day he gave Joseph a special **g**—a beautiful
Ex 29:24 and his sons to be lifted up as a special **g** to the
29:26 up in the LORD's presence as a special **g** to him.
34:20 No one is allowed to appear before me without a **g**.
Lev 3:7 If you bring a sheep as your **g**, present it to the
7:14 One of each kind of bread must be presented as a **g**
7:29 bring part of it as a special **g** to the LORD.
7:32 thigh of your peace offering to the priest as a **g**.
27:9 then your **g** to the LORD will be considered holy.
Nu 7:11 "Let each leader bring his **g** on a different day for
15:19 But you must set some aside as a **g** to the LORD.
15:20 first of the flour you grind and set it aside as a **g**,
18:7 I am giving you the priesthood as your special **g** of
18:26 a tithe of the tithe—to the LORD as a **g**.
18:28 received from the Israelites as a **g** to the LORD.
31:52 the gold that the commanders presented as a **g** to
Dt 15:14 Give him a generous farewell **g** from your flock,
16:16 and they must bring a **g** to the LORD.
26:3 'With this **g** I acknowledge that the LORD your
26:13 'I have taken the sacred **g** from my house and have
33:13 with the choice **g** of rain from the heavens,
1Sa 6:3 of Israel back, along with a **g**," they were told.
2Sa 6:19 Then he gave a **g** of food to every man and woman
11:8 David even sent a **g** to Uriah after he had left the
1Ki 9:16 He gave the city to his daughter as a wedding **g**
10:10 Then she gave the king a **g** of nine thousand
13:7 have something to eat, and I will give you a **g**."
14:3 Take him a **g** of ten loaves of bread, some cakes,
15:19 See, I am sending you a **g** of silver and gold.
2Ki 8:8 he said to Hazael, "Take a **g** to the man of God.
8:9 the finest products of Damascus as a **g** for Elisha.
12:4 a payment of vows, or a voluntary **g**.
16:8 and sent it as a **g** to the Assyrian king.
20:12 of Babylon, sent Hezekiah his best wishes and a **g**,
1Ch 16:3 Then he gave a **g** of food to every man and woman
2Ch 9:9 Then she gave the king a **g** of nine thousand
16:3 See, I am sending you a **g** of silver and gold.
Job 6:22 But why? Have I ever asked you for a **g**? Have I
35:7 If you are good, is this some great **g** to him?
42:11 And each of them brought him a **g** of money
Ps 127:3 Children are a **g** from the LORD; they are a
Pr 18:16 Giving a **g** works wonders; it may bring you before
21:14 A secret **g** calms anger; a secret bribe pacifies fury.
25:14 A person who doesn't give a promised **g** is like
Ecc 5:19 your lot in life—that is indeed a **g** from God.
SS 3:10 Its interior was a **g** of love from the young women
Isa 39:1 of Babylon, sent Hezekiah his best wishes and a **g**.
57:9 given olive oil and perfume to Molech as your **g**.
Eze 46:16 If the prince gives a **g** of land to one of his sons,
46:17 But if he gives a **g** of land to one of his servants,
Hos 10:6 as captives to Assyria, a **g** to the great king there.
Mic 1:14 Send a farewell **g** to Moresheth-gath; there is no
Zec 13:4 "No one will be boasting then of a prophetic **g**!
Mt 6:2 When you give a **g** to someone in need, don't shout
23:19 For which is greater, the **g** on the altar, or the altar that makes the **g** sacred?
Lk 6:38 Your **g** will return to you in full measure,
Jn 4:10 "If you only knew the **g** God has for you and who
14:27 "I am leaving you with a **g**—peace of mind
17:7 Now they know that everything I have is a **g** from
Ac 2:38 Then you will receive the **g** of the Holy Spirit.
3:5 lame man looked at them eagerly, expecting a **g**.
8:20 with you for thinking God's **g** can be bought!
10:45 **g** of the Holy Spirit had been poured out upon the
11:17 And since God gave these Gentiles the same **g** he
21:9 He had four unmarried daughters who had the **g** of
21:10 who also had the **g** of prophecy, arrived from
Ro 4:4 When people work, their wages are not a **g**.
4:16 is the key! God's promise is given to us as a free **g**.
5:15 our sin and God's generous **g** of forgiveness.
5:15 forgiveness to many through God's bountiful **g**.
5:16 And the result of God's gracious **g** is very different
5:16 but we have the free **g** of being accepted by God,
5:17 gracious **g** of righteousness will live in triumph
6:23 but the free **g** of God is eternal life through Christ
12:7 If your **g** is that of serving others, serve them well.
12:8 If your **g** is to encourage others, do it! If you have a **g** for showing kindness to
15:25 I must go down to Jerusalem to take a **g** to the
1Co 1:7 Now you have every spiritual **g** you need as you
7:7 God gives some the **g** of marriage, and to others he gives the **g** of singleness.
12:7 A spiritual **g** is given to each of us as a means of
12:8 to another he gives the **g** of special knowledge.
12:11 He alone decides which **g** each person should have.
12:28 do miracles, / those who have the **g** of healing,
12:30 Does everyone have the **g** of healing? Of course
13:2 If I had the **g** of prophecy, and if I knew all the
13:2 And if I had the **g** of faith so that I could speak to a
13:9 a little, and even the **g** of prophecy reveals little!
14:1 the Spirit gives, especially the **g** of prophecy.
14:2 For if your **g** is the ability to speak in tongues,
14:5 I wish you all had the **g** of speaking in tongues,
14:5 and more useful **g** than speaking in tongues,
14:13 So anyone who has the **g** of speaking in tongues
14:13 **g** of interpretation in order to tell people plainly
16:3 you choose to deliver your **g** to Jerusalem.
2Co 8:4 of sharing in the **g** for the Christians in Jerusalem.
8:20 fault with the way we are handling this generous **g**.
9:1 I really don't need to write to you about this **g** for
9:5 of me to make sure the **g** you promised is ready.
9:5 But I want it to be a willing **g**, not one given under
9:15 God for his Son—a **g** too wonderful for words!
11:9 who came from Macedonia brought me another **g**.
Gal 2:9 recognized the **g** God had given me, and they
Eph 2:8 you can't take credit for this; it is a **g** from God.
4:7 he has given each one of us a special **g** according
Php 4:17 I don't say this because I want a **g** from you.
1Ti 4:14 Do not neglect the spiritual **g** you received through
2Ti 1:6 **g** God gave you when I laid my hands on you.
1Pe 3:7 but she is your equal partner in God's **g** of new

GIFTED (6) [GIFT]

Ex 35:10 "Come, all of you who are **g** craftsmen.
36:1 and the other craftsmen whom the LORD has **g**
36:2 along with all those who were specially **g** by the
2Ch 2:12 David a wise son, **g** with skill and understanding,
Da 1:4 are **g** with knowledge and good sense, and have the
2Co 8:7 you have so much faith, such **g** speakers,

GIFTS (146) [GIFT]

Ge 12:16 Then Pharaoh gave Abram many **g** because of
24:10 He loaded ten of Abraham's camels with **g** and set
25:6 he gave **g** to the sons of his concubines and sent
30:20 "God has given me good **g** for my husband.
33:8 Jacob replied, "They are **g**, my lord, to ensure
33:11 Please take my **g**, for God has been very generous
43:11 Take them to the man as **g**—balm, honey, spices,
43:15 and the **g** and double the money and hurried to
43:25 so they prepared their **g** for Joseph's arrival at
43:26 they gave him their **g** and bowed low before him.
Ex 3:21 They will load you down with **g** so you will not
35:20 and went to their tents to prepare their **g**.
36:3 Additional **g** were brought each morning.
38:24 The people brought **g** of gold totaling about 2,200
Lev 22:2 and his sons to treat the sacred **g** that the Israelites
23:38 must be given in addition to your personal **g**,
Nu 5:9 All the sacred **g** that the Israelites bring to a priest
6:20 then lift the **g** up before the LORD in a gesture of
7:5 "Receive their **g** and use these oxen and carts for
7:10 The leaders also presented dedication **g** for the
7:10 They each placed their **g** before the altar.
18:8 "I have put the priests in charge of all the holy **g**
18:12 "I also give you the harvest **g** brought by the
18:29 of the **g** given to you as your **g** to the LORD.'
18:32 But be careful not to treat the holy **g** of the people
31:54 and Eleazar the priest accepted the **g** from the
Dt 12:6 your sacrifices, your tithes, your special **g**,
12:11 your sacrifices, your tithes, your special **g**,
12:17 nor your freewill offerings, nor your special **g**.
12:26 Take your sacred **g** and your offerings given to
17:1 to the LORD your God, for he detests such **g**.
33:16 with the best **g** of the earth and its fullness,
1Sa 6:17 to the LORD were **g** from the rulers of Ashdod,
10:27 And they despised him and refused to bring him **g**.
17:20 and set out early the next morning with the **g**.
25:35 Then David accepted her **g** and told her,
30:27 The **g** were sent to the leaders of the following
2Sa 8:10 Joram presented David with many **g** of silver,
8:11 King David dedicated all these **g** to the LORD,
19:42 And he hasn't fed us or even given us **g**!"
1Ki 7:51 Then Solomon brought all the **g** his father, David,
10:13 besides all the other customary **g** he had
10:25 everyone who came to visit brought him **g** of silver
2Ki 5:5 taking as **g** 750 pounds of silver, 150 pounds of
5:15 world except in Israel. Now please accept my **g**."
5:16 whom I serve, I will not accept any **g**."
5:16 And though Naaman urged him to take the **g**,
5:20 let this Aramean get away without accepting his **g**.
5:23 and sent two of his servants to carry the **g** for
5:24 Gehazi took the **g** from the servants and sent the men back. Then he hid the **g** inside the house.
12:7 Don't use any more **g** for your own needs.
1Ch 18:10 Joram presented David with many **g** of gold,

18:11 King David dedicated all these g to the LORD,
28:12 God's Temple, and the rooms for the dedicated g.
29:17 and I have watched your people offer their g
2Ch 5: 1 he brought in the g dedicated by his father,
9:12 g of greater value than the g she had given him.
9:24 everyone who came to visit brought him g of silver
17: 5 All the people of Judah brought g to Jehoshaphat,
17:11 Some of the Philistines brought him g and silver as
21: 3 Their father had given each of them valuable g of
31:10 "Since the people began bringing their g to the
31:12 Then all the g and tithes were faithfully brought to
31:14 the g, and the things that had been dedicated to the
31:15 They distributed the g among the families of
31:15 dividing the g fairly among young and old alike.
31:16 They also distributed the g to all males three years
31:17 And they distributed g to the priests who were
32:23 and many g for the LORD arrived at Jerusalem,
34: 9 The g were brought by people from Manasseh,
Ezr 1: 6 They gave them many choice g in addition to all
2:69 The total of their g came to 61,000 gold coins,
Ne 7:70 "Some of the family leaders gave g for the work.
8:10 and share g of food with people who have nothing
8:12 and drink at a festive meal, to share g of food,
12:44 to be in charge of the storerooms for the g,
Est 2:18 giving generous g to everyone and declaring a
9:19 when they rejoice and send g to each other.
9:22 and gladness and by giving g to each other and to
Ps 20: 3 May he remember all your g / and look favorably
45:12 The princes of Tyre will shower you with g.
68:18 of captives. / You received g from the people,
68:31 Let Egypt come with g of precious metals;
72:10 eastern kings of Sheba and Seba / will bring him g.
Pr 8:19 My g are better than the purest gold, my wages
19: 6 everyone is the friend of a person who gives g!
20:12 and eyes to see—both are g from the LORD.
22:16 or by showering g on the rich will end in poverty.
Ecc 3:13 the fruits of their labor, for these are g from God.
11: 1 Give generously, for your g will return to you later.
11: 2 Divide your g among many, for you do not know
Isa 18: 7 will receive g from this land divided by rivers,
18: 7 They will bring the g to the LORD Almighty in
Jer 31:12 because of the many g the LORD has given
Eze 16:33 You give g to your lovers, bribing them to come to
20:26 I let them pollute themselves with the very g I had
20:31 For when you offer g to them and give your little
20:39 but then don't turn around and bring g to me.
20:40 me all your offerings and choice g and sacrifices.
44:29 Their food will come from the g and sacrifices
44:30 and all the g brought to the LORD will go to the
46:17 Only the g given to the prince's sons will be
Da 2: 6 I will give you many wonderful g and honors.
2:48 to a high position and gave him many valuable g.
5:17 "Keep your g or give them to someone else,
11:38 on him gold, silver, precious stones, and costly g.
Hos 2: 8 used in worshiping the god Baal were g from me!
3: 1 turned to other gods, offering them choice g."
3: 5 and they will receive his good g in the last days.
Zec 6:10 and Jedaiah will bring g of silver and gold from the
6:11 Accept their g and make a crown from the silver
Mal 1: 8 Try giving g like that to your governor, and see
Mt 2:11 their treasure chests and gave him g of gold,
6: 4 Give your g in secret, and your Father, who knows
7:11 If you sinful people know how to give good g to
7:11 heavenly Father give good g to those who ask him.
23:18 but to swear 'by the g on the altar' is binding!
Lk 11:13 If you sinful people know how to give good g to
21: 1 he watched the rich people putting their g into the
Ac 10: 4 and g to the poor have not gone unnoticed by God!
10:31 and your g to the poor have been noticed by God!
11:30 entrusting their g to Barnabas and Saul to take to
Ro 11:28 for God has given his g to you Gentiles.
11:29 For God's g and his call can never be withdrawn.
1Co 1: 4 God for all the generous g he has given you,
1: 5 He has enriched your church with the g of
12: 4 Now there are different kinds of spiritual g, but it
12:11 and only Holy Spirit who distributes these g.
12:31 in any event, you should desire the most helpful g.
13:10 the end comes, these special g will all disappear.
14:12 Since you are so eager to have spiritual g, ask God
2Co 9:11 And when we take your g to those who need them,
9:13 will be glorifying God through your generous g.
Eph 4: 8 a crowd of captives / and gave g to his people."
4:11 He is the one who gave these g to the church:
Php 4:18 I am generously supplied with the g you sent me
Heb 2: 4 and by giving g of the Holy Spirit whenever he
5: 1 He presents their g to God and offers their
8: 3 And since every high priest is required to offer g
8: 4 since there already are priests who offer the g
9: 9 For the g and sacrifices that the priests offer are
1Pe 4:10 God has given g to each of you from his great
variety of spiritual g.

GIHON (6)

Ge 2:13 The second branch is the G, which flows around
1Ki 1:33 and my officers down to G Spring.
1:38 bodyguard took Solomon down to G Spring,
1:44 The king sent him down to G Spring with Zadok
2Ch 32:30 He blocked up the upper spring of G and brought
33:14 from west of the G Spring in the Kidron Valley to

GILALAI (1)

Ne 12:36 Azarel, Milalai, G, Maai, Nethanel, Judah,

GILBOA (7)

1Sa 28: 4 and Saul and the armies of Israel camped at G.
31: 1 Many were slaughtered on the slopes of Mount G.
31: 8 the bodies of Saul and his three sons on Mount G.
2Sa 1: 6 man answered, "I happened to be on Mount G.
1:21 O mountains of G, / let there be no dew or rain
1Ch 10: 1 Many were slaughtered on the slopes of Mount G.
10: 8 found the bodies of Saul and his sons on Mount G.

GILEAD (93) [GILEAD'S, GILEADITE, GILEADITES, JABESH-GILEAD, RAMOTH-GILEAD]

LAND OF GILEAD (15) Nu 32:29; Jos 17:5,6; 22:9,15; Jdg 10:4; 11:29; 20:1; 2Sa 17:26; 1Ki 4:19; 1Ch 2:22; 5:9,16; 26:31; Ob 1:19

Ge 31:21 the Euphrates River, heading for the territory of G.
31:23 with them seven days later in the hill country of G.
31:25 Jacob as he was camped in the hill country of G,
37:25 taking spices, balm, and myrrh from G to Egypt.
Nu 26:29 named after its ancestor G, Makir's son.
27: 1 son of G, son of Makir, son of Manasseh, son of
32: 1 and G were ideally suited for their flocks
32:26 flocks, and cattle will stay here in the towns of G.
32:29 you must give them the land of G as their property.
32:39 of Makir of the tribe of Manasseh went to G
32:40 So Moses gave G to the Makirites, descendants of
32:41 captured many of the towns in G and changed the
36: 1 Then the heads of the clan of G—descendants of
Dt 2:36 town in the gorge, and the whole area as far as G.
3:10 and all G and Bashan as far as the towns of
3:12 plus half of the hill country of G with its towns,
3:13 Then I gave the rest of G and all of Bashan—
3:15 I gave G to the clan of Makir.
3:16 and Gad I gave the area extending from G to the
4:43 Ramoth in G for the tribe of Gad; Golan in Bashan
34: 1 showed him the whole land, from G as far as Dan;
Jos 12: 2 territory included half of the present area of G,
12: 5 His kingdom included the northern half of G,
13:11 It included G, the territory of the kingdoms of
13:25 Their territory included Jazer, all the towns of G,
13:31 It also included half of G and King Og's royal
17: 1 G and Bashan on the east side of the Jordan had
17: 1 Manasseh's oldest son and was the father of G.)
17: 3 of Manasseh, Makir, and G, had no sons.
17: 5 in addition to the land of G and Bashan across the
17: 6 (The land of G was given to the rest of the male
20: 8 Ramoth in G, in the territory of the tribe of Gad;
21:38 From the tribe of Gad they received Ramoth in G
22: 9 started the journey back to their own land of G,
22:15 When they arrived in the land of G, they said to
22:32 officials left the tribes of Reuben and Gad in G
Jdg 5:17 G remained east of the Jordan. / And Dan, why did
10: 3 a man from G named Jair judged Israel for
10: 4 and they owned thirty towns in the land of G,
10: 8 River in the land of the Amorites (that is, in G).
10:17 had gathered for war and were camped in G,
10:18 The leaders of G said to each other,
10:18 first will become ruler over all the people of G."
11: 1 Now Jephthah from G was a great warrior. He was
the son of G, but his mother was a
11: 5 the leaders of G sent for Jephthah in the land of
11: 8 we will make you ruler over all the people of G."
11:11 So Jephthah went with the leaders of G, and he
11:29 and he went throughout the land of G and
Manasseh, including Mizpah in G,
12: 4 "The men of G are nothing more than rejects from
12: 5 go back across, the men of G would challenge him.
12: 7 he died, he was buried in one of the towns of G.
20: 1 from Dan to Beersheba and from the land of G,
1Sa 13: 7 and escaped into the land of Gad and G.
2Sa 2: 9 There he proclaimed Ishbosheth king over G,
17:26 and the Israelite army set up camp in the land of G.
24: 6 then to G in the land of Tahtim-hodshi and to
1Ki 2: 7 "Be kind to the sons of Barzillai from G.
4:13 in G, and in the Argob region of Bashan,
4:19 Geber son of Uri, in the land of G,
17: 1 Now Elijah, who was from Tishbe in G, told King
2Ki 10:33 including all of G, Gad, Reuben, and Manasseh.
10:33 of Aroer by the Arnon Gorge to as far north as G
15:25 With fifty men from G, Pekah assassinated the
15:29 He also conquered the regions of G, Galilee,
1Ch 2:22 who ruled twenty-three towns in the land of G.
2:23 these were descendants of Makir, the father of G.
5: 9 And since they had so many cattle in the land of G,
5:10 Hagrite settlements all along the eastern edge of G.
5:14 son of Jaroah, son of G, son of Michael, son of
5:16 The Gadites lived in the land of G, in Bashan
6:80 of Gad, they received Ramoth in G, Mahanaim,
7:14 were Asriel and Makir. Makir was the father of G.
26:31 of Hebron were found at Jazer in the land of G.)
Ezr 2:61 married one of the daughters of Barzillai from G
Ne 7:63 married one of the daughters of Barzillai from G
Ps 60: 7 G is mine, / and Manasseh is mine. / Ephraim will
108: 8 G is mine, / and Manasseh is mine. / Ephraim will
SS 4: 1 like flocks of goats frisking across the slopes of G.
6: 5 like a flock of goats frisking down the slopes of G.
Jer 8:22 Is there no medicine in G? Is there no physician
22: 6 "You are as beloved to me as fruitful G
46:11 Go up to G to get ointment, O virgin daughter of
50:19 once more on the hill country of Ephraim and G.
Eze 47:18 along the Jordan River between Israel and G,
Hos 6: 8 G is a city of sinners, tracked with footprints of
12:11 But G is filled with sinners who worship idols.
Am 1: 3 They beat down my people in G as grain is
1:13 When they attacked G to extend their borders,
Ob 1:19 the people of Benjamin will occupy the land of G.
Mic 7:14 pastures of Bashan and G as they did long ago.
Zec 10:10 and Assyria and resettle them in G and Lebanon.

GILEAD'S (2) [GILEAD]

Jdg 11: 2 G wife also had several sons, and when these half
1Ch 2:21 he married G sister, the daughter of Makir.

GILEADITE (3) [GILEAD]

Nu 26:29 The G clan, named after its ancestor Gilead,
2Sa 17:27 of Lo-debar, and by Barzillai the G from Rogelim.
19:31 Barzillai the G now arrived from Rogelim to

GILEADITES (2) [GILEAD]

Nu 26:30 These were the subclans descended from the G:
1Ch 7:17 All these were considered G, descendants of Makir

GILGAL (38) [BETH-GILGAL]

Dt 11:30 who live in the Jordan Valley, near the town of G.
Jos 4:19 from Egypt. They camped at G, east of Jericho.
4:20 It was there at G that Joshua piled up the twelve
5: 9 So that place has been called G to this day.
5:10 While the Israelites were camped at G on the
9: 6 When they arrived at the camp of Israel at G,
10: 6 of Gibeon quickly sent messengers to Joshua at G,
10: 7 So Joshua and the entire Israelite army left G
10: 9 Joshua traveled all night from G and took the
10:15 and the Israelite army returned to their camp at G.
10:43 and the Israelite army returned to their camp at G.
12:23 the city of Naphoth-dor / The king of Goyim in G
14: 6 of Jephunneh the Kenizzite, came to Joshua at G.
15: 7 valley of Achor to Debir, turning north toward G,
Jdg 2: 1 The angel of the LORD went up from G to
3:19 But when Ehud reached the stone carvings near G,
1Sa 7:16 court first at Bethel, then at G, and then at Mizpah.
10: 8 Then go down to G ahead of me and wait for me
11:14 let us all go to G to reaffirm Saul's kingship."
11:15 So they went to G, and in a solemn ceremony
13: 4 Israelite army mobilized again and met Saul at G.
13: 7 Meanwhile, Saul stayed at G, and his men were
13:15 Samuel then left G and went on his way,
13:15 They went up from G to Gibeah in the land of
15:12 up a monument to himself; then he went on to G."
15:21 to sacrifice to the LORD your God in G."
15:33 cut Agag to pieces before the LORD at G.
2Sa 19:15 the people of Judah came to G to meet him
19:40 The king then went on to G, taking Kimham with
2Ki 2: 1 Elijah and Elisha were traveling from G.
4:38 Elisha now returned to G, but there was a famine
Hos 4:15 join with those who worship me insincerely at G
9:15 LORD says, "All their wickedness began at G;
12:11 And in G, too, they sacrifice bulls; their altars are
Am 4: 4 offer your sacrifices to the idols at Bethel and G.
5: 5 go to worship the idols of Bethel, G, or Beersheba.
5: 5 For the people of G will be dragged off into exile,
Mic 6: 5 And remember your journey from Acacia to G,

GILOH (3)

Jos 15:51 Goshen, Holon, and G—eleven towns with their
2Sa 15:12 one of David's counselors who lived in G.
23:34 from Maacah; / Eliam son of Ahithophel from G;

GIMZO (1)

2Ch 28:18 Timnah with its villages, and G with its villages,

GIN [KJV] See TRAP

GINATH (2)

1Ki 16:21 Half the people tried to make Tibni son of G their
16:22 defeated the supporters of Tibni son of G.

GINNETHON (3)

Ne 10: 6 Daniel, G, Baruch,
12: 4 Iddo, G, Abijah,
12:16 Meshullam was leader of the family of G.

GIRDED [KJV] See also CLOTHED, FASTENED, FITTED, STRAPPED, WEARING

GIRGASHITES (7)

Ge 10:16 Jebusites, Amorites, G,
15:21 Amorites, Canaanites, G, and Jebusites."
Dt 7: 1 G, Amorites, Canaanites, Perizzites, Hivites,
Jos 3:10 Hittites, Hivites, Perizzites, G, Amorites,
24:11 the Canaanites, the Hittites, the G, the Hivites,
1Ch 1:14 Jebusites, Amorites, G,
Ne 9: 8 Hittites, Amorites, Perizzites, Jebusites, and G.

GIRL (43) [GIRL'S, GIRLS]

Ge 34: 4 "Get this g for me," he demanded. "I want to
34:12 I will pay it—only give me the g as my wife."
Ex 2: 8 So the g rushed home and called the baby's
21: 9 he may no longer treat her as a slave g, but he must
21:31 principle applies if the bull gores a boy or a g.
Lev 19:20 "If a man has sexual intercourse with a slave g
27: 5 a g of that age is valued at ten pieces of silver.
27: 6 a g of that age is valued at three pieces of silver.
Dt 22:21 the judges must take the g to the door of her
Ru 2: 5 asked his foreman, "Who is that g over there?"
2Sa 17:17 Arrangements had been made for a servant g to
1Ki 1: 3 searched throughout the country for a beautiful g,
1: 4 The g was very beautiful, and she waited on the
2:17 me Abishag, the g from Shunem, as my wife."

2:21 marry Abishag, the g from Shunem," she replied.
2Ki 5: 2 and among their captives was a young g who had
5: 3 One day the g said to her mistress, "I wish my
5: 4 So Naaman told the king what the young g from
Ps 123: 2 as a slave g watches her mistress for the slightest
Pr 30:23 a servant g who supplants her mistress.
Eze 23: 4 The older g was named Oholah, and her sister was
23:21 you celebrated your former days as a young g in
Mt 9:24 He said, "Go away, for the g isn't dead; she's only
9:25 Jesus went in and took the g by the hand, and she
14: 8 At her mother's urging, the g asked, "I want the
14:11 his head was brought on a tray and given to the g,
26:69 a servant g came over and said to him,
26:71 another servant g noticed him and said to those
Mk 5:40 and his three disciples into the room where the g
5:41 her hand, he said to her, "Get up, little g!"
5:42 And the g, who was twelve years old,
6:22 the king said to the g, "and I will give it to you."
6:25 So the g hurried back to the king and told him,
6:28 and gave it to the g, who took it to her mother.
7:25 Right away a woman came to him whose little g
7:30 her little g was lying quietly in bed, and the demon
14:69 The servant g saw him standing there and began
Lk 1:48 For he took notice of his lowly servant g,
8:42 only child was dying, a little g twelve years old.
8:49 home with the message, "Your little g is dead.
22:56 A servant g noticed him in the firelight and began
Ac 12:13 and a servant g named Rhoda came to open it.
16:16 of prayer, we met a demon-possessed slave g.

GIRL'S (4) [GIRL]

Ex 21: 9 And if the slave g owner arranges for her to marry
Mt 9:27 After Jesus left the g home, two blind men
Mk 5:40 Then he took the g father and mother and his three
Lk 8:51 James, John, and the little g father and mother.

GIRLS (28) [GIRL]

Ex 1:16 as they are born. Allow only the baby g to live."
1:22 the Nile River. But you may spare the baby g."
2: 5 and her servant g walked along the riverbank.
2: 5 she told one of her servant g to get it for her.
2:17 often come and chase the g and their flocks away.
2:17 to their aid, rescuing the g from the shepherds.
2:18 When the g returned to Reuel, their father,
Nu 31:18 Only the young g who are virgins may live;
31:35 and 32,000 young g.
31:40 16,000 young g, of whom 32 were the LORD's
31:46 and 16,000 young g.
1Sa 25:42 she took along five of her servant g as attendants,
2Sa 6:20 He exposed himself to the servant g like any
6:22 but I will be held in honor by the g of whom you
Job 19:15 The servant g consider me a stranger. I am like a
41: 5 like a bird, or give it to your little g to play with?
Pr 31:15 and plan the day's work for her servant g.
SS 1: 6 you fair city g, just because my complexion is
Jer 11:22 die in battle, and their little boys and g will starve.
La 2:21 young and old, boys and g, killed by the swords of
5:11 enemies rape the women and young g in Jerusalem
Eze 9: 6 and young, g and women and little children.
23: 3 Even as young g, they allowed themselves to be
Joel 3: 3 and little g for enough wine to get drunk.
Am 8:13 Beautiful g and fine young men will grow faint
Na 2: 7 and all the servant g mourn its capture.
Zec 8: 5 of the city will be filled with boys and g at play.
Mk 14:66 One of the servant g who worked for the high

GIRZITES (1)

1Sa 27: 8 raiding the Geshurites, the G, and the Amalekites

GISHPA (1)

Ne 11:21 Temple servants, whose leaders were Ziha and G,

GITTAH-HEPHER [KJV] See GATH-HEPHER

GITTAIM (2)

2Sa 4: 3 because the original people of Beeroth fled to G,
Ne 11:33 Hazor, Ramah, G,

GITTITE (1) [GITTITES]

2Sa 18: 2 son of Zeruiah, and one-third under Ittai the G.

GITTITES (2) [GITTITE]

2Sa 15:18 There were six hundred G who had come with
15:19 turned to Ittai, the captain of the G, and asked,

GIVE (1106) [GAVE, GIVEN, GIVERS, GIVES, GIVING, GOD-GIVEN, LIFE-GIVING] See Index of Articles, Etc.

GIVEN (630) [GIVE] See Index of Articles, Etc.

GIVERS (1) [GIVE]

Ps 37:21 and never repay, / but the godly are generous g.

GIVES (147) [GIVE] See Index of Articles, Etc.

GIVING (190) [GIVE] See Index of Articles, Etc.

GIZON (1)

1Ch 11:34 the sons of Jashen from G; / Jonathan son of

GLAD (53) [GLADLY, GLADNESS]

Ex 4:14 you now. And when he sees you, he will be very g.
1Ki 3:10 and was g that he had asked for wisdom.
1Ch 16:31 Let the heavens be g, and let the earth rejoice!
Ps 32:11 So rejoice in the LORD and be g, all you who
35: 9 in the LORD. / I will be g because he rescues me.
35:15 But they are g now that I am in trouble;
48:11 Let the towns of Judah be g, / for your judgments
67: 4 How g the nations will be, singing for joy,
68: 3 godly rejoice. / Let them be g in God's presence.
69:32 The humble will see their God at work and be g.
96:11 Let the heavens be g, and let the earth rejoice!
97: 1 Let the earth rejoice! / Let the farthest islands be g.
97: 8 and rejoiced, / and all the cities of Judah are g
104:15 wine to make them g, / olive oil as lotion for their
105:38 Egypt was g when they were gone, / for the dread
107:42 The godly will see these things and be g,
118:24 LORD has made. / We will rejoice and be g in it.
122: 1 I was g when they said to me, / "Let us go to the
Pr 10: 8 The wise are g to be instructed, but babbling fools
15:13 A g heart makes a happy face; a broken heart
28:12 When the godly succeed, everyone is g.
Isa 65:18 Be g; rejoice forever in my creation! And look!
66:10 Be g with her, all you who love her and mourn for
Jer 50:11 "You rejoice and are g, you plunderers of my
Hos 4: 8 to them. So the priests are g when the people sin!
7: 3 The people make the king g with their wickedness.
Joel 2:21 Be g now and rejoice because the LORD has
Mic 6: 7 for the sins of our souls? Would that make him g?
Zep 3:14 Be g and rejoice with all your heart, O daughter of
Zec 10: 7 Their children, too, will see it all and be g;
Mt 5:12 Be happy about it! Be very g! For a great reward
Lk 1:42 Elizabeth gave a g cry and exclaimed to Mary,
Jn 8:56 forward to my coming. He saw it and was g."
11:15 And for your sake, I am g I wasn't there,
Ac 13:48 they were very g and thanked the Lord for his
Ro 12:12 Be g for all God is planning for you. Be patient in
15:27 They were very g to do this because they feel they
1Co 11: 2 I am so g, dear friends, that you always keep me in
12:26 and if one part is honored, all the parts are g.
13: 6 It is never g about injustice but rejoices whenever
16:17 I am so g that Stephanas, Fortunatus, and Achaicus
2Co 2: 2 and make you sad, who is going to make me g?
7: 9 Now I am g I sent it, not because it hurt you,
12: 9 So now I am g to boast about my weaknesses,
13: 9 We are g to be weak, if you are really strong.
Eph 3:12 into God's presence, assured of his g welcome.
Php 2:28 for I know you will be g to see him, and that will
Col 1:24 I am g when I suffer for you in my body, for I am
Jas 1: 9 Christians who are poor should be g, for God has
1:10 And those who are rich should be g, for God has
1Pe 1: 6 So be truly g! There is wonderful joy ahead,
4:13 Instead, be very g—because these trials will make
Rev 19: 7 Let us be g and rejoice and honor him. For the time

GLADLY (13) [GLAD]

Ge 34:18 Hamor and Shechem g agreed,
Jdg 5: 2 leaders take charge, / and the people g follow—
5: 9 to Israel's leaders, / and to those who g followed.
8:25 "G!" they replied. They spread out a cloak,
2Ch 24:10 and they g brought their money and filled the chest
Jn 3:21 But those who do what is right come to the light g,
5:44 For you g honor each other, but you don't care
8:47 Anyone whose Father is God listens g to the words
Ro 12: 8 have a gift for showing kindness to others, do it g.
2Co 12:15 I will g spend myself and all I have for your
Gal 4:15 I know you would g have taken out your own eyes
1Ti 4: 4 of it. We may receive it g, with thankful hearts.
Jas 1: 5 wants you to do—ask him, and he will g tell you.

GLADNESS (19) [GLAD]

Nu 10:10 Blow the trumpets in times of g, too,
Est 8:16 The Jews were filled with joy and g and were
9:17 their victory with a day of feasting and g.
9:18 third day, making that their day of feasting and g.
9:22 and g and by giving gifts to each other and to the
9:22 when their sorrow was turned into g and their
Ps 40:16 all who search for you / be filled with joy and g.
70: 4 all who search for you / be filled with joy and g.
90:15 Give us g in proportion to our former misery!
100: 2 Worship the LORD with g. / Come before him,
SS 3:11 him on his wedding day, the day of his g."
Isa 16:10 Gone now is the g; gone is the joy of harvest.
24:11 its lowest ebb. G has been banished from the land.
35:10 and they will be overcome with joy and g.
51: 3 of the LORD. Joy and g will be found there.
51:11 and they will be overcome with joy and g.
Jer 48:33 Joy and g are gone from fruitful Moab. The presses
Zep 3:17 He will rejoice over you with great g. With his
Lk 1:14 You will have great joy and g, and many will

GLANCE (5) [GLANCED]

Job 40:12 Humiliate the proud with a g; walk on the wicked
Ps 104:32 The earth trembles at his g; / the mountains burst
SS 4: 9 I am overcome by one g of your eyes, by a single
Jer 46: 5 of its fighting men run without a backward g.
47: 3 without a backward g at their helpless children.

GLANCED (1) [GLANCE]

Jn 20:14 She g over her shoulder and saw someone standing

GLASS (6)

Job 41:30 Its belly is covered with scales as sharp as g.
Ecc 5:18 drink a good g of wine, and enjoy their work—
Rev 4: 6 In front of the throne was a shiny sea of g,
7: 1 in the trees, and the sea became as smooth as g.
21:18 of jasper, and the city was pure gold, as clear as g.
21:21 And the main street was pure gold, as clear as g.

GLASSES [KJV] MIRRORS

GLAZE (1)

Pr 26:23 just as a pretty g covers a common clay pot.

GLEAM (1) [GLEAMING]

Pr 4:18 The way of the righteous is like the first g of dawn,

GLEAMING (3) [GLEAM]

Eze 1: 4 The fire inside the cloud glowed like g amber.
1:27 From his waist up, he looked like g amber,
8: 2 From the waist up he looked like g amber.

GLEAN (2) [GLEANED]

Dt 24:21 Do not g the vines after they are picked, but leave
Job 24: 6 not own, and they g in the vineyards of the wicked.

GLEANED (1) [GLEAN]

Jer 6: 9 Even the few who remain in Israel will be g again,

GLEDE [KJV] See BUZZARD

GLEE (2) [GLEEFULLY]

Ps 98: 8 Let the rivers clap their hands in g! / Let the hills
Eze 25: 6 and cheered with g at the destruction of my people,

GLEEFULLY (2) [GLEE]

Ps 35:15 I am in trouble; / they g join together against me.
Eze 36: 5 me by g taking my land for themselves as plunder.

GLIDE (2) [GLIDES, GLIDING]

Dt 32:24 by poisonous snakes that g in the dust.
Isa 18: 1 of the Nile. Its winged sailboats g along the river,

GLIDES (1) [GLIDE]

Pr 30:19 how an eagle g through the sky, / how a snake

GLIDING (3) [GLIDE]

Job 26:13 and his power pierced the g serpent.
Jer 46:22 Silent as a serpent g away, Egypt flees.
Zec 5: 9 flying toward us, with wings g on the wind.

GLISTENS (2)

Job 20:25 from his body, and the arrowhead g with blood.
41:32 The water g in its wake. One would think the sea

GLITTERING (3) [GLITTERS]

Na 2: 3 Watch as their g chariots move into position,
3: 3 and g spears in the upraised arms of the cavalry!
Hab 3:11 from your arrows and the flashing of your g spear.

GLITTERS (1) [GLITTERING]

Eze 21:15 melt with terror, for the sword g at every gate.

GLOAT (9) [GLOATED]

Ps 13: 4 Don't let my enemies g, saying, "We have
22:17 bone in my body. / My enemies stare at me and g.
35:19 who hate me without cause / g over my sorrow.
38:16 I prayed, "Don't let my enemies g over me
94: 3 How long will the wicked be allowed to g?
Jer 9:23 "Let not the wise man g in his wisdom,
Mic 4:11 for your blood, eager to g over your destruction.
7: 8 Do not g over me, my enemies! For though I fall,
Hab 2:15 so that you can g over their nakedness and shame.

GLOATED (2) [GLOAT]

Ob 1:12 You shouldn't have g when they exiled your
1:13 You shouldn't have g over the destruction of your

GLOOM (18) [GLOOMY]

Job 3: 5 let the darkness and utter g claim it for its own.
10:21 before I leave for the land of darkness and utter g,
10:22 a land of utter g where confusion reigns
12:22 with light; he brings light to the deepest g.
30:28 I walk in g, without sunlight. I stand in the public
38:17 are located? Have you seen the gates of utter g?
Ps 107:10 Some sat in darkness and deepest g,
107:14 He led them from the darkness and deepest g;
Isa 25: 7 In that day he will remove the cloud of g,
29:18 and blind people will see through the g
30:11 Forget all this g. We have heard more than enough
59: 9 expected light. No wonder we are walking in the g.
Eze 30: 3 It is a day of clouds and g, a day of despair for the
Joel 2: 2 It is a day of darkness and g, a day of thick clouds
Zep 1:15 a day of darkness and g, of clouds, blackness,
Heb 12:18 a place of flaming fire, darkness, g, and whirlwind,
Jas 4: 9 be sadness instead of laughter, and g instead of joy.
Jude 1:13 heading for everlasting g and darkness.

GLOOMY (2) [GLOOM]

Job 30: 3 to the deserts and the wastelands, desolate and g.
2Pe 2: 4 in g caves and darkness until the judgment day.

GLORIFIED (3) [GLORY]

Lev 10: 3 among those who are near me. / I will be g
Isa 44:23 the LORD has redeemed Jacob and is g in Israel.
Ro 15: 7 just as Christ has accepted you; then God will be g.

GLORIFIES (1) [GLORY]

2Co 8:19 a service that g the Lord and shows our eagerness

GLORIFY (10) [GLORY]

Job 36:24 Instead, g his mighty works, singing songs of
Isa 26: 8 your laws; / our heart's desire is to g your name.
42:12 Let the coastlands g the LORD; / let them sing his
59:19 and g the name of the LORD throughout the
Da 4:37 praise and g and honor the King of heaven.
Jn 8:50 And though I have no wish to g myself, God wants to g me.
17: 1 G your Son so he can give glory back to you.
21:19 know what kind of death he would die to g God.
Rev 15: 4 Who will not fear, O Lord, and g your name?

GLORIFYING (2) [GLORY]

Lk 2:20 g and praising God for what the angels had told
2Co 9:13 You will be g God through your generous gifts.

GLORIOUS (130) [GLORY]

GLORIOUS NAME (3) 1Ch 29:13; Ne 9:5; Ps 72:19

GLORIOUS PRESENCE (20) Ex 16:7; 24:16; 29:43; 33:18,22; 40:34; Lev 9:6,23; Nu 14:10,22; 16:19,42; 20:6; 1Ki 8:11; 2Ch 5:14; 7:1,2,3; Isa 3:8; Jude 1:24

GLORIOUS STRENGTH (4) Dt 9:26,29; Ps 89:13,17

GLORIOUS THINGS (4) Ps 87:3; 118:15,16; Jn 8:54

Ex 15: 6 "Your right hand, O LORD, / is g in power.
15:11 O LORD? / Who is g in holiness like you—
16: 7 In the morning you will see the g presence of the
24:16 And the g presence of the LORD rested upon
29:43 and the Tabernacle will be sanctified by my g
33:18 "Please let me see your g presence," he said.
33:22 As my g presence passes by, I will put you in the
40:34 and the g presence of the LORD filled it.
Lev 9: 6 the g presence of the LORD will appear to you."
9:23 and the g presence of the LORD appeared to the
Nu 14:10 Then the g presence of the LORD appeared to all
14:22 They have seen my g presence and the miraculous
16:19 Then the g presence of the LORD appeared to the
16:42 and the g presence of the LORD appeared.
20: 6 Then the g presence of the LORD appeared to
Dt 9:26 from Egypt by your mighty power and g strength.
9:29 from Egypt by your mighty power and g strength.'
28:58 and if you do not fear the g and awesome name of
32: 3 the name of the LORD; / how g is our God!
2Sa 6:20 in disgust, "How g the king of Israel looked today!
1Ki 8:11 because the g presence of the LORD filled the
8:13 But I have built a g Temple for you, where you can
22: 6 right ahead! The Lord will give you a g victory!"
22:15 The LORD will give the king a g victory!"
1Ch 16:24 Publish his g deeds among the nations.
16:28 recognize that the LORD is g and strong.
22: 5 famous and g throughout the world.
29:13 our God, we thank you and praise your g name!
2Ch 5:14 because the g presence of the LORD filled the
6: 2 But I have built a g Temple for you, where you can
7: 1 and the g presence of the LORD filled the
7: 2 because the g presence of the LORD filled it.
7: 3 and the g presence of the LORD filling the
18:11 The LORD will give you a g victory!"
18:14 "Go right ahead! It will be a g victory!"
Ne 4:14 Remember the Lord, who is great and g, and fight
9: 5 Then they continued, "Praise his g name! It is far
9:10 You have a g reputation that has never been
Job 25: 5 God is so g that even the moon and stars scarcely
37: 5 God's voice is g in the thunder. We cannot
Ps 21:13 We praise you, LORD, for all your g power.
45: 3 O mighty warrior! / You are so g, so majestic!
46: 8 Come, see the g works of the LORD: / See how
50: 2 perfection of beauty, / God shines in g radiance.
66: 2 the glory of his name! / Tell the world how g he is.
66: 4 your praises, / shouting your name in g songs."
72:19 Bless his g name forever! / Let the whole earth be
73:24 me with your counsel, / leading me to a g destiny.
76: 4 You are g and more majestic / than the everlasting
78: 4 but will tell the next generation about the g deeds
78: 7 hope anew on God, / remembering his g miracles
87: 3 O city of God, / what g things are said of you!
89:13 Your right hand is lifted high in g strength.
89:17 You are their g strength. / Our power is based on
94: 1 O God of vengeance, let your g justice be seen!
96: 3 Publish his g deeds among the nations.
96: 7 recognize that the LORD is g and strong.
106: 2 Who can list the g miracles of the LORD?
106:20 They traded their g God / for a statue of a
107:22 of thanksgiving / and sing joyfully about his g acts.
118:15 The strong right arm of the LORD has done g
118:16 The strong right arm of the LORD has done g
132:18 his enemies with shame, / but he will be a g king."
145: 5 I will meditate on your majestic, g splendor
Isa 3: 8 They have offended his g presence among them.
4: 5 and clouds of fire at night, covering the g land.
6: 4 The g singing shook the Temple to its foundations,
10:18 Assyria's vast army is like a g forest, yet it will be
11:10 for the land where he lives will be a g place.
13:19 Babylon, the most g of kingdoms, the flower of
22:18 and there your g chariots will remain, broken
28: 1 but its g beauty will suddenly disappear.
28: 4 but its g beauty will suddenly disappear.
31: 7 I know the g day will come when every one of you
40:10 the Sovereign LORD is coming in all his g
42:21 LORD has magnified his law and made it truly g.
55: 5 the Holy One of Israel, have made you g."
60: 7 for my altars. In that day I will make my Temple g.
60:13 to beautify my sanctuary. My Temple will be g!
63:15 from heaven and see us from your holy, g home.
Jer 2:11 Yet my people have exchanged their g God for
13:18 for your g crowns will soon be snatched from your
17:12 we worship at your throne—eternal, high, and g!
Eze 25: 9 eastern flank and wipe out their g frontier cities—
27: 4 boundaries into the sea. Your builders made you g!
39:13 for it will be a g victory for Israel when I
Da 8: 9 and the east and toward the g land of Israel.
11:16 He will pause in the g land of Israel, intent on
11:41 He will enter the g land of Israel, and many nations
11:45 He will halt between the g holy mountain
Zec 10: 3 he will make them strong and g, like a proud
Mt 19:28 Son of Man, sit upon my g throne in the Kingdom,
25:31 angels with him, then he will sit upon his g throne.
Mk 10:37 "In your g Kingdom, we want to sit in places of
Lk 9:31 They were g to see. And they were speaking of
Jn 8:54 But it is my Father who says these g things about
Ac 2:20 before that great and g day of the Lord arrives.
7: 2 Our g God appeared to our ancestor Abraham in
Ro 1:23 And instead of worshiping the g, ever-living God,
3:23 all have sinned; all fall short of God's g standard.
6: 4 raised from the dead by the g power of the Father,
8:21 it will join God's children in g freedom from death
1Co 2: 8 they would never have crucified our g Lord.
2Co 3: 9 old covenant, which brings condemnation, was g,
3: 9 how much more g is the new covenant,
3:10 that first glory was not g at all compared with the
4: 4 so they are unable to see the g light of the Good
4: 7 So everyone can see that our g power is from God
Eph 1:12 the first to trust in Christ should praise our g God.
1:14 This is just one more reason for us to praise our g
1:17 asking God, the g Father of our Lord Jesus Christ,
1:18 and g inheritance he has given to his people.
3:16 I pray that from his g, unlimited resources he will
4: 4 and we have all been called to the same g future.
5:27 He did this to present her to himself as a g church
Php 3:21 and change them into g bodies like his own,
4:19 of me will supply all your needs from his g riches,
Col 1:11 pray that you will be strengthened with his g power
2Th 1: 9 separated from the Lord and from his g power
1Ti 1:11 that comes from the g Good News entrusted to me
2Ti 4: 8 but for all who eagerly look forward to his g
Heb 9: 5 The g cherubim were above the Ark. Their wings
Jas 2: 1 how can you claim that you have faith in our g
1Pe 1: 8 and even now you are happy with a g,
4:14 then the g Spirit of God will come upon you.
2Pe 1:17 and glory from God the Father when God's g,
2:10 daring even to scoff at the g ones without so much
2:11 never speak out disrespectfully against the g ones.
Jude 1: 8 and scoff at the power of the g ones.
1:24 and who will bring you into his g presence

GLORIOUSLY (3) [GLORY]

Ex 15: 1 "I will sing to the LORD, for he has triumphed g;
15:21 "I will sing to the LORD, for he has triumphed g;
Isa 24:23 He will rule g in Jerusalem, in the sight of all the

GLORY (291) [GLORIFIED, GLORIFIES, GLORIFY, GLORIFYING, GLORIOUS, GLORIOUSLY]

GAVE/GIVE/GIVING...GLORY (28) Jos 7:19; 1Ch 16:29; Ps 44:8; 50:15; 86:12; 96:8; Isa 24:15; 42:8; 46:13; Jer 13:16; Da 5:18; Zep 3:19; Lk 4:6; 17:18; Jn 9:24; 17:1,24; Ac 12:23; Ro 15:6,9; 2Co 1:20; Gal 1:24; 1Pe 1:21; Rev 1:6; 4:9; 11:13; 14:7; 16:9

GLORY OF (THE) GOD (24) Ps 19:1; Eze 8:4; 9:3; 10:19; 11:22; 43:2; Hos 4:7; Jn 11:4,40; Ac 7:55; Ro 5:2; 6:10,11,13; 1Co 10:31; 11:7; 2Co 3:7; 4:6; Php 2:11; Tit 2:13; Rev 11:13; 15:8; 21:11,23

GLORY OF THE LORD; THE LORD'S GLORY (2) Lk 2:9; 2Co 3:18

GLORY OF THE LORD*; THE LORD'S* GLORY (21) Ex 16:10; 24:17; 40:35; Nu 14:21; Ps 104:31; 138:5; Isa 40:5; 58:8; 60:1,2; Eze 1:28; 3:12,23; 10:4,4,18; 11:23; 43:4,5; 44:4; Hab 2:14

HIS GLORY (35) Dt 5:24; Ps 29:1; 72:19; 78:61; 85:9; 97:6; 102:15,16; 111:3; 113:4; 148:13; Isa 6:3; 35:2; Eze 43:2; Da 5:20; Mt 6:29; 25:31; Lk 12:27; Jn 1:14; 2:11; 7:39; 12:16,23; Ro 8:17,30; 9:4,23; 11:36; 2Co 3:18; Col 1:27; 3:4; 1Th 2:12; 1Pe 4:13; 5:1,4

MY GLORY (17) Ps 3:3; Isa 42:8; 43:7; 46:13; 48:11; 66:18,19,19; Jer 13:11; Eze 28:22; 39:13,21; Lk 9:26; Jn 13:31,32; 17:10,24

YOUR GLORY (15) Ps 8:1; 26:8; 57:5,11; 71:8; 76:10; 90:16; 108:5; Isa 10:16; 25:3; 60:19; 62:2; Jer 14:21; 48:18; Hab 2:16

Ex 14: 4 so I will receive great g at the expense of Pharaoh
14:17 Then I will receive great g at the expense of
16:10 they could see the awesome g of the LORD.
24:17 The awesome g of the LORD on the mountaintop
40:35 and the Tabernacle was filled with the awesome g
Nu 14:21 as surely as the earth is filled with the LORD's g,
Dt 5:24 'The LORD our God has shown us his g
Jos 7:19 "My son, give g to the LORD, the God of Israel,
1Sa 4:21 "Where is the g?"—murmuring, "Israel's g is gone."
4:22 Then she said, "The g has departed from Israel,
15:29 And he who is the G of Israel will not lie, nor will
1Ch 16:29 Give to the LORD the g he deserves! / Bring your
29:11 is the greatness, the power, the g, the victory,
Est 1: 4 display of the opulent wealth and g of his empire.
Ps 3: 3 my g, and the one who lifts my head high.
8: 1 fills the earth! / Your g is higher than the heavens.
8: 5 than God, / and you crowned us with g and honor.
19: 1 The heavens tell of the g of God. / The skies
24: 7 ancient doors, / and let the King of g enter.
24: 8 Who is the King of g? / The LORD, strong
24: 9 ancient doors, / and let the King of g enter.
24:10 Who is the King of g? / The LORD Almighty— / he is the King of g.
26: 8 LORD, / the place where your g shines.
29: 1 give honor to the LORD for his g and strength.
29: 2 Give honor to the LORD for the g of his name.
29: 3 The God of g thunders. / The LORD thunders
29: 9 In his Temple everyone shouts, "G!"
44: 8 O God, we give g to you all day long
48: 8 We had heard of the city's g, / but now we have
50:15 and I will rescue you, / and you will give me g."
57: 5 May your g shine over all the earth.
57:11 May your g shine over all the earth.
63: 2 your sanctuary / and gazed upon your power and g.
66: 2 Sing about the g of his name! / Tell the world how
71: 8 stop praising you; / I declare your g all day long.
72:19 Let the whole earth be filled with his g. / Amen
76:10 Human opposition only enhances your g, / for you
78:61 he surrendered his g into enemy hands.
80: 1 above the cherubim, / display your radiant g
84:11 our light and protector. / He gives us grace and g.
85: 9 who honor him; / our land will be filled with his g.
86:12 Lord my God. / I will give g to your name forever,
90:16 let our children see your g at work.
96: 8 Give to the LORD the g he deserves! / Bring your
97: 6 declare his righteousness; / every nation sees his g.
102:15 The kings of the earth will tremble before his g.
102:16 will rebuild Jerusalem. / He will appear in his g.
104:31 May the g of the LORD last forever!
108: 5 May your g shine over all the earth.
111: 3 Everything he does reveals his g and majesty.
113: 4 the nations; / his g is far greater than the heavens.
115: 1 Not to us, O LORD, but to you goes all the g
138: 5 for the g of the LORD is very great.
143:11 For the g of your name, O LORD, save me.
145:11 They will talk together about the g of your
145:12 and about the majesty and g of your reign.
148:13 his g towers over the earth and heaven!
149: 9 This is the g of his faithful ones.
Pr 14:28 A growing population is a king's g; a dwindling
16:31 Gray hair is a crown of g; it is gained by living a
17: 6 Grandchildren are the crowning g of the aged;
20:29 The g of the young is their strength; the gray hair
Isa 2:10 the terror of the LORD and the g of his majesty.
2:19 the terror of the LORD and the g of his majesty.
2:21 and the g of his majesty as he rises to shake the
6: 3 The whole earth is filled with his g!"
9: 1 the Jordan and the sea, will be filled with g.
10:16 proud troops, and a flaming fire will ignite your g.
14:18 "The kings of the nations lie in stately g in their
16:14 without fail, the g of Moab will be ended,
17: 3 in Aram will share the fate of Israel's departed g,"
17: 4 "In that day the g of Israel will be very dim,
21:16 the Lord, "all the g of Kedar will come to an end.
24:15 In eastern lands, give g to the LORD.
24:23 There will be such g that the brightness of the sun
25: 3 Therefore, strong nations will declare your g;
28: 5 Almighty will himself be Israel's crowning g.
35: 2 There the LORD will display his g, the splendor
40: 5 Then the g of the LORD will be revealed, and all
41:16 You will g in the Holy One of Israel.
42: 8 is my name! I will not give my g to anyone else.
43: 7 God will come, for I have made them for my g.
46:13 ready to save Jerusalem and give my g to Israel.
47: 1 For your days of g, pomp, and honor have ended.
48:11 have conquered me. I will not let them have my g!
49: 3 are my servant, Israel, and you will bring me g."
58: 8 and the g of the LORD will protect you from
60: 1 For the g of the LORD is shining upon you.
60: 2 but the g of the LORD will shine over you.
60:13 The g of Lebanon will be yours—the forests of
60:19 be your everlasting light, and he will be your g.
60:21 with my own hands in order to bring myself g.
61: 3 them like strong and graceful oaks for his own g.
62: 2 Kings will be blinded by your g.
66:11 Drink deeply of her g even as an infant drinks at its
66:18 and peoples together, and they will see my g.
66:19 sea that have not heard of my fame or seen my g.
66:19 There they will declare my g to the nations.
Jer 2:16 have utterly destroyed Israel's g and power.
13:11 "They were to be my people, my pride, my g—
13:16 Give g to the LORD your God before it is too
14:21 Do not disgrace yourself and the throne of your g.
33: 9 Then this city will bring me joy, g, and honor
48:18 Come down from your g and sit in the dust,
Eze 1:28 This was the way the g of the LORD appeared to
3:12 (May the g of the LORD be praised in his place!)
3:23 and went, and there I saw the g of the LORD,
8: 4 Suddenly, the g of the God of Israel was there,
9: 3 Then the g of the God of Israel rose up from
10: 3 and the cloud of g filled the inner courtyard.
10: 4 Then the g of the LORD rose up from above the
10: 4 The Temple was filled with this cloud of g,
10: 4 glowed brightly with the g of the LORD.

10:18 Then the **g** of the LORD moved from the door of
10:19 And the **g** of the God of Israel hovered above
11:22 and the **g** of the God of Israel hovered above them.
11:23 Then the **g** of the LORD went up from the city
24:25 their joy and **g**, their heart's desire, their dearest
28:22 and I will reveal my **g** by what happens to you.
29:21 when I will cause the ancient **g** of Israel to revive,
31:18 of Eden will you compare your strength and **g**?
39:13 for Israel when I demonstrate my **g** on that day,
39:21 "Thus, I will demonstrate my **g** among the nations.
43: 2 the **g** of the God of Israel appeared from the east.
43: 2 and the whole landscape shone with his **g**.
43: 4 And the **g** of the LORD came into the Temple
43: 5 and the **g** of the LORD filled the Temple.
44: 4 and saw that the **g** of the LORD filled the Temple
Da 4:36 to me, so did my honor and **g** and kingdom.
5:18 majesty, **g**, and honor to your predecessor,
5:20 down from his royal throne and stripped of his **g**.
Hos 4: 7 They have exchanged the **g** of God for the disgrace
9:11 The **g** of Israel will fly away like a bird, for your
10: 5 wail for it, because its **g** will be stripped away.
Am 6: 8 "I despise the pride and false **g** of Israel, and I hate
9:11 but I will rebuild its walls and restore its former **g**.
Hab 2:14 the sea, with an awareness of the **g** of the LORD.
2:16 and all your **g** will be turned to shame.
Zep 3:19 I will give **g** and renown to my former exiles,
Hag 2: 7 I will fill this place with **g**, says the LORD
2: 9 The future **g** of this Temple will be greater than its past **g**.
Zec 2: 5 And I will be the **g** inside the city!' "
2: 8 "After a period of **g**, the LORD Almighty sent
Mt 4: 8 him the nations of the world and all their **g**.
6:29 yet Solomon in all his **g** was not dressed as
16:27 will come in the **g** of my Father with his angels
24:30 on the clouds of heaven with power and great **g**.
25:31 "But when the Son of Man comes in his **g**, and all
Mk 8:38 return in the **g** of my Father with the holy angels."
13:26 Man arrive on the clouds with great power and **g**.
Lk 2: 9 and the radiance of the Lord's **g** surrounded them.
2:14 "**G** to God in the highest heaven, / and peace on
2:32 and he is the **g** of your people Israel!"
4: 6 "I will give you the **g** of these kingdoms
9:26 be ashamed of that person when I return in my **g**
9:26 and in the **g** of the Father and the holy angels.
9:32 Now they woke up and saw Jesus' **g** and the two
12:27 yet Solomon in all his **g** was not dressed as
17:18 Does only this foreigner return to give **g** to God?"
19:38 Peace in heaven / and **g** in highest heaven!"
21:27 Man arrive on the clouds with power and great **g**.
24:26 all these things before entering his time of **g**?"
Jn 1:14 And we have seen his **g**, the **g** of the only Son of the Father.
2:11 at Cana in Galilee was Jesus' first display of his **g**.
7:39 because Jesus had not yet entered into his **g**.)
9:24 and told him, "Give **g** to God by telling the truth,
11: 4 No, it is for the **g** of God. I, the Son of God, will receive **g** from this."
11:40 "Didn't I tell you that you will see God's **g** if you
12:16 But after Jesus entered into his **g**, they remembered
12:23 has come for the Son of Man to enter into his **g**.
12:28 Father, bring **g** to your name." Then a voice spoke
12:28 saying, "I have already brought it **g**, and I will do
12:41 because he was given a vision of the Messiah's **g**.
13:31 the Son of Man, to enter into my **g**, and God will receive **g** because of all that happens
13:32 And God will bring me into my **g** very soon.
14:13 because the work of the Son brings **g** to the Father.
15: 8 much fruit. This brings great **g** to my Father.
16:14 He will bring me **g** by revealing to you whatever
17: 1 Glorify your Son so he can give **g** back to you.
17: 4 I brought **g** to you here on earth by doing
17: 5 bring me into the **g** we shared before the world
17:10 you have given them back to me, so they are my **g**!
17:22 "I have given them the **g** you gave me, so that they
17:24 given me to be with me, so they can see my **g**.
17:24 You gave me the **g** because you loved me even
Ac 3:13 the God of all our ancestors who has brought **g** to
7:55 steadily upward into heaven and saw the **g** of God,
12:23 people's worship instead of giving the **g** to God.
Ro 1: 5 will believe and obey him, bringing **g** to his name.
2: 7 seeking after the **g** and honor and immortality that
2:10 But there will be **g** and honor and peace from God
3: 7 his truthfulness and brings him more **g**?"
4:20 grew stronger, and in this he brought **g** to God.
5: 2 and joyfully look forward to sharing God's **g**.
6:10 to defeat sin, and now he lives for the **g** of God.
6:11 and able to live for the **g** of God through Christ
6:13 body as a tool to do what is right for the **g** of God.
8:17 But if we are to share his **g**, we must also share his
8:18 is nothing compared to the **g** he will give us later.
8:23 the Holy Spirit within us as a foretaste of future **g**,
8:30 standing with himself, and he promised them his **g**.
9: 4 God revealed his **g** to them. He made covenants
9:23 He also has the right to pour out the riches of his **g**
11:36 exists by his power and is intended for his **g**. To him be **g** evermore. Amen.
15: 6 giving praise and **g** to God, the Father of our Lord
15: 9 so the Gentiles might also give **g** to God for his
16:27 is wise, be the **g** forever through Jesus Christ.
1Co 10:31 whatever you do, you must do all for the **g** of God.
11: 7 for man is God's **g**, made in God's own image, but woman is the **g** of man.
15:40 The **g** of the heavenly bodies is different from the
15:41 The sun has one kind of **g**, while the moon
15:43 but when they are raised, they will be full of **g**.
2Co 1:20 That is why we say "Amen" when we give **g** to
3: 7 yet it began with such **g** that the people of Israel
3: 7 For his face shone with the **g** of God, even though
3: 8 Shouldn't we expect far greater **g** when the Holy
3:10 that first **g** was not glorious at all compared with the overwhelming **g** of the new covenant.
3:11 was full of **g**, then the new covenant, which remains forever, has far greater **g**.
3:13 so the people of Israel would not see the **g** fading
3:18 so that we can be mirrors that brightly reflect the **g**
3:18 and more like him and reflect his **g** even more.
4: 4 the message we preach about the **g** of Christ,
4: 6 the **g** of God that is seen in the face of Jesus Christ.
4:15 and God will receive more and more **g**.
4:17 Yet they produce for us an immeasurably great **g**
5:13 If it seems that we are crazy, it is to bring **g** to God.
8:23 They are splendid examples of those who bring **g**
Gal 1: 5 That is why all **g** belongs to God through all the
1:24 And they gave **g** to God because of me.
Eph 3:20 Now **g** be to God! By his mighty power at work
3:21 May he be given **g** in the church and in Christ
Php 1:11 for this will bring much **g** and praise to God.
2:11 Jesus Christ is Lord, to the **g** of God the Father.
4:20 Now **g** be to God our Father forever and ever.
Col 1:27 that the riches and **g** of Christ are for you Gentiles,
1:27 this is your assurance that you will share in his **g**.
3: 4 to the whole world, you will share in all his **g**.
1Th 2:12 For he called you into his Kingdom to share his **g**.
2Th 1:10 when he comes to receive **g** and praise from his
2:14 now you can share in the **g** of our Lord Jesus
1Ti 1:17 **G** and honor to God forever and ever. He is the
2Ti 2:10 and eternal **g** in Christ Jesus to those God has
4:18 To God be the **g** forever and ever. Amen.
Tit 2:13 that wonderful event when the **g** of our great God
Heb 1: 3 The Son reflects God's own **g**, and everything
2: 7 and you crowned him with **g** and honor.
2: 9 and now is "crowned with **g** and honor"
2:10 was made—should bring his many children into **g**.
3: 3 But Jesus deserves far more **g** than Moses, just as a
13:15 of praise to God by proclaiming the **g** of his name.
13:20[-21] To him be **g** forever and ever. Amen.
1Pe 1: 7 it will bring you much praise and **g** and honor on
1:11 about Christ's suffering and his great **g** afterward.
1:21 raised Christ from the dead and gave him great **g**,
4:11 Then God will be given **g** in everything through
4:11 All **g** and power belong to him forever and ever.
4:13 sharing his **g** when it is displayed to all the world.
5: 1 will share his **g** and his honor when he returns.
5: 4 your reward will be a never-ending share in his **g**
5:10 In his kindness God called you to his eternal **g** by
2Pe 1: 3 He has called us to receive his own **g**
1:17 and **g** from God the Father when God's glorious,
3:18 To him be all **g** and honor, both now
Jude 1:24 And now, all **g** to God, who is able to keep you
1:25 All **g** to him, who alone is God our Savior,
1:25 Yes, **g**, majesty, power, and authority belong to
Rev 1: 6 Give to him everlasting **g**! He rules forever
4: 9 Whenever the living beings give **g** and honor
4:11 Lord our God, / to receive **g** and honor and power.
5:12 and strength / and honor and **g** and blessing."
5:13 also sang: / "Blessing and honor and **g** and power
7:12 They said, / "Amen! Blessing and **g** and wisdom
11:13 die was terrified and gave **g** to the God of heaven.
14: 7 "Fear God," he shouted. "Give **g** to him.
15: 8 The Temple was filled with smoke from God's **g**
16: 9 these plagues. They did not repent and give him **g**.
19: 1 from our God. **G** and power belong to him alone.
21:11 It was filled with the **g** of God and sparkled like a
21:23 or moon, for the **g** of God illuminates the city,
21:24 of the world will come and bring their **g** to it.
21:26 And all the nations will bring their **g** and honor

GLOVES (1)

Ge 27:16 She made him a pair of **g** from the hairy skin of the

GLOW (2) [GLOWED, GLOWING]

Job 18: 5 be snuffed out. The sparks of their fire will not **g**.
Rev 4: 3 And the **g** of an emerald circled his throne like a

GLOWED (3) [GLOW]

Ex 34:29 he wasn't aware that his face **g** because he had
Eze 1: 4 The fire inside the cloud **g** like gleaming amber.
10: 4 and the Temple courtyard **g** brightly with the glory

GLOWING (8) [GLOW]

2Sa 22: 9 from his mouth; / **g** coals flamed forth from him.
Ps 18: 8 from his mouth; / **g** coals flamed forth from him.
120: 4 with sharp arrows / and burned with **g** coals.
La 4: 7 Our princes were once **g** with health; they were as
Eze 1:28 All around him was a **g** halo, like a rainbow
10: 2 and take a handful of **g** coals and scatter them over
Mt 5:14 a city on a mountain, **g** in the night for all to see.
Ro 16:18 and **g** words they deceive innocent people.

GLUED (1)

Pr 17:24 Sensible people keep their eyes **g** on wisdom,

GLUTTED (2) [GLUTTON]

Jer 50:10 plundered until the attackers are **g** with plunder,"
Eze 39:19 Gorge yourselves with flesh until you are **g**;

GLUTTON (2) [GLUTTED, GLUTTONS, GLUTTONY]

Mt 11:19 and drink, and you say, 'He's a **g** and a drunkard,
Lk 7:34 and drink, and you say, 'He's a **g** and a drunkard,

GLUTTONS (2) [GLUTTON]

Pr 23:20 Do not carouse with drunkards and **g**,
Tit 1:12 are all liars; they are cruel animals and lazy **g**."

GLUTTONY (1) [GLUTTON]

Eze 16:49 laziness, and **g**, while the poor and needy suffered

GNASHES (1) [GNASHING]

Job 16: 9 He **g** his teeth at me and pierces me with his eyes.

GNASHING (7) [GNASHES]

Mt 8:12 where there will be weeping and **g** of teeth."
13:42 burn them. There will be weeping and **g** of teeth.
13:50 into the fire. There will be weeping and **g** of teeth.
22:13 where there is weeping and **g** of teeth.'
24:51 In that place there will be weeping and **g** of teeth.
25:30 where there will be weeping and **g** of teeth.'
Lk 13:28 "And there will be great weeping and **g** of teeth,

GNAT (1) [GNATS]

Mt 23:24 your water so you won't accidentally swallow a **g**,

GNATS (5) [GNAT]

Ex 8:16 The dust will turn into swarms of **g** throughout the
8:17 Suddenly, **g** infested the entire land,
8:17 All the dust in the land of Egypt turned into **g**.
8:18 And the **g** covered all the people and animals.
Ps 105:31 on the Egyptians, / and **g** swarmed across Egypt.

GNAW (1) [GNAWING]

Isa 18: 6 The wild animals will **g** at bones all winter.

GNAWING (1) [GNAW]

Job 30:17 though something were relentlessly **g** at my bones.

GO (1158) [BEGONE, GOES, GOING, GONE, WENT] See Index of Articles, Etc.

GOAD (2)

Jdg 3:31 He killed six hundred Philistines with an ox **g**.
1Sa 13:21 ounce for sharpening an ax, a sickle, or an ox **g**.)

GOAH (1)

Jer 31:39 out over the hill of Gareb and across to **G**.

GOAL (5)

Job 6:11 I do not have a **g** that encourages me to carry on.
1Co 9:26 So I run straight to the **g** with purpose in every
14: 1 Let love be your highest **g**, but also desire the
2Co 10:13 Our **g** is to stay within the boundaries of God's
Col 2: 2 My **g** is that they will be encouraged and knit

GOAT (89) [GOAT'S, GOATS, GOATS', GOATSKIN, SCAPEGOAT]

Ge 15: 9 a three-year-old female **g**, a three-year-old ram,
37:31 Then Joseph's brothers killed a **g** and dipped the
38:17 "I'll send you a young **g** from my flock,"
38:20 the Adullamite to take the young **g** back to her
38:23 "We tried our best to send her the **g**.
Ex 12: 3 must choose a lamb or a young **g** for a sacrifice.
12: 5 either a sheep or a **g**, with no physical defects.
23:19 "You must not cook a young **g** in its mother's
25: 4 purple, and scarlet yarn; fine linen; **g** hair for cloth;
26: 7 "Make heavy sheets of cloth from **g** hair to cover
34:26 "You must not cook a young **g** in its mother's
35: 6 purple, and scarlet yarn; fine linen; **g** hair for cloth;
35:23 and scarlet yarn, fine linen, or **g** hair for cloth.
35:26 their skills to spin and weave the **g** hair into cloth.
36:14 from eleven sheets of cloth made from **g** hair.
Lev 1:10 bring a male sheep or **g** with no physical defects.
3: 6 from the flock, you may bring either a **g** or a sheep.
3:12 "If you bring a **g** as your offering to the LORD,
4:23 he must bring as his offering a male **g** with no
4:28 they must bring as their offering a female **g** with
5: 6 a female from the flock, either a sheep or a **g**.
9: 3 Then tell the Israelites to take a male **g** for a sin
9:15 He slaughtered the people's **g** and presented it as
10:16 what had happened to the **g** of the sin offering,
16: 8 He is to cast sacred lots to determine which **g** will
16: 9 The **g** chosen to be sacrificed to the LORD will
16:10 The **g** chosen to be the scapegoat will be presented
16:15 "Then Aaron must slaughter the **g** as a sin offering
16:18 from the bull and the **g** on each of the altar's horns.
16:20 and the altar, he must bring the living **g** forward.
16:21 he will lay the people's sins on the head of the **g**;
16:22 the **g** will carry all the people's sins upon itself into
16:26 "The man chosen to send the **g** out into the
16:27 "The bull and **g** given as sin offerings,
17: 3 or a lamb or a **g** anywhere inside or outside the
22:19 It may be either a bull, a ram, or a male **g**.
22:27 "When a bull or a ram or a male **g** is born, it must
23:19 Then you must offer one male **g** as a sin offering
Nu 7:16 a male **g** for a sin offering;
7:22 a male **g** for a sin offering;
7:28 a male **g** for a sin offering;
7:34 a male **g** for a sin offering;
7:40 a male **g** for a sin offering;
7:46 a male **g** for a sin offering;
7:52 a male **g** for a sin offering;
7:58 a male **g** for a sin offering;

7:64 a male **g** for a sin offering;
7:70 a male **g** for a sin offering;
7:76 a male **g** for a sin offering;
7:82 a male **g** for a sin offering;
15:11 each sacrificial bull, ram, lamb, or young **g**.
15:24 and with one male **g** for a sin offering.
15:27 bring a one-year-old female **g** for a sin offering.
28:15 offer one male **g** for a sin offering to the LORD.
28:22 You must also offer a male **g** as a sin offering,
28:30 offer one male **g** to make atonement for
29: 5 you must sacrifice a male **g** as a sin offering,
29:11 You must also sacrifice one male **g** for a sin
29:16 You must also sacrifice a male **g** as a sin offering,
29:19 You must also sacrifice a male **g** as a sin offering,
29:22 You must also sacrifice a male **g** as a sin offering,
29:25 You must also sacrifice a male **g** as a sin offering,
29:28 You must also sacrifice a male **g** as a sin offering,
29:31 You must also sacrifice a male **g** as a sin offering,
29:34 You must also sacrifice one male **g** as a sin
29:38 You must also sacrifice one male **g** as a sin
31:20 and everything made of leather, **g** hair, or wood."
Dt 14: 4 the animals you may eat: the ox, the sheep, the **g**,
14: 5 the gazelle, the roebuck, the wild **g**, the ibex,
14:21 "Do not boil a young **g** in its mother's milk.
Jdg 6:19 He cooked a young **g**, and with half a bushel of
13:15 "Please stay here until we can prepare a young **g**
13:19 Then Manoah took a young **g** and a grain offering
14: 6 He did it as easily as if it were a young **g**. But he
15: 1 Samson took a young **g** as a present to his wife.
1Sa 16:20 along with a young **g** and a donkey loaded down
2Ch 11:15 where they worshiped the **g** and calf idols he had
Pr 30:31 the strutting rooster, / the male **g**, / a king as he
Isa 11: 6 the leopard and the **g** will be at peace.
Eze 43:22 sacrifice as a sin offering a young male **g** that has
43:25 "Every day for seven days a male **g**, a young bull,
45:23 A male **g** will also be given each day for a sin
Da 8: 5 suddenly a male **g** appeared from the west,
8: 5 This **g**, which had one very large horn between its
8: 7 The **g** charged furiously at the ram and struck it,
8: 7 and the **g** knocked it down and trampled it.
8: 8 The **g** became very powerful. But at the height of
8:21 The shaggy male **g** represents the king of Greece,
Lk 15:29 me even one young **g** for a feast with my friends.

GOAT'S (9) [GOAT]

Ge 27:16 and she fastened a strip of the **g** skin around his
Lev 3:13 Then the sons of Aaron will sprinkle the **g** blood
4:24 He is to lay his hand on the **g** head and slaughter it
4:26 He must burn all the **g** fat on the altar, just as is
4:31 Those who are guilty must remove all the **g** fat,
16:21 He is to lay both of his hands on the **g** head
1Sa 19:13 and put a cushion of **g** hair at its head.
19:16 idol in the bed with a cushion of **g** hair at its head.
Da 8: 7 one who could rescue the ram from the **g** power.

GOATH [KJV] See GOAH

GOATS (81) [GOAT]

Ge 26:14 He acquired large flocks of sheep and **g**,
27: 9 out to the flocks and bring me two fine young **g**.
27:13 "Just do what I tell you. Go out and get the **g**."
27:14 his mother's instructions, bringing her the two **g**.
27:16 a pair of gloves from the hairy skin of the young **g**,
30:32 all the sheep and **g** that are speckled or spotted,
30:33 flock any white sheep or **g** that are not speckled,
30:35 and removed all the male **g** that were speckled
31:10 and saw that the male **g** mating with the flock were
31:38 and **g** so they produced healthy offspring.
32: 5 donkeys, sheep, **g**, and many servants, both men
32:14 two hundred female **g**, twenty male **g**, two hundred
ewes, twenty rams,
Ex 20:24 peace offerings, your sheep and **g** and your cattle.
Lev 7:23 never eat fat, whether from oxen or sheep or **g**.
16: 5 then bring him two male **g** for a sin offering
16: 7 Then he must bring the two male **g** and present
Nu 7:17 and two oxen, five rams, five male **g**, and five
7:23 and two oxen, five rams, five male **g**, and five
7:29 and two oxen, five rams, five male **g**, and five
7:35 and two oxen, five rams, five male **g**, and five
7:41 and two oxen, five rams, five male **g**, and five
7:47 and two oxen, five rams, five male **g**, and five
7:53 and two oxen, five rams, five male **g**, and five
7:59 and two oxen, five rams, five male **g**, and five
7:65 and two oxen, five rams, five male **g**, and five
7:71 and two oxen, five rams, five male **g**, and five
7:77 and two oxen, five rams, five male **g**, and five
7:83 and two oxen, five rams, five male **g**, and five
7:87 Twelve male **g** were brought for the sin offerings.
7:88 Twenty-four young bulls, sixty rams, sixty male **g**,
15: 3 flocks of sheep and **g** or from your herds of cattle.
18:17 may not redeem the firstborn of cattle, sheep, or **g**.
31:28 donkeys, sheep, and **g** that belong to the army.
31:30 and **g** in the half that belongs to the people of
Dt 7:13 and olives, and great herds of cattle, sheep, and **g**.
32:14 the flock, / together with the fat of lambs and **g**.
32:14 He gave them choice rams and **g** from Bashan,
1Sa 10: 3 One will be bringing three young **g**, another will
24: 2 for David and his men near the rocks of the wild **g**.
25: 2 He had three thousand sheep and a thousand **g**,
25: 7 I am told that you are shearing your sheep and **g**.
1Ki 4:23 one hundred sheep or **g**, as well as deer, gazelles,
20:27 **g** in comparison to the vast Aramean forces that
2Ch 15:11 hundred oxen and seven thousand sheep and **g**.
17:11 hundred rams and seventy-seven hundred male **g**.
29:21 and seven male **g** as a sin offering for the kingdom,
29:23 The male **g** for the sin offering were then brought
29:24 The priests then killed the **g** as a sin offering
32:28 his cattle and folds for his flocks of sheep and **g**.
35: 7 and young **g** for the people's Passover offerings,
35: 8 the priests twenty-six hundred lambs and young **g**
35: 9 gave five thousand lambs and young **g** and five
Ezr 6:17 And twelve male **g** were presented as a sin offering
8:35 They also offered twelve **g** as a sin offering.
Job 39: 1 "Do you know when the mountain **g** give birth?
Ps 50: 9 your barns; / I want no more **g** from your pens.
50:13 bulls you sacrifice; / I don't need the blood of **g**.
66:15 And I will sacrifice bulls and **g**. / *Interlude*
104:18 High in the mountains are pastures for the wild **g**,
Pr 27:26 and your **g** will be sold for the price of a field.
SS 1: 8 the shepherds' tents, and there feed your young **g**.
4: 1 like flocks of **g** frisking across the slopes of
6: 5 is like a flock of **g** frisking down the slopes of
Isa 1:11 blood from your offerings of bulls and rams and **g**.
7:25 cover them. Cattle, sheep, and **g** will graze there.
13:21 the ruins, and wild **g** will come there to dance.
32:14 and **g** will graze on the hills where the watchtowers
34: 6 for killing lambs and **g** and rams for a sacrifice.
34:14 Wild **g** will bleat at one another among the ruins,
Jer 51:40 to the slaughter, like rams and **g** to be sacrificed.
Eze 27:21 and rams and **g** in trade for your goods.
34:17 and another, separating the sheep from the **g**.
39:18 lambs, **g**, and fat young bulls of Bashan!
Mt 25:32 them as a shepherd separates the sheep from the **g**.
25:33 the sheep at his right hand and the **g** at his left.
Heb 9:12 Most Holy Place, but not the blood of **g** and calves.
9:13 the blood of **g** and bulls and the ashes of a young
9:19 he took the blood of calves and **g**, along with
10: 4 for the blood of bulls and **g** to take away sins.
11:37 Some went about in skins of sheep and **g**, hungry

GOATS' (1) [GOAT]

Pr 27:27 And you will have enough **g** milk for you,

GOATSKIN (14) [GOAT, SKIN]

Ex 25: 5 tanned ram skins and fine **g** leather; acacia wood;
26:14 and over them put a layer of fine **g** leather.
35: 7 tanned ram skins and fine **g** leather; acacia wood;
35:23 Some gave tanned ram skins or fine **g** leather.
36:19 and the second was made of fine **g** leather.
39:34 the layers of tanned ram skins and fine **g** leather;
Nu 4: 6 Then they must cover the inner curtain with fine **g**
4: 6 and the **g** leather with a dark blue cloth.
4: 8 and finally a covering of fine **g** leather on top of
4:10 utensils must then be covered with fine **g** leather,
4:11 and cover this cloth with a covering of fine **g**
4:12 covered with fine **g** leather, and placed on the
4:14 and a covering of fine **g** leather must be spread
4:25 its coverings, the outer covering of fine **g** leather,

GOB (2)

2Sa 21:18 was another battle against the Philistines at **G**.
21:19 In still another battle at **G**, Elhanan son of Jair

GOBLET (2) [GOBLETS]

SS 7: 2 Your navel is as delicious as a **g** filled with wine.
Rev 17: 4 She held in her hand a gold **g** full of obscenities

GOBLETS (1) [GOBLET]

Est 1: 7 Drinks were served in gold **g** of many designs,

GOD (4536) [GOD'S, GOD-FEARING, GOD-GIVEN, GODDESS, GODFORSAKEN, GODLESS, GODLINESS, GODLY, GODS, NON-GODS]

GOD ALMIGHTY (37) Ge 17:1; 28:3; 35:11; 43:14; 48:3; Ex 6:3; 2Sa 5:10; 1Ki 19:10,14; Ps 59:5; 80:4,7,14,19; 84:8; 89:8; Jer 5:14; 15:16; 35:17; 38:17; 44:7; Eze 10:5; Hos 12:5; Am 3:13; 4:13; 5:14,15,16,27; 6:8,14; Rev 4:8; 11:17; 15:3; 16:7,14; 21:22

GOD OF HEAVEN (25) Ge 24:3,7; 2Ch 36:23; Ezr 1:2; 5:11,12; 6:9,10; 7:12,21,23; Ne 1:4,5; 2:4,20; Job 31:28; Ps 136:26; Da 2:18,19,37,44; Jnh 1:9; Heb 1:3; Rev 11:13; 16:11

GOD OF ISRAEL (221) Ex 5:1; 24:10; 32:27; 34:23; Nu 16:9; Dt 33:26; Jos 7:13,19,20; 8:30; 9:18,19; 10:40,42; 13:14,33; 14:14; 22:16,24; 24:2,23; Jdg 4:6; 5:3,5; 6:8; 11:21,23; 21:3; Ru 2:12; 1Sa 1:17; 2:30; 5:7,8,8,10,11; 6:3,5; 10:18; 14:41; 20:12; 23:10,11; 25:32,34; 2Sa 7:27; 12:7; 23:3; 1Ki 1:30,48; 8:15,17,20,23,25,26; 11:9,31; 14:7,13; 15:30; 16:13,26,33; 17:1,14; 22:53; 2Ki 9:6; 10:31; 14:25; 18:5; 19:15,20; 21:12; 22:15,18; 1Ch 4:10; 5:26; 15:12,14; 16:4,36; 22:6; 23:25; 24:19; 28:4; 2Ch 2:12; 6:4,7,10,14,16,17; 11:16; 13:5; 15:4,13; 20:19; 29:7,10; 30:1,5; 32:17; 33:16,18; 34:23,26; 36:13; Ezr 1:3; 3:2; 4:1,3; 5:1; 6:14,21,22; 7:6,15; 8:35; 9:4,15; Ps 20:1; 24:6; 41:13; 46:7,11; 59:5; 68:8,35; 69:6; 72:18; 75:9; 81:1; 84:8; 94:7; 106:48; 114:7; 146:5, Isa 2:3; 17:6; 21:10,17; 24:15; 29:23; 37:16,21; 41:17; 45:3,15; 48:1,2; 52:7,12; Jer 7:3,21; 9:15; 10:16; 11:3; 13:12; 16:9; 19:3,15; 21:4; 23:2; 24:5; 25:15,27; 27:4,21; 28:2,14; 29:4,8,21,25; 30:2; 31:23; 32:14,15,36; 33:4; 34:2,13; 35:13,17,18,19; 37:7; 38:17; 39:16; 42:9,15,18; 43:10; 44:2,7,11,25; 45:2; 46:25; 48:1; 50:18; 51:19,33; Eze 8:4; 9:3; 10:19,20; 11:22; 43:2; 44:2; Joel 2:17; Mic 4:2; Zep 2:9; Mal 2:16; Mt 15:31; Lk 1:68; Ac 10:2,22; 13:16,26

GOD OF JUSTICE (2) Isa 26:7; Mal 2:17

GOD OF PEACE (4) Ro 16:20; Php 4:9; 1Th 5:23; Heb 13:20

GOD OF SALVATION (4) Ps 18:46; 27:9; 88:1; Hab 3:18

LORD GOD ALMIGHTY (5) Rev 4:8; 11:17; 15:3; 16:7; 21:22

LORD* GOD ALMIGHTY (21) 2Sa 5:10; 1Ki 19:10,14; Ps 59:5; 80:4,19; 84:8; 89:8; Jer 5:14; 15:16; 35:17; 38:17; 44:7; Hos 12:5; Am 3:13; 4:13; 5:14,15,16; 6:8,14

SON OF GOD (41) Mt 4:3,6; 8:29; 14:33; 26:63; 27:40,43,54; Mk 1:1; 3:11; 15:39; Lk 1:35; 3:38; 4:3,9,41; 22:70; Jn 1:34,49; 3:18; 5:25; 10:36; 11:4,27; 19:7; 20:31; Ac 9:20; Ro 1:4; 2Co 1:19; Gal 2:20; Heb 4:14; 6:6; 7:3; 10:29; 1Jn 3:8; 4:15; 5:5,10,13,20; Rev 2:18

WILL OF GOD (16) Nu 22:18; 1Ch 13:2; 2Ch 10:15; Ezr 7:18; Jn 4:34; 5:30; 6:38,39; 7:17; Ac 13:36; Ro 15:32; 1Co 1:1; Eph 6:6; Col 4:12; 1Pe 4:2; 1Jn 2:17

Ge 1: 1 In the beginning **G** created the heavens
1: 2 And the Spirit of **G** was hovering over its surface.
1: 3 Then **G** said, "Let there be light," and there was
1: 4 And **G** saw that it was good. Then he separated the
1: 5 **G** called the light "day" and the darkness
1: 6 And **G** said, "Let there be space between the
1: 7 **G** made this space to separate the waters above
1: 8 And **G** called the space "sky." This happened on
1: 9 And **G** said, "Let the waters beneath the sky be
1:10 **G** named the dry ground "land" and the water
"seas." And **G** saw that it was good.
1:11 Then **G** said, "Let the land burst forth with every
1:12 and trees of like kind. And **G** saw that it was good.
1:14 And **G** said, "Let bright lights appear in the sky to
1:16 For **G** made two great lights, the sun
1:17 **G** set these lights in the heavens to light the earth,
1:18 from the darkness. And **G** saw that it was good.
1:20 And **G** said, "Let the waters swarm with fish
1:21 So **G** created great sea creatures and every sort of
1:21 every kind of bird. And **G** saw that it was good.
1:22 Then **G** blessed them, saying, "Let the fish
1:24 And **G** said, "Let the earth bring forth every kind
1:25 **G** made all sorts of wild animals, livestock,
1:25 more of its own kind. And **G** saw that it was good.
1:26 Then **G** said, "Let us make people in our image,
1:27 So **G** created people in his own image; / **G**
patterned them after himself;
1:28 **G** blessed them and told them, "Multiply and fill
1:29 And **G** said, "Look! I have given you the
1:31 Then **G** looked over all he had made, and he saw
2: 2 finished his task, **G** rested from all his work.
2: 3 And **G** blessed the seventh day and declared it
2: 4 When the LORD **G** made the heavens
2: 5 the earth, for the LORD **G** had not sent any rain.
2: 7 And the LORD **G** formed a man's body from the
2: 8 Then the LORD **G** planted a garden in Eden,
2: 9 And the LORD **G** planted all sorts of trees in the
2:15 The LORD **G** placed the man in the Garden of
2:16 But the LORD **G** gave him this warning:
2:18 And the LORD **G** said, "It is not good for the
2:19 So the LORD **G** formed from the soil every kind
2:21 So the LORD **G** caused Adam to fall into a deep
2:22 Then the LORD **G** made a woman from the rib
3: 1 of all the creatures the LORD **G** had made.
3: 1 "Did **G** really say you must not eat any of the fruit
3: 3 **G** says we must not eat it or even touch it, or we
3: 5 "**G** knows that your eyes will be opened when you
3: 5 You will become just like **G**, knowing everything,
3: 8 Toward evening they heard the LORD **G** walking
3: 9 The LORD **G** called to Adam, "Where are you?"
3:11 you that you were naked?" the LORD **G** asked.
3:13 Then the LORD **G** asked the woman,
3:14 So the LORD **G** said to the serpent,
3:21 And the LORD **G** made clothing from animal
3:22 Then the LORD **G** said, "The people have
3:23 So the LORD **G** banished Adam and his wife
3:24 the LORD **G** stationed mighty angelic beings to
4:25 "**G** has granted me another son in place of Abel,
5: 1 When **G** created people, he made them in the
likeness of **G**.
5:22 lived another 300 years in close fellowship with **G**,
5:24 He enjoyed a close relationship with **G** throughout
5:24 he disappeared because **G** took him.
6: 2 the sons of **G** saw the beautiful women of the
6: 4 for whenever the sons of **G** had intercourse with
6:12 **G** observed all this corruption in the world, and he
6:13 So **G** said to Noah, "I have decided to destroy all
6:22 So Noah did everything exactly as **G** had
7: 9 and female, just as **G** had commanded Noah.
7:16 male and female, just as **G** had commanded.
8: 1 But **G** remembered Noah and all the animals in the
8:15 Then **G** said to Noah,
9: 1 **G** blessed Noah and his sons and told them,
9: 8 Then **G** told Noah and his sons,
9:12 And **G** said, "I am giving you a sign as evidence
9:16 I will remember the eternal covenant between **G**
9:17 Then **G** said to Noah, "Yes, this is the sign of my
9:26 "May Shem be blessed by the LORD my **G**;
9:27 May **G** enlarge the territory of Japheth, / and may
14:18 the king of Salem and a priest of **G** Most High,
14:19 "Blessed be Abram by **G** Most High, / Creator of
14:20 And blessed be **G** Most High, / who has helped
14:22 **G** Most High, Creator of heaven and earth,
16:13 to her, as "the **G** who sees me," for she said,
17: 1 appeared to him and said, "I am **G** Almighty;
17: 3 fell face down in the dust. Then **G** said to him,
17: 7 And I will always be your **G** and the **G** of your
descendants after you.
17: 8 to your offspring forever. And I will be their **G**.
17: 9 "Your part of the agreement," **G** told Abraham,
17:15 Then **G** added, "Regarding Sarai, your wife—
17:18 And Abraham said to **G**, "Yes, may Ishmael enjoy

17:19 But **G** replied, "Sarah, your wife, will bear you a
17:22 That ended the conversation, and **G** left Abraham.
17:23 off their foreskins, exactly as **G** had told him.
19:29 But **G** had listened to Abraham's request and kept
20: 3 But one night **G** came to Abimelech in a dream
20: 6 "Yes, I know you are innocent," **G** replied.
20:13 When **G** sent me to travel far from my father's
20:17 Then Abraham prayed to **G**, and **G** healed
Abimelech, his wife,
21: 2 It all happened at the time **G** had said it would.
21: 4 Abraham circumcised him as **G** had commanded.
21: 6 And Sarah declared, "**G** has brought me laughter!
21:12 But **G** told Abraham, "Do not be upset over the
21:17 Then **G** heard the boy's cries, and the angel of **G**
called to Hagar from the sky,
21:17 **G** has heard the boy's cries from the place where
21:19 Then **G** opened Hagar's eyes, and she saw a well.
21:20 And **G** was with the boy as he grew up in the
21:22 "It is clear that **G** helps you in everything you
21:33 worshiped the LORD, the Eternal **G**, at that place.
22: 1 Later on **G** tested Abraham's faith and obedience.
22: 1 "Abraham!" **G** called. "Yes," he replied.
22: 3 and set out for the place where **G** had told him to
22: 8 "**G** will provide a lamb, my son,"
22: 9 When they arrived at the place where **G** had told
22:12 in any way, for now I know that you truly fear **G**.
24: 3 "Swear by the LORD, the **G** of heaven and earth,
24: 7 For the LORD, the **G** of heaven, who took me
24:12 "O LORD, **G** of my master," he prayed.
24:27 the **G** of my master, Abraham," he said.
24:42 'O LORD, the **G** of my master, Abraham, if you
24:48 praised the LORD, the **G** of my master, Abraham,
25:11 **G** poured out rich blessings on Isaac,
26:24 "I am the **G** of your father, Abraham," he said.
27:20 "Because the LORD your **G** put it in my path!"
27:28 May **G** always give you plenty of dew for healthy
28: 3 May **G** Almighty bless you and give you many
28: 4 May **G** pass on to you and your descendants the
28: 4 we now are foreigners, for **G** gave it to Abraham."
28:12 And he saw the angels of **G** going up and down on
28:13 the **G** of your grandfather Abraham and the **G** of
your father,
28:17 It is none other than the house of **G**—the gateway
28:19 He named the place Bethel—"house of **G**"—
28:20 "If **G** will be with me and protect me on this
28:21 to my father, then I will make the LORD my **G**.
28:22 pillar will become a place for worshiping **G**,
28:22 and I will give **G** a tenth of everything he gives
30: 2 Jacob flew into a rage. "Am I **G**?" he asked.
30: 6 him Dan, for she said, "**G** has vindicated me!
30:17 And **G** answered her prayers. She became pregnant
30:18 "**G** has rewarded me for giving my servant to my
30:20 "**G** has given me good gifts for my husband.
30:22 Then **G** remembered Rachel's plight and answered
30:23 to a son. "**G** has removed my shame," she said.
31: 5 "But the **G** of my father has been with me.
31: 7 But **G** has not allowed him to do me any harm.
31: 9 **G** has made me wealthy at your father's expense.
31:11 in my dream, the angel of **G** said to me, 'Jacob!'
31:13 I am the **G** you met at Bethel, the place where you
31:16 The riches **G** has given you from our father are
31:16 So go ahead and do whatever **G** has told you."
31:24 But the previous night **G** had appeared to Laban in
31:29 but the **G** of your father appeared to me last night
31:42 In fact, except for the grace of **G**—the **G** of my
grandfather Abraham,
31:42 the awe-inspiring **G** of my father, Isaac—
31:42 But **G** has seen your cruelty and my hard work.
31:50 or if you take other wives, but **G** will see it.
31:53 I call on the **G** of our ancestors—the **G** of your
grandfather Abraham and the **G** of my grandfather
Nahor—
31:53 So Jacob took an oath before the awesome **G** of his
31:54 Then Jacob presented a sacrifice to **G** and invited
32: 1 on their way again, angels of **G** came to meet him.
32: 9 "O **G** of my grandfather Abraham and my father,
32:28 because you have struggled with both **G** and men
32:30 "face of **G**"—for he said, "I have seen **G** face to
face,
33: 5 "These are the children **G** has graciously given to
33:10 your friendly smile. It is like seeing the smile of **G**!
33:11 take my gifts, for **G** has been very generous to me.
35: 1 **G** said to Jacob, "Now move on to Bethel
35: 1 the **G** who appeared to you when you fled from
35: 3 where I will build an altar to the **G** who answered
35: 5 terror from **G** came over the people in all the
35: 7 because **G** had appeared to him there at Bethel
35: 9 **G** appeared to Jacob once again when he arrived at
35: 9 after traveling from Paddan-aram. **G** blessed him
35:11 Then **G** said, "I am **G** Almighty.
35:13 Then **G** went up from the place where he had
35:14 to mark the place where **G** had spoken to him.
35:14 then poured wine over it as an offering to **G**
35:15 Jacob called the place Bethel—"house of
G"—because **G** had spoken to him there.
39: 9 a wicked thing? It would be a great sin against **G**."
41:16 "But **G** will tell you what it means and will set
41:25 "**G** was telling you what he is about to do.
41:28 for **G** has shown you what he is about to do.
41:32 it means that the matter has been decreed by **G**
41:38 man who is obviously filled with the spirit of **G**."
41:39 "Since **G** has revealed the meaning of the dreams
41:51 "**G** has made me forget all my troubles
41:52 "**G** has made me fruitful in this land of my
42:28 and said to each other, "What has **G** done to us?"
43:14 May **G** Almighty give you mercy as you go before
43:23 "Your **G**, the **G** of your ancestors, must have
43:29 me about? May **G** be gracious to you, my son."
44:16 **G** is punishing us for our sins. My lord, we have
45: 5 yourselves that you did this to me, for **G** did it.
45: 7 **G** has sent me here to keep you and your families
45: 8 Yes, it was **G** who sent me here, not you! And he
45: 9 **G** has made me master over all the land of Egypt.
46: 1 he offered sacrifices to the **G** of his father, Isaac.
46: 2 During the night **G** spoke to him in a vision.
46: 3 "I am **G**," the voice said, "the **G** of your father.
48: 3 "**G** Almighty appeared to me at Luz in the land of
48: 9 "these are the sons **G** has given me here in
48:11 but now **G** has let me see your children, too."
48:15 Then he blessed Joseph and said, "May **G**,
48:15 the **G** before whom my grandfather Abraham
48:15 the **G** who has been my shepherd all my life,
48:20 'May **G** make you as prosperous as Ephraim
48:21 but **G** will be with you and will bring you again to
49:25 May the **G** of your ancestors help you;
50:17 So we, the servants of the **G** of your father,
50:19 be afraid of me. Am I **G**, to judge and punish you?
50:20 **G** turned into good what you meant for evil.
50:24 told his brothers, "but **G** will surely come for you,
50:25 "When **G** comes to lead us back to Canaan,
Ex 1:17 But because the midwives feared **G**, they refused
1:20 So **G** blessed the midwives, and the Israelites
1:21 And because the midwives feared **G**, he gave them
2:23 and their pleas for deliverance rose up to **G**.
2:24 **G** heard their cries and remembered his covenant
3: 1 into the wilderness near Sinai, the mountain of **G**.
3: 4 **G** called to him from the bush, "Moses!
3: 5 "Do not come any closer," **G** told him. "Take off
3: 6 Then he said, "I am the **G** of your ancestors—
3: 6 the **G** of Abraham, the **G** of Isaac, and the **G** of
Jacob."
3: 6 in his hands because he was afraid to look at **G**.
3:11 am I to appear before Pharaoh?" Moses asked **G**.
3:12 Then **G** told him, "I will be with you. And this
3:12 you will return here to worship **G** at this very
3:13 'The **G** of your ancestors has sent me to you,'
3:13 They will ask, 'Which **g** are you talking about?
3:14 **G** replied, "I AM THE ONE WHO ALWAYS IS.
3:15 **G** also said, "Tell them, 'The LORD, the **G** of your
ancestors—
3:15 the **G** of Abraham, the **G** of Isaac, and the **G** of
Jacob—
3:16 Tell them, 'The LORD, the **G** of your ancestors—
3:16 the **G** of Abraham, Isaac, and Jacob—
3:18 and tell him, 'The LORD, the **G** of the Hebrews,
3:18 to offer sacrifices to the LORD our **G**.'
4: 5 realize that the LORD, the **G** of their ancestors—
4: 5 the **G** of Abraham, the **G** of Isaac, and the **G** of
Jacob—
4:16 and you will be as **G** to him, telling him what to
4:20 land of Egypt. In his hand he carried the staff of **G**.
4:27 So Aaron traveled to the mountain of **G**, where he
5: 1 "This is what the LORD, the **G** of Israel, says:
5: 3 "The **G** of the Hebrews has met with us,"
5: 3 so we can offer sacrifices to the LORD our **G**.
5: 8 into the wilderness to offer sacrifices to their **G**.
6: 2 And **G** continued, "I am the LORD.
6: 3 to Abraham, to Isaac, and to Jacob as **G** Almighty,
6: 7 you my own special people, and I will be your **G**.
6: 7 And you will know that I am the LORD your **G**
7: 1 I will make you seem like **G** to Pharaoh.
7: 9 show him a miracle to prove that **G** has sent you.
7:16 Say to him, 'The LORD, the **G** of the Hebrews,
8:10 that no one is as powerful as the LORD our **G**.
8:19 "This is the finger of **G**!" the magicians
8:25 Go ahead and offer sacrifices to your **G**," he said.
8:26 the sacrifices that we offer to the LORD our **G**
8:27 wilderness to offer sacrifices to the LORD our **G**,
8:28 sacrifices to the LORD your **G** in the wilderness.
9: 1 is what the LORD, the **G** of the Hebrews, says:
9:13 tell him, 'The LORD, the **G** of the Hebrews, says:
9:14 I will prove to you that there is no other **G** like me
9:30 I know that you still do not fear the LORD **G** as
10: 3 is what the LORD, the **G** of the Hebrews, says:
10: 7 let the Israelites go to serve the LORD their **G**!
10: 8 go and serve the LORD your **G**," he said.
10:16 "I confess my sin against the LORD your **G**
10:17 and plead with the LORD your **G** to take away
10:25 and burnt offerings to the LORD our **G**.
10:26 for the LORD our **G** from among these animals.
13:17 **G** did not lead them on the road that runs through
13:17 **G** said, "If the people are faced with a battle,
13:18 So **G** led them along a route through the
13:19 bones with them when **G** led them out of
Egypt—as he was sure **G** would.
14:19 Then the angel of **G**, who had been leading the
15: 2 He is my **G**, and I will praise him; / he is my
father's **G**, and I will exalt him!
15:26 listen carefully to the voice of the LORD your **G**
16:12 you will know that I am the LORD your **G**.' "
17: 9 I will stand at the top of the hill with the staff of **G**
18: 1 about all the wonderful things **G** had done for
18: 4 at his birth, "The **G** of my fathers was my helper;
18: 5 the people were camped near the mountain of **G**.
18:12 presented a burnt offering and gave sacrifices to **G**.
18:19 give you a word of advice, and may **G** be with you.
18:19 to be the people's representative before **G**,
18:21 honest men who fear **G** and hate bribes.
18:23 follow this advice, and if **G** directs you to do so,
19: 3 Moses climbed the mountain to appear before **G**.
19:17 Moses led them out from the camp to meet with **G**,
19:19 and **G** thundered his reply for all to hear.
20: 1 Then **G** instructed the people as follows:
20: 2 "I am the LORD your **G**, who rescued you from
20: 5 for I, the LORD your **G**, am a jealous **G** who will
not share your affection with any other **g**!
20: 7 "Do not misuse the name of the LORD your **G**.
20:10 is a day of rest dedicated to the LORD your **G**.
20:12 full life in the land the LORD your **G** will give
20:19 "You tell us what **G** says, and we will listen.
20:19 But don't let **G** speak directly to us. If he does,
20:20 "for **G** has come in this way to show you his
20:21 Moses entered into the deep darkness where **G**
21: 6 he does this, his master must present him before **G**.
21:13 But if it is an accident and **G** allows it to happen,
22: 8 **G** will determine whether or not it was the
22: 9 Both parties must come before **G** for a decision,
22: 9 and the person whom **G** declares guilty must pay
22:20 "Anyone who sacrifices to any **g** other than the
22:28 "Do not blaspheme **G** or curse anyone who rules
23:19 It must be offered to the LORD your **G**.
23:25 "You must serve only the LORD your **G**. If you
24:10 There they saw the **G** of Israel. Under his feet there
24:11 And though Israel's leaders saw **G**, he did not
24:13 his assistant Joshua climbed up the mountain of **G**.
28: 2 clothing for Aaron to show his separation to **G**—
29:45 will live among the people of Israel and be their **G**,
29:46 and they will know that I am the LORD their **G**.
29:46 I could live among them. I am the LORD their **G**.
31: 3 I have filled him with the Spirit of **G**, giving him
31:18 terms of the covenant, written by the finger of **G**.
32:11 But Moses pleaded with the LORD his **G** not to
32:12 '**G** tricked them into coming to the mountains
32:16 the words on them were written by **G** himself.
32:27 "This is what the LORD, the **G** of Israel, says:
34: 6 I am the LORD, the merciful and gracious **G**.
34:14 for he is a **G** who is passionate about his
34:23 before the Sovereign LORD, the **G** of Israel.
34:24 the LORD your **G** those three times each year.
34:26 year's crop to the house of the LORD your **G**.
35:31 The LORD has filled Bezalel with the Spirit of **G**,
Lev 4:22 does something forbidden by the LORD his **G**,
11:44 After all, I, the LORD, am your **G**. You must be
11:45 you up from the land of Egypt to be your **G**.
18: 2 the Israelites: I, the LORD, am your **G**.
18: 4 to keep my laws, for I, the LORD, am your **G**.
18:21 for you must not profane the name of your **G**.
18:30 doing any of them, for I, the LORD, am your **G**."
19: 2 be holy because I, the LORD your **G**, am holy.
19: 3 days of rest, for I, the LORD, am your **G**.
19: 4 of metal for yourselves. I, the LORD, am your **G**.
19:10 live among you, for I, the LORD, am your **G**.
19:12 a falsehood and so profane the name of your **G**.
19:14 "Show your fear of **G** by treating the deaf with
19:25 yield will be increased. I, the LORD, am your **G**.
19:31 will be defiled by them. I, the LORD, am your **G**.
19:32 "Show your fear of **G** by standing up in the
19:34 in the land of Egypt. I, the LORD, am your **G**.
19:36 I, the LORD, am your **G**, who brought you out of
20: 7 apart to be holy, for I, the LORD, am your **G**.
20:24 I, the LORD, am your **G**, who has set you apart
21: 6 They must be set apart to **G** as holy and must never
21: 6 providing **G** with his food, and they must remain
21: 7 for the priests must be set apart to **G** as holy.
21: 8 them as holy because they offer up food to your **G**.
21:12 He must not desecrate the sanctuary of his **G** by
21:12 has been made holy by the anointing oil of his **G**.
21:17 defects will not qualify to offer food to their **G**.
21:21 he has a blemish, he may not offer food to his **G**.
21:22 However, he may eat from the food offered to **G**,
22:25 foreigners to be offered as a sacrifice to your **G**.
22:33 you from Egypt, that I might be your very own **G**.
23:14 after you have brought this offering to your **G**.
23:22 living among you. I, the LORD, am your **G**."
23:28 will be made for you before the LORD your **G**,
23:40 Then rejoice before the LORD your **G** for seven
23:43 the land of Egypt. I, the LORD, am your **G**."
24:15 Those who blaspheme **G** will suffer the
24:22 who live among you. I, the LORD, am your **G**."
25:17 Show your fear of **G** by not taking advantage of
each other. I, the LORD, am your **G**.
25:36 show your fear of **G** by letting them live with you
25:38 I, the LORD, am your **G**, who brought you out of
25:38 to give you the land of Canaan and to be your **G**.
25:43 Show your fear of **G** by treating them well;
25:55 of the land of Egypt. I, the LORD, am your **G**.
26: 1 worshiped in your land. I, the LORD, am your **G**.
26:12 I will be your **G**, and you will be my people.
26:13 I, the LORD, am your **G**, who brought you from
26:44 by wiping them out. I, the LORD, am their **G**.
26:45 the nations watched. I, the LORD, am their **G**."
Nu 6: 7 because it is the symbol of their separation to **G**.
10: 9 so the LORD your **G** will remember you
10:10 The trumpets will remind the LORD your **G** of his
covenant with you. I am the LORD your **G**."
12:13 out to the LORD, "Heal her, O **G**, I beg you!"
15:40 obey all my commands and be holy to your **G**.
15:41 I am the LORD your **G** who brought you out of the
land of Egypt that I might be your **G**. I am the
LORD your **G**!' "
16: 9 Does it seem a small thing to you that the **G** of
16:22 "O **G**, the **G** and source of all life,"
21: 5 and they began to murmur against **G** and Moses.
22: 9 That night **G** came to Balaam and asked him,
22:10 So Balaam said to **G**, "Balak son of Zippor,
22:12 "Do not go with them," **G** told Balaam. "You are
22:18 do anything against the will of the LORD my **G**.
22:20 That night **G** came to Balaam and told him,
22:22 But **G** was furious that Balaam was going, so he
22:38 I will speak only the messages that **G** gives me."
23: 4 and **G** met him there. Balaam said to him, "I have

23: 8 how can I curse / those whom **G** has not cursed?
23:19 **G** is not a man, that he should lie. / He is not a
23:21 for Israel. / For the LORD their **G** is with them;
23:22 **G** has brought them out of Egypt; / he is like a
23:23 of Jacob, / 'What wonders **G** has done for Israel!'
23:27 Perhaps it will please **G** to let you curse them from
24: 2 tribe by tribe. Then the Spirit of **G** came upon him,
24: 4 who hears the words of **G**, / who sees a vision
24: 8 **G** brought them up from Egypt, / drawing them
24:16 who hears the words of **G**, / who has knowledge
24:23 "Alas, who can survive when **G** does this?
25:13 because he was zealous for his **G** and made
27:16 the **G** of the spirits of all living things,
Dt 1: 6 were at Mount Sinai, the LORD our **G** said to us,
1:10 The LORD your **G** has made you as numerous as
1:11 And may the LORD, the **G** of your ancestors,
1:17 will react, for you are judging in the place of **G**.
1:19 "Then, just as the LORD our **G** directed us,
1:20 the land that the LORD our **G** is giving us.
1:21 the **G** of your ancestors, has promised you.
1:25 And they reported that the land the LORD our **G**
1:26 against the command of the LORD your **G**
1:30 The LORD your **G** is going before you. He will
1:31 And you saw how the LORD your **G** cared for
1:32 all he did, you refused to trust the LORD your **G**,
1:41 and fight for it, as the LORD our **G** has told us.'
2: 7 The LORD your **G** has blessed everything you
2: 7 the LORD your **G** has been with you
2:29 into the land the LORD our **G** has given us.'
2:30 because the LORD your **G** made Sihon stubborn
2:33 But the LORD our **G** handed him over to us,
2:36 "The LORD our **G** helped us conquer Aroer on
2:37 all the places the LORD our **G** had commanded
3: 3 So the LORD our **G** handed King Og and all his
3:18 'Although the LORD your **G** has given you this
3:20 and when they occupy the land the LORD your **G**
3:21 'You have seen all that the LORD your **G** has
3:22 for the LORD your **G** will fight for you.'
3:24 Is there any **g** in heaven or on earth who can
4: 1 the LORD, the **G** of your ancestors, is giving you.
4: 2 I am giving you from the LORD your **G**.
4: 3 where the LORD your **G** destroyed everyone who had worshiped the **g** Baal of Peor.
4: 4 faithful to the LORD your **G** are still alive today.
4: 5 The LORD my **G** gave them to me
4: 7 For what great nation has a **g** as near to them as the
4: 7 our **G** is near to us whenever we call on him?
4:10 stood before the LORD your **G** at Mount Sinai,
4:19 The LORD your **G** designated these heavenly
4:21 your **G** is giving you as your special possession.
4:23 covenant the LORD your **G** has made with you.
4:23 for the LORD your **G** has absolutely forbidden
4:24 The LORD your **G** is a devouring fire, a jealous **G**.
4:25 This is evil in the sight of the LORD your **G**
4:29 there you will search again for the LORD your **G**.
4:30 you will finally return to the LORD your **G**
4:31 For the LORD your **G** is merciful—he will not
4:32 from the time **G** created people on the earth until
4:33 Has any nation ever heard the voice of **G** speaking
4:34 Has any other **g** taken one nation for himself by
4:34 Yet that is what the LORD your **G** did for you in
4:35 so you would realize that the LORD is **G** and that there is no other **g**.
4:39 The LORD is **G** both in heaven and on earth, and there is no other **g**!
4:40 the LORD your **G** is giving you for all time."
5: 2 the LORD our **G** made a covenant with us.
5: 6 " 'I am the LORD your **G**, who rescued you
5: 9 or bow down to them, for I, the LORD your **G**, am a jealous **G** who will not share your affection with any other **g**!
5:11 " 'Do not misuse the name of the LORD your **G**.
5:12 as the LORD your **G** has commanded you.
5:14 is a day of rest dedicated to the LORD your **G**.
5:15 and that the LORD your **G** brought you out with
5:15 That is why the LORD your **G** has commanded
5:16 as the LORD your **G** commanded you.
5:16 full life in the land the LORD your **G** will give
5:24 'The LORD our **G** has shown us his glory
5:24 Today we have seen **G** speaking to humans,
5:25 If the LORD our **G** speaks to us again, we will
5:26 Can any living thing hear the voice of the living **G**
5:27 You go and listen to what the LORD our **G** says.
5:32 obey all the commands of the LORD your **G**,
5:33 Stay on the path that the LORD your **G** has
6: 1 and regulations that the LORD your **G** told me to
6: 2 and grandchildren might fear the LORD your **G**
6: 3 the **G** of your ancestors, promised you.
6: 4 O Israel! The LORD is our **G**, the LORD alone.
6: 5 And you must love the LORD your **G** with all
6:10 "The LORD your **G** will soon bring you into the
6:13 You must fear the LORD your **G** and serve him.
6:15 for the LORD your **G**, who lives among you, is a jealous **G**.
6:16 Do not test the LORD your **G** as you did when
6:17 obey the commands of the LORD your **G**—
6:20 and regulations that the LORD our **G** has given
6:24 And the LORD our **G** commanded us to obey all
6:25 all the commands the LORD our **G** has given us.'
7: 1 "When the LORD your **G** brings you into the
7: 2 When the LORD your **G** hands these nations over
7: 6 a holy people, who belong to the LORD your **G**.
7: 6 the LORD your **G** has chosen you to be his own
7: 9 therefore, that the LORD your **G** is indeed **G**.
7: 9 He is the faithful **G** who keeps his covenant for a
7:12 the LORD your **G** will keep his covenant of
7:16 the nations the LORD your **G** hands over to you.
7:18 Just remember what the LORD your **G** did to
7:19 Remember the great terrors the LORD your **G**
7:19 The LORD your **G** will use this same power
7:20 then the LORD your **G** will send hornets to drive
7:21 for the LORD your **G** is among you, and he is a great and awesome **G**.
7:22 The LORD your **G** will drive those nations out
7:23 But the LORD your **G** will hand them over to
7:25 to you, for it is detestable to the LORD your **G**.
8: 2 Remember how the LORD your **G** led you
8: 5 the LORD your **G** disciplines you to help you.
8: 6 "So obey the commands of the LORD your **G** by
8: 7 For the LORD your **G** is bringing you into a good
8:10 praise the LORD your **G** for the good land he has
8:11 your plenty you do not forget the LORD your **G**
8:14 proud at that time and forget the LORD your **G**,
8:18 Always remember that it is the LORD your **G**
8:19 If you ever forget the LORD your **G** and follow
8:20 be destroyed for not obeying the LORD your **G**.
9: 3 But the LORD your **G** will cross over ahead of
9: 4 "After the LORD your **G** has done this for you,
9: 5 The LORD your **G** will drive these nations out
9: 6 The LORD your **G** is not giving you this good
9: 7 made the LORD your **G** out in the wilderness.
9:10 the tablets on which **G** himself had written all the
9:16 in your terrible sin against the LORD your **G**.
9:23 against the command of the LORD your **G**
10: 9 their inheritance, as the LORD your **G** told them.
10:12 what does the LORD your **G** require of you?
10:14 everything in it all belong to the LORD your **G**.
10:17 "The LORD your **G** is the **G** of gods
10:17 He is the great **G**, mighty and awesome,
10:20 You must fear the LORD your **G** and worship
10:21 He is your **G**, the one who is worthy of your
10:22 But now the LORD your **G** has made you as
11: 1 "You must love the LORD your **G** and obey all
11: 2 experienced the discipline of the LORD your **G**
11:12 a land that the LORD your **G** cares for.
11:13 and if you love the LORD your **G** with all your
11:22 show love to the LORD your **G** by walking in his
11:25 for the LORD your **G** will send fear and dread
11:27 of the LORD your **G** that I am giving you today.
11:28 if you reject the commands of the LORD your **G**
11:29 "When the LORD your **G** brings you into the
11:31 occupy the land the LORD your **G** is giving you.
12: 1 the LORD, the **G** of your ancestors, is giving you.
12: 4 "Do not worship the LORD your **G** in the way
12: 5 you must seek the LORD your **G** at the place he
12: 7 will feast in the presence of the LORD your **G**,
12: 7 because the LORD your **G** has blessed you.
12: 9 the place of rest the LORD your **G** is giving you.
12:10 and live in the land the LORD your **G** is giving
12:11 to the place the LORD your **G** will choose for his
12:12 servants in the presence of the LORD your **G**.
12:15 as many animals as the LORD your **G** gives you.
12:18 of the LORD your **G** at the place he will choose.
12:18 celebrating in the presence of the LORD your **G**
12:20 "When the LORD your **G** enlarges your territory
12:21 It might happen that the place the LORD your **G**
12:27 burnt offerings on the altar of the LORD your **G**.
12:27 poured out beside the altar of the LORD your **G**,
12:28 will be doing what pleases the LORD your **G**.
12:29 "When the LORD your **G** destroys the nations
12:31 You must not do this to the LORD your **G**.
13: 3 The LORD your **G** is testing you to see if you
13: 4 Serve only the LORD your **G** and fear him alone.
13: 5 encourage rebellion against the LORD your **G**,
13: 5 to keep you from following the LORD your **G**,
13:10 tried to draw you away from the LORD your **G**,
13:12 one of the towns the LORD your **G** is giving you
13:16 the torch as a burnt offering to the LORD your **G**.
13:18 "The LORD your **G** will be merciful only if you
14: 1 "Since you are the people of the LORD your **G**,
14: 2 have been set apart as holy to the LORD your **G**,
14:21 for you are set apart as holy to the LORD your **G**.
14:23 Bring this tithe to the place the LORD your **G**
14:23 is to teach you always to fear the LORD your **G**.
14:24 Now the place the LORD your **G** chooses for his
14:25 money to the place the LORD your **G** chooses.
14:26 feast there in the presence of the LORD your **G**
14:29 Then the LORD your **G** will bless you in all your
15: 4 for the LORD your **G** will greatly bless you in the
15: 5 of the LORD your **G** that I am giving you today.
15: 6 The LORD your **G** will bless you as he has
15: 7 arrive in the land the LORD your **G** is giving you,
15:10 and the LORD your **G** will bless you in
15:14 with which the LORD your **G** has blessed you.
15:15 of Egypt and the LORD your **G** redeemed you!
15:18 and the LORD your **G** will bless you in all you
15:19 "You must set aside for the LORD your **G** all the
15:20 LORD your **G** each year at the place he chooses.
15:21 you must not sacrifice it to the LORD your **G**.
16: 1 "In honor of the LORD your **G**, always celebrate
16: 1 for that was when the LORD your **G** brought you
16: 2 and it must be sacrificed to the LORD your **G** at
16: 5 in the towns that the LORD your **G** is giving you.
16: 6 It must be offered at the place the LORD your **G**
16: 7 and eat it in the place the LORD your **G** chooses.
16: 8 people must assemble before the LORD your **G**,
16:10 Festival of Harvest to honor the LORD your **G**.
16:11 It is a time to celebrate before the LORD your **G**
16:15 honor the LORD your **G** at the place he chooses,
16:15 for it is the LORD your **G** who gives you
16:16 They must appear before the LORD your **G** at the
16:17 the blessings given to them by the LORD your **G**.
16:18 in all the towns the LORD your **G** is giving you.
16:20 and occupy the land that the LORD your **G** is
16:21 pole beside the altar of the LORD your **G**.
16:22 for worship, for the LORD your **G** hates them.
17: 1 or defective ox or sheep to the LORD your **G**.
17: 2 in one of your towns that the LORD your **G** is
17: 2 has done evil in the sight of the LORD your **G**
17: 8 Take such cases to the place the LORD your **G**
17:12 or of the priest who represents the LORD your **G**
17:14 arrive in the land the LORD your **G** is giving you,
17:15 select as king the man the LORD your **G** chooses.
17:19 That way he will learn to fear the LORD his **G** by
18: 5 For the LORD your **G** chose the tribe of Levi out
18: 7 minister there in the name of the LORD his **G**,
18: 9 "When you arrive in the land the LORD your **G**
18:12 LORD your **G** will drive them out ahead of you.
18:13 You must be blameless before the LORD your **G**.
18:14 but the LORD your **G** forbids you to do such
18:15 "The LORD your **G** will raise up for you a
18:16 your **G** when you were assembled at Mount Sinai.
18:16 have to listen to the voice of the LORD your **G**
18:20 who claims to give a message from another **g**
19: 1 "The LORD your **G** will soon destroy the nations
19: 2 land the LORD your **G** is giving you to occupy.
19: 3 Divide the land the LORD your **G** is giving you
19: 8 "If the LORD your **G** enlarges your territory,
19: 9 if you always love the LORD your **G** and walk in
19:10 your **G** is giving you as a special possession,
19:14 "When you arrive in the land the LORD your **G**
20: 1 The LORD your **G**, who brought you safely out
20: 4 For the LORD your **G** is going with you! He will
20:13 When the LORD your **G** hands it over to you,
20:14 enemies that the LORD your **G** has given you.
20:16 your **G** is giving you as a special possession,
20:17 just as the LORD your **G** has commanded you.
20:18 you to sin deeply against the LORD your **G**.
21: 1 field in the land the LORD your **G** is giving you,
21: 5 for the LORD your **G** has chosen them to
21:10 and the LORD your **G** hands them over to you
21:23 for anyone hanging on a tree is cursed of **G**.
21:23 Do not defile the land the LORD your **G** is giving
22: 5 The LORD your **G** detests people who do this.
23: 5 (But the LORD your **G** would not listen to
23: 5 a blessing because the LORD your **G** loves you.)
23:14 for the LORD your **G** moves around in your
23:18 Do not bring to the house of the LORD your **G**
23:18 for both are detestable to the LORD your **G**.
23:20 so the LORD your **G** may bless you in everything
23:21 "When you make a vow to the LORD your **G**,
23:21 For the LORD your **G** demands that you
23:23 for you have made a vow to the LORD your **G**.
24: 4 your **G** is giving you as a special possession.
24: 9 Remember what the LORD your **G** did to Miriam
24:13 And the LORD your **G** will count it as a
24:18 and that the LORD your **G** redeemed you.
24:19 Then the LORD your **G** will bless you in all you
25:15 life in the land the LORD your **G** is giving you.
25:16 and measures are detestable to the LORD your **G**.
25:18 who were lagging behind. They had no fear of **G**.
25:19 when the LORD your **G** has given you rest from
26: 1 "When you arrive in the land the LORD your **G**
26: 2 and bring it to the place the LORD your **G**
26: 3 **G** has brought me into the land he swore to give
26: 4 and set it before the altar of the LORD your **G**.
26: 5 then say in the presence of the LORD your **G**,
26: 7 we cried out to the LORD, the **G** of our ancestors.
26:10 Then place the produce before the LORD your **G**
26:11 because of all the good things the LORD your **G**
26:13 declare in the presence of the LORD your **G**,
26:14 I have obeyed the LORD my **G** and have done
26:16 "Today the LORD your **G** has commanded you
26:17 have declared today that the LORD is your **G**.
26:19 will be a nation that is holy to the LORD your **G**,
27: 2 and enter the land the LORD your **G** is giving
27: 3 to enter the land the LORD your **G** is giving you,
27: 3 the **G** of your ancestors, promised you.
27: 5 Then build an altar there to the LORD your **G**,
27: 6 must offer burnt offerings to the LORD your **G**.
27: 7 there with great joy before the LORD your **G**.
27: 9 have become the people of the LORD your **G**.
27:10 So obey the LORD your **G** by keeping all these
28: 1 "If you fully obey the LORD your **G** by keeping
28: 1 the LORD your **G** will exalt you above all the
28: 2 all these blessings if you obey the LORD your **G**:
28: 8 The LORD your **G** will bless you in the land he is
28: 9 "If you obey the commands of the LORD your **G**
28:13 listen to these commands of the LORD your **G**
28:15 "But if you refuse to listen to the LORD your **G**
28:45 "If you refuse to listen to the LORD your **G**
28:47 Because you have not served the LORD your **G**
28:52 in the land the LORD your **G** has given you.
28:53 whom the LORD your **G** has given you.
28:58 and awesome name of the LORD your **G**,
28:62 you would not listen to the LORD your **G**.
29: 6 so you would know that he is the LORD your **G**.
29:10 are standing today before the LORD your **G**.
29:12 to enter into a covenant with the LORD your **G**.
29:13 as his people and to confirm that he is your **G**,
29:15 The LORD your **G** is making this covenant with
29:18 our **G** to worship these gods of other nations,
29:25 the **G** of their ancestors, when he brought them out
29:29 are secret things that belong to the LORD our **G**,
30: 1 to which the LORD your **G** has exiled you.
30: 2 If at that time you return to the LORD your **G**,
30: 3 then the LORD your **G** will restore your fortunes.
30: 4 the LORD your **G** will go and find you and bring
30: 6 "The LORD your **G** will cleanse your heart
30: 7 The LORD your **G** will inflict all these curses on
30: 9 The LORD your **G** will make you successful in

30:10 The LORD your **G** will delight in you if you obey
30:10 and if you turn to the LORD your **G** with all your
30:16 commanded you today to love the LORD your **G**
30:16 and the LORD your **G** will bless you and the land
30:20 Choose to love the LORD your **G** and to obey
31: 3 But the LORD your **G** himself will cross over
31: 6 of them! The LORD your **G** will go ahead of you.
31:11 before the LORD your **G** at the place he chooses.
31:12 may listen and learn to fear the LORD your **G**
31:13 and will learn to fear the LORD your **G**.
31:17 have come because **G** is no longer among us!'
31:26 the Ark of the Covenant of the LORD your **G**,
32: 3 the name of the LORD; / how glorious is our **G**!
32: 4 and fair. / He is a faithful **G** who does no wrong;
32:15 Then they abandoned the **G** who had made them;
32:18 you forgot the **G** who had given you birth.
32:39 I myself am he! / There is no **g** other than me!
32:43 and let all the angels of **G** worship him,
33: 1 This is the blessing that Moses, the man of **G**,
33:26 "There is no one like the **G** of Israel. / He rides
33:27 The eternal **G** is your refuge, / and his everlasting
Jos 1: 9 For the LORD your **G** is with you wherever you
1:11 and take possession of the land the LORD your **G**
1:13 'The LORD your **G** is giving you rest and has
1:15 possess the land the LORD your **G** is giving
1:17 And may the LORD your **G** be with you as he
2:11 For the LORD your **G** is the supreme **G** of the
3: 3 the Ark of the Covenant of the LORD your **G**,
3: 9 and listen to what the LORD your **G** says.
3:10 Today you will know that the living **G** is among
4: 5 in front of the Ark of the LORD your **G**.
4:23 For the LORD your **G** dried up the river right
4:24 and that you might fear the LORD your **G**
7:13 For this is what the LORD, the **G** of Israel, says:
7:19 to the LORD, the **G** of Israel, by telling the truth.
7:20 "I have sinned against the LORD, the **G** of Israel.
8: 7 the city, for the LORD your **G** will give it to you.
8:30 to the LORD, the **G** of Israel, on Mount Ebal.
9: 9 We have heard of the might of the LORD your **G**
9:18 had made a vow to the LORD, the **G** of Israel.
9:19 oath in the presence of the LORD, the **G** of Israel.
9:20 for **G** would be angry with us if we broke our oath.
9:23 and carry water for the house of my **G**."
9:24 because we were told that the LORD your **G**
10:19 for the LORD your **G** has given you victory over
10:40 as the LORD, the **G** of Israel, had commanded.
10:42 and their land, for the LORD, the **G** of Israel,
13:14 burned on the altar to the LORD, the **G** of Israel.
13:33 for the LORD, the **G** of Israel, had promised to be
14: 6 the man of **G**, about you and me when we were at
14: 8 my part, I followed the LORD my **G** completely.
14: 9 you wholeheartedly followed the LORD my **G**.'
14:14 followed the LORD, the **G** of Israel.
18: 3 the **G** of your ancestors, has given to you?
18: 6 **G** to decide which section will be assigned to each
22: 3 of the LORD your **G** up to the present day.
22: 4 And now the LORD your **G** has given the other
22: 5 Love the LORD your **G**, walk in all his ways,
22:16 to know why you are betraying the **G** of Israel.
22:19 There is only one true altar of the LORD our **G**.
22:20 Didn't **G** punish all the people of Israel when
22:22 "The LORD alone is **G**! The LORD alone is God!
The LORD alone is **G**!
22:24 you have to worship the LORD, the **G** of Israel?
22:29 Only the altar of the LORD our **G** that stands in
22:33 And all the Israelites were satisfied and praised **G**
22:34 between us and them that the LORD is our **G**.
23: 3 You have seen everything the LORD your **G** has
23: 3 The LORD your **G** has fought for you against
23: 5 for the LORD your **G** will drive out all the people
23: 5 of them, just as the LORD your **G** promised you.
23: 8 But be faithful to the LORD your **G** as you have
23:10 for the LORD your **G** fights for you, just as he
23:11 So be very careful to love the LORD your **G**.
23:13 then know for certain that the LORD your **G** will
23:13 this good land the LORD your **G** has given you.
23:14 promise of the LORD your **G** has come true.
23:15 But as surely as the LORD your **G** has given you
23:16 If you break the covenant of the LORD your **G**
24: 1 So they came and presented themselves to **G**.
24: 2 "This is what the LORD, the **G** of Israel, says:
24:17 For the LORD our **G** is the one who rescued us
24:18 will serve the LORD, for he alone is our **G**."
24:19 serve the LORD, for he is a holy and jealous **G**.
24:23 turn your hearts to the LORD, the **G** of Israel."
24:24 said to Joshua, "We will serve the LORD our **G**.
24:26 recorded these things in the Book of the Law of **G**.
24:27 against you if you go back on your word to **G**."
Jdg 1: 7 Now **G** has paid me back for what I did to them."
2:12 abandoned the LORD, the **G** of their ancestors,
3: 7 They forgot about the LORD their **G**, and they
3:20 and said, "I have a message for you from **G**!"
4: 6 what the LORD, the **G** of Israel, commands you:
4:23 So on that day Israel saw **G** subdue Jabin,
5: 3 will lift up my song to the LORD, the **G** of Israel.
5: 5 in the presence of the LORD, the **G** of Israel.
6: 8 "This is what the LORD, the **G** of Israel, says:
6:10 I told you, 'I am the LORD your **G**. You must not
6:20 The angel of **G** said to him, "Place the meat
6:26 Then build an altar to the LORD your **G** here on
6:31 If Baal truly is a **g**, let him defend himself
6:36 Then Gideon said to **G**, "If you are truly going to
6:39 Then Gideon said to **G**, "Please don't be angry
6:40 So that night **G** did as Gideon asked. The fleece
7:14 **G** has given Gideon son of Joash, the Israelite,
7:15 the dream and its interpretation, he thanked **G**.
8: 3 **G** gave you victory over Oreb and Zeeb,
8:33 the images of Baal, making Baal-berith their **g**.
8:34 They forgot the LORD their **G**, who had rescued
9: 7 Listen to me if you want **G** to listen to you!
9: 9 I quit producing the olive oil that blesses both **G**
9:13 I quit producing the wine that cheers both **G**
9:23 **G** stirred up trouble between Abimelech
9:24 **G** punished Abimelech and the men of Shechem
9:27 held in the temple of the local **g**, the wine flowed
9:56 **G** punished Abimelech for the evil he had done
9:57 **G** also punished the men of Shechem for all their
10:10 because we have abandoned you as our **G**
11:21 But the LORD, the **G** of Israel, gave his people
11:23 "So you see, it was the LORD, the **G** of Israel,
11:24 You keep whatever your **g** Chemosh gives you,
11:24 and we will keep whatever the LORD our **G**
13: 5 For he will be dedicated to **G** as a Nazirite from
13: 6 told her husband, "A man of **G** appeared to me!
13: 7 For your son will be dedicated to **G** as a Nazirite
13: 8 please let the man of **G** come back to us again
13: 9 **G** answered his prayer, and the angel of **G**
appeared once again to his wife
13:22 to his wife, "We will die, for we have seen **G**!"
15:19 So **G** caused water to gush out of a hollow in the
16:17 "for I was dedicated to **G** as a Nazirite from birth.
16:23 offering sacrifices and praising their **g**, Dagon.
16:23 "Our **g** has given us victory over our enemy
16:24 the people saw him, they praised their **g**, saying,
"Our **g** has delivered our enemy to us!
16:28 O **G**, please strengthen me one more time so that I
18: 5 "Ask **G** whether or not our journey will be
18:10 **G** has given us a spacious and fertile land,
18:31 as long as the Tabernacle of **G** remained at Shiloh.
20: 2 their positions in the assembly of the people of **G**.
20:18 battle the Israelites went to Bethel and asked **G**,
20:27 (In those days the Ark of the Covenant of **G** was in
21: 2 and sat in the presence of **G** until evening,
21: 3 "O LORD, **G** of Israel," they cried out,
Ru 1:16 will be my people, and your **G** will be my **G**.
2:12 May the LORD, the **G** of Israel, under whose
1Sa 1:17 May the **G** of Israel grant the request you have
2: 2 no one besides you; / there is no Rock like our **G**.
2: 3 The LORD is a **G** who knows your deeds;
2:25 another person, **G** can mediate for the guilty party.
2:30 "Therefore, the LORD, the **G** of Israel, says:
3: 3 The lamp of **G** had not yet gone out, and Samuel
was sleeping in the Tabernacle near the Ark of **G**.
3:13 because his sons are blaspheming **G** and he hasn't
3:17 And may **G** punish you if you hide anything from
4: 4 helped carry the Ark of **G** to where the battle was
4:11 The Ark of **G** was captured, and Hophni
4:13 his heart trembled for the safety of the Ark of **G**.
4:17 too. And the Ark of **G** has been captured."
4:19 When she heard that the Ark of **G** had been
4:21 because the Ark of **G** had been captured and
4:22 from Israel, for the Ark of **G** has been captured."
5: 1 After the Philistines captured the Ark of **G**,
5: 2 They carried the Ark of **G** into the temple of
5: 7 "We can't keep the Ark of the **G** of Israel here any
5: 7 We will all be destroyed along with our **g** Dagon."
5: 8 "What should we do with the Ark of the **G** of
5: 8 So they moved the Ark of the **G** of Israel to Gath.
5:10 So they sent the Ark of **G** to the city of Ekron,
5:10 "They are bringing the Ark of the **G** of Israel here
5:11 "Please send the Ark of the **G** of Israel back to its
5:11 For the plague from **G** had already begun,
6: 3 "Send the Ark of the **G** of Israel back, along with
6: 3 you will know that **G** didn't send the plague after
6: 5 Make these things to show honor to the **G** of Israel.
6: 6 They wouldn't let Israel go until **G** had ravaged
6:20 stand in the presence of the LORD, this holy **G**?"
7: 8 "Plead with the LORD our **G** to save us from the
9: 6 There is a man of **G** who lives here in this town.
9: 9 (In those days if people wanted a message from **G**,
9:10 So they started into the town where the man of **G**
9:27 have received a special message for you from **G**."
10: 3 you who are on their way to worship **G** at Bethel.
10: 5 "When you arrive at Gibeah of **G**,
10: 7 whatever you think is best, for **G** will be with you.
10: 9 and started to leave, **G** changed his heart,
10:10 Then the Spirit of **G** came upon Saul, and he,
10:18 this message from the LORD, the **G** of Israel:
10:26 a band of men whose hearts **G** had touched became
11: 6 Then the Spirit of **G** came mightily upon Saul,
12: 9 the people soon forgot about the LORD their **G**,
12:12 even though the LORD your **G** was already your
12:14 if you and your king follow the LORD your **G**,
12:19 "Pray to the LORD your **G** for us, or we will
13:13 disobeyed the command of the LORD your **G**.
14:36 is best." But the priest said, "Let's ask **G** first."
14:37 So Saul asked **G**, "Should we go after the
14:37 us defeat them?" But **G** made no reply that day.
14:41 Then Saul prayed, "O LORD, **G** of Israel,
14:44 May **G** strike me dead if you are not executed for
14:45 for he has been used of **G** to do a mighty miracle
15:15 are going to sacrifice them to the LORD your **G**.
15:21 and plunder to sacrifice to the LORD your **G** in
15:30 by going with me to worship the LORD your **G**."
16:15 "It is clear that a spirit from **G** is tormenting you,"
16:23 And whenever the tormenting spirit from **G**
17:26 he is allowed to defy the armies of the living **G**?"
17:36 for he has defied the armies of the living **G**!
17:45 the **G** of the armies of Israel, whom you have
17:46 and the whole world will know that there is a **G** in
18:10 a tormenting spirit from **G** overwhelmed Saul,
19:20 the Spirit of **G** came upon Saul's men, and they
19:23 But on the way to Naioth the Spirit of **G** came
20:12 "I promise by the LORD, the **G** of Israel,
22: 3 until I know what **G** is going to do for me?"
22:13 a sword? Why have you inquired of **G** for him?
22:15 not the first time I had consulted **G** for him!
23: 7 **G** has handed him over to me, for he has trapped
23:10 And David prayed, "O LORD, **G** of Israel,
23:11 O LORD, **G** of Israel, please tell me."
23:14 him day after day, but **G** didn't let him be found.
23:16 and encouraged him to stay strong in his faith in **G**.
25:22 May **G** deal with me severely if even one man of
25:29 you are safe in the care of the LORD your **G**,
25:32 to Abigail, "Praise the LORD, the **G** of Israel,
25:33 Thank **G** for your good sense! Bless you for
25:34 For I swear by the LORD, the **G** of Israel,
26: 8 "**G** has surely handed your enemy over to you this
28:13 "I see a **g** coming up out of the earth," she said.
28:15 and **G** has left me and won't reply by prophets
29: 9 I'm concerned, you're as perfect as an angel of **G**.
30: 6 But David found strength in the LORD his **G**.
2Sa 2:27 "**G** only knows what would have happened if you
3: 9 May **G** deal harshly with me if I don't help David
3:35 "May **G** kill me if I eat anything before
5:10 because the LORD **G** Almighty was with him.
6: 2 to Baalah of Judah to bring home the Ark of **G**,
6: 3 They placed the Ark of **G** on a new cart
6: 4 with the Ark of **G** on it, with Ahio walking in
6: 6 and Uzzah put out his hand to steady the Ark of **G**.
6: 7 and **G** struck him dead beside the Ark of **G**.
6:12 and everything he has because of the Ark of **G**."
7: 2 cedar palace, but the Ark of **G** is out in a tent!"
7:22 There is no one like you—there is no other **G**.
7:22 We have never even heard of another **g** like you!
7:23 What other nation, O **G**, have you redeemed from
7:24 and you, O LORD, became their **G**.
7:25 "And now, O LORD **G**, do as you have promised
7:26 will say, 'The LORD Almighty is **G** over Israel!'
7:27 "O LORD Almighty, **G** of Israel, I have been
7:28 For you are **G**, O Sovereign LORD. Your words
10:12 bravely to save our people and the cities of our **G**.
12: 7 The LORD, the **G** of Israel, says, 'I anointed you
12:16 David begged **G** to spare the child. He went
14:11 "Please swear to me by the LORD your **G** that
14:13 people of **G** as you have promised to do for me?
14:14 That is why **G** tries to bring us back when we have
14:17 I know that you are like an angel of **G** and can
14:17 from evil. May the LORD your **G** be with you."
14:20 But you are as wise as an angel of **G**, and you
15:24 and the Levites took the Ark of the Covenant of **G**
15:25 David instructed Zadok to take the Ark of **G** back
15:29 and Abiathar took the Ark of **G** back to the city
15:32 of the Mount of Olives where people worshiped **G**,
16:23 though it had come directly from the mouth of **G**.
18:28 and said, "Blessed be the LORD your **G**,
19:13 may **G** strike me dead if I do not appoint you as
19:27 But I know that you are like an angel of **G**, so do
21:14 After that, **G** ended the famine in the land of Israel.
22: 3 my **G** is my rock, in whom I find protection.
22: 7 out to the LORD; / yes, I called to my **G** for help.
22:22 I have not turned from my **G** to follow evil.
22:24 I am blameless before **G**; / I have kept myself from
22:30 crush an army; / with my **G** I can scale any wall.
22:31 "As for **G**, his way is perfect. / All the LORD's
22:32 For who is **G** except the LORD? / Who but our **G** is
a solid rock?
22:33 **G** is my strong fortress; / he has made my way
22:47 May **G**, the rock of my salvation, be exalted!
22:48 He is the **G** who pays back those who harm me;
23: 1 the man to whom **G** gave such wonderful success,
23: 1 David, the man anointed by the **G** of Jacob,
23: 3 The **G** of Israel spoke. / The Rock of Israel said to
23: 3 who rules righteously, / who rules in the fear of **G**,
23: 5 "It is my family **G** has chosen! / Yes, he has made
24: 3 "May the LORD your **G** let you live until there
24:23 and may the LORD your **G** accept your
24:24 to the LORD my **G** that have cost me nothing."
1Ki 1:17 you vowed to me by the LORD your **G** that my
1:30 swore to you before the LORD, the **G** of Israel."
1:36 the **G** of my lord the king, decree it to be so.
1:47 'May your **G** make Solomon's fame even greater
1:48 'Blessed be the LORD, the **G** of Israel,
2: 3 Observe the requirements of the LORD your **G**
2:23 "May **G** strike me dead if Adonijah has not sealed
3: 5 in a dream, and **G** said, "What do you want?
3: 7 O LORD my **G**, now you have made me king
3:11 So **G** replied, "Because you have asked for
3:28 **G** had given him to render decisions with justice.
4:29 **G** gave Solomon great wisdom and understanding,
5: 3 a Temple to honor the name of the LORD his **G**
5: 4 But now the LORD my **G** has given me peace on
5: 5 a Temple to honor the name of the LORD my **G**,
8:15 "Blessed be the LORD, the **G** of Israel, who has
8:17 to honor the name of the LORD, the **G** of Israel.
8:20 to honor the name of the LORD, the **G** of Israel.
8:23 He prayed, "O LORD, **G** of Israel, there is no **G**
like you in all of heaven or earth.
8:25 And now, O LORD, **G** of Israel, carry out your
8:26 Now, O **G** of Israel, fulfill this promise to your
8:27 "But will **G** really live on earth? Why,
8:28 to my prayer and my request, O LORD my **G**.
8:57 May the LORD our **G** be with us as he was with
8:59 so that the LORD our **G** may uphold my cause
8:60 all over the earth know that the LORD is **G** and that
there is no other **g**.
8:61 his people, always be faithful to the LORD our **G**.
8:65 of Shelters in the presence of the LORD their **G**.
9: 9 'Because his people forgot the LORD their **G**,
10: 9 The LORD your **G** is great indeed! He delights in
10:24 visit him and to hear the wisdom **G** had given him.

11: 4 gods instead of trusting only in the LORD his **G**,
11: 5 and Molech, the detestable **g** of the Ammonites.
11: 7 the detestable **g** of Moab, and another for Molech, the detestable **g** of the Ammonites.
11: 9 the **G** of Israel, who had appeared to him twice.
11:23 **G** also raised up Rezon son of Eliada to be an
11:31 for this is what the LORD, the **G** of Israel, says:
11:33 Chemosh, the **g** of Moab; and Molech, the **g** of the Ammonites.
12:22 But **G** said to Shemaiah, the man of **G**,
13: 1 a man of **G** from Judah went to Bethel,
13: 3 That same day the man of **G** gave a sign to prove
13: 4 King Jeroboam was very angry with the man of **G**
13: 5 just as the man of **G** had predicted in his message
13: 6 The king cried out to the man of **G**, "Please ask the LORD your **G** to restore my hand
13: 6 So the man of **G** prayed to the LORD,
13: 7 Then the king said to the man of **G**, "Come to the
13: 8 But the man of **G** said to the king, "Even if you
13:11 and told him what the man of **G** had done in Bethel
13:12 So they told their father which road the man of **G**
13:14 he rode after the man of **G** and found him sitting
13:14 "Are you the man of **G** who came from Judah?"
13:15 Then he said to the man of **G**, "Come home with
13:19 and the man of **G** ate some food and drank some
13:21 He cried out to the man of **G** from Judah, "This is
13:21 the command the LORD your **G** gave you.
13:23 Now after the man of **G** had finished eating
13:24 and the man of **G** started off again. But as he was
13:26 "It is the man of **G** who disobeyed the LORD's
13:29 So the prophet laid the body of the man of **G** on
13:31 bury me in the grave where the man of **G** is buried.
14: 7 this message from the LORD, the **G** of Israel:
14:13 the **G** of Israel, sees in the entire family of
15: 3 and his heart was not right with the LORD his **G**,
15: 4 the LORD his **G** allowed his dynasty to continue,
15:30 the **G** of Israel, by the sins he had committed
16:13 of the LORD, the **G** of Israel, with their idols.
16:26 aroused the anger of the LORD, the **G** of Israel.
16:33 the **G** of Israel, than any of the other kings of Israel
17: 1 "As surely as the LORD, the **G** of Israel, lives—the **G** whom I worship and serve—
17:12 "I swear by the LORD your **G** that I don't have a
17:14 For this is what the LORD, the **G** of Israel, says:
17:18 She then said to Elijah, "O man of **G**, what have
17:20 Elijah cried out to the LORD, "O LORD my **G**,
17:21 and cried out to the LORD, "O LORD my **G**,
17:24 "Now I know for sure that you are a man of **G**,
18:10 For I swear by the LORD your **G** that the king
18:21 If the LORD is **G**, follow him! But if Baal is **G**, then follow him!"
18:24 Then call on the name of your **g**, and I will call on
18:24 The **g** who answers by setting fire to the wood is the true **G**!"
18:25 and prepare it and call on the name of your **g**.
18:27 to shout louder," he scoffed, "for surely he is a **g**!
18:36 "O LORD, **G** of Abraham, Isaac, and Jacob,
18:36 prove today that you are **G** in Israel and that I am
18:37 are **G** and that you have brought them back to
18:39 on their faces and cried out, "The LORD is **G**! The LORD is **G**!"
19: 8 forty nights to Mount Sinai, the mountain of **G**.
19:10 "I have zealously served the LORD **G** Almighty.
19:14 "I have zealously served the LORD **G** Almighty.
20:28 Then the man of **G** went to the king of Israel
20:28 The Arameans have said that the LORD is a **g** of
21:10 two scoundrels who will accuse him of cursing **G**
21:13 accused him before all the people of cursing **G**
22:53 the **G** of Israel, just as his father had done.
2Ki 1: 2 the **g** of Ekron, to ask whether he would recover.
1: 3 'Why are you going to Baal-zebub, the **g** of Ekron,
1: 3 the king will get well? Is there no **G** in Israel?
1: 6 'Why are you going to Baal-zebub, the **g** of Ekron,
1: 6 Is there no **G** in Israel? Now, since you have done
1: 9 The captain said to him, "Man of **G**, the king has
1:10 "If I am a man of **G**, let fire come down from
1:11 The captain said to him, "Man of **G**, the king says
1:12 Elijah replied, "If I am a man of **G**, let fire come
1:12 And again the fire of **G** fell from heaven and killed
1:13 "O man of **G**, please spare my life and the lives of
1:16 the **g** of Ekron, to ask whether you will get well?
1:16 Is there no **G** in Israel? Now, since you have done
2:14 "Where is the LORD, the **G** of Elijah?"
4: 7 When she told the man of **G** what had happened,
4: 9 who stops in from time to time is a holy man of **G**.
4:16 "Please don't lie to me like that, O man of **G**."
4:21 She carried him up to the bed of the man of **G**,
4:22 and a donkey so that I can hurry to the man of **G**
4:25 As she approached the man of **G** at Mount Carmel,
4:27 But when she came to the man of **G** at the
4:27 but the man of **G** said, "Leave her alone.
4:40 had eaten a bite or two they cried out, "Man of **G**,
4:42 brought the man of **G** a sack of fresh grain
5: 7 leper to heal! Am I **G**, that I can kill and give life?
5: 8 But when Elisha, the man of **G**, heard about the
5:11 and call on the name of the LORD his **G** and heal
5:14 seven times, as the man of **G** had instructed him.
5:15 his entire party went back to find the man of **G**.
5:15 "I know at last that there is no **G** in all the world
5:17 or sacrifices to any other **g** except the LORD.
5:18 into the temple of the **g** Rimmon to worship there
6: 6 "Where did it fall?" the man of **G** asked. When he
6: 9 But immediately Elisha, the man of **G**, would warn
6:10 send word to the place indicated by the man of **G**,
6:15 When the servant of the man of **G** got up early the
6:31 "May **G** kill me if I don't execute Elisha son of
7: 2 The officer assisting the king said to the man of **G**,
7:17 So everything happened exactly as the man of **G**
7:18 The man of **G** had said to the king, "By this time
7:19 And the man of **G** had said, "You will see it
8: 2 So the woman did as the man of **G** instructed.
8: 4 talking with Gehazi, the servant of the man of **G**.
8: 7 Someone told the king that the man of **G** had
8: 8 he said to Hazael, "Take a gift to the man of **G**.
8:11 Then the man of **G** started weeping.
9: 6 "This is what the LORD, the **G** of Israel, says:
10:31 of the LORD, the **G** of Israel, with all his heart.
13:19 But the man of **G** was angry with him.
14:25 the Dead Sea, just as the LORD, the **G** of Israel,
16: 2 was pleasing in the sight of the LORD his **G**,
17: 7 other gods, sinning against the LORD their **G**,
17: 9 that were not pleasing to the LORD their **G**.
17:14 and refused to believe in the LORD their **G**.
17:16 defied all the commands of the LORD their **G**
17:19 to obey the commands of the LORD their **G**.
17:26 do not know how to worship the **G** of the land.
17:27 the religious customs of the **G** of the land."
17:30 Those from Babylon worshiped idols of their **g**
17:30 Those from Cuthah worshiped their **g** Nergal.
17:39 You must worship only the LORD your **G**.
18: 5 Hezekiah trusted in the LORD, the **G** of Israel.
18:12 they had refused to listen to the LORD their **G**.
18:22 will say, 'We are trusting in the LORD our **G**!'
18:35 What **g** of any nation has ever been able to save its
19: 4 But perhaps the LORD your **G** has heard the
19: 4 the Assyrian representative defying the living **G**
19:10 Don't let this **G** you trust deceive you with
19:15 "O LORD, **G** of Israel, you are enthroned
19:15 You alone are **G** of all the kingdoms of the earth.
19:16 words of defiance against the living **G**.
19:19 Now, O LORD our **G**, rescue us from his power;
19:19 earth will know that you alone, O LORD, are **G**."
19:20 "This is what the LORD, the **G** of Israel, says:
19:37 he was worshiping in the temple of his **g** Nisroch,
20: 5 the LORD, the **G** of your ancestor David, says:
21:12 So this is what the LORD, the **G** of Israel, says:
21:22 He abandoned the LORD, the **G** of his ancestors,
22:15 "The LORD, the **G** of Israel, has spoken!
22:18 'This is what the LORD, the **G** of Israel,
23:13 and for Chemosh, the detestable **g** of the Moabites;
23:13 for Molech, the detestable **g** of the Ammonites.
23:16 **G** as Jeroboam stood beside the altar at the
23:16 and looked up at the tomb of the man of **G** who
23:17 "It is the tomb of the man of **G** who came from
23:21 must celebrate the Passover to the LORD your **G**,
1Ch 4:10 He was the one who prayed to the **G** of Israel,
4:10 and pain!" And **G** granted him his request.
5:20 They cried out to **G** during the battle, and he
5:22 in the battle because **G** was fighting against them.
5:25 and violated their covenant with the **G** of their
5:25 They worshiped the gods of the nations that **G** had
5:26 So the **G** of Israel caused King Pul of Assyria (also
6:48 other tasks in the Tabernacle, the house of **G**.
6:49 that Moses, the servant of **G**, had given them.
9:11 Azariah was the chief officer of the house of **G**.
9:13 were responsible for ministering at the house of **G**.
9:26 for the rooms and treasuries at the house of **G**.
9:27 would spend the night around the house of **G**,
11: 2 And the LORD your **G** has told you, 'You will be
11:19 "**G** forbid that I should drink this!" he exclaimed.
12:17 then may the **G** of our ancestors see and judge
12:18 help you, / for your **G** is the one who helps you."
12:22 until he had a great army, like the army of **G**.
13: 2 and if it is the will of the LORD our **G**,
13: 3 It is time to bring back the Ark of our **G**, for we
13: 5 to join in bringing the Ark of **G** from
13: 6 to bring back the Ark of **G**, which bears the name
13: 7 They transported the Ark of **G** from the house of
13: 8 and all Israel were celebrating before **G** with all
13:10 the Ark. So Uzzah died there in the presence of **G**.
13:12 David was now afraid of **G** and asked, "How can I ever bring the Ark of **G** back into my
13:14 The Ark of **G** remained there with the family of
14:10 So David asked **G**, "Should I go out to fight the
14:11 "**G** has done it!" David exclaimed.
14:14 And once again David asked **G** what to do.
14:14 "Do not attack them straight on," **G** replied.
14:15 That will be the signal that **G** is moving ahead of
14:16 So David did what **G** commanded, and he struck
15: 1 He also prepared a place for the Ark of **G** and set
15: 2 "When we transport the Ark of **G** this time,
15:12 the **G** of Israel, to the place I have prepared for it.
15:13 the anger of the LORD our **G** burst out against us.
15:13 We failed to ask **G** how to move it in the proper
15:14 Ark of the LORD, the **G** of Israel, to Jerusalem.
15:15 Then the Levites carried the Ark of **G** on their
15:24 trumpets as they marched in front of the Ark of **G**.
15:26 because **G** was clearly helping the Levites as they
16: 1 So they brought the Ark of **G** into the special tent
16: 1 burnt offerings and peace offerings before **G**.
16: 4 and praise to the LORD, the **G** of Israel.
16:14 He is the LORD our **G**. / His rule is seen
16:35 Cry out, "Save us, O **G** of our salvation! / Gather
16:36 Blessed be the LORD, the **G** of Israel,
16:42 instruments to accompany the songs of praise to **G**.
17: 2 with what you have in mind, for **G** is with you."
17: 3 But that same night **G** said to Nathan,
17:16 the LORD and prayed, "Who am I, O LORD **G**,
17:17 And now, O **G**, in addition to everything else,
17:17 though I were someone very great, O LORD **G**!
17:20 there is no one like you—there is no other **G**.
17:20 We have never even heard of another **g** like you!
17:21 What other nation, O **G**, have you redeemed from
17:22 and you, O LORD, have become their **G**.
17:24 will say, 'The LORD Almighty is **G** over Israel!'
17:25 "O my **G**, I have been bold enough to pray this
17:26 For you are **G**, O LORD. And you have promised
19:13 bravely to save our people and the cities of our **G**.
21: 7 **G** was very displeased with the census, and he
21: 8 Then David said to **G**, "I have sinned greatly
21:15 And **G** sent an angel to destroy Jerusalem. But just
21:17 And David said to **G**, "I am the one who called for
21:17 O LORD my **G**, let your anger fall against me
21:30 But David was not able to go there to inquire of **G**,
22: 1 be the location for the Temple of the LORD **G**
22: 2 blocks of stone for building the Temple of **G**.
22: 6 to build a Temple for the LORD, the **G** of Israel.
22: 7 Temple to honor the name of the LORD my **G**,"
22:11 in building the Temple of the LORD your **G**.
22:12 that you may obey the law of the LORD your **G**
22:18 "The LORD your **G** is with you," he declared.
22:19 Now seek the LORD your **G** with all your heart.
22:19 Build the sanctuary of the LORD **G** so that you
22:19 and the holy vessels of **G** into the Temple built to
23:14 As for Moses, the man of **G**, his sons were
23:25 For David said, "The LORD, the **G** of Israel,
23:28 and served in many other ways in the house of **G**.
24: 5 for there were many qualified officials serving **G**
24:19 to the commands of the LORD, the **G** of Israel.
25: 5 for **G** had honored him with fourteen sons
25: 6 of cymbals, lyres, and harps at the house of **G**.
26: 5 (the eighth). **G** had richly blessed Obed-edom.
26:20 were in charge of the treasuries of the house of **G**
26:32 for all matters related to the things of **G**
27:24 because the anger of **G** broke out against Israel.
28: 3 but **G** said to me, 'You must not build a temple to
28: 4 "Yet the LORD, the **G** of Israel, has chosen me
28: 8 So now, with **G** as our witness, I give you this
28: 8 to obey all the commands of the LORD your **G**,
28: 9 my son, get to know the **G** of your ancestors.
28:20 the task, for the LORD **G**, my **G**, is with you.
28:21 and Levites will serve in the Temple of **G**.
29: 1 whom **G** has chosen to be the next king of Israel,
29: 1 another building—it is for the LORD **G** himself!
29: 2 much as I could for building the Temple of my **G**.
29: 3 because of my devotion to the Temple of my **G**,
29: 7 For the construction of the Temple of **G**, they gave
29:10 "O LORD, the **G** of our ancestor Israel, may you
29:13 "O our **G**, we thank you and praise your glorious
29:16 "O LORD our **G**, even these materials that we
29:17 I know, my **G**, that you examine our hearts
29:18 the **G** of our ancestors Abraham, Isaac, and Israel,
29:20 "Give praise to the LORD your **G**!"
29:20 the **G** of their ancestors, and they bowed low
2Ch 1: 1 for the LORD his **G** was with him and made him
1: 4 David had already moved the Ark of **G** from
1: 7 That night **G** appeared to Solomon in a dream
1: 8 Solomon replied to **G**, "You have been so faithful
1: 9 Now, LORD **G**, please keep your promise to
1:11 **G** said to Solomon, "Because your greatest desire
2: 4 a Temple to honor the name of the LORD my **G**.
2: 4 the other appointed festivals of the LORD our **G**.
2: 5 because our **G** is an awesome **G**,
2:12 the **G** of Israel, who made the heavens
3: 3 The foundation for the Temple of **G** was ninety
4:11 had assigned him to make for the Temple of **G**:
4:19 made all the furnishings for the Temple of **G**:
5: 1 were stored in the treasuries of the Temple of **G**.
5:14 presence of the LORD filled the Temple of **G**.
6: 4 "Blessed be the LORD, the **G** of Israel, who has
6: 7 to honor the name of the LORD, the **G** of Israel.
6:10 to honor the name of the LORD, the **G** of Israel.
6:14 He prayed, "O LORD, **G** of Israel, there is no **G** like you in all of heaven and earth.
6:16 And now, O LORD, **G** of Israel, carry out your
6:17 Now, O LORD, **G** of Israel, fulfill this promise to
6:18 "But will **G** really live on earth among people?
6:19 to my prayer and my request, O LORD my **G**.
6:40 "O my **G**, be attentive to all the prayers made to
6:41 O LORD **G**, arise and enter this resting place
6:41 May your priests, O LORD **G**, be clothed with
6:42 O LORD **G**, do not reject your anointed one.
7: 5 and all the people dedicated the Temple of **G**.
7:22 the **G** of their ancestors, who brought them out of
8:14 following the commands of David, the man of **G**.
9: 8 The LORD your **G** is great indeed! He delights in
9: 8 Because **G** loves Israel so much and desires this
9:23 visit him and to hear the wisdom **G** had given him.
10:15 This turn of events was the will of **G**, for it
11: 2 But the LORD said to Shemaiah, the man of **G**,
11:16 the **G** of Israel, followed the Levites to Jerusalem,
11:16 sacrifices to the LORD, the **G** of their ancestors.
13: 5 Don't you realize that the LORD, the **G** of Israel,
13:10 "But as for us, the LORD is our **G**, and we have
13:11 following the instructions of the LORD our **G**,
13:12 So you see, **G** is with us. He is our leader.
13:12 the **G** of your ancestors, for you will not succeed!"
13:15 **G** defeated Jeroboam and the Israelite army
13:16 and **G** handed them over to Judah in defeat.
13:18 trusted in the LORD, the **G** of their ancestors.
14: 2 and good in the sight of the LORD his **G**.
14: 4 the **G** of their ancestors, and to obey his law
14: 7 land is ours because we sought the LORD our **G**,
14:11 Then Asa cried out to the LORD his **G**,
14:11 Help us, O LORD our **G**, for we trust in you
14:11 O LORD, you are our **G**; do not let mere men
15: 1 Then the Spirit of **G** came upon Azariah son of
15: 3 For a long time, Israel was without the true **G**,
15: 4 the **G** of Israel, and sought him out, you found
15: 6 for **G** was troubling you with every kind of
15: 9 they saw that the LORD his **G** was with him.

15:12 the **G** of their ancestors, with all their heart
15:13 the **G** of Israel, would be put to death—
15:15 Eagerly they sought after **G**, and they found him.
15:18 He brought into the Temple of **G** the silver
16: 7 the king of Aram instead of in the LORD your **G**,
17: 4 He sought his father's **G** and obeyed his
18: 5 "Go ahead, for **G** will give you a great victory!"
18:13 I will say only what my **G** tells me to say."
18:31 and **G** helped him by turning the attack away from
19: 3 and you have committed yourself to seeking **G**."
19: 4 to return to the LORD, the **G** of their ancestors.
19: 7 for the LORD our **G** does not tolerate perverted
20: 6 He prayed, "O LORD, **G** of our ancestors,
20: 6 you alone are the **G** who is in heaven.
20: 7 O our **G**, did you not drive out those who lived in
20:12 O our **G**, won't you stop them? We are powerless
20:19 the **G** of Israel, with a very loud shout.
20:20 Believe in the LORD your **G**, and you will be
20:29 enemies of Israel, the fear of **G** came over them.
20:30 for his **G** had given him rest on every side.
20:33 themselves to following the **G** of their ancestors.
21:10 had abandoned the LORD, the **G** of his ancestors.
21:12 the LORD, the **G** of your ancestor David, says:
22: 7 for **G** had decided to punish Ahaziah.
22:12 Joash remained hidden in the Temple of **G** for six
23: 3 They all gathered at the Temple of **G**, where they
23: 9 to King David and were stored in the Temple of **G**.
24: 5 so that we can repair the Temple of your **G**.
24: 7 wicked Athaliah had broken into the Temple of **G**,
24: 9 the servant of **G**, had required of the Israelites in
24:13 They restored the Temple of **G** according to its
24:16 so much good in Israel for **G** and his Temple.
24:18 the **G** of their ancestors, and they worshiped
24:18 Then the anger of **G** burned against Judah
24:20 Then the Spirit of **G** came upon Zechariah son of
24:20 before the people and said, "This is what **G** says:
24:24 the **G** of their ancestors, so judgment was executed
24:27 **G** are written in *The Commentary on the Book of*
25: 7 But a man of **G** came to the king and said,
25: 8 **G** will overthrow you, for he has the power to help
25: 9 Amaziah asked the man of **G**, "But what should I
25: 9 The man of **G** replied, "The LORD is able to
25:16 "I know that **G** has determined to destroy you
25:20 for **G** was arranging to destroy him for worshiping
25:24 and all the utensils from the Temple of **G** that had
26: 5 Uzziah sought **G** during the days of Zechariah,
who instructed him in the fear of **G**.
26: 5 the king sought the LORD, **G** gave him success.
26: 7 **G** helped him not only with his wars against the
26:16 He sinned against the LORD his **G** by entering
26:18 The LORD **G** will not honor you for this!"
27: 6 careful to live in obedience to the LORD his **G**.
28: 5 That is why the LORD his **G** allowed the king of
28: 6 abandoned the LORD, the **G** of their ancestors.
28: 9 and said, "The LORD, the **G** of your ancestors,
28:10 about your own sins against the LORD your **G**?
28:24 The king took the utensils from the Temple of **G**
28:25 the anger of the LORD, the **G** of his ancestors.
29: 5 Temple of the LORD, the **G** of your ancestors.
29: 6 what was evil in the sight of the LORD our **G**.
29: 7 burnt offerings at the sanctuary of the **G** of Israel.
29:10 the **G** of Israel, so that his fierce anger will turn
29:36 because of what **G** had done for the people,
30: 1 the Passover of the LORD, the **G** of Israel.
30: 5 the Passover of the LORD, the **G** of Israel.
30: 6 the LORD, the **G** of Abraham, Isaac, and Israel,
30: 7 the **G** of their ancestors, and became an object of
30: 8 Worship the LORD your **G** so that his fierce
30: 9 For the LORD your **G** is gracious and merciful.
30:16 found in the law of Moses, the man of **G**.
30:19 to follow the LORD, the **G** of their ancestors,
30:22 their sins to the LORD, the **G** of their ancestors.
30:27 and **G** heard them from his holy dwelling in
31: 6 that had been dedicated to the LORD their **G**,
31:13 and Azariah, the chief official in the Temple of **G**.
31:14 charge of distributing the freewill offerings of **G**,
31:20 and good in the sight of the LORD his **G**.
31:21 In all that he did in the service of the Temple of **G**
31:21 Hezekiah sought his **G** wholeheartedly.
32: 8 We have the LORD our **G** to help us and to fight
32:11 'The LORD our **G** will rescue us from the king of
32:14 Name just one time when any **g**, anywhere,
32:14 What makes you think your **G** can do any better?
32:15 no **g** of any nation has ever yet been able to rescue
32:15 How much less will your **G** rescue you from my
32:16 officials further mocked the LORD **G**
32:17 sent letters scorning the LORD, the **G** of Israel.
32:17 my power, so the **G** of Hezekiah will also fail."
32:19 These officials talked about the **G** of Jerusalem as
32:20 son of Amoz cried out in prayer to **G** in heaven.
32:21 And when he entered the temple of his **g**, some of
32:29 and herds, for **G** had given him great wealth.
32:31 **G** withdrew from Hezekiah in order to test him
33: 7 the very place where **G** had told David and his son
33:12 Manasseh sought the LORD his **G** and cried out
humbly to the **G** of his ancestors.
33:13 had finally realized that the LORD alone is **G**!
33:16 of Judah to worship the LORD, the **G** of Israel.
33:17 the pagan shrines, but only to the LORD their **G**.
33:18 of the events of Manasseh's reign, his prayer to **G**,
33:18 the **G** of Israel, are recorded in *The Book of the*
33:19 the account of the way **G** answered him,
34: 3 Josiah began to seek the **G** of his ancestor David.
34: 8 to repair the Temple of the LORD his **G**.
34: 9 who served as gatekeepers at the Temple of **G**.
34:23 "The LORD, the **G** of Israel, has spoken!
34:26 'This is what the LORD, the **G** of Israel,
34:27 and humbled yourself before **G** when you heard
34:32 they renewed their covenant with **G**, the **G** of their
ancestors.
34:33 required everyone to worship the LORD their **G**.
34:33 away from the LORD, the **G** of their ancestors.
35: 3 spend your time serving the LORD your **G**
35:21 And **G** has told me to hurry! Do not interfere with
G, who is with me, or he will
35:22 to whom **G** had indeed spoken, and he would not
36: 5 did what was evil in the sight of the LORD his **G**.
36:12 did what was evil in the sight of the LORD his **G**,
36:13 refusing to turn to the LORD, the **G** of Israel.
36:15 The LORD, the **G** of their ancestors,
36:16 But the people mocked these messengers of **G**
36:17 **G** handed them all over to Nebuchadnezzar.
36:18 large and small, used in the Temple of **G**,
36:19 Then his army set fire to the Temple of **G**,
36:23 The LORD, the **G** of heaven, has given me all the
36:23 this task. May the LORD your **G** be with you!"
Ezr 1: 2 The LORD, the **G** of heaven, has given me all the
1: 3 the **G** of Israel, who lives in Jerusalem. And may
your **G** be with you!
1: 4 as well as a freewill offering for the Temple of **G**
1: 5 Then **G** stirred the hearts of the priests and Levites
3: 2 family began to rebuild the altar of the **G** of Israel
3: 2 as instructed in the law of Moses, the man of **G**.
3: 8 The construction of the Temple of **G** began in
3: 9 The workers at the Temple of **G** were supervised
4: 1 a Temple to the LORD, the **G** of Israel.
4: 2 with you, for we worship your **G** just as you do.
4: 3 the **G** of Israel, just as King Cyrus of Persia
4:24 The work on the Temple of **G** in Jerusalem had
5: 1 in the name of the **G** of Israel to the Jews in Judah
5: 2 task of rebuilding the Temple of **G** in Jerusalem.
5: 2 And the prophets of **G** were with them and helped
5: 5 But because their **G** was watching over them,
5: 8 the Temple of the great **G** in the province of Judah.
5:11 'We are the servants of the **G** of heaven and earth,
5:12 because our ancestors angered the **G** of heaven,
5:13 issued a decree that the Temple of **G** should be
5:14 had taken from the Temple of **G** in Jerusalem
5:15 and to rebuild the Temple of **G** there as it had been
5:16 and laid the foundations of the Temple of **G** in
6: 3 a decree was sent out concerning the Temple of **G**
6: 5 from the Temple of **G** in Jerusalem,
6: 7 not disturb the construction of the Temple of **G**.
6: 8 of the Jews as they rebuild this Temple of **G**.
6: 9 the burnt offerings presented to the **G** of heaven.
6:10 to offer acceptable sacrifices to the **G** of heaven
6:12 May the **G** who has chosen the city of Jerusalem as
6:14 as had been commanded by the **G** of Israel
6:16 The Temple of **G** was then dedicated with great
6:17 the dedication ceremony for the Temple of **G**,
6:18 divisions to serve at the Temple of **G** in Jerusalem,
6:21 customs to worship the LORD, the **G** of Israel.
6:22 to rebuild the Temple of **G**, the **G** of Israel.
7: 6 law of Moses, which the LORD, the **G** of Israel,
7: 6 because the gracious hand of the LORD his **G**
7: 9 for the gracious hand of his **G** was on him.
7:12 the teacher of the law of the **G** of heaven.
7:15 offering to the **G** of Israel who lives in Jerusalem.
7:16 presented for the Temple of their **G** in Jerusalem.
7:17 on the altar of the Temple of your **G** in Jerusalem.
7:18 and your colleagues feel is the will of your **G**.
7:19 to you for the service of the Temple of your **G**,
7:19 deliver them in full to the **G** of Jerusalem.
7:21 a priest and teacher of the law of the **G** of heaven.
7:23 Be careful to provide whatever the **G** of heaven
7:24 or other worker in this Temple of **G** will be
7:25 are to use the wisdom **G** has given you to appoint
7:26 Anyone who refuses to obey the law of your **G**
7:27 Praise the LORD, the **G** of our ancestors,
7:28 because the gracious hand of the LORD my **G**
8:17 us ministers for the Temple of **G** at Jerusalem.
8:18 Since the gracious hand of our **G** was on us,
8:21 all of us to fast and humble ourselves before our **G**.
8:22 "Our **G** protects all those who worship him,
8:23 and earnestly prayed that our **G** would take care of
8:25 people of Israel had presented for the Temple of **G**.
8:28 offering to the LORD, the **G** of our ancestors.
8:30 treasures to the Temple of our **G** in Jerusalem.
8:31 And the gracious hand of our **G** protected us
8:33 valuables were weighed at the Temple of our **G**
8:35 sacrificed burnt offerings to the **G** of Israel.
8:36 by supporting the people and the Temple of **G**.
9: 4 Then all who trembled at the words of the **G** of
9: 5 to my knees, lifted my hands to the LORD my **G**.
9: 6 I prayed, "O my **G**, I am utterly ashamed; I blush
9: 8 for the LORD our **G** has allowed a few of us to
9: 8 Our **G** has brightened our eyes and granted us
9: 9 but in his unfailing love our **G** did not abandon us
9: 9 that we were able to rebuild the Temple of our **G**
9:10 "And now, O our **G**, what can we say after all of
9:13 for you, our **G**, have allowed some of us to survive
9:15 O LORD, **G** of Israel, you are just. We stand
10: 1 himself to the ground in front of the Temple of **G**,
10: 2 confess that we have been unfaithful to our **G**,
10: 3 Let us now make a covenant with our **G** to divorce
10: 3 by the others who respect the commands of our **G**.
We will obey the law of **G**.
10: 6 Then Ezra left the front of the Temple of **G**
10: 9 were sitting in the square before the Temple of **G**.
10:11 the **G** of your ancestors, and do what he demands.
10:14 so that the fierce anger of our **G** may be turned
Ne 1: 4 I mourned, fasted, and prayed to the **G** of heaven.
1: 5 **G** of heaven, the great and awesome **G** who keeps
his covenant of
2: 4 can I help you?" With a prayer to the **G** of heaven,
2: 8 because the gracious hand of **G** was on me.
2:12 I had not told anyone about the plans **G** had put in
2:18 Then I told them about how the gracious hand of **G**
2:20 I replied, "The **G** of heaven will help us succeed.
4: 4 Then I prayed, "Hear us, O our **G**, for we are
4: 9 But we prayed to our **G** and guarded the city day
4:15 knew of their plans and that **G** had frustrated them,
4:20 it is sounding. Then our **G** will fight for us!"
5: 9 Should you not walk in the fear of our **G** in order
5:13 may **G** shake you from your homes and from your
5:15 But because of my fear of **G**, I did not act that
5:19 Remember, O my **G**, all that I have done for these
6:10 "Let us meet together inside the Temple of **G**
6:12 I realized that **G** had not spoken to him, but that he
6:14 Remember, O my **G**, all the evil things that Tobiah
6:16 this work had been done with the help of our **G**.
7: 2 for he was a faithful man who feared **G** more than
7: 5 So my **G** gave me the idea to call together all the
8: 6 the great **G**, and all the people chanted, "Amen!
8: 8 They read from the Book of the Law of **G**
8: 9 today is a sacred day before the LORD your **G**."
8:18 Ezra read from the Book of the Law of **G** on each
9: 3 The Book of the Law of the LORD their **G** was
9: 3 their sins and worshiping the LORD their **G**.
9: 4 on the stairs, crying out to the LORD their **G**.
9: 5 "Stand up and praise the LORD your **G**, for he
9: 7 "You are the LORD **G**, who chose Abram
9:17 But you are a **G** of forgiveness, gracious
9:18 'This is your **g** who brought you out of Egypt!'
9:31 What a gracious and merciful **G** you are!
9:32 our **G**, the great and mighty and awesome **G**,
10:28 the pagan people of the land in order to serve **G**,
10:29 They vowed to accept the curse of **G** if they failed
10:29 obey the law of **G** as issued by his servant Moses.
10:32 be enough money to care for the Temple of our **G**.
10:33 necessary for the work of the Temple of our **G**.
10:34 to be burned on the altar of the LORD our **G**,
10:36 We agree to give to **G** our oldest sons
10:36 to the priests who minister in the Temple of our **G**.
10:37 produce in the storerooms of the Temple of our **G**.
10:38 be delivered by the Levites to the Temple of our **G**
10:39 together not to neglect the Temple of our **G**."
11:11 son of Ahitub, the supervisor of the Temple of **G**;
11:16 in charge of the work outside the Temple of **G**;
12:24 just as commanded by David, the man of **G**.
12:36 instruments prescribed by David, the man of **G**.
12:40 giving thanks then proceeded to the Temple of **G**,
12:43 for **G** had given the people cause for great joy.
12:45 They performed the service of their **G**
12:46 and thanks to **G** began long ago in the days of
13: 1 ever be permitted to enter the assembly of **G**.
13: 2 though our **G** turned the curse into a blessing.
13: 4 of the storerooms of the Temple of our **G**
13: 7 a room in the courtyards of the Temple of **G**—
13:11 "Why has the Temple of **G** been neglected?"
13:14 Remember this good deed, O my **G**, and do not
13:14 that I have faithfully done for the Temple of my **G**.
13:18 so that our **G** brought the present troubles upon us
13:22 Remember this good deed also, O my **G**!
13:25 I made them swear before **G** that they would not
13:26 and **G** loved him and made him king over all
13:27 and acting unfaithfully toward **G** by marrying
13:29 Remember them, O my **G**, for they have defiled
13:31 the priests. / Remember this in my favor, O my **G**.
Job 1: 1 He feared **G** and stayed away from evil.
1: 5 have sinned and have cursed **G** in their hearts."
1: 8 He fears **G** and will have nothing to do with evil."
1: 9 Satan replied to the LORD, "Yes, Job fears **G**,
1:16 "The fire of **G** has fallen from heaven and burned
1:20 he shaved his head and fell to the ground before **G**.
1:22 In all of this, Job did not sin by blaming **G**.
2: 3 He fears **G** and will have nothing to do with evil.
2: 9 to maintain your integrity? Curse **G** and die."
2:10 we accept only good things from the hand of **G**
3: 4 Let it be lost even to **G** on high, and let it be
3:23 no future, those destined by **G** to live in distress?
4: 3 encouraged many a troubled soul to trust in **G**;
4: 6 Does your reverence for **G** give you no
4: 6 Shouldn't you believe that **G** will care for those
4: 9 They perish by a breath from **G**. They vanish in a
4:17 'Can a mortal be just and upright before **G**?
4:18 "If **G** cannot trust his own angels and has charged
5: 3 I know that fools who turn from **G** may be
5: 8 you is this: Go to **G** and present your case to him.
5:17 "But consider the joy of those corrected by **G**!
6: 8 have my request, that **G** would grant my hope.
7: 7 O **G**, remember that my life is but a breath, and I
8: 3 Does **G** twist justice? Does the Almighty twist
8: 5 But if you pray to **G** and seek the favor of the
8:13 Such is the fate of all who forget **G**. The hope of
8:20 **G** will not reject a person of integrity, nor will he
9: 2 a person be declared innocent in the eyes of **G**?
9: 3 If someone wanted to take **G** to court, would it be
9: 4 For **G** is so wise and so mighty. Who has ever
9:13 And **G** does not restrain his anger. The mightiest
9:14 that I should try to answer **G** or even reason with
9:24 and **G** blinds the eyes of the judges and lets them
9:28 For I know you will not hold me innocent, O **G**.
9:32 "**G** is not a mortal like me, so I cannot argue with
9:34 The mediator could make **G** stop beating me,
10: 2 I will say to **G**, 'Don't simply condemn me—
11: 3 When you mock **G**, shouldn't someone make you
11: 4 is pure,' and 'I am clean in the sight of **G**.'
11: 5 If only **G** would speak; if only he would tell you
11: 6 **G** is doubtless punishing you far less than you
11: 7 "Can you solve the mysteries of **G**? Can you

11:10 If **G** comes along and puts a person in prison,
12: 4 I am a man who calls on **G** and receives an answer.
12: 6 are left in peace, and those who provoke **G**—
12: 6 and **G** has them in his power—live in safety!
12:13 "But true wisdom and power are with **G**; counsel
13: 3 I want to argue my case with **G** himself.
13: 7 "Are you defending **G** by means of lies
13:15 **G** might kill me, but I cannot wait. I am going to
13:20 "O **G**, there are two things I beg of you, and I will
15: 4 Have you no fear of **G**, no reverence for him?
15:13 that you turn against **G** and say all these evil
15:15 Why, **G** doesn't even trust the angels!
15:25 For they have clenched their fists against **G**,
15:30 and the breath of **G** will destroy everything they
16: 7 "O **G**, you have ground me down and devastated
16: 9 **G** hates me and tears angrily at my flesh.
16:11 **G** has handed me over to sinners. He has tossed me
16:20 My friends scorn me, but I pour out my tears to **G**.
16:21 that someone would mediate between **G** and me,
17: 3 "You must defend my innocence, O **G**, since no
17: 6 "**G** has made a mockery of me among the people;
18:21 the place of one who rejected **G**.' "
19: 6 but it is **G** who has wronged me. I cannot defend
19: 8 **G** has blocked my way and plunged my path into
19:21 have mercy, for the hand of **G** has struck me.
19:22 Why must you persecute me as **G** does?
19:26 my body has decayed, yet in my body I will see **G**!
20:15 he swallowed. **G** won't let him keep it down.
20:23 May **G** give him a bellyful of trouble. May **G** rain
down his anger upon him.
20:29 the wicked. It is the inheritance decreed by **G**."
21: 4 "My complaint is with **G**, not with people.
21: 9 safe from every fear, and **G** does not punish them.
21:14 All this, even though they say to **G**, 'Go away.
21:17 and **G** skips them when he distributes sorrows in
21:19 you say, 'at least **G** will punish their children!'
21:19 But I say that **G** should punish the ones who sin,
21:22 "But who can teach a lesson to **G**, the supreme
22: 2 "Can a person's actions be of benefit to **G**?
22:12 "**G** is so great—higher than the heavens,
22:13 'That's why **G** can't see what I am doing!
22:17 For they said to **G**, 'Leave us alone! What can the
22:21 "Stop quarreling with **G**! If you agree with him,
22:26 delight yourself in the Almighty and look up to **G**.
22:29 you say, 'Help him up,' **G** will save the downcast.
23: 3 If only I knew where to find **G**, I would go to his
23:16 **G** has made my heart faint; the Almighty has
24:12 for help, yet **G** does not respond to their moaning.
24:22 "**G**, in his power, drags away the rich. They may
24:23 to live in security, but **G** is always watching them.
25: 2 "**G** is powerful and dreadful. He enforces peace in
25: 4 How can a mere mortal stand before **G** and claim
25: 5 **G** is so glorious that even the moon and stars
26: 7 **G** stretches the northern sky over empty space
27: 2 "I make this vow by the living **G**, who has taken
27: 3 As long as I live, while I have breath from **G**,
27: 8 For what hope do the godless have when **G** cuts
27: 9 Will **G** listen to their cry when trouble comes upon
27:10 in the Almighty? Can they call to **G** at any time?
27:13 "This is what the wicked will receive from **G**;
28:23 "**G** surely knows where it can be found,
29: 2 "I long for the years gone by when **G** took care of
29: 4 the friendship of **G** was felt in my home.
30:11 For **G** has cut the cords of my tent. He has
30:18 With a strong hand, **G** grabs my garment. He grips
30:20 "I cry to you, O **G**, but you don't answer me.
31: 2 What has **G** above chosen for us? What is our
31: 6 Let **G** judge me on the scales of justice, for he
31:14 how could I face **G**? What could I say when he
31:15 For **G** created both me and my servants.
31:23 be better than facing the judgment sent by **G**.
31:23 For if the majesty of **G** opposes me, what hope is
31:28 for it would mean I had denied the **G** of heaven.
32: 2 had sinned and that **G** was right in punishing him.
32: 3 because they had condemned **G** by their inability
32:13 'He is too wise for us. Only **G** can convince him.'
33: 4 For the Spirit of **G** has made me, and the breath of
33: 6 "Look, you and I are the same before **G**. I, too,
33:10 **G** is picking a quarrel with me, and he considers
33:12 yourself have said, '**G** is greater than any person.'
33:14 But **G** speaks again and again, though people do
33:19 Or **G** disciplines people with sickness and pain,
33:24 **G** will be gracious and say, 'Set him free. Do not
33:26 When he prays to **G**, he will be accepted. And **G**
will receive him with joy and restore him to
33:28 **G** rescued me from the grave, and now my life is
33:29 "Yes, **G** often does these things for people.
34: 5 'I am innocent, but **G** has taken away my rights.
34: 9 even said, 'Why waste time trying to please **G**?'
34:10 Everyone knows that **G** doesn't sin!
34:12 **G** will not do wrong. The Almighty cannot twist
34:14 If **G** were to take back his spirit and withdraw his
34:17 Could **G** govern if he hated justice? Are you going
34:21 "For **G** carefully watches the way people live;
34:23 to decide when to come before **G** in judgment.
34:31 "Why don't people say to **G**, 'I have sinned,
34:33 "Must **G** tailor his justice to your demands?
34:37 and blasphemy against **G** to your other sins."
35: 2 right for you to claim, 'I am righteous before **G**'?
35:10 Yet they don't ask, 'Where is **G** my Creator,
35:12 "And if they do cry out and **G** does not answer,
35:13 But it is wrong to say **G** doesn't listen, to say the
36: 2 I am saying. For I have not finished defending **G**!
36: 5 "**G** is mighty, yet he does not despise anyone!
36:11 "If they listen and obey **G**, then they will be
36:16 "**G** has led you away from danger, giving you
36:21 getting into a life of evil that **G** sent this suffering.
36:22 "Look, **G** is all-powerful. Who is a teacher like
36:26 **G** is exalted beyond what we can understand.
37:14 stop and consider the wonderful miracles of **G**!
37:15 Do you know how **G** controls the storm and causes
37:19 so much, so teach the rest of us what to say to **G**.
37:20 Should **G** be told that I want to speak? Can we
37:22 Golden splendor comes from the mountain of **G**.
38:33 the laws of the universe and how **G** rules the earth?
38:41 cry out to **G** as they wander about in hunger?
39:17 for **G** has deprived her of wisdom. He has given
40: 9 Are you as strong as **G**, and can you thunder with a
Ps 3: 2 So many are saying, / "**G** will never rescue him!"
3: 7 Arise, O LORD! / Rescue me, my **G**! / Slap all
4: 1 me when I call, / O **G** who declares me innocent.
5: 2 Listen to my cry for help, my King and my **G**,
5: 4 O **G**, you take no pleasure in wickedness;
5:10 O **G**, declare them guilty. / Let them be caught in
7: 1 I come to you for protection, O LORD my **G**.
7: 3 O LORD my **G**, if I have done wrong / or am
7: 6 my enemies! / Wake up, my **G**, and bring justice!
7: 9 deep within the mind and heart, / O righteous **G**.
7:10 **G** is my shield, / saving those whose hearts are true
7:11 **G** is a judge who is perfectly fair. / He is angry
7:12 person does not repent, / **G** will sharpen his sword;
8: 5 For you made us only a little lower than **G**,
9:17 This is the fate of all the nations who ignore **G**.
10: 4 These wicked people are too proud to seek **G**. /
They seem to think that **G** is dead.
10:11 The wicked say to themselves, "**G** isn't watching!
10:12 Arise, O LORD! / Punish the wicked, O **G**!
10:13 Why do the wicked get away with cursing **G**?
10:13 can they think, "**G** will never call us to account"?
13: 3 Turn and answer me, O LORD my **G**!
14: 1 Only fools say in their hearts, / "There is no **G**."
14: 2 with real understanding, / one who seeks for **G**.
14: 3 But no, all have turned away from **G**; / all have
14: 5 will grip them, / for **G** is with those who obey him.
16: 1 Keep me safe, O **G**, / for I have come to you for
17: 6 to you because I know you will answer, O **G**.
18: 2 my **G** is my rock, in whom I find protection.
18: 6 to the LORD; / yes, I prayed to my **G** for help.
18:21 I have not turned from my **G** to follow evil.
18:23 I am blameless before **G**; / I have kept myself from
18:28 light to my life; / my **G**, you light up my darkness.
18:29 crush an army; / with my **G** I can scale any wall.
18:30 As for **G**, his way is perfect. / All the LORD's
18:31 For who is **G** except the LORD? / Who but our **G** is
a solid rock?
18:32 **G** arms me with strength; / he has made my way
18:46 my rock! / May the **G** of my salvation be exalted!
18:47 He is the **G** who pays back those who harm me;
19: 1 The heavens tell of the glory of **G**. / The skies
19: 4 The sun lives in the heavens / where **G** placed it.
20: 1 May the **G** of Israel keep you safe from all harm.
20: 5 of your victory, / flying banners to honor our **G**.
20: 7 and weapons, / but we boast in the LORD our **G**.
22: 1 My **G**, my **G**! Why have you forsaken me?
22: 2 day I call to you, my **G**, but you do not answer.
22:10 You have been my **G** from the moment I was born.
24: 5 and have right standing with **G** their savior.
24: 6 and worship the **G** of Israel. / *Interlude*
25: 2 I trust in you, my **G**! / Do not let me be disgraced,
25: 5 and teach me, / for you are the **G** who saves me.
25:22 O **G**, ransom Israel / from all its troubles.
27: 9 me now; don't abandon me, / O **G** of my salvation!
29: 3 The **G** of glory thunders. / The LORD thunders
30: 2 O LORD my **G**, I cried out to you for help,
30:12 O LORD my **G**, I will give you thanks forever!
31: 5 Rescue me, LORD, for you are a faithful **G**.
31:14 O LORD, / saying, "You are my **G**!"
33:12 What joy for the nation whose **G** is the LORD,
35:23 Take up my case, my **G** and my Lord.
35:24 O LORD my **G**, for you give justice.
36: 1 They have no fear of **G** to restrain them.
36: 7 How precious is your unfailing love, O **G**!
38:15 You must answer for me, O Lord my **G**.
38:21 LORD. / Do not stand at a distance, my **G**.
40: 3 me a new song to sing, / a hymn of praise to our **G**.
40: 5 O LORD my **G**, you have done many miracles
40: 8 I take joy in doing your will, my **G**, / for your law
40:17 my helper and my savior. / Do not delay, O my **G**.
41:13 Bless the LORD, the **G** of Israel, / who lives
42: 1 pants for streams of water, / so I long for you, O **G**.
42: 2 I thirst for **G**, the living **G**. / When can I come
42: 3 taunt me, saying, / "Where is this **G** of yours?"
42: 4 leading a great procession to the house of **G**,
42: 5 Why so sad? / I will put my hope in **G**!
42: 6 my **G**! / Now I am deeply discouraged, / but I will
42: 8 I sing his songs, / praying to **G** who gives me life.
42: 9 "O **G** my rock," I cry, / "Why have you forsaken
42:10 They scoff, "Where is this **G** of yours?"
42:11 Why so sad? / I will put my hope in **G**!
42:11 I will praise him again— / my Savior and my **G**!
43: 1 O **G**, take up my cause! / Defend me against these
43: 2 For you are **G**, my only safe haven. / Why have
43: 4 There I will go to the altar of **G**, / to **G**—the source
of all my joy.
43: 4 I will praise you with my harp, / O **G**, my **G**!
43: 5 Why so sad? / I will put my hope in **G**!
43: 5 I will praise him again— / my Savior and my **G**!
44: 1 O **G**, we have heard it with our own ears—
44: 4 You are my King and my **G**. / You command
44: 8 O **G**, we give glory to you all day long
44:20 If we had turned away from worshiping our **G**
44:21 **G** would surely have known it, / for he knows the
45: 2 your lips. / **G** himself has blessed you forever.
45: 6 Your throne, O **G**, endures forever and ever.
45: 7 Therefore, **G**—your **G**—has anointed you,
46: 1 **G** is our refuge and strength, / always ready to help
46: 4 A river brings joy to the city of our **G**, / the sacred
46: 5 **G** himself lives in that city; it cannot be destroyed.
/ **G** will protect it at the break of day.
46: 6 **G** thunders, / and the earth melts!
46: 7 is here among us; / the **G** of Israel is our fortress.
46:10 "Be silent, and know that I am **G**! / I will be
46:11 is here among us; / the **G** of Israel is our fortress.
47: 1 your hands for joy! / Shout to **G** with joyful praise!
47: 5 **G** has ascended with a mighty shout. / The LORD
47: 6 Sing praise to **G**, sing praises; / sing praise to our
47: 7 For **G** is the King over all the earth. / Praise him
47: 8 **G** reigns above the nations, / sitting on his holy
47: 9 They join us in praising the **G** of Abraham.
47: 9 For all the kings of the earth belong to **G**.
48: 1 in the city of our **G**, / which is on his holy
48: 3 **G** himself is in Jerusalem's towers. / He reveals
48: 8 It is the city of our **G**; / he will make it safe
48: 9 O **G**, we meditate on your unfailing love / as we
48:10 As your name deserves, O **G**, / you will be praised
48:14 For that is what **G** is like. / He is our **G** forever and
ever,
49: 7 themselves from death / by paying a ransom to **G**.
49:15 But as for me, **G** will redeem my life. / He will
50: 1 The mighty **G**, the LORD, has spoken; / he has
50: 2 of beauty, / **G** shines in glorious radiance.
50: 3 Our **G** approaches with the noise of thunder.
50: 6 his justice, / for **G** himself will be the judge.
50: 7 charges against you, O Israel: / I am **G**, your **G**!
50:14 What I want instead is your true thanks to **G**;
50:16 But **G** says to the wicked: / "Recite my laws no
50:23 my path, / I will reveal to you the salvation of **G**."
51: 1 Have mercy on me, O **G**, / because of your
51:10 Create in me a clean heart, O **G**. / Renew a right
51:14 Forgive me for shedding blood, O **G** who saves;
51:17 A broken and repentant heart, O **G**, / you will not
52: 5 But **G** will strike you down once and for all.
52: 7 who do not trust in **G**. / They trust their wealth
52: 8 I am like an olive tree, / thriving in the house of **G**.
52: 9 I will praise you forever, O **G**, / for what you have
53: 1 Only fools say in their hearts, / "There is no **G**."
53: 2 **G** looks down from heaven / on the entire human
53: 2 with real understanding, / one who seeks for **G**.
53: 3 But no, all have turned away from **G**; / all have
53: 4 like bread; / they wouldn't think of praying to **G**.
53: 5 **G** will scatter the bones of your enemies.
53: 5 will put them to shame, for **G** has rejected them.
53: 6 For when **G** restores his people, / Jacob will shout
54: 1 Come with great power, O **G**, and rescue me!
54: 2 O **G**, listen to my prayer. / Pay attention to my
54: 3 to kill me. / They care nothing for **G**. / *Interlude*
54: 4 But **G** is my helper. / The Lord is the one who
55: 1 Listen to my prayer, O **G**. / Do not ignore my cry
55:14 as we walked together to the house of **G**.
55:16 But I will call on **G**, / and the LORD will rescue
55:19 **G**, who is king forever, / will hear me and will
55:19 refuse to change their ways; / they do not fear **G**.
55:23 But you, O **G**, will send the wicked / down to the
56: 1 O **G**, have mercy on me. / The enemy troops press
56: 4 O **G**, I praise your word. / I trust in **G**, so why
should I be afraid?
56: 7 in your anger, O **G**, throw them to the ground.
56: 9 will retreat. / This I know: **G** is on my side.
56:10 O **G**, I praise your word. / Yes, LORD, I praise
56:11 I trust in **G**, so why should I be afraid? / What can
56:12 I will fulfill my vows to you, O **G**, / and offer a
56:13 So now I can walk in your presence, O **G**,
57: 1 Have mercy on me, O **G**, have mercy! / I look to
57: 2 I cry out to **G** Most High, / to **G** who will fulfill
his purpose for me.
57: 3 My **G** will send forth his unfailing love
57: 5 Be exalted, O **G**, above the highest heavens!
57: 7 My heart is confident in you, O **G**; / no wonder I
57:11 Be exalted, O **G**, above the highest heavens.
58: 6 Break off their fangs, O **G**! / Smash the jaws of
58: 9 **G** will sweep them away, both young and old,
58:11 "There truly is a reward for those who live for **G**;
58:11 surely there is a **G** who judges justly here on
59: 1 Rescue me from my enemies, O **G**. / Protect me
59: 5 O LORD **G** Almighty, the **G** of Israel, / rise up
59: 9 rescue me, / for you, O **G**, are my place of safety.
59:10 In his unfailing love, my **G** will come and help me.
59:13 will know / that **G** reigns in Israel. / *Interlude*
59:17 to you I sing praises, / for you, O **G**, are my refuge,
/ the **G** who shows me unfailing love.
60: 1 You have rejected us, O **G**, and broken our
60: 6 **G** has promised this by his holiness: / "I will
60:10 Have you rejected us, O **G**? / Will you no longer
61: 1 O **G**, listen to my cry! / Hear my prayer!
61: 5 For you have heard my vows, O **G**. / You have
62: 1 I wait quietly before **G**, / for my salvation comes
62: 5 I wait quietly before **G**, / for my hope is in him.
62: 7 My salvation and my honor come from **G** alone.
62: 8 Pour out your heart to him, / for **G** is our refuge.
62:11 **G** has spoken plainly, / and I have heard it many
times: / Power, O **G**, belongs to you;
63: 1 O **G**, you are my **G**; / I earnestly search for you.
63:11 But the king will rejoice in **G**. / All who trust in
64: 1 O **G**, listen to my complaint. / Do not let me
64: 7 But **G** himself will shoot them down. / Suddenly,
64: 9 stand in awe, / proclaiming the mighty acts of **G**,
65: 1 What mighty praise, O **G**, / belongs to you in Zion.
65: 5 our prayers with awesome deeds, / O **G** our savior.
65: 9 and fertile. / The rivers of **G** will not run dry;
66: 1 Shout joyful praises to **G**, all the earth!
66: 3 Say to **G**, "How awesome are your deeds!

66: 5 Come and see what our G has done,
66: 8 Let the whole world bless our G / and sing aloud
66:10 You have tested us, O G; / you have purified us
66:16 Come and listen, all you who fear G, / and I will
66:19 But G did listen! / He paid attention to my prayer.
66:20 Praise G, who did not ignore my prayer / and did
67: 1 May G be merciful and bless us. / May his face
67: 3 May the nations praise you, O G. / Yes, may all
67: 5 May the nations praise you, O G. / Yes, may all
67: 6 its harvests, / and G, our G, will richly bless us.
67: 7 Yes, G will bless us, / and people all over the
68: 1 Arise, O G, and scatter your enemies. / Let those who hate G run for their lives.
68: 2 Let the wicked perish in the presence of G.
68: 4 Sing praises to G and to his name! / Sing loud
68: 5 of widows— / this is G, whose dwelling is holy.
68: 6 G places the lonely in families; / he sets the
68: 7 O G, when you led your people from Egypt,
68: 8 before you, the G of Sinai, / before G, the G of Israel.
68: 9 You sent abundant rain, O G, / to refresh the weary
68:10 finally settled, / and with a bountiful harvest, O G,
68:16 at Mount Zion, where G has chosen to live,
68:18 Now the LORD G will live among us here.
68:19 Praise the Lord; praise G our savior! / For each
68:20 Our G is a G who saves! / The Sovereign
68:21 But G will smash the heads of his enemies,
68:24 Your procession has come into view, O G— / the procession of my G and King
68:26 Praise G, all you people of Israel;
68:28 Summon your might, O G. / Display your power, O G, as you have in the past.
68:31 let Ethiopia bow in submission to G.
68:32 Sing to G, you kingdoms of the earth.
68:35 G is awesome in his sanctuary. / The G of Israel gives power and strength to his people. / Praise be to G!
69: 1 Save me, O G, / for the floodwaters are up to my
69: 3 with weeping, / waiting for my G to help me.
69: 5 O G, you know how foolish I am; / my sins cannot
69: 6 let me cause them to be humiliated, / O G of Israel.
69:13 In your unfailing love, O G, / answer my prayer
69:29 in pain. / Rescue me, O G, by your saving power.
69:32 The humble will see their G at work and be glad.
69:35 For G will save Jerusalem / and rebuild the towns
70: 1 Please, G, rescue me! / Come quickly, LORD,
70: 4 your salvation / repeatedly shout, "G is great!"
70: 5 am poor and needy; / please hurry to my aid, O G.
71: 4 My G, rescue me from the power of the wicked,
71:11 They say, "G has abandoned him. / Let's go
71:12 O G, don't stay away. / My G, please hurry to help me.
71:17 O G, you have taught me from my earliest
71:18 that I am old and gray, / do not abandon me, O G.
71:19 Your righteousness, O G, reaches to the highest
71:19 Who can compare with you, O G?
71:22 because you are faithful to your promises, O G.
72: 1 Give justice to the king, O G, / and righteousness
72:18 Bless the LORD G, the G of Israel, / who alone
73: 1 Truly G is good to Israel, / to those whose hearts
73:11 "Does G realize what is going on?" they ask.
73:17 Then one day I went into your sanctuary, O G,
73:26 but G remains the strength of my heart;
73:28 But as for me, how good it is to be near G!
74: 1 O G, why have you rejected us forever? / Why is
74: 8 So they burned down all the places where G was
74:10 How long, O G, will you allow our enemies to
74:12 You, O G, are my king from ages past,
74:22 Arise, O G, and defend your cause.
75: 1 We thank you, O G! / We give thanks because you
75: 2 G says, "At the time I have planned, / I will bring
75: 7 It is G alone who judges; / he decides who will rise
75: 9 as for me, I will always proclaim what G has done; / I will sing praises to the G of Israel.
75:10 For G says, "I will cut off the strength of the
76: 1 G is well known in Judah; / his name is great in
76: 6 When you rebuked them, O G of Jacob,
76: 9 You stand up to judge those who do evil, O G,
76:11 Make vows to the LORD your G, and fulfill
77: 1 I cry out to G without holding back. / Oh, that G would listen to me!
77: 3 I think of G, and I moan, / overwhelmed with
77: 9 Has G forgotten to be kind? / Has he slammed the
77:13 O G, your ways are holy. / Is there any g as mighty as you?
77:14 You are the G of miracles and wonders!
77:16 When the Red Sea saw you, O G, / its waters
78: 7 So each generation can set its hope anew on G,
78: 8 and unfaithful, / refusing to give their hearts to G.
78:18 They willfully tested G in their hearts,
78:19 They even spoke against G himself, saying, / "G can't give us food in the desert.
78:22 for they did not believe G / or trust him to care for
78:25 food of angels! / G gave them all they could hold.
78:31 the anger of G rose against them, / and he killed
78:34 When G killed some of them, the rest finally sought him. / They repented and turned to G.
78:35 Then they remembered that G was their rock,
78:58 They made G angry by building altars to other
78:59 When G heard them, he was very angry, / and he
79: 1 O G, pagan nations have conquered your land,
79: 9 Help us, O G of our salvation! / Help us for the
79:10 be allowed to scoff, / asking, "Where is their G?"
80: 1 O G, enthroned above the cherubim,
80: 3 Turn us again to yourself, O G. / Make your face
80: 4 O LORD G Almighty, / how long will you be
80: 7 Turn us again to yourself, O G Almighty.
80:14 Come back, we beg you, O G Almighty.
80:19 Turn us again to yourself, O LORD G Almighty.
81: 1 Sing praises to G, our strength. / Sing to the G of Israel.
81: 4 by the laws of Israel; / it is a law of the G of Jacob.
81: 9 You must never have a foreign g; / you must not bow down before a false g.
81:10 For it was I, the LORD your G, / who rescued
82: 1 G presides over heaven's court; / he pronounces
82: 8 Rise up, O G, and judge the earth, / for all the
83: 1 O G, don't sit idly by, / silent and inactive!
83:12 seize for our own use / these pasturelands of G!"
83:13 O my G, blow them away like whirling dust,
84: 2 and soul, / I will shout joyfully to the living G.
84: 3 O LORD Almighty, my King and my G!
84: 7 and each of them will appear before G in
84: 8 O LORD G Almighty, hear my prayer. / Listen, O G of Israel. / *Interlude*
84: 9 O G, look with favor upon the king, our protector!
84:10 would rather be a gatekeeper in the house of my G
84:11 For the LORD G is our light and protector.
85: 4 Now turn to us again, O G of our salvation.
85: 8 I listen carefully to what G the LORD is saying,
86: 2 for I serve you and trust you. / You are my G.
86: 8 Nowhere among the pagan gods is there a g like
86:10 and perform great miracles. / You alone are G.
86:12 With all my heart I will praise you, O Lord my G.
86:14 O G, insolent people rise up against me;
86:15 But you, O Lord, are a merciful and gracious G,
87: 3 O city of G, / what glorious things are said of you!
88: 1 O LORD, G of my salvation, / I have cried out to
89: 7 The highest angelic powers stand in awe of G.
89: 8 O LORD G Almighty! / Where is there anyone as
89:26 my Father, / my G, and the Rock of my salvation.'
90: T A prayer of Moses, the man of G.
90: 2 the world, / you are G, without beginning or end.
90:17 And may the Lord our G show us his approval
91: 2 of safety; / he is my G, and I am trusting him.
92:13 own house. / They flourish in the courts of our G.
94: 1 O LORD, the G to whom vengeance belongs,
94: 1 O G of vengeance, let your glorious justice be
94: 7 "and besides, the G of Israel doesn't care."
94:20 Can unjust leaders claim that G is on their side—
94:22 my G is a mighty rock where I can hide.
94:23 G will make the sins of evil people fall back upon
94:23 their sins. / The LORD our G will destroy them.
95: 3 For the LORD is a great G, / the great King
95: 7 for he is our G. / We are the people he watches
97: 7 worthless gods— / for every g must bow to him.
98: 3 The whole earth has seen the salvation of our G.
99: 5 Exalt the LORD our G! / Bow low before his
99: 8 O LORD our G, you answered them. / You were a forgiving G,
99: 9 Exalt the LORD our G / and worship at his holy
99: 9 in Jerusalem, / for the LORD our G is holy!
100: 3 Acknowledge that the LORD is G! / He made us,
102:24 But I cried to him, "My G, who lives forever,
104: 1 tell myself; / O LORD my G, how great you are!
104:21 roar for their food, / but they are dependent on G.
104:33 as I live. / I will praise my G to my last breath!
105: 7 He is the LORD our G. / His rule is seen
106:20 They traded their glorious G / for a statue of a
106:21 They forgot G, their savior, / who had done such
106:47 O LORD our G, save us! / Gather us back from
106:48 Blessed be the LORD, the G of Israel,
107:11 They rebelled against the words of G,
108: 1 My heart is confident in you, O G; / no wonder I
108: 5 Be exalted, O G, above the highest heavens.
108: 7 G has promised this by his holiness: / "I will
108:11 Have you rejected us, O G? / Will you no longer
109: 1 O G, whom I praise, / don't stand silent and aloof
109:26 Help me, O LORD my G! / Save me because of
113: 5 Who can be compared with the LORD our G,
114: 7 of the Lord, / at the presence of the G of Israel.
115: 2 Why let the nations say, / "Where is their G?"
115: 3 For our G is in the heavens, / and he does as he
116: 5 How good he is! / So merciful, this G of ours!
118:27 The LORD is G, shining upon us. / Bring forward
118:28 You are my G, and I will praise you! / You are my G, and I will exalt you!
119:115 for I intend to obey the commands of my G.
120: 3 O deceptive tongue, what will G do to you?
122: 9 For the sake of the house of the LORD our G,
123: 1 I lift my eyes to you, / O G, enthroned in heaven.
123: 2 We look to the LORD our G for his mercy,
127: 2 for food to eat; / for G gives rest to his loved ones.
135: 2 the LORD, / in the courts of the house of our G.
135: 5 that our Lord is greater than any other g.
136: 2 Give thanks to the G of gods. / His faithful love
136:21 G gave the land of these kings as an inheritance—
136:26 Give thanks to the G of heaven. / His faithful love
139:17 How precious are your thoughts about me, O G!
139:19 O G, if only you would destroy the wicked!
139:23 Search me, O G, and know my heart; / test me
140: 6 I said to the LORD, "You are my G!" / Listen,
140: 8 Do not let their evil schemes succeed, O G.
143:10 Teach me to do your will, / for you are my G.
144: 9 I will sing a new song to you, O G! / I will sing
144:15 Happy indeed are those whose G is the LORD.
145: 1 I will praise you, my G and King, / and bless your
146: 2 I will sing praises to my G even with my dying
146: 5 But happy are those who have the G of Israel as
146: 5 whose hope is in the LORD their G.
146:10 O Jerusalem, your G is King in every generation!
147: 1 How good it is to sing praises to our G!
147: 7 sing praises to our G, accompanied by harps.
147:12 the LORD, O Jerusalem! / Praise your G, O Zion!
149: 6 Let the praises of G be in their mouths, / and a
150: 1 the LORD! / Praise G in his heavenly dwelling;
Pr 2: 5 the LORD, and you will gain knowledge of G.
2:17 and ignores the covenant she made before G.
3: 4 Then you will find favor with both G and people,
11: 8 G rescues the godly from danger, but he lets the
20:25 It is dangerous to make a rash promise to G before
21:27 G loathes the sacrifice of an evil person,
24:12 For G knows all hearts, and he sees you. He keeps
30: 1 I am weary, O G; I am weary and worn out, O G.
30: 4 Who but G goes up to heaven and comes back
30: 5 Every word of G proves true. He defends all who
30: 7 O G, I beg two favors from you before I die.
Ecc 1:13 I soon discovered that G has dealt a tragic
2:24 I realized that this pleasure is from the hand of G.
2:26 G gives wisdom, knowledge, and joy to those who
2:26 G takes the wealth away and gives it to those who
3:10 various kinds of work G has given people to do.
3:11 G has made everything beautiful for its own time.
3:13 the fruits of their labor, for these are gifts from G.
3:14 And I know that whatever G does is final.
3:15 in the past. For G calls each event back in its turn.
3:17 "In due season G will judge everyone, both good
3:18 Then I realized that G allows people to continue in
5: 1 As you enter the house of G, keep your ears open
5: 1 realize that mindless offerings to G are evil.
5: 2 And don't make rash promises to G, for he is in
5: 4 So when you make a promise to G, don't delay in
5: 4 for G takes no pleasure in fools.
5: 6 That would make G angry, and he might wipe out
5: 7 is ruin in a flood of empty words. Fear G instead.
5:18 under the sun—for however long G lets them live.
5:19 And it is a good thing to receive wealth from G
5:19 your lot in life—that is indeed a gift from G.
5:20 on the past, for G has given them reasons for joy.
6: 2 G gives great wealth and honor to some people
6:10 So there's no use arguing with G about your
7:13 Notice the way G does things; then fall into line.
7:13 Don't fight the ways of G, for who can straighten
7:14 hard times strike, realize that both come from G.
7:18 but those who fear G will succeed either way.
7:26 Those who please G will escape from her,
7:29 I discovered that G created people to be upright,
8: 2 because you have vowed before G to do this.
8:12 I know that those who fear G will be better off.
8:13 never live long, good lives, for they do not fear G.
8:15 along with all the hard work G gives them.
8:17 discover everything G has created in our world,
9: 1 or not G will show them favor in this life.
9: 7 wine with a happy heart, for G approves of this!
9: 9 days of life that G has given you in this world.
9: 9 The wife G gives you is your reward for all your
11: 9 But remember that you must give an account to G
12: 7 and the spirit will return to G who gave it.
12:13 Fear G and obey his commands, for this is the duty
12:14 G will judge us for everything we do,
Isa 1:10 Listen to the law of our G, people of Israel.
2: 3 of the LORD, to the Temple of the G of Israel.
5:16 The holiness of G is displayed by his
7:13 You exhaust the patience of G as well!
7:14 and will call him Immanuel—'G is with us.'
8:10 of attack—and then die! For G is with us!' "
8:19 out the future from the dead? Why not ask your G?
8:21 fists at heaven and curse their king and their G.
9: 4 For G will break the chains that bind his people
9: 6 Mighty G, Everlasting Father, Prince of Peace.
10:21 A remnant of them will return to the Mighty G.
12: 2 See, G has come to save me. / I will trust in him
13:19 and Gomorrah when G destroyed them.
17: 6 bare of people," says the LORD, the G of Israel.
17:10 Because you have turned from the G who can save
17:13 roar like breakers on a beach, G will silence them.
17:14 of those who plunder and destroy the people of G.
19:23 their lands, and they will worship the same G.
21: 3 I grow faint when I hear what G is planning;
21:10 the LORD Almighty, the G of Israel, has said.
21:17 I, the LORD, the G of Israel, have spoken!"
22:11 are to no avail because you never ask G for help.
24: 5 for they have twisted the instructions of G,
24:15 praise the name of the LORD, the G of Israel.
25: 1 and praise your name, for you are my G.
25: 9 that day the people will proclaim, "This is our G.
25:11 G will push down Moab's people as a swimmer
26: 7 is not steep and rough. / You are a G of justice,
26: 9 long I search for you; / earnestly I seek for G.
26:13 O LORD our G, others have ruled us, / but we
26:19 Those who belong to G will live; / their bodies will
27:11 for its people have turned away from G.
28:11 G will speak to them through foreign oppressors
28:26 what to do, for G has given him understanding.
29:23 of Israel. They will stand in awe of the G of Israel.
30:18 and compassion. For the LORD is a faithful G.
30:29 But the people of G will sing a song of joy,
31: 3 For these Egyptians are mere humans, not G!
31: 8 The sword of G will strike them, and they will
32: 3 Then everyone who can see will be looking for G,
32:20 G will greatly bless his people. Wherever they
33:23 Their treasure will be divided by the people of G.
34:11 For G will bring chaos and destruction to that land.
35: 2 will display his glory, the splendor of our G.
35: 4 for your G is coming to destroy your enemies.
36: 7 will say, 'We are trusting in the LORD our G!'
36:20 What g of any nation has ever been able to save its
37: 4 But perhaps the LORD your G has heard the
37: 4 the Assyrian representative defying the living G
37:10 Don't let this G you trust deceive you with
37:16 "O LORD Almighty, G of Israel, you are

37:16 You alone are **G** of all the kingdoms of the earth.
37:17 words of defiance against the living **G**.
37:20 Now, O LORD our **G**, rescue us from his power;
37:20 earth will know that you alone, O LORD, are **G**."
37:21 "This is what the LORD, the **G** of Israel, says:
37:38 he was worshiping in the temple of his **g** Nisroch,
38: 5 the LORD, the **G** of your ancestor David, says:
40: 1 "Comfort, comfort my people," says your **G**.
40: 3 smooth road through the desert for our **G**.
40: 8 but the word of our **G** stands forever."
40: 9 Tell the towns of Judah, "Your **G** is coming!"
40:16 would not make an offering worthy of our **G**.
40:18 To whom, then, can we compare **G**? What image
40:20 Can **G** be compared to an idol that must be placed
40:21 Are you deaf to the words of **G**—the words he
40:22 It is **G** who sits above the circle of the earth.
40:27 How can you say **G** refuses to hear your case?
40:28 you know that the LORD is the everlasting **G**,
41:10 with you. Do not be dismayed, for I am your **G**.
41:13 you by your right hand—I, the LORD your **G**.
41:17 I, the **G** of Israel, will never forsake them.
42: 5 **G**, the LORD, created the heavens and stretched
43: 3 For I am the LORD, your **G**, the Holy One of
43: 7 All who claim me as their **G** will come, for I have
43:10 believe in me, and understand that I alone am **G**.
43:10 There is no other **G**; there never has been
43:12 saved you. No foreign **g** has ever done this before.
43:12 You are witnesses that I am the only **G**,"
43:13 "From eternity to eternity I am **G**. No one can
44: 6 I am the First and the Last; there is no other **G**.
44: 8 You are my witnesses—is there any other **G**?
44:10 Who but a fool would make his own **g**—an idol
44:11 mere humans—who claim they can make a **g**.
44:15 and makes himself a **g** for people to worship!
44:17 Then he takes what's left and makes his **g**:
44:17 to it. "Rescue me!" he says. "You are my **g**!"
44:19 and roast my meat. How can the rest of it be a **g**?
45: 3 the **G** of Israel, the one who calls you by name.
45: 5 I am the LORD; there is no other **G**. I have
45: 6 from east to west will know there is no other **G**.
45:14 their knees in front of you and say, '**G** is with you, and he is the only **G**.' "
45:15 Truly, O **G** of Israel, our Savior, you work in
45:18 For the LORD is **G**, and he created the heavens
45:21 For there is no other **G** but me—a just **G** and a Savior—no, not one!
45:22 to me for salvation! For I am **G**; there is no other.
46: 4 I will be your **G** throughout your lifetime—
46: 6 and gold and hire a craftsman to make a **g** from it.
46: 9 For I am **G**—I alone! I am **G**, and there is no one else like me.
48: 1 name of the LORD and call on the **G** of Israel.
48: 2 and talk about depending on the **G** of Israel,
48: 5 and metal **g** commanded it to happen!'
48:12 chosen one! I alone am **G**, the First and the Last.
48:17 I am the LORD your **G**, who teaches you what is
49: 4 the LORD's hand; I will trust **G** for my reward."
49: 5 has honored me, and my **G** has given me strength.
50:10 of light, trust in the LORD and rely on your **G**.
51:15 For I am the LORD your **G**, who stirs up the sea,
51:20 has poured out his fury; **G** has rebuked them.
51:22 the Sovereign LORD, your **G** and Defender, says:
52: 7 and salvation, the news that the **G** of Israel reigns!
52:10 ends of the earth will see the salvation of our **G**.
52:12 and the **G** of Israel will protect you from behind.
53: 4 were a punishment from **G** for his own sins!
54: 5 the Holy One of Israel, the **G** of all the earth.
54: 6 wife abandoned by her husband," says your **G**.
55: 5 because I, the LORD your **G**, the Holy One of
55: 7 Yes, turn to our **G**, for he will abundantly pardon.
57: 1 No one seems to understand that **G** is protecting
57:21 There is no peace for the wicked," says my **G**.
58: 2 a righteous nation that would never abandon its **G**.
59: 2 is a problem—your sins have cut you off from **G**.
59: 9 That is why **G** doesn't punish those who injure us.
59:12 For our sins are piled up before **G** and testify
59:13 We have turned our backs on **G**. We know how
60: 9 and it will bring great honor to the LORD your **G**,
60:19 for the LORD your **G** will be your everlasting
61: 6 be called priests of the LORD, ministers of our **G**.
61:10 I am overwhelmed with joy in the LORD my **G**!
62: 3 for all to see—a splendid crown in the hands of **G**.
62: 4 be the City of God's Delight and the Bride of **G**,
62: 5 Then **G** will rejoice over you as a bridegroom
64: 4 no ear has heard and no eye has seen a **G** like you,
65:16 or take an oath will do so by the **G** of truth.
66: 9 keep this nation from being born," says your **G**.
Jer 2:11 any nation ever exchanged its gods for another **g**,
2:11 Yet my people have exchanged their glorious **G**
2:17 the LORD your **G** when he wanted to lead you
2:19 bitter thing it is to forsake the LORD your **G**,
2:31 do my people say, 'At last we are free from **G**!
3:13 that you rebelled against the LORD your **G**
3:21 For they have forgotten the LORD their **G**
3:22 the people reply, "for you are the LORD our **G**.
3:23 Only in the LORD our **G** will Israel ever find
3:25 have always sinned against the LORD our **G**.
5: 4 They don't understand what **G** expects of them.
5: 5 the LORD's ways and what **G** requires of them."
5: 5 But the leaders, too, had utterly rejected their **G**.
5:14 this is what the LORD **G** Almighty says:
5:19 'Why is the LORD our **G** doing this to us?'
5:24 'Let us live in awe of the LORD our **G**, for he
7: 3 The LORD Almighty, the **G** of Israel, says:
7:21 what the LORD Almighty, the **G** of Israel, says:
7:23 'Obey me, and I will be your **G**, and you will be
7:28 whose people will not obey the LORD their **G**
8:14 For the LORD our **G** has decreed our destruction
9:15 what the LORD Almighty, the **G** of Israel, says:
10: 5 There stands their **g** like a helpless scarecrow in a
10:10 But the LORD is the only true **G**, the living **G**.
10:12 But **G** made the earth by his power, / and he
10:16 But the **G** of Israel is no idol! / He is the Creator of
11: 3 'This is what the LORD, the **G** of Israel, says:
11: 4 then you will be my people, and I will be your **G**."
11:13 altars for burning incense to your **g** Baal—
13:12 "So tell them, 'The LORD, the **G** of Israel, says:
13:16 Give glory to the LORD your **G** before it is too
14:22 No, it comes from you, the LORD our **G**!
15:16 for I bear your name, O LORD **G** Almighty.
16: 9 For the LORD Almighty, the **G** of Israel, says:
16:10 What is our sin against the LORD our **G**?'
16:20 Can people make their own **g**? The gods they make
19: 3 what the LORD Almighty, the **G** of Israel, says:
19:15 what the LORD Almighty, the **G** of Israel, says:
21: 4 'This is what the LORD, the **G** of Israel, says:
22: 9 the LORD their **G** by worshiping other gods.' "
22:15 in all his dealings. That is why **G** blessed him.
23: 2 the **G** of Israel, says to these shepherds:
23:23 Am I a **G** who is only in one place?"
23:25 'Listen to the dream I had from **G** last night.'
23:36 turning upside down the words of our **G**, the living **G**, the LORD Almighty.
24: 5 "This is what the LORD, the **G** of Israel, says:
24: 7 They will be my people, and I will be their **G**,
25:15 Then the LORD, the **G** of Israel, said to me,
25:27 'The LORD Almighty, the **G** of Israel, says:
26:13 and begin to obey the LORD your **G**,
26:16 spoken to us in the name of the LORD our **G**."
27: 4 what the LORD Almighty, the **G** of Israel, says:
27:21 this is what the LORD Almighty, the **G** of Israel,
28: 2 "The LORD Almighty, the **G** of Israel, says:
28:14 The LORD Almighty, the **G** of Israel, says:
29: 4 The LORD Almighty, the **G** of Israel, sends this
29: 8 The LORD Almighty, the **G** of Israel, says,
29:21 the **G** of Israel, says about your prophets—
29:25 what the LORD Almighty, the **G** of Israel, says:
30: 2 "This is what the LORD, the **G** of Israel, says:
30: 9 For my people will serve the LORD their **G**
30:22 You will be my people, and I will be your **G**."
31: 1 "I will be the **G** of all the families of Israel,
31: 6 up to Jerusalem to worship the LORD our **G**.' "
31:18 restore me, for you alone are the LORD my **G**.
31:19 I turned away from **G**, but then I was sorry.
31:22 different to happen—Israel will embrace her **G**."
31:23 what the LORD Almighty, the **G** of Israel, says:
31:33 I will be their **G**, and they will be my people.
32:14 "The LORD Almighty, the **G** of Israel, says:
32:15 For the LORD Almighty, the **G** of Israel, says:
32:18 You are the great and powerful **G**, the LORD
32:27 the LORD, the **G** of all the peoples of the world.
32:36 But this is what the LORD, the **G** of Israel, says:
32:38 They will be my people, and I will be their **G**.
33: 4 For this is what the LORD, the **G** of Israel, says:
34: 2 'This is what the LORD, the **G** of Israel, says:
34:13 "This is what the LORD, the **G** of Israel, says:
35: 4 to the sons of Hanan son of Igdaliah, a man of **G**.
35:13 "The LORD Almighty, the **G** of Israel, says:
35:17 "Therefore, the LORD **G** Almighty, the **G** of Israel,
35:18 what the LORD Almighty, the **G** of Israel, says:
35:19 LORD Almighty, the **G** of Israel, has spoken!"
37: 3 "Please pray to the LORD our **G** for us."
37: 7 "This is what the LORD, the **G** of Israel, says:
38:17 "The LORD **G** Almighty, the **G** of Israel, says:
39:16 'The LORD Almighty, the **G** of Israel, says:
40: 2 "The LORD your **G** has brought this disaster on
42: 2 "Please pray to the LORD your **G** for us.
42: 3 Beg the LORD your **G** to show us what to do
42: 4 "I will pray to the LORD your **G**, and I will tell
42: 5 "May the LORD your **G** be a faithful witness
42: 6 we will obey the LORD our **G** to whom we send
42: 9 the **G** of Israel, with your request, and this is his
42:13 "But if you refuse to obey the LORD your **G**
42:15 The LORD Almighty, the **G** of Israel, says:
42:18 "For the LORD Almighty, the **G** of Israel, says:
42:20 you sent me to pray to the LORD your **G** for you,
42:20 saying, 'Just tell us what the LORD our **G** says,
42:21 but you will not obey the LORD your **G** any
43: 1 message from the LORD their **G** to all the people,
43: 2 The LORD our **G** hasn't forbidden us to go to
43:10 'The LORD Almighty, the **G** of Israel, says:
44: 2 what the LORD Almighty, the **G** of Israel, says:
44: 7 "And now the LORD **G** Almighty, the **G** of Israel,
44:11 the LORD Almighty, the **G** of Israel, says:
44:25 The LORD Almighty, the **G** of Israel, says:
45: 2 what LORD, the **G** of Israel, says to you, Baruch:
46:25 The LORD Almighty, the **G** of Israel, says:
46:25 "I will punish Amon, the **g** of Thebes, and all the
48: 1 what the LORD Almighty, the **G** of Israel, says:
48: 7 Your **g** Chemosh, with his priests and princes,
48:46 The people of the **g** Chemosh are destroyed!
49: 3 for your **g** Molech will be exiled along with his
50: 4 "weeping and seeking the LORD their **G**.
50:18 the LORD Almighty, the **G** of Israel, says:
50:28 **G** has taken vengeance against those who
51: 5 He is still their **G**, even though their land was filled
51:10 Jerusalem everything the LORD our **G** has done.
51:19 But the **G** of Israel is no idol! / He is the Creator of
51:33 For the LORD Almighty, the **G** of Israel, says:
51:44 And I will punish Bel, the **g** of Babylon, and pull
51:56 For the LORD is a **G** who gives just punishment,
La 3:41 us lift our hearts and hands to **G** in heaven and say,
Eze 1: 1 were opened to me, and I saw visions of **G**.
7:13 For what **G** has said applies to everyone—it will
8: 3 and transported me in a vision of **G** to Jerusalem.
8: 4 Suddenly, the glory of the **G** of Israel was there,
8:14 were sitting there, weeping for the **g** Tammuz.
9: 3 Then the glory of the **G** of Israel rose up from
10: 5 cherubim sounded like the voice of **G** Almighty
10:19 And the glory of the **G** of Israel hovered above
10:20 the **G** of Israel when I was by the Kebar River.
11:20 they will truly be my people, and I will be their **G**.
11:22 and the glory of the **G** of Israel hovered above
11:24 Afterward the Spirit of **G** carried me back again to
14:11 They will be my people, and I will be their **G**,
20: 5 I swore that I, the LORD, would be her **G**.
20: 7 the Egyptian gods, for I am the LORD your **G**.'
20: 9 nations wouldn't be able to laugh at Israel's **G**,
20:19 'I am the LORD your **G**,' I told them.
20:20 sign to remind you that I am the LORD your **G**.'
28: 2 In your great pride you claim, 'I am a **g**! I sit on a
28: 2 But you are only a man and not a **g**, though you boast that you are like a **g**.
28: 6 Because you think you are as wise as a **g**,
28: 9 Will you then boast, 'I am a **g**!' to those who kill
28: 9 To them you will be no **g** but merely a man!
28:13 You were in Eden, the garden of **G**. Your clothing
28:14 You had access to the holy mountain of **G**
28:16 So I banished you from the mountain of **G**.
28:26 they will know that I am the LORD their **G**."
31: 8 than any of the other cedars in the garden of **G**.
31: 8 No tree in the garden of **G** came close to it in
31: 9 of all the other trees of Eden, the garden of **G**.
34:24 And I, the LORD, will be their **G**, and my servant
34:30 know that I, the LORD their **G**, am with them.
34:31 You are my people, and I am your **G**,
36:28 You will be my people, and I will be your **G**.
37:23 they will truly be my people, and I will be their **G**.
37:27 I will be their **G**, and they will be my people.
39:22 of Israel will know that I am the LORD their **G**.
39:23 for sin, for they acted in treachery against their **G**.
39:28 people will know that I am the LORD their **G**—
40: 2 In a vision of **G** he took me to the land of Israel
43: 2 the glory of the **G** of Israel appeared from the east.
44: 2 for the LORD, the **G** of Israel, entered here.
44: 7 my sanctuary—people who have no heart for **G**.
Da 1: 2 some of the sacred objects from the Temple of **G**
1: 2 and placed them in the treasure-house of his **g** in
1: 9 Now **G** had given the chief official great respect
1:17 **G** gave these four young men an unusual aptitude
1:17 And **G** gave Daniel special ability in understanding
2:18 He urged them to ask the **G** of heaven to show
2:19 in a vision. Then Daniel praised the **G** of heaven,
2:20 saying, / "Praise the name of **G** forever and ever,
2:23 I thank and praise you, **G** of my ancestors,
2:28 But there is a **G** in heaven who reveals secrets,
2:30 because **G** wanted you to understand what you
2:37 The **G** of heaven has given you sovereignty,
2:44 the **G** of heaven will set up a kingdom that will
2:45 "The great **G** has shown Your Majesty what will
2:47 "Truly, your **G** is the **G** of gods, the Lord over
3:15 What **g** will be able to rescue you from my power
3:17 the **G** whom we serve is able to save us.
3:26 servants of the Most High **G**, come out!
3:28 "Praise to the **G** of Shadrach, Meshach,
3:28 than serve or worship any **g** except their own **G**.
3:29 speak a word against the **G** of Shadrach, Meshach,
3:29 There is no other **g** who can rescue like this!"
4: 2 and wonders the Most High **G** has performed for
4: 8 (He was named Belteshazzar after my **g**,
5: 3 cups taken from the Temple of **G** in Jerusalem,
5:11 and wisdom as though he himself were a **g**.
5:18 the Most High **G** gave sovereignty, majesty,
5:21 until he learned that the Most High **G** rules the
5:23 But you have not honored the **G** who gives you the
5:24 So **G** has sent this hand to write a message.
5:26 **G** has numbered the days of your reign and has
6:10 just as he had always done, giving thanks to his **G**.
6:13 He still prays to his **G** three times a day."
6:16 The king said to him, "May your **G**, whom you
6:20 out in anguish, "Daniel, servant of the living **G**!
6:20 Was your **G**, whom you worship continually,
6:22 My **G** sent his angel to shut the lions' mouths
6:23 was found on him because he had trusted in his **G**.
6:26 should tremble with fear before the **G** of Daniel.
6:26 For he is the living **G**, / and he will endure forever.
9: 3 So I turned to the Lord **G** and pleaded with him in
9: 4 I prayed to the LORD my **G** and confessed:
9: 4 "O Lord, you are a great and awesome **G**!
9: 9 But the Lord our **G** is merciful and forgiving,
9:10 We have not obeyed the LORD our **G**, for we
9:11 the servant of **G**, have been poured out against us
9:13 from the LORD our **G** by turning from our sins
9:14 and the LORD our **G** is just in everything he
9:15 "O Lord our **G**, you brought lasting honor to your
9:17 "O our **G**, hear your servant's prayer! Listen as I
9:18 "O my **G**, listen to me and hear my request.
9:19 O my **G**, do not delay, for your people and your
9:20 pleading with the LORD my **G** for Jerusalem,
9:23 to tell you what it was, for **G** loves you very much.
10:11 the man said to me, "O Daniel, greatly loved of **G**,
10:12 and to humble yourself before your **G**,
10:19 he said, "for you are deeply loved by **G**.
11:32 But the people who know their **G** will be strong
11:36 and claiming to be greater than every **g** there is, even blaspheming the **G** of gods.
11:37 for the **g** beloved of women, nor for any other **g**,
11:38 of these, he will worship the **g** of fortresses—
11:38 a **g** his ancestors never knew—and lavish on him
Hos 1: 7 But I, the LORD their **G**, will show love to the
1: 9 for Israel is not my people, and I am not their **G**.

1:10 it will be said, 'You are children of the living **G**.'
1:11 when **G** will again plant his people in his land.
2: 8 and silver she used in worshiping the **g** Baal were
2:22 chorus will sing together, 'Jezreel'—'**G** plants!'
2:23 Then they will reply, 'You are our **G**!' "
3: 5 the people will return to the LORD their **G**
4: 1 no kindness, no knowledge of **G** in your land.
4: 6 Since you have forgotten the laws of your **G**,
4: 7 They have exchanged the glory of **G** for the
4:12 serving other gods and deserting their **G**.
5: 4 Your deeds won't let you return to your **G**.
6: 6 I want you to know **G**; that's more important than
7:10 yet he doesn't return to the LORD his **G** or even
8: 2 pleads with me, 'Help us, for you are our **G**!'
8: 6 It is not **G**! Therefore, it must be smashed to bits.
9: 1 For you have been unfaithful to your **G**,
9: 7 and shows only hatred for those who love **G**.
9: 8 The prophet is a watchman for my **G** over Israel,
9: 8 he goes. He faces hostility even in the house of **G**.
9: 9 **G** will not forget. He will surely punish them for
9:10 Soon they became as vile as the **g** they worshiped.
9:17 My **G** will reject the people of Israel because they
11: 9 destroy Israel, for I am **G** and not a mere mortal.
11:12 but Judah still walks with **G** and is faithful to the
12: 3 when he became a man, he even fought with **G**.
12: 4 he met **G** face to face, and **G** spoke to him—
12: 5 the LORD **G** Almighty, the LORD is his name!
12: 6 So now, come back to your **G**! Act on the
12: 6 always live in confident dependence on your **G**.
12: 9 "I am the LORD your **G**, who rescued you from
13: 4 "I am the LORD your **G**, who rescued you from
13: 4 You have no **G** but me, for there is no other savior.
13:16 of their guilt because they rebelled against their **G**.
14: 1 Return, O Israel, to the LORD your **G**, for your
Joel 1:13 the night in sackcloth, you ministers of my **G**!
1:13 no grain or wine to offer at the Temple of your **G**.
1:14 the people into the Temple of the LORD your **G**,
1:16 are no joyful celebrations in the house of our **G**.
2:13 Return to the LORD your **G**, for he is gracious
2:14 and wine to the LORD your **G** as before!
2:17 foreigners who say, 'Where is the **G** of Israel?
2:23 of Jerusalem! Rejoice in the LORD your **G**!
2:26 and you will praise the LORD your **G**, who does
2:27 of Israel and that I alone am the LORD your **G**.
3:17 the LORD your **G**, live in Zion, my holy
Am 2: 8 In the house of their **g**, they present offerings of
3:13 all Israel," says the Lord, the LORD **G** Almighty.
4:12 Prepare to meet your **G** as he comes in judgment,
4:13 his feet. The LORD **G** Almighty is his name!
5:14 Then the LORD **G** Almighty will truly be your
5:15 Perhaps even yet the LORD **G** Almighty will
5:16 is what the Lord, the LORD **G** Almighty, says:
5:26 Sakkuth your king **g** and Kaiwan your star **g**—
5:27 says the LORD, whose name is **G** Almighty.
6: 8 and this is what he, the LORD **G** Almighty, says:
6:14 nation against you," says the LORD **G** Almighty.
9:15 land I have given them," says the LORD your **G**.
Jnh 1: 6 he shouted. "Get up and pray to your **g**! Maybe he
1: 9 the **G** of heaven, who made the sea and the land."
1:14 Then they cried out to the LORD, Jonah's **G**.
2: 1 Then Jonah prayed to the LORD his **G** from
2: 6 But you, O LORD my **G**, have snatched me from
3: 8 required to wear sackcloth and pray earnestly to **G**.
3: 9 Perhaps even yet **G** will have pity on us and hold
3:10 When **G** saw that they had put a stop to their evil
4: 2 that you were a gracious and compassionate **G**,
4: 6 And the LORD **G** arranged for a leafy plant to
4: 7 But **G** also prepared a worm! The next morning at
4: 8 **G** sent a scorching east wind to blow on Jonah.
4: 9 Then **G** said to Jonah, "Is it right for you to be
Mic 2: 4 **G** has confiscated our land, / taking it from us.
3: 7 will admit that your messages were not from **G**."
4: 2 of the LORD, to the Temple of the **G** of Israel.
4: 5 we will follow the LORD our **G** forever and ever.
5: 4 in the majesty of the name of the LORD his **G**.
6: 6 Should we bow before **G** with offerings of yearling
6: 8 to love mercy, and to walk humbly with your **G**.
7: 7 I wait confidently for **G** to save me, and my **G** will certainly hear me.
7:10 saying, "Where is the LORD—that **G** of yours?"
7:17 they will come out to meet the LORD our **G**.
7:18 Where is another **G** like you, who pardons the sins
Na 1: 2 The LORD is a jealous **G**, filled with vengeance
Hab 1:11 are deeply guilty, for their own strength is their **g**."
1:12 O LORD my **G**, my Holy One, you who are
2:19 Can an idol speak for **G**? They may be overlaid
3: 3 I see **G**, the Holy One, moving across the deserts
3: 3 is filled with his praise! What a wonderful **G** he is!
3:18 I will be joyful in the **G** of my salvation.
Zep 2: 7 For the LORD their **G** will visit his people in
2: 9 the **G** of Israel, "Moab and Ammon will be
3: 2 does not trust in the LORD or draw near to its **G**.
3:17 For the LORD your **G** has arrived to live among
Hag 1:12 obeyed the message from the LORD their **G**.
1:12 whom the LORD their **G** had sent,
1:14 on the house of the LORD Almighty, their **G**.
Zec 4: 7 will shout: 'May **G** bless it! May **G** bless it!' "
6:15 obey the commands of the LORD your **G**.
8: 8 I will be faithful and just toward them as their **G**.
8:23 for we have heard that **G** is with you.' "
9: 7 All the surviving Philistines will worship our **G**
9:16 the LORD their **G** will rescue his people,
10: 6 for I am the LORD their **G**, who will hear their
11: 4 This is what the LORD my **G** says: "Go and care
12: 5 found strength in the LORD Almighty, their **G**.'
12: 8 And the royal descendants will be like **G**,
13: 9 and they will say, 'The LORD is our **G**.' "
14: 5 Then the LORD my **G** will come, and all his holy
Mal 1: 9 "Go ahead, beg **G** to be merciful to you! But when
2:10 Are we not all created by the same **G**? Then why
2:16 I hate divorce!" says the LORD, the **G** of Israel.
2:17 him by asking, "Where is the **G** of justice?"
3: 8 "Should people cheat **G**? Yet you have cheated
3:14 "You have said, 'What's the use of serving **G**?
3:15 and those who dare **G** to punish them go free of
3:18 between those who serve **G** and those who do
Mt 1:23 be called Immanuel / (meaning, **G** is with us)."
2:12 because **G** had warned them in a dream not to
3: 2 "Turn from your sins and turn to **G**,
3: 8 have really turned from your sins and turned to **G**.
3: 9 **G** can change these stones here into children of
3:11 water those who turn from their sins and turn to **G**.
3:16 and he saw the Spirit of **G** descending like a dove
4: 3 and said to him, "If you are the Son of **G**,
4: 4 their life; / they must feed on every word of **G**.' "
4: 6 and said, "If you are the Son of **G**, jump off!
4: 7 also say, 'Do not test the Lord your **G**.' "
4:10 'You must worship the Lord your **G**;
4:17 to preach, "Turn from your sins and turn to **G**,
5: 3 "**G** blesses those who realize their need for him,
5: 4 **G** blesses those who mourn, / for they will be
5: 5 **G** blesses those who are gentle and lowly,
5: 6 **G** blesses those who are hungry and thirsty for
5: 7 **G** blesses those who are merciful, / for they will be
5: 8 **G** blesses those whose hearts are pure, / for they will see **G**.
5: 9 **G** blesses those who work for peace, / for they will be called the children of **G**.
5:10 **G** blesses those who are persecuted because they live for **G**,
5:11 "**G** blesses you when you are mocked
5:20 unless you obey **G** better than the teachers of
5:23 the altar in the Temple, offering a sacrifice to **G**,
5:24 Then come and offer your sacrifice to **G**.
6:24 the other. You cannot serve both **G** and money.
6:30 And if **G** cares so wonderfully for flowers that are
6:33 and make the Kingdom of **G** your primary
8:29 at him, "Why are you bothering us, Son of **G**?
9: 3 "Blasphemy! This man talks like he is **G**!"
9: 8 They praised **G** for sending a man with such great
10:28 Fear only **G**, who can destroy both soul and body
10:41 you welcome a prophet as one who speaks for **G**,
11: 6 '**G** blesses those who are not offended by me.' "
11:20 they hadn't turned from their sins and turned to **G**.
12: 4 He went into the house of **G**, and they ate the
12:28 But if I am casting out demons by the Spirit of **G**,
12:28 then the Kingdom of **G** has arrived among you.
12:38 a miraculous sign to prove that you are from **G**."
14:33 "You really are the Son of **G**!" they exclaimed.
15: 3 violate the direct commandments of **G**?
15: 4 For instance, **G** says, 'Honor your father
15: 5 for their needs if you give the money to **G** instead.'
15: 6 you nullify the direct commandment of **G**.
15:20 defile you and make you unacceptable to **G**!"
15:31 could see again! And they praised the **G** of Israel.
15:36 the seven loaves and the fish, thanked **G** for them,
16:16 "You are the Messiah, the Son of the living **G**."
19: 4 "They record that from the beginning '**G** made
19: 6 separate them, for **G** has joined them together."
19: 8 but it was not what **G** had originally intended.
19:11 Jesus said. "Only those whom **G** helps.
19:17 Jesus replied. "Only **G** is good. But to answer
19:24 than for a rich person to enter the Kingdom of **G**!"
19:26 is impossible. But with **G** everything is possible."
21: 9 were shouting, / "Praise **G** for the Son of David!
21: 9 name of the Lord! / Praise **G** in highest heaven!"
21:15 "Praise **G** for the Son of David."
21:21 'May **G** lift you up and throw you into the sea,'
21:31 and prostitutes will get into the Kingdom of **G**
21:43 What I mean is that the Kingdom of **G** will be
22:16 You teach about the way of **G** regardless of the
22:21 everything that belongs to **G** must be given to **G**."
22:29 and you don't know the power of **G**.
22:31 after Abraham, Isaac, and Jacob had died, **G** said,
22:32 'I am the **G** of Abraham, the **G** of Isaac, and the **G** of Jacob.'
22:32 So he is the **G** of the living, not the dead."
22:37 " 'You must love the Lord your **G** with all your
23: 9 for only **G** in heaven is your spiritual Father.
23:21 you are swearing by it and by **G**, who lives in it.
23:22 you are swearing by the throne of **G** and by **G**,
26:27 he took a cup of wine and gave thanks to **G** for it.
26:28 which seals the covenant between **G** and his
26:31 the Scriptures say, / '**G** will strike the Shepherd,
26:61 'I am able to destroy the Temple of **G** and rebuild
26:63 "I demand in the name of the living **G** that you tell us whether you are the Messiah, the Son of **G**."
26:74 Peter said, "I swear by **G**, I don't know the man."
27:40 Well then, if you are the Son of **G**, save yourself
27:43 He trusted **G**—let **G** show his approval by delivering him!
27:43 For he said, 'I am the Son of **G**.' "
27:46 "My **G**, my **G**, why have you forsaken me?"
27:54 They said, "Truly, this was the Son of **G**!"
Mk 1: 1 Good News about Jesus the Messiah, the Son of **G**.
1: 2 In the book of the prophet Isaiah, **G** said, / "Look,
1: 4 from their sins and turned to **G** to be forgiven.
1:15 he announced. "The Kingdom of **G** is near!
1:24 I know who you are—the Holy One sent from **G**!"
2: 7 This is blasphemy! Who but **G** can forgive sins!"
2:12 Then they all praised **G**. "We've never seen
2:26 He went into the house of **G** (during the days when
3:11 in front of him shrieking, "You are the Son of **G**!"
4:11 to understand the secret about the Kingdom of **G**.
4:26 illustration of what the Kingdom of **G** is like:
4:30 "How can I describe the Kingdom of **G**?
5: 7 you bothering me, Jesus, Son of the Most High **G**?
7:10 For instance, Moses gave you this law from **G**:
7:11 For I have vowed to give to **G** what I could have
7:13 you break the law of **G** in order to protect your
7:23 what defile you and make you unacceptable to **G**."
8: 6 thanked **G** for them, broke them into pieces,
8:11 Testing him to see if he was from **G**,
9: 1 you see the Kingdom of **G** arrive in great power!"
9:47 It is better to enter the Kingdom of **G** half blind
10: 9 separate them, for **G** has joined them together."
10:14 For the Kingdom of **G** belongs to such as these.
10:15 of faith will never get into the Kingdom of **G**."
10:18 me good?" Jesus asked. "Only **G** is truly good.
10:23 it is for rich people to get into the Kingdom of **G**!"
10:24 it is very hard to get into the Kingdom of **G**.
10:25 than for a rich person to enter the Kingdom of **G**!"
10:27 But not with **G**. Everything is possible with **G**."
10:40 **G** has prepared those places for the ones he has
11: 9 crowds all around him were shouting, / "Praise **G**!
11:10 our ancestor David! / Praise **G** in highest heaven!"
11:22 Then Jesus said to the disciples, "Have faith in **G**.
11:23 'May **G** lift you up and throw you into the sea,'
12:14 You sincerely teach the ways of **G**. Now tell us—
12:17 everything that belongs to **G** must be given to **G**."
12:24 and you don't know the power of **G**.
12:26 Isaac, and Jacob had died, **G** said to Moses,
12:26 'I am the **G** of Abraham, the **G** of Isaac, and the **G** of Jacob.'
12:27 So he is the **G** of the living, not the dead. You have
12:29 O Israel! The Lord our **G** is the one and only Lord.
12:30 And you must love the Lord your **G** with all your
12:32 spoken the truth by saying that there is only one **G**
12:34 to him, "You are not far from the Kingdom of **G**."
13:11 Just say what **G** tells you to. Then it is not you who
13:19 horror than at any time since **G** created the world.
14:23 he took a cup of wine and gave thanks to **G** for it.
14:24 sealing the covenant between **G** and his people.
14:25 day when I drink it new in the Kingdom of **G**."
14:27 the Scriptures say, / '**G** will strike the Shepherd,
14:61 "Are you the Messiah, the Son of the blessed **G**?"
14:71 Peter said, "I swear by **G**, I don't know this man
15:34 "My **G**, my **G**, why have you forsaken me?"
15:39 he exclaimed, "Truly, this was the Son of **G**!"
15:43 (who was waiting for the Kingdom of **G** to come),
Lk 1: 2 and other eyewitnesses of what **G** has done in
1: 8 One day Zechariah was serving **G** in the Temple,
1:13 For **G** has heard your prayer, and your wife,
1:16 many Israelites to turn to the Lord their **G**.
1:19 "I am Gabriel! I stand in the very presence of **G**.
1:26 **G** sent the angel Gabriel to Nazareth, a village in
1:30 angel told her, "for **G** has decided to bless you!
1:32 And the Lord **G** will give him the throne of his
1:35 will be holy, and he will be called the Son of **G**.
1:37 For nothing is impossible with **G**."
1:42 "You are blessed by **G** above all other women,
1:47 How I rejoice in **G** my Savior!
1:64 could speak again, and he began praising **G**.
1:68 "Praise the Lord, the **G** of Israel, / because he has
1:74 our enemies, / so we can serve **G** without fear,
2:13 host of others—the armies of heaven—praising **G**:
2:14 "Glory to **G** in the highest heaven, / and peace on earth to all whom **G** favors."
2:20 and praising **G** for what the angels had told them,
2:28 He took the child in his arms and praised **G**,
2:32 He is a light to reveal **G** to the nations, / and he is
2:37 and night, worshiping **G** with fasting and prayer.
2:38 with Mary and Joseph, and she began praising **G**.
2:40 his years, and **G** placed his special favor upon him.
2:52 and he was loved by **G** and by all who knew him.
3: 2 At this time a message from **G** came to John son of
3: 3 from their sins and turned to **G** to be forgiven.
3: 6 all people will see / the salvation sent from **G**.' "
3: 8 have really turned from your sins and turned to **G**.
3: 8 **G** can change these stones here into children of
3:38 was the son of Adam. / Adam was the son of **G**.
4: 3 the Devil said to him, "If you are the Son of **G**,
4: 8 'You must worship the Lord your **G**
4: 9 and said, "If you are the Son of **G**, jump off!
4:12 also say, 'Do not test the Lord your **G**.' "
4:34 I know who you are—the Holy One sent from **G**."
4:41 his command, shouting, "You are the Son of **G**."
4:43 Good News of the Kingdom of **G** in other places,
5: 1 pressed in on him to listen to the word of **G**.
5:21 is blasphemy! Who but **G** can forgive sins?"
5:25 picked up his mat, and went home praising **G**.
5:26 And they praised **G**, saying over and over again,
6: 4 He went into the house of **G**, ate the special bread
6:12 to a mountain to pray, and he prayed to **G** all night.
6:20 and said, / "**G** blesses you who are poor, / for the Kingdom of **G** is given to you.
6:21 **G** blesses you who are hungry now, / for you will be satisfied. / **G** blesses you who weep now,
6:22 **G** blesses you who are hated and excluded
7:16 fear swept the crowd, and they praised **G**, saying,
7:16 and "We have seen the hand of **G** at work today."
7:23 '**G** blesses those who are not offended by me.' "
7:28 person in the Kingdom of **G** is greater than he is!"
7:39 If **G** had really sent him, he would know what kind
8: 1 the Good News concerning the Kingdom of **G**.
8:10 to understand the secrets of the Kingdom of **G**.
8:21 brothers are all those who hear the message of **G**
8:28 you bothering me, Jesus, Son of the Most High **G**?
8:39 and tell them all the wonderful things **G** has done
9: 2 everyone about the coming of the Kingdom of **G**
9:11 teaching them about the Kingdom of **G** and curing

9:20 Peter replied, "You are the Messiah sent from **G**!"
9:27 will not die before you see the Kingdom of **G**."
9:60 and preach the coming of the Kingdom of **G**."
9:62 then looks back is not fit for the Kingdom of **G**."
10:9 say, 'The Kingdom of **G** is near you now.'
10:11 And don't forget the Kingdom of **G** is near!'
10:16 And anyone who rejects me is rejecting **G** who
10:27 " 'You must love the Lord your **G** with all your
11:16 sign from heaven to see if he was from **G**.
11:20 But if I am casting out demons by the power of **G**,
11:20 then the Kingdom of **G** has arrived among you.
11:27 in the crowd called out, "**G** bless your mother—
11:28 even more blessed are all who hear the word of **G**
11:30 sign to the people of Nineveh that **G** had sent him.
11:30 What happens to me will be a sign that **G** has sent
11:40 Didn't **G** make the inside as well as the outside?
11:42 completely forget about justice and the love of **G**.
11:49 This is what **G** in his wisdom said about you:
12:5 Fear **G**, who has the power to kill people and
12:6 Yet **G** does not forget a single one of them.
12:20 "But **G** said to him, 'You fool! You will die this
12:21 but not have a rich relationship with **G**."
12:24 or put food in barns because **G** feeds them.
12:28 And if **G** cares so wonderfully for flowers that are
12:29 Don't worry whether **G** will provide it for you.
12:31 make the Kingdom of **G** your primary concern.
13:3 unless you turn from your evil ways and turn to **G**.
13:13 stand straight. How she praised and thanked **G**!
13:18 Then Jesus said, "What is the Kingdom of **G** like?
13:20 also asked, "What else is the Kingdom of **G** like?
13:28 and all the prophets within the Kingdom of **G**,
13:29 the world to take their places in the Kingdom of **G**.
13:33 For it wouldn't do for a prophet of **G** to be killed
14:14 **G** will reward you for inviting those who could not
14:15 it would be to have a share in the Kingdom of **G**!"
15:7 **G** than over ninety-nine others who are righteous
16:13 the other. You cannot serve both **G** and money."
16:15 look good in public, but **G** knows your evil hearts.
16:15 world honors is an abomination in the sight of **G**.
16:16 But now the Good News of the Kingdom of **G** is
17:6 'May **G** uproot you and throw you into the sea,'
17:15 back to Jesus, shouting, "Praise **G**, I'm healed!"
17:18 only this foreigner return to give glory to **G**?"
17:20 "When will the Kingdom of **G** come?"
17:20 "The Kingdom of **G** isn't ushered in with visible
17:21 over there!' For the Kingdom of **G** is among you."
18:4 'I fear neither **G** nor man,' he said to himself,
18:7 so don't you think **G** will surely give justice to his
18:11 'I thank you, **G**, that I am not a sinner like
18:13 saying, 'O **G**, be merciful to me, for I am a sinner.'
18:14 not the Pharisee, returned home justified before **G**.
18:16 For the Kingdom of **G** belongs to such as these.
18:17 of faith will never get into the Kingdom of **G**."
18:19 Jesus asked him. "Only **G** is truly good.
18:24 it is for rich people to get into the Kingdom of **G**!
18:25 than for a rich person to enter the Kingdom of **G**!"
18:27 from a human perspective is possible with **G**."
18:29 or children, for the sake of the Kingdom of **G**,
18:43 man could see, and he followed Jesus, praising **G**.
And all who saw it praised **G**, too.
19:11 that the Kingdom of **G** would begin right away.
19:37 praising **G** for all the wonderful miracles they had
19:44 because you have rejected the opportunity **G**
20:16 "But **G** forbid that such a thing should ever
20:21 others think. You sincerely teach the ways of **G**.
20:25 everything that belongs to **G** must be given to **G**."
20:36 They are children of **G** raised up to new life.
20:37 he referred to the Lord as 'the **G** of Abraham, the
G of Isaac, and the **G** of Jacob.'
20:38 So he is the **G** of the living, not the dead. They are
21:31 you can be sure that the Kingdom of **G** is near.
22:16 until it comes to fulfillment in the Kingdom of **G**."
22:18 wine again until the Kingdom of **G** has come."
22:19 and when he had thanked **G** for it, he broke it in
22:70 "Then you claim you are the Son of **G**?"
23:40 "Don't you fear **G** even when you are dying?
23:47 he praised **G** and said, "Surely this man was
23:51 and he had been waiting for the Kingdom of **G** to
24:16 because **G** kept them from recognizing him.
24:19 highly regarded by both **G** and all the people.
24:53 spent all of their time in the Temple, praising **G**.

Jn 1:1 already existed. He was with **G**, and he was **G**.
1:2 He was in the beginning with **G**.
1:6 **G** sent John the Baptist
1:12 he gave the right to become children of **G**.
1:13 passion or plan—this rebirth comes from **G**.
1:18 No one has ever seen **G**. But his only Son, who is
himself **G**, is near to the
1:29 There is the Lamb of **G** who takes away the sin of
1:33 but when **G** sent me to baptize with water, he told
1:34 to Jesus, so I testify that he is the Son of **G**."
1:36 then declared, "Look! There is the Lamb of **G**!"
1:49 "Teacher, you are the Son of **G**—
1:51 all see heaven open and the angels of **G** going up
2:18 "If you have this authority from **G**, show us a
3:2 "we all know that **G** has sent you to teach us.
3:2 Your miraculous signs are proof enough that **G** is
3:3 born again, you can never see the Kingdom of **G**."
3:5 no one can enter the Kingdom of **G** without being
3:16 "For **G** so loved the world that he gave his only
3:17 **G** did not send his Son into the world to condemn
3:18 been judged for not believing in the only Son of **G**.
3:21 so everyone can see that they are doing what **G**
3:27 "**G** in heaven appoints each person's work.
3:33 Those who believe him discover that **G** is true.
3:34 For he is sent by **G**. He speaks God's words,
3:36 but the wrath of **G** remains upon them."
4:10 "If you only knew the gift **G** has for you and who
4:24 For **G** is Spirit, so those who worship him must
4:34 "My nourishment comes from doing the will of **G**,
5:18 he had spoken of **G** as his Father, thereby making
himself equal with **G**.
5:24 and believe in **G** who sent me have eternal life.
5:25 will hear my voice—the voice of the Son of **G**.
5:30 because it is according to the will of **G** who sent
5:44 care about the honor that comes from **G** alone.
6:11 Then Jesus took the loaves, gave thanks to **G**,
6:27 For **G** the Father has sent me for that very
6:28 They replied, "What does **G** want us to do?"
6:29 Jesus told them, "This is what **G** wants you to do:
6:33 The true bread of **G** is the one who comes down
6:38 from heaven to do the will of **G** who sent me,
6:39 And this is the will of **G**, that I should not lose
6:45 in the Scriptures, 'They will all be taught by **G**.'
6:46 only I, who was sent from **G**, have seen him.)
6:69 and we know you are the Holy One of **G**."
7:16 my own ideas, but those of **G** who sent me.
7:17 Anyone who wants to do the will of **G** will know
whether my teaching is from **G**
8:40 I told you the truth I heard from **G**, but you are
8:41 out of wedlock! Our true Father is **G** himself."
8:42 Jesus told them, "If **G** were your Father,
8:42 love me, because I have come to you from **G**.
8:47 Anyone whose Father is **G** listens gladly to the
words of **G**.
8:50 no wish to glorify myself, **G** wants to glorify me.
8:54 glorious things about me. You say, 'He is our **G**,'
9:3 born blind so the power of **G** could be seen in him.
9:16 the Pharisees said, "This man Jesus is not from **G**,
9:24 and told him, "Give glory to **G** by telling the truth,
9:29 We know **G** spoke to Moses, but as for this man,
9:31 Well, **G** doesn't listen to sinners, but he is ready to
9:33 If this man were not from **G**, he couldn't do it."
10:33 because you, a mere man, have made yourself **G**."
10:34 "It is written in your own law that **G** said to
10:36 the world by the Father says, 'I am the Son of **G**'?
11:4 No, it is for the glory of **G**. I, the Son of **G**, will
receive glory from this."
11:22 But even now I know that **G** will give you
11:27 always believed you are the Messiah, the Son of **G**,
11:27 the one who has come into the world from **G**."
11:52 of all the children of **G** scattered around the world.
12:13 the road to meet him. They shouted, / "Praise **G**!
12:43 they loved human praise more than the praise of **G**.
12:44 trust me, you are really trusting **G** who sent me.
13:3 he had come from **G** and would return to **G**.
13:31 and **G** will receive glory because of all that
13:32 And **G** will bring me into my glory very soon.
14:1 "Don't be troubled. You trust **G**, now trust in me.
15:21 belong to me, for they don't know **G** who sent me.
16:2 who kill you will think they are doing **G** a service.
16:27 you love me and believe that I came from **G**.
16:30 From this we believe that you came from **G**."
17:3 to know you, the only true **G**, and Jesus Christ,
19:7 to die because he called himself the Son of **G**."
20:17 my Father and your Father, my **G** and your **G**."
20:28 "My Lord and my **G**!" Thomas exclaimed.
20:31 the Son of **G**, and that by believing in him you will
21:19 what kind of death he would die to glorify **G**.

Ac 1:3 he talked to them about the Kingdom of **G**.
2:11 about the wonderful things **G** has done!"
2:17 'In the last days, **G** said, / I will pour out my Spirit
2:22 **G** publicly endorsed Jesus of Nazareth by doing
2:24 **G** released him from the horrors of death
2:30 and he knew **G** had promised with an oath that one
2:32 whom **G** raised from the dead, and we all are
2:36 **G** has made this Jesus whom you crucified to be
2:38 of you must turn from your sins and turn to **G**,
2:39 all who have been called by the Lord our **G**."
2:47 all the while praising **G** and enjoying the goodwill
3:8 Then, walking, leaping, and praising **G**, he went
3:9 people saw him walking and heard him praising **G**.
3:13 the **G** of Abraham, the **G** of Isaac, the **G** of Jacob,
3:13 the **G** of all our ancestors who has brought glory to
3:15 killed the author of life, but **G** raised him to life.
3:18 But **G** was fulfilling what all the prophets had
3:19 Now turn from your sins and turn to **G**, so you can
3:21 as **G** promised long ago through his prophets.
3:22 'The Lord your **G** will raise up a Prophet like me
3:25 and you are included in the covenant **G** promised
3:25 For **G** said to Abraham, 'Through your
3:26 When **G** raised up his servant, he sent him first to
4:10 you crucified, but whom **G** raised from the dead.
4:19 "Do you think **G** wants us to obey you rather than
4:21 starting a riot. For everyone was praising **G**
5:4 thing like this? You weren't lying to us but to **G**."
5:29 "We must obey **G** rather than human authority.
5:30 The **G** of our ancestors raised Jesus from the dead
5:31 Then **G** put him in the place of honor at his right
5:31 and turn to **G** so their sins would be forgiven.
5:32 who is given by **G** to those who obey him."
5:39 But if it is of **G**, you will not be able to stop them.
5:39 may even find yourselves fighting against **G**."
5:41 The apostles left the high council rejoicing that **G**
6:2 our time preaching and teaching the word of **G**,
6:11 "We heard him blaspheme Moses, and even **G**."
7:2 Our glorious **G** appeared to our ancestor Abraham
7:3 **G** told him, 'Leave your native land and your
7:4 Then **G** brought him here to the land where you
7:5 But **G** gave him no inheritance here, not even one
7:5 **G** did promise, however, that eventually the whole
7:6 But **G** also told him that his descendants would
7:7 **G** told him, 'and in the end they will come out
7:8 **G** also gave Abraham the covenant of circumcision
7:9 him to be a slave in Egypt. But **G** was with him
7:10 And **G** gave him favor before Pharaoh, king of
7:10 **G** also gave Joseph unusual wisdom so that
7:17 "As the time drew near when **G** would fulfill his
7:25 Moses assumed his brothers would realize that **G**
7:32 'I am the **G** of your ancestors—the **G** of Abraham,
Isaac, and Jacob.'
7:35 so **G** sent back the same man his people had
7:37 '**G** will raise up a Prophet like me from among
7:42 Then **G** turned away from them and gave them up
7:43 the shrine of Molech, / the star **g** Rephan,
7:44 accordance with the plan shown to Moses by **G**.
7:45 the Gentile nations that **G** drove out of this land,
7:46 "David found favor with **G** and asked for the
7:46 building a permanent Temple for the **G** of Jacob.
7:55 upward into heaven and saw the glory of **G**,
8:10 of him as "the Great One—the Power of **G**."
8:12 of Good News concerning the Kingdom of **G**
8:21 no part in this, for your heart is not right before **G**.
9:20 saying, "He is indeed the Son of **G**!"
10:2 He was a devout man who feared the **G** of Israel,
10:2 and was a man who regularly prayed to **G**.
10:3 he had a vision in which he saw an angel of **G**
10:4 gifts to the poor have not gone unnoticed by **G**!
10:15 "If **G** says something is acceptable, don't say it
10:22 He is a devout man who fears the **G** of Israel
10:28 But **G** has shown me that I should never think of
10:31 and your gifts to the poor have been noticed by **G**!
10:33 waiting before **G** to hear the message the Lord has
10:34 "I see very clearly that **G** doesn't show partiality.
10:36 that there is peace with **G** through Jesus Christ,
10:38 And no doubt you know that **G** anointed Jesus of
10:38 were oppressed by the Devil, for **G** was with him.
10:40 but **G** raised him to life three days later. Then **G**
allowed him to appear,
10:41 but to us whom **G** had chosen beforehand to be his
10:42 and to testify that Jesus is ordained of **G** to be the
10:46 heard them speaking in tongues and praising **G**.
11:1 Judea that the Gentiles had received the word of **G**.
11:9 'If **G** says something is acceptable, don't say it
11:17 And since **G** gave these Gentiles the same gift he
11:18 were answered and they began praising **G**.
11:18 "**G** has also given the Gentiles the privilege of
12:22 shouting, "It is the voice of a **g**, not of a man!"
12:23 people's worship instead of giving the glory to **G**.
13:5 Jewish synagogues and preached the word of **G**.
13:7 to visit him, for he wanted to hear the word of **G**.
13:16 "and you devout Gentiles who fear the **G** of Israel,
13:17 "The **G** of this nation of Israel chose our ancestors
13:21 and **G** gave them Saul son of Kish, a man of the
13:22 But **G** removed him from the kingship
13:22 him with David, a man about whom **G** said,
13:24 to turn from sin and turn to **G** and be baptized.
13:26 and also all of you devout Gentiles who fear the **G**
13:30 But **G** raised him from the dead!
13:33 in that **G** raised Jesus. This is what the second
13:34 For **G** had promised to raise him from the dead,
13:36 served his generation according to the will of **G**,
13:37 someone whom **G** raised and whose body did not
13:39 is freed from all guilt and declared right with **G**—
13:46 "It was necessary that this Good News from **G** be
14:12 They decided that Barnabas was the Greek **g** Zeus
14:15 turn from these worthless things to the living **G**,
14:22 into the Kingdom of **G** through many tribulations.
14:26 grace of **G** for the work they had now completed.
14:27 telling all that **G** had done and how he had opened
15:4 They reported on what **G** had been doing through
15:7 you all know that **G** chose me from among you
15:8 **G**, who knows people's hearts, confirmed that he
15:12 and wonders **G** had done through them among the
15:14 Peter has told you about the time **G** first visited the
15:19 should stop troubling the Gentiles who turn to **G**,
16:10 for we could only conclude that **G** was calling us
16:14 She was a worshiper of **G**. As she listened to us,
16:17 "These men are servants of the Most High **G**,
16:25 and Silas were praying and singing hymns to **G**,
16:34 household rejoiced because they all believed in **G**.
17:13 that Paul was preaching the word of **G** in Berea,
17:23 had this inscription on it—'To an Unknown **G**.'
17:24 "He is the **G** who made the world and everything
17:27 all of this was that the nations should seek after **G**
17:29 we shouldn't think of **G** as an idol designed by
17:30 **G** overlooked people's former ignorance about
18:7 a Gentile who worshiped **G** and lived next door to
18:11 the next year and a half, teaching the word of **G**.
18:13 to worship **G** in ways that are contrary to the law."
18:21 saying, "I will come back later, **G** willing."
18:26 and explained the way of **G** more accurately.
19:4 demonstrate a desire to turn from sin and turn to **G**.
19:8 arguing persuasively about the Kingdom of **G**.
19:11 **G** gave Paul the power to do unusual miracles,
20:21 the necessity of turning from sin and turning to **G**,
20:27 for I didn't shrink from declaring all that **G** wants
20:32 "And now I entrust you to **G** and the word of his
21:19 Paul gave a detailed account of the things **G** had
21:20 After hearing this, they praised **G**. But then they
22:3 I became very zealous to honor **G** in everything I
22:14 'The **G** of our ancestors has chosen you to know
23:1 I have always lived before **G** in all good
23:3 But Paul said to him, "**G** will slap you,
24:14 I worship the **G** of our ancestors, and I firmly
24:15 I have hope in **G**, just as these men do, that he will
24:16 always try to maintain a clear conscience before **G**
24:17 to aid my people and to offer sacrifices to **G**.
26:7 that is why the twelve tribes of Israel worship **G**
26:8 Why does it seem incredible to any of you that **G**
26:18 to light, and from the power of Satan to **G**.

26:20 that all must turn from their sins and turn to **G**—
26:22 But **G** protected me so that I am still alive today to
26:29 I pray to **G** that both you and everyone here in this
27:23 For last night an angel of the **G** to whom I belong
27:24 **G** in his goodness has granted safety to everyone
27:25 So take courage! For I believe **G**. It will be just as
27:35 gave thanks to **G** before them all, and broke off a
28: 6 they changed their minds and decided he was a **g**.
28:15 Paul saw them, he thanked **G** and took courage.
28:23 He told them about the Kingdom of **G** and taught
28:28 So I want you to realize that this salvation from **G**
28:31 proclaiming the Kingdom of **G** with all boldness
Ro 1: 1 chosen by **G** to be an apostle and sent out to preach
1: 2 This Good News was promised long ago by **G**
1: 4 **G** when **G** powerfully raised him from the dead
1: 5 **G** has given us the privilege and authority to tell
Gentiles everywhere what **G**
1: 7 **G** loves you dearly, and he has called you to be his
1: 7 May grace and peace be yours from **G** our Father
1: 8 Let me say first of all that your faith in **G** is
1: 8 How I thank **G** through Jesus Christ for each one
1: 9 **G** knows how often I pray for you. Day and night I
bring you and your needs in prayer to **G**,
1:10 **G** willing, to come at last to see you.
1:16 It is the power of **G** at work, saving everyone who
1:17 This Good News tells us how **G** makes us right in
1:18 But **G** shows his anger from heaven against all
1:19 For the truth about **G** is known to them
1:19 **G** has put this knowledge in their hearts.
1:20 have seen the earth and sky and all that **G** made.
1:20 have no excuse whatsoever for not knowing **G**.
1:21 Yes, they knew **G**, but they wouldn't worship him
as **G** or even give
1:21 And they began to think up foolish ideas of what **G**
1:23 instead of worshiping the glorious, ever-living **G**,
1:24 So **G** let them go ahead and do whatever shameful
1:25 of believing what they knew was the truth about **G**,
1:25 So they worshiped the things **G** made but not the
1:26 That is why **G** abandoned them to their shameful
1:28 When they refused to acknowledge **G**,
1:30 haters of **G**, insolent, proud, and boastful.
2: 2 And we know that **G**, in his justice, will punish
2: 3 Do you think that **G** will judge and condemn
2: 4 how kind, tolerant, and patient **G** is with you?
2: 5 there is going to come a day of judgment when **G**,
2: 7 the glory and honor and immortality that **G** offers.
2:10 and honor and peace from **G** for all who do good—
2:11 For **G** does not show favoritism.
2:12 **G** will punish the Gentiles when they sin,
2:16 The day will surely come when **G**, by Jesus Christ,
2:17 You boast that all is well between yourself and **G**.
2:19 for people who are lost in darkness without **G**.
2:20 the ignorant and teach children the ways of **G**.
2:23 the law, but you dishonor **G** by breaking it.
2:24 "The world blasphemes the name of **G** because of
2:26 won't **G** give them all the rights and honors of
2:29 a true Jew is one whose heart is right with **G**.
2:29 has that kind of change seeks praise from **G**,
3: 2 were entrusted with the whole revelation of **G**.
3: 3 does that mean **G** will break his promises?
3: 4 everyone else in the world is a liar, **G** is true.
3: 5 Isn't it unfair, then, for **G** to punish us?" (That is
3: 6 If **G** is not just, how is he qualified to judge the
3: 7 "how can **G** judge and condemn me as a sinner if
3:11 one has real understanding; / no one is seeking **G**.
3:12 All have turned away from **G**; / all have gone
3:18 "They have no fear of **G** to restrain them."
3:19 to bring the entire world into judgment before **G**.
3:21 But now **G** has shown us a different way of being
3:24 Yet now **G** in his gracious kindness declares us not
3:25 For **G** sent Jesus to take the punishment for our
3:25 We are made right with **G** when we believe that
3:25 **G** was being entirely fair and just when he did not
3:27 that we have done anything to be accepted by **G**?
3:28 So we are made right with **G** through faith and not
3:29 After all, **G** is not the **G** of the Jews only, is he?
Isn't he also the **G** of the Gentiles?
3:30 There is only one **G**, and there is only one way of
4: 2 because of his good deeds that **G** accepted him?
4: 3 For the Scriptures tell us, "Abraham believed **G**,
so **G** declared him to be righteous."
4: 9 have been saying he was declared righteous by **G**
4:10 The answer is that **G** accepted him first, and
4:11 and that **G** had already accepted him and declared
4:11 They are made right with **G** by faith.
4:13 but on the new relationship with **G** that comes by
4:17 That is what the Scriptures mean when **G** told him,
4:17 because Abraham believed in the **G** who brings the
4:18 When **G** promised Abraham that he would become
4:18 **G** had also said, "Your descendants will be as
4:20 grew stronger, and in this he brought glory to **G**.
4:21 He was absolutely convinced that **G** was able to do
4:22 Abraham's faith, **G** declared him to be righteous.
4:23 that **G** declared him to be righteous—
4:24 assuring us that **G** will also declare us to be
righteous if we believe in **G**,
4:25 was raised from the dead to make us right with **G**.
5: 1 we have peace with **G** because of what Jesus
5: 5 For we know how dearly **G** loves us, because he
5: 8 But **G** showed his great love for us by sending
5:10 For since we were restored to friendship with **G** by
5:11 rejoice in our wonderful new relationship with **G**—
5:11 Christ has done for us in making us friends of **G**.
5:14 did not disobey an explicit commandment of **G**,
5:16 but we have the free gift of being accepted by **G**,
5:19 Because one person disobeyed **G**, many people
5:19 But because one other person obeyed **G**,
5:21 giving us right standing with **G** and resulting in
6: 1 so that **G** can show us more and more kindness
6:10 to defeat sin, and now he lives for the glory of **G**.
6:11 and able to live for the glory of **G** through Christ
6:13 give yourselves completely to **G** since you have
6:13 as a tool to do what is right for the glory of **G**.
6:16 or you can choose to obey **G** and receive his
6:17 Thank **G**! Once you were slaves of sin, but now
6:17 all your heart the new teaching **G** has given you.
6:22 the power of sin and have become slaves of **G**.
6:23 but the free gift of **G** is eternal life through Christ
7: 4 can produce good fruit, that is, good deeds for **G**.
7: 6 Now we can really serve **G**, not in the old way by
7: 7 am I suggesting that the law of **G** is evil?
7:25 Thank **G**! The answer is in Jesus Christ our Lord.
8: 3 But **G** put into effect a different plan to save us.
8: 3 **G** destroyed sin's control over us by giving his Son
8: 7 For the sinful nature is always hostile to **G**.
8: 8 control of their sinful nature can never please **G**.
8: 9 the Spirit if you have the Spirit of **G** living in you.
8:10 is alive because you have been made right with **G**.
8:11 The Spirit of **G**, who raised Jesus from the dead,
8:14 all who are led by the Spirit of **G** are children of **G**.
8:17 for everything **G** gives to his Son, Christ, is ours
8:19 day when **G** will reveal who his children really are.
8:23 wait anxiously for that day when **G** will give us
8:28 And we know that **G** causes everything to work
together for the good of those who love **G**
8:29 For **G** knew his people in advance, and he chose
8:31 If **G** is for us, who can ever be against us?
8:32 Since **G** did not spare even his own Son but gave
him up for us all, won't **G**, who gave us Christ,
8:33 Who dares accuse us whom **G** has chosen for his
own? Will **G**? No!
8:34 is sitting at the place of highest honor next to **G**,
8:39 love of **G** that is revealed in Christ Jesus our Lord.
9: 4 **G** revealed his glory to them. He made covenants
9: 5 Their ancestors were great people of **G**, and Christ
9: 5 And he is **G**, who rules over everything and is
9: 6 has **G** failed to fulfill his promise to the Jews?
9: 8 descendants are not necessarily children of **G**.
9: 9 For **G** had promised, "Next year I will return,
9:11 or bad, she received a message from **G**.
9:11 (This message proves that **G** chooses according to
9:14 can we say? Was **G** being unfair? Of course not!
9:15 For **G** said to Moses, / "I will show mercy to
9:16 for it. **G** will show mercy to anyone he chooses.
9:17 For the Scriptures say that **G** told Pharaoh, "I have
9:18 **G** shows mercy to some just because he wants to,
9:19 "Why does **G** blame people for not listening?
9:20 Who are you, a mere human being, to criticize **G**?
9:22 **G** has every right to exercise his judgment and his
9:25 the Gentiles, **G** says in the prophecy of Hosea,
9:26 he will say, / 'You are children of the living **G**.' "
9:30 The Gentiles have been made right with **G** by
9:31 so hard to get right with **G** by keeping the law,
9:32 Because they were trying to get right with **G** by
9:33 **G** warned them of this in the Scriptures when he
10: 1 and my prayer to **G** is that the Jewish people might
10: 2 I know what enthusiasm they have for **G**, but it is
10: 3 of getting right with **G** by trying to keep the law.
10: 4 All who believe in him are made right with **G**.
10: 5 with **G** requires obedience to all of its commands.
10: 6 But the way of getting right with **G** through faith
10: 9 and believe in your heart that **G** raised him from
10:10 in your heart that you are made right with **G**,
10:19 for even in the time of Moses, **G** had said,
10:20 And later Isaiah spoke boldly for **G**: / "I was
10:21 But regarding Israel, **G** said, / "All day long I
11: 1 I ask, then, has **G** rejected his people, the Jews?
11: 2 No, **G** has not rejected his own people, whom he
11: 2 Elijah the prophet complained to **G** about the
11: 5 for not all the Jews have turned away from **G**.
11: 7 Most of the Jews have not found the favor of **G**
11: 7 A few have—the ones **G** has chosen—but the rest
11: 8 "**G** has put them into a deep sleep.
11:13 **G** has appointed me as the apostle to the Gentiles.
11:15 For since the Jews' rejection meant that **G** offered
11:17 So now you also receive the blessing **G** has
11:20 were broken off because they didn't believe **G**,
11:21 For if **G** did not spare the branches he put there in
11:22 Notice how **G** is both kind and severe. He is severe
11:23 **G** will graft them back into the tree again.
11:24 For if **G** was willing to take you who were,
11:28 for **G** has given his gifts to you Gentiles.
11:30 Once, you Gentiles were rebels against **G**,
11:30 refused his mercy, **G** was merciful to you instead.
11:32 For **G** has imprisoned all people in their own
11:33 Oh, what a wonderful **G** we have! How great are
12: 1 I plead with you to give your bodies to **G**.
12: 2 but let **G** transform you into a new person by
12: 2 Then you will know what **G** wants you to do,
12: 3 measuring your value by how much faith **G** has
12: 6 **G** has given each of us the ability to do certain
12: 6 So if **G** has given you the ability to prophesy,
12: 6 speak out when you have faith that **G** is speaking
12: 8 If **G** has given you leadership ability,
12:12 Be glad for all **G** is planning for you. Be patient in
12:14 don't curse them; pray that **G** will bless them.
12:19 Leave that to **G**. For it is written, / "I will take
13: 1 the government, for **G** is the one who put it there.
13: 1 All governments have been placed in power by **G**.
13: 2 to obey the laws of the land are refusing to obey **G**,
13: 4 The authorities are sent by **G** to help you. But if
13: 4 The authorities are established by **G** for that very
13: 6 so they can keep on doing the work **G** intended
14: 3 condemn those who do, for **G** has accepted them.
14: 6 the Lord, since they give thanks to **G** before eating.
14: 6 also want to please the Lord and give thanks to **G**.
14:10 stand personally before the judgment seat of **G**.
14:11 and every tongue will confess allegiance to **G**.' "
14:12 of us will have to give a personal account to **G**.
14:17 For the Kingdom of **G** is not a matter of what we
14:18 serve Christ with this attitude, you will please **G**.
14:20 Don't tear apart the work of **G** over what you eat.
14:22 you are doing, but keep it between yourself and **G**.
14:23 be condemned for not acting in faith before **G**.
15: 5 May **G**, who gives this patience
15: 6 giving praise and glory to **G**, the Father of our
15: 7 Christ has accepted you; then **G** will be glorified.
15: 8 **G** is true to the promises he made to their
15: 9 so the Gentiles might also give glory to **G** for his
15:13 So I pray that **G**, who gives you hope, will keep
15:16 and offer you up as a fragrant sacrifice to **G**
15:17 Jesus has done through me in my service to **G**.
15:18 I have brought the Gentiles to **G** by my message
15:19 the miracles done through me as signs from **G**—
15:30 to join me in my struggle by praying to **G** for me.
15:31 rescued from those in Judea who refuse to obey **G**.
15:32 Then, by the will of **G**, I will be able to come to
15:33 And now may **G**, who gives us his peace, be with
16:20 The **G** of peace will soon crush Satan under your
16:25 **G** is able to make you strong, just as the Good
16:26 and as the eternal **G** has commanded,
16:27 To **G**, who alone is wise, be the glory forever
1Co 1: 1 chosen by the will of **G** to be an apostle of Christ
1: 2 We are writing to the church of **G** in Corinth,
1: 2 you who have been called by **G** to be his own holy
1: 3 May **G** our Father and the Lord Jesus Christ give
1: 4 I can never stop thanking **G** for all the generous
1: 9 **G** will surely do this for you, for he always does
1:14 I thank **G** that I did not baptize any of you except
1:18 recognize this message as the very power of **G**.
1:20 **G** has made them all look foolish and has shown
1:21 Since **G** in his wisdom saw to it that the world
1:24 But to those called by **G** to salvation, both Jews
1:24 Christ is the mighty power of **G** and the wonderful
wisdom of **G**.
1:25 This "foolish" plan of **G** is far wiser than the
1:26 or powerful, or wealthy when **G** called you.
1:27 **G** deliberately chose things the world considers
1:28 **G** chose things despised by the world,
1:29 so that no one can ever boast in the presence of **G**.
1:30 **G** alone made it possible for you to be in Christ
1:30 For our benefit **G** made Christ to be wisdom itself.
1:30 He is the one who made us acceptable to **G**.
2: 5 so that you might trust the power of **G** rather than
2: 7 the wisdom we speak of is the secret wisdom of **G**,
2: 9 what **G** has prepared / for those who love him."
2:10 because **G** has revealed them to us by his Spirit,
2:12 And **G** has actually given us his Spirit (not the
2:12 so we can know the wonderful things **G** has freely
3: 5 only servants. Through us **G** caused you to believe.
3: 6 watered it, but it was **G**, not we, who made it grow.
3: 7 but **G** is important because he is the one who
3: 9 We work together as partners who belong to **G**.
3:16 realize that all of you together are the temple of **G**
and that the Spirit of **G** lives in you?
3:17 **G** will bring ruin upon anyone who ruins this
3:19 For the wisdom of this world is foolishness to **G**.
3:19 "**G** catches those who think they are wise
3:23 and you belong to Christ, and Christ belongs to **G**.
4: 5 then **G** will give to everyone whatever praise is
4: 7 What do you have that **G** hasn't given you? And if
all you have is from **G**, why boast as though
4: 9 But sometimes I think **G** has put us apostles on
4:20 For the Kingdom of **G** is not just fancy talk;
5:13 **G** will judge those on the outside; but as the
6: 9 do wrong will have no share in the Kingdom of **G**?
6:10 of these will have a share in the Kingdom of **G**.
6:11 washed away, and you have been set apart for **G**.
6:11 You have been made right with **G** because of what
6:11 and the Spirit of our **G** have done for you.
6:13 though someday **G** will do away with both of
6:14 And **G** will raise our bodies from the dead by his
6:19 who lives in you and was given to you by **G**?
6:20 for **G** bought you with a high price. So you must
honor **G** with your body.
7: 7 **G** gives some the gift of marriage, and to others he
7:15 for **G** wants his children to live in peace.)
7:17 and continue on as you were when **G** first called
7:20 You should continue on as you were when **G**
7:23 **G** purchased you at a high price. Don't be enslaved
7:24 stay there in your new relationship with **G**.
8: 3 But the person who loves **G** is the one **G** knows
8: 4 we all know that an idol is not really a **g** and that
there is only one **G** and no other.
8: 6 But we know that there is only one **G**, the Father,
8: 6 through whom **G** made everything and through
9: 9 Do you suppose **G** was thinking only about oxen
9:16 I am compelled by **G** to do it. How terrible for me
9:17 But **G** has chosen me and given me this sacred
9:21 But I do not discard the law of **G**; I obey the law of
10: 1 **G** guided all of them by sending a cloud that
10: 5 after all this, **G** was not pleased with most of them,
10:10 for that is why **G** sent his angel of death to destroy
10:13 And **G** is faithful. He will keep the temptation
10:20 these sacrifices are offered to demons, not to **G**.
10:30 If I can thank **G** for the food and enjoy it,
10:31 you do, you must do all for the glory of **G**.
10:32 offense to Jews or Gentiles or the church of **G**.
11: 3 to her husband, and Christ is responsible to **G**.
11:12 women ever since, and everything comes from **G**.
11:13 Is it right for a woman to pray to **G** in public

11:16 and all the churches of **G** feel the same way about
11:22 Or do you really want to disgrace the church of **G**
11:25 "This cup is the new covenant between **G**
11:31 we will not be examined by **G** and judged in this
12: 3 you to know how to discern what is truly from **G**:
12: 3 No one speaking by the Spirit of **G** can curse
12: 6 There are different ways **G** works in our lives,
12: 6 but it is the same **G** who does the work through all
12:10 ability to know whether it is really the Spirit of **G**
12:18 But **G** made our bodies with many parts, and he
12:24 So **G** has put the body together in such a way that
12:28 Here is a list of some of the members that **G** has
12:30 Does **G** give all of us the ability to speak in
13:12 everything completely, just as **G** knows me now.
14: 2 you will be talking to **G** but not to people,
14:12 ask **G** for those that will be of real help to the
14:16 For if you praise **G** only in the spirit, how can
those who don't understand you praise **G**
14:18 I thank **G** that I speak in tongues more than all of
14:25 they will fall down on their knees and worship **G**,
14:25 declaring, "**G** is really here among you."
14:26 another will tell some special revelation **G** has
14:28 and speak in tongues to **G** privately.
14:33 For **G** is not a **G** of disorder but of peace,
15: 9 apostle after the way I persecuted the church of **G**.
15:10 because **G** poured out his special favor on me—
15:10 but **G** who was working through me by his grace.
15:14 preaching is useless, and your trust in **G** is useless.
15:15 And we apostles would all be lying about **G**,
15:15 for we have said that **G** raised Christ from the
15:24 when he will turn the Kingdom over to **G** the
15:27 "**G** has given him authority over all things."
15:27 it does not include **G** himself, who gave Christ his
15:28 the Son will present himself to **G**, so that **G**,
15:34 shame I say that some of you don't even know **G**.
15:38 Then **G** gives it a new body—just the kind he
15:50 and blood cannot inherit the Kingdom of **G**.
15:51 But let me tell you a wonderful secret **G** has
15:57 How we thank **G**, who gives us victory over sin
2Co 1: 1 appointed by **G** to be an apostle of Christ Jesus,
1: 2 May **G** our Father and the Lord Jesus Christ give
1: 3 All praise to the **G** and Father of our Lord Jesus
1: 3 source of every mercy and the **G** who comforts us.
1: 4 we will be able to give them the same comfort **G**
1: 5 the more **G** will shower us with his comfort
1: 6 For when **G** comforts us, it is so that we, in turn,
1: 9 rely on ourselves, but on **G** who can raise the dead.
1:11 many will give thanks to **G** because so many
1:18 As surely as **G** is true, I am not that sort of person.
1:19 because Jesus Christ, the Son of **G**, never wavers
1:20 "Amen" when we give glory to **G** through Christ.
1:21 It is **G** who gives us, along with you, the ability to
1:23 Now I call upon **G** as my witness that I am telling
2:14 But thanks be to **G**, who made us his captives
2:15 Our lives are a fragrance presented by Christ to **G**.
2:17 And we know that the **G** who sent us is watching
3: 3 and ink, but with the Spirit of the living **G**.
3: 4 because of our great trust in **G** through Christ.
3: 5 Our only power and success come from **G**.
3: 7 For his face shone with the glory of **G**,
3: 9 is the new covenant, which makes us right with **G**!
4: 1 since **G** in his mercy has given us this wonderful
4: 2 trick anyone, and we do not distort the word of **G**.
4: 2 We tell the truth before **G**, and all who are honest
4: 4 Satan, the **g** of this evil world, has blinded the
4: 4 the glory of Christ, who is the exact likeness of **G**.
4: 6 For **G**, who said, "Let there be light in the
4: 6 glory of **G** that is seen in the face of Jesus Christ.
4: 7 everyone can see that our glorious power is from **G**
4: 9 We are hunted down, but **G** never abandons us.
4:13 when he said, "I believed in **G**, and so I speak."
4:14 We know that the same **G** who raised our Lord
4:15 and **G** will receive more and more glory.
5: 1 an eternal body made for us by **G** himself and not
5: 5 **G** himself has prepared us for this, and as a
5:11 **G** knows we are sincere, and I hope you know this,
5:12 rather than having a sincere heart before **G**.
5:13 it seems that we are crazy, it is to bring glory to **G**.
5:18 All this newness of life is from **G**, who brought us
5:18 And **G** has given us the task of reconciling people
5:19 For **G** was in Christ, reconciling the world to
5:20 and **G** is using us to speak to you.
5:20 here pleading with you, "Be reconciled to **G**!"
5:21 For **G** made Christ, who never sinned, to be the
5:21 so that we could be made right with **G** through
6: 2 For **G** says, / "At just the right time, I heard you.
6: 2 Indeed, **G** is ready to help you right now.
6: 4 do we try to show that we are true ministers of **G**.
6: 8 We serve **G** whether people honor us or despise us,
6:16 and idols? For we are the temple of the living **G**.
6:16 As **G** said: / "I will live in them / and walk among
them. / I will be their **G**,
7: 1 work toward complete purity because we fear **G**.
7: 6 But **G**, who encourages those who are discouraged,
7: 9 It was the kind of sorrow **G** wants his people to
7:10 For **G** can use sorrow in our lives to help us turn
7:12 so that in the sight of **G** you could show how much
8: 1 what **G** in his kindness has done for the churches
8: 5 and to us for whatever directions **G** might give
8:12 **G** wants you to give what you have, not what you
8:16 I am thankful to **G** that he has given Titus the same
9: 7 For **G** loves the person who gives cheerfully.
9: 8 And **G** will generously provide all you need.
9:10 For **G** is the one who gives seed to the farmer
9:11 they will break out in thanksgiving to **G**.
9:12 they will joyfully express their thanksgiving to **G**.
9:13 You will be glorifying **G** through your generous
9:14 because of the wonderful grace of **G** shown
9:15 Thank **G** for his Son—a gift too wonderful for
10: 5 argument that keeps people from knowing **G**.
11: 2 I am jealous for you with the jealousy of **G**
11:11 Why? Because I don't love you? **G** knows I do.
11:31 **G**, the Father of our Lord Jesus, who is to be
12: 3 or just my spirit, I don't know; only **G** knows.
12: 7 I have received wonderful revelations from **G**.
12:12 I am truly an apostle, sent to you by **G** himself.
12:19 Christ's servants, and we know that **G** is listening.
12:21 I come, **G** will humble me again because of you.
13: 4 he now lives by the mighty power of **G**.
13: 6 we have passed the test and are approved by **G**.
13: 7 We pray to **G** that you will not do anything wrong.
13:11 Then the **G** of love and peace will be with you.
13:13 the grace of our Lord Jesus Christ, the love of **G**,
Gal 1: 1 from Jesus Christ himself and from **G** the Father,
1: 3 May grace and peace be yours from **G** our Father
1: 4 He died for our sins, just as **G** our Father planned,
1: 5 That is why all glory belongs to **G** through all the
1: 6 shocked that you are turning away so soon from **G**,
1:10 No, I am trying to please **G**. If I were still trying to
1:15 For it pleased **G** in his kindness to choose me
1:20 for I declare before **G** that I am not lying.
1:24 And they gave glory to **G** because of me.
2: 2 because **G** revealed to me that I should go.
2: 6 made no difference to me, for **G** has no favorites.)
2: 7 They saw that **G** had given me the responsibility of
2: 8 For the same **G** who worked through Peter for the
2: 9 recognized the gift **G** had given me, and they
2:16 Christians know that we become right with **G**,
2:16 that we might be accepted by **G** because of our
2:17 But what if we seek to be made right with **G**
2:19 So I died to the law so that I might live for **G**.
2:20 life in this earthly body by trusting in the Son of **G**,
2:21 I am not one of those who treats the grace of **G** as
3: 5 does **G** give you the Holy Spirit and work miracles
3: 6 In the same way, "Abraham believed **G**, so **G**
declared him righteous because of his faith."
3: 7 then, are all those who put their faith in **G**.
3: 8 the Scriptures looked forward to this time when **G**
3: 8 **G** promised this good news to Abraham long ago
3:10 law to make them right with **G** are under his curse,
3:11 it is clear that no one can ever be right with **G** by
3:14 **G** has blessed the Gentiles with the same blessing
3:16 **G** gave the promise to Abraham and his child.
3:17 The agreement **G** made with Abraham could not
3:17 430 years later when **G** gave the law to Moses. **G**
would be breaking his promise.
3:18 But **G** gave it to Abraham as a promise.
3:19 **G** gave his laws to angels to give to Moses,
3:19 who was the mediator between **G** and the people.
3:20 but **G** acted on his own when he made his promise
3:21 we could have been made right with **G** by obeying
3:23 shown to us as the way of becoming right with **G**,
3:24 through faith in Christ, we are made right with **G**.
3:26 So you are all children of **G** through faith in Christ
3:29 and now all the promises **G** gave to him belong to
4: 4 **G** sent his Son, born of a woman, subject to the
4: 5 **G** sent him to buy freedom for us who were slaves
4: 6 **G** has sent the Spirit of his Son into your hearts,
4: 6 and now you can call **G** your dear Father.
4: 8 Before you Gentiles knew **G**, you were slaves to
4: 9 And now that you have found **G** (or should I say,
now that **G** has found you),
4:10 You are trying to find favor with **G** by what you do
4:14 and cared for me as though I were an angel from **G**
4:31 free woman, acceptable to **G** because of our faith.
5: 2 on circumcision to make you right with **G**,
5: 3 If you are trying to find favor with **G** by being
5: 4 make yourselves right with **G** by keeping the law,
5: 5 promised to us who are right with **G** through faith.
5: 6 it makes no difference to **G** whether we are
5: 8 It certainly isn't **G**, for he is the one who called
5:10 **G** will judge that person, whoever it is, who has
5:21 that sort of life will not inherit the Kingdom of **G**.
6: 6 Those who are taught the word of **G** should help
6: 7 Remember that you can't ignore **G** and get away
6:14 **G** forbid that I should boast about anything except
6:16 by this principle. They are the new people of **G**.
Eph 1: 1 chosen by **G** to be an apostle of Christ Jesus.
1: 2 sent to you from **G** our Father and Jesus Christ our
1: 3 How we praise **G**, the Father of our Lord Jesus
1: 4 **G** loved us and chose us in Christ to be holy
1: 6 So we praise **G** for the wonderful kindness he has
1:11 of Christ, we have received an inheritance from **G**,
1:12 first to trust in Christ should praise our glorious **G**.
1:13 heard the truth, the Good News that **G** saves you.
1:14 one more reason for us to praise our glorious **G**.
1:16 I have never stopped thanking **G** for you. I pray for
1:17 asking **G**, the glorious Father of our Lord Jesus
1:17 so that you might grow in your knowledge of **G**.
1:22 And **G** has put all things under the authority of
2: 2 work in the hearts of those who refuse to obey **G**.
2: 4 But **G** is so rich in mercy, and he loved us so very
2: 7 so **G** can always point to us as examples of the
2: 8 **G** saved you by his special favor when you
2: 8 you can't take credit for this; it is a gift from **G**.
2:12 and you did not know the promises **G** had made to
2:12 You lived in this world without **G** and without
2:13 Though you once were far away from **G**, now you
2:16 Christ reconciled both groups to **G** by means of his
2:22 as part of this dwelling where **G** lives by his Spirit.
3: 2 **G** has given me this special ministry of
3: 3 **G** himself revealed his secret plan to me.
3: 5 **G** did not reveal it to previous generations,
3: 9 was chosen to explain to everyone this plan that **G**,
3:19 the fullness of life and power that comes from **G**.
3:20 Now glory be to **G**! By his mighty power at work
4: 1 of your calling, for you have been called by **G**.
4: 6 and there is only one **G** and Father, who is over us
4:18 they are far away from the life of **G** because they
4:32 just as **G** through Christ has forgiven you.
5: 2 And **G** was pleased, because that sacrifice was like
5: 4 not for you. Instead, let there be thankfulness to **G**.
5: 5 will inherit the Kingdom of Christ and of **G**.
5: 6 for the terrible anger of **G** comes upon all those
5:20 **G** the Father in the name of our Lord Jesus Christ.
6: 6 of Christ, do the will of **G** with all your heart.
6:17 the sword of the Spirit, which is the Word of **G**.
6:19 Ask **G** to give me the right words as I boldly
6:23 May **G** give you peace, dear friends, and love with
6:23 from **G** the Father and the Lord Jesus Christ.
Php 1: 2 May **G** our Father and the Lord Jesus Christ give
1: 3 Every time I think of you, I give thanks to my **G**.
1: 6 And I am sure that **G**, who began the good work
1: 7 We have shared together the blessings of **G**,
1: 8 **G** knows how much I love you and long for you
1:11 for this will bring much glory and praise to **G**.
1:28 that you are going to be saved, even by **G** himself.
2: 6 Though he was **G**, he did not demand and cling to
his rights as **G**.
2: 9 **G** raised him up to the heights of heaven and gave
2:11 Jesus Christ is Lord, to the glory of **G** the Father.
2:12 obeying **G** with deep reverence and fear.
2:13 For **G** is working in you, giving you the desire to
2:15 innocent lives as children of **G** in a dark world full
2:27 But **G** had mercy on him—and also on me, so that
3: 3 For we who worship **G** in the Spirit are the only
3:14 end of the race and receive the prize for which **G**,
3:15 some point, I believe **G** will make it plain to you.
3:19 Their **g** is their appetite, they brag about shameful
4: 6 Tell **G** what you need, and thank him for all he has
4: 9 me doing, and the **G** of peace will be with you.
4:18 a sweet-smelling sacrifice that is acceptable to **G**
4:19 And this same **G** who takes care of me will supply
4:20 Now glory be to **G** our Father forever and ever.
Col 1: 1 chosen by **G** to be an apostle of Christ Jesus,
1: 2 May **G** our Father give you grace and peace.
1: 3 and we give thanks to **G** the Father of our Lord
1: 9 We ask **G** to give you a complete understanding of
1:10 you will learn to know **G** better and better.
1:14 **G** has purchased our freedom with his blood
1:15 Christ is the visible image of the invisible **G**.
1:15 He existed before **G** made anything at all and is
1:16 Christ is the one through whom **G** created
1:19 For **G** in all his fullness was pleased to live in
1:20 and by him **G** reconciled everything to himself.
1:21 includes you who were once so far away from **G**.
1:22 he has brought you into the very presence of **G**,
1:23 Paul, have been appointed by **G** to proclaim it.
1:25 **G** has given me the responsibility of serving his
1:27 For it has pleased **G** to tell his people that the
1:28 and teach them with all the wisdom **G** has given
1:28 for we want to present them to **G**, perfect in their
2: 9 For in Christ the fullness of **G** lives in a human
2:12 because you trusted the mighty power of **G**,
2:13 Then **G** made you alive with Christ. He forgave all
2:15 **G** disarmed the evil rulers and authorities.
2:19 as we get our nourishment and strength from **G**.
3: 3 and your real life is hidden with Christ in **G**.
3:12 Since **G** chose you to be the holy people whom he
3:16 and spiritual songs to **G** with thankful hearts.
3:17 all the while giving thanks through him to **G** the
3:25 For **G** has no favorites who can get away with evil.
4: 3 that **G** will give us many opportunities to preach
4:11 are working with me here for the Kingdom of **G**.
4:12 for you, asking **G** to make you strong and perfect,
fully confident of the whole will of **G**.
4:18 my chains. May the grace of **G** be with you.
1Th 1: 1 you who belong to **G** the Father and the Lord Jesus
1: 2 We always thank **G** for all of you and pray for you
1: 3 As we talk to our **G** and Father about you,
1: 4 We know that **G** loves you, dear brothers
1: 8 go we find people telling us about your faith in **G**.
1: 9 away from idols to serve the true and living **G**.
1:10 Jesus, whom **G** raised from the dead.
2: 2 Yet our **G** gave us the courage to declare his Good
2: 4 by **G** to be entrusted with the Good News.
2: 4 Our purpose is to please **G**, not people. He is the
2: 5 And **G** is our witness that we were not just
2:10 and so is **G**—that we were pure and honest
2:12 and urged you to live your lives in a way that **G**
2:13 And we will never stop thanking **G** that when we
2:13 accepted what we said as the very word of **G**—
2:15 us out. They displease **G** and oppose everyone
2:16 But the anger of **G** has caught up with them at last.
3: 2 He is our co-worker for **G** and our brother in
3: 9 How we thank **G** for you! Because of you we have
great joy in the presence of **G**.
3:10 asking **G** to let us see you again to fill up anything
3:11 May **G** himself, our Father, and our Lord Jesus
3:13 and holy when you stand before **G** our Father on
4: 1 of the Lord Jesus to live in a way that pleases **G**,
4: 3 **G** wants you to be holy, so you should keep clear
4: 5 pagans do, in their ignorance of **G** and his ways.
4: 7 **G** has called us to be holy, not to live impure lives.
4: 8 is not disobeying human rules but is rejecting **G**,
4: 9 For **G** himself has taught you to love one another.
4:14 **G** will bring back with Jesus all the Christians who
4:16 of the archangel, and with the trumpet call of **G**.
5: 9 For **G** decided to save us through our Lord Jesus
5:23 Now may the **G** of peace make you holy in every
5:24 **G**, who calls you, is faithful; he will do this.

2Th 1: 1 you who belong to **G** our Father and the Lord
1: 2 May **G** our Father and the Lord Jesus Christ give
1: 3 and sisters, we always thank **G** for you, as is right,
1: 5 But **G** will use this persecution to show his justice.
1: 7 And **G** will provide rest for you who are being
1: 8 bringing judgment on those who don't know **G**
1:11 that our **G** will make you worthy of the life to
1:11 And we pray that **G**, by his power, will fulfill all
1:12 because of the undeserved favor of our **G**
2: 3 not come until there is a great rebellion against **G**
2: 4 He will exalt himself and defy every **g** there is
2: 4 He will position himself in the temple of **G**,
claiming that he himself is **G**.
2:11 So **G** will send great deception upon them,
2:13 As for us, we always thank **G** for you,
2:13 We are thankful that **G** chose you to be among the
2:16 May our Lord Jesus Christ and **G** our Father,
3: 5 into an ever deeper understanding of the love of **G**
1Ti 1: 1 appointed by the command of **G** our Savior and by
1: 2 May **G** our Father and Christ Jesus our Lord give
1: 4 they don't help people live a life of faith in **G**.
1: 8 laws are good when they are used as **G** intended.
1:11 Good News entrusted to me by our blessed **G**.
1:13 But **G** had mercy on me because I did it in
1:16 But that is why **G** had mercy on me, so that Christ
1:17 Glory and honor to **G** forever and ever. He is the
1:17 the unseen one who never dies; he alone is **G**.
1:20 to Satan so they would learn not to blaspheme **G**.
2: 3 This is good and pleases **G** our Savior,
2: 5 For there is only one **G** and one Mediator who can
reconcile **G** and people.
2: 6 This is the message that **G** gave to the world at the
2: 8 I want men to pray with holy hands lifted up to **G**,
2:10 For women who claim to be devoted to **G** should
2:13 For **G** made Adam first, and afterward he made
3:15 must conduct themselves in the household of **G**.
3:15 This is the church of the living **G**, which is the
4: 3 But **G** created those foods to be eaten with
4: 4 Since everything **G** created is good, we should not
4: 5 For we know it is made holy by the word of **G**
4:10 for our hope is in the living **G**, who is the Savior of
4:16 and **G** will save you and those who hear you.
5: 4 This is something that pleases **G** very much.
5: 5 truly alone in this world, has placed her hope in **G**.
5: 5 Night and day she asks **G** for help and spends
5:20 so that others will have a proper fear of **G**.
5:21 I solemnly command you in the presence of **G**
6: 1 so that the name of **G** and his teaching will not be
6:11 But you, Timothy, belong to **G**; so run from all
6:12 Hold tightly to the eternal life that **G** has given
6:13 And I command you before **G**, who gives life to
6:15 from heaven by the blessed and only almighty **G**,
6:17 But their trust should be in the living **G**, who richly
6:18 to share with others whatever **G** has given them.
6:20 Timothy, guard what **G** has entrusted to you.
2Ti 1: 2 May **G** our Father and Christ Jesus our Lord give
1: 3 Timothy, I thank **G** for you. He is the **G** I serve
with a clear conscience, just as
1: 6 gift **G** gave you when I laid my hands on you.
1: 7 For **G** has not given us a spirit of fear and timidity,
1: 8 With the strength **G** gives you, be ready to suffer
1: 9 It is **G** who saved us and chose us to live a holy
1:11 And **G** chose me to be a preacher, an apostle,
2: 1 be strong with the special favor **G** gives you in
2: 9 a criminal. But the word of **G** cannot be chained.
2:10 and eternal glory in Christ Jesus to those **G** has
2:15 Work hard so **G** can approve you. Be a good
2:21 you will be a utensil **G** can use for his purpose.
2:25 Perhaps **G** will change those people's hearts,
3: 2 They will be boastful and proud, scoffing at **G**,
3: 4 up with pride, and love pleasure rather than **G**.
3:16 All Scripture is inspired by **G** and is useful to teach
3:17 fully equipped for every good thing **G** wants us to
4: 1 And so I solemnly urge you before **G** and before
4: 2 Preach the word of **G**. Be persistent,
4: 5 to Christ. Complete the ministry **G** has given you.
4: 6 has already been poured out as an offering to **G**.
4:18 To **G** be the glory forever and ever. Amen.
Tit 1: 1 a slave of **G** and an apostle of Jesus Christ.
1: 1 I have been sent to bring faith to those **G** has
1: 2 which **G** promised them before the world began—
1: 3 It is by the command of **G** our Savior that I have
1: 4 May **G** the Father and Christ Jesus our Savior give
1:16 Such people claim they know **G**, but they deny
2: 5 Then they will not bring shame on the word of **G**.
2:10 Then they will make the teaching about **G** our
2:11 For the grace of **G** has been revealed,
2:12 with self-control, right conduct, and devotion to **G**,
2:13 that wonderful event when the glory of our great **G**
3: 4 But then **G** our Savior showed us his kindness
3: 8 so that everyone who trusts in **G** will be careful to
Phm 1: 3 May **G** our Father and the Lord Jesus Christ give
1: 4 I always thank **G** when I pray for you, Philemon,
1:22 for I am hoping that **G** will answer your prayers
Heb 1: 1 Long ago **G** spoke many times and in many ways
1: 2 **G** promised everything to the Son as an
1: 3 and everything about him represents **G** exactly.
1: 3 at the right hand of the majestic **G** of heaven.
1: 4 just as the name **G** gave him is far greater than
1: 5 For **G** never said to any angel what he said to
1: 5 And again **G** said, / "I will be his Father, / and he
1: 6 **G** said, "Let all the angels of **G** worship him."
1: 7 **G** calls his angels / "messengers swift as the wind,
1: 8 "Your throne, O **G**, endures forever and ever.
1: 9 Therefore **G**, your **G**, has anointed you,
1:13 And **G** never said to an angel, as he did to his Son,
1:14 They are spirits sent from **G** to care for those who
2: 2 The message **G** delivered through angels has
2: 4 and **G** verified the message by signs and wonders
2:10 And it was only right that **G**—who made
2:10 suffering of Jesus, **G** made him a perfect leader,
2:12 For he said to **G**, / "I will declare the wonder of
2:13 together with the children **G** has given me."
2:17 be our merciful and faithful High Priest before **G**.
3: 1 dear friends who belong to **G** and are bound for
3: 2 For he was faithful to **G**, who appointed him,
3: 4 a builder, but **G** is the one who made everything.
3: 5 His work was an illustration of the truths **G** would
3:12 turning you away from the living **G**.
3:13 will be deceived by sin and hardened against **G**.
3:14 trusting **G** just as firmly as when we first believed,
3:16 who were those people who rebelled against **G**,
3:17 And who made **G** angry for forty years? Wasn't it
3:18 And to whom was **G** speaking when he vowed that
4: 2 Good News—that **G** has prepared a place of rest—
4: 2 because they didn't believe what **G** told them.
4: 3 As for those who didn't believe, **G** said, / "In my
4: 4 "On the seventh day **G** rested from all his work."
4: 5 But in the other passage **G** said, "They will never
4: 6 News failed to enter because they disobeyed **G**.
4: 7 So **G** set another time for entering his place of rest,
4: 7 **G** announced this through David a long time later
4: 8 **G** would not have spoken later about another day
4: 9 is a special rest still waiting for the people of **G**.
4:10 just as **G** rested after creating the world.
4:11 For anyone who disobeys **G**, as the people of Israel
4:12 For the word of **G** is full of living power. It is
4:13 This is the **G** to whom we must explain all that we
4:14 Priest who has gone to heaven, Jesus the Son of **G**.
4:16 let us come boldly to the throne of our gracious **G**.
5: 1 other human beings in their dealings with **G**.
5: 1 He presents their gifts to **G** and offers their
5: 4 He has to be called by **G** for this work, just as
5: 5 No, he was chosen by **G**, who said to him,
5: 6 And in another passage **G** said to him, / "You are
5: 7 And **G** heard his prayers because of his reverence
for **G**.
5: 9 this way, **G** qualified him as a perfect High Priest,
5:10 And **G** designated him to be a High Priest in the
6: 1 away from evil deeds and placing our faith in **G**.
6: 3 And so, **G** willing, we will move forward to further
6: 5 who have tasted the goodness of the word of **G**
6: 6 and who then turn away from **G**. It is impossible to
6: 6 because they are nailing the Son of **G** to the cross
6: 7 a good crop for the farmer, it has the blessing of **G**.
6:10 For **G** is not unfair. He will not forget how hard
6:13 swear by, **G** took an oath in his own name, saying:
6:15 and he received what **G** had promised.
6:17 **G** also bound himself with an oath, so that those
6:18 So **G** has given us both his promise and his oath.
6:18 because it is impossible for **G** to lie.
7: 1 the city of Salem and also a priest of **G** Most High.
7: 3 remains a priest forever, resembling the Son of **G**.
7: 6 one who had already received the promises of **G**.
7:11 why did **G** need to send a different priest from the
7:19 taken its place. And that is how we draw near to **G**.
7:20 **G** took an oath that Christ would always be a
7:25 to save everyone who comes to **G** through him.
7:25 He lives forever to plead with **G** on their behalf.
7:28 law was given, **G** appointed his Son with an oath,
8: 5 to build the Tabernacle, **G** gave him this warning:
8: 6 who guarantees for us a better covenant with **G**,
8: 8 But **G** himself found fault with the old one when
8:10 so they will obey them. / I will be their **G**,
8:13 When **G** speaks of a new covenant, it means he has
9: 1 Now in that first covenant between **G** and Israel,
9: 7 which he offers to **G** to cover his own sins
9:14 lead to death so that we can worship the living **G**.
9:14 Christ offered himself to **G** as a perfect sacrifice
9:15 the one who mediates the new covenant between **G**
9:15 the eternal inheritance **G** has promised them.
9:20 "This blood confirms the covenant **G** has made
9:24 itself to appear now before **G** as our Advocate.
10: 7 I said, 'Look, I have come to do your will, O **G**—
10:10 And what **G** wants is for us to be made holy by the
10:12 But our High Priest offered himself to **G** as one
10:22 let us go right into the presence of **G**, with true
10:23 we have, for **G** can be trusted to keep his promise.
10:29 be for those who have trampled on the Son of **G**
10:31 terrible thing to fall into the hands of the living **G**.
10:39 we are not like those who turn their backs on **G**
11: 2 **G** gave his approval to people in days of old
11: 4 a more acceptable offering to **G** than Cain did.
11: 4 **G** accepted Abel's offering to show that he was a
11: 5 "suddenly he disappeared because **G** took him."
11: 5 was taken up, he was approved as pleasing to **G**.
11: 6 you see, it is impossible to please **G** without faith.
11: 6 wants to come to him must believe that there is a **G**
11: 7 He obeyed **G**, who warned him about something
11: 8 It was by faith that Abraham obeyed when **G**
11: 8 and go to another land that **G** would give him as
11: 9 And even when he reached the land **G** promised
11: 9 and Jacob, to whom **G** gave the same promise.
11:10 eternal foundations, a city designed and built by **G**.
11:11 Abraham believed that **G** would keep his promise.
11:13 died without receiving what **G** had promised them,
11:13 from a distance and welcomed the promises of **G**.
11:16 That is why **G** is not ashamed to be called their **G**,
11:17 Isaac as a sacrifice when **G** was testing him.
11:18 though **G** had promised him, "Isaac is the son
11:19 **G** was able to bring him back to life again.
11:20 He had confidence in what **G** was going to do in
11:23 They saw that **G** had given them an unusual child,
11:26 ahead to the great reward that **G** would give him.
11:31 all the others in her city who refused to obey **G**.
11:33 and received what **G** had promised them.
11:35 But others trusted **G** and were tortured,
11:35 preferring to die rather than turn from **G** and be
11:39 yet none of them received all that **G** had promised.
11:40 For **G** had far better things in mind for us that
12: 1 And let us run with endurance the race that **G** has
12: 5 forgotten the encouraging words **G** spoke to you,
12: 7 remember that **G** is treating you as his own
12: 8 If **G** doesn't discipline you as he does all of his
12:15 of you will miss out on the special favor of **G**.
12:18 as the Israelites did at Mount Sinai when **G** gave
12:19 so terrible that they begged **G** to stop speaking.
12:22 to the city of the living **G**, the heavenly Jerusalem,
12:23 You have come to **G** himself, who is the judge of
12:24 the one who mediates the new covenant between **G**
12:25 See to it that you obey **G**, the one who is speaking
12:26 When **G** spoke from Mount Sinai his voice shook
12:28 and please **G** by worshiping him with holy fear
12:29 For our **G** is a consuming fire.
13: 4 **G** will surely judge people who are immoral
13: 5 For **G** has said, / "I will never fail you. / I will
13: 7 your leaders who first taught you the word of **G**.
13:15 let us continually offer our sacrifice of praise to **G**
13:16 in need, for such sacrifices are very pleasing to **G**.
13:17 and they know they are accountable to **G**.
13:20[-21] And now, may the **G** of peace, who brought
Jas 1: 1 a slave of **G** and of the Lord Jesus Christ.
1: 5 if you want to know what **G** wants you to do—
1: 9 are poor should be glad, for **G** has honored them.
1:10 are rich should be glad, for **G** has humbled them.
1:12 **G** blesses the people who patiently endure testing.
1:12 of life that **G** has promised to those who love him.
1:13 to do wrong should ever say, "**G** is tempting me."
1:13 **G** is never tempted to do wrong, and he never
1:17 is good and perfect comes to us from **G** above,
1:21 and humbly accept the message **G** has planted in
1:25 what you heard, then **G** will bless you for doing it.
1:27 and lasting religion in the sight of **G** our Father
2: 5 Hasn't **G** chosen the poor in this world to be rich
2: 5 the kingdom **G** promised to those who love him?
2:11 For the same **G** who said, "Do not commit
2:16 and you say, "Well, good-bye and **G** bless you;
2:19 it's enough just to believe that there is one **G**?
2:21 our ancestor Abraham was declared right with **G**
2:22 he was trusting **G** so much that he was willing to
do whatever **G** told
2:23 "Abraham believed **G**, so **G** declared him to be
righteous."
2:23 He was even called "the friend of **G**."
2:24 you see, we are made right with **G** by what we do,
2:25 She was made right with **G** by her actions—
3: 1 for we who teach will be judged by **G** with greater
3: 9 those who have been made in the image of **G**.
4: 2 have what you want is that you don't ask **G** for it.
4: 4 with this world makes you an enemy of **G**?
4: 4 is to enjoy this world, you can't be a friend of **G**.
4: 5 whom **G** has placed within us, jealously longs for
4: 6 Scriptures say, / "**G** sets himself against the proud,
4: 7 So humble yourselves before **G**. Resist the Devil,
4: 8 Draw close to **G**, and **G** will draw close to you.
4:12 **G** alone, who made the law, can rightly judge
5: 9 my brothers and sisters, or **G** will judge you.
1Pe 1: 2 **G** the Father chose you long ago, and the Spirit has
1: 3 All honor to the **G** and Father of our Lord Jesus
1: 3 for it is by his boundless mercy that **G** has given us
1: 4 For **G** has reserved a priceless inheritance for his
1: 5 And **G**, in his mighty power, will protect you until
1: 7 and your faith is far more precious to **G** than mere
1:14 Obey **G** because you are his children. Don't slip
1:15 you must be holy in everything you do, just as **G**—
1:18 For you know that **G** paid a ransom to save you
1:19 of Christ, the sinless, spotless Lamb of **G**.
1:20 **G** chose him for this purpose long before the world
1:21 Through Christ you have come to trust in **G**.
1:21 And because **G** raised Christ from the dead
1:21 and hope can be placed confidently in **G**.
1:23 it comes from the eternal, living word of **G**.
2: 4 the people, but he is precious to **G** who chose him.
2: 5 And now **G** is building you, as living stones,
2: 9 This is so you can show others the goodness of **G**,
2:10 were not a people; / now you are the people of **G**.
2:12 and give honor to **G** when he comes to judge the
2:17 Love your Christian brothers and sisters. Fear **G**.
2:19 For **G** is pleased with you when, for the sake of
2:20 patient beneath the blows, **G** is pleased with you.
2:21 This suffering is all part of what **G** has called you
2:23 He left his case in the hands of **G**, who always
3: 4 a gentle and quiet spirit, which is so precious to **G**.
3: 5 They trusted **G** and accepted the authority of their
3: 9 That is what **G** wants you to do, and he will bless
3:14 for doing what is right, **G** will reward you for it.
3:17 if that is what **G** wants, than to suffer for doing
3:18 sinners that he might bring us safely home to **G**.
3:20 those who disobeyed **G** long ago when **G** waited
3:21 it is an appeal to **G** from a clean conscience.
3:22 He is seated in the place of honor next to **G**,
4: 2 but you will be anxious to do the will of **G**.
4: 5 But just remember that they will have to face **G**,
4: 6 they could still live in the spirit as **G** does.
4:10 **G** has given gifts to each of you from his great
4:11 Then speak as though **G** himself were speaking
4:11 it with all the strength and energy that **G** supplies.
4:11 Then **G** will be given glory in everything through
4:14 then the glorious Spirit of **G** will come upon you.
4:16 Praise **G** for the privilege of being called by his
4:19 and trust yourself to the **G** who made you, for he

5: 2 Care for the flock of **G** entrusted to you.
5: 2 get out of it, but because you are eager to serve **G**.
5: 5 for / "**G** sets himself against the proud,
5: 6 humble yourselves under the mighty power of **G**,
5: 7 Give all your worries and cares to **G**, for he cares
5:10 In his kindness **G** called you to his eternal glory by
5:12 and assure you that the grace of **G** is with you no
2Pe 1: 1 our **G** and Savior, who makes us right with **G**.
1: 2 May **G** bless you with his special favor
1: 2 to know Jesus, our **G** and Lord, better and better.
1: 5 A life of moral excellence leads to knowing **G**
1: 6 Knowing **G** leads to self-control. Self-control leads
1: 9 They have already forgotten that **G** has cleansed
1:10 prove that you really are among those **G** has called
1:11 And **G** will open wide the gates of heaven for you
1:17 and glory from **G** the Father when God's glorious,
1:21 Spirit who moved the prophets to speak from **G**.
2: 1 cleverly teach their destructive heresies about **G**
2: 3 But **G** condemned them long ago, and their
2: 4 For **G** did not spare even the angels when they
2: 5 And **G** did not spare the ancient world—except for
2: 5 Then **G** destroyed the whole world of ungodly
2: 7 **G** rescued Lot out of Sodom because he was a
3: 5 They deliberately forget that **G** made the heavens
3: 7 And **G** has also commanded that the heavens
3:12 the day when **G** will set the heavens on fire
3:13 a world where everyone is right with **G**.
3:14 a pure and blameless life. And be at peace with **G**.
3:15 Paul wrote to you with the wisdom **G** gave him—
1Jn 1: 2 This one who is life from **G** was shown to us,
1: 5 **G** is light and there is no darkness in him at all.
1: 6 we are lying if we say we have fellowship with **G**
1:10 we are calling **G** a liar and showing that his word
2: 1 is Jesus Christ, the one who pleases **G** completely.
2: 4 If someone says, "I belong to **G**," but doesn't
2: 6 Those who say they live in **G** should live their
2:17 But if you do the will of **G**, you will live forever.
2:29 Since we know that **G** is always right, we also
3: 1 the people who belong to this world don't know **G**,
3: 4 Those who sin are opposed to the law of **G**, for all sin opposes the law of **G**.
3: 8 But the Son of **G** came to destroy these works of
3: 9 on sinning, because they have been born of **G**.
3:10 So now we can tell who are children of **G** and who
3:10 not love other Christians does not belong to **G**.
3:20 For **G** is greater than our hearts, and he knows
3:21 is clear, we can come to **G** with bold confidence.
4: 1 them to see if the spirit they have comes from **G**.
4: 2 is the way to find out if they have the Spirit of **G**:
4: 2 a human being, that person has the Spirit of **G**.
4: 3 not acknowledge Jesus, that person is not from **G**.
4: 4 But you belong to **G**, my dear children. You have
4: 6 But we belong to **G**; that is why those who know **G** listen to us.
4: 6 If they do not belong to **G**, they do not listen to us.
4: 7 to love one another, for love comes from **G**.
4: 7 Anyone who loves is born of **G** and knows **G**.
4: 8 But anyone who does not love does not know **G**—for **G** is love.
4: 9 **G** showed how much he loved us by sending his
4:10 It is not that we loved **G**, but that he loved us
4:11 Dear friends, since **G** loved us that much,
4:12 No one has ever seen **G**. But if we love each other, **G** lives in us,
4:13 And **G** has given us his Spirit as proof that we live
4:15 All who proclaim that Jesus is the Son of **G** have **G** living in them, and they live in **G**.
4:16 We know how much **G** loves us, and we have put
4:16 **G** is love, and all who live in love live in **G**, and **G** lives in them.
4:17 And as we live in **G**, our love grows more perfect.
4:20 If someone says, "I love **G**," but hates another
4:20 how can we love **G**, whom we have not seen?
4:21 And **G** himself has commanded that we must love
5: 1 believes that Jesus is the Christ is a child of **G**.
5: 2 We know we love God's children if we love **G**
5: 3 Loving **G** means keeping his commandments,
5: 4 For every child of **G** defeats this evil world by
5: 5 are the ones who believe that Jesus is the Son of **G**.
5: 9 we can believe the testimony that comes from **G**. And **G** has testified about his Son.
5:10 All who believe in the Son of **G** know that this is
5:10 Those who don't believe this are actually calling **G**
5:10 because they don't believe what **G** has testified
5:11 And this is what **G** has testified: He has given us
5:13 I write this to you who believe in the Son of **G**,
5:16 you should pray, and **G** will give that person life.
5:19 We know that we are children of **G** and that the
5:20 And we know that the Son of **G** has come, and he
5:20 us understanding so that we can know the true **G**.
5:20 And now we are in **G** because we are in his Son,
5:20 He is the only true **G**, and he is eternal life.
2Jn 1: 3 which come from **G** our Father and from Jesus
1: 6 Love means doing what **G** has commanded us,
1: 9 of Christ, you will not have fellowship with **G**.
1:13 from the children of your sister, chosen by **G**.
3Jn 1: 5 you are doing a good work for **G** when you take
1: 6 send them on their way in a manner that pleases **G**.
1:11 those who do evil prove that they do not know **G**.
Jude 1: 1 who are called to live in the love of **G** the Father
1: 3 **G** gave this unchanging truth once for all time to
1: 6 not stay within the limits of authority **G** gave them
1: 6 **G** has kept them chained in prisons of darkness,
1:24 And now, all glory to **G**, who is able to keep you
1:25 All glory to him, who alone is **G** our Savior,
Rev 1: 1 which **G** gave him concerning the events that will
1: 2 John faithfully reported the word of **G**
1: 3 **G** blesses the one who reads this prophecy to the
1: 6 and his priests who serve before **G** his Father.
1: 8 the beginning and the end," says the Lord **G**.
1: 9 the island of Patmos for preaching the word of **G**
2: 7 will eat from the tree of life in the paradise of **G**.
2:18 This is the message from the Son of **G**, whose eyes
3: 1 from the one who has the sevenfold Spirit of **G**
3: 2 Your deeds are far from right in the sight of **G**.
3:12 will become pillars in the Temple of my **G**,
3:12 and they will be citizens in the city of my **G**—
3:12 that comes down from heaven from my **G**.
4: 5 burning flames. They are the seven spirits of **G**.
4: 8 "Holy, holy, holy is the Lord **G** Almighty—
4:11 "You are worthy, O Lord our **G**, / to receive glory
5: 6 which are the seven spirits of **G** that are sent out
5: 9 and your blood has ransomed people for **G**
5:14 elders fell down and worshiped **G** and the Lamb.
6: 9 of all who had been martyred for the word of **G**
7: 2 from the east, carrying the seal of the living **G**.
7: 3 or the trees until we have placed the seal of **G** on
7: 4 I heard how many were marked with the seal of **G**.
7:10 "Salvation comes from our **G** on the throne
7:11 fell face down before the throne and worshiped **G**.
7:12 belong to our **G** forever and forever. Amen!"
7:15 why they are standing in front of the throne of **G**,
7:17 And **G** will wipe away all their tears."
8: 2 And I saw the seven angels who stand before **G**,
8: 4 ascended up to **G** from the altar where the angel
9: 4 who did not have the seal of **G** on their foreheads.
9:13 of the gold altar that stands in the presence of **G**.
10: 6 everything in it. He said, "**G** will wait no longer.
11: 1 "Go and measure the Temple of **G** and the altar,
11:11 a half days, the spirit of life from **G** entered them,
11:13 was terrified and gave glory to the **G** of heaven.
11:16 sitting on their thrones before **G** fell on their faces
11:17 "We give thanks to you, Lord **G** Almighty,
11:19 the Temple of **G** was opened and the Ark of his
12: 5 and was caught up to **G** and to his throne.
12: 6 where **G** had prepared a place to give her care for
12:10 the salvation and power and kingdom of our **G**,
12:10 and sisters before our **G** day and night.
13: 1 on each head were names that blasphemed **G**.
13: 5 was allowed to speak great blasphemies against **G**.
13: 6 he spoke terrible words of blasphemy against **G**,
14: 3 a wonderful new song in front of the throne of **G**
14: 4 the people on the earth as a special offering to **G**
14: 7 "Fear **G**," he shouted. "Give glory to him.
15: 2 They were all holding harps that **G** had given
15: 3 the servant of **G**, and the song of the Lamb:
15: 3 marvelous are your actions, / Lord **G** Almighty.
15: 7 a gold bowl filled with the terrible wrath of **G**,
16: 7 "Yes, Lord **G** Almighty, your punishments are
16: 9 and they cursed the name of **G**, who sent all of
16:11 and they cursed the **G** of heaven for their pains
16:14 Lord on that great judgment day of **G** Almighty.
16:19 And so **G** remembered all of Babylon's sins,
16:21 They cursed **G** because of the hailstorm,
17: 3 written all over with blasphemies against **G**.
17:17 For **G** has put a plan into their minds, a plan that
17:17 and so the words of **G** will be fulfilled.
18: 5 and **G** is ready to judge her for her evil deeds.
18: 8 by fire, for the Lord **G** who judges her is mighty."
18:20 O holy people of **G** and apostles and prophets!
18:20 For at last **G** has judged her on your behalf.
19: 1 Salvation is from our **G**. Glory and power belong
19: 4 the four living beings fell down and worshiped **G**,
19: 5 "Praise our **G**, all his servants, from the least to
19: 6 For the Lord our **G**, the Almighty, reigns.
19: 8 the good deeds done by the people of **G**.)
19: 9 "These are true words that come from **G**."
19:10 For I am a servant of **G**, just like you and other
19:10 who testify of their faith in Jesus. Worship **G**.
19:13 dipped in blood, and his title was the Word of **G**.
19:15 the winepress of the fierce wrath of almighty **G**.
19:17 Gather together for the great banquet **G** has
20: 4 about Jesus, for proclaiming the word of **G**.
20: 6 but they will be priests of **G** and of Christ and will
21: 2 coming down from **G** out of heaven like a
21: 3 "Look, the home of **G** is now among his people!
21: 3 will be his people. **G** himself will be with them.
21: 7 and I will be their **G**, and they will be my children.
21:10 Jerusalem, descending out of heaven from **G**.
21:11 It was filled with the glory of **G** and sparkled like a
21:22 for the Lord **G** Almighty and the Lamb are its
21:23 or moon, for the glory of **G** illuminates the city,
22: 1 flowing from the throne of **G** and of the Lamb,
22: 3 For the throne of **G** and of the Lamb will be there,
22: 5 or sun—for the Lord **G** will shine on them.
22: 6 'The Lord **G**, who tells his prophets what the
22: 9 I am a servant of **G**, just like you and your brothers
22: 9 obey what is written in this scroll. Worship **G**!"
22:18 **G** will add to that person the plagues described in
22:19 **G** will remove that person's share in the tree of life

GOD'S (507) [GOD]

GOD'S SON (9) Jn 3:36; 5:28; Eph 4:13; 1Th 1:10; Heb 1:4; 5:8; 1Jn 5:6,12,18

GOD'S WILL (8) Ge 6:9; Ex 28:15; Mk 3:35; 1Th 5:18; 2Ti 1:1; Heb 10:36; 1Pe 2:15; 4:19

Ge 6: 9 He consistently followed **G** will and enjoyed a
6:11 Now the earth had become corrupt in **G** sight,
9: 6 a person is to kill a living being made in **G** image.
21:23 "Swear to me in **G** name that you won't deceive
32: 2 Jacob saw them, he exclaimed, "This is **G** camp!"
40: 8 "Interpreting dreams is **G** business,"
Ex 18:12 They all joined him in a sacrificial meal in **G**
18:15 "Well, the people come to me to seek **G** guidance.
18:16 I inform the people of **G** decisions and teach them
18:20 You should tell them **G** decisions, teach them **G** laws and instructions,
24:11 In fact, they shared a meal together in **G** presence!
28:15 make a chestpiece that will be used to determine **G**
32:16 These stone tablets were **G** work; the words on
Lev 2:13 offerings with salt, to remind you of **G** covenant.
Jdg 13: 6 He was like one of **G** angels, terrifying to look at.
21:18 anyone who does this will fall under **G** curse."
1Sa 30:15 "If you swear by **G** name that you will not kill me
2Sa 9: 3 I want to show **G** kindness to them in any way I
14:16 us from those who would cut us off from **G** people.
2Ki 11:12 He presented Joash with a copy of **G** covenant
1Ch 16: 6 played the trumpets regularly before the Ark of **G**
16:13 O children of Israel, **G** servant, / O descendants of Jacob, **G** chosen one.
25: 1 and Jeduthun to proclaim **G** messages to the
25: 2 who proclaimed **G** messages by the king's orders.
25: 3 who proclaimed **G** messages to the
28: 2 **G** footstool, could rest permanently.
28:12 the outside rooms, the treasuries of **G** Temple,
2Ch 1: 3 the hill at Gibeon where **G** Tabernacle was located.
15: 3 without a priest to teach them, and without **G** law.
19:10 or some other violation of **G** instructions,
20:15 this mighty army, for the battle is not yours, but **G**.
23:11 They presented Joash with a copy of **G** laws
30:12 **G** hand was on the people in the land of Judah,
30:18 even though this was contrary to **G** laws.
33: 7 carved idol he had made and set it up in **G** Temple,
35: 8 and Jehiel, the administrators of **G** Temple,
36:13 even though he had taken an oath of loyalty in **G**
Ezr 2:68 the rebuilding of **G** Temple on its original site,
5:17 issued a decree to rebuild **G** Temple in Jerusalem.
6: 5 and put into **G** Temple as they were before."
7:14 in Judah and Jerusalem, based on your **G** law,
7:20 money for anything necessary for your **G** Temple
7:23 for why should we risk bringing **G** anger against
7:25 and judges who know your **G** laws to govern all
Ne 8:12 because they had heard **G** words and understood
8:16 in their courtyards, in the courtyards of **G** Temple,
10:34 and the common people should bring wood to **G**
11:22 whose family served as singers at **G** Temple.
13: 9 and I brought back the utensils for **G** Temple,
Job 6: 4 my spirit. All **G** terrors are arrayed against me.
13: 8 in his favor? Will you argue **G** case for him?
15: 8 Were you listening at **G** secret council? Do you
15:11 "Is **G** comfort too little for you? Is his gentle word
20:24 He will try to escape, but **G** arrow will pierce him.
20:28 his house. **G** anger will descend on him in torrents.
23:11 "For I have stayed in **G** paths; I have followed his
26: 6 The underworld is naked in **G** presence. There is
27:11 "I will teach you about **G** power. I will not
32: 8 Surely it is **G** Spirit within people, the breath of the
34:28 cause the poor to cry out, catching **G** attention.
37: 2 Listen carefully to the thunder of **G** voice as it rolls
37: 5 **G** voice is glorious in the thunder. We cannot
37:10 **G** breath sends the ice, freezing wide expanses of
40: 2 You are **G** critic, but do you have the answers?"
40:19 It is a prime example of **G** amazing handiwork.
Ps 2:12 Submit to **G** royal son, or he will become angry,
24: 6 They alone may enter **G** presence / and worship
37:31 They fill their hearts with **G** law, / so they will
52: 1 of yours, / you who have disgraced **G** people?
52: 8 I trust in **G** unfailing love / forever and ever.
60:12 With **G** help we will do mighty things, / for he will
61: 7 May he reign under **G** protection forever.
68: 3 the godly rejoice. / Let them be glad in **G** presence.
68:34 Tell everyone about **G** power. / His majesty shines
69:30 Then I will praise **G** name with singing, / and I
69:32 and be glad. / Let all who seek **G** help live in joy.
78:10 They did not keep **G** covenant, / and they refused
78:41 Again and again they tested **G** patience
78:71 of Jacob's descendants— / **G** own people, Israel.
105: 6 O children of Abraham, **G** servant, / O descendants of Jacob, **G** chosen one.
106:14 ran wild, / testing **G** patience in that dry land.
108:13 With **G** help we will do mighty things, / for he will
114: 2 the land of Judah became **G** sanctuary, / and Israel
Pr 25: 2 It is **G** privilege to conceal things and the king's
30: 9 too poor, I may steal and thus insult **G** holy name.
Ecc 3:11 people cannot see the whole scope of **G** work from
3:14 **G** purpose in this is that people should fear him.
9: 1 actions of godly and wise people are in **G** hands,
11: 5 **G** ways are as hard to discern as the pathways of
Isa 14:13 ascend to heaven and set my throne above **G** stars.
26: 1 We are surrounded by the walls of **G** salvation.
26:19 sing for joy! / For **G** light of life will fall like dew
28:12 **G** people could have rest in their own land if they
35: 8 It will be only for those who walk in **G** ways;
53: 6 We have left **G** paths to follow our own.
61: 2 with it, the day of **G** anger against their enemies.
62: 4 Your new name will be the City of **G** Delight
Jer 5:13 **G** prophets are windbags full of words with no
Da 6:11 and found him praying and asking for **G** help.
11:39 Claiming this foreign **g** help, he will attack the
Jnh 2: 8 false gods turn their backs on all **G** mercies.
3: 5 The people of Nineveh believed **G** message,
Mic 3:11 can get; you priests teach **G** laws only for a price;
4: 8 As for you, O Jerusalem, the citadel of **G** people,
Zep 3: 4 Its priests defile the Temple by disobeying **G** laws.
Hag 1:12 and the whole remnant of **G** people obeyed the
1:14 high priest, and the whole remnant of **G** people.
2: 2 and to the remnant of **G** people there in the land:
Zec 8: 6 a small and discouraged remnant of **G** people.
Mal 2: 8 But not you! You have left **G** paths.

Mt 3: 7 “Who warned you to flee **G** coming judgment?
3:10 Even now the ax of **G** judgment is poised, ready to
5:18 even the smallest detail of **G** law will remain until
5:19 But anyone who obeys **G** laws and teaches them
5:34 it is a sacred vow because heaven is **G** throne.
7:13 “You can enter **G** Kingdom only through the
8:29 You have no right to torture us before **G** appointed
10: 6 but only to the people of Israel—**G** lost sheep.
13:23 the hearts of those who truly accept **G** message
14:19 toward heaven, and asked **G** blessing on the food.
15: 9 for they replace **G** commands with their own
15:24 people of Israel—**G** lost sheep—not the Gentiles.”
16:23 from a human point of view, and not from **G**.”
23:16 For you say that it means nothing to swear ‘by **G**
23:37 that kills the prophets and stones **G** messengers!
24:22 But it will be shortened for the sake of **G** chosen
24:24 so as to deceive, if possible, even **G** chosen ones.
26:26 took a loaf of bread and asked **G** blessing on it.
26:64 sitting at **G** right hand in the place of power
Mk 1:14 Jesus went to Galilee to preach **G** Good News.
3:35 Anyone who does **G** will is my brother and sister
4:14 The farmer I talked about is the one who brings **G**
4:20 and accept **G** message and produce a huge
5: 7 Most High God? For **G** sake, don't torture me!”
6:41 toward heaven, and asked **G** blessing on the food.
7: 7 for they replace **G** commands with their own
7: 8 For you ignore **G** specific laws and substitute your
7: 9 “You reject **G** laws in order to hold on to your
8:33 merely from a human point of view, not from **G**.”
10: 6 But **G** plan was seen from the beginning of
13:22 so as to deceive, if possible, even **G** chosen ones.
14:22 took a loaf of bread and asked **G** blessing on it.
14:62 sitting at **G** right hand in the place of power
16:19 and sat down in the place of honor at **G** right hand.
Lk 1: 6 Zechariah and Elizabeth were righteous in **G** eyes,
1:78 Because of **G** tender mercy, / the light from heaven
3: 7 Who warned you to flee **G** coming judgment?
3: 9 Even now the ax of **G** judgment is poised, ready to
7:29 unjust tax collectors, agreed that **G** plan was right,
7:30 and experts in religious law had rejected **G** plan for
8:11 is the meaning of the story: The seed is **G** message.
8:15 good-hearted people who hear **G** message, cling to
9:16 toward heaven, and asked **G** blessing on the food.
9:31 was about to fulfill **G** plan by dying in Jerusalem.
9:43 the people as they saw this display of **G** power.
11:50 of all **G** prophets from the creation of the world—
12: 8 that person in the presence of **G** angels.
12: 9 on earth, I will deny that person before **G** angels.
13:34 that kills the prophets and stones **G** messengers!
15:10 there is joy in the presence of **G** angels when even
21:22 For those will be days of **G** vengeance,
22:20 “This wine is the token of **G** new covenant to save
22:22 the Son of Man, must die since it is part of **G** plan.
22:69 will be sitting at **G** right hand in the place of
23:35 “let him save himself if he is really **G** Chosen
24:30 asked **G** blessing on it, broke it, then gave it to
Jn 1:17 **G** unfailing love and faithfulness came through
2:17 “Passion for **G** house burns within me.”
3:34 He speaks **G** words, for **G** Spirit is upon him
without measure or limit.
3:36 And all who believe in **G** Son have eternal life.
5:28 dead in their graves will hear the voice of **G** Son,
5:42 because I know you don't have **G** love within you.
8:47 Since you don't, it proves you aren't **G** children.”
10:35 So if those people, who received **G** message,
11:40 “Didn't I tell you that you will see **G** glory if you
16: 8 and of **G** righteousness, and of the coming
Ac 2:23 But you followed **G** prearranged plan.
2:33 throne of highest honor in heaven, at **G** right hand.
3:23 listen to that Prophet will be cut off from **G** people
4:31 And they preached **G** message with boldness.
4:33 Lord Jesus, and **G** great favor was upon them all.
6: 7 **G** message was preached in ever-widening circles.
6: 8 Stephen, a man full of **G** grace and power,
7:20 time Moses was born—a beautiful child in **G** eyes.
7:38 Moses was with the assembly of **G** people in the
7:53 You deliberately disobeyed **G** law, though you
7:55 standing in the place of honor at **G** right hand.
7:56 standing in the place of honor at **G** right hand!”
8:14 the people of Samaria had accepted **G** message,
8:20 “May your money perish with you for thinking **G**
11:23 When he arrived and saw this proof of **G** favor,
12:24 But **G** Good News was spreading rapidly,
13:23 Jesus, who is **G** promised Savior of Israel!
13:32 **G** promise to our ancestors has come true in our
13:43 men urged them, “By **G** grace, remain faithful.”
14: 2 But the Jews who spurned **G** message stirred up
15:10 Why are you now questioning **G** way by burdening
18:27 benefit to those who, by **G** grace, had believed.
20:24 the work of telling others the Good News about **G**
20:28 Be sure that you feed and shepherd **G** flock—
23: 4 to him, “Is that the way to talk to **G** high priest?”
26: 6 the fulfillment of **G** promise made to our ancestors.
26:18 their sins and be given a place among **G** people,
Ro 1:15 to you in Rome, too, to preach **G** Good News.
1:32 They are fully aware of **G** death penalty for those
2:12 even though they never had **G** written law.
2:13 For it is not merely knowing the law that brings **G**
2:13 who obey the law will be declared right in **G** sight.
2:14 when Gentiles, who do not have **G** written law,
2:15 They demonstrate that **G** law is written within
2:17 you are relying on **G** law for your special
2:20 For you are certain that in **G** law you have
2:25 is worth something only if you obey **G** law.
2:25 But if you don't obey **G** law, you are no better off
2:26 And if the Gentiles obey **G** law, won't God give
2:27 uncircumcised Gentiles who keep **G** law will be
2:27 and know so much about **G** law but don't obey it.
2:29 but a change of heart produced by **G** Spirit.
3: 5 for people will see **G** goodness when he declares
3:20 For no one can ever be made right in **G** sight by
3:20 For the more we know **G** law, the clearer it
3:22 We are made right in **G** sight when we trust in
3:23 have sinned; all fall short of **G** glorious standard.
3:25 for our sins and to satisfy **G** anger against us.
4: 2 But from **G** point of view Abraham had no basis at
4:13 that **G** promise to give the whole earth to Abraham
4:13 descendants was not based on obedience to **G** law,
4:14 if you claim that **G** promise is for those who obey
G law and think they are “good enough” in **G** sight,
4:16 is the key! **G** promise is given to us as a free gift.
4:20 Abraham never wavered in believing **G** promise.
5: 1 since we have been made right in **G** sight by faith,
5: 2 and joyfully look forward to sharing **G** glory.
5: 9 And since we have been made right in **G** sight by
5: 9 he will certainly save us from **G** judgment.
5:15 our sin and **G** generous gift of forgiveness.
5:15 brought forgiveness to many through **G** bountiful
5:16 And the result of **G** gracious gift is very different
5:17 to rule over us, but all who receive **G** wonderful,
5:18 of righteousness makes all people right in **G** sight
5:19 many people will be made right in **G** sight.
5:20 **G** law was given so that all people could see how
5:20 **G** wonderful kindness became more abundant.
5:21 to death, now **G** wonderful kindness rules instead,
6:14 you to sin. Instead, you are free by **G** grace.
6:15 So since **G** grace has set us free from the law,
7:13 It uses **G** good commandment for its own evil
7:22 I love **G** law with all my heart.
7:25 In my mind I really want to obey **G** law, but
8: 7 to God. It never did obey **G** laws, and it never will.
8:15 You should behave instead like **G** very own
8:16 in our hearts and tells us that we are **G** children.
8:20 everything on earth was subjected to **G** curse.
8:21 All creation anticipates the day when it will join **G**
8:27 for us believers in harmony with **G** own will.
8:38 and even the powers of hell can't keep **G** love
9: 4 people of Israel, chosen to be **G** special children.
9:16 So receiving **G** promise is not up to us. We can't
10: 3 For they don't understand **G** way of making people
10: 3 to keep the law. They won't go along with **G** way.
10:18 “The message of **G** creation has gone out to
11: 4 And do you remember **G** reply? He said, “You are
11: 5 A few are being saved as a result of **G** kindness in
11: 6 And if they are saved by **G** kindness, then it is not
11: 6 **G** wonderful kindness would not be what it really
11:11 Did **G** people stumble and fall beyond recovery?
11:12 because the Jews turned down **G** offer of salvation,
11:17 sharing in **G** rich nourishment of his special olive
11:29 For **G** gifts and his call can never be withdrawn.
11:31 Jews are the rebels, and **G** mercy has come to you.
11:31 But someday they too will share in **G** mercy.
12: 3 As **G** messenger, I give each of you this warning:
12:13 When **G** children are in need, be the one to help
13: 8 you will fulfill all the requirements of **G** law.
13:10 to anyone, so love satisfies all of **G** requirements.
14: 4 Who are you to condemn **G** servants? They are
15: 4 and encouragement as we wait patiently for **G**
15:15 is this reminder from me. For I am, by **G** grace,
15:19 as signs from God—all by the power of **G** Spirit.
1Co 1:22 **G** way seems foolish to the Jews because they
1:25 and **G** weakness is far stronger than the greatest of
2: 1 and brilliant ideas to tell you **G** message.
2:10 out everything and shows us even **G** deep secrets.
2:11 and no one can know **G** thoughts except **G**
2:14 can't understand these truths from **G** Spirit.
3: 9 to God. You are **G** field, **G** building—not ours.
3:10 Because of **G** special favor to me, I have laid the
3:17 For **G** temple is holy, and you Christians are that
3:18 a fool so you can become wise by **G** standards.
4: 1 have been put in charge of explaining **G** secrets.
4:19 big talkers or whether they really have **G** power.
4:20 God is not just fancy talk; it is living by **G** power.
7:19 The important thing is to keep **G** commandments.
7:30 or wealth should not keep anyone from doing **G**
7:40 and I think I am giving you counsel from **G** Spirit
8: 8 It's true that we can't win **G** approval by what we
9: 8 human opinion. Doesn't **G** law say the same thing?
11: 7 for man is **G** glory, made in **G** own image,
11:29 are eating and drinking **G** judgment upon yourself.
14:36 Do you think that the knowledge of **G** word begins
2Co 1: 1 We are writing to **G** church in Corinth and to all
1: 7 share in suffering, you will also share **G** comfort.
1:12 We have depended on **G** grace, not on our own
1:19 to you, and he is the divine Yes—**G** affirmation.
1:20 For all of **G** promises have been fulfilled in him.
2:17 We preach **G** message with sincerity and with
4:15 And as **G** grace brings more and more people to
6: 1 As **G** partners, we beg you not to reject this
marvelous message of **G** great kindness.
6: 7 the truth. **G** power has been working in us.
6:16 And what union can there be between **G** temple
10: 4 We use **G** mighty weapons, not mere worldly
10:13 Our goal is to stay within the boundaries of **G** plan
11: 7 and honored you by preaching **G** Good News to
13: 4 are weak, but we live in him and have **G** power—
Gal 1: 8 Let **G** curse fall on anyone, including myself,
1: 9 you welcomed, let **G** curse fall upon that person.
2:19 the law, I realized I could never earn **G** approval.
3:10 and obey all these commands that are written in **G**
3:18 then it would not be the result of accepting **G**
3:19 coming of the child to whom **G** promise was made.
3:21 is there a conflict between **G** law and **G** promises?
3:22 so the only way to receive **G** promise is to believe
4: 7 Now you are no longer a slave but **G** own child.
4:23 to bring about the fulfillment of **G** promise.
4:23 But the son of the freeborn wife was born as **G**
4:24 Now these two women serve as an illustration of **G**
5: 4 from Christ! You have fallen away from **G** grace.
6:16 May **G** mercy and peace be upon all those who
Eph 1: 1 It is written to **G** holy people in Ephesus, who are
1: 9 **G** secret plan has now been revealed to us; it is a
1:12 **G** purpose was that we who were the first to trust
1:14 The Spirit is **G** guarantee that he will give us
1:20 and seated him in the place of honor at **G** right
2: 3 and we were under **G** anger just like everyone else.
2: 5 (It is only by **G** special favor that you have been
2:10 For we are **G** masterpiece. He has created us anew
2:12 You were excluded from **G** people, Israel, and you
2:19 You are citizens along with all of **G** holy people.
You are members of **G** family.
3: 6 the Jews in all the riches inherited by **G** children.
3: 7 By **G** special favor and mighty power, I have been
3:10 **G** purpose was to show his wisdom in all its rich
3:12 we can now come fearlessly into **G** presence,
3:14 When I think of the wisdom and scope of **G** plan,
3:17 May your roots go down deep into the soil of **G**
3:18 as all **G** people should, how wide, how long,
4:12 Their responsibility is to equip **G** people to do his
4:13 and knowledge of **G** Son that we will be mature
4:24 you are a new person, created in **G** likeness—
4:30 And do not bring sorrow to **G** Holy Spirit by the
5: 1 Follow **G** example in everything you do,
5: 3 Such sins have no place among **G** people.
5:26 and clean, washed by baptism and **G** word.
6:11 Put on all of **G** armor so that you will be able to
6:13 Use every piece of **G** armor to resist the enemy in
6:14 of truth and the body armor of **G** righteousness.
6:19 **G** secret plan that the Good News is for the
6:20 now for preaching this message as **G** ambassador.
6:24 May **G** grace be upon all who love our Lord Jesus
Php 1: 1 It is written to all of **G** people in Philippi,
2:12 to put into action **G** saving work in your lives,
3: 9 on my own goodness or my ability to obey **G** law,
3: 9 For **G** way of making us right with himself
4: 7 If you do this, you will experience **G** peace,
Col 1: 2 It is written to **G** holy people in the city of
1: 4 in Christ Jesus and that you love all of **G** people.
1: 6 and understood the truth about **G** great kindness to
1:12 the inheritance that belongs to **G** holy people,
2: 2 because they have complete understanding of **G**
3: 1 where Christ sits at **G** right hand in the place of
3: 6 **G** terrible anger will come upon those who do such
1Th 1:10 forward to the coming of **G** Son from heaven—
2: 8 so much that we gave you not only **G** Good News
2: 9 there as we preached **G** Good News among you.
2:14 you imitated the believers in **G** churches in Judea
4: 9 love that should be shown among **G** people.
5:18 for this is **G** will for you who belong to Christ
2Th 1: 4 We proudly tell **G** other churches about your
1Ti 2: 1 plead for **G** mercy upon them, and give thanks.
3: 5 own household, how can he take care of **G** church?
6:21 such foolishness. May **G** grace be with you all.
2Ti 1: 1 is from Paul, an apostle of Christ Jesus by **G** will,
2:14 and command them in **G** name to stop fighting
2:19 But **G** truth stands firm like a foundation stone
3:17 It is **G** way of preparing us in every way,
Tit 1: 7 must live a blameless life because he is **G** minister.
3:15 who love us. May **G** grace be with you all.
Phm 1: 5 in the Lord Jesus and your love for all of **G** people.
1: 7 so often refreshed the hearts of **G** people.
Heb 1: 3 The Son reflects **G** own glory, and everything
1: 4 This shows that **G** Son is far greater than the
2: 9 Yes, by **G** grace, Jesus tasted death for everyone in
2:14 Because **G** children are human beings—made of
3: 1 think about this Jesus whom we declare to be **G**
3: 2 and was entrusted with **G** entire house.
3: 5 Moses was certainly faithful in **G** house, but only
3: 6 And we are **G** household, if we keep up our
3: 8 when they tested **G** patience in the wilderness.
4: 1 **G** promise of entering his place of rest still stands,
4: 6 So **G** rest is there for people to enter. But those
4:10 For all who enter into **G** rest will find rest from
5: 8 So even though Jesus was **G** Son, he learned
6:12 of those who are going to inherit **G** promises
6:13 For example, there was **G** promise to Abraham.
6:19 It leads us through the curtain of heaven into **G**
7:11 if the priesthood of Levi could have achieved **G**
7:15 The change in **G** law is even more evident from
7:22 Because of **G** oath, it is Jesus who guarantees the
8: 1 place of highest honor in heaven, at **G** right hand.
9:19 For after Moses had given the people all of **G** laws,
9:19 and sprinkled both the book of **G** laws and all the
10:12 down at the place of highest honor at **G** right hand.
10:21 have a great High Priest who rules over **G** people,
10:27 but the terrible expectation of **G** judgment
10:29 and enraged the Holy Spirit who brings **G** mercy to
10:36 you need now, so you will continue to do **G** will.
11: 3 that the entire universe was formed at **G** command,
11: 7 rest of the world and was made right in **G** sight.
11:17 Abraham, who had received **G** promises,
11:22 confidently spoke of **G** bringing the people of
11:25 He chose to share the oppression of **G** people
11:39 All of these people we have mentioned received **G**
12: 2 place of highest honor beside **G** throne in heaven.
12:10 But **G** discipline is always right and good for us
12:20 They staggered back under **G** command: “If even
12:23 You have come to the assembly of **G** firstborn
13: 9 Your spiritual strength comes from **G** special
13:25 May **G** grace be with you all.
Jas 1:20 Your anger can never make things right in **G** sight.

1:25 But if you keep looking steadily into **G** perfect
2:10 guilty as the person who has broken all of **G** laws.
2:13 then **G** mercy toward you will win out over his
3:13 If you are wise and understand **G** ways, live a life
3:15 and selfishness are not **G** kind of wisdom.
4:11 then you are criticizing and condemning **G** law.
1Pe 1: 1 I am writing to **G** chosen people who are living as
1: 2 May you have more and more of **G** special favor
2: 4 who is the living cornerstone of **G** temple.
2: 5 What's more, you are **G** holy priests, who offer the
2: 8 because they do not listen to **G** word or obey it,
2: 9 of priests, **G** holy nation, his very own possession.
2:10 of God. / Once you received none of **G** mercy;
2:15 It is **G** will that your good lives should silence
2:16 excuse to do evil. You are free to live as **G** slaves.
3: 7 but she is your equal partner in **G** gift of new life.
4:10 so that **G** generosity can flow through you.
4:17 and it must begin first among **G** own children.
4:17 those who have never believed **G** Good News?
4:19 So if you are suffering according to **G** will,
2Pe 1:17 and glory from God the Father when **G** glorious,
2: 5 Noah warned the world of **G** righteous judgment.
1Jn 1: 7 But if we are living in the light of **G** presence,
2: 4 but doesn't obey **G** commandments, that person is
2: 5 But those who obey **G** word really do love him.
2:14 because you are strong with **G** word living in your
3: 2 Yes, dear friends, we are already **G** children,
3: 9 Those who have been born into **G** family do not sin, because **G** life is in them.
3:10 Anyone who does not obey **G** commands and does
3:17 refuses to help—how can **G** love be in that person?
3:24 Those who obey **G** commandments live in
5: 2 We know we love **G** children if we love God
5: 6 And Jesus Christ was revealed as **G** Son by his
5:12 So whoever has **G** Son has life; whoever does not
5:18 We know that those who have become part of **G**
5:18 for **G** Son holds them securely, and the evil one
5:21 keep away from anything that might take **G** place
2Jn 1: 1 as does everyone else who knows **G** truth—
3Jn 1:11 those who do good prove that they are **G** children,
1:15 May **G** peace be with you. Your friends here send
Jude 1: 2 May you receive more and more of **G** mercy,
1: 4 saying that **G** forgiveness allows us to live
1:19 because they do not have **G** Spirit living in them.
1:21 Live in such a way that **G** love can bless you as
Rev 1: 1 An angel was sent to **G** servant John so that John could share the revelation with **G**
3:12 And I will write my **G** name on them, and they
3:14 and true witness, the ruler of **G** creation:
5: 8 filled with incense—the prayers of **G** people!
5:10 And you have caused them to become **G** kingdom
8: 3 given to him to mix with the prayers of **G** people,
10: 7 his trumpet, **G** mysterious plan will be fulfilled.
12:17 all who keep **G** commandments and confess that
13: 7 And the beast was allowed to wage war against **G**
14:10 must drink the wine of **G** wrath. It is poured out undiluted into **G** cup of wrath.
14:12 Let this encourage **G** holy people to endure
14:19 and loaded the grapes into the great winepress of **G**
15: 1 which would bring **G** wrath to completion.
15: 5 in heaven, **G** Tabernacle, was thrown wide open!
15: 8 The Temple was filled with smoke from **G** glory
16: 1 and empty out the seven bowls of **G** wrath on the
17: 6 drunk with the blood of **G** holy people who were
18:10 In one single moment **G** judgment came on her."
18:24 She was the one who slaughtered **G** people all over
20: 9 and surrounded **G** people and the beloved city.
20:12 both great and small, standing before **G** throne.

GOD* (3) [LORD* (YAHWEH)]

Isa 12: 2 The LORD **G** is my strength and my song;
26: 4 for the LORD **G** is the eternal Rock.
38:11 I said, "Never again will I see the LORD **G**

GOD-FEARING (2) [GOD, FEAR]

Ge 42:18 the third day Joseph said to them, "I am a **G** man.
Ac 17:17 to debate with the Jews and the **G** Gentiles,

GOD-GIVEN (2) [GOD, GIVE]

La 3:35 They deprived people of their **G** rights in defiance
Mic 2: 9 and stripped their children of all their **G** rights.

GOD-WARD [KJV] See (BEFORE) GOD, (IN) GOD

GODDESS (7) [GOD]

1Ki 11: 5 the **g** of the Sidonians, and Molech,
11:33 and worshiped Ashtoreth, the **g** of the Sidonians;
2Ki 23:13 for Ashtoreth, the detestable **g** of the Sidonians;
Ac 19:24 silver shrines of the Greek **g** Artemis.
19:27 I'm also concerned that the temple of the great **g**
19:27 this magnificent **g** worshiped throughout the
19:37 from the temple and have not spoken against our **g**.

GODFORSAKEN (2) [FORSAKE, GOD]

Isa 62: 4 Never again will you be called the **G** City
Eze 36:35 will say, 'This **g** land is now like Eden's garden!

GODHEAD [KJV] See GOD

GODLESS (30) [GOD]

Ge 20:11 Abraham said, "I figured this to be a **g** place.
2Sa 23: 6 But the **g** are like thorns to be thrown away,
Job 2:10 But Job replied, "You talk like a **g** woman.
8:13 forget God. The hope of the **g** comes to nothing.
8:16 The **g** seem so strong, like a lush plant growing in
13:16 that I am not **g**. If I were, I would be thrown from
15:34 For the **g** are barren. Their homes,
20: 5 and the joy of the **g** has been only temporary?
20: 6 Though the **g** man's pride reaches to the heavens
27: 8 For what hope do the **g** have when God cuts them
29:17 I broke the jaws of **g** oppressors and made them
34:30 He prevents the **g** from ruling so they cannot be a
36:13 For the **g** are full of resentment. Even when he
36:17 But you are too obsessed with judgment on the **g**.
Pr 11:10 godly succeed; they shout for joy when the **g** die.
Isa 10: 6 will enslave my people, who are a **g** nation.
49:22 "See, I will give a signal to the **g** nations.
52: 1 and **g** people will no longer enter your gates.
Hos 7: 8 "My people of Israel mingle with **g** foreigners,
Ob 1:15 near when I, the LORD, will judge the **g** nations!
Lk 18: 2 "who was a **g** man with great contempt for
1Ti 4: 7 Do not waste time arguing over **g** ideas and old
6:20 Avoid **g**, foolish discussions with those who
2Ti 2:16 Avoid **g**, foolish discussions that lead to more
Tit 2:12 And we are instructed to turn from **g** living
Heb 12:16 Make sure that no one is immoral or **g** like Esau.
1Pe 4: 3 in the past of the evil things that **g** people enjoy—
4:18 what chance will the **g** and sinners have?"
Jude 1: 4 because some **g** people have wormed their way in
1:15 and of all the insults that **g** sinners / have spoken

GODLINESS (14) [GOD]

1Ki 9: 4 for you, if you will follow me with integrity and **g**,
Pr 11: 6 The **g** of good people rescues them; the ambition
13: 6 **G** helps people all through life, while the evil are
14:34 **G** exalts a nation, but sin is a disgrace to any
15: 9 of the wicked, but he loves those who pursue **g**.
21:21 Whoever pursues **g** and unfailing love will find life, **g**, and honor.
Isa 58: 8 Your **g** will lead you forward, and the glory of the
Mt 10:41 welcome good and godly people because of their **g**,
Ac 3:12 had made this man walk by our own power and **g**?
1Ti 2: 2 can live in peace and quietness, in **g** and dignity.
5: 4 their first responsibility is to show **g** at home
2Pe 1: 6 and patient endurance leads to **g**.
1: 7 **G** leads to love for other Christians, and finally

GODLY (160) [GOD]

Dt 16:19 eyes of the wise and corrupt the decisions of the **g**.
1Sa 2: 9 He will protect his **g** ones, / but the wicked will
Job 24: 1 Why must the **g** wait for him in vain?
Ps 1: 5 Sinners will have no place among the **g**.
1: 6 For the LORD watches over the path of the **g**,
4: 3 The LORD has set apart the **g** for himself.
5:12 For you bless the **g**, O LORD, / surrounding them
12: 1 Help, O LORD, for the **g** are fast disappearing!
16: 3 The **g** people in the land / are my true heroes!
16:10 the dead / or allow your **g** one to rot in the grave.
30: 4 Sing to the LORD, all you **g** ones! / Praise his
31:18 those proud and arrogant lips that accuse the **g**.
32: 6 let all the **g** confess their rebellion to you while
33: 1 Let the **g** sing with joy to the LORD, / for it is
37:12 The wicked plot against the **g**; / they snarl at them
37:16 It is better to be **g** and have little / than to be evil
37:17 be shattered, / but the LORD takes care of the **g**.
37:21 and never repay, / but the **g** are generous givers.
37:23 The steps of the **g** are directed by the LORD.
37:25 I am old. / Yet I have never seen the **g** forsaken,
37:26 The **g** always give generous loans to others,
37:28 loves justice, / and he will never abandon the **g**.
37:29 The **g** will inherit the land / and will live there
37:30 The **g** offer good counsel; / they know what is right
37:32 Those who are evil spy on the **g**, / waiting for an
37:33 or let the **g** be condemned when they are brought
37:39 The LORD saves the **g**; / he is their fortress in
49:14 In the morning the **g** will rule over them.
55:22 of you. / He will not permit the **g** to slip and fall.
58:10 The **g** will rejoice when they see injustice avenged.
64:10 The **g** will rejoice in the LORD / and find shelter
68: 3 But let the **g** rejoice. / Let them be glad in God's
72: 7 May all the **g** flourish during his reign. / May there
75:10 but I will increase the power of the **g**."
79: 2 for the birds of heaven. / The flesh of your **g** ones
92:12 But the **g** will flourish like palm trees / and grow
97:10 hate evil! / He protects the lives of his **g** people
97:11 Light shines on the **g**, / and joy on those who do
97:12 May all who are **g** be happy in the LORD
101: 6 I will keep a protective eye on the **g**, / so they may
107:42 The **g** will see these things and be glad,
111: 1 with all my heart / as I meet with his **g** people.
112: 2 an entire generation of **g** people will be blessed.
112: 4 When darkness overtakes the **g**, light will come
118:15 of joy and victory are sung in the camp of the **g**.
118:20 the presence of the LORD, / and the **g** enter there.
125: 3 The wicked will not rule the **g**, / for then the **g** might be forced to do wrong.
132:16 agents of salvation; / its **g** people will sing for joy.
140:13 Surely the **g** are praising your name, / for they will
141: 5 The **g** strike me! / It will be a kindness!
142: 7 so I can thank you. / The **g** will crowd around me,
148:14 made his people strong, / honoring his **g** ones—
Pr 2: 7 He grants a treasure of good sense to the **g**. He is
3:32 to the LORD, but he offers his friendship to the **g**.
10: 3 The LORD will not let the **g** starve to death,
10: 6 The **g** are showered with blessings; evil people
10: 7 We all have happy memories of the **g**,
10:11 The words of the **g** lead to life; evil people cover
10:16 The earnings of the **g** enhance their lives, but evil
10:20 The words of the **g** are like sterling silver; the heart
10:21 The **g** give good advice, but fools are destroyed by
10:24 will all come true; so will the hopes of the **g**.
10:25 wicked away, but the **g** have a lasting foundation.
10:28 The hopes of the **g** result in happiness,
10:30 The **g** will never be disturbed, but the wicked will
10:31 The **g** person gives wise advice, but the tongue that
10:32 The **g** speak words that are helpful, but the wicked
11: 5 The **g** are directed by their honesty; the wicked fall
11: 8 God rescues the **g** from danger, but he lets the
11: 9 one's friends; wise discernment rescues the **g**.
11:10 The whole city celebrates when the **g** succeed;
11:18 for the moment, but the reward of the **g** will last.
11:19 **G** people find life; evil people find death.
11:21 be punished, but the children of the **g** will go free.
11:23 The **g** can look forward to happiness,
11:28 you go! But the **g** flourish like leaves in spring.
11:30 The **g** are like trees that bear life-giving fruit,
12: 3 never brings stability; only the **g** have deep roots.
12: 5 The plans of the **g** are just; the advice of the
12: 6 but the words of the **g** save lives.
12: 7 and are gone, but the children of the **g** stand firm.
12:10 The **g** are concerned for the welfare of their
12:12 each other's loot, while the **g** bear their own fruit.
12:13 by their own words, but the **g** escape such trouble.
12:21 No real harm befalls the **g**, but the wicked have
12:26 The **g** give good advice to their friends; the wicked
12:28 The way of the **g** leads to life; their path does not
13: 5 Those who are **g** hate lies; the wicked come to
13: 9 The life of the **g** is full of light and joy,
13:22 but the sinner's wealth passes to the **g**.
13:25 The **g** eat to their hearts' content, but the belly of
14: 9 but the **g** acknowledge it and seek reconciliation.
14:11 will perish, but the tent of the **g** will flourish.
14:19 the wicked will bow at the gates of the **g**.
14:32 their sins, but the **g** have a refuge when they die.
15: 6 There is treasure in the house of the **g**,
15:28 The **g** think before speaking; the wicked spout evil
16: 8 It is better to be poor and **g** than rich and dishonest.
16:31 is a crown of glory; it is gained by living a **g** life.
17:26 It is wrong to fine the **g** for being good or to punish
18:10 is a strong fortress; the **g** run to him and are safe.
20: 7 The **g** walk with integrity; blessed are their
21:15 Justice is a joy to the **g**, but it causes dismay
21:18 Sometimes the wicked are punished to save the **g**,
21:26 always greedy for more, while the **g** love to give!
23:24 The father of **g** children has cause for joy. What a
24:15 not lie in wait like an outlaw at the home of the **g**.
24:15 And don't raid the house where the **g** live.
25:26 If the **g** compromise with the wicked, it is like
28: 1 one is chasing them, but the **g** are as bold as lions.
28:12 When the **g** succeed, everyone is glad.
28:28 When the wicked meet disaster, the **g** multiply.
29: 2 When the **g** are in authority, the people rejoice.
29: 7 The **g** know the rights of the poor; the wicked
29:16 But the **g** will live to see the tyrant's downfall.
29:27 The **g** despise the wicked; the wicked despise the **g**.
Ecc 9: 1 Even though the actions of **g** and wise people are
Isa 3:10 But all will be well for those who are **g**. Tell them,
57: 1 pass away; the **g** often die before their time.
57: 2 For the **g** who die will rest in peace.
59:15 and anyone who tries to live a **g** life is soon
59:17 himself with the robes of vengeance and **g** fury.
64: 5 those who cheerfully do good, who follow **g** ways. But we are not **g**.
Jer 6:16 Look for the old, **g** way, and walk in it. Travel its
Mic 7: 2 The **g** people have all disappeared; not one
Mal 2:15 **G** children from your union. So guard yourself;
Mt 7:21 "Not all people who sound religious are really **g**.
10:41 And if you welcome good and **g** people because of
13:17 many prophets and **g** people have longed to see
13:43 Then the **g** will shine like the sun in their Father's
13:49 and separate the wicked people from the **g**,
23:29 and decorate the graves of the **g** people your
23:35 you will become guilty of murdering all the **g**
27:52 The bodies of many **g** men and women who had
Lk 1:17 and he will change disobedient minds to accept **g**
14:14 Then at the resurrection of the **g**, God will reward
16: 8 of this world are more shrewd than the **g** are.
Ac 2: 5 **G** Jews from many nations were living in
8: 2 (Some **g** people came and buried Stephen with
13:43 and **g** converts to Judaism who worshiped at the
17: 4 including a large number of **g** Greek men and also
22:12 He was a **g** man in his devotion to the law, and he
1Co 7:14 your children would not have a **g** influence,
2Co 7:11 Just see what this **g** sorrow produced in you!
9: 9 "**G** people give generously to the poor.
11:15 can also do it by pretending to be **g** ministers.
Gal 6: 1 you who are **g** should gently and humbly help that
1Ti 6: 3 and they are the foundation for a **g** life.
6:11 Pursue a **g** life, along with faith, love,
2Ti 3: 5 they will reject the power that could make them **g**.
3:12 and everyone who wants to live a **g** life in Christ
Tit 1: 1 know the truth that shows them how to live **g** lives.
1Pe 3: 1 Your **g** lives will speak to them better than any
3: 2 by watching your pure, **g** behavior.
2Pe 1: 3 gives us everything we need for living a **g** life.
2: 9 the Lord knows how to rescue **g** people from their
3:11 melt away, what holy, **g** lives you should be living!

GODS (278) [GOD]

FALSE GODS (4) Jer 13:25; 48:35; Jnh 2:8; Nah 3:4

OTHER GODS (59) Ex 18:11; 20:3; 23:13; 34:14,16,16; Dt 5:7; 7:4; 8:19; 11:16; 13:6; 17:3; 28:14; 29:26; 30:17; 31:18,20; Jos 23:16; 24:2,16,20; Jdg 2:12,17,19; 10:13; 1Sa 8:8; 1Ki 9:6,9; 11:10; 14:9; 2Ki 17:7,35,37,38; 2Ch 7:19,22;

28:25; Ps 10:16; 16:4; 78:58; Jer 1:16; 2:25; 3:6; 10:11; 16:11; 22:9; 32:29; 35:15; 44:3; 46:25; Eze 6:9; 43:7; 44:12; Hos 1:2; 3:1; 4:10,12; 6:10; 9:1

THEIR GODS (31) Ex 23:32; 34:15,15; Nu 25:2; Dt 7:16; 12:2,3,4,30,30,31,31; 20:18; 32:37; Jos 23:7; Jdg 2:3; 3:6; 1Ki 11:2,4,8; 2Ki 17:31; 1Ch 10:10; Ps 16:4; Isa 42:17; 44:9; 48:11; Eze 6:13; 20:26,28; Jnh 1:5; Ac 7:42

Ge 31:19 Rachel stole her father's household **g** and took
31:30 but why have you stolen my household **g**?"
31:32 But as for your household **g**, let the person who has
31:33 of the two concubines, but he didn't find the **g**.
31:34 Rachel had taken the household **g** and had stuffed
Ex 12:12 I will execute judgment against all the **g** of Egypt,
15:11 "Who else among the **g** is like you, O LORD?
18:11 now that the LORD is greater than all other **g**,
20: 3 "Do not worship any other **g** besides me.
23:13 never pray to or swear by any other **g**.
23:24 Do not worship the **g** of these other nations
23:32 with them and have nothing to do with their **g**.
32: 1 they said, "make us some **g** who can lead us.
32: 4 these are the **g** who brought you out of Egypt!"
32: 8 They are saying, 'These are your **g**, O Israel,
32:23 They said to me, 'Make us some **g** to lead us,
32:31 They have made **g** of gold for themselves.
34:14 You must worship no other **g**, but only the
34:15 adultery against me by sacrificing to their **g**.
34:15 will invite you to go with them to worship their **g**,
34:16 who worship other **g**, as wives for your sons.
34:16 commit adultery against me by worshiping other **g**.
34:17 You must make no **g** for yourselves at all.
Lev 19: 4 trust in idols or make **g** of metal for yourselves.
Nu 25: 2 women invited them to attend sacrifices to their **g**,
25: 2 feasting with them and worshiping the **g** of Moab.
33: 4 The LORD had defeated the **g** of Egypt that night
Dt 4:28 **g** that neither see nor hear nor eat nor smell.
5: 7 " 'Do not worship any other **g** besides me.
6:14 "You must not worship any of the **g** of
7: 4 young people away from me to worship other **g**.
7:16 Show them no mercy and do not worship their **g**.
8:19 forget the LORD your God and follow other **g**,
10:17 "The LORD your God is the God of **g** and Lord
11:16 turn away from the LORD to worship other **g**.
11:28 and turn from his way by worshiping foreign **g**.
12: 2 destroy all the places where they worship their **g**—
12: 3 Erase the names of their **g** from those places!
12: 4 in the way these pagan peoples worship their **g**.
12:30 into following their example in worshiping their **g**.
12:30 Do not say, 'How do these nations worship their **g**?
12:31 that the LORD hates, all in the name of their **g**.
12:31 their sons and daughters as sacrifices to their **g**.
13: 2 'Come, let us worship the **g** of foreign nations,'
13: 6 and says, 'Let us go worship other **g**'—
13: 6 **g** that neither you nor your ancestors have known.
13: 7 They might suggest that you worship the **g** of
13:13 astray by encouraging them to worship foreign **g**.
17: 3 by serving other **g** or by worshiping the sun,
20:18 their detestable customs in the worship of their **g**,
28:14 I am giving you today to follow after other **g**
28:36 Then in exile you will worship **g** of wood
28:64 There you will worship foreign **g** that neither you
28:64 ancestors have known, **g** made of wood and stone!
29:18 our God to worship these **g** of other nations,
29:26 and worship other **g** that were foreign to them,
29:26 **g** that the LORD had not designated for them.
30:17 you are drawn away to serve and worship other **g**,
31:16 these people will begin worshiping foreign **g**,
31:16 the **g** of the land where they are going.
31:18 sins they have committed by worshiping other **g**.
31:20 Then they will begin to worship other **g**; they will
32:12 guided them; / they lived without any foreign **g**.
32:16 stirred up his jealousy by worshiping foreign **g**;
32:17 to **g** they had not known before, / to **g** only recently arrived,
32:17 to **g** their ancestors had never feared.
32:37 Then he will ask, 'Where are their **g**, / the rocks
32:38 Where now are those **g**, / who ate the fat of their
32:38 Let those **g** arise and help you! / Let them provide
Jos 23: 7 Do not even mention the names of their **g**,
23:16 your God by worshiping and serving other **g**,
24: 2 the Euphrates River, and they worshiped other **g**.
24:15 Would you prefer the **g** your ancestors served
24:15 Or will it be the **g** of the Amorites in whose land
24:16 never forsake the LORD and worship other **g**.
24:20 If you forsake the LORD and serve other **g**,
Jdg 2: 3 and their **g** will be a constant temptation to you."
2:12 They chased after other **g**, worshiping the **g** of the people around them.
2:17 to the judges but prostituted themselves to other **g**,
2:19 They followed other **g**, worshiping and bowing
3: 6 to their sons. And the Israelites worshiped their **g**.
5: 8 When Israel chose new **g**, / war erupted at the city
6:10 You must not worship the **g** of the Amorites,
10: 6 and the **g** of Aram, Sidon, Moab, Ammon,
10:13 Yet you have abandoned me and served other **g**.
10:14 Go and cry out to the **g** you have chosen! Let them
10:16 Then the Israelites put aside their foreign **g**
18:24 "You've taken away all my **g** and my priest,
Ru 1:15 has gone back to her people and to her **g**.
1Sa 4: 7 "The **g** have come into their camp!" they cried.
4: 8 Who can save us from these mighty **g** of Israel?
4: 8 They are the same **g** who destroyed the Egyptians
6: 5 he will stop afflicting you, your **g**, and your land.
7: 3 get rid of your foreign **g** and your images of
8: 8 continually forsaken me and followed other **g**.
17:43 And he cursed David by the names of his **g**.
2Sa 7:23 drove out the nations and **g** that stood in their way.
1Ki 9: 6 and laws, and if you go and worship other **g**,
9: 9 out of Egypt, and they worshiped other **g** instead.
11: 2 they married would lead them to worship their **g**.
11: 4 they turned his heart to worship their **g** instead of
11: 8 use for burning incense and sacrificing to their **g**.
11:10 Solomon specifically about worshiping other **g**,
12:28 these are the **g** who brought you out of Egypt!"
14: 9 You have made other **g** and have made me furious
19: 2 "May the **g** also kill me if by this time tomorrow I
20:10 "May the **g** bring tragedy on me, and even worse
20:23 said to him, "The Israelite **g** are **g** of the hills;
2Ki 17: 7 of Israel because the people worshiped other **g**,
17:29 foreigners also continued to worship their own **g**.
17:31 The Avvites worshiped their **g** Nibhaz and Tartak.
17:35 "Do not worship any other **g** or bow before them
17:37 wrote for you. You must not worship any other **g**.
17:38 I made with you, and do not worship other **g**.
18:33 Have the **g** of any other nations ever saved their
18:34 What happened to the **g** of Hamath and Arpad?
18:34 And what about the **g** of Sepharvaim, Hena,
19:12 Have the **g** of other nations rescued them—
19:18 And they have thrown the **g** of these nations into
19:18 They were not **g** at all—only idols of wood
22:17 have abandoned me and worshiped pagan **g**,
23:24 the mediums and psychics, the household **g**,
1Ch 5:25 They worshiped the **g** of the nations that God had
10:10 They placed his armor in the temple of their **g**,
16:25 worthy of praise! / He is to be revered above all **g**.
16:26 The **g** of other nations are merely idols,
2Ch 7:19 have given you, and if you go and worship other **g**,
7:22 out of Egypt, and they worshiped other **g** instead.
13: 8 those gold calves that Jeroboam made as your **g**!
13: 9 can become a priest of these so-called **g** of yours!
21:11 and Judah to give themselves to pagan **g**.
25:14 He set them up as his own **g**, bowed down in front
25:15 "Why have you worshiped **g** who could not even
25:20 to destroy him for worshiping the **g** of Edom.
28:23 He offered sacrifices to the **g** of Damascus who
28:23 for he said, "These **g** helped the kings of Aram,
28:24 then set up altars to pagan **g** in every corner of
28:25 towns of Judah for offering sacrifices to other **g**.
32:13 Were any of the **g** of those nations able to rescue
32:17 "Just as the **g** of all the other nations failed to
32:19 of Jerusalem as though he were one of the pagan **g**,
33:15 Manasseh also removed the foreign **g** from the
34:25 Judah have abandoned me and worshiped pagan **g**,
Ezr 1: 7 and had placed in the temple of his own **g**.
Ps 10:16 Let those who worship other **g** be swept from the
16: 4 Those who chase after other **g** will be filled with
16: 4 their sacrifices / or even speak the names of their **g**.
44:20 or spread our hands in prayer to foreign **g**,
78:58 They made God angry by building altars to other **g**;
82: 6 I say, 'You are **g** / and children of the Most High.
86: 8 Nowhere among the pagan **g** is there a god like
95: 3 is a great God, / the great King above all **g**.
96: 4 of praise! / He is to be revered above all the **g**.
96: 5 The **g** of other nations are merely idols,
97: 7 all who brag about their worthless **g**—
97: 9 over all the earth; / you are exalted far above all **g**.
136: 2 Give thanks to the God of **g**. / His faithful love
138: 1 all my heart; / I will sing your praises before the **g**.
Isa 10:10 we have finished off many a kingdom whose **g**
10:11 So when we have defeated Samaria and her **g**,
14:13 I will preside on the mountain of the **g** far away in
16:12 They will cry to the **g** in their temples, but no one
36:18 Have the **g** of any other nations ever saved their
36:19 What happened to the **g** of Hamath and Arpad? And what about the **g** of Sepharvaim?
37:12 Have the **g** of other nations rescued them—
37:19 And they have thrown the **g** of these nations into
37:19 They were not **g** at all—only idols of wood
41:23 If you are **g**, tell what will occur in the days ahead.
42:17 But those who trust in idols, / calling them their **g**
44: 9 are those who manufacture idols to be their **g**.
45:20 their wooden idols and pray to **g** that cannot save!
46: 2 The **g** cannot protect the people, and the people cannot protect the **g**.
48:11 be able to claim that their **g** have conquered me.
57: 6 Your **g** are the smooth stones in the valleys.
57: 8 have climbed right into bed with these detestable **g**.
57: 9 into the world of the dead, to find new **g** to love.
65:11 his Temple and worship the **g** of Fate and Destiny,
Jer 1:16 for deserting me and worshiping other **g**.
2:11 Has any nation ever exchanged its **g** for another god, even though its **g** are nothing?
2:25 refuse to turn from all this running after other **g**?
2:25 I have fallen in love with these foreign **g**, and I
2:28 Why don't you call on these **g** you have made?
2:28 For you have as many **g** as there are cities
3: 6 Israel has worshiped other **g** on every hill
5: 7 They have sworn by **g** that are not **g** at all!
5:19 and gave yourselves to foreign **g** in your own land.
7: 9 worship Baal and all those other new **g** of yours,
7:18 And they give drink offerings to their other idol **g**!
8: 2 the **g** my people have loved, served,
8:19 me with their carved idols and worthless **g**?"
10: 5 Do not be afraid of such **g**, for they can neither
10: 9 Then they dress these **g** in royal purple robes made
10:11 Say this to those who worship other **g**:
10:11 "Your so-called **g**, who did not make the heavens
11:13 you have as many **g** as there are cities and towns.
13:25 you have forgotten me and put your trust in false **g**.
14:22 Can any of the foreign **g** send us rain? Does it fall
16:11 They worshiped other **g** and served them.
16:18 my land with lifeless images of their detestable **g**
16:20 The **g** they make are not real **g** at all!"
19: 4 The people burn incense to foreign **g**—idols never
19:13 you burned incense on the rooftops to your star **g**,
22: 9 the LORD their God by worshiping other **g**.' "
32:29 and by pouring out drink offerings to other **g**.
35:15 your wicked ways and to stop worshiping other **g**,
43:12 He will set fire to the temples of Egypt's **g**,
43:13 he will burn down the temples of Egypt's **g**.' "
44: 3 They burned incense and worshiped other **g**—
44: 3 **g** that neither they nor you nor any of your
44: 5 They kept right on burning incense to these **g**.
46:25 the god of Thebes, and all the other **g** of Egypt.
48:35 the pagan shrines and burn incense to their false **g**.
50: 2 Her **g** Bel and Marduk will be utterly disgraced.
Eze 6: 9 and lustful eyes that long for other **g**.
6:13 and great oak where they offered incense to their **g**,
16:20 had borne to me—and sacrificed them to your **g**.
16:36 slaughtered your children as sacrifices to your **g**,
20: 7 Do not defile yourselves with the Egyptian **g**,
20: 8 not get rid of their idols or forsake the **g** of Egypt.
20:26 give their firstborn children as offerings to their **g**
20:28 my fury as they offered up sacrifices to their **g**.
43: 7 any longer by their adulterous worship of other **g**
44:12 But they encouraged my people to worship other **g**,
Da 2:11 No one except the **g** can tell you your dream,
2:47 "Truly, your God is the God of **g**, the Lord over
3:12 defied Your Majesty by refusing to serve your **g**
3:14 that you refuse to serve my **g** or to worship the
3:18 can be sure that we will never serve your **g**
4: 8 after my god, and the spirit of the holy **g** is in him.)
4: 9 I know that the spirit of the holy **g** is in you
4:18 because the spirit of the holy **g** is in you.' "
5:11 who has within him the spirit of the holy **g**.
5:14 I have heard that you have the spirit of the **g** within
5:23 drinking wine from them while praising **g** of silver,
5:23 **g** that neither see nor hear nor know anything at
11:36 every god there is, even blaspheming the God of **g**.
11:37 He will have no regard for the **g** of his ancestors,
Hos 1: 2 against the LORD by worshiping other **g**."
3: 1 even though the people have turned to other **g**,
4:10 they have deserted the LORD to worship other **g**.
4:12 serving other **g** and deserting their God.
6:10 have defiled themselves by chasing after other **g**!
7: 9 Worshiping foreign **g** has sapped their strength,
7:14 begging foreign **g** for crops and prosperity.
9: 1 offering sacrifices to other **g** on every threshing
10: 1 more they poured it on the altars of their foreign **g**.
14: 3 again will we call the idols we have made 'our **g**.'
Am 5: 6 Your **g** in Bethel certainly won't be able to quench
5:26 No, your real interest was in your pagan **g**—
Jnh 1: 5 the desperate sailors shouted to their **g** for help
1: 7 cast lots to see which of them had offended the **g**
2: 8 Those who worship false **g** turn their backs on all
Na 1:14 I will destroy all the idols in the temples of your **g**.
3: 4 She taught them all to worship her false **g**,
Hab 1:16 "These nets are the **g** who have made us rich!"
Zep 2:11 terrify them as he destroys all the **g** in the land.
Zec 10: 2 Household **g** give false advice,
Jn 10:34 to certain leaders of the people, 'I say, you are **g**!'
10:35 who received God's message, were called '**g**,'
Ac 7:40 told Aaron, 'Make us some **g** who can lead us,
7:42 up to serve the sun, moon, and stars as their **g**!
7:43 No, your real interest was in your pagan **g**—
14:11 local dialect, "These men are **g** in human bodies!"
19:26 many people that handmade **g** aren't **g** at all.
28:11 an Alexandrian ship with the twin **g** as its
1Co 8: 5 there are many so-called **g** and many lords, both in
8: 7 they think of it as the worship of real **g**, and their
10:19 idols to whom the pagans bring sacrifices are real **g**
Gal 4: 8 you were slaves to so-called **g** that do not even

GOES (65) [GO] See Index of Articles, Etc.

GOG (9)

1Ch 5: 4 descendants of Joel were Shemaiah, **G**, Shimei,
Eze 38: 2 of man, prophesy against **G** of the land of Magog,
38: 3 from the Sovereign LORD: **G**, I am your enemy!
38:14 "Therefore, son of man, prophesy against **G**.
38:18 But when **G** invades the land of Israel,
39: 1 "Son of man, prophesy against **G**. Give him this
39: 1 I am your enemy, O **G**, ruler of the nations of
39:11 "And I will make a vast graveyard for **G** and his
Rev 20: 8 corner of the earth, which are called **G** and Magog.

GOG'S (2)

Eze 39:11 the name of the place to the Valley of **G** Hordes.
39:15 and take them to be buried in the Valley of **G**

GOIIM (2)

Ge 14: 1 King Kedorlaomer of Elam, and King Tidal of **G**
14: 9 King Kedorlaomer of Elam and the kings of **G**,

GOING (309) [GO] See Index of Articles, Etc.

GOINGS (2) [GO]

2Ki 19:27 you well— / your comings and **g** and all you do.
Isa 37:28 you well— / your comings and **g** and all you do.

GOLAN (4)

Dt 4:43 of Gad; **G** in Bashan for the tribe of Manasseh.
Jos 20: 8 and **G** in Bashan, in the land of the tribe of
21:27 **G** in Bashan (a city of refuge) and Be-eshterah.
1Ch 6:71 the town of **G** in Bashan with its pasturelands

GOLD (478) [GOLDEN, GOLDSMITH, GOLDSMITHS]

Ge 2:11 the entire land of Havilah, where g is found.
2:12 The g of that land is exceptionally pure;
13: 2 for Abram was very rich in livestock, silver, and g.
24:22 he gave her a g ring for her nose and two large g bracelets for her wrists.
24:35 a fortune in silver and g, and many servants
24:53 Then he brought out silver and g jewelry
41:42 and placed the royal g chain about his neck.
44: 8 we steal silver or g from your master's house?
Ex 3:22 Israelite women will ask for silver and g jewelry
11: 2 Egyptian neighbors for articles of silver and g."
12:35 Egyptians for clothing and articles of silver and g.
20:23 you must not make or worship idols of silver or g.
25: 3 may accept on my behalf: g, silver, and bronze;
25:11 Overlay it inside and outside with pure g, and put a molding of g all around it.
25:12 Cast four rings of g for it, and attach them to its
25:13 poles from acacia wood, and overlay them with g.
25:17 the place of atonement—out of pure g.
25:18 Then use hammered g to make two cherubim,
25:22 g cherubim that hover over the Ark of the
25:24 Overlay it with pure g and run a molding of g around it.
25:25 top edge, and put a g molding all around the rim.
25:26 Make four g rings, and put the rings at the four
25:28 poles from acacia wood and overlay them with g.
25:29 And make g plates and dishes, as well as pitchers
25:31 "Make a lampstand of pure, hammered g.
25:36 the stem, and they must be hammered from pure g.
25:38 and trays must also be made of pure g.
25:39 You will need seventy-five pounds of pure g for
26: 6 Then make fifty g clasps to fasten the loops of the
26:29 Overlay the frames with g and make g rings to support the crossbars. Overlay the crossbars with g
26:32 Hang this inner curtain on g hooks set into four posts made from acacia wood and overlaid with g.
26:37 Hang this curtain on g hooks set into five posts made from acacia wood and overlaid with g.
28: 5 and embroidered with g thread and blue,
28: 6 and skillfully embroidered with g thread and blue,
28: 8 fine linen cloth embroidered with g thread
28:11 engraves a seal. Mount the stones in g settings.
28:13 The settings are to be made of g filigree,
28:14 and two cords made of pure g will be attached to
28:15 fine linen cloth embroidered with g thread
28:20 and a jasper. All these stones will be set in g.
28:22 to the ephod, make braided cords of pure g.
28:23 Then make two g rings and attach them to the top
28:24 The two g cords will go through the rings on the
28:25 and the ends of the cords will be tied to the g
28:26 Then make two more g rings, and attach them to
28:27 And make two more g rings and attach them to the
28:33 to the hem of the robe, with g bells between them.
28:34 The g bells and pomegranates are to alternate all
28:36 "Next make a medallion of pure g.
29: 6 And place on his head the turban with the g
30: 3 the top, sides, and horns of the altar with pure g,
30: 3 and run a g molding around the entire altar.
30: 4 attach two g rings to support the carrying poles.
30: 5 are to be made of acacia wood and overlaid with g.
31: 4 He is able to create beautiful objects from g,
31: 8 the g lampstand with all its accessories; the incense
32: 2 and sons and daughters to take off their g earrings,
32: 3 obeyed Aaron and brought him their g earrings.
32: 4 Then Aaron took the g, melted it down,
32:24 So I told them, 'Bring me your g earrings.'
32:31 They have made gods of g for themselves.
35: 5 offerings to the LORD: g, silver, and bronze;
35:22 Some brought to the LORD their offerings of g—
35:22 They presented g objects of every kind to the
35:32 He is able to create beautiful objects from g,
36:13 Then fifty g clasps were made to connect the loops
36:34 The frames and crossbars were all overlaid with g.
36:34 used to hold the crossbars were made of pure g.
36:36 then attached to four g hooks set into four posts of
36:36 The posts were overlaid with g and set into four
36:38 decorated tops and bands were overlaid with g.
37: 2 It was overlaid with pure g inside and out, and it had a molding of g all the way around.
37: 3 Four g rings were fastened to its four feet,
37: 4 poles from acacia wood and overlaid them with g.
37: 6 Then, from pure g, he made the Ark's cover—
37: 7 made two figures of cherubim out of hammered g
37:11 It was overlaid with pure g, with a g molding all around the edge.
37:12 of the table, and a g molding ran around the rim.
37:13 Then he cast four rings of g and attached them to
37:15 poles of acacia wood and overlaid them with g.
37:16 Next, using pure g, he made the plates, dishes,
37:17 the lampstand, again using pure, hammered g.
37:22 the stem, and they were hammered from pure g.
37:23 the lamp snuffers, and the trays, all of pure g.
37:24 was made from seventy-five pounds of pure g.
37:26 and horns of the altar with pure g and ran a g molding around the edge.
37:27 Two g rings were placed on opposite sides,
37:28 made of acacia wood and were overlaid with g.
38:24 The people brought gifts of g totaling about 2,200
39: 2 and embroidered with g thread and blue,
39: 3 A skilled craftsman made g thread by beating g
39: 5 and g thread, just as the LORD had commanded
39: 6 shoulder-pieces of the ephod, were set in g filigree.
39: 8 and embroidered with g thread and blue,
39:13 and a jasper. Each of these gemstones was set in g.
39:15 to the ephod, they made braided cords of pure g.
39:16 They also made two g rings and attached them to
39:17 The two g cords were put through the g rings on
39:18 and the ends of the cords were tied to the g settings
39:19 Two more g rings were attached to the lower inside
39:20 Then two g rings were attached to the ephod near
39:25 Bells of pure g were placed between the
39:30 they made the sacred medallion of pure g to be
39:37 the g lampstand and its accessories; the lamp cups
39:38 the g altar; the anointing oil; the fragrant incense;
Lev 8: 9 He placed on Aaron's head the turban with the g
24: 4 The lamps on the pure g lampstand must be tended
24: 6 in the LORD's presence on the pure g table,
Nu 4:11 must also spread a dark blue cloth over the g altar
7:14 He also brought a g container weighing about four
7:20 He also brought a g container weighing about four
7:26 He also brought a g container weighing about four
7:32 He also brought a g container weighing about four
7:38 He also brought a g container weighing about four
7:44 He also brought a g container weighing about four
7:50 He also brought a g container weighing about four
7:56 He also brought a g container weighing about four
7:62 He also brought a g container weighing about four
7:68 He also brought a g container weighing about four
7:74 He also brought a g container weighing about four
7:80 He also brought a g container weighing about four
7:84 silver basins, and twelve g incense containers.
7:86 The weight of the donated g came to about three
7:86 about four ounces for each of the g containers that
8: 4 to its decorative blossoms, was made of beaten g.
22:18 were to give me a palace filled with silver and g,
24:13 were to give me a palace filled with silver and g,
31:22 Anything made of g, silver, bronze, iron, tin,
31:50 So we are presenting the items of g we captured as
31:51 and Eleazar the priest received the g from all the
31:52 the g that the commanders presented as a gift to the
31:54 and brought the g to the Tabernacle as a reminder
Dt 7:25 not desire the silver or g with which they are made.
8:13 and g have multiplied along with everything else,
9:12 and have cast an idol for themselves from g.'
9:16 There below me I could see the g calf you had
17:17 vast amounts of wealth in silver and g for himself.
29:17 detestable idols made of wood, stone, silver, and g.
Jos 6:19 Everything made from silver, g, bronze, or iron is
6:24 Only the things made from silver, g, bronze,
7:21 and a bar of g weighing more than a pound.
7:24 the silver, the robe, the bar of g, his sons,
22: 8 your silver and g, your bronze and iron, and your
Jdg 8:24 being Ishmaelites, all wore g earrings.)
8:25 and each one threw in a g earring he had gathered.
8:26 The weight of the g earrings was forty-three
8:27 Gideon made a sacred ephod from the g and put it
1Sa 6: 4 five rulers, make five g tumors and five g rats,
6: 8 and beside it place a chest containing the g rats
6: 8 place a chest containing the gold rats and g tumors.
6:11 of the LORD and the chest containing the g rats and g tumors were placed on the cart.
6:15 and the chest containing the g rats and g tumors
6:17 The five g tumors that were sent by the Philistines
6:18 The five g rats represented the five Philistine cities
2Sa 1:24 he dressed you in fine clothing and g ornaments.
8: 7 David brought the g shields of Hadadezer's
8:10 David with many gifts of silver, g, and bronze.
8:11 and g he had set apart from the other nations he
12:30 The crown was made of g and set with gems,
1Ki 6:20 Solomon overlaid its walls and ceiling with pure g.
6:21 the rest of the Temple's interior with pure g,
6:21 and he made g chains to protect the entrance to the
6:22 So he finished overlaying the entire Temple with g,
6:28 He overlaid the two cherubim with g.
6:30 The floor in both rooms was overlaid with g.
6:32 open flowers, and the doors were overlaid with g.
6:35 open flowers, and the doors were overlaid with g.
7:48 the g altar, / the g table for the Bread of the Presence,
7:49 the g lampstands, five on the south and five on the
7:49 flower decorations, lamps, and tongs, all of g,
7:50 basins, dishes, and firepans, all of pure g.
7:50 of the Temple, with their fronts overlaid with g.
7:51 the silver, the g, and the other utensils—
9:11 and g he had furnished for the construction of the
9:14 had sent Solomon nine thousand pounds of g.
9:28 brought back to Solomon some sixteen tons of g.
10: 2 huge quantities of g, and precious jewels.
10:10 gave the king a gift of nine thousand pounds of g,
10:11 (When Hiram's ships brought g from Ophir,
10:14 year Solomon received about twenty-five tons of g.
10:16 made two hundred large shields of hammered g,
10:16 each containing over fifteen pounds of g.
10:17 three hundred smaller shields of hammered g,
10:17 each containing nearly four pounds of g.
10:18 a huge ivory throne and overlaid it with pure g.
10:21 All of King Solomon's drinking cups were solid g,
10:22 loaded down with g, silver, ivory, apes,
10:25 who came to visit brought him gifts of silver and g,
12:28 of his counselors, the king made two g calves.
14: 9 and have made me furious with your g calves.
14:26 including all the g shields Solomon had made.
15:15 and g and the utensils that he and his father had
15:18 and g that was left in the treasuries of the
15:19 See, I am sending you a gift of silver and g.
20: 3 'Your silver and g are mine, and so are the best of
20: 5 you give me your silver, g, wives, and children.
20: 7 give him my wives and children and silver and g."
22:48 built a fleet of trading ships to sail to Ophir for g.
2Ki 5: 5 of silver, 150 pounds of g, and ten sets of clothing.
7: 8 carrying out silver and g and clothing and hiding it.
10:29 however, destroy the g calves at Bethel and Dan,
12:13 or other articles of g or silver for the Temple of the
12:18 along with all the g in the treasuries of the
14:14 He carried off all the g and silver and all the
16: 8 and g from the Temple of the LORD
18:14 than eleven tons of silver and about one ton of g.
18:16 Hezekiah even stripped the g from the doors of the
18:16 and from the doorposts he had overlaid with g,
20:13 the silver, the g, the spices, and the aromatic oils.
23:33 pounds of silver and 75 pounds of g as tribute.
23:35 and g demanded as tribute by Pharaoh Neco,
24:13 They cut apart all the g vessels that King Solomon
25:15 and all the other utensils made of pure g or silver.
1Ch 18: 7 David brought the g shields of Hadadezer's
18:10 Joram presented David with many gifts of g,
18:11 and g he had taken from the other nations he had
20: 2 The crown was made of g and set with gems,
21:25 So David gave Araunah six hundred pieces of g in
22:14 nearly four thousand tons of g, nearly forty
28:14 David gave instructions regarding how much g
28:15 He told Solomon the amount of g needed for the g lampstands
28:16 He designated the amount of g for the table on
28:17 David also designated the amount of g for the solid
28:17 g meat hooks used to handle the sacrificial meat
28:18 he designated the amount of refined g for the altar of incense and for the g cherubim,
29: 2 Now there is enough g, silver, bronze, iron,
29: 3 I am giving all of my own private treasures of g
29: 4 I am donating more than 112 tons of g from Ophir
29: 5 and for the other g and silver work to be done by
29: 7 they gave almost 188 tons of g, 10,000 g coins,
2Ch 1:15 and g were as plentiful in Jerusalem as stones.
2: 7 send me a master craftsman who can work with g,
2:14 He is skillful at making things from g, silver,
3: 4 the foyer and the ceiling were overlaid with pure g.
3: 5 overlaid with pure g, and decorated with carvings
3: 6 and with pure g from the land of Parvaim.
3: 7 throughout the Temple were overlaid with g,
3: 8 overlaid with about twenty-three tons of pure g.
3: 9 They used g nails that weighed about twenty
3: 9 of the upper rooms were also overlaid with pure g.
3:10 shaped like cherubim and overlaid them with g.
4: 7 then cast ten g lampstands according to the
4: 8 north wall. Then he molded one hundred g basins.
4:19 the g altar; / the tables for the Bread of the
4:20 and their lamps of pure g to burn in front of the
4:21 flower decorations, lamps, and tongs, all of pure g;
4:22 basins, dishes, and firepans, all of pure g;
4:22 and the main room of the Temple, overlaid with g.
5: 1 including all the silver and g and all the utensils.
8:18 back to Solomon almost seventeen tons of g.
9: 1 huge quantities of g, and precious jewels.
9: 9 gave the king a gift of nine thousand pounds of g,
9:10 of Hiram and Solomon brought g from Ophir,
9:13 Each year Solomon received about 25 tons of g.
9:14 and the governors of the land also brought g
9:15 made two hundred large shields of hammered g,
9:15 each containing over 15 pounds of g.
9:16 three hundred smaller shields of hammered g,
9:16 each containing about 7-1/2 pounds of g.
9:17 a huge ivory throne and overlaid it with pure g.
9:18 and there was a footstool of g attached to it.
9:20 All of King Solomon's drinking cups were solid g,
9:21 loaded down with g, silver, ivory, apes,
9:24 who came to visit brought him gifts of silver and g,
12: 9 royal palace, including all of Solomon's g shields.
13: 8 but with you are those g calves that Jeroboam
13:11 and they light the g lampstand every evening.
15:18 and g and the utensils that he and his father had
16: 2 and g from the treasuries of the LORD's Temple
16: 3 See, I am sending you a gift of silver and g.
21: 3 g, and costly items, and also the ownership of
24:14 and other vessels made of g and silver.
25:24 He carried off all the g and silver and all the
32:27 g, precious stones, and spices, and for his shields
36: 3 of 7,500 pounds of silver and 75 pounds of g.
Ezr 1: 4 their expenses by supplying them with silver and g,
1: 6 assisted by giving them vessels of silver and g,
1:10 g bowls | 30 / silver bowls | 410 / other items
1:11 5,400 g and silver items were turned over to
2:69 The total of their gifts came to 61,000 g coins,
5:14 King Cyrus returned the g and silver utensils that
6: 5 And the g and silver utensils, which were taken to
7:15 you to take with you some silver and g,
7:16 and g which you may obtain from the province of
8:25 the g, the g bowls, and the other items that the
8:26 pounds of silver utensils, / 7,500 pounds of g,
8:27 20 g bowls, equal in value to 1,000 g coins,
8:27 2 fine articles of polished bronze, as precious as g.
8:28 and g is a freewill offering to the LORD,
8:33 On the fourth day after our arrival, the silver, g,
Ne 7:70 The governor gave to the treasury 1,000 g coins,
7:70 50 g basins, and 530 robes for the priests.
7:71 gave to the treasury a total of 20,000 g coins
7:72 The rest of the people gave 20,000 g coins,
Est 1: 6 G and silver couches stood on a mosaic pavement
1: 7 Drinks were served in g goblets of many designs,
4:11 to die unless the king holds out his g scepter.
5: 2 he welcomed her, holding out the g scepter to her.
8: 4 Again the king held out the g scepter to Esther.
8:15 robe of blue and white and the great crown of g,
Job 3:15 wealthy princes whose palaces were filled with g
22:24 and throw your precious g into the river.
23:10 And when he has tested me like g in a fire, he will
28: 1 "People know how to mine silver and refine g.
28: 6 "People know how to find sapphires and g dust—

28:15 "It cannot be bought for **g** or silver.
28:16 Its value is greater than all the **g** of Ophir,
28:17 Wisdom is far more valuable than **g** and crystal.
28:17 cannot be purchased with jewels mounted in fine **g**.
28:19 for it. Its value is greater than the purest **g**.
31:24 my trust in money or felt secure because of my **g**?
42:11 of them brought him a gift of money and a **g** ring.
Ps 19:10 They are more desirable than **g**, / even the finest **g**.
21:3 You placed a crown of finest **g** on his head.
45:9 wearing jewelry of finest **g** from Ophir!
45:13 her chamber, / dressed in a gown woven with **g**.
68:13 now they are covered with silver and **g**,
72:15 the king! / May the **g** of Sheba be given to him.
105:37 safely out of Egypt, loaded with silver and **g**;
106:19 they bowed before an image made of **g**.
115:4 Their idols are merely things of silver and **g**,
119:72 more valuable to me / than millions in **g** and silver!
119:127 your commands / more than **g**, even the finest **g**.
135:15 Their idols are merely things of silver and **g**,
Pr 3:14 better than silver, and her wages are better than **g**.
8:10 rather than silver, and knowledge over pure **g**.
8:19 My gifts are better than the purest **g**, my wages
11:22 but lacks discretion is like a **g** ring in a pig's snout.
16:16 How much better to get wisdom than **g**,
17:3 Fire tests the purity of silver and **g**, but the LORD
20:15 is rarer and more valuable than **g** and rubies.
22:1 in high esteem is better than having silver or **g**.
25:12 one who heeds it as jewelry made from finest **g**.
27:21 Fire tests the purity of silver and **g**, but a person is
Ecc 2:8 I collected great sums of silver and **g**, the treasure
SS 1:11 We will make earrings of **g** for you and beads of
3:10 Its posts are of silver, its canopy is **g**, and its seat is
5:11 His head is the finest **g**, and his hair is wavy
5:14 His arms are like round bars of **g**, set with
5:15 like pillars of marble set in sockets of the finest **g**,
Isa 2:7 of silver and **g** and many horses and chariots.
2:20 They will abandon their **g** and silver idols to the
13:12 People will be as scarce as **g**—more rare than the **g** of Ophir.
13:17 and no amount of silver or **g** will buy them off.
30:22 you will destroy all your silver idols and **g** images.
31:7 when every one of you will throw away the **g** idols
39:2 the silver, the **g**, the spices, and the aromatic oils.
40:19 overlaid with **g**, and decorated with silver chains?
46:6 Some people pour out their silver and **g** and hire a
60:6 From Sheba they will bring **g** and incense for the
60:17 I will exchange your bronze for **g**, your iron for
Jer 10:4 They decorate it with **g** and silver and then fasten it
10:9 sheets of silver from Tarshish and **g** from Uphaz,
20:5 precious jewels and **g** and silver of your kings—
27:16 **g** utensils taken from my Temple will be returned
27:18 let them pray to the LORD Almighty about the **g**
48:13 as Israel was ashamed of her **g** calf at Bethel.
52:19 and all the other utensils made of pure **g** or silver.
La 4:1 How the **g** has lost its luster! Even the finest **g** has
4:2 worth their weight in **g**, are now treated like pots of
Eze 7:20 They were proud of their **g** jewelry and used it to
16:13 And so you were made beautiful with **g** and silver.
16:17 You took the very jewels and **g** and silver
27:22 jewels, and **g** in exchange for your wares.
28:4 great wealth—**g** and silver for your treasuries.
28:13 beautifully crafted for you and set in the finest **g**.
38:13 will ask, 'Who are you to rob them of silver and **g**?
Da 2:32 The head of the statue was made of fine **g**, its chest
2:35 into a heap of iron, clay, bronze, silver, and **g**.
2:38 birds under your control. You are the head of **g**.
2:45 dust the statue of iron, bronze, clay, silver, and **g**.
3:1 King Nebuchadnezzar made a **g** statue ninety feet
3:5 to worship King Nebuchadnezzar's **g** statue.
3:10 and worship the **g** statue when they hear the sound
3:12 or to worship the **g** statue you have set up."
3:14 my gods or to worship the **g** statue I have set up?
3:18 or worship the **g** statue you have set up."
5:2 he gave orders to bring in the **g** and silver cups that
5:3 So they brought these **g** cups taken from the
5:4 toasts from them to honor their idols made of **g**,
5:7 and will wear a **g** chain around his neck.
5:16 and you will wear a **g** chain around your neck.
5:23 gods of silver, **g**, bronze, iron, wood, and stone—
5:29 purple robes, a **g** chain was hung around his neck,
10:5 with a belt of pure **g** around his waist.
11:8 with him, along with priceless **g** and silver dishes.
11:38 and lavish on him **g**, silver, precious stones,
11:43 He will gain control over the **g**, silver,
Hos 2:8 Even the **g** and silver she used in worshiping the
8:4 idols for themselves from their silver and **g**,
Joel 3:5 You have taken my silver and **g** and all my
Na 2:9 Loot the silver! Plunder the **g**! There seems no end
Hab 2:19 They may be overlaid with **g** and silver, but they
Zep 1:18 and **g** will be of no use to you on that day of the
Hag 2:8 The silver is mine, and the **g** is mine,
Zec 4:2 "I see a solid **g** lampstand with a bowl of oil on
4:12 that pour out golden oil through two **g** tubes?"
6:10 of silver and **g** from the Jews exiled in Babylon.
6:11 their gifts and make a crown from the silver and **g**.
9:3 and **g** that it is as common as dust in the streets!
13:9 just as **g** and silver are refined and purified by fire.
14:14 great quantities of **g** and silver and fine clothing.
Mal 3:3 purify the Levites, refining them like **g** or silver,
Mt 2:11 their treasure chests and gave him gifts of **g**,
23:16 then you say that it is binding to swear 'by the **g** in
23:17 Which is greater, the **g**, or the Temple that makes the **g** sacred?
25:15 He gave five bags of **g** to one, two bags of **g** to another, and one bag of **g** to the last—
25:16 The servant who received the five bags of **g** began
25:17 The servant with two bags of **g** also went right to
25:18 But the servant who received the one bag of **g** dug
25:20 to whom he had entrusted the five bags of **g** said,
25:20 you gave me five bags of **g** to invest and I have
25:22 the servant who had received the two bags of **g**,
25:22 'Sir, you gave me two bags of **g** to invest,
25:24 "Then the servant with the one bag of **g** came
25:28 and give it to the one with the ten bags of **g**.
Ac 17:29 of God as an idol designed by craftsmen from **g**
1Co 3:12 anyone who builds on that foundation may use **g**,
1Ti 2:9 or by wearing **g** or pearls or expensive clothes.
2Ti 2:20 In a wealthy home some utensils are made of **g**
Heb 9:4 In that room were a **g** incense altar and a wooden
9:4 which was covered with **g** on all sides.
9:4 Inside the Ark were a **g** jar containing some
Jas 5:3 Your **g** and silver have become worthless.
1Pe 1:7 It is being tested as fire tests and purifies **g**—
1:7 your faith is far more precious to God than mere **g**.
1:18 And the ransom he paid was not mere **g** or silver.
Rev 1:12 was speaking to me, I saw seven **g** lampstands.
1:13 He was wearing a long robe with a **g** sash across
1:20 saw in my right hand and the seven **g** lampstands:
2:1 the one who walks among the seven **g** lampstands:
3:18 I advise you to buy **g** from me—**g** that has been purified by fire.
4:4 clothed in white and had **g** crowns on their heads.
5:8 a harp, and they held **g** bowls filled with incense—
8:3 Then another angel with a **g** incense burner came
8:3 to be offered on the **g** altar before the throne.
9:7 They had **g** crowns on their heads, and they had
9:13 of the **g** altar that stands in the presence of God.
9:20 continued to worship demons and idols made of **g**,
14:14 He had a **g** crown on his head and a sharp sickle in
15:6 clothed in spotless white linen with **g** belts across
15:7 a **g** bowl filled with the terrible wrath of God,
17:4 and beautiful jewelry made of **g** and precious gems
17:4 She held in her hand a **g** goblet full of obscenities
18:12 She bought great quantities of **g**, silver, jewels,
18:16 decked out with **g** and precious stones and pearls!
21:15 The angel who talked to me held in his hand a **g**
21:18 of jasper, and the city was pure **g**, as clear as glass.
21:21 And the main street was pure **g**, as clear as glass.

GOLDEN (5) [GOLD]

Job 37:22 **G** splendor comes from the mountain of God.
Pr 25:11 Timely advice is as lovely as **g** apples in a silver
Ecc 12:6 silver cord of life snaps and the **g** bowl is broken.
Jer 51:7 Babylon has been like a **g** cup in the LORD's
Zec 4:12 and what are the two olive branches that pour out **g**

GOLDSMITH (2) [GOLD, SMITHS]

Ne 3:8 a **g** by trade, who also worked on the wall.
Isa 41:7 The carver hurries the **g**, and the molder helps at

GOLDSMITHS (3) [GOLD, SMITHS]

1Ch 22:16 They are expert **g** and silversmiths and workers of
Ne 3:31 Malkijah, one of the **g**, repaired the wall as far as
3:32 The other **g** and merchants repaired the wall from

GOLGOTHA (3)

Mt 27:33 Then they went out to a place called **G** (which
Mk 15:22 And they brought Jesus to a place called **G** (which
Jn 19:17 to the place called Skull Hill (in Hebrew, **G**).

GOLIATH (15) [GOLIATH'S]

1Sa 17:4 Then **G**, a Philistine champion from Gath,
17:8 **G** stood and shouted across to the Israelites,
17:23 with them, he saw **G**, the champion from Gath,
17:40 and sling, he started across to fight **G**.
17:41 **G** walked out toward David with his shield bearer
17:44 flesh to the birds and wild animals!" **G** yelled.
17:48 As **G** moved closer to attack, David quickly ran
17:49 and **G** stumbled and fell face downward to the
17:55 As Saul watched David go out to fight **G**, he asked
17:57 After David had killed **G**, Abner brought him to
18:6 army was returning home after David had killed **G**.
21:9 "I only have the sword of **G** the Philistine,
22:10 David food and the sword of **G** the Philistine."
2Sa 21:19 from Bethlehem killed the brother of **G** of Gath.
1Ch 20:5 son of Jair killed Lahmi, the brother of **G** of Gath.

GOLIATH'S (2) [GOLIATH]

1Sa 17:51 he ran over and pulled **G** sword from its sheath.
17:54 (David took **G** head to Jerusalem, but he stored the

GOMER (8)

Ge 10:2 The descendants of Japheth were **G**, Magog,
10:3 The descendants of **G** were Ashkenaz, Riphath,
1Ch 1:5 The descendants of Japheth were **G**, Magog,
1:6 The descendants of **G** were Ashkenaz, Riphath,
Eze 38:6 **G** and all its hordes will also join you, along with
Hos 1:3 So Hosea married **G**, the daughter of Diblaim,
1:6 Soon **G** became pregnant again and gave birth to a
1:8 After **G** had weaned Lo-ruhamah, she again

GOMORRAH (24)

Ge 10:19 to Sodom, **G**, Admah, and Zeboiim, near Lasha.
13:10 before the LORD had destroyed Sodom and **G**.)
14:2 King Birsha of **G**, King Shinab of Admah,
14:3 The kings of Sodom, **G**, Admah, Zeboiim,
14:8 **G**, Admah, Zeboiim, and Bela (now called Zoar)
14:10 And as the army of the kings of Sodom and **G** fled,
14:11 victorious invaders then plundered Sodom and **G**
18:20 that the people of Sodom and **G** are extremely evil,
19:24 burning sulfur from the heavens on Sodom and **G**.
19:28 and **G** and saw columns of smoke and fumes,
Dt 29:23 It will be just like Sodom and **G**, Admah
32:32 from the vine of Sodom, / from the vineyards of **G**.
Isa 1:9 been wiped out as completely as Sodom and **G**.
1:10 act just like the rulers and people of Sodom and **G**.
13:19 like Sodom and **G** when God destroyed them.
Jer 23:14 wicked as the people of Sodom and **G** once were."
49:18 of Sodom and **G** and their neighboring towns,"
50:40 and **G** and their neighboring towns,"
Am 4:11 some of your cities, as I destroyed Sodom and **G**.
Zep 2:9 will be destroyed as completely as Sodom and **G**.
Mt 10:15 and **G** will be better off on the judgment day than
Ro 9:29 been wiped out / as completely as Sodom and **G**."
2Pe 2:6 the cities of Sodom and **G** into heaps of ashes
Jude 1:7 of Sodom and **G** and their neighboring towns,

GONE (215) [GO] See Index of Articles, Etc.

GONG (1)

1Co 13:1 only be making meaningless noise like a loud **g**

GOOD (810) [BEST, BEST-EQUIPPED, BETTER, GOOD-HEARTED, GOOD-LOOKING, GOODNESS, GOODWILL]

DO GOOD (31) Ps 34:14; 37:3,27; 125:4; Isa 1:17; 26:10; 64:5; Mt 12:12; Mk 3:4; Lk 6:9,27,33,33,35; Ro 2:10; 7:19; 2Co 9:10; Gal 4:18; 6:10; Col 1:10; 1Th 5:15; 1Ti 5:10; 6:18; Tit 2:5; 3:8,14; Heb 13:16; 1Pe 3:11,13; 3Jn 1:11; Rev 22:11

FOR HE IS GOOD (6) 1Ch 16:34; Ps 106:1; 107:1; 118:1,29; 136:1

GOOD DEED (4) Ne 13:14,22; Ac 4:9; Ro 15:28

GOOD DEEDS (30) Job 35:8; Ps 112:3,9; Isa 57:12; Eze 3:20; 33:13; Mt 5:16; 6:1; Mk 3:4; Lk 6:9,45; Jn 10:32; Ro 3:27; 4:2; 7:4; 2Co 9:9; 1Ti 5:25; Tit 2:7; 3:8; Heb 10:24; Jas 2:17,18,18,18,20,26; 3:13,17; Rev 14:13; 19:8

GOOD...EVIL; EVIL...GOOD (61) Ge 2:9,17; 3:5,22; 50:20; 1Sa 24:17; 25:21,21; 2Sa 14:17; Job 30:26; Ps 14:1; 34:14; 35:12; 36:4; 37:27; 38:20; 52:3; 53:1; 90:15; 109:5; Pr 11:27; 14:19,22; 15:3; 17:13; Isa 5:20,20; Jer 13:23; 18:11,20; Eze 33:12; Am 5:14,15; Mic 3:2; Mt 5:45; 12:34,35,35,35,35; 13:19,38; Lk 6:45,45,45; 16:15; Jn 5:29; Ro 7:13,13,13; 12:21; 2Co 4:4; 5:10; Eph 5:16; 1Th 5:15; 1Ti 6:11; Tit 2:3; 1Pe 3:10,11,16; 3Jn 1:11,11

GOOD HEALTH (3) Job 21:24; Pr 15:30; Ecc 5:19

GOOD LAND (16) Dt 1:25,35; 4:21; 6:18; 8:7,10; 9:6; 11:17; Jos 23:13,15,16; 1Ki 14:15; 2Ki 3:19,25; 1Ch 28:8; Eze 20:6

GOOD NEWS (156) 2Sa 4:10; 18:19,20,27,31; 1Ki 1:42; 1Ch 16:23; Ps 40:10; 96:2; Pr 15:30; 25:25; Isa 40:9; 52:7; 61:1; Jer 20:15; Na 1:15; Mt 4:23; 9:35; 11:5; 13:19,22; 24:14; 26:13; Mk 1:1,14,15; 4:18; 8:35; 10:29; 13:10; 14:9; 16:15; Lk 1:19; 2:10; 3:18; 4:18,43; 7:22; 8:1; 9:6; 16:16; 20:1; 22:35; Ac 8:4,12,25,35,40; 10:36; 11:15,19; 12:24; 13:32,46; 14:7,15,21; 15:7; 16:10; 20:24; 23:11; Ro 1:1,2,3,9,15,16,17; 10:15,16,17,17; 11:28; 15:16,19,20,27; 16:25; 1Co 1:17; 4:15; 9:12,14,16,18,23; 15:1,2; 2Co 2:12,14; 4:3,4; 8:18; 9:13; 10:14,16; 11:7; Gal 1:7,7,11,16; 2:5,7,14; 3:4,8; 4:13; Eph 1:13; 2:17; 3:6,7; 6:15,19; Php 1:5,7,12,16,27,27; 2:22; 4:3,15; Col 1:5,6,7,23,23; 1Th 1:5; 2:2,4,8,9,16; 3:2,6; 2Th 1:8; 2:14; 1Ti 1:11; 2Ti 1:8,10,11; 2:8,9; 4:17; Tit 1:3; Phm 1:1,13; Heb 4:2,6; 1Pe 1:12,22,25; 3:1; 4:6,17; Jude 1:3; Rev 14:6

GOOD THINGS (42) Ge 45:23; Nu 10:32; 11:4; Dt 26:11; 28:11; Jos 23:15; 1Sa 19:4; 2Sa 7:28; 19:37; 1Ch 17:26; Ne 9:25; Job 2:10; 22:18; Ps 16:2; 39:2; 81:10; 103:2,5; 107:9; 119:65; Pr 12:14; 28:10; Ecc 2:1; Jer 5:25; 8:13; 29:10,32; Zec 3:8; Mt 19:16; Lk 1:53; Ac 26:20; 2Co 9:12; Eph 2:9,10; Php 1:11; Col 3:5; 1Ti 2:10; Tit 3:5; Phm 1:6; Heb 6:4; 9:11; 10:1

GOOD WORK (6) Ne 2:18; Jn 10:33; 2Co 3:2; Php 1:6; 2Ti 2:21; 3Jn 1:5

GOOD WORKS (3) Eze 33:12; Ro 11:6; 1Ti 6:18

NOT GOOD (11) Ge 2:18; Ex 4:10; 18:17; 1Sa 2:24; Pr 19:2; 25:27,27; Jer 21:10; 44:27; Eze 11:3; Ro 6:21

WHAT IS GOOD (19) 1Sa 12:23; Job 34:4; Ps 36:3; Isa 40:14; 48:17; Hos 8:3; Am 5:14,15; Mic 6:8; Mt 12:34; 19:17; Ro 2:7; Gal 6:9; Eph 5:9; 1Th 5:21; 2Ti 3:3; Tit 2:3; 3:1; 3Jn 1:11

Ge 1:4 And God saw that it was **g**. Then he separated the
1:10 and the water "seas." And God saw that it was **g**.
1:12 and trees of like kind. And God saw that it was **g**.
1:18 from the darkness. And God saw that it was **g**.
1:21 and every kind of bird. And God saw that it was **g**.
1:25 more of its own kind. And God saw that it was **g**.
2:9 of life and the tree of the knowledge of **g** and evil.
2:17 except fruit from the tree of the knowledge of **g**
2:18 God said, "It is not **g** for the man to be alone.
3:5 like God, knowing everything, both **g** and evil."
3:22 as we are, knowing everything, both **g** and evil.
15:2 what **g** are all your blessings when I don't even
25:32 said Esau. "What **g** is my birthright to me now?"
27:4 Prepare it just the way I like it so it's savory and **g**,
27:27 "The smell of my son is the **g** smell of the open
27:28 for healthy crops and **g** harvests of grain and wine.
28:11 At sundown he arrived at a **g** place to set up camp
30:20 "God has given me **g** gifts for my husband.
40:16 saw that the first dream had such a **g** meaning,

41:31 so terrible that even the memory of the **g** years will
41:34 one-fifth of all the crops during the seven **g** years.
41:35 and grain of these **g** years into the royal
45:23 He sent his father ten donkeys loaded with the **g**
49:15 When he sees how **g** the countryside is,
50:20 God turned into **g** what you meant for evil.
Ex 3:8 and lead them out of Egypt into their own **g**
4:10 the LORD, "O Lord, I'm just not a **g** speaker.
4:14 Aaron the Levite? He is a **g** speaker. And look!
15:25 it into the water. This made the water **g** to drink.
16:24 morning the leftover food was wholesome and **g**,
18:17 "This is not **g**!" his father-in-law exclaimed.
Lev 5:4 of any kind, whether its purpose is for **g** or bad,
27:10 neither a **g** animal for a bad one nor a bad animal
for a **g** one.
27:33 must not be selected on the basis of whether it is **g**
Nu 10:32 and we will share with you all the **g** things that the
11:4 the Israelites began to crave the **g** things of Egypt,
13:19 Is it **g** or bad? Do their towns have walls or are
17:12 of Israel said to Moses, "We are as **g** as dead!
Dt 1:13 understanding, and a **g** reputation, and I will
1:14 "You agreed that my plan was a **g** one.
1:23 This seemed like a **g** idea to me, so I chose twelve
1:25 LORD our God had given us was indeed a **g** land.
1:35 to see the **g** land I swore to give your ancestors,
4:21 **g** land the LORD your God is giving you as your
6:18 Do what is right and **g** in the LORD's sight,
6:18 and occupy the **g** land that the LORD solemnly
8:7 For the LORD your God is bringing you into a **g**
8:10 praise the LORD your God for the **g** land he has
8:16 did this to humble you and test you for your own **g**.
9:6 The LORD your God is not giving you this **g** land
10:13 laws that I am giving you today for your own **g**.
11:17 Then you will quickly die in that **g** land the
19:3 Keep the roads to these cities in **g** repair so that
26:11 because of all the **g** things the LORD your God
28:11 "The LORD will give you an abundance of **g**
30:9 for the LORD will delight in being **g** to you as he
30:18 **g** life in the land you are crossing the Jordan to
Jos 14:7 I returned and gave from my heart a **g** report,
21:45 All of the **g** promises that the LORD had given
23:13 and you will be wiped out from this **g** land the
23:15 your God has given you the **g** things he promised,
23:15 He will completely wipe you out from this **g** land
23:16 and you will quickly be wiped out from the **g** land
24:20 even though he has been so **g** to you."
Jdg 8:35 Gideon), despite all the **g** he had done for Israel.
9:16 and in **g** faith by making Abimelech your king,
9:19 and in **g** faith toward Gideon and his descendants,
9:20 But if you have not acted in **g** faith, then may fire
17:8 that area of Ephraim, looking for a **g** place to live.
18:9 We have seen the land, and it is very **g**.
Ru 1:6 his people in Judah by giving them **g** crops again.
3:7 Boaz had finished his meal and was in **g** spirits,
1Sa 2:24 I hear among the LORD's people are not **g**.
12:23 And I will continue to teach you what is **g**
16:16 "Let us find a **g** musician to play the harp for you
16:18 he is brave and strong and has **g** judgment.
19:4 about David, saying many **g** things about him.
23:7 "**G**!" he exclaimed. "We've got him now!
24:17 man than I am, for you have repaid me **g** for evil.
25:15 But David's men were very **g** to us, and we never
25:21 been saying, "A lot of **g** it did to help this fellow.
25:21 was lost or stolen. But he has repaid me evil for **g**.
25:33 Thank God for your **g** sense! Bless you for keeping
26:16 This isn't **g** at all! I swear by the LORD that you
26:23 The LORD gives his own reward for doing **g**
2Sa 4:10 is dead,' thinking he was bringing me **g** news.
7:28 and you have promised these **g** things to me,
14:17 like an angel of God and can discern **g** from evil.
17:4 This plan seemed **g** to Absalom and to all the other
18:19 "Let me run to the king with the **g** news that the
18:20 "it wouldn't be **g** news to the king that his son is
18:27 "He is a **g** man and comes with **g** news,"
18:31 and said, "I have **g** news for my lord the king.
19:37 and receive whatever **g** things you want to give
19:38 "**G**," the king agreed. "Kimham will go with me,
23:15 how I would love some of that **g** water from the
1Ki 1:42 "for you are a **g** man. You must have **g** news."
8:66 because the LORD had been **g** to his servant
14:13 for this child is the only **g** thing that the LORD,
14:15 He will uproot the people of Israel from this **g** land
18:14 Elijah is here'! Sir, if I do that, I'm as **g** as dead!"
18:41 Then Elijah said to Ahab, "Go and enjoy a **g** meal!
22:43 Jehoshaphat was a **g** king, following the example
2Ki 3:19 their springs, and ruin all their **g** land with stones."
3:25 covered their **g** land with stones, stopped up the
springs, and cut down the **g** trees.
4:13 Does she want me to put in a **g** word for her to the
4:13 she replied, "my family takes **g** care of me."
12:7 it must all be spent on getting the Temple into **g**
20:19 you have given me from the LORD is **g**."
1Ch 4:41 because they wanted its **g** pastureland for their
11:17 how I would love some of that **g** water from the
16:23 Each day proclaim the **g** news that he saves.
16:34 Give thanks to the LORD, for he is **g**!
17:26 And you have promised these **g** things to me,
28:8 so that you may possess this **g** land and leave it to
29:17 You know I have done all this with **g** motives,
2Ch 5:13 "He is so **g**! / His faithful love endures forever!"
7:3 and praised the LORD, saying, / "He is so **g**!
7:10 so **g** to David and Solomon and to his people
10:7 "If you are **g** to the people and show them
14:2 and **g** in the sight of the LORD his God.
19:3 There is some **g** in you, however, for you have
20:32 Jehoshaphat was a **g** king, following the ways of
21:12 You have not followed the **g** example of your
24:16 so much **g** in Israel for God and his Temple.
30:18 "May the LORD, who is **g**, pardon those
31:20 and **g** in the sight of the LORD his God.
Ezr 3:11 they sang this song to the LORD: / "He is so **g**!
9:12 You promised that we would enjoy the **g** produce
Ne 2:18 They replied at once, "**G**! Let's rebuild the wall!"
So they began the **g** work.
9:20 You sent your **g** Spirit to instruct them, and you
9:25 They took over houses full of **g** things,
13:14 Remember this **g** deed, O my God, and do not
13:22 Remember this **g** deed also, O my God!
Est 1:21 and his princes thought this made **g** sense,
10:3 because he worked for the **g** of his people and was
Job 1:9 "Yes, Job fears God, but not without **g** reason!
2:10 Should we accept only **g** things from the hand of
5:26 You will live to a **g** old age. You will not be
12:11 Just as the mouth tastes **g** food, so the ear tests the
12:17 He leads counselors away stripped of **g** judgment;
15:3 to speak so foolishly. What **g** do such words do?
15:21 and even on **g** days they fear the attack of the
21:7 "The truth is that the wicked live to a **g** old age.
21:15 we obey him? What **g** will it do us if we pray?'
21:24 the very picture of **g** health.
21:25 in bitter poverty, never having tasted the **g** life.
22:18 forgot that he had filled their homes with **g** things,
29:18 die surrounded by my family after a long, **g** life.
30:2 A lot of **g** they are to me—those worn-out
30:26 So I looked for **g**, but evil came instead. I waited
33:26 receive him with joy and restore him to **g** standing.
34:3 'Just as the mouth tastes **g** food, the ear tests the
34:4 what is right; let us learn together what is **g**.
35:7 If you are **g**, is this some great gift to him?
35:8 and your **g** deeds affect only other people.
41:29 Clubs do no **g**, and it laughs at the swish of the
42:17 he died, an old man who had lived a long, **g** life.
Ps 13:6 to the LORD / because he has been so **g** to me.
14:1 and their actions are evil; / no one does **g**!
14:3 become corrupt. / No one does **g**, / not even one!
16:2 All the **g** things I have are from you."
25:8 The LORD is **g** and does what is right; / he shows
33:5 He loves whatever is just and **g**, / and his unfailing
34:8 Taste and see that the LORD is **g**. / Oh, the joys
34:10 trust in the LORD will never lack any **g** thing.
34:12 any of you want to live / a life that is long and **g**?
34:14 Turn away from evil and do **g**. / Work hard at
35:12 They repay me with evil for the **g** I do. / I am sick
36:3 They refuse to act wisely or do what is **g**.
36:4 sinful plots. / Their course of action is never **g**.
37:3 Trust in the LORD and do **g**. / Then you will live
37:27 Turn from evil and do **g**, / and you will live in the
37:30 The godly offer **g** counsel; / they know what is
37:37 Look at those who are honest and **g**, / for a
38:20 They repay me evil for **g** / and oppose me
39:2 there in silence— / not even speaking of **g** things—
40:10 I have not kept this **g** news hidden in my heart;
52:3 You love evil more than **g** / and lies more than
53:1 and their actions are evil; / no one does **g**!
53:3 become corrupt. / No one does **g**, / not even one!
54:6 I will praise your name, O LORD, / for it is **g**.
55:14 What **g** fellowship we enjoyed / as we walked
71:16 I will tell everyone that you alone are just and **g**.
73:1 Truly God is **g** to Israel, / to those whose hearts are
73:28 But as for me, how **g** it is to be near God! / I have
77:5 I think of the **g** old days, long since ended,
81:10 your mouth wide, and I will fill it with **g** things.
84:10 than live the **g** life in the homes of the wicked.
84:11 and glory. / No **g** thing will the LORD withhold
86:5 O Lord, you are so **g**, so ready to forgive, / so full
88:5 abandoned me to death, / and I am as **g** as dead.
90:15 our former misery! / Replace the evil years with **g**.
92:1 It is **g** to give thanks to the LORD, / to sing
92:2 It is **g** to proclaim your unfailing love in the
96:2 Each day proclaim the **g** news that he saves.
100:5 For the LORD is **g**. / His unfailing love continues
103:2 and never forget the **g** things he does for me.
103:5 He fills my life with **g** things. / My youth is
106:1 Give thanks to the LORD, for he is **g**!
107:1 Give thanks to the LORD, for he is **g**!
107:9 the thirsty / and fills the hungry with **g** things.
109:5 They return evil for **g**, / and hatred for my love.
109:21 Rescue me because you are so faithful and **g**.
111:7 All he does is just and **g**, / and all his
112:3 and their **g** deeds will never be forgotten.
112:9 Their **g** deeds will never be forgotten. / They will
116:5 How **g** he is! / So merciful, this God of ours!
116:7 rest again, / for the LORD has been so **g** to me.
118:1 Give thanks to the LORD, for he is **g**!
118:29 Give thanks to the LORD, for he is **g**!
119:17 Be **g** to your servant, / that I may live and obey
119:65 You have done many **g** things for me, LORD,
119:66 now teach me **g** judgment and knowledge.
119:68 You are **g** and do only **g**; / teach me your
119:71 The suffering you sent was **g** for me, / for it taught
125:4 O LORD, do **g** to those who are **g**,
127:1 a city, / guarding it with sentries will do no **g**.
129:4 But the LORD is **g**; / he has cut the cords used by
135:3 Praise the LORD, for the LORD is **g**;
136:1 Give thanks to the LORD, for he is **g**!
145:9 The LORD is **g** to everyone. / He showers
147:1 How **g** it is to sing praises to our God!
Pr 1:3 **g** conduct, and doing what is right, just, and fair.
2:7 He grants a treasure of **g** sense to the godly.
2:20 Follow the steps of **g** men instead, and stay on the
3:4 and people, and you will gain a **g** reputation.
3:21 don't lose sight of **g** planning and insight.
3:27 Do not withhold **g** from those who deserve it when
4:2 for I am giving you **g** guidance. Don't turn away
4:5 Learn to be wise, and develop **g** judgment.
4:7 can do! And whatever else you do, get **g** judgment.
4:10 and do as I say, and you will have a long, **g** life.
8:8 My advice is wholesome and **g**. There is nothing
8:12 "I, Wisdom, live together with **g** judgment. I know
8:14 **G** advice and success belong to me. Insight
9:4 the simple. To those without **g** judgment, she says,
9:16 the simple. To those without **g** judgment, she says,
10:21 The godly give **g** advice, but fools are destroyed by
11:3 **G** people are guided by their honesty;
11:6 The godliness of **g** people rescues them;
11:12 a neighbor; a person with **g** sense remains silent.
11:27 If you search for **g**, you will find favor; but if you
12:2 The LORD approves of those who are **g**, but he
12:8 Everyone admires a person with **g** sense, but a
12:14 People can get many **g** things by the words they
12:26 The godly give **g** advice to their friends;
13:2 **G** people enjoy the positive results of their words,
13:15 A person with **g** sense is respected; a treacherous
13:22 **G** people leave an inheritance to their
14:14 what they deserve; **g** people receive their reward.
14:19 Evil people will bow before **g** people; the wicked
14:22 but if you plan **g**, you will be granted unfailing
15:3 keeping his eye on both the evil and the **g**.
15:7 Only the wise can give **g** advice; fools cannot do
15:30 joy to the heart; **g** news makes for **g** health.
16:26 It is **g** for workers to have an appetite; an empty
17:13 If you repay evil for **g**, evil will never leave your
17:22 A cheerful heart is **g** medicine, but a broken spirit
17:26 It is wrong to fine the godly for being **g** or to
19:2 Zeal without knowledge is not **g**; a person who
19:11 People with **g** sense restrain their anger; they earn
20:5 Though **g** advice lies deep within a person's heart,
20:8 all the evidence, distinguishing the bad from the **g**.
20:18 Plans succeed through **g** counsel; don't go to war
21:5 **G** planning and hard work lead to prosperity,
22:1 Choose a **g** reputation over great riches, for being
22:18 For it is **g** to keep these sayings deep within
24:3 by wisdom and becomes strong through **g** sense.
24:13 My child, eat honey, for it is **g**, and the honeycomb
25:10 Then you will never regain your **g** reputation.
25:25 **G** news from far away is like cold water to the
25:27 Just as it is not **g** to eat too much honey, it is not **g**
for people to think about all the honors
28:10 their own trap, but the honest will inherit **g** things.
28:21 Showing partiality is never **g**, yet some will do
Ecc 2:1 Let's look for the '**g** things' in life." But I found
2:2 "What **g** does it do to seek only pleasure?"
3:17 both **g** and bad, for all their deeds."
5:12 always worrying and seldom get a **g** night's sleep.
5:18 Even so, I have noticed one thing, at least, that is **g**.
5:18 It is **g** for people to eat well, drink a **g** glass of
wine, and enjoy their work—
5:19 And it is a **g** thing to receive wealth from God and
the **g** health to enjoy it.
7:1 A **g** reputation is more valuable than the most
7:4 while the fool thinks only about having a **g** time
7:10 Don't long for "the **g** old days," for you don't
7:11 Being wise is as **g** as being rich; in fact, it is better.
7:15 including the fact that some **g** people die young
7:16 So don't be too **g** or too wise! Why destroy
7:20 not a single person in all the earth who is always **g**
8:13 never live long, **g** lives, for they do not fear God.
8:14 **g** people are often treated as though they were **g**.
9:2 whether they are righteous or wicked, **g** or bad,
9:2 **G** people receive the same treatment as sinners,
9:3 That is why people are not more careful to be **g**.
9:18 of war, but one sinner can destroy much that is **g**.
10:11 It does no **g** to charm a snake after it has bitten
12:14 including every secret thing, whether **g** or bad.
Isa 1:17 Learn to do **g**. Seek justice. Help the oppressed.
1:26 Afterward I will give you **g** judges and wise
5:20 certain for those who say that evil is **g** and **g** is evil;
16:12 in anguish to their idols, but it will do them no **g**.
23:18 not be hoarded but will be used to provide **g** food
25:6 It will be a delicious feast of **g** food, with clear,
25:10 For the LORD's **g** hand will rest on Jerusalem.
26:10 kindness to the wicked does not make them do **g**.
30:24 and donkeys that till the ground will eat **g** grain,
32:8 But **g** people will be generous to others and will be
38:16 Lord, your discipline is **g**, / for it leads to life
38:17 Yes, it was **g** for me to suffer this anguish,
39:8 you have given me from the LORD is **g**."
40:9 Messenger of **g** news, shout to Zion from the
40:14 Does he need instruction about what is **g** or what is
41:7 "**G**," they say. "It's coming along fine."
41:23 and fear. Do something, whether **g** or bad!
45:7 I am the one who sends **g** times and bad times.
48:17 who teaches you what is **g** and leads you along the
52:7 are the feet of those who bring **g** news of peace
53:10 But it was the LORD's **g** plan to crush him
55:2 Why pay for food that does you no **g**? Listen,
55:2 and I will tell you where to get food that is **g** for
56:1 "Do what is right and **g**, for I am coming soon to
57:12 "Now I will expose your so-called **g** deeds that
58:4 What **g** is fasting when you keep on fighting
59:8 true peace is or what it means to be just and **g**.
61:1 because the LORD has appointed me to bring **g**
64:5 You welcome those who cheerfully do **g**,
65:8 "For just as **g** grapes are found among a cluster of
65:8 there are some **g** grapes there!'), so I will not
66:1 Could you ever build me a temple as **g** as that?
66:14 Everyone will see the **g** hand of the LORD on his
Jer 2:18 What **g** to you are the waters of the Nile
2:30 I have punished your children, but it did them no **g**.
3:16 "you will no longer wish for 'the **g** old days' when
4:2 and begin to live **g**, honest lives and uphold justice,

4: 3 Do not waste your **g** seed among thorns.
4:30 It will do you no **g**! Your allies despise you
5:25 Your sin has robbed you of all these **g** things.
8:13 All the **g** things I prepared for them will soon be
10: 5 for they can neither harm you nor do you any **g**."
11:16 olive tree, beautiful to see and full of **g** fruit.
12:13 They have worked hard, but it has done them no **g**.
13:10 will become like this linen belt—**g** for nothing!
13:23 Neither can you start doing **g**, for you always do
18:11 I am planning disaster against you instead of **g**.
18:15 They have stumbled off the ancient highways of **g**,
18:20 Should they repay evil for **g**? They have set a trap
20:15 the messenger who told my father, "**G** news—
21:10 decided to bring disaster and not **g** upon this city,
24: 3 I replied, "Figs, some very **g** and some very bad."
24: 5 The **g** figs represent the exiles I sent from Judah to
24: 6 I have sent them into captivity for their own **g**.
29:10 and do for you all the **g** things I have promised,
29:11 "They are plans for **g** and not for disaster, to give
29:32 None of his descendants will see the **g** things I will
31:12 the **g** crops of wheat, wine, and oil, and the healthy
32:25 paying **g** money for it before these witnesses—
32:39 their own **g** and for the **g** of all their descendants.
32:40 with them, promising not to stop doing **g** for them.
32:41 I will rejoice in doing **g** to them and will faithfully
32:42 so I will do all the **g** I have promised them.
33: 5 The men of this city are already as **g** as dead,
33: 9 The people of the world will see the **g** I do for my
33:11 to the LORD Almighty, for the LORD is **g**.
33:14 for Israel and Judah all the **g** I have promised them.
35: 7 you will live long, **g** lives in the land.'
37: 9 yourselves that the Babylonians are gone for **g**.
44:27 watch over you to bring you disaster and not **g**.
La 3:25 The LORD is wonderfully **g** to those who wait for
3:26 So it is **g** to wait quietly for salvation from the
3:27 And it is **g** for the young to submit to the yoke of
Eze 3:20 If **g** people turn bad and don't listen to my
3:20 Their previous **g** deeds won't help them, and I will
11: 3 to the people, 'Is it not a **g** time to build houses?
14:16 Sovereign LORD swears that it would do no **g**—
16:54 for your sins make them feel **g** in comparison.
17: 8 this even though it was already planted in **g** soil
17:10 It will die in the same **g** soil where it had grown
18:26 When righteous people turn from being **g** and start
20: 6 a **g** land, a land flowing with milk and honey,
30:22 his arms—the **g** arm along with the broken one—
33:12 The **g** works of righteous people will not save them
33:13 then none of their **g** deeds will be remembered.
34:14 I will give them **g** pastureland on the high hills of
36:29 I will give you **g** crops, and I will abolish famine in
Da 1: 4 are gifted with knowledge and **g** sense, and have
Hos 3: 5 and they will receive his **g** gifts in the last days.
8: 3 The people of Israel have rejected what is **g**,
10:12 I said, 'Plant the **g** seeds of righteousness, and you
Am 5:12 You oppress **g** people by taking bribes and deprive
5:14 Do what is **g** and run from evil—that you may live!
5:15 Hate evil and love what is **g**; remodel your courts
Jnh 1:14 you have sent this storm upon him for your own **g**
Mic 2: 7 do what is right, you would find my words to be **g**.
3: 2 but you are the very ones who hate **g** and love evil.
6: 8 the LORD has already told you what is **g**,
Na 1: 7 The LORD is **g**. When trouble comes, he is a
1:15 A messenger is coming over the mountains with **g**
Zep 3:20 I will give you a **g** name, a name of distinction
Zec 3: 8 You are symbols of the **g** things to come.
Mal 2: 6 they walked with me, living **g** and righteous lives,
Mt 3:10 every tree that does not produce **g** fruit will be
4:23 preaching everywhere the **G** News about the
5:13 the earth. But what **g** is salt if it has lost its flavor?
5:16 same way, let your **g** deeds shine out for all to see,
5:29 So if your eye—even if it is your **g** eye—
5:45 For he gives his sunlight to both the evil and the **g**,
5:46 you love only those who love you, what **g** is that?
6: 1 Don't do your **g** deeds publicly, to be admired,
7:11 If you sinful people know how to give **g** gifts to
7:11 how much more will your heavenly Father give **g**
7:17 A healthy tree produces **g** fruit, and an unhealthy
7:18 A **g** tree can't produce bad fruit, and a bad tree
can't produce **g** fruit.
7:19 So every tree that does not produce **g** fruit is
9:13 not those who think they are already **g** enough."
9:35 and announcing the **G** News about the Kingdom.
10:41 And if you welcome **g** and godly people because of
11: 5 and the **G** News is being preached to the poor.
12:12 a sheep! Yes, it is right to do **g** on the Sabbath."
12:33 Make a tree **g**, and its fruit will be **g**. Make a
12:34 How could evil men like you speak what is **g**
12:35 A **g** person produces **g** words from a **g** heart,
13:19 those who hear the **G** News about the Kingdom
13:22 represents those who hear and accept the **G** News,
13:23 The **g** soil represents the hearts of those who truly
13:24 is like a farmer who planted **g** seed in his field.
13:27 the field where you planted that **g** seed is full of
13:37 Son of Man, am the farmer who plants the **g** seed.
13:38 and the **g** seed represents the people of the
13:48 sit down, sort the **g** fish into crates, and throw the
16: 3 You are **g** at reading the weather signs in the sky,
19:16 what **g** things must I do to have eternal life?"
19:17 "Why ask me about what is **g**?" Jesus replied.
"Only God is **g**. But to answer your
22:10 **g** and bad alike, and the banquet hall was filled
24:14 And the **G** News about the Kingdom will be
24:46 and finds that the servant has done a **g** job,
25:21 of praise. 'Well done, my **g** and faithful servant.
25:23 master said, 'Well done, my **g** and faithful servant.
26:10 "Why berate her for doing such a **g** thing to me?
26:13 wherever the **G** News is preached throughout the
Mk 1: 1 Here begins the **G** News about Jesus the Messiah,
1:14 Jesus went to Galilee to preach God's **G** News.
1:15 Turn from your sins and believe this **G** News!"
2:17 not those who think they are already **g** enough."
3: 4 "Is it legal to do **g** deeds on the Sabbath,
4:18 represents those who hear and accept the **G** News,
4:20 But the **g** soil represents those who hear and accept
6:20 knowing that he was a **g** and holy man,
7:29 "**G** answer!" he said. "And because you have
8:35 life for my sake and for the sake of the **G** News,
9:50 Salt is **g** for seasoning. But if it loses its flavor,
10:17 up to Jesus, knelt down, and asked, "**G** Teacher,
10:18 "Why do you call me **g**?" Jesus asked. "Only God
is truly **g**.
10:29 or property, for my sake and for the **G** News,
13:10 And the **G** News must first be preached to every
14: 6 Why berate her for doing such a **g** thing to me?
14: 9 wherever the **G** News is preached throughout the
16:15 all the world and preach the **G** News to everyone,
Lk 1:19 It was he who sent me to bring you this **g** news!
1:53 He has satisfied the hungry with **g** things / and sent
2:10 "I bring you **g** news of great joy for everyone!
3: 9 every tree that does not produce **g** fruit will be
3:18 as he announced the **G** News to the people.
4:18 for he has appointed me to preach **G** News to the
4:43 "I must preach the **G** News of the Kingdom of
5:32 with those who think they are already **g** enough."
6: 9 Is it legal to do **g** deeds on the Sabbath, or is it a
6:27 love your enemies. Do **g** to those who hate you.
6:33 And if you do **g** only to those who do **g** to you,
6:34 only to those who can repay you, what **g** is that?
6:35 "Love your enemies! Do **g** to them! Lend to them!
6:39 "What **g** is it for one blind person to lead another?
6:43 "A **g** tree can't produce bad fruit, and a bad tree
can't produce **g** fruit.
6:45 A **g** person produces **g** deeds from a **g** heart,
7:22 and the **G** News is being preached to the poor.
8: 1 and villages to announce the **G** News concerning
8:15 But the **g** soil represents honest,
9: 6 preaching the **G** News and healing the sick.
11:13 If you sinful people know how to give **g** gifts to
12:43 and finds that the servant has done a **g** job,
14:34 "Salt is **g** for seasoning. But if it loses its flavor,
14:35 Flavorless salt is **g** neither for the soil nor for
15:16 the pods he was feeding the pigs looked **g** to him.
16:15 he said to them, "You like to look **g** in public,
16:16 But now the **G** News of the Kingdom of God is
18:18 "**G** teacher, what should I do to get eternal life?"
18:19 "Why do you call me **g**?" Jesus asked him. "Only
God is truly **g**.
19:18 "The next servant also reported a **g** gain—
20: 1 and preaching the **G** News in the Temple,
22:35 "When I sent you out to preach the **G** News
23:50 Now there was a **g** and righteous man named
Jn 1:46 "Can anything **g** come from there?" "Just come
4:36 The harvesters are paid **g** wages, and the fruit they
5:29 Those who have done **g** will rise to eternal life,
6: 9 two fish. But what **g** is that with this huge crowd?"
7:18 who seek to honor the one who sent them are **g**
8:39 of Abraham, you would follow his **g** example.
10:11 "I am the **g** shepherd. The **g** shepherd lays down
his life for the sheep.
10:14 "I am the **g** shepherd; I know my own sheep,
10:32 For which one of these **g** deeds are you killing
10:33 They replied, "Not for any **g** work, but for
11:13 They thought Jesus meant Lazarus was having a **g**
Ac 4: 9 because we've done a **g** deed for a crippled man?
7:49 Could you ever build me a temple as **g** as that?'
8: 4 everywhere preaching the **G** News about Jesus.
8:12 But now the people believed Philip's message of **G**
8:25 along the way to preach the **G** News to them,
8:35 then used many others to tell him the **G** News
8:40 He preached the **G** News there and in every city
10:33 I sent for you at once, and it was **g** of you to come.
10:36 I'm sure you have heard about the **G** News for the
10:38 Then Jesus went around doing **g** and healing all
11:15 "Well, I began telling them the **G** News, but just
11:19 They preached the **G** News, but only to Jews.
11:24 Barnabas was a **g** man, full of the Holy Spirit
12:24 But God's **G** News was spreading rapidly,
13:10 sort of trickery and villainy, enemy of all that is **g**,
13:32 and I are here to bring you this **G** News.
13:46 "It was necessary that this **G** News from God be
14: 7 and they preached the **G** News there.
14:15 We have come to bring you the **G** News that you
14:17 and **g** crops and giving you food and joyful
14:21 After preaching the **G** News in Derbe and making
15: 7 so that they could hear the **G** News and believe.
15:25 So it seemed **g** to us, having unanimously agreed
15:28 "For it seemed **g** to the Holy Spirit and to us to lay
16:10 God was calling us to preach the **G** News there.
20:24 the work of telling others the **G** News about God's
23: 1 I have always lived before God in all **g**
23:11 you must preach the **G** News in Rome."
26:20 and prove they have changed by the **g** things they
27:12 Phoenix was a **g** harbor with only a southwest
27:34 "Please eat something now for your own **g**.
Ro 1: 1 to be an apostle and sent out to preach his **G** News.
1: 2 This **G** News was promised long ago by God
1: 3 It is the **G** News about his Son, Jesus, who came as
1: 9 heart by telling others the **G** News about his Son.
1:13 I want to work among you and see **g** results,
1:15 to you in Rome, too, to preach God's **G** News.
1:16 For I am not ashamed of this **G** News about Christ.
1:17 This **G** News tells us how God makes us right in
2: 7 eternal life to those who persist in doing what is **g**,
2:10 and honor and peace from God for all who do **g**—
3: 5 "But," some say, "our sins serve a **g** purpose,
3:10 As the Scriptures say, / "No one is **g**— / not even
3:12 gone wrong. / No one does **g**, / not even one."
3:27 because our acquittal is not based on our **g** deeds.
4: 2 because of his **g** deeds that God accepted him?
4:14 and think they are "**g** enough" in God's sight,
5: 3 and trials, for we know that they are **g** for us—
5: 7 Now, no one is likely to die for a **g** person,
5: 7 be willing to die for a person who is especially **g**.
6:21 It was not **g**, since now you are ashamed of the
7: 4 you can produce **g** fruit, that is, **g** deeds for God.
7:10 So the **g** law, which was supposed to show me the
7:11 it took the **g** law and used it to make me guilty of
7:12 But still, the law itself is holy and right and **g**.
7:13 Did the law, which is **g**, cause my doom?
7:13 Sin used what was **g** to bring about my
7:13 It uses God's **g** commandment for its own evil
7:14 The law is **g**, then. The trouble is not with the law
7:16 bad conscience shows that I agree that the law is **g**.
7:19 When I want to do **g**, I don't. And when I try not to
8:28 to work together for the **g** of those who love God
9:11 were born, before they had done anything **g** or bad,
9:12 not according to our **g** or bad works.) She was told,
9:32 and being **g** instead of by depending on faith.
10:15 "How beautiful are the feet of those who bring **g**
10:16 But not everyone welcomes the **G** News, for Isaiah
10:17 comes from listening to this message of **G**
News—the **G** News about Christ.
11: 6 by God's kindness, then it is not by their **g** works.
11:24 wild olive tree and graft you into his own **g** tree—
11:28 Many of the Jews are now enemies of the **G** News.
12: 2 and you will know how **g** and pleasing and perfect
12: 7 If you are a teacher, do a **g** job of teaching.
12: 9 Hate what is wrong. Stand on the side of the **g**.
12:21 get the best of you, but conquer evil by doing **g**.
15:16 I bring you the **G** News and offer you up as a
15:19 I have fully presented the **G** News of Christ all the
15:20 My ambition has always been to preach the **G**
15:27 of the **G** News from the Jewish Christians,
15:28 this money and completed this **g** deed of theirs,
16:10 to Apelles, a **g** man whom Christ approves.
16:21 my relatives, send you their **g** wishes.
16:25 able to make you strong, just as the **G** News says.
1Co 1:17 send me to baptize, but to preach the **G** News—
4:15 Christ Jesus when I preached the **G** News to you.
6:12 But I reply, "Not everything is **g** for you."
7: 1 in your letter. Yes, it is **g** to live a celibate life.
7:31 **g** use of them without becoming attached to them,
9:11 We have planted **g** spiritual seed among you.
9:12 an obstacle in the way of the **G** News about Christ.
9:14 the Lord gave orders that those who preach the **G**
9:16 For preaching the **G** News is not something I can
9:18 It is the satisfaction I get from preaching the **G**
9:23 I do all this to spread the **G** News, and in doing
10:24 Don't think only of your own **g**. Think of other
11:17 For it sounds as if more harm than **g** is done when
13: 2 but didn't love others, what **g** would I be?
13: 2 it move, without love I would be no **g** to anybody.
14: 5 so that the whole church can get some **g** out of it.
15: 1 of the **G** News I preached to you before.
15: 2 And it is this **G** News that saves you if you firmly
15:33 for "bad company corrupts **g** character."
2Co 2:12 when I came to the city of Troas to preach the **G**
2:14 and to spread the **G** News like a sweet perfume.
3: 1 Are we beginning again to tell you how **g** we are?
3: 2 can read it and recognize our **g** work among you.
4: 3 If the **G** News we preach is veiled from anyone,
4: 4 so they are unable to see the glorious light of the **G**
5:10 will each receive whatever we deserve for the **g**
8:18 in all the churches as a preacher of the **G** News.
9: 9 the poor. / Their **g** deeds will never be forgotten."
9:10 he will give you many opportunities to do **g**,
9:12 So two **g** things will happen—the needs of the
9:13 that you are obedient to the **G** News of Christ.
10:14 all the way to you with the **G** News of Christ.
10:16 and preach the **G** News in other places that are far
11: 7 and honored you by preaching God's **G** News to
12:10 Since I know it is all for Christ's **g**, I am quite
12:15 spend myself and all I have for your spiritual **g**,
Gal 1: 7 that pretends to be the **G** News but is not the **G**
News at all.
1:11 I solemnly assure you that the **G** News of salvation
1:16 so that I could proclaim the **G** News about Jesus to
2: 5 We wanted to preserve the truth of the **G** News for
2: 7 of preaching the **G** News to the Gentiles,
2:14 they were not following the truth of the **G** News,
3: 4 You have suffered so much for the **G** News.
3: 8 God promised this **g** news to Abraham long ago
4:13 when I first brought you the **G** News of Christ.
4:17 to win your favor are not doing it for your **g**.
4:18 Now it's wonderful if you are eager to do **g**,
6: 9 So don't get tired of doing what is **g**. Don't get
6:10 we should do **g** to everyone, especially to our
Eph 1: 9 designed long ago according to his **g** pleasure.
1:13 heard the truth, the **G** News that God saves you.
2: 9 Salvation is not a reward for the **g** things we have
2:10 so that we can do the **g** things he planned for us
2:17 He has brought this **G** News of peace to you
3: 6 Both groups have believed the **G** News, and both
3: 7 privilege of serving him by spreading this **G** News.
4:29 Let everything you say be **g** and helpful, so that
5: 9 For this light within you produces only what is **g**
5:16 Make the most of every opportunity for doing **g** in
6: 8 Lord will reward each one of us for the **g** we do,
6:15 put on the peace that comes from the **G** News,
6:19 secret plan that the **G** News is for the Gentiles,
Php 1: 5 **G** News about Christ from the time you first heard

1: 6 sure that God, who began the **g** work within you,
1: 7 defending the truth and telling others the **G** News.
1:11 those **g** things that are produced in your life by
1:12 to me here has helped to spread the **G** News.
1:16 the Lord brought me here to defend the **G** News.
1:27 you must live in a manner worthy of the **G** News
1:27 side by side, fighting together for the **G** News.
2: 3 don't live to make a **g** impression on others.
2:22 he has helped me in preaching the **G** News.
3: 1 of telling you this. I am doing this for your own **g**.
4: 3 worked hard with me in telling others the **G** News.
4:15 me financial help when I brought you the **G** News
Col 1: 5 ever since you first heard the truth of the **G** News.
1: 6 This same **G** News that came to you is going out
1: 7 was the one who brought you the **G** News.
1:10 and please the Lord, and you will continually do **g**,
1:23 you received when you heard the **G** News.
1:23 The **G** News has been preached all over the world,
3: 5 Don't be greedy for the **g** things of this life,
1Th 1: 5 For when we brought you the **G** News, it was not
2: 2 Yet our God gave us the courage to declare his **G**
2: 4 approved by God to be entrusted with the **G** News.
2: 8 so much that we gave you not only God's **G** News
2: 9 there as we preached God's **G** News among you.
2:16 by trying to keep us from preaching the **G** News to
3: 2 and our brother in proclaiming the **G** News of
3: 6 bringing the **g** news that your faith and love are as
5:15 but always try to do **g** to each other and to
5:21 test everything that is said. Hold on to what is **g**.
2Th 1: 8 and on those who refuse to obey the **G** News of
1:11 will fulfill all your **g** intentions and faithful deeds.
2:14 He called you to salvation when we told you the **G**
2:16 favor gave us everlasting comfort and **g** hope,
2:17 and give you strength in every **g** thing you do
3:13 dear brothers and sisters, never get tired of doing **g**.
1Ti 1: 8 We know these laws are **g** when they are used as
1:11 that comes from the glorious **G** News entrusted to
2: 3 This is **g** and pleases God our Savior,
2:10 make themselves attractive by the **g** things they do.
3: 2 live wisely, and have a **g** reputation.
4: 4 Since everything God created is **g**, we should not
5:10 by everyone because of the **g** she has done.
5:10 are in trouble? Has she always been ready to do **g**?
5:25 everyone knows how much **g** some people do,
5:25 but there are others whose **g** deeds won't be known
6:11 all these evil things, and follow what is right and **g**.
6:12 Fight the **g** fight for what we believe. Hold tightly
6:13 who gave a **g** testimony before Pontius Pilate,
6:18 Tell them to use their money to do **g**. They should
be rich in **g** works and should give
6:19 up their treasure as a **g** foundation for the future
2Ti 1: 8 with me for the proclamation of the **G** News.
1:10 us the way to everlasting life through the **G** News.
1:11 an apostle, and a teacher of this **G** News.
2: 3 along with me, as a **g** soldier of Christ Jesus.
2: 8 raised from the dead. This is the **G** News I preach.
2: 9 And because I preach this **G** News, I am suffering
2:15 Be a **g** worker, one who does not need to be
2:21 ready for the Master to use you for every **g** work.
3: 3 they will be cruel and have no interest in what is **g**.
3:17 fully equipped for every **g** thing God wants us to
4: 2 and encourage your people with **g** teaching.
4: 7 I have fought a **g** fight, I have finished the race,
4:17 that I might preach the **G** News in all its fullness
Tit 1: 3 And now at the right time he has revealed this **G**
1: 6 An elder must be well thought of for his **g** life.
1: 8 guests in his home and must love all that is **g**.
1:16 and disobedient, worthless for doing anything **g**.
2: 3 Instead, they should teach others what is **g**.
2: 5 and be pure, to take care of their homes, to do **g**,
2: 7 example to them by doing **g** deeds of every kind.
2:10 show themselves to be entirely trustworthy and **g**.
3: 1 should be obedient, always ready to do what is **g**.
3: 5 not because of the **g** things we did, but because of
3: 8 in God will be careful to do **g** deeds all the time.
3: 8 These things are **g** and beneficial for everyone.
3:14 They must learn to do **g** by helping others who
Phm 1: 1 in prison for preaching the **G** News about Christ
1: 6 of all the **g** things we can do for Christ.
1:13 I am in these chains for preaching the **G** News,
Heb 4: 2 For this **G** News—that God has prepared a place of
4: 2 But it did them no **g** because they didn't believe
4: 6 But those who formerly heard the **G** News failed to
6: 4 those who have experienced the **g** things of heaven
6: 7 that falls on it and bears a **g** crop for the farmer,
9:11 High Priest over all the **g** things that have come.
10: 1 not the reality of the **g** things Christ has done for
10:12 to God as one sacrifice for sins, **g** for all time.
10:24 one another to outbursts of love and **g** deeds.
11:38 They were too **g** for this world. They wandered
12:10 But God's discipline is always right and **g** for us
13: 7 Think of all the **g** that has come from their lives,
13:16 Don't forget to do **g** and to share what you have
Jas 1:17 Whatever is **g** and perfect comes to us from God
2: 3 special attention and a **g** seat to the rich person,
2: 8 it is **g** when you truly obey our Lord's royal
2:16 person any food or clothing. What **g** does that do?
2:17 Faith that doesn't show itself by **g** deeds is no faith
2:18 "Some people have faith; others have **g** deeds."
2:18 "I can't see your faith if you don't have **g** deeds,
2:18 but I will show you my faith through my **g** deeds."
2:20 that faith that does not result in **g** deeds is useless?
2:26 a spirit, so also faith is dead without **g** deeds.
3:13 so that only **g** deeds will pour forth.
3:13 And if you don't brag about the **g** you do, then you
3:17 It is full of mercy and **g** deeds. It shows no
5: 6 and killed **g** people who had no power to defend
5:11 we see how the Lord's plan finally ended in **g**,
1Pe 1:12 And now this **G** News has been announced by
1:22 sins when you accepted the truth of the **G** News.
1:25 And that word is the **G** News that was preached to
2: 1 and deceit. Don't just pretend to be **g**!
2:15 It is God's will that your **g** lives should silence
3: 1 even those who refuse to accept the **G** News.
3:10 "If you want a happy life and **g** days,
3:11 Turn away from evil and do **g**. / Work hard at
3:13 will want to harm you if you are eager to do **g**?
3:16 they will be ashamed when they see what a **g** life
3:17 Remember, it is better to suffer for doing **g**, if that
4: 6 That is why the **G** News was preached even to
4:17 those who have never believed God's **G** News?
5: 3 to your care, but lead them by your **g** example.
5: 6 power of God, and in his **g** time he will honor you.
2Pe 2: 7 because he was a **g** man who was sick of all the
3Jn 1: 5 you are doing a **g** work for God when you take
1:11 bad example influence you. Follow only what is **g**.
1:11 Remember that those who do **g** prove that they are
Jude 1: 3 urging you to defend the truth of the **G** News.
Rev 2: 6 But there is this about you that is **g**: You hate the
14: 6 carrying the everlasting **G** News to preach to the
14:13 and trials; for their **g** deeds follow them!"
19: 8 (Fine linen represents the **g** deeds done by the
22:11 to be vile; the one who is **g**, continue to do **g**;

GOOD-BYE (12)

Ge 24:59 So they said **g** to Rebekah and sent her away with
31:28 my daughters and grandchildren and tell them **g**?
Ex 18:27 Soon after this, Moses said **g** to his father-in-law,
Ru 1: 9 Then she kissed them **g**, and they all broke down
1:14 and Orpah kissed her mother-in-law **g**.
1Sa 20:41 in tears as they embraced each other and said **g**,
1Ki 19:20 "First let me go and kiss my father and mother **g**,
Lk 9:61 follow you, but first let me say **g** to my family."
Ac 18:18 and then said **g** to the Christians and sailed for the
20: 1 Then he said **g** and left for Macedonia.
2Co 2:13 So I said **g** and went on to Macedonia to find him.
Jas 2:16 and you say, "Well, **g** and God bless you;

GOOD-HEARTED (1) [GOOD, HEART]

Lk 8:15 **g** people who hear God's message, cling to it,

GOOD-LOOKING (1) [GOOD, LOOK]

Da 1: 4 only strong, healthy, and **g** young men," he said.

GOODLIER, GOODLIEST, GOODLY

[KJV] See also BEAUTIFUL, BEST, FAIR, FINE, HANDSOME, LOVELY, MAJESTIC, PRECIOUS, NOBLE

GOODMAN [KJV] See FOREMAN, HOMEOWNER, HUSBAND, OWNER

GOODNESS (28) [GOOD]

Ex 33:19 "I will make all my **g** pass before you,
2Ch 6:41 and may your saints rejoice in your **g**.
12:12 And there was still **g** in the land of Judah.
Ne 9:35 you even though you showered your **g** on them.
Ps 23: 6 Surely your **g** and unfailing love will pursue me
27:13 Yet I am confident that I will see the LORD's **g**
31:19 Your **g** is so great! / You have stored up great
35:28 Then I will tell everyone of your justice and **g**,
92:15 He is my rock! / There is nothing but **g** in him!"
119:40 your commandments! / Renew my life with your **g**.
145: 7 Everyone will share the story of your wonderful **g**;
Isa 63: 7 I will rejoice in his great **g** to Israel, which he has
Jer 2: 7 you into a fruitful land to enjoy its bounty and **g**,
Eze 18:20 Righteous people will be rewarded for their own **g**,
18:24 All their previous **g** will be forgotten, and they will
Ac 27:24 God in his **g** has granted safety to everyone sailing
Ro 3: 5 for people will see God's **g** when he declares us
14:17 but of living a life of **g** and peace and joy in the
15:14 fully convinced, dear friends, that you are full of **g**.
2Co 6:14 How can **g** be a partner with wickedness? How can
Gal 5:22 love, joy, peace, patience, kindness, **g**, faithfulness,
Php 3: 9 I no longer count on my own **g** or my ability to
Heb 6: 5 who have tasted the **g** of the word of God
Jas 1:18 In his **g** he chose to make us his own children by
3:13 live a life of steady **g** so that only good deeds will
3:18 will plant seeds of peace and reap a harvest of **g**.
1Pe 2: 9 This is so you can show others the **g** of God,
2Pe 1: 3 He has called us to receive his own glory and **g**!

GOODS (24)

Ge 14:16 the **g** that had been taken, Abram's nephew Lot
14:20 Then Abram gave Melchizedek a tenth of all the **g**
14:21 But you may keep for yourself all the **g** you have
14:24 But give a share of the **g** to my allies—Aner,
40:17 In the top basket were all kinds of bakery **g** for
Ex 22: 7 someone entrusts money or **g** to a neighbor,
Lev 19:36 Your containers for measuring dry **g** or liquids
Dt 6:11 The houses will be richly stocked with **g** you did
Jos 7:22 ran to the tent and found the stolen **g** hidden there,
8: 2 But this time you may keep the captured **g**
11:14 And the Israelites took all the captured **g** and cattle
Jdg 5:30 'They are dividing the captured **g** they found—
Ezr 7:26 banishment, confiscation of **g**, or imprisonment."
8:21 protect us, our children, and our **g** as we traveled.
Job 20:26 A wildfire will devour his **g**, consuming all he has
Isa 60:16 and mighty nations will bring the best of their **g** to
Jer 49:29 and their household **g** and camels will be taken
Eze 27: 9 Ships came with **g** from every land to barter for
27:14 things were exchanged for your manufactured **g**.
27:18 Damascus traded for your rich variety of **g**,
27:21 and rams and goats in trade for your **g**.
38:13 their cattle and seize their **g** and make them poor?'
Rev 18:11 for her, for there is no one left to buy their **g**.
18:12 every kind of perfumed wood, ivory **g**,

GOODWILL (2) [GOOD, WILL]

Ge 33: 8 "They are gifts, my lord, to ensure your **g**."
Ac 2:47 praising God and enjoying the **g** of all the people.

GOPHER [KJV] See RESINOUS (WOOD)

GORE (4) [GORED, GORES]

Ex 21:36 if the bull was known from past experience to **g**,
Dt 33:17 He will **g** distant nations, / driving them to the ends
1Ki 22:11 With these horns you will **g** the Arameans to
2Ch 18:10 With these horns you will **g** the Arameans to

GORED (1) [GORE]

Ex 21:29 that the owner knew the bull had **g** people in the

GORES (3) [GORE]

Ex 21:28 "If a bull **g** a man or woman to death, the bull
21:31 "The same principle applies if the bull **g** a boy
21:32 But if the bull **g** a slave, either male or female,

GORGE (17) [GORGED, GORGING]

Dt 2:24 "Then the LORD said, 'Now cross the Arnon **G**!
2:36 us conquer Aroer on the edge of the Arnon **G**,
2:36 the town in the **g**, and the whole area as far as
3: 8 from the Arnon **G** to Mount Hermon.
3:12 the territory beyond Aroer along the Arnon **G**,
3:16 from Gilead to the middle of the Arnon **G**,
4:48 Aroer at the edge of the Arnon **G** to Mount Sirion,
Jos 12: 1 Their territory extended from the Arnon **G** to
12: 2 included Aroer, on the edge of the Arnon **G**,
12: 2 and extended from the middle of the Arnon **G** to
13: 9 **G** (including the town in the middle of the **g**)
13:16 **G** (including the town in the middle of the **g**)
2Ki 10:33 of Aroer by the Arnon **G** to as far north as Gilead
Eze 32: 4 and the wild animals of the whole earth will **g**
39:19 **G** yourselves with flesh until you are glutted;

GORGED (1) [GORGE]

Rev 19:21 And all the vultures of the sky **g** themselves on the

GORGEOUS (1)

Jdg 5:30 There are **g** robes for Sisera, / and colorful,

GORGEOUS [KJV] See also ROYAL

GORGING (1) [GORGE]

Job 20:21 Nothing is left after he finishes **g** himself;

GOSHEN (14)

Ge 45:10 You will live in the land of **G** so you can be near
46:28 to meet Joseph and get directions to the land of **G**.
46:29 his chariot and traveled to **G** to meet his father.
46:34 him this, he will let you live here in the land of **G**,
47: 1 and they are now in the land of **G**."
47: 4 We request permission to live in the land of **G**."
47: 6 the best land of Egypt—the land of **G** will be fine.
47:27 So the people of Israel settled in the land of **G** in
50: 8 and flocks and herds in the land of **G**.
Ex 8:22 But it will be very different in the land of **G**,
9:26 all Egypt without hail that day was the land of **G**,
Jos 10:41 Kadesh-barnea to Gaza and from **G** to Gibeon.
11:16 the hill country, the Negev, the land of **G**,
15:51 **G**, Holon, and Giloh—eleven towns with their

GOSPEL (2)

2Co 11: 4 or a different kind of **g** than the one you believed.
Gal 1: 9 If anyone preaches any other **g** than the one you

GOSSIP (10) [GOSSIPING]

Lev 19:16 "Do not spread slanderous **g** among your people.
Ps 41: 6 are my friends, / but all the while they gather **g**,
69:12 I am the favorite topic of town **g**, / and all the
Pr 11:13 A **g** goes around revealing secrets, but those who
16:28 seeds of strife; **g** separates the best of friends.
20:19 A **g** tells secrets, so don't hang around with
25:10 or others may accuse you of **g**. Then you will never
26:20 lack of fuel, and quarrels disappear when **g** stops.
Ro 1:29 fighting, deception, malicious behavior, and **g**.
2Co 12:20 of anger, selfishness, backstabbing, **g**, conceit,

GOSSIPING (2) [GOSSIP]

Pr 25:23 the north brings rain, so a **g** tongue causes anger!
1Ti 5:13 and spend their time **g** from house to house,

GOT (106) [GET]

Ge 13: 8 "This arguing between our herdsmen has **g** to
18: 2 He **g** up and ran to meet them, welcoming them by
18:16 Then the men **g** up from their meal and started on
19:33 So that night they **g** him drunk, and the older
19:35 So that night they **g** him drunk again,
20: 8 Abimelech **g** up early the next morning and hastily
21:14 So Abraham **g** up early the next morning,

22: 3 The next morning Abraham g up early. He saddled
25:30 (This was how Esau g his other name, Edom—
27:42 But someone g wind of what Esau was planning
28:18 The next morning he g up very early. He took the
31:55 Laban g up early the next morning, and he kissed
32:22 But during the night Jacob g up and sent his two
43:22 We have no idea how the money g into our sacks."
Ex 2: 1 and woman from the tribe of Levi g married.
2: 3 she g a little basket made of papyrus reeds
32: 6 So the people g up early the next morning to
Lev 24:10 and an Egyptian father g into a fight with one of
Nu 14:40 So they g up early the next morning and set out for
16:25 So Moses g up and rushed over to the tents of
22:13 The next morning Balaam g up and told Balak's
Jos 6:12 Joshua g up early the next morning, and the priests
6:15 On the seventh day the Israelites g up at dawn
15:18 As she g down off her donkey, Caleb asked her,
Jdg 1:14 As she g down off her donkey, Caleb asked her,
3:25 a long delay, they became concerned and g a key.
6:38 When Gideon g up the next morning, he squeezed
7: 1 and his army g up early and went as far as the
7: 6 All the others g down on their knees and drank
8: 8 and asked for food, but he g the same answer.
15: 6 Philistines went and g the woman and her father
16: 3 Then he g up, took hold of the city gates with its
19: 7 The man g up to leave, but his father-in-law kept
19:29 When he g home, he took a knife and cut his
Ru 1: 6 and her daughters-in-law g ready to leave Moab to
3:14 but she g up before it was light enough for people
1Sa 1:19 The entire family g up early the next morning
3:15 then g up and opened the doors of the Tabernacle
9:26 So Saul g ready, and he and Samuel left the house
19:18 So David g away and went to Ramah to see
23: 7 "Good!" he exclaimed. "We've g him now!
25:23 she quickly g off her donkey and bowed low
26:12 and Abishai g away without anyone seeing them
28:23 so he finally yielded and g up from the ground
30:18 David g back everything the Amalekites had taken,
2Sa 11: 2 Late one afternoon David g out of bed after taking
11:13 Then David invited him to dinner and g him drunk.
12:20 Then David g up from the ground, washed himself,
15: 2 He g up early every morning and went out to the
15: 3 would say, "You've really g a strong case here!
18: 9 thick branches of a great oak, his head g caught.
18:23 and g to Mahanaim ahead of the man from Cush.
1Ki 3:20 Then she g up in the night and took my son from
19: 1 When Ahab g home, he told Jezebel what Elijah
19: 8 So he g up and ate and drank, and the food gave
2Ki 1:15 Go with him." So Elijah g up and went to the king.
3:22 But when they g up the next morning, the sun was
4:35 Elisha g up and walked back and forth in the room
6:15 When the servant of the man of God g up early the
7:12 The king g out of bed in the middle of the night
9:16 Then Jehu g into a chariot and rode to Jezreel to
2Ch 20:26 which g its name that day because the people
23: 1 He g up his courage and made a pact with five
29:12 Then these Levites g right to work: / From the clan
Job 2:11 they g together and traveled from their homes to
Ps 40:15 for they said, "Aha! We've g him now!"
70: 3 for they said, "Aha! We've g him now!"
Jer 36:17 "But first, tell us how you g these messages.
Eze 3:23 So I g up and went, and there I saw the glory of the
42:17 the north side and g the same measurement.
Da 6:20 When he g there, he called out in anguish,
8:27 Afterward I g up and performed my duties for the
Hos 10: 1 But the more wealth the people g, the more they
12: 8 No one can say I g it by cheating! My record is
Jnh 1: 3 But Jonah g up and went in the opposite direction
Zec 11: 8 I g rid of their three evil shepherds in a single
Mt 8:15 Then she g up and prepared a meal for him.
8:23 Then Jesus g into the boat and started across the
9: 9 said to him. So Matthew g up and followed him.
13: 2 He g into a boat, where he sat and taught as the
15:39 and he g into a boat and crossed over to the region
25: 7 "All the bridesmaids g up and prepared their
Mk 1:31 and she g up and prepared a meal for them.
2:14 Jesus said to him. So Levi g up and followed him.
4: 1 a large crowd along the shore that he g into a boat
5:18 When Jesus g back into the boat, the man who had
8:10 he g into a boat with his disciples and crossed over
8:13 So he g back into the boat and left them, and he
Lk 4:39 She g up at once and prepared a meal for them.
5:28 So Levi g up, left everything, and followed him.
8:22 of the lake." So they g into a boat and started out.
Jn 6:17 they g into the boat and headed out across the lake
6:24 they g into the boats and went across to
10:39 tried to arrest him, but he g away and left them.
11:20 When Martha g word that Jesus was coming,
13: 4 So he g up from the table, took off his robe,
20: 4 The other disciple outran Peter and g there first.
21: 9 When they g there, they saw that a charcoal fire
Ac 5:37 He g some people to follow him, but he was killed,
9:18 regained his sight. Then he g up and was baptized.
10:27 So Cornelius g up, and they talked together
14:20 around him, he g up and went back into the city.
15: 6 and church elders g together to decide this
16:18 This went on day after day until Paul g.
23:12 The next morning a group of Jews g together
2Co 11:33 a window in the city wall, and that's how I g away!

GOTTEN (5) [GET]

2Sa 19:41 g to do most of the work in helping him cross the
Job 26: 4 Where have you g all these wise sayings?
Hos 12: 8 "I am rich, and I've g it all by myself!
Mk 5:26 she had to pay them, but she had g no better.
1Th 3: 5 I was afraid that the Tempter had g the best of you

GOUGE (4) [GOUGED]

1Sa 11: 2 I will g out the right eye of every one of you as a
Mt 5:29 causes you to lust, g it out and throw it away.
18: 9 eye causes you to sin, g it out and throw it away.
Mk 9:47 And if your eye causes you to sin, g it out. It is

GOUGED (4) [GOUGE]

Jdg 16:21 So the Philistines captured him and g out his eyes.
2Ki 25: 7 Then they g out Zedekiah's eyes, bound him in
Jer 39: 7 Then he g out Zedekiah's eyes, bound him in
52:11 Then they g out Zedekiah's eyes, bound him in

GOURD [KJV] See (LEAFY) PLANT

GOURDS (4)

1Ki 6:18 and the paneling was decorated with carvings of g
7:24 just below its rim by two rows of decorative g.
7:24 There were about six g per foot all the way around,
2Ki 4:39 and came back with a pocketful of wild g.

GOVERN (12) [GOVERNED, GOVERNING, GOVERNMENT, GOVERNMENTS, GOVERNOR, GOVERNOR'S, GOVERNORS, GOVERNS]

Ge 1:18 to g the day and the night, and to separate the light
49:16 "Dan will g his people / like any other tribe in
Jdg 13:12 what kind of rules should g the boy's life
1Sa 8:20 Our king will g us and lead us into battle."
1Ki 3: 9 so that I can g your people well
3: 9 For who by himself is able to g this great nation of
2Ch 1:10 for who is able to g this great nation of yours?"
1:11 and knowledge to properly g my people,
Ezr 7:25 and judges who know your God's laws to g all the
Job 34:17 Could God g if he hated justice? Are you going to
Ps 67: 4 singing for joy, / because you g them with justice
Mic 3:11 You rulers g for the bribes you can get; you priests

GOVERNED (2) [GOVERN]

2Ki 15: 5 of the royal palace, and he g the people of the land.
2Ch 26:21 of the royal palace, and he g the people of the land.

GOVERNING (2) [GOVERN]

1Ki 3:11 "Because you have asked for wisdom in g my
Ne 7: 2 I gave the responsibility of g Jerusalem to my

GOVERNMENT (23) [GOVERN]

Ge 41:48 in Egypt and stored them for the g in nearby cities.
1Ki 9:22 g officials, officers in his army, commanders of his
Est 3: 9 and I will give 375 tons of silver to the g
Pr 28: 2 is moral rot within a nation, its g topples easily.
Isa 9: 6 is given to us. And the g will rest on his shoulders.
9: 7 His ever expanding, peaceful g will never end.
54:14 You will live under a g that is just and fair.
Mt 22:17 Is it right to pay taxes to the Roman g or not?"
27: 1 persuade the Roman g to sentence Jesus to death.
Mk 12:14 is it right to pay taxes to the Roman g or not?
Lk 3:13 no more taxes than the Roman g requires you to."
20:22 is it right to pay taxes to the Roman g or not?"
23: 2 telling them not to pay their taxes to the Roman g
23:19 part in an insurrection in Jerusalem against the g.)
Jn 4:46 There was a g official in the city of Capernaum
Ac 19:40 of being charged with rioting by the Roman g,
24: 5 world to riots and rebellions against the Roman g.
25: 8 the Jewish laws or the Temple or the Roman g."
28:17 in Jerusalem and handed over to the Roman g,
Ro 13: 1 Obey the g, for God is the one who put it there.
13: 5 So you must obey the g for two reasons: to keep
13: 6 For g workers need to be paid so they can keep on
Tit 3: 1 Remind your people to submit to the g and its

GOVERNMENTS (1) [GOVERN]

Ro 13: 1 it there. All g have been placed in power by God.

GOVERNOR (68) [GOVERN]

Ge 42: 6 Since Joseph was g of all Egypt and in charge of
1Ki 4:19 And there was one g over the land of Judah.
22:26 to Amon, the g of the city, and to my son Joash.
2Ki 23: 8 entrance to the gate of Joshua, the g of Jerusalem.
25:22 and grandson of Shaphan as g over the people left
25:23 the king of Babylon had appointed Gedaliah as g,
2Ch 18:25 to Amon, the g of the city, and to my son Joash.
34: 8 Maaseiah the g of Jerusalem, and Joah son of
Ezr 2:63 The g would not even let them eat the priests'
4: 8 Rehum the g and Shimshai the court secretary
4:17 "To Rehum the g, Shimshai the court secretary,
5: 3 g of the province west of the Euphrates,
5: 6 This is the letter that Tattenai the g,
5:14 whom King Cyrus appointed as g of Judah.
6: 6 g of the province west of the Euphrates River,
6: 7 and do not hinder the g of Judah and the leaders of
6:13 g of the province west of the Euphrates River,
Ne 3: 7 the headquarters of the g of the province west of
5:14 for the entire twelve years that I was g of Judah—
7:65 The g would not even let them eat the priests'
7:70 The g gave to the treasury 1,000 gold coins,
8: 9 Then Nehemiah the g, Ezra the priest and scribe,
10: 1 Nehemiah the g, the son of Hacaliah.
12:26 and in the days of Nehemiah the g and of Ezra the
Pr 6: 7 they have no prince, g, or ruler to make them work,
Jer 40: 5 He has been appointed g of Judah by the king of
40: 7 g over the poor people who were left behind in
40:11 a few people in Judah and that Gedaliah was the g,
41: 2 whom the king of Babylon had appointed g.
41:18 the g appointed by the Babylonian king.
Hag 1: 1 g of Judah, and to Jeshua son of Jehozadak,
1:14 g of Judah, Jeshua son of Jehozadak, the high
2: 2 g of Judah, and to Jeshua son of Jehozadak,
2:21 "Tell Zerubbabel, the g of Judah, that I am about
Mal 1: 8 Try giving gifts like that to your g, and see how
Mt 27: 2 bound him and took him to Pilate, the Roman g.
27:11 Jesus was standing before Pilate, the Roman g.
27:11 the g asked him. Jesus replied, "Yes, it is as you
27:21 So when the g asked again, "Which of these two
28:14 If the g hears about it, we'll stand up for you
Mk 15: 1 bound Jesus and took him to Pilate, the Roman g.
Lk 2: 2 first census taken when Quirinius was g of Syria.)
3: 1 Pilate was g over Judea; Herod Antipas was ruler
19:17 so you will be g of ten cities as your reward.'
19:19 the king said. 'You can be g over five cities.'
20:20 something that could be reported to the Roman g
23: 1 council took Jesus over to Pilate, the Roman g.
Jn 18:28 he was taken to the headquarters of the Roman g.
18:29 So Pilate, the g, went out to them and asked,
Ac 4:27 Herod Antipas, Pontius Pilate the g, the Gentiles,
7:10 so that Pharaoh appointed him g over all of Egypt
13: 7 He had attached himself to the g, Sergius Paulus,
13: 7 The g invited Barnabas and Saul to visit him,
13: 8 and urged the g to pay no attention to what Saul
13: 8 He was trying to turn the g away from the
13:12 When the g saw what had happened, he believed
18:12 But when Gallio became g of Achaia, some Jews
18:12 and brought him before the g for judgment.
23:24 for Paul to ride, and get him safely to G Felix."
23:25 Then he wrote this letter to the g:
23:26 Claudius Lysias, to his Excellency, G Felix.
23:33 they presented Paul and the letter to G Felix.
23:35 myself when your accusers arrive," the g told him.
23:35 Then the g ordered him kept in the prison at
24: 2 against Paul in the following address to the g:
24:10 The g motioned for him to rise and speak.
26:30 Then the king, the g, Bernice, and all the others
2Co 11:32 the g under King Aretas kept guards at the city

GOVERNOR'S (5) [GOVERN]

Ne 5:18 Yet I refused to claim the g food allowance
Mt 27:14 Jesus said nothing, much to the g great surprise.
27:15 Now it was the g custom to release one prisoner to
27:27 Some of the g soldiers took Jesus into their
Mk 15: 6 Now it was the g custom to release one prisoner

GOVERNORS (18) [GOVERN]

1Ki 4: 5 Azariah son of Nathan presided over the district g.
4: 7 Solomon also had twelve district g who were over
4: 8 These are the names of the twelve g: / Ben-hur,
4:27 The district g faithfully provided food for King
10:15 all the kings of Arabia, and the g of the land.
2Ch 9:14 and the g of the land also brought gold and silver
Ezr 8:36 and the g of the province west of the Euphrates
Ne 2: 7 give me letters to the g of the province west of the
2: 9 When I came to the g of the province west of the
5:15 This was quite a contrast to the former g who had
Est 3:12 to the princes, the g of the respective provinces,
8: 9 wrote a decree to the Jews and to the princes, g,
9: 3 commanders of the provinces, the princes, the g,
Da 3: 2 prefects, g, advisers, counselors, judges,
3:27 Then the princes, prefects, g, and advisers crowded
Mt 10:18 And you must stand trial before g and kings
Mk 13: 9 You will be accused before g and kings of being
Lk 21:12 accused before kings and g of being my followers.

GOVERNS (1) [GOVERN]

Job 36:31 By his mighty acts he g the people, giving them

GOWN (1) [GOWNS]

Ps 45:13 her chamber, / dressed in a g woven with gold.

GOWNS (2) [GOWN]

Pr 31:22 She dresses like royalty in g of finest cloth.
Isa 3:22 party clothes, g, capes, and purses;

GOYIM (1)

Jos 12:23 the city of Naphoth-dor / The king of G in Gilgal

GOZAN (5)

2Ki 17: 6 along the banks of the Habor River in G,
18:11 in Halah, along the banks of the Habor River in G,
19:12 such nations as G, Haran, Rezeph, and the people
1Ch 5:26 Habor, Hara, and the G River, where they remain
Isa 37:12 such nations as G, Haran, Rezeph, and the people

GRAB (4) [GRABBED, GRABBING, GRABS]

1Sa 21: 8 so urgent that I didn't even have time to g a
2Ki 6: 7 "G it," Elisha said to him. And the man reached
Isa 21: 5 Quick! G your shields and prepare for battle!
Mk 14:51 in a linen nightshirt. When the mob tried to g him,

GRABBED (19) [GRAB]

Ge 39:12 She came and g him by his shirt, demanding,
Ex 4: 4 So Moses reached out and g it, and it became a
1Sa 15:27 Saul g at him to try to hold him back and tore his
2Sa 2:16 Each one g his opponent by the hair and thrust his
4: 4 the capital, the child's nurse g him and fled.
13:11 he g her and demanded, "Come to bed with me,
2Ki 6: 7 said to him. And the man reached out and g it.

Mt 14:31 Instantly Jesus reached out his hand and **g** him.
18:28 He **g** him by the throat and demanded instant
21:35 But the farmers **g** his servants, beat one, killed one,
21:39 So they **g** him, took him out of the vineyard,
26:50 Then the others **g** Jesus and arrested him.
27:30 And they spit on him and **g** the stick and beat him
Mk 12:3 But the farmers **g** the servant, beat him up,
12:8 So they **g** him and murdered him and threw his
14:46 Then the others **g** Jesus and arrested him.
Ac 16:19 so they **g** Paul and Silas and dragged them before
18:17 The mob had **g** Sosthenes, the leader of the
21:27 and roused a mob against him. They **g** him,

GRABBING (1) [GRAB]
Dt 25:11 her husband by **g** the testicles of the other man,

GRABS (2) [GRAB]
Job 18:9 A trap **g** them by the heel. A noose tightens around
30:18 With a strong hand, God **g** my garment. He grips

GRACE (57) [GRACIOUS, GRACIOUSLY]
Ge 31:42 In fact, except for the **g** of God—the God of my
Ezr 9:8 now we have been given a brief moment of **g**,
Ps 84:11 our light and protector. / He gives us **g** and glory.
Pr 1:9 What you learn from them will crown you with **g**
Isa 60:10 my anger, I will have mercy on you through my **g**.
Joel 2:23 For the rains he sends are an expression of his **g**.
Zec 12:10 "Then I will pour out a spirit of **g** and prayer on
Ac 6:8 Stephen, a man full of God's **g** and power,
13:43 men urged them, "By God's **g**, remain faithful."
14:3 preaching boldly about the **g** of the Lord.
14:26 and where they had been committed to the **g** of
15:40 sent them off, entrusting them to the Lord's **g**.
18:27 benefit to those who, by God's **g**, had believed.
20:32 now I entrust you to God and the word of his **g**—
Ro 1:7 May **g** and peace be yours from God our Father
6:14 you to sin. Instead, you are free by God's **g**.
6:15 So since God's **g** has set us free from the law,
15:15 is this reminder from me. For I am, by God's **g**,
16:20 May the **g** of our Lord Jesus Christ be with you.
1Co 1:3 and the Lord Jesus Christ give you his **g** and peace.
15:10 but God who was working through me by his **g**.
16:23 May the **g** of the Lord Jesus be with you.
2Co 1:2 and the Lord Jesus Christ give you his **g** and peace.
1:12 We have depended on God's **g**, not on our own
4:15 And as God's **g** brings more and more people to
9:14 because of the wonderful **g** of God shown through
13:13 May the **g** of our Lord Jesus Christ, the love of
Gal 1:3 May **g** and peace be yours from God our Father
2:21 I am not one of those who treats the **g** of God as
5:4 from Christ! You have fallen away from God's **g**.
6:18 may the **g** of our Lord Jesus Christ be with you all.
Eph 1:2 May **g** and peace be yours, sent to you from God
6:24 May God's **g** be upon all who love our Lord Jesus
Php 1:2 and the Lord Jesus Christ give you **g** and peace.
4:23 May the **g** of the Lord Jesus Christ be with your
Col 1:2 May God our Father give you **g** and peace.
4:18 my chains. May the **g** of God be with you.
1Th 1:1 Lord Jesus Christ. May his **g** and peace be yours.
5:28 And may the **g** of our Lord Jesus Christ be with all
2Th 1:2 and the Lord Jesus Christ give you **g** and peace.
3:18 May the **g** of our Lord Jesus Christ be with you all.
1Ti 1:2 our Father and Christ Jesus our Lord give you **g**,
6:21 such foolishness. May God's **g** be with you all.
2Ti 1:2 our Father and Christ Jesus our Lord give you **g**,
4:22 the Lord be with your spirit. **G** be with you all.
Tit 1:4 and Christ Jesus our Savior give you **g** and peace.
2:11 For the **g** of God has been revealed,
3:15 who love us. May God's **g** be with you all.
Phm 1:3 and the Lord Jesus Christ give you **g** and peace.
1:25 The **g** of the Lord Jesus Christ be with your spirit.
Heb 2:9 Yes, by God's **g**, Jesus tasted death for everyone in
4:16 and we will find **g** to help us when we need it.
13:25 May God's **g** be with you all.
1Pe 5:12 and assure you that the **g** of God is with you no
2Jn 1:3 May **g**, mercy, and peace, which come from God
Rev 1:4 **G** and peace from the one who is, who always was,
22:21 The **g** of the Lord Jesus be with you all.

GRACEFUL (3) [GRACEFULLY]
Ps 144:12 May our daughters be like **g** pillars,
Pr 5:19 She is a loving doe, a **g** deer. Let her breasts satisfy
Isa 61:3 them like strong and **g** oaks for his own glory.

GRACEFULLY (1) [GRACEFUL]
SS 6:13 as she moves so **g** between two lines of dancers?"

GRACIOUS (40) [GRACE]
Ge 43:29 told me about? May God be **g** to you, my son."
Ex 34:6 I am the LORD, the merciful and **g** God.
Nu 6:25 May the LORD smile on you / and be **g** to you.
2Sa 1:23 How beloved and **g** were Saul and Jonathan!
12:22 'Perhaps the LORD will be **g** to me and let the
2Ki 13:23 But the LORD was **g** to the people of Israel,
2Ch 30:9 For the LORD your God is **g** and merciful.
Ezr 7:6 because the **g** hand of the LORD his God was on
7:9 on August 4, for the **g** hand of his God was on him.
7:28 because the **g** hand of the LORD my God was on
8:18 Since the **g** hand of our God was on us, they sent
8:31 And the **g** hand of our God protected us and saved
Ne 2:8 because the **g** hand of God was on me.
2:18 Then I told them about how the **g** hand of God had
9:17 **g** and merciful, slow to become angry, and full of
9:31 them forever. What a **g** and merciful God you are!
Job 33:24 God will be **g** and say, 'Set him free. Do not make
Ps 45:2 handsome of all. / **G** words stream from your lips.
86:15 But you, O Lord, are a merciful and **g** God,
103:8 The LORD is merciful and **g**; / he is slow to get
111:4 he performs? / How **g** and merciful is our LORD!
143:10 May your **g** Spirit lead me forward / on a firm
145:13 is faithful in all he says; / he is **g** in all he does.
Pr 22:11 loves a pure heart and **g** speech is the king's friend.
Isa 30:19 weep no more. He will be **g** if you ask for help.
Jer 21:2 Perhaps the LORD will be **g** and do a mighty
Joel 2:13 to the LORD your God, for he is **g** and merciful.
Jnh 4:2 I knew that you were a **g** and compassionate God,
Lk 4:22 and were amazed by the **g** words that fell from his
Jn 1:16 he brought to us—one **g** blessing after another!
Ro 3:24 Yet now God in his **g** kindness declares us not
5:16 And the result of God's **g** gift is very different
5:17 **g** gift of righteousness will live in triumph over sin
2Co 8:4 and again for the **g** privilege of sharing in the gift
8:7 now I want you to excel also in this **g** ministry of
12:9 Each time he said, "My **g** favor is all you need.
Col 4:6 Let your conversation be **g** and effective so that
1Ti 1:14 Oh, how kind and **g** the Lord was! He filled me
Heb 4:16 So let us come boldly to the throne of our **g** God.
1Pe 1:10 They prophesied about this **g** salvation prepared

GRACIOUSLY (3) [GRACE]
Ge 33:5 "These are the children God has **g** given to me,"
Hos 14:2 Say to him, "Forgive all our sins and **g** receive us,
Heb 12:24 which **g** forgives instead of crying out for

GRADUALLY (1)
Ge 8:3 So the flood **g** began to recede. After 150 days,

GRAFF(ED) [KJV] See GRAFT, GRAFTED

GRAFT (3) [GRAFTED]
Ro 11:23 God will **g** them back into the tree again.
11:24 wild olive tree and **g** you into his own good tree—
11:24 he will be far more eager to **g** the Jews back into

GRAFTED (2) [GRAFT]
Ro 11:17 were branches from a wild olive tree, were **g** in.
11:18 But you must be careful not to brag about being **g**

GRAIN (288) [GRAINFIELDS, GRAINS, GRANARIES]

GRAIN OFFERING (64) Ex 40:29; Lev 2:1,4,5,6,8,9,10, 14,15; 5:13; 6:14,18,20,21; 7:9,37; 9:4,17; 10:12; 14:20,21, 31; 23:13; Nu 4:16; 6:17; 8:8; 15:4,9,24; 28:5,8,9,31; 29:11, 14,16,18,19,21,22,24,25,27,28, 30,31,33,34,37,38; Jdg 13:19, 23; 2Ki 16:13,15,15; 1Ch 21:23; Eze 45:24,25; 46:5,7,11, 14,15

GRAIN OFFERINGS (54) Ex 30:9; Lev 2:11,13,13; 6:23; 7:10; 23:18,37; Nu 6:15; 7:13,19,25,31,37,43,49,55,61,67, 73,79,87; 18:9; 28:12,20,28; 29:3,6,9,39; Jos 22:23,29; 1Ki 8:64; 1Ch 23:29; 2Ch 7:7; Ezr 7:17; Ne 10:33,37; 13:5,9; Isa 43:23; 57:6; Jer 14:12; 17:26; 33:18; 41:5; Eze 42:13; 44:29; 45:15,17; 46:20; Am 5:22; Heb 10:5,8

Ge 2:5 there were no plants or **g** growing on the earth,
9:3 for food, just as I have given you **g** and vegetables.
26:12 He harvested a hundred times more **g** than he
27:28 for healthy crops and good harvests of **g** and wine.
27:37 I have guaranteed him an abundance of **g**
37:7 "We were out in the field tying up bundles of **g**.
41:5 This time he saw seven heads of **g** on one stalk,
41:22 This time there were seven heads of **g** on one stalk,
41:26 and the seven plump heads of **g** both represent
41:27 and the seven withered heads of **g** represent seven
41:35 and **g** of these good years into the royal
41:49 There was so much **g**, like sand on the seashore,
41:54 but in Egypt there was plenty of **g** in the
41:56 up the storehouses and sold **g** to the Egyptians.
41:57 lands also came to Egypt to buy **g** from Joseph
42:1 When Jacob heard that there was **g** available in
42:2 I have heard there is **g** in Egypt. Go down and buy
42:3 ten older brothers went down to Egypt to buy **g**.
42:6 of all Egypt and in charge of the sale of the **g**,
42:7 they replied. "We have come to buy **g**."
42:19 The rest of you may go on home with **g** for your
42:25 ordered his servants to fill the men's sacks with **g**,
42:26 So they loaded up their donkeys with the **g**
42:27 and one of them opened his sack to get some **g** to
42:33 and take **g** for your families and go on home.
42:34 you may come as often as you like to buy **g**.' "
42:35 of each one was the bag of money paid for the **g**.
43:2 When the **g** they had brought from Egypt was
43:21 The money we had used to pay for the **g** was there
43:22 We also have additional money to buy more **g**.
44:1 "Fill each of their sacks with as much **g** as they
44:2 youngest brother's sack, along with his **g** money."
44:26 of the **g** unless our youngest brother is with us.'
45:23 and ten donkeys loaded with **g** and all kinds of
47:14 the money in Egypt and Canaan in exchange for **g**,
47:19 Just give us **g** so that our lives may be saved
Ex 22:5 must pay damages in the form of high-quality **g**
22:6 destroying the sheaves or the standing **g**,
30:9 any burnt offerings, **g** offerings, or drink offerings.
40:29 On it he offered a burnt offering and a **g** offering,
Lev 2:1 "When you bring a **g** offering to the LORD,
2:4 present some kind of baked bread as a **g** offering,
2:5 If your **g** offering is cooked on a griddle, it must be
2:6 and pour oil on it; it is a kind of **g** offering.
2:8 "No matter how a **g** offering has been prepared
2:9 The priests will take a token portion of the **g**
2:10 The rest of the **g** offering will be given to Aaron
2:11 "Do not use yeast in any of the **g** offerings you
2:13 Season all your **g** offerings with salt, to remind you
2:13 Never forget to add salt to your **g** offerings.
2:14 "If you present a **g** offering to the LORD from
2:14 bring kernels of new **g** that have been roasted on a
2:15 Since it is a **g** offering, put olive oil on it
2:16 token portion of the roasted **g** mixed with olive oil,
5:13 belong to the priest, just as with the **g** offering."
6:14 "These are the instructions regarding the **g**
6:18 generation to generation, may eat of the **g** offering,
6:20 they must bring to the LORD a **g** offering of two
6:21 You must present this **g** offering, and it will be
6:23 All such **g** offerings of the priests must be entirely
7:9 Any **g** offering that has been baked in an oven,
7:10 All other **g** offerings, whether flour mixed with
7:37 the **g** offering, the sin offering, the guilt offering,
9:4 and flour mixed with olive oil for a **g** offering.
9:17 He also brought the **g** offering, burning a handful
10:12 "Take what is left of the **g** offering after the
11:37 If the dead body falls on seed **g** to be planted in the
14:20 and offer it on the altar along with the **g** offering.
14:21 of choice flour mixed with olive oil as a **g** offering
14:31 to be presented along with the **g** offering.
19:9 do not harvest the **g** along the edges of your fields,
23:10 some **g** from the first portion of your **g** harvest.
23:13 A **g** offering must accompany it consisting of three
23:14 Do not eat any bread or roasted **g** or fresh kernels
23:15 the day the bundle of **g** was lifted up as an
23:16 and bring an offering of new **g** to the LORD.
23:18 together with the accompanying **g** offerings
23:22 do not harvest the **g** along the edges of your fields,
23:37 whole burnt offerings and **g** offerings,
26:5 harvest will extend until it is time to plant **g** again.
27:30 whether **g** or fruit, belongs to the LORD and must
27:31 to redeem the LORD's tenth of the fruit or **g**,
Nu 4:16 the fragrant incense, the daily **g** offering,
6:15 along with their prescribed **g** offerings and drink
6:17 The priest must also make the prescribed **g**
7:13 These were both filled with **g** offerings of choice
7:19 These were both filled with **g** offerings of choice
7:25 These were both filled with **g** offerings of choice
7:31 These were both filled with **g** offerings of choice
7:37 These were both filled with **g** offerings of choice
7:43 These were both filled with **g** offerings of choice
7:49 These were both filled with **g** offerings of choice
7:55 These were both filled with **g** offerings of choice
7:61 These were both filled with **g** offerings of choice
7:67 These were both filled with **g** offerings of choice
7:73 These were both filled with **g** offerings of choice
7:79 These were both filled with **g** offerings of choice
7:87 along with their prescribed **g** offerings.
8:8 and a **g** offering of choice flour mixed with olive
15:4 whoever brings it must also give to the LORD a **g**
15:9 then the **g** offering accompanying it must include
15:20 as you do with the first **g** from the threshing floor.
15:24 and it must be offered along with the prescribed **g**
18:9 including the **g** offerings, sin offerings, and guilt
18:12 the LORD—the best of the olive oil, wine, and **g**.
18:27 as though it were the first **g** from your own
20:5 This land has no **g**, figs, grapes, or pomegranates.
28:5 With each lamb you must offer a **g** offering of two
28:8 lamb in the evening with the same **g** offering
28:9 They must be accompanied by a **g** offering of three
28:12 These will be accompanied by **g** offerings of
28:20 These will be accompanied by **g** offerings of
28:26 when you present the first of your new **g** to the
28:28 These will be accompanied by **g** offerings of
28:31 burnt offering and its accompanying **g** offering.
29:3 These must be accompanied by **g** offerings of
29:6 and they must be given with their prescribed **g**
29:9 **g** offerings of choice flour mixed with olive oil—
29:11 and the regular daily burnt offering with its **g**
29:14 a **g** offering of choice flour mixed with olive oil—
29:16 burnt offering with its accompanying **g** offering
29:18 must be accompanied by the prescribed **g** offering
29:19 burnt offering with its accompanying **g** offering
29:21 must be accompanied by the prescribed **g** offering
29:22 burnt offering with its accompanying **g** offering
29:24 must be accompanied by the prescribed **g** offering
29:25 burnt offering with its accompanying **g** offering
29:27 must be accompanied by the prescribed **g** offering
29:28 burnt offering with its accompanying **g** offering
29:30 must be accompanied by the prescribed **g** offering
29:31 burnt offering with its accompanying **g** offering
29:33 must be accompanied by the prescribed **g** offering
29:34 burnt offering with its accompanying **g** offering
29:37 must be accompanied by the prescribed **g** offering
29:38 burnt offering with its accompanying **g** offering
29:39 burnt offerings, **g** offerings, drink offerings,
Dt 7:13 you will have large crops of **g**, grapes, and olives,
11:14 their proper seasons so you can harvest crops of **g**,
12:17 neither the tithe of your **g** and new wine and olive
14:23 This applies to your tithes of **g**, new wine,
16:9 seven weeks from the beginning of your **g** harvest.
16:13 after the **g** has been threshed and the grapes have
18:4 must also give to the priests the first share of the **g**,
23:25 pluck a few heads of your neighbor's **g** by hand,
24:19 and forget to bring in a bundle of **g** from your
25:4 not keep an ox from eating as it treads out the **g**.
28:8 you do and will fill your storehouses with **g**.
28:51 They will leave you no **g**, new wine, olive oil,
33:28 Jacob in security, / in a land of **g** and wine,
Jos 5:11 and roasted **g** harvested from the land.
22:23 burnt offerings or **g** offerings or peace offerings.
22:29 altar for burnt offerings, **g** offerings, or sacrifices.

Jdg 6:11 of a winepress to hide the **g** from the Midianites.
13:19 Then Manoah took a young goat and a **g** offering
13:23 have accepted our burnt offering and **g** offering.
15: 5 He burned all their **g** to the ground,
15: 5 including the **g** still in piles and all that had been
16:21 bronze chains and made to grind **g** in the prison.
Ru 2: 2 "Let me go out into the fields to gather leftover **g**
2: 3 So Ruth went out to gather **g** behind the harvesters.
2: 7 She asked me this morning if she could gather **g**
2: 8 Stay right here with us when you gather **g**;
2:15 "Let her gather **g** right among the sheaves without
2:17 and when she beat out the **g** that evening, it came
2:19 "Where did you gather all this **g** today?
2:23 and gathered **g** with them until the end of the
3: 2 and he's been very kind by letting you gather **g**
3: 7 he lay down beside the heap of **g** and went to
1Sa 17:17 "Take this half-bushel of roasted **g** and these ten
23: 1 were at Keilah stealing **g** from the threshing floors.
25:18 five dressed sheep, nearly a bushel of roasted **g**,
2Sa 17:19 the top of the well with **g** on it to dry in the sun;
17:28 wheat and barley flour, roasted **g**, beans, lentils,
1Ki 8:64 He offered burnt offerings, **g** offerings, and the fat
2Ki 4:42 brought the man of God a sack of fresh **g**
4:42 barley bread made from the first **g** of his harvest.
7: 1 and ten quarts of barley **g** will cost only half an
7:16 and ten quarts of barley **g** were sold for half an
7:18 and ten quarts of barley **g** will cost half an ounce of
16:13 king presented a burnt offering and a **g** offering,
16:15 the evening **g** offering, the king's burnt offering
and **g** offering,
18:32 a country with bountiful harvests of **g** and wine,
1Ch 21:23 And take the wheat for the **g** offering. I will give it
23:29 the choice flour for the **g** offerings, the wafers
2Ch 7: 7 the burnt offerings, **g** offerings, and sacrificial fat.
31: 5 and generously with the first of their crops and **g**,
32:28 He also constructed many storehouses for his **g**,
Ezr 7:17 and the appropriate **g** offerings and drink offerings,
Ne 5:10 have been lending the people money and **g**,
5:11 charged on their money, **g**, wine, and olive oil."
10:31 or **g** to be sold on the Sabbath or on any other holy
10:33 for the regular **g** offerings and burnt offerings;
10:37 bring the best of our flour and other **g** offerings,
10:39 and the Levites must bring these offerings of **g**,
13: 5 previously been used for storing the **g** offerings,
13: 5 and tithes of **g**, new wine, olive oil,
13: 9 the **g** offerings, and the frankincense.
13:12 people of Judah began bringing their tithes of **g**,
13:15 They were also bringing in bundles of **g**
Job 24:24 be gone like all others, withered like heads of **g**.
39:12 it to return, bringing your **g** to the threshing floor?
Ps 4: 7 than those who have abundant harvests of **g**
65: 9 not run dry; / they provide a bountiful harvest of **g**,
65:13 of sheep, / and the valleys are carpeted with **g**.
Pr 3:10 Then he will fill your barns with **g**, and your vats
11:26 People curse those who hold their **g** for higher
27:22 even though you grind them like **g** with mortar
Isa 3:14 filling your barns with **g** extorted from helpless
5:10 of seed will yield only one measure of **g**."
23: 3 They brought you **g** from Egypt and harvests from
27:12 gather them together one by one like handpicked **g**.
28:28 Bread **g** is easily crushed, so he doesn't keep on
30:24 and donkeys that till the ground will eat good **g**,
36:17 a country with bountiful harvests of **g** and wine,
43:23 and wearied you with my requests for **g** offerings
55:10 They cause the **g** to grow, producing seed for the
57: 6 worship them with drink offerings and **g** offerings.
62: 8 warriors come and take away your **g** and wine.
66: 3 they sacrifice a lamb or bring an offering of **g**,
Jer 4:11 It is not a gentle breeze useful for winnowing **g**.
9:22 like dung, or like bundles of **g** after the harvest.
14:12 present their burnt offerings and **g** offerings to me,
15: 7 I will winnow you like **g** at the gates of your cities
17:26 They will bring their **g** offerings, incense,
33:18 and **g** offerings and sacrifices to me."
41: 5 and had brought along **g** offerings and incense.
Eze 42:13 And they will use these rooms to store the **g**
44:29 the **g** offerings, the sin offerings, and the guilt
44:30 The first samples of each **g** harvest and the first of
45:15 These will be the **g** offerings, burnt offerings,
45:17 burnt offerings, **g** offerings, drink offerings,
45:24 The prince will provide a half bushel of flour as a **g**
45:25 the burnt offering, and the **g** offering, along with
46: 5 He will present a **g** offering of a half bushel of
46: 7 must bring a half bushel of flour for a **g** offering.
46:11 the **g** offering will be a half bushel of flour with
46:14 a **g** offering must also be given to the LORD—
46:15 The lamb, the **g** offering, and the olive oil must be
46:20 and bake the flour from the **g** offerings into bread.
Hos 2: 8 everything she has—the **g**, the wine, the olive oil.
2: 9 and ripened **g** I generously provided each harvest
2:22 the earth will answer the thirsty cries of the **g**,
8: 7 The stalks of wheat wither, producing no **g**. And if
there is any **g**, foreigners will eat it.
10:11 a trained heifer accustomed to treading out the **g**—
14: 7 They will flourish like **g** and blossom like
Joel 1: 9 There is no **g** or wine to offer at the Temple of the
1:10 The **g**, the wine, and the olive oil are gone.
1:13 There is no **g** or wine to offer at the Temple of
1:17 die in the parched ground, and the **g** crops fail.
2:14 give you so much that you will be able to offer **g**
2:19 I am sending you **g** and wine and olive oil,
2:24 threshing floors will again be piled high with **g**,
Am 1: 3 They beat down my people in Gilead as **g** is
2:13 as a wagon groans when it is loaded down with **g**.
5:22 not accept your burnt offerings and **g** offerings.
8: 5 You measure out your **g** in false measures
9: 9 by the other nations as **g** is sifted in a sieve,
9:13 "when the **g** and grapes will grow faster than they
Mic 4:12 and trampled like bundles of **g** on a threshing floor.
6:10 by dishonestly measuring out **g** in short measures.
Hag 1:11 a drought to wither the **g** and grapes and olives
2:19 before you have harvested your **g** and before the
Zec 5: 6 He replied, "It is a basket for measuring **g**, and it
9:17 and women will thrive on the abundance of **g**
12: 6 or like a burning torch among sheaves of **g**.
Mt 3:12 He is ready to separate the chaff from the **g** with
3:12 storing the **g** in his barn but burning the chaff with
12: 1 breaking off heads of wheat and eating the **g**.
12: 2 It's against the law to work by harvesting **g** on the
13:18 of the story I told about the farmer sowing **g**:
13:26 When the crop began to grow and produce **g**,
Mk 2:24 It's against the law to work by harvesting **g** on the
4: 7 out the tender blades so that it produced no **g**.
4:28 heads of wheat are formed, and finally the **g** ripens.
4:29 And as soon as the **g** is ready, the farmer comes
Lk 3:17 He is ready to separate the chaff from the **g** with
3:17 storing the **g** in his barn but burning the chaff with
6: 2 It's against the law to work by harvesting **g** on the
Ac 7:12 Jacob heard that there was still **g** in Egypt, so he
1Co 9: 9 not keep an ox from eating as it treads out the **g**."
9:10 and thresh the **g** expect a share of the harvest,
1Ti 5:18 not keep an ox from eating as it treads out the **g**."
Heb 10: 5 did not want animal sacrifices and **g** offerings.
10: 8 or **g** offerings or animals burned on the altar
Rev 18:22 no industry of any kind, and no more milling of **g**.

GRAINFIELDS (4) [GRAIN, FIELD]

Isa 17: 5 Israel will be abandoned like the **g** in the valley of
Mt 12: 1 Jesus was walking through some **g** on the Sabbath.
Mk 2:23 Sabbath day as Jesus was walking through some **g**,
Lk 6: 1 Sabbath day as Jesus was walking through some **g**,

GRAINS (6) [GRAIN]

Ge 3:18 and thistles for you, though you will eat of its **g**.
Jdg 7:12 Their camels were like **g** of sand on the seashore—
1Sa 13: 5 and as many warriors as the **g** of sand along the
Ps 139:18 even count them; / they outnumber the **g** of sand!
Jer 15: 8 "There will be more widows than the **g** of sand
Lk 6: 1 rubbed off the husks in their hands, and ate the **g**.

GRANARIES (3) [GRAIN]

Ge 41:49 After seven years, the **g** were filled to overflowing.
Jer 50:26 Break open her **g**. Crush her walls and houses into
Joel 1:17 The barns and **g** stand empty and abandoned.

GRAND (3) [GRANDLY]

Ps 49:14 will rot in the grave, / far from their **g** estates.
Isa 5:12 furnish lovely music and wine at your **g** parties;
Hos 2:22 And the whole **g** chorus will sing together,

GRANDCHILDREN (23) [CHILD]

Ge 21:23 that you won't deceive me, my children, or my **g**.
31:28 kiss my daughters and **g** and tell them good-bye?
31:43 and these children are my **g**, and these flocks
31:43 what can I do now to my own daughters and **g**?
31:55 he kissed his daughters and **g** and blessed them.
36:12 These were all **g** of Esau's wife Adah.
36:13 These were all **g** of Esau's wife Basemath.
36:15 and **g** became the leaders of different clans.
45:10 so you can be near me with all your children and **g**,
Ex 1: 7 But their descendants had many children and **g**.
10: 2 and **g** about the marvelous things I am doing
Dt 4: 9 be sure to pass them on to your children and **g**.
4:25 when you have children and **g** and have lived in
6: 2 and **g** might fear the LORD your God as long as
Job 18:19 They will have neither children nor **g**, nor any
21: 8 children grow to maturity, and they enjoy their **g**.
42:16 living to see four generations of his children and **g**.
Ps 128: 6 May you live to enjoy your **g**. / And may Israel
Pr 13:22 Good people leave an inheritance to their **g**,
17: 6 **G** are the crowning glory of the aged; parents are
Jer 29: 6 Then find spouses for them, and have many **g**.
Eze 37:25 and their **g** after them will live there forever,
1Ti 5: 4 But if she has children or **g**, their first

GRANDDAUGHTER (8) [DAUGHTER]

Ge 36: 2 the daughter of Anah and **g** of Zibeon the Hivite.
36:14 the daughter of Anah and **g** of Zibeon.
36:39 the daughter of Matred and **g** of Mezahab.
Lev 18:10 "Do not have sexual intercourse with your **g**,
18:17 and her daughter or marry both a woman and her **g**,
2Ki 8:26 mother was Athaliah, a **g** of King Omri of Israel.
1Ch 1:50 the daughter of Matred and **g** of Me-zahab.
2Ch 22: 2 mother was Athaliah, a **g** of King Omri of Israel.

GRANDDAUGHTERS (1) [DAUGHTER]

Ge 46: 7 sons and daughters, grandsons and **g**—all his

GRANDFATHER (16) [FATHER]

Ge 28: 2 to Paddan-aram, to the house of your **g** Bethuel,
28:13 the God of your **g** Abraham and the God of your
31: 3 of your father and **g** and to your relatives there,
31:42 the God of my **g** Abraham, the awe-inspiring God
31:53 the God of your **g** Abraham and the God of my **g**
Nahor—
32: 9 "O God of my **g** Abraham and my father, Isaac—
48:15 the God before whom my **g** Abraham and my
48:16 and the names of my **g** Abraham and my father,
49:29 with my father and **g** in the cave in Ephron's field.
49:32 It is the cave that my **g** Abraham bought from the
Ru 4:17 He became the father of Jesse and the **g** of David.
2Sa 9: 7 you all the land that once belonged to your **g** Saul,
13:37 Absalom fled to his **g**, Talmai son of Ammihud,
16: 3 'Today I will get back the kingdom of my **g**
2Ch 21:12 Jehoshaphat, or your **g** King Asa of Judah.

GRANDFATHER'S (1) [FATHER]

Ge 48:12 Joseph took the boys from their **g** knees, and he

GRANDLY (1) [GRAND]

Job 39:13 "The ostrich flaps her wings **g**, but they are no

GRANDMOTHER (4) [MOTHER]

1Ki 15:10 His **g** was Maacah, the daughter of Absalom.
15:13 He even deposed his **g** Maacah from her position
2Ch 15:16 King Asa even deposed his **g** Maacah from her
2Ti 1: 5 the faith of your mother, Eunice, and your **g**, Lois.

GRANDPARENTS (2) [PARENT]

Ge 24:24 she replied. "My **g** are Nahor and Milcah.
Jer 6:11 of young men, and on husbands and wives and **g**.

GRANDSON (48) [SON]

Ge 11:31 and his **g** Lot (his son Haran's child)
29: 5 know a man there named Laban, the **g** of Nahor?"
Ex 31: 2 Bezalel son of Uri, **g** of Hur, of the tribe of Judah.
35:30 Bezalel son of Uri, **g** of Hur, of the tribe of Judah.
38:22 Bezalel son of Uri, **g** of Hur, of the tribe of Judah,
Nu 25: 7 son of Eleazar and **g** of Aaron the priest saw this,
25:11 and **g** of Aaron the priest has turned my anger
Jdg 8:22 You and your son and your **g** will be our rulers,
20:28 son of Eleazar and **g** of Aaron was the priest.)
1Sa 1: 1 He was the son of Jeroham and **g** of Elihu,
9: 1 He was the son of Abiel and **g** of Zeror,
14: 3 Ahitub was the son of Phinehas and the **g** of Eli,
2Sa 9: 6 he was Jonathan's son and Saul's **g**.
9: 9 "I have given your master's **g** everything that
19:24 Now Mephibosheth, Saul's **g**, arrived from
21: 7 who was Saul's **g**, because of the oath David
1Ki 15:18 to Ben-hadad son of Tabrimmon and **g** of Hezion,
2Ki 9: 2 and find Jehu son of Jehoshaphat and **g** of Nimshi.
9:14 and **g** of Nimshi formed a conspiracy against King
14: 8 king Jehoash, the son of Jehoahaz and **g** of Jehu:
22: 3 sent Shaphan son of Azaliah and **g** of Meshullam,
22:14 the wife of Shallum son of Tikvah and **g** of Harhas,
25:22 and **g** of Shaphan as governor over the people left
25:25 Ishmael son of Nethaniah and **g** of Elishama,
2Ch 1: 5 and **g** of Hur was still at Gibeon in front of the
22: 9 the people said, "He was the **g** of Jehoshaphat—
25:17 king Jehoash, the son of Jehoahaz and **g** of Jehu:
34:22 the wife of Shallum son of Tikvah and **g** of Harhas,
Ne 3: 4 and **g** of Hakkoz repaired the next section of wall.
3: 4 Meshullam son of Berekiah and **g** of Meshezabel,
3:21 and **g** of Hakkoz rebuilt another section of the wall
3:23 and **g** of Ananiah repaired the sections next to their
6:10 visit Shemaiah son of Delaiah and **g** of Mehetabel,
12:23 down to the days of Johanan, the **g** of Eliashib.
13:13 son of Zaccur and **g** of Mattaniah as their assistant.
Isa 7: 1 the reign of Ahaz son of Jotham and **g** of Uzziah,
Jer 27: 7 serve him and his son and his **g** until his time is up.
32:12 them to Baruch son of Neriah and **g** of Mahseiah.
35: 3 and **g** of Habazziniah and all his brothers
36:11 and **g** of Shaphan heard the messages from the
36:14 **g** of Shelemiah, and great-grandson of Cushi,
37:13 was Irijah son of Shelemiah and **g** of Hananiah.
39:14 care of Gedaliah son of Ahikam and **g** of Shaphan,
40: 5 to Gedaliah son of Ahikam and **g** of Shaphan.
41: 1 Ishmael son of Nethaniah and **g** of Elishama,
51:59 Seraiah son of Neriah and **g** of Mahseiah, when he
Zec 1: 1 prophet Zechariah son of Berekiah and **g** of Iddo.
1: 7 prophet Zechariah son of Berekiah and **g** of Iddo.

GRANDSONS (5) [SON]

Ge 46: 7 sons and daughters, **g** and granddaughters—all his
Jdg 12:14 He had forty sons and thirty **g**, who rode on
2Sa 21: 6 let seven of Saul's sons or **g** be handed over to us,
1Ch 8:40 They had many sons and **g**—150 in all.
26: 8 of Obed-edom, including their sons and **g**—

GRANT (21) [GRANTED, GRANTING, GRANTS]

Ge 19:21 "All right," the angel said, "I will **g** your request.
1Sa 1:17 May the God of Israel **g** the request you have
2Sa 7:29 For when you **g** a blessing to your servant,
1Ki 2:33 and may the LORD **g** peace to David and his
8:43 heaven where you live, and **g** what they ask of you.
1Ch 17:27 For when you **g** a blessing, O LORD, it is an
2Ch 6:33 heaven where you live, and **g** what they ask of you.
Ne 1:11 Please **g** me success now as I go to ask the king for
Est 5: 8 is pleased with me and wants to **g** my request,
7: 3 is pleased with me and wants to **g** my request,
Job 6: 8 might have my request, that God would **g** my hope.
Ps 20: 4 May he **g** your heart's desire / and fulfill all your
85: 7 O LORD, / and **g** us your salvation.
86:11 **G** me purity of heart, / that I may honor you.
144:10 For you **g** victory to kings! / You are the one who
Isa 26:12 LORD, you will **g** us peace, / for all we have
Jer 16:13 idols all you like—and I will **g** you no favors!
Eze 36:37 and I am ready to **g** them their requests.
Lk 18: 8 I tell you, he will **g** justice to them quickly!
22:29 has granted me a Kingdom, I now **g** you the right
Jn 16:23 and he will **g** your request because you use my

GRANTED (18) [GRANT]
Ge 4:25 "God has g me another son in place of Abel,
19:19 and saved my life, and you have g me such mercy.
39:21 too, and he g Joseph favor with the chief jailer.
1Sa 12:13 asked for him, and the LORD has g your request.
2Sa 14:22 your approval, for you have g me this request!"
1Ch 4:10 all trouble and pain!" And God g him his request.
Ezr 9: 8 our eyes and g us some relief from our slavery.
Ne 2: 8 And the king g these requests, because the gracious
Est 9:12 It will be g to you; tell me and I will do it."
Ps 21: 4 to preserve his life, / and you have g his request.
Pr 14:22 you will be g unfailing love and faithfulness.
Isa 63: 7 which he has g according to his mercy and love.
Mt 15:28 to her, "your faith is great. Your request is g."
Lk 22:29 And just as my Father has g me a Kingdom,
Jn 5:26 and he has g his Son to have life in himself.
15: 7 you may ask any request you like, and it will be g!
Ac 12:21 and an appointment with Herod was g.
27:24 God in his goodness has g safety to everyone

GRANTING (1) [GRANT]
Ps 16:11 me the way of life, / g me the joy of your presence

GRANTS (3) [GRANT]
Pr 2: 6 For the LORD g wisdom! From his mouth come
2: 7 He g a treasure of good sense to the godly. He is
Eze 18: 8 And suppose he g loans without interest,

GRAPE (10) [GRAPE-PICKING, GRAPES, GRAPEVINE, GRAPEVINES]
Lev 19:10 It is the same with your g crop—do not strip every
26: 5 Your threshing season will extend until the g
26: 5 and your g harvest will extend until it is time to
Nu 6: 3 not drink other fermented drinks or fresh g juice,
6: 4 from a grapevine, not even the g seeds or skins.
SS 7: 8 Now may your breasts be like g clusters,
Isa 24: 7 The g harvest will fail, and there will be no wine.
Mt 21:33 around it, dug a pit for pressing out the g juice,
21:34 At the time of the g harvest he sent his servants to
Mk 12: 1 around it, dug a pit for pressing out the g juice,

GRAPE-PICKING (2) [GRAPE, PICK]
Mk 12: 2 At g time he sent one of his servants to collect his
Lk 20:10 At g time, he sent one of his servants to collect his

GRAPES (67) [GRAPE]
Ge 40:10 and soon there were clusters of ripe g.
40:11 so I took the g and squeezed the juice into it.
Ex 22: 5 pay damages in the form of high-quality grain or g.
Lev 19:10 do not strip every last bunch of g from the vines,
19:10 and do not pick up the g that fall to the ground.
25: 5 or process the g that grow on your unpruned vines.
25:11 and do not process the g that grow on your
Nu 6: 3 grape juice, and they must not eat g or raisins.
13:20 to be the season for harvesting the first ripe g.)
13:23 they cut down a cluster of g so large that it took
13:24 because of the cluster of g they had cut there.
20: 5 This land has no grain, figs, g, or pomegranates.
Dt 7:13 g, and olives, and great herds of cattle, sheep,
11:14 crops of grain, g for wine, and olives for oil.
16:13 has been threshed and the g have been pressed.
22: 9 you are forbidden to use either the g from the
23:24 "You may eat your fill of g from your neighbor's
24:21 This also applies to the g in your vineyard. Do not
24:21 but leave any remaining g for the foreigners,
28:39 but you will not drink the wine or eat the g,
32:14 drank the finest wine, / made from the juice of g.
32:32 Their g are poison, / and their clusters are bitter.
Jdg 8: 2 Aren't the last g of Ephraim's harvest better than
13:14 She must not eat g or raisins, drink wine or any
1Ch 27:27 Zabdi from Shepham was responsible for the g
Ne 13:15 g, figs, and all sorts of produce to Jerusalem to sell.
Job 15:33 They will be like a vine whose g are harvested
Isa 5: 2 Then he waited for a harvest of sweet g,
5: 2 but the g that grew were wild and sour.
5: 4 Why did my vineyard give me wild g
16:10 The treading out of g in the winepresses has ceased
17:11 but you will never pick any g from them.
18: 5 your attack, while your plans are ripening like g,
24:13 the tree or the few g left on the vine after harvest,
63: 2 so red, as if you have been treading out g?
63: 3 I have trampled my enemies as if they were g.
65: 8 "For just as good g are found among a cluster of
65: 8 there are some good g there!'), so I will not destroy
Jer 5:17 herds of cattle. Yes, they will eat your g and figs.
6: 9 vine a second time to pick the g that were missed."
8:13 I will take away their rich harvests of figs and g.
25:30 the harvesters do as they crush juice from the g.
31:29 'The parents eat sour g, but their children's mouths
31:30 those who eat the sour g will be the ones whose
40:10 Harvest the g and summer fruits and olives,
40:12 Judean countryside to gather a great harvest of g
48:32 He has harvested your g and summer fruits.
48:33 No one treads the g with shouts of joy. There is
49: 9 Those who harvest g always leave a few for the
La 1:15 The Lord has trampled his beloved city as g are
Eze 18: 2 'The parents have eaten sour g, but their children's
Hos 2:22 of the grain, the g, and the olive trees for moisture.
9: 2 The g you gather will not quench your thirst.
9:10 found you, it was like finding fresh g in the desert!
Joel 1: 5 All the g are ruined, and all your new wine is
Am 9:13 and g will grow faster than they can be harvested.
Ob 1: 5 Those who harvest g always leave a few for the
Mic 6:15 You will trample the g but get no juice to make
7: 1 Not a cluster of g or a single fig can be found to
Hab 3:17 have no blossoms, and there are no g on the vine;
Hag 1:11 the grain and g and olives and all your other crops,
Mal 3:11 Your g will not shrivel before they are ripe,"
Mt 7:16 You don't pick g from thornbushes, or figs from
Lk 6:44 grow on thornbushes or g on bramble bushes.
Rev 14:18 "Use your sickle now to gather the clusters of g
14:19 and loaded the g into the great winepress of God's
14:20 And the g were trodden in the winepress outside

GRAPEVINE (8) [GRAPE, VINE]
Ge 49:11 He ties his foal to a g, / the colt of his donkey to a
Nu 6: 4 to eat or drink anything that comes from a g,
Jdg 9:12 "Then they said to the g, 'You be our king!'
9:13 But the g replied, 'Should I quit producing the
Isa 16: 8 Moab was once like a spreading g. Her tendrils
Eze 15: 2 "Son of man, how does a g compare to a tree?
Hag 2:19 you have harvested your grain and before the g,
Jas 3:12 you pick olives from a fig tree or figs from a g?

GRAPEVINES (14) [GRAPE, VINE]
Dt 8: 8 It is a land of wheat and barley, of g, fig trees,
Jdg 15: 5 He also destroyed their g and olive trees.
Ps 78:47 He destroyed their g with hail / and shattered their
105:33 He ruined their g and fig trees / and shattered all
SS 2:13 The fig trees are budding, and the g are in blossom.
2:15 of your love, for the g are all in blossom."
6:11 I wanted to see whether the g were budding yet,
Isa 17:10 can hide you. You may plant the finest imported g,
Eze 15: 6 The people of Jerusalem are like g growing among
Hos 14: 7 They will flourish like grain and blossom like g.
Joel 1: 7 They have destroyed my g and fig trees,
1:12 The g and the fig trees have all withered.
2:22 fig trees and g will flourish once more.
Zec 8:12 among you. The g will be heavy with fruit.

GRASP (7) [GRASPING]
1Sa 14:47 Now when Saul had secured his g on Israel's
1Ki 20:33 The men were quick to g at this straw of hope,
Ps 82: 4 deliver them from the g of evil people.
Jer 34: 3 You will not escape his g but will be taken into
Eze 13:21 the magic veils and save my people from your g.
13:23 For I will rescue my people from your g.
Lk 18:34 and they failed to g what he was talking about.

GRASPING (2) [GRASP]
Ge 25:26 Then the other twin was born with his hand g
Lev 1:17 Then, g the bird by its wings, the priest will tear

GRASS (57) [GRASS-EATING, GRASSES, GRASSY]
Ge 1:11 "Let the land burst forth with every sort of g
Nu 22: 4 devour everything in sight, like an ox devours g!"
Dt 29:23 and nothing growing, not even a blade of g.
32: 2 like dew. / My words will fall like rain on tender g,
2Sa 23: 4 like the refreshing rains that bring tender g from
1Ki 18: 5 and valley to see if we can find enough g to save at
2Ki 19:26 easy prey for you. / They are as helpless as the g,
19:26 They are like g sprouting on a housetop,
Job 5:25 your descendants will be as plentiful as g!
6: 5 Wild donkeys bray when they find no green g,
13:25 by the wind? Would you chase a dry stalk of g?
38:27 parched ground and makes the tender g spring up?
39: 8 where it searches for every blade of g.
40:15 I made it, just as I made you. It eats g like an ox.
Ps 37: 2 For like g, they soon fade away. / Like springtime
72:16 they do in Lebanon, / sprouting up like g in a field.
90: 5 or like g that springs up in the morning.
102: 4 My heart is sick, withered like g, / and I have lost
102:11 as the evening shadows. / I am withering like g.
103:15 Our days on earth are like g; / like wildflowers,
104:14 You cause g to grow for the cattle. / You cause
129: 6 May they be as useless as g on a rooftop,
147: 8 and makes the green g grow in mountain pastures.
Pr 19:12 like a lion's roar, but his favor is like dew on the g.
SS 1:16 sight you are, my love, as we lie here on the g,
Isa 11: 7 And lions will eat g as the livestock do.
27:10 the houses abandoned, the streets covered with g.
35: 7 Marsh g and reeds and rushes will flourish where
37:27 easy prey for you. / They are as helpless as the g,
37:27 They are like g sprouting on a housetop,
40: 6 "Shout that people are like the g that dies away.
40: 7 The g withers, and the flowers fade beneath the
40: 8 The g withers, and the flowers fade, but the word
44: 4 They will thrive like watered g, like willows on a
47:14 But they are as useless as dried g burning in a fire.
51:12 mere humans, who wither like the g and disappear?
58: 5 bowing your heads like a blade of g in the wind.
Jer 12: 4 Even the g in the fields has withered. The wild
14: 5 abandons her newborn fawn because there is no g.
14: 6 They strain their eyes looking for g to eat, but there
Da 4:15 of iron and bronze and surrounded by tender g.
4:23 of iron and bronze and surrounded by tender g.
4:23 Let him eat g with the animals of the field for
4:25 You will eat g like a cow, and you will be
4:32 the wild animals, and you will eat g like a cow.
4:33 He ate g like a cow, and he was drenched with the
5:21 He ate g like a cow, and he was drenched with the
Am 1: 2 All the g on Mount Carmel withers and dies."
Mic 5: 7 sent by the LORD or like rain falling on the g,
Mt 14:19 Then he told the people to sit down on the g.
Mk 6:39 the crowd to sit down in groups on the green g.
Jas 1:11 The hot sun rises and dries up the g; the flower
5:18 The g turned green, and the crops began to grow
1Pe 1:24 prophet says, / "People are like g that dies away;
1:24 The g withers, / and the flowers fall away.
Rev 8: 7 of the trees were burned, and all the g was burned.
9: 4 They were told not to hurt the g or plants or trees

GRASS-EATING (1) [EAT, GRASS]
Ps 106:20 traded their glorious God / for a statue of a g ox!

GRASSES (2) [GRASS]
Ge 1:30 And I have given all the g and other green plants to
Pr 27:25 crop appears, and the mountain g are gathered in,

GRASSHOPPER (1) [GRASSHOPPERS]
Ps 109:23 at dusk; / I am falling like a g that is brushed aside.

GRASSHOPPERS (5) [GRASSHOPPER]
Lev 11:22 locusts of all varieties, crickets, bald locusts, and g.
Nu 13:33 We felt like g next to them, and that's what we
Isa 40:22 The people below must seem to him like g!
Jer 46:23 the LORD, "for they are more numerous than g.
Na 3:15 will be no escape, even if you multiply like g.

GRASSY (2) [GRASS]
Isa 15: 6 The g banks are scorched, and the tender plants are
Jn 6:10 five thousand—sat down on the g slopes.

GRATEFUL (4) [GRATITUDE]
Ps 119:108 LORD, accept my g thanks / and teach me your
Jnh 4: 6 his discomfort, and Jonah was very g for the plant.
Ac 24: 3 And for all of this we are very g to you.
Php 4:10 How g I am, and how I praise the Lord that you are

GRATING (7)
Ex 27: 4 Make a bronze g, with a metal ring at each corner.
27: 5 Fit the g halfway down into the firebox, resting it
35:16 the bronze g of the altar and its carrying poles
38: 4 Next he made a bronze g that rested on a ledge
38: 5 Four rings were cast for each side of the g to
38:30 and for the bronze altar with its bronze g and altar
39:39 bronze altar; the bronze g; its poles and utensils;

GRATITUDE (1) [GRATEFUL]
2Ki 4:37 She fell at his feet, overwhelmed with g. Then she

GRAVE (88) [GRAVECLOTHES, GRAVES, GRAVESIDE, GRAVEYARD]
Ge 35:20 Jacob set up a stone monument over her g, and it
42:38 you would bring my gray head down to the g in
44:29 you would bring my gray head down to the g in
44:31 for bringing his gray head down to the g in sorrow.
Nu 16:30 their belongings, and they go down alive into the g,
16:33 So they went down alive into the g, along with
19:16 or if someone touches a human bone or a g,
19:18 or who died naturally, or has touched a g.
Dt 32:22 and burns to the depths of the g. / It devours the
Jdg 8:32 and he was buried in the g of his father, Joash,
1Sa 2: 6 he brings some down to the g but raises others up.
2Sa 3:31 himself walked behind the procession to the g.
22: 6 The g wrapped its ropes around me; / death itself
1Ki 13:22 your body will not be buried in the g of your
13:30 He laid the body in his own g, crying out in grief,
13:31 bury me in the g where the man of God is buried.
Job 3:22 relief when they finally die, when they find the g.
10:19 would have gone directly from the womb to the g.
17: 1 and I am near death. The g is ready to receive me.
17:13 I might go to the g and make my bed in darkness.
17:14 And I might call the g my father, and the worm my
17:16 No, my hope will go down with me to the g.
21:13 in prosperity; then they go down to the g in peace.
21:32 When they are carried to the g, an honor guard
27:15 Those who survive will be brought down to the g
33:18 He keeps them from the g, from crossing over the
33:28 God rescued me from the g, and now my life is
33:30 He rescues them from the g so they may live in the
Ps 5: 9 Their talk is foul, like the stench from an open g.
6: 5 remembers you? / Who can praise you from the g?
9:17 The wicked will go down to the g. / This is the fate
16:10 the dead / or allow your godly one to rot in the g.
18: 5 The g wrapped its ropes around me; / death itself
30: 3 You brought me up from the g, O LORD.
30: 9 will you gain if I die, / if I sink down into the g? / Can my dust praise you from the g?
31:17 wicked be disgraced; / let them lie silent in the g.
49: 9 to live forever / and never see the g.
49:11 The g is their eternal home, / where they will stay
49:14 Like sheep, they are led to the g, / where death will
49:14 Their bodies will rot in the g, / far from their grand
49:17 Their wealth will not follow them into the g.
55:15 enemies by surprise; / let the g swallow them alive,
88:11 Can those in the g declare your unfailing love?
89:48 No one can escape the power of the g. / *Interlude*
115:17 for they have gone into the silence of the g.
116: 3 my throat; / the terrors of the g overtook me.
143: 3 He forces me to live in darkness like those in the g.
Pr 1:12 Let's swallow them alive as the g swallows its
5: 5 go down to death; her steps lead straight to the g.
7:27 Her house is the road to the g. Her bedroom is the
9:18 realize that her former guests are now in the g.
15:24 wise leads to life above; they leave the g behind.
28:17 tormented conscience will drive him into the g.
30:16 the g, / the barren womb, / the thirsty desert,

Ecc 9:10 For when you go to the g, there will be no work
10: 5 world go by. Kings and rulers make a g mistake
SS 8: 6 as death, and its jealousy is as enduring as the g.
Isa 5:14 The g is licking its chops in anticipation of
14:19 but your body is thrown from the g like a discarded
14:19 you will be dumped into a mass g with those killed
28:15 avoid death and have made a deal to dodge the g.
28:18 and I will overturn your deal to dodge the g.
53: 9 like a criminal; he was put in a rich man's g.
Jer 17:13 They will be buried in a dry and dusty g, for they
20:17 my mother's womb, that her body had been my g!
26:23 a sword and had him buried in an unmarked g.)
Eze 24:17 but only quietly. Let there be no wailing at her g.
31:15 When Assyria went down into the g, I made the
31:16 for I sent it down to the g with all the others like it.
31:17 They had gone down to the g—all those nations
32:21 Down in the g mighty leaders will mockingly
32:27 who went down to the g with their weapons—
Hos 13:14 Should I ransom them from the g? Should I redeem
13:14 O g, bring forth your plagues! For I will not relent!
Na 1:14 I am preparing a g for you because you are
Jn 11:17 he was told that Lazarus had already been in his g
11:31 they assumed she was going to Lazarus's g to
11:38 was deeply troubled. Then they came to the g.
Ac 2:27 the dead / or allow your Holy One to rot in the g.
2:31 the dead and that his body would not rot in the g.
13:35 'You will not allow your Holy One to rot in the g.'
Ro 3:13 "Their talk is foul, like the stench from an open g.
1Co 15:15 for we have said that God raised Christ from the g,
Rev 1:18 and ever! And I hold the keys of death and the g.
6: 8 of its rider, who was followed around by the G.
20:13 and death and the g gave up the dead in them.
20:14 and the g were thrown into the lake of fire.

GRAVECLOTHES (1) [CLOTHE, GRAVE]

Jn 11:44 And Lazarus came out, bound in g, his face

GRAVED, GRAVEN [KJV] See CARVED, ENGRAVED, IDOL, IMAGE, WRITTEN

GRAVEL (2)

Pr 20:17 bread tastes sweet, but it turns to g in the mouth.
La 3:16 He has made me grind my teeth on g. He has rolled

GRAVES (18) [GRAVE]

Ex 14:11 Weren't there enough g for us in Egypt? Why did
Nu 11:34 called Kibroth-hattaavah—"the g of craving"—
2Ch 34: 4 and scattered over the g of those who had
Isa 14:18 kings of the nations lie in stately glory in their g,
65: 4 At night they go out among the g and secret places
Jer 7:32 in Topheth that there won't be room for all the g.
8: 1 "the enemy will break open the g of the kings
8: 1 and the g of the priests, prophets, and common
Eze 32:22 "Assyria lies there surrounded by the g of all its
32:23 Their g are in the depths of the pit, and they are
32:25 surrounded by the g of all their people.
32:26 are there, surrounded by the g of all their hordes.
37:12 I will open your g of exile and cause you to rise
Mt 23:29 and decorate the g of the godly people your
Lk 11:44 will be for you. For you are like hidden g in a field.
Jn 5:28 the time is coming when all the dead in their g will
1Th 4:15 rise to meet him ahead of those who are in their g.
4:16 the Christians who have died will rise from their g.

GRAVESIDE (1) [GRAVE]

2Sa 3:32 and the king and all the people wept at his g.

GRAVEYARD (2) [GRAVE]

Jer 31:40 including the g and ash dump in the valley, and all
Eze 39:11 "And I will make a vast g for Gog and his hordes

GRAVITY [KJV] See RESPECT

GRAY (6) [GRAY-HAIRED, GRAYING]

Ge 42:38 you would bring my g head down to the grave in
44:29 you would bring my g head down to the grave in
44:31 We will be responsible for bringing his g head
Ps 71:18 Now that I am old and g, / do not abandon me,
Pr 16:31 G hair is a crown of glory; it is gained by living a
20:29 the g hair of experience is the splendor of the old.

GRAY-HAIRED (2) [GRAY, HAIR]

1Sa 12: 2 of my own sons, and I stand here, an old, g man.
Job 15:10 side are aged, g men much older than your father!

GRAYHEADED [KJV] See GRAY HEAD, GRAY-HAIRED

GRAYING (1) [GRAY]

Hos 7: 9 Israel is like an old man with g hair, unaware of

GRAZE (11) [GRAZES, GRAZING]

Ex 22: 5 owner lets it stray into someone else's field to g,
34: 3 even let the flocks or herds g near the mountain."
Dt 11:15 give you lush pastureland for your cattle to g in,
SS 6: 2 to his spice beds, to g and to gather the lilies.
Isa 7:25 cover them. Cattle, sheep, and goats will g there.
11: 7 The cattle will g among bears. Cubs and calves
17: 2 Sheep will g in the streets and lie down unafraid.
27:10 Cattle will g there, chewing on twigs and branches.
32:14 and goats will g on the hills where the watchtowers
32:20 Their flocks and herds will g in green pastures.
Eze 32:13 all your flocks and herds that g beside the streams.

GRAZES (1) [GRAZE]

SS 6: 3 and my lover is mine. He g among the lilies!"

GRAZING (6) [GRAZE]

Ge 29: 7 you water the flocks so they can get back to g?"
36:24 the wilderness while he was g his father's donkeys.
41: 2 up out of the river and began g along its bank.
41:18 up out of the river and began g along its bank.
Ex 22: 5 "If an animal is g in a field or vineyard
Isa 49: 9 g in green pastures and on hills that were

GREASE [KJV] See STUPID

GREASED (1)

Pr 27:16 to stop the wind or hold something with g hands.

GREAT (769) [GREATER, GREATEST, GREATLY, GREATNESS]

GREAT CITY (16) Ge 11:4; Jer 22:8; 51:47; Da 4:30; Am 6:2; Jnh 1:2; 3:2; 4:11; Rev 14:8; 16:19; 17:18; 18:2,10,16, 19,21

GREAT CROWD (8) 2Sa 13:34; Jer 44:15; Mk 8:1; 9:14; 10:46; Lk 1:10; 7:11; Jn 6:5

GREAT GOD (6) Dt 10:17; Ezr 5:8; Ne 8:6; Ps 95:3; Da 2:45; Tit 2:13

GREAT JOY (23) Dt 16:15; 27:7; 1Ch 12:40; 29:22; 2Ch 30:21,26; Ezr 6:16,22; Ne 8:12,17; 12:43; Ps 35:27; Jer 15:16; Mt 28:8; Lk 1:14; 2:10; 24:52; Ac 2:46; 8:8; 15:31; Php 2:29; 1Th 3:9; Jude 1:24

GREAT KING (15) 2Ki 18:19,28; Ezr 5:11; Ps 47:2; 48:2; 95:3; Ecc 9:14; Isa 36:4,13; Jer 22:15; Hos 5:13; 8:10; 10:6; Mal 1:14; Mt 5:35

GREAT POWER (24) Ex 13:9,16; 15:16; 32:11; Ne 1:10; Job 30:21; Ps 20:6; 54:1; 66:7; 79:11; 111:6; Ecc 4:1; 8:4; Jer 21:5; 27:5; 32:17,21; Jnh 1:16; Mal 1:5; Mk 9:1; 13:26; Jas 5:16; Rev 6:15; 11:17

GREAT SEA (5) Ge 1:21; Job 26:12; Ps 89:10; Da 7:2; Am 9:3

GREAT THING (3) 1Sa 12:16; 2Ki 5:13; Lk 8:39

GREAT THINGS (12) Jdg 2:7; 1Sa 12:7; 25:31; 2Sa 7:21; 2Ki 8:4; 1Ch 17:19; Ps 106:21; Jer 45:5; Joel 2:20,21; Mk 5:20; Lk 1:49

Ge 1:16 For God made two g lights, the sun and the moon,
1:21 So God created g sea creatures and every sort of
4:13 "My punishment is too g for me to bear!
8:17 so they can breed and reproduce in g numbers."
11: 3 "let's make g piles of burnt brick and collect
11: 4 Let's build a g city with a tower that reaches to the
12: 2 I will cause you to become the father of a g nation.
15: 1 for I will protect you, and your reward will be g."
15:14 and in the end they will come away with g wealth.
15:18 all the way from the border of Egypt to the g
17:20 I will cause him to multiply and become a g nation.
18:18 "For Abraham will become a g and mighty nation,
19: 3 He set a g feast before them, complete with fresh
20: 8 had happened, g fear swept through the crowd.
20: 9 making me and my kingdom guilty of this g sin?
21:18 for I will make a g nation from his descendants."
24:35 blessed my master richly; he has become a g man.
26:10 and you would have made us guilty of g sin."
26:14 large flocks of sheep and goats, g herds of cattle,
26:24 and they will become a g nation.
26:30 So Isaac prepared a g feast for them, and they ate
28: 3 And may your descendants become a g assembly
35:11 the earth! Become a g nation, even many nations.
39: 9 a wicked thing? It would be a g sin against God."
41:29 The next seven years will be a period of g
41:30 so g that all the prosperity will be forgotten
45: 7 families alive so that you will become a g nation.
46: 3 for I will see to it that you become a g nation there.
48: 7 So with g sorrow I buried her there beside the road
48:19 "Manasseh, too, will become a g people, but his
50: 7 with a g number of Pharaoh's counselors
50: 9 So a g number of chariots, cavalry, and people
50:10 they held a very g and solemn funeral,
50:17 'Forgive your brothers for the g evil they did to
Ex 6: 6 you with mighty power and g acts of judgment.
7: 4 the forces of Israel out with g acts of judgment.
8:14 They were piled into g heaps, and a terrible stench
11: 3 and Moses was considered a very g man in the
13: 6 you will celebrate a g feast to the LORD.
13: 9 who rescued you from Egypt with g power.
13:16 who brought you out of Egypt with g power."
14: 4 so I will receive g glory at the expense of Pharaoh
14:17 Then I will receive g glory at the expense of
15:16 Because of your g power, / they will be silent like
31: 3 giving him g wisdom, intelligence, and skill in all
32:10 Moses, into a g nation instead of them."
32:11 brought from the land of Egypt with such g power
32:29 of this, he will now give you a g blessing."
32:35 And the LORD sent a g plague upon the people
35:31 giving him g wisdom, intelligence, and skill in all
Lev 11:17 the little owl, the cormorant, the g owl,
11:29 the mole, the mouse, the g lizard of all varieties,
22: 2 gifts that the Israelites set apart for me with g care,
Nu 14: 2 Their voices rose in a g chorus of complaint
14:17 prove that your power is as g as you have claimed
21:18 which princes dug, / which g leaders hollowed out
33: 4 gods of Egypt that night with g acts of judgment!
Dt 1: 7 and all the way to the g Euphrates River.
1: 9 'You are too g a burden for me to carry all by
1:17 those who are rich; be fair to lowly and g alike.
1:19 we left Mount Sinai and traveled through the g
2: 7 and has watched your every step through this g
3:24 or on earth who can perform such g deeds as
4: 7 For what g nation has a god as near to them as the
4: 8 And what g nation has laws and regulations as fair
4:32 See if anything as g as this has ever happened
4:36 He let you see his g fire here on earth so he could
4:37 and personally brought you out of Egypt with a g
7:13 and bless you and make you into a g nation.
7:13 and olives, and g herds of cattle, sheep, and goats.
7:19 Remember the g terrors the LORD your God sent
7:21 is among you, and he is a g and awesome God.
8:15 Do not forget that he led you through the g
10:17 He is the g God, mighty and awesome, who shows
13:17 have compassion on you and make you a g nation,
14:16 the little owl, the g owl, the white owl,
16:15 This festival will be a time of g joy for all.
27: 7 and feast there with g joy before the LORD your
28:63 "Just as the LORD has found g pleasure in
29: 3 all the g tests of strength, the miraculous signs,
29:28 In g anger and fury the LORD uprooted his
30:16 If you do this, you will live and become a g nation,
31:21 Then g disasters will come down on them, and this
Jos 3: 5 for tomorrow the LORD will do g wonders
3: 7 "Today I will begin to make you g in the eyes of
4:14 That day the LORD made Joshua g in the eyes of
7: 9 then what will happen to the honor of your g
7:26 They piled a g heap of stones over Achan,
8:29 They piled a g heap of stones over him that can
10:10 and the Israelites slaughtered them in g numbers at
11: 8 The Israelites chased them as far as G Sidon
14:12 as scouts we found the Anakites living there in g,
14:15 been named after Arba, a g hero of the Anakites.)
17: 1 to the family of Makir because he was a g warrior.
22: 8 "Share with your relatives back home the g wealth
23: 9 "For the LORD has driven out g and powerful
Jdg 2: 7 those who had seen all the g things the LORD
5:15 But in the tribe of Reuben / there was g indecision.
5:16 In the tribe of Reuben / there was g indecision.
10: 9 and Ephraim. The Israelites were in g distress.
11: 1 Now Jephthah from Gilead was a g warrior.
11:36 for the LORD has given you a g victory over your
15: 8 So he attacked the Philistines with g fury
15:18 "You have accomplished this g victory by the
16:23 The Philistine leaders held a g festival,
18: 7 And they lived a g distance from Sidon and had no
18:28 for they lived a g distance from Sidon and had no
Ru 4:11 May you be g in Ephrathah and famous in
1Sa 1:16 For I have been praying out of g anguish
4:10 The slaughter was g; thirty thousand Israelite men
5: 9 with a plague of tumors, and there was a g panic.
5:11 and g fear was sweeping across the city.
6: 9 the LORD who brought this g disaster upon us.
7: 6 in a g ceremony, drew water from a well
9:22 Samuel brought Saul and his servant into the g hall
12: 7 of all the g things the LORD has done for you
12:16 and see the g thing the LORD is about to do.
12:22 chosen people, for that would dishonor his g name.
14:48 He did g deeds and conquered the Amalekites,
17:52 Then the Israelites gave a g shout of triumph
19: 5 and how the LORD brought a g victory to Israel
19:22 went to Ramah and arrived at the g well in Secu.
23:25 he went even farther into the wilderness to the g
25:31 And when the LORD has done these g things for
26:15 "Well, Abner, you're a g man, aren't you?"
26:25 You will do heroic deeds and be a g conqueror."
30:19 small or g, son or daughter, or anything else that
2Sa 3:20 twenty men, David entertained them with a g feast.
3:38 "Do you not realize that a g leader and a g man has fallen today in Israel?
5:12 and had made his kingdom g for the sake of his
6:12 and brought the Ark to the City of David with a g
7:21 you have done all these g things and have shown
7:22 "How g you are, O Sovereign LORD! There is
7:23 You made a g name for yourself when you rescued
9: 6 he bowed low in g fear and said, "I am your
12:14 But you have given the enemies of the LORD g
13:34 Then the watchman on the Jerusalem wall saw a g
14: 2 from Tekoa who had a reputation for g wisdom.
18: 7 There was a g slaughter, and twenty thousand men
18: 9 but as he rode beneath the thick branches of a g
18:17 pit in the forest and piled a g heap of stones over it.
20: 8 As they arrived at the g stone in Gibeon,
22:13 A g brightness shone before him, / and bolts of
22:36 of your salvation; / your help has made me g.
22:51 You give g victories to your king; / you show
23:10 and the LORD gave him a g victory that day.
23:12 So the LORD brought about a g victory.
23:21 he killed a g Egyptian warrior who was armed with
24:14 into the hands of the LORD, for his mercy is g.
1Ki 3: 6 And you have continued this g kindness to him
3: 8 a nation so g they are too numerous to count!
3: 9 For who by himself is able to govern this g nation
3:15 Then he invited all his officials to a g banquet.
3:28 and the people were awed as they realized the g
4:13 including sixty g fortified cities with gates barred
4:29 God gave Solomon g wisdom and understanding,
4:33 from the g cedar of Lebanon to the tiny hyssop that
5: 7 a wise son to be king of the g nation of Israel."
5:12 So the LORD gave g wisdom to Solomon just as
7: 2 The g cedar ceiling beams rested on four rows of
7:12 The walls of the g courtyard were built so that
8:41 and come from distant lands to worship your g

10: 2 and a **g** caravan of camels loaded with spices,
10: 9 The LORD your God is **g** indeed! He delights in
10:10 and **g** quantities of spices and precious jewels.
12:30 This became a **g** sin, for the people worshiped
13:34 This became a **g** sin and resulted in the destruction
20:21 and the Arameans were killed in a **g** slaughter.
2Ki 3:27 As a result, the anger against Israel was **g**, so they
5: 1 him the LORD had given Aram **g** victories.
5:13 if the prophet had told you to do some **g** thing,
6:14 So one night the king of Aram sent a **g** army with
6:23 So the king made a **g** feast for them and then sent
6:25 As a result there was a **g** famine in the city. After a
7: 6 of horses and the sounds of a **g** army approaching.
8: 4 "Tell me some stories about the **g** things Elisha
8:13 a nobody like me ever accomplish such a **g** feat?"
10:19 for I am going to offer a **g** sacrifice to Baal.
10:29 the **g** sin that Jeroboam son of Nebat had led Israel
17:21 the LORD and made them commit a **g** sin.
18:19 "This is what the **g** king of Assyria says: What are
18:28 "Listen to this message from the **g** king of
21:15 For they have done **g** evil in my sight and have
23:26 because of all the **g** evils of King Manasseh,
25:16 water carts, and the Sea was too **g** to be weighed.
1Ch 5:24 Each of these men had a **g** reputation as a warrior
9:26 all Levites, were in an office of **g** trust,
11:14 So the LORD saved them by giving them a **g**
12:22 day more men joined David until he had a **g** army,
12:40 There was **g** joy throughout the land of Israel.
14: 2 and had made his kingdom very **g** for the sake of
15:25 covenant up to Jerusalem with a **g** celebration.
16:25 **G** is the LORD! He is most worthy of praise!
17:17 You speak as though I were someone very **g**,
17:19 you have done all these **g** things and have made
17:21 You made a **g** name for yourself when you rescued
21:13 the hands of the LORD, for his mercy is very **g**.
22: 8 'You have killed many men in the **g** battles you
26: 6 Obed-edom's son Shemaiah had sons with **g** ability
26: 6 who earned positions of **g** authority in the clan.
27:32 to the king, a man of **g** insight, and a scribe.
29: 2 iron, and wood, as well as **g** quantities of onyx,
29:12 and it is at your discretion that people are made **g**
29:22 and drank in the LORD's presence with **g** joy that
2Ch 1:10 for who is able to govern this **g** nation of yours?"
4:18 Such **g** quantities of bronze were used that its
6:32 come from distant lands to worship your **g** name
8: 1 and the **g** building projects of the LORD's
9: 1 and a **g** caravan of camels loaded with spices,
9: 8 The LORD your God is **g** indeed! He delights in
9: 9 and **g** quantities of spices and precious jewels.
18: 1 Now Jehoshaphat enjoyed **g** riches and high
18: 2 who prepared a **g** banquet for him and his officials.
18: 2 They butchered **g** numbers of sheep and oxen for
18: 5 "Go ahead, for God will give you a **g** victory!"
21:19 His people did not build a **g** fire to honor him at his
23:13 were leading the people in a **g** celebration.
25:10 with Judah, and they returned home in a **g** rage.
25:13 and carrying off **g** quantities of plunder.
26:10 because he kept **g** herds of livestock in the foothills
26:11 This **g** army of fighting men had been mustered
28:13 Our guilt is already **g**, and the LORD's fierce
29:35 and a **g** deal of fat from the many peace offerings.
30: 5 The people had not been celebrating it in **g**
30:21 of Unleavened Bread for seven days with **g** joy.
30:26 There was **g** joy in the city, for Jerusalem had not
31: 6 their God, and they piled them up in **g** heaps.
32: 8 He may have a **g** army, but they are just men.
32:29 and herds, for God had given him **g** wealth.
Ezr 3:11 Then all the people gave a **g** shout,
4:10 greetings from the rest of the people whom the **g**
5: 8 the Temple of the **g** God in the province of Judah.
5: 8 The work is going forward with **g** energy
5:11 built here many years ago by a **g** king of Israel.
6:16 then dedicated with **g** joy by the people of Israel,
6:22 There was **g** joy throughout the land
9: 7 Our whole history has been one of **g** sin. That is
9:13 because of our wickedness and our **g** guilt.
Ne 1: 3 They are in **g** trouble and disgrace. The wall of
1: 5 the **g** and awesome God who keeps his covenant of
1:10 the people you rescued by your **g** power and might.
1:11 success now as I go to ask the king for a **g** favor.
3:27 who repaired another section opposite the **g**
4:14 Remember the Lord, who is **g** and glorious,
6: 3 "I am doing a **g** work! I cannot stop to come
8: 6 the **g** God, and all the people chanted, "Amen!
8:12 and to celebrate with **g** joy because they had heard
8:17 of the festival, and everyone was filled with **g** joy!
9:19 But in your **g** mercy you did not abandon them to
9:22 "Then you helped our ancestors conquer **g**
9:27 In **g** mercy, you sent them deliverers who rescued
9:31 But in your **g** mercy, you did not destroy them
9:32 our God, the **g** and mighty and awesome God,
9:32 **G** trouble has come upon us and upon our kings
9:37 them at their pleasure, and we are in **g** misery.
12:43 for God had given the people cause for **g** joy.
13:22 Have compassion on me according to your **g**
Est 4: 3 there was **g** mourning among the Jews.
5:11 and boasted to them about his **g** wealth and his
8:15 robe of blue and white and the **g** crown of gold,
8:17 the Jews rejoiced and had a **g** celebration
10: 2 His **g** achievements and the full account of the
10: 3 He was very **g** among the Jews, who held him in
Job 2:13 for they saw that his suffering was too **g** for words.
3:14 famous for their **g** construction projects.
5: 9 For he does **g** works too marvelous to understand.
9:10 His **g** works are too marvelous to understand.
21:33 A **g** funeral procession goes to the cemetery.
22:12 "God is so **g**—higher than the heavens,
24:24 And though they are **g** now, in a moment they will
26:12 By his skill he crushed the **g** sea monster.
30:21 toward me. You persecute me with your **g** power.
33: 7 I am not some **g** person to make you nervous
34:19 He doesn't care how **g** a person may be, and he
35: 7 If you are good, is this some **g** gift to him?
Ps 18:35 supports me; / your gentleness has made me **g**.
18:50 You give **g** victories to your king; / you show
19: 5 after his wedding. / It rejoices like a **g** athlete
19:11 there is **g** reward for those who obey them.
19:13 Then I will be free of guilt / and innocent of **g** sin.
20: 6 his holy heaven / and rescue him by his **g** power.
21: 5 Your victory brings him **g** honor, / and you have
31: 2 rescue me quickly. / Be for me a **g** rock of safety,
31:19 Your goodness is so **g**! / You have stored up **g**
blessings for those who
33:16 a king, / nor is **g** strength enough to save a warrior.
35:27 But give **g** joy to those / who have stood with me
35:27 Let them continually say, "**G** is the LORD,
40:10 I have told everyone in the **g** assembly
40:16 repeatedly shout, "The LORD is **g**!"
42: 4 leading a **g** procession to the house of God,
42: 4 it was the sound of a **g** celebration!
45:12 People of **g** wealth will entreat your favor.
47: 2 is awesome. / He is the **g** King of all the earth.
48: 1 How **g** is the LORD, / and how much we should
48: 2 the holy mountain, / is the city of the **g** King!
49: 6 They trust in their wealth / and boast of **g** riches.
50: 3 in his way, / and a **g** storm rages around him.
51: 1 Because of your **g** compassion, / blot out the stain
54: 1 Come with **g** power, O God, and rescue me!
66: 7 For by his **g** power he rules forever. / He watches
66:12 But you brought us to a place of **g** abundance.
68:27 Then comes a **g** throng of rulers from Judah
70: 4 love your salvation / repeatedly shout, "God is **g**!"
76: 1 is well known in Judah; / his name is **g** in Israel.
79:11 Demonstrate your **g** power by saving those
86: 9 Lord; / they will praise your **g** and holy name.
86:10 For you are **g** and perform **g** miracles.
86:13 for your love for me is very **g**. / You have rescued
89:10 You are the one who crushed the **g** sea monster.
92: 5 O LORD, what **g** miracles you do! / And how
95: 3 the LORD is a **g** God, / the **g** King above all gods.
96: 4 **G** is the LORD! He is most worthy of praise!
99: 3 Let them praise your **g** and awesome name.
103:11 is as **g** as the height of the heavens above the earth.
104: 1 I tell myself; / O LORD my God, how **g** you are!
104:25 teeming with life of every kind, / both **g** and small.
105:38 they were gone, / for the dread of them was **g**.
105:39 and gave them a **g** fire to light the darkness.
106:21 who had done such **g** things in Egypt—
107: 8 Let them praise the LORD for his **g** love / and for
107:15 Let them praise the LORD for his **g** love / and for
107:21 Let them praise the LORD for his **g** love / and for
107:31 Let them praise the LORD for his **g** love / and for
111: 6 He has shown his **g** power to his people / by giving
115:13 those who fear the LORD, / both **g** and small.
119:156 LORD, how **g** is your mercy; / in your justice,
119:162 in your word / like one who finds a **g** treasure.
119:165 Those who love your law have **g** peace / and do not
131: 1 I don't concern myself with matters too **g**
135:10 He struck down **g** nations / and slaughtered mighty
138: 5 for the glory of the LORD is very **g**.
138: 6 Though the LORD is **g**, he cares for the humble,
139: 6 is too wonderful for me, / too **g** for me to know!
140:11 Cause disaster to fall with **g** force on the violent.
143: 5 the days of old. / I ponder all your **g** works.
145: 3 **G** is the LORD! He is most worthy of praise!
147: 5 How **g** is our Lord! His power is absolute!
148:13 For his name is very **g**; / his glory towers over the
Pr 9: 2 She has prepared a **g** banquet, mixed the wines,
14:16 fools plunge ahead with **g** confidence.
14:29 Those who control their anger have **g**
15:16 the LORD than to have **g** treasure with turmoil.
17: 1 A dry crust eaten in peace is better than a **g** feast
22: 1 Choose a good reputation over **g** riches, for being
24:10 you fail under pressure, your strength is not very **g**.
25: 6 with the king or push for a place among the **g**.
Ecc 2: 7 I also owned **g** herds and flocks, more than any of
2: 8 I collected **g** sums of silver and gold, the treasure
2:10 I even found **g** pleasure in hard work, an additional
4: 1 The oppressors have **g** power, and the victims are
6: 2 God gives **g** wealth and honor to some people
8: 4 The king's command is backed by **g** power.
9:14 and a **g** king came with his army and besieged it.
10: 4 A quiet spirit can overcome even **g** mistakes.
10: 6 if they give foolish people **g** authority, and if they
10:10 Since a dull ax requires **g** strength,
SS 8: 5 gave you birth, where in **g** pain she delivered you.
Isa 2:16 He will destroy the **g** trading ships and all the
3:13 He is the **g** prosecuting attorney, presenting his
5: 8 Your homes are built on **g** estates so you can be
5:13 The **g** and honored among them will starve,
5:14 Her **g** and lowly will be swallowed up, with all her
6: 3 In a **g** chorus they sang, "Holy, holy, holy is the
7:17 The mighty king of Assyria will come with his **g**
9: 2 The people who walk in darkness will see a **g**
9: 3 Israel will again be **g**, and its people will rejoice as
12: 6 For **g** is the Holy One of Israel who lives among
16:11 My sorrow for Kir-hareseth will be very **g**.
21: 5 Look! They are preparing a **g** feast. They are
23: 5 hears the news about Tyre, there will be **g** sorrow.
24:20 and will not rise again, for its sins are very **g**.
26:15 LORD! / You have made our nation **g**;
27:12 He will bring them to his **g** threshing floor—
27:13 In that day the **g** trumpet will sound. Many who
28: 6 He will give **g** courage to their warriors who stand
28:29 and he gives the farmer **g** wisdom.
29: 6 them with thunder and earthquake and **g** noise,
31: 2 In his wisdom, the LORD will send **g** disaster;
33: 5 Though the LORD is very **g** and lives in heaven,
34: 6 the LORD will offer a **g** sacrifice in the rich city
36: 4 "This is what the **g** king of Assyria says: What are
36:13 "Listen to this message from the **g** king of
40:23 He judges the **g** people of the world and brings
43: 2 When you go through deep waters and **g** trouble,
50:11 from me: You will soon lie down in **g** torment.
51: 2 But when I blessed him, he became a **g** nation."
53:12 give him the honors of one who is mighty and **g**,
54: 7 but with **g** compassion I will take you back.
54:13 all your citizens, and their prosperity will be **g**.
55:13 This miracle will bring **g** honor to the LORD's
57: 5 You worship your idols with **g** passion beneath
58:14 I will give you **g** honor and give you your full
60: 9 and it will bring **g** honor to the LORD your God,
63: 7 I will rejoice in his **g** goodness to Israel, which he
66: 4 I will send **g** troubles against them—all the things
Jer 4:31 I hear a **g** cry, like that of a woman giving birth to
5: 6 For their rebellion is **g**, and their sins are many.
5:27 evil plots. And the result? Now they are **g** and rich.
6:22 "See a **g** army marching from the north!
6:22 A **g** nation is rising against you from far-off lands.
10: 6 For you are **g**, and your name is full of power.
10:18 you from this land and pour **g** troubles upon you.
10:19 My wound is desperate, and my grief is **g**.
10:22 Hear the terrifying roar of **g** armies as they roll
14: 2 in mourning, and a **g** cry rises from Jerusalem.
15:16 They bring me **g** joy and are my heart's delight,
16: 6 Both the **g** and the lowly will die in this land.
18: 9 certain nation or kingdom, making it strong and **g**,
20:11 But the LORD stands beside me like a **g** warrior.
21: 5 I myself will fight against you with **g** power,
22: 8 'Why did the LORD destroy such a **g** city?'
22:15 "But a beautiful palace does not make a **g** king!
25:14 and **g** kings will enslave the Babylonians,
25:32 A **g** whirlwind of fury is rising from the most
26:18 A **g** forest will grow on the hilltop,
27: 5 By my **g** power I have made the earth and all its
27: 7 But then many nations and **g** kings will conquer
30:14 For your sins are many, and your guilt is **g**.
30:15 because your sins are many and your guilt is **g**.
30:19 and make of them a **g** and honored nation.
31: 8 about to give birth. A **g** company will return!
31: 9 their faces, and I will lead them home with **g** care.
32:17 have made the heavens and earth by your **g** power.
32:18 You are the **g** and powerful God, the LORD
32:19 have all wisdom and do **g** and mighty miracles.
32:20 And you have continued to do **g** miracles in Israel
32:20 You have made your name very **g**, as it is today.
32:21 with **g** power and overwhelming terror.
40:12 Judean countryside to gather a **g** harvest of grapes
44:15 a **g** crowd of all the Judeans living in Pathros,
44:18 we have been in **g** trouble and have suffered the
44:26 I have sworn by my **g** name, says the LORD,
45: 5 Are you seeking **g** things for yourself? Don't do it!
45: 5 I will bring **g** disaster upon all these people,
46:21 and run, for it is a day of **g** disaster for Egypt, a
time of **g** punishment.
48:29 have heard of the pride of Moab, for it is very **g**.
49:37 My fierce anger will bring **g** disaster upon the
50: 9 I am raising up an army of **g** nations from the
50:22 cry be heard in the land, a shout of **g** destruction.
50:41 "Look! A **g** army is marching from the north!
50:41 A **g** nation and many kings are rising against you
51: 9 her judgment will be so **g** it cannot be measured.
51:13 a **g** center of commerce, but your end has come.
51:34 He has swallowed us like a **g** monster and filled his
51:41 is fallen—**g** Babylon, praised throughout the earth!
51:47 time is surely coming when I will punish this **g** city
51:54 the sound of **g** destruction from the land of the
52:20 twelve bulls beneath it was too **g** to be measured.
La 1:15 At his command a **g** army has come to crush my
3:23 **G** is his faithfulness; his mercies begin afresh each
Eze 1: 4 I saw a **g** storm coming toward me from the north,
4:16 It will be weighed out with **g** care and eaten
6:13 and **g** oak where they offered incense to their gods,
8: 6 Do you see the **g** sins the people of Israel are doing
9: 9 sins of the people of Israel and Judah are very **g**.
13:11 **g** hailstones and mighty winds will knock it down.
13:13 with a **g** flood of anger, and with hailstones of
16:29 You added to your lovers by embracing that **g**
17: 3 A **g** eagle with broad wings full of many-colored
17: 7 But then another **g** eagle with broad wings and full
17:15 sending ambassadors to Egypt to request a **g** army
20:33 I will rule you with an iron fist in **g** anger and with
21:14 to symbolize the **g** massacre they will face!
23:24 wagons, and a **g** army fully prepared for attack.
26: 7 against Tyre with his cavalry, chariots, and **g** army.
26:19 waves of enemy attack. **G** seas will swallow you.
27: 5 You were like a **g** ship built of the finest cypress
27:10 Lydia, and Libya served in your **g** army.
27:10 and helmets on your walls, giving you **g** honor.
28: 2 In your **g** pride you claim, 'I am a god! I sit on a
28: 4 and understanding you have amassed **g** wealth—
28:16 Your **g** wealth filled you with violence, and you
29: 3 you **g** monster, lurking in the streams of the Nile.
29:15 never again **g** enough to rise above its neighbors.
30: 9 **G** panic will come upon them on that day of
31: 3 You are as Assyria was—a **g** and mighty nation.
31: 5 This **g** tree towered above all the other trees around
31: 6 All the **g** nations of the world lived in its shadow.
36:23 I will show how holy my **g** name is—the name you
36:30 I will give you **g** harvests from your fruit trees
37:10 and stood up on their feet—a **g** army of them.

39:17 to them: Gather together for my **g** sacrificial feast.
Da 1: 9 Now God had given the chief official **g** respect for
2:10 And no king, however **g** and powerful, has ever
2:35 became a **g** mountain that covered the whole earth.
2:39 another **g** kingdom, inferior to yours, will rise to
2:39 that kingdom has fallen, yet a third **g** kingdom,
2:40 there will be a fourth **g** kingdom, as strong as iron.
2:45 "The **g** God has shown Your Majesty what will
4: 3 How **g** are his signs, / how powerful his wonders!
4: 9 and that no mystery is too **g** for you to solve.
4:22 For you have grown strong and **g**; your greatness
4:30 he said, "Just look at this **g** city of Babylon!
5: 1 King Belshazzar gave a **g** feast for a thousand of
5:19 made him so **g** that people of all races and nations
6: 3 Because of his **g** ability, the king made plans to
7: 2 saw a **g** storm churning the surface of a **g** sea,
7: 6 had four heads. **G** authority was given to this beast.
8: 4 its victims. It did as it pleased and became very **g**.
8: 9 came a small horn whose power grew very **g**.
8:22 with four kings, none of them as **g** as the first.
9: 4 "O Lord, you are a **g** and awesome God!
9:15 your people from Egypt in a **g** display of power.
10: 1 times of war and **g** hardship—and Daniel
10: 4 as I was standing beside the **g** Tigris River,
11: 5 than he and will rule his kingdom with **g** strength.
11:11 Then the king of the south, in **g** anger, will rally
11:22 Before him **g** armies will be swept away,
11:25 and raise a **g** army against the king of the south.
11:28 of the north will then return home with **g** riches.
11:44 and he will set out in **g** anger to destroy many as he
Hos 1:10 when Israel will prosper and become a **g** nation.
5:13 Israel turned to Assyria, to the **g** king there,
7: 1 "I wanted to heal Israel, but its sins were far too **g**.
8:10 Then they will writhe under the burden of the **g**
8:14 "Israel has built **g** palaces, and Judah has fortified
10: 6 go as captives to Assyria, a gift to the **g** king there.
10:13 believing that **g** armies could make your nation
10:15 that fate, Bethel, because of your **g** wickedness.
Joel 2: 2 army appears! How **g** and powerful they are!
2:20 the land." Surely the LORD has done **g** things!
2:21 and rejoice because the LORD has done **g** things.
2:25 It was I who sent this **g** destroying army against
2:31 and the moon will turn bloodred before that **g**
Am 6: 2 Then go to the **g** city of Hamath and on down to
6: 5 and you fancy yourselves to be **g** musicians,
6:11 homes both **g** and small will be smashed to pieces.
7: 4 I saw him preparing to punish his people with a **g**
9: 3 I will send the **g** sea serpent after them to bite
Jnh 1: 2 "Get up and go to the **g** city of Nineveh!
1:16 The sailors were awestruck by the LORD's **g**
1:17 Now the LORD had arranged for a **g** fish to
2: 2 "I cried out to the LORD in my **g** trouble,
3: 2 "Get up and go to the **g** city of Nineveh,
4:11 Shouldn't I feel sorry for such a **g** city?"
Mic 3:12 A **g** forest will grow on the hilltop,
Na 1: 3 LORD is slow to get angry, but his power is **g**,
2:11 Where now is that **g** Nineveh, lion of the nations,
Zep 1: 7 The LORD has prepared his people for a **g**
1:10 And a **g** crashing sound will come from the
2:13 He will destroy Assyria and make its **g** capital,
2:15 "In all the world there is no city as **g** as I,"
3:17 He will rejoice over you with **g** gladness. With his
Zec 14:13 be terrified, stricken by the LORD with **g** panic.
14:14 **g** quantities of gold and silver and fine clothing.
Mal 1: 5 the LORD's **g** power reaches far beyond our
1:11 For my name is **g** among the nations,"
1:14 For I am a **g** king," says the LORD Almighty,
3:10 so **g** you won't have enough room to take it in!
4: 5 I am sending you the prophet Elijah before the **g**
Mt 4:16 people who sat in darkness / have seen a **g** light.
5:12 Be very glad! For a **g** reward awaits you in heaven.
5:19 and teaches them will be **g** in the Kingdom of
5:35 for Jerusalem is the city of the **g** King.
9: 8 They praised God for sending a man with such **g**
9:36 He felt **g** pity for the crowds that came,
9:36 because their problems were so **g** and they didn't
9:37 "The harvest is so **g**, but the workers are so few.
12:40 For as Jonah was in the belly of the **g** fish for three
13:46 When he discovered a pearl of **g** value, he sold
13:56 live right here among us. What makes him so **g**?"
15:28 "Woman," Jesus said to her, "your faith is **g**.
22: 2 a king who prepared a **g** wedding feast for his son.
24:24 and perform **g** miraculous signs and wonders
24:30 on the clouds of heaven with power and **g** glory.
27:14 said nothing, much to the governor's **g** surprise.
27:60 Then he rolled a **g** stone across the entrance as he
28: 2 Suddenly there was a **g** earthquake, because an
28: 8 were very frightened but also filled with **g** joy,
Mk 1:34 So Jesus healed **g** numbers of sick people who had
4:39 the wind stopped, and there was a **g** calm.
5:20 and began to tell everyone about the **g** things Jesus
5:26 She had suffered a **g** deal from many doctors
6:15 was a prophet like the other **g** prophets of the past.
8: 1 About this time another **g** crowd had gathered,
9: 1 you see the Kingdom of God arrive in **g** power!"
9:14 At the foot of the mountain they found a **g** crowd
10:46 his disciples left town, a **g** crowd was following.
12:37 And the crowd listened to him with **g** interest.
13:26 the Son of Man arrive on the clouds with **g** power
Lk 1:10 being burned, a **g** crowd stood outside, praying.
1:14 You will have **g** joy and gladness, and many will
1:15 for he will be **g** in the eyes of the Lord. He must
1:32 He will be very **g** and will be called the Son of the
1:49 is holy, / and he has done **g** things for me.
2:10 "I bring you good news of **g** joy for everyone!
5: 1 **g** crowds pressed in on him to listen to the word of
5:26 Everyone was gripped with **g** wonder and awe.
6:23 leap for joy! For a **g** reward awaits you in heaven.
6:35 Then your reward from heaven will be very **g**,
7:11 the village of Nain, with a **g** crowd following him.
7:16 **G** fear swept the crowd, and they praised God,
8:37 them alone, for a **g** wave of fear swept over them.
8:39 So he went all through the city telling about the **g**
10: 2 "The harvest is so **g**, but the workers are so few.
12:32 For it gives your Father **g** happiness to give you
13:28 "And there will be **g** weeping and gnashing of
14:16 "A man prepared a **g** feast and sent out many
14:25 **G** crowds were following Jesus. He turned around
15:14 a **g** famine swept over the land, and he began to
15:27 calf we were fattening and has prepared a **g** feast.
16:26 And besides, there is a **g** chasm separating us.
18: 2 "who was a godless man with **g** contempt for
18: 9 Then Jesus told this story to some who had **g**
19: 6 and took Jesus to his house in **g** excitement
21:11 There will be **g** earthquakes, and there will be
21:11 and **g** miraculous signs in the heavens.
21:12 this occurs, there will be a time of **g** persecution.
21:23 For there will be **g** distress in the land and wrath
21:27 Man arrive on the clouds with power and **g** glory.
22:25 the kings and **g** men order their people around,
22:44 his sweat fell to the ground like **g** drops of blood.
23:27 **G** crowds trailed along behind, including many
24:52 then returned to Jerusalem filled with **g** joy.
Jn 6: 5 Jesus soon saw a **g** crowd of people climbing the
8:55 If I said otherwise, I would be as **g** a liar as you!
13:21 Now Jesus was in **g** anguish of spirit, and he
15: 8 much fruit. This brings **g** glory to my Father.
Ac 2:20 before that **g** and glorious day of the Lord arrives.
2:46 and shared their meals with **g** joy and generosity—
4:29 and give your servants **g** boldness in their
4:33 Lord Jesus, and God's **g** favor was upon them all.
5:11 **G** fear gripped the entire church and all others who
5:36 fellow Theudas, who pretended to be someone **g**.
7:11 There was **g** misery for our ancestors, as they ran
8: 1 A **g** wave of persecution began that day,
8: 8 So there was **g** joy in that city.
8: 9 there for many years, claiming to be someone **g**.
8:10 to the greatest, often spoke of him as "the **G** One—
8:13 and he was amazed by the **g** miracles and signs
8:27 a eunuch of **g** authority under the queen of
11:26 for a full year, teaching **g** numbers of people.
11:28 **g** famine was coming upon the entire Roman
12:18 there was a **g** commotion among the soldiers about
12:22 The people gave him a **g** ovation, shouting, "It is
14: 1 and preached with such power that a **g** number of
15:31 And there was **g** joy throughout the church that day
16:26 Suddenly, there was a **g** earthquake, and the prison
18:25 and talked to others with **g** enthusiasm
18:27 he proved to be of **g** benefit to those who,
19:27 I'm also concerned that the temple of the **g**
19:28 began shouting, "**G** is Artemis of the Ephesians!"
19:34 up for two hours: "**G** is Artemis of the Ephesians! **G** is Artemis of the Ephesians!"
19:35 official guardian of the temple of the **g** Artemis,
21:30 rocked by these accusations, and a **g** riot followed.
23: 9 So a **g** clamor arose. Some of the teachers of
25:23 and Bernice arrived at the auditorium with **g** pomp,
27: 7 and after **g** difficulty we finally neared Cnidus.
27: 8 We struggled along the coast with **g** difficulty
27:16 where with **g** difficulty we hoisted aboard the
Ro 1:14 For I have a **g** sense of obligation to people in our
5: 8 But God showed his **g** love for us by sending
9: 5 Their ancestors were **g** people of God, and Christ
9:32 They stumbled over the **g** rock in their path.
11:13 as the apostle to the Gentiles. I lay **g** stress on this,
11:33 How **g** are his riches and wisdom and knowledge!
15:29 I come, Christ will give me a **g** blessing for you.
1Co 1: 8 and he will keep you free from all blame on the **g**
3:15 work is burned up, the builder will suffer **g** loss.
15:20 He has become the first of a **g** harvest of those who
16: 9 for there is a wide-open door for a **g** work here,
2Co 3: 4 because of our **g** trust in God through Christ.
4:15 people to Christ, there will be **g** thanksgiving,
4:17 Yet they produce for us an immeasurably **g** glory
6: 1 reject this marvelous message of God's **g** kindness.
7: 4 confidence in you, and my pride in you is **g**.
9:10 and he will produce a **g** harvest of generosity in
Gal 2: 6 their reputation as **g** leaders made no difference to
4: 1 and leaves **g** wealth for his young children,
Eph 1: 5 Jesus Christ. And this gave him **g** pleasure.
3:19 though it is so **g** you will never fully understand it.
5:32 This is a **g** mystery, but it is an illustration of the
Php 1:30 and you know that I am still in the midst of this **g**
2:29 Welcome him with Christian love and with **g** joy,
Col 1: 6 and understood the truth about God's **g** kindness to
1: 8 He is the one who told us about the **g** love for
1Th 3: 9 Because of you we have **g** joy in the presence of
2Th 2: 3 For that day will not come until there is a **g**
2:11 So God will send **g** deception upon them, and they
1Ti 1:16 of his **g** patience with even the worst sinners.
3:16 Without question, this is the **g** mystery of our faith:
6: 6 Yet true religion with contentment is **g** wealth.
2Ti 2: 2 Teach these **g** truths to trustworthy people who are
4: 8 will give me on that **g** day of his return.
Tit 2:13 that wonderful event when the glory of our **g** God
3: 7 declared us not guilty because of his **g** kindness.
Heb 2: 3 **g** salvation that was announced by the Lord Jesus
4:14 That is why we have a **g** High Priest who has gone
6:11 Our **g** desire is that you will keep right on loving
7: 1 home after winning a **g** battle against many kings,
7: 4 Consider then how **g** this Melchizedek was.
7: 4 Even Abraham, the **g** patriarch of Israel,
7: 4 recognized how **g** Melchizedek was by giving him
9:11 He has entered that **g**, perfect sanctuary in heaven,
10:21 And since we have a **g** High Priest who rules over
10:35 Remember the **g** reward it brings you!
11:26 for he was looking ahead to the **g** reward that God
13:20[-21] Jesus is the **g** Shepherd of the sheep
Jas 3: 5 it can do. A tiny spark can set a **g** forest on fire.
5: 9 will judge you. For look! The **g** Judge is coming.
5:11 We give **g** honor to those who endure under
5:16 The earnest prayer of a righteous person has **g**
1Pe 1:11 about Christ's suffering and his **g** glory afterward.
1:21 raised Christ from the dead and gave him **g** glory,
4:10 God has given gifts to each of you from his **g**
5: 8 out for attacks from the Devil, your **g** enemy.
1Jn 2:22 And who is the **g** liar? The one who says that Jesus
Jude 1:24 glorious presence innocent of sin and with **g** joy.
Rev 2:13 "I know that you live in the city where that **g**
3:10 I will protect you from the **g** time of testing that
6:12 broke the sixth seal, and there was a **g** earthquake.
6:15 the people with **g** power, and every slave and every
6:17 For the **g** day of their wrath has come, and who
7: 9 too **g** to count, from every nation and tribe
7:14 "These are the ones coming out of the **g**
8: 3 And a **g** quantity of incense was given to him to
8: 8 and a **g** mountain of fire was thrown into the sea.
8:10 and a **g** flaming star fell out of the sky,
9:14 "Release the four angels who are bound at the **g**
10: 3 And he gave a **g** shout, like the roar of a lion.
11:17 for now you have assumed your **g** power
11:19 there was a **g** hailstorm, and the world was shaken
12: 1 Then I witnessed in heaven an event of **g**
12: 9 This **g** dragon—the ancient serpent called the
12:12 For the Devil has come down to you in **g** anger,
12:14 But she was given two wings like those of a **g**
13: 2 him his own power and throne and **g** authority.
13: 4 "Is there anyone as **g** as the beast?"
13: 5 Then the beast was allowed to speak **g** blasphemies
13:14 He ordered the people of the world to make a **g**
13:16 **g** and small, rich and poor, slave and free—
14: 2 sound from heaven like the roaring of a **g** waterfall
14: 3 This **g** choir sang a wonderful new song in front of
14: 8 shouting, "Babylon is fallen—that **g** city is fallen
14:19 and loaded the grapes into the **g** winepress of
15: 1 significant event, and it was **g** and marvelous.
15: 3 "**G** and marvelous are your actions, / Lord God
16:12 Then the sixth angel poured out his bowl on the **g**
16:14 the Lord on that **g** judgment day of God Almighty.
16:19 The **g** city of Babylon split into three pieces,
17: 1 judgment that is going to come on the **g** prostitute,
17: 5 "Babylon the **G**, Mother of All Prostitutes
17:18 the **g** city that rules over the kings of the earth."
18: 1 angel come down from heaven with **g** authority,
18: 2 "Babylon is fallen—that **g** city is fallen!
18: 9 and enjoyed her **g** luxury will mourn for her as
18:10 will stand at a distance, terrified by her **g** torment.
18:10 how terrible for Babylon, that **g** city!
18:12 She bought **g** quantities of gold, silver, jewels,
18:15 will stand at a distance, terrified by her **g** torment.
18:16 "How terrible, how terrible for that **g** city!
18:19 throw dust on their heads to show their **g** sorrow.
18:19 will say, "How terrible, how terrible for the **g** city! She made us all rich from her **g** wealth.
18:21 angel picked up a boulder as large as a **g** millstone.
18:21 it into the ocean and shouted, "Babylon, the **g** city,
19: 2 He has punished the **g** prostitute who corrupted the
19:17 Gather together for the **g** banquet God has
19:18 of all humanity, both free and slave, small and **g**."
20:11 And I saw a **g** white throne, and I saw the one who
20:12 I saw the dead, both **g** and small, standing before
21:10 So he took me in spirit to a **g**, high mountain,

GREAT-GRANDSON (1) [SON]

Jer 36:14 and **g** of Cushi, to ask Baruch to come and read the

GREATER (125) [GREAT]

Ge 1:16 The **g** one, the sun, presides during the day;
48:19 but his younger brother will become even **g**.
49:26 be **g** than the blessings of the eternal mountains,
Ex 18:11 I know now that the LORD is **g** than all other
Nu 14:12 Then I will make you into a nation far **g**
16: 3 What right do you have to act as though you are **g**
24: 7 Their king will be **g** than Agag; / their kingdom
Dt 4:38 He drove out nations far **g** than you, so he could
7: 7 because you were larger or **g** than other nations,
9: 1 to occupy the land belonging to nations much **g**
11:23 though they are much **g** and stronger than you.
20: 1 and chariots and an army **g** than your own,
26:19 you do, he will make you **g** than any other nation.
Jos 19:28 Rehob, Hammon, Kanah, and as far as **G** Sidon.
2Sa 13:16 "To reject me now is a **g** wrong than what you
1Ki 1:37 and may he make Solomon's reign even **g** than
1:47 'May your God make Solomon's fame even **g** than
1:47 and may Solomon's kingdom be even **g** than
10: 7 and prosperity are far **g** than what I was told.
2Ki 7:13 it won't be a **g** loss than if they stay here and die
1Ch 29:25 and he gave Solomon even **g** wealth and honor
2Ch 2: 5 our God is an awesome God, **g** than any other.
9: 6 of it! Your wisdom is far **g** than what I was told.
9:12 gifts of **g** value than the gifts she had given him.
32: 7 mighty army, for there is a power far **g** on our side!
Ne 8:13 and Levites met with Ezra to go over the law in **g**
9: 5 glorious name! It is far **g** than we can think or say.
Job 28:16 Its value is **g** than all the gold of Ophir, **g** than precious onyx stone or sapphires.
28:19 exchanged for it. Its value is **g** than the purest gold.
33:12 you yourself have said, 'God is **g** than any person.'
Ps 4: 7 You have given me **g** joy / than those who have
71:21 You will restore me to even **g** honor / and comfort

113: 4 the nations; / his glory is far g than the heavens.
135: 5 that our Lord is g than any other god.
Ecc 1:16 I have g wisdom and knowledge than any of
1:18 For the g my wisdom, the g my grief.
2: 9 So I became g than any of the kings who ruled in
Isa 7:17 You will soon experience g terror than has been
10:10 whose gods were far g than those in Jerusalem
10:15 Can the ax boast g power than the person who uses
10:15 Is the saw g than the person who saws? Can a whip
28:22 scoff no more, or your punishment will be even g.
29:16 He is the Potter, and he is certainly g than you.
56: 5 and a name far g than the honor they would have
La 4: 6 The guilt of my people is g than that of Sodom,
Eze 8: 6 and you will see even g sins than these!"
8:13 "Come, and I will show you g sins than these!"
8:15 "But I will show you even g sins than these!"
16:57 But now your g wickedness has been exposed to
21:29 And now it will fall with even g force on the
23:19 She turned to even g prostitution, remembering her
Da 4:36 of my kingdom, with even g honor than before.
7:20 This was the horn that seemed g than the others
11:13 a fully equipped army far g than the one he lost.
11:36 and claiming to be g than every god there is,
11:37 for he will boast that he is g than them all.
12: 1 Then there will be a time of anguish g than any
Hos 4:18 Their love for shame is g than their love for honor.
Hag 2: 9 The future glory of this Temple will be g than its
Zec 12: 7 and the royal line of David will not have g honor
Mt 3:11 But someone is coming soon who is far g than I
3:11 so much g that I am not even worthy to be his
10:24 "A student is not g than the teacher. A servant is not g than the master.
11:11 have ever lived, none is g than John the Baptist.
11:11 person in the Kingdom of Heaven is g than he is!
12: 6 there is one here who is even g than the Temple!
12:41 And now someone g than Jonah is here—and you
12:42 And now someone g than Solomon is here—
23:17 Which is g, the gold, or the Temple that makes the
23:19 For which is g, the gift on the altar, or the altar that
24:21 For that will be a time of g horror than anything
Mk 1: 7 "Someone is coming soon who is far g than I am—
1: 7 so much g that I am not even worthy to be his
12:31 No other commandment is g than these."
12:40 Because of this, their punishment will be the g."
13:19 For those will be days of g horror than at any time
Lk 3:16 but someone is coming soon who is g than I am—
3:16 so much g that I am not even worthy to be his
6:40 A student is not g than the teacher. But the student
7:28 of all who have ever lived, none is g than John.
7:28 person in the Kingdom of God is g than he is!"
11:31 And now someone g than Solomon is here—
11:32 And now someone g than Jonah is here—and you
16:10 a little, you won't be honest with g responsibilities.
20:47 Because of this, their punishment will be the g."
Jn 1:15 'Someone is coming who is far g than I am,
1:30 'Soon a man is coming who is far g than I am,
1:50 the fig tree? You will see g things than this."
3:30 He must become g and g, and I must become
3:31 has come from above and is g than anyone else.
4:12 are you g than our ancestor Jacob who gave us this
5:20 and the Son will do far g things than healing this
5:36 But I have a g witness than John—my teachings
8:53 Are you g than our father Abraham, who died? Are you g than the prophets, who died?
13:16 How true it is that a servant is not g than the
14:12 and even g works, because I am going to be with
14:28 now I can go to the Father, who is g than I am.
15: 3 You have already been pruned for g fruitfulness by
15:20 'A servant is not g than the master.' Since they
19:11 So the one who brought me to you has the g sin."
Ac 15:28 and to us to lay no g burden on you than these
22: 2 in their own language, the silence was even g.
Ro 11:12 think how much g a blessing the world will share
1Co 9:12 shouldn't we have an even g right to be supported?
14: 5 For prophecy is a g and more useful gift than
2Co 3: 8 Shouldn't we expect far g glory when the Holy
3:11 which remains forever, has far g glory.
Heb 1: 4 This shows that God's Son is far g than the angels,
1: 4 just as the name God gave him is far g than their
6:13 Since there was no one g to swear by, God took an
6:16 they call on someone g than themselves to hold
7: 7 the person who has the power to bless is always g
7: 8 But Melchizedek is g than they are, because we are
Jas 3: 1 for we who teach will be judged by God with g
2Pe 1:19 we have even g confidence in the message
2:11 even though they are far g in power and strength
1Jn 3:20 For God is g than our hearts, and he knows
4: 4 because the Spirit who lives in you is g than the
3Jn 1: 4 I could have no g joy than to hear that my children
Rev 16:18 And there was an earthquake g than ever before in

GREATEST (45) [GREAT]

Nu 24:20 this prophecy: / "Amalek was the g of nations,
Jdg 20:44 Eighteen thousand of Benjamin's g warriors died
2Sa 13:13 And you would be called one of the g fools in
23: 8 the three g warriors among David's men.
2Ki 23: 2 the prophets—all the people from the least to the g.
25:26 all the people of Judah, from the least to the g,
1Ch 11:11 the three g warriors among David's men.
2Ch 1:11 "Because your g desire is to help your people,
34:30 the Levites—all the people from the g to the least.
Est 1: 5 and officials—from the g to the least.
Ps 62: 9 From the g to the lowliest— / all are nothing in his
Isa 14:17 Is this the king who demolished the world's g
47: 8 bragging as if you were the g in the world!
Jer 6:13 "From the least to the g, they trick others to get
8:10 From the least to the g, they trick others to get
31: 7 Shout for the g of nations! Shout out with praise
31:34 For everyone, from the least to the g, will already
42: 1 all the people, from the least to the g, approached
42: 8 and for all the people, from the least to the g.
44:12 and famine. All will die, from the least to the g.
Ob 1:11 your relatives in Israel during their time of g need.
Jnh 3: 5 and from the g to the least, they decided to go
Mt 18: 1 "Which of us is g in the Kingdom of Heaven?"
18: 4 this little child is the g in the Kingdom of Heaven.
19:30 who are considered least here will be the g then.
22:38 This is the first and g commandment.
23:11 The g among you must be a servant.
Mk 9:34 had been arguing about which of them was the g.
10:31 who are considered least here will be the g then."
Lk 2:34 But he will be the g joy to many others.
9:46 among them as to which of them would be the g.
9:48 sent me. Whoever is the least among you is the g."
22:24 as to who would be the g in the coming Kingdom.
22:26 those who are the g should take the lowest rank,
Jn 15:13 the g love is shown when people lay down their
Ac 8:10 The Samaritan people, from the least to the g,
26:22 tell these facts to everyone, from the least to the g.
1Co 1:25 and God's weakness is far stronger than the g of
12:23 less honorable are those we clothe with the g care.
13:13 faith, hope, and love—and the g of these is love.
2Co 2: 3 by the very ones who ought to give me the g joy.
Heb 8:11 For everyone, from the least to the g, / will already
Rev 11:18 all who fear your name, from the least to the g.
18:23 her merchants, who were the g in the world,
19: 5 our God, all his servants, from the least to the g,

GREATLY (49) [GREAT]

Ge 13:13 and sinned g against the LORD.
39: 2 and blessed him g as he served in the home of his
Dt 15: 4 for the LORD your God will g bless you in the
Jdg 7:11 are saying, and you will be g encouraged.
1Sa 6:19 And the people mourned g because of what the
2Sa 24:10 "I have sinned g and shouldn't have taken the
1Ch 21: 8 "I have sinned g and shouldn't have taken the
29:23 David, and he prospered g, and all Israel obeyed
2Ch 29:36 And Hezekiah and all the people rejoiced g
32: 8 for us!" These words g encouraged the people.
Ezr 6:14 and they were g encouraged by the preaching of
Ne 9:33 We have sinned g, and you gave us only what we
Job 20: 2 "I must reply because I am g disturbed.
Ps 18:14 his lightning flashed, and they were g confused.
76: 7 No wonder you are g feared! / Who can stand
Pr 31:11 can trust her, and she will g enrich his life.
31:30 but a woman who fears the LORD will be g
Isa 32:20 God will g bless his people. Wherever they plant
Jer 3: 9 and stone. So now the land has been g defiled.
31:27 "when I will g increase the population
32:35 What an incredible evil, causing Judah to sin so g!
La 1: 8 Jerusalem has sinned g, so she has been tossed
Eze 11: 8 I will expose you to the war you so g fear,
22:26 so that my holy name is g dishonored among them.
25:12 The people of Edom have sinned g by avenging
30:19 And so I will g punish Egypt, and they will know
36:10 I will g increase the population of Israel,
36:11 but your flocks and herds will also g multiply.
Da 4: 5 But one night I had a dream that g frightened me;
8:27 but I was g troubled by the vision and could not
10:11 the man said to me, "O Daniel, g loved of God,
Mic 7:17 They will fear him g, trembling in terror at his
Zec 9: 9 Rejoice g, O people of Zion! Shout in triumph,
Mal 2: 5 and they g revered me and stood in awe of my
Mt 14: 6 Herodias' daughter performed a dance that g
26:22 G distressed, one by one they began to ask him,
Mk 6:22 and performed a dance that g pleased them all.
14:19 G distressed, one by one they began to ask him,
Lk 13:30 Some who are despised now will be g honored
13:30 and some who are g honored now will be despised
22: 2 without starting a riot, a possibility they g feared.
Ac 6: 7 The number of believers g increased in Jerusalem,
7:17 the number of our people in Egypt g increased.
19:17 and the name of the Lord Jesus was g honored.
20:12 taken home unhurt, and everyone was g relieved.
2Co 7: 4 You have g encouraged me; you have made me
10:15 and that our work among you will be g enlarged.
1Th 3: 7 So we have been g comforted, dear friends, in all
Rev 2:22 and she will suffer g with all who commit adultery

GREATNESS (26) [GREAT]

Ge 11: 4 that reaches to the skies—a monument to our g!
Ex 15: 7 In the g of your majesty, / you overthrew those
Dt 3:24 You have only begun to show me your g
5:24 LORD our God has shown us his glory and g,
11: 2 your God or seen his g and awesome power.
1Ch 16: 8 Give thanks to the LORD and proclaim his g.
29:11 Yours, O LORD, is the g, the power, the glory,
Est 10: 2 and the full account of the g of Mordecai,
Job 23: 6 Would he merely argue with me in his g? No,
37: 5 We cannot comprehend the g of his power.
Ps 34: 3 Come, let us tell of the LORD's g; / let us exalt
79:13 praising your g from generation to generation.
105: 1 Give thanks to the LORD and proclaim his g.
135: 5 I know the g of the LORD— / that our Lord is
145: 3 most worthy of praise! / His g is beyond discovery!
145: 6 will be on every tongue; / I will proclaim your g.
150: 2 him for his mighty works; / praise his unequaled g!
Isa 10:14 By my g I have robbed their nests of riches
23: 9 your pride and show his contempt for all human g.
63: 1 in royal robes, marching in the g of his strength?
La 3:32 he also shows compassion according to the g of his
Eze 31: 2 his people: To whom would you compare your g?
38:23 Thus will I show my g and holiness, and I will
Da 4:22 your g reaches up to heaven, and your rule to the
7:27 and g of all the kingdoms under heaven will be
Eph 1:19 incredible g of his power for us who believe him.

GRECIA(NS) [KJV] See GREECE, GREEK(S), GREEK-SPEAKING

GREECE (14) [GREEK-SPEAKING, GREEK, GREEKS]

Isa 66:19 (who are famous as archers), to Tubal and G,
Eze 27:13 Merchants from G, Tubal, and Meshech brought
Da 8:21 The shaggy male goat represents the king of G,
10:20 then against the spirit prince of the kingdom of G.
11: 2 stir up everyone to war against the kingdom of G.
Ac 16: 9 He saw a man from Macedonia in northern G,
20: 2 he passed through. Then he traveled down to G,
Ro 15:26 the believers in G have eagerly taken up an
1Co 16:15 were the first to become Christians in G,
2Co 1: 1 in Corinth and to all the Christians throughout G.
9: 2 in G were ready to send an offering a year ago.
11:10 I will never stop boasting about this all over G.
1Th 1: 7 became an example to all the Christians in G.
1: 8 even beyond G, for wherever we go we find

GREED (10) [GREEDILY, GREEDY]

Pr 28:25 G causes fighting; trusting the LORD leads to
Jer 22:17 "But you! You are full of selfish g and dishonesty!
Hab 2: 5 In their g they have gathered up many nations
Mt 23:25 you are filthy—full of g and self-indulgence!
Mk 7:22 adultery, g, wickedness, deceit, eagerness for
Lk 11:39 you are still filthy—full of g and wickedness!
Ro 1:29 sin, g, hate, envy, murder, fighting, deception,
Eph 4:19 lives are filled with all kinds of impurity and g.
5: 3 no sexual immorality, impurity, or g among you.
2Pe 2: 3 In their g they will make up clever lies to get hold

GREEDILY (3) [GREED]

Ps 57: 4 who g devour human prey— / whose teeth pierce
Isa 28: 4 It will be g snatched up, as an early fig is hungrily
Lk 11:41 So give to the needy what you g possess, and you

GREEDY (18) [GREED]

1Sa 8: 3 not like their father, for they were g for money.
Job 20:20 He was always g but never satisfied. Of all the
Ps 10: 3 they praise the g and curse the LORD.
Pr 1:19 Such is the fate of all who are g for gain. It ends up
21:26 They are always g for more, while the godly love
28:22 A g person tries to get rich quick, but it only leads
Isa 56:11 And they are as g as dogs, never satisfied. They are
57:17 I was angry and punished these g people.
Lk 12:15 "Beware! Don't be g for what you don't have.
1Co 5:10 or who are g or are swindlers or idol worshipers.
5:11 or is g, or worships idols, or is abusive, or a
6:10 thieves, g people, drunkards, abusers,
Eph 5: 5 or g person will inherit the Kingdom of Christ
5: 5 For a g person is really an idolater who worships
Col 3: 5 Don't be g for the good things of this life, for that
1Ti 3: 8 be heavy drinkers and must not be g for money.
Tit 1: 7 not be a heavy drinker, violent, or g for money.
2Pe 2:14 They train themselves to be g; they are doomed

GREEK (14) [GREECE]

Da 8:21 its eyes represents the first king of the G Empire.
8:22 G Empire will break into four sections with four
Jn 19:20 Latin, and G, so that many people could read it.
Ac 6: 1 Those who spoke G complained against those who
9:36 in Joppa named Tabitha (which in G is Dorcas).
13: 8 the sorcerer (as his name means in G), interfered
14:12 They decided that Barnabas was the G god Zeus
16: 1 was a Jewish believer, but whose father was a G.
16: 3 for everyone knew that his father was a G.
17: 4 including a large number of godly G men and also
17:12 as did some of the prominent G women and many
19:24 silver shrines of the G goddess Artemis.
21:37 "Do you know G?" the commander asked,
Rev 9:11 his name in Hebrew is *Abaddon,* and in G,

GREEK-SPEAKING (1) [GREECE, SPEAK]

Ac 9:29 He debated with some G Jews, but they plotted to

GREEKS (8) [GREECE]

Eze 27:19 G from Uzal came to trade for your merchandise.
Joel 3: 6 sold the people of Judah and Jerusalem to the G,
Zec 9:13 and like a warrior, I will brandish it against the G.
Jn 12:20 Some G who had come to Jerusalem to attend the
Ac 18: 4 trying to convince the Jews and G alike.
19:10 both Jews and G—heard the Lord's message.
19:17 quickly all through Ephesus, to Jews and G alike.
1Co 1:22 And it is foolish to the G because they believe only

GREEN (45) [GREENERY]

Ge 1:30 and other g plants to the animals and birds for their
Ex 10:15 Not one g thing remained, neither tree nor plant,
Lev 13:49 or the leather has turned bright g or a reddish color,
14:37 If he finds bright g or reddish streaks on the walls
Dt 12: 2 up on the hills, and under every g tree.
1Ki 14:23 poles on every high hill and under every g tree.
2Ki 16: 4 and on the hills and under every g tree.
17:10 at the top of every hill and under every g tree.
19:26 as the grass, / as easily trampled as tender g shoots.
2Ch 28: 4 and on the hills and under every g tree.

Job 6: 5 Wild donkeys bray when they find no **g** grass,
Ps 23: 2 He lets me rest in **g** meadows; / he leads me beside
92: 14 still produce fruit; / they will remain vital and **g**.
105: 35 They ate up everything **g** in the land,
147: 8 and makes the **g** grass grow in mountain pastures.
Isa 32: 20 Their flocks and herds will graze in **g** pastures.
35: 2 The deserts will become as **g** as the mountains of
37: 27 as the grass, / as easily trampled as tender **g** shoots.
49: 9 grazing in **g** pastures and on hills that were
53: 2 up in the LORD's presence like a tender **g** shoot,
57: 5 your idols with great passion beneath every **g** tree.
Jer 2: 20 On every hill and under every **g** tree, you have
3: 6 other gods on every hill and under every **g** tree.
3: 13 against him by worshiping idols under every **g** tree.
17: 2 beneath every **g** tree and on every high hill.
17: 8 Their leaves stay **g**, and they go right on producing
22: 6 me as fruitful Gilead and the **g** forests of Lebanon.
Eze 6: 13 on every hill and mountain and under every **g** tree
17: 24 It is I who makes the **g** tree wither and gives new
19: 10 planted by the water's edge. / It had lush, **g** foliage
20: 28 on every high hill and under every **g** tree they saw!
20: 47 every tree will be burned—**g** and dry trees alike.
Da 4: 12 It had fresh **g** leaves, and it was loaded with fruit
4: 21 It had fresh **g** leaves, and it was loaded with fruit
Hos 14: 8 I am like a tree that is always **g**, giving my fruit to
Joel 2: 22 animals of the field! The pastures will soon be **g**.
Am 7: 2 the locusts ate everything in sight that was **g**.
Mic 7: 14 and rule your people; lead your flock in **g** pastures.
Na 1: 4 and Carmel fade, and the **g** forests of Lebanon wilt.
Mk 6: 39 told the crowd to sit down in groups on the **g** grass.
Lk 23: 31 For if these things are done when the tree is **g**,
Jn 10: 9 Wherever they go, they will find **g** pastures.
Jas 5: 18 The grass turned **g**, and the crops began to grow
Rev 6: 8 and saw a horse whose color was pale **g** like a
6: 13 Then the stars of the sky fell to the earth like **g** figs

GREENERY (2) [GREEN]

Isa 19: 7 All the **g** along the riverbank will wither and blow
42: 15 and hills / and bring a blight on all their **g**.

GREET (21) [GREETED, GREETING, GREETINGS]

Ge 48: 2 he gathered his strength and sat up in bed to **g** him.
Jdg 11: 31 out of my house to **g** me when I return in triumph.
11: 35 What a tragedy that you came out to **g** me.
1Sa 10: 4 They will **g** you and offer you two of the loaves,
17: 22 and hurried out to the ranks to **g** his brothers.
2Sa 19: 20 the very first person in all Israel to **g** you."
20: 8 As he stepped forward to **g** Amasa, he secretly
Mk 9: 15 he came toward them, and then they ran to **g** him.
Lk 10: 4 of sandals. And don't stop to **g** anyone on the road.
Ro 16: 3 **G** Priscilla and Aquila. They have been co-workers
16: 5 meets in their home. **G** my dear friend Epenetus.
16: 11 **G** Herodion, my relative. **G** the Christians in the household of Narcissus.
16: 13 **G** Rufus, whom the Lord picked out to be his very
16: 16 **G** each other in Christian love. All the churches of
1Co 16: 19 The churches here in the province of Asia **g** you
16: 20 The other believers here have asked me to **g** you for them. **G** each other in Christian love.
2Co 13: 12 **G** each other in Christian love. All the Christians
1Th 5: 26 **G** each other in Christian love.
1Pe 5: 14 **G** each other in Christian love. Peace be to all of

GREETED (15) [GREET]

Ge 29: 13 he rushed out to meet him and **g** him warmly.
Ex 4: 27 of God, where he found Moses and **g** him warmly.
18: 7 He bowed to him respectfully and **g** him warmly.
Jdg 18: 15 where the young Levite lived, and **g** him kindly.
Ru 2: 4 Boaz arrived from Bethlehem and **g** the harvesters.
1Sa 15: 13 Samuel finally found him, Saul **g** him cheerfully.
30: 21 too tired to go with them, David **g** them joyfully.
2Sa 17: 27 he was warmly **g** by Shobi son of Nahash of
2Ki 10: 15 After they had **g** each other, Jehu said to him,
Ezr 4: 9 They **g** the king for all their colleagues—the judges
Lk 1: 40 She entered the house and **g** Elizabeth.
1: 44 When you came in and **g** me, my baby jumped for
22: 47 Judas walked over to Jesus and **g** him with a kiss.
24: 33 When they arrived, they were **g** with the report,
Ac 21: 7 where we **g** the believers but stayed only one day.

GREETING (8) [GREET]

Pr 27: 14 If you shout a pleasant **g** to your neighbor too early
Mt 26: 48 arrest when I go over and give him the kiss of **g**."
Mk 14: 44 to arrest when I go over and give him the kiss of **g**.
Lk 1: 41 At the sound of Mary's **g**, Elizabeth's child leaped
7: 45 You didn't give me a kiss of **g**, but she has kissed
1Co 16: 21 Here is my **g**, which I write with my own hand—
Col 4: 18 Here is my **g** in my own handwriting—PAUL.
2Th 3: 17 Now here is my **g**, which I write with my own

GREETINGS (43) [GREET]

Ge 32: 4 master Esau: 'Humble **g** from your servant Jacob!
Ezr 4: 10 They also sent **g** from the rest of the people whom
4: 18 "**G**. The letter you sent has been translated
5: 7 "**G** to King Darius.
7: 12 "**G** from Artaxerxes, the king of kings, to Ezra the
Mt 26: 49 "**G**, Teacher!" he exclaimed and gave him the
28: 9 And as they went, Jesus met them. "**G**!" he said.
Lk 1: 28 Gabriel appeared to her and said, "**G**,
11: 43 and the respectful **g** from everyone as you walk
Ac 15: 23 Gentile believers in Antioch, Syria, and Cilicia. **G**!
21: 19 After **g** were exchanged, Paul gave a detailed
23: 26 to his Excellency, Governor Felix. **G**!
Ro 16: 5 Please give my **g** to the church that meets in their
16: 6 Give my **g** to Mary, who has worked so hard for
16: 7 Christians before I did. Please give them my **g**.
16: 10 Give my **g** to Apelles, a good man whom Christ
16: 14 And please give my **g** to Asyncritus, Phlegon,
16: 15 Give my **g** to Philologus, Julia, Nereus and his
16: 16 All the churches of Christ send you their **g**.
16: 22 for Paul, send my **g**, too, as a Christian brother.
16: 23 sends you his **g**, and so does Quartus,
2Co 13: 12 All the Christians here send you their **g**.
Gal 1: 2 All the Christians here join me in sending **g** to the
Php 4: 21 Give my **g** to all the Christians there. The brothers who are with me here send you their **g**.
4: 22 And all the other Christians send their **g**, too,
Col 4: 10 sends you his **g**, and so does Mark,
4: 11 Jesus (the one we call Justus) also sends his **g**.
4: 12 a servant of Christ Jesus, sends you his **g**.
4: 14 Dear Doctor Luke sends his **g**, and so does Demas.
4: 15 Please give my **g** to our Christian brothers
2Ti 4: 19 Give my **g** to Priscilla and Aquila and those living
4: 21 Eubulus sends you **g**, and so do Pudens, Linus,
Tit 3: 15 Everybody here sends **g**. Please give my **g** to all of the believers who love
Phm 1: 23 my fellow prisoner in Christ Jesus, sends you his **g**.
Heb 13: 24 Give my **g** to all your leaders and to the other
13: 24 The Christians from Italy send you their **g**.
Jas 1: 1 Jewish Christians scattered among the nations. **G**!
1Pe 5: 13 Your sister church here in Rome sends you **g**,
2Jn 1: 13 **G** from the children of your sister, chosen by God.
3Jn 1: 15 be with you. Your friends here send you their **g**.
1: 15 Please give my personal **g** to each of our friends

GREW (70) [GROW]

Ge 4: 2 When they **g** up, Abel became a shepherd,
4: 26 When Seth **g** up, he had a son and named him
21: 8 As time went by and Isaac **g** and was weaned,
21: 20 And God was with the boy as he **g** up in the
25: 27 As the boys **g** up, Esau became a skillful hunter,
26: 33 the town that **g** up there has been called
38: 6 When his oldest son, Er, **g** up, Judah arranged his
47: 27 to prosper there, and their population **g** rapidly.
Ex 19: 19 As the horn blast **g** louder and louder,
Nu 21: 4 But the people **g** impatient along the way,
Dt 32: 15 the people **g** heavy, plump, and stuffed!
Jdg 1: 28 When the Israelites **g** stronger, they forced the
2: 10 another generation **g** up who did not acknowledge
11: 2 and when these half brothers **g** up, they chased
13: 24 And the LORD blessed him as he **g** up.
1Sa 2: 21 Samuel **g** up in the presence of the LORD.
2: 26 Meanwhile, as young Samuel **g** taller, he also
3: 19 As Samuel **g** up, the LORD was with him,
8: 1 As Samuel **g** old, he appointed his sons to be
14: 19 and confusion in the Philistine camp **g** louder
31: 3 The fighting **g** very fierce around Saul,
2Sa 10: 5 the men to stay at Jericho until their beards **g** out,
12: 3 raised that little lamb, and it **g** up with his children.
16: 14 and all who were with him **g** weary along the way,
1Ki 11: 19 Pharaoh **g** very fond of Hadad, and he gave him a
17: 17 He **g** worse and worse, and finally he died.
1Ch 10: 3 The fighting **g** very fierce around Saul,
19: 5 the men to stay at Jericho until their beards **g** out,
2Ch 13: 21 Abijah of Judah **g** more and more powerful.
Ne 9: 25 So they ate until they were full and **g** fat
Est 7: 6 Haman **g** pale with fright before the king
Job 26: 12 By his power the sea **g** calm. By his skill he
Ps 39: 2 the turmoil within me **g** to the bursting point.
39: 3 My thoughts **g** hot within me / and began to burn,
Isa 5: 2 but the grapes that **g** were wild and sour.
7: 25 go to the fertile hillsides where the gardens once **g**,
38: 14 My eyes **g** tired of looking to heaven for help.
53: 2 My servant **g** up in the LORD's presence like a
55: 13 will grow. Where briers **g**, myrtles will sprout up.
57: 10 You **g** weary in your search, but you never gave
Eze 16: 7 You **g** up and became a beautiful jewel.
16: 7 Your breasts became full, and your hair **g**,
17: 6 It took root there and **g** into a low, spreading vine.
17: 6 toward the eagle, and its roots **g** down beneath it.
31: 5 It prospered and **g** long thick branches because of
Da 4: 11 The tree **g** very tall and strong, reaching high into
5: 9 So the king **g** even more alarmed, and his face
8: 8 In the large horn's place **g** four prominent horns
8: 9 came a small horn whose power **g** very great.
10: 8 My strength left me, my face **g** deathly pale,
Jnh 4: 8 And as the sun **g** hot, God sent a scorching east
4: 8 The sun beat down on his head until he **g** faint
Mt 13: 26 began to grow and produce grain, the weeds also **g**.
Mk 4: 27 the seeds sprouted and **g** without the farmer's help,
Lk 1: 80 John **g** up and became strong in spirit. Then he
2: 40 There the child **g** up healthy and strong. He was
2: 52 So Jesus **g** both in height and in wisdom, and he
8: 8 This seed **g** and produced a crop one hundred times
12: 1 the crowds **g** until thousands were milling about
Jn 6: 18 them as they rowed, and the sea **g** very rough.
Ac 9: 31 and Samaria, and it **g** in strength and numbers.
16: 5 strengthened in their faith and **g** daily in numbers.
21: 35 the mob **g** so violent the soldiers had to lift Paul to
23: 10 The shouting **g** louder and louder, and the men
Ro 4: 20 In fact, his faith **g** stronger, and in this he brought
9: 10 When he **g** up, he married Rebekah, who gave
1Co 13: 11 But when I **g** up, I put away childish things.
Heb 11: 24 It was by faith that Moses, when he **g** up,
Rev 18: 1 and the earth **g** bright with his splendor.
22: 2 On each side of the river **g** a tree of life,

GREY(HEADED) [KJV] See GRAY, GRAY-HAIRED

GREYHOUND [KJV] See ROOSTER

GRIDDLE (4)

Lev 2: 5 If your grain offering is cooked on a **g**, it must be
6: 21 It must be cooked on a **g** with olive oil, and it must
7: 9 or cooked on a **g** belongs to the priest who presents
Eze 4: 3 Then take an iron **g** and place it between you

GRIEF (44) [GRIEF-STRICKEN, GRIEVE, GRIEVED, GRIEVES, GRIEVING, GRIEVOUS]

1Sa 2: 33 Those who are left alive will live in sadness and **g**,
4: 12 his clothes and put dust on his head to show his **g**.
2Sa 19: 2 As the troops heard of the king's deep **g** for his
1Ki 13: 30 his own grave, crying out in **g**, "Oh, my brother!"
Job 1: 20 Job stood up and tore his robe in **g**. Then he shaved
2: 12 into the air over their heads to demonstrate their **g**.
14: 22 They are absorbed in their own pain and **g**."
16: 5 that helps you. I would try to take away your **g**.
16: 6 my **g** remains no matter how I defend myself.
Ps 6: 7 My vision is blurred by **g**; / my eyes are worn out
10: 14 But you do see the trouble and **g** they cause.
31: 10 I am dying from **g**; / my years are shortened by
38: 6 and racked with pain. / My days are filled with **g**.
119: 28 I weep with **g**; / encourage me by your word.
Pr 10: 1 joy to a father; a foolish child brings **g** to a mother.
14: 13 heavy heart; when the laughter ends, the **g** remains.
15: 27 Dishonest money brings **g** to the whole family,
17: 25 A foolish child brings **g** to a father and bitterness
Ecc 1: 18 For the greater my wisdom, the greater my **g**.
2: 23 Their days of labor are filled with pain and **g**;
11: 10 So banish **g** and pain, but remember that youth,
Isa 17: 11 Your only harvest will be a load of **g** and incurable
24: 16 But my heart is heavy with **g**. I am discouraged,
32: 11 your pretty clothes, and wear sackcloth in your **g**.
53: 3 a man of sorrows, acquainted with bitterest **g**.
53: 10 good plan to crush him and fill him with **g**.
54: 6 For the LORD has called you back from your **g**—
Jer 8: 18 My **g** is beyond healing; my heart is broken.
8: 21 of my people. I am stunned and silent, mute with **g**.
10: 19 My wound is desperate, and my **g** is great.
14: 3 confused and desperate, covering their heads in **g**.
La 1: 1 Like a widow broken with **g**, she sits alone in her
3: 32 Though he brings **g**, he also shows compassion
Eze 13: 22 with your lies, when I didn't want them to suffer **g**.
27: 31 They shave their heads in **g** because of you
Joel 2: 13 Don't tear your clothing in your **g**; instead,
Mic 4: 6 who are lame, who have been exiles, filled with **g**.
Mt 17: 23 And the disciples' hearts were filled with **g**.
26: 38 "My soul is crushed with **g** to the point of death.
Mk 14: 34 "My soul is crushed with **g** to the point of death.
Lk 22: 45 only to find them asleep, exhausted from **g**.
Jn 16: 20 but your **g** will suddenly turn to wonderful joy
Ro 9: 2 heart is filled with bitter sorrow and unending **g**
Jas 4: 9 Let there be sorrow and deep **g**. Let there be

GRIEF-STRICKEN (1) [GRIEF]

Lk 23: 27 trailed along behind, including many **g** women.

GRIEVE (6) [GRIEF]

Ecc 3: 4 a time to laugh. / A time to **g** and a time to dance.
La 3: 20 never forget this awful time, as I **g** over my loss.
Eze 7: 12 they find or for sellers to **g** over their losses,
Zec 12: 10 They will **g** bitterly for him as for a firstborn son
Jn 16: 20 You will **g**, but your grief will suddenly turn to
2Co 12: 21 And I will have to **g** because many of you who

GRIEVED (7) [GRIEF]

Jdg 10: 16 served the LORD. And he was **g** by their misery.
Job 30: 25 those in trouble? Was I not deeply **g** for the needy?
Ps 35: 13 Yet when they were ill, / I **g** for them. / I even
78: 40 in the desert / and **g** his heart in the wilderness.
Isa 63: 10 they rebelled against him and **g** his Holy Spirit.
Eze 6: 9 They will recognize how **g** I am by their unfaithful
Jn 21: 17 Peter was **g** that Jesus asked the question a third

GRIEVES (1) [GRIEF]

Ps 116: 15 ones are precious to him; / it **g** him when they die.

GRIEVING (2) [GRIEF]

Ps 35: 14 or family, / as if I were **g** for my own mother.
Mk 16: 10 and found the disciples, who were **g** and weeping.

GRIEVOUS (1) [GRIEF]

Zec 12: 11 **g** mourning of Hadad-rimmon in the valley of

GRILLED (1)

Lk 11: 53 From that time on they **g** him with many hostile

GRIND (9) [GRINDING]

Nu 15: 20 Present a cake from the first of the flour you **g**
Jdg 16: 21 bronze chains and made to **g** grain in the prison.
Ps 112: 10 They will **g** their teeth in anger; / they will slink
Pr 27: 22 even though you **g** them like grain with mortar
Isa 3: 15 How dare you **g** my people into the dust like that!"
47: 2 Take heavy millstones and **g** the corn.
La 2: 16 They scoff and **g** their teeth and say, "We have
3: 16 He has made me **g** my teeth on gravel. He has
Mk 9: 18 at the mouth and **g** his teeth and become rigid.

GRINDING (3) [GRIND]
Nu 11: 8 and made flour by **g** it with hand mills or pounding
Mt 24:41 Two women will be **g** flour at the mill; one will be
Lk 17:35 Two women will be **g** flour together at the mill;

GRIP (11) [GRIPPED, GRIPS]
Ex 15:14 anguish will **g** the people of Philistia.
1Ki 2:46 So the kingdom was now firmly in Solomon's **g**.
2Ki 15:19 gain his support in tightening his **g** on royal power.
Ps 14: 5 Terror will **g** them, / for God is with those who
53: 5 But then terror will **g** them, / terror like they have
101: 8 and free the city of the LORD from their **g**.
Isa 14: 6 blows of rage and held the nations in your angry **g**.
Mic 4:10 he will redeem you from the **g** of your enemies.
Ac 2:24 to life again, for death could not keep him in its **g**.
2Th 2:15 and keep a strong **g** on everything we taught you
Heb 12:12 So take a new **g** with your tired hands and stand

GRIPPED (14) [GRIP]
Ge 42:35 for the grain. Terror **g** them, as it did their father.
Job 4:14 Fear **g** me; I trembled and shook with terror.
41:25 When it rises, the mighty are afraid, **g** by terror.
Ps 48: 6 They were **g** with terror, / like a woman writhing
Jer 6:24 Fear and pain have **g** us, like that of a woman
49:24 and pain have **g** her as they do a woman giving
50:43 Fear and pain have **g** him, like that of a woman
Da 5: 6 Such terror **g** him that his knees knocked together
Mic 4: 9 Pain has **g** you like it does a woman in labor.
Mk 1:27 Amazement **g** the audience, and they began to
Lk 5:26 Everyone was **g** with great wonder and awe.
9:34 over them; and terror **g** them as it covered them.
9:43 Awe **g** the people as they saw this display of God's
Ac 5:11 Great fear **g** the entire church and all others who

GRIPS (4) [GRIP]
Job 23:15 in his presence. When I think of it, terror **g** me.
30:18 my garment. He **g** me by the collar of my tunic.
Isa 13: 8 Fear **g** them with terrible pangs, like those of a
Joel 2: 6 Fear **g** all the people; every face grows pale with

GRISLED [KJV] See SPOTTED, DAPPLED-GRAY

GROAN (17) [GROANED, GROANING, GROANINGS, GROANS]
Job 23: 2 is still a bitter one, and I try hard not to **g** aloud.
35: 9 to them. They **g** beneath the power of the mighty.
Ps 90: 9 beneath your wrath. / We end our lives with a **g**.
Pr 5:11 Afterward you will **g** in anguish when disease
29: 2 But when the wicked are in power, they **g**.
Jer 22:23 but soon you will cry and **g** in anguish—
La 1: 4 The city gates are silent, her priests **g**, her young
1: 8 All she can do is **g** and hide her face.
1:11 Her people **g** as they search for bread. They have
Eze 21: 6 "Son of man, **g** before the people! **G** before them with bitter anguish and a broken
21: 7 'I **g** because of the terrifying news I have heard.
Am 2:13 "So I will make you **g** as a wagon groans when it
Mic 4:10 Writhe and **g** in terrible pain, you people of
Ro 8:23 also **g** to be released from pain and suffering.
2Co 5: 4 Our dying bodies make us **g** and sigh, but it's not
Jas 5: 1 weep and **g** with anguish because of all the terrible

GROANED (7) [GROAN]
Ex 2:23 But the Israelites still **g** beneath their burden of
1Sa 31: 4 Saul **g** to his armor bearer, "Take your sword
1Ki 22:34 out of here!" Ahab **g** to the driver of his chariot.
1Ch 10: 4 Saul **g** to his armor bearer, "Take your sword
2Ch 18:33 out of here!" Ahab **g** to the driver of his chariot.
Ps 32: 3 I was weak and miserable, / and I **g** all day long.
Jnh 1:10 they heard this. "Oh, why did you do it?" they **g**.

GROANING (6) [GROAN]
Ps 5: 1 hear me as I pray; / pay attention to my **g**.
102: 5 Because of my **g**, / I am reduced to skin and bones.
Isa 21: 2 and the **g** of all the nations she enslaved will end.
Eze 30:24 and he will lie there mortally wounded, **g** in pain.
Mal 2:13 weeping and **g** because he pays no attention to
Ro 8:22 For we know that all creation has been **g** as in the

GROANINGS (1) [GROAN]
Ro 8:26 But the Holy Spirit prays for us with **g** that cannot

GROANS (11) [GROAN]
Ex 6: 5 You can be sure that I have heard the **g** of the
Job 3:24 I cannot eat for sighing; my **g** pour out like water.
24:12 The **g** of the dying rise from the city,
Ps 12: 5 to the helpless, / and I have heard the **g** of the poor.
38: 8 My **g** come from an anguished heart.
102:20 to hear the **g** of the prisoners, / to release those
Jer 51:52 The **g** of her wounded people will be heard
La 1:18 is right," she **g**, "for I rebelled against him.
1:21 "Others heard my **g**, but no one turned to comfort
1:22 all my sins. My **g** are many, and my heart is faint."
Am 2:13 "So I will make you groan as a wagon **g** when it is

GROOM (4) [GROOMS]
Mt 9:15 guests mourn while celebrating with the **g**?
Mk 2:19 wedding guests fast while celebrating with the **g**?
2:19 They can't fast while they are with the **g**.
Lk 5:34 wedding guests fast while celebrating with the **g**?

GROOMED (1)
Jer 5:28 They are well fed and well **g**, and there is no limit

GROOMS (1) [GROOM]
Rev 18:23 There will be no happy voices of brides and **g**.

GROPE (5) [GROPING]
Dt 28:29 You will **g** around in broad daylight, just like a
Job 5:14 They **g** in the daylight as though they were blind;
12:25 They **g** in the darkness without a light. He makes
32:11 to your arguments, listening to you **g** for words.
Isa 59:10 No wonder we **g** like blind people and stumble

GROPING (1) [GROPE]
Dt 28:29 just like a blind person **g** in the darkness,

GROSS (1)
Eze 23:20 She lusted after lovers whose attentions were **g**

GROSS [KJV] See also HARDENED, TERRIBLE

GROUND (266) [AGROUND, GROUNDLESS, GROUNDS, UNDERGROUND]
Ge 1: 9 be gathered into one place so dry **g** may appear."
1:10 God named the dry **g** "land" and the water
2: 6 But water came up out of the **g** and watered all the
2: 7 God formed a man's body from the dust of the **g**
3:17 I told you not to eat, I have placed a curse on the **g**.
3:19 Then you will return to the **g** from which you
3:23 and he sent Adam out to cultivate the **g** from which
4:10 your brother's blood cries out to me from the **g**!
4:11 You are hereby banished from the **g** you have
5:29 of farming this **g** that the LORD has cursed."
7:17 covering the **g** and lifting the boat high above the
7:18 As the waters rose higher and higher above the **g**,
8: 8 he sent out a dove to see if it could find dry **g**.
17:17 Then Abraham bowed down to the **g**, but he
18: 2 welcoming them by bowing low to the **g**.
19: 1 Then he welcomed them and bowed low to the **g**.
24:26 The man fell down to the **g** and worshiped the
24:52 Abraham's servant bowed to the **g** and worshiped
28:13 Isaac. The **g** you are lying on belongs to you.
38: 9 he spilled the semen on the **g** to keep her from
42: 6 bowed low before him, with their faces to the **g**.
44:14 brothers arrived, and they fell to the **g** before him.
Ex 3: 5 off your sandals, for you are standing on holy **g**."
4: 3 "Throw it down on the **g**," the LORD told him.
4: 9 from the Nile River and pour it out on the dry **g**.
8:21 with them, and the **g** will be covered with them.
9:32 because they had not yet sprouted from the **g**.
10: 5 so many that you won't be able to see the **g**.
10:15 of the whole country, making the **g** look black.
14:16 all the people of Israel will walk through on dry **g**.
14:22 people of Israel walked through the sea on dry **g**,
16:14 thin flakes, white like frost, covered the **g**.
16:22 there was twice as much as usual on the **g**—
16:25 the LORD. There will be no food on the **g** today.
16:26 There will be no food on the **g** for you on that
16:29 Do not pick up food from the **g** on that day."
32:19 terrible anger, he threw the stone tablets to the **g**,
32:20 he **g** it into powder and mixed it with water.
34: 8 Moses immediately fell to the **g** and worshiped.
Lev 5: 2 or an animal that scurries along the **g**—
9:24 they shouted with joy and fell face down on the **g**.
11:20 all swarming insects that walk along the **g**.
11:29 The small animals that scurry or creep on the **g**,
11:41 detestable any animal that scurries along the **g**;
11:44 any of these animals that scurry along the **g**.
19:10 and do not pick up the grapes that fall to the **g**.
Nu 11: 8 The people gathered it from the **g** and made flour
11:31 were quail flying about three feet above the **g**.
14: 5 and Aaron fell face down on the **g** before the
15:21 LORD each year from the first of your **g** flour.
16: 4 he threw himself down with his face to the **g**.
16:22 But Moses and Aaron fell face down on the **g**.
16:30 and the **g** opens up and swallows them and all their
16:31 when the **g** suddenly split open beneath them.
16:45 But Moses and Aaron fell face down on the **g**.
20: 6 the Tabernacle, where they fell face down on the **g**.
22:31 Balaam fell face down on the **g** before him.
Dt 9:17 I raised the stone tablets and dashed them to the **g**.
9:21 and I melted it in the fire and **g** it into fine dust.
12:16 the blood. You must pour it out on the **g** like water.
12:24 Instead, pour out the blood on the **g** like water.
15:23 the blood. You must pour it out on the **g** like water.
22: 6 "If you find a bird's nest on the **g** or in a tree
26:10 of the first crops you have given me from the **g**.'
28:56 she would not so much as touch her feet to the **g**—
Jos 1: 5 No one will be able to stand their **g** against you as
3:17 **g** in the middle of the riverbed as the people passed
3:17 until everyone had crossed the Jordan on dry **g**.
4:22 is where the Israelites crossed the Jordan on dry **g**.'
5:14 Joshua fell with his face to the **g** in reverence.
5:15 "Take off your sandals, for this is holy **g**."
7:21 They are hidden in the **g** beneath my tent,
7:23 Then they laid them on the **g** in the presence of the
24:32 in the parcel of **g** Jacob had bought from the sons
Jdg 4:21 the tent peg through his temple and into the **g**,
5:22 Then the horses' hooves hammered the **g**,
6:37 is wet with dew in the morning but the **g** is dry,
6:39 This time let the fleece remain dry while the **g**
6:40 in the morning, but the **g** was covered with dew.
9:40 and the **g** was covered with dead bodies all the way
9:45 leveled the city, and scattered salt all over the **g**.
13:20 his wife saw this, they fell with their faces to the **g**.
15: 5 He burned all their grain to the **g**,
15:15 up a donkey's jawbone that was lying on the **g**
15:19 water to gush out of a hollow in the **g** at Lehi,
16: 3 and lifted them, bar and all, right out of the **g**.
18:27 killed all the people and burned the town to the **g**.
1Sa 4: 5 shout of joy was so loud that it made the **g** shake!
5: 3 Dagon had fallen with his face to the **g** in front of
14:25 even though they found honeycomb on the **g** in the
17:49 Goliath stumbled and fell face downward to the **g**.
19:24 his clothes and lay on the **g** all day and all night,
20:41 David bowed to Jonathan with his face to the **g**.
25:41 She bowed low to the **g** and responded, "Yes,
26: 7 with his spear stuck in the **g** beside his head.
26: 8 I'll pin him to the **g**, and I won't need to strike
28:14 that it was Samuel, and he fell to the **g** before him.
28:20 Saul fell full length on the **g**, paralyzed with fright
28:23 so he finally yielded and got up from the **g** and sat
30: 1 raid into the Negev and had burned Ziklag to the **g**.
2Sa 1: 2 He fell to the **g** before David in deep respect.
2:23 his back. He stumbled to the **g** and died there.
8: 2 He made the people lie down on the **g** in a row,
9: 8 Mephibosheth fell to the **g** before the king.
12:16 went without food and lay all night on the bare **g**.
12:20 Then David got up from the **g**, washed himself,
13:31 tore his robe, and fell prostrate on the **g**.
14:14 Our lives are like water spilled out on the **g**,
14:22 Joab fell to the **g** before the king and blessed him
17:12 can descend on him like the dew that falls to the **g**,
18:28 He bowed low with his face to the **g** and said,
20:10 with it so that his insides gushed out onto the **g**.
22:43 I **g** them as fine as the dust of the earth; / I swept
23:12 but Shammah held his **g** in the middle of the field
23:20 Then, despite the snow and slippery **g**, he caught
24:20 and bowed before the king with his face to the **g**.
1Ki 13: 3 and its ashes will be poured out on the **g**."
18: 7 him at once and fell to the **g** before him.
18:42 top of Mount Carmel and fell to the **g** and prayed.
2Ki 2: 8 and the two of them went across on dry **g**!
4:27 she fell to the **g** before him and caught hold of his
8:12 kill their young men, dash their children to the **g**,
13:18 up the other arrows and strike them against the **g**."
13:18 king picked them up and struck the **g** three times.
13:19 "You should have struck the **g** five or six times!"
23: 6 Then he **g** the pole to dust and threw the dust in the
1Ch 11:14 and David held their **g** in the middle of the field
11:22 Then, despite the snow and slippery **g**, he caught
21:16 and fell down with their faces to the **g**.
21:21 threshing floor and bowed to the **g** before David.
2Ch 7: 3 they fell face down on the **g** and worshiped
8:11 of the LORD has been there, and it is holy **g**."
20:18 Jehoshaphat bowed down with his face to the **g**.
20:24 there were dead bodies lying on the **g** for as far as
Ezr 10: 1 and throwing himself to the **g** in front of the
Ne 8: 6 worshiped the LORD with their faces to the **g**.
Job 1:20 he shaved his head and fell to the **g** before God.
2:13 Then they sat on the **g** with him for seven days
16: 7 you have **g** me down and devastated my family.
16:13 me without mercy. The **g** is wet with my blood.
18:10 A snare lies hidden in the **g**. A rope lies coiled on
38:27 Who sends the rain that satisfies the parched **g**
39:24 Fiercely it paws the **g** and rushes forward into
41:30 They tear up the **g** as it drags through the mud.
Ps 7: 5 Let them trample me into the **g**. / Let my honor be
17:11 me down, surround me, / and throw me to the **g**.
18:42 I **g** them as fine as dust carried by the wind.
40: 2 the mud and the mire. / He set my feet on solid **g**
56: 7 in your anger, O God, throw them to the **g**.
58: 7 May they disappear like water into thirsty **g**.
65:10 You drench the plowed **g** with rain,
74: 7 They set the sanctuary on fire, burning it to the **g**.
80: 9 You cleared the **g** for us, / and we took root
137: 7 "Destroy it!" they yelled. / "Level it to the **g**!"
143: 3 has chased me. / He has knocked me to the **g**.
147:16 he scatters frost upon the **g** like ashes.
SS 3: 6 from the deserts like a cloud of smoke along the **g**?
Isa 2:19 his enemies will crawl with fear into holes in the **g**.
3:26 will be like a ravaged woman, huddled on the **g**.
5: 6 wild place. / I will not prune the vines or hoe the **g**.
7:24 vast brier patch, a hunting **g** overrun by wildlife.
21: 9 All the idols of Babylon lie broken on the **g**!"
22:25 so firm. It will come out and fall to the **g**.
25:12 walls of Moab will be demolished and **g** to dust.
28: 2 they will burst upon it and dash it to the **g**.
28:18 enemy floods in, you will be trampled into the **g**.
30:24 and donkeys that till the **g** will eat good grain,
34: 9 burning pitch, and the **g** will be covered with fire.
35: 7 The parched **g** will become a pool, and springs of
41: 3 on safely, though he is walking over unfamiliar **g**.
41:18 fed by springs will flow across the dry, parched **g**.
53: 2 sprouting from a root in dry and sterile **g**.
55:10 the heavens and stay on the **g** to water the earth.
63: 6 and made them stagger and fall to the **g**."
Jer 4: 3 and Jerusalem: "Plow up the hard **g** of your hearts!
8: 2 and spread them out on the **g** before the sun,
8: 2 or buried but will be scattered on the **g** like dung.
12: 5 If you stumble and fall on open **g**, what will you do
14: 2 "Judah wilts; her businesses have **g** to a halt.
14: 2 All the people sit on the **g** in mourning, and a great
14: 4 The **g** is parched and cracked for lack of rain.
14:17 with a sword and lies mortally wounded on the **g**.
16: 4 and they will lie scattered on the **g** like dung.
25:33 They will be scattered like dung on the **g**.
37: 8 and capture this city and burn it to the **g**.
37:10 from their tents and burn this city to the **g**!"

38:18 to the Babylonians, and they will burn it to the g."
51:58 wide walls of Babylon will be leveled to the g,
La 2:9 Jerusalem's gates have sunk into the g. All their
2:10 The leaders of Jerusalem sit on the g in silence,
Eze 1:15 I saw four wheels on the g beneath them,
17:5 "Then he planted one of its seedlings in fertile g
19:12 and thrown down to the g. / The desert wind dried
19:13 in the wilderness, / where the g is hard and dry.
26:16 They will sit on the g trembling with horror at
28:18 I let it burn you to ashes on the g in the sight of all
29:5 You will lie unburied on the open g, for I have
30:4 and those who are slaughtered will cover the g.
30:11 Egypt until slaughtered Egyptians cover the g.
30:22 and I will make his sword clatter to the g.
31:12 the nations—cut it down and left it fallen on the g.
36:9 Your g will be tilled and your crops planted.
37:2 They were scattered everywhere across the g.
39:11 who travel there will be blocked by this burial g,
44:4 and I fell to the g with my face in the dust.
45:1 6-2/3 miles wide. The entire area will be holy g.
Da 2:46 Then King Nebuchadnezzar bowed to the g before
3:5 bow to the g to worship King Nebuchadnezzar's
3:7 bowed to the g and worshiped the statue that King
4:15 But leave the stump and the roots in the g,
4:23 But leave the stump and the roots in the g,
4:26 But the stump and the roots were left in the g.
7:4 it was left standing with its two hind feet on the g,
8:5 the land so swiftly that it didn't even touch the g.
8:10 and stars to the g and trampling them.
8:17 I became so terrified that I fell to the g.
8:18 I fainted and lay there with my face to the g.
10:9 I fainted and lay there with my face to the g.
10:15 I looked down at the g, unable to say a word.
Hos 2:18 the birds and the animals that scurry along the g
10:11 Israel and Judah must now break up the hard g;
10:12 Plow up the hard g of your hearts, for now is the
13:16 their little ones dashed to death against the g,
Joel 1:17 The seeds die in the parched g, and the grain crops
Am 2:15 The archers will fail to stand their g. The swiftest
3:14 horns of the altar will be cut off and fall to the g.
5:2 never to rise again! / She lies forsaken on the g,
9:5 The g rises like the Nile River at floodtime, and
Zep 1:17 and your bodies will lie there rotting on the g."
Zec 9:4 Tyre will be set on fire and burned to the g.
Mt 10:29 can fall to the g without your Father knowing it.
13:22 The thorny g represents those who hear and accept
15:35 So Jesus told all the people to sit down on the g.
17:6 disciples were terrified and fell face down on the g.
25:18 received the one bag of gold dug a hole in the g
26:39 went on a little farther and fell face down on the g,
Mk 4:18 The thorny g represents those who hear and accept
8:6 So Jesus told all the people to sit down on the g.
9:18 it throws him violently to the g and makes him
9:20 and he fell to the g, writhing and foaming at the
14:35 went on a little farther and fell face down on the g.
Lk 5:12 he fell to the g, face down in the dust, begging to
8:14 The thorny g represents those who hear and accept
8:28 he shrieked and fell to the g before him, screaming,
9:14 "Just tell them to sit down on the g in groups of
9:42 the demon knocked him to the g and threw him
17:16 He fell face down on the g at Jesus' feet,
19:44 They will crush you to the g, and your children
22:44 his sweat fell to the g like great drops of blood.
Jn 4:5 near the parcel of g that Jacob gave to his son
9:6 Then he spit on the g, made mud with the saliva,
18:6 he said, "I am he," they all fell backward to the g!
Ac 7:33 off your sandals, for you are standing on holy g.
9:4 He fell to the g and heard a voice saying to him,
9:8 As Saul picked himself up off the g, he found that
22:7 I fell to the g and heard a voice saying to me,
1Co 9:22 I try to find common g with everyone so that I
10:1 all safely through the waters of the sea on dry g.
15:36 When you put a seed into the g, it doesn't grow
15:37 And what you put in the g is not the plant that will
2Co 11:12 But I will continue doing this to cut the g out from
Eph 6:14 Stand your g, putting on the sturdy belt of truth
Heb 6:7 When the g soaks up the rain that falls on it
11:29 through the Red Sea as though they were on dry g.
11:38 and mountains, hiding in caves and holes in the g.
Rev 16:10 And his subjects g their teeth in anguish,

GROUNDLESS (1) [GROUND]

Ps 4:2 How long will you make these g accusations?

GROUNDS (4) [GROUND]

2Ki 11:16 her out to the gate where horses enter the palace g,
2Ch 23:15 her out to the gate where horses enter the palace g,
Da 6:5 "Our only chance of finding g for accusing Daniel
Mt 24:1 As Jesus was leaving the Temple g, his disciples

GROUP (67) [GROUP'S, GROUPS, REGROUPED]

Ge 31:23 he gathered a g of his relatives and set out in hot
32:8 He thought, "If Esau attacks one g,
32:16 each g of animals by itself, separated by a distance
32:17 these instructions to the men leading the first g:
37:25 It was a g of Ishmaelite traders taking spices,
Nu 10:25 The tribe of Dan headed this g,
20:22 The whole community of Israel left Kadesh as a g
Jos 8:33 One g stood at the foot of Mount Gerizim,
8:33 Each g faced the other, and between them stood
Jdg 7:5 In one g put all those who cup water in their hands
7:5 In the other g put all those who kneel down
7:18 As soon as my g blows the rams' horns, those of
9:37 And another g is coming down the road past the
9:44 and his g stormed the city gate to keep the men of
20:33 When the main g of Israelite warriors reached
2Sa 8:2 groups to be executed for every one g to be spared.
23:13 an elite g among David's fighting men) went down
1Ki 10:2 She arrived in Jerusalem with a large g of
20:35 the LORD instructed one of the g of prophets to
2Ki 2:3 The g of prophets from Bethel came to Elisha
2:5 Then the g of prophets from Jericho came to Elisha
2:7 Fifty men from the g of prophets also went
2:15 When the g of prophets from Jericho saw what
2:23 a g of boys from the town began mocking
4:38 One day as the g of prophets was seated before
4:42 "Give it to the g of prophets so they can eat."
4:43 "Give it to the g of prophets so they can eat,
6:1 One day the g of prophets came to Elisha and told
9:1 had summoned a member of the g of prophets.
19:31 from Jerusalem, a g of survivors from Mount Zion.
1Ch 11:15 an elite g among David's fighting men) went down
16:5 Asaph, the leader of this g, sounded the cymbals.
16:19 few in number, / a tiny g of strangers in Canaan.
16:38 This g included Obed-edom (son of Jeduthun),
24:19 Each g carried out its duties in the house of the
26:14 for the east gate went to Meshelemiah and his g.
27:6 David's elite military g known as the Thirty.
2Ch 9:1 She arrived with a large g of attendants and a great
Ezr 2:59 Another g returned to Jerusalem at this time from
2:60 This g consisted of the families of Delaiah, Tobiah,
8:20 a g of Temple workers first instituted by King
Ne 3:17 Next was a g of Levites working under the
7:61 "Another g returned to Jerusalem at this time from
7:62 This g included the families of Delaiah, Tobiah,
12:40 together with the g of leaders who were with me.
Ps 105:12 few in number, / a tiny g of strangers in Canaan.
Isa 30:29 as when a flutist leads a g of pilgrims to
37:32 from Jerusalem, a g of survivors from Mount Zion.
60:22 The tiniest g will become a mighty nation. I,
Eze 42:1 and came to a g of rooms against the north wall of
42:2 This g of structures, whose entrance opened
Zec 13:9 I will bring that g through the fire and make them
Mt 11:16 These people are like a g of children playing a
21:36 So the landowner sent a larger g of his servants to
22:23 a g of Jews who say there is no resurrection after
Mk 9:38 we told him to stop because he isn't one of our g."
12:18 a g of Jews who say there is no resurrection after
Lk 7:32 They are like a g of children playing a game in the
9:49 We tried to stop him because he isn't in our g."
20:27 a g of Jews who say there is no resurrection after
24:22 Then some women from our g of his followers
24:37 But the whole g was terribly frightened,
Ac 2:47 And each day the Lord added to their g those who
6:5 This idea pleased the whole g, and they chose the
23:12 The next morning a g of Jews got together
Gal 1:1 I was not appointed by any g or by human
5:20 is wrong except those in your own little g,

GROUP'S (1) [GROUP]

Nu 26:54 each g inheritance reflecting the size of its

GROUPS (40) [GROUP]

Ge 10:25 of the world were divided into different language g
Ex 6:16 of Levi, listed according to their family g.
6:25 the Levite clans, listed according to their family g.
18:21 Appoint them as judges over g of one thousand,
18:25 They were put in charge of g of one thousand,
Nu 2:2 and the various g will camp beneath their family
3:20 the Levite clans, listed according to their family g.
26:56 by lot among the larger and smaller tribal g."
Jos 8:33 officers, and judges, were divided into two g.
Jdg 7:5 the LORD told him, "Divide the men into two g.
7:16 He divided the three hundred men into three g
7:20 Then all three g blew their horns and broke their
9:34 and his men went by night and split into four g,
9:43 he divided his men into three g and set an ambush
9:44 while Abimelech's other two g cut them down in
1Sa 29:2 were leading out their troops in g of one hundred
2Sa 2:13 The two g sat down there, facing each other from
8:2 and he measured them off in g with a length of
8:2 He measured off two g to be executed for every
1Ki 16:21 now the people of Israel were divided into two g.
2Ki 1:14 the fire from heaven has destroyed the first two g.
5:2 Now g of Aramean raiders had invaded the land of
11:6 These three g will all guard the palace.
13:20 G of Moabite raiders used to invade the land each
17:24 And the king of Assyria transported g of people
17:29 But these various g of foreigners also continued to
1Ch 1:19 of the world were divided into different language g
23:24 the leaders of their family g, registered carefully by
24:1 the priests, were divided into g for service.
24:3 David divided Aaron's descendants into g
24:4 Eleazar's descendants were divided into sixteen g
24:5 All tasks were assigned to the various g by means
2Ch 35:12 burnt offerings among the people by their family g,
Zec 12:12 with the husbands and wives in separate g.
Mk 6:39 Then Jesus told the crowd to sit down in g on the
6:40 So they sat in g of fifty or a hundred.
Lk 9:14 "Just tell them to sit down on the ground in g of
Eph 2:15 creating in himself one new person from the two g.
2:16 Christ reconciled both g to God by means of his
3:6 Both g have believed the Good News, and both are

GROVE (9) [GROVES]

Ge 13:18 Then Abram moved his camp to the oak g owned
14:13 who was camped at the oak g belonging to Mamre
18:1 was camped near the oak g belonging to Mamre.
SS 6:11 "I went down into the g of nut trees and out to the
Mt 26:36 Then Jesus brought them to an olive g called
Mk 14:32 And they came to an olive g called Gethsemane,
Jn 18:1 with his disciples and entered a g of olive trees.
18:3 lanterns, and weapons, they arrived at the olive g.
18:26 "Didn't I see you out there in the olive g with

GROVEL (1)

Ge 3:14 You will g in the dust as long as you live,

GROVES (11) [GROVE]

Ex 23:11 The same applies to your vineyards and olive g.
Nu 24:6 They spread before me like g of palms,
Jos 24:13 I gave you vineyards and olive g for food,
1Sa 8:14 and vineyards and olive g and give them to his
2Ki 5:26 and clothing and olive g and vineyards and sheep
1Ch 27:28 from Geder was in charge of the king's olive g
Ne 5:11 You must restore their fields, vineyards, olive g,
9:25 with cisterns already dug and vineyards and olive g
Job 29:6 and my olive g poured out streams of olive oil.
Ecc 2:6 collect the water to irrigate my many flourishing g.
Isa 1:29 offered sacrifices to idols in your g of sacred oaks.

GROW (112) [GREW, GROWERS, GROWING, GROWN, GROWS, GROWTH, OVERGROWN]

Ge 1:11 And let there be trees that g seed-bearing fruit.
3:18 It will g thorns and thistles for you, though you
6:1 When the human population began to g rapidly on
26:13 a rich man, and his wealth only continued to g.
45:6 These two years of famine will g to seven,
Lev 23:40 leafy branches and willows that g by the streams.
25:5 And don't store away the crops that g naturally
25:5 or process the grapes that g on your unpruned
25:11 or store away any of the crops that g naturally,
25:11 and do not process the grapes that g on your
Nu 6:5 That is why they must let their hair g long.
6:11 vow that day and let their hair begin to g again.
15:19 you will eat from the crops that g there. But you
Dt 28:33 about will eat the crops you worked so hard to g.
28:40 You will g olive trees throughout your land,
33:14 with the riches that g in the sun, / and the bounty
Jdg 16:22 But before long his hair began to g back.
Ru 1:11 Can I still give birth to other sons who could g up
1:13 Would you wait for them to g up and refuse to
1Ki 17:14 the LORD sends rain and the crops g again!"
2Ki 4:34 And the child's body began to g warm again!
2Ch 31:7 and the heaps continued to g until early autumn.
Job 8:11 "Can papyrus reeds g where there is no marsh?
8:17 Its roots g down through a pile of rocks to hold it
14:7 hope that it will sprout again and g new branches.
14:21 They never know if their sons g up in honor
18:6 The light in their tent will g dark. The lamp
21:7 live to a good old age. They g old and wealthy.
21:8 They live to see their children g to maturity,
31:40 then let thistles g on that land instead of wheat
39:4 Their young g up in the open fields, then leave
Ps 49:16 So don't be dismayed when the wicked g rich,
52:7 and g more and more bold in their wickedness."
69:23 and let their bodies g weaker and weaker.
73:26 My health may fail, and my spirit may g weak,
84:7 They will continue to g stronger, / and each of
90:12 most of our time, / so that we may g in wisdom.
92:12 and g strong like the cedars of Lebanon.
104:14 You cause grass to g for the cattle. / You cause
plants to g for people to use.
147:8 and makes the green grass g in mountain pastures.
Pr 4:1 your father's instruction. Pay attention and g wise,
15:32 if you listen to correction, you g in understanding.
30:9 For if I g rich, I may deny you and say, "Who is
Ecc 8:13 Their days will never g long like the evening
11:6 variety of crops, for you never know which will g
12:1 Honor him in your youth before you g old and no
12:3 tremble with age, and your strong legs will g weak.
Isa 6:13 but the stump will be a holy seed that will g
11:1 Out of the stump of David's family will g a shoot
17:11 and they may g so well that they blossom on the
21:3 I g faint when I hear what God is planning; I am
34:13 will overrun its palaces; nettles will g in its forts.
40:31 They will run and not g weary. They will walk
55:10 They cause the grain to g, producing seed for the
55:13 Where once there were thorns, cypress trees will g.
Jer 2:21 How did you g into this corrupt wild vine?
26:18 A great forest will g on the hilltop,
La 3:4 He has made my skin and flesh g old. He has
5:17 are sick and weary, and our eyes g dim with tears.
Eze 17:5 where it would g as quickly as a willow tree.
17:8 plenty of water so it could g into a splendid vine
17:9 Should I let this vine g and prosper? No! I will pull
17:24 down the tall tree and helps the short tree to g tall.
31:4 watered it and helped it to g tall and luxuriant.
44:20 "They must neither let their hair g too long nor
47:12 All kinds of fruit trees will g along both sides of
Da 8:3 even though it had begun to g later than the shorter
Hos 2:12 I will let them g into tangled thickets, where only
9:12 Even if your children do survive to g up, I will take
10:8 Thorns and thistles will g up around them.
Joel 2:10 The sun and moon g dark, and the stars no longer
3:15 The sun and moon will g dark, and the stars will no
Am 8:13 and fine young men will g faint and weary,
9:13 and grapes will g faster than they can be harvested.
Jnh 4:6 LORD God arranged for a leafy plant to g there,
Mic 3:12 A great forest will g on the hilltop,
Zec 10:8 their population will g again to its former size.
Mt 6:28 Look at the lilies and how they g. They don't work
13:26 When the crop began to g and produce grain,

13:30 Let both **g** together until the harvest. Then I will
24:12 and the love of many will **g** cold.
Lk 6:44 Figs never **g** on thornbushes or grapes on bramble
8:6 This seed began to **g**, but soon it withered and died
8:14 of this life. And so they never **g** into maturity.
12:27 "Look at the lilies and how they **g**. They don't
Ac 18:23 and helping them to **g** in the Lord.
Ro 1:11 with you that will help you **g** strong in the Lord.
11:10 and let their backs **g** weaker and weaker."
1Co 3:6 watered it, but it was God, not we, who made it **g**.
3:7 because he is the one who makes the seed **g**.
14:3 But one who prophesies is helping others **g** in the
15:36 it doesn't **g** into a plant unless it dies first.
15:37 you put in the ground is not the plant that will **g**,
2Co 5:2 We **g** weary in our present bodies, and we long for
10:15 we hope that your faith will **g** and that our work
Gal 4:1 are not much better off than slaves until they **g** up,
Eph 1:17 so that you might **g** in your knowledge of God.
4:16 it helps the other parts **g**, so that the whole body is
Php 1:25 so I will continue with you so that you will **g**
Col 2:7 Let your roots **g** down into him and draw up
2:7 so you will **g** in faith, strong and vigorous in the
2:19 and we **g** only as we get our nourishment
1Th 3:12 And may the Lord make your love **g** and overflow
Heb 1:12 you are always the same; / you will never **g** old."
Jas 1:3 faith is tested, your endurance has a chance to **g**.
1:4 So let it **g**, for when your endurance is fully
5:18 grass turned green, and the crops began to **g** again.
1Pe 2:2 so that you can **g** into the fullness of your
2Pe 1:7 and finally you will **g** to have genuine love for
1:8 The more you **g** like this, the more you will
3:18 But **g** in the special favor and knowledge of our

GROWERS (1) [GROW]

Joel 1:11 Wail, all you vine **g**! Weep, because the wheat

GROWING (18) [GROW]

Ge 2:5 there were no plants or grain **g** on the earth,
30:14 Reuben found some mandrakes **g** in a field
Ex 1:20 continued to multiply, **g** more and more powerful.
Dt 29:23 and salt, with nothing planted and nothing **g**,
Jos 13:1 old man, the LORD said to him, "You are **g** old,
1Sa 14:31 from Micmash to Aijalon, **g** more and more faint.
Job 8:16 so strong, like a lush plant **g** in the sunshine,
Pr 14:28 A **g** population is a king's glory; a dwindling
Ecc 6:5 Yet he would have had more peace than he has in **g**
Eze 15:6 The people of Jerusalem are like grapevines **g**
19:13 Now the vine is **g** in the wilderness,
47:7 many trees were now **g** on both sides of the river!
Da 4:20 You saw a tree **g** very tall and strong,
Mt 8:18 When Jesus noticed how large the crowd was **g**,
Mk 9:25 Jesus saw that the crowd of onlookers was **g**,
Eph 4:16 the whole body is healthy and **g** and full of love.
Php 1:9 and that you will keep on **g** in your knowledge
2Th 1:3 and you are all **g** in love for each other.

GROWL (3)

Isa 5:30 The enemy nations will **g** over their victims like
59:11 We **g** like hungry bears; we moan like mournful
Am 3:4 Does a young lion **g** in its den without first

GROWN (16) [GROW]

Ge 30:29 many years, and how your flocks and herds have **g**.
38:14 Tamar was aware that Shelah had **g** up, but they
41:48 Joseph took a portion of all the crops **g** in Egypt
47:26 receive one-fifth of all the crops **g** on his land.
Ex 2:11 Many years later, when Moses had **g** up, he went
Lev 13:37 and black hair has **g** in the affected area,
Jos 5:7 those who had **g** up to take their fathers' places.
1Ki 12:8 opinion of the young men who had **g** up with him
2Ch 10:8 opinion of the young men who had **g** up with him
Job 14:8 Though its roots have **g** old in the earth and its
Ps 129:6 on a rooftop, / turning yellow when only half **g**,
Isa 43:22 refuse to ask for my help. You have **g** tired of me!
Eze 17:10 It will die in the same good soil where it had **g**
Da 4:22 For you have **g** strong and great; your greatness
Eph 4:13 Son that we will be mature and full **g** in the Lord,
Rev 18:3 and merchants throughout the world have **g** rich as

GROWS (23) [GROW]

Lev 13:23 But if the area **g** no larger and does not spread,
25:6 produce that **g** naturally during the Sabbath year.
25:12 eat the produce that **g** naturally in the fields that
Dt 32:32 Their vine **g** from the vine of Sodom,
1Ki 4:33 to the tiny hyssop that **g** from cracks in a wall.
10:27 the sycamore wood that **g** in the foothills of Judah.
2Ki 19:29 This year you will eat only what **g** up by itself,
2Ch 1:15 the sycamore wood that **g** in the foothills of Judah.
9:27 the sycamore wood that **g** in the foothills of Judah.
Ps 74:23 have said. / Their uproar of rebellion **g** ever louder.
Pr 13:11 quickly disappears; wealth from hard work **g**.
Ecc 4:16 But then the next generation **g** up and rejects him!
Isa 37:30 This year you will eat only what **g** up by itself,
40:28 Creator of all the earth? He never **g** faint or weary.
Jer 6:29 The refining fire **g** hotter. But it will never purify
15:9 The mother of seven **g** faint and gasps for breath;
Eze 18:10 "But suppose that man has a son who **g** up to be a
Joel 2:6 **g** grips all the people; every face **g** pale with fright.
Mt 13:32 and **g** into a tree where birds can come and find
Mk 4:32 it **g** to become one of the largest of plants,
Lk 13:19 it **g** and becomes a tree, and the birds come
1Co 15:38 A different kind of plant **g** from each kind of seed.
1Jn 4:17 And as we live in God, our love **g** more perfect.

GROWTH (2) [GROW]

Lev 22:22 injured, mutilated, or that has a **g**, an open sore,
SS 6:11 and out to the valley to see the new **g** brought on

GRUDGE (2) [BEGRUDGING, GRUDGINGLY]

Lev 19:18 "Never seek revenge or bear a **g** against anyone,
Mk 11:25 first forgive anyone you are holding a **g** against,

GRUDGINGLY (1) [GRUDGE]

1Pe 5:2 Watch over it willingly, not **g**—not for what you

GRUMBLE (3) [GRUMBLED, GRUMBLERS]

Ge 31:1 learned that Laban's sons were beginning to **g**.
1Co 10:10 And don't **g** as some of them did, for that is why
Jas 5:9 Don't **g** about each other, my brothers and sisters,

GRUMBLED (4) [GRUMBLE]

Ex 17:2 So once more the people **g** and complained to
Jos 9:18 The people of Israel **g** against their leaders
Ps 106:25 Instead, they **g** in their tents / and refused to obey
Lk 19:7 gone to be the guest of a notorious sinner," they **g**.

GRUMBLERS (1) [GRUMBLE]

Jude 1:16 These people are **g** and complainers,

GUARANTEE (11) [GUARANTEED, GUARANTEEING, GUARANTEES]

Ge 17:2 by which I will **g** to make you into a mighty
43:9 I personally **g** his safety. If I don't bring him back
Jos 2:12 since I have helped you. Give me some **g** that
2:14 "We offer our own lives as a **g** for your safety,"
2:17 they left, the men told her, "We can **g** your safety
Ps 119:122 Please **g** a blessing for me. / Don't let those who
Pr 6:1 or **g** the debt of someone you hardly know—
22:26 or put up a **g** for someone else's loan.
Isa 9:7 commitment of the LORD Almighty will **g** this!
2Co 5:5 for this, and as a **g** he has given us his Holy Spirit.
Eph 1:14 The Spirit is God's **g** that he will give us

GUARANTEED (2) [GUARANTEE]

Ge 27:37 I have **g** him an abundance of grain and wine—
Ps 111:9 He has **g** his covenant with them forever.

GUARANTEEING (2) [GUARANTEE]

Pr 11:15 **G** a loan for a stranger is dangerous; it is better to
Eph 4:30 **g** that you will be saved on the day of redemption.

GUARANTEES (6) [GUARANTEE]

Pr 20:16 Be sure to get collateral from anyone who **g** the
20:16 Get a deposit if someone **g** the debt of a foreigner.
27:13 Be sure to get collateral from anyone who **g** the
27:13 Get a deposit if someone **g** the debt of an
Heb 7:22 it is Jesus who **g** the effectiveness of this better
8:6 for he is the one who **g** for us a better covenant

GUARD (111) [BODYGUARD, BODYGUARDS, GUARDED, GUARDIAN, GUARDIANS, GUARDING, GUARDROOM, GUARDS, SAFEGUARD]

Ge 37:36 of Egypt. Potiphar was captain of the palace **g**.
39:1 of Egypt. Potiphar was the captain of the palace **g**.
40:3 in the palace of Potiphar, the captain of the **g**.
41:10 imprisoned us in the palace of the captain of the **g**.
41:12 man who was a servant of the captain of the **g**.
Nu 1:53 The Levites are responsible to stand **g** around the
8:26 Levites by performing **g** duty at the Tabernacle,
10:25 They served as the rear **g** for all the tribal camps.
Jdg 7:19 after the changing of the **g**, when Gideon
1Sa 25:13 and two hundred remained behind to **g** their
30:24 who go to battle and those who **g** the equipment."
2Sa 20:7 and Joab set out after Sheba with an elite **g** from
1Ki 8:25 'If your descendants **g** their behavior as you have
14:27 and he entrusted them to the care of the palace **g**
20:39 He said, '**G** this man; if for any reason he gets
2Ki 6:10 of God, warning the people there to be on their **g**.
11:5 duty on the Sabbath are to **g** the royal palace itself.
11:6 Another third of you are to stand **g** at the Sur Gate.
11:6 the final third must stand **g** behind the palace **g**.
11:6 These three groups will all **g** the palace.
11:7 must stand **g** for the king at the LORD's Temple.
25:8 Nebuzaradan, captain of the **g**, an official of the
25:10 Then the captain of the **g** supervised the entire
25:11 Nebuzaradan, captain of the **g**, then took as exiles
25:12 But the captain of the **g** allowed some of the
25:15 Nebuzaradan, captain of the **g**, also took the
25:18 The captain of the **g** took with him as prisoners
1Ch 9:27 the house of God, since it was their duty to **g** it.
15:23 Berekiah and Elkanah were chosen to **g** the Ark.
15:24 Obed-edom and Jehiah were chosen to **g** the Ark.
26:13 They were assigned by families for **g** duty at the
26:16 up to the Temple. **G** duties were divided evenly.
2Ch 6:16 'If your descendants **g** their behavior and obey my
Ezr 8:29 **G** these treasures well until you present them,
Ne 3:25 from the king's house beside the court of the **g**.
4:13 I stationed the people to stand **g** by families,
4:16 worked while the other half stood **g** with spears,
4:21 to sunset. And half the men were always on **g**.
4:22 and their servants could go on **g** duty at night as
12:39 on to the Sheep Gate and stopped at the **G** Gate.
13:19 I also sent some of my own servants to **g** the gates
13:22 and to **g** the gates in order to preserve the holiness
Job 7:12 Am I a sea monster that you place a **g** on me?
21:32 to the grave, an honor **g** keeps watch at their tomb.
36:21 Be on **g**! Turn back from evil, for it was to prevent
40:24 No one can catch it off **g** or put a ring in its nose
Ps 16:5 my cup of blessing. / You **g** all that is mine.
17:8 **G** me as the apple of your eye. / Hide me in the
Pr 4:6 she will protect you. Love her, and she will **g** you.
4:13 **G** them, for they will lead you to a fulfilled life.
4:23 Above all else, **g** your heart, for it affects
7:2 **G** my teachings as your most precious possession.
Isa 42:6 I will **g** and support you, for I have given you to
Jer 32:2 in the courtyard of the **g** in the royal palace.
33:1 was still confined in the courtyard of the **g**,
37:21 he was imprisoned in the courtyard of the **g** in the
38:13 Jeremiah was returned to the courtyard of the **g**—
38:28 of the **g** until the day Jerusalem was captured.
39:4 and his royal **g** saw the Babylonians in the city
39:9 Then Nebuzaradan, the captain of the **g**, sent to
39:13 So Nebuzaradan, the captain of the **g**,
40:1 captain of the **g**, had released him at Ramah.
40:2 The captain of the **g** called for Jeremiah and said,
41:10 care in Mizpah by Nebuzaradan, captain of the **g**.
43:6 the captain of the **g**, had left with Gedaliah.
51:12 Reinforce the **g** and station the watchmen.
52:12 Nebuzaradan, captain of the **g**, an official of the
52:14 Then the captain of the **g** supervised the entire
52:15 Nebuzaradan, captain of the **g**, then took as exiles
52:19 Nebuzaradan, captain of the **g**, also took the small
52:24 The captain of the **g** took with him as prisoners
52:30 his captain of the **g**, who took 745 more—
Eze 40:7 There were **g** alcoves on each side built into the
40:10 There were three **g** alcoves on each side of the
40:12 In front of each of the **g** alcoves was a 21-inch
40:13 between the back walls of facing **g** alcoves;
40:16 narrowed inward through the walls of the **g** alcoves
40:21 too, there were three **g** alcoves on each side,
40:21 wide between the back walls of facing **g** alcoves.
40:25 wide between the back walls of facing **g** alcoves.
40:29 Its **g** alcoves, dividing walls, and foyer were the
40:33 Its **g** alcoves, dividing walls, and foyer were the
40:36 The **g** alcoves, dividing walls, and foyer of this
Da 2:14 When Arioch, the commander of the king's **g**,
8:25 defeating many by catching them off **g**.
12:1 the archangel who stands **g** over your nation,
Zec 9:8 I will **g** my Temple and protect it from invading
Mal 2:7 The priests' lips should **g** knowledge, and people
2:15 So **g** yourself; remain loyal to the wife of your
2:16 "So **g** yourself; always remain loyal to your
3:11 for I will **g** them from insects and disease.
Mt 27:36 Then they sat around and kept **g** as he hung there.
Mk 14:44 of greeting. Then you can take him away under **g**."
Lk 4:10 'He orders his angels to protect and **g** you.
22:4 and captains of the Temple **g** to discuss the best
22:52 to the leading priests and captains of the Temple **g**
Ac 4:1 the leading priests, the captain of the Temple **g**,
5:24 When the captain of the Temple **g** and the leading
12:4 placing him under the **g** of four squads of four
12:6 with others standing **g** at the prison gate.
12:10 They passed the first and second **g** posts and came
1Co 16:13 Be on **g**. Stand true to what you believe.
2Co 8:20 By traveling together we will **g** against any
Php 1:13 including all the soldiers in the palace **g**,
4:7 His peace will **g** your hearts and minds as you live
1Th 5:6 So be on your **g**, not asleep like the others.
2Th 3:3 will make you strong and **g** you from the evil one.
1Ti 6:20 Timothy, **g** what God has entrusted to you.
2Ti 1:12 and I am sure that he is able to **g** what I have
1:14 carefully **g** what has been entrusted to you.

GUARDED (12) [GUARD]

Dt 32:10 he **g** them as his most precious possession.
33:9 and **g** your covenant. / They were more loyal to
1Sa 26:15 So why haven't you **g** your master the king when
1Ch 9:19 just as their ancestors had **g** the Tabernacle in the
2Ch 35:15 The gatekeepers **g** the gates and did not need to
Ne 4:9 But we prayed to our God and **g** the city day
11:19 and 172 of their associates, who **g** the gates.
Est 6:2 two of the eunuchs who **g** the door to the king's
Jn 17:12 I **g** them so that not one was lost, except the one
Ac 28:16 own private lodging, though he was **g** by a soldier.
Gal 3:23 of becoming right with God, we were **g** by the law.
Rev 21:12 and high, with twelve gates **g** by twelve angels.

GUARDIAN (6) [GUARD]

Eze 28:14 and anointed you as the mighty angelic **g**.
28:16 I expelled you, O mighty **g**, from your place
Ac 19:35 "Everyone knows that Ephesus is the official **g** of
Gal 3:24 The law was our **g** and teacher to lead us until
3:25 has come, we no longer need the law as our **g**.
1Pe 2:25 have turned to your Shepherd, the **G** of your souls.

GUARDIANS (3) [GUARD]

2Ki 10:1 of the people, and to the **g** of King Ahab's sons.
10:5 with the other leaders and the **g** of the king's sons,
Gal 4:2 They have to obey their **g** until they reach

GUARDING (8) [GUARD]

Ge 3:24 flashed back and forth, **g** the way to the tree of life.
2Ki 12:9 The priests **g** the entrance put all of the people's
1Ch 9:19 were responsible for **g** the entrance to the
9:21 responsible for **g** the entrance to the Tabernacle.
9:23 were responsible for **g** the entrance to the house of

Ps 127: 1 protects a city, / g it with sentries will do no good.
Mt 28:11 some of the men who had been g the tomb went to
Lk 2: 8 fields outside the village, g their flocks of sheep.

GUARDROOM (2) [GUARD]

1Ki 14:28 carry them along and then return them to the g.
2Ch 12:11 carry them along and then return them to the g.

GUARDS (47) [GUARD]

Jos 6: 9 Armed g marched both in front of the priests
6:13 Armed g marched both in front of the priests with
10:18 and place g at the entrance to keep the kings inside.
1Ki 14:28 the g would carry them along and then return them
2Ki 10:25 he commanded his g and officers, "Go in and kill
10:25 and the g and officers dragged their bodies outside.
11: 4 and the g to come to the Temple of the LORD.
11:11 The g stationed themselves around the king,
11:13 When Athaliah heard all the noise made by the g
11:18 Jehoiada the priest stationed g at the Temple of the
11:19 the commanders, the Carite mercenaries, the g,
11:19 They went through the gate of the g and into the
2Ch 12:11 the g would carry them along and then return them
23:10 He stationed the g around the king, with their
Ne 4:13 So I placed armed g behind the lowest parts of the
4:23 nor my servants, nor the g who were with me—
7: 3 Appoint the residents of Jerusalem to act as g,
Est 2:21 who were g at the door of the king's private
Job 3:18 are at ease in death, with no g to curse them.
Ps 34: 7 For the angel of the LORD g all who fear him,
Pr 2: 8 He g the paths of justice and protects those who
Eze 12:14 I will scatter his servants and g to the four winds
22:30 rebuild the wall of righteousness that g the land.
44:11 They may still be Temple g and gatemen, and they
Mt 26:58 He went in, sat with the g, and waited to see what
27:65 "Take g and secure it the best you can."
27:66 So they sealed the tomb and posted g to protect it.
28: 4 The g shook with fear when they saw him,
28:15 So the g accepted the bribe and said what they
Mk 14:54 For a while he sat with the g, warming himself by
14:65 And even the g were hitting him as they led him
Lk 11:21 who is completely armed, g his palace, it is safe—
22:55 The g lit a fire in the courtyard and sat around it,
22:63 Now the g in charge of Jesus began mocking
Jn 7:32 and the leading priests sent Temple g to arrest
7:45 The Temple g who had been sent to arrest him
7:46 heard anyone talk like this!" the g responded.
18: 3 Roman soldiers and Temple g to accompany him.
18:12 and the Temple g arrested Jesus and tied him up.
18:18 The g and the household servants were standing
18:22 One of the Temple g standing there struck Jesus on
19: 6 the leading priests and Temple g began shouting,
Ac 5:22 But when the Temple g went to the jail, the men
5:23 "The jail was locked, with the g standing outside,
5:26 The captain went with his Temple g and arrested
12:19 Herod interrogated the g and sentenced them to
2Co 11:32 the governor under King Aretas kept g at the city

GUDGODAH (1)

Dt 10: 7 Then they journeyed to G, and from there to

GUERRILLA (3)

Jer 40: 7 The leaders of the Judean g bands in the
40:13 and the other g leaders came to Gedaliah at
41:11 and the rest of the g leaders heard what Ishmael

GUESS (1)

1Sa 21: 4 which I g you can have if your young men have

GUEST (18) [GUESTS]

Jdg 19:23 For this man is my g, and such a thing would be
1Sa 9:23 the piece that had been set aside for the g of honor.
21:15 Why should I let someone like this be my g?"
2Sa 12: 4 One day a g arrived at the home of the rich man.
12: 4 man's lamb and killed it and served it to his g."
15:19 for you are a g in Israel, a foreigner in exile.
Ps 23: 5 You welcome me as a g, / anointing my head with
39:12 Don't ignore my tears. / For I am your g—
Mk 6:10 each village, be a g in only one home," he said.
14:14 Where is the g room where I can eat the Passover
Lk 5:29 a banquet in his home with Jesus as the g of honor.
9: 4 you enter each village, be a g in only one home.
19: 5 For I must be a g in your home today."
19: 7 "He has gone to be the g of a notorious sinner,"
22:11 Where is the g room where I can eat the Passover
Jn 2: 1 The next day Jesus' mother was a g at a wedding
Ro 16:23 I am his g, and the church meets here in his home.
Phm 1:22 Please keep a g room ready for me, for I am

GUESTCHAMBER [KJV] See GUEST (ROOM)

GUESTS (30) [GUEST]

Ge 19: 2 home to wash your feet, and be my g for the night.
24:25 food for the camels, and we have a room for g."
Ex 3:22 their Egyptian neighbors and their neighbors' g.
1Sa 9:13 The g won't start until he arrives to bless the
9:22 the table, honoring them above the thirty special g.
2Sa 15:11 two hundred men from Jerusalem with him as g,
1Ki 1:41 Adonijah and his g heard the celebrating
1:49 Then all of Adonijah's g jumped up in panic from
2: 7 Make them permanent g of the king, for they took
Pr 9:18 But the men don't realize that her former g are
Mt 9:10 invited Jesus and his disciples to be his dinner g,
9:15 "Should the wedding g mourn while celebrating
14: 9 he didn't want to back down in front of his g,
22: 3 Many g were invited, and when the banquet was
22: 5 But the g he had invited ignored them and went
22: 8 and the g I invited aren't worthy of the honor.
22:10 bad alike, and the banquet hall was filled with g.
22:11 But when the king came in to meet the g,
Mk 2:15 invited Jesus and his disciples to be his dinner g,
2:19 "Do wedding g fast while celebrating with the
6:26 was embarrassed to break his oath in front of his g.
Lk 5:29 Levi's fellow tax collectors and other g were there.
5:34 "Do wedding g fast while celebrating with the
14:10 you will be honored in front of all the other g.
14:17 he sent his servant around to notify the g that it
Ac 10:23 So Peter invited the men to be his g for the night.
16:15 of her household, and she asked us to be her g.
Ro 12:13 And get into the habit of inviting g home for
1Ti 3: 2 He must enjoy having g in his home and must be
Tit 1: 8 He must enjoy having g in his home and must love

GUIDANCE (11) [GUIDE]

Ex 18:15 "Well, the people come to me to seek God's g.
1Ch 10:14 instead of asking the LORD for g. So the LORD
2Ch 20: 3 alarmed by this news and sought the LORD for g.
Ps 119:19 here on earth; / I need the g of your commands.
Pr 1: 5 And let those who understand receive g
4: 2 for I am giving you good g. Don't turn away from
24: 6 So don't go to war without wise g; victory depends
29:18 When people do not accept divine g, they run wild.
Ecc 12:11 The collected sayings of the wise are like g from a
Zep 1: 6 They no longer ask for the LORD's g or seek my
Mal 2: 8 Your 'g' has caused many to stumble into sin.

GUIDE (26) [GUIDANCE, GUIDED, GUIDEPOSTS, GUIDES, GUIDING]

Ge 24:42 mission a success, please g me in a special way.
33:15 "at least let me leave some of my men to g
Ex 15:13 have ransomed. / You will g them in your strength
Nu 10:32 be our g and we will share with you all the good
Jos 3: 4 never traveled this way before, they will g you.
1Sa 30:15 me back to my master, then I will g you to them."
Job 38:32 or g the constellation of the Bear with her cubs
Ps 32: 8 "I will g you along the best pathway for your life.
43: 3 Send out your light and your truth; / let them g me.
48:14 and ever, / and he will be our g until we die.
119:98 for your commands are my constant g.
119:133 G my steps by your word, / so I will not be
139:10 even there your hand will g me, / and your strength
Pr 3:17 She will g you down delightful paths; all her ways
26: 3 G a horse with a whip, a donkey with a bridle,
Ecc 7:23 All along I have tried my best to let wisdom g my
Isa 42: 6 And you will be a light to g all nations to me.
45:13 my righteous purpose, and I will g all his actions.
58:11 The LORD will g you continually, watering your
Jer 3: 4 you have been my g since the days of my youth.
3:15 who will g you with knowledge and understanding.
Mic 2:13 will lead you; the LORD himself will g you."
Zec 10: 2 without a shepherd to protect and g them.
Lk 1:79 of death, / and to g us to the path of peace."
Jn 16:13 Spirit of truth comes, he will g you into all truth.
Ro 2:19 You are convinced that you are a g for the blind

GUIDED (10) [GUIDE]

Ex 13:21 The LORD g them by a pillar of cloud during the
Dt 32:12 The LORD alone g them; / they lived without any
Job 10:10 You g my conception and formed me in the womb.
Ps 78:26 and g the south wind by his mighty power.
Pr 4:12 If you live a life g by wisdom, you won't limp
11: 3 Good people are g by their honesty;
Hos 12:13 of Egypt by a prophet, who g and protected them.
Ac 1:16 who g the Temple police to arrest Jesus.
1Co 10: 1 God g all of them by sending a cloud that moved
Jas 2: 4 doesn't this discrimination show that you are g by

GUIDEPOSTS (1) [GUIDE]

Jer 31:21 "Set up road signs; put up g. Mark well the path

GUIDES (7) [GUIDE]

Ps 16: 7 I will bless the LORD who g me; / even at night
23: 3 renews my strength. / He g me along right paths,
Mt 15:14 They are blind g leading the blind, and if one blind
person g another, they will both
23:16 "Blind g! How terrible it will be for you! For you
23:24 Blind g! You strain your water so you won't
Lk 16:16 and the messages of the prophets were your g.

GUIDING (8) [GUIDE]

Ex 16:10 Within the g cloud, they could see the awesome
Dt 1:33 g you by a pillar of fire at night and a pillar of
2Sa 6: 3 and Ahio, Abinadab's sons, were g the cart
1Ch 13: 7 Abinadab on a new cart, with Uzzah and Ahio g it.
Ps 73:24 You will keep on g me with your counsel,
78:52 of sheep, / g them safely through the wilderness.
Isa 42:16 a new path, / g them along an unfamiliar way.
Mt 2: 9 the star appeared to them, g them to Bethlehem.

GUILE [KJV] See also DECEIT, FRAUD, TREACHERY, TRICKERY

GUILT (94) [GUILTY]

Ex 28:38 thus bearing the g connected with any errors
28:43 Thus they will not incur g and die. This law is
Lev 4: 3 priest sins, bringing g upon the entire community,
5: 5 "When any of the people become aware of their g
5:15 LORD a ram from the flock as their g offering.
5:16 for them with the ram sacrificed as a g offering,
5:17 When they become aware of their g,
5:18 to the priest a ram from the flock as a g offering.
5:19 This is a g offering, for they have been guilty of an
6: 5 When they realize their g, they must restore the
6: 6 They must then bring a g offering to the priest,
6:17 Like the sin offering and the g offering, it is most
7: 1 "These are the instructions for the g offering,
7: 2 The animal sacrificed as a g offering must be
7: 5 to the LORD made by fire. It is a g offering.
7: 7 "For both the sin offering and the g offering,
7:37 the grain offering, the sin offering, the g offering,
10:17 It was given to you for removing the g of the
14:12 and offer them as a g offering by lifting them up
14:13 the g offering will be given to the priest.
14:14 then take some of the blood from the g offering
14:17 in addition to the blood of the g offering.
14:21 lambs must bring one male lamb for a g offering,
14:21 The g offering will be presented by lifting it up,
14:24 The priest will take the lamb for the g offering,
14:25 Then the priest will slaughter the lamb for the g
14:28 in addition to the blood of the g offering.
19:21 must bring a ram as a g offering and present it to
19:22 LORD with the sacrificial ram of the g offering,
20:17 his sister, he will suffer the consequences of his g.
22:16 The negligent priest would bring g upon the people
24:15 God will suffer the consequences of their g
Nu 5:24 the curse and cause bitter suffering in cases of g.
5:31 The husband will be innocent of any g in this
6:11 he will make atonement for the g they incurred
6:12 bring a one-year-old male lamb for a g offering.
9:13 They will suffer the consequences of their g.
15:31 cut off and suffer the consequences of their g."
18: 9 the grain offerings, sin offerings, and g offerings—
30:15 he will suffer the consequences of her g."
Dt 19:13 Purge the g of murder from Israel so all may go
21: 8 Do not charge your people Israel with the g of
21: 8 Then they will be absolved of the g of this person's
21: 9 you will cleanse the g of murder from your
22: 8 That way you will not bring the g of bloodshed on
24: 4 You must not bring g upon the land the LORD
1Sa 6: 3 "Send a g offering so the plague will stop. Then,
6: 4 "What sort of g offering should we send?"
6:17 g offering to the LORD were gifts from the rulers
1Ki 2:31 This will remove the g of his senseless murders
2Ki 12:16 the money that was contributed for g offerings
2Ch 28:13 "We cannot afford to add to our sins and g.
28:13 Our g is already great, and the LORD's fierce
Ezr 9: 6 our heads, and our g has reached to the heavens.
9:13 because of our wickedness and our great g.
9:15 We stand before you in our g as nothing but an
10:19 and they each acknowledged their g by offering a
ram as a g offering.
Ne 4: 5 Do not ignore their g. Do not blot out their sins,
Job 6:29 Stop assuming my g, for I am righteous. Don't be
7:21 Why not just pardon my sin and take away my g?
10: 6 that you are in a hurry to probe for my g, to search
20:27 The heavens will reveal his g, and the earth will
22: 5 because of your wickedness! Your g has no limit!
31:33 as people normally do, hiding my g in a closet?
Ps 19:13 Then I will be free of g / and innocent of great sin.
32: 5 you forgave me! All my g is gone. / *Interlude*
38: 4 My g overwhelms me— / it is a burden too heavy
51: 2 Wash me clean from my g. / Purify me from my
51: 9 looking at my sins. / Remove the stain of my g.
85: 2 You have forgiven the g of your people— / yes,
Pr 14: 9 Fools make fun of g, but the godly acknowledge it
Isa 1: 4 They are loaded down with a burden of g. They are
3: 9 their faces gives them away and displays their g.
6: 7 Now your g is removed, and your sins are
53: 6 Yet the LORD laid on him the g and sins of us
Jer 2:22 You are stained with g that cannot be washed
3:13 Only acknowledge your g. Admit that you rebelled
30:14 For your sins are many, and your g is great.
30:15 because your sins are many and your g is great.
La 4: 6 The g of my people is greater than that of Sodom,
Eze 21:24 Again and again your g cries out against you,
40:39 the burnt offerings, sin offerings, and g offerings.
42:13 and g offerings because these rooms are holy.
44:29 the sin offerings, and the g offerings.
46:20 the priests will cook the meat from the g offerings
Da 9:24 to bring an end to sin, to atone for g, to bring in
Hos 4:15 Israel is a prostitute, may Judah avoid such g.
5: 5 against her; she will stumble under her load of g.
5:15 I will return to my place until they admit their g
13:16 of Samaria must bear the consequences of their g
Ac 13:39 Everyone who believes in him is freed from all g
2Ti 3: 6 women who are burdened with the g of sin
Heb 10: 2 and their feelings of g would have disappeared.

GUILTY (119) [GUILT]

Ge 18:23 "Will you destroy both innocent and g alike?
18:25 do such a thing, destroying the innocent with the g.
18:25 be treating the innocent and the g exactly the same!
20: 9 making me and my kingdom g of this great sin?
26:10 and you would have made us g of great sin."
37:26 That would just give us a g conscience.
Ex 22: 2 the person who killed the thief is not g.
22: 3 the one who killed the thief is g of murder.
22: 9 and the person whom God declares g must pay
23: 7 I will not allow anyone g of this to go free.
Lev 4:13 the community's notice, all the people will be g.
4:22 he will be g even if he sinned unintentionally.

4:27 they will be g even if they sinned unintentionally.
4:31 Those who are g must remove all the goat's fat,
4:35 Those who are g must remove all the sheep's fat,
5: 2 will be considered ceremonially unclean and g,
5: 3 they will be considered g as soon as they become
5: 4 they will be considered g even if they were not
5:10 the priest will make atonement for those who are g,
5:13 the priest will make atonement for those who are g,
5:18 the priest will make atonement for those who are g,
5:19 for they have been g of an offense against the
6: 4 If they have sinned in any of these ways and are g,
17: 4 that person will be g of a capital offense.
19:17 so you will not be held g for their crimes.
20: 4 to Molech and refuse to execute the g parents,
20: 9 be put to death. They are g of a capital offense.
20:11 must die, for they are g of a capital offense.
20:12 contrary to nature and are g of a capital offense.
20:13 a detestable act and are g of a capital offense.
20:16 Both must die, for they are g of a capital offense.
20:19 Both parties are g of a capital offense.
20:20 and woman involved are g of a capital offense
20:21 his brother, and the g couple will remain childless.
20:27 death by stoning. They are g of a capital offense."
Nu 5: 6 by doing wrong to another person, they are g.
5:15 an offering of inquiry to find out if she is g.
5:18 bitter water that brings a curse to those who are g.
15:27 the g person must bring a one-year-old female goat
15:28 The priest will make atonement for the g person
18:22 they come too near, they will be judged g and die.
18:32 You will not be considered g for accepting the
35:31 for the life of someone judged g of murder
Dt 13:10 Stone the g ones to death because they have tried
15: 9 out to the LORD, you will be considered g of sin.
17: 8 whether someone is g of murder or only of
22:24 The woman is g because she did not scream for
23:21 all your vows. If you don't, you will be g of sin.
Jos 7:14 will point out the tribe to which the g man belongs.
7:14 its clans, and the LORD will point out the g clan.
7:14 and the LORD will point out the g family.
7:14 each member of the g family must come one by
Jdg 21:22 And you are not g of breaking the vow since you
1Sa 2:25 another person, God can mediate for the g party.
14:41 please show us who is g and who is innocent.
14:41 Are Jonathan and I g, or is the sin among the
14:41 And Jonathan and Saul were chosen as the g ones,
14:42 And Jonathan was shown to be the g one.
24:15 judge which of us is right and punish the g one.
2Sa 3:29 Joab and his family are the g ones. May his family
11:11 I swear that I will never be g of acting like that."
14:32 if he finds me g of anything, then let him execute
21: 1 and his family are g of murdering the Gibeonites."
1Ki 2:33 and his descendants be forever g of these murders,
8:32 Punish the g party and acquit the one who is
21:26 He was especially g because he worshiped idols
2Ch 6:23 Punish the g party, and acquit the one who is
19:10 and them. Do this and you will not be g.
Ezr 10:23 These are the Levites who were g: Jozabad,
10:24 This is the singer who was g: Eliashib. These are the gatekeepers who were g:
10:25 These are the other people of Israel who were g:
Job 9:20 my own mouth would pronounce me g.
9:29 Whatever happens, I will be found g. So what's the
10: 7 Although you know I am not g, no one can rescue
10:15 If I am g, too bad for me. And even if I'm
31: 7 my eyes have seen, or if I am g of any other sin,
Ps 5:10 O God, declare them g. / Let them be caught in
7: 3 if I have done wrong / or am g of injustice,
35:24 Declare me "not g," O LORD my God, for you
68:21 crushing the skulls of those who love their g ways.
79: 8 Oh, do not hold us g for our former sins! / Let your
109: 7 is called for judgment, / let him be pronounced g.
Pr 17:15 The LORD despises those who acquit the g
18: 5 It is wrong for a judge to favor the g or condemn
21: 8 The g walk a crooked path; the innocent travel a
24:25 blessings are showered on those who convict the g.
Isa 29:21 Those who make the innocent g by their false
46: 8 "Do not forget this, you g ones.
50: 9 LORD is on my side! Who will declare me g?
Jer 2: 3 All who harmed my people were considered g,
3:11 "Even faithless Israel is less g than treacherous
Eze 22: 4 you are g of both murder and idolatry. Your day of
Hos 10: 2 people are fickle; they are g and must be punished.
Na 1: 3 is great, and he never lets the g go unpunished.
Hab 1:11 But they are deeply g, for their own strength is
Mt 12: 7 aren't g if you knew the meaning of this Scripture:
23:35 you will become g of murdering all the godly
26:66 "G!" they shouted. "He must die!"
Jn 9:41 you were blind, you wouldn't be g," Jesus replied.
9:41 "But you remain g because you claim you can see.
15:22 They would not be g if I had not come and spoken
15:24 no one else could do, they would not be counted g.
18:38 and told them, "He is not g of any crime.
19: 4 but understand clearly that I find him not g."
19: 6 crucify him," Pilate said. "I find him not g."
Ac 17: 7 They are all g of treason against Caesar, for they
25: 8 Paul denied the charges. "I am not g," he said.
25:10 be tried right here. You know very well I am not g.
Ro 3:24 God in his gracious kindness declares us not g.
5:16 by God, even though we are g of many sins.
7:11 the good law and used it to make me g of death.
1Co 11:27 that person is g of sinning against the body
Gal 2:18 I make myself g if I rebuild the old system I
3:19 It was given to show people how g they are.
1Ti 5:12 Then they would be g of breaking their previous
Tit 3: 7 He declared us not g because of his great kindness.
Jas 2: 9 a sin, for you are g of breaking that law.
2:10 g as the person who has broken all of God's laws.

GULP (1) [GULPS]

Job 39:30 Its nestlings g down blood, for it feeds on the

GULPS (1) [GULP]

Pr 19:28 of justice; the mouth of the wicked g down evil.

GUNI (4) [GUNITE]

Ge 46:24 of Naphtali were Jahzeel, G, Jezer, and Shillem.
Nu 26:48 The Gunite clan, named after its ancestor G.
1Ch 5:15 Ahi son of Abdiel, son of G, was the leader of their
7:13 of Naphtali were Jahzeel, G, Jezer, and Shillem.

GUNITE (1) [GUNI]

Nu 26:48 The G clan, named after its ancestor Guni.

GUR (2)

2Ki 9:27 they shot Ahaziah in his chariot at the Ascent of G,
2Ch 26: 7 but also in his battles with the Arabs of G and in

GUSH (7) [GUSHED, GUSHES, GUSHING]

Nu 24: 7 Water will g out in buckets; / their offspring are
Dt 8: 7 with springs that g forth in the valleys and hills.
Jdg 15:19 So God caused water to g out of a hollow in the
Ps 74:15 You caused the springs and streams to g forth,
104:10 so streams g down from the mountains.
119:136 Rivers of tears g from my eyes / because people
Isa 35: 6 Springs will g forth in the wilderness, and streams

GUSHED (7) [GUSH]

Ex 17: 6 was told; and as the leaders looked on, water g out.
Nu 20:11 the rock twice with the staff, and water g out.
2Sa 20:10 with it so that his insides g out onto the ground.
1Ki 18:28 with knives and swords until the blood g out.
Ps 105:41 He opened up a rock, and water g out / to form a
Isa 48:21 divided the rock, and water g out for them to drink.
Rev 12:16 and swallowing the river that g out from the mouth

GUSHES (1) [GUSH]

Ps 78:20 Yes, he can strike a rock so water g out, / but he

GUSHING (4) [GUSH]

Ge 8: 2 The underground water sources ceased their g,
26:19 also dug in the Gerar Valley and found a g spring.
Ps 78:15 to give them plenty of water, as from a g spring.
Eze 32: 6 I will drench the earth with your g blood all the

GUTTER (6)

2Sa 22:43 dust of the earth; / I swept them into the g like dirt.
Ps 18:42 by the wind. / I swept them into the g like dirt.
La 1: 9 Now she lies in the g with no one to lift her out.
Eze 43:13 There is a g all around the altar 21 inches wide
43:14 From the g the altar rises 3-1/2 feet to a ledge that
43:17 with a 21-inch g and a 10-1/2-inch curb all around

GUZZLE (1)

Pr 31: 4 And it is not for kings, O Lemuel, to g wine.

H

HA (2) [AHA]

Eze 26: 2 has rejoiced over the fall of Jerusalem, saying, 'H!
Mk 15:29 "H! Look at you now!" they yelled at him.

HAAHASHTARI (1)

1Ch 4: 6 gave birth to Ahuzzam, Hepher, Temeni, and H.

HABAIAH [KJV] See also HOBAIAH

HABAKKUK (2)

Hab 1: 1 This is the message that the prophet H received
3: 1 This prayer was sung by the prophet H:

HABAZZINIAH (1)

Jer 35: 3 and grandson of H and all his brothers and sons—

HABERGEONS [KJV] See COATS OF MAIL

HABIT (2)

Zec 8:17 And stop this h of swearing to things that are false.
Ro 12:13 And get into the h of inviting guests home for

HABITATION [KJV] See also ANCESTORS, CAMP, DWELLING, FOLD, LIVE, PLACE, REFUGE, STRONGHOLD, THRONE, TOWN

HABOR (3)

2Ki 17: 6 along the banks of the H River in Gozan,
18:11 in Halah, along the banks of the H River in Gozan,
1Ch 5:26 H, Hara, and the Gozan River, where they remain

HACALIAH (2)

Ne 1: 1 These are the memoirs of Nehemiah son of H.
10: 1 Nehemiah the governor, the son of H.

HACMONITE (3)

2Sa 23: 8 The first was Jashobeam the H, who was
1Ch 11:11 The first was Jashobeam the H, who was
27:32 Jehiel the H was responsible to teach the king's

HAD (508 of 2647) [HAVE] See also Index of Articles, Etc.

Ge 4:22 Tubal-cain h a sister named Naamah.
4:26 When Seth grew up, he h a son and named him
5: 4 Adam lived another 800 years, and he h other sons
5: 7 Seth lived another 807 years, and he h other sons
5:10 Enosh lived another 815 years, and he h other sons
5:13 Kenan lived another 840 years, and he h other
5:16 Mahalalel lived 830 years, and he h other sons
5:19 Jared lived another 800 years, and he h other sons
5:22 in close fellowship with God, and he h other sons
5:26 Methuselah lived another 782 years, and he h other
5:30 Lamech lived 595 years, and he h other sons
5:32 By the time Noah was 500 years old, he h three
6: 4 for whenever the sons of God h intercourse with
6:10 Noah h three sons: Shem, Ham, and Japheth.
10:25 Eber h two sons. The first was named Peleg—
11:11 Shem lived another 500 years and h other sons
11:13 Arphaxad lived another 403 years and h other sons
11:15 Shelah lived another 403 years and h other sons
11:17 Eber lived another 430 years and h other sons
11:19 Peleg lived another 209 years and h other sons
11:21 Reu lived another 207 years and h other sons
11:23 Serug lived another 200 years and h other sons
11:25 Nahor lived another 119 years and h other sons
11:27 Nahor, and Haran; and Haran h a son named Lot.
11:29 brother Haran. (Milcah h a sister named Iscah.)
16: 1 But Sarai, Abram's wife, h no children. So Sarai
22:24 Nahor h four other children from his concubine
24:19 for your camels, too, until they have h enough!"
24:29 Now Rebekah h a brother named Laban.
24:54 Then they h supper, and the servant and the men
26:26 One day Isaac h visitors from Gerar.
28: 9 daughters, in addition to the wives he already h.
29:16 Now Laban h two daughters: Leah, who was
29:17 Leah h pretty eyes, but Rachel was beautiful in
29:32 So Leah became pregnant and h a son. She named
29:33 She soon became pregnant again and h another son
29:34 Again she became pregnant and h a son.
29:35 Once again she became pregnant and h a son.
30: 8 "I have h an intense struggle with my sister,
30:19 Then she became pregnant again and h a sixth son.
30:30 You h little indeed before I came, and your wealth
31:10 During the mating season, I h a dream and saw
36: 4 Esau and Adah h a son named Eliphaz. Esau and Basemath h a son named Reuel.
36: 5 Esau and Oholibamah h sons named Jeush, Jalam,
36:12 Eliphaz h another son named Amalek, born to
36:14 Esau also h sons through Oholibamah,
37: 5 One night Joseph h a dream and promptly reported
37: 9 Then Joseph h another dream and told his brothers
38: 3 She became pregnant and h a son, and Judah
38: 4 Then Judah's wife h another son, and she named
38: 5 when she h a third son, she named him Shelah.
38: 9 So whenever he h intercourse with Tamar,
38:21 "We've never h a prostitute here," they replied.
38:27 Tamar's delivery arrived, and she h twin sons.
39:13 she saw that she h his shirt and that he had fled,
39:17 "That Hebrew slave you've h around here tried to
39:23 The chief jailer h no more worries after that,
40: 5 One night the cup-bearer and the baker each h a dream, and each dream h its own meaning.
40: 8 And they replied, "We both h dreams last night,
40:10 It h three branches that began to bud and blossom,
40:16 saw that the first dream h such a good meaning,
41: 5 Soon he fell asleep again and h a second dream.
41:11 One night the chief baker and I each h a dream, and each dream h a meaning.
41:15 "I h a dream last night," Pharaoh told him,
41:22 "A little later I h another dream. This time there
42: 9 he remembered the dreams he had h many years
42:24 chose Simeon from among them and h him tied up
43: 6 did you ever tell him you h another brother?"
43: 7 and he asked us if we h another brother so we told
44:16 we and our brother who h your cup in his sack."
44:19 asked us, my lord, if we h a father or a brother.
44:27 said to us, 'You know that my wife h two sons,
Ex 1: 5 In all, Jacob h seventy direct descendants.
1: 7 But their descendants h many children and
2:16 the priest of Midian h seven daughters who came
2:22 Later they h a baby boy, and Moses named him
9:21 those who h no respect for the word of the LORD
12:39 out of Egypt and h no time to wait for bread to rise.
16: 3 At least there we h plenty to eat. But now you
16:18 By gathering two quarts for each person, everyone h just enough. Those who gathered a lot h nothing left over, and those who gathered only a little h enough. Each family h just what it needed.
16:20 then it was full of maggots and h a terrible smell.
17:11 staff with his hands, the Israelites h the advantage.

21: 4 and they **h** sons or daughters, then the man will be
33: 18 Moses **h** one more request. "Please let me see your
35: 24 And those who **h** acacia wood brought it.
37: 2 and it **h** a molding of gold all the way around.
37: 18 The lampstand **h** six branches, three going out
38: 17 Each post **h** a bronze base, and all the hooks and
Lev 13: 18 "If anyone has **h** a boil on the skin that has started
15: 33 who has **h** a bodily discharge of any kind; and for
dealing with a man who has **h** intercourse with a
20: 17 Since the man has **h** intercourse with his sister,
21: 3 who was dependent because she **h** no husband.
21: 10 "The high priest, who has **h** the anointing oil
23: 43 their ancestors **h** to live in shelters when I rescued
24: 10 a man who **h** an Israelite mother and an Egyptian
Nu 3: 4 Since they **h** no sons, this left only Eleazar and
3: 17 Levi **h** three sons, who were named Gershon,
3: 38 Aaron and his sons, who **h** the final responsibility
11: 5 And we **h** all the cucumbers, melons, leeks, onions,
11: 18 "If only we **h** meat to eat! Surely we were better
22: 29 Balaam shouted. "If I **h** a sword with me, I would
26: 33 Hepher's son, Zelophehad, **h** no sons, but his
26: 46 Asher also **h** a daughter named Serah.
27: 4 of our father disappear just because he **h** no sons?
Dt 2: 36 No town **h** walls too strong for us.
25: 18 who were lagging behind. They **h** no fear of God.
29: 6 You **h** no bread or wine or other strong drink,
Jos 5: 4 Joshua **h** to circumcise them because all the men
7: 24 everything he **h**, and they brought them to the
8: 20 was filling the sky, and they **h** nowhere to go.
11: 23 the tribes. So the land finally **h** rest from war.
14: 15 of the Anakites.) / And the land **h** rest from war.
17: 3 who was a descendant of Manasseh, Makir, and
Gilead, **h** no sons. Instead, he **h** five daughters.
19: 47 But the tribe of Dan **h** trouble taking possession of
21: 42 of these towns **h** pasturelands surrounding it.
Jdg 1: 7 Adoni-bezek said, "I once **h** seventy kings with
1: 19 the plains because the people there **h** iron chariots.
3: 2 of Israelites who **h** no experience in battle.
4: 3 Sisera, who **h** nine hundred iron chariots,
7: 13 The man said, "I **h** this dream, and in my dream a
8: 18 they replied. "They all **h** the look of a king's son."
8: 30 He **h** seventy sons, for he **h** many wives.
8: 31 He also **h** a concubine in Shechem, who bore him
11: 2 Gilead's wife also **h** several sons, and when these
11: 3 Soon he **h** a large band of rebels following him.
12: 9 and he **h** thirty sons and thirty daughters.
12: 14 He **h** forty sons and thirty grandsons, who rode on
13: 2 unable to become pregnant, and they **h** no children.
17: 6 In those days Israel **h** no king, so the people did
18: 1 Now in those days Israel **h** no king. And the tribe
18: 7 a great distance from Sidon and **h** no allies nearby.
18: 28 a great distance from Sidon and **h** no allies nearby.
19: 1 Now in those days Israel **h** no king. There was a
19: 6 down together and **h** something to eat and drink.
19: 8 this afternoon." So they **h** another day of feasting.
19: 21 they washed their feet, they **h** supper together.
20: 17 Israel **h** 400,000 warriors armed with swords,
21: 25 In those days Israel **h** no king, so the people did
1Sa 1: 2 Elkanah **h** two wives, Hannah and Peninnah.
Peninnah **h** children, while Hannah did not.
2: 12 were scoundrels who **h** no respect for the LORD
3: 7 he had never **h** a message from the LORD before.
4: 7 We have never **h** to face anything like this before!
6: 7 and find two cows that have just **h** calves.
13: 20 they **h** to take them to a Philistine blacksmith.
13: 22 So none of the people of Israel **h** a sword or spear,
14: 4 To reach the Philistine outpost, Jonathan **h** to go
14: 49 He also **h** two daughters: Merab, who was older,
17: 12 an old man at that time, and he **h** eight sons in all.
17: 50 only a stone and sling. And since he **h** no sword,
18: 10 this happened. But Saul, who **h** a spear in his hand,
18: 25 Saul **h** in mind was that David would be killed in
19: 17 "I **h** to," Michal replied. "He threatened to kill me
20: 9 "You know that if I **h** the slightest notion my
24: 19 his enemy get away when he **h** him in his power?
25: 2 He **h** three thousand sheep and a thousand goats,
25: 37 As a result he **h** a stroke, and he lay on his bed
30: 12 because he hadn't **h** anything to eat or drink for
2Sa 4: 4 (Saul's son Jonathan **h** a son named Mephibosheth
5: 13 concubines, and he **h** many sons and daughters.
9: 10 Ziba, who **h** fifteen sons and twenty servants,
9: 12 Mephibosheth **h** a young son named Mica.
13: 1 David's son Absalom **h** a beautiful sister named
13: 3 Now Amnon **h** a very crafty friend—his cousin
14: 2 woman from Tekoa who **h** a reputation for great
14: 6 "My two sons **h** a fight out in the field. And since
14: 27 He **h** three sons and one daughter. His daughter's
1Ki 1: 4 But the king **h** no sexual relations with her.
1: 44 They **h** him ride on the king's own mule,
3: 12 such as no one else has ever **h** or ever will have!
3: 18 Three days later, she also **h** a baby. We were alone;
4: 7 Solomon also **h** twelve district governors who
4: 25 each family **h** its own home and garden.
4: 26 Solomon **h** four thousand stalls for his chariot
7: 3 It **h** a cedar roof supported by forty-five rafters
7: 20 Each capital on the two pillars **h** two hundred
7: 30 Each of these carts **h** four bronze wheels and
7: 31 The top of each cart **h** a circular frame for the basin
7: 46 The king **h** them cast in clay molds in the Jordan
10: 2 they talked about everything she **h** on her mind.
10: 19 The throne **h** six steps and a rounded back.
10: 22 The king **h** a fleet of trading ships that sailed with
10: 26 He **h** fourteen hundred chariots and twelve
11: 3 He **h** seven hundred wives and three hundred
19: 4 "I have **h** enough, LORD," he said. "Take my life,
21: 1 King Ahab **h** a palace in Jezreel, and near the
2Ki 4: 17 And at that time the following year she **h** a son,
5: 1 The king of Aram **h** high admiration for Naaman,
7: 13 One of his officers replied, "We **h** better send out
10: 1 Now Ahab **h** seventy sons living in the city of
13: 5 Israel lived in safety again as they **h** in former
23: 4 The king **h** all these things burned outside
25: 21 the king of Babylon **h** them all put to death.
1Ch 1: 19 Eber **h** two sons. The first was named Peleg—
2: 3 Judah **h** three sons through Bathshua, a Canaanite
2: 4 Later Judah **h** twin sons through Tamar,
2: 4 Perez and Zerah. So Judah **h** five sons in all.
2: 16 Zeruiah **h** three sons named Abishai, Joab, and
2: 17 an Ishmaelite, and they **h** a son named Amasa.
2: 18 Hezron's son Caleb **h** two wives named Azubah
2: 19 married Ephrathah, and they **h** a son named Hur.
2: 21 the daughter of Makir. They **h** a son named Segub.
2: 26 Jerahmeel **h** a second wife named Atarah.
2: 31 Appaim **h** a son named Ishi. The son of Ishi was
Sheshan. Sheshan **h** a descendant named Ahlai.
2: 32 Shammai's brother, Jada, **h** two sons named Jether
2: 33 but Jonathan **h** two sons named Peleth and Zaza.
2: 34 Sheshan **h** no sons, though he did have daughters.
He also **h** an Egyptian servant named Jarha.
2: 35 the wife of Jarha, and they **h** a son named Attai.
2: 49 and Gibea). Caleb also **h** a daughter named Acsah.
3: 6 David also **h** nine other sons: Ibhar, Elishua,
3: 9 concubines. David also **h** a daughter named Tamar.
3: 19 Hananiah. He also **h** a daughter named Shelomith.
4: 5 Ashhur (the father of Tekoa) **h** two wives, named
4: 27 Shimei **h** sixteen sons and six daughters, but none
of his brothers **h** large families. So Simeon's tribe
5: 9 since they **h** so many cattle in the land of Gilead,
5: 24 Each of these men **h** a great reputation as a warrior
7: 4 for all five of them **h** many wives and many sons.
7: 15 was Zelophehad, who **h** only daughters.
7: 24 Ephraim **h** a daughter named Sheerah. She built
7: 30 Ishvi, and Beriah. They **h** a sister named Serah.
7: 32 Shomer, and Hotham. They **h** a sister named Shua.
8: 8 and Baara, he **h** children in the land of Moab.
8: 38 Azel **h** six sons: Azrikam, Bokeru, Ishmael,
8: 39 Azel's brother Eshek **h** three sons: Ulam (the
8: 40 They **h** many sons and grandsons—150 in all.
9: 44 Azel **h** six sons, and their names were Azrikam,
11: 42 the Reubenite leader who **h** thirty men with him;
12: 22 more men joined David until he **h** a great army,
12: 27 family of Aaron, who **h** 3,700 under his command.
14: 3 in Jerusalem, and they **h** many sons and daughters.
23: 11 as a single family because neither **h** many sons.
23: 17 Eliezer **h** only one son, Rehabiah, the family
leader. Rehabiah **h** numerous descendants.
23: 24 Each **h** to be twenty years old or older to qualify
24: 2 died before their father did, and they **h** no sons.
24: 28 the leader was Eleazar, though he **h** no sons.
25: 3 Jeduthun **h** six sons: Gedaliah, Zeri, Jeshaiah,
26: 6 Obed-edom's son Shemaiah **h** sons with great
27: 1 for one month and **h** twenty-four thousand troops.
28: 12 also gave Solomon all the plans he **h** in mind for
2Ch 1: 12 such as no other king has ever **h** before you or will
3: 12 In the same way, the second figure **h** one wing
4: 17 The king **h** them cast in clay molds in the Jordan
7: 9 On the eighth day they **h** a closing ceremony, for
9: 2 they talked about everything she **h** on her mind.
9: 18 The throne **h** six steps, and there was a footstool
9: 21 The king **h** a fleet of trading ships manned by the
9: 25 Solomon **h** four thousand stalls for his chariot
11: 19 Mahalath **h** three sons—Jeush, Shemariah,
11: 21 In all, he **h** eighteen wives and sixty concubines,
13: 21 He married fourteen wives and **h** twenty-two sons
14: 8 King Asa **h** an army of 300,000 warriors from the
14: 8 He also **h** an army of 280,000 warriors from the
24: 3 Jehoiada chose two wives for Joash, and he **h** sons
25: 5 found that he **h** an army of 300,000 men twenty
26: 10 He **h** many workers who cared for his farms and
26: 11 Uzziah **h** an army of well-trained warriors, ready
26: 21 So King Uzziah **h** leprosy until the day he died.
26: 23 So Uzziah died, and since he **h** leprosy, he was
30: 17 the Levites **h** to slaughter their Passover lambs for
31: 10 we have **h** enough to eat and plenty to spare, for
32: 27 He **h** to build special treasury buildings for his
36: 15 for he **h** compassion on his people and his Temple.
36: 17 They **h** no pity on the people, killing both young
Ezr 10: 44 Each of these men **h** a pagan wife, and some even
h children by these wives.
Ne 4: 18 All the builders **h** a sword belted to their side.
5: 8 who have **h** to sell themselves to pagan foreigners,
5: 8 And they **h** nothing to say in their defense.
9: 35 Even while they **h** their own kingdom, they did
13: 13 These men **h** an excellent reputation, and it was
Est 2: 7 This man **h** a beautiful and lovely young cousin,
6: 1 That night the king **h** trouble sleeping, so he
8: 17 **h** a great celebration and declared a public festival
Job 1: 2 He **h** seven sons and three daughters.
1: 4 Every year when Job's sons **h** birthdays,
1: 21 The LORD gave me everything I **h**, / and the LORD
20: 3 I have **h** to endure your insults, but now my spirit
29: 12 need and the orphans who **h** no one to help them.
29: 22 And after I spoke, they **h** nothing to add, for my
31: 35 "If only I **h** someone who would listen to me and
32: 5 But when he saw that they **h** no further reply,
42: 12 For now he **h** fourteen thousand sheep, six
Ps 55: 6 Oh, how I wish I **h** wings like a dove; / then I
106: 30 Phinehas **h** the courage to step in, / and the plague
116: 3 Death **h** its hands around my throat; / the terrors of
123: 3 have mercy, / for we have **h** our fill of contempt.
123: 4 We have **h** our fill of the scoffing of the proud
Pr 23: 5 riches can disappear as though they **h** the wings of
Ecc 2: 8 both men and women, and **h** many beautiful
concubines. I **h** everything a man could desire!
6: 4 in darkness. He wouldn't even have **h** a name,
6: 5 Yet he would have **h** more peace than he has in
Isa 8: 3 my wife, and she became pregnant and **h** a son.
14: 17 greatest cities and **h** no mercy on his prisoners?'
40: 15 the islands as though they **h** no weight at all.
48: 18 Then you would have **h** peace flowing like a
Jer 11: 19 I **h** no idea that they were planning to kill me!
20: 2 arrested Jeremiah the prophet and **h** him whipped
23: 25 say, 'Listen to the dream I **h** from God last night.'
26: 23 a sword and **h** him buried in an unmarked grave.)
30: 15 I have **h** to punish you because your sins are many
31: 20 "I **h** to punish him, but I still love him. I long for
35: 8 We have never **h** a drink of wine since then, nor
37: 14 Jeremiah protested. "I **h** no intention of doing any
37: 15 were furious with Jeremiah and **h** him flogged and
40: 15 Johanan **h** a private conference with Gedaliah
42: 10 for all the punishment I have **h** to bring upon you.
44: 17 For in those days we **h** plenty to eat, and we were
well off and **h** no troubles!
45: 3 Haven't I **h** enough pain already? And now the
48: 9 Oh, that Moab **h** wings so she could fly away, for
52: 27 the king of Babylon **h** them all put to death.
La 5: 21 to you again! Give us back the joys we once **h**!
Eze 1: 6 that each **h** four faces and two pairs of wings.
1: 10 Each **h** a human face in the front, the face of a lion
1: 11 Each **h** two pairs of outstretched wings—one pair
1: 16 each wheel **h** a second wheel turning crosswise
1: 23 wings, and each **h** two wings covering its body.
2: 5 they will know they have **h** a prophet among them.
10: 8 (All the cherubim **h** what looked like human hands
10: 9 Each of the four cherubim **h** a wheel beside him,
10: 10 each wheel **h** a second wheel turning crosswise
10: 12 The cherubim **h** eyes all over their bodies,
10: 14 Each of the four cherubim **h** four faces—the first
10: 21 for each **h** four faces and four wings and what
10: 22 they traveled straight ahead, just as the others **h**.
16: 5 No one **h** the slightest interest in you; no one
17: 8 planted in good soil and **h** plenty of water so it
19: 10 It **h** lush, green foliage / because of the abundant
28: 14 You **h** access to the holy mountain of God and
31: 8 No cypress **h** branches equal to it; no plane tree **h**
boughs to compare. No tree in the garden of God
37: 8 their bodies, but they still **h** no breath in them.
40: 10 Each **h** the same measurements, and the dividing
40: 25 It **h** windows along the walls as the others did,
40: 26 This gateway also **h** a stairway of seven steps
40: 28 He measured it and found that it **h** the same
40: 29 It also **h** windows along its walls and in the foyer
40: 31 It **h** palm tree decorations on its columns, and
40: 32 He measured it and found that it **h** the same
40: 34 It **h** palm tree decorations on its columns, and
40: 35 He measured it and found that it **h** the same
40: 36 foyer of this gateway **h** the same measurements as
40: 37 and it **h** palm tree decorations on the columns.
41: 23 Place and the Most Holy Place **h** double doorways,
42: 5 the upper levels **h** to allow space for walkways in
42: 11 and it **h** the same entrances and doors.
Da 2: 1 Nebuchadnezzar **h** a dream that disturbed him so
2: 3 he said, "I have **h** a dream that troubles me.
4: 5 But one night I **h** a dream that greatly frightened
4: 12 It **h** fresh green leaves, and it was loaded with fruit
4: 18 that was the dream that I, King Nebuchadnezzar, **h**.
4: 21 It **h** fresh green leaves, and it was loaded with fruit
5: 23 have **h** these cups from his Temple brought before
7: 1 Daniel **h** a dream and saw visions as he lay in his
7: 5 and it **h** three ribs in its mouth between its teeth.
7: 6 It **h** four wings like birds' wings on its back, and it
h four heads. Great authority was given to this
7: 7 from any of the other beasts, and it **h** ten horns.
7: 8 This little horn **h** eyes like human eyes and a
7: 20 and **h** human eyes and a mouth that was boasting
8: 5 goat, which **h** one very large horn between its eyes,
10: 1 Daniel (also known as Belteshazzar) **h** another
11: 4 nor will the kingdom hold the authority it once **h**.
Mt 4: 23 he healed people who **h** every kind of sickness and
7: 29 for he taught as one who **h** real authority—quite
9: 20 a woman who had **h** a hemorrhage for twelve
12: 11 And he answered, "If you **h** one sheep, and it fell
13: 6 died because the roots **h** no nourishment in the
14: 14 he **h** compassion on them and healed their sick.
16: 21 his disciples plainly that he **h** to go to Jerusalem,
17: 20 "I assure you, even if you **h** faith as small as a
17: 25 But before he **h** a chance to speak, Jesus asked
18: 25 and everything he **h** be sold to pay the debt.
18: 30 He **h** the man arrested and jailed until the debt
18: 33 on your fellow servant, just as I **h** mercy on you?'
19: 22 went sadly away because he **h** many possessions.
22: 12 without wedding clothes?' And the man **h** no reply.
26: 6 at the home of Simon, a man who **h** leprosy.
27: 19 I **h** a terrible nightmare about him last night."
Mk 1: 22 for he taught as one who **h** real authority—quite
1: 34 people who **h** many different kinds of diseases,
1: 45 He **h** to stay out in the secluded places, and people
3: 30 because they were saying he **h** an evil spirit.
4: 6 the roots **h** no nourishment in the shallow soil.
5: 25 a woman in the crowd who had **h** a hemorrhage
5: 26 and had spent everything she **h** to pay them, but
6: 34 he **h** compassion on them because they were like
10: 22 went sadly away because he **h** many possessions.
14: 3 at the home of Simon, a man who **h** leprosy.
Lk 1: 7 They **h** no children because Elizabeth was barren,
2: 4 of King David, he **h** to go to Bethlehem in Judea,
8: 43 who had **h** a hemorrhage for twelve years. She had
spent everything she **h** on doctors and still could
12: 16 "A rich man **h** a fertile farm that produced fine
14: 6 Again they **h** no answer.
15: 4 "If you **h** one hundred sheep, and one of them

15:11 Jesus told them this story: "A man **h** two sons.
15:32 We **h** to celebrate this happy day. For your brother
16: 8 "The rich man **h** to admire the dishonest rascal for
16:25 'Son, remember that during your lifetime you **h** everything you wanted, and Lazarus **h** nothing.
17: 6 "Even if you **h** faith as small as a mustard seed,"
18: 9 this story to some who **h** great self-confidence and
Jn 4: 4 He **h** to go through Samaria on the way.
4:18 for you have **h** five husbands, and you aren't even
7:13 But no one **h** the courage to speak favorably about
13: 5 and to wipe them with the towel he **h** around him.
19: 1 Pilate **h** Jesus flogged with a lead-tipped whip.
Ac 2:44 together constantly and shared everything they **h**.
4:13 were ordinary men who had **h** no special training.
4:14 there among them, the council **h** nothing to say.
4:32 was not their own; they shared everything they **h**.
5:13 join them, though everyone **h** high regard for them.
5:34 But one member **h** a different perspective. He was
5:40 They called in the apostles and **h** them flogged.
7: 5 and his descendants—though he **h** no children yet.
7:21 When at last they **h** to abandon him, Pharaoh's
8: 6 Crowds listened intently to what he **h** to say
10: 3 One afternoon about three o'clock, he **h** a vision in
12: 2 He **h** the apostle James (John's brother) killed
14: 9 noticed him and realized he **h** faith to be healed.
15:24 but they **h** no such instructions from us.
16: 9 That night Paul **h** a vision. He saw a man from
17:18 He also **h** a debate with some of the Epicurean and
17:23 And one of them **h** this inscription on it—'To an
19:20 spread widely and **h** a powerful effect.
19:24 silversmith who **h** a large business manufacturing
20:21 I have **h** one message for Jews and Gentiles alike
21: 9 He **h** four unmarried daughters who **h** the gift of prophecy.
21:10 named Agabus, who also **h** the gift of prophecy,
21:35 the soldiers **h** to lift Paul to their shoulders to
22:11 and **h** to be led into Damascus by my companions.
22:30 He **h** Paul brought in before them to try to find out
26:11 Many times I **h** them whipped in the synagogues
27: 7 We **h** several days of rough sailing, and after great
27:37 began eating—for that is the number we **h** aboard.
28:19 even though I **h** no desire to press charges against
28:21 We have **h** no letters from Judea or reports from
Ro 2:12 even though they never **h** God's written law.
4: 2 If so, he would have **h** something to boast about. But from God's point of view Abraham **h** no basis
4:11 a sign that Abraham already **h** faith and that God
4:12 of faith Abraham **h** before he was circumcised.
9: 7 counted," though Abraham **h** other children, too.
1Co 3: 1 I **h** to talk as though you belonged to this world or
3: 2 I **h** to feed you with milk and not with solid food,
4:15 For even if you **h** ten thousand others to teach you
12:19 strange thing a body would be if it **h** only one part!
13: 2 If I **h** the gift of prophecy, and if I knew all the
13: 2 And if I **h** the gift of faith so that I could speak to
14: 5 I wish you all **h** the gift of speaking in tongues,
2Co 3:18 And all of us have **h** that veil removed so that we
4:13 same kind of faith the psalmist **h** when he said,
8:15 "Those who gathered a lot **h** nothing left over, and those who gathered only a little **h** enough."
Gal 2: 6 of the church who were there **h** nothing to add to
2:11 when Peter came to Antioch, I **h** to oppose him
4: 1 though they actually own everything their father **h**.
4:22 The Scriptures say that Abraham **h** two sons, one
Php 2: 5 attitude should be the same that Christ Jesus **h**.
2:27 But God **h** mercy on him—and also on me, so that
Col 2:18 even though they say they have **h** visions about
1Th 2: 7 As apostles of Christ we certainly **h** a right to
2Th 2: 2 Even if they claim to have **h** a vision, a revelation,
1Ti 1:13 But God **h** mercy on me because I did it in
1:16 But that is why God **h** mercy on me, so that Christ
Heb 2:14 the power of the Devil, who **h** the power of death.
7:23 When one priest died, another **h** to take his place.
9:23 **h** to be purified by the blood of animals. But the
9:26 he would have **h** to die again and again, ever since
10:34 You knew you **h** better things waiting for you in
11:20 He **h** confidence in what God was going to do in
11:40 For God **h** far better things in mind for us that
Jas 5: 6 who **h** no power to defend themselves against you.
1Pe 1:10 they **h** many questions as to what it all could mean.
2: 3 now that you have **h** a taste of the Lord's kindness.
4: 1 must arm yourselves with the same attitude he **h**,
4: 3 You have **h** enough in the past of the evil things
1Jn 2: 7 for it is an old one you have always **h**, right from
2Jn 1: 5 not a new commandment, but one we **h** from the
Rev 4: 4 They were all clothed in white and **h** gold crowns
4: 7 The first of these living beings **h** the form of a lion; the second looked like an ox; the third **h** a human face; and the fourth **h** the form of an eagle
4: 8 Each of these living beings **h** six wings, and their
5: 6 He **h** seven horns and seven eyes, which are the
5: 8 Each one **h** a harp, and they held gold bowls filled
9: 7 They **h** gold crowns on their heads, and they **h** human faces.
9:10 They **h** tails that sting like scorpions, with power
9:19 For their tails **h** heads like snakes, with the power
13: 1 It **h** seven heads and ten horns, with ten crowns on
13: 2 but it **h** bear's feet and a lion's mouth! And the
13:11 He **h** two horns like those of a lamb, and he spoke
14: 1 and with him were 144,000 who **h** his name and
14:14 He **h** a gold crown on his head and a sharp sickle
14:17 the Temple in heaven, and he also **h** a sharp sickle.
16: 2 sores broke out on everyone who **h** the mark of the
16: 5 I heard the angel who **h** authority over all water
17: 2 The rulers of the world have **h** immoral relations
17: 3 sitting on a scarlet beast that **h** seven heads and ten
21:14 The wall of the city **h** twelve foundation stones,

HADAD (15) [BEN-HADAD, HADAD'S, HADAD-RIMMON]

Ge 25:15 **H**, Tema, Jetur, Naphish, and Kedemah.
36:35 **H** son of Bedad became king and ruled from the
36:36 When **H** died, Samlah from the city of Masrekah
36:39 **H** became king and ruled from the city of Pau.
1Ki 11:14 Then the LORD raised up **H** the Edomite,
11:17 But **H** and a few of his father's royal officials had fled. (**H** was a very small child at the time.)
11:19 Pharaoh grew very fond of **H**, and he gave him a
11:21 When the news reached **H** in Egypt that David
11:25 and he made trouble, just as **H** did.
1Ch 1:30 Mishma, Dumah, Massa, **H**, Tema,
1:46 **H** son of Bedad became king and ruled from the
1:47 When **H** died, Samlah from the city of Masrekah
1:50 **H** became king and ruled from the city of Pau.
1:51 Then **H** died. The clan leaders of Edom were

HADAD'S (1) [HADAD]

Ge 36:39 **H** wife was Mehetabel, the daughter of Matred

HADAD-RIMMON (1) [HADAD, RIMMON]

Zec 12:11 grievous mourning of **H** in the valley of Megiddo.

HADADEZER (16) [HADADEZER'S]

2Sa 8: 3 David also destroyed the forces of **H** son of Rehob,
8: 3 when **H** marched out to strengthen his control
8: 5 Arameans from Damascus arrived to help **H**,
8: 9 heard that David had destroyed the army of **H**,
8:10 **H** and Toi had long been enemies, and there had
8:12 and from **H** son of Rehob, king of Zobah.
10:16 by **H** from the other side of the Euphrates River.
10:19 When **H** and his Aramean allies realized they had
1Ki 11:23 Rezon had fled from his master, King **H** of Zobah,
11:24 After David conquered **H**, Rezon and his men fled
1Ch 18: 3 Then David destroyed the forces of King **H** of
18: 3 when **H** marched out to strengthen his control
18: 5 Arameans from Damascus arrived to help **H**,
18: 9 David had destroyed the army of King **H** of Zobah,
18:10 **H** and Toi had long been enemies, and there had
19:19 When the servants of **H** realized they had been

HADADEZER'S (6) [HADADEZER]

2Sa 8: 7 David brought the gold shields of **H** officers to
8: 8 along with a large amount of bronze from **H** cities
10:16 of Shobach, the commander of all **H** forces.
1Ch 18: 7 David brought the gold shields of **H** officers to
18: 8 along with a large amount of bronze from **H** cities
19:16 of Shobach, the commander of all **H** forces.

HADASHAH (1)

Jos 15:37 Also included were Zenan, **H**, Migdal-gad,

HADASSAH (1) [ESTHER]

Est 2: 7 man had a beautiful and lovely young cousin, **H**,

HADID (3)

Ezr 2:33 The citizens of Lod, **H**, and Ono | 725
Ne 7:37 The citizens of Lod, **H**, and Ono | 721
11:34 **H**, Zeboim, Neballat,

HADLAI (1)

2Ch 28:12 Jehizkiah son of Shallum, and Amasa son of **H**—

HADN'T (17) [HAVE, NOT] See Index of Articles, Etc.

HADORAM (2)

Ge 10:27 **H**, Uzal, Diklah,
1Ch 1:21 **H**, Uzal, Diklah,

HAELEPH (1)

Jos 18:28 Zela, **H**, Jebus (that is, Jerusalem), Gibeah,

HAFT [KJV] See HANDLE

HAGAB (1)

Ezr 2:46 **H**, Shalmai, Hanan,

HAGABAH (2)

Ezr 2:45 Lebanah, **H**, Akkub,
Ne 7:48 Lebanah, **H**, Shalmai,

HAGAR (14) [HAGAR'S]

Ge 16: 1 took her servant, an Egyptian woman named **H**,
16: 3 took **H** the Egyptian servant and gave her to
16: 4 So Abram slept with **H**, and she became pregnant.
16: 4 When **H** knew she was pregnant, she began to treat
16: 6 So Sarai treated her harshly, and **H** ran away.
16: 7 The angel of the LORD found **H** beside a desert
16: 8 The angel said to her, "**H**, Sarai's servant,
16:13 Thereafter, **H** referred to the LORD, who had
16:15 So **H** gave Abram a son, and Abram named him
21: 9 the son of Abraham and her Egyptian servant **H**—
21:17 and the angel of God called to **H** from the sky, "**H**, what's wrong?
25:12 the son of Abraham through **H**, Sarah's Egyptian
Gal 4:24 **H**, the slave-wife, represents Mount Sinai where

HAGAR'S (3) [HAGAR]

Ge 21:13 But I will make a nation of the descendants of **H**
21:14 and strapped a container of water to **H** shoulders.
21:19 Then God opened **H** eyes, and she saw a well.

HAGARENES, HAGARITE(S) [KJV] See HAGRITE(S)

HAGGAI (11)

Ezr 5: 1 At that time the prophets **H** and Zechariah son of
6:14 encouraged by the preaching of the prophets **H**
Hag 1: 1 the LORD gave a message through the prophet **H**
1: 3 LORD sent this message through the prophet **H**:
1:12 It had been delivered by the prophet **H**,
1:13 Then **H**, the LORD's messenger, gave the people
2: 1 sent another message through the prophet **H**.
2:10 the LORD sent this message to the prophet **H**:
2:13 Then **H** asked, "But if someone becomes
2:14 Then **H** said, "That is how it is with this people
2:20 The LORD sent this second message to **H** on

HAGGEDOLIM (1)

Ne 11:14 Their chief officer was Zabdiel son of **H**.

HAGGERI [KJV] See HAGRI

HAGGI (2) [HAGGITE]

Ge 46:16 **H**, Shuni, Ezbon, Eri, Arodi, and Areli.
Nu 26:15 The Haggite clan, named after its ancestor **H**.

HAGGIAH (1)

1Ch 6:30 Shimea, **H**, and Asaiah.

HAGGITE (1) [HAGGI]

Nu 26:15 The **H** clan, named after its ancestor Haggi.

HAGGITH (4) [HAGGITH'S]

2Sa 3: 4 The fourth was Adonijah, whose mother was **H**.
1Ki 1: 5 time David's son Adonijah, whose mother was **H**,
2:13 One day Adonijah, whose mother was **H**, came to
1Ch 3: 2 The fourth was Adonijah, whose mother was **H**.

HAGGITH'S (1) [HAGGITH]

1Ki 1:11 asked her, "Did you realize that **H** son, Adonijah,

HAGGLES (1)

Pr 20:14 The buyer **h** over the price, saying,

HAGRI (1) [HAGRITE, HAGRITES]

1Ch 11:38 Joel, the brother of Nathan; / Mibhar son of **H**;

HAGRITE (2) [HAGRI]

1Ch 5:10 Then they moved into the **H** settlements all along
27:31 Jaziz the **H** was in charge of the king's sheep.

HAGRITES (6) [HAGRI]

1Ch 5:10 of Saul, the Reubenites defeated the **H** in battle.
5:19 They waged war against the **H**, the Jeturites,
5:20 in him. So the **H** and all their allies were defeated.
5:21 The plunder taken from the **H** included 50,000
5:22 Many of the **H** were killed in the battle
Ps 83: 6 these Edomites and Ishmaelites, / Moabites and **H**,

HAI [KJV] See AI

HAIL (22) [HAILSTONES, HAILSTORM]

Ex 9:19 or animal left outside will die beneath the **h**.' "
9:22 and cause the **h** to fall throughout Egypt,
9:23 and the LORD sent thunder and **h**, and lightning
9:24 with such severe **h** and continuous lightning.
9:26 The only spot in all Egypt without **h** that day was
9:28 the LORD to end this terrifying thunder and **h**.
9:29 to the LORD. Then the thunder and **h** will stop.
9:33 all at once the thunder and **h** stopped,
Jos 10:11 The **h** killed more of the enemy than the Israelites
Job 38:22 Have you seen where the **h** is made and stored?
Ps 18:12 the clouds, / raining down **h** and burning coals.
78:47 He destroyed their grapevines with **h**
78:48 He abandoned their cattle to the **h**, / their livestock
105:32 Instead of rain, he sent murderous **h**, / and flashes
147:17 He hurls the **h** like stones. / Who can stand against
148: 8 fire and **h**, snow and storm, / wind and weather
Hag 2:17 and **h** to destroy all the produce of your labor.
Mt 27:29 they knelt before him in mockery, yelling, "**H**!
Mk 15:18 Then they saluted, yelling, "**H**! King of the
Jn 12:13 the name of the Lord! / **H** to the King of Israel!"
19: 3 "**H**! King of the Jews!" they mocked, and they hit
Rev 8: 7 and **h** and fire mixed with blood were thrown

HAILSTONES (5) [HAIL]

Isa 30:30 with cloudbursts, thunderstorms, and huge **h**,
Eze 13:11 great **h** and mighty winds will knock it down.
13:13 with a great flood of anger, and with **h** of fury.
38:22 will send torrential rain, **h**, fire, and burning sulfur!
Rev 16:21 and **h** weighing seventy-five pounds fell from the

HAILSTORM (11) [HAIL]

Ex 9:18 So tomorrow at this time I will send a **h** worse than
9:23 The LORD sent a tremendous **h** against all the

10: 5 They will devour everything that escaped the **h**,
10: 12 the land and eat all the crops still left after the **h**."
10: 15 all the fruit on the trees that had survived the **h**.
Jos 10: 11 the LORD destroyed them with a terrible **h** that
Isa 28: 2 Like a mighty **h** and a torrential rain, they will
28: 17 but since it is made of lies, a **h** will knock it down.
Rev 11: 19 there was a great **h**, and the world was shaken by a
16: 21 There was a terrible **h**, and hailstones weighing
16: 21 They cursed God because of the **h**, which was a

HAIR (93) [GRAY-HAIRED, HAIRS, HAIRSBREADTH, HAIRSTYLES, HAIRY, WHITE-HAIRED]

Ge 25: 25 so much **h** that one would think he was wearing a
Ex 25: 4 and scarlet yarn; fine linen; goat **h** for cloth;
26: 7 "Make heavy sheets of cloth from goat **h** to cover
35: 6 and scarlet yarn; fine linen; goat **h** for cloth;
35: 23 and scarlet yarn, fine linen, or goat **h** for cloth.
35: 26 their skills to spin and weave the goat **h** into cloth.
36: 14 from eleven sheets of cloth made from goat **h**.
Lev 10: 6 "Do not mourn by letting your **h** hang loose
13: 3 If the **h** in the affected area has turned white
13: 4 and if the **h** in the spot has not turned white,
13: 10 If the priest sees that some **h** has turned white
13: 20 and if the **h** in the affected area has turned white,
13: 21 But if the priest sees that there is no white **h** in the
13: 25 If the **h** in the affected area turns white
13: 26 But if the priest discovers that there is no white **h**
13: 30 and fine yellow **h** is found in the affected area,
13: 31 and there is no black **h** in the affected area,
13: 32 area has not spread and no yellow **h** has appeared,
13: 33 the infected person must shave off all **h** except the **h** on the affected area.
13: 36 even without checking for yellow **h**.
13: 37 and black **h** has grown in the affected area,
13: 40 "If a man loses his **h** and his head becomes bald,
13: 41 And if he loses **h** on his forehead, he simply has a
13: 45 tear their clothing and allow their **h** to hang loose.
14: 8 shaving off all their **h**, and bathing themselves in
14: 9 seventh day, they must again shave off all their **h**,
14: 9 including the **h** of the beard and eyebrows,
19: 27 "Do not trim off the **h** on your temples or clip the
21: 10 must never let his **h** hang loose or tear his clothing.
Nu 5: 18 he must unbind her **h** and place the offering of
6: 5 "They must never cut their **h** throughout the time
6: 5 That is why they must let their **h** grow long.
6: 7 They must not defile the **h** on their head, because it
6: 9 "If their **h** is defiled because someone suddenly
6: 11 vow that day and let their **h** begin to grow again.
6: 18 "Then the Nazirites will shave their **h** at the
31: 20 and everything made of leather, goat **h**, or wood."
Dt 14: 1 or shave the **h** above your foreheads for the sake of
Jdg 13: 5 give birth to a son, and his **h** must never be cut.
16: 13 "If you weave the seven braids of my **h** into the
16: 13 Delilah wove the seven braids of his **h** into the
16: 14 and yanked his **h** away from the loom
16: 17 "My **h** has never been cut," he confessed, "for I
16: 19 and she called in a man to shave off his **h**,
16: 22 But before long his **h** began to grow back.
1Sa 1: 11 dedicated to the LORD, his **h** will never be cut."
14: 45 not one **h** on his head will be touched,
19: 13 and put a cushion of goat's **h** at its head.
19: 16 in the bed with a cushion of goat's **h** at its head.
2Sa 2: 16 Each one grabbed his opponent by the **h** and thrust
14: 11 "not a **h** on your son's head will be disturbed!"
14: 26 He cut his **h** only once a year, and then only
2Ki 9: 30 her eyelids and fixed her **h** and sat at a window.
Ezr 9: 3 my clothing, pulled **h** from my head and beard,
Ne 13: 25 I beat some of them and pulled out their **h**.
Job 18: 4 You may tear your **h** out in anger, but will that
Pr 16: 31 Gray **h** is a crown of glory; it is gained by living a
20: 29 the gray **h** of experience is the splendor of the old.
SS 4: 1 Your **h** falls in waves, like flocks of goats frisking
5: 2 with dew, my **h** with the wetness of the night.'
5: 11 is the finest gold, and his **h** is wavy and black.
6: 5 Your **h**, as it falls across your face, is like a flock
7: 5 and the sheen of your **h** radiates royalty.
Isa 3: 24 ropes for sashes, and their well-set **h** will fall out.
46: 4 your lifetime—until your **h** is white with age.
Eze 5: 1 Use a scale to weigh the **h** into three equal parts.
5: 3 Keep just a bit of the **h** and tie it up in your robe.
8: 3 what seemed to be a hand and took me by the **h**.
16: 7 Your breasts became full, and your **h** grew,
44: 20 "They must neither let their **h** grow too long nor
Da 3: 27 Not a **h** on their heads was singed, and their
4: 33 He lived this way until his **h** was as long as eagles'
7: 9 was as white as snow, his **h** like whitest wool.
Hos 7: 9 Israel is like an old man with graying **h**,
Mt 3: 4 John's clothes were woven from camel **h**, and he
5: 36 my head!' for you can't turn one **h** white or black.
6: 17 when you fast, comb your **h** and wash your face.
Mk 1: 6 His clothes were woven from camel **h**, and he
Lk 7: 38 fell on his feet, and she wiped them off with her **h**.
7: 44 them with her tears and wiped them with her **h**.
21: 18 But not a **h** of your head will perish!
Jn 11: 2 on the Lord's feet and wiped them with her **h**.
12: 3 Jesus' feet with it and wiped his feet with her **h**.
Ac 27: 34 own good. For not a **h** of your heads will perish."
1Co 11: 6 wear a head covering, she should cut off all her **h**.
11: 6 And since it is shameful for a woman to have her **h**
11: 14 that it's disgraceful for a man to have long **h**?
11: 15 And isn't it obvious that long **h** is a woman's pride
1Ti 2: 9 attention to themselves by the way they fix their **h**
Rev 1: 14 His head and his **h** were white like wool, as white
9: 8 Their **h** was long like the **h** of a woman,

HAIRS (5) [HAIR]

Ps 40: 12 They are more numerous than the **h** on my head.
69: 4 are more numerous than the **h** on my head.
Eze 5: 4 Then take a few of these **h** out and throw them into
Mt 10: 30 And the very **h** on your head are all numbered.
Lk 12: 7 And the very **h** on your head are all numbered.

HAIRSBREADTH (1) [HAIR]

Jdg 20: 16 could sling a rock and hit a target within a **h**,

HAIRSTYLES (1) [HAIR]

1Pe 3: 3 about the outward beauty that depends on fancy **h**,

HAIRY (4) [HAIR]

Ge 27: 11 Think how **h** Esau is and how smooth my skin is!
27: 16 She made him a pair of gloves from the **h** skin of
27: 23 because Jacob's hands felt **h** just like Esau's.
2Ki 1: 8 They replied, "He was a **h** man, and he wore a

HAKILAH (3)

1Sa 23: 19 is in the strongholds of Horesh on the hill of **H**,
26: 1 "David is hiding on the hill of **H**, which overlooks
26: 3 Saul camped along the road beside the hill of **H**,

HAKKATAN (1)

Ezr 8: 12 of Azgad: Johanan son of **H** and 110 other men.

HAKKOZ (5)

1Ch 24: 10 The seventh lot fell to **H**. / The eighth lot fell to
Ezr 2: 61 families of priests—Hobaiah, **H**, and Barzillai—
Ne 3: 4 and grandson of **H** repaired the next section of
3: 21 and grandson of **H** rebuilt another section of the
7: 63 Hobaiah, **H**, and Barzillai—also returned to

HAKUPHA (2)

Ezr 2: 51 Bakbuk, **H**, Harhur,
Ne 7: 53 Bakbuk, **H**, Harhur,

HALAH (3)

2Ki 17: 6 They were settled in colonies in **H**, along the banks
18: 11 Israelites to Assyria and put them in colonies in **H**,
1Ch 5: 26 The Assyrians exiled them to **H**, Habor, Hara,

HALAK (2)

Jos 11: 17 territory now extended all the way from Mount **H**,
12: 7 Baal-gad in the valley of Lebanon to Mount **H**,

HALE [KJV] See REACHES

HALF (122) [HALF-BAKED, HALF-BURNED, HALF-BUSHEL, HALF-SHARE, HALF-TRIBE, HALFWAY, HALVES]

Ge 8: 5 Two and a **h** months later, as the waters continued
8: 13 years old, ten and a **h** months after the flood began,
15: 10 by side. He did not, however, divide the birds in **h**.
37: 2 he often tended his father's flocks with his **h**
48: 10 Now Jacob was **h** blind because of his age
Ex 21: 35 Each will also own **h** of the dead bull.
24: 6 Moses took **h** the blood from these animals
24: 6 The other **h** he splashed against the altar.
26: 12 An extra **h** sheet of this roof covering will be left
Lev 6: 20 **h** to be offered in the morning and **h** to be offered in the evening.
18: 9 have sexual intercourse with your sister or **h** sister,
18: 11 of any of your father's wives; she is your **h** sister.
Nu 15: 6 flour mixed with two and a **h** pints of olive oil,
15: 7 give two and a **h** pints of wine for a drink offering.
28: 14 two and a **h** pints for the ram, and one quart for
31: 27 and give **h** to the men who fought the battle and **h** to the rest of the people.
31: 29 Give this share of their **h** to Eleazar the priest as an
31: 30 and goats in the **h** that belongs to the people of
31: 36 So the **h** of the plunder given to the fighting men
31: 42 The **h** of the plunder belonging to the people of
31: 42 which Moses had separated from the **h** belonging
32: 33 and **h** the tribe of Manasseh son of Joseph the
34: 13 up among the nine and a **h** remaining tribes.
34: 14 and **h** the tribe of Manasseh have already received
Dt 3: 12 plus **h** of the hill country of Gilead with its towns,
Jos 3: 4 Stay about a **h** mile behind them, keeping a clear
12: 2 This territory included **h** of the present area of
12: 5 His kingdom included the northern **h** of Gilead,
13: 8 **H** the tribe of Manasseh and the tribes of Reuben
13: 25 the towns of Gilead, and **h** of the land of Ammon,
13: 31 It also included **h** of Gilead and King Og's royal
14: 2 and a **h** tribes received their inheritance by means
14: 3 and a **h** tribes on the east side of the Jordan River.
22: 7 The other **h** of the tribe was given land west of the
Jdg 6: 19 and with **h** a bushel of flour he baked some bread
9: 5 one stone, they killed all seventy of his **h** brothers.
11: 2 and when these **h** brothers grew up, they chased
16: 25 **H** drunk by now, the people demanded, "Bring out
Ru 2: 17 the grain that evening, it came to about **h** a bushel.
1Sa 1: 24 and **h** a bushel of flour and some wine.
14: 14 and their bodies were scattered over about **h** an
2Sa 2: 11 he ruled as king of Judah for seven and a **h** years.
10: 4 and shaved off **h** of each man's beard,
13: 1 And Amnon, her **h** brother, fell desperately in love
18: 3 we have to turn and run—and even if **h** of us die—
19: 40 and **h** the army of Israel escorted him across the
1Ki 3: 25 child in two and give **h** to each of these women!"
7: 14 He was **h** Israelite, since his mother was a widow
10: 7 Truly I had not heard the **h** of it! Your wisdom
13: 8 "Even if you gave me **h** of everything you own,
16: 9 who commanded **h** of the royal chariots,
16: 21 **H** the people tried to make Tibni son of Ginath their king, while the other **h** supported Omri.
2Ki 7: 1 five quarts of fine flour will cost only **h** an ounce
7: 1 and ten quarts of barley grain will cost only **h** an
7: 16 flour were sold that day for **h** an ounce of silver,
7: 16 and ten quarts of barley grain were sold for **h** an
7: 18 five quarts of fine flour will cost **h** an ounce of
7: 18 and ten quarts of barley grain will cost **h** an ounce
1Ch 2: 52 were Haroeh, **h** the Manahathites,
2: 54 the other **h** of the Manahathites, the Zorites,
3: 4 in Hebron, where he reigned seven and a **h** years.
11: 23 Egyptian warrior who was seven and a **h** feet tall
2Ch 9: 6 my own eyes. Truly I had not heard the **h** of it!
Ne 3: 9 of Hur, the leader of **h** the district of Jerusalem,
3: 12 He was the leader of the other **h** of the district of
3: 16 of Azbuk, the leader of **h** the district of Beth-zur.
3: 17 the leader of **h** the district of Keilah,
3: 18 the leader of the other **h** of the district of Keilah.
4: 6 At last the wall was completed to **h** its original
4: 16 only **h** my men worked while the other **h** stood
4: 21 to sunset. And **h** the men were always on guard.
12: 32 and **h** the leaders of Judah followed them,
12: 38 I followed them, with the other **h** of the people,
13: 24 **h** their children spoke in the language of Ashdod
Est 1: 10 when King Xerxes was **h** drunk with wine, he told
5: 3 I will give it to you, even if it is **h** the kingdom!"
5: 6 I will give it to you, even if it is **h** the kingdom!"
7: 2 I will give it to you, even if it is **h** the kingdom!"
Job 42: 12 So the LORD blessed Job in the second **h** of his
Ps 106: 2 the LORD? / Who can ever praise him **h** enough?
129: 6 on a rooftop, / turning yellow when only **h** grown,
Isa 44: 19 I burned **h** of it for heat and used it to bake my
Jer 39: 2 Two and a **h** years later, on July 18,
Eze 16: 51 "Even Samaria did not commit **h** your sins.
45: 24 The prince will provide a **h** bushel of flour as a
46: 5 He will present a grain offering of a **h** bushel of
46: 5 He is to offer one gallon of olive oil for each **h**
46: 7 With the young bull he must bring a **h** bushel of
46: 7 With the ram he must bring another **h** bushel of
46: 7 With each **h** bushel of flour he must offer one
46: 11 the grain offering will be a **h** bushel of flour with
46: 11 another **h** bushel of flour with each ram, and as
46: 11 One gallon of oil is to be given with each **h** bushel
46: 14 and a **h** quarts of flour with a third of a gallon of
Da 7: 25 under his control for a time, times, and **h** a time.
9: 27 but after **h** this time, he will put an end to the
12: 7 "It will go on for a time, times, and **h** a time.
Zec 14: 2 **H** the population will be taken away into captivity,
14: 2 and **h** will be left among the ruins of the city.
14: 4 for **h** the mountain will move toward the north and **h** toward the south.
14: 8 **h** toward the Dead Sea and **h** toward the Mediterranean,
Mt 10: 29 Not even a sparrow, worth only **h** a penny, can fall
18: 9 It is better to enter heaven **h** blind than to have two
Mk 6: 23 you whatever you ask, up to **h** of my kingdom!"
9: 47 It is better to enter the Kingdom of God **h** blind
Lk 4: 25 for three and a **h** years and hunger stalked the land.
10: 30 beat him up, and left him **h** dead beside the road.
19: 8 "I will give **h** my wealth to the poor, Lord,
Ac 1: 12 so they walked the **h** mile back to Jerusalem.
18: 11 So Paul stayed there for the next year and a **h**,
Heb 11: 37 Some died by stoning, and some were sawed in **h**;
Jas 5: 17 none fell for the next three and a **h** years!
Rev 8: 1 there was silence throughout heaven for about **h** an
11: 9 And for three and a **h** days all peoples, tribes,
11: 11 But after three and a **h** days, the spirit of life from
12: 14 from the dragon for a time, times, and **h** a time.

HALF-BAKED (1) [BAKE, HALF]

Hos 7: 8 Now they have become as worthless as a **h** cake!

HALF-BURNED (1) [BURN, HALF]

Am 4: 11 Those of you who survived were like **h** sticks

HALF-BUSHEL (1) [BUSHEL, HALF]

1Sa 17: 17 "Take this **h** of roasted grain and these ten loaves

HALF-SHARE (1) [HALF, SHARE]

Nu 31: 47 From the **h** given to the people, Moses took one of

HALF-TRIBE (31) [HALF, TRIBE]

Dt 3: 13 Og's former kingdom—to the **h** of Manasseh.
29: 8 and to the **h** of Manasseh as their inheritance.
Jos 1: 12 the tribes of Reuben, Gad, and the **h** of Manasseh.
4: 12 and the **h** of Manasseh led the Israelites across the
12: 6 the tribes of Reuben, Gad, and the **h** of Manasseh.
13: 7 among the nine tribes and the **h** of Manasseh."
13: 29 area to the families of the **h** of Manasseh.
16: 9 villages in the territory of the **h** of Manasseh.
17: 1 The next allotment of land was given to the **h** of
18: 7 and the **h** of Manasseh won't receive any more
21: 5 of Ephraim, Dan, and the **h** of Manasseh.
21: 6 Asher, Naphtali, and the **h** of Manasseh in Bashan.
21: 25 The **h** of Manasseh allotted the following towns
21: 27 with their pasturelands from the **h** of Manasseh:
22: 1 the tribes of Reuben, Gad, and the **h** of Manasseh.
22: 7 Now Moses had given the land of Bashan to the **h**
22: 9 and the **h** of Manasseh left the rest of Israel at

22:10 and the **h** of Manasseh built a very large altar near
22:13 the tribes of Reuben, Gad, and the **h** of Manasseh.
22:15 the tribes of Reuben, Gad, and the **h** of Manasseh,
22:21 and the **h** of Manasseh answered these high
22:30 Gad, and the **h** of Manasseh, they were satisfied.
1Ch 5:18 the armies of Reuben, Gad, and the **h** of Manasseh.
5:23 The **h** of Manasseh spread through the land from
5:26 Gad, and the **h** of Manasseh as captives.
6:61 of the **h** of Manasseh by means of sacred lots.
6:70 towns from the territory of the **h** of Manasseh:
6:71 **h** of Manasseh the town of Golan in Bashan with
12:31 From the **h** of Manasseh west of the Jordan,
12:37 of Reuben and Gad and the **h** of Manasseh lived—
26:32 tribes of Reuben and Gad and the **h** of Manasseh.

HALFWAY (4) [HALF]

Ex 26:28 The middle crossbar, **h** up the frames, will run all
27:5 Fit the grating **h** down into the firebox, resting it
36:33 The middle crossbar of the five was **h** up the
38:4 rested on a ledge about **h** down into the firebox.

HALHUL (1)

Jos 15:58 In addition, there were **H**, Beth-zur, Gedor,

HALI (1)

Jos 19:25 included these towns: Helkath, **H**, Beten, Acshaph,

HALL (11) [HALLS]

1Sa 9:22 brought Saul and his servant into the great **h**
1Ki 7:6 He also built the **H** of Pillars, which was 75 feet
7:7 There was also the **H** of the Throne, also known as the **H** of Judgment,
7:8 quarters surrounded a courtyard behind this **h**;
Est 5:1 court of the palace, just across from the king's **h**.
Pr 1:21 the main street, and to those in front of city **h**.
SS 2:4 He brings me to the banquet **h**, so everyone can see
Da 5:10 what was happening, she hurried to the banquet **h**.
Mt 22:10 bad alike, and the banquet **h** was filled with guests.
Ac 19:9 Then he began preaching daily at the lecture **h** of

HALLELUJAH (4)

Rev 19:1 the sound of a vast crowd in heaven shouting, "**H**!
19:3 Again and again their voices rang, "**H**! The smoke
19:4 sitting on the throne. They cried out, "Amen! **H**!"
19:6 "**H**! For the Lord our God, the Almighty, reigns.

HALLOHESH (2)

Ne 3:12 Shallum son of **H** and his daughters repaired the
10:24 **H**, Pilha, Shobek,

HALLOW(ED) [KJV] See (SET) APART, DEDICATE, HONORED, HOLY, PRESENTED, SANCTIFY

HALLS (1) [HALL]

Am 5:15 is good; remodel your courts into true **h** of justice.

HALLUCINATIONS (1)

Pr 23:33 You will see **h**, and you will say crazy things.

HALO (1)

Eze 1:28 All around him was a glowing **h**, like a rainbow

HALOHESH [KJV] See HALLOHESH

HALT (2)

Jer 14:2 "Judah wilts; her businesses have ground to a **h**.
Da 11:45 He will **h** between the glorious holy mountain

HALVES (5) [HALF]

Ge 15:10 one down the middle and laid the **h** side by side.
15:17 and a flaming torch pass between the **h** of the
SS 4:3 cheeks behind your veil are like pomegranate **h**—
6:7 cheeks behind your veil are like pomegranate **h**—
Jer 34:18 you walked between its **h** to solemnize your vows.

HAM (17) [HAM'S]

Ge 5:32 he had three sons: Shem, **H**, and Japheth.
6:10 Noah had three sons: Shem, **H**, and Japheth.
7:13 his wife and his sons—Shem, **H**, and Japheth—
9:18 Shem, **H**, and Japheth, the three sons of Noah,
9:18 their father. (**H** is the ancestor of the Canaanites.)
9:22 **H**, the father of Canaan, saw that his father was
9:24 he learned what **H**, his youngest son, had done,
9:25 he cursed the descendants of Canaan, the son of **H**:
10:1 of Shem, **H**, and Japheth, the three sons of Noah.
10:6 The descendants of **H** were Cush, Mizraim, Put,
10:20 These were the descendants of **H**,
14:5 the Zuzites in **H**, the Emites in the plain of
1Ch 1:4 The sons of Noah were Shem, **H**, and Japheth.
1:8 The descendants of **H** were Cush, Mizraim, Put,
4:41 destroyed the homes of the descendants of **H**
Ps 105:23 Jacob lived as a foreigner in the land of **H**.
105:27 the Egyptians, / and miracles in the land of **H**.

HAM'S (1) [HAM]

1Ch 4:40 Some of **H** descendants had been living in the

HAMAN (39) [HAMAN'S]

Est 3:1 King Xerxes promoted **H** son of Hammedatha the
3:2 All the king's officials would bow down before **H**
3:4 So they spoke to **H** about this to see if he would
3:5 When **H** saw that Mordecai would not bow down
3:8 Then **H** approached King Xerxes and said,
3:10 and giving it to **H** son of Hammedatha the
3:11 the king told **H**, "but go ahead and do as you like
3:12 On April 17 **H** called in the king's secretaries
3:15 Then the king and **H** sat down to drink, but the city
4:7 and told him how much money **H** had promised to
5:4 and **H** come today to a banquet I have prepared for
5:5 and said, "Tell **H** to come quickly to a banquet,
5:5 So the king and **H** went to Esther's banquet.
5:8 please come with **H** tomorrow to the banquet I will
5:9 What a happy man **H** was as he left the banquet!
5:12 Then **H** added, "And that's not all! Queen Esther
5:14 This pleased **H** immensely, and he ordered the
6:4 **H** had just arrived in the outer court of the palace
6:5 attendants replied to the king, "**H** is out there."
6:6 So **H** came in, and the king said, "What should I
6:6 **H** thought to himself, "Whom would the king
6:10 the king said to **H**. "Hurry and get the robe
6:11 So **H** took the robe and put it on Mordecai,
6:12 but **H** hurried home dejected and completely
6:13 When **H** told his wife, Zeresh, and all his friends
6:14 the king's eunuchs arrived to take **H** to the banquet
7:1 So the king and **H** went to Queen Esther's banquet.
7:6 Esther replied, "This wicked **H** is our enemy."
7:6 **H** grew pale with fright before the king and queen.
7:7 But **H** stayed behind to plead for his life with
7:9 "**H** has set up a gallows that stands seventy-five
7:9 "Then hang **H** on it!" the king ordered.
7:10 So they hanged **H** on the gallows he had set up for
8:1 that same day King Xerxes gave the estate of **H**,
8:2 which he had taken back from **H**—and gave it to
8:7 the Jew, "I have given Esther the estate of **H**,
9:10 the ten sons of **H** son of Hammedatha, the enemy
9:24 **H** son of Hammedatha the Agagite, the enemy of
9:25 and **H** and his sons were hanged on the gallows.

HAMAN'S (9) [HAMAN]

Est 5:14 So **H** wife, Zeresh, and all his friends suggested,
7:8 his attendants covered **H** face, signaling his doom.
8:2 appointed Mordecai to be in charge of **H** property.
8:3 and begging him with tears to stop **H** evil plot
8:5 send out a decree reversing **H** orders to destroy the
9:12 in the fortress of Susa alone and also **H** ten sons.
9:13 and have the bodies of **H** ten sons hung from the
9:14 They also hung the bodies of **H** ten sons from the
9:25 he issued a decree causing **H** evil plot to backfire,

HAMATH (24) [HAMATH-ZOBAH, HAMATHITES, LEBO-HAMATH]

2Sa 8:9 When King Toi of **H** heard that David had
2Ki 14:28 how he recovered for Israel both Damascus and **H**,
17:24 Cuthah, Avva, **H**, and Sepharvaim and resettled
17:30 god Nergal. And those from **H** worshiped Ashima.
18:34 What happened to the gods of **H** and Arpad?
19:13 What happened to the king of **H** and the king of
23:33 of **H** to prevent him from ruling from Jerusalem.
25:21 And there at Riblah, in the land of **H**, the king of
1Ch 18:3 forces of King Hadadezer of Zobah, as far as **H**,
18:9 When King Toi of **H** heard that David had
2Ch 8:4 and built towns in the region of **H** as supply
Isa 10:9 did Carchemish. **H** will fall before us as Arpad did.
11:11 Upper Egypt, Ethiopia, Elam, Babylonia, **H**,
36:19 What happened to the gods of **H** and Arpad?
37:13 What happened to the king of **H** and the king of
Jer 39:5 of Babylon, who was at Riblah in the land of **H**.
49:23 "The towns of **H** and Arpad are struck with fear,
52:9 in the land of **H**, where sentence was passed
52:27 And there at Riblah in the land of **H**, the king of
Eze 47:16 which are on the border between Damascus and **H**,
47:17 on the border between **H** to the north
48:1 on the border of Damascus, with **H** to the north.
Am 6:2 Then go to the great city of **H** and on down to the
Zec 9:2 Doom is certain for **H**, near Damascus, and for the

HAMATH-ZOBAH (1) [HAMATH]

2Ch 8:3 that Solomon fought against the city of **H**

HAMATHITES (2) [HAMATH]

Ge 10:18 Arvadites, Zemarites, and **H**.
1Ch 1:16 Arvadites, Zemarites, and **H**.

HAMMATH (2)

Jos 19:35 territory were Ziddim, Zer, **H**, Rakkath, Kinnereth,
1Ch 2:55 All these were Kenites who descended from **H**,

HAMMEDATHA (4)

Est 3:1 King Xerxes promoted Haman son of **H** the
3:10 and giving it to Haman son of **H** the Agagite—
9:10 the ten sons of Haman son of **H**, the enemy of the
9:24 Haman son of **H** the Agagite, the enemy of the

HAMMER (7) [HAMMERED, SLEDGEHAMMERS]

Nu 16:38 then **h** the metal of the incense burners into a sheet
Jdg 4:21 Jael quietly crept up to him with a **h** and tent peg.
5:26 her right hand she reached for the workman's **h**.
1Ki 6:7 entire structure was built without the sound of **h**,
Jer 10:4 and then fasten it securely with **h** and nails
23:29 "Is it not like a mighty **h** that smashes rock to
50:23 Babylon, the mightiest **h** in all the earth,

HAMMERED (12) [HAMMER]

Ex 25:18 Then use **h** gold to make two cherubim, and place
25:31 "Make a lampstand of pure, **h** gold. The entire
25:36 with the stem, and they must be **h** from pure gold.
37:7 He made two figures of cherubim out of **h** gold
37:17 he made the lampstand, again using pure, **h** gold.
37:22 with the stem, and they were **h** from pure gold.
Nu 16:39 and they were **h** out into a sheet of metal to cover
Jdg 5:22 Then the horses' hooves **h** the ground,
1Ki 10:16 made two hundred large shields of **h** gold,
10:17 He also made three hundred smaller shields of **h**
2Ch 9:15 made two hundred large shields of **h** gold,
9:16 He also made three hundred smaller shields of **h**

HAMMOLEKETH (1)

1Ch 7:18 Makir's sister **H** gave birth to Ishhod, Abiezer,

HAMMON (2)

Jos 19:28 Abdon, Rehob, **H**, Kanah, and as far as Greater
1Ch 6:76 **H**, and Kiriathaim, each with its pasturelands.

HAMMOTH-DOR (1)

Jos 21:32 in Galilee (a city of refuge), **H**, and Kartan—

HAMMUEL (1)

1Ch 4:26 The descendants of Mishma were **H**, Zaccur,

HAMONAH (1)

Eze 39:16 (There will be a town there named **H**—

HAMOR (10)

Ge 33:19 the land he camped on from the family of **H**,
34:2 Shechem son of **H** the Hivite, saw her, he took her
34:6 Meanwhile, **H**, Shechem's father, came out to
34:8 **H** told Jacob and his sons, "My son Shechem is
34:13 But Dinah's brothers deceived Shechem and **H**
34:18 **H** and Shechem gladly agreed,
34:26 including **H** and Shechem. They rescued Dinah
Jos 24:32 the sons of **H** for one hundred pieces of silver.
Jdg 9:28 Serve the men of **H**, who are Shechem's true
Ac 7:16 had bought from the sons of **H** in Shechem.

HAMUEL [KJV] See HAMMUEL

HAMUL (3) [HAMULITES]

Ge 46:12 of Canaan.) The sons of Perez were Hezron and **H**.
Nu 26:21 The Hamulites, named after their ancestor **H**.
1Ch 2:5 The sons of Perez were Hezron and **H**.

HAMULITES (1) [HAMUL]

Nu 26:21 The **H**, named after their ancestor Hamul.

HAMUTAL (3)

2Ki 23:31 His mother was **H**, the daughter of Jeremiah from
24:18 His mother was **H**, the daughter of Jeremiah from
Jer 52:1 His mother's name was **H**, the daughter of

HANAMEL (4)

Jer 32:7 "Your cousin **H** son of Shallum will come and say
32:8 he would, **H** came and visited me in the prison.
32:9 paying **H** seventeen pieces of silver for it.
32:12 I did all this in the presence of my cousin **H**,

HANAN (12) [BAAL-HANAN, BEN-HANAN]

1Ch 8:23 Abdon, Zicri, **H**,
8:38 Bokeru, Ishmael, Sheariah, Obadiah, and **H**.
9:44 Bokeru, Ishmael, Sheariah, Obadiah, and **H**.
11:43 **H** son of Maacah; / Joshaphat from Mithna;
Ezr 2:46 Hagab, Shalmai, **H**,
Ne 7:49 **H**, Giddel, Gahar,
8:7 Hodiah, Maaseiah, Kelita, Azariah, Jozabad, **H**,
10:10 Shebaniah, Hodiah, Kelita, Pelaiah, **H**,
10:22 Pelatiah, **H**, Anaiah,
10:26 Ahiah, **H**, Anan,
13:13 And I appointed **H** son of Zaccur and grandson of
Jer 35:4 the room assigned to the sons of **H** son of Igdaliah,

HANANEL (4)

Ne 3:1 which they dedicated, and the Tower of **H**.
12:39 past the Fish Gate and the Tower of **H**, and went
Jer 31:38 for me, from the Tower of **H** to the Corner Gate.
Zec 14:10 and from the Tower of **H** to the king's

HANANI (12)

1Ki 16:1 to King Baasha by the prophet Jehu son of **H**:
16:7 and his family through the prophet Jehu son of **H**.
1Ch 25:4 Jerimoth, Hananiah, **H**, Eliathah, Geddalti,
25:25 The eighteenth lot fell to **H** and twelve of his sons
2Ch 16:7 At that time **H** the seer came to King Asa and told
16:10 so angry with **H** for saying this that he threw him
19:2 Jehu son of **H** the seer went out to meet him.
20:34 are recorded in *The Record of Jehu Son of H*,
Ezr 10:20 From the family of Immer: **H** and Zebadiah.
Ne 1:2 **H**, one of my brothers, came to visit me with some
7:2 of governing Jerusalem to my brother **H**,
12:36 Milalai, Gilalai, Maai, Nethanel, Judah, and **H**.

HANANIAH (28) [SHADRACH]

1Ch 3:19 The sons of Zerubbabel were Meshullam and **H**.
3:21 The sons of **H** were Pelatiah and Jeshaiah.
8:24 **H**, Elam, Anthothijah,
25:4 Shubael, Jerimoth, **H**, Hanani, Eliathah, Geddalti,
25:23 The sixteenth lot fell to **H** and twelve of his sons
2Ch 26:11 They were under the direction of **H**, one of the
Ezr 10:28 family of Bebai: Jehohanan, **H**, Zabbai, and Athlai.
Ne 3:8 Beyond him was **H**, a manufacturer of perfumes.
3:30 Next **H** son of Shelemiah and Hanun, the sixth son
7:2 along with **H**, the commander of the fortress,
10:23 Hoshea, **H**, Hasshub,
12:12 **H** was leader of the family of Jeremiah.
12:41 Miniamin, Micaiah, Elioenai, Zechariah, and **H**—
Jer 28:1 **H** son of Azzur, a prophet from Gibeon,
28:5 Jeremiah responded to **H** as they stood in front of
28:10 Then **H** the prophet took the yoke off Jeremiah's
28:11 And **H** said again to the crowd that had gathered,
28:13 "Go and tell **H**, 'This is what the LORD says:
28:15 Then Jeremiah the prophet said to **H**, "Listen, **H**!
28:17 Two months later, **H** died.
36:12 Gemariah son of Shaphan, Zedekiah son of **H**,
37:13 was Irijah son of Shelemiah and grandson of **H**.
Da 1:6 Daniel, **H**, Mishael, and Azariah were four of the
1:7 **H** was called Shadrach. / Mishael was called
1:11 to look after Daniel, **H**, Mishael, and Azariah.
1:19 him as much as Daniel, **H**, Mishael, and Azariah.
2:17 Then Daniel went home and told his friends **H**,

HAND (357) [HAND-TO-HAND, HAND-WASHING, HANDED, HANDFUL, HANDFULS, HANDING, HANDMADE, HANDS, HANDWRITING, LEFT-HANDED, RIGHT-HAND, UNDERHANDED]

FROM...HAND (12) Lev 14:28; Nu 5:25; Dt 26:4; 2Sa 23:21; 1Ki 11:31; 1Ch 11:23; 28:19; Job 2:10; Ps 39:10; Ecc 2:24; Jer 25:15; Rev 5:7

HAND OF...GOD (12) Ezr 7:6,9,28; 8:18,31; Ne 2:8,18; Job 2:10; 19:21; Ecc 2:24; Lk 7:16; Heb 1:3

HAND OF THE...LORD*/LORD (6) 1Ch 28:19; Ezr 7:6,28; Isa 66:14; Eze 1:3; Lk 1:66

INTO...HAND (3) Lev 14:15,26; Ps 31:5

LEFT HAND (12) Ge 48:13,14; Lev 14:15,17,26; Jdg 3:21; 5:26; 2Sa 20:10; 1Ch 12:2; SS 2:6; 8:3; Mt 6:3

MIGHTY HAND (1) Ps 17:14

RIGHT HAND (65) Ge 48:13,14,17,18; Ex 15:6,6; Lev 8:23; 14:14,17,25,28; Dt 33:2; Jdg 5:26; 2Sa 20:9; 1Ki 2:19; Ps 18:35; 21:8; 48:10; 63:8; 73:23; 74:11; 89:13; 110:1,5; 137:5; Pr 3:16; SS 2:6; 8:3; Isa 41:10,13; 45:1; 48:13; Jer 22:24; Zec 3:1; Mt 6:3; 22:44; 25:33; 26:64; 27:29; Mk 12:36; 14:62; 16:19; Lk 6:6; 20:42; 22:69; Ac 2:33,34; 3:7; 5:31; 7:55,56; Eph 1:20; Col 3:1; Heb 1:3,13; 8:1; 10:12; Rev 1:16,17,20; 2:1; 5:1,7; 10:5; 13:16

Ge 8:9 and Noah held out his **h** and drew the dove back
19:16 the angels seized his **h** and the hands of his wife
25:26 Then the other twin was born with his **h** grasping
38:28 were being born, one of them reached out his **h**,
38:29 But then he drew back his **h**, and the other baby
40:11 I was holding Pharaoh's wine cup in my **h**, so I
40:11 into it. Then I placed the cup in Pharaoh's **h**."
41:44 but no one will move a **h** or a foot in the entire
48:13 the boys so Ephraim was at Jacob's left **h** and Manasseh was at his right **h**.
48:14 So his right **h** was on the head of Ephraim, and his left **h** was on the head of Manasseh,
48:17 his father had laid his right **h** on Ephraim's head.
48:18 over here is older. Put your right **h** on his head."
Ex 4:2 asked him, "What do you have there in your **h**?"
4:6 said to Moses, "Put your **h** inside your robe."
4:6 it out again, his **h** was white as snow with leprosy.
4:7 "Now put your **h** back into your robe again,"
4:20 land of Egypt. In his **h** he carried the staff of God.
6:1 "When he feels my powerful **h** upon him, he will
9:22 said to Moses, "Lift your **h** toward the sky,
10:12 "Raise your **h** over the land of Egypt to bring on
10:21 "Lift your **h** toward heaven, and a deep
10:22 So Moses lifted his **h** toward heaven, and there
14:21 Then Moses raised his **h** over the sea,
14:26 said to Moses, "Raise your **h** over the sea again.
14:27 sun began to rise, Moses raised his **h** over the sea.
15:6 "Your right **h**, O LORD, / is glorious in power. / Your right **h**, O LORD,
15:12 You raised up your **h**, / and the earth swallowed
17:9 the top of the hill with the staff of God in my **h**."
17:11 his hands, the Amalekites gained the upper **h**.
21:24 Similarly, the payment must be **h** for **h**, foot for
21:29 Suppose, on the other **h**, that the owner knew the
33:22 and cover you with my **h** until I have passed.
33:23 Then I will remove my **h**, and you will see me
36:5 "We have more than enough materials on **h** now
Lev 1:4 Lay your **h** on its head so the LORD will accept it
3:2 Lay your **h** on the animal's head, and slaughter it
3:8 by laying your **h** on its head and slaughtering it at
3:13 lay your **h** on its head, and slaughter it at the
4:4 lay his **h** on the bull's head, and slaughter it there
4:24 He is to lay his **h** on the goat's head and slaughter
4:29 They are to lay a **h** on the head of the sin offering
4:33 They are to lay a **h** on the head of the sin offering
8:23 the thumb of his right **h**, and the big toe of his right
14:14 on the thumb of the right **h**, and on the big toe of
14:15 of the olive oil into the palm of his own left **h**.
14:17 then put some of the oil remaining in his left **h** on
14:17 on the thumb of the right **h**, and on the big toe of
14:18 The oil remaining in the priest's **h** will then be
14:25 on the thumb of the right **h**, and on the big toe of
14:26 of the olive oil into the palm of his own left **h**.
14:28 then put some of the olive oil from his **h** on the
14:28 on the thumb of the right **h**, and on the big toe of
14:29 The oil that is still in the priest's **h** will then be
21:19 or has a broken foot or **h**,
Nu 5:25 take the jealousy offering from the woman's **h**,
11:8 and made flour by grinding it with **h** mills
20:11 Then Moses raised his **h** and struck the rock twice
22:23 standing in the road with a drawn sword in his **h**.
22:31 in the roadway with a drawn sword in his **h**.
Dt 2:15 The LORD had lifted his **h** against them until all
2:31 I have begun to **h** King Sihon and his land over to
7:23 But the LORD your God will **h** them over to you.
15:9 a loan because the year of release is close at **h**.
19:21 for eye, tooth for tooth, **h** for **h**, foot for foot.
23:25 pluck a few heads of your neighbor's grain by **h**,
25:12 her **h** must be cut off without pity.
26:4 The priest will then take the basket from your **h**
28:13 not the tail, and you will always have the upper **h**.
30:14 The message is very close at **h**; it is on your lips
31:5 The LORD will **h** over to you the people who live
32:40 Now I raise my **h** to heaven / and declare,
33:2 with flaming fire at his right **h**.
Jos 2:19 will be killed—not a **h** will be laid on any of them.
5:13 and saw a man facing him with sword in **h**.
Jdg 3:21 Ehud reached with his left **h**, pulled out the dagger
5:26 Then with her left **h** she reached for a tent peg,
5:26 and with her right **h** she reached for the workman's
6:21 touched the meat and bread with the staff in his **h**,
15:12 to tie you up and **h** you over to the Philistines."
15:13 will tie you up and **h** you over to the Philistines,"
16:26 said to the servant who was leading him by the **h**,
Ru 4:7 to remove his sandal and **h** it to the other party.
1Sa 7:13 the LORD's powerful **h** was raised against the
12:15 then his **h** will be as heavy upon you as it was
17:57 him to Saul with the Philistine's head still in his **h**.
18:10 this happened. But Saul, who had a spear in his **h**,
23:20 and we will catch him and **h** him over to you!"
24:11 Look, my father, at what I have in my **h**. It is a
25:8 give us any provisions you might have on **h**."
28:19 the LORD will **h** you and the army of Israel over
2Sa 5:19 Will you **h** them over to me?" The LORD
6:6 and Uzzah put out his **h** to steady the Ark of God.
15:5 Instead, he took them by the **h** and embraced them.
20:9 and took him by the beard with his right **h** as
20:10 Amasa didn't notice the dagger in his left **h**,
20:21 If you **h** him over to me, we will leave the city in
21:20 a huge man with six fingers on each **h** and six toes
23:6 for they tear the **h** that touches them.
23:10 He killed Philistines until his **h** was too tired to lift
23:21 Benaiah wrenched the spear from the Egyptian's **h**
1Ki 2:19 brought for his mother, and she sat at his right **h**.
11:31 'I am about to tear the kingdom from the **h** of
13:4 But instantly the king's **h** became paralyzed in that
13:6 "Please ask the LORD your God to restore my **h**
13:6 and the king's **h** became normal again.
18:44 "I saw a little cloud about the size of a **h** rising
20:13 enemy forces? Today I will **h** them all over to you.
2Ki 5:11 "I expected him to wave his **h** over the leprosy
10:15 "If you are," Jehu said, "then give me your **h**."
10:15 So Jehonadab put out his **h**, and Jehu helped him
11:8 for the king and keep your weapons in **h**.
13:16 Then Elisha told the king of Israel to put his **h** on
18:21 breaks beneath your weight and pierces your **h**.
21:14 and I will **h** them over as plunder for their enemies.
1Ch 11:23 Benaiah wrenched the spear from the Egyptian's **h**
12:2 or sling stones with their left **h** as well as their
13:9 and Uzzah put out his **h** to steady the Ark.
13:10 him dead because he had laid his **h** on the Ark.
14:10 Will you **h** them over to me?" The LORD
20:6 a huge man with six fingers on each **h** and six toes
28:19 "was given to me in writing from the **h** of the
29:12 Power and might are in your **h**, and it is at your
2Ch 15:5 to travel. Problems troubled the nation on every **h**.
23:7 for the king and keep your weapons in **h**.
30:12 God's **h** was on the people in the land of Judah,
Ezr 7:6 because the gracious **h** of the LORD his God was
7:9 for the gracious **h** of his God was on him.
7:14 based on your God's law, which is in your **h**.
7:28 because the gracious **h** of the LORD my God was
8:18 Since the gracious **h** of our God was on us,
8:31 And the gracious **h** of our God protected us
Ne 2:8 because the gracious **h** of God was on me.
2:18 Then I told them about how the gracious **h** of God
4:17 on their work with one **h** supporting their load and one **h** holding a weapon.
6:5 servant came with an open letter in his **h**,
Job 2:10 Should we accept only good things from the **h** of
6:9 I wish he would reach out his **h** and kill me.
7:1 person's life is long and hard, like that of a hired **h**,
12:10 For the life of every living thing is in his **h**,
13:21 Remove your **h** from me, and don't terrify me with
19:21 have mercy, for the **h** of God has struck me.
21:5 be stunned. Put your **h** over your mouth in shock.
30:18 With a strong **h**, God grabs my garment. He grips
34:20 the mighty are removed without human **h**.
40:4 I will put my **h** over my mouth in silence.
41:8 If you lay a **h** on it, you will never forget the battle
Ps 13:2 How long will my enemy have the upper **h**?
17:14 Save me by your mighty **h**, O LORD,
18:35 Your right **h** supports me; / your gentleness has
21:8 Your strong right **h** will seize all those who hate
31:5 I entrust my spirit into your **h**. / Rescue me,
32:4 and night your **h** of discipline was heavy on me.
37:24 will not fall, / for the LORD holds them by the **h**.
39:5 My life is no longer than the width of my **h**.
39:10 I am exhausted by the blows from your **h**.
48:10 Your strong right **h** is filled with victory.
58:2 are crooked; / you **h** out violence instead of justice.
63:8 your strong right **h** holds me securely.
73:23 I still belong to you; / you are holding my right **h**.
74:11 Why do you hold back your strong right **h**?
75:8 For the LORD holds a cup in his **h**; / it is full of
76:5 of death. / No warrior could lift a **h** against us.
82:2 "How long will you judges **h** down unjust
89:13 Powerful is your arm! / Strong is your **h**!
89:13 Your right **h** is lifted high in glorious strength.
104:28 You open your **h** to feed them, and they are
110:1 said to my Lord, / "Sit in honor at my right **h**
110:5 The Lord stands at your right **h** to protect you.
136:12 He acted with a strong **h** and powerful arm.
137:5 let my right **h** forget its skill upon the harp.
139:5 You place your **h** of blessing on my head.
139:10 even there your **h** will guide me, / and your
145:16 When you open your **h**, / you satisfy the hunger
Pr 3:16 She offers you life in her right **h**, and riches
5:9 and **h** over to merciless people everything you
30:32 about it—cover your mouth with your **h** in shame.
31:20 She extends a helping **h** to the poor and opens her
Ecc 2:24 Then I realized that this pleasure is from the **h** of
7:17 On the other **h**, don't be too wicked either—
SS 2:6 His left **h** is under my head, and his right **h** embraces me.
8:3 Your left **h** would be under my head and your right **h** would embrace me.
Isa 10:5 of my anger. Its military power is a club in my **h**.
10:15 Can a whip strike unless a **h** is moving it? Can a
11:8 a little child will put its **h** in a nest of deadly
11:15 He will wave his **h** over the Euphrates River,
14:27 his plans? When his **h** moves, who can stop him?"
19:4 I will **h** Egypt over to a hard, cruel master, to a
23:11 The LORD holds out his **h** over the seas.
25:10 For the LORD's good **h** will rest on Jerusalem.
36:6 breaks beneath your weight and pierces your **h**.
40:12 Who else has held the oceans in his **h**? Who has
41:10 I will uphold you with my victorious right **h**.
41:13 I am holding you by your right **h**—I, the LORD
44:20 this idol that I'm holding in my **h**, a lie?"
45:1 his anointed one, whose right **h** he will empower.
48:13 It was my **h** that laid the foundations of the earth.
48:13 The palm of my right **h** spread out the heavens
49:2 He has hidden me in the shadow of his **h**. I am like
49:4 Yet I leave it all in the LORD's **h**; I will trust
49:16 See, I have written your name on my **h**.
51:16 in your mouth and hidden you safely within my **h**.
62:8 "I will never again **h** you over to your enemies.
63:12 when Moses lifted up his **h**, establishing his
64:8 you are the potter. We are all formed by your **h**.
66:14 Everyone will see the good **h** of the LORD on his
Jer 5:31 and the priests rule with an iron **h**.
15:9 I will **h** over to the enemy to be killed,"
15:13 I will **h** over their wealth and treasures as plunder
15:17 I sat alone because your **h** was on me. I burst with
18:6 As the clay is in the potter's **h**, so are you in my **h**.
20:4 I will **h** the people of Judah over to the king of
21:7 I will **h** them over to King Nebuchadnezzar of
22:24 Even if you were the signet ring on my right **h**,
22:25 I will **h** you over to those who seek to kill you,
25:15 "Take from my **h** this cup filled to the brim with
31:32 with their ancestors when I took them by the **h**
32:3 I am about to **h** this city over to the king of
32:28 I will **h** this city over to the Babylonians and to
34:2 I am about to **h** this city over to the king of
34:21 I will **h** over King Zedekiah of Judah and his
38:16 or **h** you over to the men who want you dead."
38:19 "for the Babylonians will **h** me over to the Judeans
46:26 I will **h** them over to those who want them killed—
La 3:3 against me. Day and night his **h** is heavy upon me.
5:7 but they died before the **h** of judgment fell.
Eze 1:3 and I felt the **h** of the LORD take hold of me.
2:9 Then I looked and saw a **h** reaching out to me,
8:3 He put out what seemed to be a **h** and took me by
9:2 faces north, each carrying a battle club in his **h**.
10:7 Then one of the cherubim reached out his **h**
11:9 and **h** you over to foreigners who will carry out my
21:5 My sword is in my **h**, and it will not return to its
21:27 the right to judge it. Then I will **h** it over to him.
21:31 I will **h** you over to cruel men who are skilled in
23:24 And I will **h** you over to them so they can do with
23:28 I will surely **h** you over to your enemies, to those
23:46 and **h** them over to be terrorized and plundered.
25:10 And I will **h** Moab over to nomads from the
25:14 By the **h** of my people of Israel, I will accomplish
30:12 the Nile River and **h** the land over to wicked men.
30:24 arms of Babylon's king and put my sword in his **h**.
30:25 And when I put my sword in the **h** of Babylon's
36:7 I have raised my **h** and sworn an oath that those
37:17 Now hold them together in your **h** as one stick.
37:19 to Judah. I will make them one stick in my **h**.'
40:3 He was holding in his **h** a measuring tape and a
44:12 So I have raised my **h** and taken an oath that they
Da 5:5 **h** writing on the plaster wall of the king's palace,
5:5 The king himself saw the **h** as it wrote,
5:24 So God has sent this **h** to write a message.
10:10 Just then a **h** touched me and lifted me,
Hos 11:3 Israel how to walk, leading him along by the **h**.
Am 5:19 he leans his **h** against a wall in his house—
Zep 3:15 For the LORD will remove his **h** of judgment
Zec 2:1 I saw a man with a measuring line in his **h**.
3:1 Satan was there at the angel's right **h**,

4: 10 to see the plumb line in Zerubbabel's **h**.
Mt 5: 30 And if your **h**—even if it is your stronger **h**—causes you to sin,
6: 3 don't tell your left **h** what your right **h** is doing.
8: 15 But when Jesus touched her **h**, the fever left her.
9: 18 again if you just come and lay your **h** upon her."
9: 25 Jesus went in and took the girl by the **h**, and she
12: 10 where he noticed a man with a deformed **h**.
12: 13 Then he said to the man, "Reach out your **h**."
12: 13 The man reached out his **h**, and it became normal,
14: 31 Instantly Jesus reached out his **h** and grabbed him.
15: 2 "They ignore our tradition of ceremonial **h**
18: 8 So if your **h** or foot causes you to sin, cut it off
20: 19 Then they will **h** him over to the Romans to be
22: 13 'Bind him **h** and foot and throw him out into the
22: 44 said to my Lord, / Sit in honor at my right **h**
25: 33 He will place the sheep at his right **h** and the goats
26: 64 sitting at God's right **h** in the place of power
27: 29 and they placed a stick in his right **h** as a scepter.
Mk 1: 31 and as he took her by the **h** and helped her to sit
3: 1 and noticed a man with a deformed **h**.
3: 2 Would he heal the man's **h** on the Sabbath? If he
3: 5 Then he said to the man, "Reach out your **h**."
3: 5 The man reached out his **h**, and it became normal
5: 41 Holding her **h**, he said to her, "Get up, little girl!"
7: 2 the usual Jewish ritual of **h** washing before eating.
8: 23 Jesus took the blind man by the **h** and led him out
9: 27 But Jesus took him by the **h** and helped him to his
9: 43 If your **h** causes you to sin, cut it off. It is better to enter heaven with only one **h** than to
10: 33 sentence him to die and **h** him over to the Romans.
12: 36 said to my Lord, / Sit in honor at my right **h**
14: 62 sitting at God's right **h** in the place of power
16: 19 sat down in the place of honor at God's right **h**.
Lk 1: 66 For the **h** of the Lord is surely upon him in a
4: 40 diseases were, the touch of his **h** healed every one.
6: 6 a man with a deformed right **h** was in the
6: 8 He said to the man with the deformed **h**, "Come
6: 10 and then said to the man, "Reach out your **h**."
6: 10 The man reached out his **h**, and it became normal
7: 16 and "We have seen the **h** of God at work today."
8: 54 Then Jesus took her by the **h** and said in a loud
9: 62 "Anyone who puts a **h** to the plow and then looks
20: 42 said to my Lord, / Sit in honor at my right **h**
22: 69 will be sitting at God's right **h** in the place of
Jn 7: 30 but no one laid a **h** on him, because his time had
10: 12 A hired **h** will run when he sees a wolf coming.
10: 13 The hired **h** runs away because he is merely hired
19: 42 the Passover and since the tomb was close at **h**,
20: 25 and place my **h** into the wound in his side."
20: 27 my hands. Put your **h** into the wound in my side.
Ac 2: 33 throne of highest honor in heaven, at God's right **h**.
2: 34 said to my Lord, / Sit in honor at my right **h**
3: 7 Then Peter took the lame man by the right **h**
5: 31 him in the place of honor at his right **h** as Prince
7: 55 standing in the place of honor at God's right **h**.
7: 56 standing in the place of honor at God's right **h**!"
9: 9 So his companions led him by the **h** to Damascus.
9: 41 He gave her his **h** and helped her up. Then he
13: 11 And now the Lord has laid his **h** of punishment
13: 11 around begging for someone to take his **h**
13: 16 So Paul stood, lifted his **h** to quiet them,
26: 1 So Paul, with a gesture of his **h**, started his
28: 3 driven out by the heat, fastened itself onto his **h**.
Ro 10: 8 the Scriptures say, "The message is close at **h**;
1Co 12: 15 am not a part of the body because I am not a **h**,"
12: 21 The eye can never say to the **h**, "I don't need
16: 21 is my greeting, which I write with my own **h**—
Eph 1: 20 of honor at God's right **h** in the heavenly realms.
Col 3: 1 where Christ sits at God's right **h** in the place of
2Th 3: 17 my greeting, which I write with my own **h**—
Heb 1: 3 he sat down in the place of honor at the right **h** of
1: 13 as he did to his Son, / "Sit in honor at my right **h**
8: 1 place of highest honor in heaven, at God's right **h**.
8: 9 with their ancestors / when I took them by the **h**
10: 12 at the place of highest honor at God's right **h**.
Rev 1: 16 He held seven stars in his right **h**, and a sharp
1: 17 But he laid his right **h** on me and said, "Don't be
1: 20 meaning of the seven stars you saw in my right **h**
2: 1 the one who holds the seven stars in his right **h**,
5: 1 And I saw a scroll in the right **h** of the one who
5: 7 and took the scroll from the right **h** of the one
6: 5 and its rider was holding a pair of scales in his **h**.
10: 2 And in his **h** was a small scroll, which he had
10: 5 the sea and on the land lifted his right **h** to heaven.
13: 16 to be given a mark on the right **h** or on the
14: 9 or who accepts his mark on the forehead or the **h**
14: 14 gold crown on his head and a sharp sickle in his **h**.
17: 4 She held in her **h** a gold goblet full of obscenities
20: 1 to the bottomless pit and a heavy chain in his **h**.
21: 15 The angel who talked to me held in his **h** a gold

HAND-TO-HAND (2) [HAND]

2Sa 2: 14 of our warriors put on an exhibition of **h** combat."
Zec 14: 13 They will fight against each other in **h** combat;

HAND-WASHING (1) [HAND, WASH]

Mk 7: 5 For they eat without first performing the **h**

HANDED (62) [HAND]

Lev 9: 13 They **h** the animal to him piece by piece,
Dt 2: 33 But the LORD our God **h** him over to us, and we
3: 3 So the LORD our God **h** King Og and all his
4: 44 This is the law that Moses **h** down to the Israelites.
9: 11 the LORD **h** me the two stone tablets with the
19: 12 and **h** over to the dead person's avenger to be
Jdg 2: 14 so he **h** them over to marauders who stole their
3: 8 and he **h** them over to King Cushan-rishathaim of
4: 2 So the LORD **h** them over to King Jabin of
6: 1 So the LORD **h** them over to the Midianites for
6: 13 abandoned us and **h** us over to the Midianites."
10: 7 and he **h** them over to the Philistines
13: 1 so the LORD **h** them over to the Philistines,
1Sa 23: 7 God has **h** him over to me, for he has trapped
26: 8 "God has surely **h** your enemy over to you this
2Sa 18: 28 who has **h** over the rebels who dared to stand
21: 6 seven of Saul's sons or grandsons be **h** over to us,
2Ki 18: 30 This city will never be **h** over to the Assyrian
1Ch 6: 32 following all the regulations **h** down to them.
16: 12 the miracles, and the judgments he **h** down,
22: 18 He has **h** them over to me, and they are now
2Ch 13: 16 and God **h** them over to Judah in defeat.
16: 8 on the LORD, and he **h** them all over to you.
28: 14 and **h** over the plunder in the sight of all the
36: 17 and sick. God **h** them all over to Nebuchadnezzar.
Ne 9: 27 So you **h** them over to their enemies. But in their
Job 16: 11 God has **h** me over to sinners. He has tossed me
Ps 31: 8 You have not **h** me over to my enemy / but have
78: 3 and know, / stories our ancestors **h** down to us.
78: 50 Egyptians' lives / but **h** them over to the plague.
105: 5 the miracles and the judgments he **h** down,
106: 41 He **h** them over to pagan nations, / and those who
118: 18 me severely, / but he has not **h** me over to death.
Isa 23: 13 The Assyrians have **h** Babylon over to the wild
36: 15 This city will never be **h** over to the Assyrian
Jer 32: 12 and I **h** them to Baruch son of Neriah and grandson
32: 24 the city has been **h** over to the Babylonians,
38: 3 The city of Jerusalem will surely be **h** over to the
38: 18 This city will be **h** over to the Babylonians,
38: 20 "You won't be **h** over to them if you choose to
46: 24 she will be **h** over to men from the north."
Eze 16: 27 I **h** you over to your enemies, the Philistines,
23: 9 And so I **h** her over to her Assyrian lovers,
25: 10 from the eastern deserts, just as I **h** over Ammon.
31: 11 I **h** it over to a mighty nation that destroyed it as its
Mt 5: 25 into court, **h** over to an officer, and thrown in jail.
10: 17 For you will be **h** over to the courts and beaten in
22: 19 coin used for the tax." When they **h** him the coin,
Mk 12: 16 When they **h** it to him, he asked, "Whose picture
13: 9 You will be **h** over to the courts and beaten in the
Lk 4: 17 the messages of Isaiah the prophet was **h** to him,
4: 20 the scroll, **h** it back to the attendant, and sat down.
10: 35 The next day he **h** the innkeeper two pieces of
12: 58 and **h** over to an officer and thrown in jail.
18: 32 He will be **h** over to the Romans to be mocked,
24: 20 and **h** him over to be condemned to death,
Jn 18: 30 "We wouldn't have **h** him over to you if he
Ac 3: 13 This is the same Jesus whom you **h** over
6: 14 and change the customs Moses **h** down to us."
28: 17 in Jerusalem and **h** over to the Roman government,
Ro 4: 25 He was **h** over to die because of our sins, and he
Rev 15: 7 And one of the four living beings **h** each of the

HANDFUL (13) [HAND]

Lev 2: 2 and he will take a **h** of the flour mixed with olive
5: 12 who will scoop out a **h** as a token portion.
6: 15 The priest on duty will take a **h** of the choice flour
6: 16 After burning this **h**, the rest of the flour will
9: 17 grain offering, burning a **h** of the flour on the altar,
10: 12 "Take what is left of the grain offering after the **h**
Nu 5: 26 He will take a **h** as a token portion and burn it on
1Ki 17: 12 And I have only a **h** of flour left in the jar and a
20: 10 to provide more than a **h** for each of my soldiers."
Jer 37: 10 leaving only a **h** of wounded survivors, they would
44: 14 of returning home to Judah, only a **h** will escape."
Eze 10: 2 and take a **h** of glowing coals and scatter them
Da 11: 23 With a mere **h** of followers, he will become strong.

HANDFULS (3) [HAND]

Pr 8: 26 made the earth and fields and the first **h** of soil.
Eze 13: 19 You turn my people away from me for a few **h** of
Ac 22: 23 off their coats, and tossed **h** of dust into the air.

HANDING (2) [HAND]

2Ki 17: 20 He punished them by **h** them over to their attackers
Ob 1: 14 **h** them over to their enemies in that terrible time of

HANDIWORK (2) [WORK]

Job 14: 15 and you would yearn for me, your **h**.
40: 19 It is a prime example of God's amazing **h**. Only its

HANDKERCHIEFS (1)

Ac 19: 12 so that even when **h** or cloths that had touched his

HANDLE (15) [HANDLED, HANDLING]

Ex 18: 18 This job is too heavy a burden for you to **h** all by
Nu 18: 7 must personally **h** all the sacred service associated
Dt 1: 17 that are too difficult for you, and I will **h** them.'
19: 5 them swings an ax and the ax head flies off the **h**,
Jdg 3: 22 so deep that the **h** disappeared beneath the king's
2Sa 21: 19 The **h** of his spear was as thick as a weaver's
1Ki 8: 64 altar in the LORD's presence was too small to **h**
1Ch 20: 5 The **h** of Lahmi's spear was as thick as a weaver's
28: 17 solid gold meat hooks used to **h** the sacrificial meat
2Ch 7: 7 because the bronze altar he had built could not **h**
Pr 20: 22 this wrong." Wait for the LORD to **h** the matter.
Mk 16: 18 They will be able to **h** snakes with safety, and if
Lk 16: 1 "A rich man hired a manager to **h** his affairs,
1Co 3: 2 because you couldn't **h** anything stronger.
Col 2: 21 "Don't **h**, don't eat, don't touch."

HANDLED (2) [HANDLE]

2Ch 31: 20 King Hezekiah **h** the distribution throughout all
Da 2: 14 Daniel **h** the situation with wisdom and discretion.

HANDLING (5) [HANDLE]

Da 6: 4 for some fault in the way Daniel was **h** his affairs,
Mt 25: 21 You have been faithful in **h** this small amount,
25: 23 You have been faithful in **h** this small amount,
Lk 23: 47 When the captain of the Roman soldiers **h** the
2Co 8: 20 find fault with the way we are **h** this generous gift.

HANDMADE (1) [HAND, MAKE]

Ac 19: 26 this man Paul has persuaded many people that **h**

HANDMAID (1) [MAID]

Ps 116: 16 yes, I am your servant, the son of your **h**,

HANDMAID [KJV] See also GIRL, MAID, SERVANT, SLAVE, WOMAN

HANDPICKED (1) [PICK]

Isa 27: 12 will gather them together one by one like **h** grain.

HANDS (288) [HAND]

FROM...HANDS (10) Ex 29:25; Jdg 7:6; Isa 49:24; 51:22; Jer 15:21; Eze 39:3; Hos 2:10; Hab 3:4; Ac 7:53; Rev 10:10

HANDS ON (42) Ge 34:28; 48:14; Ex 29:10,15,19; Lev 4:15; 8:14,18,22; 16:21; 24:14; Nu 8:10,12; 27:18,23; Dt 34:9; Jdg 16:29; 19:27; 2Ki 4:34; 13:16; 2Ch 29:23; Est 3:6; Jer 2:37; Mt 19:13,15; Mk 5:23; 6:5; 7:32; 8:23; 10:16; 16:18; Ac 6:6; 8:19; 9:12,17; 13:3; 19:6; 27:19; 28:8; 1Ti 4:14; 2Ti 1:6; 1Jn 5:18

HUMAN HANDS (19) Ex 19:13; 2Sa 24:14; 2Ki 19:18; 1Ch 21:13; 2Ch 32:19; Ps 115:4; 135:15; Isa 37:19; Eze 1:8; 10:8,21; Hos 13:2; Mk 14:58,58; Ac 7:48; 17:25; 2Co 5:1; Heb 8:2; 9:11

INTO THE HANDS (10) Jdg 15:18; 2Sa 24:14; 1Ch 21:13; Job 16:11; Isa 51:23; Eze 10:7; Mt 26:45; Mk 14:41; Lk 24:7; Heb 10:31

Ge 19: 16 his hand and the **h** of his wife and two daughters
27: 22 but the **h** are Esau's," Isaac said to himself.
27: 23 because Jacob's **h** felt hairy just like Esau's.
34: 28 everything they could lay their **h** on, both inside
48: 14 as he reached out to lay his **h** on the boys' heads.
Ex 3: 6 he hid his face in his **h** because he was afraid to
9: 29 the city, I will lift my **h** and pray to the LORD.
9: 33 As he lifted his **h** to the LORD, all at once the
12: 11 and carry your walking sticks in your **h**.
13: 9 like a mark branded on your **h** or your forehead.
13: 16 ceremony will be like a mark branded on your **h**
15: 17 the sanctuary, O Lord, that your **h** have made.
17: 11 As long as Moses held up the staff with his **h**,
17: 11 But whenever he lowered his **h**, the Amalekites
17: 12 stood on each side, holding up his **h** until sunset.
19: 13 They must not be touched by human **h**.'
29: 10 and Aaron and his sons will lay their **h** on its head.
29: 15 and his sons must lay their **h** on the head of one of
29: 19 have Aaron and his sons lay their **h** on its head
29: 24 Put all these in the **h** of Aaron and his sons to be
29: 25 Afterward take the bread from their **h**, and burn it
30: 19 Aaron and his sons will wash their **h** and feet there
32: 15 He held in his **h** the two stone tablets inscribed
34: 4 told him, carrying the two stone tablets in his **h**.
40: 31 and Aaron and Aaron's sons washed their **h**
Lev 4: 15 The leaders must then lay their **h** on the bull's head
7: 30 Present it to him with your own **h** as an offering
8: 14 and Aaron and his sons laid their **h** on its head
8: 18 and Aaron and his sons laid their **h** on its head
8: 22 Aaron and his sons laid their **h** on its head
8: 24 the thumb of their right **h**, and the big toe of their
9: 22 Aaron raised his **h** toward the people and blessed
15: 11 If the man touches you without first rinsing his **h**,
16: 12 after filling both his **h** with fragrant incense,
16: 21 He is to lay both of his **h** on the goat's head
24: 14 and tell all those who heard him to lay their **h** on
Nu 5: 18 in her **h** to determine whether or not her husband's
6: 19 and put them all into the Nazirite's **h**.
8: 10 the people of Israel must lay their **h** on them.
8: 12 "Next the Levites will lay their **h** on the heads of
24: 10 He angrily clapped his **h** and shouted, "I called
27: 18 who has the Spirit in him, and lay your **h** on him.
27: 23 Moses laid his **h** on him and commissioned him to
Dt 6: 8 Tie them to your **h** as a reminder, and wear them
7: 2 When the LORD your God **h** these nations over
7: 16 all the nations the LORD your God **h** over to you.
9: 15 holding in my **h** the two stone tablets of the
11: 18 Tie them to your **h** as a reminder, and wear them
20: 13 When the LORD your God **h** it over to you,
21: 6 **h** over the young cow whose neck was broken.
21: 7 they must say, 'Our **h** did not shed this blood,
21: 10 and the LORD your God **h** them over to you
33: 3 love the people; / all your holy ones are in your **h**.
34: 9 spirit of wisdom, for Moses had laid his **h** on him.
Jdg 4: 9 victory over Sisera will be at the **h** of a woman."
7: 5 In one group put all those who cup water in their **h**
7: 6 Only three hundred of the men drank from their **h**.
7: 20 They held the blazing torches in their left **h**
7: 20 and the horns in their right **h** and shouted,
14: 6 and he ripped the lion's jaws apart with his bare **h**.
14: 9 He scooped some of the honey into his **h** and ate it

15:18 of thirst and fall into the **h** of these pagan people?"
16:26 by the hand, "Place my **h** against the two pillars.
16:29 Then Samson put his **h** on the center pillars of the
19:27 was lying face down, with her **h** on the threshold.
1Sa 5: 4 This time his head and **h** had broken off and were
14:13 So they climbed up using both **h** and feet,
20:42 and each other's children into the LORD's **h**
25:26 and taking vengeance into your own **h**,
25:33 and carrying out vengeance with my own **h**.
2Sa 3:34 Your **h** were not bound; / your feet were not
4:12 They cut off their **h** and feet and hung their bodies
13:19 And then, with her face in her **h**, she went away
19: 4 The king covered his face with his **h** and kept on
24:14 "But let us fall into the **h** of the LORD, for his
mercy is great. Do not let me fall into human **h**."
1Ki 8:22 Then Solomon stood with his **h** lifted toward
8:24 and today you have fulfilled it with your own **h**.
8:38 or sorrow, raising their **h** toward this Temple,
8:54 where he had been kneeling with his **h** raised
18: 9 you are sending me to my death at the **h** of Ahab?
2Ki 4:34 on the child's eyes, and his **h** on the child's **h**.
9:35 they found only her skull, her feet, and her **h**.
11:12 and all the people clapped their **h** and shouted,
13:16 and Elisha laid his own **h** on the king's **h**.
19:18 only idols of wood and stone shaped by human **h**.
1Ch 21:13 "But let me fall into the **h** of the LORD,
21:13 is very great. Do not let me fall into human **h**."
2Ch 6:12 Then Solomon stood with his **h** spread out before
6:13 then he knelt down and lifted his **h** toward heaven.
6:15 and today you have fulfilled it with your own **h**.
6:29 or sorrow, raising their **h** toward this Temple,
29:23 the assembly of people, who laid their **h** on them.
32:19 he were one of the pagan gods, made by human **h**.
Ezr 9: 5 to my knees, lifted my **h** to the LORD my God.
Ne 8: 6 Amen!" as they lifted their **h** toward heaven.
9:37 The lush produce of this land piles up in the **h** of
Est 3: 6 So he decided it was not enough to lay **h** on
Job 5:18 he also bandages. He strikes, but his **h** also heal.
9:24 The whole earth is in the **h** of the wicked, and God
9:30 and cleanse my **h** with lye to make them absolutely
10: 3 the work of your own **h**, while sending joy
10: 8 " 'You formed me with your **h**; you made me,
11:13 your heart and lift up your **h** to him in prayer!
13:14 I will take my life in my **h** and say what I really
14: 6 We are like hired **h**, so let us finish the task you
16:11 He has tossed me into the **h** of the wicked.
22:30 even sinners will be rescued by your pure **h**."
29: 9 stood in silence and put their **h** over their mouths.
36:32 He fills his **h** with lightning bolts. He hurls each at
Ps 9:13 See how I suffer at the **h** of those who hate me.
18:24 because of the innocence of my **h** in his sight.
22:16 in on me. / They have pierced my **h** and feet.
24: 4 Only those whose **h** and hearts are pure, / who do
26: 6 I wash my **h** to declare my innocence. / I come to
26:10 Their **h** are dirty with wicked schemes, / and they
27:12 Do not let me fall into their **h**. / For they accuse me
28: 2 as I lift my **h** toward your holy sanctuary.
28: 5 or for what his **h** have made. / So he will tear them
31:15 My future is in your **h**. / Rescue me from those
44:20 our God / or spread our **h** in prayer to foreign gods,
47: 1 Come, everyone, and clap your **h** for joy!
58: 7 Make their weapons useless in their **h**.
63: 4 as long as I live, / lifting up my **h** to you in prayer.
66: 9 Our lives are in his **h**, / and he keeps our feet from
77: 2 long I pray, with **h** lifted toward heaven, pleading.
78:61 he surrendered his glory into enemy **h**.
78:72 with a true heart / and led them with skillful **h**.
81: 6 I will free your **h** from their heavy tasks.
81:14 How soon my **h** would be upon their foes!
88: 9 O LORD; / I lift my pleading **h** to you for mercy.
91:12 They will hold you with their **h** / to keep you from
95: 5 for he made it. / His **h** formed the dry land, too.
98: 8 Let the rivers clap their **h** in glee! / Let the hills
102:25 the earth, / and the heavens are the work of your **h**.
115: 4 things of silver and gold, / shaped by human **h**.
115: 7 or feel with their **h**, / or walk with their feet,
116: 3 Death had its **h** around my throat; / the terrors of
127: 4 young man / are like sharp arrows in a warrior's **h**.
134: 2 Lift your **h** in holiness, / and bless the LORD.
135:15 things of silver and gold, / shaped by human **h**.
140: 4 O LORD, keep me out of the **h** of the wicked.
141: 2 to you, / and my upraised **h** as an evening offering.
149: 6 be in their mouths, / and a sharp sword in their **h**—
Pr 6:10 little more slumber, a little folding of the **h** to rest
6:17 a lying tongue, / **h** that kill the innocent,
12:14 the work of their **h** also gives them many benefits.
14: 1 a foolish woman tears hers down with her own **h**.
21:25 people will be their ruin, for their **h** refuse to work.
24:33 little more slumber, a little folding of the **h** to rest
27:16 to stop the wind or hold something with greased **h**.
28: 8 It will end up in the **h** of someone who is kind to
31:19 Her **h** are busy spinning thread, her fingers
Ecc 7:26 Her passion is a trap, and her soft **h** will bind you.
9: 1 actions of godly and wise people are in God's **h**,
SS 5: 5 My **h** dripped with perfume, my fingers with
Isa 1:15 From now on, when you lift up your **h** in prayer,
1:15 For your **h** are covered with the blood of your
17: 8 for help or worship what their own **h** have made.
25:11 as a swimmer pushes down water with his **h**.
31: 7 and silver images that your sinful **h** have made.
35: 3 With this news, strengthen those who have tired **h**,
37:19 only idols of wood and stone shaped by human **h**.
44: 5 Some will write the LORD's name on their **h**
45:11 Do you give me orders about the work of my **h**?
45:12 to live on it. With my **h** I stretched out the heavens.
47: 6 their punishment by letting them fall into your **h**.
49:24 Who can snatch the plunder of war from the **h** of a
51:22 "See, I am taking the terrible cup from your **h**.
51:23 But I will put that cup into the **h** of those who
53:10 and the LORD's plan will prosper in his **h**.
55:12 and the trees of the field will clap their **h**!
59: 3 Your **h** are the **h** of murderers, and your
60:21 for I will plant them there with my own **h** in order
62: 3 The LORD will hold you in his **h** for all to see—a
splendid crown in the **h** of God.
66: 2 My **h** have made both heaven and earth, and they
Jer 2:37 you will be led into exile with your **h** on your
15:21 wicked men. I will rescue you from their cruel **h**."
17: 4 I have reserved for you will slip out of your **h**,
30: 6 **h** pressed against their sides like women about to
48:37 They slash their **h** and put on clothes made of
51: 7 has been like a golden cup in the LORD's **h**,
51:56 are captured, and their weapons break in their **h**.
La 1:14 gave me to my enemies; I am helpless in their **h**.
2:19 water to the Lord. Lift up your **h** to him in prayer.
3:41 us lift our hearts and **h** to God in heaven and say,
Eze 1: 8 Beneath each of their wings I could see human **h**.
6:11 Clap your **h** in horror, and stamp your feet.
7:17 Everyone's **h** will be feeble; their knees will be as
7:27 and the people's **h** will tremble with fear.
10: 7 He put the coals into the **h** of the man in linen
10: 8 (All the cherubim had what looked like human **h**
10:12 including their **h**, their backs, and their wings.
10:21 and what looked like human **h** under their wings.
12: 7 I dug through the wall with my **h** and went out into
21:14 prophesy to them and clap your **h** vigorously.
21:17 I, too, will clap my **h**, and I will satisfy my fury.
22:13 "But now I clap my **h** in indignation over your
28:10 You will die like an outcast at the **h** of foreigners.
32:23 everywhere are now dead at the **h** of their enemies.
39: 3 I will knock your weapons from your **h** and leave
Da 10:10 and lifted me, still trembling, to my **h** and knees.
12: 7 raised both his **h** toward heaven and took this
Hos 2:10 No one will be able to rescue her from my **h**.
8: 6 This calf you worship was crafted by your own **h**!
13: 2 images shaped skillfully with human **h**.
Mic 5:13 will never again worship the work of your own **h**.
7: 3 They go about their evil deeds with both **h**.
Na 3:19 All who hear of your destruction will clap their **h**
Hab 2:18 foolish to trust in something made by your own **h**!
3: 4 Rays of brilliant light flash from his **h**. He rejoices
3:10 mighty deep cried out, lifting its **h** to the LORD.
Mt 4: 6 protect you. / And they will hold you with their **h**
15:20 Eating with unwashed **h** could never defile you
16:21 He would suffer at the **h** of the leaders
17:12 soon the Son of Man will also suffer at their **h**."
18: 8 into the unquenchable fire with both of your **h**
19:13 so he could lay his **h** on them and pray for them.
19:15 And he put his **h** on their heads and blessed them
26:45 the Son of Man, am betrayed into the **h** of sinners.
27:24 bowl of water and washed his **h** before the crowd,
Mk 5:23 "Please come and place your **h** on her; heal her
6: 5 them except to place his **h** on a few sick people
7: 3 until they have poured water over their cupped **h**,
7: 4 market unless they have immersed their **h** in water.
7:32 and the people begged Jesus to lay his **h** on the
8:23 on the man's eyes, he laid his **h** on him and asked,
8:25 Then Jesus placed his **h** over the man's eyes again.
9:43 go into the unquenchable fires of hell with two **h**.
10:16 and placed his **h** on their heads and blessed them.
14:41 the Son of Man, am betrayed into the **h** of sinners.
14:58 'I will destroy this Temple made with human **h**,
14:58 I will build another, made without human **h**.' "
16:18 They will be able to place their **h** on the sick
Lk 1:53 good things / and sent the rich away with empty **h**.
4:11 And they will hold you with their **h** / to keep you
6: 1 rubbed off the husks in their **h**, and ate the grains.
23:46 "Father, I entrust my spirit into your **h**!"
24: 7 that the Son of Man must be betrayed into the **h** of
24:39 Look at my **h**. Look at my feet. You can see that
24:40 As he spoke, he held out his **h** for them to see,
24:50 and lifting his **h** to heaven, he blessed them.
Jn 13: 9 "Then wash my **h** and head as well, Lord, not just
20:20 As he spoke, he held out his **h** for them to see.
20:25 believe it unless I see the nail wounds in his **h**,
20:27 to Thomas, "Put your finger here and see my **h**.
21:18 But when you are old, you will stretch out your **h**,
Ac 6: 6 who prayed for them as they laid their **h** on them.
7:48 High doesn't live in temples made by human **h**.
7:53 though you received it from the **h** of angels."
7:57 Then they put their **h** over their ears, and drowning
8:17 and John laid their **h** upon these believers,
8:18 the apostles placed their **h** upon people's heads,
8:19 he exclaimed, "so that when I lay my **h** on people,
9:12 and laying his **h** on him so that he can see again."
9:17 He laid his **h** on him and said, "Brother Saul,
13: 3 the men laid their **h** on them and sent them on their
17:25 and human **h** can't serve his needs—for he has no
19: 6 Then when Paul laid his **h** on them, the Holy Spirit
20:34 You know that these **h** of mine have worked to pay
21:11 Paul's belt and bound his own feet and **h** with it.
27:19 and anything else they could lay their **h** on.
28: 8 for him, and laying his **h** on him, he healed him.
1Co 4:12 We have worked wearily with our own **h** to earn
5: 5 cast this man out of the church and into Satan's **h**,
2Co 5: 1 made for us by God himself and not by human **h**.
Eph 4:28 Begin using your **h** for honest work, and then give
1Th 4:11 your own business and working with your **h**,
1Ti 2: 8 I want men to pray with holy **h** lifted up to God,
4:14 when the elders of the church laid their **h** on you.
2Ti 1: 6 gift God gave you when I laid my **h** on you.
Heb 1:10 the earth, / and the heavens are the work of your **h**.
6: 2 the laying on of **h**, the resurrection of the dead,
8: 2 that was built by the Lord and not by human **h**.
9:11 not made by human **h** and not part of this created
10:31 It is a terrible thing to fall into the **h** of the living
12:12 So take a new grip with your tired **h** and stand firm
Jas 4: 8 Wash your **h**, you sinners; purify your hearts,
1Pe 2:23 He left his case in the **h** of God, who always
1Jn 1: 1 our own eyes and touched him with our own **h**.
5:18 and the evil one cannot get his **h** on them.
Rev 7: 9 clothed in white and held palm branches in their **h**.
10:10 So I took the little scroll from the **h** of the angel,
20: 4 nor accepted his mark on their forehead or their **h**.

HANDSOME (11)

Ge 39: 6 Now Joseph was a very **h** and well-built young
1Sa 9: 2 His son Saul was the most **h** man in Israel—head
16:12 for him. He was ruddy and **h**, with pleasant eyes.
2Sa 14:25 Now no one in Israel was as **h** as Absalom.
1Ki 1: 6 Adonijah was a very **h** man and had been born
Ps 45: 2 You are the most **h** of all. / Gracious words stream
Eze 23: 6 captains and commanders dressed in **h** blue,
23:12 those **h** young men on fine horses, those captains
and commanders in **h** uniforms—
23:15 **H** belts encircled their waists, and flowing turbans
23:23 **h** young captains, commanders, chariot officers,

HANDSTAVES [KJV] See JAVELINS

HANDWRITING (3) [HAND, WRITE]

Gal 6:11 I use as I write these closing words in my own **h**.
Col 4:18 Here is my greeting in my own **h**—PAUL.
Phm 1:19 I, Paul, write this in my own **h**: "I will repay it."

HANDYWORK [KJV] See CRAFTSMANSHIP

HANES (1)

Isa 30: 4 For though his power extends to Zoan and **H**,

HANG (19) [HANGED, HANGING, HANGINGS, HANGS, HUNG, OVERHANGING]

Ex 26:12 will be left to **h** over the back of the Tabernacle,
26:13 and the covering will **h** down an extra eighteen
26:31 "Across the inside of the Tabernacle **h** a special
26:32 **H** this inner curtain on gold hooks set into four
26:37 **H** this curtain on gold hooks set into five posts
40: 8 and **h** the curtain for the courtyard entrance.
Lev 10: 6 "Do not mourn by letting your hair **h** loose or by
13:45 tear their clothing and allow their hair to **h** loose.
21:10 must never let his hair **h** loose or tear his clothing.
Dt 28:66 Your lives will **h** in doubt. You will live night
Est 5:14 and in the morning ask the king to **h** Mordecai on
6: 4 to **h** Mordecai from the gallows he had prepared.
7: 9 He intended to use it to **h** Mordecai, the man who
7: 9 "Then **h** Haman on it!" the king ordered.
Pr 3:21 sight of good planning and insight. **H** on to them,
20:19 so don't **h** around with someone who talks too
Isa 33:23 The enemies' sails **h** loose on broken masts with
La 2:10 The young women of Jerusalem **h** their heads in
Eze 15: 3 for making things, like pegs to **h** up pots and pans?

HANGED (8) [HANG]

Dt 21:22 of death and is executed and then **h** on a tree,
2Sa 17:23 set his affairs in order, and **h** himself.
Est 2:23 found to be true, the two men were **h** on a gallows.
7:10 So they **h** Haman on the gallows he had set up for
8: 7 and he has been **h** on the gallows because he tried
9:25 and Haman and his sons were **h** on the gallows.
La 5:12 Our princes are being **h** by their thumbs,
Mt 27: 5 floor of the Temple and went out and **h** himself.

HANGING (9) [HANG]

Dt 21:23 same day, for anyone **h** on a tree is cursed of God.
Jos 2:18 only if you leave this scarlet rope **h** from the
2:21 leaving the scarlet rope **h** from the window.
Job 18: 6 The lamp **h** above them will be quenched.
Ps 137: 2 **h** them on the branches of the willow trees.
Lk 23:39 One of the criminals **h** beside him scoffed,
23:45 the thick veil **h** in the Temple was torn apart.
Jn 19:31 The Jewish leaders didn't want the victims **h** there
Ac 28: 4 The people of the island saw it **h** there and said to

HANGINGS (1) [HANG]

Est 1: 6 with beautifully woven white and blue linen **h**,

HANGS (4) [HANG]

Job 26: 7 sky over empty space and **h** the earth on nothing.
Ps 119:109 My life constantly **h** in the balance, / but I will not
Pr 29: 3 but if he **h** around with prostitutes, his wealth is
Isa 25: 7 the shadow of death that **h** over the earth.

HANIEL [KJV] See HANNIEL

HANNAH (16)

1Sa 1: 2 Elkanah had two wives, **H** and Peninnah.
1: 2 Peninnah had children, while **H** did not.
1: 5 But he gave **H** a special portion because he loved
1: 6 But Peninnah made fun of **H** because the LORD
1: 7 Peninnah would taunt **H** as they went to the
1: 7 **H** would finally be reduced to tears and would not
1: 8 "What's the matter, **H**?" Elkanah would ask.
1: 9 **H** went over to the Tabernacle after supper to pray
1:10 **H** was in deep anguish, crying bitterly as she

1:19 When Elkanah slept with **H**, the LORD
1:22 But **H** did not go. She told her husband,
1:24 **H** took him to the Tabernacle in Shiloh.
1:26 "Sir, do you remember me?" **H** asked. "I am the
2:1 Then **H** prayed: / "My heart rejoices in the
2:11 and **H** returned home to Ramah without Samuel.
2:21 And the LORD gave **H** three sons and two

HANNATHON (1)
Jos 19:14 The northern boundary of Zebulun passed **H**

HANNIEL (2)
Nu 34:23 Manasseh son of Joseph | **H** son of Ephod
1Ch 7:39 The sons of Ulla were Arah, **H**, and Rizia.

HANOCH (6) [HANOCHITE]
Ge 25:4 sons were Ephah, Epher, **H**, Abida, and Eldaah.
46:9 The sons of Reuben were **H**, Pallu, Hezron,
Ex 6:14 oldest son, included **H**, Pallu, Hezron, and Carmi.
Nu 26:5 The Hanochite clan, named after its ancestor **H**.
1Ch 1:33 Midian were Ephah, Epher, **H**, Abida, and Eldaah.
5:3 son of Israel, were **H**, Pallu, Hezron, and Carmi.

HANOCHITE (1) [HANOCH]
Nu 26:5 The **H** clan, named after its ancestor Hanoch.

HANUKKAH (1)
Jn 10:22 and Jesus was in Jerusalem at the time of **H**.

HANUN (12) [HANUN'S]
2Sa 10:1 the Ammonites died, and his son **H** became king.
10:2 "I am going to show complete loyalty to **H**
10:2 to express sympathy to **H** about his father's death.
10:4 So **H** seized David's ambassadors and shaved off
1Ch 19:1 the Ammonites died, and his son **H** became king.
19:2 "I am going to show complete loyalty to **H**
19:2 to express sympathy to **H** about his father's death.
19:4 So **H** seized David's ambassadors and shaved their
19:6 so **H** and the Ammonites sent thirty-eight tons of
19:7 troops that **H** had recruited from his own towns.
Ne 3:13 led by **H**, rebuilt the Valley Gate, hung its doors,
3:30 Next Hananiah son of Shelemiah and **H**, the sixth

HANUN'S (2) [HANUN]
2Sa 10:3 **H** advisers said to their master, "Do you really
1Ch 19:3 **H** advisers said to him, "Do you really think these

HAPHARAIM (1)
Jos 19:19 **H**, Shion, Anaharath,

HAPLY [KJV] See EVEN, OTHERWISE, PERHAPS

HAPPEN (144) [HAPPENED, HAPPENING, HAPPENS]
Ge 41:28 This will **h** just as I have described it, for God has
41:32 by God and that he will make these events **h** soon.
42:38 If anything should **h** to him, you would bring my
49:1 and I will tell you what is going to **h** to you in the
Ex 2:4 at a distance, watching to see what would **h** to him.
8:23 This miraculous sign will **h** tomorrow.' "
21:13 But if it is an accident and God allows it to **h**,
Nu 16:40 the same thing would **h** to him as happened to
35:24 If this should **h**, the assembly must follow these
Dt 2:14 For the LORD had vowed that this could not **h**
12:21 It might **h** that the place the LORD your God
18:22 something in the LORD's name and it does not **h**,
21:7 hands did not shed this blood, nor did we see it **h**.
30:1 "Suppose all these things **h** to you—the blessings
Jos 7:9 then what will **h** to the honor of your great name?"
Jdg 6:27 He knew what would **h** if they found out who had
1Sa 11:7 "This is what will **h** to the oxen of anyone who
28:10 nothing bad will **h** to you for doing this."
1Ki 14:3 jar of honey, and ask him what will **h** to the boy."
14:14 family of Jeroboam. This will **h** today, even now!
21:29 It will **h** to his sons; I will destroy all his
2Ki 7:2 "That couldn't **h** even if the LORD opened the
7:2 But Elisha replied, "You will see it **h**, but you
7:19 "That couldn't **h** even if the LORD opened the
7:19 And the man of God had said, "You will see it **h**,
10:10 through his servant Elijah that this would **h**."
17:23 just as all his prophets had warned would **h**.
19:25 Long ago I planned what I am now causing to **h**,
19:31 passion of the LORD Almighty will make this **h**!
Est 3:13 This was scheduled to **h** nearly a year later on
Job 37:13 He causes things to **h** on earth, either as a
Ps 10:6 say to themselves, "Nothing bad will ever **h** to us!
37:35 I myself have seen it **h**— / proud and evil people
Ecc 6:12 And who can tell what will **h** in the future after we
8:7 people avoid what they don't know is going to **h**?
10:14 But who can really know what is going to **h**?
Isa 7:7 LORD says: This invasion will never **h**,
8:6 and are rejoicing over what will **h** to King Rezin
14:24 sworn this oath: "It will all **h** as I have planned.
20:6 They will say, 'If this can **h** to Egypt, what chance
37:26 Long ago I planned what I am now causing to **h**,
37:32 passion of the LORD Almighty will make this **h**!
41:26 "Who but I have told you this would **h**? Who else
44:7 Who else can tell you what is going to **h** in the
44:25 events to **h** that are contrary to their predictions.
45:21 What idol ever told you they would **h**? Was it not
46:10 Only I can tell you what is going to **h** even before
48:3 and again I warned you about what was going to **h**
48:5 wooden image and metal god commanded it to **h**!'
48:16 I have always told you plainly what would **h**
Jer 2:21 "How could this **h**? When I planted you, I chose a
26:19 we kill Jeremiah, who knows what will **h** to us?"
31:22 will cause something new and different to **h**—
33:3 remarkable secrets about what is going to **h** here.
37:7 who sent you to ask me what is going to **h**,
40:15 "What will **h** then to the Judeans who have
44:29 that all I have threatened will **h** to you and that I
La 3:37 Can anything **h** without the Lord's permission?
Eze 5:5 This is an illustration of what will **h** to Jerusalem.
6:10 when I predicted that all this would **h** to them.
12:11 are a demonstration of what will soon **h** to them,
16:16 Unbelievable! How could such a thing ever **h**?
20:32 But what you have in mind will never **h**.
33:33 But when all these terrible things **h** to them—
38:16 land like a cloud. This will **h** in the distant future.
39:8 Everything will **h** just as I have declared it.
Da 2:28 King Nebuchadnezzar what will **h** in the future.
2:29 of mysteries has shown you what is going to **h**.
2:45 has shown Your Majesty what will **h** in the future.
4:19 in this dream would **h** to your enemies,
4:24 and what the Most High has declared will **h** to you.
4:28 But all these things did **h** to King Nebuchadnezzar.
8:19 "I am here to tell you what will **h** later in the time
8:26 But none of these things will **h** for a long time,
10:1 It concerned events certain to **h** in the future—
10:14 Now I am here to explain what will **h** to your
12:6 long will it be until these shocking events **h**?"
Am 9:10 all those who say, 'Nothing bad will **h** to us.'
Jnh 4:3 because nothing I predicted is going to **h**."
4:5 as he waited to see if anything would **h** to the city.
Hab 2:3 But these things I plan won't **h** right away. Slowly,
Zec 6:15 All this will **h** if you carefully obey the commands
14:7 Only the LORD knows how this could **h**!
Mt 9:8 Fear swept through the crowd as they saw this **h**
9:29 and said, "Because of your faith, it will **h**."
10:25 how much more will it **h** to you, the members of
16:21 and he told them what would **h** to him there.
16:22 Lord," he said. "This will never **h** to you!"
20:17 and told them what was going to **h** to him.
21:21 you up and throw you into the sea,' and it will **h**.
24:33 you see the events I've described beginning to **h**,
24:36 the day or the hour when these things will **h**,
24:39 People didn't realize what was going to **h** until the
26:54 be fulfilled that describe what must **h** now?"
26:58 and waited to see what was going to **h** to Jesus.
28:6 been raised from the dead, just as he said would **h**.
Mk 10:32 everything that was about to **h** to him in Jerusalem.
13:9 But when these things begin to **h**, watch out!
13:19 God created the world. And it will never **h** again.
13:29 you see the events I've described beginning to **h**,
13:32 knows the day or hour when these things will **h**,
13:33 And since you don't know when they will **h**,
Lk 1:18 said to the angel, "How can I know this will **h**?
17:37 "Lord, where will this **h**?" the disciples asked.
20:16 "But God forbid that such a thing should ever **h**,"
21:28 So when all these things begin to **h**, stand straight
22:49 When the other disciples saw what was about to **h**,
23:31 the tree is green, what will **h** when it is dry?"
Jn 1:34 I saw this **h** to Jesus, so I testify that he is the Son
3:12 when I tell you about things that **h** here on earth,
5:14 or something even worse may **h** to you."
11:45 with Mary believed in Jesus when they saw this **h**.
14:29 I have told you these things before they **h** so that
you will believe when they do **h**.
16:4 telling you these things now, so that when they **h**,
16:20 and mourn over what is going to **h** to me,
18:4 Jesus fully realized all that was going to **h** to him.
Ac 8:24 "that these terrible things won't **h** to me!"
26:22 what the prophets and Moses said would **h**—
Ro 11:20 think highly of yourself, but fear what could **h**.
1Co 8:10 You see, this is what can **h**: Weak Christians who
15:52 It will **h** in a moment, in the blinking of an eye,
2Co 9:12 So two good things will **h**—the needs of the
Eph 1:11 and all things **h** just as he decided long ago.
Php 2:23 as soon as I find out what is going to **h** to me here.
1Th 3:3 you know that such troubles are going to **h** to us
4:13 I want you to know what will **h** to the Christians
5:1 to write to you about how and when all this will **h**,
Heb 2:8 is left out. But we have not yet seen all of this **h**.
11:1 assurance that what we hope for is going to **h**.
Jas 4:14 How do you know what will **h** tomorrow? For your
1Pe 1:11 wondered when and to whom all this would **h**.
1:12 They were told that these things would not **h**
1:12 the angels are eagerly watching these things **h**.
2Pe 2:6 He made them an example of what will **h** to
3:14 while you are waiting for these things to **h**,
Rev 1:1 gave him concerning the events that will **h** soon.
1:3 For the time is near when these things will **h**.
1:19 are now happening and the things that will **h** later.
4:1 and I will show you what must **h** after these
8:13 because of what will **h** when the last three angels
10:7 It will **h** just as he announced it to his servants the
18:23 This will **h** because her merchants, who were the
22:6 has sent his angel to tell you what will **h** soon.' "

HAPPENED (212) [HAPPEN]
Ge 1:8 called the space "sky." This **h** on the second day.
1:13 This all **h** on the third day.
1:19 This all **h** on the fourth day.
1:23 This all **h** on the fifth day.
1:31 excellent in every way. This all **h** on the sixth day.
11:10 was born. This **h** two years after the Flood.
14:10 As it **h**, the valley was filled with tar pits. And as
16:3 (This **h** ten years after Abram first arrived in the
20:8 When he told them what had **h**, great fear swept
21:2 old age. It all **h** at the time God had said it would.
24:28 ran home to tell her family about all that had **h**.
26:1 struck the land, as had **h** before in Abraham's time.
32:32 from near the hip, in memory of what **h** that night.
39:22 and over everything that **h** in the prison.
41:13 and everything **h** just as he said it would. I was
42:21 "This has all **h** because of what we did to Joseph
42:29 in the land of Canaan and told him all that had **h**.
Ex 2:16 Now it **h** that the priest of Midian had seven
16:22 the people came and asked Moses why this had **h**.
22:10 and there is no eyewitness to report just what **h**.
32:1 We don't know what has **h** to him."
32:23 for something has **h** to this man Moses, who led us
Lev 10:16 When Moses demanded to know what had **h** to the
10:19 he said. "This kind of thing has also **h** to me.
Nu 11:25 rested upon them, but that was the only time this **h**.
12:10 snow with leprosy. When Aaron saw what had **h**,
13:20 (It **h** to be the season for harvesting the first ripe
16:40 the same thing would happen to him as **h** to Korah
33:38 This **h** on a day in midsummer, during the fortieth
Dt 2:23 A similar thing **h** when the Caphtorites from Crete
4:32 See if anything as great as this has ever **h** before.
29:25 'This **h** because the people of the land broke the
Jos 2:23 and reported to Joshua all that had **h** to them.
9:1 kings west of the Jordan heard about what had **h**.
9:3 But when the people of Gibeon heard what had **h**
11:1 When King Jabin of Hazor heard what had **h**,
20:4 the leaders at the city gate and explain what **h**.
22:32 the land of Canaan to tell the Israelites what had **h**.
Jdg 6:13 "if the LORD is with us, why has all this **h** to us?
6:38 And it **h** just that way. When Gideon got up the
9:46 lived in the tower of Shechem heard what had **h**,
14:19 But Samson was furious about what had **h**, and he
17:8 He **h** to stop at Micah's house as he was traveling
18:28 allies nearby. This **h** in the valley near Beth-rehob.
20:3 then asked how this terrible crime had **h**.
21:3 God of Israel," they cried out, "why has this **h**?
Ru 2:3 And as it **h**, she found herself working in a field
3:16 Naomi asked, "What **h**, my daughter?"
1Sa 4:13 When the messenger arrived and told what had **h**,
4:16 there this very day." "What **h**?" Eli demanded.
4:18 When the messenger mentioned what had **h** to the
5:4 But the next morning the same thing **h**—the idol
6:18 the field of Joshua as a reminder of what **h** there.
18:6 But something **h** when the victorious Israelite army
18:10 began to play the harp, as he did whenever this **h**.
18:11 and escaped. This **h** another time, too,
19:7 Jonathan called David and told him what had **h**.
19:21 When Saul heard what had **h**, he sent other troops,
19:21 too, prophesied! The same thing **h** a third time!
24:3 But as it **h**, David and his men were hiding in that
25:37 when he was sober, she told him what had **h**.
27:11 This **h** again and again while he was living among
30:3 the ruins and realized what had **h** to their families,
2Sa 1:4 "What **h**?" David demanded. "Tell me how the
1:6 young man answered, "I **h** to be on Mount Gilboa.
2:24 When Joab and Abishai found out what had **h**,
2:27 "God only knows what would have **h** if you hadn't
10:5 When David heard what had **h**, he sent messengers
12:19 saw them whispering, he realized what had **h**.
13:21 When King David heard what had **h**, he was very
18:10 One of David's men saw what had **h** and told Joab,
1Ki 12:24 for what has **h** is my doing!' " So they obeyed the
13:11 As it **h**, there was an old prophet living in Bethel,
16:10 This **h** in the twenty-seventh year of King Asa's
16:13 This **h** because of the sins of Baasha and his son
16:34 This all **h** according to the message from the
2Ki 2:15 the group of prophets from Jericho saw what **h**,
4:7 When she told the man of God what had **h**, he said
4:31 and laid the staff on the child's face, but nothing **h**.
6:10 there to be on their guard. This **h** several times.
7:10 to the city and told the gatekeepers what had **h**—
7:12 the night and told his officers, "I know what has **h**.
7:14 and the king sent scouts to see what had **h** to the
7:17 So everything **h** exactly as the man of God had
18:34 What **h** to the gods of Hamath and Arpad?
19:13 What **h** to the king of Hamath and the king of
19:13 What **h** to the kings of Sepharvaim, Hena,
23:16 This **h** just as the LORD had promised through
24:3 These disasters **h** to Judah according to the
1Ch 19:5 When David heard what had **h**, he sent messengers
29:30 and everything that **h** to him and to Israel and to all
2Ch 11:4 for what has **h** is my doing!' " So they obeyed the
16:8 Don't you remember what **h** to the Ethiopians
22:8 he **h** to meet some of Judah's officials
Ne 13:4 Before this had **h**, Eliashib the priest, who had
Est 1:1 This **h** in the days of King Xerxes, who reigned
6:4 Now, as it **h**, Haman had just arrived in the outer
6:13 Zeresh, and all his friends what had **h**, they said,
9:1 hoped to destroy them, but quite the opposite **h**.
9:12 that here, what has **h** in the rest of the provinces?
9:28 nor would the memory of what **h** ever die out
Job 3:25 What I always feared has **h** to me. What I dreaded
Ps 44:17 All this has **h** despite our loyalty to you. / We have
105:45 All this **h** so they would follow his principles
114:5 What **h**, Jordan River, that you turned away?
Ecc 1:11 We don't remember what **h** in those former times.
Isa 19:12 What has **h** to your wise counselors, Pharaoh?
36:19 What **h** to the gods of Hamath and Arpad?
37:13 What **h** to the king of Hamath and the king of
37:13 What **h** to the kings of Sepharvaim, Hena,
41:22 "Let them try to tell us what **h** long ago or what
Jer 5:30 "A horrible and shocking thing has **h** in this land—
9:13 "This has **h** because my people have abandoned
32:24 Everything has **h** just as you said it would.

36: 9 This **h** on the day of sacred fasting held in late
40: 3 the LORD and disobeyed him. That is why it **h**.
41: 6 "Oh, come and see what has **h** to Gedaliah!"
44: 23 The very reason all these terrible things have **h** to
48: 19 to those who flee from Moab, 'What has **h** there?'
La 2: 11 spirit poured out, as I see what has **h** to my people.
4: 13 Yet it **h** because of the sins of her prophets
5: 1 LORD, remember everything that has **h** to us.
Eze 1: 2 This **h** during the fifth year of King Jehoiachin's
23: 11 "Yet even though Oholibah saw what had **h** to
24: 26 come to you in Babylon and tell you what has **h**.
34: 10 and I will hold them responsible for what has **h** to
Da 2: 15 a harsh decree?" So Arioch told him all that had **h**.
2: 17 Mishael, and Azariah what had **h**.
9: 12 been a disaster like the one that **h** in Jerusalem.
12: 7 come to an end, all these things will have **h**."
Joel 1: 2 your history, has anything like this ever **h** before?
Am 6: 2 Go over to Calneh and see what **h** there. Then go
Zep 3: 6 There are no survivors to even tell what **h**.
Zec 1: 6 my servants the prophets **h** to your ancestors,
Mt 1: 22 All of this **h** to fulfill the Lord's message through
8: 13 "Go on home. What you have believed has **h**."
8: 33 telling everyone what **h** to the demon-possessed
9: 33 "Nothing like this has ever **h** in Israel!"
14: 12 and buried it. Then they told Jesus what had **h**.
18: 31 They went to the king and told him what had **h**.
27: 54 were terrified by the earthquake and all that had **h**.
28: 11 to the leading priests and told them what had **h**.
Mk 1: 27 and they began to discuss what had **h**.
1: 45 the news, telling everyone what had **h** to him.
5: 11 There **h** to be a large herd of pigs feeding on the
5: 16 Those who had seen what **h** to the man and to the
5: 33 trembling at the realization of what had **h** to her,
5: 43 commanded them not to tell anyone what had **h**,
6: 29 When John's disciples heard what had **h**,
15: 42 This all **h** on Friday, the day of preparation,
Lk 1: 65 and the news of what had **h** spread throughout the
2: 15 Let's see this wonderful thing that has **h**,
2: 17 Then the shepherds told everyone what had **h**
5: 8 When Simon Peter realized what had **h**, he fell to
5: 14 Jesus instructed him not to tell anyone what had **h**.
8: 35 for they wanted to see for themselves what had **h**.
8: 36 Then those who had seen what **h** told the others
8: 50 But when Jesus heard what had **h**, he said to Jairus,
8: 56 Jesus insisted that they not tell anyone what had **h**.
9: 36 anyone what they had seen until long after this **h**.
11: 30 What **h** to him was a sign to the people of Nineveh
17: 32 Remember what **h** to Lot's wife!
20: 11 owner sent another servant, but the same thing **h**;
20: 12 A third man was sent and the same thing **h**. He,
23: 7 and Herod **h** to be in Jerusalem at the time.
23: 47 soldiers handling the executions saw what had **h**,
23: 48 that came to see the crucifixion saw all that had **h**,
24: 4 trying to think what could have **h** to it.
24: 9 eleven disciples—and everyone else—what had **h**.
24: 10 several others. They told the apostles what had **h**,
24: 12 then he went home again, wondering what had **h**.
24: 14 they were talking about everything that had **h**.
24: 18 all the things that have **h** there the last few days."
24: 19 "The things that **h** to Jesus, the man from
24: 21 come to rescue Israel. That all **h** three days ago.
Jn 5: 9 But this miracle **h** on the Sabbath day.
9: 10 They asked, "Who healed you? What **h**?"
9: 14 Now as it **h**, Jesus had healed the man on a
9: 35 When Jesus heard what had **h**, he found the man
19: 36 These things **h** in fulfillment of the Scriptures that
21: 1 beside the Sea of Galilee. This is how it **h**.
Ac 1: 12 apostles were at the Mount of Olives when this **h**,
3: 11 there in awe of the wonderful thing that had **h**.
4: 27 "That is what has **h** here in this city! For Herod
5: 7 later his wife came in, not knowing what had **h**.
5: 11 entire church and all others who heard what had **h**.
10: 8 He told them what had **h** and sent them off to
10: 37 You know what **h** all through Judea, beginning in
11: 4 Then Peter told them exactly what had **h**.
11: 10 "This **h** three times before the sheet and all it
11: 22 When the church at Jerusalem heard what had **h**,
12: 11 Peter finally realized what had **h**. "It's really
12: 17 for them to quiet down and told them what had **h**
12: 17 "Tell James and the other brothers what **h**,"
12: 18 among the soldiers about what had **h** to Peter.
13: 12 When the governor saw what had **h**, he believed
17: 17 daily in the public square to all who **h** to be there.
19: 17 The story of what **h** spread quickly all through
28: 8 As it **h**, Publius's father was ill with fever
Ro 4: 17 This **h** because Abraham believed in the God who
1Co 10: 1 what **h** to our ancestors in the wilderness long ago.
10: 6 These events **h** as a warning to us, so that we
10: 11 All these events **h** to them as examples for us.
2Co 7: 7 and how sorry you were about what had **h**,
Gal 1: 15 But then something **h**! For it pleased God in his
1: 16 When all this **h** to me, I did not rush out to consult
Php 1: 12 that everything that has **h** to me here has helped to
2Ti 3: 9 fools they are, just as **h** with Jannes and Jambres.
Heb 10: 3 But just the opposite **h**. Those yearly sacrifices
11: 7 who warned him about something that had never **h**
Jas 2: 23 And so it **h** just as the Scriptures say:
Rev 12: 10 "It has **h** at last—the salvation and power

HAPPENING (35) [HAPPEN]

Ge 25: 22 about it. "Why is this **h** to me?" she asked.
Ex 3: 16 over you and have seen what is **h** to you in Egypt.
1Sa 5: 7 When the people realized what was **h**, they cried
2Sa 10: 17 When David heard what was **h**, he mobilized all
18: 29 lot of commotion. But I didn't know what was **h**."
1Ki 15: 21 As soon as Baasha of Israel heard what was **h**,
2Ki 9: 27 When King Ahaziah of Judah saw what was **h**,
11: 13 hurried to the LORD's Temple to see what was **h**.
1Ch 19: 17 When David heard what was **h**, he mobilized all
2Ch 16: 5 As soon as Baasha of Israel heard what was **h**,
23: 12 hurried to the LORD's Temple to see what was **h**.
Ne 4: 11 were saying, "Before they know what's **h**,
Est 2: 11 ask about Esther and to find out what was **h** to her.
Ps 64: 8 All who see it **h** will shake their heads in scorn.
73: 11 "Is the Most High even aware of what is **h**?"
Isa 22: 1 What is **h**? Why is everyone running to the
Jer 13: 22 You may ask yourself, "Why is all this **h** to me?"
26: 10 When the officials of Judah heard what was **h**,
Da 5: 10 But when the queen mother heard what was **h**,
Mic 1: 5 And why is this **h**? Because of the sins
Mt 21: 32 And even when you saw this **h**, you refused to turn
26: 56 But this is all **h** to fulfill the words of the prophets
Mk 3: 21 When his family heard what was **h**, they tried to
9: 21 "How long has this been **h**?" Jesus asked the
10: 14 But when Jesus saw what was **h**, he was very
14: 49 But these things are **h** to fulfill what the Scriptures
Lk 7: 39 the Pharisee who was the host saw what was **h**
18: 36 noise of a crowd going past, he asked what was **h**.
Ac 3: 24 every prophet spoke about what is **h** today.
12: 9 it was a vision. He didn't realize it was really **h**.
14: 14 But when Barnabas and Paul heard what was **h**,
19: 26 And this is **h** not only here in Ephesus
Heb 12: 11 No discipline is enjoyable while it is **h**—it is
1Pe 4: 12 as if something strange were **h** to you.
Rev 1: 19 both the things that are now **h** and the things that

HAPPENS (46) [HAPPEN]

Ex 22: 3 But if it **h** in daylight, the one who killed the thief
Dt 17: 15 If this **h**, be sure that you select as king the man the
21: 12 If this **h**, you may take her to your home,
22: 23 sexual intercourse with her. If this **h** within a town,
25: 9 'This is what **h** to a man who refuses to raise up a
Ru 3: 18 be patient, my daughter, until we hear what **h**.
1Sa 9: 8 We can at least offer it to him and see what **h**!"
24: 21 swear to me by the LORD that when that **h** you
2Sa 14: 20 and you understand everything that **h** among us!"
15: 21 that I will go wherever you go, no matter what **h**—
15: 28 Let me know what **h** in Jerusalem before I
18: 22 with Joab, "Whatever **h**, please let me go, too."
2Ki 7: 13 If something **h** to them, it won't be a greater loss
Est 6: 9 'This is what **h** to those the king wishes to
6: 11 "This is what **h** to those the king wishes to
Job 9: 29 Whatever **h**, I will be found guilty. So what's the
21: 21 are dead, they will not care what **h** to their family.
Ps 52: 7 "Look what **h** to mighty warriors / who do not
142: 4 one will help me; / no one cares a bit what **h** to me.
Isa 42: 9 I will tell you the future before it **h**."
46: 10 tell you what is going to happen even before it **h**.
Jer 38: 26 If this **h**, just tell them you begged me not to send
Eze 5: 15 They will see what **h** when the LORD turns
12: 25 For I am the LORD! What I threaten always **h**.
15: 7 When this **h**, you will know that I am the LORD.
20: 38 And when that **h**, you will know that I am the
28: 22 and I will reveal my glory by what **h** to you.
37: 13 When this **h**, O my people, you will know that I
38: 16 and my holiness will be displayed by what **h** to
Hag 2: 12 and **h** to brush against some bread or stew,
2: 23 But when this **h**, says the LORD Almighty,
Zec 6: 15 And when this **h**, you will know my messages
Mt 27: 64 If that **h**, we'll be worse off than we were at first."
Lk 6: 23 "When that **h**, rejoice! Yes, leap for joy! For a
11: 30 What **h** to me will be a sign that God has sent me,
12: 59 And if that **h**, you won't be free again until you
Jn 13: 19 so that when it **h** you will believe I am the
13: 31 God will receive glory because of all that **h** to me.
1Co 15: 54 When this **h**—when our perishable earthly bodies
Php 1: 27 But whatever **h** to me, you must live in a manner
3: 1 Whatever **h**, dear friends, may the Lord give you
1Th 5: 18 No matter what **h**, always be thankful, for this is
2Th 3: 16 always give you his peace no matter what **h**.
Heb 10: 35 this confident trust in the Lord, no matter what **h**.
1Pe 5: 7 and cares to God, for he cares about what **h** to you.
5: 12 that the grace of God is with you no matter what **h**.

HAPPIER (1) [HAPPY]

Lk 15: 7 heaven will be **h** over one lost sinner who returns

HAPPILY (2) [HAPPY]

Ecc 9: 9 Live **h** with the woman you love through all the
Php 4: 11 for I have learned how to get along **h** whether I

HAPPINESS (20) [HAPPY]

Dt 24: 5 for one year, bringing **h** to the wife he has married.
Job 31: 25 Does my **h** depend on my wealth and all that I
Ps 86: 4 Give me **h**, O Lord, / for my life depends on you.
119: 35 your commands, / for that is where my **h** is found.
Pr 10: 28 The hopes of the godly result in **h**,
11: 23 The godly can look forward to **h**, while the wicked
29: 17 and they will give you **h** and peace of mind.
Ecc 2: 3 I hoped to experience the only **h** most people find
5: 10 How absurd to think that wealth brings true **h**!
8: 15 That way they will experience some **h** along with
10: 19 A party gives laughter, and wine gives **h**,
Isa 65: 18 And look! I will create Jerusalem as a place of **h**.
Jer 31: 24 shepherds alike will live together in peace and **h**.
Lk 6: 24 you who are rich, / for you have your only **h** now.
6: 28 Pray for the **h** of those who curse you. Pray for
12: 32 For it gives your Father great **h** to give you the
Ro 4: 6 describing the **h** of an undeserving sinner who is
1Co 7: 30 **H** or sadness or wealth should not keep anyone
2Co 2: 3 Surely you know that my **h** depends on your **h**.

HAPPIZZEZ (1)

1Ch 24: 15 lot fell to Hezir. / The eighteenth lot fell to **H**.

HAPPY (91) [HAPPIER, HAPPILY, HAPPINESS]

Ge 21: 8 Abraham gave a big party to celebrate the **h**
30: 13 The other women will consider me **h** indeed!"
45: 16 Pharaoh was very **h** to hear this and so were his
Ex 2: 21 Moses was **h** to accept the invitation, and he
Dt 16: 14 This festival will be a **h** time of rejoicing with your
Jdg 18: 20 The young priest was quite **h** to go with them,
1Sa 11: 15 and Saul and all the Israelites were very **h**.
19: 5 You were certainly **h** about it then. Why should
21: 11 But Achish's officers weren't **h** about his being
1Ki 8: 66 and they were all joyful and **h** because the LORD
10: 8 How **h** these people must be! What a privilege for
2Ch 7: 10 They were all joyful and **h** because the LORD
9: 7 How **h** these people must be! What a privilege for
15: 15 All were **h** about this covenant, for they had
Est 5: 9 What a **h** man Haman was as he left the banquet!
Job 8: 6 he will rise up and restore your **h** home.
22: 19 "Now the righteous will be **h** to see the wicked
Ps 68: 11 and throngs of women shout the **h** news.
84: 4 How **h** are those who can live in your house,
84: 5 **H** are those who are strong in the LORD,
84: 12 LORD Almighty, / **h** are those who trust in you.
89: 15 **H** are those who hear the joyful call to worship,
94: 12 **H** are those whom you discipline, LORD,
97: 12 May all who are godly be **h** in the LORD
106: 3 **H** are those who deal justly with others
112: 1 **H** are those who fear the LORD. / Yes, **h** are those
who delight in doing what he
113: 9 woman a home, / so that she becomes a **h** mother.
119: 1 **H** are people of integrity, / who follow the law of
119: 2 **H** are those who obey his decrees / and search for
119: 56 This is my **h** way of life: / obeying your
127: 5 How **h** is the man whose quiver is full of them!
128: 1 How **h** are those who fear the LORD— / all who
128: 2 How **h** you will be! How rich your life!
137: 8 be destroyed. / **H** is the one who pays you back
137: 9 **H** is the one who takes your babies / and smashes
144: 15 Yes, **h** are those who have it like this!
144: 15 **H** indeed are those whose God is the LORD.
146: 5 But **h** are those who have the God of Israel as their
Pr 3: 13 **H** is the person who finds wisdom and gains
3: 18 who embrace her; **h** are those who hold her tightly.
8: 31 And how **h** I was with what he created—his wide
8: 32 listen to me, for **h** are all who follow my ways.
8: 34 "**H** are those who listen to me, watching for me
10: 7 We all have **h** memories of the godly, but the name
15: 13 A glad heart makes a **h** face; a broken heart
15: 15 for the **h** heart, life is a continual feast.
16: 20 will prosper; those who trust the LORD will be **h**.
23: 25 parents joy! May she who gave you birth be **h**.
24: 17 fall into trouble. Don't be **h** when they stumble.
27: 11 how **h** I will be if you turn out to be wise!
29: 18 they run wild. But whoever obeys the law is **h**.
Ecc 3: 12 that there is nothing better for people than to be **h**
3: 22 nothing better for people than to be **h** in their work.
9: 7 Eat your food and drink your wine with a **h** heart,
10: 17 **H** is the land whose king is a nobleman and whose
SS 1: 4 O my king." / "How **h** we are for him!
Isa 16: 10 The **h** singing in the vineyards will be heard no
24: 8 the **h** cries of celebration will be heard no more.
32: 13 Your joyful homes and **h** cities will be gone.
57: 6 are your inheritance. Does all this make me **h**?
Jer 7: 34 I will put an end to the **h** singing and laughter in
12: 1 so prosperous? Why are evil people so **h**?
16: 9 I will put an end to the **h** singing and laughter in
25: 10 I will take away your **h** singing and laughter.
31: 4 You will again be **h** and dance merrily with
La 1: 21 they were **h** to see what you had done.
Zep 3: 17 He will exult over you by singing a **h** song."
Zec 10: 7 and their hearts will be **h** as if by wine.
Mt 5: 12 Be **h** about it! Be very glad! For a great reward
11: 17 'We played wedding songs and you weren't **h**,
Lk 7: 32 'We played wedding songs and you weren't **h**,
15: 32 We had to celebrate this **h** day. For your brother
Jn 14: 28 If you really love me, you will be very **h** for me,
Ro 12: 15 When others are **h**, be **h** with them. If they are
15: 13 will keep you **h** and full of peace as you believe in
15: 32 I will be able to come to you with a **h** heart,
16: 19 This makes me very **h**. I want you to see clearly
2Co 7: 4 you have made me **h** despite all our troubles.
7: 13 we were especially delighted to see how **h** Titus
7: 16 I am very **h** now because I have complete
Php 2: 2 Then make me truly **h** by agreeing wholeheartedly
2: 18 And you should be **h** about this and rejoice with
Col 2: 5 And I am very **h** because you are living as you
1Pe 1: 8 and even now you are **h** with a glorious,
3: 10 "If you want a **h** life and good days,
4: 14 Be **h** if you are insulted for being a Christian,
2Jn 1: 4 How **h** I was to meet some of your children
3Jn 1: 3 and made me very **h** by telling me about your
Rev 18: 23 There will be no **h** voices of brides and grooms.

HARA (1)

1Ch 5: 26 Habor, **H**, and the Gozan River, where they remain

HARADAH (2)

Nu 33: 24 They left Mount Shepher and camped at **H**.
33: 25 They left **H** and camped at Makheloth.

HARAN (20) [BETH-HARAN, HARAN'S]

Ge 11: 26 he became the father of Abram, Nahor, and **H**.

11:27 Terah was the father of Abram, Nahor, and **H**; and **H** had a son named Lot.
11:28 But while **H** was still young, he died in Ur of the
11:29 married Milcah, the daughter of their brother **H**.
11:31 But they stopped instead at the village of **H**
11:32 Terah lived for 205 years and died while still at **H**.
12: 4 Abram was seventy-five years old when he left **H**.
12: 5 all the people who had joined his household at **H**—
27:43 you should do. Flee to your uncle Laban in **H**.
28:10 Jacob left Beersheba and traveled toward **H**.
29: 4 "Where do you live?" "At **H**," they said.
2Ki 19:12 such nations as Gozan, **H**, Rezeph, and the people
1Ch 2:46 Caleb's concubine Ephah gave birth to **H**, Moza, and Gazez. **H** was the father of Gazez.
23: 9 of Shimei were Shelomoth, Haziel, and **H**.
Isa 37:12 such nations as Gozan, **H**, Rezeph, and the people
Eze 27:23 **H**, Canneh, Eden, Sheba, Asshur, and Kilmad
Ac 7: 2 Abraham in Mesopotamia before he moved to **H**.
7: 4 the Chaldeans and lived in **H** until his father died.

HARAN'S (1) [HARAN]

Ge 11:31 and his grandson Lot (his son **H** child)

HARAR (5)

2Sa 23:11 Next in rank was Shammah son of Agee from **H**.
23:33 Jonathan son of Shagee from **H**; / Ahiam son of Sharar from **H**;
1Ch 11:34 from Gizon; / Jonathan son of Shagee from **H**;
11:35 Ahiam son of Sharar from **H**; / Eliphal son of Ur;

HARASS (3) [HARASSED, HARASSING]

Nu 33:55 They will **h** you in the land where you live.
Ps 119:161 Powerful people **h** me without cause, / but my
Isa 29:20 Those who intimidate and **h** will be gone, and all

HARASSED (1) [HARASS]

Ge 49:23 attacked by archers, / who shot at him and **h** him.

HARASSING (1) [HARASS]

Jn 5:16 So the Jewish leaders began **h** Jesus for breaking

HARBONA (2)

Est 1:10 Biztha, **H**, Bigtha, Abagtha, Zethar, and Carcas,
7: 9 Then **H**, one of the king's eunuchs, said,

HARBOR (8) [HARBORING, HARBORS]

Ge 49:13 and will be a **h** for ships; / his borders will extend
Ps 107:30 that stillness / as he brought them safely into **h**!
Isa 2:16 great trading ships and all the small boats in the **h**.
23: 1 Weep for your **h** at Tyre because it is gone!
Jer 4:14 be saved. How long will you **h** your evil thoughts?
Ac 21: 3 it on our left, and landed at the **h** of Tyre, in Syria,
27:12 And since Fair Havens was an exposed **h**—a poor
27:12 Phoenix was a good **h** with only a southwest

HARBORING (1) [HARBOR]

Dt 19: 4 kills a neighbor without **h** any previous hatred,

HARBORS (1) [HARBOR]

Jdg 5:17 sat unmoved at the seashore, / remaining in his **h**.

HARD (154) [HARD-HEARTED, HARD-WON, HARDEN, HARDENED, HARDER, HARDHEADED, HARDNESS, HARDSHIP, HARDSHIPS, HARDWORKING]

Ge 4:12 crops for you, no matter how **h** you work!
18:14 Is anything too **h** for the LORD? About a year
31: 6 You know how **h** I have worked for your father,
31:42 But God has seen your cruelty and my **h** work.
33:13 too. If they are driven too **h**, they may die.
35:17 After a very **h** delivery, the midwife finally
47: 9 Jacob replied, "I have lived for 130 **h** years,
Ex 2:11 and he saw how **h** they were forced to work.
7:13 however, remained **h** and stubborn.
7:22 So Pharaoh's heart remained **h** and stubborn.
9:35 But Pharaoh's heart remained **h** and stubborn.
15: 8 in the middle of the sea the waters became **h**.
18:26 They brought the **h** cases to Moses, but they
21:12 "Anyone who hits a person **h** enough to cause
Lev 26:19 as iron and the earth beneath as **h** as bronze.
Dt 17: 8 "Suppose a case arises in a local court that is too **h**
28:23 and the earth beneath will be as **h** as iron.
28:33 about will eat the crops you worked so **h** to grow.
32:13 from the cliffs, / with olive oil from the **h** rock.
Jos 9:13 and sandals are worn out from our long, **h** trip."
Ru 2: 7 She has been **h** at work ever since, except for a few
2:16 her pick them up, and don't give her a **h** time!"
2Sa 12: 3 but a little lamb he had worked **h** to buy.
19:18 and worked **h** ferrying the king's household across
1Ki 10: 1 the LORD, she came to test him with **h** questions.
10: 3 nothing was too **h** for the king to explain to her.
12: 4 "Your father was a **h** master," they said.
12:10 if you think he was **h** on you, just wait and see
1Ch 22:14 "I have worked **h** to provide materials for building
2Ch 9: 1 she came to Jerusalem to test him with **h** questions.
9: 2 nothing was too **h** for him to explain to her.
10: 4 "Your father was a **h** master," they said.
10:10 if you think he was **h** on you, just wait and see
24:13 So the men in charge of the renovation worked **h**,
36:13 Zedekiah was a **h** and stubborn man, refusing to
Ne 4: 6 the entire city, for the people had worked very **h**.
Job 6:12 Do I have strength as **h** as stone? Is my body made
7: 1 A person's life is long and **h**, like that of a hired
23: 2 is still a bitter one, and I try **h** not to groan aloud.
38:30 For the water turns to ice as **h** as rock,
41:23 Its flesh is **h** and firm, not soft and fat.
41:24 Its heart is as **h** as rock, as **h** as a millstone.
Ps 34:14 do good. / Work **h** at living in peace with others.
37:19 They will survive through **h** times; / even in
60: 3 You have been very **h** on us, / making us drink
65:11 even the **h** pathways overflow with abundance.
107:12 That is why he broke them with **h** labor; / they fell,
127: 2 It is useless for you to work so **h** / from early
Pr 6: 8 they labor **h** all summer, gathering food for the
10: 4 Lazy people are soon poor; **h** workers get rich.
10: 5 A wise youth works **h** all summer; a youth who
12:11 **H** work means prosperity; only fools idle away
12:24 Work **h** and become a leader; be lazy and become
13: 4 but those who work **h** will prosper and be satisfied.
13:11 quickly disappears; wealth from **h** work grows.
21: 5 Good planning and **h** work lead to prosperity,
28:19 **H** workers have plenty of food; playing around
31:17 She is energetic and strong, a **h** worker.
Ecc 1: 3 What do people get for all their **h** work?
1:17 So I worked **h** to distinguish wisdom from
2:10 I even found great pleasure in **h** work,
2:11 at everything I had worked so **h** to accomplish,
2:18 I am disgusted that I must leave the fruits of my **h**
2:19 everything I have gained by my skill and **h** work.
2:20 So I turned in despair from **h** work. It was not the
2:22 So what do people get for all their **h** work?
3: 9 What do people really get for all their **h** work?
4: 6 better to be lazy and barely survive than to work **h**,
4: 8 yet who works **h** to gain as much wealth as he can.
5:12 People who work **h** sleep well, whether they eat
5:16 so they depart. All their **h** work is for nothing.
7:14 But when **h** times strike, realize that both come
8:15 along with all the **h** work God gives them.
8:17 in our world, no matter how **h** they work at it.
9:12 People can never predict when **h** times might
11: 5 God's ways are as **h** to discern as the pathways of
Isa 19: 4 I will hand Egypt over to a **h**, cruel master, to a
Jer 4: 3 "Plow up the **h** ground of your hearts!
6:28 are as insolent as bronze, as **h** and cruel as iron.
12:13 They have worked **h**, but it has done them no
32:17 by your great power. Nothing is too **h** for you!
32:27 the peoples of the world. Is anything too **h** for me?
La 3:65 Give them **h** and stubborn hearts, and then let your
4: 8 sticks to their bones; it is as dry and **h** as wood.
Eze 3: 8 I have made you as **h** and stubborn as they are.
3: 9 I have made you as **h** as rock! So don't be afraid of
19:13 in the wilderness, / where the ground is **h** and dry.
29:18 so **h** against Tyre that the warriors' heads were
Hos 10:11 and Judah must now break up the **h** ground;
10:12 Plow up the **h** ground of your hearts, for now is the
13:15 It will blow **h** against the people of Ephraim,
Am 9: 1 so **h** that the foundation will shake.
Hab 2:13 will turn to ashes? They work so **h**, but all in vain!
Hag 1:11 to ruin everything you have worked so **h** to get."
Zec 7:12 They made their hearts as **h** as stone, so they could
Mal 1:13 You say, 'It's too **h** to serve the LORD,' and you
Mt 13:19 The seed that fell on the **h** path represents those
19:23 it is very **h** for a rich person to get into the
25:24 gold came and said, 'Sir, I know you are a **h** man,
25:26 You think I'm a **h** man, do you, harvesting crops I
Mk 3: 5 because he was deeply disturbed by their **h** hearts.
4:15 The seed that fell on the **h** path represents those
6:48 rowing **h** and struggling against the wind
6:52 for their hearts were **h** and they did not believe.
8:17 or understand? Are your hearts too **h** to take it in?
10:23 "How **h** it is for rich people to get into the
10:24 it is very **h** to get into the Kingdom of God.
Lk 1:15 He must never touch wine or **h** liquor, and he will
5: 5 "we worked **h** all last night and didn't catch a
6:40 But the student who works **h** will become like the
8:12 The seed that fell on the **h** path represents those
13:24 Work **h** to get in, because many will try to enter,
15:29 'All these years I've worked **h** for you and never
18:24 "How **h** it is for rich people to get into the
19:21 I was afraid because you are a **h** man to deal with,
19:22 '**H**, am I? If you knew so much about me and how
24:25 so **h** to believe all that the prophets wrote in the
Jn 6:60 his disciples said, "This is very **h** to understand.
Ac 20:35 of how you can help the poor by working **h**.
26:14 It is **h** for you to fight against my will.'
Ro 9:16 We can't get it by choosing it or working **h** for it.
9:31 so **h** to get right with God by keeping the law,
11:25 Some of the Jews have **h** hearts, but this will last
15:26 in Jerusalem, who are going through such **h** times.
16: 6 to Mary, who has worked so **h** for your benefit.
16:12 to dear Persis, who has worked so **h** for the Lord.
1Co 3: 8 according to their own **h** work.
9: 1 because of my **h** work that you are in the Lord?
2Co 5:11 of the Lord that we work so **h** to persuade others.
8: 2 been going through much trouble and **h** times,
Gal 1:14 and I tried as **h** as possible to follow all the old
4:11 I am afraid that all my **h** work for you was worth
Eph 6: 6 Work **h**, but not just to please your masters when
Php 4: 3 for they worked **h** with me in telling others the
Col 1:29 I work very **h** at this, as I depend on Christ's
3:23 Work **h** and cheerfully at whatever you do,
1Th 2: 9 and sisters, how **h** we worked among you?
2:17 we tried very **h** to come back because of our
5:12 They work **h** among you and warn you against all
2Th 3: 6 and doesn't follow the tradition of **h** work we gave
3: 8 We worked **h** day and night so that we would not
1Ti 4:10 We work **h** and suffer much in order that people
5:17 especially those who work **h** at both preaching
2Ti 2:15 Work **h** so God can approve you. Be a good
Heb 5:11 seem to listen, so it's **h** to make you understand.
6:10 He will not forget how **h** you have worked for him
1Pe 3:11 do good. / Work **h** at living in peace with others.
2Pe 1:10 work **h** to prove that you really are among those
1:15 So I will work **h** to make these things clear to you.
2:10 He is especially **h** on those who follow their own
3:16 Some of his comments are **h** to understand,
2Jn 1: 8 the prize for which we have been working so **h**.
Rev 2: 2 I have seen your **h** work and your patient

HARD-HEARTED (5) [HARD, HEART]

Dt 15: 7 giving you, do not be **h** or tightfisted toward them.
Eze 2: 4 They are a **h** and stubborn people. But I am
3: 7 For the whole lot of them are **h** and stubborn.
Mt 19: 8 divorce as a concession to your **h** wickedness,
Mk 10: 5 only as a concession to your **h** wickedness.

HARD-WON (1) [HARD, WIN]

Isa 65:22 as trees and will have time to enjoy their **h** gains.

HARDEN (7) [HARD]

Ex 14: 4 And once again I will **h** Pharaoh's heart, and he
14:17 Yet I will **h** the hearts of the Egyptians, and they
Ps 95: 8 "Don't **h** your hearts as Israel did at Meribah,
Isa 6:10 **H** the hearts of these people. Close their ears,
Heb 3: 8 Don't **h** your hearts against him / as Israel did
3:15 Don't **h** your hearts against him / as Israel did
4: 7 to his voice. / Don't **h** your hearts against him."

HARDENED (12) [HARD]

Ex 8:15 saw that the frogs were gone, he **h** his heart.
8:32 But Pharaoh **h** his heart again and refused to let the
10:27 So the LORD **h** Pharaoh's heart once more,
11:10 the LORD **h** his heart so he wouldn't let the
Jos 11:20 For the LORD **h** their hearts and caused them to
Da 5:20 But when his heart and mind were **h** with pride,
Mt 13:15 For the hearts of these people are **h**, / and their ears
Jn 12:40 and **h** their hearts— / so their eyes cannot see,
Ac 28:27 For the hearts of these people are **h**, / and their ears
2Co 3:14 But the people's minds were **h**, and even to this
Eph 4:18 shut their minds and **h** their hearts against him.
Heb 3:13 of you will be deceived by sin and **h** against God.

HARDER (6) [HARD]

2Sa 11:25 Fight **h** next time, and conquer the city!"
Pr 18:19 It's **h** to make amends with an offended friend than
Jnh 1:13 the sailors tried even **h** to row the boat ashore.
1Co 15:10 For I have worked **h** than all the other apostles,
2Co 11:23 I have worked **h**, been put in jail more often,
1Ti 6: 2 You should work all the **h** because you are helping

HARDHEADED (1) [HARD]

Isa 48: 4 are as unbending as iron. You are as **h** as bronze.

HARDLY (9)

Ge 48:10 was half blind because of his age and could **h** see.
Nu 16:31 He had **h** finished speaking the words when the
2Ki 10:18 "Ahab **h** worshiped Baal at all compared to the
Pr 6: 1 or guarantee the debt of someone you **h** know—
Isa 40:24 They **h** get started, barely taking root, when he
Jer 32:23 They have **h** done one thing you told them to!
Da 10:17 My strength is gone, and I can **h** breathe."
Lk 9:39 and injuring him. It **h** ever leaves him alone.
1Co 5: 1 I can **h** believe the report about the sexual

HARDNESS (1) [HARD]

Ecc 8: 1 Wisdom lights up a person's face, softening its **h**.

HARDSHIP (5) [HARD]

Dt 15:18 "Do not consider it a **h** when you release your
26: 7 He heard us and saw our **h**, toil, and oppression.
Ps 71:20 You have allowed me to suffer much **h**, / but you
Da 10: 1 times of war and great **h**—and Daniel understood
2Ti 2:12 If we endure **h**, / we will reign with him. / If we

HARDSHIPS (6) [HARD]

Nu 11: 1 began to complain to the LORD about their **h**;
20:14 You know all the **h** we have been through,
Ne 9:32 do not let all the **h** we have suffered be as nothing
2Co 6: 4 endure troubles and **h** and calamities of every kind.
12:10 and with insults, **h**, persecutions, and calamities.
2Th 1: 4 in all the persecutions and **h** you are suffering.

HARDWORKING (1) [HARD, WORK]

2Ti 2: 6 **H** farmers are the first to enjoy the fruit of their

HARE (2)

Lev 11: 6 and the **h**, so they also may never be eaten.
Dt 14: 7 may not eat the camel, the **h**, or the rock badger.

HAREM (8)

Ge 12:15 the pharaoh, and she was taken into his **h**.
Est 2: 3 beautiful young women into the royal **h** at Susa.
2: 8 was brought to the king's **h** at the fortress of Susa
2: 9 and her maids into the best place in the **h**.
2:11 near the courtyard of the **h** to ask about Esther
2:14 the next morning she was brought to the second **h**,
2:15 the advice of Hegai, the eunuch in charge of the **h**.
2:19 young women had been transferred to the second **h**

HAREPH (1)
1Ch 2:51 of Bethlehem), and **H** (the father of Beth-gader).

HARETH [KJV] See HERETH

HARHAIAH (1)
Ne 3: 8 Next was Uzziel son of **H**, a goldsmith by trade,

HARHAS (2)
2Ki 22:14 wife of Shallum son of Tikvah and grandson of **H**,
2Ch 34:22 wife of Shallum son of Tikvah and grandson of **H**,

HARHUR (2)
Ezr 2:51 Bakbuk, Hakupha, **H**,
Ne 7:53 Bakbuk, Hakupha, **H**,

HARIM (12)
1Ch 24: 8 The third lot fell to **H**. / The fourth lot fell to
Ezr 2:32 The citizens of **H** | 320
2:39 The family of **H** | 1,017
10:21 From the family of **H**: Maaseiah, Elijah, Shemaiah,
10:31 From the family of **H**: Eliezer, Ishijah, Malkijah,
Ne 3:11 Then came Malkijah son of **H** and Hasshub son of
7:35 The citizens of **H** | 320
7:42 The family of **H** | 1,017
10: 5 **H**, Meremoth, Obadiah,
10:27 Malluch, **H**, and Baanah.
12: 3 Shecaniah, **H**, Meremoth,
12:15 Adna was leader of the family of **H**. / Helkai was

HARIPH (1)
Ne 10:19 **H**, Anathoth, Nebai,

HARLOT [KJV] See PROSTITUTE(D), WHORE

HARM (70) [HARMED, HARMFUL, HARMING, HARMLESS, HARMS]
Ge 26:29 Swear that you will not **h** us, just as we did not **h** you.
31: 7 But God has not allowed him to do me any **h**.
31:52 I will not cross this line to **h** you, and you will not cross it to **h** me.
42: 4 however, for fear some **h** might come to him.
44:29 his brother from me, too, and any **h** comes to him,
48:16 and the angel who has kept me from all **h**—may he
Ex 21:22 If no further **h** results, then the person responsible
21:23 But if any **h** results, then the offender must be
Dt 33:12 and preserves them from every **h**."
1Sa 19: 4 "He's never done anything to **h** you.
24: 9 listen to the people who say I am trying to **h** you?
24:10 For I said, 'I will never **h** him—he is the LORD's
24:11 This proves that I am not trying to **h** you and that I
24:12 you are trying to do to me, but I will never **h** you.
24:13 evil deeds.' So you can be sure I will never **h** you.
25:15 to us, and we never suffered any **h** from them.
26:21 my son, and I will no longer try to **h** you,
2Sa 18:12 'For my sake, please don't **h** young Absalom.'
22:48 He is the God who pays back those who **h** me;
24: 1 and he caused David to **h** them by taking a census.
1Ki 18: 9 "what **h** have I done to you that you are sending
2Ki 4:41 go ahead and eat." And then it did not **h** them!
25:24 that the Babylonian officials meant them no **h**.
Ne 6: 2 of Ono. But I realized they were plotting to **h** me,
Est 9: 2 against anyone who might try to **h** them.
Job 1:10 and his home and his property from **h**.
1:12 he possesses, but don't **h** him physically."
2: 3 even though you persuaded me to **h** him without
31:29 to ruin or become excited when **h** came their way?
Ps 15: 3 or **h** their neighbors / or speak evil of their friends.
18:47 He is the God who pays back those who **h** me;
20: 1 May the God of Israel keep you safe from all **h**.
34:20 For the LORD protects them from **h**— / not one of
37: 8 Do not envy others— / it only leads to **h**.
52: 4 You love to say things that **h** others, / you liar!
56: 5 they spend their days plotting ways to **h** me.
71:13 and shame cover / those who want to **h** me.
Pr 1:33 to me will live in peace and safety, unafraid of **h**."
12:21 No real **h** befalls the godly, but the wicked have
13:20 whoever walks with fools will suffer **h**.
15:32 If you reject criticism, you only **h** yourself; but if
19:23 LORD gives life, security, and protection from **h**.
21:10 Evil people love to **h** others; their neighbors get no
28:18 The honest will be rescued from **h**, but those who
Ecc 5:13 Riches are sometimes hoarded to the **h** of the
Jer 7: 6 worshiping idols as you now do to your own **h**.
10: 5 for they can neither **h** you nor do you any good."
23:17 evil desires, they say, 'No **h** will come your way!'
25: 6 the idols you have made. Then I will not **h** you.'
49: 4 your wealth and thought no one could ever **h** you.
Eze 11: 3 Inside it we will be like meat—safe from all **h**.'
44:19 so they do not **h** the people by transmitting
Da 11:27 Seeking nothing but each other's **h**, these kings
Hos 2:18 scurry along the ground so that they will not **h** you.
Mic 3:11 "No **h** can come to us," you say, "for the LORD
Zec 7:10 And do not make evil plans to **h** each other.
8:17 Do not make evil plots to **h** each other. And stop
Mal 3:15 who dare God to punish them go free of **h**.' "
Mk 3: 4 deeds on the Sabbath, or is it a day for doing **h**?
Lk 6: 9 deeds on the Sabbath, or is it a day for doing **h**?
Ac 18:10 and no one will **h** you because many people here in
28: 6 had waited a long time and saw no **h** come to him,
1Co 11:17 For it sounds as if more **h** than good is done when
2Ti 4:14 Alexander the coppersmith has done me much **h**,
1Pe 3:13 who will want to **h** you if you are eager to do
2Pe 2:13 Their destruction is their reward for the **h** they
Rev 11: 5 If anyone tries to **h** them, fire flashes from the
11: 5 This is how anyone who tries to **h** them must die.

HARMED (8) [HARM]
Lev 6: 5 a penalty of 20 percent to the person they have **h**.
1Sa 25: 7 we never **h** them, and nothing was ever stolen from
1Ki 1:52 "If he proves himself to be loyal, he will not be **h**.
Jer 2: 3 All who **h** my people were considered guilty,
La 3:52 My enemies, whom I have never **h**, chased me like
Lk 18: 3 appealing for justice against someone who had **h**
2Co 7: 9 to have, so you were not **h** by us in any way.
Phm 1:18 If he has **h** you in any way or stolen anything from

HARMFUL (5) [HARM]
Pr 10: 6 evil people cover up their **h** intentions.
10:11 lead to life; evil people cover up their **h** intentions.
16:29 their companions, leading them down a **h** path.
25:18 Telling lies about others is as **h** as hitting them
1Ti 6: 9 and **h** desires that plunge them into ruin

HARMING (4) [HARM]
Eze 46:20 and **h** the people by transmitting holiness to
Joel 3: 2 There I will judge them for **h** my people,
Lk 17: 2 punishment in store for **h** one of these little ones.
1Ti 1:13 down his people, **h** them in every way I could.

HARMLESS (4) [HARM]
Lev 13:39 the patch is only a pale white, this is a **h** skin rash,
Isa 30: 7 promises are worthless! I call her the **H** Dragon.
Mt 7:15 of false prophets who come disguised as **h** sheep,
10:16 Be as wary as snakes and **h** as doves.

HARMONY (14)
Ps 92: 3 by the harp and lute / and the **h** of the lyre.
133: 1 how pleasant, / when brothers live together in **h**!
133: 2 For **h** is as precious as the fragrant anointing oil
133: 3 **H** is as refreshing as the dew from Mount Hermon
Zec 6:13 and there will be perfect **h** between the two.
Ro 8:27 for the Spirit pleads for us believers in **h** with
12:16 Live in **h** with each other. Don't try to act
14:19 let us aim for **h** in the church and try to build each
15: 5 help you live in complete **h** with each other—
1Co 1:10 Let there be real **h** so there won't be divisions in
12:25 This makes for **h** among the members, so that all
2Co 6:15 What **h** can there be between Christ and the Devil?
13:11 Live in **h** and peace. Then the God of love
Col 3:14 Love is what binds us all together in perfect **h**.

HARMS (5) [HARM]
Ge 26:11 "Anyone who **h** this man or his wife will die!"
31:53 to punish either one of us who **h** the other."
La 3:38 it not the Most High who helps one and **h** another?
Zec 2: 8 'Anyone who **h** you **h** my most precious

HARNEPHER (1)
1Ch 7:36 sons of Zophah were Suah, **H**, Shual, Beri, Imrah,

HARNESS (2) [HARNESSED]
Jer 46: 4 **H** the horses, and prepare to mount them. Put on
Zec 14:20 On that day even the **h** bells of the horses will be

HARNESSED (1) [HARNESS]
Dt 22:10 "Do not plow with an ox and a donkey **h** together.

HAROD (4)
Jdg 7: 1 got up early and went as far as the spring of **H**.
2Sa 23:25 Shammah from **H**; / Elika from **H**;
1Ch 11:27 Shammah from **H**; / Helez from Pelon;

HAROEH (1)
1Ch 2:52 of Kiriath-jearim) were **H**, half the Manahathites,

HAROSHETH-HAGGOYIM (3)
Jdg 4: 2 of his army was Sisera, who lived in **H**.
4:13 and they marched from **H** to the Kishon River.
4:16 the enemy and their chariots all the way to **H**,

HARP (34) [HARPISTS, HARPS]
Ge 4:21 the first musician—the inventor of the **h** and flute.
1Sa 10: 5 They will be playing a **h**, a tambourine, a flute,
16:16 "Let us find a good musician to play the **h** for you
16:16 The **h** music will quiet you, and you will soon be
16:18 to Saul, "The son of Jesse is a talented **h** player.
16:23 from God troubled Saul, David would play the **h**.
18:10 David began to play the **h**, as he did whenever this
19: 9 him again. As David played his **h** for the king,
2Ki 3:15 Now bring me someone who can play the **h**."
3:15 While the **h** was being played, the power of the
1Ch 25: 3 God's messages to the accompaniment of the **h**,
Job 21:12 They sing with tambourine and **h**. They make
30:31 My **h** plays sad music, and my flute accompanies
Ps 33: 2 make music for him on the ten-stringed **h**.
33: 3 to him; / play skillfully on the **h** and sing with joy.
43: 4 I will praise you with my **h**, / O God, my God!
49: 4 and solve riddles with inspiration from a **h**.
57: 8 Wake up, my soul! / Wake up, O **h** and lyre!
71:22 Then I will praise you with music on the **h**,
81: 2 the tambourine. / Play the sweet lyre and the **h**.
92: 3 accompanied by the **h** and lute / and the harmony
98: 5 Sing your praise to the LORD with the **h**, / with the **h** and melodious song,
108: 2 Wake up, O **h** and lyre! / I will waken the dawn
137: 5 let my right hand forget its skill upon the **h**.
144: 9 I will sing your praises with a ten-stringed **h**.
149: 3 with dancing, / accompanied by tambourine and **h**.
150: 3 of the trumpet; / praise him with the lyre and **h**!
Isa 23:16 she will take a **h**, walk the streets, and sing her
24: 8 The melodious chords of the **h** will be silent.
Da 3: 5 flute, zither, lyre, **h**, pipes, and other instruments,
Am 6: 5 You sing idle songs to the sound of the **h**, and you
1Co 14: 7 Even musical instruments like the flute or the **h**,
Rev 5: 8 Each one had a **h**, and they held gold bowls filled

HARPISTS (1) [HARP]
Rev 14: 2 It was like the sound of many **h** playing together.

HARPOON (1)
Job 41: 7 Will its hide be hurt by darts, or its head by a **h**?

HARPS (22) [HARP]
Ge 31:27 joyful singing accompanied by tambourines and **h**.
2Sa 6: 5 lyres, **h**, tambourines, castanets, and cymbals.
1Ki 10:12 and to construct **h** and lyres for the musicians.
1Ch 13: 8 lyres, **h**, tambourines, cymbals, and trumpets.
15:16 to the accompaniment of lyres, **h**, and cymbals.
15:21 Jeiel, and Azaziah were chosen to play the **h**.
15:28 of cymbals, and loud playing on **h** and lyres.
16: 5 and Jeiel. They played the **h** and lyres.
25: 1 God's messages to the accompaniment of **h**,
25: 6 of cymbals, lyres, and **h** at the house of God.
2Ch 5:12 east side of the altar playing cymbals, **h**, and lyres.
9:11 and to construct **h** and lyres for the musicians.
20:28 They marched into Jerusalem to the music of **h**,
29:25 Temple of the LORD with cymbals, **h**, and lyres.
Ne 12:27 and with the music of cymbals, lyres, and **h**.
Ps 45: 8 with ivory, / you are entertained by the music of **h**.
147: 7 sing praises to our God, accompanied by **h**.
Isa 5:12 the **h**, lyres, tambourines, and flutes are superb!
30:32 keep time with the music of tambourines and **h**.
Eze 26:13 No more will the sound of **h** be heard among your
Rev 15: 2 They were all holding **h** that God had given them.
18:22 heard there—no more **h**, songs, flutes, or trumpets.

HARSH (15) [HARSHER, HARSHLY]
Ge 31:50 I won't know about it if you are **h** to my daughters
Ex 3: 7 I have heard their cries for deliverance from their **h**
Dt 28:33 suffer under constant oppression and **h** treatment.
2Sa 19:43 and the men of Judah were very **h** in their replies.
1Ki 12: 4 "Lighten the **h** labor demands and heavy taxes that
12:11 Yes, my father was **h** on you, but I'll be even
12:14 He told the people, "My father was **h** on you,
2Ch 10: 4 "Lighten the **h** labor demands and heavy taxes that
10:11 Yes, my father was **h** on you, but I'll be even
10:14 He told the people, "My father was **h** on you,
Job 39:16 She is **h** toward her young, as if they were not her
Pr 15: 1 turns away wrath, but **h** words stir up anger.
Da 2:15 "Why has the king issued such a **h** decree?"
Eph 4:31 of all bitterness, rage, anger, **h** words, and slander,
1Pe 2:18 are kind and reasonable, but even if they are **h**.

HARSHA (2) [TEL-HARSHA]
Ezr 2:52 Bazluth, Mehida, **H**,
Ne 7:54 Bazluth, Mehida, **H**,

HARSHER (4) [HARSH]
1Ki 12:11 my father was harsh on you, but I'll be even **h**!
12:14 "My father was harsh on you, but I'll be even **h**!
2Ch 10:11 my father was harsh on you, but I'll be even **h**!
10:14 "My father was harsh on you, but I'll be even **h**!

HARSHLY (13) [HARSH]
Ge 16: 6 So Sarai treated her **h**, and Hagar ran away.
Dt 28:48 They will oppress you **h** until you are destroyed.
2Sa 3: 9 May God deal **h** with me if I don't help David get
1Ki 12:13 But Rehoboam spoke **h** to them, for he rejected
2Ch 10:13 But Rehoboam spoke **h** to them, for he rejected
Job 19: 3 You should be ashamed of dealing with me so **h**.
Ps 31:23 to him, / but he **h** punishes all who are arrogant.
Isa 53: 7 He was oppressed and treated **h**, yet he never said
Mk 14: 5 the money to the poor!" And they scolded her **h**.
2Co 13:10 hoping that I won't need to deal **h** with you when I
Php 3: 6 Yes, in fact I **h** persecuted the church.
Col 3:19 must love your wives and never treat them **h**.
1Ti 5: 1 Never speak **h** to an older man, but appeal to him

HART [KJV] See DEER, STAG

HARUM (1)
1Ch 4: 8 Zobebah, and all the families of Aharhel son of **H**.

HARUMAPH (1)
Ne 3:10 Next Jedaiah son of **H** repaired the wall beside his

HARUPH (1)
1Ch 12: 5 Bealiah, Shemariah, and Shephatiah from **H**;

HARUZ (1)
2Ki 21:19 was Meshullemeth, the daughter of **H** from Jotbah.

HARVEST (138) [HARVESTED, HARVESTER, HARVESTERS, HARVESTING, HARVESTS, HARVESTTIME]

Ge 4: 3 At **h** time Cain brought to the LORD a gift of his
8: 22 there will be springtime and **h**, cold and heat,
30: 14 One day during the wheat **h**, Reuben found some
45: 6 during which there will be neither plowing nor **h**.
47: 24 Then when you **h** it, a fifth of your crop will
49: 11 his clothes in wine / because his **h** is so plentiful.
Ex 23: 10 "Plant and **h** your crops for six years,
23: 11 Then let the poor among you **h** any volunteer crop
23: 16 You must also celebrate the Festival of **H**,
23: 16 when you bring me the first crops of your **h**.
23: 16 you are to celebrate the Festival of the Final **H** at the end of the **h** season.
23: 19 "As you **h** each of your crops, bring me a choice sample of the first day's **h**.
34: 21 even during the seasons of plowing and **h**.
34: 22 of **H** with the first crop of the wheat **h**,
34: 22 and celebrate the Festival of the Final **H** at the end of the **h** season.
Lev 2: 14 to the LORD from the first portion of your **h**,
19: 9 "When you **h** your crops, do not **h** the grain along the edges of your fields,
23: 10 land I am giving you and you **h** your first crops,
23: 10 some grain from the first portion of your grain **h**.
23: 22 "When you **h** the crops of your land, do not **h** the grain along the edges of your fields,
25: 3 and prune your vineyards and **h** your crops,
25: 20 we are not allowed to plant or **h** crops that year?'
25: 22 you will eat from the old crop until the new **h**
26: 5 threshing season will extend until the grape **h**,
26: 5 and your grape **h** will extend until it is time to
26: 10 the previous year to make room for each new **h**.
Nu 18: 12 "I also give you the **h** gifts brought by the people
18: 27 The LORD will consider this to be your **h**
28: 26 "On the first day of the Festival of **H**, when you
Dt 11: 14 in their proper seasons so you can **h** crops of grain,
14: 22 one-tenth of all the crops you **h** each year.
16: 9 seven weeks from the beginning of your grain **h**.
16: 10 Then you must celebrate the Festival of **H** to honor
16: 13 must be observed for seven days at the end of the **h**
16: 16 the Festival of **H**, and the Festival of Shelters.
23: 25 grain by hand, but you may not **h** it with a sickle.
26: 2 put some of the first produce from each **h** into a
28: 38 "You will plant much but **h** little, for locusts will
Jos 3: 15 Now it was the **h** season, and the Jordan was
Jdg 8: 2 Aren't the last grapes of Ephraim's **h** better than
9: 27 During the annual **h** festival at Shechem, held in
15: 1 Later on, during the wheat **h**, Samson took a young
Ru 1: 22 in Bethlehem at the beginning of the barley **h**.
2: 21 and stay with his harvesters until the entire **h** is
2: 22 Stay with his workers right through the whole **h**.
2: 23 grain with them until the end of the barley **h**.
2: 23 Then she worked with them through the wheat **h**,
1Sa 8: 12 will be forced to plow in his fields and **h** his crops,
8: 15 He will take a tenth of your **h** and distribute it
12: 17 not rain at this time of the year during the wheat **h**.
2Sa 21: 9 them died together at the beginning of the barley **h**.
21: 10 on a rock and stayed there the entire **h** season.
2Ki 4: 42 of barley bread made from the first grain of his **h**.
19: 29 in the third year you will plant crops and **h** them;
2Ch 8: 13 the Passover celebration, the Festival of **H**,
Ne 10: 35 the first part of every **h** to the LORD's Temple—
12: 44 for the gifts, the first part of the **h**, and the tithes.
13: 31 and that the first part of the **h** was collected for the
Job 4: 8 plant trouble and cultivate evil will **h** the same.
24: 6 They **h** a field they do not own, and they glean in
31: 8 then let someone else **h** the crops I have planted,
Ps 65: 9 not run dry; / they provide a bountiful **h** of grain,
65: 11 You crown the year with a bountiful **h**;
68: 10 finally settled, / and with a bountiful **h**, O God,
78: 46 to caterpillars; / their **h** was consumed by locusts.
107: 37 plant their vineyards, / and **h** their bumper crops.
126: 5 who plant in tears / will **h** with shouts of joy.
126: 6 their seed, / but they sing as they return with the **h**.
Pr 20: 4 in the right season, you will have no food at the **h**.
22: 8 Those who plant seeds of injustice will **h** disaster,
26: 1 any more than snow with summer or rain with **h**.
Ecc 3: 2 and a time to die. / A time to plant and a time to **h**.
Isa 1: 8 shelter in a vineyard or field after the **h** is over.
5: 2 Then he waited for a **h** of sweet grapes,
5: 4 more could I have done / to cultivate a rich **h**?
16: 10 Gone now is the gladness; gone is the joy of **h**.
16: 10 has ceased forever. I have ended all their **h** joys.
17: 5 the grainfields in the valley of Rephaim after the **h**.
17: 6 like the stray olives left on the tree after the **h**.
17: 11 Your only **h** will be a load of grief and incurable
18: 4 dew forms on an autumn morning during the **h**."
24: 7 The grape **h** will fail, and there will be no wine.
24: 13 the tree or the few grapes left on the vine after **h**,
32: 10 fruit crop will fail, and the **h** will never take place.
37: 30 in the third year you will plant crops and **h** them;
Jer 8: 20 "The **h** is finished, and the summer is gone,"
9: 22 like dung, or like bundles of grain after the **h**.
12: 13 They will **h** a crop of shame, for the fierce anger of
40: 10 **H** the grapes and summer fruits and olives,
40: 12 Judean countryside to gather a great **h** of grapes
49: 9 Those who **h** grapes always leave a few for the
51: 33 be trampled. In just a little while her **h** will begin."
Eze 25: 4 They will **h** all your fruit and steal your livestock.
44: 30 The first samples of each grain **h** and the first of
45: 13 bushel of wheat or barley for every sixty you **h**,
Hos 2: 9 and ripened grain I generously provided each **h**
6: 11 a **h** of punishment is also waiting for you,
8: 7 have planted the wind and will **h** the whirlwind.
10: 12 of righteousness, and you will **h** a crop of my love.
Joel 3: 13 Now let the sickle do its work, for the **h** is ripe.
Ob 1: 5 Those who **h** grapes always leave a few for the
Mic 6: 15 You will plant crops but not **h** them. You will
7: 1 I feel like the fruit picker after the **h** who can find
Hag 1: 9 And when you brought your **h** home, I blew it
Mt 6: 26 They don't need to plant or **h** or put food in barns
9: 37 "The **h** is so great, but the workers are so few.
9: 38 So pray to the Lord who is in charge of the **h**;
13: 23 accept God's message and produce a huge **h**—
13: 30 Let both grow together until the **h**. Then I will tell
13: 39 The **h** is the end of the world, and the harvesters
21: 34 At the time of the grape **h** he sent his servants to
21: 41 will give him his share of the crop after each **h**."
Mk 4: 20 and accept God's message and produce a huge **h**—
Lk 8: 15 cling to it, and steadily produce a huge **h**.
10: 2 "The **h** is so great, but the workers are so few.
10: 2 Pray to the Lord who is in charge of the **h**, and ask
12: 24 They don't need to plant or **h** or put food in barns
Jn 4: 35 ripening all around us and are ready now for the **h**.
4: 36 and the fruit they **h** is people brought to eternal
4: 38 I sent you to **h** where you didn't plant; others had
4: 38 already done the work, and you will gather the **h**."
12: 24 many new kernels—a plentiful **h** of new lives.
1Co 9: 10 and thresh the grain expect a share of the **h**,
15: 20 He has become the first of a great **h** of those who
2Co 9: 10 and he will produce a great **h** of generosity in you.
Gal 6: 8 sinful desires will **h** the consequences of decay
6: 8 But those who live to please the Spirit will **h**
6: 9 for we will reap a **h** of blessing at the appropriate
Heb 12: 11 But afterward there will be a quiet **h** of right living
Jas 3: 18 will plant seeds of peace and reap a **h** of goodness.
5: 7 They patiently wait for the precious **h** to ripen.
Rev 14: 15 the sickle, for the time has come for you to **h**;

HARVESTED (15) [HARVEST]

Ge 26: 12 He **h** a hundred times more grain than he planted,
Lev 23: 39 after you have **h** all the produce of the land,
Jos 5: 11 and roasted grain **h** from the land.
2Ki 8: 6 including the value of any crops that had been **h**
Job 5: 26 old age. You will not be **h** until the proper time!
15: 33 They will be like a vine whose grapes are **h** before
Ps 105: 44 and they **h** crops that others had planted.
Pr 27: 25 After the hay is **h**, the new crop appears,
Jer 48: 32 you bare! He has **h** your grapes and summer fruits.
Am 7: 1 This was after the king's share had been **h** from the
9: 13 and grapes will grow faster than they can be **h**.
Hag 1: 6 You have planted much but **h** little. You have food
2: 16 hoped for a twenty-bushel crop, you **h** only ten.
2: 19 before you have **h** your grain and before the
Rev 14: 16 sickle over the earth, and the whole earth was **h**.

HARVESTER (3) [HARVEST]

Ps 129: 7 ignored by the **h**, / despised by the binder.
Jer 6: 9 as when a **h** checks each vine a second time to pick
Jn 4: 36 What joy awaits both the planter and the **h** alike!

HARVESTERS (14) [HARVEST]

Lev 19: 9 of your fields, and do not pick up what the **h** drop.
23: 22 of your fields, and do not pick up what the **h** drop.
Ru 2: 3 So Ruth went out to gather grain behind the **h**.
2: 4 Boaz arrived from Bethlehem and greeted the **h**.
2: 4 he said. "The LORD bless you!" the **h** replied.
2: 7 this morning if she could gather grain behind the **h**.
2: 14 So she sat with his **h**, and Boaz gave her food—
2: 21 and stay with his **h** until the entire harvest is
2Ki 4: 18 out to visit his father, who was working with the **h**.
Jer 25: 30 like the **h** do as they crush juice from the grapes.
50: 16 all those who plant crops; send all the **h** away.
Mt 13: 30 Then I will tell the **h** to sort out the weeds and burn
13: 39 is the end of the world, and the **h** are the angels.
Jn 4: 36 The **h** are paid good wages, and the fruit they

HARVESTING (12) [HARVEST]

Nu 13: 20 (It happened to be the season for **h** the first ripe
Dt 24: 19 "When you are **h** your crops and forget to bring in
Ru 2: 9 See which part of the field they are **h**, and
1Sa 6: 13 The people of Beth-shemesh were **h** wheat in the
Jer 12: 13 My people have planted wheat but are **h** thorns.
Mt 12: 2 It's against the law to work by **h** grain on the
25: 24 **h** crops you didn't plant and gathering crops you
25: 26 **h** crops I didn't plant and gathering crops I didn't
Mk 2: 24 It's against the law to work by **h** grain on the
Lk 6: 2 It's against the law to work by **h** grain on the
19: 21 what isn't yours and **h** crops you didn't plant.'
Jn 4: 35 Do you think the work of **h** will not begin until the

HARVESTS (23) [HARVEST]

Ge 27: 28 for healthy crops and good **h** of grain and wine.
Lev 25: 16 land is actually selling you a certain number of **h**.
Dt 11: 17 the sky and hold back the rain, and your **h** will fail.
16: 15 is the LORD your God who gives you bountiful **h**
30: 9 and your fields will produce abundant **h**,
2Ki 18: 32 a country with bountiful **h** of grain and wine,
Job 5: 5 Their **h** are stolen, and their wealth satisfies the
Ps 4: 7 than those who have abundant **h** of grain and wine.
67: 6 Then the earth will yield its **h**, / and God, our God,
Isa 16: 9 their summer fruits and **h** have all been destroyed.
23: 3 you grain from Egypt and **h** from along the Nile.
30: 23 There will be wonderful **h** and plenty of
36: 17 a country with bountiful **h** of grain and wine,
Jer 5: 17 They will eat your **h** and your children's bread,
5: 24 each spring and fall, assuring us of plentiful **h**.'
8: 13 I will take away their rich **h** of figs and grapes.
Eze 36: 30 I will give you great **h** from your fruit trees
Hos 9: 2 So now your **h** will be too small to feed you.
10: 1 The richer the **h** they brought in, the more
Hag 1: 9 You hoped for rich **h**, but they were poor.
Mk 4: 29 is ready, the farmer comes and **h** it with a sickle."
Jn 4: 37 'One person plants and someone else **h**.'
1Co 9: 7 And have you ever heard of a farmer who **h** his

HARVESTTIME (4) [HARVEST]

Lev 2: 12 and honey to the offerings presented at **h**,
2Sa 23: 13 Once during **h**, when David was at the cave of
Isa 9: 3 and its people will rejoice as people rejoice at **h**.
Jude 1: 12 They are like trees without fruit at **h**.

HAS (215 of 2109) [HAVE] See also Index of Articles, Etc.

Ge 39: 9 No one here **h** more authority than I do!
Ex 12: 20 Wherever you live, eat only bread that **h** no yeast
22: 19 "Anyone who **h** sexual relations with an animal
23: 18 never be offered together with bread that **h** yeast
35: 33 carving wood. In fact, he **h** every necessary skill.
Lev 11: 7 pig may not be eaten, for though it **h** split hooves,
11: 9 you may eat whatever **h** both fins and scales,
13: 29 "If anyone, whether a man or woman, **h** an open
13: 38 "If anyone, whether a man or woman, **h** shiny
13: 41 on his forehead, he simply **h** a bald forehead;
14: 35 'It looks like my house **h** some kind of disease.'
15: 2 man who **h** a genital discharge is ceremonially
15: 7 if you touch the man who **h** the unclean discharge.
15: 16 "Whenever a man **h** an emission of semen,
15: 19 "Whenever a woman **h** her menstrual period,
15: 24 If a man **h** sexual intercourse with her during this
19: 20 "If a man **h** sexual intercourse with a slave girl
20: 11 If a man **h** intercourse with his father's wife,
20: 12 If a man **h** intercourse with his daughter-in-law,
20: 14 If a man **h** intercourse with both a woman and her
20: 15 "If a man **h** sexual intercourse with an animal, he
20: 17 "If a man **h** sexual intercourse with his sister, the
20: 18 If a man **h** intercourse with a woman suffering
20: 19 "If a man **h** sexual intercourse with his aunt,
20: 20 If a man **h** intercourse with his uncle's wife,
21: 18 No one who **h** a defect may come near to me,
21: 19 or **h** a broken foot or hand,
21: 20 or **h** a humped back or is a dwarf, or **h** a defective eye, or **h** oozing sores or scabs on his skin, or **h** damaged testicles.
21: 21 Since he **h** a blemish, he may not offer food to his
22: 13 becomes a widow or is divorced and **h** no children
22: 21 must offer an animal that **h** no physical defects of
22: 22 that is blind, injured, mutilated, or that **h** a growth,
22: 24 If an animal **h** damaged testicles or is castrated,
25: 27 then that person **h** the right to redeem it from the
25: 29 who sells a house inside a walled city **h** the right
Nu 5: 2 from the camp who **h** a contagious skin disease or
19: 2 to bring you a red heifer that **h** no physical defects
20: 5 This land **h** no grain, figs, grapes, or pomegranates.
22: 19 to see if the LORD **h** anything else to say to me."
23: 23 no sorcery **h** any power against Israel.
24: 16 of God, / who **h** knowledge from the Most High,
27: 8 'If a man dies and **h** no sons, then give his
27: 9 And if he **h** no daughters, turn his inheritance over
27: 10 If he **h** no brothers, give his inheritance to his
27: 11 But if his father **h** no brothers, pass on his
27: 18 "Take Joshua son of Nun, who **h** the Spirit in him,
Dt 4: 7 For what great nation **h** a god as near to them as
4: 8 And what great nation **h** laws and regulations as
14: 6 "Any animal that **h** split hooves and chews the cud
14: 8 pig may not be eaten, for though it **h** split hooves,
14: 9 you may eat whatever **h** both fins and scales.
15: 21 But if this firstborn animal **h** any defect, such as
18: 8 offerings, even if he **h** a private source of income.
21: 15 "Suppose a man **h** two wives, but he loves one and
21: 18 "Suppose a man **h** a stubborn, rebellious son who
22: 23 be married, and he **h** sexual intercourse with her.
24: 12 If your neighbor is poor and **h** only a cloak to give
27: 20 'Cursed is anyone who **h** sexual intercourse with
27: 21 'Cursed is anyone who **h** sexual intercourse with
27: 22 'Cursed is anyone who **h** sexual intercourse with
27: 23 'Cursed is anyone who **h** sexual intercourse with
28: 55 because he **h** nothing else to eat during the siege
33: 17 Joseph **h** the strength and majesty of a young bull;
Jos 2: 11 No one **h** the courage to fight after hearing such
7: 15 be burned with fire, along with everything he **h**,
Ru 4: 17 women said, "Now at last Naomi **h** a son again!"
1Sa 2: 5 The barren woman now **h** seven children; / but the
14: 6 He can win a battle whether he **h** many warriors or
14: 33 by eating meat that still **h** blood in it."
16: 18 he is brave and strong and **h** good judgment.
2Sa 3: 29 cursed with a man who **h** open sores or leprosy or
6: 12 blessed Obed-edom's home and everything he **h**
18: 25 and the king replied, "If he is alone, he **h** news."
1Ki 2: 22 he **h** Abiathar the priest and Joab son of Zeruiah
18: 22 of the LORD who is left, but Baal **h** 450 prophets.
22: 8 Jehoshaphat said. "Let's hear what he **h** to say."
2Ki 19: 3 but the mother **h** no strength to deliver it.
18: 7 Jehoshaphat said. "Let's hear what he **h** to say."
25: 8 for he **h** the power to help or to frustrate."
Ezr 10: 14 Everyone who **h** a pagan wife will come at the
Job 1: 11 But take away everything he **h**, and he will surely
2: 4 A man will give up everything he **h** to save his life.
9: 19 As for strength, he **h** it. As for justice, who can
12: 6 and God **h** them in his power—live in safety!
26: 2 How you have saved a person who **h** no strength!
Ps 41: 8 "Whatever he **h**, it is fatal," they say. / "He will

111: 9 What a holy, awe-inspiring name he **h**!
119:96 Even perfection **h** its limits, / but your commands
Ps 10: 2 Ill-gotten gain **h** no lasting value, but right living
15:19 A lazy person **h** trouble all through life; the path
17:16 to educate a fool who **h** no heart for wisdom.
23:24 The father of godly children **h** cause for joy.
23:29 Who **h** anguish? Who **h** sorrow? Who is always fighting? Who is always complaining? Who **h** unnecessary bruises? Who **h** bloodshot eyes?
24: 7 When the leaders gather, the fool **h** nothing to say.
30:15 The leech **h** two suckers that cry out, "More,
31:21 She **h** no fear of winter for her household because
Ecc 6: 5 than he **h** in growing up to be an unhappy man.
7: 3 for sadness **h** a refining influence on us.
8: 8 None of us **h** the power to prevent the day of our
SS 8:11 "Solomon **h** a vineyard at Baal-hamon, which he
Isa 2: 7 Israel **h** vast treasures of silver and gold and many
5: 1 My beloved **h** a vineyard / on a rich and fertile hill.
8:18 the plans the LORD Almighty **h** for his people.
9:17 That is why the Lord **h** no joy in the young men
30:11 We are tired of listening to what he **h** to say."
37: 3 be born, but the mother **h** no strength to deliver it.
44:13 Now he **h** a wonderful idol that cannot even move
46: 7 It **h** no power to get anyone out of trouble.
54: 1 who could bear no children now **h** more than all
Jer 9:20 of the LORD; open your ears to what he **h** to say.
29: 7 held captive, for if Babylon **h** peace, so will you."
30:15 your punishment—this wound that **h** no cure?
La 1: 3 nations and **h** no place of rest. Her enemies have chased her down, and she **h** nowhere to turn.
Eze 18:10 "But suppose that man **h** a son who grows up to be
18:14 in turn, **h** a son who sees his father's wickedness
21:27 until the one appears who **h** the right to judge it.
43:22 a young male goat that **h** no physical defects.
43:23 young bull that **h** no defects and a perfect ram
Da 2:20 and ever, / for he alone **h** all wisdom and power.
4:35 He **h** the power to do as he pleases / among the
5:11 who **h** within him the spirit of the holy gods.
5:12 **h** a sharp mind and is filled with divine knowledge
Hos 2: 8 that it was I who gave her everything she **h**—
Joel 1: 2 history, **h** anything like this ever happened before?
Am 3: 5 Does a bird ever get caught in a trap that **h** no bait?
Ob 1: 8 everyone who **h** wisdom and understanding.
Jnh 4:11 But Nineveh **h** more than 120,000 people living in
Mic 6: 2 He **h** a case against his people Israel! He will
Mt 5:23 remember that someone **h** something against you,
15:22 For my daughter **h** a demon in her, and it is
17:15 my son, because he **h** seizures and suffers terribly.
18:12 "If a shepherd **h** one hundred sheep, and one
Mk 1:27 "It **h** such authority! Even evil spirits obey his
10: 4 "He said a man merely **h** to write his wife an
12:44 she, poor as she is, has given everything she **h**."
Lk 12: 5 Fear God, who **h** the power to kill people and then
15: 8 "Or suppose a woman **h** ten valuable silver coins
21: 4 she, poor as she is, has given everything she **h**."
Jn 4:10 "If you only knew the gift God **h** for you and who
5:26 The Father **h** life in himself, and he has granted
6:47 anyone who believes in me already **h** eternal life.
10:13 merely hired and **h** no real concern for the sheep.
10:20 Some of them said, "He **h** a demon, or he's crazy.
14:30 of this world approaches. He **h** no power over me,
16:15 All that the Father **h** is mine; this is what I mean
19:11 the one who brought me to you **h** the greater sin."
Ac 17:25 hands can't serve his needs—for he **h** no needs.
23:17 He **h** something important to tell him."
23:18 man to you because he **h** something to tell you."
25:11 neither you nor anyone else **h** a right to turn me
Ro 1:17 "It is through faith that a righteous person **h** life."
2:29 Whoever **h** that kind of change seeks praise from
3: 2 Yes, being a Jew **h** many advantages. First of all,
3:11 No one **h** real understanding; / no one is seeking
6: 9 Death no longer **h** any power over him.
9:22 God **h** every right to exercise his judgment and his power, but he also **h** the right to be very patient
9:23 He also **h** the right to pour out the riches of his
11:23 into the tree again. He **h** the power to do it.
12: 4 have many parts and each part **h** a special function,
12: 5 one body, and each of us **h** different work to do.
14: 2 But another believer who **h** a sensitive conscience
1Co 7:12 If a Christian man **h** a wife who is an unbeliever
7:13 Christian woman **h** a husband who is an unbeliever
7:33 He **h** to think about his earthly responsibilities and
7:36 because he **h** trouble controlling his passions and
9: 7 What soldier **h** to pay his own expenses?
12:12 The human body **h** many parts, but the many parts
12:14 the body **h** many different parts, not just one part.
14:13 So anyone who **h** the gift of speaking in tongues
15:41 The sun **h** one kind of glory, while the moon and
15:48 Every human being **h** an earthly body just like
2Co 3:11 which remains forever, **h** far greater glory.
Gal 2: 6 made no difference to me, for God **h** no favorites.)
3:11 "It is through faith that a righteous person **h** life."
4:27 now **h** more than all the other women!"
Eph 6: 9 the same Master in heaven, and he **h** no favorites.
Col 3:25 For God **h** no favorites who can get away with evil.
1Ti 4: 8 Physical exercise **h** some value, but spiritual
5: 3 church should care for any widow who **h** no one
5: 4 But if she **h** children or grandchildren, their first
5:16 If a Christian woman **h** relatives who are widows,
6: 4 Such a person **h** an unhealthy desire to quibble
Heb 3: 4 For every house **h** a builder, but God is the one
5: 3 That is why he **h** to offer sacrifices, both for their
5: 4 He **h** to be called by God for this work, just as
6: 7 good crop for the farmer, it **h** the blessing of God.
7: 7 the person who **h** the power to bless is always
Jas 1: 3 faith is tested, your endurance **h** a chance to grow.
4:12 He alone **h** the power to save or to destroy.
5:16 The earnest prayer of a righteous person **h** great
1Pe 1:17 to whom you pray **h** no favorites when he judges.
1Jn 1:10 and showing that his word **h** no place in our hearts.
2:23 anyone who confesses the Son **h** the Father also.
3:17 But if one of you **h** money enough to live well
4: 2 a human being, that person **h** the Spirit of God.
4: 3 Such a person **h** the spirit of the Antichrist.
4: 6 know if someone **h** the Spirit of truth or the spirit
4:18 Such love **h** no fear because perfect love expels all
5:12 So whoever **h** God's Son **h** life; whoever does not
Rev 2:12 from the one who **h** a sharp two-edged sword:
3: 1 from the one who **h** the sevenfold Spirit of God
3: 7 He is the one who **h** the key of David. He opens
12:12 in great anger, and he knows that he **h** little time."
13:18 Let the one who **h** understanding solve the number
14:18 Then another angel, who **h** power to destroy the
21:23 And the city **h** no need of sun or moon, for the

HASADIAH (1)

1Ch 3:20 Ohel, Berekiah, **H**, and Jushab-hesed.

HASENUAH [KJV] See HASSENUAH

HASHABIAH (16)

1Ch 6:45 **H**, Amaziah, Hilkiah,
9:14 son of Azrikam, son of **H**, a descendant of Merari;
25: 3 Gedaliah, Zeri, Jeshaiah, Shimei, **H**,
25:19 The twelfth lot fell to **H** and twelve of his sons
26:30 From the clan of Hebron came **H**. He and his
27:17 Levi | **H** son of Kemuel / Aaron (the priests)
2Ch 35: 9 his brothers Shemaiah and Nethanel, and **H**, Jeiel,
Ezr 8:19 They also sent **H**, together with Jeshaiah from the
8:24 the priests—Sherebiah, **H**, and ten other priests—
10:25 Ramiah, Izziah, Malkijah, Mijamin, Eleazar, **H**,
Ne 3:17 Then came **H**, the leader of half the district of
10:11 Mica, Rehob, **H**,
11:15 son of Azrikam, son of **H**, son of Bunni;
11:22 son of **H**, son of Mattaniah, son of Mica,
12:21 **H** was leader of the family of Hilkiah.
12:24 **H**, Sherebiah, Jeshua, Binnui, Kadmiel, and other

HASHABNAH (1)

Ne 10:25 Rehum, **H**, Maaseiah,

HASHABNEIAH (2)

Ne 3:10 own house, and next to him was Hattush son of **H**.
9: 5 Jeshua, Kadmiel, Bani, **H**, Sherebiah, Hodiah,

HASHBADDANAH (1)

Ne 8: 4 Mishael, Malkijah, Hashum, **H**, Zechariah,

HASHMONAH (2)

Nu 33:29 They left Mithcah and camped at **H**.
33:30 They left **H** and camped at Moseroth.

HASHUB [KJV] See HASSHUB

HASHUBAH (1)

1Ch 3:20 His five other sons were **H**, Ohel, Berekiah,

HASHUM (5)

Ezr 2:19 The family of **H** | 223
10:33 From the family of **H**: Mattenai, Mattattah, Zabad,
Ne 7:22 The family of **H** | 328
8: 4 Mishael, Malkijah, **H**, Hashbaddanah, Zechariah,
10:18 Hodiah, **H**, Bezai,

HASHUPHA [KJV] See HASUPHA

HASN'T (16) [HAVE, NOT] See Index of Articles, Etc.

HASSENAAH (1)

Ne 3: 3 The Fish Gate was built by the sons of **H**. They did

HASSENUAH (2)

1Ch 9: 7 son of Meshullam, son of Hodaviah, son of **H**;
Ne 11: 9 who was assisted by Judah son of **H**,

HASSHUB (5)

1Ch 9:14 Levites who returned were Shemaiah son of **H**,
Ne 3:11 Malkijah son of Harim and **H** son of Pahath-moab,
3:23 After them, Benjamin, **H**, and Azariah son of
10:23 Hoshea, Hananiah, **H**,
11:15 Shemaiah son of **H**, son of Azrikam, son of

HASTE (1) [HASTEN, HASTILY, HASTY]

Na 2: 5 they stumble in their **h**, rushing to the walls to set

HASTEN (2) [HASTE]

Job 30:13 and do everything they can to **h** my calamity,
Jn 19:31 so they asked Pilate to **h** their deaths by ordering

HASTEN [KJV] See also CHOOSE, CHOSE, ENJOYMENT, HASTE, HURRY, QUICKLY, WATCHING

HASTILY (5) [HASTE]

Ge 20: 8 and **h** called a meeting of all his servants.
41:14 at once, and he was brought **h** from the dungeon.
Ex 8:25 Pharaoh **h** called for Moses and Aaron. "All right!
2Ki 13:21 So they **h** threw the body they were burying into
Jn 11:31 house trying to console Mary saw her leave so **h**,

HASTY (3) [HASTE]

Ge 43:30 Then Joseph made a **h** exit because he was
Pr 14:29 those with a **h** temper will make mistakes.
21: 5 lead to prosperity, but **h** shortcuts lead to poverty.

HASUPHA (2)

Ezr 2:43 servants returned from exile: / Ziha, **H**, Tabbaoth,
Ne 7:46 servants returned from exile: / Ziha, **H**, Tabbaoth,

HATACH [KJV] See HATHACH

HATCH (1) [HATCHES, HATCHING]

Isa 34:15 She will **h** her young and cover them with her

HATCHES (1) [HATCH]

Jer 17:11 Like a bird that **h** eggs she has not laid, so are

HATCHING (2) [HATCH]

Ps 36: 4 They lie awake at night, **h** sinful plots.
Am 7:10 "Amos is **h** a plot against you right here on your

HATE (101) [HATED, HATEFUL, HATERS, HATES, HATING, HATRED]

Ge 37: 5 to his brothers, causing them to **h** him even more.
Ex 18:21 honest men who fear God and **h** bribes.
20: 5 I do not leave unpunished the sins of those who **h**
Nu 21: 5 nothing to drink. And we **h** this wretched manna!"
Dt 1:27 in your tents and said, 'The LORD must **h** us,
5: 9 I do not leave unpunished the sins of those who **h**
7:10 hesitate to punish and destroy those who **h** him.
32:41 on my enemies / and repay those who **h** me.
Jdg 14:16 in tears and said, "You don't love me; you **h** me!
1Sa 27:12 "By now the people of Israel must **h** him bitterly.
2Sa 5: 8 those 'lame' and 'blind' Jebusites. How I **h** them."
13:15 Then suddenly Amnon's love turned to **h**, and he
19: 6 You seem to love those who **h** you and **h** those who love you.
1Ki 22: 8 is still one prophet of the LORD, but I **h** him.
2Ch 18: 7 is still one prophet of the LORD, but I **h** him.
19: 2 the wicked and love those who **h** the LORD?"
Job 7:16 I **h** my life. I do not want to go on living. Oh,
8:22 Those who **h** you will be clothed with shame,
9:31 I would be so filthy my own clothing would **h** me.
Ps 5: 5 stand in your presence, / for you **h** all who do evil.
9:13 See how I suffer at the hands of those who **h** me.
21: 8 Your strong right hand will seize all those who **h**
25:19 enemies I have, / and how viciously they **h** me!
26: 5 I **h** the gatherings of those who do evil, / and I
31: 6 I **h** those who worship worthless idols. / I trust in
34:21 and those who **h** the righteous will be punished.
35:19 Don't let those who **h** me without cause
38:19 they **h** me though I have done nothing against
41: 7 All who **h** me whisper about me,
44: 7 it is you who humbles those who **h** us.
45: 7 You love what is right and **h** what is wrong.
68: 1 Let those who **h** God run for their lives.
69: 4 Those who **h** me without cause / are more
69:14 any deeper! / Rescue me from those who **h** me,
81:15 Those who **h** the LORD would cringe before him;
86:17 Then those who **h** me will be put to shame,
89:23 before him / and destroy those who **h** him.
97:10 You who love the LORD, **h** evil! / He protects the
101: 3 anything vile and vulgar. / I **h** all crooked dealings;
118: 7 I will look in triumph at those who **h** me.
119:85 These arrogant people who **h** your law / have dug
119:104 no wonder I **h** every false way of life.
119:113 I **h** those who are undecided about you, / but my
119:128 is right. / That is why I **h** every false way.
119:158 I **h** these traitors / because they care nothing for
119:163 I **h** and abhor all falsehood, / but I love your law.
120: 6 tired of living here / among people who **h** peace.
129: 5 May all who **h** Jerusalem / be turned back in
139:21 O LORD, shouldn't I **h** those who **h** you?
139:22 Yes, I **h** them with complete hatred, / for your
Pr 8: 7 for I speak the truth and **h** every kind of deception.
8:13 All who fear the LORD will **h** evil. That is why I **h** pride, arrogance, corruption,
8:36 injured themselves. All who **h** me love death."
9: 8 bother rebuking mockers; they will only **h** you.
12: 1 must love discipline; it is stupid to **h** correction.
13: 5 Those who are godly **h** lies; the wicked come to
15:17 you love is better than steak with someone you **h**.
15:27 the whole family, but those who **h** bribes will live.
26:24 People with **h** in their hearts may sound pleasant
29:10 The bloodthirsty **h** the honest, but the upright seek
Ecc 2:17 So now I **h** life because everything done here
3: 8 A time to love and a time to **h**. / A time for war
Isa 1:14 I **h** all your festivals and sacrifices. I cannot stand
61: 8 love justice. I **h** robbery and wrongdoing.
66: 5 "Your close relatives **h** you and throw you out for
Jer 14:19 rejected Judah? Do you really **h** Jerusalem?
44: 4 'Don't do these horrible things that I **h** so much.'
Eze 6: 9 Then at last they will **h** themselves for all their
20:43 and **h** yourselves because of the evil you have
36:31 and **h** yourselves for all the evil things you did.
Hos 9:15 began at Gilgal; there I began to **h** them.

Am 5:10 How you **h** honest judges! How you despise
5:15 **H** evil and love what is good; remodel your courts
5:21 "I **h** all your show and pretense—the hypocrisy of
6:8 false glory of Israel, and I **h** their beautiful homes.
Mic 3:2 but you are the very ones who **h** good and love
3:9 of Israel! You **h** justice and twist all that is right.
Zec 8:17 are false. I **h** all these things, says the LORD."
Mal 2:16 "For I **h** divorce!" says the LORD, the God of
Mt 5:43 'Love your neighbor' and **h** your enemy.
6:24 For you will **h** one and love the other, or be
10:22 And everyone will **h** you because of your
24:10 turn away from me and betray and **h** each other.
Mk 13:13 And everyone will **h** you because of your
Lk 1:71 saved from our enemies / and from all who **h** us.
6:27 love your enemies. Do good to those who **h** you.
16:13 For you will **h** one and love the other, or be
21:17 And everyone will **h** you because of your
Jn 3:20 They **h** the light because they want to sin in the
7:7 The world can't **h** you, but it does **h** me because I accuse it of sin and evil.
15:21 The people of the world will **h** you because you
Ro 1:29 sin, greed, **h**, envy, murder, fighting, deception,
7:15 but I don't do it. Instead, I do the very thing I **h**.
12:9 Really love them. **H** what is wrong. Stand on the
Heb 1:9 You love what is right and **h** what is wrong.
Rev 2:6 You **h** the deeds of the immoral Nicolaitans,
17:16 kings who will reign with him—all **h** the prostitute.

HATED (37) [HATE]

Ge 27:41 Esau **h** Jacob because he had stolen his blessing,
37:4 But his brothers **h** Joseph because of their father's
37:8 And they **h** him all the more for his dream
Dt 9:18 you had sinned by doing what the LORD **h**,
9:28 might say, "He destroyed them because he **h** them;
Jdg 11:7 "Aren't you the ones who **h** me and drove me
15:2 "I really thought you **h** her," her father explained,
1Sa 13:4 the Philistines now **h** the Israelites more than ever.
2Sa 13:15 and he **h** her even more than he had loved her.
13:22 he **h** Amnon deeply because of what he had done
22:18 from those who **h** me and were too strong for me.
22:41 them turn and run; / I have destroyed all who **h** me.
1Ki 11:25 Rezon **h** Israel intensely and continued to reign in
Est 9:5 and did as they pleased with those who **h** them.
9:16 killing seventy-five thousand of those who **h** them.
Job 34:17 Could God govern if he **h** justice? Are you going
Ps 18:17 from those who **h** me and were too strong for me.
18:40 them turn and run; / I have destroyed all who **h** me.
106:41 and those who **h** them ruled over them.
Pr 1:29 For they **h** knowledge and chose not to fear the
5:12 and you will say, "How I **h** discipline! If only I
14:17 do foolish things, and schemers are **h**.
Isa 60:15 you were once despised and **h** and rebuffed by all,
Jer 12:8 so I have treated them as though I **h** them.
15:10 that I had died at birth! I am **h** everywhere I go.
Eze 16:37 both those you loved and those you **h**—
Zec 11:8 with these sheep—this nation—and they **h** me, too.
Mt 24:9 You will be **h** all over the world because of your
Lk 6:22 God blesses you who are **h** and excluded
19:14 But his people **h** him and sent a delegation after
Jn 8:44 from the beginning and has always **h** the truth.
15:18 hates you, remember it **h** me before it **h** you.
15:24 they saw all that I did and yet **h** both of us—
15:25 the Scriptures said: 'They **h** me without cause.'
Tit 3:3 of evil and envy. We **h** others, and they **h** us.

HATEFUL (1) [HATE]

Ps 109:3 They are all around me with their **h** words,

HATEFUL [KJV] See also DREADFUL, HATED

HATERS (1) [HATE]

Ro 1:30 **h** of God, insolent, proud, and boastful.

HATES (24) [HATE]

Ex 23:5 If you see the donkey of someone who **h** you
Dt 12:31 committed many detestable acts that the LORD **h**,
16:22 for worship, for the LORD your God **h** them.
19:11 "But suppose someone **h** a neighbor
Job 16:9 God **h** me and tears angrily at my flesh.
39:7 It **h** the noise of the city, and it has no driver to
Ps 11:5 the wicked. / He **h** everyone who loves violence.
Pr 6:16 There are six things the LORD **h**—no,
11:1 The LORD **h** cheating, but he delights in honesty.
11:20 The LORD **h** people with twisted hearts, but he
12:22 The LORD **h** those who don't keep their word,
15:8 The LORD **h** the sacrifice of the wicked, but he
15:10 severely punished; whoever **h** correction will die.
26:28 A lying tongue **h** its victims, and flattery causes
28:16 but a king will have a long reign if he **h** dishonesty
Jn 15:18 "When the world **h** you, remember it hated me
15:19 you to come out of the world, and so it **h** you.
15:23 Anyone who **h** me **h** my Father, too.
17:14 And the world **h** them because they do not belong
Eph 5:29 No one **h** his own body but lovingly cares for it,
1Jn 3:13 dear brothers and sisters, if the world **h** you.
3:15 Anyone who **h** another Christian is really a
4:20 "I love God," but **h** another Christian,

HATHACH (8)

Est 4:5 Then Esther sent for **H**, one of the king's eunuchs
4:6 So **H** went out to Mordecai in the square in front of
4:8 Mordecai gave **H** a copy of the decree issued in
4:8 of all Jews, and he asked **H** to show it to Esther.
4:8 He also asked **H** to explain it to her and to urge her
4:9 So **H** returned to Esther with Mordecai's message.
4:10 Then Esther told **H** to go back and relay this
4:12 So **H** gave Esther's message to Mordecai.

HATHATH (1)

1Ch 4:13 Othniel's sons were **H** and Meonothai.

HATING (1) [HATE]

Ecc 9:6 loving, **h**, envying—is all long gone.

HATIPHA (2)

Ezr 2:54 Neziah, and **H**.
Ne 7:56 Neziah, and **H**.

HATITA (2)

Ezr 2:42 Ater, Talmon, Akkub, **H**, and Shobai | 139
Ne 7:45 Ater, Talmon, Akkub, **H**, and Shobai | 138

HATRED (13) [HATE]

Lev 19:17 "Do not nurse **h** in your heart for any of your
Dt 19:4 kills a neighbor without harboring any previous **h**,
Ps 55:8 far away from this wild storm of **h**.
77:10 blessings of the Most High have changed to **h**."
109:5 They return evil for good, / and **h** for my love.
139:22 Yes, I hate them with complete **h**, / for your
Pr 10:12 **H** stirs up quarrels, but love covers all offenses.
10:18 To hide **h** is to be a liar; to slander is to be a fool.
26:26 While their **h** may be concealed by trickery,
Eze 23:29 They will deal with you in **h** and rob you of all you
35:5 Your continual **h** for the people of Israel led you to
35:11 punish you for all your acts of anger, envy, and **h**.
Hos 9:7 with sin and shows only **h** for those who love God.

HATTIL (2)

Ezr 2:57 Shephatiah, **H**, Pokereth-hazzebaim, and Ami.
Ne 7:59 Shephatiah, **H**, Pokereth-hazzebaim, and Ami.

HATTUSH (5)

1Ch 3:22 and his sons, **H**, Igal, Bariah, Neariah,
Ezr 8:3 From the family of David: **H** son of Shecaniah.
Ne 3:10 and next to him was **H** son of Hashabneiah.
10:4 **H**, Shebaniah, Malluch,
12:2 Amariah, Malluch, **H**,

HAUGHTINESS (3) [HAUGHTY]

Pr 16:18 Pride goes before destruction, and **h** before a fall.
18:12 **H** goes before destruction; humility precedes
Isa 13:11 the arrogance of the proud and the **h** of the mighty.

HAUGHTY (7) [HAUGHTINESS]

1Sa 2:3 "Stop acting so proud and **h**! / Don't speak with
Ps 131:1 my heart is not proud; / my eyes are not **h**.
Pr 6:17 **h** eyes, / a lying tongue, / hands that kill the
21:4 **H** eyes, a proud heart, and evil actions are all sin.
21:24 Mockers are proud and **h**; they act with boundless
Jer 48:29 of her loftiness, her arrogance, and her **h** heart.
Lk 1:51 How he scatters the proud and **h** ones!

HAUL (2) [HAULED]

Eze 32:3 to catch you in my net and **h** you out of the water.
Jn 4:15 and I won't have to come here to **h** water."

HAULED (1) [HAUL]

Isa 46:1 Bel and Nebo, are being **h** away on ox carts.

HAUNT (3) [HAUNTED, HAUNTS]

Ps 51:3 my shameful deeds— / they **h** me day and night.
Isa 34:13 The ruins will become a **h** for jackals and a home
Jer 10:22 will be destroyed and will become a **h** for jackals.

HAUNTED (5) [HAUNT]

Isa 13:21 The houses will be **h** by howling creatures.
34:11 It will be **h** by the horned owl, the hawk,
Jer 9:11 says the LORD. "It will be a place **h** by jackals.
51:37 will become a heap of rubble, **h** by jackals.
La 5:18 is empty and desolate, a place **h** by jackals.

HAUNTS (3) [HAUNT]

Job 30:16 now my heart is broken. Depression **h** my days.
38:15 The light disturbs the **h** of the wicked, and it stops
Pr 4:15 Avoid their **h**. Turn away and go somewhere else,

HAURAN (2)

Eze 47:16 and finally to Hazer-hatticon, on the border of **H**.
47:18 "The eastern border starts at a point between **H**

HAVE (1047 of 4502) [HAD, HADN'T, HASN'T, HAVE, HAVEN'T, HAVING, I'VE, WE'VE, YOU'D] See also Index of Articles, Etc.

Ge 9:4 must never eat animals that still **h** their lifeblood
9:7 Now you must **h** many children and repopulate the
11:30 Now Sarai was not able to **h** any children.
12:12 is his wife. Let's kill him; then we can **h** her!'
15:2 what good are all your blessings when I don't even **h** a son? Since I don't **h** a son, Eliezer of
15:3 so one of my servants will **h** to be my heir."
15:4 you will **h** a son of your own to inherit everything
16:2 Perhaps I can **h** children through her." And Abram
17:17 Sarah is ninety; how could she **h** a baby?"
18:10 I will return, and your wife Sarah will **h** a son."
18:12 worn-out woman like me **h** a baby?" she thought.
18:13 did she say, 'Can an old woman like me **h** a baby?'
18:14 as I told you, I will return, and Sarah will **h** a son."
19:5 Bring them out so we can **h** sex with them."
19:8 Look—I **h** two virgin daughters. Do with them as
19:12 "Do you **h** any other relatives here in the city?"
19:31 And our father will soon be too old to **h** children.
20:12 she is my sister—we both **h** the same father,
20:13 go, **h** the kindness to say that you are my sister.' "
20:17 women of the household, so they could **h** children.
21:7 would have dreamed that I would ever **h** a baby?
21:10 inheritance with my son, Isaac. I won't **h** it!"
21:26 "And I **h** no idea who is responsible. Why didn't
22:7 "We **h** the wood and the fire," said the boy, "but
23:4 Please let me **h** a piece of land for a burial plot."
23:9 to let me **h** the cave of Machpelah, down at the
23:9 I may **h** a permanent burial place for my family."
24:23 "Would your father **h** any room to put us up for
24:25 Yes, we **h** plenty of straw and food for the camels, and we **h** a room for guests."
24:31 we **h** a room all ready for you and a place prepared
26:28 So we decided we should **h** a treaty, a covenant
27:31 "I'm back, Father, and I **h** the wild game. Sit up
29:27 the bridal week is over, and you can **h** Rachel, too
29:31 Leah was unloved, the LORD let her **h** a child,
31:8 said I could **h** the streaked ones, then all the lambs
31:43 and these flocks and all that you **h**—all are mine.
33:9 "Brother, I **h** plenty," Esau answered. "Keep what you **h**."
33:11 I **h** more than enough." Jacob continued to insist,
33:13 and the flocks and herds **h** their young, too.
34:11 be kind to me, and let me **h** her as my wife,"
35:17 exclaimed, "Don't be afraid—you **h** another son!"
38:9 But Onan was not willing to **h** a child who would
38:22 village had claimed they didn't **h** a prostitute there.
39:6 With Joseph there, he didn't **h** a worry in the world
40:14 And please **h** some pity on me when you are back
41:35 **H** them gather all the food and grain of these good
41:40 my people. Only I will **h** a rank higher than yours."
42:16 If it turns out that you don't **h** a younger brother,
43:6 "Why did you **h** to treat me with such cruelty?"
43:22 We also **h** additional money to buy more grain. We **h** no idea how the money got into our sacks."
44:20 We said, 'Yes, we **h** a father, an old man, and a
45:10 your flocks and herds, and all that you **h**.
47:6 And if any of them **h** special skills, put them in
47:18 We **h** nothing left but our bodies and land.
50:20 He brought me to the high position I **h** today so I
Ex 1:19 They **h** their babies so quickly that we cannot get
4:2 asked him, "What do you **h** there in your hand?"
5:8 single brick. They obviously don't **h** enough to do.
5:17 just lazy! You obviously don't **h** enough to do.
7:2 Aaron everything I say to you and **h** him announce
10:26 We will **h** to choose our sacrifices for the LORD
14:14 You won't **h** to lift a finger in your defense!"
16:12 'In the evening you will **h** meat to eat, and in the
19:9 Then they will always **h** confidence in you."
19:10 and tomorrow, and **h** them wash their clothing.
21:30 The owner will **h** to pay whatever is demanded.
23:32 "Make no treaties with them and **h** nothing to do
25:32 It will **h** six branches, three branches going out
28:3 Instruct all those who **h** special skills as tailors to
36:5 "We **h** more than enough materials on hand now
Lev 3:1 you offer to the LORD must **h** no physical defects.
3:6 male or female, and it must **h** no physical defects.
5:15 The animal must **h** no physical defects, and it must
5:18 The animal must **h** no physical defects, and it must
7:18 It will **h** no value as a sacrifice, and you will
7:18 if you eat it, you will **h** to answer for your sin.
11:3 include those that **h** completely divided hooves
11:4 because they either **h** split hooves or chew the cud,
11:4 though it chews the cud, it does not **h** split hooves.
11:10 marine animals that do not **h** both fins and scales.
11:12 not **h** both fins and scales is strictly forbidden to
11:27 walk on all fours, those that **h** paws are unclean
14:36 he must **h** the house emptied so everything inside
18:6 "You must never **h** sexual intercourse with a close
18:7 mother; you must never **h** intercourse with her.
18:8 Do not **h** sexual intercourse with any of your
18:9 "Do not **h** sexual intercourse with your sister or
18:10 "Do not **h** sexual intercourse with your
18:11 Do not **h** sexual intercourse with the daughter of
18:12 Do not **h** intercourse with your aunt, your father's
18:13 Do not **h** sexual intercourse with your aunt, your
18:15 Do not **h** sexual intercourse with your
18:16 Do not **h** intercourse with your brother's wife; this
18:17 "Do not **h** sexual intercourse with both a woman
18:23 in order to **h** intercourse with it; this is a terrible
20:16 approaches a male animal to **h** intercourse with it,
21:17 his descendants who **h** physical defects will not
22:4 "If any of the priests **h** a contagious skin disease
22:11 And if his slaves **h** children, they also may share
24:3 must arrange to **h** the lamps tended continually,
25:5 unpruned vines. The land is to **h** a year of total rest.
25:32 "The Levites always **h** the right to redeem any
26:10 You will **h** such a surplus of crops that you will
26:26 so the bread from one oven will **h** to be stretched
26:26 even if you **h** food to eat, you will not be satisfied.
26:37 You will **h** no power to stand before your enemies.
Nu 1:52 Each tribe of Israel will **h** a designated camping
5:28 unharmed and will still be able to **h** children.
7:5 the Levites according to the work they **h** to do."
11:6 day after day we **h** nothing to eat but this manna!"
11:17 along with you, so you will not **h** to carry it alone.

11:18 for tomorrow they will **h** meat to eat. Tell them,
11:18 LORD will give you meat, and you will **h** to eat it.
13:19 Do their towns **h** walls or are they unprotected?
14:34 will discover what it is like to **h** me for an enemy.'
16: 3 What right do you **h** to act as though you are
22:38 "I have come, but I **h** no power to say just anything
28:31 all the animals you sacrifice **h** no physical defects.
32: 5 please let us **h** this land as our property instead of
Dt 1:13 Choose some men from each tribe who **h** wisdom,
4:25 when you **h** children and grandchildren and have
5:29 Oh, that they would always **h** hearts like this, that
6: 3 and you will **h** many children in the land flowing
7:13 you will **h** large crops of grain, grapes, and olives,
10: 9 That is why the Levites **h** no share or inheritance
11: 8 so you may **h** strength to go in and occupy the land
11:15 to graze in, and you yourselves will **h** plenty to eat.
12:12 for they will **h** no inheritance of land as their own.
13: 1 or those who **h** dreams about the future, and they
13: 8 they do this, do not give in or listen, and **h** no pity.
13:17 He will **h** compassion on you and make you a
14: 7 if the animal doesn't **h** both, it may not be eaten.
14: 7 They chew the cud but do not **h** split hooves.
14:10 marine animals that do not **h** both fins and scales.
14:27 community, for they **h** no inheritance as you do.
14:29 Give it to the Levites, who **h** no inheritance among
17:14 'We ought to **h** a king like the other nations
18: 2 They will **h** no inheritance of their own among the
18:16 You begged that you might never again **h** to listen
19:12 must **h** the murderer brought back from the city of
22: 8 "Every new house you build must **h** a barrier
22:30 "A man must not **h** intercourse with his father's
23:13 Each of you must **h** a spade as part of your
26:12 so that they will **h** enough to eat in your towns.
28:13 not the tail, and you will always **h** the upper hand.
28:41 You will **h** sons and daughters, but you will not
28:54 will **h** no compassion for his own brother, his
28:57 She will **h** nothing else to eat during the siege and
30: 3 He will **h** mercy on you and gather you back from
Jos 8: 8 as the LORD has commanded. You **h** your orders."
17:16 Jezreel **h** iron chariots—they are too strong for us."
17:18 even though they are strong and **h** iron chariots."
18:10 to determine which tribe should **h** each section.
19:50 For the LORD had said he could **h** any town he
22:24 'What right do you **h** to worship the LORD,
22:25 You **h** no claim to the LORD.' And your
22:27 **h** the right to worship the LORD at his sanctuary
22:27 able to say to ours, 'You **h** no claim to the LORD.'
22:28 of the relationship both of us **h** with the LORD.'
Jdg 3:19 to Eglon and said, "I **h** a secret message for you."
3:20 and said, "I **h** a message for you from God!"
6:14 "Go with the strength you **h** and rescue Israel from
7: 2 "You **h** too many warriors with you. If I let all of
8:24 However, I **h** one request. Each of you can give
11:38 and wept because she would never **h** children.
13: 3 "Even though you have been unable to **h** children,
17: 3 I will **h** an image carved and an idol cast."
17:13 said, "because I **h** a Levite serving as my priest."
19:19 even though we **h** everything we need. We **h** straw
19:22 is staying with you so we can **h** sex with him."
21:22 Let them **h** your daughters, for we didn't find
Ru 4: 5 she can **h** children who will carry on her
4:10 This way she can **h** a son to carry on the family
1Sa 1: 8 Why be so sad just because you **h** no children?
You **h** me—isn't that better than having ten sons?"
2: 1 Now I **h** an answer for my enemies, / as I delight
2: 5 but the woman with many children will **h** no more.
2:36 among the priests so we will **h** enough to eat.' "
4:20 "You **h** a baby boy!" But she did not answer or
8: 5 Give us a king like all the other nations **h**."
9: 7 we don't **h** anything to offer him," Saul replied.
"Even our food is gone, and we don't **h** a thing to
9: 8 the servant said, "I **h** one small silver piece.
10: 3 another will **h** three loaves of bread, and the third
14: 1 go over to where the Philistines **h** their outpost."
16:11 Samuel asked, "Are these all the sons you **h**?"
18:21 "I **h** a way for you to become my son-in-law after
21: 3 me five loaves of bread or anything else you **h**."
21: 4 "We don't **h** any regular bread," the priest replied.
21: 4 the holy bread, which I guess you can **h** if your
21: 8 "Do you **h** a spear or sword? The king's business
was so urgent that I didn't even **h** time to grab a
21: 9 "I only **h** the sword of Goliath the Philistine,
21:15 We already **h** enough of them around here!
23:23 even if I **h** to search every hiding place in Judah!"
24:11 Look, my father, at what I **h** in my hand. It is a
25: 8 give us any provisions you might **h** on hand."
25:24 my lord. Please listen to what I **h** to say.
25:31 Then you won't **h** to carry on your conscience the
27:12 Now he will **h** to stay here and serve me forever!"
28: 8 "I **h** to talk to a man who has died," he said.
29: 9 But my commanders are afraid to **h** you with them
30:22 go with us, so they can't **h** any of the plunder.
2Sa 2:14 "Let's **h** a few of our warriors put on an exhibition
2:22 be able to face your brother Joab if I **h** to kill you!"
7: 3 "Go ahead and do what you **h** in mind, for the
10: 9 Joab saw that he would **h** to fight on two fronts,
14: 7 of the family is demanding, 'Let us **h** your son.
14: 7 But if I do that, I will **h** no one left, and my
15: 3 It's too bad the king doesn't **h** anyone to hear it.
16:11 Shouldn't this relative of Saul **h** even more reason
17:10 even the bravest of them, though they **h** the heart
17:11 That way you will **h** an army as numerous as the
17:13 you will **h** the entire army of Israel there at your
18: 3 "If we **h** to turn and run—and even if half of us
18:18 for he had said, "I **h** no son to carry on my name."
18:26 The king replied, "He also will **h** news."
18:31 and said, "I **h** good news for my lord the king.
19:30 "I am content just to **h** you back again, my lord!"
19:43 "So we **h** ten times as much right to the king as
20: 1 and shouted, "We **h** nothing to do with David.
1Ki 2:14 In fact, I **h** a favor to ask of you." / "What is it?"
2:16 So now I **h** just one favor to ask of you. Please
2:20 "I **h** one small request to make of you," she said.
3:12 such as no one else has ever had or ever will **h**!
3:16 came to the king to **h** an argument settled.
5: 4 on every side, and I **h** no enemies and all is well.
9: 5 never fail to **h** a successor on the throne of Israel.'
11:36 His son will **h** one tribe so that the descendants of
12:16 We **h** no share in Jesse's son! Let's go home,
13: 7 to the palace with me and **h** something to eat,
14: 6 Then he told her, "I **h** bad news for you.
14:13 will **h** a proper burial, for this child is the only
17:12 that I don't **h** a single piece of bread in the house.
And I **h** only a handful of flour left in the jar
18:27 "You'll **h** to shout louder," he scoffed, "for surely
20: 4 my lord," Ahab replied. "All that I **h** is yours!"
21:15 sell you? Well, you can **h** it now! He's dead!"
2Ki 1:17 Since Ahaziah did not **h** a son to succeed him,
2:19 "We **h** a problem, my lord," they told him.
3:17 You will **h** plenty for yourselves and for your
4: 2 "Tell me, what do you **h** in the house?"
4:10 he will **h** a place to stay whenever he comes by."
4:14 "She doesn't **h** a son, and her husband is an old
4:28 "It was you, my lord, who said I would **h** a son.
6:27 "I **h** neither food nor wine to give you."
9: 5 "I **h** a message for you, Commander," he said.
10: 2 you **h** at your disposal chariots, horses, a fortified
19: 7 his land, where I will **h** him killed with a sword.' "
19:26 That is why their people **h** so little power / and are
20:17 The time is coming when everything you **h**—all
22: 4 and **h** him count the money the gatekeepers have
22: 6 Also **h** them buy the timber and the cut stone
1Ch 2:34 Sheshan had no sons, though he did **h** daughters.
17: 2 "Go ahead with what you **h** in mind, for God is
19:10 Joab saw that he would **h** to fight on two fronts,
22: 9 But you will **h** a son who will experience peace
22:15 You **h** many skilled stonemasons and carpenters
29:14 Everything we **h** has come from you, and we give
2Ch 6:15 and today you **h** fulfilled it with your own hands.
7:18 never fail to **h** a successor who rules over Israel.'
10:16 We **h** no share in Jesse's son! Let's go home,
11:23 and arranged for each of them to **h** several wives.
19:11 "Amariah the high priest will **h** final say in all
19:11 tribe of Judah, will **h** final say in all civil cases.
31:11 Hezekiah decided to **h** storerooms prepared in the
32: 8 He may **h** a great army, but they are just men. We
h the LORD our God to help us and to fight our
35:21 king of Judah? I **h** no quarrel with you today!
Ezr 4: 3 "You may **h** no part in this work, for we **h** nothing
in common. We alone will build the Temple for
Ne 2:20 But you **h** no stake or claim in Jerusalem."
5: 2 They were saying, "We **h** such large families.
9:10 You **h** a glorious reputation that has never been
9:37 They **h** power over us and our cattle. We serve
13:22 **H** compassion on me according to your great and
Est 1: 8 who wished could **h** as much as they pleased,
6: 9 **H** the prince shout as they go, 'This is what
Job 1: 8 He fears God and will **h** nothing to do with evil."
2: 3 He fears God and will **h** nothing to do with evil.
3: 7 Let that night be barren. Let it **h** no joy.
3:26 I **h** no peace, no quietness. I **h** no rest; instead,
5:16 And so at last the poor **h** hope, and the fangs of
5:21 and will **h** no fear of destruction when it comes.
6: 5 Don't I **h** a right to complain? Wild donkeys bray
6: 5 no green grass, and oxen low when they **h** no food.
6: 8 "Oh, that I might **h** my request, that God would
6:11 But I do not **h** the strength to endure. I do not **h** a
goal that encourages me to carry on.
6:12 Do I **h** strength as hard as stone? Is my body made
9:15 Even if I were innocent, I would **h** no defense.
10:20 I **h** only a little time left, so leave me alone—that I
may **h** a little moment of comfort
11:18 You will **h** courage because you will **h** hope. You
will be protected and will rest in safety.
11:18 You will **h** courage because you will **h** hope.
13:12 Your statements **h** about as much value as ashes.
15: 4 **H** you no fear of God, no reverence for him?
15: 8 secret council? Do you **h** a monopoly on wisdom?
15:30 the breath of God will destroy everything they **h**.
18: 3 we are cattle? Do you think we **h** no intelligence?
18:19 They will **h** neither children nor grandchildren,
19:21 "**H** mercy on me, my friends, **h** mercy, for the
hand of God has struck me.
21:16 so I will **h** nothing to do with that kind of thinking.
22: 8 and that those who are privileged **h** a right to it!
22:18 so I will **h** nothing to do with that kind of thinking.
24:21 of the childless who **h** no protecting sons.
24:22 They may rise high, but they **h** no assurance in life.
27: 3 As long as I live, while I **h** breath from God,
27: 8 For what hope do the godless **h** when God cuts
27:14 If they **h** a multitude of children, their children
27:16 "Evil people may **h** all the money in the world,
30:13 knowing full well that I **h** no one to help me.
33: 1 "Listen, Job, to what I **h** to say.
33: 2 Now that I **h** begun to speak, let me continue.
34: 2 Pay attention, you who **h** knowledge.
34:10 "Listen to me, you who **h** understanding.
34:27 They **h** no respect for any of his ways.
35: 6 sin again and again, what effect will it **h** on him?
38: 3 because I **h** some questions for you, and you must
38:28 "Does the rain **h** a father? Where does dew come
40: 2 You are God's critic, but do you **h** the answers?"
40: 5 said too much already. I **h** nothing more to say."
40: 7 because I **h** some questions for you, and you must
42: 4 I **h** some questions for you, and you must answer
Ps 1: 5 Sinners will **h** no place among the godly.
3: 1 O LORD, I **h** so many enemies; / so many are
4: 1 my distress. / **H** mercy on me and hear my prayer.
4: 7 those who **h** abundant harvests of grain and wine.
6: 2 **H** compassion on me, LORD, for I am weak. / Heal
9:13 LORD, **h** mercy on me. / See how I suffer at the
13: 2 How long will my enemy **h** the upper hand?
16: 2 my Master! / All the good things I **h** are from you."
17:14 May they **h** their punishment in full. / May their
21:10 face of the earth; / they will never **h** descendants.
23: 1 The LORD is my shepherd; / I **h** everything I need.
24: 5 and **h** right standing with God their savior.
25:16 Turn to me and **h** mercy on me, / for I am alone
25:19 See how many enemies I **h**, / and how viciously
30:10 Hear me, LORD, and **h** mercy on me. / Help me,
31: 9 **H** mercy on me, LORD, for I am in distress.
34: 9 for those who honor him will **h** all they need.
35:25 Don't let them say, "Look! We **h** what we wanted!
36: 1 They **h** no fear of God to restrain them.
37:16 It is better to be godly and **h** little / than to be evil
37:19 even in famine they will **h** more than enough.
37:38 the wicked will be destroyed; / they **h** no future.
40: 4 who **h** no confidence in the proud,
41: 4 "O LORD," I prayed, "**h** mercy on me. / Heal me,
41:10 LORD, **h** mercy on me. / Make me well again, so I
42: 3 Day and night, I **h** only tears for food, / while my
50: 8 I **h** no complaint about your sacrifices
51: 1 **H** mercy on me, O God, / because of your
56: 1 O God, **h** mercy on me. / The enemy troops press
57: 1 **H** mercy on me, O God, **h** mercy! / I look to you
72:12 help the oppressed, who **h** no one to defend them.
73: 7 These fat cats **h** everything / their hearts could
73:25 Whom **h** I in heaven but you? / I desire you more
81: 9 You must never **h** a foreign god; / you must not
84: 9 protector! / **H** mercy on the one you **h** anointed.
86:16 Look down and **h** mercy on me. / Give strength to
94:15 and those who are upright will **h** a reward.
101: 3 dealings; / I will **h** nothing to do with them.
102:13 You will arise and **h** mercy on Jerusalem—
112: 9 They will **h** influence and honor.
115: 5 They cannot talk, though they **h** mouths, / or see,
though they **h** eyes!
116: 2 down and listens, / I will pray as long as I **h** breath!
119:42 Then I will **h** an answer for those who taunt me,
119:80 then I will never **h** to be ashamed.
119:96 has its limits, / but your commands **h** no limit.
119:99 Yes, I **h** more insight than my teachers, / for I am
119:165 Those who love your law **h** great peace / and do
123: 3 **H** mercy on us, LORD, **h** mercy, / for we have had
our fill of contempt.
125: 5 who do evil. / And let Israel **h** quietness and peace.
128: 6 And may Israel **h** quietness and peace.
135:14 his people / and **h** compassion on his servants.
135:16 They cannot talk, though they **h** mouths, / or see,
though they **h** eyes!
144:15 Yes, happy are those who **h** it like this! / Happy
146: 5 But happy are those who **h** the God of Israel as
Pr 2:21 land, and those who **h** integrity will remain in it.
4:10 and do as I say, and you will **h** a long, good life.
4:19 Those who follow it **h** no idea what they are
6: 3 your pride; go and beg to **h** your name erased.
6: 7 Even though they **h** no prince, governor, or ruler
6:34 and he will **h** no mercy in his day of vengeance.
8: 6 Listen to me! For I **h** excellent things to tell you.
10: 7 We all **h** happy memories of the godly,
10: 9 People with integrity **h** firm footing, but those
10:25 wicked away, but the godly **h** a lasting foundation.
11:20 but he delights in those who **h** integrity.
12: 3 never brings stability; only the godly **h** deep roots.
12: 9 a servant than to be self-important but **h** no food.
12:21 the godly, but the wicked **h** their fill of trouble.
13: 3 Those who control their tongue will **h** a long life;
14:20 their neighbors, while the rich **h** many "friends."
14:29 who control their anger **h** great understanding;
14:32 but the godly **h** a refuge when they die.
15:16 It is better to **h** little with fear for the LORD than to
h great treasure with turmoil.
15:21 Foolishness brings joy to those who **h** no sense;
16:26 It is good for workers to **h** an appetite; an empty
16:32 it is better to **h** self-control than to conquer a city.
18: 2 Fools **h** no interest in understanding; they only
19:19 If you rescue them once, you will **h** to do it again.
20: 4 he right season, you will **h** no food at the harvest.
21:20 The wise **h** wealth and luxury, but fools spend
22: 2 The rich and the poor **h** this in common:
23: 8 you will **h** to take back your words of appreciation
23:18 For surely you **h** a future ahead of you; your hope
23:24 What a pleasure it is to **h** wise children.
23:35 When will I wake up so I can **h** another drink?"
24:14 you will **h** a bright future, and your hopes will not
24:20 the evil **h** no future; their light will be snuffed out.
27:10 you won't **h** to ask your relatives for assistance.
27:27 will **h** enough goats' milk for you, your family,
28:14 Blessed are those who **h** a tender conscience,
28:16 a king will **h** a long reign if he hates dishonesty
28:19 Hard workers **h** plenty of food; playing around
29:13 The poor and the oppressor **h** this in common—
29:14 A king who is fair to the poor will **h** a long reign.
30:27 Locusts—they **h** no king, / but they march like an
31:21 her household because all of them **h** warm clothes.
31:27 does not **h** to bear the consequences of laziness.
Ecc 1:16 I **h** greater wisdom and knowledge than any of
3:19 So people **h** no real advantage over the animals.
4: 1 The oppressors **h** great power, and the victims are
5:10 Those who love money will never **h** enough.
5:11 The more you **h**, the more people come to help

6: 3 A man might **h** a hundred children and live to be
6: 7 for food, but they never seem to **h** enough.
6: 8 do wise people really **h** any advantage over fools?
6: 9 Enjoy what you **h** rather than desiring what you
don't **h**. Just dreaming about nice things is
9: 3 choose their own mad course, for they **h** no hope.
9: 5 They **h** no further reward, nor are they remembered
9: 6 They no longer **h** a part in anything here on earth.
10: 15 that they **h** no strength for even the simplest tasks.
SS 4: 8 where lions **h** their dens and panthers prowl.
8: 8 "We **h** a little sister too young for breasts.
Isa 1: 19 and let me help you, then you will **h** plenty to eat.
1: 26 and wise counselors like the ones you used to **h**.
3: 6 "Since you **h** a cloak, you be our leader!
3: 7 I don't **h** any extra food or clothes. Don't ask me
5: 8 who buy up property so others **h** no place to live.
7: 21 farmer will be fortunate to **h** a cow and two sheep
8: 18 I and the children the LORD has given me **h** names
13: 18 They will **h** no mercy on helpless babies and will
14: 1 But the LORD will **h** mercy on the descendants of
14: 26 I **h** a plan for the whole earth, for my mighty
17: 7 Creator and **h** respect for the Holy One of Israel.
19: 9 The weavers will **h** no flax or cotton, for the crops
20: 6 this can happen to Egypt, what chance do we **h**?
22: 21 He will **h** your royal robes, your title, and your
23: 4 "Now I am childless; I **h** no sons or daughters."
26: 19 Yet we **h** this assurance: / Those who belong to
28: 12 God's people could **h** rest in their own land if they
28: 20 For you **h** no place of refuge—the bed you have
30: 15 is your strength. But you would **h** none of it.
33: 8 before witnesses. They **h** no respect for anyone.
33: 16 to them, and they will **h** water in abundance.
35: 3 With this news, strengthen those who **h** tired
hands, and encourage those who **h** weak knees.
37: 7 his land, where I will **h** him killed with a sword.' "
37: 27 That is why their people **h** so little power
39: 6 The time is coming when everything you **h**—all
42: 22 They are fair game for all and **h** no one to protect
43: 8 Bring out the people who **h** eyes but are blind,
who **h** ears but are deaf.
43: 26 and you can present your case if you **h** one.
47: 13 You **h** more than enough advisers, astrologers, and
48: 11 have conquered me. I will not let them **h** my glory!
48: 16 happen so you would **h** no trouble understanding."
49: 13 and will **h** compassion on them in their sorrow.
50: 2 Is it because I **h** no power to rescue? No, that is
53: 5 He was beaten that we might **h** peace. He was
53: 10 he will **h** a multitude of children, many heirs.
54: 8 But with everlasting love I will **h** compassion on
55: 1 Come and drink—even if you **h** no money! Come,
55: 7 Let them turn to the LORD that he may **h** mercy on
56: 12 "We will get some wine and **h** a party. Let's all
57: 11 I have not corrected you that you **h** no fear of me?
57: 19 May they **h** peace, both near and far, for I will heal
60: 10 my anger, I will **h** mercy on you through my grace.
65: 8 destroy all Israel. For I still **h** true servants there.
65: 22 and will **h** time to enjoy their hard-won gains.
66: 2 "I will bless those who **h** humble and contrite
Jer 2: 28 For you **h** as many gods as there are cities and
2: 31 We won't **h** anything to do with him anymore!'
4: 22 "They are senseless children who **h** no
4: 22 wrong, but they **h** no talent at all for doing right!"
5: 21 Listen, you foolish and senseless people—who **h**
eyes but do not see, who **h** ears but do not hear.
5: 21 Listen, you foolish and senseless people—who **h**
eyes but do not see, who **h** ears but do not hear.
5: 22 Do you **h** no respect for me? Why do you not
5: 23 "But my people **h** stubborn and rebellious hearts.
6: 20 Your sacrifices **h** no sweet fragrance for me."
8: 8 "We are wise because we **h** the law of the LORD,"
9: 26 the people of Israel also **h** uncircumcised hearts."
10: 14 all people are foolish / and **h** no knowledge at all!
10: 14 they are frauds. / They **h** no life or power in them.
11: 13 you **h** as many gods as there are cities and towns.
12: 15 But afterward I will return and **h** compassion on
16: 2 "Do not marry or **h** children in this place.
18: 18 We **h** our own priests and wise men and prophets.
19: 9 Then those trapped inside will **h** to eat their own
20: 15 who told my father, "Good news—you **h** a son!"
23: 17 'Don't worry! The LORD says you will **h** peace!'
23: 32 and they **h** no message at all for my people,"
23: 34 'I **h** a prophecy from the LORD,' I will punish that
26: 9 "What right do you **h** to prophesy in the LORD's
26: 19 They begged him to **h** mercy on them.
29: 6 Marry, and **h** children. Then find spouses for them,
and **h** many grandchildren. Multiply!
29: 11 For I know the plans I **h** for you," says the LORD.
30: 10 Israel will return and will **h** peace and quiet in
30: 21 They will **h** their own ruler again, and he will not
31: 20 I long for him and surely will **h** mercy on him.
32: 7 By law you **h** the right to buy it before it is offered
32: 8 By law you **h** the right to buy it before it is offered
32: 19 You **h** all wisdom and do great and mighty
33: 17 David will forever **h** a descendant sitting on the
33: 21 Only then will he no longer **h** a descendant to
33: 26 restore them to their land and **h** mercy on them."
35: 5 before them and invited them to **h** a drink,
35: 19 of Recab will always **h** descendants who serve me.
36: 30 He will **h** no heirs to sit on the throne of David.
37: 17 "Do you **h** any messages from the LORD?"
38: 22 will taunt you, saying, 'What fine friends you **h**!
46: 27 Israel will return and will **h** peace and quiet, and
51: 17 all people are foolish / and **h** no knowledge at all!
51: 17 they are frauds. / They **h** no life or power in them.
La 1: 16 My children **h** no future, for the enemy has
5: 4 We **h** to pay for water to drink, and even firewood
Eze 9: 5 forehead is not marked. Show no mercy; **h** no pity!
9: 10 So I will not spare them or **h** any pity on them.
16: 30 "What a sick heart you **h**, says the Sovereign LORD
18: 6 he does not commit adultery or **h** intercourse with
20: 32 But what you **h** in mind will never happen.
21: 13 the Sovereign LORD asks: What chance do they **h**?
22: 10 sleep with their fathers' wives and **h** intercourse
22: 30 wouldn't **h** to destroy the land, but I found no one.
29: 19 plundering everything they **h** to pay his army.
32: 15 wipe out everything you **h** and strike down all
32: 25 They **h** a resting place among the slaughtered,
33: 30 'Come on, let's **h** some fun! Let's go hear the
33: 31 But they **h** no intention of doing what I tell them.
34: 19 All they **h** to drink is water that you have fouled.
36: 7 nations will soon **h** their turn at suffering shame.
36: 35 The ruined cities now **h** strong walls, and they are
37: 24 their king, and they will **h** only one shepherd.
39: 25 I will **h** mercy on Israel, for I am jealous for my
42: 6 did not **h** supporting columns as in the courtyards,
43: 25 None of these animals may **h** physical defects of
44: 7 my sanctuary—people who **h** no heart for God.
44: 28 "As to property, the priests will not **h** any, for I
48: 33 will **h** gates named for Simeon, Issachar, and
Da 1: 4 and **h** the poise needed to serve in the royal palace.
1: 10 I am afraid the king will **h** me beheaded for
4: 16 him **h** the mind of an animal instead of a human.
5: 11 this man was found to **h** insight, understanding,
5: 14 I have heard that you **h** the spirit of the gods
10: 11 listen carefully to what I **h** to say to you. Stand up,
11: 12 and will **h** many thousands of his enemies killed.
11: 37 He will **h** no regard for the gods of his ancestors,
Hos 3: 3 During this time, you will not **h** sexual intercourse
4: 10 big business as prostitutes, they will **h** no children,
10: 3 Then they will say, "We **h** no king because we
13: 4 You **h** no God but me, for there is no other savior.
13: 15 Every precious thing they **h** will be plundered and
Joel 1: 20 cry out to you because they **h** no water to drink.
2: 26 Once again you will **h** all the food you want,
3: 4 "What do you **h** against me, Tyre and Sidon and
Am 5: 11 and steal what little they **h** through taxes and
5: 15 LORD God Almighty will **h** mercy on his people
5: 18 But you **h** no idea what you are wishing for.
Jnh 1: 6 Maybe he will **h** mercy on us and spare our lives."
3: 9 Perhaps even yet God will **h** pity on us and hold
Mic 2: 1 of the wicked schemes you **h** power to accomplish.
2: 5 people will **h** no say in how the land is divided.
2: 7 Will the LORD **h** patience with such behavior?
4: 9 **H** you no king to lead you? He is dead! **H** you no
wise people to counsel you? All are gone!
6: 14 You will eat but never **h** enough. Your hunger
7: 19 Once again you will **h** compassion on us. You will
Nah 1: 12 "Even though the Assyrians **h** many allies, they
1: 14 "You will **h** no more children to carry on your
Hab 1: 14 Are we but creeping things that **h** no leader to
2: 7 They will turn on you and take all you **h**, while
3: 17 Even though the fig trees **h** no blossoms, and there
Zep 1: 13 They will never **h** a chance to live in the new
3: 7 thought, 'Surely they will **h** reverence for me now!
Hag 1: 6 You **h** food to eat, but not enough to fill you up.
You **h** wine to drink, but not enough to satisfy
your thirst. You **h** clothing to wear, but not
Zec 2: 4 people that it won't **h** room enough for everyone!
3: 5 could he also **h** a clean turban on his head?"
11: 5 Even the shepherds **h** no compassion for them.
11: 6 I will no longer **h** pity on the inhabitants of the
12: 7 will not **h** greater honor than the rest of Judah.
14: 17 the King, the LORD Almighty, will **h** no rain.
Mal 3: 10 so great you won't **h** enough room to take it in!
Mt 1: 21 she will **h** a son, and you are to name him Jesus,
6: 23 If the light you think you **h** is really darkness, how
6: 25 everyday life—whether you **h** enough food, drink,
6: 30 he more surely care for you? You **h** so little faith!
7: 3 in your friend's eye when you **h** a log in your own?
8: 4 leprosy, so everyone will **h** proof of your healing."
8: 9 officers and I **h** authority over my soldiers.
8: 20 Jesus said, "Foxes **h** dens to live in, and birds **h**
nests, but I, the Son of Man, **h** no home of my own
8: 26 "Why are you afraid? You **h** so little faith!"
8: 29 You **h** no right to torture us before God's
9: 6 Son of Man, **h** the authority on earth to forgive sins
9: 27 shouting, "Son of David, **h** mercy on us!"
13: 12 will **h** an abundance of knowledge. But to those
who are not listening, even what they **h** will be
13: 21 but they wilt as soon as they **h** problems or are
14: 17 "We **h** only five loaves of bread and two fish!"
14: 31 "You don't **h** much faith," Jesus said. "Why did
15: 22 pleading, "**H** mercy on me, O Lord, Son of David!
15: 32 for three days, and they **h** nothing left to eat.
15: 34 asked, "How many loaves of bread do you **h**?"
16: 8 "You **h** so little faith! Why are you worried about
17: 15 "Lord, **h** mercy on my son, because he has seizures
17: 20 "You didn't **h** enough faith," Jesus told them.
18: 9 blind than to **h** two eyes and be thrown into hell.
18: 33 Shouldn't you **h** mercy on your fellow servant,
19: 16 what good things must I do to **h** eternal life?"
19: 21 go and sell all you **h** and give the money to the
poor, and you will **h** treasure in heaven.
19: 29 times as much in return and will **h** eternal life.
20: 23 "But I **h** no right to say who will sit on the thrones
20: 30 shouting, "Lord, Son of David, **h** mercy on us!"
20: 31 louder, "Lord, Son of David, **h** mercy on us!"
21: 21 if you **h** faith and don't doubt, you can do things
22: 24 and **h** a child who will be the brother's heir.'
23: 8 call you 'Rabbi,' for you **h** only one teacher,
25: 9 others replied, 'We don't **h** enough for all of us.
25: 27 my money into the bank so I could **h** some interest.
25: 29 they will **h** an abundance. But from those who are
unfaithful, even what little they **h** will be taken
26: 11 You will always **h** the poor among you, but I will
26: 35 Peter insisted. "Not even if I **h** to die with you!
26: 62 these charges? What do you **h** to say for yourself?"
Mk 1: 44 leprosy, so everyone will **h** proof of your healing."
2: 10 Son of Man, **h** the authority on earth to forgive sins
4: 17 but they wilt as soon as they **h** problems or are
4: 40 are you so afraid? Do you still not **h** faith in me?"
6: 31 Jesus and his apostles didn't even **h** time to eat.
6: 38 "How much food do you **h**?" he asked. "Go and
6: 38 reported, "We **h** five loaves of bread and two fish."
8: 2 for three days, and they **h** nothing left to eat.
8: 5 "How many loaves of bread do you **h**?" he asked.
8: 18 'You **h** eyes—can't you see? You **h** ears—can't
you hear?' Don't you remember anything at all?
9: 22 **H** mercy on us and help us. Do something if you
9: 47 blind than to **h** two eyes and be thrown into hell,
9: 50 You must **h** the qualities of salt among yourselves
10: 15 who doesn't **h** their kind of faith will never get into
10: 21 "Go and sell all you **h** and give the money to the
poor, and you will **h** treasure in heaven.
10: 30 And in the world to come they will **h** eternal life.
10: 40 but I **h** no right to say who will sit on the thrones
10: 47 shout out, "Jesus, Son of David, **h** mercy on me!"
10: 48 shouted louder, "Son of David, **h** mercy on me!"
11: 22 Then Jesus said to the disciples, "**H** faith in God.
11: 24 pray for anything, and if you believe, you will **h** it.
12: 19 widow and **h** a child who will be the brother's heir.
12: 38 to **h** everyone bow to them as they walk in the
14: 7 You will always **h** the poor among you, and you
14: 31 Peter insisted. "Not even if I **h** to die with you!
14: 60 these charges? What do you **h** to say for yourself?"
15: 45 fact, and Pilate told Joseph he could **h** the body.
Lk 1: 14 You will **h** great joy and gladness, and many will
1: 31 and **h** a son, and you are to name him Jesus.
1: 34 the angel, "But how can I **h** a baby? I am a virgin."
3: 11 replied, "If you **h** two coats, give one to the poor.
If you **h** food, share it with those who are hungry."
5: 14 leprosy, so everyone will **h** proof of your healing."
5: 24 Son of Man, **h** the authority on earth to forgive sins
6: 9 Jesus said to his critics, "I **h** a question for you.
6: 24 who are rich, / for you **h** your only happiness now.
6: 30 Give what you **h** to anyone who asks you for it;
6: 41 in your friend's eye when you **h** a log in your own?
7: 8 officers, and I **h** authority over my soldiers.
7: 40 said to the Pharisee, "I **h** something to say to you."
8: 18 they think they **h** will be taken away from them."
9: 13 "We **h** only five loaves of bread and two fish.
9: 53 The people of the village refused to **h** anything to
9: 58 But Jesus replied, "Foxes **h** dens to live in, and
birds **h** nests, but I, the Son of Man, **h** no home of
my own, not even a place to lay my head."
11: 6 arrived for a visit, and I **h** nothing for him to eat.'
11: 35 the light you think you **h** is not really darkness.
12: 15 "Beware! Don't be greedy for what you don't **h**.
12: 18 Then I'll **h** room enough to store everything.
12: 19 you **h** enough stored away for years to come.
12: 21 wealth but not **h** a rich relationship with God."
12: 22 whether you **h** enough food to eat or clothes to
12: 28 he more surely care for you? You **h** so little faith!
12: 33 "Sell what you **h** and give to those in need.
12: 33 And the purses of heaven **h** no holes in them.
14: 9 will **h** to take whatever seat is left at the foot of the
14: 10 'Friend, we **h** a better place than this for you!'
14: 15 it would be to **h** a share in the Kingdom of God!"
15: 17 'At home even the hired men **h** food enough to
15: 30 you celebrate by killing the finest calf we **h**.'
15: 31 and I are very close, and everything I **h** is yours.
16: 3 and I don't **h** the strength to go out and dig ditches,
16: 4 And then I'll **h** plenty of friends to take care of me
16: 24 rich man shouted, 'Father Abraham, **h** some pity!
16: 28 I **h** five brothers, and I want him to warn them
16: 28 so they won't **h** to come here when they die.'
17: 13 crying out, "Jesus, Master, **h** mercy on us!"
18: 8 return, how many will I find who **h** faith?"
18: 17 who doesn't **h** their kind of faith will never get into
18: 22 "Sell all you **h** and give the money to the poor, and
you will **h** treasure in heaven. Then come,
18: 38 shouting, "Jesus, Son of David, **h** mercy on me!"
18: 39 shouted louder, "Son of David, **h** mercy on me!"
19: 26 even what little they **h** will be taken away.
20: 28 widow and **h** a child who will be the brother's heir.
20: 46 and to **h** everyone bow to them as they walk in the
22: 31 "Simon, Simon, Satan has asked to **h** all of you,
22: 35 you did not **h** money, a traveler's bag, or extra
22: 36 And if you don't **h** a sword, sell your clothes and
22: 38 "Lord," they replied, "we **h** two swords among us."
22: 71 "What need do we **h** for other witnesses?"
23: 16 I will **h** him flogged, but then I will release him."
24: 26 Messiah would **h** to suffer all these things before
24: 39 ghosts don't **h** bodies, as you see that I do!"
24: 41 he asked them, "Do you **h** anything here to eat?"
Jn 1: 22 sent us. What do you **h** to say about yourself?"
1: 25 or the Prophet, what right do you **h** to baptize?"
2: 3 the problem. "They **h** no more wine," she told him.
2: 18 "What right do you **h** to do these things?" the
Jewish leaders demanded. "If you **h** this authority
3: 15 everyone who believes in me will **h** eternal life.
3: 16 believes in him will not perish but **h** eternal life.
3: 36 And all who believe in God's Son **h** eternal life.
4: 9 Jews refuse to **h** anything to do with Samaritans.
4: 11 "But sir, you don't **h** a rope or a bucket," she said,
4: 17 "I don't **h** a husband," the woman replied.
4: 17 Jesus said, "You're right! You don't **h** a husband—
4: 18 for you **h** had five husbands, and you aren't even
4: 32 "No," he said, "I **h** food you don't know about."
5: 7 "for I **h** no one to help me into the pool when the
5: 24 and believe in God who sent me **h** eternal life.

5:26 and he has granted his Son to **h** life in himself.
5:36 But I **h** a greater witness than John—my teachings
5:38 and you do not **h** his message in your hearts,
5:42 because I know you don't **h** God's love within you.
6:40 see his Son and believe in him should **h** eternal life
6:53 his blood, you cannot **h** eternal life within you.
6:54 eat my flesh and drink my blood **h** eternal life,
6:68 You alone **h** the words that give eternal life."
8:12 because you will **h** the light that leads to life."
8:16 am not alone—I **h** with me the Father who sent me.
8:26 I **h** much to say about you and much to condemn,
8:49 "No," Jesus said, "I **h** no demon in me. For I honor
8:50 though I **h** no wish to glorify myself, God wants to
10:16 I **h** other sheep, too, that are not in this sheepfold.
10:17 I lay down my life that I may **h** it back again.
10:18 For I **h** the right to lay it down when I want to and
11: 9 They can see because they **h** the light of this world.
12: 8 You will always **h** the poor among you, but I will
14:30 "I don't **h** much more time to talk to you, because
15:22 But now they **h** no excuse for their sin.
16:22 You **h** sorrow now, but I will see you again;
16:24 you will receive, and you will **h** abundant joy.
16:33 I have told you all this so that you may **h** peace in
me. Here on earth you will **h** many trials and
17: 3 And this is the way to **h** eternal life—to know you,
17: 7 they know that everything I **h** is a gift from you,
18:39 you **h** a custom of asking me to release someone
19:10 "Don't you realize that I **h** the power to release you
19:11 Then Jesus said, "You would **h** no power over me
19:15 "We **h** no king but Caesar," the leading priests
20:31 and that by believing in him you will **h** life.
21:12 "Now come and **h** some breakfast!" Jesus said.
Ac 3: 6 But Peter said, "I don't **h** any money for you. But
I'll give you what I **h**. In the name of Jesus Christ
8:19 "Let me **h** this power, too," he exclaimed, "so that
8:21 You can **h** no part in this, for your heart is not right
10:43 in him will **h** their sins forgiven through his name."
13: 2 and Saul for the special work I **h** for them."
13:15 if you **h** any word of encouragement for us, come
13:28 but they asked Pilate to **h** him killed anyway.
19:38 If Demetrius and the craftsmen **h** a case against
21:23 We **h** four men here who have taken a vow and
21:24 and pay for them to **h** their heads shaved.
21:37 to the commander, "May I **h** a word with you?"
22:16 Get up and be baptized, and **h** your sins washed
24:15 I **h** hope in God, just as these men do, that he will
24:19 to bring charges if they **h** anything against me!
25:26 we examine him, I might **h** something to write.
26: 7 and they share the same hope I **h**. Yet, O king,
they say it is wrong for me to **h** this hope!
28:16 Paul was permitted to **h** his own private lodging,
Ro 1:14 For I **h** a great sense of obligation to people in our
1:20 they **h** no excuse whatsoever for not knowing God.
1:26 the women turned against the natural way to **h** sex
2: 1 But you are just as bad, and you **h** no excuse!
2:12 the Jews when they sin, for they do **h** the law.
2:14 when Gentiles, who do not **h** God's written law,
2:20 in God's law you **h** complete knowledge and truth.
3:18 "They **h** no fear of God to restrain them."
3:31 only when we **h** faith do we truly fulfill the law.
4:11 is the spiritual father of those who **h** faith but
4:12 but only if they **h** the same kind of faith Abraham
4:15 to avoid breaking the law is to **h** no law to break!)
4:16 Jewish customs, if we **h** faith like Abraham's.
4:19 Sarah, his wife, had never been able to **h** children.
5: 1 we **h** peace with God because of what Jesus Christ
5:16 but we **h** the free gift of being accepted by God,
7: 8 If there were no law, sin would not **h** that power.
8: 9 You are controlled by the Spirit if you **h** the Spirit
8: 9 (And remember that those who do not **h** the Spirit
8:12 you **h** no obligation whatsoever to do what your
8:23 we **h** the Holy Spirit within us as a foretaste of
8:24 For if you already **h** something, you don't need to
8:25 if we look forward to something we don't **h** yet,
8:35 Does it mean he no longer loves us if we **h** trouble
9: 4 They **h** the privilege of worshiping him and
9: 9 "Next year I will return, and Sarah will **h** a son."
9:21 doesn't he **h** a right to use the same lump of clay
10: 2 I know what enthusiasm they **h** for God, but it is
10:12 They all **h** the same Lord, who generously gives
11: 4 I **h** seven thousand others who have never bowed
11:14 to make the Jews want what you Gentiles **h**, and in
11:25 Some of the Jews **h** hard hearts, but this will last
11:32 disobedience so he could **h** mercy on everyone.
11:33 Oh, what a wonderful God we **h**! How great are
11:35 give him so much that he would **h** to pay it back?
12: 4 Just as our bodies **h** many parts and each part has
12: 6 speak out when you **h** faith that God is speaking
12: 8 If you **h** money, share it generously. If God has
12: 8 And if you **h** a gift for showing kindness to others,
14: 5 Each person should **h** a personal conviction about
14: 6 Those who **h** a special day for worshiping the
14:12 each of us will **h** to give a personal account to God.
14:22 You may **h** the faith to believe that there is
14:23 if people **h** doubts about whether they should eat
1Co 1: 7 Now you **h** every spiritual gift you need as you
2:14 who **h** the Spirit can understand what the Spirit
2:15 We who **h** the Spirit understand these things, but
2:16 these things, for we **h** the mind of Christ.
4: 7 What do you **h** that God hasn't given you? And if
all you **h** is from God, why boast as though you
4: 8 You think you already **h** everything you need!
4:11 many beatings, and we **h** no homes of our own.
4:15 about Christ, you **h** only one spiritual father.
4:19 big talkers or whether they really **h** God's power.
5: 1 I am told that you **h** a man in your church who is
5:10 You would **h** to leave this world to avoid people
6: 1 When you **h** something against another Christian,
6: 4 If you **h** legal disputes about such matters, why do
6: 7 To **h** such lawsuits at all is a real defeat for you.
6: 9 who do wrong will **h** no share in the Kingdom of
6:10 none of these will **h** a share in the Kingdom of
7: 2 sexual immorality, each man should **h** his own
wife, and each woman should **h** her own husband.
7:10 Now, for those who are married I **h** a command
7:12 I do not **h** a direct command from the Lord.
7:14 your children would not **h** a godly influence, but
7:25 I do not **h** a command from the Lord for them.
7:27 If you **h** a wife, do not end the marriage. If you do
not **h** a wife, do not get married.
9: 1 Do I not **h** as much freedom as anyone else?
9: 4 Don't we **h** the right to live in your homes and
9: 5 Don't we **h** the right to bring a Christian wife
9: 6 Or is it only Barnabas and I who **h** to work to
9: 7 harvests his crop and doesn't **h** the right to eat
9:12 we **h** an even greater right to be supported?
9:17 and given me this sacred trust, and I **h** no choice.
9:21 When I am with the Gentiles who do not **h** the
11: 6 since it is shameful for a woman to **h** her hair cut
11:14 that it's disgraceful for a man to **h** long hair?
11:16 all I can say is that we **h** no other custom than this,
11:22 Don't you **h** your own homes for eating and
12:11 He alone decides which gift each person should **h**.
12:24 and care are given to those parts that **h** less dignity.
12:28 those who **h** the gift of healing, / those who can
12:29 Does everyone **h** the power to do miracles?
12:30 Does everyone **h** the gift of healing? Of course not.
13: 3 If I gave everything I **h** to the poor and even
14:12 Since you are so eager to **h** spiritual gifts, ask God
14:31 In this way, all who prophesy will **h** a turn to speak
14:35 If they **h** any questions to ask, let them ask their
15:19 And if we **h** hope in Christ only for this life,
15:35 dead be raised? What kind of bodies will they **h**?"
15:38 gives it a new body—just the kind he wants it to **h**.
15:41 while the moon and stars each **h** another kind.
2Co 4:13 to preach because we **h** the same kind of faith the
5: 1 we will **h** a home in heaven, an eternal body made
5: 4 it's not that we want to die and **h** no bodies at all.
6: 7 We **h** righteousness as our weapon, both to attack
6:10 Our hearts ache, but we always **h** joy. We are
6:10 We own nothing, and yet we **h** everything.
7: 1 Because we **h** these promises, dear friends, let us
7: 4 I **h** the highest confidence in you, and my pride in
7: 9 but because the pain caused you to **h** remorse and
7: 9 the kind of sorrow God wants his people to **h**, so
7:16 now because I **h** complete confidence in you.
8: 7 you **h** so much faith, such gifted speakers, such
8:11 Give whatever you can according to what you **h**.
8:12 how much you are able to give. God wants you to
give what you **h**, not what you don't **h**.
8:14 Right now you **h** plenty and can help them.
8:16 given Titus the same enthusiasm for you that I **h**.
9: 8 Then you will always **h** everything you need and
10: 2 but when I come I may **h** to be very bold with
10:13 But we will not boast of authority we do not **h**.
11: 9 And when I was with you and didn't **h** enough to
11:20 they make you their slaves, take everything you **h**,
11:28 I **h** the daily burden of how the churches are
12: 6 I **h** plenty to boast about and would be no fool in
12:14 I don't want what you **h**; I want you. And anyway,
12:15 spend myself and all I **h** for your spiritual good,
12:18 For we both **h** the same Spirit and walk in each
12:21 I will **h** to grieve because many of you who sinned
13: 4 but we live in him and **h** God's power—the power
Gal 4: 2 They **h** to obey their guardians until they reach
6:10 Whenever we **h** the opportunity, we should do
Eph 3: 6 The Gentiles **h** an equal share with the Jews in all
3:18 And may you **h** the power to understand, as all
4: 4 We are all one body, we **h** the same Spirit,
5: 3 Such sins **h** no place among God's people.
6: 9 remember, you both **h** the same Master in heaven,
Php 1:17 Those others do not **h** pure motives as they preach
1:26 you will **h** even more reason to boast about what
2:20 I **h** no one else like Timothy, who genuinely cares
2:24 And I **h** confidence from the Lord that I myself
2:27 so that I would not **h** such unbearable sorrow.
3: 4 Yet I could **h** confidence in myself if anyone
could. If others **h** reason for confidence in their
own efforts, I **h** even more!
3: 8 counting it all as garbage, so that I may **h** Christ
4:10 but for a while you didn't **h** the chance to help me.
4:11 to get along happily whether I **h** much or little.
4:18 At the moment I **h** all I need—more than I need!
Col 1:11 so that you will **h** all the patience and endurance
2: 2 I want them to **h** full confidence because they **h**
complete understanding of God's secret plan,
2:23 But they **h** no effect when it comes to conquering
3: 5 **H** nothing to do with sexual sin, impurity, lust,
4: 1 Remember that you also **h** a Master—in heaven.
4: 6 so that you will **h** the right answer for everyone.
1Th 3: 9 of you we **h** great joy in the presence of God.
4:13 not be full of sorrow like people who **h** no hope.
2Th 3: 9 It wasn't that we didn't **h** the right to ask you to
1Ti 2:12 I do not let women teach men or **h** authority over
3: 2 self-control, live wisely, and **h** a good reputation.
3: 8 must be people who are respected and **h** integrity.
5:14 these younger widows to marry again, **h** children,
5:20 church so that others will **h** a proper fear of God.
6: 8 if we **h** enough food and clothing, let us be content.
2Ti 1: 5 for you **h** the faith of your mother, Eunice,
1:13 live in the faith and love that you **h** in Christ Jesus.
3: 3 they will slander others and **h** no self-control; they
will be cruel and **h** no interest in what is good.
Tit 1: 9 He must **h** a strong and steadfast belief in the
2: 2 They must **h** strong faith and be filled with love
2: 8 ashamed because they won't **h** anything bad to say
2:15 You **h** the authority to do this, so don't let anyone
3:10 After that, **h** nothing more to do with that person.
3:14 For our people should not **h** unproductive lives.
3:14 to do good by helping others who **h** urgent needs.
Phm 1:15 for a little while so you could **h** him back forever.
Heb 2:11 Jesus and the ones he makes holy **h** the same
4:14 That is why we **h** a great High Priest who has
5: 2 For he is subject to the same weaknesses they **h**.
10:21 And since we **h** a great High Priest who rules over
10:23 let us hold tightly to the hope we say we **h**, for
10:38 I will **h** no pleasure in anyone who turns away."
10:39 their fate. We **h** faith that assures our salvation.
11:11 together with Abraham was able to **h** a child.
11:12 Abraham, who was too old to **h** any children—
13: 5 the love of money; be satisfied with what you **h**.
13:10 We **h** an altar from which the priests in the Temple
on earth **h** no right to eat.
13:16 and to share what you **h** with those in need,
Jas 2: 1 that you **h** faith in our glorious Lord Jesus Christ if
2:14 you **h** faith if you don't prove it by your actions?
2:17 So you see, it isn't enough just to **h** faith. Faith
2:18 "Some people **h** faith; others **h** good deeds." I say,
"I can't see your faith if you don't **h** good deeds,
4: 2 You want what you don't **h**, so you scheme and
kill to get it. You are jealous for what others **h**,
4: 2 you don't **h** what you want is that you don't ask
4:12 So what right do you **h** to condemn your neighbor?
5:13 And those who **h** reason to be thankful should
5:14 elders of the church and **h** them pray over them,
1Pe 1: 2 May you **h** more and more of God's special favor
1:22 Now you can **h** sincere love for each other as
4: 5 But just remember that they will **h** to face God,
4:13 afterward you will **h** the wonderful joy of sharing
4:18 what chance will the godless and sinners **h**?"
2Pe 1: 1 you who share the same precious faith we **h**,
1: 7 you will grow to **h** genuine love for everyone.
1:19 Because of that, we **h** even greater confidence in
3:15 Lord is waiting so that people **h** time to be saved.
1Jn 1: 3 heard, so that you may **h** fellowship with us.
1: 6 we are lying if we say we **h** fellowship with God
1: 7 we **h** fellowship with each other, and the blood of
1: 8 If we say we **h** no sin, we are only fooling
2:15 that you do not **h** the love of the Father in you.
2:23 Anyone who denies the Son doesn't **h** the Father
3:15 that murderers don't **h** eternal life within them.
4: 1 them to see if the spirit they **h** comes from God.
4: 2 This is the way to find out if they **h** the Spirit of
4: 9 world so that we might **h** eternal life through him.
4:15 proclaim that Jesus is the Son of God **h** God living
5: 7 So we **h** these three witnesses—
5:12 So whoever has God's Son has life; whoever does
not **h** his Son does not **h** life.
5:13 of God, so that you may know you **h** eternal life.
2Jn 1: 9 of Christ, you will not **h** fellowship with God.
1: 9 you will **h** fellowship with both the Father and the
1:12 I **h** much more to say to you, but I don't want to
3Jn 1: 4 I could **h** no greater joy than to hear that my
1:13 I **h** much to tell you, but I don't want to do it in a
Jude 1:19 by natural instinct because they do not **h** God's
Rev 2: 4 But I **h** this complaint against you. You don't love
2:14 And yet I **h** a few complaints against you.
2:15 same way, you **h** some Nicolaitans among you—
2:20 But I **h** this complaint against you. You are
2:24 But I also **h** a message for the rest of you in
2:25 that you hold tightly to what you **h** until I come.
2:28 They will **h** the same authority I received from my
3: 1 you **h** a reputation for being alive—but you are
3: 8 You **h** little strength, yet you obeyed my word and
3:11 Hold on to what you **h**, so that no one will take
3:12 Temple of my God, and they will never **h** to leave
3:12 they will **h** my new name inscribed upon them.
3:17 You say, 'I am rich. I **h** everything I want. I don't
9: 4 who did not **h** the seal of God on their foreheads.
11: 6 They **h** power to shut the skies so that no rain will
11: 6 And they **h** the power to turn the rivers and oceans
13:10 here is your opportunity to **h** endurance and faith.
14:11 and ever, and they will **h** no relief day or night,

HAVEN (1) [HAVENS]

Ps 43: 2 For you are God, my only safe **h**. / Why have you

HAVEN'T (48) [HAVE, NOT] See Index of Articles, Etc.

HAVENS (3) [HAVEN]

Ac 27: 8 with great difficulty and finally arrived at Fair **H**,
27:12 And since Fair **H** was an exposed harbor—a poor
27:21 listened to me in the first place and not left Fair **H**.

HAVILAH (7)

Ge 2:11 which flows around the entire land of **H**,
10: 7 Cush were Seba, **H**, Sabtah, Raamah, and Sabteca.
10:29 Ophir, **H**, and Jobab.
25:18 were scattered across the country from **H** to Shur,
1Sa 15: 7 Then Saul slaughtered the Amalekites from **H** all
1Ch 1: 9 Cush were Seba, **H**, Sabtah, Raamah, and Sabteca.
1:23 Ophir, **H**, and Jobab. All these were descendants of

HAVING (43 of 60) [HAVE] See also Index of Articles, Etc.

Ge 16: 2 "The LORD has kept me from **h** any children,"
18:11 old, and Sarah was long past the age of **h** children,

29:35 the LORD!" And then she stopped **h** children.
30: 1 When Rachel saw that she wasn't **h** any children,
31:35 Rachel explained. "I'm **h** my monthly period."
37:22 That way he will die without our **h** to touch him."
38: 9 to keep her from **h** a baby who would belong to
41:32 As for **h** the dream twice, it means that the matter
Ex 19:15 And until then, abstain from **h** sexual intercourse."
Lev 15:18 After **h** sexual intercourse, both the man and the
18: 7 Do not violate your father by **h** sexual intercourse
18:14 your father's brother, by **h** sexual intercourse with
18:19 "Do not violate a woman by **h** sexual intercourse
18:20 "Do not defile yourself by **h** sexual intercourse
18:23 "A man must never defile himself by **h** sexual
Dt 4:42 killed someone without **h** any previous hostility
1Sa 1: 8 You have me—isn't that better than **h** ten sons?"
2Sa 11: 4 the purification rites after **h** her menstrual period.)
12: 6 poor man for the one he stole and for **h** no pity."
21: 5 to keep us from **h** any place at all in Israel.
Ne 5:18 because the people were already **h** a difficult time.
12:46 The custom of **h** choir directors to lead the choirs
Pr 22: 1 held in high esteem is better than **h** silver or gold.
24: 6 guidance; victory depends on **h** many counselors.
Ecc 7: 4 the fool thinks only about **h** a good time now.
Isa 56: 5 would have received by **h** sons and daughters.
Jer 2:19 to forsake the LORD your God, **h** no fear of him.
Eze 1:12 forward in all directions without **h** to turn around.
32:31 find that he is not alone in **h** his entire army killed,
Zec 4: 2 seven lamps, each one **h** seven spouts with wicks.
Mt 6:31 "So don't worry about **h** enough food or drink or
16: 8 Why are you worried about **h** no food?
Mk 8:17 "Why are you so worried about **h** no food?
Lk 1:25 "He has taken away my disgrace of **h** no children!"
Jn 11:13 Lazarus was **h** a good night's rest, but Jesus meant
Ro 1:27 instead of **h** normal sexual relationships with
3:19 for its purpose is to keep people from **h** excuses
2Co 5:12 answer those who brag about **h** a spectacular
ministry rather than **h** a sincere heart before God.
8:13 give so much that you suffer from **h** too little.
10: 8 put to shame by **h** my work among you destroyed.
1Ti 3: 2 He must enjoy **h** guests in his home and must be
Tit 1: 8 He must enjoy **h** guests in his home and must love

HAVOCK [KJV] See DEVASTATE

HAVOTH-JAIR [KJV] See TOWNS (OF JAIR)

HAWK (2) [HAWKS, NIGHTHAWK]

Job 39:26 "Are you the one who makes the **h** soar
Isa 34:11 horned owl, the **h**, the screech owl, and the raven.

HAWKS (2) [HAWK]

Lev 11:16 the nighthawk, the seagull, **h** of all kinds,
Dt 14:15 the nighthawk, the seagull, **h** of all kinds,

HAY (2)

Pr 27:25 After the **h** is harvested, the new crop appears,
1Co 3:12 may use gold, silver, jewels, wood, **h**, or straw.

HAZAEL (24) [HAZAEL'S]

1Ki 19:15 you arrive there, anoint **H** to be king of Aram.
19:17 Anyone who escapes from **H** will be killed by
2Ki 8: 8 When the king heard the news, he said to **H**,
8: 9 So **H** loaded down forty camels with the finest
8:11 Elisha stared at **H** with a fixed gaze until **H**
8:12 "What's the matter, my lord?" **H** asked him.
8:13 Then **H** replied, "How could a nobody like me
8:14 When **H** went back, the king asked him,
8:14 And **H** replied, "He told me that you will surely
8:15 But the next day **H** took a blanket, soaked it in
8:15 he died. Then **H** became the next king of Aram.
8:28 his war against King **H** of Aram at Ramoth-gilead.
9:14 defending Israel against the forces of King **H** of
10:32 King **H** conquered several sections of the country
12:17 About this time King **H** of Aram went to war
12:18 He sent them all to **H**, along with all the gold in the
12:18 So **H** called off his attack on Jerusalem.
13: 3 and he allowed King **H** of Aram and his son
13:22 King **H** of Aram had oppressed Israel during the
13:24 King **H** of Aram died, and his son Ben-hadad
13:25 **H** the towns that **H** had taken from Jehoash's
father,
2Ch 22: 5 They went out to fight King **H** of Aram at

HAZAEL'S (1) [HAZAEL]

Am 1: 4 So I will send down fire on King **H** palace,

HAZAIAH (1)

Ne 11: 5 son of **H**, son of Adaiah, son of Joiarib, son of

HAZAR-ADDAR (1) [ADDAR]

Nu 34: 4 from which it will go to **H**, and on to Azmon.

HAZAR-ENAN (4)

Nu 34: 9 and Ziphron to **H**. This will be your northern
34:10 "The eastern boundary will start at **H** and run
Eze 47:17 border will run from the Mediterranean to **H**,
48: 1 then runs on to **H** on the border of Damascus,

HAZAR-GADDAH (1)

Jos 15:27 **H**, Heshmon, Beth-pelet,

HAZAR-SHUAL (4)

Jos 15:28 **H**, Beersheba, Biziothiah,
19: 3 **H**, Balah, Ezem,
1Ch 4:28 They lived in Beersheba, Moladah, **H**,
Ne 11:27 **H**, Beersheba with its villages,

HAZAR-SUSAH (1)

Jos 19: 5 Ziklag, Beth-marcaboth, **H**,

HAZAR-SUSIM (1)

1Ch 4:31 Beth-marcaboth, **H**, Beth-biri, and Shaaraim.

HAZARDED [KJV] See RISKED

HAZARHATTICON [KJV] See HAZER-HATTICON

HAZARMAVETH (2)

Ge 10:26 was the ancestor of Almodad, Sheleph, **H**, Jerah,
1Ch 1:20 was the ancestor of Almodad, Sheleph, **H**, Jerah,

HAZAZON-TAMAR (2) [EN-GEDI, TAMAR]

Ge 14: 7 the Amalekites, and also the Amorites living in **H**.
2Ch 20: 2 They are already at **H**." (This was another name

HAZEL [KJV] See ALMOND

HAZELELPONI [KJV] See HAZZELELPONI

HAZER-HATTICON (1)

Eze 47:16 between Damascus and Hamath, and finally to **H**,

HAZERIM [KJV] See VILLAGES

HAZEROTH (6)

Nu 11:35 From there the Israelites traveled to **H**, where they
12: 1 While they were at **H**, Miriam and Aaron criticized
12:16 Then they left **H** and camped in the wilderness of
33:17 They left Kibroth-hattaavah and camped at **H**.
33:18 They left **H** and camped at Rithmah.
Dt 1: 1 between Paran on one side and Tophel, Laban, **H**,

HAZIEL (1)

1Ch 23: 9 of Shimei were Shelomoth, **H**, and Haran.

HAZO (1)

Ge 22:22 Kesed, **H**, Pildash, Jidlaph, and Bethuel.

HAZOR (16) [BAAL-HAZOR, EN-HAZOR, HAZOR'S, HAZOR-HADATTAH, KERIOTH-HEZRON]

Jos 11: 1 When King Jabin of **H** heard what had happened,
11:10 Joshua then turned back and captured **H** and killed
11:10 (**H** had at one time been the capital of the
11:13 burn any of the cities built on mounds except **H**.
12:19 The king of Madon / The king of **H**
15:23 Kedesh, **H**, Ithnan,
15:25 Hazor-hadattah, Kerioth-hezron (that is, **H**),
19:36 Adamah, Ramah, **H**,
Jdg 4: 2 the LORD handed them over to King Jabin of **H**,
4:17 family was on friendly terms with King Jabin of **H**.
1Ki 9:15 and the cities of **H**, Megiddo, and Gezer.
2Ki 15:29 of Ijon, Abel-beth-maacah, Janoah, Kedesh, and **H**.
Ne 11:33 **H**, Ramah, Gittaim,
Jer 49:28 given concerning Kedar and the kingdoms of **H**,
49:30 "Hide yourselves in deep caves, you people of **H**,
49:33 "**H** will be inhabited by jackals, and it will be

HAZOR'S (1) [HAZOR]

1Sa 12: 9 the general of **H** army, and by the Philistines

HAZOR-HADATTAH (1) [HAZOR]

Jos 15:25 **H**, Kerioth-hezron (that is, Hazor),

HAZZELELPONI (1)

1Ch 4: 3 were Jezreel, Ishma, Idbash, **H** (his daughter),

HE (8267) [HE'LL, HE'S, HIM, HIS] See Index of Articles, Etc.

HE'LL (3) [HE, WILL] See Index of Articles, Etc.

HE'S (29) [BE, HE] See Index of Articles, Etc.

HEAD (231) [AHEAD, EMPTY-HEADED, FIGUREHEAD, HARDHEADED, HEADBANDS, HEADCLOTH, HEADDRESSES, HEADED, HEADING, HEADQUARTERS, HEADS, HOTHEAD, HOTHEADS]

Ge 3:15 He will crush your **h**, and you will strike his heel."
24:48 "Then I bowed my **h** and worshiped the LORD.
40:16 "there were three baskets of pastries on my **h**.
40:19 Three days from now Pharaoh will cut off your **h**
42:38 you would bring my gray **h** down to the grave in
44:29 you would bring my gray **h** down to the grave in
44:31 We will be responsible for bringing his gray **h**
48:14 So his right hand was on the **h** of Ephraim,
48:14 and his left hand was on the **h** of Manasseh,
48:17 his father had laid his right hand on Ephraim's **h**.
48:17 So he lifted it to place it on Manasseh's **h** instead.
48:18 over here is older. Put your right hand on his **h**."
49:26 These blessings will fall on the **h** of Joseph,
Ex 12: 9 roast it all, including the **h**, legs, and internal
28:32 with an opening for Aaron's **h** in the middle of it.
29: 6 And place on his **h** the turban with the gold
29: 7 Then take the anointing oil and pour it over his **h**.
29:10 and his sons will lay their hands on its **h**.
29:15 and his sons must lay their hands on the **h** of one
29:17 Set them alongside the **h** and the other pieces of
29:19 have Aaron and his sons lay their hands on its **h**
39:23 with an opening for Aaron's **h** in the middle of it.
Lev 1: 4 Lay your hand on its **h** so the LORD will accept it
1: 8 including its **h** and fat, on the wood fire.
1:12 including the **h** and fat, on top of the wood fire on
1:15 twist off its **h**, and burn the **h** on the altar.
3: 2 Lay your hand on the animal's **h**, and slaughter it
3: 8 by laying your hand on its **h** and slaughtering it at
3:13 lay your hand on its **h**, and slaughter it at the
4: 4 lay his hand on the bull's **h**, and slaughter it there
4:11 its hide, meat, **h**, legs, internal organs, and dung—
4:15 leaders must then lay their hands on the bull's **h**
4:24 He is to lay his hand on the goat's **h** and slaughter
4:29 They are to lay a hand on the **h** of the sin offering
4:33 They are to lay a hand on the **h** of the sin offering
5: 8 its neck but without severing its **h** from the body.
8: 9 He placed on Aaron's **h** the turban with the gold
8:12 he poured some of the anointing oil on Aaron's **h**,
8:14 and Aaron and his sons laid their hands on its **h**
8:18 and Aaron and his sons laid their hands on its **h**
8:20 Next he cut the ram into pieces and burned the **h**,
8:22 Aaron and his sons laid their hands on its **h**
9:13 including the **h**, and he burned each part on the
13:12 someone's skin, covering the body from **h** to foot.
13:29 or woman, has an open sore on the **h** or chin,
13:30 The infection is a contagious skin disease of the **h**
13:40 "If a man loses his hair and his **h** becomes bald,
13:42 infection appears on the front or the back of his **h**,
14:18 then be poured over the healed person's **h**.
14:29 hand will then be poured over the person's **h**.
16: 4 around his waist and put the linen turban on his **h**.
16:21 He is to lay both of his hands on the goat's **h**
16:21 he will lay the people's sins on the **h** of the goat;
21:10 who has had the anointing oil poured on his **h**
24:14 all those who heard him to lay their hands on his **h**.
Nu 6: 7 They must not defile the hair on their **h**, because it
6:19 After each Nazirite's **h** has been shaved, the priest
Dt 19: 5 swings an ax and the ax **h** flies off the handle,
21:12 where she must shave her **h**, cut her fingernails,
28:13 the LORD will make you the **h** and not the tail,
28:35 The LORD will cover you from **h** to foot with
28:44 They will be the **h**, and you will be the tail!
33:16 May these blessings rest on Joseph's **h**,
33:20 is poised there like a lion / to tear off an arm or a **h**.
Jdg 5:26 She hit Sisera, crushing his **h**. / She pounded the
tent peg through his **h**,
9:53 down a millstone that landed on Abimelech's **h**
16:17 If my **h** were shaved, my strength would leave me,
16:19 Delilah lulled Samson to sleep with his **h** in her
1Sa 4:12 his clothes and put dust on his **h** to show his grief.
5: 4 This time his **h** and hands had broken off and were
9: 2 **h** and shoulders taller than anyone else in the land.
9:22 the great hall and placed them at the **h** of the table,
10: 1 a flask of olive oil and poured it over Saul's **h**.
10:23 and he stood **h** and shoulders above anyone else.
14:45 not one hair on his **h** will be touched,
16:13 oil he had brought and poured it on David's **h**.
17:46 conquer you, and I will kill you and cut off your **h**.
17:51 David used it to kill the giant and cut off his **h**.
17:54 (David took Goliath's **h** to Jerusalem, but he stored
17:57 Abner brought him to Saul with the Philistine's **h**
19:13 and put a cushion of goat's hair at its **h**.
19:16 in the bed with a cushion of goat's hair at its **h**.
26: 7 with his spear stuck in the ground beside his **h**.
26:12 the spear and jug of water that were near Saul's **h**.
26:16 and the jug of water that were beside his **h**?"
31: 9 So they cut off Saul's **h** and stripped off his armor.
2Sa 1: 2 and put dirt on his **h** to show that he was in
4: 7 they cut off his **h** as he lay there on his bed.
4: 7 Taking his **h** with them, they fled across the Jordan
4: 8 at Hebron and presented Ishbosheth's **h** to David.
4: 8 "Here is the **h** of Ishbosheth, the son of your
4:12 Then they took Ishbosheth's **h** and buried it in
12:30 David removed the crown from the king's **h**, and it
was placed on David's own **h**.
13:19 now Tamar tore her robe and put ashes on her **h**.
14:11 "not a hair on your son's **h** will be disturbed!"
14:25 From **h** to foot, he was the perfect specimen of a
15:30 His **h** was covered and his feet were bare as a sign
15:32 and put dirt on his **h** as a sign of mourning.
16: 9 "Let me go over and cut off his **h**!"
18: 9 the thick branches of a great oak, his **h** got caught.
20:21 "we will throw his **h** over the wall to you."
20:22 and they cut off Sheba's **h** and threw it out to Joab.
1Ki 1:39 from the sacred tent and poured it on Solomon's **h**.
1:47 Then the king bowed his **h** in worship as he lay in
2:37 surely die; your blood will be on your own **h**."
2Ki 4:19 he complained, "My **h** hurts! My **h** hurts!"
6: 5 of them was chopping, his ax **h** fell into the river.
6: 6 Then the ax **h** rose to the surface and floated.
6:25 After a while even a donkey's **h** sold for two
9: 3 and pour the oil over his **h**. Say to him, 'This is

9: 6 the young prophet poured the oil over Jehu's **h**
11:12 the king's son, and placed the crown on his **h**.
19:21 of Jerusalem / scoffs and shakes her **h** as you flee.
1Ch 7:40 Each of these descendants of Asher was the **h** of an
10: 9 So they stripped off Saul's armor and cut off his **h**.
10:10 and they fastened his **h** to the wall in the temple of
15:22 Kenaniah, the **h** Levite, was chosen as the choir
20: 2 he removed the crown from the king's **h**, and it was placed on David's own **h**.
2Ch 23:11 the king's son, and placed the crown on his **h**.
Ezr 9: 3 tore my clothing, pulled hair from my **h** and beard,
Est 1:11 Vashti to him with the royal crown on her **h**.
2:17 with her that he set the royal crown on her **h**
6: 8 the king's own horse with a royal emblem on its **h**.
Job 1:20 Then he shaved his **h** and fell to the ground before
2: 7 Job with a terrible case of boils from **h** to foot.
10:15 and misery so that I can't hold my **h** high.
10:16 And if I hold my **h** high, you hunt me like a lion
16: 4 my criticisms against you and shake my **h** at you.
19: 9 of my honor and removed the crown from my **h**.
20: 6 to the heavens and though his **h** touches the clouds,
41: 7 its hide be hurt by darts, or its **h** by a harpoon?
Ps 3: 3 my glory, and the one who lifts my **h** high.
21: 3 You placed a crown of finest gold on his **h**.
23: 5 welcome me as a guest, / anointing my **h** with oil.
27: 6 Then I will hold my **h** high, / above my enemies
40:12 They are more numerous than the hairs on my **h**.
69: 4 are more numerous than the hairs on my **h**.
133: 2 that was poured over Aaron's **h**, / that ran down his
139: 5 You place your hand of blessing on my **h**.
Pr 4: 9 She will place a lovely wreath on your **h**; she will
SS 2: 6 His left hand is under my **h**, and his right hand
5: 2 My **h** is soaked with dew, my hair with the wetness
5:11 His **h** is the finest gold, and his hair is wavy
7: 5 Your **h** is as majestic as Mount Carmel,
8: 3 Your left hand would be under my **h** and your right
Isa 1: 5 Your **h** is injured, and your heart is sick.
1: 6 You are sick from **h** to foot—covered with bruises,
3:23 linen garments, **h** ornaments, and shawls.
9:14 the LORD will destroy both the **h** and the tail,
9:15 The leaders of Israel are the **h**, and the lying
37:22 of Jerusalem / scoffs and shakes her **h** as you flee.
59:17 and placed the helmet of salvation on his **h**.
Jer 7:29 O Jerusalem, shave your **h** in mourning, and weep
La 3:54 The water flowed above my **h**, and I cried out,
Eze 5: 1 and use it as a razor to shave your **h** and beard.
16:12 for your ears, and a lovely crown for your **h**.
24:17 Do not uncover your **h** or take off your sandals.
Da 2:32 The **h** of the statue was made of fine gold, its chest
2:38 birds under your control. You are the **h** of gold.
4:36 and I was reestablished as **h** of my kingdom,
7:20 asked about the ten horns on the fourth beast's **h**
Jnh 2: 5 and seaweed wrapped itself around my **h**.
4: 6 and soon it spread its broad leaves over Jonah's **h**,
4: 8 The sun beat down on his **h** until he grew faint
Hab 3:13 the wicked and laid bare their bones from **h** to toe.
Zec 3: 5 could he also have a clean turban on his **h**?"
3: 5 So they put a clean priestly turban on his **h**
6:11 Then put the crown on the **h** of Jeshua son of
Mt 5:36 Don't even swear, 'By my **h**!' for you can't turn
8:20 home of my own, not even a place to lay my **h**."
10:30 And the very hairs on your **h** are all numbered.
14: 8 "I want the **h** of John the Baptist on a tray!"
14:11 and his **h** was brought on a tray and given to the
23: 6 And how they love to sit at the **h** table at banquets
26: 7 jar of expensive perfume and poured it over his **h**.
27:29 a crown of long, sharp thorns and put it on his **h**,
27:30 and grabbed the stick and beat him on the **h** with it.
27:37 was fastened to the cross above Jesus' **h**,
Mk 2: 4 so they dug through the clay roof above his **h**.
4:38 at the back of the boat with his **h** on a cushion.
6:24 mother told her, "Ask for John the Baptist's **h**!"
6:25 "I want the **h** of John the Baptist, right now,
6:27 sent an executioner to the prison to cut off John's **h**
6:28 brought his **h** on a tray, and gave it to the girl,
6:45 the boat and **h** out across the lake to Bethsaida,
12: 4 but they beat him over the **h** and treated him
14: 3 broke the seal and poured the perfume over his **h**.
15:17 a crown of long, sharp thorns and put it on his **h**.
15:19 And they beat him on the **h** with a stick, spit on
15:26 was fastened to the cross above Jesus' **h**,
Lk 7:46 neglected the courtesy of olive oil to anoint my **h**,
9:58 home of my own, not even a place to lay my **h**."
12: 7 And the very hairs on your **h** are all numbered.
13:25 but when the **h** of the house has locked the door,
14: 7 the dinner were trying to sit near the **h** of the table,
14: 8 to a wedding feast, don't always **h** for the best seat.
21:18 But not a hair of your **h** will perish!
Jn 13: 9 "Then wash my hands and **h** as well, Lord,
19: 2 a crown of long, sharp thorns and put it on his **h**,
19:30 Then he bowed his **h** and gave up his spirit.
20: 7 while the cloth that had covered Jesus' **h** was
20:12 She saw two white-robed angels sitting at the **h**
Ac 18:18 Paul had shaved his **h** according to Jewish custom,
1Co 11: 4 A man dishonors Christ if he covers his **h** while
11: 5 or prophesies without a covering on her **h**, for this is the same as shaving her **h**.
11: 6 Yes, if she refuses to wear a **h** covering, she should
11: 6 for a woman to have her hair cut or her **h** shaved,
11: 7 A man should not wear anything on his **h** when
11:10 So a woman should wear a covering on her **h** as a
11:13 to pray to God in public without covering her **h**?
12:21 The **h** can't say to the feet, "I don't need you."
Eph 4:15 like Christ, who is the **h** of his body, the church.
5:23 For a husband is the **h** of his wife as Christ is the **h** of his body,
Col 1:18 Christ is the **h** of the church, which is his body.
2:19 they are not connected to Christ, the **h** of the body.
1Pe 2:13 accept all authority—the king as **h** of state,
5: 4 And when the **h** Shepherd comes, your reward will
Rev 1:14 His **h** and his hair were white like wool, as white
6: 2 carried a bow, and a crown was placed on his **h**.
10: 1 surrounded by a cloud, with a rainbow over his **h**.
12: 1 her feet, and a crown of twelve stars on her **h**.
13: 1 And written on each **h** were names that
14:14 He had a gold crown on his **h** and a sharp sickle in
19:12 flames of fire, and on his **h** were many crowns.

HEADBANDS (1) [HEAD]

Isa 3:18 their ornaments, **h**, and crescent necklaces;

HEADCLOTH (1) [CLOTH, HEAD]

Jn 11:44 bound in graveclothes, his face wrapped in a **h**.

HEADDRESSES (3) [DRESS, HEAD]

Ex 28:40 sashes, and **h** to give them dignity and respect.
29: 9 with their woven sashes and their **h**. They will
39:28 The turban, the **h**, and the underclothes were all

HEADED (17) [HEAD]

Ex 4:20 them on a donkey, and **h** back to the land of Egypt.
Nu 10:14 The tribes that camped with Judah **h** the march
10:25 The tribe of Dan **h** this group, under the leadership
Dt 1:19 and **h** toward the hill country of the Amorites.
3: 1 "Next we **h** for the land of Bashan, where King
Jdg 19:10 and **h** in the direction of Jebus (that is,
1Sa 29:11 So David **h** back into the land of the Philistines,
Pr 28:14 but the stubborn are **h** for serious trouble.
Jer 4: 7 a destroyer of nations. And it is **h** for your land!
39: 4 the king's garden and **h** toward the Jordan Valley.
Da 8: 6 **h** toward the two-horned ram that I had seen
Mt 14:13 But the crowds heard where he was **h** and followed
Lk 22:52 and the other leaders who **h** the mob.
Jn 6:17 and **h** out across the lake toward Capernaum.
17:12 not one was lost, except the one **h** for destruction,
Ac 16: 7 of Mysia, they **h** for the province of Bithynia,
27:40 the rudders, raised the foresail, and **h** toward shore.

HEADING (2) [HEAD]

Ge 31:21 the Euphrates River, **h** for the territory of Gilead.
Jude 1:13 **h** for everlasting gloom and darkness.

HEADQUARTERS (6) [HEAD]

Ne 3: 7 the **h** of the governor of the province west of the
Mt 27:27 of the governor's soldiers took Jesus into their **h**
Mk 15:16 The soldiers took him into their **h** and called out
Jn 18:28 Then he was taken to the **h** of the Roman governor.
19: 9 He took Jesus back into the **h** again and asked him,
Ac 23:35 ordered him kept in the prison at Herod's **h**.

HEADS (112) [HEAD]

Ge 41: 5 This time he saw seven **h** of grain on one stalk,
41: 6 seven more **h** appeared on the stalk,
41: 7 And these thin **h** swallowed up the seven plump, well-formed **h**!
41:22 This time there were seven **h** of grain on one stalk, and all seven **h** were plump and full.
41:23 Then out of the same stalk came seven withered **h**,
41:24 And the withered **h** swallowed up the plump ones!
41:26 and the seven plump **h** of grain both represent
41:27 and the seven withered **h** of grain represent seven
48:14 as he reached out to lay his hands on the boys' **h**.
Ex 4:31 for them, they all bowed their **h** and worshiped.
12:27 destroy us.' " Then all the people bowed their **h**
Lev 21: 5 "The priests must never shave their **h**,
26:13 so you can walk free with your **h** held high.
Nu 1:16 These tribal leaders, **h** of their own families,
6: 9 must wait for seven days and then shave their **h**.
8:12 "Next the Levites will lay their hands on the **h** of
36: 1 Then the **h** of the clan of Gilead—descendants of
Dt 23:25 And you may pluck a few **h** of your neighbor's
32:42 the captives, / and the **h** of the enemy leaders." '
Jos 7: 6 tore their clothing in dismay, threw dust on their **h**,
Jdg 7:25 Afterward the Israelites brought the **h** of Oreb
Ru 2:16 And pull out some **h** of barley from the bundles
2Sa 15:30 And the people who were with him covered their **h**
1Ki 20:31 by wearing sackcloth and putting ropes on our **h**.
2Ki 10: 6 bring the **h** of the king's sons to me at Jezreel at
10: 7 They placed their **h** in baskets and presented them
10: 8 "They have brought the **h** of the king's sons."
1Ch 9:13 They were **h** of clans and very able men.
9:34 These were the **h** of Levite families and were listed
Ezr 9: 6 For our sins are piled higher than our **h**, and our
Ne 4: 4 May their scoffing fall back on their own **h**,
9: 1 dressed in sackcloth and sprinkled dust on their **h**.
11:13 242 of his associates, who were **h** of their families.
12:23 The **h** of the Levite families were recorded in *The*
Job 2:12 and threw dust into the air over their **h** to
24:24 be gone like all others, withered like **h** of grain.
Ps 7:16 violence for others, / but it falls on their own **h**.
22: 7 mocks me. / They sneer and shake their **h**, saying,
64: 8 All who see it happening will shake their **h** in
68:21 But God will smash the **h** of his enemies,
74:13 your strength / and smashed the sea monster's **h**.
74:14 You crushed the **h** of Leviathan / and let the desert
109:25 when they see me, they shake their **h**.
110: 6 and fill them with their dead; / he will shatter **h**
140:10 Let burning coals fall down on their **h**, / or throw
Pr 25:22 You will heap burning coals on their **h**,
Isa 3:17 will send a plague of scabs to ornament their **h**.
15: 2 They will shave their **h** in sorrow and cut off their
22:12 He told you to shave your **h** in sorrow for your sins
58: 5 bowing your **h** like a blade of grass in the wind.
Jer 2:37 will be led into exile with your hands on your **h**,
13:18 crowns will soon be snatched from your **h**."
14: 3 confused and desperate, covering their **h** in grief.
14: 4 The farmers are afraid; they, too, cover their **h**.
16: 6 will not cut themselves or shave their **h** in sadness.
18:16 and shake their **h** in amazement at its utter
23:19 a whirlwind that swirls down on the **h** of the
30:23 a driving wind that swirls down on the **h** of the
48:37 They shave their **h** and beards in mourning.
La 2:10 They throw dust on their **h** in sorrow and despair.
2:10 The young women of Jerusalem hang their **h** in
5:16 The garlands have fallen from our **h**. Disaster has
Eze 1:26 Above the surface over their **h** was what looked
7:18 They will shave their **h** in sorrow and remorse.
8:11 so there was a thick cloud of incense above their **h**.
10: 1 the crystal surface over the **h** of the cherubim.
10:11 They went straight in the direction in which their **h**
23:15 their waists, and flowing turbans crowned their **h**.
23:42 on your wrists and beautiful crowns on your **h**.
24:23 Your **h** must remain covered, and your sandals
27:30 They weep bitterly as they throw dust on their **h**
27:31 They shave their **h** in grief because of you
27:36 of the nations / shake their **h** at the sight of you,
29:18 so hard against Tyre that the warriors' **h** were
32:27 their bodies, and their swords beneath their **h**.
Da 3:27 Not a hair on their **h** was singed, and their clothing
7: 6 like birds' wings on its back, and it had four **h**.
Am 8:10 and shave your **h** as signs of sorrow,
Ob 1:15 All your evil deeds will fall back on your own **h**.
Mic 1:16 Shave your **h** in sorrow, for the children you love
Hab 3:13 You crushed the **h** of the wicked and laid bare their
Mt 11:21 and throwing ashes on their **h** to show their
12: 1 so they began breaking off **h** of wheat and eating
19:15 And he put his hands on their **h** and blessed them
23:36 will break upon the **h** of this very generation.
27:39 by shouted abuse, shaking their **h** in mockery.
Mk 2:23 his disciples began breaking off **h** of wheat.
4:28 then the **h** of wheat are formed, and finally the
10:16 and placed his hands on their **h** and blessed them.
15:29 by shouted abuse, shaking their **h** in mockery.
Lk 6: 1 his disciples broke off **h** of wheat, rubbed off the
10:13 and throwing ashes on their **h** to show their
Ac 8:18 the apostles placed their hands upon people's **h**,
18: 6 and said, "Your blood be upon your own **h**—
21:23 taken a vow and are preparing to shave their **h**.
21:24 and pay for them to have their **h** shaved.
27:34 own good. For not a hair of your **h** will perish."
Rev 4: 4 clothed in white and had gold crowns on their **h**.
9: 7 They had gold crowns on their **h**, and they had
9:17 The horses' **h** were like the **h** of lions, and fire
9:19 For their tails had **h** like snakes, with the power to
12: 3 I saw a large red dragon with seven **h** and ten horns, with seven crowns on his **h**.
13: 1 It had seven **h** and ten horns, with ten crowns on
13: 3 I saw that one of the **h** of the beast seemed
17: 3 a woman sitting on a scarlet beast that had seven **h**
17: 7 and of the beast with seven **h** and ten horns.
17: 9 The seven **h** of the beast represent the seven hills
18:19 And they will throw dust on their **h** to show their

HEADSTONE [KJV] See FINAL (STONE)

HEADWATERS (1) [WATER]

Isa 18: 1 the land of Ethiopia, which lies at the **h** of the Nile.

HEADWINDS (1) [WIND]

Ac 27: 4 we encountered **h** that made it difficult to keep the

HEADY [KJV] See RECKLESS

HEAL (60) [HEALED, HEALING, HEALINGS, HEALS]

Lev 13:16 if the open sores **h** and turn white like the rest of
13:18 has had a boil on the skin that has started to **h**,
Nu 12:13 out to the LORD, "**H** her, O God, I beg you!"
2Ki 5: 3 in Samaria. He would **h** him of his leprosy."
5: 6 I want you to **h** him of his leprosy."
5: 7 and said, "This man sends me a leper to **h**!
5:11 call on the name of the LORD his God and **h** me!
20: 5 I will **h** you, and three days from now you will get
20: 8 will the LORD give to prove that he will **h** me
2Ch 7:14 and will forgive their sins and **h** their land.
Job 5:18 he also bandages. He strikes, but his hands also **h**.
Ps 6: 2 **H** me, LORD, for my body is in agony.
41: 4 on me. / **H** me, for I have sinned against you."
Ecc 3: 3 A time to kill and a time to **h**. / A time to tear
Isa 19:22 and he will listen to their pleas and **h** them.
30:26 So it will be when the LORD begins to **h** his
57:18 have seen what they do, but I will **h** them anyway!
57:19 both near and far, for I will **h** them all,"
Jer 3:22 back to me, and I will **h** your wayward hearts."
17:14 O LORD, you alone can **h** me; you alone can
30:17 will give you back your health and **h** your wounds,
33: 6 the time will come when I will **h** Jerusalem's
La 2:13 your wound is as deep as the sea. Who can **h** you?
Eze 30:21 His arm has not been put in a cast so that it may **h**.
47: 8 The waters of this stream will **h** the salty waters of
Hos 6: 1 He has torn us in pieces; now he will **h** us. He has
7: 1 "I wanted to **h** Israel, but its sins were far too
14: 4 "Then I will **h** you of your idolatry
Mic 1: 9 For my people's wound is far too deep to **h**.
Zec 11:16 the young, nor **h** the injured, nor feed the healthy.

Mt 8: 7 Jesus said, "I will come and **h** him."
10: 1 and to **h** every kind of disease and illness.
10: 8 **H** the sick, raise the dead, cure those with leprosy,
13: 15 and they cannot turn to me / and let me **h** them.'
17: 16 him to your disciples, but they couldn't **h** him."
Mk 3: 2 Would he **h** the man's hand on the Sabbath?
5: 23 pleading with him to **h** his little daughter. "She is
5: 23 place your hands on her; **h** her so she can live."
6: 5 place his hands on a few sick people and **h** them.
7: 32 begged Jesus to lay his hands on the man to **h** him.
8: 22 and they begged him to touch and **h** the man.
9: 17 "Teacher, I brought my son for you to **h** him.
16: 18 able to place their hands on the sick and **h** them."
Lk 4: 23 quote me that proverb, 'Physician, **h** yourself'—
4: 38 a high fever. "Please **h** her," everyone begged.
6: 7 see whether Jesus would **h** the man on the Sabbath,
7: 3 Jewish leaders to ask him to come and **h** his slave.
9: 1 authority to cast out demons and to **h** all diseases.
9: 2 coming of the Kingdom of God and to **h** the sick.
10: 9 and **h** the sick. As you **h** them, say, 'The Kingdom of God is near
14: 3 is it permitted in the law to **h** people on the
17: 17 Jesus asked, "Didn't I **h** ten men? Where are the
Jn 4: 47 him to come to Capernaum with him to **h** his son,
9: 26 did he do?" they asked. "How did he **h** you?"
12: 40 and they cannot turn to me / and let me **h** them."
Ac 28: 27 and they cannot turn to me / and let me **h** them.'
1Co 12: 9 and to someone else he gives the power to **h** the
Jas 5: 15 And their prayer offered in faith will **h** the sick,
Rev 22: 2 The leaves were used for medicine to **h** the

HEALED (99) [HEAL]

Ge 20: 17 prayed to God, and God **h** Abimelech, his wife,
Lev 13: 37 grown in the affected area, then the infection has **h**.
14: 2 Those who have been **h** must be brought to the
14: 3 If the priest finds that someone has been **h** of the
14: 14 and put it on the tip of the **h** person's right ear,
14: 17 his left hand on the tip of the **h** person's right ear,
14: 18 hand will then be poured over the **h** person's head.
14: 20 and the **h** person will be ceremonially clean.
Jos 5: 8 they rested in the camp until they were **h**.
2Ki 5: 10 will be restored, and you will be **h** of leprosy."
5: 12 Why shouldn't I wash in them and be **h**?"
5: 14 as healthy as a young child's, and he was **h**!
2Ch 30: 20 listened to Hezekiah's prayer and **h** the people.
32: 24 who **h** him and gave him a miraculous sign.
Ps 107: 20 He spoke, and they were **h**— / snatched from the
Isa 38: 20 Think of it—the LORD has **h** me! / I will sing his
53: 5 have peace. He was whipped, and we were **h**!
Jer 51: 8 and give her medicine. Perhaps she can yet be **h**.
Eze 47: 9 abound in the Dead Sea, for its waters will be **h**.
Mt 4: 23 And he **h** people who had every kind of sickness
4: 24 so that the sick were soon coming to be **h** from as
4: 24 were epileptics, or were paralyzed—he **h** them all.
8: 3 Jesus touched him. "I want to," he said. "Be **h**!"
8: 4 of Moses for those who have been **h** of leprosy.
8: 8 from where you are, and my servant will be **h**!
8: 13 And the young servant was **h** that same hour.
8: 16 he commanded them to leave; and he **h** all the sick.
9: 6 your mat, and go on home, because you are **h**!"
9: 21 "If I can just touch his robe, I will be **h**."
9: 22 you well." And the woman was **h** at that moment.
9: 35 he **h** people of every sort of disease and illness.
12: 15 followed him. He **h** all the sick among them,
12: 22 He **h** the man so that he could both speak and see.
14: 14 and he had compassion on them and **h** their sick.
14: 35 soon people were bringing all their sick to be **h**.
14: 36 fringe of his robe, and all who touched it were **h**.
15: 28 is granted." And her daughter was instantly **h**.
15: 30 and they laid them before Jesus. And he **h** them all.
19: 2 crowds followed him there, and he **h** their sick.
21: 14 came to him, and he **h** them there in the Temple.
Mk 1: 34 So Jesus **h** great numbers of sick people who had
1: 40 and knelt in front of Jesus, begging to be **h**.
1: 41 Jesus touched him. "I want to," he said. "Be **h**!"
1: 42 Instantly the leprosy disappeared—the man was **h**.
1: 44 of Moses for those who have been **h** of leprosy,
2: 11 your mat, and go on home, because you are **h**!"
5: 28 "If I can just touch his clothing, I will be **h**."
5: 29 and she could feel that she had been **h**!
5: 34 made you well. Go in peace. You have been **h**."
6: 13 cast out many demons and **h** many sick people,
6: 56 fringe of his robe, and all who touched it were **h**.
7: 29 have answered so well, I have **h** your daughter."
10: 52 said to him, "Go your way. Your faith has **h** you."
Lk 4: 27 of the prophet Elisha, who **h** Naaman, a Syrian,
4: 40 diseases were, the touch of his hand **h** every one.
5: 12 the ground, face down in the dust, begging to be **h**.
5: 13 touched the man. "I want to," he said. "Be **h**!"
5: 14 of Moses for those who have been **h** of leprosy,
5: 15 to hear him preach and to be **h** of their diseases.
5: 24 your mat, and go on home, because you are **h**!"
6: 18 They had come to hear him and to be **h**, and Jesus
7: 7 from where you are, and my servant will be **h**.
7: 10 to his house, they found the slave completely **h**.
8: 2 along with some women he had **h** and from whom
8: 36 others how the demon-possessed man had been **h**.
8: 47 touched him and that she had been immediately **h**.
9: 42 But Jesus rebuked the evil spirit and **h** the boy.
13: 12 and said, "Woman, you are **h** of your sickness!"
13: 14 indignant that Jesus had **h** her on the Sabbath day.
13: 14 "Come on those days to be **h**, not on the
14: 4 the sick man and **h** him and sent him away.
17: 15 One of them, when he saw that he was **h**,
17: 15 back to Jesus, shouting, "Praise God, I'm **h**!"
18: 42 "All right, you can see! Your faith has **h** you."
22: 51 the place where the man's ear had been and **h** him.
Jn 5: 9 Instantly, the man was **h**! He rolled up the mat
5: 11 He replied, "The man who **h** me said to me,
5: 15 and told them it was Jesus who had **h** him.
6: 2 because they saw his miracles as he **h** the sick.
9: 10 They asked, "Who **h** you? What happened?"
9: 14 as it happened, Jesus had **h** the man on a Sabbath.
9: 21 but we don't know how he can see or who **h** him.
9: 30 "He **h** my eyes, and yet you don't know anything
11: 37 But some said, "This man **h** a blind man.
Ac 3: 7 the man's feet and anklebones were **h**
3: 16 "The name of Jesus has **h** this man—and you
4: 9 Do you want to know how he was **h**?
4: 10 and to all the people of Israel that he was **h** in the
4: 14 But since the man who had been **h** was standing
5: 16 those possessed by evil spirits, and they were all **h**.
8: 7 many who had been paralyzed or lame were **h**.
9: 34 and make your bed!" And he was **h** instantly.
14: 9 Paul noticed him and realized he had faith to be **h**.
19: 12 they were **h** of their diseases, and any evil spirits
28: 8 for him, and laying his hands on him, he **h** him.
Jas 5: 16 and pray for each other so that you may be **h**.
1Pe 2: 24 for what is right. You have been **h** by his wounds!
Rev 13: 3 beyond recovery—but the fatal wound was **h**!
13: 12 the first beast, whose death-wound had been **h**.

HEALING (33) [HEAL]

Pr 6: 15 destroyed suddenly, broken beyond all hope of **h**.
12: 18 cutting remarks, but the words of the wise bring **h**.
13: 17 into trouble, but a reliable messenger brings **h**.
Isa 6: 10 understand with their hearts, and turn to me for **h**."
19: 22 will strike Egypt in a way that will bring **h**.
58: 8 Yes, your **h** will come quickly. Your godliness will
Jer 8: 15 We hoped for a time of **h**, but found only terror.
8: 18 My grief is beyond **h**; my heart is broken.
8: 22 Why is there no **h** for the wounds of my people?
14: 19 Why have you wounded us past all hope of **h**?
14: 19 We hoped for a time of **h** but found only terror.
46: 11 But your many medicines will bring you no **h**.
Eze 47: 12 The fruit will be for food and the leaves for **h**."
Na 3: 19 There is no **h** for your wound; your injury is fatal.
Mal 4: 2 the Sun of Righteousness will rise with **h** in his
Mt 8: 4 of leprosy, so everyone will have proof of your **h**."
12: 10 "Is it legal to work by **h** on the Sabbath day?"
Mk 1: 44 of leprosy, so everyone will have proof of your **h**."
5: 30 Jesus realized at once that **h** power had gone out
Lk 5: 14 of leprosy, so everyone will have proof of your **h**."
5: 17 And the Lord's **h** power was strongly with Jesus.
6: 19 because **h** power went out from him, and they were
8: 46 touched me, for I felt **h** power go out from me."
9: 6 preaching the Good News and **h** the sick.
13: 32 and doing miracles of **h** today and tomorrow;
Jn 5: 20 and the Son will do far greater things than **h** this
7: 21 "I worked on the Sabbath by **h** a man,
Ac 3: 16 Faith in Jesus' name has caused this **h** before your
4: 22 the **h** of a man who had been lame for more than
4: 30 Send your **h** power; may miraculous signs
10: 38 and **h** all who were oppressed by the Devil,
1Co 12: 28 who do miracles, / those who have the gift of **h**,
12: 30 Does everyone have the gift of **h**? Of course not.

HEALINGS (1) [HEAL]

Mk 3: 10 There had been many **h** that day. As a result,

HEALS (7) [HEAL]

Ex 15: 26 the Egyptians; for I am the LORD who **h** you."
Lev 15: 13 "When the man's discharge **h**, he must count off a
Dt 32: 39 and gives life; / I am the one who wounds and **h**;
Ps 103: 3 He forgives all my sins / and **h** all my diseases.
147: 3 He **h** the brokenhearted, / binding up their wounds.
Mk 7: 37 He even **h** those who are deaf and mute."
Ac 9: 34 Peter said to him, "Aeneas, Jesus Christ **h** you!

HEALTH (19) [HEALTHIER, HEALTHY, HEALTHY-LOOKING]

Ex 18: 7 They asked about each other's **h** and then went to
Job 2: 5 But take away his **h**, and he will surely curse you
21: 24 the very picture of good **h**.
Ps 30: 2 I cried out to you for help, / and you restored my **h**.
38: 3 body is sick; / my **h** is broken because of my sins.
38: 7 fever burns within me, / and my **h** is broken.
73: 26 My **h** may fail, and my spirit may grow weak,
119: 93 for you have used them to restore my joy and **h**.
Pr 3: 8 Then you will gain renewed **h** and vitality.
4: 22 and radiant **h** to anyone who discovers their
15: 4 Gentle words bring life and **h**; a deceitful tongue
15: 30 joy to the heart; good news makes for good **h**.
Ecc 5: 19 wealth from God and the good **h** to enjoy it.
6: 2 but then he doesn't give them the **h** to enjoy it.
Isa 38: 16 your discipline is good, / for it leads to life and **h**. / You have restored my **h**
66: 14 your heart will rejoice. Vigorous **h** will be yours!
Jer 30: 17 I will give you back your **h** and heal your wounds,
La 4: 7 Our princes were once glowing with **h**; they were

HEALTHIER (1) [HEALTH]

Da 1: 15 Daniel and his three friends looked **h** and better

HEALTHY (21) [HEALTH]

Ge 27: 28 May God always give you plenty of dew for **h**
31: 38 your sheep and goats so they produced **h** offspring.
Ex 4: 7 it out this time, it was as **h** as the rest of his body.
23: 25 you with food and water, and I will keep you **h**.
2Ki 5: 14 And his flesh became as **h** as a young child's,
2Ch 36: 17 both young and old, men and women, **h** and sick.
Job 33: 25 Then his body will become as **h** as a child's,
Ps 73: 4 a painless life; / their bodies are so **h** and strong.
128: 3 your table / as vigorous and **h** as young olive trees.
Pr 16: 24 like honey—sweet to the soul and **h** for the body.
Isa 58: 11 your life when you are dry and keeping you **h**,
Jer 31: 12 of wheat, wine, and oil, and the **h** flocks and herds.
Da 1: 4 "Select only strong, **h**, and good-looking young
Zec 11: 16 the young, nor heal the injured, nor feed the **h**.
Mt 7: 17 A **h** tree produces good fruit, and an unhealthy tree
9: 12 Jesus replied, "**H** people don't need a doctor—
Mk 2: 17 he told them, "**H** people don't need a doctor—
Lk 2: 40 There the child grew up **h** and strong. He was
5: 31 answered them, "**H** people don't need a doctor—
Eph 4: 16 so that the whole body is **h** and growing and full of
3Jn 1: 2 and that your body is as **h** as I know your soul is.

HEALTHY-LOOKING (2) [HEALTH, LOOK]

Ge 41: 2 **h** cows suddenly came up out of the river
41: 18 **h** cows came up out of the river and began grazing

HEAP (30) [HEAPING, HEAPS]

Ge 31: 46 his men to gather stones and pile them up in a **h**.
31: 51 This **h** of stones and this pillar
Lev 4: 12 He will burn it all on a wood fire in the ash **h**.
Dt 32: 23 I will **h** disasters upon them / and shoot them down
Jos 3: 13 and the river will pile up there in one **h**."
7: 26 They piled a great **h** of stones over Achan,
8: 29 They piled a great **h** of stones over him that can
Ru 3: 7 he lay down beside the **h** of grain and went to
2Sa 18: 17 in the forest and piled a great **h** of stones over it.
Ps 39: 6 We **h** up wealth for someone else to spend.
79: 1 holy Temple / and made Jerusalem a **h** of ruins.
Pr 25: 22 You will **h** burning coals on their heads,
SS 7: 2 is lovely, like a **h** of wheat set about with lilies.
Isa 3: 6 you be our leader! Take charge of this **h** of ruins!"
17: 1 will disappear! It will become a **h** of ruins.
23: 13 down its palaces, and turned it into a **h** of rubble.
Jer 9: 11 "I will make Jerusalem into a **h** of ruins,"
49: 2 It will become a desolate **h**, and the neighboring
49: 13 will become an object of horror and a **h** of rubble;
51: 25 am finished, you will be nothing but a **h** of rubble.
51: 37 and Babylon will become a **h** of rubble, haunted by
Eze 22: 31 I will **h** on them the full penalty for all their sins,
24: 5 the flock and **h** fuel on the fire beneath the pot.
24: 10 Yes, **h** on the wood! Let the fire roar to make the
Da 2: 35 The whole statue collapsed into a **h** of iron, clay,
Hos 5: 9 punishment comes, you will become a **h** of rubble.
Jnh 3: 6 himself in sackcloth and sat on a **h** of ashes.
Mic 1: 6 will make the city of Samaria a **h** of rubble.
Mal 2: 3 festival sacrifices, and I will add you to the dung **h**.
Lk 6: 49 that house, it will crumble into a **h** of ruins."

HEAPING (1) [HEAP]

2Ch 32: 16 and his servant Hezekiah, **h** insult upon insult.

HEAPS (17) [HEAP]

Ex 8: 14 They were piled into great **h**, and a terrible stench
Jdg 15: 16 the jawbone of a donkey, / I've made **h** on **h**!
2Ki 10: 8 "Pile them in two **h** at the entrance of the city
19: 25 that you should crush fortified cities into **h** of
2Ch 31: 6 their God, and they piled them up in great **h**.
31: 7 and the **h** continued to grow until early autumn.
Isa 25: 2 You turn mighty cities into **h** of ruins. Cities with
37: 26 that you should crush fortified cities into **h** of
Jer 50: 26 Crush her walls and houses into **h** of rubble.
Da 2: 5 and your houses will be demolished into **h** of
3: 29 and their houses will be crushed into **h** of rubble.
Hos 12: 11 their altars are lined up like the **h** of stone along
Na 3: 3 the streets—dead bodies, **h** of bodies, everywhere.
Zep 1: 3 I will reduce the wicked to **h** of rubble, along with
2Pe 2: 6 the cities of Sodom and Gomorrah into **h** of ashes
Rev 16: 19 and cities around the world fell into **h** of rubble.

HEAR (324) [HEARD, HEARING, HEARS, HEARSAY, OVERHEARD]

Ge 21: 6 All who **h** about this will laugh with me.
45: 16 Pharaoh was very happy to **h** this and so were his
Ex 4: 11 or not speak, **h** or not **h**, see or not see?
15: 14 The nations will **h** and tremble; / anguish will grip
16: 9 and **h** his reply to your complaints.' "
18: 13 Moses sat as usual to **h** the people's complaints
19: 9 so the people themselves can **h** me as I speak to
19: 13 until they **h** one long blast from the ram's horn.
19: 19 and God thundered his reply for all to **h**.
22: 27 me for help, then I will **h**, for I am very merciful.
Nu 14: 13 "But what will the Egyptians think when they **h**
23: 18 "Rise up, Balak, and listen! / **H** me, son of Zippor.
Dt 2: 25 When they **h** reports about you, they will tremble
4: 6 When they **h** about these laws, they will exclaim,
4: 28 gods that neither see nor **h** nor eat nor smell.
4: 36 He let you **h** his voice from heaven so he could
5: 26 Can any living thing **h** the voice of the living God
6: 4 "**H**, O Israel! The LORD is our God, the LORD
9: 1 "**H**, O Israel! Today you are about to cross the
13: 11 Then all Israel will **h** about it and be afraid,
13: 12 "Suppose you **h** in one of the towns the LORD
17: 4 When you **h** about it, investigate the matter
17: 9 and the judge on duty will **h** the case and decide
17: 13 Then everyone will **h** about it and be afraid to act
19: 20 Those who **h** about it will be afraid to do such an
21: 21 and all Israel will **h** about it and be afraid.
29: 4 that understand, nor eyes that see, nor ears that **h**!
29: 19 Let none of those who **h** the warnings of this curse

30:12 and bring it down so we can **h** and obey it?'
30:13 the sea to bring it to us so we can **h** and obey it?'
31:13 who have not known these laws will **h** them
32: 1 and I will speak! / **H**, O earth, the words that I say!
33: 7 "O LORD, **h** the cry of Judah / and bring them
Jos 6: 5 When you **h** the priests give one long blast on the
7: 9 and all the other people living in the land **h** about
Jdg 5:16 to **h** the shepherds whistle for their flocks?
5:28 Why don't we **h** the sound of chariot wheels?'
14:13 "All right," they agreed, "let's **h** your riddle."
Ru 3:18 be patient, my daughter, until we **h** what happens.
1Sa 2:24 The reports I **h** among the LORD's people are not
4:13 Eli was waiting beside the road to **h** the news of
7:17 home at Ramah, and he would **h** cases there, too.
15:14 all the bleating of sheep and lowing of cattle I **h**?"
20:21 If you **h** me tell him, 'They're on this side,'
29: 6 with us, but the other Philistine rulers won't **h** of it.
2Sa 5:24 When you **h** a sound like marching feet in the tops
15: 3 It's too bad the king doesn't have anyone to **h** it.
15:10 "As soon as you **h** the trumpets," his message
19:35 and I cannot **h** the musicians as they play.
22:45 before me; / as soon as they **h** of me, they submit.
1Ki 7: 7 where Solomon sat to **h** legal matters.
8:28 **H** the cry and the prayer that your servant is
8:29 May you always **h** the prayers I make toward this
8:30 May you **h** the humble and earnest requests from
8:30 Yes, **h** us from heaven where you live, and when you **h**, forgive.
8:32 then **h** from heaven and judge between your
8:34 then **h** from heaven and forgive their sins
8:36 then **h** from heaven and forgive the sins of your
8:39 then **h** from heaven where you live, and forgive.
8:41 "And when foreigners **h** of you and come from
8:42 for they will **h** of you and of your mighty miracles
8:43 then **h** from heaven where you live, and grant what
8:45 then **h** their prayers from heaven and uphold their
8:49 then **h** their prayers from heaven where you live.
8:52 **H** and answer them whenever they cry out to you.
10:24 visit him and to **h** the wisdom God had given him.
12:12 and all the people returned to **h** Rehoboam's
18:41 a good meal! For I **h** a mighty rainstorm coming!"
22: 8 Jehoshaphat said. "Let's **h** what he has to say."
2Ki 7: 1 Elisha replied, "**H** this message from the LORD!
7: 6 army of Aram to **h** the clatter of speeding chariots
18:26 in Hebrew, for the people on the wall will **h**."
18:27 "My master wants everyone in Jerusalem to **h** this,
19:16 Listen to me, O LORD, and **h**! Open your eyes,
21:12 and Judah that the ears of those who **h** about it will
1Ch 14:15 When you **h** a sound like marching feet in the tops
2Ch 6:19 **H** the cry and the prayer that your servant is
6:20 May you always **h** the prayers I make toward this
6:21 May you **h** the humble and earnest requests from
6:21 Yes, **h** us from heaven where you live, and when you **h**, forgive.
6:23 then **h** from heaven and judge between your
6:25 then **h** from heaven and forgive their sins
6:27 then **h** from heaven and forgive the sins of your
6:30 then **h** from heaven where you live, and forgive.
6:32 "And when foreigners **h** of you and your mighty
6:33 then **h** from heaven where you live, and grant what
6:35 then **h** their prayers from heaven and uphold their
6:39 then **h** their prayers from heaven where you live.
7:14 I will **h** from heaven and will forgive their sins
9:23 visit him and to **h** the wisdom God had given him.
10:12 and all the people returned to **h** Rehoboam's
18: 7 Jehoshaphat said. "Let's **h** what he has to say."
20: 9 to you to save us, and you will **h** us and rescue us.'
Ne 1:11 O Lord, please **h** my prayer! Listen to the prayers
4: 4 Then I prayed, "**H** us, O our God, for we are being
4:20 When you **h** the blast of the trumpet, rush to
Est 1:18 will **h** what the queen did and will start talking to
Job 13:17 closely to what I am about to say. **H** me out.
22:27 You will pray to him, and he will **h** you, and you
31:13 if I have refused to **h** their complaints,
33:32 I want to **h** it, for I am anxious to see you justified.
34:34 people will tell me, and wise people will **h** me say,
39:20 a locust? Its majestic snorting is something to **h**!
Ps 4: 1 my distress. / Have mercy on me and **h** my prayer.
5: 1 O LORD, **h** me as I pray; / pay attention to my
17: 1 O LORD, **h** my plea for justice. / Listen to my cry
18:44 As soon as they **h** of me, they submit;
19:11 They are a warning to those who **h** them; / there is
20: 5 May we shout for joy when we **h** of your victory,
22: 2 Every night you **h** my voice, but I find no relief.
22:30 Our children will **h** about the wonders of the Lord.
22:31 They will **h** about everything he has done.
30:10 **H** me, LORD, and have mercy on me. / Help me,
35: 3 Let me **h** you say, / "I am your salvation!"
38: 9 know what I long for, Lord; / you **h** my every sigh.
38:14 I choose to **h** nothing, / and I make no reply.
39:12 **H** my prayer, O LORD! / Listen to my cries for
42: 7 I **h** the tumult of the raging seas / as your waves
44:16 All we **h** are the taunts of our mockers. / All we
55:19 is king forever, / will **h** me and will humble them.
61: 1 O God, listen to my cry! / **H** my prayer!
83: 2 Don't you **h** the tumult of your enemies?
84: 8 O LORD God Almighty, **h** my prayer. / Listen,
86: 1 Bend down, O LORD, and **h** my prayer;
86: 6 to my prayer, O LORD; / **h** my urgent cry.
88: 2 Now **h** my prayer; / listen to my cry.
89: 1 Young and old will **h** of your faithfulness.
89:15 Happy are those who **h** the joyful call to worship,
94: 4 **H** their arrogance! / How these evildoers boast!
102: 1 LORD, **h** my prayer! / Listen to my plea!
102:20 to **h** the groans of the prisoners, / to release those
115: 6 They cannot **h** with their ears, / or smell with their
119:149 In your faithful love, O LORD, **h** my cry;
130: 2 **H** my cry, O Lord. / Pay attention to my prayer.
135:17 They cannot **h** with their ears / or smell with their
138: 4 O LORD, / for all of them will **h** your words.
142: 6 **H** my cry, / for I am very low. / Rescue me from
143: 1 **H** my prayer, O LORD; / listen to my plea!
143: 8 Let me **h** of your unfailing love to me in the
Pr 8: 1 calls out! **H** as understanding raises her voice!
20:12 Ears to **h** and eyes to see—both are gifts from the
23:12 attune your ears to **h** words of knowledge.
Ecc 1: 8 No matter how much we **h**, we are not content.
7:21 you may **h** your servant laughing at you.
SS 2: 8 "Ah, I **h** him—my lover! Here he comes,
2:14 Let me see you; let me **h** your voice. For your
8:13 can listen to your voice. Let me **h** it, too!"
Isa 1: 2 **H**, O heavens! Listen, O earth! This is what the
6: 9 'You will **h** my words, but you will not
6:10 **h** with their ears, understand with their hearts,
13: 4 **H** the noise on the mountains! Listen, as the armies
21: 3 I grow faint when I **h** what God is planning;
24:16 **H** them singing praises to the Righteous One!
29:18 In that day deaf people will **h** words read from a
30:21 and you will **h** a voice say, "This is the way;
32: 3 and those who can **h** will listen to his voice.
34: 1 Let the world and everything in it **h** my words.
36:11 in Hebrew, for the people on the wall will **h**."
36:12 "My master wants everyone in Jerusalem to **h** this,
37:17 Listen to me, O LORD, and **h**! Open your eyes,
40: 3 I **h** the voice of someone shouting, "Make a
40:27 How can you say God refuses to **h** your case?
42:20 to act on it. You **h**, but you don't really listen."
51: 4 **H** me, Israel, for my law will be proclaimed,
58: 2 every day and seem delighted to **h** my laws.
59: 1 is not becoming deaf. He can **h** you when you call.
66: 5 **H** this message from the LORD, and tremble at
Jer 4:31 I **h** a great cry, like that of a woman giving birth to
5:21 but do not see, who have ears but do not **h**.
6:10 I speak? Their ears are closed, and they cannot **h**.
7:26 people have not listened to me or even tried to **h**.
8: 6 I listen to their conversations, and what do I **h**?
9:19 **H** the people of Jerusalem crying in despair,
10: 1 **H** the word of the LORD, O Israel!
10:22 **H** the terrifying roar of great armies as they roll
12:11 made it an empty wasteland; I **h** its mournful cry.
19: 3 that the ears of those who **h** about it will ring!
23:18 the LORD well enough to **h** what he is saying?
25: 4 but you have not listened or even tried to **h**.
38:25 My officials may **h** that I spoke to you. Then they
47: 3 **H** the clatter of hooves and the rumble of wheels
48:39 How it is broken! **H** the wailing! See the shame of
51:46 But do not panic when you **h** the first rumor of
51:54 **H** the cry of Babylon, the sound of great
Eze 12: 2 They could **h** me if they would listen, but they
20:47 **H** the word of the LORD! I will set you on fire,
25: 3 **H** the word of the Sovereign LORD! Because you
33: 4 Then if those who **h** the alarm refuse to take
33:30 Let's go **h** the prophet tell us what the LORD is
33:32 They **h** what you say, but they don't do it!
34: 7 you shepherds, **h** the word of the LORD:
34: 9 you shepherds, **h** the word of the LORD.
36: 1 O mountains of Israel, **h** the word of the LORD!
36: 4 of Israel, **h** the word of the Sovereign LORD.
36:37 I am ready to **h** Israel's prayers for these blessings,
Da 3: 5 When you **h** the sound of the horn, flute, zither,
3:10 and worship the gold statue when they **h** the sound
3:15 and worship the statue I have made when you **h** the
5:23 gods that neither see nor **h** nor know anything at
7:11 because I could **h** the little horn's boastful speech.
9:17 "O our God, **h** your servant's prayer! Listen as I
9:18 "O my God, listen to me and **h** my request.
9:19 "O Lord, **h**. O Lord, forgive. O Lord, listen
Hos 4: 1 **H** the word of the LORD, O people of Israel!
5: 1 "**H** this, you priests and all of Israel's leaders!
Joel 1: 2 **H** this, you leaders of the people! Everyone listen!
Am 6:10 the name of the LORD. He might **h** you!"
Mic 7: 7 God to save me, and my God will certainly **h** me.
Na 3: 2 **H** the crack of the whips as the chariots rush
3:19 All who **h** of your destruction will clap their hands
Zec 1:14 angel said to me, "Shout this message for all to **h**:
7:12 so they could not **h** the law or the messages that
10: 6 I am the LORD their God, who will **h** their cries.
11: 3 **H** the young lions roaring, for their thickets in the
Mt 3: 5 Valley went out to the wilderness to **h** him preach.
10:27 in your ears, shout from the housetops for all to **h**!
11: 5 the lame walk, the lepers are cured, the deaf **h**,
11:15 Anyone who is willing to **h** should listen
12:42 because she came from a distant land to **h** the
13: 9 Anyone who is willing to **h** should listen
13:13 They **h** what I say, but they don't really **h**,
13:14 of Isaiah, which says: / 'You will **h** my words,
13:15 people are hardened, / and their ears cannot **h**,
13:15 so their eyes cannot see, / and their ears cannot **h**,
13:16 because they see; and your ears, because they **h**.
13:17 longed to see and **h** what you have seen and heard,
13:19 those who **h** the Good News about the Kingdom
13:20 The rocky soil represents those who **h** the message
13:22 The thorny ground represents those who **h**
13:43 Anyone who is willing to **h** should listen
21:16 "Do you **h** what these children are saying?"
24:14 the whole world, so that all nations will **h** it;
27:13 "Don't you **h** their many charges against you?"
Mk 1: 5 traveled out into the wilderness to see and **h** John.
4: 9 "Anyone who is willing to **h** should listen
4:12 They **h** my words, / but they don't understand.
4:15 the hard path represents those who **h** the message,
4:16 The rocky soil represents those who **h** the message
4:18 The thorny ground represents those who **h**
4:20 But the good soil represents those who **h**
4:23 Anyone who is willing to **h** should listen
4:24 And be sure to pay attention to what you **h**.
7:14 Then Jesus called to the crowd to come and **h**.
7:35 Instantly the man could **h** perfectly and speak
8:18 can't you see? You have ears—can't you **h**?'
12:29 '**H**, O Israel! The Lord our God is the one and only
Lk 5:15 and vast crowds came to **h** him preach and to be
6:18 They had come to **h** him and to be healed,
7:22 the lame walk, the lepers are cured, the deaf **h**,
8: 4 that had gathered from many towns to **h** him:
8: 8 "Anyone who is willing to **h** should listen
8:10 but they don't really see; / they **h** what I say,
8:12 the hard path represents those who **h** the message,
8:13 The rocky soil represents those who **h** the message
8:14 The thorny ground represents those who **h**
8:15 good-hearted people who **h** God's message,
8:18 So be sure to pay attention to what you **h**. To those
8:21 and my brothers are all those who **h** the message of
9: 9 "so who is this man about whom I **h** such strange
10:24 longed to see and **h** what you have seen and heard,
11:28 "But even more blessed are all who **h** the word of
11:31 because she came from a distant land to **h** the
12: 3 will be shouted from the housetops for all to **h**!
14:35 Anyone who is willing to **h** should listen
16: 2 'What's this I **h** about your stealing from me?
21: 9 And when you **h** of wars and insurrections,
21:38 The crowds gathered early each morning to **h** him.
Jn 3: 8 Just as you can **h** the wind but can't tell where it
4:41 long enough for many of them to **h** his message
5:25 in fact it is here, when the dead will **h** my voice—
5:28 dead in their graves will **h** the voice of God's Son,
9:27 Didn't you listen? Why do you want to **h** it again?
9:31 but he is ready to **h** those who worship him and do
10: 3 and the sheep **h** his voice and come to him.
11:42 You always **h** me, but I said it out loud for the sake
Ac 2: 6 and they were bewildered to **h** their own languages
2: 8 and yet we **h** them speaking the languages of the
2:11 And we all **h** these people speaking in our own
2:33 to pour out upon us, just as you see and **h** today.
4:29 And now, O Lord, **h** their threats, and give your
9:14 And we **h** that he is authorized by the leading
10:33 waiting before God to **h** the message the Lord has
13: 7 to visit him, for he wanted to **h** the word of God.
13:27 though they **h** the prophets' words read every
13:44 turned out to **h** them preach the word of the Lord.
15: 7 so that they could **h** the Good News and believe.
17:32 others said, "We want to **h** more about this later."
21:22 For they will certainly **h** that you have come.
22: 9 with me saw the light but didn't **h** the voice.
22:14 and to see the Righteous One and **h** him speak.
23:35 "I will **h** your case myself when your accusers
25:22 "I'd like to **h** the man myself," Agrippa said.
28:22 But we want to **h** what you believe, for the only
28:26 and say to my people, / You will **h** my words,
28:27 people are hardened, / and their ears cannot **h**,
28:27 so their eyes cannot see, / and their ears cannot **h**,
Ro 10:14 And how can they **h** about him unless someone
11: 8 not see, / and closed their ears so they do not **h**."
1Co 11:18 I **h** that there are divisions among you when you
12:17 whole body were an eye—then how would you **h**?
14:23 and **h** everyone talking in an unknown language,
Eph 4:29 will be an encouragement to those who **h** them.
Php 1:27 I come and see you again or only **h** about you,
2Th 3:11 Yet we **h** that some of you are living idle lives,
1Ti 4:16 and God will save you and those who **h** you.
2Ti 2:14 are useless, and they can ruin those who **h** them.
4: 3 who will tell them whatever they want to **h**.
4:17 News in all its fullness for all the Gentiles to **h**.
Jas 5: 4 **H** the cries of the field workers whom you have
3Jn 1: 4 I could have no greater joy than to **h** that my
Rev 2: 7 "Anyone who is willing to **h** should listen to the
2:11 "Anyone who is willing to **h** should listen to the
2:17 "Anyone who is willing to **h** should listen to the
2:29 Anyone who is willing to **h** should listen to the
3: 6 Anyone who is willing to **h** should listen to the
3:13 Anyone who is willing to **h** should listen to the
3:20 If you **h** me calling and open the door, I will come
3:22 Anyone who is willing to **h** should listen to the
9:20 and wood—idols that neither see nor **h** nor walk!
13: 9 Anyone who is willing to **h** should listen

HEARD (550) [HEAR]

Ge 3: 8 Toward evening they **h** the LORD God walking
3:10 He replied, "I **h** you, so I hid. I was afraid
16:11 for the LORD has **h** about your misery.
18:20 "I have **h** that the people of Sodom and Gomorrah
21:17 Then God **h** the boy's cries, and the angel of God
21:17 God has **h** the boy's cries from the place where
21:26 "This is the first I've **h** of it," Abimelech said.
22:20 Soon after this, Abraham **h** that Milcah, his brother
24:30 and when he **h** her story, he rushed out to the
28: 6 Esau **h** that his father had blessed Jacob and sent
29:13 As soon as Laban **h** about Jacob's arrival,
29:33 "The LORD **h** that I was unloved and has given
30: 6 He has **h** my request and given me a son."
37:17 I **h** your brothers say they were going to Dothan."
39:15 When he **h** my loud cries, he ran and left his shirt
41:15 But I have **h** that you can interpret dreams, and that
42: 1 When Jacob **h** that there was grain available in
42: 2 I have **h** there is grain in Egypt. Go down and buy
42:21 We saw his terror and anguish and **h** his pleadings,
45: 2 His sobs could be **h** throughout the palace,
48: 2 When Jacob **h** that Joseph had arrived, he gathered
Ex 2:15 And sure enough, when Pharaoh **h** about it,
2:24 God **h** their cries and remembered his covenant
3: 6 When Moses **h** this, he hid his face in his hands

3: 7 I have **h** their cries for deliverance from their harsh
6: 5 You can be sure that I have **h** the groans of the
11: 6 Then a loud wail will be **h** throughout the land of
12:30 and loud wailing was **h** throughout the land of
16: 7 He has **h** your complaints, which are against the
16: 9 for he has **h** all your complaints against him.
16:12 "I have **h** the people's complaints. Now tell them,
18: 1 He had **h** about how the LORD had brought them
18: 9 Jethro was delighted when he **h** about all that the
20:18 When the people **h** the thunder and the loud blast
32:17 When Joshua **h** the noise of the people shouting
33: 4 When the people **h** these stern words, they went
Lev 10:20 And when Moses **h** this, he approved.
24:14 and tell all those who **h** him to lay their hands on
Nu 7:89 he **h** the voice speaking to him from between the
11: 1 and when the LORD **h** them, his anger blazed
11:10 Moses **h** all the families standing in front of their
11:18 'The LORD has **h** your whining and complaints:
12: 2 spoken through us, too?" But the LORD **h** them.
14:15 the nations that have **h** of your fame will say,
14:27 I have **h** everything the Israelites have been saying.
14:28 I live, I will do to you the very things I **h** you say.
16: 4 When Moses **h** what they were saying, he threw
16:34 All of the people of Israel fled as they **h** their
20:16 he **h** us and sent an angel who brought us out of
21: 1 **h** that the Israelites were approaching on the road
21: 3 The LORD **h** their request and gave them victory
22:36 When King Balak **h** that Balaam was on the way,
33:40 **h** that the people of Israel were approaching his
Dt 1:34 "When the LORD **h** your complaining,
4:12 You **h** his words but didn't see his form; there was
4:33 Has any nation ever **h** the voice of God speaking
5:23 But when you **h** the voice from the darkness,
5:24 and we have **h** his voice from the heart of the fire.
5:28 "The LORD **h** your request and said to me, 'I have
h what the people have said to you,
9: 2 You've **h** the saying, 'Who can stand up to the
26: 7 He **h** us and saw our hardship, toil, and oppression.
28:33 A foreign nation you have never **h** about will eat
Jos 2:10 For we have **h** how the LORD made a dry path
5: 1 **h** how the LORD had dried up the Jordan River
6:20 When the people **h** the sound of the horns,
9: 1 Now all the kings west of the Jordan **h** about what
9: 3 But when the people of Gibeon **h** what had
9: 9 We have **h** of the might of the LORD your God
9:10 We have also **h** what he did to the two Amorite
10: 1 **h** that Joshua had captured and completely
10: 2 and his people became very afraid when they **h** all
10:17 When Joshua **h** that they had been found,
11: 1 When King Jabin of Hazor **h** what had happened,
22:11 When the rest of Israel **h** they had built the altar at
22:30 and the high officials **h** this from the tribes of
24:27 "This stone has **h** everything the LORD said to
Jdg 7:15 When Gideon **h** the dream and its interpretation,
8: 3 When the men of Ephraim **h** Gideon's answer,
9: 7 When Jotham **h** about this, he climbed to the top of
9:30 the city, **h** what Gaal was saying, he was furious.
9:42 the fields to battle. When Abimelech **h** about it,
9:46 in the tower of Shechem **h** what had happened,
17: 2 "I **h** you curse the thief who stole eleven hundred
Ru 1: 6 Then Naomi **h** in Moab that the LORD had
2:11 I have **h** how you left your father and mother
1Sa 4:19 When she **h** that the Ark of God had been captured
7: 7 When the Philistine rulers **h** that all Israel had
9:16 on my people in mercy and have **h** their cry."
10:11 When his friends **h** about it, they exclaimed,
14:27 But Jonathan had not **h** his father's command,
15:11 so deeply moved when he **h** this that he cried out
17:11 When Saul and the Israelites **h** this, they were
17:25 And have you **h** about the huge reward the king
17:28 Eliab, **h** David talking to the men, he was angry.
18:20 and Saul was delighted when he **h** about it.
19:21 When Saul **h** what had happened, he sent other
21:12 David **h** these comments and was afraid of what
22: 7 of Benjamin!" Saul shouted when he **h** the news.
23:10 I have **h** that Saul is planning to come and destroy
23:11 And will Saul actually come as I have **h**?
23:25 When David **h** that Saul and his men were
25: 4 When David **h** that Nabal was shearing his sheep,
25:39 When David **h** that Nabal was dead, he said,
31:11 But when the people of Jabesh-gilead **h** what the
2Sa 1:11 tore their clothes in sorrow when they **h** the news.
2: 4 When David **h** that the men of Jabesh-gilead had
3:28 When David **h** about it, he declared, "I vow by the
4: 1 When Ishbosheth **h** about Abner's death at
5:17 When the Philistines **h** that David had been
7:22 We have never even **h** of another god like you!
8: 9 When King Toi of Hamath **h** that David had
10: 5 When David **h** what had happened, he sent
10: 7 When David **h** about this, he sent Joab
10:17 When David **h** what was happening, he mobilized
11:10 When David **h** what Uriah had done, he summoned
11:26 When Bathsheba **h** that her husband was dead,
13:21 When King David **h** what had happened, he was
18: 5 And all the troops **h** the king give this order to his
18:12 "We all **h** the king say to you and Abishai
19: 2 As the troops **h** of the king's deep grief for his son,
19:11 For I have **h** that all Israel is ready, and only you
22: 7 He **h** me from his sanctuary; / my cry reached his
1Ki 1:41 Adonijah and his guests **h** the celebrating
1:41 When Joab **h** the sound of trumpets, he asked,
2:28 When Joab **h** about Adonijah's death, he ran to the
2:41 Solomon **h** that Shimei had left Jerusalem and had
9: 3 to him, "I have **h** your prayer and your request.
10: 1 When the queen of Sheba **h** of Solomon's
10: 6 "Everything I **h** in my country about your
10: 7 Truly I had not **h** the half of it! Your wisdom
12: 2 When Jeroboam son of Nebat **h** of Solomon's
13:26 When the old prophet **h** the report, he said, "It is
14: 6 So when Ahijah **h** her footsteps at the door,
15:21 As soon as Baasha of Israel **h** what was happening,
16:16 **h** that Zimri had assassinated the king, they chose
17:22 The LORD **h** Elijah's prayer, and the life of the
19:13 When Elijah **h** it, he wrapped his face in his cloak
20:31 we have **h** that the kings of Israel are very
21:15 When Jezebel **h** the news, she said to Ahab,
21:27 When Ahab **h** this message, he tore his clothing,
2Ki 3:21 when the people of Moab **h** about the three armies
5: 8 the man of God, **h** about the king's reaction,
6:30 When the king **h** this, he tore his clothes in despair.
8: 8 When the king **h** the news, he said to Hazael,
9:30 the queen mother, **h** that Jehu had come to Jezreel,
11:13 When Athaliah **h** all the noise made by the guards
13: 4 the LORD's help, and the LORD **h** his prayer.
19: 1 When King Hezekiah **h** their report, he tore his
19: 4 But perhaps the LORD your God has **h** the
19:20 I have **h** your prayer about King Sennacherib of
19:25 'But have you not **h**? / It was I, the LORD,
19:28 arrogance against me, / which I have **h** for myself,
20: 2 When Hezekiah **h** this, he turned his face to the
20: 5 says: I have **h** your prayer and seen your tears.
20:12 for he had **h** that Hezekiah had been very sick.
22:11 When the king **h** what was written in the Book of
22:18 says concerning the message you have just **h**:
22:19 LORD when you **h** what I said against this city
22:19 So I have indeed **h** you, says the LORD.
1Ch 10:11 But when the people of Jabesh-gilead **h** what the
14: 8 When the Philistines **h** that David had been
17:20 We have never even **h** of another god like you!
18: 9 When King Toi of Hamath **h** that David had
19: 5 When David **h** what had happened, he sent
19: 8 When David **h** about this, he sent Joab and all his
19:17 When David **h** what was happening, he mobilized
2Ch 7:12 "I have **h** your prayer and have chosen this
9: 1 When the queen of Sheba **h** of Solomon's
9: 5 "Everything I **h** in my country about your
9: 6 with my own eyes. Truly I had not **h** the half of it!
10: 2 When Jeroboam son of Nebat **h** of Solomon's
15: 8 When Asa **h** this message from Azariah the
16: 5 As soon as Baasha of Israel **h** what was happening,
20:29 When the surrounding kingdoms **h** that the
23:12 When Athaliah **h** the noise of the people running
30:27 and God **h** them from his holy dwelling in heaven.
34:19 When the king **h** what was written in the law,
34:26 says concerning the message you have just **h**:
34:27 and humbled yourself before God when you **h**
34:27 So I have indeed **h** you, says the LORD.
Ezr 3:13 loud commotion that could be **h** far in the distance.
4: 1 and Benjamin **h** that the exiles were rebuilding a
8:23 God would take care of us, and he **h** our prayer.
9: 3 When I **h** this, I tore my clothing, pulled hair from
Ne 1: 4 When I **h** this, I sat down and wept. In fact,
2:10 and Tobiah the Ammonite official **h** of my arrival,
2:19 Tobiah, and Geshem the Arab **h** of our plan,
4: 7 and Ashdodites **h** that the work was going ahead
4:15 When our enemies **h** that we knew of their plans
5: 6 When I **h** their complaints, I was very angry.
6:16 our enemies and the surrounding nations **h** about it,
8:12 because they had **h** God's words and understood
9: 9 and you **h** their cries from beside the Red Sea.
9:27 they cried to you, and you **h** them from heaven.
12:43 and the joy of the people of Jerusalem could be **h**
Est 2:22 But Mordecai **h** about the plot and passed the
Job 2:11 When they **h** of the tragedy he had suffered,
15:18 men who have **h** the same thing from their fathers,
16: 2 "I have **h** all this before. What miserable
28:22 'We have **h** a rumor of where wisdom can be
29:11 "All who **h** of me praised me. All who saw me
33: 8 said it in my hearing. I have **h** your very words.
42: 5 "I had **h** about you before, but now I have seen
Ps 6: 8 you who do evil, / for the LORD has **h** my crying.
6: 9 The LORD has **h** my plea; / the LORD will
12: 5 the helpless, / and I have **h** the groans of the poor.
18: 6 He **h** me from his sanctuary; / my cry reached his
22: 5 You **h** their cries for help and saved them.
27: 8 My heart has **h** you say, "Come and talk with
28: 6 the LORD! / For he has **h** my cry for mercy.
31:13 I have **h** the many rumors about me, / and I am
31:22 But you **h** my cry for mercy / and answered my
34: 6 out to the LORD in my suffering, and he **h** me.
40: 1 to help me, / and he turned to me and **h** my cry.
44: 1 O God, we have **h** it with our own ears—
48: 8 We had **h** of the city's glory, / but now we have
61: 5 For you have **h** my vows, O God. / You have given
62:11 has spoken plainly, / and I have **h** it many times:
66:14 yes, the sacred vows you **h** me make / when I was
78: 3 stories we have **h** and know, / stories our ancestors
78:21 When the LORD **h** them, he was angry. / The fire
78:59 When God **h** them, he was very angry, / and he
81: 5 to set us free. / I **h** an unknown voice that said,
92:11 with my own ears I have **h** the defeat of my wicked
97: 8 Jerusalem has **h** and rejoiced, / and all the cities of
132: 6 We **h** that the Ark was in Ephrathah; / then we
SS 5: 2 awakened in a dream. I **h** the voice of my lover.
Isa 5: 3 you have **h** the case; you be the judges.
5: 7 but instead he **h** cries of oppression.
5: 9 With my own ears I **h** him say, "Many beautiful
6: 8 Then I **h** the Lord asking, "Whom should I send as
15: 4 cities of Heshbon and Elealeh will be **h** far away,
15: 5 Their crying can be **h** all along the road to
16: 6 the proud land we have **h** so much about?
16:10 The happy singing in the vineyards will be **h** no
23: 1 it is gone! The rumors you **h** in Cyprus are all true.
24: 8 the happy cries of celebration will be **h** no more.
30:11 We have **h** more than enough about your 'Holy
30:30 And the LORD will make his majestic voice **h**.
37: 1 When King Hezekiah **h** their report, he tore his
37: 4 But perhaps the LORD your God has **h** the
37:26 'But have you not **h**? / It was I, the LORD,
37:29 arrogance against me, / which I have **h** for myself,
38: 2 When Hezekiah **h** this, he turned his face to the
38: 5 says: I have **h** your prayer and seen your tears.
39: 1 He had **h** that Hezekiah had been very sick
40:21 Have you never **h** or understood? Are you deaf to
40:28 Have you never **h** or understood? Don't you know
48: 6 You have **h** my predictions and seen them fulfilled,
48: 6 not mentioned before, secrets you have not yet **h**.
52:15 they will understand what they had not **h** about.
64: 4 no ear has **h** and no eye has seen a God like you,
65:19 sound of weeping and crying will be **h** no more.
66: 8 has ever seen or **h** of anything as strange as this?
66:19 and to all the lands beyond the sea that have not **h**
Jer 2:10 See if anyone has ever **h** of anything as strange as
3:21 Voices are **h** high on the windswept mountains,
4:19 For I have **h** the blast of enemy trumpets
6:24 We have **h** reports about the enemy, and we are
7:28 from among them; it is no longer **h** on their lips.
7:34 and brides will no longer be **h** in the towns of
8:16 The snorting of the enemies' warhorses can be **h**
8:19 of my people; it can be **h** all across the land.
9:10 the lowing of cattle is **h** no more; the birds
14:14 and revelations they have never seen or **h**.
16: 9 of bridegrooms and brides will no longer be **h**.
18:13 LORD said, "Has anyone ever **h** of such a thing,
18:22 Let screaming be **h** from their homes as warriors
20: 1 of the LORD, **h** what Jeremiah was saying.
20:10 I have **h** the many rumors about me. They call me
23:25 "I have **h** these prophets say, 'Listen to the dream
25:10 of bridegrooms and brides will no longer be **h**.
26:10 When the officials of Judah **h** what was happening,
26:11 "You have **h** with your own ears what a traitor he
26:15 LORD sent me to speak every word you have **h**."
26:21 army officers and officials **h** what he was saying,
26:21 But Uriah **h** about the plot and escaped to Egypt.
30: 5 I have **h** the people crying; there is only fear
31:15 "A cry of anguish is **h** in Ramah—mourning
31:18 I have **h** Israel saying, 'You disciplined me
32: 8 Then I knew for sure that the message I had **h** was
33:10 Judah's other towns, there will be **h** once more
33:11 voices of bridegrooms and brides will be **h** again,
33:24 "Have you **h** what people are saying?—
36:11 and grandson of Shaphan **h** the messages from the
36:16 "We must tell the king what we have **h**,"
36:24 any signs of fear or repentance at what they **h**.
37: 5 When the Babylonian army **h** about it,
38: 1 and Pashhur son of Malkijah **h** what Jeremiah had
38: 7 palace official, **h** that Jeremiah was in the cistern.
40: 7 **h** that the king of Babylon had appointed Gedaliah
40:11 and the other nearby countries **h** that the king of
41: 4 before anyone had **h** about Gedaliah's murder,
41:11 and the rest of the guerrilla leaders **h** what Ishmael
41:18 do when they **h** that Ishmael had killed Gedaliah,
46:12 The nations have **h** of your shame. The earth is
48:29 We have **h** of the pride of Moab, for it is very
48:34 their awful cries of terror can be **h** from Heshbon
49:14 I have **h** a message from the LORD that an
49:21 and its cry of despair will be **h** all the way to the
49:23 for they have **h** the news of their destruction.
49:29 taken away. Everywhere shouts of panic will be **h**:
50:22 "Let the battle cry be **h** in the land, a shout of
50:46 and her cry of despair will be **h** around the world.
51:52 The groans of her wounded people will be **h**
La 1:21 "Others **h** my groans, but no one turned to comfort
1:21 When my enemies **h** of my troubles, they were
3:56 and you **h** me! You listened to my pleading; you **h**
my weeping!
3:61 LORD, you have **h** the vile names they call me.
Eze 1:28 the dust, and I **h** someone's voice speaking to me.
3:12 me up, and I **h** a loud rumbling sound behind me.
9: 5 Then I **h** the LORD say to the other men,
10: 5 and could be **h** clearly in the outer courtyard.
10:13 I **h** someone refer to the wheels as "the whirling
19: 4 Then the nations **h** about him, / and he was trapped
19: 7 in the land trembled in fear / when they **h** him roar.
19: 9 in captivity, / so his voice could never again be **h**
21: 7 'I groan because of the terrifying news I have **h**.
26:13 No more will the sound of harps be **h** among your
33: 5 They **h** the warning but wouldn't listen,
35:12 have **h** every contemptuous word you spoke
35:13 you boasted proudly against me, and I have **h** it all!
43: 6 And I **h** someone speaking to me from within the
Da 2:12 The king was furious when he **h** this, and he sent
5:10 But when the queen mother **h** what was happening,
5:14 I have **h** that you have the spirit of the gods within
7: 5 And I **h** a voice saying to it, "Get up!
8:13 Then I **h** two of the holy ones talking to each other.
8:16 And I **h** a human voice calling out from the Ulai
10: 9 When I **h** him speak, I fainted and lay there with
10:12 your God, your request has been **h** in heaven.
12: 8 I **h** what he said, but I did not understand what he
Am 1: 2 This is his report of what he saw and **h**:
7:10 the priest of Bethel, **h** what Amos was saying,
Ob 1: 1 We have **h** a message from the LORD that an
Jnh 1:10 The sailors were terrified when they **h** this. "Oh,
2: 2 the world of the dead, and LORD, you **h** me!
3: 6 When the king of Nineveh **h** what Jonah was
Na 2:13 will the voices of your proud messengers be **h**."
Hab 3: 2 I have **h** all about you, LORD, and I am filled
3:16 I trembled inside when I **h** all this; my lips
Zep 2: 8 "I have **h** the taunts of the people of Moab
Zec 8: 9 You have **h** what the prophets have been saying

8:23 with you, for we have **h** that God is with you.’ ”
Mt 2:18 “A cry of anguish is **h** in Ramah— / weeping
4:12 When Jesus **h** that John had been arrested, he left
5:21 “You have **h** that the law of Moses says, ‘Do not
5:27 “You have **h** that the law of Moses says, ‘Do not
5:31 “You have **h** that the law of Moses says, ‘A man
5:33 “Again, you have **h** that the law of Moses says,
5:38 “You have **h** that the law of Moses says, ‘If an eye
5:43 “You have **h** that the law of Moses says,
8:10 When Jesus **h** this, he was amazed. Turning to the
9:12 When he **h** this, Jesus replied, “Healthy people
9:23 noticed the noisy crowds and **h** the funeral music.
11:2 **h** about all the things the Messiah was doing.
11:4 and tell him about what you have **h** and seen—
12:24 But when the Pharisees **h** about the miracle,
13:17 longed to see and hear what you have seen and **h**,
14:1 When Herod Antipas **h** about Jesus,
14:13 As soon as Jesus **h** the news, he went off by
14:13 But the crowds **h** where he was headed
19:22 But when the young man **h** this, he went sadly
20:24 When the ten other disciples **h** what James
20:30 When they **h** that Jesus was coming that way,
21:15 and **h** even the little children in the Temple
21:45 When the leading priests and Pharisees **h** Jesus,
22:33 When the crowds **h** him, they were impressed with
22:34 But when the Pharisees **h** that he had silenced the
26:65 other witnesses? You have all **h** his blasphemy.
Mk 2:17 When Jesus **h** this, he told them, “Healthy people
3:21 When his family **h** what was happening, they tried
5:27 She had **h** about Jesus, so she came up behind him
6:2 and many who **h** him were astonished.
6:14 Herod Antipas, the king, soon **h** about Jesus,
6:16 When Herod **h** about Jesus he said, “John, the man
6:29 When John’s disciples **h** what had happened,
7:25 She had **h** about Jesus, and now she came and fell
8:11 When the Pharisees **h** that Jesus had arrived,
8:12 When he **h** this, he sighed deeply and said,
10:47 When Bartimaeus **h** that Jesus from Nazareth was
10:49 When Jesus **h** him, he stopped and said, “Tell him
11:14 your fruit again!” And the disciples **h** him say it.
11:18 and teachers of religious law **h** what Jesus had
14:11 The leading priests were delighted when they **h**
14:58 “We **h** him say, ‘I will destroy this Temple made
14:64 You have all **h** his blasphemy. What is your
Lk 1:13 For God has **h** your prayer, and your wife,
1:44 my baby jumped for joy the instant I **h** your voice!
1:66 Everyone who **h** about it reflected on these events
2:18 All who **h** the shepherds’ story were astonished,
2:47 And all who **h** him were amazed at his
4:28 When they **h** this, the people in the synagogue
7:3 When the officer **h** about Jesus, he sent some
7:9 When Jesus **h** this, he was amazed. Turning to the
7:22 to John and tell him what you have seen and **h**—
7:29 When they **h** this, all the people,
7:37 A certain immoral woman **h** he was there
8:47 The whole crowd **h** her explain why she had
8:50 But when Jesus **h** what had happened, he said to
9:54 When James and John **h** about it, they said to
10:24 longed to see and hear what you have seen and **h**,
12:3 Whatever you have said in the dark will be **h** in the
15:25 he **h** music and dancing in the house,
18:23 But when the man **h** this, he became sad
18:26 Those who **h** this said, “Then who in the world
18:36 When he **h** the noise of a crowd going past,
18:40 When Jesus **h** him, he stopped and ordered that the
20:19 of religious law and the leading priests **h** this story,
22:71 they shouted. “We ourselves **h** him say it.”
23:8 because he had **h** about him and had been hoping
24:18 **h** about all the things that have happened there the
Jn 1:40 was one of these men who had **h** what John said
3:32 He tells what he has seen and **h**, but how few
4:1 Jesus learned that the Pharisees had **h**, “Jesus is
4:42 we believe because we have **h** him ourselves,
4:47 When he **h** that Jesus had come from Judea
5:37 You have never **h** his voice or seen him face to
7:15 The Jewish leaders were surprised when they **h**
7:32 When the Pharisees **h** that the crowds were
7:40 When the crowds **h** him say this, some of them
7:46 “We have never **h** anyone talk like this!”
8:9 When the accusers **h** this, they slipped away one
8:26 For I say only what I have **h** from the one who sent
8:30 Then many who **h** him say these things believed in
8:40 I told you the truth I **h** from God, but you are
9:35 When Jesus **h** what had happened, he found the
9:40 The Pharisees who were standing there **h** him
10:6 Those who **h** Jesus use this illustration didn’t
11:4 But when Jesus **h** about it he said,
12:9 When all the people **h** of Jesus’ arrival,
12:18 because they had **h** about this mighty miracle.
12:29 When the crowd **h** the voice, some thought it was
16:13 his own ideas; he will be telling you what he has **h**.
18:20 I have been **h** by people everywhere, and I teach
18:21 Ask those who **h** me. They know what I said.”
19:8 When Pilate **h** this, he was more frightened than
21:7 When Simon Peter **h** that it was the Lord, he put
Ac 2:6 When they **h** this sound, they came running to see
3:9 people saw him walking and **h** him praising God.
4:4 But many of the people who **h** their message
4:20 about the wonderful things we have seen and **h**.”
5:5 As soon as Ananias **h** these words, he fell to the
5:5 and died. Everyone who **h** about it was terrified.
5:11 and all others who **h** what had happened.
5:24 of the Temple guard and the leading priests **h** this,
6:11 saying, “We **h** him blaspheme Moses, and even
6:14 We have **h** him say that this Jesus of Nazareth will
7:12 Jacob **h** that there was still grain in Egypt, so he
7:29 When Moses **h** that, he fled the country and lived
7:34 I have **h** their cries. So I have come to rescue them.
8:14 When the apostles back in Jerusalem **h** that the
8:30 and **h** the man reading from the prophet Isaiah;
9:4 He fell to the ground and **h** a voice saying to him,
9:7 for they **h** the sound of someone’s voice, but they
9:13 “I’ve **h** about the terrible things this man has done
9:21 All who **h** him were amazed. “Isn’t this the same
9:30 When the believers **h** about it, however, they took
9:38 But they had **h** that Peter was nearby at Lydda,
10:31 He told me, ‘Cornelius, your prayers have been **h**,
10:36 I’m sure you have **h** about the Good News for the
10:44 the Holy Spirit fell upon all who had **h** the
10:46 for they **h** them speaking in tongues and praising
11:7 And I **h** a voice say, ‘Get up, Peter; kill and eat
11:18 When the others **h** this, all their objections were
11:22 When the church at Jerusalem **h** what had
13:48 When the Gentiles **h** this, they were very glad
14:14 when Barnabas and Paul **h** what was happening,
17:32 When they **h** Paul speak of the resurrection of a
18:26 and Aquila **h** him preaching boldly in the
19:2 We haven’t even **h** that there is a Holy Spirit.”
19:5 As soon as they **h** this, they were baptized in the
19:10 both Jews and Greeks—**h** the Lord’s message.
19:26 As you have seen and **h**, this man Paul has
21:12 When we **h** this, we who were traveling with him,
22:2 When they **h** him speaking in their own language,
22:7 I fell to the ground and **h** a voice saying to me,
22:15 telling the whole world what you have seen and **h**.
22:29 withdrew when they **h** he was a Roman citizen,
23:16 But Paul’s nephew **h** of their plan and went to the
26:14 and I **h** a voice saying to me in Aramaic, ‘Saul,
28:15 The believers in Rome had **h** we were coming,
28:21 They replied, “We have **h** nothing against you.
Ro 10:14 believe in him if they have never **h** about him?
10:18 Have they actually **h** the message? Yes, they have:
15:20 News where the name of Christ has never been **h**,
15:21 and those who have never **h** of him will
1Co 2:9 when they say, / “No eye has seen, no ear has **h**,
9:7 And have you ever **h** of a farmer who harvests his
2Co 6:2 For God says, / “At just the right time, I **h** you.
12:4 and **h** things so astounding that they cannot be
Gal 3:2 after you believed the message you **h** about Christ.
3:5 because you believe the message you **h** about
Eph 1:13 And now you also have **h** the truth, the Good News
1:15 Ever since I first **h** of your strong faith in the Lord
4:21 Since you have **h** all about him and have learned
Php 1:5 about Christ from the time you first **h** it until now.
2:26 and he was very distressed that you **h** he was ill.
4:9 learned from me and **h** from me and saw me doing,
Col 1:4 for we have **h** that you trust in Christ Jesus and that
1:5 as you have been ever since you first **h** the truth of
1:6 just as it changed yours that very first day you **h**
1:9 praying for you ever since we first **h** about you.
1:23 you received when you **h** the Good News.
2Ti 2:2 You have **h** me teach many things that have been
Heb 2:1 must listen very carefully to the truth we have **h**,
2:3 It was passed on to us by those who **h** him speak,
3:16 against God, even though they **h** his voice?
4:6 But those who formerly **h** the Good News failed to
5:7 And God **h** his prayers because of his reverence for
12:7 Whoever **h** of a child who was never disciplined?
12:19 For they **h** an awesome trumpet blast and a voice
Jas 1:25 if you do what it says and don’t forget what you **h**,
1Pe 3:7 treat her as you should, your prayers will not be **h**.
2Pe 1:18 We ourselves **h** the voice when we were there with
2:8 by the wickedness he saw and **h** day after day.
1Jn 1:1 existed from the beginning is the one we have **h**
1:3 about what we ourselves have actually seen and **h**,
2:7 one another—is the same message you **h** before.
2:18 You have **h** that the Antichrist is coming,
3:11 This is the message we have **h** from the beginning:
4:3 You have **h** that he is going to come into the
2Jn 1:6 love one another, just as you **h** from the beginning.
Rev 1:10 Suddenly, I **h** a loud voice behind me, a voice that
3:3 Go back to what you **h** and believed at first;
4:1 and the same voice I had **h** before spoke to me
5:11 and I **h** the singing of thousands and millions of
5:13 And then I **h** every creature in heaven and on earth
6:3 I **h** the second living being say, “Come!”
6:5 third seal, I **h** the third living being say, “Come!”
6:7 I **h** the fourth living being say, “Come!”
7:4 And I **h** how many were marked with the seal of
8:13 And I **h** a single eagle crying loudly as it flew
9:13 and I **h** a voice speaking from the four horns of the
9:16 I **h** an announcement of how many there were.
12:10 Then I **h** a loud voice shouting across the heavens,
14:2 And I **h** a sound from heaven like the roaring of a
14:13 And I **h** a voice from heaven saying, “Write this
16:1 Then I **h** a mighty voice shouting from the Temple
16:5 And I **h** the angel who had authority over all water
16:7 And I **h** a voice from the altar saying, “Yes,
18:4 Then I **h** another voice calling from heaven,
18:22 Never again will the sound of music be **h** there—
19:1 I **h** the sound of a vast crowd in heaven shouting,
19:6 Then I **h** again what sounded like the shout of a
21:3 I **h** a loud shout from the throne, saying, “Look,
22:8 John, am the one who saw and **h** all these things.
22:8 And when I saw and **h** these things, I fell down to

HEARING (19) [HEAR]

Ge 39:19 After **h** his wife’s story, Potiphar was furious!
Jos 2:11 No one has the courage to fight after **h** such things.
1Sa 1:13 Seeing her lips moving but **h** no sound, he thought
2:23 “I have been **h** reports from the people about the
17:27 “What you have been **h** is true. That is the reward
Job 23:6 me in his greatness? No, he would give me a fair **h**.
33:8 “You have said it in my **h**. I have heard your very
Da 4:19 Upon **h** this, Daniel (also known as Belteshazzar)
6:14 **H** this, the king was very angry with himself for
Am 8:11 or water but of **h** the words of the LORD.
Zec 1:12 Upon **h** this, the angel of the LORD prayed this
7:11 and put their fingers in their ears to keep from **h**.
Lk 14:15 **H** this, a man sitting at the table with Jesus
Jn 7:51 it legal to convict a man before he is given a **h**?”
11:41 to heaven and said, “Father, thank you for **h** me.
Ac 21:20 After **h** this, they praised God. But then they said,
24:22 adjourned the **h** and said, “Wait until Lysias,
26:2 that you are the one **h** my defense against all these
Phm 1:5 because I keep **h** of your trust in the Lord Jesus

HEARKEN, HEARKENED, HEARKENETH, HEARKENING [KJV] See AGREED, CONSENT, HEAR, HEEDED, LISTEN, LISTENED

HEARS (28) [HEAR]

Nu 24:4 who **h** the words of God, / who sees a vision from
24:16 who **h** the words of God, / who has knowledge
30:4 and her father **h** of the vow or pledge but says
30:5 her fulfill the vow or pledge on the day he **h** of it,
30:7 and raises no objections on the day he **h** of it,
30:8 her vow or impulsive pledge on the day he **h** of it,
30:11 If her husband **h** of it and does nothing to stop her,
30:12 husband refuses to accept it on the day he **h** of it,
30:14 But if he says nothing on the day he **h** of it, then he
1Sa 16:2 can I do that? If Saul **h** about it, he will kill me.”
Ne 6:6 “Geshem tells me that everywhere he goes he **h**
Job 12:11 tastes good food, so the ear tests the words it **h**.
19:7 “I cry out for help, but no one **h** me. I protest,
34:3 tastes good food, the ear tests the words it **h**.’
34:28 God’s attention. Yes, he **h** the cries of the needy.
Ps 34:17 The LORD **h** his people when they call to him for
55:17 aloud in my distress, / and the LORD **h** my voice.
69:33 For the LORD **h** the cries of his needy ones;
116:1 I love the LORD because he **h** / and answers my
145:19 he **h** their cries for help and rescues them.
Pr 15:29 the wicked, but he **h** the prayers of the righteous.
Isa 23:5 When Egypt **h** the news about Tyre, there will be
Mt 7:26 But anyone who **h** my teaching and ignores it is
28:14 If the governor **h** about it, we’ll stand up for you
Jn 6:45 Everyone who **h** and learns from the Father comes
12:47 If anyone **h** me and doesn’t obey me, I am not his
Rev 22:17 “Come.” Let each one who **h** them say, “Come.”
22:18 And I solemnly declare to everyone who **h** the

HEARSAY (1) [HEAR]

Isa 11:3 never judge by appearance, false evidence, or **h**.

HEART (316) [BROKENHEARTED, EVIL-HEARTED, GOOD-HEARTED, HARD-HEARTED, HEART’S, HEARTBROKEN, HEARTFELT, HEARTLESS, HEARTS, HEARTS’, TENDERHEARTED, WHOLEHEARTED, WHOLEHEARTEDLY]

Ge 6:6 was sorry he had ever made them. It broke his **h**.
Ex 2:6 the baby boy. His helpless cries touched her **h**.
3:20 and strike at the **h** of Egypt with all kinds of
7:13 Pharaoh’s **h**, however, remained hard
7:22 So Pharaoh’s **h** remained hard and stubborn.
8:15 saw that the frogs were gone, he hardened his **h**.
8:19 But Pharaoh’s **h** remained hard and stubborn.
8:22 and that I have power even in the **h** of your land.
8:32 But Pharaoh hardened his **h** again and refused to
9:7 he found it to be true, his **h** remained stubborn.
10:27 So the LORD hardened Pharaoh’s **h** once more,
11:10 the LORD hardened his **h** so he wouldn’t let the
14:4 And once again I will harden Pharaoh’s **h**, and he
28:29 **h** when he goes into the presence of the LORD in
28:30 to be carried over Aaron’s **h** when he goes into the
Lev 19:17 “Do not nurse hatred in your **h** for any of your
Dt 4:29 And if you search for him with all your **h** and soul,
5:4 The LORD spoke to you face to face from the **h**
5:22 a loud voice to all of you from the **h** of the fire,
5:24 and we have heard his voice from the **h** of the fire.
5:26 the voice of the living God from the **h** of the fire
6:5 must love the LORD your God with all your **h**,
10:4 **h** of the fire on the mountain as you were
10:12 to love and worship him with all your **h** and soul,
11:13 if you love the LORD your God with all your **h**
11:16 “But do not let your **h** turn away from the LORD
13:3 is testing you to see if you love him with all your **h**
20:3 you go out to fight today! Do not lose **h** or panic.
28:32 Your **h** will break as you long for them,
28:65 And the LORD will cause your **h** to tremble,
30:6 “The LORD your God will cleanse your **h**
30:6 so that you will love him with all your **h** and soul,
30:10 if you turn to the LORD your God with all your **h**
30:14 it is on your lips and in your **h** so that you can obey
30:17 But if your **h** turns away and you refuse to listen,
32:46 “Take to **h** all the words I have given you today.
Jos 5:1 they lost **h** and were paralyzed with fear.
14:7 I returned and gave from my **h** a good report,
22:5 and serve him with all your **h** and all your soul.”
Jdg 5:9 My **h** goes out to Israel’s leaders, / and to those
11:35 “My daughter!” he cried out. “My **h** is breaking!
1Sa 1:15 and I was pouring out my **h** to the LORD.
2:1 “My **h** rejoices in the LORD! / Oh,
4:13 for his **h** trembled for the safety of the Ark of God.

10: 9 and started to leave, God changed his **h**,
12:20 now that you worship the LORD with all your **h**
13:14 the LORD has sought out a man after his own **h**.
2Sa 3:21 be able to rule over everything your **h** desires."
17:10 though they have the **h** of a lion, will be paralyzed
18:14 and plunged them into Absalom's **h** as he dangled
1Ki 2: 4 and follow me faithfully with all their **h** and soul,
8:39 they deserve, for you alone know the human **h**.
8:48 Then if they turn to you with their whole **h**
11: 3 sure enough, they led his **h** away from the LORD.
11: 4 they turned his **h** to worship their gods instead of
11: 9 for his **h** had turned away from the LORD,
11:37 and you will rule over all that your **h** desires.
14: 8 my commands and followed me with all his **h**
15: 3 and his **h** was not right with the LORD his God, as the **h** of his ancestor David had been.
2Ki 9:24 The arrow pierced his **h**, and he sank down dead in
10:31 of the LORD, the God of Israel, with all his **h**.
23: 3 regulations, and laws with all his **h** and soul.
23:25 who turned to the LORD with all his **h** and soul
1Ch 22:13 and courageous; do not be afraid or lose **h**!
22:19 Now seek the LORD your God with all your **h**.
28: 9 Worship and serve him with your whole **h**
28: 9 For the LORD sees every **h** and understands
2Ch 6:30 they deserve, for you alone know the human **h**.
6:38 Then if they turn to you with their whole **h**
7:16 My eyes and my **h** will always be here.
12: 7 When the LORD saw their change of **h**, he gave
12:14 for he did not seek the LORD with all his **h**.
15:12 God of their ancestors, with all their **h** and soul.
22: 9 a man who sought the LORD with all his **h**."
32:31 to test him and to see what was really in his **h**.
34:31 regulations, and laws with all his **h** and soul.
36:22 the **h** of Cyrus to put this proclamation into writing
Ezr 1: 1 the **h** of Cyrus to put this proclamation into writing
Ne 1:11 Put it into his **h** to be kind to me." In those days I
2:12 about the plans God had put in my **h** for Jerusalem.
Job 11:13 "If only you would prepare your **h** and lift up your
13:11 Doesn't his majesty strike terror into your **h**?
22:22 Listen to his instructions, and store them in your **h**.
23:12 but have treasured his word in my **h**.
23:16 God has made my **h** faint; the Almighty has
30:16 "And now my **h** is broken. Depression haunts my
30:27 My **h** is troubled and restless. Days of affliction
31: 7 or if my **h** has lusted for what my eyes have seen,
31: 9 "If my **h** has been seduced by a woman, or if I
31:27 and been secretly enticed in my **h** to worship
37: 1 "My **h** pounds as I think of this. It leaps within
41:24 Its **h** is as hard as rock, as hard as a millstone.
Ps 6: 3 I am sick at **h**. / How long, O LORD, until you
7: 9 For you look deep within the mind and **h**,
9: 1 I will thank you, LORD, with all my **h**; / I will
13: 2 in my soul, / with sorrow in my **h** every day?
16: 7 who guides me; / even at night my **h** instructs me.
16: 9 No wonder my **h** is filled with joy, / and my mouth
17: 1 to my prayer, / for it comes from an honest **h**.
17: 3 my thoughts and examined my **h** in the night.
19: 8 of the LORD are right, / bringing joy to the **h**.
19:12 How can I know all the sins lurking in my **h**?
19:14 the words of my mouth and the thoughts of my **h**
22:14 of joint. / My **h** is like wax, / melting within me.
27: 3 army surrounds me, / my **h** will know no fear.
27: 8 My **h** has heard you say, "Come and talk with
27: 8 And my **h** responds, "LORD, I am coming."
28: 7 I trust in him with all my **h**. / He helps me, and my **h** is filled with joy.
34: 2 in the LORD; / let all who are discouraged take **h**.
35:10 I will praise him from the bottom of my **h**:
37:15 But they will be stabbed through the **h** with their
38: 8 My groans come from an anguished **h**.
38:10 My **h** beats wildly, my strength fails, / and I am
40: 8 my God, / for your law is written on my **h**."
40:10 I have not kept this good news hidden in my **h**;
42: 4 My **h** is breaking / as I remember how it used to
44:21 known it, / for he knows the secrets of every **h**.
45: 1 My **h** overflows with a beautiful thought! / I will
45:10 to me, O royal daughter; take to **h** what I say.
51: 6 But you desire honesty from the **h**, / so you can
51:10 Create in me a clean **h**, O God. / Renew a right
51:17 A broken and repentant **h**, O God, / you will not
55: 4 My **h** is in anguish. / The terror of death
55:21 words are as smooth as cream, / but in his **h** is war.
57: 7 My **h** is confident in you, O God; / no wonder I
61: 2 cry to you for help, / for my **h** is overwhelmed.
62: 8 Pour out your **h** to him, / for God is our refuge.
64: 6 Yes, the human **h** and mind are cunning.
66:18 If I had not confessed the sin in my **h**, / my Lord
69:20 Their insults have broken my **h**, / and I am in
73:13 Was it for nothing that I kept my **h** pure / and kept
73:26 but God remains the strength of my **h**;
78:40 in the desert / and grieved his **h** in the wilderness.
78:72 He cared for them with a true **h** / and led them with
86:11 Grant me purity of **h**, / that I may honor you.
86:12 With all my **h** I will praise you, O Lord my God.
89:50 I carry in my **h** the insults of so many people.
102: 4 My **h** is sick, withered like grass, / and I have lost
103: 1 with my whole **h**, I will praise his holy name.
107:43 Those who are wise will take all this to **h**;
108: 1 My **h** is confident in you, O God; / no wonder I
109:22 For I am poor and needy, / and my **h** is full of pain.
111: 1 I will thank the LORD with all my **h**
116:19 in the house of the LORD, / in the **h** of Jerusalem.
119:11 I have hidden your word in my **h**, / that I might not
119:34 your law; / I will put it into practice with all my **h**.
119:58 With all my **h** I want your blessings. / Be merciful
119:69 in truth I obey your commandments with all my **h**.
119:145 I pray with all my **h**; answer me, LORD! / I will
119:161 but my **h** trembles only at your word.
131: 1 LORD, my **h** is not proud; / my eyes are not
138: 1 I give you thanks, O LORD, with all my **h**;
139: 1 O LORD, you have examined my **h** / and know
139:23 Search me, O God, and know my **h**; / test me
Pr 2:10 For wisdom will enter your **h**, and knowledge will
3: 1 I have taught you. Store my commands in your **h**,
3: 3 like a necklace; write them deep within your **h**.
3: 5 Trust in the LORD with all your **h**; do not depend
4: 4 My father told me, "Take my words to **h**.
4:21 my words. Let them penetrate deep within your **h**,
4:23 Above all else, guard your **h**, for it affects
6:18 a **h** that plots evil, / feet that race to do wrong,
6:21 Keep their words always in your **h**. Tie them
7: 3 as a reminder. Write them deep within your **h**.
7:10 approached him, dressed seductively and sly of **h**.
7:23 awaiting the arrow that would pierce its **h**. He was
10:20 are like sterling silver; the **h** of a fool is worthless.
13:12 Hope deferred makes the **h** sick, but when dreams
14:10 Each **h** knows its own bitterness, and no one else
14:13 Laughter can conceal a heavy **h**; when the laughter
14:33 Wisdom is enshrined in an understanding **h**;
15:11 How much more does he know the human **h**!
15:13 A glad **h** makes a happy face; a broken **h** crushes the spirit.
15:15 for the happy **h**, life is a continual feast.
15:30 A cheerful look brings joy to the **h**; good news
17: 3 of silver and gold, but the LORD tests the **h**.
17:16 tuition to educate a fool who has no **h** for wisdom.
17:20 The crooked **h** will not prosper; the twisted tongue
17:22 A cheerful **h** is good medicine, but a broken spirit
18: 8 rumors are—but they sink deep into one's **h**.
20: 5 Though good advice lies deep within a person's **h**,
20: 9 Who can say, "I have cleansed my **h**; I am pure
20:30 cleanses away evil; such discipline purifies the **h**.
21: 1 The king's **h** is like a stream of water directed by
21: 2 what is right, but the LORD examines the **h**.
21: 4 Haughty eyes, a proud **h**, and evil actions are all
22:11 Anyone who loves a pure **h** and gracious speech is
22:15 A youngster's **h** is filled with foolishness,
22:17 words of the wise; apply your **h** to my instruction.
23:16 my **h** will thrill when you speak what is right
23:19 and be wise. Keep your **h** on the right course.
23:26 O my son, give me your **h**. May your eyes delight
25:20 Singing cheerful songs to a person whose **h** is
26:22 rumors are—but they sink deep into one's **h**.
26:23 Smooth words may hide a wicked **h**, just as a
27:19 is reflected in water, so the **h** reflects the person.
27:23 and put your **h** into caring for your herds,
Ecc 3:11 He has planted eternity in the human **h**, but even
7: 7 wise people into fools, and bribes corrupt the **h**.
9: 7 Eat your food and drink your wine with a happy **h**,
SS 4: 9 You have ravished my **h**, my treasure, my bride.
5: 2 as I was sleeping, my **h** awakened in a dream.
5: 4 to unlatch the door, and my **h** thrilled within me.
8: 6 Place me like a seal over your **h**, or like a seal on
Isa 1: 5 Your head is injured, and your **h** is sick.
15: 5 My **h** weeps for Moab. Its people flee to Zoar
19: 3 The Egyptians will lose **h**, and I will confuse their
19:10 The weavers and all the workers will be sick at **h**.
19:19 will be an altar to the LORD in the **h** of Egypt,
21: 4 My mind reels; my **h** races. The sleep I once
24:16 But my **h** is heavy with grief. I am discouraged,
40:11 the lambs in his arms, holding them close to his **h**.
62: 1 I love Zion, because my **h** yearns for Jerusalem,
66:14 When you see these things, your **h** will rejoice.
Jer 3:15 And I will give you leaders after my own **h**,
4:18 your own medicine. It has pierced you to the **h**!"
4:19 My **h**, my **h**—I writhe in pain! My **h** pounds within me! I cannot be still.
5:24 They do not say from the **h**, 'Let us live in awe of
8:18 My grief is beyond healing; my **h** is broken.
12: 3 But as for me, LORD, you know my **h**. You see
17: 9 "The human **h** is most deceitful and desperately
20: 9 in his name, his word burns in my **h** like a fire.
21: 4 I will bring your enemies right into the **h** of this
23: 9 My **h** is broken because of the false prophets,
32:39 And I will give them one **h** and mind to worship
48:29 of her loftiness, her arrogance, and her haughty **h**.
48:31 my **h** is broken for the men of Kir-hareseth.
48:36 My **h** moans like a flute for Moab
La 1:20 My **h** is broken and my soul despairs, for I have
1:22 my sins. My groans are many, and my **h** is faint."
2:11 My **h** is broken, my spirit poured out, as I see what
3:13 He shot his arrows deep into my **h**.
3:51 My **h** is breaking over the fate of all the women of
Eze 3:10 let all my words sink deep into your own **h** first.
11:19 And I will give them singleness of **h** and put a new
16:30 "What a sick **h** you have, says the Sovereign
18:31 and get for yourselves a new **h** and a new spirit.
21: 6 before them with bitter anguish and a broken **h**.
21: 7 it comes true, the boldest **h** will melt with fear;
27:26 You are shipwrecked in the **h** of the sea!
28: 2 a god! I sit on a divine throne in the **h** of the sea.'
28: 8 and you will die there on your island home in the **h**
28:17 Your **h** was filled with pride because of all your
36:26 And I will give you a new **h** with new and right
36:26 I will take out your stony **h** of sin and give you a new, obedient **h**.
44: 7 into my sanctuary—people who have no **h** for God.
Da 5:20 But when his **h** and mind were hardened with
10:19 Be at peace; take **h** and be strong!" As he spoke
Hos 11: 8 My **h** is torn within me, and my compassion
Jnh 2: 3 ocean depths, and I sank down to the **h** of the sea.
Zep 3:14 Be glad and rejoice with all your **h**, O daughter of
Zec 8: 9 LORD Almighty says: Take **h** and finish the task!
Mal 2: 2 Listen to me and take it to **h**. Honor my name,"
Mt 5:28 has already committed adultery with her in his **h**.
6:21 treasure is, there your **h** and thoughts will also be.
9: 2 Jesus said to the paralyzed man, "Take **h**, son!
12:34 For whatever is in your **h** determines what you say.
12:35 good person produces good words from a good **h**,
12:35 an evil person produces evil words from an evil **h**.
12:40 will be in the **h** of the earth for three days and three
15:18 But evil words come from an evil **h** and defile the
15:19 For from the **h** come evil thoughts, murder,
18:35 to forgive your brothers and sisters in your **h**."
22:37 must love the Lord your God with all your **h**,
Mk 7:19 Food doesn't come in contact with your **h**, but only
7:21 For from within, out of a person's **h**, come evil
11:23 that you really believe and do not doubt in your **h**.
12:30 you must love the Lord your God with all your **h**,
12:33 I know it is important to love him with all my **h**
Lk 2:19 but Mary quietly treasured these things in her **h**
2:51 and his mother stored all these things in her **h**.
6:45 good person produces good deeds from a good **h**,
6:45 an evil person produces evil deeds from an evil **h**.
6:45 Whatever is in your **h** determines what you say.
7:13 Lord saw her, his **h** overflowed with compassion.
10:27 must love the Lord your God with all your **h**,
12:34 treasure is, there your **h** and thoughts will also be.
Jn 1:18 who is himself God, is near to the Father's **h**;
14:27 am leaving you with a gift—peace of mind and **h**.
16:33 But take **h**, because I have overcome the world."
Ac 1:24 "O Lord," they said, "you know every **h**.
2:26 No wonder my **h** is filled with joy, / and my mouth
4:32 All the believers were of one **h** and mind, and they
5: 3 Peter said, "Ananias, why has Satan filled your **h**?
7:51 You are heathen at **h** and deaf to the truth.
8:21 no part in this, for your **h** is not right before God.
13:22 'David son of Jesse is a man after my own **h**,
16:14 As she listened to us, the Lord opened her **h**,
21:13 "Why all this weeping? You are breaking my **h**!
Ro 1: 9 whom I serve with all my **h** by telling others the
2:29 a true Jew is one whose **h** is right with God.
2:29 but a change of **h** produced by God's Spirit.
6:17 but now you have obeyed with all your **h** the new
7:22 I love God's law with all my **h**.
9: 2 My **h** is filled with bitter sorrow and unending
10: 1 the longing of my **h** and my prayer to God is that
10: 8 is close at hand; it is on your lips and in your **h**."
10: 9 and believe in your **h** that God raised him from the
10:10 For it is by believing in your **h** that you are made
15:32 I will be able to come to you with a happy **h**,
2Co 5:12 ministry rather than having a sincere **h** before God.
Eph 6: 6 slaves of Christ, do the will of God with all your **h**.
Php 1: 4 and I make my requests with a **h** full of joy
1: 7 of you, for you have a very special place in my **h**.
2: 2 and working together with one **h** and purpose.
Col 2: 5 though I am far away from you, my **h** is with you.
4: 2 to prayer with an alert mind and a thankful **h**.
1Ti 1: 5 would be filled with love that comes from a pure **h**,
Phm 1:12 him back to you, and with him comes my own **h**.
1Jn 3:15 hates another Christian is really a murderer at **h**.

HEART'S (10) [HEART]

1Ki 9:19 He built to his **h** content in Jerusalem and Lebanon
2Ch 8: 6 He built to his **h** content in Jerusalem and Lebanon
Job 17:11 hopes have disappeared. My **h** desires are broken.
Ps 20: 4 May he grant your **h** desire / and fulfill all your
21: 2 For you have given him his **h** desire; / you have
37: 4 the LORD, / and he will give you your **h** desires.
119:111 are my treasure; / they are truly my **h** delight.
Isa 26: 8 your laws; / our **h** desire is to glorify your name.
Jer 15:16 They bring me great joy and are my **h** delight,
Eze 24:25 their joy and glory, their **h** desire, their dearest

HEARTBROKEN (1) [BREAK, HEART]

2Co 2: 4 **H**, I cried over it. I didn't want to hurt you, but I

HEARTFELT (1) [FEEL, HEART]

Pr 27: 9 The **h** counsel of a friend is as sweet as perfume

HEARTH (2)

Isa 47:14 them at all. Their **h** is not a place to sit for warmth.
Eze 43:15 The top of the altar, the **h**, rises still 7 feet higher,

HEARTILY (2)

Ne 10:29 now all **h** bound themselves with an oath.
1Co 16:19 in the province of Asia greet you **h** in the Lord,

HEARTLESS (3) [HEART]

Dt 28:50 and **h** nation that shows no respect for the old
Hab 1:17 Will they succeed forever in their **h** conquests?
Ro 1:31 break their promises, and are **h** and unforgiving.

HEARTS (211) [HEART]

Ex 14:17 Yet I will harden the **h** of the Egyptians, and they
35:21 If their **h** were stirred and they desired to do so,
35:22 and women came, all whose **h** were willing.
Lev 26:41 then at last their disobedient **h** will be humbled,
Dt 5:29 Oh, that they would always have **h** like this,
10:16 cleanse your sinful **h** and stop being stubborn.
30: 6 and the **h** of all your descendants so that you will
Jos 2:11 No wonder our **h** have melted in fear! No one has
11:20 For the LORD hardened their **h** and caused them
23:14 Deep in your **h** you know that every promise of the
24:23 and turn your **h** to the LORD, the God of Israel."
1Sa 10:26 a band of men whose **h** God had touched became
2Sa 15: 6 Absalom stole the **h** of all the people of Israel.

1Ch 29:17 that you examine our **h** and rejoice when you find
2Ch 15:15 for they had entered into it with all their **h**.
16: 9 those whose **h** are fully committed to him.
19: 9 the LORD, with integrity and with undivided **h**.
29:31 and those whose **h** were willing brought burnt
Ezr 1: 5 Then God stirred the **h** of the priests and Levites
Job 1: 5 have sinned and have cursed God in their **h**."
13:10 in your **h** you slant your testimony in his favor.
15:35 and evil, and their **h** give birth only to deceit."
17: 9 and those with pure **h** will become stronger
29:13 And I caused the widows' **h** to sing for joy.
Ps 7:10 saving those whose **h** are true and right.
12: 2 speaking with flattering lips and insincere **h**.
14: 1 Only fools say in their **h**, / "There is no God."
15: 2 what is right, / speaking the truth from sincere **h**.
22:26 Their **h** will rejoice with everlasting joy.
24: 4 Only those whose hands and **h** are pure, / who do
28: 3 to their neighbors / while planning evil in their **h**.
32:11 Shout for joy, all you whose **h** are pure!
33:15 He made their **h**, / so he understands everything
33:21 In him our **h** rejoice, / for we are trusting in his
36: 1 Sin whispers to the wicked, deep within their **h**.
36:10 who love you; / give justice to those with honest **h**.
37:31 They fill their **h** with God's law, / so they will
44:18 Our **h** have not deserted you. / We have not strayed
45: 5 Your arrows are sharp, / piercing your enemies' **h**.
53: 1 Only fools say in their **h**, / "There is no God."
62: 4 friendly to my face, / but they curse me in their **h**.
65: 3 Though our **h** are filled with sins, / you forgive
73: 1 God is good to Israel, / to those whose **h** are pure.
73: 7 cats have everything / their **h** could ever wish for!
78: 8 and unfaithful, / refusing to give their **h** to God.
78:18 They willfully tested God in their **h**,
78:37 Their **h** were not loyal to him. / They did not keep
95: 8 "Don't harden your **h** as Israel did at Meribah,
95:10 'They are a people whose **h** turn away from me.
119: 2 his decrees / and search for him with all their **h**.
119:70 Their **h** are dull and stupid, / but I delight in your
125: 4 who are good, / whose **h** are in tune with you.
140: 2 those who plot evil in their **h** / and stir up trouble
Pr 6:14 Their perverted **h** plot evil. They stir up trouble
7:25 Don't let your **h** stray away toward her.
11:20 The LORD hates people with twisted **h**, but he
12:20 Deceit fills **h** that are plotting evil; joy fills **h** that are planning peace!
24:12 For God knows all **h**, and he sees you. He keeps
26:24 People with hate in their **h** may sound pleasant
26:25 to be kind, their **h** are full of all kinds of evil.
Ecc 10: 2 The **h** of the wise lead them to do right,
10: 2 and the **h** of the foolish lead them to do evil.
Isa 6:10 Harden the **h** of these people. Close their ears,
6:10 hear with their ears, understand with their **h**,
7: 2 So the **h** of the king and his people trembled with
13: 7 is paralyzed with fear. Even the strongest **h** melt
19: 1 The **h** of the Egyptians melt with fear.
19:17 the name of Israel will strike deep terror in their **h**,
29:13 honor me with their lips, but their **h** are far away.
47:12 Ask them to help you strike terror into the **h** of
51: 7 right from wrong and cherish my law in your **h**.
57:15 and give new courage to those with repentant **h**.
60: 5 eyes will shine, and your **h** will thrill with joy,
63:17 Why have you given us stubborn **h** so we no
66: 2 will bless those who have humble and contrite **h**,
Jer 3:22 back to me, and I will heal your wayward **h**."
4: 3 "Plow up the hard ground of your **h**!
4: 4 Cleanse your minds and **h** before the LORD,
4: 8 on clothes of mourning and weep with broken **h**,
4:14 cleanse your **h** that you may be saved.
5:23 "But my people have stubborn and rebellious **h**.
7:24 following the stubborn desires of their evil **h**.
9:26 the people of Israel also have uncircumcised **h**."
11:20 and you examine the deepest thoughts of **h**
12: 2 but in their **h** they give you no credit at all.
14:14 speak foolishness made up in their own lying **h**.
17: 1 inscribed with a diamond point on their stony **h**,
17: 5 and turn their **h** away from the LORD.
17:10 search all **h** and examine secret motives.
20:12 and you examine the deepest thoughts of **h**
24: 7 I will give them **h** that will recognize me as the
31:33 in their minds, and I will write them on their **h**.
32:40 I will put a desire in their **h** to worship me,
49:23 Their **h** are troubled like a wild sea in a raging
La 2:19 and cry out. Pour out your **h** like water to the Lord.
3:41 Let us lift our **h** and hands to God in heaven
3:65 Give them hard and stubborn **h**, and then let your
5:15 The joy of our **h** has ended; our dancing has turned
5:17 Our **h** are sick and weary, and our eyes grow dim
Eze 6: 9 recognize how grieved I am by their unfaithful **h**
11:19 I will take away their **h** of stone and give them tender **h** instead,
14: 3 of man, these leaders have set up idols in their **h**.
14: 4 the people of Israel who set up idols in their **h**
14: 5 and **h** of all my people who have turned from me
14: 7 who reject me and set up idols in their **h** so they
20:16 my Sabbath days. Their **h** were given to their idols.
21:15 Let their **h** melt with terror, for the sword glitters at
32: 9 that you have never seen, I will disturb many **h**.
32:23 These mighty men who once struck terror in the **h**
32:26 They once struck terror into the **h** of all people.
33:31 their mouths, but their **h** seek only after money.
Hos 7: 6 Their **h** blaze like a furnace with intrigue.
7:14 They do not cry out to me with sincere **h**. Instead,
10: 2 The **h** of the people are fickle; they are guilty
10:12 Plow up the hard ground of your **h**, for now is the
Joel 2:12 Give me your **h**. Come with fasting, weeping,
2:13 your clothing in your grief; instead, tear your **h**."
Na 2:10 of its wealth. **H** melt in horror, and knees shake.
Zec 7:12 They made their **h** as hard as stone, so they could
10: 7 and their **h** will be happy as if by wine.
10: 7 and be glad; their **h** will rejoice in the LORD.
Mal 4: 6 His preaching will turn the **h** of parents to their
4: 6 and the **h** of children to their parents.
Mt 5: 8 God blesses those whose **h** are pure, / for they will
13:15 For the **h** of these people are hardened, / and their
13:15 ears cannot hear, / and their **h** cannot understand,
13:19 and snatches the seed away from their **h**.
13:23 The good soil represents the **h** of those who truly
15: 8 me with their words, / but their **h** are far away.
17:23 And the disciples' **h** were filled with grief.
23:28 but inside your **h** are filled with hypocrisy
Mk 3: 5 because he was deeply disturbed by their hard **h**.
6:52 for their **h** were hard and they did not believe.
7: 7 honor me with their lips, / but their **h** are far away.
8:17 or understand? Are your **h** too hard to take it in?
Lk 1:17 He will turn the **h** of the fathers to their children,
2:35 the deepest thoughts of many **h** will be revealed.
16:15 to look good in public, but God knows your evil **h**.
24:32 "Didn't our **h** feel strangely warm as he talked
Jn 5:38 and you do not have his message in your **h**,
8:37 my message does not find a place in your **h**.
12:40 and hardened their **h**— / so their eyes cannot see, / and their **h** cannot understand,
Ac 14:17 and good crops and giving you food and joyful **h**."
15: 8 God, who knows people's **h**, confirmed that he
15: 9 for he also cleansed their **h** through faith.
28:27 For the **h** of these people are hardened, / and their
28:27 ears cannot hear, / and their **h** cannot understand,
Ro 1:19 God has put this knowledge in their **h**.
1:24 and do whatever shameful things their **h** desired.
2:14 they show that in their **h** they know right from
5: 5 because he has given us the Holy Spirit to fill our **h**
8:16 For his Holy Spirit speaks to us deep in our **h**
8:27 And the Father who knows all **h** knows what the
11:25 Some of the Jews have hard **h**, but this will last
1Co 3: 6 My job was to plant the seed in your **h**,
2Co 1:22 **h** as the first installment of everything he will give
3: 2 Your lives are a letter written in our **h**,
3: 3 It is carved not on stone, but on human **h**.
3:15 their **h** are covered with that veil, and they do not
6:10 Our **h** ache, but we always have joy. We are poor,
6:11 spoken honestly with you. Our **h** are open to you.
6:13 as I would to my own children. Open your **h** to us!
7: 2 Please open your **h** to us. We have not done wrong
7: 3 for I said before that you are in our **h** forever.
Gal 4: 6 God has sent the Spirit of his Son into your **h**,
Eph 1:18 I pray that your **h** will be flooded with light so that
2: 2 He is the spirit at work in the **h** of those who refuse
2:11 though it affected only their bodies and not their **h**.
3:17 and more at home in your **h** as you trust in him.
4:18 shut their minds and hardened their **h** against him.
5: 8 For though your **h** were once full of darkness,
5:19 making music to the Lord in your **h**.
Php 2: 1 in the Spirit? Are your **h** tender and sympathetic?
4: 7 His peace will guard your **h** and minds as you live
Col 3:15 let the peace that comes from Christ rule in your **h**.
3:16 their richness, live in your **h** and make you wise.
3:16 and spiritual songs to God with thankful **h**.
1Th 2: 4 He is the one who examines the motives of our **h**.
2:17 you for a little while (though our **h** never left you),
3:13 a result, Christ will make your **h** strong, blameless,
2Th 2:17 comfort your **h** and give you strength in every
1Ti 4: 4 of it. We may receive it gladly, with thankful **h**.
2Ti 2:22 of those who call on the Lord with pure **h**.
2:25 Perhaps God will change those people's **h**,
Tit 1:15 Everything is pure to those whose **h** are pure.
Phm 1: 7 so often refreshed the **h** of God's people.
Heb 3: 8 Don't harden your **h** against him / as Israel did
3:10 and I said, / 'Their **h** always turn away from me.
3:12 Make sure that your own **h** are not evil
3:15 Don't harden your **h** against him / as Israel did
4: 7 to his voice. / Don't harden your **h** against him."
8:10 understand them, / and I will write them on their **h**
9:14 will purify our **h** from deeds that lead to death
10:16 says the Lord: / I will put my laws in their **h**
10:22 the presence of God, with true **h** fully trusting him.
Jas 1:21 accept the message God has planted in your **h**,
3:14 and there is selfish ambition in your **h**,
4: 8 you sinners; purify your **h**, you hypocrites.
5: 5 Now your **h** are nice and fat, ready for the
1Pe 1:22 really do love each other intensely with all your **h**.
3: 8 loving one another with tender **h** and humble
2Pe 1:19 and his brilliant light shines in your **h**.
1Jn 1:10 and showing that his word has no place in our **h**.
2:14 you are strong with God's word living in your **h**,
3:20 even if our **h** condemn us. For God is greater than our **h**, and he knows
5:21 anything that might take God's place in your **h**.
2Jn 1: 2 truth that lives in us and will be in our **h** forever.

HEARTS' (2) [HEART]

Ps 12: 4 They say, "We will lie to our **h** content. / Our lips
Pr 13:25 The godly eat to their **h** content, but the belly of

HEAT (22) [HEATED, HEATEDLY, HEATS]

Ge 8:22 cold and **h**, winter and summer, day and night."
31:40 I worked for you through the scorching **h** of the
Dt 28:22 with scorching **h** and drought, and with blight
Job 6:17 the water disappears. The brook vanishes in the **h**.
24:19 sinners just as drought and **h** consume snow.
30: 4 and they burn the roots of shrubs for **h**.
37:18 he makes the skies reflect the **h** like a giant mirror.
Ps 19: 6 to the other end. / Nothing can hide from its **h**.
32: 4 strength evaporated like water in the summer **h**.
Pr 25:13 are as refreshing as snow in the **h** of summer.
Isa 4: 6 It will be a shelter from daytime **h** and a hiding
18: 4 as quietly as the **h** rises on a summer day, or as the
25: 4 you are a shelter from the rain and the **h**.
25: 5 or like the relentless **h** of the desert. But you
44:19 I burned half of it for **h** and used it to bake my
Jer 17: 8 Such trees are not bothered by the **h** or worried by
Eze 22:20 I will melt you down in the **h** of my fury, just as
22:22 and you will melt like silver in fierce **h**. Then you
Mt 20:12 paid us who worked all day in the scorching **h**.'
Ac 28: 3 a poisonous snake, driven out by the **h**,
Rev 7:16 be fully protected from the scorching noontime **h**.
16: 9 Everyone was burned by this blast of **h**, and they

HEATED (1) [HEAT]

Da 3:19 He commanded that the furnace be **h** seven times

HEATEDLY (1) [HEAT]

Jdg 8: 1 the Midianites?" And they argued **h** with Gideon.

HEATH [KJV] See HIDE, SHRUBS

HEATHEN (1)

Ac 7:51 You are **h** at heart and deaf to the truth.

HEATS (1) [HEAT]

Ps 58: 9 and old, / faster than a pot **h** on an open flame.

HEAVE (OFFERING) [KJV] See PRESENT

HEAVEN (479) [HEAVEN'S, HEAVENLY, HEAVENS]

ARMY(IES) OF HEAVEN (6) 1Ki 22:19; 2Ch 18:18; Ps 148:2; Da 8:12; Lk 2:13; Rev 19:14

DOWN FROM HEAVEN (28) 2Sa 22:17; 1Ki 18:38; 2Ki 1:10,12; 2Ch 7:1; Ps 14:2; 18:16; 33:13; 53:2; 80:14; 85:11; 144:7; Isa 63:15; La 3:50; Da 4:13,23,31; Mt 28:2; Lk 17:29; Jn 6:33,38,42; 1Th 4:16; 2Pe 1:17; Rev 3:12; 10:1; 18:1; 20:1

FATHER IN HEAVEN (11) Mt 5:45,48; 6:1,9; 7:21; 10:32,33; 12:50; 16:17; 18:19; Mk 11:25

GOD OF HEAVEN (25) Ge 24:3,7; 2Ch 36:23; Ezr 1:2; 5:11,12; 6:9,10; 7:12,21,23; Ne 1:4,5; 2:4,20; Job 31:28; Ps 136:26; Da 2:18,19,37,44; Jnh 1:9; Heb 1:3; Rev 11:13; 16:11

HEAVEN...EARTH; EARTH...HEAVEN (97) Ge 14:19,22; 24:3; 28:12; Ex 31:17; Dt 3:24; 4:19,26,36,39; 30:19; 31:28; 1Sa 2:10; 1Ki 8:23,43; 1Ch 21:16; 2Ch 6:14,33; 20:6; 36:23; Ezr 1:2; 5:11; Ne 9:6; Ps 11:4; 50:4; 69:34; 73:25; 76:8; 85:11; 102:19; 115:15; 134:3; 135:6; 146:6; 148:13; Pr 25:3; Ecc 5:2; Isa 14:12; 26:21; 66:1,2; Jer 25:30; Da 4:22,35; Mic 1:3; Zec 6:5; Mt 5:18; 6:10; 10:32,33; 11:25; 16:19,19,19; 18:18,18,19; 23:9; 24:30,31,35; 28:18; Mk 13:27,31; Lk 2:14; 10:21; 16:17; 21:33; Jn 3:12,13,31; Ac 4:24; 7:49,50; 14:15; 17:24; 1Co 8:5; 13:1; 15:47,49; Eph 1:10; 3:15; Php 2:10; Col 1:16,20; 3:2; Jas 5:12; Rev 1:7; 5:3,13; 10:6; 13:13; 14:7; 18:1; 20:9; 21:1,1

KINGDOM OF HEAVEN (33) Mt 3:2; 4:17; 5:3,10,19,19,20; 7:21; 8:11; 10:7; 11:11,12; 13:11,24,31,33,44,45,47,52; 16:19; 18:1,3,4,23; 19:12,14,23; 20:1; 22:2; 23:13; 25:1,14

LORD OF HEAVEN (4) Da 5:23; Mt 11:25; Lk 10:21; Ac 17:24

STARS OF HEAVEN (3) Ex 32:13; 2Ch 33:3,5

UNDER HEAVEN (7) Ex 17:14; Dt 9:14; 25:19; 29:20; Job 41:11; Ecc 3:1; Da 7:27

Ge 14:19 by God Most High, / Creator of **h** and earth.
14:22 God Most High, Creator of **h** and earth,
22:11 the angel of the LORD shouted to him from **h**,
22:15 of the LORD called again to Abraham from **h**,
24: 3 "Swear by the LORD, the God of **h** and earth,
24: 7 For the LORD, the God of **h**, who took me from
28:12 dreamed of a stairway that reached from earth to **h**.
28:17 other than the house of God—the gateway to **h**!"
Ex 10:21 "Lift your hand toward **h**, and a deep
10:22 So Moses lifted his hand toward **h**, and there was
16: 4 I'm going to rain down food from **h** for you.
17:14 will blot out every trace of Amalek from under **h**."
20:22 are witnesses that I have spoken to you from **h**.
31:17 For in six days the LORD made **h** and earth,
32:13 your descendants as numerous as the stars of **h**.
Dt 3:24 Is there any god in **h** or on earth who can perform
4:19 see the sun, moon, and stars—all the forces of **h**—
4:26 "Today I call **h** and earth as witnesses against you.
4:36 He let you hear his voice from **h** so he could
4:39 The LORD is God both in **h** and on earth,
9:14 destroy them and erase their name from under **h**.
17: 3 the sun, the moon, or any of the forces of **h**,
25:19 and erase their memory from under **h**.
26:15 Look down from your holy dwelling place in **h**
29:20 the LORD will erase their names from under **h**.
30:12 It is not up in **h**, so distant that you must ask,
30:12 'Who will go to **h** and bring it down so we can
30:19 I call on **h** and earth to witness the choice you
31:28 of your tribes so that I can speak to them and call **h**
32:40 Now I raise my hand to **h** / and declare, "As surely
Jdg 5:20 The stars fought from **h**. / The stars in their orbits
1Sa 2:10 He thunders against them from **h**; / the LORD
7:10 spoke with a mighty voice of thunder from **h**,
2Sa 22:14 The LORD thundered from **h**; / the Most High
22:17 "He reached down from **h** and rescued me;

1Ki 8:22 Then Solomon stood with his hands lifted toward **h**
8:23 there is no God like you in all of **h** or earth.
8:30 Yes, hear us from **h** where you live, and when you
8:32 then hear from **h** and judge between your
8:34 then hear from **h** and forgive their sins and return
8:36 then hear from **h** and forgive the sins of your
8:39 then hear from **h** where you live, and forgive.
8:43 then hear from **h** where you live, and grant what
8:45 then hear their prayers from **h** and uphold their
8:49 then hear their prayers from **h** where you live.
8:54 had been kneeling with his hands raised toward **h**.
18:38 the fire of the LORD flashed down from **h**
22:19 on his throne with all the armies of **h** around him,
2Ki 1:10 let fire come down from **h** and destroy you
1:10 Then fire fell from **h** and killed them all.
1:12 let fire come down from **h** and destroy you
1:12 And again the fire of God fell from **h** and killed
1:14 See how the fire from **h** has destroyed the first two
2:1 When the LORD was about to take Elijah up to **h**
2:11 and Elijah was carried by a whirlwind into **h**.
7:2 even if the LORD opened the windows of **h**!"
7:19 even if the LORD opened the windows of **h**!"
17:16 and worshiped Baal and all the forces of **h**.
21:3 He also bowed before all the forces of **h**
21:5 He built these altars for all the forces of **h** in both
23:4 to worship Baal, Asherah, and all the forces of **h**.
23:5 the constellations, and to all the forces of **h**.
1Ch 21:16 saw the angel of the LORD standing between **h**
21:26 the LORD answered him by sending fire from **h**
27:23 to make the Israelites as numerous as the stars in **h**.
2Ch 6:13 then he knelt down and lifted his hands toward **h**.
6:14 there is no God like you in all of **h** and earth.
6:21 Yes, hear us from **h** where you live, and when you
6:23 then hear from **h** and judge between your
6:25 then hear from **h** and forgive their sins and return
6:27 then hear from **h** and forgive the sins of your
6:30 then hear from **h** where you live, and forgive.
6:33 then hear from **h** where you live, and grant what
6:35 then hear their prayers from **h** and uphold their
6:39 then hear their prayers from **h** where you live.
7:1 fire flashed down from **h** and burned up the burnt
7:14 I will hear from **h** and will forgive their sins
18:18 on his throne with all the armies of **h** on his right
20:6 our ancestors, you alone are the God who is in **h**.
28:9 killing them without mercy, and all **h** is disturbed.
30:27 and God heard them from his holy dwelling in **h**.
32:20 Isaiah son of Amoz cried out in prayer to God in **h**.
33:3 He also bowed before all the stars of **h**
33:5 He put these altars for the stars of **h** in both
36:23 The LORD, the God of **h**, has given me all the
Ezr 1:2 The LORD, the God of **h**, has given me all the
5:11 'We are the servants of the God of **h** and earth,
5:12 because our ancestors angered the God of **h**,
6:9 for the burnt offerings presented to the God of **h**.
6:10 able to offer acceptable sacrifices to the God of **h**
7:12 the priest, the teacher of the law of the God of **h**.
7:21 is a priest and teacher of the law of the God of **h**.
7:23 Be careful to provide whatever the God of **h**
Ne 1:4 I mourned, fasted, and prayed to the God of **h**.
1:5 God of **h**, the great and awesome God who keeps
2:4 can I help you?" With a prayer to the God of **h**,
2:20 But I replied, "The God of **h** will help us succeed.
8:6 Amen!" as they lifted their hands toward **h**.
9:6 to everything, and all the angels of **h** worship you.
9:13 down on Mount Sinai and spoke to them from **h**.
9:15 "You gave them bread from **h** when they were
9:20 and you did not stop giving them bread from **h**
9:27 they cried to you, and you heard them from **h**.
9:28 you again for help, you listened once more from **h**.
Job 1:16 "The fire of God has fallen from **h** and burned up
16:19 Even now my witness is in **h**. My advocate is there
22:14 He is way up there, walking on the vault of **h**.'
26:11 The foundations of **h** tremble at his rebuke.
31:28 for it would mean I had denied the God of **h**.
33:23 "But if a special messenger from **h** is there to
36:29 the clouds and the thunder that rolls forth from **h**?
38:37 all the clouds? Who can tilt the water jars of **h**,
41:11 and remain safe? Everything under **h** is mine.
Ps 2:4 But the one who rules in **h** laughs. / The Lord
11:4 in his holy Temple; / the LORD still rules from **h**.
14:2 The LORD looks down from **h** / on the entire
18:13 The LORD thundered from **h**; / the Most High
18:16 He reached down from **h** and rescued me;
20:6 He will answer him from his holy **h** / and rescue
33:13 The LORD looks down from **h** / and sees the
50:4 **H** and earth will be his witnesses / as he judges his
53:2 God looks down from **h** / on the entire human race;
57:3 He will send help from **h** to save me, / rescuing me
69:34 Praise him, O **h** and earth, / the seas and all that
73:25 Whom have I in **h** but you? / I desire you more
76:8 From **h** you sentenced your enemies; / the earth
77:2 long I pray, with hands lifted toward **h**, pleading.
78:23 the skies to open— / he opened the doors of **h**—
78:24 for them to eat. / He gave them bread from **h**.
79:2 as food for the birds of **h**. / The flesh of your godly
80:14 Look down from **h** and see our plight.
85:11 the earth, / and righteousness smiles down from **h**.
89:5 All **h** will praise your miracles, LORD;
89:6 For who in all of **h** can compare with the LORD?
89:29 his throne will be as endless as the days of **h**.
102:19 He looked to the earth from **h**
105:40 them quail; / he gave them manna—bread from **h**.
115:15 be blessed by the LORD, / who made **h** and earth.
119:89 Forever, O LORD, / your word stands firm in **h**.
123:1 I lift my eyes to you, / O God, enthroned in **h**.
134:3 May the LORD, who made **h** and earth,
135:6 throughout all **h** and earth, / and on the seas
136:26 Give thanks to the God of **h**. / His faithful love
139:8 If I go up to **h**, you are there; / if I go down to the
144:7 Reach down from **h** and rescue me; / deliver me
146:6 He is the one who made **h** and earth, / the sea,
148:2 all his angels! / Praise him, all the armies of **h**!
148:13 very great; / his glory towers over the earth and **h**!
150:1 heavenly dwelling; / praise him in his mighty **h**!
Pr 25:3 No one can discover the height of **h**, the depth of
30:4 Who but God goes up to **h** and comes back down?
Ecc 3:1 a season for every activity under **h**.
5:2 for he is in **h**, and you are only here on earth.
Isa 8:21 they will rage and shake their fists at **h** and curse
14:12 "How you are fallen from **h**, O shining star,
14:13 'I will ascend to **h** and set my throne above God's
26:21 The LORD is coming from **h** to punish the people
32:15 at last the Spirit is poured down upon us from **h**.
33:5 Though the LORD is very great and lives in **h**,
38:14 My eyes grew tired of looking to **h** for help.
63:15 look down from **h** and see us from your holy,
66:1 "**H** is my throne, and the earth is my footstool.
66:2 My hands have made both **h** and earth, and they
Jer 7:18 and make cakes to offer to the Queen of **H**.
25:30 against his own land from his holy dwelling in **h**.
44:17 We will burn incense to the Queen of **H**
44:18 since we quit burning incense to the Queen of **H**
44:19 suppose that we were worshiping the Queen of **H**,
44:25 up your devotion and sacrifices to the Queen of **H**,
La 1:13 "He has sent fire from **h** that burns in my bones.
2:1 lies in the dust, thrown down from the heights of **h**.
3:41 us lift our hearts and hands to God in **h** and say,
3:50 until the LORD looks down from **h** and sees.
Da 2:18 He urged them to ask the God of **h** to show them
2:19 in a vision. Then Daniel praised the God of **h**,
2:28 But there is a God in **h** who reveals secrets, and he
2:37 The God of **h** has given you sovereignty, power,
2:44 the God of **h** will set up a kingdom that will never
4:13 a messenger, a holy one, coming down from **h**.
4:15 Now let him be drenched with the dew of **h**,
4:22 your greatness reaches up to **h**, and your rule to the
4:23 a holy one, coming down from **h** and saying,
4:23 Let him be drenched with the dew of **h**.
4:25 and you will be drenched with the dew of **h**.
4:26 back again when you have learned that **h** rules.
4:31 a voice called down from **h**, "O King
4:33 like a cow, and he was drenched with the dew of **h**.
4:34 had passed, I, Nebuchadnezzar, looked up to **h**.
4:35 among the angels of **h** / and with those who live on
4:37 praise and glorify and honor the King of **h**.
5:21 like a cow, and he was drenched with the dew of **h**,
5:23 For you have defied the Lord of **h** and have had
7:13 looked like a man coming with the clouds of **h**.
7:27 and greatness of all the kingdoms under **h** will be
8:12 But the army of **h** was restrained from destroying
10:12 before your God, your request has been heard in **h**.
12:7 raised both his hands toward **h** and took this
Hos 7:16 They look everywhere except to **h**, to the Most
14:5 I will be to Israel like a refreshing dew from **h**.
Jnh 1:9 the God of **h**, who made the sea and the land."
Mic 1:3 He leaves his throne in **h** and comes to earth,
Zec 6:5 "These are the four spirits of **h** who stand before
Mal 3:10 "I will open the windows of **h** for you.
Mt 3:2 turn to God, because the Kingdom of **H** is near."
3:17 And a voice from **h** said, "This is my beloved Son,
4:17 turn to God, because the Kingdom of **H** is near."
5:3 for him, / for the Kingdom of **H** is given to them.
5:10 they live for God, / for the Kingdom of **H** is theirs.
5:12 Be very glad! For a great reward awaits you in **h**.
5:18 I assure you, until **h** and earth disappear,
5:19 you will be the least in the Kingdom of **H**.
5:19 teaches them will be great in the Kingdom of **H**.
5:20 you can't enter the Kingdom of **H** at all!
5:34 If you say, 'By **h**!' it is a sacred vow because **h** is God's throne.
5:45 will be acting as true children of your Father in **h**.
5:48 to be perfect, even as your Father in **h** is perfect.
6:1 you will lose the reward from your Father in **h**.
6:9 Pray like this: / Our Father in **h**, / may your name
6:10 your will be done here on earth, / just as it is in **h**.
6:20 Store your treasures in **h**, where they will never
7:21 but they still won't enter the Kingdom of **H**.
7:21 decisive issue is whether they obey my Father in **h**.
8:11 Isaac, and Jacob at the feast in the Kingdom of **H**.
10:7 and announce to them that the Kingdom of **H** is
10:32 acknowledge that person before my Father in **h**.
10:33 I will deny that person before my Father in **h**.
11:11 person in the Kingdom of **H** is greater than he is!
11:12 the Kingdom of **H** has been forcefully advancing,
11:23 people of Capernaum, will you be exalted to **h**?
11:25 "O Father, Lord of **h** and earth, thank you for
12:50 Anyone who does the will of my Father in **h** is my
13:11 to understand the secrets of the Kingdom of **H**,
13:24 "The Kingdom of **H** is like a farmer who planted
13:31 "The Kingdom of **H** is like a mustard seed planted
13:33 "The Kingdom of **H** is like yeast used by a woman
13:44 "The Kingdom of **H** is like a treasure that a man
13:45 the Kingdom of **H** is like a pearl merchant on the
13:47 the Kingdom of **H** is like a fishing net that is
13:52 **H** is like a person who brings out of the storehouse
14:19 the five loaves and two fish, looked up toward **h**,
16:1 him to show them a miraculous sign from **h**.
16:17 because my Father in **h** has revealed this to you.
16:19 And I will give you the keys of the Kingdom of **H**.
16:19 Whatever you lock on earth will be locked in **h**,
16:19 whatever you open on earth will be opened in **h**."
16:22 and corrected him. "**H** forbid, Lord," he said.
18:1 "Which of us is greatest in the Kingdom of **H**?"
18:3 you will never get into the Kingdom of **H**.
18:4 this little child is the greatest in the Kingdom of **H**.
18:8 It is better to enter **h** crippled or lame than to be
18:9 It is better to enter **h** half blind than to have two
18:10 For I tell you that in **h** their angels are always in
18:18 Whatever you prohibit on earth is prohibited in **h**,
18:18 and whatever you allow on earth is allowed in **h**.
18:19 anything you ask, my Father in **h** will do it for you.
18:23 the Kingdom of **H** can be compared to a king who
19:12 not to marry for the sake of the Kingdom of **H**.
19:14 For the Kingdom of **H** belongs to such as these."
19:21 money to the poor, and you will have treasure in **h**.
19:23 for a rich person to get into the Kingdom of **H**.
20:1 "For the Kingdom of **H** is like the owner of an
21:9 the name of the Lord! / Praise God in highest **h**!"
21:25 "Did John's baptism come from **h** or was it merely
21:25 "If we say it was from **h**, he will ask why we
22:2 "The Kingdom of **H** can be illustrated by the story
22:30 won't be married. They will be like the angels in **h**.
23:9 for only God in **h** is your spiritual Father.
23:13 For you won't let others enter the Kingdom of **H**,
23:22 And when you swear 'by **h**,' you are swearing by
24:29 from the sky, / and the powers of **h** will be shaken.
24:30 Son of Man arrive on the clouds of **h** with power
24:31 ones from the farthest ends of the earth and **h**.
24:35 **H** and earth will disappear, but my words will
24:36 not even the angels in **h** or the Son himself.
25:1 "The Kingdom of **H** can be illustrated by the story
25:14 the Kingdom of **H** can be illustrated by the story of
26:64 of power and coming back on the clouds of **h**."
28:2 because an angel of the Lord came down from **h**
28:18 "I have been given complete authority in **h** and on
Mk 1:11 And a voice came from **h** saying, "You are my
6:41 the five loaves and two fish, looked up toward **h**,
7:34 And looking up to **h**, he sighed and commanded,
8:11 "Give us a miraculous sign from **h** to prove
9:43 It is better to enter **h** with only one hand than to go
9:45 It is better to enter **h** with only one foot than to be
10:21 money to the poor, and you will have treasure in **h**.
11:10 of our ancestor David! / Praise God in highest **h**!"
11:25 so that your Father in **h** will forgive your sins,
11:30 "Did John's baptism come from **h** or was it merely
11:31 "If we say it was from **h**, he will ask why we
12:25 won't be married. They will be like the angels in **h**.
13:25 from the sky, / and the powers of **h** will be shaken.
13:27 from the farthest ends of the earth and **h**.
13:31 **H** and earth will disappear, but my words will
13:32 not even the angels in **h** or the Son himself.
14:62 of power and coming back on the clouds of **h**."
16:19 he was taken up into **h** and sat down in the place of
Lk 1:78 the light from **h** is about to break upon us,
2:13 host of others—the armies of **h**—praising God:
2:14 "Glory to God in the highest **h**, / and peace on
2:15 When the angels had returned to **h**, the shepherds
3:22 And a voice from **h** said, "You are my beloved
6:23 leap for joy! For a great reward awaits you in **h**.
6:35 Then your reward from **h** will be very great,
9:16 the five loaves and two fish, looked up toward **h**,
9:51 As the time drew near for his return to **h**,
9:54 should we order down fire from **h** to burn them
10:15 people of Capernaum, will you be exalted to **h**?
10:18 "I saw Satan falling from **h** as a flash of lightning!
10:20 your names are registered as citizens of **h**."
10:21 and said, "O Father, Lord of **h** and earth,
11:16 others asked for a miraculous sign from **h** to see if
12:33 in need. This will store up treasure for you in **h**!
12:33 And the purses of **h** have no holes in them.
13:24 "The door to **h** is narrow. Work hard to get in,
15:7 **h** will be happier over one lost sinner who returns
15:18 "Father, I have sinned against both **h** and you,
15:21 'Father, I have sinned against both **h** and you,
16:9 your generosity stores up a reward for you in **h**.
16:11 who will trust you with the true riches of **h**?
16:17 It is stronger and more permanent than **h** and earth.
17:29 Then fire and burning sulfur rained down from **h**
18:13 and dared not even lift his eyes to **h** as he prayed.
18:22 money to the poor, and you will have treasure in **h**.
19:38 Peace in **h** / and glory in highest **h**!"
20:4 "Did John's baptism come from **h**, or was it
20:5 "If we say it was from **h**, he will ask why we
21:33 **H** and earth will disappear, but my words will
22:43 Then an angel from **h** appeared and strengthened
24:49 Spirit comes and fills you with power from **h**."
24:50 and lifting his hands to **h**, he blessed them.
24:51 blessing them, he left them and was taken up to **h**.
Jn 1:32 saw the Holy Spirit descending like a dove from **h**
1:51 you will all see **h** open and the angels of God
3:6 but the Holy Spirit gives new life from **h**.
3:12 possibly believe if I tell you what is going on in **h**?
3:13 have come to earth and will return to **h** again.
3:19 The light from **h** came into the world, but they
3:27 "God in **h** appoints each person's work.
3:31 to the things of earth, but he has come from **h**.
6:31 'Moses gave them bread from **h** to eat.' "
6:32 assure you, Moses didn't give them bread from **h**.
6:32 And now he offers you the true bread from **h**.
6:33 bread of God is the one who comes down from **h**
6:38 For I have come down from **h** to do the will of
6:41 because he had said, "I am the bread from **h**."
6:42 How can he say, 'I came down from **h**'?"
6:50 the bread from **h** gives eternal life to everyone who
6:51 I am the living bread that came down out of **h**.
6:58 I am the true bread from **h**. Anyone who eats this
6:62 if you see me, the Son of Man, return to **h** again?
11:41 Then Jesus looked up to **h** and said, "Father,
12:28 Then a voice spoke from **h**, saying, "I have
17:1 he looked up to **h** and said, "Father, the time has
Ac 1:2 until the day he ascended to **h** after giving his

1:11 Jesus has been taken away from you into **h**.
1:22 by John until the day he was taken from us into **h**.
2: 2 there was a sound from **h** like the roaring of a
2:33 Now he sits on the throne of highest honor in **h**,
2:34 For David himself never ascended into **h**, yet he
3:21 For he must remain in **h** until the time for the final
4:12 There is no other name in all of **h** for people to call
4:24 Sovereign Lord, Creator of **h** and earth, the sea,
7:49 '**H** is my throne, / and the earth is my footstool.
7:50 Didn't I make everything in **h** and earth?'
7:55 gazed steadily upward into **h** and saw the glory of
9: 3 a brilliant light from **h** suddenly beamed down
10:16 Then the sheet was pulled up again to **h**.
11: 9 "But the voice from **h** came again, 'If God says
11:10 and all it contained was pulled back up to **h**.
14:15 who made **h** and earth, the sea, and everything in
17:24 Since he is Lord of **h** and earth, he doesn't live in
19:35 whose image fell down to us from **h**.
22: 6 about noon a very bright light from **h** suddenly
26:13 a light from **h** brighter than the sun shone down on
26:19 I was not disobedient to that vision from **h**.
Ro 1:18 But God shows his anger from **h** against all sinful,
10: 6 "You don't need to go to **h**" (to find Christ
1Co 1:22 because they want a sign from **h** to prove it is true.
8: 5 and many lords, both in **h** and on earth.
13: 1 If I could speak in any language in **h** or on earth
15:47 while Christ, the second man, came from **h**.
15:49 so we will someday be like Christ, the man from **h**.
2Co 5: 1 we will have a home in **h**, an eternal body made
12: 2 I was caught up into the third **h** fourteen years ago.
Gal 1: 8 Even if an angel comes from **h** and preaches any
Eph 1:10 authority of Christ—everything in **h** and on earth.
3:15 the Creator of everything in **h** and on earth.
6: 9 remember, you both have the same Master in **h**,
Php 1:27 of the Good News about Christ, as citizens of **h**.
2: 9 God raised him up to the heights of **h** and gave him
2:10 will bow, in **h** and on earth and under the earth,
3:14 through Christ Jesus, is calling us up to **h**.
3:20 But we are citizens of **h**, where the Lord Jesus
Col 1: 5 because you are looking forward to the joys of **h**—
1:16 the one through whom God created everything in **h**
1:20 He made peace with everything in **h** and on earth
3: 1 with Christ, set your sights on the realities of **h**,
3: 2 Let **h** fill your thoughts. Do not think only about
4: 1 Remember that you also have a Master—in **h**.
1Th 1:10 forward to the coming of God's Son from **h**—
4:16 For the Lord himself will come down from **h** with
2Th 1: 7 also for us when the Lord Jesus appears from **h**.
1Ti 3:16 believed on in the world / and was taken up into **h**.
6:15 For at the right time Christ will be revealed from **h**
Heb 1: 3 of honor at the right hand of the majestic God of **h**.
3: 1 friends who belong to God and are bound for **h**,
4:14 we have a great High Priest who has gone to **h**,
6: 4 those who have experienced the good things of **h**
6:19 It leads us through the curtain of **h** into God's
7:26 he has been given the highest place of honor in **h**.
8: 1 Priest sat down in the place of highest honor in **h**,
8: 5 that is only a copy, a shadow of the real one in **h**.
9:11 He has entered that great, perfect sanctuary in **h**,
9:23 in it—which were copies of things in **h**—
9:23 But the real things in **h** had to be purified with far
9:24 For Christ has entered into **h** itself to appear now
9:24 for that was merely a copy of the real Temple in **h**.
9:25 Nor did he enter **h** to offer himself again and again,
11: 5 It was by faith that Enoch was taken up to **h**
12: 2 place of highest honor beside God's throne in **h**.
12:23 firstborn children, whose names are written in **h**.
12:23 redeemed in **h** who have now been made perfect.
12:25 if we reject the One who speaks to us from **h**!
13:14 we are looking forward to our city in **h**, which is
Jas 3:17 But the wisdom that comes from **h** is first of all
5:12 never take an oath, by **h** or earth or anything else.
1Pe 1: 4 It is kept in **h** for you, pure and undefiled,
1:12 to you in the power of the Holy Spirit sent from **h**.
3:22 Now Christ has gone to **h**. He is seated in the place
2Pe 1:11 And God will open wide the gates of **h** for you to
1:17 majestic voice called down from **h**, "This is my
Rev 1: 7 Look! He comes with the clouds of **h**.
2:17 eat of the manna that has been hidden away in **h**.
3:12 the new Jerusalem that comes down from **h** from
4: 1 Then as I looked, I saw a door standing open in **h**,
4: 2 and I saw a throne in **h** and someone sitting on it!
5: 3 But no one in **h** or on earth or under the earth was
5:13 And then I heard every creature in **h** and on earth
8: 1 there was silence throughout **h** for about half an
10: 1 I saw another mighty angel coming down from **h**,
10: 4 about to write. But a voice from **h** called to me:
10: 5 on the sea and on the land lifted his right hand to **h**.
10: 6 who created **h** and everything in it, the earth
10: 8 Then the voice from **h** called to me again: "Go
11:12 Then a loud voice shouted from **h**, "Come up
11:12 And they rose to **h** in a cloud as their enemies
11:13 die was terrified and gave glory to the God of **h**.
11:15 and there were loud voices shouting in **h**:
11:19 Then, in **h**, the Temple of God was opened
12: 1 Then I witnessed in **h** an event of great
12: 3 I witnessed in **h** another significant event.
12: 7 Then there was war in **h**. Michael and the angels
12: 8 the dragon lost the battle and was forced out of **h**.
13: 6 slandering his name and all who live in **h**, who are
13:13 such as making fire flash down to earth from **h**
14: 2 And I heard a sound from **h** like the roaring of a
14: 7 Worship him who made **h** and earth, the sea,
14:13 And I heard a voice from **h** saying, "Write this
14:17 another angel came from the Temple in **h**,
15: 1 Then I saw in **h** another significant event, and it
15: 5 Then I looked and saw that the Temple in **h**,
16:11 and they cursed the God of **h** for their pains
16:17 shout came from the throne of the Temple in **h**,
18: 1 angel come down from **h** with great authority,
18: 4 Then I heard another voice calling from **h**,
18: 5 For her sins are piled as high as **h**, and God is
18:20 But you, O **h**, rejoice over her fate. And you also
19: 1 I heard the sound of a vast crowd in **h** shouting,
19:11 Then I saw **h** opened, and a white horse was
19:14 The armies of **h**, dressed in pure white linen,
20: 1 Then I saw an angel come down from **h** with the
20: 9 But fire from **h** came down on the attacking armies
21: 1 Then I saw a new **h** and a new earth, for the old **h**
and the old earth had disappeared.
21: 2 coming down from God out of **h** like a beautiful
21:10 Jerusalem, descending out of **h** from God.

HEAVEN'S (5) [HEAVEN]

Ps 82: 1 God presides over **h** court; / he pronounces
Da 8:11 He even challenged the Commander of **h** armies
8:13 will the Temple and **h** armies be trampled on?"
Heb 10:19 we can boldly enter **h** Most Holy Place because of
Jas 1:17 to us from God above, who created all **h** lights.

HEAVENLY (37) [HEAVEN]

HEAVENLY FATHER (12) Mt 5:16; 6:14,26,32; 7:11; 15:13; 18:10,35; Lk 11:13; Heb 12:9; 1Pe 1:17; 1Jn 3:1

Dt 4:19 The LORD your God designated these **h** bodies
Job 25: 3 Who is able to count his **h** army? Does his light not
Ps 102:19 from his **h** sanctuary. / He looked to the earth
104:13 You send rain on the mountains from your **h** home,
136: 7 Give thanks to him who made the **h** lights—
150: 1 Praise the LORD! / Praise God in his **h** dwelling;
Da 8:10 to the heavens where it attacked the **h** armies,
8:10 throwing some of the **h** beings and stars to the
Mt 5:16 to see, so that everyone will praise your **h** Father.
6:14 sin against you, your **h** Father will forgive you.
6:26 food in barns because your **h** Father feeds them.
6:32 Your **h** Father already knows all your needs,
7:11 how much more will your **h** Father give good gifts
15:13 "Every plant not planted by my **h** Father will be
18:10 angels are always in the presence of my **h** Father.
18:14 it is not my **h** Father's will that even one of these
18:35 "That's what my **h** Father will do to you if you
Lk 11:13 how much more will your **h** Father give the Holy
1Co 15:40 The glory of the **h** bodies is different from the
15:48 but our **h** bodies will be just like Christ's.
15:53 be transformed into **h** bodies that will never die.
15:54 transformed into **h** bodies that will never die—
2Co 5: 2 and we long for the day when we will put on our **h**
5: 3 without bodies, but we will put on new **h** bodies.
Gal 4:26 the free woman, represents the **h** Jerusalem.
Eph 1: 3 us with every spiritual blessing in the **h** realms
1:20 place of honor at God's right hand in the **h** realms.
2: 6 and we are seated with him in the **h** realms—
3:10 to all the rulers and authorities in the **h** realms.
6:12 and against wicked spirits in the **h** realms.
2Ti 4:18 and will bring me safely to his **h** Kingdom.
Heb 11:16 they were looking for a better place, a **h** homeland.
11:16 their God, for he has prepared a **h** city for them.
12: 9 cheerfully submit to the discipline of our **h** Father
12:22 to the city of the living God, the **h** Jerusalem,
1Pe 1:17 And remember that the **h** Father to whom you pray
1Jn 3: 1 See how very much our **h** Father loves us, for he

HEAVENS (166) [HEAVEN]

HEAVENS...EARTH; EARTH...HEAVEN (93) Ge 1:1,17; 2:1,4,4; 49:25; Ex 20:11; Dt 4:32; 10:14; 32:1; 33:13; Jos 2:11; 2Sa 22:8; 1Ki 8:27; 2Ki 19:15; 1Ch 16:31; 29:11; 2Ch 2:12; 6:18; Ne 9:6; Job 20:27; 28:24; Ps 8:1; 19:4; 57:5,11; 68:8; 73:9; 89:11; 96:11; 102:25; 103:11; 108:5; 113:6; 115:16; 121:2; 124:8; 147:8; Pr 3:19; Isa 1:2; 13:13; 24:21; 37:16; 40:12,22; 42:5; 44:23,24; 45:8,12,18; 48:13; 49:13; 55:9,10; 65:17; 66:22; Jer 4:23,28; 10:11,12,13; 23:24; 31:37; 32:17; 33:2; 51:15,16,48; Eze 32:4; Da 6:27; Joel 2:10,30; 3:16; Am 9:6; Hab 3:3; Hag 1:10; 2:6,21; Zec 12:1; Mt 24:30; Lk 21:26; Ac 2:19; 1Co 15:40; Heb 1:10; 12:26; 2Pe 3:5,7,10,13; Rev 12:10,12,12

Ge 1: 1 In the beginning God created the **h** and the earth.
1:17 God set these lights in the **h** to light the earth,
2: 1 So the creation of the **h** and the earth
2: 4 This is the account of the creation of the **h**
2: 4 When the LORD God made the **h** and the earth,
15: 5 "Look up into the **h** and count the stars if you can.
19:24 and burning sulfur from the **h** on Sodom
49:25 bless you / with the blessings of the **h** above,
Ex 20:11 For in six days the LORD made the **h**, the earth,
24:10 a pavement of brilliant sapphire, as clear as the **h**.
Dt 4:32 Then search from one end of the **h** to the other.
10:14 The highest **h** and the earth and everything in it all
28:12 rich treasury in the **h** to bless all the work you do.
32: 1 "Listen, O **h**, and I will speak! / Hear, O earth,
32:43 "Rejoice with him, O **h**, / and let all the angels of
33:13 with the choice gift of rain from the **h**, / and water
33:26 He rides across the **h** to help you, / across the skies
33:28 of grain and wine, / while the **h** drop down dew.
Jos 2:11 your God is the supreme God of the **h** above
2Sa 22: 8 and trembled; / the foundations of the **h** shook;
22:10 He opened the **h** and came down; / dark storm
1Ki 8:27 Why, even the highest **h** cannot contain you.
2Ki 19:15 of the earth. You alone created the **h** and the earth.
1Ch 16:26 are merely idols, / but the LORD made the **h**!
16:31 Let the **h** be glad, and let the earth rejoice!
29:11 Everything in the **h** and on earth is yours,
2Ch 2: 6 Not even the highest **h** can contain him!
2:12 the God of Israel, who made the **h** and the earth!
6:18 Why, even the highest **h** cannot contain you.
7:13 At times I might shut up the **h** so that no rain falls,
Ezr 9: 6 than our heads, and our guilt has reached to the **h**.
Ne 9: 6 You made the skies and the **h** and all the stars.
Job 9: 8 He alone has spread out the **h** and marches on the
11: 8 Such knowledge is higher than the **h**—but who are
14:12 Until the **h** are no more, they will not wake up nor
15:15 Even the **h** cannot be absolutely pure in his sight.
20: 6 Though the godless man's pride reaches to the **h**
20:27 The **h** will reveal his guilt, and the earth will give
22:12 higher than the **h**, higher than the farthest stars.
25: 2 and dreadful. He enforces peace in the **h**.
26:13 His Spirit made the **h** beautiful, and his power
28:24 looks throughout the whole earth, under all the **h**.
37: 3 It rolls across the **h**, and his lightning flashes out in
38:29 of the ice? Who gives birth to the frost from the **h**?
38:32 of the Bear with her cubs across the **h**?
Ps 8: 1 fills the earth! / Your glory is higher than the **h**.
18: 9 He opened the **h** and came down; / dark storm
19: 1 The **h** tell of the glory of God. / The skies display
19: 4 The sun lives in the **h** / where God placed it.
19: 6 The sun rises at one end of the **h** / and follows its
33: 6 LORD merely spoke, / and the **h** were created.
36: 5 Your unfailing love, O LORD, is as vast as the **h**;
50: 6 Then let the **h** proclaim his justice, / for God
57: 5 Be exalted, O God, above the highest **h**!
57:10 For your unfailing love is as high as the **h**.
57:11 Be exalted, O God, above the highest **h**.
68: 8 the earth trembled, and the **h** poured rain
68:33 Sing to the one who rides across the ancient **h**,
68:34 down on Israel; / his strength is mighty in the **h**.
71:19 O God, reaches to the highest **h**.
73: 9 They boast against the very **h**, / and their words
75: 5 Don't lift your fists in defiance at the **h** / or speak
78:26 He released the east wind in the **h** / and guided the
89: 2 Your faithfulness is as enduring as the **h**.
89:11 The **h** are yours, and the earth is yours;
92: 8 But you are exalted in the **h**. / You, O LORD,
96: 5 are merely idols, / but the LORD made the **h**!
96:11 Let the **h** be glad, and let the earth rejoice!
97: 6 The **h** declare his righteousness; / every nation sees
102:25 of the earth, / and the **h** are the work of your hands.
103:11 is as great as the height of the **h** above the earth.
103:19 The LORD has made the **h** his throne;
104: 2 You stretch out the starry curtain of the **h**;
107:26 Their ships were tossed to the **h** / and sank again to
108: 4 For your unfailing love is higher than the **h**.
108: 5 Be exalted, O God, above the highest **h**.
113: 4 the nations; / his glory is far greater than the **h**.
113: 6 Far below him are the **h** and the earth. / He stoops
115: 3 For our God is in the **h**, / and he does as he wishes.
115:16 The **h** belong to the LORD, / but he has given the
121: 2 from the LORD, / who made the **h** and the earth!
124: 8 from the LORD, / who made the **h** and the earth.
136: 5 Give thanks to him who made the **h** so skillfully.
144: 5 Bend down the **h**, LORD, and come down.
147: 8 He covers the **h** with clouds, / provides rain for the
148: 1 the LORD! / Praise the LORD from the **h**!
Pr 3:19 the earth; by understanding he established the **h**.
8:27 "I was there when he established the **h**, when he
Isa 1: 2 Hear, O **h**! Listen, O earth! This is what the
13:10 The **h** will be black above them. No light will
13:13 For I will shake the **h**, and the earth will move
14:14 I will climb to the highest **h** and be like the Most
24:18 Destruction falls on you from the **h**. The world is
24:21 the LORD will punish the fallen angels in the **h**
34: 4 The **h** above will melt away and disappear like a
34: 5 And when my sword has finished its work in the **h**,
37:16 of the earth. You alone created the **h** and the earth.
40:12 Who has measured off the **h** with his fingers?
40:22 He is the one who spreads out the **h** like a curtain
40:26 Look up into the **h**. Who created all the stars?
42: 5 the LORD, created the **h** and stretched them out.
44:23 Sing, O **h**, for the LORD has done this wondrous
44:24 who made all things. I alone stretched out the **h**.
45: 8 Open up, O **h**, and pour out your righteousness.
45:12 to live on it. With my hands I stretched out the **h**.
45:18 and he created the **h** and earth and put everything
48:13 The palm of my right hand spread out the **h** above.
49:13 Sing for joy, O **h**! Rejoice, O earth! Burst into
55: 9 For just as the **h** are higher than the earth, so are
55:10 "The rain and snow come down from the **h**
64: 1 that you would burst from the **h** and come down!
65:17 I am creating new **h** and a new earth—
66:22 "As surely as my new **h** and earth will remain,
Jer 2:12 The **h** are shocked at such a thing and shrink back
4:23 I looked at the **h**, and there was no light.
4:28 earth will mourn, the **h** will be draped in black,
10:11 so-called gods, who did not make the **h** and earth,
10:12 He has stretched out the **h** / by his understanding.
10:13 When he speaks, there is thunder in the **h**.
23:24 Am I not everywhere in all the **h** and earth?"
31:37 Just as the **h** cannot be measured
32:17 You have made the **h** and earth by your great
33: 2 "The LORD, the Maker of the **h** and earth—
51:15 He has stretched out the **h** / by his understanding.
51:16 When he speaks, there is thunder in the **h**.
51:48 The **h** and earth will rejoice, for out of the north
51:53 Though Babylon reaches as high as the **h**,
La 3:66 destroying them from beneath the LORD's **h**.
Eze 1: 1 the **h** were opened to me, and I saw visions of God.
32: 4 All the birds of the **h** will land on you, and the wild
32: 7 I blot you out, I will veil the **h** and darken the stars.
Da 4:11 reaching high into the **h** for all the world to see.
4:20 reaching high into the **h** for all the world to see.
6:27 and wonders / in the **h** and on earth.
8:10 His power reached to the **h** where it attacked the

Joel 2:10 earth quakes as they advance, and the **h** tremble.
2:30 "I will cause wonders in the **h** and on the earth—
3:16 and the earth and **h** will begin to shake.
Am 9: 2 Even if they climb up into the **h**, I will bring them
9: 6 upper stories of the LORD's home are in the **h**,
Hab 3: 3 His brilliant splendor fills the **h**, and the earth is
Hag 1:10 That is why the **h** have withheld the dew
2: 6 In just a little while I will again shake the **h**
2:21 that I am about to shake the **h** and the earth.
Zec 12: 1 who stretched out the **h**, laid the foundations of the
Mt 3:16 the **h** were opened and he saw the Spirit of God
24:30 the coming of the Son of Man will appear in the **h**,
Mk 1:10 he saw the **h** split open and the Holy Spirit
Lk 3:21 was baptized. As he was praying, the **h** opened,
21:11 and great miraculous signs in the **h**.
21:26 because the stability of the very **h** will be broken
Ac 2:19 And I will cause wonders in the **h** above
7:56 I see the **h** opened and the Son of Man standing in
1Co 15:40 There are bodies in the **h**, and there are bodies on
Eph 4:10 is the one who ascended higher than all the **h**,
Heb 1:10 of the earth, / and the **h** are the work of your hands.
12:26 I will shake not only the earth but the **h** also."
2Pe 3: 5 They deliberately forget that God made the **h** by
3: 7 And God has also commanded that the **h**
3:10 Then the **h** will pass away with a terrible noise,
3:12 the day when God will set the **h** on fire
3:13 But we are looking forward to the new **h** and new
Rev 12:10 Then I heard a loud voice shouting across the **h**,
12:12 Rejoice, O **h**! And you who live in the **h**, rejoice!
14: 6 And I saw another angel flying through the **h**,

HEAVIER (2) [HEAVY]

Job 6: 3 they would be **h** than all the sands of the sea.
Pr 27: 3 but the resentment caused by a fool is **h** than both.

HEAVILY (1) [HEAVY]

Ecc 8: 6 even as people's troubles lie **h** upon them.

HEAVING (1)

Eze 32: 2 **h** around in your own rivers, stirring up mud with

HEAVY (53) [HEAVIER, HEAVILY]

Ge 29: 2 But a **h** stone covered the mouth of the well.
Ex 1:11 hoping to wear them down under **h** burdens.
3: 9 the Egyptians have oppressed them with **h** tasks.
3:19 Egypt will not let you go except under **h** pressure.
18:18 This job is too **h** a burden for you to handle all by
23: 5 who hates you struggling beneath a **h** load,
26: 7 "Make **h** sheets of cloth from goat hair to cover
Nu 11:14 all these people by myself! The load is far too **h**!
Dt 32:15 the people grew **h**, plump, and stuffed!
Jdg 20:34 so **h** that Benjamin didn't realize the impending
1Sa 12:15 then his hand will be as **h** upon you as it was upon
17: 7 The shaft of his spear was as **h** and thick as a
2Sa 14:26 then only because it was too **h** to carry around.
1Ki 12: 4 and **h** taxes that your father imposed on us.
18:45 A **h** wind brought a terrific rainstorm, and Ahab
2Ki 17: 3 so Israel was forced to pay **h** annual tribute to
2Ch 10: 4 and **h** taxes that your father imposed on us.
13:17 Abijah and his army inflicted **h** losses on them;
21:14 your wives, and all that is yours with a **h** blow.
Ne 5:15 governors who had laid **h** burdens on the people,
Ps 32: 4 and night your hand of discipline was **h** on me.
38: 4 overwhelms me— / it is a burden too **h** to bear.
81: 6 I will free your hands from their **h** tasks.
88: 7 Your anger lies **h** on me; / wave after wave engulfs
Pr 14:13 Laughter can conceal a **h** heart; when the laughter
25:20 Singing cheerful songs to a person whose heart is **h**
27: 3 A stone is **h** and sand is weighty,
Ecc 11: 3 When the clouds are **h**, the rains come down.
Isa 24:16 But my heart is **h** with grief. I am discouraged,
28:27 A **h** sledge is never used on dill; rather, it is beaten
47: 2 Take **h** millstones and grind the corn.
47: 6 You have forced even the elderly to carry **h**
64: 5 We are constant sinners, so your anger is **h** on us.
La 3: 3 against me. Day and night his hand is **h** upon me.
3: 7 and I cannot escape. He has bound me in **h** chains.
5:13 and the children stagger under **h** loads of wood.
Eze 13:11 A **h** rainstorm will undermine it; great hailstones
27:26 Your mighty vessel flounders in the **h** eastern gale.
33:10 You are saying, 'Our sins are **h** upon us; we are
36: 8 But the mountains of Israel will produce **h** crops of
Hos 10:11 Now I will put a **h** yoke on her tender neck.
Zec 5: 7 When the **h** lead cover was lifted off the basket,
5: 8 her back into the basket and closed the **h** lid again.
8:12 among you. The grapevines will be **h** with fruit.
12: 3 On that day I will make Jerusalem a **h** stone,
Mt 11:28 all of you who are weary and carry **h** burdens,
14:24 wind had risen, and they were fighting **h** waves.
Lk 12:50 and I am under a **h** burden until it is accomplished.
1Ti 3: 3 He must not be a **h** drinker or be violent. He must
3: 8 They must not be **h** drinkers and must not be
Tit 1: 7 he must not be a **h** drinker, violent, or greedy for
2: 3 speaking evil of others and must not be **h** drinkers.
Rev 20: 1 key to the bottomless pit and a **h** chain in his hand.

HEBER (9) [HEBER'S, HEBERITES]

Ge 46:17 named Serah. Beriah's sons were **H** and Malkiel.
Nu 26:45 The Heberites, named after their ancestor **H**.
Jdg 4:11 Now **H** the Kenite, a descendant of Moses'
4:17 ran to the tent of Jael, the wife of **H** the Kenite,
5:24 "Most blessed is Jael, / the wife of **H** the Kenite.
1Ch 4:18 **H** (the father of Soco), and Jekuthiel (the father of
7:31 The sons of Beriah were **H** and Malkiel (the father
7:32 The sons of **H** were Japhlet, Shomer, and Hotham.
8:17 Zebadiah, Meshullam, Hizki, **H**,

HEBER'S (1) [HEBER]

Jdg 4:17 because **H** family was on friendly terms with King

HEBERITES (1) [HEBER]

Nu 26:45 The **H**, named after their ancestor Heber.

HEBREW (29) [HEBREWS, HEBREWS']

Ge 14:13 the men who escaped came and told Abram the **H**,
39:14 "My husband has brought this **H** slave here to
39:17 "That **H** slave you've had around here tried to
41:12 We told the dreams to a young **H** man who was a
Ex 1:15 gave this order to the **H** midwives, Shiphrah
1:16 "When you help the **H** women give birth, kill all
1:19 they told him, "the **H** women are very strong.
2: 6 "He must be one of the **H** children," she said.
2: 7 and find one of the **H** women to nurse the baby for
2:11 he saw an Egyptian beating one of the **H** slaves.
2:13 his people again, he saw two **H** men fighting.
21: 2 "If you buy a **H** slave, he is to serve for only six
22:25 "If you lend money to a fellow **H** in need, do not
1Sa 4: 6 "What's all the shouting about in the **H** camp?"
2Ki 18:26 Don't speak in **H**, for the people on the wall will
18:28 and shouted in **H** to the people on the wall,
2Ch 32:18 **H** language to the people gathered on the walls of
Isa 19:18 They will even begin to speak the **H** language.
36:11 Don't speak in **H**, for the people on the wall will
36:13 and shouted in **H** to the people on the wall,
Jer 34: 9 He had ordered all the people to free their **H**
34:14 I told them that every **H** slave must be freed after
Jnh 1: 9 And Jonah answered, "I am a **H**, and I worship the
Jn 19:13 platform that is called the Stone Pavement (in **H**,
19:17 Jesus went to the place called Skull Hill (in **H**,
19:20 and the sign was written in **H**, Latin, and Greek,
Ac 6: 1 Greek complained against those who spoke **H**,
Rev 9:11 his name in **H** is *Abaddon,* and in Greek,
16:16 their armies to a place called *Armageddon* in **H**.

HEBREWS (13) [HEBREW]

Ge 40:15 the land of the **H**, and now I'm here in jail, but I
43:32 because Egyptians despise **H** and refuse to eat with
Ex 3:18 and tell him, 'The LORD, the God of the **H**,
5: 3 "The God of the **H** has met with us,"
7:16 Say to him, 'The LORD, the God of the **H**,
9: 1 'This is what the LORD, the God of the **H**, says:
9:13 and tell him, 'The LORD, the God of the **H**, says:
10: 3 "This is what the LORD, the God of the **H**, says:
1Sa 13:19 fear they would make swords and spears for the **H**.
14:11 "Look! The **H** are crawling out of their holes!"
14:21 Even the **H** who had gone over to the Philistine
29: 3 "What are these **H** doing here?"
2Co 11:22 They say they are **H**, do they? So am I. And they

HEBREWS' (1) [HEBREW]

1Sa 4: 9 we will become the **H** slaves just as they have been

HEBRON (74) [HEBRONITES, KIRIATH-ARBA]

Ge 13:18 to the oak grove owned by Mamre, which is at **H**.
23: 2 she died at Kiriath-arba (now called **H**) in the land
23:19 the cave of Machpelah, near Mamre, which is at **H**.
35:27 which is near Kiriath-arba (now called **H**),
37:14 to Shechem from his home in the valley of **H**.
Ex 6:18 of Kohath included Amram, Izhar, **H**, and Uzziel.
Nu 3:19 of his descendants, Amram, Izhar, **H**, and Uzziel.
3:27 descended from Amram, Izhar, **H**, and Uzziel.
13:22 passed first through the Negev and arrived at **H**,
13:22 (The ancient town of **H** was founded seven years
Jos 10: 3 Hoham of **H**, Piram of Jarmuth, Japhia of Lachish,
10:23 of Jerusalem, **H**, Jarmuth, Lachish, and Eglon.
10:36 After leaving Eglon, they attacked **H**,
10:39 Debir just as they had destroyed Libnah and **H**.
11:21 who lived in the hill country of **H**, Debir, Anab,
12:10 The king of Jerusalem / The king of **H**
14:13 of Jephunneh and gave **H** to him as an inheritance.
14:14 **H** still belongs to the descendants of Caleb son of
14:15 (Previously **H** had been called Kiriath-arba.
15:13 So Caleb was given the city of Arba (that is, **H**),
15:54 Humtah, Kiriath-arba (that is, **H**), and Zior—
20: 7 and Kiriath-arba (that is, **H**), in the hill country of
21:11 Kiriath-arba (that is, **H**), in the hill country of
21:13 **H** (a city of refuge for those who accidentally
Jdg 1:10 Judah marched against the Canaanites in **H**
1:20 The city of **H** was given to Caleb as Moses had
16: 3 all the way to the top of the hill across from **H**.
1Sa 30:31 **H**, and all the other places they had visited.
2Sa 2: 1 should I go to?" And the LORD replied, "**H**."
2: 3 to Judah, and they settled near the town of **H**.
2:11 David made **H** his capital, and he ruled as king of
2:13 Joab son of Zeruiah led David's troops from **H**,
2:32 they traveled all night and reached **H** at daybreak.
3: 2 These were the sons who were born to David in **H**:
3: 5 These sons were all born to David in **H**.
3:19 Then he went to **H** to tell David that all the people
3:20 When Abner came to **H** with his twenty men,
3:27 When Abner arrived at **H**, Joab took him aside at
3:32 They buried Abner in **H**, and the king and all the
4: 1 When Ishbosheth heard about Abner's death at **H**,
4: 8 They arrived at **H** and presented Ishbosheth's head
4:12 and hung their bodies beside the pool in **H**.
4:12 and buried it in Abner's tomb in **H**.
5: 1 Then all the tribes of Israel went to David at **H**
5: 3 So there at **H**, David made a covenant with the
5: 5 He had reigned over Judah from **H** for seven years
5:13 After moving from **H** to Jerusalem, David married
15: 7 "Let me go to **H** to offer a sacrifice to the LORD
15: 8 I promised to sacrifice to him in **H** if he would
15: 9 and fulfill your vow." So Absalom went to **H**.
15:10 know that Absalom has been crowned king in **H**."
1Ki 2:11 seven of them in **H** and thirty-three in Jerusalem.
1Ch 2:42 Caleb's second son was Mareshah, the father of **H**.
2:43 The sons of **H** were Korah, Tappuah, Rekem,
3: 1 These were the sons who were born to David in **H**:
3: 4 These six sons were born to David in **H**, where he
6: 2 of Kohath were Amram, Izhar, **H**, and Uzziel.
6:18 of Kohath included Amram, Izhar, **H**, and Uzziel.
6:55 This included **H** and its surrounding pasturelands
6:57 **H** (a city of refuge), Libnah, Jattir, Eshtemoa,
11: 1 Then all Israel went to David at **H** and told him,
11: 3 So there at **H** David made a covenant with the
12:23 numbers of armed warriors who joined David at **H**.
12:38 All these men came in battle array to **H** with the
15: 9 There were 80 descendants of **H**, with Eliel as their
23:12 of Kohath included Amram, Izhar, **H**, and Uzziel.
23:19 The descendants of **H** included Jeriah (the family
24:23 From the descendants of **H**, Jeriah was the leader,
26:23 that descended from Amram, Izhar, **H**, and Uzziel:
26:30 From the clan of **H** came Hashabiah. He and his
26:31 Also from the clan of **H** came Jeriah, who was the
26:31 and capable men from the clan of **H** were found at
29:27 seven years from **H** and thirty-three years from
2Ch 11:10 Zorah, Aijalon, and **H**. These became the fortified

HEBRONITES (2) [HEBRON]

Nu 26:58 The Libnites, the **H**, the Mahlites, the Mushites,
1Ch 26:31 who was the leader of the **H** according to the

HEDGE (1) [HEDGES]

Mic 7: 4 the straightest is more crooked than a **h** of thorns.

HEDGES (3) [HEDGE]

Jer 49: 3 Weep and wail, hiding in the **h**, for your god
Na 3:17 crowding together in the **h** to survive the cold.
Lk 14:23 'Go out into the country lanes and behind the **h**

HEEDED (1) [HEEDS]

Pr 29:19 the words may be understood, but they are not **h**.

HEEDS (1) [HEEDED]

Pr 25:12 Valid criticism is as treasured by the one who **h** it

HEEL (3) [HEELS]

Ge 3:15 will crush your head, and you will strike his **h**."
25:26 twin was born with his hand grasping Esau's **h**.
Job 18: 9 A trap grabs them by the **h**. A noose tightens

HEELS (2) [HEEL]

Ge 49:17 viper along the path, / that bites the horse's **h**
La 5: 5 Those who pursue us are at our **h**; we are

HEGAI (3) [HEGAI'S]

Est 2: 3 **H**, the eunuch in charge, will see that they are all
2: 9 **H** was very impressed with Esther and treated her
2:15 she accepted the advice of **H**, the eunuch in charge

HEGAI'S (1) [HEGAI]

Est 2: 8 harem at the fortress of Susa and placed in **H** care.

HEIFER (10)

Ge 15: 9 LORD told him, "Bring me a three-year-old **h**,
Nu 19: 2 Tell the people of Israel to bring you a red **h** that
19: 5 As Eleazar watches, the **h** must be burned—
19: 6 and throw them into the fire where the **h** is
19: 9 clean will gather up the ashes of the **h**
19:10 The man who gathers up the ashes of the **h** must
Jdg 14:18 Samson replied, "If you hadn't plowed with my **h**,
1Sa 16: 2 "Take a **h** with you," the LORD replied,
Hos 4:16 Israel is as stubborn as a **h**, so the LORD will put
10:11 "Israel is like a trained **h** accustomed to treading

HEIGHT (12) [HEIGHTS]

1Sa 16: 7 "Don't judge by his appearance or **h**, for I have
Ezr 6: 3 Its **h** will be ninety feet, and its width will be
Ne 4: 6 At last the wall was completed to half its original **h**
Ps 103:11 is as great as the **h** of the heavens above the earth.
Pr 25: 3 No one can discover the **h** of heaven, the depth of
Eze 19:11 It stood out because of its **h** / and because of its
43:13 wide around its edge. And this is the **h** of the altar:
Da 8: 8 But at the **h** of its power, its large horn was broken
8:23 when their sin is at its **h**, a fierce king, a master of
11: 4 But at the **h** of his power, his kingdom will be
Lk 2:52 So Jesus grew both in **h** and in wisdom, and he
Rev 21:16 its length and width and **h** were each 1,400 miles.

HEIGHTS (14) [HEIGHT]

Nu 21:28 in Moab; / it destroyed the rulers of the Arnon **h**.
2Sa 22:34 a deer, / leading me safely along the mountain **h**.
Job 39:27 Is it at your command that the eagle rises to the **h**
Ps 18:33 a deer, / leading me safely along the mountain **h**.
68:18 When you ascended to the **h**, / you led a crowd of
Pr 9: 3 She calls out from the **h** overlooking the city.
9:14 She sits in her doorway on the **h** overlooking the
Ecc 12: 5 You will be afraid of **h** and of falling, white-haired

Jer 31:12 and sing songs of joy on the **h** of Jerusalem.
51:25 my fist against you, to roll you down from the **h**.
La 2: 1 lies in the dust, thrown down from the **h** of heaven.
Eze 36: 2 saying, 'Aha! Now the ancient **h** belong to us!'
Eph 4: 8 the Scriptures say, / "When he ascended to the **h**,
Php 2: 9 God raised him up to the **h** of heaven and gave him

HEIR (16) [INHERIT]

Ge 15: 3 so one of my servants will have to be my **h**."
15: 4 said to him, "No, your servant will not be your **h**,
38: 8 Her first son from you will be your brother's **h**."
38: 9 to have a child who would not be his own **h**.
Ps 89:29 I will preserve an **h** for him; / his throne will be as
Isa 11:10 In that day the **h** to David's throne will be a banner
Eze 26: 2 routes to the east has been broken, and I am the **h**!
Mt 21:38 to one another, 'Here comes the **h** to this estate.
22:24 and have a child who will be the brother's **h**.'
Mk 12: 7 to one another, 'Here comes the **h** to this estate.
12:19 and have a child who will be the brother's **h**.
Lk 20:14 said to each other, 'Here comes the **h** to this estate.
20:28 and have a child who will be the brother's **h**.
Ro 15:12 Isaiah said, / "The **h** to David's throne will come,
Rev 5: 5 of Judah, the **h** to David's throne, has conquered.
22:16 both the source of David and the **h** to his throne.

HEIRS (5) [INHERIT]

Jdg 21:17 There must be **h** for the survivors so that an entire
Isa 53:10 he will have a multitude of children, many **h**.
Jer 36:30 He will have no **h** to sit on the throne of David.
Zec 8:12 in Judah and Israel the **h** of these blessings.
Gal 3:29 You are his **h**, and now all the promises God gave

HELAH (2)

1Ch 4: 5 of Tekoa) had two wives, named **H** and Naarah.
4: 7 **H** gave birth to Zereth, Izhar, Ethnan,

HELAM (2)

2Sa 10:16 These troops arrived at **H** under the command of
10:17 crossed the Jordan River, and led the army to **H**.

HELBAH (1)

Jdg 1:31 Sidon, Ahlab, Aczib, **H**, Aphik, and Rehob.

HELBON (1)

Eze 27:18 bringing wine from **H** and white wool from Zahar.

HELD (86) [HOLD]

Ge 8: 9 and Noah **h** out his hand and drew the dove back
9:23 and Japheth took a robe, **h** it over their shoulders,
39: 9 He has **h** back nothing from me except you,
39:20 into the prison where the king's prisoners were **h**.
50:10 they **h** a very great and solemn funeral,
Ex 16:36 manna was an omer, which **h** about two quarts.)
17:11 As long as Moses **h** up the staff with his hands,
21:28 a case, however, the owner will not be **h** liable.
27:10 They will be **h** up by twenty bronze posts that fit
27:10 The curtains will be **h** up with silver hooks
27:11 150 feet of curtains **h** up by twenty posts fitted into
32:15 He **h** in his hands the two stone tablets inscribed
37:19 Each of the six branches **h** a cup shaped like an
39:21 the chestpiece was **h** securely to the ephod above
Lev 5: 1 they will be **h** responsible and be subject to
5:17 is done unintentionally, they will be **h** responsible.
17:16 your clothes and bathe, you will be **h** responsible."
19:17 so you will not be **h** guilty for their crimes.
26:13 so you can walk free with your heads **h** high.
Nu 5:31 but his wife will be **h** accountable for her sin.' "
15:34 They **h** him in custody because they did not know
18: 1 and your relatives from the tribe of Levi will be **h**
18: 1 and your sons alone will be **h** liable for violations
18:23 and they will be **h** responsible for any offenses
Dt 19:10 and you will not be **h** responsible for murder.
Jos 2:19 they will be killed, and we cannot be **h** to our oath.
Jdg 7:20 They **h** the blazing torches in their left hands
9:27 **h** in the temple of the local god, the wine flowed
16:23 The Philistine leaders **h** a great festival,
21: 5 **h** our council in the presence of the LORD at
21:19 of the annual festival of the LORD **h** in Shiloh,
1Sa 8: 2 and Abijah, his oldest sons, **h** court in Beersheba.
9: 6 He is **h** in high honor by all the people
2Sa 6:22 but I will be **h** in honor by the girls of whom you
23:12 but Shammah **h** his ground in the middle of the
1Ki 12:32 **h** on a day in midautumn, similar to the annual
2Ki 4:20 took him home, and his mother **h** him on her lap.
8:15 in water, and **h** it over the king's face until he died.
1Ch 11:14 and David **h** their ground in the middle of the field
26:26 **h** all the things dedicated to the LORD by King
2Ch 32:27 Hezekiah was very wealthy and **h** in high esteem.
Ne 8:14 in shelters during the festival to be **h** that month.
8:18 Then on October 15 they **h** a solemn assembly,
Est 1: 5 and was **h** at Susa in the courtyard of the palace
1:14 and **h** the highest positions in the empire.
8: 4 Again the king **h** out the gold scepter to Esther.
10: 3 great among the Jews, who **h** him in high esteem,
Job 32: 6 so I **h** back and did not dare to tell you what I
Ps 21: 2 you have **h** back nothing that he requested.
78:38 destroy them all. / Many a time he **h** back his anger
Pr 5:22 An evil man is **h** captive by his own sins; they are
22: 1 for being **h** in high esteem is better than having
SS 3: 4 A little while later I found him and **h** him. I didn't
7: 5 A king is **h** captive in your queenly tresses.
Isa 14: 6 blows of rage and **h** the nations in your angry grip.
40:12 Who else has **h** the oceans in his hand? Who has
Jer 26:19 Then the LORD **h** back the terrible disaster he
29: 7 Pray to the LORD for that city where you are **h**
36: 9 This happened on the day of sacred fasting **h** in
Eze 2: 9 saw a hand reaching out to me, and it **h** a scroll.
8:11 Each of them **h** an incense burner, so there was a
16:56 In your proud days you **h** Sodom in contempt.
19: 9 They **h** him in captivity, / so his voice could never
20:14 But again I **h** back in order to protect the honor of
20:17 and **h** back from destroying them in the wilderness.
33: 9 die in their sins, but you will not be **h** responsible.
Zec 10:11 of distress, for the waves of the sea will be **h** back.
Mt 28: 9 they ran to him, **h** his feet, and worshiped him.
Lk 5:29 Soon Levi **h** a banquet in his home with Jesus as
11:50 "And you of this generation will be **h** responsible
13:16 in which Satan has **h** her for eighteen years?"
24:40 As he spoke, he **h** out his hands for them to see,
Jn 2: 6 and **h** twenty to thirty gallons each.
19:29 put it on a hyssop branch, and **h** it up to his lips.
20:20 As he spoke, he **h** out his hands for them to see,
Ac 8:23 you are full of bitterness and **h** captive by sin."
2Co 4: 7 is **h** in perishable containers, that is, in our weak
2Ti 2:26 For they have been **h** captive by him to do
Jas 5: 4 The wages you **h** back cry out against you.
Rev 1:16 He **h** seven stars in his right hand, and a sharp
5: 8 a harp, and they **h** gold bowls filled with incense—
7: 9 in white and **h** palm branches in their hands.
9:14 And the voice spoke to the sixth angel who **h** the
17: 4 She **h** in her hand a gold goblet full of obscenities
21: 9 Then one of the seven angels who **h** the seven
21:15 The angel who talked to me **h** in his hand a gold

HELDAI (2)

Zec 6:10 "**H**, Tobijah, and Jedaiah will bring gifts of silver
6:14 **H**, Tobijah, Jedaiah, and Josiah son of

HELECH (1)

Eze 27:11 and from **H** stood on your walls as sentinels.

HELED (3)

2Sa 23:29 **H** son of Baanah from Netophah; / Ithai son of
1Ch 11:30 from Netophah; / **H** son of Baanah from Netophah;
27:15 **H**, a descendant of Othniel from Netophah,

HELEK (2) [HELEKITES]

Nu 26:30 The Helekites, named after their ancestor **H**.
Jos 17: 2 Abiezer, **H**, Asriel, Shechem, Hepher,

HELEKITES (1) [HELEK]

Nu 26:30 The **H**, named after their ancestor Helek.

HELEM (1)

1Ch 7:35 The sons of his brother **H** were Zophah, Imna,

HELEPH (1)

Jos 19:33 Its boundary ran from **H**, from the oak at

HELEZ (5)

2Sa 23:26 **H** from Pelon; / Ira son of Ikkesh from Tekoa;
1Ch 2:39 Azariah was the father of **H**. / **H** was the father of
Eleasah.
11:27 Shammah from Harod; / **H** from Pelon;
27:10 **H**, a descendant of Ephraim from Pelon,

HELI (2)

Lk 3:23 as the son of Joseph. / Joseph was the son of **H**.
3:24 **H** was the son of Matthat. / Matthat was the son of

HELIOPOLIS (5)

Ge 41:45 the daughter of Potiphera, priest of **H**.
41:50 Asenath, the daughter of Potiphera, priest of **H**.
46:20 was Asenath, daughter of Potiphera, priest of **H**.
Isa 19:18 One of these will be **H**, the City of the Sun.
Eze 30:17 The young men of **H** and Bubastis will die in

HELKAI (1)

Ne 12:15 **H** was leader of the family of Meremoth.

HELKATH (2) [HUKOK]

Jos 19:25 included these towns: **H**, Hali, Beten, Acshaph,
21:31 **H**, and Rehob—four towns and their pasturelands.

HELL (19)

Job 31:12 It is a devastating fire that destroys to **h**. It would
Pr 2:18 her house leads to death; it is the road to **h**.
Mt 5:22 curse someone, you are in danger of the fires of **h**.
5:29 body than for your whole body to be thrown into **h**.
5:30 body than for your whole body to be thrown into **h**.
7:13 The highway to **h** is broad, and its gate is wide for
10:28 who can destroy both soul and body in **h**.
16:18 and all the powers of **h** will not conquer it.
18: 9 blind than to have two eyes and be thrown into **h**.
23:15 then you turn him into twice the son of **h** as you
23:33 of vipers! How will you escape the judgment of **h**?
Mk 9:43 into the unquenchable fires of **h** with two hands.
9:45 one foot than to be thrown into **h** with two feet.
9:47 blind than to have two eyes and be thrown into **h**,
Lk 12: 5 power to kill people and then throw them into **h**.
Ro 8:38 and even the powers of **h** can't keep God's love
Jas 3: 6 flame of destruction, for it is set on fire by **h** itself.
5: 3 were counting on will eat away your flesh in **h**.
2Pe 2: 4 he threw them into **h**, in gloomy caves

HELLO (3)

Ro 16: 8 Say **h** to Ampliatus, whom I love as one of the
16:12 Say **h** to Tryphena and Tryphosa, the Lord's
16:23 Gaius says **h** to you. I am his guest, and the church

HELM [KJV] See RUDDER

HELMET (5) [HELMETS]

1Sa 17: 5 He wore a bronze **h** and a coat of mail that
17:38 his own armor—a bronze **h** and a coat of mail.
Isa 59:17 and placed the **h** of salvation on his head.
Eph 6:17 Put on salvation as your **h**, and take the sword of
1Th 5: 8 and wearing as our **h** the confidence of our

HELMETS (3) [HELMET]

2Ch 26:14 spears, **h**, coats of mail, bows, and sling stones.
Jer 46: 4 Put on your **h**, sharpen your spears, and prepare
Eze 27:10 They hung their shields and **h** on your walls,

HELMSMEN (4)

Eze 27: 8 your **h** were skilled men from Tyre itself.
27:27 your riches and wares, your sailors and **h**,
27:28 "Your cities by the sea tremble as your **h** cry out
27:29 the sailors and **h** come to stand on the shore.

HELON (5)

Nu 1: 9 Zebulun | Eliab son of **H**
2: 7[-8] Zebulun | Eliab son of **H** | 57,400
7:24 On the third day Eliab son of **H**, leader of the tribe
7:29 This was the offering brought by Eliab son of **H**.
10:16 The tribe of Zebulun was led by Eliab son of **H**.

HELP (448) [HELPED, HELPER, HELPFUL, HELPING, HELPLESS, HELPLESSLY, HELPS]

Ge 2:18 I will make a companion who will **h** him."
4: 1 birth to Cain, and she said, "With the LORD's **h**,
24:12 **H** me to accomplish the purpose of my journey.
37:22 Reuben was secretly planning to **h** Joseph escape,
49:25 May the God of your ancestors **h** you;
Ex 1:16 "When you **h** the Hebrew women give birth,
2: 9 the princess told her. "I will pay you for your **h**."
2:23 They cried out for **h**, and their pleas for
4:12 I will **h** you speak well, and I will tell you what to
4:15 I will **h** both of you to speak clearly, and I will tell
14:10 to panic, and they cried out to the LORD for **h**.
15:25 So Moses cried out to the LORD for **h**,
18:14 have been standing here all day to get your **h**."
18:22 They will **h** you carry the load, making the task
22:23 and they cry out to me, then I will surely **h** them.
22:27 return it and your neighbor cries out to me for **h**,
23: 5 do not walk by. Instead, stop and offer to **h**.
23:31 I will **h** you defeat the people now living in the
35:29 and woman who wanted to **h** in the work the
Nu 11: 2 The people screamed to Moses for **h**; and when he
15:40 The tassels will **h** you remember that you must
21: 2 "If you will **h** us conquer these people, we will
22: 5 message to request that Balaam come to **h** him:
34:18 Also enlist one leader from each tribe to **h** them
Dt 2:24 Look, I will **h** you defeat Sihon the Amorite,
2:30 and defiant so he could **h** you defeat them,
8: 5 the LORD your God disciplines you to **h** you.
22: 4 Go and **h** your neighbor get it to its feet!
22:24 woman is guilty because she did not scream for **h**.
23: 6 try to **h** the Ammonites or the Moabites in any
28:31 to your enemies, and no one will be there to **h** you.
28:32 as you long for them, but nothing you do will **h**.
32:38 Let those gods arise and **h** you! / Let them provide
33: 7 their cause; / **h** them against their enemies!"
33:26 He rides across the heavens to **h** you,
Jos 1:14 must lead the other tribes across the Jordan to **h**
10: 4 "Come and **h** me destroy Gibeon," he urged them,
10:33 had arrived with his army to **h** defend the city.
Jdg 1: 3 Then we will **h** you conquer your territory."
3: 9 But when Israel cried out to the LORD for **h**,
3:15 But when Israel cried out to the LORD for **h**,
4: 3 Then the Israelites cried out to the LORD for **h**.
5:23 because they did not come to **h** the LORD,
5:23 to **h** the LORD against the mighty warriors.'
6: 6 Then the Israelites cried out to the LORD for **h**.
6:17 Gideon replied, "If you are truly going to **h** me,
6:37 then I will know that you are going to **h** me rescue
11: 6 be our commander! **H** us fight the Ammonites!"
12: 1 "Why didn't you call for us to **h** you fight against
12: 2 "You failed to **h** us in our struggle against
Ru 2: 9 **h** yourself to the water they have drawn from the
2:14 over here and **h** yourself to some of our food.
1Sa 1:23 and may the LORD **h** you keep your promise."
7: 9 He pleaded with the LORD to **h** Israel,
7:12 "the stone of **h**"—for he said, "Up to this point
8:18 are demanding, but the LORD will not **h** you."
12:21 back to worshiping worthless idols that cannot **h**
13:12 and I haven't even asked for the LORD's **h**!'
14: 6 "Perhaps the LORD will **h** us, for nothing can
14:10 That will be the LORD's sign that he will **h** us
14:12 "for the LORD will **h** us defeat them!"
14:37 Will you **h** us defeat them?" But God made no
19:17 "He threatened to kill me if I didn't **h** him."
23: 4 to Keilah, for I will **h** you conquer the Philistines."
25:21 been saying, "A lot of good it did to **h** this fellow.
2Sa 1: 7 me to come to him. 'How can I **h**?' I asked him.
3: 9 May God deal harshly with me if I don't **h** David
3:12 and I will **h** turn the entire nation of Israel over to
8: 5 When Arameans from Damascus arrived to **h**

10:11 then come over and **h** me," Joab told his brother.
10:11 are too strong for you, I will come and **h** you.
10:19 the Arameans were afraid to **h** the Ammonites.
14: 4 in front of him and cried out, "O king! **H** me!"
16:19 I helped your father, and now I will **h** you!"
18: 3 stay here in the city and send us **h** if we need it."
22: 7 out to the LORD; / yes, I called to my God for **h**.
22:36 of your salvation; / your **h** has made me great.
22:42 They called for **h**, but no one came to rescue them.
1Ki 1: 7 and they agreed to **h** him become king.
15:22 **h** to carry away the building stones and timbers
20:28 of the plains. So I will **h** you defeat this vast army.
2Ki 3: 7 Will you **h** me fight him?" And Jehoshaphat
4: 2 "What can I do to **h** you?" Elisha asked.
6:26 called to him, "Please **h** me, my lord the king!"
6:27 "If the LORD doesn't **h** you, what can I do?"
13: 4 Then Jehoahaz prayed for the LORD's **h**,
14:26 and how they had absolutely no one to **h** them.
17: 4 of Egypt to **h** him shake free of Assyria's power
18:24 even with the **h** of Egypt's chariots and horsemen?
23:29 went to the Euphrates River to **h** the king of
1Ch 12:17 and said, "If you have come in peace to **h** me,
12:18 be with you, / and success to all who **h** you,
18: 5 When Arameans from Damascus arrived to **h**
19:12 then come over and **h** me," Joab told his brother.
19:12 the Ammonites are too strong for you, I will **h** you.
19:19 the Arameans were no longer willing to **h** the
24: 3 With the **h** of Zadok, who was a descendant of
29: 3 of gold and silver to **h** in the construction.
2Ch 1:11 "Because your greatest desire is to **h** your people,
2: 8 at cutting timber. I will send my men to **h** them.
13:10 and the Levites alone may **h** them in their work.
13:14 and the rear, they cried out to the LORD for **h**.
14:11 but you can **h** the powerless against the mighty!
14:11 **H** us, O LORD our God, for we trust in you
16:12 he did not seek the LORD's **h** but sought **h** only from his physicians.
19: 2 "Why should you **h** the wicked and love those
20:12 know what to do, but we are looking to you for **h**."
25: 7 with Israel. He will not **h** those people of Ephraim!
25: 8 for he has the power to **h** or to frustrate."
28:16 the king of Assyria for **h** against his enemies.
28:21 of Assyria as tribute. But even this did not **h** him.
28:23 so they will **h** me, too, if I sacrifice to them."
32: 8 We have the LORD our God to **h** us and to fight
33:13 to him and was moved by his request for **h**.
35: 5 and **h** the families assigned to you as they bring
35: 6 and prepare to **h** those who come.
Ezr 6: 8 Moreover I hereby decree that you are to **h** these
9:12 and not to **h** those nations in any way.
Ne 2: 4 The king asked, "Well, how can I **h** you?" With a
2:20 I replied, "The God of heaven will **h** us succeed.
3: 5 from Tekoa, though their leaders refused to **h**.
6:16 this work had been done with the **h** of our God.
9:28 Yet whenever your people cried to you again for **h**,
Job 5: 1 "You may cry for **h**, but no one listens. You may turn to the angels, but they give you no **h**.
5: 4 Their children are abandoned far from **h**, with no
6:21 You, too, have proved to be of no **h**. You have
11:19 lie down unafraid, and many will look to you for **h**.
16: 6 And it does not **h** if I refuse to speak.
19: 7 "I cry out for **h**, but no one hears me. I protest,
22:29 someone is brought low and you say, '**H** him up,'
24:12 rise from the city, and the wounded cry for **h**,
24:21 They refuse to **h** the needy widows.
29:12 and the orphans who had no one to **h** them.
30:13 knowing full well that I have no one to **h** me.
30:24 would turn against the needy when they cry for **h**.
30:28 I stand in the public square and cry for **h**.
31:16 "Have I refused to **h** the poor or crushed the hopes of widows who looked to me for **h**?
36:13 punishes them, they refuse to cry out to him for **h**.
Ps 5: 2 Listen to my cry for **h**, my King and my God,
7: 9 of the ungodly, / but **h** all those who obey you.
9:12 He does not ignore those who cry to him for **h**.
12: 1 **H**, O LORD, for the godly are fast disappearing!
17: 1 hear my plea for justice. / Listen to my cry for **h**.
18: 6 out to the LORD; / yes, I prayed to my God for **h**.
18:41 They called for **h**, but no one came to rescue them.
20: 2 May he send you **h** from his sanctuary
20: 9 to our king, O LORD! / Respond to our cry for **h**.
22: 1 so distant? / Why do you ignore my cries for **h**?
22: 5 You heard their cries for **h** and saved them.
22:11 for trouble is near, / and no one else can **h** me.
22:24 walked away. / He has listened to their cries for **h**.
25:15 My eyes are always looking to the LORD for **h**.
28: 1 Please **h** me; don't refuse to answer me. / For if
28: 2 to my prayer for mercy / as I cry out to you for **h**,
30: 2 O LORD my God, I cried out to you for **h**,
30:10 and have mercy on me. / **H** me, O LORD."
31:17 O LORD, / for I call out to you for **h**.
31:22 my cry for mercy / and answered my call for **h**.
33:20 Only he can **h** us, protecting us like a shield.
34: 5 Those who look to him for **h** will be radiant with
34:15 who do right; / his ears are open to their cries for **h**.
34:17 hears his people when they call to him for **h**.
37: 5 do to the LORD. / Trust him, and he will **h** you.
38:22 Come quickly to **h** me, O Lord my savior.
39:12 my prayer, O LORD! / Listen to my cries for **h**!
40: 1 I waited patiently for the LORD to **h** me, / and he
40:13 rescue me! / Come quickly, LORD, and **h** me.
44:26 Come and **h** us! / Save us because of your
46: 1 always ready to **h** in times of trouble.
50:18 When you see a thief, you **h** him, / and you spend
50:22 or I will tear you apart, / and no one will **h** you.
51:18 Look with favor on Zion and **h** her;
54: 7 and **h** me to triumph over my enemies.
55: 1 to my prayer, O God. / Do not ignore my cry for **h**!
56: 9 On the very day I call to you for **h**, / my enemies
56:12 O God, / and offer a sacrifice of thanks for your **h**.
57: 3 He will send **h** from heaven to save me,
59: 4 to kill me. / Rise up and **h** me! Look on my plight!
59:10 In his unfailing love, my God will come and **h** me.
60:11 Oh, please **h** us against our enemies, / for all human **h** is useless.
60:12 With God's **h** we will do mighty things, / for he
61: 2 From the ends of the earth, / I will cry to you for **h**,
66:17 For I cried out to him for **h**, / praising him as I
69: 3 I am exhausted from crying for **h**; / my throat is
69: 3 with weeping, / waiting for my God to **h** me.
69:32 and be glad. / Let all who seek God's **h** live in joy.
70: 1 rescue me! / Come quickly, LORD, and **h** me.
71:11 and get him, / for there is no one to **h** him now."
71:12 don't stay away. / My God, please hurry to **h** me.
71:14 But I will keep on hoping for you to **h** me;
72: 2 **H** him judge your people in the right way;
72: 4 **H** him to defend the poor, / to rescue the children
72:12 he will **h** the oppressed, who have no one to defend
77: 3 and I moan, / overwhelmed with longing for his **h**.
79: 9 **H** us, O God of our salvation! / **H** us for the honor of your name. / Oh, save us
86: 1 hear my prayer; / answer me, for I need your **h**.
86:17 to shame, / for you, O LORD, **h** and comfort me.
88: 9 my tears. / Each day I beg for your **h**, O LORD;
89:19 and said, / "I have given **h** to a warrior.
89:43 sword useless / and have refused to **h** him in battle.
99: 6 They cried to the LORD for **h**, / and he answered
102:13 to pity her, / now is the time you promised to **h**.
107: 6 "LORD, **h**!" they cried in their trouble, / and he
107:13 "LORD, **h**!" they cried in their trouble, / and he
107:19 "LORD, **h**!" they cried in their trouble, / and he
107:28 "LORD, **h**!" they cried in their trouble, / and he
108:12 Oh, please **h** us against our enemies, / for all human **h** is useless.
108:13 With God's **h** we will do mighty things, / for he
109:26 **H** me, O LORD my God! / Save me because of
118: 7 Yes, the LORD is for me; he will **h** me. / I will
119:27 **H** me understand the meaning of your
119:32 If you will **h** me, / I will run to follow your
119:39 **H** me abandon my shameful ways; / your laws are
119:144 **h** me to understand them, that I may live.
119:147 I cry out for **h** and put my hope in your words.
119:173 Stand ready to **h** me, / for I have chosen to follow
121: 1 to the mountains— / does my **h** come from there?
121: 2 My **h** comes from the LORD, / who made the
124: 8 Our **h** is from the LORD, / who made the heavens
130: 1 depths of despair, O LORD, / I call for your **h**.
140:12 But I know the LORD will surely **h** those they
141: 1 Please hurry! / Listen when I cry to you for **h**!
141: 8 I look to you for **h**, O Sovereign LORD. / You are
142: 4 I look for someone to come and **h** me, / but no one
142: 4 No one will **h** me; / no one cares a bit what
145:15 All eyes look to you for **h**; / you give them their
145:19 he hears their cries for **h** and rescues them.
146: 3 in powerful people; / there is no **h** for you there.
Pr 1: 2 and to **h** them understand wise sayings.
1:28 "I will not answer when they cry for **h**.
3:27 who deserve it when it's in your power to **h** them.
3:28 If you can **h** your neighbor now, don't say,
3:28 "Come back tomorrow, and then I'll **h** you."
8:16 Rulers lead with my **h**, and nobles make righteous
11: 4 Riches won't **h** on the day of judgment, but right
14:21 one's neighbors; blessed are those who **h** the poor.
14:31 their Maker, but those who **h** the poor honor him.
17:17 and a brother is born to **h** in time of need.
19:17 If you **h** the poor, you are lending to the LORD—
30: 8 First, **h** me never to tell a lie. Second, give me
31:12 She will not hinder him but **h** him all her life.
Ecc 4:10 If one person falls, the other can reach out and **h**.
4:15 Everyone is eager to **h** such a youth, even to **h** him take the throne.
5:11 you have, the more people come to **h** you spend it.
SS 6: 1 has your lover gone? We will **h** you find him."
Isa 1: 4 One of Israel, cutting themselves off from his **h**.
1:17 Learn to do good. Seek justice. **H** the oppressed.
1:19 If you will only obey me and let me **h** you,
2:22 as frail as breath. How can they be of **h** to anyone?
3: 7 "No!" he will reply. "I can't **h**. I don't have any
8:17 I will wait for the LORD to **h** us, though he has
10: 3 To whom will you turn for **h**? Where will your
10: 4 I will not **h** you. You will stumble along as
14: 2 The nations of the world will **h** the LORD's
16: 3 "**H** us," they cry. "Defend us against our
17: 8 They will no longer ask their idols for **h** or worship
19:15 or poor, important or unknown, can offer any **h**.
19:20 When the people cry to the LORD for **h** against
22:11 are to no avail because you never ask God for **h**.
30: 2 you have gone down to Egypt to find **h**.
30: 5 your shame. He will not **h** you even one little bit."
30:16 You said, 'No, we will get our **h** from Egypt.
30:18 Blessed are those who wait for him to **h** them.
30:19 no more. He will be gracious if you ask for **h**.
31: 1 is certain for those who look to Egypt for **h**,
31: 3 and fall among those they are trying to **h**.
36: 9 even with the **h** of Egypt's chariots and horsemen?
38:14 My eyes grew tired of looking to heaven for **h**. / I am in trouble, Lord. **H** me!"
41:10 I am your God. I will strengthen you. I will **h** you.
41:13 I say to you, 'Do not be afraid. I am here to **h** you.
41:14 you are, O Israel, don't be afraid, for I will **h** you.
41:27 the first to tell Jerusalem, 'Look! **H** is on the way!'
43:22 "But, my dear people, you refuse to ask for my **h**.
44:10 his own god—an idol that cannot **h** him one bit!
44:20 He is trusting something that can give him no **h** at
44:21 made you, and I will not forget to **h** you.
47:12 Ask them to **h** you strike terror into the hearts of
47:14 You will get no **h** from them at all.
47:15 will slip away and disappear, unable to **h**.
48:15 send him on this errand and will **h** him succeed.
49: 8 to you. On the day of salvation, I will **h** you.
51:18 Not one of your children is left alive to **h** you
57:13 do anything for you when you cry to them for **h**.
58: 7 and do not hide from relatives who need your **h**.
58:10 Feed the hungry and **h** those in trouble. Then your
59:16 He was amazed to see that no one intervened to **h**
63: 3 the winepress alone; no one was there to **h** me.
63: 5 I looked, but no one came to **h** my people. I was
63:17 Return and **h** us, for we are your servants and your
64:12 all this, LORD, must you still refuse to **h** us?
Jer 2:36 you flit from one ally to another asking for **h**.
2:37 you trust. You will not succeed despite their **h**.
4:31 pleading for **h**, prostrate before their murderers.
7:14 this Temple that you trust for **h**, this place that I
7:16 or pray for them, and don't beg me to **h** them,
10:20 home is gone, and no one is left to **h** me rebuild it.
14: 7 **h** us for the sake of your own reputation.
14:22 can do such things. So we will wait for you to **h** us.
15: 1 me pleading for these people, I wouldn't **h** them.
15:18 Your **h** seems as uncertain as a seasonal brook.
18:19 LORD, **h** me! Listen to what they are planning to
21: 2 "Please ask the LORD to **h** us.
21:12 **H** those who have been robbed; rescue them from
22: 3 **H** those who have been robbed; rescue them from
22:16 and **h** were given to the poor and needy,
22:20 they are all destroyed. Not one is left to **h** you.
30:13 There is no one to **h** you or bind up your injury. You are beyond the **h** of any medicine.
37: 7 to return to Egypt, though he came here to **h** you.
41:14 from Mizpah escaped and began to **h** Johanan.
49: 5 and no one will **h** your exiles as they flee.
49:11 too, will be able to depend on me for **h**."
La 1: 2 Among all her lovers, there is no one left to **h** her.
1: 7 fell to her enemy, and there was no one to **h** her.
1:17 Jerusalem pleads for **h**, but no one comforts her.
1:19 "I begged my allies for **h**, but they betrayed me.
4: 6 disaster struck in a moment with no one to **h** them.
4:17 were looking to nations that could offer no **h** at all.
Eze 3:20 Their previous good deeds won't **h** them, and I
14: 4 into sin and then come to a prophet asking for **h**.
17:17 and all his mighty army will fail to **h** Israel when
20: 3 How dare you come to ask for my **h**? As surely as
20:31 Should I listen to you or **h** you, O people of Israel?
29: 6 like a reed when Israel looked to you for **h**.
29:16 will no longer be tempted to trust in Egypt for **h**.
36: 9 I am concerned for you, and I will come to **h** you.
39:13 Everyone in Israel will **h**, for it will be a glorious
44:11 for burnt offerings and be present to **h** the people.
Da 4:18 tell me what it means, for no one else can **h** me.
6:11 and found him praying and asking for God's **h**.
8: 4 and no one could stand against it or **h** its victims.
9:18 We do not ask because we deserve **h**, but
10:13 one of the archangels, came to **h** me,
10:21 (There is no one to **h** me against these spirit
11:34 persecutions are going on, a little **h** will arrive,
11:39 Claiming this foreign god's **h**, he will attack the
11:45 run out, and there will be no one to **h** him.
Hos 1: 7 from their enemies without any **h** from weapons
5:13 king there, but he could neither **h** nor cure them.
5:15 until they admit their guilt and look to me for **h**.
7: 7 one after another, and no one cries out to me for **h**.
8: 2 Israel pleads with me, '**H** us, for you are our God!'
13:10 is your king? Why don't you call on him for **h**?
Joel 1:19 LORD, **h** us! The fire has consumed the pastures
Am 6: 1 popular in Israel, you to whom the people go for **h**.
9: 4 to bring disaster upon them and not to **h** them."
Ob 1: 7 They will **h** to chase you from your land. They will
1:11 refusing to lift a finger to **h** when foreign invaders
Jnh 1: 5 the desperate sailors shouted to their gods for **h**
Mic 1:14 kings of Israel, for it promised **h** it could not give.
3: 4 Then you beg the LORD for **h** in times of
6: 4 I sent Moses, Aaron, and Miriam to **h** you.
7: 7 As for me, I look to the LORD for his **h**. I wait
7:14 **H** them to live in peace and prosperity.
Hab 1: 2 How long, O LORD, must I call for **h**? But you
3: 2 begin again to **h** us, as you did in years gone by.
Mt 7: 4 let me **h** you get rid of that speck in your eye,'
9:36 so great and they didn't know where to go for **h**.
15:24 "I was sent only to **h** the people of Israel—
15:25 worshiped him and pleaded again, "Lord, **h** me!"
23: 4 and never lift a finger to **h** ease the burden.
25:44 or naked or sick or in prison, and not **h** you?'
25:45 when you refused to **h** the least of these my
25:45 and sisters, you were refusing to **h** me.'
Mk 4:27 seeds sprouted and grew without the farmer's **h**,
7:11 people to say to their parents, 'Sorry, I can't **h** you.
7:27 "First I should **h** my own family, the Jews.
9:22 trying to kill him. Have mercy on us and **h** us.
9:24 "I do believe, but **h** me not to doubt!"
14: 7 and you can **h** them whenever you want to.
Lk 4:25 widows in Israel who needed **h** in Elijah's time,
4:27 than the many lepers in Israel who needed **h**."
5: 7 A shout for **h** brought their partners in the other
6:42 let me **h** you get rid of that speck in your eye,'
7: 4 begged Jesus to come with them and **h** the man.
7: 4 "If anyone deserves your **h**, it is he," they said,
10:40 I do all the work? Tell her to come and **h** me."
11: 7 and we are all in bed. I can't **h** you this time.'
11:46 and you never lift a finger to **h** ease the burden.
22: 5 They were delighted that he was ready to **h** them,
Jn 5: 7 "for I have no one to **h** me into the pool when the
10:32 direction I have done many things to **h** the people.

Ac 2:23 With the **h** of lawless Gentiles, you nailed him to
16: 9 pleading with him, "Come over here and **h** us."
20:35 of how you can **h** the poor by working hard.
21:28 yelling, "Men of Israel! **H**! This is the man who
Ro 1:11 with you that will **h** you grow strong in the Lord.
4:10 But how did his faith **h** him? Was he declared
5: 3 they are good for us—they **h** us learn to endure.
7:17 But I can't **h** myself, because it is sin inside me
10: 6 (to find Christ and bring him down to **h** you).
12:13 children are in need, be the one to **h** them out.
13: 4 The authorities are sent by God to **h** you. But if
14: 4 The Lord's power will **h** them do as they should.
15: 5 **h** you live in complete harmony with each other—
15:27 they feel the least they can do in return is **h** them
16: 2 **H** her in every way you can, for she has helped
1Co 4:17 reason I am sending Timothy—to **h** you do this.
7:35 I want you to do whatever will **h** you serve the
12:28 have the gift of healing, / those who can **h** others,
14: 6 in an unknown language, how would that **h** you?
14: 6 or some teaching—that is what will **h** you.
14:12 ask God for those that will be of real **h** to the
14:17 no doubt, but it doesn't **h** the other people present.
14:19 **h** others than ten thousand words in an unknown
16:17 They have been making up for the **h** you weren't
2Co 6: 2 Indeed, God is ready to **h** you right now.
7:10 For God can use sorrow in our lives to **h** us turn
8:14 Right now you have plenty and can **h** them.
8:19 glorifies the Lord and shows our eagerness to **h**.
8:23 say that he is my partner who works with me to **h**
9: 2 For I know how eager you are to **h**, and I have
11: 9 have enough to live on, I did not ask you to **h** me.
Gal 2:10 suggested was that we remember to **h** the poor,
5: 2 you right with God, then Christ cannot **h** you.
6: 1 and humbly **h** that person back onto the right path.
6: 3 If you think you are too important to **h** someone in
6: 6 Those who are taught the word of God should **h**
Php 2:25 And he was your messenger to **h** me in my need.
4: 3 I ask you, my true teammate, to **h** these women,
4:10 but for a while you didn't have the chance to **h** me.
4:13 For I can do everything with the **h** of Christ who
4:15 me financial **h** when I brought you the Good News
4:16 Even when I was in Thessalonica you sent **h** more
1Ti 1: 4 they don't **h** people live a life of faith in God.
5: 5 Night and day she asks God for **h** and spends much
2Ti 1:14 With the **h** of the Holy Spirit who lives within us,
Tit 3:13 Do everything you can to **h** Zenas the lawyer
Phm 1:14 And I didn't want you to **h** because you were
Heb 2:16 We all know that Jesus came to **h** the descendants
of Abraham, not to **h** the angels.
2:18 he is able to **h** us when we are being tempted.
4:16 and we will find grace to **h** us when we need it.
13: 9 about food, which don't **h** those who follow them.
13:15 With Jesus' **h**, let us continually offer our sacrifice
1Pe 4:11 Are you called to **h** others? Do it with all the
5:12 I have written this short letter to you with the **h** of
1Jn 3:17 sees a brother or sister in need and refuses to **h**—
3Jn 1:10 he also tells others not to **h** them.
1:10 And when they do **h**, he puts them out of the

HELPED (57) [HELP]

Ge 14:20 who has **h** you conquer your enemies."
Ex 2:17 Then he **h** them draw water for their flocks.
Dt 2:22 He had similarly **h** the descendants of Esau at
2:36 "The LORD our God **h** us conquer Aroer on the
Jos 2:12 be kind to me and my family since I have **h** you.
21:44 for the LORD **h** them conquer all their enemies.
Jdg 20:35 So the LORD **h** Israel defeat Benjamin, and that
Ru 2:19 May the LORD bless the one who **h** you!"
3:15 barley into the cloak and **h** her put it on her back.
1Sa 4: 4 **h** carry the Ark of God to where the battle was
7:12 he said, "Up to this point the LORD has **h** us!"
19: 4 He has always **h** you in any way he could.
19:12 So she **h** him climb out through a window, and he
30:23 He has kept us safe and **h** us defeat the enemy.
2Sa 16:19 I **h** your father, and now I will help you!"
1Ki 5:18 Men from the city of Gebal **h** Solomon's
2Ki 10:15 put out his hand, and Jehu **h** him into the chariot.
1Ch 12:21 They **h** David chase down bands of raiders,
23:28 **h** perform the ceremonies of purification,
2Ch 18:31 and God **h** him by turning the attack away from
24:24 the LORD **h** them conquer the much larger army
26: 7 God **h** him not only with his wars against the
26:15 for the LORD **h** him wonderfully until he became
28:23 for he said, "These gods **h** the kings of Aram,
29:34 so their relatives the Levites **h** them until the work
Ezr 3: 9 They were **h** in this task by the Levites of the
5: 2 the prophets of God were with them and **h** them.
6:22 so that he **h** them to rebuild the Temple of God,
Ne 9:22 "Then you **h** our ancestors conquer great
Est 9: 3 and the royal officials **h** the Jews for fear of
Job 26: 2 "How you have **h** the powerless! How you have
29:12 For I **h** the poor in their need and the orphans who
29:13 I **h** those who had lost hope, and they blessed me.
Ps 63: 7 I think how much you have **h** me; / I sing for joy in
94:17 Unless the LORD had **h** me, / I would soon have
107:12 they fell, and no one **h** them rise again.
118:13 to kill me, O my enemy, / but the LORD **h** me.
Jer 51: 9 We would have **h** her if we could, but nothing can
Eze 13: 5 They have not **h** it to stand firm in battle on the
16: 7 And I **h** you to thrive like a plant in the field.
31: 4 watered it and **h** it to grow tall and luxuriant.
Da 8:18 roused me with a touch and **h** me to my feet.
Na 3: 9 The nations of Put and Libya also **h** and supported
Mk 1:31 and as he took her by the hand and **h** her to sit up,
9:27 Jesus took him by the hand and **h** him to his feet,
Lk 1:54 And how he has **h** his servant Israel! / He has not
Ac 3: 7 took the lame man by the right hand and **h** him up.
9:41 He gave her his hand and **h** her up. Then he called
Ro 16: 2 for she has **h** many in their needs, including me.
2Co 6: 2 On the day of salvation, I **h** you." Indeed, God is
Php 1:12 that everything that has happened to me here has **h**
2:22 he has **h** me in preaching the Good News.
1Ti 5:10 Has she **h** those who are in trouble? Has she
2Ti 1:18 And you know how much he **h** me at Ephesus.
Phm 1:13 and he would have **h** me on your behalf.
Heb 10:33 and sometimes you **h** others who were suffering
Rev 12:16 But the earth **h** her by opening its mouth

HELPER (16) [HELP]

Ex 18: 4 at his birth, "The God of my fathers was my **h**;
1Sa 2:11 And the boy became the LORD's **h**, for he
2:18 though only a boy, was the LORD's **h**.
Ps 27: 9 You have always been my **h**. / Don't leave me
40:17 You are my **h** and my savior. / Do not delay,
54: 4 But God is my **h**. / The Lord is the one who keeps
70: 5 to my aid, O God. / You are my **h** and my savior;
115: 9 trust the LORD! / He is your **h**; he is your shield.
115:10 trust the LORD! / He is your **h**; he is your shield.
115:11 trust the LORD! / He is your **h**; he is your shield.
146: 5 are those who have the God of Israel as their **h**,
Hos 13: 9 to be destroyed, O Israel, though I am your **h**.
Am 5:14 the LORD God Almighty will truly be your **h**,
Eph 6:21 loved brother and faithful **h** in the Lord's work,
Col 4: 7 He is a faithful **h** who serves the Lord with me.
Heb 13: 6 we can say with confidence, / "The Lord is my **h**,

HELPFUL (7) [HELP]

1Sa 3:19 and everything Samuel said was wise and **h**.
Job 22: 2 to God? Can even a wise person be **h** to him?
Pr 10:32 The godly speak words that are **h**, but the wicked
1Co 10:23 allowed to do anything"—but not everything is **h**.
12:31 in any event, you should desire the most **h** gifts.
Eph 4:29 Let everything you say be good and **h**, so that your
2Ti 4:11 with you when you come, for he will be **h** to me.

HELPING (27) [HELP]

Nu 8:22 to perform their duties, **h** Aaron and his sons.
Dt 28:63 "Just as the LORD has found great pleasure in **h**
1Sa 17:15 and **h** his father with the sheep in Bethlehem.
2Sa 14: 9 if you are criticized for **h** me like this."
19:18 across the river, **h** them in every way they could.
19:41 to do most of the work in **h** him cross the Jordan.
1Ch 12:31 18,000 men were sent for the express purpose of **h**
15:26 because God was clearly **h** the Levites as they
2Ch 28:20 he oppressed King Ahaz instead of **h** him.
Ne 2:10 someone had come who was interested in **h** Israel.
8: 8 being read, **h** the people understand each passage.
Job 22: 9 You must have sent widows away without **h** them
Ps 35:27 is the LORD, / who enjoys **h** his servant."
Pr 31:20 She extends a **h** hand to the poor and opens her
Jer 44:19 without our husbands knowing it and **h** us?
Eze 44:14 and **h** the people in a general way.
Mt 12:30 Anyone who isn't **h** me opposes me, and anyone
Lk 11:23 "Anyone who isn't **h** me opposes me, and anyone
Ac 9:36 always doing kind things for others and **h** the poor.
18:23 encouraging them and **h** them to grow in the Lord.
1Co 12: 7 to each of us as a means of **h** the entire church.
14: 3 But one who prophesies is **h** others grow in the
2Co 1:11 will rescue us because you are **h** by praying for us.
9: 2 that stirred up many of them to begin **h**.
Col 1: 7 faithful servant, and he is **h** us in your place.
1Ti 6: 2 because you are **h** another believer by your efforts.
Tit 3:14 They must learn to do good by **h** others who have

HELPLESS (49) [HELP]

Ex 2: 6 found the baby boy. His **h** cries touched her heart.
Nu 14: 9 They are only **h** prey to us! They have no
2Ki 19:26 easy prey for you. / They are as **h** as the grass,
Ne 5: 5 and we are **h** to do anything about it, for our fields
Job 6:13 No, I am utterly **h**, without any chance of success.
Ps 9:12 For he who avenges murder cares for the **h**.
10: 8 They are always searching / for some **h** victim.
10: 9 they crouch silently, / waiting to pounce on the **h**.
10:10 The **h** are overwhelmed and collapse; / they fall
10:12 Punish the wicked, O God! / Do not forget the **h**!
10:14 and punish them. / The **h** put their trust in you.
10:17 LORD, you know the hopes of the **h**. / Surely you
12: 5 "I have seen violence done to the **h**,
35:10 Who else rescues the weak and **h** from the strong?
82: 4 Rescue the poor and **h**; / deliver them from the
88:15 I stand **h** and desperate before your terrors.
Pr 31: 9 Yes, speak up for the poor and **h**, and see that they
Ecc 4: 1 oppressors have great power, and the victims are **h**.
Isa 1: 8 the harvest is over. It is as **h** as a city under siege.
3:14 filling your barns with grain extorted from **h**
13:18 They will have no mercy on **h** babies and will
33:24 "We are sick and **h**," for the LORD will forgive
37:27 easy prey for you. / They are as **h** as the grass,
51:20 and lie in the streets, **h** as antelopes caught in a net.
57:13 so **h** that a breath of wind can knock them down!
58: 9 "Stop oppressing the **h** and stop making false
Jer 10: 5 There stands their god like a **h** scarecrow in a
12: 3 Drag these people away like **h** sheep to be
14: 9 Are you also confused? Are you **h** to save us?
26:14 As for me, I am **h** and in your power—do with me
47: 3 without a backward glance at their **h** children.
La 1:14 and gave me to my enemies; I am **h** in their hands.
3:11 tore me with his claws, leaving me **h** and desolate.
Eze 7:27 The king and the prince will stand **h**, weeping in
18:12 oppresses the poor and **h**, steals from debtors by
35: 5 Israel led you to butcher them when they were **h**,
39: 3 your weapons from your hands and leave you **h**.
Da 8: 7 Now the ram was **h**, and the goat knocked it down
Hos 4:16 and unprotected, like a **h** lamb in an open field.
Joel 2:17 'Where is the God of Israel? He must be **h**!' "
Am 2: 7 They trample **h** people in the dust and deny justice
8: 5 to end so you can get back to cheating the **h**.
Mic 5: 8 And the other nations will be like **h** sheep, with no
Na 3:13 Your troops will be as weak and **h** as women.
Hab 2: 7 take all you have, while you stand trembling and **h**.
Zep 1:17 I will make you as **h** as a blind man searching for a
3:19 I will save the weak and **h** ones; I will bring
Ro 5: 6 When we were utterly **h**, Christ came at just the
Rev 18: 7 'I am queen on my throne. I am no **h** widow.

HELPLESSLY (2) [HELP]

Isa 13: 8 They look **h** at one another as the flames of the
Eze 16: 6 saw you there, **h** kicking about in your own blood.

HELPS (21) [HELP]

Ge 21:22 "It is clear that God **h** you in everything you do,"
Ex 31:13 It **h** you to remember that I am the LORD,
1Ch 12:18 help you, / for your God is the one who **h** you."
Job 16: 5 I would do. I would speak in a way that **h** you.
Ps 28: 7 He **h** me, and my heart is filled with joy.
37:40 The LORD **h** them, / rescuing them from the
145:14 The LORD **h** the fallen / and lifts up those bent
Pr 13: 6 Godliness **h** people all through life, while the evil
Ecc 10:10 That's the value of wisdom; it **h** you succeed.
Isa 41: 7 the goldsmith, and the molder **h** at the anvil.
44: 2 The LORD who made you and **h** you says:
50: 7 Because the Sovereign LORD **h** me, I will not be
La 3:38 Is it not the Most High who **h** one and harms
4:16 has scattered them, and he no longer **h** them.
Eze 17:24 down the tall tree and **h** the short tree to grow tall.
18:17 **h** the poor, does not lend money at interest,
Mt 19:11 Jesus said. "Only those whom God **h**.
Ro 8:26 And the Holy Spirit **h** us in our distress. For we
15: 2 If we do what **h** them, we will build them up in the
Eph 4:16 it **h** the other parts grow, so that the whole body is
Php 1:19 pray for me and as the Spirit of Jesus Christ **h** me,

HEM (5) [HEMMED, HEMS]

Ex 28:33 scarlet yarn, and attach them to the **h** of the robe,
28:34 are to alternate all the way around the **h**.
39:25 between the pomegranates along the **h** of the robe,
39:26 and pomegranates alternating all around the **h**.
Zec 8:23 and languages around the world will clutch at the **h**

HEMAN (15) [HEMAN'S]

Ge 36:22 The sons of Lotan were Hori and **H**. Lotan's sister
1Ki 4:31 including Ethan the Ezrahite and **H**, Calcol,
1Ch 1:39 The sons of Lotan were Hori and **H**. Lotan's sister
2: 6 Zerah were Zimri, Ethan, **H**, Calcol, and Darda—
6:33 **H** the musician was from the clan of Kohath.
15:17 So the Levites appointed **H** son of Joel, Asaph son
15:19 **H**, Asaph, and Ethan were chosen to sound the
16:41 David also appointed **H**, Jeduthun, and the others
25: 1 then appointed men from the families of Asaph, **H**,
25: 5 All these were the sons of **H**, the king's seer,
25: 6 Jeduthun, and **H** reported directly to the king.
2Ch 5:12 Asaph, **H**, Jeduthun, and all their sons
29:14 From the family of **H**: Jehiel and Shimei.
35:15 by David, Asaph, **H**, and Jeduthun, the king's seer.
Ps 88: T of Affliction." A psalm of **H** the Ezrahite. A song.

HEMAN'S (3) [HEMAN]

1Ch 6:39 **H** first assistant was Asaph from the clan of
6:44 **H** second assistant was Ethan from the clan of
25: 4 **H** sons were Bukkiah, Mattaniah, Uzziel, Shubael,

HEMATH [KJV] See HAMMATH, LEBO-HAMATH

HEMDAN (2)

Ge 36:26 The sons of Dishon were **H**, Eshban, Ithran,
1Ch 1:41 The sons of Dishon were **H**, Eshban, Ithran,

HEMLOCK [KJV] See POISON, POISONOUS (WEEDS)

HEMMED (1) [HEM]

Ps 22:12 of bulls; / fierce bulls of Bashan have **h** me in!

HEMORRHAGE (4)

Lev 20:18 has intercourse with a woman suffering from a **h**,
Mt 9:20 a woman who had had a **h** for twelve years came
Mk 5:25 in the crowd who had had a **h** for twelve years.
Lk 8:43 in the crowd who had had a **h** for twelve years.

HEMS (1) [HEM]

Nu 15:38 you must make tassels for the **h** of your clothing

HEN (2)

Mt 23:37 as a **h** protects her chicks beneath her wings,
Lk 13:34 as a **h** protects her chicks beneath her wings,

HENA (3)

2Ki 18:34 what about the gods of Sepharvaim, **H**, and Ivvah?
19:13 to the kings of Sepharvaim, **H**, and Ivvah?"
Isa 37:13 to the kings of Sepharvaim, **H**, and Ivvah?"

HENADAD (4)

Ezr 3: 9 in this task by the Levites of the family of **H**.
Ne 3:18 line were his countrymen led by Binnui son of **H**,
3:24 Next was Binnui son of **H**, who rebuilt another
10: 9 of Azaniah, Binnui from the family of **H**, Kadmiel,

HENCE [KJV] See AWAY, LEAVE, PLACE

HENOCH [KJV] See HANOCH

HEPHER (8) [GATH-HEPHER, HEPHER'S, HEPHERITES]

Nu 26:32 The Hepherites, named after their ancestor **H**.
27: 1 Their father, Zelophehad, was the son of **H**,
Jos 12:17 The king of Tappuah / The king of **H**
17: 2 Abiezer, Helek, Asriel, Shechem, **H**, and Shemida.
17: 3 However, Zelophehad son of **H**, who was a
1Ki 4:10 including Socoh and all the land of **H**.
1Ch 4: 6 birth to Ahuzzam, **H**, Temeni, and Haahashtari.
11:36 **H** from Mekerah; / Ahijah from Pelon;

HEPHER'S (1) [HEPHER]

Nu 26:33 **H** son, Zelophehad, had no sons, but his

HEPHERITES (1) [HEPHER]

Nu 26:32 The **H**, named after their ancestor Hepher.

HEPHZIBAH (1)

2Ki 21: 1 in Jerusalem fifty-five years. His mother was **H**.

HER (1408) [SHE] See Index of Articles, Etc.

HERALD (2)

Ps 85:13 Righteousness goes as a **h** before him,
Da 3: 4 a **h** shouted out, "People of all races and nations

HERBS (2)

Ex 12: 8 evening everyone must eat roast lamb with bitter **h**
Nu 9:11 They must eat the lamb at that time with bitter **h**

HERD (17) [HERDING, HERDS, HERDSMAN, HERDSMEN]

Ge 18: 7 Then Abraham ran out to the **h** and chose a fat calf
Lev 1: 3 sacrifice for a whole burnt offering is from the **h**,
3: 1 you want to present a peace offering from the **h**,
22:21 bring a peace offering to the LORD from the **h**
22:28 on the same day, whether from the **h** or the flock.
Dt 16: 2 sacrifice may be from either the flock or the **h**,
32:14 He fed them curds from the **h** and milk from the
Jdg 6:25 "Take the second best bull from your father's **h**,
Ps 22:12 My enemies surround me like a **h** of bulls;
68:30 this **h** of bulls among the weaker calves.
Mt 8:30 A large **h** of pigs was feeding in the distance,
8:31 "If you cast us out, send us into that **h** of pigs."
8:32 and the whole **h** plunged down the steep hillside
Mk 5:11 There happened to be a large **h** of pigs feeding on
5:13 and the entire **h** of two thousand pigs plunged
Lk 8:32 A large **h** of pigs was feeding on the hillside
8:33 and the whole **h** plunged down the steep hillside

HERDING (1) [HERD]

Ge 34: 5 but his sons were out in the fields **h** cattle so he did

HERDS (55) [HERD]

Ge 13: 6 with all their flocks and **h** living so close together.
24:35 has given him flocks of sheep and **h** of cattle,
26:14 large flocks of sheep and goats, great **h** of cattle,
30:29 and how your flocks and **h** have grown.
32: 7 along with the flocks and **h** and camels, into two
33: 8 what were all the flocks and **h** I met as I came?"
33:13 and the flocks and **h** have their young, too.
33:17 a house and made shelters for his flocks and **h**.
34:28 They seized all the flocks and **h** and donkeys—
45:10 and grandchildren, your flocks and **h**,
46:32 them their flocks and **h** and everything they own.'
47: 1 came with all their flocks and **h** and possessions,
47:17 Soon all the horses, flocks, **h**, and donkeys of
50: 8 and flocks and **h** in the land of Goshen.
Ex 9: 6 didn't lose a single animal from their flocks and **h**.
10: 9 take our sons and daughters and our flocks and **h**.
10:24 he said. "But let your flocks and **h** stay here.
10:25 "we must take our flocks and **h** for sacrifices
12:32 Take your flocks and **h**, and be gone. Go, but give
12:38 went with them, along with the many flocks and **h**.
34: 3 even let the flocks or **h** graze near the mountain."
Lev 1: 2 you must bring animals from your flocks and **h**.
27:32 owns every tenth animal counted off from your **h**
Nu 11:22 Even if we butchered all our flocks and **h**,
15: 3 flocks of sheep and goats or from your **h** of cattle.
32: 1 Gilead were ideally suited for their flocks and **h**,
32: 4 It is ideally suited for all our flocks and **h**.
Dt 7:13 and olives, and great **h** of cattle, sheep, and goats.
8:13 and **h** have become very large and your silver
12: 6 of the firstborn animals of your flocks and **h**.
12:17 olive oil, nor the firstborn of your flocks and **h**,
14:23 and the firstborn males of your flocks and **h**.
14:25 you may sell the tithe portion of your crops and **h**
15:19 God all the firstborn males from your flocks and **h**.
15:19 Do not use the firstborn of your **h** to work your
28: 4 You will be blessed with fertile **h** and flocks.
28:18 You will be cursed with infertile **h** and flocks.
Jos 14: 4 the surrounding pasturelands for their flocks and **h**.
22: 8 Share with them your large **h** of cattle, your silver
1Sa 30:20 up all the flocks and **h** and drove them on ahead.
2Ch 26:10 because he kept great **h** of livestock in the foothills
32:29 built many towns and acquired vast flocks and **h**,
Ne 10:36 and the firstborn of all our **h** and flocks,
Ps 107:38 large families there, / and their **h** of cattle increase.
Pr 27:23 and put your heart into caring for your **h**,
Ecc 2: 7 I also owned great **h** and flocks, more than any of
Isa 32:14 **H** of donkeys and goats will graze on the hills
32:20 Their flocks and **h** will graze in green pastures.
65:10 the valley of Achor will be a place to pasture **h**.
Jer 3:24 their flocks and **h**, their sons and daughters—
5:17 your flocks of sheep and your **h** of cattle.
31:12 wine, and oil, and the healthy flocks and **h**.
Eze 32:13 all your flocks and **h** that graze beside the streams.
36:11 but your flocks and **h** will also greatly multiply.
Hos 5: 6 their flocks and **h** to offer sacrifices to the LORD.

HERDSMAN (1) [HERD]

1Sa 21: 7 Now Doeg the Edomite, Saul's chief **h**, was there

HERDSMEN (9) [HERD]

Ge 4:20 He became the first of the **h** who live in tents.
13: 7 So an argument broke out between the **h** of Abram
13: 8 "This arguing between our **h** has got to stop,"
26:20 they said, and they argued over it with Isaac's **h**.
32:19 Jacob gave the same instructions to each of the **h**
2Ch 14:15 They also attacked the camps of **h** and captured
Mt 8:33 The **h** fled to the nearby city, telling everyone what
Mk 5:14 The **h** fled to the nearby city and the surrounding
Lk 8:34 When the **h** saw it, they fled to the nearby city

HERE (678) [HERE'S, HEREBY]

Ge 12:19 **H** is your wife! Take her and be gone!"
13: 9 If you want that area over there, then I'll stay **h**.
15:16 your descendants will return **h** to this land,
18: 3 he said, "if it pleases you, stop **h** for a while.
19: 2 "we'll just spend the night out **h** in the city
19:12 "Do you have any other relatives **h** in the city?"
19:15 your wife and your two daughters who are **h**.
19:15 Get out of **h** right now, or you will be caught in the
22: 1 God called. "Yes," he replied. "**H** I am."
22: 5 "Stay **h** with the donkey," Abraham told the
23: 4 "**H** I am, a stranger in a foreign land, with no
23:11 **H** in the presence of my people, I give it to you.
24:13 See, **h** I am, standing beside this spring,
24:31 Why do you stand **h** outside the village when we
24:38 I was to come to his relatives **h** in this far-off land,
24:38 I was told to bring back a young woman from **h** to
24:43 **H** I am, standing beside this spring. I will say to
24:50 "The LORD has obviously brought you **h**,
24:51 **H** is Rebekah; take her and go. Yes, let her be the
25:13 **H** is a list, by their names and clans, of Ishmael's
26: 3 Do as I say, and stay **h** in this land. If you do,
27: 4 it's savory and good, and bring it **h** for me to eat.
27:19 **H** is the wild game, cooked the way you like it.
27:21 Then Isaac said to Jacob, "Come over **h**. I want to
27:26 "Come **h** and kiss me, my son."
27:35 But Isaac said, "Your brother was **h**, and he
29: 6 **h** comes his daughter Rachel with the sheep."
29: 8 watering until all the flocks and shepherds are **h**,"
30:27 that the LORD has blessed me because you are **h**.
31:14 There's nothing for us **h**—none of our father's
31:37 Set it out **h** in front of us, before our relatives,
34:10 the land is open to you! Settle **h** and trade with us.
34:15 But **h** is a solution. If every man among you will
34:16 we will intermarry with you and live **h** and unite
34:21 "Let's invite them to live **h** among us and ply their
34:22 But they will consider staying **h** only on one
34:23 let's agree to this so they will settle **h** among us."
37:17 the man told him, "but they are no longer **h**.
37:19 "**H** comes that dreamer!" they exclaimed.
37:22 Let's just throw him alive into this pit **h**.
38:21 "We've never had a prostitute **h**," they replied.
39: 9 No one **h** has more authority than I do! He has held
39:14 "My husband has brought this Hebrew slave **h** to
39:17 "That Hebrew slave you've had around **h** tried to
40: 8 but there is no one **h** to tell us what they mean."
40:14 me to Pharaoh, and ask him to let me out of **h**.
40:15 the land of the Hebrews, and now I'm **h** in jail,
42:15 leave Egypt unless your youngest brother comes **h**.
42:16 I'll keep the rest of you **h**, bound in prison.
42:28 "My money is **h** in my sack!" They were filled
42:33 Leave one of your brothers **h** with me, and take
43:21 in our sacks. **H** it is; we have brought it back again.
44:21 And you said to us, 'Bring him **h** so I can see him.'
44:33 my lord, let me stay **h** as a slave instead of the boy,
45: 4 "Come over **h**," he said. So they came closer.
45: 5 He sent me **h** ahead of you to preserve your lives.
45: 7 God has sent me **h** to keep you and your families
45: 8 Yes, it was God who sent me **h**, not you! And he
45:13 Tell my father how I am honored **h** in Egypt.
45:18 all of their families, and to come **h** to Egypt to live.
45:19 and little ones and to bring your father **h**.
46: 2 Jacob!" he called. "**H** I am," Jacob replied.
46:34 he will let you live **h** in the land of Goshen,
47: 1 "My father and my brothers are **h** from Canaan.
47: 4 We have come to live **h** in Egypt, for there is no
47: 5 "Now that your family has joined you **h**,
48: 5 who were born **h** in the land of Egypt before I
48: 9 "these are the sons God has given me **h** in Egypt."
48:18 "No, Father," he said, "this one over **h** is older.
Ex 3: 4 him from the bush, "Moses! Moses!" "**H** I am!"
3:12 you will return **h** to worship God at this very
5: 5 Look, there are many people **h** in Egypt, and you
8:25 to your God," he said. "But do it **h** in this land.
8:26 If we offer them **h** where they can see us, they will
10:24 he said. "But let your flocks and herds stay **h**.
10:28 "Get out of **h**!" Pharaoh shouted at Moses.
14:11 "Why did you bring us out **h** to die in the
14:12 was far better than dying out **h** in the wilderness!"
14:25 "Let's get out of **h**!" the Egyptians shouted.
17: 3 Why did you bring us **h**? We, our children, and our
18:14 The people have been standing **h** all day to get
19:21 They must not come up **h** to see the LORD,
19:24 or the people cross the boundaries to come up **h**.
21: 1 "**H** are some other instructions you must present
24: 1 "Come up **h** to me, and bring along Aaron, Nadab,
24:14 "Stay **h** and wait for us until we come back.
24:14 consult with Aaron and Hur, who are **h** with you."
25: 3 **H** is a list of items you may accept on my behalf:
25:40 to the pattern I have shown you **h** on the mountain.
32: 1 who brought us **h** from Egypt, has disappeared.
32:26 on the LORD's side, come over **h** and join me."
33:21 "Stand **h** on this rock beside me.
38:21 **H** is an inventory of the materials used in building
Lev 11: 4 eat the animals named **h** because they either have
27: 3 **h** is the scale of values to be used. A man between
Nu 9: 8 "Wait **h** until I have received instructions for you
11:20 who is **h** among you, and you have complained to
11:21 "There are 600,000 foot soldiers **h** with me,
13:27 and honey. **H** is some of its fruit as proof.
14: 2 had died in Egypt, or even **h** in the wilderness!"
14: 3 as slaves! Let's get out of **h** and return to Egypt!"
14:29 You will all die **h** in this wilderness! Because you
14:35 against me. They will all die **h** in this wilderness!"
16:13 with milk and honey, to kill us **h** in this wilderness,
16:16 "Come **h** tomorrow and present yourself before
16:16 with all your followers. Aaron will also be **h**.
19: 2 "**H** is another ritual law required by the LORD:
20: 5 us leave Egypt and bring us **h** to this terrible place?
21: 5 "Why have you brought us out of Egypt to die **h** in
21: 5 "There is nothing to eat **h** and nothing to drink.
22: 8 "Stay **h** overnight," Balaam said. "In the morning
22:19 But stay **h** one more night to see if the LORD has
23: 1 said to King Balak, "Build me seven altars **h**,
23: 3 said to Balak, "Stand **h** by your burnt offerings,
23:15 "Stand **h** by your burnt offering while I go to meet
24:11 Now get out of **h**! Go back home! I had planned to
32: 6 "Do you mean you want to stay back **h** while your
32:14 But **h** you are, a brood of sinners, doing exactly the
32:17 families will stay in the fortified cities we build **h**,
32:19 We would rather live **h** on the east side where we
32:26 and cattle will stay **h** in the towns of Gilead.
32:32 but our inheritance of land will be **h** on this side of
Dt 1:27 bringing us **h** from Egypt to be slaughtered by
1:31 cared for you again and again **h** in the wilderness,
3:20 then you may return **h** to the land I have given
4:22 the land, I will die **h** on this side of the river.
4:36 He let you see his great fire **h** on earth so he could
5:31 But you stay **h** with me so I can give you all my
11: 5 cared for you in the wilderness until you arrived **h**.
22:17 But **h** is the proof of my daughter's virginity.'
29: 7 When we came **h**, King Sihon of Heshbon
29:12 You are standing **h** today to enter into a covenant
Jos 1:14 and cattle may remain **h** on the east side of the
1:15 then may you settle **h** on the east side of the Jordan
2: 2 "Some Israelites have come **h** tonight to spy out
2: 3 They are spies sent **h** to discover the best way to
2: 4 the two men, replied, "The men were **h** earlier,
2:18 and all your relatives—must be **h** inside the house.
9:22 in a distant land when you live right **h** among us?
10:32 **H**, too, the entire population was slaughtered,
18: 8 lots in the presence of the LORD **h** at Shiloh."
24:18 and the other nations living **h** in the land.
Jdg 4:20 anybody comes and asks you if there is anyone **h**,
6:18 "I will stay **h** until you return."
6:26 Then build an altar to the LORD your God **h** on
8:15 said to the leaders, "**H** are Zebah and Zalmunna.
8:15 When we were **h** before, you taunted me, saying,
11:26 Israel has been living **h** all this time, spread across
13:10 "The man who appeared to me the other day is **h**
13:15 "Please stay **h** until we can prepare a young goat
17: 2 Well, **h** they are. I was the one who took them."
17:10 "Stay **h** with me," Micah said, "and you can be a
18: 3 him aside and asked him, "Who brought you **h**,
18: 3 and what are you doing? Why are you **h**?"
18:14 "There is a shrine **h** with a sacred ephod,
19:24 **H**, take my virgin daughter and this man's
Ru 2: 8 Stay right **h** with us when you gather grain;
2:11 and your own land to live **h** among complete
2:14 "Come over **h** and help yourself to some of our
3:13 Stay **h** tonight, and in the morning I will talk to
3:13 I will marry you! Now lie down **h** until morning."
3:14 "No one must know that a woman was **h** at the
4: 1 Boaz called out to him, "Come over **h**, friend.
4: 4 then buy it **h** in the presence of these witnesses.
4:10 and to inherit the family property **h** in his
1Sa 1:14 "Must you come **h** drunk?" he demanded.
1:23 "Stay **h** for now, and may the LORD help you
1:26 "I am the woman who stood **h** several years ago
3: 5 He jumped up and ran to Eli. "**H** I am. What do
3: 6 jumped up and ran to Eli. "**H** I am," he said.
3: 8 jumped up and ran to Eli. "**H** I am," he said.
3:16 "Samuel, my son." "**H** I am," Samuel replied.
5: 7 "We can't keep the Ark of the God of Israel **h** any
5:10 "They are bringing the Ark of the God of Israel **h**
6:20 cried out. "Where can we send the Ark from **h**?"
6:21 the Ark of the LORD. Please come **h** and get it!"
9: 6 There is a man of God who lives **h** in this town.
9:11 and his servant asked, "Is the seer **h** today?"

9:20 And I am **h** to tell you that you and your family are
9:27 After the servant was gone, Samuel said, "Stay **h**,
11:12 over us? Bring them **h**, and we will kill them!"
12: 2 own sons, and I stand **h**, an old, gray-haired man.
12: 7 Now stand **h** quietly before the LORD as I
12:13 All right, **h** is the king you have chosen. Look him
12:16 "Now stand **h** and see the great thing the LORD
14:12 "Come on up **h**, and we'll teach you a lesson!"
14:17 "Find out who isn't **h**," Saul ordered. And when
14:18 Saul shouted to Ahijah, "Bring the ephod **h**!"
14:33 Saul said. "Find a large stone and roll it over **h**.
14:34 'Bring the cattle and sheep **h** to kill them and drain
14:38 I want all my army commanders to come **h**.
14:40 Then Saul said, "Jonathan and I will stand over **h**,
16:17 me someone who plays well and bring him **h**."
17:28 "What are you doing around **h** anyway?"
17:44 "Come over **h**, and I'll give your flesh to the birds
20:26 Yes, that must be why he's not **h**."
20:27 "Why hasn't the son of Jesse been **h** for dinner
20:29 so I told him he could go. That's why he isn't **h**."
21: 2 "He told me not to tell anyone why I am **h**.
21: 9 that if you want it, for there is nothing else **h**."
21:15 We already have enough of them around **h**!
22: 3 and mother live **h** under royal protection until I
22: 7 "Listen **h**, you men of Benjamin!" Saul shouted
22:13 revolt against me and to come **h** and attack me?"
22:23 Stay **h** with me, and I will protect you with my
23: 3 David's men said, "We're afraid even **h** in Judah.
23:10 to come and destroy Keilah because I am **h**.
25:27 And **h** is a present I have brought to you and your
26:11 and his jug of water and then get out of **h**!"
26:22 "**H** is your spear, O king," David replied.
27: 5 the country towns instead of **h** in the royal city."
27:12 Now he will have to stay **h** and serve me forever!"
28:19 and you and your sons will be **h** with me.
29: 3 "What are these Hebrews doing **h**?"
30:26 "**H** is a present for you, taken from the LORD's
2Sa 1: 9 'Come over **h** and put me out of my misery,
2:22 Again Abner shouted to him, "Get away from **h**!
4: 8 "**H** is the head of Ishbosheth, the son of your
5: 6 "You'll never get in **h**," the Jebusites taunted.
7: 2 "**H** I am living in this beautiful cedar palace,
9: 7 and you may live **h** with me at the palace!"
9:10 But Mephibosheth will live **h** at the palace with
10: 3 "Do you really think these men are coming **h** to
11:12 "Well, stay **h** tonight," David told him,
13: 9 "Everyone get out of **h**," Amnon told his servants.
13:10 the food into my bedroom and feed it to me **h**."
13:15 had loved her. "Get out of **h**!" he snarled at her.
14:19 "Did Joab send you **h**?" And the woman replied,
15: 3 would say, "You've really got a strong case **h**!
15:27 king told Zadok the priest, "Look, **h** is my plan.
16: 7 "Get out of **h**, you murderer, you scoundrel!"
16:18 "I'm **h** because I work for the man who is chosen
16:21 for he has left them **h** to keep the house.
17:20 She replied, "They were **h**, but they crossed the
18: 3 and it is better that you stay **h** in the city and send
18:26 He shouted down, "**H** comes another one!"
18:30 "Wait **h**," the king told him. So Ahimaaz stepped
19: 7 not a single one of them will remain **h** tonight.
19:20 That is why I have come **h** today, the very first
19:37 But **h** is my son Kimham. Let him go with you
20:16 to me, Joab. Come over **h** so I can talk to you."
24:22 "**H** are oxen for the burnt offering, and you can
1Ki 1:23 told him, "Nathan the prophet is **h** to see you."
1:35 When you bring him back **h**, he will sit on my
2:30 But Joab answered, "No, I will die **h**."
2:36 "Build a house **h** in Jerusalem and live there.
3: 8 And **h** I am among your own chosen people,
8:33 on your name and pray to you **h** in this Temple,
10: 7 I didn't believe it until I arrived **h** and saw it with
10: 8 What a privilege for your officials to stand **h** day
11:22 Pharaoh asked him. "What do you lack **h**?
13: 2 the pagan shrines who come **h** to burn incense,
13:16 to eat any food or drink any water **h** in this place.
14: 5 "Jeroboam's wife will come **h**, pretending to be
17:18 Have you come **h** to punish my sins by killing my
18: 8 "Now go and tell your master I am **h**."
18:10 And each time when he was told, 'Elijah isn't **h**,'
18:11 you say, 'Go and tell your master that Elijah is **h**'!
18:14 you say, 'Go and tell your master that Elijah is **h**'!
18:30 Then Elijah called to the people, "Come over **h**!"
19: 9 said to him, "What are you doing **h**, Elijah?"
19:13 And a voice said, "What are you doing **h**, Elijah?"
22:34 "Get me out of **h**!" Ahab groaned to the driver of
2Ki 2: 2 And Elijah said to Elisha, "Stay **h**, for the LORD
2: 4 Then Elijah said to Elisha, "Stay **h**,
2: 6 Then Elijah said to Elisha, "Stay **h**,
3:10 "The LORD has brought the three of us **h** to let
3:11 officers replied, "Elisha son of Shaphat is **h**.
3:13 For it was the LORD who called us three kings **h**
4:36 she came in, Elisha said, "**H**, take your son!"
5: 8 and he will learn that there is a true prophet **h** in
7: 3 "Why should we sit **h** waiting to die?" they asked
7: 4 "We will starve if we stay **h**, and we will starve if
7:13 it won't be a greater loss than if they stay **h** and die
8: 5 "**H** is the woman now, and this is her son—
9:26 'I solemnly swear that I will repay him **h** on
10:23 sure that only those who worship Baal are **h**.
11:15 Do not kill her **h** in the Temple of the LORD."
18:22 in Judah worship only at the altar **h** in Jerusalem?
19:29 "**H** is the proof that the LORD will protect this
21: 7 "My name will be honored **h** forever in this
1Ch 11: 5 of Jebus said to David, "You will never get in **h**!"
11:11 **H** is the record of David's mightiest men: The first
12:20 **H** is a list of the men from Manasseh who defected
17: 1 "**H** I am living in this beautiful cedar palace,
19: 3 "Do you really think these men are coming **h** to
21:23 "**H** are oxen for the burnt offerings, and you can
25: 1 **H** is a list of their names and their work:
29:15 We are **h** for only a moment, visitors and strangers
2Ch 6:24 on your name and pray to you **h** in this Temple,
7:16 My eyes and my heart will always be **h**.
9: 6 I didn't believe it until I arrived **h** and saw it with
9: 7 What a privilege for your officials to stand **h** day
18:33 "Get me out of **h**!" Ahab groaned to the driver of
20: 8 Your people settled **h** and built this Temple for
23:14 Do not kill her **h** in the Temple of the LORD."
28:13 "You must not bring the prisoners **h**!"
32: 4 "Why should the kings of Assyria come **h** and find
33: 7 "My name will be honored **h** forever in this
Ezr 2: 1 **H** is the list of the Jewish exiles of the provinces
4: 2 since King Esarhaddon of Assyria brought us **h**."
4:12 "Please be informed that the Jews who came **h** to
5:11 and we are rebuilding the Temple that was built **h**
8: 1 **H** is a list of the family leaders and the genealogies
10:13 rainy season, so we cannot stay out **h** much longer.
Ne 4: 5 for they have provoked you to anger **h** in the
7: 6 "**H** is the list of the Jewish exiles of the provinces
9:36 "So now today we are slaves **h** in the land of
11: 3 **H** is a list of the names of the provincial officials
12: 1 **H** is the list of the priests and Levites who had
13:21 to them and said, "What are you doing out **h**,
Est 7: 8 "Will he even assault the queen right **h** in the
9:12 If they have done that **h**, what has happened in the
Job 16:15 **H** I sit in sackcloth. I have surrendered, and I sit in
28:14 is not **h**,' says the ocean. 'Nor is it **h**,' says the sea.
38:11 will you come. **H** your proud waves must stop!'
Ps 27:13 while I am **h** in the land of the living.
46: 7 The LORD Almighty is **h** among us; / the God of
46:11 The LORD Almighty is **h** among us; / the God of
50: 7 **H** are my charges against you, O Israel: / I am
58:11 surely there is a God who judges justly **h** on
68:18 Now the LORD God will live among us **h**.
74: 2 And remember Jerusalem, your home **h** on earth.
87: 5 "Everyone has become a citizen **h**."
103:16 we are gone— / as though we had never been **h**.
104:25 **H** is the ocean, vast and wide, / teeming with life
116: 9 in the LORD's presence / as I live **h** on earth!
119:19 I am but a foreigner **h** on earth; / I need the
120: 6 I am tired of living **h** / among people who hate
122: 2 And now we are standing **h** / inside your gates,
122: 4 the LORD's people— / make their pilgrimage **h**.
122: 5 **H** stand the thrones where judgment is given,
132:14 "I will live **h**, for this is the place I desired.
132:17 **H** I will increase the power of David;
135:21 be praised from Zion, / for he lives **h** in Jerusalem.
140:11 Don't let liars prosper **h** in our land.
Pr 1:23 Come **h** and listen to me! I'll pour out the spirit of
6:12 **H** is a description of worthless and wicked people:
7:15 looking for! I came out to find you, and **h** you are!
11:31 If the righteous are rewarded **h** on earth, how much
24:23 **H** are some further sayings of the wise: It is wrong
Ecc 1: 6 The wind blows south and north, **h** and there,
2:17 because everything done **h** under the sun is
3:22 That is why they are **h**! No one will bring them
5: 2 for he is in heaven, and you are only **h** on earth.
8: 9 I have thought deeply about all that goes on **h** in
9: 6 They no longer have a part in anything **h** on earth.
9:13 **H** is another bit of wisdom that has impressed me
12:13 **H** is my final conclusion: Fear God and obey his
SS 1:16 sight you are, my love, as we lie **h** on the grass,
2: 8 **H** he comes, leaping on the mountains
2:13 Yes, spring is **h**! Arise, my beloved, my fair one,
5: 1 "I am **h** in my garden, my treasure, my bride!
Isa 13: 4 The LORD Almighty has brought them **h** to form
17: 9 Amorites abandoned when the Israelites came **h**
21: 9 at last—look! **H** come the chariots and warriors!"
30:21 "This is the way; turn around and walk **h**."
33:14 "can live **h** in the presence of this all-consuming
33:15 The ones who can live **h** are those who are honest
34: 1 Come **h** and listen, O nations of the earth.
36: 7 in Judah worship only at the altar **h** in Jerusalem?
37:30 "**H** is the proof that the LORD will protect this
41:13 I say to you, 'Do not be afraid. I am **h** to help you.
49:20 and say, 'We need more room! It's crowded **h**!'
49:21 I was left **h** all alone. Who bore these children?
50: 1 Is that why you are not **h**? Is your mother gone
57: 3 come **h**, you witches' children, you offspring of
58: 9 will answer. 'Yes, I am **h**,' he will quickly reply.
65: 1 not looking for me. To them I have said, 'I am **h**!'
Jer 2:36 "First **h**, then there—you flit from one ally to
3:14 one from **h** and two from there, from wherever you
7: 2 the LORD! Listen to it, all of you who worship **h**!
7: 4 because the Temple of the LORD is **h**.
7: 8 because the Temple is **h** you will never suffer?
7:10 and then come **h** and stand before me in my
8:14 the people will say, 'Why should we wait **h** to die?
14: 9 to save us? You are right **h** among us, LORD.
16: 3 LORD says about the children born **h** in this city
17:25 of David sitting on the throne **h** in Jerusalem.
21:13 are safe on our mountain! No one can touch us **h**."
22: 4 of David sitting on the throne **h** in Jerusalem.
23:11 I have seen their despicable acts right **h** in my own
24: 6 well treated, and I will bring them back **h** again.
27:20 King Nebuchadnezzar of Babylon left them **h**
29:16 and all those still living **h** in Jerusalem—
29:28 Jeremiah sent a letter **h** to Babylon, predicting that
29:28 because we will be **h** to eat the fruit for many
30: 3 and they will possess it and live **h** again.
31:21 my virgin Israel; return to your cities **h**.
31:27 and multiply the number of cattle **h** in Israel
32:15 Someday people will again own property **h** in this
32:44 in the land of Benjamin and **h** in Jerusalem,
33: 3 secrets about what is going to happen **h**.
35:11 to move to Jerusalem. That is why we are **h**."
35:15 so that you might live in peace **h** in the land I gave
36: 5 "I am a prisoner **h** and unable to go to the Temple.
37: 7 to return to Egypt, though he came **h** to help you.
40: 4 But if you don't want to come, you may stay **h**.
40: 9 "Stay **h**, and serve the king of Babylon," he said,
42:10 'Stay **h** in this land. If you do, I will build you up
42:12 him kind, so he will let you stay **h** in your land.'
42:13 LORD your God and say, 'We will not stay **h**,'
43: 3 so we will stay **h** and be killed by the Babylonians
43: 9 the entrance of Pharaoh's palace **h** in Tahpanhes.
43:10 king of Babylon, **h** to Egypt.
44: 7 or child among you who has come **h** from Judah,
44: 8 incense to the idols you have made **h** in Egypt?
44:12 of Judah that insisted on coming **h** to Egypt,
44:12 They will fall **h** in Egypt, killed by war
44:29 will happen to you and that I will punish you **h**:
51:62 so that neither people nor animals will remain **h**.
La 1:16 No one is **h** to comfort me; any who might
2:16 have we awaited this day, and it is finally **h**!"
Eze 7: 2 The end is **h**! Wherever you look—east, west,
7:10 "The day of judgment is **h**; your destruction
7:12 Yes, the time has come; the day is **h**! There is no
9: 6 the mark. Begin your task right **h** at the Temple."
14:22 and they will come **h** to join you as exiles in
21:25 prince of Israel, your final day of reckoning is **h**!
26:20 a position of respect **h** in the land of the living.
30: 3 for the terrible day is almost **h**—the day of the
40: 4 You have been brought **h** so I can show you many
40:21 **H**, too, there were three guard alcoves on each
40:23 **H** on the north side, just as on the east, there was
40:27 And **h** again, directly opposite the outer gateway,
43: 7 I will remain **h** forever, living among the people of
44: 2 for the LORD, the God of Israel, entered **h**.
46:20 They will do it **h** to avoid carrying the sacrifices
48: 1 "**H** is the list of the tribes of Israel and the territory
Da 3:26 of the Most High God, come out! Come **h**!"
8:19 "I am **h** to tell you what will happen later in the
9:22 I have come **h** to give you insight
9:23 I am **h** to tell you what it was, for God loves you
10:14 Now I am **h** to explain what will happen to your
12: 4 Many will rush **h** and there, and knowledge will
Hos 9: 3 You may no longer stay **h** in this land of the
9: 7 has come; the day of payment is almost **h**.
Joel 2:27 Then you will know that I am **h** among my people
Am 5:18 who say, "If only the day of the LORD were **h**!
7:10 "Amos is hatching a plot against you right **h** on
7:12 "Get out of **h**, you seer! Go on back to the land of
7:13 Don't bother us **h** in Bethel with your prophecies,
7:13 especially not **h** where the royal sanctuary is!"
8:12 running **h** and going there, but they will not find it.
Ob 1: 3 'Who can ever reach us way up **h**?' you ask
Mic 3:11 to us," you say, "for the LORD is **h** among us."
7: 4 coming swiftly now. Your time of punishment is **h**.
Zec 3: 7 of my presence along with these others standing **h**.
6:12 **H** is the man called the Branch. He will branch out
8:18 **H** is another message that came to me from the
Mal 2:13 **H** is another thing you do. You cover the
Mt 3: 9 God can change these stones **h** into children of
4:10 "Get out of **h**, Satan," Jesus told him.
6:10 May your will be done **h** on earth, / just as it is in
6:19 "Don't store up treasures **h** on earth, where they
6:30 so wonderfully for flowers that are **h** today
10: 2 **H** are the names of the twelve apostles:
10:32 "If anyone acknowledges me publicly **h** on earth,
10:33 But if anyone denies me **h** on earth, I will deny
11:23 had been done in Sodom, it would still be **h** today.
12: 6 there is one **h** who is even greater than the Temple!
12:41 And now someone greater than Jonah is **h**—
12:42 And now someone greater than Solomon is **h**—
13:18 "Now **h** is the explanation of the story I told about
13:24 **H** is another story Jesus told: "The Kingdom of
13:31 **H** is another illustration Jesus used:
13:56 All his sisters live right **h** among us. What makes
14:18 "Bring them **h**," he said.
14:27 "It's all right," he said. "I am **h**! Don't be
15:32 They have been **h** with me for three days, and they
15:33 "And where would we get enough food out **h** in
16:28 And I assure you that some of you standing **h** right
17:20 'Move from **h** to there,' and it would move.
18:19 If two of you agree down **h** on earth concerning
19:30 and those who are considered least **h** will be the
20:28 came **h** not to be served but to serve others,
21: 2 its colt beside it. Untie them and bring them **h**.
21:38 to one another, '**H** comes the heir to this estate.
22:12 'how is it that you are **h** without wedding clothes?'
22:19 **H**, show me the Roman coin used for the tax."
23: 9 And don't address anyone **h** on earth as 'Father,'
24:23 'Look, **h** is the Messiah,' or 'There he is,'
24:26 Or, 'Look, he is hiding **h**,' don't believe it!
25:25 lose your money, so I hid it in the earth and **h** it is.'
26:11 but I will not be **h** with you much longer.
26:36 and he said, "Sit **h** while I go on ahead to pray."
26:38 to the point of death. Stay **h** and watch with me."
26:46 Up, let's be going. See, my betrayer is **h**!"
28: 6 He isn't **h**! He has been raised from the dead,
Mk 1: 1 **H** begins the Good News about Jesus the Messiah,
4:26 "**H** is another illustration of what the Kingdom of
5: 9 because there are many of us **h** inside this man."
6: 3 and Simon. And his sisters live right **h** among us."
6:50 "It's all right," he said. "I am **h**! Don't be
8: 2 They have been **h** with me for three days, and they
8: 4 to find enough food for them **h** in the wilderness?"
9: 1 "I assure you that some of you standing **h** right
10:31 and those who are considered least **h** will be the
10:45 came **h** not to be served but to serve others,

10:49 he stopped and said, "Tell him to come **h**."
11: 2 that has never been ridden. Untie it and bring it **h**.
12: 7 to one another, '**H** comes the heir to this estate.
12:38 **H** are some of the other things he taught them at
13:21 'Look, **h** is the Messiah,' or, 'There he is,'
14: 7 want to. But I will not be **h** with you much longer.
14:18 betray me, one of you who is **h** eating with me."
14:32 and Jesus said, "Sit **h** while I go and pray."
14:34 to the point of death. Stay **h** and watch with me."
14:42 Up, let's be going. See, my betrayer is **h**!"
16: 6 the Nazarene, who was crucified. He isn't **h**!
Lk 3: 7 **H** is a sample of John's preaching to the crowds
3: 8 God can change these stones **h** into children of
4:23 'Why don't you do miracles **h** in your hometown
6: 8 "Come and stand **h** where everyone can see."
6:13 twelve of them to be apostles. **H** are their names:
7:44 said to Simon, "Look at this woman kneeling **h**.
9:12 There is nothing to eat **h** in this deserted place."
9:27 And I assure you that some of you standing **h** right
9:41 I be with you and put up with you? Bring him **h**."
10:35 'I'll pay the difference the next time I am **h**.'
10:40 that my sister just sits **h** while I do all the work?
11:31 And now someone greater than Solomon is **h**—
11:32 And now someone greater than Jonah is **h**—
12: 8 If anyone acknowledges me publicly **h** on earth,
12: 9 But if anyone denies me **h** on earth, I will deny
12:28 so wonderfully for flowers that are **h** today
12:54 to form in the west, you say, '**H** comes a shower.'
13:31 "Get out of **h** if you want to live, because Herod
14: 9 The host will say, 'Let this person sit **h** instead.'
15:17 food enough to spare, and **h** I am, dying of hunger!
16: 3 I'm through **h**, and I don't have the strength to go
16: 7 '**H**,' the manager said, 'take your bill and replace it
16:24 Send Lazarus over **h** to dip the tip of his finger in
16:25 So now he is **h** being comforted, and you are in
16:26 Anyone who wanted to cross over to you from **h** is
16:28 so they won't have to come **h** when they die.'
17:21 You won't be able to say, '**H** it is!' or 'It's over
19:27 and execute them right **h** in my presence.' "
19:30 that has never been ridden. Untie it and bring it **h**.
20:14 said to each other, '**H** comes the heir to this estate.
20:34 Jesus replied, "Marriage is for people **h** on earth.
21:25 And down **h** on earth the nations will be in turmoil,
22:21 "But **h** at this table, sitting among us as a friend,
22:27 by his servants. But not **h**! For I am your servant.
24: 6 He isn't **h**! He has risen from the dead! Don't you
24:41 he asked them, "Do you have anything **h** to eat?"
24:49 But stay **h** in the city until the Holy Spirit comes
Jn 1:14 became human and lived **h** on earth among us.
1:26 but right **h** in the crowd is someone you do not
1:47 Jesus said, "**H** comes an honest man—
2:16 he told them, "Get these things out of **h**.
3:12 I tell you about things that happen **h** on earth,
3:26 is going over there instead of coming **h** to us."
3:28 I am **h** to prepare the way for him—that is all.
4:15 and I won't have to come **h** to haul water."
4:20 while we Samaritans claim it is **h** at Mount
4:21 no longer matter whether you worship the Father **h**
4:23 and is already **h** when true worshipers will worship
5:25 in fact it is **h**, when the dead will hear my voice—
6: 9 "There's a young boy **h** with five barley loaves
6:20 but he called out to them, "I am **h**! Don't be
6:25 they asked, "Teacher, how did you get **h**?"
7:26 But **h** he is, speaking in public, and they say
7:33 But Jesus told them, "I will be **h** a little longer.
8:42 from God. I am not **h** on my own, but he sent me.
9: 5 But while I am still **h** in the world, I am the light of
11:21 Martha said to Jesus, "Lord, if you had been **h**,
11:28 told her, "The Teacher is **h** and wants to see you."
11:32 at his feet and said, "Lord, if you had been **h**,
11:42 out loud for the sake of all these people standing **h**,
12: 8 but I will not be **h** with you much longer."
13:10 you are clean, but that isn't true of everyone **h**."
15:13 And **h** is how to measure it—the greatest love is
16:32 But the time is coming—in fact, it is already **h**—
16:33 **H** on earth you will have many trials and sorrows.
17: 4 I brought glory to you **h** on earth by doing
17:12 During my time **h**, I have kept them safe. I guarded
18:35 and their leading priests brought you **h**.
19: 5 the purple robe. And Pilate said, "**H** is the man!"
19:14 And Pilate said to the people, "**H** is your king!"
20:27 to Thomas, "Put your finger **h** and see my hands.
21:24 who saw these events and recorded them **h**.
Ac 1:11 why are you standing **h** staring at the sky?
1:13 **H** is the list of those who were present: / Peter,
2: 9 **H** we are—Parthians, Medes, Elamites,
2:29 and was buried, and his tomb is still **h** among us.
4:27 "That is what has happened **h** in this city!
7: 4 Then God brought him **h** to the land where you
7: 5 But God gave him no inheritance **h**, not even one
9:21 "And we understand that he came **h** to arrest them
10:33 Now **h** we are, waiting before God to hear the
11:12 These six brothers **h** accompanied me, and we
13:32 and I are **h** to bring you this Good News.
15:24 "We understand that some men from **h** have
16: 9 pleading with him, "Come over **h** and help us."
16:28 Paul shouted to him, "Don't do it! We are all **h**!"
17: 6 and now they are **h** disturbing our city,"
18:10 because many people **h** in this city belong to me."
19:26 And this is happening not only **h** in Ephesus
19:37 You have brought these men **h**, but they have
21:21 Our Jewish Christians **h** at Jerusalem have been
21:23 We have four men **h** who have taken a vow and are
22: 3 and educated **h** in Jerusalem under Gamaliel.
22:18 for the people **h** won't believe you when you give
23:11 Just as you have told the people about me **h** in
24:19 and they ought to be **h** to bring charges if they
24:20 Ask these men **h** what wrongdoing the Jewish high
25:10 official Roman court, so I ought to be tried right **h**.
25:14 "There is a prisoner **h**," he told him, "whose case
25:17 "When they came **h** for the trial, I called the case
26:29 and everyone **h** in this audience might become the
28:20 I asked you to come **h** today so we could get
28:21 or reports from anyone who has arrived **h**.
Ro 13:12 is almost gone; the day of salvation will soon be **h**.
16:23 I am his guest, and the church meets **h** in his home.
1Co 6: 3 able to resolve ordinary disagreements **h** on earth.
12:28 **H** is a list of some of the members that God has
14:25 declaring, "God is really **h** among you."
16: 8 I will be staying **h** at Ephesus until the Festival of
16: 9 for there is a wide-open door for a great work **h**,
16:17 Fortunatus, and Achaicus have come **h**.
16:17 making up for the help you weren't **h** to give me.
16:19 The churches **h** in the province of Asia greet you
16:20 The other believers **h** have asked me to greet you
16:21 **H** is my greeting, which I write with my own
2Co 5: 9 whether we are **h** in this body or away from this
5:20 as though Christ himself were **h** pleading with you,
6: 9 We live close to death, but **h** we are, still alive.
13:12 All the Christians **h** send you their greetings.
Gal 1: 2 All the Christians **h** join me in sending greetings to
5:23 **H** there is no conflict with the law.
Eph 3:13 because of what they are doing to me **h**.
Php 1:12 that everything that has happened to me **h** has
1:13 For everyone **h**, including all the soldiers in the
1:14 many of the Christians **h** have gained confidence
1:16 for they know the Lord brought me **h** to defend the
2:23 soon as I find out what is going to happen to me **h**.
3:19 and all they think about is this life **h** on earth.
4:21 The brothers who are with me **h** send you their
Col 3: 2 Do not think only about things down **h** on earth.
4: 3 also for you Gentiles. That is why I am **h** in chains.
4:11 they are working with me **h** for the Kingdom of
4:18 **H** is my greeting in my own handwriting—PAUL.
2Th 3:17 Now **h** is my greeting, which I write with my own
1Ti 1:18 Timothy, my son, **h** are my instructions for you,
2Ti 1:12 And that is why I am suffering **h** in prison. But I
1:15 all the Christians who came **h** from the province of
4:21 Hurry so you can get **h** before winter.
Tit 3:15 Everybody **h** sends greetings. Please give my
Phm 1:10 a believer as a result of my ministry **h** in prison.
1:13 I really wanted to keep him **h** with me while I am
Heb 2:13 And in the same context he said, "**H** I am—
5: 7 While Jesus was **h** on earth, he offered prayers
8: 1 **H** is the main point: Our High Priest sat down in
8: 4 If he were **h** on earth, he would not even be a
8: 5 the design I have shown you **h** on the mountain."
9: 1 for worship and a sacred tent **h** on earth.
11:13 no more than foreigners and nomads **h** on earth.
13:23 If he comes **h** soon, I will bring him with me to see
Jas 4:13 Look **h**, you people who say, "Today or tomorrow
4:14 morning fog—it's **h** a little while, then it's gone.
5: 1 Look **h**, you rich people, weep and groan with
1Pe 1:17 of him during your time as foreigners **h** on earth.
2:11 and sisters, you are foreigners and aliens **h**.
5:13 Your sister church **h** in Rome sends you greetings,
2Pe 1:14 shown me that my days **h** on earth are numbered
1Jn 2:18 Dear children, the last hour is **h**. You have heard
4: 3 going to come into the world, and he is already **h**.
4:17 because we are like Christ **h** in this world.
3Jn 1: 6 They have told the church **h** of your friendship
1:15 with you. Your friends **h** send you their greetings.
Jude 1:19 Now they are **h**, and they are the ones who are
Rev 3:20 "Look! **H** I stand at the door and knock. If you
4: 1 The voice said, "Come up **h**, and I will show you
11:12 a loud voice shouted from heaven, "Come up **h**!"
13:10 for **h** is your opportunity to have endurance
22:18 If anyone adds anything to what is written **h**,

HERE'S (4) [BE, HERE]
1Sa 18:21 "**H** another chance to see him killed by the
Ac 21:23 "**H** our suggestion. We have four men here who
1Co 10:25 **H** what you should do. You may eat any meat that
Gal 3:15 Dear friends, **h** an example from everyday life.

HEREAFTER [KJV] See also AFTER, AGAIN, LATER, LONGER

HEREBY (6) [HERE]
Ge 4:11 You are **h** banished from the ground you have
41:40 I **h** appoint you to direct this project. You will
41:41 "I **h** put you in charge of the entire land of
Ezr 6: 8 Moreover I **h** decree that you are to help these
7:14 and my Council of Seven **h** instruct you to conduct
7:21 **h** send this decree to all the treasurers in the

HEREIN [KJV] See HERE

HERES (2)
Jdg 1:35 The Amorites were determined to stay in Mount **H**,
8:13 After this, Gideon returned by way of **H** Pass.

HERESH (1)
1Ch 9:15 Bakbakkar; **H**; Galal; Mattaniah son of Mica,

HERESIES (1)
2Pe 2: 1 They will cleverly teach their destructive **h** about

HERETH (1)
1Sa 22: 5 land of Judah." So David went to the forest of **H**.

HERETICK [KJV] See (CAUSING) DIVISIONS

HERETOFORE [KJV] See BEFORE

HERITAGE (1) [INHERIT]
Ps 106: 5 let me praise you with those who are your **h**.

HERMAS (1)
Ro 16:14 Phlegon, Hermes, Patrobas, **H**, and the other

HERMES (2)
Ac 14:12 that Paul, because he was the chief speaker, was **H**.
Ro 16:14 Phlegon, **H**, Patrobas, Hermas, and the other

HERMOGENES (1)
2Ti 1:15 have deserted me; even Phygelus and **H** are gone.

HERMON (16) [BAAL-HERMON, SENIR, SIRION]
Dt 3: 8 Jordan River—from the Arnon Gorge to Mount **H**.
3: 9 (Mount **H** is called Sirion by the Sidonians;
4:48 Gorge to Mount Sirion, also called Mount **H**.
Jos 11: 3 the Hivites in the towns on the slopes of Mount **H**,
11:17 to Baal-gad at the foot of Mount **H** in the valley of
12: 1 extended from the Arnon Gorge to Mount **H**
12: 5 He ruled a territory stretching from Mount **H** to
13: 5 from Baal-gad beneath Mount **H** to Lebo-hamath;
13:11 kingdoms of Geshur and Maacah, all of Mount **H**,
1Ch 5:23 from Bashan to Baal-hermon, Senir, and Mount **H**.
Ps 29: 6 like a calf / and Mount **H** to leap like a young bull.
42: 6 from Mount **H**, the source of the Jordan,
89:12 Mount Tabor and Mount **H** praise your name.
133: 3 is as refreshing as the dew from Mount **H**
SS 4: 8 from Mount Senir and Mount **H**, where lions have
Jer 18:14 flowing streams from the crags of Mount **H** ever

HERO (3) [HERO'S, HEROES, HEROIC]
Jos 14:15 been named after Arba, a great **h** of the Anakites.)
Jdg 6:12 the LORD appeared to him and said, "Mighty **h**,
Ps 52: 1 You call yourself a **h**, do you? / Why boast about

HERO'S (1) [HERO]
2Sa 18:11 you with ten pieces of silver and a **h** belt!"

HEROD (49) [HEROD'S]
Mt 2: 1 of Bethlehem in Judea, during the reign of King **H**.
2: 3 **H** was deeply disturbed by their question, as was
2: 7 Then **H** sent a private message to the wise men,
2:12 had warned them in a dream not to return to **H**.
2:13 because **H** is going to try to kill the child."
2:16 **H** was furious when he learned that the wise men
2:19 When **H** died, an angel of the Lord appeared in a
14: 1 When **H** Antipas heard about Jesus,
14: 3 For **H** had arrested and imprisoned John as a favor
14: 4 John kept telling **H**, "It is illegal for you to marry
14: 5 **H** would have executed John, but he was afraid of
14: 6 But at a birthday party for **H**, Herodias' daughter
22:16 along with the supporters of **H**, to ask him this
Mk 1:14 Later on, after John was arrested by **H** Antipas,
3: 6 and met with the supporters of **H** to discuss plans
6:14 **H** Antipas, the king, soon heard about Jesus,
6:16 When **H** heard about Jesus he said, "John, the man
6:17 For **H** had sent soldiers to arrest and imprison John
6:17 his brother Philip's wife, but **H** had married her.
6:18 John kept telling **H**, "It is illegal for you to marry
6:20 And **H** respected John, knowing that he was a
6:20 **H** was disturbed whenever he talked with John,
8:15 "Beware of the yeast of the Pharisees and of **H**."
12:13 and supporters of **H** to try to trap Jesus into saying
Lk 1: 5 Zechariah, who lived when **H** was king of Judea.
3: 1 over Judea; **H** Antipas was ruler over Galilee;
3:19 John also publicly criticized **H** Antipas, ruler of
3:20 So **H** put John in prison, adding this sin to his
9: 7 When reports of Jesus' miracles reached **H**
9: 9 "I beheaded John," **H** said, "so who is this man
13:31 to live, because **H** Antipas wants to kill you!"
23: 7 that he was, Pilate sent him to **H** Antipas,
23: 7 and **H** happened to be in Jerusalem at the time.
23: 8 **H** was delighted at the opportunity to see Jesus,
23:11 Now **H** and his soldiers began mocking
23:12 **H** and Pilate, who had been enemies before,
23:15 **H** came to the same conclusion and sent him back
Ac 4:27 For **H** Antipas, Pontius Pilate the governor,
12: 1 About that time King **H** Agrippa began to
12: 3 When **H** saw how much this pleased the Jewish
12:11 Lord has sent his angel and saved me from **H**
12:19 **H** Agrippa ordered a thorough search for him.
12:19 **H** interrogated the guards and sentenced them to
12:19 Afterward **H** left Judea to stay in Caesarea for a
12:20 Now **H** was very angry with the people of Tyre
12:21 and an appointment with **H** was granted.
12:21 **H** put on his royal robes, sat on his throne,
12:23 an angel of the Lord struck **H** with a sickness,
13: 1 Manaen (the childhood companion of King **H**

HEROD'S (12) [HEROD]
Mt 2:15 and they stayed there until **H** death. This fulfilled
2:17 **H** brutal action fulfilled the prophecy of Jeremiah:
2:22 But when he learned that the new ruler was **H** son
14: 3 Herodias (the former wife of **H** brother Philip).
Mk 6:19 but without **H** approval she was powerless.
6:21 It was **H** birthday, and he gave a party for his

Lk 8: 3 Joanna, the wife of Chuza, **H** business manager;
23: 7 because Galilee was under **H** jurisdiction,
Ac 12: 4 **H** intention was to bring Peter out for public trial
12:20 because their cities were dependent upon **H**
12:20 made friends with Blastus, **H** personal assistant,
23:35 ordered him kept in the prison at **H** headquarters.

HERODIAS (5) [HERODIAS']

Mt 14: 3 and imprisoned John as a favor to his wife **H** (the
Mk 6:17 to arrest and imprison John as a favor to **H**.
6:19 **H** was enraged and wanted John killed in revenge,
6:22 also named **H**, came in and performed a dance that
Lk 3:19 ruler of Galilee, for marrying **H**, his brother's wife,

HERODIAS' (2) [HERODIAS]

Mt 14: 6 **H** daughter performed a dance that greatly pleased
Mk 6:21 **H** chance finally came. It was Herod's birthday,

HERODION (1)

Ro 16:11 Greet **H**, my relative. Greet the Christians in the

HEROES (11) [HERO]

Ge 6: 4 they gave birth to children who became the **h**
2Sa 1:19 dead on the hills! / How the mighty **h** have fallen!
1:25 How the mighty **h** have fallen in battle!
1:27 How the mighty **h** have fallen! / Stripped of their
Ps 16: 3 the land / are my true **h**! / I take pleasure in them!
SS 4: 4 of David, jeweled with the shields of a thousand **h**.
Isa 3: 2 the **h**, soldiers, judges, prophets, diviners, elders,
5:22 Destruction is certain for those who are **h** when it
32: 5 In that day ungodly fools will not be **h**.
Jer 48:14 "You used to boast, 'We are **h**, mighty men of
Eze 32:27 They are not buried in honor like the fallen **h** of the

HEROIC (5) [HERO]

Ge 10: 8 descendants was Nimrod, who became a **h** warrior.
1Sa 26:25 You will do **h** deeds and be a great conqueror."
2Sa 23:20 He did many **h** deeds, which included killing two
1Ch 1:10 who was known across the earth as a **h** warrior.
11:22 He did many **h** deeds, which included killing two

HERONS (2)

Lev 11:19 the stork, **h** of all kinds, the hoopoe, and the bat.
Dt 14:18 the stork, **h** of all kinds, the hoopoe, and the bat.

HERS (3) [SHE] See Index of Articles, Etc.

HERSELF (28) [SELF, SHE] See Index of Articles, Etc.

HESED [KJV] See BEN-HESED

HESHBON (37)

Nu 21:25 including the city of **H** and its surrounding
21:26 **H** had been the capital of King Sihon of the
21:27 "Come to **H**, city of Sihon! / May it be restored
21:28 A fire flamed forth from **H**, / a blaze from the city
21:30 destroyed them, / all the way from **H** to Dibon.
21:34 to King Sihon of the Amorites, who ruled in **H**."
32: 3 Dibon, Jazer, Nimrah, **H**, Elealeh, Sebam, Nebo,
32:37 The people of Reuben built the towns of **H**,
Dt 1: 4 who had ruled in **H**, and King Og of Bashan,
2:24 king of **H**, and I will give you his land.
2:26 to King Sihon of **H** with this proposal of peace:
3: 2 King Sihon of the Amorites, who ruled in **H**.'
3: 6 just as we had destroyed King Sihon of **H**.
4:46 occupied by the Amorites under King Sihon of **H**.
29: 7 King Sihon of **H** and King Og of Bashan came out
Jos 9:10 King Sihon of **H** and King Og of Bashan (who
12: 2 of the Amorites, who lived in **H**, was defeated.
12: 5 of which was in the territory of King Sihon of **H**.
13:10 who reigned in **H**, and extended as far as the
13:17 It included **H** and the other towns on the plain—
13:21 Sihon was the Amorite king who had reigned in **H**
13:26 It extended from **H** to Ramath-mizpeh
13:27 and the rest of the kingdom of King Sihon of **H**.
21:39 **H**, and Jazer—four towns with their pasturelands.
Jdg 11:19 to King Sihon of the Amorites, who ruled from **H**,
11:26 spread across the land from **H** to Aroer and in all
1Ch 6:81 **H**, and Jazer, each with its pasturelands.
Ne 9:22 completely took over the land of King Sihon of **H**
SS 7: 4 Your eyes are like the sparkling pools in **H** by the
Isa 15: 4 The cries from the cities of **H** and Elealeh will be
16: 8 Weep for the abandoned farms of **H**
16: 9 My tears will flow for **H** and Elealeh, for their
Jer 48: 2 In **H** plans have been completed to destroy her.
48:34 their awful cries of terror can be heard from **H**
48:45 "The people flee as far as **H** but are unable to go
48:45 For a fire comes from **H**, King Sihon's ancestral
49: 3 "Cry out, O **H**, for the town of Ai is destroyed.

HESHMON (1)

Jos 15:27 Hazar-gaddah, **H**, Beth-pelet,

HESITATE (4) [HESITATED, HESITATION]

Dt 7:10 But he does not **h** to punish and destroy those who
Jdg 18: 9 You should not **h** to go and take possession of it.
Mt 10:10 Don't **h** to accept hospitality, because those who
Lk 10: 7 Don't **h** to accept hospitality, because those who

HESITATED (1) [HESITATE]

Ge 19:16 When Lot still **h**, the angels seized his hand

HESITATION (1) [HESITATE]

Ac 10:20 Go down and go with them without **h**. All is well,

HETHLON (2)

Eze 47:15 border will run from the Mediterranean toward **H**,
48: 1 Its boundary line follows the **H** road to

HEW [KJV] See CARVE, CUT, PREPARE

HEWER(S) [KJV] See also CHOP, STONECUTTERS, CRAFTSMAN, WOODSMEN

HEWN (3)

1Ki 6:36 of cedar beams after every three layers of **h** stone.
7:12 of cedar beams after every three layers of **h** stone,
Eze 40:42 There were also four tables of **h** stone for

HEZEKI [KJV] See HIZKI

HEZEKIAH (133) [HEZEKIAH'S]

2Ki 16:20 of David. Then his son **H** became the next king.
18: 1 **H** son of Ahaz began to rule over Judah in the third
18: 5 **H** trusted in the LORD, the God of Israel.
18: 7 and **H** was successful in everything he did.
18:14 King **H** sent this message to the king of Assyria at
18:15 King **H** used all the silver stored in the Temple of
18:16 **H** even stripped the gold from the doors of the
18:17 with a huge army to confront King **H** in Jerusalem.
18:18 They summoned King **H**, but the king sent these
18:19 representative sent this message to King **H**:
18:22 But isn't he the one who was insulted by King **H**?
18:22 Didn't **H** tear down his shrines and altars and make
18:29 what the king says: Don't let King **H** deceive you.
18:31 "Don't listen to **H**! These are the terms the king of
18:32 "Don't listen to **H** when he tries to mislead you by
18:36 not answer because **H** had told them not to speak.
18:37 son of Asaph, the royal historian, went back to **H**.
19: 1 When King **H** heard their report, he tore his
19: 3 They told him, "This is what King **H** says: This is
19: 9 he sent this message back to **H** in Jerusalem:
19:10 "This message is for King **H** of Judah. Don't let
19:14 After **H** received the letter and read it, he went up
19:15 And **H** prayed this prayer before the LORD:
19:20 Then Isaiah son of Amoz sent this message to **H**:
19:29 Then Isaiah said to **H**, "Here is the proof that the
20: 1 About that time **H** became deathly ill,
20: 2 When **H** heard this, he turned his face to the wall
20: 5 "Go back to **H**, the leader of my people. Tell him,
20: 7 it over the boil." They did this, and **H** recovered!
20: 8 Meanwhile, **H** had said to Isaiah, "What sign will
20:10 "The shadow always moves forward," **H** replied.
20:12 king of Babylon, sent **H** his best wishes and a gift,
for he had heard that **H** had been very sick.
20:13 **H** welcomed the Babylonian envoys and showed
20:13 in his palace or kingdom that **H** did not show them.
20:14 Then Isaiah the prophet went to King **H** and asked
20:14 **H** replied, "They came from the distant land of
20:15 Isaiah asked. "They saw everything," **H** replied.
20:16 Then Isaiah said to **H**, "Listen to this message
20:19 Then **H** said to Isaiah, "This message you have
20:21 When **H** died, his son Manasseh became the next
21: 3 the pagan shrines his father, **H**, had destroyed.
1Ch 3:13 Ahaz, **H**, Manasseh,
4:41 But during the reign of King **H** of Judah,
2Ch 28:27 Then his son **H** became the next king.
29: 1 **H** was twenty-five years old when he became the
29: 3 **H** reopened the doors of the Temple of the LORD
29:18 Then the Levites went to King **H** and gave him this
29:20 Early the next morning King **H** gathered the city
29:25 King **H** then stationed the Levites at the Temple of
29:27 Then **H** ordered that the burnt offering be placed
29:30 King **H** and the officials ordered the Levites to
29:31 Then **H** declared, "The dedication ceremony has
29:36 And **H** and all the people rejoiced greatly
30: 1 King **H** now sent word to all Israel and Judah,
30:18 But King **H** prayed for them, and they were
30:18 For **H** said, "May the LORD, who is good,
30:22 **H** encouraged the Levites for the skill they
30:24 King **H** gave the people one thousand bulls
31: 2 **H** then organized the priests and Levites into
31: 8 When **H** and his officials came and saw these huge
31: 9 this come from?" **H** asked the priests and Levites.
31:11 **H** decided to have storerooms prepared in the
31:13 These appointments were made by King **H**
31:20 King **H** handled the distribution throughout all
31:21 the commands, **H** sought his God wholeheartedly.
32: 1 After **H** had faithfully carried out this work,
32: 2 When **H** realized that Sennacherib also intended to
32: 5 Then **H** further strengthened his defenses by
32: 6 Then **H** encouraged them with this address:
32: 9 sent officials to Jerusalem with this message for **H**
32:11 **H** has said, 'The LORD our God will rescue us
32:11 Surely **H** is misleading you, sentencing you to
32:12 Surely you must realize that **H** is the very person
32:15 Don't let **H** fool you! Don't let him deceive you
32:16 further mocked the LORD God and his servant **H**,
32:17 from my power, so the God of **H** will also fail."
32:20 Then King **H** and the prophet Isaiah son of Amoz
32:22 That is how the LORD rescued **H** and the people
32:23 then on King **H** became highly respected among
32:23 with valuable presents for King **H**, too.
32:24 About that time, **H** became deathly ill. He prayed
32:25 But **H** did not respond appropriately to the
32:26 Then **H** repented of his pride, and the people of
32:27 **H** was very wealthy and held in high esteem.
32:31 God withdrew from **H** in order to test him and to
32:33 When **H** died, he was buried in the upper area of
33: 3 He rebuilt the pagan shrines his father **H** had
Ezr 2:16 The family of Ater (descendants of **H**) | 98
Ne 7:21 The family of Ater (descendants of **H**) | 98
10:17 Ater, **H**, Azzur,
Pr 25: 1 collected by the advisers of King **H** of Judah.
Isa 1: 1 during the reigns of Uzziah, Jotham, Ahaz, and **H**
36: 2 from Lachish to confront King **H** in Jerusalem.
36: 4 representative sent this message to King **H**:
36: 7 But isn't he the one who was insulted by King **H**?
36: 7 Didn't **H** tear down his shrines and altars and make
36:14 what the king says: Don't let King **H** deceive you.
36:16 "Don't listen to **H**! These are the terms the king of
36:18 "Don't let **H** mislead you by saying, 'The LORD
36:21 not answer because **H** had told them not to speak.
36:22 son of Asaph, the royal historian, went back to **H**.
37: 1 When King **H** heard their report, he tore his
37: 3 They told him, "This is what King **H** says: This is
37: 9 he sent this message back to **H** in Jerusalem:
37:10 "This message is for King **H** of Judah. Don't let
37:14 After **H** received the letter and read it, he went up
37:15 And **H** prayed this prayer before the LORD:
37:21 Then Isaiah son of Amoz sent this message to **H**:
37:30 Then Isaiah said to **H**, "Here is the proof that the
38: 1 About that time **H** became deathly ill,
38: 2 When **H** heard this, he turned his face to the wall
38: 5 "Go back to **H** and tell him, 'This is what the
38: 9 When King **H** was well again, he wrote this poem
38:21 and spread it over the boil, and **H** will recover."
38:22 And **H** had asked, "What sign will prove that I
39: 1 king of Babylon, sent **H** his best wishes and a gift.
39: 1 He had heard that **H** had been very sick and that he
39: 2 **H** welcomed the Babylonian envoys and showed
39: 2 in his palace or kingdom that **H** did not show them.
39: 3 Then Isaiah the prophet went to King **H** and asked
39: 3 **H** replied, "They came from the distant land of
39: 4 asked Isaiah. "They saw everything," **H** replied.
39: 5 Then Isaiah said to **H**, "Listen to this message
39: 8 Then **H** said to Isaiah, "This message you have
Jer 15: 4 Because of the wicked things Manasseh son of **H**,
26:18 prophesied during the reign of King **H** of Judah.
26:19 But did King **H** and the people kill him for saying
Hos 1: 1 Jotham, Ahaz, and **H** were kings of Judah,
Mic 1: 1 when Jotham, Ahaz, and **H** were kings of Judah.
Zep 1: 1 son of Gedaliah, son of Amariah, son of **H**.
Mt 1: 9 was the father of Ahaz. / Ahaz was the father of **H**.
1:10 **H** was the father of Manasseh. / Manasseh was the

HEZEKIAH'S (12) [HEZEKIAH]

2Ki 18: 9 During the fourth year of **H** reign, which was the
18:10 during the sixth year of King **H** reign and the ninth
18:13 In the fourteenth year of King **H** reign,
19: 5 After King **H** officials delivered the king's
20: 7 Then Isaiah said to **H** servants, "Make an ointment
20:20 The rest of the events in **H** reign,
2Ch 30:20 And the LORD listened to **H** prayer and healed
32:26 anger did not come against them during **H** lifetime.
32:32 The rest of the events of **H** reign and his acts of
Isa 36: 1 In the fourteenth year of King **H** reign,
37: 5 After King **H** officials delivered the king's
38:21 Isaiah had said to **H** servants, "Make an ointment

HEZION (1)

1Ki 15:18 Ben-hadad son of Tabrimmon and grandson of **H**,

HEZIR (2)

1Ch 24:15 The seventeenth lot fell to **H**. / The eighteenth lot
Ne 10:20 Magpiash, Meshullam, **H**,

HEZRAI [KJV] See HEZRO

HEZRO (2)

2Sa 23:35 **H** from Carmel; / Paarai from Arba;
1Ch 11:37 **H** from Carmel; / Paarai son of Ezbai;

HEZRON (19) [HEZRON'S, HEZRONITE, HEZRONITES]

Ge 46: 9 sons of Reuben were Hanoch, Pallu, **H**, and Carmi.
46:12 of Canaan.) The sons of Perez were **H** and Hamul.
Ex 6:14 oldest son, included Hanoch, Pallu, **H**, and Carmi.
Nu 26: 6 The Hezronite clan, named after its ancestor **H**.
26:21 The Hezronites, named after their ancestor **H**.
Jos 15: 3 of Zin and went south of Kadesh-barnea to **H**.
Ru 4:18 their ancestor Perez: / Perez was the father of **H**.
4:19 **H** was the father of Ram. / Ram was the father of
1Ch 2: 5 The sons of Perez were **H** and Hamul.
2: 9 The sons of **H** were Jerahmeel, Ram, and Caleb.
2:21 When **H** was sixty years old, he married Gilead's
2:24 Soon after **H** died in the town of Caleb-ephrathah,
2:25 the oldest son of **H**, were Ram (the oldest), Bunah,
4: 1 of Judah were Perez, **H**, Carmi, Hur, and Shobal.
5: 3 son of Israel, were Hanoch, Pallu, **H**, and Carmi.
Mt 1: 3 Perez was the father of **H**. / **H** was the father of
Ram.
Lk 3:33 Arni was the son of **H**. / **H** was the son of Perez.

HEZRON'S (1) [HEZRON]

1Ch 2:18 **H** son Caleb had two wives named Azubah

HEZRONITE (1) [HEZRON]

Nu 26: 6 The **H** clan, named after its ancestor Hezron.

HEZRONITES (1) [HEZRON]

Nu 26:21 The **H**, named after their ancestor Hezron.

HID (24) [HIDE]

Ge 3: 8 the garden, so they **h** themselves among the trees.
3:10 He replied, "I heard you, so I **h**. I was afraid
Ex 3: 6 he **h** his face in his hands because he was afraid to
Jos 10:16 five kings escaped and **h** in a cave at Makkedah.
Jdg 9: 5 But the youngest brother, Jotham, escaped and **h**.
1Sa 20:19 go to the place where you **h** before,
20:24 So David **h** himself in the field, and when the new
2Sa 17:18 where a man **h** them inside a well in his courtyard.
1Ki 18:13 I **h** a hundred of them in two caves and supplied
20:30 Ben-hadad fled into the city and **h** in a secret room.
2Ki 5:24 the men back. Then he **h** the gifts inside the house.
1Ch 21:20 His four sons, who were with him, ran away and **h**.
2Ch 22:11 **h** the child so that Athaliah could not murder him.
Jer 13: 5 and **h** it at the Euphrates as the LORD had
La 3:10 He **h** like a bear or a lion, waiting to attack me.
4:19 If we **h** in the wilderness, they were waiting for us
Mt 13:44 he **h** it again and sold everything he owned to get
25:18 and **h** the master's money for safekeeping.
25:25 your money, so I **h** it in the earth and here it is.'
Lk 19:20 amount of money and said, 'I **h** it and kept it safe.
Jn 8:59 But Jesus **h** himself from them and left the
Heb 11:23 It was by faith that Moses' parents **h** him for three
Jas 2:25 when she **h** those messengers and sent them safely
Rev 6:15 all **h** themselves in the caves and among the rocks

HIDDEKEL [KJV] See TIGRIS

HIDDEN (58) [HIDE]

Ex 2: 2 baby he was and kept him **h** for three months.
Dt 33:19 riches of the sea / and the **h** treasures of the sand."
Jos 2: 4 Rahab, who had **h** the two men, replied, "The men
2: 6 up to the roof and **h** them beneath piles of flax.)
6:25 because she had **h** the spies Joshua sent to Jericho.
7:11 about it and **h** the things among their belongings.
7:13 **H** among you, O Israel, are things set apart for the
7:21 They are **h** in the ground beneath my tent,
7:22 ran to the tent and found the stolen goods **h** there,
Jdg 3:16 it to his right thigh, keeping it **h** under his clothing.
16: 9 She had **h** some men in one of the rooms of her
2Sa 17: 9 He has probably already **h** in some pit or cave.
1Ki 18: 4 Obadiah had **h** one hundred of them in two caves.
2Ki 6:29 your son so we can eat him,' but she had **h** him."
7:12 they have left their camp and have **h** in the fields.
11: 3 and his nurse remained **h** in the Temple of the
2Ch 22:12 Joash remained **h** in the Temple of God for six
Job 3:21 They search for death more eagerly than for **h**
18:10 A snare lies **h** in the ground. A rope lies coiled on
23: 9 I do not see him in the north, for he is **h**. I turn to
28:11 trickling streams and bring to light the **h** treasures.
28:21 For it is **h** from the eyes of all humanity.
40:21 It lies down under the lotus plants, **h** by the reeds.
Ps 19:12 in my heart? / Cleanse me from these **h** faults.
40:10 I have not kept this good news **h** in my heart;
55:12 arrogantly insult me— / I could have **h** from them.
69: 5 how foolish I am; / my sins cannot be **h** from you.
78: 2 I will teach you **h** lessons from our past—
119:11 I have **h** your word in my heart, / that I might not
Pr 2: 4 them as you would for lost money or **h** treasure.
20:27 the human spirit, exposing every **h** motive.
27: 5 An open rebuke is better than **h** love!
Isa 45: 3 And I will give you treasures **h** in the darkness—
49: 2 He has **h** me in the shadow of his hand. I am like a
51:16 in your mouth and **h** you safely within my hand.
Jer 13: 7 and dug it out of the hole where I had **h** it.
18:22 a pit for me, and they have **h** traps along my path.
36:26 and Jeremiah. But the LORD had **h** them.
41: 8 barley, oil, and honey that they had **h** away.
43:10 I will set his throne on these stones that I have **h**.
La 3:44 You have **h** yourself in a cloud so our prayers
Eze 8: 8 into the wall and uncovered a door to a **h** room.
10: 8 looked like human hands **h** beneath their wings.)
28: 3 than Daniel and think no secret is **h** from you.
Da 2:22 and knows what lies **h** in darkness,
Mt 13:35 I will explain mysteries **h** since the creation of the
13:44 is like a treasure that a man discovered **h** in a field.
Mk 4:22 "Everything that is now **h** or secret will eventually
Lk 8:17 For everything that is **h** or secret will eventually be
9:45 Its significance was **h** from them, so they could not
11:44 will be for you. For you are like **h** graves in a field.
18:34 Its significance was **h** from them, and they failed
19:42 But now it is too late, and peace is **h** from you.
Jn 12:36 Jesus went away and was **h** from them.
1Co 2: 7 wisdom of God, which was **h** in former times,
Col 2: 3 In him lie **h** all the treasures of wisdom
3: 3 and your real life is **h** with Christ in God.
Rev 2:17 eat of the manna that has been **h** away in heaven.

HIDE (92) [HID, HIDDEN, HIDEOUT, HIDES, HIDING]

Ge 18:17 "Should I **h** my plan from Abraham?"
Ex 2: 3 But when she could no longer **h** him, she got a
Lev 4:11 its **h**, meat, head, legs, internal organs, and dung—
7: 8 the **h** of the sacrificed animal also belongs to the
8:17 rest of the bull, including its **h**, meat, and dung,
9:11 The meat and the **h**, however, he burned outside
13:48 some woolen or linen fabric, the **h** of an animal,
13:49 area in the clothing, the animal **h**, the fabric,
Nu 19: 5 must be burned—its **h**, meat, blood, and dung.
Dt 28:57 She will **h** from them the afterbirth and the new
31:18 At that time I will **h** my face from them on account
Jos 2:16 "**H** there for three days until the men who are
7:19 tell me what you have done. Don't **h** it from me."
8: 4 "**H** in ambush close behind the city and be ready
Jdg 6:11 of a winepress to **h** the grain from the Midianites.
9:32 by night with an army and **h** out in the fields.
21:20 still needed wives, "Go and **h** in the vineyards.
1Sa 3:17 And may God punish you if you **h** anything from
13: 6 lost their nerve entirely and tried to **h** in caves,
20: 2 I know he wouldn't **h** something like this from me.
20: 5 but tomorrow I'll **h** in the field and stay there until
2Sa 14:19 Nobody can **h** anything from you. Yes, Joab sent
1Ki 17: 3 and **h** by Kerith Brook at a place east of where it
2Ki 11: 2 and his nurse in a bedroom to **h** him from Athaliah,
Job 14:13 "I wish you would **h** me with the dead and forget
24: 4 kicked aside; the needy must **h** together for safety.
31:33 Have I tried to **h** my sins as people normally do,
34:22 No darkness is thick enough to **h** the wicked from
37: 8 The wild animals **h** in the rocks or in their dens.
41: 7 Will its **h** be hurt by darts, or its head by a
41:13 Who can strip off its **h**, and who can penetrate its
Ps 10: 1 Why do you **h** when I need you the most?
17: 8 of your eye. / **H** me in the shadow of your wings.
19: 6 to the other end. / Nothing can **h** from its heat.
27: 5 troubles come; / he will **h** me in his sanctuary.
27: 9 Do not **h** yourself from me. / Do not reject your
31:20 You **h** them in the shelter of your presence,
32: 5 and stopped trying to **h** them. / I said to myself,
57: 1 I will **h** beneath the shadow of your wings
69:17 Don't **h** from your servant; / answer me quickly,
78: 4 We will not **h** these truths from our children
89:46 long will this go on? / Will you **h** yourself forever?
94:22 my God is a mighty rock where I can **h**.
119:19 of your commands. / Don't **h** them from me!
119:95 Though the wicked **h** along the way to kill me,
139:11 I could ask the darkness to **h** me / and the light
139:12 but even in darkness I cannot **h** from you. / To you
143: 9 from my enemies, LORD; / I run to you to **h** me.
Pr 1:11 "Come and join us. Let's **h** and kill someone!
10:18 To **h** hatred is to be a liar; to slander is to be a fool.
26:23 Smooth words may **h** a wicked heart, just as a
28:28 When the wicked take charge, people **h**.
Isa 2:10 **H** from the terror of the LORD and the glory of
2:19 They will **h** in caves in the rocks from the terror of
2:21 and **h** among the jagged rocks at the tops of cliffs.
16: 4 **H** them from our enemies until the terror is past."
17:10 God who can save you—the Rock who can **h** you.
21:13 O caravans from Dedan, **h** in the deserts of Arabia.
26:20 **H** until the LORD's anger against your enemies
26:21 The earth will no longer **h** those who have been
29:15 Destruction is certain for those who try to **h** their
50: 6 I do not **h** from shame, for they mock me and spit
58: 7 and do not **h** from relatives who need your help.
Jer 2:32 Does a bride **h** her wedding dress? No!
4:29 They **h** in the bushes and run for the mountains.
10:10 at his anger. The nations **h** before his wrath.
13: 4 Euphrates River. **H** it there in a hole in the rocks."
13: 6 and get the linen belt that I told you to **h** there."
16:17 I see every sin. They cannot hope to **h** from me.
23:24 Can anyone **h** from me? Am I not everywhere in
25:35 You will find no place to **h**; there will be no way to
36:19 "You and Jeremiah should both **h**," the officials
38:14 the king said. "And don't try to **h** the truth."
42: 4 everything he says. I will **h** nothing from you."
48: 6 Flee for your lives! **H** in the wilderness!
49: 8 and flee! **H** in deep caves, you people of Dedan!
49:10 land of Edom, and there will be no place left to **h**.
49:16 live in a rock fortress and **h** high in the mountains.
49:30 "**H** yourselves in deep caves, you people of Hazor,
La 1: 8 All she can do is groan and **h** her face.
Eze 7:22 I will **h** my eyes as these robbers invade my
21:24 You don't even try to **h** it! Wherever you go,
Da 10: 7 but they were suddenly terrified and ran away to **h**.
Am 9: 3 Even if they **h** at the very top of Mount Carmel,
9: 3 Even if they **h** at the bottom of the ocean, I will
Na 3:11 You will **h** for fear of the attacking enemy.
Mt 5:15 Don't **h** your light under a basket! Instead, put it
Lk 11:52 For you **h** the key to knowledge from the people.
Jn 7: 4 "You can't become a public figure if you **h** like
Heb 4:13 Nothing in all creation can **h** from him.
Rev 6:16 and **h** us from the face of the one who sits on the
20:11 from his presence, but they found no place to **h**.

HIDEOUS (1)

Eze 8:10 with all kinds of snakes, lizards, and **h** creatures.

HIDEOUT (1) [HIDE]

Rev 18: 2 She has become the **h** of demons and evil spirits,

HIDES (4) [HIDE]

Lev 16:27 This includes the animals' **h**, the internal organs,
Job 34:29 But when he **h** his face, who can find him?
Pr 23:28 She **h** and waits like a robber, looking for another
Lk 11:33 "No one lights a lamp and then **h** it or puts it

HIDING (42) [HIDE]

Dt 7:20 to drive out the few survivors still **h** from you!
31:17 I will abandon them, **h** my face from them,
Jos 10:27 and thrown into the cave where they had been **h**.
Jdg 6: 2 where they made **h** places for themselves in caves
9:35 gates when Abimelech and his army came out of **h**.
9:43 he and his men jumped up from their **h** places
16:12 The men were **h** in the room as before, and again
20:33 Then the Israelites **h** in ambush west of Gibeah
20:36 to give those **h** in ambush more room to maneuver.
20:37 Then those who were in **h** rushed in from all sides
1Sa 10:22 LORD replied, "He is **h** among the baggage."
14:22 the men who were **h** in the hills joined the chase
19: 2 "you must find a **h** place out in the fields.
20:41 David came out from where he had been **h** near the
23:19 to him. "We know where David is **h**," they said.
23:23 Discover his **h** places, and come back with a more
23:23 even if I have to search every **h** place in Judah!"
24: 3 David and his men were **h** in that very cave!
26: 1 "David is **h** on the hill of Hakilah,
26: 3 hill of Hakilah, near Jeshimon, where David was **h**.
1Ki 22:25 when you find yourself **h** in some secret room!"
2Ki 7: 8 carrying out silver and gold and clothing and **h** it.
25:19 And of the people still **h** in the city, he took an
1Ch 12: 1 at Ziklag while he was **h** from Saul son of Kish.
2Ch 18:24 when you find yourself **h** in some secret room!"
22: 9 and they found him **h** in the city of Samaria.
Job 31:33 sins as people normally do, **h** my guilt in a closet?
Ps 17:12 like young lions in **h**, waiting for their chance.
32: 7 For you are my **h** place; / you protect me from
54: T and said to Saul, "We know where David is **h**."
Pr 28:12 When the wicked take charge, people go into **h**.
SS 2:14 "My dove is **h** behind some rocks, behind an
Isa 4: 6 daytime heat and a **h** place from storms and rain.
Jer 5:26 lie in wait for victims like a hunter **h** in a blind.
49: 3 Weep and wail, **h** in the hedges, for your god
52:25 And of the people still **h** in the city, he took an
Eze 33:27 Those **h** in the forts and caves will die of disease.
Mt 11:25 thank you for **h** the truth from those who think
24:26 and look. Or, 'Look, he is **h** here,' don't believe it!
Lk 10:21 thank you for **h** the truth from those who think
Ac 23:21 There are more than forty men **h** along the way
Heb 11:38 and mountains, **h** in caves and holes in the ground.

HIEL (1)

1Ki 16:34 It was during his reign that **H**, a man from Bethel,

HIERAPOLIS (1)

Col 4:13 and also for the Christians in Laodicea and **H**.

HIGH (309) [HIGH-QUALITY, HIGH-RANKING, HIGH-SOUNDING, HIGHER, HIGHEST, HIGHLANDS, HIGHLY]

GOD MOST HIGH (6) Ge 14:18,19,20,22; Ps 57:2; Heb 7:1

HIGH PLACE(S) (4) 1Ki 12:31; Eze 20:29,29; Mic 1:3

HIGH PRIEST (90) Ex 29:30; Lev 4:3,21; 16:32; 21:10,13; Nu 35:25,28,28,32; Dt 10:6; Jos 20:6; 2Ki 12:10; 22:4,8; 23:4; 1Ch 6:10; 2Ch 19:11; 24:6,11; 26:17; 31:10; 34:9,14; Ezr 7:5; Ne 3:1,20; 12:1,10,12; 13:28; Hag 1:1,12,14; 2:2,4; Zec 3:1,8; 6:11; Mt 26:3,57,62,63,65; Mk 2:26; 14:60,61,63, 66; Jn 11:49,51; 18:13,15,19,22,24,26; Ac 4:6,6; 5:17,21,28; 7:1; 9:1; 22:5; 23:2,4,5; 24:1; Heb 2:17; 3:1; 4:14,15; 5:1,4,5,9,10; 6:20; 7:26; 8:1,3,3,6; 9:7,11,25; 10:12,21; 13:11

MOST HIGH (57) Ge 14:18,19,20,22; Nu 24:16; Dt 32:8; 2Sa 22:14; Ps 7:8,17; 9:2; 18:13; 21:7; 46:4; 47:2; 50:14; 57:2; 73:11; 77:10; 78:17,35,56; 82:6; 83:18; 87:5; 91:1,9; 92:1; 97:9; 107:11; Isa 14:14; La 3:35,38; Da 3:26; 4:2,17,24, 25,32,34; 5:18,21; 7:18,22,25,25,27; Hos 7:16; 11:7; Mk 5:7; Lk 1:32,35,76; 6:35; 8:28; Ac 7:48; 16:17; Heb 7:1

MOST HIGH GOD (7) Da 3:26; 4:2; 5:18,21; Mk 5:7; Lk 8:28; Ac 16:17

ON HIGH (6) Job 3:4; 16:19; 31:2; Ps 113:5; Isa 33:16; 41:18

Ge 6:15 Make it 450 feet long, 75 feet wide, and 45 feet **h**.
7:17 the ground and lifting the boat **h** above the earth.
8: 9 no place to land because the water was still too **h**.
14:18 the king of Salem and a priest of God Most **H**,
14:19 "Blessed be Abram by God Most **H**, / Creator of
14:20 And blessed be God Most **H**, / who has helped you
14:22 God Most **H**, Creator of heaven and earth,
50:20 He brought me to the **h** position I have today
Ex 25:10 3-3/4 feet long, 2-1/4 feet wide, and 2-1/4 feet **h**.
25:23 3 feet long, 1-1/2 feet wide, and 2-1/4 feet **h**.
26:16 Each frame must be 15 feet **h** and 2-1/4 feet wide.
27: 1 7-1/2 feet wide, 7-1/2 feet long, and 4-1/2 feet **h**.
27:18 and 75 feet wide, with curtain walls 7-1/2 feet **h**,
29:30 Whoever is the next **h** priest after Aaron will wear
30: 2 It must be eighteen inches square and three feet **h**,
36:21 Each frame was 15 feet **h** and 2-1/4 feet wide.
37: 1 3-3/4 feet long, 2-1/4 feet wide, and 2-1/4 feet **h**.
37:10 3 feet long, 1-1/2 feet wide, and 2-1/4 feet **h**.
37:25 It was eighteen inches square and three feet **h**,
38: 1 It was 7-1/2 feet square at the top and 4-1/2 feet **h**.
38:18 It was 30 feet long and 7-1/2 feet **h**, just like the
Lev 4: 3 "If the **h** priest sins, bringing guilt upon the entire
4:21 just as is done with the sin offering for the **h** priest.
16:32 **h** priest who serves in place of his ancestor Aaron.
21:10 "The **h** priest, who has had the anointing oil
21:13 "The **h** priest must marry a virgin.
26:13 so you can walk free with your heads held **h**.
Nu 24:16 of God, / who has knowledge from the Most **H**,
35:25 in a city of refuge until the death of the **h** priest.
35:28 the city of refuge until the death of the **h** priest.
35:28 But after the death of the **h** priest, the slayer may

35:32 to his property before the death of the **h** priest.
Dt 1:28 and that the walls of their towns rise **h** into the sky!
3:5 These were all fortified cities with **h** walls
10:6 His son Eleazar became the **h** priest in his place.
12:2 **h** on the mountains, up on the hills, and under
32:8 When the Most **H** assigned lands to the nations,
Jos 20:6 **h** priest who was in office at the time of the
22:14 In this delegation were ten **h** officials of Israel,
22:21 and the half-tribe of Manasseh answered these **h**
22:30 and the **h** officials heard this from the tribes of
22:32 and the ten **h** officials left the tribes of Reuben
1Sa 9:6 He is held in **h** honor by all the people
2Sa 22:3 my **h** tower, my savior, the one who saves me from
22:14 from heaven; / the Most **H** gave a mighty shout.
1Ki 4:2 and these were his **h** officials: / Azariah son of
6:2 was 90 feet long, 30 feet wide, and 45 feet **h**.
6:6 The complex was three stories **h**, the bottom floor
6:10 Each story of the complex was 7-1/2 feet **h**.
6:20 was 30 feet long, 30 feet wide, and 30 feet **h**.
7:2 It was 150 feet long, 75 feet wide, and 45 feet **h**.
12:31 Jeroboam built shrines at the pagan **h** places
14:23 up sacred pillars and Asherah poles on every **h** hill
2Ki 5:1 The king of Aram had **h** admiration for Naaman,
12:10 and the **h** priest counted the money that had been
22:4 "Go up to Hilkiah the **h** priest and have him count
22:8 Hilkiah the **h** priest said to Shaphan the court
23:4 Then the king instructed Hilkiah the **h** priest
25:17 capital on top of each pillar was 7-1/2 feet **h**
1Ch 6:10 the **h** priest at the Temple built by Solomon in
2Ch 3:4 pure gold. The roof of the foyer was thirty feet **h**.
4:1 altar 30 feet long, 30 feet wide, and 15 feet **h**.
6:13 and 4-1/2 feet **h** and had placed it at the center of
18:1 Jehoshaphat enjoyed great riches and **h** esteem,
19:11 "Amariah the **h** priest will have final say in all
24:6 So the king called for Jehoiada the **h** priest
24:11 and an officer of the **h** priest counted the money
26:17 Azariah the **h** priest went in after him with eighty
31:10 And Azariah the **h** priest, from the family of
32:27 Hezekiah was very wealthy and held in **h** esteem.
33:14 around the hill of Ophel, where it was built very **h**.
34:9 They gave Hilkiah the **h** priest the money that had
34:14 As Hilkiah the **h** priest was recording the money
Ezr 7:5 son of Eleazar, son of Aaron the **h** priest.
Ne 3:1 Then Eliashib the **h** priest and the other priests
3:20 to the door of the home of Eliashib the **h** priest.
8:4 Ezra the scribe stood on a **h** wooden platform that
12:1 son of Shealtiel and Jeshua the **h** priest:
12:10 Jeshua the **h** priest was the father of Joiakim.
12:12 Now when Joiakim was **h** priest, the family leaders
12:22 and the priests in the days of the following **h**
13:28 One of the sons of Joiada son of Eliashib the **h**
Est 1:14 seven **h** officials of Persia and Media.
10:3 great among the Jews, who held him in **h** esteem,
Job 3:4 Let it be lost even to God on **h**, and let it be
6:19 With **h** hopes, the caravans from Tema and from
10:15 and misery so that I can't hold my head **h**.
10:16 And if I hold my head **h**, you hunt me like a lion
16:19 witness is in heaven. My advocate is there on **h**.
24:22 They may rise **h**, but they have no assurance in
31:2 What is our inheritance from the Almighty on **h**?
35:5 up into the sky and see the clouds **h** above you.
Ps 3:3 my glory, and the one who lifts my head **h**.
7:7 before you. / Sit on your throne **h** above them.
7:8 O LORD, / for I am innocent, O Most **H**!
7:17 sing praise to the name of the LORD Most **H**.
9:2 I will sing praises to your name, O Most **H**.
18:13 from heaven; / the Most **H** gave a mighty shout.
21:7 The unfailing love of the Most **H** will keep him
27:5 He will place me out of reach on a **h** rock.
27:6 Then I will hold my head **h**, / above my enemies
40:12 too many to count! / They pile up so **h**
46:4 city of our God, / the sacred home of the Most **H**.
47:2 For the LORD Most **H** is awesome. / He is the
49:2 **H** and low, / rich and poor—listen!
50:14 I want you to fulfill your vows to the Most **H**.
57:2 I cry out to God Most **H**, / to God who will fulfill
57:10 For your unfailing love is as **h** as the heavens.
62:4 They plan to topple me from my **h** position.
68:15 mountains of Bashan / stretch **h** into the sky.
69:27 Pile their sins up **h**, / and don't let them go free.
73:11 "Is the Most **H** even aware of what is
77:10 that the blessings of the Most **H** have changed to
78:17 rebelling against the Most **H** in the desert.
78:35 their rock, / that their redeemer was the Most **H**.
78:56 They rebelled against the Most **H** / and refused to
82:6 'You are gods / and children of the Most **H**.
83:18 that you alone are the Most **H**, supreme over all the
87:5 And the Most **H** will personally bless this city.
89:13 Your right hand is lifted **h** in glorious strength.
91:1 Those who live in the shelter of the Most **H**
91:9 your refuge, / if you make the Most **H** your shelter,
92:1 to the LORD, / to sing praises to the Most **H**.
97:9 For you, O LORD, are most **h** over all the earth;
104:18 **H** in the mountains are pastures for the wild goats,
107:11 of God, / scorning the counsel of the Most **H**.
113:4 For the LORD is **h** above the nations; / his glory
113:5 the LORD our God, / who is enthroned on **h**?
148:4 Praise him, vapors **h** above the clouds!
Pr 18:11 they imagine it is a **h** wall of safety.
22:1 for being held in **h** esteem is better than having
Isa 2:14 He will level the **h** mountains and hills.
2:15 He will break down every **h** tower and wall.
10:33 army of Assyria—officers and **h** officials alike.
13:2 against Babylon to destroy the palaces of the **h**
14:14 to the highest heavens and be like the Most **H**.'
22:19 "I will pull you down from your **h** position.
25:12 The **h** walls of Moab will be demolished
30:33 the Assyrian king; it has been piled **h** with wood.
33:16 These are the ones who will dwell on **h**. The rocks
40:31 They will fly **h** on wings like eagles. They will run
41:18 I will open up rivers for them on **h** plateaus.
57:15 The **h** and lofty one who inhabits eternity, the Holy
57:15 "I live in that **h** and holy place with those whose
Jer 3:21 Voices are heard **h** on the windswept mountains,
5:1 "Look **h** and low; search throughout the city!
17:2 beneath every green tree and on every **h** hill.
17:12 worship at your throne—eternal, **h**, and glorious!
18:14 Does the snow ever melt **h** up in the mountains of
44:3 all their wickedness, my anger rose **h** against them.
49:16 live in a rock fortress and hide **h** in the mountains.
51:53 Though Babylon reaches as **h** as the heavens,
51:58 to the ground, and her **h** gates will be burned.
52:22 capital on top of each pillar was 7-1/2 feet **h**
La 3:9 He has blocked my path with a **h** stone wall.
3:35 their God-given rights in defiance of the Most **H**.
3:38 Is it not the Most **H** who helps one and harms
Eze 1:26 And **h** above this throne was a figure whose
20:28 they offered sacrifices and incense on every **h** hill
20:29 'What is this **h** place where you are going?'
20:29 has been called Bamah—'**h** place'—ever since.)
31:3 deep forest shade with its top **h** among the clouds.
31:10 and because it set itself so **h** above the others,
34:14 I will give them good pastureland on the **h** hills of
40:2 of Israel and set me down on a very **h** mountain.
40:5 the wall was 10-1/2 feet thick and 10-1/2 feet **h**.
40:42 each 31-1/2 inches square and 21 inches **h**.
41:8 for the side rooms. This terrace was 10-1/2 feet **h**.
41:22 made of wood, 3-1/2 feet square and 5-1/4 feet **h**.
42:3 The two blocks were built three levels **h** and stood
Da 2:48 Then the king appointed Daniel to a **h** position
3:26 servants of the Most **H** God, come out!
4:2 and wonders the Most **H** God has performed for
4:11 reaching **h** into the heavens for all the world to see.
4:17 the Most **H** rules over the kingdoms of the world
4:20 reaching **h** into the heavens for all the world to see.
4:24 and what the Most **H** has declared will happen to
4:25 until you learn that the Most **H** rules over the
4:32 until you learn that the Most **H** rules over the
4:34 and I praised and worshiped the Most **H**
5:18 the Most **H** God gave sovereignty, majesty, glory,
5:21 until he learned that the Most **H** God rules the
7:18 the holy people of the Most **H** will be given the
7:22 judged in favor of the holy people of the Most **H**.
7:25 He will defy the Most **H** and wear down the holy people of the Most **H**.
7:27 will be given to the holy people of the Most **H**.
Hos 7:16 look everywhere except to heaven, to the Most **H**.
11:7 They call me the Most **H**, but they don't truly
Joel 2:24 The threshing floors will again be piled **h** with
Ob 1:3 and make your home **h** in the mountains.
1:4 Though you soar as **h** as eagles and build your nest
Mic 1:3 and comes to earth, walking on the **h** places.
Hab 3:15 with your horses, and the mighty waters piled **h**.
Hag 1:1 and to Jeshua son of Jehozadak, the **h** priest.
1:12 of Shealtiel, Jeshua son of Jehozadak, the **h** priest,
1:14 of Judah, Jeshua son of Jehozadak, the **h** priest,
2:2 and to Jeshua son of Jehozadak, the **h** priest,
2:4 Jeshua son of Jehozadak, the **h** priest
Zec 3:1 Then the angel showed me Jeshua the **h** priest
3:8 Listen to me, O Jeshua the **h** priest, and all you
6:11 the head of Jeshua son of Jehozadak, the **h** priest.
Mt 4:8 Next the Devil took him to the peak of a very **h**
8:14 Peter's mother-in-law was in bed with a **h** fever.
14:30 But when he looked around at the **h** waves, he was
17:1 James and John, and led them up a **h** mountain.
26:3 meeting at the residence of Caiaphas, the **h** priest,
26:51 and slashed off an ear of the **h** priest's servant.
26:57 the **h** priest, where the teachers of religious law
26:58 and eventually came to the courtyard of the **h**
26:59 and the entire **h** council were trying to find
26:62 Then the **h** priest stood up and said to Jesus,
26:63 Then the **h** priest said to him, "I demand in the
26:65 Then the **h** priest tore his clothing to show his
Mk 1:30 Simon's mother-in-law was sick in bed with a **h**
2:26 God (during the days when Abiathar was **h** priest),
4:37 **H** waves began to break into the boat until it was
5:7 you bothering me, Jesus, Son of the Most **H** God?
14:47 and slashed off an ear of the **h** priest's servant.
14:53 Jesus was led to the **h** priest's home where the
14:54 then slipped inside the gates of the **h** priest's
14:55 and the entire **h** council were trying to find
14:60 Then the **h** priest stood up before the others
14:61 Then the **h** priest asked him, "Are you the
14:63 Then the **h** priest tore his clothing to show his
14:66 One of the servant girls who worked for the **h**
15:1 the entire **h** council—met to discuss their next step.
15:43 an honored member of the **h** council, Joseph from
Lk 1:32 and will be called the Son of the Most **H**.
1:35 and the power of the Most **H** will overshadow you.
1:76 will be called the prophet of the Most **H**,
3:2 Annas and Caiaphas were the **h** priests. At this
4:38 Simon's mother-in-law very sick with a **h** fever.
6:35 you will truly be acting as children of the Most **H**,
8:28 you bothering me, Jesus, Son of the Most **H** God?
22:50 And one of them slashed at the **h** priest's servant
22:54 and led him to the **h** priest's residence,
22:66 religious law. Jesus was led before this **h** council,
23:50 He was a member of the Jewish **h** council,
Jn 11:47 and Pharisees called the **h** council together to
11:49 Caiaphas, who was **h** priest that year, said,
11:51 came from Caiaphas in his position as **h** priest.
18:10 off the right ear of Malchus, the **h** priest's servant.
18:13 father-in-law of Caiaphas, the **h** priest that year.
18:15 That other disciple was acquainted with the **h**
18:19 the **h** priest began asking Jesus about his followers
18:22 "Is that the way to answer the **h** priest?"
18:24 bound Jesus and sent him to Caiaphas, the **h** priest.
18:26 But one of the household servants of the **h** priest,
Ac 4:6 Annas the **h** priest was there, along with Caiaphas,
4:6 Alexander, and other relatives of the **h** priest.
5:13 join them, though everyone had **h** regard for them.
5:17 The **h** priest and his friends, who were Sadducees,
5:21 When the **h** priest and his officials arrived, they convened the **h** council,
5:28 the **h** priest demanded. "Instead, you have filled
5:33 the **h** council was furious and decided to kill them.
5:41 The apostles left the **h** council rejoicing that God
6:12 and brought him before the **h** council.
7:1 Then the **h** priest asked Stephen, "Are these
7:48 the Most **H** doesn't live in temples made by human
9:1 the Lord's followers, so he went to the **h** priest.
16:17 "These men are servants of the Most **H** God,
22:5 The **h** priest and the whole council of leaders can
22:30 priests into session with the Jewish **h** council.
23:1 Gazing intently at the **h** council, Paul began:
23:2 Instantly Ananias the **h** priest commanded those
23:4 to him, "Is that the way to talk to God's **h** priest?"
23:5 I didn't realize he was the **h** priest," Paul replied,
23:6 Paul realized that some members of the **h** council
23:15 and the **h** council should tell the commander to
23:20 bring Paul before the Jewish **h** council tomorrow,
23:28 Then I took him to their **h** council to try to find out
24:1 Five days later Ananias, the **h** priest, arrived with
24:20 Ask these men here what wrongdoing the Jewish **h**
Ro 8:39 Whether we are **h** above the sky or in the deepest
16:2 her in the Lord, as one who is worthy of **h** honor.
1Co 6:20 for God bought you with a **h** price. So you must
7:23 God purchased you at a **h** price. Don't be enslaved
Eph 3:18 God's people should, how wide, how long, how **h**,
Heb 2:17 be our merciful and faithful **H** Priest before God.
3:1 we declare to be God's Messenger and **H** Priest.
4:14 That is why we have a great **H** Priest who has gone
4:15 This **H** Priest of ours understands our weaknesses,
5:1 Now a **h** priest is a man chosen to represent other
5:4 And no one can become a **h** priest simply
5:5 Christ did not exalt himself to become **H** Priest.
5:9 this way, God qualified him as a perfect **H** Priest,
5:10 And God designated him to be a **H** Priest in the
6:20 He has become our eternal **H** Priest in the line of
7:1 the city of Salem and also a priest of God Most **H**.
7:26 He is the kind of **h** priest we need because he is
7:27 offer sacrifices every day like the other **h** priests.
7:28 Those who were **h** priests under the law of Moses
8:1 Our **H** Priest sat down in the place of highest
8:3 And since every **h** priest is required to offer gifts
8:3 our **H** Priest must make an offering, too.
8:6 But our **H** Priest has been given a ministry that is
9:7 But only the **h** priest goes into the Most Holy
9:11 So Christ has now become the **H** Priest over all the
9:25 like the earthly **h** priest who enters the Most Holy
10:12 But our **H** Priest offered himself to God as one
10:21 And since we have a great **H** Priest who rules over
13:11 the **h** priest brought the blood of animals into the
Rev 14:20 about 180 miles long and as **h** as a horse's bridle.
18:5 For her sins are piled as **h** as heaven, and God is
19:17 shouting to the vultures flying **h** in the sky:
21:10 **h** mountain, and he showed me the holy city,
21:12 Its walls were broad and **h**, with twelve gates

HIGH-QUALITY (1) [HIGH, QUALITY]

Ex 22:5 owner must pay damages in the form of **h** grain

HIGH-RANKING (1) [HIGH, RANK]

Eze 23:23 commanders, chariot officers, and other **h** officers,

HIGH-SOUNDING (2) [HIGH, SOUND]

1Co 1:17 and not with clever speeches and **h** ideas, for fear
Col 2:8 and **h** nonsense that come from human thinking

HIGHER (23) [HIGH]

Ge 7:18 As the waters rose **h** and **h** above the ground,
41:40 my people. Only I will have a rank **h** than yours."
Ex 24:18 into the cloud as he climbed **h** up the mountain.
Lev 25:16 The more the years, the **h** the price; the fewer the
Ezr 9:6 For our sins are piled **h** than our heads, and our
Job 11:8 Such knowledge is **h** than the heavens—but who
22:12 **h** than the heavens, **h** than the farthest stars.
Ps 8:1 fills the earth! / Your glory is **h** than the heavens.
108:4 For your unfailing love is **h** than the heavens.
Pr 11:26 People curse those who hold their grain for **h**
Ecc 5:8 For every official is under orders from **h** up,
Isa 55:9 For just as the heavens are **h** than the earth, so are my ways **h** than your ways and my thoughts **h** than your thoughts.
Eze 31:14 though it be **h** than the clouds, for all are doomed.
41:7 to the narrowing of the Temple wall as it rose **h**.
43:15 The top of the altar, the hearth, rises still 7 feet **h**,
Da 3:30 and Abednego to even **h** positions in the province
Lk 10:35 'If his bill runs **h** than that,' he said, 'I'll pay the
Jn 6:15 make him king, so he went **h** into the hills alone.
Eph 4:10 is the one who ascended **h** than all the heavens,

HIGHEST (41) [HIGH]

Ge 7:19 the water covered even the **h** mountains on the
7:20 standing more than twenty-two feet above the **h**
Dt 10:14 The **h** heavens and the earth and everything in it all
1Ki 8:27 Why, even the **h** heavens cannot contain you.
2Ki 19:23 I have conquered the **h** mountains— / yes,

2Ch 2: 6 Not even the **h** heavens can contain him!
6: 18 Why, even the **h** heavens cannot contain you.
Est 1: 14 and held the **h** positions in the empire.
Job 29: 10 The **h** officials of the city stood quietly,
Ps 57: 5 Be exalted, O God, above the **h** heavens!
57: 11 Be exalted, O God, above the **h** heavens.
71: 19 O God, reaches to the **h** heavens.
89: 7 The **h** angelic powers stand in awe of God.
108: 5 Be exalted, O God, above the **h** heavens.
137: 6 if I don't make Jerusalem my **h** joy.
Isa 14: 14 I will climb to the **h** heavens and be like the Most
17: 6 Only two or three remain in the **h** branches, four
22: 22 house of David—the **h** position in the royal court.
37: 24 I have conquered the **h** mountains— / yes,
64: 3 you did awesome things beyond our **h**
Eze 17: 3 He took hold of the **h** branch of a cedar tree
17: 22 and I will plant it on the top of Israel's **h** mountain.
Da 5: 7 He will become the third **h** ruler in the kingdom!"
5: 16 You will become the third **h** ruler in the
5: 29 and he was proclaimed the third **h** ruler in the
Mt 4: 5 him to Jerusalem, to the **h** point of the Temple,
21: 9 the name of the Lord! / Praise God in **h** heaven!"
Mk 11: 10 of our ancestor David! / Praise God in **h** heaven!"
Lk 2: 14 "Glory to God in the **h** heaven, / and peace on
4: 9 to the **h** point of the Temple, and said, "If you are
19: 38 Peace in heaven / and glory in **h** heaven!"
Ac 2: 33 Now he sits on the throne of **h** honor in heaven,
Ro 5: 2 Christ has brought us into this place of **h** privilege
8: 34 and is sitting at the place of **h** honor next to God,
1Co 14: 1 Let love be your **h** goal, but also desire the special
2Co 7: 4 I have the **h** confidence in you, and my pride in
8: 5 Best of all, they went beyond our **h** hopes, for their
Heb 1: 3 and he has been given the **h** place of honor in
8: 1 Our High Priest sat down in the place of **h** honor in
10: 12 Then he sat down at the place of **h** honor at God's
12: 2 Now he is seated in the place of **h** honor beside

HIGHLANDS (1) [HIGH, LAND]

Dt 32: 13 He made them ride over the **h**; / he let them feast

HIGHLIGHTS (1)

Ro 3: 7 and condemn me as a sinner if my dishonesty **h** his

HIGHLY (16) [HIGH]

Ge 34: 19 Shechem was a **h** respected member of his family,
1Sa 22: 14 and a **h** honored member of your household!
2Ch 17: 5 so he became very wealthy and **h** esteemed.
32: 23 then on King Hezekiah became **h** respected among
Ps 47: 9 earth belong to God. / He is **h** honored everywhere.
Ecc 2: 21 to earn it. This is not only foolish but **h** unfair.
Isa 44: 9 These **h** valued objects are really worthless.
52: 13 my servant will prosper; he will be **h** exalted.
Mic 5: 4 for he will be **h** honored all around the world.
Lk 7: 2 Now the **h** valued slave of a Roman officer was
24: 19 **h** regarded by both God and all the people.
Ro 11: 20 Don't think **h** of yourself, but fear what could
2Co 8: 18 He is **h** praised in all the churches as a preacher of
12: 6 I don't want anyone to think more **h** of me than
1Th 5: 13 Think **h** of them and give them your wholehearted
3Jn 1: 12 But everyone speaks **h** of Demetrius, even truth

HIGHMINDED [KJV] See PROUD, PUFFED, THINK (HIGHLY)

HIGHWAY (6) [HIGHWAYS]

Isa 11: 16 He will make a **h** from Assyria for the remnant
19: 23 day Egypt and Assyria will be connected by a **h**.
35: 8 It will be named the **H** of Holiness.
40: 3 "Make a **h** for the LORD through the wilderness.
62: 10 Go out! Prepare the **h** for my people to return!
Mt 7: 13 The **h** to hell is broad, and its gate is wide for the

HIGHWAYS (2) [HIGHWAY]

Isa 49: 11 for them. The **h** will be raised above the valleys.
Jer 18: 15 They have stumbled off the ancient **h** of good,

HILKIAH (34)

2Ki 18: 18 Eliakim son of **H**, the palace administrator,
18: 26 Then Eliakim son of **H**, Shebna, and Joah said to
18: 37 Then Eliakim son of **H**, the palace administrator,
22: 4 "Go up to **H** the high priest and have him count
22: 8 **H** the high priest said to Shaphan the court
22: 8 Then **H** gave the scroll to Shaphan, and he read it.
22: 10 to the king, "**H** the priest has given me a scroll."
22: 12 Then he gave these orders to **H** the priest,
22: 14 So **H** the priest, Ahikam, Acbor, Shaphan,
23: 4 Then the king instructed **H** the high priest
23: 24 **H** the priest had found in the LORD's Temple.
1Ch 6: 13 Shallum was the father of **H**. / **H** was the father of Azariah.
6: 45 Hashabiah, Amaziah, **H**,
9: 11 Azariah son of **H**, son of Meshullam, son of
26: 11 His other sons included **H** (the second),
2Ch 34: 9 They gave **H** the high priest the money that had
34: 14 As **H** the high priest was recording the money
34: 15 **H** said to Shaphan the court secretary, "I have
34: 15 Then **H** gave the scroll to Shaphan.
34: 18 to the king, "**H** the priest has given me a scroll."
34: 20 Then he gave these orders to **H**, Ahikam son of
34: 22 So **H** and the other men went to the newer
35: 8 **H**, Zechariah, and Jehiel, the administrators of
Ezr 7: 1 was the son of Seraiah, son of Azariah, son of **H**,
Ne 8: 4 Shema, Anaiah, Uriah, **H**, and Maaseiah.
11: 11 and Seraiah son of **H**, son of Meshullam, son of
12: 7 Sallu, Amok, **H**, and Jedaiah. These were the
12: 21 Hashabiah was leader of the family of **H**.
Isa 22: 20 then I will call my servant Eliakim son of **H** to
36: 3 Eliakim son of **H**, the palace administrator,
36: 22 Then Eliakim son of **H**, the palace administrator,
Jer 1: 1 These are the words of Jeremiah son of **H**, one of
29: 3 Elasah son of Shaphan and Gemariah son of **H**,

HILL (150) [FOOTHILLS, HILLS, HILLSIDE, HILLSIDES, HILLTOP, HILLTOPS]

Ge 12: 8 and set up camp in the **h** country between Bethel
31: 23 He caught up with them seven days later in the **h**
31: 25 Jacob as he was camped in the **h** country of Gilead,
36: 8 known as Edom) settled in the **h** country of Seir.
36: 9 the Edomites, who live in the **h** country of Seir.
Ex 17: 9 I will stand at the top of the **h** with the staff of God
17: 10 Aaron, and Hur went to the top of a nearby **h**.
Nu 13: 17 "Go northward through the Negev into the **h**
13: 29 Jebusites, and Amorites live in the **h** country.
14: 40 and set out for the **h** country of Canaan.
14: 44 But the people pushed ahead toward the **h** country
23: 3 to me." So Balaam went alone to the top of a **h**,
Dt 1: 7 Go to the **h** country of the Amorites and to all the
1: 7 the Jordan Valley, the **h** country, the western
1: 19 and headed toward the **h** country of the Amorites.
1: 41 thinking it would be easy to conquer the **h** country.
1: 43 and arrogantly went into the **h** country to fight.
2: 3 'You have been wandering around in this **h**
2: 5 for I have given them all the **h** country around
2: 37 the Jabbok River and the towns in the **h** country—
3: 12 plus half of the **h** country of Gilead with its towns,
3: 25 the beautiful **h** country and the Lebanon
Jos 2: 16 "Escape to the **h** country," she told them.
2: 22 The spies went up into the **h** country and stayed
2: 23 Then the two spies came down from the **h** country,
9: 1 Hivites, and Jebusites, who lived in the **h** country,
10: 6 For all the Amorite kings who live in the **h** country
10: 40 the kings and people of the **h** country, the Negev,
11: 2 all the kings of the northern **h** country; the kings in
11: 3 the Perizzites; the kings in the Jebusite **h** country;
11: 16 the **h** country, the Negev, the land of Goshen,
11: 21 who lived in the **h** country of Hebron, Debir,
11: 21 and the entire **h** country of Judah and Israel.
12: 8 including the **h** country, the western foothills,
13: 6 and all the **h** country from Lebanon to
13: 19 Sibmah, Zereth-shahar on the **h** above the valley,
14: 12 So I'm asking you to give me the **h** country that
15: 11 then proceeded to the slope of the **h** north of
15: 48 Judah also received the following towns in the **h**
16: 1 the wilderness and into the **h** country of Bethel.
17: 15 "If the **h** country of Ephraim is not large enough
17: 16 They said, "The **h** country is not enough for us,
17: 18 The forests of the **h** country will be yours as well.
18: 12 then west through the **h** country and the wilderness
18: 13 to the top of the **h** south of Lower Beth-horon.
18: 14 then ran south along the western edge of the **h**
19: 50 He chose Timnath-serah in the **h** country of
20: 7 Kedesh of Galilee, in the **h** country of Naphtali;
20: 7 Shechem, in the **h** country of Ephraim;
20: 7 (that is, Hebron), in the **h** country of Judah.
21: 11 (that is, Hebron), in the **h** country of Judah,
24: 4 To Esau I gave the **h** country of Seir, while Jacob
24: 30 at Timnath-serah in the **h** country of Ephraim,
24: 33 He was buried in the **h** country of Ephraim,
Jdg 1: 9 to fight the Canaanites living in the **h** country,
1: 19 and they took possession of the **h** country.
1: 34 the Amorites forced them into the **h** country
2: 9 at Timnath-serah in the **h** country of Ephraim,
3: 3 and the Hivites living in the **h** country of Lebanon
3: 27 When he arrived in the **h** country of Ephraim,
4: 5 and Bethel in the **h** country of Ephraim,
6: 26 an altar to the LORD your God here on this **h**,
7: 1 north of them in the valley near the **h** of Moreh.
7: 24 Gideon also sent messengers throughout the **h**
10: 1 but lived in the town of Shamir in the **h** country of
12: 15 in Ephraim, in the **h** country of the Amalekites.
15: 17 the jawbone; and the place was named Jawbone **H**.
16: 3 and carried them all the way to the top of the **h**
17: 1 A man named Micah lived in the **h** country of
18: 2 When these warriors arrived in the **h** country of
18: 13 Then they went up into the **h** country of Ephraim
19: 1 in a remote area of the **h** country of Ephraim.
19: 16 He was from the **h** country of Ephraim, but he was
19: 18 home to a remote area in the **h** country of Ephraim,
1Sa 1: 1 who lived in Ramah in the **h** country of Ephraim.
9: 4 and traveled all through the **h** country of Ephraim,
9: 11 As they were climbing a **h** toward the town,
9: 12 to take part in a public sacrifice up on the **h**.
9: 13 and catch him before he goes up the **h** to eat.
9: 14 was coming out toward them to climb the **h**.
9: 19 "Go on up the **h** ahead of me to the place of
10: 5 of prophets coming down from the altar on the **h**.
10: 13 finished prophesying, he climbed the **h** to the altar.
13: 2 with him to Micmash and the **h** country of Bethel.
22: 6 sitting beneath a tamarisk tree on the **h** at Gibeah,
23: 14 of the wilderness and in the **h** country of Ziph.
23: 19 "He is in the strongholds of Horesh on the **h** of
26: 1 "David is hiding on the **h** of Hakilah,
26: 3 Saul camped along the road beside the **h** of
26: 13 David climbed the **h** opposite the camp until he
2Sa 2: 24 down as they arrived at the **h** of Ammah near Giah,
2: 25 regrouped there at the top of the **h** to take a stand.
13: 34 from the Horonaim road along the side of the **h**."
16: 1 David was just past the top of the **h** when Ziba,
20: 21 Sheba son of Bicri from the **h** country of Ephraim,
1Ki 4: 8 Ben-hur, in the **h** country of Ephraim.
5: 15 eighty thousand stonecutters in the **h** country,
12: 25 then built up the city of Shechem in the **h** country
14: 23 sacred pillars and Asherah poles on every high **h**
16: 24 Then Omri bought the **h** now known as Samaria
2Ki 1: 9 They found him sitting on top of a **h**. The captain
5: 22 from the **h** country of Ephraim have just arrived.
5: 24 But when they arrived at the **h**, Gehazi took the
17: 10 and Asherah poles at the top of every **h**
23: 16 he noticed several tombs in the side of the **h**.
1Ch 6: 67 Shechem (a city of refuge in the **h** country of
16: 39 the Tabernacle of the LORD on the **h** of Gibeon,
21: 29 in the wilderness were located at the **h** of Gibeon.
2Ch 1: 3 Then Solomon led the entire assembly to the **h** at
1: 13 Jerusalem from the Tabernacle at the **h** of Gibeon,
2: 2 eighty thousand stonecutters in the **h** country,
2: 18 80,000 as stonecutters in the **h** country, and 3,600
13: 4 When the army of Judah arrived in the **h** country
15: 8 and in the towns he had captured in the **h** country
19: 4 traveling from Beersheba to the **h** country of
21: 11 He had built pagan shrines in the **h** country of
27: 3 extensive rebuilding on the wall at the **h** of Ophel.
27: 4 He built towns in the **h** country of Judah
33: 14 and continuing around the **h** of Ophel, where it
33: 15 He tore down all the altars he had built on the **h**
Ne 3: 26 and the Temple servants living on the **h** of Ophel,
3: 28 The priests repaired the wall up the **h** from the
11: 21 were Ziha and Gishpa, all lived on the **h** of Ophel.
Ps 15: 1 Who may enter your presence on your holy **h**?
SS 4: 6 mountain of myrrh and to the **h** of frankincense.
Isa 5: 1 My beloved has a vineyard / on a rich and fertile **h**.
30: 25 of water flowing down every mountain and **h**.
Jer 2: 20 On every **h** and under every green tree, you have
3: 6 Israel has worshiped other gods on every **h**
4: 15 From Dan and the **h** country of Ephraim,
17: 2 beneath every green tree and on every high **h**.
17: 26 western foothills and the **h** country and the Negev,
31: 6 will shout from the **h** country of Ephraim,
31: 39 A measuring line will be stretched out over the **h**
32: 44 in the towns of Judah and in the **h** country,
33: 13 flocks will prosper in the towns of the **h** country,
50: 19 and to be satisfied once more on the **h** country of
Eze 6: 13 on every **h** and mountain and under every green
20: 28 they offered sacrifices and incense on every high **h**
34: 26 and their homes around my holy **h** to be a blessing.
43: 12 The entire top of the **h** where the Temple is built is
Mic 1: 4 like wax in a fire, like water pouring down a **h**.
Mal 1: 3 and I rejected Esau and devastated his **h** country.
Mt 15: 29 the Sea of Galilee and climbed a **h** and sat down.
27: 33 to a place called Golgotha (which means Skull **H**).
Mk 15: 22 to a place called Golgotha (which means Skull **H**).
Lk 1: 39 A few days later Mary hurried to the **h** country of
4: 29 and took him to the edge of the **h** on which the city
Jn 6: 5 soon saw a great crowd of people climbing the **h**,
19: 17 Jesus went to the place called Skull **H** (in Hebrew,

HILLEL (1)

Jdg 12: 13 After Elon died, Abdon son of **H**, from Pirathon,

HILLS (83) [HILL]

Ge 10: 30 from Mesha toward the eastern **h** of Sephar.
31: 54 Afterward they spent the night there in the **h**.
49: 26 reaching to the utmost bounds of the everlasting **h**.
Nu 14: 45 and the Canaanites who lived in those **h** came
23: 7 the king of Moab brought me from the eastern **h**.
23: 9 them from the cliff tops; / I watch them from the **h**.
Dt 1: 24 They crossed into the **h** and came to the valley of
8: 7 with springs that gush forth in the valleys and **h**.
8: 9 common as sand, and copper is abundant in the **h**.
11: 11 It is a land of **h** and valleys with plenty of rain—
12: 2 high on the mountains, up on the **h**, and under
33: 15 and the abundance from the everlasting **h**;
Jdg 3: 27 Then he led a band of Israelites down from the **h**.
9: 36 "It's just the shadows of the **h** that look like
9: 37 "No, people are coming down from the **h**.
11: 37 But first let me go up and roam in the **h** and weep
11: 38 She and her friends went into the **h** and wept
1Sa 14: 22 the men who were hiding in the **h** joined the chase
17: 3 and Israelites faced each other on opposite **h**,
2Sa 1: 19 Your pride and joy, O Israel, lies dead on the **h**!
1: 25 fallen in battle! / Jonathan lies dead upon the **h**.
1Ki 20: 23 said to him, "The Israelite gods are gods of the **h**;
20: 28 have said that the LORD is a god of the **h**
2Ki 16: 4 and on the **h** and under every green tree.
2Ch 28: 4 and on the **h** and under every green tree.
33: 15 also removed the foreign gods from the **h**
Ne 8: 15 telling the people to go to the **h** to get branches
Job 15: 7 Were you born before the **h** were made?
Ps 50: 10 are mine, / and I own the cattle on a thousand **h**.
72: 3 yield prosperity for all, / and may the **h** be fruitful,
78: 54 holy land, / to this land of **h** he had won for them.
98: 8 in glee! / Let the **h** sing out their songs of joy
114: 4 skipped like rams, / the little **h** like lambs!
114: 6 did you skip like rams? / Why, little **h**, like lambs?
148: 9 mountains and all **h**, / fruit trees and all cedars,
Pr 8: 25 Before the mountains and the **h** were formed,
SS 2: 8 leaping on the mountains and bounding over the **h**.
Isa 2: 14 He will level the high mountains and **h**.
5: 25 The **h** tremble, and the rotting bodies of his people
32: 14 and goats will graze on the **h** where the
40: 4 Fill the valleys and level the **h**. Straighten out the
40: 12 or has weighed out the mountains and the **h**?
42: 15 I will level the mountains and **h** / and bring a blight
49: 9 green pastures and on **h** that were previously bare.
54: 10 For the mountains may depart and the **h** disappear,
55: 12 The mountains and **h** will burst into song,

65: 7 incense on the mountains and insulted me on the **h**.
Jer 3:23 worship of idols and our religious orgies on the **h**
4:24 I looked at the mountains and **h**, and they trembled
13:27 idol worship out in the fields and on the **h**.
14: 6 The wild donkeys stand on the bare **h** panting like
48: 5 Her refugees will climb the **h** of Luhith,
Eze 6: 3 the mountains and **h** and to the ravines and valleys:
32: 5 I will cover the **h** with your flesh and fill the
34: 6 They have wandered through the mountains and **h**,
34:14 I will give them good pastureland on the high **h** of
35: 8 Your **h**, your valleys, and your streams will be
36: 4 He speaks to the **h** and mountains, ravines
36: 6 prophesy to the **h** and mountains, the ravines
Hos 4:13 They go up into the **h** to burn incense in the
10: 8 mountains to bury them and the **h** to fall on them.
Joel 3:18 with sweet wine, and the **h** will flow with milk.
Am 3: 9 "Take your seats now on the **h** around Samaria,
9:13 Then the terraced vineyards on the **h** of Israel will
Mic 6: 1 and **h** be called to witness your complaints.
Na 1: 5 the mountains quake, and the **h** melt away;
Hab 3: 6 the everlasting mountains and levels the eternal **h**.
Zep 1:10 crashing sound will come from the surrounding **h**.
Hag 1: 8 Now go up into the **h**, bring down timber,
1:11 I have called for a drought on your fields and **h**—
Mt 14:23 Afterward he went up into the **h** by himself to
18:12 and go out into the **h** to search for the lost one?
24:16 "Then those in Judea must flee to the **h**.
Mk 5: 5 he would wander among the tombs and in the **h**,
6:46 Afterward he went up into the **h** by himself to
13:14 "Then those in Judea must flee to the **h**.
Lk 1:65 had happened spread throughout the Judean **h**.
3: 5 Fill in the valleys, / and level the mountains and **h**!
21:21 Then those in Judea must flee to the **h**. Let those in
23:30 mountains to fall on them and the **h** to bury them.
Jn 6: 3 Then Jesus went up into the **h** and sat down with
6:15 make him king, so he went higher into the **h** alone.
Rev 17: 9 The seven heads of the beast represent the seven **h**

HILLSIDE (9) [HILL]

1Sa 7: 1 They took it to the **h** home of Abinadab
2Sa 6: 3 and brought it from the **h** home of Abinadab.
16:13 and Shimei kept pace with them on a nearby **h**,
2Ki 6:17 he saw that the **h** around Elisha was filled with
Mt 8:32 and the whole herd plunged down the steep **h** into
Mk 5:11 to be a large herd of pigs feeding on the **h** nearby.
5:13 pigs plunged down the steep **h** into the lake,
Lk 8:32 A large herd of pigs was feeding on the **h** nearby,
8:33 and the whole herd plunged down the steep **h** into

HILLSIDES (3) [HILL]

2Ch 26:10 both on the **h** and in the fertile valleys.
Ps 65:12 a lush pasture, / and the **h** blossom with joy.
Isa 7:25 No one will go to the fertile **h** where the gardens

HILLTOP (3) [HILL]

Pr 8: 2 She stands on the **h** and at the crossroads.
Jer 26:18 A great forest will grow on the **h**,
Mic 3:12 A great forest will grow on the **h**,

HILLTOPS (3) [HILL]

Jdg 9:25 of Shechem set an ambush for Abimelech on the **h**
9:36 there are people coming down from the **h**!"
Isa 16:12 On the **h** the people of Moab will pray in anguish

HIM (3969) [HE] See Index of Articles, Etc.

HIMSELF (326) [HE, SELF] See Index of Articles, Etc.

HIND (2)

Lev 11:21 These include insects that jump with their **h** legs:
Da 7: 4 and it was left standing with its two **h** feet on the

HIND [KJV] See also DEER, DOE

HINDER (4) [HINDERED, HINDERS, HINDRANCE]

Ge 24:56 But he said, "Don't **h** my return. The LORD has
1Sa 14: 6 will help us, for nothing can **h** the LORD.
Ezr 6: 7 and do not **h** the governor of Judah and the leaders
Pr 31:12 She will not **h** him but help him all her life.

HINDERED (1) [HINDER]

2Co 6: 3 We try to live in such a way that no one will be **h**

HINDERMOST [KJV] See LAST, LEAST

HINDERS (1) [HINDER]

Heb 12: 1 especially the sin that so easily **h** our progress.

HINDMOST [KJV] See REAR, LAGGING

HINDRANCE (1) [HINDER]

Rev 16:12 east could march their armies westward without **h**.

HINGED (1) [HINGES]

1Ki 6:34 and each door was **h** to fold back upon itself.

HINGES (1) [HINGED]

Pr 26:14 As a door turns back and forth on its **h**, so the lazy

HINNOM (12) [BEN-HINNOM]

Jos 15: 8 then passed through the valley of the son of **H**,
15: 8 to the top of the mountain above the valley of **H**,
18:16 of the mountain beside the valley of the son of **H**,
18:16 From there it went down the valley of **H**,
2Ch 28: 3 He offered sacrifices in the valley of the son of **H**,
33: 6 own sons in the fire in the valley of the son of **H**.
Ne 11:30 all the way from Beersheba to the valley of **H**.
Jer 7:31 shrines of Topheth in the valley of the son of **H**,
7:32 be called Topheth or the valley of the son of **H**,
19: 2 Go out into the valley of the son of **H** by the
19: 6 be called Topheth or the valley of the son of **H**,
32:35 pagan shrines to Baal in the valley of the son of **H**,

HIP (3) [HIPS]

Ge 32:25 he struck Jacob's **h** and knocked it out of joint at
32:31 he left Peniel, and he was limping because of his **h**.
32:32 the people of Israel don't eat meat from near the **h**,

HIPPOPOTAMUS (1)

Job 40:15 "Take a look at the mighty **h**. I made it, just as I

HIPS (1) [HIP]

Ge 3: 7 So they strung fig leaves together around their **h** to

HIRAH (5)

Ge 38: 1 to Adullam, where he visited a man named **H**.
38:12 and his friend **H** the Adullamite went to Timnah to
38:20 Judah asked his friend **H** the Adullamite to take the
38:20 pledges he had given her, but **H** couldn't find her.
38:22 So **H** returned to Judah and told him that he

HIRAM (21) [HIRAM'S]

2Sa 5:11 Then King **H** of Tyre sent messengers to David,
5:11 a palace. **H** also sent many cedar logs for lumber.
1Ki 5: 1 King **H** of Tyre had always been a loyal friend of
5: 1 of Israel, **H** sent ambassadors to congratulate him.
5: 2 Then Solomon sent this message back to **H**:
5: 7 When **H** received Solomon's message, he was very
5:10 So **H** produced for Solomon as much cedar
5:12 And **H** and Solomon made a formal alliance of
9:11 to King **H** of Tyre as payment for all the cedar
9:12 **H** came from Tyre to see the towns Solomon had
9:13 So **H** called that area Cabul—"worthless"—
9:14 **H** had sent Solomon nine thousand pounds of gold.
9:27 **H** sent experienced crews of sailors to sail the
1Ch 14: 1 Now King **H** of Tyre sent messengers to David,
14: 1 a palace. **H** also sent many cedar logs for lumber.
2Ch 2: 3 Solomon also sent this message to King **H** at Tyre:
2:11 King **H** sent this letter of reply to Solomon:
8: 2 to rebuilding the towns that King **H** had given him,
8:18 **H** sent him ships commanded by his own officers
9:10 (When the crews of **H** and Solomon brought gold
9:21 of trading ships manned by the sailors sent by **H**.

HIRAM'S (3) [HIRAM]

1Ki 5:18 and **H** builders prepare the timber and stone for the
10:11 (When **H** ships brought gold from Ophir, they also
10:22 had a fleet of trading ships that sailed with **H** fleet.

HIRE (11) [HIRED, HIRES, HIRING]

Lev 25:50 whatever it would cost to **h** a servant for that
Dt 23: 4 they tried to **h** Balaam son of Beor from Pethor in
Jdg 9: 4 which he used to **h** some soldiers who agreed to
2Ki 22: 6 They will need to **h** carpenters, builders,
1Ch 19: 6 sent thirty-eight tons of silver to **h** chariots
2Ch 25: 6 He also paid about 7,500 pounds of silver to **h**
25: 7 and said, "O king, do not **h** troops from Israel,
25: 9 "But what should I do about the silver I paid to **h**
Isa 46: 6 and gold and **h** a craftsman to make a god from it.
Mt 20: 1 early one morning to **h** workers for his vineyard.
Lk 15:15 He persuaded a local farmer to **h** him to feed his

HIRED (36) [HIRE]

Ex 12:45 **H** servants and visiting foreigners may not eat it.
Lev 19:13 "Always pay your **h** workers promptly.
22:10 lives in a priest's home or is one of his **h** servants.
25: 6 your male and female slaves, your **h** servants,
25:40 Treat them instead as **h** servants or as resident
25:53 The foreigner must treat them as servants **h** on a
Dt 15:18 the services worth double the wages of **h** workers,
2Sa 10: 6 so they **h** twenty thousand Aramean mercenaries
15: 1 and he **h** fifty footmen to run ahead of him.
2Ki 7: 6 "The king of Israel has **h** the Hittites
1Ch 19: 7 They also **h** thirty-two thousand chariots
2Ch 24:12 who **h** masons and carpenters to restore the
24:12 They also **h** metalworkers, who made articles of
25:10 So Amaziah discharged the **h** troops and sent them
25:13 the **h** troops that Amaziah had sent home raided
34:11 they **h** carpenters and masons and purchased cut
Ezr 3: 7 Then they **h** masons and carpenters and bought
Ne 6:12 because Tobiah and Sanballat had **h** him.
13: 2 Instead, they **h** Balaam to curse them, though our
Job 7: 1 person's life is long and hard, like that of a **h** hand,
14: 6 We are like **h** hands, so let us finish the task you
Ecc 2: 8 I **h** wonderful singers, both men and women,
Isa 7:20 these Assyrians you have **h** to protect you—
Eze 22:12 There are **h** murderers, loan racketeers,
44: 8 for you have **h** foreigners to take charge of my
Mt 20: 4 So he **h** them, telling them he would pay them
20: 7 "They replied, 'Because no one **h** us.'
20: 9 When those **h** at five o'clock were paid,
20:10 When those **h** earlier came to get their pay,
Mk 1:20 in the boat with the **h** men and went with him.
Lk 15:17 'At home even the **h** men have food enough to
15:19 called your son. Please take me on as a **h** man." '
16: 1 "A rich man **h** a manager to handle his affairs,
Jn 10:12 A **h** hand will run when he sees a wolf coming.
10:13 The **h** hand runs away because he is merely **h**

HIRELING [KJV] See also HIRED, LABORERS

HIRES (1) [HIRE]

Pr 26:10 An employer who **h** a fool or a bystander is like an

HIRING (1) [HIRE]

Hos 9: 1 to your God, **h** yourselves out like prostitutes,

HIS (5676) [HE] See Index of Articles, Etc.

HISSED (1)

Ge 3: 4 "You won't die!" the serpent **h**.

HISTORIAN (9) [HISTORY]

2Sa 8:16 Jehoshaphat son of Ahilud was the royal **h**.
20:24 Jehoshaphat son of Ahilud was the royal **h**.
1Ki 4: 3 Jehoshaphat son of Ahilud was the royal **h**.
2Ki 18:18 court secretary, and Joah son of Asaph, the royal **h**.
18:37 and Joah son of Asaph, the royal **h**, went back to
1Ch 18:15 Jehoshaphat son of Ahilud was the royal **h**.
2Ch 34: 8 of Jerusalem, and Joah son of Joahaz, the royal **h**,
Isa 36: 3 court secretary, and Joah son of Asaph, the royal **h**.
36:22 and Joah son of Asaph, the royal **h**, went back to

HISTORICAL (1) [HISTORY]

Est 6: 1 so he ordered an attendant to bring the **h** records of

HISTORY (63) [HISTORIAN, HISTORICAL]

Ge 5: 1 This is the **h** of the descendants of Adam.
6: 9 This is the **h** of Noah and his family. Noah was a
10: 1 This is the **h** of the families of Shem, Ham,
11:10 This is the **h** of Shem's family. When Shem was
11:27 This is the **h** of Terah's family. Terah was the
25:12 This is the **h** of the descendants of Ishmael, the son
25:19 This is the **h** of the family of Isaac, the son of
36: 1 This is the **h** of the descendants of Esau (also
37: 2 This is the **h** of Jacob's family. When Joseph was
Ex 9:18 a hailstorm worse than any in all of Egypt's **h**.
9:24 Never in all the **h** of Egypt had there been a storm
10: 6 Never in the **h** of Egypt has there been a plague
10:14 It was the worst locust plague in Egyptian **h**,
Dt 4:32 "Search all of **h**, from the time God created people
1Ki 14:19 are recorded in *The Book of the **H** of the Kings*
14:29 in *The Book of the **H** of the Kings of Judah.*
15: 7 ***H** of the Kings of Judah.* There was constant war
15:23 ***H** of the Kings of Judah.* In his old age his feet
15:31 in *The Book of the **H** of the Kings of Israel.*
16: 5 in *The Book of the **H** of the Kings of Israel.*
16:14 in *The Book of the **H** of the Kings of Israel.*
16:20 in *The Book of the **H** of the Kings of Israel.*
16:27 in *The Book of the **H** of the Kings of Israel.*
22:39 in *The Book of the **H** of the Kings of Israel.*
22:45 in *The Book of the **H** of the Kings of Judah.*
2Ki 1:18 in *The Book of the **H** of the Kings of Israel.*
8:23 in *The Book of the **H** of the Kings of Judah.*
10:34 in *The Book of the **H** of the Kings of Israel.*
12:19 in *The Book of the **H** of the Kings of Judah.*
13: 8 are recorded in *The Book of the **H** of the Kings*
13:12 are recorded in *The Book of the **H** of the Kings*
14:15 are recorded in *The Book of the **H** of the Kings*
14:18 in *The Book of the **H** of the Kings of Judah.*
14:28 are recorded in *The Book of the **H** of the Kings*
15: 6 in *The Book of the **H** of the Kings of Judah.*
15:11 in *The Book of the **H** of the Kings of Israel.*
15:15 are recorded in *The Book of the **H** of the Kings*
15:21 in *The Book of the **H** of the Kings of Israel.*
15:26 in *The Book of the **H** of the Kings of Israel.*
15:31 in *The Book of the **H** of the Kings of Israel.*
15:36 in *The Book of the **H** of the Kings of Judah.*
16:19 and his deeds are recorded in *The Book of the **H***
20:20 are recorded in *The Book of the **H** of the Kings*
21:17 are recorded in *The Book of the **H** of the Kings*
21:25 in *The Book of the **H** of the Kings of Judah.*
23:28 in *The Book of the **H** of the Kings of Judah.*
24: 5 in *The Book of the **H** of the Kings of Judah.*
Ezr 4:15 because of its long **h** of sedition against the kings
9: 7 Our whole **h** has been one of great sin. That is why
Ne 12:23 in *The Book of **H*** down to the days of Johanan,
Est 2:23 This was all duly recorded in *The Book of the **H***
10: 2 are recorded in *The Book of the **H** of the Kings of*
Ps 107:43 they will see in our **h** the faithful love of the
Ecc 1: 9 **H** merely repeats itself. It has all been done before.
Isa 23: 7 What a **h** was yours! Think of all the colonists you
46: 9 do not forget the things I have done throughout **h**.
Jer 30: 7 In all **h** there has never been such a time of terror.
48:11 "From her earliest **h**, Moab has lived in peace.
Eze 21:32 will be utterly wiped out, your memory lost to **h**.
Da 9:12 Never in all **h** has there been a disaster like the one
Joel 1: 2 In all your **h**, has anything like this ever happened
Ob 1:16 will drink and stagger and disappear from **h**,
Rev 16:18 an earthquake greater than ever before in human **h**.

HIT (23) [HITS, HITTING]

Ex 7:17 I will **h** the water of the Nile with this staff,
7:20 Moses raised his staff and **h** the water of the Nile.

Jdg 5:26 She **h** Sisera, crushing his head. / She pounded the
7:13 It **h** a tent, turned it over, and knocked it flat!"
20:16 sling a rock and **h** a target within a hairsbreadth,
1Sa 17:49 from his sling and **h** the Philistine in the forehead.
1Ki 19:11 and a mighty windstorm **h** the mountain.
22:34 and the arrow **h** the king of Israel between the
2Ch 18:33 and the arrow **h** the king of Israel between the
35:23 But the enemy archers **h** King Josiah with their
Job 1:19 in from the desert and **h** the house on all sides.
Pr 23:35 And you will say, "They **h** me, but I didn't feel it.
Isa 47:11 will arise so fast that you won't know what **h** you.
Da 6:24 and tore them apart before they even **h** the floor of
Mt 26:67 they spit in Jesus' face and **h** him with their fists.
26:68 to us, you Messiah! Who **h** you that time?"
Mk 14:65 they blindfolded him and **h** his face with their fists.
14:65 "Who **h** you that time, you prophet?" they jeered.
Lk 22:64 They blindfolded him, then they **h** him and asked, "Who **h** you that time,
Jn 18:23 for it. Should you **h** a man for telling the truth?"
19:3 they mocked, and they **h** him with their fists.
Ac 27:41 But the ship **h** a shoal and ran aground. The bow of

HITCH (3) [HITCHED]

1Sa 6:7 **H** the cows to the cart, but shut their calves away
Job 39:10 Can you **h** a wild ox to a plow? Will it plow a field
La 1:14 "He wove my sins into ropes to **h** me to a yoke of

HITCHED (1) [HITCH]

1Sa 6:10 Two cows with newborn calves were **h** to the cart,

HITHER [KJV] See HERE

HITHERTO [KJV] See PREVIOUSLY, SINCE, STILL

HITS (5) [HIT]

Ex 21:12 "Anyone who **h** a person hard enough to cause
21:18 and one **h** the other with a stone or fist,
21:26 "If an owner **h** a male or female slave in the eye
Nu 35:21 Or if someone angrily **h** another person with a fist
35:22 or throws something that unintentionally **h** another

HITTING (5) [HIT]

Ex 2:13 "What are you doing, **h** your neighbor like that?"
Pr 25:18 Telling lies about others is as harmful as **h** them
Mk 5:5 in the hills, screaming and **h** himself with stones.
14:65 And even the guards were **h** him as they led him
Lk 9:39 at the mouth. It is always **h** and injuring him.

HITTITE (19) [HITTITES]

Ge 23:3 leaving her body, he went to the **H** elders and said,
23:18 in the presence of the **H** elders at the city gate.
25:9 in the field of Ephron son of Zohar the **H**.
26:34 woman named Judith, the daughter of Beeri the **H**.
26:34 married Basemath, the daughter of Elon the **H**.
27:46 "I'm sick and tired of these local **H** women.
36:2 Adah, the daughter of Elon the **H**;
49:30 which Abraham bought from Ephron the **H** for a
50:13 burial place in the field of Ephron the **H**,
1Sa 26:6 David asked Ahimelech the **H** and Abishai son of
2Sa 11:3 daughter of Eliam and the wife of Uriah the **H**."
11:6 David sent word to Joab: "Send me Uriah the **H**."
11:21 Then tell him, 'Uriah the **H** was killed, too.' "
11:24 of our men were killed, including Uriah the **H**."
23:39 Uriah the **H**. There were thirty-seven in all.
1Ki 15:5 except in the affair concerning Uriah the **H**.
1Ch 11:41 Uriah the **H**; / Zabad son of Ahlai;
Eze 16:3 Your father was an Amorite and your mother a **H**!
16:45 Truly your mother must have been a **H** and your

HITTITES (33) [HITTITE]

Ge 10:15 Canaan was also the ancestor of the **H**,
15:20 **H**, Perizzites, Rephaites,
23:5 The **H** replied to Abraham,
23:20 and the cave were sold to Abraham by the **H** as a
25:10 was the field Abraham had purchased from the **H**,
49:32 that my grandfather Abraham bought from the **H**."
Ex 3:8 **H**, Amorites, Perizzites, Hivites, and Jebusites live.
3:17 **H**, Amorites, Perizzites, Hivites, and Jebusites—
13:5 **H**, Amorites, Hivites, and Jebusites.
23:23 **H**, Perizzites, Canaanites, Hivites, and Jebusites,
23:28 of you to drive out the Hivites, Canaanites, and **H**.
33:2 Amorites, **H**, Perizzites, Hivites, and Jebusites.
34:11 the Amorites, Canaanites, **H**, Perizzites, Hivites,
Nu 13:29 Amalekites live in the Negev, and the **H**, Jebusites,
Dt 7:1 the **H**, Girgashites, Amorites, Canaanites,
20:17 You must completely destroy the **H**, Amorites,
Jos 1:4 Sea on the west, and all the land of the **H**.'
3:10 **H**, Hivites, Perizzites, Girgashites, Amorites,
9:1 (These were the kings of the **H**, Amorites,
11:3 the kings of the Amorites; the kings of the **H**;
12:8 The people who lived in this region were the **H**,
24:11 the Perizzites, the Canaanites, the **H**,
Jdg 1:26 Later the man moved to the land of the **H**,
3:5 **H**, Amorites, Perizzites, Hivites, and Jebusites,
1Ki 9:20 **H**, Perizzites, Hivites, and Jebusites.
10:29 of these were then resold to the kings of the **H**
11:1 Ammon, Edom, Sidon, and from among the **H**.
2Ki 7:6 "The king of Israel has hired the **H** and Egyptians
1Ch 1:13 Canaan was also the ancestor of the **H**,
2Ch 1:17 of these were then resold to the kings of the **H**
8:7 including **H**, Amorites, Perizzites, Hivites,
Ezr 9:1 **H**, Perizzites, Jebusites, Ammonites, Moabites,
Ne 9:8 **H**, Amorites, Perizzites, Jebusites, and Girgashites.

HIVITE (2) [HIVITES]

Ge 34:2 Shechem son of Hamor the **H**, saw her, he took her
36:2 of Anah and granddaughter of Zibeon the **H**.

HIVITES (23) [HIVITE]

Ge 10:17 **H**, Arkites, Sinites,
Ex 3:8 Hittites, Amorites, Perizzites, **H**, and Jebusites
3:17 Hittites, Amorites, Perizzites, **H**, and Jebusites—
13:5 Hittites, Amorites, **H**, and Jebusites.
23:23 Hittites, Perizzites, Canaanites, **H**, and Jebusites,
23:28 I will send hornets ahead of you to drive out the **H**,
33:2 Amorites, Hittites, Perizzites, **H**, and Jebusites.
34:11 the Amorites, Canaanites, Hittites, Perizzites, **H**,
Dt 7:1 Girgashites, Amorites, Canaanites, Perizzites, **H**,
20:17 Amorites, Canaanites, Perizzites, **H**, and Jebusites,
Jos 3:10 Hittites, **H**, Perizzites, Girgashites, Amorites,
9:1 Amorites, Canaanites, Perizzites, **H**, and Jebusites,
9:7 The Israelites replied to these **H**, "How do we
11:3 and the **H** in the towns on the slopes of Mount
11:19 peace with the Israelites except the **H** of Gibeon.
12:8 the Amorites, the Canaanites, the Perizzites, the **H**,
24:11 the Canaanites, the Hittites, the Girgashites, the **H**,
Jdg 3:3 and the **H** living in the hill country of Lebanon
3:5 Hittites, Amorites, Perizzites, **H**, and Jebusites,
2Sa 24:7 of Tyre, and all the cities of the **H** and Canaanites.
1Ki 9:20 Hittites, Perizzites, **H**, and Jebusites.
1Ch 1:15 **H**, Arkites, Sinites,
2Ch 8:7 Amorites, Perizzites, **H**, and Jebusites.

HIZKI (1)

1Ch 8:17 Zebadiah, Meshullam, **H**, Heber,

HIZKIAH (1)

1Ch 3:23 sons of Neariah were Elioenai, **H**, and Azrikam—

HO [KJV] See COME

HOAR [KJV] See WHITE

HOARDED (2)

Ecc 5:13 Riches are sometimes **h** to the harm of the saver,
Isa 23:18 Her wealth will not be **h** but will be used to

HOARY [KJV] See ELDERLY, FROST, GRAY-HAIRED, WHITE

HOBAB (3)

Nu 10:29 his brother-in-law, **H** son of Reuel the Midianite,
10:30 But **H** replied, "No, I will not go. I must return to
Jdg 4:11 a descendant of Moses' brother-in-law **H**,

HOBAH (1)

Ge 14:15 but Abram chased them to **H**, north of Damascus.

HOBAIAH (2)

Ezr 2:61 families of priests—**H**, Hakkoz, and Barzillai—
Ne 7:63 **H**, Hakkoz, and Barzillai—also returned to

HOD (1)

1Ch 7:37 Bezer, **H**, Shamma, Shilshah, Ithran, and Beera.

HODAIAH, HODIJAH [KJV] See HODIAH

HODAVIAH (6)

1Ch 3:24 The sons of Elioenai were **H**, Eliashib, Pelaiah,
5:24 Epher, Ishi, Eliel, Azriel, Jeremiah, **H**, and Jahdiel.
9:7 son of Meshullam, son of **H**, son of Hassenuah;
Ezr 2:40 families of Jeshua and Kadmiel (descendants of **H**)
3:9 and Kadmiel and his sons, all descendants of **H**.
Ne 7:43 families of Jeshua and Kadmiel (descendants of **H**)

HODESH (1)

1Ch 8:9 **H**, his new wife, gave birth to Jobab, Zibia, Mesha,

HODIAH (5) [HODIAH'S]

Ne 8:7 **H**, Maaseiah, Kelita, Azariah, Jozabad, Hanan,
9:5 Bani, Hashabneiah, Sherebiah, **H**, Shebaniah,
10:10 Shebaniah, **H**, Kelita, Pelaiah, Hanan,
10:13 **H**, Bani, and Beninu.
10:18 **H**, Hashum, Bezai,

HODIAH'S (1) [HODIAH]

1Ch 4:19 **H** wife was the sister of Naham. One of her sons

HOE (1)

Isa 5:6 I will not prune the vines or **h** the ground.

HOGLAH (4) [BETH-HOGLAH]

Nu 26:33 names were Mahlah, Noah, **H**, Milcah, and Tirzah.
27:1 Mahlah, Noah, **H**, Milcah, and Tirzah.
36:11 Mahlah, Tirzah, **H**, Milcah, and Noah all married
Jos 17:3 names were Mahlah, Noah, **H**, Milcah, and Tirzah.

HOHAM (1)

Jos 10:3 **H** of Hebron, Piram of Jarmuth, Japhia of Lachish,

HOISED [KJV] See RAISED

HOISTED (1)

Ac 27:16 where with great difficulty we **h** aboard the

HOLD (108) [HELD, HOLDING, HOLDS]

Ge 34:21 For the land is large enough to **h** them, and we can
Ex 4:4 Then the LORD told him, "Take **h** of its tail."
5:1 for they must go out into the wilderness to **h** a
14:16 **h** it out over the water, and a path will open up
17:12 Moses' arms finally became too tired to **h** up the
22:29 "Do not **h** anything back when you give me the
25:33 Each of the six branches will **h** a cup shaped like
28:28 This will **h** the chestpiece securely to the ephod
36:34 The rings used to **h** the crossbars were made of
37:14 These were made to **h** the carrying poles in place.
37:27 beneath the molding, to **h** the carrying poles.
38:10 were silver hooks and rods to **h** up the curtains.
38:17 and the rods to **h** up the curtains were solid silver.
38:31 and all the tent pegs used to **h** the curtains of the
Lev 23:8 all their regular work to **h** a sacred assembly."
Nu 36:9 each tribe of Israel must **h** on to its allotted
Dt 11:17 He will shut up the sky and **h** back the rain,
Jdg 4:5 She would **h** court under the Palm of Deborah,
13:25 the Spirit of the LORD began to take **h** of him.
16:3 got up, took **h** of the city gates with its two posts,
1Sa 3:18 told Eli everything; he didn't **h** anything back.
15:27 Saul grabbed at him to try to **h** him back and tore
2Sa 22:49 You **h** me safe beyond the reach of my enemies;
1Ki 1:50 sacred tent and caught **h** of the horns of the altar.
2:28 the LORD and caught **h** of the horns of the altar.
7:26 It could **h** about 11,000 gallons of water.
7:38 was 6 feet across and could **h** 220 gallons of water.
18:32 the altar large enough to **h** about three gallons.
2Ki 4:27 to the ground before him and caught **h** of his feet.
23:26 and he did not **h** back his fierce anger from them.
2Ch 4:5 It could **h** about 16,500 gallons of water.
24:22 see what they are doing and **h** them accountable!"
Job 8:15 They try to **h** it fast, but it will not endure.
8:17 Its roots grow down through a pile of rocks to **h** it
9:28 For I know you will not **h** me innocent, O God.
10:15 and misery so that I can't **h** my head high.
10:16 And if I **h** my head high, you hunt me like a lion
30:15 They **h** me in contempt, and my prosperity has
38:31 "Can you **h** back the movements of the stars?
Ps 18:48 You **h** me safe beyond the reach of my enemies;
27:6 Then I will **h** my head high, / above my enemies
27:10 mother abandon me, / the LORD will **h** me close.
40:11 don't **h** back your tender mercies from me.
74:11 Why do you **h** back your strong right hand?
78:25 food of angels! / God gave them all they could **h**.
79:8 Oh, do not **h** us guilty for our former sins!
91:12 They will **h** you with their hands / to keep you
119:51 The proud **h** me in utter contempt, / but I do not
Pr 3:18 embrace her; happy are those who **h** her tightly.
5:22 his own sins; they are ropes that catch and **h** him.
7:5 Let them **h** you back from an affair with an
11:26 People curse those who **h** their grain for higher
27:16 stop the wind or **h** something with greased hands.
Ecc 8:8 None of us can **h** back our spirit from departing.
SS 7:8 up into the palm tree and take **h** of its branches.'
Isa 5:22 who boast about all the liquor they can **h**.
22:6 drive the chariots. The men of Kir **h** up the shields.
48:9 I will **h** back my anger and not wipe you out.
62:3 The LORD will **h** you in his hands for all to see—
Jer 2:13 cracked cisterns that can **h** no water at all!
15:7 of your cities and take away everything you **h** dear.
26:10 and sat down at the New Gate of the Temple to **h**
48:10 who **h** back their swords from shedding blood!
50:33 Their captors **h** them and refuse to let them go.
La 2:14 They did not try to **h** you back from exile by
4:20 we could **h** our own against any nation on earth!
Eze 1:3 and I felt the hand of the LORD take **h** of me.
3:14 and turmoil, but the LORD's **h** on me was strong.
3:18 And I will **h** you responsible, demanding your
3:20 and I will **h** you responsible, demanding your
3:22 Then the LORD took **h** of me, and he said to me,
8:1 in my home, the Sovereign LORD took **h** of me.
13:10 and these prophets are trying to **h** it together by
17:3 He took **h** of the highest branch of a cedar tree
20:37 and **h** you to the terms of the covenant.
24:14 The time has come and I won't **h** back; I will not
30:21 a splint to make it strong enough to **h** a sword.
33:6 their sins, but I will **h** the watchman accountable.
33:8 but I will **h** you responsible for their deaths.
33:22 The previous evening the LORD had taken **h** of
34:10 and I will **h** them responsible for what has
37:1 The LORD took **h** of me, and I was carried away
37:17 Now **h** them together in your hand as one stick.
37:20 Then **h** out the sticks you have inscribed,
40:1 the fall of Jerusalem—the LORD took **h** of me.
Da 11:4 nor will the kingdom **h** the authority it once had.
Jnh 1:5 all this time Jonah was sound asleep down in the **h**.
1:14 And don't **h** us responsible for his death, because it
3:9 and **h** back his fierce anger from destroying us."
Mic 5:7 rain falling on the grass, which no one can **h** back.
Mt 4:6 protect you. / And they will **h** you with their hands
Mk 7:9 "You reject God's laws in order to **h** on to your
Lk 4:11 And they will **h** you with their hands / to keep you
Gal 5:7 Who has interfered with you to **h** you back from
Eph 4:15 Instead, we will **h** to the truth in love,
Php 2:16 **H** tightly to the word of life, so that when Christ
1Th 5:21 test everything that is said. **H** on to what is good.
1Ti 6:12 **H** tightly to the eternal life that God has given you,
6:19 for the future so that they may take **h** of real life.

2Ti 1:13 **H** on to the pattern of right teaching you learned
Heb 6:16 they call on someone greater than themselves to **h**
6:18 for we can **h** on to his promise with confidence.
10:23 let us **h** tightly to the hope we say we have,
2Pe 2:3 In their greed they will make up clever lies to get **h**
Rev 1:18 and ever! And I **h** the keys of death and the grave.
2:25 except that you **h** tightly to what you have until I
3:3 at first; **h** to it firmly and turn to me again.
3:11 **H** on to what you have, so that no one will take

HOLDING (41) [HOLD]

Ge 39:12 She was left **h** it as he ran from the house.
40:11 I was **h** Pharaoh's wine cup in my hand, so I took
Ex 17:12 stood on each side, **h** up his hands until sunset.
39:40 of the courtyard and the posts and bases **h** them up;
Nu 5:18 **h** the jar of bitter water that brings a curse to those
Dt 9:15 **h** in my hands the two stone tablets of the
Jos 8:26 For Joshua kept **h** out his spear until everyone who
1Sa 22:6 **h** his spear and surrounded by his officers.
2Sa 19:11 that all Israel is ready, and only you are **h** out.
1Ki 7:43 the ten water carts **h** the ten basins,
2Ki 4:16 "Next year at about this time you will be **h** a son
2Ch 4:14 the water carts **h** the basins,
26:19 refused to set down the incense burner he was **h**.
Ne 4:17 supporting their load and one hand **h** a weapon.
Est 5:2 he welcomed her, **h** out the gold scepter to her.
Job 15:26 **H** their strong shields, they defiantly charge
20:13 He savored it, **h** it long in his mouth.
29:10 of the city stood quietly, **h** their tongues in respect.
Ps 73:23 Yet I still belong to you; / you are **h** my right hand.
77:1 I cry out to God without **h** back. / Oh, that God
Isa 40:11 the lambs in his arms, **h** them close to his heart.
41:13 I am **h** you by your right hand—I, the LORD your
44:20 this thing, this idol that I'm **h** in my hand, a lie?"
Jer 6:11 Yes, I am weary of **h** it in! "I will pour out my
14:1 explaining why he was **h** back the rain:
20:9 It's like a fire in my bones! I am weary of **h** it in!
38:7 At that time the king was **h** court at the Benjamin
Eze 40:3 He was **h** in his hand a measuring tape and a
Mt 27:48 **h** it up to him on a stick so he could drink.
Mk 5:41 **H** her hand, he said to her, "Get up, little girl!"
11:25 first forgive anyone you are **h** a grudge against,
15:36 **h** it up to him on a stick so he could drink.
Ac 3:11 where he was **h** tightly to Peter and John.
2Th 2:6 And you know what is **h** him back, for he can be
2:7 and it will remain secret until the one who is **h** it
Heb 6:6 again by rejecting him, **h** him up to public shame.
Rev 6:5 and its rider was **h** a pair of scales in his hand.
7:1 **h** back the four winds from blowing upon the
15:1 Seven angels were **h** the seven last plagues,
15:2 They were all **h** harps that God had given them.
15:6 The seven angels who were **h** the bowls of the

HOLDS (17) [HOLD]

Est 4:11 to die unless the king **h** out his gold scepter.
Job 12:15 If he **h** back the rain, the earth becomes a desert.
Ps 33:4 For the word of the LORD **h** true,
37:24 will not fall, / for the LORD **h** them by the hand.
63:8 behind you; / your strong right hand **h** me securely.
75:8 For the LORD **h** a cup in his hand; / it is full of
Pr 29:11 vent to anger, but a wise person quietly **h** it back.
30:4 comes back down? Who **h** the wind in his fists?
Isa 23:11 The LORD **h** out his hand over the seas.
41:22 us what happened long ago or what the future **h**.
47:13 stand up and save you from what the future **h**.
Ro 7:4 The law no longer **h** you in its power, because you
Col 1:17 else began, and he **h** all creation together.
1Jn 5:18 for God's Son **h** them securely, and the evil one
Rev 2:1 This is the message from the one who **h** the seven
20:6 For them the second death **h** no power, but they
22:6 Lord God, who tells his prophets what the future **h**,

HOLE (9) [HOLES]

Dt 23:13 you must dig a **h** with the spade and cover the
2Ki 12:9 Then Jehoiada the priest bored a **h** in the lid of a
Jer 13:4 Euphrates River. Hide it there in a **h** in the rocks."
13:7 and dug it out of the **h** where I had hidden it.
Eze 12:5 Dig a **h** through the wall while they are watching
12:12 leave Jerusalem at night through a **h** in the wall,
Mt 9:16 the old cloth, leaving an even bigger **h** than before.
25:18 received the one bag of gold dug a **h** in the ground
Mk 2:21 the old cloth, leaving an even bigger **h** than before.

HOLES (8) [HOLE]

Jdg 5:11 to the village musicians gathered at the watering **h**.
1Sa 13:6 tried to hide in caves, **h**, rocks, tombs, and cisterns.
14:11 "Look! The Hebrews are crawling out of their **h**!"
Isa 2:19 his enemies will crawl with fear into **h** in the
Mic 7:17 Like snakes crawling from their **h**, they will come
Hag 1:6 you were putting them in pockets filled with **h**!
Lk 12:33 And the purses of heaven have no **h** in them.
Heb 11:38 hiding in caves and **h** in the ground.

HOLIDAY (2) [HOLIDAYS]

Est 8:17 and declared a public festival and **h**.
9:19 celebrate an annual festival and **h** in late winter,

HOLIDAYS (1) [HOLIDAY]

Hos 7:5 "On royal **h**, the princes get drunk. The king

HOLIER (1) [HOLY]

Isa 65:5 too close or you will defile me! I am **h** than you!'

HOLILY [KJV] See PURE

HOLINESS (38) [HOLY]

Ex 15:11 O LORD? / Who is glorious in **h** like you—
15:13 in your strength / to the place where your **h** dwells.
Lev 16:19 Israel's defilement and return it to its former **h**.
21:9 defiling her father's **h** as well as herself, she must
Nu 20:12 to demonstrate my **h** to the people of Israel,
20:13 and where he demonstrated his **h** among them.
27:14 you failed to demonstrate my **h** to them at the
Dt 32:51 You failed to demonstrate my **h** to the people of
Ne 13:22 and to guard the gates in order to preserve the **h** of
Ps 29:2 Worship the LORD in the splendor of his **h**.
60:6 God has promised this by his **h**: / "I will divide up
89:35 sworn an oath to David, / and in my **h** I cannot lie:
93:5 The nature of your reign, O LORD, is **h** forever.
98:1 He has won a mighty victory / by his power and **h**.
108:7 God has promised this by his **h**: / "I will divide up
134:2 Lift your hands in **h**, / and bless the LORD.
Isa 5:16 The **h** of God is displayed by his righteousness.
29:23 they will recognize the **h** of the Holy One of Israel.
35:8 It will be named the Highway of **H**.
Eze 20:41 And I will display my **h** in you as all the nations
28:22 judgment against you and reveal my **h** among you,
28:25 I will reveal to the nations of the world my **h**
36:23 And when I reveal my **h** through you before their
38:16 and my **h** will be displayed by what happens to
38:23 Thus will I show my greatness and **h**, and I will
39:27 my **h** will be displayed to the nations.
43:12 this is the basic law of the Temple: absolute **h**!
44:19 so they do not harm the people by transmitting **h** to
46:20 and harming the people by transmitting **h** to
Am 4:2 The Sovereign LORD has sworn this by his **h**:
Lk 1:75 in **h** and righteousness forever.
Ro 6:22 Now you do those things that lead to **h** and result
1Co 7:14 For the Christian wife brings **h** to her marriage,
7:14 and the Christian husband brings **h** to his marriage.
1Th 4:4 will control your body and live in **h** and honor—
1Ti 2:15 by continuing to live in faith, love, **h**, and modesty.
Heb 12:10 for us because it means we will share in his **h**.
Rev 22:11 to do good; and the one who is holy, continue in **h**.

HOLLOW (4) [HOLLOWED]

Ex 27:8 The altar must be **h**, made from planks. Be careful
38:7 The altar was **h** and was made from planks.
Jdg 15:19 So God caused water to gush out of a **h** in the
Jer 52:21 They were **h**, with walls 3 inches thick.

HOLLOWED (1) [HOLLOW]

Nu 21:18 which princes dug, / which great leaders **h** out

HOLON (4)

Jos 15:51 Goshen, **H**, and Giloh—eleven towns with their
21:15 **H**, Debir,
1Ch 6:58 **H**, Debir,
Jer 48:21 out on them all—on **H** and Jahaz and Mephaath,

HOLPEN [KJV] See ALLIED, HELP(ED)

HOLY (699) [HOLIER, HOLINESS]

HOLY CITY (11) Ne 11:1,18; Ps 2:6; Isa 48:2; 52:1; Da 9:24; Mt 27:53; Rev 11:2; 21:2,10; 22:19

HOLY MOUNTAIN (24) Ps 3:4; 43:3; 48:1,2; 87:1; 99:9; Isa 11:9; 27:13; 56:7; 57:13; 65:25; 66:20; Jer 31:23; Eze 20:40; 28:14; Da 9:16,20; 11:45; Joel 2:1; 3:17; Ob 1:16; Zep 3:11; Zec 8:3; 2Pe 1:18

HOLY NAME (25) Lev 20:3; 22:2,32; 1Ch 16:10,35; 29:16; Ps 30:4; 33:21; 74:7; 86:9; 97:12; 103:1; 105:3; 106:47; 145:21; Pr 30:9; Eze 20:39; 22:26; 36:20,21,22; 39:7; 43:7,8; Am 2:7

HOLY ONE (56) Nu 16:7; 2Ki 19:22; Job 6:10; Ps 71:22; 78:41; 89:18; Pr 9:10; 30:3; Isa 1:4; 5:19,24; 8:13; 10:17,20; 12:6; 17:7; 29:19,23; 30:11,12,15; 31:1; 37:23; 40:25; 41:14, 16,20; 43:3,14,15; 45:11; 47:4; 48:17; 49:7,7; 54:5; 55:5; 57:15; 60:9,14; Jer 50:29; 51:5; Eze 39:7; Da 4:13,23; Hos 11:9,12; Hab 1:12; 3:3; Mk 1:24; Lk 4:34; Jn 6:69; 10:36; Ac 2:27; 13:35; Rev 16:5

HOLY ONES (5) Dt 33:3; Da 4:17; 8:13; Zec 14:5; Jude 1:14

HOLY PEOPLE (30) Ex 22:31; Dt 7:6; 28:9; Isa 4:3; 52:11; 62:12; 63:18; Da 7:18,21,22,22,25,27; 8:24; 12:7; 1Co 1:2; Eph 1:1; 2:19; Col 1:2,12,26; 3:12; 2Th 1:10; Jude 1:3; Rev 11:18; 13:7; 14:12; 16:6; 17:6; 18:20

HOLY PLACE (77) Ex 26:33,33,34; 27:21; 28:29,35,43; 29:30; 31:11; 35:12,19; 39:1,34,41; 40:3,22,24,26; Lev 4:6; 6:30; 10:18; 16:2,16,17,20,23,27,33; 24:3; Nu 28:7; 1Ki 6:16,17,21,22; 7:49,50; 8:6,8; 1Ch 6:49; 2Ch 3:8,10,14; 4:20,22; 5:7,9,11; Ezr 9:8; Ps 24:3; Isa 57:15; 63:18; Eze 41:1,2,3,4,15,15,17,20,21,21,23,23,25; 42:14; 45:3; Da 9:24; Ob 1:17; Mt 24:15; Heb 9:2,3,7,8,12,25; 10:19; 13:11

HOLY SPIRIT (155) Ps 51:11; Isa 63:10,11; Mt 1:18,20; 3:11; 4:1; 12:31,32; 22:43; 28:19; Mk 1:8,10,12; 3:29; 12:36; 13:11; Lk 1:15,35,41,67; 2:25,26; 3:16,22; 4:1; 10:21; 11:13; 12:10,12; 24:49,49; Jn 1:32,33,33; 3:6; 14:17,26; 20:22; Ac 1:2,5,8,16; 2:4,4,33,38; 4:8,25,31; 5:3,32; 6:3,5; 7:51,55; 8:15,16,17,18,19,29; 9:17,31; 10:19,38,44,45,47; 11:12,15, 16,24; 13:2,4,9,52; 15:8,28; 16:6; 19:2,2,6,21; 20:22,23,28; 21:4,11; 28:25; Ro 1:4; 5:5; 8:5,6,13,16,23,26,26; 9:1; 14:17; 15:13,16,30; 1Co 2:4; 6:19; 12:1,3,4,11; 2Co 1:22; 3:6,8; 5:5; 6:6; 13:13; Gal 3:2,2,5,14; 4:29; 5:16,17,18,22,25; Eph 1:13; 2:18; 3:5,16; 4:3,30; 5:18; 6:18; Col 1:8; 1Th 1:5,6; 4:8; 5:19; 1Ti 4:1; 2Ti 1:14; Tit 3:5; Heb 2:4; 3:7; 6:4; 9:8; 10:15,29; Jas 4:5; 1Pe 1:12; 2Pe 1:21; 1Jn 2:20,27; 3:24; Jude 1:20

HOLY TEMPLE (10) 1Ch 29:3; Ps 11:4; 65:4; 79:1; 138:2; Jnh 2:4,7; Mic 1:2; Hab 2:20; Eph 2:21

HOLY THINGS (5) Lev 5:16; 1Ch 23:13; Eze 22:8,26; 44:13

MOST HOLY (62) Ex 26:33,34; 27:21; 29:44; 30:36; 35:12; 39:34; 40:3,10; Lev 2:3,10; 4:6; 6:17,25,29; 7:1,6; 10:12; 14:13; 16:2,16,17,20,23,27,33; 21:22; 24:3,9; Nu 18:9,9,10,10; 1Ki 6:16,17,21,22; 7:49,50; 8:6; 1Ch 6:49; 23:13; 2Ch 3:8,10,14; 4:20,22; 5:7; Eze 41:4,15,17,21,23; 42:13; 45:3; Da 9:24; Heb 9:3,7,8,12,25; 10:19

MOST HOLY PLACE (42) Ex 26:33,34; 27:21; 35:12; 39:34; 40:3; Lev 4:6; 16:2,16,17,20,23,27,33; 24:3; 1Ki 6:16,17,21,22; 7:49,50; 8:6; 1Ch 6:49; 2Ch 3:8,10,14; 4:20,22; 5:7; Eze 41:4,15,17,21,23; 45:3; Da 9:24; Heb 9:3,7,8,12,25; 10:19

Ge 2:3 And God blessed the seventh day and declared it **h**,
Ex 3:5 your sandals, for you are standing on **h** ground."
16:23 as a day of rest, a **h** Sabbath to the LORD.
19:6 will be to me a kingdom of priests, my **h** nation.'
20:8 to observe the Sabbath day by keeping it **h**.
20:11 blessed the Sabbath day and set it apart as **h**.
20:25 a tool, for that would make them unfit for **h** use.
22:31 "You are my own **h** people. Therefore, do not eat
26:33 This curtain will separate the **H** Place from the Most **H** Place.
26:34 the Ark of the Covenant inside the Most **H** Place.
27:21 curtain of the Most **H** Place in the Tabernacle.
28:29 into the presence of the LORD in the **H** Place.
28:35 he enters the **H** Place to minister to the LORD,
28:36 SET APART AS **H** TO THE LORD.
28:41 Set them apart as **h** so they can serve as my priests.
28:43 or approach the altar in the **H** Place to perform
29:21 and their clothing will be set apart as **h** to the
29:27 "Set aside as **h** the parts of the ordination ram that
29:30 to minister in the Tabernacle and the **H** Place.
29:33 not eat them, for these things are set apart and **h**.
29:34 it must be burned. It may not be eaten, for it is **h**.
29:36 atonement for it; make it **h** by anointing it with oil.
29:37 After that, the altar will be exceedingly **h**,
29:37 and whatever touches it will become **h**.
29:44 I will make the Tabernacle and the altar most **h**,
29:44 and I will set apart Aaron and his sons as **h**,
30:10 for this is the LORD's supremely **h** altar."
30:25 Blend these ingredients into a **h** anointing oil.
30:29 Sanctify them to make them entirely **h**. After this, whatever touches them will become **h**.
30:31 of Israel, 'This will always be my **h** anointing oil.
30:32 It is **h**, and you must treat it as **h**.
30:35 refine it to produce a pure and **h** incense.
30:36 with you in the Tabernacle. This incense is most **h**.
30:37 for the LORD, and you must treat it as **h**.
31:10 **h** garments for Aaron the priest,
31:11 and the special incense for the **H** Place.
31:13 that I am the LORD, who makes you **h**.
31:14 Yes, keep the Sabbath day, for it is **h**. Anyone who
31:15 Because the LORD considers it a **h** day,
35:2 of total rest, a **h** day that belongs to the LORD.
35:12 the inner curtain to enclose the Ark in the Most **H**
35:19 priests to wear while ministering in the **H** Place;
35:21 and its furnishings and for the **h** garments.
39:1 clothing to be worn while ministering in the **H**
39:30 SET APART AS **H** TO THE LORD.
39:34 the inner curtain that enclosed the Most **H** Place;
39:41 to be worn while ministering in the **H** Place—
39:41 the **h** garments for Aaron the priest and for his
40:3 to enclose the Ark within the Most **H** Place.
40:9 and on all its furnishings to make them **h**.
40:10 Then the altar will become most **h**.
40:11 large washbasin and its pedestal to make them **h**.
40:13 Clothe Aaron with the **h** garments and anoint him,
40:22 along the north side of the **H** Place, just outside the
40:24 from the table on the south side of the **H** Place.
40:26 in the **H** Place in front of the inner curtain.
Lev 2:3 It will be considered a most **h** part of the offerings
2:10 It will be considered a most **h** part of the offerings
4:6 in front of the inner curtain of the Most **H** Place.
5:16 then make restitution for whatever **h** things they
6:17 the sin offering and the guilt offering, it is most **h**.
6:18 or anything that touches this food will become **h**."
6:25 The animal given as a sin offering is most **h**
6:27 who touches the sacrificial meat will become **h**,
6:29 family may eat of this offering, for it is most **h**.
6:30 atonement in the **H** Place for the people's sins,
7:1 instructions for the guilt offering, which is most **h**.
7:6 it must be eaten in a sacred place, for it is most **h**.
8:10 and everything in it, thus making them **h**.
8:11 and the washbasin and its pedestal, making them **h**.
8:12 thus anointing him and making him **h** for his work.
8:15 he set the altar apart as **h** and made atonement for
8:30 he made Aaron and his sons and their clothing **h**.
10:3 meant when he said, / 'I will show myself **h**
10:10 You are to distinguish between what is **h** and what
10:12 in it, and eat it beside the altar, for it is most **h**.
10:17 he demanded. "It is a **h** offering! It was given to
10:18 Since the animal's blood was not taken into the **H**
11:44 am your God. You must be **h** because I am **h**.
11:45 You must therefore be **h** because I am **h**.
12:4 she must not touch anything that is **h**.
14:13 will be given to the priest. It is a most **h** offering.
16:2 "Warn your brother Aaron not to enter the Most **H**
16:16 he will make atonement for the Most **H** Place,
16:17 goes in to make atonement for the Most **H** Place.
16:20 finished making atonement for the Most **H** Place,

16:23 he wore when he entered the Most **H** Place,
16:27 whose blood Aaron brought into the Most **H** Place
16:32 He will put on the **h** linen garments
16:33 and make atonement for the Most **H** Place,
19: 2 must be **h** because I, the LORD your God, am **h**.
19: 8 you will answer for the sin of profaning what is **h**
20: 3 and profaned my **h** name by giving their children
20: 7 So set yourselves apart to be **h**, for I, the LORD,
20: 8 for I am the LORD, who makes you **h**.
20:26 You must be **h** because I, the LORD, am **h**.
21: 6 They must be set apart to God as **h** and must never
21: 6 God with his food, and they must remain **h**.
21: 7 for the priests must be set apart to God as **h**.
21: 8 You must treat them as **h** because they offer up
21: 8 You must consider them **h** because I, the LORD, am **h**, and I make you **h**.
21:12 because he has been made **h** by the anointing oil of
21:15 because I, the LORD, have made him **h**."
21:22 including the **h** offerings and the most **h** offerings.
21:23 the altar, for this would desecrate my **h** places. I am the LORD who makes them **h**."
22: 2 with great care, so they do not profane my **h** name.
22: 9 I am the LORD who makes them **h**.
22:16 I am the LORD, who makes them **h**."
22:32 Do not treat my **h** name as common and ordinary.
22:32 I must be treated as **h** by the people of Israel. It is I, the LORD, who makes you **h**.
23: 3 of complete rest, a **h** day to assemble for worship.
23: 4 the **h** occasions to be observed at the proper time
23:20 These offerings are **h** to the LORD and will
24: 3 inner curtain of the Most **H** Place in the Tabernacle
24: 9 for they represent a most **h** portion of the offerings
25:10 This year will be set apart as **h**, a time to proclaim
25:12 and you must observe it as a special and **h** time.
27: 9 then your gift to the LORD will be considered **h**.
27:10 and the substitute will be considered **h**.
27:21 it will be **h**, a field specially set apart for the
27:28 in this way has been set apart for the LORD as **h**.
27:30 to the LORD and must be set apart to him as **h**.
27:32 and flocks. They are set apart to him as **h**.
27:33 and the substituted one will be considered **h**
Nu 5:17 He must take some **h** water in a clay jar and mix it
6: 5 for they are **h** and set apart to the LORD.
6:20 These are **h** portions for the priest, along with the
7: 1 he anointed it and set it apart as **h**, along with all
15:40 must obey all my commands and be **h** to your God.
16: 5 will show us who belongs to him and who is **h**.
16: 5 allow those who are chosen to enter his **h** presence.
16: 7 will see whom the LORD chooses as his **h** one.
16:37 all the incense burners from the fire, for they are **h**.
16:38 for these burners have become **h** because they
18: 8 "I have put the priests in charge of all the **h** gifts
18: 9 You are allotted the portion of the most **h** offerings
18: 9 From all the most **h** offerings—including the grain
18:10 You must eat it as a most **h** offering. All the males
18:10 may eat of it, and you must treat it as most **h**.
18:17 They are **h** and have been set apart for the LORD.
18:19 I am giving you all these **h** offerings that the
18:32 But be careful not to treat the **h** gifts of the people
28: 7 poured out in the **H** Place as an offering to the
28:25 you must call another **h** assembly of the people.
28:26 you must call a **h** assembly of the people.
29: 7 you must call another **h** assembly of all the people.
29:12 you must call yet another **h** assembly of all the
29:35 call all the people to another **h** assembly.
31: 6 They carried along the **h** objects of the sanctuary
Dt 5:12 " 'Observe the Sabbath day by keeping it **h**,
7: 6 For you are a **h** people, who belong to the LORD
14: 2 You have been set apart as **h** to the LORD your
14:21 for you are set apart as **h** to the LORD your God.
23:14 The camp must be **h**, for the LORD your God
26:15 Look down from your **h** dwelling place in heaven
26:19 You will be a nation that is **h** to the LORD your
28: 9 the LORD will establish you as his **h** people as he
33: 3 love the people; / all your **h** ones are in your hands.
Jos 5:15 "Take off your sandals, for this is **h** ground."
24:19 to serve the LORD, for he is a **h** and jealous God.
1Sa 2: 2 No one is **h** like the LORD! / There is no one
6:20 stand in the presence of the LORD, this **H** God?"
21: 4 "But there is the **h** bread, which I guess you can
21: 6 food available, the priest gave him the **h** bread—
1Ki 6:16 the Most **H** Place—at the far end of the Temple.
6:17 outside the Most **H** Place, was 60 feet long.
6:21 chains to protect the entrance to the Most **H** Place.
6:22 including the altar that belonged to the Most **H**
7:49 in front of the Most **H** Place, the flower
7:50 the doors for the entrances to the Most **H** Place
8: 6 the Most **H** Place—and placed it beneath the wings
8: 8 main room—the **H** Place—but not from outside it.
2Ki 4: 9 who stops in from time to time is a **h** man of God.
19:22 proud condescension? / It was the **H** One of Israel!
1Ch 6:49 all the other duties related to the Most **H** Place.
16:10 Exult in his **h** name; / O worshipers of the LORD,
16:29 Worship the LORD in all his **h** splendor
16:35 among the nations, / so we can thank your **h** name
22:19 and the **h** vessels of God into the Temple built to
23:13 were set apart to dedicate the most **h** things,
29: 3 I have already collected for his **h** Temple.
29:16 a Temple to honor your **h** name come from you!
2Ch 3: 8 The Most **H** Place was thirty feet wide,
3:10 with gold. These were placed in the Most **H** Place.
3:14 Across the entrance of the Most **H** Place,
4:20 to burn in front of the Most **H** Place as prescribed;
4:22 the doors for the entrances to the Most **H** Place
5: 7 the Most **H** Place—and placed it beneath the wings
5: 9 main room—the **H** Place—but not from outside it.
5:11 Then the priests left the **H** Place. All the priests
8:11 of the LORD has been there, and it is **h** ground."
13:11 They place the Bread of the Presence on the **h**
20:21 to the LORD and praising him for his **h** splendor.
23: 6 Temple of the LORD, for they are set apart as **h**.
30: 8 Come to his Temple which he has set apart as **h**
30:27 and God heard them from his **h** dwelling in
35: 5 Then stand in your appointed **h** places and help the
35:13 and they boiled the **h** offerings in pots, kettles,
Ezr 8:28 and these treasures have been set apart as **h** to the
9: 2 So the **h** race has become polluted by these mixed
9: 8 He has given us security in this **h** place. Our God
Ne 9:14 You instructed them concerning the laws of your **h**
10:31 to be sold on the Sabbath or on any other **h** day,
10:33 and the annual festivals; for the **h** offerings;
11: 1 were living in Jerusalem, the **h** city, at this time.
11:18 In all, there were 284 Levites in the **h** city.
Job 6:10 the pain, I have not denied the words of the **H** One.
Ps 2: 6 king on the throne / in Jerusalem, my **h** city."
3: 4 and he answered me from his **h** mountain.
11: 4 But the LORD is in his **h** Temple; / the LORD
15: 1 Who may enter your presence on your **h** hill?
20: 6 He will answer him from his **h** heaven / and rescue
22: 3 Yet you are **h**. / The praises of Israel surround your
24: 3 of the LORD? / Who may stand in his **h** place?
28: 2 as I lift my hands toward your **h** sanctuary.
30: 4 all you godly ones! / Praise his **h** name.
33:21 hearts rejoice, / for we are trusting in his **h** name.
43: 3 guide me. / Let them lead me to your **h** mountain,
47: 8 reigns above the nations, / sitting on his **h** throne.
48: 1 the city of our God, / which is on his **h** mountain!
48: 2 Mount Zion, the **h** mountain, / is the city of the
51:11 and don't take your **H** Spirit from me.
65: 4 to bring near, / those who live in your **h** courts.
65: 4 What joys await us / inside your **h** Temple.
68: 5 of widows— / this is God, whose dwelling is **h**.
71:22 I will sing for you with a lyre, / O **H** One of Israel.
74: 7 They utterly defiled the place that bears your **h**
77:13 O God, your ways are **h**. / Is there any god as
78:41 God's patience / and frustrated the **H** One of Israel.
78:54 He brought them to the border of his **h** land,
79: 1 They have defiled your **h** Temple
86: 9 Lord; / they will praise your great and **h** name.
87: 1 On the **h** mountain stands the city founded by the
89:18 and he, the **H** One of Israel, has given us our king.
89:20 servant David. / I have anointed him with my **h** oil.
96: 9 Worship the LORD in all his **h** splendor. / Let all
97:12 be happy in the LORD / and praise his **h** name!
99: 3 your great and awesome name. / Your name is **h**!
99: 5 our God! / Bow low before his feet, for he is **h**!
99: 9 and worship at his **h** mountain in Jerusalem, / for the LORD our God is **h**!
103: 1 with my whole heart, I will praise his **h** name.
105: 3 Exult in his **h** name; / O worshipers of the LORD,
106:16 and envious of Aaron, the LORD's **h** priest.
106:47 among the nations, / so we can thank your **h** name
110: 3 will serve you willingly. / Arrayed in **h** garments,
111: 9 What a **h**, awe-inspiring name he has!
138: 2 I bow before your **h** Temple as I worship. / I will
145:21 and everyone on earth will bless his **h** name
Pr 9:10 Knowledge of the **H** One results in understanding.
30: 3 human wisdom, nor do I know the **H** One.
30: 9 too poor, I may steal and thus insult God's **h** name.
Isa 1: 4 They have despised the **H** One of Israel,
4: 3 the destruction of Jerusalem, will be a **h** people.
5:19 They even mock the **H** One of Israel and say,
5:24 They have despised the word of the **H** One of
6: 3 In a great chorus they sang, "**H**, **h**, **h** is the LORD Almighty!
6:13 but the stump will be a **h** seed that will grow
8:13 He alone is the **H** One. If you fear him, you need
10:17 The LORD, the Light of Israel and the **H** One,
10:20 Judah will trust the LORD, the **H** One of Israel.
11: 9 Nothing will hurt or destroy in all my **h** mountain.
12: 6 For great is the **H** One of Israel who lives among
17: 7 and have respect for the **H** One of Israel.
27:13 to worship the LORD on his **h** mountain.
29:19 Those who are poor will rejoice in the **H** One of
29:23 they will recognize the holiness of the **H** One of
30:11 We have heard more than enough about your '**H**
30:12 This is the reply of the **H** One of Israel:
30:15 The Sovereign LORD, the **H** One of Israel, says,
30:29 sing a song of joy, like the songs at the **h** festivals.
31: 1 of looking to the LORD, the **H** One of Israel.
37:23 proud condescension? / It was the **H** One of Israel!
40:25 compare me? Who is my equal?" asks the **H** One.
41:14 your Redeemer. I am the **H** One of Israel.'
41:16 You will glory in the **H** One of Israel.
41:20 it is the LORD, the **H** One of Israel, who did it.
43: 3 your God, the **H** One of Israel, your Savior.
43:14 LORD your Redeemer, the **H** One of Israel, says:
43:15 your **H** One, Israel's Creator and King.
45:11 the LORD, the Creator and **H** One of Israel, says:
47: 4 is the LORD Almighty, is the **H** One of Israel.
48: 2 even though you call yourself the **h** city and talk
48:17 your Redeemer, the **H** One of Israel, says:
49: 7 The LORD, the Redeemer and **H** One of Israel,
49: 7 the **H** One of Israel, chooses you."
52: 1 O **h** city of Jerusalem, for unclean and godless
52:10 The LORD will demonstrate his **h** power before
52:11 You are the LORD's **h** people. Purify yourselves,
54: 5 He is your Redeemer, the **H** One of Israel, the God
55: 5 the LORD your God, the **H** One of Israel,
56: 4 this to the eunuchs who keep my Sabbath days **h**,
56: 7 I will bring them also to my **h** mountain of
57:13 will possess the land and inherit my **h** mountain.
57:15 one who inhabits eternity, the **H** One, says this:
57:15 and **h** place with those whose spirits are contrite
58:13 "Keep the Sabbath day **h**. Don't pursue your own
58:13 and speak of it with delight as the LORD's **h** day.
60: 9 the **H** One of Israel, for he will fill you with
60:14 of the LORD, and Zion of the **H** One of Israel.
62:12 They will be called the **H** People and the People
63:10 they rebelled against him and grieved his **H** Spirit.
63:11 Where is the one who sent his **H** Spirit to be
63:15 look down from heaven and see us from your **h**,
63:18 How briefly your **h** people possessed the **h**
64:10 Your **h** cities are destroyed; even Jerusalem is a
64:11 The **h**, beautiful Temple where our ancestors
65:25 one will be hurt or destroyed on my **h** mountain.
66:20 They will bring them to my **h** mountain in
Jer 2: 3 In those days Israel was **h** to the LORD, the first
17:22 do your work on the Sabbath, but make it a **h** day.
17:24 or work on the Sabbath day, and if you keep it **h**,
17:27 not listen to me and refuse to keep the Sabbath **h**,
23: 9 because of the **h** words the LORD has spoken
25:30 his own land from his **h** dwelling in heaven.
31:23 bless you—O righteous home, O **h** mountain!'
31:40 as far as the Horse Gate—will be **h** to the LORD.
50:29 for she has defied the LORD, the **H** One of Israel.
51: 5 was filled with sin against the **H** One of Israel."
La 2: 6 The LORD has blotted out all memory of the **h**
Eze 20:12 that I, the LORD, had set them apart to be **h**,
20:20 and keep my Sabbath days **h**, for they are a sign to
20:39 to me. Such desecration of my **h** name must stop!
20:40 For on my **h** mountain, says the Sovereign
22: 8 Inside your walls you despise my **h** things
22:26 have violated my laws and defiled my **h** things.
22:26 To them there is no difference between what is **h**
22:26 so that my **h** name is greatly dishonored among
28:14 You had access to the **h** mountain of God
34:26 and their homes around my **h** hill to be a blessing.
36:20 the nations, they brought dishonor to my **h** name.
36:21 Then I was concerned for my **h** name, which had
36:22 I am doing it to protect my **h** name, which you
36:23 I will show how **h** my great name is—the name
37:28 have set Israel apart for myself to be **h**."
39: 7 I will make known my **h** name among my people
39: 7 know that I am the LORD, the **H** One of Israel.
39:25 on Israel, for I am jealous for my **h** reputation!
41: 1 After that, the man brought me into the **H** Place,
41: 2 The **H** Place itself was 70 feet long and 35 feet
41: 3 went into the inner room at the end of the **H** Place.
41: 4 "This," he told me, "is the Most **H** Place."
41:15 The **H** Place, the Most **H** Place, and the foyer of
41:17 The space above the door leading into the Most **H**
41:20 the walls, including the outer wall of the **H** Place.
41:21 square columns at the entrance to the **H** Place,
41:21 and the ones at the entrance of the Most **H** Place
41:23 Both the **H** Place and the Most **H** Place had double doorways,
41:25 The doors leading into the **H** Place were decorated
42:13 the Temple from the north and south are **h**.
42:13 to the LORD will eat the most **h** offerings.
42:13 and guilt offerings because these rooms are **h**.
42:14 When the priests leave the **H** Place, they must not
42:14 while ministering because these clothes are **h**.
42:20 it to separate the **h** places from the common.
43: 7 and their kings will not defile my **h** name any
43: 8 They defiled my **h** name by such wickedness,
43:12 entire top of the hill where the Temple is built is **h**.
43:26 for the altar, thus setting it apart for **h** use.
44:13 not touch any of my **h** things or the **h** offerings,
44:23 teach my people the difference between what is **h**
44:24 see to it that the Sabbath is set apart as a **h** day.
45: 1 a section of it for the LORD as his **h** portion.
45: 1 6-2/3 miles wide. The entire area will be **h** ground.
45: 3 Within it the sanctuary of the Most **H** Place will be
45: 4 This area will be a **h** land, set aside for the priests
48:14 for it belongs to the LORD; it is set apart as **h**.
Da 4: 8 my god, and the spirit of the **h** gods is in him.)
4: 9 I know that the spirit of the **h** gods is in you
4:13 I saw a messenger, a **h** one, coming down from
4:17 by the messengers; it is commanded by the **h** ones.
4:18 because the spirit of the **h** gods is in you.' "
4:23 a **h** one, coming down from heaven and saying,
5:11 who has within him the spirit of the **h** gods.
7:18 the **h** people of the Most High will be given the
7:21 this horn was waging war against the **h** people
7:22 and judged in favor of the **h** people of the Most
7:22 Then the time arrived for the **h** people to take over
7:25 and wear down the **h** people of the Most High.
7:27 will be given to the **h** people of the Most High.
8:13 Then I heard two of the **h** ones talking to each
8:24 powerful leaders and devastate the **h** people.
9:16 from your city of Jerusalem, your **h** mountain.
9:20 LORD my God for Jerusalem, his **h** mountain.
9:24 your people and your **h** city to put down rebellion,
9:24 prophetic vision, and to anoint the Most **H** Place.
11:28 set himself against the people of the **h** covenant,
11:30 vent his anger against the people of the **h** covenant
11:45 He will halt between the glorious **h** mountain
12: 7 When the shattering of the **h** people has finally
Hos 11: 9 I am the **H** One living among you, and I will not
11:12 still walks with God and is faithful to the **H** One.
Joel 2: 1 Sound the alarm on my **h** mountain! Let everyone
3:17 LORD your God, live in Zion, my **h** mountain.
3:17 Jerusalem will be **h** forever, and foreign armies
Am 2: 7 with the same woman, corrupting my **h** name.
Ob 1:16 Just as you swallowed up my people on my **h**
1:17 a refuge for those who escape; it will be a **h** place.
Jnh 2: 4 How will I ever again see your **h** Temple?'
2: 7 And my earnest prayer went out to you in your **h**
Mic 1: 2 against you; the Lord speaks from his **h** Temple.
Hab 1:12 O LORD my God, my **H** One, you who are

2:20 But the LORD is in his **h** Temple. Let all the
3:3 I see God, the **H** One, moving across the deserts
Zep 3:11 There will be no pride on my **h** mountain.
Hag 2:12 If one of you is carrying a **h** sacrifice in his robes
2:12 or any other kind of food, will it also become **h**?"
Zec 2:12 will be the LORD's inheritance in the **h** land,
2:13 for he is springing into action from his **h**
7:6 And even now in your **h** festivals, you don't think
8:3 LORD Almighty will be called the **H** Mountain.
14:5 my God will come, and all his **h** ones with him.
14:20 SET APART AS H TO THE LORD.
14:21 and Judah will be set apart as **h** to the LORD
Mt 1:18 still a virgin, she became pregnant by the **H** Spirit.
1:20 within her has been conceived by the **H** Spirit.
3:11 He will baptize you with the **H** Spirit and with fire.
4:1 by the **H** Spirit to be tempted there by the Devil.
7:6 "Don't give what is **h** to unholy people.
12:31 except blasphemy against the **H** Spirit, which can
12:32 but blasphemy against the **H** Spirit will never be
22:43 speaking under the inspiration of the **H** Spirit,
24:15 that causes desecration standing in the **h** place"—
27:53 left the cemetery, went into the **h** city of Jerusalem,
28:19 name of the Father and the Son and the **H** Spirit.
Mk 1:8 but he will baptize you with the **H** Spirit!"
1:10 and the **H** Spirit descending like a dove on him.
1:12 Immediately the **H** Spirit compelled Jesus to go
1:24 I know who you are—the **H** One sent from God!"
3:29 but anyone who blasphemes against the **H** Spirit
6:20 knowing that he was a good and **h** man,
8:38 in the glory of my Father with the **h** angels."
12:36 speaking under the inspiration of the **H** Spirit,
13:11 it is not you who will be speaking, but the **H** Spirit.
Lk 1:15 hard liquor, and he will be filled with the **H** Spirit,
1:35 angel replied, "The **H** Spirit will come upon you,
1:35 So the baby born to you will be **h**, and he will be
1:41 and Elizabeth was filled with the **H** Spirit.
1:49 For he, the Mighty One, is **h**, / and he has done
1:67 was filled with the **H** Spirit and gave this
1:70 as he promised / through his **h** prophets long ago.
2:25 He was filled with the **H** Spirit, and he eagerly
2:26 The **H** Spirit had revealed to him that he would not
3:16 He will baptize you with the **H** Spirit and with fire.
3:22 and the **H** Spirit descended on him in the form of a
4:1 Then Jesus, full of the **H** Spirit, left the Jordan
4:14 to Galilee, filled with the **H** Spirit's power.
4:34 I know who you are—the **H** One sent from God."
9:26 and in the glory of the Father and the **h** angels.
10:21 Then Jesus was filled with the joy of the **H** Spirit
11:13 Father give the **H** Spirit to those who ask him."
12:10 but anyone who speaks blasphemies against the **H**
12:12 for the **H** Spirit will teach you what needs to be
24:49 "And now I will send the **H** Spirit, just as my
24:49 But stay here in the city until the **H** Spirit comes
Jn 1:32 "I saw the **H** Spirit descending like a dove from
1:33 'When you see the **H** Spirit descending and resting
1:33 He is the one who baptizes with the **H** Spirit.'
3:6 but the **H** Spirit gives new life from heaven.
5:1 returned to Jerusalem for one of the Jewish **h** days.
6:69 and we know you are the **H** One of God."
10:36 why do you call it blasphemy when the **H** One
14:17 He is the **H** Spirit, who leads into all truth.
14:26 and by the Counselor I mean the **H** Spirit—he will
17:11 **H** Father, keep them and care for them—all those
17:17 and **h** by teaching them your words of truth.
20:22 on them and said to them, "Receive the **H** Spirit.
Ac 1:2 apostles further instructions from the **H** Spirit.
1:5 a few days you will be baptized with the **H** Spirit."
1:8 But when the **H** Spirit has come upon you,
1:16 This was predicted long ago by the **H** Spirit,
2:4 And everyone present was filled with the **H** Spirit
2:4 as the **H** Spirit gave them this ability.
2:27 the dead / or allow your **H** One to rot in the grave.
2:33 gave him the **H** Spirit to pour out upon us, just as
2:38 Then you will receive the gift of the **H** Spirit.
3:14 You rejected this **h**, righteous one, and instead
4:8 Then Peter, filled with the **H** Spirit, said to them,
4:25 you spoke long ago by the **H** Spirit through our
4:27 against Jesus, your **h** servant, whom you anointed.
4:30 and wonders be done through the name of your **h**
4:31 and they were all filled with the **H** Spirit.
5:3 You lied to the **H** Spirit, and you kept some of the
5:32 are witnesses of these things and so is the **H** Spirit,
6:3 and are full of the **H** Spirit and wisdom.
6:5 Stephen (a man full of faith and the **H** Spirit),
7:33 off your sandals, for you are standing on **h** ground.
7:51 to the truth. Must you forever resist the **H** Spirit?
7:55 But Stephen, full of the **H** Spirit, gazed steadily
8:15 for these new Christians to receive the **H** Spirit.
8:16 The **H** Spirit had not yet come upon any of them,
8:17 these believers, and they received the **H** Spirit.
8:18 When Simon saw that the **H** Spirit was given when
8:19 hands on people, they will receive the **H** Spirit!"
8:29 The **H** Spirit said to Philip, "Go over and walk
9:17 your sight back and be filled with the **H** Spirit."
9:31 fear of the Lord and in the comfort of the **H** Spirit.
10:19 puzzling over the vision, the **H** Spirit said to him,
10:22 A **h** angel instructed him to send for you so you
10:38 God anointed Jesus of Nazareth with the **H** Spirit
10:44 the **H** Spirit fell upon all who had heard the
10:45 **H** Spirit had been poured out upon the Gentiles,
10:47 now that they have received the **H** Spirit just as we
11:12 The **H** Spirit told me to go with them and not to
11:15 as I was getting started, the **H** Spirit fell on them,
11:16 but you will be baptized with the **H** Spirit.'
11:24 a good man, full of the **H** Spirit and strong in faith.
13:2 worshiping the Lord and fasting, the **H** Spirit said,
13:4 Sent out by the **H** Spirit, Saul and Barnabas went
13:9 also known as Paul, filled with the **H** Spirit,
13:35 'You will not allow your **H** One to rot in the
13:52 were filled with joy and with the **H** Spirit.
15:8 he accepts Gentiles by giving them the **H** Spirit,
15:28 "For it seemed good to the **H** Spirit and to us to
16:6 because the **H** Spirit had told them not to go into
19:2 "Did you receive the **H** Spirit when you
19:2 We haven't even heard that there is a **H** Spirit."
19:6 the **H** Spirit came on them, and they spoke in other
19:21 Afterward Paul felt impelled by the **H** Spirit to go
20:22 drawn there irresistibly by the **H** Spirit,
20:23 except that the **H** Spirit has told me in city after
20:28 over whom the **H** Spirit has appointed you as
21:4 These disciples prophesied through the **H** Spirit
21:11 Then he said, "The **H** Spirit declares, 'So shall the
28:25 "The **H** Spirit was right when he said to our
Ro 1:2 by God through his prophets in the **h** Scriptures.
1:4 raised him from the dead by means of the **H** Spirit.
5:5 because he has given us the **H** Spirit to fill our
6:19 slaves of righteousness so that you will become **h**.
7:12 But still, the law itself is **h** and right and good.
8:5 but those who are controlled by the **H** Spirit think
8:6 But if the **H** Spirit controls your mind, there is life
8:13 But if through the power of the **H** Spirit you turn
8:16 For his **H** Spirit speaks to us deep in our hearts
8:23 although we have the **H** Spirit within us as a
8:26 And the **H** Spirit helps us in our distress. For we
8:26 But the **H** Spirit prays for us with groanings that
9:1 and the **H** Spirit confirm that what I am saying is
11:16 since Abraham and the other patriarchs were **h**,
their children will also be **h**.
11:16 For if the roots of the tree are **h**, the branches will
12:1 Let them be a living and **h** sacrifice—the kind he
14:5 some think one day is more **h** than another day,
14:17 life of goodness and peace and joy in the **H** Spirit.
15:13 with hope through the power of the **H** Spirit.
15:16 might be pure and pleasing to him by the **H** Spirit.
15:30 of your love for me, given to you by the **H** Spirit.
1Co 1:2 you who have been called by God to be his own **h**
1:2 He made you **h** by means of Christ Jesus, just as he
1:30 He made us pure and **h**, and he gave himself to
2:4 but the **H** Spirit was powerful among you.
3:17 For God's temple is **h**, and you Christians are that
6:19 know that your body is the temple of the **H** Spirit,
12:1 I will write about the special abilities the **H** Spirit
12:3 to say, "Jesus is Lord," except by the **H** Spirit.
12:4 but it is the same **H** Spirit who is the source of
12:11 and only **H** Spirit who distributes these gifts.
2Co 1:22 **H** Spirit in our hearts as the first installment of
3:6 in death; in the new way, the **H** Spirit gives life.
3:8 Shouldn't we expect far greater glory when the **H**
5:5 and as a guarantee he has given us his **H** Spirit.
6:6 our sincere love, and the power of the **H** Spirit.
13:13 and the fellowship of the **H** Spirit be with you all.
Gal 3:2 Did you receive the **H** Spirit by keeping the law?
3:2 for the **H** Spirit came upon you only after you
3:5 does God give you the **H** Spirit and work miracles
3:14 and we Christians receive the promised **H** Spirit
4:29 And we who are born of the **H** Spirit are
5:16 to live according to your new life in the **H** Spirit.
5:17 which is just opposite from what the **H** Spirit
5:18 But when you are directed by the **H** Spirit, you are
5:22 But when the **H** Spirit controls our lives, he will
5:25 If we are living now by the **H** Spirit, let us follow
the **H** Spirit's leading in every part of
Eph 1:1 It is written to God's **h** people in Ephesus, who are
1:4 God loved us and chose us in Christ to be **h**
1:13 he identified you as his own by giving you the **H**
2:18 may come to the Father through the same **H** Spirit
2:19 You are citizens along with all of God's **h** people.
2:21 joined together, becoming a **h** temple for the Lord.
3:5 but now he has revealed it by the **H** Spirit to his **h**
apostles
3:16 you mighty inner strength through his **H** Spirit.
4:3 Always keep yourselves united in the **H** Spirit,
4:24 created in God's likeness—righteous, **h**, and true.
4:30 And do not bring sorrow to God's **H** Spirit by the
5:18 Instead, let the **H** Spirit fill and control you.
5:26 to make her **h** and clean, washed by baptism
5:27 Instead, she will be **h** and without fault.
6:18 and on every occasion in the power of the **H** Spirit.
Col 1:2 It is written to God's **h** people in the city of
1:8 love for others that the **H** Spirit has given you.
1:12 the inheritance that belongs to God's **h** people,
1:22 and you are **h** and blameless as you stand before
1:26 but now it has been revealed to his own **h** people.
2:16 or for not celebrating certain **h** days or new-moon
3:12 Since God chose you to be the **h** people whom he
1Th 1:5 for the **H** Spirit gave you full assurance that what
1:6 So you received the message with joy from the **H**
3:13 and **h** when you stand before God our Father on
4:3 God wants you to be **h**, so you should keep clear of
4:7 God has called us to be **h**, not to live impure lives.
4:8 but is rejecting God, who gives his **H** Spirit to you.
5:19 Do not stifle the **H** Spirit.
5:23 Now may the God of peace make you **h** in every
2Th 1:10 to receive glory and praise from his **h** people.
2:13 that came through the Spirit who makes you **h**
1Ti 1:9 who consider nothing sacred and defile what is **h**,
2:8 I want men to pray with **h** hands lifted up to God,
4:1 Now the **H** Spirit tells us clearly that in the last
4:5 For we know it is made **h** by the word of God
5:21 and the **h** angels to obey these instructions without
2Ti 1:9 is God who saved us and chose us to live a **h** life.
1:14 With the help of the **H** Spirit who lives within us,
3:15 You have been taught the **h** Scriptures from
Tit 3:5 and gave us a new life through the **H** Spirit.
Heb 2:4 and by giving gifts of the **H** Spirit whenever he
2:11 and the ones he makes **h** have the same Father.
3:7 That is why the **H** Spirit says, / "Today you must
6:4 good things of heaven and shared in the **H** Spirit,
7:26 high priest we need because he is **h** and blameless,
9:2 a table, and loaves of **h** bread on the table. This
was called the **H** Place.
9:3 was the second room called the Most **H** Place.
9:7 But only the high priest goes into the Most **H**
9:8 By these regulations the **H** Spirit revealed that the
9:8 **H** Place was not open to the people as long as the
9:12 Once for all time he took blood into that Most **H**
9:25 like the earthly high priest who enters the Most **H**
10:10 And what God wants is for us to be made **h** by the
10:14 perfected forever all those whom he is making **h**.
10:15 And the **H** Spirit also testifies that this is so.
10:19 we can boldly enter heaven's Most **H** Place
10:29 and enraged the **H** Spirit who brings God's mercy
12:14 with everyone, and seek to live a clean and **h** life,
12:14 for those who are not **h** will not see the Lord.
12:28 and please God by worshiping him with **h** fear
13:11 of animals into the **H** Place as a sacrifice for sin,
13:12 to make his people **h** by shedding his own blood.
Jas 4:5 Scriptures mean when they say that the **H** Spirit,
1Pe 1:2 chose you long ago, and the Spirit has made you **h**.
1:12 you in the power of the **H** Spirit sent from heaven.
1:15 But now you must be **h** in everything you do,
1:15 as God—who chose you to be his children—is **h**.
1:16 has said, "You must be **h** because I am **h**."
2:5 What's more, you are God's **h** priests, who offer
2:9 God's **h** nation, his very own possession.
3:5 That is the way the **h** women of old made
2Pe 1:18 when we were there with him on the **h** mountain.
1:21 It was the **H** Spirit who moved the prophets to
2:21 then reject the **h** commandments that were given to
3:2 and understand what the **h** prophets said long ago
3:11 what **h**, godly lives you should be living!
1Jn 2:20 not like that, for the **H** Spirit has come upon you,
2:27 But you have received the **H** Spirit, and he lives
3:24 he lives in us because the **H** Spirit lives in us.
Jude 1:3 unchanging truth once for all time to his **h** people.
1:14 the Lord is coming / with thousands of his **h** ones.
1:20 build your lives on the foundation of your **h** faith.
1:20 And continue to pray as you are directed by the **H**
Rev 3:7 This is the message from the one who is **h**
4:8 "**H**, **h**, **h** is the Lord God Almighty—
6:10 the Lord and said, "O Sovereign Lord, **h** and true,
11:2 They will trample the **h** city for 42 months.
11:18 You will reward your prophets and your **h** people,
13:7 was allowed to wage war against God's **h** people
14:10 and burning sulfur in the presence of the **h** angels
14:12 Let this encourage God's **h** people to endure
15:4 For you alone are **h**. / All nations will come
16:5 O **H** One, who is and who always was.
16:6 For your **h** people and your prophets have been
17:6 drunk with the blood of God's **h** people who were
18:20 O **h** people of God and apostles and prophets!
20:6 and **h** are those who share in the first resurrection.
21:2 And I saw the **h** city, the new Jerusalem,
21:10 and he showed me the **h** city, Jerusalem,
22:11 and the one who is **h**, continue in holiness.
22:19 and in the **h** city that are described in this book.

HOLYDAY [KJV] See CELEBRATION, HOLY DAYS

HOME (485) [HOMELAND, HOMELESS, HOMELESSNESS, HOMEOWNER, HOMES, HOMETOWN]

Ge 14:11 and Gomorrah and began their long journey **h**,
19:2 he said, "come to my **h** to wash your feet,
19:3 But Lot insisted, so at last they went **h** with him.
20:13 God sent me to travel far from my father's **h**,
21:32 and they returned **h** to the land of the Philistines.
22:19 young men and traveled **h** again to Beersheba,
24:5 find a young woman who will travel so far from **h**?
24:28 The young woman ran **h** to tell her family about all
24:32 So the man went **h** with Laban, and Laban
24:38 relatives here in this far-off land, to his father's **h**.
24:62 Meanwhile, Isaac, whose **h** was in the Negev,
25:27 was the kind of person who liked to stay at **h**.
25:28 because of the wild game he brought **h**,
25:29 Esau arrived **h** exhausted and hungry from a hunt.
26:31 Then Isaac sent them **h** again in peace.
29:13 Laban then brought him **h**, and Jacob told him his
30:16 as Jacob was coming **h** from the fields,
30:25 Jacob said to Laban, "I want to go back **h**.
31:30 and you long intensely for your childhood **h**,
31:55 and blessed them. Then he returned **h**.
32:10 When I left **h**, I owned nothing except a walking
35:27 So Jacob came **h** to his father Isaac in Mamre,
37:14 and Joseph traveled to Shechem from his **h** in the
38:1 this time, Judah left **h** and moved to Adullam,
38:11 again at that time but to return to her parents' **h**.
38:11 his two brothers.) So Tamar went **h** to her parents.
38:19 Afterward she went **h**, took off her veil, and put on
39:2 and blessed him greatly as he served in the **h** of his
39:16 with her, and when her husband came **h** that night,
42:19 The rest of you may go on **h** with grain for your
42:26 up their donkeys with the grain and started for **h**.
42:33 and take grain for your families and go on **h**.
43:5 don't let Benjamin go, we may as well stay at **h**.
43:21 as we were returning **h**, we stopped for the night
44:14 Joseph was still at **h** when Judah and his brothers
44:17 The rest of you may go **h** to your father."

Ex 2: 8 So the girl rushed **h** and called the baby's mother.
2: 9 "Take this child **h** and nurse him for me,"
2: 9 So the baby's mother took her baby **h** and nursed
2: 20 leave him there? Go and invite him **h** for a meal!"
4: 18 Then Moses went back **h** and talked it over with
8: 3 Every **h** in Egypt will be filled with them.
8: 24 flies in Pharaoh's palace and in every **h** in Egypt.
12: 23 the doorframe, the LORD will pass over your **h**.
15: 17 the place you have made as your **h**, O LORD,
18: 23 and all these people will go **h** in peace."
Lev 22: 10 even if the person lives in a priest's **h** or is one of
22: 13 and she returns to live in her father's **h**,
Nu 22: 13 got up and told Balak's officials, "Go on **h**!
22: 34 I will go back **h** if you are against my going."
24: 11 Now get out of here! Go back **h**! I had planned to
30: 3 under oath while she is still living at her father's **h**,
30: 10 and living in her husband's **h** when she makes a
30: 16 a father and a young daughter who still lives at **h**.
Dt 6: 7 Talk about them when you are at **h** and when you
7: 26 Do not bring any detestable objects into your **h**,
11: 19 Talk about them when you are at **h** and when you
12: 17 "But your offerings must not be eaten at **h**—
12: 21 his name to be honored is a long way from your **h**.
12: 21 and you may eat the meat at your **h** as I have
14: 24 to be honored might be a long way from your **h**.
15: 22 Instead, use it for food for your family at **h**.
20: 5 a new house but not yet dedicated it? If so, go **h**!
20: 6 If so, go **h**! You might die in battle, and someone
20: 7 Well, go **h** and get married! You might die in the
20: 8 If you are, go **h** before you frighten anyone else.'
21: 12 If this happens, you may take her to your **h**,
21: 13 Then she must remain in your **h** for a full month,
22: 21 must take the girl to the door of her father's **h**,
22: 21 being promiscuous while living in her parents' **h**.
24: 5 He must be free to be at **h** for one year,
33: 18 May the people of Issachar prosper at **h** in their
Jos 20: 6 the one found innocent is free to return **h**."
22: 4 So go **h** now to the land Moses, the servant of the
22: 6 So Joshua blessed them and sent them **h**.
22: 8 "Share with your relatives back **h** the great wealth
Jdg 3: 18 Ehud sent **h** those who had carried the tax money.
5: 16 Why did you sit at **h** among the sheepfolds—
5: 17 And Dan, why did he stay **h**? / Asher sat unmoved
6: 19 Gideon hurried **h**. He cooked a young goat,
7: 3 and go **h**.' " Twenty-two thousand of them went **h**,
7: 7 victory over the Midianites. Send all the others **h**."
7: 8 rams' horns of the other warriors and sent them **h**.
8: 29 Then Gideon son of Joash returned **h**.
9: 5 He took the soldiers to his father's **h** at Ophrah,
11: 34 When Jephthah returned **h** to Mizpah,
11: 39 When she returned **h**, her father kept his vow,
14: 2 When he returned **h**, he told his father and mother,
14: 19 and he went back **h** to live with his father
16: 31 They took him back **h** and buried him between
18: 2 they came to Micah's **h** and spent the night there.
18: 22 tribe of Dan were quite a distance from Micah's **h**,
18: 26 for him to attack, he turned around and went **h**.
19: 1 One day he brought **h** a woman from Bethlehem in
19: 2 and returned to her father's **h** in Bethlehem.
19: 16 That evening an old man came **h** from his work in
19: 18 "We are on our way **h** to a remote area in the hill
19: 21 So he took them **h** with him and fed their donkeys.
19: 28 So he put her body on his donkey and took her **h**.
19: 29 When he got **h**, he took a knife and cut his
20: 8 and replied, "Not one of us will return **h**.
21: 21 and each of you can take one of them **h** to be your
Ru 1: 21 but the LORD has brought me **h** empty.
3: 1 it's time that I found a permanent **h** for you,
4: 11 woman who is now coming into your **h** like Rachel
4: 13 Boaz married Ruth and took her **h** to live with him.
1Sa 1: 19 They returned **h** to Ramah. When Elkanah
1: 23 So she stayed **h** and nursed the baby.
2: 11 and Hannah returned **h** to Ramah without Samuel.
2: 20 Before they returned **h**, Eli would bless Elkanah
7: 1 They took it to the hillside **h** of Abinadab
7: 17 Then he would return to his **h** at Ramah, and he
8: 22 Then Samuel agreed and sent the people **h**.
9: 5 of Zuph, and Saul said to his servant, "Let's go **h**.
10: 25 the LORD. Then Samuel sent the people **h** again.
10: 26 When Saul returned to his **h** at Gibeah, a band of
13: 2 the army of Israel and sent the rest of the men **h**.
14: 46 the Philistines, and the Philistines returned **h**.
15: 34 Then Samuel went **h** to Ramah, and Saul returned
18: 2 him at the palace and wouldn't let him return **h**.
18: 6 was returning **h** after David had killed Goliath.
19: 9 But one day as Saul was sitting at **h**,
20: 6 tell him I asked permission to go **h** to Bethlehem
23: 18 Then Jonathan returned **h**, while David stayed at
23: 24 So the men of Ziph returned **h** ahead of Saul.
24: 22 So David promised, and Saul went **h**. But David
25: 1 his funeral. They buried him near his **h** at Ramah.
25: 35 accepted her gifts and told her, "Return **h** in peace.
25: 36 When Abigail arrived **h**, she found that Nabal had
26: 19 For you have driven me from my **h**, so I can no
26: 21 Come back **h**, my son, and I will no longer try to
26: 25 Then David went away, and Saul returned **h**.
27: 9 and clothing before returning **h** to see King
28: 8 Then he went to the woman's **h** at night,
30: 1 and his men arrived **h** at their town of Ziklag,
2Sa 2: 30 Meanwhile, Joab and his men also returned **h**.
3: 16 Then Abner told him, "Go back **h**!" So Palti
4: 5 went to Ishbosheth's **h** around noon as he was
5: 9 So David made the fortress his **h**, and he called it
6: 2 He led them to Baalah of Judah to bring **h** the Ark
6: 3 and brought it from the hillside **h** of Abinadab.
6: 10 He took it instead to the **h** of Obed-edom of Gath.
6: 12 "The LORD has blessed Obed-edom's **h**
6: 19 and a cake of raisins. Then everyone went **h**.
6: 20 When David returned **h** to bless his family,
7: 6 My **h** has always been a tent, moving from one
9: 4 Ziba told him, "at the **h** of Makir son of Ammiel."
9: 5 sent for him and brought him from Makir's **h**.
11: 4 having her menstrual period.) Then she returned **h**.
11: 8 Then he told Uriah, "Go on **h** and relax."
11: 9 But Uriah wouldn't go **h**. He stayed that night at
11: 10 Why didn't you go **h** last night after being away
11: 11 How could I go **h** to wine and dine and sleep with
11: 13 then he couldn't get Uriah to go **h** to his wife.
12: 4 One day a guest arrived at the **h** of the rich man.
12: 15 After Nathan returned to his **h**, the LORD made
14: 8 "Go **h**, and I'll see to it that no one touches him."
14: 13 because you have refused to bring **h** your own
19: 39 and embraced him, Barzillai returned to his own **h**.
20: 1 Come on, you men of Israel, let's all go **h**!"
1Ki 1: 53 and Solomon dismissed him, saying, "Go on **h**."
2: 26 the priest, "Go back to your **h** in Anathoth.
2: 34 and Joab was buried at his **h** in the wilderness.
4: 25 each family had its own **h** and garden.
5: 14 be one month in Lebanon and two months at **h**.
8: 66 the festival was over, Solomon sent the people **h**.
11: 18 who gave them a **h**, food, and some land.
11: 22 have we disappointed you that you want to go **h**?"
11: 22 he replied. "But even so, I must return **h**."
12: 16 Let's go **h**, Israel! Look out for your own house,
12: 16 O David!" So the people of Israel returned **h**.
12: 24 Go back **h**, for what has happened is my doing!' "
12: 24 obeyed the message of the LORD and went **h**,
13: 10 So he left Bethel and went **h** another way.
13: 11 and his sons came **h** and told him what the man of
13: 15 of God, "Come **h** with me and eat some food."
13: 18 'Bring him **h** with you, and give him food to eat
13: 19 and drank some water at the prophet's **h**.
14: 4 So Jeroboam's wife went to Ahijah's **h** at Shiloh.
14: 12 "Go on **h**, and when you enter the city, the child
14: 17 died just as she walked through the door of her **h**.
16: 9 in Tirzah, Elah was getting drunk at the **h** of Arza,
17: 20 on this widow who has opened her **h** to me,
18: 44 tell him, 'Climb into your chariot and go back **h**.
19: 1 When Ahab got **h**, he told Jezebel what Elijah had
20: 43 So the king of Israel went **h** to Samaria angry
21: 4 So Ahab went **h** angry and sullen because of
22: 17 master has been killed. Send them **h** in peace.' "
22: 36 ran through his troops: "It's all over—return **h**!"
2Ki 4: 19 one of the servants, "Carry him **h** to his mother."
4: 20 So the servant took him **h**, and his mother held him
4: 30 I won't go **h** unless you go with me."
5: 17 from this place, and I will take it back **h** with me.
5: 19 in peace," Elisha said. So Naaman started **h** again.
6: 22 and drink and send them **h** again to their master."
6: 23 feast for them and then sent them **h** to their king.
14: 10 Be content with your victory and stay at **h**!
14: 12 of Israel, and its army scattered and fled for **h**.
19: 7 from Assyria telling him that he is needed at **h**.
19: 36 He went **h** to his capital of Nineveh and stayed
1Ch 11: 7 David made the fortress his **h**, and that is why it is
13: 13 He took it instead to the **h** of Obed-edom of Gath.
15: 25 and the generals of the army went to the **h** of
16: 43 and David returned **h** to bless his family.
17: 5 My **h** has always been a tent, moving from one
2Ch 2: 6 But who can really build him a worthy **h**?
7: 10 end of the celebration, Solomon sent the people **h**.
7: 16 this Temple and set it apart to be my **h** forever.
10: 16 Let's go **h**, Israel! Look out for your own house, O
David!" So all Israel returned **h**.
11: 4 Go back **h**, for what has happened is my doing!' "
18: 16 master has been killed. Send them **h** in peace.' "
19: 1 When King Jehoshaphat of Judah arrived safely **h**
23: 8 Jehoiada the priest did not let anyone go **h** after
25: 10 with Judah, and they returned **h** in a great rage.
25: 13 the hired troops that Amaziah had sent **h** raided
25: 19 your conquest of Edom, but my advice is to stay **h**.
25: 22 of Israel, and its army scattered and fled for **h**.
28: 9 in Samaria when the army of Israel returned **h**.
32: 21 So Sennacherib returned **h** in disgrace to his own
36: 18 The king also took **h** to Babylon all the utensils,
Ne 3: 20 to the door of the **h** of Eliashib the high priest.
6: 10 grandson of Mehetabel, who was confined to his **h**.
Est 1: 22 that every man should be the ruler of his **h**.
2: 20 just as she did when she was living in his **h**.
5: 10 However, he restrained himself and went on **h**.
6: 12 but Haman hurried **h** dejected and completely
Job 1: 10 and his **h** and his property from harm.
1: 14 a messenger arrived at Job's **h** with this news:
1: 18 daughters were feasting in their oldest brother's **h**.
5: 24 You will know that your **h** is kept safe. When you
7: 10 They are gone forever from their **h**—never to be
8: 6 he will rise up and restore your happy **h**.
8: 15 They cling to their **h** for security, but it won't last.
18: 15 The **h** of the wicked will disappear beneath a fiery
18: 19 nor any survivor in their **h** country.
18: 21 They will say, 'This was the **h** of a wicked person,
24: 8 and they huddle against the rocks for want of a **h**.
29: 4 early years, the friendship of God was felt in my **h**.
38: 20 Can you take it to its **h**? Do you know how to get
38: 24 origin of light? Where is the **h** of the east wind?
39: 6 placed it in the wilderness; its **h** is the wasteland.
39: 28 on the cliffs, making its **h** on a distant, rocky crag.
42: 11 former friends came and feasted with him in his **h**.
Ps 46: 4 city of our God, / the sacred **h** of the Most High.
49: 11 The grave is their eternal **h**, / where they will stay
52: 5 and for all. / He will pull you from your **h**
55: 15 them alive, / for evil makes its **h** within them.
74: 2 And remember Jerusalem, your **h** here on earth.
76: 2 Jerusalem is where he lives; / Mount Zion is his **h**.
84: 3 Even the sparrow finds a **h** there, / and the swallow
90: 1 through all the generations / you have been our **h**!
101: 2 I will lead a life of integrity / in my own **h**.
104: 3 you lay out the rafters of your **h** in the rain clouds.
104: 13 send rain on the mountains from your heavenly **h**,
105: 36 Then he killed the oldest child in each Egyptian **h**,
113: 9 He gives the barren woman a **h**, / so that she
128: 3 be like a fruitful vine, / flourishing within your **h**.
132: 3 "I will not go **h**; / I will not let myself rest.
132: 13 has chosen Jerusalem; / he has desired it as his **h**.
132: 14 "This is my **h** where I will live forever," he said.
135: 8 He destroyed the firstborn in each Egyptian **h**,
Pr 3: 33 but his blessing is on the **h** of the upright.
7: 11 was the brash, rebellious type who never stays at **h**.
7: 19 for my husband is not **h**. He's away on a long trip.
8: 34 me daily at my gates, waiting for me outside my **h**!
9: 4 "Come **h** with me," she urges the simple.
9: 16 "Come **h** with me," she urges the simple.
15: 31 you will be at **h** among the wise.
21: 9 an attic than with a contentious wife in a lovely **h**.
24: 15 Do not lie in wait like an outlaw at the **h** of the
25: 24 an attic than with a contentious wife in a lovely **h**.
27: 8 A person who strays from **h** is like a bird that
Ecc 12: 5 And as you near your everlasting **h**, the mourners
SS 3: 4 him go until I had brought him to my childhood **h**,
8: 2 I would bring you to my childhood **h**, and there
Isa 1: 21 Once the **h** of justice and righteousness, she is now
1: 26 Then Jerusalem will again be called the **H** of
15: 3 From every **h** will come the sound of weeping.
18: 2 Go **h**, swift messengers! Take a message to your
23: 1 O ships of Tarshish, returning **h** from distant lands!
23: 14 O ships of Tarshish, for your **h** port is destroyed!
24: 10 in chaos; every **h** is locked to keep out looters.
26: 20 Go **h**, my people, and lock your doors! Hide until
32: 18 My people will live in safety, quietly at **h**.
33: 5 he will make Jerusalem his **h** of justice
34: 13 become a haunt for jackals and a **h** for ostriches.
37: 7 from Assyria telling him that he is needed at **h**.
37: 37 He went **h** to his capital of Nineveh and stayed
43: 19 through the wilderness for my people to come **h**.
50: 2 why the house is silent and empty when I come **h**?
52: 8 see the LORD bringing his people **h** to Jerusalem.
52: 11 you who carry **h** the vessels of the LORD.
54: 2 your house; build an addition; spread out your **h**!
60: 4 "Look and see, for everyone is coming **h**!
60: 4 your little daughters will be carried **h**.
60: 9 reserved to bring the people of Israel **h**.
63: 15 from heaven and see us from your holy, glorious **h**.
Jer 3: 12 come **h** to me again, for I am merciful.
3: 14 "Return **h**, you wayward children,"
10: 20 My **h** is gone, and no one is left to help me rebuild
12: 15 I will bring them **h** to their own lands again,
29: 10 I have promised, and I will bring you **h** again.
29: 14 sent you and bring you **h** again to your own land."
30: 3 I will bring them **h** to this land that I gave to their
30: 10 For I will bring you **h** again from distant lands,
30: 18 When I bring you **h** again from your captivity
31: 9 their faces, and I will lead them **h** with great care.
31: 12 They will come **h** and sing songs of joy on the
31: 23 bless you—O righteous **h**, O holy mountain!'
39: 14 of Shaphan, who was to take him back to his **h**.
44: 14 fled to Egypt with dreams of returning **h** to Judah,
46: 27 For I will bring you **h** again from distant lands,
48: 38 Crying and sorrow will be in every Moabite **h**
48: 45 comes from Heshbon, King Sihon's ancestral **h**,
50: 5 the way to Jerusalem and will start back **h** again.
50: 8 land of the Babylonians. Lead my people **h** again.
50: 19 And I will bring Israel **h** again to her own land,
50: 39 It will be a **h** for the wild animals of the desert.
51: 50 far-off land, and think about your **h** in Jerusalem."
La 1: 20 streets the sword kills, and at **h** there is only death.
2: 2 Without mercy the Lord has destroyed every **h** in
Eze 8: 1 while the leaders of Judah were in my **h**,
12: 3 on your back and leave your **h** to go on a journey.
20: 41 When I bring you **h** from exile, you will be as
20: 42 Then when I have brought you **h** to the land I
28: 8 and you will die there on your island **h** in the heart
29: 13 **h** again from the nations to which they have been
34: 13 I will bring them back **h** to their own land of Israel
34: 16 strayed away, and I will bring them safely **h** again.
36: 8 and they will be coming **h** again soon!
36: 24 all the nations and bring you **h** again to your land.
37: 14 and you will live and return **h** to your own land.
37: 21 I will bring them **h** to their own land from the
37: 27 I will make my **h** among them. I will be their God,
39: 26 and treachery against me after they come **h** to live
39: 27 When I bring them **h** from the lands of their
39: 28 away to exile and responsible for bringing them **h**.
Da 2: 17 Then Daniel went **h** and told his friends Hananiah,
6: 10 he went **h** and knelt down as usual in his upstairs
11: 28 of the north will then return **h** with great riches.
11: 30 scare him off, and he will withdraw and return **h**.
Hos 9: 4 There, far from **h**, you will not be allowed to pour
11: 11 And I will bring them **h** again," says the LORD.
Joel 3: 21 will make my **h** in Jerusalem with my people."
Am 9: 6 The upper stories of the LORD's **h** are in the
Ob 1: 3 and make your **h** high in the mountains.
Jnh 4: 2 "Didn't I say before I left **h** that you would do
Mic 2: 8 ragged as men who have just come **h** from battle.
2: 10 This is no longer your land and **h**, for you have
4: 7 They are weak and far from **h**, but I will make
Zep 3: 20 I will gather you together and bring you **h** again.
Hag 1: 9 And when you brought your harvest **h**, I blew it
Zec 3: 10 each of you will invite your neighbor into your **h**
6: 10 meet them at the **h** of Josiah son of Zephaniah.
8: 8 I will bring them **h** again to live safely in
10: 9 they will survive and come **h** again to Israel.

13: 6 he will say, 'I was wounded at the **h** of friends!'
Mt 1:24 He brought Mary **h** to be his wife,
2:12 it was time to leave, they went **h** another way,
8: 8 I am not worthy to have you come into my **h**.
8:13 Then Jesus said to the Roman officer, "Go on **h**.
8:20 but I, the Son of Man, have no **h** of my own,
8:21 "Lord, first let me return **h** and bury my father."
9: 6 and said, "Stand up, take your mat, and go on **h**,
9: 7 And the man jumped up and went **h**!
9:19 and the disciples were going to the official's **h**,
9:23 When Jesus arrived at the official's **h**, he noticed
9:27 After Jesus left the girl's **h**, two blind men
10:11 and stay in his **h** until you leave for the next town.
10:12 When you are invited into someone's **h**, give it
10:13 If it turns out to be a worthy **h**, let your blessing
12:25 A city or **h** divided against itself is doomed.
12:44 So it returns and finds its former **h** empty, swept,
14:22 other side of the lake while he sent the people **h**.
15:39 Then Jesus sent the people **h**, and he got into a
25:35 I was a stranger, and you invited me into your **h**.
25:43 a stranger, and you didn't invite me into your **h**.
26: 6 Jesus was in Bethany at the **h** of Simon,
26:57 had arrested Jesus led him to the **h** of Caiaphas,
Mk 1:29 they went over to Simon and Andrew's **h**,
2:11 "Stand up, take your mat, and go on **h**,
3:21 was happening, they tried to take him **h** with them.
3:25 A **h** divided against itself is doomed.
5:19 But Jesus said, "No, go **h** to your friends, and tell
5:35 messengers arrived from Jairus' **h** with the
5:38 When they came to the **h** of the synagogue leader,
6:10 each village, be a guest in only one **h**," he said.
6:45 the lake to Bethsaida, while he sent the people **h**.
7:30 And when she arrived **h**, her little girl was lying
8: 3 And if I send them **h** without feeding them,
8: 9 that day, and he sent them **h** after they had eaten.
8:26 Jesus sent him **h**, saying, "Don't go back into the village on your way **h**."
13:34 with that of a man who left **h** to go on a trip.
14: 3 Jesus was in Bethany at the **h** of Simon,
14:53 Jesus was led to the high priest's **h** where the
Lk 1:23 term of service was over, and then he returned **h**.
1:56 three months and then went back to her own **h**.
2: 4 to go to Bethlehem in Judea, David's ancient **h**.
2:39 of the Lord, they returned **h** to Nazareth in Galilee.
2:43 celebration was over, they started **h** to Nazareth,
4:16 he came to the village of Nazareth, his boyhood **h**,
4:38 the synagogue that day, Jesus went to Simon's **h**,
5:24 and said, "Stand up, take your mat, and go on **h**,
5:25 picked up his mat, and went **h** praising God.
5:29 Soon Levi held a banquet in his **h** with Jesus as the
7: 6 "Lord, don't trouble yourself by coming to my **h**,
7:36 One of the Pharisees asked Jesus to come to his **h**
7:44 When I entered your **h**, you didn't offer me water
8:41 at Jesus' feet, begging him to come **h** with him.
8:49 a messenger arrived from Jairus' **h** with the
9: 4 you enter each village, be a guest in only one **h**.
9:58 but I, the Son of Man, have no **h** of my own,
9:59 "Lord, first let me return **h** and bury my father."
10: 5 "Whenever you enter a **h**, give it your blessing.
10: 7 enter a town, don't move around from **h** to **h**.
10:38 woman named Martha welcomed them into her **h**.
11:17 with itself is doomed. A divided **h** is also doomed.
11:25 and finds that its former **h** is all swept and clean.
11:37 one of the Pharisees invited him **h** for a meal.
14: 1 One Sabbath day Jesus was in the **h** of a leader of
15: 5 then you would joyfully carry it **h** on your
15:17 'At **h** even the hired men have food enough to
15:18 I will go **h** to my father and say, "Father, I have
15:20 "So he returned **h** to his father. And while he was
15:25 When he returned **h**, he heard music and dancing
16:27 Father Abraham, send him to my father's **h**.
18:14 not the Pharisee, returned **h** justified before God.
19: 5 For I must be a guest in your **h** today."
19: 9 "Salvation has come to this **h** today,
23:48 all that had happened, they went **h** in deep sorrow.
23:56 Then they went **h** and prepared spices
24:12 then he went **h** again, wondering what had
24:29 since it was getting late. So he went **h** with them.
Jn 4:50 Then Jesus told him, "Go back **h**. Your son will
4:50 And the man believed Jesus' word and started **h**.
7:53 Then the meeting broke up and everybody went **h**.
11:20 she went to meet him. But Mary stayed at **h**.
12: 1 Jesus arrived in Bethany, the **h** of Lazarus—
14: 2 There are many rooms in my Father's **h**, and I am
19:27 And from then on this disciple took her into his **h**.
20:10 Then they went **h**.
Ac 1:20 where it says, 'Let his **h** become desolate, with no
7:20 His parents cared for him at **h** for three months.
10:25 As Peter entered his **h**, Cornelius fell to the floor
10:28 laws for me to come into a Gentile **h** like this.
10:32 He is staying in the **h** of Simon, a leatherworker
11: 3 "You entered the **h** of Gentiles and even ate with
11:12 and we soon arrived at the **h** of the man who had
11:13 told us how an angel had appeared to him in his **h**
12:12 After a little thought, he went to the **h** of Mary,
16:15 to the Lord," she said, "come and stay at my **h**."
16:40 Paul and Silas then returned to the **h** of Lydia,
17: 5 They attacked the **h** of Jason, searching for Paul
17: 7 "And Jason has let them into his **h**. They are all
20:12 Meanwhile, the young man was taken **h** unhurt,
21: 6 Then we went aboard, and they returned **h**.
21: 8 and stayed at the **h** of Philip the Evangelist,
21:16 and they took us to the **h** of Mnason, a man
27: 2 We left on a boat whose **h** port was Adramyttium;
Ro 12:13 And get into the habit of inviting guests **h** for
16: 5 my greetings to the church that meets in their **h**.
16:23 I am his guest, and the church meets here in his **h**.
1Co 10:27 If someone who isn't a Christian asks you **h** for
11:34 eat at **h** so you won't bring judgment upon
14:35 questions to ask, let them ask their husbands at **h**,
16:19 and all the others who gather in their **h** for church
2Co 5: 1 we will have a **h** in heaven, an eternal body made
5: 6 live in these bodies we are not at **h** with the Lord.
5: 8 for then we will be at **h** with the Lord.
Eph 3:17 and more at **h** in your hearts as you trust in him.
Php 2:26 Now I am sending him **h** again, for he has been
1Ti 3: 2 He must enjoy having guests in his **h** and must be
5: 4 their first responsibility is to show godliness at **h**
2Ti 2:20 In a wealthy **h** some utensils are made of gold
Tit 1: 8 He must enjoy having guests in his **h** and must
Heb 7: 1 When Abraham was returning **h** after winning a
11: 8 Abraham obeyed when God called him to leave **h**
13:14 For this world is not our **h**; we are looking forward
1Pe 3:18 for sinners that he might bring us safely **h** to God.
4: 9 Cheerfully share your **h** with those who need a
Rev 21: 3 "Look, the **h** of God is now among his people!

HOMEBORN [KJV] See NATIVE-BORN

HOMELAND (16) [HOME]

Ge 24: 4 Go instead to my **h**, to my relatives, and find a
40:15 For I was kidnapped from my **h**, the land of the
Ru 1: 6 got ready to leave Moab to return to her **h**.
2Sa 7:10 And I have provided a permanent **h** for my people
1Ch 17: 9 And I have provided a permanent **h** for my people
Ps 45:10 I say. / Forget your people and your **h** far away.
Jer 42:18 And you will never see your **h** again.'
46:16 'Come, let's go back to our **h** where we were born.
50:12 But your **h** will be overwhelmed with shame
Eze 11:18 "When the people return to their **h**, they will
12:12 his face, and his eyes will never see his **h** again.
38:15 You will come from your **h** in the distant north
Joel 3: 6 to the Greeks, who took them far from their **h**.
Am 7:17 become captives in exile, far from their **h**."
Ob 1:20 Jerusalem exiled in the north will return to their **h**
Heb 11:16 they were looking for a better place, a heavenly **h**.

HOMELESS (6) [HOME]

Ge 4:12 From now on you will be a **h** fugitive on the earth,
Job 31:19 Whenever I saw someone who was **h** and without
Ps 107: 4 Some wandered in the desert, / lost and **h**.
Isa 16: 2 The women of Moab are left like **h** birds at the
Hos 9:17 They will be wanderers, **h** among the nations.
Lk 8:27 **H** and naked, he had lived in a cemetery for a long

HOMELESSNESS (1) [HOME]

La 3:19 of my suffering and **h** is bitter beyond words.

HOMEOWNER (3) [HOME, OWN]

Mt 24:43 A **h** who knew exactly when a burglar was coming
Mk 13:35 For you do not know when the **h** will return—
Lk 12:39 A **h** who knew exactly when a burglar was coming

HOMER (2)

Eze 45:11 The **h** will be your standard unit for measuring
45:11 and the bath will each measure one-tenth of a **h**.

HOMES (99) [HOME]

Ge 45:17 and return quickly to their **h** in Canaan.
Ex 7:19 wooden bowls and stone pots in the people's **h**."
8:21 Your **h** will be filled with them, and the ground
10: 6 and the **h** of your officials and all the houses of
12:15 you must remove every trace of yeast from your **h**.
12:19 there must be no trace of yeast in your **h**.
12:27 for he passed over the **h** of the Israelites in Egypt.
13: 7 there must be no yeast in your **h** or anywhere
35: 3 Do not even light fires in your **h** on that day."
Lev 7:26 Even in your **h**, you must never eat the blood of
Nu 24: 5 O Jacob; / how lovely are your **h**, O Israel!
24:25 Then Balaam and Balak returned to their **h**.
32:18 We will not return to our **h** until all the people of
35: 3 These towns will be their **h**, and the surrounding
Dt 8:12 and prosperous and have built fine **h** to live in,
19: 1 will displace them and settle in their towns and **h**.
Jdg 9:55 was dead, they disbanded and returned to their **h**.
21:14 Then the men of Benjamin returned to their **h**,
21:24 and families, and they returned to their own **h**.
Ru 1: 8 "Go back to your mothers' **h** instead of coming
1:12 No, my daughters, return to your parents' **h**,
2Sa 18:17 over it. And the army of Israel fled to their **h**.
19: 8 who supported Absalom had fled to their **h**.
20:22 from the attack, and they all returned to their **h**.
1Ki 20: 6 to search your palace and the **h** of your people.
1Ch 4:41 and completely destroyed the **h** of the descendants
16:43 Then all the people returned to their **h**, and David
2Ch 11:14 The Levites even abandoned their **h** and property
28:21 and from the **h** of his officials and gave them to the
31: 1 the Israelites returned to their own towns and **h**.
Ne 4:14 fight for your friends, your families, and your **h**!"
5: 3 vineyards, and **h** to get food during the famine."
5:11 olive groves, and **h** to them this very day.
5:13 may God shake you from your **h** and from your
7: 3 regular posts and some in front of their own **h**."
11: 3 live in their own **h** in the various towns of Judah,
Job 2:11 got together and traveled from their **h** to comfort
15:34 Their **h**, enriched through bribery, will be
20:19 and left them destitute. He foreclosed on their **h**.
21: 9 Their **h** are safe from every fear, and God does not
22:18 But they forgot that he had filled their **h** with good
Ps 49:16 and their **h** become ever more splendid.
69:25 May their **h** become desolate / and their tents be
78:55 by lot. / He settled the tribes of Israel into their **h**.
84:10 than live the good life in the **h** of the wicked.
104:17 their nests, / and the storks make their **h** in the firs.
109:10 may they be evicted from their ruined **h**.
Pr 21:12 knows what is going on in the **h** of the wicked;
30:26 but they make their **h** among the rocky cliffs.
Ecc 2: 4 I also tried to find meaning by building huge **h** for
Isa 5: 8 Your **h** are built on great estates so you can be
5: 9 "Many beautiful **h** will stand deserted, the owners
13:16 Their **h** will be sacked and their wives raped by the
32:13 Your joyful **h** and happy cities will be gone.
58: 7 and to welcome poor wanderers into your **h**.
65: 3 They burn incense on the rooftops of their **h**.
Jer 5:27 filled with birds, their **h** are filled with evil plots.
6:12 Their **h** will be turned over to their enemies,
9:19 our land, because our **h** have been torn down.' "
18:22 Let screaming be heard from their **h** as warriors
25:10 will fail, and all your **h** will stand silent and dark.
29: 5 "Build **h**, and plan to stay. Plant gardens, and eat
29:28 He said we should build **h** and plan to stay for
49:20 will be dragged off, and their **h** will be empty.
50:45 will be dragged off, and their **h** will be empty.
La 5: 2 been turned over to strangers, our **h** to foreigners.
Eze 7:24 the most ruthless of nations to occupy their **h**.
12:11 for they will be driven from their **h** and sent away
16:41 They will burn your **h** and punish you in front of
23:47 butcher their sons and daughters and burn their **h**.
26:12 They will destroy your lovely **h** and dump your
28:26 in Israel and build their **h** and plant their vineyards.
34:26 and their **h** around my holy hill to be a blessing.
44:30 to the priests so the LORD will bless your **h**.
45: 4 They will use it for their **h**, and my Temple will be
45: 9 out of their land! Stop expelling them from their **h**!
48:15 **h**, pasturelands, and common lands, with a city at
Hos 9: 6 your treasures of silver; brambles will fill your **h**.
Am 3:15 And I will destroy the beautiful **h** of the wealthy—
6: 8 false glory of Israel, and I hate their beautiful **h**.
6:11 **h** both great and small will be smashed to pieces.
Ob 1:13 looting their **h** and making yourselves rich at their
Mic 2: 9 You have evicted women from their **h** and stripped
4: 4 Everyone will live quietly in their own **h** in peace
6:10 The **h** of the wicked are filled with treasures
Na 2:12 your city and your **h** with captives and plunder.
Zep 1: 9 who steal and kill to fill their masters' **h** with loot.
1:13 by the enemy, whose **h** will be ransacked.
1:13 They will never have a chance to live in the new **h**
Lk 18:28 "We have left our **h** and followed you."
Ac 2:46 met in **h** for the Lord's Supper, and shared their
5:42 And every day, in the Temple and in their **h**,
20:20 telling you the truth, either publicly or in your **h**.
1Co 4:11 many beatings, and we have no **h** of our own.
9: 4 Don't we have the right to live in your **h** and share
11:22 Don't you have your own **h** for eating
1Ti 5:14 have children, and take care of their own **h**.
2Ti 3: 6 are the kind who work their way into people's **h**
Tit 2: 5 and be pure, to take care of their **h**, to do good,

HOMETOWN (14) [HOME, TOWN]

Dt 19:12 the leaders of the murderer's **h** must have the
Jdg 8:27 ephod from the gold and put it in Ophrah, his **h**.
Ru 4:10 and to inherit the family property here in his **h**.
1Sa 11: 4 Saul's **h**, and told the people about their plight,
28: 3 He was buried in Ramah, his **h**. And Saul had
2Sa 17:23 went to his **h**, set his affairs in order, and hanged
Mt 13:54 He returned to Nazareth, his **h**. When he taught
13:57 prophet is honored everywhere except in his own **h**
Mk 6: 1 and returned with his disciples to Nazareth, his **h**.
6: 4 prophet is honored everywhere except in his own **h**
Lk 4:23 'Why don't you do miracles here in your **h** like
4:24 the truth is, no prophet is accepted in his own **h**.
Jn 1:44 Philip was from Bethsaida, Andrew and Peter's **h**.
Ac 9:30 him to Caesarea and sent him on to his **h** of Tarsus.

HOMOSEXUAL (1) [HOMOSEXUALITY, HOMOSEXUALS]

Lev 20:13 "The penalty for **h** acts is death to both parties.

HOMOSEXUALITY (1) [HOMOSEXUAL]

Lev 18:22 "Do not practice **h**; it is a detestable sin.

HOMOSEXUALS (2) [HOMOSEXUAL]

1Co 6: 9 are idol worshipers, adulterers, male prostitutes, **h**,
1Ti 1:10 for **h** and slave traders, for liars and oath breakers,

HONEST (54) [HONESTLY, HONESTY]

Ge 30:33 it easy for you to see whether or not I have been **h**.
42:11 We are all brothers and **h** men, sir! We are not
42:31 But we said, 'We are **h** men, not spies.
42:33 'This is the way I will find out if you are **h** men.
42:34 Then I will know that you are **h** men and not spies.
Ex 18:21 **h** men who fear God and hate bribes.
23: 7 Never put an innocent or **h** person to death. I will
Dt 25:14 and you must use full and **h** measures.
25:15 Yes, use **h** weights and measures, so that you will
1Ki 3: 6 because he was **h** and true and faithful to you.
2Ki 12:15 because they were **h** and faithful workers.
22: 7 of the money they receive, for they are **h** people."
Ne 13:13 and it was their job to make **h** distributions to their
Job 6:25 **H** words are painful, but what do your criticisms
23: 7 Fair and **h** people can reason with him, so I would
29:14 All I did was just and **h**. Righteousness covered me
36: 4 I am telling you the **h** truth, for I am a man of
Ps 17: 1 to my prayer, / for it comes from an **h** heart.
36:10 who love you; / give justice to those with **h** hearts.

37:37 Look at those who are **h** and good, / for a
Pr 12:17 An **h** witness tells the truth; a false witness tells
17:26 for being good or to punish nobles for being **h**!
19: 1 to be poor and **h** than to be a fool and dishonest.
24:26 It is an honor to receive an **h** reply.
28: 6 It is better to be poor and **h** than rich and crooked.
28:10 their own trap, but the **h** will inherit good things.
28:18 The **h** will be rescued from harm, but those who
29:10 The bloodthirsty hate the **h**, but the upright seek out the **h**.
Isa 8: 2 son of Jeberekiah, both known as **h** men,
32: 1 king is coming! And **h** princes will rule under him.
33:15 The ones who can live here are those who are **h**
59: 4 No one cares about being fair and **h**. Their lawsuits
Jer 4: 2 and begin to live good, **h** lives and uphold justice,
5: 1 If you can find even one person who is just and **h**,
Eze 18: 8 from injustice, is **h** and fair when judging others,
45:10 You must use only **h** weights and scales, **h** dry volume measures, and **h** liquid volume measures.
Da 6: 4 He was faithful and **h** and always responsible.
Am 2: 6 They have perverted justice by selling **h** people for
5:10 How you hate **h** judges! How you despise people
Mt 22:16 this question: "Teacher, we know how **h** you are.
Mk 12:14 these men said, "we know how **h** you are.
Lk 8:15 But the good soil represents **h**,
16:10 you won't be **h** with greater responsibilities.
20:20 the leaders sent secret agents pretending to be **h**
Jn 1:47 Jesus said, "Here comes an **h** man—
Ro 12: 3 Be **h** in your estimate of yourselves,
2Co 1:12 and a clear conscience that we have been **h**
4: 2 the truth before God, and all who are **h** know that.
6: 8 or praise us. We are **h**, but they call us impostors.
Eph 4:28 Begin using your hands for **h** work, and then give
1Th 2:10 that we were pure and **h** and faultless toward all of

HONESTLY (3) [HONEST]

Pr 16:13 with righteous lips; he loves those who speak **h**.
Zec 7: 9 Judge fairly and **h**, and show mercy and kindness
2Co 6:11 Corinthian friends! We have spoken **h** with you.

HONESTY (9) [HONEST]

Ps 25:21 May integrity and **h** protect me, / for I put my hope
27:11 to live, O LORD. / Lead me along the path of **h**,
32: 2 of sin, / whose lives are lived in complete **h**!
51: 6 But you desire **h** from the heart, / so you can teach
Pr 11: 1 The LORD hates cheating, but he delights in **h**.
11: 3 Good people are guided by their **h**;
11: 5 The godly are directed by their **h**; the wicked fall
Jer 5: 3 LORD, you are searching for **h**. You struck your
Lk 3:13 "Show your **h**," he replied. "Make sure you

HONEY (62) [HONEYCOMB]

Ge 43:11 balm, **h**, spices, myrrh, pistachio nuts,
Ex 3: 8 It is a land flowing with milk and **h**—the land
3:17 a land flowing with milk and **h**." '
13: 5 your ancestors—a land flowing with milk and **h**.
16:31 like coriander seed, and it tasted like **h** cakes.
33: 3 Theirs is a land flowing with milk and **h**. But I will
Lev 2:11 or **h** may be burned as an offering to the LORD
2:12 and **h** to the offerings presented at harvesttime,
20:24 inherit their land, a land flowing with milk and **h**.
Nu 13:27 a land flowing with milk and **h**.
14: 8 It is a rich land flowing with milk and **h**, and he
16:13 a land flowing with milk and **h**, to kill us here in
16:14 and **h** or given us an inheritance of fields
Dt 6: 3 many children in the land flowing with milk and **h**,
8: 8 fig trees, pomegranates, olives, and **h**.
11: 9 their descendants—a land flowing with milk and **h**!
26: 9 and gave us this land flowing with milk and **h**!
26:15 have given us—a land flowing with milk and **h**—
27: 3 a land flowing with milk and **h**, just as the
31:20 their ancestors—a land flowing with milk and **h**.
32:13 He nourished them with **h** from the cliffs,
Jos 5: 6 sworn to give us—a land flowing with milk and **h**.
Jdg 14: 8 a swarm of bees had made some **h** in the carcass.
14: 9 He scooped some of the **h** into his hands and ate it
14: 9 But he didn't tell them he had taken the **h** from the
14:18 "What is sweeter than **h**? / What is stronger than a
1Sa 14:26 They didn't even touch the **h** because they all
14:27 a stick into a piece of honeycomb and ate the **h**.
14:29 I feel now that I have eaten this little bit of **h**.
14:43 "I tasted a little **h**," Jonathan admitted.
2Sa 17:29 **h**, butter, sheep, and cheese for David and those
1Ki 14: 3 of ten loaves of bread, some cakes, and a jar of **h**,
2Ki 18:32 and wine, bread and vineyards, olive trees and **h**—
2Ch 31: 5 of their crops and grain, new wine, olive oil, **h**,
Job 20:17 streams of olive oil or rivers of milk and **h**.
Ps 19:10 sweeter than **h**, / even **h** dripping from the comb.
81:16 I would satisfy you with wild **h** from the rock."
119:103 your words to my taste; / they are sweeter than **h**.
Pr 5: 3 The lips of an immoral woman are as sweet as **h**,
16:24 Kind words are like **h**—sweet to the soul
24:13 My child, eat **h**, for it is good, and the honeycomb
25:16 Do you like **h**? Don't eat too much of it, or it will
25:27 Just as it is not good to eat too much **h**, it is not
27: 7 **H** seems tasteless to a person who is full, but even
SS 4:11 my bride, are as sweet as **h**. Yes, **h** and cream are
5: 1 with my spices and eat my honeycomb with my **h**.
Isa 7:15 the time this child is old enough to eat curds and **h**,
7:22 and wild **h** because that is all the land will produce.
Jer 11: 5 to give you a land flowing with milk and **h**—
32:22 long before—a land flowing with milk and **h**.
41: 8 barley, oil, and **h** that they had hidden away.
Eze 3: 3 he said. And when I ate it, it tasted as sweet as **h**.
16:13 ate the finest foods—fine flour, **h**, and olive oil—
16:19 the fine flour and oil and **h** I had given you,
20: 6 a good land, a land flowing with milk and **h**,
20:15 a land flowing with milk and **h**, the most beautiful
27:17 wheat from Minnith, early figs, **h**, oil, and balm.
Mt 3: 4 a leather belt; his food was locusts and wild **h**.
Mk 1: 6 a leather belt; his food was locusts and wild **h**.
Rev 10: 9 "At first it will taste like **h**, but when you swallow

HONEYCOMB (4) [HONEY]

1Sa 14:25 even though they found **h** on the ground in the
14:27 and he dipped a stick into a piece of **h** and ate the
Pr 24:13 for it is good, and the **h** is sweet to the taste.
SS 5: 1 with my spices and eat my **h** with my honey.

HONOR (278) [HONORABLE, HONORABLY, HONORED, HONORING, HONORS]

Ge 30:20 Now he will **h** me, for I have given him six sons."
47:29 swear most solemnly that you will **h** this, my last
49: 3 You are first on the list in rank and **h**.
Ex 5: 1 wilderness to hold a religious festival in my **h**.' "
20:12 "**H** your father and mother. Then you will live a
23:14 year you must celebrate three festivals in my **h**.
Dt 5:16 " '**H** your father and mother, as the LORD your
16: 1 "In **h** of the LORD your God, always celebrate
16:10 the Festival of Harvest to **h** the LORD your God.
16:15 For seven days celebrate this festival to **h** the
26:19 Then you will receive praise, **h**, and renown.
Jos 7: 9 then what will happen to the **h** of your great
24:14 "So **h** the LORD and serve him wholeheartedly.
Jdg 4: 9 you have made this choice, you will receive no **h**.
9:16 Have you treated my father with the **h** he deserves?
13:17 For when all this comes true, we want to **h** you."
17: 3 In **h** of my son, I will have an image carved and an
1Sa 2: 8 them like princes, / placing them in seats of **h**.
2:29 Why do you **h** your sons more than me—for you
2:30 But I will **h** only those who **h** me, and I will
6: 5 Make these things to show **h** to the God of Israel.
9: 6 He is held in high **h** by all the people
9:23 the piece that had been set aside for the guest of **h**.
15:30 at least **h** me before the leaders and before my
21:11 "Isn't he the one the people **h** with dances,
2Sa 6:22 but I will be held in **h** by the girls of whom you
10: 3 think these men are coming here to **h** your father?
19:36 Just to go across the river with you is all the **h** I
1Ki 3:13 give you what you did not ask for—riches and **h**!
5: 3 was not able to build a Temple to **h** the name of
5: 5 So I am planning to build a Temple to **h** the name
5: 5 your throne, will build the Temple to **h** my name.'
8:16 where a temple should be built to **h** my name.
8:17 wanted to build this Temple to **h** the name of the
8:18 'It is right for you to want to build the Temple to **h**
8:20 I have built this Temple to **h** the name of the
8:48 and toward this Temple I have built to **h** your
9: 7 I will reject this Temple that I have set apart to **h**
10: 1 which brought **h** to the name of the LORD,
14:21 all the tribes of Israel as the place to **h** his name.
16:24 on it and called the city Samaria in **h** of Shemer.
21: 9 and prayer and give Naboth a place of **h**.
2Ki 19:34 For my own **h** and for the sake of my servant
20: 6 I will do this to defend my **h** and for the sake of
1Ch 16:27 **H** and majesty surround him; / strength and beauty
19: 3 think these men are coming here to **h** your father?
22: 7 "I wanted to build a Temple to **h** the name of the
22: 8 you will not be the one to build a Temple to **h** my
22:10 He is the one who will build a Temple to **h** my
22:19 into the Temple built to **h** the LORD's name."
28: 3 'You must not build a temple to **h** my name,
29:12 Riches and **h** come from you alone, for you rule
29:16 a Temple to **h** your holy name come from you!
29:25 Solomon even greater wealth and **h** than his father.
29:28 old age, having enjoyed long life, wealth, and **h**.
2Ch 1:11 and **h** or the death of your enemies or even a long
1:12 and **h** such as no other king has ever had before
2: 4 I am about to build a Temple to **h** the name of the
6: 5 where a temple should be built to **h** my name.
6: 7 wanted to build this Temple to **h** the name of the
6: 8 'It is right for you to want to build the Temple to **h**
6:10 I have built this Temple to **h** the name of the
6:38 and toward this Temple I have built to **h** your
7:20 I will reject this Temple that I have set apart to **h**
12:13 all the tribes of Israel as the place to **h** his name.
16:14 at his funeral the people built a huge fire in his **h**.
21:19 His people did not build a great fire to **h** him at his
26:18 The LORD God will not **h** you for this!"
Ezr 6:12 as the place to **h** his name destroy any king
Est 2:18 he gave a banquet in Esther's **h** for all his princes
6: 6 "What should I do to **h** a man who truly pleases
6: 6 "Whom would the king wish to **h** more than me?"
6: 7 So he replied, "If the king wishes to **h** someone,
6: 9 is what happens to those the king wishes to **h**!' "
6:11 is what happens to those the king wishes to **h**!"
Job 14:21 They never know if their sons grow up in **h** or sink
19: 9 He has stripped me of my **h** and removed the
21:32 to the grave, an **h** guard keeps watch at their tomb.
Ps 7: 5 Let my **h** be left in the dust. / *Interlude*
8: 5 than God, / and you crowned us with glory and **h**.
15: 4 and **h** the faithful followers of the LORD
20: 5 hear of your victory, / flying banners to **h** our God.
21: 5 Your victory brings him great **h**, / and you have
22:23 **H** him, all you descendants of Jacob! / Show him
23: 3 me along right paths, / bringing **h** to his name.
25:11 For the **h** of your name, O LORD, / forgive my
29: 1 Give **h** to the LORD, you angels; / give **h** to the LORD for his glory and strength.
29: 2 Give **h** to the LORD for the glory of his name.
31: 3 For the **h** of your name, lead me out of this peril.
31:19 You have stored up great blessings for those who **h**
34: 9 for those who **h** him will have all they need.
37:34 his path. / He will **h** you, giving you the land.
45:11 delights in your beauty; / **h** him, for he is your lord.
45:17 I will bring **h** to your name in every generation.
60: 4 But you have raised a banner for those who **h**
62: 7 My salvation and my **h** come from God alone.
63: 4 I will **h** you as long as I live, / lifting up my hands
69:30 with singing, / and I will **h** him with thanksgiving.
71:21 You will restore me to even greater **h**
79: 9 Help us for the **h** of your name. / Oh, save us
85: 9 Surely his salvation is near to those who **h** him;
86:11 Grant me purity of heart, / that I may **h** you.
91:15 them in trouble. / I will rescue them and **h** them.
96: 6 **H** and majesty surround him; / strength and beauty
104: 1 you are! / You are robed with **h** and with majesty;
106: 8 he saved them— / to defend the **h** of his name
110: 1 said to my Lord, / "Sit in **h** at my right hand
112: 9 be forgotten. / They will have influence and **h**.
119:38 of your promise, / which is for those who **h** you.
119:48 I **h** and love your commands. / I meditate on your
138: 2 promises are backed / by all the **h** of your name.
147:11 the LORD's delight is in those who **h** him,
149: 5 Let the faithful rejoice in this **h**. / Let them sing for
Pr 1: 9 will crown you with grace and clothe you with **h**.
3: 9 **H** the LORD with your wealth and with the best
3:16 life in her right hand, and riches and **h** in her left.
3:22 they fill you with life and bring you **h** and respect.
3:35 The wise inherit **h**, but fools are put to shame!
4: 8 she will exalt you. Embrace her and she will **h** you.
5: 9 you will lose your **h** and hand over to merciless
8:18 Unending riches, **h**, wealth, and justice are mine to
14:31 their Maker, but those who help the poor **h** him.
15:33 teaches a person to be wise; humility precedes **h**.
18:12 goes before destruction; humility precedes **h**.
20: 3 Avoiding a fight is a mark of **h**; only fools insist on
21:21 and unfailing love will find life, godliness, and **h**.
22: 4 fear of the LORD lead to riches, **h**, and long life.
24:26 It is an **h** to receive an honest reply.
26: 1 **H** doesn't go with fools any more than snow with
29:23 Pride ends in humiliation, while humility brings **h**.
Ecc 6: 2 God gives great wealth and **h** to some people
8:10 I have seen wicked people buried with **h**.
10: 1 can outweigh a pound of wisdom and **h**.
12: 1 **H** him in your youth before you grow old and no
Isa 22:23 He will bring **h** to his family name, for I will drive
22:24 and he will bring **h** to even the lowliest members
25: 1 O LORD, I will **h** and praise your name, for you
29:13 They **h** me with their lips, but their hearts are far
37:35 For my own **h** and for the sake of my servant
40:16 fuel to consume a sacrifice large enough to **h** him.
43:21 and they will someday **h** me before the whole
47: 1 For your days of glory, pomp, and **h** have ended.
48: 9 Yet for my own sake and for the **h** of my name,
55:13 This miracle will bring great **h** to the LORD's
56: 2 Blessed are those who **h** my Sabbath days of rest
56: 5 and a name far greater than the **h** they would have
58:13 **H** the LORD in everything you do, and don't
58:14 I will give you great **h** and give you your full share
60: 9 and it will bring great **h** to the LORD your God,
Jer 3:17 All nations will come there to **h** the LORD.
7:12 where I once put the Tabernacle to **h** my name.
7:14 I will now destroy this Temple that was built to **h**
13:11 my people, my pride, my glory—an **h** to my name.
33: 9 glory, and **h** before all the nations of the earth!
Eze 20: 9 do it, for I acted to protect the **h** of my name.
20:14 But again I held back in order to protect the **h** of
20:22 **h** of my name among the nations who had seen my
27:10 and helmets on your walls, giving you great **h**.
32:27 They are not buried in **h** like the fallen heroes of
35:11 And I will bring **h** to my name by what I do to you.
43: 7 or by raising monuments in **h** of their dead kings.
43: 9 and the sacred pillars erected to **h** their kings,
Da 2:37 has given you sovereignty, power, strength, and **h**.
4:36 to me, so did my **h** and glory and kingdom.
4:36 of my kingdom, with even greater **h** than before.
4:37 praise and glorify and **h** the King of heaven.
5: 4 They drank toasts from them to **h** their idols made
5: 7 it means will be dressed in purple robes of royal **h**
5:16 you will be clothed in purple robes of royal **h**,
5:18 majesty, glory, and **h** to your predecessor,
5:19 He honored those he wanted to **h** and disgraced
7:14 He was given authority, **h**, and royal power over
9:15 you brought lasting **h** to your name by rescuing
11:39 He will **h** those who submit to him,
Hos 4:18 love for shame is greater than their love for **h**.
5: 7 For they have betrayed the **h** of the LORD,
11: 7 call me the Most High, but they don't truly **h** me.
Joel 2:18 his people and be indignant for the **h** of his land!
Mic 7:12 People from many lands will come and **h** you—
Na 2: 2 but the LORD will restore its **h** and power again.
Hag 2:23 says the LORD Almighty, I will **h** you,
Zec 6:13 and he will receive royal **h** and will rule as king
6:14 the Temple of the LORD to **h** those who gave it—
12: 7 and the royal line of David will not have greater **h**
Mal 1: 6 but where are the **h** and respect I deserve?
1:11 sweet incense and pure offerings in **h** of my name.
2: 2 **H** my name," says the LORD Almighty, "or I
Mt 15: 4 God says, '**H** your father and mother,'
15: 5 'You don't need to **h** your parents by caring for
15: 8 'These people **h** me with their words, / but their
19:19 **H** your father and mother. Love your neighbor as
20:21 will you let my two sons sit in places of **h** next to
22: 8 and the guests I invited aren't worthy of the **h**.
22:44 said to my Lord, / Sit in **h** at my right hand

Mk 7: 7 'These people **h** me with their lips, / but their
7:10 '**H** your father and mother,' and 'Anyone who
10:19 Do not cheat. **H** your father and mother.' "
10:37 we want to sit in places of **h** next to you,"
12:36 said to my Lord, / Sit in **h** at my right hand
12:39 And how they love the seats of **h** in the
16:19 and sat down in the place of **h** at God's right hand.
Lk 1:43 What an **h** this is, that the mother of my Lord
5:29 a banquet in his home with Jesus as the guest of **h**.
7: 6 to my home, for I am not worthy of such an **h**.
11:43 For how you love the seats of **h** in the synagogues
18:20 not testify falsely. **H** your father and mother.' "
20:42 said to my Lord, / Sit in **h** at my right hand
20:46 And how they love the seats of **h** in the
Jn 5:23 so that everyone will **h** the Son, just as they **h** the Father.
5:23 But if you refuse to **h** the Son, then you are
5:44 For you gladly **h** each other, but you don't care about the **h** that comes from
7:18 but those who seek to **h** the one who sent them are
8:49 in me. For I **h** my Father—and you dishonor me.
12: 2 A dinner was prepared in Jesus' **h**. Martha served,
12:26 And if they follow me, the Father will **h** them.
Ac 2:33 Now he sits on the throne of highest **h** in heaven,
2:34 said to my Lord, / Sit in **h** at my right hand
5:31 Then God put him in the place of **h** at his right
7:55 and he saw Jesus standing in the place of **h** at
7:56 and the Son of Man standing in the place of **h** at
22: 3 I became very zealous to **h** God in everything I
Ro 2: 7 seeking after the glory and **h** and immortality that
2:10 But there will be glory and **h** and peace from God
8:34 and is sitting at the place of highest **h** next to God,
13: 7 and give respect and **h** to all to whom it is due.
14: 6 day for worshiping the Lord are trying to **h** him.
14: 6 who eat all kinds of food do so to **h** the Lord,
16: 2 her in the Lord, as one who is worthy of high **h**.
1Co 6:20 a high price. So you must **h** God with your body.
12:24 put the body together in such a way that extra **h**
16:18 You must give proper **h** to all who serve so well.
2Co 6: 8 We serve God whether people **h** us or despise us,
Eph 1:20 and seated him in the place of **h** at God's right
6: 2 "**H** your father and mother." This is the first of
6: 3 If you **h** your father and mother, "you will live a
Php 1:20 and that my life will always **h** Christ, whether I
2:29 with great joy, and be sure to **h** people like him.
Col 1:10 Then the way you live will always **h** and please the
3: 1 Christ sits at God's right hand in the place of **h**
1Th 4: 4 will control your body and live in holiness and **h**—
5:12 **h** those who are your leaders in the Lord's work.
2Th 1:12 Then everyone will give **h** to the name of our Lord
1Ti 1:17 Glory and **h** to God forever and ever. He is the
6:16 ever will. To him be **h** and power forever. Amen.
Heb 1: 3 he sat down in the place of **h** at the right hand of
1:13 as he did to his Son, / "Sit in **h** at my right hand
2: 7 and you crowned him with glory and **h**.
2: 9 and now is "crowned with glory and **h**"
5: 4 a high priest simply because he wants such an **h**.
7:26 and he has been given the highest place of **h** in
8: 1 Our High Priest sat down in the place of highest **h**
10:12 Then he sat down at the place of highest **h** at God's
12: 2 Now he is seated in the place of highest **h** beside
13: 4 Give **h** to marriage, and remain faithful to one
Jas 4:10 on him, he will lift you up and give you **h**.
5:11 We give great **h** to those who endure under
1Pe 1: 3 All **h** to the God and Father of our Lord Jesus
1: 7 and **h** on the day when Jesus Christ is revealed to
2:12 and give **h** to God when he comes to judge the
2:14 all who do wrong and to **h** those who do right.
3: 7 you husbands must give **h** to your wives.
3:22 He is seated in the place of **h** next to God, and all
5: 1 will share his glory and his **h** when he returns.
5: 4 will be a never-ending share in his glory and **h**.
5: 6 power of God, and in his good time he will **h** you.
2Pe 1:17 And he received **h** and glory from God the Father
3:18 To him be all glory and **h**, both now
Rev 4: 9 Whenever the living beings give glory and **h**
4:11 Lord our God, / to receive glory and **h** and power.
5:12 and strength / and **h** and glory and blessing."
5:13 also sang: / "Blessing and **h** and glory and power
7:12 and thanksgiving and **h** and power and strength
19: 7 Let us be glad and rejoice and **h** him. For the time
21:26 nations will bring their glory and **h** into the city.

HONORABLE (13) [HONOR]

Ge 42:19 We'll see how **h** you really are. Only one of you
Ru 3:11 for everyone in town knows you are an **h** woman.
Isa 3: 3 army officers, **h** citizens, advisers,
3: 5 and nobodies will sneer at **h** people.
Lk 1: 1 Most **h** Theophilus: Many people have written
Ac 7: 2 "Brothers and **h** fathers, listen to me.
Ro 12:17 in such a way that everyone can see you are **h**.
1Co 12:23 And the parts we regard as less **h** are those we
2Co 8:21 We are careful to be **h** before the Lord, but we also want everyone else to know we are **h**.
Php 4: 8 Fix your thoughts on what is true and **h** and right.
1Ti 3: 1 wants to be an elder, he desires an **h** responsibility.
1Pe 2:12 they will see your **h** behavior, and they will believe

HONORABLY (3) [HONOR]

Jdg 9:16 "Now make sure you have acted **h** and in good
9:19 If you have acted **h** and in good faith toward
Heb 13:18 is clear and we want to live **h** in everything we do.

HONORED (71) [HONOR]

Ge 23: 6 "Certainly, for you are an **h** prince among us.
45:13 Tell my father how I am **h** here in Egypt. Tell him
Dt 12: 5 from among all the tribes for his name to be **h**.
12:11 your God will choose for his name to be **h**.
12:21 for his name to be **h** is a long way from your home.
14:23 LORD your God chooses for his name to be **h**,
14:24 to be **h** might be a long way from your home.
16: 2 God at the place he chooses for his name to be **h**.
16: 6 your God will choose for his name to be **h**.
16:11 God at the place he chooses for his name to be **h**.
26: 2 LORD your God chooses for his name to be **h**.
1Sa 22:14 and a highly **h** member of your household!
2Sa 7:26 And may your name be **h** forever so that all the
19:28 but instead you have **h** me among those who eat at
23:23 He was more **h** than the other members of the
1Ki 9: 3 have built so that my name will be **h** there forever.
2Ki 21: 4 where the LORD had said his name should be **h**.
21: 7 "My name will be **h** here forever in this Temple
23:27 and the Temple where my name was to be **h**."
1Ch 11:25 He was more **h** than the other members of the
17:18 What more can I say about the way you have **h**
17:24 and **h** forever so that all the world will say,
25: 5 for God had **h** him with fourteen sons and three
2Ch 20: 9 presence before this Temple where your name is **h**.
32:33 and all Judah and Jerusalem **h** him at his death.
33: 4 the LORD had said his name should be **h** forever.
33: 7 "My name will be **h** here forever in this Temple
Ne 1: 9 to the place I have chosen for my name to be **h**.'
Est 8:16 with joy and gladness and were **h** everywhere.
Job 29: 7 city gate and took my place among the **h** leaders.
Ps 46:10 know that I am God! / I will be **h** by every nation. / I will be **h** throughout the world."
47: 9 earth belong to God. / He is highly **h** everywhere.
Pr 13:18 and disgrace; if you accept criticism, you will be **h**.
Isa 5:13 The great and **h** among them will starve,
43: 4 you are precious to me. You are **h**, and I love you.
43:23 You have not **h** me with sacrifices, though I have
44: 5 and will take the **h** name of Israel as their own.
49: 5 The LORD has **h** me, and my God has given me
61: 9 will be known and **h** among the nations.
66: 5 'Let the LORD be **h**!' they scoff. 'Be joyful in
Jer 25:29 the city where my own name is **h**.
30:19 my people and make of them a great and **h** nation.
La 1: 8 All who once **h** her now despise her, for they have
4:16 The priests and leaders are no longer **h**
Eze 20:44 when I have **h** my name by treating you mercifully
Da 4:34 the Most High and **h** the one who lives forever.
5:19 He **h** those he wanted to honor and disgraced those
5:23 But you have not **h** the God who gives you the
Mic 5: 4 for he will be highly **h** all around the world.
Hag 1: 8 Then I will take pleasure in it and be **h**,
Mal 1:11 But my name is **h** by people of other nations from
Mt 6: 9 Our Father in heaven, / may your name be **h**.
13:57 "A prophet is **h** everywhere except in his own
Mk 6: 4 "A prophet is **h** everywhere except in his own
15:43 an **h** member of the high council, Joseph from
Lk 11: 2 you should pray: / "Father, may your name be **h**.
13:30 Some who are despised now will be greatly **h** then;
13:30 and some who are greatly **h** now will be despised
14:10 Then you will be **h** in front of all the other guests.
14:11 proud will be humbled, but the humble will be **h**."
18:14 proud will be humbled, but the humble will be **h**."
Jn 4:44 "A prophet is **h** everywhere except in his own
Ac 19:17 and the name of the Lord Jesus was greatly **h**.
1Co 12:26 with it, and if one part is **h**, all the parts are glad.
2Co 11: 7 and **h** you by preaching God's Good News to you
Eph 3:13 am suffering, so you should feel **h** and encouraged.
2Th 1:12 because of you, and you will be **h** along with him.
3: 1 will spread rapidly and be **h** wherever it goes,
Heb 1: 6 when he presented his **h** Son to the world,
Jas 1: 9 who are poor should be glad, for God has **h** them.

HONORING (9) [HONOR]

1Sa 9:22 of the table, **h** them above the thirty special guests.
1Ki 3: 2 for a temple **h** the name of the LORD had not yet
Ezr 7:28 such unfailing love to me by **h** me before the king,
Ne 1:11 to the prayers of those of us who delight in **h** you.
Ps 148:14 He has made his people strong, / **h** his godly ones
Pr 26: 8 **H** a fool is as foolish as tying a stone to a
Jn 5:23 then you are certainly not **h** the Father who sent
Ro 12:10 genuine affection, and take delight in **h** each other.
1Co 11:29 not **h** the body of Christ, you are eating

HONORS (12) [HONOR]

Est 5:11 He bragged about the **h** the king had given him
Job 29:20 New **h** are constantly bestowed on me, and my
Ps 50:23 But giving thanks is a sacrifice that truly **h** me.
Pr 25:27 it is not good for people to think about all the **h**
29:12 If a ruler **h** liars, all his advisers will be wicked.
Isa 53:12 I will give him the **h** of one who is mighty
Jer 7:11 which **h** my name, is a den of thieves?
Da 2: 6 I will give you many wonderful gifts and **h**.
Mal 1: 6 "A son **h** his father, and a servant respects his
Lk 16:15 What this world **h** is an abomination in the sight of
Ac 28:10 As a result we were showered with **h**, and when
Ro 2:26 them all the rights and **h** of being his own people?

HOOF (1) [HOOVES]

Ex 10:26 must go with us; not a **h** can be left behind.

HOOK (4) [HOOKS]

2Ki 19:28 heard for myself, / I will put my **h** in your nose
Job 41: 1 "Can you catch a crocodile with a **h** or put a noose
Isa 37:29 heard for myself, / I will put my **h** in your nose
Am 4: 2 one of you will be dragged away like a fish on a **h**!

HOOKS (28) [HOOK]

Ex 26:32 Hang this inner curtain on gold **h** set into four
26:37 Hang this curtain on gold **h** set into five posts
27: 3 The ash buckets, shovels, basins, meat **h**,
27:10 The curtains will be held up with silver **h** attached
27:11 fitted into bronze bases, with silver **h** and rods.
27:17 must be connected by silver rods, using silver **h**.
36:36 then attached to four gold **h** set into four posts of
36:38 This curtain was connected by five **h** to five posts.
38: 3 ash buckets, shovels, basins, meat **h**, and firepans.
38:10 and there were silver **h** and rods to hold up the
38:11 bronze posts and bases and with silver **h** and rods.
38:12 by ten posts and bases and with silver **h** and rods.
38:17 a bronze base, and all the **h** and rods were silver.
38:19 and the **h** and rods were also made of silver.
38:28 was used to make the rods and **h** and to overlay the
Nu 4:14 the firepans, **h**, shovels, basins, and all the
1Ch 28:17 gold meat **h** used to handle the sacrificial meat
2Ch 4:16 the pots, the shovels, the meat **h**, and all the related
Isa 2: 4 into plowshares and their spears into pruning **h**.
19: 8 Those who fish with **h** and those who use nets will
Eze 19: 9 With **h**, they dragged him into a cage / and brought
29: 4 I will put **h** in your jaws and drag you out on the
38: 4 and put **h** into your jaws to lead you out to your
40:43 There were **h**, each three inches long, fastened to
Joel 3:10 into swords and your pruning **h** into spears.
Am 4: 2 when you will be led away with **h** in your noses.
Mic 4: 3 into plowshares and their spears into pruning **h**.
Hab 1:15 Must we be strung up on their **h** and dragged out in

HOOPOE (2)

Lev 11:19 the stork, herons of all kinds, the **h**, and the bat.
Dt 14:18 the stork, herons of all kinds, the **h**, and the bat.

HOOTING (1)

Zep 2:14 ruins of its palaces, **h** from the gaping windows.

HOOVES (17) [HOOF]

Lev 11: 3 include those that have completely divided **h**
11: 4 because they either have split **h** or chew the cud,
11: 4 though it chews the cud, it does not have split **h**.
11: 7 for though it has split **h**, it does not chew the cud.
11:26 "Any animal that has divided but unsplit **h** or that
Dt 14: 6 "Any animal that has split **h** and chews the cud
14: 7 They chew the cud but do not have split **h**.
14: 8 for though it has split **h**, it does not chew the cud.
Jdg 5:22 Then the horses' **h** hammered the ground,
2Ki 9:33 And Jehu trampled her body under his horses' **h**.
Ps 69:31 an ox / or presenting a bull with its horns and **h**.
Isa 5:28 Sparks will fly from their horses' **h** as the wheels
Jer 47: 3 Hear the clatter of **h** and the rumble of wheels as
Eze 26:10 The **h** of his cavalry will choke the city with dust,
Mic 4:13 "For I will give you iron horns and bronze **h**,
Na 3: 2 Wheels rumble, horses' **h** pound, and chariots
Zec 11:16 the meat of the fattest sheep and tear off their **h**.

HOPE (131) [HOPED, HOPEFUL, HOPELESS, HOPELESSLY, HOPES, HOPING]

Ru 2:13 "I **h** I continue to please you, sir," she replied.
2Sa 16:21 you have insulted him beyond **h** of reconciliation,
1Ki 2:20 of you," she said. "I **h** you won't turn me down."
20:33 The men were quick to grasp at this straw of **h**,
Ezr 10: 2 of the land. But there is **h** for Israel in spite of this.
Job 3: 9 Let it **h** for light, but in vain; may it never see the
5:16 And so at last the poor have **h**, and the fangs of the
6: 8 have my request, that God would grant my **h**.
7: 6 shuttle flying back and forth. They end without **h**.
8:13 forget God. The **h** of the godless comes to nothing.
11:18 You will have courage because you will have **h**.
11:20 But the wicked will lose **h**. They have no escape. Their **h** becomes despair."
14: 7 there is **h** that it will sprout again and grow new
14:14 This thought would give me **h**, and through my
14:19 wash away the soil, so you destroy people's **h**.
17:15 But where then is my **h**? Can anyone find it?
17:16 No, my **h** will go down with me to the grave.
19:10 and I am finished. He has destroyed my **h**.
27: 8 For what **h** do the godless have when God cuts
29:13 I helped those who had lost **h**, and they blessed
31:23 if the majesty of God opposes me, what **h** is there?
Ps 25: 5 who saves me. / All day long I put my **h** in you.
25:21 and honesty protect me, / for I put my **h** in you.
31:24 all you who put your **h** in the LORD!
33:22 surround us, LORD, / for our **h** is in you alone.
39: 7 Lord, where do I put my **h**? / My only **h** is in you.
40:11 My only **h** is in your unfailing love
42: 5 Why so sad? / I will put my **h** in God!
42:11 Why so sad? / I will put my **h** in God!
43: 5 Why so sad? / I will put my **h** in God!
62: 5 I wait quietly before God, / for my **h** is in him.
65: 5 our savior. / You are the **h** of everyone on earth,
71: 5 O Lord, you alone are my **h**. / I've trusted you,
78: 7 So each generation can set its **h** anew on God,
94:19 your comfort gave me renewed **h** and cheer.
119:43 of truth from me, / for my only **h** is in your laws.
119:49 your promise to me, / for it is my only **h**.
119:74 a cause for joy, / for I have put my **h** in your word.
119:81 your salvation; / but I have put my **h** in your word.
119:114 and my shield; / your word is my only source of **h**.
119:116 that I may live! / Do not let my **h** be crushed.
119:147 I cry out for help and put my **h** in your words.
130: 5 am counting on him. / I have put my **h** in his word.
130: 7 O Israel, **h** in the LORD; / for with the LORD
131: 3 O Israel, put your **h** in the LORD— / now

143: 4 I am losing all **h**; / I am paralyzed with fear.
146: 5 their helper, / whose **h** is in the LORD their God.
147: 11 those who put their **h** in his unfailing love.
Pr 6: 15 broken beyond all **h** of healing.
13: 12 **H** deferred makes the heart sick, but when dreams
19: 18 Discipline your children while there is **h**. If you
23: 18 ahead of you; your **h** will not be disappointed.
26: 12 There is more **h** for fools than for people who
29: 20 There is more **h** for a fool than for someone who
Ecc 9: 3 choose their own mad course, for they have no **h**.
9: 4 There is **h** only for the living. For as they say,
Isa 8: 17 from the people of Israel. My only **h** is in him.
38: 18 can no longer **h** in your faithfulness.
42: 3 those who are weak or quench the smallest **h**.
51: 1 "Listen to me, all who **h** for deliverance—all who
Jer 14: 8 O **H** of Israel, our Savior in times of trouble!
14: 19 Why have you wounded us past all **h** of healing?
16: 17 I see every sin. They cannot **h** to hide from me.
17: 6 shrubs in the desert, with no **h** for the future.
17: 7 and have made the LORD their **h** and confidence.
17: 13 O LORD, the **h** of Israel, all who turn away from
17: 17 me now! You alone are my **h** in the day of disaster.
19: 11 of Judah and Jerusalem beyond all **h** of repair.
28: 6 I **h** the LORD does everything you say.
28: 6 I **h** he does bring back from Babylon the treasures
29: 11 and not for disaster, to give you a future and a **h**.
31: 17 There is **h** for your future," says the LORD.
50: 7 their place of rest, the **h** of their ancestors.'
La 2: 14 they painted false pictures, filling you with false **h**.
3: 21 Yet I still dare to **h** when I remember this:
3: 24 is my inheritance; therefore, I will **h** in him!"
3: 29 down in the dust; then at last there is **h** for them.
Eze 7: 3 No **h** remains, for I will unleash my anger against
37: 11 'We have become old, dry bones—all **h** is gone.'
Hos 2: 15 the Valley of Trouble into a gateway of **h**.
Am 5: 20 a dark and hopeless day, without a ray of joy or **h**.
Jnh 2: 7 "When I had lost all **h**, I turned my thoughts once
Mic 1: 14 gift to Moresheth-gath; there is no **h** of saving it.
Zec 9: 12 place of safety, all you prisoners, for there is yet **h**!
Mt 12: 20 those who are weak, / or quench the smallest **h**,
12: 21 And his name will be the **h** / of all the world."
Ac 2: 26 my mouth shouts his praises! / My body rests in **h**.
23: 6 because my **h** is in the resurrection of the dead!"
24: 15 I have **h** in God, just as these men do, that he will
26: 7 and day, and they share the same **h** I have.
26: 7 O king, they say it is wrong for me to have this **h**!
27: 20 the sun and the stars, until at last all **h** was gone.
28: 20 this chain because I believe that the **h** of Israel—
Ro 8: 24 already have something, you don't need to **h** for it.
15: 4 They give us **h** and encouragement as we wait
15: 13 So I pray that God, who gives you **h**, will keep you
15: 13 May you overflow with **h** through the power of the
1Co 13: 13 faith, **h**, and love—and the greatest of these is love.
15: 19 And if we have **h** in Christ only for this life,
2Co 1: 13 I **h** someday you will fully understand us,
5: 11 knows we are sincere, and I **h** you know this, too.
10: 2 I **h** it won't be necessary, but when I come I may
10: 15 we **h** that your faith will grow and that our work
11: 1 I **h** you will be patient with me as I keep on talking
13: 6 I **h** you recognize that we have passed the test
Eph 2: 12 lived in this world without God and without **h**.
3: 20 more than we would ever dare to ask or **h**.
Php 1: 20 and **h** that I will never do anything that causes me
2: 19 Jesus is willing, I **h** to send Timothy to you soon.
2: 23 I **h** to send him to you just as soon as I find out
3: 15 I **h** all of you who are mature Christians will agree
1Th 2: 19 After all, what gives us **h** and joy, and what is our
4: 13 not be full of sorrow like people who have no **h**.
2Th 2: 16 favor gave us everlasting comfort and good **h**,
1Ti 1: 1 of God our Savior and by Christ Jesus our **h**.
3: 14 to you now, even though I **h** to be with you soon,
4: 10 for our **h** is in the living God, who is the Savior of
5: 5 truly alone in this world, has placed her **h** in God.
2Ti 4: 16 I **h** it will not be counted against them.
Heb 3: 6 and remain confident in our **h** in Christ.
6: 11 in order to make certain that what you **h** for will
7: 19 and now a better **h** has taken its place.
10: 23 let us hold tightly to the **h** we say we have,
11: 1 It is the confident assurance that what we **h** for is
11: 35 They placed their **h** in the resurrection to a better
1Pe 1: 21 your faith and **h** can be placed confidently in God.
3: 15 And if you are asked about your Christian **h**,
2Jn 1: 12 For I **h** to visit you soon and to talk with you face
3Jn 1: 14 For I **h** to see you soon, and then we will talk face

HOPED (12) [HOPE]

Ge 32: 20 "Perhaps," Jacob **h**, "he will be friendly to us."
Est 9: 1 the enemies of the Jews had **h** to destroy them,
Ecc 2: 3 I **h** to experience the only happiness most people
Jer 8: 15 We **h** for peace, but no peace came. We **h** for a time of healing, but found only terror.
14: 19 We **h** for peace, but no peace came. We **h** for a time of healing but found only terror.
18: 4 the jar he was making did not turn out as he had **h**,
La 3: 18 Everything I had **h** for from the LORD is lost!"
Hag 1: 9 You **h** for rich harvests, but they were poor.
2: 16 When you **h** for a twenty-bushel crop,
Ac 24: 26 He also **h** that Paul would bribe him, so he sent for

HOPEFUL (1) [HOPE]

1Co 13: 7 Love never gives up, never loses faith, is always **h**,

HOPELESS (2) [HOPE]

Eze 24: 12 But it's **h**; the corruption remains. So throw it into
Am 5: 20 the day of the LORD will be a dark and **h** day,

HOPELESSLY (1) [HOPE]

Eph 4: 17 longer as the ungodly do, for they are **h** confused.

HOPES (21) [HOPE]

1Sa 9: 20 and your family are the focus of all Israel's **h**."
2Ki 4: 28 a son. And didn't I tell you not to raise my **h**?"
Job 6: 19 With high **h**, the caravans from Tema and from
6: 20 but finding none, their **h** are dashed.
17: 11 My days are over. My **h** have disappeared.
31: 16 or crushed the **h** of widows who looked to me for
Ps 9: 18 the **h** of the poor will not always be crushed.
10: 17 LORD, you know the **h** of the helpless.
112: 10 in anger; / they will slink away, their **h** thwarted.
Pr 10: 24 will all come true; so will the **h** of the godly.
10: 28 The **h** of the godly result in happiness,
11: 7 When the wicked die, their **h** all perish, for they
24: 14 a bright future, and your **h** will not be cut short.
Jer 23: 16 they prophesy to you, filling you with futile **h**.
Eze 19: 5 mother lion saw / that all her **h** for him were gone,
Da 2: 9 You have conspired to tell me lies in **h** that
Zec 9: 5 and so will Ekron, for their **h** will be dashed.
Jn 5: 45 accuse you! Yes, Moses, on whom you set your **h**.
Ac 16: 19 Her masters' **h** of wealth were now shattered,
Ro 15: 12 the Gentiles. / They will place their **h** on him."
2Co 8: 5 Best of all, they went beyond our highest **h**,

HOPHNI (5)

1Sa 1: 3 time were the two sons of Eli—**H** and Phinehas.
2: 34 two sons, **H** and Phinehas, to die on the same day!
4: 4 **H** and Phinehas, the sons of Eli, helped carry the
4: 11 and **H** and Phinehas, the two sons of Eli,
4: 17 Your two sons, **H** and Phinehas, were killed, too.

HOPHRA (2)

Jer 37: 5 At this time the army of Pharaoh **H** of Egypt
44: 30 I will turn Pharaoh **H**, king of Egypt, over to his

HOPING (11) [HOPE]

Ge 32: 5 my coming, **h** that you will be friendly to us.' "
Ex 1: 11 **h** to wear them down under heavy burdens.
Ne 6: 13 They were **h** to intimidate me and make me sin by
Ps 69: 13 **h** this is the time you will show me favor.
71: 14 But I will keep on **h** for you to help me; / I will
Jnh 1: 3 **h** that by going away to the west he could escape
Mt 12: 10 (They were, of course, **h** he would say yes, so they
Lk 23: 8 and had been **h** for a long time to see him perform
Ac 12: 11 and from what the Jews were **h** to do to me!"
2Co 13: 10 **h** that I won't need to deal harshly with you when I
Phm 1: 22 for I am **h** that God will answer your prayers

HOPPING (2)

Joel 1: 4 After them came the **h** locusts, and
2: 25 the swarming locusts, and the **h** locusts.

HOR (11)

Nu 20: 22 left Kadesh as a group and arrived at Mount **H**.
20: 23 and Aaron at Mount **H** on the border of the land of
20: 25 Now take Aaron and his son Eleazar up Mount **H**.
20: 27 The three of them went up Mount **H** together as
21: 4 Then the people of Israel set out from Mount **H**,
33: 37 They left Kadesh and camped at Mount **H**,
33: 38 While they were at the foot of Mount **H**,
33: 39 was 123 years old when he died there on Mount **H**.
33: 41 the Israelites left Mount **H** and camped at
34: 7 Mediterranean Sea and run eastward to Mount **H**,
Dt 32: 50 died on Mount **H** and joined his ancestors.

HOR-HAGGIDGAD (2)

Nu 33: 32 They left Bene-jaakan and camped at **H**.
33: 33 They left **H** and camped at Jotbathah.

HORAM (1)

Jos 10: 33 King **H** of Gezer had arrived with his army to help

HORDE (6) [HORDES]

Nu 22: 5 "A vast **h** of people has arrived from Egypt.
22: 11 'A vast **h** of people has come from Egypt and has
2Ch 14: 11 your name that we have come against this vast **h**.
Eze 38: 4 and cavalry and make you a vast and mighty **h**,
38: 9 and all your allies—a vast and awesome **h**—
39: 16 which means '**h**.') And so the land will finally be

HORDES (22) [HORDE]

Ex 8: 2 I will send vast **h** of frogs across your entire land
Jdg 6: 5 These enemy **h**, coming with their cattle and tents
Ps 78: 45 to consume them / and **h** of frogs to ruin them.
105: 34 He spoke, and **h** of locusts came— / locusts
Isa 7: 19 They will come in vast **h**, spreading across the
13: 16 be sacked and their wives raped by the attacking **h**.
47: 12 "Call out the demon **h** you have worshiped all
Eze 30: 10 of Babylon, I will destroy the **h** of Egypt.
31: 18 will be the fate of Pharaoh and all his teeming **h**.
32: 12 the pride of Egypt, and all its **h** will be destroyed.
32: 16 Let all the nations mourn for Egypt and its **h**.
32: 18 weep for the **h** of Egypt and for the other mighty
32: 24 "Elam lies there buried with its **h** who descended
32: 26 are there, surrounded by the graves of all their **h**.
32: 32 and his **h** will lie there among the outcasts who
38: 6 Gomer and all its **h** will also join you, along with
38: 22 punish you and your **h** with disease and bloodshed;
39: 4 and all your vast **h** will die on the mountains.
39: 11 for Gog and his **h** in the Valley of the Travelers,
39: 11 the name of the place to the Valley of Gog's **H**.
39: 15 take them to be buried in the Valley of Gog's **H**.
Hab 1: 9 Their **h** advance like a wind from the desert,

HOREM (1)

Jos 19: 38 Yiron, Migdal-el, **H**, Beth-anath,

HORESH (3)

1Sa 23: 15 One day near **H**, David received the news that Saul
23: 18 Jonathan returned home, while David stayed at **H**.
23: 19 "He is in the strongholds of **H** on the hill of

HORI (3) [HORITE, HORITES]

Ge 36: 22 The sons of Lotan were **H** and Heman.
Nu 13: 5 Simeon | Shaphat son of **H**
1Ch 1: 39 The sons of Lotan were **H** and Heman.

HORITE (4) [HORI]

Ge 36: 20 names of the tribes that descended from Seir the **H**,
36: 21 These were the **H** clans, the descendants of Seir,
36: 29 So the leaders of the **H** clans were Lotan, Shobal,
36: 30 The **H** clans are named after their clan leaders,

HORITES (3) [HORI]

Ge 14: 6 and the **H** in Mount Seir, as far as El-paran at the
Dt 2: 12 In earlier times the **H** had lived at Mount Seir,
2: 22 for he destroyed the **H** so they could settle there in

HORIZON (3)

Job 15: 29 possessions will no longer spread across the **h**.
26: 10 He created the **h** when he separated the waters;
Pr 8: 27 the heavens, when he drew the **h** on the oceans.

HORMAH (9)

Nu 14: 45 and attacked them and chased them as far as **H**.
21: 3 and the place has been called **H** ever since.
Dt 1: 44 and battered you all the way from Seir to **H**.
Jos 12: 14 The king of **H** / The king of Arad
15: 30 Eltolad, Kesil, **H**,
19: 4 Eltolad, Bethul, **H**,
Jdg 1: 17 destroyed the town. So the town was named **H**.
1Sa 30: 30 **H**, Bor-ashan, Athach,
1Ch 4: 30 Bethuel, **H**, Ziklag,

HORN (25) [HORN'S, HORNED, HORNS, TWO-HORNED]

Ex 19: 13 until they hear one long blast from the ram's **h**.
19: 16 There was a long, loud blast from a ram's **h**,
19: 19 As the **h** blast grew louder and louder,
20: 18 heard the thunder and the loud blast of the **h**,
27: 2 Make a **h** at each of the four corners of the altar
Jos 6: 4 walk ahead of the Ark, each carrying a ram's **h**.
6: 6 to walk in front of it, each carrying a ram's **h**."
Jdg 6: 34 He blew a ram's **h** as a call to arms, and the men of
7: 16 and gave each man a ram's **h** and a clay jar with a
1Sa 16: 1 Now fill your **h** with olive oil and go to
Ps 98: 6 with trumpets and the sound of the ram's **h**.
Eze 43: 15 with a **h** rising up from each of the four corners.
Da 3: 5 When you hear the sound of the **h**, flute, zither,
7: 8 suddenly another small **h** appeared among them.
7: 8 This little **h** had eyes like human eyes and a mouth
7: 20 and the little **h** that came up afterward
7: 20 This was the **h** that seemed greater than the others
7: 21 this **h** was waging war against the holy people
8: 5 which had one very large **h** between its eyes,
8: 8 the height of its power, its large **h** was broken off.
8: 9 From one of the prominent horns came a small **h**
8: 12 The **h** succeeded in everything it did.
8: 21 and the large **h** between its eyes represents the first
8: 22 **h** show that the Greek Empire will break into four
Hos 5: 8 "Blow the ram's **h** in Gibeah! Sound the alarm in

HORN'S (2) [HORN]

Da 7: 11 because I could hear the little **h** boastful speech.
8: 8 In the large **h** place grew four prominent horns

HORNED (1) [HORN]

Isa 34: 11 It will be haunted by the **h** owl, the hawk,

HORNETS (3)

Ex 23: 28 I will send **h** ahead of you to drive out the Hivites,
Dt 7: 20 then the LORD your God will send **h** to drive out
Jos 24: 12 And I sent **h** ahead of you to drive out the two

HORNS (77) [HORN]

Ge 22: 13 looked up and saw a ram caught by its **h** in a bush.
Ex 27: 2 of the altar so the **h** and altar are all one piece. Overlay the altar and its **h** with bronze.
29: 12 Smear some of its blood on the **h** of the altar with
30: 2 with **h** at the corners carved from the same piece of
30: 3 the top, sides, and **h** of the altar with pure gold,
30: 10 **h** the blood from the offering made for the
37: 25 with its corner **h** made from the same piece of
37: 26 and **h** of the altar with pure gold and ran a gold
38: 2 There were four **h**, one at each of the four corners,
Lev 4: 7 The priest will put some of the blood on the **h** of
4: 18 then put some of the blood on the **h** of the incense
4: 25 put it on the **h** of the altar of burnt offerings,
4: 30 put the blood on the **h** of the altar of burnt
4: 34 put it on the **h** of the altar of burnt offerings,

8:15 and with his finger he put it on the four **h** of the
9: 9 his finger into it and put it on the **h** of the altar.
16:18 from the bull and the goat on each of the altar's **h**.
Dt 33:17 a young bull; / his power is like the **h** of a wild ox.
Jos 6: 4 the city seven times, with the priests blowing the **h**.
6: 5 you hear the priests give one long blast on the **h**,
6: 8 the seven priests with the rams' **h** started marching
6: 8 of the LORD, blowing the **h** as they marched.
6: 9 the Ark, with the priests continually blowing the **h**.
6:13 The seven priests with the rams' **h** marched in
6:13 in front of the Ark of the LORD, blowing their **h**.
6:13 marched both in front of the priests with the **h**
6:13 All this time the priests were sounding their **h**.
6:16 as the priests sounded the long blast on their **h**,
6:20 When the people heard the sound of the **h**,
Jdg 7: 8 and rams' **h** of the other warriors and sent them
7:18 As soon as my group blows the rams' **h**, those of
7:18 of you on the other sides of the camp blow your **h**
7:19 they blew the **h** and broke their clay jars.
7:20 Then all three groups blew their **h** and broke their
7:20 and the **h** in their right hands and shouted,
7:22 When the three hundred Israelites blew their **h**,
1Ki 1:50 sacred tent and caught hold of the **h** of the altar.
1:51 that Adonijah had seized the **h** of the altar
2:28 the LORD and caught hold of the **h** of the altar.
22:11 of Kenaanah, made some iron **h** and proclaimed,
22:11 With these **h** you will gore the Arameans to
1Ch 15:28 the blowing of **h** and trumpets, the crashing of
2Ch 15:14 the LORD with trumpets blaring and **h** sounding.
18:10 of Kenaanah, made some iron **h** and proclaimed,
18:10 With these **h** you will gore the Arameans to
Ps 22:21 lions' jaws, / and from the **h** of these wild oxen.
69:31 an ox / or presenting a bull with its **h** and hooves.
Jer 48:25 Her **h** have been cut off, and her arms have been
Eze 43:20 of its blood and smear it on the four **h** of the altar,
Da 7: 7 from any of the other beasts, and it had ten **h**.
7: 8 As I was looking at the **h**, suddenly another small
7: 8 Three of the first **h** were wrenched out, roots
7:20 I also asked about the ten **h** on the fourth beast's
7:20 up afterward and destroyed three of the other **h**.
7:24 Its ten **h** are ten kings that will rule that empire.
8: 3 I saw in front of me a ram with two long **h**
8: 3 One of the **h** was longer than the other,
8: 7 at the ram and struck it, breaking off both its **h**.
8: 8 In the large horn's place grew four prominent **h**
8: 9 From one of the prominent **h** came a small horn
8:22 The four prominent **h** that replaced the one large
Am 3:14 The **h** of the altar will be cut off and fall to the
Mic 4:13 "For I will give you iron **h** and bronze hooves,
Zec 1:18 Then I looked up and saw four animal **h**.
1:19 "These **h** represent the world powers that scattered
1:21 "The blacksmiths have come to terrify the four **h**
Rev 5: 6 He had seven **h** and seven eyes, which are the
9:13 and I heard a voice speaking from the four **h** of the
12: 3 saw a large red dragon with seven heads and ten **h**,
13: 1 seven heads and ten **h**, with ten crowns on its **h**.
13:11 He had two **h** like those of a lamb, and he spoke
17: 3 on a scarlet beast that had seven heads and ten **h**,
17: 7 and of the beast with seven heads and ten **h**.
17:12 His ten **h** are ten kings who have not yet risen to
17:16 The scarlet beast and his ten **h**—which represent

HORONAIM (5)

2Sa 13:34 "I see a crowd of people coming from the **H** road
Isa 15: 5 Their crying can be heard all along the road to **H**.
Jer 48: 3 And then the roar of battle will surge against **H**,
48: 5 while cries of terror rise from **H** below.
48:34 from Zoar all the way to **H** and Eglath-shelishiyah.

HORONITE (2) [BETH-HORON]

Ne 2:10 But when Sanballat the **H** and Tobiah the
13:28 priest had married a daughter of Sanballat the **H**,

HORRIBLE (15) [HORROR]

Lev 18:17 and to do this would be a **h** wickedness.
Jos 7:15 of the LORD and has done a **h** thing in Israel."
Jdg 19:30 "Such a **h** crime has not been committed since
2Sa 12: 9 the word of the LORD and done this **h** deed?
Jer 5:30 "A **h** and shocking thing has happened in this
7:31 I have never commanded such a **h** deed; it never
19: 5 I have never commanded such a **h** deed; it never
32:35 I have never commanded such a **h** deed; it never
44: 4 'Don't do these **h** things that I hate so much.'
Eze 27:36 at the sight of you, / for you have come to a **h** end
Hos 6:10 Yes, I have seen a **h** thing in Israel: My people
Mt 21:41 "He will put the wicked men to a **h** death
24:29 "Immediately after those **h** days end, / the sun will
Mk 13:24 "At that time, after those **h** days end, / the sun will
Rev 16: 2 and poured out his bowl over the earth, and **h**,

HORRIFIED (4) [HORROR]

Job 18:20 are appalled at their fate; people in the east are **h**.
Ps 40:15 Let them be **h** by their shame, / for they said,
70: 3 Let them be **h** by their shame, / for they said,
Jer 50:13 All who pass by will be **h** and will gasp at the

HORROR (33) [HORRIBLE, HORRIFIED, HORRORS]

Ge 15:12 He saw a terrifying vision of darkness and **h**.
Dt 18:12 Anyone who does these things is an object of **h**
28:25 You will be an object of **h** to all the kingdoms of
28:37 You will become an object of **h**, a proverb and a
2Sa 13:31 His advisers also tore their clothes in **h** and sorrow.
2Ki 21:12 ears of those who hear about it will tingle with **h**.
2Ch 29: 8 of dread, **h**, and ridicule, as you can so plainly see.
Isa 21: 3 Sharp pangs of **h** are upon me, like the pangs of a
66:24 All who pass by will view them with utter **h**."
Jer 2:12 at such a thing and shrink back in **h** and dismay,
4: 9 and the prophets will be struck with **h**."
15: 4 I will make my people an object of **h** to all the
24: 9 I will make them an object of **h** and evil to every
25: 9 and make you an object of **h** and contempt and a
25:18 an object of **h**, contempt, and cursing.
29:18 an object of damnation, **h**, contempt, and mockery.
42:18 an object of damnation, **h**, cursing, and mockery.
44:12 an object of damnation, **h**, cursing, and mockery.
49:13 "that Bozrah will become an object of **h** and a
49:17 "Edom will be an object of **h**. All who pass by
51:37 It will be an object of **h** and contempt, without a
Eze 5:15 become an object of mockery and taunting and **h**.
6:11 Clap your hands in **h**, and stamp your feet. Cry out,
7:18 in sackcloth; **h** and shame will cover them.
26:16 They will sit on the ground trembling with **h** at
27:35 Their kings are filled with **h** / and look on with
Na 2:10 of its wealth. Hearts melt in **h**, and knees shake.
3: 7 All who see you will shrink back in **h** and say,
Mt 24:21 For that will be a time of greater **h** than anything
26:65 the high priest tore his clothing to show his **h**,
Mk 13:19 For those will be days of greater **h** than at any time
14:33 and he began to be filled with **h** and deep distress.
14:63 Then the high priest tore his clothing to show his **h**

HORRORS (8) [HORROR]

Dt 28:46 These **h** will serve as a sign and warning among
28:67 because of your terror at the awesome **h** you see
Mt 11:21 "What **h** await you, Korazin and Bethsaida!
24: 8 But all this will be only the beginning of the **h** to
Mk 13: 8 But all this will be only the beginning of the **h** to
Lk 10:13 "What **h** await you, Korazin and Bethsaida!
21:36 you may escape these **h** and stand before the Son
Ac 2:24 God released him from the **h** of death and raised

HORSE (29) [HORSE'S, HORSEMEN, HORSES, HORSES', WARHORSE, WARHORSES]

Ex 15: 1 he has thrown both **h** and rider into the sea.
15:21 he has thrown both **h** and rider into the sea."
2Ki 14:20 They brought him back to Jerusalem on a **h**,
23:11 **h** statues that the former kings of Judah had
2Ch 25:28 They brought him back to Jerusalem on a **h**,
Ne 3:28 The priests repaired the wall up the hill from the **H**
Est 6: 8 as well as the king's own **h** with a royal emblem
6: 9 him through the city square on the king's own **h**.
6:10 "Hurry and get the robe and my **h**, and do just as
6:11 it on Mordecai, placed him on the king's own **h**,
Job 39:18 up to run, she passes the swiftest **h** with its rider.
39:19 "Have you given the **h** its strength or clothed its
Ps 32: 9 Do not be like a senseless **h** or mule / that needs a
147:10 The strength of a **h** does not impress him;
Pr 26: 3 Guide a **h** with a whip, a donkey with a bridle,
Jer 8: 6 the path of sin as swiftly as a **h** rushing into battle!
31:40 Kidron Valley on the east as far as the **H** Gate—
51:21 destroying the **h** and rider, the chariot
Zec 1: 8 I saw a man sitting on a red **h** that was standing
12: 4 I will cause every **h** to panic and every rider to lose
Jas 3: 3 We can make a large **h** turn around and go
Rev 6: 2 I looked up and saw a white **h**. Its rider carried a
6: 4 And another **h** appeared, a red one. Its rider was
6: 5 And I looked up and saw a black **h**, and its rider
6: 8 and saw a **h** whose color was pale green like a
19:11 heaven opened, and a white **h** was standing there.
19:11 And the one sitting on the **h** was named Faithful
19:19 in order to fight against the one sitting on the **h**
19:21 out of the mouth of the one riding the white **h**.

HORSE'S (2) [HORSE]

Ge 49:17 viper along the path, / that bites the **h** heels
Rev 14:20 about 180 miles long and as high as a **h** bridle.

HORSELEACH [KJV] See LEECH

HORSEMEN (15) [HORSE, MAN]

1Sa 13: 5 six thousand **h**, and as many warriors as the grains
2Sa 10:18 seven hundred charioteers and forty thousand **h**,
2Ki 18:23 If you can find two thousand **h** in your entire army,
18:24 even with the help of Egypt's chariots and **h**?
2Ch 12: 3 sixty thousand **h**, and a countless army of foot
16: 8 their vast army, with all of their chariots and **h**?
Ezr 8:22 and **h** to accompany us and protect us from
Ne 2: 9 had sent along army officers and **h** to protect me.
Isa 36: 8 If you can find two thousand **h** in your entire army,
36: 9 even with the help of Egypt's chariots and **h**?
Eze 26:11 His **h** will trample every street in the city.
Hab 1: 8 at dusk. Their **h** race forward from distant places.
Zec 10: 5 they will overthrow even the **h** of the enemy.
Ac 23:23 Also take two hundred spearmen and seventy **h**.
23:32 next morning, while the **h** took him on to Caesarea.

HORSES (114) [HORSE]

Ge 47:17 Soon all the **h**, flocks, herds, and donkeys of Egypt
Ex 9: 3 will send a deadly plague to destroy your **h**,
14: 9 all his **h**, chariots, and charioteers—were used in
14:23 all of Pharaoh's **h**, chariots, and charioteers—
15:19 When Pharaoh's **h**, chariots, and charioteers
Dt 11: 4 to the armies of Egypt and to their **h** and chariots—
17:16 The king must not build up a large stable of **h** for
17:16 must never send his people to Egypt to buy **h** there,
20: 1 and you face **h** and chariots and an army greater
Jos 11: 4 along with a vast array of **h** and chariots,
11: 6 be dead. Cripple their **h** and burn their chariots."
11: 9 Then Joshua crippled the **h** and burned all the
24: 6 the Egyptians chased after you with chariots and **h**.
2Sa 8: 4 he crippled all but one hundred of the chariot **h**.
15: 1 After this, Absalom bought a chariot and **h**, and he
1Ki 1: 5 So he provided himself with chariots and **h**
4:26 stalls for his chariot **h** and twelve thousand **h**.
4:28 and straw for the royal **h** in the stables.
9:19 cities where his chariots and **h** could be kept.
10:25 of silver and gold, clothing, weapons, spices, **h**,
10:26 Solomon built up a huge force of chariots and **h**.
10:26 fourteen hundred chariots and twelve thousand **h**.
10:28 Solomon's **h** were imported from Egypt and from
10:29 and **h** could be bought for 150 pieces of silver.
18: 5 find enough grass to save at least some of my **h**
20: 1 by the chariots and **h** of thirty-two allied kings.
20:20 King Ben-hadad and a few others escaped on **h**.
20:21 However, the other **h** and chariots were destroyed,
20:25 Give us the same number of **h**, chariots, and men,
22: 4 to command. Even my **h** are at your service."
2Ki 2:11 a chariot of fire appeared, drawn by **h** of fire.
3: 7 to command. Even my **h** are at your service."
5: 9 So Naaman went with his **h** and chariots
6:14 with many chariots and **h** to surround the city.
6:15 and went outside, there were troops, **h**,
6:17 that the hillside around Elisha was filled with **h**
7: 6 and the galloping of **h** and the sounds of a great
7: 7 their tents, **h**, donkeys, and everything else,
7:10 The **h** and donkeys were tethered and the tents
7:13 Let them take five of the remaining **h**. If something
7:14 So two chariots with **h** were prepared, and the king
9:23 Then King Joram reined the chariot **h** around
9:33 her blood spattered against the wall and on the **h**.
10: 2 disposal chariots, **h**, a fortified city, and weapons.
11:16 and led her out to the gate where **h** enter the palace
18:23 he will give you two thousand **h** for them to ride
1Ch 18: 4 he crippled all but one hundred of the chariot **h**.
2Ch 1:14 fourteen hundred chariots and twelve thousand **h**.
1:16 Solomon's **h** were imported from Egypt and from
1:17 and **h** could be bought for 150 pieces of silver.
8: 6 cities where his chariots and **h** could be kept.
9:24 of silver and gold, clothing, weapons, spices, **h**,
9:25 stalls for his chariot **h** and twelve thousand **h**.
9:28 Solomon's **h** were imported from Egypt and many
23:15 and led her out to the gate where **h** enter the palace
Ezr 2:66 They took with them 736 **h**, 245 mules,
Ne 7:68 They took with them 736 **h**, 245 mules,
Est 8:10 who rode **h** especially bred for the king's service.
8:14 the messengers rode out swiftly on **h** bred for the
Ps 76: 6 O God of Jacob, / their **h** and chariots stood still.
Pr 21:31 The **h** are prepared for battle, but the victory
Isa 2: 7 of silver and gold and many **h** and chariots.
21: 7 sound the alert when he sees chariots drawn by **h**
30:16 They will give us swift **h** for riding into battle.'
31: 3 Their **h** are puny flesh, not mighty spirits!
36: 8 he will give you two thousand **h** for them to ride
43:17 mighty army of Egypt with all its chariots and **h**.
66:20 They will ride on **h**, in chariots and wagons,
Jer 4:13 are like whirlwinds; his **h** are swifter than eagles.
12: 5 men makes you tired, how will you race against **h**?
17:25 among the people of Judah in chariots and on **h**,
22: 4 ride through the palace gates in chariots and on **h**,
46: 4 Harness the **h**, and prepare to mount them. Put on
46: 9 you **h** and chariots and mighty warriors of Egypt!
50:37 When it strikes her **h** and chariots, her allies from
51:27 Appoint a leader, and bring a multitude of **h**!
Eze 17:15 to Egypt to request a great army and many **h**.
23: 6 in handsome blue, dashing about on their **h**.
23:12 those handsome young men on fine **h**,
23:23 and other high-ranking officers, riding their **h**.
26:10 and your walls will shake as the **h** gallop through
27:14 Togarmah came riding **h**, chariot **h**, and mules.
39:20 feast on **h**, riders, and valiant warriors,
Joel 2: 4 They look like tiny **h**, and they run as fast.
Am 2:15 Even warriors on **h** won't be able to outrun the
4:10 your young men in war and slaughtered all your **h**.
6:12 Can **h** gallop over rocks? Can oxen be used to
Mic 5:10 destroy all your weapons—your **h** and chariots.
Hab 1: 8 Their **h** are swifter than leopards. They are a fierce
3:15 You trampled the sea with your **h**, and the mighty
Hag 2:22 The **h** will fall, and their riders will kill each other.
Zec 1: 8 Behind him were red, brown, and white **h**,
1: 9 with me, "My lord, what are all those **h** for?"
6: 2 chariot was pulled by red **h**, the second by black **h**,
6: 3 the third by white **h**, and the fourth by dappled-gray **h**.
6: 6 The chariot with black **h** is going north, the chariot with white **h** is going west, and the chariot with dappled-gray **h** is going
6: 7 The powerful **h** were eager to be off, to patrol back
12: 4 of Judah, but I will blind the **h** of her enemies.
14:15 This same plague will strike the **h**, mules, camels,
14:20 On that day even the harness bells of the **h** will be
Ac 23:24 Provide **h** for Paul to ride, and get him safely to
Rev 9: 7 The locusts looked like **h** armed for battle.
9:17 I saw the **h** and the riders sitting on them.
9:18 burning sulfur that came from the mouths of the **h**.
18:13 fine flour, wheat, cattle, sheep, **h**, chariots,
19:14 in pure white linen, followed him on white **h**.
19:18 captains, and strong warriors; of **h** and their riders;

HORSES' (5) [HORSE]

Jdg 5:22 Then the **h** hooves hammered the ground,
2Ki 9:33 And Jehu trampled her body under his **h** hooves.

Isa 5:28 Sparks will fly from their **h** hooves as the wheels
Na 3:2 Wheels rumble, **h** hooves pound, and chariots
Rev 9:17 The **h** heads were like the heads of lions, and fire

HOSAH (4) [HOSAH'S]

Jos 19:29 of Tyre and came to the Mediterranean Sea at **H**.
1Ch 16:38 **H**, and sixty-eight other Levites as gatekeepers.
26:10 **H**, of the Merari clan, appointed Shimri as the
26:16 Shuppim and **H** were assigned the west gate

HOSAH'S (1) [HOSAH]

1Ch 26:11 **H** sons and relatives, who served as gatekeepers,

HOSEA (6)

Hos 1:1 The LORD gave these messages to **H** son of
1:2 LORD first began speaking to Israel through **H**,
1:3 So **H** married Gomer, the daughter of Diblaim,
1:3 and she became pregnant and gave **H** a son.
1:6 And the LORD said to **H**, "Name your daughter
Ro 9:25 the Gentiles, God says in the prophecy of **H**,

HOSHAIAH (3)

Ne 12:32 **H** and half the leaders of Judah followed them,
Jer 42:1 Johanan son of Kareah and Jezaniah son of **H**,
43:2 Azariah son of **H** and Johanan son of Kareah

HOSHAMA (1)

1Ch 3:18 Malkiram, Pedaiah, Shenazzar, Jekamiah, **H**,

HOSHEA (7) [HOSHEA'S, JOSHUA]

Nu 13:8 Ephraim | **H** son of Nun
2Ki 15:30 Then **H** son of Elah conspired against Pekah
17:1 **H** son of Elah began to rule over Israel in the
17:3 of Assyria attacked and defeated King **H**,
17:4 Then **H** conspired against the king of Assyria by
1Ch 27:20 Ephraim | **H** son of Azaziah / Manasseh (west)
Ne 10:23 **H**, Hananiah, Hasshub,

HOSHEA'S (5) [HOSHEA]

Nu 13:16 By this time Moses had changed **H** name to
2Ki 17:6 Finally, in the ninth year of King **H** reign,
18:1 Judah in the third year of King **H** reign in Israel.
18:9 which was the seventh year of King **H** reign in
18:10 and the ninth year of King **H** reign in Israel,

HOSPITALITY (4)

Mt 10:10 Don't hesitate to accept **h**, because those who work
25:38 Or a stranger and show you **h**? Or naked and give
Lk 10:7 Don't hesitate to accept **h**, because those who work
Heb 13:2 Don't forget to show **h** to strangers, for some who

HOST (8)

Lk 2:13 the angel was joined by a vast **h** of others—
7:39 When the Pharisee who was the **h** saw what was
11:38 His **h** was amazed to see that he sat down to eat
14:9 The **h** will say, 'Let this person sit here instead.'
14:10 Then when your **h** sees you, he will come and say,
14:12 Then he turned to his **h**. "When you put on a
Jn 2:10 "Usually a **h** serves the best wine first," he said.
Rev 20:8 a mighty **h**, as numberless as sand along the shore.

HOSTAGES (2)

2Ki 14:14 He also took **h** and returned to Samaria.
2Ch 25:24 along with **h**, and then returned to Samaria.

HOSTILE (11) [HOSTILITY]

Lev 26:21 "If even then you remain **h** toward me and refuse
26:24 then I myself will be **h** toward you, and I will
26:27 still refuse to listen and still remain **h** toward me,
26:40 ancestors for betraying me and being **h** toward me.
2Sa 22:27 but to the wicked you show yourself **h**.
Ps 18:26 but to the wicked you show yourself **h**.
59:5 the God of Israel, / rise up to punish **h** nations.
59:8 you laugh at them. / You scoff at all the **h** nations.
118:10 Though **h** nations surrounded me, / I destroyed
Lk 11:53 From that time on they grilled him with many **h**
Ro 8:7 For the sinful nature is always **h** to God. It never

HOSTILITY (11) [HOSTILE]

Lev 26:23 a lesson from this and continue your **h** toward me,
26:28 then I will give full vent to my **h**. I will punish you
26:41 when I have given full expression to my **h**
Nu 35:20 So if in premeditated **h** someone pushes another
35:22 pushes another person without premeditated **h**,
Dt 4:42 having any previous **h** could flee for safety.
Ps 78:49 them his fierce anger— / all his fury, rage, and **h**.
Hos 9:8 he goes. He faces **h** even in the house of God.
Gal 5:20 **h**, quarreling, jealousy, outbursts of anger,
Eph 2:14 He has broken down the wall of **h** that used to
2:16 and our **h** toward each other was put to death.

HOT (22) [HOT-TEMPERED, HOTBED, HOTHEAD, HOTHEADS, HOTTER, HOTTEST, RED-HOT]

Ge 31:23 a group of his relatives and set out in **h** pursuit.
36:24 This is the Anah who discovered the **h** springs in
Ex 16:21 And as the sun became **h**, the food they had not
Dt 8:15 and scorpions, where it was so **h** and dry.
Jos 9:12 "This bread was **h** from the ovens when we left.
1Ki 19:6 and saw some bread baked on **h** stones
Job 6:17 But when the **h** weather arrives, the water
Ps 39:3 My thoughts grew **h** within me / and began to
Pr 6:28 Can he walk on **h** coals and not blister his feet?
26:21 A quarrelsome person starts fights as easily as **h**
SS 1:6 and sent me out to tend the vineyards in the **h** sun.
Isa 32:2 and as the cool shadow of a large rock in a **h**
66:15 of his anger and the flaming fire of his **h** rebuke.
Jer 36:30 lie unburied—exposed to **h** days and frosty nights.
Da 3:22 had demanded such a **h** fire in the furnace,
Hos 7:4 They are like an oven that is kept **h** even while the
Jnh 4:8 And as the sun grew **h**, God sent a scorching east
Mt 13:6 but they soon wilted beneath the **h** sun and died
Mk 4:6 but it soon wilted beneath the **h** sun and died
Lk 8:13 but they wilt when the **h** winds of testing blow.
Jas 1:11 The **h** sun rises and dries up the grass; the flower
Rev 3:15 the things you do, that you are neither **h** nor cold.

HOT-TEMPERED (1) [HOT, TEMPER]

Pr 29:22 A **h** person starts fights and gets into all kinds of

HOTBED (1) [HOT]

Ezr 4:19 past been a **h** of insurrection against many kings.

HOTHAM (2)

1Ch 7:32 The sons of Heber were Japhlet, Shomer, and **H**.
11:44 Shama and Jeiel, the sons of **H**, from Aroer;

HOTHEAD (1) [HEAD, HOT]

Pr 15:18 A **h** starts fights; a cool-tempered person tries to

HOTHEADS (1) [HEAD, HOT]

Isa 32:4 Even the **h** among them will be full of sense

HOTHIR (2)

1Ch 25:4 Romamti-ezer, Joshbekashah, Mallothi, **H**,
25:28 The twenty-first lot fell to **H** and twelve of his sons

HOTTER (2) [HOT]

Jer 6:29 The refining fire grows **h**. But it will never purify
Da 3:19 the furnace be heated seven times **h** than usual.

HOTTEST (1) [HOT]

Ne 7:3 "Do not leave the gates open during the **h** part of

HOUGH(ED) [KJV] See CRIPPLE(D)

HOUND (1) [HOUNDED, HOUNDING]

Ps 56:2 My slanderers **h** me constantly, / and many are

HOUNDED (2) [HOUND]

Ps 109:16 and needy, / and he **h** the brokenhearted to death.
Ac 26:11 so violently opposed to them that I even **h** them in

HOUNDING (1) [HOUND]

Ac 22:4 **h** some to death, binding and delivering both men

HOUR (28) [HOURS]

Jdg 10:14 Let them rescue you in your **h** of distress!"
Pr 10:5 a youth who sleeps away the **h** of opportunity
Jer 44:10 To this very **h** you have shown no remorse
Da 4:33 That very same **h** the prophecy was fulfilled,
Mic 2:8 Yet to this very **h** my people rise against me!
Mt 8:13 And the young servant was healed that same **h**.
20:12 'Those people worked only one **h**, and yet you've
24:36 the day or the **h** when these things will happen,
25:13 you do not know the day or **h** of my return.
26:40 you stay awake and watch with me even one **h**?
Mk 13:32 knows the day or **h** when these things will happen,
14:35 the awful **h** awaiting him might pass him by.
14:37 you stay awake and watch with me even one **h**?
Lk 17:30 it will be 'business as usual' right up to the **h** when
22:15 "I have looked forward to this **h** with deep
22:59 About an **h** later someone else insisted, "This must
24:33 And within the **h** they were on their way back to
Jn 13:1 Jesus knew that his **h** had come to leave this world
Ac 16:33 That same **h** the jailer washed their wounds,
22:13 your sight.' And that very **h** I could see him!
1Co 4:11 To this very **h** we go hungry and thirsty,
15:30 risking our lives, facing death **h** by **h**?
1Jn 2:18 Dear children, the last **h** is here. You have heard
Rev 8:1 was silence throughout heaven for about half an **h**.
9:15 the four angels who had been prepared for this **h**
11:13 And in the same **h** there was a terrible earthquake
18:19 great wealth. And now in a single **h** it is all gone."

HOURS (10) [HOUR]

Ex 1:14 and mortar and to work long **h** in the fields.
1Ch 9:33 there since they were on duty at all **h**.
Ne 9:3 their God was read aloud to them for about three **h**.
9:3 Then for three more **h** they took turns confessing
Ps 90:4 years are as yesterday! / They are like a few **h**!
Pr 23:30 It is the one who spends long **h** in the taverns,
Jn 11:9 "There are twelve **h** of daylight every day.
18:28 Jesus' trial before Caiaphas ended in the early **h** of
Ac 5:7 About three **h** later his wife came in, not knowing
19:34 started shouting again and kept it up for two **h**:

HOUSE (319) [HOUSEHOLD, HOUSEHOLDS, HOUSES, HOUSETOP, HOUSETOPS, HOUSING, STOREHOUSE, STOREHOUSES, TREASURE-HOUSE, TREASURE-HOUSES]

FATHER'S HOUSE (7) Ge 12:1; 24:7; Jdg 11:7; 14:15; 19:3; Lk 2:49; Jn 2:16

HOUSE OF DAVID (2) Ne 12:37; Isa 22:22

HOUSE OF...GOD (28) Ge 28:17,19; 35:15; Ex 34:26; Dt 23:18; Jos 9:23; 1Ch 6:48; 9:11,13,26,27; 23:28; 25:6; 26:20; Ps 42:4; 52:8; 55:14; 84:10; 122:9; 135:2; Ecc 5:1; Hos 9:8; Joel 1:16; Am 2:8; Hag 1:14; Mt 12:4; Mk 2:26; Lk 6:4

HOUSE OF THE LORD* (23) Ex 34:26; Dt 23:18; 1Ch 6:31; 9:23; 23:24,28,32; 24:19; 25:6; 26:12,22,27; 29:8; Ps 23:6; 27:4; 116:19; 118:26; 122:1,9; 134:1; 135:2; Jer 29:26; Hag 1:14

LORD'S HOUSE (2) Jos 6:24; Hag 1:2

MY HOUSE (12) Lev 14:35; Dt 26:13; Jdg 11:31; Pr 7:6; Isa 56:5,7; Eze 23:39; Hos 3:3; Hag 1:4,8,9; Ac 10:30

THIS HOUSE (2) Jos 2:19; Hag 2:3

Ge 12:1 your country, your relatives, and your father's **h**,
19:4 came from all over the city and surrounded the **h**.
24:7 who took me from my father's **h** and my native
27:15 which were there in the **h**, and dressed Jacob with
28:2 to the **h** of your grandfather Bethuel,
28:17 It is none other than the **h** of God—the gateway to
28:19 He named the place Bethel—"**h** of God"—
33:17 There he built himself a **h** and made shelters for
34:26 They rescued Dinah from Shechem's **h**
35:15 Jacob called the place Bethel—"**h** of God"—
39:11 around when he was doing his work inside the **h**.
39:12 She was left holding it as he ran from the **h**.
44:8 we steal silver or gold from your master's **h**?
Ex 12:7 and sides of the doorframe of the **h** where the lamb
12:22 no one is allowed to leave the **h** until morning.
12:30 There was not a single **h** where someone had not
12:46 All who eat the lamb must eat it together in one **h**.
20:17 "Do not covet your neighbor's **h**. Do not covet
22:2 "If a thief is caught in the act of breaking into a **h**
22:7 and they are stolen from the neighbor's **h**.
34:26 each year's crop to the **h** of the LORD your God.
Lev 14:35 The owner of such a **h** must then go to the priest
14:35 'It looks like my **h** has some kind of disease.'
14:36 Before the priest examines the **h**, he must have the **h** emptied so everything inside
14:36 Then the priest will go in and inspect the **h**.
14:37 or reddish streaks on the walls of the **h**
14:38 he will leave the **h** and lock it up for seven days.
14:39 If the mildew on the walls of the **h** has spread,
14:41 Next the inside walls of the entire **h** must be
14:44 the priest must return and inspect the **h** again.
14:44 with an infectious mildew, and the **h** is defiled.
14:46 Anyone who enters the **h** while it is closed will be
14:47 who sleep or eat in the **h** must wash their clothing.
14:48 then he will pronounce the **h** clean
14:49 To purify the **h** the priest will need two birds,
14:51 and he will sprinkle the **h** seven times.
14:52 After he has purified the **h** in this way,
14:53 this way, the priest will make atonement for the **h**,
14:55 whether in clothing, in a **h**,
25:29 "Anyone who sells a **h** inside a walled city has the
25:30 then the **h** within the walled city will become the
25:31 But a **h** in a village—a settlement without fortified
25:31 Such a **h** may be redeemed at any time and must be
25:32 **h** they have sold within the cities belonging to
27:14 "If you dedicate a **h** to the LORD, the priest must
27:15 If you wish to redeem the **h**, you must pay the
27:15 20 percent. Then the **h** will again belong to you.
Nu 12:7 servant Moses. He is entrusted with my entire **h**.
Dt 5:21 Do not covet your neighbor's **h** or land, male
6:9 Write them on the doorposts of your **h** and on your
11:20 Write them on the doorposts of your **h** and on your
16:4 Let no yeast be found in any **h** throughout your
20:5 'Has anyone just built a new **h** but not yet
20:5 and someone else would dedicate your **h**!
22:8 "Every new **h** you build must have a barrier
23:18 Do not bring to the **h** of the LORD your God any
24:10 do not enter your neighbor's **h** to claim the
26:13 'I have taken the sacred gift from my **h** and have
28:30 You will build a **h**, but someone else will live in it.
Jos 2:1 and came to the **h** of a prostitute named Rahab
2:3 "Bring out the men who have come into your **h**.
2:15 since Rahab's **h** was built into the city wall,
2:18 and all your relatives—must be here inside the **h**.
2:19 But we swear that no one inside this **h** will be
6:17 the prostitute and the others in her **h** will be spared,
6:22 Go to the prostitute's **h** and bring her out,
6:24 iron were kept for the treasury of the LORD's **h**.
6:25 and her relatives who were with her in the **h**,
9:23 chop wood and carry water for the **h** of my God."
Jdg 11:7 who hated me and drove me from my father's **h**?
11:31 out of my **h** to greet me when I return in triumph.
12:1 We are going to burn down your **h** with you in it!"
14:15 or we will burn down your father's **h** with you in
16:9 had hidden some men in one of the rooms of her **h**,
17:4 and an idol. And these were placed in Micah's **h**.
17:8 He happened to stop at Micah's **h** as he was
17:12 as his personal priest, and he lived in Micah's **h**.
18:13 country of Ephraim and came to the **h** of Micah.
18:15 So the five men went over to Micah's **h**,
19:3 When he arrived at her father's **h**, she took him
19:22 of the wicked men in the town surrounded the **h**.
19:26 At daybreak the woman returned to the **h** where
19:26 She collapsed at the door of the **h** and lay there
20:5 some of the leaders of Gibeah surrounded the **h**,

1Sa 9:18 "Can you please tell me where the seer's **h** is?"
9:25 Samuel took Saul up to the roof of the **h**
9:26 got ready, and he and Samuel left the **h** together.
15:34 to Ramah, and Saul returned to his **h** at Gibeah.
19:11 Then Saul sent troops to watch David's **h**.
19:15 lies there!" And he sent them back to David's **h**.
2Sa 4:11 men who have killed an innocent man in his own **h**
5:8 "The blind and the lame may not enter the **h**."
7:11 LORD declares that he will build a **h** for you—
7:13 He is the one who will build a **h**—a temple—
7:27 because you have revealed that you will build a **h**
12:8 I gave you his **h** and his wives and the kingdoms of
13:7 and sent Tamar to Amnon's **h** to prepare some
13:8 When Tamar arrived at Amnon's **h**, she went to
13:20 Tamar lived as a desolate woman in Absalom's **h**.
14:24 "Absalom may go to his own **h**, but he must never
16:21 for he has left them here to keep the **h**.
20:3 he had left to keep **h** should be placed in seclusion.
1Ki 2:36 "Build a **h** here in Jerusalem and live there.
3:17 them began, "this woman and I live in the same **h**.
3:17 birth to a baby while she was with me in the **h**.
3:18 We were alone; there were only two of us in the **h**.
12:16 Israel! Look out for your own **h**, O David!"
16:18 he went into the citadel of the king's **h** and burned
17:12 that I don't have a single piece of bread in the **h**.
2Ki 4:2 "Tell me, what do you have in the **h**?"
4:4 Then go into your **h** with your sons and shut the
5:9 and chariots and waited at the door of Elisha's **h**.
5:24 the men back. Then he hid the gifts inside the **h**.
6:32 Elisha was sitting in his **h** at a meeting with the
7:17 of God had predicted when the king came to his **h**.
8:3 she went to see the king about getting back her **h**
9:6 So Jehu left the others and went into the **h**.
15:5 the day of his death; he lived in a **h** by himself.
1Ch 6:31 at the **h** of the LORD after he put the Ark there.
6:48 various other tasks in the Tabernacle, the **h** of God.
9:11 Azariah was the chief officer of the **h** of God.
9:13 They were responsible for ministering at the **h** of
9:23 were responsible for guarding the entrance to the **h**
9:23 of the LORD, the **h** that was formerly a tent.
9:26 for the rooms and treasuries at the **h** of God.
9:27 They would spend the night around the **h** of God,
13:7 They transported the Ark of God from the **h** of
17:10 I declare that the LORD will build a **h** for you—
17:12 He is the one who will build a **h**—a temple—
17:25 because you have revealed that you will build a **h**
23:24 or older to qualify for service in the **h** of the
23:28 of Aaron, as they served at the **h** of the LORD.
23:28 and served in many other ways in the **h** of God.
23:32 out their duties of service at the **h** of the LORD.
24:19 Each group carried out its duties in the **h** of the
25:6 fathers as they made music at the **h** of the LORD.
25:6 of cymbals, lyres, and harps at the **h** of God.
26:12 other Levites, they served at the **h** of the LORD.
26:20 were in charge of the treasuries of the **h** of God
26:22 were in charge of the treasuries of the **h** of the
26:27 gained in battle to maintain the **h** of the LORD.
29:8 which were deposited in the treasury of the **h** of
2Ch 10:16 Israel! Look out for your own **h**, O David!"
Ezr 6:11 in any way will have a beam pulled from their **h**.
6:11 and their **h** will be reduced to a pile of rubble.
Ne 2:8 for the city walls, and for a **h** for myself."
3:10 of Harumaph repaired the wall beside his own **h**,
3:16 as the water reservoir and the **H** of the Warriors.
3:21 the door of Eliashib's **h** to the side of the **h**.
3:24 section of the wall from Azariah's **h** to the buttress
3:25 from the king's **h** beside the court of the guard.
3:28 doing the section immediately opposite his own **h**.
3:29 of Immer also rebuilt the wall next to his own **h**,
3:30 son of Berekiah rebuilt the wall next to his own **h**.
12:37 They passed the **h** of David and then proceeded to
Job 1:13 and daughters were dining at the oldest brother's **h**,
1:19 swept in from the desert and hit the **h** on all sides.
1:19 The **h** collapsed, and all your children are dead.
20:28 A flood will sweep away his **h**. God's anger will
Ps 5:7 Because of your unfailing love, I can enter your **h**;
23:6 of my life, / and I will live in the **h** of the LORD
27:4 is to live in the **h** of the LORD all the days of my
36:8 You feed them from the abundance of your own **h**,
42:4 leading a great procession to the **h** of God,
52:8 I am like an olive tree, / thriving in the **h** of God.
55:14 as we walked together to the **h** of God.
59:T soldiers to watch David's **h** in order to kill him.
69:9 Passion for your **h** burns within me, / so those who
84:4 How happy are those who can live in your **h**,
84:10 I would rather be a gatekeeper in the **h** of my God
92:13 For they are transplanted into the LORD's own **h**.
116:19 in the **h** of the LORD, / in the heart of Jerusalem.
118:26 We bless you from the **h** of the LORD.
122:1 said to me, / "Let us go to the **h** of the LORD."
122:9 For the sake of the **h** of the LORD our God,
127:1 Unless the LORD builds a **h**, / the work of the
132:5 until I find a place to build a **h** for the LORD,
134:1 you who serve as night watchmen in the **h** of the
135:2 you who serve in the **h** of the LORD, / in the courts of the **h** of our God.
Pr 2:18 Entering her **h** leads to death; it is the road to hell.
3:33 The curse of the LORD is on the **h** of the wicked,
5:8 Run from her! Don't go near the door of her **h**!
6:31 even if it means selling everything in his **h** to pay it
7:6 I was looking out the window of my **h** one day
7:8 He was crossing the street near the **h** of an
7:8 He was strolling down the path by her **h**
7:27 Her **h** is the road to the grave. Her bedroom is the
9:1 Wisdom has built her spacious **h** with seven
14:1 A wise woman builds her **h**; a foolish woman tears
14:11 The **h** of the wicked will perish, but the tent of the
15:6 There is treasure in the **h** of the godly,
15:25 The LORD destroys the **h** of the proud, but he
17:13 repay evil for good, evil will never leave your **h**.
24:3 A **h** is built by wisdom and becomes strong
24:15 And don't raid the **h** where the godly live.
24:27 Develop your business first before building your **h**.
Ecc 5:1 As you enter the **h** of God, keep your ears open
Isa 22:22 I will give him the key to the **h** of David—
50:2 Is that why the **h** is silent and empty when I come
54:2 "Enlarge your **h**; build an addition; spread out
56:5 in my **h**, within my walls—a memorial and a name
56:7 and will fill them with joy in my **h** of prayer.
56:7 because my Temple will be called a **h** of prayer for
Jer 29:26 as the priest in charge of the **h** of the LORD.
37:15 and imprisoned in the **h** of Jonathan the secretary.
37:15 Jonathan's **h** had been converted into a prison.
37:20 Don't send me back to the dungeon in the **h** of
Eze 3:24 to me and said, "Go, shut yourself up in your **h**.
12:4 as they are watching, leave your **h** in the evening,
23:39 to worship! They came in and defiled my **h**!
Da 6:11 The officials went together to Daniel's **h** and found
Hos 3:3 "You must live in my **h** for many days and stop
9:8 he goes. He faces hostility even in the **h** of God.
Joel 1:16 There are no joyful celebrations in the **h** of our
Am 2:8 In the **h** of their god, they present offerings of wine
5:19 the bear, he leans his hand against a wall in his **h**—
6:9 If there are ten men left in one **h**, they will all die.
6:10 goes into the **h** to carry away a dead body, he will
9:11 It is now like a **h** in ruins, but I will rebuild its
Mic 2:2 When you want someone's **h**, you take it by fraud
Hag 1:2 time has not yet come to rebuild the LORD's **h**—
1:4 living in luxurious houses while my **h** lies in ruins?
1:8 into the hills, bring down timber, and rebuild my **h**.
1:9 Because my **h** lies in ruins, says the LORD
1:14 and began their work on the **h** of the LORD
2:3 Is there anyone who can remember this **h**—
Zec 5:4 I am sending this curse into the **h** of every thief
5:4 and into the **h** of everyone who swears falsely by
5:4 And my curse will remain in that **h** until it is
Mt 2:11 They entered the **h** where the child and his mother,
7:24 is wise, like a person who builds a **h** on solid rock.
7:25 floodwaters rise and the winds beat against that **h**,
7:26 it is foolish, like a person who builds a **h** on sand.
7:27 and floods come and the winds beat against that **h**,
8:14 When Jesus arrived at Peter's **h**,
9:28 They went right into the **h** where he was staying,
12:4 He went into the **h** of God, and they ate the special
12:29 You can't enter a strong man's **h** and rob him
12:29 first tying him up. Only then can his **h** be robbed!
13:1 Jesus left the **h** and went down to the shore,
13:36 leaving the crowds outside, Jesus went into the **h**.
17:25 Then he went into the **h** to talk to Jesus about it.
23:38 your **h** is left to you, empty and desolate.
24:17 A person outside the **h** must not go inside to pack.
24:43 stay alert and not permit the **h** to be broken into.
26:18 the Passover meal with my disciples at your **h**.' "
26:58 came to the courtyard of the high priest's **h**.
27:17 As the crowds gathered before Pilate's **h** that
Mk 2:2 Soon the **h** where he was staying was so packed
2:26 He went into the **h** of God (during the days when
3:20 When Jesus returned to the **h** where he was
3:27 You can't enter a strong man's **h** and rob him
3:27 first tying him up. Only then can his **h** be robbed!
3:31 and brothers arrived at the **h** where he was
7:17 Then Jesus went into a **h** to get away from the
9:28 when Jesus was alone in the **h** with his disciples,
9:33 and his disciples settled in the **h** where they would
10:10 when he was alone with his disciples in the **h**,
10:29 "I assure you that everyone who has given up **h**
11:4 the colt standing in the street, tied outside a **h**.
13:15 A person outside the **h** must not go back into the **h** to pack.
14:14 At the **h** he enters, say to the owner, 'The Teacher
Lk 1:40 She entered the **h** and greeted Elizabeth.
2:49 have known that I would be in my Father's **h**."
6:4 He went into the **h** of God, ate the special bread
6:48 It is like a person who builds a **h** on a strong
6:48 When the floodwaters rise and break against the **h**,
6:49 and doesn't obey is like a person who builds a **h**
6:49 When the floods sweep down against that **h**,
7:6 But just before they arrived at the **h**, the officer
7:10 And when the officer's friends returned to his **h**,
8:16 where they can be seen by those entering the **h**.
8:51 When they arrived at the **h**, Jesus wouldn't let
8:52 The **h** was filled with people weeping and wailing,
11:5 "Suppose you went to a friend's **h** at midnight,
12:39 coming would not permit the **h** to be broken into.
13:25 but when the head of the **h** has locked the door,
13:35 And now look, your **h** is left to you empty.
14:23 anyone you find to come, so that the **h** will be full.
15:8 and look in every corner of the **h** and sweep every
15:22 Bring the finest robe in the **h** and put it on him.
15:25 he heard music and dancing in the **h**,
17:31 On that day a person outside the **h** must not go into the **h** to pack.
18:29 everyone who has given up **h** or wife or brothers
19:6 and took Jesus to his **h** in great excitement and joy.
22:10 will meet you. Follow him. At the **h** he enters,
Jn 2:16 Don't turn my Father's **h** into a marketplace!"
2:17 "Passion for God's **h** burns within me."
11:31 When the people who were at the **h** trying to
12:3 with her hair. And the **h** was filled with fragrance.
Ac 1:13 Then they went to the upstairs room of the **h** where
2:2 and it filled the **h** where they were meeting.
8:3 He went from **h** to **h**, dragging out both men
9:11 "Go over to Straight Street, to the **h** of Judas.
10:17 Just then the men sent by Cornelius found the **h**
10:22 so you can go to his **h** and give him a message."
10:30 "Four days ago I was praying in my **h** at three
11:11 Caesarea arrived at the **h** where I was staying.
16:34 Then he brought them into his **h** and set a meal
19:16 them with such violence that they fled from the **h**,
28:23 day a large number of people came to Paul's **h**.
28:30 the next two years, Paul lived in his own rented **h**.
Eph 2:20 We are his **h**, built on the foundation of the
Col 4:15 and to Nympha and those who meet in her **h**.
1Ti 5:13 and spend their time gossiping from **h** to **h**,
Phm 1:2 am also writing to the church that meets in your **h**.
Heb 3:2 and was entrusted with God's entire **h**.
3:3 just as a person who builds a fine **h** deserves more praise than the **h** itself.
3:4 For every **h** has a builder, but God is the one who
3:5 Moses was certainly faithful in God's **h**, but only
2Jn 1:10 don't invite him into your **h** or encourage him in

HOUSEHOLD (101) [HOUSE]

Ge 12:5 and all the people who had joined his **h** at Haran—
12:17 LORD sent a terrible plague upon Pharaoh's **h**
12:20 and his wife, with all their **h** and belongings.
14:14 he called together the men born into his **h**, 318 of
15:2 a son, Eliezer of Damascus, a servant in my **h**,
17:12 but also to the servants born in your **h**
17:23 and every other male in his **h** and circumcised
17:27 along with all the other men and boys of the **h**,
20:7 can be sure that you and your entire **h** will die."
20:17 his wife, and the other women of the **h**,
24:2 day Abraham said to the man in charge of his **h**,
31:19 Rachel stole her father's **h** gods and took them
31:30 but why have you stolen my **h** gods?"
31:32 But as for your **h** gods, let the person who has
31:34 Rachel had taken the **h** gods and had stuffed them
32:1 As Jacob and his **h** started on their way again,
32:7 He divided his **h**, along with the flocks and herds
32:10 a walking stick, and now my **h** fills two camps!
33:17 Jacob and his **h** traveled on to Succoth.
35:2 So Jacob told everyone in his **h**, "Destroy your
36:6 his wives, children, **h** servants, cattle, and flocks—
39:4 Potiphar soon put Joseph in charge of his entire **h**
39:5 All his **h** affairs began to run smoothly, and his
39:8 master trusts me with everything in his entire **h**.
40:20 he gave a banquet for all his officials and **h** staff.
41:40 You will manage my **h** and organize all my people.
43:16 he said to the manager of his **h**, "These men will
43:19 they went over to the man in charge of Joseph's **h**.
43:23 Don't worry about it," the **h** manager told them.
44:1 these instructions to the man in charge of his **h**:
44:2 So the **h** manager did as he was told.
44:4 Joseph said to his **h** manager, "Chase after them
45:8 manager of his entire **h** and ruler over all Egypt.
45:11 and your **h** will come to utter poverty.' "
50:8 also took his brothers and the entire **h** of Jacob.
Ex 16:16 The LORD says that each **h** should gather as
20:10 On that day no one in your **h** may do any kind of
23:12 It will also allow the people of your **h**,
Dt 5:14 On that day no one in your **h** may do any kind of
14:26 of the LORD your God and celebrate with your **h**.
22:8 on your **h** if someone falls from the roof.
26:11 the LORD your God has given to you and your **h**.
Jdg 6:27 was afraid of the other members of his father's **h**
17:5 and he made a sacred ephod and some **h** idols.
18:14 some **h** idols, a carved image, and a cast idol.
18:17 the sacred ephod, the **h** idols, and the cast idol.
18:19 tribe of Israel than just for the **h** of one man?"
18:20 sacred ephod, the **h** idols, and the carved image.
1Sa 22:14 and a highly honored member of your **h**!
25:22 one man of his **h** is still alive tomorrow morning!"
2Sa 6:11 and the LORD blessed him and his entire **h**.
9:12 all the members of Ziba's **h** were Mephibosheth's
12:11 will cause your own **h** to rebel against you.
15:16 So the king and his **h** set out at once. He left no
19:18 and worked hard ferrying the king's **h** across the
1Ki 4:7 providing food from the people for the king's **h**.
5:9 to you. You can pay me with food for my **h**."
5:11 payment of 100,000 bushels of wheat for his **h**
2Ki 23:24 the mediums and psychics, the **h** gods,
1Ch 13:14 and the LORD blessed him and his entire **h**.
Job 19:15 The members of my **h** have forgotten me.
Ps 105:21 Joseph was put in charge of all the king's **h**;
Pr 31:15 gets up before dawn to prepare breakfast for her **h**
31:21 She has no fear of winter for her **h** because all of
31:27 She carefully watches all that goes on in her **h**
Ecc 2:7 and women, and others were born into my **h**.
Jer 20:6 and all your **h** will go as captives to Babylon.
20:8 from the LORD have made me a **h** joke.
49:29 and their **h** goods and camels will be taken away.
Da 11:26 Those of his own **h** will bring his downfall.
Mic 7:6 Your enemies will be right in your own **h**.
Zec 10:2 **H** gods give false advice, fortune-tellers predict
Mt 10:25 And since I, the master of the **h**, have been called
10:25 more will it happen to you, the members of the **h**!
10:36 Your enemies will be right in your own **h**!
24:45 can give the responsibility of managing his **h**
Lk 12:42 master gives the responsibility of managing his **h**
Jn 4:53 And the officer and his entire **h** believed in Jesus.
18:18 and the **h** servants were standing around a charcoal
18:26 But one of the **h** servants of the high priest,
Ac 10:2 who feared the God of Israel, as did his entire **h**.
10:7 Cornelius called two of his **h** servants and a devout
11:14 will tell you how you and all your **h** will be saved!'
16:15 was baptized along with other members of her **h**,
16:31 and you will be saved, along with your entire **h**."
16:32 of the Lord with him and all who lived in his **h**.
16:33 and everyone in his **h** were immediately baptized.

16:34 He and his entire **h** rejoiced because they all
18: 8 the synagogue, and all his **h** believed in the Lord.
Ro 16:10 And give my best regards to the members of the **h**
16:11 Greet the Christians in the **h** of Narcissus.
1Co 1:11 For some members of Chloe's **h** have told me
1:16 (Oh yes, I also baptized the **h** of Stephanas. I don't
16:15 and his **h** were the first to become Christians in
1Ti 3: 5 For if a man cannot manage his own **h**, how can he
3:12 and he must manage his children and **h** well.
3:15 people must conduct themselves in the **h** of God.
5: 8 especially those living in the same **h**, have denied
2Ti 4:19 and those living at the **h** of Onesiphorus.
Heb 3: 6 the faithful Son, was in charge of the entire **h**.
3: 6 And we are God's **h**, if we keep up our courage

HOUSEHOLDS (4) [HOUSE]

Ge 46:31 And Joseph said to his brothers and to all their **h**,
47:24 to feed yourselves, your **h**, and your little ones."
Nu 16:32 along with their **h** and the followers who were
Dt 11: 6 along with their **h** and tents and every living thing

HOUSES (51) [HOUSE]

Ex 8: 3 They will come up out of the river and into your **h**,
8: 9 pray that you and your **h** will be rid of the frogs.
8:13 The frogs in the **h**, the courtyards, and the fields all
10: 6 the homes of your officials and all the **h** of Egypt.
Lev 14:34 I may contaminate some of your **h** with an
25:33 all **h** within the Levitical cities—must be returned
Dt 6:11 The **h** will be richly stocked with goods you did
2Ki 23: 7 He also tore down the **h** of the shrine prostitutes
25: 9 the royal palace, and all the **h** of Jerusalem.
Ne 3:23 Ananiah repaired the sections next to their own **h**.
7: 4 And only a few **h** were scattered throughout the
8:16 used them to build shelters on the roofs of their **h**,
9:25 They took over **h** full of good things, with cisterns
Job 15:28 They will live in abandoned **h** that are ready to
24:16 They break into **h** at night and sleep in the
27:18 The **h** built by the wicked are as fragile as a
Pr 1:13 we'll get! We'll fill our **h** with all kinds of things!
19:14 can provide their sons with an inheritance of **h**
Isa 6:11 Until their **h** are deserted and the whole country is
13:21 The **h** will be haunted by howling creatures.
22:10 You check the **h** and tear some down to get stone
27:10 cities will be silent and empty, the **h** abandoned,
54:11 and make the walls of your **h** from precious jewels.
65:21 people will live in the **h** they build and eat the fruit
65:22 when invaders took the **h** and confiscated the
Jer 2:34 them even though they didn't break into your **h**!
19:13 Yes, all the **h** in Jerusalem, including the palace of
19:13 all the **h** where you burned incense on the rooftops
32:15 and will buy and sell **h** and vineyards and fields."
32:29 They will burn down all these **h**, where the people
33: 4 Though you have torn down the **h** of this city
35: 7 And do not build **h** or plant crops or vineyards,
35: 9 We haven't built **h** or owned vineyards or farms
50:26 Crush her walls and **h** into heaps of rubble.
51:30 The invaders have burned the **h** and broken down
52:13 the royal palace, and all the **h** of Jerusalem.
Eze 11: 3 say to the people, 'Is it not a good time to build **h**?
33:30 They talk about you in their **h** and whisper about
Da 2: 5 and your **h** will be demolished into heaps of
3:29 and their **h** will be crushed into heaps of rubble.
Joel 2: 9 They enter all the **h**, climbing like thieves through
Am 3:15 their winter mansions and their summer **h**, too—
5:11 you will never live in the beautiful stone **h** you are
Hab 2:11 The very stones in the walls of your **h** cry out
Zep 2: 7 They will lie down to rest in the abandoned **h** in
Hag 1: 4 "Why are you living in luxurious **h** while my
1: 9 while you are all busy building your own fine **h**.
Zec 14: 2 be taken, the **h** plundered, and the women raped.
Mt 19:29 And everyone who has given up **h** or brothers
Mk 10:30 **h**, brothers, sisters, mothers, children,
Ac 4:34 because people who owned land or **h** sold them

HOUSETOP (2) [HOUSE]

2Ki 19:26 They are like grass sprouting on a **h**,
Isa 37:27 They are like grass sprouting on a **h**,

HOUSETOPS (2) [HOUSE]

Mt 10:27 in your ears, shout from the **h** for all to hear!
Lk 12: 3 doors will be shouted from the **h** for all to hear!

HOUSING (1) [HOUSE]

Ne 3:31 repaired the wall as far as the **h** for the Temple

HOVER (4) [HOVERED, HOVERING, HOVERS]

Ex 25:22 gold cherubim that **h** over the Ark of the Covenant.
33: 9 and **h** at the entrance while the LORD spoke with
Isa 5:30 A cloud of darkness and sorrow will **h** over Israel.
31: 5 The LORD Almighty will **h** over Jerusalem as a

HOVERED (4) [HOVER]

Nu 10:34 on each day, the cloud of the LORD **h** over them.
Eze 10:18 the door of the Temple and **h** above the cherubim.
10:19 And the glory of the God of Israel **h** above them.
11:22 and the glory of the God of Israel **h** above them.

HOVERING (2) [HOVER]

Ge 1: 2 And the Spirit of God was **h** over its surface.
Isa 6: 2 **H** around him were mighty seraphim, each with six

HOVERS (3) [HOVER]

Nu 14:14 your people in the pillar of cloud that **h** over them.
Dt 32:11 eagle that rouses her chicks / and **h** over her young,
Isa 31: 5 hover over Jerusalem as a bird **h** around its nest.

HOW (921) [HOWEVER, SOMEHOW]

Ge 3:13 asked the woman, "**H** could you do such a thing?"
4:12 crops for you, no matter **h** hard you work!
15: 8 **h** can I be sure that you will give it to me?"
17:17 "**H** could I become a father at the age of one
17:17 Sarah is ninety; **h** could she have a baby?"
18:12 "**H** could a worn-out woman like me have a
19:20 let me go there instead; don't you see **h** small it is?
23: 8 "Since this is **h** you feel, be so kind as to ask
25:30 (This was **h** Esau got his other name, Edom—
26:10 "**H** could you treat us this way!"
26:29 And now look **h** the LORD has blessed you!"
27:11 Think **h** hairy Esau is and **h** smooth my skin is!
27:20 "**H** were you able to find it so quickly, my son?"
29: 6 "**H** is he?" Jacob asked. "He's well
29:15 because we are relatives. **H** much do you want?"
30:11 named him Gad, for she said, "**H** fortunate I am!"
30:28 **H** much do I owe you? Whatever it is, I'll pay it."
30:29 "You know **h** faithfully I've served you through
30:29 and **h** your flocks and herds have grown.
30:40 This is **h** he built his flock from Laban's.
31: 6 You know **h** hard I have worked for your father,
37:14 "Go and see **h** your brothers and the flocks are
38:16 "**H** much will you pay me?" Tamar asked.
38:29 "**H** did you break out first?" And ever after,
39: 9 his wife. **H** could I ever do such a wicked thing?
42: 9 You have come to see **h** vulnerable our land has
42:12 "You have come to discover **h** vulnerable the
42:15 This is **h** I will test your story. I swear by the life
42:19 We'll see **h** honorable you really are. Only one of
43: 7 **H** could we have known he would say, 'Bring me
43:22 We have no idea **h** the money got into our sacks."
43:27 He asked them **h** they had been getting along, and
then he said, "**H** is your father—
44:16 my lord, what can we say to you? **H** can we plead?
H can we prove our innocence?
44:34 For **h** can I return to my father if the boy is not
45:13 Tell my father **h** I am honored here in Egypt.
47: 8 "**H** old are you?" Pharaoh asked him.
49:15 When he sees **h** good the countryside is, / **h**
pleasant the land,
Ex 2:11 and he saw **h** hard they were forced to work.
2:18 "**H** did you get the flocks watered so quickly
3: 9 and I have seen **h** the Egyptians have oppressed
3:11 "**H** can you expect me to lead the Israelites out of
6:12 **H** can I expect Pharaoh to listen? I'm no orator!"
10: 3 says: **H** long will you refuse to submit to me?
10: 7 to him. "**H** long will you let these disasters go on?
12: 4 on the size of each family and **h** much they can eat.
14:30 This was **h** the LORD rescued Israel from the
16:28 "**H** long will these people refuse to obey my
18: 1 He had heard about **h** the LORD had brought
18: 8 and **h** the LORD had delivered his people from
18:20 and show them **h** to conduct their lives.
19: 4 You know **h** I brought you to myself and carried
29:35 "This is **h** you will ordain Aaron and his sons to
32: 5 When Aaron saw **h** excited the people were about
32: 9 "I have seen **h** stubborn and rebellious these
32:21 "**H** did they ever make you bring such terrible sin
33:16 **h** will anyone ever know that your people and I
33:16 **H** else will they know we are special and distinct
Lev 2: 8 "No matter **h** a grain offering has been prepared
13:59 This is **h** the priest will determine whether these
18:24 because this is **h** the people I am expelling from
Nu 6:27 This is **h** Aaron and his sons will designate the
8:26 This is **h** you will assign duties to the Levites."
12: 7 But that is not **h** I communicate with my servant
13:20 **H** is the soil? Is it fertile or poor? Are there many
14:11 to Moses, "**H** long will these people reject me?
14:27 "**H** long will this wicked nation complain about
22: 3 And when they saw **h** many Israelites there were,
23: 8 But **h** can I curse / those whom God has not
cursed? / **H** can I condemn
24: 5 **H** beautiful are your tents, O Jacob; / **h** lovely are
your homes, O Israel!
26: 2 to find out **h** many of each family are of military
27:21 This is **h** Joshua and the rest of the community of
28:24 this is **h** you will prepare the food offerings to be
Dt 1:12 But **h** can I settle all your quarrels and problems by
1:17 Don't be afraid of **h** they will react, for you are
1:28 **H** can we go on? Our scouts have demoralized us
1:31 And you saw **h** the LORD your God cared for
7:17 '**H** can we ever conquer these nations that are
8: 2 Remember **h** the LORD your God led you
9: 7 "Remember **h** angry you made the LORD your
9: 8 Remember **h** angry you made the LORD at
9:16 **H** quickly you had turned from the path the
9:19 **H** I feared for you, for the LORD was ready to
11: 4 **h** he drowned them in the Red Sea as they were
11: 4 and **h** he has kept them devastated to this very day!
11: 5 They didn't see **h** the LORD cared for you in the
12: 8 whatever you please, but that is not **h** it will be
12:30 not say, '**H** do these nations worship their gods?
15: 2 This is **h** it must be done. Creditors must cancel the
18:21 '**H** will we know whether the prophecy is from the
29:16 "Surely you remember **h** we lived in the land of
29:16 and **h** we traveled through the lands of enemy
31:27 For I know **h** rebellious and stubborn you are.
31:27 **H** much more rebellious will you be after my
32: 3 the name of the LORD; / **h** glorious is our God!
32: 4 God who does no wrong; / **h** just and upright he is!
32:30 **H** could one person chase a thousand of them,
33:29 **H** blessed you are, O Israel! / Who else is like you,
Jos 2:10 For we have heard **h** the LORD made a dry path
5: 1 heard **h** the LORD had dried up the Jordan River
9: 7 "**H** do we know you don't live nearby?
18: 3 "**H** long are you going to wait before taking
22:16 **H** could you turn away from the LORD and build
Jdg 2:17 **H** quickly they turned away from the path of their
6:15 Gideon replied, "**h** can I rescue Israel?
8:28 That is the story of **h** Israel subdued Midian,
16: 5 so strong and **h** he can be overpowered and tied up
16:10 Now please tell me **h** you can be tied up securely."
16:13 Won't you please tell me **h** you can be tied up
16:15 "**H** can you say you love me when you don't
20: 3 then asked **h** this terrible crime had happened.
21: 7 **H** can we find wives for the few who remain,
21:16 "**H** can we find wives for the few who remain,
Ru 2:11 I have heard **h** you left your father and mother
1Sa 2: 1 the LORD! / Oh, **h** the LORD has blessed me!
6: 2 the LORD? Tell us **h** to return it to its own land."
8: 9 but solemnly warn them about **h** a king will treat
8:11 "This is **h** a king will treat you," Samuel said.
10:11 **H** did the son of Kish become a prophet?"
10:27 men who complained, "**H** can this man save us?"
12:17 Then you will realize **h** wicked you have been in
13:13 "**H** foolish!" Samuel exclaimed. "You have
14:29 See **h** much better I feel now that I have eaten this
14:30 think **h** many more we could have killed!"
16: 2 But Samuel asked, "**H** can I do that? If Saul hears
17:18 See **h** your brothers are getting along, and bring
18:23 "**H** can a poor man from a humble family afford
18:28 When the king realized **h** much the LORD was
with David and **h** much Michal loved him,
19: 5 and **h** the LORD brought a great victory to Israel
20: 1 **H** have I offended your father that he is
20:10 "**H** will I know whether or not your father is
20:12 and let you know at once **h** he feels about you.
21: 5 even on ordinary trips, **h** much more on this one!"
28:21 When the woman saw **h** distraught he was,
2Sa 1: 4 "Tell me **h** the battle went." The man replied,
1: 5 "**H** do you know that Saul and Jonathan are
1: 7 me to come to him. '**H** can I help?' I asked him.
1:19 on the hills! / **H** the mighty heroes have fallen!
1:23 **H** beloved and gracious were Saul and Jonathan!
1:25 **H** the mighty heroes have fallen in battle!
1:26 **H** I weep for you, my brother Jonathan! / Oh, **h**
much I loved you!
1:27 **H** the mighty heroes have fallen! / Stripped of their
5: 8 those 'lame' and 'blind' Jebusites. **H** I hate them."
6: 9 "**H** can I ever bring the Ark of the LORD back
6:20 "**H** glorious the king of Israel looked today!
7:22 "**H** great you are, O Sovereign LORD! There is
8:14 This was another example of **h** the LORD made
10: 6 Now the people of Ammon realized **h** seriously
11: 7 David asked him **h** Joab and the army were getting
along and **h** the war was progressing.
11:11 **H** could I go home to wine and dine and sleep with
12:31 That is **h** he dealt with the people of all the
13:26 **h** about sending my brother Amnon instead?"
14: 1 Joab realized **h** much the king longed to see
14:19 "My lord the king, **h** can I deny it?
17:10 your father is and **h** courageous his warriors are.
17:21 And they told him **h** Ahithophel had advised that
19:20 I know **h** much I sinned. That is why I have come
19:28 who eat at your own table! So **h** can I complain?"
20: 9 "**H** are you, my cousin?" Joab said and took him
23:15 **h** I would love some of that good water from the
24: 2 so that I may know **h** many people there are."
1Ki 1: 1 and no matter **h** many blankets covered him,
2: 9 and you will know **h** to arrange a bloody death for
2:22 "**H** can you possibly ask me to give Abishag to
8:27 contain you. **H** much less this Temple I have built!
10: 4 When the queen of Sheba realized **h** wise Solomon
10: 8 **H** happy these people must be! What a privilege
11:22 **H** have we disappointed you that you want to go
11:28 and when Solomon saw **h** industrious he was,
12: 6 he asked. "**H** should I answer these people?"
12: 9 "**H** should I answer these people who want me to
14:19 of Jeroboam's reign, all his wars and **h** he ruled,
17:16 For no matter **h** much they used, there was always
18:21 "**H** long are you going to waver between two
20: 7 to them, "Look **h** this man is stirring up trouble!
20:14 Ahab asked, "**H** will he do it?" And the prophet
21:29 "Do you see **h** Ahab has humbled himself before
22:16 "**H** many times must I demand that you speak only
22:22 " '**H** will you do this?' the LORD asked.
2Ki 1:14 See **h** the fire from heaven has destroyed the first
4: 1 is dead, and you know **h** he feared the LORD.
8:13 "**H** could a nobody like me ever accomplish such
9:22 "**H** can there be peace as long as the idolatry
10:16 with me, and see **h** devoted I am to the LORD."
13: 4 The LORD could see **h** terribly the king of Aram
14:26 and **h** they had absolutely no one to help them.
14:28 and **h** he recovered for Israel both Damascus
17:26 do not know **h** to worship the God of the land.
17:28 and taught the new residents **h** to worship the
18:24 **h** can you think of challenging even the weakest
20: 3 **h** I have always tried to be faithful to you and do
20:20 the extent of his power and **h** he built a pool
1Ch 11:17 **h** I would love some of that good water from the
13:12 "**H** can I ever bring the Ark of God back into my
15:13 We failed to ask God **h** to move it in the proper
18:13 This was another example of **h** the LORD made
19: 6 Now the people of Ammon realized **h** seriously
20: 3 That is **h** he dealt with the people of all the
21: 2 me the totals so I may know **h** many there are."
24: 1 This is **h** Aaron's descendants, the priests,

28:14 David gave instructions regarding **h** much gold
28:15 and lamps, depending on **h** each would be used.
2Ch 6:18 contain you. **H** much less this Temple I have built!
9: 3 When the queen of Sheba realized **h** wise Solomon
9: 7 **H** happy these people must be! What a privilege
10: 6 he asked. "**H** should I answer these people?"
10: 9 "**H** should I answer these people who want me to
12: 8 so that they can learn **h** much better it is to serve
18:15 "**H** many times must I demand that you speak only
18:20 and said, 'I can do it!' " '**H** will you do this?'
20:11 Now see **h** they reward us! For they have come to
24:22 That was **h** King Joash repaid Jehoiada for his love
25: 8 you will be defeated no matter **h** well you fight.
32:15 **H** much less will your God rescue you from my
32:22 That is **h** the LORD rescued Hezekiah
Ezr 10: 4 for it is your duty to tell us **h** to proceed in setting
Ne 1: 2 and about **h** things were going in Jerusalem.
2: 4 The king asked, "Well, **h** can I help you?" With a
2: 6 beside him, asked, "**H** long will you be gone?
2:18 Then I told them about **h** the gracious hand of God
5: 8 **H** often must we redeem them?" And they had
9:10 for you knew **h** arrogantly the Egyptians were
13:27 **H** could you even think of committing this sinful
Est 4: 7 and told him **h** much money Haman had promised
5:11 and **h** he had been promoted over all the other
6: 2 In those records he discovered an account of **h**
8: 1 for Esther had told the king **h** they were related.
8: 6 For **h** can I endure to see my people and my family
Job 1:10 in everything he does. Look **h** rich he is!
4:19 **h** much less will he trust those made of clay!
6: 6 And **h** tasteless is the uncooked white of an egg!
8: 2 "**H** long will you go on like this? Your words are a
9: 2 But **h** can a person be declared innocent in the eyes
13: 3 Oh, **h** I long to speak directly to the Almighty.
14: 1 "**H** frail is humanity! **H** short is life, and **h** full of trouble!
14: 5 You know **h** many months we will live, and we are
15:16 **H** much less pure is a corrupt and sinful person
16: 6 my grief remains no matter **h** I defend myself.
17: 2 by mockers. I watch **h** bitterly they taunt me.
17:12 is day and day is night; **h** they pervert the truth!
18: 2 "**H** long before you stop talking? Speak sense if
19: 2 "**H** long will you torture me? **H** long will you try to break me with your words?
19:28 "**H** dare you go on persecuting me, saying,
21:34 "**H** can you comfort me? All your explanations are
22:13 **H** can he judge through the thick darkness?
25: 4 **H** can a mere mortal stand before God and claim to
25: 6 **H** much less are mere people, who are but worms
26: 2 "**H** you have helped the powerless! **H** you have saved a person who has no strength!
26: 3 **H** you have enlightened my stupidity! What wise
28: 1 "People know **h** to mine silver and refine gold.
28: 2 They know **h** to dig iron from the earth and smelt
28: 3 They know **h** to put light into darkness and explore
28: 6 "People know **h** to find sapphires and gold dust—
28: 9 People know **h** to tear apart flinty rocks
28:25 and determined **h** much rain should fall.
31:14 **h** could I face God? What could I say when he
34:19 He doesn't care **h** great a person may be, and he
35: 3 of living a righteous life? **H** will it benefit me?'
36:30 See **h** he spreads the lightning around him and **h** it lights up the depths of the sea.
37:15 Do you know **h** God controls the storm and causes
37:16 Do you understand **h** he balances the clouds with
38: 5 Do you know **h** its dimensions were determined
38:20 take it to its home? Do you know **h** to get there?
38:33 the laws of the universe and **h** God rules the earth?
39: 2 Do you know **h** many months they carry their
40: 4 "I am nothing—**h** could I ever find the answers?
Ps 4: 2 **H** long will you people ruin my reputation?
4: 2 **H** long will you make these groundless
4: 2 **H** long will you pursue lies? / *Interlude*
6: 3 at heart. / **H** long, O LORD, until you restore me?
9:13 See **h** I suffer at the hands of those who hate me.
10:13 **H** can they think, "God will never call us to
13: 1 O LORD, **h** long will you forget me? Forever? / **H** long will you look the other way?
13: 2 **H** long must I struggle with anguish in my soul,
13: 2 **H** long will my enemy have the upper hand?
19:12 **H** can I know all the sins lurking in my heart?
21: 1 **H** the king rejoices in your strength, O LORD!
25:19 See **h** many enemies I have, / and **h** viciously they hate me!
27:11 Teach me **h** to live, O LORD. / Lead me along
35:17 **H** long, O Lord, will you look on and do nothing?
36: 2 they cannot see **h** wicked they really are.
36: 7 **H** precious is your unfailing love, O God!
39: 4 remind me **h** brief my time on earth will be.
41: 5 "**H** soon will he die and be forgotten?" they ask.
42: 4 heart is breaking / as I remember **h** it used to be:
46: 8 See **h** he brings destruction upon the world
48: 1 **H** great is the LORD, / and **h** much we should praise him
55: 6 Oh, **h** I wish I had wings like a dove; / then I
55: 8 **H** quickly I would escape— / far away from this
58: 5 snake charmers, / no matter **h** skillfully they play.
63: 3 love is better to me than life itself; / **h** I praise you!
63: 7 I think **h** much you have helped me; / I sing for joy
64: 5 and plan **h** to set their traps. / "Who will ever
66: 2 glory of his name! / Tell the world **h** glorious he is.
66: 3 Say to God, "**H** awesome are your deeds!
67: 4 **H** glad the nations will be, singing for joy,
69: 5 O God, you know **h** foolish I am; / my sins cannot
71:15 for I am overwhelmed by **h** much you have done
73:21 Then I realized **h** bitter I had become, / **h** pained I had been by all I had seen.
73:28 But as for me, **h** good it is to be near God! / I have
74: 3 see **h** the enemy has destroyed your sanctuary.
74:10 **H** long, O God, will you allow our enemies to
74:18 See **h** these enemies scoff at you, LORD.
74:22 Remember **h** these fools insult you all day long.
78:40 **h** often they rebelled against him in the desert
78:42 and **h** he rescued them from their enemies.
79: 5 O LORD, **h** long will you be angry with us? Forever? / **H** long will your jealousy burn like fire?
80: 4 **h** long will you be angry and reject our prayers?
81:14 **H** quickly I would then subdue their enemies!
81:14 **H** soon my hands would be upon their foes!
82: 2 "**H** long will you judges hand down unjust
82: 2 **H** long will you shower special favors on the
84: 1 **H** lovely is your dwelling place, / O LORD
84: 4 **H** happy are those who can live in your house,
89:46 O LORD, **h** long will this go on? / Will you hide
89:46 **H** long will your anger burn like fire?
89:47 Remember **h** short my life is, / **h** empty and futile
89:50 Consider, Lord, **h** your servants are disgraced!
90:13 come back to us! / **H** long will you delay?
91: 8 you will see **h** the wicked are punished.
92: 5 miracles you do! / And **h** deep are your thoughts.
92:10 as a wild bull. / **H** refreshed I am by your power!
94: 3 **H** long, O LORD? / **H** long will the wicked be
94: 4 Hear their arrogance! / **H** these evildoers boast!
103:14 For he understands **h** weak we are; / he knows we
104: 1 I tell myself; / O LORD my God, **h** great you are!
106:13 Yet **h** quickly they forgot what he had done!
107:38 **H** he blesses them! / They raise large families
111: 2 **H** amazing are the deeds of the LORD! / All who
111: 4 **H** gracious and merciful is our LORD!
116: 5 **H** kind the LORD is! **H** good he is!
119: 9 **H** can a young person stay pure? / By obeying
119:47 **H** I delight in your commands! / **H** I love them!
119:84 **H** long must I wait? / When will you punish those
119:97 Oh, **h** I love your law! / I think about it all day
119:103 **H** sweet are your words to my taste; / they are
119:156 LORD, **h** great is your mercy; / in your justice,
119:159 See **h** I love your commandments, LORD.
120: 3 do to you? / **H** will he increase your punishment?
120: 5 **H** I suffer among these scoundrels of Meshech!
127: 5 **H** happy is the man whose quiver is full of them!
128: 1 **H** happy are those who fear the LORD— / all who
128: 2 **H** happy you will be! **H** rich your life!
133: 1 **H** wonderful it is, **h** pleasant, / when brothers
137: 4 But **h** can we sing the songs of the LORD
139:14 workmanship is marvelous—and **h** well I know it.
139:17 **H** precious are your thoughts about me, O God!
147: 1 **H** good it is to sing praises to our God! / **H** delightful and **h** right!
147: 5 **H** great is our Lord! His power is absolute!
147:10 **h** puny in his sight is the strength of a man.
147:15 his orders to the world— / **h** swiftly his word flies!
Pr 1:22 "**H** long will you go on being simpleminded?
1:22 **H** long will you mockers relish your mocking?
1:22 **H** long will you fools fight the facts?
2: 9 and you will know **h** to find the right course of
5:12 and you will say, "**H** I hated discipline! If only I
6: 9 But you, lazybones, **h** long will you sleep?
8: 5 **H** naive you are! Let me give you common sense.
8:31 And **h** happy I was with what he created—his wide
9: 6 and begin to live; learn **h** to be wise."
11:31 **h** much more true that the wicked and the sinner
15:11 **H** much more does he know the human heart!
16:16 **H** much better to get wisdom than gold,
16:33 the dice, but the LORD determines **h** they fall.
19: 7 **h** much more will their friends avoid them.
20:24 **H** can we understand the road we travel? It is the
21:30 Human plans, no matter **h** wise or well advised,
23: 7 They are always thinking about **h** much it costs.
23:15 My child, **h** I will rejoice if you become wise.
27:11 **h** happy I will be if you turn out to be wise!
30:19 **h** an eagle glides through the sky, / **h** a snake slithers on a rock, / **h** a ship navigates the ocean, / **h** a man loves a woman.
30:20 Equally amazing is **h** an adulterous woman can
Ecc 1: 8 No matter **h** much we see, we are never satisfied.
1: 8 No matter **h** much we hear, we are not content.
1:10 **H** do you know it didn't already exist long ago?
2:19 gained by my skill and hard work. **H** meaningless!
3:19 real advantage over the animals. **H** meaningless!
4:11 from each other. But **h** can one be warm alone?
5:10 **H** absurd to think that wealth brings true
6: 8 being wise and knowing **h** to act in front of others?
6:12 who knows **h** our days can best be spent?
7:22 For you know **h** often you yourself have laughed at
8: 1 **H** wonderful to be wise, to be able to analyze
8: 7 **h** can people avoid what they don't know is going
8:10 **H** strange that they were the very ones who
8:17 in our world, no matter **h** hard they work at it.
9:15 wise man living there who knew **h** to save the
SS 1: 3 **H** fragrant your cologne, and **h** pleasing your
1: 4 O my king." / "**H** happy we are for him!
1:10 **H** lovely are your cheeks, with your earrings
1:10 **H** stately is your neck, accented with a long string
1:15 "**H** beautiful you are, my beloved, **h** beautiful!
2: 4 so everyone can see **h** much he loves me.
2:13 **H** delicious they smell! Yes, spring is here! Arise,
4: 1 "**H** beautiful you are, my beloved, **h** beautiful!
4: 3 a ribbon of scarlet. Oh, **h** beautiful your mouth!
4:10 **H** sweet is your love, my treasure, my bride! **H** much better it is than wine!
7: 1 "**H** beautiful are your sandaled feet, O queenly
7: 6 "Oh, **h** delightful you are, my beloved; **h** pleasant for utter delight!
8:13 **h** wonderful that your companions can listen to
Isa 1:18 "No matter **h** deep the stain of your sins, I can
1:21 See **h** Jerusalem, once so faithful, has become a
2:22 as frail as breath. **H** can they be of help to anyone?
3: 9 not one bit ashamed. **H** terrible it will be for them!
3:15 **H** dare you grind my people into the dust like
6:11 Then I said, "Lord, **h** long must I do this?"
12: 4 the world what he has done. / Oh, **h** mighty he is!
14:12 "**H** you are fallen from heaven, O shining star,
20: 5 **H** dismayed will be the Philistines, who counted
21:11 "Watchman, **h** much longer until morning?
23: 7 **H** can this silent ruin be all that is left of your once
24: 1 See **h** he is scattering the people over the face of
29:12 they will say, "Sorry, we don't know **h** to read."
29:16 **H** stupid can you be? He is the Potter, and he is
33:18 and estimated **h** much plunder they would get from
36: 9 **h** can you think of challenging even the weakest
38: 3 **h** I have always tried to be faithful to you and do
40:27 **h** can you say the LORD does not see your
40:27 **H** can you say God refuses to hear your case?
42:18 "Oh, **h** deaf and blind you are toward me!
44: 9 **H** foolish are those who manufacture idols to be
44:19 and roast my meat. **H** can the rest of it be a god?
45: 9 Does the pot exclaim, '**H** clumsy can you be!'?
45:10 **H** terrible it would be if a newborn baby said to its
48: 4 "I know **h** stubborn and obstinate you are.
52: 7 **H** beautiful on the mountains are the feet of those
57:11 **H** is it that you don't even remember me or think
59:13 We know **h** unfair and oppressive we have been,
63:18 **H** briefly your holy people possessed the holy
64: 1 **H** the mountains would quake in your presence!
64: 3 And oh, **h** the mountains quaked!
64: 5 is heavy on us. **H** can people like us be saved?
Jer 2: 2 I remember **h** eager you were to please me as a
2: 2 **h** you loved me and followed me even through the
2:21 "**H** could this happen? When I planted you,
2:21 **H** did you grow into this corrupt wild vine?
2:23 But **h** can you say that? Go and look in any valley
2:33 "**H** you plot and scheme to win your lovers.
4:13 **H** terrible it will be! Our destruction is sure!
4:14 **H** long will you harbor your evil thoughts?
4:21 **H** long must this go on? **H** long must I be surrounded by war and death?
5: 7 "**H** can I pardon you? For even your children have
7:18 Watch **h** the children gather wood and the fathers
7:18 See **h** the women knead dough and make cakes to
8: 8 " '**H** can you say, "We are wise because we have
9:20 daughters to wail; teach one another **h** to lament.
12: 4 **H** long must this land weep? Even the grass in the
12: 5 makes you tired, **h** will you race against horses?
12: 6 not trust them, no matter **h** pleasantly they speak.
13: 9 This illustrates **h** I will rot away the pride of Judah
13:12 you don't need to tell us **h** prosperous we will be!'
13:21 **H** will you feel when the LORD sets your foreign
13:27 Jerusalem! **H** long will it be before you are pure?"
15: 5 for you? Who will even bother to ask **h** you are?
17: 9 desperately wicked. Who really knows **h** bad it is?
23:26 **H** long will this go on? If they are prophets,
31:22 **H** long will you wander, my wayward daughter?
32:24 "See **h** the siege ramps have been built against the
35:13 'Come and learn a lesson about **h** to obey me.
36:17 "But first, tell us **h** you got these messages.
47: 5 **h** long will you lament and mourn?
47: 7 But **h** can it be still when the LORD has sent it on
48:17 See **h** the strong scepter is broken, **h** the beautiful
48:39 **H** it is broken! Hear the wailing! See the shame of
49:12 the innocent must suffer, **h** much more must you!
50: 6 and cannot remember **h** to get back to the fold.
50:28 as they declare in Jerusalem **h** the LORD our God
51:41 "**H** Babylon is fallen—great Babylon,
La 1: 4 women are crying—**h** bitterly Jerusalem weeps!
1:11 look," she mourns, "and see **h** I am despised.
2:13 O virgin daughter of Zion, **h** can I comfort you?
4: 1 **H** the gold has lost its luster! Even the finest gold
4: 2 See **h** the precious children of Jerusalem,
Eze 4: 3 and demonstrate **h** the enemy will attack
6: 9 They will recognize **h** grieved I am by their
12:16 so they can confess to their captors about **h** wicked
14:21 **H** terrible it will be when all four of these
14:22 You will see with your own eyes **h** wicked they
15: 2 of man, **h** does a grapevine compare to a tree?
16:16 Unbelievable! **H** could such a thing ever happen?
20: 3 **H** dare you come to ask for my help? As surely as
20: 4 Make them realize **h** loathsome the actions of their
22:14 **H** strong and courageous will you be in my day of
26:17 once ruler of the sea, / **h** you have been destroyed!
29:16 Egypt's shattered condition will remind Israel of **h**
33:10 upon us; we are wasting away! **H** can we survive?'
36:23 I will show **h** holy my great name is—the name
Da 1:13 see **h** we look compared to the other young men
4: 3 **H** great are his signs, / **h** powerful his wonders!
4:19 **h** I wish the events foreshadowed in this dream
8:13 "**H** long will the events of this vision last?
8:13 **H** long will the rebellion that causes desecration
8:13 **H** long will the Temple and heaven's armies be
9:18 See **h** your city lies in ruins—for everyone knows
10:17 **H** can someone like me, your servant, talk to you,
12: 6 "**H** long will it be until these shocking events
12: 8 So I asked, "**H** will all this finally end, my lord?"
Hos 5:13 "When Israel and Judah saw **h** sick they were,
7: 9 unaware of **h** weak and old he has become.
7:13 "**H** terrible it will be for my people who have
8: 5 **H** long will you be incapable of innocence?
10: 1 **H** prosperous Israel is—a luxuriant vine loaded
11: 3 It was I who taught Israel **h** to walk, leading him
11: 8 "Oh, **h** can I give you up, Israel? **H** can I let you
11: 8 **H** can I destroy you like Admah and Zeboiim?
13:13 being born. **H** stubborn they are! **H** foolish!

Joel 1:15 from the Almighty. **H** terrible that day will be!
1:18 **H** the animals moan with hunger! The cattle
2:2 army appears! **H** great and powerful they are!
Am 5:10 **H** you hate honest judges! **H** you despise people who tell the truth!
5:18 **H** terrible it will be for you who say, "If only the
5:23 not listen to your music, no matter **h** lovely it is.
6:1 **H** terrible it will be for you who lounge in luxury
6:2 than they were, and look at **h** they were destroyed.
6:4 **H** terrible it will be for you who sprawl on ivory
6:12 but that's **h** stupid you are when you turn justice
8:10 only son had died. **H** very bitter that day will be!
Jnh 1:2 because I have seen **h** wicked its people are."
1:6 "**H** can you sleep at a time like this?" he shouted.
2:4 **H** will I ever again see your holy Temple?'
4:2 I knew **h** easily you could cancel your plans for
Mic 2:1 **H** terrible it will be for you who lie awake at night,
2:5 and the LORD's people will have no say in **h** the
6:5 **h** King Balak of Moab tried to have you cursed
6:5 and **h** Balaam son of Beor blessed you instead?
6:11 And **h** can I tolerate all your merchants who use
7:3 **H** skilled they are at using them! Officials
Na 3:1 **H** terrible it will be for Nineveh, the city of murder
3:6 with filth and show the world **h** vile you really are.
Hab 1:2 **H** long, O LORD, must I call for help? But you
2:1 will say to me and **h** he will answer my complaint.
2:9 "**H** terrible it will be for you who get rich by
2:12 "**H** terrible it will be for you who build cities with
2:15 "**H** terrible it will be for you who make your
2:18 **H** foolish to trust in something made by your own
2:19 **H** terrible it will be for you who beg lifeless
Zep 2:5 And **h** terrible it will be for you Philistines who
2:15 But now, look **h** it has become an utter ruin,
3:1 **H** terrible it will be for rebellious,
Hag 1:5 Consider **h** things are going for you!
1:7 Consider **h** things are going for you!
2:3 In comparison, **h** does it look to you now?
2:14 "That is **h** it is with this people and this nation,
2:15 consider **h** things were going for you before you
Zec 1:12 **H** long will it be until you again show mercy to
2:2 to see **h** wide and **h** long it is."
9:17 **H** wonderful and beautiful they will be! The young
11:16 This will illustrate **h** I will give this nation a
14:7 Only the LORD knows **h** this could happen!
Mal 1:2 But you retort, "Really? **H** have you loved us?"
1:6 you ask, '**H** have we ever despised your name?'
1:7 "Then you ask, '**H** have we defiled the sacrifices?'
1:8 that to your governor, and see **h** pleased he is!"
2:17 you ask. "**H** have we wearied him?"
3:7 '**H** can we return when we have never gone away?'
3:13 do you mean? **H** have we spoken against you?'
Mt 1:18 Now this is **h** Jesus the Messiah was born.
4:19 and I will show you **h** to fish for people!"
5:47 your friends, **h** are you different from anyone else?
6:23 is really darkness, **h** deep that darkness will be!
6:28 Look at the lilies and **h** they grow. They don't
7:2 it will be used to measure **h** you are judged.
7:4 **H** can you think of saying, 'Friend, let me help you
7:11 If you sinful people know **h** to give good gifts to
7:11 **h** much more will your heavenly Father give good
8:18 When Jesus noticed **h** large the crowd was
10:25 **h** much more will it happen to you, the members of
11:16 "**H** shall I describe this generation? These people
12:12 And **h** much more valuable is a person than a
12:34 **H** could evil men like you speak what is good
15:34 "**H** many loaves of bread do you have?"
16:11 **H** could you even think I was talking about food?
16:26 And **h** do you benefit if you gain the whole world
17:17 **H** long must I be with you until you believe?
17:17 **H** long must I put up with you? Bring the boy to
18:7 "**H** terrible it will be for anyone who causes others
18:7 but **h** terrible it will be for the person who does the
18:21 **h** often should I forgive someone who sins against
21:20 and asked, "**H** did the fig tree wither so quickly?"
22:12 '**h** is it that you are here without wedding clothes?'
22:16 "Teacher, we know **h** honest you are.
22:45 him Lord, **h** can he be his son at the same time?"
23:6 And **h** they love to sit at the head table at banquets
23:13 "**H** terrible it will be for you teachers of religious
23:15 **h** terrible it will be for you teachers of religious
23:16 "Blind guides! **H** terrible it will be for you!
23:19 **H** blind! For which is greater, the gift on the altar,
23:23 "**H** terrible it will be for you teachers of religious
23:25 "**H** terrible it will be for you teachers of religious
23:27 "**H** terrible it will be for you teachers of religious
23:29 "**H** terrible it will be for you teachers of religious
23:33 of vipers! **H** will you escape the judgment of hell?
23:37 **H** often I have wanted to gather your children
24:19 **H** terrible it will be for pregnant women and for
25:19 and called them to give an account of **h** they had
26:4 to discuss **h** to capture Jesus secretly and put him
26:15 "**H** much will you pay me to betray Jesus to
26:24 long ago. But **h** terrible it will be for my betrayer.
26:54 **h** would the Scriptures be fulfilled that describe
27:1 and other leaders met again to discuss **h** to
Mk 1:17 and I will show you **h** to fish for people!"
3:23 way of illustration, "**H** can Satan cast out Satan?
3:26 if Satan is fighting against himself, **h** can he stand?
4:13 **h** will you understand all the others I am going to
4:30 "**H** can I describe the Kingdom of God?
5:19 has done for you and **h** merciful he has been."
5:31 **H** can you ask, 'Who touched me?' "
6:38 "**H** much food do you have?" he asked. "Go
8:4 "**H** are we supposed to find enough food for them
8:5 "**H** many loaves of bread do you have?" he asked.
8:19 **H** many baskets of leftovers did you pick up
8:20 **h** many large baskets of leftovers did you pick
8:36 And **h** do you benefit if you gain the whole world
9:19 **H** long must I be with you until you believe?
9:19 **H** long must I put up with you? Bring the boy to
9:21 "**H** long has this been happening?" Jesus asked
9:50 if it loses its flavor, **h** do you make it salty again?
10:23 "**H** hard it is for rich people to get into the
11:18 Jesus had done, they began planning **h** to kill him.
12:14 these men said, "we know **h** honest you are.
12:37 him Lord, **h** can he be his son at the same time?"
12:39 And **h** they love the seats of honor in the
13:17 **H** terrible it will be for pregnant women and for
14:21 long ago. But **h** terrible it will be for my betrayer.
15:39 officer who stood facing him saw **h** he had died,
Lk 1:18 said to the angel, "**H** can I know this will happen?
1:25 "**H** kind the Lord is!" she exclaimed. "He has
1:34 Mary asked the angel, "But **h** can I have a baby?
1:46 Mary responded, / "Oh, **h** I praise the Lord.
1:47 **H** I rejoice in God my Savior!
1:51 **H** he scatters the proud and haughty ones!
1:54 And **h** he has helped his servant Israel! / He has
1:77 You will tell his people **h** to find salvation
2:12 And this is **h** you will recognize him: You will find
4:22 "**H** can this be?" they asked. "Isn't this Joseph's
6:42 **H** can you think of saying, 'Friend, let me help you
7:31 "**H** shall I describe this generation?" Jesus asked.
8:36 **h** the demon-possessed man had been healed.
9:25 And **h** do you benefit if you gain the whole world
9:31 And they were speaking of **h** he was about to
9:41 "**h** long must I be with you and put up with you?
10:23 "**H** privileged you are to see what you have seen.
10:26 does the law of Moses say? **H** do you read it?"
11:2 He said, "This is **h** you should pray: / "Father,
11:13 If you sinful people know **h** to give good gifts to
11:13 **h** much more will your heavenly Father give the
11:18 to cast out his demons, **h** can his kingdom survive?
11:42 "But **h** terrible it will be for you Pharisees!
11:43 "**H** terrible it will be for you Pharisees! For **h** you love the seats of honor in the
11:44 Yes, **h** terrible it will be for you. For you are like
11:46 "**h** terrible it will be for you experts in religious
11:47 **H** terrible it will be for you! For you build tombs
11:52 "**H** terrible it will be for you experts in religious
12:15 Real life is not measured by **h** much we own."
12:27 "Look at the lilies and **h** they grow. They don't
12:56 You know **h** to interpret the appearance of the
13:13 stand straight. **H** she praised and thanked God!
13:18 is the Kingdom of God like? **H** can I illustrate it?
13:34 **H** often I have wanted to gather your children
14:29 of funds. And then **h** everyone would laugh at you!
14:34 if it loses its flavor, **h** do you make it salty again?
16:5 He asked the first one, '**H** much do you owe him?'
16:7 " 'And **h** much do you owe my employer?'
17:1 but **h** terrible it will be for the person who does the
17:5 the Lord, "We need more faith; tell us **h** to get it."
18:8 return, **h** many will I find who have faith?"
18:24 "**H** hard it is for rich people to get into the
19:22 If you knew so much about me and **h** tough I am,
19:47 leaders of the people began planning **h** to kill him.
20:44 him Lord, **h** can he be his son at the same time?"
20:46 And **h** they love the seats of honor in the
21:14 So don't worry about **h** to answer the charges
21:23 **H** terrible it will be for pregnant women and for
22:22 But **h** terrible it will be for my betrayer!"
22:48 But Jesus said, "Judas, **h** can you betray me,
24:35 Then the two from Emmaus told their story of **h**
24:35 and **h** they had recognized him as he was breaking
Jn 1:48 "**H** do you know about me?" Nathanael asked.
2:4 "**H** does that concern you and me?" Jesus asked.
3:4 "**H** can an old man go back into his mother's
3:8 so you can't explain **h** people are born of the
3:12 **h** can you possibly believe if I tell you what is
3:28 You yourselves know **h** plainly I told you that I am
3:32 and heard, but **h** few believe what he tells them!
4:12 **H** can you offer better water than he and his sons
5:6 Jesus saw him and knew **h** long he had been ill,
5:47 what he wrote, **h** will you believe what I say?"
6:25 they asked, "Teacher, **h** did you get here?"
6:42 **H** can he say, 'I came down from heaven'?"
6:52 "**H** can this man give us his flesh to eat?"
6:60 very hard to understand. **H** can anyone accept it?"
7:15 "**H** does he know so much when he hasn't studied
7:27 But **h** could he be? For we know where this man
8:57 **H** can you say you have seen Abraham?"
9:16 "But **h** could an ordinary sinner do such
9:19 your son? Was he born blind? If so, **h** can he see?"
9:21 but we don't know **h** he can see or who healed
9:26 did he do?" they asked. "**H** did he heal you?"
10:24 "**H** long are you going to keep us in suspense?
11:36 standing nearby said, "See **h** much he loved him."
11:49 priest that year, said, "**H** can you be so stupid?
12:33 He said this to indicate **h** he was going to die.
13:16 **H** true it is that a servant is not greater than the
13:33 **h** brief are these moments before I must go away
14:4 you know where I am going and **h** to get there."
14:5 where you are going, so **h** can we know the way?"
15:13 And here is **h** to measure it—the greatest love is
21:1 beside the Sea of Galilee. This is **h** it happened.
Ac 2:7 "**H** can this be?" they exclaimed. "These people
3:16 this man—and you know **h** lame he was before.
4:9 Do you want to know **h** he was healed?
4:21 because they didn't know **h** to punish them without
5:4 **H** could you do a thing like this? You weren't
5:9 "**H** could the two of you even think of doing a
8:31 The man replied, "**H** can I, when there is no one to
9:16 And I will show him **h** much he must suffer for
9:27 and told them **h** Saul had seen the Lord on the way
9:27 and **h** he boldly preached in the name of Jesus in
11:13 He told us **h** an angel had appeared to him in his
11:14 He will tell you **h** you and all your household will
12:3 When Herod saw **h** much this pleased the Jewish
12:17 and **h** the Lord had led him out of jail.
14:27 and **h** he had opened the door of faith to the
15:36 to see **h** the new believers are getting along."
16:17 and they have come to tell you **h** to be saved."
20:35 And I have been a constant example of **h** you can
21:20 **h** many thousands of Jews have also believed,
25:20 I was perplexed as to **h** to conduct an investigation
Ro 1:8 **H** I thank God through Jesus Christ for each one of
1:9 God knows **h** often I pray for you. Day and night I
1:17 This Good News tells us **h** God makes us right in
2:4 Don't you realize **h** kind, tolerant, and patient God
2:4 Can't you see **h** kind he has been in giving you
3:6 is not just, **h** is he qualified to judge the world?
3:7 "**h** can God judge and condemn me as a sinner if
4:10 But **h** did his faith help him? Was he declared
5:5 For we know **h** dearly God loves us, because he
5:20 so that all people could see **h** sinful they were.
6:2 we have died to sin, **h** can we continue to live in it?
7:13 But **h** can that be? Did the law, which is good,
7:13 So we can see **h** terrible sin really is.
7:25 is in Jesus Christ our Lord. So you see **h** it is:
8:26 what we should pray for, nor **h** we should pray.
10:14 But **h** can they call on him to save them unless
10:14 And **h** can they believe in him if they have never
10:14 And **h** can they hear about him unless someone
10:15 And **h** will anyone go and tell them without being
10:15 "**H** beautiful are the feet of those who bring good
11:12 think **h** much greater a blessing the world will
11:15 **h** much more wonderful their acceptance will be.
11:22 Notice **h** God is both kind and severe. He is severe
11:33 **H** great are his riches and wisdom and knowledge!
11:33 **H** impossible it is for us to understand his
12:2 and you will know **h** good and pleasing and perfect
12:3 measuring your value by **h** much faith God has
13:11 Another reason for right living is that you know **h**
1Co 1:18 I know very well **h** foolish the message of the
2:16 **H** could they? For, / "Who can know what the
5:6 **H** terrible that you should boast about your
7:32 the Lord's work and thinking **h** to please him.
7:33 his earthly responsibilities and **h** to please his wife.
7:34 and **h** to please her husband.
9:16 by God to do it. **H** terrible for me if I didn't do it!
12:3 So I want you to know **h** to discern what is truly
12:17 whole body were an eye—then **h** would you hear?
12:17 were just one big ear, **h** could you smell anything?
14:6 in an unknown language, **h** would that help you?
14:8 **h** will the soldiers know they are being called to
14:9 **h** will they know what you mean?
14:16 **h** can those who don't understand you praise God
14:16 **H** can they join you in giving thanks when they
15:35 But someone may ask, "**H** will the dead be raised?
15:57 **H** we thank God, who gives us victory over sin
2Co 1:12 That is **h** we have acted toward everyone,
1:24 to tell you exactly **h** to put your faith into practice.
2:4 **H** painful it was to write that letter! Heartbroken,
2:4 but I wanted you to know **h** very much I love you.
2:9 I wrote to you as I did to find out **h** far you would
3:1 Are we beginning again to tell you **h** good we are?
3:9 **h** much more glorious is the new covenant,
5:16 human being. **H** differently I think about him now!
6:14 **H** can goodness be a partner with wickedness? **H** can light live with darkness?
6:15 **H** can a believer be a partner with an unbeliever?
7:7 When he told me **h** much you were looking
7:7 and **h** sorry you were about what had happened,
7:7 and **h** loyal your love is for me, I was filled with
7:12 so that in the sight of God you could show **h** much
7:13 we were especially delighted to see **h** happy Titus
7:14 I had told him **h** proud I was of you—and you
8:9 You know **h** full of love and kindness our Lord
8:12 it isn't important **h** much you are able to give.
8:22 and has shown **h** earnest he is on many occasions.
9:2 For I know **h** eager you are to help, and I have
9:7 You must each make up your own mind as to **h**
10:12 these other men who tell you **h** important they are!
11:28 I have the daily burden of **h** the churches are
11:30 I would rather boast about the things that show **h**
11:33 a window in the city wall, and that's **h** I got away!
12:17 But **h**? Did any of the men I sent to you take
Gal 1:13 **h** I violently persecuted the Christians.
3:12 **H** different from this way of faith is the way of
3:19 It was given to show people **h** guilty they are.
4:20 **H** I wish I were there with you right now, so that I
Eph 1:3 **H** we praise God, the Father of our Lord Jesus
3:18 **h** wide, **h** long, **h** high, and **h** deep his love really
5:13 on them, it becomes clear **h** evil these things are.
5:15 So be careful **h** you live, not as fools but as those
6:21 will tell you all about **h** I am getting along.
6:22 He will let you know **h** we are, and he will
Php 1:8 God knows **h** much I love you and long for you
2:19 he can cheer me up by telling me **h** you are getting
2:22 But you know **h** Timothy has proved himself.
4:10 **H** grateful I am, and **h** I praise the Lord that you
4:11 for I have learned **h** to get along happily whether I
4:12 I know **h** to live on almost nothing or with
Col 2:1 I want you to know **h** much I have agonized for
4:7 loved brother, will tell you **h** I am getting along.
4:8 on this special trip to let you know **h** we are doing
1Th 1:9 and **h** you turned away from idols to serve the true
1:10 And they speak of **h** you are looking forward to the
2:2 You know **h** badly we had been treated at Philippi
2:2 we came to you and **h** much we suffered there.
2:9 and sisters, **h** hard we worked among you?
3:9 **H** we thank God for you! Because of you we have

5: 1 I really don't need to write to you about **h**
2Th 2: 1 and **h** we will be gathered together to meet him.
1Ti 1:12 **H** thankful I am to Christ Jesus our Lord for
1:14 Oh, **h** kind and gracious the Lord was! He filled
3: 5 **h** can he take care of God's church?
3:15 you will know **h** people must conduct themselves
5:25 everyone knows **h** much good some people do,
2Ti 1:18 And you know **h** much he helped me at Ephesus.
3:10 But you know what I teach, Timothy, and **h** I live,
3:10 You know my faith and **h** long I have suffered.
3:11 You know **h** much persecution and suffering I
3:11 You know all about **h** I was persecuted in Antioch,
Tit 1: 1 the truth that shows them **h** to live godly lives.
Heb 6:10 He will not forget **h** hard you have worked for him
6:10 and **h** you have shown your love to him by caring
7: 4 Consider then **h** great this Melchizedek was.
7: 4 recognized **h** great Melchizedek was by giving him
7:19 taken its place. And that is **h** we draw near to God.
9:14 Just think **h** much more the blood of Christ will
10:29 Think **h** much more terrible the punishment will be
10:32 Remember **h** you remained faithful even though it
11:32 Well, **h** much more do I need to say? It would take
12:10 us for a few years, doing the best they knew **h**.
12:25 **h** terrible our danger if we reject the One who
Jas 2: 1 **h** can you claim that you have faith in our glorious
4:14 **H** do you know what will happen tomorrow?
5:11 From his experience we see **h** the Lord's plan
1Pe 2:12 Be careful **h** you live among your unbelieving
2Pe 2: 9 the Lord knows **h** to rescue godly people from
1Jn 2: 3 And **h** can we be sure that we belong to him?
3: 1 See **h** very much our heavenly Father loves us,
3:17 to help—**h** can God's love be in that person?
4: 6 That is **h** we know if someone has the Spirit of
4: 9 God showed **h** much he loved us by sending his
4:16 We know **h** much God loves us, and we have put
4:20 **h** can we love God, whom we have not seen?
2Jn 1: 4 **H** happy I was to meet some of your children
Jude 1:11 **H** terrible it will be for them! For they follow the
Rev 2: 5 Look **h** far you have fallen from your first love!
2:14 who showed Balak **h** to trip up the people of Israel.
6:10 **h** long will it be before you judge the people who
7: 4 And I heard **h** many were marked with the seal of
9:16 I heard an announcement of **h** many there were.
11: 5 This is **h** anyone who tries to harm them must die.
18:10 They will cry out, "**H** terrible, **h** terrible for
Babylon, that great city!
18:16 "**H** terrible, **h** terrible for that great city!
18:19 will say, "**H** terrible, **h** terrible for the great city!

HOWBEIT [KJV] See BUT, FORMERLY, HOWEVER, NEVERTHELESS, RATHER, SINCE, THOUGH, YET

HOWEVER (106) [HOW]

Ge 15:10 side by side. He did not, **h**, divide the birds in half.
35:18 the baby's father, **h**, called him Benjamin.
39:11 One day, **h**, no one else was around when he was
40:23 Pharaoh's cup-bearer, **h**, promptly forgot all about
42: 4 Benjamin, go with them, **h**, for fear some harm
Ex 2:17 This time, **h**, Moses came to their aid,
7:13 Pharaoh's heart, **h**, remained hard and stubborn.
13:13 its neck. **H**, you must redeem every firstborn son.
21:14 **H**, if someone deliberately attacks and kills
21:21 **h**, then the owner should not be punished,
21:28 In such a case, **h**, the owner will not be held liable.
21:30 **H**, the dead person's relatives may accept payment
34:20 its neck. **H**, you must redeem every firstborn son.
Lev 6:16 It must, **h**, be baked without yeast and eaten in a
6:30 If, **h**, the blood of a sin offering has been taken into
7:16 "**H**, if you bring an offering to fulfill a vow
9:11 The meat and the hide, **h**, he burned outside the
10: 6 **H**, the rest of the Israelites, your relatives,
11: 4 You may not, **h**, eat the animals named here
11:10 You may not, **h**, eat marine animals that do not
11:21 **H**, there are some exceptions that you may eat.
11:36 "**H**, if the dead body of such an animal falls into a
13:16 **H**, if the open sores heal and turn white like the
13:31 **H**, if the priest's examination reveals that the
13:42 **H**, if a reddish white infection appears on the front
13:57 at a later time, **h**, the mildew is clearly spreading,
14: 8 **H**, they must still remain outside their tents for
19:21 The man, **h**, must bring a ram as a guilt offering
21:22 **H**, he may eat from the food offered to God,
22:11 **H**, if the priest buys slaves with his own money,
25:12 You may, **h**, eat the produce that grows naturally
25:44 "**H**, you may purchase male or female slaves from
26:14 "**H**, if you do not listen to me or obey my
27:27 **H**, if it is the firstborn of a ceremonially unclean
27:28 "**H**, anything specially set apart by the LORD—
Nu 18:17 "**H**, you may not redeem the firstborn of cattle,
26:11 **H**, the sons of Korah did not die that day.
30: 9 If, **h**, a woman is a widow or is divorced, she must
Dt 2:37 **H**, we stayed away from the Ammonites along the
3:19 Your wives, children, and numerous livestock, **h**,
14:10 You may not, **h**, eat marine animals that do not
15: 3 This release from debt, **h**, applies only to your
23:22 **H**, it is not a sin to refrain from making a vow.
Jos 2:20 If you betray us, **h**, we are not bound by this oath
11:13 **H**, Joshua did not burn any of the cities built on
16:10 They did not drive the Canaanites out of Gezer, **h**,
17: 3 **H**, Zelophehad son of Hepher, who was a
17:13 Later on, **h**, when the Israelites became strong
18: 7 **H**, the Levites will not receive any land. Their role
22:13 First, **h**, they sent a delegation led by Phinehas son
Jdg 1:21 The tribe of Benjamin, **h**, failed to drive out the
8:24 **H**, I have one request. Each of you can give me an
13:16 **H**, you may prepare a burnt offering as a sacrifice
1Ki 20:21 **H**, the other horses and chariots were destroyed,
22:34 An Aramean soldier, **h**, randomly shot an arrow at
22:43 During his reign, **h**, he failed to remove all the
2Ki 5:18 **H**, may the LORD pardon me in this one thing.
6:24 Some time later, **h**, King Ben-hadad of Aram
8:21 Jehoram's army, **h**, deserted him and fled.
10:29 He did not, **h**, destroy the gold calves at Bethel
12:16 **H**, the money that was contributed for guilt
14: 6 **H**, he did not kill the children of the assassins,
2Ch 18:33 An Aramean soldier, **h**, randomly shot an arrow at
19: 3 There is some good in you, **h**, for you have
20:33 During his reign, **h**, he failed to remove all the
21: 3 **H**, Jehoram became king because he was the
25: 4 **H**, he did not kill the children of the assassins,
30:11 **H**, some from Asher, Manasseh, and Zebulun
32:31 **H**, when ambassadors arrived from Babylon to ask
33:17 **H**, the people still sacrificed at the pagan shrines,
Ezr 2:59 **H**, they could not prove that they or their families
3:12 The others, **h**, were shouting for joy.
5:13 **H**, King Cyrus of Babylon, during the first year of
Ne 7:61 **H**, they could not prove that they or their families
11:21 **H**, the Temple servants, whose leaders were Ziha
Est 5:10 **H**, he restrained himself and went on home.
Ecc 2:26 Even this, **h**, is meaningless, like chasing the wind.
5:18 do under the sun—for **h** long God lets them live.
Isa 7: 1 city withstood the attack, **h**, and was not taken.
28: 7 Now, **h**, Israel is being led by drunks! The priests
Eze 18:24 **H**, if righteous people turn to sinful ways and start
44:15 "**H**, the Levitical priests of the family of Zadok
Da 2:10 And no king, **h** great and powerful, has ever asked
11:10 **H**, the sons of the king of the north will assemble a
Zep 3: 7 **h** much I punish them, they continue their evil
Mt 17:27 **H**, we don't want to offend them, so go down to
24:36 "**H**, no one knows the day or the hour when these
Mk 13:32 "**H**, no one knows the day or hour when these
Lk 24:12 **H**, Peter ran to the tomb to look. Stooping,
Jn 6:37 **H**, those the Father has given me will come to me,
6:50 **H**, the bread from heaven gives eternal life to
19:34 One of the soldiers, **h**, pierced his side with a
Ac 2:24 **H**, God released him from the horrors of death
7: 5 God did promise, **h**, that eventually the whole
7:48 **H**, the Most High doesn't live in temples made by
9:30 **h**, they took him to Caesarea and sent him on to his
11:20 **H**, some of the believers who went to Antioch
18:25 **H**, he knew only about John's baptism.
25:25 **H**, he appealed his case to the emperor, and I
Ro 3: 8 If you follow that kind of thinking, **h**, you might as
1Co 7:28 **H**, I am trying to spare you the extra problems that
8: 7 **H**, not all Christians realize this. Some are
12:31 First, **h**, let me tell you about something else that is
14:22 prophecy, **h**, is for the benefit of believers,
Eph 4: 7 **H**, he has given each one of us a special gift
1Pe 4:15 If you suffer, **h**, it must not be for murder, stealing,

HOWL (3) [HOWLING, HOWLS]

Job 30: 7 They sound like animals as they **h** among the
Isa 13:22 Hyenas will **h** in its fortresses, and jackals will
Mic 1: 8 I will **h** like a jackal and wail like an ostrich.

HOWLING (2) [HOWL]

Dt 32:10 them in a desert land, / in an empty, **h** wasteland.
Isa 13:21 The houses will be haunted by **h** creatures.

HOWLS (1) [HOWL]

Isa 34:14 mingle there with hyenas, their **h** filling the night.

HUBBAH (1)

1Ch 7:34 sons of Shomer were Ahi, Rohgah, **H**, and Aram.

HUBS (1)

1Ki 7:33 rims, and **h** were all cast from molten bronze.

HUCKSTERS (1)

2Co 2:17 You see, we are not like those **h**—and there are

HUDDLE (2) [HUDDLED]

Job 24: 8 and they **h** against the rocks for want of a home.
30: 7 they **h** together for shelter beneath the nettles.

HUDDLED (1) [HUDDLE]

Isa 3:26 will be like a ravaged woman, **h** on the ground.

HUGE (44)

Nu 13:32 go to live there. All the people we saw were **h**.
Jos 24:26 he took a **h** stone and rolled it beneath the oak tree
1Sa 17: 7 An armor bearer walked ahead of him carrying a **h**
17:25 And have you heard about the **h** reward the king
2Sa 21:20 a **h** man with six fingers on each hand and six toes
1Ki 7: 9 All these buildings were built entirely from **h**,
7:10 Some of the **h** foundation stones were 15 feet long,
10: 2 **h** quantities of gold, and precious jewels.
10:18 Then the king made a **h** ivory throne and overlaid
10:26 Solomon built up a **h** force of chariots and horses.
2Ki 18:17 a **h** army to confront King Hezekiah in Jerusalem.
1Ch 20: 6 a **h** man with six fingers on each hand and six toes
2Ch 1:14 Solomon built up a **h** military force,
7: 8 **h** crowds gathered from all the tribes of Israel.
9: 1 **h** quantities of gold, and precious jewels.
9:17 Then the king made a **h** ivory throne and overlaid
16:14 and at his funeral the people built a **h** fire in his
30:13 so a **h** crowd assembled at Jerusalem in midspring
31: 8 and his officials came and saw these **h** piles,
32: 4 They organized a **h** work crew to stop the flow of
Ecc 2: 4 I also tried to find meaning by building **h** homes
Isa 30:30 with cloudbursts, thunderstorms, and **h** hailstones,
36: 2 **h** army from Lachish to confront King Hezekiah in
Jer 22:14 'I will build a magnificent palace with **h** rooms
Eze 1: 4 driving before it a **h** cloud that flashed with
Da 2:31 in your vision you saw in front of you a **h**
7: 3 Then four **h** beasts came up out of the water,
7: 7 and crushed its victims with **h** iron teeth
7:17 "These four **h** beasts represent four kingdoms that
Mt 13:23 accept God's message and produce a **h** harvest—
17:14 of the mountain, a **h** crowd was waiting for them.
20:29 left the city of Jericho, a **h** crowd followed behind.
Mk 1:33 And a **h** crowd of people from all over Capernaum
3: 7 followed by a **h** crowd from all over Galilee,
4:20 accept God's message and produce a **h** harvest—
Lk 8:15 cling to it, and steadily produce a **h** harvest.
9:37 come down the mountain, a **h** crowd met Jesus.
Jn 6: 2 And a **h** crowd kept following him wherever he
6: 9 But what good is that with this **h** crowd?"
12:12 through the city. A **h** crowd of Passover visitors
Heb 12: 1 since we are surrounded by such a **h** crowd of
Jas 3: 4 And a tiny rudder makes a **h** ship turn wherever
Rev 9: 2 smoke poured out as though from a **h** furnace,
19: 6 again what sounded like the shout of a **h** crowd,

HUKKOK (1)

Jos 19:34 boundary ran past Aznoth-tabor, then to **H**,

HUKOK (1) [HELKATH]

1Ch 6:75 **H**, and Rehob, each with its pasturelands.

HUL (2)

Ge 10:23 of Aram were Uz, **H**, Gether, and Mash.
1Ch 1:17 of Aram were Uz, **H**, Gether, and Mash.

HULDAH (2)

2Ki 22:14 section of Jerusalem to consult with the prophet **H**.
2Ch 34:22 section of Jerusalem to consult with the prophet **H**.

HULL (1)

Ac 27:17 we banded the ship with ropes to strengthen the **h**.

HUMAN (170) [HUMANITY, HUMANLY, HUMANS]

HUMAN BEING (9) Jos 10:14; Da 7:4; Mt 16:17; Ac 10:26; Ro 9:20; 1Co 15:48; 2Co 5:16; Heb 2:14; 1Jn 4:2

HUMAN BEINGS (3) Ac 14:15; Heb 2:14; 5:1

HUMAN HANDS (19) Ex 19:13; 2Sa 24:14; 2Ki 19:18; 1Ch 21:13; 2Ch 32:19; Ps 115:4; 135:15; Isa 37:19; Eze 1:8; 10:8,21; Hos 13:2; Mk 14:58,58; Ac 7:48; 17:25; 2Co 5:1; Heb 8:2; 9:11

HUMAN HEART (6) 1Ki 8:39; 2Ch 6:30; Ps 64:6; Pr 15:11; Ecc 3:11; Jer 17:9

Ge 5: 2 and he blessed them and called them "**h**."
6: 1 When the **h** population began to grow rapidly on
6: 2 the sons of God saw the beautiful women of the **h**
6: 4 the sons of God had intercourse with **h** women,
6: 7 "I will completely wipe out this **h** race that I have
Ex 19:13 They must not be touched by **h** hands.'
Lev 5: 3 "Or if they come into contact with any source of **h**
7:21 whether it is **h** defilement or an unclean animal,
Nu 18:15 firstborn of every mother, whether **h** or animal,
19:11 "All those who touch a dead **h** body will be
19:16 or if someone touches a **h** bone or a grave,
19:18 in the tent, or anyone who has touched a **h** bone,
23:19 He is not a **h**, that he should change his mind.
Dt 32: 8 to the nations, / when he divided up the **h** race,
Jos 10:14 LORD answered such a request from a **h** being.
1Sa 15:29 for he is not **h** that he should change his mind!"
26:19 But if this is simply a **h** scheme, then may those
2Sa 24:14 mercy is great. Do not let me fall into **h** hands."
1Ki 8:39 they deserve, for you alone know the **h** heart.
13: 2 burn incense, and **h** bones will be burned on you."
2Ki 19:18 only idols of wood and stone shaped by **h** hands.
23:14 Then he desecrated these places by scattering **h**
23:20 and he burned **h** bones on the altars to desecrate
1Ch 21:13 is very great. Do not let me fall into **h** hands."
2Ch 6:30 they deserve, for you alone know the **h** heart.
32:19 he were one of the pagan gods, made by **h** hands.
Job 10: 4 Are your eyes only those of a **h**? Do you see things
10: 5 Is your lifetime merely **h**? Is your life so short
11:12 any more than a wild donkey can bear **h** offspring!
15:14 Can a mortal be pure? Can a **h** be just?
34:20 the mighty are removed without **h** hand.
Ps 9:20 O LORD. / Let them know they are merely **h**.
14: 2 looks down from heaven / on the entire **h** race;
33:13 down from heaven / and sees the whole **h** race.
39: 5 a moment to you; / **h** existence is but a breath."
39:11 **H** existence is as frail as breath. / *Interlude*
53: 2 looks down from heaven / on the entire **h** race;
57: 4 who greedily devour **h** prey— / whose teeth pierce
60:11 us against our enemies, / for all **h** help is useless.
64: 6 Yes, the **h** heart and mind are cunning.
76:10 **H** opposition only enhances your glory, / for you
89:47 my life is, / how empty and futile this **h** existence!
108:12 us against our enemies, / for all **h** help is useless.
109:15 but may his name be cut off from **h** memory.
115: 4 things of silver and gold, / shaped by **h** hands.
135:15 things of silver and gold, / shaped by **h** hands.
Pr 8:31 he created—his wide world and all the **h** family!

15:11 How much more does he know the **h** heart!
18:14 The **h** spirit can endure a sick body, but who can
20:27 The LORD's searchlight penetrates the **h** spirit,
21:30 **H** plans, no matter how wise or well advised,
27:20 are never satisfied, so **h** desire is never satisfied.
30: 2 I am too ignorant to be **h**, and I lack common
30: 3 I have not mastered **h** wisdom, nor do I know the
Ecc 1:13 that God has dealt a tragic existence to the **h** race.
3:11 He has planted eternity in the **h** heart, but even so,
3:21 For who can prove that the **h** spirit goes upward
Isa 23: 9 and show his contempt for all **h** greatness.
29:13 to nothing more than **h** laws learned by rote.
29:14 I will show that **h** wisdom is foolish and even the
37:19 only idols of wood and stone shaped by **h** hands.
41: 4 directing the affairs of the **h** race as each new
51:13 Will you remain in constant dread of **h** oppression?
57: 5 You slaughter your children as **h** sacrifices down
66: 3 an ox, it is no more acceptable than a **h** sacrifice.
Jer 17: 9 "The **h** heart is most deceitful and desperately
Eze 1: 5 of the cloud came four living beings that looked **h**,
1: 7 Their legs were straight like **h** legs, but their feet
1: 8 Beneath each of their wings I could see **h** hands.
1:10 Each had a **h** face in the front, the face of a lion on
4:12 bake it over a fire using dried **h** dung as fuel
4:14 must I be defiled by using **h** dung?
4:15 your bread with cow dung instead of **h** dung."
10: 8 (All the cherubim had what looked like **h** hands
10:14 first was the face of an ox, the second was a **h** face,
10:21 and what looked like **h** hands under their wings.
Da 4:16 let him have the mind of an animal instead of a **h**.
4:25 You will be driven from **h** society, and you will
4:32 You will be driven from **h** society. You will live in
4:33 and Nebuchadnezzar was driven from **h** society.
5: 5 At that very moment they saw the fingers of a **h**
5:21 He was driven from **h** society. He was given the
6: 7 days anyone who prays to anyone, divine or **h**—
6:12 days anyone who prays to anyone, divine or **h**—
7: 4 with its two hind feet on the ground, like a **h** being. And a **h** mind was given to it.
7: 8 This little horn had eyes like **h** eyes and a mouth
7:20 and had **h** eyes and a mouth that was boasting
8:16 And I heard a **h** voice calling out from the Ulai
8:25 but he will be broken, though not by **h** power.
Hos 13: 2 to worship—images shaped skillfully with **h** hands.
Mt 16:17 to you. You did not learn this from any **h** being.
16:23 You are seeing things merely from a **h** point of
21:25 baptism come from heaven or was it merely **h**?"
21:26 But if we say it was merely **h**, we'll be mobbed,
24:22 is shortened, the entire **h** race will be destroyed.
Mk 8:33 You are seeing things merely from a **h** point of
11:30 baptism come from heaven or was it merely **h**?
11:32 But do we dare say it was merely **h**?" For they
13:20 of calamity, the entire **h** race will be destroyed.
14:58 'I will destroy this Temple made with **h** hands,
14:58 I will build another, made without **h** hands.' "
Lk 18:27 "What is impossible from a **h** perspective is
20: 4 baptism come from heaven, or was it merely **h**?"
20: 6 But if we say it was merely **h**, the people will stone
Jn 1:13 This is not a physical birth resulting from **h**
1:14 So the Word became **h** and lived here on earth
2:25 No one needed to tell him about **h** nature.
3: 6 Humans can reproduce only **h** life, but the Holy
6:63 gives eternal life. **H** effort accomplishes nothing.
8:15 You judge me with all your **h** limitations, but I am
12:43 For they loved **h** praise more than the praise of
Ac 5:29 "We must obey God rather than **h** authority.
7:48 the Most High doesn't live in temples made by **h**
10:26 and said, "Stand up! I'm a **h** being like you!"
14:11 local dialect, "These men are gods in **h** bodies!"
14:15 We are merely **h** beings like yourselves!
17:25 and **h** hands can't serve his needs—for he has no
Ro 5:12 When Adam sinned, sin entered the entire **h** race.
8: 3 He sent his own Son in a **h** body like ours,
9: 5 and Christ himself was a Jew as far as his **h** nature
9:20 Who are you, a mere **h** being, to criticize God?
1Co 1:19 As the Scriptures say, / "I will destroy **h** wisdom
1:21 the world would never find him through **h** wisdom,
1:25 plan of God is far wiser than the wisest of **h** plans,
1:25 is far stronger than the greatest of **h** strength.
2: 5 trust the power of God rather than **h** wisdom.
2:13 we tell you this, we do not use words of **h** wisdom.
9: 8 And this isn't merely **h** opinion. Doesn't God's
12:12 The **h** body has many parts, but the many parts
15:44 They are natural **h** bodies now, but when they are
15:48 Every **h** being has an earthly body just like
2Co 3: 3 It is carved not on stone, but on **h** hearts.
5: 1 made for us by God himself and not by **h** hands.
5:16 that way, as though he were merely a **h** being.
10: 2 those who think we act from purely **h** motives.
10: 3 We are **h**, but we don't wage war with **h** plans and methods.
11:18 And since others boast about their **h** achievements,
Gal 1: 1 was not appointed by any group or by **h** authority.
1:11 which I preach is not based on mere **h** reasoning
3: 3 trying to become perfect by your own **h** effort?
4:23 The son of the slave-wife was born in a **h** attempt
Php 2: 7 humble position of a slave and appeared in **h** form.
2: 8 And in **h** form he obediently humbled himself even
3: 3 We put no confidence in **h** effort. Instead, we boast
4: 7 which is far more wonderful than the **h** mind can
Col 1:22 through his death on the cross in his own **h** body.
2: 8 and high-sounding nonsense that come from **h**
2: 9 For in Christ the fullness of God lives in a **h** body,
2:22 Such rules are mere **h** teaching about things that
1Th 4: 8 to live by these rules is not disobeying **h** rules
1Ti 6:16 in light so brilliant that no **h** can approach him.
Heb 2:14 Because God's children are **h** beings—made of
2:14 became flesh and blood by being born in **h** form.
2:14 For only as a **h** being could he die, and only by
5: 1 represent other **h** beings in their dealings with God.
5: 2 And because he is **h**, he is able to deal gently with
7:28 the law of Moses were limited by **h** weakness.
8: 2 that was built by the Lord and not by **h** hands.
9:11 not made by **h** hands and not part of this created
Jas 5:17 Elijah was as **h** as we are, and yet when he prayed
2Pe 2:16 when his donkey rebuked him with a **h** voice.
1Jn 4: 2 acknowledges that Jesus Christ became a **h** being,
5: 9 Since we believe **h** testimony, surely we can
Rev 4: 7 second looked like an ox; the third had a **h** face;
9: 7 gold crowns on their heads, and they had **h** faces.
16:18 an earthquake greater than ever before in **h** history.
18:13 and slaves—yes, she even traded in **h** lives.
21:17 feet thick (the angel used a standard **h** measure).

HUMANITY (16) [HUMAN]

Job 7: 1 "Is this not the struggle of all **h**? A person's life is
7:20 What have I done to you, O watcher of all **h**?
12:10 living thing is in his hand, and the breath of all **h**.
14: 1 "How frail is **h**! How short is life, and how full of
28:21 For it is hidden from the eyes of all **h**.
28:28 And this is what he says to all **h**: 'The fear of the
34:15 life would cease, and **h** would turn again to dust.
Ps 36: 7 is your unfailing love, O God! / All **h** finds shelter
50: 1 he has summoned all **h** from east to west!
115:16 to the LORD, / but he has given the earth to all **h**.
Isa 66:23 "All **h** will come to worship me from week to
Zep 1: 3 along with the rest of **h**," says the LORD.
Zec 2:13 Be silent before the LORD, all **h**, for he is
9: 1 and the city of Damascus, for the eyes of all **h**,
Ac 15:17 so that the rest of **h** might find the Lord,
Rev 19:18 and of all **h**, both free and slave, small and great."

HUMANLY (3) [HUMAN]

Mt 19:26 looked at them intently and said, "**H** speaking,
Mk 10:27 looked at them intently and said, "**H** speaking,
Ro 4: 1 Abraham was, **h** speaking, the founder of our

HUMANS (15) [HUMAN]

Ge 6: 3 "My Spirit will not put up with **h** for such a long
Dt 5:24 Today we have seen God speaking to **h**, and yet we
Ps 8: 4 think of us, / mere **h** that you should care for us?
144: 3 notice us, / mere **h** that you should care for us?
Ecc 3:19 For **h** and animals both breathe the same air,
Isa 2:22 Stop putting your trust in mere **h**. They are as frail
31: 3 For these Egyptians are mere **h**, not God!
44:11 in shame, along with all these craftsmen—mere **h**—
51:12 So why are you afraid of mere **h**, who wither like
Jer 17: 5 "Cursed are those who put their trust in mere **h**
La 3:39 Then why should we, mere **h**, complain when we
Da 4:17 to anyone he chooses—even to the lowliest of **h**."
Zec 12: 1 of the earth, and formed the spirit within **h**.
Jn 3: 6 **H** can reproduce only human life, but the Holy
1Co 15:39 of flesh—whether of **h**, animals, birds, or fish.

HUMBLE (56) [HUMBLED, HUMBLES, HUMBLING, HUMBLY, HUMILIATE, HUMILIATED, HUMILIATION, HUMILITY]

Ge 32: 4 '**H** greetings from your servant Jacob!
Lev 23:27 On that day you must **h** yourselves, gather for a
23:32 for you, and on that day you must **h** yourselves.
Nu 12: 3 Now Moses was more **h** than any other person on
Dt 8:16 He did this to **h** you and test you for your own
1Sa 18:23 "How can a poor man from a **h** family afford the
2Sa 22:28 You rescue those who are **h**, / but your eyes are on
1Ki 8:30 May you hear the **h** and earnest requests from me
20:31 So let's **h** ourselves by wearing sackcloth
2Ch 6:21 May you hear the **h** and earnest requests from me
7:14 who are called by my name will **h** themselves
33:23 his father, he did not **h** himself before the LORD.
36:12 and he refused to **h** himself in the presence of the
Ezr 8:21 for all of us to fast and **h** ourselves before our God.
Job 5:11 He gives prosperity to the poor and **h**, and he takes
Ps 18:27 You rescue those who are **h**, / but you humiliate
25: 9 He leads the **h** in what is right, / teaching them his
55:19 is king forever, / will hear me and will **h** them.
68:30 **H** those who demand tribute from us.
69:32 The **h** will see their God at work and be glad.
110: 1 in honor at my right hand / until I **h** your enemies,
138: 6 Though the LORD is great, he cares for the **h**,
147: 6 The LORD supports the **h**, / but he brings the
149: 4 in his people; / he crowns the **h** with salvation.
Pr 3:34 mocks at mockers, but he shows favor to the **h**.
Isa 29:19 The **h** will be filled with fresh joy from the
57:15 place with those whose spirits are contrite and **h**.
57:15 I refresh the **h** and give new courage to those with
58: 5 You **h** yourselves by going through the motions of
66: 2 "I will bless those who have **h** and contrite hearts,
Da 4:37 and true, and he is able to **h** those who are proud."
10:12 and to **h** yourself before your God,
Zep 2: 3 all you who are **h**, all you who uphold justice.
3:12 Those who are left will be the lowly and the **h**,
Zec 9: 9 He is righteous and victorious, yet he is **h**,
Mt 11:29 Let me teach you, because I am **h** and gentle,
18: 4 anyone who becomes as **h** as this little child is the
21: 5 is coming to you. / He is **h**, riding on a donkey—
22:44 until I **h** your enemies beneath your feet.'
23:12 and those who **h** themselves will be exalted.
Mk 12:36 until I **h** your enemies beneath your feet.'
Lk 14:11 proud will be humbled, but the **h** will be honored."
18:14 proud will be humbled, but the **h** will be honored."
20:43 until I **h** your enemies, / making them a footstool
Ac 2:34 in honor at my right hand / until I **h** your enemies,
2Co 12:21 when I come, God will **h** me again because of you.
Eph 4: 2 Be **h** and gentle. Be patient with each other,
Php 2: 3 Be **h**, thinking of others as better than yourself.
2: 7 he took the **h** position of a slave and appeared in
Col 2:18 These people claim to be so **h**, but their sinful
Heb 1:13 in honor at my right hand / until I **h** your enemies,
Jas 4: 6 against the proud, / but he shows favor to the **h**."
4: 7 So **h** yourselves before God. Resist the Devil,
1Pe 3: 8 loving one another with tender hearts and **h** minds.
5: 5 against the proud, / but he shows favor to the **h**."
5: 6 So **h** yourselves under the mighty power of God,

HUMBLED (28) [HUMBLE]

Lev 26:41 then at last their disobedient hearts will be **h**,
Dt 8: 3 he **h** you by letting you go hungry and then feeding
2Sa 8: 1 and **h** the Philistines by conquering Gath,
1Ki 21:29 "Do you see how Ahab has **h** himself before me?
2Ki 22:19 and **h** yourself before the LORD when you heard
1Ch 18: 1 and **h** the Philistines by conquering Gath
2Ch 12: 6 and the leaders of Israel **h** themselves and said,
12: 7 "Since the people have **h** themselves, I will not
12:12 Because Rehoboam **h** himself, the LORD's anger
30:11 and Zebulun **h** themselves and went to Jerusalem.
32:26 and the people of Jerusalem **h** themselves.
34:27 and **h** yourself before God when you heard what I
34:27 You **h** yourself and tore your clothing in despair
Job 30:11 He has **h** me, so they have thrown off all restraint.
Isa 2: 9 So now everyone will be **h** and brought low.
5:15 be brought down to the dust; the proud will be **h**.
9: 1 The land of Zebulun and Naphtali will soon be **h**,
Jer 6:15 They will be **h** beneath my punishing anger,"
8:12 They will be **h** when they are punished,
Da 5:22 and you knew all this, yet you have not **h** yourself.
Zec 1:21 to terrify the four horns that scattered and **h** Judah.
Mt 23:12 But those who exalt themselves will be **h**,
Lk 14:11 For the proud will be **h**, but the humble will be
18:14 For the proud will be **h**, but the humble will be
2Co 11: 7 Did I do wrong when I **h** myself and honored you
Php 2: 8 And in human form he obediently **h** himself even
Heb 10:13 There he waits until his enemies are **h** as a
Jas 1:10 who are rich should be glad, for God has **h** them.

HUMBLES (3) [HUMBLE]

Ps 44: 7 our enemies; / it is you who **h** those who hate us.
Isa 26: 5 He **h** the proud / and brings the arrogant city to the
1Co 15:25 For Christ must reign until he **h** all his enemies

HUMBLING (2) [HUMBLE]

Dt 8: 2 **h** you and testing you to prove your character,
2Ch 28:19 The LORD was **h** Judah because of King Ahaz of

HUMBLY (9) [HUMBLE]

2Ch 33:12 and cried out **h** to the God of his ancestors.
Pr 16:19 It is better to live **h** with the poor than to share
Isa 38:15 Now I will walk **h** throughout my years
Mic 6: 8 to love mercy, and to walk **h** with your God.
Zep 2: 3 who uphold justice. Walk **h** and do what is right.
Ac 20:19 I have done the Lord's work **h**—yes, and with
Gal 6: 1 and **h** help that person back onto the right path.
1Ti 5:10 to strangers? Has she served other Christians **h**?
Jas 1:21 and **h** accept the message God has planted in your

HUMILIATE (7) [HUMBLE]

Dt 25: 3 more than forty lashes would publicly **h** your
1Sa 31: 4 these pagan Philistines run me through and **h** me."
2Sa 22:28 but your eyes are on the proud to **h** them.
1Ch 10: 4 before these pagan Philistines come and **h** me."
Job 40:12 **H** the proud with a glance; walk on the wicked
Ps 18:27 those who are humble, / but you **h** the proud.
35: 4 **H** and disgrace those trying to kill me; / turn them

HUMILIATED (22) [HUMBLE]

Dt 21:14 sell her or treat her as a slave, for you have **h** her.
26: 6 and **h** us by making us their slaves,
Ne 6:16 nations heard about it, they were frightened and **h**.
Est 6:12 Haman hurried home dejected and completely **h**.
6:13 this man who has **h** you—is a Jew, you will never
Ps 35:26 be **h** and disgraced. / May those who triumph over
40:14 who try to destroy me / be **h** and put to shame.
69: 6 Don't let me cause them to be **h**, / O God of Israel.
70: 2 who try to destroy me / be **h** and put to shame.
71:24 who tried to hurt me / has been shamed and **h**.
Isa 30: 3 in trusting Pharaoh, you will be **h** and disgraced.
45:16 All who make idols will be **h** and disgraced.
45:17 They will never again be **h** and disgraced
Jer 15: 9 She sits childless now, disgraced and **h**. And those
20:11 defeat me. They will be shamed and thoroughly **h**.
46:24 Egypt will be **h**; she will be handed over to men
48: 1 The city of Kiriathaim will be **h** and captured;
48: 1 the fortress will be **h** and broken down.
La 1: 8 for they have seen her stripped naked and **h**.
Mal 2: 9 you despised and **h** in the eyes of all the people.
Ac 8:33 He was **h** and received no justice. / Who can speak
2Co 9: 4 I would be **h**—and so would you—if some

HUMILIATION (8) [HUMBLE]

Job 19: 5 overcome me, using my **h** as evidence of my sin,
Ps 44:15 We can't escape the constant **h**; / shame is written
69: 7 for your sake; / **h** is written all over my face.
69:19 know the insults I endure— / the **h** and disgrace.
71:13 May **h** and shame cover / those who want to harm

109:29 Make their **h** obvious to all; / clothe my accusers
Pr 29:23 Pride ends in **h**, while humility brings honor.
Eze 32:24 and share the **h** of those who have gone to the

HUMILITY (11) [HUMBLE]

Lev 23:29 Anyone who does not spend that day in **h** will be
Ps 45:4 ride out to victory, / defending truth, **h**, and justice.
Pr 11:2 Pride leads to disgrace, but with **h** comes wisdom.
15:33 teaches a person to be wise; **h** precedes honor.
18:12 goes before destruction; **h** precedes honor.
22:4 True **h** and fear of the LORD lead to riches,
29:23 Pride ends in humiliation, while **h** brings honor.
Col 2:23 strong devotion, **h**, and severe bodily discipline.
3:12 kindness, **h**, gentleness, and patience.
Tit 3:2 they should be gentle and show true **h** to everyone.
1Pe 5:5 And all of you, serve each other in **h**, for

HUMPED (1)

Lev 21:20 or has a **h** back or is a dwarf, or has a defective

HUMTAH (1)

Jos 15:54 **H**, Kiriath-arba (that is, Hebron), and Zior—

HUNDRED (167) [100]

Ge 15:13 and they will be oppressed as slaves for four **h**
17:17 could I become a father at the age of one **h**?"
21:5 Abraham was one **h** years old at the time.
21:16 and sat down by herself about a **h** yards away.
23:15 "the land is worth four **h** pieces of silver, but what
23:16 four **h** pieces of silver, as was publicly agreed.
26:12 He harvested a **h** times more grain than he planted,
32:6 way to meet Jacob—with an army of four **h** men!
32:14 two **h** female goats, twenty male goats, two **h** ewes, twenty rams,
33:1 Jacob saw Esau coming with his four **h** men.
33:19 Shechem's father, for a **h** pieces of silver.
45:22 five changes of clothes and three **h** pieces of silver!
Ex 14:7 He took with him six **h** of Egypt's best chariots,
18:21 over groups of one thousand, one **h**, fifty, and ten.
18:25 of groups of one thousand, one **h**, fifty, and ten.
Lev 26:8 Five of you will chase a **h**, and a **h** of you will chase ten thousand!
Nu 31:28 Set apart one out of every five **h** as the LORD's
Dt 1:15 some for a **h**, some for fifty, and some for ten.
22:19 They will fine him one **h** pieces of silver, for he
Jos 7:21 two **h** silver coins, and a bar of gold weighing
24:32 from the sons of Hamor for one **h** pieces of silver.
Jdg 3:31 He killed six **h** Philistines with an ox goad.
4:3 Sisera, who had nine **h** iron chariots,
4:13 he called for all nine **h** of his iron chariots and all
7:6 Only three **h** of the men drank from their hands.
7:7 "With these three **h** men I will rescue you
7:8 them home. But he kept the three **h** men with him.
7:16 He divided the three **h** men into three groups
7:19 and the one **h** men with him reached the outer edge
7:22 When the three **h** Israelites blew their horns,
8:4 then crossed the Jordan River with his three **h** men,
11:26 But now after three **h** years you make an issue of
15:4 Then he went out and caught three **h** foxes. He tied
16:5 Then each of us will give you eleven **h** pieces of
17:2 "I heard you curse the thief who stole eleven **h**
17:4 So his mother took two **h** of the silver coins to a
18:11 So six **h** warriors from the tribe of Dan set out
18:16 As the six **h** warriors from the tribe of Dan stood
20:15 to join the seven **h** warriors who lived there.
20:16 Seven **h** of Benjamin's warriors were left-handed,
20:47 leaving only six **h** men who escaped to the rock of
21:12 **h** young virgins who had never slept with a man,
21:14 and the four **h** women of Jabesh-gilead who were
1Sa 13:15 who were still with him, he found only six **h** left!
14:2 and his six **h** men were camped on the outskirts of
14:20 and his six **h** men rushed out to the battle
18:25 for the bride price is one **h** Philistine foreskins!
18:27 and his men went out and killed two **h** Philistines
22:2 until David was the leader of about four **h** men.
23:13 about six **h** of them now—left Keilah and began
25:13 Four **h** men started off with David, and two **h** remained behind to guard their
25:18 She quickly gathered two **h** loaves of bread,
25:18 one **h** raisin cakes, and two **h** fig cakes.
27:2 So David took his six **h** men and their families
29:2 were leading out their troops in groups of one **h**
30:9 So David and his six **h** men set out, and they soon
30:10 But two **h** of the men were too exhausted to cross
30:10 so David continued the pursuit with his four **h**
30:17 None of the Amalekites escaped except four **h**
30:21 and met the two **h** men who had been too tired to
2Sa 2:31 But three **h** and sixty of Abner's men, all from the
3:14 for I bought her with the lives of one **h**
8:4 David captured seventeen **h** charioteers and twenty
8:4 he crippled all but one **h** of the chariot horses.
10:18 This time David's forces killed seven **h** charioteers
15:11 He took two **h** men from Jerusalem with him as
15:18 There were six **h** Gittites who had come with
15:22 So Ittai and his six **h** men and their families went
16:1 He was leading two donkeys loaded with two **h**
16:1 one **h** clusters of raisins, one **h** bunches of summer fruit, and a skin of wine.
23:8 He once used his spear to kill eight **h** enemy
23:18 He once used his spear to kill three **h** enemy
24:3 **h** times as many people in your kingdom as there
1Ki 4:23 one **h** sheep or goats, as well as deer, gazelles,
5:16 and thirty-six **h** foremen to supervise the work.
7:20 Each capital on the two pillars had two **h**
7:42 four **h** pomegranates that hung from the chains on
10:16 King Solomon made two **h** large shields of
10:17 He also made three **h** smaller shields of hammered
10:26 He had fourteen **h** chariots and twelve thousand
11:3 He had seven **h** wives and three **h** concubines.
18:4 Obadiah had hidden one **h** of them in two caves.
18:13 I hid a **h** of them in two caves and supplied them
22:6 about four **h** of them, and asked them,
2Ki 3:26 he led seven **h** of his warriors in a desperate
4:43 "Feed one **h** people with only this?" But Elisha
14:13 Then Jehoash ordered his army to demolish six **h**
1Ch 4:42 Five **h** of these invaders from the tribe of Simeon
11:11 He once used his spear to kill three **h** enemy
11:20 He once used his spear to kill three **h** enemy
12:14 The weakest among them could take on a **h** regular
18:4 he crippled all but one **h** of the chariot horses.
21:3 increase the number of his people a **h** times over!
21:25 So David gave Araunah six **h** pieces of gold in
26:30 and his relatives—seventeen **h** capable men—
26:32 There were twenty-seven **h** capable men among
2Ch 1:14 which included fourteen **h** chariots and twelve
2:2 in the hill country, and thirty-six **h** foremen.
3:16 He also made one **h** decorative pomegranates
4:8 the north wall. Then he molded one **h** gold basins.
4:13 four **h** pomegranates that hung from the chains on
9:15 King Solomon made two **h** large shields of
9:16 He also made three **h** smaller shields of hammered
12:3 He came with twelve **h** chariots, sixty thousand
14:9 with an army of a million men and three **h** chariots.
15:11 seven **h** oxen and seven thousand sheep and goats.
17:11 and the Arabs brought seventy-seven **h** rams and seventy-seven **h** male goats.
18:5 his prophets, four **h** of them, and asked them,
25:23 Then Jehoash ordered his army to demolish six **h**
26:12 Twenty-six **h** clan leaders commanded these
29:32 one **h** rams, and two **h** lambs for burnt offerings.
29:33 They also brought six **h** bulls and three thousand
35:8 gave the priests twenty-six **h** lambs and young
35:8 and three **h** bulls as Passover offerings.
35:9 and five **h** bulls to the Levites for their Passover
Ezr 6:17 one **h** young bulls, two **h** rams, and four **h** lambs were sacrificed.
Ne 3:1 building the wall as far as the Tower of the **H**,
3:13 They also repaired the fifteen **h** feet of wall to the
12:39 of Hananel, and went on to the Tower of the **H**.
Est 9:6 They killed five **h** people in the fortress of Susa.
9:12 "The Jews have killed five **h** people in the fortress
9:15 on March 8 and killed three **h** more people,
Job 1:3 three thousand camels, five **h** teams of oxen, and five **h** female donkeys,
Pr 17:10 understanding than a **h** lashes on the back of a fool.
Ecc 6:3 A man might have a **h** children and live to be very
8:12 But even though a person sins a **h** times and still
SS 8:12 And I will give two **h** pieces of silver to those who
Isa 65:20 No longer will people be considered old at one **h**!
Jer 52:23 and a total of one **h** on the network around the top.
Eze 45:15 and one sheep for every two **h** in your flocks in
Da 7:10 to him, and a **h** million stood to attend him.
8:14 "It will take twenty-three **h** evenings
8:26 "This vision about the twenty-three **h** evenings
Am 5:3 a thousand men to battle, only a **h** will return.
5:3 When a town sends a **h**, only ten will come back
Mt 13:8 and even a **h** times as much as had been planted.
13:23 or even a **h** times as much as had been planted."
18:12 "If a shepherd has one **h** sheep, and one wanders
19:29 will receive a **h** times as much in return and will
Mk 4:8 and even a **h** times as much as had been planted."
4:20 or even a **h** times as much as had been planted."
6:40 So they sat in groups of fifty or a **h**.
10:30 a **h** times over, houses, brothers, sisters, mothers,
Lk 7:41 five **h** pieces of silver to one and fifty pieces to the
8:8 and produced a crop one **h** times as much as had
15:4 "If you had one **h** sheep, and one of them strayed
16:6 'I owe him eight **h** gallons of olive oil.'
16:6 that bill and write another one for four **h** gallons.'
16:7 and replace it with one for only eight **h** bushels.'
Jn 21:8 the shore, for they were only out about three **h** feet.
Ac 5:36 About four **h** others joined him, but he was killed,
7:6 would be mistreated as slaves for four **h** years.
23:23 "Get two **h** soldiers ready to leave for Caesarea at
23:23 Also take two **h** spearmen and seventy horsemen.
Ro 4:19 he was too old to be a father at the age of one **h**
1Co 15:6 he was seen by more than five **h** of his followers at

HUNG (24) [HANG]

Ex 40:33 Then he **h** the curtains forming the courtyard
Jos 8:29 Joshua **h** the king of Ai on a tree and left him there
10:26 five kings and **h** them on five trees until evening.
2Sa 4:12 and **h** their bodies beside the pool in Hebron.
1Ki 7:42 four hundred pomegranates that **h** from the chains
7:42 were **h** around the capitals on top of the pillars),
2Ch 3:14 Solomon **h** a curtain made of fine linen and blue,
4:13 four hundred pomegranates that **h** from the chains
4:13 were **h** around the capitals on top of the pillars),
Ne 3:3 laid the beams, **h** the doors, and put the bolts
3:13 **h** its doors, and installed the bolts and bars.
3:14 he **h** the doors and installed the bolts and bars.
3:15 He rebuilt it, roofed it, **h** its doors, and installed its
6:1 though we had not yet **h** the doors in the gates—
7:1 was finished and I had **h** the doors in the gates,
Est 9:13 and have the bodies of Haman's ten sons **h** from
9:14 They also **h** the bodies of Haman's ten sons from
Eze 27:10 They **h** their shields and helmets on your walls,
27:11 Their shields **h** on your walls, perfecting your
Da 5:29 purple robes, a gold chain was **h** around his neck,
Mt 27:36 Then they sat around and kept guard as he **h** there.
Lk 19:48 because all the people **h** on every word he said.
Gal 3:13 When he was **h** on the cross, he took upon himself
3:13 "Cursed is everyone who is **h** on a tree."

HUNGER (17) [HUNGRY, HUNGRILY]

1Sa 28:20 He was also faint with **h**, for he had eaten nothing
Job 17:5 own advantage, so let their children faint with **h**.
18:12 Their vigor is depleted by **h**, and calamity waits for
30:3 They are gaunt with **h** and flee to the deserts
38:41 young cry out to God as they wander about in **h**?
Ps 145:16 you satisfy the **h** and thirst of every living thing.
Isa 49:10 They will neither **h** nor thirst. The searing sun
Jer 38:9 He will soon die of **h**, for almost all the bread in
La 2:19 Plead for your children as they faint with **h** in the
4:9 sword are far better off than those who die of **h**,
Joel 1:18 How the animals moan with **h**! The cattle wander
Am 4:6 "I brought **h** to every city and famine to every
Mic 6:14 Your **h** pangs and emptiness will still remain.
7:1 or a single fig can be found to satisfy my **h**.
Lk 4:25 for three and a half years and **h** stalked the land.
6:25 for a time of awful **h** is before you.
15:17 food enough to spare, and here I am, dying of **h**!

HUNGRILY (1) [HUNGER]

Isa 28:4 snatched up, as an early fig is **h** picked and eaten.

HUNGRY (69) [HUNGER]

Ge 25:29 Esau arrived home exhausted and **h** from a hunt.
29:7 "They'll be **h** if you stop so early in the day."
Dt 8:3 he humbled you by letting you go **h** and
28:48 You will be left **h**, thirsty, naked, and lacking in
1Sa 14:31 But **h** as they were, they chased and killed the
2Sa 17:29 "You must all be very tired and **h** and thirsty after
2Ki 18:27 The people will become so **h** and thirsty that they
Ne 9:15 gave them bread from heaven when they were **h**
Job 22:7 refused water for the thirsty and food for the **h**.
31:17 my food and refused to share it with **h** orphans?
31:31 My servants have never let others go **h**.
Ps 17:12 They are like **h** lions, eager to tear me apart—
34:10 Even strong young lions sometimes go **h**,
50:12 If I were **h**, I would not mention it to you, / for all
107:5 **H** and thirsty, / they nearly died.
107:9 the thirsty / and fills the **h** with good things.
107:36 He brings the **h** to settle there / and build their
146:7 and food to the **h**. / The LORD frees the
Pr 13:25 hearts' content, but the belly of the wicked goes **h**.
15:14 A wise person is **h** for truth, while the fool feeds
19:15 A lazy person sleeps soundly—and goes **h**.
25:21 If your enemies are **h**, give them food to eat.
27:7 is full, but even bitter food tastes sweet to the **h**.
Isa 8:21 people will be led away as captives, weary and **h**.
8:21 And because they are **h**, they will rage and shake
9:20 neighbors to steal food, but they will still be **h**.
29:8 A **h** person dreams of eating but is still **h**.
32:6 they deprive the **h** of food and give no water to the
36:12 The people will become so **h** and thirsty that they
44:12 His work makes him **h** and thirsty, weak and faint.
55:10 producing seed for the farmer and bread for the **h**.
58:7 I want you to share your food with the **h** and to
58:10 Feed the **h** and help those in trouble. Then your
59:11 We growl like **h** bears; we moan like mournful
Eze 18:7 not rob the poor but instead gives food to the **h**
18:16 And suppose this son feeds the **h**, provides clothes
34:21 and **h** flock until they are scattered to distant lands.
34:29 so my people will never again go **h** or be shamed
Hos 4:10 They will eat and still be **h**. Though they do a big
13:8 I will tear you apart and devour you like a **h** lion.
Mt 4:2 and forty nights he ate nothing and became very **h**.
5:6 God blesses those who are **h** and thirsty for justice,
12:1 His disciples were **h**, so they began breaking off
12:3 David did when he and his companions were **h**?
15:32 I don't want to send them away **h**, or they will
21:18 as Jesus was returning to Jerusalem, he was **h**,
25:35 For I was **h**, and you fed me. I was thirsty, and you
25:37 'Lord, when did we ever see you **h** and feed you?
25:42 For I was **h**, and you didn't feed me. I was thirsty,
25:44 when did we ever see you **h** or thirsty or a stranger
Mk 2:25 David did when he and his companions were **h**?
11:12 as they were leaving Bethany, Jesus felt **h**.
Lk 1:53 He has satisfied the **h** with good things / and sent
3:11 If you have food, share it with those who are **h**."
4:2 He ate nothing all that time and was very **h**.
6:3 David did when he and his companions were **h**?
6:21 God blesses you who are **h** now, / for you will be
15:16 so **h** that even the pods he was feeding the pigs
Jn 6:35 No one who comes to me will ever be **h** again.
Ac 10:10 and he was **h**. But while lunch was being prepared,
Ro 8:35 or are **h** or cold or in danger or threatened with
12:20 "If your enemies are **h**, feed them. / If they are
1Co 4:11 To this very hour we go **h** and thirsty,
11:21 As a result, some go **h** while others get drunk.
11:34 If you are really **h**, eat at home so you won't bring
2Co 11:27 Often I have been **h** and thirsty and have gone
Heb 11:37 and goats, **h** and oppressed and mistreated.
Rev 7:16 They will never again be **h** or thirsty, and they will

HUNT (11) [HUNTED, HUNTER, HUNTER'S, HUNTERS, HUNTING, HUNTS]

Ge 25:29 Esau arrived home exhausted and hungry from a **h**.
27:3 the open country, and **h** some wild game for me.
27:5 So when Esau left to **h** for the wild game,
1Sa 26:2 and went to **h** him down in the wilderness of Ziph.
26:20 Why does he **h** me down like a partridge on the
Job 10:16 you **h** me like a lion and display your awesome
Ps 31:15 Rescue me from those who **h** me down

119:86 Protect me from those who **h** me down without
Pr 16:27 Scoundrels **h** for scandal; their words are a
Isa 15: 9 Lions will **h** down the survivors, both those who
La 5: 9 We must **h** for food in the wilderness at the risk of

HUNTED (4) [HUNT]
1Sa 23:14 Saul **h** him day after day, but God didn't let him be
Isa 13:14 rushing back to their own lands like **h** deer,
2Co 4: 9 We are **h** down, but God never abandons us.
1Ti 1:13 I **h** down his people, harming them in every way I

HUNTER (6) [HUNT]
Ge 10: 9 He was a mighty **h** in the LORD's sight.
10: 9 "like Nimrod, a mighty **h** in the LORD's sight."
25:27 As the boys grew up, Esau became a skillful **h**,
Job 41: 9 The **h** who attempts it will be thrown down.
Pr 6: 5 Save yourself like a deer escaping from a **h**,
Jer 5:26 lie in wait for victims like a **h** hiding in a blind.

HUNTER'S (1) [HUNT]
Ps 124: 7 We escaped like a bird from a **h** trap. / The trap is

HUNTERS (2) [HUNT]
Ps 10: 9 Like **h** they capture their victims / and drag them
Jer 16:16 "I am sending for **h** who will search for them in

HUNTING (8) [HUNT]
Ge 27:30 had left his father, Esau returned from his **h** trip.
Lev 17:13 If you go **h** and kill an animal or bird that is
1Sa 24:11 even though you have been **h** for me to kill me.
27: 1 Then Saul will stop **h** for me, and I will finally be
27: 4 David had fled to Gath, so he stopped **h** for him.
Ps 55: 3 bring trouble on me, / **h** me down in their anger.
Isa 7:24 vast brier patch, a **h** ground overrun by wildlife.
Zep 3: 3 Its leaders are like roaring lions **h** for their

HUNTS (1) [HUNT]
Job 39:29 From there it **h** its prey, keeping watch with

HUPHAM (1) [HUPHAMITE]
Nu 26:39 The Huphamite clan, named after its ancestor **H**.

HUPHAMITE (1) [HUPHAM]
Nu 26:39 The **H** clan, named after its ancestor Hupham.

HUPPAH (1)
1Ch 24:13 The thirteenth lot fell to **H**. / The fourteenth lot fell

HUPPIM (3)
Ge 46:21 Gera, Naaman, Ehi, Rosh, Muppim, **H**, and Ard.
1Ch 7:12 The sons of Ir were Shuppim and **H**. Hushim was
7:15 Makir found wives for **H** and Shuppim.

HUR (15) [BEN-HUR]
Ex 17:10 Aaron, and **H** went to the top of a nearby hill.
17:12 So Aaron and **H** found a stone for him to sit on.
24:14 consult with Aaron and **H**, who are here with
31: 2 son of Uri, grandson of **H**, of the tribe of Judah.
35:30 son of Uri, grandson of **H**, of the tribe of Judah.
38:22 Bezalel son of Uri, grandson of **H**, of the tribe of
Nu 31: 8 Evi, Rekem, Zur, **H**, and Reba—died in the battle.
Jos 13:21 Evi, Rekem, Zur, **H**, and Reba—princes living in
1Ch 2:19 married Ephrathah, and they had a son named **H**.
2:20 **H** was the father of Uri. Uri was the father of
2:50 The sons of **H**, the oldest son of Caleb's wife
4: 1 Judah were Perez, Hezron, Carmi, **H**, and Shobal.
4: 4 These were the descendants of **H** (the firstborn of
2Ch 1: 5 and grandson of **H** was still at Gibeon in front of
Ne 3: 9 Rephaiah son of **H**, the leader of half the district of

HURAI (2)
2Sa 23:30 Benaiah from Pirathon; / **H** from Nahale-gaash;
1Ch 11:32 **H** from near Nahale-gaash;

HURAM (9)
1Ki 7:13 then asked for a man named **H** to come from Tyre,
7:15 **H** cast two bronze pillars, each 27 feet tall and 18
7:21 **H** set the pillars at the entrance of the Temple,
7:23 Then **H** cast a large round tank, 15 feet across from
7:27 **H** also made ten bronze water carts, each 6 feet
7:38 **H** also made ten bronze basins, one for each cart.
7:40 So at last **H** completed everything King Solomon
7:45 **H** made for Solomon were made of burnished
1Ch 8: 5 Gera, Shephuphan, and **H**.

HURAM-ABI (4)
2Ch 2:13 "I am sending you a master craftsman named **H**.
4:11 **H** also made the necessary pots, shovels,
4:11 So at last **H** completed everything King Solomon
4:16 **H** made all these things out of burnished bronze

HURI (1)
1Ch 5:14 These were all descendants of Abihail son of **H**,

HURL (4) [HURLED, HURLS]
2Ch 26:15 and **h** stones from the towers and the corners of the
Ps 35:15 even know; / they **h** slander at me continually.
Isa 22:17 the LORD is about to seize you and **h** you away.
Zec 9: 4 and **h** its fortifications into the Mediterranean Sea.

HURLED (7) [HURL]
1Sa 17:49 he **h** it from his sling and hit the Philistine in the
18:11 suddenly **h** it at David, intending to pin him to the
19:10 Saul **h** his spear at David in an attempt to kill him.
20:33 Then Saul **h** his spear at Jonathan, intending to kill
Ne 9:11 then you **h** their enemies into the depths of the sea.
Ps 79:12 on our neighbors / for the scorn they have **h** at you.
136:15 but he **h** Pharaoh and his army into the sea.

HURLS (2) [HURL]
Job 36:32 hands with lightning bolts. He **h** each at its target.
Ps 147:17 He **h** the hail like stones. / Who can stand against

HURRICANE (1)
Eze 27:26 oarsmen are rowing your ship of state into a **h**!

HURRIED (20) [HURRY]
Ge 19:27 and **h** out to the place where he had stood in the
29: 1 Jacob **h** on, finally arriving in the land of the east.
43:15 and the gifts and double the money and **h** to Egypt,
Jos 4:10 Meanwhile, the people **h** across the riverbed.
Jdg 6:19 Gideon **h** home. He cooked a young goat, and with
1Sa 17:22 and **h** out to the ranks to greet his brothers.
25:34 hurting you, that if you had not **h** out to meet me,
28:24 had been fattening a calf, so she **h** out and killed it.
2Sa 17:21 crawled out of the well and **h** on to King David.
19:16 **h** across with the men of Judah to welcome King
2Ki 4:31 Gehazi **h** on ahead and laid the staff on the child's
11:13 she **h** to the LORD's Temple to see what was
2Ch 23:12 she **h** to the LORD's Temple to see what was
Ezr 4:23 they **h** to Jerusalem and forced the Jews to stop
Est 6:12 but Haman **h** home dejected and completely
Ps 114: 3 Red Sea saw them coming and **h** out of their way!
Da 5:10 what was happening, she **h** to the banquet hall.
6:19 the next morning, the king **h** out to the lions' den.
Mk 6:25 So the girl **h** back to the king and told him,
Lk 1:39 A few days later Mary **h** to the hill country of

HURRIEDLY (1) [HURRY]
Jos 8:14 and all his army **h** went out early the next morning

HURRIES (2) [HURRY]
Ecc 1: 5 The sun rises and sets and **h** around to rise again.
Isa 41: 7 The carver **h** the goldsmith, and the molder helps

HURRY (38) [HURRIED, HURRIEDLY, HURRIES, HURRYING]
Ge 18: 7 a fat calf and told a servant to **h** and butcher it.
19:15 "**H**," they said to Lot. "Take your wife and your
19:22 But **h**! For I can do nothing until you are there."
45: 9 "**H**, return to my father and tell him, 'This is what
Ex 8:28 don't go too far away. Now **h**, and pray for me."
11: 8 bowing low. 'Please leave!' they will beg. '**H**!
Dt 16: 3 you did when you escaped from Egypt in such a **h**.
Jos 2: 5 If you **h**, you can probably catch up with them."
1Sa 9:13 **H** and catch him before he goes up the hill to eat.
20:38 **H**, **h**, don't wait." So the boy quickly gathered
2Sa 15:14 or it will be too late!" David urged his men. "**H**!
1Ki 18:44 Then Elijah shouted, "**H** to Ahab and tell him,
18:44 If you don't **h**, the rain will stop you!' "
2Ki 4:22 and a donkey so that I can **h** to the man of God
4:24 saddled the donkey and said to the servant, "**H**!
2Ch 35:21 And God has told me to **h**! Do not interfere with
Est 6:10 "**H** and get the robe and my horse, and do just as
Job 10: 6 that you are in a **h** to probe for my guilt, to search
Ps 70: 5 I am poor and needy; / please **h** to my aid, O God.
71:12 don't stay away. / My God, please **h** to help me.
114: 5 Red Sea, that made you **h** out of their way?
119:60 I will **h**, without lingering, / to obey your
141: 1 O LORD, I am calling to you. Please **h**!
Pr 1:16 rush to commit crimes. They **h** to commit murder.
25: 8 don't be in a **h** to go to court. You might go down
Isa 5:19 One of Israel and say, "**H** up and do something!
52:12 You will not leave in a **h**, running for your lives.
Mic 2: 1 and **h** to carry out any of the wicked schemes you
Zec 2: 4 The other angel said, "**H**, and say to that young
Mt 22: 4 meats have been cooked. Everything is ready. **H**!'
Jn 13:27 into him. Then Jesus told him, "**H**. Do it now."
Ac 17:15 a message for Silas and Timothy to **h** and join him.
22:18 I saw a vision of Jesus saying to me, '**H**!
1Co 11:21 For I am told that some of you **h** to eat your own
1Ti 5:22 Never be in a **h** about appointing an elder. Do not
2Ti 4:21 **H** so you can get here before winter.
2Pe 3:12 should look forward to that day and **h** it along—

HURRYING (1) [HURRY]
Ac 20:16 He was **h** to get to Jerusalem, if possible,

HURT (33) [HURTING, HURTS]
Ge 22:12 "Do not **h** the boy in any way, for now I know that
Ex 21:22 they **h** a pregnant woman so her child is born
Lev 24:20 Whatever anyone does to **h** another person must be
Nu 16:15 and I have never **h** a single one of them."
1Sa 20: 3 'I won't tell Jonathan—why should I **h** him?'
2Sa 20: 6 "That troublemaker Sheba is going to **h** us more
1Ch 16:22 I have chosen, / and do not **h** my prophets."
Job 41: 7 Will its hide be **h** by darts, or its head by a
Ps 59: 7 fly from their lips. / "Who can **h** us?" they sneer.
69:26 they scoff at the pain of those you have **h**.
71:24 all day long, / for everyone who tried to **h** me
105:15 I have chosen, / and do not **h** my prophets."
121: 6 The sun will not **h** you by day, / nor the moon at
Pr 9: 7 Anyone who rebukes the wicked will get **h**.
Ecc 8: 9 where people have the power to **h** each other.
Isa 11: 9 Nothing will **h** or destroy in all my holy mountain.
42:24 Who allowed Israel to be robbed and **h**? Was it not
65:25 no one will be **h** or destroyed on my holy
Jer 7:19 "Most of all, they **h** themselves, to their own
8:21 I weep for the **h** of my people. I am stunned
39:12 "See that he isn't **h**," he had said. "Look after
Da 3:25 in the fire. They aren't even **h** by the flames!
6:22 the lions' mouths so that they would not **h** me,
Mt 13:29 "He replied, 'No, you'll **h** the wheat if you do.
Mk 16:18 if they drink anything poisonous, it won't **h** them.
Lk 6:28 of those who curse you. Pray for those who **h** you.
2Co 2: 4 I didn't want to **h** you, but I wanted you to know
2: 5 trouble **h** your entire church more than he **h** me.
7: 9 not because it **h** you, but because the pain caused
Rev 2:11 Whoever is victorious will not be **h** by the second
7: 3 Don't **h** the land or the sea or the trees until we
9: 4 They were told not to **h** the grass or plants or trees

HURTING (7) [HURT]
1Sa 25:34 the God of Israel, who has kept me from **h** you,
Ps 94: 5 oppress your people, LORD, / **h** those you love.
Pr 29:24 If you assist a thief, you are only **h** yourself.
Jer 7:19 Am I the one they are **h**?" asks the LORD.
La 3:33 For he does not enjoy **h** people or causing them
Lk 4:35 then it left him without **h** him further.
Ac 7:26 'you are brothers. Why are you **h** each other?'

HURTS (6) [HURT]
Ex 23: 8 A bribe always **h** the cause of the person who is in
1Sa 14:29 "A command like that only **h** us.
2Ki 4:19 he complained, "My head **h**! My head **h**!"
Ps 15: 4 and keep their promises even when it **h**.
Jer 30:20 before me, and I will punish anyone who **h** them.

HUSBAND (112) [HUSBAND'S, HUSBANDS]
Ge 3: 6 She also gave some to her **h**, who was with her.
3:16 And though your desire will be for your **h**, he will
18:12 "And when my master—my **h**—is also so old?"
20: 7 Now return her to her **h**, and he will pray for you,
29:32 noticed my misery, and now my **h** will love me."
29:34 "Surely now my **h** will feel affection for me,
30:15 "Wasn't it enough that you stole my **h**?
30:18 me for giving my servant to my **h** as a wife."
30:20 she said, "God has given me good gifts for my **h**.
39:14 "My **h** has brought this Hebrew slave here to
39:16 with her, and when her **h** came home that night,
Ex 21:22 damages in the amount the woman's **h** demands
Lev 21: 3 sister who was dependent because she had no **h**.
21: 4 As a **h** among his relatives, he must not defile
Nu 5:12 a man's wife goes astray and is unfaithful to her **h**.
5:14 If her **h** becomes jealous and suspicious of his
5:15 the **h** must bring his wife to the priest with an
5:27 she has defiled herself by being unfaithful to her **h**,
5:29 woman defiles herself by being unfaithful to her **h**,
5:30 the **h** must present his wife before the LORD,
5:31 The **h** will be innocent of any guilt in this matter,
30: 7 If her **h** learns of her vow or pledge and raises no
30: 8 But if her **h** refuses to accept her vow or impulsive
30:11 If her **h** hears of it and does nothing to stop her,
30:12 But if her **h** refuses to accept it on the day he hears
30:13 So her **h** may either confirm or nullify any vows
Dt 24: 3 and the second **h** also divorces her or dies,
24: 4 the former **h** may not marry her again, for she has
25:11 and the wife of one tries to rescue her **h** by
28:56 will be cruel to the **h** she loves and to her own son
Jdg 13: 6 The woman ran and told her **h**, "A man of God
13: 9 in the field. But her **h**, Manoah, was not with her.
13:10 So she quickly ran and told her **h**, "The man who
14:15 "Get the answer to the riddle from your **h**,
19: 3 her **h** took a servant and an extra donkey to
19:26 returned to the house where her **h** was staying.
19:27 When her **h** opened the door to leave, he found her
20: 4 the **h** of the woman who had been murdered,
Ru 1: 5 This left Naomi alone, without her **h** or sons.
2: 1 who was a relative of Naomi's **h**, Elimelech.
2:11 your mother-in-law since the death of your **h**.
2:20 his kindness to us as well as to your dead **h**.
4:10 a son to carry on the family name of her dead **h**
1Sa 1:22 She told her **h**, "Wait until the baby is weaned.
2:19 and brought it to him when she came with her **h** for
4:19 and that her **h** and father-in-law were dead,
4:21 and because her **h** and her father-in-law were dead.
25:19 But she didn't tell her **h** what she was doing.
25:35 "Return home in peace. We will not kill your **h**."
2Sa 3:15 So Ishbosheth took Michal away from her **h** Palti
11:26 When Bathsheba heard that her **h** was dead,
17: 3 the people back to you as a bride returns to her **h**.
1Ki 14: 7 Give your **h**, Jeroboam, this message from the
2Ki 4: 1 cried out to him, "My **h** who served you is dead,
4: 9 She said to her **h**, "I am sure this man who stops in
4:14 doesn't have a son, and her **h** is an old man."
4:22 She sent a message to her **h**: "Send one of the
4:26 'Is everything all right with you, with your **h**,
Ps 45:11 For your royal **h** delights in your beauty;
Pr 2:17 She has abandoned her **h** and ignores the covenant
6:34 For the woman's **h** will be furious in his jealousy,
7:19 for my **h** is not home. He's away on a long trip.
30:23 a bitter woman who finally gets a **h**, / a servant girl
31:11 Her **h** can trust her, and she will greatly enrich his
31:23 Her **h** is well known, for he sits in the council
31:28 Her children stand and bless her. Her **h** praises her:
Isa 54: 5 for your Creator will be your **h**. The LORD
54: 6 you were a young wife abandoned by her **h**,"

Jer 3:14 says the LORD, "for I am your **h**.
3:20 have been like a faithless wife who leaves her **h**,"
31:32 though I loved them as a **h** loves his wife,"
Eze 16:32 wife who takes in strangers instead of her own **h**.
16:45 For your mother loathed her **h** and her children,
Hos 2: 2 she is no longer my wife, and I am no longer her **h**.
2: 7 'I might as well return to my **h** because I was
2:16 "you will call me 'my **h**' instead of 'my master.'
5: 3 You have left me as a prostitute leaves her **h**;
Mt 1:16 Jacob was the father of Joseph, the **h** of Mary.
Mk 10:12 And if a woman divorces her **h** and remarries,
Lk 2:36 for her **h** had died when they had been married
Jn 4:16 "Go and get your **h**," Jesus told her.
4:17 "I don't have a **h**," the woman replied. Jesus said, "You're right! You don't have a **h**—
Ac 5: 8 the price you and your **h** received for your land?"
5: 9 that door are the young men who buried your **h**,
5:10 they carried her out and buried her beside her **h**.
Ro 7: 2 the law binds her to her **h** as long as he is alive.
7: 3 So while her **h** is alive, she would be committing
7: 3 But if her **h** dies, she is free from that law and does
1Co 7: 2 own wife, and each woman should have her own **h**.
7: 3 The **h** should not deprive his wife of sexual
7: 3 married woman, nor should the wife deprive her **h**.
7: 4 The wife gives authority over her body to her **h**,
7: 4 and the **h** also gives authority over his body to his
7: 5 to this rule would be the agreement of both **h**
7:10 but from the Lord. A wife must not leave her **h**.
7:11 go back to him. And the **h** must not leave his wife.
7:13 And if a Christian woman has a **h** who is an
7:14 and the Christian **h** brings holiness to his marriage.
7:15 (But if the **h** or wife who isn't a Christian
7:15 In such cases the Christian **h** or wife is not
7:34 earthly responsibilities and how to please her **h**.
7:39 A wife is married to her **h** as long as he lives.
7:39 If her **h** dies, she is free to marry whomever she
11: 3 to Christ, a woman is responsible to her **h**,
11: 5 But a woman dishonors her **h** if she prays
2Co 11: 2 For I promised you as a pure bride to one **h**,
Eph 5:23 For a **h** is the head of his wife as Christ is the head
5:33 he loves himself, and the wife must respect her **h**.
1Ti 5: 9 is at least sixty years old and was faithful to her **h**.
1Pe 3: 6 For instance, Sarah obeyed her **h**, Abraham,
Rev 21: 2 of heaven like a beautiful bride prepared for her **h**.

HUSBAND'S (8) [HUSBAND]

Nu 5:18 or not her **h** suspicions are justified.
5:20 But if you have gone astray while under your **h**
30:10 and living in her **h** home when she makes a vow
Dt 25: 5 her **h** brother must marry her and fulfill the duties
25: 7 'My **h** brother refuses to preserve his brother's
Ru 4: 5 she can have children who will carry on her **h**
2Sa 14: 7 and my **h** name and family will disappear from the
Pr 12: 4 A worthy wife is her **h** joy and crown; a shameful

HUSBANDMAN [KJV] See FARMER(S), GARDENER

HUSBANDS (29) [HUSBAND]

Ru 1: 8 LORD reward you for your kindness to your **h**
1:11 to other sons who could grow up to be your **h**?
Est 1:17 Women everywhere will begin to despise their **h**
1:18 and will start talking to their **h** the same way.
1:20 **h** everywhere, whatever their rank, will receive
Jer 6:11 young men, and on **h** and wives and grandparents.
14:16 **H**, wives, sons, and daughters—all will be gone.
44:19 without our **h** knowing it and helping us?
Eze 16:45 for they despised their **h** and their children.
Am 4: 1 and who are always asking your **h** for another
Zec 12:12 by itself, with the **h** and wives in separate groups.
12:14 Judah will mourn separately, **h** and wives apart.
Jn 4:18 for you have had five **h**, and you aren't even
1Co 7:16 You wives must remember that your **h** might be
7:16 And you **h** must remember that your wives might
7:29 so **h** should not let marriage be their major
14:35 any questions to ask, let them ask their **h** at home,
Eph 5:22 You wives will submit to your **h** as you do to the
5:24 so you wives must submit to your **h** in everything.
5:25 And you **h** must love your wives with the same
5:28 **h** ought to love their wives as they love their own
Col 3:18 You wives must submit to your **h**, as is fitting for
3:19 And you **h** must love your wives and never treat
Tit 2: 4 must train the younger women to love their **h**
2: 5 to do good, and to be submissive to their **h**.
1Pe 3: 1 you wives must accept the authority of your **h**,
3: 5 trusted God and accepted the authority of their **h**.
3: 6 what is right without fear of what your **h** might do.
3: 7 same way, you **h** must give honor to your wives.

HUSH (3) [HUSHED]

Ne 8:11 too, quieted the people, telling them, "**H**!
Am 6:10 person will answer, "No!" Then he will say, "**H**!
Lk 18:39 The crowds ahead of Jesus tried to **h** the man,

HUSHAH (6)

2Sa 21:18 As they fought, Sibbecai from **H** killed Saph,
23:27 Abiezer from Anathoth; / Sibbecai from **H**;
1Ch 4: 4 (the father of Gedor), and Ezer (the father of **H**).
11:29 Sibbecai from **H**; / Zalmon from Ahoah;
20: 4 As they fought, Sibbecai from **H** killed Saph,
27:11 Sibbecai, a descendant of Zerah from **H**,

HUSHAI (11) [HUSHAI'S]

2Sa 15:32 David found **H** the Arkite waiting for him.
15:32 **H** had torn his clothing and put dirt on his head as
15:37 So David's friend **H** returned to Jerusalem,
16:16 When David's friend **H** the Arkite arrived, he went
16:18 is chosen by the LORD and by Israel," **H** replied.
17: 5 But then Absalom said, "Bring in **H** the Arkite.
17: 6 When **H** arrived, Absalom told him what
17: 7 "Well," **H** replied, "this time I think Ahithophel
17:15 Then **H** reported to Zadok and Abiathar,
1Ki 4:16 Baana son of **H**, in Asher and in Aloth.
1Ch 27:33 royal adviser. **H** the Arkite was the king's friend.

HUSHAI'S (1) [HUSHAI]

2Sa 17:14 "**H** advice is better than Ahithophel's."

HUSHAM (4)

Ge 36:34 **H** from the land of the Temanites became king.
36:35 When **H** died, Hadad son of Bedad became king
1Ch 1:45 **H** from the land of the Temanites became king.
1:46 When **H** died, Hadad son of Bedad became king

HUSHED (1) [HUSH]

Job 4:16 was a form before my eyes, and a **h** voice said,

HUSHIM (4) [SHUHAM]

Ge 46:23 The son of Dan was **H**.
1Ch 7:12 and Huppim. **H** was the son of Aher.
8: 8 After Shaharaim divorced his wives **H** and Baara,
8:11 Shaharaim's wife **H** had already given birth to

HUSK [KJV] See (GRAPE) SKINS, GRAIN

HUSKS (1)

Lk 6: 1 rubbed off the **h** in their hands, and ate the grains.

HUZ [KJV] See UZ

HUZZAB [KJV] See DECREED

HYENAS (2)

Isa 13:22 **H** will howl in its fortresses, and jackals will make
34:14 animals of the desert will mingle there with **h**,

HYMENAEUS (2)

1Ti 1:20 **H** and Alexander are two examples of this. I turned
2Ti 2:17 like cancer. **H** and Philetus are examples of this.

HYMN (4) [HYMNS]

Ps 40: 3 me a new song to sing, / a **h** of praise to our God.
137: 3 Our tormentors requested a joyful **h**: / "Sing us
Mt 26:30 Then they sang a **h** and went out to the Mount of
Mk 14:26 Then they sang a **h** and went out to the Mount of

HYMNS (5) [HYMN]

Ne 12:46 choir directors to lead the choirs in **h** of praise
Am 5:23 Away with your **h** of praise! They are only noise to
Ac 16:25 and Silas were praying and singing **h** to God,
Eph 5:19 Then you will sing psalms and **h** and spiritual
Col 3:16 Sing psalms and **h** and spiritual songs to God with

HYPOCRISY (7) [HYPOCRITE, HYPOCRITES]

Am 5:21 the **h** of your religious festivals and solemn
Mt 23:28 but inside your hearts are filled with **h**
Mk 12:15 Jesus saw through their **h** and said, "Who are you
Lk 12: 1 of the yeast of the Pharisees—beware of their **h**.
Gal 2:13 the other Jewish Christians followed Peter's **h**,
2:13 Barnabas was influenced to join them in their **h**.
1Pe 2: 1 Be done with **h** and jealousy and backstabbing.

HYPOCRITE (3) [HYPOCRISY]

Mt 7: 5 **H**! First get rid of the log from your own eye,
Lk 6:42 **H**! First get rid of the log from your own eye;
13:15 But the Lord replied, "You **h**! You work on the

HYPOCRITES (19) [HYPOCRISY]

Ps 26: 4 I do not spend time with liars / or go along with **h**.
Isa 9:17 For they are all **h**, speaking wickedness with lies.
29:14 Because of this, I will do wonders among these **h**.
Eze 14:10 False prophets and **h**—evil people who claim to
Mt 6: 2 someone in need, don't shout about it as the **h** do—
6: 5 don't be like the **h** who love to pray publicly on
6:16 as the **h** do, who try to look pale and disheveled
15: 7 You **h**! Isaiah was prophesying about you when he
22:18 Jesus knew their evil motives. "You **h**!" he said.
23:13 teachers of religious law and you Pharisees. **H**!
23:23 teachers of religious law and you Pharisees. **H**!
23:25 **H**! You are so careful to clean the outside of the
23:27 teachers of religious law and you Pharisees. **H**!
23:29 teachers of religious law and you Pharisees. **H**!
24:51 tear the servant apart and banish him with the **h**.
Mk 7: 6 Jesus replied, "You **h**! Isaiah was prophesying
Lk 12:56 You **h**! You know how to interpret the appearance
1Ti 4: 2 These teachers are **h** and liars. They pretend to be
Jas 4: 8 your hands, you sinners; purify your hearts, you **h**.

HYSSOP (11)

Ex 12:22 Then take a cluster of **h** branches and dip it into the
12:22 Strike the **h** against the top and sides of the
Lev 14: 4 some cedarwood, a scarlet cloth, and a **h** branch.
14: 6 the cedarwood, the scarlet cloth, and the **h** branch,
14:49 some cedarwood, a scarlet cloth, and a **h** branch.
14:51 dip the cedarwood, the **h** branch, the scarlet cloth,
Nu 19: 6 a **h** branch, and scarlet thread and throw them into
19:18 who is ceremonially clean must take a **h** branch
1Ki 4:33 from the great cedar of Lebanon to the tiny **h** that
Jn 19:29 put it on a **h** branch, and held it up to his lips.
Heb 9:19 using branches of **h** bushes and scarlet wool.

I

I (9352) [I'LL, I'M, I'VE, ME, MINE, MYSELF] See Index of Articles, Etc.

I AM (61 of 1200)

Ge 17: 1 "**I am** God Almighty; serve me faithfully
Ex 3:14 God replied, "**I AM** THE ONE WHO ALWAYS IS. Just tell them, '**I AM** has sent me to you.' "
Ps 46:10 "Be silent, and know that **I am** God!
Isa 41:10 Don't be afraid, for **I am** with you. Do not be dismayed, for **I am** your God.
43: 3 For **I am** the LORD, your God, the Holy One of Israel, your Savior.
43:11 **I am** the LORD, and there is no other Savior.
43:15 **I am** the LORD, your Holy One, Israel's Creator and King.
44: 6 **I am** the First and the Last; there is no other God.
Jer 3:14 "Return home, you wayward children," says the LORD, "for **I am** your husband.
32:27 "**I am** the LORD, the God of all the peoples of the world. Is anything too hard for me?
Mt 16:15 Then he asked them, "Who do you say **I am**?"
28:20 And be sure of this: **I am** with you always, even to the end of the age."
Mk 8:29 Then Jesus asked, "Who do you say **I am**?"
14:62 Jesus said, "**I am**, and you will see me, the Son of Man, sitting at God's right hand in the place of power and coming back on the clouds of heaven."
Jn 6:35 Jesus replied, "**I am** the bread of life.
6:41 he had said, "**I am** the bread from heaven."
6:48 Yes, **I am** the bread of life!
6:51 **I am** the living bread that came down out of heaven.
8:12 Jesus said to the people, "**I am** the light of the world.
8:24 for unless you believe that **I am** who I say **I am**, you will die in your sins."
8:28 So Jesus said, "When you have lifted up the Son of Man on the cross, then you will realize that **I am** he and that I do nothing on my own,
9: 5 But while **I am** still here in the world, **I am** the light of the world."
10: 7 "I assure you, **I am** the gate for the sheep," he said.
10: 9 Yes, **I am** the gate. Those who come in through me will be saved.
10:11 "**I am** the good shepherd. The good shepherd lays down his life for the sheep.
10:14 "**I am** the good shepherd; I know my own sheep,
10:36 by the Father says, '**I am** the Son of God'?
11:25 Jesus told her, "**I am** the resurrection and the life.
13:19 I tell you this now, so that when it happens you will believe **I am** the Messiah.
14: 6 Jesus told him, "**I am** the way, the truth, and the life. No one can come to the Father except through me.
14:10 Don't you believe that **I am** in the Father and the Father is in me?
14:11 Just believe that **I am** in the Father and the Father is in me.
14:20 When **I am** raised to life again, you will know that **I am** in my Father, and you are in me, and **I am** in you.
15: 1 "**I am** the true vine, and my Father is the gardener.
15: 5 "Yes, **I am** the vine; you are the branches.
18: 5 "**I am** he," Jesus said.
18: 6 And as he said, "**I am** he," they all fell backward to the ground!
18: 8 "I told you that **I am** he," Jesus said.
Ac 9: 5 And the voice replied, "**I am** Jesus, the one you are persecuting!
18:10 For **I am** with you, and no one will harm you because many people here in this city belong to me."
22: 8 And he replied, '**I am** Jesus of Nazareth, the one you are persecuting.'
26:15 "And the Lord replied, '**I am** Jesus, the one you are persecuting.
Rev 1: 8 "**I am** the Alpha and the Omega—the beginning and the end," says the Lord God. "**I am** the one who is, who always was, and who is still to come, the Almighty One."
1:17 "Don't be afraid! **I am** the First and the Last.
1:18 **I am** the living one who died. Look, **I am** alive forever and ever!
3:11 Look, **I am** coming quickly.
21: 6 And he also said, "It is finished! **I am** the Alpha and the Omega—the Beginning and the End.
22: 7 "Look, **I am** coming soon!

22:12 "See, **I am** coming soon, and my reward is with me,
22:13 **I am** the Alpha and the Omega, the First and the Last, the Beginning and the End."
22:16 **I am** both the source of David and the heir to his throne. **I am** the bright morning star."
22:20 "Yes, **I am** coming soon!"

I'D (5) [I, WOULD] See Index of Articles, Etc.

I'LL (80) [I, WILL] See Index of Articles, Etc.

I'M (75) [BE, I] See Index of Articles, Etc.

I'VE (28) [HAVE, I] See Index of Articles, Etc.

IBEX (1)
Dt 14: 5 the roebuck, the wild goat, the **i**, the antelope,

IBHAR (3)
2Sa 5:15 **I**, Elishua, Nepheg, Japhia,
1Ch 3: 6 David also had nine other sons: **I**, Elishua, Elpelet,
14: 5 **I**, Elishua, Elpelet,

IBLEAM (3)
Jos 17:11 Beth-shan, **I**, Dor (that is, Naphoth-dor), Endor,
Jdg 1:27 Taanach, Dor, **I**, Megiddo, and their surrounding
2Ki 9:27 Ahaziah in his chariot at the Ascent of Gur, near **I**.

IBNEIAH (1)
1Ch 9: 8 **I** son of Jeroham; Elah son of Uzzi, son of Micri;

IBNIJAH (1)
1Ch 9: 8 son of Shephatiah, son of Reuel, son of **I**.

IBRI (1)
1Ch 24:27 the leaders were Beno, Shoham, Zaccur, and **I**.

IBSAM (1)
1Ch 7: 2 Rephaiah, Jeriel, Jahmai, **I**, and Shemuel.

IBZAN (2)
Jdg 12: 8 After Jephthah, **I** became Israel's judge. He lived
12: 9 to marry his sons. **I** judged Israel for seven years.

ICE (5)
Job 6:16 when it is swollen with **i** and melting snow.
37:10 God's breath sends the **i**, freezing wide expanses of
38:29 Who is the mother of the **i**? Who gives birth to the
38:30 For the water turns to **i** as hard as rock,
Ps 147:18 it all melts. / He sends his winds, and the **i** thaws.

ICHABOD (1) [ICHABOD'S]
1Sa 4:21 She named the child **I**—"Where is the glory?"—

ICHABOD'S (1) [ICHABOD]
1Sa 14: 3 Ahijah was the son of Ahitub, **I** brother.

ICONIUM (6)
Ac 13:51 of their feet against them and went to the city of **I**.
14: 1 In **I**, Paul and Barnabas went together to the
14:19 Now some Jews arrived from Antioch and **I**
14:21 returned again to Lystra, **I**, and Antioch of Pisidia,
16: 2 well thought of by the believers in Lystra and **I**,
2Ti 3:11 how I was persecuted in Antioch, **I**, and Lystra—

IDALAH (1)
Jos 19:15 Nahalal, Shimron, **I**, and Bethlehem—

IDBASH (1)
1Ch 4: 3 Ishma, **I**, Hazzelelponi (his daughter),

IDDO (13)
1Ki 4:14 Ahinadab son of **I**, in Mahanaim.
1Ch 6:21 Joah, **I**, Zerah, and Jeatherai.
27:21 Manasseh (east) | **I** son of Zechariah / Benjamin
2Ch 9:29 and also in *The Visions of **I** the Seer,* concerning
12:15 and in *The Record of **I** the Seer,* which are part
13:22 are recorded in *The Commentary of **I** the*
Ezr 5: 1 and Zechariah son of **I** prophesied in the name of
6:14 of the prophets Haggai and Zechariah son of **I**.
8:17 I sent them to **I**, the leader of the Levites at
Ne 12: 4 **I**, Ginnethon, Abijah,
12:16 Zechariah was leader of the family of **I**.
Zec 1: 1 Zechariah son of Berekiah and grandson of **I**.
1: 7 Zechariah son of Berekiah and grandson of **I**.

IDEA (10) [IDEAS]
Ge 21:26 "And I have no **i** who is responsible.
43:22 We have no **i** how the money got into our sacks."
Dt 1:23 This seemed like a good **i** to me, so I chose twelve
Ne 7: 5 So my God gave me the **i** to call together all the
Pr 4:19 Those who follow it have no **i** what they are
Jer 11:19 I had no **i** that they were planning to kill me!
Am 5:18 But you have no **i** what you are wishing for.
Jn 14: 5 "We haven't any **i** where you are going, so how
Ac 6: 5 This **i** pleased the whole group, and they chose the
2Co 8:10 a year ago, for you were the first to propose this **i**,

IDEALLY (2)
Nu 32: 1 and Gilead were **i** suited for their flocks and herds,
32: 4 of Israel. It is **i** suited for all our flocks and herds.

IDEAS (15) [IDEA]
Ps 101: 4 I will reject perverse **i** / and stay away from every
Pr 18:15 Intelligent people are always open to new **i**. In fact,
Jer 23:36 people are using it to give authority to their own **i**,
Jn 7:16 So Jesus told them, "I'm not teaching my own **i**,
7:18 Those who present their own **i** are looking for
16:13 He will not be presenting his own **i**; he will be
Ac 17:18 "This babbler has picked up some strange **i**."
17:21 to spend all their time discussing the latest **i**.)
Ro 1:21 And they began to think up foolish **i** of what God
1Co 1:17 and not with clever speeches and high-sounding **i**,
1:19 and discard their most brilliant **i**."
2: 1 and brilliant **i** to tell you God's message.
2Co 10: 5 With these weapons we conquer their rebellious **i**,
1Ti 4: 7 Do not waste time arguing over godless **i** and old
Heb 13: 9 So do not be attracted by strange, new **i**.

IDENTICAL (4) [IDENTIFY]
1Ki 6:25 The two cherubim were **i** in shape and size;
Eze 40:10 and the dividing walls separating them were also **i**.
40:22 and the palm tree decorations were **i** to those in the
42:11 and doors. The dimensions of each were **i**.

IDENTIFICATION (2) [IDENTIFY]
Ge 38:18 She replied, "I want your **i** seal, your cord,
38:25 "The man who owns this **i** seal and walking stick

IDENTIFIED (10) [IDENTIFY]
Ge 10:20 **i** according to their tribes, languages, territories,
10:31 **i** according to their tribes, languages, territories,
Nu 33: 2 **i** by the different places they stopped along the
Mt 12:33 "A tree is **i** by its fruit. Make a tree good, and its
Lk 6:22 because you are **i** with me, the Son of Man.
6:44 A tree is **i** by the kind of fruit it produces.
Jn 18: 5 Judas was standing there with them when Jesus **i**
2Co 1:22 and he has **i** us as his own by placing the Holy
Eph 1:13 he **i** you as his own by giving you the Holy Spirit,
4:30 Remember, he is the one who has **i** you as his own,

IDENTIFY (4) [IDENTICAL, IDENTIFICATION, IDENTIFIED, IDENTITY]
Ge 37:32 beautiful robe to their father and asked him to **i** it.
Ecc 10: 3 You can **i** fools just by the way they walk down the
Mt 7:16 the way they act, just as you can **i** a tree by its fruit.
7:20 the way to **i** a tree or a person is by the kind of fruit

IDENTITY (2) [IDENTIFY]
Eze 17:14 with Babylon could Israel maintain her national **i**.
Ac 7:13 they went, Joseph revealed his **i** to his brothers,

IDIOT (1)
Mt 5:22 If you say to your friend, 'You **i**,' you are in

IDLE (4) [IDLENESS, IDLY]
Pr 12:11 means prosperity; only fools **i** away their time.
Am 6: 5 You sing **i** songs to the sound of the harp, and you
Mt 12:36 on judgment day of every **i** word you speak.
2Th 3:11 Yet we hear that some of you are living **i** lives,

IDLENESS (1) [IDLE]
2Th 3: 6 Stay away from any Christian who lives in **i**

IDLY (3) [IDLE]
Ps 83: 1 O God, don't sit **i** by, / silent and inactive!
Isa 58:13 and don't follow your own desires or talk **i**.
Hab 1:13 in any form, stand **i** by while they swallow us up?

IDOL (60) [IDOLATER, IDOLATERS, IDOLATROUS, IDOLATRY, IDOLS]
Ex 23:33 they will infect you with their sin of **i** worship,
32: 8 They have made an **i** shaped like a calf, and they
Dt 9:12 and have cast an **i** for themselves from gold.'
Jdg 17: 3 I will have an image carved and an **i** cast."
17: 4 who made them into an image and an **i**.
18:14 some household idols, a carved image, and a cast **i**.
18:17 sacred ephod, the household idols, and the cast **i**.
1Sa 5: 2 of Dagon and placed it beside the **i** of Dagon.
5: 3 the Ark of the LORD! So they set the **i** up again.
5: 4 the **i** had fallen face down before the Ark of the
19:13 Then she took an **i** and put it in his bed, covered it
19:16 they discovered that it was only an **i** in the bed
2Ki 23:24 and every other kind of **i** worship, both in
2Ch 33: 7 Manasseh even took a carved **i** he had made
33:15 from the hills and the **i** from the LORD's Temple.
Ne 9:18 even though they made an **i** shaped like a calf
Isa 40:19 Can he be compared to an **i** formed in a mold,
40:20 Or is a poor person's wooden **i** better? Can God be compared to an **i** that must be placed
44:10 his own god—an **i** that cannot help him one bit!
44:13 Now he has a wonderful **i** that cannot even move
44:15 He makes an **i** and bows down and praises it!
44:17 he takes what's left and makes his god: a carved **i**!
44:19 The person who made the **i** never stops to reflect,
44:20 this **i** that I'm holding in my hand, a lie?"
45:21 and state your proofs that **i** worship pays.
45:21 What **i** ever told you they would happen? Was it
66: 3 they burn incense, it is as if they had blessed an **i**.
Jer 2:27 To an **i** chiseled out of stone they say, 'You are my
7:18 And they give drink offerings to their other **i** gods!
10: 3 and foolish. They cut down a tree and carve an **i**.
10:16 But the God of Israel is no **i**! / He is the Creator of
13:27 and your abominable **i** worship out in the fields
48:13 At last Moab will be ashamed of her **i** Chemosh,
51:19 But the God of Israel is no **i**! / He is the Creator of
Eze 8: 3 where there is a large **i** that has made the LORD
8: 5 stood the **i** that had made the LORD so angry.
11:18 they will remove every trace of their detestable **i**
20:29 (This **i** shrine has been called Bamah—
22: 9 You are filled with **i** worshipers and people who
43: 8 They put their **i** altars right next to mine with only
Hos 8: 5 I reject this calf—this **i** you have made.
9:10 for Baal-peor, giving themselves to that shameful **i**.
10: 5 The people of Samaria tremble for their calf **i** at
10: 6 This **i** they love so much will be carted away with
10: 6 because its people have trusted in this **i**.
Mic 1:13 in Judah to follow Israel in the sin of **i** worship,
5:14 and destroy the cities where your **i** temples stand.
Hab 2:19 Can an **i** speak for God? They may be overlaid
Zec 13: 2 I will get rid of every trace of **i** worship throughout
Ac 7:41 So they made an **i** shaped like a calf, and they
17:29 we shouldn't think of God as an **i** designed by
1Co 5:10 or who are greedy or are swindlers or **i** worshipers.
6: 9 who are **i** worshipers, adulterers, male prostitutes,
8: 4 we all know that an **i** is not really a god and that
8:10 this food will see you eating in the temple of an **i**.
8:10 by eating food that has been dedicated to the **i**.
10:28 warns you that this meat has been offered to an **i**.
Rev 21: 8 practice witchcraft, and **i** worshipers, and all liars—
22:15 sexually immoral, the murderers, the **i** worshipers,

IDOLATER (1) [IDOL]
Eph 5: 5 For a greedy person is really an **i** who worships the

IDOLATERS (1) [IDOL]
Eze 33:26 Murderers! **I**! Adulterers! Should the land belong

IDOLATROUS (1) [IDOL]
Zep 1: 4 I will put an end to all the **i** priests, so that even the

IDOLATRY (29) [IDOL]
Nu 31: 2 on the Midianites for leading the Israelites into **i**.
1Ki 15:26 continuing the sins of **i** that Jeroboam had led
15:34 continuing the sins of **i** that Jeroboam had led
16:19 continuing the sins of **i** that Jeroboam had led
16:26 continuing the sins of **i** that Jeroboam had led
22:52 son of Nebat, who had led Israel into the sin of **i**.
2Ki 3: 3 Nevertheless he continued in the sins of **i** that
9:22 "How can there be peace as long as the **i**
10:31 He refused to turn from the sins of **i** that Jeroboam
13: 2 continuing the sins of **i** that Jeroboam son of Nebat
13:11 He refused to turn from the sins of **i** that Jeroboam
14:24 He refused to turn from the sins of **i** that Jeroboam
15: 9 He refused to turn from the sins of **i** that Jeroboam
15:18 he refused to turn from the sins of **i** that Jeroboam
15:24 He refused to turn from the sins of **i** that Jeroboam
15:28 He refused to turn from the sins of **i** that Jeroboam
17:22 They did not turn from these sins of **i**
21:11 before Israel. He has led the people of Judah into **i**.
Jer 5:23 turned against me and have chosen to practice **i**.
Eze 22: 4 you are guilty of both murder and **i**. Your day of
23:48 I will put an end to lewdness and **i** in the land,
24:13 It is the filth and corruption of your lewdness and **i**.
Hos 4:17 Leave her alone because she is married to **i**.
14: 4 "Then I will heal you of your **i** and faithlessness,
Mic 1: 5 Where is the center of **i** in Judah? In Jerusalem,
Ro 2:22 You condemn **i**, but do you steal from pagan
Gal 5:20 **i**, participation in demonic activities, hostility,
Col 3: 5 greedy for the good things of this life, for that is **i**.
Rev 21:27 no one who practices shameful **i** and dishonesty—

IDOLS (244) [IDOL]
Ge 35: 2 "Destroy your **i**, wash yourselves, and put on
35: 4 So they gave Jacob all their **i** and their earrings,
Ex 20: 4 "Do not make **i** of any kind, whether in the shape
20:23 you must not make or worship **i** of silver or gold.
23:24 conquer them and break down their shameful **i**.
Lev 19: 4 Do not put your trust in **i** or make gods of metal for
26: 1 "Do not make **i** or set up carved images,
26:30 leave your corpses piled up beside your lifeless **i**,
Dt 4:23 You will break it if you make **i** of any shape
4:25 do not corrupt yourselves by making **i** of any kind.
4:28 you will worship **i** made from wood and stone,
5: 8 " 'Do not make **i** of any kind, whether in the
7: 5 Cut down their Asherah poles and burn their **i**.
7:25 "You must burn their **i** in fire, and do not desire
12: 3 their Asherah poles and cut down their carved **i**.
27:15 who carves or casts **i** and secretly sets them up.
27:15 These **i**, the work of craftsmen, are detestable to
29:17 You have seen their detestable **i** made of wood,
32:21 they have provoked my fury with useless **i**.
Jos 24:14 Put away forever the **i** your ancestors worshiped
24:23 Joshua said, "destroy the **i** among you,
Jdg 3:26 Ehud escaped, passing the **i** on his way to Seirah.
17: 5 and he made a sacred ephod and some household **i**.
18:14 some household **i**, a carved image, and a cast idol.
18:17 sacred ephod, the household **i**, and the cast idol.
18:20 the household **i**, and the carved image.
18:27 Then, with Micah's **i** and his priest, the men of
1Sa 12:21 Don't go back to worshiping worthless **i** that

15: 23 and stubbornness is as bad as worshiping **i**.
2Sa 5: 21 The Philistines had abandoned their **i** there,
1Ki 12: 29 He placed these calf **i** at the southern and northern
15: 12 and removed all the **i** his ancestors had made.
16: 13 of the LORD, the God of Israel, with their **i**.
21: 26 because he worshiped **i** just as the Amorites had
2Ki 11: 18 demolished the altars and smashed the **i** to pieces,
17: 12 Yes, they worshiped **i**, despite the LORD's
17: 15 They worshiped worthless **i** and became worthless
17: 29 they placed their **i** at the pagan shrines that the
17: 30 Those from Babylon worshiped **i** of their god
17: 41 worshiped the LORD, they also worshiped their **i**.
19: 18 only **i** of wood and stone shaped by human hands.
21: 21 worshiping the same **i** that his father had
1Ch 10: 9 proclaimed the news of Saul's death before their **i**
14: 12 The Philistines had abandoned their **i** there,
16: 26 The gods of other nations are merely **i**,
2Ch 11: 15 they worshiped the goat and calf **i** he had made.
15: 8 and removed all the **i** in the land of Judah
21: 13 led the people of Jerusalem and Judah to worship **i**,
23: 17 They demolished the altars and smashed the **i**,
24: 18 and they worshiped Asherah poles and **i** instead!
25: 14 he brought with him **i** taken from the people of
33: 19 and set up Asherah poles and **i** before he repented.
33: 22 and sacrificed to all the **i** his father had made.
34: 3 Asherah poles, and the carved **i** and cast images.
34: 4 the carved **i**, and the cast images were smashed
34: 7 the Asherah poles, and he crushed the **i** into dust.
34: 33 So Josiah removed all detestable **i** from the entire
Ps 24: 4 and hearts are pure, / who do not worship **i**
31: 6 I hate those who worship worthless **i**. / I trust in the
40: 4 in the proud, / or in those who worship **i**.
78: 58 to other gods; / they made him jealous with their **i**.
96: 5 The gods of other nations are merely **i**,
97: 7 Those who worship **i** are disgraced— / all who
106: 36 They worshiped their **i**, / and this led to their
106: 38 By sacrificing them to the **i** of Canaan,
106: 39 and their love of **i** was adultery in the LORD's
115: 4 Their **i** are merely things of silver and gold,
135: 15 Their **i** are merely things of silver and gold,
Isa 1: 29 sacrifices to **i** in your groves of sacred oaks.
2: 8 The land is filled with **i**. The people bow down
2: 18 **I** will be utterly abolished and destroyed.
2: 20 their gold and silver **i** to the moles and bats.
16: 12 the people of Moab will pray in anguish to their **i**,
17: 8 They will no longer ask their **i** for help or worship
19: 1 riding on a swift cloud. The **i** of Egypt tremble.
19: 3 They will plead with their **i** for wisdom. They will
21: 9 All the **i** of Babylon lie broken on the ground!"
30: 22 Then you will destroy all your silver **i** and gold
31: 7 when every one of you will throw away the gold **i**
37: 19 only **i** of wood and stone shaped by human hands.
41: 7 The craftsmen rush to make new **i**. The carver
41: 21 "Can your **i** make such claims as these? Let them
41: 28 Not one of your **i** told you this. Not one gave any
41: 29 Your **i** are all as empty as the wind.
42: 8 I will not share my praise with carved **i**.
42: 17 But those who trust in **i**, / calling them their gods—
43: 9 Which of their **i** has ever foretold such things?
44: 9 How foolish are those who manufacture **i** to be
44: 9 that this is so, for their **i** neither see nor know.
44: 11 All who worship **i** will stand before the LORD in
45: 16 All who make **i** will be humiliated and disgraced.
45: 20 fools they are who carry around their wooden **i**
46: 1 The **i** of Babylon, Bel and Nebo, are being hauled
46: 2 Both the **i** and the ones carrying them are bowed
48: 5 That way, you could never say, 'My **i** did it.
48: 14 "Have any of your **i** ever told you this? Come,
57: 5 You worship your **i** with great passion beneath
57: 7 on the mountaintops by worshiping **i** there,
57: 8 you have set up your **i** and worship them instead of
57: 8 for you are loving these **i** instead of loving me.
57: 13 Let's see if your **i** can do anything for you when
65: 3 to my face by worshiping **i** in their sacred gardens.
Jer 1: 16 they worship **i** that they themselves have made!
2: 5 They worshiped foolish **i**, only to become foolish
2: 11 have exchanged their glorious God for worthless **i**!
2: 20 have prostituted yourselves by bowing down to **i**.
3: 9 adultery by worshiping **i** made of wood
3: 13 him by worshiping **i** under every green tree.
3: 23 Our worship of **i** and our religious orgies on the
4: 1 "If you will throw away your detestable **i** and go
7: 6 and if you stop worshiping **i** as you now do to your
7: 30 "They have set up their abominable **i** right in my
8: 19 why have they angered me with their carved **i**
10: 8 The wisest of people who worship **i** are stupid
10: 9 materials to skillful craftsmen who make their **i**.
10: 14 They make **i**, but the **i** will disgrace their makers,
10: 15 **I** are worthless; they are lies! / The time is coming
11: 10 have refused to listen to me and are worshiping **i**.
11: 12 people of Judah and Jerusalem will pray to their **i**
11: 12 But the **i** will not save them when disaster strikes!
13: 10 stubbornly follow their own desires and worship **i**.
16: 13 There you can worship **i** all you like—and I will
16: 19 were foolish, for they worshiped worthless **i**.
18: 15 they have deserted me and turned to worthless **i**.
19: 4 **i** never before worshiped by this generation,
19: 13 drink offerings were poured out to your **i**.' "
23: 27 just as their ancestors did by worshiping the **i** of
25: 6 Do not make me angry by worshiping the **i** you
25: 7 "You made me furious by worshiping your **i**,
32: 34 They have set up their abominable **i** right in my
43: 12 burning all their **i** and carrying away the people as
44: 8 Why arouse my anger by burning incense to the **i**
44: 15 knew that their wives had burned incense to **i**—
44: 21 and all the people were burning incense to **i** in the
44: 23 because you have burned incense to **i** and sinned
50: 2 Her images and **i** will be shattered. Her gods Bel
50: 38 Because the whole land is filled with **i**,
51: 17 They make **i**, but the **i** will disgrace their makers,
51: 18 **I** are worthless; they are lies! / The time is coming
51: 47 when I will punish this great city and all her **i**.
51: 52 "but the time is coming when Babylon's **i** will be
Eze 5: 9 Because of your detestable **i**, I will punish you
5: 11 because you have defiled my Temple with **i**
6: 4 I will kill your people in front of your **i**.
6: 5 I will lay your corpses in front of your **i** and scatter
6: 6 your altars, your **i**, your incense altars,
6: 13 When their dead lie scattered among their **i**
7: 20 and used it to make vile and detestable **i**.
8: 10 I also saw the various **i** worshiped by the people of
8: 12 of Israel are doing with their **i** in dark rooms?
11: 21 But as for those who long for **i**, I will repay them
14: 3 of man, these leaders have set up **i** in their hearts.
14: 4 will punish the people of Israel who set up **i** in
14: 5 have turned from me to worship their detestable **i**.
14: 6 Repent and turn away from your **i**, and stop all
14: 7 who reject me and set up **i** in their hearts so they
16: 16 the lovely things I gave you to make shrines for **i**,
16: 18 embroidered clothes I gave you to cover your **i**.
16: 21 also slaughter my children by sacrificing them to **i**?
16: 24 and put altars to **i** in every town square.
16: 31 street corner and your altars to **i** in every square.
16: 36 and because you have worshiped detestable **i**,
16: 39 down your pagan shrines and the altars to your **i**.
18: 6 he has not feasted in the mountains before Israel's **i**
18: 11 worships **i** on the mountains, commits adultery,
18: 12 worships **i** and takes part in loathsome practices,
18: 15 Suppose this son refuses to worship **i** on the
20: 7 Then I said to them, 'Each of you, get rid of your **i**.
20: 8 They did not get rid of their **i** or forsake the gods
20: 16 Sabbath days. Their hearts were given to their **i**.
20: 18 parents' footsteps, defiling themselves with their **i**.
20: 24 and longing for the **i** of their ancestors.
20: 30 prostituting yourselves by worshiping detestable **i**?
20: 32 all around us, who serve **i** of wood and stone.'
20: 39 go right ahead and worship your **i**, but then don't
22: 3 doomed and damned—city of **i**, filthy and foul—
23: 7 of Assyria, worshiping their **i** and defiling herself.
23: 30 to other nations, defiling yourself with all their **i**.
23: 37 adultery by worshiping **i** and murder by burning
23: 39 that they murdered their children in front of their **i**,
23: 49 repaid for all your prostitution—your worship of **i**.
30: 13 I will smash the **i** of Egypt and the images at
33: 25 you worship **i**, and you murder the innocent.
36: 18 polluted the land with murder and by worshiping **i**,
36: 25 be washed away, and you will no longer worship **i**.
37: 23 stop polluting themselves with their detestable **i**
43: 9 Now let them put away their **i** and the sacred
44: 10 **i** must bear the consequences of their
44: 15 in the Temple when Israel abandoned me for **i**.
Da 5: 4 They drank toasts from them to honor their **i** made
11: 8 he will carry back their **i** with him, along with
Hos 3: 4 and without sacrifices, temple, priests, or even **i**!
4: 7 exchanged the glory of God for the disgrace of **i**.
4: 12 Longing after **i** has made them foolish. They have
4: 13 They offer sacrifices to **i** on the tops of mountains.
4: 19 will die in shame because they offer sacrifices to **i**.
5: 1 people into a snare by worshiping the **i** at Mizpah
5: 11 because they are determined to worship **i**.
8: 4 By making **i** for themselves from their silver
10: 1 the more beautiful the statues and **i** they built.
10: 2 down their foreign altars and smash their many **i**.
11: 2 to the images of Baal and burning incense to **i**.
12: 11 But Gilead is filled with sinners who worship **i**.
13: 2 Now they keep on sinning by making silver **i** to
13: 2 to these," they cry, "and kiss the calf **i**!"
14: 3 Never again will we call the **i** we have made 'our
14: 8 "O Israel, stay away from **i**! I am the one who
Am 4: 4 and offer your sacrifices to the **i** at Bethel
5: 5 Don't go to worship the **i** of Bethel, Gilgal,
8: 14 those who worship and swear by the **i** of Samaria,
Mic 4: 5 Even though the nations around us worship **i**,
5: 13 I will destroy all your **i** and sacred pillars, so you
Na 1: 14 I will destroy all the **i** in the temples of your gods.
Hab 2: 18 you gained by worshiping all your man-made **i**?
2: 19 be for you who beg lifeless wooden **i** to save you.
Zec 13: 2 so that even the names of the **i** will be forgotten.
Mal 2: 11 sanctuary by marrying women who worship **i**.
Ac 15: 20 them to abstain from eating meat sacrificed to **i**,
15: 29 You must abstain from eating food offered to **i**,
17: 16 he was deeply troubled by all the **i** he saw
17: 30 everyone everywhere to turn away from **i**
21: 25 They should not eat food offered to **i**, nor consume
Ro 1: 23 they worshiped **i** made to look like mere people,
1Co 5: 11 or is greedy, or worships **i**, or is abusive, or a
8: 1 let's talk about food that has been sacrificed to **i**.
8: 4 Should we eat meat that has been sacrificed to **i**?
8: 7 Some are accustomed to thinking of **i** as being real,
8: 7 so when they eat food that has been offered to **i**,
10: 7 or worship **i** as some of them did.
10: 14 So, my dear friends, flee from the worship of **i**.
10: 19 Am I saying that the **i** to whom the pagans bring
10: 25 Don't ask whether or not it was offered to **i**,
12: 2 and swept along in worshiping speechless **i**.
2Co 6: 16 union can there be between God's temple and **i**?
1Th 1: 9 and how you turned away from **i** to serve the true
1Pe 4: 3 and wild parties, and their terrible worship of **i**.
Rev 2: 14 He taught them to worship **i** by eating food offered
offered to **i**
2: 20 She is encouraging them to worship **i**, eat food
offered to **i**, and commit sexual sin.
9: 20 continued to worship demons and **i** made of gold,
9: 20 and wood—**i** that neither see nor hear nor walk!

IDUMEA (1)

Mk 3: 8 Jerusalem, **I**, from east of the Jordan River,

IEZER (1) [IEZERITES]

Nu 26: 30 The Iezerites, named after their ancestor **I**.

IEZERITES (1) [IEZER]

Nu 26: 30 The **I**, named after their ancestor Iezer.

IF (1932) See Index of Articles, Etc.

IGAL (3)

Nu 13: 7 Issachar | **I** son of Joseph
2Sa 23: 36 **I** son of Nathan from Zobah; / Bani from Gad;
1Ch 3: 22 and his sons, Hattush, **I**, Bariah, Neariah,

IGDALIAH (1)

Jer 35: 4 the room assigned to the sons of Hanan son of **I**,

IGEAL [KJV] See IGAL

IGNITE (2) [IGNITES, IGNITING]

Ps 7: 13 his deadly weapons / and **i** his flaming arrows.
Isa 10: 16 proud troops, and a flaming fire will **i** your glory.

IGNITES (1) [IGNITE]

Dt 32: 22 its crops / and **i** the foundations of the mountains.

IGNITING (1) [IGNITE]

Ps 39: 3 within me / and began to burn, / **i** a fire of words:

IGNOMINY [KJV] See DISGRACE

IGNORANCE (9) [IGNORE]

Job 4: 21 Their tent collapses; they die in **i**.
42: 3 is this that questions my wisdom with such **i**?'
Isa 44: 18 Such stupidity and **i**! Their eyes are closed,
Eze 45: 20 year for anyone who has sinned through error or **i**.
Ac 3: 17 I realize that what you did to Jesus was done in **i**;
17: 30 God overlooked people's former **i** about these
1Th 4: 5 as the pagans do, in their **i** of God and his ways.
1Ti 1: 13 had mercy on me because I did it in **i** and unbelief.
Heb 9: 7 and the sins the people have committed in **i**.

IGNORANT (15) [IGNORE]

Job 37: 19 to God. We are too **i** to make our own arguments.
38: 2 "Who is this that questions my wisdom with such **i**
Ps 73: 22 I was so foolish and **i**— / I must have seemed like a
82: 5 But these oppressors know nothing; / they are so **i**!
92: 6 Only an **i** person would not know this! / Only a
Pr 9: 13 and brash. She is **i** and doesn't even know it.
30: 2 I am too **i** to be human, and I lack common sense.
Isa 40: 21 he gave before the world began? Are you so **i**?
Jer 5: 4 "But what can we expect from the poor and **i**?
Jn 7: 49 These **i** crowds do, but what do they know about
Ro 2: 20 You think you can instruct the **i** and teach children
1Ti 6: 4 teaches anything different is both conceited and **i**.
2Ti 2: 23 in foolish, **i** arguments that only start fights.
Heb 5: 2 with the people, though they are **i** and wayward.
2Pe 3: 16 and those who are **i** and unstable have twisted his

IGNORE (27) [IGNORANCE, IGNORANT, IGNORED, IGNORES, IGNORING]

Ex 23: 8 for a bribe makes you **i** something that you clearly
Lev 20: 4 And if the people of the community **i** this offering
Ne 4: 5 Do not **i** their guilt. Do not blot out their sins,
Ps 9: 12 He does not **i** those who cry to him for help.
9: 17 This is the fate of all the nations who **i** God.
22: 1 so distant? / Why do you **i** my cries for help?
39: 12 Don't **i** my tears. / For I am your guest—
44: 24 Why do you **i** our suffering and oppression?
50: 22 Repent, all of you who **i** me, / or I will tear you
55: 1 to my prayer, O God. / Do not **i** my cry for help!
66: 20 Praise God, who did not **i** my prayer / and did not
Pr 3: 11 don't **i** it when the LORD disciplines you,
8: 33 Listen to my counsel and be wise. Don't **i** it.
10: 17 to life, but those who **i** it will lead others astray.
13: 18 If you **i** criticism, you will end in poverty
Isa 2: 9 The LORD cannot simply **i** their sins!
Jer 18: 18 spread rumors about him and **i** what he says."
La 4: 3 They **i** their children's cries, like the ostriches of
Eze 3: 27 will listen, but some will **i** you, for they are rebels.
Am 7: 8 this plumb line. I will no longer **i** all their sins.
Mt 15: 2 "They **i** our tradition of ceremonial hand washing
15: 14 so **i** them. They are blind guides leading the blind,
23: 23 but you **i** the important things of the law—
Mk 7: 8 For you **i** God's specific laws and substitute your
Gal 6: 7 Remember that you can't **i** God and get away with
Tit 2: 15 so don't let anyone **i** you or disregard what you
Heb 12: 5 don't **i** it when the Lord disciplines you,

IGNORED (15) [IGNORE]

Jdg 2: 20 with their ancestors and have **i** my commands,
1Sa 10: 27 and refused to bring him gifts. But Saul **i** them.
2Ch 33: 10 and his people, but they **i** all his warnings.
Ezr 9: 10 of this? For once again we have **i** your commands!
Ps 22: 24 For he has not **i** the suffering of the needy.
31: 12 I have been **i** as if I were dead, / as if I were a
129: 7 **i** by the harvester, / despised by the binder.
Pr 1: 25 You **i** my advice and rejected the correction I

21:13 of the poor will be **i** in their own time of need.
Jer 2: 8 The judges **i** me, the rulers turned against me,
Eze 20:16 **i** my will for them, and violated my Sabbath days.
22: 7 Fathers and mothers are contemptuously **i**.
Mt 22: 5 But the guests he had invited **i** them and went
Mk 5:36 But Jesus **i** their comments and said to Jairus,
Lk 18: 4 The judge **i** her for a while, but eventually she

IGNORES (3) [IGNORE]
Pr 2:17 and **i** the covenant she made before God.
28: 9 The prayers of a person who **i** the law are despised.
Mt 7:26 anyone who hears my teaching and **i** it is foolish,

IGNORING (1) [IGNORE]
Ps 58: 5 **i** the tunes of the snake charmers, / no matter how

II (11) [TWO]
2Ki 13:13 Then his son Jeroboam **I** became the next king.
14:16 Then his son Jeroboam **I** became the next king.
14:23 Jeroboam **I**, the son of Jehoash, began to rule over
14:25 Jeroboam **I** recovered the territories of Israel
14:27 he used Jeroboam **I**, the son of Jehoash, to save
14:28 The rest of the events in the reign of Jeroboam **I**
14:29 When Jeroboam **I** died, he was buried with his
15: 1 year of the reign of King Jeroboam **I** of Israel.
15: 8 Zechariah son of Jeroboam **I** began to rule over
Ne 12:22 During the reign of Darius **I** of Persia, a list was
Am 1: 1 when Uzziah was king of Judah and Jeroboam **I**,

IIM (1)
Jos 15:29 Baalah, **I**, Ezem,

IJE-ABARIM [KJV] See IYE-ABARIM

IJON (3)
1Ki 15:20 They conquered the towns of **I**, Dan,
2Ki 15:29 and he captured the towns of **I**, Abel-beth-maacah,
2Ch 16: 4 They conquered the towns of **I**, Dan,

IKKESH (3)
2Sa 23:26 Helez from Pelon; / Ira son of **I** from Tekoa;
1Ch 11:28 Ira son of **I** from Tekoa; / Abiezer from Anathoth;
27: 9 Ira son of **I** from Tekoa was commander of the

ILL (12) [ILLNESS]
2Sa 12:15 the LORD made Bathsheba's baby deathly **i**.
13: 2 so obsessed with Tamar that he became **i**.
2Ki 20: 1 About that time Hezekiah became deathly **i**,
2Ch 32:24 About that time, Hezekiah became deathly **i**.
Ps 35:13 Yet when they were **i**, / I grieved for them.
Isa 38: 1 About that time Hezekiah became deathly **i**,
Lk 9:11 the Kingdom of God and curing those who were **i**.
Jn 5: 6 Jesus saw him and knew how long he had been **i**,
Ac 9:37 About this time she became **i** and died. Her friends
28: 8 Publius's father was **i** with fever and dysentery.
Php 2:26 and he was very distressed that you heard he was **i**.
2:27 And he surely was **i**; in fact, he almost died.

ILL-GOTTEN (2) [GET]
Job 20:10 from the poor, for he must give back his **i** wealth.
Pr 10: 2 **I** gain has no lasting value, but right living can

ILL-TEMPERED (2) [TEMPER]
1Sa 25:17 He's so **i** that no one can even talk to him!"
25:25 I know Nabal is a wicked and **i** man; please don't

ILLEGAL (3)
Mt 14: 4 kept telling Herod, "It is **i** for you to marry her."
Mk 6:18 "It is **i** for you to marry your brother's wife."
Jn 5:10 on the Sabbath! It's **i** to carry that sleeping mat!"

ILLEGITIMATE (2)
Dt 23: 2 "Those of **i** birth and their descendants for ten
Heb 12: 8 it means that you are **i** and are not really his

ILLNESS (6) [ILL]
2Ki 13:14 When Elisha was in his last **i**, King Jehoash of
20: 1 are going to die. You will not recover from this **i**."
Isa 38: 1 are going to die. You will not recover from this **i**."
Mt 4:24 And whatever their **i** and pain, or if they were
9:35 he healed people of every sort of disease and **i**.
10: 1 evil spirits and to heal every kind of disease and **i**.

ILLUMINATES (1)
Rev 21:23 of sun or moon, for the glory of God **i** the city,

ILLUSTRATE (11) [ILLUSTRATED, ILLUSTRATES, ILLUSTRATION, ILLUSTRATIONS]
Hos 1: 2 This will **i** the way my people have been untrue to
Zec 11:16 This will **i** how I will give this nation a shepherd
Mt 12:29 Let me **i** this. You can't enter a strong man's house
22: 1 Jesus told them several other stories to **i** the
Mk 3:27 Let me **i** this. You can't enter a strong man's house
4:30 Kingdom of God? What story should I use to **i** it?
Lk 13:18 is the Kingdom of God like? How can I **i** it?
15:11 To **i** the point further, Jesus told them this story:
18: 1 One day Jesus told his disciples a story to **i** their
Ro 7: 2 Let me **i**. When a woman marries, the law binds
1Co 4: 6 and myself to **i** what I've been saying.

ILLUSTRATED (3) [ILLUSTRATE]
Mt 22: 2 "The Kingdom of Heaven can be **i** by the story of
25: 1 "The Kingdom of Heaven can be **i** by the story of
25:14 the Kingdom of Heaven can be **i** by the story of a

ILLUSTRATES (2) [ILLUSTRATE]
Jer 13: 9 This **i** how I will rot away the pride of Judah
Hos 3: 4 This **i** that Israel will be a long time without a king

ILLUSTRATION (23) [ILLUSTRATE]
Eze 5: 5 This is an **i** of what will happen to Jerusalem.
24: 3 Then show these rebels an **i**; give them a message
Mt 13:31 Here is another **i** Jesus used: "The Kingdom of
13:33 Jesus also used this **i**: "The Kingdom of Heaven is
Mk 3:23 called them over and said to them by way of **i**,
4:26 "Here is another **i** of what the Kingdom of God is
12:12 Jewish leaders wanted to arrest him for using this **i**
Lk 5:36 Then Jesus gave them this **i**: "No one tears a piece
6:39 Then Jesus gave the following **i**: "What good is it
10:30 Jesus replied with an **i**: "A Jewish man was
11: 5 teaching them more about prayer, he used this **i**:
12:16 And he gave an **i**: "A rich man had a fertile farm
12:41 "Lord, is this **i** just for us or for everyone?"
13: 6 Then Jesus used this **i**: "A man planted a fig tree
14:16 Jesus replied with this **i**: "A man prepared a great
15: 3 So Jesus used this **i**:
21:29 Then he gave them this **i**: "Notice the fig tree,
Jn 10: 6 Those who heard Jesus use this **i** didn't understand
Ro 6:19 I speak this way, using the **i** of slaves and masters,
Gal 4:24 Now these two women serve as an **i** of God's two
Eph 5:32 but it is an **i** of the way Christ and the church are
Heb 3: 5 His work was an **i** of the truths God would reveal
9: 9 This is an **i** pointing to the present time.

ILLUSTRATIONS (3) [ILLUSTRATE]
Job 36: 3 I will give you many **i** of the righteousness of my
Mt 13:34 and **i** like these when speaking to the crowds.
Mk 4:33 and **i** to teach the people as much as they were able

ILLYRICUM (1)
Ro 15:19 Christ all the way from Jerusalem clear over into **I**.

IMAGE (22) [IMAGES]
Ge 1:26 Then God said, "Let us make people in our **i**,
1:27 So God created people in his own **i**;
5: 3 was born, and Seth was the very **i** of his father.
9: 6 a person is to kill a living being made in God's **i**.
Dt 4:16 yourselves by making a physical **i** in any form—
Jdg 17: 3 my son, I will have an **i** carved and an idol cast."
17: 4 a silversmith, who made them into an **i** and an idol.
18:14 some household idols, a carved **i**, and a cast idol.
18:17 five spies entered the shrine and took the carved **i**,
18:20 the household idols, and the carved **i**.
18:30 Then they set up the carved **i**, and they appointed
18:31 So Micah's carved **i** was worshiped by the tribe of
Ps 106:19 they bowed before an **i** made of gold.
Isa 40:18 What **i** might we find to resemble him?
48: 5 My wooden **i** and metal god commanded it to
Jer 2:27 To an **i** carved from a piece of wood they say,
44:19 and making cakes marked with her **i**, without our
Da 3: 3 and were standing before the **i** King
Ac 19:35 whose **i** fell down to us from heaven.
1Co 11: 7 for man is God's glory, made in God's own **i**,
Col 1:15 Christ is the visible **i** of the invisible God.
Jas 3: 9 against those who have been made in the **i** of God.

IMAGES (35) [IMAGE]
Ex 34:13 pillars they worship, and cut down their carved **i**.
Lev 26: 1 "Do not make idols or set up carved **i**,
Nu 33:52 You must destroy all their carved and molten **i**
Jdg 2:11 in the LORD's sight and worshiped the **i** of Baal.
2:13 the LORD to serve Baal and the **i** of Ashtoreth.
3: 7 and they worshiped the **i** of Baal and the Asherah
8:33 prostituted themselves by worshiping the **i** of Baal,
10: 6 They worshiped **i** of Baal and Ashtoreth,
10:10 you as our God and have served the **i** of Baal."
1Sa 7: 3 rid of your foreign gods and your **i** of Ashtoreth.
7: 4 So the Israelites destroyed their **i** of Baal
12:10 and worshiping the **i** of Baal and Ashtoreth.
1Ki 18:18 and have worshiped the **i** of Baal instead.
2Ch 17: 3 early years and did not worship the **i** of Baal.
24: 7 the Temple of the LORD to worship the **i** of Baal.
28: 2 kings of Israel and cast **i** for the worship of Baal.
33: 3 He constructed altars for the **i** of Baal and set up
34: 3 the Asherah poles, and the carved idols and cast **i**.
34: 4 He saw to it that the altars for the **i** of Baal
34: 4 and the cast **i** were smashed and scattered over the
Isa 30:22 you will destroy all your silver idols and gold **i**.
31: 7 and silver **i** that your sinful hands have made.
Jer 2:23 not true! We haven't worshiped the **i** of Baal!'
9:14 their own desires and worshiped the **i** of Baal,
16:18 because they have defiled my land with lifeless **i** of
50: 2 Her **i** and idols will be shattered. Her gods Bel
Eze 30:13 smash the idols of Egypt and the **i** at Memphis.
Hos 2:13 when she burned incense to her **i** of Baal, put on
2:17 O Israel, I will cause you to forget your **i** of Baal;
11: 2 offering sacrifices to the **i** of Baal and burning
13: 2 to worship—**i** shaped skillfully with human hands.
Am 5:26 Kaiwan your star god—the **i** you yourselves made.
Mic 1: 7 All her carved **i** will be smashed to pieces. All her
Hab 2:19 You ask speechless stone **i** to tell you what to do.
Ac 7:43 god Rephan, / and the **i** you made to worship them.

IMAGINABLE (1) [IMAGINE]
Jude 1:18 in life is to enjoy themselves in every evil way **i**.

IMAGINARY (1) [IMAGINE]
Jer 23:32 Their **i** dreams are flagrant lies that lead my people

IMAGINATIONS (2) [IMAGINE]
Eze 13: 3 the false prophets who are following their own **i**
13:17 against the women who prophesy from their own **i**.

IMAGINE (6) [IMAGINABLE, IMAGINARY, IMAGINATIONS, IMAGINED, IMAGINING]
Job 37:23 We cannot **i** the power of the Almighty, yet he is
Pr 18:11 they **i** it is a high wall of safety.
Isa 55: 8 my ways are far beyond anything you could **i**.
Eze 16:19 **I** it! You set before them as a lovely sacrifice the
Mt 10:34 "Don't **i** that I came to bring peace to the earth!
1Jn 3: 2 and we can't even **i** what we will be like when

IMAGINED (1) [IMAGINE]
1Co 2: 9 eye has seen, no ear has heard, / and no mind has **i**

IMAGINING (2) [IMAGINE]
Ne 6: 9 **i** that they could break our resolve and stop the
Ps 41: 7 hate me whisper about me, / **i** the worst for me.

IMITATE (3) [IMITATED, IMITATING]
Lev 18: 3 I am taking you. You must not **i** their way of life.
Dt 18: 9 be very careful not to **i** the detestable customs of
2Ki 17:15 disobeying the LORD's command not to **i** them.

IMITATED (6) [IMITATE]
1Ki 14:24 The people **i** the detestable practices of the pagan
2Ki 16: 3 He **i** the detestable practices of the pagan nations
17: 8 They had **i** the practices of the pagan nations the
2Ch 28: 3 He **i** the detestable practices of the pagan nations
1Th 1: 6 In this way, you **i** both us and the Lord.
2:14 you **i** the believers in God's churches in Judea

IMITATING [IMITATE] (2)
2Ki 21: 2 **i** the detestable practices of the pagan nations
2Ch 33: 2 **i** the detestable practices of the pagan nations

IMLAH (4)
1Ki 22: 8 bad news for me! His name is Micaiah son of **I**."
22: 9 and said, "Quick! Go and get Micaiah son of **I**."
2Ch 18: 7 bad news for me! His name is Micaiah son of **I**."
18: 8 and said, "Quick! Go and get Micaiah son of **I**."

IMMANUEL (2) [IMMANUEL'S]
Isa 7:14 She will give birth to a son and will call him **I**—
Mt 1:23 will give birth to a son, / and he will be called **I**

IMMANUEL'S (1) [IMMANUEL]
Isa 8: 8 It will submerge **I** land from one end to the other.

IMMEASURABLY (2)
Jer 51:53 and though she increases her strength **i**, I will send
2Co 4:17 Yet they produce for us an **i** great glory that will

IMMEDIATE (1) [IMMEDIATELY]
1Sa 18: 1 There was an **i** bond of love between them,

IMMEDIATELY (61) [IMMEDIATE]
Ge 21:19 She **i** filled her water container and gave the boy a
Ex 9:20 They **i** brought their livestock and servants in from
34: 8 Moses **i** fell to the ground and worshiped.
Lev 11:25 you must **i** wash your clothes, and you will remain
11:28 move its carcass, you must **i** wash your clothes,
Nu 12: 4 So **i** the LORD called to Moses, Aaron,
Dt 9:12 'Go down **i** because the people you led out of
1Sa 20:22 of you,' then it will mean that you must leave **i**,
22:11 King Saul **i** sent for Ahimelech and all his family,
2Sa 16:16 the Arkite arrived, he went **i** to see Absalom.
1Ki 15:29 He **i** killed all the descendants of King Jeroboam,
16:11 Zimri **i** killed the entire royal family of Baasha,
18:38 **I** the fire of the LORD flashed down from heaven
21:16 So Ahab **i** went down to the vineyard to claim it.
2Ki 6: 9 But **i** Elisha, the man of God, would warn the king
2Ch 31: 5 The people responded **i** and generously with the
Ezr 3: 3 Then they **i** began to sacrifice burnt offerings on
7:26 and the law of the king will be punished **i** by death,
Ne 3:28 each one doing the section **i** opposite his own
13: 3 all those of mixed ancestry were **i** expelled from
13:11 I **i** confronted the leaders and demanded,
Est 1:13 He **i** consulted with his advisers, who knew all the
2: 4 to the king, so he put the plan into effect **i**.
Eze 3:17 a message from me, pass it on to the people **i**.
Da 3: 6 Anyone who refuses to obey will **i** be thrown into a
3:15 you will be thrown **i** into the blazing furnace.
Mt 2:21 So Joseph returned **i** to Israel with Jesus and his
4:22 They **i** followed him, leaving the boat and their
14:22 **I** after this, Jesus made his disciples get back into
21: 3 'The Lord needs them,' and he will **i** send them."
21:19 bear fruit again!" And **i** the fig tree withered up.
24: 6 these things must come, but the end won't follow **i**.
24:29 "**I** after those horrible days end, / the sun will be

25:16 the five bags of gold began i to invest the money
26:74 I don't know the man." And i the rooster crowed.
Mk 1:12 I the Holy Spirit compelled Jesus to go into the
1:20 too, and i they left their father, Zebedee,
5:29 I the bleeding stopped, and she could feel that she
5:42 twelve years old, i stood up and walked around!
6:45 I after this, Jesus made his disciples get back into
8:10 I after this, he got into a boat with his disciples
13: 7 these things must come, but the end won't follow i.
14:43 And i, as he said this, Judas, one of the twelve
14:72 And i the rooster crowed the second time.
Lk 4:39 and i her temperature returned to normal.
5:25 And i, as everyone watched, the man jumped to his
8:44 the fringe of his robe. I, the bleeding stopped.
8:47 had touched him and that she had been i healed.
8:55 that moment her life returned, and she i stood up!
20:19 they wanted to arrest Jesus i because they realized
21: 9 things must come, but the end won't follow i."
Jn 6:21 him in, and i the boat arrived at their destination!
11:29 So Mary i went to him.
11:57 that anyone seeing Jesus must report him i
18:27 Again Peter denied it. And i a rooster crowed.
Ac 5:21 the Temple about daybreak and i began teaching.
9:20 And i he began preaching about Jesus in the
16:33 and everyone in his household were i baptized.
21:30 and i the gates were closed behind him.
21:32 He i called out his soldiers and officers and ran
23:30 of a plot to kill him, I i sent him on to you.

IMMEMORIAL (1)

Ps 93: 2 O LORD, has been established from time i.

IMMENSE (2) [IMMENSELY]

2Ch 2: 9 An i amount of timber will be needed,
Mt 13: 2 where an i crowd soon gathered. He got into a

IMMENSELY (1) [IMMENSE]

Est 5:14 This pleased Haman i, and he ordered the gallows

IMMER (10)

1Ch 9:12 son of Meshullam, son of Meshillemith, son of I.
24:14 lot fell to Bilgah. / The sixteenth lot fell to I.
Ezr 2:37 The family of I 1,052
2:59 of Tel-melah, Tel-harsha, Kerub, Addan, and I.
10:20 From the family of I: Hanani and Zebadiah.
Ne 3:29 Next Zadok son of I also rebuilt the wall next to
7:40 The family of I 1,052
7:61 of Tel-melah, Tel-harsha, Kerub, Addan, and I.
11:13 son of Ahzai, son of Meshillemoth, son of I;
Jer 20: 1 Now Pashhur son of I, the priest in charge of the

IMMERSED (1)

Mk 7: 4 the market unless they have i their hands in water.

IMMIGRANTS (1)

Eze 47:23 All these i are to be given land within the territory

IMMORAL (24) [IMMORALITY]

Ezr 6:21 turned from their i customs to worship the LORD,
Job 36:14 They die young after wasting their lives in i living.
Pr 2:16 Wisdom will save you from the i woman,
5: 3 The lips of an i woman are as sweet as honey,
5:20 Why be captivated, my son, with an i woman,
6:24 and this teaching will keep you from the i woman,
7: 5 Let them hold you back from an affair with an i
7: 8 He was crossing the street near the house of an i
22:14 The mouth of an i woman is a deep pit;
Jer 11:15 where they have done so many i things?
Lk 7:37 A certain i woman heard he was there and brought
Ro 13:13 or in adultery and i living, or in fighting
Eph 4:19 and they have given themselves over to i ways.
5: 5 You can be sure that no i, impure, or greedy person
1Ti 1:10 These laws are for people who are sexually i,
Heb 12:16 Make sure that no one is i or godless like Esau.
13: 4 God will surely judge people who are i and those
Jude 1: 4 saying that God's forgiveness allows us to live i
1: 8 from their dreams, live i lives, defy authority,
Rev 2: 6 You hate the deeds of the i Nicolaitans, just as I
17: 2 The rulers of the world have had i relations with
18: 9 And the rulers of the world who took part in her i
21: 8 and the corrupt, and murderers, and the i,
22:15 the sorcerers, the sexually i, the murderers, the idol

IMMORALITY (25) [IMMORAL]

La 1: 9 She defiled herself with i with no thought of the
Mt 15:19 murder, adultery, all other sexual i, theft, lying,
Mk 7:21 come evil thoughts, sexual i, theft, murder,
Ac 15:20 from sexual i, and from consuming blood or eating
15:29 the meat of strangled animals, and from sexual i.
21:25 and they should stay away from all sexual i."
1Co 5: 1 I can hardly believe the report about the sexual i
6:13 But our bodies were not made for sexual i.
6:18 For sexual i is a sin against your own body.
7: 2 But because there is so much sexual i, each man
10: 8 And we must not engage in sexual i as some of
2Co 12:21 sexual i, and eagerness for lustful pleasure.
Gal 5:19 sexual i, impure thoughts, eagerness for lustful
Eph 5: 3 Let there be no sexual i, impurity, or greed among
1Pe 4: 3 their i and lust, their feasting and drunkenness
2Pe 2: 2 will follow their evil teaching and shameful i.
2: 7 he was a good man who was sick of all the i
Jude 1: 7 which were filled with sexual i and every kind of
Rev 2:21 to repent, but she would not turn away from her i.
9:21 or their witchcraft or their i or their thefts.
14: 8 made them drink the wine of her passionate i."
17: 2 world have been made drunk by the wine of her i."
17: 4 full of obscenities and the impurities of her i.
18: 3 the nations have drunk the wine of her passionate i.
19: 2 great prostitute who corrupted the earth with her i,

IMMORTALITY (1)

Ro 2: 7 after the glory and honor and i that God offers.

IMMUNE (3)

Nu 5:19 may you be i from the effects of this bitter water
Dt 29:19 the warnings of this curse consider themselves i,
Jer 1:18 For see, today I have made you i to their attacks.

IMMUTABILITY, IMMUTABLE [KJV] See NEVER (CHANGE), UNCHANGEABLE

IMNA (1)

1Ch 7:35 brother Helem were Zophah, I, Shelesh, and Amal.

IMNAH (4) [IMNITE]

Ge 46:17 The sons of Asher were I, Ishvah, Ishvi,
Nu 26:44 The Imnite clan, named after its ancestor I.
1Ch 7:30 The sons of Asher were I, Ishvah, Ishvi,
2Ch 31:14 Kore son of I the Levite, who was the gatekeeper

IMNITE (1) [IMNAH]

Nu 26:44 The I clan, named after its ancestor Imnah.

IMPALE (1) [IMPALED]

Ge 40:19 will cut off your head and i your body on a pole.

IMPALED (2) [IMPALE]

Ge 40:22 but he sentenced the chief baker to be i on a pole,
41:13 and the chief baker was executed and i on a pole."

IMPARTIAL (3)

Job 13: 8 You should be i witnesses, but will you slant your
Mt 22:16 You are i and don't play favorites.
Mk 12:14 honest you are. You are i and don't play favorites.

IMPATIENT (4)

Nu 21: 4 of Edom. But the people grew i along the way,
Job 21: 4 is with God, not with people. No wonder I'm so i.
Ps 37:34 Don't be i for the LORD to act! / Travel steadily
Zec 11: 8 But I became i with these sheep—this nation—

IMPEDIMENT (1)

Mk 7:32 A deaf man with a speech i was brought to him,

IMPELLED (1)

Ac 19:21 Afterward Paul felt i by the Holy Spirit to go over

IMPENDING (1)

Jdg 20:34 so heavy that Benjamin didn't realize the i disaster.

IMPENETRABLE (1)

Job 23:17 is all around me; thick, i darkness is everywhere.

IMPERFECTLY (1)

1Co 13:12 Now we see things i as in a poor mirror, but

IMPERIAL (1) [EMPIRE]

Ac 27: 1 officer named Julius, a captain of the I Regiment.

IMPLACABLE [KJV] See HEARTLESS

IMPLEMENTS (1)

Eze 40:42 and other i and the sacrificial animals.

IMPLORE (1)

Job 41: 3 Will it beg you for mercy or i you for pity?

IMPORT (1) [IMPORTED]

Ro 13: 7 Pay your taxes and i duties, and give respect

IMPORTANCE (1) [IMPORTANT]

Heb 6: 1 again with the i of turning away from evil deeds

IMPORTANT (53) [IMPORTANCE, SELF-IMPORTANT]

Ex 18:22 Anything that is too i or too complicated can be
19:15 "Get ready for an i event two days from now.
1Sa 9:21 and my family is the least i of all the families of
1Ki 3: 4 The most i of these altars was at Gibeon,
2Ki 10:11 relatives living in Jezreel and all his i officials,
25: 9 He destroyed all the i buildings in the city.
Pr 4: 7 Getting wisdom is the most i thing you can do!
18:16 works wonders; it may bring you before i people!
Ecc 7:12 but it's i to know that only wisdom can save your
12:11 spur students to action and emphasize i truths.
Isa 2: 2 in Jerusalem will become the most i place on earth.
19:15 in Egypt, whether rich or poor, i or unknown,
Jer 27:20 along with all the other i people of Judah
38: 7 Ebed-melech the Ethiopian, an i palace official,
52:13 He destroyed all the i buildings in the city.
Hos 6: 6 to know God; that's more i than burnt offerings.
Am 9: 7 "Do you Israelites think you are more i to me than
Mic 4: 1 in Jerusalem will become the most i place on earth.
Mt 19:30 many who seem to be i now will be the least i then,
22:36 which is the most i commandment in the law of
22:39 A second is equally i: 'Love your neighbor as
23:23 but you ignore the i things of the law—
23:23 but you should not leave undone the more i things.
Mk 10:31 many who seem to be i now will be the least i then,
12:28 "Of all the commandments, which is the most i?"
12:29 Jesus replied, "The most i commandment is this:
12:31 The second is equally i: 'Love your neighbor as
12:33 And I know it is i to love him with all my heart
12:33 This is more i than to offer all of the burnt
Lk 11:42 but you should not leave undone the more i things.
Jn 13:16 Nor are messengers more i than the one who sends
Ac 17: 4 Greek men and also many i women of the city.
21:39 am a Jew from Tarsus in Cilicia, which is an i city.
23:17 the commander. He has something i to tell him."
Ro 12:16 Don't try to act i, but enjoy the company of
1Co 1:28 to bring to nothing what the world considers i,
3: 7 The ones who do the planting or watering aren't i,
3: 7 but God is i because he is the one who makes the
7:19 The i thing is to keep God's commandments.
8: 1 While knowledge may make us feel i, it is love that
12:22 and least i are really the most necessary.
15: 3 I passed on to you what was most i and what had
15:11 The i thing is that you believed what we preached
2Co 8:12 to give, it isn't i how much you are able to give.
10:12 as these other men who tell you how i they are!
Gal 5: 6 What is i is faith expressing itself in love.
6: 3 If you think you are too i to help someone in need,
Php 3: 7 I once thought all these things were so very i,
Col 3:14 And the most i piece of clothing you must wear is
1Ti 4: 8 some value, but spiritual exercise is much more i,
1Pe 4: 8 Most i of all, continue to show deep love for each

IMPORTED (7) [IMPORT]

Jos 7:21 For I saw a beautiful robe i from Babylon,
1Ki 10:28 Solomon's horses were i from Egypt and from
2Ch 1:16 Solomon's horses were i from Egypt and from
9:28 Solomon's horses were i from Egypt and many
Pr 7:16 with colored sheets of finest linen i from Egypt.
SS 3: 9 for himself from wood i from Lebanon's forests.
Isa 17:10 hide you. You may plant the finest i grapevines,

IMPORTUNITY [KJV] See (KEEP) KNOCKING

IMPOSE (1) [IMPOSED, IMPOSING]

Dt 17:11 the sentence they i must be fully executed;

IMPOSED (5) [IMPOSE]

1Ki 12: 4 and heavy taxes that your father i on us.
12: 9 want me to lighten the burdens i by my father?"
2Ch 10: 4 and heavy taxes that your father i on us.
10: 9 want me to lighten the burdens i by my father?"
Est 10: 1 King Xerxes i tribute throughout his empire,

IMPOSING (1) [IMPOSE]

Nu 20:20 and marched out to meet them with an i force.

IMPOSSIBLE (22)

Ge 11: 6 what they will do later. Nothing will be i for them!
Ex 14:25 began to come off, making their chariots i to drive.
2Sa 13: 2 and it seemed i that he could ever fulfill his love
Da 2:11 This is an i thing the king requires. No one except
Mic 3: 6 cover you, making it i for you to predict the future.
Zec 8: 6 All this may seem i to you now, a small
8: 6 But do you think this is i for me, the LORD
Mt 14:17 "I!" they exclaimed. "We have only five loaves
17:20 to there,' and it would move. Nothing would be i."
19:26 them intently and said, "Humanly speaking, it is i.
23: 4 They crush you with i religious demands and never
Mk 10:27 them intently and said, "Humanly speaking, it is i.
Lk 1:37 For nothing is i with God."
9:13 Jesus said, "You feed them." "I!" they protested.
11:46 For you crush people beneath i religious demands,
18:27 "What is i from a human perspective is possible
Ro 4:18 even though such a promise seemed utterly i!
11:33 How i it is for us to understand his decisions
Heb 6: 4 For it is i to restore to repentance those who were
6: 6 It is i to bring such people to repentance again
6:18 are unchangeable because it is i for God to lie.
11: 6 So, you see, it is i to please God without faith.

IMPOSTORS (2)

2Co 6: 8 or praise us. We are honest, but they call us i.
2Ti 3:13 But evil people and i will flourish. They will go on

IMPOTENT [KJV] See SICK, CRIPPLED

IMPOVERISHED (1) [POOR]

Ps 107:39 When they decrease in number and become i

IMPREGNABLE (1)

Pr 18:11 The rich think of their wealth as an i defense;

IMPRESS (1) [IMPRESSED, IMPRESSION, IMPRESSIVE]
Ps 147:10 The strength of a horse does not **i** him; / how puny

IMPRESSED (7) [IMPRESS]
Est 2:9 Hegai was very **i** with Esther and treated her
Ps 106:7 in Egypt / were not **i** by the LORD's miracles.
Pr 3:7 Don't be **i** with your own wisdom. Instead,
Ecc 9:13 Here is another bit of wisdom that has **i** me as I
Isa 58:3 fasted before you!' they say. 'Why aren't you **i**?
Da 1:19 and none of them **i** him as much as Daniel,
Mt 22:33 crowds heard him, they were **i** with his teaching.

IMPRESSION (2) [IMPRESS]
Lk 19:11 he told a story to correct the **i** that the Kingdom of
Php 2:3 be selfish; don't live to make a good **i** on others.

IMPRESSIVE (3) [IMPRESS]
1Ki 9:8 And though this Temple is **i** now, it will become an
2Ch 7:21 And though this Temple is **i** now, it will become an
Ps 107:24 power in action, / his **i** works on the deepest seas.

IMPRISON (2) [PRISON]
Job 40:13 them in the dust. **I** them in the world of the dead.
Mk 6:17 soldiers to arrest and **i** John as a favor to Herodias.

IMPRISONED (13) [PRISON]
Ge 41:10 and you **i** us in the palace of the captain of the
Isa 42:22 they have been robbed, enslaved, **i**, and trapped.
58:6 I want calls you to free those who are wrongly **i**
Jer 32:2 and Jeremiah was **i** in the courtyard of the guard in
37:4 Jeremiah had not yet been **i**, so he could come
37:15 and **i** in the house of Jonathan the secretary.
37:18 or the people that I should be **i** like this?
37:21 he was **i** in the courtyard of the guard in the royal
Jnh 2:6 was locked out of life and **i** in the land of the dead.
Mt 14:3 and **i** John as a favor to his wife Herodias (the
Ac 12:4 and **i** him, placing him under the guard of four
22:19 'they certainly know that I **i** and beat those in
Ro 11:32 For God has **i** all people in their own disobedience

IMPRISONMENT (5) [PRISON]
Ezr 7:26 by death, banishment, confiscation of goods, or **i**."
Isa 51:14 **I**, starvation, and death will not be your fate!
Ac 23:29 certainly nothing worthy of **i** or death.
26:31 man hasn't done anything worthy of death or **i**."
Php 1:14 And because of my **i**, many of the Christians here

IMPROPER (1)
1Co 14:35 for it is **i** for women to speak in church meetings.

IMPROVE (1) [IMPROVEMENT]
Jas 1:23 in a mirror but doing nothing to **i** your appearance.

IMPROVEMENT (1) [IMPROVE]
Rev 2:19 And I can see your constant **i** in all these things.

IMPUDENT [KJV] See BRAZEN, HARD-HEARTED

IMPULSIVE (2)
Nu 30:6 takes a vow or makes an **i** pledge and later marries.
30:8 her vow or **i** pledge on the day he hears of it,

IMPURE (8) [IMPURITIES, IMPURITY]
Dt 23:9 against your enemies, stay away from everything **i**.
Job 14:4 Who can create purity in one born **i**? No one!
Isa 64:6 We are all infected and **i** with sin. When we
Ac 10:28 shown me that I should never think of anyone as **i**.
Gal 5:19 sexual immorality, **i** thoughts, eagerness for lustful
Eph 5:5 You can be sure that no immoral, **i**, or greedy
1Th 2:3 preaching with any deceit or **i** purposes or trickery.
4:7 God has called us to be holy, not to live **i** lives.

IMPURITIES (2) [IMPURE]
Isa 1:25 and skim off your slag. I will remove all your **i**.
Rev 17:4 full of obscenities and the **i** of her immorality.

IMPURITY (9) [IMPURE]
Lev 15:24 her menstrual **i** will be transmitted to him.
18:19 with her during her period of menstrual **i**.
20:21 If a man marries his brother's wife, it is an act of **i**.
Mt 23:27 inside with dead people's bones and all sorts of **i**.
Ro 6:19 you let yourselves be slaves of **i** and lawlessness.
2Co 12:21 you who sinned earlier have not repented of your **i**,
Eph 4:19 Their lives are filled with all kinds of **i** and greed.
5:3 be no sexual immorality, **i**, or greed among you.
Col 3:5 to do with sexual sin, **i**, lust, and shameful desires.

IMPUTE(D), IMPUTETH, IMPUTING [KJV] See COUNT(ED) COUNTING, CREDIT, DECLARED, GUILTY, RECKONING

IMRAH (1)
1Ch 7:36 of Zophah were Suah, Harnepher, Shual, Beri, **I**,

IMRI (2)
1Ch 9:4 son of Omri, son of **I**, son of Bani, a descendant of
Ne 3:2 to them, and beyond them was Zaccur son of **I**.

IN (9921) [INMOST, INNER, INNERMOST, INSIDE, INSIDES, INTO, WITHIN] See Index of Articles, Etc.

INABILITY (1)
Job 32:3 because they had condemned God by their **i** to

INACTIVE (1)
Ps 83:1 O God, don't sit idly by, / silent and **i**!

INAUGURATE (1)
Est 9:27 the Jews throughout the realm agreed to **i** this

INCANTATION (2)
Ac 19:13 The **i** they used was this: "I command you by
19:19 had been practicing magic brought their **i** books

INCAPABLE (1)
Hos 8:5 against you. How long will you be **i** of innocence?

INCENSE (164) [FRANKINCENSE]
Ex 25:6 spices for the anointing oil and the fragrant **i**;
30:1 a small altar out of acacia wood for burning **i**.
30:6 Place the **i** altar just outside the inner curtain,
30:7 the lamps, he must burn fragrant **i** on the altar.
30:8 he must again burn **i** in the LORD's presence.
30:9 Do not offer any unholy **i** on this altar, or any burnt
30:27 the lampstand and all its accessories, the **i** altar,
30:34 LORD's instructions to Moses concerning the **i**:
30:35 Using the usual techniques of the **i** maker, refine it to produce a pure and holy **i**.
30:36 with you in the Tabernacle. This **i** is most holy.
30:37 Never make this **i** for yourselves. It is reserved for
31:8 gold lampstand with all its accessories; the **i** altar;
31:11 anointing oil; and the special **i** for the Holy Place.
35:8 spices for the anointing oil and the fragrant **i**;
35:15 the **i** altar and its carrying poles; the anointing oil and fragrant **i**;
35:28 for the light, the anointing oil, and the fragrant **i**.
37:25 The **i** altar was made of acacia wood. It was
37:29 oil for anointing the priests and the fragrant **i**,
37:29 using the techniques of the most skilled **i** maker.
39:38 the gold altar; the anointing oil; the fragrant **i**;
40:5 "Place the **i** altar just outside the inner curtain,
40:26 He also placed the **i** altar in the Tabernacle,
40:27 On it he burned the fragrant **i** made from sweet
Lev 2:1 are to pour olive oil on it and sprinkle it with **i**.
2:2 together with all the **i**, and burn this token portion
2:15 put olive oil on it and sprinkle it with **i**.
2:16 together with all the **i**, and burn it as an offering
4:7 **i** altar that stands in the LORD's presence in the
4:18 then put some of the blood on the horns of the **i**
5:11 must not mix it with olive oil or put any **i** on it.
6:15 has been mixed with olive oil and sprinkled with **i**.
10:1 and Abihu put coals of fire in their **i** burners and sprinkled **i** over it.
16:12 he will fill an **i** burner with burning coals from the
16:12 Then, after filling both his hands with fragrant **i**,
16:12 will carry the burner and **i** behind the inner curtain.
16:13 he will put the **i** on the burning coals so that a cloud of **i** will rise over the Ark's cover—
26:30 your pagan shrines and cut down your **i** altars.
26:31 and I will take no pleasure in your offerings of **i**.
Nu 4:16 the fragrant **i**, the daily grain offering,
7:14 about four ounces, which was filled with **i**.
7:20 about four ounces, which was filled with **i**.
7:26 about four ounces, which was filled with **i**.
7:32 about four ounces, which was filled with **i**.
7:38 about four ounces, which was filled with **i**.
7:44 about four ounces, which was filled with **i**.
7:50 about four ounces, which was filled with **i**.
7:56 about four ounces, which was filled with **i**.
7:62 about four ounces, which was filled with **i**.
7:68 about four ounces, which was filled with **i**.
7:74 about four ounces, which was filled with **i**.
7:80 about four ounces, which was filled with **i**.
7:84 twelve silver basins, and twelve gold **i** containers.
7:86 each of the gold containers that were filled with **i**.
16:6 and all your followers must do this: Take **i** burners,
16:7 and burn **i** in them tomorrow before the LORD.
16:17 Be sure that each of your 250 followers brings an **i** burner with **i** on it,
16:17 the LORD. Aaron will also bring his **i** burner."
16:18 So these men came with their **i** burners,
16:18 placed burning coals and **i** on them,
16:35 and burned up the 250 men who were offering **i**.
16:37 the priest to pull all the **i** burners from the fire,
16:37 they are holy. Also tell him to scatter the burning **i**
16:38 then hammer the metal of the **i** burners into a sheet
16:39 So Eleazar the priest collected the 250 bronze **i**
16:40 should ever enter the LORD's presence to burn **i**.
16:46 take an **i** burner and place burning coals on it from
16:46 Lay **i** on it and carry it quickly among the people to
16:47 but Aaron burned the **i** and made atonement for
Dt 33:10 to Israel. / They will present **i** before you
1Sa 2:28 to offer sacrifices on my altar, to burn **i**, and to
1Ki 3:3 offered sacrifices and burned **i** at the local altars.
9:25 He also burned **i** to the LORD. And so he finished
11:8 shrines for all his foreign wives to use for burning **i**
12:33 for Israel, and he went up to the altar to burn **i**.
13:2 from the pagan shrines who come here to burn **i**,
22:43 people still offered sacrifices and burned **i** there.
2Ki 12:3 people still offered sacrifices and burned **i** there.
14:4 where the people offered sacrifices and burned **i**.
15:4 where the people offered sacrifices and burned **i**.
15:35 where the people offered sacrifices and burned **i**.
16:4 and burned **i** at the pagan shrines and on the hills
17:11 They burned **i** at the shrines, just like the nations
18:4 of Israel had begun to worship it by burning **i** to it.
23:5 for they had burned **i** at the pagan shrines
23:5 They had also offered **i** to Baal, and to the sun,
23:8 where they had burned **i**, from Geba to Beersheba.
1Ch 6:49 on the altar of burnt offering and the altar of **i**,
9:29 such as choice flour, wine, olive oil, **i**, and spices.
9:30 it was the priests who prepared the spices and **i**.
28:18 the amount of refined gold for the altar of **i**
2Ch 2:4 It will be a place set apart to burn **i** and sweet
13:11 and fragrant **i** to the LORD every morning
14:5 as well as the **i** altars from every one of Judah's
26:16 and personally burning **i** on the altar.
26:18 "It is not for you, Uzziah, to burn **i** to the LORD.
26:19 and refused to set down the **i** burner he was
26:19 priests before the **i** altar in the LORD's Temple,
28:4 and burned **i** at the pagan shrines and on the hills
29:7 They stopped burning **i** and presenting burnt
30:14 They took away all the **i** altars and threw them into
34:4 images of Baal and their **i** altars were torn down.
34:7 He cut down the **i** altars throughout the land of
Ps 141:2 Accept my prayer as **i** offered to you, / and my
Pr 27:9 counsel of a friend is as sweet as perfume and **i**.
SS 4:14 myrrh and aloes, perfume from every **i** tree,
Isa 1:13 The **i** you bring me is a stench in my nostrils!
17:8 Asherah poles or burn **i** on the altars they built.
27:9 won't be an Asherah pole or **i** altar left standing.
43:23 you with my requests for grain offerings and **i**.
43:24 You have not brought me fragrant **i** or pleased me
60:6 bring gold and **i** for the worship of the LORD.
65:3 They burn **i** on the rooftops of their homes.
65:7 "For they also burned **i** on the mountains
66:3 When they burn **i**, it is as if they had blessed an
Jer 6:20 There is no use now in offering me sweet **i** from
11:12 will pray to their idols and offer **i** before them.
11:13 of shame—altars for burning **i** to your god Baal—
11:17 provoking my anger by offering **i** to Baal."
17:26 They will bring their grain offerings, **i**,
19:4 The people burn **i** to foreign gods—idols never
19:13 all the houses where you burned **i** on the rooftops
32:29 my fury to rise by offering **i** to Baal on the rooftops
34:5 They will burn **i** in your memory, just as they did
41:5 and had brought along grain offerings and **i**.
44:3 They burned **i** and worshiped other gods—
44:5 They kept right on burning **i** to these gods.
44:8 Why arouse my anger by burning **i** to the idols you
44:15 who knew that their wives had burned **i** to idols—
44:17 We will burn **i** to the Queen of Heaven
44:18 But ever since we quit burning **i** to the Queen of
44:21 and all the people were burning **i** to idols in the
44:23 because you have burned **i** to idols and sinned
48:35 at the pagan shrines and burn **i** to their false gods.
Eze 6:4 be demolished, and your **i** altars will be smashed.
6:6 pagan shrines, your altars, your idols, your **i** altars,
6:13 and great oak where they offered **i** to their gods,
8:11 Each of them held an **i** burner, so there was a thick cloud of **i** above their heads.
16:18 Then you used my oil and **i** to worship them.
20:28 they offered sacrifices and **i** on every high hill
20:28 They brought their perfumes and **i** and poured out
20:41 be as pleasing to me as an offering of perfumed **i**.
23:41 and put my **i** and my oil on a table that was spread
Da 2:46 to offer sacrifices and burn sweet **i** before him.
Hos 2:13 when she burned **i** to her images of Baal, put on
4:13 They go up into the hills to burn **i** in the pleasant
11:2 to the images of Baal and burning **i** to idols.
Hab 1:16 will worship their nets and burn **i** in front of them.
Mal 1:11 All around the world they offer sweet **i** and pure
Lk 1:9 the sanctuary and burn **i** in the Lord's presence.
1:10 While the **i** was being burned, a great crowd stood
1:11 Lord appeared, standing to the right of the **i** altar.
Heb 9:4 In that room were a gold **i** altar and a wooden chest
Rev 5:8 had a harp, and they held gold bowls filled with **i**—
8:3 Then another angel with a gold **i** burner came
8:3 And a great quantity of **i** was given to him to mix
8:4 The smoke of the **i**, mixed with the prayers of the
8:5 Then the angel filled the **i** burner with fire from the
18:13 spice, **i**, myrrh, frankincense, wine, olive oil,

INCH (1) [10-1/2-INCH, 21-INCH, INCHES]
2Co 6:9 We have been beaten within an **i** of our lives.

INCHES (21) [INCH]
Ge 6:16 all the way around the boat, 18 **i** below the roof.
Ex 25:25 Put a rim about three **i** wide around the top edge,
26:13 will hang down an extra eighteen **i** on each side.
28:16 two folds of cloth, forming a pouch nine **i** square.
30:2 It must be eighteen **i** square and three feet high,
37:12 A rim about 3 **i** wide was attached along the edges
37:25 It was eighteen **i** square and three feet high,
39:9 It was doubled over to form a pouch, nine **i** square.
Jdg 3:16 a double-edged dagger that was eighteen **i** long,
1Ki 7:26 The walls of the Sea were about three **i** thick,
7:35 Around the top of each cart there was a rim 9 **i**
2Ch 4:5 The walls of the Sea were about three **i** thick,
Jer 52:21 They were hollow, with walls 3 **i** thick.
Eze 40:42 each 31-1/2 **i** square and 21 **i** high.

40:43 There were hooks, each three **i** long, fastened to
43:13 There is a gutter all around the altar 21 **i** wide and 21 **i** deep, with a curb 9 **i** wide around its edge.
43:14 surrounds the altar; this lower ledge is 21 **i** wide.
43:14 the upper ledge; this upper ledge is also 21 **i** wide.

INCIDENT (2) [INCIDENTALLY]
Nu 16:49 in addition to those who had died in the **i** involving
Jn 1:28 This **i** took place at Bethany, a village east of the

INCIDENTALLY (1) [INCIDENT]
Dt 3:11 (**I**, King Og of Bashan was the last of the giant

INCITE (1) [INCITED, INCITING]
Ac 24:12 nor did I **i** a riot in any synagogue or on the streets

INCITED (3) [INCITE]
Nu 14:36 Then the ten scouts who had **i** the rebellion against
16:2 They **i** a rebellion against Moses, involving 250
Ac 13:50 and they **i** a mob against Paul and Barnabas

INCITING (2) [INCITE]
Jdg 9:31 and now they are **i** the city to rebel against you.
Ac 24:5 a man who is constantly **i** the Jews throughout the

INCLOSE [KJV] See SHUT

INCLUDE (15) [INCLUDED, INCLUDES, INCLUDING]
Lev 11:3 **i** those that have completely divided hooves
11:21 These **i** insects that jump with their hind legs:
Nu 1:47 But this total did not **i** the Levites.
1:49 do not **i** them when you count the rest of the
15:9 then the grain offering accompanying it must **i** five
Dt 26:11 Remember to **i** the Levites and the foreigners
Jos 13:7 **I** all this territory as Israel's inheritance when you
1Ki 10:15 This did not **i** the additional revenue he received
1Ch 21:6 But Joab did not **i** the tribes of Levi and Benjamin
29:30 These accounts **i** the mighty deeds of his reign
2Ch 9:14 This did not **i** the additional revenue he received
Jer 26:2 Give them my entire message; **i** every word.
Eze 48:22 So the prince's land will **i** everything between the
Mt 1:17 All those listed above **i** fourteen generations from
1Co 15:27 it does not **i** God himself, who gave Christ his

INCLUDED (77) [INCLUDE]
Ge 23:17 This **i** the field, the cave that was in it, and all the
Ex 6:14 oldest son, **i** Hanoch, Pallu, Hezron, and Carmi.
6:15 The descendants of Simeon **i** Jemuel, Jamin,
6:17 The descendants of Gershon **i** Libni and Shimei,
6:18 The descendants of Kohath **i** Amram, Izhar,
6:19 The descendants of Merari **i** Mahli and Mushi.
6:21 The descendants of Izhar **i** Korah, Nepheg,
6:22 The descendants of Uzziel **i** Mishael, Elzaphan,
6:24 The descendants of Korah **i** Assir, Elkanah,
38:26 This **i** all the men who were twenty years old
Nu 4:35 The count **i** all the men between thirty and fifty
4:39 The count **i** all the men between thirty and fifty
4:43 The count **i** all the men between thirty and fifty
26:62 But the Levites were not **i** in the total census figure
Dt 23:1 he may not be **i** in the assembly of the LORD.
23:2 may not be **i** in the assembly of the LORD.
23:3 may be **i** in the assembly of the LORD.
Jos 12:1 and **i** all the land east of the Jordan Valley.
12:2 His kingdom **i** Aroer, on the edge of the Arnon
12:2 This territory **i** half of the present area of Gilead,
12:5 His kingdom **i** the northern half of Gilead,
13:10 It also **i** all the towns of King Sihon of the
13:11 It **i** Gilead, the territory of the kingdoms of Geshur
13:17 It **i** Heshbon and the other towns on the plain—
13:21 The land of Reuben also **i** all the towns of the plain
13:25 Their territory **i** Jazer, all the towns of Gilead,
13:31 It also **i** half of Gilead and King Og's royal cities
15:37 Also **i** were Zenan, Hadashah, Migdal-gad,
15:45 The territory of the tribe of Judah also **i** all the
15:46 and **i** the towns near Ashdod with their
15:47 It also **i** Ashdod with its towns and villages
15:52 Also **i** were the towns of Arab, Dumah, Eshan,
19:2 Simeon's inheritance **i** Beersheba, Sheba,
19:7 It also **i** Ain, Rimmon, Ether, and Ashan—
19:15 The towns in these areas **i** Kattath, Nahalal,
19:18 Its boundaries **i** the following towns: Jezreel,
19:25 Its boundaries **i** these towns: Helkath, Hali, Beten,
19:29 Sea at Hosah. The territory also **i** Mehebel, Aczib,
19:35 The fortified cities **i** in this territory were Ziddim,
19:41 The towns within Dan's inheritance **i** Zorah,
1Sa 14:49 Saul's sons **i** Jonathan, Ishbosheth, and Malkishua.
2Sa 23:20 which **i** killing two of Moab's mightiest warriors.
23:24 Other members of the Thirty **i**: / Asahel,
2Ki 25:23 These **i** Ishmael son of Nethaniah, Johanan son of
1Ch 3:5 The sons born to David in Jerusalem **i** Shimea,
4:34 Other descendants of Simeon **i** Meshobab,
5:21 The plunder taken from the Hagrites **i** 50,000
6:17 The descendants of Gershon **i** Libni and Shimei.
6:18 The descendants of Kohath **i** Amram, Izhar,
6:19 The descendants of Merari **i** Mahli and Mushi.
6:55 This **i** Hebron and its surrounding pasturelands in
7:11 and their descendants **i** 17,200 men available for
7:28 of Ephraim lived in the territory that **i** Bethel
8:1 in order of age, **i** Bela (the oldest), Ashbel, Aharah,
11:22 which **i** killing two of Moab's mightiest warriors.
11:26 These were also **i** among David's mighty men:
12:27 This **i** Jehoiada, leader of the family of Aaron,
12:28 This also **i** Zadok, a young warrior,
16:38 This group **i** Obed-edom (son of Jeduthun), Hosah,
23:12 The descendants of Kohath **i** Amram, Izhar,
23:14 man of God, his sons were **i** with the tribe of Levi.
23:16 The descendants of Gershom **i** Shebuel, the family
23:18 The descendants of Izhar **i** Shelomith, the family
23:19 The descendants of Hebron **i** Jeriah (the family
23:20 The descendants of Uzziel **i** Micah (the family
23:21 The descendants of Merari **i** Mahli and Mushi.
25:6 Their responsibilities **i** the playing of cymbals,
26:11 His other sons **i** Hilkiah (the second), Tebaliah (the
2Ch 1:14 which **i** fourteen hundred chariots and twelve
17:7 These officials **i** Ben-hail, Obadiah, Zechariah,
20:34 which is **i** in *The Book of the Kings of Israel.*
32:32 which is **i** in *The Book of the Kings of Judah*
Ne 7:62 This group **i** the families of Delaiah, Tobiah,
8:2 which **i** the men and women and all the children
12:25 This **i** Mattaniah, Bakbukiah, and Obadiah.
Jer 43:6 Also **i** were the prophet Jeremiah and Baruch.
Ac 3:25 and you are **i** in the covenant God promised to

INCLUDES (12) [INCLUDE]
Ex 20:10 This **i** you, your sons and daughters, your male
29:27 This **i** the breast and the thigh that were lifted up
Lev 3:3 by fire. This **i** the fat around the internal organs,
3:9 This **i** the fat of the entire tail cut off near the
3:14 This part **i** the fat around the internal organs,
11:42 This **i** all animals that slither along on their bellies,
16:27 This **i** the animals' hides, the internal organs,
Dt 5:14 This **i** you, your sons and daughters, your male
Jos 13:4 and **i** the five Philistine cities of Gaza, Ashdod,
2Ch 33:19 **i** a list of the locations where he built pagan shrines
2Co 10:13 for us, and this plan **i** our working there with you.
Col 1:21 This **i** you who were once so far away from God.

INCLUDING (125) [INCLUDE]
Ge 34:26 **i** Hamor and Shechem. They rescued Dinah from
Ex 10:5 escaped the hailstorm, **i** all the trees in the fields.
12:9 roast it all, **i** the head, legs, and internal organs.
23:12 **i** your slaves and visitors, to be refreshed.
27:19 **i** all the tent pegs used to support the Tabernacle
29:14 Then take the carcass (**i** the skin and the dung)
29:22 **i** the fat tail and the fat that covers the internal
35:11 **i** the sacred tent and its coverings, the clasps,
Lev 1:8 of the animal, **i** its head and fat, on the wood fire.
1:12 **i** the head and fat, on top of the wood fire on the
7:3 offer all its fat on the altar, **i** the fat from the tail,
8:17 The rest of the bull, **i** its hide, meat, and dung,
8:25 Next he took the fat, **i** the fat from the tail, the fat
9:13 **i** the head, and he burned each part on the altar.
14:9 **i** the hair of the beard and eyebrows, and wash
21:22 **i** the holy offerings and the most holy offerings.
25:45 **i** those who have been born in your land.
Nu 15:26 **i** the foreigners living among you, for the entire
17:6 tribal leaders, **i** Aaron, brought Moses a staff.
18:9 **i** the grain offerings, sin offerings, and guilt
21:25 **i** the city of Heshbon and its surrounding villages.
31:26 taken in the battle, **i** the people and animals.
Dt 3:17 **i** the Jordan River and its eastern banks,
Jos 8:35 **i** the women and children and the foreigners who
10:28 city of Makkedah, killing everyone in it, **i** the king.
12:8 **i** the hill country, the western foothills, the Jordan
13:4 **i** Mearah (which belongs to the Sidonians),
13:6 **i** all the land of the Sidonians.
13:9 Gorge (**i** the town in the middle of the gorge)
13:16 Gorge (**i** the town in the middle of the gorge)
13:30 **i** all of Bashan, all the former kingdom of King
19:8 **i** all the villages as far south as Baalath-beer (also
24:2 Your ancestors, **i** Terah, the father of Abraham
24:11 **i** the Amorites, the Perizzites, the Canaanites,
Jdg 8:26 not **i** the crescents and pendants, the royal clothing
11:29 land of Gilead and Manasseh, **i** Mizpah in Gilead,
15:5 **i** the grain still in piles and all that had been
21:10 to kill everyone there, **i** women and children.
1Sa 14:15 in the field, **i** even the outposts and raiding parties.
2Sa 10:18 and forty thousand horsemen, **i** Shobach,
11:24 Some of our men were killed, **i** Uriah the Hittite."
13:27 finally agreed to let all his sons attend, **i** Amnon.
19:17 **i** Ziba, the servant of Saul, and Ziba's fifteen sons
1Ki 4:10 in Arubboth, **i** Socoh and all the land of Hepher.
4:13 **i** the Towns of Jair (named for Jair son of
4:13 **i** sixty great fortified cities with gates barred with
4:19 **i** the territories of King Sihon of the Amorites
4:31 **i** Ethan the Ezrahite and Heman, Calcol,
6:22 **i** the altar that belonged to the Most Holy Place.
9:20 **i** Amorites, Hittites, Perizzites, Hivites,
11:41 rest of the events in Solomon's reign, **i** his wisdom,
14:26 **i** all the gold shields Solomon had made.
2Ki 8:6 **i** the value of any crops that had been harvested
10:33 **i** all of Gilead, Gad, Reuben, and Manasseh.
13:8 and all his deeds, **i** the extent of his power,
13:12 **i** the extent of his power and his war with King
14:15 **i** the extent of his power and his war with King
14:28 all his deeds, **i** the extent of his power, his wars,
15:15 of the events in Shallum's reign, **i** his conspiracy,
16:15 the offerings of the people, **i** their drink offerings.
20:20 **i** the extent of his power and how he built a pool
21:17 and all his deeds, **i** the sins he committed,
24:14 **i** all the princes and the best of the soldiers,
1Ch 3:9 the sons of David, not **i** the sons of his concubines.
9:5 from the Shilonite clan, **i** Asaiah (the oldest)
13:1 **i** the generals and captains of his army.
13:2 **i** the priests and Levites in their towns
19:18 **i** Shobach, the commander of their army.
26:8 of Obed-edom, **i** their sons and grandsons—
28:11 **i** the treasuries, the upstairs rooms, the inner
2Ch 5:1 **i** all the silver and gold and all the utensils.
8:7 **i** Hittites, Amorites, Perizzites, Hivites,
12:3 foot soldiers, **i** Libyans, Sukkites, and Ethiopians.
12:9 of the royal palace, **i** all of Solomon's gold shields.
13:19 some of his towns, **i** Bethel, Jeshanah, and Ephron,
13:22 the events of Abijah's reign, **i** his words and deeds,
17:8 **i** Shemaiah, Nethaniah, Zebadiah, Asahel,
21:17 value in the royal palace, **i** his sons and his wives.
24:14 **i** ladles and other vessels made of gold and silver.
27:7 of Jotham's reign, **i** his wars and other activities,
30:25 **i** the priests, the Levites, all who came from the
31:18 **i** the little babies, the wives, and the sons
36:8 **i** all the evil things he did and everything found
Ezr 3:8 **i** Zerubbabel son of Shealtiel, Jeshua son of
7:13 **i** the priests and Levites, may volunteer to return to
Est 3:13 young and old, **i** women and children—must be
8:9 of all the peoples of the empire, **i** the Jews.
Ecc 7:15 **i** the fact that some good people die young
12:14 we do, **i** every secret thing, whether good or bad.
Isa 20:2 "Take off all your clothes, **i** your sandals."
32:7 **i** all the lies they use to oppress the poor in the
Jer 10:16 that exists, / **i** Israel, his own special possession.
19:13 **i** the palace of Judah's kings, will become like
31:40 **i** the graveyard and ash dump in the valley, and all
39:8 the Babylonians burned Jerusalem, **i** the palace,
42:1 **i** Johanan son of Kareah and Jezaniah son of
44:24 Then Jeremiah said to them all, **i** the women,
51:19 **i** his people, his own special possession.
Eze 10:12 **i** their hands, their backs, and their wings.
41:13 The courtyard around the building, **i** its walls,
41:15 to the west, **i** its two walls, was also 175 feet wide.
41:20 top of the walls, **i** the outer wall of the Holy Place.
43:11 **i** its entrances and doors—and everything else
44:9 **i** those who live among the people of Israel,
48:20 This entire area—**i** the sacred lands and the city—
Da 9:7 **i** the people of Judah and Jerusalem and all Israel,
11:22 armies will be swept away, **i** a covenant prince.
Zec 9:1 **i** the people of Israel, are on the LORD.
Mk 3:28 you that any sin can be forgiven, **i** blasphemy;
15:40 watching from a distance, **i** Mary Magdalene,
16:7 and give this message to his disciples, **i** Peter:
Lk 7:29 all the people, **i** the unjust tax collectors,
22:66 **i** the leading priests and the teachers of religious
23:27 trailed along behind, **i** many grief-stricken women.
23:49 **i** the women who had followed him from Galilee,
Jn 12:42 Many people, **i** some of the Jewish leaders,
Ac 15:4 by the whole church, **i** the apostles and elders.
15:17 of humanity might find the Lord, / **i** the Gentiles—
17:4 **i** a large number of godly Greek men and also
21:5 the entire congregation, **i** wives and children,
Ro 8:23 his children, **i** the new bodies he has promised us.
16:2 for she has helped many in their needs, **i** me.
Gal 1:8 Let God's curse fall on anyone, **i** myself,
Php 1:13 everyone here, **i** all the soldiers in the palace guard,
Rev 20:12 And the books were opened, **i** the Book of Life.

INCOME (6)
Dt 18:8 and offerings, even if he has a private source of **i**.
2Ch 31:4 bring the prescribed portion of their **i** to the priests
Pr 14:4 stays clean, but no **i** comes from an empty stable.
Mt 23:23 are careful to tithe even the tiniest part of your **i**,
Lk 11:42 are careful to tithe even the tiniest part of your **i**,
18:12 I fast twice a week, and I give you a tenth of my **i**.'

INCOMPLETE (1)
1Co 13:12 All that I know now is partial and **i**, but then I will

INCORRUPTIBLE, INCORRUPTION [KJV] See ETERNAL, FOREVER

INCREASE (13) [EVER-INCREASING, INCREASED, INCREASES, INCREASING]
Ge 1:22 fill the oceans. Let the birds **i** and fill the earth."
1Ch 21:3 "May the LORD **i** the number of his people a
Ps 75:10 the wicked, / but I will **i** the power of the godly."
107:38 large families there, / and their herds of cattle **i**.
120:3 God do to you? / How will he **i** your punishment?
132:17 Here I will **i** the power of David; / my anointed one
Ecc 1:18 my grief. To **i** knowledge only increases sorrow.
Jer 23:3 own fold, and they will be fruitful and **i** in number.
31:27 "when I will greatly **i** the population and multiply
Eze 22:25 They **i** the number of widows in the land.
36:10 I will greatly **i** the population of Israel,
Da 11:5 "The king of the south will **i** in power, but one of
12:4 will rush here and there, and knowledge will **i**."

INCREASED (8) [INCREASE]
Ge 30:30 before I came, and your wealth has **i** enormously.
30:43 As a result, Jacob's flocks **i** rapidly, and he became
Ex 23:30 until your population has **i** enough to fill the land.
Lev 19:25 In this way, its yield will be **i**. I, the LORD,
Ac 6:7 The number of believers greatly **i** in Jerusalem,
7:17 the number of our people in Egypt greatly **i**.
2Co 8:22 because of his **i** confidence in you.
1Ti 3:13 and will have **i** confidence in their faith in Christ

INCREASES (6) [INCREASE]
1Sa 2:10 to his king; / he **i** the might of his anointed one."
Ps 62:10 by extortion or robbery. / And if your wealth **i**,
107:41 and **i** their families like vast flocks of sheep.
Pr 29:16 When the wicked are in authority, sin **i**.
Ecc 1:18 my grief. To increase knowledge only **i** sorrow.
Jer 51:53 and though she **i** her strength immeasurably,

INCREASING (2) [INCREASE]
Ex 6: 9 They had become too discouraged by the i burden
Eze 16:26 fanning the flames of my anger with your i

INCREDIBLE (5)
Pr 5:23 he will be lost because of his i folly.
Jer 32:35 What an i evil, causing Judah to sin so greatly!
Ac 26: 8 Why does it seem i to any of you that God can
Eph 1:19 I pray that you will begin to understand the i
2: 7 so God can always point to us as examples of the i

INCREDULOUS (1)
Isa 29: 9 Are you amazed and i? Do you not believe it?

INCUR (1) [INCURRED]
Ex 28:43 Thus they will not i guilt and die. This law is

INCURABLE (6)
Dt 28:35 will cover you from head to foot with i boils.
Job 34: 6 My suffering is i, even though I have not sinned.'
Isa 17:11 Your only harvest will be a load of grief and i pain.
Jer 10:19 grief is great. My sickness is i, but I must bear it.
15:18 my suffering continue? Why is my wound so i?
30:12 Yours is an i bruise, a terrible wound.

INCURRED (1) [INCUR]
Nu 6:11 he will make atonement for the guilt they i from

INDECENT (1)
2Sa 6:20 He exposed himself to the servant girls like any i

INDECISION (2)
Jdg 5:15 But in the tribe of Reuben / there was great i.
5:16 In the tribe of Reuben / there was great i.

INDEED (47)
Ge 30:13 The other women will consider me happy i!"
30:30 You had little i before I came, and your wealth has
50:21 I, I myself will take care of you and your
Ex 33:17 "I will i do what you have asked, for you have
Lev 13:17 the affected areas have i turned completely white,
Nu 13:27 sent us to see, and it is i a magnificent country—
16:47 The plague i had already begun, but Aaron burned
Dt 1:25 LORD our God had given us was i a good land.
7: 9 therefore, that the LORD your God is i God.
32:36 "I, the LORD will judge his people, / and he will
33: 3 I, you love the people; / all your holy ones are in
1Ki 10: 9 The LORD your God is great i! He delights in
2Ki 4:32 When Elisha arrived, the child was i dead,
14:10 You have i destroyed Edom and are very proud
22:19 So I have i heard you, says the LORD.
2Ch 9: 8 The LORD your God is great i! He delights in
13: 8 Your army is vast i, but with you are those gold
34:27 So I have i heard you, says the LORD.
35:22 to whom God had i spoken, and he would not turn
Ezr 4:19 and have i found that Jerusalem has in times past
Ps 93: 1 I, the LORD is robed in majesty and armed with
121: 4 I, he who watches over Israel / never tires
144:15 Happy i are those whose God is the LORD.
Ecc 5:19 accept your lot in life—that is i a gift from God.
7: 6 I, a fool's laughter is quickly gone, like thorns
8: 7 I, how can people avoid what they don't know is
12:10 I, the Teacher taught the plain truth, and he did
Isa 41: 2 victory at every step? Who, i, but the LORD?
42:16 Yes, I will i do these things; / I will not forsake
Jer 12: 9 And i, they are surrounded by vultures. Bring on
Da 3:24 "Yes," they said, "we did i, Your Majesty."
Mal 2: 2 I, I have already cursed them, because you have
Mt 17:11 "Elijah is i coming first to set everything in order.
20:23 "You will i drink from it," he told them. "But I
Mk 9:12 "Elijah is i coming first to set everything in order.
10:39 "You will i drink from my cup and be baptized
Lk 23:29 'Fortunate i are the women who are childless,
Jn 2:23 many people were convinced that he was i the
4:42 what you told us. He is i the Savior of the world."
5:28 I, the time is coming when all the dead in their
8:36 So if the Son sets you free, you will i be free.
Ac 9:20 the synagogues, saying, "He is i the Son of God!"
9:22 refute his proofs that Jesus was i the Messiah.
2Co 6: 2 I, God is ready to help you right now.
1Th 4:10 I, your love is already strong toward all the
Jas 2: 8 Yes i, it is good when you truly obey our Lord's
Rev 14:13 Yes, says the Spirit, they are blessed i, for they will

INDEPENDENCE (2) [INDEPENDENT]
2Ki 1: 1 the nation of Moab declared its i from Israel.
Hos 1: 5 I will put an end to Israel's i by breaking its

INDEPENDENT (4) [INDEPENDENCE]
2Ki 8:22 Edom has been i from Judah to this day. The town
2Ch 21:10 Edom has been i from Judah to this day. The town
1Co 11:11 women are not i of men, and men are not i of women.

INDESCRIBABLE (1)
Dt 28:59 both you and your children with i plagues.

INDIA (2)
Est 1: 1 who reigned over 127 provinces stretching from I
8: 9 all the 127 provinces stretching from I to Ethiopia.

INDICATE (4) [INDICATED]
Lev 13:15 because open sores i the presence of a contagious
Mt 24:28 carcass nearby, so these signs i that the end is near.
Lk 17:37 so these signs i that the end is near."
Jn 12:33 He said this to i how he was going to die.

INDICATED (2) [INDICATE]
Nu 26:53 proportion to their populations, as i by the census.
2Ki 6:10 would send word to the place i by the man of God,

INDIFFERENCE (1) [INDIFFERENT]
Rev 3:19 everyone I love. Be diligent and turn from your i.

INDIFFERENT (4) [INDIFFERENCE]
Ge 25:34 i to the fact that he had given up his birthright.
Zep 1:12 i to the LORD, thinking he will do nothing at all
Heb 2: 3 What makes us think that we can escape if we are i
6:12 Then you will not become spiritually dull and i.

INDIGNANT (9) [INDIGNATION]
Job 36:33 his presence; the storm announces his i anger.
Joel 2:18 pity his people and be i for the honor of his land!
Mt 9:11 The Pharisees were i. "Why does your teacher eat
20:24 heard what James and John had asked, they were i.
21:15 God for the Son of David." But they were i
26: 8 The disciples were i when they saw this. "What a
Mk 10:41 what James and John had asked, they were i.
14: 4 Some of those at the table were i. "Why was this
Lk 13:14 But the leader in charge of the synagogue was i

INDIGNATION (7) [INDIGNANT]
Isa 30:30 With angry i he will bring down his mighty arm on
Jer 15:17 your hand was on me. I burst with i at their sins.
Eze 13:13 away your whitewashed wall with a storm of i,
22:13 "But now I clap my hands in i over your dishonest
22:24 In the day of my i, you will become like an
Jn 11:33 he was moved with i and was deeply troubled.
2Co 7:11 such i, such alarm, such longing to see me,

INDISPUTABLE (1)
Ac 19:36 Since this is an i fact, you shouldn't be disturbed,

INDIVIDUAL (1) [INDIVIDUALLY]
Nu 15:27 "If the unintentional sin is committed by an i,

INDIVIDUALLY (1) [INDIVIDUAL]
1Co 3: 8 Yet they will be rewarded i, according to their own

INDUCTED (1)
Lev 6:22 they will be i into office by offering this same

INDULGE (5) [INDULGED, INDULGES, SELF-INDULGENCE, SELF-INDULGENT]
Ro 13:14 and don't think of ways to i your evil desires.
1Co 5: 9 I told you not to associate with people who i in
5:10 But I wasn't talking about unbelievers who i in
6: 9 Those who i in sexual sin, who are idol worshipers,
2Pe 2:13 They love to i in evil pleasures in broad daylight.

INDULGED (3) [INDULGE]
Ex 32: 6 and drinking, and i themselves in pagan revelry.
Ro 1:26 to have sex and instead i in sex with each other.
1Co 10: 7 and they i themselves in pagan revelry."

INDULGES (1) [INDULGE]
1Co 5:11 who claims to be a Christian yet i in sexual sin,

INDUSTRIOUS (1) [INDUSTRY]
1Ki 11:28 young man, and when Solomon saw how i he was,

INDUSTRY (1) [INDUSTRIOUS]
Rev 18:22 There will be no i of any kind, and no more milling

INEFFECTIVE (1)
Job 41:28 it flee. Stones shot from a sling are as i as straw.

INEVITABLE (1) [INEVITABLY]
Mt 18: 7 Temptation to do wrong is i, but how terrible it

INEVITABLY (1) [INEVITABLE]
Ro 7:21 I want to do what is right, I i do what is wrong.

INEXCUSABLE [KJV] See (NO) EXCUSE

INEXPERIENCED (3)
1Ch 22: 5 David said, "My son Solomon is still young and i,
29: 1 to be the next king of Israel, is still young and i.
2Ch 13: 7 he was young and i and could not stand up to them.

INEXPRESSIBLE (1)
1Pe 1: 8 and even now you are happy with a glorious, i joy.

INFAMOUS (2)
Jer 23:40 and your name will be i throughout the ages.' "
Eze 22: 5 O i city, filled with confusion, you will be mocked

INFANT (4) [INFANTS]
2Ki 11: 2 of King Jehoram, took Ahaziah's i son, Joash,
2Ch 22:11 of King Jehoram, took Ahaziah's i son, Joash,
Ps 22: 9 and led me to trust you when I was a nursing i.
Isa 66:11 Drink deeply of her glory even as an i drinks at its

INFANTS (4) [INFANT]
Dt 32:25 and young women, / both i and the aged.
Ps 8: 2 You have taught children and nursing i / to give
Mt 21:16 have taught children and i to give you praise.' "
1Co 3: 1 or as though you were i in the Christian life.

INFECT (2) [INFECTED, INFECTION, INFECTIOUS]
Ex 23:33 they will i you with their sin of idol worship,
Gal 5: 9 But it takes only one wrong person among you to i

INFECTED (12) [INFECT]
Lev 13: 4 the priest will put the i person in quarantine for
13: 7 the i person must return to be examined again.
13:13 the priest must examine the i person to see if the
13:14 the i person will be pronounced ceremonially
13:26 then the priest is to put the i person in quarantine
13:30 the priest must pronounce the i person
13:33 the i person must shave off all hair except the hair
13:36 he must pronounce the i person ceremonially
13:37 then pronounce the i person ceremonially clean.
13:44 the man is i with a contagious skin disease and is
Isa 1: 6 covered with bruises, welts, and i wounds—
64: 6 We are all i and impure with sin. When we proudly

INFECTION (11) [INFECT]
Lev 13:30 the priest must examine the i. If it appears to be
13:30 The i is a contagious skin disease of the head
13:31 if the priest's examination reveals that the i is only
13:32 and if the i does not appear to be more than
13:34 and he will examine the i again on the seventh day.
13:35 But if the i begins to spread after the person is
13:36 If the i has spread, he must pronounce the infected
13:37 But if it appears that the i has stopped spreading
13:37 grown in the affected area, then the i has healed.
13:42 if a reddish white i appears on the front or the back
13:44 him ceremonially unclean because of the i.

INFECTIOUS (10) [INFECT]
Lev 13:47 "Now suppose an i mildew contaminates some
13:49 it is contaminated with an i mildew and must be
13:51 the material is clearly contaminated by an i mildew
13:52 because it has been contaminated by an i mildew.
13:59 "These are the instructions for dealing with i
14:34 I may contaminate some of your houses with an i
14:44 the walls are clearly contaminated with an i
14:48 house clean because the i mildew is clearly gone.
14:54 kinds of contagious skin disease and i mildew,
14:57 with any contagious skin disease or i mildew,

INFERIOR (3)
Da 2:39 another great kingdom, i to yours, will rise to take
2Co 11: 5 But I don't think I am i to these "super apostles."
12:11 for I am not at all i to these "super apostles,"

INFERTILE (4) [INFERTILITY]
Nu 5:21 LORD's curse is upon you when he makes you i.
5:22 brings the curse enter your body and make you i."
5:27 She will become i, and her name will become a
Dt 28:18 You will be cursed with i herds and flocks.

INFERTILITY (3) [INFERTILE]
Ge 20:18 For the LORD had stricken all the women with i
Ex 23:26 will be no miscarriages or i among your people,
2Ki 2:21 It will no longer cause death or i."

INFESTED (1)
Ex 8:17 Suddenly, gnats i the entire land,

INFIDEL [KJV] See UNBELIEVER(S)

INFINITE [KJV] See BEYOND (COMPREHENSION), NO (LIMIT), WITHOUT (LIMIT)

INFINITELY (1)
Eph 3:20 he is able to accomplish i more than we would ever

INFLAMED (1) [INFLAMMATION]
Jer 51:39 And while they lie i with all their wine, I will

INFLAMMATION (1) [INFLAMED]
Dt 28:22 fever, and i, with scorching heat and drought,

INFLICT (5) [INFLICTED]
Lev 26:21 I will i you with seven more disasters for your sins.
Dt 28:55 the siege that your enemy will i on all your towns.
28:57 and terrible distress that your enemy will i on all
30: 7 The LORD your God will i all these curses on
Ps 119:36 your decrees; / do not i me with love for money!

INFLICTED (5) [INFLICT]

Lev 24:19 must be dealt with according to the injury **i**—
2Ch 13:17 Abijah and his army **i** heavy losses on them;
28: 5 defeated Ahaz and **i** many casualties on his army.
Eze 25:17 And when I have **i** my revenge, then they will
39:21 Everyone will see the punishment I have **i** on them

INFLUENCE (9) [INFLUENCED, INFLUENTIAL]

Ps 112: 9 never be forgotten. / They will have **i** and honor.
Ecc 7: 3 than laughter, for sadness has a refining **i** on us.
Jer 15:19 You are to **i** them; do not let them **i** you!
Da 11: 6 but she will lose her **i** over him, and so will her
Mic 7: 3 The people with money and **i** pay them off,
Ac 19:27 temple of the great goddess Artemis will lose its **i**
1Co 7:14 Otherwise, your children would not have a godly **i**,
3Jn 1:11 Dear friend, don't let this bad example **i** you.

INFLUENCED (3) [INFLUENCE]

1Ki 21:25 sight as did Ahab, for his wife, Jezebel, **i** him.
Lk 20:21 what is right and are not **i** by what others think.
Gal 2:13 and even Barnabas was **i** to join them in their

INFLUENTIAL (6) [INFLUENCE]

Ru 2: 1 a wealthy and **i** man in Bethlehem named Boaz,
1Sa 9: 1 Kish was a rich, **i** man from the tribe of Benjamin.
Eze 17:13 of loyalty. He also exiled Israel's most **i** leaders,
Lk 19: 2 He was one of the most **i** Jews in the Roman
Ac 8:11 He was very **i** because of the magic he performed.
13:50 Then the Jewish leaders stirred up both the **i**

INFORM (5) [INFORMATION, INFORMED, INFORMING]

Ge 32: 5 I have sent these messengers to **i** you of my
Ex 18:16 I **i** the people of God's decisions and teach them
Dt 32: 7 Ask your father and he will **i** you. / Inquire of your
2Sa 11: 5 she was pregnant, she sent a message to **i** David.
Ezr 5: 8 We wish to **i** you that we went to the construction

INFORMATION (3) [INFORM]

Ezr 4:14 dishonored in this way, we have sent you this **i**.
Est 2:22 about the plot and passed the **i** on to Queen Esther.
Ac 23:20 pretending they want to get some more **i**.

INFORMED (6) [INFORM]

Ex 5:10 So the slave drivers and foremen **i** the people:
Ezr 4:12 "Please be **i** that the Jews who came here to
Est 9:11 when the king was **i** of the number of people killed
Da 3: 8 the astrologers went to the king and **i** on the Jews.
Lk 13: 1 About this time Jesus was **i** that Pilate had
Ac 23:30 But when I was **i** of a plot to kill him,

INFORMING (1) [INFORM]

2Ki 6:11 Who has been **i** the king of Israel of my plans?"

INFURIATED (3)

Ps 112:10 The wicked will be **i** when they see this.
Jer 32:30 They have **i** me with all their evil deeds,"
Ac 7:54 The Jewish leaders were **i** by Stephen's accusation,

INGREDIENTS (1)

Ex 30:25 Blend these **i** into a holy anointing oil.

INHABITANT (2) [INHABITANTS, INHABITED, INHABITS]

Jer 44:22 a desolate ruin without a single **i**—as it is today.
51:29 Babylon will be left desolate without a single **i**.

INHABITANTS (6) [INHABITANT]

Nu 14:14 They will tell this to the **i** of this land, who are well
Dt 13:15 attack that town and completely destroy all its **i**,
1Ch 8:13 living in Aijalon, and they drove out the **i** of Gath.
11: 4 where the Jebusites, original **i** of the land, lived.
Ne 9:30 So once again you allowed the pagan **i** of the land
Zec 11: 6 I will no longer have pity on the **i** of the land,"

INHABITED (6) [INHABITANT]

Ge 12: 6 At that time, the area was **i** by Canaanites.
Ne 9:24 the Canaanites, who **i** the land, were powerless!
Jer 49:33 "Hazor will be **i** by jackals, and it will be desolate
50:39 "Soon this city of Babylon will be **i** by ostriches
Da 2:38 He has made you the ruler over all the **i** world
Zec 14:10 and will be **i** all the way from the Benjamin Gate

INHABITS (1) [INHABITANT]

Isa 57:15 The high and lofty one who **i** eternity, the Holy

INHERIT (29) [HEIR, HEIRS, HERITAGE, INHERITANCE, INHERITED]

Ge 15: 2 a servant in my household, will **i** all my wealth.
15: 4 for you will have a son of your own to **i** everything
48: 5 They will **i** from me just as Reuben and Simeon
48: 6 The land they **i** will be within the territories of
Lev 20:24 But I have promised that you will **i** their land,
Nu 36: 8 in line to **i** property must marry within their tribe,
Ru 4:10 and to **i** the family property here in his hometown.
2Sa 14: 7 He doesn't deserve to **i** his family's property.'
Ps 17:14 in full. / May their children **i** more of the same,
25:13 and their children will **i** the Promised Land.
37:22 Those blessed by the LORD will **i** the land,
37:29 The godly will **i** the land / and will live there
69:36 The descendants of those who obey him will **i** the
Pr 3:35 The wise **i** honor, but fools are put to shame!
8:21 Those who love me **i** wealth, for I fill their
11:29 Those who bring trouble on their families **i** only
28:10 their own trap, but the honest will **i** good things.
Isa 57:13 me will possess the land and **i** my holy mountain.
61: 7 you will **i** a double portion of prosperity
65: 9 Those I choose will **i** it and serve me there.
Jer 49: 1 Are there no descendants of Israel to **i** the land of
Mt 25:34 **i** the Kingdom prepared for you from the
1Co 15:50 that flesh and blood cannot **i** the Kingdom of God.
Gal 5:21 that anyone living that sort of life will not **i** the
Eph 5: 5 or greedy person will **i** the Kingdom of Christ
Tit 3: 7 And now we know that we will **i** eternal life.
Heb 6:12 of those who are going to **i** God's promises
Jas 2: 5 Aren't they the ones who will **i** the kingdom God
Rev 21: 7 All who are victorious will **i** all these blessings,

INHERITANCE (149) [INHERIT]

Ge 21:10 He is not going to share the family **i** with my son,
Lev 14:34 arrive in Canaan, the land I am giving you as an **i**,
25: 2 you have entered the land I am giving you as an **i**,
25:46 passing them on to your children as a permanent **i**.
Nu 16:14 and honey or given us an **i** of fields and vineyards.
18:20 "You priests will receive no **i** of land or share of
18:20 the people of Israel. I am your **i** and your share.
18:23 But the Levites will receive no **i** of land among the
18:24 That is why I said they would receive no **i** of land
26:54 each group's **i** reflecting the size of its population.
26:55 and define the **i** of each ancestral tribe by means of
26:56 Each **i** must be assigned by lot among the larger
26:62 because they were not given an **i** of land when it
27: 7 You must give them an **i** of land along with their
27: 8 and has no sons, then give his **i** to his daughters.
27: 9 he has no daughters, turn his **i** over to his brothers.
27:10 has no brothers, give his **i** to his father's brothers.
27:11 pass on his **i** to the nearest relative in his clan.
32:17 battle until we have brought them safely to their **i**.
32:18 the people of Israel have received their **i** of land.
32:19 on the east side where we have received our **i**."
32:22 side of the Jordan will be your **i** from the LORD.
32:32 but our **i** of land will be here on this side of the
33:54 A larger **i** of land will be allotted to each of the
33:54 and a smaller **i** will be allotted to each of the
34:14 of Manasseh have already received their **i** of land
35: 8 Each tribe will give in proportion to its **i**."
36: 2 You were told by the LORD to give the **i** of our
36: 3 their **i** of land will go with them to the tribe into
36: 4 their **i** of land will be added to that of the new
36: 7 for the **i** of every tribe must remain fixed as it was
36: 9 No **i** may pass from one tribe to another; each tribe of Israel must hold on to its allotted **i** of
36:12 their **i** of land remained within their ancestral tribe.
Dt 5:31 them in the land I am giving to them as their **i**.' "
10: 9 or **i** reserved for them among the other Israelite
10: 9 The LORD himself is their **i**, as the LORD your
12:12 for they will have no **i** of land as their own.
14:27 in your community, for they have no **i** as you do.
14:29 Give it to the Levites, who have no **i** among you,
18: 1 be given an **i** of land like the other tribes in Israel.
18: 1 given to the LORD by fire, for that is their **i**.
18: 2 They will have no **i** of their own among the
18: 2 The LORD himself is their **i**, just as he promised
21:16 When the man divides the **i**, he may not give the larger **i** to his younger son,
29: 8 and to the half-tribe of Manasseh as their **i**.
31: 7 are the one who will deliver it to them as their **i**.
Jos 12: 7 allotted this land to the tribes of Israel as their **i**,
13: 7 Include all this territory as Israel's **i** when you
13: 8 and Gad had already received their **i** on the east
13:14 their **i** came from the offerings burned on the altar
13:23 and villages in this area were given as an **i** to the
13:28 and villages in this area were given as an **i** to the
13:33 the God of Israel, had promised to be their **i**.
14: 2 and a half tribes received their **i** by means of
14: 3 Moses had already given an **i** of land to the two
14:13 son of Jephunneh and gave Hebron to him as an **i**.
15:20 This was the **i** given to the families of the tribe of
16: 4 Manasseh and Ephraim, received their **i**.
16: 5 to the families of the tribe of Ephraim as their **i**.
16: 5 The eastern boundary of their **i** began at
16: 8 This is the **i** given to the families of the tribe of
17: 4 "The LORD commanded Moses to give us an **i**
17: 4 So Joshua gave them an **i** along with their uncles,
17: 5 a result, Manasseh's **i** came to ten parcels of land,
17: 6 received an **i** along with the male descendants.
18: 2 seven tribes who had not yet been allotted their **i**.
18: 4 a written report of their proposed divisions of the **i**.
18: 7 Their role as priests of the LORD is their **i**.
18: 7 for they have already received their **i**,
18:20 This was the **i** for the families of the tribe of
18:28 This was the **i** given to the families of the tribe of
19: 1 Their **i** was surrounded by Judah's territory.
19: 2 Simeon's **i** included Beersheba, Sheba, Moladah,
19: 8 This was the **i** of the families of the tribe of
19: 9 Their **i** came from part of what had been given to
19: 9 So the tribe of Simeon received an **i** within the
19:10 The boundary of Zebulun's **i** started at Sarid.
19:16 This was the **i** of the families of the tribe of
19:23 This was the **i** of the families of the tribe of
19:31 This was the **i** of the families of the tribe of Asher.
19:39 This was the **i** of the families of the tribe of
19:41 The towns within Dan's **i** included Zorah, Eshtaol,
19:48 This was the **i** of the families of the tribe of Dan—
19:49 gave a special piece of land to Joshua as his **i**.
19:51 and the tribal leaders gave as an **i** to the tribes of
21: 3 their **i** the following towns with their pasturelands.
23: 4 I have allotted to you as an **i** all the land of the
24:28 Joshua sent the people away, each to his own **i**.
Jdg 11: 2 "You will not get any of our father's **i**," they said,
21:23 and carried them off to the land of their own **i**.
1Ki 21: 3 "The LORD forbid that I should give you the **i**
1Ch 28: 8 and leave it to your children as a permanent **i**.
2Ch 20:11 us out of your land, which you gave us as an **i**.
Ezr 9:12 and leave this prosperity to our children as an **i**
Ne 11:20 family **i** was located in any of the towns of Judah.
Job 20:29 that awaits the wicked. It is the **i** decreed by God."
27:13 receive from God; this is their **i** from the Almighty.
31: 2 for us? What is our **i** from the Almighty on high?
Ps 2: 8 Only ask, and I will give you the nations as your **i**,
16: 5 LORD, you alone are my **i**, my cup of blessing.
16: 6 given me is a pleasant land. / What a wonderful **i**!
47: 4 He chose the Promised Land as our **i**, / the proud
61: 5 You have given me an **i** reserved for those who
78:55 nations before them; / he gave them their **i** by lot.
135:12 He gave their land as an **i**, / a special possession to
136:21 God gave the land of these kings as an **i**—
Pr 13:22 Good people leave an **i** to their grandchildren,
17: 2 the master's shameful sons and will share their **i**.
19:14 Parents can provide their sons with an **i** of houses
20:21 An **i** obtained early in life is not a blessing in the
Isa 57: 6 and grain offerings. They, not I, are your **i**.
58:14 and give you your full share of the **i** I promised to
Jer 2: 7 my land and corrupted the **i** I had promised you.
3:18 to the land I gave their ancestors as an **i** forever.
3:19 you this beautiful land—the finest **i** in the world.
12:14 "As for all the evil nations reaching out for the **i** I
12:15 to their own lands again, each nation to its own **i**.
16:18 and filled my **i** with their evil deeds."
17: 4 The wonderful **i** I have reserved for you will slip
La 3:24 I say to myself, "The LORD is my **i**; therefore,
5: 2 Our **i** has been turned over to strangers, our homes
Eze 35:15 You rejoiced at the desolation of Israel's **i**. Now I
36:12 to walk on you once again, and you will be their **i**.
44:28 the priests will not have any, for I alone am their **i**.
47:14 and it will now come to you as your **i**.
47:22 Distribute the land as an **i** for yourselves and for
47:22 to you, and they will receive an **i** among the tribes.
48:29 allotments that will be set aside for each tribe's **i**,
Da 12:13 you will rise again to receive the **i** set aside for
Joel 3: 2 for scattering my **i** among the nations, and for
Ob 1:17 people of Israel will come back to reclaim their **i**.
Mic 2: 2 No one's family or **i** is safe with you around!
Zec 2:12 The land of Judah will be the LORD's **i** in the
Mal 1: 3 I turned Esau's **i** into a desert for jackals."
Ac 7: 5 But God gave him no **i** here, not even one square
13:19 in Canaan and gave their land to Israel as an **i**.
20:32 and give you an **i** with all those he has set apart for
Gal 3:18 For if the **i** could be received only by keeping the
4:30 not share the family **i** with the free woman's son."
Eph 1:11 because of Christ, we have received an **i** from God,
1:18 a rich and glorious **i** he has given to his people.
Col 1:12 who has enabled you to share the **i** that belongs to
3:24 Remember that the Lord will give you an **i** as your
Heb 1: 2 God promised everything to the Son as an **i**,
9:15 so that all who are invited can receive the eternal **i**
11: 8 to another land that God would give him as his **i**.
1Pe 1: 4 For God has reserved a priceless **i** for his children.

INHERITED (8) [INHERIT]

Lev 25:25 go bankrupt and are forced to sell some **i** land,
27:28 whether a person, an animal, or an **i** field—
Nu 36: 7 None of the **i** land may pass from tribe to tribe,
Jos 14: 1 The remaining tribes of Israel **i** land in Canaan as
24:30 They buried him in the land he had **i**,
Jdg 2: 9 They buried him in the land he had **i**,
Eph 3: 6 with the Jews in all the riches **i** by God's children.
1Pe 1:18 you from the empty life you **i** from your ancestors.

INIQUITY (4) [INIQUITIES]

Ex 34: 9 but please pardon our **i** and our sins.
Job 10:14 and if I sinned, you would not forgive my **i**.
11:14 Get rid of your sins and leave all **i** behind you.
14:17 sealed in a pouch, and you would cover over my **i**.

INITIALS (1)

Ex 39: 6 the tribes of Israel, just as **i** are engraved on a seal.

INITIATE (1)

Dt 13: 9 You must be the one to **i** the execution; then all the

INJURE (7) [INJURED, INJURES, INJURIES, INJURING, INJURY]

Ex 21:24 an eye is injured, **i** the eye of the person who did it.
Pr 22:23 their defender. He will **i** anyone who injures them.
Isa 59: 9 That is why God doesn't punish those who **i** us.
Mt 5:38 an eye is injured, **i** the eye of the person who did it.
Lk 10:19 and scorpions and crush them. Nothing will **i** you.
Rev 7: 2 four angels who had been given power to **i** land
9:19 had heads like snakes, with the power to **i** people.

INJURED (15) [INJURE]

Ex 21:19 If the **i** person is later able to walk again, even with
21:24 If an eye is **i**, injure the eye of the person who did
21:35 bull injures a neighbor's bull and the **i** bull dies,
22:10 or any other animal, but it dies or is **i** or gets away,
22:14 an animal from a neighbor and it is **i** or killed,

Lev 22:22 **i**, mutilated, or that has a growth, an open sore,
2Ki 1: 2 at his palace in Samaria, and he was seriously **i**.
Pr 8:36 But those who miss me have **i** themselves. All who
Isa 1: 5 Your head is **i**, and your heart is sick.
28:13 They will be **i**, trapped, and captured.
Eze 34:16 I will bind up the **i** and strengthen the weak.
Hos 6: 1 He has **i** us; now he will bandage our wounds.
Zec 11:16 after the young, nor heal the **i**, nor feed the healthy.
Mt 5:38 'If an eye is **i**, injure the eye of the person who did
Ac 19:16 that they fled from the house, naked and badly **i**.

INJURES (3) [INJURE]
Ex 21:35 "If someone's bull **i** a neighbor's bull
Lev 24:19 "Anyone who **i** another person must be dealt with
Pr 22:23 their defender. He will injure anyone who **i** them.

INJURIES (1) [INJURE]
Ac 27:10 shipwreck, loss of cargo, **i**, and danger to our

INJURING (1) [INJURE]
Lk 9:39 foams at the mouth. It is always hitting and **i** him.

INJURY (8) [INJURE]
Ex 21:18 other with a stone or fist, causing **i** but not death.
21:19 the assailant must pay for time lost because of the **i**
21:23 the offender must be punished according to the **i**.
Lev 24:19 must be dealt with according to the **i** inflicted—
Ps 69:26 To those you have punished, they add insult to **i**;
Jer 30:13 There is no one to help you or bind up your **i**.
Na 3:19 There is no healing for your wound; your **i** is fatal.
Ac 27:21 You would have avoided all this **i** and loss.

INJUSTICE (11)
Ps 7: 3 my God, if I have done wrong / or am guilty of **i**,
58:10 The godly will rejoice when they see **i** avenged.
94:20 their side— / leaders who permit **i** by their laws?
Pr 13:23 may produce much food, but **i** sweeps it all away.
22: 8 Those who plant seeds of **i** will harvest disaster,
Jer 22:13 he builds **i** into its walls and oppression into its
Eze 9: 9 land is full of murder; the city is filled with **i**.
11: 7 but the victims of your **i** are the pieces of meat.
18: 8 stays away from **i**, is honest and fair when judging
1Co 6: 7 Why not just accept the **i** and leave it at that?
13: 6 It is never glad about **i** but rejoices whenever the

INK (2)
Jer 36:18 and I wrote down his words with **i** on this scroll."
2Co 3: 3 It is written not with pen and **i**, but with the Spirit

INKHORN [KJV] See WRITER'S CASE

INLAID (2)
Eze 27: 6 coasts of Cyprus. Then they **i** it with ivory.
Rev 21:19 was built on foundation stones **i** with twelve gems:

INLAND (1)
Ac 13:14 and Paul traveled **i** to Antioch of Pisidia.

INMOST (1) [IN, MOST]
Ps 51: 6 so you can teach me to be wise in my **i** being.

INN (2) [INNKEEPER]
Lk 2: 7 there was no room for them in the village **i**.
10:34 the man on his own donkey and took him to an **i**,

INNER (87) [IN]
Ex 26:32 Hang this **i** curtain on gold hooks set into four
26:33 When the **i** curtain is in place, put the Ark of the
26:35 the room from each other outside the **i** curtain.
27:21 The lampstand will be placed outside the **i** curtain
30: 6 Place the incense altar just outside the **i** curtain,
35:12 the **i** curtain to enclose the Ark in the Most Holy
36:35 The **i** curtain was made of fine linen cloth,
38:27 and for the posts supporting the **i** curtain required
39:34 the **i** curtain that enclosed the Most Holy Place;
40: 3 and install the **i** curtain to enclose the Ark within
40: 5 "Place the incense altar just outside the **i** curtain,
40:21 and set up the **i** curtain to shield it from view,
40:22 side of the Holy Place, just outside the **i** curtain.
40:26 in the Holy Place in front of the **i** curtain.
Lev 4: 6 in front of the **i** curtain of the Most Holy Place.
4:17 times before the LORD in front of the **i** curtain.
16: 2 Place behind the **i** curtain whenever he chooses;
16:12 carry the burner and incense behind the **i** curtain.
16:15 the people and bring its blood behind the **i** curtain.
21:23 he must never go behind the **i** curtain or come near
24: 3 Aaron will set it up outside the **i** curtain of the
Nu 3:31 the **i** curtain, and all the equipment related to their
4: 5 enter the Tabernacle first to take down the **i** curtain
4: 6 Then they must cover the **i** curtain with fine
18: 7 with the altar and everything within the **i** curtain.
1Ki 6:16 He partitioned off an **i** sanctuary—the Most Holy
6:19 Solomon prepared the **i** sanctuary in the rear of the
6:20 This **i** sanctuary was 30 feet long, 30 feet wide,
6:23 Within the **i** sanctuary Solomon placed two
6:27 Solomon placed them side by side in the **i**
6:27 while their **i** wings touched at the center of the
6:29 All the walls of the **i** sanctuary and the main room
6:31 For the entrance to the **i** sanctuary, Solomon made
6:36 The walls of the **i** courtyard were built so that there
7:12 just like the walls of the **i** courtyard of the
8: 6 covenant into the **i** sanctuary of the Temple—
8:10 As the priests came out of the **i** sanctuary, a cloud
1Ch 28:11 the treasuries, the upstairs rooms, the **i** rooms,
28:11 and the **i** sanctuary where the Ark's cover—
2Ch 3: 4 The **i** walls of the foyer and the ceiling were
5: 7 covenant into the **i** sanctuary of the Temple—
Est 4:11 **i** court without being invited is doomed to die
5: 1 royal robes and entered the **i** court of the palace,
5: 2 When he saw Queen Esther standing there in the **i**
Ps 139:13 You made all the delicate, **i** parts of my body
Jer 35: 2 Take them into one of the **i** rooms, and offer them
Eze 8: 3 I was taken to the north gate of the **i** courtyard of
8:16 Then he brought me into the **i** courtyard of the
10: 3 and the cloud of glory filled the **i** courtyard.
40: 7 The gateway's **i** threshold, which led to the foyer at the **i** end of the gateway
40: 9 This foyer was at the **i** end of the gateway
40:19 outer courtyard between the outer and **i** gateways;
40:22 and the foyer was at the **i** end of the gateway
40:23 **i** courtyard directly opposite this outer gateway.
40:27 was another gateway that led into the **i** courtyard.
40:28 to the south gateway leading into the **i** courtyard.
40:30 (The foyers of the gateways leading into the **i**
40:32 me to the east gateway leading to the **i** courtyard.
40:35 to the north gateway leading to the **i** courtyard.
40:38 A door led from the foyer of the **i** gateway on the
40:44 Inside the **i** courtyard there were two one-room
40:45 "The building beside the north **i** gate is for the
40:46 The building beside the south **i** gate is for the
40:47 Then the man measured the **i** courtyard and found
41: 3 Then he went into the **i** room at the end of the Holy
41: 3 extended 12-1/4 feet to the corners of the **i** room.
41: 4 The **i** room was 35 feet square. "This," he told
41:10 and the row of rooms along the outer wall of the **i**
41:14 The **i** courtyard to the east of the Temple was also
41:16 The **i** walls of the Temple were paneled with wood
42: 1 of rooms against the north wall of the **i** courtyard.
42: 3 overlooked the 35-foot width of the **i** courtyard.
42: 8 extended for only 87-1/2 feet, while the **i** block—
42:10 just south of the **i** courtyard between the Temple
42:12 in the wall facing the doors of the **i** block of rooms,
43: 5 took me up and brought me into the **i** courtyard,
44:17 When they enter the gateway to the **i** courtyard,
44:17 They must wear no wool while on duty in the **i**
44:21 never drink wine before entering the **i** courtyard.
44:27 and enters the **i** courtyard and the sanctuary,
45:19 and the gateposts at the entrance to the **i** courtyard.
46: 1 The east gateway of the **i** wall will be closed
46:12 the east gateway to the **i** courtyard will be opened
Ac 16:24 he took no chances but put them into the **i** dungeon
Eph 3:16 unlimited resources he will give you mighty **i**
Heb 6:19 the curtain of heaven into God's **i** sanctuary.

INNERMOST (1) [IN, MOST]
Heb 4:12 cutting deep into our **i** thoughts and desires.

INNKEEPER (1) [INN]
Lk 10:35 The next day he handed the **i** two pieces of silver

INNOCENCE (18) [INNOCENT]
Ge 20: 5 'Yes, he is my brother.' I acted in complete **i**!"
44:16 How can we plead? How can we prove our **i**?
Ex 22:11 then take an oath of **i** in the presence of the
2Sa 22:21 doing right; / he compensated me because of my **i**.
22:25 me for doing right, / because of my **i** in his sight.
1Ki 8:31 and is required to take an oath of **i** in front of the
2Ch 6:22 and is required to take an oath of **i** in front of the
Job 11:15 Then your face will brighten in **i**. You will be
17: 3 "You must defend my **i**, O God, since no one else
27: 5 that you are right; until I die, I will defend my **i**.
27: 6 I will maintain my **i** without wavering.
32: 1 further to him because he kept insisting on his **i**.
Ps 18:20 doing right; / he compensated me because of my **i**.
18:24 because of the **i** of my hands in his sight.
26: 6 I wash my hands to declare my **i**. / I come to your
37: 6 He will make your **i** as clear as the dawn,
59: 4 Despite my **i**, they prepare to kill me. / Rise up
Hos 8: 5 against you. How long will you be incapable of **i**?

INNOCENT (101) [INNOCENCE]
Ge 18:23 "Will you destroy both **i** and guilty alike?
18:24 Suppose you find fifty **i** people there within the
18:25 do such a thing, destroying the **i** with the guilty.
18:25 you would be treating the **i** and the guilty exactly
18:26 LORD replied, "If I find fifty **i** people in Sodom,
20: 4 her yet, so he said, "Lord, will you kill an **i** man?
20: 6 "Yes, I know you are **i**," God replied. "That is
Ex 21:19 even with a crutch, the assailant will be **i**.
23: 7 Never put an **i** or honest person to death. I will not
Nu 5:31 The husband will be **i** of any guilt in this matter,
Dt 1:39 I will give the land to your **i** children. You were
19:10 That way you will prevent the death of **i** people in
21: 8 Israel with the guilt of murdering an **i** person.'
27:25 'Cursed is anyone who accepts payment to kill an **i**
Jos 20: 6 and be tried by the community and found **i**.
20: 6 Then the one declared **i** because the death was
20: 6 After that, the one found **i** is free to return home."
1Sa 14:41 please show us who is guilty and who is **i**.
14:41 as the guilty ones, and the people were declared **i**.
19: 5 Why should you murder an **i** man like David?
26: 9 For who can remain **i** after attacking the LORD's
2Sa 3:28 and my people are **i** of this crime against Abner.
4:11 men who have killed an **i** man in his own house
24:17 But these people are **i**—what have they done?
1Ki 2: 9 But that oath does not make him **i**. You are a wise
8:32 Punish the guilty party and acquit the one who is **i**.
2Ki 21:16 Manasseh also murdered many **i** people until
21:16 was filled from one end to the other with **i** blood.
24: 4 He had filled Jerusalem with **i** blood,
1Ch 12:17 come to betray me to my enemies when I am **i**,
21:17 But these people are **i**—what have they done?
2Ch 6:23 Punish the guilty party, and acquit the one who is **i**.
Job 4: 7 "Stop and think! Does the **i** person perish?
9: 2 But how can a person be declared **i** in the eyes of
9:15 Even if I were **i**, I would have no defense. I could
9:20 Though I am **i**, my own mouth would pronounce
9:21 "I am **i**, but it makes no difference to me—
9:22 **I** or wicked, it is all the same to him. That is why I
9:23 He laughs when a plague suddenly kills the **i**.
9:28 For I know you will not hold me **i**, O God.
10:15 And even if I'm **i**, I am filled with shame
11: 2 of words? Is a person proved **i** just by talking a lot?
13:18 I have prepared my case; I will be proved **i**.
16:17 Yet I am **i**, and my prayer is pure.
17: 8 they see me. The **i** are aroused against the ungodly.
22:19 and the **i** will laugh them to scorn.
23:10 me like gold in a fire, he will pronounce me **i**.
27:17 that clothing, and the **i** will divide all that money.
33: 9 You said, 'I am pure; I am **i**; I have not sinned.
34: 5 For Job has said, 'I am **i**, but God has taken away
34: 6 I am **i**, but they call me a liar. My suffering is
36: 7 His eyes never leave the **i**, but he establishes
Ps 4: 1 me when I call, / O God who declares me **i**.
7: 8 O LORD, / for I am **i**, O Most High!
10: 8 lurk in dark alleys, / murdering the **i** who pass by.
15: 5 who refuse to accept bribes to testify against the **i**.
17: 2 Declare me **i**, / for you know those who do right.
19:13 Then I will be free of guilt / and **i** of great sin.
26: 1 Declare me **i**, O LORD, / for I have acted with
35:20 don't talk of peace; / they plot against **i** people
37:18 Day by day the LORD takes care of the **i**,
41:12 You have preserved my life because I am **i**;
64: 4 They shoot from ambush at the **i**,
94:21 attack the righteous / and condemn the **i** to death.
106:38 They shed **i** blood, / the blood of their sons
Pr 1:11 Let's hide and kill someone! Let's ambush the **i**!
6:17 a lying tongue, / hands that kill the **i**,
17:15 those who acquit the guilty and condemn the **i**.
18: 5 for a judge to favor the guilty or condemn the **i**.
21: 8 walk a crooked path; the **i** travel a straight road.
24:24 "You are **i**," will be cursed by many people
24:28 Do not testify spitefully against **i** neighbors;
Isa 1:15 hands are covered with the blood of your **i** victims.
5:23 They let the wicked go free while punishing the **i**.
29:21 Those who make the **i** guilty by their false
29:21 and tell lies to tear down the **i** will be no more.
Jer 2:34 Your clothing is stained with the blood of the **i**
19: 4 And they have filled this place with the blood of **i**
22: 3 orphans, and widows. Stop murdering the **i**!
22:17 You murder the **i**, oppress the poor, and reign
26:15 rest assured that you will be killing an **i** man!
49:12 "If the **i** must suffer, how much more must you!
La 4:13 who defiled the city by shedding **i** blood.
Eze 16:52 In comparison, you make your sisters seem **i**!
22:25 They devour **i** people, seizing treasures
33:25 in it, you worship idols, and you murder the **i**.
Da 6:22 not hurt me, for I have been found **i** in his sight.
Joel 3:19 they attacked Judah and killed her **i** people.
Mt 27: 4 he declared, "for I have betrayed an **i** man."
27:19 "Leave that **i** man alone, because I had a terrible
27:24 saying, "I am **i** of the blood of this man.
Lk 23:14 on this point in your presence and find him **i**.
23:47 he praised God and said, "Surely this man was **i**."
Ac 18: 6 "Your blood be upon your own heads—I am **i**.
25:11 But if I am **i**, neither you nor anyone else has a
Ro 3: 5 goodness when he declares us sinners to be **i**.
16:18 and glowing words they deceive **i** people.
16:19 see clearly what is right and to stay **i** of any wrong.
1Co 14:20 Be **i** as babies when it comes to evil, but be mature
Php 2:15 **i** lives as children of God in a dark world full of
Jude 1:24 and who will bring you into his glorious presence **i**

INNUMERABLE (2)
1Ch 22: 4 He also provided **i** cedar logs, for the men of Tyre
Ps 139:17 are your thoughts about me, O God! / They are **i**!

INORDINATE [KJV] See LUST

INQUIRE (2) [INQUIRED, INQUIRY]
Dt 32: 7 **I** of your elders, and they will tell you.
1Ch 21:30 But David was not able to go there to **i** of God,

INQUIRED (4) [INQUIRE]
Ge 38:18 he **i**. She replied, "I want your identification seal,
1Sa 22:13 and a sword? Why have you **i** of God for him?
Est 6: 4 the king **i**. Now, as it happened, Haman had just
Isa 65: 1 "People who never before **i** about me are now

INQUIRY (3) [INQUIRE]
Nu 5:15 an offering of **i** to find out if she is guilty.
5:18 must unbind her hair and place the offering of **i**—
Ezr 7:14 you to conduct an **i** into the situation in Judah

INQUISITION [KJV] See AVENGES, INVESTIGATION, QUESTIONED

INSANE (4)
1Sa 21:13 So he pretended to be **i**, scratching on doors
Ps 34: T regarding the time he pretended to be **i** in front of

Ac 26:24 Suddenly, Festus shouted, "Paul, you are **i**.
26:25 But Paul replied, "I am not **i**, Most Excellent

INSCRIBE (3) [INSCRIBED, INSCRIPTION]

Ex 28:36 techniques of an engraver, **i** it with these words:
Nu 17: 2 and **i** each tribal leader's name on his staff.
17: 3 **I** Aaron's name on the staff of the tribe of Levi,

INSCRIBED (16) [INSCRIBE]

Ex 24:12 tablets of stone that I have **i** with my instructions
25:16 place inside it the stone tablets **i** with the terms of
25:21 Place inside the Ark the stone tablets **i** with the
31:18 he gave him the two stone tablets **i** with the terms
32:15 He held in his hands the two stone tablets **i** with
32:15 They were **i** on both sides, front and back.
34:29 the stone tablets **i** with the terms of the covenant,
39:30 of an engraver, they **i** it with these words:
40:20 He placed inside the Ark the stone tablets **i** with
Dt 9: 9 **i** with the covenant that the LORD had made with
9:11 the two stone tablets with the covenant **i** on them.
Job 19:23 Oh, that they could be **i** on a monument,
Jer 17: 1 **i** with a diamond point on their stony hearts,
Eze 37:20 Then hold out the sticks you have **i**, so the people
Zec 14:20 bells of the horses will be **i** with these words:
Rev 3:12 And they will have my new name **i** upon them.

INSCRIPTION (3) [INSCRIBE]

Zec 3: 9 I will engrave an **i** on it, says the LORD
Ac 17:23 And one of them had this **i** on it—'To an Unknown
2Ti 2:19 truth stands firm like a foundation stone with this **i**:

INSECTS (7)

Ge 7:14 along with birds and flying **i** of every kind.
Lev 11:20 "You are to consider detestable all swarming **i** that
11:21 These include **i** that jump with their hind legs:
11:23 consider detestable all other swarming **i** that walk
Dt 14:19 "All flying **i** are ceremonially unclean for you
28:42 Swarms of **i** will destroy your trees and crops.
Mal 3:11 for I will guard them from **i** and disease.

INSERT (2) [INSERTED]

Ex 28:30 **I** into the pocket of the chestpiece the Urim
Nu 4: 8 Then they must **i** the carrying poles into the table.

INSERTED (2) [INSERT]

Ex 38: 7 These poles were **i** into the rings at the side of the
1Ki 6: 6 So the beams were not **i** into the walls themselves.

INSIDE (103) [IN]

Ge 6:14 from resinous wood and seal it with tar, **i** and out.
6:16 Then put three decks **i** the boat—bottom, middle,
8: 9 Noah held out his hand and drew the dove back **i**.
34:28 hands on, both **i** the town and outside in the fields.
39:11 around when he was doing his work **i** the house.
43:16 this noon. Take them **i** and prepare a big feast."
Ex 4: 6 said to Moses, "Put your hand **i** your robe."
25:11 Overlay it **i** and outside with pure gold, and put a
25:16 place **i** it the stone tablets inscribed with the terms
25:21 Place **i** the Ark the stone tablets inscribed with the
26:31 "Across the **i** of the Tabernacle hang a special
26:34 on top of the Ark of the Covenant **i** the Most Holy
28:26 and attach them to the two lower **i** corners of the
33: 8 would all watch Moses until he disappeared **i**.
33:11 **I** the Tent of Meeting, the LORD would speak to
37: 2 It was overlaid with pure gold **i** and out, and it had
39:19 Two more gold rings were attached to the lower **i**
40: 3 Place the Ark of the Covenant **i**, and install the
40:20 He placed **i** the Ark the stone tablets inscribed with
Lev 8: 8 on Aaron and put the Urim and the Thummim **i** it.
13:55 whether it is contaminated on the **i** or outside.
14: 8 and may return to live **i** the camp.
14:36 so everything **i** will not be pronounced unclean.
14:41 Next the **i** walls of the entire house must be
16:17 No one else is allowed **i** the Tabernacle while
17: 3 or a lamb or a goat anywhere **i** or outside the camp
25:29 "Anyone who sells a house **i** a walled city has the
Nu 19:14 and those who were **i** when the death occurred,
35:28 The slayer should have stayed **i** the city of refuge
Dt 20:11 then all the people **i** will serve you in forced labor.
32:25 the sword will bring death, / and **i**, terror will strike
Jos 2:18 and all your relatives—must be here **i** the house.
2:19 But we swear that no one **i** this house will be
8:22 Then the Israelites who were **i** the city came out
8:24 they went back and finished off everyone **i**.
10:18 place guards at the entrance to keep the kings **i**.
Jdg 9:51 But there was a strong tower **i** the city,
19: 3 she took him **i**, and her father welcomed him.
1Sa 26: 5 were sleeping **i** a ring formed by the slumbering
2Sa 6:17 The Ark of the LORD was placed **i** the special
17:18 where a man hid them **i** a well in his courtyard.
1Ki 6:15 The entire **i**, from floor to ceiling, was paneled
7:19 The capitals on the columns **i** the foyer were
2Ki 5:24 the men back. Then he hid the gifts **i** the house.
10:24 So they were all **i** the temple to offer sacrifices
16:18 constructed **i** the palace for use on the Sabbath day,
23: 7 prostitutes that were **i** the Temple of the LORD,
Ne 6:10 "Let us meet together **i** the Temple of God
8: 1 as one person at the square just **i** the Water Gate.
8: 3 He faced the square just **i** the Water Gate from
8:16 or in the squares just **i** the Water Gate
Ps 65: 4 What joys await us / **i** your holy Temple.
122: 2 we are standing here / **i** your gates, O Jerusalem.
Jer 19: 9 Then those trapped **i** will have to eat their own
41: 7 But as soon as they were all **i** the town, Ishmael
Eze 1: 4 The fire **i** the cloud glowed like gleaming amber.
7:15 Those who stay **i** will die of famine and disease.
11: 3 **I** it we will be like meat—safe from all harm.'
11:11 pot for you, and you will not be the meat, safe **i**.
22: 8 **I** your walls you despise my holy things
40:14 He measured the dividing walls all along the **i** of
40:41 four **i** and four outside, where the sacrifices were
40:44 **I** the inner courtyard there were two one-room
41:19 The figures were carved all along the **i** of the
44: 3 Only the prince himself may sit **i** this gateway to
46: 2 He will worship **i** the gateway passage and then go
46:23 Along the **i** of these walls was a ledge of stone
Jnh 1:17 And Jonah was **i** the fish for three days and three
2: 1 Then Jonah prayed to the LORD his God from **i**
Hab 2:19 overlaid with gold and silver, but they are lifeless **i**.
3:16 I trembled **i** when I heard all this; my lips quivered
Zec 2: 5 the LORD. And I will be the glory **i** the city!' "
5: 7 lifted off the basket, there was a woman sitting **i** it.
Mt 23: 5 extra wide prayer boxes with Scripture verses **i**,
23:25 of the cup and the dish, but **i** you are filthy—
23:26 First wash the **i** of the cup, and then the outside
23:27 but filled on the **i** with dead people's bones
23:28 but **i** your hearts are filled with hypocrisy
24:17 A person outside the house must not go **i** to pack.
26:59 **I**, the leading priests and the entire high council
Mk 5: 9 because there are many of us here **i** this man."
5:39 He went **i** and spoke to the people. "Why all this
14:54 then slipped **i** the gates of the high priest's
14:55 **I**, the leading priests and the entire high council
Lk 11:39 of the cup and the dish, but **i** you are still filthy—
11:40 Didn't God make the **i** as well as the outside?
Jn 5: 2 **I** the city, near the Sheep Gate, was the pool of
18:19 **I**, the high priest began asking Jesus about his
18:33 Then Pilate went back **i** and called for Jesus to be
20: 6 Then Simon Peter arrived and went **i**. He also
Ac 10:27 and went **i** where the others were assembled.
11: 6 When I looked **i** the sheet, I saw all sorts of small
12:14 opening the door, she ran back **i** and told everyone,
19:32 **I**, the people were all shouting, some one thing
21:37 As Paul was about to be taken **i**, he said to the
22:24 The commander brought Paul **i** and ordered him
Ro 7:17 because it is sin **i** me that makes me do these evil
1Co 5:12 but it certainly is your job to judge those **i** the
2Co 7: 5 conflict from every direction, and **i** there was fear.
Heb 9: 4 **I** the Ark were a gold jar containing some manna,
Rev 4: 8 and their wings were covered with eyes, **i** and out.
5: 1 There was writing on the **i** and the outside of the
11:19 and the Ark of his Covenant could be seen **i** the

INSIDES (1) [IN]

2Sa 20:10 with it so that his **i** gushed out onto the ground.

INSIGHT (14)

1Ch 27:32 to the king, a man of great **i**, and a scribe.
Job 12:20 trusted adviser, and he removes the **i** of the elders.
34:35 'Job speaks without knowledge; his words lack **i**.'
Ps 19: 8 of the LORD are clear, / giving **i** to life.
49: 3 words are wise, / and my thoughts are filled with **i**.
119:99 Yes, I have more **i** than my teachers, / for I am
Pr 2: 3 Cry out for **i** and understanding.
3:21 My child, don't lose sight of good planning and **i**.
7: 4 a sister; make **i** a beloved member of your family.
8:14 and success belong to me. **I** and strength are mine.
Da 5:11 this man was found to have **i**, understanding,
5:14 the gods within you and that you are filled with **i**,
9:22 I have come here to give you **i** and understanding.
Ac 13: 7 a man of considerable **i** and understanding.

INSIGNIFICANCE (1) [INSIGNIFICANT]

Job 14:21 know if their sons grow up in honor or sink to **i**.

INSIGNIFICANT (4) [INSIGNIFICANCE]

Ps 119:141 I am **i** and despised, / but I don't forget your
Mic 7:16 They will be embarrassed that their power is so **i**.
Mt 11:11 Yet even the most **i** person in the Kingdom of
Lk 7:28 Yet even the most **i** person in the Kingdom of God

INSINCERE (1) [INSINCERELY]

Ps 12: 2 speaking with flattering lips and **i** hearts.

INSINCERELY (1) [INSINCERE]

Hos 4:15 do not join with those who worship me **i** at Gilgal

INSIST (15) [INSISTED, INSISTENT, INSISTING, INSISTS]

Ge 33:11 Jacob continued to **i**, so Esau finally accepted
2Sa 24:24 the king replied to Araunah, "No, I **i** on buying it,
1Ch 21:24 to Araunah, "No, I **i** on paying what it is worth.
Pr 20: 3 fight is a mark of honor; only fools **i** on quarreling.
Jer 27:13 "Why do you **i** on dying—you and your people?
42:14 and if you **i** on going to live in Egypt where you
42:15 the God of Israel, says: 'If you **i** on going to Egypt,
42:22 and disease in Egypt, where you **i** on going."
Eze 20:39 If you **i**, go right ahead and worship your idols,
Mt 17:10 "Why do the teachers of religious law **i** that Elijah
Mk 9:11 "Why do the teachers of religious law **i** that Elijah
Jn 4:20 why is it that you Jews **i** that Jerusalem is the only
1Ti 4:11 Teach these things and **i** that everyone learn them.
Tit 1:10 This is especially true of those who **i** on
3: 8 I want you to **i** on them so that everyone who trusts

INSISTED (20) [INSIST]

Ge 19: 3 But Lot **i**, so at last they went home with him.
23:13 "No, listen to me," he **i**. "I will buy it from you.
25:33 So Jacob **i**, "Well then, swear to me right now that
33:15 is no reason for you to be so kind to me," Jacob **i**.
42:12 "Yes, you are!" he **i**. "You have come to discover
42:14 But Joseph **i**, "As I said, you are spies!
47:31 "Swear that you will do it," Jacob **i**. So Joseph
Ru 1:14 But Ruth **i** on staying with Naomi.
1Sa 15:20 "But I did obey the LORD," Saul **i**. "I carried
29: 9 But Achish **i**, "As far as I'm concerned, you're as
2Sa 24: 4 But the king **i** that they take the census, so Joab
1Ki 11: 2 their gods. Yet Solomon **i** on loving them anyway.
2Ki 5:23 all means, take 150 pounds of silver," Naaman **i**.
1Ch 21: 4 But the king **i** that Joab take the census, so Joab
Jer 44:12 I will take this remnant of Judah that **i** on coming
Mt 26:35 "No!" Peter **i**. "Not even if I have to die with
Mk 14:31 "No!" Peter **i**. "Not even if I have to die with
Lk 8:56 but Jesus **i** that they not tell anyone what had
22:59 About an hour later someone else **i**, "This must be
Ac 12:15 When she **i**, they decided, "It must be his angel."

INSISTENT (1) [INSIST]

Ge 19:15 At dawn the next morning the angels became **i**.

INSISTING (2) [INSIST]

Job 32: 1 further to him because he kept **i** on his innocence.
Col 2:18 Don't let anyone condemn you by **i** on self-denial.

INSISTS (4) [INSIST]

Dt 25: 8 If he still **i** that he doesn't want to marry her,
Jer 42:17 That is the fate awaiting every one of you who **i** on
Ac 25:19 called Jesus who died, but whom Paul **i** is alive.
1Co 7:15 or wife who isn't a Christian **i** on leaving,

INSOLENCE (5) [INSOLENT]

Isa 14: 4 man has been destroyed. Yes, your **i** is ended.
16: 6 so much about? Its pride and **i** are all gone now!
Jer 48:30 I know about her **i**," says the LORD, "but her
Da 11:18 from another land will put an end to his **i**
Hos 7:16 by their enemies because of their **i** toward me.

INSOLENT (3) [INSOLENCE]

Ps 86:14 O God, **i** people rise up against me;
Jer 6:28 They are as **i** as bronze, as hard and cruel as iron.
Ro 1:30 haters of God, **i**, proud, and boastful.

INSOMUCH [KJV] See also BECAUSE, POSSIBLE, RESULT

INSPECT (10) [INSPECTED, INSPECTING, INSPECTION]

Lev 13:51 On the seventh day the priest must **i** it again.
13:55 Then the priest must **i** the object again. If he sees
14:36 Then the priest will go in and **i** the house.
14:44 the priest must return and **i** the house again. If he
Ne 2:13 and over to the Dung Gate to **i** the broken walls
Ps 48:12 Go, **i** the city of Jerusalem. / Walk around
Pr 31:16 She goes out to **i** a field and buys it; with her
Isa 22: 9 You **i** the walls of Jerusalem to see what needs to
Eze 21:21 They will **i** the livers of their animal sacrifices.
Lk 14:18 said he had just bought a field and wanted to **i** it,

INSPECTED (2) [INSPECT]

Ex 39:43 Moses **i** all their work and blessed them because it
2Ki 16:12 he **i** the altar and made offerings on it.

INSPECTING (1) [INSPECT]

Ne 2:15 **i** the wall before I turned back and entered again at

INSPECTION (4) [INSPECT]

Ge 41:46 he made a tour of **i** throughout the land.
Lev 14:39 the seventh day the priest must return for another **i**.
14:48 "But if the priest returns for his **i** and finds that the
Ne 3:31 and merchants, opposite the **I** Gate.

INSPIRATION (3) [INSPIRE]

Ps 49: 4 and solve riddles with **i** from a harp.
Mt 22:43 speaking under the **i** of the Holy Spirit, call him
Mk 12:36 speaking under the **i** of the Holy Spirit, said,

INSPIRE (5) [INSPIRATION, INSPIRED]

1Ki 22:22 will go out and **i** all Ahab's prophets to speak lies.'
2Ch 18:21 will go out and **i** all Ahab's prophets to speak lies.'
Ps 65: 8 the sun rises to where it sets, / you **i** shouts of joy.
Jer 49:16 You are proud that you **i** fear in others. And you
Zec 13: 2 false prophets and the unclean spirits that **i** them.

INSPIRED (3) [INSPIRE]

Hos 9: 7 "The **i** men are mad!" So they taunt, for the nation
Jn 11:51 He didn't think of it himself; he was **i** to say it.
2Ti 3:16 All Scripture is **i** by God and is useful to teach us

INSTALL (2) [INSTALLED, INSTALLING, INSTALLMENT]

Ex 40: 3 and **i** the inner curtain to enclose the Ark within
Isa 7: 6 and **i** the son of Tabeel as Judah's king.'

INSTALLED (8) [INSTALL]
Jdg 17: 5 Then he **i** one of his sons as the priest.
1Ki 2:35 and he **i** Zadok the priest to take the place of
2Ki 23:34 Pharaoh Neco then **i** Eliakim, another of Josiah's
24:17 Then the king of Babylon **i** Mattaniah,
Ne 3: 6 set up the doors, and **i** the bolts and bars.
3:13 hung its doors, and **i** the bolts and bars.
3:14 he hung the doors and **i** the bolts and bars.
3:15 roofed it, hung its doors, and **i** its bolts and bars.

INSTALLING (1) [INSTALL]
2Ch 8: 5 rebuilding their walls and **i** barred gates.

INSTALLMENT (1) [INSTALL]
2Co 1:22 hearts as the first **i** of everything he will give us.

INSTANCE (11) [INSTANCES]
Dt 17: 8 for **i**, whether someone is guilty of murder or only
1Sa 2:22 He knew, for **i**, that his sons were seducing the
Eze 33:15 For **i**, they might give back a borrower's pledge,
Mt 15: 4 For **i**, God says, 'Honor your father and mother,'
Mk 7:10 For **i**, Moses gave you this law from God:
Ac 4:36 For **i**, there was Joseph, the one the apostles
15:15 what the prophets predicted. For **i**, it is written:
Ro 14: 2 For **i**, one person believes it is all right to eat
1Co 7:18 For **i**, a man who was circumcised before he
Jas 2: 2 For **i**, suppose someone comes into your meeting
1Pe 3: 6 For **i**, Sarah obeyed her husband, Abraham,

INSTANCES (1) [INSTANCE]
Job 13: 1 "Look, I have seen many **i** such as you describe.

INSTANT (7) [INSTANTLY]
Ge 44:18 for I know you could have me killed in an **i**,
Ps 2:12 your pursuits— / for his anger can flare up in an **i**.
73:19 In an **i** they are destroyed, / swept away by terrors.
Isa 29: 6 In an **i**, I, the LORD Almighty, will come against
30:13 In an **i** it will collapse and come crashing down.
Mt 18:28 him by the throat and demanded **i** payment.
Lk 1:44 my baby jumped for joy the **i** I heard your voice!

INSTANTLY (28) [INSTANT]
Ge 42: 7 Joseph recognized them **i**, but he pretended to be a
Nu 16:21 from these people so that I may **i** destroy them!"
16:45 from these people so that I can **i** destroy them!"
1Ki 13: 4 But **i** the king's hand became paralyzed in that
Isa 30:19 He will respond **i** to the sound of your cries.
Mt 8: 3 "Be healed!" And **i** the leprosy disappeared.
9:33 Jesus cast out the demon, and **i** the man could talk.
14:31 **I** Jesus reached out his hand and grabbed him.
15:28 is granted." And her daughter was **i** healed.
20:34 for them and touched their eyes. **I** they could see!
26:53 of angels to protect us, and he would send them **i**?
Mk 1:42 **I** the leprosy disappeared—the man was healed.
7:35 **I** the man could hear perfectly and speak plainly!
9:24 The father **i** replied, "I do believe, but help me not
10:52 has healed you." And **i** the blind man could see!
Lk 1:64 **I** Zechariah could speak again, and he began
5:13 "Be healed!" And **i** the leprosy disappeared.
13:13 Then he touched her, and **i** she could stand straight.
18:43 **I** the man could see, and he followed Jesus,
Jn 5: 9 **I**, the man was healed! He rolled up the mat
Ac 5:10 **I**, she fell to the floor and died. When the young
9:18 **I** something like scales fell from Saul's eyes,
9:34 Get up and make your bed!" And he was healed **i**.
12:23 **I**, an angel of the Lord struck Herod with a
13:11 **I** mist and darkness fell upon him, and he began
16:18 to come out of her," he said. And **i** it left her.
23: 2 **I** Ananias the high priest commanded those close
Rev 4: 2 And **i** I was in the Spirit, and I saw a throne in

INSTEAD (256)
Ge 11:31 But they stopped **i** at the village of Haran
19:20 Please let me go there **i**; don't you see how small it
24: 4 Go **i** to my homeland, to my relatives, and find a
24:38 **I**, I was to come to his relatives here in this far-off
26:17 Isaac moved to the Gerar Valley and lived there **i**.
27:10 can eat it and bless you **i** of Esau before he dies."
27:12 and then he'll curse me **i** of blessing me."
28: 2 **I**, go at once to Paddan-aram, to the house of your
44:33 my lord, let me stay here as a slave **i** of the boy,
48:17 So he lifted it to place it on Manasseh's head **i**.
Ex 16:22 the ground—four quarts for each person **i** of two.
23: 5 do not walk by. **I**, stop and offer to help.
23:24 **I**, you must utterly conquer them and break down
32:10 make you, Moses, into a great nation **i** of them."
34:13 **I**, you must break down their pagan altars,
Lev 23:25 **I**, you are to present offerings to the LORD by
25:36 **I**, show your fear of God by letting them live with
25:40 Treat them **i** as hired servants or as resident
Nu 15:39 and that you are to obey his commands **i** of
21:23 **I**, he mobilized his entire army and attacked Israel
23:11 to curse my enemies. **I**, you have blessed them!"
24: 1 **I**, he turned and looked out toward the wilderness,
24:10 my enemies! **I**, you have blessed them three times.
32: 5 please let us have this land as our property **i** of
Dt 1:38 **I**, your assistant, Joshua son of Nun, will lead the
1:43 **I**, you again rebelled against the LORD's
7: 5 **I**, you must break down their pagan altars
9:27 but remember **i** your servants Abraham, Isaac,
12:24 **I**, pour out the blood on the ground like water.
15: 8 **I**, be generous and lend them whatever they need.
15:20 **I**, you and your family must eat these animals in
15:22 **I**, use it for food for your family at home.
18: 1 **I**, the priests and Levites will eat from the
23: 4 **I**, they tried to hire Balaam son of Beor from
25: 5 **I**, her husband's brother must marry her and fulfill
Jos 11:20 and caused them to fight the Israelites **i** of asking
13:14 **I**, as the LORD had promised them,
17: 3 and Gilead, had no sons. **I**, he had five daughters.
22:31 **I**, you have rescued Israel from being destroyed by
23: 5 You will live there **i** of them, just as the LORD
23:13 **I**, they will be a snare and a trap to you, a pain in
24:10 **I**, I made Balaam bless you, and so I rescued you
Jdg 1:33 **I**, the Canaanites dominated the land where they
2: 2 in this land; **i**, you were to destroy their altars.
11:20 **I**, he mobilized his army at Jahaz and attacked
15: 2 sister is more beautiful than she is. Marry her **i**."
20: 9 **I**, we will draw lots to decide who will attack
20:14 **I**, they came from their towns and gathered at
Ru 1: 8 "Go back to your mothers' homes **i** of coming
1:20 "**I**, call me Mara, for the Almighty has made life
1Sa 10:19 you have rejected me and said, 'We want a king **i**!'
27: 5 we would rather live in one of the country towns **i**
28: 8 by wearing ordinary clothing **i** of his royal robes.
2Sa 5:23 "**I**, circle around behind them and attack them near
6:10 He took it **i** to the home of Obed-edom of Gath.
12: 4 But **i** of killing a lamb from his own flocks for
12:28 so you will get credit for the victory **i** of me."
13:26 how about sending my brother Amnon **i**?"
15: 5 **I**, he took them by the hand and embraced them.
17:15 had said and what he himself had suggested **i**.
18:33 If only I could have died **i** of you! O Absalom,
19:28 but **i** you have honored me among those who eat at
23:16 to drink it. **I**, he poured it out before the LORD.
1Ki 1:18 But **i**, Adonijah has become the new king, and you
2:15 were turned, and everything went to my brother **i**;
3: 7 now you have made me king **i** of my father,
8:19 be the one to do it. One of your sons will build it **i**.'
9: 9 out of Egypt, and they worshiped other gods **i**.
9:22 **I**, he assigned them to serve as fighting men,
11: 4 they turned his heart to worship their gods **i** of
12: 8 and **i** asked the opinion of the young men who had
12:27 They will kill me and make him their king **i**."
18:18 and have worshiped the images of Baal **i**.
20:42 and your people will die **i** of his people."
2Ki 14: 3 **I**, he followed the example of his father, Joash.
16: 3 **I**, he followed the example of the kings of Israel,
17:34 They follow their former practices **i** of truly
18:12 **I**, they had violated his covenant—all the laws the
18:32 a land of plenty. Choose life **i** of death!
20:10 Hezekiah replied. "Make it go backward **i**."
1Ch 10:14 **i** of asking the LORD for guidance.
11:18 to drink it. **I**, he poured it out before the LORD.
12:23 They were all eager to see David become king **i** of
13:13 He took it **i** to the home of Obed-edom of Gath.
14:14 "**I**, circle around behind them and attack them near
2Ch 6: 9 be the one to do it. One of your sons will build it **i**.'
7:22 out of Egypt, and they worshiped other gods **i**.
8: 9 **I**, he assigned them to serve as fighting men,
10: 8 and **i** asked the opinion of the young men who had
16: 7 in the king of Aram **i** of in the LORD your God,
17: 4 and obeyed his commands **i** of following the
21:13 **I**, you have been as evil as the kings of Israel.
24:18 and they worshiped Asherah poles and idols **i**!
28: 2 **I**, he followed the example of the kings of Israel
28:20 he oppressed King Ahaz **i** of helping him.
28:23 But **i**, they led to his ruin and the ruin of all Israel.
33:23 before the LORD. **I**, Amon sinned even more.
35:22 **I**, he led his army into battle on the plain of
Ezr 9: 9 **I**, he caused the kings of Persia to treat us
Ne 2:15 So I went up the Kidron Valley **i**,
9:17 **I**, they rebelled and appointed a leader to take them
13: 2 **I**, they hired Balaam to curse them, though our
Est 2: 4 pleases you most will be made queen **i** of Vashti."
2:17 on her head and declared her queen **i** of Vashti.
Job 3:26 I have no rest; **i**, only trouble comes."
9:18 catch my breath, but fills me **i** with bitter sorrows.
14:16 would count my steps, **i** of watching for my sins.
30:26 So I looked for good, but evil came **i**. I waited for
30:29 But **i**, I am considered a brother to jackals and a
31:40 then let thistles grow on that land **i** of wheat and
weeds **i** of barley."
36:24 **I**, glorify his mighty works, singing songs of
Ps 25: 7 look **i** through the eyes of your unfailing love,
50:14 What I want **i** is your true thanks to God; / I want
52: 7 They trust their wealth **i** / and grow more and more
55:13 **I**, it is you—my equal, / my companion and close
58: 2 are crooked; / you hand out violence **i** of justice.
69:21 But **i**, they give me poison for food; / they offer me
74:21 **I**, let these poor and needy ones give praise to your
78:68 He chose **i** the tribe of Judah, / Mount Zion,
102: 9 I eat ashes **i** of my food. / My tears run down into
105:32 **I** of rain, he sent murderous hail, / and flashes of
106: 7 **I**, they rebelled against him at the Red Sea.
106:25 **I**, they grumbled in their tents / and refused to obey
106:35 **I**, they mingled among the pagans / and adopted
Pr 2:20 Follow the steps of good men **i**, and stay on the
3: 7 **I**, fear the LORD and turn your back on evil.
Ecc 5: 7 Dreaming all the time **i** of working is foolishness.
5: 7 there is ruin in a flood of empty words. Fear God **i**.
9: 3 **I**, they choose their own mad course, for they have
Isa 3:24 **I** of smelling of sweet perfume, they will stink.
3:24 They will wear rough sackcloth **i** of rich robes.
5: 7 yield a crop of justice, / but **i** he found bloodshed.
5: 7 but **i** he heard cries of oppression.
14:15 But **i**, you will be brought down to the place of the
22:13 But **i**, you dance and play; you slaughter sacrificial
28:27 rolled on cummin; **i**, it is beaten softly with a flail.
30:12 what I tell you and trust **i** in oppression and lies,
31: 1 and chariots **i** of looking to the LORD,
33:20 **I**, you will see Zion as a place of worship
43:24 **I**, you have burdened me with your sins
57: 8 have set up your idols and worship them **i** of me.
57: 8 for you are loving these idols **i** of loving me.
61: 3 joy **i** of mourning, praise **i** of despair.
61: 7 **I** of shame and dishonor, you will inherit a double
Jer 7:24 their evil hearts. They went backward **i** of forward.
9:14 **I**, they have stubbornly followed their own desires
11: 8 **I**, they stubbornly followed their own evil desires.
16:15 **I**, they will say, 'As surely as the LORD lives,
18:11 I am planning disaster against you **i** of good.
22:10 **I**, weep for the captive king being led away!
23: 2 "**I** of leading my flock to safety, you have deserted
23: 8 **I**, they will say, 'As surely as the LORD lives,
23:14 They encourage those who are doing evil **i** of
33:26 **I**, I will restore them to their land and have mercy
37:21 **I**, he was imprisoned in the courtyard of the guard
48:34 **I**, their awful cries of terror can be heard from
La 2:14 **I**, they painted false pictures, filling you with false
3:40 **I**, let us test and examine our ways. Let us turn
Eze 4:15 "You may bake your bread with cow dung **i** of
11:12 **i**, you have copied the sins of the nations around
11:19 their hearts of stone and give them tender hearts **i**,
13: 6 **I**, they have lied and said, 'My message is from the
16:15 so you trusted **i** in your fame and beauty.
16:32 you are an adulterous wife who takes in strangers **i**
16:34 No one pays you; **i**, you pay them!
18: 7 does not rob the poor but **i** gives food to the hungry
18:16 but **i** is fair to debtors and does not rob them.
23: 5 "Then Oholah lusted after other lovers **i** of me,
34: 2 shepherds who feed yourselves **i** of your flocks.
34: 4 **I**, you have ruled them with force and cruelty.
44:20 it off completely. **I**, they must trim it regularly.
Da 1: 8 chief official for permission to eat other things **i**.
1:16 the attendant fed them only vegetables **i** of the rich
4:16 let him have the mind of an animal **i** of a human.
11:38 **I** of these, he will worship the god of fortresses—
Hos 2:16 "you will call me 'my husband' **i** of 'my master.'
7:14 **I**, they sit on their couches and wail. They cut
Joel 2:13 your clothing in your grief; **i**, tear your hearts."
2:14 sending you a blessing **i** of this terrible curse.
Am 5:24 **I**, I want to see a mighty flood of justice, a river of
Jnh 1:13 **I**, the sailors tried even harder to row the boat
Mic 6: 5 and how Balaam son of Beor blessed you **i**?
Zec 8:13 but **i** get on with rebuilding the Temple!
11:16 **I**, this shepherd will eat the meat of the fattest
Mt 4:13 But **i** of going to Nazareth, he went to Capernaum,
5:15 a basket! **I**, put it on a stand and let it shine for all.
7: 9 ask for a loaf of bread, do you give them a stone **i**?
9:31 But **i**, they spread his fame all over the region.
15: 5 for their needs if you give the money to God **i**.'
Mk 15:11 mob to demand the release of Barabbas **i** of Jesus.
Lk 4:26 He was sent **i** to a widow of Zarephath—
5:33 that Jesus' disciples were feasting **i** of fasting.
11:11 children ask for a fish, do you give them a snake **i**?
11:33 **I**, it is put on a lampstand to give light to all who
14: 9 The host will say, 'Let this person sit here **i**.'
14:10 "Do this **i**—sit at the foot of the table. Then when
14:13 **I**, invite the poor, the crippled, the lame,
15:12 of your estate now, **i** of waiting until you die.'
18:13 **I**, he beat his chest in sorrow, saying, 'O God,
20:26 **I**, they were amazed by his answer, and they were
Jn 3:26 And everybody is going over there **i** of coming
16: 6 **I**, you are very sad.
Ac 3:14 and **i** demanded the release of a murderer.
5:28 "**I**, you have filled all Jerusalem with your
12:14 she was so overjoyed that, **i** of opening the door,
12:23 because he accepted the people's worship **i** of
16: 8 So **i**, they went on through Mysia to the city of
17: 6 dragged out Jason and some of the other believers **i**
Ro 1:22 Claiming to be wise, they became utter fools **i**.
1:23 And **i** of worshiping the glorious, ever-living God,
1:25 **I** of believing what they knew was the truth about
1:26 to have sex and **i** indulged in sex with each other.
1:27 **i** of having normal sexual relationships with
5:21 to death, now God's wonderful kindness rules **i**,
6:13 **I**, give yourselves completely to God since you
6:14 enslaves you to sin. **I**, you are free by God's grace.
7:10 me the way of life, **i** gave me the death penalty.
7:15 but I don't do it. **I**, I do the very thing I hate.
8: 4 follow our sinful nature but **i** follow the Spirit.
8:15 You should behave **i** like God's very own children,
9:32 the law and being good **i** of by depending on faith.
10: 3 **I**, they are clinging to their own way of getting
11:30 Jews refused his mercy, God was merciful to you **i**.
12:20 **I**, do what the Scriptures say: / "If your enemies
14:13 Decide **i** to live in such a way that you will not put
1Co 1:27 **I**, God deliberately chose things the world
6: 1 **i** of taking it to other Christians to decide who is
6: 6 But **i**, one Christian sues another—right in front of
6: 8 But **i**, you yourselves are the ones who do wrong
2Co 5:15 **I**, they will live to please Christ, who died and was
10:15 **I**, we hope that your faith will grow and that our
Gal 5:15 But if **i** of showing love among yourselves you are
Eph 4:15 **I**, we will hold to the truth in love, becoming more
4:23 **I**, there must be a spiritual renewal of your
4:32 **I**, be kind to each other, tenderhearted,
5: 4 are not for you. **I**, let there be thankfulness to God.
5:11 of evil and darkness; **i**, rebuke and expose them.
5:18 your life. **I**, let the Holy Spirit fill and control you.
5:27 other blemish. **I**, she will be holy and without fault.
Php 3: 3 **I**, we boast about what Christ Jesus has done for
4: 6 worry about anything; **i**, pray about everything.
Tit 2: 3 **I**, they should teach others what is good.
3: 2 **I**, they should be gentle and show true humility to
Heb 5:12 **I**, you need someone to teach you again the basic

6: 1 Let us go on **i** and become mature in our
6: 12 **I**, you will follow the example of those who are
7: 11 **i** of from the line of Levi and Aaron?
11: 25 He chose to share the oppression of God's people **i**
12: 24 which graciously forgives **i** of crying out for
Jas 4: 9 Let there be sadness **i** of laughter, and gloom **i** of joy.
1Pe 3: 9 **I**, pay them back with a blessing. That is what God
3: 15 **I**, you must worship Christ as Lord of your life.
4: 13 **I**, be very glad—because these trials will make you

INSTINCT (3) [INSTINCTIVELY, INSTINCTS]

Job 38: 36 Who gives intuition and **i**?
2Pe 2: 12 creatures of **i**, who are born to be caught
Jude 1: 19 They live by natural **i** because they do not have

INSTINCTIVELY (2) [INSTINCT]

Ro 1: 19 For the truth about God is known to them **i**.
2: 14 have God's written law, **i** follow what the law says,

INSTINCTS (1) [INSTINCT]

Jude 1: 10 Like animals, they do whatever their **i** tell them,

INSTITUTED (3)

1Ki 12: 32 Jeroboam also **i** a religious festival in Bethel,
12: 33 He **i** a religious festival for Israel, and he went up
Ezr 8: 20 a group of Temple workers first **i** by King David.

INSTRUCT (13) [INSTRUCTED, INSTRUCTING, INSTRUCTION, INSTRUCTIONS, INSTRUCTS]

Ex 28: 3 **I** all those who have special skills as tailors to
Nu 6: 23 "**I** Aaron and his sons to bless the people of Israel
35: 2 "**I** the people of Israel to give to the Levites from
Dt 4: 10 'Summon the people before me, and I will **i** them.
4: 36 you hear his voice from heaven so he could **i** you.
1Ch 21: 18 Then the angel of the LORD told Gad to **i** David
Ezr 7: 14 and my Council of Seven hereby **i** you to conduct
Ne 9: 20 You sent your good Spirit to **i** them, and you did
Est 6: 9 **I** one of the king's most noble princes to dress the
Job 12: 8 Speak to the earth, and it will **i** you. Let the fish of
Ps 105: 22 He could **i** the king's aides as he pleased
Ac 8: 31 "How can I, when there is no one to **i** me?"
Ro 2: 20 You think you can **i** the ignorant and teach children

INSTRUCTED (59) [INSTRUCT]

Ge 12: 4 So Abram departed as the LORD had **i** him,
44: 6 and spoke to them in the way he had been **i**.
50: 16 to Joseph: "Before your father died, he **i** us
Ex 12: 35 And the people of Israel did as Moses had **i**
17: 14 Then the LORD **i** Moses, "Write this down as a
20: 1 Then God **i** the people as follows:
24: 1 Then the LORD **i** Moses: "Come up here to me,
31: 6 so they can make all the things I have **i** you to
34: 18 just as I **i** you, at the appointed time each year in
Nu 2: 34 their banners exactly as the LORD had **i** them.
8: 23 The LORD also **i** Moses,
36: 2 the LORD **i** you to divide the land by sacred lot
Dt 1: 16 I **i** the judges, 'You must be perfectly fair at all
2: 1 just as the LORD had **i** me, and we wandered
Jos 2: 1 He **i** them, "Spy out the land on the other side of
9: 11 So our leaders and our people **i** us, 'Prepare for a
9: 24 because we were told that the LORD your God **i**
11: 9 and burned all the chariots, as the LORD had **i**.
11: 23 of the entire land, just as the LORD had **i** Moses.
15: 13 The LORD **i** Joshua to assign some of Judah's
20: 2 to designate the cities of refuge, as I **i** Moses.
21: 2 "The LORD **i** Moses to give us towns to live in
1Sa 9: 23 then **i** the cook to bring Saul the finest cut of meat,
13: 8 as Samuel had **i** him earlier, but Samuel still didn't
16: 4 So Samuel did as the LORD **i** him. When he
2Sa 11: 15 The letter **i** Joab, "Station Uriah on the front lines
15: 25 David **i** Zadok to take the Ark of God back into the
20: 3 he **i** that the ten concubines he had left to keep
20: 4 Then the king **i** Amasa to mobilize the army of
1Ki 5: 5 my God, just as he **i** my father that I should do.
11: 2 The LORD had clearly **i** his people not to
20: 35 the LORD **i** one of the group of prophets to say to
2Ki 5: 14 himself seven times, as the man of God had **i** him.
8: 2 So the woman did as the man of God **i**. She took
10: 22 And Jehu **i** the keeper of the wardrobe, "Be sure
12: 2 LORD's sight because Jehoiada the priest **i** him.
16: 16 Uriah the priest did just as King Ahaz **i** him.
23: 4 Then the king **i** Hilkiah the high priest
1Ch 15: 15 its carrying poles, just as the LORD had **i** Moses.
22: 6 and **i** him to build a Temple for the LORD,
2Ch 23: 18 of Moses, and to sing and rejoice as David had **i**.
26: 5 days of Zechariah, who **i** him in the fear of God.
Ezr 3: 2 on it, as **i** in the law of Moses, the man of God.
5: 15 The king **i** him to return the utensils to their place
Ne 8: 7 and Pelaiah—**i** the people who were standing there.
9: 14 You **i** them concerning the laws of your holy
Est 1: 8 for the king had **i** his staff to let everyone decide
Pr 10: 8 The wise are glad to be **i**, but babbling fools fall
Jer 9: 12 Who has been **i** by the LORD and can explain it
13: 5 and hid it at the Euphrates as the LORD had **i** me.
Mt 8: 18 he **i** his disciples to cross to the other side of the
Mk 3: 9 Jesus **i** his disciples to bring around a boat and to
Lk 5: 14 Then Jesus **i** him not to tell anyone what had
9: 3 he **i** them, "nor a traveler's bag, nor food,
Ac 10: 22 A holy angel **i** him to send for you so you can go to
Col 4: 10 And as you were **i** before, make Mark welcome if
Tit 1: 5 and appoint elders in each town as I **i** you.
2: 12 And we are **i** to turn from godless living and sinful
Rev 22: 10 Then he **i** me, "Do not seal up the prophetic words

INSTRUCTING (2) [INSTRUCT]

Ne 2: 7 **i** them to let me travel safely through their
2: 8 of the king's forest, **i** him to give me timber.

INSTRUCTION (20) [INSTRUCT]

Dt 33: 3 They follow in your steps / and accept your **i**.
Pr 1: 3 people will receive **i** in discipline, good conduct,
4: 1 My children, listen to me. Listen to your father's **i**.
5: 13 Why didn't I pay attention to those who gave me **i**?
8: 10 "Choose my **i** rather than silver, and knowledge
16: 20 Those who listen to **i** will prosper; those who trust
16: 21 and **i** is appreciated if it's well presented.
19: 20 Get all the advice and **i** you can, and be wise the
19: 27 If you stop listening to **i**, my child, you have turned
21: 11 mockers punished; a wise person learns from **i**.
22: 17 to the words of the wise; apply your heart to my **i**.
23: 12 Commit yourself to **i**; attune your ears to hear
Isa 29: 24 and those who constantly complain will accept **i**.
40: 14 Does he need **i** about what is good or what is best?
42: 4 distant lands beyond the sea will wait for his **i**."
Da 11: 33 "Those who are wise will give **i** to many. But for a
Mal 2: 7 and people should go to them for **i**,
Eph 6: 4 up with the discipline and **i** approved by the Lord.
1Ti 1: 5 The purpose of my **i** is that all the Christians there
Heb 6: 2 You don't need further **i** about baptisms, the laying

INSTRUCTIONS (187) [INSTRUCT]

Ge 24: 9 a solemn oath that he would follow Abraham's **i**.
27: 14 So Jacob followed his mother's **i**, bringing her the
32: 17 He gave these **i** to the men leading the first group:
32: 19 Jacob gave the same **i** to each of the herdsmen
42: 25 but he also gave secret **i** to return each brother's
44: 1 Joseph gave these **i** to the man in charge of his
Ex 12: 1 Now the LORD gave the following **i** to Moses
12: 24 these **i** are permanent and must be observed by you
12: 50 So the people of Israel followed all the LORD's **i**
13: 9 Let it remind you always to keep the LORD's **i** in
13: 11 And remember these **i** when the LORD brings
14: 1 Then the LORD gave these **i** to Moses:
16: 4 them in this to see whether they will follow my **i**.
16: 28 these people refuse to obey my commands and **i**?"
18: 16 of God's decisions and teach them his laws and **i**."
18: 20 God's decisions, teach them God's laws and **i**,
19: 3 "Give these **i** to the descendants of Jacob,
21: 1 "Here are some other **i** you must present to Israel:
23: 13 "Be sure to obey all my **i**. And remember,
23: 21 Pay attention to him, and obey all of his **i**. Do not
23: 22 if you are careful to obey him, following all my **i**,
24: 4 Moses carefully wrote down all the LORD's **i**.
24: 12 the tablets of stone that I have inscribed with my **i**
30: 34 These were the LORD's **i** to Moses concerning
31: 11 They must follow exactly all the **i** I have given
31: 12 The LORD then gave these further **i** to Moses:
34: 27 LORD said to Moses, "Write down all these **i**,
34: 32 and Moses gave them the **i** the LORD had given
34: 34 Then he would give the people whatever **i** the
35: 1 "You must obey these **i** from the LORD.
39: 42 of Israel followed all of the LORD's **i** to Moses.
Lev 1: 2 "Give the following **i** to the Israelites:
4: 2 "Give the Israelites the following **i** for dealing
6: 9 and his sons the following **i** regarding the whole
6: 14 "These are the **i** regarding the grain offering.
6: 25 and his sons these further **i** regarding the sin
7: 1 "These are the **i** for the guilt offering, which is
7: 11 "These are the **i** regarding the different kinds of
7: 23 "Give the Israelites these **i**: You must never eat
7: 29 "Give these further **i** to the Israelites: When you
7: 37 These are the **i** for the whole burnt offering,
7: 38 The LORD gave these **i** to Moses on Mount Sinai
8: 4 So Moses followed the LORD's **i**, and all the
9: 6 "When you have followed these **i** from the
11: 2 "Give the following **i** to the Israelites:
11: 46 "These are the **i** regarding the land animals,
12: 1 said to Moses, "Give these **i** to the Israelites:
12: 7 These are the **i** to be followed after the birth of a
13: 59 "These are the **i** for dealing with infectious
14: 2 "The following **i** must be followed by those
14: 32 These are the **i** for cleansing those who have
14: 54 "These are the **i** for dealing with the various kinds
14: 57 These **i** must be followed when dealing with any
15: 2 "Give these further **i** to the Israelites: Any man
15: 7 The same **i** apply if you touch the man who has the
15: 32 These are the **i** for dealing with a man who has
16: 3 the sanctuary area, he must follow these **i** fully.
16: 13 the Covenant. If he follows these **i**, he will not die.
16: 34 Moses followed all these **i** that the LORD had
20: 2 "Give the Israelites these **i**, which apply to those
21: 24 So Moses gave these **i** to Aaron and his sons
22: 9 Warn all the priests to follow these **i** carefully;
22: 18 and his sons and all the Israelites these **i**,
23: 2 "Give the Israelites **i** regarding the LORD's
23: 10 to give these **i** to the Israelites: "When you arrive
23: 24 to give these **i** to the Israelites: "On the appointed
23: 44 So Moses gave these **i** regarding the annual
24: 23 After Moses gave all these **i** to the Israelites,
25: 2 "Give these **i** to the Israelites: When you have
26: 46 and **i** that the LORD gave to the Israelites through
27: 2 "Give the following **i** to the Israelites: If you make
Nu 2: 1 Then the LORD gave these **i** to Moses and Aaron:
5: 1 The LORD gave these **i** to Moses:
5: 6 "Give these **i** to the people of Israel: If any of the
6: 1 to the people of Israel and give them these **i**:
8: 20 carefully following all the LORD's **i** to Moses.
9: 1 The LORD gave these **i** to Moses in early spring,
9: 8 "Wait here until I have received **i** for you from the
13: 17 Moses gave the men these **i** as he sent them out to
15: 1 The LORD told Moses to give these **i** to the
15: 11 "These are the **i** for what is to accompany each
15: 13 to the LORD, you must follow all these **i**.
15: 16 The same **i** and regulations will apply both to you
15: 18 "Give the people of Israel the following **i**:
16: 40 Thus, the LORD's **i** to Moses were carried out.
17: 6 So Moses gave the **i** to the people of Israel,
18: 5 If you follow these **i**, the LORD's anger will
18: 8 The LORD gave these further **i** to Aaron: "I have
20: 24 because the two of you rebelled against my **i**
23: 2 Balak followed his **i**, and the two of them
26: 3 and Eleazar the priest issued these census **i** to the
27: 14 for you both rebelled against my **i** in the wilderness
28: 1 to Moses, "Give these **i** to the people of Israel:
28: 2 the appointed times and offered according to my **i**.
29: 40 So Moses gave all of these **i** to the people of Israel,
32: 25 are your servants and will follow your **i** exactly.
34: 2 "Give these **i** to the Israelites: When you come
Dt 1: 18 And at that time I gave you **i** about everything you
5: 32 LORD your God, following his **i** in every detail.
20: 15 But these **i** apply only to distant towns, not to the
21: 9 By following these **i** and doing what is right in the
24: 8 and follow the **i** of the Levitical priests;
31: 25 he gave these **i** to the Levites who carried the Ark
32: 47 These **i** are not mere words—they are your life!
33: 10 to Jacob; / let them give your **i** to Israel.
Jos 3: 3 giving these **i** to the people: "When you see the
3: 8 Give these **i** to the priests who are carrying the Ark
4: 10 the middle of the river until all of the LORD's **i**,
8: 31 He followed the **i** that Moses the LORD's servant
8: 33 This was all done according to the **i** Moses,
10: 27 Joshua gave **i** for the bodies of the kings to be
11: 15 carefully obeying all of the LORD's **i** to Moses.
14: 5 in strict accordance with the LORD's **i** to Moses.
23: 6 Be very careful to follow all the **i** written in the
Jdg 13: 8 and give us more **i** about this son who is to be
13: 13 "Be sure your wife follows the **i** I gave her.
Ru 3: 6 that night and followed the **i** of her mother-in-law.
1Sa 6: 10 So these **i** were carried out. Two cows with
10: 8 When I arrive, I will give you further **i**."
15: 24 I have disobeyed your **i** and the LORD's
28: 18 because you did not obey his **i** concerning the
1Ki 3: 3 the LORD and followed all the **i** of his father,
17: 9 there who will feed you. I have given her my **i**."
21: 11 and other leaders followed the **i** Jezebel had
2Ki 10: 30 "You have done well in following my **i** to destroy
16: 11 built an altar just like it by following the king's **i**,
17: 34 the LORD and obeying the laws, regulations, **i**,
17: 37 Be careful to obey all the laws, regulations, **i**,
1Ch 15: 2 Then he issued these **i**: "When we transport the
21: 19 So David obeyed the **i** the LORD had given him
22: 11 and give you success as you follow his **i** in
23: 27 It was according to David's final **i** that all the
28: 13 The king also gave Solomon the **i** concerning the
28: 14 David gave **i** regarding how much gold and silver
2Ch 13: 11 We are following the **i** of the LORD our God,
19: 6 and he gave them these **i**: "Always think carefully
19: 9 These were his **i** to them: "You must always act in
19: 10 a murder case or some other violation of God's **i**,
23: 6 The rest of the people must obey the LORD's **i**
23: 18 of the LORD, following all the **i** given by David.
24: 5 the priests and Levites and gave them these **i**:
24: 8 So now Joash gave **i** for a chest to be made and set
29: 15 They were careful to follow all the LORD's **i** in
33: 8 all the **i**, laws, and regulations given through
35: 4 following the written **i** of King David of Israel and the **i** of his son Solomon.
35: 6 Follow all the **i** that the LORD gave through
35: 12 according to the **i** recorded in the Book of Moses.
Ezr 6: 18 following all the **i** recorded in the Book of Moses.
Ne 9: 13 You gave them regulations and **i** that were just,
9: 14 to obey all your commands, laws, and **i**.
Job 22: 22 Listen to his **i**, and store them in your heart.
Pr 2: 1 My child, listen to me and treasure my **i**.
4: 4 my words to heart. Follow my **i** and you will live.
4: 13 Carry out my **i**; don't forsake them. Guard them,
31: 26 are wise, and kindness is the rule when she gives **i**.
Isa 24: 5 for they have twisted the **i** of God, violated his
30: 9 who refuse to pay any attention to the LORD's **i**.
Jer 6: 19 refuse to listen to me. They have rejected all my **i**.
9: 13 because my people have abandoned the **i** I gave
35: 18 Jehonadab in every respect, following all his **i**.
38: 27 But Jeremiah followed the king's **i**, and they left
44: 23 refusing to obey him and follow his **i**, laws,
Eze 20: 13 They wouldn't obey my **i** even though obedience
20: 19 told them. 'Follow my laws, pay attention to my **i**,
20: 21 They refused to keep my laws and follow my **i**,
20: 24 They scorned my **i** by violating my Sabbath days
44: 24 And the priests themselves must obey my **i**
47: 13 "Follow these **i** for dividing the land for the twelve
Mal 4: 4 "Remember to obey the **i** of my servant Moses,
Mt 10: 5 Jesus sent the twelve disciples out with these **i**:
11: 1 When Jesus had finished giving these **i** to his
Mk 10: 5 "He wrote those **i** only as a concession to your
13: 34 He gave each of his employees **i** about the work
16: S Then they reported all these **i** briefly to Peter
Lk 5: 15 Yet despite Jesus' **i**, the report of his power spread
10: 2 These were his **i** to them: "The harvest is so great,
Jn 2: 8 the master of ceremonies." So they followed his **i**.
12: 49 The Father who sent me gave me his own **i** as to
12: 50 And I know his **i** lead to eternal life; so I say
Ac 1: 2 his chosen apostles further **i** from the Holy Spirit.
15: 24 with their teaching, but they had no such **i** from us.

1Co 11:34 I'll give you i about the other matters after I arrive.
Php 2:12 so careful to follow my i when I was with you.
1Ti 1:18 Timothy, my son, here are my i for you, based on
5:7 Give these i to the church so that the widows you
5:21 and the holy angels to obey these i without taking

INSTRUCTS (1) [INSTRUCT]

Ps 16:7 who guides me; / even at night my heart i me.

INSTRUMENT (8) [INSTRUMENTS]

Ps 6:T of David, to be accompanied by an eight-stringed i.
8:T psalm of David, to be accompanied by a stringed i.
12:T of David, to be accompanied by an eight-stringed i.
81:T psalm of Asaph, to be accompanied by a stringed i.
84:T of Korah, to be accompanied by a stringed i.
Isa 41:15 You will be a new threshing i with many sharp
Eze 33:32 with a beautiful voice or plays fine music on an i.
Ac 9:15 For Saul is my chosen i to take my message to the

INSTRUMENTS (27) [INSTRUMENT]

Ge 4:22 to work with metal, forging i of bronze and iron.
2Sa 6:5 singing songs and playing all kinds of musical i—
1Ch 13:8 singing and playing all kinds of musical i—
16:42 and other i to accompany the songs of praise to
23:5 the LORD with the musical i I have made."
2Ch 5:13 cymbals, and other i, they raised their voices
7:6 i King David had made for praising the LORD.
9:11 Never before had there been such beautiful i in
23:13 Singers with musical i were leading the people in a
29:26 positions around the Temple with the i of David,
29:27 accompanied by the trumpets and other i of David,
30:21 priests sang to the LORD, accompanied by loud i.
Ne 12:36 They used the musical i prescribed by David,
Ps 4:T psalm of David, to be accompanied by stringed i.
54:T is hiding." To be accompanied by stringed i.
55:T psalm of David, to be accompanied by stringed i.
61:T psalm of David, to be accompanied by stringed i.
67:T A psalm, to be accompanied by stringed i. A song.
76:T psalm of Asaph, to be accompanied by stringed i.
150:4 praise him with stringed i and flutes!
Isa 38:20 I will sing his praises with i / every day of my life
Da 3:5 the horn, flute, zither, lyre, harp, pipes, and other i,
3:7 So at the sound of the musical i, all the people,
3:10 statue when they hear the sound of the musical i.
3:15 made when you hear the sound of the musical i,
Hab 3:19 This prayer is to be accompanied by stringed i.)
1Co 14:7 Even musical i like the flute or the harp,

INSULT (18) [INSULTED, INSULTING, INSULTS]

Ge 39:14 has brought this Hebrew slave here to i us!"
2Ki 19:3 This is a day of trouble, i, and disgrace.
2Ch 32:16 and his servant Hezekiah, heaping i upon i.
Job 19:3 Ten times now you have meant to i me.
Ps 55:12 It is not my foes who so arrogantly i me—
69:9 so those who i you are also insulting me.
69:26 To those you have punished, they add i to injury;
74:22 Remember how these fools i you all day long.
119:22 Don't let them scorn and i me, / for I have obeyed
Pr 14:31 Those who oppress the poor i their Maker,
17:5 Those who mock the poor i their Maker; those who
30:9 too poor, I may steal and thus i God's holy name.
Isa 37:3 This is a day of trouble, i, and disgrace.
65:3 All day long they i me to my face by worshiping
La 2:15 They scoff and i Jerusalem, saying, "Is this the
Ro 15:3 "Those who i you are also insulting me."
Jas 2:6 And yet, you i the poor man! Isn't it the rich who

INSULTED (12) [INSULT]

1Sa 25:14 the wilderness to talk to our master, and he i them.
2Sa 16:21 Then all Israel will know that you have i him
2Ki 18:22 But isn't he the one who was i by King Hezekiah?
Pr 12:16 but a wise person stays calm when i.
Isa 36:7 But isn't he the one who was i by King Hezekiah?
65:7 incense on the mountains and i me on the hills.
Jer 51:51 "We are i and disgraced because the LORD's
Lk 11:45 "you have i us, too, in what you just said."
Ac 18:6 But when the Jews opposed him and i him,
Heb 10:29 Such people have i and enraged the Holy Spirit
1Pe 2:23 He did not retaliate when he was i. When he
4:14 Be happy if you are i for being a Christian, for

INSULTING (5) [INSULT]

2Sa 5:8 When the i message from the defenders of the city
2Ki 19:22 'Whom do you think you have been i
Ps 69:9 within me, / so those who insult you are also i me.
Isa 37:23 'Whom do you think you have been i
Ro 15:3 "Those who insult you are also i me."

INSULTS (12) [INSULT]

Job 20:3 I have had to endure your i, but now my spirit
Ps 69:19 You know the i I endure— / the humiliation
69:20 Their i have broken my heart, / and I am in despair.
89:50 I carry in my heart the i of so many people.
Pr 18:23 The poor plead for mercy; the rich answer with i.
22:10 and fighting, quarrels, and i will disappear.
Isa 25:8 He will remove forever all i and mockery against
La 3:30 strike them. Let them accept the i of their enemies.
Mt 27:44 crucified with him also shouted the same i at him.
Lk 22:65 And they threw all sorts of terrible i at him.
2Co 12:10 I am quite content with my weaknesses and with i,
Jude 1:15 and of all the i that godless sinners / have spoken

INSURRECTION (4) [INSURRECTIONS]

Ezr 4:19 times past been a hotbed of i against many kings.
Mk 15:7 convicted along with others for murder during an i.
Lk 23:19 and for taking part in an i in Jerusalem against the
23:25 the man in prison for i and murder.

INSURRECTIONS (1) [INSURRECTION]

Lk 21:9 And when you hear of wars and i, don't panic.

INTACT (1)

1Sa 5:4 the doorway. Only the trunk of his body was left i.

INTEGRITY (28)

Dt 32:20 they are a twisted generation, / children without i.
2Sa 22:26 to those with i you show i.
1Ki 9:4 for you, if you will follow me with i and godliness,
1Ch 29:17 our hearts and rejoice when you find i there.
2Ch 19:9 of the LORD, with i and with undivided hearts.
Job 1:1 He was blameless, a man of complete i. He feared
1:8 finest man in all the earth—a man of complete i.
2:3 finest man in all the earth—a man of complete i.
2:3 And he has maintained his i, even though you
2:9 to him, "Are you still trying to maintain your i?
8:6 if you are pure and live with complete i, he will
8:20 God will not reject a person of i, nor will he make
31:6 me on the scales of justice, for he knows my i.
Ps 18:25 to those with i you show i.
25:21 May i and honesty protect me, / for I put my hope
26:1 me innocent, O LORD, / for I have acted with i;
101:2 my aid? / I will lead a life of i / in my own home.
111:8 forever true, / to be obeyed faithfully and with i.
119:1 Happy are people of i, / who follow the law of the
Pr 2:7 is their shield, protecting those who walk with i.
2:21 in the land, and those who have i will remain in it.
10:9 People with i have firm footing, but those who
11:20 twisted hearts, but he delights in those who have i.
20:7 The godly walk with i; blessed are their children
1Ti 3:8 must be people who are respected and have i.
Tit 2:7 Let everything you do reflect the i and seriousness

INTELLIGENCE (5) [INTELLIGENT]

Ex 31:3 giving him great wisdom, i, and skill in all kinds of
35:31 giving him great wisdom, i, and skill in all kinds of
36:1 and i will construct and furnish the Tabernacle,
Dt 4:6 your wisdom and i to the surrounding nations.
Job 18:3 think we are cattle? Do you think we have no i?

INTELLIGENT (3) [INTELLIGENCE]

Job 32:8 of the Almighty within them, that makes them i.
Pr 17:28 when they keep their mouths shut, they seem i.
18:15 I people are always open to new ideas. In fact,

INTEND (6) [INTENDED, INTENDING, INTENDS, INTENT, INTENTION, INTENTIONS, INTENTLY]

Ge 38:11 (But Judah didn't really i to do this because he was
2Sa 14:32 me back from Geshur if he didn't i to see me.
Ps 119:115 for I i to obey the commands of my God.
Eze 20:30 Do you i to keep prostituting yourselves by
Hos 10:4 and make promises they don't i to keep.
Ac 5:28 about Jesus, and you i to blame us for his death!"

INTENDED (16) [INTEND]

Ge 24:21 or not she was the one the LORD i him to meet.
Nu 24:1 By now Balaam realized that the LORD i to bless
25:11 So I have stopped destroying all Israel as I had i to
Dt 19:19 the accuser will receive the punishment i for the
23:5 He turned the i curse into a blessing
Jdg 15:1 He i to sleep with her, but her father wouldn't let
2Ch 32:2 When Hezekiah realized that Sennacherib also i to
Est 7:9 He i to use it to hang Mordecai, the man who
Pr 26:2 an unfair curse will not land on its i victim.
Zec 11:4 "Go and care for a flock that is i for slaughter.
11:7 So I cared for the flock i for slaughter—the flock
Mt 19:8 but it was not what God had originally i.
Lk 4:29 the city was built. They i to push him over the cliff,
Ro 11:36 exists by his power and is i for his glory.
13:6 so they can keep on doing the work God i them to
1Ti 1:8 these laws are good when they are used as God i.

INTENDING (3) [INTEND]

1Sa 18:11 hurled it at David, i to pin him to the wall.
20:33 Saul hurled his spear at Jonathan, i to kill him.
Php 1:17 i to make my chains more painful to me.

INTENDS (1) [INTEND]

Ex 23:2 "Do not join a crowd that i to do evil. When you

INTENSE (6) [INTENSELY]

Ge 3:16 "You will bear children with i pain and suffering.
30:8 she said, "I have had an i struggle with my sister,
Dt 28:59 These plagues will be i and without relief,
Ps 74:1 so i against the sheep of your own pasture?
Ac 22:11 "I was blinded by the i light and had to be led into
1Th 2:17 because of our i longing to see you again.

INTENSELY (3) [INTENSE]

Ge 31:30 must go, and you long i for your childhood home,
1Ki 11:25 Rezon hated Israel i and continued to reign in
1Pe 1:22 So see to it that you really do love each other i

INTENT (3) [INTEND]

Job 10:13 " 'Yet your real motive—I know this was your i—
Isa 56:11 their own path, all of them i on personal gain.
Da 11:16 in the glorious land of Israel, i on destroying it.

INTENTION (3) [INTEND]

Jer 37:14 "I had no i of doing any such thing."
Eze 33:31 But they have no i of doing what I tell them.
Ac 12:4 Herod's i was to bring Peter out for public trial

INTENTIONS (11) [INTEND]

Ex 10:10 little ones along! I can see through your wicked i.
33:13 show me your i so I will understand you more fully
1Sa 16:7 the LORD looks at a person's thoughts and i."
2Sa 15:11 with him as guests, but they knew nothing of his i.
Ps 33:11 stand firm forever; / his i can never be shaken.
Pr 6:13 signaling their true i to their friends by making
10:6 evil people cover up their harmful i.
10:11 lead to life; evil people cover up their harmful i.
Zec 1:15 but the nations punished them far beyond my i.
2Th 1:11 will fulfill all your good i and faithful deeds.
Rev 2:23 searches out the thoughts and i of every person.

INTENTLY (9) [INTEND]

SS 6:13 do you gaze so i at this young woman of Shulam,
Mt 19:26 Jesus looked at them i and said,
Mk 8:25 As the man stared i, his sight was completely
10:27 Jesus looked at them i and said,
Lk 4:20 Everyone in the synagogue stared at him i.
Jn 1:42 Looking i at Simon, Jesus said, "You are Simon,
Ac 3:4 Peter and John looked at him i and Peter said,
8:6 Crowds listened i to what he had to say because of
23:1 Gazing i at the high council, Paul began:

INTERCEDE (3) [INTERCEDED]

1Sa 2:25 if someone sins against the LORD, who can i?
2Sa 14:29 Then Absalom sent for Joab to ask him to i for
Job 33:23 messenger from heaven is there to i for a person,

INTERCEDED (1) [INTERCEDE]

Isa 53:12 He bore the sins of many and i for sinners.

INTERCOURSE (43)

Ge 6:4 for whenever the sons of God had i with human
38:9 So whenever he had i with Tamar, he spilled the
Ex 19:15 And until then, abstain from having sexual i."
Lev 15:18 After having sexual i, both the man and the woman
15:24 If a man has sexual i with her during this time,
15:33 and for dealing with a man who has had i with a
18:6 "You must never have sexual i with a close
18:7 Do not violate your father by having sexual i with
18:7 is your mother; you must never have i with her.
18:8 Do not have sexual i with any of your father's
18:9 "Do not have sexual i with your sister or half
18:10 "Do not have sexual i with your granddaughter,
18:11 Do not have sexual i with the daughter of any of
18:12 Do not have i with your aunt, your father's sister,
18:13 Do not have sexual i with your aunt, your mother's
18:14 father's brother, by having sexual i with his wife;
18:15 Do not have sexual i with your daughter-in-law;
18:16 Do not have i with your brother's wife; this would
18:17 "Do not have sexual i with both a woman and her
18:19 "Do not violate a woman by having sexual i with
18:20 "Do not defile yourself by having sexual i with
18:23 defile himself by having sexual i with an animal,
18:23 herself to a male animal in order to have i with it;
19:20 "If a man has sexual i with a slave girl who is
20:11 If a man has i with his father's wife, both the man
20:12 If a man has i with his daughter-in-law, both must
20:14 If a man has i with both a woman and her mother,
20:15 "If a man has sexual i with an animal, he must be
20:16 If a woman approaches a male animal to have i
20:17 "If a man has sexual i with his sister, the daughter
20:17 Since the man has had i with his sister, he will
20:18 If a man has i with a woman suffering from a
20:19 "If a man has sexual i with his aunt, whether his
20:20 If a man has i with his uncle's wife, he has violated
Dt 22:23 to be married, and he has sexual i with her.
22:30 "A man must not have i with his father's wife,
27:20 'Cursed is anyone who has sexual i with his
27:21 'Cursed is anyone who has sexual i with an
27:22 'Cursed is anyone who has sexual i with his sister,
27:23 'Cursed is anyone who has sexual i with his
Eze 18:6 or have i with a woman during her menstrual
22:10 and have i with women who are menstruating.
Hos 3:3 this time, you will not have sexual i with anyone,

INTEREST (25) [INTERESTED, INTERESTING, INTERESTS]

Ge 12:13 will treat me well because of their i in you,
Ex 22:25 in need, do not be like a money lender, charging i.
Lev 25:36 or charge i on the money you lend them.
25:37 do not charge your relatives i on anything you lend
Dt 23:19 "Do not charge i on the loans you make to a
23:19 food, or anything else that may be loaned with i.
23:20 You may charge i to foreigners, but not to
Ne 5:7 by charging them i when they borrow money!"
5:11 Repay the i you charged on their money, grain,
Est 3:8 the king. So it is not in the king's i to let them live.
Ps 15:5 Those who do not charge i on the money they lend,
Pr 18:2 Fools have no i in understanding; they only want to
28:8 A person who makes money by charging i will lose

Eze 16: 5 No one had the slightest **i** in you; no one pitied you
18: 8 And suppose he grants loans without **i**, stays away
18: 13 and lends money at **i**. Should such a sinful person
18: 17 helps the poor, does not lend money at **i**, and obeys
Am 5: 26 No, your real **i** was in your pagan gods—
Mt 25: 27 my money into the bank so I could have some **i**.
Mk 12: 37 And the crowd listened to him with great **i**.
Lk 19: 23 in the bank so I could at least get some **i** on it?'
Ac 7: 43 No, your real **i** was in your pagan gods—
Gal 6: 14 my **i** in this world died long ago, and the world's **i** in me is also long dead.
2Ti 3: 3 they will be cruel and have no **i** in what is good.

INTERESTED (2) [INTEREST]
Ne 2: 10 someone had come who was **i** in helping Israel.
Php 2: 4 but be **i** in others, too, and what they are doing.

INTERESTING (1) [INTEREST]
Ecc 12: 10 taught the plain truth, and he did so in an **i** way.

INTERESTS (5) [INTEREST]
Pr 27: 18 workers who protect their employer's **i** will be
Isa 58: 13 Don't pursue your own **i** on that day, but enjoy the
Da 6: 2 the princes and to watch out for the king's **i**.
Ro 16: 18 our Lord; they are serving their own personal **i**.
1Co 7: 34 His **i** are divided. In the same way, a woman who

INTERFERE (1) [INTERFERED, INTERFERING]
2Ch 35: 21 Do not **i** with God, who is with me, or he will

INTERFERED (2) [INTERFERE]
Ac 13: 8 **i** and urged the governor to pay no attention to
Gal 5: 7 Who has **i** with you to hold you back from

INTERFERING (1) [INTERFERE]
Pr 26: 17 Yanking a dog's ears is as foolish as **i** in someone

INTERIOR (6)
Ge 6: 14 Then construct decks and stalls throughout its **i**.
1Ki 6: 21 Then he overlaid the rest of the Temple's **i** with
2Ch 3: 8 Its **i** was overlaid with about twenty-three tons of
SS 3: 10 Its **i** was a gift of love from the young women of
Eze 42: 12 and another on the east at the end of the **i** walkway.
Ac 19: 1 in Corinth, Paul traveled through the **i** provinces.

INTERLUDE (71)
Ps 3: 2 are saying, / "God will never rescue him!" /*I*
3: 4 and he answered me from his holy mountain. /*I*
3: 8 May your blessings rest on your people. /*I*
4: 2 How long will you pursue lies? /*I*
4: 4 Think about it overnight and remain silent. /*I*
7: 5 the ground. / Let my honor be left in the dust. /*I*
9: 16 trapped themselves in their own snares. / *Quiet I*
9: 20 Let them know they are merely human. /*I*
20: 3 and look favorably on your burnt offerings. /*I*
21: 2 you have held back nothing that he requested. /*I*
24: 6 and worship the God of Israel. /*I*
24: 10 LORD Almighty— / he is the King of glory. /*I*
32: 4 evaporated like water in the summer heat. /*I*
32: 5 And you forgave me! All my guilt is gone. /*I*
32: 7 You surround me with songs of victory. /*I*
39: 5 to you; / human existence is but a breath." /*I*
39: 11 Human existence is as frail as breath. /*I*
44: 8 day long / and constantly praise your name. /*I*
46: 3 the mountains tremble as the waters surge! /*I*
46: 7 among us; / the God of Israel is our fortress. /*I*
46: 11 among us; / the God of Israel is our fortress. /*I*
47: 4 of Jacob's descendants, whom he loves. /*I*
48: 8 city of our God; / he will make it safe forever. /*I*
49: 13 they will be remembered as being so wise. /*I*
49: 15 He will snatch me from the power of death. /*I*
50: 6 for God himself will be the judge. /*I*
52: 3 more than good / and lies more than truth. /*I*
52: 5 and drag you from the land of the living. /*I*
54: 3 trying to kill me. / They care nothing for God. /*I*
55: 7 fly far away / to the quiet of the wilderness. /*I*
55: 19 will hear me and will humble them. /*I*
57: 3 *I* / My God will send forth his unfailing love
57: 6 but they themselves have fallen into it. /*I*
59: 5 Show no mercy to wicked traitors. /*I*
59: 13 world will know / that God reigns in Israel. /*I*
60: 4 a rallying point in the face of attack. /*I*
61: 4 safe beneath the shelter of your wings! /*I*
62: 4 to my face, / but they curse me in their hearts. /*I*
62: 8 out your heart to him, / for God is our refuge. /*I*
66: 4 shouting your name in glorious songs." /*I*
66: 7 of the nations; / let no rebel rise in defiance. /*I*
66: 15 And I will sacrifice bulls and goats. /*I*
67: 1 May his face shine with favor upon us. /*I*
67: 4 and direct the actions of the whole world. /*I*
68: 7 when you marched through the wilderness, /*I*
68: 19 For each day he carries us in his arms. /*I*
68: 32 of the earth. / Sing praises to the Lord. /*I*
75: 3 I am the one who keeps its foundations firm. /*I*
76: 3 and swords and weapons of his foes. /*I*
76: 9 and to rescue the oppressed of the earth. /*I*
77: 3 overwhelmed with longing for his help. /*I*
77: 9 Has he slammed the door on his compassion? /*I*
77: 15 of Jacob and of Joseph by your might. /*I*
81: 7 you complained that there was no water. /*I*
82: 2 you shower special favors on the wicked? /*I*
83: 8 and is allied with the descendants of Lot. /*I*
84: 4 in your house, / always singing your praises. /*I*
84: 8 hear my prayer. / Listen, O God of Israel. /*I*
85: 2 yes, you have covered all their sins. /*I*
87: 3 of God, / what glorious things are said of you! /*I*
87: 6 one has become a citizen of Jerusalem." /*I*
88: 7 heavy on me; / wave after wave engulfs me. /*I*
88: 10 Do the dead get up and praise you? /*I*
89: 4 sit on your throne from now until eternity.' " /*I*
89: 37 the moon, / my faithful witness in the sky!" /*I*
89: 45 before his time / and publicly disgraced him. /*I*
89: 48 No one can escape the power of the grave. /*I*
140: 3 the poison of a viper drips from their lips. /*I*
140: 5 they have placed traps all along the way. /*I*
140: 8 Do not let their evil schemes succeed, O God. /*I*
143: 6 I thirst for you as parched land thirsts for rain. /*I*

INTERMARRIAGE (1) [MARRY]
Da 2: 43 by forming alliances with each other through **i**.

INTERMARRIED (1) [MARRY]
Jdg 3: 6 and they **i** with them. Israelite sons married their

INTERMARRY (6) [MARRY]
Ge 34: 16 we will **i** with you and live here and unite with you
34: 21 large enough to hold them, and we can **i** with them.
Dt 7: 3 Do not **i** with them, and don't let your daughters
Jos 23: 12 and **i** with the survivors of these nations remaining
1Ki 11: 2 instructed his people not to **i** with those nations,
Ne 13: 25 their children **i** with the pagan people of the land.

INTERMARRYING (1) [MARRY]
Ezr 9: 14 and **i** with people who do these detestable things.

INTERMEDIARY (1)
Dt 5: 5 I stood as an **i** between you and the LORD,

INTERNAL (18)
Ex 12: 9 roast it all, including the head, legs, and **i** organs.
29: 13 Take all the fat that covers the **i** organs,
29: 17 up the ram and wash off the **i** organs and the legs.
29: 22 the fat tail and the fat that covers the **i** organs.
Lev 1: 9 But the **i** organs and legs must first be washed with
1: 13 The **i** organs and legs must first be washed with
3: 3 by fire. This includes the fat around the **i** organs,
3: 9 off near the backbone, the fat around the **i** organs,
3: 14 This part includes the fat around the **i** organs,
4: 8 must remove all the fat around the bull's **i** organs,
4: 11 its hide, meat, head, legs, **i** organs, and dung—
7: 3 the fat from the tail, the fat around the **i** organs,
8: 16 He took all the fat around the **i** organs, the lobe of
8: 21 After washing the **i** organs and the legs with water,
8: 25 the fat around the **i** organs, the lobe of the liver,
9: 14 Then he washed the **i** organs and the legs and also
9: 19 the fat from the tail and from around the **i** organs—
16: 27 the animals' hides, the **i** organs, and the dung.

INTERNATIONAL (2) [NATION]
Isa 2: 4 The LORD will settle **i** disputes. All the nations
Mic 4: 3 The LORD will settle **i** disputes. All the nations

INTERPRET (11) [INTERPRETATION, INTERPRETATIONS, INTERPRETED, INTERPRETER, INTERPRETERS, INTERPRETING, INTERPRETS]
Ge 41: 15 But I have heard that you can **i** dreams, and that is
Dt 18: 10 or sorcery, or allow them to **i** omens,
Ecc 8: 1 to be wise, to be able to analyze and **i** things.
Da 5: 12 He can **i** dreams, explain riddles, and solve
Lk 12: 56 You know how to **i** the appearance of the earth and the sky, but you can't **i** these present times.
1Co 12: 10 and another is given the ability to **i** what is being
12: 30 Can everyone **i** unknown languages? No!
14: 26 while another will **i** what is said.
14: 27 and someone must be ready to **i** what they are
14: 28 But if no one is present who can **i**, they must be

INTERPRETATION (3) [INTERPRET]
Jdg 7: 15 When Gideon heard the dream and its **i**, he thanked
Mal 2: 9 but have shown partiality in your **i** of the law."
1Co 14: 13 **i** in order to tell people plainly what has been said.

INTERPRETATIONS (1) [INTERPRET]
Da 5: 16 I am told that you can give **i** and solve difficult

INTERPRETED (2) [INTERPRET]
Dt 17: 11 After they have **i** the law and reached a verdict,
Ac 17: 2 and for three Sabbaths in a row he **i** the Scriptures

INTERPRETER (1) [INTERPRET]
Ge 42: 23 for he had been speaking to them through an **i**.

INTERPRETERS (3) [INTERPRET]
Jer 27: 9 fortune-tellers, **i** of dreams, mediums,
Zec 10: 2 and **i** of dreams pronounce comfortless falsehoods.
Mt 23: 2 and the Pharisees are the official **i** of the

INTERPRETING (2) [INTERPRET]
Ge 40: 8 "**I** dreams is God's business," Joseph replied.
Ne 8: 9 and the Levites who were **i** for the people said to

INTERPRETS (1) [INTERPRET]
1Co 14: 5 unless someone **i** what you are saying so that the

INTERROGATE (1) [INTERROGATED]
Ac 22: 29 The soldiers who were about to **i** Paul quickly

INTERROGATED (1) [INTERROGATE]
Ac 12: 19 Herod **i** the guards and sentenced them to death.

INTERRUPTED (3)
1Ki 3: 22 Then the other woman **i**, "It certainly was your
2Ch 25: 16 But the king **i** him and said, "Since when have I
Ac 26: 28 Agrippa **i** him. "Do you think you can make me a

INTERVENED (1)
Isa 59: 16 He was amazed to see that no one **i** to help the

INTERVIEW (2) [INTERVIEWED]
Mt 2: 9 After this **i** the wise men went their way.
15: 1 law now arrived from Jerusalem to **i** Jesus.

INTERVIEWED (1) [INTERVIEW]
Ecc 7: 28 Just one out of every thousand men I **i** can be said

INTERWOVEN (2) [WEAVE]
1Ki 7: 17 with seven sets of latticework and **i** chains.
2Ch 3: 16 He made a network of **i** chains and used them to

INTESTINAL (2) [INTESTINES]
2Ch 21: 15 You yourself will be stricken with a severe **i**
21: 18 LORD struck Jehoram with the severe **i** disease.

INTESTINES (1) [INTESTINAL]
Ac 1: 18 and falling there, he burst open, spilling out his **i**.

INTIMACY (2)
1Co 7: 3 husband should not deprive his wife of sexual **i**,
7: 5 and wife to refrain from sexual **i** for a limited time,

INTIMIDATE (5)
Ne 6: 9 They were just trying to **i** us, imagining that they
6: 13 They were hoping to **i** me and make me sin by
6: 14 and all the prophets like her who have tried to **i**
6: 19 And Tobiah sent many threatening letters to **i** me.
Isa 29: 20 Those who **i** and harass will be gone, and all those

INTIMIDATED (1)
Php 1: 28 Don't be **i** by your enemies. This will be a sign to

INTO (1342) [IN] See Index of Articles, Etc.

INTOLERABLE (1)
Am 7: 10 What he is saying is **i**. It will lead to rebellion all

INTOXICATING (1)
Zec 12: 2 and Judah like an **i** drink to all the nearby nations

INTREAT(ED), INTREATIES, INTREATY [KJV] See also ASK, DEMAND, ENTREAT, IMPLORE, INSULTED, MISTREATED, PRAY, PRAYED, REQUEST, SEEK

INTRIGUE (3)
Da 8: 23 a fierce king, a master of **i**, will rise to power.
11: 21 and take over the kingdom by flattery and **i**.
Hos 7: 6 Their hearts blaze like a furnace with **i**. Their plot

INTRODUCED (2) [INTRODUCTION]
2Ki 17: 8 as well as the practices the kings of Israel had **i**.
Ac 7: 13 identity to his brothers, and they were **i** to Pharaoh.

INTRODUCTION (1) [INTRODUCED]
2Ki 5: 5 "I will send a letter of **i** for you to carry to the king

INTRUSION (1)
Lev 16: 2 whenever he chooses; the penalty for **i** is death.

INTUITION (1)
Job 38: 36 Who gives **i** and instinct?

INVADE (16) [INVADED, INVADERS, INVADES, INVADING, INVASION]
Ex 23: 27 my terror upon all the people whose lands you **i**,
1Sa 7: 13 and didn't **i** Israel again for a long time.
2Ki 5: 7 He is only trying to find an excuse to **i** us again."
13: 20 Groups of Moabite raiders used to **i** the land each
1Ch 5: 26 to **i** the land and lead away the people of Reuben,
2Ch 20: 10 You would not let our ancestors **i** those nations
Isa 7: 6 'We will **i** Judah and throw its people into panic.
8: 4 the king of Assyria will **i** both Damascus
Eze 7: 22 I will hide my eyes as these robbers **i** my treasured
Da 11: 9 "Later the king of the north will **i** the realm of the
11: 29 "Then at the appointed time he will once again **i**
11: 40 He will **i** various lands and sweep through them
Mic 5: 5 When the Assyrians **i** our land and break through

5: 6 when they pour over the borders to **i** our land.
Na 1:15 for your enemies from Nineveh will never **i** your
Hab 3:16 day when disaster will strike the people who **i** us.

INVADED (15) [INVADE]
Dt 2:23 thing happened when the Caphtorites from Crete **i**
1Ki 15:17 King Baasha of Israel **i** Judah and fortified Ramah
2Ki 5: 2 Now groups of Aramean raiders had **i** the land of
15:19 Then King Tiglath-pileser of Assyria **i** the land.
17: 5 Then the king of Assyria **i** the entire land, and for
18:25 do you think we have **i** your land without the
24: 1 King Nebuchadnezzar of Babylon **i** the land of
1Ch 4:41 the leaders of Simeon **i** it and completely destroyed
2Ch 16: 1 King Baasha of Israel **i** Judah and fortified Ramah
24:23 They **i** Judah and Jerusalem and killed all the
28:17 The armies of Edom had again **i** Judah and taken
32: 1 this work, King Sennacherib of Assyria **i** Judah.
Isa 6:13 a remnant—survive, it will be **i** again and burned.
36:10 do you think we have **i** your land without the
Joel 1: 6 A vast army of locusts has **i** my land. It is a terrible

INVADERS (6) [INVADE]
Ge 14:11 The victorious **i** then plundered Sodom
1Ch 4:42 Five hundred of these **i** from the tribe of Simeon
Ps 55:10 Its walls are patrolled day and night against **i**,
Isa 65:22 when **i** took the houses and confiscated the
Jer 51:30 The **i** have burned the houses and broken down the
Ob 1:11 refusing to lift a finger to help when foreign **i**

INVADES (1) [INVADE]
Eze 38:18 But when Gog **i** the land of Israel,

INVADING (7) [INVADE]
Isa 43:14 "For your sakes I will send an **i** army against
Jer 13:22 you have been raped and destroyed by **i** armies.
19: 7 and Jerusalem and let **i** armies slaughter them.
46:22 The **i** army marches in; they come against her with
Hos 13:16 They will be killed by an **i** army, their little ones
Zep 2: 8 mocking my people and **i** their borders.
Zec 9: 8 will guard my Temple and protect it from **i** armies.

INVALID (1)
Nu 30: 5 then all her vows and pledges will become **i**.

INVASION (2) [INVADE]
Isa 7: 7 Sovereign LORD says: This **i** will never happen,
Eze 14:15 "Or suppose I were to send an **i** of dangerous wild

INVENTING (3) [INVENTOR]
Jer 23:26 they are prophets of deceit, **i** everything they say.
Eze 13: 2 speak against the false prophets of Israel who are **i**
Ro 1:30 They are forever **i** new ways of sinning and are

INVENTOR (1) [INVENTING]
Ge 4:21 the first musician—the **i** of the harp and flute.

INVENTORY (1)
Ex 38:21 Here is an **i** of the materials used in building the

INVEST (5) [INVESTMENTS]
Mt 25:14 and gave them money to **i** for him while he was
25:16 bags of gold began immediately to **i** the money
25:20 you gave me five bags of gold to **i** and I have
25:22 the report, 'Sir, you gave me two bags of gold to **i**,
Lk 19:13 and gave them ten pounds of silver to **i** for him

INVESTIGATE (3) [INVESTIGATED, INVESTIGATION]
Dt 17: 4 When you hear about it, **i** the matter thoroughly.
Jos 9:17 The Israelites set out at once to **i** and reached their
Ezr 10:16 December 29, the leaders sat down to **i** the matter.

INVESTIGATED (1) [INVESTIGATE]
Lk 1: 3 Having carefully **i** all of these accounts from the

INVESTIGATION (2) [INVESTIGATE]
Est 2:23 When an **i** was made and Mordecai's story was
Ac 25:20 I was perplexed as to how to conduct an **i** of this

INVESTMENTS (1) [INVEST]
Ecc 5:14 or they are put into risky **i** that turn sour,

INVINCIBLE (1)
Ps 24: 8 strong and mighty, / the LORD, **i** in battle.

INVISIBLE (3)
Ro 1:20 They can clearly see his **i** qualities—his eternal
Col 1:15 Christ is the visible image of the **i** God. He existed
Heb 11:27 because he kept his eyes on the one who is **i**.

INVITATION (6) [INVITE]
Ex 2:21 Moses was happy to accept the **i**, and he settled
Nu 22:37 "Did I not send you an urgent **i**? Why didn't you
2Ch 30: 1 and he wrote letters of **i** to Ephraim and Manasseh.
Pr 25: 7 It is better to wait for an **i** than to be sent to the end
Lk 7:36 a meal, so Jesus accepted the **i** and sat down to eat.
1Co 10:27 for dinner, go ahead; accept the **i** if you want to.

INVITATIONS (1) [INVITE]
Lk 14:16 "A man prepared a great feast and sent out many **i**.

INVITE (22) [INVITATION, INVITATIONS, INVITED, INVITES, INVITING]
Ge 34: 9 We **i** you to let your daughters marry our sons,
34:21 "Let's **i** them to live here among us and ply their
Ex 2:20 leave him there? Go and **i** him home for a meal!"
34:15 they will **i** you to go with them to worship their
Jdg 14:15 Did you **i** us to this party just to make us poor?"
1Sa 16: 3 **I** Jesse to the sacrifice, and I will show you which
1Ki 1:10 But he did not **i** Nathan the prophet, or Benaiah,
1:19 the army. But he did not **i** your servant Solomon.
1Ch 13: 2 Let us **i** them to come and join us.
Pr 9: 3 She has sent her servants to **i** everyone to come.
Isa 1: 5 Why do you continue to **i** punishment? Must you
Jer 30:21 I will **i** him to approach me, says the LORD,
35: 2 and **i** them to the LORD's Temple.
Eze 23:16 so she sent messengers to Babylonia to **i** them to
Zec 3:10 each of you will **i** your neighbor into your home to
Mt 22: 9 out to the street corners and **i** everyone you see.'
25:43 a stranger, and you didn't **i** me into your home.
Lk 14:12 he said, "don't **i** your friends, brothers, relatives,
14:13 Instead, **i** the poor, the crippled, the lame,
14:21 into the streets and alleys of the city and **i** the poor,
2Jn 1:10 don't **i** him into your house or encourage him in
Rev 3:21 I will **i** everyone who is victorious to sit with me

INVITED (46) [INVITE]
Ge 29:22 So Laban **i** everyone in the neighborhood to
31:54 a sacrifice to God and **i** everyone to a feast.
39: 7 began to desire him and **i** him to sleep with her.
Ex 35: 5 Everyone is **i** to bring these offerings to the
Nu 25: 2 These women **i** them to attend sacrifices to their
Jdg 14:11 Thirty young men from the town were **i** to be his
1Sa 9:24 "I was saving it for you even before I **i** these
16: 5 purification rite for Jesse and his sons and **i** them,
2Sa 11:13 Then David **i** him to dinner and got him drunk.
13:23 Absalom **i** all the king's sons to come to a feast.
1Ki 1: 9 He **i** all his brothers—the other sons of King
1:19 and he has **i** all your sons and Abiathar the priest
1:25 and he has **i** your sons to attend the celebration.
1:25 He also **i** Joab, the commander of the army,
1:26 But I myself, your servant, was not **i**; neither were
3:15 Then he **i** all his officials to a great banquet.
20:33 Ben-hadad arrived, Ahab **i** him up into his chariot!
2Ki 4: 8 woman lived there, and she **i** him to eat some food.
Est 1: 3 He **i** all the military officers of Media and Persia,
4:11 **i** is doomed to die unless the king holds out his
5:12 Queen Esther **i** only me and the king himself to the
5:12 And she has **i** me to dine with her and the king
Job 1: 4 they **i** their brothers and sisters to join them for a
Jer 30:21 the LORD, for who would dare to come unless **i**?
35: 5 of wine before them and **i** them to have a drink,
41: 1 Gedaliah **i** them to dinner. While they were eating,
La 2:22 "You have **i** terrors from all around as though you
Mt 9:10 That night Matthew **i** Jesus and his disciples to be
10:12 When you are **i** into someone's home, give it your
22: 3 Many guests were **i**, and when the banquet was
22: 5 But the guests he had **i** ignored them and went
22: 8 and the guests I **i** aren't worthy of the honor.
25:35 I was a stranger, and you **i** me into your home.
Mk 2:15 That night Levi **i** Jesus and his disciples to be his
Lk 11:37 one of the Pharisees **i** him home for a meal.
14: 8 "If you are **i** to a wedding feast, don't always head
14: 8 someone more respected than you has also been **i**?
14:24 For none of those I **i** first will get even the
16: 5 "So he **i** each person who owed money to his
Jn 2: 2 and his disciples were also **i** to the celebration.
Ac 10:23 So Peter **i** the men to be his guests for the night.
13: 7 The governor **i** Barnabas and Saul to visit him,
28:14 who **i** us to stay with them seven days.
1Co 1: 9 and he is the one who **i** you into this wonderful
Heb 9:15 so that all who are **i** can receive the eternal
Rev 19: 9 Blessed are those who are **i** to the wedding feast of

INVITES (2) [INVITE]
Pr 10:14 but the babbling of a fool **i** trouble.
17:19 loves sin; anyone who speaks boastfully **i** disaster.

INVITING (4) [INVITE]
2Ch 30: 5 **i** everyone to come to Jerusalem to celebrate the
Lk 14:12 For they will repay you by **i** you back.
14:14 God will reward you for **i** those who could not
Ro 12:13 And get into the habit of **i** guests home for dinner

INVOKE (2) [INVOKED]
Isa 65:16 All who **i** a blessing or take an oath will do so by
Jer 44:26 None of you may **i** my name or use this oath:

INVOKED (1) [INVOKE]
Jos 6:26 At that time Joshua **i** this curse: / "May the curse

INVOLVED (8) [INVOLVES, INVOLVING]
Lev 20:20 the man and woman **i** are guilty of a capital offense
Nu 15:26 for the entire population was **i** in the sin.
1Sa 26:19 then may those **i** be cursed by the LORD.
Ezr 10:13 for many of us are **i** in this extremely sinful affair.
Pr 23: 3 don't desire all the delicacies—deception may be **i**.
Isa 3: 7 any extra food or clothes. Don't ask me to get **i**!"
2Ti 2:23 Again I say, don't get **i** in foolish,
Tit 3: 9 Do not get **i** in foolish discussions about spiritual

INVOLVES (3) [INVOLVED]
Lev 27: 9 "If your vow **i** giving a clean animal—one that is
27:11 But if your vow **i** an unclean animal—one that is
Nu 4:27 whether it **i** moving or doing other work.

INVOLVING (5) [INVOLVED]
Nu 16: 2 **i** 250 other prominent leaders, all members of the
16:49 in addition to those who had died in the incident **i**
Dt 17: 8 or a case **i** different kinds of assault.
2Ch 35:18 **i** all the priests and Levites, all the people of
Ac 18:14 if this were a case **i** some wrongdoing or a serious

INWARD (2)
2Sa 5: 9 around the city, starting at the Millo and working **i**.
Eze 40:16 There were recessed windows that narrowed **i**

IPHDEIAH (1)
1Ch 8:25 **I**, and Penuel were the sons of Shashak.

IPHTAH (1) [IPHTAH-EL]
Jos 15:43 **I**, Ashnah, Nezib,

IPHTAH-EL (2) [IPHTAH]
Jos 19:14 passed Hannathon and ended at the valley of **I**.
19:27 and ran as far as Zebulun in the valley of **I**,

IR (2)
Nu 24:19 rise in Jacob / who will destroy the survivors of **I**."
1Ch 7:12 The sons of **I** were Shuppim and Huppim.

IR-NAHASH (1)
1Ch 4:12 and Tehinnah. Tehinnah was the father of **I**.

IR-SHEMESH (1)
Jos 19:41 Dan's inheritance included Zorah, Eshtaol, **I**,

IRA (6)
2Sa 20:26 **I** the Jairite was David's personal priest.
23:26 Helez from Pelon; / **I** son of Ikkesh from Tekoa;
23:38 **I** from Jattir; / Gareb from Jattir;
1Ch 11:28 **I** son of Ikkesh from Tekoa; / Abiezer from
11:40 **I** from Jattir; / Gareb from Jattir;
27: 9 **I** son of Ikkesh from Tekoa was commander of the

IRAD (2)
Ge 4:18 Enoch was the father of **I**. / **I** was the father of Mehujael.

IRAM (2)
Ge 36:43 Magdiel, and **I**. These are the names of the clans of
1Ch 1:54 Magdiel, and **I**. These were the clan leaders of

IRI (1)
1Ch 7: 7 of Bela were Ezbon, Uzzi, Uzziel, Jerimoth, and **I**.

IRIJAH (2)
Jer 37:13 The sentry making the arrest was **I** son of
37:14 But **I** wouldn't listen, and he took Jeremiah before

IRON (86) [IRON-SMELTING, IRONS]
Ge 4:22 with metal, forging instruments of bronze and **i**.
Lev 26:19 spirit by making the skies above as unyielding as **i**
Nu 31:22 made of gold, silver, bronze, **i**, tin, or lead—
35:16 and kills another person with a piece of **i**,
Dt 3:11 His **i** bed was more than thirteen feet long and six
8: 9 It is a land where **i** is as common as stone,
27: 6 Do not shape the stones with an **i** tool. On the altar
28:23 and the earth beneath will be as hard as **i**.
33:25 May the bolts of your gates be of **i** and bronze;
Jos 6:19 or **i** is sacred to the LORD and must be brought
6:24 or **i** were kept for the treasury of the LORD's
8:31 are uncut and have not been shaped with **i** tools."
17:16 and the valley of Jezreel have **i** chariots—
17:18 even though they are strong and have **i** chariots."
22: 8 your silver and gold, your bronze and **i**, and your
Jdg 1:19 the plains because the people there had **i** chariots.
4: 3 Sisera, who had nine hundred **i** chariots,
4:13 he called for all nine hundred of his **i** chariots
1Sa 17: 7 tipped with an **i** spearhead that weighed fifteen
1Ki 6: 7 ax, or any other **i** tool at the building site.
22:11 of Kenaanah, made some **i** horns and proclaimed,
1Ch 22: 3 David provided large amounts of **i** for the nails that
22:14 and so much **i** and bronze that it cannot be
22:16 and silversmiths and workers of bronze and **i**.
29: 2 there is enough gold, silver, bronze, **i**, and wood,
29: 7 675 tons of bronze, and about 3,750 tons of **i**.
2Ch 2: 7 who can work with gold, silver, bronze, and **i**;
2:14 at making things from gold, silver, bronze, and **i**.
18:10 of Kenaanah, made some **i** horns and proclaimed,
24:12 who made articles of **i** and bronze for the
Job 19:24 carved with an **i** chisel and filled with lead,
28: 2 They know how to dig **i** from the earth and smelt
40:18 bones are tubes of bronze. Its limbs are bars of **i**.
41:27 To the crocodile, **i** is nothing but straw, and bronze
Ps 2: 9 You will break them with an **i** rod / and smash
105:18 feet with fetters / and placed his neck in an **i** collar.
107:16 prison gates of bronze; / he cut apart their bars of **i**.
149: 8 with shackles / and their leaders with **i** chains,
Pr 18:19 separate friends like a gate locked with **i** bars.
27:17 As **i** sharpens **i**, a friend sharpens a friend.

Isa 45: 2 down gates of bronze and cut through bars of i.
48: 4 you are. Your necks are as unbending as i.
60:17 your i for silver, your wood for bronze, and your stones for i.
Jer 1:18 be captured, like an i pillar or a bronze wall.
5:31 and the priests rule with an i hand.
6:28 are as insolent as bronze, as hard and cruel as i.
15:12 Can a man break a bar of i from the north, or a bar
17: 1 or with an i chisel on the corners of their altars.
28:13 but you have replaced it with a yoke of i.
28:14 I have put a yoke of i on the necks of all these
Eze 4: 3 Then take an i griddle and place it between you
11: 3 Our city is like an i pot. Inside it we will be like
11: 7 This city is an i pot, but the victims of your
11:11 No, this city will not be an i pot for you, and you
20:33 I will rule you with an i fist in great anger and with
22:18 a useless mixture of copper, tin, i, and lead.
22:20 just as copper, tin, i, and lead are melted down in a
27:12 your wares in exchange for silver, i, tin, and lead.
27:19 Wrought i, cassia, and calamus were bartered for
Da 2:33 its legs were of i, and its feet were a combination of i and clay.
2:34 It struck the feet of i and clay, smashing them to
2:35 The whole statue collapsed into a heap of i, clay,
2:40 there will be a fourth great kingdom, as strong as i.
2:40 just as i smashes and crushes everything it strikes.
2:41 and toes you saw that were a combination of i
2:42 Some parts of it will be as strong as i, and others as
2:43 This mixture of i and clay also shows that these
2:43 this will not succeed, just as i and clay do not mix.
2:45 crushing to dust the statue of i, bronze, clay,
4:15 bound with a band of i and bronze and surrounded
4:23 bound with a band of i and bronze and surrounded
5: 4 made of gold, silver, bronze, i, wood, and stone.
5:23 gods of silver, gold, bronze, i, wood, and stone—
7: 7 and crushed its victims with huge i teeth
7:19 It devoured and crushed its victims with i teeth
Am 1: 3 as grain is threshed with threshing sledges of i.
Mic 4:13 "For I will give you i horns and bronze hooves,
Ac 12:10 guard posts and came to the i gate to the street,
Rev 2:27 They will rule the nations with an i rod and smash
9: 9 They wore armor made of i, and their wings roared
12: 5 to a boy who was to rule all nations with an i rod.
18:12 made of expensive wood, bronze, i, and marble.
19:15 He ruled them with an i rod, and he trod the

IRON-SMELTING (1) [IRON]

1Ki 8:51 whom you brought out of the i furnace of Egypt.

IRONS (1) [IRON]

Jer 29:26 claims to be a prophet in the stocks and neck i.

IRPEEL (1)

Jos 18:27 Rekem, I, Taralah,

IRRATIONAL (1)

Ecc 2:17 because everything done here under the sun is so i.

IRRELIGIOUS (1)

Ecc 9: 2 ceremonially clean or unclean, religious or i.

IRRESISTIBLY (1)

Ac 20:22 drawn there i by the Holy Spirit, not knowing what

IRREVERENT (1)

Job 34: 7 a man as arrogant as Job, with his thirst for i talk?

IRREVOCABLE (2)

Ge 27:33 and I blessed him with an i blessing before you
Gal 3:15 as no one can set aside or amend an i agreement,

IRRIGATE (1) [IRRIGATION]

Ecc 2: 6 I built reservoirs to collect the water to i my many

IRRIGATION (1) [IRRIGATE]

Dt 11:10 and dug out i ditches with your foot as in a

IRRITABLE (1) [IRRITATE]

1Co 13: 5 Love is not i, and it keeps no record of when it has

IRRITATE (1) [IRRITABLE]

Gal 5:26 or i one another, or be jealous of one another.

IRU (1)

1Ch 4:15 The sons of Caleb son of Jephunneh were I,

IS (6473) [BE] See Index of Articles, Etc.

ISAAC (139) [ISAAC'S]

Ge 17:19 You will name him I, and I will confirm my
17:21 But my covenant is with I, who will be born to you
21: 3 And Abraham named his son I.
21: 4 Eight days after I was born, Abraham circumcised
21: 8 As time went by and I grew and was weaned,
21: 9 and her Egyptian servant Hagar—making fun of I.
21:10 to share the family inheritance with my son, I.
21:12 for I is the son through whom your descendants
22: 2 your only son—yes, I, whom you love so much—
22: 3 two of his servants with him, along with his son I.
22: 7 I said, "Father?" "Yes, my son,"
22: 9 Then he tied I up and laid him on the altar over the
24: 4 my relatives, and find a wife there for my son I."
24: 5 then take I there to live among your relatives?"
24:37 not let I marry one of the local Canaanite women.
24:62 Meanwhile, I, whose home was in the Negev,
24:64 When Rebekah looked up and saw I, she quickly
24:66 Then the servant told I the whole story.
24:67 And I brought Rebekah into his mother's tent,
25: 5 Abraham left everything he owned to his son I.
25: 6 and sent them off to the east, away from I.
25: 9 His sons I and Ishmael buried him in the cave of
25:11 God poured out rich blessings on I,
25:19 This is the history of the family of I, the son of
25:20 When I was forty years old, he married Rebekah,
25:21 I pleaded with the LORD to give Rebekah a child
25:26 I was sixty years old when the twins were born.
25:28 I loved Esau in particular because of the wild game
26: 1 So I moved to Gerar, where Abimelech, king of
26: 6 So I stayed in Gerar.
26: 8 looked out a window and saw I fondling Rebekah.
26: 9 Abimelech called for I and exclaimed, "She is
26: 9 would kill me to get her from me," I replied.
26:16 And Abimelech asked I to leave the country.
26:17 So I moved to the Gerar Valley and lived there
26:18 I renamed them, using the names Abraham had
26:20 So I named the well "Argument," because they
26:21 was a fight over it. So I named it "Opposition."
26:22 So I called it "Room Enough," for he said,
26:23 From there I moved to Beersheba,
26:25 Then I built an altar there and worshiped the
26:26 One day I had visitors from Gerar.
26:27 "Why have you come?" I asked them. "This is
26:30 So I prepared a great feast for them, and they ate
26:31 Then I sent them home again in peace.
26:33 So I named the well "Oath," and from that time to
26:35 But Esau's wives made life miserable for I
27: 1 When I was old and almost blind, he called for
27: 2 "I am an old man now," I said, "and I expect
27:14 a delicious meat dish, just the way I liked it.
27:20 I asked, "How were you able to find it so quickly,
27:21 Then I said to Jacob, "Come over here. I want to
27:22 Jacob went over to his father, and I touched him.
27:22 but the hands are Esau's," I said to himself.
27:23 like Esau's. So I pronounced his blessing on Jacob.
27:25 Then I said, "Now, my son, bring me the meat.
27:25 Jacob took the food over to his father, and I ate it.
27:25 drank the wine that Jacob served him. Then I said,
27:27 And when I caught the smell of his clothes, he was
27:30 As soon as I had blessed Jacob, and almost before
27:32 But I asked him, "Who are you?" "Why, it's me,
27:33 I began to tremble uncontrollably and said,
27:35 But I said, "Your brother was here, and he tricked
27:37 I said to Esau, "I have made Jacob your master
27:39 His father, I, said to him, "You will live off the
27:46 Then Rebekah said to I, "I'm sick and tired of
28: 1 So I called for Jacob, blessed him, and said,
28: 5 So I sent Jacob away, and he went to Paddan-aram
28:13 and the God of your father, I.
31:18 to the land of Canaan, where his father, I, lived.
31:42 the awe-inspiring God of my father, I—
31:53 God of his father, I, to respect the boundary line.
32: 9 God of my grandfather Abraham and my father, I
35:12 pass on to you the land I gave to Abraham and I.
35:27 So Jacob came home to his father I in Mamre,
35:28 I lived for 180 years,
46: 1 he offered sacrifices to the God of his father, I.
48:15 my grandfather Abraham and my father, I, walked,
48:16 of my grandfather Abraham and my father, I.
49:31 There I and his wife, Rebekah, are buried.
50:24 to the descendants of Abraham, I, and Jacob."
Ex 2:24 his covenant promise to Abraham, I, and Jacob.
3: 6 the God of Abraham, the God of I, and the God of
3:15 the God of Abraham, the God of I, and the God of
3:16 the God of Abraham, I, and Jacob—
4: 5 the God of Abraham, the God of I, and the God of
6: 3 I appeared to Abraham, to I, and to Jacob as God
6: 8 the land I swore to give to Abraham, I, and Jacob.
32:13 with your servants—Abraham, I, and Jacob.
33: 1 land I solemnly promised Abraham, I, and Jacob.
Lev 26:42 with I, and with Abraham, and I will remember the
Nu 32:11 I, and Jacob, for they have not obeyed me
Dt 1: 8 I, and Jacob, and to all their descendants.'
6:10 to give your ancestors Abraham, I, and Jacob.
9: 5 sworn to your ancestors Abraham, I, and Jacob.
9:27 instead your servants Abraham, I, and Jacob.
29:13 he swore to your ancestors Abraham, I, and Jacob.
30:20 to give your ancestors Abraham, I, and Jacob."
34: 4 land I promised on oath to Abraham, I, and Jacob,
Jos 24: 3 I gave him many descendants through his son I.
24: 4 To I I gave Jacob and Esau. To Esau I gave the hill
1Ki 18:36 "O LORD, God of Abraham, I, and Jacob,
2Ki 13:23 of his covenant with Abraham, I, and Jacob.
1Ch 1:28 The sons of Abraham were I and Ishmael.
1:34 Abraham was the father of I. The sons of I were Esau and Israel.
16:16 made with Abraham / and the oath he swore to I.
29:18 the God of our ancestors Abraham, I, and Israel,
2Ch 30: 6 to the LORD, the God of Abraham, I, and Israel,
Ps 105: 9 made with Abraham / and the oath he swore to I.
Jer 33:26 will rule the descendants of Abraham, I, and Jacob.
Mt 1: 2 Abraham was the father of I. / I was the father of Jacob.
8:11 all over the world and sit down with Abraham, I,
22:31 after Abraham, I, and Jacob had died, God said,
22:32 of Abraham, the God of I, and the God of Jacob.'
Mk 12:26 I, and Jacob had died, God said to Moses,
12:26 of Abraham, the God of I, and the God of Jacob.'
Lk 3:34 Jacob was the son of I. / I was the son of Abraham.
13:28 of teeth, for you will see Abraham, I, Jacob,
20:37 Long after Abraham, I, and Jacob had died,
20:37 of Abraham, the God of I, and the God of Jacob.'
Ac 3:13 God of Abraham, the God of I, the God of Jacob,
7: 8 And so I, Abraham's son, was circumcised when
7: 8 I became the father of Jacob, and Jacob was the
7:32 the God of Abraham, I, and Jacob.'
Ro 9: 7 "I is the son through whom your descendants will
9:10 This son was our ancestor I. When he grew up,
11:28 because of his promises to Abraham, I, and Jacob.
Gal 4:28 and sisters, are children of the promise, just like I.
4:29 just as I, the child of promise, was persecuted by
Heb 11: 9 And so did I and Jacob, to whom God gave the
11:17 It was by faith that Abraham offered I as a
11:17 was ready to sacrifice his only son, I,
11:18 "I is the son through whom your descendants will
11:19 Abraham assumed that if I died, God was able to
11:20 It was by faith that I blessed his two sons, Jacob
Jas 2:21 because of what he did when he offered his son I

ISAAC'S (8) [ISAAC]

Ge 22: 6 the wood for the burnt offering on I shoulders,
24:14 let her be the one you have appointed as I wife.
25:21 So the LORD answered I prayer, and his wife
26:12 That year I crops were tremendous! He harvested a
26:15 and they filled up all of I wells with earth.
26:20 they said, and they argued over it with I herdsmen.
26:21 I men then dug another well, but again there was a
26:32 That very day I servants came and told him about a

ISAIAH (59) [ISAIAH'S]

2Ki 19: 2 dressed in sackcloth, to the prophet I son of Amoz.
19: 5 officials delivered the king's message to I,
19:20 Then I son of Amoz sent this message to
19:29 Then I said to Hezekiah, "Here is the proof that
20: 1 and the prophet I son of Amoz went to visit him.
20: 4 But before I had left the middle courtyard,
20: 7 Then I said to Hezekiah's servants, "Make an
20: 8 Meanwhile, Hezekiah had said to I, "What sign
20: 9 I replied, "This is the sign that the LORD will
20:11 So I asked the LORD to do this, and he caused
20:14 Then I the prophet went to King Hezekiah
20:15 I asked. "They saw everything,"
20:16 Then I said to Hezekiah, "Listen to this message
20:19 Then Hezekiah said to I, "This message you have
2Ch 26:22 to end, are recorded by the prophet I son of Amoz.
32:20 and the prophet I son of Amoz cried out in prayer
32:32 *I Son of Amoz*, which is included in *The Book of*
Isa 1: 1 and Jerusalem came to I son of Amoz during the
2: 1 This is another vision that I son of Amoz saw
7: 3 Then the LORD said to I, "Go out to meet King
7:13 Then I said, "Listen well, you royal family of
13: 1 I son of Amoz received this message concerning
20: 2 the LORD told I son of Amoz, "Take off all your
20: 2 I did as he was told and walked around naked
20: 3 "My servant I has been walking around naked
37: 2 dressed in sackcloth, to the prophet I son of Amoz.
37: 5 officials delivered the king's message to I,
37:21 Then I son of Amoz sent this message to
37:30 Then I said to Hezekiah, "Here is the proof that
38: 1 and the prophet I son of Amoz went to visit him.
38: 4 Then this message came to I from the LORD:
38:21 I had said to Hezekiah's servants, "Make an
39: 3 Then I the prophet went to King Hezekiah
39: 4 asked I. "They saw everything,"
39: 5 Then I said to Hezekiah, "Listen to this message
39: 8 Then Hezekiah said to I, "This message you have
Mt 3: 3 I had spoken of John when he said, / "He is a
8:17 This fulfilled the word of the Lord through I,
12:17 This fulfilled the prophecy of I concerning him:
13:14 This fulfills the prophecy of I, which says:
15: 7 I was prophesying about you when he said,
Mk 1: 2 In the book of the prophet I, God said, / "Look,
7: 6 I was prophesying about you when he said,
Lk 3: 4 I had spoken of John when he said, / "He is a
4:17 The scroll containing the messages of I the prophet
Jn 1:23 John replied in the words of I: / "I am a voice
12:38 This is exactly what I the prophet had predicted:
12:39 But the people couldn't believe, for as I also said,
12:41 I was referring to Jesus when he made this
Ac 8:28 was reading aloud from the book of the prophet I.
8:30 and heard the man reading from the prophet I;
8:34 "Was I talking about himself or someone else?"
28:25 he said to our ancestors through I the prophet,
Ro 9:27 Concerning Israel, I the prophet cried out,
9:29 And I said in another place, / "If the Lord
10:16 for I the prophet said, "Lord, who has believed our
10:20 And later I spoke boldly for God: / "I was found
15:12 And the prophet I said, / "The heir to David's
Gal 4:27 That is what I meant when he prophesied,

ISAIAH'S (1) [ISAIAH]

Mt 4:14 This fulfilled I prophecy:

ISCAH (1)

Ge 11:29 their brother Haran. (Milcah had a sister named I.)

ISCARIOT (11) [JUDAS]

Mt 10: 4 (the Zealot), / Judas I (who later betrayed him).
26:14 Then Judas I, one of the twelve disciples, went to
Mk 3:19 Judas I (who later betrayed him).
14:10 Then Judas I, one of the twelve disciples, went to
Lk 6:16 (son of James), / Judas I (who later betrayed him).

22: 3 Then Satan entered into Judas **I**, who was one of
Jn 6: 71 son of Simon **I**, one of the Twelve, who would
12: 4 But Judas **I**, one of his disciples—the one who
13: 2 son of Simon **I**, to carry out his plan to betray
13: 26 had dipped it, he gave it to Judas, son of Simon **I**.
14: 22 Judas (not Judas **I**, but the other disciple with that

ISHBAH (1)

1Ch 4: 17 Shammai, and **I** (the father of Eshtemoa).

ISHBAK (2)

Ge 25: 2 Jokshan, Medan, Midian, **I**, and Shuah.
1Ch 1: 32 Jokshan, Medan, Midian, **I**, and Shuah.

ISHBI-BENOB (1)

2Sa 21: 16 **I** was a descendant of the giants; his bronze

ISHBOSHETH (10) [ISHBOSHETH'S]

1Sa 14: 49 Saul's sons included Jonathan, **I**, and Malkishua.
2Sa 2: 8 had already gone to Mahanaim with Saul's son **I**.
2: 9 There he proclaimed **I** king over Gilead, Jezreel,
2: 10 **I** was forty years old when he became king, and he
3: 7 One day **I**, Saul's son, accused Abner of sleeping
3: 11 **I** didn't dare say another word because he was
3: 14 David then sent this message to **I**, Saul's son:
3: 15 So **I** took Michal away from her husband Palti son
4: 1 When **I** heard about Abner's death at Hebron,
4: 8 "Here is the head of **I**, the son of your enemy Saul

ISHBOSHETH'S (6) [ISHBOSHETH]

2Sa 2: 12 One day Abner led some of **I** troops from
4: 2 and Recab, who were captains of **I** raiding parties.
4: 5 went to **I** home around noon as he was taking a
4: 6 went into **I** bedroom, and stabbed him in the
4: 8 arrived at Hebron and presented **I** head to David.
4: 12 Then they took **I** head and buried it in Abner's

ISHHOD (1)

1Ch 7: 18 Makir's sister Hammoleketh gave birth to **I**,

ISHI (5)

1Ch 2: 31 but Appaim had a son named **I**. The son of **I** was Sheshan.
4: 20 The descendants of **I** were Zoheth and Ben-zoheth.
4: 42 Neariah, Rephaiah, and Uzziel—all sons of **I**.
5: 24 Epher, **I**, Eliel, Azriel, Jeremiah, Hodaviah,

ISHIJAH (1)

Ezr 10: 31 Eliezer, **I**, Malkijah, Shemaiah, Shimeon,

ISHMA (1)

1Ch 4: 3 **I**, Idbash, Hazzelelponi (his daughter),

ISHMAEL (42) [ISHMAEL'S, ISHMAELITE, ISHMAELITES]

Ge 16: 11 You are to name him **I**, for the LORD has heard
16: 15 Hagar gave Abram a son, and Abram named him **I**.
17: 18 to God, "Yes, may **I** enjoy your special blessing!"
17: 20 As for **I**, I will bless him also, just as you have
17: 23 On that very day Abraham took his son **I** and every
17: 25 and **I** his son was thirteen.
21: 9 But Sarah saw **I**—the son of Abraham and her
21: 11 upset Abraham very much because **I** was his son.
25: 9 and **I** buried him in the cave of Machpelah,
25: 12 This is the history of the descendants of **I**, the son
25: 16 These twelve sons of **I** became the founders of
25: 17 **I** finally died at the age of 137 and joined his
25: 18 The clans descended from **I** camped close to one
28: 9 was the sister of Nebaioth and the daughter of **I**,
36: 3 who was the daughter of **I** and the sister of
2Ki 25: 23 These included **I** son of Nethaniah, Johanan son of
25: 25 **I** son of Nethaniah and grandson of Elishama,
1Ch 1: 28 The sons of Abraham were Isaac and **I**.
1: 29 The sons of **I** were Nebaioth (the oldest), Kedar,
1: 31 Naphish, and Kedemah. These were the sons of **I**.
8: 38 Azrikam, Bokeru, **I**, Sheariah, Obadiah,
9: 44 Bokeru, **I**, Sheariah, Obadiah, and Hanan.
2Ch 19: 11 Zebadiah son of **I**, a leader from the tribe of Judah,
23: 1 **I** son of Jehohanan, Azariah son of Obed,
Ezr 10: 22 Elioenai, Maaseiah, **I**, Nethanel, Jozabad,
Jer 40: 8 **I** son of Nethaniah, Johanan and Jonathan, sons of
40: 14 has sent **I** son of Nethaniah to assassinate you?"
40: 15 with Gedaliah and volunteered to kill **I** secretly.
40: 16 to do any such thing, for you are lying about **I**."
41: 1 **I** son of Nethaniah and grandson of Elishama,
41: 2 **I** and his ten men suddenly drew their swords
41: 6 **I** left Mizpah to meet them, weeping as he went.
41: 7 **I** and his men killed all but ten of them and threw
41: 8 The other ten had talked **I** into letting them go by
41: 9 The cistern where **I** dumped the bodies of the men
41: 9 of Israel. **I** son of Nethaniah filled it with corpses.
41: 10 **I** made captives of the king's daughters
41: 11 and the rest of the guerrilla leaders heard what **I**
41: 13 The people **I** had captured shouted for joy when
41: 15 **I** and eight of his men escaped from Johanan into
41: 18 do when they heard that **I** had killed Gedaliah,
Gal 4: 29 as Isaac, the child of promise, was persecuted by **I**,

ISHMAEL'S (4) [ISHMAEL]

Ge 25: 13 is a list, by their names and clans, of **I** descendants:
25: 18 **I** descendants were scattered across the country
28: 9 So he visited his uncle **I** family and married one of **I** daughters,

ISHMAELITE (7) [ISHMAEL]

Ge 37: 25 It was a group of **I** traders taking spices, balm,
37: 27 Let's sell Joseph to those **I** traders. Let's not be
37: 28 of silver, and the **I** traders took him along to Egypt.
39: 1 Now when Joseph arrived in Egypt with the **I**
2Sa 17: 25 His father was Jether, an **I**. His mother,
1Ch 2: 17 an **I**, and they had a son named Amasa.
27: 30 Obil the **I** was in charge of the camels.

ISHMAELITES (2) [ISHMAEL]

Jdg 8: 24 (The enemies, being **I**, all wore gold earrings.)
Ps 83: 6 these Edomites and **I**, / Moabites and Hagrites,

ISHMAIAH (2)

1Ch 12: 4 **I** from Gibeon, a famous warrior and leader among
27: 19 Zebulun | **I** son of Obadiah / Naphtali | Jeremoth

ISHMEELITE(S) [KJV] See ISHMAELITE, ISHMAELITES

ISHMERAI (1)

1Ch 8: 18 **I**, Izliah, and Jobab were the sons of Elpaal.

ISHPAH (1)

1Ch 8: 16 Michael, **I**, and Joha were the sons of Beriah.

ISHPAN (1)

1Ch 8: 22 **I**, Eber, Eliel,

ISHTOB [KJV] See TOB

ISHVAH (2)

Ge 46: 17 sons of Asher were Imnah, **I**, Ishvi, and Beriah.
1Ch 7: 30 sons of Asher were Imnah, **I**, Ishvi, and Beriah.

ISHVI (3) [ISHVITE]

Ge 46: 17 sons of Asher were Imnah, Ishvah, **I**, and Beriah.
Nu 26: 44 The Ishvite clan, named after its ancestor **I**.
1Ch 7: 30 sons of Asher were Imnah, Ishvah, **I**, and Beriah.

ISHVITE (1) [ISHVI]

Nu 26: 44 The **I** clan, named after its ancestor Ishvi.

ISLAND (25) [ISLANDS]

Eze 26: 5 The **i** of Tyre will become uninhabited. It will be a
26: 14 I will make your **i** a bare rock, a place for
26: 17 'O famous **i** city, / once ruler of the sea,
27: 25 Your **i** warehouse was filled to the brim!
28: 8 and you will die there on your **i** home in the heart
Ac 4: 36 the tribe of Levi and came from the **i** of Cyprus.
13: 4 of Seleucia and then sailed for the **i** of Cyprus.
13: 6 the entire **i** until finally they reached Paphos,
16: 11 and sailed straight across to the **i** of Samothrace,
20: 15 The next day we passed the **i** of Kios.
20: 15 The following day, we crossed to the **i** of Samos.
21: 1 Ephesian elders, we sailed straight to the **i** of Cos.
21: 3 We sighted the **i** of Cyprus, passed it on our left,
27: 4 so we sailed north of Cyprus between the **i**
27: 16 We sailed behind a small **i** named Cauda,
27: 26 But we will be shipwrecked on an **i**."
28: 1 we learned that we were on the **i** of Malta.
28: 2 The people of the **i** were very kind to us. It was
28: 4 The people of the **i** saw it hanging there and said to
28: 7 belonging to Publius, the chief official of the **i**.
28: 9 Then all the other sick people on the **i** came
28: 11 set sail on another ship that had wintered at the **i**—
Tit 1: 5 I left you on the **i** of Crete so you could complete
Rev 1: 9 I was exiled to the **i** of Patmos for preaching the
16: 20 And every **i** disappeared, and all the mountains

ISLANDS (5) [ISLAND]

Ps 72: 10 The western kings of Tarshish and the **i** / will bring
97: 1 Let the earth rejoice! / Let the farthest **i** be glad.
Isa 40: 15 He picks up the **i** as though they had no weight at
Eze 26: 18 your fall. / The **i** are dismayed as you pass away.'
Rev 6: 14 all of the mountains and all of the **i** disappeared.

ISMAIAH [KJV] See ISHMAIAH

ISMAKIAH (1)

2Ch 31: 13 Asahel, Jerimoth, Jozabad, Eliel, **I**, Mahath,

ISN'T (94) [BE, NOT] See Index of Articles, Etc.

ISOLATED (1) [ISOLATION]

Lev 13: 54 to be washed and then **i** for seven more days.

ISOLATION (2) [ISOLATED]

Lev 13: 46 and must live in **i** outside the camp.
2Ch 26: 21 He lived in **i**, excluded from the Temple of the

ISPAH [KJV] See ISHPAH

ISRAEL (2117) [EL-ELOHE-ISRAEL, ISRAEL'S, ISRAELITE, ISRAELITES, ISRAELITES']

ALL ISRAEL (88) Lev 25:33; Nu 20:29; 25:11; Dt 13:11; 21:21; 27:9; 31:7; 34:12; Jos 6:18; 22:22; 1Sa 7:2,7; 10:24; 11:2; 18:16; 25:1; 26:15; 28:3; 30:25; 2Sa 5:5; 6:15; 8:15; 10:17; 12:12; 15:13; 16:21; 17:10; 19:11,20; 21:5; 1Ki 1:20; 3:28; 4:1,7; 5:13; 8:62,63,65; 11:42; 12:1,16,18,20; 14:13,16; 21:22; 22:17; 2Ki 10:21; 1Ch 9:1; 11:1,4,10; 12:38; 13:6,8; 14:8; 15:28; 18:14; 19:17; 28:4,8; 29:23,26; 2Ch 1:2; 7:6; 9:30; 10:1,3,16,16; 12:1; 18:16; 28:23; 29:24,24; 30:1,5; Ne 7:73; 13:26; Isa 65:8; Eze 5:4,13; Da 9:7,11; Am 3:13; Zec 12:12; Mal 4:4; Ro 11:26

ASSEMBLY OF ISRAEL (5) Dt 31:30; 33:4; Jdg 21:24; 1Ki 12:3; 1Ch 13:2

GOD OF ISRAEL (221) Ex 5:1; 24:10; 32:27; 34:23; Nu 16:9; Dt 33:26; Jos 7:13,19,20; 8:30; 9:18,19; 10:40,42; 13:14,33; 14:14; 22:16,24; 24:2,23; Jdg 4:6; 5:3,5; 6:8; 11:21,23; 21:3; Ru 2:12; 1Sa 1:17; 2:30; 5:7,8,8,10,11; 6:3,5; 10:18; 14:41; 20:12; 23:10,11; 25:32,34; 2Sa 7:27; 12:7; 23:3; 1Ki 1:30,48; 8:15,17,20,23,25,26; 11:9,31; 14:7,13; 15:30; 16:13,26,33; 17:1,14; 22:53; 2Ki 9:6; 10:31; 14:25; 18:5; 19:15,20; 21:12; 22:15,18; 1Ch 4:10; 5:26; 15:12,14; 16:4,36; 22:6; 23:25; 24:19; 28:4; 2Ch 2:12; 6:4,7,10,14, 16,17; 11:16; 13:5; 15:4,13; 20:19; 29:7,10; 30:1,5; 32:17; 33:16,18; 34:23,26; 36:13; Ezr 1:3; 3:2; 4:1,3; 5:1; 6:14,21, 22; 7:6,15; 8:35; 9:4,15; Ps 20:1; 24:6; 41:13; 46:7,11; 59:5; 68:8,35; 69:6; 72:18; 75:9; 81:1; 84:8; 94:7; 106:48; 114:7; 146:5; Isa 2:3; 17:6; 21:10,17; 24:15; 29:23; 37:16,21; 41:17; 45:3,15; 48:1,2; 52:7,12; Jer 7:3,21; 9:15; 10:16; 11:3; 13:12; 16:9; 19:3,15; 21:4; 23:2; 24:5; 25:15,27; 27:4,21; 28:2,14; 29:4,8,21,25; 30:2; 31:23; 32:14,15,36; 33:4; 34:2,13; 35:13,17,18,19; 37:7; 38:17; 39:16; 42:9,15,18; 43:10; 44:2,7,11,25; 45:2; 46:25; 48:1; 50:18; 51:19,33; Eze 8:4; 9:3; 10:19,20; 11:22; 43:2; 44:2; Joel 2:17; Mic 4:2; Zep 2:9; Mal 2:16; Mt 15:31; Lk 1:68; Ac 10:2,22; 13:16,26

ISRAEL AND JUDAH (43) 1Sa 18:16; 2Sa 5:5; 11:11; 12:8; 24:1; 1Ki 1:35; 2Ki 17:13; 23:22; 2Ch 27:7; 30:1,6; 34:21; 35:27; 36:8; Isa 5:7; 7:17; 8:14; 10:20; 11:13; 65:9; Jer 5:11,20; 11:10,17; 30:3,4; 31:27,31; 32:30,32; 33:14; 50:4,33; 51:5; Eze 9:9; 35:10; Hos 5:13,14; 6:4; 10:11; Am 3:1; Mic 1:5; Heb 8:8

JUDAH AND ISRAEL (18) Jos 11:21; 2Sa 3:37; 1Ki 4:20,25; 2Ch 16:11; 25:26; 28:26; 32:32; 35:18; Jer 3:18; 13:11; 33:7,24; Eze 27:17; Hos 1:11; Zec 8:12,13; 11:14

KING OF ISRAEL (73) 1Sa 15:1,17,26,35; 16:1; 23:17; 24:14; 26:20; 2Sa 5:3,17; 6:20; 12:7; 19:22; 1Ki 5:1; 15:28; 19:16; 20:11,28,32,32,33,41,43; 21:7; 22:9,18,29,31,32,33, 34,44; 2Ki 3:4,5,10,13; 5:5,6,7; 6:9,10,11,12,21,26; 7:6; 13:16; 15:25; 1Ch 11:3; 12:38; 29:1; 2Ch 18:8,17,28,30,31, 32,33; 29:27; Ezr 5:11; Pr 1:1; Ecc 1:12; Isa 41:21; Eze 17:16,18; Hos 1:1; 10:15; Am 1:1; Zep 3:15; Mt 27:42; Mk 15:32; Jn 1:49; 12:13

KING OVER (ALL) ISRAEL (14) 2Sa 3:10; 5:12; 1Ki 1:34; 4:1; 12:20; 14:14; 2Ki 9:3,12; 1Ch 14:2,8; 23:1; 28:4,4; Ne 13:26

KINGS OF ISRAEL (42) 1Ki 14:19; 15:31; 16:5,14,20, 27,33; 20:31; 22:39; 2Ki 1:18; 3:12; 8:18; 10:30,34; 13:8,12; 14:15,28,29; 15:11,12,15,21,26,31; 16:3; 17:2,8; 23:19,22; 1Ch 9:1; 2Ch 20:34; 21:6,13; 27:7; 28:2; 33:18; 35:18,27; 36:8; Isa 7:16; Mic 1:14

LAND OF ISRAEL (42) Nu 18:21; Jos 11:22; Jdg 20:6; 1Sa 13:19; 28:3; 2Sa 21:14; 2Ki 5:2; 6:23; 8:3; 1Ch 12:40; 21:12; 2Ch 2:17; 30:25; 34:7,33; Isa 6:12; 11:11; 33:9; 49:8; Jer 3:14; 24:10; La 2:3; Eze 11:17; 18:2; 20:38; 34:13; 37:12,25; 38:8,18,19; 40:2; 48:1,23; Da 8:9; 11:16,41; Ob 1:13; Na 2:2; Mt 2:20; 8:10; Lk 7:9

MEN OF ISRAEL (23) Ex 34:23; Nu 1:18,45; 26:2,4; Dt 20:3; 29:10; Jos 9:6; 1Sa 7:11; 11:8; 13:6; 14:24; 2Sa 2:17; 19:41; 20:1,2; Ezr 2:2; 9:2; Ne 7:7; Hos 4:18; Ac 5:35; 7:26; 21:28

MOUNTAINS OF ISRAEL (13) Eze 6:2,3; 19:9; 33:28; 34:13; 35:12; 36:1,3,4,8,11; 39:2,17

PEOPLE ISRAEL (46) Dt 21:8,8; 26:15; 1Sa 10:1; 2Sa 5:2, 12; 7:7,8,10; 1Ki 8:16,30,33,36,43,52,56,59,66; 14:7; 16:2; 1Ch 11:2; 14:2; 17:7,9; 2Ch 6:5,21,24,27,33; 7:10; 31:8; 35:3; Ne 1:6; Ps 79:7; 135:12; Isa 1:3; 56:8; 58:1; Jer 10:25; 12:14; 30:7; 31:36; La 4:3; Mic 6:2; Mt 2:6; Lk 2:32

PEOPLE OF ISRAEL (410) Ge 32:32; 47:27; 48:20; Ex 3:9,13,18; 5:6; 6:5,11,13,26; 7:2; 9:26; 10:23; 11:3; 12:28,33, 35,37,40,50,51; 14:8,9,10,16,19,22,29,31; 15:1,19,22; 16:6, 17,35; 17:1,7,8; 19:3; 20:22; 25:2,8,22; 27:20,21; 28:12,38; 29:28,43,45; 30:12,31; 31:13,16; 34:30; 35:29; 39:7,42; 40:36,38; Lev 10:14; 15:31; 16:5; 17:14; 22:32; 24:2,15; 25:42,46,55; Nu 1:53; 2:34; 3:12,38,42,45,45; 5:2,6,12; 6:1, 23; 8:6,10,11,14,16,17; 9:17,17,22; 11:4; 13:26; 14:5; 15:1, 18,32,38; 16:9,34,38; 17:6,12; 18:5,8,19,20,32; 19:2,9,10; 20:1,12,13,14,24; 21:2,4,31; 22:1,41; 24:2; 25:4,13; 26:62,63; 27:8,12,14; 28:1; 29:40; 31:16,30,42,54; 32:4,7,9,18,22; 33:3, 40; 35:2,8,10,34; 36:2,13; Dt 1:1,5; 4:45; 5:1; 10:6; 27:14; 31:1,11,19,23,26; 32:9,49,51,52; 33:1; 34:8,9; Jos 4:7; 5:1; 8:33; 9:11,18,26,27; 10:4,12; 11:23; 22:20; 23:1; 24:1; Jdg 11:16,17; 1Sa 2:22,27,32; 3:20; 4:1; 7:3,16; 10:17; 13:22; 15:6; 27:12; 2Sa 3:19,21; 6:5; 15:6; 24:1,4; 1Ki 3:2; 6:1,13; 8:9; 9:7; 12:16,20; 14:15,18; 16:21; 18:19; 19:10,14; 2Ki 3:3; 8:12; 13:23; 17:6,9,11,22,24; 18:4; 1Ch 6:64; 13:5; 16:17; 2Ch 5:10; 6:11; 7:3,20; 13:12; 30:6,21; Ezr 6:16,21; 7:6,7,10, 13; 8:25,35; 9:1; 10:5,25; Ne 13:18; Ps 68:26; 103:7; 105:10, 24; 115:12; 122:4; 148:14; Isa 1:10; 2:5,6; 8:17; 9:9; 10:22; 14:1; 29:22; 33:24; 45:17,19; 48:20; 49:5,6; 60:9; 62:11; 65:9; Jer 3:20; 5:11; 7:15; 9:26; 11:17; 16:14,15; 23:7,8,13; 30:3; 31:2,31,33; 32:22; 50:4,33; 51:49; Eze 3:1,4,7; 4:3;

6:11; 7:7; 8:6,10; 9:9; 11:5; 12:6,9,10,27; 13:4; 14:4,6,11; 17:2; 18:25,29,29,30,31; 20:13,27,30,31,39,40,44; 22:18,24; 24:21; 25:14; 28:25; 33:7,10,11,20; 34:30; 35:5; 36:17,22,32; 37:11,21; 39:7,12, 22; 40:4; 43:7,10; 44:6,6,9; 45:16,17,22; 48:11; Hos 1:6; 4:1; 5:11; 7:8,11; 8:3,8,9,13; 9:1,16,17; 12:1, 14; Joel 2:27; 3:16; Am 2:6,11; 3:1; 4:12; 5:1; 6:14; 7:11,17; 8:2; 9:14; Ob 1:17; Mic 5:3,9; Zep 3:13; Zec 9:1; 10:7; Mt 10:6; 15:24; 21:5; 27:9; Jn 12:15; Ac 2:22; 3:12,26; 4:10,27; 5:31; 7:23,37,38; 9:15; 10:36; 13:16,31; Ro 9:4,27; 10:19; 11:2; 2Co 3:7,13; Heb 4:11; 8:8,10; 11:22,28,29,30; 12:25; Rev 2:14

SONS OF ISRAEL (9) Ge 50:25; Ex 13:2,19; Nu 3:41,46, 49,50; 8:18; 1Ch 2:1

TRIBE OF ISRAEL (9) Nu 1:52; 31:4,5; 36:9; Jdg 18:19; 19:29; 21:5,17; Eze 48:31

TRIBES OF ISRAEL (49) Ge 49:28; Ex 24:4; 28:9,21,29; 39:6,14; Nu 10:4; 30:1; 36:8; Dt 29:21; 33:5; Jos 7:16; 12:7; 14:1; 19:51; 21:1; Jdg 20:2; 21:15; 1Sa 15:17; 2Sa 5:1; 19:9; 1Ki 8:16; 11:32; 12:19; 14:21; 18:31; 2Ki 21:7; 1Ch 27:16, 22; 29:6; 2Ch 6:5; 7:8; 10:19; 11:13; 12:13; 33:7; Ezr 6:17; Ps 78:55; Eze 37:16; 45:1; 47:13,21; 48:1; Mt 19:28; Lk 22:30; Ac 26:7; Rev 7:4; 21:12

Ge 32:28 “It is now I, because you have struggled with both
32:32 That is why even today the people of I don’t eat
35:10 is no longer Jacob; you will now be called I.”
36:31 who ruled in Edom before there were kings in I:
47:27 So the people of I settled in the land of Goshen in
48:20 “The people of I will use your names to bless each
49: 2 O sons of Jacob; / listen to I, your father.
49: 7 their descendants / throughout the nation of I.
49:16 will govern his people / like any other tribe in I.
49:24 One of Jacob, / the Shepherd, the Rock of I.
49:28 These are the twelve tribes of I, and these are the
50:25 Then Joseph made the sons of I swear an oath,
Ex 3: 9 The cries of the people of I have reached me,
3:13 “If I go to the people of I and tell them,
3:16 “Now go and call together all the leaders of I.
3:18 “The leaders of the people of I will accept your
4:22 is what the LORD says: I is my firstborn son.
4:29 to Egypt and called the leaders of I to a meeting.
5: 1 “This is what the LORD, the God of I, says:
5: 2 the LORD that I should listen to him and let I go?
5: 2 I don’t know the LORD, and I will not let I go.”
5: 6 and foremen he had set over the people of I:
6: 5 sure that I have heard the groans of the people of I,
6:11 and tell him to let the people of I leave Egypt.”
6:13 and to demand that he let the people of I leave
6:26 “Lead all the people of I out of the land of Egypt,
7: 2 He will demand that the people of I be allowed to
7: 4 after which I will lead the forces of I out with great
9:26 the land of Goshen, where the people of I lived.
10:23 But there was light as usual where the people of I
11: 3 the Egyptians to look favorably on the people of I,
12:15 festival will be cut off from the community of I.
12:19 this week will be cut off from the community of I.
12:21 Then Moses called for the leaders of I and said,
12:28 So the people of I did just as the LORD had
12:33 All the Egyptians urged the people of I to get out
12:35 And the people of I did as Moses had instructed
12:37 That night the people of I left Rameses and started
12:40 The people of I had lived in Egypt for 430 years.
12:47 The whole community of I must celebrate this
12:50 So the people of I followed all the LORD’s
12:51 LORD began to lead the people of I out of Egypt,
13: 2 “Dedicate to me all the firstborn sons of I
13:19 for Joseph had made the sons of I swear that they
14: 8 and he chased after the people of I who had
14: 9 The Egyptians caught up with the people of I as
14:10 the people of I could see them in the distance,
14:16 Then all the people of I will walk through on dry
14:19 of God, who had been leading the people of I,
14:22 So the people of I walked through the sea on dry
14:25 “The LORD is fighting for I against us!”
14:29 The people of I had walked through the middle of
14:30 This was how the LORD rescued I from the
14:31 When the people of I saw the mighty power that
15: 1 and the people of I sang this song to the LORD:
15:19 But the people of I had walked through on dry
15:22 Then Moses led the people of I away from the Red
16: 2 the whole community of I spoke bitterly against
16: 6 and Aaron called a meeting of all the people of I
16: 9 to Aaron, “Say this to the entire community of I:
16:17 So the people of I went out and gathered this
16:35 So the people of I ate manna for forty years until
17: 1 the people of I left the Sin Desert and moved from
17: 5 Then call some of the leaders of I and walk on
17: 7 because the people of I argued with Moses
17: 8 While the people of I were still at Rephidim,
18: 8 the LORD had done to rescue I from Pharaoh
18: 9 had done for I as he brought them out of Egypt.
18:10 He has rescued I from the power of Egypt!
18:12 Aaron and the leaders of I came out to meet him.
18:25 He chose capable men from all over I and made
19: 3 to the descendants of Jacob, the people of I:
20:22 said to Moses, “Say this to the people of I:
21: 1 are some other instructions you must present to I:
23:17 every man in I must appear before the Sovereign
24: 4 the altar, one for each of the twelve tribes of I.
24: 9 and seventy of the leaders of I went up the
24:10 There they saw the God of I. Under his feet there
25: 2 “Tell the people of I that everyone who wants to
25: 8 “I want the people of I to build me a sacred
25:22 I will give you my commands for the people of I.
27:20 “Tell the people of I to bring you pure olive oil for
27:21 This is a permanent law for the people of I, and it
28: 9 and engrave on them the names of the tribes of I.
28:12 the ephod as memorial stones for the people of I.
28:21 Each stone will represent one of the tribes of I,
28:29 Aaron will carry the names of the tribes of I on the
28:38 regarding the sacred offerings of the people of I.
29:28 whenever the people of I offer up peace offerings
29:43 I will meet the people of I there,
29:45 I will live among the people of I and be their God,
30:12 “Whenever you take a census of the people of I,
30:31 And say to the people of I, ‘This will always be
31:13 “Tell the people of I to keep my Sabbath day,
31:16 The people of I must keep the Sabbath day forever.
32: 4 The people exclaimed, “O I, these are the gods
32: 8 They are saying, ‘These are your gods, O I,
32:27 “This is what the LORD, the God of I, says:
34:23 Three times each year all the men of I must appear before the Sovereign LORD, the God of I.
34:27 the terms of my covenant with you and with I.”
34:30 and the people of I saw the radiance of Moses’
35:29 So the people of I—every man and woman who
39: 6 were engraved with the names of the tribes of I,
39: 7 to the LORD concerning the people of I.
39:14 each with the name of one of the twelve tribes of I.
39:42 So the people of I followed all of the LORD’s
40:36 the people of I would set out on their journey,
40:38 fire in the cloud so all the people of I could see it.
Lev 4:21 This is a sin offering for the entire community of I.
4:27 “If any of the citizens of I do something forbidden
8: 3 Then call the entire community of I to meet you
9: 1 together Aaron and his sons and the leaders of I.
10: 6 will be angry with the whole community of I.
10:14 of the peace offerings presented by the people of I.
15:31 you will keep the people of I separate from things
16: 5 The people of I must then bring him two male
16:27 into the Most Holy Place to make atonement for I,
17:14 That is why I have told the people of I never to eat
18:29 things will be cut off from the community of I.
19: 2 “Say this to the entire community of I: You must
22:32 I must be treated as holy by the people of I. It is I,
24: 2 “Command the people of I to provide you with
24:15 Say to the people of I: Those who blaspheme God
24:16 be stoned to death by the whole community of I.
25:33 the Levites are the only property they own in all I.
25:42 The people of I are my servants, whom I brought
25:46 but the people of I, your relatives, must never be
25:55 For the people of I are my servants, whom I
Nu 1: 2 “Take a census of the whole community of I by
1:18 called together the whole community of I on that
1:18 The men of I twenty years old or older were
1:44 by Moses and Aaron and the twelve leaders of I,
1:45 all the men of I who were twenty years old or older
1:52 Each tribe of I will have a designated camping area
1:53 of I protection from the LORD’s fierce anger.
2:32 the troops of I listed by their families totaled
2:34 So the people of I did everything just as the
3:12 for all the firstborn sons of the people of I.
3:13 I set apart for myself all the firstborn in I of both
3:38 for the sanctuary on behalf of the people of I.
3:40 “Now count all the firstborn sons in I who are one
3:41 for me as substitutes for the firstborn sons of I;
3:41 the firstborn livestock of the whole nation of I.”
3:42 counted the firstborn sons of the people of I,
3:45 in place of the firstborn sons of the people of I.
3:45 for the firstborn livestock of the people of I.
3:46 To redeem the 273 firstborn sons of I who are in
3:49 sons of I who exceeded the number of Levites.
3:50 of I came to about thirty-four pounds in weight.
4:46 and the leaders of I counted all the Levites by their
5: 2 “Command the people of I to remove anyone from
5: 6 “Give these instructions to the people of I: If any
5:12 “Say to the people of I: ‘Suppose a man’s wife
6: 1 “Speak to the people of I and give them these
6:23 and his sons to bless the people of I with this
7: 2 Then the leaders of I—the tribal leaders who had
7:84 brought by the leaders of I at the time it was
8: 6 set the Levites apart from the rest of the people of I
8: 9 Then assemble the whole community of I
8:10 the people of I must lay their hands on them.
8:11 LORD as a special offering from the people of I,
8:14 the Levites apart from the rest of the people of I,
8:16 “Of all the people of I, the Levites are reserved for
8:17 For all the firstborn males among the people of I
8:18 the Levites in place of all the firstborn sons of I.
8:20 and the whole community of I dedicated the
9:13 will be cut off from the community of I for failing
9:17 over the sacred tent, the people of I followed it.
9:17 wherever the cloud settled, the people of I camped.
9:22 the people of I stayed in camp and did not move
10: 4 then only the leaders of the tribes of I will come to
10:29 the LORD has given wonderful promises to I!”
10:36 O LORD, to the countless thousands of I!”
11: 4 and the people of I also began to complain.
11:16 “Summon before me seventy of the leaders of I.
11:30 Moses returned to the camp with the leaders of I.
13: 2 the land of Canaan, the land I am giving to I.
13: 3 He sent out twelve men, all tribal leaders of I,
13:26 and the people of I at Kadesh in the wilderness of
14: 5 face down on the ground before the people of I.
14: 7 They said to the community of I, “The land we
15: 1 Moses to give these instructions to the people of I:
15:18 “Give the people of I the following instructions:
15:25 make atonement for the whole community of I,
15:26 The whole community of I will be forgiven,
15:32 One day while the people of I were in the
15:38 “Say to the people of I:
16: 3 Everyone in I has been set apart by the LORD,
16: 9 Does it seem a small thing to you that the God of I
16: 9 I to be near him as you serve in the LORD’s
16:34 All of the people of I fled as they heard their
16:38 then serve as a warning to the people of I.”
17: 6 So Moses gave the instructions to the people of I,
17:12 Then the people of I said to Moses, “We are as
18: 5 will never again blaze against the people of I.
18: 8 holy gifts that are brought to me by the people of I.
18:19 offerings that the people of I bring to the LORD.
18:20 of land or share of property among the people of I.
18:21 Tabernacle with the tithes from the entire land of I.
18:32 of the people of I as though they were common.
19: 2 Tell the people of I to bring you a red heifer that
19: 9 They will be kept there for the people of I to use in
19:10 This is a permanent law for the people of I and any
19:13 and will be cut off from the community of I.
20: 1 In early spring the people of I arrived in the
20:12 to demonstrate my holiness to the people of I,
20:13 because it was where the people of I argued with
20:14 message is from your relatives, the people of I:
20:21 Because Edom refused to allow I to pass through their country, I was forced to turn around.
20:22 The whole community of I left Kadesh as a group
20:24 will not enter the land I am giving the people of I,
20:29 Aaron had died, all I mourned for him thirty days.
21: 2 Then the people of I made this vow to the LORD:
21: 4 Then the people of I set out from Mount Hor,
21:23 his entire army and attacked I in the wilderness,
21:25 So I captured all the towns of the Amorites
21:31 So the people of I occupied the territory of the
21:35 And I was victorious and killed King Og, his sons,
21:35 survivor remained. Then I occupied their land.
22: 1 Then the people of I traveled to the plains of Moab
22: 7 took money with them to pay Balaam to curse I.
22:41 From there he could see the people of I spread out
23:13 There you will see only a portion of the nation of I.
23:21 is in sight for Jacob; / no trouble is in store for I.
23:23 touch Jacob; / no sorcery has any power against I.
23:23 of Jacob, / ‘What wonders God has done for I!’
24: 1 realized that the LORD intended to bless I,
24: 2 where he saw the people of I camped, tribe by
24: 5 O Jacob; / how lovely are your homes, O I!
24: 9 Like a lion, I crouches and lies down; / like a
24: 9 Blessed is everyone who blesses you, O I,
24:17 rise from Jacob; / a scepter will emerge from I.
24:18 be conquered, / while I continues on in triumph.
25: 3 Before long I was joining in the worship of Baal of
25: 4 fierce anger will turn away from the people of I.”
25:11 So I have stopped destroying all I as I had intended
25:13 his God and made atonement for the people of I.”
26: 2 “Take a census of all the men of I who are twenty
26: 3 At that time the entire nation of I was camped on
26: 3 issued these census instructions to the leaders of I:
26: 4 “Count all the men of I twenty years old
26: 4 This is the census record of all the descendants of I
26:10 This served as a warning to the entire nation of I.
26:62 in the total census figure of the people of I
26:63 So these are the census figures of the people of I as
27: 8 Moreover announce this to the people of I: ‘If a
27:12 look out over the land I have given the people of I.
27:14 When the people of I rebelled, you failed to
27:20 so the whole community of I will obey him.
27:21 and the rest of the community of I will discover
28: 1 “Give these instructions to the people of I:
29:40 gave all of these instructions to the people of I,
30: 1 Moses summoned the leaders of the tribes of I
31: 4 From each tribe of I, send one thousand men into
31: 5 they chose one thousand men from each tribe of I,
31:12 the priest, and to the whole community of I,
31:16 and caused the people of I to rebel against the
31:30 goats in the half that belongs to the people of I.
31:42 half of the plunder belonging to the people of I,
31:54 to the LORD that the people of I belong to him.
32: 4 has conquered this whole area for the people of I.
32: 7 I from going across to the land the LORD has
32: 9 they discouraged the people of I from entering the
32:13 “The LORD was furious with I and made them
32:14 You are making the LORD even angrier with I.
32:18 people of I have received their inheritance of land.
32:22 to the LORD and to the rest of the people of I.
32:28 to Eleazar, Joshua, and the tribal leaders of I.
33: 3 The people of I left defiantly, in full view of all the
33:40 heard that the people of I were approaching his
35: 1 While I was camped beside the Jordan on the
35: 2 “Instruct the people of I to give to the Levites
35: 8 will come from the property of the people of I.
35:10 “Say this to the people of I: ‘When you cross the
35:34 the LORD, who lives among the people of I.’ ”
36: 1 and the family leaders of I with a petition.
36: 2 the land by sacred lot among the people of I.
36: 8 The daughters throughout the tribes of I who are in
36: 9 each tribe of I must hold on to its allotted
36:13 I through Moses while they were camped on the
Dt 1: 1 I while they were in the wilderness east of the
1: 5 So Moses addressed the people of I while they
2:12 from the land that the LORD had assigned to I.)
4: 1 “And now, I, listen carefully to these laws
4:45 and regulations that Moses gave to the people of I
4:47 I conquered his land and that of King Og of
4:48 So I conquered all the area from Aroer at the edge
5: 1 Moses called all the people of I together and said,
6: 3 Listen closely, I, to everything I say. Be careful to
6: 4 “Hear, O I! The LORD is our God, the LORD
9: 1 “Hear, O I! Today you are about to cross the
10: 6 “The people of I set out from the wells of the
10:12 “And now, I, what does the LORD your God
13:11 Then all I will hear about it and be afraid, and such
16:16 “Each year every man in I must celebrate these

17: 4 is true that this detestable thing has been done in **I**,
17:12 be put to death. Such evil must be purged from **I**.
17:20 descendants will reign for many generations in **I**.
18: 1 an inheritance of land like the other tribes in **I**.
18: 6 so desires may come from any town in **I**,
19:13 Purge the guilt of murder from **I** so all may go well
20: 3 He will say, 'Listen to me, all you men of **I**!
21: 8 forgive your people **I** whom you have redeemed.
21: 8 Do not charge your people **I** with the guilt of
21:21 and all **I** will hear about it and be afraid.
22:19 pieces of silver, for he falsely accused a virgin of **I**.
22:21 She has committed a disgraceful crime in **I** by
22:22 In this way, the evil will be cleansed from **I**.
25: 6 so that his name will not be forgotten in **I**.
25: 7 refuses to preserve his brother's name in **I**—
26:15 and bless your people **I** and the land you have
27: 1 and the leaders of **I** charged the people as follows:
27: 9 and the Levitical priests addressed all **I** as follows: "O **I**, be quiet and listen!
27:14 Then the Levites must shout to all the people of **I**:
29:10 your judges, your officers, all the men of **I**—
29:15 and also with all future generations of **I**.
29:21 LORD will separate them from all the tribes of **I**,
31: 1 finished saying these things to all the people of **I**,
31: 7 and as all **I** watched he said to him, "Be strong
31: 9 of the LORD's covenant, and to the leaders of **I**.
31:11 you must read this law to all the people of **I** when
31:19 words of this song, and teach it to the people of **I**.
31:23 You must bring the people of **I** into the land I
31:26 so it may serve as a witness against the people of **I**.
31:30 Moses recited this entire song to the assembly of **I**:
32: 9 For the people of **I** belong to the LORD;
32:15 But **I** soon became fat and unruly; / the people
32:28 "**I** is a nation that lacks sense; / the people are
32:45 Moses had finished reciting these words to **I**,
32:49 the land I am giving to the people of **I** as their own
32:51 demonstrate my holiness to the people of **I** there.
32:52 not enter the land I am giving to the people of **I**."
33: 1 of God, gave to the people of **I** before his death:
33: 4 the special possession of the assembly of **I**.
33: 5 The LORD became king in **I**— / when the leaders
33: 5 people assembled, / when the tribes of **I** gathered."
33:10 to Jacob; / let them give your instructions to **I**.
33:21 and obeyed his regulations for **I**."
33:26 "There is no one like the God of **I**. / He rides
33:28 So **I** will live in safety, / prosperous Jacob in
33:29 How blessed you are, O **I**! / Who else is like you,
34: 8 The people of **I** mourned thirty days for Moses on
34: 9 So the people of **I** obeyed him and did everything
34:12 and terrifying acts in the sight of all **I**.
Jos 1:10 Joshua then commanded the leaders of **I**,
4: 7 as a permanent memorial among the people of **I**."
5: 1 up the Jordan River so the people of **I** could cross,
5: 3 and circumcised the entire male population of **I** at
6:18 and you will bring trouble on all **I**.
6:23 whole family to a safe place near the camp of **I**.
7: 1 But **I** was unfaithful concerning the things set apart
7: 6 and the leaders of **I** tore their clothing in dismay,
7: 8 am I to say, now that **I** has fled from its enemies?
7:11 **I** has sinned and broken my covenant! They have
7:12 For now **I** has been set apart for destruction.
7:13 For this is what the LORD, the God of **I**, says:
7:13 Hidden among you, O **I**, are things set apart for the
7:15 of the LORD and has done a horrible thing in **I**."
7:16 Joshua brought the tribes of **I** before the LORD,
7:19 to the LORD, the God of **I**, by telling the truth.
7:20 "I have sinned against the LORD, the God of **I**.
8: 3 So Joshua and the army of **I** set out to attack Ai.
8:10 started toward Ai, accompanied by the leaders of **I**.
8:30 altar to the LORD, the God of **I**, on Mount Ebal.
8:33 the LORD, had given for blessing the people of **I**.
9: 6 When they arrived at the camp of **I** at Gilgal, they told Joshua and the men of **I**,
9:11 Go meet with the people of **I** and declare our
9:15 and the leaders of **I** ratified their agreement with a
9:18 had made a vow to the LORD, the God of **I**.
9:18 The people of **I** grumbled against their leaders
9:19 oath in the presence of the LORD, the God of **I**.
9:26 Joshua did not allow the people of **I** to kill them.
9:27 and water carriers for the people of **I** and for the
10: 1 learned that the Gibeonites had made peace with **I**
10: 4 have made peace with Joshua and the people of **I**."
10:12 to the LORD in front of all the people of **I**.
10:14 The LORD fought for **I** that day. Never before
10:21 After that, no one dared to speak a word against **I**.
10:40 just as the LORD, the God of **I**, had commanded.
10:42 and their land, for the LORD, the God of **I**,
11: 4 their warriors and uniting to fight against **I**.
11: 5 around the water near Merom to fight against **I**.
11:16 and the mountains and lowlands of **I**.
11:21 Anab, and the entire hill country of Judah and **I**.
11:22 Not one was left in all the land of **I**, though some
11:23 He gave it to the people of **I** as their special
12: 7 (Joshua allotted this land to the tribes of **I** as their
12: 8 and the Jebusites.) These are the kings **I** defeated:
13: 6 So be sure to give this land to **I** as a special
13:14 burned on the altar to the LORD, the God of **I**.
13:33 for the LORD, the God of **I**, had promised to be
14: 1 The remaining tribes of **I** inherited land in Canaan
14:10 even while **I** wandered in the wilderness.
14:14 wholeheartedly followed the LORD, the God of **I**.
19:51 **I** by casting sacred lots in the presence of the
21: 1 son of Nun, and the leaders of the other tribes of **I**.
21:43 So the LORD gave to **I** all the land he had sworn
21:45 promises that the LORD had given **I** came true.
22: 9 and the half-tribe of Manasseh left the rest of **I** at
22:11 When the rest of **I** heard they had built the altar at
22:14 In this delegation were ten high officials of **I**,
22:14 and each a leader within the family divisions of **I**.
22:16 to know why you are betraying the God of **I**.
22:20 Didn't God punish all the people of **I** when Achan,
22:22 But the LORD knows, and let all **I** know, too,
22:24 do you have to worship the LORD, the God of **I**?
22:31 you have rescued **I** from being destroyed by the
23: 1 and the LORD had given the people of **I** rest from
23: 2 all the elders, leaders, judges, and officers of **I**.
24: 1 Then Joshua summoned all the people of **I** to
24: 2 "This is what the LORD, the God of **I**, says:
24: 9 of Zippor, king of Moab, started a war against **I**.
24:23 and turn your hearts to the LORD, the God of **I**."
24:31 **I** served the LORD throughout the lifetime of
24:31 experienced all that the LORD had done for **I**.
Jdg 2: 7 seen all the great things the LORD had done for **I**.
2:10 or remember the mighty things he had done for **I**.
2:14 This made the LORD burn with anger against **I**,
2:15 Every time **I** went out to battle, the LORD fought
2:17 Yet **I** did not listen to the judges but prostituted
2:18 Whenever the LORD placed a judge over **I**,
2:20 So the LORD burned with anger against **I**.
2:22 I did this to test **I**—to see whether or not they
3: 5 So **I** lived among the Canaanites, Hittites,
3: 8 Then the LORD burned with anger against **I**,
3: 9 But when **I** cried out to the LORD for help,
3:12 LORD gave King Eglon of Moab control over **I**.
3:13 Eglon attacked **I** and took possession of Jericho.
3:15 But when **I** cried out to the LORD for help,
3:30 So Moab was conquered by **I** that day, and the land
3:31 After Ehud, Shamgar son of Anath rescued **I**.
4: 4 was a prophet who had become a judge in **I**.
4: 6 is what the LORD, the God of **I**, commands you:
4:23 So on that day **I** saw God subdue Jabin,
4:24 And from that time on **I** became stronger
5: 3 I will lift up my song to the LORD, the God of **I**.
5: 5 shook in the presence of the LORD, the God of **I**.
5: 7 There were few people left in the villages of **I**— / until Deborah arose as a mother for **I**.
5: 8 When **I** chose new gods, / war erupted at the city
5: 8 could be seen / among forty thousand warriors in **I**!
5:11 the LORD, / and the victories of his villagers in **I**.
6: 3 Amalek, and the people of the east would attack **I**,
6: 6 So **I** was reduced to starvation by the Midianites.
6: 8 "This is what the LORD, the God of **I**, says:
6:14 you have and rescue **I** from the Midianites.
6:15 "But Lord," Gideon replied, "how can I rescue **I**?
6:33 the people of the east formed an alliance against **I**
6:36 "If you are truly going to use me to rescue **I** as
6:37 are going to help me rescue **I** as you promised."
8:28 That is the story of how **I** subdued Midian,
8:35 Gideon), despite all the good he had done for **I**.
9:22 After Abimelech had ruled over **I** for three years,
10: 1 of Puah and descendant of Dodo, came to rescue **I**.
10: 3 a man from Gilead named Jair judged **I** for
10: 7 So the LORD burned with anger against **I**,
11: 4 this time, the Ammonites began their war against **I**.
11:12 demanding to know why **I** was being attacked.
11:15 **I** did not steal any land from Moab or Ammon.
11:16 When the people of **I** arrived at Kadesh on their
11:17 So the people of **I** stayed in Kadesh.
11:19 "Then **I** sent messengers to King Sihon of the
11:20 But King Sihon didn't trust **I** to pass through his
11:21 But the LORD, the God of **I**, gave his people
11:21 So **I** took control of all the land of the Amorites,
11:23 "So you see, it was the LORD, the God of **I**,
11:23 away the land from the Amorites and gave it to **I**.
11:25 Did he try to make a case against **I** for disputed
11:26 **I** has been living here all this time, spread across
11:27 decide today which of us is right—**I** or Ammon."
11:33 as Abel-keramim. Thus **I** subdued the Ammonites.
11:39 she died a virgin. So it has become a custom in **I**
12: 9 to marry his sons. Ibzan judged **I** for seven years.
12:11 became Israel's judge. He judged **I** for ten years.
13: 5 from birth. He will rescue **I** from the Philistines."
14: 4 the Philistines, who ruled over **I** at that time.
17: 6 In those days **I** had no king, so the people did
18: 1 Now in those days **I** had no king. And the tribe of
18:19 Isn't it better to be a priest for an entire tribe of **I**
19: 1 Now in those days **I** had no king. There was a man
19:29 Then he sent one piece to each tribe of **I**.
19:30 crime has not been committed since **I** left Egypt.
20: 2 leaders of all the people and all the tribes of **I**—
20: 6 and sent the pieces throughout the land of **I**,
20: 7 the entire community of **I** must decide what should
20:10 for this shameful thing they have done in **I**."
20:13 so we can execute them and purge **I** of this evil."
20:17 **I** had 400,000 warriors armed with swords,
20:35 So the LORD helped **I** defeat Benjamin, and that
20:45 but **I** killed five thousand of them along the road.
21: 3 "O LORD, God of **I**," they cried out, "why has
21: 5 "Was any tribe of **I** not represented when we held
21:15 the LORD had left this gap in the tribes of **I**.
21:17 so that an entire tribe of **I** will not be lost forever.
21:24 So the assembly of **I** departed by tribes
21:25 In those days **I** had no king, so the people did
Ru 1: 1 In the days when the judges ruled in **I**, a man from
2:12 May the LORD, the God of **I**, under whose wings
4: 7 In those days it was the custom in **I** for anyone
4:11 from whom all the nation of **I** descended!
4:14 a family redeemer today! May he be famous in **I**.
1Sa 1:17 May the God of **I** grant the request you have asked
2:22 of what his sons were doing to the people of **I**.
2:27 when the people of **I** were slaves in Egypt?
2:30 "Therefore, the LORD, the God of **I**, says:
2:32 envy as I pour out prosperity on the people of **I**.
3:11 to Samuel, "I am about to do a shocking thing in **I**.
3:20 All the people of **I** from one end of the land to the
4: 1 Samuel's words went out to all the people of **I**.
4: 1 At that time **I** was at war with the Philistines.
4: 2 Philistines attacked and defeated the army of **I**,
4: 3 the army of **I** retreated to their camp, and their
4: 8 Who can save us from these mighty gods of **I**?
4: 8 with plagues when **I** was in the wilderness.
4:10 fought desperately, and **I** was defeated again.
4:17 "**I** has been defeated," the messenger replied.
4:18 was old and very fat. He had led **I** for forty years.
4:22 Then she said, "The glory has departed from **I**,
5: 7 "We can't keep the Ark of the God of **I** here any
5: 8 should we do with the Ark of the God of **I**?"
5: 8 So they moved the Ark of the God of **I** to Gath.
5:10 "They are bringing the Ark of the God of **I** here to
5:11 "Please send the Ark of the God of **I** back to its
6: 3 "Send the Ark of the God of **I** back, along with a
6: 5 Make these things to show honor to the God of **I**.
6: 6 They wouldn't let **I** go until God had ravaged them
7: 2 all **I** mourned because it seemed that the LORD
7: 3 Then Samuel said to all the people of **I**, "If you
7: 7 When the Philistine rulers heard that all **I** had
7: 9 He pleaded with the LORD to help **I**,
7:11 The men of **I** chased them from Mizpah to
7:13 and didn't invade **I** again for a long time.
7:14 that the Philistines had captured were restored to **I**,
7:14 And there was also peace between **I**
7:16 He judged the people of **I** at each of these places.
8: 1 he appointed his sons to be judges over **I**.
8: 4 the leaders of **I** met at Ramah to discuss the matter
9: 2 His son Saul was the most handsome man in **I**—
9:16 Anoint him to be the leader of my people, **I**.
9:21 I'm only from Benjamin, the smallest tribe in **I**,
10: 1 has appointed you to be the leader of his people **I**.
10:17 Later Samuel called all the people of **I** to meet
10:18 them this message from the LORD, the God of **I**:
10:24 No one in all **I** is his equal!" And all the people
11: 2 eye of every one of you as a disgrace to all **I**!"
11: 3 us seven days to send messengers throughout **I**!"
11: 7 and sent the messengers to carry them throughout **I**
11: 8 he found that there were 300,000 men of **I**,
11:13 for today the LORD has rescued **I**!"
13: 2 three thousand special troops from the army of **I**
13: 3 quickly among the Philistines that **I** was in revolt,
13: 3 so Saul sounded the call to arms throughout **I**.
13: 6 When the men of **I** saw the vast number of enemy
13:13 have established your kingdom over **I** forever.
13:19 There were no blacksmiths in the land of **I** in those
13:22 So none of the people of **I** had a sword or spear,
14:23 So the LORD saved **I** that day, and the battle
14:24 Now the men of **I** were worn out that day,
14:39 I vow by the name of the LORD who rescued **I**
14:41 Then Saul prayed, "O LORD, God of **I**,
14:45 "Should Jonathan, who saved **I** today, die?
14:48 saving **I** from all those who had plundered them.
15: 1 "I anointed you king of **I** because the LORD told
15: 2 for opposing **I** when they came from Egypt.
15: 6 For you were kind to the people of **I** when they
15:17 are you not the leader of the tribes of **I**? The LORD has anointed you king of **I**.
15:26 he has rejected you from being the king of **I**."
15:28 The LORD has torn the kingdom of **I** from you
15:29 And he who is the Glory of **I** will not lie, nor will
15:35 was sorry he had ever made Saul king of **I**.
16: 1 I have rejected him as king of **I**. Now fill your horn
17: 4 out of the Philistine ranks to face the forces of **I**.
17:10 I defy the armies of **I**! Send me a man who will
17:23 shouting his challenge to the army of **I**.
17:25 "He comes out each day to challenge **I**.
17:26 and putting an end to his abuse of **I**?"
17:45 the God of the armies of **I**, whom you have defied.
17:46 the whole world will know that there is a God in **I**!
18:16 But all **I** and Judah loved David because he was
18:18 and what is my family in **I** that I should be the
19: 5 and how the LORD brought a great victory to **I** as
20:12 "I promise by the LORD, the God of **I**,
23:10 And David prayed, "O LORD, God of **I**, I have
23:11 O LORD, God of **I**, please tell me."
23:17 You are going to be the king of **I**, and I will be
23:27 Saul that the Philistines were raiding **I** again.
24: 2 three thousand special troops from throughout **I**
24:14 Who is the king of **I** trying to catch anyway?
24:20 to be king, and **I** will flourish under your rule.
25: 1 Samuel died, and all **I** gathered for his funeral.
25:30 done all he promised and has made you leader of **I**,
25:32 to Abigail, "Praise the LORD, the God of **I**,
25:34 For I swear by the LORD, the God of **I**, who has
26:15 "Where in all **I** is there anyone as mighty?
26:20 Why has the king of **I** come out to search for a
27:12 "By now the people of **I** must hate him bitterly.
28: 1 mustered their armies for another war with **I**.
28: 3 Samuel had died, and all **I** had mourned for him.
28: 3 all mediums and psychics from the land of **I**.
28: 4 and Saul and the armies of **I** camped at Gilboa.
28:19 and the army of **I** over to the Philistines tomorrow,
28:19 The LORD will bring the entire army of **I** down
29: 3 the man who ran away from King Saul of **I**.
29: 5 about whom the women of **I** sing in their dances,
30:25 From then on David made this a law for all of **I**,
31: 1 Now the Philistines attacked **I**,
2Sa 1:12 and for the LORD's army and the nation of **I**,
1:19 Your pride and joy, O **I**, lies dead on the hills!
1:24 O women of **I**, weep for Saul, / for he dressed you
2: 9 the land of the Ashurites, and all the rest of **I**.
2:17 and the men of **I** had been defeated by the forces of
2:28 and his men stopped chasing the troops of **I**.
3:10 I should set him up as king over **I** as well as Judah,

3:12 and I will help turn the entire nation of **I** over to
3:17 Abner had consulted with the leaders of **I**.
3:19 went to Hebron to tell David that all the people of **I**
3:21 me go and call all the people of **I** to your side.
3:37 and **I** knew that David was not responsible for
3:38 great leader and a great man has fallen today in **I**?
5: 1 Then all the tribes of **I** went to David at Hebron
5: 2 was our king, you were the one who really led **I**.
5: 2 'You will be the shepherd of my people **I**.
5: 3 David made a covenant with the leaders of **I**
before the LORD. And they anointed him king of **I**.
5: 5 and from Jerusalem he reigned over all **I** and Judah
5:12 realized that the LORD had made him king over **I**
5:12 his kingdom great for the sake of his people **I**.
5:17 heard that David had been anointed king of **I**,
6: 5 and all the people of **I** were celebrating before the
6:15 and all **I** brought up the Ark of the LORD with
6:19 gave a gift of food to every man and woman in **I**:
6:20 "How glorious the king of **I** looked today!
6:21 He appointed me as the leader of **I**, the people of
7: 7 to Israel's leaders, the shepherds of my people **I**.
7: 8 I chose you to lead my people **I** when you were
7:10 provided a permanent homeland for my people **I**,
7:23 What other nation on earth is like **I**? What other
7:24 You made **I** your people forever, and you,
7:26 will say, 'The LORD Almighty is God over **I**!'
7:27 "O LORD Almighty, God of **I**, I have been bold
8:15 David reigned over all **I** and was fair to everyone.
10:15 now realized that they were no match for **I**.
10:17 he mobilized all **I**, crossed the Jordan River,
10:19 allies realized they had been defeated by **I**,
11:11 "The Ark and the armies of **I** and Judah are living
12: 7 The LORD, the God of **I**, says, 'I anointed you king
of **I** and saved you from the
12: 8 and his wives and the kingdoms of **I** and Judah.
12:12 I will do this to you openly in the sight of all **I**.' "
13:12 what a serious crime it is to do such a thing in **I**.
13:13 you would be called one of the greatest fools in **I**.
14:25 Now no one in **I** was as handsome as Absalom.
15: 6 Absalom stole the hearts of all the people of **I**.
15:10 he sent secret messengers to every part of **I** to stir
15:13 "All **I** has joined Absalom in a conspiracy against
15:19 for you are a guest in **I**, a foreigner in exile.
16:18 the man who is chosen by the LORD and by **I**,"
16:21 Then all **I** will know that you have insulted him
17: 4 good to Absalom and to all the other leaders of **I**.
17:10 For all **I** knows what a mighty man your father is
17:11 "I suggest that you mobilize the entire army of **I**,
17:13 you will have the entire army of **I** there at your
17:14 Then Absalom and all the leaders of **I** said,
17:24 Absalom had mobilized the entire army of **I**
18:16 and his men returned from chasing the army of **I**.
18:17 over it. And the army of **I** fled to their homes.
19: 9 And throughout the tribes of **I** there was much
19:11 For I have heard that all **I** is ready, and only you
19:20 the very first person in all **I** to greet you."
19:22 but for celebration! I am once again the king of **I**!"
19:40 and half the army of **I** escorted him across the
19:41 But the men of **I** complained to the king that the
19:43 "But there are ten tribes in **I**," the others replied.
20: 1 Come on, you men of **I**, let's all go home!"
20: 2 So the men of **I** deserted David and followed
20:14 Sheba had traveled across **I** to mobilize his own
20:19 I am one who is peace loving and faithful in **I**.
21: 2 They were not part of **I** but were all that was left of
21: 2 **I** had sworn not to kill them, but Saul, in his zeal,
21: 5 to keep us from having any place at all in **I**.
21:14 After that, God ended the famine in the land of **I**.
21:15 Once again the Philistines were at war with **I**.
21:17 Why should we risk snuffing out the light of **I**?"
21:21 defied and taunted **I**. But he was killed by
23: 1 the God of Jacob, / David, the sweet psalmist of **I**.
23: 3 The God of **I** spoke. / The Rock of **I** said to me:
24: 1 again the anger of the LORD burned against **I**,
24: 1 "Go and count the people of **I** and Judah,"
24: 4 and his officers went out to count the people of **I**.
24: 9 There were 800,000 men of military age in **I**
24:15 So the LORD sent a plague upon **I** that morning,
1Ki 1:20 all **I** is waiting for your decision as to who will
1:30 I swore to you before the LORD, the God of **I**."
1:34 Nathan the prophet are to anoint him king over **I**.
1:35 for I have appointed him to be ruler over **I**
1:48 'Blessed be the LORD, the God of **I**, who today
2: 4 one of them will always sit on the throne of **I**.'
2:11 He had reigned over **I** for forty years, seven of
2:32 commander of the army of **I**, and Amasa son of
3: 2 At that time the people of **I** sacrificed their
3:28 the king's decision spread quickly throughout all **I**,
4: 1 So Solomon was king over all **I**,
4: 7 had twelve district governors who were over all **I**.
4:20 and **I** were as numerous as the sand on the
4:25 all of Judah and **I** lived in peace and safety.
5: 1 that David's son Solomon was the new king of **I**,
5: 7 a wise son to be king of the great nation of **I**."
5:13 enlisted thirty thousand laborers from all **I**.
6: 1 This was 480 years after the people of **I** were
6:13 I will live among the people of **I** and never forsake
8: 1 and families of **I** to assemble in Jerusalem.
8: 3 When all the leaders of **I** arrived, the priests picked
8: 5 and the entire community of **I** sacrificed sheep
8: 9 people of **I** as they were leaving the land of Egypt.
8:14 to the entire community of **I** standing before him
8:15 "Blessed be the LORD, the God of **I**, who has
8:16 'From the day I brought my people **I** out of Egypt,
8:16 I have never chosen a city among the tribes of **I** as
8:17 to honor the name of the LORD, the God of **I**.
8:20 to honor the name of the LORD, the God of **I**.
8:22 the LORD in front of the entire community of **I**.
8:23 He prayed, "O LORD, God of **I**, there is no God
8:25 And now, O LORD, God of **I**, carry out your
8:25 as you have done, they will always reign over **I**.'
8:26 Now, O God of **I**, fulfill this promise to your
8:30 and your people **I** when we pray toward this place.
8:33 "If your people **I** are defeated by their enemies
8:36 forgive the sins of your servants, your people **I**.
8:43 and fear you, just as your own people **I** do.
8:52 to my requests and to the requests of your people **I**.
8:53 **I** from among all the nations of the earth to be your
8:55 this blessing over the entire community of **I**:
8:56 the LORD who has given rest to his people **I**,
8:59 uphold my cause and the cause of his people **I**,
8:62 and all **I** with him offered sacrifices to the LORD.
8:63 and all **I** dedicated the Temple of the LORD.
8:65 and all **I** celebrated the Festival of Shelters in the
8:66 been good to his servant David and to his people **I**.
9: 5 establish the throne of your dynasty over **I** forever.
9: 5 never fail to have a successor on the throne of **I**.'
9: 7 then I will uproot the people of **I** from this land I
9: 7 I will make **I** an object of mockery and ridicule
9:21 These were descendants of the nations that **I** had
10: 9 in you and has placed you on the throne of **I**.
10: 9 Because the LORD loves **I** with an eternal love,
11: 9 the God of **I**, who had appeared to him twice.
11:25 Rezon hated **I** intensely and continued to reign in
11:31 for this is what the LORD, the God of **I**, says:
11:32 which I have chosen out of all the tribes of **I**.
11:37 And I will place you on the throne of **I**, and you
11:38 for you as I did for David, and I will give **I** to you.
11:42 Solomon ruled in Jerusalem over all **I** for forty
12: 1 where all **I** had gathered to make him king.
12: 3 The leaders of **I** sent for Jeroboam, and the whole
assembly of **I** went to speak with
12:16 When all **I** realized that the king had rejected their
12:16 Let's go home, **I**! Look out for your own house, O
David!" So the people of **I** returned home.
12:18 to restore order, but all **I** stoned him to death.
12:19 The northern tribes of **I** have refused to be ruled by
12:20 When the people of **I** learned of Jeroboam's return
12:20 called an assembly and made him king over all **I**.
12:21 to fight against the army of **I** and to restore the
12:28 O **I**, these are the gods who brought you out of
12:29 calf idols at the southern and northern ends of **I**—
12:33 He instituted a religious festival for **I**, and he went
14: 7 this message from the LORD, the God of **I**:
14: 7 and made you ruler over my people **I**.
14:13 All **I** will mourn for him and bury him. He is the
14:13 the God of **I**, sees in the entire family of Jeroboam.
14:14 And the LORD will raise up a king over **I** who
14:15 Then the LORD will shake **I** like a reed whipped
14:15 He will uproot the people of **I** from this good land
14:16 He will abandon **I** because Jeroboam sinned
14:16 and made all of **I** sin along with him."
14:18 When the people of **I** buried him, they mourned for
14:19 in *The Book of the History of the Kings of* **I**.
14:20 Jeroboam reigned in **I** twenty-two years.
14:21 all the tribes of **I** as the place to honor his name.
15: 1 in the eighteenth year of Jeroboam's reign in **I**.
15: 9 in the twentieth year of Jeroboam's reign in **I**.
15:16 between King Asa of Judah and King Baasha of **I**.
15:17 King Baasha of **I** invaded Judah and fortified
15:19 Break your treaty with King Baasha of **I** so that he
15:20 King Asa's request and sent his armies to attack **I**.
15:21 As soon as Baasha of **I** heard what was happening,
15:25 Nadab son of Jeroboam began to rule over **I** in the
15:25 Asa's reign in Judah. He reigned in **I** two years.
15:26 sins of idolatry that Jeroboam had led **I** to commit.
15:28 reign in Judah, and he became the next king of **I**.
15:30 the God of **I**, by the sins he had committed and the
sins he had led **I** to commit.
15:31 in *The Book of the History of the Kings of* **I**.
15:32 constant war between Asa and King Baasha of **I**.
15:33 Baasha began to rule over **I** in the third year of
15:34 sins of idolatry that Jeroboam had led **I** to commit.
16: 2 out of the dust to make you ruler of my people **I**,
16: 5 in *The Book of the History of the Kings of* **I**.
16: 8 Elah son of Baasha began to rule over **I** from
16: 8 Asa's reign in Judah. He reigned in **I** two years.
16:13 and because of all the sins they led **I** to commit,
16:13 anger of the LORD, the God of **I**, with their idols.
16:14 in *The Book of the History of the Kings of* **I**.
16:15 Zimri began to rule over **I** from Tirzah in the
16:15 When the army of **I**, which was then engaged in
16:17 So Omri led the army of **I** away from Gibbethon to
16:19 sins of idolatry that Jeroboam had led **I** to commit.
16:20 in *The Book of the History of the Kings of* **I**.
16:21 But now the people of **I** were divided into two
16:23 Omri began to rule over **I** in the thirty-first year of
16:26 sins of idolatry that Jeroboam had led **I** to commit.
16:26 he aroused the anger of the LORD, the God of **I**.
16:27 in *The Book of the History of the Kings of* **I**.
16:29 Ahab son of Omri began to rule over **I** in the
16:33 the God of **I**, than any of the other kings of **I**
before him.
17: 1 "As surely as the LORD, the God of **I**, lives—
17:14 For this is what the LORD, the God of **I**, says:
18:18 "I have made no trouble for **I**," Elijah replied.
18:19 Now bring all the people of **I** to Mount Carmel,
18:31 one to represent each of the tribes of **I**,
18:36 prove today that you are God in **I** and that I am
19:10 But the people of **I** have broken their covenant
19:14 But the people of **I** have broken their covenant
19:16 Then anoint Jehu son of Nimshi to be king of **I**,
19:18 Yet I will preserve seven thousand others in **I** who
20: 2 the city to relay this message to King Ahab of **I**:
20:11 The king of **I** sent back this answer: "A warrior
20:26 up the Aramean army and marched out against **I**,
20:27 **I** then mustered its army, set up supply lines,
20:28 Then the man of God went to the king of **I**
20:31 we have heard that the kings of **I** are very merciful.
20:32 and ropes and went to the king of **I** and begged,
20:32 'Please let me live!' " The king of **I** responded,
20:33 "Go and get him," the king of **I** told them.
20:41 and the king of **I** recognized him as one of the
20:43 So the king of **I** went home to Samaria angry
21: 7 "Are you the king of **I** or not?" Jezebel asked.
21:21 male descendants, slave or free alike, survive in **I**!
21:22 made him very angry and have led all of **I** into sin.
22: 1 three years there was no war between Aram and **I**.
22: 2 Jehoshaphat of Judah went to visit King Ahab of **I**.
22: 9 So the king of **I** called one of his officials and said,
22:10 King Ahab of **I** and King Jehoshaphat of Judah,
22:17 "In a vision I saw all **I** scattered on the mountains,
22:18 I tell you?" the king of **I** said to Jehoshaphat.
22:26 King Ahab of **I** then ordered, "Arrest Micaiah
22:29 So the king of **I** and King Jehoshaphat of Judah led
22:31 "Attack only the king of **I**!"
22:32 after him. "There is the king of **I**!" they shouted.
22:33 the charioteers realized he was not the king of **I**,
22:34 and the arrow hit the king of **I** between the joints
22:39 in *The Book of the History of the Kings of* **I**.
22:41 Judah in the fourth year of King Ahab's reign in **I**.
22:44 Jehoshaphat also made peace with the king of **I**.
22:51 Ahaziah son of Ahab began to rule over **I** in the
22:52 son of Nebat, who had led **I** into the sin of idolatry.
22:53 the God of **I**, just as his father had done.
2Ki 1: 1 nation of Moab declared its independence from **I**.
1: 3 the king will get well? Is there no God in **I**?
1: 6 Is there no God in **I**? Now, since you have done
1:16 Is there no God in **I**? Now, since you have done
1:18 in *The Book of the History of the Kings of* **I**.
2:12 My father! The chariots and charioteers of **I**!"
3: 1 Ahab's son Joram began to rule over **I** in the
3: 3 son of Nebat had led the people of **I** to commit.
3: 4 They used to pay the king of **I** an annual tribute of
3: 5 the king of Moab rebelled against the king of **I**.
3: 6 So King Joram mustered the army of **I**
3:10 "What should we do?" the king of **I** cried out.
3:12 So the kings of **I**, Judah, and Edom went to consult
3:13 want no part of you," Elisha said to the king of **I**.
3:24 the army of **I** rushed out and attacked the
3:24 The army of **I** chased them into the land of Moab,
3:27 As a result, the anger against **I** was great, so they
5: 2 of Aramean raiders had invaded the land of **I**,
5: 4 told the king what the young girl from **I** had said.
5: 5 of introduction for you to carry to the king of **I**."
5: 6 The letter to the king of **I** said: "With this letter I
5: 7 When the king of **I** read it, he tore his clothes in
5: 8 he will learn that there is a true prophet here in **I**."
5:12 better than all the rivers of **I** put together?
5:15 that there is no God in all the world except in **I**.
6: 8 When the king of Aram was at war with **I**,
6: 9 the man of God, would warn the king of **I**,
6:10 So the king of **I** would send word to the place
6:11 Who has been informing the king of **I** of my
6:12 "Elisha, the prophet in **I**, tells the king of **I** even
the words you speak in the
6:21 When the king of **I** saw them, he shouted to Elisha,
6:23 Aramean raiders stayed away from the land of **I**.
6:26 One day as the king of **I** was walking along the
6:32 **I** when the king sent a messenger to summon him.
7: 6 "The king of **I** has hired the Hittites and Egyptians
8: 1 for the LORD has called for a famine on **I** that
8: 3 the famine ended she returned to the land of **I**,
8:12 the terrible things you will do to the people of **I**.
8:16 Judah in the fifth year of King Joram's reign in **I**.
8:18 Jehoram followed the example of the kings of **I**
8:25 in the twelfth year of King Joram's reign in **I**.
8:26 was Athaliah, a granddaughter of King Omri of **I**.
8:28 Ahaziah joined King Joram of **I** in his war against
9: 3 I anoint you to be the king over **I**.' Then open the
9: 6 "This is what the LORD, the God of **I**, says:
9: 6 I anoint you king over the LORD's people, **I**.
9: 8 wiped out—every male, slave and free alike, in **I**.
9:12 command he had been anointed king over **I**.
9:14 defending **I** against the forces of King Hazael of
9:21 Then King Joram of **I** and King Ahaziah of Judah
9:29 in the eleventh year of King Joram's reign in **I**.
10:21 He sent messengers throughout all **I** summoning
10:28 Jehu destroyed every trace of Baal worship from **I**.
10:29 the great sin that Jeroboam son of Nebat had led **I**
10:30 be the kings of **I** down to the fourth generation."
10:31 law of the LORD, the God of **I**, with all his heart.
10:31 sins of idolatry that Jeroboam had led **I** to commit.
10:34 in *The Book of the History of the Kings of* **I**.
10:36 Jehu reigned over **I** from Samaria for twenty-eight
12: 1 Judah in the seventh year of King Jehu's reign in **I**.
13: 1 Jehoahaz son of Jehu began to rule over **I** in the
13: 2 that Jeroboam son of Nebat had led **I** to commit.
13: 3 So the LORD was very angry with **I**, and he
13: 4 how terribly the king of Aram was oppressing **I**.
13: 5 Then **I** lived in safety again as they had in former
13: 8 in *The Book of the History of the Kings of* **I**.
13:10 Jehoash son of Jehoahaz began to rule over **I** in the
13:11 that Jeroboam son of Nebat had led **I** to commit.
13:12 in *The Book of the History of the Kings of* **I**.
13:14 King Jehoash of **I** visited him and wept over him.
13:14 The chariots and charioteers of **I**!" he cried.
13:16 Then Elisha told the king of **I** to put his hand on
13:22 King Hazael of Aram had oppressed **I** during the
13:23 But the LORD was gracious to the people of **I**,
14: 1 the second year of the reign of King Jehoash of **I**.

14: 9 But King Jehoash of I replied to King Amaziah of
14: 11 so King Jehoash of I mobilized his army against
14: 12 Judah was routed by the army of I, and its army
14: 13 King Jehoash of I captured King Amaziah of
14: 15 in *The Book of the History of the Kings of I.*
14: 17 fifteen years after the death of King Jehoash of I.
14: 23 began to rule over I in the fifteenth year of King
14: 24 that Jeroboam son of Nebat had led I to commit.
14: 25 Jeroboam II recovered the territories of I between
14: 25 the Dead Sea, just as the LORD, the God of I,
14: 26 LORD saw the bitter suffering of everyone in I,
14: 27 said he would blot out the name of I completely,
14: 28 and how he recovered for I both Damascus
14: 28 in *The Book of the History of the Kings of I.*
14: 29 he was buried with his ancestors, the kings of I.
15: 1 year of the reign of King Jeroboam II of I.
15: 8 Zechariah son of Jeroboam II began to rule over I
15: 9 that Jeroboam son of Nebat had led I to commit.
15: 11 in *The Book of the History of the Kings of I.*
15: 12 "Your descendants will be kings of I down to the
15: 13 Shallum son of Jabesh began to rule over I in the
15: 15 in *The Book of the History of the Kings of I.*
15: 17 Menahem son of Gadi began to rule over I in the
15: 18 that Jeroboam son of Nebat had led I to commit.
15: 20 Menahem extorted the money from the rich of I,
15: 20 So the king of Assyria turned from attacking I
15: 21 in *The Book of the History of the Kings of I.*
15: 23 Pekahiah son of Menahem began to rule over I in
15: 24 that Jeroboam son of Nebat had led I to commit.
15: 25 at Samaria. Pekah then became the next king of I.
15: 26 in *The Book of the History of the Kings of I.*
15: 27 Pekah son of Remaliah began to rule over I in the
15: 28 that Jeroboam son of Nebat had led I to commit.
15: 29 King Tiglath-pileser of Assyria attacked I again,
15: 30 He began to rule over I in the twentieth year of
15: 31 in *The Book of the History of the Kings of I.*
15: 32 in the second year of King Pekah's reign in I.
15: 37 of Aram and King Pekah of I to attack Judah.
16: 1 in the seventeenth year of King Pekah's reign in I.
16: 3 Instead, he followed the example of the kings of I,
16: 5 and King Pekah of I declared war on Ahaz.
16: 7 me from the attacking armies of Aram and I."
17: 1 Hoshea son of Elah began to rule over I in the
17: 2 but not as much as the kings of I who ruled before
17: 3 so I was forced to pay heavy annual tribute to
17: 6 and the people of I were exiled to Assyria.
17: 7 This disaster came upon the nation of I
17: 8 as well as the practices the kings of I had
17: 9 The people of I had also secretly done many things
17: 11 So the people of I had done many evil things,
17: 13 his prophets and seers to warn both I and Judah:
17: 19 They walked down the same evil paths that I had
17: 20 So the LORD rejected all the descendants of I.
17: 21 For when the LORD tore I away from the
17: 21 Then Jeroboam drew I away from following the
17: 22 And the people of I persisted in all the evil ways of
17: 23 So I was carried off to the land of Assyria,
17: 24 in the towns of Samaria, replacing the people of I.
17: 24 took over Samaria and the other towns of I.
17: 26 I do not know how to worship the God of the land.
17: 27 one of the exiled priests from Samaria back to I.
17: 29 at the pagan shrines that the people of I had built.
17: 34 of Jacob, whose name he changed to I.
18: 1 Judah in the third year of King Hoshea's reign in I.
18: 4 because the people of I had begun to worship it by
18: 5 Hezekiah trusted in the LORD, the God of I.
18: 9 was the seventh year of King Hoshea's reign in I,
18: 9 King Shalmaneser of Assyria attacked I and began
18: 10 and the ninth year of King Hoshea's reign in I,
19: 15 "O LORD, God of I, you are enthroned between
19: 20 "This is what the LORD, the God of I, says:
19: 22 proud condescension? / It was the Holy One of I!
21: 3 an Asherah pole, just as King Ahab of I had done.
21: 7 I have chosen from among all the other tribes of I.
21: 11 than the Amorites, who lived in this land before I.
21: 12 So this is what the LORD, the God of I, says:
22: 15 to them, "The LORD, the God of I, has spoken!
22: 18 'This is what the LORD, the God of I,
23: 13 where King Solomon of I had built shrines for
23: 15 son of Nebat had made when he led I into sin.
23: 19 They had been built by the various kings of I
23: 22 like that since the time when the judges ruled in I,
23: 22 throughout all the years of the kings of I
23: 27 "I will destroy Judah just as I have destroyed I.
24: 13 that King Solomon of I had placed in the Temple.
1Ch 1: 34 father of Isaac. The sons of Isaac were Esau and I.
1: 43 who ruled in Edom before there were kings in I:
2: 1 The sons of I were Reuben, Simeon, Levi, Judah,
2: 7 brought disaster on I by taking plunder that had
4: 10 He was the one who prayed to the God of I,
5: 1 The oldest son of I was Reuben. But since he
5: 3 the oldest son of I, were Hanoch, Pallu, Hezron,
5: 17 of King Jotham of Judah and King Jeroboam of I.
5: 26 So the God of I caused King Pul of Assyria (also
6: 38 Izhar, Kohath, Levi, and I.
6: 49 They made atonement for I by following all the
6: 64 So the people of I assigned all these towns
7: 29 The descendants of Joseph son of I lived in these
9: 1 All I was listed in the genealogical record in *The Book of the Kings of I.*
10: 1 Now the Philistines attacked I,
11: 1 Then all I went to David at Hebron and told him,
11: 2 was our king, you were the one who really led I.
11: 2 'You will be the shepherd of my people I.
11: 3 covenant with the leaders of I before the LORD.
11: 3 They anointed him king of I, just as the LORD
11: 4 Then David and all I went to Jerusalem (or Jebus,
11: 10 Together with all I, they determined to make
11: 10 just as the LORD had promised concerning I.
12: 32 of the times and knew the best course for I to take.
12: 38 the single purpose of making David the king of I.
12: 38 In fact, all I agreed that David should be their king.
12: 40 There was great joy throughout the land of I.
13: 2 Then he addressed the entire assembly of I as
13: 5 So David summoned all the people of I, from one
13: 6 and all I went to Baalah of Judah (also called
13: 8 and all I were celebrating before God with all their
14: 2 realized that the LORD had made him king over I
14: 2 his kingdom very great for the sake of his people I.
14: 8 heard that David had been anointed king over all I,
15: 12 the God of I, to the place I have prepared for it.
15: 14 the Ark of the LORD, the God of I, to Jerusalem.
15: 25 Then David and the leaders of I and the generals of
15: 28 So all I brought up the Ark of the LORD's
16: 3 gave a gift of food to every man and woman in I:
16: 4 and praise to the LORD, the God of I.
16: 13 O children of I, God's servant, / O descendants of
16: 17 to the people of I as a never-ending treaty:
16: 36 Blessed be the LORD, the God of I,
16: 40 in the law of the LORD, which he had given to I.
17: 7 I chose you to lead my people I when you were
17: 9 provided a permanent homeland for my people I,
17: 21 What other nation on earth is like I? What other
17: 22 You chose I to be your people forever, and you,
17: 24 will say, 'The LORD Almighty is God over I!'
18: 14 David reigned over all I and was fair to everyone.
19: 16 now realized that they were no match for I,
19: 17 he mobilized all I, crossed the Jordan River,
19: 19 of Hadadezer realized they had been defeated by I,
20: 7 defied and taunted I. But he was killed by
21: 1 Satan rose up against I and caused David to take a
21: 3 all your servants? Why must you cause I to sin?"
21: 4 so Joab traveled throughout I to count the people.
21: 5 There were 1,100,000 men of military age in I,
21: 7 with the census, and he punished I for it.
21: 12 brings devastation throughout the land of I.
21: 14 So the LORD sent a plague upon I, and seventy
21: 16 and the leaders of I put on sackcloth to show their
22: 2 orders to call together the foreigners living in I,
22: 6 to build a Temple for the LORD, the God of I.
22: 9 I will give peace and quiet to I during his reign.
22: 10 establish the throne of his kingdom over I forever.'
22: 12 the law of the LORD your God as you rule over I.
22: 13 and regulations that the LORD gave to I through
22: 17 Then David ordered all the leaders of I to assist
23: 1 he appointed his son Solomon to be king over I.
23: 2 David summoned all the political leaders of I,
23: 25 For David said, "The LORD, the God of I,
24: 19 to the commands of the LORD, the God of I.
26: 29 as public administrators and judges throughout I.
27: 16 The following were the tribes of I and their
27: 22 Jeroham These were the leaders of the tribes of I.
27: 24 because the anger of God broke out against I.
27: 25 throughout the towns, villages, and fortresses of I.
28: 4 "Yet the LORD, the God of I, has chosen me
28: 4 all my father's family to be king over I forever.
28: 4 LORD was pleased to make me king over all I.
28: 5 to succeed me on the throne of his kingdom of I.
28: 8 I give you this charge for all I, the LORD's
29: 1 whom God has chosen to be the next king of I,
29: 6 the leaders of the tribes of I, the generals
29: 10 "O LORD, God of our ancestor I, may you
29: 18 the God of our ancestors Abraham, Isaac, and I,
29: 21 and many other sacrifices on behalf of I.
29: 23 and he prospered greatly, and all I obeyed him.
29: 25 so the entire nation of I stood in awe of him,
29: 26 So David son of Jesse reigned over all I.
29: 27 He ruled I for forty years in all, seven years from
29: 30 and everything that happened to him and to I
2Ch 1: 2 He called together all I—the generals and captains
1: 13 at the hill of Gibeon, and he reigned over I.
2: 4 He has commanded I to do these things forever.
2: 12 the God of I, who made the heavens and the earth!
2: 14 the son of a woman from Dan in I; his father is
2: 17 took a census of all foreigners in the land of I,
5: 2 and families of I to assemble in Jerusalem.
5: 4 When all the leaders of I arrived, the Levites
5: 6 and the entire community of I sacrificed sheep
5: 10 covenant with the people of I after they left Egypt.
6: 3 to the entire community of I standing before him
6: 4 "Blessed be the LORD, the God of I, who has
6: 5 I have never chosen a city among the tribes of I as
6: 5 Nor have I chosen a king to lead my people I.
6: 7 to honor the name of the LORD, the God of I.
6: 10 to honor the name of the LORD, the God of I.
6: 11 that the LORD made with the people of I."
6: 12 the LORD in front of the entire community of I.
6: 14 He prayed, "O LORD, God of I, there is no God
6: 16 And now, O LORD, God of I, carry out your
6: 16 as you have done, they will always reign over I.'
6: 17 Now, O LORD, God of I, fulfill this promise to
6: 21 and your people I when we pray toward this place.
6: 24 "If your people I are defeated by their enemies
6: 27 forgive the sins of your servants, your people I.
6: 33 and fear you, just as your own people I do.
7: 3 When all the people of I saw the fire coming down
7: 6 the priests blew the trumpets, while all I stood.
7: 8 with huge crowds gathered from all the tribes of I.
7: 10 so good to David and Solomon and to his people I.
7: 18 never fail to have a successor who rules over I.'
7: 20 then I will uproot the people of I from this land of
8: 8 These were descendants of the nations that I had
9: 8 Because God loves I so much and desires this
9: 30 Solomon ruled in Jerusalem over all I for forty
10: 1 where all I had gathered to make him king.
10: 3 The leaders of I sent for Jeroboam, and he and all I went together to speak with Rehoboam.
10: 16 When all I realized that the king had rejected their
10: 16 Let's go home, I! Look out for your own house, O David!" So all I returned home.
10: 19 The northern tribes of I have refused to be ruled by
11: 1 to fight against the army of I and to restore the
11: 13 and Levites living among the northern tribes of I
11: 16 From all over I, those who sincerely wanted to
11: 16 the God of I, followed the Levites to Jerusalem,
12: 1 of the LORD, and all I followed him in this sin.
12: 6 and the leaders of I humbled themselves and said,
12: 13 all the tribes of I as the place to honor his name.
13: 1 in the eighteenth year of Jeroboam's reign in I.
13: 3 mustered 800,000 courageous men from I.
13: 5 Don't you realize that the LORD, the God of I,
13: 5 and his descendants the throne of I forever?
13: 12 O people of I, do not fight against the LORD,
13: 18 So Judah defeated I because they trusted in the
13: 20 So Jeroboam of I never regained his power during
15: 3 For a long time, I was without the true God,
15: 4 the God of I, and sought him out, you found him.
15: 13 the LORD, the God of I, would be put to death—
15: 17 shrines were not completely removed from I,
16: 1 King Baasha of I invaded Judah and fortified
16: 3 Break your treaty with King Baasha of I so that he
16: 4 King Asa's request and sent his armies to attack I.
16: 5 As soon as Baasha of I heard what was happening,
16: 11 in *The Book of the Kings of Judah and I.*
17: 1 Judah to stand against any attack from I.
17: 4 of following the practices of the kingdom of I.
18: 1 his son to marry the daughter of King Ahab of I.
18: 8 So the king of I called one of his officials and said,
18: 9 King Ahab of I and King Jehoshaphat of Judah,
18: 16 "In a vision I saw all I scattered on the mountains,
18: 17 I tell you?" the king of I said to Jehoshaphat.
18: 19 'Who can entice King Ahab of I to go into battle
18: 25 King Ahab of I then ordered, "Arrest Micaiah
18: 28 So the king of I and King Jehoshaphat of Judah led
18: 30 to his charioteers: "Attack only the king of I!"
18: 31 after him. "There is the king of I!" they shouted.
18: 32 as the charioteers realized he was not the king of I,
18: 33 and the arrow hit the king of I between the joints
19: 8 and clan leaders in I to serve as judges in
20: 10 ancestors invade those nations when I left Egypt,
20: 19 the LORD, the God of I, with a very loud shout.
20: 29 himself had fought against the enemies of I,
20: 34 which is included in *The Book of the Kings of I.*
20: 35 of Judah made an alliance with King Ahaziah of I,
21: 4 all his brothers and some of the other leaders of I.
21: 6 Jehoram followed the example of the kings of I
21: 13 Instead, you have been as evil as the kings of I.
21: 13 Judah to worship idols, just as King Ahab did in I.
22: 2 was Athaliah, a granddaughter of King Omri of I.
22: 5 with King Joram, the son of King Ahab of I.
24: 6 levied this tax on the community of I in order to
24: 16 so much good in I for God and his Temple.
25: 6 to hire 100,000 experienced fighting men from I.
25: 7 and said, "O king, do not hire troops from I, for the LORD is not with I.
25: 9 I do about the silver I paid to hire the army of I?"
25: 18 But King Jehoash of I replied to King Amaziah of
25: 21 So King Jehoash of I mobilized his army against
25: 22 Judah was routed by the army of I, and its army
25: 23 King Jehoash of I captured King Amaziah of
25: 25 fifteen years after the death of King Jehoash of I.
25: 26 in *The Book of the Kings of Judah and I.*
27: 7 are recorded in *The Book of the Kings of I*
28: 2 he followed the example of the kings of I and cast
28: 5 The armies of I also defeated Ahaz and inflicted
28: 8 The armies of I captured 200,000 women
28: 9 in Samaria when the army of I returned home.
28: 12 Then some of the leaders of I—Azariah son of
28: 13 LORD's fierce anger is already turned against I."
28: 23 they led to his ruin and the ruin of all I.
28: 26 in *The Book of the Kings of Judah and I.*
29: 7 burnt offerings at the sanctuary of the God of I.
29: 10 the God of I, so that his fierce anger will turn away
29: 24 on the altar to make atonement for the sins of all I.
29: 24 and sin offering should be made for all I.
29: 27 and other instruments of David, king of I.
30: 1 King Hezekiah now sent word to all I and Judah,
30: 1 celebrate the Passover of the LORD, the God of I.
30: 5 So they sent a proclamation throughout all I,
30: 5 celebrate the Passover of the LORD, the God of I.
30: 6 messengers were sent throughout I and Judah.
30: 6 "O people of I, return to the LORD, the God of Abraham, Isaac, and I,
30: 21 So the people of I who were present in Jerusalem
30: 25 the Levites, all who came from the land of I,
31: 6 The people who had moved to Judah from I,
31: 8 they thanked the LORD and his people I!
32: 17 also sent letters scorning the LORD, the God of I.
32: 32 in *The Book of the Kings of Judah and I.*
33: 7 I have chosen from among all the other tribes of I.
33: 16 of Judah to worship the LORD, the God of I.
33: 18 the God of I, are recorded in *The Book of the Kings of I.*
34: 7 down the incense altars throughout the land of I
34: 9 Ephraim, and from all the remnant of I, as well as
34: 21 for me and for all the remnant of I and Judah.
34: 23 to them, "The LORD, the God of I, has spoken!
34: 26 'This is what the LORD, the God of I,
34: 33 all detestable idols from the entire land of I
35: 3 apart to serve the LORD and were teachers in I:
35: 3 serving the LORD your God and his people I.

35: 4 the written instructions of King David of I
35:18 None of the kings of I had ever kept a Passover as
35:18 of Jerusalem, and people from all over Judah and I.
35:27 are recorded in *The Book of the Kings of I*
36: 8 are recorded in *The Book of the Kings of I*
36:13 refusing to turn to the LORD, the God of I.
36:23 the LORD's people may return to I for this task.
Ezr 1: 3 the LORD, the God of I, who lives in Jerusalem.
2: 2 This is the number of the men of I who returned
2:59 that they or their families were descendants of I.
3: 2 his family began to rebuild the altar of the God of I
3:11 so good! / His faithful love for I endures forever!"
4: 1 rebuilding a Temple to the LORD, the God of I.
4: 3 Jeshua, and the other leaders of I replied,
4: 3 the God of I, just as King Cyrus of Persia
5: 1 in the name of the God of I to the Jews in Judah
5:11 was built here many years ago by a great king of I.
6:14 as had been commanded by the God of I
6:16 then dedicated with great joy by the people of I,
6:17 as a sin offering for the twelve tribes of I.
6:21 The Passover meal was eaten by the people of I
6:21 customs to worship the LORD, the God of I.
6:22 them to rebuild the Temple of God, the God of I.
7: 6 the law of Moses, which the LORD, the God of I, had given to the people of I.
7: 7 Some of the people of I, as well as some of the
7:10 teach those laws and regulations to the people of I.
7:11 taught the commands and laws of the LORD to I:
7:13 "I decree that any of the people of I in my
7:15 an offering to the God of I who lives in Jerusalem.
7:28 And I gathered some of the leaders of I to return
8:18 of Mahli, who was a descendant of Levi son of I.
8:25 and the people of I had presented for the Temple
8:29 and the leaders of I at the storerooms of the
8:35 captivity sacrificed burnt offerings to the God of I.
8:35 They presented twelve oxen for the people of I,
9: 1 came to me and said, "Many of the people of I,
9: 2 For the men of I have married women from these
9: 4 Then all who trembled at the words of the God of I
9:15 O LORD, God of I, you are just. We stand before
10: 1 Temple of God, a large crowd of people from I—
10: 2 of the land. But there is hope for I in spite of this.
10: 5 and all the people of I swear that they would do as
10:25 These are the other people of I who were guilty:
Ne 1: 6 see me praying night and day for your people I.
2:10 had come who was interested in helping I.
7: 7 This is the number of men of I who returned from
7:61 that they or their families were descendants of I.
7:73 that is to say, all I—settled in their own towns."
8: 1 which the LORD had given for I to obey.
10:33 and for the sin offerings to make atonement for I.
13:18 I by permitting the Sabbath to be desecrated in this
13:26 "Wasn't this exactly what led King Solomon of I
13:26 and God loved him and made him king over all I.
Ps 14: 7 would come from Mount Zion to rescue I!
14: 7 Jacob will shout with joy, and I will rejoice.
20: 1 May the God of I keep you safe from all harm.
22: 3 are holy. / The praises of I surround your throne.
22:23 Show him reverence, all you descendants of I!
24: 6 and worship the God of I. / *Interlude*
25:22 O God, ransom I / from all its troubles.
28: 9 your people! / Bless I, your special possession!
41:13 Bless the LORD, the God of I, / who lives forever
46: 7 is here among us; / the God of I is our fortress.
46:11 is here among us; / the God of I is our fortress.
50: 7 Here are my charges against you, O I: / I am God,
53: 6 would come from Mount Zion to rescue I!
53: 6 Jacob will shout with joy, and I will rejoice.
59: 5 O LORD God Almighty, the God of I, / rise up to
59:13 will know / that God reigns in I. / *Interlude*
68: 8 the God of Sinai, / before God, the God of I.
68:12 while the women of I divide the plunder.
68:26 Praise God, all you people of I;
68:34 God's power. / His majesty shines down on I;
68:35 The God of I gives power and strength to his
69: 6 let me cause them to be humiliated, / O God of I.
71:22 I will sing for you with a lyre, / O Holy One of I.
72:18 Bless the LORD God, the God of I, / who alone
73: 1 Truly God is good to I, / to those whose hearts are
75: 9 God has done; / I will sing praises to the God of I.
76: 1 is well known in Judah; / his name is great in I.
78: 5 issued his decree to Jacob; / he gave his law to I.
78:21 against Jacob. / Yes, his anger rose against I,
78:41 God's patience / and frustrated the Holy One of I.
78:55 by lot. / He settled the tribes of I into their homes.
78:59 he was very angry, / and he rejected I completely.
78:71 of Jacob's descendants— / God's own people, I.
79: 7 For they have devoured your people I,
80: 1 Please listen, O Shepherd of I, / you who lead I like a flock.
81: 1 praises to God, our strength. / Sing to the God of I.
81: 4 For this is required by the laws of I; / it is a law of
81: 5 He made it a decree for I / when he attacked Egypt
81: 8 you stern warnings. / O I, if you would only listen!
81:11 people wouldn't listen. / I did not want me around.
81:13 Oh, that I would follow me, walking in my paths!
83: 4 "Come," they say, "let us wipe out I as a nation.
84: 8 hear my prayer. / Listen, O God of I. / *Interlude*
85: 1 on your land! / You have restored the fortunes of I.
87: 2 city of Jerusalem / more than any other city in I.
89:18 and he, the Holy One of I, has given us our king.
94: 7 "and besides, the God of I doesn't care."
95: 8 "Don't harden your hearts as I did at Meribah,
98: 3 his promise to love and be faithful to I.
99: 4 acted with justice / and righteousness throughout I.
103: 7 to Moses / and his deeds to the people of I.
105:10 to the people of I as a never-ending treaty:
105:23 Then I arrived in Egypt; / Jacob lived as a
105:24 And the LORD multiplied the people of I
106: 9 He led I across the sea bottom that was as dry as a
106:34 I failed to destroy the nations in the land,
106:48 Blessed be the LORD, the God of I,
114: 2 God's sanctuary, / and I became his kingdom.
114: 7 of the Lord, / at the presence of the God of I.
115: 9 O I, trust the LORD! / He is your helper; he is
115:12 He will bless the people of I / and the family of
118: 2 Let the congregation of I repeat: / "His faithful
121: 4 Indeed, he who watches over I / never tires
122: 4 All the people of I—the LORD's people—
124: 1 LORD had not been on our side— / let I now say—
125: 5 who do evil. / And let I have quietness and peace.
128: 6 And may I have quietness and peace.
129: 1 enemies have persecuted me— / let I now say—
130: 7 O I, hope in the LORD; / for with the LORD
130: 8 He himself will free I / from every kind of sin.
131: 3 O I, put your hope in the LORD— / now
132: 2 the LORD. / He vowed to the Mighty One of I,
132: 5 a sanctuary for the Mighty One of I."
135: 4 Jacob for himself, / I for his own special treasure.
135:12 a special possession to his people I.
135:19 O I, praise the LORD! / O priests of Aaron,
136:11 He brought I out of Egypt. / His faithful love
136:14 He led I safely through, / His faithful love endures
136:22 a special possession to his servant I. / His faithful
146: 5 But happy are those who have the God of I as their
147: 2 and bringing the exiles back to I.
147:19 his words to Jacob, / his principles and laws to I.
148:14 the people of I who are close to him.
149: 2 O I, rejoice in your Maker. / O people of
Pr 1: 1 the proverbs of Solomon, David's son, king of I.
Ecc 1:12 I, the Teacher, was king of I, and I lived in
Isa 1: 3 and appreciate his care, but not my people I.
1: 4 They have despised the Holy One of I,
1:10 Listen to the LORD, you leaders of I! Listen to the law of our God, people of I.
1:24 the LORD Almighty, the Mighty One of I, says,
2: 3 of the LORD, to the Temple of the God of I.
2: 5 Come, people of I, let us walk in the light of the
2: 6 The LORD has rejected the people of I
2: 7 I has vast treasures of silver and gold and many
3:14 "You have ruined I, which is my vineyard.
4: 2 But in the future, I—the branch of the LORD—
5: 7 I and Judah are his pleasant garden. / He expected
5:19 They even mock the Holy One of I and say,
5:24 They have despised the word of the Holy One of I.
5:30 A cloud of darkness and sorrow will hover over I.
6:12 distant lands and the entire land of I lies deserted.
6:13 I will remain a stump, like a tree that is cut down,
7: 1 by King Rezin of Aram and King Pekah of I,
7: 2 "Aram is allied with I against us!" So the hearts
7: 5 the kings of Aram and I are coming against you.
7: 8 As for I, within sixty-five years it will be crushed
7: 9 I is no stronger than its capital, Samaria.
7:16 you fear so much—the kings of I and Aram—
7:17 years since Solomon's empire was divided into I
8:14 But to I and Judah he will be a stone that causes
8:17 though he has turned away from the people of I.
9: 3 I will again be great, and its people will rejoice as
9: 8 The Lord has spoken out against that braggart I,
9: 9 and the people of I and Samaria will soon discover
9:12 With bared fangs, they will devour I. But even
9:15 The leaders of I are the head, and the lying
10:17 The LORD, the Light of I and the Holy One,
10:20 Then at last those left in I and Judah will trust the LORD, the Holy One of I.
10:22 But though the people of I are as numerous as the
11:11 returning them to the land of I from Assyria,
11:12 He will raise a flag among the nations for I to rally
11:13 Then at last the jealousy between I and Judah will
11:16 just as he did for I long ago when they returned
12: 6 For great is the Holy One of I who lives among
13: 2 waving as the enemy attacks. Cheer them on, O I!
14: 1 of Jacob. I will be his special people once again.
14: 1 them there and become a part of the people of I.
14: 2 Those who captured I will be captured, and I will rule over its enemies.
14:25 I will break the Assyrians when they are in I;
17: 3 The fortified cities of I will also be destroyed,
17: 4 "In that day the glory of I will be very dim,
17: 5 I will be abandoned like the grainfields in the
17: 6 Yes, I will be stripped bare of people," says the LORD, the God of I.
17: 7 and have respect for the Holy One of I.
17:14 In the evening I waits in terror, but by dawn its
19:17 Just to speak the name of I will strike deep terror
19:24 And I will be their ally. The three will be together, and I will be a blessing to them.
19:25 have made. Blessed be I, my special possession!"
21:10 the LORD Almighty, the God of I, has said.
21:17 I, the LORD, the God of I, have spoken!"
24:15 praise the name of the LORD, the God of I.
27: 4 My anger against I will be gone. If I find briers
27: 6 I will bud and blossom and fill the whole earth
27: 7 Has the LORD punished I in the same way he has
27: 8 but he has punished I only a little. He has exiled
27:11 I is a foolish and stupid nation, for its people have
28: 1 the pride and joy of the drunkards of I!
28: 3 the pride and joy of the drunkards of I—
28: 7 Now, however, I is being led by drunks!
29:19 who are poor will rejoice in the Holy One of I.
29:22 who redeemed Abraham, says to the people of I,
29:23 will recognize the holiness of the Holy One of I. They will stand in awe of the God of I.
30:11 more than enough about your 'Holy One of I.'
30:12 This is the reply of the Holy One of I:
30:15 The Sovereign LORD, the Holy One of I, says,
30:29 the mountain of the LORD—to the Rock of I.
31: 1 of looking to the LORD, the Holy One of I.
32: 2 He will shelter I from the storm and the wind.
33: 9 All the land of I is in trouble. Lebanon has been
33:24 The people of I will no longer say, "We are sick
34: 8 when Edom will be paid back for all it did to I.
37:16 "O LORD Almighty, God of I, you are
37:21 "This is what the LORD, the God of I, says:
37:23 proud condescension? / It was the Holy One of I!
40:27 O I, how can you say the LORD does not see
41: 8 "But as for you, I my servant, Jacob my chosen
41:14 you are, O I, don't be afraid, for I will help you.
41:14 your Redeemer. I am the Holy One of I.'
41:16 You will glory in the Holy One of I.
41:17 I, the God of I, will never forsake them.
41:20 that it is the LORD, the Holy One of I, who did it.
41:21 they can do!" says the LORD, the King of I.
42:16 I will lead blind I down a new path, / guiding them
42:24 Who allowed I to be robbed and hurt? Was it not
43: 1 But now, O I, the LORD who created you says:
43: 3 your God, the Holy One of I, your Savior.
43: 6 and daughters back to I from the distant corners of
43:10 "But you are my witnesses, O I!"
43:14 LORD your Redeemer, the Holy One of I, says:
43:21 I have made I for myself, and they will someday
43:28 and assigned I a future of complete destruction
44: 1 listen to me, Jacob my servant, I my chosen one.
44: 2 do not be afraid. O I, my chosen one, do not fear.
44: 5 and will take the honored name of I as their own.
44:21 "Pay attention, O I, for you are my servant.
44:23 LORD has redeemed Jacob and is glorified in I.
45: 3 the God of I, the one who calls you by name.
45: 4 for the sake of Jacob my servant, I my chosen one.
45:11 the LORD, the Creator and Holy One of I, says:
45:15 Truly, O God of I, our Savior, you work in strange
45:17 But the LORD will save the people of I with
45:19 And I did not tell the people of I to ask me for
45:25 In the LORD all the generations of I will be
46: 3 "Listen to me, all you who are left in I. I created
46:13 am ready to save Jerusalem and give my glory to I.
47: 4 is the LORD Almighty, is the Holy One of I.
48: 1 who are called by the name of I and born into the
48: 1 the name of the LORD and call on the God of I.
48: 2 holy city and talk about depending on the God of I,
48:12 to me, O family of Jacob, I my chosen one!
48:17 your Redeemer, the Holy One of I, says:
48:20 LORD has redeemed his servants, the people of I.
49: 3 He said to me, "You are my servant, I, and you
49: 5 who commissioned me to bring his people of I
49: 6 "You will do more than restore the people of I to
49: 7 The LORD, the Redeemer and Holy One of I,
49: 7 faithful LORD, the Holy One of I, chooses you."
49: 8 I will give you as a token and pledge to I.
49: 8 This will prove that I will reestablish the land of I
49:26 your Savior and Redeemer, the Mighty One of I."
51: 3 The LORD will comfort I again and make her
51: 4 Hear me, I, for my law will be proclaimed, and my
51:16 I am the one who says to I, 'You are mine!' "
52: 7 and salvation, the news that the God of I reigns!
52:12 and the God of I will protect you from behind.
54: 5 He is your Redeemer, the Holy One of I, the God
55: 5 the LORD your God, the Holy One of I,
56: 8 who brings back the outcasts of I, says:
56: 8 I will bring others, too, besides my people I."
58: 1 of a trumpet blast. Tell my people I of their sins!
59:20 "to buy back those in I who have turned from their
60: 8 "And what do I see flying like clouds to I,
60: 9 reserved to bring the people of I home.
60: 9 the Holy One of I, for he will fill you with
60:14 City of the LORD, and Zion of the Holy One of I.
60:16 your Savior and Redeemer, the Mighty One of I.
61: 3 To all who mourn in I, he will give beauty for
62:11 "Tell the people of I, 'Look, your Savior is
63: 7 I will rejoice in his great goodness to I, which he
63:11 "Where is the one who brought I through the sea,
65: 8 good grapes there!'), so I will not destroy all I.
65: 9 I will preserve a remnant of the people of I and of
Jer 2: 3 In those days I was holy to the LORD, the first of
2: 4 people of Jacob—all you families of I!
2:14 "Why has I become a nation of slaves? Why has
2:26 a thief, I feels shame only when she gets caught.
2:31 of the LORD! Have I been like a desert to I?
3: 6 said to me, "Have you seen what fickle I does?
3: 6 I has worshiped other gods on every hill and under
3: 8 She saw that I had divorced faithless I and sent her
3: 9 I treated it all so lightly—she thought nothing of
3:11 "Even faithless I is less guilty than treacherous
3:12 Therefore, go and say these words to I, 'This is
3:12 O I, my faithless people, come home to me again,
3:14 I will bring you again to the land of I—one from
3:18 and I will return together from exile in the north.
3:20 But you have betrayed me, you people of I!
3:23 Only in the LORD our God will I ever find
4: 1 "O I, come back to me," says the LORD.
5:11 The people of I and Judah are full of treachery
5:15 O I, I will bring a distant nation against you,"
5:20 "Make this announcement to I and to Judah:
6: 9 Even the few who remain in I will be gleaned
7: 3 The LORD Almighty, the God of I, says:
7:15 just as I did your relatives, the people of I.'
7:21 is what the LORD Almighty, the God of I, says:
9:15 to what the LORD Almighty, the God of I, says:
9:26 the people of I also have uncircumcised hearts."
10: 1 Hear the word of the LORD, O I!
10:16 But the God of I is no idol! / He is the Creator of

10:16 including **I**, his own special possession.
10:25 For they have utterly devoured your people **I**,
11: 3 'This is what the LORD, the God of **I**, says:
11:10 **I** and Judah have both broken the covenant I made
11:17 For the people of **I** and Judah have done evil,
12:14 out for the inheritance I gave my people **I**,
13:11 so I created Judah and **I** to cling to me,"
13:12 "So tell them, 'The LORD, the God of **I**, says:
14: 8 O Hope of **I**, our Savior in times of trouble!
16: 9 For the LORD Almighty, the God of **I**, says:
16:14 who rescued the people of **I** from the land of
16:15 who brought the people of **I** back to their own land
17:13 O LORD, the hope of **I**, all who turn away from
18: 6 "O **I**, can I not do to you as this potter has done to
18:13 My virgin **I** has done something too terrible to
19: 3 is what the LORD Almighty, the God of **I**, says:
19: 4 " 'For **I** has forsaken me and turned this valley
19:15 is what the LORD Almighty, the God of **I**, says:
21: 4 'This is what the LORD, the God of **I**, says:
23: 2 the LORD, the God of **I**, says to these shepherds:
23: 6 day Judah will be saved, and **I** will live in safety.
23: 7 who rescued the people of **I** from the land of
23: 8 who brought the people of **I** back to their own land
23:13 prophesied by Baal and led my people of **I** into sin.
24: 5 "This is what the LORD, the God of **I**, says:
24:10 disease until they have vanished from the land of **I**,
25:11 **I** and her neighboring lands will serve the king of
25:15 Then the LORD, the God of **I**, said to me,
25:27 'The LORD Almighty, the God of **I**, says:
27: 4 is what the LORD Almighty, the God of **I**, says:
27:21 this is what the LORD Almighty, the God of **I**,
28: 2 "The LORD Almighty, the God of **I**, says:
28:14 The LORD Almighty, the God of **I**, says: I have
29: 4 The LORD Almighty, the God of **I**, sends this
29: 8 The LORD Almighty, the God of **I**, says,
29:21 the God of **I**, says about your prophets—
29:25 is what the LORD Almighty, the God of **I**, says:
30: 2 "This is what the LORD, the God of **I**, says:
30: 3 when I will restore the fortunes of my people of **I**
30: 4 This is the message the LORD gave concerning **I**
30: 7 It will be a time of trouble for my people **I**. Yet in
30:10 do not be dismayed, **I**, says the LORD.
30:10 **I** will return and will have peace and quiet in their
31: 1 "I will be the God of all the families of **I**,
31: 2 I will again come to give rest to the people of **I**."
31: 3 Long ago the LORD said to **I**: "I have loved you,
31: 4 I will rebuild you, my virgin **I**. You will again be
31: 7 "Sing with joy for **I**! Shout for the greatest of
31: 7 'Save your people, O LORD, the remnant of **I**!'
31:11 For the LORD has redeemed **I** from those too
31:18 I have heard **I** saying, 'You disciplined me
31:20 "Is not **I** still my son, my darling child?"
31:21 Come back again, my virgin **I**; return to your cities
31:22 and different to happen—**I** will embrace her God."
31:23 is what the LORD Almighty, the God of **I**, says:
31:27 and multiply the number of cattle here in **I**
31:31 I will make a new covenant with the people of **I**
31:33 I will make with the people of **I** on that day,"
31:36 "I am as likely to reject my people **I** as I am to do
32:14 "The LORD Almighty, the God of **I**, says:
32:15 For the LORD Almighty, the God of **I**, says:
32:20 And you have continued to do great miracles in **I**
32:21 "You brought **I** out of Egypt with mighty signs
32:22 You gave the people of **I** this land that you had
32:30 **I** and Judah have done nothing but wrong since
32:32 "The sins of **I** and Judah—the sins of the people of
32:36 But this is what the LORD, the God of **I**, says:
33: 4 For this is what the LORD, the God of **I**, says:
33: 7 the fortunes of Judah and **I** and rebuild their cities.
33:14 when I will do for **I** and Judah all the good I have
33:17 have a descendant sitting on the throne of **I**.
33:24 chose Judah and **I** and then abandoned them!'
33:24 and saying that **I** is not worthy to be counted as a
34: 2 'This is what the LORD, the God of **I**, says:
34:13 "This is what the LORD, the God of **I**, says:
35:13 "The LORD Almighty, the God of **I**, says:
35:17 the LORD God Almighty, the God of **I**, says:
35:18 is what the LORD Almighty, the God of **I**, says:
35:19 LORD Almighty, the God of **I**, have spoken!"
36: 2 and write down all my messages against **I**, Judah,
37: 7 "This is what the LORD, the God of **I**, says:
38:17 "The LORD God Almighty, the God of **I**, says:
39:16 'The LORD Almighty, the God of **I**, says:
41: 9 to protect himself against King Baasha of **I**.
42: 9 the God of **I**, with your request, and this is his
42:15 The LORD Almighty, the God of **I**, says: 'If you
42:18 "For the LORD Almighty, the God of **I**, says:
43:10 'The LORD Almighty, the God of **I**, says:
44: 2 is what the LORD Almighty, the God of **I**, says:
44: 7 the LORD God Almighty, the God of **I**, asks you:
44:11 the LORD Almighty, the God of **I**, says:
44:25 The LORD Almighty, the God of **I**, says: You
45: 2 is what LORD, the God of **I**, says to you, Baruch:
46:25 The LORD Almighty, the God of **I**, says: "I will
46:27 Jacob, my servant; do not be dismayed, **I**.
46:27 **I** will return and will have peace and quiet,
48: 1 is what the LORD Almighty, the God of **I**, says:
48:13 as **I** was ashamed of her gold calf at Bethel.
48:27 Did you not make **I** the object of your ridicule?
49: 1 Are there no descendants of **I** to inherit the land of
49: 2 Then **I** will come and take back the land you took
50: 4 "Then the people of **I** and Judah will join
50:18 the LORD Almighty, the God of **I**, says:
50:19 And I will bring **I** home again to her own land,
50:20 the LORD, "no sin will be found in **I** or in Judah,
50:29 for she has defied the LORD, the Holy One of **I**.
50:33 "The people of **I** and Judah have been wronged.
50:34 He will defend them and give them rest again in **I**.
51: 5 For the LORD Almighty has not forsaken **I**
51: 5 was filled with sin against the Holy One of **I**."
51:19 But the God of **I** is no idol! / He is the Creator of
51:33 For the LORD Almighty, the God of **I**, says:
51:49 "Just as Babylon killed the people of **I** and others
La 2: 2 mercy the Lord has destroyed every home in **I**.
2: 3 All the strength of **I** vanishes beneath his fury.
2: 3 He consumes the whole land of **I** like a raging fire.
2: 5 Yes, the Lord has vanquished **I** like an enemy.
4: 3 the jackals feed their young, but not my people **I**.
Eze 2: 3 he said, "I am sending you to the nation of **I**,
3: 1 Then go and give its message to the people of **I**."
3: 4 of man, go to the people of **I** with my messages.
3: 7 I am sending you to the people of **I**, but they won't
3:17 of man, I have appointed you as a watchman for **I**.
4: 3 This will be a warning to the people of **I**.
4: 4 your left side and place the sins of **I** on yourself.
4:13 **I** will eat defiled bread in the Gentile lands,
5: 4 then spread from this remnant and destroy all of **I**.
5:13 all **I** will know that I, the LORD, have spoken to
6: 2 look over toward the mountains of **I** and prophesy
6: 3 Give the mountains of **I** this message from the
6:11 because of all the evil that the people of **I** have
7: 2 this is what the Sovereign LORD says to **I**:
7: 7 O people of **I**, the day of your destruction is
8: 4 Suddenly, the glory of the God of **I** was there,
8: 6 Do you see the great sins the people of **I** are doing
8:10 saw the various idols worshiped by the people of **I**.
8:11 Seventy leaders of **I** were standing there with
8:12 have you seen what the leaders of **I** are doing with
9: 3 Then the glory of the God of **I** rose up from
9: 8 against Jerusalem wipe out everyone left in **I**?"
9: 9 "The sins of the people of **I** and Judah are very
10:19 And the glory of the God of **I** hovered above them.
10:20 the God of **I** when I was by the Kebar River.
11: 5 "This is what the LORD says to the people of **I**:
11:10 will be slaughtered all the way to the borders of **I**,
11:11 I will judge you even to the borders of **I**,
11:13 are you going to kill everyone in **I**?"
11:17 and I will give you the land of **I** once again.
11:22 and the glory of the God of **I** hovered above them.
12: 6 of these actions will be a sign for the people of **I**."
12: 9 "Son of man, these rebels, the people of **I**,
12:10 Zedekiah in Jerusalem and for all the people of **I**.'
12:19 the Sovereign LORD concerning those living in **I**
12:22 "Son of man, what is that proverb they quote in **I**:
12:24 and misleading predictions about peace in **I**.
12:25 There will be no more delays, you rebels of **I**!
12:27 "Son of man, the people of **I** are saying,
13: 2 speak against the false prophets of **I** who are
13: 4 "O people of **I**, these prophets of yours are like
13: 9 they will be banished from the community of **I**.
14: 1 Then some of the leaders of **I** visited me, and while
14: 4 will punish the people of **I** who set up idols in their
14: 6 give the people of **I** this message from the
14: 9 and cut them off from the community of **I**.
14:11 the people of **I** will learn not to stray from me,
14:23 these things are not being done to **I** without cause,
17: 2 "Son of man, tell this story to the people of **I**.
17:12 "Say to these rebels of **I**: Don't you understand the
17:14 so **I** would not become strong again and revolt.
17:14 Only by keeping her treaty with Babylon could **I**
17:15 Can **I** break her sworn treaties like that and get
17:16 the king of **I** will die in Babylon,
17:17 and all his mighty army will fail to help **I** when the
17:18 For the king of **I** broke his treaty after swearing to
17:21 And all the best warriors of **I** will be killed in
18: 2 "Why do you quote this proverb in the land of **I**:
18: 3 you will not say this proverb anymore in **I**.
18:25 Lord isn't being just!' Listen to me, O people of **I**.
18:29 And yet the people of **I** keep saying, 'The Lord is
18:29 O people of **I**, it is you who are unjust, not I.
18:30 I will judge each of you, O people of **I**,
18:31 new spirit. For why should you die, O people of **I**?
19: 1 "Sing this funeral song for the princes of **I**:
19: 9 could never again be heard / on the mountains of **I**.
20: 1 some of the leaders of **I** came to request a message
20: 3 give the leaders of **I** this message from the
20: 5 When I chose **I** and revealed myself to her in
20:13 "But the people of **I** rebelled against me, and they
20:27 give the people of **I** this message from the
20:30 give the people of **I** this message from the
20:31 Should I listen to you or help you, O people of **I**?
20:38 are in exile, but they will never enter the land of **I**.
20:39 "As for you, O people of **I**, this is what the
20:40 the people of **I** will someday worship me, and I
20:44 will know that I am the LORD, O people of **I**,
21: 2 and prophesy against **I** and her sanctuaries.
21: 3 I am your enemy, O **I**, and I am about to unsheath
21:25 "O you corrupt and wicked prince of **I**, your final
22: 6 "Every leader in **I** who lives within your walls is
22:18 the people of **I** are the worthless slag that remains
22:24 "Son of man, give the people of **I** this message:
24:21 I was told to give this message to the people of **I**.
25: 3 mocked **I** in her desolation, and laughed at Judah
25:14 By the hand of my people of **I**, I will accomplish
27:17 Judah and **I** traded for your wares, offering wheat
28:25 The people of **I** will again live in their own land,
28:26 They will live safely in **I** and build their homes
29: 6 for you collapsed like a reed when **I** looked to you
29: 7 **I** leaned on you, but like a cracked staff,
29:16 "Then **I** will no longer be tempted to trust in
29:16 Egypt's shattered condition will remind **I** of how
29:16 Then **I** will know that I alone am the Sovereign
29:21 when I will cause the ancient glory of **I** to revive,
33: 7 I am making you a watchman for the people of **I**.
33:10 "Son of man, give the people of **I** this message:
33:11 Turn! Turn from your wickedness, O people of **I**!
33:20 O people of **I**, you are saying, 'The Lord is not
33:28 The mountains of **I** will be so ruined that no one
34: 2 prophesy against the shepherds, the leaders of **I**.
34:13 I will bring them back home to their own land of **I**
34:13 I will feed them on the mountains of **I** and by the
34:14 give them good pastureland on the high hills of **I**.
34:30 the people of **I**, are my people, says the Sovereign
35: 5 Your continual hatred for the people of **I** led you to
35:10 you said, 'The lands of **I** and Judah will be ours.
35:12 word you spoke against the mountains of **I**.
36: 1 O mountains of **I**, hear the word of the LORD!
36: 3 give the mountains of **I** this message from the
36: 4 Therefore, O mountains of **I**, hear the word of the
36: 6 and mountains, the ravines and valleys of **I**.
36: 8 But the mountains of **I** will produce heavy crops of
36:10 I will greatly increase the population of **I**,
36:11 O mountains of **I**, I will bring people to live on you
36:13 saying, '**I** is a land that devours her own people!'
36:17 when the people of **I** were living in their own land,
36:22 give the people of **I** this message from the
36:28 "And you will live in **I**, the land I gave your
36:32 O my people of **I**, you should be utterly ashamed
37:11 of man, these bones represent the people of **I**.
37:12 Then I will bring you back to the land of **I**.
37:16 'This stick represents the northern tribes of **I**.'
37:21 I will gather the people of **I** from among the
37:25 They will live in the land of **I** where their ancestors
37:28 have set **I** apart for myself to be holy."
38: 8 future you will swoop down on the land of **I**,
38:11 '**I** is an unprotected land filled with unwalled
38:18 But when Gog invades the land of **I**,
38:19 I promise a mighty shaking in the land of **I** on that
38:21 I will summon the sword against you throughout **I**,
39: 2 turn you and drive you toward the mountains of **I**,
39: 7 make known my holy name among my people of **I**.
39: 7 know that I am the LORD, the Holy One of **I**.
39: 9 "Then the people in the towns of **I** will go out
39:12 It will take seven months for the people of **I** to
39:13 Everyone in **I** will help, for it will be a glorious victory for **I** when I
39:17 Come from far and near to the mountains of **I**,
39:22 And from that time on the people of **I** will know
39:23 then know why **I** was sent away to exile—
39:25 I will have mercy on **I**, for I am jealous for my
40: 2 In a vision of God he took me to the land of **I**
40: 4 Then you will return to the people of **I** and tell
43: 2 the glory of the God of **I** appeared from the east.
43: 7 remain here forever, living among the people of **I**.
43:10 describe to the people of **I** the Temple I have
44: 2 for the LORD, the God of **I**, entered here.
44: 6 And give these rebels, the people of **I**, this message
44: 6 O people of **I**, enough of your disgusting sins!
44: 9 including those who live among the people of **I**,
44:10 **I** strayed away from me to worship idols must bear
44:12 worship other gods, causing **I** to fall into deep sin.
44:15 in the Temple when **I** abandoned me for idols.
44:22 their wives only from among the virgins of **I**
45: 1 "When you divide the land among the tribes of **I**,
45: 6 set aside to be a city where anyone in **I** can come
45: 9 Enough, you princes of **I**! Stop all your violence
45:15 sheep for every two hundred in your flocks in **I**.
45:16 All the people of **I** must join the prince in bringing
45:17 offerings to make reconciliation for the people of **I**.
45:22 as a sin offering for himself and the people of **I**.
47:13 for dividing the land for the twelve tribes of **I**:
47:18 runs southward along the Jordan River between **I**
47:21 land within these boundaries among the tribes of **I**.
48: 1 "Here is the list of the tribes of **I** and the territory
48: 1 all the way across the land of **I** from east to west.
48:11 and did not go astray when the people of **I**
48:21 directions to the eastern and western borders of **I**.
48:23 and it extends across the entire land of **I** from east
48:31 be three gates, each one named after a tribe of **I**.
Da 8: 9 and the east and toward the glorious land of **I**.
9: 7 the people of Judah and Jerusalem and all **I**,
9:11 All **I** has disobeyed your law and turned away,
11:16 He will pause in the glorious land of **I**, intent on
11:41 He will enter the glorious land of **I**, and many
Hos 1: 1 and Jeroboam son of Jehoash was king of **I**.
1: 2 When the LORD first began speaking to **I**
1: 6 for I will no longer show love to the people of **I**
1: 9 for **I** is not my people, and I am not their God.
1:10 Yet the time will come when **I** will prosper
1:11 people of Judah and **I** will unite under one leader,
2: 2 "But now, call **I** to account, for she is no longer
2:17 O **I**, I will cause you to forget your images of Baal;
3: 1 For the LORD still loves **I** even though the
3: 4 This illustrates that **I** will be a long time without a
4: 1 Hear the word of the LORD, O people of **I**!
4: 5 false prophets. And I will destroy your mother, **I**.
4:15 "Though **I** is a prostitute, may Judah avoid such
4:16 **I** is as stubborn as a heifer, so the LORD will put
4:18 The men of **I** finish up their drinking bouts and off
5: 3 I know what you are like, O **I**! You have left me as
5: 5 "The arrogance of **I** testifies against her; she will
5: 9 One thing is certain, **I**: When your day of
5:11 The people of **I** will be crushed and broken by my
5:12 I will destroy **I** as a moth consumes wool. I will
5:13 "When **I** and Judah saw how sick they were,
5:13 **I** turned to Assyria, to the great king there,
5:14 I will tear at **I** and Judah as a lion rips apart its
6: 4 "O **I** and Judah, what should I do with you?"
6:10 Yes, I have seen a horrible thing in **I**: My people
7: 1 "I wanted to heal **I**, but its sins were far too great.
7: 8 "My people of **I** mingle with godless foreigners,

7: 9 I is like an old man with graying hair, unaware of
7:11 "The people of I have become like silly,
8: 2 Now I pleads with me, 'Help us, for you are our
8: 3 The people of I have rejected what is good,
8: 8 The people of I have been swallowed up; they lie
8: 9 The people of I have sold themselves to many
8:11 "I has built many altars to take away sin, but these
8:13 The people of I love their rituals of sacrifice,
8:14 "I has built great palaces, and Judah has fortified
9: 1 O people of I, do not rejoice as others do. For you
9: 7 Soon I will know this all too well. "The prophets
9: 8 The prophet is a watchman for my God over I,
9:10 The LORD says, "O I, when I first found you,
9:11 The glory of I will fly away like a bird, for your
9:13 I have watched I become as beautiful and pleasant
9:13 But now I will bring out her children to be
9:16 The people of I are stricken. Their roots are dried
9:17 My God will reject the people of I because they
10: 1 How prosperous I is—a luxuriant vine loaded with
10: 6 I will be laughed at and shamed because its people
10: 9 The LORD says, "O I, ever since that awful
10:11 "I is like a trained heifer accustomed to treading
10:11 I and Judah must now break up the hard ground;
10:15 the king of I will be completely destroyed.
11: 1 "When I was a child, I loved him as a son, and I
11: 3 It was I who taught I how to walk, leading him
11: 4 I led I along with my ropes of kindness and love.
11: 8 "Oh, how can I give you up, I? How can I let you
11: 9 I will not completely destroy I, for I am God
11:12 I surrounds me with lies and deceit, but Judah still
12: 1 The people of I feed on the wind; they chase after
12: 8 I boasts, "I am rich, and I've gotten it all by
12:14 But the people of I have bitterly provoked the
13: 9 to be destroyed, O I, though I am your helper.
14: 1 Return, O I, to the LORD your God, for your sins
14: 5 I will be to I like a refreshing dew from heaven.
14: 8 "O I, stay away from idols! I am the one who
Joel 2:17 foreigners who say, 'Where is the God of I?
2:27 will know that I am here among my people of I
3:16 But to his people of I, the LORD will be a
Am 1: 1 and Jeroboam II, the son of Jehoash, was king of I.
1: 9 They broke their treaty of brotherhood with I,
2: 6 "The people of I have sinned again and again,
2:11 Can you deny this, my people of I?"
3: 1 has spoken against you, O people of I and Judah—
3:13 and announce it throughout all I," says the Lord,
3:14 "On the very day I punish I for its sins, I will
4:12 God as he comes in judgment, you people of I!"
5: 1 Listen, you people of I! Listen to this funeral song
5: 2 "The virgin I has fallen, / never to rise again!
5: 4 this is what the LORD says to the family of I:
5: 6 If you don't, he will roar through I like a fire,
5:25 during the forty years in the wilderness, I?
6: 1 You are famous and popular in I, you to whom the
6: 8 "I despise the pride and false glory of I, and I hate
6:14 "O people of I, I am about to bring an enemy
7: 2 Unless you relent, I will not survive, for we are
7: 5 Unless you relent, I will not survive, for we are
7: 9 and the temples of I will be destroyed,
7:11 and the people of I will be sent away into
7:15 and told me, 'Go and prophesy to my people in I.'
7:16 You say, 'Don't prophesy against I.
7:17 And the people of I will certainly become captives
8: 2 "This fruit represents my people of I—
8: 7 sworn this oath by his own name, the Pride of I:
9: 8 am watching this sinful nation of I, and I will
9: 8 I will never completely destroy the family of I,"
9: 9 "For I have commanded that I be persecuted by
9:12 And I will possess what is left of Edom and all the
9:13 Then the terraced vineyards on the hills of I will
9:14 I will bring my exiled people of I back from
Ob 1:10 of the violence you did to your close relatives in I.
1:11 For you deserted your relatives in I during their
1:13 You shouldn't have plundered the land of I when
1:15 As you have done to I, so it will be done to you.
1:17 And the people of I will come back to reclaim their
1:18 At that time I will be a raging fire, and Edom,
1:20 The exiles of I will return to their land and occupy
Mic 1: 5 Because of the sins and rebellion of I and Judah.
1:13 You were the first city in Judah to follow I in the
1:14 The town of Aczib has deceived the kings of I,
1:15 And the leaders of I will go to Adullam.
2: 7 Should you talk that way, O family of I?
2:12 "Someday, O I, I will gather the few of you who
3: 1 Listen, you leaders of I! You are supposed to know
3: 9 Listen to me, you leaders of I! You hate justice
4: 2 of the LORD, to the Temple of the God of I.
5: 1 With a rod they will strike the leader of I in the
5: 2 Yet a ruler of I will come from you, one whose
5: 3 The people of I will be abandoned to their enemies
5: 7 Then the few left in I will go out among the
5: 8 The remnant of I will go out among the nations
5: 9 The people of I will stand up to their foes, and all
6: 2 He has a case against his people I!
7:11 In that day, I, your cities will be rebuilt, and your
Na 2: 2 For the land of I lies empty and broken after your
Hab 3:14 like a whirlwind, thinking I would be easy prey.
Zep 2: 9 the God of I, "Moab and Ammon will be
3:13 The people of I who survive will do no wrong to
3:14 Sing, O daughter of Zion; shout aloud, O I!
3:15 the King of I, will live among you!
Zec 1:17 The towns of I will again overflow with prosperity,
1:19 powers that scattered Judah, I, and Jerusalem."
8:12 remnant in Judah and I the heirs of these blessings.
8:13 and I had become symbols of what it means to be
9: 1 including the people of I, are on the LORD.
9:10 I will remove the battle chariots from I
9:13 Judah is my bow, and I is my arrow! Jerusalem is
10: 6 "I will strengthen Judah and save I; I will
10: 7 The people of I will become like mighty warriors,
10: 9 they will survive and come home again to I.
11:14 the bond of unity between Judah and I was broken.
12: 1 This message concerning the fate of I came from
12:12 "All I will weep in profound sorrow, each family
Mal 1: 1 This is the message that the LORD gave to I
2:11 In Judah, in I, and in Jerusalem there is treachery,
2:12 May the LORD cut off from the nation of I every
2:16 I hate divorce!" says the LORD, the God of I.
4: 4 that I gave him on Mount Sinai for all I.
Mt 2: 6 who will be the shepherd for my people I.' "
2:20 take the child and his mother back to the land of I,
2:21 So Joseph returned immediately to I with Jesus
8:10 I haven't seen faith like this in all the land of I!
9:33 "Nothing like this has ever happened in I!"
10: 6 but only to the people of I—God's lost sheep.
10:23 return before you have reached all the towns of I.
15:24 "I was sent only to help the people of I—
15:31 could see again! And they praised the God of I.
19:28 on twelve thrones, judging the twelve tribes of I.
21: 5 "Tell the people of I, / 'Look, your King is
27: 9 price at which he was valued by the people of I—
27:42 he can't save himself! So he is the king of I, is he?
Mk 12:29 'Hear, O I! The Lord our God is the one and only
15:32 Let this Messiah, this king of I, come down from
Lk 1:33 And he will reign over I forever; his Kingdom will
1:54 And how he has helped his servant I! / He has not
1:68 "Praise the Lord, the God of I, / because he has
1:80 wilderness until he began his public ministry to I.
2:25 expected the Messiah to come and rescue I.
2:32 the nations, / and he is the glory of your people I!"
2:34 to Mary, "This child will be rejected by many in I,
4:25 "Certainly there were many widows in I who
4:27 rather than the many lepers in I who needed help."
7: 9 I haven't seen faith like this in all the land of I!"
22:30 will sit on thrones, judging the twelve tribes of I.
24:21 he was the Messiah who had come to rescue I.
Jn 1:31 with water in order to point him out to I."
1:47 "Here comes an honest man—a true son of I."
1:49 you are the Son of God—the King of I!"
11:52 that Jesus' death would be not for I only,
12:13 in the name of the Lord! / Hail to the King of I!"
12:15 "Don't be afraid, people of I. / Look, your King is
Ac 1: 6 are you going to free I now and restore our
2:22 "People of I, listen! God publicly endorsed Jesus
2:36 So let it be clearly known by everyone in I that
3:12 "People of I," he said, "what is so astounding
3:26 up his servant, he sent him first to you people of I,
4:10 and to all the people of I that he was healed in the
4:27 and the people of I were all united against Jesus,
5:21 the high council, along with all the elders of I.
5:31 He did this to give the people of I an opportunity
5:35 "Men of I, take care what you are planning to do
7:23 he decided to visit his relatives, the people of I.
7:24 he saw an Egyptian mistreating a man of I.
7:26 visited them again and saw two men of I fighting.
7:37 "Moses himself told the people of I, 'God will
7:38 He was the mediator between the people of I
7:42 during those forty years in the wilderness, I?
9:15 and to kings, as well as to the people of I.
10: 2 He was a devout man who feared the God of I,
10:22 He is a devout man who fears the God of I and is
10:36 heard about the Good News for the people of I—
10:39 we apostles are witnesses of all he did throughout I
13:16 "People of I," he said, "and you devout Gentiles who fear the God of I,
13:17 "The God of this nation of I chose our ancestors
13:19 and gave their land to I as an inheritance.
13:23 Jesus, who is God's promised Savior of I!
13:24 the need for everyone in I to turn from sin
13:26 all of you devout Gentiles who fear the God of I—
13:31 these are his witnesses to the people of I.
21:28 yelling, "Men of I! Help! This is the man who
26: 7 that is why the twelve tribes of I worship God
28:20 this chain because I believe that the hope of I—
Ro 9: 4 They are the people of I, chosen to be God's
9:27 Concerning I, Isaiah the prophet cried out,
9:27 "Though the people of I are as numerous as the
10:19 But did the people of I really understand? Yes,
10:21 But regarding I, God said, / "All day long I
11: 2 prophet complained to God about the people of I
11:26 And so all I will be saved. Do you remember what
11:26 and he will turn I from all ungodliness.
1Co 10:18 And think about the nation of I; all who eat the
10:22 Do you dare to rouse the Lord's jealousy as I did?
2Co 3: 7 yet it began with such glory that the people of I
3:13 so the people of I would not see the glory fading
Eph 2:12 You were excluded from God's people, I, and you
Heb 3: 8 hearts against him / as I did when they rebelled,
3:15 hearts against him / as I did when they rebelled."
4:11 who disobeys God, as the people of I did, will fall.
7: 4 Even Abraham, the great patriarch of I,
8: 8 a new covenant / with the people of I and Judah.
8:10 with the people of I on that day, says the Lord:
9: 1 Now in that first covenant between God and I,
11:22 of God's bringing the people of I out of Egypt.
11:28 commanded the people of I to keep the Passover
11:29 It was by faith that the people of I went right
11:30 It was by faith that the people of I marched around
12:25 For if the people of I did not escape when they
2Pe 2: 1 But there were also false prophets in I, just as there
Jude 1: 5 the Lord rescued the whole nation of I from Egypt,
Rev 2:14 who showed Balak how to trip up the people of I.
7: 4 144,000 who were sealed from all the tribes of I:
21:12 And the names of the twelve tribes of I were

ISRAEL'S (82) [ISRAEL]

Ex 5: 1 After this presentation to I leaders, Moses
6:14 These are the ancestors of clans from some of I
6:14 I oldest son, included Hanoch, Pallu, Hezron,
9: 4 Not a single one of I livestock will die!' "
24: 1 Nadab, Abihu, and seventy of I leaders.
24:11 And though I leaders saw God, he did not destroy
Lev 4:22 "If one of I leaders does something forbidden by
16:19 he will cleanse it from I defilement and return it to
Nu 1: 1 during the second year after I departure from
9: 1 during the second year after I departure from
10:11 during the second year after I departure from
17: 2 wooden staffs, one from each of I ancestral tribes,
23: 7 Jacob for me! / Come and announce I doom.'
23:10 Who can count even a fourth of I people?
25: 5 So Moses ordered I judges to execute everyone
33:38 during the fortieth year after I departure from
Jos 13: 7 Include all this territory as I inheritance when you
Jdg 3:10 LORD came upon him, and he became I judge.
5: 2 "When I leaders take charge, / and the people
5: 9 My heart goes out to I leaders, / and to those who
10: 2 He was I judge for twenty-three years. When he
10:17 in Gilead, preparing to attack I army at Mizpah.
12: 7 Jephthah was I judge for six years. When he died,
12: 8 After Jephthah, Ibzan became I judge. He lived in
12:11 After him, Elon from Zebulun became I judge.
12:13 son of Hillel, from Pirathon, became I judge.
12:14 seventy donkeys. He was I judge for eight years.
15:20 Samson was I judge for twenty years,
16:31 Samson had been I judge for twenty years.
18:29 I son, but it had originally been called Laish.
1Sa 4:21 is the glory?"—murmuring, "I glory is gone."
7: 6 So it was at Mizpah that Samuel became I judge.
7:15 Samuel continued as I judge for the rest of his life.
9:20 and your family are the focus of all I hopes."
14:47 Now when Saul had secured his grasp on I throne,
2Sa 7: 7 And I have never once complained to I leaders,
1Ki 11:25 Rezon was I bitter enemy for the rest of Solomon's
16:17 away from Gibbethon to attack Tirzah, I capital.
18:17 "So it's you, is it—I troublemaker?" Ahab asked
2Ki 1: 2 One day I new king, Ahaziah, fell through the
10:32 the LORD began to reduce the size of I territory.
14: 8 One day Amaziah sent this challenge to I king
1Ch 17: 6 And I never once complained to I leaders,
22: 1 and the place of the altar for I burnt offerings!"
2Ch 13:17 there were 500,000 casualties among I finest
25:17 King Amaziah of Judah sent this challenge to I
28: 6 I king, killed 120,000 of Judah's troops
Ps 68:26 of Israel; / praise the LORD, the source of I life.
78:31 he struck down the finest of I young men.
SS 3: 7 with sixty of I mightiest men surrounding it.
Isa 17: 3 The few left in Aram will share the fate of I
27: 9 The LORD did this to purge away I sin. When he
27:10 I fortified cities will be silent and empty,
28: 5 Then at last the LORD Almighty will himself be I
30: 8 then stand until the end of time as a witness to I
43:15 the LORD, your Holy One, I Creator and King.
44: 6 I King and Redeemer, the LORD Almighty,
Jer 2:16 have utterly destroyed I glory and power.
3:21 the weeping and pleading of I people.
31: 9 For I am I father, and Ephraim is my oldest child.
La 2: 1 The fairest of I cities lies in the dust, thrown down
Eze 4: 5 You will bear I sins for 390 days—one day for
7:14 "The trumpets call I army to mobilize, but no one
13: 9 I will blot their names from I record books,
17:13 He also exiled I most influential leaders,
17:15 this man of I royal family rebelled against
17:22 and I will plant it on the top of I highest mountain.
18: 6 and he has not feasted in the mountains before I
20: 9 nations wouldn't be able to laugh at I God,
28:24 No longer will I scornful neighbors prick and tear
35:15 You rejoiced at the desolation of I inheritance.
36: 1 "Son of man, prophesy to I mountains. Give them
36:37 I am ready to hear I prayers for these blessings,
38:17 when I announced through I prophets that in future
Hos 1: 5 I will put an end to I independence by breaking its
5: 1 "Hear this, you priests and all of I leaders! Listen,
9: 7 The time of I punishment has come; the day of
10: 8 shrines of Aven, the place of I sin, will crumble.
Am 3: 9 and witness the scandalous spectacle of all I
Ob 1:11 You acted as though you were one of I enemies.
Mic 1: 5 Who is to blame for I rebellion? Samaria,
3: 8 fearlessly pointing out I sin and rebellion.

ISRAELITE (105) [ISRAEL]

Ex 1:22 "Throw all the newborn I boys into the Nile River.
3:22 The I women will ask for silver and gold jewelry
5:14 Then they whipped the I foremen in charge of the
5:15 So the I foremen went to Pharaoh and pleaded with
5:19 the I foremen could see that they were in serious
11: 2 Tell all the I men and women to ask their Egyptian
12:49 whether a native-born I or a foreigner who has
14:20 The cloud settled between the I and Egyptian
14:20 turned into a pillar of fire, lighting the I camp.
Lev 4:13 "If the entire I community does something
17: 3 If any I sacrifices a bull or a lamb or a goat
17:10 whether an I or a foreigner living among you,
24:10 One day a man who had an I mother and an
24:10 father got into a fight with one of the I men.
24:11 this son of an I woman blasphemed the LORD's
24:16 Any I or foreigner among you who blasphemes the
25:25 If any of your I relatives go bankrupt and are
25:35 "If any of your I relatives fall into poverty
25:39 "If any of your I relatives go bankrupt and sell
25:47 and if some of your I relatives go bankrupt and sell
25:53 foreigner to treat any of your I relatives ruthlessly.

Nu 16:25 and Abiram, followed closely by the **I** leaders.
25: 6 then one of the **I** men brought a Midianite woman
25:14 The **I** man killed with the Midianite woman was
26:51 So the total number of **I** men counted in the census
31: 9 Then the **I** army captured the Midianite women
Dt 3:18 armed and ready to protect your **I** relatives.
10: 9 or inheritance reserved for them among the other **I**
15:12 "If an **I** man or woman voluntarily becomes your
17:15 You must appoint a fellow **I**, not a foreigner.
23:17 "No **I** man or woman may ever become a temple
23:19 charge interest on the loans you make to a fellow **I**,
24: 7 "If anyone kidnaps a fellow **I** and treats him as a
25:11 "If two **I** men are fighting and the wife of one tries
Jos 2: 1 Then Joshua secretly sent out two spies from the **I**
3: 2 days later, the **I** leaders went through the camp
8:15 and the **I** army fled toward the wilderness as
8:24 When the **I** army finished killing all the men
9:14 So the **I** leaders examined their bread, but they did
10: 7 So Joshua and the entire **I** army left Gilgal and set
10:15 and the **I** army returned to their camp at Gilgal.
10:20 So Joshua and the **I** army continued the slaughter
10:34 Then Joshua and the **I** army went to Eglon
10:43 and the **I** army returned to their camp at Gilgal.
11:17 The **I** territory now extended all the way from
12: 7 and the **I** armies defeated on the west side of the
17: 4 Joshua son of Nun, and the **I** leaders and said,
18: 1 Now that the land was under **I** control, the entire **I** assembly gathered at Shiloh and set up
21:41 and pasturelands within **I** territory given to the
Jdg 3: 6 **I** sons married their daughters, and **I** daughters were given in marriage to their
7:14 God has given Gideon son of Joash, the **I**,
7:15 Then he returned to the **I** camp and shouted,
11:40 for young **I** women to go away for four days each
20:33 When the main group of **I** warriors reached
21:13 The **I** assembly sent a peace delegation to the little
21:16 So the **I** leaders asked, "How can we find wives
1Sa 4: 1 The **I** army was camped near Ebenezer,
4:10 was great; thirty thousand **I** men died that day.
4:17 "Thousands of **I** troops are dead on the battlefield.
7:14 The **I** towns near Ekron and Gath that the
11: 1 King Nahash of Ammon led his army against the **I**
13: 4 So the entire **I** army mobilized again and met Saul
14: 3 No one realized that Jonathan had left the **I** camp.
17:16 the Philistine giant strutted in front of the **I** army.
17:19 with Saul and the **I** army at the valley of Elah,
17:20 He arrived at the outskirts of the camp just as the **I**
17:21 Soon the **I** and Philistine forces stood facing each
17:24 As soon as the **I** army saw him, they began to run
17:53 Then the **I** army returned and plundered the
18: 6 But something happened when the victorious **I**
2Sa 1: 2 a man arrived from the **I** battlefront.
1: 3 "I escaped from the **I** camp," the man replied.
2:26 call off your men from chasing their **I** brothers?"
10: 7 he sent Joab and the entire **I** army to fight them.
11: 1 and the **I** army to destroy the Ammonites.
11:17 And Uriah was killed along with several other **I**
12:26 and the **I** army were successfully ending their siege
17:26 and the **I** army set up camp in the land of Gilead.
18: 7 and the **I** troops were beaten back by David's men.
23: 9 the Philistines when the entire **I** army had fled.
23:11 Israelites in a field full of lentils. The **I** army fled,
1Ki 7:14 He was half **I**, since his mother was a widow from
11:15 the **I** army had killed nearly every male in Edom.
15:27 and the **I** army were laying siege to the Philistine
20: 1 They went to besiege Samaria, the **I** capital,
20:20 Each **I** soldier killed his Aramean opponent,
20:23 said to him, "The **I** gods are gods of the hills;
20:27 But the **I** army looked like two little flocks of goats
22:34 however, randomly shot an arrow at the **I** troops,
2Ki 3:24 When they arrived at the **I** camp, the army of Israel
13:25 on three occasions, and so recovered the **I** towns.
1Ch 11:13 place in a field full of barley, and the **I** army fled.
12:19 Some men from Manasseh defected from the **I**
20: 1 Joab led the **I** army in successful attacks against
26:30 were put in charge of the **I** lands west of the Jordan
27: 1 This is the list of **I** generals and captains, and their
27:34 by Abiathar. Joab was commander of the **I** army.
2Ch 13: 4 and shouted to Jeroboam and the **I** army:
13:15 God defeated Jeroboam and the **I** army and routed
13:16 The **I** army fled from Judah, and God handed them
18:33 however, randomly shot an arrow at the **I** troops,
Ne 9: 2 Those of **I** descent separated themselves from all
Hos 13: 1 because the other **I** tribes looked up to them.

ISRAELITES (407) [ISRAEL]

ALL THE ISRAELITES (30) Ex 14:26; Lev 16:17; 17:2; 21:24; 22:18; Nu 3:8; 8:19; 14:10; 36:8; Dt 29:2; Jos 3:1,7; 4:14; 7:23,24,25; 8:33; 22:33; Jdg 8:27; 10:8; 14:3; 20:1,11, 26; 1Sa 2:14; 11:15; 1Ch 13:2; 15:3; 2Ch 11:3; 35:17

Ge 46: 8 These are the names of the **I**, the descendants of
Ex 1: 9 "These **I** are becoming a threat to us because there
1:11 So the Egyptians made the **I** their slaves and put
1:12 oppressed them, the more quickly the **I** multiplied!
1:14 They were ruthless with the **I**, forcing them to
1:20 and the **I** continued to multiply, growing more
2:11 grown up, he went out to visit his people, the **I**,
2:23 But the **I** still groaned beneath their burden of
2:25 He looked down on the **I** and felt deep concern for
3:10 You will lead my people, the **I**, out of Egypt."
3:11 "How can you expect me to lead the **I** out of
3:12 When you have brought the **I** out of Egypt,
6: 6 "Therefore, say to the **I**: 'I am the LORD, and I
7: 5 Egyptians my power and force them to let the **I** go,
8:22 different in the land of Goshen, where the **I** live.
9: 4 make a distinction between the property of the **I**
9: 6 but the **I** didn't lose a single animal from their
10: 7 Please let the **I** go to serve the LORD their God!
11: 7 But among the **I** it will be so peaceful that not even
11: 7 a distinction between the Egyptians and the **I**.
11:10 his heart so he wouldn't let the **I** leave the country.
12:27 for he passed over the homes of the **I** in Egypt.
12:34 The **I** took with them their bread dough made
12:36 caused the Egyptians to look favorably on the **I**,
12:36 and they gave the **I** whatever they asked for.
12:38 Many people who were not **I** went with them,
13:18 and the **I** left Egypt like a marching army.
14: 3 Then Pharaoh will think, 'Those **I** are confused.
14: 4 So the **I** camped there as they were told.
14: 5 When word reached the king of Egypt that the **I**
14:17 and they will follow the **I** into the sea.
14:20 to the Egyptians, and they couldn't find the **I**.
14:26 When all the **I** were on the other side, the LORD
14:28 Of all the Egyptians who had chased the **I** into the
14:30 And the **I** could see the bodies of the Egyptians
16:15 The **I** were puzzled when they saw it. "What is
17: 9 Moses commanded Joshua, "Call the **I** to arms,
17:11 the staff with his hands, the **I** had the advantage.
18: 1 God had done for Moses and his people, the **I**.
19: 1 The **I** arrived in the wilderness of Sinai exactly two
19: 6 my holy nation.' Give this message to the **I**."
24:17 The **I** at the foot of the mountain saw an awesome
30:16 It will bring you, the **I**, to the LORD's attention,
33: 6 they left Mount Sinai, the **I** wore no more jewelry.
39:32 The **I** had done everything just as the LORD had
Lev 1: 2 "Give the following instructions to the **I**:
4: 2 "Give the **I** the following instructions for dealing
7:23 "Give the **I** these instructions: You must never eat
7:29 "Give these further instructions to the **I**:
7:34 share of the peace offerings brought by the **I**.
7:36 The LORD commanded that the **I** were to give
7:38 **I** to bring their offerings to the LORD in the
9: 3 Then tell the **I** to take a male goat for a sin offering
10: 6 However, the rest of the **I**, your relatives,
10:11 And you must teach the **I** all the laws that the
11: 2 "Give the following instructions to the **I**:
12: 1 said to Moses, "Give these instructions to the **I**:
15: 2 "Give these further instructions to the **I**: Any man
16:16 because of the defiling sin and rebellion of the **I**.
16:17 atonement for himself, his family, and all the **I**.
16:21 confess over it all the sins and rebellion of the **I**.
16:29 for you, and it applies to those who are **I** by birth,
16:34 to make atonement for the **I** once each year."
17: 2 and all the **I** these commands from the LORD:
17: 5 This rule will stop the **I** from sacrificing animals in
17: 8 which applies both to **I** and to the foreigners living
17:12 That is why I said to the **I**: 'You and the foreigners
17:13 "And this command applies both to **I** and to the
17:15 "And this command also applies both to **I**
18: 2 "Say this to your people, the **I**: I, the LORD,
18:26 This applies both to you who are **I** by birth and to
20: 2 "Give the **I** these instructions, which apply to those who are **I** by birth as well as
21:24 instructions to Aaron and his sons and to all the **I**.
22: 2 and his sons to treat the sacred gifts that the **I** set
22: 3 they approach the sacred food presented by the **I**,
22:15 sacred offerings brought to the LORD by the **I**
22:18 and his sons and all the **I** these instructions,
22:18 which apply to those who are **I** by birth as well as
23: 2 "Give the **I** instructions regarding the LORD's
23:10 to give these instructions to the **I**: "When you
23:24 to give these instructions to the **I**:
23:34 "Tell the **I** to begin the Festival of Shelters on the
23:42 all of you who are **I** by birth must live in shelters.
23:43 This will remind each new generation of **I** that
23:44 the annual festivals of the LORD to the **I**.
24: 8 behalf of the **I** as a continual part of the covenant.
24:22 "These same regulations apply to **I** by birth
24:23 After Moses gave all these instructions to the **I**,
25: 2 "Give these instructions to the **I**: When you have
25:54 If any **I** have not been redeemed by the time the
26:46 and instructions that the LORD gave to the **I**
27: 2 "Give the following instructions to the **I**: If you
27:34 gave to the **I** through Moses on Mount Sinai.
Nu 1:49 not include them when you count the rest of the **I**.
1:54 So the **I** did everything just as the LORD had
2: 9 the way whenever the **I** travel to a new campsite.
2:16 tribes will be second in line whenever the **I** travel.
2:31 They are to bring up the rear whenever the **I** move
3: 8 serving in the Tabernacle on behalf of all the **I**.
3:12 "I have chosen the Levites from among the **I** as
5: 4 So the **I** did just as the LORD had commanded
5: 9 All the sacred gifts that the **I** bring to a priest will
6:27 and his sons will designate the **I** as my people,
8:16 for myself in place of all the firstborn sons of the **I**;
8:19 And of all the **I**, I have assigned the Levites to
8:19 will serve in the Tabernacle on behalf of the **I**
9: 1 and the rest of the **I** were in the wilderness of
9: 2 "Tell the **I** to celebrate the Passover at the proper
9: 7 offering at the proper time with the rest of the **I**?"
9:10 "Say to the **I**: 'If any of the people now or in
9:19 the **I** stayed for a long time, just as the LORD
10:12 So the **I** set out from the wilderness of Sinai
11: 4 with the **I** began to crave the good things of Egypt,
11:35 From there the **I** traveled to Hazeroth, where they
13:24 At that time the **I** renamed the valley Eshcol—
13:32 discouraging reports about the land among the **I**:
14:10 appeared to all the **I** from above the Tabernacle.
14:27 I have heard everything the **I** have been saying.
14:39 When Moses reported the LORD's words to the **I**,
15:13 If you native **I** want to present an offering by fire
15:15 Native **I** and foreigners are the same before the
15:29 This same law applies both to native **I**
15:30 whether native **I** or foreigners,
16:40 This would warn the **I** that no unauthorized man—
18: 6 from among the **I** to be your special assistants.
18:11 "All the other offerings presented to me by the **I**
18:22 **I** other than the priests and Levites are to stay
18:23 will receive no inheritance of land among the **I**,
18:24 receive no inheritance of land among the **I**."
18:26 'When you receive the tithes from the **I**, give a
18:28 tithe received from the **I** as a gift to the LORD.
20:19 The **I** answered, "We will stay on the main road.
21: 1 heard that the **I** were approaching on the road to
21: 1 So he attacked the **I** and took some of them as
21: 3 The **I** completely destroyed them and their towns,
21:10 The **I** traveled next to Oboth and camped there.
21:16 From there the **I** traveled to Beer, which is the well
21:17 There the **I** sang this song: / "Spring up, O well!
21:18 Then the **I** left the wilderness and proceeded on
21:21 The **I** now sent ambassadors to King Sihon of the
21:24 But the **I** slaughtered them and occupied their land
22: 2 knew what the **I** had done to the Amorites.
22: 3 And when they saw how many **I** there were,
24:14 But first let me tell you what the **I** will do to your
25: 1 While the **I** were camped at Acacia, some of the
25: 2 and soon the **I** were feasting with them
25: 8 So the plague against the **I** was stopped,
25:11 **I** by displaying passionate zeal among them on my
26:62 of land when it was divided among the **I**.
27:11 The **I** must observe this as a general legal
31: 2 on the Midianites for leading the **I** into idolatry.
32:17 and lead our fellow **I** into battle until we have
33: 1 This is the itinerary the **I** followed as they marched
33: 5 leaving Rameses, the **I** set up camp at Succoth.
33:41 The **I** left Mount Hor and camped at Zalmonah.
33:51 "Speak to the **I** and tell them: 'When you cross the
34: 2 "Give these instructions to the **I**: When you come
34:13 Then Moses told the **I**, "This is the territory you
34:29 the dividing of the land of Canaan among the **I**."
35:15 These cities are for the protection of **I**,
36: 5 So Moses gave the **I** this command from the
36: 8 so that all the **I** will keep their ancestral property.
Dt 1: 3 But forty years after the **I** left Mount Sinai, on a
1: 3 in midwinter, Moses gave these speeches to the **I**,
1:16 be perfectly fair at all times, not only to fellow **I**,
3:20 the LORD has given security to the rest of the **I**,
4:44 This is the law that Moses handed down to the **I**.
4:46 by Moses and the **I** as they came up from Egypt.
15: 2 cancel the loans they have made to their fellow **I**.
15: 3 from debt, however, applies only to your fellow **I**
15:11 freely with the poor and with other **I** in need.
18: 2 will have no inheritance of their own among the **I**.
18:15 you a prophet like me from among your fellow **I**,
18:18 up a prophet like you from among their fellow **I**.
23:20 You may charge interest to foreigners, but not to **I**,
24:14 whether fellow **I** or foreigners living in your
29: 1 with the **I** while they were in the land of Moab,
29: 2 Moses summoned all the **I** and said to them,
31:22 down the words of the song and taught it to the **I**.
32:51 For both of you broke faith with me among the **I** at
Jos 2: 2 "Some **I** have come here tonight to spy out the
3: 1 the next morning Joshua and all the **I** left Acacia
3: 7 begin to make you great in the eyes of all the **I**.
3: 9 So Joshua told the **I**, "Come and listen to what the
4:12 and the half-tribe of Manasseh led the **I** across the
4:14 LORD made Joshua great in the eyes of all the **I**,
4:21 Then Joshua said to the **I**, "In the future,
4:22 'This is where the **I** crossed the Jordan on dry
5: 2 "Use knives of flint to make the **I** a circumcised
5: 6 The **I** wandered in the wilderness for forty years
5:10 While the **I** were camped at Gilgal on the plains of
5:12 So from that time on the **I** ate from the crops of
6: 1 tightly shut because the people were afraid of the **I**.
6:15 On the seventh day the **I** got up at dawn
6:20 and the **I** charged straight into the city from every
6:24 Then the **I** burned the city and everything in it.
6:25 to Jericho. And she lives among the **I** to this day.
7: 1 so the LORD was very angry with the **I**.
7: 5 chased the **I** from the city gate as far as the
7: 5 The **I** were paralyzed with fear at this turn of
7:12 That is why the **I** are running from their enemies in
7:23 the tent and brought them to Joshua and all the **I**.
7:24 Then Joshua and all the **I** took Achan, the silver,
7:25 And all the **I** stoned Achan and his family
8: 6 'The **I** are running away from us as they did
8:14 When the king of Ai saw the **I** across the valley,
8:14 and attacked the **I** at a place overlooking the
8:17 left in Ai or Bethel who did not chase after the **I**,
8:20 For the **I** who had fled in the direction of the
8:21 and the other **I** saw that the ambush had succeeded
8:22 Then the **I** who were inside the city came out
8:27 for the **I** kept these for themselves, as the LORD
8:29 At sunset the **I** took down the body and threw it in
8:32 And as the **I** watched, Joshua copied the law of
8:33 Then all the **I**—foreigners and citizens alike—
8:35 and the foreigners who lived among the **I**.
9: 2 their armies to fight against Joshua and the **I**.
9: 7 The **I** replied to these Hivites, "How do we know
9:17 The **I** set out at once to investigate and reached
9:18 But the **I** did not attack the towns, for their leaders
9:21 So the **I** kept their promise to the Gibeonites.
10:10 and the **I** slaughtered them in great numbers at
10:10 Then the **I** chased the enemy along the road to
10:11 The hail killed more of the enemy than the **I** killed
10:12 On the day the LORD gave the **I** victory over the
10:13 and moon stood still until the **I** had defeated their
10:21 Then the **I** returned safely to their camp at
10:29 Then Joshua and the **I** went to Libnah and attacked
10:31 Joshua and the **I** went to Lachish and attacked it.

11: 8 The **I** chased them as far as Great Sidon
11: 11 The **I** completely destroyed every living thing in
11: 14 And the **I** took all the captured goods and cattle of
11: 19 No one in this region made peace with the **I** except
11: 20 and caused them to fight the **I** instead of asking for
12: 6 and the **I** had destroyed the people of King Sihon
13: 6 "I will drive these people out of the land for the **I**.
13: 13 But the **I** failed to drive out the people of Geshur
13: 13 so they continue to live among the **I** to this day.
13: 22 The **I** also killed Balaam the magician, the son of
17: 13 however, when the **I** became strong enough,
19: 49 the **I** gave a special piece of land to Joshua as his
20: 2 "Now tell the **I** to designate the cities of refuge,
20: 9 These cities were set apart for **I** as well as the
21: 8 So the **I** obeyed the LORD's command to Moses
21: 9 The **I** gave the following towns from the tribes of
22: 32 and returned to the land of Canaan to tell the **I**
22: 33 And all the **I** were satisfied and praised God
24: 32 which the **I** had brought along with them when
Jdg 1: 1 After Joshua died, the **I** asked the LORD,
1: 6 but the **I** soon captured him and cut off his thumbs
1: 28 When the **I** grew stronger, they forced the
2: 1 up from Gilgal to Bokim with a message for the **I**.
2: 4 the LORD finished speaking, the **I** wept loudly.
2: 7 And the **I** served the LORD throughout the
2: 11 Then the **I** did what was evil in the LORD's sight
2: 16 Then the LORD raised up judges to rescue the **I**
3: 1 **I** who had not participated in the wars of Canaan.
3: 2 He did this to teach warfare to generations of **I**
3: 4 These people were left to test the **I**—to see whether
3: 6 to their sons. And the **I** worshiped their gods.
3: 7 The **I** did what was evil in the LORD's sight.
3: 8 And the **I** were subject to Cushan-rishathaim for
3: 12 Once again the **I** did what was evil in the
3: 14 And the **I** were subject to Eglon of Moab for
3: 15 The **I** sent Ehud to deliver their tax money to King
3: 27 Then he led a band of **I** down from the hills.
3: 28 And the **I** took control of the shallows of the
4: 1 the **I** again did what was evil in the LORD's
4: 3 ruthlessly oppressed the **I** for twenty years.
4: 3 Then the **I** cried out to the LORD for help.
4: 5 and the **I** came to her to settle their disputes.
6: 1 Again the **I** did what was evil in the LORD's
6: 2 so cruel that the **I** fled to the mountains,
6: 3 Whenever the **I** planted their crops,
6: 4 They left the **I** with nothing to eat, taking all the
6: 6 Then the **I** cried out to the LORD for help.
6: 8 the LORD sent a prophet to the **I**. He said,
7: 2 the **I** will boast to me that they saved themselves
7: 22 When the three hundred **I** blew their horns,
7: 25 Afterward the **I** brought the heads of Oreb
8: 22 Then the **I** said to Gideon, "Be our ruler! You
8: 27 But soon all the **I** prostituted themselves by
8: 33 the **I** prostituted themselves by worshiping the
10: 6 Again the **I** did evil in the LORD's sight.
10: 8 For eighteen years they oppressed all the **I** east of
10: 9 and Ephraim. The **I** were in great distress.
10: 15 But the **I** pleaded with the LORD and said,
10: 16 Then the **I** put aside their foreign gods and served
11: 13 "When the **I** came out of Egypt,
13: 1 Again the **I** did what was evil in the LORD's
14: 3 in our tribe or among all the **I** you could marry?
19: 12 can't stay in this foreign city where there are no **I**.
20: 1 Then all the **I**, from Dan to Beersheba and from the
20: 3 The **I** then asked how this terrible crime had
20: 11 So all the **I** were united, and they gathered together
20: 12 The **I** sent messengers to the tribe of Benjamin,
20: 14 their towns and gathered at Gibeah to fight the **I**.
20: 18 Before the battle the **I** went to Bethel and asked
20: 19 So the **I** left early the next morning and camped
20: 21 and killed twenty-two thousand **I** in the field that
20: 22 But the **I** took courage and assembled at the same
20: 25 of Benjamin killed another eighteen thousand **I**,
20: 26 Then all the **I** went up to Bethel and wept in the
20: 27 And the **I** went up seeking direction from the
20: 28 The **I** asked the LORD, "Should we fight against
20: 29 So the **I** set an ambush all around Gibeah.
20: 31 as they had done before, they began to kill the **I**.
20: 31 About thirty **I** died in the open fields and along the
20: 32 But the **I** had agreed in advance to run away
20: 33 Then the **I** hiding in ambush west of Gibeah
20: 35 and that day the **I** killed 25,100 of Benjamin's
20: 36 The **I** had retreated from Benjamin's warriors in
20: 39 which was the signal for the **I** to turn and attack
20: 39 time Benjamin's warriors had killed about thirty **I**,
20: 41 the **I** turned and attacked. At this point Benjamin's
20: 42 but the **I** chased after them and killed them.
20: 43 The **I** surrounded the Benjaminites and were
20: 48 Then the **I** returned and slaughtered every living
21: 1 The **I** had vowed at Mizpah never to give their
21: 6 The **I** felt deep sadness for Benjamin and said,
1Sa 2: 14 All the **I** who came to worship at Shiloh were
4: 5 When the **I** saw the Ark of the Covenant of the
7: 4 So the **I** destroyed their images of Baal
7: 7 The **I** were badly frightened when they learned that
7: 10 into such confusion that the **I** defeated them.
11: 15 and Saul and all the **I** were very happy.
12: 8 "When the **I** were in Egypt and cried out to the
13: 4 that the Philistines now hated the **I** more than ever.
13: 20 So whenever the **I** needed to sharpen their
14: 18 Ahijah was wearing the ephod in front of the **I**.
14: 21 joined in with Saul, Jonathan, and the rest of the **I**.
14: 52 The **I** fought constantly with the Philistines
17: 3 and **I** faced each other on opposite hills,
17: 8 Goliath stood and shouted across to the **I**, "Do you
17: 11 When Saul and the **I** heard this, they were terrified
17: 52 Then the **I** gave a great shout of triumph
29: 1 at Aphek, and the **I** camped at the spring in Jezreel.
31: 1 the Philistines attacked Israel, forcing the **I** to flee.
31: 7 When the **I** on the other side of the Jezreel Valley
2Sa 7: 6 from the day I brought the **I** out of Egypt until
10: 18 But again the Arameans fled from the **I**. This time
19: 8 the **I** who supported Absalom had fled to their
21: 4 "And we don't want to see the **I** executed in
23: 11 at Lehi and attacked the **I** in a field full of lentils.
1Ki 9: 20 still some people living in the land who were not **I**,
9: 22 But Solomon did not conscript any of the **I** for
11: 15 to bury some **I** who had died in battle.
12: 17 But Rehoboam continued to rule over the **I** who
12: 24 Do not fight against your relatives, the **I**. Go back
14: 24 LORD had driven from the land ahead of the **I**.
20: 20 The **I** chased them, but King Ben-hadad and a few
20: 29 The **I** killed 100,000 Aramean foot soldiers in one
21: 26 LORD had driven from the land ahead of the **I**.
2Ki 13: 5 So the LORD raised up a deliverer to rescue the **I**
13: 21 Once when some **I** were burying a man, they spied
16: 3 LORD had driven from the land ahead of the **I**.
17: 14 But the **I** would not listen. They were as stubborn
18: 11 At that time the king of Assyria deported the **I** to
21: 2 LORD had driven from the land ahead of the **I**.
21: 8 If the **I** will obey my commands—the whole law
21: 9 LORD had destroyed when the **I** entered the land.
1Ch 10: 1 the Philistines attacked Israel, forcing the **I** to flee.
10: 7 When the **I** in the Jezreel Valley saw that their
13: 2 let us send messages to all the **I** throughout the
15: 3 Then David summoned all the **I** to Jerusalem to
17: 5 from the day I brought the **I** out of Egypt until
19: 18 But again the Arameans fled from the **I**. This time
21: 1 and caused David to take a census of the **I**.
27: 23 because the LORD had promised to make the **I** as
2Ch 8: 2 Hiram had given him, and he settled **I** in them.
8: 7 still some people living in the land who were not **I**,
8: 9 But Solomon did not conscript any of the **I** for
10: 17 But Rehoboam continued to rule over the **I** who
10: 18 to restore order, but the **I** stoned him to death.
11: 3 of Judah, and to all the **I** in Judah and Benjamin:
24: 9 of God, had required of the **I** in the wilderness.
28: 3 LORD had driven from the land ahead of the **I**.
31: 1 the **I** who attended went to all the towns of Judah,
31: 1 the **I** returned to their own towns and homes.
33: 2 LORD had driven from the land ahead of the **I**.
33: 8 If the **I** will obey my commands—
33: 9 LORD had destroyed when the **I** entered the land.
35: 17 All the **I** present in Jerusalem celebrated Passover
Ezr 3: 1 early autumn, when the **I** had settled in their towns,
Ne 7: 73 when the **I** had settled in their towns,
8: 14 **I** should live in shelters during the festival to be
8: 17 The **I** had not celebrated this way since the days of
11: 20 and the rest of the **I** lived wherever their family
13: 2 For they had not been friendly to the **I** when they
Ps 105: 25 Then he turned the Egyptians against the **I**,
114: 1 When the **I** escaped from Egypt—
Isa 17: 9 the Amorites abandoned when the **I** came here
Jer 7: 12 because of all the wickedness of my people, the **I**.
50: 17 "The **I** are like sheep that have been scattered by
Eze 14: 7 both **I** and foreigners, who reject me and set up
47: 22 They will be just like native-born **I** to you,
Hos 2: 23 "At that time I will plant a crop of **I** and raise
12: 13 the **I**, out of Egypt by a prophet, who guided
Am 1: 11 chased down their relatives, the **I**, with swords.
3: 12 So it will be when the **I** in Samaria are rescued
4: 5 This is the kind of thing you **I** love to do,"
9: 7 "Do you **I** think you are more important to me
Mt 8: 12 But many **I**—those for whom the Kingdom was
Lk 1: 16 And he will persuade many **I** to turn to the Lord
2Co 11: 22 So am I. And they say they are **I**? So am I.
Heb 12: 18 as the **I** did at Mount Sinai when God gave them

ISRAELITES' (2) [ISRAEL]

Ex 9: 7 it was true that none of the **I** animals were dead.
Nu 18: 24 because I have given them the **I** tithes, which have

ISSACHAR (41)

Ge 30: 18 She named him **I**, for she said, "God has rewarded
35: 23 oldest son), Simeon, Levi, Judah, **I**, and Zebulun.
46: 13 The sons of **I** were Tola, Puah, Jashub,
49: 14 "**I** is a strong beast of burden, / resting among the
Ex 1: 3 **I**, Zebulun, Benjamin,
Nu 1: 8 **I** | Nethanel son of Zuar
1: 28[-29] **I** | 54,400
2: 3[-4] "The divisions of Judah, **I**, and Zebulun are to
2: 5[-6] **I** | Nethanel son of Zuar | 54,400
7: 18 leader of the tribe of **I**, presented his offering.
10: 15 The tribe of **I** was led by Nethanel son of Zuar.
13: 7 **I** | Igal son of Joseph
26: 23 These were the clans descended from the sons of **I**:
26: 25 The men from all the clans of **I** numbered 64,300.
34: 26 **I** | Paltiel son of Azzan
Dt 27: 12 the tribes of Simeon, Levi, Judah, **I**, Joseph,
33: 18 Moses said this about the tribes of Zebulun and **I**:
33: 18 May the people of **I** prosper at home in their tents.
Jos 17: 10 of Asher, and to the east was the territory of **I**.
17: 11 The following towns within the territory of **I**
19: 17 of land went to the families of the tribe of **I**.
19: 23 was the inheritance of the families of the tribe of **I**.
21: 6 received thirteen towns from the tribes of **I**,
21: 28 From the tribe of **I** they received Kishion,
Jdg 5: 15 The princes of **I** were with Deborah and Barak.
10: 1 He was from the tribe of **I** but lived in the town of
1Ki 4: 17 Jehoshaphat son of Paruah, in **I**.
15: 27 from the tribe of **I**, plotted against Nadab
1Ch 2: 1 were Reuben, Simeon, Levi, Judah, **I**, Zebulun,
6: 62 sacred lots thirteen towns from the territories of **I**,
6: 72 From the territory of **I**, they were given Kedesh,
7: 1 The four sons of **I** were Tola, Puah, Jashub,
7: 5 from all the clans of the tribe of **I** was 87,000.
12: 32 From the tribe of **I**, there were 200 leaders of the
12: 40 And people from as far away as **I**, Zebulun,
26: 5 Ammiel (the sixth), **I** (the seventh), and Peullethai
27: 18 (a brother of David) / **I** | Omri son of Michael
2Ch 30: 18 of those who came from Ephraim, Manasseh, **I**,
Eze 48: 25 Next is the territory of **I** with the same eastern
48: 33 will have gates named for Simeon, **I**, and Zebulun.
Rev 7: 7 from Levi | 12,000 / from **I** | 12,000

ISSHIAH (6)

1Ch 7: 3 of Izrahiah were Michael, Obadiah, Joel, and **I**.
12: 6 Elkanah, **I**, Azarel, Joezer, and Jashobeam,
23: 20 Micah (the family leader) and **I** (the second).
24: 21 the descendants of Rehabiah, the leader was **I**.
24: 25 along with **I**, the brother of Micah.
24: 25 From the descendants of **I**, the leader was

ISSUE (9) [ISSUED]

Dt 4: 14 time that the LORD commanded me to **i** the laws
Jdg 11: 26 But now after three hundred years you make an **i**
Ezr 4: 21 **i** orders to have these people stop their work.
Est 1: 19 we suggest that you **i** a written decree, a law of the
3: 9 Your Majesty, **i** a decree that they be destroyed,
Isa 10: 1 for the unjust judges, for those who **i** unfair laws.
Da 6: 8 And let Your Majesty **i** and sign this law so it
Mt 7: 21 The decisive **i** is whether they obey my Father in
1Co 11: 17 But now when I mention this next **i**, I cannot praise

ISSUED (25) [ISSUE]

Nu 25: 4 The LORD **i** the following command to Moses:
26: 3 and Eleazar the priest **i** these census instructions to
Jos 10: 18 he **i** this command: "Cover the opening of the cave
1Ki 22: 31 Now the king of Aram had **i** these orders to his
2Ki 23: 21 King Josiah then **i** this order to all the people:
1Ch 15: 2 Then he **i** these instructions: "When we transport
2Ch 18: 30 Now the king of Aram had **i** these orders to his
35: 3 He **i** this order to the Levites, who had been set
Ezr 5: 13 **i** a decree that the Temple of God should be
5: 17 **i** a decree to rebuild God's Temple in Jerusalem.
6: 1 So King Darius **i** orders that a search be made in
6: 12 destroys this Temple. I, Darius, have **i** this decree.
Ne 10: 29 to obey the law of God as **i** by his servant Moses.
Est 3: 14 A copy of this decree was to be **i** in every province
4: 8 Mordecai gave Hathach a copy of the decree **i** in
8: 14 The same decree was also **i** at the fortress of Susa.
9: 25 he **i** a decree causing Haman's evil plot to backfire,
Ps 78: 5 For he **i** his decree to Jacob; / he gave his law to
148: 5 for he **i** his command, and they came into being.
Isa 9: 5 In that day of peace, battle gear will no longer be **i**.
Da 2: 15 "Why has the king **i** such a harsh decree?"
3: 10 You **i** a decree requiring all the people to bow
4: 6 So I **i** an order calling in all the wise men of
Mt 14: 9 in front of his guests, he **i** the necessary orders.
27: 58 And Pilate **i** an order to release it to him.

ISUAH [KJV] See ISHVAH

ISUI [KJV] See ISHVI

IT (4851) [IT'S, ITS, ITSELF] See Index of Articles, Etc.

IT'S (81) [BE, IT] See Index of Articles, Etc.

ITALIAN (1) [ITALY]

Ac 10: 1 who was a captain of the **I** Regiment.

ITALY (5) [ITALIAN]

Ac 18: 2 who had recently arrived from **I** with his wife,
18: 2 They had been expelled from **I** as a result of
27: 1 When the time came, we set sail for **I**. Paul
27: 6 ship from Alexandria that was bound for **I**,
Heb 13: 24 The Christians from **I** send you their greetings.

ITCH (1)

Dt 28: 27 boils of Egypt and with tumors, scurvy, and the **i**,

ITEM (2) [ITEMS]

Lev 6: 2 an **i** entrusted to their safekeeping has been lost
6: 3 Or suppose they find a lost **i** and lie about it,

ITEMS (22) [ITEM]

Ge 38: 18 So Judah gave these **i** to her. She then let him sleep
Ex 25: 3 Here is a list of **i** you may accept on my behalf:
28: 5 These **i** must be made of fine linen cloth
Nu 4: 26 are responsible for transporting all these **i**.
31: 50 So we are presenting the **i** of gold we captured as
1Ch 9: 29 the **i** in the sanctuary, and the supplies such as
26: 28 and his relatives also cared for the **i** dedicated to
26: 28 All the other dedicated **i** were in their care, too.
28: 13 And he gave specifications for the **i** in the
28: 14 and silver should be used to make the necessary **i**.
2Ch 21: 3 gold, and costly **i**, and also the ownership of some
28: 21 Ahaz took valuable **i** from the LORD's Temple,
32: 27 and spices, and for his shields and other valuable **i**.
Ezr 1: 7 King Cyrus himself brought out the valuable **i**
1: 8 to count these **i** and present them to Sheshbazzar,
1: 9 These were the **i** Cyrus donated: / silver trays
1: 10 bowls | 30 / silver bowls | 410 / other **i** | 1,000

1:11 and silver **i** were turned over to Sheshbazzar to
5:14 These **i** were taken from that temple and delivered
8:25 and the other **i** that the king, his council,
Ne 10:33 It will also provide for the other **i** necessary for the
Eze 18: 7 not keeping the **i** given in pledge by poor debtors,

ITHAI (2)
2Sa 23:29 **I** son of Ribai from Gibeah (from the tribe of
1Ch 11:31 **I** son of Ribai from Gibeah (from the tribe of

ITHAMAR (19) [ITHAMAR'S]
Ex 6:23 and she bore him Nadab, Abihu, Eleazar, and **I**.
28: 1 Aaron, and his sons, Nadab, Abihu, Eleazar, and **I**,
38:21 and **I** son of Aaron the priest served as recorder.
Lev 10: 6 Moses said to Aaron and his sons Eleazar and **I**,
10:12 to Aaron and his remaining sons, Eleazar and **I**,
10:16 a result, he became very angry with Eleazar and **I**,
Nu 3: 2 were Nadab (the firstborn), Abihu, Eleazar, and **I**.
3: 4 and **I** to serve as priests with their father,
4:28 They will be directly responsible to **I** son of Aaron
4:33 They are directly responsible to **I** son of Aaron the
7: 8 All their work was done under the leadership of **I**
26:60 To Aaron were born Nadab, Abihu, Eleazar, and **I**.
1Ch 6: 3 sons of Aaron were Nadab, Abihu, Eleazar, and **I**.
24: 1 sons of Aaron were Nadab, Abihu, Eleazar, and **I**.
24: 2 only Eleazar and **I** were left to carry on as priests.
24: 3 and of Ahimelech, who was a descendant of **I**,
24: 5 from among the descendants of both Eleazar and **I**.
24: 6 of Eleazar and **I** took turns casting lots.
Ezr 8: 2 Gershom. / From the family of **I**: Daniel.

ITHAMAR'S (1) [ITHAMAR]
1Ch 24: 4 were divided into sixteen groups and **I** into eight,

ITHIEL (1)
Ne 11: 7 son of Maaseiah, son of **I**, son of Jeshaiah;

ITHLAH (1)
Jos 19:42 Shaalabbin, Aijalon, **I**,

ITHMAH (1)
1Ch 11:46 and Joshaviah, the sons of Elnaam; / **I** from Moab;

ITHNAN (1)
Jos 15:23 Kedesh, Hazor, **I**,

ITHRAN (3)
Ge 36:26 of Dishon were Hemdan, Eshban, **I**, and Keran.
1Ch 1:41 of Dishon were Hemdan, Eshban, **I**, and Keran.
7:37 Bezer, Hod, Shamma, Shilshah, **I**, and Beera.

ITHREAM (2)
2Sa 3: 5 The sixth was **I**, whose mother was David's wife
1Ch 3: 3 The sixth was **I**, whose mother was Eglah.

ITHRITES (1)
1Ch 2:53 the **I**, Puthites, Shumathites, and Mishraites,

ITINERARY (1)
Nu 33: 1 This is the **i** the Israelites followed as they marched

ITS (947) [IT] See Index of Articles, Etc.

ITSELF (49) [IT, SELF] See Index of Articles, Etc.

ITTAH-KAZIN [KJV] See ETH-KAZIN

ITTAI (6)
2Sa 15:19 Then the king turned to **I**, the captain of the
15:21 But **I** said to the king, "I vow by the LORD
15:22 So **I** and his six hundred men and their families
18: 2 son of Zeruiah, and one-third under **I** the Gittite.
18: 5 king gave this command to Joab, Abishai, and **I**:
18:12 all heard the king say to you and Abishai and **I**,

ITUREA (1)
Lk 3: 1 his brother Philip was ruler over **I** and Traconitis;

IVORY (13)
1Ki 10:18 Then the king made a huge **i** throne and overlaid it
10:22 down with gold, silver, **i**, apes, and peacocks.
22:39 events in Ahab's reign and the story of the **i** palace
2Ch 9:17 Then the king made a huge **i** throne and overlaid it
9:21 down with gold, silver, **i**, apes, and peacocks.
Ps 45: 8 aloes, and cassia. / In palaces decorated with **i**,
SS 5:14 His body is like bright **i**, aglow with sapphires.
7: 4 Your neck is as stately as an **i** tower. Your eyes are
Eze 27: 6 coasts of Cyprus. Then they inlaid it with **i**.
27:15 they brought payment in **i** tusks and ebony wood.
Am 3:15 summer houses, too—all their palaces filled with **i**.
6: 4 How terrible it will be for you who sprawl on **i**
Rev 18:12 every kind of perfumed wood, **i** goods,

IVVAH (3)
2Ki 18:34 what about the gods of Sepharvaim, Hena, and **I**?
19:13 to the kings of Sepharvaim, Hena, and **I**?"
Isa 37:13 to the kings of Sepharvaim, Hena, and **I**?"

IYE-ABARIM (3)
Nu 21:11 Then they went on to **I**, in the wilderness on the
33:44 left Oboth and camped at **I** on the border of Moab.
33:45 They left **I** and camped at Dibon-gad.

IZHAR (14)
Ex 6:18 of Kohath included Amram, **I**, Hebron, and Uzziel.
6:21 The descendants of **I** included Korah, Nepheg,
Nu 3:19 of his descendants, Amram, **I**, Hebron, and Uzziel.
3:27 descended from Amram, **I**, Hebron, and Uzziel.
16: 1 One day Korah son of **I**, a descendant of Kohath
1Ch 4: 7 Helah gave birth to Zereth, **I**, Ethnan,
6: 2 of Kohath were Amram, **I**, Hebron, and Uzziel.
6:18 of Kohath included Amram, **I**, Hebron, and Uzziel.
6:38 **I**, Kohath, Levi, and Israel.
23:12 of Kohath included Amram, **I**, Hebron, and Uzziel.
23:18 The descendants of **I** included Shelomith,
24:22 From the descendants of **I**, the leader was
26:23 descended from Amram, **I**, Hebron, and Uzziel:
26:29 From the clan of **I** came Kenaniah. He and his sons

IZLIAH (1)
1Ch 8:18 Ishmerai, **I**, and Jobab were the sons of Elpaal.

IZRAHIAH (2)
1Ch 7: 3 The son of Uzzi was **I**. The sons of **I** were Michael,

IZRAHITE (1)
1Ch 27: 8 Shammah the **I** was commander of the fifth

IZZIAH (1)
Ezr 10:25 Ramiah, **I**, Malkijah, Mijamin, Eleazar,

J

JAAKAN (1) [BENE-JAAKAN]
Dt 10: 6 of Israel set out from the wells of the people of **J**

JAAKOBAH (1)
1Ch 4:36 Elioenai, **J**, Jeshohaiah, Asaiah, Adiel, Jesimiel,

JAALAH (2)
Ezr 2:56 **J**, Darkon, Giddel,
Ne 7:58 **J**, Darkon, Giddel,

JAAR (1)
Ps 132: 6 then we found it in the distant countryside of **J**.

JAARESHIAH (1)
1Ch 8:27 **J**, Elijah, and Zicri were the sons of Jeroham.

JAASIEL (2)
1Ch 11:47 Eliel and Obed; / **J** from Zobah.
27:21 son of Zechariah / Benjamin | **J** son of Abner

JAASU (1)
Ezr 10:37 Mattaniah, Mattenai, and **J**.

JAAZANIAH (5)
2Ki 25:23 and **J** son of the Maacathite, and all their men.
Jer 35: 3 So I went to see **J** son of Jeremiah and grandson of
40: 8 **J** son of the Maacathite, and all their men.
Eze 8:11 there with **J** son of Shaphan in the middle.
11: 1 Among them were **J** son of Azzur and Pelatiah son

JAAZIAH (2)
1Ch 24:26 From the descendants of **J**, the leader was Beno.
24:27 From the descendants of Merari through **J**,

JAAZIEL (1) [AZIEL]
1Ch 15:18 Zechariah, **J**, Shemiramoth, Jehiel, Unni, Eliab,

JABAL (1)
Ge 4:20 Adah gave birth to a baby named **J**. He became the

JABBOK (8)
Ge 32:22 and eleven sons across the **J** River.
Nu 21:24 their land from the Arnon River to the **J** River.
Dt 2:37 we stayed away from the Ammonites along the **J**
3:16 all the way to the **J** River on the Ammonite
Jos 12: 2 from the middle of the Arnon Gorge to the **J** River,
12: 2 area of Gilead, which lies north of the **J** River.
Jdg 11:13 they stole my land from the Arnon River to the **J**
11:22 from the Arnon River to the **J** River, and from the

JABESH (10) [JABESH-GILEAD]
1Sa 11: 1 But the citizens of **J** asked for peace. "Make a
11: 3 replied the leaders of **J**. "If none of our relatives
11: 5 So they told him about the message from **J**.
11:10 The men of **J** then told their enemies,
31:12 They brought them to **J**, where they burned the
31:13 and buried them beneath the tamarisk tree at **J**,
2Ki 15:10 Then Shallum son of **J** conspired against
15:13 Shallum son of **J** began to rule over Israel in the
1Ch 10:12 the bodies of Saul and his three sons back to **J**.
10:12 they buried their remains beneath the oak tree at **J**,

JABESH-GILEAD (13) [GILEAD, JABESH]
Jdg 21: 8 And they discovered that no one from **J** had
21: 9 counted all the people, no one from **J** was present.
21:10 So they sent twelve thousand warriors to **J** with
21:12 Among the residents of **J** they found four hundred
21:14 and the four hundred women of **J** who were spared
21:22 find enough wives for them when we destroyed **J**.
1Sa 11: 1 Ammon led his army against the Israelite city of **J**.
11: 9 So Saul sent the messengers back to **J** to say,
31:11 But when the people of **J** heard what the
2Sa 2: 4 When David heard that the men of **J** had buried
21:12 he went to the people of **J** and asked for the bones
21:12 it was the people of **J** who had retrieved their
1Ch 10:11 But when the people of **J** heard what the

JABEZ (3)
1Ch 2:55 and the families of scribes living at **J**—
4: 9 There was a man named **J** who was more
4: 9 His mother named him **J** because his birth had

JABIN (6) [JABIN'S]
Jos 11: 1 When King **J** of Hazor heard what had happened,
Jdg 4: 2 So the LORD handed them over to King **J** of
4:17 was on friendly terms with King **J** of Hazor.
4:23 So on that day Israel saw God subdue **J**,
4:24 became stronger and stronger against King **J**,
Ps 83: 9 or as you did to Sisera and **J** at the Kishon River.

JABIN'S (1) [JABIN]
Jdg 4: 7 I will lure Sisera, commander of **J** army,

JABNEEL (2)
Jos 15:11 It passed **J** and ended at the Mediterranean Sea.
19:33 **J**, and as far as Lakkum, ending at the Jordan

JABNEH (1)
2Ch 26: 6 and broke down the walls of Gath, **J**, and Ashdod.

JACAN (1)
1Ch 5:13 Meshullam, Sheba, Jorai, **J**, Zia, and Eber.

JACINTH (3)
Ex 28:19 The third row will contain a **j**, an agate, and an
39:12 In the third row were a **j**, an agate, and an
Rev 21:20 the eleventh **j**, the twelfth amethyst.

JACKAL (1) [JACKAL'S, JACKALS]
Mic 1: 8 I will howl like a **j** and wail like an ostrich.

JACKAL'S (1) [JACKAL]
Ne 2:13 went out through the Valley Gate, past the **J** Well,

JACKALS (16) [JACKAL]
Job 30:29 I am considered a brother to **j** and a companion to
Ps 63:10 will die by the sword / and become the food of **j**.
Isa 13:22 and **j** will make their dens in its palaces.
34:13 The ruins will become a haunt for **j** and a home for
35: 7 and rushes will flourish where desert **j** once lived.
43:20 the **j** and ostriches, too, for giving them water in
Jer 9:11 says the LORD. "It will be a place haunted by **j**.
10:22 will be destroyed and will become a haunt for **j**.
14: 6 stand on the bare hills panting like thirsty **j**.
49:33 "Hazor will be inhabited by **j**, and it will be
50:39 of Babylon will be inhabited by ostriches and **j**.
51:37 will become a heap of rubble, haunted by **j**.
La 4: 3 Even the **j** feed their young, but not my people
5:18 is empty and desolate, a place haunted by **j**.
Eze 13: 4 these prophets of yours are like **j** digging around in
Mal 1: 3 I turned Esau's inheritance into a desert for **j**."

JACKET (1)
Pr 25:20 is as bad as stealing someone's **j** in cold weather

JACOB (314) [JACOB'S]
GOD OF JACOB (11) Ex 3:6,15; 4:5; 2Sa 23:1; Ps 76:6; 81:4; Mt 22:32; Mk 12:26; Lk 20:37; Ac 3:13; 7:46
SERVANT JACOB (8) Ge 32:4,18,20; 1Ch 16:13; Ps 105:6; Isa 41:8; Eze 28:25; 37:25
Ge 25:26 So they called him **J**. Isaac was sixty years old
25:27 while **J** was the kind of person who liked to stay at
25:28 game he brought home, but Rebekah favored **J**.
25:29 One day when **J** was cooking some stew,
25:30 Esau said to **J**, "I'm starved! Give me some of that
25:31 **J** replied, "All right, but trade me your birthright
25:33 So **J** insisted, "Well then, swear to me right now
25:34 Then **J** gave Esau some bread and lentil stew.
27: 6 she said to her son **J**, "I overheard your father
27:11 "But Mother!" **J** replied. "He won't be fooled
27:14 So **J** followed his mother's instructions,
27:15 were there in the house, and dressed **J** with them.
27:18 **J** carried the platter of food to his father and said,

27:18 my son," he answered. "Who is it—Esau or J?"
27:19 J replied, "It's Esau, your older son. I've done as
27:20 LORD your God put it in my path!" J replied.
27:21 Then Isaac said to J, "Come over here. I want to
27:22 So J went over to his father, and Isaac touched
27:23 But he did not recognize J because Jacob's hands
27:23 like Esau's. So Isaac pronounced his blessing on J.
27:24 son Esau?" he asked. "Yes, of course," J replied.
27:25 So J took the food over to his father, and Isaac ate
it. He also drank the wine that J served him.
27:27 So J went over and kissed him. And when Isaac
27:30 As soon as Isaac had blessed J, and almost before
J had left his father,
27:36 Esau said bitterly, "No wonder his name is J,
27:37 "I have made J your master and have declared that
27:41 Esau hated J because he had stolen his blessing,
27:41 will soon be dead and gone. Then I will kill J."
27:42 She sent for J and told him, "Esau is threatening
27:46 I'd rather die than see J marry one of them."
28: 1 So Isaac called for J, blessed him, and said,
28: 5 So Isaac sent J away, and he went to Paddan-aram
28: 6 Esau heard that his father had blessed J and sent
28: 6 and that he had warned J not to marry a Canaanite
28: 7 He also knew that J had obeyed his parents
28:10 J left Beersheba and traveled toward Haran.
28:11 J found a stone for a pillow and lay down to sleep.
28:16 Then J woke up and said, "Surely the LORD is
28:20 Then J made this vow: "If God will be with me
29: 1 J hurried on, finally arriving in the land of the east.
29: 4 J went over to the shepherds and asked them,
29: 6 J asked. "He's well and prosperous. Look,
29: 7 J asked. "They'll be hungry if you stop so early in
29:10 J went over to the well and rolled away the stone
29:11 Then J kissed Rachel, and tears came to his eyes.
29:13 then brought him home, and J told him his story.
29:14 After J had been there about a month,
29:18 Since J was in love with Rachel, he told her father,
29:20 So J spent the next seven years working to pay for
29:21 "I have fulfilled my contract," J said to Laban.
29:22 to celebrate with J at a wedding feast.
29:23 when it was dark, Laban took Leah to J,
29:25 But when J woke up in the morning—it was Leah!
29:25 "What sort of trick is this?" J raged at Laban.
29:28 So J agreed to work seven more years. A week
after J had married Leah, Laban gave him
29:30 So J slept with Rachel, too, and he loved her more
30: 1 me children, or I'll die!" she exclaimed to J.
30: 2 J flew into a rage. "Am I God?" he asked. "He is
30: 4 him Bilhah to be his wife, and J slept with her.
30: 7 became pregnant again and gave J a second son.
30: 9 so she gave her servant, Zilpah, to J to be his wife.
30:16 as J was coming home from the fields,
30:16 roots my son has found." So J slept with her.
30:25 J said to Laban, "I want to go back home.
30:29 J replied, "You know how faithfully I've served
30:31 J replied, "Don't give me anything at all. Just do
30:36 took them three days' distance from where J was.
30:36 Meanwhile, J stayed and cared for Laban's flock.
30:37 Now J took fresh shoots from poplar, almond,
30:40 J added them to his own flock, thus separating the
30:41 J set up the peeled branches in front of them.
31: 1 But J soon learned that Laban's sons were
31: 1 "J has robbed our father!" they said. "All his
31: 2 And J began to notice a considerable cooling in
31: 3 Then the LORD said to J, "Return to the land of
31: 4 J called Rachel and Leah out to the field where he
31:11 in my dream, the angel of God said to me, 'J!'
31:17 So J put his wives and children on camels.
31:21 J took all his possessions with him and crossed the
31:24 "Be careful about what you say to J!" he was
31:25 So when Laban caught up with J as he was
31:29 and told me, 'Be careful about what you say to J!'
31:31 rushed away because I was afraid," J answered.
31:32 But J didn't know that Rachel had taken them.
31:36 Then J became very angry. "What did you find?"
31:43 Then Laban replied to J, "These women are my
31:45 So J took a stone and set it up as a monument.
31:46 J and Laban then sat down beside the pile of
31:53 So J took an oath before the awesome God of his
31:54 Then J presented a sacrifice to God and invited
32: 1 As J and his household started on their way again,
32: 2 When J saw them, he exclaimed, "This is God's
32: 3 J now sent messengers to his brother, Esau,
32: 4 'Humble greetings from your servant J!
32: 6 the news that Esau was on his way to meet J—
32: 7 J was terrified at the news. He divided his
32: 9 Then J prayed, "O God of my grandfather
32:13 J stayed where he was for the night and prepared a
32:18 You should reply, 'These belong to your servant J.
32:19 J gave the same instructions to each of the
32:20 'Your servant J is right behind us.' " Jacob's plan
32:20 "Perhaps," J hoped, "he will be friendly to us."
32:21 sent on ahead, and J spent that night in the camp.
32:22 But during the night J got up and sent his two
32:24 This left J all alone in the camp, and a man came
32:26 But J panted, "I will not let you go unless you
32:27 is your name?" the man asked. He replied, "J."
32:28 "Your name will no longer be J," the man told
32:29 J asked him. "Why do you ask?" the man replied.
Then he blessed J there.
32:30 J named the place Peniel—"face of God"—
33: 1 J saw Esau coming with his four hundred men.
33: 2 J now arranged his family into a column, with his
33: 3 Then J went on ahead. As he approached his
33: 5 God has graciously given to me," J replied.
33: 8 J replied, "They are gifts, my lord, to ensure your
33:10 "No, please accept them," J said, "for what a
33:11 J continued to insist, so Esau finally accepted
33:13 But J replied, "You can see, my lord, that some of
33:15 no reason for you to be so kind to me," J insisted.
33:17 J and his household traveled on to Succoth.
33:19 J bought the land he camped on from the family of
34: 5 Word soon reached J that his daughter had been
34: 6 came out to discuss the matter with J.
34: 8 Hamor told J and his sons, "My son Shechem is
34:30 Afterward J said to Levi and Simeon, "You have
35: 1 God said to J, "Now move on to Bethel and settle
35: 2 So J told everyone in his household,
35: 4 So they gave J all their idols and their earrings,
35: 7 J built an altar there and named it El-bethel,
35: 9 God appeared to J once again when he arrived at
35:10 and said, "Your name is no longer J; you will now
35:13 went up from the place where he had spoken to J.
35:14 J set up a stone pillar to mark the place where God
35:15 J called the place Bethel—"house of God"—
35:20 J set up a stone monument over her grave, and it
35:21 J then traveled on and camped beyond the tower of
35:22 father's concubine, and someone told J about it.
35:22 These are the names of the twelve sons of J:
35:26 These were the sons born to J at Paddan-aram.
35:27 So J came home to his father Isaac in Mamre,
35:29 in death. Then his sons, Esau and J, buried him.
36: 6 of Canaan—and moved away from his brother, J.
37: 1 So J settled again in the land of Canaan, where his
37: 3 Now J loved Joseph more than any of his other
37:13 had been gone for some time, J said to Joseph,
37:14 and the flocks are getting along," J said.
37:14 So J sent him on his way, and Joseph traveled to
37:34 Then J tore his clothes and put on sackcloth.
42: 1 When J heard that there was grain available in
42: 4 J wouldn't let Joseph's younger brother,
42:29 J, in the land of Canaan and told him all that had
42:36 J exclaimed, "You have deprived me of my
42:38 But J replied, "My son will not go down with you,
43: 2 J said to his sons, "Go again and buy us a little
43: 6 J moaned. "Why did you have to treat me with
43:11 So their father, J, finally said to them, "If it can't
45:21 So the sons of J did as they were told. Joseph gave
45:25 returned to their father, J, in the land of Canaan.
45:26 J was stunned at the news—he couldn't believe it.
45:28 Then J said, "It must be true! My son Joseph is
46: 1 So J set out for Egypt with all his possessions.
46: 2 "J! J!" he called. "Here I am," J replied.
46: 5 So J left Beersheba, and his sons brought him to
46: 6 J and his entire family arrived in Egypt—
46: 8 the descendants of J, who went with him to Egypt:
46:15 These are the sons of J who were born to Leah in
46:18 These sixteen were descendants of J through
46:22 These fourteen were the descendants of J and his
46:25 These seven were the descendants of J through
46:28 J sent Judah on ahead to meet Joseph and get
46:30 Then J said to Joseph, "Now let me die, for I have
47: 7 J, and presented him to Pharaoh, and J blessed
Pharaoh.
47: 9 J replied, "I have lived for 130 hard years, but I
47:10 Then J blessed Pharaoh again before he left.
47:28 J lived for seventeen years after his arrival in
47:31 "Swear that you will do it," J insisted. So Joseph
47:31 and J bowed in worship as he leaned on his staff.
48: 2 When J heard that Joseph had arrived, he gathered
48: 3 J said to Joseph, "God Almighty appeared to me
48: 8 Then J looked over at the two boys. "Are these
48: 9 And J said, "Bring them over to me, and I will
48:10 Now J was half blind because of his age and could
48:10 close to him, and J kissed and embraced them.
48:11 Then J said to Joseph, "I never thought I would
48:14 But J crossed his arms as he reached out to lay his
48:20 So J blessed the boys that day with this blessing:
48:20 In this way, J put Ephraim ahead of Manasseh.
48:21 Then J said to Joseph, "I am about to die, but God
49: 1 Then J called together all his sons and said,
49: 2 "Come and listen, O sons of J; / listen to Israel,
49:24 by the Mighty One of J, / the Shepherd, the Rock
49:28 and these are the blessings with which J blessed
49:29 Then J told them, "Soon I will die. Bury me with
49:33 Then when J had finished this charge to his sons,
50: 8 took his brothers and the entire household of J.
50:24 give to the descendants of Abraham, Isaac, and J."
Ex 1: 1 These are the sons of J who went with their father
1: 5 in Egypt. In all, J had seventy direct descendants.
2:24 his covenant promise to Abraham, Isaac, and J.
3: 6 of Abraham, the God of Isaac, and the God of J."
3:15 of Abraham, the God of Isaac, and the God of J—
3:16 the God of Abraham, Isaac, and J—
4: 5 of Abraham, the God of Isaac, and the God of J—
6: 3 to Abraham, to Isaac, and to J as God Almighty,
6: 8 the land I swore to give to Abraham, Isaac, and J.
19: 3 "Give these instructions to the descendants of J,
32:13 with your servants—Abraham, Isaac, and J.
33: 1 land I solemnly promised Abraham, Isaac, and J.
Lev 26:42 Then I will remember my covenant with J,
Nu 23: 7 'Come,' he said, 'curse J for me! / Come
23:21 No misfortune is in sight for J; / no trouble is in
23:23 No curse can touch J; / no sorcery has any power
against Israel. / For now it will be said of J,
24: 5 How beautiful are your tents, O J; / how lovely are
24:17 far in the distant future. / A star will rise from J;
24:19 A ruler will rise in J / who will destroy the
32:11 Isaac, and J, for they have not obeyed me
Dt 1: 8 Isaac, and J, and to all their descendants.'
6:10 to give your ancestors Abraham, Isaac, and J.
9: 5 sworn to your ancestors Abraham, Isaac, and J.
9:27 instead your servants Abraham, Isaac, and J.
26: 5 'My ancestor J was a wandering Aramean who
29:13 he swore to your ancestors Abraham, Isaac, and J.
30:20 to give your ancestors Abraham, Isaac, and J."
32: 9 belong to the LORD; / J is his special possession.
33:10 Now let them teach your regulations to J;
33:28 Israel will live in safety, / prosperous J in security,
34: 4 land I promised on oath to Abraham, Isaac, and J,
Jos 24: 4 To Isaac I gave J and Esau. To Esau I gave the hill
24: 4 while J and his children went down into Egypt.
24:32 in the parcel of ground J had bought from the sons
2Sa 23: 1 David, the man anointed by the God of J,
1Ki 18:36 "O LORD, God of Abraham, Isaac, and J,
2Ki 13:23 of his covenant with Abraham, Isaac, and J.
17:34 and commands he gave the descendants of J,
17:35 had made a covenant with the descendants of J
1Ch 16:13 O descendants of J, God's chosen one.
16:17 He confirmed it to J as a decree, / to the people of
Ps 14: 7 J will shout with joy, and Israel will rejoice.
22:23 Honor him, all you descendants of J! / Show him
53: 6 J will shout with joy, and Israel will rejoice.
76: 6 When you rebuked them, O God of J, / their horses
77:15 the descendants of J and of Joseph by your might.
78: 5 For he issued his decree to J; / he gave his law to
78:21 The fire of his wrath burned against J. / Yes,
81: 4 by the laws of Israel; / it is a law of the God of J.
105: 6 O descendants of J, God's chosen one.
105:10 He confirmed it to J as a decree, / to the people of
105:23 J lived as a foreigner in the land of Ham.
114: 1 when the family of J left that foreign land—
135: 4 For the LORD has chosen J for himself,
147:19 He has revealed his words to J, / his principles
Isa 14: 1 LORD will have mercy on the descendants of J.
41: 8 as for you, Israel my servant, J my chosen one,
44: 1 "But now, listen to me, J my servant, Israel my
44: 2 O J, my servant, do not be afraid. O Israel,
44: 5 Others will say, 'I am a descendant of J.'
44:23 For the LORD has redeemed J and is glorified in
45: 4 It is for the sake of J my servant, Israel my chosen
48: 1 "Listen to me, O family of J, who are called by
48:12 "Listen to me, O family of J, Israel my chosen
58:14 your full share of the inheritance I promised to J,
63:16 Even if Abraham and J would disown us, LORD,
Jer 2: 4 Listen to the word of the LORD, people of J—
30:10 "So do not be afraid, J, my servant; do not be
33:26 I will never abandon the descendants of J
33:26 will rule the descendants of Abraham, Isaac, and J.
46:27 "But do not be afraid, J, my servant; do not be
46:28 Fear not, J, my servant," says the LORD, "for I
Eze 28:25 in their own land, the land I gave my servant J.
37:25 their ancestors lived, the land I gave my servant J.
Hos 12: 2 He is about to punish J for all his deceitful ways.
12: 3 Before J was born, he struggled with his brother;
12:12 J fled to the land of Aram and earned a wife by
Mic 7:20 an oath to our ancestors Abraham and J long ago.
Mal 1: 2 showed my love for you by loving your ancestor J.
3: 6 That is why you descendants of J are not already
Mt 1: 2 Isaac was the father of J. / J was the father of
Judah and his brothers.
1:15 father of Matthan. / Matthan was the father of J.
1:16 J was the father of Joseph, the husband of Mary.
8:11 and J at the feast in the Kingdom of Heaven.
22:31 after Abraham, Isaac, and J had died, God said,
22:32 of Abraham, the God of Isaac, and the God of J.'
Mk 12:26 Isaac, and J had died, God said to Moses,
12:26 of Abraham, the God of Isaac, and the God of J.'
Lk 3:34 Judah was the son of J. / J was the son of Isaac.
13:28 of teeth, for you will see Abraham, Isaac, J,
20:37 Long after Abraham, Isaac, and J had died,
20:37 of Abraham, the God of Isaac, and the God of J.'
Jn 4: 5 near the parcel of ground that J gave to his son
4:12 are you greater than our ancestor J who gave us
Ac 3:13 God of Abraham, the God of Isaac, the God of J,
7: 8 Isaac became the father of J, and J was the father
of the twelve patriarchs of the
7: 9 "These sons of J were very jealous of their brother
7:12 J heard that there was still grain in Egypt, so he
7:14 Then Joseph sent for his father, J, and all his
7:15 So J went to Egypt. He died there, as did all his
7:32 the God of Abraham, Isaac, and J.'
7:46 of building a permanent Temple for the God of J.
Ro 9:13 of the Scriptures, "I loved J, but I rejected Esau."
11:28 because of his promises to Abraham, Isaac, and J.
Heb 11: 9 And so did Isaac and J, to whom God gave the
11:20 faith that Isaac blessed his two sons, J and Esau.
11:21 It was by faith that J, when he was old and dying,

JACOB'S (31) [JACOB]

Ge 27:22 "The voice is J, but the hands are Esau's,"
27:23 because J hands felt hairy just like Esau's.
29:13 As soon as Laban heard about J arrival, he rushed
30:42 belonged to Laban, and the stronger ones were J.
30:43 As a result, J flocks increased rapidly, and he
31:25 of Gilead, he set up his camp not far from J.
31:33 Laban went first into J tent to search there,
31:47 in Laban's language and Galeed in J.
32:20 'Your servant Jacob is right behind us.' " J plan
32:25 he struck J hip and knocked it out of joint at the
34: 7 He arrived just as J sons were coming in from the
34: 7 Shechem had done a disgraceful thing against J
34:27 Then all of J sons plundered the town
35:23 The sons of Leah were Reuben (J oldest son),
37: 2 This is the history of J family. When Joseph was
42: 5 So J sons arrived in Egypt along with others to buy
46: 8 went with him to Egypt: Reuben was J oldest son.
46:15 J descendants through Leah numbered thirty-three.
46:19 The sons of J wife Rachel were Joseph
46:26 So the total number of J direct descendants who

46:27 there were seventy members of **J** family in the land
48:13 positioned the boys so Ephraim was at **J** left hand
50:12 So **J** sons did as he had commanded them.
Nu 23:10 Who can count **J** descendants, as numerous as
26: 5 the clans descended from Reuben, **J** oldest son:
1Ch 7:13 They were all descendants of **J** wife Bilhah.
Ps 47: 4 the proud possession of **J** descendants, whom he
78:71 and made him the shepherd of **J** descendants—
Hos 12:13 Then the LORD led **J** descendants, the Israelites,
Mal 1: 2 your ancestor Jacob. Yet Esau was **J** brother,
Jn 4: 6 **J** well was there; and Jesus, tired from the long

JADA (2)
1Ch 2:28 The sons of Onam were Shammai and **J**. The sons
2:32 Shammai's brother, **J**, had two sons named Jether

JADAH (4)
1Ch 8:36 Ahaz was the father of **J**. / **J** was the father of Alemeth, Azmaveth, and Zimri.
9:42 Ahaz was the father of **J**. / **J** was the father of Alemeth, Azmaveth, and Zimri.

JADDAI (1)
Ezr 10:43 Jeiel, Mattithiah, Zabad, Zebina, **J**, Joel,

JADDUA (3)
Ne 10:21 Meshezabel, Zadok, **J**,
12:11 father of Johanan. / Johanan was the father of **J**.
12:22 high priests: Eliashib, Joiada, Johanan, and **J**.

JADON (1)
Ne 3: 7 **J** from Meronoth, and people from Gibeon

JAEL (7)
Jdg 4:17 Meanwhile, Sisera ran to the tent of **J**, the wife of
4:18 **J** went out to meet Sisera and said to him,
4:21 **J** quietly crept up to him with a hammer and tent
4:22 came looking for Sisera, **J** went out to meet him.
5: 6 of Shamgar son of Anath, and in the days of **J**,
5:24 "Most blessed is **J**, / the wife of Heber the Kenite.
5:25 Sisera asked for water, / and **J** gave him milk.

JAGGED (1)
Isa 2:21 and hide among the **j** rocks at the tops of cliffs.

JAGUR (1)
Jos 15:21 of Edom in the extreme south are Kabzeel, Eder, **J**,

JAH [KJV] See LORD*

JAHATH (8)
1Ch 4: 2 Shobal's son Reaiah was the father of **J**.
4: 2 **J** was the father of Ahumai and Lahad. These were
6:20 descendants of Gershon were Libni, **J**, Zimmah,
6:43 **J**, Gershon, and Levi.
23:10 Four other descendants of Shimei were **J**, Ziza,
23:11 **J** was the family leader, and Ziza was next. Jeush
24:22 the descendants of Shelomith, the leader was **J**.
2Ch 34:12 workers served faithfully under the leadership of **J**

JAHAZ (9)
Nu 21:23 in the wilderness, engaging them in battle at **J**.
Dt 2:32 declared war on us and mobilized his forces at **J**.
Jos 13:18 **J**, Kedemoth, Mephaath,
21:36 From the tribe of Reuben they received Bezer, **J**,
Jdg 11:20 he mobilized his army at **J** and attacked them.
1Ch 6:78 they received Bezer (a desert town), **J**,
Isa 15: 4 and Elealeh will be heard far away, even in **J**!
Jer 48:21 out on them all—on Holon and **J** and Mephaath,
48:34 heard from Heshbon clear across to Elealeh and **J**;

JAHAZIEL (6)
1Ch 12: 4 Jeremiah, **J**, Johanan, and Jozabad from Gederah;
16: 6 The priests, Benaiah and **J**, played the trumpets
23:19 Amariah (the second), **J** (the third), and Jekameam
24:23 **J** was third, and Jekameam was fourth.
2Ch 20:14 His name was **J** son of Zechariah, son of Benaiah,
Ezr 8: 5 of Zattu: Shecaniah son of **J** and 300 other men.

JAHDAI (1)
1Ch 2:47 The sons of **J** were Regem, Jotham, Geshan,

JAHDIEL (1)
1Ch 5:24 Ishi, Eliel, Azriel, Jeremiah, Hodaviah, and **J**.

JAHDO (1)
1Ch 5:14 of Michael, son of Jeshishai, son of **J**, son of Buz.

JAHLEEL (2) [JAHLEELITE]
Ge 46:14 The sons of Zebulun were Sered, Elon, and **J**.
Nu 26:26 The Jahleelite clan, named after its ancestor **J**.

JAHLEELITE (1) [JAHLEEL]
Nu 26:26 The **J** clan, named after its ancestor Jahleel.

JAHMAI (1)
1Ch 7: 2 Rephaiah, Jeriel, **J**, Ibsam, and Shemuel.

JAHZEEL (3) [JAHZEELITE]
Ge 46:24 The sons of Naphtali were **J**, Guni, Jezer,
Nu 26:48 The Jahzeelite clan, named after its ancestor **J**.
1Ch 7:13 The sons of Naphtali were **J**, Guni, Jezer,

JAHZEELITE (1) [JAHZEEL]
Nu 26:48 The **J** clan, named after its ancestor Jahzeel.

JAHZEIAH (1)
Ezr 10:15 and **J** son of Tikvah opposed this course of action,

JAHZERAH (1)
1Ch 9:12 son of **J**, son of Meshullam, son of Meshillemith,

JAIL (16) [JAILED, JAILER]
Ge 40:15 the land of the Hebrews, and now I'm here in **j**,
Mt 5:25 handed over to an officer, and thrown in **j**.
Lk 12:58 and handed over to an officer and thrown in **j**.
Ac 5:18 They arrested the apostles and put them in the **j**.
5:19 opened the gates of the **j**, and brought them out.
5:22 But when the Temple guards went to the **j**, the men
5:23 "The **j** was locked, with the guards standing
8: 3 out both men and women to throw them into **j**.
12:17 and how the Lord had led him out of **j**.
16:39 They came to the **j** and apologized to them.
20:23 the Holy Spirit has told me in city after city that **j**
25:21 So I ordered him back to **j** until I could arrange to
2Co 6: 5 have been beaten, been put in **j**, faced angry mobs,
11:23 I have worked harder, been put in **j** more often,
Heb 10:34 suffered along with those who were thrown into **j**.
13:23 to know that our brother Timothy is now out of **j**.

JAILED (6) [JAIL]
Da 11:33 die by fire and sword, or they will be **j** and robbed.
Mt 18:30 and **j** until the debt could be paid in full.
Ac 4: 3 since it was already evening, **j** them until morning.
5:25 that the men they had **j** were out in the Temple,
16:37 have publicly beaten us without trial and **j** us—
21:13 For I am ready not only to be **j** at Jerusalem

JAILER (9) [JAIL]
Ge 39:21 and he granted Joseph favor with the chief **j**.
39:22 the **j** put Joseph in charge of all the other prisoners
39:23 The chief **j** had no more worries after that,
Ac 16:23 The **j** was ordered to make sure they didn't escape.
16:27 The **j** woke up to see the prison doors wide open.
16:29 the **j** called for lights and ran to the dungeon
16:33 That same hour the **j** washed their wounds, and he
16:35 the city officials sent the police to tell the **j**,
16:36 So the **j** told Paul, "You and Silas are free to

JAIR (16) [JAIRITE]
Nu 32:41 The people of **J**, another clan of the tribe of
32:41 changed the name of that region to the Towns of **J**.
Dt 3:14 **J**, a leader from the tribe of Manasseh,
3:14 **J** renamed this region after himself, calling it the Towns of **J**, as it is still known
Jos 13:30 of King Og, and the sixty towns of **J** in Bashan.
Jdg 10: 3 a man from Gilead named **J** judged Israel for
10: 4 of Gilead, which are still called the Towns of **J**.
10: 5 When **J** died, he was buried in Kamon.
2Sa 21:19 Elhanan son of **J** from Bethlehem killed the
1Ki 4:13 including the Towns of **J** (named for **J** son of
1Ch 2:22 Segub was the father of **J**, who ruled twenty-three
2:23 (Later Geshur and Aram captured the Towns of **J**
20: 5 Elhanan son of **J** killed Lahmi, the brother of
Est 2: 5 there was a certain Jew named Mordecai son of **J**.

JAIRITE (1) [JAIR]
2Sa 20:26 Ira the **J** was David's personal priest.

JAIRUS (4) [JAIRUS']
Mk 5:22 whose name was **J**, came and fell down before
5:36 But Jesus ignored their comments and said to **J**,
Lk 8:41 And now a man named **J**, a leader of the local
8:50 what had happened, he said to **J**, "Don't be afraid.

JAIRUS' (2) [JAIRUS]
Mk 5:35 messengers arrived from **J** home with the message,
Lk 8:49 a messenger arrived from **J** home with the

JAKAN [KJV] See JAAKAN

JAKEH (1)
Pr 30: 1 The message of Agur son of **J**. An oracle. I am

JAKIM (2)
1Ch 8:19 **J**, Zicri, Zabdi,
24:12 lot fell to Eliashib. / The twelfth lot fell to **J**.

JAKIN (8) [JAKINITE]
Ge 46:10 were Jemuel, Jamin, Ohad, **J**, Zohar, and Shaul.
Ex 6:15 Jamin, Ohad, **J**, Zohar, and Shaul (whose mother
Nu 26:12 The Jakinite clan, named after its ancestor **J**.
1Ki 7:21 He named the one on the south **J**, and the one on
1Ch 9:10 the priests who returned were Jedaiah, Jehoiarib, **J**,
24:17 The twenty-first lot fell to **J**. / The twenty-second
2Ch 3:17 He named the one on the south **J**, and the one on
Ne 11:10 From the priests: Jedaiah son of Joiarib; **J**;

JAKINITE (1) [JAKIN]
Nu 26:12 The **J** clan, named after its ancestor Jakin.

JALAM (4)
Ge 36: 5 Oholibamah had sons named Jeush, **J**, and Korah.
36:14 of Zibeon. Their names were Jeush, **J**, and Korah.
36:18 the leaders of the clans of Jeush, **J**, and Korah.
1Ch 1:35 of Esau were Eliphaz, Reuel, Jeush, **J**, and Korah.

JALON (1)
1Ch 4:17 sons of Ezrah were Jether, Mered, Epher, and **J**.

JAMBRES (2)
2Ti 3: 8 the truth just as Jannes and **J** fought against Moses.
3: 9 fools they are, just as happened with Jannes and **J**.

JAMES (44) [JAMES'S]
Mt 4:21 **J** and John, sitting in a boat with their father,
10: 2 Andrew (Peter's brother), / **J** (son of Zebedee),
10: 3 Matthew (the tax collector), / **J** (son of Alphaeus),
13:55 and his brothers—**J**, Joseph, Simon, and Judas.
17: 1 Jesus took Peter and the two brothers, **J** and John,
20:20 Then the mother of **J** and John, the sons of
20:24 When the ten other disciples heard what **J**
26:37 He took Peter and Zebedee's two sons, **J** and John,
27:56 Mary (the mother of **J** and Joseph), and Zebedee's wife, the mother of **J** and John.
Mk 1:19 **J** and John, in a boat mending their nets.
1:29 Andrew's home, and **J** and John were with them.
3:17 **J** and John (the sons of Zebedee, but Jesus
3:18 Matthew, / Thomas, / **J** (son of Alphaeus),
5:37 anyone go with him except Peter and **J** and John.
6: 3 the son of Mary and brother of **J**, Joseph, Judas,
9: 2 Six days later Jesus took Peter, **J**, and John to the
10:35 Then **J** and John, the sons of Zebedee, came over
10:41 When the ten other disciples discovered what **J**
13: 3 Peter, **J**, John, and Andrew came to him privately
14:33 He took Peter, **J**, and John with him, and he began
15:40 Mary (the mother of **J** the younger and of Joseph),
16: 1 and Salome and Mary the mother of **J** went out
Lk 5:10 His partners, **J** and John, the sons of Zebedee,
6:14 called him Peter), / Andrew (Peter's brother), / **J**,
6:15 Matthew, / Thomas, / **J** (son of Alphaeus),
6:16 Judas (son of **J**), / Judas Iscariot (who later
8:51 **J**, John, and the little girl's father and mother.
9:28 Jesus took Peter, **J**, and John to a mountain to pray.
9:54 When **J** and John heard about it, they said to Jesus,
24:10 Joanna, Mary the mother of **J**, and several others.
Ac 1:13 Peter, / John, / **J**, / Andrew, / Philip, / Thomas, / Bartholomew, / Matthew, / **J** (son of Alphaeus), / Simon (the Zealot), / and Judas (son of **J**).
12: 2 He had the apostle **J** (John's brother) killed with a
12:17 "Tell **J** and the other brothers what happened,"
15:13 **J** stood and said, "Brothers, listen to me.
21:18 The next day Paul went in with us to meet with **J**,
1Co 15: 7 Then he was seen by **J** and later by all the apostles.
Gal 1:19 And the only other apostle I met at that time was **J**,
2: 9 In fact, **J**, Peter, and John, who were known as
2:12 when some Jewish friends of **J** came,
Jas 1: 1 This letter is from **J**, a slave of God and of the
Jude 1: 1 a slave of Jesus Christ and a brother of **J**.

JAMES'S (1) [JAMES]
Mt 10: 2 James (son of Zebedee), / John (**J** brother),

JAMIN (6) [JAMINITE]
Ge 46:10 were Jemuel, **J**, Ohad, Jakin, Zohar, and Shaul.
Ex 6:15 **J**, Ohad, Jakin, Zohar, and Shaul (whose mother
Nu 26:12 The Jaminite clan, named after its ancestor **J**.
1Ch 2:27 oldest son of Jerahmeel, were Maaz, **J**, and Eker.
4:24 Simeon were Nemuel, **J**, Jarib, Zerah, and Shaul.
Ne 8: 7 Jeshua, Bani, Sherebiah, **J**, Akkub, Shabbethai,

JAMINITE (1) [JAMIN]
Nu 26:12 The **J** clan, named after its ancestor Jamin.

JAMLECH (1)
1Ch 4:34 included Meshobab, **J**, Joshah son of Amaziah,

JANAI (1)
1Ch 5:12 along with **J** and Shaphat.

JANGLING [KJV] See ARGUING

JANIM (1)
Jos 15:53 **J**, Beth-tappuah, Aphekah,

JANNAI (2)
Lk 3:24 Melki was the son of **J**. / **J** was the son of Joseph.

JANNES (2)
2Ti 3: 8 And these teachers fight the truth just as **J**
3: 9 they are, just as happened with **J** and Jambres.

JANOAH (3)
Jos 16: 6 eastward past Taanath-shiloh to the east of **J**.
16: 7 From **J** it turned southward to Ataroth and Naarah,
2Ki 15:29 of Ijon, Abel-beth-maacah, **J**, Kedesh, and Hazor.

JANUARY (6)

2Ki 25: 1 So on **J** 15, during the ninth year of Zedekiah's
Jer 39: 1 It was in **J** during the ninth year of King
52: 4 So on **J** 15, during the ninth year of Zedekiah's
Eze 24: 1 On **J** 15, during the ninth year of King
29: 1 On **J** 7, during the tenth year of King Jehoiachin's
33:21 On **J** 8, during the twelfth year of our captivity,

JAPHETH (12)

Ge 5:32 years old, he had three sons: Shem, Ham, and **J**.
6:10 Noah had three sons: Shem, Ham, and **J**.
7:13 with his wife and his sons—Shem, Ham, and **J**—
9:18 Shem, Ham, and **J**, the three sons of Noah,
9:23 Shem and **J** took a robe, held it over their
9:25 of servants / to the descendants of Shem and **J**."
9:27 May God enlarge the territory of **J**, / and may he
10: 1 of Shem, Ham, and **J**, the three sons of Noah.
10: 2 The descendants of **J** were Gomer, Magog, Madai,
10:21 were also born to Shem, the older brother of **J**.
1Ch 1: 4 The sons of Noah were Shem, Ham, and **J**.
1: 5 The descendants of **J** were Gomer, Magog, Madai,

JAPHIA (5)

Jos 10: 3 Hoham of Hebron, Piram of Jarmuth, **J** of Lachish,
19:12 and from there to Daberath and up to **J**.
2Sa 5:15 Ibhar, Elishua, Nepheg, **J**,
1Ch 3: 7 Nogah, Nepheg, **J**,
14: 6 Nogah, Nepheg, **J**,

JAPHLET (2) [JAPHLETITES]

1Ch 7:32 The sons of Heber were **J**, Shomer, and Hotham.
7:33 The sons of **J** were Pasach, Bimhal, and Ashvath.

JAPHLETITES (1) [JAPHLET]

Jos 16: 3 to the territory of the **J** as far as Lower Beth-horon,

JAPHO [KJV] See JOPPA

JAR (28) [JARS]

Nu 5:17 He must take some holy water in a clay **j** and mix
5:18 holding the **j** of bitter water that brings a curse to
19:17 the ashes from the burnt purification offering in a **j**
Jdg 7:16 man a ram's horn and a clay **j** with a torch in it.
1Ki 14: 3 ten loaves of bread, some cakes, and a **j** of honey,
17:12 And I have only a handful of flour left in the **j**
19: 6 some bread baked on hot stones and a **j** of water!
2Ki 4: 6 "Bring me another **j**," she said to one of her sons.
Ecc 12: 6 Don't wait until the water **j** is smashed at the
Isa 29:16 Does a **j** ever say, "The potter who made me is
Jer 18: 4 But the **j** he was making did not turn out as he had
18: 4 so the potter squashed the **j** into a lump of clay
19: 1 The LORD said to me, "Go and buy a clay **j**.
19:10 Jeremiah, smash the **j** you brought with you.
19:11 As this **j** lies shattered, so I will shatter the people
32:14 and put them into a pottery **j** to preserve them for a
48:12 I will send troublemakers to pour her from her **j**.
They will pour her out, then shatter the **j**!
Eze 4: 9 and spelt, and mix them together in a storage **j**.
4:11 Then measure out a **j** of water for each day,
Mt 26: 7 a woman came in with a beautiful **j** of expensive
Mk 14: 3 a woman came in with a beautiful **j** of expensive
Lk 7:37 and brought a beautiful **j** filled with expensive
Jn 4:28 The woman left her water **j** beside the well
12: 3 Then Mary took a twelve-ounce **j** of expensive
19:29 A **j** of sour wine was sitting there, so they soaked a
Ro 9:21 the same lump of clay to make one **j** for decoration
Heb 9: 4 Inside the Ark were a gold **j** containing some

JAREB [KJV] See GREAT (KING)

JARED (7)

Ge 5:15 Mahalalel was 65 years old, his son **J** was born.
5:16 After the birth of **J**, Mahalalel lived 830 years,
5:18 When **J** was 162 years old, his son Enoch was
5:19 **J** lived another 800 years, and he had other sons
1Ch 1: 2 Kenan, Mahalalel, **J**,
Lk 3:37 Enoch was the son of **J**. / **J** was the son of
Mahalalel.

JARHA (2)

1Ch 2:34 He also had an Egyptian servant named **J**.
2:35 gave one of his daughters to be the wife of **J**,

JARIB (3)

1Ch 4:24 Simeon were Nemuel, Jamin, **J**, Zerah, and Shaul.
Ezr 8:16 Ariel, Shemaiah, Elnathan, **J**, Elnathan, Nathan,
10:18 his brothers: Maaseiah, Eliezer, **J**, and Gedaliah.

JARMUTH (6) [REMETH]

Jos 10: 3 Hoham of Hebron, Piram of **J**, Japhia of Lachish,
10:23 kings of Jerusalem, Hebron, **J**, Lachish, and Eglon.
12:11 The king of **J** / The king of Lachish
15:35 **J**, Adullam, Socoh, Azekah,
21:29 **J**, and En-gannim—four towns with their
Ne 11:29 They were also in En-rimmon, Zorah, **J**,

JAROAH (1)

1Ch 5:14 son of **J**, son of Gilead, son of Michael, son of

JARS (14) [JAR]

Nu 4: 9 lamp snuffers, trays, and special **j** of olive oil.
Jdg 7:19 they blew the horns and broke their clay **j**.
7:20 all three groups blew their horns and broke their **j**.
1Ki 18:33 Then he said, "Fill four large **j** with water,
2Ki 4: 3 "Borrow as many empty **j** as you can from your
4: 4 Pour olive oil from your flask into the **j**, setting the
j aside as they are filled."
4: 5 Her sons brought many **j** to her, and she filled one
Job 38:37 all the clouds? Who can tilt the water **j** of heaven,
Isa 29:16 greater than you. You are only the **j** he makes!
Jer 18: 2 down to the shop where clay pots and **j** are made.
Jn 2: 7 Jesus told the servants, "Fill the **j** with water."
2: 7 When the **j** had been filled to the brim,
Ro 9:21 When a potter makes **j** out of clay, doesn't he have

JASHAR (2)

Jos 10:13 Is this event not recorded in *The Book of J*?
2Sa 1:18 of the Bow, and it is recorded in *The Book of J*.

JASHEN (2)

2Sa 23:32 Eliahba from Shaalbon; / the sons of **J**;
1Ch 11:34 the sons of **J** from Gizon; / Jonathan son of Shagee

JASHER [KJV] See JASHAR

JASHOBEAM (4)

2Sa 23: 8 The first was **J** the Hacmonite, who was
1Ch 11:11 The first was **J** the Hacmonite, who was
12: 6 Elkanah, Isshiah, Azarel, Joezer, and **J**, who were
27: 2 **J** son of Zabdiel was commander of the first

JASHUB (4) [JASHUBITE]

Ge 46:13 sons of Issachar were Tola, Puah, **J**, and Shimron.
Nu 26:24 The Jashubite clan, named after its ancestor **J**.
1Ch 7: 1 sons of Issachar were Tola, Puah, **J**, and Shimron.
Ezr 10:29 Meshullam, Malluch, Adaiah, **J**, Sheal,

JASHUBI-LEHEM (1)

1Ch 4:22 Joash, and Saraph, who ruled over Moab and **J**.

JASHUBITE (1) [JASHUB]

Nu 26:24 The **J** clan, named after its ancestor Jashub.

JASON (5)

Ac 17: 5 They attacked the home of **J**, searching for Paul
17: 6 they dragged out **J** and some of the other believers
17: 7 "And **J** has let them into his home. They are all
17: 9 But the officials released **J** and the other believers
Ro 16:21 and Lucius, **J**, and Sosipater, my relatives,

JASPER (7)

Ex 28:20 fourth row will contain a beryl, an onyx, and a **j**.
39:13 In the fourth row were a beryl, an onyx, and a **j**.
Eze 28:13 beryl, onyx, **j**, sapphire, turquoise, and emerald—
Rev 4: 3 was as brilliant as gemstones—**j** and carnelian.
21:11 sparkled like a precious gem, crystal clear like **j**.
21:18 The wall was made of **j**, and the city was pure
21:19 the first was **j**, the second sapphire, the third agate,

JATHNIEL (1)

1Ch 26: 2 (the second), Zebadiah (the third), **J** (the fourth),

JATTIR (8)

Jos 15:48 towns in the hill country: Shamir, **J**, Socoh,
21:14 **J**, Eshtemoa,
1Sa 30:27 and his men had been: Bethel, Ramoth-negev, **J**,
2Sa 23:38 Ira from **J**; / Gareb from **J**;
1Ch 6:57 Hebron (a city of refuge), Libnah, **J**, Eshtemoa,
11:40 Ira from **J**; / Gareb from **J**;

JAVAN (4)

Ge 10: 2 Magog, Madai, **J**, Tubal, Meshech, and Tiras.
10: 4 The descendants of **J** were Elishah, Tarshish,
1Ch 1: 5 Magog, Madai, **J**, Tubal, Meshech, and Tiras.
1: 7 The descendants of **J** were Elishah, Tarshish,

JAVELIN (4) [JAVELINS]

1Sa 17: 6 and he slung a bronze **j** over his back.
17:45 "You come to me with sword, spear, and **j**,
Job 39:23 arrows rattle against it, and the spear and **j** flash.
Ps 35: 3 Lift up your spear and **j** / and block the way of my

JAVELINS (2) [JAVELIN]

Job 41:29 do no good, and it laughs at the swish of the **j**.
Eze 39: 9 and large shields, bows and arrows, **j** and spears,

JAW (3) [JAWBONE, JAWS]

1Sa 17:35 turns on me, I catch it by the **j** and club it to death.
Job 41: 1 a crocodile with a hook or put a noose around its **j**?
41: 2 a rope through the nose or pierce its **j** with a spike?

JAWBONE (5) [JAW]

Jdg 15:15 Then he picked up a donkey's **j** that was lying on
15:16 And Samson said, / "With the **j** of a donkey,
15:16 made heaps on heaps! / With the **j** of a donkey,
15:17 When he finished speaking, he threw away the **j**;
and the place was named **J** Hill.

JAWS (9) [JAW]

Jdg 14: 6 and he ripped the lion's **j** apart with his bare hands.
Job 29:17 I broke the **j** of godless oppressors and made them
41:14 Who could pry open its **j**? For its teeth are terrible!
Ps 9:13 who hate me. / Snatch me back from the **j** of death.
22:21 Snatch me from the lions' **j**, / and from the horns
58: 6 O God! / Smash the **j** of these lions, O LORD!
Eze 29: 4 I will put hooks in your **j** and drag you out on the
38: 4 and put hooks into your **j** to lead you out to your
Jnh 2: 6 have snatched me from the yawning **j** of death!

JAZER (12)

Nu 21:32 After Moses sent men to explore the **J** area,
32: 1 So when they saw that the lands of **J** and Gilead
32: 3 Dibon, **J**, Nimrah, Heshbon, Elealeh, Sebam,
32:35 Atroth-shophan, **J**, Jogbehah,
Jos 13:25 Their territory included **J**, all the towns of Gilead,
21:39 Heshbon, and **J**—four towns with their
2Sa 24: 5 in the direction of Gad. Then they went on to **J**,
1Ch 6:81 Heshbon, and **J**, each with its pasturelands.
26:31 of Hebron were found at **J** in the land of Gilead.)
Isa 16: 8 Her tendrils spread out as far as **J** and trailed out
16: 9 So I wail and lament for **J** and the vineyards of
Jer 48:32 I will weep for you even more than I did for **J**.

JAZIZ (1)

1Ch 27:31 **J** the Hagrite was in charge of the king's sheep.

JEALOUS (32) [JEALOUSLY, JEALOUSY]

Ge 26:14 Soon the Philistines became **j** of him,
30: 1 having any children, she became **j** of her sister.
37:11 But while his brothers were **j** of Joseph, his father
Ex 20: 5 am a **j** God who will not share your affection with
Nu 5:14 If her husband becomes **j** and suspicious of his
11:29 But Moses replied, "Are you **j** for my sake?
Dt 4:24 The LORD your God is a devouring fire, a **j** God.
5: 9 am a **j** God who will not share your affection with
6:15 your God, who lives among you, is a **j** God.
Jos 24:19 to serve the LORD, for he is a holy and **j** God.
1Sa 18: 9 So from that time on Saul kept a **j** eye on David.
18:12 and he was **j** because the LORD had left him
Ps 78:58 to other gods; / they made him **j** with their idols.
106:16 The people in the camp were **j** of Moses
Pr 12:12 Thieves are **j** of each other's loot, while the godly
Eze 5:13 the LORD, have spoken to them in my **j** anger.
16:38 I will cover you with blood in my **j** fury.
16:42 you will be spent, and my **j** anger will subside.
23:25 I will turn my **j** anger against you, and they will
36: 5 My **j** anger is on fire against these nations,
39:25 mercy on Israel, for I am **j** for my holy reputation!
Na 1: 2 The LORD is a **j** God, filled with vengeance
Ac 7: 9 "These sons of Jacob were very **j** of their brother
13:45 the Jewish leaders saw the crowds, they were **j**;
17: 5 But the Jewish leaders were **j**, so they gathered
Ro 11:11 and then the Jews would be **j** and want it for
1Co 3: 3 You are **j** of one another and quarrel with each
13: 4 and kind. Love is not **j** or boastful or proud
2Co 11: 2 I am **j** for you with the jealousy of God himself.
Gal 5:26 or irritate one another, or be **j** of one another.
Jas 3:14 But if you are bitterly **j** and there is selfish
4: 2 You are **j** for what others have, and you can't

JEALOUSLY (1) [JEALOUS]

Jas 4: 5 has placed within us, **j** longs for us to be faithful?

JEALOUSY (31) [JEALOUS]

Nu 5:15 with olive oil or frankincense, for it is a **j** offering
5:18 and place the offering of inquiry—the **j** offering—
5:25 " 'Then the priest will take the **j** offering from the
5:29 " 'This is the ritual law for dealing with **j**. If a
5:30 or if a man is overcome with **j** and suspicion that
Dt 29:20 His anger and **j** will burn against them.
32:16 They stirred up his **j** by worshiping foreign gods;
32:21 They have roused my **j** by worshiping non-gods;
32:21 Now I will rouse their **j** by blessing other nations;
Job 5: 2 resentment destroys the fool, and **j** kills the simple.
Ps 79: 5 Forever? / How long will your **j** burn like fire?
Pr 6:34 For the woman's husband will be furious in his **j**,
14:30 A relaxed attitude lengthens life; **j** rots it away.
27: 4 but who can survive the destructiveness of **j**?
SS 8: 6 as death, and its **j** is as enduring as the grave.
Isa 11:13 Then at last the **j** between Israel and Judah will
Eze 38:19 For in my **j** and blazing anger, I promise a mighty
Zep 1:18 the whole land will be devoured by the fire of his **j**.
3: 8 All the earth will be devoured by the fire of my **j**.
Ac 5:17 who were Sadducees, reacted with violent **j**.
Ro 10:19 "I will rouse your **j** by blessing other nations.
13:13 in adultery and immoral living, or in fighting and **j**.
1Co 10:22 Do you dare to rouse the Lord's **j** as Israel did?
2Co 11: 2 I am jealous for you with the **j** of God himself.
12:20 **j**, outbursts of anger, selfishness, backstabbing,
Gal 5:20 hostility, quarreling, **j**, outbursts of anger,
Php 1:15 Some are preaching out of **j** and rivalry. But others
1Ti 6: 4 This stirs up arguments ending in **j**, fighting,
Jas 3:15 For **j** and selfishness are not God's kind of
3:16 For wherever there is **j** and selfish ambition,
1Pe 2: 1 Be done with hypocrisy and **j** and backstabbing.

JEARIM (1) [KESALON]

Jos 15:10 town of Kesalon on the northern slope of Mount **J**,

JEATHERAI (1)

1Ch 6:21 Joah, Iddo, Zerah, and **J**.

JEBEREKIAH (1)
Isa 8: 2 I asked Uriah the priest and Zechariah son of **J**,

JEBUS (5) [JEBUSITE, JEBUSITES, JERUSALEM]
Jos 18:28 Zela, Haeleph, **J** (that is, Jerusalem), Gibeah,
Jdg 19:10 and headed in the direction of **J** (that is,
19:11 It was late in the day when they reached **J**,
1Ch 11: 4 Then David and all Israel went to Jerusalem (or **J**,
11: 5 The people of **J** said to David, "You will never get

JEBUSITE (7) [JEBUS]
Jos 11: 3 of the Perizzites; the kings in the **J** hill country;
Jdg 19:11 too late to travel; let's stay in this **J** city tonight."
2Sa 24:16 was by the threshing floor of Araunah the **J**.
24:18 LORD on the threshing floor of Araunah the **J**."
1Ch 21:15 standing by the threshing floor of Araunah the **J**.
21:18 the LORD at the threshing floor of Araunah the **J**.
2Ch 3: 1 was built on the threshing floor of Araunah the **J**,

JEBUSITES (34) [JEBUS]
Ge 10:16 **J**, Amorites, Girgashites,
15:21 Amorites, Canaanites, Girgashites, and **J**."
Ex 3: 8 Hittites, Amorites, Perizzites, Hivites, and **J** live.
3:17 Hittites, Amorites, Perizzites, Hivites, and **J**—
13: 5 the Canaanites, Hittites, Amorites, Hivites, and **J**.
23:23 Hittites, Perizzites, Canaanites, Hivites, and **J**,
33: 2 Amorites, Hittites, Perizzites, Hivites, and **J**.
34:11 Canaanites, Hittites, Perizzites, Hivites, and **J**.
Nu 13:29 Amalekites live in the Negev, and the Hittites, **J**,
Dt 7: 1 Amorites, Canaanites, Perizzites, Hivites, and **J**.
20:17 Amorites, Canaanites, Perizzites, Hivites, and **J**,
Jos 3:10 Hivites, Perizzites, Girgashites, Amorites, and **J**.
9: 1 Amorites, Canaanites, Perizzites, Hivites, and **J**,
12: 8 the Perizzites, the Hivites, and the **J**.)
15: 8 along the southern slopes of the **J**, where the city
15:63 But the tribe of Judah could not drive out the **J**,
15:63 so the **J** live there among the people of Judah to
18:16 crossing south of the slope where the **J** lived,
24:11 the Hittites, the Girgashites, the Hivites, and the **J**.
Jdg 1:21 of Benjamin, however, failed to drive out the **J**,
1:21 So to this day the **J** live in Jerusalem among the
3: 5 Hittites, Amorites, Perizzites, Hivites, and **J**,
2Sa 5: 6 led his troops to Jerusalem to fight against the **J**.
5: 6 "You'll never get in here," the **J** taunted.
5: 6 keep you out!" For the **J** thought they were safe.
5: 8 into the city and destroy those 'lame' and 'blind' **J**.
1Ki 9:20 Hittites, Perizzites, Hivites, and **J**.
1Ch 1:14 **J**, Amorites, Girgashites,
11: 4 (or Jebus, as it used to be called), where the **J**,
11: 6 "Whoever leads the attack against the **J** will
2Ch 8: 7 Amorites, Perizzites, Hivites, and **J**.
Ezr 9: 1 Hittites, Perizzites, **J**, Ammonites, Moabites,
Ne 9: 8 Hittites, Amorites, Perizzites, **J**, and Girgashites.
Zec 9: 7 Ekron will join my people, just as the **J** once did.

JECHONIAS [KJV] See JEHOIACHIN

JECOLIAH (2)
2Ki 15: 2 fifty-two years. His mother was **J**, from Jerusalem.
2Ch 26: 3 fifty-two years. His mother was **J**, from Jerusalem.

JEDAIAH (13)
1Ch 4:37 son of Allon, son of **J**, son of Shimri, son of
9:10 Among the priests who returned were **J**, Jehoiarib,
24: 7 first lot fell to Jehoiarib. / The second lot fell to **J**.
Ezr 2:36 The family of **J** (through the line of Jeshua)
Ne 3:10 Next **J** son of Harumaph repaired the wall beside
7:39 The family of **J** (through the line of Jeshua)
11:10 From the priests: **J** son of Joiarib; Jakin;
12: 6 Shemaiah, Joiarib, **J**,
12: 7 Sallu, Amok, Hilkiah, and **J**. These were the
12:19 of Joiarib. / Uzzi was leader of the family of **J**.
12:21 Nethanel was leader of the family of **J**.
Zec 6:10 and **J** will bring gifts of silver and gold from the
6:14 Heldai, Tobijah, **J**, and Josiah son of Zephaniah."

JEDIAEL (6)
1Ch 7: 6 Three of Benjamin's sons were Bela, Beker, and **J**.
7:10 The son of **J** was Bilhan. The sons of Bilhan were
7:11 They were the leaders of the clans of **J**, and their
11:45 **J** son of Shimri; / Joha, his brother, from Tiz;
12:20 Adnah, Jozabad, **J**, Michael, Jozabad, Elihu,
26: 2 **J** (the second), Zebadiah (the third), Jathniel (the

JEDIDAH (1)
2Ki 22: 1 His mother was **J**, the daughter of Adaiah from

JEDIDIAH (1) [SOLOMON]
2Sa 12:25 Nathan the prophet that his name should be **J**—

JEDUTHUN (15)
1Ch 9:16 Obadiah son of Shemaiah, son of Galal, son of **J**;
16:38 This group included Obed-edom (son of **J**), Hosah,
16:41 David also appointed Heman, **J**, and the others
16:42 And the sons of **J** were appointed as gatekeepers.
25: 1 and **J** to proclaim God's messages to the
25: 3 **J** had six sons: Gedaliah, Zeri, Jeshaiah, Shimei,
25: 3 They worked under the direction of their father, **J**,
25: 6 Asaph, **J**, and Heman reported directly to the king.
2Ch 5:12 Asaph, Heman, **J**, and all their sons and brothers—
29:14 From the family of **J**: Shemaiah and Uzziel.
35:15 by David, Asaph, Heman, and **J**, the king's seer.
Ne 11:17 and Abda son of Shammua, son of Galal, son of **J**.
Ps 39: T For **J**, the choir director: A psalm of David.
62: T For **J**, the choir director: A psalm of David.
77: T For **J**, the choir director: A psalm of Asaph.

JEER (2) [JEERED, JEERS]
Job 16:10 People **j** and laugh at me. They slap my cheek in
La 2:15 All who pass by **j** at you. They scoff and insult

JEERED (1) [JEER]
Mk 14:65 "Who hit you that time, you prophet?" they **j**.

JEERS (1) [JEER]
Job 27:23 But everyone **j** at them and mocks them.

JEEZER [KJV] See IEZER

JEEZERITES [KJV] See IEZERITES

JEGAR-SAHADUTHA (1) [GALEED]
Ge 31:47 which is **J** in Laban's language and Galeed in

JEHALLELEL (2)
1Ch 4:16 The sons of **J** were Ziph, Ziphah, Tiria, and Asarel.
2Ch 29:12 of Merari: Kish son of Abdi and Azariah son of **J**.

JEHDEIAH (2)
1Ch 24:20 From the descendants of Shebuel, the leader was **J**.
27:30 **J** from Meronoth was in charge of the donkeys.

JEHEZKEL (1)
1Ch 24:16 lot fell to Pethahiah. / The twentieth lot fell to **J**.

JEHIAH (1)
1Ch 15:24 Obed-edom and **J** were chosen to guard the Ark.

JEHIEL (16)
1Ch 15:18 **J**, Unni, Eliab, Benaiah, Maaseiah, Mattithiah,
15:20 Aziel, Shemiramoth, **J**, Unni, Eliab, Maaseiah,
16: 5 **J**, Mattithiah, Eliab, Benaiah, Obed-edom,
23: 8 Three of the descendants of Libni were **J** (the
26:21 of Libni in the clan of Gershon, **J** was the leader.
26:22 The sons of **J**, Zetham and his brother Joel, were in
27:32 **J** the Hacmonite was responsible to teach the
29: 8 of the house of the LORD under the care of **J**,
2Ch 21: 2 were Azariah, **J**, Zechariah, Azariahu, Michael,
29:14 From the family of Heman: **J** and Shimei.
31:13 The supervisors under them were **J**, Azaziah,
35: 8 Hilkiah, Zechariah, and **J**, the administrators of
Ezr 8: 9 of Joab: Obadiah son of **J** and 218 other men.
10: 2 Then Shecaniah son of **J**, a descendant of Elam,
10:21 Maaseiah, Elijah, Shemaiah, **J**, and Uzziah.
10:26 Mattaniah, Zechariah, **J**, Abdi, Jeremoth,

JEHIZKIAH (1)
2Ch 28:12 **J** son of Shallum, and Amasa son of Hadlai—

JEHOADAH [KJV] See JADAH

JEHOADDIN (2)
2Ki 14: 2 His mother was **J**, from Jerusalem.
2Ch 25: 1 His mother was **J**, from Jerusalem.

JEHOAHAZ (20) [JEHOAHAZ'S]
2Ki 10:35 in Samaria. Then his son **J** became the next king.
13: 1 **J** son of Jehu began to rule over Israel in the
13: 4 Then **J** prayed for the LORD's help,
13: 9 When **J** died, he was buried in Samaria with his
13:10 Jehoash son of **J** began to rule over Israel in the
13:22 oppressed Israel during the entire reign of King **J**.
13:25 Then Jehoash son of **J** recaptured from Ben-hadad
13:25 that Hazael had taken from Jehoash's father, **J**.
14: 8 king Jehoash, the son of **J** and grandson of Jehu:
23:30 Then the people anointed his son **J** and made him
23:31 **J** was twenty-three years old when he became
23:33 Pharaoh Neco put **J** in prison at Riblah in the land
23:34 **J** was taken to Egypt as a prisoner, where he died.
1Ch 3:15 Zedekiah (the third), and **J** (the fourth).
2Ch 25:17 king Jehoash, the son of **J** and grandson of Jehu:
36: 1 Then the people of the land took Josiah's son **J**
36: 2 **J** was twenty-three years old when he became
36: 4 the brother of **J**, as the next king of Judah
36: 4 Then Neco took **J** to Egypt as a prisoner.
Jer 22:11 For this is what the LORD says about **J**,

JEHOAHAZ'S (2) [JEHOAHAZ]
2Ki 13: 7 **J** army was reduced to fifty mounted troops,
13: 8 The rest of the events in **J** reign and all his deeds,

JEHOASH (24) [JEHOASH'S]
2Ki 13: 9 his ancestors. Then his son **J** became the next king.
13:10 **J** son of Jehoahaz began to rule over Israel in the
13:13 When **J** died, he was buried with his ancestors in
13:14 King **J** of Israel visited him and wept over him.
13:25 Then **J** son of Jehoahaz recaptured from
13:25 **J** defeated Ben-hadad on three occasions, and
14: 1 in the second year of the reign of King **J** of Israel.
14: 8 day Amaziah sent this challenge to Israel's king **J**,
14: 9 But King **J** of Israel replied to King Amaziah of
14:11 so King **J** of Israel mobilized his army against
14:13 King **J** of Israel captured King Amaziah of Judah
14:13 Then **J** ordered his army to demolish six hundred
14:16 When **J** died, he was buried with his ancestors in
14:17 for fifteen years after the death of King **J** of Israel.
14:23 Jeroboam II, the son of **J**, began to rule over Israel
14:27 he used Jeroboam II, the son of **J**, to save them.
2Ch 25:17 of Judah sent this challenge to Israel's king **J**,
25:18 But King **J** of Israel replied to King Amaziah of
25:21 So King **J** of Israel mobilized his army against
25:23 King **J** of Israel captured King Amaziah of Judah
25:23 Then **J** ordered his army to demolish six hundred
25:25 for fifteen years after the death of King **J** of Israel.
Hos 1: 1 and Jeroboam son of **J** was king of Israel.
Am 1: 1 was king of Judah and Jeroboam II, the son of **J**,

JEHOASH'S (3) [JEHOASH]
2Ki 13:12 The rest of the events in **J** reign and all his deeds,
13:25 the towns that Hazael had taken from **J** father,
14:15 The rest of the events in **J** reign,

JEHOHANAN (9)
1Ch 26: 3 Elam (the fifth), **J** (the sixth), and Eliehoenai (the
2Ch 17:15 Next in command was **J**, who commanded 280,000
23: 1 Ishmael son of **J**, Azariah son of Obed,
28:12 Azariah son of **J**, Berekiah son of Meshillemoth,
Ezr 10: 6 of God and went to the room of **J** son of Eliashib.
10:28 family of Bebai: **J**, Hananiah, Zabbai, and Athlai.
Ne 6:18 because his son **J** was married to the daughter of
12:13 of Ezra. / **J** was leader of the family of Amariah.
12:42 Eleazar, Uzzi, **J**, Malkijah, Elam, and Ezer.

JEHOIACHIN (29) [JEHOIACHIN'S]
2Ki 24: 6 Jehoiakim died, his son **J** became the next king.
24: 8 **J** was eighteen years old when he became king,
24: 9 **J** did what was evil in the LORD's sight, just as
24:12 Then King **J**, along with his advisers, nobles,
24:12 of Nebuchadnezzar's reign, he took **J** prisoner.
24:15 Nebuchadnezzar led King **J** away as a captive to
25:27 He was kind to **J** and released him from prison on
25:28 He spoke pleasantly to **J** and gave him preferential
25:29 He supplied **J** with new clothes to replace his
1Ch 3:16 Jehoiakim was succeeded by his son **J**; he, in turn,
3:17 The sons of **J**, who was taken prisoner by the
2Ch 36: 8 *and Judah.* Then his son **J** became the next king.
36: 9 **J** was eighteen years old when he became king,
36: 9 **J** did what was evil in the LORD's sight.
36:10 **J** was summoned to Babylon by King
Est 2: 6 along with King **J** of Judah and many others.
Jer 22:24 abandon you, **J** son of Jehoiakim, king of Judah.
22:28 "Why is this man **J** like a discarded, broken dish?
22:30 Let the record show that this man **J** was childless,
24: 1 After King Nebuchadnezzar of Babylon exiled **J**
27:20 left them here when he exiled **J** son of Jehoiakim,
28: 4 And I will bring back **J** son of Jehoiakim, king of
29: 2 This was after King **J**, the queen mother, the court
37: 1 Zedekiah son of Josiah succeeded **J** son of
52:31 He was kind to **J** and released him from prison on
52:32 He spoke pleasantly to **J** and gave him preferential
52:33 He supplied **J** with new clothes to replace his
Mt 1:11 Josiah was the father of **J** and his brothers (born at
1:12 Babylonian exile: / **J** was the father of Shealtiel.

JEHOIACHIN'S (15) [JEHOIACHIN]
2Ki 24:10 During **J** reign, the officers of King
24:17 installed Mattaniah, **J** uncle, as the next king,
25:27 In the thirty-seventh year of King **J** exile in
2Ch 36:10 And Nebuchadnezzar appointed **J** uncle, Zedekiah,
Jer 52:31 In the thirty-seventh year of King **J** exile in
Eze 1: 2 This happened during the fifth year of King **J**
8: 1 during the sixth year of King **J** captivity,
20: 1 during the seventh year of King **J** captivity,
24: 1 during the ninth year of King **J** captivity,
26: 1 during the twelfth year of King **J** captivity,
29: 1 during the tenth year of King **J** captivity,
29:17 during the twenty-seventh year of King **J** captivity,
30:20 during the eleventh year of King **J** captivity,
31: 1 during the eleventh year of King **J** captivity,
32: 1 during the twelfth year of King **J** captivity,

JEHOIADA (51) [JEHOIADA'S]
2Sa 8:18 Benaiah son of **J** was captain of the king's
20:23 Benaiah son of **J** was commander of the king's
23:20 There was also Benaiah son of **J**, a valiant warrior
1Ki 1: 8 Benaiah son of **J**, Nathan the prophet, Shimei,
1:26 Zadok the priest, Benaiah son of **J**, nor Solomon.
1:32 Nathan the prophet, and Benaiah son of **J**."
1:36 "Amen!" Benaiah son of **J** replied.
1:38 the priest, Nathan the prophet, Benaiah son of **J**,
1:44 Nathan the prophet, and Benaiah son of **J**,
2:25 So King Solomon ordered Benaiah son of **J** to
2:29 he sent Benaiah son of **J** to execute him.
2:34 So Benaiah son of **J** returned to the sacred tent
2:46 Benaiah son of **J** took Shimei outside and killed
4: 4 Benaiah son of **J** was commander of the army.
2Ki 11: 4 **J** the priest summoned the commanders, the Carite
11: 5 **J** told them, "This is what you must do. A third of
11: 9 So the commanders did everything just as **J** the
11: 9 off duty. They brought them all to **J** the priest,
11:12 Then **J** brought out Joash, the king's son,
11:15 Then **J** the priest ordered the commanders who
11:17 Then **J** made a covenant between the LORD
11:18 **J** the priest stationed guards at the Temple of the
12: 2 LORD's sight because **J** the priest instructed him.
12: 7 So King Joash called for **J** and the other priests

12: 9 Then **J** the priest bored a hole in the lid of a large
1Ch 11:22 There was also Benaiah son of **J**, a valiant warrior
12:27 This included **J**, leader of the family of Aaron,
18:17 Benaiah son of **J** was captain of the king's
27: 5 Benaiah son of **J** the priest was commander of the
27:34 Ahithophel was succeeded by **J** son of Benaiah
2Ch 22:11 In this way, Jehosheba, the wife of **J** the priest,
23: 1 year of Athaliah's reign, **J** the priest decided to act.
23: 3 **J** said to them, "The time has come for the king's
23: 8 and the people did everything just as **J** the priest
23: 8 **J** the priest did not let anyone go home after their
23: 9 Then **J** supplied the commanders with the spears
23:11 Then **J** and his sons brought out Joash, the king's
23:14 Then **J** the priest ordered the commanders who
23:16 Then **J** made a covenant between himself
23:18 **J** now put the Levitical priests in charge of the
24: 2 sight throughout the lifetime of **J** the priest.
24: 3 **J** chose two wives for Joash, and he had sons
24: 6 So the king called for **J** the high priest and asked
24:12 and **J** gave the money to the construction
24:14 brought the remaining money to the king and **J**.
24:14 of the LORD during the lifetime of **J** the priest.
24:15 **J** lived to a very old age, finally dying at 130.
24:20 of God came upon Zechariah son of **J** the priest.
24:22 That was how King Joash repaid **J** for his love
24:25 to kill him for murdering the son of **J** the priest.
Jer 29:26 'The LORD has appointed you to replace **J** as the

JEHOIADA'S (1) [JEHOIADA]

2Ch 24:17 But after **J** death, the leaders of Judah came

JEHOIAKIM (33) [JEHOIAKIM'S]

2Ki 23:34 of his father, and he changed Eliakim's name to **J**.
23:35 **J** collected a tax from the people of Judah,
23:36 **J** was twenty-five years old when he became king,
24: 1 **J** surrendered and paid him tribute for three years
24: 6 When **J** died, his son Jehoiachin became the next
24:19 was evil in the LORD's sight, just as **J** had done.
1Ch 3:15 **J** (the second), Zedekiah (the third), and Jehoahaz
3:16 **J** was succeeded by his son Jehoiachin; he, in turn,
2Ch 36: 4 and he changed Eliakim's name to **J**.
36: 5 **J** was twenty-five years old when he became king,
36: 6 and he bound **J** in chains and led him away to
Jer 1: 3 King **J**, until the eleventh year of King Zedekiah's
22:13 the LORD says, "Destruction is certain for **J**,
22:18 LORD's decree of punishment against King **J**,
22:24 abandon you, Jehoiachin son of **J**, king of Judah.
24: 1 of Babylon exiled Jehoiachin son of **J**,
26: 1 the LORD early in the reign of **J** son of Josiah,
26:21 When King **J** and the army officers and officials
26:22 Then King **J** sent Elnathan son of Acbor to Egypt
26:23 took him prisoner and brought him back to King **J**.
27:20 left them here when he exiled Jehoiachin son of **J**,
28: 4 And I will bring back Jehoiachin son of **J**, king of
35: 1 Jeremiah when **J** son of Josiah was king of Judah:
36: 1 During the fourth year that **J** son of Josiah was
36: 9 during the fifth year of the reign of **J** son of Josiah.
36:28 again just as you did on the scroll King **J** burned.
36:30 Now this is what the LORD says about King **J** of
36:32 been on the scroll King **J** had burned in the fire.
37: 1 Jehoiachin son of **J** as the king of Judah.
45: 1 in the fourth year of the reign of **J** son of Josiah,
46: 2 in the fourth year of the reign of **J** son of Josiah,
52: 2 was evil in the LORD's sight, just as **J** had done.
Da 1: 2 The Lord gave him victory over King **J** of Judah.

JEHOIAKIM'S (5) [JEHOIAKIM]

2Ki 24: 1 During **J** reign, King Nebuchadnezzar of Babylon
24: 5 The rest of the events in **J** reign and all his deeds
2Ch 36: 8 The rest of the events of **J** reign, including all the
Jer 25: 1 during the fourth year of **J** reign over Judah.
Da 1: 1 During the third year of King **J** reign in Judah,

JEHOIARIB (2)

1Ch 9:10 the priests who returned were Jedaiah, **J**, Jakin,
24: 7 The first lot fell to **J**. / The second lot fell to

JEHONADAB (10)

2Ki 10:15 When Jehu left there, he met **J** son of Recab,
10:15 "Yes, I am," **J** replied. "If you are," Jehu said,
10:15 So **J** put out his hand, and Jehu helped him into the
10:16 I am to the LORD." So **J** rode along with him.
10:23 Then Jehu went into the temple of Baal with **J** son
Jer 35: 6 because **J** son of Recab, our ancestor, gave us this
35:10 and have fully obeyed all the commands of **J**,
35:14 because their ancestor **J** told them not to.
35:18 You have obeyed your ancestor **J** in every respect,
35:19 **J** son of Recab will always have descendants who

JEHONATHAN (2)

2Ch 17: 8 Asahel, Shemiramoth, **J**, Adonijah, Tobijah,
Ne 12:18 **J** was leader of the family of Shemaiah.

JEHORAM (29) [JEHORAM'S]

1Ki 22:50 of David. Then his son **J** became the next king.
2Ki 1:17 This took place in the second year of the reign of **J**
8:16 **J** son of King Jehoshaphat of Judah began to rule
8:17 **J** was thirty-two years old when he became king,
8:18 But **J** followed the example of the kings of Israel
8:18 So **J** did what was evil in the LORD's sight.
8:21 So **J** went with all his chariots to attack the town of
8:24 When **J** died, he was buried with his ancestors in
8:25 Ahaziah son of **J** began to rule over Judah in the
11: 2 the daughter of King **J**, took Ahaziah's infant son,
12:18 **J**, and Ahaziah, the previous kings of Judah,
1Ch 3:11 **J**, Ahaziah, Joash,
2Ch 17: 8 He also sent out the priests, Elishama and **J**.
21: 1 of David. Then his son **J** became the next king.
21: 3 **J** became king because he was the oldest.
21: 4 But when **J** had become solidly established as
21: 5 **J** was thirty-two years old when he became king,
21: 6 But **J** followed the example of the kings of Israel
21: 6 So **J** did what was evil in the LORD's sight.
21: 9 So **J** went to attack Edom with his full army
21:10 because **J** had abandoned the LORD, the God of
21:12 Then Elijah the prophet wrote **J** this letter:
21:16 who lived near the Ethiopians, to attack **J**.
21:18 It was after this that the LORD struck **J** with the
21:20 **J** was thirty-two years old when he became king,
22: 1 So Ahaziah son of **J** reigned as king of Judah.
22:11 the daughter of King **J**, took Ahaziah's infant son,
Mt 1: 8 Jehoshaphat was the father of **J**. / **J** was the father of Uzziah.

JEHORAM'S (6) [JEHORAM]

2Ki 8:20 During **J** reign, the Edomites revolted against
8:21 **J** army, however, deserted him and fled.
8:23 The rest of the events in **J** reign and all his deeds
2Ch 21: 2 **J** brothers—the other sons of Jehoshaphat—
21: 8 During **J** reign, the Edomites revolted against
22: 1 made Ahaziah, **J** youngest son, their next king.

JEHOSHAPHAT (80) [JEHOSHAPHAT'S]

2Sa 8:16 the army. **J** son of Ahilud was the royal historian.
20:24 **J** son of Ahilud was the royal historian.
1Ki 4: 3 **J** son of Ahilud was the royal historian.
4:17 **J** son of Paruah, in Issachar.
15:24 of David. Then his son **J** became the next king.
22: 2 King **J** of Judah went to visit King Ahab of Israel.
22: 4 Then he turned to **J** and asked, "Will you join me
22: 4 And **J** replied to King Ahab, "Why, of course!
22: 5 Then **J** added, "But first let's find out what the
22: 7 But **J** asked, "Isn't there a prophet of the LORD
22: 8 "You shouldn't talk like that," **J** said. "Let's hear
22:10 King Ahab of Israel and King **J** of Judah,
22:18 "Didn't I tell you?" the king of Israel said to **J**.
22:29 and King **J** of Judah led their armies against
22:30 Now King Ahab said to **J**, "As we go into battle,
22:32 So when the Aramean charioteers saw **J** in his
22:32 of Israel!" they shouted. But when **J** cried out,
22:41 **J** son of Asa began to rule over Judah in the fourth
22:43 **J** was a good king, following the example of his
22:44 **J** also made peace with the king of Israel.
22:48 **J** also built a fleet of trading ships to sail to Ophir
22:49 At that time Ahaziah son of Ahab proposed to **J**,
22:49 with your men." But **J** refused the offer.
22:50 When **J** died, he was buried with his ancestors in
2Ki 1:17 in the second year of the reign of Jehoram son of **J**,
3: 7 the way, he sent this message to King **J** of Judah:
3: 7 And **J** replied, "Why, of course! You and I are
3: 8 Then **J** asked, "What route will we take?"
3:11 But King **J** of Judah asked, "Is there no prophet of
3:12 **J** said, "Then the LORD will speak through
3:14 you except for my respect for King **J** of Judah.
8:16 Jehoram son of King **J** of Judah began to rule over
9: 2 and find Jehu son of **J** and grandson of Nimshi.
9:14 So Jehu son of **J** and grandson of Nimshi formed a
12:18 King Joash collected all the sacred objects that **J**,
1Ch 3:10 of Solomon were Rehoboam, Abijah, Asa, **J**,
18:15 the army. **J** son of Ahilud was the royal historian.
2Ch 17: 1 Then **J**, Asa's son, became the next king.
17: 3 The LORD was with **J** because he followed the
17: 5 All the people of Judah brought gifts to **J**, so he
17: 7 **J** sent out his officials to teach in all the towns of
17:10 so that none of them declared war on **J**.
17:12 So **J** became more and more powerful and built
17:19 besides those **J** stationed in the fortified cities
18: 1 Now **J** enjoyed great riches and high esteem,
18: 2 Then Ahab enticed **J** to join forces with him to
18: 3 And **J** replied, "Why, of course! You and I are
18: 4 Then **J** added, "But first let's find out what the
18: 6 But **J** asked, "Isn't there a prophet of the LORD
18: 7 "You shouldn't talk like that," **J** said. "Let's hear
18: 9 King Ahab of Israel and King **J** of Judah,
18:17 "Didn't I tell you?" the king of Israel said to **J**.
18:28 and King **J** of Judah led their armies against
18:29 Now King Ahab said to **J**, "As we go into battle,
18:31 So when the Aramean charioteers saw **J** in his
18:31 But **J** cried out to the LORD to save him,
19: 1 When King **J** of Judah arrived safely home to
19: 4 So **J** lived in Jerusalem, but he went out among the
19: 8 **J** appointed some of the Levites and priests
20: 1 and some of the Meunites declared war on **J**.
20: 2 Messengers came and told **J**, "A vast army from
20: 3 **J** was alarmed by this news and sought the LORD
20: 5 **J** stood before the people of Judah and Jerusalem
20:15 He said, "Listen, King **J**! Listen, all you people of
20:18 Then King **J** bowed down with his face to the
20:20 On the way **J** stopped and said, "Listen to me,
20:25 King **J** and his men went out to gather the plunder.
20:27 they returned to Jerusalem, with **J** leading them,
20:31 So **J** ruled over the land of Judah. He was
20:32 **J** was a good king, following the ways of his
20:35 King **J** of Judah made an alliance with King
20:37 of Dodavahu from Mareshah prophesied against **J**.
21: 1 When **J** died, he was buried with his ancestors in
21: 2 the other sons of **J**—were Azariah, Jehiel,
21:12 **J**, or your grandfather King Asa of Judah.
22: 9 the people said, "He was the grandson of **J**—
Joel 3: 2 gather the armies of the world into the valley of **J**.
3:12 Let them march to the valley of **J**. There I,
Mt 1: 8 Asaph was the father of **J**. / **J** was the father of

JEHOSHAPHAT'S (6) [JEHOSHAPHAT]

1Ki 22:45 The rest of the events in **J** reign, the extent of his
22:51 in the seventeenth year of King **J** reign in Judah.
2Ki 3: 1 in the eighteenth year of King **J** reign in Judah.
2Ch 17: 5 So the LORD established **J** control over the
20:30 So **J** kingdom was at peace, for his God had given
20:34 The rest of the events of **J** reign, from beginning to

JEHOSHEBA (4)

2Ki 11: 2 But Ahaziah's sister **J**, the daughter of King
11: 2 **J** put Joash and his nurse in a bedroom to hide him
2Ch 22:11 But Ahaziah's sister **J**, the daughter of King
22:11 In this way, **J**, the wife of Jehoiada the priest,

JEHOSHUA [KJV] See HOSHEA

JEHOSHUAH [KJV] See JOSHUA

JEHOVAH [KJV] See LORD*

JEHOVAH-JIREH [KJV] See THE LORD* (WILL PROVIDE)

JEHOVAH-NISSI [KJV] See THE LORD* (IS MY BANNER)

JEHOVAH-SHALOM [KJV] See THE LORD* (IS PEACE)

JEHOZABAD (4)

2Ki 12:21 Jozacar son of Shimeath and **J** son of Shomer—
1Ch 26: 4 **J** (the second), Joah (the third), Sacar (the fourth),
2Ch 17:18 Next in command was **J**, who commanded 180,000
24:26 and **J**, the son of a Moabite woman named

JEHOZADAK (12)

1Ch 6:14 the father of Seraiah. / Seraiah was the father of **J**,
Ezr 3: 2 Then Jeshua son of **J** with his fellow priests
3: 8 Jeshua son of **J** and his fellow priests, and all the
5: 2 and Jeshua son of **J** responded by beginning the
10:18 From the family of Jeshua son of **J** and his
Ne 12:26 son of **J**, and in the days of Nehemiah the governor
Hag 1: 1 of Judah, and to Jeshua son of **J**, the high priest.
1:12 son of Shealtiel, Jeshua son of **J**, the high priest,
1:14 governor of Judah, Jeshua son of **J**, the high priest,
2: 2 of Judah, and to Jeshua son of **J**, the high priest,
2: 4 Take courage, Jeshua son of **J**, the high priest.
Zec 6:11 Then put the crown on the head of Jeshua son of **J**,

JEHU (76) [JEHU'S]

1Ki 16: 1 to King Baasha by the prophet **J** son of Hanani:
16: 7 and his family through the prophet **J** son of
16:12 as the LORD had promised through the prophet **J**.
19:16 Then anoint **J** son of Nimshi to be king of Israel,
19:17 who escapes from Hazael will be killed by **J**,
19:17 and those who escape **J** will be killed by Elisha!
2Ki 9: 2 and find **J** son of Jehoshaphat and grandson of
9: 5 he found **J** sitting in a meeting with the other army
9: 5 **J** asked. "For you, Commander," he replied.
9: 6 So **J** left the others and went into the house.
9:11 **J** went back to his fellow officers, and one of them
9:11 know the way such a man babbles on," **J** replied.
9:12 So **J** told them what the man had said and that at
9:13 and blew a trumpet, shouting, "**J** is king!"
9:14 So **J** son of Jehoshaphat and grandson of Nimshi
9:15 So **J** told the men with him, "Since you want me
9:16 Then **J** got into a chariot and rode to Jezreel to find
9:17 The watchman on the tower of Jezreel saw **J**
9:18 So a rider went out to meet **J** and said, "The king
9:18 **J** replied, "What do you know about peace?
9:19 Again **J** answered, "What do you know about
9:20 It must be **J** son of Nimshi, for he is driving
9:21 of Judah rode out in their chariots to meet **J**.
9:22 Joram demanded, "Do you come in peace, **J**?"
9:22 **J** replied, "How can there be peace as long as the
9:24 Then **J** drew his bow and shot Joram between the
9:25 **J** said to Bidkar, his officer, "Throw him into the
9:27 **J** rode after him, shouting, "Shoot him, too!"
9:30 the queen mother, heard that **J** had come to Jezreel,
9:31 When **J** entered the gate of the palace, she shouted
9:32 **J** looked up and saw her at the window
9:33 "Throw her down!" **J** yelled. So they threw her
9:33 And **J** trampled her body under his horses'
9:34 Then **J** went into the palace and ate and drank.
9:36 When they returned and told **J**, he stated,
10: 1 So **J** wrote a letter and sent copies to Samaria,
10: 5 of the king's sons, sent this message to **J**:
10: 6 **J** responded with a second letter: "If you are on
10: 7 heads in baskets and presented them to **J** at Jezreel.
10: 8 A messenger went to **J** and said, "They have
10: 8 So **J** ordered, "Pile them in two heaps at the
10:11 Then **J** killed all of Ahab's relatives living in
10:12 Then **J** set out for Samaria. Along the way,
10:14 "Take them alive!" **J** shouted to his men.
10:15 When **J** left there, he met Jehonadab son of Recab,
10:15 After they had greeted each other, **J** said to him,
10:15 "If you are," **J** said, "then give me your hand."
10:15 put out his hand, and **J** helped him into the chariot.

10:16 Then **J** said, "Now come with me, and see how
10:17 When **J** arrived in Samaria, he killed everyone
10:18 Then **J** called a meeting of all the people of the
10:20 Then **J** ordered, "Prepare a solemn assembly to
10:22 And **J** instructed the keeper of the wardrobe,
10:23 Then **J** went into the temple of Baal with
10:23 **J** said to the worshipers of Baal, "Make sure that
10:24 Now **J** had surrounded the building with eighty of
10:25 As soon as **J** had finished sacrificing the burnt
10:28 **J** destroyed every trace of Baal worship from
10:30 Nonetheless the LORD said to **J**, "You have
10:31 But **J** did not obey the law of the LORD, the God
10:35 When **J** died, he was buried with his ancestors in
10:36 **J** reigned over Israel from Samaria for
13: 1 Jehoahaz son of **J** began to rule over Israel in the
14: 8 the son of Jehoahaz and grandson of **J**
15:12 So the LORD's message to **J** came true:
1Ch 2:38 Obed was the father of **J**. / **J** was the father of
4:35 Joel, **J** son of Joshibiah, son of Seraiah, son of
12: 3 sons of Azmaveth; / Beracah and **J** from Anathoth;
2Ch 19: 2 **J** son of Hanani the seer went out to meet him.
20:34 are recorded in *The Record of J Son of Hanani,*
22: 7 went out with Joram to meet **J** son of Nimshi,
22: 8 While **J** was executing judgment against the family
22: 8 who were attending Ahaziah. So **J** killed them all.
22: 9 They brought him to **J**, who killed him.
25:17 the son of Jehoahaz and grandson of **J**:

JEHU'S (7) [JEHU]
2Ki 9: 6 Then the young prophet poured the oil over **J** head
10:19 But **J** plan was to destroy all the worshipers of
10:25 Then **J** men went into the fortress of the temple of
10:34 The rest of the events in **J** reign and all his deeds
12: 1 Judah in the seventh year of King **J** reign in Israel.
2Ch 22: 9 Then **J** men searched for Ahaziah, and they found
Hos 1: 4 for I am about to punish King **J** dynasty to avenge

JEHUBBAH [KJV] See HUBBAH

JEHUCAL (2)
Jer 37: 3 King Zedekiah sent **J** son of Shelemiah
38: 1 Gedaliah son of Pashhur, **J** son of Shelemiah,

JEHUD (1)
Jos 19:45 **J**, Bene-berak, Gath-rimmon,

JEHUDI (4)
Jer 36:14 the officials sent **J** son of Nethaniah, grandson of
36:21 The king sent **J** to get the scroll. **J** brought it from
Elishama's room and read it to
36:23 Whenever **J** finished reading three or four

JEHUDIJAH [KJV] See (WOMAN OF) JUDAH

JEIEL (13) [JEIEL'S]
1Ch 5: 7 genealogy by their clans: **J** (the leader), Zechariah,
8:29 **J** (the father of Gibeon) lived in Gibeon.
9:35 **J** (the father of Gibeon) lived in Gibeon.
11:44 Shama and **J**, the sons of Hotham, from Aroer;
15:18 Mikneiah, and the gatekeepers, Obed-edom and **J**.
15:21 Mattithiah, Eliphelehu, Mikneiah, Obed-edom, **J**,
16: 5 then **J**, Shemiramoth, Jehiel, Mattithiah, Eliab,
Benaiah, Obed-edom, and **J**.
2Ch 20:14 son of Benaiah, son of **J**, son of Mattaniah,
26:11 men had been mustered and organized by **J**,
29:13 Shimri and **J**. / From the family of Asaph:
35: 9 and Nethanel, and Hashabiah, **J**, and Jozabad—
Ezr 10:43 **J**, Mattithiah, Zabad, Zebina, Jaddai, Joel,

JEIEL'S (2) [JEIEL]
1Ch 8:30 **J** other sons were Zur, Kish, Baal, Ner, Nadab,
9:36 **J** other sons were Zur, Kish, Baal, Ner, Nadab,

JEKABZEEL (1)
Ne 11:25 Dibon with its villages, and **J** with its villages.

JEKAMEAM (2)
1Ch 23:19 Jahaziel (the third), and **J** (the fourth).
24:23 Jahaziel was third, and **J** was fourth.

JEKAMIAH (3)
1Ch 2:41 Shallum was the father of **J**. / **J** was the father of
Elishama.
3:18 Malkiram, Pedaiah, Shenazzar, **J**, Hoshama,

JEKUTHIEL (1)
1Ch 4:18 (the father of Soco), and **J** (the father of Zanoah)

JEMIMAH (1)
Job 42:14 He named his first daughter **J**, the second Keziah,

JEMUEL (2) [NEMUEL]
Ge 46:10 The sons of Simeon were **J**, Jamin, Ohad, Jakin,
Ex 6:15 The descendants of Simeon included **J**, Jamin,

JEOPARDED [KJV] See RISKED

JEPHTHAH (24) [JEPHTHAH'S]
Jdg 11: 1 Now **J** from Gilead was a great warrior. He was
11: 2 half brothers grew up, they chased **J** off the land.
11: 3 So **J** fled from his brothers and lived in the land of
11: 5 the leaders of Gilead sent for **J** in the land of Tob.
11: 7 But **J** said to them, "Aren't you the ones who
11: 9 **J** said, "If I come with you and if the LORD
11:11 So **J** went with the leaders of Gilead, and he
11:11 **J** repeated what he had said to the leaders.
11:12 Then **J** sent messengers to the king of Ammon,
11:14 **J** sent this message back to the Ammonite king:
11:15 "This is what **J** says: Israel did not steal any land
11:29 At that time the Spirit of the LORD came upon **J**,
11:30 And **J** made a vow to the LORD. He said,
11:32 So **J** led his army against the Ammonites,
11:34 When **J** returned home to Mizpah, his daughter—
11:38 "You may go," **J** said. And he let her go away for
12: 1 over to Zaphon. They sent this message to **J**:
12: 2 of the dispute, but you refused to come!" **J** said.
12: 4 So **J** called out his army and attacked the men of
12: 5 **J** captured the shallows of the Jordan,
12: 7 **J** was Israel's judge for six years. When he died,
12: 8 After **J**, Ibzan became Israel's judge. He lived in
1Sa 12:11 Barak, **J**, and Samuel to save you, and you lived in
Heb 11:32 Barak, Samson, **J**, David, Samuel, and all the

JEPHTHAH'S (3) [JEPHTHAH]
Jdg 11:13 The king of Ammon answered **J** messengers,
11:28 But the king of Ammon paid no attention to **J**
11:40 days each year to lament the fate of **J** daughter.

JEPHUNNEH (15)
Nu 13: 6 Judah | Caleb son of **J**
14: 6 Joshua son of Nun and Caleb son of **J**, tore their
14:30 The only exceptions will be Caleb son of **J**
26:65 The only exceptions were Caleb son of **J**
32:12 The only exceptions are Caleb son of **J** the
34:19 the names of the leaders: / Judah | Caleb son of **J**
Dt 1:36 except Caleb son of **J**. He will see this land
Jos 14: 6 led by Caleb son of **J** the Kenizzite, came to
14:13 So Joshua blessed Caleb son of **J** and gave Hebron
14:14 to the descendants of Caleb son of **J** the Kenizzite
15:13 assign some of Judah's territory to Caleb son of **J**.
21:12 surrounding villages were given to Caleb son of **J**.
1Ch 4:15 The sons of Caleb son of **J** were Iru, Elah,
6:56 and outlying areas were given to Caleb son of **J**.
7:38 The sons of Jether were **J**, Pispah, and Ara.

JERAH (2)
Ge 10:26 ancestor of Almodad, Sheleph, Hazarmaveth, **J**,
1Ch 1:20 ancestor of Almodad, Sheleph, Hazarmaveth, **J**,

JERAHMEEL (8) [JERAHMEELITES]
1Ch 2: 9 The sons of Hezron were **J**, Ram, and Caleb.
2:25 The sons of **J**, the oldest son of Hezron, were Ram
2:26 **J** had a second wife named Atarah. She was the
2:27 the oldest son of **J**, were Maaz, Jamin, and Eker.
2:33 and Zaza. These were all descendants of **J**.
2:42 the brother of **J**, was Mesha, the father of Ziph.
24:29 From the descendants of Kish, the leader was **J**.
Jer 36:26 Then the king commanded his son **J**, Seraiah son

JERAHMEELITES (2) [JERAHMEEL]
1Sa 27:10 the south of Judah, the **J**, and the Kenites."
30:29 Racal, the towns of the **J**, the towns of the Kenites,

JERED (1)
1Ch 4:18 who became the mother of **J** (the father of Gedor),

JEREMAI (1)
Ezr 10:33 Mattenai, Mattattah, Zabad, Eliphelet, **J**,

JEREMIAH (153) [JEREMIAH'S]
2Ki 23:31 was Hamutal, the daughter of **J** from Libnah.
24:18 was Hamutal, the daughter of **J** from Libnah.
1Ch 5:24 Epher, Ishi, Eliel, Azriel, **J**, Hodaviah, and Jahdiel.
12: 4 **J**, Jahaziel, Johanan, and Jozabad from Gederah;
12:10 Mishmannah was fourth. / **J** was fifth.
12:13 **J** was tenth. / Macbannai was eleventh.
2Ch 35:25 The prophet **J** composed funeral songs for Josiah,
36:12 to humble himself in the presence of the prophet **J**,
36:21 So the message of the LORD spoken through **J**
Ne 10: 2 Seraiah, Azariah, **J**,
12: 1 and Jeshua the high priest: / Seraiah, **J**, Ezra,
12:12 Hananiah was leader of the family of **J**.
12:34 Judah, Benjamin, Shemaiah, **J**,
Jer 1: 1 These are the words of **J** son of Hilkiah, one of the
1: 2 The LORD first gave messages to **J** during the
1:11 Then the LORD said to me, "Look, **J**! What do
6:27 "**J**, I have made you a tester of metals, that you
7: 1 The LORD gave another message to **J**. He said,
7:16 "Pray no more for these people, **J**. Do not weep
8: 4 "**J**, say to the people, 'This is what the LORD
11: 1 The LORD gave another message to **J**. He said,
11:14 "Pray no more for these people, **J**. Do not weep
14: 1 This message came to **J** from the LORD,
14:17 "Now, **J**, say this to them: 'Night and day my eyes
15:11 The LORD replied, "All will be well with you, **J**.
18: 1 The LORD gave another message to **J**. He said,
18:11 **J**, go and warn all Judah and Jerusalem.
18:18 people said, "Come on, let's find a way to stop **J**.
19:10 "As these men watch, **J**, smash the jar you brought
19:14 Then **J** returned from Topheth where he had
20: 1 Temple of the LORD, heard what **J** was saying.
20: 2 So he arrested **J** the prophet and had him whipped
20: 3 Pashhur finally released him, **J** said, "Pashhur,
21: 1 The LORD spoke through **J** when King Zedekiah
21: 1 the priest, to speak with him. They begged **J**,
21: 3 **J** replied, "Go back to King Zedekiah and tell him,
24: 3 the LORD said to me, "What do you see, **J**?"
25: 1 This message for all the people of Judah came to **J**
25: 2 **J** the prophet said to the people in Judah
25:13 all the penalties announced by **J** against the
26: 1 This message came to **J** from the LORD early in
26: 7 and all the people listened to **J** as he spoke in front
26: 8 But when **J** had finished his message,
26:12 Then **J** spoke in his own defense. "The LORD
26:19 If we kill **J**, who knows what will happen to us?"
26:20 terrible disaster against the city and nation as **J** did.
26:24 Ahikam son of Shaphan also stood with **J**
27: 1 This message came to **J** from the LORD early in
28: 5 **J** responded to Hananiah as they stood in front of
28:11 of Babylon." At that, **J** left the Temple area.
28:12 afterward the LORD gave this message to **J**:
28:15 Then **J** the prophet said to Hananiah, "Listen,
29: 1 **J** wrote a letter from Jerusalem to the elders,
29:27 So why have you done nothing to stop **J** from
29:28 **J** sent a letter here to Babylon, predicting that our
29:29 Shemaiah's letter, he took it to **J** and read it to him.
29:30 Then the LORD gave this message to **J**:
30: 1 The LORD gave another message to **J**. He said,
30: 2 for the record everything I have said to you, **J**.
32: 1 The following message came to **J** from the
32: 2 and **J** was imprisoned in the courtyard of the guard
32:26 Then this message came to **J** from the LORD:
33: 1 While **J** was still confined in the courtyard of the
33:19 Then this message came to **J** from the LORD:
33:23 The LORD gave another message to **J**. He said,
34: 1 At that time this message came to **J** from the
34: 6 So **J** the prophet delivered the message to King
34: 8 This message came to **J** from the LORD after
34:12 So the LORD gave them this message through **J**:
35: 1 This is the message the LORD gave **J** when
35: 3 So I went to see Jaazaniah son of **J** and grandson
35:12 Then the LORD gave this message to **J**:
35:18 Then **J** turned to the Recabites and said, "This is
36: 1 king in Judah, the LORD gave this message to **J**:
36: 4 **J** sent for Baruch son of Neriah, and as **J** dictated,
36: 5 Then **J** said to Baruch, "I am a prisoner here
36: 8 Baruch did as **J** told him and read these messages
36:17 these messages. Did they come directly from **J**?"
36:18 "**J** dictated them to me word by word,
36:19 "You and **J** should both hide," the officials told
36:26 Shelemiah son of Abdeel to arrest Baruch and **J**.
36:27 the LORD gave **J** another message.
36:32 Then **J** took another scroll and dictated again to his
37: 2 land listened to what the LORD said through **J**.
37: 3 Zephaniah the priest, son of Maaseiah, to ask **J**,
37: 4 **J** had not yet been imprisoned, so he could come
37: 6 Then the LORD gave this message to **J**:
37:12 **J** started to leave the city on his way to the land of
37:14 "That's not true!" **J** protested. "I had no intention
37:14 wouldn't listen, and he took **J** before the officials.
37:15 They were furious with **J** and had him flogged
37:16 **J** was put into a dungeon cell, where he remained
37:17 Later King Zedekiah secretly requested that **J**
37:17 "Yes, I do!" said **J**. "You will be defeated by the
37:18 Then **J** asked the king, "What crime have I
37:21 So King Zedekiah commanded that **J** not be
37:21 The king also commanded that **J** be given a loaf of
37:21 left in the city. So **J** was put in the palace prison.
38: 1 and Pashhur son of Malkijah heard what **J** had
38: 6 So the officials took **J** from his cell and lowered
38: 6 of mud at the bottom, and **J** sank down into it.
38: 7 palace official, heard that **J** was in the cistern.
38: 9 evil thing in putting **J** the prophet into the cistern.
38:10 and pull **J** out of the cistern before he dies."
38:11 to the cistern and lowered them to **J** on a rope.
38:12 Ebed-melech called down to **J**, "Put these rags
38:12 you from the ropes." Then when **J** was ready,
38:13 So **J** was returned to the courtyard of the guard—
38:14 One day King Zedekiah sent for **J** to meet him at
38:15 **J** said, "If I tell you the truth, you will kill me.
38:17 Then **J** said to Zedekiah, "The LORD God
38:20 **J** replied, "You won't be handed over to them if
38:24 Then Zedekiah said to **J**, "Don't tell anyone you
38:27 it wasn't long before the king's officials came to **J**
38:27 But **J** followed the king's instructions, and they
38:27 No one had overheard the conversation between **J**
38:28 And **J** remained a prisoner in the courtyard of the
39:11 Nebuchadnezzar had told Nebuzaradan to find **J**.
39:14 sent messengers to bring **J** out of the prison.
39:14 So **J** stayed in Judah among his own people.
39:15 The LORD had given the following message to **J**
40: 1 The LORD gave a message to **J** after
40: 1 He had found **J** bound in chains among the
40: 2 The captain of the guard called for **J** and said,
40: 5 Then Nebuzaradan gave **J** some food and money
40: 6 So **J** returned to Gedaliah son of Ahikam at
42: 2 **J** the prophet. They said, "Please pray to the
42: 4 "All right," **J** replied. "I will pray to the LORD
42: 5 Then they said to **J**, "May the LORD your God
42: 7 Ten days later, the LORD gave his reply to **J**.
43: 1 When **J** had finished giving this message from the
43: 2 of Kareah and all the other proud men said to **J**,
43: 6 Also included were the prophet **J** and Baruch.
43: 8 the LORD gave another message to **J**.
44: 1 This is the message **J** received concerning the
44:15 the southern region of Egypt—answered **J**,
44:20 Then **J** said to all of them, men and women alike,
44:24 Then **J** said to them all, including the women,
45: 1 The prophet **J** gave a message to Baruch son of

45: 1 after Baruch had written down everything **J** had
46: 1 The following messages were given to **J** the
46: 13 Then the LORD gave the prophet **J** this message
47: 1 This is the LORD's message to the prophet **J**
49: 34 **J** from the LORD at the beginning of the reign of
50: 1 The LORD gave **J** the prophet this message
51: 59 The prophet **J** gave this message to Zedekiah's
51: 60 **J** had recorded on a scroll all the terrible disasters
52: 1 name was Hamutal, the daughter of **J** from Libnah.
Da 9: 2 word of the LORD, as recorded by **J** the prophet,
Mt 2: 17 Herod's brutal action fulfilled the prophecy of **J**:
16: 14 and others say **J** or one of the other prophets."
27: 9 This fulfilled the prophecy of **J** that says,

JEREMIAH'S (8) [JEREMIAH]

2Ch 36: 22 the LORD fulfilled **J** prophecy by stirring the
Ezr 1: 1 the LORD fulfilled **J** prophecy by stirring the
Jer 28: 10 Then Hananiah the prophet took the yoke off **J**
29: 3 to Nebuchadnezzar. This is what **J** letter said:
36: 10 Baruch read **J** words to all the people from the
36: 27 After the king had burned **J** scroll, the LORD
48: 47 This is the end of **J** prophecy concerning Moab.
51: 64 bring upon her.' " This is the end of **J** messages.

JEREMIAS, JEREMY [KJV] See JEREMIAH

JEREMOTH (6)

1Ch 7: 8 Joash, Eliezer, Elioenai, Omri, **J**, Abijah,
8: 14 Ahio, Shashak, **J**,
27: 19 son of Obadiah / Naphtali | **J** son of Azriel
Ezr 10: 26 Mattaniah, Zechariah, Jehiel, Abdi, **J**, and Elijah.
10: 27 Elioenai, Eliashib, Mattaniah, **J**, Zabad, and Aziza.
10: 29 Malluch, Adaiah, Jashub, Sheal, and **J**.

JERIAH (4)

1Ch 23: 19 The descendants of Hebron included **J** (the family
24: 23 From the descendants of Hebron, **J** was the leader,
26: 31 Also from the clan of Hebron came **J**, who was the
26: 32 hundred capable men among the relatives of **J**.

JERIBAI (1)

1Ch 11: 46 **J** and Joshaviah, the sons of Elnaam;

JERICHO (69)

Nu 22: 1 camped east of the Jordan River, across from **J**.
26: 3 of Moab beside the Jordan River, across from **J**.
26: 63 of Moab beside the Jordan River, across from **J**.
31: 12 of Moab beside the Jordan River, across from **J**.
33: 48 of Moab beside the Jordan River, across from **J**.
33: 50 the Jordan River on the plains of Moab opposite **J**,
34: 15 the east side of the Jordan River, across from **J**."
35: 1 of Moab, across from **J**, the LORD said to Moses,
36: 13 of Moab beside the Jordan River, across from **J**.
Dt 32: 49 and climb Mount Nebo, which is across from **J**.
34: 1 and climbed Pisgah Peak, which is across from **J**.
34: 3 the Negev; the Jordan Valley with **J**—the city of
Jos 2: 1 side of the Jordan River, especially around **J**."
2: 2 But someone told the king of **J**, "Some Israelites
2: 3 So the king of **J** sent orders to Rahab: "Bring out
2: 13 when **J** is conquered, you will let me live,
3: 16 Then all the people crossed over near the city of **J**.
4: 13 and they crossed over to the plains of **J** in the
4: 19 from Egypt. They camped at Gilgal, east of **J**.
5: 10 Israelites were camped at Gilgal on the plains of **J**,
5: 13 As Joshua approached the city of **J**, he looked up
6: 1 Now the gates of **J** were tightly shut
6: 2 "I have given you **J**, its king, and all its mighty
6: 20 Suddenly, the walls of **J** collapsed,
6: 25 because she had hidden the spies Joshua sent to **J**.
6: 26 who tries to rebuild the city of **J**. / At the cost of
7: 2 Joshua sent some of his men from **J** to spy out the
8: 2 You will destroy them as you destroyed **J** and its
9: 3 people of Gibeon heard what had happened to **J**
10: 1 just as he had destroyed the city of **J** and killed its
10: 28 king of Makkedah as he had killed the king of **J**.
10: 30 king of Libnah just as he had killed the king of **J**.
12: 9 The king of **J** / The king of Ai, near Bethel
13: 32 plains of Moab, across the Jordan River, east of **J**.
16: 1 of Joseph extended from the Jordan River near **J**,
16: 1 east of the waters of **J**, through the wilderness
16: 7 southward to Ataroth and Naarah, touched **J**,
18: 12 went north of the slope of **J**, then west through the
18: 21 tribe of Benjamin. / **J**, Beth-hoglah, Emek-keziz,
20: 8 On the east side of the Jordan River, across from **J**,
24: 11 you crossed the Jordan River and came to **J**, the men of **J** fought against you.
Jdg 1: 16 When the tribe of Judah left **J**, the Kenites,
3: 13 Eglon attacked Israel and took possession of **J**.
2Sa 10: 5 he sent messengers to tell the men to stay at **J** until
1Ki 16: 34 his reign that Hiel, a man from Bethel, rebuilt **J**.
16: 34 concerning **J** spoken by Joshua son of Nun.
2Ki 2: 4 for the LORD has told me to go to **J**."
2: 4 never leave you." So they went on together to **J**.
2: 5 Then the group of prophets from **J** came to Elisha
2: 15 When the group of prophets from **J** saw what
2: 18 Elisha was still at **J** when they returned. "Didn't I
2: 19 Now the leaders of the town of **J** visited Elisha.
2: 23 Elisha left **J** and went up to Bethel. As he was
25: 5 after them and caught the king on the plains of **J**,
1Ch 6: 78 of Reuben, east of the Jordan River opposite **J**,
19: 5 he sent messengers to tell the men to stay at **J** until
2Ch 28: 15 back to their own land—to **J**, the city of palms.
Ezr 2: 34 The citizens of **J** | 345
Ne 3: 2 People from the city of **J** worked next to them,
7: 36 The citizens of **J** | 345
Jer 39: 5 chased the king and caught him on the plains of **J**.
52: 8 and caught King Zedekiah on the plains of **J**,
Mt 20: 29 As Jesus and the disciples left the city of **J**, a huge
Mk 10: 46 And so they reached **J**. Later, as Jesus and his
Lk 10: 30 man was traveling on a trip from Jerusalem to **J**,
18: 35 As they approached **J**, a blind beggar was sitting
19: 1 Jesus entered **J** and made his way through the
Heb 11: 30 the people of Israel marched around **J** seven days,

JERIEL (1)

1Ch 7: 2 Rephaiah, **J**, Jahmai, Ibsam, and Shemuel.

JERIMOTH (8)

1Ch 7: 7 sons of Bela were Ezbon, Uzzi, Uzziel, **J**, and Iri.
12: 5 Eluzai, **J**, Bealiah, Shemariah, and Shephatiah
23: 23 The three sons of Mushi were Mahli, Eder, and **J**.
24: 30 of Mushi, the leaders were Mahli, Eder, and **J**.
25: 4 Uzziel, Shubael, **J**, Hananiah, Hanani, Eliathah,
25: 22 The fifteenth lot fell to **J** and twelve of his sons
2Ch 11: 18 the daughter of David's son **J** and of Abihail,
31: 13 Azaziah, Nahath, Asahel, **J**, Jozabad, Eliel,

JERIOTH (1)

1Ch 2: 18 son Caleb had two wives named Azubah and **J**.

JEROBOAM (97) [JEROBOAM'S]

1Ki 11: 26 Another rebel leader was **J** son of Nebat, one of
11: 28 **J** was a very capable young man, and when
11: 29 One day as **J** was leaving Jerusalem, the prophet
11: 31 Then he said to **J**, "Take ten of these pieces,
11: 40 Solomon tried to kill **J**, but he fled to King Shishak
12: 2 When **J** son of Nebat heard of Solomon's death,
12: 3 The leaders of Israel sent for **J**, and the whole
12: 12 **J** and all the people returned to hear Rehoboam's
12: 15 for it fulfilled the LORD's message to **J** son of
12: 25 **J** then built up the city of Shechem in the hill
12: 26 **J** thought to himself, "Unless I am careful,
12: 31 **J** built shrines at the pagan high places
12: 32 **J** also instituted a religious festival in Bethel,
12: 33 **J** offered sacrifices on the altar at Bethel.
13: 1 and he arrived there just as **J** was approaching the
13: 4 King **J** was very angry with the man of God for
13: 33 even after this, **J** did not turn from his evil ways.
14: 2 So **J** told his wife, "Disguise yourself so that no
14: 6 at the door, he called out, "Come in, wife of **J**!
14: 7 Give your husband, **J**, this message from the
14: 13 the God of Israel, sees in the entire family of **J**.
14: 14 a king over Israel who will destroy the family of **J**.
14: 16 He will abandon Israel because **J** sinned and made
14: 20 **J** reigned in Israel twenty-two years.
14: 20 When **J** died, his son Nadab became the next king.
14: 30 There was constant war between Rehoboam and **J**.
15: 6 between Abijam and **J** throughout Abijam's reign.
15: 7 There was constant war between Abijam and **J**.
15: 25 Nadab son of **J** began to rule over Israel in the
15: 26 continuing the sins of idolatry that **J** had led Israel
15: 29 immediately killed all the descendants of King **J**,
15: 29 just as the LORD had promised concerning **J** by
15: 30 because **J** had aroused the anger of the LORD,
15: 34 the LORD's sight and followed the example of **J**,
15: 34 continuing the sins of idolatry that **J** had led Israel
16: 2 but you have followed the evil example of **J**.
16: 3 just as I destroyed the descendants of **J** son of
16: 7 just like the family of **J**, and also because Baasha had destroyed the family of **J**.
16: 19 the LORD's sight and followed the example of **J**,
16: 19 continuing the sins of idolatry that **J** had led Israel
16: 26 He followed the example of **J**, continuing the sins of idolatry that **J** had led Israel
16: 31 And as though it were not enough to live like **J**,
21: 22 your family as he did the family of **J** son of Nebat
22: 52 and mother and the example of **J** son of Nebat,
2Ki 3: 3 **J** son of Nebat had led the people of Israel to
9: 9 Ahab as I destroyed the families of **J** son of Nebat
10: 29 the great sin that **J** son of Nebat had led Israel to
10: 31 He refused to turn from the sins of idolatry that **J**
13: 2 He followed the example of **J** son of Nebat,
13: 2 continuing the sins of idolatry that **J** son of Nebat
13: 6 continued to sin, following the evil example of **J**.
13: 11 He refused to turn from the sins of idolatry that **J**
13: 13 Then his son **J II** became the next king.
14: 16 Then his son **J II** became the next king.
14: 23 **J II**, the son of Jehoash, began to rule over Israel in
14: 23 in Judah. **J** reigned in Samaria forty-one years.
14: 24 He refused to turn from the sins of idolatry that **J**
14: 25 **J II** recovered the territories of Israel between
14: 27 he used **J II**, the son of Jehoash, to save them.
14: 28 The rest of the events in the reign of **J II** and all his
14: 29 When **J II** died, he was buried with his ancestors,
15: 1 year of the reign of King **J II** of Israel.
15: 8 Zechariah son of **J II** began to rule over Israel in
15: 9 He refused to turn from the sins of idolatry that **J**
15: 18 he refused to turn from the sins of idolatry that **J**
15: 24 He refused to turn from the sins of idolatry that **J**
15: 28 He refused to turn from the sins of idolatry that **J**
17: 21 of David, they chose **J** son of Nebat as their king.
17: 21 Then **J** drew Israel away from following the
17: 22 people of Israel persisted in all the evil ways of **J**.
23: 15 the pagan shrine that **J** son of Nebat had made
23: 16 of God as **J** stood beside the altar at the festival.
1Ch 5: 17 days of King Jotham of Judah and King **J** of Israel.
2Ch 9: 29 *of Iddo the Seer,* concerning **J** son of Nebat.
10: 2 When **J** son of Nebat heard of Solomon's death,
10: 3 The leaders of Israel sent for **J**, and he and all
10: 12 **J** and all the people returned to hear Rehoboam's
10: 15 **J** son of Nebat by the prophet Ahijah from Shiloh.
11: 4 message of the LORD and did not fight against **J**.
11: 14 because **J** and his sons would not allow them to
11: 15 **J** appointed his own priests to serve at the pagan
12: 15 and **J** were continually at war with each other.
13: 2 Then war broke out between Abijah and **J**.
13: 3 while **J** mustered 800,000 courageous men from
13: 4 and shouted to **J** and the Israelite army:
13: 6 Yet **J** son of Nebat, who was a mere servant of
13: 8 but with you are those gold calves that **J** made as
13: 13 **J** had secretly sent part of his army around behind
13: 15 God defeated **J** and the Israelite army and routed
13: 20 So **J** of Israel never regained his power during
Hos 1: 1 of Judah, and **J** son of Jehoash was king of Israel.
Am 1: 1 when Uzziah was king of Judah and **J II**, the son of
7: 9 and I will bring the dynasty of King **J** to a sudden
7: 10 Amos was saying, he rushed a message to King **J**:
7: 11 '**J** will soon be killed and the people of Israel will

JEROBOAM'S (12) [JEROBOAM]

1Ki 12: 20 When the people of Israel learned of **J** return from
13: 34 and resulted in the destruction of **J** kingdom
14: 1 At that time **J** son Abijah became very sick.
14: 4 So **J** wife went to Ahijah's home at Shiloh. He was
14: 5 "**J** wife will come here, pretending to be someone
14: 12 Then Ahijah said to **J** wife, "Go on home,
14: 17 So **J** wife returned to Tirzah, and the child died
14: 19 The rest of the events of **J** reign, all his wars
15: 1 Judah in the eighteenth year of **J** reign in Israel.
15: 9 Judah in the twentieth year of **J** reign in Israel.
2Ch 13: 1 Judah in the eighteenth year of **J** reign in Israel.
13: 19 Abijah and his army pursued **J** troops and captured

JEROHAM (10)

1Sa 1: 1 He was the son of **J** and grandson of Elihu,
1Ch 6: 27 Eliab, **J**, Elkanah, and Samuel.
6: 34 Elkanah, **J**, Eliel, Toah,
8: 27 Jaareshiah, Elijah, and Zicri were the sons of **J**.
9: 8 Ibneiah son of **J**; Elah son of Uzzi, son of Micri;
9: 12 Other returning priests were Adaiah son of **J**,
12: 7 Joelah and Zebadiah, sons of **J** from Gedor.
27: 22 Dan | Azarel son of **J** These were the leaders of
2Ch 23: 1 Azariah son of **J**, Ishmael son of Jehohanan,
Ne 11: 12 Also, there was Adaiah son of **J**, son of Pelaliah,

JERUBBAAL (3) [GIDEON]

Jdg 6: 32 From then on Gideon was called **J**, which means
7: 1 So **J** (that is, Gideon) and his army got up early
8: 35 Nor did they show any loyalty to the family of **J**

JERUEL (1)

2Ch 20: 16 of the valley that opens into the wilderness of **J**.

JERUSALEM (1018) [ARIEL, JEBUS, JERUSALEM'S, SALEM]

DAUGHTER(S) OF JERUSALEM (4) 2Ki 19:21; Isa 37:22; La 2:13; Zep 3:14; Lk 23:28

JERUSALEM AND JUDAH (11) 2Ki 21:12; 24:20; 2Ch 21:11,13; Isa 3:1; 5:3; 22:21; Jer 40:1; 52:3; Zec 12:2; 14:21

JUDAH AND JERUSALEM (53) 2Ki 23:1,2; 1Ch 6:15; 2Ch 2:7; 11:14; 20:5,15,17,18,20; 24:9,18,23; 28:10; 29:8; 32:12,25,33; 33:9; 34:3,5,29,30; 35:24; 36:4,10; Ezr 4:6; 5:1; 7:14; 9:9; 10:7; Isa 1:1; 2:1; 3:8; Jer 4:3; 11:2,9,12; 13:9; 18:11; 19:7,11; 25:2; 27:20; 35:13,17; 36:31; 44:9; Da 9:7; Joel 3:1,6; Zep 1:4; Mal 3:4

LIVE IN JERUSALEM (5) Jdg 1:21; 2Sa 19:33; 1Ch 23:25; Isa 30:19; Zec 8:3

LIVED IN JERUSALEM (9) 2Sa 14:28; 1Ki 2:38; 1Ch 8:28; 9:34; 2Ch 19:4; Ne 11:6; Ecc 1:12; 2:7; Lk 2:25

STREETS OF JERUSALEM (9) Jer 7:17,34; 11:6; 14:16; 33:10; 44:6,17,21; Eze 9:4

Jos 10: 1 Now Adoni-zedek, king of **J**, heard that Joshua
10: 3 So King Adoni-zedek of **J** sent messengers to
10: 23 the kings of **J**, Hebron, Jarmuth, Lachish,
12: 10 The king of **J** / The king of Hebron
15: 8 of the Jebusites, where the city of **J** is located.
15: 63 drive out the Jebusites, who lived in the city of **J**,
18: 28 Zela, Haeleph, Jebus (that is, **J**), Gibeah,
Jdg 1: 7 to them." They took him to **J**, and he died there.
1: 8 The men of Judah attacked **J** and captured it,
1: 21 to drive out the Jebusites, who were living in **J**.
1: 21 So to this day the Jebusites live in **J** among the
19: 10 and headed in the direction of Jebus (that is, **J**).
1Sa 17: 54 (David took Goliath's head to **J**, but he stored the
2Sa 5: 5 and from **J** he reigned over all Israel and Judah for
5: 6 then led his troops to **J** to fight against the
5: 13 After moving from Hebron to **J**, David married
5: 14 are the names of David's sons who were born in **J**:
8: 7 the gold shields of Hadadezer's officers to **J**,
9: 13 in both feet, moved to **J** to live at the palace.
10: 14 After the battle was over, Joab returned to **J**.
11: 1 the city of Rabbah. But David stayed behind in **J**.
11: 12 So Uriah stayed in **J** that day and the next.
11: 22 So the messenger went to **J** and gave a complete
12: 31 Then David and his army returned to **J**.
13: 30 As they were on the way back to **J**, this report
13: 34 Then the watchman on the **J** wall saw a great
14: 23 went to Geshur and brought Absalom back to **J**.
14: 28 Absalom lived in **J** for two years without getting to
15: 8 to him in Hebron if he would bring me back to **J**."
15: 11 He took two hundred men from **J** with him as

15:13 A messenger soon arrived in **J** to tell King David,
15:14 and the city of **J** will be spared from disaster."
15:28 Let me know what happens in **J** before I disappear
15:34 Return to **J** and tell Absalom, 'I will now be your
15:37 So David's friend Hushai returned to **J**,
16: 3 "He stayed in **J**," Ziba replied. "He said,
16:15 Meanwhile, Absalom and his men arrived at **J**,
17:20 looked for them without success and returned to **J**.
19:15 So the king started back to **J**. And when he arrived
19:19 "Forget the terrible thing I did when you left **J**.
19:24 Saul's grandson, arrived from **J** to meet the king.
19:24 nor trimmed his beard since the day the king left **J**.
19:33 "Come across with me and live in **J**," the king
20: 2 and escorted him from the Jordan River to **J**.
20: 3 When the king arrived at his palace in **J**,
20:22 to their homes. Joab returned to the king at **J**.
24: 8 and twenty days and then returned to **J**.
24:16 But as the death angel was preparing to destroy **J**,
1Ki 1:40 And all the people returned with Solomon to **J**,
2:11 seven of them in Hebron and thirty-three in **J**.
2:36 told him, "Build a house here in **J** and live there.
2:38 So Shimei lived in **J** for a long time.
2:40 When he had found them, he took them back to **J**.
2:41 Solomon heard that Shimei had left **J** and had gone
3:15 He returned to **J** and stood before the Ark of the
8: 1 the tribes and families of Israel to assemble in **J**.
9:15 the royal palace, the Millo, the wall of **J**,
9:19 He built to his heart's content in **J** and Lebanon
10: 2 She arrived in **J** with a large group of attendants
10:26 them in the chariot cities, and some near him in **J**.
10:27 The king made silver as plentiful in **J** as stones.
10:29 Egyptian chariots delivered to **J** could be
11: 7 On the Mount of Olives, east of **J**, he even built a
11:13 the sake of my servant David and for the sake of **J**,
11:29 One day as Jeroboam was leaving **J**, the prophet
11:32 the sake of my servant David and for the sake of **J**,
11:36 of David my servant will continue to reign in **J**,
11:42 Solomon ruled in **J** over all Israel for forty years.
12:18 he quickly jumped into his chariot and fled to **J**.
12:21 When Rehoboam arrived at **J**, he mobilized the
12:27 When they go to **J** to offer sacrifices at the Temple
12:28 "It is too much trouble for you to worship in **J**.
14:21 became king, and he reigned seventeen years in **J**,
14:25 King Shishak of Egypt came up and attacked **J**.
15: 2 He reigned in **J** three years. His mother was
15: 4 and he gave Abijam a son to rule after him in **J**.
15:10 He reigned in **J** forty-one years. His grandmother
22:42 and he reigned in **J** twenty-five years.
2Ki 8:17 he became king, and he reigned in **J** eight years.
8:26 he became king, and he reigned in **J** one year.
9:28 His officials took him by chariot to **J**, where they
12: 1 He reigned in **J** forty years. His mother was
12:17 and captured it. Then he turned to attack **J**.
12:18 royal palace. So Hazael called off his attack on **J**.
14: 2 and he reigned in **J** twenty-nine years.
14: 2 His mother was Jehoaddin, from **J**.
14:13 of Judah at Beth-shemesh and marched on to **J**.
14:19 was a conspiracy against Amaziah's life in **J**,
14:20 They brought him back to **J** on a horse, and he was
15: 2 became king, and he reigned in **J** fifty-two years.
His mother was Jecoliah, from **J**.
15:33 he became king, and he reigned in **J** sixteen years.
16: 2 he became king, and he reigned in **J** sixteen years.
16: 5 on Ahaz. They besieged **J** but did not conquer it.
18: 2 and he reigned in **J** twenty-nine years.
18:17 with a huge army to confront King Hezekiah in **J**.
18:22 in Judah worship only at the altar here in **J**?
18:27 "My master wants everyone in **J** to hear this,
18:35 makes you think that the LORD can rescue **J**?"
19: 8 the Assyrian representative left **J** and went to
19: 9 he sent this message back to Hezekiah in **J**:
19:10 that **J** will not be captured by the king of Assyria.
19:21 The daughter of **J** / scoffs and shakes her head as
19:31 For a remnant of my people will spread out from **J**,
19:32 His armies will not enter **J** to shoot their arrows.
21: 1 became king, and he reigned in **J** fifty-five years.
21: 7 be honored here forever in this Temple and in **J**—
21:12 I will bring such disaster on **J** and Judah that the
21:13 I will judge **J** by the same standard I used for
21:13 I will wipe away the people of **J** as one wipes a
21:16 **J** was filled from one end to the other with
21:19 he became king, and he reigned in **J** two years.
22: 1 became king, and he reigned in **J** thirty-one years.
22:14 and Asaiah went to the newer Mishneh section of **J**
23: 1 the king summoned all the leaders of Judah and **J**.
23: 2 of the LORD with all the people of Judah and **J**,
23: 4 The king had all these things burned outside **J** on
23: 5 throughout Judah and even in the vicinity of **J**.
23: 6 and took it outside **J** to the Kidron Valley,
23: 8 Josiah brought back to **J** all the priests of the
23: 8 entrance to the gate of Joshua, the governor of **J**.
23: 9 not allowed to serve at the LORD's altar in **J**,
23:13 king also desecrated the pagan shrines east of **J**
23:20 altars to desecrate them. Finally, he returned to **J**.
23:23 This Passover was celebrated to the LORD in **J**
23:24 both in **J** and throughout the land of Judah.
23:27 from my presence and reject my chosen city of **J**
23:30 took his body back in a chariot from Megiddo to **J**
23:31 he became king, and he reigned in **J** three months.
23:33 land of Hamath to prevent him from ruling from **J**.
23:36 he became king, and he reigned in **J** eleven years.
24: 4 He had filled **J** with innocent blood,
24: 8 he became king, and he reigned in **J** three months.
24: 8 was Nehushta, the daughter of Elnathan from **J**.
24:10 Nebuchadnezzar of Babylon came up against **J**
24:14 took ten thousand captives from **J**,
24:18 he became king, and he reigned in **J** eleven years.
24:20 finally banished the people of **J** and Judah from his
25: 1 of Babylon led his entire army against **J**.
25: 2 **J** was kept under siege until the eleventh year of
25: 8 an official of the Babylonian king, arrived in **J**.
25: 9 the royal palace, and all the houses of **J**.
25:10 Babylonian army as they tore down the walls of **J**.
1Ch 3: 4 Then David moved the capital to **J**, where he
3: 5 The sons born to David in **J** included Shimea,
6:10 high priest at the Temple built by Solomon in **J**.
6:15 and **J** into captivity under Nebuchadnezzar.
6:32 Solomon built the Temple of the LORD in **J**.
8:28 listed in their tribal genealogy. They all lived in **J**.
8:32 All these families lived near each other in **J**.
9: 3 Ephraim, and Manasseh came and settled in **J**.
9:34 All these men lived in **J**. They were the heads of
9:38 All these families lived near each other in **J**.
11: 4 Then David and all Israel went to **J** (or Jebus,
11: 8 surrounding area, while Joab rebuilt the rest of **J**.
14: 3 Then David married more wives in **J**, and they had
14: 4 are the names of David's sons who were born in **J**:
15: 3 Then David summoned all the Israelites to **J** to
15:14 the Ark of the LORD, the God of Israel, to **J**.
15:25 covenant up to **J** with a great celebration.
15:28 of the LORD's covenant to **J** with shouts of joy,
18: 7 the gold shields of Hadadezer's officers to **J**,
19:15 and retreated into the city. Then Joab returned to **J**.
20: 1 and destroyed it. But David had stayed behind in **J**.
20: 3 Then David and his army returned to **J**.
21: 4 Israel to count the people. Then he returned to **J**
21:15 And God sent an angel to destroy **J**. But just as the
21:16 earth with his sword drawn, stretched out over **J**.
23:25 has given us peace, and he will always live in **J**.
28: 1 David summoned all his officials to **J**—the leaders
29:27 years from Hebron and thirty-three years from **J**.
2Ch 1: 4 to the special tent he had prepared for it in **J**.
1:13 Then Solomon returned to **J** from the Tabernacle
1:14 them in the chariot cities, and some near him in **J**.
1:15 silver and gold were as plentiful in **J** as stones.
1:17 Egyptian chariots delivered to **J** could be
2: 7 of Judah and **J** who were selected by my father,
2:16 From there you can transport the logs up to **J**."
3: 1 the Temple of the LORD in **J** on Mount Moriah,
5: 2 the tribes and families of Israel to assemble in **J**.
6: 6 But now I have chosen **J** as that city, and David as
8: 6 He built to his heart's content in **J** and Lebanon
9: 1 she came to **J** to test him with hard questions.
9:25 them in the chariot cities, and some near him in **J**.
9:27 The king made silver as plentiful in **J** as stones.
9:30 Solomon ruled in **J** over all Israel for forty years.
10:18 he quickly jumped into his chariot and fled to **J**.
11: 1 When Rehoboam arrived at **J**, he mobilized the
11: 5 Rehoboam remained in **J** and fortified various
11:14 and property and moved to Judah and **J**,
11:16 the God of Israel, followed the Levites to **J**,
12: 2 King Shishak of Egypt attacked **J** in the fifth year
12: 4 fortified cities and then advanced to attack **J**.
12: 5 who had all fled to **J** because of Shishak.
12: 7 I will not use Shishak to pour out my anger on **J**.
12: 9 So King Shishak of Egypt came to **J** and took
12:13 King Rehoboam firmly established himself in **J**
12:13 became king, and he reigned seventeen years in **J**,
13: 2 He reigned in **J** three years. His mother was
14:15 and camels before finally returning to **J**.
15:10 The people gathered at **J** in late spring,
17:13 and stationed an army of seasoned troops at **J**.
17:19 These were the troops stationed in **J** to serve the
19: 1 Jehoshaphat of Judah arrived safely home to **J**,
19: 4 So Jehoshaphat lived in **J**, but he went out among
19: 8 and clan leaders in Israel to serve as judges in **J** for
20: 4 So people from all the towns of Judah came to **J** to
20: 5 and **J** in front of the new courtyard at the Temple
20:15 Listen, all you people of Judah and **J**!
20:17 He is with you, O people of Judah and **J**. Do not be
20:18 And all the people of Judah and **J** did the same,
20:20 "Listen to me, all you people of Judah and **J**!
20:27 Then they returned to **J**, with Jehoshaphat leading
20:28 They marched into **J** to the music of harps, lyres,
20:31 and he reigned in **J** twenty-five years.
21: 5 he became king, and he reigned in **J** eight years.
21:11 and had led the people of **J** and Judah to give
21:13 You have led the people of **J** and Judah to worship
21:20 he became king, and he reigned in **J** eight years.
22: 1 Then the people of **J** made Ahaziah,
22: 2 he became king, and he reigned in **J** one year.
23: 2 and clan leaders in Judah's towns to come to **J**.
24: 1 he became king, and he reigned in **J** forty years.
24: 6 Temple taxes from the towns of Judah and from **J**?
24: 9 a proclamation was sent throughout Judah and **J**,
24:18 burned against Judah and **J** because of their sin.
24:23 They invaded Judah and **J** and killed all the leaders
25: 1 and he reigned in **J** twenty-nine years.
25: 1 His mother was Jehoaddin, from **J**.
25:23 Judah at Beth-shemesh and brought him back to **J**.
25:27 there was a conspiracy against his life in **J**, and he
25:28 They brought him back to **J** on a horse, and he was
26: 3 became king, and he reigned in **J** fifty-two years.
His mother was Jecoliah, from **J**.
26: 9 Uzziah built fortified towers in **J** at the Corner
26:15 he produced machines mounted on the walls of **J**,
27: 1 he became king, and he reigned in **J** sixteen years.
27: 8 he became king, and he reigned in **J** sixteen years.
28: 1 he became king, and he reigned in **J** sixteen years.
28:10 to make slaves of these people from Judah and **J**.
28:24 set up altars to pagan gods in every corner of **J**.
28:27 he was buried in **J** but not in the royal cemetery.
29: 1 of Judah, and he reigned in **J** twenty-nine years.
29: 8 the LORD's anger has fallen upon Judah and **J**.
30: 1 at **J** to celebrate the Passover of the LORD,
30: 2 and all the community of **J** decided to celebrate
30: 3 and the people had not yet assembled at **J**.
30: 5 inviting everyone to come to **J** to celebrate the
30:11 and Zebulun humbled themselves and went to **J**.
30:13 so a huge crowd assembled at **J** in midspring to
30:14 set to work and removed the pagan altars from **J**.
30:21 So the people of Israel who were present in **J**
30:26 for **J** had not seen a celebration like this one since
31: 4 he required the people in **J** to bring the prescribed
32: 2 realized that Sennacherib also intended to attack **J**,
32: 9 sent officials to **J** with this message for Hezekiah
32:10 makes you think you can survive my siege of **J**?
32:12 and **J** to worship at only the one altar at the
32:19 These officials talked about the God of **J** as though
32:22 and the people of **J** from King Sennacherib of
32:23 and many gifts for the LORD arrived at **J**,
32:25 anger came against him and against Judah and **J**.
32:26 his pride, and the people of **J** humbled themselves.
32:33 and all Judah and **J** honored him at his death.
33: 1 became king, and he reigned in **J** fifty-five years.
33: 7 be honored here forever in this Temple and in **J**—
33: 9 and **J** to do even more evil than the pagan nations
33:13 So the LORD let Manasseh return to **J** and to his
33:15 the Temple stood and all the altars that were in **J**,
33:21 he became king, and he reigned in **J** two years.
34: 1 became king, and he reigned in **J** thirty-one years.
34: 3 in the twelfth year, he began to purify Judah and **J**,
34: 5 on their own altars, and so he purified Judah and **J**.
34: 7 the land of Israel and then returned to **J**.
34: 8 Maaseiah the governor of **J**, and Joah son of
34: 9 as from all Judah, Benjamin, and the people of **J**.
34:22 section of **J** to consult with the prophet Huldah.
34:29 the king summoned all the leaders of Judah and **J**.
34:30 of Judah and **J** and the priests and the Levites—
34:32 And he required everyone in **J** and the people of
34:32 As the people of **J** did this, they renewed their
35: 1 in **J** on the appointed day in early spring.
35:17 All the Israelites present in **J** celebrated Passover
35:18 all the priests and Levites, all the people of **J**,
35:24 Then they brought him back to **J**, where he died.
35:24 And all Judah and **J** mourned for him.
36: 1 son Jehoahaz and made him the next king in **J**.
36: 4 of Jehoahaz, as the next king of Judah and **J**,
36: 5 he became king, and he reigned in **J** eleven years.
36: 6 Then King Nebuchadnezzar of Babylon came to **J**
36: 9 but he reigned in **J** only three months and ten days.
36:10 Zedekiah, to be the next king in Judah and **J**.
36:11 he became king, and he reigned in **J** eleven years.
36:14 desecrating the Temple of the LORD in **J**.
36:19 broke down the walls of **J**, burned all the palaces,
36:23 He has appointed me to build him a Temple at **J** in
Ezr 1: 2 He has appointed me to build him a Temple at **J** in
1: 3 All of you who are his people may return to **J** in
1: 3 of the LORD, the God of Israel, who lives in **J**.
1: 4 as a freewill offering for the Temple of God in **J**."
1: 5 and Benjamin to return to **J** to rebuild the Temple
1: 7 had taken from the LORD's Temple in **J**
1:11 to **J** when the exiles returned there from Babylon.
2: 1 provinces who returned from their captivity to **J**
2:59 Another group returned to **J** at this time from the
2:61 Hakkoz, and Barzillai—also returned to **J**.
2:68 they arrived at the Temple of the LORD in **J**,
2:70 of the common people settled in villages near **J**.
3: 1 the people assembled together as one person in **J**.
3: 8 during the second year after they arrived in **J**.
4: 6 of accusation against the people of Judah and **J**.
4: 8 telling King Artaxerxes about the situation in **J**.
4:12 to **J** from Babylon are rebuilding this rebellious
4:19 and have indeed found that **J** has in times past
4:20 Powerful kings have ruled over **J** and the entire
4:23 they hurried to **J** and forced the Jews to stop
4:24 The work on the Temple of God in **J** had stopped,
5: 1 of the God of Israel to the Jews in Judah and **J**.
5: 2 the task of rebuilding the Temple of God in **J**.
5: 3 and their colleagues soon arrived in **J** and asked,
5:14 had taken from the Temple of God in **J**
5:15 him to return the utensils to their place in **J**
5:16 and laid the foundations of the Temple of God in **J**.
5:17 ever issued a decree to rebuild God's Temple in **J**.
6: 3 was sent out concerning the Temple of God at **J**.
6: 5 by Nebuchadnezzar from the Temple of God in **J**,
6: 5 will be taken back to **J** and put into God's Temple
6: 9 Give the priests in **J** whatever is needed in the way
6:12 May the God who has chosen the city of **J** as the
6:18 divisions to serve at the Temple of God in **J**,
7: 6 He came up to **J** from Babylon, and the king gave
7: 7 traveled up to **J** with him in the seventh year of
7: 8 Ezra arrived in **J** in August of that year.
7: 9 left Babylon on April 8 and came to **J** on August 4,
7:13 and Levites, may volunteer to return to **J** with you.
7:14 an inquiry into the situation in Judah and **J**,
7:15 as an offering to the God of Israel who lives in **J**.
7:16 that are presented for the Temple of their God in **J**.
7:17 on the altar of the Temple of your God in **J**.
7:19 of your God, deliver them in full to the God of **J**.
7:27 want to beautify the Temple of the LORD in **J**!
7:28 some of the leaders of Israel to return with me to **J**.
8:17 to send us ministers for the Temple of God at **J**.
8:29 at the storerooms of the LORD's Temple in **J**."
8:30 these treasures to the Temple of our God in **J**.
8:31 at the Ahava Canal on April 19 and started off to **J**.
8:32 So at last we arrived safely in **J**, where we rested
9: 9 He has given us a protective wall in Judah and **J**.
10: 7 and **J** that all the returned exiles should come to **J**.
10: 9 people of Judah and Benjamin had gathered in **J**.
Ne 1: 2 the captivity and about how things were going in **J**.

1: 3 The wall of **J** has been torn down, and the gates
2: 11 Three days after my arrival at **J**,
2: 12 about the plans God had put in my heart for **J**.
2: 17 Let us rebuild the wall of **J** and rid ourselves of
2: 20 this wall. But you have no stake or claim in **J**."
3: 8 They left out a section of **J** as far as the Broad
3: 9 son of Hur, the leader of half the district of **J**,
3: 12 was the leader of the other half of the district of **J**.
4: 8 They all made plans to come and fight against **J**
4: 22 everyone living outside the walls to move into **J**.
6: 7 appointed prophets to prophesy about you in **J**,
7: 2 I gave the responsibility of governing **J** to my
7: 3 Appoint the residents of **J** to act as guards,
7: 6 provinces who returned from their captivity to **J**
7: 61 "Another group returned to **J** at this time from the
7: 63 Hakkoz, and Barzillai—also returned to **J**.
8: 15 made throughout their towns and especially in **J**,
11: 1 Now the leaders of the people were living in **J**,
11: 2 everyone who volunteered to resettle in **J**.
11: 3 names of the provincial officials who came to **J**.
11: 4 the people from Judah and Benjamin resettled in **J**.
11: 6 also 468 descendants of Perez who lived in **J**—
11: 22 The chief officer of the Levites in **J** was Uzzi son
12: 27 During the dedication of the new wall of **J**,
12: 27 asked to come to **J** to assist in the ceremonies.
12: 28 The singers were brought together from **J** and its
12: 29 the singers had built their own villages around **J**.
12: 43 and the joy of the people of **J** could be heard far
13: 6 I was not in **J** at that time, for I had returned to the
13: 7 When I arrived back in **J** and learned the extent of
13: 15 grapes, figs, and all sorts of produce to **J** to sell.
13: 16 Sabbath to the people of Judah—and in **J** at that!
13: 20 with a variety of wares camped outside **J** once
Est 2: 6 He had been exiled from **J** to Babylon by King
Ps 2: 6 chosen king on the throne / in **J**, my holy city."
9: 11 Sing praises to the LORD who reigns in **J**.
20: 2 from his sanctuary / and strengthen you from **J**.
48: 12 Go, inspect the city of **J**. / Walk around and count
51: 18 favor on Zion and help her; / rebuild the walls of **J**.
68: 29 the earth are bringing tribute / to your Temple in **J**.
69: 35 For God will save **J** / and rebuild the towns of
74: 2 And remember **J**, your home here on earth.
76: 2 **J** is where he lives; / Mount Zion is his home.
79: 1 your holy Temple / and made **J** a heap of ruins.
79: 3 Blood has flowed like water all around **J**; / no one
84: 5 who set their minds on a pilgrimage to **J**.
84: 7 and each of them will appear before God in **J**.
87: 2 He loves the city of **J** / more than any other city in
87: 4 They have all become citizens of **J**!
87: 5 And it will be said of **J**, / "Everyone has become a
87: 6 he will say, "This one has become a citizen of **J**."
87: 7 people will sing, / "The source of my life is in **J**!"
97: 8 **J** has heard and rejoiced, / and all the cities of
99: 2 The LORD sits in majesty in **J**, / supreme above
99: 9 our God / and worship at his holy mountain in **J**,
102: 13 You will arise and have mercy on **J**— / and now is
102: 16 For the LORD will rebuild **J**. / He will appear in
102: 21 fame will be celebrated in Zion, / his praises in **J**,
110: 2 will extend your powerful dominion from **J**;
116: 19 in the house of the LORD, / in the heart of **J**.
120: T A song for the ascent to **J**.
121: T A song for the ascent to **J**.
122: T A song for the ascent to **J**. A psalm of David.
122: 2 now we are standing here / inside your gates, O **J**.
122: 3 **J** is a well-built city, / knit together as a single unit.
122: 6 Pray for the peace of **J**. / May all who love this city
122: 7 O **J**, may there be peace within your walls
122: 9 our God, / I will seek what is best for you, O **J**.
123: T A song for the ascent to **J**.
124: T A song for the ascent to **J**. A psalm of David.
125: T A song for the ascent to **J**.
125: 2 Just as the mountains surround and protect **J**,
126: T A song for the ascent to **J**.
126: 1 When the LORD restored his exiles to **J**, / it was
127: T A song for the ascent to **J**. A psalm of Solomon.
128: T A song for the ascent to **J**.
128: 5 May you see **J** prosper as long as you live.
129: T A song for the ascent to **J**.
129: 5 May all who hate **J** / be turned back in shameful
130: T A song for the ascent to **J**.
131: T A song for the ascent to **J**. A psalm of David.
132: T A song for the ascent to **J**.
132: 13 For the LORD has chosen **J**; / he has desired it as
133: T A song for the ascent to **J**. A psalm of David.
134: T A song for the ascent to **J**.
134: 3 who made heaven and earth, / bless you from **J**.
135: 21 be praised from Zion, / for he lives here in **J**.
137: 1 of Babylon, we sat and wept / as we thought of **J**.
137: 3 joyful hymn: / "Sing us one of those songs of **J**!"
137: 5 If I forget you, O **J**, / let my right hand forget its
137: 6 remember you, / if I don't make **J** my highest joy.
137: 7 on the day the armies of Babylon captured **J**.
146: 10 O **J**, your God is King in every generation!
147: 2 The LORD is rebuilding **J** / and bringing the
147: 12 Praise the LORD, O **J**! / Praise your God,
149: 2 in your Maker. / O people of **J**, exult in your King.
Ecc 1: 1 of the Teacher, King David's son, who ruled in **J**.
1: 12 the Teacher, was king of Israel, and I lived in **J**.
1: 16 I am wiser than any of the kings who ruled in **J**
2: 7 more than any of the kings who lived in **J** before
2: 9 than any of the kings who ruled in **J** before me.
SS 1: 5 "I am dark and beautiful, O women of **J**, tanned as
2: 7 "Promise me, O women of **J**, by the swift gazelles
3: 5 "Promise me, O women of **J**, by the swift gazelles
3: 10 was a gift of love from the young women of **J**."
3: 11 to look upon King Solomon, O young women of **J**.
5: 8 "Make this promise to me, O women of **J**! If you
5: 16 Such, O women of **J**, is my lover, my friend."
6: 4 Yes, as beautiful as **J**! You are as majestic as an
8: 4 "I want you to promise, O women of **J**, not to
Isa 1: 1 and **J** came to Isaiah son of Amoz during the
1: 8 **J** stands abandoned like a watchman's shelter in a
1: 21 See how **J**, once so faithful, has become a
1: 26 Then **J** will again be called the Home of Justice
1: 27 the repentant people of **J** will be redeemed.
2: 1 Isaiah son of Amoz saw concerning Judah and **J**:
2: 2 the Temple of the LORD in **J** will become the
2: 3 and his word will go out from **J**.
3: 1 the supplies of food and water from **J** and Judah.
3: 8 Judah and **J** will lie in ruins because they speak out
3: 16 Next the LORD will judge the women of **J**,
3: 26 The gates of **J** will weep and mourn. The city will
4: 3 who have survived the destruction of **J**, will be a
4: 4 will wash the moral filth from the women of **J**.
4: 4 He will cleanse **J** of its bloodstains by a spirit of
4: 5 Then the LORD will provide shade for **J** and all
5: 3 "Now, you people of **J** and Judah, / you have
5: 14 The grave is licking its chops in anticipation of **J**,
5: 26 of the earth, and they will come racing toward **J**.
7: 1 **J** was attacked by King Rezin of Aram and King
7: 6 Then we will fight our way into **J** and install the
8: 14 And for the people of **J** he will be a trap that
10: 10 whose gods were far greater than those in **J**
10: 11 and her gods, we will destroy **J** with hers.' "
10: 12 king of Assyria to accomplish his purposes in **J**,
10: 24 "My people in **J**, do not be afraid of the Assyrians
10: 32 of that day. He shakes his fist at Mount Zion in **J**.
12: 6 Let all the people of **J** shout his praise with joy!
14: 32 Tell them that the LORD has built **J**, and that the
16: 1 Moab's refugees at Sela send lambs to **J** as a token
18: 7 will bring the gifts to the LORD Almighty in **J**,
22: 1 This message came to me concerning **J**: What is
22: 5 The walls of **J** have been broken, and cries of
22: 9 You inspect the walls of **J** to see what needs to be
22: 21 And he will be a father to the people of **J**
24: 23 He will rule gloriously in **J**, in the sight of all the
25: 6 In **J**, the LORD Almighty will spread a wonderful
25: 10 For the LORD's good hand will rest on **J**.
27: 13 and Egypt will return to **J** to worship the LORD
28: 14 from the LORD, you scoffing rulers in **J**.
28: 16 "Look! I am placing a foundation stone in **J**.
29: 2 For **J** will become as her name Ariel means—
29: 3 your enemy, surrounding **J** and attacking its walls.
29: 7 All the nations fighting against **J** will vanish like a
29: 8 will dream of a victorious conquest over **J**,
30: 19 O people of Zion, who live in **J**, you will weep no
30: 29 as when a flutist leads a group of pilgrims to **J**—
31: 5 The LORD Almighty will hover over **J** as a bird
31: 9 says the LORD, whose flame burns brightly in **J**.
33: 4 so **J** will strip the fallen army of Assyria!
33: 5 he will make **J** his home of justice
33: 20 You will see **J**, a city quiet and secure.
35: 10 been ransomed by the LORD will return to **J**,
36: 2 from Lachish to confront King Hezekiah in **J**.
36: 7 in Judah worship only at the altar here in **J**?
36: 12 "My master wants everyone in **J** to hear this,
36: 20 makes you think that the LORD can rescue **J**?"
37: 8 the Assyrian representative left **J** and went to
37: 9 he sent this message back to Hezekiah in **J**:
37: 10 that **J** will not be captured by the king of Assyria.
37: 22 The daughter of **J** / scoffs and shakes her head as
37: 32 For a remnant of my people will spread out from **J**,
37: 33 His armies will not enter **J** to shoot their arrows.
40: 2 "Speak tenderly to **J**. Tell her that her sad days are
40: 9 Shout louder to **J**—do not be afraid. Tell the towns
41: 27 I was the first to tell **J**, 'Look! Help is on the way!'
44: 26 When they say **J** will be saved and the towns of
44: 28 He will command that **J** be rebuilt and that the
46: 13 I am ready to save **J** and give my glory to Israel.
49: 14 Yet **J** says, "The LORD has deserted us;
51: 11 been ransomed by the LORD will return to **J**,
51: 17 Wake up, wake up, O **J**! You have drunk enough
52: 1 O holy city of **J**, for unclean and godless people
52: 2 Rise from the dust, O **J**. Remove the slave bands
52: 8 see the LORD bringing his people home to **J**.
52: 9 Let the ruins of **J** break into joyful song,
52: 9 has comforted his people. He has redeemed **J**.
54: 1 Break forth into loud and joyful song, O **J**,
56: 7 I will bring them also to my holy mountain of **J**
59: 20 "The Redeemer will come to **J**,"
60: 1 "Arise, **J**! Let your light shine for all the nations to
62: 1 I love Zion, because my heart yearns for **J**,
62: 5 O **J**, just as a young man cares for his bride.
62: 6 O **J**, I have posted watchmen on your walls;
62: 7 Give the LORD no rest until he makes **J** the
62: 8 The LORD has sworn to **J** by his own strength:
62: 12 And **J** will be known as the Desirable Place
64: 10 are destroyed; even **J** is a desolate wilderness.
65: 18 And look! I will create **J** as a place of happiness.
65: 19 I will rejoice in **J** and delight in my people.
66: 7 the birth pains even begin, **J** gives birth to a son.
66: 10 "Rejoice with **J**! Be glad with her, all you who
66: 11 Delight in **J**! Drink deeply of her glory even as an
66: 12 and prosperity will overflow **J** like a river,"
66: 20 They will bring them to my holy mountain in **J** as
Jer 1: 3 the people of **J** were taken away as captives.
1: 15 armies of the kingdoms of the north to come to **J**.
3: 17 In that day **J** will be known as The Throne of the
4: 3 the LORD says to the people of Judah and **J**:
4: 5 "Shout to **J** and to all Judah! Tell them to sound
4: 6 Send a signal toward **J**: 'Flee now! Do not delay!'
4: 10 by what you said, for you promised peace for **J**.
4: 11 when the LORD will say to the people of **J**,
4: 14 O **J**, cleanse your hearts that you may be saved.
4: 16 "Warn the surrounding nations and announce to **J**:
4: 17 They surround **J** like watchmen surrounding a
5: 1 "Run up and down every street in **J**,"
6: 1 your lives, you people of Benjamin! Flee from **J**!
6: 2 O **J**, you are my beautiful and delicate daughter—
6: 6 Build ramps against the walls of **J**. This is the city
6: 8 This is your last warning, **J**! If you do not listen,
6: 11 "I will pour out my fury over **J**, even on children
6: 23 marching in battle formation to destroy you, **J**."
7: 17 the towns of Judah and in the streets of **J**?
7: 29 O **J**, shave your head in mourning, and weep alone
7: 34 the happy singing and laughter in the streets of **J**.
8: 19 "Has the LORD abandoned **J**?" the people ask.
9: 11 "I will make **J** into a heap of ruins,"
9: 19 Hear the people of **J** crying in despair, 'We are
11: 2 and **J** about the terms of their covenant with me.
11: 6 "Broadcast this message in the streets of **J**.
11: 9 against me among the people of Judah and **J**.
11: 12 the people of Judah and **J** will pray to their idols
11: 13 to your god Baal—are along every street in **J**.
13: 9 how I will rot away the pride of Judah and **J**.
13: 27 and on the hills. Your destruction is sure, **J**!
14: 2 ground in mourning, and a great cry rises from **J**.
14: 16 their bodies will be thrown out into the streets of **J**,
14: 19 completely rejected Judah? Do you really hate **J**?
15: 4 Manasseh son of Hezekiah, king of Judah, did in **J**,
15: 5 "Who will feel sorry for you, **J**? Who will weep
17: 19 said to me, "Go and stand in the gates of **J**,
17: 20 all you people of Judah and everyone living in **J**.
17: 25 descendant of David sitting on the throne here in **J**.
17: 26 And from all around **J**, from the towns of Judah
17: 27 through the gates of **J** just as on other days,
18: 11 Jeremiah, go and warn all Judah and **J**.
19: 3 the LORD, you kings of Judah and citizens of **J**!
19: 7 and **J** and let invading armies slaughter them.
19: 8 I will wipe **J** from the face of the earth, making it a
19: 11 people of Judah and **J** beyond all hope of repair.
19: 13 Yes, all the houses in **J**, including the palace of
20: 5 And I will let your enemies plunder **J**.
21: 9 Everyone who stays in **J** will die from war, famine,
21: 13 I will fight against this city of **J** that boasts,
22: 4 descendant of David sitting on the throne here in **J**.
22: 19 dragged out of **J** and dumped outside the gate!
23: 14 But now I see that the prophets of **J** are even
24: 1 figs placed in front of the LORD's Temple in **J**.
24: 8 his officials, all the people left in **J**, and those who
25: 2 the prophet said to the people in Judah and **J**,
25: 18 I went to **J** and the other towns of Judah, and their
25: 29 I have begun to punish **J**, the city where my own
26: 6 And I will make **J** an object of cursing in every
26: 9 do you mean, saying that **J** will be destroyed?"
26: 18 like an open field; **J** will be reduced to rubble!
27: 3 through their ambassadors to King Zedekiah in **J**.
27: 18 and in the king's palace and in the palaces of **J**.
27: 20 with all the other important people of Judah and **J**.
27: 22 But someday I will bring them back to **J** again."
29: 1 Jeremiah wrote a letter from **J** to the elders, priests,
29: 2 and all the craftsmen had been deported from **J**.
29: 4 to all the captives he has exiled to Babylon from **J**:
29: 16 David's throne and all those still living here in **J**—
29: 25 you sent copies to the other priests and people in **J**.
30: 17 are called an outcast—'**J** for whom nobody cares.'
30: 18 restore your fortunes, **J** will be rebuilt on her ruins.
31: 6 let us go up to **J** to worship the LORD our
31: 12 and sing songs of joy on the heights of **J**.
31: 38 the LORD, "when all **J** will be rebuilt for me,
32: 2 **J** was under siege from the Babylonian army,
32: 32 the sins of the people of **J**, the kings, the officials,
32: 44 in the land of Benjamin and here in **J**, in the towns
33: 10 Yet in the empty streets of **J** and Judah's other
33: 13 the Negev, the land of Benjamin, the vicinity of **J**,
33: 16 day Judah will be saved, and **J** will live in safety.
34: 1 and he fought against **J** and the towns of Judah.
34: 7 At this time the Babylonian army was besieging **J**,
34: 19 whether you are officials of Judah or **J**,
35: 11 and Aramean armies. So we decided to move to **J**.
35: 13 Go and say to the people in Judah and **J**, 'Come
35: 17 and **J** all the disasters I have threatened."
36: 31 of Judah and **J** all the disasters I have promised,
37: 5 heard about it, they withdrew from their siege of **J**.
37: 11 When the Babylonian army left **J** because of
38: 2 Everyone who stays in **J** will die from war, famine,
38: 3 The city of **J** will surely be handed over to the
38: 28 of the guard until the day **J** was captured.
39: 1 and his army returned to besiege **J**.
39: 8 Meanwhile, the Babylonians burned **J**,
40: 1 Jeremiah bound in chains among the captives of **J**
42: 18 and fury were poured out on the people of **J**,
44: 2 You saw what I did to **J** and to all the towns of
44: 6 fire on the towns of Judah and into the streets of **J**,
44: 9 and your wives committed in Judah and **J**?
44: 13 punish them in Egypt just as I punished them in **J**,
44: 17 done in the towns of Judah and in the streets of **J**.
44: 21 idols in the towns of Judah and in the streets of **J**?
50: 5 They will ask the way to **J** and will start back
50: 28 as they declare in **J** how the LORD our God has
51: 10 let us announce in **J** everything the LORD our
51: 24 all the wrong they have done to my people in **J**,"
51: 35 all the violence she did to us," say the people of **J**.
51: 35 paid in full for all the blood they spilled," says **J**.
51: 36 The LORD says to **J**, "I will be your lawyer to
51: 50 in a far-off land, and think about your home in **J**."
52: 1 he became king, and he reigned in **J** eleven years.
52: 3 finally banished the people of **J** and Judah from his
52: 4 of Babylon led his entire army against **J**.
52: 5 **J** was kept under siege until the eleventh year of
52: 12 an official of the Babylonian king, arrived in **J**.

52:13 the royal palace, and all the houses of **J**.
52:14 Babylonian army as they tore down the walls of **J**.
La 1:4 The roads to **J** are in mourning, no longer filled
1:4 young women are crying—how bitterly **J** weeps!
1:5 for the LORD has punished **J** for her many sins.
1:6 All the beauty and majesty of **J** are gone.
1:7 and wandering, **J** remembers her ancient splendor.
1:8 **J** has sinned greatly, so she has been tossed away
1:17 **J** pleads for help, but no one comforts her.
2:1 Lord in his anger has cast a dark shadow over **J**.
2:2 anger he has broken down the fortress walls of **J**.
2:4 His fury is poured out like fire on beautiful **J**.
2:5 He has brought unending sorrow and tears to **J**.
2:8 LORD was determined to destroy the walls of **J**.
2:10 The leaders of **J** sit on the ground in silence,
2:10 The young women of **J** hang their heads in shame.
2:13 O daughter of **J**, to what can I compare your
2:15 They scoff and insult **J**, saying, "Is this the city
2:17 He has destroyed **J** without mercy and caused her
2:18 Cry aloud before the Lord, O walls of **J**! Let your
2:20 "O LORD, think about this!" **J** cries. "You are
3:51 is breaking over the fate of all the women of **J**.
4:2 See how the precious children of **J**, worth their
4:11 He started a fire in **J** that burned the city to its
4:12 an enemy could march through the gates of **J**.
4:22 O **J**, your punishment will end; you will soon
5:11 Our enemies rape the women and young girls in **J**
5:18 For **J** is empty and desolate, a place haunted by
Eze 4:1 of you. Then draw a map of the city of **J** on it.
4:3 and demonstrate how the enemy will attack **J**.
4:7 continue your demonstration of the siege of **J**.
4:16 of man, I will cause food to be very scarce in **J**.
5:2 Place a third of it at the center of your map of **J**.
5:5 This is an illustration of what will happen to **J**.
7:23 by terrible crimes. **J** is filled with violence.
8:3 the sky and transported me in a vision of God to **J**.
9:4 "Walk through the streets of **J** and put a mark on
9:8 Will your fury against **J** wipe out everyone left in
11:9 I will drive you out of **J** and hand you over to
11:15 the people still left in **J** are talking about their
11:24 And so ended the vision of my visit to **J**.
12:10 These actions contain a message for Zedekiah in **J**
12:12 "Even Zedekiah will leave **J** at night through a
12:19 LORD concerning those living in Israel and **J**:
13:16 peace would come to **J** when there was no peace.
14:21 four of these fearsome punishments fall upon **J**—
14:22 you will feel better about what I have done to **J**.
15:6 The people of **J** are like grapevines growing
16:2 "Son of man, confront **J** with her loathsome sins.
17:12 The king of Babylon came to **J**, took away her
17:17 when the king of Babylon lays siege to **J** again
21:2 look toward **J** and prophesy against Israel and her
21:20 Rabbah, and the other to Judah and fortified **J**.
21:21 the fork, uncertain whether to attack **J** or Rabbah.
21:22 Then they will decide to turn toward **J**!
21:23 The people of **J** will think it is a mistake,
22:2 "Son of man, are you ready to judge **J**? Are you
22:19 worthless slag, I will bring you to my crucible in **J**.
23:4 I am speaking of Samaria and **J**, for Oholah is
Samaria and Oholibah is **J**.
24:2 king of Babylon is beginning his attack against **J**.
24:6 Destruction is certain for **J**, the city of murderers!
24:9 Destruction is certain for **J**, the city of murderers!
24:26 And on that day a refugee from **J** will come to you
26:2 Tyre has rejoiced over the fall of **J**, saying, 'Ha!
33:21 a man who had escaped from **J** came to me
40:1 fourteen years after the fall of **J**—the LORD took
43:3 Kebar River and then when he came to destroy **J**.
Da 1:1 King Nebuchadnezzar of Babylon came to **J**
5:2 had taken from the Temple in **J**, so that he and his
5:3 gold cups taken from the Temple of God in **J**,
6:10 his upstairs room, with its windows open toward **J**.
9:2 that **J** must lie desolate for seventy years.
9:7 including the people of Judah and **J** and all Israel,
9:12 been a disaster like the one that happened in **J**.
9:16 turn your furious anger away from your city of **J**,
9:16 All the neighboring nations mock **J** and your
9:20 pleading with the LORD my God for **J**, his holy
9:25 is given to rebuild **J** until the Anointed One comes.
9:25 **J** will be rebuilt with streets and strong defenses,
Joel 2:1 Blow the trumpet in **J**! Sound the alarm on my
2:15 Blow the trumpet in **J**! Announce a time of fasting;
2:23 Rejoice, you people of **J**! Rejoice in the LORD
2:32 There will be people on Mount Zion in **J** who
3:1 when I restore the prosperity of Judah and **J**,"
3:6 have sold the people of Judah and **J** to the Greeks,
3:16 voice will roar from Zion and thunder from **J**,
3:17 **J** will be holy forever, and foreign armies will
3:20 and **J** will endure through all future generations.
3:21 will make my home in **J** with my people."
Am 1:2 his Temple on Mount Zion; he thunders from **J**!
2:5 and all the fortresses of **J** will be destroyed."
6:1 and think you are secure in **J** and Samaria!
Ob 1:11 carried off their wealth and cast lots to divide up **J**.
1:17 "But **J** will become a refuge for those who escape;
1:20 The captives from **J** exiled in the north will return
1:21 Deliverers will go up to Mount Zion in **J** to rule
Mic 1:1 The messages concerned both Samaria and **J**,
1:5 is the center of idolatry in Judah? In **J**, its capital!
1:9 It has reached into Judah, even to the gates of **J**.
1:12 LORD's judgment reaches even to the gates of **J**.
1:13 in the sin of idol worship, and so you led **J** into sin.
3:10 You are building **J** on a foundation of murder
3:12 like an open field; **J** will be reduced to rubble!
4:1 the Temple of the LORD in **J** will become the
4:2 and his word will go out from **J**.
4:7 will rule from **J** as their king forever."
4:8 As for you, O **J**, the citadel of God's people,
4:8 The kingship will be restored to my precious **J**.
4:10 Writhe and groan in terrible pain, you people of **J**,
4:13 "Rise up and destroy the nations, O **J**!"
5:1 your troops! The enemy is laying siege to **J**.
6:9 are wise! His voice is calling out to everyone in **J**:
Zep 1:4 "I will crush Judah and **J** with my fist and destroy
3:1 polluted **J**, the city of violence and crime.
3:14 and rejoice with all your heart, O daughter of **J**!
3:16 On that day the announcement to **J** will be,
Zec 1:12 for seventy years now you have been angry with **J**
1:14 My love for **J** and Mount Zion is passionate
1:16 I have returned to show mercy to **J**. My Temple
1:16 and plans will be made for the reconstruction of **J**.' "
1:17 again comfort Zion and choose **J** as his own.' "
1:19 world powers that scattered Judah, Israel, and **J**."
2:2 He replied, "I am going to measure **J**, to see how
2:4 '**J** will someday be so full of people that it won't
2:5 For I, myself, will be a wall of fire around **J**,
2:7 Escape to **J**, you who are exiled in Babylon!"
2:10 The LORD says, "Shout and rejoice, O **J**, for I
2:12 and he will once again choose **J** to be his own city.
3:2 Yes, the LORD, who has chosen **J**, rebukes you.
7:7 proclaimed through the prophets years ago when **J**
8:2 and strong; I am consumed with passion for **J**!
8:3 I am returning to Mount Zion, and I will live in **J**.
8:3 Then **J** will be called the Faithful City;
8:8 I will bring them home again to live safely in **J**.
8:15 Neither will I change my decision to bless **J**
8:20 and cities around the world will travel to **J**.
8:21 'Let us go to **J** to ask the LORD to bless us
8:22 will come to **J** to seek the LORD Almighty
9:9 Shout in triumph, O people of **J**! Look, your king
9:10 chariots from Israel and the warhorses from **J**,
9:13 **J** is my sword, and like a warrior, I will brandish it
12:2 I will make **J** and Judah like an intoxicating drink
12:2 nearby nations that send their armies to besiege **J**.
12:3 On that day I will make **J** a heavy stone, a burden
12:5 'The people of **J** have found strength in the
12:6 and left, while the people living in **J** remain secure.
12:7 before **J**, so that the people of **J** and the royal line
12:8 that day the LORD will defend the people of **J**;
12:9 is to destroy all the nations that come against **J**.
12:10 on the family of David and on all the people of **J**.
12:11 and mourning in **J** on that day will be like the
13:1 for the dynasty of David and for the people of **J**,
14:2 day I will gather all the nations to fight against **J**.
14:4 on the Mount of Olives, which faces **J** on the east.
14:8 that day life-giving waters will flow out from **J**,
14:10 from Geba, north of Judah, to Rimmon, south of **J**,
14:10 But **J** will be raised up in its original place and will
14:11 And **J** will be filled, safe at last, never again to be
14:12 a plague on all the nations that fought against **J**.
14:14 Judah, too, will be fighting at **J**. The wealth of all
14:16 the enemies of **J** who survive the plague will go up
to **J** each year to worship the King,
14:17 that refuses to come to **J** to worship the King,
14:21 every cooking pot in **J** and Judah will be set apart
Mal 2:11 In Judah, in Israel, and in **J** there is treachery,
3:4 brought to him by the people of Judah and **J**,
Mt 2:1 some wise men from eastern lands arrived in **J**,
2:3 deeply disturbed by their question, as was all of **J**.
3:5 People from **J** and from every section of Judea
4:5 Then the Devil took him to **J**, to the highest point
4:25 the Ten Towns, **J**, from all over Judea,
5:35 the earth is his footstool. And don't swear, 'By **J**!'
for **J** is the city of the great King.
15:1 and teachers of religious law now arrived from **J** to
16:21 to tell his disciples plainly that he had to go to **J**,
20:17 As Jesus was on the way to **J**, he took the twelve
20:18 "When we get to **J**," he said, "the Son of Man
21:1 As Jesus and the disciples approached **J**, they came
21:10 The entire city of **J** was stirred as he entered.
21:18 as Jesus was returning to **J**, he was hungry,
23:37 "O **J**, **J**, the city that kills the prophets
27:53 left the cemetery, went into the holy city of **J**,
Mk 1:5 People from **J** and from all over Judea traveled out
3:8 **J**, Idumea, from east of the Jordan River, and even
3:22 of religious law who had arrived from **J** said,
7:1 and teachers of religious law arrived from **J** to
10:32 They were now on the way to **J**, and Jesus was
10:32 everything that was about to happen to him in **J**.
10:33 "When we get to **J**," he told them, "the Son of
11:1 As Jesus and his disciples approached **J**, they came
11:11 So Jesus came to **J** and went into the Temple.
11:15 When they arrived back in **J**, Jesus entered the
11:27 By this time they had arrived in **J** again. As Jesus
14:13 So Jesus sent two of them into **J** to make the
15:41 and many other women had come with him to **J**.
16:12 to two who were walking from **J** into the country,
Lk 2:22 so his parents took him to **J** to present him to the
2:25 there was a man named Simeon who lived in **J**.
2:38 for the promised King to come and deliver **J**.
2:41 Every year Jesus' parents went to **J** for the
2:43 home to Nazareth, but Jesus stayed behind in **J**.
2:45 they went back to **J** to search for him there.
4:9 Then the Devil took him to **J**, to the highest point
5:17 village in all Galilee and Judea, as well as from **J**.)
6:17 There were people from all over Judea and from **J**
9:31 he was about to fulfill God's plan by dying in **J**.
9:51 his return to heaven, Jesus resolutely set out for **J**.
9:53 do with Jesus because he had resolved to go to **J**.
10:30 "A Jewish man was traveling on a trip from **J** to
10:38 and the disciples continued on their way to **J**,
13:1 Galilee as they were sacrificing at the Temple in **J**.
13:4 fell on them? Were they the worst sinners in **J**?
13:22 teaching as he went, always pressing on toward **J**.
13:33 do for a prophet of God to be killed except in **J**!
13:34 "O **J**, **J**, the city that kills the prophets
17:11 As Jesus continued on toward **J**, he reached the
18:31 Jesus told them, "As you know, we are going to **J**.
19:11 And because he was nearing **J**, he told a story to
19:28 After telling this story, Jesus went on toward **J**,
19:41 But as they came closer to **J** and Jesus saw the city
21:20 "And when you see **J** surrounded by armies,
21:21 Let those in **J** escape, and those outside the city
21:24 And **J** will be conquered and trampled down by the
22:10 He replied, "As soon as you enter **J**, a man
23:5 he goes, all over Judea, from Galilee to **J**!"
23:7 and Herod happened to be in **J** at the time.
23:19 and for taking part in an insurrection in **J** against
23:28 Jesus turned and said to them, "Daughters of **J**,
24:13 to the village of Emmaus, seven miles out of **J**.
24:18 "You must be the only person in **J** who hasn't
24:33 within the hour they were on their way back to **J**,
24:47 of repentance to all the nations, beginning in **J**:
24:52 and then returned to **J** filled with great joy.
Jn 1:19 and Temple assistants from **J** to ask John whether
2:13 annual Passover celebration, and Jesus went to **J**.
2:23 Because of the miraculous signs he did in **J** at the
3:22 Afterward Jesus and his disciples left **J**, but they
4:20 why is it that you Jews insist that **J** is the only
4:21 whether you worship the Father here or in **J**.
4:45 for they had been in **J** at the Passover celebration
5:1 Afterward Jesus returned to **J** for one of the Jewish
7:25 Some of the people who lived there in **J** said
10:22 and Jesus was in **J** at the time of Hanukkah.
11:18 was only a few miles down the road from **J**,
11:54 his public ministry among the people and left **J**.
11:55 and many people from the country arrived in **J**
12:12 the news that Jesus was on the way to **J** swept
12:20 Some Greeks who had come to **J** to attend the
Ac 1:4 "Do not leave **J** until the Father sends you what he
1:8 in **J**, throughout Judea, in Samaria, and to the ends
1:12 so they walked the half mile back to **J**.
1:19 his death spread rapidly among all the people of **J**,
2:5 Godly Jews from many nations were living in **J** at
2:14 all of you, fellow Jews and residents of **J**!
4:5 and elders and teachers of religious law met in **J**.
4:16 and everybody in **J** knows about it.
5:16 Crowds came in from the villages around **J**,
5:28 you have filled all **J** with your teaching about
6:7 The number of believers greatly increased in **J**,
8:1 began that day, sweeping over the church in **J**,
8:4 But the believers who had fled **J** went everywhere
8:14 When the apostles back in **J** heard that the people
8:25 the Lord in Samaria, Peter and John returned to **J**.
8:26 "Go south down the desert road that runs from **J**
8:27 of Ethiopia. The eunuch had gone to **J** to worship,
9:2 both men and women—back to **J** in chains.
9:13 things this man has done to the believers in **J**!
9:21 Jesus' followers with such devastation in **J**?"
9:26 When Saul arrived in **J**, he tried to meet with the
9:28 and after that he was constantly with them in **J**,
10:39 witnesses of all he did throughout Israel and in **J**.
11:2 But when Peter arrived back in **J**, some of the
11:19 the believers who had fled from **J** during the
11:22 When the church at **J** heard what had happened,
11:27 some prophets traveled from **J** to Antioch.
11:30 and Saul to take to the elders of the church in **J**.
12:25 and Saul had finished their mission in **J**,
13:13 There John Mark left them and returned to **J**.
13:27 The people in **J** and their leaders fulfilled prophecy
13:31 those who had gone with him from Galilee to **J**—
15:2 Finally, Paul and Barnabas were sent to **J**,
15:3 The church sent the delegates to **J**, and they
15:4 When they arrived in **J**, Paul and Barnabas were
15:22 and the whole church in **J** chose delegates,
15:23 is from the apostles and elders, your brothers in **J**.
15:33 and then Judas and Silas were sent back to **J**,
16:4 as decided by the apostles and elders in **J**.
18:22 there he went up and visited the church at **J** and
19:21 to Macedonia and Achaia before returning to **J**.
20:16 He was hurrying to get to **J**, if possible,
20:22 "And now I am going to **J**, drawn there irresistibly
21:4 the Holy Spirit that Paul should not go on to **J**.
21:11 of this belt be bound by the Jewish leaders in **J**
21:12 the local believers, begged Paul not to go on to **J**.
21:13 For I am ready not only to be jailed at **J** but also to
21:15 afterward we packed our things and left for **J**.
21:17 All the believers in **J** welcomed us cordially.
21:18 and all the elders of the **J** church were present.
21:21 Our Jewish Christians here at **J** have been told that
21:31 of the Roman regiment that all **J** was in an uproar.
22:3 brought up and educated here in **J** under Gamaliel.
22:5 me to bring the Christians from there to **J**,
22:17 "One day after I returned to **J**, I was praying in the
22:18 Leave **J**, for the people here won't believe you
22:21 "But the Lord said to me, 'Leave **J**, for I will send
23:11 as you have told the people about me here in **J**,
24:11 ago that I arrived in **J** to worship at the Temple.
24:17 I returned to **J** with money to aid my people
25:1 to take over his new responsibilities, he left for **J**,
25:3 They asked Festus as a favor to transfer Paul to **J**.
25:7 the Jewish leaders from **J** gathered around
25:9 "Are you willing to go to **J** and stand trial before
25:15 When I was in **J**, the leading priests and other
25:20 be willing to stand trial on these charges in **J**.
25:24 demanded both by the local Jews and by those in **J**.
26:4 earliest childhood among my own people and in **J**.
26:10 I caused many of the believers in **J** to be sent to
26:20 then in **J** and throughout all Judea, and also to the
28:17 I was arrested in **J** and handed over to the Roman
Ro 9:33 "I am placing a stone in **J** that causes people to

11:26 "A Deliverer will come from **J**, / and he will turn
15:19 Christ all the way from **J** clear over into Illyricum.
15:25 I must go down to **J** to take a gift to the Christians
15:26 eagerly taken up an offering for the Christians in **J**.
1Co 16:1 the money being collected for the Christians in **J**:
16:3 messengers you choose to deliver your gift to **J**.
2Co 8:4 of sharing in the gift for the Christians in **J**.
8:19 to accompany us as we take the offering to **J**—
9:1 write to you about this gift for the Christians in **J**.
9:12 the needs of the Christians in **J** will be met,
Gal 1:17 nor did I go up to **J** to consult with those who were
1:18 later that I finally went to **J** for a visit with Peter
2:1 Then fourteen years later I went back to **J** again,
4:25 And now **J** is just like Mount Sinai in Arabia,
4:26 the free woman, represents the heavenly **J**.
Heb 12:22 to the city of the living God, the heavenly **J**,
1Pe 2:6 Scriptures express it, / "I am placing a stone in **J**,
Rev 3:12 the new **J** that comes down from heaven from my
11:8 And their bodies will lie in the main street of **J**,
21:2 And I saw the holy city, the new **J**, coming down
21:10 high mountain, and he showed me the holy city, **J**,

JERUSALEM'S (18) [JERUSALEM]

2Ki 14:13 his army to demolish six hundred feet of **J** wall,
24:15 and officials, the queen mother, and all **J** elite.
2Ch 25:23 his army to demolish six hundred feet of **J** wall,
Ps 9:14 Save me, so I can praise you publicly at **J** gates,
48:3 God himself is in **J** towers. / He reveals himself as
Isa 49:16 Ever before me is a picture of **J** walls in ruins.
66:8 But by the time **J** birth pains begin, the baby will
Jer 2:2 "Go and shout in **J** streets: 'This is what the
4:31 It is the cry of **J** people gasping for breath,
17:21 Stop carrying on your trade at **J** gates on the
23:15 because of **J** prophets that wickedness fills this
33:6 the time will come when I will heal **J** damage
La 1:1 **J** streets, once bustling with people, are now silent.
2:7 He has given **J** palaces to her enemies.
2:9 **J** gates have sunk into the ground. All their locks
Eze 36:38 flocks that fill **J** streets at the time of her festivals.
Zep 1:12 "I will search with lanterns in **J** darkest corners to
Zec 8:4 old men and women will walk **J** streets with a cane

JERUSHA (2)

2Ki 15:33 His mother was **J**, the daughter of Zadok.
2Ch 27:1 His mother was **J**, the daughter of Zadok.

JESHAIAH (7) [JESHAIAH'S]

1Ch 3:21 The sons of Hananiah were Pelatiah and **J**.
25:3 Gedaliah, Zeri, **J**, Shimei, Hashabiah,
25:15 The eighth lot fell to **J** and twelve of his sons
26:25 were Rehabiah, **J**, Joram, Zicri, and Shelomoth.
Ezr 8:7 of Elam: **J** son of Athaliah and 70 other men.
8:19 together with **J** from the descendants of Merari,
Ne 11:7 son of Maaseiah, son of Ithiel, son of **J**;

JESHAIAH'S (1) [JESHAIAH]

1Ch 3:21 were Pelatiah and Jeshaiah. **J** son was Rephaiah.

JESHANAH (2)

1Sa 7:12 and placed it between the towns of Mizpah and **J**.
2Ch 13:19 of his towns, including Bethel, **J**, and Ephron,

JESHARELAH [KJV] See ASARELAH

JESHEBEAB (1)

1Ch 24:13 lot fell to Huppah. / The fourteenth lot fell to **J**.

JESHER (1)

1Ch 2:18 Azubah's sons were named **J**, Shobab, and Ardon.

JESHIMON (4)

1Sa 23:19 hill of Hakilah, which is in the southern part of **J**.
23:24 of Maon in the Arabah Valley south of **J**.
26:1 hiding on the hill of Hakilah, which overlooks **J**."
26:3 hill of Hakilah, near **J**, where David was hiding.

JESHISHAI (1)

1Ch 5:14 son of Michael, son of **J**, son of Jahdo, son of Buz.

JESHOHAIAH (1)

1Ch 4:36 Jaakobah, **J**, Asaiah, Adiel, Jesimiel, Benaiah,

JESHUA (41) [JESHUA'S, JOSHUA]

1Ch 24:11 The ninth lot fell to **J**. / The tenth lot fell to
2Ch 31:15 Miniamin, **J**, Shemaiah, Amariah, and Shecaniah.
Ezr 2:2 **J**, Nehemiah, Seraiah, Reelaiah, Mordecai,
2:6 The family of Pahath-moab (descendants of **J**
2:36 The family of Jedaiah (through the line of **J**)
2:40 The families of **J** and Kadmiel (descendants of
3:2 Then **J** son of Jehozadak with his fellow priests
3:8 **J** son of Jehozadak and his fellow priests, and all
3:9 Temple of God were supervised by **J** with his sons
4:3 But Zerubbabel, **J**, and the other leaders of Israel
5:2 and **J** son of Jehozadak responded by beginning
8:33 along with Jozabad son of **J** and Noadiah son of
10:18 From the family of **J** son of Jehozadak and his
Ne 3:19 Next to them, Ezer son of **J**, the leader of Mizpah,
7:7 **J**, Nehemiah, Seraiah, Reelaiah, Nahamani,
7:11 The family of Pahath-moab (descendants of **J**
7:39 The family of Jedaiah (through the line of **J**)
7:43 The families of **J** and Kadmiel (descendants of
8:7 **J**, Bani, Sherebiah, Jamin, Akkub, Shabbethai,
9:4 Their names were **J**, Bani, Kadmiel, Shebaniah,
9:5 **J**, Kadmiel, Bani, Hashabneiah, Sherebiah,
10:9 The Levites who signed were **J** son of Azaniah,
11:26 They also lived in **J**, Moladah, Beth-pelet,
12:1 Zerubbabel son of Shealtiel and **J** the high priest:
12:7 of the priests and their associates in the days of **J**.
12:8 The Levites who had returned with them were **J**,
12:10 **J** the high priest was the father of Joiakim.
12:24 Hashabiah, Sherebiah, **J**, Binnui, Kadmiel,
12:26 These all served in the days of Joiakim son of **J**,
Hag 1:1 and to **J** son of Jehozadak, the high priest.
1:12 of Shealtiel, **J** son of Jehozadak, the high priest,
1:14 of Judah, **J** son of Jehozadak, the high priest,
2:2 and to **J** son of Jehozadak, the high priest,
2:4 Take courage, **J** son of Jehozadak, the high priest.
Zec 3:1 Then the angel showed me **J** the high priest
3:1 the angel's right hand, accusing **J** of many things.
3:4 And turning to **J** he said, "See, I have taken away
3:6 the angel of the LORD spoke very solemnly to **J**
3:8 Listen to me, O **J** the high priest, and all you other
3:9 Now look at the jewel I have set before **J**, a single
6:11 Then put the crown on the head of **J** son of

JESHUA'S (1) [JESHUA]

Zec 3:3 **J** clothing was filthy as he stood there before the

JESIAH [KJV] See ISSHIAH

JESIMIEL (1)

1Ch 4:36 Jaakobah, Jeshohaiah, Asaiah, Adiel, **J**, Benaiah,

JESSE (35) [JESSE'S]

SON OF JESSE (13) 1Sa 16:18; 20:27,31; 25:10; 2Sa 20:1; 23:1; 1Ch 10:14; 12:18; 29:26; 2Ch 11:18; Ps 72:20; Lk 3:32; Ac 13:22

Ru 4:17 He became the father of **J** and the grandfather of
4:22 Obed was the father of **J**. / **J** was the father of David.
1Sa 16:1 Find a man named **J** who lives there, for I have
16:3 Invite **J** to the sacrifice, and I will show you which
16:5 Then Samuel performed the purification rite for **J**
16:8 Then **J** told his son Abinadab to step forward
16:9 Next **J** summoned Shammah, but Samuel said,
16:10 But Samuel said to **J**, "The LORD has not
16:11 "There is still the youngest," **J** replied.
16:12 So **J** sent for him. He was ruddy and handsome,
16:18 to Saul, "The son of **J** is a talented harp player.
16:19 So Saul sent messengers to **J** to say, "Send me
16:20 **J** responded by sending David to Saul, along with
16:22 Then Saul sent word to **J** asking, "Please let David
17:12 Now David was the son of a man named **J**,
17:12 **J** was an old man at that time, and he had eight
17:17 One day **J** said to David, "Take this half-bushel of
17:58 And David replied, "His name is **J**, and we live in
20:27 "Why hasn't the son of **J** been here for dinner
20:31 As long as that son of **J** is alive, you'll never be
25:10 "Who does this son of **J** think he is?
2Sa 20:1 We want no part of this son of **J**. Come on,
23:1 "David, the son of **J**, speaks— / David, the man to
1Ch 2:12 was the father of Obed. / Obed was the father of **J**.
10:14 and turned his kingdom over to David son of **J**.
12:18 We are on your side, son of **J**. / Peace
29:26 So David son of **J** reigned over all Israel.
2Ch 11:18 (Eliab was one of David's brothers, a son of **J**.)
Ps 72:20 (This ends the prayers of David son of **J**.)
Mt 1:5 (his mother was Ruth). / Obed was the father of **J**.
1:6 **J** was the father of King David. / David was the
Lk 3:32 David was the son of **J**. / **J** was the son of Obed.
Ac 13:22 'David son of **J** is a man after my own heart,

JESSE'S (6) [JESSE]

1Sa 16:10 In the same way all seven of **J** sons were presented
17:13 **J** three oldest sons—Eliab, Abinadab,
17:14 David was the youngest of **J** sons. Since David's
1Ki 12:16 We have no share in **J** son! Let's go home, Israel!
1Ch 2:13 **J** first son was Eliab, his second was Abinadab,
2Ch 10:16 We have no share in **J** son! Let's go home, Israel!

JESTING [KJV] See (COARSE) JOKES

JESUI [KJV] See ISHVI

JESUITES [KJV] See ISHVITE

JESURUN [KJV] See ISRAEL

JESUS (1420) [JESUS']

CHRIST JESUS (87) Ac 24:24; Ro 3:24; 6:3,11,23; 8:1,2, 34,39; 15:5,16,17; 16:3; 1Co 1:2,4,30; 4:15,17; 16:24; 2Co 1:1; 4:5; Gal 2:4,16; 3:14,26,28; 4:14; 5:6,24; Eph 1:1,1; 2:6, 7,10,13,20; 3:1,6,11,21; Php 1:1,1,6,8,26; 2:5; 3:3,8,12,14; 4:7,19; Col 1:1,4; 2:6; 4:12; 1Th 2:14; 5:18; 1Ti 1:1,1,2,12, 14,15,16; 2:5; 3:13; 4:6; 5:21; 6:13; 2Ti 1:1,1,2,9,10,13; 2:1, 3,10; 3:12,15; 4:1; Tit 1:4; Phm 1:1,9,23

JESUS CHRIST (135) Jn 1:17; 17:3; Ac 2:38; 3:6; 4:10; 8:12; 9:34; 10:36,48; 11:17; 15:26; 16:18; 28:31; Ro 1:4,6,7, 8; 2:16; 3:22; 5:1,11,15,17,21; 7:25; 13:14; 15:6,30; 16:20,25, 27; 1Co 1:2,3,7,8,9,10; 2:2; 3:11; 6:11; 8:6; 15:31,57; 2Co 1:2,3,19; 4:6; 8:9; 13:5,13; Gal 1:1,3,12; 2:16; 3:22; 6:14,18; Eph 1:2,3,5,17; 5:20; 6:23,24; Php 1:2,11,19; 2:11,21; 3:20; 4:23; Col 1:3; 1Th 1:1,3; 5:9,23,28; 2Th 1:1,2,12; 2:1,14,16; 3:6,12,18; 1Ti 6:3,14; 2Ti 2:8; Tit 1:1; 2:13; 3:6; Phm 1:3,25; Heb 10:10; 13:8,20; Jas 1:1; 2:1,7; 1Pe 1:1,2,3,3,7,13; 2:5; 4:11; 5:10; 2Pe 1:1,1,8,11,14,16; 2:20; 3:18; 1Jn 1:1,3; 2:1; 3:23; 4:2; 5:6,20; 2Jn 1:3,7; Jude 1:1,1,4,17,21,25; Rev 1:1,2,5

JESUS OF NAZARETH (12) Mt 26:71; Mk 1:24; Lk 4:34; 18:37; Jn 18:5,7; 19:19; Ac 2:22; 6:14; 10:38; 22:8; 26:9

LORD JESUS (102) Mk 16:19; Lk 24:3; Ac 1:21; 4:33; 7:59; 8:16; 9:17; 11:17,20; 15:11,26; 16:31; 19:5,13,17; 20:21,24,35; 21:13; 28:31; Ro 1:7; 5:11; 13:14; 14:14; 15:6, 30; 16:20; 1Co 1:3,7,8,10; 5:4,4; 6:11; 8:6; 11:23; 15:31; 16:23; 2Co 1:2,3,14; 4:14; 8:9; 11:31; 13:13; Gal 1:3; 6:14, 18; Eph 1:3,15,17; 5:20; 6:23,24; Php 1:2; 2:19; 3:20; 4:23; Col 1:3; 3:17; 1Th 1:3; 2:15,19; 3:11,13; 4:1,2; 5:9,23,28; 2Th 1:1,2,7,8,12,12; 2:1,8,14,16; 3:6,12,18; 1Ti 6:3,14; Phm 1:3,5,25; Heb 2:3; 13:20; Jas 1:1; 2:1; 1Pe 1:3; 2Pe 1:8,14,16; Jude 1:4,17,21; Rev 22:20,21

LORD JESUS CHRIST (59) Ac 11:17; 15:26; 28:31; Ro 1:7; 5:11; 13:14; 15:6,30; 16:20; 1Co 1:3,7,8,10; 6:11; 8:6; 15:31; 2Co 1:2,3; 8:9; 13:13; Gal 1:3; 6:14,18; Eph 1:3,17; 5:20; 6:23,24; Php 1:2; 3:20; 4:23; Col 1:3; 1Th 1:3; 5:9,23, 28; 2Th 1:2,12; 2:1,14,16; 3:6,12,18; 1Ti 6:3,14; Phm 1:3,25; Jas 1:1; 2:1; 1Pe 1:3; 2Pe 1:8,14,16; Jude 1:4,17,21

NAME OF JESUS (11) Ac 2:38; 3:6,16; 5:40,41; 8:12; 9:27; 10:48; 16:18; 1Co 1:2; Php 2:10

Mt 1:1 This is a record of the ancestors of **J** the Messiah,
1:16 Mary was the mother of **J**, who is called the
1:18 Now this is how **J** the Messiah was born.
1:21 she will have a son, and you are to name him **J**,
1:25 until her son was born. And Joseph named him **J**.
2:1 **J** was born in the town of Bethlehem in Judea,
2:21 So Joseph returned immediately to Israel with **J**
3:13 Then **J** went from Galilee to the Jordan River to be
3:15 But **J** said, "It must be done, because we must do
3:16 After his baptism, as **J** came up out of the water,
4:1 Then **J** was led out into the wilderness by the Holy
4:4 But **J** told him, "No! The Scriptures say,
4:7 **J** responded, "The Scriptures also say, 'Do not
4:10 "Get out of here, Satan," **J** told him.
4:11 Devil went away, and angels came and cared for **J**.
4:12 When **J** heard that John had been arrested, he left
4:17 From then on, **J** began to preach, "Turn from your
4:18 One day as **J** was walking along the shore beside
4:19 **J** called out to them, "Come, be my disciples,
4:23 **J** traveled throughout Galilee teaching in the
5:1 **J** went up the mountainside with his disciples
7:28 After **J** finished speaking, the crowds were amazed
8:1 Large crowds followed **J** as he came down the
8:2 Suddenly, a man with leprosy approached **J**.
8:3 **J** touched him. "I want to," he said. "Be healed!"
8:4 Then **J** said to him, "Go right over to the priest
8:5 When **J** arrived in Capernaum, a Roman officer
8:7 **J** said, "I will come and heal him."
8:10 When **J** heard this, he was amazed. Turning to the
8:13 Then **J** said to the Roman officer, "Go on home.
8:14 When **J** arrived at Peter's house,
8:15 But when **J** touched her hand, the fever left her.
8:16 many demon-possessed people were brought to **J**.
8:18 When **J** noticed how large the crowd was growing,
8:20 But **J** said, "Foxes have dens to live in, and birds
8:22 But **J** told him, "Follow me now! Let those who
8:23 Then **J** got into the boat and started across the lake
8:24 waves breaking into the boat. But **J** was sleeping.
8:26 And **J** answered, "Why are you afraid? You have
8:28 When **J** arrived on the other side of the lake in the
8:32 "All right, go!" **J** commanded them.
8:34 The entire town came out to meet **J**, but they
9:1 **J** climbed into a boat and went back across the
9:2 **J** said to the paralyzed man, "Take heart, son!
9:4 **J** knew what they were thinking, so he asked them,
9:6 Then **J** turned to the paralyzed man and said,
9:9 As **J** was going down the road, he saw Matthew
9:9 "Come, be my disciple," **J** said to him.
9:10 That night Matthew invited **J** and his disciples to
9:12 When he heard this, **J** replied, "Healthy people
9:14 One day the disciples of John the Baptist came to **J**
9:15 **J** responded, "Should the wedding guests mourn
9:18 As **J** was saying this, the leader of a synagogue
9:19 As **J** and the disciples were going to the official's
9:22 **J** turned around and said to her, "Daughter,
9:23 When **J** arrived at the official's home, he noticed
9:25 **J** went in and took the girl by the hand, and she
9:27 After **J** left the girl's home, two blind men
9:28 and **J** asked them, "Do you believe I can make
9:30 **J** sternly warned them, "Don't tell anyone about
9:33 So **J** cast out the demon, and instantly the man
9:35 **J** traveled through all the cities and villages of that
10:1 **J** called his twelve disciples to him and gave them
10:5 **J** sent the twelve disciples out with these
11:1 When **J** had finished giving these instructions to
11:2 was doing. So he sent his disciples to ask **J**,
11:4 **J** told them, "Go back to John and tell him about
11:7 had gone, **J** began talking about him to the crowds.
11:20 Then **J** began to denounce the cities where he had
11:25 Then **J** prayed this prayer: "O Father, Lord of
11:28 Then **J** said, "Come to me, all of you who are
12:1 At about that time **J** was walking through some
12:3 But **J** said to them, "Haven't you ever read in the
12:10 The Pharisees asked **J**, "Is it legal to work by
12:14 called a meeting and discussed plans for killing **J**.
12:15 But **J** knew what they were planning. He left that
12:22 both blind and unable to talk, was brought to **J**.
12:23 "Could it be that **J** is the Son of David,
12:25 **J** knew their thoughts and replied, "Any kingdom
12:38 of religious law and Pharisees came to **J** and said,
12:39 But **J** replied, "Only an evil, faithless generation
12:46 As **J** was speaking to the crowd, his mother

12:47 Someone told **J**, "Your mother and your brothers
12:48 **J** asked, "Who is my mother? Who are my
13: 1 **J** left the house and went down to the shore,
13:24 Here is another story **J** told: "The Kingdom of
13:31 Here is another illustration **J** used: "The Kingdom
13:33 **J** also used this illustration: "The Kingdom of
13:34 **J** always used stories and illustrations like these
13:36 leaving the crowds outside, **J** went into the house.
13:53 When **J** had finished telling these stories, he left
13:57 Then **J** told them, "A prophet is honored
14: 1 When Herod Antipas heard about **J**,
14:12 and buried it. Then they told **J** what had happened.
14:13 As soon as **J** heard the news, he went off by
14:16 But **J** replied, "That isn't necessary—you feed
14:22 **J** made his disciples get back into the boat
14:25 About three o'clock in the morning **J** came to
14:27 But **J** spoke to them at once. "It's all right,"
14:29 "All right, come," **J** said. So Peter went over the
side of the boat and walked on the water toward **J**.
14:31 Instantly **J** reached out his hand and grabbed him.
14:31 "You don't have much faith," **J** said.
15: 1 law now arrived from Jerusalem to interview **J**.
15: 3 **J** replied, "And why do you, by your traditions,
15:10 Then **J** called to the crowds and said, "Listen to
15:13 **J** replied, "Every plant not planted by my
15:15 Then Peter asked **J**, "Explain what you meant
15:16 "Don't you understand?" **J** asked him.
15:21 **J** then left Galilee and went north to the region of
15:23 But **J** gave her no reply—not even a word.
15:28 "Woman," **J** said to her, "your faith is great.
15:29 **J** returned to the Sea of Galilee and climbed a hill
15:30 physical difficulties, and they laid them before **J**.
15:32 Then **J** called his disciples to him and said, "I feel
15:34 **J** asked, "How many loaves of bread do you
15:35 So **J** told all the people to sit down on the ground.
15:39 Then **J** sent the people home, and he got into a
16: 4 prophet Jonah." Then **J** left them and went away.
16: 6 "Watch out!" **J** warned them. "Beware of the
16: 8 **J** knew what they were thinking, so he said,
16:13 When **J** came to the region of Caesarea Philippi,
16:17 **J** replied, "You are blessed, Simon son of John,
16:21 then on **J** began to tell his disciples plainly that he
16:23 **J** turned to Peter and said, "Get away from me,
16:24 Then **J** said to the disciples, "If any of you wants
17: 1 Six days later **J** took Peter and the two brothers,
17: 3 and Elijah appeared and began talking with **J**.
17: 7 **J** came over and touched them. "Get up," he said,
17: 8 And when they looked, they saw only **J** with them.
17: 9 they descended the mountain, **J** commanded them,
17:11 **J** replied, "Elijah is indeed coming first to set
17:14 for them. A man came and knelt before **J** and said,
17:17 **J** replied, "You stubborn, faithless people!
17:18 Then **J** rebuked the demon in the boy, and it left
17:19 Afterward the disciples asked **J** privately,
17:20 "You didn't have enough faith," **J** told them.
17:22 **J** told them, "The Son of Man is going to be
17:25 Then he went into the house to talk to **J** about it.
17:25 to speak, **J** asked him, "What do you think, Peter?
17:26 "Well, then," **J** said, "the citizens are free!
18: 1 About that time the disciples came to **J** and asked,
18: 2 **J** called a small child over to him and put the child
18:22 "No!" **J** replied, "seventy times seven!
19: 1 After **J** had finished saying these things, he left
19: 4 "Haven't you read the Scriptures?" **J** replied.
19: 8 **J** replied, "Moses permitted divorce as a
19:11 "Not everyone can accept this statement," **J** said.
19:13 Some children were brought to **J** so he could lay
19:14 But **J** said, "Let the children come to me.
19:16 Someone came to **J** with this question: "Teacher,
19:17 **J** replied. "Only God is good. But to answer your
19:18 "Which ones?" the man asked. And **J** replied:
19:21 **J** told him, "If you want to be perfect, go and sell
19:23 Then **J** said to his disciples, "I tell you the truth,
19:26 **J** looked at them intently and said,
19:28 And **J** replied, "I assure you that when I, the Son
20:17 As **J** was on the way to Jerusalem, he took the
20:20 the sons of Zebedee, came to **J** with her sons.
20:22 But **J** told them, "You don't know what you are
20:25 But **J** called them together and said, "You know
20:29 As **J** and the disciples left the city of Jericho,
20:30 When they heard that **J** was coming that way,
20:32 **J** stopped in the road and called, "What do you
20:34 **J** felt sorry for them and touched their eyes.
21: 1 As **J** and the disciples approached Jerusalem,
21: 1 the Mount of Olives. **J** sent two of them on ahead.
21: 6 The two disciples did as **J** said.
21: 8 crowd spread their coats on the road ahead of **J**,
21:11 And the crowds replied, "It's **J**, the prophet from
21:12 **J** entered the Temple and began to drive out the
21:16 and asked **J**, "Do you hear what these children are
21:16 "Yes," **J** replied. "Haven't you ever read the
21:18 as **J** was returning to Jerusalem, he was hungry,
21:21 Then **J** told them, "I assure you, if you have faith
21:23 When **J** returned to the Temple and began
21:24 things if you answer one question," **J** replied.
21:27 And **J** responded, "Then I won't answer your
21:31 of course." Then **J** explained his meaning:
21:40 the owner of the vineyard returns," **J** asked,
21:42 Then **J** asked them, "Didn't you ever read this in
21:45 When the leading priests and Pharisees heard **J**,
21:46 because the crowds considered **J** to be a prophet.
22: 1 **J** told them several other stories to illustrate the
22:15 **J** into saying something for which they could
22:18 But **J** knew their evil motives. "You hypocrites!"
22:29 **J** replied, "Your problem is that you don't know
22:37 **J** replied, " 'You must love the Lord your God
22:41 by the Pharisees, **J** asked them a question:
22:43 **J** responded, "Then why does David,
23: 1 Then **J** said to the crowds and to his disciples,
24: 1 As **J** was leaving the Temple grounds, his disciples
24: 3 Later, **J** sat on the slopes of the Mount of Olives.
24: 4 **J** told them, "Don't let anyone mislead you.
26: 1 When **J** had finished saying these things, he said to
26: 4 to discuss how to capture **J** secretly and put him to
26: 6 **J** was in Bethany at the home of Simon,
26:10 But **J** replied, "Why berate her for doing such a
26:15 "How much will you pay me to betray **J** to you?"
26:16 looking for the right time and place to betray **J**.
26:17 the disciples came to **J** and asked,
26:19 So the disciples did as **J** told them and prepared
26:20 **J** sat down at the table with the twelve disciples.
26:25 And **J** told him, "You have said it yourself."
26:26 **J** took a loaf of bread and asked God's blessing on
26:31 "Tonight all of you will desert me," **J** told them.
26:34 "Peter," **J** replied, "the truth is, this very night,
26:36 Then **J** brought them to an olive grove called
26:49 So Judas came straight to **J**. "Greetings,
26:50 **J** said, "My friend, go ahead and do what you
26:50 Then the others grabbed **J** and arrested him.
26:51 One of the men with **J** pulled out a sword
26:52 "Put away your sword," **J** told him. "Those who
26:55 Then **J** said to the crowd, "Am I some dangerous
26:57 Then the people who had arrested **J** led him to the
26:58 and waited to see what was going to happen to **J**.
26:59 trying to find witnesses who would lie about **J**,
26:62 Then the high priest stood up and said to **J**, "Well,
26:63 But **J** remained silent. Then the high priest said to
26:64 **J** replied, "Yes, it is as you say. And in the future
26:69 "You were one of those with **J** the Galilean."
26:71 "This man was with **J** of Nazareth."
27: 1 the Roman government to sentence **J** to death.
27: 3 realized that **J** had been condemned to die,
27:11 Now **J** was standing before Pilate, the Roman
27:11 asked him. **J** replied, "Yes, it is as you say."
27:12 their accusations against him, **J** remained silent.
27:14 But **J** said nothing, much to the governor's great
27:17 Barabbas, or **J** who is called the Messiah?"
27:18 that the Jewish leaders had arrested **J** out of envy.)
27:20 to be released and for **J** to be put to death.
27:22 "what should I do with **J** who is called the
27:26 He ordered **J** flogged with a lead-tipped whip,
27:27 Some of the governor's soldiers took **J** into their
27:37 It read: "This is **J**, the King of the Jews."
27:41 religious law, and the other leaders also mocked **J**.
27:46 **J** called out with a loud voice, "*Eli, Eli,*
27:50 Then **J** shouted out again, and he gave up his
27:55 **J** to care for him were watching from a distance.
28: 5 "I know you are looking for **J**, who was crucified.
28: 9 And as they went, **J** met them. "Greetings!"
28:10 Then **J** said to them, "Don't be afraid! Go tell my
28:16 going to the mountain where **J** had told them to go.
28:18 **J** came and told his disciples, "I have been given
Mk 1: 1 Here begins the Good News about **J** the Messiah,
1: 9 One day **J** came from Nazareth in Galilee, and he
1:10 And when **J** came up out of the water, he saw the
1:12 Immediately the Holy Spirit compelled **J** to go into
1:14 **J** went to Galilee to preach God's Good News.
1:16 One day as **J** was walking along the shores of the
1:17 **J** called out to them, "Come, be my disciples,
1:19 A little farther up the shore **J** saw Zebedee's sons,
1:21 **J** and his companions went to the town of
1:24 "Why are you bothering us, **J** of Nazareth?
1:25 **J** cut him short. "Be silent! Come out of the
1:29 After **J** and his disciples left the synagogue,
1:30 a high fever. They told **J** about her right away.
1:32 and demon-possessed people were brought to **J**.
1:34 So **J** healed great numbers of sick people who had
1:35 The next morning **J** awoke long before daybreak
1:40 A man with leprosy came and knelt in front of **J**,
1:41 Moved with pity, **J** touched him. "I want to,"
1:43 Then **J** sent him on his way and told him sternly,
1:45 such crowds soon surrounded **J** that he couldn't
2: 1 Several days later **J** returned to Capernaum,
2: 4 They couldn't get to **J** through the crowd, so they
2: 4 the sick man on his mat, right down in front of **J**.
2: 5 their faith, **J** said to the paralyzed man, "My son,
2: 8 **J** knew what they were discussing among
2:10 Then **J** turned to the paralyzed man and said,
2:13 Then **J** went out to the lakeshore again and taught
2:14 "Come, be my disciple," **J** said to him. So Levi
2:15 That night Levi invited **J** and his disciples to be his
2:15 of this kind among the crowds that followed **J**.)
2:17 When **J** heard this, he told them, "Healthy people
2:18 One day some people came to **J** and asked,
2:19 **J** replied, "Do wedding guests fast while
2:23 One Sabbath day as **J** was walking through some
2:24 But the Pharisees said to **J**, "They shouldn't be
2:25 But **J** replied, "Haven't you ever read in the
3: 1 **J** went into the synagogue again and noticed a man
3: 3 **J** said to the man, "Come and stand in front of
3: 6 supporters of Herod to discuss plans for killing **J**.
3: 7 **J** and his disciples went out to the lake,
3: 9 **J** instructed his disciples to bring around a boat
3:12 But **J** strictly warned them not to say who he was.
3:13 Afterward **J** went up on a mountain and called the
3:17 but **J** nicknamed them "Sons of Thunder"),
3:20 When **J** returned to the house where he was
3:23 **J** called them over and said to them by way of
3:32 There was a crowd around **J**, and someone said,
3:33 **J** replied, "Who is my mother? Who are my
4: 1 Once again **J** began teaching by the lakeshore.
4:10 when **J** was alone with the twelve disciples
4:21 Then **J** asked them, "Would anyone light a lamp
4:26 **J** also said, "Here is another illustration of what
4:30 **J** asked, "How can I describe the Kingdom of
4:35 As evening came, **J** said to his disciples,
4:38 **J** was sleeping at the back of the boat with his head
5: 2 Just as **J** was climbing from the boat, a man
5: 6 When **J** was still some distance away, the man saw
5: 6 He ran to meet **J** and fell down before him.
5: 7 you bothering me, **J**, Son of the Most High God?
5: 8 For **J** had already said to the spirit, "Come out of
5: 9 Then **J** asked, "What is your name?"
5:13 **J** gave them permission. So the evil spirits came
5:15 A crowd soon gathered around **J**, but they were
5:17 and the crowd began pleading with **J** to go away
5:18 When **J** got back into the boat, the man who had
5:19 But **J** said, "No, go home to your friends, and tell
5:20 and began to tell everyone about the great things **J**
5:21 When **J** went back across to the other side of the
5:24 **J** went with him, and the crowd thronged behind.
5:27 She had heard about **J**, so she came up behind him
5:30 **J** realized at once that healing power had gone out
5:36 But **J** ignored their comments and said to Jairus,
5:37 Then **J** stopped the crowd and wouldn't let anyone
5:38 **J** saw the commotion and the weeping and wailing.
5:43 **J** commanded them not to tell anyone what had
6: 1 **J** left that part of the country and returned with his
6: 4 Then **J** told them, "A prophet is honored
6: 6 Then **J** went out from village to village, teaching.
6:14 Herod Antipas, the king, soon heard about **J**,
6:15 Others thought **J** was the ancient prophet Elijah.
6:16 When Herod heard about **J** he said, "John,
6:30 The apostles returned to **J** from their ministry tour
6:31 Then **J** said, "Let's get away from the crowds for
6:31 so many people coming and going that **J**
6:37 But **J** said, "You feed them." "With what?"
6:39 Then **J** told the crowd to sit down in groups on the
6:41 **J** took the five loaves and two fish, looked up
6:45 **J** made his disciples get back into the boat
6:47 in the middle of the lake, and **J** was alone on land.
6:50 But **J** spoke to them at once. "It's all right,"
7: 1 religious law arrived from Jerusalem to confront **J**.
7: 6 **J** replied, "You hypocrites! Isaiah was
7:14 Then **J** called to the crowd to come and hear.
7:17 Then **J** went into a house to get away from the
7:24 Then **J** left Galilee and went north to the region of
7:25 She had heard about **J**, and now she came and fell
7:27 **J** told her, "First I should help my own family,
7:31 **J** left Tyre and went to Sidon, then back to the Sea
7:32 and the people begged **J** to lay his hands on the
7:33 **J** led him to a private place away from the crowd.
7:36 **J** told the crowd not to tell anyone, but the more he
8: 1 of food again. **J** called his disciples and told them,
8: 6 So **J** told all the people to sit down on the ground.
8: 7 so **J** also blessed these and told the disciples to
8:11 When the Pharisees heard that **J** had arrived,
8:15 As they were crossing the lake, **J** warned them,
8:17 **J** knew what they were thinking, so he said,
8:22 some people brought a blind man to **J**, and they
8:23 **J** took the blind man by the hand and led him out
8:25 Then **J** placed his hands over the man's eyes again.
8:26 **J** sent him home, saying, "Don't go back into the
8:27 **J** and his disciples left Galilee and went up to the
8:29 Then **J** asked, "Who do you say I am?"
8:30 But **J** warned them not to tell anyone about him.
8:31 Then **J** began to tell them that he, the Son of Man,
8:33 **J** turned and looked at his disciples and then said
9: 1 **J** went on to say, "I assure you that some of you
9: 2 Six days later **J** took Peter, James, and John to the
9: 4 and Moses appeared and began talking with **J**.
9: 8 and Elijah were gone, and only **J** was with them.
9:12 **J** responded, "Elijah is indeed coming first to set
9:15 The crowd watched **J** in awe as he came toward
9:19 **J** said to them, "You faithless people! How long
9:20 But when the evil spirit saw **J**, it threw the child
9:21 **J** asked the boy's father. He replied, "Since he
9:23 "What do you mean, 'If I can'?" **J** asked.
9:25 When **J** saw that the crowd of onlookers was
9:27 But **J** took him by the hand and helped him to his
9:28 when **J** was alone in the house with his disciples,
9:29 **J** replied, "This kind can be cast out only by
9:30 through Galilee. **J** tried to avoid all publicity
9:33 **J** and his disciples settled in the house where they
9:33 **J** asked them, "What were you discussing out on
9:38 John said to **J**, "Teacher, we saw a man using your
9:39 "Don't stop him!" **J** said. "No one who performs
10: 1 Then **J** left Capernaum and went southward to the
10: 3 did Moses say about divorce?" **J** asked them.
10: 5 But **J** responded, "He wrote those instructions
10:13 One day some parents brought their children to **J**
10:14 But when **J** saw what was happening, he was very
10:17 a man came running up to **J**, knelt down,
10:18 call me good?" **J** asked. "Only God is truly good.
10:21 **J** felt genuine love for this man as he looked at
10:23 **J** looked around and said to his disciples,
10:24 But **J** said again, "Dear children, it is very hard to
10:27 **J** looked at them intently and said,
10:29 And **J** replied, "I assure you that everyone who
10:32 to Jerusalem, and **J** was walking ahead of them.
10:32 **J** once more began to describe everything that was
10:38 But **J** answered, "You don't know what you are
10:39 And **J** said, "You will indeed drink from my cup
10:42 So **J** called them together and said, "You know
10:46 Later, as **J** and his disciples left town, a great
10:46 was sitting beside the road as **J** was going by.
10:47 When Bartimaeus heard that **J** from Nazareth was
10:47 shout out, "**J**, Son of David, have mercy on me!"
10:49 When **J** heard him, he stopped and said, "Tell him
10:50 threw aside his coat, jumped up, and came to **J**.
10:51 **J** asked. "Teacher," the blind man said, "I want

10:52 And **J** said to him, "Go your way. Your faith has
10:52 man could see! Then he followed **J** down the road.
11: 1 As **J** and his disciples approached Jerusalem,
11: 1 the Mount of Olives. **J** sent two of them on ahead.
11: 6 They said what **J** had told them to say, and they
11: 7 Then they brought the colt to **J** and threw their
11: 8 crowd spread their coats on the road ahead of **J**,
11:11 So **J** came to Jerusalem and went into the Temple.
11:12 as they were leaving Bethany, **J** felt hungry.
11:14 Then **J** said to the tree, "May no one ever eat your
11:15 **J** entered the Temple and began to drive out the
11:18 and teachers of religious law heard what **J** had
11:19 That evening **J** and the disciples left the city.
11:21 Peter remembered what **J** had said to the tree on
11:22 Then **J** said to the disciples, "Have faith in God.
11:27 As **J** was walking through the Temple area,
11:29 things if you answer one question," **J** replied.
11:33 And **J** responded, "Then I won't answer your
12: 1 Then **J** began telling them stories: "A man planted
12: 9 **J** asked. "I'll tell you—he will come and kill them
12:13 and supporters of Herod to try to trap **J** into saying
12:15 **J** saw through their hypocrisy and said, "Who are
12:17 "Well, then," **J** said, "give to Caesar what
12:24 **J** replied, "Your problem is that you don't know
12:28 He realized that **J** had answered well, so he asked,
12:29 **J** replied, "The most important commandment is
12:34 Realizing this man's understanding, **J** said to him,
12:35 Later, as **J** was teaching the people in the Temple,
12:41 **J** went over to the collection box in the Temple
13: 1 As **J** was leaving the Temple that day, one of his
13: 2 **J** replied, "These magnificent buildings will be
13: 3 **J** sat on the slopes of the Mount of Olives across
13: 5 **J** replied, "Don't let anyone mislead you,
14: 1 looking for an opportunity to capture **J** secretly
14: 3 **J** was in Bethany at the home of Simon,
14: 6 But **J** replied, "Leave her alone. Why berate her
14:10 went to the leading priests to arrange to betray **J** to
14:11 looking for the right time and place to betray **J**.
14:13 So **J** sent two of them into Jerusalem to make the
14:16 the city and found everything just as **J** had said,
14:17 In the evening **J** arrived with the twelve disciples.
14:18 **J** said, "The truth is, one of you will betray me,
14:22 **J** took a loaf of bread and asked God's blessing on
14:27 "All of you will desert me," **J** told them.
14:30 "Peter," **J** replied, "the truth is, this very night,
14:32 and **J** said, "Sit here while I go and pray."
14:39 Then **J** left them again and prayed, repeating his
14:45 As soon as they arrived, Judas walked up to **J**.
14:46 Then the others grabbed **J** and arrested him.
14:48 **J** asked them, "Am I some dangerous criminal,
14:53 **J** was led to the high priest's home where the
14:55 to find witnesses who would testify against **J**,
14:60 high priest stood up before the others and asked **J**,
14:61 **J** made no reply. Then the high priest asked him,
14:62 **J** said, "I am, and you will see me, the Son of
14:67 and then said, "You were one of those with **J**,
15: 1 They bound **J** and took him to Pilate, the Roman
15: 2 Pilate asked **J**, "Are you the King of the Jews?"
J replied, "Yes, it is as you say."
15: 5 But **J** said nothing, much to Pilate's surprise.
15:10 that the leading priests had arrested **J** out of envy.)
15:11 to demand the release of Barabbas instead of **J**.
15:15 He ordered **J** flogged with a lead-tipped whip,
15:22 And they brought **J** to a place called Golgotha
15:31 and teachers of religious law also mocked **J**.
15:32 who were being crucified with **J** ridiculed him.
15:34 Then, at that time **J** called out with a loud voice,
15:37 Then **J** uttered another loud cry and breathed his
15:41 They had been followers of **J** and had cared for
15:44 Pilate couldn't believe that **J** was already dead,
16: 6 You are looking for **J**, the Nazarene, who was
16: 7 including Peter: **J** is going ahead of you to Galilee.
16: 9 It was early on Sunday morning when **J** rose from
16:11 But when she told them that **J** was alive and she
16:19 When the Lord **J** had finished talking with them,
16: S Afterward **J** himself sent them out from east to
Lk 1:31 and have a son, and you are to name him **J**.
2:21 when the baby was circumcised, he was named **J**,
2:27 and Joseph came to present the baby **J** to the Lord
2:33 Mary were amazed at what was being said about **J**.
2:38 She talked about **J** to everyone who had been
2:42 When **J** was twelve years old, they attended the
2:43 to Nazareth, but **J** stayed behind in Jerusalem.
2:52 So **J** grew both in height and in wisdom, and he
3:21 were being baptized, **J** himself was baptized.
3:23 **J** was about thirty years old when he began his
3:23 **J** was known as the son of Joseph. / Joseph was the
4: 1 Then **J**, full of the Holy Spirit, left the Jordan
4: 4 But **J** told him, "No! The Scriptures say,
4: 8 **J** replied, "The Scriptures say, / 'You must
4:12 **J** responded, "The Scriptures also say, 'Do not
4:13 When the Devil had finished tempting **J**, he left
4:14 Then **J** returned to Galilee, filled with the Holy
4:31 Then **J** went to Capernaum, a town in Galilee,
4:33 a man possessed by a demon began shouting at **J**,
4:34 Why are you bothering us, **J** of Nazareth?
4:35 **J** cut him short. "Be silent!" he told the demon.
4:38 the synagogue that day, **J** went to Simon's home,
4:40 the village brought sick family members to **J**.
4:42 Early the next morning **J** went out into the
5: 1 One day as **J** was preaching on the shore of the Sea
5: 3 **J** asked Simon, its owner, to push it out into the
5: 8 he fell to his knees before **J** and said, "Oh, Lord,
5:10 also amazed. **J** replied to Simon, "Don't be afraid!
5:11 as they landed, they left everything and followed **J**.
5:12 **J** met a man with an advanced case of leprosy.
5:12 When the man saw **J**, he fell to the ground,
5:13 **J** reached out and touched the man. "I want to,"
5:14 Then **J** instructed him not to tell anyone what had
5:16 But **J** often withdrew to the wilderness for prayer.
5:17 One day while **J** was teaching, some Pharisees
5:17 And the Lord's healing power was strongly with **J**.
5:18 They tried to push through the crowd to **J**,
5:19 into the crowd, still on his mat, right in front of **J**.
5:20 Seeing their faith, **J** said to the man, "Son,
5:22 **J** knew what they were thinking, so he asked them,
5:24 Then **J** turned to the paralyzed man and said,
5:27 Later, as **J** left the town, he saw a tax collector
5:27 "Come, be my disciple!" **J** said to him.
5:29 Soon Levi held a banquet in his home with **J** as the
5:31 **J** answered them, "Healthy people don't need a
5:34 **J** asked, "Do wedding guests fast while
5:36 Then **J** gave them this illustration: "No one tears a
6: 1 One Sabbath day as **J** was walking through some
6: 3 **J** replied, "Haven't you ever read in the Scriptures
6: 5 And **J** added, "I, the Son of Man, am master even
6: 6 hand was in the synagogue while **J** was teaching.
6: 7 and the Pharisees watched closely to see whether **J**
6: 8 But **J** knew their thoughts. He said to the man with
6: 9 Then **J** said to his critics, "I have a question for
6:11 the enemies of **J** were wild with rage and began to
6:12 One day soon afterward **J** went to a mountain to
6:17 the disciples stood with **J** on a large, level area,
6:18 and to be healed, and **J** cast out many evil spirits.
6:20 Then **J** turned to his disciples and said,
6:39 Then **J** gave the following illustration:
7: 1 When **J** had finished saying all this, he went back
7: 3 When the officer heard about **J**, he sent some
7: 4 So they earnestly begged **J** to come with them
7: 6 So **J** went with them. But just before they arrived
7: 9 When **J** heard this, he was amazed. Turning to the
7:11 Soon afterward **J** went with his disciples to the
7:15 around him! And **J** gave him back to his mother.
7:17 The report of what **J** had done that day spread all
7:18 the Baptist told John about everything **J** was doing.
7:20 John's two disciples found **J** and said to him,
7:24 After they left, **J** talked to the crowd about John.
7:31 **J** asked. "With what will I compare them?
7:36 One of the Pharisees asked **J** to come to his home
7:36 so **J** accepted the invitation and sat down to eat.
7:39 said to himself, "This proves that **J** is no prophet.
7:40 Then **J** spoke up and answered his thoughts.
7:41 Then **J** told him this story: "A man loaned money
7:43 canceled the larger debt." "That's right," **J** said.
7:48 Then **J** said to the woman, "Your sins are
7:50 And **J** said to the woman, "Your faith has saved
8: 1 Not long afterward **J** began a tour of the nearby
8: 3 contributing from their own resources to support **J**
8: 4 One day **J** told this story to a large crowd that had
8:20 Someone told **J**, "Your mother and your brothers
8:21 **J** replied, "My mother and my brothers are all
8:22 One day **J** said to his disciples, "Let's cross over
8:23 On the way across, **J** lay down for a nap, and while
8:24 So **J** rebuked the wind and the raging waves.
8:27 As **J** was climbing out of the boat, a man who was
8:28 As soon as he saw **J**, he shrieked and fell to the
8:28 you bothering me, **J**, Son of the Most High God?
8:29 For **J** had already commanded the evil spirit to
8:30 **J** asked. "Legion," he replied—for the man was
8:31 The demons kept begging **J** not to send them into
8:32 them enter into the pigs. **J** gave them permission.
8:35 A crowd soon gathered around **J**, for they wanted
8:37 And all the people in that region begged **J** to go
8:37 So **J** returned to the boat and left, crossing back to
8:38 demon possessed begged to go, too, but **J** said,
8:39 telling about the great thing **J** had done for him.
8:40 On the other side of the lake the crowds received **J**
8:42 As **J** went with him, he was surrounded by the
8:44 She came up behind **J** and touched the fringe of his
8:45 **J** asked. Everyone denied it, and Peter said,
8:46 But **J** told him, "No, someone deliberately
8:47 When the woman realized that **J** knew, she began
8:50 But when **J** heard what had happened, he said to
8:51 **J** wouldn't let anyone go in with him except Peter,
8:54 Then **J** took her by the hand and said in a loud
8:55 Then **J** told them to give her something to eat.
8:56 but **J** insisted that they not tell anyone what had
9: 1 One day **J** called together his twelve apostles
9:10 they told **J** everything they had done.
9:13 But **J** said, "You feed them." "Impossible!"
9:14 ground in groups of about fifty each," **J** replied.
9:16 **J** took the five loaves and two fish, looked up
9:18 One day as **J** was alone, praying, he came over to
9:21 **J** warned them not to tell anyone about this.
9:28 About eight days later **J** took Peter, James,
9:30 and Elijah, appeared and began talking with **J**.
9:36 When the voice died away, **J** was there alone.
9:37 had come down the mountain, a huge crowd met **J**.
9:41 "You stubborn, faithless people," **J** said,
9:42 But **J** rebuked the evil spirit and healed the boy.
9:43 things he was doing, **J** said to his disciples,
9:47 But **J** knew their thoughts, so he brought a little
9:49 John said to **J**, "Master, we saw someone using
9:50 But **J** said, "Don't stop him! Anyone who is not
9:51 return to heaven, **J** resolutely set out for Jerusalem.
9:53 of the village refused to have anything to do with **J**
9:54 and John heard about it, they said to **J**, "Lord,
9:55 But **J** turned and rebuked them.
9:57 As they were walking along someone said to **J**,
9:58 But **J** replied, "Foxes have dens to live in,
9:60 **J** replied, "Let those who are spiritually dead care
9:62 But **J** told him, "Anyone who puts a hand to the
10:21 Then **J** was filled with the joy of the Holy Spirit
10:25 law stood up to test **J** by asking him this question:
10:26 **J** replied, "What does the law of Moses say?
10:28 "Right!" **J** told him. "Do this and you will live!"
10:29 so he asked **J**, "And who is my neighbor?"
10:30 **J** replied with an illustration: "A Jewish man was
10:36 the man who was attacked by bandits?" **J** asked.
10:37 Then **J** said, "Yes, now go and do the same."
10:38 As **J** and the disciples continued on their way to
10:40 She came to **J** and said, "Lord, doesn't it seem
11: 1 Once when **J** had been out praying, one of his
11:14 One day **J** cast a demon out of a man who couldn't
11:16 Trying to test **J**, others asked for a miraculous sign
11:29 As the crowd pressed in on **J**, he said, "These are
11:37 As **J** was speaking, one of the Pharisees invited
11:46 "Yes," said **J**, "how terrible it will be for you
11:53 As **J** finished speaking, the Pharisees and teachers
12: 1 **J** turned first to his disciples and warned them,
12:14 **J** replied, "Friend, who made me a judge over you
12:22 Then turning to his disciples, **J** said, "So I tell you,
12:54 Then **J** turned to the crowd and said, "When you
13: 1 About this time **J** was informed that Pilate had
13: 6 Then **J** used this illustration: "A man planted a fig
13:10 One Sabbath day as **J** was teaching in a
13:12 When **J** saw her, he called her over and said,
13:14 indignant that **J** had healed her on the Sabbath day.
13:18 Then **J** said, "What is the Kingdom of God like?
13:22 **J** went through the towns and villages, teaching as
13:32 **J** replied, "Go tell that fox that I will keep on
14: 1 One Sabbath day **J** was in the home of a leader of
14: 3 **J** asked the Pharisees and experts in religious law,
14: 4 **J** touched the sick man and healed him and sent
14: 7 When **J** noticed that all who had come to the
14:15 a man sitting at the table with **J** exclaimed,
14:16 **J** replied with this illustration: "A man prepared a
14:25 Great crowds were following **J**. He turned around
15: 1 notorious sinners often came to listen to **J** teach.
15: 3 So **J** used this illustration:
15:11 illustrate the point further, **J** told them this story:
16: 1 **J** told this story to his disciples: "A rich man hired
16:19 **J** said, "There was a certain rich man who was
17: 1 One day **J** said to his disciples, "There will always
17:11 As **J** continued on toward Jerusalem, he reached
17:13 crying out, "**J**, Master, have mercy on us!"
17:15 came back to **J**, shouting, "Praise God,
17:17 **J** asked, "Didn't I heal ten men? Where are the
17:19 And **J** said to the man, "Stand up and go.
17:20 One day the Pharisees asked **J**, "When will the
17:20 **J** replied, "The Kingdom of God isn't ushered in
17:37 **J** replied, "Just as the gathering of vultures shows
18: 1 One day **J** told his disciples a story to illustrate
18: 9 Then **J** told this story to some who had great
18:15 day some parents brought their little children to **J**
18:16 Then **J** called for the children and said to the
18:18 Once a religious leader asked **J** this question:
18:19 me good?" **J** asked him. "Only God is truly good.
18:22 "There is still one thing you lack," **J** said.
18:24 **J** watched him go and then said to his disciples,
18:29 "Yes," **J** replied, "and I assure you,
18:31 **J** told them, "As you know, we are going to
18:37 They told him that **J** of Nazareth was going by.
18:38 "**J**, Son of David, have mercy on me!"
18:39 The crowds ahead of **J** tried to hush the man,
18:40 When **J** heard him, he stopped and ordered that the
18:41 Then **J** asked the man, "What do you want me to
18:42 And **J** said, "All right, you can see! Your faith has
18:43 man could see, and he followed **J**, praising God.
19: 1 **J** entered Jericho and made his way through the
19: 3 He tried to get a look at **J**, but he was too short to
19: 5 When **J** came by, he looked up at Zacchaeus
19: 6 and took **J** to his house in great excitement
19: 9 **J** responded, "Salvation has come to this home
19:11 The crowd was listening to everything **J** said.
19:28 telling this story, **J** went on toward Jerusalem,
19:32 So they went and found the colt, just as **J** had said.
19:35 So they brought the colt to **J** and threw their
19:36 spread out their coats on the road ahead of **J**.
19:41 came closer to Jerusalem and **J** saw the city ahead,
19:45 Then **J** entered the Temple and began to drive out
20: 1 One day as **J** was teaching and preaching the Good
20: 8 And **J** responded, "Then I won't answer your
20: 9 Now **J** turned to the people again and told them
20:15 of the vineyard will do to those farmers?" **J** asked.
20:17 **J** looked at them and said, "Then what do the
20:19 they wanted to arrest **J** immediately because they
20:20 They tried to get **J** to say something that could be
20:20 to the Roman governor so he would arrest **J**.
20:34 **J** replied, "Marriage is for people here on earth.
20:41 Then **J** presented them with a question. "Why is
21: 1 While **J** was in the Temple, he watched the rich
21: 5 the memorial decorations on the walls. But **J** said,
21:37 Every day **J** went to the Temple to teach, and each
22: 4 guard to discuss the best way to betray **J** to them.
22: 6 So he began looking for an opportunity to betray **J**
22: 8 **J** sent Peter and John ahead and said, "Go
22:13 to the city and found everything just as **J** had said,
22:14 Then at the proper time **J** and the twelve apostles
22:15 **J** said, "I have looked forward to this hour with
22:25 **J** told them, "In this world the kings and great
22:34 But **J** said, "Peter, let me tell you something.
22:35 Then **J** asked them, "When I sent you out to
22:39 **J** left the upstairs room and went as usual to the
22:47 Judas walked over to **J** and greeted him with a
22:48 But **J** said, "Judas, how can you betray me,
22:51 But **J** said, "Don't resist anymore." And he
22:52 Then **J** spoke to the leading priests and captains of
22:63 Now the guards in charge of **J** began mocking
22:66 of religious law. **J** was led before this high council,
23: 1 Then the entire council took **J** over to Pilate,

23: 3 of the Jews?" **J** replied, "Yes, it is as you say."
23: 8 Herod was delighted at the opportunity to see **J**,
23: 9 He asked **J** question after question, but **J** refused to answer.
23:11 and his soldiers began mocking and ridiculing **J**.
23:20 argued with them, because he wanted to release **J**.
23:24 So Pilate sentenced **J** to die as they demanded.
23:25 But he delivered **J** over to them to do as they
23:26 As they led **J** away, Simon of Cyrene, who was forced to follow **J** and carry his cross.
23:28 But **J** turned and said to them, "Daughters of
23:33 **J** on the center cross, and the two criminals on
23:34 **J** said, "Father, forgive these people, because they
23:42 Then he said, "**J**, remember me when you come
23:43 And **J** replied, "I assure you, today you will be
23:46 Then **J** shouted, "Father, I entrust my spirit into
24: 3 but they couldn't find the body of the Lord **J**.
24:15 **J** himself came along and joined them and began
24:19 "What things?" **J** asked. "The things that happened to **J**, the man from
24:23 and they had seen angels who told them **J** is alive!
24:25 Then **J** said to them, "You are such foolish
24:27 Then **J** quoted passages from the writings of
24:28 the end of their journey. **J** would have gone on,
24:33 and the other followers of **J** were gathered.
24:35 **J** had appeared to them as they were walking along
24:36 **J** himself was suddenly standing there among
24:50 Then **J** led them to Bethany, and lifting his hands
Jn 1:17 and faithfulness came through **J** Christ.
1:29 The next day John saw **J** coming toward him
1:34 I saw this happen to **J**, so I testify that he is the
1:36 As **J** walked by, John looked at him and
1:37 Then John's two disciples turned and followed **J**.
1:38 **J** looked around and saw them following.
1:40 who had heard what John said and then followed **J**.
1:42 Then Andrew brought Simon to meet **J**.
1:42 **J** said, "You are Simon, the son of John—
1:43 The next day **J** decided to go to Galilee. He found
1:45 His name is **J**, the son of Joseph from Nazareth."
1:47 As they approached, **J** said, "Here comes an
1:48 And **J** replied, "I could see you under the fig tree
1:50 **J** asked him, "Do you believe all this just
2: 2 **J** and his disciples were also invited to the
2: 4 "How does that concern you and me?" **J** asked.
2: 7 **J** told the servants, "Fill the jars with water."
2:13 Passover celebration, and **J** went to Jerusalem.
2:15 **J** made a whip from some ropes and chased them
2:19 "All right," **J** replied. "Destroy this temple,
2:21 But by "this temple," **J** meant his body.
2:22 And they believed both **J** and the Scriptures.
2:24 But **J** didn't trust them, because he knew what
3: 2 came to speak with **J**. "Teacher," he said, "we all
3: 3 **J** replied, "I assure you, unless you are born again,
3: 5 **J** replied, "The truth is, no one can enter the
3:10 **J** replied, "You are a respected Jewish teacher,
3:22 Afterward **J** and his disciples left Jerusalem,
4: 1 **J** learned that the Pharisees had heard, "**J** is baptizing and making more disciples than
4: 2 (though **J** himself didn't baptize them—
4: 6 and **J**, tired from the long walk, sat wearily beside
4: 7 and **J** said to her, "Please give me a drink."
4: 9 She said to **J**, "You are a Jew, and I am a
4:10 **J** replied, "If you only knew the gift God has for
4:13 **J** replied, "People soon become thirsty again after
4:16 "Go and get your husband," **J** told her.
4:17 the woman replied. **J** said, "You're right!
4:21 **J** replied, "Believe me, the time is coming when it
4:26 Then **J** told her, "I am the Messiah!"
4:31 Meanwhile, the disciples were urging **J** to eat.
4:34 Then **J** explained: "My nourishment comes from
4:39 Many Samaritans from the village believed in **J**
4:43 end of the two days' stay, **J** went on into Galilee.
4:47 When he heard that **J** had come from Judea
4:47 He found **J** and begged him to come to Capernaum
4:48 **J** asked, "Must I do miraculous signs and wonders
4:50 Then **J** told him, "Go back home. Your son will
4:53 Then the father realized it was the same time that **J**
4:53 the officer and his entire household believed in **J**.
5: 1 Afterward **J** returned to Jerusalem for one of the
5: 6 When **J** saw him and knew how long he had been
5: 8 **J** told him, "Stand up, pick up your sleeping mat,
5:13 didn't know, for **J** had disappeared into the crowd.
5:14 But afterward **J** found him in the Temple and told
5:15 and told them it was **J** who had healed him.
5:16 So the Jewish leaders began harassing **J** for
5:17 But **J** replied, "My Father never stops working,
5:19 **J** replied, "I assure you, the Son can do nothing by
6: 1 After this, **J** crossed over the Sea of Galilee,
6: 3 Then **J** went up into the hills and sat down with his
6: 5 **J** soon saw a great crowd of people climbing the
6:10 "Tell everyone to sit down," **J** ordered. So all of
6:11 Then **J** took the loaves, gave thanks to God,
6:12 **J** told his disciples, "so that nothing is wasted."
6:15 **J** saw that they were ready to take him by force
6:17 But as darkness fell and **J** still hadn't come back,
6:19 or four miles out when suddenly they saw **J**
6:22 began gathering on the shore, waiting to see **J**.
6:24 When the crowd saw that **J** wasn't there, nor his
6:26 **J** replied, "The truth is, you want to be with me
6:29 **J** told them, "This is what God wants you to do:
6:32 **J** said, "I assure you, Moses didn't give them
6:35 **J** replied, "I am the bread of life. No one who
6:42 They said, "This is **J**, the son of Joseph. We know
6:43 But **J** replied, "Don't complain about what I said.
6:53 So **J** said again, "I assure you, unless you eat the
6:61 **J** knew within himself that his disciples were
6:64 (For **J** knew from the beginning who didn't
6:67 Then **J** turned to the Twelve and asked, "Are you
6:70 Then **J** said, "I chose the twelve of you, but one is
7: 1 After this, **J** stayed in Galilee, going from village
7: 6 **J** replied, "Now is not the right time for me to go.
7: 9 So **J** remained in Galilee.
7:10 **J** also went, though secretly, staying out of public
7:14 **J** went up to the Temple and began to teach.
7:16 So **J** told them, "I'm not teaching my own ideas,
7:21 **J** replied, "I worked on the Sabbath by healing a
7:28 While **J** was teaching in the Temple, he called out,
7:32 the leading priests sent Temple guards to arrest **J**.
7:33 But **J** told them, "I will be here a little longer.
7:37 **J** stood and shouted to the crowds, "If you are
7:39 because **J** had not yet entered into his glory.)
7:50 Nicodemus, the leader who had met with **J** earlier,
8: 1 **J** returned to the Mount of Olives,
8: 4 "Teacher," they said to **J**, "this woman was
8: 6 but **J** stooped down and wrote in the dust with his
8: 9 until only **J** was left in the middle of the crowd
8:10 Then **J** stood up again and said to her, "Where are
8:11 And **J** said, "Neither do I. Go and sin no more."
8:12 **J** said to the people, "I am the light of the world.
8:14 **J** told them, "These claims are valid even though I
8:19 **J** answered, "Since you don't know who I am,
8:20 **J** made these statements while he was teaching in
8:21 Later **J** said to them again, "I am going away.
8:25 **J** replied, "I am the one I have always claimed to
8:28 So **J** said, "When you have lifted up the Son of
8:31 **J** said to the people who believed in him, "You are
8:34 **J** replied, "I assure you that everyone who sins is a
8:39 "No," **J** replied, "for if you were children of
8:42 **J** told them, "If God were your Father, you would
8:49 "No," **J** said, "I have no demon in me. For I
8:54 **J** answered, "If I am merely boasting about
8:58 **J** answered, "The truth is, I existed before
8:59 But **J** hid himself from them and left the Temple.
9: 1 As **J** was walking along, he saw a man who had
9: 3 of his sins or his parents' sins," **J** answered.
9:11 "The man they call **J** made mud and smoothed it
9:14 as it happened, **J** had healed the man on a Sabbath.
9:16 the Pharisees said, "This man **J** is not from God,
9:22 who had announced that anyone saying **J** was the
9:24 telling the truth, because we know **J** is a sinner."
9:35 When **J** heard what had happened, he found the
9:37 "You have seen him," **J** said, "and he is speaking
9:38 the man said, "I believe!" And he worshiped **J**.
9:39 Then **J** told him, "I have come to judge the world.
9:41 you were blind, you wouldn't be guilty," **J** replied.
10: 6 Those who heard **J** use this illustration didn't
10:22 and **J** was in Jerusalem at the time of Hanukkah.
10:25 **J** replied, "I have already told you, and you don't
10:32 **J** said, "At my Father's direction I have done
10:34 **J** replied, "It is written in your own law that God
11: 3 So the two sisters sent a message to **J** telling him,
11: 4 But when **J** heard about it he said,
11: 5 Although **J** loved Martha, Mary, and Lazarus,
11: 9 **J** replied, "There are twelve hours of daylight
11:13 They thought **J** meant Lazarus was having a good night's rest, but **J** meant Lazarus had died.
11:16 fellow disciples, "Let's go, too—and die with **J**."
11:17 When **J** arrived at Bethany, he was told that
11:20 When Martha got word that **J** was coming,
11:21 Martha said to **J**, "Lord, if you had been here,
11:23 **J** told her, "Your brother will rise again."
11:25 **J** told her, "I am the resurrection and the life.
11:30 Now **J** had stayed outside the village, at the place
11:32 When Mary arrived and saw **J**, she fell down at his
11:33 When **J** saw her weeping and saw the other people
11:35 Then **J** wept.
11:38 And again **J** was deeply troubled. Then they came
11:39 "Roll the stone aside," **J** told them. But Martha,
11:40 **J** responded, "Didn't I tell you that you will see
11:41 Then **J** looked up to heaven and said, "Father,
11:43 Then **J** shouted, "Lazarus, come out!"
11:44 **J** told them, "Unwrap him and let him go!"
11:45 Mary believed in **J** when they saw this happen.
11:46 to the Pharisees and told them what **J** had done.
11:51 This prophecy that **J** should die for the entire
11:54 **J** stopped his public ministry among the people
11:56 They wanted to see **J**, and as they talked in the
11:57 that anyone seeing **J** must report him immediately
12: 1 **J** arrived in Bethany, the home of Lazarus—
12: 7 **J** replied, "Leave her alone. She did it in
12: 9 to see Lazarus, the man **J** had raised from the dead.
12:11 of the people had deserted them and believed in **J**.
12:12 the news that **J** was on the way to Jerusalem swept
12:14 **J** found a young donkey and sat on it,
12:16 But after **J** entered into his glory, they remembered
12:17 Those in the crowd who had seen **J** call Lazarus
12:21 in Galilee. They said, "Sir, we want to meet **J**."
12:22 Andrew about it, and they went together to ask **J**.
12:23 **J** replied, "The time has come for the Son of Man
12:30 Then **J** told them, "The voice was for your benefit,
12:35 **J** replied, "My light will shine out for you just a
12:36 **J** went away and was hidden from them.
12:41 Isaiah was referring to **J** when he made this
12:44 **J** shouted to the crowds, "If you trust me, you are
13: 1 **J** knew that his hour had come to leave this world
13: 2 of Simon Iscariot, to carry out his plan to betray **J**.
13: 3 **J** knew that the Father had given him authority
13: 7 **J** replied, "You don't understand now why I am
13: 8 **J** replied, "But if I don't wash you, you won't
13:10 **J** replied, "A person who has bathed all over does
13:11 For **J** knew who would betray him. That is what he
13:21 Now **J** was in great anguish of spirit, and he
13:23 One of Jesus' disciples, the one **J** loved, was sitting next to **J** at the table.
13:25 Leaning toward **J**, he asked, "Lord, who is it?"
13:26 **J** said, "It is the one to whom I give the bread
13:27 into him. Then **J** told him, "Hurry. Do it now."
13:28 None of the others at the table knew what **J** meant.
13:29 some thought **J** was telling him to go and pay for
13:31 **J** said, "The time has come for me, the Son of
13:36 And **J** replied, "You can't go with me now,
13:38 **J** answered, "Die for me? No, before the rooster
14: 6 **J** told him, "I am the way, the truth, and the life.
14: 9 **J** replied, "Philip, don't you even yet know who I
14:23 **J** replied, "All those who love me will do what I
16:19 **J** realized they wanted to ask him, so he said,
16:31 **J** asked, "Do you finally believe?
17: 1 When **J** had finished saying all these things,
17: 3 to know you, the only true God, and **J** Christ,
18: 1 **J** crossed the Kidron Valley with his disciples
18: 2 because **J** had gone there many times with his
18: 4 **J** fully realized all that was going to happen to
18: 5 "**J** of Nazareth," they replied. "I am he," **J** said.
18: 5 Judas was standing there with them when **J**
18: 7 And again they replied, "**J** of Nazareth."
18: 8 "I told you that I am he," **J** said. "And since I am
18:11 But **J** said to Peter, "Put your sword back into its
18:12 and the Temple guards arrested **J** and tied him up.
18:15 so he was allowed to enter the courtyard with **J**.
18:19 the high priest began asking **J** about his followers
18:20 **J** replied, "What I teach is widely known,
18:22 One of the Temple guards standing there struck **J**
18:23 **J** replied, "If I said anything wrong, you must give
18:24 Then Annas bound **J** and sent him to Caiaphas,
18:26 I see you out there in the olive grove with **J**?"
18:33 back inside and called for **J** to be brought to him.
18:34 **J** replied, "Is this your own question, or did others
18:36 Then **J** answered, "I am not an earthly king.
18:37 say that I am a king, and you are right," **J** said.
19: 1 Then Pilate had **J** flogged with a lead-tipped whip.
19: 5 Then **J** came out wearing the crown of thorns
19: 9 He took **J** back into the headquarters again
19: 9 "Where are you from?" But **J** gave no answer.
19:11 Then **J** said, "You would have no power over me
19:13 they said this, Pilate brought **J** out to them again.
19:16 Then Pilate gave **J** to them to be crucified. / So they took **J** and led him away.
19:17 **J** went to the place called Skull Hill (in Hebrew,
19:18 with him, one on either side, with **J** between them.
19:19 that read, "**J** of Nazareth, the King of the Jews."
19:20 The place where **J** was crucified was near the city;
19:23 When the soldiers had crucified **J**, they divided his
19:26 When **J** saw his mother standing there beside the
19:28 **J** knew that everything was now finished, and to
19:30 When **J** had tasted it, he said, "It is finished!"
19:32 and broke the legs of the two men crucified with **J**.
19:33 But when they came to **J**, they saw that he was
19:38 who had been a secret disciple of **J** (because he
19:39 the man who had come to **J** at night, also came,
19:42 since the tomb was close at hand, they laid **J** there.
20: 2 and the other disciple, the one whom **J** loved.
20:12 and foot of the place where the body of **J** had been
20:14 behind her. It was **J**, but she didn't recognize him.
20:15 "Why are you crying?" **J** asked her. "Who are
20:16 "Mary!" **J** said. She turned toward him
20:17 "Don't cling to me," **J** said, "for I haven't yet
20:19 Suddenly, **J** was standing there among them!
20:24 the Twin), was not with the others when **J** came.
20:26 as before, **J** was standing among them.
20:29 Then **J** told him, "You believe because you have
20:31 so that you may believe that **J** is the Messiah,
21: 1 Later **J** appeared again to the disciples beside the
21: 4 At dawn the disciples saw **J** standing on the beach,
21: 7 Then the disciple whom **J** loved said to Peter,
21:10 some of the fish you've just caught," **J** said.
21:12 "Now come and have some breakfast!" **J** said.
21:13 Then **J** served them the bread and the fish.
21:14 This was the third time **J** had appeared to his
21:15 After breakfast **J** said to Simon Peter, "Simon son
21:15 I love you." "Then feed my lambs," **J** told him.
21:16 **J** repeated the question: "Simon son of John,
21:16 love you." "Then take care of my sheep," **J** said.
21:17 Peter was grieved that **J** asked the question a third
21:17 know I love you." **J** said, "Then feed my sheep.
21:19 **J** said this to let him know what kind of death he
21:19 die to glorify God. Then **J** told him, "Follow me."
21:20 and saw the disciple **J** loved following them—
21:20 the one who had leaned over to **J** during supper
21:21 Peter asked **J**, "What about him, Lord?"
21:22 **J** replied, "If I want him to remain alive until I
21:23 But that isn't what **J** said at all. He only said,
21:25 And I suppose that if all the other things **J** did were
Ac 1: 1 In my first book I told you about everything **J**
1: 6 When the apostles were with **J**, they kept asking
1:11 **J** has been taken away from you into heaven.
1:14 along with Mary the mother of **J**, several other women, and the brothers of **J**.
1:16 who guided the Temple police to arrest **J**.
1:21 with us all the time that we were with the Lord **J**—
2:22 God publicly endorsed **J** of Nazareth by doing
2:32 "This prophecy was speaking of **J**, whom God
2:36 made this **J** whom you crucified to be both Lord
2:38 and be baptized in the name of **J** Christ for the
3: 6 In the name of **J** Christ of Nazareth, get up
3:13 has brought glory to his servant **J** by doing this.
3:13 This is the same **J** whom you handed over
3:16 "The name of **J** has healed this man—and you
3:17 I realize that what you did to **J** was done in
3:20 and he will send **J** your Messiah to you again.
4: 2 and John were claiming, on the authority of **J**,
4:10 in the name and power of **J** Christ from Nazareth,

4:11 For **J** is the one referred to in the Scriptures,
4:13 also recognized them as men who had been with **J**.
4:18 told them never again to speak or teach about **J**.
4:27 and the people of Israel were all united against **J**,
4:30 be done through the name of your holy servant **J**."
4:33 powerful witness to the resurrection of the Lord **J**,
5:28 filled all Jerusalem with your teaching about **J**,
5:30 The God of our ancestors raised **J** from the dead
5:40 them never again to speak in the name of **J**,
5:41 them worthy to suffer dishonor for the name of **J**.
5:42 "The Messiah you are looking for is **J**."
6:14 We have heard him say that this **J** of Nazareth will
7:55 and he saw **J** standing in the place of honor at
7:59 Stephen prayed, "Lord **J**, receive my spirit."
8:4 everywhere preaching the Good News about **J**.
8:12 the Kingdom of God and the name of **J** Christ.
8:16 had only been baptized in the name of the Lord **J**.
8:35 many others to tell him the Good News about **J**.
9:5 And the voice replied, "I am **J**, the one you are
9:17 hands on him and said, "Brother Saul, the Lord **J**,
9:20 And immediately he began preaching about **J** in
9:22 refute his proofs that **J** was indeed the Messiah.
9:27 and how he boldly preached in the name of **J** in
9:34 Peter said to him, "Aeneas, **J** Christ heals you!
10:36 that there is peace with God through **J** Christ,
10:38 And no doubt you know that God anointed **J** of
10:38 Then **J** went around doing good and healing all
10:42 and to testify that **J** is ordained of God to be the
10:48 for them to be baptized in the name of **J** Christ.
11:17 he gave us when we believed in the Lord **J** Christ,
11:20 began preaching to Gentiles about the Lord **J**.
13:23 **J**, who is God's promised Savior of Israel!
13:27 fulfilled prophecy by condemning **J** to death.
13:33 in that God raised **J**. This is what the second psalm
is talking about when it says concerning **J**,
13:38 In this man **J** there is forgiveness for your sins.
15:11 the same way, by the special favor of the Lord **J**."
15:26 risked their lives for the sake of our Lord **J** Christ.
16:7 but again the Spirit of **J** did not let them go.
16:18 "I command you in the name of **J** Christ to come
16:31 "Believe on the Lord **J** and you will be saved,
17:3 "This **J** I'm telling you about is the Messiah."
17:7 for they profess allegiance to another king, **J**."
17:18 When he told them about **J** and his resurrection,
18:5 "The Messiah you are looking for is **J**."
18:25 others with great enthusiasm and accuracy about **J**.
18:28 to them, "The Messiah you are looking for is **J**."
19:4 John himself told the people to believe in **J**,
19:5 they were baptized in the name of the Lord **J**.
19:13 out evil spirits tried to use the name of the Lord **J**.
19:13 "I command you by **J**, whom Paul preaches,
19:15 the spirit replied, "I know **J**, and I know Paul.
19:17 and the name of the Lord **J** was greatly honored.
20:21 and turning to God, and of faith in our Lord **J**.
20:24 it for doing the work assigned me by the Lord **J**—
20:35 You should remember the words of the Lord **J**:
21:13 but also to die for the sake of the Lord **J**."
22:8 And he replied, 'I am **J** of Nazareth, the one you
22:18 I saw a vision of **J** saying to me, 'Hurry!
24:24 listened as he told them about faith in Christ **J**.
25:19 and about someone called **J** who died,
26:9 I could to oppose the followers of **J** of Nazareth.
26:15 "And the Lord replied, 'I am **J**, the one you are
28:23 and taught them about **J** from the Scriptures—
28:31 all boldness and teaching about the Lord **J** Christ.
Ro 1:1 This letter is from Paul, **J** Christ's slave, chosen by
1:3 Good News about his Son, **J**, who came as a man,
1:4 And **J** Christ our Lord was shown to be the Son of
1:6 those who have been called to belong to **J** Christ,
1:7 yours from God our Father and the Lord **J** Christ.
1:8 How I thank God through **J** Christ for each one of
2:16 by **J** Christ, will judge everyone's secret life.
3:22 when we trust in **J** Christ to take away our sins.
3:24 He has done this through Christ **J**, who has freed
3:25 For God sent **J** to take the punishment for our sins
3:25 with God when we believe that **J** shed his blood,
3:26 to be right in his sight because they believe in **J**.
4:24 who brought **J** our Lord back from the dead.
5:1 because of what **J** Christ our Lord has done for us.
5:11 because of what our Lord **J** Christ has done for us
5:15 But this other man, **J** Christ, brought forgiveness
5:17 over sin and death through this one man, **J** Christ.
5:21 and resulting in eternal life through **J** Christ our
6:3 and were baptized to become one with Christ **J**,
6:11 able to live for the glory of God through Christ **J**.
6:23 of God is eternal life through Christ **J** our Lord.
7:25 Thank God! The answer is in **J** Christ our Lord.
8:1 no condemnation for those who belong to Christ **J**.
8:2 Christ **J** from the power of sin that leads to death.
8:11 of God, who raised **J** from the dead, lives in you.
8:34 Will Christ **J**? No, for he is the one who died for us
8:39 love of God that is revealed in Christ **J** our Lord.
10:9 For if you confess with your mouth that **J** is Lord
13:14 But let the Lord **J** Christ take control of you,
14:14 sure on the authority of the Lord **J** that no food,
15:5 each with the attitude of Christ **J** toward the other.
15:6 and glory to God, the Father of our Lord **J** Christ.
15:16 a special messenger from Christ **J** to you Gentiles.
15:17 **J** has done through me in my service to God.
15:30 I urge you in the name of our Lord **J** Christ to join
16:3 have been co-workers in my ministry for Christ **J**.
16:20 May the grace of our Lord **J** Christ be with you.
16:25 It is the message about **J** Christ and his plan for
16:27 is wise, be the glory forever through **J** Christ.
1Co 1:1 by the will of God to be an apostle of Christ **J**,
1:2 He made you holy by means of Christ **J**, just as he
1:2 whoever calls upon the name of **J** Christ, our Lord
1:3 and the Lord **J** Christ give you his grace and peace.
1:4 he has given you, now that you belong to Christ **J**.
1:7 eagerly wait for the return of our Lord **J** Christ.
1:8 on the great day when our Lord **J** Christ returns.
1:9 friendship with his Son, **J** Christ our Lord.
1:10 I appeal to you by the authority of the Lord **J**
1:30 alone made it possible for you to be in Christ **J**.
2:2 For I decided to concentrate only on **J** Christ
3:11 foundation than the one we already have—**J** Christ
4:15 For I became your father in Christ **J** when I
4:17 He will remind you of what I teach about Christ **J**
5:4 in the name of the Lord **J**. You are to call a
5:4 and the power of the Lord **J** will be with you as
6:11 right with God because of what the Lord **J** Christ
8:6 And there is only one Lord, **J** Christ,
9:1 Haven't I seen **J** our Lord with my own eyes?
11:23 he was betrayed, the Lord **J** took a loaf of bread,
12:3 No one speaking by the Spirit of God can curse **J**,
12:3 and no one is able to say, "**J** is Lord," except by
15:31 This is as certain as my pride in what the Lord **J**
15:57 over sin and death through **J** Christ our Lord!
16:23 May the grace of the Lord **J** be with you.
16:24 My love to all of you in Christ **J**.
2Co 1:1 appointed by God to be an apostle of Christ **J**,
1:2 and the Lord **J** Christ give you his grace and peace.
1:3 praise to the God and Father of our Lord **J** Christ.
1:14 Then on the day when our Lord **J** comes back
1:19 because **J** Christ, the Son of God, never wavers
4:5 about ourselves; we preach Christ **J**, the Lord.
4:5 your servants because of what **J** has done for us.
4:6 the glory of God that is seen in the face of **J** Christ.
4:10 bodies of ours constantly share in the death of **J**
4:10 so that the life of **J** may also be seen in our bodies.
4:11 under constant danger of death because we serve **J**,
4:11 so that the life of **J** will be obvious in our dying
4:14 We know that the same God who raised our Lord **J**
will also raise us with **J**
8:9 full of love and kindness our Lord **J** Christ was.
11:4 even if they preach about a different **J** than the one
11:31 God, the Father of our Lord **J**, who is to be praised
13:5 If you cannot tell that **J** Christ is among you,
13:13 May the grace of our Lord **J** Christ, the love of
Gal 1:1 My call is from **J** Christ himself and from God the
Father, who raised **J** from the dead.
1:3 from God our Father and from the Lord **J** Christ.
1:12 For my message came by a direct revelation from **J**
1:16 so that I could proclaim the Good News about **J** to
2:4 came to spy on us and see our freedom in Christ **J**.
2:16 what the law commands, but by faith in **J** Christ.
2:16 So we have believed in Christ **J**, that we might be
3:1 For you used to see the meaning of **J** Christ's
3:14 Through the work of Christ **J**, God has blessed the
3:22 to receive God's promise is to believe in **J** Christ.
3:26 are all children of God through faith in Christ **J**.
3:28 For you are all Christians—you are one in Christ **J**.
4:14 I were an angel from God or even Christ **J** himself.
5:6 For when we place our faith in Christ **J**, it makes
5:24 Those who belong to Christ **J** have nailed the
6:14 anything except the cross of our Lord **J** Christ.
6:17 bear on my body the scars that show I belong to **J**.
6:18 may the grace of our Lord **J** Christ be with you all.
Eph 1:1 chosen by God to be an apostle of Christ **J**.
1:1 in Ephesus, who are faithful followers of Christ **J**.
1:2 to you from God our Father and **J** Christ our Lord.
1:3 we praise God, the Father of our Lord **J** Christ,
1:5 family by bringing us to himself through **J** Christ.
1:15 since I first heard of your strong faith in the Lord **J**
1:17 the glorious Father of our Lord **J** Christ,
2:6 all because we are one with Christ **J**.
2:7 as shown in all he has done for us through Christ **J**.
2:10 He has created us anew in Christ **J**, so that we can
2:13 But now you belong to Christ **J**. Though you once
2:20 And the cornerstone is Christ **J** himself.
3:1 am a prisoner of Christ **J** because of my preaching
3:6 together the promise of blessings through Christ **J**.
3:11 and it has now been carried out through Christ **J**
3:21 and in Christ **J** forever and ever through endless
4:21 about him and have learned the truth that is in **J**,
5:20 to God the Father in the name of our Lord **J** Christ.
6:23 from God the Father and the Lord **J** Christ.
6:24 May God's grace be upon all who love our Lord **J**
Php 1:1 letter is from Paul and Timothy, slaves of Christ **J**.
1:1 who believe in Christ **J**, and to the elders
1:2 and the Lord **J** Christ give you grace and peace.
1:6 on that day when Christ **J** comes back again.
1:8 for you with the tender compassion of Christ **J**.
1:11 things that are produced in your life by **J** Christ—
1:19 pray for me and as the Spirit of **J** Christ helps me,
1:26 to boast about what Christ **J** has done for me.
2:5 Your attitude should be the same that Christ **J** had.
2:10 so that at the name of **J** every knee will bow,
2:11 and every tongue will confess that **J** Christ is Lord,
2:19 If the Lord **J** is willing, I hope to send Timothy to
2:21 and not for what matters to **J** Christ.
3:3 we boast about what Christ **J** has done for us.
3:8 the priceless gain of knowing Christ **J** my Lord.
3:12 when I will finally be all that Christ **J** saved me for
3:14 through Christ **J**, is calling us up to heaven.
3:20 citizens of heaven, where the Lord **J** Christ lives.
4:7 your hearts and minds as you live in Christ **J**.
4:19 which have been given to us in Christ **J**.
4:23 May the grace of the Lord **J** Christ be with your
Col 1:1 chosen by God to be an apostle of Christ **J**,
1:3 and we give thanks to God the Father of our Lord **J**
1:4 for we have heard that you trust in Christ **J**
2:6 just as you accepted Christ **J** as your Lord,
3:17 or say, let it be as a representative of the Lord **J**,
4:11 **J** (the one we call Justus) also sends his greetings.
4:12 Epaphras, from your city, a servant of Christ **J**,
1Th 1:1 belong to God the Father and the Lord **J** Christ.
1:3 anticipation of the return of our Lord **J** Christ.
1:10 from heaven—**J**, whom God raised from the dead.
2:14 because of their belief in Christ **J**, suffered from
2:15 own prophets, and some even killed the Lord **J**.
2:19 before our Lord **J** when he comes back again.
3:11 and our Lord **J** make it possible for us to come to
3:13 Lord **J** comes with all those who belong to him.
4:1 we urge you in the name of the Lord **J** to live in a
4:2 what we taught you in the name of the Lord **J**.
4:14 For since we believe that **J** died and was raised to
life again, we also believe that when **J** comes,
4:14 God will bring back with **J** all the Christians who
5:9 For God decided to save us through our Lord **J**
5:18 this is God's will for you who belong to Christ **J**.
5:23 until that day when our Lord **J** Christ comes again.
5:28 And may the grace of our Lord **J** Christ be with all
2Th 1:1 belong to God our Father and the Lord **J** Christ.
1:2 and the Lord **J** Christ give you grace and peace.
1:7 and also for us when the Lord **J** appears from
1:8 who refuse to obey the Good News of our Lord **J**.
1:12 everyone will give honor to the name of our Lord **J**
1:12 undeserved favor of our God and Lord, **J** Christ.
2:1 you about the coming again of our Lord **J** Christ
2:8 whom the Lord **J** will consume with the breath of
2:14 now you can share in the glory of our Lord **J**
2:16 May our Lord **J** Christ and God our Father,
3:6 command with the authority of our Lord **J** Christ:
3:12 In the name of the Lord **J** Christ we appeal to such
3:18 May the grace of our Lord **J** Christ be with you all.
1Ti 1:1 This letter is from Paul, an apostle of Christ **J**,
1:1 of God our Savior and by Christ **J** our hope.
1:2 our Father and Christ **J** our Lord give you grace,
1:12 How thankful I am to Christ **J** our Lord for
1:14 me completely with faith and the love of Christ **J**.
1:15 Christ **J** came into the world to save sinners—
1:16 so that Christ **J** could use me as a prime example
2:5 reconcile God and people. He is the man Christ **J**.
3:13 have increased confidence in their faith in Christ **J**.
4:6 be doing your duty as a worthy servant of Christ **J**,
5:21 command you in the presence of God and Christ **J**
6:3 wholesome teachings of the Lord **J** Christ,
6:13 who gives life to all, and before Christ **J**,
6:14 with you from now until our Lord **J** Christ returns.
2Ti 1:1 is from Paul, an apostle of Christ **J** by God's will,
1:1 the life he has promised through faith in Christ **J**.
1:2 our Father and Christ **J** our Lord give you grace,
1:9 show his love and kindness to us through Christ **J**.
1:10 all of this plain to us by the coming of Christ **J**,
1:13 live in the faith and love that you have in Christ **J**.
2:1 with the special favor God gives you in Christ **J**.
2:3 along with me, as a good soldier of Christ **J**.
2:8 Never forget that **J** Christ was a man born into
2:10 and eternal glory in Christ **J** to those God has
3:12 live a godly life in Christ **J** will suffer persecution.
3:15 the salvation that comes by trusting in Christ **J**.
4:1 urge you before God and before Christ **J**—
Tit 1:1 a slave of God and an apostle of **J** Christ.
1:4 and Christ **J** our Savior give you grace and peace.
2:13 the glory of our great God and Savior, **J** Christ,
3:6 upon us because of what **J** Christ our Savior did.
Phm 1:1 for preaching the Good News about Christ **J**,
1:3 and the Lord **J** Christ give you grace and peace.
1:5 because I keep hearing of your trust in the Lord **J**
1:9 an old man, now in prison for the sake of Christ **J**.
1:23 Epaphras, my fellow prisoner in Christ **J**,
1:25 The grace of the Lord **J** Christ be with your spirit.
Heb 1:5 For God never said to any angel what he said to **J**:
2:3 that was announced by the Lord **J** himself?
2:9 What we do see is **J**, who "for a little while was
2:9 **J** tasted death for everyone in all the world.
2:10 Through the suffering of **J**, God made him a
2:11 So now **J** and the ones he makes holy have the
2:11 That is why **J** is not ashamed to call them his
2:14 **J** also became flesh and blood by being born in
2:16 We all know that **J** came to help the descendants
2:17 it was necessary for **J** to be in every respect like
3:1 think about this **J** whom we declare to be God's
3:3 But **J** deserves far more glory than Moses, just as a
4:14 Priest who has gone to heaven, **J** the Son of God.
5:7 While **J** was here on earth, he offered prayers
5:8 So even though **J** was God's Son, he learned
6:20 **J** has already gone in there for us. He has become
7:21 Only to **J** did he say, / "The Lord has taken an
7:22 it is **J** who guarantees the effectiveness of this
7:24 But **J** remains a priest forever; his priesthood will
7:27 But **J** did this once for all when he sacrificed
10:10 sacrifice of the body of **J** Christ once for all time.
10:19 Most Holy Place because of the blood of **J**.
12:2 We do this by keeping our eyes on **J**, on whom our
12:24 You have come to **J**, the one who mediates the
13:8 **J** Christ is the same yesterday, today, and forever.
13:12 So also **J** suffered and died outside the city gates in
13:20[-21] who brought again from the dead our Lord **J**,
13:20[-21] in you, through the power of **J** Christ,
13:20[-21] **J** is the great Shepherd of the sheep by an
Jas 1:1 a slave of God and of the Lord **J** Christ.
2:1 **J** Christ if you favor some people more than
2:7 Aren't they the ones who slander **J** Christ,
1Pe 1:1 This letter is from Peter, an apostle of **J** Christ.
1:2 you have obeyed **J** Christ and are cleansed by his
1:3 honor to the God and Father of our Lord **J** Christ,
1:3 because **J** Christ rose again from the dead.
1:7 and honor on the day when **J** Christ is revealed to
1:13 that will come to you at the return of **J** Christ.

2: 5 sacrifices that please him because of J Christ.
3:21 which now saves you by the power of J Christ's
4:11 will be given glory in everything through J Christ.
5:10 you to his eternal glory by means of J Christ.
2Pe 1: 1 from Simon Peter, a slave and apostle of J Christ.
1: 1 faith given to us by J Christ, our God and Savior,
1: 2 and wonderful peace as you come to know J,
1: 3 As we know J better, his divine power gives us
1: 8 and useful in your knowledge of our Lord J Christ.
1:11 eternal Kingdom of our Lord and Savior J Christ.
1:14 But the Lord J Christ has shown me that my days
1:16 we told you about the power of our Lord J Christ
2:20 and Savior J Christ and then get tangled up with
3: 4 "J promised to come back, did he? Then where is
3:18 and knowledge of our Lord and Savior J Christ.
1Jn 1: 1 our own hands. He is J Christ, the Word of life.
1: 3 is with the Father and with his Son, J Christ.
1: 7 and the blood of J, his Son, cleanses us from every
2: 1 He is J Christ, the one who pleases God
2:12 because your sins have been forgiven because of J.
2:22 The one who says that J is not the Christ.
3: 5 And you know that J came to take away our sins,
3:23 J Christ, and love one another, just as he
4: 2 If a prophet acknowledges that J Christ became a
4: 3 If a prophet does not acknowledge J, that person is
4:15 All who proclaim that J is the Son of God have
5: 1 Everyone who believes that J is the Christ is a
5: 5 are the ones who believe that J is the Son of God.
5: 6 And J Christ was revealed as God's Son by his
5:20 we are in God because we are in his Son, J Christ.
2Jn 1: 3 from God our Father and from J Christ his Son,
1: 7 They do not believe that J Christ came to earth in a
Jude 1: 1 a slave of J Christ and a brother of James.
1: 1 the love of God the Father and the care of J Christ.
1: 4 turned against our only Master and Lord, J Christ.
1:17 must remember what the apostles of our Lord J
1:21 Lord J Christ in his mercy is going to give you.
1:25 alone is God our Savior, through J Christ our Lord.
Rev 1: 1 This is a revelation from J Christ, which God gave
1: 2 the word of God and the testimony of J Christ—
1: 5 and from J Christ, who is the faithful witness to
1: 9 In J we are partners in suffering and in the
1: 9 preaching the word of God and speaking about J.
6:11 full number of the servants of J had been martyred.
12:17 and confess that they belong to J.
14:12 the end, obeying his commands and trusting in J."
17: 6 of God's holy people who were witnesses for J.
19:10 and other believers who testify of their faith in J.
19:10 of prophecy is to give a clear witness for J."
20: 4 had been beheaded for their testimony about J,
22:16 "I, J, have sent my angel to give you this message
22:20 "Yes, I am coming soon!" Amen! Come, Lord J!
22:21 The grace of the Lord J be with you all.

JESUS' (69) [JESUS]

Mt 16: 1 and Sadducees came to test J claims by asking him
17: 2 J appearance changed so that his face shone like
19:10 J disciples then said to him, "Then it is better not
26:67 Then they spit in J face and hit him with their fists.
26:75 Suddenly, J words flashed through Peter's mind:
27:32 from Cyrene, and they forced him to carry J cross.
27:37 A signboard was fastened to the cross above J
27:53 after J resurrection. They left the cemetery,
27:57 a rich man from Arimathea who was one of J
27:58 went to Pilate and asked for J body. And Pilate
28:13 'J disciples came during the night while we were
Mk 3: 2 it was the Sabbath, J enemies watched him closely.
3:31 J mother and brothers arrived at the house where
7: 2 They noticed that some of J disciples failed to
9: 2 As the men watched, J appearance changed,
11:18 the people were so enthusiastic about J teaching.
14:12 J disciples asked him, "Where do you want us to
14:72 Suddenly, J words flashed through Peter's mind:
15:21 just then, and they forced him to carry J cross.
15:26 A signboard was fastened to the cross above J
15:43 his courage and went to Pilate to ask for J body.
15:46 and taking J body down from the cross,
15:47 and Mary the mother of Joseph saw where J body
16: 1 and purchased burial spices to put on J body.
Lk 2:39 When J parents had fulfilled all the requirements
2:41 Every year J parents went to Jerusalem for the
5:15 Yet despite J instructions, the report of his power
5:30 of religious law complained bitterly to J disciples,
5:33 The religious leaders complained that J disciples
8:19 Once when J mother and brothers came to see him,
8:35 been possessed by demons sitting quietly at J feet,
8:41 the local synagogue, came and fell down at J feet,
9: 7 When reports of J miracles reached Herod
9:32 Now they woke up and saw J glory and the two
17:16 He fell face down on the ground at J feet,
22: 2 of religious law were actively plotting J murder.
22:56 she said, "This man was one of J followers!"
22:59 "This must be one of J disciples because he is a
23:23 the crowd shouted louder and louder for J death,
23:49 But J friends, including the women who had
23:52 He went to Pilate and asked for J body.
24:13 That same day two of J followers were walking to
24:24 and sure enough, J body was gone, just as the
Jn 2: 1 The next day J mother was a guest at a wedding
2: 3 so J mother spoke to him about the problem.
2:11 This miraculous sign at Cana in Galilee was J first
4:50 And the man believed J word and started home.
4:54 This was J second miraculous sign in Galilee after
7: 3 and J brothers urged him to go to Judea for the
11:52 It was a prediction that J death would be not for
11:53 time on the Jewish leaders began to plot J death.
12: 2 A dinner was prepared in J honor. Martha served,
12: 3 and she anointed J feet with it and wiped his feet
12: 9 When all the people heard of J arrival,
13:23 One of J disciples, the one Jesus loved, was sitting
18:17 asked Peter, "Aren't you one of J disciples?"
18:28 J trial before Caiaphas ended in the early hours of
18:32 This fulfilled J prediction about the way he would
19:25 Standing near the cross were J mother, and his
19:38 asked Pilate for permission to take J body down.
19:40 Together they wrapped J body in a long linen cloth
20: 7 while the cloth that had covered J head was folded
20:30 J disciples saw him do many other miraculous
Ac 1:22 Whoever is chosen will join us as a witness of J
2: 1 day of Pentecost, seven weeks after J resurrection,
3:16 Faith in J name has caused this healing before your
4:17 We'll warn them not to speak to anyone in J name
9:21 "Isn't this the same man who persecuted J
Heb 13:15 With J help, let us continually offer our sacrifice

JETHER (10)

Jdg 8:20 Turning to J, his oldest son, he said, "Kill them!"
8:20 But J did not draw his sword, for he was only a
2Sa 17:25 His father was J, an Ishmaelite. His mother,
1Ki 2: 5 Abner son of Ner and Amasa son of J.
2:32 of the army of Israel, and Amasa son of J,
1Ch 2:17 Abigail married a man named J, an Ishmaelite,
2:32 Jada, had two sons named J and Jonathan. J died without children,
4:17 The sons of Ezrah were J, Mered, Epher,
7:38 The sons of J were Jephunneh, Pispah, and Ara.

JETHETH (2)

Ge 36:40 in the places named for them: Timna, Alvah, J,
1Ch 1:51 The clan leaders of Edom were Timna, Alvah, J,

JETHLAH [KJV] See ITHLAH

JETHRO (11) [REUEL]

Ex 3: 1 J, the priest of Midian, and he went deep into the
4:18 Moses went back home and talked it over with J,
4:18 are still alive." "Go with my blessing," J replied.
18: 1 Word soon reached J, the priest of Midian
18: 2 Zipporah, and his two sons to live with J,
18: 5 J now came to visit Moses, and he brought Moses'
18: 6 Moses was told, "J, your father-in-law, has come
18: 9 J was delighted when he heard about all that the
18:10 "Praise be to the LORD," J said, "for he has
18:12 Then J presented a burnt offering and gave
18:12 As J was doing this, Aaron and the leaders of

JETUR (2) [JETURITES]

Ge 25:15 Hadad, Tema, J, Naphish, and Kedemah.
1Ch 1:31 J, Naphish, and Kedemah. These were the sons of

JETURITES (1) [JETUR]

1Ch 5:19 the J, the Naphishites, and the Nodabites.

JEUEL (2)

1Ch 9: 6 the Zerahite clan, J returned with his relatives.
Ezr 8:13 Eliphelet, J, Shemaiah, and 60 other men.

JEUSH (9)

Ge 36: 5 Esau and Oholibamah had sons named J, Jalam,
36:14 of Zibeon. Their names were J, Jalam, and Korah.
36:18 Oholibamah became the leaders of the clans of J,
1Ch 1:35 of Esau were Eliphaz, Reuel, J, Jalam, and Korah.
7:10 The sons of Bilhan were J, Benjamin, Ehud,
8:39 Ulam (the oldest), J (the second), and Eliphelet
23:10 of Shimei were Jahath, Ziza, J, and Beriah.
23:11 J and Beriah were counted as a single family
2Ch 11:19 had three sons—J, Shemariah, and Zaham.

JEUZ (1)

1Ch 8:10 J, Sakia, and Mirmah. These sons all became the

JEW (33) [JEW'S, JEWISH, JEWS, JEWS', JUDAISM]

Est 2: 5 Now at the fortress of Susa there was a certain J
3: 4 since Mordecai had told them he was a J.
3: 6 Since he had learned that Mordecai was a J,
5:13 the J just sitting there at the palace gate."
6:10 and do just as you have said for Mordecai the J,
6:13 is a J, you will never succeed in your plans against
8: 7 Xerxes said to Queen Esther and Mordecai the J,
9:29 daughter of Abihail, along with Mordecai the J,
9:31 decreed by both Mordecai the J and Queen Esther.
10: 3 Mordecai the J became the prime minister,
Jn 3:25 At that time a certain J began an argument with
4: 9 She said to Jesus, "You are a J, and I am a
18:35 "Am I a J?" Pilate asked. "Your own people
Ac 18: 2 There he became acquainted with a J named
18:24 Meanwhile, a J named Apollos, an eloquent
19:34 But when the crowd realized he was a J,
21:39 Paul replied, "I am a J from Tarsus in Cilicia,
22: 3 "I am a J, born in Tarsus, a city in Cilicia, and I
Ro 2: 9 on sinning—for the J first and also for the Gentile.
2:10 do good—for the J first and also for the Gentile.
2:17 If you are a J, you are relying on God's law for
2:28 For you are not a true J just because you were born
2:29 a true J is one whose heart is right with God.
3: 1 Then what's the advantage of being a J? Is there
3: 2 Yes, being a J has many advantages. First of all,
9: 5 and Christ himself was a J as far as his human
9: 6 not everyone born into a Jewish family is truly a J!
10:12 J and Gentile are the same in this respect. They all
11: 1 Remember that I myself am a J, a descendant of
Gal 2:14 "Since you, a J by birth, have discarded the
3:28 There is no longer J or Gentile, slave or free,
Php 3: 5 So I am a real J if there ever was one!
Col 3:11 it doesn't matter if you are a J or a Gentile,

JEW'S (1) [JEW]

Zec 8:23 the world will clutch at the hem of one J robe.

JEWEL (2) [JEWELED, JEWELERS, JEWELRY, JEWELS]

Eze 16: 7 You grew up and became a beautiful j.
Zec 3: 9 Now look at the j I have set before Jeshua, a single

JEWELED (3) [JEWEL]

Ps 73: 6 They wear pride like a j necklace, / and their
SS 4: 4 of David, j with the shields of a thousand heroes.
Eze 21:26 Take off your j crown, says the Sovereign LORD.

JEWELERS (1) [JEWEL]

Ex 35:35 The LORD has given them special skills as j,

JEWELRY (17) [JEWEL]

Ge 24:53 Then he brought out silver and gold j and lovely
Ex 3:22 The Israelite women will ask for silver and gold j
33: 4 and refused to wear their j and ornaments.
33: 5 Remove your j and ornaments until I decide what
33: 6 left Mount Sinai, the Israelites wore no more j.
Nu 31:51 all kinds of j and crafted objects.
Est 2:13 or j she wanted to enhance her beauty.
Ps 45: 9 the queen, / wearing j of finest gold from Ophir!
Pr 25:12 by the one who heeds it as j made from finest gold.
Jer 2:32 Does a young woman forget her j? Does a bride
4:30 you dress up in your most beautiful clothing and j?
Eze 7:20 They were proud of their gold j and used it to
16:11 I gave you lovely j, bracelets, and beautiful
27:16 embroidery, fine linen, and j of coral and rubies.
Jas 2: 2 meeting dressed in fancy clothes and expensive j,
1Pe 3: 3 fancy hairstyles, expensive j, or beautiful clothes.
Rev 17: 4 and beautiful j made of gold and precious gems

JEWELS (27) [JEWEL]

1Ki 10: 2 with spices, huge quantities of gold, and precious j.
10:10 and great quantities of spices and precious j.
10:11 rich cargoes of almug wood and precious j.
1Ch 29: 2 other precious stones, costly j, and all kinds of fine
2Ch 3: 6 of the Temple were decorated with beautiful j
9: 1 with spices, huge quantities of gold, and precious j.
9: 9 and great quantities of spices and precious j.
9:10 rich cargoes of almug wood and precious j.
Job 28:17 It cannot be purchased with j mounted in fine gold.
SS 1:10 is your neck, accented with a long string of j.
5:12 doves beside brooks of water; they are set like j.
7: 1 Your rounded thighs are like j, the work of a
Isa 3:21 their rings, j,
49:18 "they will be like j or bridal ornaments for you to
54:11 and make the walls of your houses from precious j.
61:10 in his wedding suit or a bride with her j.
Jer 20: 5 the precious j and gold and silver of your kings—
La 4: 7 they were as clean as snow and as elegant as j.
Eze 16:17 You took the very j and gold and silver ornaments
16:39 They will strip you and take your beautiful j,
23:26 They will strip you of your beautiful clothes and j.
23:40 your eyelids, and put on your finest j for them.
27:22 of spices, j, and gold in exchange for your wares.
Hos 2:13 put on her earrings and j, and went out looking for
Zec 9:16 They will sparkle in his land like j in a crown.
1Co 3:12 may use gold, silver, j, wood, hay, or straw.
Rev 18:12 silver, j, pearls, fine linen, purple dye, silk,

JEWISH (126) [JEW]

Ezr 1: 4 Those who live in any place where J survivors are
2: 1 Here is the list of the J exiles of the provinces who
6:14 So the J leaders continued their work, and they
9: 1 But then the J leaders came to me and said,
Ne 5: 8 J relatives who have had to sell themselves to
5:17 even though I regularly fed 150 J officials at my
7: 6 "Here is the list of the J exiles of the provinces
Mt 27:18 (He knew very well that the J leaders had arrested
Mk 7: 2 the usual J ritual of hand washing before eating.
12:12 The J leaders wanted to arrest him for using this
Lk 1: 5 It all begins with a J priest, Zechariah, who lived
7: 3 he sent some respected J leaders to ask him to
10:30 "A J man was traveling on a trip from Jerusalem
10:31 "By chance a J priest came along; but when he
11:38 the ceremonial washing required by J custom.
23:50 He was a member of the J high council,
Jn 1:19 This was the testimony of John when the J leaders
2: 6 they were used for J ceremonial purposes and held
2:18 the J leaders demanded. "If you have this
3: 1 a J religious leader named Nicodemus, a Pharisee,
3:10 Jesus replied, "You are a respected J teacher,
5: 1 returned to Jerusalem for one of the J holy days.
5:10 So the J leaders objected. They said to the man
5:15 Then the man went to find the J leaders and told
5:16 So the J leaders began harassing Jesus for breaking
5:18 So the J leaders tried all the more to kill him.
7: 1 He wanted to stay out of Judea where the J leaders
7:11 The J leaders tried to find him at the festival
7:13 for they were afraid of getting in trouble with the J

7:15 The **J** leaders were surprised when they heard him.
7:35 The **J** leaders were puzzled by this statement.
8:22 The **J** leaders asked, "Is he planning to commit
9:18 The **J** leaders wouldn't believe he had been blind,
9:22 said this because they were afraid of the **J** leaders,
10:24 The **J** leaders surrounded him and asked,
10:31 Once again the **J** leaders picked up stones to kill
11: 8 "only a few days ago the **J** leaders in Judea were
11:53 So from that time on the **J** leaders began to plot
12:42 Many people, including some of the **J** leaders,
13:33 cannot come to me—just as I told the **J** leaders.
18:14 Caiaphas was the one who had told the other **J**
18:31 to execute someone," the **J** leaders replied.
18:36 have fought when I was arrested by the **J** leaders.
19: 7 The **J** leaders replied, "By our laws he ought to
19:12 but the **J** leaders told him, "If you release this
19:31 The **J** leaders didn't want the victims hanging
19:38 disciple of Jesus (because he feared the **J** leaders),
19:40 cloth with the spices, as is the **J** custom of burial.
20:19 because they were afraid of the **J** leaders.
Ac 6: 5 and Nicolas of Antioch (a Gentile convert to the **J**
6: 7 and many of the **J** priests were converted, too.
7: 8 the father of the twelve patriarchs of the **J** nation.
7:54 The **J** leaders were infuriated by Stephen's
9:23 After a while the **J** leaders decided to kill him.
10:14 my life eaten anything forbidden by our **J** laws."
10:28 "You know it is against the **J** laws for me to come
10:45 The **J** believers who came with Peter were amazed
11: 2 some of the **J** believers criticized him.
11: 8 'I have never eaten anything forbidden by our **J**
12: 3 When Herod saw how much this pleased the **J**
13: 5 they went to the **J** synagogues and preached the
13: 6 where they met a **J** sorcerer, a false prophet named
13:39 with God—something the **J** law could never do.
13:45 But when the **J** leaders saw the crowds, they were
13:50 Then the **J** leaders stirred up both the influential
15: 1 "Unless you keep the ancient **J** custom of
15:21 For these laws of Moses have been preached in **J**
16: 1 a young disciple whose mother was a **J** believer,
17: 1 to Thessalonica, where there was a **J** synagogue.
17: 5 But the **J** leaders were jealous, so they gathered
18:15 a question of words and names and your **J** laws,
18:18 Paul had shaved his head according to **J** custom,
21:11 'So shall the owner of this belt be bound by the **J**
21:21 Our **J** Christians here at Jerusalem have been told
21:21 their children or follow other **J** customs.
21:24 all false and that you yourself observe the **J** laws.
21:28 and tells everybody to disobey the **J** laws.
22: 3 At his feet I learned to follow our **J** laws
22: 5 For I received letters from them to our **J** brothers
22:30 leading priests into session with the **J** high council.
23:20 to bring Paul before the **J** high council tomorrow,
24: 1 arrived with some of the **J** leaders and the lawyer
24:10 that you have been a judge of **J** affairs for many
24:14 and I firmly believe the **J** law and everything
24:20 Ask these men here what wrongdoing the **J** high
24:24 Felix came with his wife, Drusilla, who was **J**.
24:27 because Felix wanted to gain favor with the **J**
25: 2 leading priests and other **J** leaders met with him
25: 7 the **J** leaders from Jerusalem gathered around
25: 8 "I have committed no crime against the **J** laws
25:15 and other **J** leaders pressed charges against him
26: 2 against all these accusations made by the **J** leaders,
26: 3 for I know you are an expert on **J** customs
26: 4 "As the **J** leaders are well aware, I was given a
thorough **J** training from my earliest
28:17 he called together the local **J** leaders.
28:19 But when the **J** leaders protested the decision,
Ro 2:25 The **J** ceremony of circumcision is worth
2:28 true Jew just because you were born of **J** parents
or because you have gone through the **J** ceremony
3: 1 Is there any value in the **J** ceremony of
4: 1 humanly speaking, the founder of our **J** nation.
4:16 to receive it, whether or not we follow **J** customs,
9: 3 for my people, my **J** brothers and sisters. I would
9: 6 for not everyone born into a **J** family is truly a
10: 1 and my prayer to God is that the **J** people might be
15:27 blessings of the Good News from the **J** Christians,
1Co 9:20 When I am with those who follow the **J** laws,
9:21 I am with the Gentiles who do not have the **J** law,
Gal 1:13 You know what I was like when I followed the **J**
2: 4 force us, like slaves, to follow their **J** regulations.
2:12 when some **J** friends of James came,
2:13 Then the other **J** Christians followed Peter's
2:14 have discarded the **J** laws and are living like a
2:14 these Gentiles obey the **J** laws you abandoned?
2:16 And yet we **J** Christians know that we become
Eph 2:15 By his death he ended the whole system of **J** law
Php 3: 5 having been born into a pure-blooded **J** family that
3: 5 who demand the strictest obedience to the **J** law.
3: 6 And I obeyed the **J** law so carefully that I was
Col 4:11 These are the only **J** Christians among my
Tit 1:14 They must stop listening to **J** myths
3: 9 or in quarrels and fights about obedience to **J** laws.
Heb 7: 8 In the case of **J** priests, tithes are paid to men who
13:11 Under the system of **J** laws, the high priest brought
Jas 1: 1 It is written to **J** Christians scattered among the

JEWRY [KJV] See JUDAH, JUDEA

JEWS (199) [JEW]

ALL (THE) JEWS (10) Est 3:6,13; 4:8,16; Ac 10:22; 18:2,28; 21:21; 22:12; Ro 11:5

KING OF THE JEWS (18) Mt 2:2; 27:11,29,37; Mk 15:2,9,12,18,26; Lk 23:3,37,38; Jn 18:33,39; 19:3,19,21,21

Ezr 4:12 "Please be informed that the **J** who came here to
4:13 for the **J** will then refuse to pay their tribute,
4:23 to Jerusalem and forced the **J** to stop building.
5: 1 in the name of the God of Israel to the **J** in Judah
5: 5 the leaders of the **J** were not prevented from
6: 3 It must be rebuilt on the site where **J** used to offer
6: 7 of Judah and the leaders of the **J** in their work.
6: 8 leaders of the **J** as they rebuild this Temple of God.
Ne 1: 2 I asked them about the **J** who had survived the
4: 1 the wall. He flew into a rage and mocked the **J**,
4: 2 this bunch of poor, feeble **J** think they are doing?
4:12 The **J** who lived near the enemy came and told us
5: 1 wives raised a cry of protest against their fellow **J**.
6: 6 and the **J** are planning to rebel and that is why you
10:31 and to cancel the debts owed to us by other **J**.
Est 3: 6 he decided to destroy all the **J** throughout the
3:10 of Hammedatha the Agagite—the enemy of the **J**.
3:13 The letters decreed that all **J**—young and old,
3:13 The property of the **J** would be given to those who
4: 3 there was great mourning among the **J**.
4: 7 into the royal treasury for the destruction of the **J**.
4: 8 issued in Susa that called for the death of all **J**,
4:13 there in the palace when all other **J** are killed.
4:14 deliverance for the **J** will arise from some other
4:16 "Go and gather together all the **J** of Susa and fast
8: 1 of Haman, the enemy of the **J**, to Queen Esther.
8: 3 with tears to stop Haman's evil plot against the **J**.
8: 5 the **J** throughout all the provinces of the king.
8: 7 on the gallows because he tried to destroy the **J**.
8: 8 and send a message to the **J** in the king's name,
8: 9 they wrote a decree to the **J** and to the princes,
8: 9 of all the peoples of the empire, including the **J**.
8:11 The king's decree gave the **J** in every city
8:13 That way the **J** would be ready on that day to take
8:16 The **J** were filled with joy and gladness and were
8:17 the **J** rejoiced and had a great celebration
8:17 And many of the people of the land became **J**
8:17 for they feared what the **J** might do to them.
9: 1 the enemies of the **J** had hoped to destroy them,
9: 2 The **J** gathered in their cities throughout all the
9: 3 and the royal officials helped the **J** for fear of
9: 5 But the **J** went ahead on the appointed day
9:10 of Haman son of Hammedatha, the enemy of the **J**.
9:12 "The **J** have killed five hundred people in the
9:13 give the **J** in Susa permission to do again
9:15 Then the **J** at Susa gathered together on March 8
9:16 the other **J** throughout the king's provinces had
9:18 But the **J** at Susa continued killing their enemies
9:19 rural **J** living in unwalled villages celebrate an
9:20 these events and sent letters to the **J** near and far,
9:22 This would commemorate a time when the **J**
9:23 So the **J** adopted Mordecai's suggestion and began
9:24 the enemy of the **J**, had plotted to crush
9:27 the **J** throughout the realm agreed to inaugurate
9:27 it on to their descendants and to all who became **J**.
9:28 would never cease to be celebrated among the **J**,
9:30 and security were sent to the **J** throughout the 127
10: 3 He was very great among the **J**, who held him in
Da 3: 8 astrologers went to the king and informed on the **J**.
3:12 But there are some **J**—Shadrach, Meshach,
Zec 6:10 of silver and gold from the **J** exiled in Babylon.
Mt 2: 2 "Where is the newborn king of the **J**? We have
22:23 a group of **J** who say there is no resurrection after
27:11 Roman governor. "Are you the King of the **J**?"
27:29 him in mockery, yelling, "Hail! King of the **J**!"
27:37 It read: "This is Jesus, the King of the **J**."
28:15 Their story spread widely among the **J**, and they
Mk 7: 3 (The **J**, especially the Pharisees, do not eat until
7:27 "First I should help my own family, the **J**.
12:18 a group of **J** who say there is no resurrection after
15: 2 Pilate asked Jesus, "Are you the King of the **J**?"
15: 9 "Should I give you the King of the **J**?"
15:12 I do with this man you call the King of the **J**?"
15:18 Then they saluted, yelling, "Hail! King of the **J**!"
15:26 charge against him. It read: "The King of the **J**."
Lk 7: 5 "for he loves the **J** and even built a synagogue for
19: 2 He was one of the most influential **J** in the Roman
20:27 a group of **J** who say there is no resurrection after
23: 3 So Pilate asked him, "Are you the King of the **J**?"
23:37 "If you are the King of the **J**, save yourself!"
23:38 him with these words: "This is the King of the **J**."
Jn 4: 9 for **J** refuse to have anything to do with
4:20 why is it that you **J** insist that Jerusalem is the only
4:22 one you worship, while we **J** know all about him,
for salvation comes through the **J**.
7:35 the country and going to the **J** in other lands,
18:33 "Are you the King of the **J**?" he asked him.
18:39 if you want me to, I'll release the King of the **J**."
19: 3 "Hail! King of the **J**!" they mocked, and they hit
19:19 that read, "Jesus of Nazareth, the King of the **J**."
19:21 "Change it from 'The King of the **J**' to 'He said, I
am King of the **J**.' "
Ac 2: 5 Godly **J** from many nations were living in
2:10 visitors from Rome (both **J** and converts to
2:14 all of you, fellow **J** and residents of Jerusalem!
6: 9 They were **J** from Cyrene, Alexandria, Cilicia,
9:22 and the **J** in Damascus couldn't refute his proofs
9:29 He debated with some Greek-speaking **J**, but they
10:22 the God of Israel and is well respected by all the **J**.
11:19 They preached the Good News, but only to **J**.
12:11 and from what the **J** were hoping to do to me!"
13:43 Many **J** and godly converts to Judaism who
13:46 this Good News from God be given first to you **J**.
14: 1 with such power that a great number of both **J**
14: 2 But the **J** who spurned God's message stirred up
14: 4 Some sided with the **J**, and some with the apostles.
14: 5 A mob of Gentiles and **J**, along with their leaders,
14:19 Now some **J** arrived from Antioch and Iconium
16: 3 In deference to the **J** of the area, he arranged for
16:20 whole city is in an uproar because of these **J**!"
17:12 As a result, many **J** believed, as did some of the
17:13 But when some **J** in Thessalonica learned that Paul
17:17 He went to the synagogue to debate with the **J**
18: 2 Claudius Caesar's order to deport all **J** from Rome.
18: 4 trying to convince the **J** and Greeks alike.
18: 5 his full time preaching and testifying to the **J**,
18: 6 But when the **J** opposed him and insulted him,
18:12 some **J** rose in concerted action against Paul
18:14 turned to Paul's accusers and said, "Listen, you **J**,
18:19 he went to the synagogue to debate with the **J**.
18:28 He refuted all the **J** with powerful arguments in
19:10 both **J** and Greeks—heard the Lord's message.
19:13 A team of **J** who were traveling from town to town
19:17 quickly all through Ephesus, to **J** and Greeks alike.
19:33 Alexander was thrust forward by some of the **J**,
20: 3 he discovered a plot by some **J** against his life,
20:19 the trials that came to me from the plots of the **J**.
20:21 I have had one message for **J** and Gentiles alike—
21:20 how many thousands of **J** have also believed,
21:21 **J** living in the Gentile world to turn their backs on
21:27 The seven days were almost ended when some **J**
22:12 and he was well thought of by all the **J** of
23:12 The next morning a group of **J** got together
23:20 "Some **J** are going to ask you to bring Paul before
23:27 This man was seized by some **J**, and they were
24: 2 you have given peace to us **J** and have enacted
24: 5 a man who is constantly inciting the **J** throughout
24: 9 Then the other **J** chimed in, declaring that
24:19 But some **J** from the province of Asia were there—
25: 9 Then Festus, wanting to please the **J**, asked him,
25:24 man whose death is demanded both by the local **J**
26:21 Some **J** arrested me in the Temple for preaching
26:23 and be the first to rise from the dead as a light to **J**
Ro 1:16 everyone who believes—**J** first and also Gentiles.
2:12 And he will punish the **J** when they sin, for they do
2:27 be much better off than you **J** who are circumcised
3: 2 the **J** were entrusted with the whole revelation of
3: 9 Well then, are we **J** better than others? No, not at
3: 9 whether **J** or Gentiles, are under the power of sin.
3:29 After all, God is not the God of the **J** only, is he?
3:30 only by faith, whether they are **J** or Gentiles.
4: 9 Now then, is this blessing only for the **J**, or is it for
9: 6 has God failed to fulfill his promise to the **J**?
9:24 he selected, both from the **J** and from the Gentiles.
9:31 But the **J**, who tried so hard to get right with God
10:18 But what about the **J**? Have they actually heard the
11: 1 I ask, then, has God rejected his people, the **J**?
11: 5 for not all the **J** have turned away from God.
11: 7 Most of the **J** have not found the favor of God they
11:11 and then the **J** would be jealous and want it for
11:12 because the **J** turned down God's offer of
11:12 the world will share when the **J** finally accept it.
11:14 for I want to find a way to make the **J** want what
11:17 some of the **J**, have been broken off.
11:20 those branches, the **J**, were broken off
11:23 And if the **J** turn from their unbelief, God will
11:24 he will be far more eager to graft the **J** back into
11:25 Some of the **J** have hard hearts, but this will last
11:28 Many of the **J** are now enemies of the Good News.
11:28 Yet the **J** are still his chosen people because of his
11:30 but when the **J** refused his mercy, God was
11:31 And now, in the same way, the **J** are the rebels,
15: 8 Remember that Christ came as a servant to the **J** to
15:10 O you Gentiles, / along with his people, the **J**."
1Co 1:22 God's way seems foolish to the **J** because they
1:23 the **J** are offended, and the Gentiles say it's all
1:24 both **J** and Gentiles, Christ is the mighty power of
9:20 When I am with the **J**, I become one of them
10:32 Don't give offense to **J** or Gentiles or the church of
12:13 Some of us are **J**, some are Gentiles, some are
2Co 11:24 Five different times the **J** gave me thirty-nine
11:26 my own people, the **J**, as well as from the Gentiles.
Gal 1:14 I was one of the most religious **J** of my own age,
2: 7 given Peter the responsibility of preaching to the **J**.
2: 8 **J** worked through me for the benefit of the
2: 9 while they continued their work with the **J**.
2:15 You and I are **J** by birth, not 'sinners' like the
5:11 as some say I do—why would the **J** persecute me?
Eph 2:11 were called "the uncircumcised ones" by the **J**,
2:14 For Christ himself has made peace between us **J**
2:15 His purpose was to make peace between **J**
2:17 far away from him, and to us **J** who were near.
2:18 Now all of us, both **J** and Gentiles, may come to
3: 6 The Gentiles have an equal share with the **J** in all
3:10 They will see this when **J** and Gentiles are joined
1Th 2:14 Christ Jesus, suffered from their own people, the **J**.
2:15 For some of the **J** had killed their own prophets,
Rev 2: 9 They say they are **J**, but they really aren't
3: 9 those liars who say they are **J** but are not—to come

JEWS' (1) [JEW]

Ro 11:15 For since the **J** rejection meant that God offered

JEZANIAH (1)

Jer 42: 1 Johanan son of Kareah and **J** son of Hoshaiah,

JEZEBEL (18) [JEZEBEL'S]

1Ki 16:31 he married **J**, the daughter of King Ethbaal of the
18: 4 Once when **J** had tried to kill all the LORD's
18:13 about the time when **J** was trying to kill the
18:19 prophets of Asherah, who are supported by **J**."
19: 1 he told **J** what Elijah had done and that he had

19: 2 So **J** sent this message to Elijah: "May the gods
21: 5 his wife, **J**, asked him. "What has made you
21: 7 **J** asked. "Get up and eat and don't worry about it.
21:11 and other leaders followed the instructions **J** had
21:14 The city officials then sent word to **J**, "Naboth has
21:15 When **J** heard the news, she said to Ahab,
21:23 will eat the body of your wife, **J**, at the city wall.
21:25 sight as did Ahab, for his wife, **J**, influenced him.
2Ki 9: 7 all the LORD's servants who were killed by **J**.
9:10 Dogs will eat Ahab's wife, **J**, at the plot of land in
9:22 witchcraft of your mother, **J**, are all around us?"
9:30 When **J**, the queen mother, heard that Jehu had
Rev 2:20 that **J** who calls herself a prophet—to lead my

JEZEBEL'S (1) [JEZEBEL]

2Ki 9:36 'At the plot of land in Jezreel, dogs will eat **J** flesh.

JEZER (3) [JEZERITE]

Ge 46:24 of Naphtali were Jahzeel, Guni, **J**, and Shillem.
Nu 26:49 The Jezerite clan, named after its ancestor **J**.
1Ch 7:13 of Naphtali were Jahzeel, Guni, **J**, and Shillem.

JEZERITE (1) [JEZER]

Nu 26:49 The **J** clan, named after its ancestor Jezer.

JEZIAH [KJV] See IZZIAH

JEZIEL (1)

1Ch 12: 3 **J** and Pelet, sons of Azmaveth; / Beracah and Jehu

JEZLIAH [KJV] See IZLIAH

JEZOAR [KJV] See IZHAR

JEZRAHIAH (1)

Ne 12:42 and clearly under the direction of **J** the choir

JEZREEL (44)

Jos 15:56 **J**, Jokdeam, Zanoah,
17:16 and the valley of **J** have iron chariots—
19:18 the following towns: **J**, Kesulloth, Shunem,
Jdg 6:33 and crossed the Jordan, camping in the valley of **J**.
1Sa 25:43 David also married Ahinoam from **J**, making both
27: 3 Ahinoam of **J** and Abigail of Carmel,
29: 1 and the Israelites camped at the spring in **J**.
29:11 while the Philistine army went on to **J**.
30: 5 David's two wives, Ahinoam of **J** and Abigail,
31: 7 When the Israelites on the other side of the **J**
2Sa 2: 2 David's wives were Ahinoam from **J** and Abigail,
2: 9 **J**, Ephraim, Benjamin, the land of the Ashurites,
3: 2 was Amnon, whose mother was Ahinoam of **J**.
4: 4 and Jonathan were killed at the battle of **J**.
1Ki 4:12 all of Beth-shan near Zarethan below **J**,
18:45 a terrific rainstorm, and Ahab left quickly for **J**.
18:46 of Ahab's chariot all the way to the entrance of **J**.
21: 1 King Ahab had a palace in **J**, and near the palace
21:18 He will be at Naboth's vineyard in **J**,
21:23 The LORD has also told me that the dogs of **J**
2Ki 8:29 he returned to **J** to recover from his wounds.
9:10 Jezebel, at the plot of land in **J**, and no one will
9:15 and had returned to **J** to recover from his wounds.)
9:15 don't let anyone escape to **J** to report what we
9:16 got into a chariot and rode to **J** to find King Joram,
9:17 The watchman on the tower of **J** saw Jehu and his
9:21 him at the field that had belonged to Naboth of **J**.
9:25 "Throw him into the field of Naboth of **J**.
9:30 the queen mother, heard that Jehu had come to **J**,
9:36 'At the plot of land in **J**, dogs will eat Jezebel's
9:37 body will be scattered like dung on the field of **J**,
10: 6 bring the heads of the king's sons to me at **J** at
10: 7 heads in baskets and presented them to Jehu at **J**.
10:11 Then Jehu killed all of Ahab's relatives living in **J**
1Ch 3: 1 was Amnon, whose mother was Ahinoam of **J**.
4: 3 The descendants of Etam were **J**, Ishma, Idbash,
10: 7 When the Israelites in the **J** Valley saw that their
2Ch 22: 6 Joram returned to **J** to recover from his wounds,
22: 6 and King Ahaziah of Judah went to **J** to visit him.
Hos 1: 4 And the LORD said, "Name the child **J**, for I am
1: 4 dynasty to avenge the murders he committed at **J**.
1: 5 by breaking its military power in the **J** Valley."
1:11 What a day that will be—the day of **J**—when God
2:22 the whole grand chorus will sing together, '**J**'—

JIBSAM [KJV] See IBSAM

JIDLAPH (1)

Ge 22:22 Kesed, Hazo, Pildash, **J**, and Bethuel.

JIMNA(H) [KJV] See IMNAH

JIMNITES [KJV] See IMNITE

JIPHTAH [KJV] See IPHTAH

JIPHTHAH-EL [KJV] See IPHTAH-EL

JOAB (129) [JOAB'S, ATROTH-BETH-JOAB]

2Sa 2:13 **J** son of Zeruiah led David's troops from Hebron,
2:14 Then Abner suggested to **J**, "Let's have a few of
2:14 of hand-to-hand combat." "All right," **J** agreed.
2:18 **J**, Abishai, and Asahel, the three sons of Zeruiah,
2:22 I will never be able to face your brother **J** if I have
2:24 When **J** and Abishai found out what had happened,
2:26 Abner shouted down to **J**, "Must we always solve
2:27 Then **J** said, "God only knows what would have
2:28 So **J** blew his trumpet, and his men stopped
2:30 Meanwhile, **J** and his men also returned home.
2:30 When **J** counted his casualties, he discovered that
2:32 **J** and his men took Asahel's body to Bethlehem
3:22 **J** and some of David's troops returned from a raid,
3:23 When **J** was told that Abner had just been there
3:26 **J** then left David and sent messengers to catch up
3:27 **J** took him aside at the gateway as if to speak with
3:29 **J** and his family are the guilty ones. May his
3:30 So **J** and his brother Abishai killed Abner
3:31 Then David said to **J** and all those who were with
3:39 these two sons of Zeruiah—**J** and Abishai—
8:16 **J** son of Zeruiah was commander of the army.
10: 7 he sent **J** and the entire Israelite army to fight
10: 9 When **J** saw that he would have to fight on two
10:11 then come over and help me," **J** told his brother.
10:13 When **J** and his troops attacked, the Arameans
10:14 After the battle was over, **J** returned to Jerusalem.
11: 1 David sent **J** and the Israelite army to destroy the
11: 6 So David sent word to **J**: "Send me Uriah the
11: 7 David asked him how **J** and the army were getting
11:11 and **J** and his officers are camping in the open
11:14 So the next morning David wrote a letter to **J**
11:15 The letter instructed **J**, "Station Uriah on the front
11:16 So **J** assigned Uriah to a spot close to the city wall
11:18 Then **J** sent a battle report to David.
11:25 "Well, tell **J** not to be discouraged," David said.
12:26 **J** and the Israelite army were successfully ending
12:27 **J** sent messengers to tell David, "I have fought
14: 1 **J** realized how much the king longed to see
14: 3 am about to tell you." Then **J** told her what to say.
14:19 "Did **J** send you here?" And the woman replied,
14:19 from you. Yes, **J** sent me and told me what to say.
14:21 So the king sent for **J** and told him, "All right,
14:22 **J** fell to the ground before the king and blessed
14:23 Then **J** went to Geshur and brought Absalom back
14:29 Then Absalom sent for **J** to ask him to intercede
for him, but **J** refused to come.
14:29 for him a second time, but again **J** refused to come.
14:31 Then **J** came to Absalom and demanded,
14:33 So **J** told the king what Absalom had said. Then at
17:25 replacing **J**, who had been commander under
18: 2 One-third were placed under **J**, one-third under
18: 5 And the king gave this command to **J**, Abishai,
18:10 of David's men saw what had happened and told **J**,
18:11 "What?" **J** demanded. "You saw him there
18:14 "Enough of this nonsense," **J** said. Then he took
18:16 Then **J** blew the trumpet, and his men returned
18:20 "No," **J** told him, "it wouldn't be good news to
18:21 Then **J** said to a man from Cush, "Go tell the king
18:22 But Ahimaaz continued to plead with **J**,
18:22 too." "Why should you go, my son?" **J** replied.
18:23 he begged. **J** finally said, "All right, go ahead."
18:29 Ahimaaz replied, "When **J** told me to come,
19: 1 Word soon reached **J** that the king was weeping
19: 5 Then **J** went to the king's room and said to him,
19:13 you as commander of my army in place of **J**."
20: 7 and **J** set out after Sheba with an elite guard from
20: 8 **J** was wearing his uniform with a dagger strapped
20: 9 **J** said and took him by the beard with his right
20:10 and **J** stabbed him in the stomach with it so that his
20:10 **J** did not need to strike again, and Amasa soon
20:10 **J** and his brother Abishai left him lying there
20:11 "If you are for **J** and David, come and follow **J**."
20:13 everyone went on with **J** to capture Sheba.
20:16 But a wise woman in the city called out to **J**,
"Listen to me, **J**.
20:17 he approached, the woman asked, "Are you **J**?"
20:20 And **J** replied, "Believe me, I don't want to
20:22 and they cut off Sheba's head and threw it out to **J**.
20:22 to their homes. **J** returned to the king at Jerusalem.
20:23 **J** once again became the commander of David's
23:18 Abishai son of Zeruiah, the brother of **J**,
24: 2 So the king said to **J**, the commander of his army,
24: 3 But **J** replied to the king, "May the LORD your
24: 4 so **J** and his officers went out to count the people
24: 9 **J** reported the number of people to the king.
1Ki 1: 7 Adonijah took **J** son of Zeruiah and Abiathar the
1:19 invited all your sons and Abiathar the priest and **J**,
1:25 He also invited **J**, the commander of the army,
1:41 When **J** heard the sound of trumpets, he asked,
2: 5 You know that **J** son of Zeruiah murdered my two
2:22 the priest and **J** son of Zeruiah on his side."
2:28 **J** had also joined Adonijah's revolt.
2:28 When **J** heard about Adonijah's death, he ran to
2:30 into the sacred tent of the LORD and said to **J**,
2:30 But **J** answered, "No, I will die here." So Benaiah
2:30 returned to the king and told him what **J** had said.
2:33 May **J** and his descendants be forever guilty of
2:34 of Jehoiada returned to the sacred tent and killed **J**,
2:34 and **J** was buried at his home in the wilderness.
2:35 Benaiah to command the army in place of **J**,
11:15 Years before, David had gone to Edom with **J**,
11:16 **J** and the army had stayed there for six months,
11:21 that David and his commander **J** were both dead,
1Ch 2:16 had three sons named Abishai, **J**, and Asahel.
4:14 Seraiah was the father of **J**, the founder of the
11: 6 And **J**, the son of David's sister Zeruiah,
11: 8 while **J** rebuilt the rest of Jerusalem.
11:20 Abishai, the brother of **J**, was the leader of the
18:15 **J** son of Zeruiah was commander of the army.
19: 8 he sent **J** and all his warriors to fight them.
19:10 When **J** saw that he would have to fight on two
19:12 then come over and help me," **J** told his brother.
19:14 When **J** and his troops attacked, the Arameans
19:15 into the city. Then **J** returned to Jerusalem.
20: 1 **J** led the Israelite army in successful attacks
21: 2 David gave these orders to **J** and his commanders:
21: 3 But **J** replied, "May the LORD increase the
21: 4 But the king insisted that **J** take the census, so **J**
traveled throughout Israel to count the people.
21: 6 But **J** did not include the tribes of Levi
26:28 of Kish, Abner son of Ner, and **J** son of Zeruiah.
27: 7 Asahel, the brother of **J**, was commander of the
27:24 **J** began the census but never finished it
27:34 **J** was commander of the Israelite army.
Ezr 2: 6 of Pahath-moab (descendants of Jeshua and **J**)
8: 9 From the family of **J**: Obadiah son of Jehiel
Ne 7:11 of Pahath-moab (descendants of Jeshua and **J**)
Ps 60: T and **J** returned and killed twelve thousand

JOAB'S (14) [JOAB]

1Sa 26: 6 the Hittite and Abishai son of Zeruiah, **J** brother.
2Sa 14:30 "Go and set fire to **J** barley field, the field next to
17:25 (Amasa was **J** cousin. His father was Jether,
17:25 of Nahash, was the sister of **J** mother, Zeruiah.)
18: 2 one-third under **J** brother Abishai son of Zeruiah,
18:15 Ten of **J** young armor bearers then surrounded
20: 7 set out after Sheba with an elite guard from **J** army
20:11 One of **J** young officers shouted to Amasa's
20:12 and **J** officer saw that a crowd was gathering
20:15 When **J** forces arrived, they attacked
23:24 of the Thirty included: / Asahel, **J** brother;
23:37 Naharai from Beeroth (**J** armor bearer);
1Ch 11:26 Asahel, **J** brother; / Elhanan son of Dodo from
11:39 Naharai from Beeroth (**J** armor bearer);

JOAH (11)

2Ki 18:18 and **J** son of Asaph, the royal historian.
18:26 Shebna, and **J** said to the king's representative,
18:37 and **J** son of Asaph, the royal historian, went back
1Ch 6:21 **J**, Iddo, Zerah, and Jeatherai.
26: 4 **J** (the third), Sacar (the fourth), Nethanel (the
2Ch 29:12 **J** son of Zimmah and Eden son of **J**.
34: 8 and **J** son of Joahaz, the royal historian,
Isa 36: 3 and **J** son of Asaph, the royal historian.
36:11 Shebna, and **J** said to the king's representative,
36:22 and **J** son of Asaph, the royal historian, went back

JOAHAZ (1)

2Ch 34: 8 and Joah son of **J**, the royal historian,

JOANAN (2)

Lk 3:27 Joda was the son of **J**. / **J** was the son of Rhesa.

JOANNA (2)

Lk 8: 3 **J**, the wife of Chuza, Herod's business manager;
24:10 **J**, Mary the mother of James, and several others.

JOASH (48) [JOASH'S]

Jdg 6:11 which belonged to **J** of the clan of Abiezer.
6:11 Gideon son of **J** had been threshing wheat at the
6:29 they learned that it was Gideon, the son of **J**.
6:30 "Bring out your son," they shouted to **J**.
6:31 But **J** shouted to the mob, "Why are you
7:14 God has given Gideon son of **J**, the Israelite,
8:29 Then Gideon son of **J** returned home.
8:32 and he was buried in the grave of his father, **J**,
1Ki 22:26 to Amon, the governor of the city, and to my son **J**.
2Ki 11: 2 of King Jehoram, took Ahaziah's infant son, **J**,
11: 2 Jehosheba put **J** and his nurse in a bedroom to hide
11: 3 **J** and his nurse remained hidden in the Temple of
11:12 Then Jehoiada brought out **J**, the king's son,
11:12 He presented **J** with a copy of God's covenant
11:21 **J** was seven years old when he became king.
12: 1 **J** began to rule over Judah in the seventh year of
12: 2 All his life **J** did what was pleasing in the
12: 4 One day King **J** said to the priests, "Collect all the
12: 7 So King **J** called for Jehoiada and the other priests
12:18 King **J** collected all the sacred objects that
12:21 **J** was buried with his ancestors in the City of
14: 1 Amaziah son of **J** began to rule over Judah in the
14: 3 Instead, he followed the example of his father, **J**.
1Ch 3:11 Jehoram, Ahaziah, **J**,
4:22 **J**, and Saraph, who ruled over Moab
7: 8 **J**, Eliezer, Elioenai, Omri, Jeremoth, Abijah,
12: 3 his brother **J** was second-in-command.
27:28 **J** was responsible for the supplies of olive oil.
2Ch 18:25 to Amon, the governor of the city, and to my son **J**.
22:11 of King Jehoram, took Ahaziah's infant son, **J**,
22:11 She put **J** and his nurse in a bedroom. In this way,
22:12 **J** remained hidden in the Temple of God for six
23: 3 where they made a covenant with **J**, the young
23:11 Then Jehoiada and his sons brought out **J**,
23:11 They presented **J** with a copy of God's laws
24: 1 **J** was seven years old when he became king,
24: 2 **J** did what was pleasing in the LORD's sight
24: 3 Jehoiada chose two wives for **J**, and he had sons
24: 4 **J** decided to repair and restore the Temple of the
24: 8 So now **J** gave instructions for a chest to be made
24:17 leaders of Judah came and bowed before King **J**
24:21 to kill Zechariah, and by order of King **J** himself,
24:22 That was how King **J** repaid Jehoiada for his love
24:23 of the year, the Aramean army marched against **J**.
24:24 so judgment was executed against **J**.
24:25 Arameans withdrew, leaving **J** severely wounded.
24:27 The complete story about the sons of **J**,
24:27 When **J** died, his son Amaziah became the next

JOASH'S (4) [JOASH]

2Ki 12: 6 But by the twenty-third year of **J** reign, the priests
12:19 The rest of the events in **J** reign and all his deeds
13: 1 in the twenty-third year of King **J** reign in Judah.
13:10 in the thirty-seventh year of King **J** reign in Judah.

JOB (71) [JOB'S, JOBS]

Ge 41:38 they discussed who should be appointed for the **j**,
Ex 18:18 This **j** is too heavy a burden for you to handle all
36: 5 to complete the **j** the LORD has given us to do!"
Jdg 8:21 said to Gideon, "Don't ask a boy to do a man's **j**!
2Sa 12:28 Now bring the rest of the army and finish the **j**,
1Ch 9:27 It was also their **j** to open the gates every morning.
Ne 13:13 and it was their **j** to make honest distributions to
Job 1: 1 There was a man named **J** who lived in the land of
1: 5 lasted several days—**J** would purify his children.
1: 5 For **J** said to himself, "Perhaps my children have
1: 8 asked Satan, "Have you noticed my servant **J**?
1: 9 Satan replied to the LORD, "Yes, **J** fears God,
1:20 **J** stood up and tore his robe in grief. Then he
1:22 In all of this, **J** did not sin by blaming God.
2: 3 asked Satan, "Have you noticed my servant **J**?
2: 7 and he struck **J** with a terrible case of boils from
2: 8 Then **J** scraped his skin with a piece of broken
2:10 But **J** replied, "You talk like a godless woman.
2:10 So in all this, **J** said nothing wrong.
2:12 When they saw **J** from a distance, they scarcely
3: 1 At last **J** spoke, and he cursed the day of his birth.
4: 1 Then Eliphaz the Temanite replied to **J**:
6: 1 Then **J** spoke again:
8: 1 Then Bildad the Shuhite replied to **J**:
9: 1 Then **J** spoke again:
11: 1 Then Zophar the Naamathite replied to **J**:
12: 1 Then **J** spoke again:
16: 1 Then **J** spoke again:
19: 1 Then **J** spoke again:
21: 1 Then **J** spoke again:
23: 1 Then **J** spoke again:
26: 1 Then **J** spoke again:
27: 1 **J** continued speaking:
29: 1 **J** continued speaking:
32: 2 because **J** refused to admit that he had sinned
32:12 but not one of you has refuted **J** or answered his
32:14 If **J** had been arguing with me, I would not answer
33: 1 "Listen, **J**, to what I have to say.
33:31 Mark this well, **J**. Listen to me, and let me say
34: 5 For **J** has said, 'I am innocent, but God has taken
34: 7 "Has there ever been a man as arrogant as **J**,
34:35 '**J** speaks without knowledge; his words lack
34:36 **J**, you deserve the maximum penalty for the
35:16 **J**, you have protested in vain. You have spoken
37:14 "Listen, **J**; stop and consider the wonderful
38: 1 Then the LORD answered **J** from the whirlwind:
40: 1 Then the LORD said to **J**,
40: 3 Then **J** replied to the LORD,
40: 6 Then the LORD answered **J** from the whirlwind:
42: 1 Then **J** replied to the LORD:
42: 7 After the LORD had finished speaking to **J**,
42: 7 in what you said about me, as my servant **J** was.
42: 8 young bulls and seven rams and go to my servant **J**
42: 8 My servant **J** will pray for you, and I will accept
42: 8 in what you said about me, as my servant **J** was."
42:10 When **J** prayed for his friends, the LORD
42:12 So the LORD blessed **J** in the second half of his
42:13 He also gave **J** seven more sons and three more
42:15 no other women as lovely as the daughters of **J**.
42:16 **J** lived 140 years after that, living to see four
Jer 17:16 I have not abandoned my **j** as a shepherd for your
Eze 14:14 Even if Noah, Daniel, and **J** were there,
14:20 Even if Noah, Daniel, and **J** were living there,
Hos 10:11 to treading out the grain—an easy **j** that she loves.
Mt 24:46 and finds that the servant has done a good **j**,
Lk 12:43 and finds that the servant has done a good **j**,
Ro 12: 7 If you are a teacher, do a good **j** of teaching.
1Co 3: 6 My **j** was to plant the seed in your hearts,
5:12 but it certainly is your **j** to judge those inside the
Jas 4:11 the law is right or wrong. Your **j** is to obey it.
5:11 **J** is an example of a man who endured patiently.

JOB'S (10) [JOB]

Job 1: 4 Every year when **J** sons had birthdays, they invited
1: 5 God in their hearts." This was **J** regular practice.
1:13 One day when **J** sons and daughters were dining at
1:14 a messenger arrived at **J** home with this news:
2:11 Three of **J** friends were Eliphaz the Temanite,
31:40 and weeds instead of barley." **J** words are ended.
32: 1 **J** three friends refused to reply further to him
32: 3 He was also angry with **J** three friends
32: 3 God by their inability to answer **J** arguments.
42: 9 and the LORD accepted **J** prayer.

JOBAB (9)

Ge 10:29 Ophir, Havilah, and **J**.
36:33 **J** son of Zerah from Bozrah became king.
36:34 When **J** died, Husham from the land of the
Jos 11: 1 King **J** of Madon; the king of Shimron; the king of
1Ch 1:23 Ophir, Havilah, and **J**. All these were descendants
1:44 **J** son of Zerah from Bozrah became king.
1:45 When **J** died, Husham from the land of the
8: 9 new wife, gave birth to **J**, Zibia, Mesha, Malcam,
8:18 Ishmerai, Izliah, and **J** were the sons of Elpaal.

JOBS (3) [JOB]

1Sa 2:36 'give us **j** among the priests so we will have
2Ch 31:17 or older who were listed according to their **j**
Zec 8:10 there were no **j** and no wages for either people

JOCHEBED (3)

Ex 6:20 Amram married his father's sister **J**, and she bore
Nu 26:59 and Amram's wife was named **J**. She also was a
26:59 Amram and **J** became the parents of Aaron,

JODA (2)

Lk 3:26 was the son of Josech. / Josech was the son of **J**.
3:27 **J** was the son of Joanan. / Joanan was the son of

JOED (1)

Ne 11: 7 son of **J**, son of Pedaiah, son of Kolaiah, son of

JOEL (21)

1Sa 8: 2 **J** and Abijah, his oldest sons, held court in
1Ch 4:35 **J**, Jehu son of Joshibiah, son of Seraiah, son of
5: 4 The descendants of **J** were Shemaiah, Gog,
5: 8 and Bela son of Azaz, son of Shema, son of **J**.
5:12 **J** was the leader in the land of Bashan,
6:28 The sons of Samuel were **J** (the older) and Abijah
6:33 His genealogy was traced back through **J**, Samuel,
6:36 Elkanah, **J**, Azariah, Zephaniah,
7: 3 of Izrahiah were Michael, Obadiah, **J**, and Isshiah.
11:38 **J**, the brother of Nathan; / Mibhar son of Hagri;
15: 7 from the clan of Gershon, with **J** as their leader.
15:11 Uriel, Asaiah, **J**, Shemaiah, Eliel, and Amminadab.
15:17 So the Levites appointed Heman son of **J**,
23: 8 were Jehiel (the family leader), Zetham, and **J**.
26:22 The sons of Jehiel, Zetham and his brother **J**,
27:20 of Azaziah / Manasseh (west) | **J** son of Pedaiah
2Ch 29:12 Mahath son of Amasai and **J** son of Azariah.
Ezr 10:43 Jeiel, Mattithiah, Zabad, Zebina, Jaddai, **J**,
Ne 11: 9 Their chief officer was **J** son of Zicri, who was
Joel 1: 1 The LORD gave this message to **J** son of Pethuel.
Ac 2:16 was predicted centuries ago by the prophet **J**:

JOELAH (1)

1Ch 12: 7 **J** and Zebadiah, sons of Jeroham from Gedor.

JOEZER (1)

1Ch 12: 6 Elkanah, Isshiah, Azarel, **J**, and Jashobeam,

JOGBEHAH (2)

Nu 32:35 Atroth-shophan, Jazer, **J**,
Jdg 8:11 around by the caravan route east of Nobah and **J**,

JOGLI (1)

Nu 34:22 Dan | Bukki son of **J**

JOHA (2)

1Ch 8:16 Michael, Ishpah, and **J** were the sons of Beriah.
11:45 Jediael son of Shimri; / **J**, his brother, from Tiz;

JOHANAN (27)

2Ki 25:23 Ishmael son of Nethaniah, **J** son of Kareah,
1Ch 3:15 The sons of Josiah were **J** (the oldest),
3:24 Eliashib, Pelaiah, Akkub, **J**, Delaiah, and Anani—
6: 9 the father of Azariah. / Azariah was the father of **J**.
6:10 **J** was the father of Azariah, the high priest at the
12: 4 Jeremiah, Jahaziel, **J**, and Jozabad from Gederah;
12:12 **J** was eighth. / Elzabad was ninth.
Ezr 8:12 of Azgad: **J** son of Hakkatan and 110 other men.
Ne 12:11 Joiada was the father of **J**. / **J** was the father of
12:22 high priests: Eliashib, Joiada, **J**, and Jaddua.
12:23 in *The Book of History* down to the days of **J**,
Jer 40: 8 son of Nethaniah, **J** and Jonathan, sons of Kareah,
40:13 **J** son of Kareah and the other guerrilla leaders
40:15 Later **J** had a private conference with Gedaliah
40:15 we let him come and murder you?" **J** asked.
40:16 But Gedaliah said to **J**, "I forbid you to do any
41:11 But when **J** son of Kareah and the rest of the
41:13 had captured shouted for joy when they saw **J**
41:14 captives from Mizpah escaped and began to help **J**.
41:15 and eight of his men escaped from **J** into the land
41:16 Then **J** son of Kareah and his officers led away all
42: 1 including **J** son of Kareah and Jezaniah son of
42: 8 So he called for **J** son of Kareah and the army
43: 2 Azariah son of Hoshaiah and **J** son of Kareah
43: 4 So **J** and all the army officers and all the people
43: 5 **J** and his officers took with them all the people

JOHN (161) [JOHN'S]

Mt 3: 1 In those days **J** the Baptist began preaching in the
3: 3 Isaiah had spoken of **J** when he said, / "He is a
3:13 Galilee to the Jordan River to be baptized by **J**.
3:14 But **J** didn't want to baptize him. "I am the one
3:15 everything that is right." So then **J** baptized him.
4:12 When Jesus heard that **J** had been arrested, he left
4:21 James and **J**, sitting in a boat with their father,
9:14 One day the disciples of **J** the Baptist came to
10: 2 James (son of Zebedee), / **J** (James's brother),
11: 2 **J** the Baptist, who was now in prison, heard about
11: 4 "Go back to **J** and tell him about what you have
11:10 **J** is the man to whom the Scriptures refer when
11:11 have ever lived, none is greater than **J** the Baptist.
11:12 And from the time **J** the Baptist began preaching
11:13 For before **J** came, all the teachings of the
11:18 For **J** the Baptist didn't drink wine and he often
14: 2 "This must be **J** the Baptist come back to life
14: 3 and imprisoned **J** as a favor to his wife Herodias
14: 4 **J** kept telling Herod, "It is illegal for you to marry
14: 5 Herod would have executed **J**, but he was afraid of
14: 5 because all the people believed **J** was a prophet.
14: 8 "I want the head of **J** the Baptist on a tray!"
14:10 So **J** was beheaded in the prison,
16:14 "Well," they replied, "some say **J** the Baptist,
16:17 Jesus replied, "You are blessed, Simon son of **J**,
17: 1 Jesus took Peter and the two brothers, James and **J**,
17:13 realized he had been speaking of **J** the Baptist.
20:20 Then the mother of James and **J**, the sons of
20:24 other disciples heard what James and **J** had asked,
21:32 For **J** the Baptist came and showed you the way to
26:37 took Peter and Zebedee's two sons, James and **J**,
27:56 and Zebedee's wife, the mother of James and **J**.
Mk 1: 4 This messenger was **J** the Baptist. He lived in the
1: 5 traveled out into the wilderness to see and hear **J**.
1: 9 and he was baptized by **J** in the Jordan River.
1:14 Later on, after **J** was arrested by Herod Antipas,
1:19 James and **J**, in a boat mending their nets.
1:29 Andrew's home, and James and **J** were with them.
3:17 James and **J** (the sons of Zebedee, but Jesus
5:37 anyone go with him except Peter and James and **J**.
6:14 "This must be **J** the Baptist come back to life
6:16 "**J**, the man I beheaded, has come back from the
6:17 to arrest and imprison **J** as a favor to Herodias.
6:18 **J** kept telling Herod, "It is illegal for you to marry
6:19 was enraged and wanted **J** killed in revenge,
6:20 And Herod respected **J**, knowing that he was a
6:20 Herod was disturbed whenever he talked with **J**,
6:24 mother told her, "Ask for **J** the Baptist's head!"
6:25 "I want the head of **J** the Baptist, right now,
6:27 it to him. The soldier beheaded **J** in the prison,
8:28 "Well," they replied, "some say **J** the Baptist,
9: 2 took Peter, James, and **J** to the top of a mountain.
9:38 **J** said to Jesus, "Teacher, we saw a man using
10:35 Then James and **J**, the sons of Zebedee, came over
10:41 disciples discovered what James and **J** had asked,
11:32 since everyone thought that **J** was a prophet.
13: 3 Peter, James, **J**, and Andrew came to him privately
14:33 He took Peter, James, and **J** with him, and he
Lk 1:13 will bear you a son! And you are to name him **J**.
1:60 But Elizabeth said, "No! His name is **J**!"
1:63 to everyone's surprise he wrote, "His name is **J**!"
1:80 **J** grew up and became strong in spirit. Then he
3: 2 At this time a message from God came to **J** son of
3: 3 Then **J** went from place to place on both sides of
3: 4 Isaiah had spoken of **J** when he said, / "He is a
3:11 **J** replied, "If you have two coats, give one to the
3:14 **J** replied, "Don't extort money, and don't accuse
3:15 and they were eager to know whether **J** might be
3:16 **J** answered their questions by saying, "I baptize
3:18 **J** used many such warnings as he announced the
3:19 **J** also publicly criticized Herod Antipas, ruler of
3:20 So Herod put **J** in prison, adding this sin to his
5:10 His partners, James and **J**, the sons of Zebedee,
5:33 "**J** the Baptist's disciples always fast and pray,"
6:14 him Peter), / Andrew (Peter's brother), / James, / **J**,
7:18 The disciples of **J** the Baptist told **J** about
7:18 was doing. So **J** called for two of his disciples,
7:20 and said to him, "**J** the Baptist sent us to ask,
7:22 "Go back to **J** and tell him what you have seen
7:24 After they left, Jesus talked to the crowd about **J**.
7:27 **J** is the man to whom the Scriptures refer when
7:28 of all who have ever lived, none is greater than **J**.
7:29 plan was right, for they had been baptized by **J**.
7:33 For **J** the Baptist didn't drink wine and he often
8:51 James, **J**, and the little girl's father and mother.
9: 7 "This is **J** the Baptist come back to life again."
9: 9 "I beheaded **J**," Herod said, "so who is this man
9:19 "Well," they replied, "some say **J** the Baptist,
9:28 took Peter, James, and **J** to a mountain to pray.
9:49 **J** said to Jesus, "Master, we saw someone using
9:54 When James and **J** heard about it, they said to
11: 1 teach us to pray, just as **J** taught his disciples."
16:16 "Until **J** the Baptist began to preach, the laws of
22: 8 Jesus sent Peter and **J** ahead and said, "Go
Jn 1: 6 God sent **J** the Baptist
1: 8 **J** himself was not the light; he was only a witness
1:15 **J** pointed him out to the people. He shouted to the
1:19 This was the testimony of **J** when the Jewish
1:19 and Temple assistants from Jerusalem to ask **J**
1:23 **J** replied in the words of Isaiah: / "I am a voice
1:26 **J** told them, "I baptize with water, but right here
1:28 east of the Jordan River, where **J** was baptizing.
1:29 The next day **J** saw Jesus coming toward him
1:32 Then **J** said, "I saw the Holy Spirit descending
1:35 **J** was again standing with two of his disciples.
1:36 **J** looked at him and then declared, "Look!
1:40 was one of these men who had heard what **J** said
1:42 Jesus said, "You are Simon, the son of **J**—
3:23 At this time **J** the Baptist was baptizing at Aenon,
3:24 This was before **J** was put into prison.
3:27 **J** replied, "God in heaven appoints each person's
4: 1 is baptizing and making more disciples than **J**"
5:33 you sent messengers to listen to **J** the Baptist,
5:35 **J** shone brightly for a while, and you benefited
5:36 But I have a greater witness than **J**—my teachings
10:40 to stay near the place where **J** was first baptizing.
10:41 "**J** didn't do miracles," they remarked to one
21:15 "Simon son of **J**, do you love me more than
21:16 "Simon son of **J**, do you love me?" "Yes, Lord,"
21:17 he asked him, "Simon son of **J**, do you love me?"
Ac 1: 5 **J** baptized with water, but in just a few days you
1:13 Peter, / **J**, / James, / Andrew, / Philip, / Thomas,
1:22 from the time he was baptized by **J** until the day he
3: 1 and **J** went to the Temple one afternoon to take
3: 3 When he saw Peter and **J** about to enter, he asked

3: 4 Peter and **J** looked at him intently and Peter said,
3:11 where he was holding tightly to Peter and **J**.
4: 1 While Peter and **J** were speaking to the people,
4: 2 very disturbed that Peter and **J** were claiming,
4: 6 was there, along with Caiaphas, **J**, Alexander,
4:13 amazed when they saw the boldness of Peter and **J**,
4:15 they sent Peter and **J** out of the council chamber
4:19 But Peter and **J** replied, "Do you think God wants
4:23 Peter and **J** found the other believers and told them
8:14 God's message, they sent Peter and **J** there.
8:17 and **J** laid their hands upon these believers,
8:25 in Samaria, Peter and **J** returned to Jerusalem.
10:37 beginning in Galilee after **J** the Baptist began
11:16 '**J** baptized with water, but you will be baptized
12:12 went to the home of Mary, the mother of **J** Mark,
12:25 they returned to Antioch, taking **J** Mark with them.
13: 5 of God. (**J** Mark went with them as their assistant.)
13:13 There **J** Mark left them and returned to Jerusalem.
13:24 **J** the Baptist preached the need for everyone in
13:25 As **J** was finishing his ministry he asked, 'Do you
15:37 Barnabas agreed and wanted to take along **J** Mark.
15:38 since **J** Mark had deserted them in Pamphylia
15:39 Barnabas took **J** Mark with him and sailed for
19: 3 he asked. And they replied, "The baptism of **J**."
19: 4 **J** himself told the people to believe in Jesus, the one **J** said would come later."
Gal 2: 9 In fact, James, Peter, and **J**, who were known as
2Jn 1: 1 This letter is from **J**, the Elder. It is written to
3Jn 1: 1 This letter is from **J**, the Elder. It is written to
Rev 1: 1 An angel was sent to God's servant **J** so that **J** could share the revelation with God's
1: 2 **J** faithfully reported the word of God
1: 4 This letter is from **J** to the seven churches in the
1: 9 I am **J**, your brother. In Jesus we are partners in
22: 8 I, **J**, am the one who saw and heard all these

JOHN'S (21) [JOHN]

Mt 3: 4 **J** clothes were woven from camel hair, and he
11: 7 When **J** disciples had gone, Jesus began talking
14:12 **J** disciples came for his body and buried it.
21:25 "Did **J** baptism come from heaven or was it
Mk 2:18 **J** disciples and the Pharisees sometimes fasted.
2:18 "Why do **J** disciples and the Pharisees fast,
6:27 So he sent an executioner to the prison to cut off **J**
6:29 When **J** disciples heard what had happened,
11:30 "Did **J** baptism come from heaven or was it
Lk 3: 7 Here is a sample of **J** preaching to the crowds that
7:20 **J** two disciples found Jesus and said to him,
7:22 Then he told **J** disciples, "Go back to John and tell
7:30 plan for them, for they had refused **J** baptism.
20: 4 "Did **J** baptism come from heaven, or was it
Jn 1:37 Then **J** two disciples turned and followed Jesus.
3:25 with **J** disciples over ceremonial cleansing.
3:26 **J** disciples came to him and said, "Teacher,
5:34 though I have reminded you about **J** testimony
Ac 12: 2 He had the apostle James (**J** brother) killed with a
18:25 However, he knew only about **J** baptism.
19: 4 "**J** baptism was to demonstrate a desire to turn

JOIADA (5)

Ne 3: 6 The Old City Gate was repaired by **J** son of Paseah
12:10 father of Eliashib. / Eliashib was the father of **J**.
12:11 **J** was the father of Johanan. / Johanan was the
12:22 high priests: Eliashib, **J**, Johanan, and Jaddua.
13:28 One of the sons of **J** son of Eliashib the high priest

JOIAKIM (4)

Ne 12:10 Jeshua the high priest was the father of **J**. / **J** was the father of Eliashib.
12:12 Now when **J** was high priest, the family leaders of
12:26 These all served in the days of **J** son of Jeshua,

JOIARIB (5)

Ezr 8:16 I also sent for **J** and Elnathan, who were very wise
Ne 11: 5 son of Hazaiah, son of Adaiah, son of **J**, son of
11:10 From the priests: Jedaiah son of **J**; Jakin;
12: 6 Shemaiah, **J**, Jedaiah,
12:19 Mattenai was leader of the family of **J**. / Uzzi was

JOIN (70) [JOINED, JOINING, JOINS, REJOINS]

Ge 46:31 have all come from the land of Canaan to **j** me.
Ex 1:10 they will **j** our enemies and fight against us.
10: 9 We must all **j** together in a festival to the
23: 2 "Do not **j** a crowd that intends to do evil.
26: 3 **J** five of these sheets together into one set;
26: 3 then **j** the other five sheets into a second set.
26: 9 **J** five of these together into one set, and **j** the other
32:26 on the LORD's side, come over here and **j** me."
Nu 18: 4 The Levites must **j** with you to fulfill their
20:24 "The time has come for Aaron to **j** his ancestors in
20:26 his son. Aaron will die there and **j** his ancestors."
31: 2 After that, you will die and **j** your ancestors."
Dt 13: 9 initiate the execution; then all the people must **j** in.
17: 7 the first stones, and then all the people will **j** in.
31:16 "You are about to die and **j** your ancestors.
32:50 die there on the mountain and **j** your ancestors,
Jos 22:19 land is defiled, then **j** us on our side of the river,
Jdg 1: 3 "**J** with us to fight against the Canaanites living in
20:15 to **j** the seven hundred warriors who lived there.
1Sa 10: 8 I will **j** you there to sacrifice burnt offerings
16:22 "Please let David **j** my staff, for I am very pleased
28: 1 and your men will be expected to **j** me in battle."
1Ki 22: 4 "Will you **j** me in fighting against
1Ch 12:18 So David let them **j** him, and he made them
13: 2 Let us invite them to come and **j** us.
13: 5 to **j** in bringing the Ark of God from
2Ch 18: 2 Then Ahab enticed Jehoshaphat to **j** forces with
18: 3 "Will you **j** me in fighting against
18: 3 to command. We will certainly **j** you in battle."
Job 1: 4 and sisters to **j** them for a celebration.
Ps 1: 1 or stand around with sinners, / or **j** in with scoffers.
26: 5 who do evil, / and I refuse to **j** in with the wicked.
35:15 in trouble; / they gleefully **j** together against me.
47: 9 They **j** us in praising the God of Abraham.
98: 7 his praise! / Let the earth and all living things **j** in.
Pr 1:11 They may say, "Come and **j** us. Let's hide and kill
Isa 11:14 They will **j** forces to swoop down on Philistia to
14: 1 and **j** them there and become a part of the people
41: 7 Carefully they **j** the parts together, then fasten the
42:11 **J** in the chorus, you desert towns; / let the villages
Jer 31:13 the men—old and young—will **j** in the celebration.
50: 4 the people of Israel and Judah will **j** together,"
Eze 2: 8 Do not **j** them in being a rebel. Open your mouth,
14:22 and they will come here to **j** you as exiles in
37:19 I will take the northern tribes and **j** them to Judah.
38: 5 Persia, Ethiopia, and Libya will **j** you, too, with all
38: 6 Gomer and all its hordes will also **j** you, along with
45:16 All the people of Israel must **j** the prince in
Da 11:14 Lawless ones among your own people will **j** them
11:34 though many who **j** them will not be sincere.
Hos 4:15 do not **j** with those who worship me insincerely at
Zec 2:11 Many nations will **j** themselves to the LORD on
9: 7 And the Philistines of Ekron will **j** my people,
Mt 20: 7 'Then go on out and **j** the others in my vineyard.'
Ac 1:22 Whoever is chosen will **j** us as a witness of Jesus'
5:13 No one else dared to **j** them, though everyone had
16: 3 so Paul wanted him to **j** them on their journey.
17:15 message for Silas and Timothy to hurry and **j** him.
20:13 to Assos, where he had arranged for us to **j** him,
21:24 and **j** them in the purification ceremony,
Ro 8:21 All creation anticipates the day when it will **j**
15: 6 Then all of you can **j** together with one voice,
15:30 I urge you in the name of our Lord Jesus Christ to **j**
1Co 6:15 which belongs to Christ, and **j** it to a prostitute?
14:16 How can they **j** you in giving thanks when they
Gal 1: 2 All the Christians here **j** me in sending greetings to
2:13 and even Barnabas was influenced to **j** them in
1Pe 4: 4 you no longer **j** them in the wicked things they do,
Jude 1:12 When these people **j** you in fellowship meals

JOINED (61) [JOIN]

Ge 2:24 leaves his father and mother and is **j** to his wife,
12: 5 and all the people who had **j** his household at
25:17 died at the age of 137 and **j** his ancestors in death.
47: 5 to Joseph, "Now that your family has **j** you here,
Ex 18:12 They all **j** him in a sacrificial meal in God's
26:17 on each frame so they can be **j** to the next frame.
28: 7 **j** at the shoulders with two shoulder-pieces.
36:10 Five of these sheets were **j** together to make one
36:13 Thus the Tabernacle was **j** together in one piece.
36:16 The craftsmen **j** five of these sheets together to
36:16 and the six remaining sheets were **j** to make a
36:18 the roof covering was **j** together in one piece.
36:22 on each frame so they could be **j** to the next frame.
Nu 25: 5 everyone who had **j** in worshiping Baal of Peor.
Dt 32:50 died on Mount Hor and **j** his ancestors.
Jdg 1:17 Then Judah **j** with Simeon to fight against the
7:23 who **j** in the chase after the fleeing army of
1Sa 14:21 to the Philistine army revolted and **j** in with Saul,
14:22 the men who were hiding in the hills **j** the chase
17:13 had already **j** Saul's army to fight the Philistines.
22: 1 Soon his brothers and other relatives **j** him there.
2Sa 10:16 they were **j** by additional Aramean troops
15:12 Soon many others also **j** Absalom,
15:13 "All Israel has **j** Absalom in a conspiracy against
1Ki 2:28 Absalom earlier, Joab had also **j** Adonijah's revolt.
11:18 and went to Paran, where others **j** them.
2Ki 3: 9 The king of Edom and his troops **j** them, and all
8:28 Ahaziah **j** King Joram of Israel in his war against
25:23 Gedaliah as governor, they **j** him at Mizpah.
1Ch 12: 1 The following men **j** David at Ziklag while he was
12:19 and **j** David when he went with the Philistines to
12:22 Day after day more men **j** David until he had a
12:23 These are the numbers of armed warriors who **j**
19: 7 where they were **j** by the Ammonite troops that
2Ch 5:12 They were **j** by 120 priests who were playing
13: 7 Then a whole gang of scoundrels **j** him,
Ps 48: 4 The kings of the earth **j** forces / and advanced
83: 8 Assyria has **j** them, too, / and is allied with the
106:28 Then our ancestors **j** in the worship of Baal at
Jer 15:17 I never **j** the people in their merry feasts. I sat
Eze 47:22 and for the foreigners who have **j** you and are
Mt 19: 5 leaves his father and mother and is **j** to his wife,
19: 6 one separate them, for God has **j** them together."
23:30 'We never would have **j** them in killing the
Mk 10: 7 leaves his father and mother and is **j** to his wife,
10: 9 one separate them, for God has **j** them together."
Lk 2:13 Suddenly, the angel was **j** by a vast host of others
22:55 and sat around it, and Peter **j** them there.
24:15 Jesus himself came along and **j** them and began
Jn 15: 7 But if you stay **j** to me and my words remain in
Ac 2:42 They **j** with the other believers and devoted
5:36 About four hundred others **j** him, but he was killed,
17:34 but some **j** him and became believers.
20:14 He **j** us there and we sailed together to Mitylene.
28:15 Others **j** us at The Three Taverns. When Paul saw
1Co 6:17 But the person who is **j** to the Lord becomes one
Eph 2:21 We who believe are carefully **j** together,
2:22 Through him you Gentiles are also **j** together as
3:10 and Gentiles are **j** together in his church.
5:31 leaves his father and mother and is **j** to his wife,
Col 2:19 For we are **j** together in his body by his strong

JOINING (4) [JOIN]

Ge 25: 8 he died at a ripe old age, **j** his ancestors in death.
35:29 he died at a ripe old age, **j** his ancestors in death.
Nu 25: 3 Before long Israel was **j** in the worship of Baal of
Rev 20:10 burns with sulfur, **j** the beast and the false prophet.

JOINS (1) [JOIN]

1Co 6:16 And don't you know that if a man **j** himself to a

JOINT (3) [JOINTS]

Ge 32:25 Jacob's hip and knocked it out of **j** at the socket.
Ps 22:14 out like water, / and all my bones are out of **j**.
Eze 29: 7 you gave way, and her back was thrown out of **j**.

JOINTS (2) [JOINT]

1Ki 22:34 and the arrow hit the king of Israel between the **j** of
2Ch 18:33 and the arrow hit the king of Israel between the **j** of

JOKDEAM (1)

Jos 15:56 Jezreel, **J**, Zanoah,

JOKE (2) [JOKES, JOKING]

Ps 80: 6 neighboring nations. / Our enemies treat us as a **j**.
Jer 20: 8 from the LORD have made me a household **j**.

JOKES (2) [JOKE]

Ps 44:14 You have made us the butt of their **j**; / we are
Eph 5: 4 Obscene stories, foolish talk, and coarse **j**—

JOKIM (1)

1Ch 4:22 **J**, the people of Cozeba, Joash, and Saraph,

JOKING (3) [JOKE]

Ge 19:14 But the young men thought he was only **j**.
43: 3 "The man wasn't **j** when he warned that we
Pr 26:19 who lies to a friend and then says, "I was only **j**."

JOKMEAM (2) [KIBZAIM]

1Ki 4:12 from Beth-shan to Abel-meholah and over to **J**.
1Ch 6:68 **J**, Beth-horon,

JOKNEAM (4)

Jos 12:22 The king of Kedesh / The king of **J** in Carmel
19:11 and proceeding to the brook east of **J**.
21:34 towns from the tribe of Zebulun: **J**, Kartah,
1Ch 6:77 from the territory of Zebulun the towns of **J**,

JOKSHAN (3) [JOKSHAN'S]

Ge 25: 2 him Zimran, **J**, Medan, Midian, Ishbak, and Shuah.
1Ch 1:32 **J**, Medan, Midian, Ishbak, and Shuah. / The sons of **J** were Sheba and Dedan.

JOKSHAN'S (1) [JOKSHAN]

Ge 25: 3 **J** two sons were Sheba and Dedan.

JOKTAN (6)

Ge 10:25 and dispersed. His brother's name was **J**.
10:26 **J** was the ancestor of Almodad, Sheleph,
10:30 The descendants of **J** lived in the area extending
1Ch 1:19 and dispersed. His brother's name was **J**.
1:20 **J** was the ancestor of Almodad, Sheleph,
1:23 and Jobab. All these were descendants of **J**.

JOKTHEEL (2) [SELA]

Jos 15:38 Dilean, Mizpeh, **J**,
2Ki 14: 7 He also conquered Sela and changed its name to **J**,

JONA [KJV] See JOHN

JONADAB (5)

2Sa 13: 3 Amnon had a very crafty friend—his cousin **J**.
13: 4 One day **J** said to Amnon, "What's the trouble?
13: 5 "Well," **J** said, "I'll tell you what to do. Go back
13:32 But just then **J**, the son of David's brother Shimea,
13:35 "Look!" **J** told the king. "There they are now!

JONAH (30) [JONAH'S]

2Ki 14:25 of Israel, had promised through **J** son of Amittai,
Jnh 1: 1 The LORD gave this message to **J** son of Amittai:
1: 3 But **J** got up and went in the opposite direction in
1: 5 And all this time **J** was sound asleep down in the
1: 7 terrible storm. When they did this, **J** lost the toss.
1: 9 And **J** answered, "I am a Hebrew, and I worship
1:12 "Throw me into the sea," **J** said, "and it will
1:15 Then the sailors picked **J** up and threw him into
1:17 LORD had arranged for a great fish to swallow **J**.
1:17 And **J** was inside the fish for three days and three
2: 1 Then **J** prayed to the LORD his God from inside
2:10 Then the LORD ordered the fish to spit up **J** on
3: 1 Then the LORD spoke to **J** a second time:
3: 3 This time **J** obeyed the LORD's command
3: 4 On the day **J** entered the city, he shouted to the
3: 6 When the king of Nineveh heard what **J** was
4: 1 This change of plans upset **J**, and he became very
4: 5 Then **J** went out to the east side of the city

4: 6 and **J** was very grateful for the plant.
4: 8 God sent a scorching east wind to blow on **J**.
4: 9 Then God said to **J**, "Is it right for you to be angry
4: 9 "Yes," **J** retorted, "even angry enough to die!"
Mt 12:39 sign I will give them is the sign of the prophet **J**.
12:40 For as **J** was in the belly of the great fish for three
12:41 because they repented at the preaching of **J**.
12:41 And now someone greater than **J** is here—and you
16: 4 sign I will give them is the sign of the prophet **J**."
Lk 11:29 sign I will give them is the sign of the prophet **J**.
11:32 because they repented at the preaching of **J**.
11:32 And now someone greater than **J** is here—and you

JONAH'S (2) [JONAH]

Jnh 1:14 Then they cried out to the LORD, **J** God.
4: 6 and soon it spread its broad leaves over **J** head,

JONAM (2)

Lk 3:30 Joseph was the son of **J**. / **J** was the son of Eliakim.

JONAN [KJV] See JONAM

JONAS [KJV] See JONAH

JONATHAN (113) [JONATHAN'S]

Jdg 18:30 and they appointed **J** son of Gershom,
1Sa 13: 2 The other thousand went with Saul's son **J** to
13: 3 **J** attacked and defeated the garrison of Philistines
13:16 Saul and **J** and the troops with them were staying
13:22 Israel had a sword or spear, except for Saul and **J**.
14: 1 One day **J** said to the young man who carried his
14: 1 But **J** did not tell his father what he was doing.
14: 3 No one realized that **J** had left the Israelite camp.
14: 4 **J** had to go down between two rocky cliffs that
14: 6 to see those pagans," **J** said to his armor bearer.
14: 8 "All right then," **J** told him. "We will cross over
14:12 Then they shouted to **J**, "Come on up here,
14:12 climb right behind me," **J** said to his armor bearer,
14:13 and the Philistines fell back as **J** and his armor
14:17 they found that **J** and his armor bearer were gone.
14:21 Philistine army revolted and joined in with Saul, **J**,
14:27 But **J** had not heard his father's command, and he
14:29 **J** exclaimed. "A command like that only hurts us.
14:39 sinner will surely die, even if it is my own son **J**!"
14:40 Then Saul said, "**J** and I will stand over here,
14:41 Are **J** and I guilty, or is the sin among the others?"
14:41 And **J** and Saul were chosen as the guilty ones,
14:42 Then Saul said, "Now choose between me and **J**."
14:42 And **J** was shown to be the guilty one.
14:43 demanded of **J**. "I tasted a little honey," **J** admitted.
14:44 "Yes, **J**," Saul said, "you must die! May God
14:45 the people broke in and said to Saul, "Should **J**,
14:45 So the people rescued **J**, and he was not put to
14:49 Saul's sons included **J**, Ishbosheth, and Malkishua.
18: 1 talking with Saul, he met **J**, the king's son.
18: 3 And **J** made a special vow to be David's friend,
19: 1 his servants and his son **J** to assassinate David.
19: 1 But **J**, because of his close friendship with David,
19: 4 The next morning **J** spoke with his father about
19: 4 "Please don't sin against David," **J** pleaded.
19: 6 So Saul listened to **J** and vowed, "As surely as the
19: 7 Afterward **J** called David and told him what had
20: 1 now fled from Naioth in Ramah and found **J**.
20: 2 "That's not true!" **J** protested. "I'm sure he's not
20: 3 Then David took an oath before **J** and said,
20: 3 so he has said to himself, 'I won't tell **J**—
20: 4 "Tell me what I can do!" **J** exclaimed.
20: 9 "Never!" **J** exclaimed. "You know that if I had
20:11 "Come out to the field with me," **J** replied.
20:12 Then **J** told David, "I promise by the LORD,
20:16 So **J** made a covenant with David, saying,
20:17 And **J** made David reaffirm his vow of friendship
20:17 for **J** loved David as much as he loved himself.
20:18 Then **J** said, "Tomorrow we celebrate the new
20:25 with **J** sitting opposite him and Abner beside him.
20:27 place was empty again the next day, Saul asked **J**,
20:28 **J** replied, "David earnestly asked me if he could
20:30 Saul boiled with rage at **J**. "You stupid son of a
20:32 "But what has he done?" **J** demanded.
20:33 Then Saul hurled his spear at **J**, intending to kill
20:33 So at last **J** realized that his father was really
20:34 **J** left the table in fierce anger and refused to eat all
20:35 **J** went out into the field and took a young boy with
20:36 So the boy ran, and **J** shot an arrow beyond him.
20:37 **J** shouted, "The arrow is still ahead of you.
20:39 understand what **J** meant; only **J** and David knew.
20:40 Then **J** gave his bow and arrows to the boy
20:41 Then David bowed to **J** with his face to the
20:42 At last **J** said to David, "Go in peace, for we have
20:42 Then David left, and **J** returned to the city.
23:16 **J** went to find David and encouraged him to stay
23:17 "Don't be afraid," **J** reassured him. "My father
23:18 Then **J** returned home, while David stayed at
31: 2 three of his sons—**J**, Abinadab, and Malkishua.
2Sa 1: 4 and Saul and his son **J** have been killed."
1: 5 "How do you know that Saul and **J** are dead?"
1:12 and wept and fasted all day for Saul and his son **J**,
1:17 David composed a funeral song for Saul and **J**.
1:22 Both Saul and **J** killed their strongest foes;
1:23 How beloved and gracious were Saul and **J**!
1:25 have fallen in battle! / **J** lies dead upon the hills.
1:26 How I weep for you, my brother **J**! / Oh,
4: 4 (Saul's son **J** had a son named Mephibosheth,
4: 4 and **J** were killed at the battle of Jezreel.
9: 1 for he had promised **J** that he would show kindness
9: 7 kind to you because of my vow to your father, **J**.
15:27 city with your son Ahimaaz and Abiathar's son **J**.
15:36 and **J** to find me and tell me what is going on."
17:17 **J** and Ahimaaz had been staying at En-rogel
17:20 they asked her, "Have you seen Ahimaaz and **J**?"
21: 7 oath David and **J** had sworn before the LORD.
21:12 and asked for the bones of Saul and his son **J**.
21:12 and **J** had died in a battle with the Philistines,
21:13 So David brought the bones of Saul and **J**, as well
21:21 But he was killed by **J**, the son of David's brother
23:33 **J** son of Shagee from Harar; / Ahiam son of Sharar
1Ki 1:42 still speaking, **J** son of Abiathar the priest arrived.
1:43 "Not at all!" **J** replied. "Our lord King David has
1Ch 2:32 Jada, had two sons named Jether and **J**.
2:33 but **J** had two sons named Peleth and Zaza.
8:33 Saul was the father of **J**, Malkishua, Abinadab,
8:34 **J** was the father of Meribbaal. Meribbaal was the
9:39 Saul was the father of **J**, Malkishua, Abinadab,
9:40 **J** was the father of Meribbaal. Meribbaal was the
10: 2 three of his sons—**J**, Abinadab, and Malkishua.
11:34 Jashen from Gizon; / **J** son of Shagee from Harar;
20: 7 But he was killed by **J**, the son of David's brother
27:25 **J** son of Uzziah was in charge of the regional
27:32 **J**, David's uncle, was a wise counselor to the king,
Ezr 8: 6 family of Adin: Ebed son of **J** and 50 other men.
10:15 Only **J** son of Asahel and Jahzeiah son of Tikvah
Ne 12:14 **J** was leader of the family of Malluch.
12:35 Then came Zechariah son of **J**, son of Shemaiah,
Jer 37:15 and imprisoned in the house of **J** the secretary.
37:20 back to the dungeon in the house of **J** the secretary,
40: 8 son of Nethaniah, Johanan and **J**, sons of Kareah,

JONATHAN'S (5) [JONATHAN]

2Sa 9: 3 Ziba replied, "Yes, one of **J** sons is still alive,
9: 6 he was **J** son and Saul's grandson.
21: 7 David spared **J** son Mephibosheth, who was Saul's
Jer 37:15 **J** house had been converted into a prison.
38:26 you begged me not to send you back to **J** dungeon,

JOPPA (12)

Jos 19:46 also Rakkon along with the territory across from **J**.
2Ch 2:16 rafts down the coast of the Mediterranean Sea to **J**.
Ezr 3: 7 along the coast of the Mediterranean Sea to **J**,
Jnh 1: 3 He went down to the seacoast, to the port of **J**,
Ac 9:36 There was a believer in **J** named Tabitha (which in
9:43 And Peter stayed a long time in **J**, living with
10: 5 Now send some men down to **J** to find a man
10: 8 them what had happened and sent them off to **J**.
10:23 accompanied by some other believers from **J**.
10:32 Now send some men to **J** and summon Simon
11: 5 "One day in **J**," he said, "while I was praying,
11:13 'Send messengers to **J** to find Simon Peter.

JORAH (2)

Ezr 2:18 The family of **J** | 112
Ne 7:24 The family of **J** | 112

JORAI (1)

1Ch 5:13 Meshullam, Sheba, **J**, Jacan, Zia, and Eber.

JORAM (30) [JORAM'S]

2Sa 8:10 he sent his son **J** to congratulate David on his
8:10 **J** presented David with many gifts of silver,
2Ki 1:17 to succeed him, his brother **J** became the next king.
3: 1 Ahab's son **J** began to rule over Israel in the
3: 6 So King **J** mustered the army of Israel
3: 8 attack from the wilderness of Edom," **J** replied.
3:13 of your father and mother!" But King **J** said, "No!
8:16 Joram's reign in Israel. **J** was the son of Ahab.
8:25 reign in Israel. King **J** was the son of Ahab.
8:28 Ahaziah joined King **J** of Israel in his war against
8:28 When King **J** was wounded in the battle,
8:29 While **J** was there, King Ahaziah of Judah went to
9:14 of Nimshi formed a conspiracy against King **J**.
9:14 (Now **J** had been with the army at Ramoth-gilead,
9:15 But **J** had been wounded in the fighting and had
9:16 into a chariot and rode to Jezreel to find King **J**.
9:17 and his company approaching, so he shouted to **J**,
9:17 if they are coming in peace," King **J** shouted back.
9:21 Get my chariot ready!" King **J** commanded.
9:21 Then King **J** of Israel and King Ahaziah of Judah
9:22 King **J** demanded, "Do you come in peace,
9:23 Then King **J** reined the chariot horses around
9:24 drew his bow and shot **J** between the shoulders.
1Ch 18:10 he sent his son **J** to congratulate David on his
18:10 **J** presented David with many gifts of gold, silver,
26:25 were Rehabiah, Jeshaiah, **J**, Zicri, and Shelomoth.
2Ch 22: 5 evil advice, Ahaziah made an alliance with King **J**,
22: 5 and the Arameans wounded **J** in the battle.
22: 6 **J** returned to Jezreel to recover from his wounds,
22: 7 went out with **J** to meet Jehu son of Nimshi,

JORAM'S (4) [JORAM]

2Ki 3:11 One of King **J** officers replied, "Elisha son of
8:16 Judah in the fifth year of King **J** reign in Israel.
8:25 Judah in the twelfth year of King **J** reign in Israel.
9:29 in the eleventh year of King **J** reign in Israel.

JORDAN (211)

Ge 13:10 Lot took a long look at the fertile plains of the **J**
13:11 land for himself—the **J** Valley to the east of them.
50:10 near the **J** River, they held a very great and solemn
Nu 13:29 of the Mediterranean Sea and along the **J** Valley."
22: 1 the plains of Moab and camped east of the **J** River,
26: 3 camped on the plains of Moab beside the **J** River,
26:63 the priest on the plains of Moab beside the **J** River,
31:12 camped on the plains of Moab beside the **J** River,
32: 5 instead of giving us land across the **J** River."
32:19 not want any of the land on the other side of the **J**.
32:21 and if your troops cross the **J** until the LORD has
32:22 And the land on the east side of the **J** will be your
32:29 to fight the LORD's battles cross the **J** with you,
32:32 We will cross the **J** into Canaan fully armed to
32:32 of land will be here on this side of the **J**."
33:48 and camped on the plains of Moab beside the **J**
33:49 Along the **J** River they camped from
33:50 While they were camped near the **J** River on the
33:51 'When you cross the **J** River into the land of
34:12 and then along the **J** River to the Dead Sea.
34:15 on the east side of the **J** River, across from
35: 1 While Israel was camped beside the **J** on the plains
35:10 'When you cross the **J** into the land of Canaan,
35:14 three on the east side of the **J** River and three on
36:13 camped on the plains of Moab beside the **J** River,
Dt 1: 1 they were in the wilderness east of the **J** River.
1: 1 They were camped in the **J** Valley near Suph,
1: 5 they were in the land of Moab east of the **J** River.
1: 7 the **J** Valley, the hill country, the western foothills,
2:29 Let us pass through until we cross the **J** into the
3: 8 land of the two Amorite kings east of the **J** River—
3:17 They also received the **J** Valley,
3:17 including the **J** River and its eastern banks,
3:18 command to the tribes that will live east of the **J**:
3:18 all your fighting men must cross the **J**, armed
3:20 your God is giving them across the **J** River,
3:21 same to all the kingdoms on the west side of the **J**.
3:25 Please let me cross the **J** to see the wonderful land
3:27 every direction, but you may not cross the **J** River.
3:28 for he will lead the people across the **J**.
4:21 He vowed that I would never cross the **J** River into
4:22 Though you will cross the **J** to occupy the land,
4:26 from the land you are crossing the **J** to occupy.
4:41 set apart three cities of refuge east of the **J** River,
4:46 in the valley near Beth-peor east of the **J** River.
4:47 of Bashan—the two Amorite kings east of the **J**.
4:49 And they took the eastern bank of the **J** Valley as
9: 1 Today you are about to cross the **J** River to occupy
11:30 (These two mountains are west of the **J** River in
11:30 the land of the Canaanites who live in the **J** Valley,
11:31 For you are about to cross the **J** to occupy the land
12:10 You will soon cross the **J** River and live in the land
27: 2 When you cross the **J** River and enter the land the
27: 4 When you cross the **J**, set up these stones at Mount
27:12 "When you cross the **J** River, the tribes of
30:18 good life in the land you are crossing the **J** to
31: 2 The LORD has told me that I will not cross the **J**
31:13 live in the land you are crossing the **J** to occupy."
32:47 the land you are crossing the **J** River to occupy."
34: 3 the Negev; the **J** Valley with Jericho—the city of
Jos 1: 2 you must lead my people across the **J** River into
1:11 In three days you will cross the **J** River and take
1:14 and cattle may remain here on the east side of the **J**
1:14 must lead the other tribes across the **J** to help them
1:15 then may you settle here on the east side of the **J**
2: 1 "Spy out the land on the other side of the **J** River,
2: 7 to the shallow crossing places of the **J** River.
2:10 and Og, the two Amorite kings east of the **J** River,
2:23 down from the hill country, crossed the **J** River,
3: 1 left Acacia and arrived at the banks of the **J** River,
3: 8 'When you reach the banks of the **J** River, take a
3:11 the whole earth, will lead you across the **J** River!
3:14 When the people set out to cross the **J**, the priests
3:15 and the **J** was overflowing its banks.
3:17 They waited there until everyone had crossed the **J**
4: 3 the priests are standing in the middle of the **J**
4: 5 and told them, "Go into the middle of the **J**,
4: 7 'They remind us that the **J** River stopped flowing
4: 8 They took twelve stones from the middle of the **J**
4: 9 memorial of twelve stones in the middle of the **J**,
4:12 of Manasseh led the Israelites across the **J**,
4:18 the **J** River flooded its banks as before.
4:19 The people crossed the **J** on the tenth day of the
4:20 piled up the twelve stones taken from the **J** River.
4:22 'This is where the Israelites crossed the **J** on dry
5: 1 When all the Amorite kings west of the **J** and all
5: 1 heard how the LORD had dried up the **J** River
7: 7 why did you bring us across the **J** River if you are
8:14 the Israelites at a place overlooking the **J** Valley.
9: 1 Now all the kings west of the **J** heard about what
9:10 did to the two Amorite kings east of the **J** River—
11: 2 the kings in the **J** Valley south of Galilee;
11:16 the **J** Valley, and the mountains and lowlands of
12: 1 These are the kings east of the **J** River who had
12: 1 and included all the land east of the **J** Valley.
12: 3 Sihon also controlled the **J** Valley as far north as
12: 7 Israelite armies defeated on the west side of the **J**,
12: 8 the **J** Valley, the mountain slopes,
13: 8 received their inheritance on the east side of the **J**,
13:23 The **J** River marked the western boundary for the
13:27 The **J** River was the western border, extending as
13:32 plains of Moab, across the **J** River, east of Jericho.
14: 3 and a half tribes on the east side of the **J** River.
15: 5 along the Dead Sea to the mouth of the **J** River.
15: 5 bay where the **J** River empties into the Dead Sea,
16: 1 of Joseph extended from the **J** River near Jericho,
16: 7 touched Jericho, and ended at the **J** River.
17: 1 and Bashan on the east side of the **J** had already
17: 2 Land on the west side of the **J** was allotted to the
17: 5 the land of Gilead and Bashan across the **J** River,
18: 7 gave them on the east side of the **J** River."

18:12 The northern boundary began at the **J** River,
18:18 north side of the slope overlooking the **J** Valley.
18:19 Dead Sea, which is the southern end of the **J** River.
18:20 The eastern boundary was the **J** River. This was
19:22 and Beth-shemesh, ending at the **J** River—
19:33 and as far as Lakkum, ending at the **J** River.
19:34 of Asher on the west, and the **J** River on the east.
20: 8 On the east side of the **J** River, across from
22: 4 gave you on the east side of the **J** River.
22: 7 Bashan to the half-tribe of Manasseh east of the **J**.
22: 7 other half of the tribe was given land west of the **J**.
22:10 before they crossed the **J** River, Reuben, Gad,
22:10 altar near the **J** River at a place called Geliloth.
22:11 had built the altar at Geliloth west of the **J** River,
22:25 The LORD has placed the **J** River as a barrier
23: 4 from the **J** River to the Mediterranean Sea in the
24: 8 the land of the Amorites on the east side of the **J**.
24:11 "When you crossed the **J** River and came to
Jdg 3:28 of the shallows of the **J** River across from Moab,
5:17 Gilead remained east of the **J**. / And Dan, why did
6:33 formed an alliance against Israel and crossed the **J**,
7:24 Cut them off at the shallows of the **J** River at
7:25 of Oreb and Zeeb to Gideon, who was by the **J**.
8: 4 then crossed the **J** River with his three hundred
10: 8 of the **J** River in the land of the Amorites (that is,
10: 9 Ammonites also crossed to the west side of the **J**
11:13 River to the Jabbok River and all the way to the **J**.
11:22 the Jabbok River, and from the wilderness to the **J**.
12: 5 Jephthah captured the shallows of the **J**,
12: 6 and kill him at the shallows of the **J** River.
1Sa 13: 7 Some of them crossed the **J** River and escaped into
31: 7 and beyond the **J** saw that their army had been
2Sa 2:29 and his men retreated through the **J** Valley.
2:29 They crossed the **J** River, traveling all through the
4: 7 they fled across the **J** Valley through the night.
10:17 he mobilized all Israel, crossed the **J** River, and led
15:28 I will stop at the shallows of the **J** River and wait
16:14 so they rested when they reached the **J** River.
17:16 and urge him not to stay at the shallows of the **J**
17:21 "Quick!" they told him, "cross the **J** tonight!"
17:22 and all the people with him went across the **J** River
17:24 and was leading his troops across the **J** River.
18:23 Ahimaaz took a shortcut across the plain of the **J**
19:15 And when he arrived at the **J** River, the people of
19:17 They rushed down to the **J** to arrive ahead of the
19:31 from Rogelim to conduct the king across the **J**.
19:39 So all the people crossed the **J** with the king.
19:41 to do most of the work in helping him cross the **J**.
20: 2 and escorted him from the **J** River to Jerusalem.
24: 5 First they crossed the **J** and camped at Aroer,
1Ki 2: 8 When he came down to meet me at the **J** River,
7:46 The king had them cast in clay molds in the **J**
17: 3 Brook at a place east of where it enters the **J** River.
2Ki 2: 6 for the LORD has told me to go to the **J** River."
2: 7 as Elijah and Elisha stopped beside the **J** River.
2:13 and returned to the bank of the **J** River.
5:10 and wash yourself seven times in the **J** River.
5:14 So Naaman went down to the **J** River and dipped
6: 2 Let's go down to the **J** River, where there are
6: 4 When they arrived at the **J**, they began cutting
7:15 They went all the way to the **J** River, following a
10:33 east of the **J** River, including all of Gilead, Gad,
25: 4 across the fields, in the direction of the **J** Valley.
1Ch 6:62 from the Bashan area of Manasseh, east of the **J**.
6:78 of Reuben, east of the **J** River opposite Jericho,
12:15 They crossed the **J** River during its seasonal
12:31 From the half-tribe of Manasseh west of the **J**,
12:37 From the east side of the **J** River—where the tribes
19:17 he mobilized all Israel, crossed the **J** River,
26:30 in charge of the Israelite lands west of the **J** River.
26:32 King David sent them to the east side of the **J**
2Ch 4:17 The king had them cast in clay molds in the **J**
Job 40:23 not even when the swelling **J** rushes down upon it.
Ps 42: 6 from Mount Hermon, the source of the **J**,
114: 3 their way! / The water of the **J** River turned away.
114: 5 What happened, **J** River, that you turned away?
Isa 9: 1 which lies along the road that runs between the **J**
Jer 12: 5 what will you do in the thickets near the **J**?
39: 4 the king's garden and headed toward the **J** Valley.
49:19 I will come like a lion from the thickets of the **J**,
50:44 "I will come like a lion from the thickets of the **J**,
52: 7 across the fields, in the direction of the **J** Valley.
Eze 47: 8 "This river flows east through the desert into the **J**
47:18 and runs southward along the **J** River between
Zec 11: 3 for their thickets in the **J** Valley have been
Mt 3: 5 and from all over the **J** Valley went out to the
3: 6 their sins, he baptized them in the **J** River.
3:13 Then Jesus went from Galilee to the **J** River to be
4:15 of Naphtali, / beside the sea, beyond the **J** River—
4:25 from all over Judea, and from east of the **J** River.
19: 1 of Judea and into the area east of the **J** River.
Mk 1: 5 their sins, he baptized them in the **J** River.
1: 9 and he was baptized by John in the **J** River.
3: 8 Jerusalem, Idumea, from east of the **J** River,
10: 1 of Judea and into the area east of the **J** River.
Lk 3: 3 from place to place on both sides of the **J** River,
4: 1 Then Jesus, full of the Holy Spirit, left the **J** River.
Jn 1:28 a village east of the **J** River, where John was
3:26 the man you met on the other side of the **J** River,
10:40 He went beyond the **J** River to stay near the place

JORIM (2)
Lk 3:29 Eliezer was the son of **J**. / **J** was the son of Matthat.

JORKEAM (1)
1Ch 2:44 the father of Raham. Raham was the father of **J**.

JOSABAD [KJV] See JOZABAD

JOSAPHAT [KJV] See JEHOSHAPHAT

JOSE [KJV] See JOSHUA

JOSECH (2)
Lk 3:26 Semein was the son of **J**. / **J** was the son of Joda.

JOSEDECH [KJV] See JEHOZADAK

JOSEPH (250) [BARNABAS, JOSEPH'S]
Ge 30:24 And she named him **J**, for she said,
30:25 Soon after **J** was born to Rachel, Jacob said to
33: 2 and her children next, and Rachel and **J** last.
33: 7 Finally, Rachel and **J** came and made their bows.
35:24 The sons of Rachel were **J** and Benjamin.
37: 2 When **J** was seventeen years old, he often tended
37: 2 But **J** reported to his father some of the bad things
37: 3 Now Jacob loved **J** more than any of his other
37: 3 because **J** had been born to him in his old age.
37: 3 So one day he gave **J** a special gift—a beautiful
37: 4 But his brothers hated **J** because of their father's
37: 5 One night **J** had a dream and promptly reported the
37: 9 Then **J** had another dream and told his brothers
37:11 But while his brothers were jealous of **J**, his father
37:13 they had been gone for some time, Jacob said to **J**,
37:13 send you to them." "I'm ready to go," **J** replied.
37:14 and **J** traveled to Shechem from his home in the
37:16 "For my brothers and their flocks," **J** replied.
37:17 So **J** followed his brothers to Dothan and found
37:22 Reuben was secretly planning to help **J** escape,
37:23 So when **J** arrived, they pulled off his beautiful
37:27 Let's sell **J** to those Ishmaelite traders. Let's not be
37:28 his brothers pulled **J** out of the pit and sold him for
37:29 time later, Reuben returned to get **J** out of the pit.
37:29 When he discovered that **J** was missing, he tore his
37:33 and eaten him. Surely **J** has been torn in pieces!"
37:36 in Egypt, the traders sold **J** to Potiphar,
39: 1 Now when **J** arrived in Egypt with the Ishmaelite
39: 2 The LORD was with **J** and blessed him greatly as
39: 3 and realized that the LORD was with **J**,
39: 4 So **J** naturally became quite a favorite with him.
39: 4 Potiphar soon put **J** in charge of his entire
39: 5 From the day **J** was put in charge, the LORD
39: 6 So Potiphar gave **J** complete administrative
39: 6 With **J** there, he didn't have a worry in the world,
39: 6 Now **J** was a very handsome and well-built young
39: 8 But **J** refused. "Look," he told her, "my master
39:12 **J** tore himself away, but as he did, his shirt came
39:20 He took **J** and threw him into the prison where the
39:21 But the LORD was with **J** there, too, and he
granted **J** favor with the chief jailer.
39:22 the jailer put **J** in charge of all the other prisoners
39:23 after that, because **J** took care of everything.
40: 3 and he put them in the prison where **J** was,
40: 4 and Potiphar assigned **J** to take care of them.
40: 6 The next morning **J** noticed the dejected look on
40: 8 dreams is God's business," **J** replied.
40:12 "I know what the dream means," **J** said.
40:16 such a good meaning, he told his dream to **J**, too.
40:18 "I'll tell you what it means," **J** told him.
40:22 to be impaled on a pole, just as **J** had predicted.
40:23 however, promptly forgot all about **J**,
41:14 Pharaoh sent for **J** at once, and he was brought
41:16 "It is beyond my power to do this," **J** replied.
41:25 dreams mean the same thing," **J** told Pharaoh.
41:38 Pharaoh said, "Who could do it better than **J**?
41:39 Turning to **J**, Pharaoh said, "Since God has
41:41 And Pharaoh said to **J**, "I hereby put you in charge
41:43 Pharaoh also gave **J** the chariot of his
41:43 So **J** was put in charge of all Egypt.
41:44 And Pharaoh said to **J**, "I am the king, but no one
41:45 So **J** took charge of the entire land of Egypt.
41:46 And when **J** left Pharaoh's presence, he made a
41:48 **J** took a portion of all the crops grown in Egypt
41:50 two sons were born to **J** and his wife, Asenath,
41:51 **J** named his older son Manasseh, for he said,
41:52 **J** named his second son Ephraim, for he said,
41:54 years of famine began, just as **J** had predicted.
41:55 "Go to **J** and do whatever he tells you."
41:56 **J** opened up the storehouses and sold grain to the
41:57 lands also came to Egypt to buy grain from **J**
42: 6 Since **J** was governor of all Egypt and in charge of
42: 7 **J** recognized them instantly, but he pretended to be
42: 8 didn't recognize him, but **J** recognized them.
42:14 But **J** insisted, "As I said, you are spies!
42:18 On the third day **J** said to them, "I am a
42:21 all happened because of what we did to **J** long ago.
42:23 they didn't know that **J** understood them as he was
42:25 **J** then ordered his servants to fill the men's sacks
42:36 **J** has disappeared, Simeon is gone, and now you
42:38 not go down with you, for his brother **J** is dead,
43:15 to Egypt, where they presented themselves to **J**.
43:16 When **J** saw that Benjamin was with them, he said
43:26 When **J** came, they gave him their gifts and bowed
43:29 **J** asked, "Is this your youngest brother, the one
43:30 Then **J** made a hasty exit because he was
43:32 **J** ate by himself, and his brothers were served at a
43:33 **J** told each of his brothers where to sit, and to their
44: 1 **J** gave these instructions to the man in charge of
44: 4 **J** said to his household manager, "Chase after
44:14 **J** was still at home when Judah and his brothers
44:15 "What were you trying to do?" **J** demanded.
44:17 "No," **J** said. "Only the man who stole the cup
45: 1 **J** could stand it no longer. "Out, all of you!"
45: 3 "I am **J**!" he said to his brothers. "Is my father
45: 3 They were stunned to realize that **J** was standing
45: 4 And he said again, "I am **J**, your brother whom
45: 9 and tell him, 'This is what your son **J** says:
45:12 Then **J** said, "You can see for yourselves, and
45:12 so can my brother Benjamin, that I really am **J**!
45:15 Then **J** kissed each of his brothers and wept over
45:17 Pharaoh said to **J**, "Tell your brothers to load their
45:21 **J** gave them wagons, as Pharaoh had commanded,
45:26 "**J** is still alive!" they told him. "And he is ruler
45:27 he saw the wagons loaded with the food sent by **J**,
45:28 My son **J** is alive! I will go and see him before I
46: 4 But you will die in Egypt with **J** at your side."
46:19 The sons of Jacob's wife Rachel were **J**
46:27 **J** also had two sons who had been born in Egypt.
46:28 Jacob sent Judah on ahead to meet **J** and get
46:29 **J** prepared his chariot and journeyed to Goshen to
46:29 As soon as **J** arrived, he embraced his father
46:30 Then Jacob said to **J**, "Now let me die, for I have
46:31 And **J** said to his brothers and to all their
47: 1 So **J** went to see Pharaoh and said, "My father
47: 2 **J** took five of his brothers with him and presented
47: 5 And Pharaoh said to **J**, "Now that your family has
47: 7 Then **J** brought his father, Jacob, and presented
47:11 So **J** assigned the best land of Egypt—the land of
47:12 And **J** furnished food to his father and brothers in
47:14 **J** collected all the money in Egypt and Canaan in
47:15 of money, they came to **J** crying again for food.
47:16 "Well, then," **J** replied, "since your money is
47:17 So they gave their livestock to **J** in exchange for
47:20 So **J** bought all the land of Egypt for Pharaoh.
47:23 Then **J** said to the people, "See, I have bought you
47:26 **J** then made it a law throughout the land of Egypt
47:29 he called for his son **J** and said to him, "If you are
47:30 my ancestors." So **J** promised that he would.
47:31 So **J** gave his oath, and Jacob bowed in worship as
48: 1 word came to **J** that his father was failing rapidly.
48: 1 So **J** went to visit him, and he took with him his
48: 2 When Jacob heard that **J** had arrived, he gathered
48: 3 Jacob said to **J**, "God Almighty appeared to me at
48: 9 "Yes," **J** told him, "these are the sons God has
48:10 So **J** brought the boys close to him, and Jacob
48:11 Then Jacob said to **J**, "I never thought I would see
48:12 **J** took the boys from their grandfather's knees,
48:15 Then he blessed **J** and said, "May God, the God
48:17 But **J** was upset when he saw that his father had
48:21 Then Jacob said to **J**, "I am about to die, but God
49:22 "**J** is a fruitful tree, / a fruitful tree beside a
49:26 These blessings will fall on the head of **J**,
50: 1 **J** threw himself on his father and wept over him
50: 2 Then **J** told his morticians to embalm the body.
50: 4 **J** approached Pharaoh's advisers and asked them
50: 7 So **J** went, with a great number of Pharaoh's
50: 8 **J** also took his brothers and the entire household of
50: 9 of chariots, cavalry, and people accompanied **J**.
50:14 Then **J** returned to Egypt with his brothers and all
50:15 "Now **J** will pay us back for all the evil we did to
50:16 So they sent this message to **J**: "Before your father
50:17 When **J** received the message, he broke down
50:19 But **J** told them, "Don't be afraid of me. Am I
50:22 So **J** and his brothers and their families continued
to live in Egypt. **J** was 110 years old when he died.
50:24 "Soon I will die," **J** told his brothers, "but God
50:25 Then **J** made the sons of Israel swear an oath,
50:26 So **J** died at the age of 110. They embalmed him,
Ex 1: 5 **J** was already down in Egypt. In all, Jacob had
1: 6 In time, **J** and each of his brothers died,
1: 8 to the throne of Egypt who knew nothing about **J**
13:19 Moses took the bones of **J** with him, for **J** had
made the sons of Israel swear that they
Nu 1:10 Ephraim son of **J** | Elishama son of Ammihud
1:10 Manasseh son of **J** | Gamaliel son of Pedahzur
1:32[-33] Ephraim son of **J** | 40,500
1:34[-35] Manasseh son of **J** | 32,200
13: 7 Issachar | Igal son of **J**
13:11 Manasseh son of **J** | Gaddi son of Susi
26:28 Two clans were descended from **J** through
26:37 and Ephraim were all descendants of **J**.
27: 1 son of Makir, son of Manasseh, son of **J**.
32:33 and half the tribe of Manasseh son of **J** the
34:23 Manasseh son of **J** | Hanniel son of Ephod
34:24 Ephraim son of **J** | Kemuel son of Shiphtan
36: 1 descendants of Makir, son of Manasseh, son of **J**—
36: 5 the LORD: "The men of the tribe of **J** are right.
36:12 They married into the clans of Manasseh son of **J**.
Dt 27:12 the tribes of Simeon, Levi, Judah, Issachar, **J**,
33:13 Moses said this about the tribes of **J**: / "May their
33:17 **J** has the strength and majesty of a young bull;
Jos 14: 4 The tribe of **J** had become two separate tribes—
16: 1 The allotment to the descendants of **J** extended
17:14 The descendants of **J** came to Joshua and asked,
17:17 of Ephraim and Manasseh, the descendants of **J**,
18:11 previously assigned to the tribes of Judah and **J**.
24:32 The bones of **J**, which the Israelites had brought
24:32 of Ephraim and Manasseh, the descendants of **J**.
Jdg 1:22 The descendants of **J** attacked the town of Bethel,
1:35 but when the descendants of **J** became stronger,
1Ch 2: 2 Dan, **J**, Benjamin, Naphtali, Gad, and Asher.
5: 1 birthright was given to the sons of his brother **J**.
5: 2 for the nation, but the birthright belonged to **J**.
7:29 The descendants of **J** son of Israel lived in these
25: 2 there were Zaccur, **J**, Nethaniah, and Asarelah.
25: 9 The first lot fell to **J** of the Asaph clan and twelve
Ezr 10:42 Shallum, Amariah, and **J**.
Ne 12:14 **J** was leader of the family of Shecaniah.
Ps 77:15 the descendants of Jacob and of **J** by your might.

105:17 ahead of them— / J, who was sold as a slave.
105:21 J was put in charge of all the king's household;
Eze 47:13 The tribe of J will be given two shares of land.
48:32 the gates will be named for J, Benjamin, and Dan.
Mt 1:16 Jacob was the father of J, the husband of Mary.
1:18 His mother, Mary, was engaged to be married to J.
1:19 J, her fiancé, being a just man, decided to break the
1:20 "J, son of David," the angel said, "do not be
1:24 When J woke up, he did what the angel of the
1:25 until her son was born. And J named him Jesus.
2:13 an angel of the Lord appeared to J in a dream.
2:14 That night J left for Egypt with the child
2:19 an angel of the Lord appeared in a dream to J in
2:21 So J returned immediately to Israel with Jesus
13:55 and his brothers—James, J, Simon, and Judas.
27:56 Mary (the mother of James and J), and Zebedee's
27:57 As evening approached, J, a rich man from
27:59 J took the body and wrapped it in a long linen
Mk 6:3 and brother of James, J, Judas, and Simon.
15:40 Mary (the mother of James the younger and of J),
15:43 J from Arimathea (who was waiting for the
15:45 the fact, and Pilate told J he could have the body.
15:46 J bought a long sheet of linen cloth, and taking
15:47 and Mary the mother of J saw where Jesus' body
Lk 1:27 She was engaged to be married to a man named J,
2:4 And because J was a descendant of King David,
2:16 They ran to the village and found Mary and J.
2:27 and J came to present the baby Jesus to the Lord as
2:33 J and Mary were amazed at what was being said
2:38 along just as Simeon was talking with Mary and J,
3:23 Jesus was known as the son of J. / J was the son of
3:24 was the son of Jannai. / Jannai was the son of J.
3:25 J was the son of Mattathias. / Mattathias was the
3:30 Judah was the son of J. / J was the son of Jonam.
23:50 Now there was a good and righteous man named J.
Jn 1:45 His name is Jesus, the son of J from Nazareth."
4:5 the parcel of ground that Jacob gave to his son J.
6:42 They said, "This is Jesus, the son of J. We know
19:38 Afterward J of Arimathea, who had been a secret
Ac 1:23 J called Barsabbas (also known as Justus)
4:36 For instance, there was J, the one the apostles
7:9 sons of Jacob were very jealous of their brother J,
7:10 God also gave J unusual wisdom so that Pharaoh
7:13 they went, J revealed his identity to his brothers,
7:14 Then J sent for his father, Jacob, and all his
7:18 to the throne of Egypt who knew nothing about J.
Heb 11:22 And it was by faith that J, when he was about to
Rev 7:8 from Zebulun | 12,000 / from J | 12,000

JOSEPH'S (30) [JOSEPH]

Ge 37:12 J brothers went to pasture their father's flocks at
37:18 When J brothers saw him coming, they recognized
37:21 But Reuben came to J rescue. "Let's not kill
37:31 Then J brothers killed a goat and dipped the robe
37:32 in the field," they told him. "It's J robe, isn't it?"
39:5 the LORD began to bless Potiphar for J sake.
41:37 J suggestions were well received by Pharaoh
41:42 Then Pharaoh placed his own signet ring on J
42:3 So J ten older brothers went down to Egypt to buy
42:4 Jacob wouldn't let J younger brother, Benjamin,
42:8 J brothers didn't recognize him, but Joseph
43:17 man did as he was told and took them to J palace.
43:19 they went over to the man in charge of J
43:25 so they prepared their gifts for J arrival at noon.
43:34 Their food was served to them from J own table.
44:12 J servant began searching the oldest brother's
45:16 soon reached Pharaoh: "J brothers have come!"
45:27 But when they had given him J messages,
46:20 J sons, born in the land of Egypt, were Manasseh
50:6 Pharaoh agreed to J request. "Go and bury your
50:10 with a seven-day period of mourning for J father.
50:15 their father was dead, J brothers became afraid.
Dt 33:16 May these blessings rest on J head,
Jos 16:4 The families of J sons, Manasseh and Ephraim,
17:1 of Manasseh, the descendants of J older son.
18:5 territory in the south and J territory in the north.
Ps 78:67 But he rejected J descendants; / he did not choose
105:19 to fulfill his word, / the LORD tested J character.
Lk 4:22 can this be?" they asked. "Isn't this J son?"
Heb 11:21 blessed each of J sons and bowed in worship as he

JOSHAH (1)

1Ch 4:34 included Meshobab, Jamlech, J son of Amaziah,

JOSHAPHAT (2)

1Ch 11:43 Hanan son of Maacah; / J from Mithna;
15:24 J, Nethanel, Amasai, Zechariah, Benaiah,

JOSHAVIAH (1)

1Ch 11:46 from Mahavah; / Jeribai and J, the sons of Elnaam;

JOSHBEKASHAH (2)

1Ch 25:4 Geddalti, Romamti-ezer, J, Mallothi, Hothir,
25:24 The seventeenth lot fell to J and twelve of his sons

JOSHIBIAH (1)

1Ch 4:35 Joel, Jehu son of J, son of Seraiah, son of Asiel,

JOSHUA (202) [HOSHEA, JESHUA, JOSHUA'S]

Ex 17:9 Moses commanded J, "Call the Israelites to arms,
17:10 So J did what Moses had commanded. He led his
17:13 J and his troops were able to crush the army of
17:14 down as a permanent record, and announce it to J:
24:13 and his assistant J climbed up the mountain of
32:17 When J heard the noise of the people shouting
33:11 but the young man who assisted him, J son of Nun,
Nu 11:28 J son of Nun, who had been Moses' personal
13:16 this time Moses had changed Hoshea's name to J.
14:6 J son of Nun and Caleb son of Jephunneh,
14:10 the whole community began to talk about stoning J
14:30 will be Caleb son of Jephunneh and J son of Nun.
14:38 the land, only J and Caleb remained alive.
26:65 were Caleb son of Jephunneh and J son of Nun.
27:18 The LORD replied, "Take J son of Nun, who has
27:21 is needed, J will stand before Eleazar the priest,
27:21 This is how J and the rest of the community of
27:22 and presented J to Eleazar the priest and the whole
32:12 son of Jephunneh the Kenizzite and J son of Nun,
32:28 orders to Eleazar, J, and the tribal leaders of Israel.
34:17 the people: Eleazar the priest and J son of Nun.
Dt 1:38 Instead, your assistant, J son of Nun, will lead the
3:21 "At that time I said to J, 'You have seen all that
3:28 But commission J and encourage him, for he will
31:3 J is your new leader, and he will go with you,
31:7 Then Moses called for J, and as all Israel watched
31:14 Call J and take him with you to the Tabernacle,
31:14 So Moses and J went and presented themselves at
31:23 Then the LORD commissioned J son of Nun with
32:44 So Moses came with J son of Nun and recited all
34:9 Now J son of Nun was full of the spirit of wisdom,
Jos 1:1 the LORD spoke to J son of Nun,
1:10 J then commanded the leaders of Israel,
1:12 Then J called together the tribes of Reuben,
1:16 They answered J, "We will do whatever you
2:1 Then J secretly sent out two spies from the
2:23 and reported to J all that had happened to them.
3:1 Early the next morning J and all the Israelites left
3:5 Then J told the people, "Purify yourselves,
3:6 In the morning J said to the priests, "Lift up the
3:7 The LORD told J, "Today I will begin to make
3:9 So J told the Israelites, "Come and listen to what
4:1 were safely across the river, the LORD said to J,
4:4 So J called together the twelve men
4:8 So the men did as J told them. They took twelve
4:8 each tribe, just as the LORD had commanded J.
4:9 J also built another memorial of twelve stones in
4:10 which Moses had given to J, were carried out.
4:14 That day the LORD made J great in the eyes of
4:15 The LORD had said to J,
4:17 So J gave the command.
4:20 It was there at Gilgal that J piled up the twelve
4:21 Then J said to the Israelites, "In the future,
5:2 At that time the LORD told J, "Use knives of
5:3 So J made flint knives and circumcised the entire
5:4 J had to circumcise them because all the men who
5:7 So J circumcised their sons who had not been
5:9 Then the LORD said to J, "Today I have rolled
5:13 As J approached the city of Jericho, he looked up
5:13 J went up to him and asked, "Are you friend
5:14 J fell with his face to the ground in reverence.
5:14 "I am at your command," J said. "What do you
5:15 for this is holy ground." And J did as he was told.
6:2 But the LORD said to J, "I have given you
6:6 So J called together the priests and said, "Take up
6:8 After J spoke to the people, the seven priests with
6:10 "Do not shout; do not even talk," J commanded.
6:12 J got up early the next morning, and the priests
6:16 on their horns, J commanded the people, "Shout!
6:22 Then J said to the two spies, "Keep your promise.
6:25 So J spared Rahab the prostitute and her relatives
6:25 because she had hidden the spies J sent to Jericho.
6:26 At that time J invoked this curse: / "May the curse
6:27 So the LORD was with J, and his name became
7:2 J sent some of his men from Jericho to spy out the
7:3 they returned, they told J, "It's a small town,
7:6 J and the leaders of Israel tore their clothing in
7:7 Then J cried out, "Sovereign LORD, why did
7:10 But the LORD said to J, "Get up! Why are you
7:16 Early the next morning J brought the tribes of
7:19 Then J said to Achan, "My son, give glory to the
7:22 So J sent some men to make a search. They ran to
7:23 the tent and brought them to J and all the Israelites.
7:24 Then J and all the Israelites took Achan, the silver,
7:25 Then J said to Achan, "Why have you brought
8:1 Then the LORD said to J, "Do not be afraid
8:3 So J and the army of Israel set out to attack Ai.
8:3 J chose thirty thousand fighting men and sent
8:9 But J remained among the people in the camp that
8:10 Early the next morning J roused his men
8:12 That night J sent five thousand men to lie in
8:13 of the city. J himself spent that night in the valley.
8:15 J and the Israelite army fled toward the wilderness
8:18 Then the LORD said to J, "Point your spear
8:18 give you the city." J did as he was commanded.
8:19 As soon as J gave the signal, the men in ambush
8:21 When J and the other Israelites saw that the
8:23 the king of Ai was taken alive and brought to J.
8:26 For J kept holding out his spear until everyone
8:27 for themselves, as the LORD had commanded J.
8:29 J hung the king of Ai on a tree and left him there
8:30 Then J built an altar to the LORD, the God of
8:32 J copied the law of Moses onto the stones of the
8:34 J then read to them all the blessings and curses
9:2 quickly combined their armies to fight against J
9:4 They sent ambassadors to J, loading their donkeys
9:6 Israel at Gilgal, they told J and the men of Israel,
9:8 your servants." "But who are you?" J demanded.
9:15 Then J went ahead and signed a peace treaty with
9:22 But J called together the Gibeonite leaders
9:26 J did not allow the people of Israel to kill them.
10:1 heard that J had captured and completely
10:4 "for they have made peace with J and the people
10:6 The men of Gibeon quickly sent messengers to J at
10:7 So J and the entire Israelite army left Gilgal
10:8 "Do not be afraid of them," the LORD said to J,
10:9 J traveled all night from Gilgal and took the
10:12 J prayed to the LORD in front of all the people of
10:15 Then J and the Israelite army returned to their
10:17 When J heard that they had been found,
10:20 So J and the Israelite army continued the slaughter
10:22 Then J said, "Remove the rocks covering the
10:24 J told the captains of his army, "Come and put
10:25 ever be afraid or discouraged," J told his men.
10:26 Then J killed each of the five kings and hung them
10:27 J gave instructions for the bodies of the kings to be
10:28 That same day J completely destroyed the city of
10:29 Then J and the Israelites went to Libnah
10:30 Then J killed the king of Libnah just as he had
10:31 J and the Israelites went to Lachish and attacked it.
10:34 Then J and the Israelite army went to Eglon
10:40 So J conquered the whole region—the kings
10:41 J slaughtered them from Kadesh-barnea to Gaza
10:42 In a single campaign J conquered all these kings
10:43 Then J and the Israelite army returned to their
11:6 Then the LORD said to J, "Do not be afraid of
11:7 So J and his warriors traveled to the water near
11:9 Then J crippled the horses and burned all the
11:10 J then turned back and captured Hazor and killed
11:11 person was spared. And then J burned the city.
11:12 J slaughtered all the other kings and their people,
11:13 J did not burn any of the cities built on mounds
11:15 his servant Moses, so Moses commanded J.
11:15 And J did as he was told, carefully obeying all of
11:16 So J conquered the entire region—the hill country,
11:17 J killed all the kings of those territories,
11:21 J destroyed all the descendants of Anak,
11:23 So J took control of the entire land, just as the
12:7 The following is a list of the kings J
12:7 (J allotted this land to the tribes of Israel as their
13:1 When J was an old man, the LORD said to him,
14:1 the priest, J son of Nun, and the tribal leaders.
14:6 of Jephunneh the Kenizzite, came to J at Gilgal.
14:6 Caleb said to J, "Remember what the LORD said
14:13 So J blessed Caleb son of Jephunneh and gave
15:13 The LORD instructed J to assign some of Judah's
17:4 J son of Nun, and the Israelite leaders and said,
17:4 So J gave them an inheritance along with their
17:14 The descendants of Joseph came to J and asked,
17:15 J replied, "If the hill country of Ephraim is not
17:17 Then J said to the tribes of Ephraim
18:3 Then J asked them, "How long are you going to
18:8 J commanded them, "Go and survey the land.
18:9 Then they returned to J in the camp at Shiloh.
18:10 J cast sacred lots in the presence of the LORD to
19:49 the Israelites gave a special piece of land to J as
19:51 the territories that Eleazar the priest, J son of Nun,
20:1 The LORD said to J,
21:1 J son of Nun, and the leaders of the other tribes of
22:1 Then J called together the tribes of Reuben,
22:6 So J blessed them and sent them home.
22:7 the Jordan. As J sent them away, he blessed them
23:1 from all their enemies. J, who was now very old,
24:1 Then J summoned all the people of Israel to
24:2 J said to the people, "This is what the LORD,
24:19 Then J said to the people, "You are not able to
24:21 But the people answered J, saying, "No, we are
24:22 "You are accountable for this decision," J said.
24:23 "All right then," J said, "destroy the idols among
24:24 The people said to J, "We will serve the LORD
24:25 So J made a covenant with the people that day at
24:26 J recorded these things in the Book of the Law of
24:27 J said to all the people, "This stone has heard
24:28 Then J sent the people away, each to his own
24:29 Soon after this, J son of Nun, the servant of the
24:31 served the LORD throughout the lifetime of J
Jdg 1:1 After J died, the Israelites asked the LORD,
2:6 After J sent the people away, each of the tribes left
2:7 served the LORD throughout the lifetime of J
2:8 Then J son of Nun, the servant of the LORD,
2:21 I will no longer drive out the nations that J left
2:23 the nations out or allow J to conquer them all.
1Sa 6:14 The cart came into the field of a man named J
6:18 still stands in the field of J as a reminder of what
1Ki 16:34 concerning Jericho spoken by J son of Nun.
2Ki 23:8 the shrines at the entrance to the gate of J,
1Ch 7:27 Nun, and J.
Ne 8:17 celebrated this way since the days of J son of Nun.
Lk 3:29 Er was the son of J. / J was the son of Eliezer.
Ac 7:45 when J led the battles against the Gentile nations
Heb 4:8 rest was not the land of Canaan, where J led them.

JOSHUA'S (1) [JOSHUA]

Jos 10:33 But J men killed him and destroyed his entire

JOSIAH (56) [JOSIAH'S]

1Ki 13:2 A child named J will be born into the dynasty of
2Ki 21:24 and they made his son J the next king.
21:26 of Uzza. Then his son J became the next king.
22:1 J was eight years old when he became king,
22:3 King J sent Shaphan son of Azaliah and grandson
23:8 J brought back to Jerusalem all the priests of the
23:12 J tore down the altars that the kings of Judah had
23:15 J crushed the stones to dust and burned the
23:16 Then as J was looking around, he noticed several
23:16 Then J turned and looked up at the tomb of the

23:17 **J** asked. And the people of the town told him,
23:18 **J** replied, "Leave it alone. Don't disturb his
23:19 Then **J** demolished all the buildings at the pagan
23:21 King **J** then issued this order to all the people:
23:24 **J** also exterminated the mediums and psychics,
23:25 Never before had there been a king like **J**,
23:29 While **J** was king, Pharaoh Neco, king of Egypt,
23:29 King **J** marched out with his army to fight him,
1Ch 3:14 Amon, and **J**.
3:15 The sons of **J** were Johanan (the oldest),
2Ch 33:25 and they made his son **J** the next king.
34:1 **J** was eight years old when he became king,
34:3 **J** began to seek the God of his ancestor David.
34:8 the Temple, **J** appointed Shaphan son of Azaliah,
34:33 So **J** removed all detestable idols from the entire
35:1 Then **J** announced that the Passover of the LORD
35:2 **J** also assigned the priests to their duties
35:7 Then **J** contributed from his personal property
35:16 on the altar of the LORD, as King **J** had ordered.
35:18 kings of Israel had ever kept a Passover as **J** did,
35:20 After **J** had finished restoring the Temple,
35:20 and **J** and his army marched out to fight him.
35:21 But King Neco sent ambassadors to **J** with this
35:22 But **J** refused to listen to Neco, to whom God had
35:23 But the enemy archers hit King **J** with their arrows
35:24 So they lifted **J** out of his chariot and placed him in
35:25 prophet Jeremiah composed funeral songs for **J**,
Jer 3:6 During the reign of King **J**, the LORD said to me,
22:11 who succeeded his father, King **J**, and was taken
22:15 Why did your father, **J**, reign so long? Because he
22:18 who succeeded his father, **J**, on the throne:
25:3 from the thirteenth year of **J** son of Amon, king of
26:1 LORD early in the reign of Jehoiakim son of **J**,
27:1 the LORD early in the reign of Zedekiah son of **J**,
35:1 when Jehoiakim son of **J** was king of Judah:
36:1 During the fourth year that Jehoiakim son of **J** was
36:2 Begin with the first message back in the days of **J**,
36:9 the fifth year of the reign of Jehoiakim son of **J**.
37:1 Zedekiah son of **J** succeeded Jehoiachin son of
45:1 the fourth year of the reign of Jehoiakim son of **J**,
46:2 the fourth year of the reign of Jehoiakim son of **J**,
Zep 1:1 when **J** son of Amon was king of Judah.
Zec 6:10 meet them at the home of **J** son of Zephaniah.
6:14 Heldai, Tobijah, Jedaiah, and **J** son of Zephaniah."
Mt 1:10 the father of Amos. / Amos was the father of **J**.
1:11 **J** was the father of Jehoiachin and his brothers

JOSIAH'S (9) [JOSIAH]

2Ki 23:23 during the eighteenth year of King **J** reign.
23:28 The rest of the events in **J** reign and all his deeds
23:30 **J** officers took his body back in a chariot from
23:34 then installed Eliakim, another of **J** sons,
2Ch 35:19 took place in the eighteenth year of **J** reign.
35:26 The rest of the events of **J** reign and his acts of
36:1 Then the people of the land took **J** son Jehoahaz
Jer 1:2 during the thirteenth year of King **J** reign in Judah.
1:3 to give messages throughout the reign of **J** son,

JOSIPHIAH (1)

Ezr 8:10 of Bani: Shelomith son of **J** and 160 other men.

JOSTLE (1)

Joel 2:8 They never **j** each other; each moves in exactly the

JOT [KJV] See SMALLEST (DETAIL)

JOTBAH (1)

2Ki 21:19 was Meshullemeth, the daughter of Haruz from **J**.

JOTBATHAH (3)

Nu 33:33 They left Hor-haggidgad and camped at **J**.
33:34 They left **J** and camped at Abronah.
Dt 10:7 and from there to **J**, a land with brooks of water.

JOTHAM (27) [JOTHAM'S]

Jdg 9:5 But the youngest brother, **J**, escaped and hid.
9:7 When **J** heard about this, he climbed to the top of
9:21 Then **J** escaped and lived in Beer because he was
9:57 So the curse of **J** son of Gideon came true.
2Ki 15:5 The king's son **J** was put in charge of the royal
15:7 of David. Then his son **J** became the next king.
15:30 over Israel in the twentieth year of **J** son of Uzziah.
15:32 **J** son of Uzziah began to rule over Judah in the
15:34 **J** did what was pleasing in the LORD's sight,
15:38 When **J** died, he was buried with his ancestors in
16:1 Ahaz son of **J** began to rule over Judah in the
1Ch 2:47 were Regem, **J**, Geshan, Pelet, Ephah, and Shaaph.
3:12 Amaziah, Uzziah, **J**,
5:17 records during the days of King **J** of Judah
2Ch 26:21 His son **J** was put in charge of the royal palace,
26:23 to the kings. Then his son **J** became the next king.
27:1 **J** was twenty-five years old when he became king,
27:2 **J** did not enter the Temple of the LORD.
27:3 **J** rebuilt the Upper Gate to the LORD's Temple
27:5 **J** waged war against the Ammonites
27:6 King **J** became powerful because he was careful to
Isa 1:1 the reigns of Uzziah, **J**, Ahaz, and Hezekiah—
7:1 During the reign of Ahaz son of **J** and grandson of
Hos 1:1 **J**, Ahaz, and Hezekiah were kings of Judah,
Mic 1:1 to Micah of Moresheth during the years when **J**,
Mt 1:9 Uzziah was the father of **J**. / **J** was the father of Ahaz.

JOTHAM'S (2) [JOTHAM]

2Ki 15:36 The rest of the events in **J** reign and all his deeds
2Ch 27:7 The rest of the events of **J** reign, including his wars

JOURNEY (37) [JOURNEYED, JOURNEYS]

Ge 14:11 and Gomorrah and began their long **j** home,
18:5 Please stay awhile before continuing on your **j**."
21:14 up early the next morning, prepared food for the **j**,
22:4 On the third day of the **j**, Abraham saw the place in
24:12 Help me to accomplish the purpose of my **j**.
28:20 and protect me on this **j** and give me food
31:18 and set out on his **j** to the land of Canaan,
42:25 his sack. He also gave them provisions for their **j**.
44:3 and set out on their **j** with their loaded donkeys.
45:21 and he supplied them with provisions for the **j**.
45:23 and all kinds of other food to be eaten on his **j**.
Ex 3:18 Let us go on a three-day **j** into the wilderness to
4:24 On the **j**, when Moses and his family had stopped
12:11 you eat this meal, as though prepared for a long **j**.
40:36 the people of Israel would set out on their **j**,
Nu 9:10 or if they are on a **j** and cannot be present at the
Dt 6:7 you are at home and when you are away on a **j**,
11:19 you are at home and when you are away on a **j**,
28:68 a **j** I promised you would never again make.
Jos 9:11 and our people instructed us, 'Prepare for a long **j**.
14:11 strong now as I was when Moses sent me on that **j**,
22:9 They started the **j** back to their own land of Gilead,
Jdg 11:16 on their **j** from Egypt after crossing the Red Sea,
18:5 God whether or not our **j** will be successful."
18:6 "For the LORD will go ahead of you on your **j**."
Ru 1:19 So the two of them continued on their **j**. When they
1Ki 19:7 eat some more, for there is a long **j** ahead of you."
Ezr 1:4 them with silver and gold, supplies for the **j**,
1:6 them vessels of silver and gold, supplies for the **j**,
8:21 We prayed that he would give us a safe **j**
Eze 12:3 on your back and leave your home to go on a **j**.
Da 11:28 doing much damage before continuing his **j**.
Mic 6:5 And remember your **j** from Acacia to Gilgal,
Lk 24:28 they were nearing Emmaus and the end of their **j**.
Jn 4:46 In the course of his **j** through Galilee, he arrived at
Ac 14:26 where their **j** had begun and where they had been
16:3 so Paul wanted him to join them on their **j**.

JOURNEYED (3) [JOURNEY]

Ex 16:1 Then they left Elim and **j** into the Sin Desert,
Dt 10:7 Then they **j** to Gudgodah, and from there to
Jn 6:31 our ancestors ate manna while they **j** through the

JOURNEYS (1) [JOURNEY]

Ex 40:38 could see it. This continued throughout all their **j**.

JOY (275) [JOYFUL, JOYFULLY, JOYOUS, JOYOUSLY, JOYS, OVERJOYED, REJOICE, REJOICED, REJOICES, REJOICING]

Ge 30:13 named him Asher, for she said, "What **j** is mine!
45:14 Weeping with **j**, he embraced Benjamin,
Lev 9:24 they shouted with **j** and fell face down on the
Dt 16:15 This festival will be a time of great **j** for all.
27:7 and feast there with great **j** before the LORD your
28:47 you have not served the LORD your God with **j**
Jdg 9:19 his descendants, then may you find **j** in Abimelech, and may he find **j** in you.
11:34 playing on a tambourine and dancing for **j**.
1Sa 4:5 their shout of **j** was so loud that it made the ground
11:9 What **j** there was throughout the city when that
18:6 and danced for **j** with tambourines and cymbals.
30:16 eating and drinking and dancing with **j** because of
2Sa 1:19 Your pride and **j**, O Israel, lies dead on the hills!
6:21 act like a fool in order to show my **j** in the LORD.
19:2 the **j** of that day's victory was turned into deep
1Ki 1:40 to Jerusalem, playing flutes and shouting for **j**.
1Ch 12:40 There was great **j** throughout the land of Israel.
15:28 LORD's covenant to Jerusalem with shouts of **j**,
15:29 she saw King David dancing and leaping for **j**,
16:32 Let the fields and their crops burst forth with **j**!
29:9 to the LORD, and King David was filled with **j**.
29:22 and drank in the LORD's presence with great **j**
2Ch 20:27 full of **j** that the LORD had given them victory
30:21 of Unleavened Bread for seven days with great **j**.
30:26 There was great **j** in the city, for Jerusalem had not
Ezr 3:12 The others, however, were shouting for **j**.
6:16 then dedicated with great **j** by the people of Israel,
6:22 There was great **j** throughout the land
Ne 8:10 and sad, for the **j** of the LORD is your strength!"
8:12 and to celebrate with great **j** because they had
8:17 the festival, and everyone was filled with great **j**!
12:43 for God had given the people cause for great **j**.
12:43 and the **j** of the people of Jerusalem could be heard
Est 8:16 The Jews were filled with **j** and gladness and were
9:22 was turned into gladness and their mourning into **j**.
Job 3:7 Let that night be barren. Let it have no **j**.
5:17 "But consider the **j** of those corrected by God!
8:21 mouth with laughter and your lips with shouts of **j**.
10:3 while sending **j** and prosperity to the wicked?
20:5 and the **j** of the godless has been only temporary?
20:18 not be rewarded. His wealth will bring him no **j**.
29:13 And I caused the widows' hearts to sing for **j**.
33:26 And God will receive him with **j** and restore him to
38:7 stars sang together and all the angels shouted for **j**?
Ps 2:12 But what **j** for all who find protection in him!
4:7 You have given me greater **j** / than those who have
5:11 so all who love your name may be filled with **j**.
9:2 I will be filled with **j** because of you. / I will sing
14:7 Jacob will shout with **j**, and Israel will rejoice.
16:9 No wonder my heart is filled with **j**, / and my
16:11 way of life, / granting me the **j** of your presence
19:8 of the LORD are right, / bringing **j** to the heart.
20:5 May we shout for **j** when we hear of your victory,
21:1 He shouts with **j** because of your victory.
21:6 You have given him the **j** of being in your
22:26 Their hearts will rejoice with everlasting **j**.
27:6 Tabernacle I will offer sacrifices with shouts of **j**,
28:7 He helps me, and my heart is filled with **j**.
30:5 go on all night, / but **j** comes with the morning.
30:11 my clothes of mourning and clothed me with **j**,
31:7 I am overcome with **j** because of your unfailing
32:1 Oh, what **j** for those / whose rebellion is forgiven,
32:2 Yes, what **j** for those / whose record the LORD
32:11 Shout for **j**, all you whose hearts are pure!
33:1 Let the godly sing with **j** to the LORD, / for it is
33:3 to him; / play skillfully on the harp and sing with **j**.
33:12 What **j** for the nation whose God is the LORD,
34:5 who look to him for help will be radiant with **j**;
35:27 But give great **j** to those / who have stood with me
40:8 I take **j** in doing your will, my God, / for your law
40:16 who search for you / be filled with **j** and gladness.
42:4 house of God, / singing for **j** and giving thanks—
43:4 the altar of God, / to God—the source of all my **j**.
45:7 pouring out the oil of **j** on you more than on
46:4 A river brings **j** to the city of our God, / the sacred
47:1 Come, everyone, and clap your hands for **j**!
51:8 Oh, give me back my **j** again; / you have broken
51:12 Restore to me again the **j** of your salvation,
53:6 Jacob will shout with **j**, and Israel will rejoice.
59:16 I will shout with **j** each morning because of your
60:6 by his holiness: / "I will divide up Shechem with **j**.
63:5 richest of foods. / I will praise you with songs of **j**.
63:7 I sing for **j** in the shadow of your protecting wings.
65:4 What **j** for those you choose to bring near,
65:8 sun rises to where it sets, / you inspire shouts of **j**.
65:12 a lush pasture, / and the hillsides blossom with **j**.
65:13 carpeted with grain. / They all shout and sing for **j**!
67:4 How glad the nations will be, singing for **j**,
68:3 glad in God's presence. / Let them be filled with **j**.
68:6 he sets the prisoners free and gives them **j**.
69:32 and be glad. / Let all who seek God's help live in **j**.
70:4 who search for you / be filled with **j** and gladness.
71:23 I will shout for **j** and sing your praises, / for you
77:2 pleading. / There can be no **j** for me until he acts.
90:14 so we may sing for **j** to the end of our lives.
92:4 I sing for **j** because of what you have done.
96:12 Let the fields and their crops burst forth with **j**!
97:11 shines on the godly, / and **j** on those who do right.
98:4 all the earth; / break out in praise and sing for **j**!
98:8 in glee! / Let the hills sing out their songs of **j**
100:1 Shout with **j** to the LORD, O earth!
100:2 with gladness. / Come before him, singing with **j**.
105:36 Egyptian home, / the pride and **j** of each family.
105:43 So he brought his people out of Egypt with **j**,
106:5 Let me rejoice in the **j** of your people; / let me
108:7 by his holiness: / "I will divide up Shechem with **j**.
118:15 Songs of **j** and victory are sung in the camp of the
119:74 May all who fear you find in me a cause for **j**,
119:92 If your law hadn't sustained me with **j**, / I would
119:93 for you have used them to restore my **j** and health.
119:143 bear down on me, / I find **j** in your commands.
126:2 We were filled with laughter, / and we sang for **j**.
126:3 LORD has done amazing things for us! / What **j**!
126:5 who plant in tears / will harvest with shouts of **j**.
132:9 of salvation; / may your loyal servants sing for **j**.
132:16 of salvation; / its godly people will sing for **j**.
137:6 if I don't make Jerusalem my highest **j**.
145:7 they will sing with **j** of your righteousness.
149:5 Let them sing for **j** as they lie on their beds.
Pr 2:10 your heart, and knowledge will fill you with **j**.
10:1 A wise child brings **j** to a father; a foolish child
11:10 they shout for **j** when the godless die.
12:4 A worthy wife is her husband's **j** and crown;
12:20 plotting evil; **j** fills hearts that are planning peace!
13:9 The life of the godly is full of light and **j**,
13:12 but when dreams come true, there is life and **j**.
14:10 and no one else can fully share its **j**.
15:2 The wise person makes learning a **j**; fools spout
15:20 Sensible children bring **j** to their father;
15:21 Foolishness brings **j** to those who have no sense;
15:30 A cheerful look brings **j** to the heart; good news
17:21 of a fool; there is no **j** for the father of a rebel.
21:15 Justice is a **j** to the godly, but it causes dismay
23:24 The father of godly children has cause for **j**.
23:25 So give your parents **j**! May she who gave you
29:3 The man who loves wisdom brings **j** to his father,
29:6 by sin, but the righteous escape, shouting for **j**.
Ecc 2:10 I took. I did not restrain myself from any **j**.
2:26 knowledge, and **j** to those who please him.
5:20 on the past, for God has given them reasons for **j**.
Isa 9:3 They will shout with **j** like warriors dividing the
9:17 That is why the Lord has no **j** in the young men
12:3 With **j** you will drink deeply from the fountain of
12:6 all the people of Jerusalem shout his praise with **j**!
16:10 Gone now is the gladness; gone is the **j** of harvest.
24:11 crying out for wine. **J** has reached its lowest ebb.
24:14 But all who are left will shout and sing for **j**.
26:19 who sleep in the earth / will rise up and sing for **j**!
28:1 the pride and **j** of the drunkards of Israel!
28:3 the pride and **j** of the drunkards of Israel—
28:5 will be the pride and **j** of the remnant of his people.
29:19 The humble will be filled with fresh **j** from the
30:29 But the people of God will sing a song of **j**,
30:29 You will be filled with **j**, as when a flutist leads a
35:2 will be an abundance of flowers and singing and **j**!

35:10 return to Jerusalem, singing songs of everlasting **j**.
35:10 and they will be overcome with **j** and gladness.
41:16 And the **j** of the LORD will fill you to
42:11 of Kedar rejoice! / Let the people of Sela sing for **j**;
49:13 Sing for **j**, O heavens! Rejoice, O earth! Burst into
51: 3 of the LORD. **J** and gladness will be found there.
51:11 return to Jerusalem, singing songs of everlasting **j**.
51:11 and they will be overcome with **j** and gladness.
52: 8 The watchmen shout and sing with **j**, for before
55:12 You will live in **j** and peace. The mountains
56: 7 and will fill them with **j** in my house of prayer.
60: 5 eyes will shine, and your hearts will thrill with **j**,
60:15 You will be a **j** to all generations, for I will make
61: 3 **j** instead of mourning, praise instead of despair.
61: 7 a double portion of prosperity and everlasting **j**.
61:10 I am overwhelmed with **j** in the LORD my God!
62: 5 Your children will care for you with **j**,
65:14 in sorrow and despair, while my servants sing for **j**.
65:18 of happiness. Her people will be a source of **j**.
Jer 15:16 They bring me great **j** and are my heart's delight,
30:19 There will be **j** and songs of thanksgiving, and I
31: 7 "Sing with **j** for Israel! Shout for the greatest of
31: 7 Shout out with praise and **j**: 'Save your people,
31: 9 Tears of **j** will stream down their faces, and I will
31:12 and sing songs of **j** on the heights of Jerusalem.
31:13 The young women will dance for **j**, and the men—
31:13 I will turn their mourning into **j**. I will comfort
31:25 given rest to the weary and **j** to the sorrowing."
33: 9 Then this city will bring me **j**, glory, and honor
33:11 the sounds of **j** and laughter. The joyful voices of
41:13 The people Ishmael had captured shouted for **j**
48:33 **J** and gladness are gone from fruitful Moab.
48:33 No one treads the grapes with shouts of **j**. There is shouting, yes, but not of **j**.
49:25 That famous city, a city of **j**, will be forsaken!
La 2:15 in All the World,' and '**J** of All the Earth'?"
5:15 The **j** of our hearts has ended; our dancing has
Eze 7: 7 It will ring with shouts of anguish, not shouts of **j**.
24:25 their **j** and glory, their heart's desire, their dearest
Joel 1:12 have dried up. All **j** has dried up with them.
Am 5:20 and hopeless day, without a ray of **j** or hope.
8:10 and your songs of **j** will be turned to weeping.
Na 3:19 hear of your destruction will clap their hands for **j**.
Zec 8:19 They will become festivals of **j** and celebration for
Mal 4: 2 go free, leaping with **j** like calves let out to pasture.
Mt 2:10 When they saw the star, they were filled with **j**!
13:20 those who hear the message and receive it with **j**.
28: 8 were very frightened but also filled with great **j**,
Mk 4:16 those who hear the message and receive it with **j**.
Lk 1:14 You will have great **j** and gladness, and many will
1:44 my baby jumped for **j** the instant I heard your
2:10 "I bring you good news of great **j** for everyone!
2:34 But he will be the greatest **j** to many others.
6:21 for the time will come when you will laugh with **j**.
6:23 "When that happens, rejoice! Yes, leap for **j**!
8:13 soil represents those who hear the message with **j**.
10:21 Then Jesus was filled with the **j** of the Holy Spirit
15:10 there is **j** in the presence of God's angels when
19: 6 took Jesus to his house in great excitement and **j**.
24:41 stood there doubting, filled with **j** and wonder.
24:52 then returned to Jerusalem filled with great **j**.
Jn 3:29 and I am filled with **j** at his success.
4:36 What **j** awaits both the planter and the harvester
15:11 told you this so that you will be filled with my **j**. Yes, your **j** will overflow!
16:20 but your grief will suddenly turn to wonderful **j**
16:21 her anguish gives place to **j** because she has
16:22 you will rejoice, and no one can rob you of that **j**.
16:24 and you will receive, and you will have abundant **j**.
17:13 I was with them so they would be filled with my **j**.
20:20 They were filled with **j** when they saw their Lord!
Ac 2:26 No wonder my heart is filled with **j**, / and my
2:28 and you will give me wonderful **j** in your
2:46 and shared their meals with great **j**
8: 8 So there was great **j** in that city.
11:23 saw this proof of God's favor, he was filled with **j**,
13:52 And the believers were filled with **j** and with the
15: 3 They told them—much to everyone's **j**—
15:31 And there was great **j** throughout the church that
Ro 4: 7 what **j** for those whose disobedience is forgiven,
4: 8 Yes, what **j** for those / whose sin is no longer
14:17 life of goodness and peace and **j** in the Holy Spirit.
1Co 11:15 it obvious that long hair is a woman's pride and **j**?
2Co 1:24 so you will be full of **j** as you stand firm in your
2: 3 the very ones who ought to give me the greatest **j**.
6:10 Our hearts ache, but we always have **j**. We are
7: 7 His presence was a **j**, but so was the news he
7: 7 how loyal your love is for me, I was filled with **j**!
8: 2 their wonderful **j** and deep poverty have
Gal 5:22 love, **j**, peace, patience, kindness, goodness,
Eph 3: 8 I was chosen for this special **j** of telling the
Php 1: 4 and I make my requests with a heart full of **j**
1:25 you will grow and experience the **j** of your faith.
2:17 and I want to share my **j** with all of you.
2:29 Welcome him with Christian love and with great **j**,
3: 1 dear friends, may the Lord give you **j**.
4: 1 for you are my **j** and the reward for my work.
4: 4 Always be full of **j** in the Lord. I say it again—
Col 1:11 and endurance you need. May you be filled with **j**,
1Th 1: 6 So you received the message with **j** from the Holy
2:19 After all, what gives us hope and **j**, and what is our
2:19 you will bring us much **j** as we stand together
2:20 For you are our pride and **j**.
3: 6 He reports that you remember our visit with **j**
3: 9 Because of you we have great **j** in the presence of
2Ti 1: 4 And I will be filled with **j** when we are together
Phm 1: 7 I myself have gained much **j** and comfort from
Heb 1: 9 pouring out the oil of **j** on you more than on
10:34 owned was taken from you, you accepted it with **j**.
12: 2 because of the **j** he knew would be his afterward.
Jas 1: 2 comes your way, let it be an opportunity for **j**.
4: 9 sadness instead of laughter, and gloom instead of **j**.
1Pe 1: 6 There is wonderful **j** ahead, even though it is
1: 8 now you are happy with a glorious, inexpressible **j**.
4:13 and afterward you will have the wonderful **j** of
1Jn 1: 4 writing these things so that our **j** will be complete.
2Jn 1:12 with you face to face. Then our **j** will be complete.
3Jn 1: 4 I could have no greater **j** than to hear that my
Jude 1:24 glorious presence innocent of sin and with great **j**.

JOYFUL (29) [JOY]

Ge 31:27 with **j** singing accompanied by tambourines
1Ki 8:66 and they were all **j** and happy because the LORD
1Ch 15:16 and musicians to sing **j** songs to the
2Ch 7:10 They were all **j** and happy because the LORD had
Ezr 3:13 The **j** shouting and weeping mingled together in a
Ps 5:11 in you rejoice; / let them sing **j** praises forever.
30:11 You have turned my mourning into **j** dancing.
45:15 What a **j**, enthusiastic procession / as they enter the
47: 1 your hands for joy! / Shout to God with **j** praise!
66: 1 Shout **j** praises to God, all the earth!
77: 6 when my nights were filled with **j** songs. / I search
89:15 Happy are those who hear the **j** call to worship,
98: 6 Make a **j** symphony before the LORD, the King!
137: 3 Our tormentors requested a **j** hymn: / "Sing us one
Isa 32:13 Your **j** homes and happy cities will be gone.
52: 9 Let the ruins of Jerusalem break into **j** song,
54: 1 Break forth into loud and **j** song, O Jerusalem,
66: 5 the LORD be honored!' they scoff. 'Be **j** in him!'
Jer 7:34 The **j** voices of bridegrooms and brides will no
16: 9 The **j** voices of bridegrooms and brides will no
25:10 The **j** voices of bridegrooms and brides will no
33:11 The **j** voices of bridegrooms and brides will be
Joel 1:16 There are no **j** celebrations in the house of our
Hab 3:18 the LORD! I will be **j** in the God of my salvation.
Ac 14:17 and good crops and giving you food and **j** hearts."
Gal 4:15 Where is that **j** spirit we felt together then?
4:27 Break forth into loud and **j** song,
1Th 5:16 Always be **j**.
Heb 12:22 and to thousands of angels in **j** assembly.

JOYFULLY (12) [JOY]

1Sa 30:21 too tired to go with them, David greeted them **j**.
2Sa 22:50 you among the nations; / I will sing **j** to your name.
2Ch 30:23 seven days, so they celebrated **j** for another week.
Ps 18:49 you among the nations; / I will sing **j** to your name.
51:14 who saves; / then I will **j** sing of your forgiveness.
84: 2 body and soul, / I will shout **j** to the living God.
107:22 of thanksgiving / and sing **j** about his glorious acts.
Lk 10:17 disciples returned, they **j** reported to him, "Lord,
15: 5 then you would **j** carry it home on your shoulders.
Ro 5: 2 and **j** look forward to sharing God's glory.
2Co 9:12 and they will **j** express their thanksgiving to God.
Heb 13:17 Give them reason to do this **j** and not with sorrow.

JOYOUS (9) [JOY]

Nu 28:17 On the following day a **j**, seven-day festival will
1Ki 1:40 The celebration was so **j** and noisy that the earth
2Ch 29:30 So they offered **j** praise and bowed down in
Ne 12:27 They were to take part in the **j** occasion with their
12:43 Many sacrifices were offered on that **j** day,
Ps 95: 1 Let us give a **j** shout to the rock of our salvation!
Isa 14: 8 and the cedars of Lebanon—sing out this **j** song:
23: 7 this silent ruin be all that is left of your once **j** city?
Jer 33:11 along with the **j** songs of people bringing

JOYOUSLY (1) [JOY]

1Ch 29:17 your people offer their gifts willingly and **j**.

JOYS (12) [JOY]

Ps 1: 1 Oh, the **j** of those / who do not follow the advice of
34: 8 is good. / Oh, the **j** of those who trust in him!
40: 4 Oh, the **j** of those who trust the LORD,
41: 1 Oh, the **j** of those who are kind to the poor.
65: 4 What **j** await us / inside your holy Temple.
Isa 16:10 has ceased forever. I have ended all their harvest **j**.
24: 7 All the **j** of life will be gone. The grape harvest
29: 9 Gone are the **j** of wine and song; strong drink now
La 5:21 back to you again! Give us back the **j** we once had!
Mic 2:11 "I'll preach to you the **j** of wine and drink!"
2Co 4:18 soon be over, but the **j** to come will last forever.
Col 1: 5 because you are looking forward to the **j** of

JOZABAD (10)

1Ch 12: 4 Jeremiah, Jahaziel, Johanan, and **J** from Gederah;
12:20 Adnah, **J**, Jediael, Michael, **J**, Elihu,
2Ch 31:13 Azaziah, Nahath, Asahel, Jerimoth, **J**, Eliel,
35: 9 and Nethanel, and Hashabiah, Jeiel, and **J**—
Ezr 8:33 along with **J** son of Jeshua and Noadiah son of
10:22 Elioenai, Maaseiah, Ishmael, Nethanel, **J**,
10:23 **J**, Shimei, Kelaiah (also called Kelita), Pethahiah,
Ne 8: 7 Hodiah, Maaseiah, Kelita, Azariah, **J**, Hanan,
11:16 Shabbethai and **J**, who were in charge of the work

JOZACAR (2)

2Ki 12:21 The assassins were **J** son of Shimeath
2Ch 24:26 The assassins were **J**, the son of an Ammonite

JUBAL (1)

Ge 4:21 His brother's name was **J**, the first musician—

JUBILEE (24)

Lev 25:10 It will be a **j** year for you, when each of you
25:11 Yes, the fiftieth year will be a **j** for you.
25:12 It will be a **j** year for you, and you must observe it
25:13 In the Year of **J** each of you must return to the
25:15 be based on the number of years since the last **j**.
25:15 only for the crop years left until the next Year of **J**.
25:27 on the number of years until the next Year of **J**.
25:28 belong to the new owner until the next Year of **J**.
25:28 In the **j** year, the land will be returned to the
25:30 be returned to the original owner in the Year of **J**.
25:31 be returned to the original owner in the Year of **J**.
25:33 Levitical cities—must be returned in the Year of **J**.
25:40 and they will serve you only until the Year of **J**.
25:50 the number of years left until the next Year of **J**—
25:52 If only a few years remain until the Year of **J**,
25:54 been redeemed by the time the Year of **J** arrives,
27:17 field is dedicated to the LORD in the Year of **J**,
27:18 But if the field is dedicated after the Year of **J**,
27:18 proportion to the years left until the next Year of **J**.
27:21 When the field is released in the Year of **J**, it will
27:23 value based on the years until the next Year of **J**.
27:24 In the Year of **J** the field will be released to the
Nu 36: 4 Then when the Year of **J** comes, their inheritance
Eze 46:17 the servant may keep it only until the Year of **J**,

JUDAH (816) [JUDAH'S, JUDEA, JUDEAN, JUDEANS, OHOLIBAH]

ALL JUDAH (7) 2Ki 22:13; 2Ch 31:20; 32:33; 34:9; 35:24; Jer 4:5; 18:11

CITIES OF JUDAH (7) 2Ki 18:13; 2Ch 11:10; 17:2; 33:14; Ps 97:8; Isa 36:1; Jer 34:7

ISRAEL AND JUDAH (43) 1Sa 18:16; 2Sa 5:5; 11:11; 12:8; 24:1; 1Ki 1:35; 2Ki 17:13; 23:22; 2Ch 27:7; 30:1,6; 34:21; 35:27; 36:8; Isa 5:7; 7:17; 8:14; 10:20; 11:13; 65:9; Jer 5:11,20; 11:10,17; 30:3,4; 31:27,31; 32:30,32; 33:14; 50:4,33; 51:5; Eze 9:9; 35:10; Hos 5:13,14; 6:4; 10:11; Am 3:1; Mic 1:5; Heb 8:8

JERUSALEM AND JUDAH (11) 2Ki 21:12; 24:20; 2Ch 21:11,13; Isa 3:1; 5:3; 22:21; Jer 40:1; 52:3; Zec 12:2; 14:21

JUDAH AND BENJAMIN (18) 1Ki 12:21,23; 2Ch 11:1,3,10,12,23; 15:2,8,9; 25:5; Ezr 1:5; 4:1; 10:9; Ne 11:1,4; Jer 17:26; Eze 48:22

JUDAH AND ISRAEL (18) Jos 11:21; 2Sa 3:37; 1Ki 4:20,25; 2Ch 16:11; 25:26; 28:26; 32:32; 35:18; Jer 3:18; 13:11; 33:7,24; Eze 27:17; Hos 1:11; Zec 8:12,13; 11:14

JUDAH AND JERUSALEM (53) 2Ki 23:1,2; 1Ch 6:15; 2Ch 2:7; 11:14; 20:5,15,17,18,20; 24:9,18,23; 28:10; 29:8; 32:12,25,33; 33:9; 34:3,5,29,30; 35:24; 36:4,10; Ezr 4:6; 5:1; 7:14; 9:9; 10:7; Isa 1:1; 2:1; 3:8; Jer 4:3; 11:2,9,12; 13:9; 18:11; 19:7,11; 25:2; 27:20; 35:13,17; 36:31; 44:9; Da 9:7; Joel 3:1,6; Zep 1:4; Mal 3:4

KING OF JUDAH (30) 2Sa 2:11; 1Ki 12:23; 2Ki 1:17; 22:18; 2Ch 11:3; 22:1; 29:1; 34:26; 35:21; 36:4; Isa 16:1; Jer 15:4; 22:1,2,24; 24:1; 25:3; 26:1; 27:1,20; 28:1,4; 32:1; 34:4; 35:1; 37:1,7; 46:2; Am 1:1; Zep 1:1

KINGS OF JUDAH (31) 1Sa 27:6; 1Ki 14:29; 15:7,23; 22:45; 2Ki 8:23; 12:18,19; 14:18; 15:6,36; 16:19; 20:20; 21:17,25; 23:5,11,12,28; 24:5; 2Ch 16:11; 25:26; 28:26; 32:32; 34:11; Isa 1:1; Jer 17:20; 19:3,4; Hos 1:1; Mic 1:1

LAND OF JUDAH (21) Dt 34:2; Ru 1:2; 1Sa 17:12; 22:5; 30:16; 1Ki 4:19; 2Ki 18:5; 23:24; 24:1; 2Ch 11:23; 12:12; 15:8; 17:2; 20:31; 30:12; 36:23; Ezr 1:2; Ps 114:2; Isa 26:1; Am 7:12; Zec 2:12

PEOPLE OF JUDAH (87) Jos 15:63; Jdg 1:19; 2Sa 1:18; 2:7; 19:15; 1Ki 4:20; 12:23; 14:22; 2Ki 14:10,21; 16:6; 17:19; 21:11,16; 23:2,35; 25:21,26; 1Ch 6:15; 9:1; 2Ch 14:4,7; 15:2,9; 17:5; 20:5,15,17,18,20; 24:24; 25:19; 26:1; 31:6; 33:9,16; 34:25,30; Ezr 4:4,6; 10:9; Ne 4:10,16; 11:25,30; 12:44; 13:12,16; Isa 8:6; 11:12; Jer 1:18; 3:18; 4:3; 7:30; 9:26; 11:2,9,12,13; 13:19; 17:20,25; 19:11; 20:4; 25:1; 26:18; 27:20; 31:23; 36:3,31; 43:9,10; 52:27; Eze 8:17; 25:12; Da 9:7; Hos 1:7,11; Joel 3:6,8; Am 2:4; Mic 1:16; Na 1:15; Zec 8:15,19; 12:4; Mal 3:4

TOWNS OF JUDAH (41) Jos 15:21; 1Ki 12:17; 2Ki 23:8; 2Ch 10:17; 17:7,9; 20:4; 24:5,6; 25:13; 28:25; 31:1; Ezr 2:1,70; Ne 7:6; 11:1,3,20; Ps 48:11; 69:35; Isa 40:9; 44:26; Jer 1:15; 4:16; 7:17,34; 9:11; 10:22; 17:26; 25:18; 32:44; 33:13; 34:1,22; 44:2,6,17,21; La 5:11; Zec 1:12; 7:7

TRIBE OF JUDAH (31) Ex 31:2; 35:30; 38:22; Nu 7:12; Dt 33:7; Jos 7:1,16; 14:6; 15:1,12,20,45,63; 18:14; Jdg 1:16; 2Sa 2:4,10; 1Ki 12:20; 2Ki 17:18; 1Ch 4:27; 9:6; 12:24; 28:4; 2Ch 14:8; 19:11; Ne 11:4; Ps 78:68; Da 1:6; Zep 2:7; Heb 7:14; Rev 5:5

Ge 29:35 She named him **J**, for she said, "Now I will praise
35:23 Simeon, Levi, **J**, Issachar, and Zebulun.
37:26 **J** said to the others, "What can we gain by killing
38: 1 this time, **J** left home and moved to Adullam,
38: 3 and had a son, and **J** named the boy Er.
38: 6 **J** arranged his marriage to a young woman named
38: 8 Then **J** said to Er's brother Onan, "You must
38:11 Then **J** told Tamar, his daughter-in-law, not to
38:11 (But **J** didn't really intend to do this because he
38:12 **J** and his friend Hirah the Adullamite went to
38:15 **J** noticed her as he went by and thought she was a
38:17 you a young goat from my flock," **J** promised.
38:18 So **J** gave these items to her. She then let him sleep
38:20 **J** asked his friend Hirah the Adullamite to take the
38:22 So Hirah returned to **J** and told him that he
38:23 "Then let her keep the pledges!" **J** exclaimed.

38:24 word reached **J** that Tamar, his daughter-in-law,
38:24 "Bring her out and burn her!" **J** shouted.
38:26 **J** admitted that they were his and said, "She is
38:26 son Shelah." But **J** never slept with Tamar again.
43:3 But **J** said, "The man wasn't joking when he
43:8 **J** said to his father, "Send the boy with me,
44:14 Joseph was still at home when **J** and his brothers
44:16 And **J** said, "Oh, my lord, what can we say to
44:18 Then **J** stepped forward and said, "My lord,
46:12 The sons of **J** were Er, Onan, Shelah, Perez,
46:28 Jacob sent **J** on ahead to meet Joseph and get
49:8 "**J**, your brothers will praise you. / You will defeat
49:9 **J** is a young lion / that has finished eating its prey.
49:10 The scepter will not depart from **J**, / nor the ruler's
Ex 1:2 Reuben, Simeon, Levi, **J**,
31:2 son of Uri, grandson of Hur, of the tribe of **J**.
35:30 son of Uri, grandson of Hur, of the tribe of **J**.
38:22 son of Uri, grandson of Hur, of the tribe of **J**,
Nu 1:7 **J** | Nahshon son of Amminadab
1:26[-27] **J** | 74,600
2:3[-4] "The divisions of **J**, Issachar, and Zebulun are
2:3[-4] **J** | Nahshon son of Amminadab | 74,600
7:12 leader of the tribe of **J**, presented his offering.
10:14 The tribes that camped with **J** headed the march
13:6 **J** | Caleb son of Jephunneh
26:19 **J** had two sons, Er and Onan, who had died in the
26:22 The men from all the clans of **J** numbered 76,500.
34:19 names of the leaders: / **J** | Caleb son of Jephunneh
Dt 27:12 the tribes of Simeon, Levi, **J**, Issachar, Joseph,
33:7 Moses said this about the tribe of **J**: / "O LORD, hear the cry of **J** / and bring them
34:2 all the land of **J**, extending to the Mediterranean
Jos 7:1 of Zimri, of the clan of Zerah, and of the tribe of **J**.
7:16 the LORD, and the tribe of **J** was singled out.
7:17 Then the clans of **J** came forward, and the clan of
11:21 Anab, and the entire hill country of **J** and Israel.
14:6 A delegation from the tribe of **J**, led by Caleb son
15:1 The land assigned to the families of the tribe of **J**
15:12 are the boundaries for the families of the tribe of **J**.
15:20 inheritance given to the families of the tribe of **J**.
15:21 The towns of **J** situated along the borders of Edom
15:33 in the western foothills were also given to **J**:
15:45 The territory of the tribe of **J** also included all the
15:48 **J** also received the following towns in the hill
15:63 But the tribe of **J** could not drive out the Jebusites,
15:63 so the Jebusites live there among the people of **J** to
18:11 the territory previously assigned to the tribes of **J**
18:14 one of the towns belonging to the tribe of **J**.
19:9 came from part of what had been given to **J**
19:9 received an inheritance within the territory of **J**.
20:7 (that is, Hebron), in the hill country of **J**.
21:4 that were originally assigned to the tribes of **J**,
21:9 gave the following towns from the tribes of **J**
21:11 (that is, Hebron), in the hill country of **J**,
Jdg 1:2 The LORD answered, "**J**, for I have given them
1:3 The leaders of **J** said to their relatives from the
1:3 So the men of Simeon went with **J**.
1:4 When the men of **J** attacked, the LORD gave
1:8 The men of **J** attacked Jerusalem and captured it,
1:10 **J** marched against the Canaanites in Hebron
1:16 When the tribe of **J** left Jericho, the Kenites,
1:16 traveled with them into the wilderness of **J**.
1:17 Then **J** joined with Simeon to fight against the
1:18 **J** captured the cities of Gaza, Ashkelon,
1:19 The LORD was with the people of **J**, and they
10:9 to the west side of the Jordan and attacked **J**,
15:9 The Philistines retaliated by setting up camp in **J**
15:10 The men of **J** asked the Philistines, "Why have
15:11 So three thousand men of **J** went down to get
15:12 But the men of **J** told him, "We have come to tie
17:7 One day a young Levite from Bethlehem in **J**
17:9 he replied, "I am a Levite from Bethlehem in **J**,
18:12 camped at a place west of Kiriath-jearim in **J**,
19:1 a woman from Bethlehem in **J** to be his concubine.
19:18 "We have been in Bethlehem in **J**," the man
20:18 The LORD answered, "**J** is to go first."
Ru 1:1 a man from Bethlehem in **J** left the country
1:2 were Ephrathites from Bethlehem in the land of **J**.
1:6 his people in **J** by giving them good crops again.
1:7 they took the road that would lead them back to **J**.
4:12 of our ancestor Perez, the son of Tamar and **J**."
1Sa 11:8 men of Israel, in addition to 30,000 from **J**.
15:4 200,000 troops in addition to 10,000 men from **J**.
17:1 and camped between Socoh in **J** and Azekah at
17:12 an Ephrathite from Bethlehem in the land of **J**.
18:16 But all Israel and **J** loved David because he was
22:5 the stronghold and return to the land of **J**."
22:6 The news of his arrival in **J** soon reached Saul.
23:3 David's men said, "We're afraid even here in **J**.
23:23 even if I have to search every hiding place in **J**!"
27:6 (which still belongs to the kings of **J** to this day),
27:10 "Against the south of **J**, the Jerahmeelites,
30:14 the territory of **J**, and the land of Caleb, and we
30:16 had taken from the Philistines and the land of **J**.
30:26 David sent part of the plunder to the leaders of **J**,
2Sa 1:18 commanded that it be taught to all the people of **J**.
2:1 asked the LORD, "Should I move back to **J**?"
2:3 and his men and their families all moved to **J**,
2:4 to David and crowned him king over the tribe of **J**.
2:7 my strong and loyal subjects like the people of **J**,
2:10 Meanwhile, the tribe of **J** remained loyal to David.
2:11 and he ruled as king of **J** for seven and a half
3:10 I should set him up as king over Israel as well as **J**,
3:37 So everyone in **J** and Israel knew that David was
5:5 He had reigned over **J** from Hebron for seven
5:5 reigned over all Israel and **J** for thirty-three years.
6:2 He led them to Baalah of **J** to bring home the Ark
11:11 and the armies of Israel and **J** are living in tents,
12:8 and his wives and the kingdoms of Israel and **J**.
19:11 and Abiathar, the priests, to say to the leaders of **J**,
19:14 Then Amasa convinced all the leaders of **J**,
19:15 the people of **J** came to Gilgal to meet him
19:16 hurried across with the men of **J** to welcome King
19:40 All the army of **J** and half the army of Israel
19:41 **J** had gotten to do most of the work in helping him
19:42 "Why not?" the men of **J** replied. "The king is
19:43 and the men of **J** were very harsh in their replies.
20:2 But the men of **J** stayed with their king
20:4 Amasa to mobilize the army of **J** within three days
24:1 "Go and count the people of Israel and **J**,"
24:7 Finally, they went south to **J** as far as Beersheba.
24:9 men of military age in Israel and 500,000 in **J**.
1Ki 1:9 of King David—and all the royal officials of **J**.
1:35 have appointed him to be ruler over Israel and **J**."
2:32 Amasa son of Jether, commander of the army of **J**.
4:19 And there was one governor over the land of **J**.
4:20 The people of **J** and Israel were as numerous as the
4:25 all of **J** and Israel lived in peace and safety.
10:27 the sycamore wood that grows in the foothills of **J**.
12:17 rule over the Israelites who lived in the towns of **J**.
12:20 So only the tribe of **J** remained loyal to the family
12:21 he mobilized the armies of **J** and Benjamin—
12:23 king of **J**, and to all the people of **J** and Benjamin,
12:27 again give their allegiance to King Rehoboam of **J**.
12:32 similar to the annual Festival of Shelters in **J**.
13:1 a man of God from **J** went to Bethel,
13:9 and do not return to **J** by the same way you
13:14 "Are you the man of God who came from **J**?"
13:17 and do not return to **J** by the same way you
13:21 He cried out to the man of God from **J**, "This is
14:21 Rehoboam son of Solomon was king in **J**.
14:22 the people of **J** did what was evil in the LORD's
14:29 in *The Book of the History of the Kings of **J**.*
15:1 Abijam began to rule over **J** in the eighteenth year
15:7 *of **J***. There was constant war between Abijam
15:9 Asa began to rule over **J** in the twentieth year of
15:16 There was constant war between King Asa of **J**
15:17 King Baasha of Israel invaded **J** and fortified
15:17 from entering or leaving King Asa's territory in **J**.
15:22 Then King Asa sent an order throughout **J**,
15:23 *of **J***. In his old age his feet became diseased.
15:25 Israel in the second year of King Asa's reign in **J**.
15:28 Nadab in the third year of King Asa's reign in **J**,
15:33 Israel in the third year of King Asa's reign in **J**.
16:8 in the twenty-sixth year of King Asa's reign in **J**.
16:10 the twenty-seventh year of King Asa's reign in **J**.
16:15 the twenty-seventh year of King Asa's reign in **J**,
16:23 in the thirty-first year of King Asa's reign in **J**.
16:29 in the thirty-eighth year of King Asa's reign in **J**.
19:3 He went to Beersheba, a town in **J**, and he left his
22:2 King Jehoshaphat of **J** went to visit King Ahab of
22:10 King Ahab of Israel and King Jehoshaphat of **J**,
22:29 and King Jehoshaphat of **J** led their armies against
22:41 Jehoshaphat son of Asa began to rule over **J** in the
22:45 in *The Book of the History of the Kings of **J**.*
22:51 seventeenth year of King Jehoshaphat's reign in **J**.
2Ki 1:17 the reign of Jehoram son of Jehoshaphat, king of **J**.
3:1 eighteenth year of King Jehoshaphat's reign in **J**.
3:7 he sent this message to King Jehoshaphat of **J**:
3:11 But King Jehoshaphat of **J** asked, "Is there no
3:12 So the kings of Israel, **J**, and Edom went to consult
3:14 except for my respect for King Jehoshaphat of **J**.
8:16 Jehoram son of King Jehoshaphat of **J** began to
8:16 **J** in the fifth year of King Joram's reign in Israel.
8:19 But the LORD was not willing to destroy **J**,
8:20 the Edomites revolted against **J** and crowned their
8:22 Edom has been independent from **J** to this day.
8:23 in *The Book of the History of the Kings of **J**.*
8:25 Ahaziah son of Jehoram began to rule over **J** in the
8:29 was there, King Ahaziah of **J** went to visit him.
9:16 King Ahaziah of **J** was there, too, for he had gone
9:21 and King Ahaziah of **J** rode out in their chariots to
9:27 When King Ahaziah of **J** saw what was happening,
9:29 Ahaziah's reign over **J** had begun in the eleventh
10:13 he met some relatives of King Ahaziah of **J**.
11:1 When Athaliah, the mother of King Ahaziah of **J**,
12:1 Joash began to rule over **J** in the seventh year of
12:18 Jehoram, and Ahaziah, the previous kings of **J**,
12:19 in *The Book of the History of the Kings of **J**.*
13:1 in the twenty-third year of King Joash's reign in **J**.
13:10 the thirty-seventh year of King Joash's reign in **J**.
13:12 of his power and his war with King Amaziah of **J**,
14:1 Amaziah son of Joash began to rule over **J** in the
14:9 Israel replied to King Amaziah of **J** with this story:
14:10 will bring disaster on you and the people of **J**?"
14:11 mobilized his army against King Amaziah of **J**.
14:11 drew up their battle lines at Beth-shemesh in **J**.
14:12 **J** was routed by the army of Israel, and its army
14:13 captured King Amaziah of **J** at Beth-shemesh
14:15 of his power and his war with King Amaziah of **J**,
14:17 King Amaziah of **J** lived on for fifteen years after
14:18 in *The Book of the History of the Kings of **J**.*
14:21 The people of **J** then crowned Amaziah's
14:22 rebuilt the town of Elath and restored it to **J**.
14:23 in the fifteenth year of King Amaziah's reign in **J**.
14:28 and Hamath, which had belonged to **J**,
15:1 Uzziah son of Amaziah began to rule over **J** in the
15:6 in *The Book of the History of the Kings of **J**.*
15:8 the thirty-eighth year of King Uzziah's reign in **J**.
15:13 in the thirty-ninth year of King Uzziah's reign in **J**.
15:17 in the thirty-ninth year of King Uzziah's reign in **J**.
15:23 in the fiftieth year of King Uzziah's reign in **J**.
15:27 the fifty-second year of King Uzziah's reign in **J**.
15:32 Jotham son of Uzziah began to rule over **J** in the
15:36 in *The Book of the History of the Kings of **J**.*
15:37 of Aram and King Pekah of Israel to attack **J**.
16:1 Ahaz son of Jotham began to rule over **J** in the
16:6 He drove out the people of **J** and sent Edomites to
16:19 in *The Book of the History of the Kings of **J**.*
17:1 Israel in the twelfth year of King Ahaz's reign in **J**.
17:13 his prophets and seers to warn both Israel and **J**:
17:18 Only the tribe of **J** remained in the land.
17:19 But even the people of **J** refused to obey the
18:1 Hezekiah son of Ahaz began to rule over **J** in the
18:5 was never another king like him in the land of **J**,
18:13 of Assyria came to attack the fortified cities of **J**
18:22 and make everyone in **J** worship only at the altar
19:10 "This message is for King Hezekiah of **J**.
19:30 And you who are left in **J**, who have escaped the
20:20 in *The Book of the History of the Kings of **J**.*
21:11 "King Manasseh of **J** has done many detestable
21:11 He has led the people of **J** into idolatry.
21:12 and **J** that the ears of those who hear about it will
21:16 to the sin that he caused the people of **J** to commit,
21:17 in *The Book of the History of the Kings of **J**.*
21:25 in *The Book of the History of the Kings of **J**.*
22:13 the LORD for me and for the people and for all **J**.
22:18 "But go to the king of **J** who sent you to seek the
23:1 Then the king summoned all the leaders of **J**
23:2 the Temple of the LORD with all the people of **J**
23:5 had been appointed by the previous kings of **J**,
23:5 burned incense at the pagan shrines throughout **J**
23:8 the LORD, who were living in other towns of **J**.
23:11 that the former kings of **J** had dedicated to the sun.
23:12 Josiah tore down the altars that the kings of **J** had
23:17 is the tomb of the man of God who came from **J**
23:22 all the years of the kings of Israel and **J**.
23:24 both in Jerusalem and throughout the land of **J**.
23:26 the LORD's anger burned against **J** because of all
23:27 "I will destroy **J** just as I have destroyed Israel.
23:28 in *The Book of the History of the Kings of **J**.*
23:33 He also demanded that **J** pay 7,500 pounds of
23:35 Jehoiakim collected a tax from the people of **J**,
24:1 Nebuchadnezzar of Babylon invaded the land of **J**.
24:2 and Ammonite raiders against **J** to destroy it,
24:3 These disasters happened to **J** according to the
24:3 He had decided to remove **J** from his presence
24:5 in *The Book of the History of the Kings of **J**.*
24:20 and **J** from his presence and sent them into exile.
25:12 people to stay behind in **J** to care for the vineyards
25:21 So the people of **J** were sent into exile from their
25:22 of Shaphan as governor over the people left in **J**.
25:26 Then all the people of **J**, from the least to the
1Ch 2:1 were Reuben, Simeon, Levi, **J**, Issachar, Zebulun,
2:3 **J** had three sons through Bathshua, a Canaanite
2:4 Later **J** had twin sons through Tamar, his widowed
2:4 were Perez and Zerah. So **J** had five sons in all.
2:10 was the father of Nahshon, a leader of **J**.
4:1 Some of the descendants of **J** were Perez, Hezron,
4:18 Mered also married a woman of **J**, who became the
4:27 tribe never became as large as the tribe of **J**.
4:41 But during the reign of King Hezekiah of **J**,
5:2 It was the descendants of **J** that became the most
5:17 records during the days of King Jotham of **J**
6:15 into exile when the LORD sent the people of **J**
6:55 and its surrounding pasturelands in **J**,
6:65 The towns in the territories of **J**, Simeon,
9:1 The people of **J** were exiled to Babylon
9:3 People from the tribes of **J**, Benjamin, Ephraim,
9:4 son of Bani, a descendant of Perez son of **J**.
9:6 In all, 690 families from the tribe of **J** returned.
12:16 and **J** came to David at the stronghold.
12:24 From the tribe of **J**, there were 6,800 warriors
13:6 and all Israel went to Baalah of **J** (also called
21:5 men of military age in Israel, and 470,000 in **J**.
27:18 **J** | Elihu (a brother of David) / Issachar | Omri
27:28 and sycamore-fig trees in the foothills of **J**.
28:4 For he has chosen the tribe of **J** to rule, and from among the families of **J**, he chose my
2Ch 1:15 the sycamore wood that grows in the foothills of **J**.
2:7 engraver who can work with the craftsmen of **J**
9:11 had there been such beautiful instruments in **J**.)
9:27 the sycamore wood that grows in the foothills of **J**.
10:17 rule over the Israelites who lived in the towns of **J**.
11:1 he mobilized the armies of **J** and Benjamin—
11:3 king of **J**, and to all the Israelites in **J** and Benjamin:
11:5 and fortified various cities for the defense of **J**.
11:10 These became the fortified cities of **J**
11:12 So only **J** and Benjamin remained under his
11:14 and property and moved to **J** and Jerusalem,
11:17 This strengthened the kingdom of **J**, and for three
11:23 them in the fortified cities throughout the land of **J**
12:12 And there was still goodness in the land of **J**.
13:1 Abijah began to rule over **J** in the eighteenth year
13:3 **J**, led by King Abijah, fielded 400,000 seasoned
13:4 When the army of **J** arrived in the hill country of
13:13 army around behind the men of **J** to ambush them.
13:14 When **J** realized that they were being attacked
13:15 and the men of **J** began to shout. At the sound of
13:15 and routed them before Abijah and the army of **J**.
13:16 The Israelite army fled from **J**, and God handed them over to **J** in defeat.
13:18 So **J** defeated Israel because they trusted in the
13:21 Abijah of **J** grew more and more powerful.
14:4 He commanded the people of **J** to seek the
14:6 able to build up the fortified cities throughout **J**.
14:7 Asa told the people of **J**, "Let us build towns
14:8 an army of 300,000 warriors from the tribe of **J**,
14:9 Once an Ethiopian named Zerah attacked **J** with an
14:12 in the presence of Asa and the army of **J**,

14:13 and the army of J carried off vast quantities of
15: 2 "Listen, all you people of J and Benjamin!
15: 7 And now, you men of J, be strong and courageous,
15: 8 and removed all the idols in the land of J
15: 9 Then Asa called together all the people of J
15: 9 Many had moved to J during Asa's reign when
16: 1 King Baasha of Israel invaded J and fortified
16: 1 from entering or leaving King Asa's territory in J.
16: 6 Then King Asa called out all the men of J to carry
16:11 are recorded in *The Book of the Kings of J*
17: 1 He strengthened J to stand against any attack from
17: 2 He stationed troops in all the fortified cities of J,
17: 2 he assigned additional garrisons to the land of J
17: 5 Jehoshaphat's control over the kingdom of J.
17: 5 All the people of J brought gifts to Jehoshaphat,
17: 7 sent out his officials to teach in all the towns of J.
17: 9 and traveled around through all the towns of J,
17:12 and built fortresses and store cities throughout J.
17:14 From J, there were 300,000 troops organized in
17:19 stationed in the fortified cities throughout J.
18: 9 King Ahab of Israel and King Jehoshaphat of J,
18:28 and King Jehoshaphat of J led their armies against
19: 1 When King Jehoshaphat of J arrived safely home
19:11 son of Ishmael, a leader from the tribe of J,
20: 3 He also gave orders that everyone throughout J
20: 4 So people from all the towns of J came to
20: 5 Jehoshaphat stood before the people of J
20:13 As all the men of J stood before the LORD with
20:15 Listen, all you people of J and Jerusalem!
20:17 He is with you, O people of J and Jerusalem.
20:18 And all the people of J and Jerusalem did the
20:20 Early the next morning the army of J went out into
20:20 "Listen to me, all you people of J and Jerusalem!
20:24 So when the army of J arrived at the lookout point
20:31 So Jehoshaphat ruled over the land of J. He was
20:35 King Jehoshaphat of J made an alliance with King
21: 8 the Edomites revolted against J and crowned their
21:10 Edom has been independent from J to this day.
21:11 He had built pagan shrines in the hill country of J
21:11 and J to give themselves to pagan gods.
21:12 Jehoshaphat, or your grandfather King Asa of J.
21:13 led the people of Jerusalem and J to worship idols,
21:17 They marched against J, broke down its defenses,
22: 1 So Ahaziah son of Jehoram reigned as king of J.
22: 6 and King Ahaziah of J went to Jezreel to visit him.
22:10 When Athaliah, the mother of King Ahaziah of J,
23: 2 These men traveled secretly throughout J
24: 5 "Go at once to all the towns of J and collect the
24: 6 and collect the Temple taxes from the towns of J
24: 9 Then a proclamation was sent throughout J
24:17 the leaders of J came and bowed before King
24:18 Then the anger of God burned against J
24:23 They invaded J and Jerusalem and killed all the
24:24 helped them conquer the much larger army of J.
24:24 The people of J had abandoned the LORD,
25: 5 assigning leaders to each clan from J
25:10 This made them angry with J, and they returned
25:13 raided several of the towns of J between Samaria
25:17 King Amaziah of J sent this challenge to Israel's
25:18 Israel replied to King Amaziah of J with this story:
25:19 will bring disaster on you and the people of J?"
25:21 mobilized his army against King Amaziah of J.
25:21 drew up their battle lines at Beth-shemesh in J.
25:22 J was routed by the army of Israel, and its army
25:23 captured King Amaziah of J at Beth-shemesh
25:25 King Amaziah of J lived on for fifteen years after
25:26 are recorded in *The Book of the Kings of J*
26: 1 The people of J then crowned Amaziah's
26: 2 rebuilt the town of Elath and restored it to J.
26:10 he kept great herds of livestock in the foothills of J
27: 4 He built towns in the hill country of J
27: 7 in *The Book of the Kings of Israel and J.*
28: 8 and children from J and took tremendous amounts
28: 9 was angry with J and let you defeat them.
28:10 are planning to make slaves of these people from J
28:16 About that time King Ahaz of J asked the king of
28:17 The armies of Edom had again invaded J and taken
28:18 had raided towns located in the foothills of J
28:19 The LORD was humbling J because of King Ahaz
of J,
28:25 He made pagan shrines in all the towns of J for
28:26 are recorded in *The Book of the Kings of J*
29: 1 years old when he became the king of J,
29: 8 That is why the LORD's anger has fallen upon J
29:21 for the kingdom, for the Temple, and for J.
30: 1 King Hezekiah now sent word to all Israel and J,
30: 6 messengers were sent throughout Israel and J.
30:12 God's hand was on the people in the land of J,
30:25 The entire assembly of J rejoiced,
30:25 came to the festival, and all those who lived in J.
31: 1 Israelites who attended went to all the towns of J,
31: 6 The people who had moved to J from Israel,
31: 6 and the people of J themselves, brought in the
31:20 Hezekiah handled the distribution throughout all J,
32: 1 this work, King Sennacherib of Assyria invaded J.
32:12 He commanded J and Jerusalem to worship at only
32:25 came against him and against J and Jerusalem.
32:32 which is included in *The Book of the Kings of J*
32:33 and all J and Jerusalem honored him at his death.
33: 9 But Manasseh led the people of J and Jerusalem to
33:14 military officers in all of the fortified cities of J.
33:16 He also encouraged the people of J to worship the
34: 3 twelfth year, he began to purify J and Jerusalem,
34: 5 own altars, and so he purified J and Jerusalem.
34: 9 as well as from all J, Benjamin, and the people of
34:11 They restored what earlier kings of J had allowed
34:21 for me and for all the remnant of Israel and J.
34:25 For the people of J have abandoned me
34:26 "But go to the king of J who sent you to seek the
34:29 Then the king summoned all the leaders of J
34:30 the Temple of the LORD with all the people of J
35:18 of Jerusalem, and people from all over J and Israel.
35:21 "What do you want with me, king of J? I have no
35:24 And all J and Jerusalem mourned for him.
35:27 in *The Book of the Kings of Israel and J.*
36: 3 who demanded a tribute from J of 7,500 pounds of
36: 4 of Jehoahaz, as the next king of J and Jerusalem,
36: 8 *and J.* Then his son Jehoiachin became the next
36:10 Zedekiah, to be the next king in J and Jerusalem.
36:23 build him a Temple at Jerusalem in the land of J.
Ezr 1: 2 build him a Temple at Jerusalem in the land of J.
1: 3 in J to rebuild this Temple of the LORD,
1: 5 and Levites and the leaders of the tribes of J
1: 8 the leader of the exiles returning to J.
2: 1 captivity to Jerusalem and to the other towns of J.
2:64 So a total of 42,360 people returned to J,
2:70 to the other towns of J from which they had come.
4: 1 The enemies of J and Benjamin heard that the
4: 4 and frighten the people of J to keep them from
4: 6 the enemies of J wrote him a letter of accusation
against the people of J
4: 7 the enemies of J, led by Bishlam, Mithredath,
5: 1 in the name of the God of Israel to the Jews in J
5: 8 the Temple of the great God in the province of J.
5:14 whom King Cyrus appointed as governor of J.
6: 7 and do not hinder the governor of J and the leaders
7:14 you to conduct an inquiry into the situation in J
9: 9 He has given us a protective wall in J
10: 7 Then a proclamation was made throughout J
10: 9 all the people of J and Benjamin had gathered in
10:23 (also called Kelita), Pethahiah, J, and Eliezer.
Ne 1: 2 with some other men who had just arrived from J.
1: 3 well for those who returned to the province of J.
2: 5 send me to J to rebuild the city where my
2: 7 safely through their territories on my way to J.
4:10 Then the people of J began to complain that the
4:16 stationed themselves behind the people of J
5:14 the entire twelve years that I was governor of J—
6: 7 in Jerusalem, saying, 'Look! There is a king in J!'
6:17 and forth between Tobiah and the officials of J.
6:18 For many in J had sworn allegiance to him
7: 5 record of those who had first returned to J.
7: 6 captivity to Jerusalem and to the other towns of J.
7:66 "So a total of 42,360 people returned to J,
11: 1 A tenth of the people from the other towns of J
11: 3 live in their own homes in the various towns of J,
11: 4 but some of the people from J and Benjamin
11: 4 From the tribe of J: Athaiah son of Uzziah, son of
11: 9 who was assisted by J son of Hassenuah,
11:20 inheritance was located in any of the towns of J.
11:24 son of Meshezabel, a descendant of Zerah son of J,
11:25 Some of the people of J lived in Kiriath-arba with
11:30 So the people of J were living all the way from
11:36 Some of the Levites who lived in J were sent to
12: 8 Binnui, Kadmiel, Sherebiah, J, and Mattaniah,
12:31 I led the leaders of J to the top of the wall
12:32 Hoshaiah and half the leaders of J followed them,
12:34 J, Benjamin, Shemaiah, Jeremiah,
12:36 Azarel, Milalai, Gilalai, Maai, Nethanel, J,
12:44 for all the people of J valued the priests
13:12 And once more all the people of J began bringing
13:15 One Sabbath day I saw some men of J treading
13:16 were selling it on the Sabbath to the people of J—
13:17 So I confronted the leaders of J, "Why are you
13:23 of the men of J had married women from Ashdod,
13:24 and could not speak the language of J at all.
Est 2: 6 along with King Jehoiachin of J and many others.
Ps 48:11 Let the towns of J be glad, / for your judgments
60: 7 my warriors, / and J will produce my kings.
63: T a time when David was in the wilderness of J.
68:27 Then comes a great throng of rulers from J
69:35 and rebuild the towns of J. / His people will live
76: 1 God is well known in J; / his name is great in
78:68 He chose instead the tribe of J, / Mount Zion,
97: 8 and rejoiced, / and all the cities of J are glad
108: 8 my warriors, / and J will produce my kings.
114: 2 the land of J became God's sanctuary, / and Israel
Pr 25: 1 collected by the advisers of King Hezekiah of J.
Isa 1: 1 These visions concerning J and Jerusalem came to
1: 1 Jotham, Ahaz, and Hezekiah—all kings of J.
2: 1 vision that Isaiah son of Amoz saw concerning J
3: 1 supplies of food and water from Jerusalem and J.
3: 8 J and Jerusalem will lie in ruins because they
5: 3 "Now, you people of Jerusalem and J, / you have
5: 7 Israel and J are his pleasant garden. / He expected
7: 6 'We will invade J and throw its people into panic.
7:17 Solomon's empire was divided into Israel and J.
8: 6 "The people of J have rejected my gentle care
8: 8 will overflow all its channels and sweep into J.
8:14 and J he will be a stone that causes people to
9:21 will feed on Manasseh, and both will devour J.
10:20 last those left in Israel and J will trust the LORD,
11:12 He will gather the scattered people of J from the
11:13 at last the jealousy between Israel and J will end.
16: 1 Jerusalem as a token of alliance with the king of J.
22:21 will be a father to the people of Jerusalem and J.
26: 1 everyone in the land of J will sing this song:
36: 1 of Assyria came to attack the fortified cities of J
36: 7 and make everyone in J worship only at the altar
37:10 "This message is for King Hezekiah of J.
37:31 And you who are left in J, who have escaped the
40: 9 Tell the towns of J, "Your God is coming!"
44:26 and the towns of J will be lived in once again,
48: 1 by the name of Israel and born into the family of J.
65: 9 of the people of Israel and of J to possess my land.
Jer 1: 2 the thirteenth year of King Josiah's reign in J.
1: 3 the eleventh year of King Zedekiah's reign in J.
1:15 will attack its walls and all the other towns of J.
1:18 or people of J will be able to stand against you.
2:28 as many gods as there are cities and towns in J.
3: 7 And though her faithless sister J saw this,
3: 8 But now J, too, has left me and given herself to
3:10 her faithless sister J has never sincerely returned to
3:11 faithless Israel is less guilty than treacherous J!
3:18 In those days the people of J and Israel will return
4: 3 This is what the LORD says to the people of J
4: 5 "Shout to Jerusalem and to all J! Tell them to
4:16 raising a battle cry against the towns of J.
5:11 of Israel and J are full of treachery against me,"
5:20 "Make this announcement to Israel and to J:
7: 2 'O J, listen to this message from the LORD!
7:17 see what they are doing throughout the towns of J
7:30 "The people of J have sinned before my very
7:34 brides will no longer be heard in the towns of J.
8: 1 open the graves of the kings and officials of J,
9:11 The towns of J will be ghost towns, with no one
9:26 live in distant places, and yes, even the people of J.
10:22 The towns of J will be destroyed and will become
11: 2 "Remind the people of J and Jerusalem about the
11: 9 a conspiracy against me among the people of J
11:10 and J have both broken the covenant I made with
11:12 Then the people of J and Jerusalem will pray to
11:13 Look now, people of J, you have as many gods as
11:17 For the people of Israel and J have done evil,
12:14 I will uproot them from their lands just as J will be
13: 9 This illustrates how I will rot away the pride of J
13:11 so I created J and Israel to cling to me,"
13:19 The people of J will be taken away as captives.
14: 2 "J wilts; her businesses have ground to a halt.
14:19 LORD, have you completely rejected J? Do you
15: 4 son of Hezekiah, king of J, did in Jerusalem,
17:20 you kings of J and all you people of J
17:25 will always ride among the people of J in chariots
17:26 from the towns of J and Benjamin,
18:11 Jeremiah, go and warn all J and Jerusalem.
19: 3 you kings of J and citizens of Jerusalem!
19: 4 by their ancestors, or by the kings of J,
19: 7 For I will upset the battle plans of J and Jerusalem
19:11 so I will shatter the people of J and Jerusalem
20: 4 I will hand the people of J over to the king of
21: 2 of Babylon has begun his attack on J.
21:11 "Say to the royal family of J, 'Listen to this
22: 1 "Go over and speak directly to the king of J.
22: 2 you king of J, sitting on David's throne.
22:24 Jehoiachin son of Jehoiakim, king of J.
22:30 will ever sit on the throne of David to rule in J.
23: 6 In that day J will be saved, and Israel will live in
24: 1 king of J, to Babylon along with the princes of J
24: 5 The good figs represent the exiles I sent from J to
24: 8 "represent King Zedekiah of J, his officials,
25: 1 This message for all the people of J came to
25: 1 during the fourth year of Jehoiakim's reign over J.
25: 2 Jeremiah the prophet said to the people in J
25: 3 year of Josiah son of Amon, king of J, until now—
25:18 I went to Jerusalem and the other towns of J,
26: 1 in the reign of Jehoiakim son of Josiah, king of J.
26: 2 who have come there to worship from all over J.
26:10 When the officials of J heard what was happening,
26:18 prophesied during the reign of King Hezekiah of J.
26:18 He told the people of J, 'This is what the LORD
27: 1 in the reign of Zedekiah son of Josiah, king of J.
27:12 repeated this same message to King Zedekiah of J.
27:20 king of J, to Babylon, along with all the other
27:20 along with all the other important people of J
28: 1 the fourth year of the reign of Zedekiah, king of J
28: 4 bring back Jehoiachin son of Jehoiakim, king of J,
29: 2 queen mother, the court officials, the leaders of J,
30: 3 restore the fortunes of my people of Israel and J.
30: 4 message the LORD gave concerning Israel and J:
31:23 the people of J and its cities will again say,
31:27 multiply the number of cattle here in Israel and J.
31:31 a new covenant with the people of Israel and J.
32: 1 the tenth year of the reign of Zedekiah, king of J.
32:12 the deed, and all the men of J who were there.
32:30 Israel and J have done nothing but wrong since
32:32 "The sins of Israel and J—the sins of the people of
32:35 an incredible evil, causing J to sin so greatly!
32:44 in the towns of J and in the hill country,
32:44 in the foothills of J and in the Negev, too.
33: 7 I will restore the fortunes of J and Israel
33:13 the foothills of J, the Negev, the land of Benjamin,
33:13 the vicinity of Jerusalem, and all the towns of J.
33:14 for Israel and J all the good I have promised them.
33:16 In that day J will be saved, and Jerusalem will live
33:24 'The LORD chose J and Israel and
34: 1 he fought against Jerusalem and the towns of J.
34: 2 "Go to King Zedekiah of J, and tell him, 'This is
34: 4 promise from the LORD, O Zedekiah, king of J.
34: 6 delivered the message to King Zedekiah of J.
34: 7 the only cities of J with their walls still standing.
34:19 whether you are officials of J or Jerusalem,
34:21 I will hand over King Zedekiah of J and his
34:22 I will see to it that all the towns of J are destroyed
35: 1 when Jehoiakim son of Josiah was king of J:
35:13 Go and say to the people in J and Jerusalem,
35:17 I will send upon J and Jerusalem all the disasters I
36: 1 year that Jehoiakim son of Josiah was king in J,
36: 2 messages against Israel, J, and the other nations.
36: 3 Perhaps the people of J will repent if they see in
36: 6 On that day people will be there from all over J.
36: 9 People from all over J came to attend the services

36:30 what the LORD says about King Jehoiakim of **J**:
36:31 I will pour out on them and on all the people of **J**
37: 1 Jehoiachin son of Jehoiakim as the king of **J**.
37: 5 of Egypt appeared at the southern border of **J**.
37: 7 Tell the king of **J**, who sent you to ask me what is
39: 6 as they killed his sons and all the nobles of **J**.
39:10 Nebuzaradan left a few of the poorest people in **J**,
39:14 So Jeremiah stayed in **J** among his own people.
40: 1 and **J** who were being sent to exile in Babylon.
40: 5 He has been appointed governor of **J** by the king
40: 6 and lived in **J** with the few who were still left in
40: 7 over the poor people who were left behind in **J**,
40:11 that the king of Babylon had left a few people in **J**
40:12 they began to return to **J** from the places to which
42:15 this is what the LORD says to the remnant of **J**.
42:19 "Listen, you remnant of **J**. The LORD has told
43: 4 to obey the LORD's command to stay in **J**.
43: 9 "While the people of **J** are watching, bury large
43:10 Then say to the people of **J**, 'The LORD
44: 2 what I did to Jerusalem and to all the towns of **J**.
44: 6 fury boiled over and fell like fire on the towns of **J**
44: 7 or child among you who has come here from **J**,
44: 9 the sins of the kings and queens of **J**, and the sins
44: 9 and your wives committed in **J** and Jerusalem?
44:12 I will take this remnant of **J** that insisted on
44:14 fled to Egypt with dreams of returning home to **J**,
44:17 and princes have always done in the towns of **J**
44:21 were burning incense to idols in the towns of **J**
44:24 all you citizens of **J** who live in Egypt.
44:28 will escape death and return to **J** from Egypt.
44:30 just as I turned King Zedekiah of **J** over to King
46: 2 the king of **J**, on the occasion of the battle of
49:34 the beginning of the reign of King Zedekiah of **J**.
50: 4 the people of Israel and **J** will join together,"
50:20 the LORD, "no sin will be found in Israel or in **J**,
50:33 "The people of Israel and **J** have been wronged.
51: 5 LORD Almighty has not forsaken Israel and **J**.
51:59 when he went to Babylon with King Zedekiah of **J**.
52: 3 and **J** from his presence and sent them into exile.
52:10 they also killed all the other leaders of **J**.
52:16 people to stay behind in **J** to care for the vineyards
52:27 So the people of **J** were sent into exile from their
La 1: 3 **J** has been led away into captivity, afflicted
5:11 girls in Jerusalem and throughout the towns of **J**.
Eze 8: 1 while the leaders of **J** were in my home,
8:17 "Is it nothing to the people of **J** that they commit
9: 9 sins of the people of Israel and **J** are very great.
21:20 Rabbah, and the other to **J** and fortified Jerusalem.
25: 3 and laughed at **J** as she went away into exile,
25: 8 Because the people of Moab have said that **J** is just
25:12 by avenging themselves against the people of **J**.
25:15 The people of Philistia have acted against **J** out of
27:17 **J** and Israel traded for your wares, offering wheat
33:24 the scattered remnants of **J** living among the
35:10 you said, 'The lands of Israel and **J** will be ours.
37:16 'This stick represents **J** and its allied tribes.'
37:19 I will take the northern tribes and join them to **J**.
48: 7 and then **J**, all of whose boundaries extend from
48: 8 "South of **J** is the land set aside for a special
48:22 everything between the territories allotted to **J**
48:31 the second for **J**, and the third for Levi.
Da 1: 1 the third year of King Jehoiakim's reign in **J**,
1: 2 Lord gave him victory over King Jehoiakim of **J**.
1: 6 of the young men chosen, all from the tribe of **J**.
2:25 "I have found one of the captives from **J** who will
5:13 who was exiled from **J** by my predecessor,
6:13 "That man Daniel, one of the captives from **J**,
9: 7 including the people of **J** and Jerusalem and all
Hos 1: 1 Jotham, Ahaz, and Hezekiah were kings of **J**,
1: 7 their God, will show love to the people of **J**.
1:11 Then the people of **J** and Israel will unite under
4:15 Israel is a prostitute, may **J** avoid such guilt.
4:15 O **J**, do not join with those who worship me
5: 5 under her load of guilt. **J**, too, will fall with her.
5:10 "The leaders of **J** have become as bad as thieves.
5:13 "When Israel and **J** saw how sick they were,
5:14 will tear at Israel and **J** as a lion rips apart its prey.
6: 4 "O Israel and **J**, what should I do with you?"
6:11 "O **J**, a harvest of punishment is also waiting for
8:14 has built great palaces, and **J** has fortified its cities.
10:11 Israel and **J** must now break up the hard ground;
11:12 but **J** still walks with God and is faithful to the
12: 2 Now the LORD is bringing a lawsuit against **J**.
Joel 3: 1 when I restore the prosperity of **J** and Jerusalem,"
3: 6 You have sold the people of **J** and Jerusalem to the
3: 8 sell your sons and daughters to the people of **J**,
3:18 Water will fill the dry streambeds of **J**, and a
3:19 because they attacked **J** and killed her innocent
3:20 "But **J** will remain forever, and Jerusalem will
Am 1: 1 to Amos, a shepherd from the town of Tekoa in **J**.
1: 1 when Uzziah was king of **J** and Jeroboam II,
2: 4 "The people of **J** have sinned again and again,
2: 5 So I will send down fire on **J**, and all the fortresses
3: 1 has spoken against you, O people of Israel and **J**—
7:12 Go on back to the land of **J** and do your preaching
Ob 1:19 Those living in the foothills of **J** will possess the
Mic 1: 1 when Jotham, Ahaz, and Hezekiah were kings of **J**.
1: 5 Because of the sins and rebellion of Israel and **J**.
1: 5 Where is the center of idolatry in **J**? In Jerusalem,
1: 9 It has reached into **J**, even to the gates of
1:13 You were the first city in **J** to follow Israel in the
1:16 Weep, you people of **J**! Shave your heads in
5: 2 Bethlehem Ephrathah, are only a small village in **J**.
Na 1:15 Celebrate your festivals, O people of **J**, and fulfill
Zep 1: 1 when Josiah son of Amon was king of **J**.
1: 4 "I will crush **J** and Jerusalem with my fist
1: 8 "I will punish the leaders and princes of **J** and all
2: 7 The few survivors of the tribe of **J** will pasture
Hag 1: 1 governor of **J**, and to Jeshua son of Jehozadak,
1:14 governor of **J**, Jeshua son of Jehozadak, the high
2: 2 governor of **J**, and to Jeshua son of Jehozadak,
2:21 "Tell Zerubbabel, the governor of **J**, that I am
Zec 1:12 been angry with Jerusalem and the towns of **J**.
1:19 horns represent the world powers that scattered **J**,
1:21 terrify the four horns that scattered and humbled **J**.
2:12 The land of **J** will be the LORD's inheritance in
7: 7 and the towns of **J** were bustling with people,
7: 7 and the foothills of **J** were populated areas?' "
8:12 Once more I will make the remnant in **J** and Israel
8:13 **J** and Israel had become symbols of what it means
8:15 my decision to bless Jerusalem and the people of **J**.
8:19 festivals of joy and celebration for the people of **J**.
9: 7 our God and be adopted as a new clan in **J**.
9:13 **J** is my bow, and Israel is my arrow! Jerusalem is
10: 3 Almighty has arrived to look after his flock of **J**;
10: 4 From **J** will come the cornerstone, the tent peg,
10: 6 "I will strengthen **J** and save Israel; I will
11:14 to show that the bond of unity between **J** and Israel
12: 2 and **J** like an intoxicating drink to all the nearby
12: 4 I will watch over the people of **J**, but I will blind
12: 5 And the clans of **J** will say to themselves,
12: 6 "On that day I will make the clans of **J** like a
12: 7 The LORD will give victory to the rest of **J** first,
12: 7 will not have greater honor than the rest of **J**.
12:14 Each of the surviving families from **J** will mourn
14: 5 the earthquake in the days of King Uzziah of **J**.
14:10 north of **J**, to Rimmon, south of Jerusalem,
14:14 **J**, too, will be fighting at Jerusalem. The wealth of
14:21 and **J** will be set apart as holy to the LORD
Mal 2:11 In **J**, in Israel, and in Jerusalem there is treachery,
2:11 for the men of **J** have defiled the LORD's
3: 4 the offerings brought to him by the people of **J**
Mt 1: 2 Jacob was the father of **J** and his brothers.
1: 3 **J** was the father of Perez and Zerah (their mother
2: 6 'O Bethlehem of **J**, / you are not just a lowly
village in **J**,
Lk 3:30 Simeon was the son of **J**. / **J** was the son of Joseph.
3:33 was the son of Perez. / Perez was the son of **J**.
3:34 **J** was the son of Jacob. / Jacob was the son of
Heb 7:14 What I mean is, our Lord came from the tribe of **J**,
7:14 and Moses never mentioned **J** in connection with
8: 8 a new covenant / with the people of Israel and **J**.
Rev 5: 5 Look, the Lion of the tribe of **J**, the heir to David's
7: 5 from **J** | 12,000 / from Reuben | 12,000

JUDAH'S (28) [JUDAH]

Ge 38: 4 Then **J** wife had another son, and she named him
38:12 In the course of time **J** wife died. After the time of
Nu 2: 9 So the total of all the troops on **J** side of the camp
26:20 But the following clans descended from **J**
Jos 15:13 The LORD instructed Joshua to assign some of **J**
18: 5 excluding **J** territory in the south and Joseph's
19: 1 Their inheritance was surrounded by **J** territory.
19: 9 to Judah because **J** territory was too large for them.
2Sa 2: 4 Then **J** leaders came to David and crowned him
1Ch 4:21 Shelah was one of **J** sons. The descendants of
2Ch 12: 4 Shishak conquered **J** fortified cities and
12: 5 then met with Rehoboam and **J** leaders,
14: 5 as well as the incense altars from every one of **J**
17:13 He stored numerous supplies in **J** towns
21: 3 and also the ownership of some of **J** fortified
22: 8 he happened to meet some of **J** officials
22:10 she set out to destroy the rest of **J** royal family.
23: 2 and clan leaders in **J** towns to come to Jerusalem.
28: 6 killed 120,000 of **J** troops because they had
36:17 The Babylonians killed **J** young men, even chasing
Isa 7: 6 and install the son of Tabeel as **J** king.'
22: 8 **J** defenses have been stripped away. You run to
Jer 19:13 including the palace of **J** kings, will become like
27:21 kept in the Temple and in the palace of **J** king:
33:10 the empty streets of Jerusalem and **J** other towns,
Eze 4: 6 side for 40 days—one day for each year of **J** sin.
Da 1: 3 to bring to the palace some of the young men of **J**
Hos 5:12 I will sap **J** strength as dry rot weakens wood.

JUDAISM (2) [JEW]

Ac 2:10 visitors from Rome (both Jews and converts to **J**),
13:43 and godly converts to **J** who worshiped at the

JUDAS (46) [JUDAS'S]

Mt 10: 4 (the Zealot), / **J** Iscariot (who later betrayed him).
13:55 and his brothers—James, Joseph, Simon, and **J**.
26:14 Then **J** Iscariot, one of the twelve disciples,
26:16 **J** began looking for the right time and place to
26:25 **J**, the one who would betray him, also asked,
26:47 And even as he said this, **J**, one of the twelve
26:48 **J** had given them a prearranged signal: "You will
26:49 So **J** came straight to Jesus. "Greetings, Teacher!"
27: 3 When **J**, who had betrayed him, realized that Jesus
27: 5 Then **J** threw the money onto the floor of the
Mk 3:19 **J** Iscariot (who later betrayed him).
6: 3 and brother of James, Joseph, **J**, and Simon.
14:10 Then **J** Iscariot, one of the twelve disciples,
14:43 And immediately, as he said this, **J**, one of the
14:44 **J** had given them a prearranged signal: "You will
14:45 As soon as they arrived, **J** walked up to Jesus.
Lk 6:16 **J** (son of James), / **J** Iscariot (who later betrayed
him).
22: 3 Then Satan entered into **J** Iscariot, who was one of
22:47 even as he said this, a mob approached, led by **J**,
22:47 **J** walked over to Jesus and greeted him with a kiss.
22:48 But Jesus said, "**J**, how can you betray me,
Jn 6:71 He was speaking of **J**, son of Simon Iscariot,
12: 4 But **J** Iscariot, one of his disciples—the one who
13: 2 and the Devil had already enticed **J**, son of Simon
13:26 dipped it, he gave it to **J**, son of Simon Iscariot.
13:27 As soon as **J** had eaten the bread, Satan entered
13:29 Since **J** was their treasurer, some thought Jesus
13:30 So **J** left at once, going out into the night.
13:31 As soon as **J** left the room, Jesus said, "The time
14:22 **J** (not **J** Iscariot, but the other disciple with
18: 2 **J**, the betrayer, knew this place, because Jesus had
18: 3 and Pharisees had given **J** a battalion of Roman
18: 5 **J** was standing there with them when Jesus
Ac 1:13 Simon (the Zealot), / and **J** (son of James).
1:16 for the Scriptures to be fulfilled concerning **J**,
1:17 **J** was one of us, chosen to share in the ministry
1:18 (**J** bought a field with the money he received for
1:25 as an apostle to replace **J** the traitor in this
5:37 at the time of the census, there was **J** of Galilee.
9:11 "Go over to Straight Street, to the house of **J**.
15:22 **J** (also called Barsabbas) and Silas.
15:27 So we are sending **J** and Silas to tell you what we
15:32 Then **J** and Silas, both being prophets,
15:33 and then **J** and Silas were sent back to Jerusalem,

JUDAS'S (1) [JUDAS]

Ac 1:21 "So now we must choose someone else to take **J**

JUDE (1)

Jude 1: 1 This letter is from **J**, a slave of Jesus Christ and a

JUDEA (46) [JUDAH]

Eze 24:21 and daughters in **J** will be slaughtered by the
Mt 2: 1 Jesus was born in the town of Bethlehem in **J**,
3: 5 People from Jerusalem and from every section of **J**
4:12 had been arrested, he left **J** and returned to Galilee.
4:25 the Ten Towns, Jerusalem, from all over **J**,
19: 1 left Galilee and went southward to the region of **J**
24:16 "Then those in **J** must flee to the hills.
Mk 1: 5 and from all over **J** traveled out into the wilderness
3: 7 followed by a huge crowd from all over Galilee, **J**,
10: 1 and went southward to the region of **J**
13:14 "Then those in **J** must flee to the hills.
Lk 1: 5 Zechariah, who lived when Herod was king of **J**.
1:39 days later Mary hurried to the hill country of **J**,
2: 4 he had to go to Bethlehem in **J**, David's ancient
3: 1 Pilate was governor over **J**; Herod Antipas was
4:44 preaching in synagogues throughout **J**.
5:17 showed up from every village in all Galilee and **J**,
6:17 There were people from all over **J** and from
7:17 of what Jesus had done that day spread all over **J**
21:21 Then those in **J** must flee to the hills. Let those in
23: 5 he goes, all over **J**, from Galilee to Jerusalem!"
23:51 He was from the town of Arimathea in **J**, and he
Jn 3:22 but they stayed in **J** for a while and baptized there.
4: 3 So he left **J** to return to Galilee.
4:47 When he heard that Jesus had come from **J**
4:54 miraculous sign in Galilee after coming from **J**.
7: 1 He wanted to stay out of **J** where the Jewish
7: 3 and Jesus' brothers urged him to go to **J** for the
11: 7 he said to his disciples, "Let's go to **J** again."
11: 8 "only a few days ago the Jewish leaders in **J** were
Ac 1: 8 in Jerusalem, throughout **J**, in Samaria, and to the
2: 9 **J**, Cappadocia, Pontus, the province of Asia,
8: 1 and all the believers except the apostles fled into **J**
9:31 The church then had peace throughout **J**, Galilee,
10:37 You know what happened all through **J**,
11: 1 and other believers in **J** that the Gentiles had
11:29 Antioch decided to send relief to the believers in **J**,
12:19 Afterward Herod left **J** to stay in Caesarea for a
15: 1 some men from **J** arrived and began to teach the
21:10 who also had the gift of prophecy, arrived from **J**.
26:20 then in Jerusalem and throughout all **J**, and also to
28:21 We have had no letters from **J** or reports from
Ro 15:31 Pray that I will be rescued from those in **J** who
2Co 1:16 Then you could send me on my way to **J**.
Gal 1:22 And still the Christians in the churches in **J** didn't
1Th 2:14 you imitated the believers in God's churches in **J**

JUDEAN (13) [JUDAH]

Jos 12: 8 mountain slopes, the **J** wilderness, and the Negev.
2Sa 3: 8 "Am I a **J** dog to be kicked around like this?"
2Ki 25:19 he took an officer of the **J** army, five of the king's
Jer 29:22 so that whenever the **J** exiles want to curse
34: 9 No one was to keep a fellow **J** in bondage.
40: 7 The leaders of the **J** guerrilla bands in the
40:12 then went out into the **J** countryside to gather a
41: 3 they went out and slaughtered all the **J** officials
52:25 he took an officer of the **J** army, seven of the
Eze 1: 1 while I was with the **J** exiles beside the Kebar
3:15 Then I came to the colony of **J** exiles in Tel-abib,
Mt 3: 1 the Baptist began preaching in the **J** wilderness.
Lk 1:65 what had happened spread throughout the **J** hills.

JUDEANS (9) [JUDAH]

2Ki 25:25 and everyone with him, both **J** and Babylonians.
Jer 38:19 "for the Babylonians will hand me over to the **J**
40:11 When the **J** in Moab, Ammon, Edom,
40:15 will happen then to the **J** who have returned?
44: 1 **J** living in northern Egypt in the cities of Migdol,
44:15 a great crowd of all the **J** living in Pathros,
44:26 from the LORD, all you **J** now living in Egypt:
44:26 be spoken by any of the **J** in the land of Egypt.
Eze 11:24 me back again to Babylonia, to the **J** in exile there.

JUDGE (145) [JUDGE'S, JUDGED, JUDGES, JUDGING, JUDGMENT, JUDGMENTS]

Ge 18:25 Should not the J of all the earth do what is right?"
50:19 be afraid of me. Am I God, to j and punish you?
Ex 2:14 "Who appointed you to be our prince and j?
5:21 "May the LORD j you for getting us into this
Lev 19:15 "Always j your neighbors fairly, neither favoring
Dt 16:18 They will j the people fairly throughout the land.
17:9 and the j on duty will hear the case and decide
17:12 arrogant enough to reject the verdict of the j
25:2 the j will command him to lie down and be beaten
32:36 "Indeed, the LORD will j his people, / and he
Jdg 2:18 Whenever the LORD placed a j over Israel,
2:18 he was with that j and rescued the people from
2:19 But when the j died, the people returned to their
3:10 LORD came upon him, and he became Israel's j.
4:4 was a prophet who had become a j in Israel.
10:2 He was Israel's j for twenty-three years. When he
11:27 Let the LORD, who is j, decide today which of us
12:7 Jephthah was Israel's j for six years. When he
12:8 After Jephthah, Ibzan became Israel's j. He lived
12:11 After him, Elon from Zebulun became Israel's j.
12:13 son of Hillel, from Pirathon, became Israel's j.
12:14 seventy donkeys. He was Israel's j for eight years.
15:20 Samson was Israel's j for twenty years,
16:31 Samson had been Israel's j for twenty years.
1Sa 2:3 and he will j you for what you have done.
7:6 So it was at Mizpah that Samuel became Israel's j.
7:15 Samuel continued as Israel's j for the rest of his
16:7 "Don't j by his appearance or height, for I have
16:7 People j by outward appearance, but the LORD
24:15 May the LORD j which of us is right and punish
2Sa 15:4 I wish I were the j. Then people could bring their
1Ki 8:32 hear from heaven and j between your servants—
2Ki 21:13 I will j Jerusalem by the same standard I used for
1Ch 12:17 then may the God of our ancestors see and j you."
16:33 the LORD! / For he is coming to j the earth.
2Ch 6:23 hear from heaven and j between your servants—
19:6 Remember that you do not j to please people
19:7 Fear the LORD and j with care, for the LORD
Job 21:22 who can teach a lesson to God, the supreme J?
22:13 How can he j through the thick darkness?
23:7 reason with him, so I would be acquitted by my J.
31:6 Let God j me on the scales of justice, for he knows
34:17 Are you going to condemn the almighty J?
Ps 7:11 God is a j who is perfectly fair. / He is angry with
9:8 He will j the world with justice / and rule the
37:33 be condemned when they are brought before the j.
50:6 proclaim his justice, / for God himself will be the j.
58:1 meaning of the word? / Do you j the people fairly?
62:12 O Lord, is yours. / Surely you j all people
72:2 Help him j your people in the right way;
76:9 You stand up to j those who do evil, O God,
82:8 Rise up, O God, and j the earth, / for all the nations
94:2 Arise, O j of the earth. / Sentence the proud to the
96:10 and cannot be shaken. / He will j all peoples fairly.
96:13 He is coming to j the earth. / He will j the world
98:9 For the LORD is coming to j the earth.
98:9 He will j the world with justice, / and the nations
Pr 16:10 with divine wisdom; he must never j unfairly.
18:5 It is wrong for a j to favor the guilty or condemn
24:12 And he will j all people according to what they
24:24 A j who says to the wicked, "You are innocent,"
Ecc 3:17 "In due season God will j everyone, both good
12:14 God will j us for everything we do,
Isa 3:16 Next the LORD will j the women of Jerusalem,
11:3 He will never j by appearance, false evidence,
26:9 for God. / For only when you come to j the earth
33:22 For the LORD is our j, our lawgiver, and our
Jer 21:12 Give justice to the people you j! Help those who
25:31 He will j all the people of the earth,
50:21 the land of rebels, a land that I will j!
La 3:59 done to me, LORD. Be my j, and prove me right.
Eze 11:11 I will j you even to the borders of Israel,
18:4 For all people are mine to j—both parents
18:30 "Therefore, I will j each of you, O people of
20:35 of the nations, and there I will j you face to face.
20:36 I will j you there just as I did your ancestors in the
21:27 until the one appears who has the right to j it.
22:2 "Son of man, are you ready to j Jerusalem?
22:2 Are you ready to j this city of murderers?
23:45 But righteous people will j these sister cities for
33:20 But I will j each of you according to your deeds."
34:17 I will j between one sheep and another,
34:20 I will surely j between the fat sheep
34:22 And I will j between one sheep and another.
Da 7:9 put in place and the Ancient One sat down to j.
Joel 3:2 There I will j them for harming my people,
Ob 1:15 when I, the LORD, will j the godless nations!
Zec 7:9 J fairly and honestly, and show mercy
Mal 3:3 He will sit and j like a refiner of silver,
Mt 12:27 too, so they will j you for what you have said.
16:27 and will j all people according to their deeds.
Lk 11:19 too, so they will j you for what you have said.
12:14 who made me a j over you to decide such things as
12:58 try to settle the matter before it reaches the j,
18:2 "There was a j in a certain city," he said,
18:4 The j ignored her for a while, but eventually she
18:6 the Lord said, "Learn a lesson from this evil j.
Jn 5:27 And he has given him authority to j all mankind
5:30 I j as I am told. And my judgment is absolutely
8:15 You j me with all your human limitations, but I am
8:50 God wants to glorify me. Let him be the j.
9:39 Then Jesus told him, "I have come to j the world.
12:47 hears me and doesn't obey me, I am not his j—
12:47 for I have come to save the world and not to j it.
18:31 take him away and j him by your own laws,"
Ac 7:27 'Who made you a ruler and j over us?' he asked.
7:35 'Who made you a ruler and j over us?'
10:42 that Jesus is ordained of God to be the j of all—
18:15 you take care of it. I refuse to j such matters."
23:3 What kind of j are you to break the law yourself by
24:10 that you have been a j of Jewish affairs for many
Ro 2:3 Do you think that God will j and condemn others
2:3 for doing them and not j you when you do them,
2:5 of judgment when God, the just j of all the world,
2:6 will j all people according to what they have done.
2:16 by Jesus Christ, will j everyone's secret life.
3:6 God is not just, how is he qualified to j the world?
3:7 "how can God j and condemn me as a sinner if my
1Co 5:12 It isn't my responsibility to j outsiders, but it
certainly is your job to j those inside the
5:13 God will j those on the outside; but as the
6:2 someday we Christians are going to j the world?
6:2 And since you are going to j the world, can't you
6:3 Don't you realize that we Christians will j angels?
Gal 5:10 God will j that person, whoever it is, who has been
2Ti 4:1 who will someday j the living and the dead when
4:8 of righteousness that the Lord, the righteous J,
4:14 but the Lord will j him for what he has done.
4:16 The first time I was brought before the j, no one
Heb 10:30 He also said, / "The Lord will j his own people."
12:23 come to God himself, who is the j of all people.
13:4 God will surely j people who are immoral
Jas 4:11 But you are not a j who can decide whether the law
4:12 who made the law, can rightly j among us.
5:9 my brothers and sisters, or God will j you. For
look! The great J is coming.
1Pe 1:17 He will j or reward you according to what you do.
2:12 and give honor to God when he comes to j the
4:5 who will j everyone, both the living and the dead.
Rev 6:10 how long will it be before you j the people who
11:18 It is time to j the dead and reward your servants.
14:7 to him. For the time has come when he will sit as j.
18:5 and God is ready to j her for her evil deeds.
20:4 sitting on them had been given the authority to j.

JUDGE'S (1) [JUDGE]

Jdg 2:18 from their enemies throughout the j lifetime.

JUDGED (31) [JUDGE]

Ex 18:26 but they j the smaller matters themselves.
Nu 18:22 If they come too near, they will be j guilty and die.
35:31 payment for the life of someone j guilty of murder
Jdg 10:3 a man from Gilead named Jair j Israel for
12:9 to marry his sons. Ibzan j Israel for seven years.
12:11 became Israel's judge. He j Israel for ten years.
1Sa 7:16 He j the people of Israel at each of these places.
Ps 9:4 For you have j in my favor; / from your throne,
you have j with fairness.
9:19 defy you! / Let the nations be j in your presence!
Jer 32:4 and taken to the king of Babylon to be j
34:3 You will stand before the king of Babylon to be j
Eze 24:14 You will be j on the basis of all your wicked
Da 7:22 and j in favor of the holy people of the Most High.
Mt 7:1 "Stop judging others, and you will not be j.
7:2 it will be used to measure how you are j.
Lk 6:37 "Stop judging others, and you will not be j.
Jn 3:18 But those who do not trust him have already been j
12:48 and my message will be j at the day of judgment
16:11 because the prince of this world has already been j.
Ac 13:46 and j yourselves unworthy of eternal life—
1Co 11:31 we will not be examined by God and j in this way.
11:32 But when we are j and disciplined by the Lord,
2Co 5:10 For we must all stand before Christ to be j.
1Ti 5:24 sinful lives, and everyone knows they will be j.
Jas 2:12 remember that you will be j by the law of love,
3:1 for we who teach will be j by God with greater
1Pe 4:17 And if even we Christians must be j, what terrible
Rev 18:20 For at last God has j her on your behalf.
20:12 And the dead were j according to the things written
20:13 in them. They were all j according to their deeds.

JUDGES (63) [JUDGE]

Ex 18:21 Appoint them as j over groups of one thousand,
18:25 all over Israel and made them j over the people.
21:22 the woman's husband demands and the j approve.
Nu 25:5 So Moses ordered Israel's j to execute everyone
Dt 1:15 and appointed them to serve as j and officials over
1:16 I instructed the j, 'You must be perfectly fair at all
16:18 "Appoint j and officials for each of your tribes in
19:17 and j who are on duty before the LORD.
21:2 and j must determine which town is nearest the
22:17 Then they must spread the cloth before the j.
22:18 The j must then punish the man.
22:21 the j must take the girl to the door of her father's
25:1 and the j declare that one is right and the other is
29:10 your tribal leaders, your j, your officers,
Jos 8:33 along with the leaders, officers, and j, were divided
23:2 all the elders, leaders, j, and officers of Israel.
24:1 along with their elders, leaders, j, and officers.
Jdg 2:16 Then the LORD raised up j to rescue the
2:17 Yet Israel did not listen to the j but prostituted
Ru 1:1 In the days when the j ruled in Israel, a man from
1Sa 2:10 from heaven; / the LORD j throughout the earth.
8:1 grew old, he appointed his sons to be j over Israel.
2Sa 7:11 from the time I appointed j to rule my people.
2Ki 23:22 like that since the time when the j ruled in Israel,
1Ch 17:10 from the time I appointed j to rule my people.
23:4 Six thousand are to serve as officials and j.
26:29 as public administrators and j throughout Israel.
2Ch 1:2 the j, and all the political and clan leaders.
19:5 He appointed j throughout the nation in all the
19:8 and clan leaders in Israel to serve as j in Jerusalem
Ezr 4:9 the j and local leaders, the people of Tarpel,
7:25 and j who know your God's laws to govern all the
10:14 scheduled time with the leaders and j of his city,
Job 9:24 and God blinds the eyes of the j and lets them be
12:17 stripped of good judgment; he drives j to madness.
22:4 your reverence for him that he accuses and j you?
31:28 If so, I should be punished by the j, for it would
Ps 50:4 and earth will be his witnesses / as he j his people:
58:11 surely there is a God who j justly here on earth."
75:7 It is God alone who j; / he decides who will rise
82:1 heaven's court; / he pronounces judgment on the j:
82:2 "How long will you j hand down unjust decisions?
148:11 the earth and all people, / rulers and j of the earth,
Pr 20:8 When a king j, he carefully weighs all the
Isa 1:26 Afterward I will give you good j and wise
3:2 the heroes, soldiers, j, prophets, diviners, elders,
5:3 and Judah, / you have heard the case; you be the j.
10:1 Destruction is certain for the unjust j, for those
28:6 He will give a longing for justice to their j. He will
40:23 He j the great people of the world and brings them
Jer 2:8 The j ignored me, the rulers turned against me,
Eze 44:24 "They will serve as j to resolve any disagreements
Da 3:2 prefects, governors, advisers, counselors, j,
Am 5:10 How you hate honest j! How you despise people
Mic 7:3 Officials and j alike demand bribes. The people
Zep 3:3 Its j are like ravenous wolves at evening time,
Ac 13:20 j ruled until the time of Samuel the prophet.
19:38 are in session and the j can take the case at once.
1Co 6:4 why do you go to outside j who are not respected
1Pe 1:17 to whom you pray has no favorites when he j.
2:23 his case in the hands of God, who always j fairly.
Rev 18:8 by fire, for the Lord God who j her is mighty."
19:11 and True. For he j fairly and then goes to war.

JUDGING (9) [JUDGE]

Dt 1:17 they will react, for you are j in the place of God.
Eze 18:8 from injustice, is honest and fair when j others,
Mt 7:1 "Stop j others, and you will not be judged.
7:2 Whatever measure you use in j others, it will be
19:28 sit on twelve thrones, j the twelve tribes of Israel.
Lk 6:37 "Stop j others, and you will not be judged.
22:30 you will sit on thrones, j the twelve tribes of Israel.
Jn 8:15 all your human limitations, but I am not j anyone.
Ac 17:31 For he has set a day for j the world with justice by

JUDGMENT (158) [JUDGE]

DAY OF JUDGMENT (15) Ps 37:13; Pr 11:4; Eze 7:10; 39:8; Hos 10:15; Am 6:3; Zep 1:8; Mal 4:1; Jn 12:48; Ro 2:5; Jas 5:3; 2Pe 2:9; 3:7; 1Jn 4:17; Jude 1:6

GOOD JUDGMENT (8) 1Sa 16:18; Job 12:17; Ps 119:66; Pr 4:5,7; 8:12; 9:4,16

Ex 6:6 redeem you with mighty power and great acts of j.
7:4 lead the forces of Israel out with great acts of j.
12:12 I will execute j against all the gods of Egypt,
Lev 24:11 So the man was brought to Moses for j.
Nu 33:4 the gods of Egypt that night with great acts of j!
35:24 these regulations in making a j between the slayer
1Sa 3:13 I have warned him continually that j is coming for
16:18 only that; he is brave and strong and has good j.
2Sa 15:2 When people brought a case to the king for j,
1Ki 7:7 the Hall of the Throne, also known as the Hall of J,
20:40 king replied. "You have determined your own j."
2Ch 19:6 "Always think carefully before pronouncing j.
22:8 While Jehu was executing j against the family of
24:24 of their ancestors, so j was executed against Joash.
Job 12:17 He leads counselors away stripped of good j;
19:29 your attitude. Then you will know that there is j."
24:1 doesn't the Almighty open the court and bring j?
31:23 That would be better than facing the j sent by God.
34:23 to mortals to decide when to come before God in j.
36:17 But you are too obsessed with j on the godless.
Ps 1:5 They will be condemned at the time of j.
7:8 The LORD passes j on the nations. / Declare me
9:7 reigns forever, / executing j from his throne.
17:14 and may the j continue to their children's children.
32:6 that they may not drown in the floodwaters of j.
37:13 just laughs, / for he sees their day of j coming.
51:4 in what you say, / and your j against me is just.
75:8 He pours the wine out in j, / and all the wicked
76:10 your glory, / for you use it as a sword of j.
82:1 heaven's court; / he pronounces j on the judges:
82:3 "Give fair j to the poor and the orphan;
94:15 J will come again for the righteous, / and those
109:7 When his case is called for j, / let him be
119:66 now teach me good j and knowledge.
122:5 Here stand the thrones where j is given,
149:9 to execute the j written against them. / This is the
Pr 4:5 Learn to be wise, and develop good j. Don't forget
4:7 you can do! And whatever else you do, get good j.
8:12 "I, Wisdom, live together with good j. I know
9:4 the simple. To those without good j, she says,
9:16 the simple. To those without good j, she says,
11:4 Riches won't help on the day of j, but right living
17:18 It is poor j to co-sign a friend's note, to become
24:23 It is wrong to show favoritism when passing j.
Isa 3:14 the princes will be the first to feel the LORD's j.
4:4 its bloodstains by a spirit of j that burns like fire.
22:14 That is the j of the Lord, the LORD Almighty.
34:10 This j on Edom will never end; the smoke of its
49:2 He made my words of j as sharp as a sword.
63:5 vengeance alone; unaided, I passed down j.
Jer 1:16 I will pronounce j on my people for all their evil—

23: 2 Now I will pour out j on you for the evil you have
25:31 His cry of j will reach the ends of the earth,
39: 5 There the king of Babylon pronounced j upon
48:21 J has been poured out on them all—on Holon
48:44 for the time of your j has come," says the LORD.
49:12 not go unpunished! You must drink this cup of j!
51: 9 for her j will be so great it cannot be measured.
La 5: 7 who sinned, but they died before the hand of j fell.
Eze 7:10 "The day of j is here; your destruction awaits!
20: 4 of man, bring j against them and condemn them.
20:22 I withdrew my j against them to protect the honor
23:48 and my j will be a warning to others not to follow
25:11 same way, I will bring my j down on the Moabites.
25:13 I will raise my fist of j against Edom.
25:16 I will raise my fist of j against the land of the
28:22 When I bring j against you and reveal my holiness
32:20 against them. Egypt will be dragged away to its j.
39: 8 That day of j will come, says the Sovereign
Da 1:20 In all matters requiring wisdom and balanced j,
7:26 "But then the court will pass j, and all his power
Hos 5: 1 These words of j are for you: You are doomed!
5:11 of Israel will be crushed and broken by my j
6: 5 My j will strike you as surely as day follows night.
10:15 When the day of j dawns, the king of Israel will be
Joel 3:12 the LORD, will sit to pronounce j on them all.
Am 4:12 Prepare to meet your God as he comes in j,
6: 3 but your actions only bring the day of j closer.
Jnh 1: 2 Announce my j against it because I have seen how
3: 2 and deliver the message of j I have given you."
Mic 1:12 but only bitterness awaits them as the LORD's j
7: 4 But your j day is coming swiftly now. Your time
Hab 2:16 Drink from the cup of the LORD's j, and all your
Zep 1: 7 for the awesome day of the LORD's j has come.
1: 8 "On that day of j," says the LORD, "I will
2: 2 before j begins and your opportunity is blown
2: 5 in the land of Canaan, for this j is against you, too!
3:15 For the LORD will remove his hand of j and will
Mal 4: 1 "The day of j is coming, burning like a furnace.
Mt 3: 7 "Who warned you to flee God's coming j?
3:10 Even now the ax of God's j is poised, ready to
5:21 If you commit murder, you are subject to j.'
5:22 you are angry with someone, you are subject to j!
7:22 On j day many will tell me, 'Lord, Lord,
10:15 and Gomorrah will be better off on the j day than
11:22 and Sidon will be better off on the j day than you!
11:24 Sodom will be better off on the j day than you."
12:36 that you must give an account on j day of every
12:41 will rise up against this generation on j day
12:42 will also rise up against this generation on j day
23:33 Sons of vipers! How will you escape the j of hell?
23:36 all the accumulated j of the centuries will break
27:19 Just then, as Pilate was sitting on the j seat,
Lk 3: 7 Who warned you to flee God's coming j?
3: 9 Even now the ax of God's j is poised, ready to
10:12 will be better off than such a town on the j day.
10:14 and Sidon will be better off on the j day than you.
11:31 Sheba will rise up against this generation on j day
11:32 will rise up against this generation on j day
Jn 3:18 "There is no j awaiting those who trust him.
3:19 Their j is based on this fact: The light from heaven
5:22 And the Father leaves all j to his Son,
5:29 and those who have continued in evil will rise to j.
5:30 And my j is absolutely just, because it is according
8:16 my j would be correct in every respect because I
12:31 The time of j for the world has come,
12:48 and my message will be judged at the day of j by
16: 8 and of God's righteousness, and of the coming j.
16:11 J will come because the prince of this world has
19:13 Then Pilate sat down on the j seat on the platform
Ac 15:19 so my j is that we should stop troubling the
18:12 and brought him before the governor for j.
24:25 and self-control and the j to come,
Ro 2: 5 For there is going to come a day of j when God,
3:19 and to bring the entire world into j before God.
5: 9 of Christ, he will certainly save us from God's j.
9:22 God has every right to exercise his j and his power,
9:22 very patient with those who are the objects of his j
14:10 each of us will stand personally before the j seat of
1Co 3:13 But there is going to come a time of testing at the j
4: 3 I don't even trust my own j on this point.
5: 3 the one who has done this, I have already passed j
11:29 you are eating and drinking God's j upon yourself.
11:34 so you won't bring j upon yourselves when you
2Co 2: 6 most of you were united in your j against him.
1Th 1:10 has rescued us from the terrors of the coming j.
2Th 1: 8 bringing j on those who don't know God and on
Heb 6: 2 the resurrection of the dead, and eternal j.
9:27 each person dies only once and after that comes j,
10:27 forward to but the terrible expectation of God's j
Jas 2:13 toward you will win out over his j against you.
5: 3 will stand as evidence against you on the day of j.
1Pe 4:17 For the time has come for j, and it must begin first
2Pe 2: 4 in gloomy caves and darkness until the j day.
2: 5 Noah warned the world of God's righteous j.
2: 9 punishing the wicked right up until the day of j.
3: 7 the earth will be consumed by fire on the day of j,
3:10 the earth and everything on it will be exposed to j.
1Jn 4:17 So we will not be afraid on the day of j, but we can
4:18 If we are afraid, it is for fear of j, and this shows
Jude 1: 6 in prisons of darkness, waiting for the day of j.
1:15 He will bring the people of the world / to j.
1:23 others by snatching them from the flames of j.
Rev 14:18 the vines of the earth, for they are fully ripe for j."
16: 5 "You are just in sending this j, O Holy One,
16:14 the Lord on that great j day of God Almighty.
17: 1 "and I will show you the j that is going to come on
18:10 In one single moment God's j came on her."

JUDGMENTS (8) [JUDGE]

1Ch 16:12 has done, / the miracles, and the j he handed down,
Ps 48:11 Let the towns of Judah be glad, / for your j are just.
105: 5 has done, / the miracles and the j he handed down,
119:120 I tremble in fear of you; / I fear your j.
Pr 8:16 lead with my help, and nobles make righteous j.
Eze 11: 9 to foreigners who will carry out my j against you.
Da 9:11 solemn curses and j written in the law of Moses,
Rev 19: 2 His j are just and true. He has punished the great

JUDITH (1)

Ge 26:34 of forty, Esau married a young woman named J,

JUG (11) [JUGS]

Ge 24:15 Rebekah arrived with a water j on her shoulder.
24:16 down to the spring, filled her j, and came up again.
24:18 and she quickly lowered the j for him to drink.
24:20 So she quickly emptied the j into the watering
24:45 I saw Rebekah coming along with her water j on
24:45 down to the spring and drew water and filled the j.
24:46 She quickly lowered the j from her shoulder
1Sa 26:11 we'll take his spear and his j of water and then get
26:12 the spear and j of water that were near Saul's head.
26:16 and the j of water that were beside his head?"
1Ki 17:12 and a little cooking oil in the bottom of the j.

JUGS (1) [JUG]

Jer 35: 5 I set cups and j of wine before them and invited

JUICE (7)

Ge 40:11 so I took the grapes and squeezed the j into it.
Nu 6: 3 not drink other fermented drinks or fresh grape j,
Dt 32:14 drank the finest wine, / made from the j of grapes.
Jer 25:30 like the harvesters do as they crush j from the
Mic 6:15 trample the grapes but get no j to make your wine.
Mt 21:33 around it, dug a pit for pressing out the grape j,
Mk 12: 1 around it, dug a pit for pressing out the grape j,

JULIA (1)

Ro 16:15 J, Nereus and his sister, and to Olympas and all the

JULIUS (2)

Ac 27: 1 placed in the custody of an army officer named J,
27: 3 J was very kind to Paul and let him go ashore to

JULY (4)

2Ki 25: 3 By J 18 of Zedekiah's eleventh year, the famine in
Jer 39: 2 Two and a half years later, on J 18,
52: 6 By J 18 of Zedekiah's eleventh year, the famine in
Eze 1: 1 On J 31 of my thirtieth year, while I was with the

JUMP (7) [JUMPED, JUMPING, JUMPS]

Lev 11:21 These include insects that j with their hind legs:
Jos 8: 7 Then you will j up from your ambush and take
Mt 4: 6 and said, "If you are the Son of God, j off!
Lk 4: 9 and said, "If you are the Son of God, j off!
Ac 23:21 than forty men hiding along the way ready to j him
27:43 Then he ordered all who could swim to j overboard
1Co 4: 5 So be careful not to j to conclusions before the

JUMPED (26) [JUMP]

Nu 25: 7 the priest saw this, he j up and left the assembly.
Jos 8:19 the men in ambush j up and poured into the city.
Jdg 9:43 he and his men j up from their hiding places
20:33 ambush west of Gibeah j up from where they were
1Sa 3: 5 He j up and ran to Eli. "Here I am. What do you
3: 6 "Samuel!" Again Samuel j up and ran to Eli.
3: 8 and once more Samuel j up and ran to Eli.
18:11 But David j aside and escaped. This happened
2Sa 13:29 Then the other sons of the king j on their mules
13:31 The king j up, tore his robe, and fell prostrate on
1Ki 1:49 Then all of Adonijah's guests j up in panic from
12:18 he quickly j into his chariot and fled to Jerusalem.
2Ki 13:21 the dead man revived and j to his feet!
2Ch 10:18 he quickly j into his chariot and fled to Jerusalem.
Est 7: 7 Then the king j to his feet in a rage and went out
SS 5: 5 I j up to open it. My hands dripped with perfume,
Da 3:24 Nebuchadnezzar j up in amazement and exclaimed
Mt 9: 7 And the man j up and went home!
Mk 2:12 The man j up, took the mat, and pushed his way
10:50 threw aside his coat, j up, and came to Jesus.
Lk 1:44 my baby j for joy the instant I heard your voice!
5:25 the man j to his feet, picked up his mat,
Jn 21: 7 for work), j into the water, and swam ashore.
Ac 3: 8 He j up, stood on his feet, and began to walk!
14:10 And the man j to his feet and started walking.
23: 9 were Pharisees j up to argue that Paul was all right.

JUMPING (1) [JUMP]

Lk 4:29 J up, they mobbed him and took him to the edge of

JUMPS (1) [JUMP]

Job 39:18 But whenever she j up to run, she passes the

JUNE (2)

Est 8: 9 So on J 25 the king's secretaries were summoned.
Eze 31: 1 On J 21, during the eleventh year of King

JUNIA (1)

Ro 16: 7 Then there are Andronicus and J, my relatives,

JUPITER [KJV] See HEAVEN, ZEUS

JURISDICTION (1)

Lk 23: 7 because Galilee was under Herod's j,

JUSHAB-HESED (1)

1Ch 3:20 were Hashubah, Ohel, Berekiah, Hasadiah, and J.

JUST (871) [JUSTICE, JUSTIFIED, JUSTIFY, JUSTLY]

Ge 3: 5 You will become j like God, knowing everything,
7: 9 and female, j as God had commanded Noah.
7:16 male and female, j as God had commanded.
9: 3 j as I have given you grain and vegetables.
11: 6 "If they can accomplish this when they have j
11: 6 political unity, j think of what they will do later.
17: 4 I will make you the father of not j one nation,
17:20 I will bless him also, j as you have asked.
18:14 a year from now, j as I told you, I will return,
18:19 the way of the LORD and do what is right and j.
19: 2 "we'll j spend the night out here in the city
21:12 Do j as Sarah says, for Isaac is the son through
24:11 kneel down beside a well j outside the village.
26: 3 j as I solemnly promised Abraham, your father.
26:29 you will not harm us, j as we did not harm you.
27: 4 Prepare it j the way I like it so it's savory
27:13 "J do what I tell you. Go out and get the goats."
27:14 a delicious meat dish, j the way Isaac liked it.
27:23 because Jacob's hands felt hairy j like Esau's.
27:33 "Then who was it that j served me wild game?
29:14 "J think, my very own flesh and blood!"
29:15 "You shouldn't work for me without pay j
30:31 J do one thing, and I'll go back to work for you.
33:18 and they set up camp j outside the town.
34: 7 He arrived j as Jacob's sons were coming in from
34:22 one of us men must be circumcised, j as they are.
37:22 Let's j throw him alive into this pit here.
37:25 Then, j as they were sitting down to eat,
37:26 That would j give us a guilty conscience.
40:22 to be impaled on a pole, j as Joseph had predicted.
41:13 and everything happened j as he said it would.
41:28 This will happen j as I have described it, for God
41:54 years of famine began, j as Joseph had predicted.
44:18 "My lord, let me say j this one word to you.
47:11 and brothers, j as Pharaoh had commanded.
47:19 J give us grain so that our lives may be saved
48: 5 They will inherit from me j as Reuben and Simeon
48: 7 j a short distance from Ephrath (that is,
49: 6 murdered men, / and they crippled oxen j for sport.
Ex 2:20 "Did you j leave him there? Go and invite him
3:14 J tell them, 'I AM has sent me to you.' "
4: 1 They'll j say, 'The LORD never appeared to
4:10 the LORD, "O Lord, I'm j not a good speaker.
5:11 But you must produce j as many bricks as before!"
5:13 your daily quota of bricks, j as you did before!"
5:17 But Pharaoh replied, "You're j lazy!
7: 6 and Aaron did j as the LORD had commanded
7:10 and they performed the miracle j as the LORD
7:13 refused to listen, j as the LORD had predicted.
7:20 and Aaron did j as the LORD had commanded
7:22 and Aaron, j as the LORD had predicted.
8:15 and Aaron, j as the LORD had predicted.
8:17 and Aaron did j as the LORD had commanded
8:19 listen to them, j as the LORD had predicted.
8:24 And the LORD did j as he had said. There were
8:27 the LORD our God, j as he has commanded us."
9: 6 and he did it, j as he had said. The next morning all
9:12 he refused to listen, j as the LORD had predicted.
9:35 let the people leave, j as the LORD had predicted.
10: 8 "But tell me, j whom do you want to take along?"
11: 1 "I will send j one more disaster on Pharaoh
12:28 So the people of Israel did j as the LORD had
12:48 They will be treated j as if they had been born
14:13 J stand where you are and watch the LORD
16:18 two quarts for each person, everyone had j enough.
16:18 had enough. Each family had j what it needed.
16:34 did this, j as the LORD had commanded Moses.
17: 6 Moses did j as he was told; and as the leaders
22:10 and there is no eyewitness to report j what
23: 3 do not slant your testimony in favor of a person j
23:15 made without yeast, j as I commanded you before.
27: 8 Be careful to build it j as you were shown on the
30: 6 Place the incense altar j outside the inner curtain,
34:18 j as I instructed you, at the appointed time each
36: 1 the Tabernacle, j as the LORD has commanded."
38:18 feet high, j like the curtains of the courtyard walls.
38:22 j as the LORD had commanded Moses.
39: 1 j as the LORD had commanded Moses.
39: 5 j as the LORD had commanded Moses.
39: 6 tribes of Israel, j as initials are engraved on a seal.
39: 7 All this was done j as the LORD had commanded
39:21 All this was done j as the LORD had commanded
39:26 j as the LORD had commanded Moses.
39:29 j as the LORD had commanded Moses.
39:31 blue cord, j as the LORD had commanded Moses.
39:32 The Israelites had done everything j as the LORD
40: 5 "Place the incense altar j outside the inner curtain,
40:19 roof layers, j as the LORD had commanded him.
40:21 it from view, j as the LORD had commanded.
40:22 side of the Holy Place, j outside the inner curtain.
40:23 the LORD, j as the LORD had commanded.
40:25 j as the LORD had commanded.
40:27 sweet spices, j as the LORD had commanded.
40:29 a grain offering, j as the LORD had commanded.
40:32 and wash, j as the LORD had commanded Moses.

Lev 4:10 **j** as is done with the bull or cow sacrificed as a
4:21 **j** as is done with the sin offering for the high priest.
4:26 fat on the altar, **j** as is done with the peace offering.
4:31 the goat's fat, **j** as is done with the peace offering.
4:35 **j** as is done with a sheep presented as a peace
5:12 He will burn this flour on the altar **j** like any other
5:13 belong to the priest, **j** as with the grain offering."
8:9 at its front, **j** as the LORD had commanded him.
8:13 **j** as the LORD had commanded him.
8:17 the camp, **j** as the LORD had commanded Moses.
8:21 All this was done **j** as the LORD had commanded
8:29 **j** as the LORD had commanded him.
8:31 of ordination offerings, **j** as I commanded you.
9:5 **j** as Moses had commanded, and the whole
9:7 for the people, **j** as the LORD has commanded."
9:10 **j** as the LORD had commanded Moses.
9:15 **j** as he had done previously for himself.
9:21 to the LORD, **j** as Moses had commanded.
10:15 **j** as the LORD has commanded."
12:2 **j** as she is defiled during her menstrual period.
12:5 **j** as she is defiled during her menstrual period.
15:26 **j** as it would be during her normal menstrual
16:15 front of the Ark, **j** as he did with the bull's blood.
24:23 to death, **j** as the LORD had commanded Moses.
Nu 1:19 **j** as the LORD had commanded Moses. So Moses
1:54 So the Israelites did everything **j** as the LORD
2:34 So the people of Israel did everything **j** as the
3:16 counted them, **j** as the LORD had commanded.
3:42 people of Israel, **j** as the LORD had commanded.
4:37 **j** as the LORD had commanded through Moses.
4:41 counted them, **j** as the LORD had commanded.
4:45 **j** as the LORD had commanded through Moses.
4:49 **j** as the LORD had commanded through Moses.
4:49 **j** as the LORD had commanded Moses.
5:4 So the Israelites did **j** as the LORD had
8:3 **j** as the LORD had commanded Moses.
9:5 **j** as the LORD had commanded Moses.
9:19 for a long time, **j** as the LORD commanded.
11:19 And it won't be for **j** a day or two, or for five
14:19 **j** as you have forgiven them ever since they left
15:36 to death, **j** as the LORD had commanded Moses.
18:18 **j** like the breast and right thigh that are presented
22:17 ask of me. **J** come and curse these people for me!"
22:38 have come, but I have no power to say **j** anything.
25:6 **J** then one of the Israelite men brought a Midianite
26:4 and older, **j** as the LORD commanded Moses."
27:4 Why should the name of our father disappear **j**
27:11 **j** as the LORD commanded Moses.' "
27:23 **j** as the LORD had commanded through Moses.
29:40 of Israel, **j** as the LORD had commanded him.
31:7 They attacked Midian **j** as the LORD had
31:41 the priest, **j** as the LORD had directed him.
31:47 All this was done **j** as the LORD had commanded
32:27 over to fight for the LORD, **j** as you have said."
Dt 1:19 "Then, **j** as the LORD our God directed us,
1:30 will fight for you, **j** as you saw him do in Egypt.
1:31 in the wilderness, **j** as a father cares for his child.
2:1 **j** as the LORD had instructed me, and we
3:2 Treat him **j** as you treated King Sihon of the
3:6 **j** as we had destroyed King Sihon of Heshbon.
4:2 you from the LORD your God. **J** obey them.
6:3 flowing with milk and honey, **j** as the LORD,
6:19 in your land, **j** as the LORD said you would.
7:18 **J** remember what the LORD your God did to
7:26 then you will be set apart for destruction **j** like
8:5 So you should realize that **j** as a parent disciplines
8:20 **J** as the LORD has destroyed other nations in
9:3 and drive them out, **j** as the LORD has promised.
10:5 I had made, **j** as the LORD commanded me.
12:13 Be careful not to sacrifice your burnt offerings **j**
12:15 you want, **j** as you do now with gazelle and deer.
12:22 that meat, **j** as you do now with gazelle and deer.
13:17 **j** as he solemnly promised your ancestors.
15:22 or unclean, **j** as anyone may eat a gazelle or deer.
18:2 himself is their inheritance, **j** as he promised them.
18:7 **j** like his fellow Levites who are serving the
19:15 of a crime on the testimony of **j** one witness.
20:5 'Has anyone **j** built a new house but not yet
20:6 Has anyone **j** planted a vineyard but not yet eaten
20:7 Has anyone **j** become engaged? Well, go home
20:17 **j** as the LORD your God has commanded you.
24:6 or even **j** the upper millstone, as a pledge,
26:13 orphans, and widows, **j** as you commanded me.
26:15 **j** as you solemnly promised our ancestors.'
26:18 his own special treasure, **j** as he promised, and that
26:19 holy to the LORD your God, **j** as he promised."
27:3 flowing with milk and honey, **j** as the LORD,
28:29 **j** like a blind person groping in the darkness,
28:63 "**J** as the LORD has found great pleasure in
29:13 confirm that he is your God, **j** as he promised you,
29:23 It will be **j** like Sodom and Gomorrah, Admah
31:3 and he will go with you, **j** as the LORD promised.
31:4 **j** as he destroyed Sihon and Og, the kings of the
32:4 work is perfect. / Everything he does is **j** and fair.
32:4 God who does no wrong; / how **j** and upright he is!
32:50 **j** as Aaron, your brother, died on Mount Hor
34:5 in the land of Moab, **j** as the LORD had said.
34:9 and did everything **j** as the LORD had
Jos 1:17 We will obey you **j** as we obeyed Moses. And may
3:7 know that I am with you, **j** as I was with Moses.
4:8 **j** as the LORD had commanded Joshua.
4:12 across the Jordan, **j** as Moses had directed.
4:23 **j** as he did at the Red Sea when he dried it up until
7:22 **j** as Achan had said, with the silver buried beneath
10:1 **j** as he had destroyed the city of Jericho and killed
10:30 Then Joshua killed the king of Libnah **j** as he had
10:32 entire population was slaughtered, **j** as at Libnah.
10:37 And **j** as they had done at Eglon, they completely
10:39 They completely destroyed Debir **j** as they had
10:40 **j** as the LORD, the God of Israel,
11:12 **j** as Moses, the servant of the LORD,
11:23 entire land, **j** as the LORD had instructed Moses.
13:6 a special possession, **j** as I have commanded you.
13:25 as far as the town of Aroer **j** west of Rabbah.
14:9 'The land of Canaan on which you were **j** walking
14:12 drive them out of the land, **j** as the LORD said."
21:44 **j** as he had solemnly promised their ancestors.
23:5 of them, **j** as the LORD your God promised you.
23:10 your God fights for you, **j** as he has promised.
Jdg 2:15 bringing them defeat, **j** as he promised.
6:38 And it happened **j** that way. When Gideon got up
7:8 Now the Midianite camp was in the valley **j** below
7:13 Gideon crept up **j** as a man was telling his friend
7:17 When I come to the edge of the camp, do **j** as I do.
7:19 It was **j** after midnight, after the changing of the
9:9 **j** to wave back and forth over the trees?'
9:11 'Should I quit producing my sweet fruit **j** to wave
9:13 **j** to wave back and forth over the trees?'
9:18 to be your king **j** because he is your relative.
9:36 "It's **j** the shadows of the hills that look like
14:15 Did you invite us to this party **j** to make us poor?"
18:16 from the tribe of Dan stood **j** outside the gate,
18:19 of Israel than **j** for the household of one man?"
Ru 3:18 Naomi said to her, "**J** be patient, my daughter,
1Sa 1:8 Why be so sad **j** because you have no children?
2:18 He wore a linen tunic **j** like that of a priest.
3:2 who was almost blind by now, had **j** gone to bed.
4:9 we will become the Hebrews' slaves **j** as they have
4:16 said to Eli, "I have **j** come from the battlefront—
6:4 gold rats, **j** like those that have ravaged your land.
6:7 new cart, and find two cows that have **j** had calves.
7:10 **J** as Samuel was sacrificing the burnt offering,
9:6 But the servant said, "I've **j** thought of something!
9:12 He has **j** arrived to take part in a public sacrifice up
9:18 **J** then Saul approached Samuel at the gateway
13:10 **J** as Saul was finishing with the burnt offering,
14:15 And **j** then an earthquake struck, and everyone was
17:20 He arrived at the outskirts of the camp **j** as the
17:28 and dishonesty. You **j** want to see the battle!"
20:2 hide something like this from me. It **j** isn't so!"
21:6 It had **j** been replaced that day with fresh bread.
22:2 in trouble or in debt or who were **j** discontented—
23:26 **J** as Saul and his men began to close in on David
25:21 David had **j** been saying, "A lot of good it did to
25:25 to him. He is a fool, **j** as his name suggests.
28:17 The LORD has done **j** as he said he would.
30:14 the land of Caleb, and we had **j** burned Ziklag."
2Sa 2:24 The sun was **j** going down as they arrived at the
3:10 I should **j** go ahead and give David the rest of
3:22 But **j** after Abner left, Joab and some of David's
3:23 When Joab was told that Abner had **j** been there
7:8 my people Israel when you were **j** a shepherd boy,
11:4 (She had **j** completed the purification rites after
13:13 Please, **j** speak to the king about it, and he will let
13:32 But **j** then Jonadab, the son of David's brother
13:35 they are now! Your sons are coming, **j** as I said."
15:34 **j** as I was your father's adviser in the past.'
15:37 to Jerusalem, getting there **j** as Absalom arrived.
16:1 David was **j** past the top of the hill when Ziba,
16:23 Ahithophel's advice, **j** as David had done.
19:30 "I am content **j** to have you back again, my lord!"
19:36 **J** to go across the river with you is all the honor I
21:4 David asked. "**J** tell me and I will do it for you."
1Ki 1:30 **j** as I swore to you before the LORD, the God of
1:41 and shouting **j** as they were finishing their banquet.
1:43 "Our lord King David has **j** declared Solomon
1:45 They have **j** returned, and the whole city is
2:16 So now I have **j** one favor to ask of you.
5:5 **j** as he instructed my father that I should do.
5:12 So the LORD gave great wisdom to Solomon **j** as
7:12 **j** like the walls of the inner courtyard of the
7:24 The Sea was encircled **j** below its rim by two rows
8:43 and fear you, **j** as your own people Israel do.
8:56 given rest to his people Israel, **j** as he promised.
8:61 his laws and commands, **j** as you are doing today."
11:25 and he made trouble, **j** as Hadad did.
12:10 was hard on you, **j** wait and see what I'll be like!
12:12 Rehoboam's decision, **j** as the king had requested.
13:1 and he arrived there **j** as Jeroboam was
13:5 **j** as the man of God had predicted in his message
13:18 "I am a prophet, too, **j** as you are.
14:17 and the child died **j** as she walked through the door
15:29 **j** as the LORD had promised concerning
16:3 **j** as I destroyed the descendants of Jeroboam son
16:7 **j** like the family of Jeroboam, and also
17:12 I was **j** gathering a few sticks to cook this last
17:16 **j** as the LORD had promised through Elijah.
21:19 dogs will lick your blood outside the city **j** as they
21:26 because he worshiped idols **j** as the Amorites had
22:36 **J** as the sun was setting, the cry ran through his
22:38 the king's blood, **j** as the LORD had promised.
22:53 the God of Israel, **j** as his father had done.
2Ki 1:17 **j** as the LORD had promised through Elijah.
2:16 "**j** say the word and fifty of our strongest men will
2:22 remained wholesome ever since, **j** as Elisha said.
4:17 following year she had a son, **j** as Elisha had said.
4:44 and some left over, **j** as the LORD had promised.
5:22 from the hill country of Ephraim have **j** arrived.
7:16 an ounce of silver, **j** as the LORD had promised.
8:4 The king had **j** said, "Tell me some stories about
9:26 him out on Naboth's field, **j** as the LORD said."
9:31 You are **j** like Zimri, who murdered his master!"
10:17 **j** as the LORD had promised through Elijah.
11:9 So the commanders did everything **j** as Jehoiada
14:9 But **j** then a wild animal came by and stepped on
14:25 the Dead Sea, **j** as the LORD, the God of Israel,
15:3 LORD's sight, **j** as his father, Amaziah, had done.
15:34 LORD's sight, **j** as his father Uzziah had done.
16:11 Uriah built an altar **j** like it by following the king's
16:16 Uriah the priest did **j** as King Ahaz instructed him.
17:11 **j** like the nations the LORD had driven from the
17:23 **j** as all his prophets had warned would happen.
18:3 LORD's sight, **j** as his ancestor David had done.
18:27 wants everyone in Jerusalem to hear this, not **j** you.
18:35 Name **j** one! So what makes you think that the
19:17 destroyed all these nations, **j** as the message says.
21:3 Asherah pole, **j** as King Ahab of Israel had done.
21:20 **j** as his father, Manasseh, had done.
22:16 and its people, **j** as I stated in the scroll you read.
22:18 says concerning the message you have **j** heard:
23:16 This happened **j** as the LORD had promised
23:17 and predicted the very things that you have **j** done
23:19 in the towns of Samaria, **j** as he had done at Bethel.
23:27 "I will destroy Judah **j** as I have destroyed Israel.
23:32 in the LORD's sight, **j** as his ancestors had done.
23:37 in the LORD's sight, **j** as his ancestors had done.
24:2 **j** as the LORD had promised through his
24:9 evil in the LORD's sight, **j** as his father had done.
24:19 in the LORD's sight, **j** as Jehoiakim had done.
1Ch 9:19 **j** as their ancestors had guarded the Tabernacle in
11:3 **j** as the LORD had promised through Samuel.
11:10 **j** as the LORD had promised concerning Israel.
12:23 instead of Saul, **j** as the LORD had promised.
15:15 **j** as the LORD had instructed Moses.
17:7 my people Israel when you were **j** a shepherd boy,
21:15 But **j** as the angel was preparing to destroy it,
29:1 for the Temple he will build is not **j** another
2Ch 4:3 The Sea was encircled **j** below its rim by two rows
4:16 of the LORD, **j** as King Solomon had requested.
6:33 and fear you, **j** as your own people Israel do.
10:10 was hard on you, **j** wait and see what I'll be like!
10:12 Rehoboam's decision, **j** as the king had requested.
13:9 your own priests, **j** like the pagan nations.
18:34 Then **j** as the sun was setting he died.
20:25 so much plunder that it took them three days **j** to
21:13 to worship idols, **j** as King Ahab did in Israel.
22:4 evil in the LORD's sight, **j** as Ahab had done.
23:8 and the people did everything **j** as Jehoiada the
25:18 But **j** then a wild animal came by and stepped on
26:4 LORD's sight, **j** as his father, Amaziah, had done.
27:2 LORD's sight, **j** as his father, Uzziah, had done.
29:2 LORD's sight, **j** as his ancestor David had done.
29:15 of the LORD, **j** as the king had commanded.
30:10 But most of the people **j** laughed at the messengers
32:8 He may have a great army, but they are **j** men.
32:14 Name **j** one time when any god, anywhere,
32:17 "**J** as the gods of all the other nations failed to
33:22 LORD's sight, **j** as his father Manasseh had done.
34:26 says concerning the message you have **j** heard:
36:21 for seventy years, **j** as the prophet had said.
Ezr 3:10 praise the LORD, **j** as King David had prescribed.
4:2 with you, for we worship your God **j** as you do.
4:3 **j** as King Cyrus of Persia commanded us."
9:7 captured, robbed, and disgraced, **j** as we are today.
9:15 O LORD, God of Israel, you are **j**. We stand
Ne 1:2 came to visit me with some other men who had **j**
5:2 We need more money **j** so we can buy the food we
5:5 the same family, and our children are **j** like theirs.
5:5 Yet we must sell our children into slavery **j** to get
6:9 They were **j** trying to intimidate us, imagining that
6:15 **j** fifty-two days after we had begun.
8:1 as one person at the square **j** inside the Water Gate.
8:3 He faced the square **j** inside the Water Gate from
8:16 or in the squares **j** inside the Water Gate
9:13 gave them regulations and instructions that were **j**,
9:33 Every time you punished us you were being **j**.
10:36 of all our herds and flocks, **j** as the law requires.
12:24 **j** as commanded by David, the man of God.
Est 1:7 of royal wine, **j** as the king had commanded.
2:20 **j** as she did when she was living in his home.
4:14 but that you have been elevated to the palace for **j**
5:1 court of the palace, **j** across from the king's hall.
5:13 the Jew **j** sitting there at the palace gate."
6:4 Haman had **j** arrived in the outer court of the
6:10 and do **j** as you have said for Mordecai the Jew,
7:8 **j** as the king returned from the palace garden.
9:31 **j** as they had decided for themselves and their
Job 4:17 'Can a mortal be **j** and upright before God? Can a
7:9 **J** as a cloud dissipates and vanishes, those who die
7:21 Why not **j** pardon my sin and take away my guilt?
8:8 "**J** ask the former generation. Pay attention to the
11:2 Is a person proved innocent **j** by talking a lot?
12:4 I am a **j** and blameless man, yet they laugh at me.
12:11 **J** as the mouth tastes good food, so the ear tests the
15:14 Can a mortal be pure? Can a human be **j**?
20:11 He was **j** a young man, but his bones will lie in the
24:5 the poor must spend all their time **j** getting enough
24:19 Death consumes sinners **j** as drought and heat
29:14 All I did was **j** and honest. Righteousness covered
34:3 '**J** as the mouth tastes good food, the ear tests the
37:23 yet he is so **j** and merciful that he does not oppress
40:15 I made it, **j** as I made you. It eats grass like an ox.
Ps 7:17 I will thank the LORD because he is **j**; / I will
33:5 He loves whatever is **j** and good, / and his
37:13 But the Lord **j** laughs, / for he sees their day of
39:5 An entire lifetime is **j** a moment to you;
48:11 towns of Judah be glad, / for your judgments are **j**.
49:10 must finally die, / **j** like the foolish and senseless,
51:4 what you say, / and your judgment against me is **j**.
62:3 To them I'm **j** a broken-down wall / or a tottering
71:2 Save me from my enemies, for you are **j**.

71:16 I will tell everyone that you alone are j and good.
92:15 They will declare, "The LORD is j! / He is my
111:7 All he does is j and good, / and all his
115:8 And those who make them are j like them,
119:58 your blessings. / Be merciful j as you promised.
119:62 At midnight I rise to thank you / for your j laws.
119:65 good things for me, LORD, / j as you promised.
119:76 comfort me, / j as you promised me, your servant.
119:107 restore my life again, j as you promised.
119:121 my enemies, / for I have done what is j and right.
119:160 words are true; / all your j laws will stand forever.
119:164 you seven times a day / because all your laws are j.
123:2 j as servants keep their eyes on their master,
125:2 J as the mountains surround and protect Jerusalem,
131:2 j as a small child is quiet with its mother.
135:18 And those who make them are j like them,
Pr 1:3 good conduct, and doing what is right, j, and fair.
2:9 Then you will understand what is right, j, and fair,
3:12 j as a father corrects a child in whom he delights.
5:16 your springs in public, having sex with j anyone?
7:14 offered my sacrifices and j finished my vows.
8:15 of me, kings reign, and rulers make j laws.
12:5 The plans of the godly are j; the advice of the
21:3 The LORD is more pleased when we do what is j
21:7 Because the wicked refuse to do what is j,
22:7 J as the rich rule the poor, so the borrower is
23:16 heart will thrill when you speak what is right and j.
25:7 publicly disgraced! J because you see something,
25:27 J as it is not good to eat too much honey, it is not
26:18 J as damaging as a mad man shooting a lethal
26:23 j as a pretty glaze covers a common clay pot.
27:20 J as Death and Destruction are never satisfied,
29:4 A j king gives stability to his nation, but one who
30:8 nor riches! Give me j enough to satisfy my needs.
Ecc 2:13 than foolishness, j as light is better than darkness.
2:15 Both of them die. J as the fool will die, so will I.
5:3 J as being too busy gives you nightmares, being a
6:9 J dreaming about nice things is meaningless;
7:28 J one out of every thousand men I interviewed can
10:3 You can identify fools j by the way they walk
SS 1:6 fair city girls, j because my complexion is so dark.
Isa 1:10 You act j like the rulers and people of Sodom
1:27 Because the LORD is j and righteous,
2:6 practice magic and divination, j like the Philistines.
7:2 trembled with fear, j as trees shake in a storm.
9:4 j as he did when he destroyed the army of Midian
10:9 We will destroy Calno j as we did Carchemish.
10:9 And we will destroy Samaria j as we did
10:24 they oppress you j as the Egyptians did long ago.
11:16 j as he did for Israel long ago when they returned
16:5 one who always does what is j and right.
17:14 This is the j reward of those who plunder
19:17 J to speak the name of Israel will strike deep terror
28:26 The farmer knows j what to do, for God has given
31:4 and noise. It j goes right on eating.
32:10 In a short time—in j a little more than a year—
33:4 J as locusts strip the fields and vines, so Jerusalem
34:4 j as withered leaves and fruit fall from a tree.
36:12 wants everyone in Jerusalem to hear this, not j you.
36:20 Name j one! So what makes you think that the
37:18 destroyed all these nations, j as the message says.
41:24 who chooses you becomes filthy, j like you!
44:19 stops to reflect, "Why, it's j a block of wood!
45:21 but me—a j God and a Savior—no, not one!
49:8 "At j the right time, I will respond to you.
54:9 "J as I swore in the time of Noah that I would
54:14 You will live under a government that is j and fair.
55:9 For j as the heavens are higher than the earth,
56:1 "Be j and fair to all," says the LORD. "Do what
59:8 true peace is or what it means to be j and good.
62:5 O Jerusalem, j as a young man cares for his bride.
65:8 "For j as good grapes are found among a cluster of
Jer 2:36 in Egypt will let you down, j as Assyria did before.
5:1 If you can find even one person who is j
7:14 So j as I destroyed Shiloh, I will now destroy this
7:15 j as I did your relatives, the people of Israel.'
9:24 and understand that I am the LORD who is j
11:20 O LORD Almighty, you are j, and you examine
12:14 I will uproot them from their lands j as Judah will
12:16 'As surely as the LORD lives' (j as they taught
13:24 j as chaff is scattered by the winds blowing in from
17:27 through the gates of Jerusalem j as on other days,
19:15 this city and its surrounding towns j as I promised,
22:3 Be fair-minded and j. Do what is right!
22:15 Because he was j and right in all his dealings.
23:5 He will do what is j and right throughout the land.
23:27 j as their ancestors did by worshiping the idols of
25:14 the Babylonians, j as they enslaved my people.
31:37 J as the heavens cannot be measured
32:8 Then, j as the LORD had said he would,
32:24 Everything has happened j as you said it would.
32:42 J as I have sent all these calamities upon them,
33:15 and he will do what is j and right throughout the
34:5 in your memory, j as they did for your ancestors.
34:18 I will cut you apart j as you cut apart the calf when
36:10 This room was j off the upper courtyard of the
36:28 and write everything again j as you did on the
38:26 j tell them you begged me not to send you back to
40:3 j as he said he would. For these people have sinned
42:18 'J as my anger and fury were poured out on the
42:20 saying, 'J tell us what the LORD our God says,
44:13 I will punish them in Egypt j as I punished them in
44:17 and sacrifice to her j as much as we like—
44:17 j as we and our ancestors did before us, and as our
44:30 j as I turned King Zedekiah of Judah over to King
50:18 and his land, j as I punished the king of Assyria.
50:40 I will destroy it j as I destroyed Sodom
51:33 In j a little while her harvest will begin."
51:49 "J as Babylon killed the people of Israel
51:56 For the LORD is a God who gives j punishment,
52:2 in the LORD's sight, j as Jehoiakim had done.
La 2:17 But it is the LORD who did it j as he warned.
4:22 But Edom, your punishment is j beginning;
Eze 3:23 j as I had seen it in my first vision by the Kebar
5:3 Keep j a bit of the hair and tie it up in your robe.
8:4 was there, j as I had seen it before in the valley.
10:22 were j like the faces of the beings I had seen at the
10:22 they traveled straight ahead, j as the others had.
12:4 j as captives do when they begin a long march to
18:5 "Suppose a certain man is j and does what is
18:9 Anyone who does these things is j and will surely
18:21 begin to obey my laws and do what is j and right,
18:25 "Yet you say, 'The Lord isn't being j!' Listen to
18:27 obey the law, and do what is j and right, they will
20:30 Do you plan to pollute yourselves j as your
20:36 I will judge you there j as I did your ancestors in
22:20 j as copper, tin, iron, and lead are melted down in a
22:25 Your princes plot conspiracies j as lions stalk their
23:13 was going, defiling herself j like her older sister.
23:18 disgusted with Oholibah, j as I was with her sister,
23:33 of sorrow and distress, j as your sister Samaria did.
25:8 have said that Judah is j like all the other nations,
25:10 the eastern deserts, j as I handed over Ammon.
32:2 but you are really j a sea monster, heaving around
33:14 they turn from their sins and do what is j and right.
33:16 for they have done what is j and right, and they
33:17 "Your people are saying, 'The Lord is not j,' but it
is they who are not j.
33:19 from their wickedness and do what is j and right,
33:20 of Israel, you are saying, 'The Lord is not j.'
34:26 which will come j when they are needed.
37:7 So I spoke these words, j as he told me.
37:14 You will see that I have done everything j as I
39:8 Everything will happen j as I have declared it.
40:20 There was a gateway on the north j like the one on
40:23 Here on the north side, j as on the east, there was
41:25 carved cherubim and palm trees j as on the walls.
42:10 j south of the inner courtyard between the Temple
42:10 These rooms were arranged j like the rooms on the
42:11 j like the complex on the north side of the Temple.
43:3 This vision was j like the others I had seen, first by
43:22 for the altar again, j as you did with the young bull.
45:9 and oppression and do what is j and right.
46:12 and he will offer his sacrifices j as he does on
47:10 fill the Dead Sea, j as they fill the Mediterranean!
47:22 They will be j like native-born Israelites to you,
48:23 Benjamin's territory lies j south of the prince's
48:27 The territory of Gad is j south of Zebulun with the
Da 2:6 J tell me the dream and what it means!"
2:40 j as iron smashes and crushes everything it strikes.
2:43 this will not succeed, j as iron and clay do not mix.
4:30 he said, "J look at this great city of Babylon!
4:37 All his acts are j and true, and he is able to humble
6:10 j as he had always done, giving thanks to his God.
9:7 faces are covered with shame, j as you see us now.
9:14 and the LORD our God is j in everything he does.
10:10 J then a hand touched me and lifted me,
Hos 4:5 j as you might at night, and so will your false
6:2 In j a short time, he will restore us so we can live
9:4 j as food touched by a person in mourning is
10:14 j as they did when Shalman destroyed Beth-arbel.
Joel 2:32 in Jerusalem who escape, j as the LORD has said.
Am 5:14 truly be your helper, j as you have claimed he is.
6:13 And j as stupid is this bragging about your
7:14 I'm j a shepherd, and I take care of fig trees.
Ob 1:16 J as you swallowed up my people on my holy
Jnh 4:3 J kill me now, LORD! I'd rather be dead than
Mic 2:8 making them as ragged as men who have j come
2:11 That's j the kind of prophet you would like!
Na 2:8 someone shouts, but the people j keep on running.
Hab 1:13 You are perfectly j in this. But will you,
Hag 2:5 j as I promised when you came out of Egypt.
2:6 In j a little while I will again shake the heavens
Zec 1:6 happened to your ancestors, j as I said they would.
8:8 I will be faithful and j toward them as their God.
8:16 Render verdicts in your courts that are j and that
9:7 will join my people, j as the Jebusites once did.
9:16 his people, j as a shepherd rescues his sheep.
13:9 j as gold and silver are refined and purified by fire.
Mt 1:19 Joseph, her fiancé, being a j man, decided to break
2:6 of Judah, / you are not j a lowly village in Judah,
3:9 Don't j say, 'We're safe—we're the descendants of
5:37 J say a simple, 'Yes, I will,' or 'No, I won't.'
5:45 and he sends rain on the j and on the unjust,
6:10 will be done here on earth, / j as it is in heaven.
6:12 j as we have forgiven those who have sinned
7:16 they act, j as you can identify a tree by its fruit.
8:8 J say the word from where you are, and my servant
8:27 The disciples j sat there in awe. "Who is this?"
9:18 "My daughter has j died," he said, "but you can
bring her back to life again if you j
9:21 for she thought, "If I can j touch his robe, I will be
12:13 and it became normal, j like the other one.
13:40 "J as the weeds are separated out and burned,
13:55 He's j a carpenter's son, and we know Mary,
15:12 you offended the Pharisees by what you j said?"
18:33 on your fellow servant, j as I had mercy on you?'
20:12 and yet you've paid them j as much as you paid us
21:3 what you are doing, j say, 'The Lord needs them,'
24:28 J as the gathering of vultures shows there is a
24:33 J so, when you see the events I've described
26:43 for they j couldn't keep their eyes open.
27:19 J then, as Pilate was sitting on the judgment seat,
28:6 raised from the dead, j as he said would happen.
Mk 5:2 J as Jesus was climbing from the boat, a man
5:28 "If I can j touch his clothing, I will be healed."
5:36 and said to Jairus, "Don't be afraid. J trust me."
6:3 He's j the carpenter, the son of Mary and brother
9:13 badly mistreated, j as the Scriptures predicted."
11:3 j say, 'The Lord needs it and will return it
13:11 J say what God tells you to. Then it is not you who
13:29 J so, when you see the events I've described
14:16 the city and found everything j as Jesus had said,
14:40 for they j couldn't keep their eyes open.
14:68 out into the entryway. J then, a rooster crowed.
15:21 was coming in from the country j then,
16:2 j at sunrise, they came to the tomb.
16:7 see him there, j as he told you before he died!"
Lk 1:70 j as he promised / through his holy prophets long
2:20 they had seen the child, j as the angel had said.
2:38 She came along j as Simeon was talking with Mary
3:8 Don't j say, 'We're safe—we're the descendants of
6:36 j as your Father is compassionate.
7:6 But j before they arrived at the house, the officer
7:7 J say the word from where you are, and my servant
8:50 be afraid. J trust me, and she will be all right."
9:14 "J tell them to sit down on the ground in groups of
10:20 But don't rejoice j because evil spirits obey you;
10:40 doesn't it seem unfair to you that my sister j sits
11:1 teach us to pray, j as John taught his disciples."
11:4 j as we forgive those who have sinned against us.
11:6 'A friend of mine has j arrived for a visit, and I
11:45 "you have insulted us, too, in what you j said."
12:38 come in the middle of the night or j before dawn.
12:41 is this illustration j for us or for everyone?"
14:18 One said he had j bought a field and wanted to
14:19 Another said he had j bought five pair of oxen
14:20 Another had j been married, so he said he couldn't
16:4 I know j the thing! And then I'll have plenty of
17:7 taking care of sheep, he doesn't j sit down and eat.
17:37 "J as the gathering of vultures shows there is a
18:7 Even he rendered a j decision in the end, so don't
19:31 what you are doing, j say, 'The Lord needs it.' "
19:32 they went and found the colt, j as Jesus had said.
21:31 J so, when you see the events I've described taking
22:13 the city and found everything j as Jesus had said,
22:29 And j as my Father has granted me a Kingdom,
23:26 who was coming in from the country j then,
24:24 Jesus' body was gone, j as the women had said."
24:36 And j as they were telling about it, Jesus himself
24:49 will send the Holy Spirit, j as my Father promised.
Jn 1:46 "J come and see for yourself," Philip said.
1:50 "Do you believe all this j because I told you I had
3:8 J as you can hear the wind but can't tell where it
4:27 J then his disciples arrived. They were astonished
4:42 him ourselves, not j because of what you told us.
5:21 the dead anyone he wants to, j as the Father does.
5:23 will honor the Son, j as they honor the Father.
5:30 And my judgment is absolutely j, because it is
8:45 I tell the truth, you j naturally don't believe me!
10:15 j as my Father knows me and I know the Father.
12:35 "My light will shine out for you j a little while
13:9 my hands and head as well, Lord, not j my feet!"
13:33 cannot come to me—j as I told the Jewish leaders.
13:34 J as I have loved you, you should love each other.
14:11 J believe that I am in the Father and the Father is
14:19 In j a little while the world will not see me again,
15:10 j as I obey my Father and remain in his love.
16:16 "In j a little while I will be gone, and you won't
16:16 Then, j a little while after that, you will see me
16:19 I said in j a little while I will be gone, and you
16:19 Then, j a little while after that, you will see me
17:11 given me—so that they will be united j as we are.
17:14 they do not belong to the world, j as I do not.
17:21 they will be one, j as you and I are one, Father—
17:21 that j as you are in me and I am in you, so they will
21:10 "Bring some of the fish you've j caught,"
Ac 1:5 but in j a few days you will be baptized with the
1:11 And someday, j as you saw him go, he will
2:33 to pour out upon us, j as you see and hear today.
5:9 J outside that door are the young men who buried
10:17 J then the men sent by Cornelius found the house
10:47 now that they have received the Holy Spirit j as we
11:11 J then three men who had been sent from Caesarea
11:15 but j as I was getting started, the Holy Spirit fell
on them, j as he fell on us at the beginning.
13:28 They found no j cause to execute him, but they
15:8 giving them the Holy Spirit, j as he gave him to us.
18:3 with them, for they were tentmakers j as he was.
18:14 But j as Paul started to make his defense,
18:24 had j arrived in Ephesus from Alexandria in Egypt.
19:27 I'm not j talking about the loss of public respect
22:3 God in everything I did, j as all of you are today.
23:11 J as you have told the people about me here in
24:15 I have hope in God, j as these men do, that he will
27:25 For I believe God. It will be j as he said.
Ro 1:13 j as I have done among other Gentiles.
2:1 But you are j as bad, and you have no excuse!
2:5 judgment when God, the j judge of all the world,
2:28 For you are not a true Jew j because you were born
3:3 but j because they broke their promises, does that
3:6 If God is not j, how is he qualified to judge the
3:25 and j when he did not punish those who sinned in
3:26 and j in this present time when he declares sinners
4:23 to be righteous—wasn't j for Abraham's benefit.
5:6 Christ came at j the right time and died for us
5:21 So j as sin ruled over all people and brought them
6:4 And j as Christ was raised from the dead by the
8:11 And j as he raised Christ from the dead, he will
9:7 J the fact that they are descendants of Abraham
9:18 God shows mercy to some j because he wants to,

9:30 what shall we say about these things? **J** this:
11:18 Remember, you are **j** a branch, not the root.
12: 4 **J** as our bodies have many parts and each part has
12: 9 Don't **j** pretend that you love others. Really love
15: 1 but we cannot **j** go ahead and do them to please
15: 7 So accept each other **j** as Christ has accepted you;
16:25 able to make you strong, **j** as the Good News says.
1Co 1: 2 Christ Jesus, **j** as he did all Christians everywhere
1: 9 do this for you, for he always does **j** what he says,
4:19 out whether these arrogant people are **j** big talkers
4:20 For the Kingdom of God is not **j** fancy talk; it is
6: 7 Why not **j** accept the injustice and leave it at that?
6:11 There was a time when some of you were **j** like
6:14 **j** as he raised our Lord from the dead.
7: 7 could get along without marrying, **j** as I do.
7: 8 to widows—it's better to stay unmarried, **j** as I am.
7:26 I think it is best to remain **j** as you are.
9:10 **J** as farm workers who plow fields and thresh the
9:19 This means I am not bound to obey people **j**
10:33 I don't **j** do what I like or what is best for me,
11: 1 should follow my example, **j** as I follow Christ's.
11:23 and I pass it on to you **j** as I received it.
12:14 the body has many different parts, not **j** one part.
12:17 Or if your whole body were **j** one big ear,
12:18 and he has put each part **j** where he wants it.
13:12 everything completely, **j** as God knows me now.
14:34 They should be submissive, **j** as the law says.
15: 3 Christ died for our sins, **j** as the Scriptures said.
15:21 **j** as death came into the world through a man,
15:38 gives it a new body—**j** the kind he wants it to have.
15:39 And **j** as there are different kinds of seeds
15:44 For **j** as there are natural bodies, so also there are
15:48 Every human being has an earthly body **j** like
15:48 but our heavenly bodies will be **j** like Christ's.
15:49 **J** as we are now like Adam, the man of the earth,
16: 7 This time I don't want to make **j** a short visit
16:10 He is doing the Lord's work, **j** as I am.
2Co 2:17 are many of them—who preach **j** to make money.
6: 2 For God says, / "At **j** the right time, I heard you.
7:11 **J** see what this godly sorrow produced in you!
8:11 to completion **j** as enthusiastically as you began it.
9: 3 But I am sending these brothers **j** to be sure that
10: 7 You must recognize that we belong to Christ **j** as
10: 9 Now this is not **j** an attempt to frighten you by my
10:11 this must realize that we will be **j** as demanding
11: 3 to Christ, **j** as Eve was deceived by the serpent.
11:12 of those who boast that their work is **j** like ours.
12: 3 Whether my body was there or **j** my spirit, I don't
12:19 Perhaps you think we are saying all this **j** to defend
13: 2 I again warn them and all others, **j** as I did before,
Gal 1: 4 He died for our sins, **j** as God our Father planned,
2: 7 **j** as he had given Peter the responsibility of
3: 4 was it? Are you now going to **j** throw it all away?
3:15 **J** as no one can set aside or amend an irrevocable
4:25 And now Jerusalem is **j** like Mount Sinai in
4:28 are children of the promise, **j** like Isaac.
4:29 **j** as Isaac, the child of promise, was persecuted by
5:17 which is **j** opposite from what the Holy Spirit
6:12 you to be circumcised are doing it for **j** one reason.
Eph 1:11 and all things happen **j** as he decided long ago.
1:14 This is **j** one more reason for us to praise our
2: 2 You used to live **j** like the rest of the world, full of
2: 3 and we were under God's anger **j** like everyone
3: 8 **J** think! Though I did nothing to deserve it,
4:32 **j** as God through Christ has forgiven you.
5:29 **j** as Christ cares for his body, which is the church.
6: 6 but not **j** to please your masters when they are
6:22 I am sending him to you for **j** this purpose. He will
Php 2:23 I hope to send him to you **j** as soon as I find out
Col 1: 6 **j** as it changed yours that very first day you heard
2: 6 **j** as you accepted Christ Jesus as your Lord,
3:22 all the time, not **j** when they are watching you.
4: 1 You slave owners must be **j** and fair to your slaves.
1Th 2: 2 been treated at Philippi **j** before we came to you
2: 5 And God is our witness that we were not **j**
2:13 you didn't think of the words we spoke as being **j**
3: 6 Now Timothy has **j** returned, bringing the good
3: 6 and that you want to see us **j** as much as we want
3:12 everyone else, **j** as our love overflows toward you.
4:11 with your hands, **j** as we commanded you before.
5:11 and build each other up, **j** as you are already doing.
2Th 3: 1 wherever it goes, **j** as when it came to you.
1Ti 6: 5 the truth. To them religion is **j** a way to get rich.
2Ti 1: 3 with a clear conscience, **j** as my ancestors did.
2: 5 **j** as an athlete either follows the rules or is
3: 8 And these teachers fight the truth **j** as Jannes
3: 9 they are, **j** as happened with Jannes and Jambres.
4: 8 And the prize is not **j** for me but for all who
Phm 1: 9 but because of our love, I prefer **j** to ask you.
1:16 He is no longer **j** a slave; he is a beloved brother,
Heb 1: 4 **j** as the name God gave him is far greater than their
3: 2 **j** as Moses served faithfully and was entrusted with
3: 3 **j** as a person who builds a fine house deserves
3:14 trusting God **j** as firmly as when we first believed,
4: 2 has been announced to us **j** as it was to them.
4:10 **j** as God rested after creating the world.
5: 4 to be called by God for this work, **j** as Aaron was.
9:14 **J** think how much more the blood of Christ will
9:27 And **j** as it is destined that each person dies only
10: 3 But **j** the opposite happened. Those yearly
10: 7 **j** as it is written about me in the Scriptures.' "
10:37 "For in **j** a little while, / the Coming One will
Jas 1:22 it is a message to obey, not **j** to listen to.
1:23 For if you **j** listen and don't obey, it is like looking
1:26 control your tongue, you are **j** fooling yourself,
2:17 So you see, it isn't enough **j** to have faith.
2:19 Do you still think it's enough **j** to believe that there
2:23 And so it happened **j** as the Scriptures say:
2:26 **J** as the body is dead without a spirit, so also faith
5:12 **J** say a simple yes or no, so that you will not sin
1Pe 1:15 you must be holy in everything you do, **j** as God—
2: 1 and deceit. Don't **j** pretend to be good!
4: 5 But **j** remember that they will have to face God,
2Pe 2: 1 **j** as there will be false teachers among you.
2:18 they lure back into sin those who have **j** escaped
3:15 This is **j** as our beloved brother Paul wrote to you
3:16 he meant, **j** as they do the other parts of Scripture—
1Jn 1: 7 **j** as Christ is, then we have fellowship with each
1: 9 he is faithful and **j** to forgive us and to cleanse us
3: 3 this will keep themselves pure, **j** as Christ is pure.
3:18 let us stop **j** saying we love each other;
3:23 and love one another, **j** as he commanded us.
2Jn 1: 4 **j** as we have been commanded by the Father.
1: 6 one another, **j** as you heard from the beginning.
Rev 2: 6 the deeds of the immoral Nicolaitans, **j** as I do.
3:21 **j** as I was victorious and sat with my Father on his
10: 7 It will happen **j** as he announced it to his servants
15: 3 Lord God Almighty. / **J** and true are your ways,
16: 5 "You are **j** in sending this judgment, O Holy One,
16: 6 murderers blood to drink. It is their **j** reward."
16: 7 God Almighty, your punishments are true and **j**."
19: 2 His judgments are **j** and true. He has punished the
19:10 **j** like you and other believers who testify of their
22: 9 of God, **j** like you and your brothers the prophets,

JUSTICE (148) [JUST]

Ex 18:26 men were constantly available to administer **j**.
23: 6 "Do not twist **j** against people simply because they
Dt 10:18 He gives **j** to orphans and widows. He shows love
16:19 You must never twist **j** or show partiality.
16:20 Let true **j** prevail, so you may live and occupy the
24:17 "True **j** must be given to foreigners living among
32:41 my flashing sword / and begin to carry out **j**,
33:21 were assembled, / they carried out the LORD's **j**
1Sa 8: 3 for money. They accepted bribes and perverted **j**.
2Sa 15: 4 their problems to me, and I would give them **j**!"
1Ki 3:28 God had given him to render decisions with **j**.
10: 9 so you can rule with **j** and righteousness."
2Ch 9: 8 so you can rule with **j** and righteousness."
19: 7 the LORD our God does not tolerate perverted **j**,
19:11 The Levites will assist you in making sure that **j** is
Job 8: 3 Does God twist **j**? Does the Almighty twist what is
9:19 he has it. As for **j**, who can challenge him?
19: 7 but no one hears me. I protest, but there is no **j**.
29:14 covered me like a robe, and I wore **j** like a turban.
31: 6 Let God judge me on the scales of **j**, for he knows
32: 9 not wise. Sometimes the aged do not understand **j**.
34:12 will not do wrong. The Almighty cannot twist **j**.
34:17 Could God govern if he hated **j**? Are you going to
34:33 "Must God tailor his **j** to your demands? But you
35:14 He will bring about **j** if you will only wait.
36: 6 not let the wicked live but gives **j** to the afflicted.
36:17 on the godless. Don't worry, **j** will be upheld.
40: 8 Are you going to discredit my **j** and condemn me
Ps 7: 6 of my enemies! / Wake up, my God, and bring **j**!
9: 8 He will judge the world with **j** / and rule the
9:16 The LORD is known for his **j**. / The wicked have
10:18 You will bring **j** to the orphans and the oppressed,
11: 7 For the LORD is righteous, and he loves **j**.
17: 1 O LORD, hear my plea for **j**. / Listen to my cry
35:24 "not guilty," O LORD my God, for you give **j**.
35:28 Then I will tell everyone of your **j** and goodness,
36: 6 mighty mountains, / your **j** like the ocean depths.
36:10 who love you; / give **j** to those with honest hearts.
37: 6 and the **j** of your cause will shine like the noonday
37:28 For the LORD loves **j**, / and he will never
40: 9 I have told all your people about your **j**. / I have
45: 4 out to victory, / defending truth, humility, and **j**.
45: 6 and ever. / Your royal power is expressed in **j**.
50: 6 Then let the heavens proclaim his **j**, / for God
58: 1 **J**—do you rulers know the meaning of the word?
58: 2 are crooked; / you hand out violence instead of **j**.
67: 4 singing for joy, / because you govern them with **j**
72: 1 Give **j** to the king, O God, / and righteousness to
75: 2 I have planned, / I will bring **j** against the wicked.
89:14 on two strong pillars—righteousness and **j**.
94: 1 O God of vengeance, let your glorious **j** be seen!
97: 2 and **j** are the foundation of his throne.
97: 8 of Judah are glad / because of your **j**, LORD!
98: 9 He will judge the world with **j**, / and the nations
99: 4 Mighty king, lover of **j**, / you have established
fairness. / You have acted with **j**
101: 1 I will sing of your love and **j**. / I will praise you,
103: 6 and **j** to all who are treated unfairly.
119:142 Your **j** is eternal, / and your law is perfectly true.
119:149 O LORD, hear my cry; / in your **j**, save my life.
119:156 is your mercy; / in your **j**, give me back my life.
146: 7 who gives **j** to the oppressed / and food to the
Pr 2: 8 He guards the paths of **j** and protects those who are
8:18 honor, wealth, and **j** are mine to distribute.
8:20 I walk in righteousness, in paths of **j**.
16:12 despises wrongdoing, for his rule depends on his **j**.
17:23 The wicked accept secret bribes to pervert **j**.
19:28 A corrupt witness makes a mockery of **j**; the mouth
21:15 **J** is a joy to the godly, but it causes dismay among
25: 5 and his reign will be made secure by **j**.
28: 5 Evil people don't understand **j**, but those who
29:26 the ruler's favor, but **j** comes from the LORD.
31: 5 and be unable to give **j** to those who are oppressed.
31: 8 ensure **j** for those who are perishing.
31: 9 for the poor and helpless, and see that they get **j**.
Ecc 5: 8 and **j** being miscarried throughout the land,
5: 8 and matters of **j** only get lost in red tape
Isa 1:17 Learn to do good. Seek **j**. Help the oppressed.
1:21 Once the home of **j** and righteousness, she is now
1:26 Then Jerusalem will again be called the Home of **J**
5: 7 He expected them to yield a crop of **j**, / but instead
5:16 But the LORD Almighty is exalted by his **j**.
5:23 They take bribes to pervert **j**. They let the wicked
9: 7 and **j** from the throne of his ancestor David.
10: 2 deprive the poor, the widows, and the orphans of **j**.
26: 7 path is not steep and rough. / You are a God of **j**,
28: 6 He will give a longing for **j** to their judges. He will
28:17 "I will take the measuring line of **j** and the plumb
29:21 And those who use trickery to pervert **j** and tell lies
32:16 **J** will rule in the wilderness and righteousness in
33: 5 he will make Jerusalem his home of **j**
42: 1 my Spirit upon him. He will reveal **j** to the nations.
42: 3 He will bring full **j** to all who have been wronged.
50: 8 He who gives me **j** is near. Who will dare to
51: 4 and my **j** will become a light to the nations.
51: 5 My mercy and **j** are coming soon. Your salvation
54:17 who tells lies in court will be brought to **j**.
59:11 We look for **j**, but it is nowhere to be found.
59:14 who are righteous, and **j** is nowhere to be found.
59:15 and was displeased to find that there was no **j**.
59:16 in to save them with his mighty power and **j**.
61: 8 "For I, the LORD, love **j**. I hate robbery
61:11 The Sovereign LORD will show his **j** to the
Jer 4: 2 and begin to live good, honest lives and uphold **j**,
5:28 They refuse **j** to orphans and deny the rights of the
12: 1 you always give me **j** when I bring a case before
21:12 Give **j** to the people you judge! Help those who
22:16 He made sure that **j** and help were given to the
La 3:36 They perverted **j** in the courts. Do they think the
Eze 22:29 rob the needy, and deprive foreigners of **j**.
34:16 and powerful. I will feed them, yes—feed them **j**!
Hos 2:19 showing you righteousness and **j**, unfailing love
10: 4 So perverted **j** springs up among them like
12: 6 Act on the principles of love and **j**, and always live
Am 2: 6 They have perverted **j** by selling honest people for
2: 7 in the dust and deny **j** to those who are oppressed.
5: 7 You twist **j**, making it a bitter pill for the poor
5:12 and deprive the poor of **j** in the courts.
5:15 is good; remodel your courts into true halls of **j**.
5:24 Instead, I want to see a mighty flood of **j**, a river of
6:12 but that's how stupid you are when you turn **j** into
Mic 3: 8 I am filled with **j** and might, fearlessly pointing out
3: 9 of Israel! You hate **j** and twist all that is right.
7: 3 pay them off, and together they scheme to twist **j**.
Hab 1: 4 and useless, and there is no **j** given in the courts.
1: 4 and **j** is perverted with bribes and trickery.
2: 6 'You thieves! At last **j** has caught up with you!
Zep 2: 3 all you who are humble, all you who uphold **j**.
3: 5 Day by day his **j** is more evident, but no one takes
Mal 2:17 wearied him by asking, "Where is the God of **j**?"
3: 5 who deprive the foreigners living among you of **j**,
Mt 5: 6 God blesses those who are hungry and thirsty for **j**,
12:18 upon him, / and he will proclaim **j** to the nations.
12:20 until he brings full **j** with his final victory.
23:23 important things of the law—**j**, mercy, and faith.
Lk 11:42 but you completely forget about **j** and the love of
18: 3 appealing for **j** against someone who had harmed
18: 5 I'm going to see that she gets **j**, because she is
18: 7 so don't you think God will surely give **j** to his
18: 8 I tell you, he will grant **j** to them quickly!
Ac 8:33 He was humiliated and received no **j**. / Who can
17:31 For he has set a day for judging the world with **j** by
28: 4 he escaped the sea, **j** will not permit him to live."
Ro 2: 2 And we know that God, in his **j**, will punish
2Th 1: 5 But God will use this persecution to show his **j**.
1: 6 and in his **j** he will punish those who persecute
Heb 7: 2 His name means "king of **j**." He is also "king of
11:33 these people overthrew kingdoms, ruled with **j**,

JUSTIFIED (6) [JUST]

Nu 5:18 or not her husband's suspicions are **j**.
Job 33:32 I want to hear it, for I am anxious to see you **j**.
Isa 45:25 the LORD all the generations of Israel will be **j**,
Mt 12:37 either you will be **j** by them or you will be
Lk 18:14 not the Pharisee, returned home **j** before God.
2Co 8:24 to all the churches that our boasting about you is **j**.

JUSTIFY (1) [JUST]

Lk 10:29 The man wanted to **j** his actions, so he asked Jesus,

JUSTLE [KJV] See RACE

JUSTLY (2) [JUST]

Ps 58:11 surely there is a God who judges **j** here on earth."
106: 3 Happy are those who deal **j** with others

JUSTUS (3) [TITIUS]

Ac 1:23 Joseph called Barsabbas (also known as **J**)
18: 7 After that he stayed with Titius **J**, a Gentile who
Col 4:11 Jesus (the one we call **J**) also sends his greetings.

JUTTAH (3)

Jos 15:55 Besides these, there were Maon, Carmel, Ziph, **J**,
21:16 Ain, **J**, and Beth-shemesh—nine towns from these
1Ch 6:59 Ain, **J**, and Beth-shemesh.

K

KABZEEL (3)

Jos 15:21 the borders of Edom in the extreme south are **K**,
2Sa 23:20 Benaiah son of Jehoiada, a valiant warrior from **K**.
1Ch 11:22 Benaiah son of Jehoiada, a valiant warrior from **K**.

KADESH (18) [EN-MISHPAT, KADESH-BARNEA, MERIBAH-KADESH]

Ge 14: 7 they swung around to En-mishpat (now called **K**)
16:14 and it can still be found between **K** and Bered.
20: 1 and settled for a while between **K** and Shur at a
Nu 13:26 and the people of Israel at **K** in the wilderness of
20: 1 arrived in the wilderness of Zin and camped at **K**.
20:14 While Moses was at **K**, he sent ambassadors to the
20:16 Now we are camped at **K**, a town on the border of
20:22 The whole community of Israel left **K** as a group
27:14 (These are the waters of Meribah at **K** in the
33:36 and camped at **K** in the wilderness of Zin.
33:37 They left **K** and camped at Mount Hor,
Dt 1:46 So you stayed there at **K** for a long time.
32:51 waters of Meribah at **K** in the wilderness of Zin.
Jdg 11:16 When the people of Israel arrived at **K** on their
11:17 through either. So the people of Israel stayed in **K**.
Ps 29: 8 desert quake; / the LORD shakes the desert of **K**.
Eze 47:19 go west from Tamar to the waters of Meribah at **K**
48:28 runs from Tamar to the waters of Meribah at **K**

KADESH-BARNEA (10) [KADESH]

Nu 32: 8 did when I sent them from **K** to explore the land.
34: 4 Its southernmost point will be **K**, from which it
Dt 1: 2 only eleven days to travel from Mount Sinai to **K**,
1:19 country of the Amorites. When we arrived at **K**,
2:14 arrived at **K** until we finally crossed Zered Brook!
9:23 And at **K** the LORD sent you out with this
Jos 10:41 Joshua slaughtered them from **K** to Gaza and from
14: 6 of God, about you and me when we were at **K**.
14: 7 sent me from **K** to explore the land of Canaan.
15: 3 wilderness of Zin and went south of **K** to Hezron.

KADMIEL (8)

Ezr 2:40 of Jeshua and **K** (descendants of Hodaviah)
3: 9 with his sons and relatives, and **K** and his sons,
Ne 7:43 of Jeshua and **K** (descendants of Hodaviah)
9: 4 Bani, **K**, Shebaniah, Bunni, Sherebiah, Bani,
9: 5 Jeshua, **K**, Bani, Hashabneiah, Sherebiah, Hodiah,
10: 9 of Azaniah, Binnui from the family of Henadad, **K**,
12: 8 Binnui, **K**, Sherebiah, Judah, and Mattaniah,
12:24 Hashabiah, Sherebiah, Jeshua, Binnui, **K**,

KADMONITES (1)

Ge 15:19 the land of the Kenites, Kenizzites, **K**,

KAIN (1)

Jos 15:57 **K**, Gibeah, and Timnah—ten towns with their

KAIWAN (1)

Am 5:26 Sakkuth your king god and **K** your star god—

KALLAI (1)

Ne 12:20 **K** was leader of the family of Sallu. / Eber was

KAMON (1)

Jdg 10: 5 When Jair died, he was buried in **K**.

KANAH (3)

Jos 16: 8 following the **K** Ravine to the Mediterranean Sea.
17: 9 side of the **K** Ravine to the Mediterranean Sea.
19:28 Abdon, Rehob, Hammon, **K**, and as far as Greater

KAREAH (8)

2Ki 25:23 Ishmael son of Nethaniah, Johanan son of **K**,
Jer 40: 8 of Nethaniah, Johanan and Jonathan, sons of **K**,
40:13 Johanan son of **K** and the other guerrilla leaders
41:11 But when Johanan son of **K** and the rest of the
41:16 Then Johanan son of **K** and his officers led away
42: 1 including Johanan son of **K** and Jezaniah son of
42: 8 So he called for Johanan son of **K** and the army
43: 2 Azariah son of Hoshaiah and Johanan son of **K**

KARKA (1)

Jos 15: 3 it went up to Addar, where it turned toward **K**.

KARKOR (1)

Jdg 8:10 and Zalmunna were in **K** with a remnant of 15,000

KARNAIM (1)

Am 6:13 "Didn't we take **K** by our own strength

KARTAH (2)

Jos 21:34 towns from the tribe of Zebulun: Jokneam, **K**,
1Ch 6:77 **K**, Rimmono, and Tabor, each with its

KARTAN (1)

Jos 21:32 Galilee (a city of refuge), Hammoth-dor, and **K**—

KATTATH (1)

Jos 19:15 The towns in these areas included **K**, Nahalal,

KEBAR (8)

Eze 1: 1 while I was with the Judean exiles beside the **K**
1: 3 there beside the **K** River in the land of the
3:15 of Judean exiles in Tel-abib, beside the **K** River.
3:23 just as I had seen it in my first vision by the **K**
10:15 same living beings I had seen beside the **K** River.
10:20 the God of Israel when I was by the **K** River.
10:22 just like the faces of the beings I had seen at the **K**,
43: 3 first by the **K** River and then when he came to

KEDAR (11)

Ge 25:13 was Nebaioth, followed by **K**, Abdeel, Mibsam,
1Ch 1:29 were Nebaioth (the oldest), **K**, Adbeel, Mibsam,
Ps 120: 5 It pains me to live with these people from **K**!
SS 1: 5 women of Jerusalem, tanned as the dark tents of **K**.
Isa 21:16 the Lord, "all the glory of **K** will come to an end.
42:11 you desert towns; / let the villages of **K** rejoice!
60: 7 The flocks of **K** will be given to you, and the rams
Jer 2:10 to the land of Cyprus; go east to the land of **K**.
49:28 This message was given concerning **K**
49:28 is what the LORD says: "Advance against **K**!
Eze 27:21 and the princes of **K** brought lambs and rams

KEDEMAH (2)

Ge 25:15 Hadad, Tema, Jetur, Naphish, and **K**.
1Ch 1:31 Jetur, Naphish, and **K**. These were the sons of

KEDEMOTH (4)

Dt 2:26 "Then from the wilderness of **K** I sent
Jos 13:18 Jahaz, **K**, Mephaath,
21:37 **K**, and Mephaath—four towns with their
1Ch 6:79 **K**, and Mephaath, each with its pasturelands.

KEDESH (12)

Jos 12:22 The king of **K** / The king of Jokneam in Carmel
15:23 **K**, Hazor, Ithnan,
19:37 **K**, Edrei, En-hazor,
20: 7 **K** of Galilee, in the hill country of Naphtali;
21:32 From the tribe of Naphtali they received **K** in
Jdg 4: 6 who lived in **K** in the land of Naphtali.
4: 9 of a woman." So Deborah went with Barak to **K**.
4:10 At **K**, Barak called together the tribes of Zebulun
4:11 pitched his tent by the Oak of Zaanannim, near **K**.
2Ki 15:29 of Ijon, Abel-beth-maacah, Janoah, **K**, and Hazor.
1Ch 6:72 territory of Issachar, they were given **K**, Daberath,
6:76 they were given **K** in Galilee, Hammon,

KEDORLAOMER (5) [KEDORLAOMER'S]

Ge 14: 1 King Arioch of Ellasar, King **K** of Elam, and King
14: 4 twelve years they had all been subject to King **K**,
14: 5 One year later, **K** and his allies arrived.
14: 9 against King **K** of Elam and the kings of Goiim,
14:17 As Abram returned from his victory over **K** and his

KEDORLAOMER'S (2) [KEDORLAOMER]

Ge 14:14 He chased after **K** army until he caught up with
14:15 **K** army fled, but Abram chased them to Hobah,

KEENLY (1)

Jer 13:27 I am **k** aware of your adultery and lust, and your

KEEP (358) [KEEPER, KEEPING, KEEPS, KEPT, SAFEKEEPING]

Ge 4: 9 "Am I supposed to **k** track of him wherever he
6:18 But I solemnly swear to **k** you safe in the boat,
6:19 into the boat with you to **k** them alive during the
11: 4 and **k** us from scattering all over the world."
14:21 But you may **k** for yourself all the goods you have
17:10 covenant that you and your descendants must **k**:
18:19 and their families to **k** the way of the LORD
31:49 "May the LORD **k** watch between us to make
31:49 **k** this treaty when we are out of each other's sight.
33: 9 Esau answered. "**K** what you have."
38: 9 he spilled the semen on the ground to **k** her from
38:23 "Then let her **k** the pledges!" Judah exclaimed.
38:26 because I didn't **k** my promise to let her marry my
41:49 that the people could not **k** track of the amount.
42:16 I'll **k** the rest of you here, bound in prison.
45: 7 God has sent me here to **k** you and your families
47:24 **K** four-fifths for yourselves, and use it to plant the
Ex 13: 9 Let it remind you always to **k** the LORD's
16:19 Moses told them, "Do not **k** any of it overnight."
16:32 and **k** it forever as a treasured memorial of the
19: 5 Now if you will obey me and **k** my covenant,
20:20 now on, let your fear of him **k** you from sinning!"
21:34 pay in full for the dead animal but then gets to **k** it.
21:36 yet its owner failed to **k** it under control,
21:36 pay in full for the dead bull but then gets to **k** it.
23: 7 "**K** far away from falsely charging anyone with
23:25 you with food and water, and I will **k** you healthy.
25:30 You must always **k** the special Bread of the
27:21 and his sons will **k** the lamps burning in the
29:26 as a special gift to him. Afterward **k** it for yourself.
31:13 "Tell the people of Israel to **k** my Sabbath day,
31:14 Yes, **k** the Sabbath day, for it is holy. Anyone who
31:16 The people of Israel must **k** the Sabbath day
Lev 15:31 you will **k** the people of Israel separate from things
18: 4 all my regulations and be careful to **k** my laws,
19:30 "**K** my Sabbath days of rest and show reverence
20: 8 **K** all my laws and obey them, for I am the
22:31 "You must faithfully **k** all my commands by
23:16 **K** counting until the day after the seventh Sabbath,
25:18 in the land, **k** my laws and obey my regulations.
26: 2 You must **k** my Sabbath days of rest and show
26: 3 "If you **k** my laws and are careful to obey my
Nu 5:10 Each priest may **k** the sacred donations that he
11:13 They **k** complaining and saying, 'Give us meat!'
31:18 virgins may live; you may **k** them for yourselves.
32:20 "If you **k** your word and arm yourselves for the
32:23 But if you fail to **k** your word, then you will have
36: 8 so that all the Israelites will **k** their ancestral
Dt 4:13 his covenant, which he commanded you to **k**—
4:39 So remember this and **k** it firmly in mind:
7:12 the LORD your God will **k** his covenant of
10: 1 and make a sacred chest of wood to **k** them in.
13: 5 Since they try to **k** you from following the LORD
13:17 **K** none of the plunder that has been set apart for
13:18 and **k** all the commands I am giving you today,
17:19 He must always **k** this copy of the law with him
19: 3 **K** the roads to these cities in good repair so that
20:14 But you may **k** for yourselves all the women,
20:18 This will **k** the people of the land from teaching
22: 2 owner is, **k** it until the owner comes looking for it;
24:12 to give as security, do not **k** the cloak overnight.
25: 4 "Do not **k** an ox from eating as it treads out the
27: 1 "**K** all these commands that I am giving you
28:41 have sons and daughters, but you will not **k** them,
30: 8 and **k** all the commands I am giving you today.
30:10 and **k** the commands and laws written in this Book
30:16 love the LORD your God and to **k** his commands,
Jos 2:14 we will **k** our promise when the LORD gives us
6:22 Joshua said to the two spies, "**K** your promise.
8: 2 But this time you may **k** the captured goods
10:18 and place guards at the entrance to **k** the kings
Jdg 7:17 Then he said to them, "**K** your eyes on me.
9:44 and his group stormed the city gate to **k** the men of
11:24 You **k** whatever your god Chemosh gives you,
11:24 and we will **k** whatever the LORD our God gives
Ru 4: 5 her husband's name and **k** the land in the family."
1Sa 1:23 and may the LORD help you **k** your promise."
2:23 things you are doing. Why do you **k** sinning?
5: 7 "We can't **k** the Ark of the God of Israel here any
20:23 And may the LORD make us **k** our promises to
2Sa 5: 6 "Even the blind and lame could **k** you out!"
7:11 And I will **k** you safe from all your enemies.
15:16 ten of his concubines to **k** the palace in order.
16:21 for he has left them here to **k** the house.
20: 3 had left to **k** house should be placed in seclusion.
21: 5 to **k** us from having any place at all in Israel.
22:37 a wide path for my feet / to **k** them from slipping.
1Ki 1: 1 many blankets covered him, he could not **k** warm.
1: 2 She will lie in your arms and **k** you warm."
2: 3 **K** each of the laws, commands, regulations,
2: 4 then the LORD will **k** the promise he made to
6:12 if you **k** all my laws and regulations and obey all
8: 5 Ark in such numbers that no one could **k** count!
8:23 You **k** your promises and show unfailing love to
2Ki 6:32 When he arrives, shut the door and **k** him out.
11: 8 for the king and **k** your weapons in hand.
22: 7 to **k** account of the money they receive,
1Ch 4:10 all that I do, and **k** me from all trouble and pain!"
16:11 and for his strength, / and **k** on searching.
2Ch 1: 9 please **k** your promise to David my father,
5: 6 Ark in such numbers that no one could **k** count!
6:14 You **k** your promises and show unfailing love to
23: 7 for the king and **k** your weapons in hand.
23:19 **k** those who were ceremonially unclean from
Ezr 4: 4 and frighten the people of Judah to **k** them from
Ne 5:13 my robe and said, "If you fail to **k** your promise,
Est 2:20 Esther continued to **k** her nationality and family
3:11 "**K** the money," the king told Haman, "but go
4:14 If you **k** quiet at a time like this, deliverance for
Job 4: 2 say a word? For who could **k** from speaking out?
6:24 I want is a reasonable answer—then I will **k** quiet.
7:11 "I cannot **k** from speaking. I must express my
14: 3 Must you **k** an eye on such a frail creature
20:15 wealth he swallowed. God won't let him **k** it down.
24: 5 spend all their time just getting enough to **k** body
31:20 me for providing wool clothing to **k** them warm?
33:33 to me. **K** silent and I will teach you wisdom!"
36:19 and mighty efforts **k** you from distress?
Ps 4: 8 for you alone, O LORD, will **k** me safe.
15: 4 and **k** their promises even when it hurts.
16: 1 **K** me safe, O God, / for I have come to you for
18:36 a wide path for my feet / to **k** them from slipping.
19:13 **K** me from deliberate sins! / Don't let them control
20: 1 May the God of Israel **k** you safe from all harm.
21: 7 The unfailing love of the Most High will **k** him
25:10 all those who **k** his covenant and obey his decrees.
32: 9 that needs a bit and bridle to **k** it under control."
34:13 watch your tongue! / **K** your lips from telling lies!
37:28 abandon the godly. / He will **k** them safe forever,
50:23 If you **k** to my path, / I will reveal to you the
51: 9 Don't **k** looking at my sins. / Remove the stain of
56: 8 You **k** track of all my sorrows. / You have
69:13 But I **k** right on praying to you, LORD,
71:14 But I will **k** on hoping for you to help me; / I will
73:24 You will **k** on guiding me with your counsel,
78:10 They did not **k** God's covenant, / and they refused
78:37 not loyal to him. / They did not **k** his covenant.

88:13 I cry out to you. / I will **k** on pleading day by day.
89:31 not obey my decrees / and fail to **k** my commands,
91:12 to **k** you from striking your foot on a stone.
101: 6 I will **k** a protective eye on the godly, / so they
105: 4 and for his strength, / and **k** on searching.
116:14 I will **k** my promises to the LORD
116:18 I will **k** my promises to the LORD
119: 4 charged us / to **k** your commandments carefully.
119:29 **K** me from lying to myself; / give me the privilege
119:44 I will **k** on obeying your law / forever and forever.
119:95 kill me, / I will quietly **k** my mind on your decrees.
119:112 I am determined to **k** your principles,
123: 2 just as servants **k** their eyes on their master,
140: 4 O LORD, **k** me out of the hands of the wicked.
141: 3 of what I say, O LORD, / and **k** my lips sealed.
141: 9 **K** me out of the traps they have set for me,
Pr 2:11 watch over you. Understanding will **k** you safe.
3:23 They **k** you safe on your way and **k** your feet from
3:26 He will **k** your foot from being caught in a trap.
4:27 get sidetracked; **k** your feet from following evil.
6:21 **K** their words always in your heart. Tie them
6:24 and this teaching will **k** you from the immoral
11:13 but those who are trustworthy can **k** a confidence.
12:22 The LORD hates those who don't **k** their word,
14: 3 but the words of the wise **k** them out of trouble.
17:24 Sensible people **k** their eyes glued on wisdom,
17:28 Even fools are thought to be wise when they **k**
17:28 when they **k** their mouths shut, they seem
19:16 **K** the commandments and **k** your life;
20:13 **K** your eyes open, and there will be plenty to eat!
21:23 If you **k** your mouth shut, you will stay out of
22:18 For it is good to **k** these sayings deep within
22:24 **K** away from angry, short-tempered people,
23:19 and be wise. **K** your heart on the right course.
Ecc 3: 6 to lose. / A time to **k** and a time to throw away.
5: 1 of God, **k** your ears open and your mouth shut!
5: 4 in fools. **K** all the promises you make to him.
12: 4 are gone, **k** your lips tightly closed when you eat!
Isa 1:12 Why do you **k** parading through my courts with
1:20 But if you **k** turning away and refusing to listen,
8:14 He will **k** you safe. But to Israel and Judah he will
19:21 will make promises to the LORD and **k** them.
24:10 in chaos; every home is locked to **k** out looters.
26: 3 You will **k** in perfect peace all who trust in you,
26:10 They **k** doing wrong and take no notice of the
27: 3 day and night I will watch to **k** enemies away.
28:28 is easily crushed, so he doesn't **k** on pounding it.
29:15 who try to **k** him in the dark concerning what they
30:32 his people will **k** time with the music of
44:16 of the tree to roast his meat and to **k** himself warm.
56: 2 And blessed are those who **k** themselves from
56: 4 For I say this to the eunuchs who **k** my Sabbath
58: 3 You **k** right on oppressing your workers.
58: 4 What good is fasting when you **k** on fighting
58:13 "**K** the Sabbath day holy. Don't pursue your own
62: 9 You raised it, and you will **k** it,
66: 9 I would never **k** this nation from being born,"
Jer 2: 9 my case against you and will **k** on accusing you,
3: 5 and **k** right on doing all the evil you can."
6:20 **K** your expensive perfumes! I cannot accept your
7: 7 this land that I gave to your ancestors to **k** forever.
8: 5 Then why do these people **k** going along their
11: 5 so I could **k** my promise to your ancestors to give
13:14 or compassion **k** me from destroying them.' "
15:21 I will certainly **k** you safe from these wicked men.
16:11 They abandoned me. They did not **k** my law.
17:15 "What is this 'message from the LORD' you **k**
17:24 or work on the Sabbath day, and if you **k** it holy,
17:27 not listen to me and refuse to **k** the Sabbath holy,
23:17 They **k** saying to these rebels who despise my
23:35 You should **k** asking each other, 'What is the
27:14 Do not listen to the false prophets who **k** telling
34: 9 No one was to **k** a fellow Judean in bondage.
36:22 of the palace, sitting in front of a fire to **k** warm.
39:18 trusted me, I will preserve your life and **k** you safe.
50: 2 "Tell the whole world, and **k** nothing back!
51:46 For rumors will **k** coming year by year.
Eze 3:19 If you warn them and they **k** on sinning and refuse
5: 3 **K** just a bit of the hair and tie it up in your robe.
16:60 Yet I will **k** the covenant I made with you when
18:29 And yet the people of Israel **k** saying, 'The Lord is
20:11 keeping them. Yes, all those who **k** them will live!
20:20 and **k** my Sabbath days holy, for they are a sign to
20:21 They refused to **k** my laws and follow my
20:30 Do you intend to **k** prostituting yourselves by
33:24 of Judah living among the ruined cities **k** saying,
34:18 Is it not enough for you to **k** the best of the
36:20 and he couldn't **k** them safe in his own land!'
37:24 They will obey my regulations and **k** my laws.
38: 7 **K** all the armies around you mobilized, and take
46:17 the servant may **k** it only until the Year of Jubilee,
47: 6 He told me to **k** in mind what I had seen, then he
Da 5:17 "**K** your gifts or give them to someone else,
9: 4 love to those who love you and **k** your commands.
12: 4 But you, Daniel, **k** this prophecy a secret; seal up
Hos 10: 4 and make promises they don't intend to **k**.
13: 2 Now they **k** on sinning by making silver idols to
Am 4: 4 **K** on disobeying—your sins are mounting up!
5:13 So those who are wise will **k** quiet, for it is an evil
Mic 6:16 "The only laws you **k** are those of evil King Omri;
Na 2: 1 and **k** a sharp watch for the enemy attack to begin!
2: 8 someone shouts, but the people just **k** on running.
Hag 1: 6 clothing to wear, but not enough to **k** you warm.
Zec 7:11 and put their fingers in their ears to **k** from hearing.
Mt 4: 6 to **k** you from striking your foot on a stone.' "
7: 7 "**K** on asking, and you will be given what you ask
for. **K** on looking, and you will find. **K** on
11: 3 or should we **k** looking for someone else?"
16:25 If you try to **k** your life for yourself, you will lose
19:17 you can receive eternal life if you **k** the
26:41 **K** alert and pray. Otherwise temptation will
26:43 for they just couldn't **k** their eyes open.
Mk 7:24 He tried to **k** it secret that he was there, but he
8:12 "Why do you people **k** demanding a miraculous
8:35 If you try to **k** your life for yourself, you will lose
13:33 when they will happen, stay alert and **k** watch.
13:35 So **k** a sharp lookout! For you do not know when
14:38 **K** alert and pray. Otherwise, temptation will
14:40 for they just couldn't **k** their eyes open.
Lk 4:11 to **k** you from striking your foot on a stone.' "
7:19 or should we **k** looking for someone else?"
7:20 or should we **k** looking for someone else?' "
9:24 If you try to **k** your life for yourself, you will lose
11: 8 if you **k** knocking long enough, he will get up
11: 9 **k** on asking, and you will be given what you ask
for. **K** on looking, and you will find. **K** on
13:32 "Go tell that fox that I will **k** on casting out
18: 7 him day and night? Will he **k** putting them off?
21:36 **K** a constant watch. And pray that, if possible,
Jn 8:31 "You are truly my disciples if you **k** obeying my
10:24 "How long are you going to **k** us in suspense?
11:37 Why couldn't he **k** Lazarus from dying?"
12:25 Those who despise their life in this world will **k** it
17:11 Holy Father, **k** them and care for them—all those
17:15 of the world, but to **k** them safe from the evil one.
17:26 revealed you to them and will **k** on revealing you.
Ac 2:24 to life again, for death could not **k** him in its grip.
15: 1 "Unless you **k** the ancient Jewish custom of
24:23 He ordered an officer to **k** Paul in custody but to
27: 4 that made it difficult to **k** the ship on course,
Ro 2:27 uncircumcised Gentiles who **k** God's law will be
3:19 for its purpose is to **k** people from having excuses
6: 1 should we **k** on sinning so that God can show us
8:13 For if you **k** on following it, you will perish.
8:38 and even the powers of hell can't **k** God's love
10: 3 of getting right with God by trying to **k** the law.
11:27 And then I will **k** my covenant with them
13: 5 to **k** from being punished and to **k** a clear
conscience.
13: 6 so they can **k** on doing the work God intended
14:22 you are doing, but **k** it between yourself and God.
15:13 will **k** you happy and full of peace as you believe
1Co 1: 8 He will **k** you strong right up to the end, and he
will **k** you free from all blame on the great
4:11 and thirsty, without enough clothes to **k** us warm.
7:19 The important thing is to **k** God's commandments.
7:30 or wealth should not **k** anyone from doing God's
9: 9 "Do not **k** an ox from eating as it treads out the
10:13 He will **k** the temptation from becoming so strong
11: 2 that you always **k** me in your thoughts and you are
2Co 4: 9 knocked down, but we get up again and **k** going.
11: 1 I hope you will be patient with me as I **k** on talking
11:27 with cold, without enough clothing to **k** me warm.
12: 7 But to **k** me from getting puffed up, I was given a
12: 7 Satan to torment me and **k** me from getting proud.
Gal 2: 9 They encouraged us to **k** preaching to the Gentiles,
2:19 For when I tried to **k** the law, I realized I could
3:11 can ever be right with God by trying to **k** the law.
4:29 are persecuted by those who want us to **k** the law,
6:13 circumcision don't really **k** the whole law.
Eph 4: 3 Always **k** yourselves united in the Holy Spirit,
6:20 But pray that I will **k** on speaking boldly for him,
Php 1: 9 and that you will **k** on growing in your knowledge
3:12 But I **k** working toward that day when I will finally
4: 9 **K** putting into practice all you learned from me
Col 2:20 So why do you **k** on following rules of the world,
1Th 1: 9 for they themselves **k** talking about the wonderful
2:16 by trying to **k** us from preaching the Good News to
3: 3 and to **k** you from becoming disturbed by the
4: 3 to be holy, so you should **k** clear of all sexual sin.
5:17 **K** on praying.
5:22 **K** away from every kind of evil.
2Th 1:11 And so we **k** on praying for you, that our God will
2:15 and **k** a strong grip on everything we taught you
1Ti 1:19 faith in Christ, and always **k** your conscience clear.
4:16 **K** a close watch on yourself and on your teaching.
5:18 "Do not **k** an ox from eating as it treads out the
5:22 participate in the sins of others. **K** yourself pure.
2Ti 2:21 If you **k** yourself pure, you will be a utensil God
4: 5 But you should **k** a clear mind in every situation.
Phm 1: 5 because I **k** hearing of your trust in the Lord Jesus
1:13 I really wanted to **k** him here with me while I am
1:22 Please **k** a guest room ready for me, for I am
Heb 3: 6 if we **k** up our courage and remain confident in our
6:11 Our great desire is that you will **k** right on loving
10:23 we have, for God can be trusted to **k** his promise.
11:11 Abraham believed that God would **k** his promise.
11:28 commanded the people of Israel to **k** the Passover
Jas 1:25 But if you **k** looking steadily into God's perfect
5:13 you suffering? They should **k** on praying about it.
1Pe 2:11 So I warn you to **k** away from evil desires
3:10 **k** your tongue from speaking evil, / and **k** your lips
from telling lies.
3:16 and respectful way. **K** your conscience clear.
4:19 **k** on doing what is right, and trust yourself to the
2Pe 1:12 I plan to **k** on reminding you of these things—
1:13 I believe I should **k** on reminding you of these
1Jn 3: 3 And all who believe this will **k** themselves pure,
3: 6 But those who **k** on sinning have never known him
3: 8 But when people **k** on sinning, it shows they
3: 9 So they can't **k** on sinning, because they have been
5:21 **k** away from anything that might take God's place
Jude 1:24 glory to God, who is able to **k** you from stumbling,
Rev 4: 8 after day and night after night they **k** on saying,
10: 4 "**K** secret what the seven thunders said. Do not
12:17 all who **k** God's commandments and confess that
16:15 who **k** their robes ready so they will not need to

KEEPER (4) [KEEP]

1Sa 17:22 David left his things with the **k** of supplies
2Ki 10:22 And Jehu instructed the **k** of the wardrobe,
22:14 grandson of Harhas, the **k** of the Temple wardrobe.
2Ch 34:22 grandson of Harhas, the **k** of the Temple wardrobe.

KEEPING (29) [KEEP]

Ge 43:31 his face and came out, **k** himself under control.
Ex 20: 8 "Remember to observe the Sabbath day by **k** it
32:32 if not, then blot me out of the record you are **k**."
Dt 5:12 " 'Observe the Sabbath day by **k** it holy,
7: 8 because he was **k** the oath he had sworn to your
27:10 So obey the LORD your God by **k** all these
28: 1 "If you fully obey the LORD your God by **k** all
Jos 3: 4 **k** a clear distance between you and the Ark.
Jdg 3:16 it to his right thigh, **k** it hidden under his clothing.
1Sa 25:33 Bless you for **k** me from murdering the man
1Ki 9: 4 my commands and **k** my laws and regulations,
2Ki 23: 3 He pledged to obey the LORD by **k** all his
2Ch 30: 4 This plan for **k** the Passover seemed right to the
34:31 He pledged to obey the LORD by **k** all his
Job 39:29 there it hunts its prey, **k** watch with piercing eyes.
Ps 119:80 May I be blameless in **k** your principles; / then I
Pr 15: 3 **k** his eye on both the evil and the good.
Isa 58:11 your life when you are dry and **k** you healthy,
Eze 17:14 Only by **k** her treaty with Babylon could Israel
18: 7 not **k** the items given in pledge by poor debtors,
20:11 I gave them my laws so they could live by **k** them.
Ro 9:31 so hard to get right with God by **k** the law,
9:32 they were trying to get right with God by **k** the law
Gal 2:21 For if we could be saved by **k** the law, then there
3: 2 Did you receive the Holy Spirit by **k** the law?
3:18 For if the inheritance could be received only by **k**
5: 4 to make yourselves right with God by **k** the law,
Heb 12: 2 We do this by **k** our eyes on Jesus, on whom our
1Jn 5: 3 Loving God means **k** his commandments,

KEEPS (26) [KEEP]

Dt 7: 9 He is the faithful God who **k** his covenant for a
Ne 1: 5 and awesome God who **k** his covenant of unfailing
9:32 who **k** his covenant of unfailing love,
Job 21:32 to the grave, an honor guard **k** watch at their tomb.
33:17 them to change their minds; he **k** them from pride.
33:18 He **k** them from the grave, from crossing over the
Ps 33:19 from death / and **k** them alive in times of famine.
41: 2 and **k** them alive. / He gives them prosperity
54: 4 is my helper. / The Lord is the one who **k** me alive!
55:18 He rescues me and **k** me safe / from the battle
66: 9 in his hands, / and he **k** our feet from stumbling.
75: 3 I am the one who **k** its foundations firm.
121: 7 The LORD **k** you from all evil / and preserves
121: 8 The LORD **k** watch over you as you come
138: 6 the humble, / but he **k** his distance from the proud.
146: 6 He is the one who **k** every promise forever,
Pr 24:12 He **k** watch over your soul, and he knows you
Isa 21:11 Someone from Edom **k** calling to me, "Watchman,
Eze 18:19 For if the child does what is right and **k** my laws,
Lk 9:39 An evil spirit **k** seizing him, making him scream.
11:29 and this evil generation **k** asking me to show them
Ro 2: 9 and calamity for everyone who **k** on sinning—
1Co 3:13 through the fire to see whether or not it **k** its value.
13: 5 and it **k** no record of when it has been wronged.
2Co 10: 5 proud argument that **k** people from knowing God.
Jas 2:10 And the person who **k** all of the laws except one is

KEHELATHAH (2)

Nu 33:22 They left Rissah and camped at **K**.
33:23 They left **K** and camped at Mount Shepher.

KEILAH (18)

Jos 15:44 **K**, Aczib, and Mareshah—nine towns with their
1Sa 23: 1 were at **K** stealing grain from the threshing floors.
23: 2 "Yes, go and save **K**," the LORD told him.
23: 3 We certainly don't want to go to **K** to fight the
23: 4 and again the LORD replied, "Go down to **K**,
23: 5 So David and his men went to **K**. They slaughtered
23: 5 all their livestock and rescued the people of **K**.
23: 6 Abiathar the priest went to **K** with David,
23: 7 Saul soon learned that David was at **K**. "Good!"
23: 8 So Saul mobilized his entire army to march to **K**
23:10 planning to come and destroy **K** because I am here.
23:11 Will the men of **K** surrender me to him? And will
23:12 "Will these men of **K** really betray me and my
23:13 left **K** and began roaming the countryside.
23:13 David had escaped, so he didn't go to **K** after all.
1Ch 4:19 One of her sons was the father of **K** the Garmite,
Ne 3:17 the leader of half the district of **K**,
3:18 the leader of the other half of the district of **K**.

KELAIAH (1) [KELITA]

Ezr 10:23 Jozabad, Shimei, **K** (also called Kelita), Pethahiah,

KELAL (1)

Ezr 10:30 Adna, **K**, Benaiah, Maaseiah, Mattaniah, Bezalel,

KELITA (3) [KELAIAH]

Ezr 10:23 Jozabad, Shimei, Kelaiah (also called **K**),
Ne 8: 7 Hodiah, Maaseiah, **K**, Azariah, Jozabad, Hanan,
10:10 Shebaniah, Hodiah, **K**, Pelaiah, Hanan,

KELUB (2)
1Ch 4:11 **K** (the brother of Shuhah) was the father of Mehir.
27:26 Ezri son of **K** was in charge of the field workers

KELUHI (1)
Ezr 10:35 Benaiah, Bedeiah, **K**,

KEMUEL (3)
Ge 22:21 was Buz, followed by **K** (the father of Aram),
Nu 34:24 Ephraim son of Joseph | **K** son of Shiphtan
1Ch 27:17 Levi | Hashabiah son of **K** / Aaron (the priests)

KENAANAH (5)
1Ki 22:11 One of them, Zedekiah son of **K**, made some iron
22:24 Then Zedekiah son of **K** walked up to Micaiah
1Ch 7:10 Benjamin, Ehud, **K**, Zethan, Tarshish,
2Ch 18:10 One of them, Zedekiah son of **K**, made some iron
18:23 Then Zedekiah son of **K** walked up to Micaiah

KENAN (7)
Ge 5:9 When Enosh was 90 years old, his son **K** was born.
5:10 After the birth of **K**, Enosh lived another 815
5:12 When **K** was 70 years old, his son Mahalalel was
5:13 **K** lived another 840 years, and he had other sons
1Ch 1:2 **K**, Mahalalel, Jared,
Lk 3:37 the son of Mahalalel. / Mahalalel was the son of **K**.
3:38 **K** was the son of Enosh. / Enosh was the son of

KENANI (1)
Ne 9:4 Shebaniah, Bunni, Sherebiah, Bani, and **K**.

KENANIAH (3)
1Ch 15:22 **K**, the head Levite, was chosen as the choir leader
15:27 carried the Ark, the singers, and **K** the song leader.
26:29 From the clan of Izhar came **K**. He and his sons

KENATH (2) [NOBAH]
Nu 32:42 a man named Nobah captured the town of **K**
1Ch 2:23 and also took **K** and its sixty surrounding villages.)

KENAZ (11)
Ge 36:11 Eliphaz were Teman, Omar, Zepho, Gatam, and **K**.
36:15 leaders of the clans of Teman, Omar, Zepho, **K**,
36:42 **K**, Teman, Mibzar,
Jos 15:17 Othniel, the son of Caleb's brother **K**, was the one
Jdg 1:13 Othniel, the son of Caleb's younger brother **K**,
3:9 the son of Caleb's younger brother, **K**.
3:11 land for forty years. Then Othniel son of **K** died.
1Ch 1:36 Omar, Zepho, Gatam, **K**, and Amalek, who was
1:53 **K**, Teman, Mibzar,
4:13 The sons of **K** were Othniel and Seraiah.
4:15 were Iru, Elah, and Naam. The son of Elah was **K**.

KENEZITE [KJV] See KENIZZITE(S)

KENITE (3) [KENITES]
Jdg 4:11 Now Heber the **K**, a descendant of Moses'
4:17 ran to the tent of Jael, the wife of Heber the **K**,
5:24 "Most blessed is Jael, / the wife of Heber the **K**.

KENITES (9) [KENITE]
Ge 15:19 the land of the **K**, Kenizzites, Kadmonites,
Nu 24:21 Then he looked over at the **K** and prophesied:
24:22 But the **K** will be destroyed / when Assyria takes
Jdg 1:16 When the tribe of Judah left Jericho, the **K**,
1Sa 15:6 Saul sent this message to the **K**: "Move away from
15:6 up from Egypt." So the **K** packed up and left.
27:10 the south of Judah, the Jerahmeelites, and the **K**."
30:29 the towns of the Jerahmeelites, the towns of the **K**,
1Ch 2:55 All these were **K** who descended from Hammath,

KENIZZITE (3) [KENIZZITES]
Nu 32:12 only exceptions are Caleb son of Jephunneh the **K**
Jos 14:6 led by Caleb son of Jephunneh the **K**, came to
14:14 the descendants of Caleb son of Jephunneh the **K**

KENIZZITES (1) [KENIZZITE]
Ge 15:19 the land of the Kenites, **K**, Kadmonites,

KEPHAR-AMMONI (1)
Jos 18:24 **K**, Ophni, and Geba—twelve towns with their

KEPHIRAH (4)
Jos 9:17 were Gibeon, **K**, Beeroth, and Kiriath-jearim.
18:26 Mizpeh, **K**, Mozah,
Ezr 2:25 peoples of Kiriath-jearim, **K**, and Beeroth | 743
Ne 7:29 peoples of Kiriath-jearim, **K**, and Beeroth | 743

KEPT (142) [KEEP]
Ge 6:20 and small alike, will come to you to be **k** alive.
16:2 "The LORD has **k** me from having any
19:29 had listened to Abraham's request and **k** Lot safe,
20:6 "That is why I **k** you from sinning against me;
24:20 She **k** carrying water to the camels until they had
39:10 She **k** putting pressure on him day after day,
39:10 and he **k** out of her way as much as possible.
39:16 She **k** the shirt with her, and when her husband
48:16 and the angel who has **k** me from all harm—
Ex 2:2 baby he was and **k** him hidden for three months.
12:17 for you, to be **k** from generation to generation.
16:20 them didn't listen and **k** some of it until morning.
21:29 in the past, yet the bull was not **k** under control.
27:20 the lampstand, so it can be **k** burning continually.
27:21 of Israel, and it must be **k** by all future generations.
30:21 to be **k** from generation to generation."
34:25 lamb may be **k** over until the following morning.
Lev 6:9 and the altar fire must be **k** burning all night.
6:12 Meanwhile, the fire on the altar must be **k** burning;
6:13 the fire must be **k** burning on the altar at all times.
10:9 for you, and it must be **k** by all future generations.
17:7 law for them, to be **k** generation after generation.
23:41 for you, and it must be **k** by all future generations.
24:2 the lampstand, so it can be **k** burning continually.
24:3 for you, and it must be **k** by all future generations.
Nu 18:9 of the most holy offerings that is **k** from the fire.
19:9 They will be **k** there for the people of Israel to use
20:9 He took the staff from the place where it was **k**
24:11 but the LORD has **k** you from your reward."
33:2 Moses **k** a written record of their progress.
Dt 3:7 But we **k** all the livestock for ourselves and took
11:4 and how he has **k** them devastated to this very day!
Jos 4:23 your eyes, and he **k** it dry until you were all across,
6:24 or iron were **k** for the treasury of the LORD's
8:26 For Joshua **k** holding out his spear until everyone
8:27 for the Israelites **k** these for themselves,
9:21 So the Israelites **k** their promise to the Gibeonites.
14:10 the LORD has **k** me alive and well as he
Jdg 7:8 But he **k** the three hundred men with him.
11:39 her father **k** his vow, and she died a virgin.
13:1 who **k** them in subjection for forty years.
14:17 with him and **k** it up for the rest of the celebration.
16:2 They **k** quiet during the night, saying to
19:7 but his father-in-law **k** urging him to stay, so he
1Sa 15:9 Agag's life and **k** the best of the sheep and cattle,
18:2 From that day on Saul **k** David with him at the
18:9 So from that time on Saul **k** a jealous eye on
23:25 in the wilderness of Maon. But Saul **k** after him.
25:26 since the LORD has **k** you from murdering
25:34 the God of Israel, who has **k** me from hurting you,
25:39 paid back Nabal and **k** me from doing it myself.
27:1 But David **k** thinking to himself, "Someday Saul
30:23 He has **k** us safe and helped us defeat the enemy.
2Sa 2:21 But Asahel refused and **k** right on chasing Abner.
13:27 But Absalom **k** on pressing the king until he finally
16:13 and Shimei **k** pace with them on a nearby hillside,
18:9 His mule **k** going and left him dangling in the air.
19:4 covered his face with his hands and **k** on weeping,
22:22 For I have **k** the ways of the LORD; / I have not
22:24 blameless before God; / I have **k** myself from sin.
1Ki 2:43 Then why haven't you **k** your oath to the LORD
8:15 who has **k** the promise he made to my father,
8:24 You have **k** your promise to your servant David,
9:19 cities where his chariots and horses could be **k**.
11:11 "Since you have not **k** my covenant and have
2Ki 2:17 But they **k** urging him until he was embarrassed,
25:2 Jerusalem was **k** under siege until the eleventh
1Ch 28:11 Ark's cover—the place of atonement—would be **k**.
2Ch 6:4 who has **k** the promise he made to my father,
6:15 You have **k** your promise to your servant David,
8:6 cities where his chariots and horses could be **k**.
26:10 because he **k** great herds of livestock in the
35:18 None of the kings of Israel had ever **k** a Passover
Ezr 9:1 have not **k** themselves separate from the other
Ne 6:19 They **k** telling me what a wonderful man Tobiah
Est 9:28 and **k** from generation to generation
Job 5:24 You will know that your home is **k** safe. When you
22:6 then **k** the clothing he gave you as a pledge.
32:1 to him because he **k** insisting on his innocence.
Ps 17:4 which have **k** me from going along with cruel
18:21 For I have **k** the ways of the LORD; / I have not
18:23 blameless before God; / I have **k** myself from sin.
30:3 You **k** me from falling into the pit of death.
31:21 He **k** me safe when my city was under attack.
40:10 I have not **k** this good news hidden in my heart;
56:13 me from death; / you have **k** my feet from slipping.
73:13 Was it for nothing that I **k** my heart pure / and **k** myself from doing wrong?
78:17 Yet they **k** on with their sin, / rebelling against the
78:32 But in spite of this, the people **k** on sinning.
78:53 He **k** them safe so they were not afraid;
119:100 than my elders, / for I have **k** your commandments.
130:3 LORD, if you **k** a record of our sins, / who,
Jer 7:24 They **k** on doing whatever they wanted,
27:21 says about the precious things **k** in the Temple
44:5 They **k** right on burning incense to these gods.
52:5 Jerusalem was **k** under siege until the eleventh
La 3:22 By his mercies we have been **k** from complete
Eze 44:8 You have not **k** the laws I gave you concerning
Da 7:11 I **k** watching until the fourth beast was killed
7:28 was pale with fear, but I **k** these things to myself.
Hos 7:4 They are like an oven that is **k** hot even while the
Am 4:7 "I **k** the rain from falling when you needed it the
Zec 8:19 and times of mourning you have **k** in early
Mt 14:4 John **k** telling Herod, "It is illegal for you to marry
27:36 Then they sat around and **k** guard as he hung there.
Mk 5:32 But he **k** on looking around to see who had done it.
6:18 John **k** telling Herod, "It is illegal for you to marry
6:20 and holy man, so he **k** him under his protection.
6:41 he **k** giving the bread and fish to the disciples to
9:10 So they **k** it to themselves, but they often asked
Lk 7:38 Then she **k** kissing his feet and putting perfume on
8:31 The demons **k** begging Jesus not to send them into
9:16 he **k** giving the bread and fish to the disciples to
19:20 amount of money and said, 'I hid it and **k** it safe.
19:40 He replied, "If they **k** quiet, the stones along the
24:16 because God **k** them from recognizing him.
Jn 2:10 But you have **k** the best until now!"
3:23 and people **k** coming to him for baptism.
6:2 And a huge crowd **k** following him wherever he
7:11 at the festival and **k** asking if anyone had seen him.
8:7 They **k** demanding an answer, so he stood up again
9:9 And the beggar **k** saying, "I am the same man!"
17:6 you gave them to me; and they have **k** your word.
17:12 During my time here, I have **k** them safe. I guarded
Ac 1:6 they **k** asking him, "Lord, are you going to free
5:3 and you **k** some of the money for yourself.
19:24 goddess Artemis. He **k** many craftsmen busy.
19:34 started shouting again and **k** it up for two hours:
22:20 I **k** the coats they laid aside as they stoned him.'
23:35 Then the governor ordered him **k** in the prison at
Ro 10:21 but they **k** disobeying me and arguing with me."
16:25 a plan **k** secret from the beginning of time.
2Co 11:32 the governor under King Aretas **k** guards at the
Gal 3:23 We were **k** in protective custody, so to speak,
Eph 3:9 of all things, had **k** secret from the beginning.
Col 1:26 This message was **k** secret for centuries
1Th 5:23 and body be **k** blameless until that day when our
Heb 11:27 Moses **k** right on going because he **k** his eyes on the one who is invisible.
1Pe 1:4 It is **k** in heaven for you, pure and undefiled,
Jude 1:6 God has **k** them chained in prisons of darkness,

KERAN (2)
Ge 36:26 of Dishon were Hemdan, Eshban, Ithran, and **K**.
1Ch 1:41 of Dishon were Hemdan, Eshban, Ithran, and **K**.

KERCHIEFS [KJV] See (MAGIC) VEILS

KEREN-HAPPUCH (1)
Job 42:14 the second Keziah, and the third **K**.

KERETHITES (2)
1Sa 30:14 We were on our way back from raiding the **K** in
Eze 25:16 I will wipe out the **K** and utterly destroy the people

KERIOTH (2)
Jer 48:24 and on **K** and Bozrah—all the cities of Moab,
Am 2:2 and all the fortresses in **K** will be destroyed.

KERIOTH-HEZRON (1) [HAZOR]
Jos 15:25 Hazor-hadattah, **K** (that is, Hazor),

KERITH (2)
1Ki 17:3 and hide by **K** Brook at a place east of where it
17:5 LORD had told him and camped beside **K** Brook.

KERNEL (3) [KERNELS]
Ge 41:5 on one stalk, with every **k** well formed and plump.
Am 9:9 is sifted in a sieve, yet not one true **k** will be lost.
Jn 12:24 truth is, a **k** of wheat must be planted in the soil.

KERNELS (3) [KERNEL]
Lev 2:14 bring **k** of new grain that have been roasted on a
23:14 or fresh **k** on that day until after you have brought
Jn 12:24 But its death will produce many new **k**—a plentiful

KEROS (2)
Ezr 2:44 **K**, Siaha, Padon,
Ne 7:47 **K**, Siaha, Padon,

KERUB (2)
Ezr 2:59 of Tel-melah, Tel-harsha, **K**, Addan, and Immer.
Ne 7:61 of Tel-melah, Tel-harsha, **K**, Addan, and Immer.

KESALON (1) [JEARIM]
Jos 15:10 passed along to the town of **K** on the northern

KESED (1)
Ge 22:22 **K**, Hazo, Pildash, Jidlaph, and Bethuel.

KESIL (1)
Jos 15:30 Eltolad, **K**, Hormah,

KESULLOTH (1) [KISLOTH-TABOR]
Jos 19:18 included the following towns: Jezreel, **K**, Shunem,

KETTLE (4) [KETTLES]
Lev 6:28 If a bronze **k** is used, it must be scoured and rinsed
2Ki 4:38 "Put on a large **k** and make some stew for these
4:39 and put them into the **k** without realizing they were
4:41 Then he threw it into the **k** and said, "Now it's all

KETTLES (2) [KETTLE]
2Ch 35:13 **k**, and pans, and brought them out quickly
Mk 7:4 their ceremony of washing cups, pitchers, and **k**.)

KETURAH (4)
Ge 25:1 Now Abraham married again. **K** was his new wife,
25:4 were all descendants of Abraham through **K**.
1Ch 1:32 The sons of **K**, Abraham's concubine,
1:33 these were sons of Abraham by his concubine **K**.

KEY (8) [KEYS]
Jdg 3:25 a long delay, they became concerned and got a **k**.

Isa 22:22 I will give him the **k** to the house of David—
33: 6 The fear of the LORD is the **k** to this treasure.
Lk 11:52 For you hide the **k** to knowledge from the people.
Ro 4:16 So that's why faith is the **k**! God's promise is
Rev 3: 7 and true. He is the one who has the **k** of David.
9: 1 and he was given the **k** to the shaft of the
20: 1 down from heaven with the **k** to the bottomless pit

KEYS (2) [KEY]

Mt 16:19 And I will give you the **k** of the Kingdom of
Rev 1:18 and ever! And I hold the **k** of death and the grave.

KEZIAH (1)

Job 42:14 the second **K**, and the third Keren-happuch.

KEZIB (1)

Ge 38: 5 the time of Shelah's birth, they were living at **K**.

KIBROTH-HATTAAVAH (4)

Nu 11:34 So that place was called **K**—"the graves of
33:16 They left the wilderness of Sinai and camped at **K**.
33:17 They left **K** and camped at Hazeroth.
Dt 9:22 the LORD angry at Taberah, Massah, and **K**.

KIBZAIM (1) [JOKMEAM]

Jos 21:22 **K**, and Beth-horon—four towns.

KICKED (3) [KICKING]

2Sa 3: 8 "Am I a Judean dog to be **k** around like this?"
Job 24: 4 The poor are **k** aside; the needy must hide together
Jer 31:19 then I was sorry. I **k** myself for my stupidity!

KICKING (2) [KICKED]

Eze 16: 6 you there, helplessly **k** about in your own blood.
16:22 lay naked in a field, **k** about in your own blood.

KIDNAPPED (2) [KIDNAPPER]

Ge 40:15 For I was **k** from my homeland, the land of the
Jdg 21:23 They **k** the women who took part in the celebration

KIDNAPPER (1) [KIDNAPPED, KIDNAPPERS, KIDNAPS]

Dt 24: 7 treats him as a slave or sells him, the **k** must die.

KIDNAPPERS (1) [KIDNAPPER]

Ex 21:16 "**K** must be killed, whether they are caught in

KIDNAPS (1) [KIDNAPPER]

Dt 24: 7 "If anyone **k** a fellow Israelite and treats him as a

KIDNEYS (15)

Ex 29:13 long lobe of the liver and the two **k** with their fat,
29:22 the two **k** with their fat, and the right thigh.
Lev 3: 4 the two **k** with the fat around them near the loins,
3: 4 of the liver, which is to be removed with the **k**.
3:10 the two **k** with the fat around them near the loins,
3:10 of the liver, which is to be removed with the **k**.
3:15 the two **k** with the fat around them near the loins,
3:15 of the liver, which is to be removed with the **k**.
4: 9 the two **k** with the fat around them near the loins,
7: 4 the two **k** with the fat around them near the loins,
7: 4 of the liver, which is to be removed with the **k**.
8:16 the lobe of the liver, and the two **k** and their fat,
8:25 the lobe of the liver, and the two **k** with their fat,
9:10 Then he burned on the altar the fat, the **k**,
9:19 along with the **k** and the lobe of the liver.

KIDRON (13) [SHAVEH]

2Sa 15:23 They crossed the **K** Valley and then went out
1Ki 2:37 On the day you cross the **K** Valley, you will surely
15:13 cut down the pole and burned it in the **K** Valley.
2Ki 23: 4 outside Jerusalem on the terraces of the **K** Valley,
23: 6 and took it outside Jerusalem to the **K** Valley,
23:12 to bits and scattered the pieces in the **K** Valley.
2Ch 15:16 the pole, broke it up, and burned it in the **K** Valley.
29:16 From there the Levites carted it all out to the **K**
30:14 incense altars and threw them into the **K** Valley.
33:14 from west of the Gihon Spring in the **K** Valley to
Ne 2:15 So I went up the **K** Valley instead,
Jer 31:40 and all the fields out to the **K** Valley on the east as
Jn 18: 1 Jesus crossed the **K** Valley with his disciples

KIDS (1)

Isa 5:17 among the ruins; lambs and **k** will pasture there.

KILEAB (2)

2Sa 3: 3 The second was **K**, whose mother was Abigail,
1Ch 3: 1 The second was **K**, whose mother was Abigail

KILION (3)

Ru 1: 2 was Naomi. Their two sons were Mahlon and **K**.
1: 5 both Mahlon and **K** died. This left Naomi alone,
4: 9 all the property of Elimelech, **K**, and Mahlon.

KILL (285) [KILLED, KILLING, KILLS]

Ge 4:14 All who see me will try to **k** me!"
4:15 The LORD replied, "They will not **k** you, for I
4:15 on Cain to warn anyone who might try to **k** him.
9: 5 Animals that **k** people must die, and any person
9: 6 for to **k** a person is to **k** a living being made in
9:11 never to send another flood to **k** all living creatures
12:12 is his wife. Let's **k** him; then we can have her!'
20: 4 so he said, "Lord, will you **k** an innocent man?
20:11 'They will want my wife and will **k** me to get her.'
22:10 and lifted it up to **k** his son as a sacrifice to the
26: 7 He thought they would **k** him to get her,
26: 9 "Because I was afraid someone would **k** me to get
27:41 will soon be dead and gone. Then I will **k** Jacob."
27:42 and told him, "Esau is threatening to **k** you.
32:11 I am afraid that he is coming to **k** me, along with
37:18 him in the distance and made plans to **k** him.
37:20 let's **k** him and throw him into a deep pit.
37:21 to Joseph's rescue. "Let's not **k** him," he said.
38:25 But as they were taking her out to **k** her, she sent
42:37 "You may **k** my two sons if I don't bring
Ex 1:16 give birth, **k** all the boys as soon as they are born.
2:14 Do you plan to **k** me as you killed that Egyptian
4:19 for all those who wanted to **k** you are dead."
4:23 be warned! I will **k** your firstborn son!' "
4:24 LORD confronted Moses and was about to **k** him.
5:21 You have given them an excuse to **k** us!"
12:12 and **k** all the firstborn sons and firstborn male
22:24 forth against you, and I will **k** you with the sword.
32:12 so he could **k** them and wipe them from the face of
34:20 you must **k** the donkey by breaking its neck.
Lev 17:13 If you go hunting and **k** an animal or bird that is
26:22 I will release wild animals that will **k** your children
Nu 16:13 and honey, to **k** us here in this wilderness,
22:29 "If I had a sword with me, I would **k** you!"
31:17 Now **k** all the boys and all the women who have
Dt 19: 6 and **k** the person who caused the death.
20:13 God hands it over to you, **k** every man in the town.
27:25 'Cursed is anyone who accepts payment to **k** an
Jos 7: 7 River if you are going to let the Amorites **k** us?
9:26 Joshua did not allow the people of Israel to **k** them.
Jdg 8:19 I wouldn't **k** you if you hadn't killed them."
8:20 to Jether, his oldest son, he said, "**K** them!"
9:54 young armor bearer, "Draw your sword and **k** me!
12: 6 and **k** him at the shallows of the Jordan River.
13:23 his wife said, "If the LORD were going to **k** us,
15:12 "But promise that you won't **k** me yourselves."
15:13 the Philistines," they replied. "We won't **k** you."
16: 2 the light of morning comes, we will **k** him."
18:25 they might get angry and **k** you and your family."
20: 5 planning to **k** me, and they raped my concubine
20:31 had done before, they began to **k** the Israelites.
21:10 to Jabesh-gilead with orders to **k** everyone there,
1Sa 5:10 bringing the Ark of the God of Israel here to **k** us,
5:11 Israel back to its own country, or it will **k** us all."
11:12 over us? Bring them here, and we will **k** them!"
14: 9 they say to us, 'Stay where you are or we'll **k** you,'
14:34 'Bring the cattle and sheep here to **k** them
16: 2 can I do that? If Saul hears about it, he will **k** me."
17: 9 If your man is able to **k** me, then we will be your slaves. But if I **k** him, you will be our slaves!
17:46 and I will **k** you and cut off your head.
17:51 David used it to **k** the giant and cut off his head.
18:17 and let them **k** him rather than doing it myself."
19: 5 the time he risked his life to **k** the Philistine giant
19:10 Saul hurled his spear at David in an attempt to **k**
19:11 They were told to **k** David when he came out the
19:15 Saul ordered, "so I can **k** him as he lies there!"
19:17 "He threatened to **k** me if I didn't help him."
20: 1 your father that he is so determined to **k** me?"
20: 7 then you will know he was planning to **k** me.
20: 8 or **k** me yourself if I have sinned against your
20: 9 slightest notion my father was planning to **k** you,
20:13 may the LORD **k** me if I don't warn you so you
20:31 be king. Now go and get him so I can **k** him!"
20:33 hurled his spear at Jonathan, intending to **k** him.
20:33 that his father was really determined to **k** David.
22: 8 own son—encouraging David to try and **k** me!"
22:17 "**K** these priests of the LORD, for they are allies
22:17 But Saul's men refused to **k** the LORD's priests.
22:23 own life, for the same person wants to **k** us both."
23:15 on the way to Ziph to search for him and **k** him.
24: 7 rebuked his men and did not let them **k** Saul.
24:10 and some of my men told me to **k** you, but I spared
24:11 a piece of your robe! I cut it off, but I didn't **k** you.
24:11 even though you have been hunting for me to **k**
24:21 that when that happens you will not **k** my family
25:35 home in peace. We will not **k** your husband."
26: 9 "No!" David said. "Don't **k** him. For who can
26:11 But the LORD forbid that I should **k** the one he
26:15 master the king when someone came to **k** him?
26:23 and I refused to **k** you even when the LORD
30:15 "If you swear by God's name that you will not **k**
31: 4 and **k** me before these pagan Philistines run me
2Sa 1:14 "Were you not afraid to **k** the LORD's anointed
1:15 Then David said to one of his men, "**K** him!"
2:22 able to face your brother Joab if I have to **k** you!"
3:35 "May God **k** me if I eat anything before
4: 8 the son of your enemy Saul who tried to **k** you.
4:12 So David ordered his young men to **k** them,
13:28 until Amnon gets drunk; then at my signal, **k** him!
16:11 the other officers, "My own son is trying to **k** me.
17: 2 will run away. Then I will **k** only the king,
18:11 "You saw him there and didn't **k** him?
21: 2 Israel had sworn not to **k** them, but Saul, in his
21:16 He had cornered David and was about to **k** him.
23: 8 He once used his spear to **k** eight hundred enemy
23:18 He once used his spear to **k** three hundred enemy
1Ki 1:51 "Let Solomon swear today that he will not **k** me!"
2: 8 I swore by the LORD that I would not **k** him.
2:26 You deserve to die, but I will not **k** you now,
2:31 "**K** him there beside the altar and bury him.
3:26 Give her the child—please do not **k** him!"
3:27 Then the king said, "Do not **k** him, but give the
11:40 Solomon tried to **k** Jeroboam, but he fled to King
12:27 They will **k** me and make him their king instead."
13:26 his word by causing the lion to attack and **k** him."
14:10 bring disaster on your dynasty and **k** all your sons,
16: 9 half of the royal chariots, made plans to **k** him.
18: 4 Once when Jezebel had tried to **k** all the LORD's
18:12 Ahab comes and cannot find you, he will **k** me.
18:13 about the time when Jezebel was trying to **k** the
19: 2 "May the gods also **k** me if by this time tomorrow
19:10 am left, and now they are trying to **k** me, too."
19:14 am left, and now they are trying to **k** me, too."
20:36 a lion will **k** you as soon as you leave me."
2Ki 5: 7 leper to heal! Am I God, that I can **k** and give life?
6:21 shouted to Elisha, "My father, should I **k** them?"
6:22 "Do we **k** prisoners of war? Give them food
6:29 next day I said, '**K** your son so we can eat him,'
6:31 "May God **k** me if I don't execute Elisha son of
6:32 the leaders, "A murderer has sent a man to **k** me.
7: 4 But if they **k** us, we would have died anyway."
8:12 **k** their young men, dash their children to the
10:25 his guards and officers, "Go in and **k** all of them.
11:15 the Temple, and **k** anyone who tries to rescue her.
11:15 Do not **k** her here in the Temple of the LORD."
14: 6 he did not **k** the children of the assassins,
17:25 the LORD sent lions among them to **k** some of
1Ch 11:11 He once used his spear to **k** three hundred enemy
11:20 He once used his spear to **k** three hundred enemy
2Ch 23:14 the Temple, and **k** anyone who tries to rescue her.
23:14 Do not **k** her here in the Temple of the LORD."
24:21 Then the leaders plotted to **k** Zechariah, and by
24:25 But his own officials decided to **k** him for
25: 4 he did not **k** the children of the assassins,
Ne 4:11 down on them and **k** them and end their work."
6:10 Your enemies are coming to **k** you tonight."
Est 7: 4 and I have been sold to those who would **k**,
8:11 They were allowed to **k**, slaughter, and annihilate
Job 6: 9 I wish he would reach out his hand and **k** me.
13:15 God might **k** me, but I cannot wait. I am going to
20:16 suck the poison of snakes. The viper will **k** him.
24:14 The murderer rises in the early dawn to **k** the poor
Ps 35: 4 Humiliate and disgrace those trying to **k** me;
37:14 string their bows / to **k** the poor and the oppressed,
37:32 spy on the godly, / waiting for an excuse to **k** them.
54: 3 are attacking me; / violent men are trying to **k** me.
56: 6 on me— / watching my every step, eager to **k** me.
59: T soldiers to watch David's house in order to **k** him.
59: 4 Despite my innocence, they prepare to **k** me.
59:11 Don't **k** them, for my people soon forget such
62: 3 against one man— / all of them trying to **k** me.
71:10 against me. / They are plotting together to **k** me.
86:14 up against me; / violent people are trying to **k** me.
94: 6 They **k** widows and foreigners / and murder
106:26 he swore / that he would **k** them in the wilderness,
118:13 You did your best to **k** me, O my enemy,
119:95 Though the wicked hide along the way to **k** me,
141: 8 You are my refuge; don't let them **k** me.
Pr 1:11 "Come and join us. Let's hide and **k** someone!
6:17 a lying tongue, / hands that **k** the innocent,
18:21 for the tongue can **k** or nourish life.
Ecc 3: 3 A time to **k** and a time to heal. / A time to tear
Isa 7:18 you like flies. Like bees, they will sting and **k**.
14:21 **K** the children of this sinner! Do not let them rise
33:11 Your own breath will turn to fire and **k** you.
Jer 4:30 no good! Your allies despise you and will **k** you.
6:25 The enemy is everywhere, and they are ready to **k**.
9: 8 peace to their neighbors while planning to **k** them.
11:19 I had no idea that they were planning to **k** me!
11:19 "Let's **k** him, so his name will be forgotten
11:21 They said they would **k** me if I did not stop
15: 3 "I will send the sword to **k**, the dogs to drag away,
15:15 Don't let them **k** me! Be merciful to me and give
18:20 They have set a trap to **k** me, though I pleaded for
20:17 for he did not **k** me at birth. Oh, that I had died in
22:25 I will hand you over to those who seek to **k** you,
26: 8 the Temple mobbed him. "**K** him!" they shouted.
26:15 But if you **k** me, rest assured that you will be
26:19 and the people **k** him for saying this?
26:19 If we **k** Jeremiah, who knows what will happen to
26:21 he was saying, the king sent someone to **k** him.
34:20 will give you to your enemies, and they will **k** you.
38:15 "If I tell you the truth, you will **k** me.
38:16 I will not **k** you or hand you over to the men who
38:25 talking about. If you don't tell us, we will **k** you.'
40:15 and volunteered to **k** Ishmael secretly.
44:30 of Egypt, over to his enemies who want to **k** him,
50:21 Pursue, **k**, and completely destroy them, as I have
La 2: 4 His strength is used against them to **k** their finest
Eze 6: 4 I will **k** your people in front of your idols.
9: 5 and **k** everyone whose forehead is not marked.
9: 6 **K** them all—old and young, girls and women
9: 7 "Fill its courtyards with the bodies of those you **k**!
11:13 are you going to **k** everyone in Israel?"
13:19 to listen to lies, you **k** those who should not die,
14:15 animals to devastate the land and **k** the people.
21:22 they will go against the gates, shouting for the **k**.
23:47 enemies will stone them and **k** them with swords.
28: 9 then boast, 'I am a god!' to those who **k** you?
Da 2:13 men were sent to find and **k** Daniel and his friends.
2:14 commander of the king's guard, came to **k** them,
2:24 Daniel said to him, "Don't **k** the wise men.
5:19 He killed those he wanted to **k** and spared those he
Hos 4: 2 You curse and lie and **k** and steal and commit
7: 7 They **k** their kings one after another, and no one
Am 9: 4 I will command the sword to **k** them there.

Jnh 4:3 Just **k** me now, LORD! I'd rather be dead than
Zep 1:9 and **k** to fill their masters' homes with loot.
Hag 2:22 horses will fall, and their riders will **k** each other.
Mt 2:13 because Herod is going to try to **k** the child."
2:16 He sent soldiers to **k** all the boys in and around
2:20 because those who were trying to **k** the child are
10:28 "Don't be afraid of those who want to **k** you.
10:28 They can only **k** your body; they cannot touch your
21:38 let's **k** him and get the estate for ourselves!'
23:34 You will **k** some by crucifixion and whip others in
Mk 9:22 him fall into the fire or into water, trying to **k** him.
10:34 spit on him, beat him with their whips, and **k** him,
11:18 Jesus had done, they began planning how to **k** him.
12:7 Let's **k** him and get the estate for ourselves!'
12:9 he will come and **k** them all and lease the vineyard
Lk 11:49 and they will **k** some and persecute the others.'
12:4 don't be afraid of those who want to **k** you.
12:4 They can only **k** the body; they cannot do any
12:5 who has the power to **k** people and then throw
13:31 to live, because Herod Antipas wants to **k** you!"
15:23 And **k** the calf we have been fattening in the pen.
18:33 They will whip him and **k** him, but on the third day
19:47 leaders of the people began planning how to **k** him.
20:14 Let's **k** him and get the estate for ourselves!'
20:16 he will come and **k** them all and lease the vineyard
22:2 But they wanted to **k** him without starting a riot,
23:18 "**K** him, and release Barabbas to us!"
Jn 5:18 So the Jewish leaders tried all the more to **k** him.
7:19 the law of Moses! In fact, you are trying to **k** me."
7:20 demon possessed! Who's trying to **k** you?"
7:25 "Isn't this the man they are trying to **k**?
8:37 And yet some of you are trying to **k** me
8:40 truth I heard from God, but you are trying to **k** me.
8:59 At that point they picked up stones to **k** him.
10:10 The thief's purpose is to steal and **k** and destroy.
10:31 again the Jewish leaders picked up stones to **k** him.
11:8 the Jewish leaders in Judea were trying to **k** you.
12:10 Then the leading priests decided to **k** Lazarus,
16:2 and the time is coming when those who **k** you will
Ac 5:26 for they were afraid the people would **k** them if
5:33 high council was furious and decided to **k** them.
7:28 'Are you going to **k** me as you killed that Egyptian
9:23 After a while the Jewish leaders decided to **k** him.
10:13 said to him, "Get up, Peter; **k** and eat them."
11:7 heard a voice say, 'Get up, Peter; **k** and eat them.'
16:27 had escaped, so he drew his sword to **k** himself.
21:31 As they were trying to **k** him, word reached the
21:36 followed behind shouting, "**K** him, **k** him!"
22:22 with such a fellow! **K** him! He isn't fit to live!"
23:15 his case more fully. We will **k** him on the way."
23:21 hiding along the way ready to jump him and **k** him.
23:21 have vowed not to eat or drink until they **k** him.
23:27 and they were about to **k** him when I arrived with
23:30 But when I was informed of a plot to **k** him,
25:3 (Their plan was to waylay and **k** him.)
25:11 has a right to turn me over to these men to **k** me.
26:21 Temple for preaching this, and they tried to **k** me.
27:42 The soldiers wanted to **k** the prisoners to make
Ro 11:3 am left, and now they are trying to **k** me, too."
Heb 11:28 so that the angel of death would not **k** their
Jas 4:2 you don't have, so you scheme and **k** to get it.
1Jn 3:12 and killed his brother. And why did he **k** him?
Rev 6:8 to **k** with the sword and famine and disease
9:5 They were told not to **k** them but to torture them
9:15 and year were turned loose to **k** one-third of all the
11:7 against them. He will conquer them and **k** them.

KILLED (394) [KILL]

Ge 4:8 together there, Cain attacked and **k** his brother.
4:23 I have **k** a youth who attacked and wounded me.
4:25 me another son in place of Abel, the one Cain **k**."
9:5 must die, and any person who murders must be **k**.
15:10 Abram took all these and **k** them. He cut each one
31:39 If any were attacked and **k** by wild animals,
34:30 they will come and crush us. We will all be **k**!"
37:31 Then Joseph's brothers **k** a goat and dipped the
44:18 for I know you could have me **k** in an instant,
Ex 2:12 Moses **k** the Egyptian and buried him in the sand.
2:14 Do you plan to kill me as you **k** that Egyptian
2:15 he gave orders to have Moses arrested and **k**.
9:15 I could have **k** you all by now. I could have
12:27 And though he **k** the Egyptians, he spared our
12:29 And at midnight the LORD **k** all the firstborn
12:29 Even the firstborn of their livestock were **k**.
13:13 the donkey must be **k** by breaking its neck.
13:15 so the LORD **k** all the firstborn males throughout
16:3 "It would have been better if the LORD had **k** us
21:16 "Kidnappers must be **k**, whether they are caught in
21:29 it must be stoned, and the owner must also be **k**.
22:2 act of breaking into a house and is **k** in the process,
22:2 the person who **k** the thief is not guilty.
22:3 the one who **k** the thief is guilty of murder.
22:14 an animal from a neighbor and it is injured or **k**,
22:31 that has been attacked and **k** by a wild animal.
Lev 7:24 or **k** by a wild animal may never be eaten,
17:15 that died a natural death or was **k** by a wild animal,
20:15 he must be put to death, and the animal must be **k**.
24:18 in full—a live animal for the animal that was **k**.
Nu 3:13 From the day I **k** all the firstborn sons of the
8:17 I set them apart for myself on the night I **k** all the
11:15 I'd rather you **k** me than treat me like this.
14:16 to give them, so he **k** them in the wilderness.'
16:41 saying, "You two have **k** the LORD's people!"
19:16 the corpse of someone who was **k** with a sword
19:18 or has touched a person who was **k** or who died
21:35 And Israel was victorious and **k** King Og, his sons,
22:33 I would certainly have **k** you by now and spared
25:14 The Israelite man **k** with the Midianite woman was
25:18 who was **k** on the day of the plague at Peor."
31:7 had commanded Moses, and they **k** all the men.
31:8 They also **k** Balaam son of Beor with the sword.
31:19 And all of you who have **k** anyone or touched a
33:4 whom the LORD had **k** the night before.
35:6 where a person who has accidentally **k** someone
35:11 to flee to if they have **k** someone accidentally.
35:12 The slayer must not be **k** before being tried by the
Dt 3:3 and all his people over to us, and we **k** them all.
4:42 where anyone who had accidentally **k** someone
19:3 so that anyone who has **k** someone can flee there
19:12 handed over to the dead person's avenger to be **k**.
20:5 You might be **k** in the battle, and someone else
22:22 both he and the other man's wife must be **k**.
Jos 2:19 If they go out into the street, they will be **k**, and we
2:19 we swear that no one inside this house will be **k**—
7:5 and they **k** about thirty-six who were retreating
10:1 and completely destroyed Ai and **k** its king,
10:1 he had destroyed the city of Jericho and **k** its king.
10:11 The hail **k** more of the enemy than the Israelites **k**
with the sword.
10:26 Then Joshua **k** each of the five kings and hung
10:28 He **k** the king of Makkedah as he had **k** the
10:30 Then Joshua **k** the king of Libnah just as he had **k**
the king of Jericho.
10:33 But Joshua's men **k** him and destroyed his entire
10:39 And they **k** everyone in it, leaving no survivors.
11:10 turned back and captured Hazor and **k** its king.
11:14 cities for themselves, but they **k** all the people.
11:17 Joshua **k** all the kings of those territories,
11:21 He **k** them all and completely destroyed their
12:1 the kings east of the Jordan River who had been **k**
13:21 and was **k** by Moses along with the chiefs of
13:22 The Israelites also **k** Balaam the magician, the son
20:3 protected from the relatives of the one who was **k**,
20:9 Anyone who accidentally **k** another person could
20:9 they could escape being **k** in revenge prior to
21:13 of refuge for those who accidentally **k** someone),
21:21 of refuge for those who accidentally **k** someone),
Jdg 1:4 and they **k** ten thousand enemy warriors at the
1:25 and they **k** everyone in the city except for this man
3:29 and **k** about ten thousand of their strongest
3:31 He **k** six hundred Philistines with an ox goad.
7:22 Those who were not **k** fled to places as far away as
8:10 of the east—for 120,000 had already been **k**.
8:17 the tower of Peniel and **k** all the men in the town.
8:18 and Zalmunna, "The men you **k** at Tabor—
8:19 I wouldn't kill you if you hadn't **k** them."
8:21 So Gideon **k** them both and took the royal
9:5 one stone, they **k** all seventy of his half brothers.
9:40 Many of Shechem's warriors were **k**,
9:45 He **k** the people, leveled the city, and scattered salt
9:54 Don't let it be said that a woman **k** Abimelech!"
12:6 So forty-two thousand Ephraimites were **k** at that
14:19 of Ashkelon, **k** thirty men, took their belongings,
15:8 the Philistines with great fury and **k** many of them.
15:15 on the ground and **k** a thousand Philistines with it.
15:16 jawbone of a donkey, / I've **k** a thousand men!"
16:24 The one who **k** so many of us is now in our
16:30 So he **k** more people when he died than he had
18:27 They attacked and **k** all the people and burned the
20:21 and **k** twenty-two thousand Israelites in the field
20:25 but the men of Benjamin **k** another eighteen
20:35 and that day the Israelites **k** 25,100 of Benjamin's
20:37 in from all sides and **k** everyone in the town.
20:39 By that time Benjamin's warriors had **k** about
20:42 but the Israelites chased after them and **k** them.
20:45 but Israel **k** five thousand of them along the road.
20:45 They continued the chase until they had **k** another
1Sa 4:11 and Phinehas, the two sons of Eli, were **k**.
4:17 Your two sons, Hophni and Phinehas, were **k**, too.
6:14 up the wood of the cart for a fire and **k** the cows
6:19 But the LORD **k** seventy men from Beth-shemesh
14:13 and his armor bearer **k** them right and left.
14:14 They **k** about twenty men in all, and their bodies
14:30 think how many more we could have **k**!"
14:31 and **k** the Philistines all day from Micmash to
15:33 "As your sword has **k** the sons of many mothers,
17:57 After David had **k** Goliath, Abner brought him to
18:6 was returning home after David had **k** Goliath.
18:7 This was their song: / "Saul has **k** his thousands,
18:21 "Here's another chance to see him **k** by the
18:25 in mind was that David would be **k** in the fight.
18:27 his men went out and **k** two hundred Philistines
19:6 surely as the LORD lives, David will not be **k**."
20:13 But if he is angry and wants you **k**,
21:9 whom you **k** in the valley of Elah," the priest
21:11 singing, 'Saul has **k** his thousands, and David his
22:18 So Doeg turned on them and **k** them,
22:19 the city of the priests, and **k** the priests' families—
22:21 When he told David that Saul had **k** the priests of
24:18 put me in a place where you could have **k** me,
28:9 "Are you trying to get me **k**?" the woman
28:24 been fattening a calf, so she hurried out and **k** it.
29:5 'Saul has **k** his thousands, and David his ten
31:2 Saul and his sons, and they **k** three of his sons—
2Sa 1:4 and Saul and his son Jonathan have been **k**."
1:10 "So I **k** him," the Amalekite told David, "for I
1:15 thrust his sword into the Amalekite and **k** him.
1:16 "for you yourself confessed that you **k** the
1:22 Both Saul and Jonathan **k** their strongest foes;
2:31 all from the tribe of Benjamin, had been **k**.
3:27 and **k** Abner in revenge for killing his brother
3:30 So Joab and his brother Abishai **k** Abner
3:30 because Abner had **k** their brother Asahel at the
4:4 and Jonathan were **k** at the battle of Jezreel.
4:10 good news. But I seized him and **k** him at Ziklag.
4:11 men who have **k** an innocent man in his own house
8:5 David **k** twenty-two thousand of them.
10:18 This time David's forces **k** seven hundred
11:15 is fiercest. Then pull back so that he will be **k**."
11:17 And Uriah was **k** along with several other Israelite
11:21 Wasn't Gideon's son Abimelech **k** at Thebez by a
11:21 Then tell him, 'Uriah the Hittite was **k**, too.' "
11:24 Some of our men were **k**, including Uriah the
12:4 man's lamb and **k** it and served it to his guest."
13:30 "Absalom has **k** all your sons; not one is left
13:32 and said, "No, not all your sons have been **k**!
14:6 no one was there to stop it, one of them was **k**.
17:21 Ahithophel had advised that he be captured and **k**.
18:8 because of the forest than were **k** by the sword.
18:15 then surrounded Absalom and **k** him.
21:17 of Zeruiah came to his rescue and **k** the Philistine.
21:18 As they fought, Sibbecai from Hushah **k** Saph,
21:19 Elhanan son of Jair from Bethlehem **k** the brother
21:21 But he was **k** by Jonathan, the son of David's
21:22 but they were **k** by David and his warriors.
23:10 He **k** Philistines until his hand was too tired to lift
23:20 and slippery ground, he caught the lion and **k** it.
23:21 he **k** a great Egyptian warrior who was armed with
23:21 spear from the Egyptian's hand and **k** him with it.
1Ki 2:34 of Jehoiada returned to the sacred tent and **k** Joab,
2:46 son of Jehoiada took Shimei outside and **k** him.
11:15 the Israelite army had **k** nearly every male in
13:24 he was traveling along, a lion came out and **k** him.
15:28 Baasha **k** Nadab in the third year of King Asa's
15:29 He immediately **k** all the descendants of King
16:10 Zimri walked in and struck him down and **k** him.
16:11 Zimri immediately **k** the entire royal family of
16:22 So Tibni was **k**, and Omri became the next king.
18:40 them down to the Kishon Valley and **k** them there.
19:2 failed to take your life like those whom you **k**."
19:10 your altars, and **k** every one of your prophets.
19:14 your altars, and **k** every one of your prophets.
19:17 Anyone who escapes from Hazael will be **k** by
19:17 and those who escape Jehu will be **k** by Elisha!
19:21 Elisha then returned to his oxen, **k** them, and used
20:20 Each Israelite soldier **k** his Aramean opponent,
20:21 and the Arameans were **k** in a great slaughter.
20:29 The Israelites **k** 100,000 Aramean foot soldiers in
20:30 but the wall fell on them and **k** another 27,000.
20:36 when he had gone, a lion attacked and **k** him.
22:17 And the LORD said, 'Their master has been **k**.
22:20 against Ramoth-gilead so that he can be **k** there?'
2Ki 1:10 Then fire fell from heaven and **k** them all.
1:12 the fire of God fell from heaven and **k** them all.
3:23 "The three armies have attacked and **k** each other!
9:7 and all the LORD's servants who were **k** by
10:7 the leaders **k** all seventy of the king's sons.
10:9 one who conspired against my master and **k** him.
But who **k** all these?
10:11 Then Jehu **k** all of Ahab's relatives living in
10:14 of them and **k** them at the well of Beth-eked.
10:17 he **k** everyone who was left there from Ahab's
10:25 So they **k** them all with their swords,
11:2 rest of the king's children, who were about to be **k**.
11:8 person who approaches you must be **k**.
11:16 enter the palace grounds, and she was **k** there.
11:18 and they **k** Mattan the priest of Baal in front of the
11:20 because Athaliah had been **k** at the king's palace.
13:7 The king of Aram had **k** the others like they were
14:7 It was Amaziah who **k** ten thousand Edomites in
14:19 sent assassins after him, and they **k** him there.
15:16 He **k** the entire population and ripped open the
16:9 resettling them in Kir. They also **k** King Rezin.
19:7 where I will have him **k** with a sword.' "
19:35 the Assyrian camp and **k** 185,000 Assyrian troops.
19:37 and Sharezer **k** him with their swords.
21:24 But the people of the land **k** all those who had
23:29 but King Neco **k** him when they met at Megiddo.
25:7 made Zedekiah watch as all his sons were **k**.
1Ch 2:3 Er, was a wicked man, so the LORD **k** him.
4:41 They **k** everyone who lived there and took the land
5:22 Many of the Hagrites were **k** in the battle
7:21 And Elead were **k** trying to steal livestock from the
10:2 Saul and his sons, and they **k** three of his sons—
10:14 So the LORD **k** him and turned his kingdom over
11:22 and slippery ground, he caught the lion and **k** it.
11:23 he **k** an Egyptian warrior who was seven and a half
11:23 spear from the Egyptian's hand and **k** him with it.
18:5 David **k** twenty-two thousand of them.
19:18 This time David's forces **k** seven thousand
20:4 As they fought, Sibbecai from Hushah **k** Saph,
20:5 Elhanan son of Jair **k** Lahmi, the brother of Goliath
20:7 But he was **k** by Jonathan, the son of David's
20:8 but they were **k** by David and his warriors.
22:8 'You have **k** many men in the great battles you
2Ch 18:16 And the LORD said, 'Their master has been **k**.
18:19 against Ramoth-gilead so that he can be **k** there?'
20:23 allies from Mount Seir and **k** every one of them.
21:4 he **k** all his brothers and some of the other leaders
21:13 And you have even **k** your own brothers, men who
22:1 The marauding bands of Arabs had **k** all the older
22:8 who were attending Ahaziah. So Jehu **k** them all.
22:9 They brought him to Jehu, who **k** him.
22:11 rest of the king's children, who were about to be **k**.
23:7 person who enters the Temple must be **k**.
23:15 enter the palace grounds, and they **k** her there.
23:17 and they **k** Mattan the priest of Baal in front of the
23:21 the city was peaceful because Athaliah had been **k**.
24:23 and Jerusalem and **k** all the leaders of the nation.
25:11 where they **k** ten thousand Edomite troops from

25:16 Be quiet now before I have you **k**!" So the prophet
25:27 sent assassins after him, and they **k** him there.
28: 6 **k** 120,000 of Judah's troops because they had
28: 7 warrior from Ephraim, **k** Maaseiah, the king's son;
29: 9 Our fathers have been **k** in battle, and our sons
29:22 So they **k** the bulls, and the priests took the blood
29:22 Next they **k** the rams and sprinkled their blood on
29:24 The priests then **k** the goats as a sin offering
32:21 some of his own sons **k** him there with a sword.
33:25 But the people of the land **k** all those who had
36:17 The Babylonians **k** Judah's young men,
Ezr 9: 7 We have been **k**, captured, robbed, and disgraced,
Ne 9:26 they **k** the prophets who encouraged them to return
Est 3:13 must be **k**, slaughtered, and annihilated on a single
3:13 of the Jews would be given to those who **k** them.
4:13 there in the palace when all other Jews are **k**.
9: 5 They **k** and annihilated their enemies and did as
9: 6 They **k** five hundred people in the fortress of Susa.
9: 7 They also **k** Parshandatha, Dalphon, Aspatha,
9:11 of the number of people **k** in the fortress of Susa,
9:12 "The Jews have **k** five hundred people in the
9:15 on March 8 and **k** three hundred more people,
Job 1:15 They stole all the animals and **k** all the farmhands.
1:17 have stolen your camels and **k** your servants.
Ps 44:22 For your sake we are **k** every day; / we are being
60: T and **k** twelve thousand Edomites in the Valley of
78:31 rose against them, / and he **k** their strongest men;
78:34 When God **k** some of them, the rest finally sought
78:51 He **k** the oldest son in each Egyptian family,
78:63 Their young men were **k** by fire; / their young
105:36 Then he **k** the oldest child in each Egyptian home,
136:10 Give thanks to him who **k** the firstborn of Egypt.
136:18 He **k** powerful kings— / His faithful love endures
Pr 22:13 I might meet a lion in the street and be **k**!"
Isa 14:19 you will be dumped into a mass grave with those **k**
22: 2 are lying everywhere, **k** by famine and disease.
29:20 will be gone, and all those who plot evil will be **k**.
37: 7 where I will have him **k** with a sword.' "
37:36 the Assyrian camp and **k** 185,000 Assyrian troops.
37:38 and Sharezer **k** him with their swords.
49:21 For most of my children were **k**, and the rest were
66:16 by his sword, and many will be **k** by the LORD.
Jer 2:30 You yourselves have **k** your prophets as a lion kills
2:34 You **k** them even though they didn't break into
9:21 our mansions. It has **k** off the flower of our youth:
15: 9 I will hand over to the enemy to be **k**,"
18:21 in a plague, and let their young men be **k** in battle!
26:23 The king then **k** Uriah with a sword and had him
26:24 the court not to turn him over to the mob to be **k**.
34: 4 what the LORD says: 'You will not be **k** in war
39: 6 He made Zedekiah watch as they **k** his sons
41: 2 men suddenly drew their swords and **k** Gedaliah,
41: 7 Ishmael and his men **k** all but ten of them
41:18 do when they heard that Ishmael had **k** Gedaliah,
43: 3 so we will stay here and be **k** by the Babylonians
44:12 They will fall here in Egypt, **k** by war and famine.
46:26 I will hand them over to those who want them **k**—
49:26 Her warriors will all be **k**," says the LORD
50:30 Her warriors will all be **k**," says the LORD.
51:49 "Just as Babylon **k** the people of Israel and others
51:49 throughout the world, so must her people be **k**.
52:10 made Zedekiah watch as all his sons were **k**;
52:10 they also **k** all the other leaders of Judah.
La 2:21 boys and girls, **k** by the swords of the enemy.
2:21 You have **k** them in your anger, slaughtering them
2:22 The enemy has **k** all the children I bore
4: 9 Those **k** by the sword are far better off than those
Eze 6:12 And anyone who survives will be **k** by famine.
7:15 Any who leave the city walls will be **k** by enemy
14:19 and the plague **k** people and animals alike.
17:21 And all the best warriors of Israel will be **k** in
23:10 They stripped her and **k** her and took away her
32:29 they also lie among those **k** by the sword,
32:31 that he is not alone in having his entire army **k**,
Da 3:22 and **k** the soldiers as they threw the three men in!
5:19 He **k** those he wanted to kill and spared those he
5:30 very night Belshazzar, the Babylonian king, was **k**.
7:11 I kept watching until the fourth beast was **k** and its
9:26 the Anointed One will be **k**, appearing to have
11:12 and will have many thousands of his enemies **k**.
11:26 His army will be swept away, and many will be **k**.
Hos 7:16 Their leaders will be **k** by their enemies because of
13:16 They will be **k** by an invading army, their little
Joel 3:19 they attacked Judah and **k** her innocent people.
Am 1: 8 and the few Philistines still left will be **k**.
4:10 I **k** your young men in war and slaughtered all
7:11 'Jeroboam will soon be **k** and the people of Israel
7:17 in this city, and your sons and daughters will be **k**.
Na 2:13 The finest of your youth will be **k** in battle.
Hab 1:14 Are we but fish to be caught and **k**? Are we
Zec 9: 5 Gaza will be conquered and its king **k**,
11: 9 If you die, you die. If you are **k**, you are **k**.
Mt 10:21 rise against their parents and cause them to be **k**.
16:21 He would be **k**, and he would be raised on the third
17:23 He will be **k**, but three days later he will be raised
21:35 his servants, beat one, **k** one, and stoned another.
23:29 you build tombs for the prophets your ancestors **k**
24: 9 "Then you will be arrested, persecuted, and **k**.
26:52 "Those who use the sword will be **k** by the sword.
Mk 6:19 was enraged and wanted John **k** in revenge,
8:31 He would be **k**, and three days later he would rise
9:31 He will be **k**, but three days later he will rise from
12: 5 The next servant he sent was **k**. Others who were
sent were either beaten or **k**,
13:12 rise against their parents and cause them to be **k**.
Lk 9:22 I will be **k**, but three days later I will be raised
11:47 for the very prophets your ancestors **k** long ago.
11:51 who was **k** between the altar and the sanctuary.
13:33 For it wouldn't do for a prophet of God to be **k**
15:27 'and your father has **k** the calf we were fattening
21:16 will betray you. And some of you will be **k**.
21:24 They will be brutally **k** by the sword or sent away
Ac 3:15 You **k** the author of life, but God raised him to life.
5:30 from the dead after you **k** him by crucifying him.
5:36 four hundred others joined him, but he was **k**,
5:37 got some people to follow him, but he was **k**, too,
7:28 'Are you going to kill me as you **k** that Egyptian
7:52 They even **k** the ones who predicted the coming of
12: 2 the apostle James (John's brother) **k** with a sword.
13:28 but they asked Pilate to have him **k** anyway.
22:20 And when your witness Stephen was **k**, I was
23:12 oath to neither eat nor drink until they had **k** Paul.
23:14 oath to neither eat nor drink until we have **k** Paul.
Ro 8:36 Scriptures say, "For your sake we are **k** every day;
11: 3 they have **k** your prophets and torn down your
1Th 2:15 For some of the Jews had **k** their own prophets,
and some even **k** the Lord Jesus.
Heb 11:37 were sawed in half; others were **k** with the sword.
Jas 5: 6 and **k** good people who had no power to defend
2Pe 2:12 of instinct, who are born to be caught and **k**.
1Jn 3:12 who belonged to the evil one and **k** his brother.
Jude 1:11 follow the evil example of Cain, who **k** his brother.
Rev 5: 6 I looked and I saw a Lamb that had been **k** but was
5: 9 For you were **k**, and your blood has ransomed
5:12 "The Lamb is worthy—the Lamb who was **k**.
9:18 One-third of all the people on earth were **k** by
13: 8 which belongs to the Lamb who was **k** before the
13:10 Those who are destined for death will be **k**.
16: 6 your holy people and your prophets have been **k**,
19:21 Their entire army was **k** by the sharp sword that

KILLING (47) [KILL]

Ge 37:26 to the others, "What can we gain by **k** our brother?
Ex 32:27 **k** even your brothers, friends, and neighbors."
32:29 for you obeyed him even though it meant **k** your
Dt 19: 5 the ax head flies off the handle, **k** the other person.
Jos 8:22 came out and started **k** the enemy from the rear.
8:24 When the Israelite army finished **k** all the men
10:10 at Azekah and Makkedah, **k** them along the way.
10:28 of Makkedah, **k** everyone in it, including the king.
20: 3 for the relatives may seek to avenge the **k**.
20: 5 If the relatives of the victim come to avenge the **k**,
Jdg 1: 8 **k** all its people and setting the city on fire.
4:16 to Harosheth-haggoyim, **k** all of Sisera's warriors.
7:25 two Midianite generals, **k** Oreb at the rock of Oreb,
9:18 his descendants, **k** his seventy sons on one stone.
1Sa 4: 2 defeated the army of Israel, **k** four thousand men.
14:20 to the battle and found the Philistines **k** each other.
17:26 "What will a man get for **k** this Philistine
17:27 hearing is true. That is the reward for **k** the giant."
30: 2 and everyone else but without **k** anyone.
2Sa 3:27 and killed Abner in revenge for **k** his brother
12: 4 But instead of **k** a lamb from his own flocks for
18:13 And if I had betrayed the king by **k** his son—
23:20 which included **k** two of Moab's mightiest
1Ki 9:16 **k** the Canaanite population and burning it down.
11:16 the army had stayed there for six months, **k** them.
17:18 Have you come here to punish my sins by **k** my
21:19 Isn't **k** Naboth bad enough? Must you rob him,
1Ch 11:22 which included **k** two of Moab's mightiest
2Ch 24:22 Jehoiada for his love and loyalty—by **k** his son.
25:13 **k** three thousand people and carrying off great
28: 9 But you have gone too far, **k** them without mercy,
36:17 **k** both young and old, men and women, healthy
Est 9:16 **k** seventy-five thousand of those who hated them.
9:18 But the Jews at Susa continued **k** their enemies on
Isa 34: 6 with fat as though it had been used for **k** lambs
Jer 26:15 rest assured that you will be **k** an innocent man!
Eze 9: 6 So they began by **k** the seventy leaders.
35: 7 **k** off all who try to escape and any who return.
Ob 1:14 at the crossroads, **k** those who tried to escape.
Mt 12:14 called a meeting and discussed plans for **k** Jesus.
22: 6 and treated them shamefully, even **k** some of them.
23:30 'We never would have joined them in **k** the
Mk 3: 6 supporters of Herod to discuss plans for **k** Jesus.
Lk 15:30 you celebrate by **k** the finest calf we have.'
Jn 10:32 For which one of these good deeds are you **k** me?"
Ac 7:24 to his defense and avenged him, **k** the Egyptian.
8: 1 Saul was one of the official witnesses at the **k** of

KILLS (26) [KILL]

Ge 4:24 If anyone who **k** Cain is to be punished seven
Ex 21:14 someone deliberately attacks and **k** another person,
21:29 If this is true and if the bull **k** someone, it must be
22: 1 who steals an ox or sheep and then **k** or sells it.
Lev 24:18 "Anyone who **k** another person's animal must pay
24:21 "Whoever **k** an animal must make full restitution,
24:21 but whoever **k** another person must be put to death.
Nu 35:15 Anyone who accidentally **k** someone may flee
35:16 and **k** another person with a piece of iron,
35:17 and **k** another person with a large stone,
35:18 and **k** another person with a wooden weapon.
35:27 relative finds him outside the city limits and **k** him,
Dt 19: 4 "If someone accidentally **k** a neighbor without
27:24 'Cursed is anyone who **k** another person in secret.'
32:39 I am the one who **k** and gives life; / I am the one
Jos 20: 3 Anyone who **k** another person unintentionally can
1Sa 17:25 reward the king has offered to anyone who **k** him?
2Sa 11:25 David said. "The sword **k** one as well as another!
Job 5: 2 destroys the fool, and jealousy **k** the simple.
9:23 He laughs when a plague suddenly **k** the innocent.
Isa 31: 4 "When a lion, even a young one, **k** a sheep,
Jer 2:30 have killed your prophets as a lion **k** its prey.
12:12 The sword of the LORD **k** people from one end
La 1:20 In the streets the sword **k**, and at home there is
Mt 23:37 the city that **k** the prophets and stones God's
Lk 13:34 the city that **k** the prophets and stones God's

KILMAD (1)

Eze 27:23 Asshur, and **K** came with their merchandise, too.

KILNS (1)

2Sa 12:31 picks, and axes, and to work in the brick **k**.

KIMHAM (3)

2Sa 19:37 But here is my son **K**. Let him go with you
19:38 "**K** will go with me, and I will do for him
19:40 then went on to Gilgal, taking **K** with him.

KINAH (1)

Jos 15:22 **K**, Dimonah, Adadah,

KIND (189) [KINDLY, KINDNESS, KINDS]

EVERY KIND (40) Ge 1:20,21,24; 2:19; 6:19; 7:3,3,14,14; 34:29; Ex 34:7; 35:22; Nu 14:18; 1Ch 12:37; 22:15; 28:21; 2Ch 15:6; Ps 104:25; 130:8; 144:13; Pr 8:7; 20:10; Eze 47:10; Hos 6:9; Mt 4:23; 10:1; 13:47; Mk 7:19; Ro 1:29; 1Co 1:5; 15:24; 2Co 6:4; 1Th 5:22; 2Th 2:10; Tit 2:7,14; Jas 3:16; Jude 1:7; Rev 11:6; 18:12

Ge 1:12 and their seeds produced plants and trees of like **k**.
1:20 Let the skies be filled with birds of every **k**."
1:21 and every sort of fish and every **k** of bird.
1:24 "Let the earth bring forth every **k** of animal—
1:25 each able to reproduce more of its own **k**.
2:19 So the LORD God formed from the soil every **k**
6:19 Bring a pair of every **k** of animal—a male and a
6:20 Pairs of each **k** of bird and each **k** of animal,
7: 3 Then select seven pairs of every **k** of bird.
7: 3 and a female in each pair to ensure that every **k** of
7:14 With them in the boat were pairs of every **k** of
7:14 along with birds and flying insects of every **k**.
19:19 "You have been so **k** to me and saved my life,
20: 9 this great sin? This **k** of thing should not be done!
23: 8 you feel, be so **k** as to ask Ephron son of Zohar
24:27 "The LORD has been so **k** and faithful to
25:27 while Jacob was the **k** of person who liked to stay
33:15 "There is no reason for you to be so **k** to me,"
34:11 "Please be **k** to me, and let me have her as my
34:29 all the women and children and wealth of every **k**.
37: 4 They couldn't say a **k** word to him.
44: 7 "What **k** of people do you think we are, that you
49: 5 "Simeon and Levi are two of a **k**— / men of
Ex 12:16 No work of any **k** may be done on these days
20: 4 "Do not make idols of any **k**, whether in the shape
20:10 no one in your household may do any **k** of work.
34: 7 love to many thousands by forgiving every **k** of sin
34:15 "Do not make treaties of any **k** with the people
35:22 They presented gold objects of every **k** to the
Lev 2: 4 "When you present some **k** of baked bread as a
2: 6 and pour oil on it; it is a **k** of grain offering.
5: 4 "Or if they make a rash vow of any **k**, whether its
7:14 One of each **k** of bread must be presented as a gift
10: 1 him a different **k** of fire than he had commanded.
10:19 he said. "This **k** of thing has also happened to me.
14: 4 using two wild birds of a **k** permitted for food,
14:35 'It looks like my house has some **k** of disease.'
15:33 who has had a bodily discharge of any **k**;
16: 1 who died when they burned a different **k** of fire
22: 4 or any **k** of discharge that makes them
22:21 an animal that has no physical defects of any **k**.
23:30 among you who does any **k** of work on that day.
24:20 does to hurt another person must be paid back in **k**.
Nu 3: 4 a different **k** of fire than he had commanded.
13:19 What **k** of land do they live in? Is it good or bad?
14:18 forgiving every **k** of sin and rebellion.
26:61 a different **k** of fire than he had commanded.
Dt 4:25 not corrupt yourselves by making idols of any **k**.
5: 8 " 'Do not make idols of any **k**, whether in the
5:14 no one in your household may do any **k** of work.
Jos 2:12 Now swear to me by the LORD that you will be **k**
15:19 You have been **k** enough to give me land in the
Jdg 1:15 You have been **k** enough to give me land in the
13:12 what **k** of rules should govern the boy's life
Ru 2:10 "Why are you being so **k** to me?" she asked.
3: 2 and he's been very **k** by letting you gather grain
1Sa 15: 6 For you were **k** to the people of Israel when they
24:18 Yes, you have been wonderfully **k** to me today,
25: 8 So would you please be **k** to us, since we have
2Sa 9: 7 I've asked you to come so that I can be **k** to you
1Ki 2: 7 "Be **k** to the sons of Barzillai from Gilead.
3: 6 "You were wonderfully **k** to my father, David,
9:13 "What **k** of towns are these, my brother?"
18:26 answer us!" But there was no reply of any **k**.
2Ki 4:13 "Tell her that we appreciate the **k** concern she has
23:24 and every other **k** of idol worship, both in
25:27 He was **k** to Jehoiachin and released him from
1Ch 12:37 there were 120,000 troops armed with every **k** of
22:15 and craftsmen of every **k** available to you.
28:21 Others with skills of every **k** will volunteer,
2Ch 1: 8 "You have been so faithful and **k** to my father,
15: 6 for God was troubling you with every **k** of
Ezr 7:24 of God will be required to pay taxes of any **k**.'
Ne 1:11 Put it into his heart to be **k** to me." In those days I
Job 6:14 "One should be **k** to a fainting friend, but you
21:16 so I will have nothing to do with that **k** of thinking.
22:18 so I will have nothing to do with that **k** of thinking.
32:14 with me, I would not answer with that **k** of logic!

Ps 35:16 They mock me with the worst **k** of profanity,
41: 1 Oh, the joys of those who are **k** to the poor.
77: 9 Has God forgotten to be **k**? / Has he slammed the
89:28 I will love him and be **k** to him forever;
104:25 vast and wide, / teeming with life of every **k**,
109:12 Let no one be **k** to him; / let no one pity his
116: 5 How **k** the LORD is! How good he is!
130: 8 He himself will free Israel / from every **k** of sin.
144:13 May our farms be filled / with crops of every **k**.
145: 8 The LORD is **k** and merciful, / slow to get angry,
Pr 8: 7 for I speak the truth and hate every **k** of deception.
11:17 Your own soul is nourished when you are **k**,
16:24 **K** words are like honey—sweet to the soul
20:10 The LORD despises double standards of every **k**.
26:25 Though they pretend to be **k**, their hearts are full of
28: 8 It will end up in the hands of someone who is **k** to
SS 8: 6 Love flashes like fire, the brightest **k** of flame.
Isa 58: 4 This **k** of fasting will never get you anywhere with
58: 6 the **k** of fasting I want calls you to free those who
Jer 32:18 You are loving and **k** to thousands, though children
38: 4 That **k** of talk will undermine the morale of the
42:12 I will be merciful to you by making him **k**, so he
51:39 I will prepare a different **k** of feast for them.
52:31 He was **k** to Jehoiachin and released him from
Eze 18:14 but decides against that **k** of life.
43:25 these animals may have physical defects of any **k**.
47:10 Fish of every **k** will fill the Dead Sea, just as they
Hos 6: 9 the road to Shechem and practice every **k** of sin.
Am 4: 5 This is the **k** of thing you Israelites love to do,"
Mic 2:11 That's just the **k** of prophet you would like!
Hag 2:12 or stew, wine or oil, or any other **k** of food,
Zec 1:13 And the LORD spoke **k** and comforting words to
Mal 1: 9 But when you bring that **k** of offering, why should
Mt 4:23 And he healed people who had every **k** of sickness
5:47 If you are **k** only to your friends, how are you
7:20 or a person is by the **k** of fruit that is produced.
10: 1 and to heal every **k** of disease and illness.
13:47 thrown into the water and gathers fish of every **k**.
20:15 my money? Should you be angry because I am **k**?'
Mk 2:15 (There were many people of this **k** among the
7:19 he showed that every **k** of food is acceptable.)
9:29 "This **k** can be cast out only by prayer."
10:15 anyone who doesn't have their **k** of faith will never
12:40 to cover up the **k** of people they really are,
Lk 1:25 "How **k** the Lord is!" she exclaimed. "He has
1:58 and relatives that the Lord had been very **k** to her,
6:34 Even sinners will lend to their own **k** for a full
6:35 for he is **k** to the unthankful and to those who are
6:44 A tree is identified by the **k** of fruit it produces.
7:39 he would know what **k** of woman is touching him.
18:17 anyone who doesn't have their **k** of faith will never
20:47 to cover up the **k** of people they really are,
Jn 21:19 Jesus said this to let him know what **k** of death he
Ac 9:36 She was always doing **k** things for others
23: 3 What **k** of judge are you to break the law yourself
25:20 as to how to conduct an investigation of this **k**,
27: 3 Julius was very **k** to Paul and let him go ashore to
28: 2 The people of the island were very **k** to us. It was
Ro 1:29 Their lives became full of every **k** of wickedness,
2: 4 Don't you realize how **k**, tolerant, and patient God
2: 4 Can't you see how **k** he has been in giving you
2:29 Whoever has that **k** of change seeks praise from
3: 8 If you follow that **k** of thinking, however,
4:12 but only if they have the same **k** of faith Abraham
11:22 Notice how God is both **k** and severe. He is severe
11:22 but **k** to you as you continue to trust in his
12: 1 a living and holy sacrifice—the **k** he will accept.
1Co 1: 5 the gifts of eloquence and every **k** of knowledge.
2: 6 but not the **k** of wisdom that belongs to this world,
2: 6 and not the **k** that appeals to the rulers of this
3:13 day to see what **k** of work each builder has done.
13: 4 Love is patient and **k**. Love is not jealous
14:20 and wise in understanding matters of this **k**.
15:24 having put down all enemies of every **k**.
15:35 dead be raised? What **k** of bodies will they have?"
15:38 gives it a new body—just the **k** he wants it to have.
15:38 A different **k** of plant grows from each **k** of
15:41 The sun has one **k** of glory, while the moon and
stars each have another **k**.
2Co 4:13 because we have the same **k** of faith the psalmist
6: 4 and hardships and calamities of every **k**.
7: 9 It was the **k** of sorrow God wants his people to
7:10 We will never regret that **k** of sorrow.
7:10 But sorrow without repentance is the **k** that results
11: 4 or a different **k** of gospel than the one you
Gal 5:22 our lives, he will produce this **k** of fruit in us:
Eph 4:32 Instead, be **k** to each other, tenderhearted,
Col 1:10 you will continually do good, **k** things for others.
1Th 5:22 Keep away from every **k** of evil.
2Th 2:10 He will use every **k** of wicked deception to fool
1Ti 1:14 Oh, how **k** and gracious the Lord was! He filled
5:10 up her children well? Has she been **k** to strangers?
2Ti 2:17 This **k** of talk spreads like cancer. Hymenaeus
2:24 must not quarrel but must be **k** to everyone.
3: 6 They are the **k** who work their way into people's
Tit 2: 1 promote the **k** of living that reflects right teaching.
2: 7 example to them by doing good deeds of every **k**.
2:14 He gave his life to free us from every **k** of sin,
Heb 7:26 He is the **k** of high priest we need because he is
Jas 2:14 by your actions? That **k** of faith can't save anyone.
3:14 brag about being wise. That is the worst **k** of lie.
3:15 and selfishness are not God's **k** of wisdom.
3:16 there you will find disorder and every **k** of evil.
1Pe 2:18 not only if they are **k** and reasonable, but even if
5: 9 are going through the same **k** of suffering you are.
Jude 1: 7 and every **k** of sexual perversion.
Rev 11: 6 and to send every **k** of plague upon the earth as
18:12 every **k** of perfumed wood, ivory goods,
18:22 There will be no industry of any **k**, and no more

KINDLE (1) [KINDLED, KINDLING]

Job 41:21 Yes, its breath would **k** coals, for flames shoot

KINDLED (1) [KINDLE]

Jer 17: 4 For you have **k** my anger into a roaring fire that

KINDLING (2) [KINDLE]

Isa 27:11 and used for **k** beneath the cooking pots.
Jer 5:14 that will burn them up as if they were **k** wood.

KINDLY (9) [KIND]

Ge 32: 9 to my relatives, and you promised to treat me **k**.
32:12 But you promised to treat me **k** and to multiply my
50:21 And he spoke very **k** to them, reassuring them.
Jdg 18:15 where the young Levite lived, and greeted him **k**.
Ru 2:13 "You have comforted me by speaking so **k** to me,
Est 2: 9 was very impressed with Esther and treated her **k**.
Ps 142: 7 godly will crowd around me, / for you treat me **k**."
Lk 7:42 so he **k** forgave them both, canceling their debts.
Ac 24: 4 **k** give me your attention for only a moment as I

KINDNESS (67) [KIND]

Ge 20:13 have the **k** to say that you are my sister.' "
24:12 "Give me success and show **k** to my master,
24:14 By this I will know that you have shown **k** to my
24:49 will you or won't you show true **k** to my master?
44: 4 'Why have you repaid an act of **k** with such evil?
Ex 33:19 I will show **k** to anyone I choose, and I will show
Ru 1: 8 And may the LORD reward you for your **k** to
2:11 and **k** you have shown your mother-in-law since
2:20 "He is showing his **k** to us as well as to your dead
1Sa 20: 8 Show me this **k** as my sworn friend—for we made
24:19 May the LORD reward you well for the **k** you
2Sa 9: 1 promised Jonathan that he would show **k** to them.
9: 3 I want to show God's **k** to them in any way I can."
9: 8 "Should the king show such **k** to a dead dog like
1Ki 3: 6 And you have continued this great **k** to him today
2Ch 10: 7 "If you are good to the people and show them **k**
32:25 did not respond appropriately to the **k** shown him,
Ps 42: 6 deeply discouraged, / but I will remember your **k**—
106: 7 They soon forgot his many acts of **k** to them.
106:46 He even caused their captors / to treat them with **k**.
109:16 For he refused all **k** to others; / he persecuted the
141: 5 It will be a **k**! / If they reprove me, it is soothing
145:17 in everything he does; / he is filled with **k**.
Pr 3: 3 Never let loyalty and **k** get away from you!
12:10 their animals, but even the **k** of the wicked is cruel.
23: 8 back your words of appreciation for their '**k**.'
31:26 and **k** is the rule when she gives instructions.
Isa 26:10 Your **k** to the wicked does not make them do good.
Hos 4: 1 "There is no faithfulness, no **k**, no knowledge of
11: 4 I led Israel along with my ropes of **k** and love.
Joel 2:13 He is filled with **k** and is eager not to punish you.
Zep 2: 7 For the LORD their God will visit his people in **k**
Zec 7: 9 and show mercy and **k** to one another.
Ac 20:24 others the Good News about God's wonderful **k**
Ro 3:24 Yet now God in his gracious **k** declares us not
5:20 God's wonderful **k** became more abundant.
5:21 to death, now God's wonderful **k** rules instead,
6: 1 can show us more and more **k** and forgiveness?
11: 5 A few are being saved as a result of God's **k** in
11: 6 And if they are saved by God's **k**, then it is not by
11: 6 God's wonderful **k** would not be what it really is—
11:22 but kind to you as you continue to trust in his **k**.
12: 8 And if you have a gift for showing **k** to others,
1Co 7:25 But the Lord in his **k** has given me wisdom that
2Co 6: 1 to reject this marvelous message of God's great **k**.
6: 6 our patience, our **k**, our sincere love,
8: 1 what God in his **k** has done for the churches in
8: 9 how full of love and **k** our Lord Jesus Christ was.
10: 1 the gentleness and **k** that Christ himself would use,
Gal 1:15 For it pleased God in his **k** to choose me and call
5:22 love, joy, peace, patience, **k**, goodness,
Eph 1: 6 So we praise God for the wonderful **k** he has
1: 7 so rich in **k** that he purchased our freedom through
1: 8 He has showered his **k** on us, along with all
2: 7 the incredible wealth of his favor and **k** toward us,
Php 4:17 to receive a well-earned reward because of your **k**.
Col 1: 6 and understood the truth about God's great **k** to
3:12 **k**, humility, gentleness, and patience.
2Ti 1: 9 to show his love and **k** to us through Christ Jesus.
1:16 May the Lord show special **k** to Onesiphorus
1:18 May the Lord show him special **k** on the day of
Tit 3: 4 But then God our Savior showed us his **k** and love.
3: 7 He declared us not guilty because of his great **k**.
Phm 1: 7 because your **k** has so often refreshed the hearts of
1:10 My plea is that you show **k** to Onesimus. I think of
1Pe 2: 3 now that you have had a taste of the Lord's **k**.
5:10 In his **k** God called you to his eternal glory by

KINDRED(S) [KJV] See BIRTH, FAMILY, FELLOW, KINSMAN, RACE, RELATIVE(S), TRIBE(S)

KINDS (54) [KIND]

Ge 1:11 The seeds will then produce the **k** of plants
7: 8 With them were all the various **k** of animals—
7:21 wild animals, all **k** of small animals,
8:19 And all the various **k** of animals and birds came
40:17 In the top basket were all **k** of bakery goods for
45:23 and all **k** of other food to be eaten on his journey.
Ex 3:20 and strike at the heart of Egypt with all **k** of
29: 3 Place these various **k** of bread in a single basket,
31: 3 intelligence, and skill in all **k** of crafts.
35:31 intelligence, and skill in all **k** of crafts.
Lev 7:11 **k** of peace offerings that may be presented to the
7:12 must be accompanied by various **k** of bread—
11:14 the buzzard, kites of all **k**,
11:15 ravens of all **k**,
11:16 the nighthawk, the seagull, hawks of all **k**,
11:19 the stork, herons of all **k**, the hoopoe, and the bat.
14:54 with the various **k** of contagious skin disease
19:19 "Do not breed your cattle with other **k** of animals.
19:19 Do not plant your field with two **k** of seed.
19:19 Do not wear clothing woven from two different **k**
Nu 31:51 all **k** of jewelry and crafted objects.
Dt 14:13 the buzzard, kites of all **k**,
14:14 ravens of all **k**,
14:15 the nighthawk, the seagull, hawks of all **k**,
14:18 the stork, herons of all **k**, the hoopoe, and the bat.
17: 8 or a case involving different **k** of assault.
2Sa 6: 5 and playing all **k** of musical instruments—
1Ki 4:33 He could speak with authority about all **k** of plants,
1Ch 13: 8 singing and playing all **k** of musical instruments—
29: 2 costly jewels, and all **k** of fine stone and marble.
Ne 5:18 ten days we needed a large supply of all **k** of wine.
13:16 Tyre bringing in fish and all **k** of merchandise.
Pr 1:13 we'll get! We'll fill our houses with all **k** of things!
26:25 to be kind, their hearts are full of all **k** of evil.
29:22 person starts fights and gets into all **k** of sin.
Ecc 2: 5 and parks, filling them with all **k** of fruit trees.
3:10 the various **k** of work God has given people to do.
Jer 15: 3 "I will send four **k** of destroyers against them,"
Eze 8:10 and saw the walls engraved with all **k** of snakes,
27:22 of Sheba and Raamah came with all **k** of spices,
47:12 All **k** of fruit trees will grow along both sides of
Zep 2:14 Owls of many **k** will live among the ruins of its
Mk 1:34 sick people who had many different **k** of diseases,
Ro 7: 8 and aroused all **k** of forbidden desires within me!
14: 6 Those who eat all **k** of food do so to honor the
1Co 12: 4 Now there are different **k** of spiritual gifts, but it is
12: 5 There are different **k** of service in the church,
15:39 And just as there are different **k** of seeds and
plants, so also there are different **k** of flesh—
Gal 5:21 drunkenness, wild parties, and other **k** of sin.
Eph 4:19 Their lives are filled with all **k** of impurity
1Ti 6:10 For the love of money is at the root of all **k** of evil.
Tit 3: 9 These **k** of things are useless and a waste of time.
Jas 3: 7 People can tame all **k** of animals and birds

KINE [KJV] See CATTLE, HERD

KING (2293) [KING'S, KINGDOM, KINGDOMS, KINGS, KINGS', KINGSHIP]

GREAT KING (15) 2Ki 18:19,28; Ezr 5:11; Ps 47:2; 48:2; 95:3; Ecc 9:14; Isa 36:4,13; Jer 22:15; Hos 5:13; 8:10; 10:6; Mal 1:14; Mt 5:35

KING DAVID (60) 2Sa 3:31,38; 6:12,16; 7:18; 8:11; 13:21; 15:13; 17:17,21; 19:11,16; 20:21; 21:2; 1Ki 1:1,6,9,13,31,32,43,47; 2:44; 2Ki 11:10; 1Ch 4:31; 7:2; 15:29; 17:16; 18:11; 24:31; 26:26,32; 29:1,9,24; 2Ch 1:1; 3:1; 5:1; 7:6; 23:9; 29:25; 35:4; Ezr 3:10; 8:20; Am 6:5; Zec 12:8; Mt 1:1,6,17; 12:3; Mk 2:25; Lk 1:27; 2:4; 6:3; Jn 7:42; Ac 1:16; 2:25; 4:25; 7:45; Ro 4:6

KING HEZEKIAH (36) 2Ki 18:14,15,17,18,19,22,29; 19:1,3,10; 20:14; 1Ch 4:41; 2Ch 29:18,20,25,30; 30:1,18,24; 31:13,20; 32:20,23,23; Pr 25:1; Isa 36:2,4,7,14; 37:1,3,10; 38:9; 39:3; Jer 26:18,19

KING NEBUCHADNEZZAR (58) 2Ki 24:1,10,14; 25:1,22; 2Ch 36:6,10,13; Ezr 1:7; 2:1; 5:12; Ne 7:6; Est 2:6; Jer 21:2,7; 22:25; 24:1; 25:1,9; 27:6,20; 28:3,11,14; 29:1; 32:1; 34:1; 35:11; 37:1; 39:1,5,11; 44:30; 46:2,26; 49:28,30; 50:17; 51:34; 52:4; Eze 26:7; 29:18; 30:10; Da 1:1,18; 2:28,46; 3:1,3,7,9; 4:1,18,27,28,31; 5:11,13

KING OF ASSYRIA (49) 2Ki 15:20; 16:18; 17:4,4,5,24,26,27; 18:7,11,14,14,17,19,23,28,31,33; 19:10,32,37; 20:6; 23:29; 2Ch 28:16,21; 32:7,11; Ezr 6:22; Isa 7:17; 8:4,7; 10:7,12,12,16; 20:4,6; 36:2,4,8,13,16,18; 37:10,33,38; 38:6; Jer 50:17,18

KING OF BABYLON (65) 2Ki 20:12; 24:7,17,20; 25:6,7,11,20,21,23,24; 2Ch 36:17; Isa 14:4; 39:1; Jer 20:4; 21:4,10; 25:11,12,26; 27:9,11,12,14,17; 28:2,4; 29:22; 32:3,4,28,36; 34:2,3,21; 36:29; 37:17,19; 38:3,23; 39:5; 40:5,7,9,11; 41:2; 42:11; 43:10; 50:18,43; 52:3,9,10,15,26,27; Eze 17:12,17; 19:9; 21:21,23; 24:2; 29:19; 30:25; 32:11

KING OF EGYPT (27) Ge 37:36; 39:1; 41:46; Ex 1:15; 2:23; 3:18,19; 6:13; 14:5; 1Ki 3:1; 9:16; 2Ki 17:4; 23:29; 24:7; 2Ch 36:3,4; Isa 19:11; Jer 44:30; 46:2,17; Eze 29:3; 30:21,22,24; 31:2; 32:2; Ac 7:10

KING OF ISRAEL (73) 1Sa 15:1,17,26,35; 16:1; 23:17; 24:14; 26:20; 2Sa 5:3,17; 6:20; 12:7; 19:22; 1Ki 5:1; 15:28; 19:16; 20:11,28,32,32,33,41,43; 21:7; 22:9,18,29,31,32,33,34,44; 2Ki 3:4,5,10,13; 5:5,6,7; 6:9,10,11,12,21,26; 7:6; 13:16; 15:25; 1Ch 11:3; 12:38; 29:1; 2Ch 18:8,17,28,30,31,32,33; 29:27; Ezr 5:11; Pr 1:1; Ecc 1:12; Isa 41:21; Eze 17:16,18; Hos 1:1; 10:15; Am 1:1; Zep 3:15; Mt 27:42; Mk 15:32; Jn 1:49; 12:13

KING OF JUDAH (30) 2Sa 2:11; 1Ki 12:23; 2Ki 1:17; 22:18; 2Ch 11:3; 22:1; 29:1; 34:26; 35:21; 36:4; Isa 16:1; Jer 15:4; 22:1,2,24; 24:1; 25:3; 26:1; 27:1,20; 28:1,4; 32:1; 34:4; 35:1; 37:1,7; 46:2; Am 1:1; Zep 1:1

KING OF KINGS (4) Ezr 7:12; Eze 26:7; 1Ti 6:15; Rev 19:16

KING OF THE JEWS (18) Mt 2:2; 27:11,29,37; Mk 15:2,9,12,18,26; Lk 23:3,37,38; Jn 18:33,39; 19:3,19,21,21

KING OVER (ALL) ISRAEL (15) 2Sa 3:10; 5:12; 1Ki 1:34; 4:1; 12:20; 14:14; 2Ki 9:3,6,12; 1Ch 14:2,8; 23:1; 28:4,4; Ne 13:26

KING SOLOMON (42) 1Ki 1:34,39,53; 2:17,19,23,25,29; 4:21,27; 5:13; 6:2; 7:13,14,40,51; 8:5; 9:26; 10:13,16,23; 11:1; 12:2; 2Ki 23:13; 24:13; 25:16; 1Ch 29:24; 2Ch 4:11,16; 5:6; 7:5; 8:10; 9:12,15,22; 10:2; Ezr 2:55; Ne 7:57; 13:26; SS 3:9,11; Jer 52:20

MY LORD THE KING (18) 1Sa 24:8; 26:17,19; 29:8; 2Sa 14:19; 16:9; 18:31; 19:19,26,35; 1Ki 1:20,36; 2:38; 20:9; 2Ki 6:26; Jer 37:20; 38:9; Da 1:10

Ge 12:15 they sang her praises to their **k**, the pharaoh,
14: 1 **K** Amraphel of Babylonia, **K** Arioch of Ellasar, **K** Kedorlaomer of Elam, and **K** Tidal of Goiim
14: 2 fought against **K** Bera of Sodom, **K** Birsha of Gomorrah, **K** Shinab of Admah, **K** Shemeber of Zeboiim, and the **k** of Bela (now called Zoar).
14: 4 For twelve years they had all been subject to **K**
14: 9 against **K** Kedorlaomer of Elam and the kings of
14:17 the **k** of Sodom came out to meet him in the valley
14:18 the **k** of Salem and a priest of God Most High,
14:21 The **k** of Sodom told him, "Give back my people
20: 2 So **K** Abimelech sent for her and had her brought
26: 1 where Abimelech, **k** of the Philistines, lived.
26: 8 some time later, Abimelech, **k** of the Philistines,
26:26 **K** Abimelech arrived with his adviser, Ahuzzath,
36:33 Jobab son of Zerah from Bozrah became **k**.
36:34 Husham from the land of the Temanites became **k**.
36:35 Hadad son of Bedad became **k** and ruled from the
36:36 Samlah from the city of Masrekah became **k**.
36:37 city of Rehoboth on the Euphrates River became **k**.
36:38 Shaul died, Baal-hanan son of Acbor became **k**.
36:39 Hadad became **k** and ruled from the city of Pau.
37: 8 "So you are going to be our **k**, are you?"
37:36 to Potiphar, an officer of Pharaoh, the **k** of Egypt.
39: 1 of the personal staff of Pharaoh, the **k** of Egypt.
41:44 And Pharaoh said to Joseph, "I am the **k**, but no
41:46 he entered the service of Pharaoh, the **k** of Egypt.
Ex 1: 8 Then a new **k** came to the throne of Egypt who
1:11 of Pithom and Rameses as supply centers for the **k**.
1:15 Then Pharaoh, the **k** of Egypt, gave this order to
1:17 they refused to obey the **k** and allowed the boys to
1:18 Then the **k** called for the midwives. "Why have
2:23 Years passed, and the **k** of Egypt died.
3:18 Then all of you must go straight to the **k** of Egypt
3:19 "But I know that the **k** of Egypt will not let you go
6:13 and Aaron to return to Pharaoh, **k** of Egypt,
14: 5 When word reached the **k** of Egypt that the
Nu 20:14 he sent ambassadors to the **k** of Edom with this
20:18 But the **k** of Edom said, "Stay out of my land
20:20 But the **k** of Edom replied, "Stay out! You may
21: 1 The Canaanite **k** of Arad, who lived in the Negev,
21:21 The Israelites now sent ambassadors to **K** Sihon of
21:23 But **K** Sihon refused to let them cross his land.
21:26 Heshbon had been the capital of **K** Sihon of the
21:26 He had conquered a former Moabite **k** and seized
21:29 his daughters as captives of Sihon, the Amorite **k**.
21:33 but **K** Og of Bashan and all his people attacked
21:34 You will do the same to him as you did to **K** Sihon
21:35 And Israel was victorious and killed **K** Og,
22: 2 Balak son of Zippor, the Moabite **k**, knew what the
22: 4 The **k** of Moab said to the leaders of Midian,
22: 4 like an ox devours grass!" So Balak, **k** of Moab,
22:10 said to God, "Balak son of Zippor, **k** of Moab,
22:14 So the Moabite officials returned to **K** Balak
22:36 When **K** Balak heard that Balaam was on the way,
22:40 where the **k** sacrificed cattle and sheep. He sent
23: 1 Balaam said to **K** Balak, "Build me seven altars
23: 5 Then the LORD gave Balaam a message for **K**
23: 6 the **k** was standing beside his burnt offerings with
23: 7 the **k** of Moab brought me from the eastern hills.
23:11 Then **K** Balak demanded of Balaam, "What have
23:13 Then **K** Balak told him, "Come with me to
23:15 Then Balaam said to the **k**, "Stand here by your
23:17 So Balaam returned to the place where the **k**
23:21 God is with them; / he has been proclaimed their **k**.
23:27 Then **K** Balak said to Balaam, "Come, I will take
24: 7 Their **k** will be greater than Agag; / their kingdom
24:10 **K** Balak flew into a rage against Balaam.
32:33 of Joseph the territory of **K** Sihon of the Amorites and the land of **K** Og of Bashan—
33:40 It was then that the Canaanite **k** of Arad, who lived
Dt 1: 4 This was after he had defeated **K** Sihon of the
1: 4 who had ruled in Heshbon, and **K** Og of Bashan,
2:24 **k** of Heshbon, and I will give you his land.
2:26 to **K** Sihon of Heshbon with this proposal of peace:
2:30 But **K** Sihon refused to allow you to pass through,
2:31 I have begun to hand **K** Sihon and his land over to
2:32 Then **K** Sihon declared war on us and mobilized
3: 1 where **K** Og and his army attacked us at Edrei.
3: 2 Treat him just as you treated **K** Sihon of the
3: 3 So the LORD our God handed **K** Og and all his
3: 6 just as we had destroyed **K** Sihon of Heshbon.
3:11 **K** Og of Bashan was the last of the giant
4:46 by the Amorites under **K** Sihon of Heshbon.
4:47 conquered his land and that of **K** Og of Bashan—
17:14 'We ought to have a **k** like the other nations
17:15 be sure that you select as **k** the man the LORD
17:16 The **k** must not build up a large stable of horses for
17:17 The **k** must not take many wives for himself,
17:18 "When he sits on the throne as **k**, he must copy
28:36 and the **k** you crowned to a nation unknown to you
29: 7 **K** Sihon of Heshbon and **K** Og of Bashan came out
33: 5 The LORD became **k** in Israel—
Jos 2: 2 But someone told the **k** of Jericho,
2: 3 So the **k** of Jericho sent orders to Rahab:
6: 2 "I have given you Jericho, its **k**, and all its mighty
8: 1 for I have given to you the **k** of Ai, his people,
8: 2 destroy them as you destroyed Jericho and its **k**.
8:14 When the **k** of Ai saw the Israelites across the
8:23 Only the **k** of Ai was taken alive and brought to
8:29 Joshua hung the **k** of Ai on a tree and left him
9:10 **K** Sihon of Heshbon and **K** Og of Bashan (who
10: 1 Now Adoni-zedek, **k** of Jerusalem, heard that
10: 1 and completely destroyed Ai and killed its **k**,
10: 1 had destroyed the city of Jericho and killed its **k**.
10: 3 So **K** Adoni-zedek of Jerusalem sent messengers to
10:28 killing everyone in it, including the **k**.
10:28 He killed the **k** of Makkedah as he had killed the **k** of Jericho.
10:30 too, the LORD gave them the city and its **k**.
10:30 Then Joshua killed the **k** of Libnah just as he had killed the **k** of Jericho.
10:33 **K** Horam of Gezer had arrived with his army to
10:39 They captured the city, its **k**, and all of its
11: 1 When **K** Jabin of Hazor heard what had happened,
11: 1 **K** Jobab of Madon; the **k** of Shimron; the **k** of Acshaph;
11:10 turned back and captured Hazor and killed its **k**.
12: 2 **K** Sihon of the Amorites, who lived in Heshbon,
12: 4 **K** Og of Bashan, the last of the Rephaites, lived at
12: 5 the other portion of which was in the territory of **K**
12: 6 and the Israelites had destroyed the people of **K** Sihon and **K** Og.
12: 9 The **k** of Jericho / The **k** of Ai, near Bethel
12:10 The **k** of Jerusalem / The **k** of Hebron
12:11 The **k** of Jarmuth / The **k** of Lachish
12:12 The **k** of Eglon / The **k** of Gezer
12:13 The **k** of Debir / The **k** of Geder
12:14 The **k** of Hormah / The **k** of Arad
12:15 The **k** of Libnah / The **k** of Adullam
12:16 The **k** of Makkedah / The **k** of Bethel
12:17 The **k** of Tappuah / The **k** of Hepher
12:18 The **k** of Aphek / The **k** of Lasharon
12:19 The **k** of Madon / The **k** of Hazor
12:20 The **k** of Shimron-meron / The **k** of Acshaph
12:21 The **k** of Taanach / The **k** of Megiddo
12:22 The **k** of Kedesh / The **k** of Jokneam in Carmel
12:23 The **k** of Dor in the city of Naphoth-dor / The **k** of Goyim in Gilgal
12:24 The **k** of Tirzah. In all, thirty-one kings and their
13:10 It also included all the towns of **K** Sihon of the
13:12 and all the territory of **K** Og of Bashan, who had
13:12 **K** Og was the last of the Rephaites, for Moses had
13:21 Sihon was the Amorite **k** who had reigned in
13:27 and the rest of the kingdom of **K** Sihon of
13:30 all of Bashan, all the former kingdom of **K** Og,
13:31 and **K** Og's royal cities of Ashtaroth and Edrei.
24: 9 Then Balak son of Zippor, **k** of Moab, started a
Jdg 1: 5 While at Bezek they encountered **K** Adoni-bezek
3: 8 and he handed them over to **K** Cushan-rishathaim
3:10 He went to war against **K** Cushan-rishathaim of
3:12 so the LORD gave **K** Eglon of Moab control over
3:15 to deliver their tax money to **K** Eglon of Moab.
3:19 So the **k** commanded his servants to be silent
3:20 you from God!" As **K** Eglon rose from his seat,
3:25 But when the **k** didn't come out after a long delay,
4: 2 So the LORD handed them over to **K** Jabin of Hazor, a Canaanite **k**.
4:17 was on friendly terms with **K** Jabin of Hazor.
4:23 day Israel saw God subdue Jabin, the Canaanite **k**.
4:24 became stronger and stronger against **K** Jabin,
9: 6 the pillar at Shechem and made Abimelech their **k**.
9: 8 Once upon a time the trees decided to elect a **k**. First they said to the olive tree, 'Be our **k**!'
9:10 "Then they said to the fig tree, 'You be our **k**!'
9:12 "Then they said to the grapevine, 'You be our **k**!'
9:14 to the thornbush and said, 'Come, you be our **k**!'
9:15 'If you truly want to make me your **k**, come
9:16 and in good faith by making Abimelech your **k**,
9:18 to be your **k** just because he is your relative.
11:12 Then Jephthah sent messengers to the **k** of
11:13 The **k** of Ammon answered Jephthah's
11:14 sent this message back to the Ammonite **k**:
11:17 they sent messengers to the **k** of Edom asking for
11:17 Then they asked the **k** of Moab for similar
11:19 "Then Israel sent messengers to **K** Sihon of the
11:20 But **K** Sihon didn't trust Israel to pass through his
11:21 of Israel, gave his people victory over **K** Sihon.
11:25 any better than Balak son of Zippor, **k** of Moab?
11:28 But the **k** of Ammon paid no attention to
17: 6 In those days Israel had no **k**, so the people did
18: 1 Now in those days Israel had no **k**. And the tribe of
19: 1 Now in those days Israel had no **k**. There was a
21:25 In those days Israel had no **k**, so the people did
1Sa 2:10 the earth. / He gives mighty strength to his **k**;
8: 5 Give us a **k** like all the other nations have."
8: 7 They don't want me to be their **k** any longer.
8: 9 but solemnly warn them about how a **k** will treat
8:11 "This is how a **k** will treat you," Samuel said.
8:11 "The **k** will draft your sons into his army
8:13 The **k** will take your daughters from you and force
8:18 you will beg for relief from this **k** you are
8:19 "Even so, we still want a **k**," they said.
8:20 Our **k** will govern us and lead us into battle."
8:22 "Do as they say, and give them a **k**."
10:16 tell his uncle that Samuel had anointed him to be **k**.
10:19 have rejected me and said, 'We want a **k** instead!'
10:24 "This is the man the LORD has chosen as your **k**.
10:24 And all the people shouted, "Long live the **k**!"
10:25 the people what the rights and duties of a **k** were.
11: 1 **K** Nahash of Ammon led his army against the
11:15 ceremony before the LORD they crowned him **k**.
12: 1 "I have done as you asked and given you a **k**.
12: 9 and by the Philistines and the **k** of Moab.
12:12 the **k** of Ammon, you came to me and said that you
12:12 and said that you wanted a **k** to reign over you,
12:12 though the LORD your God was already your **k**.
12:13 All right, here is the **k** you have chosen. Look him
12:14 if you and your **k** follow the LORD your God,
12:17 you have been in asking the LORD for a **k**!"
12:19 now we have added to our sins by asking for a **k**."
12:25 continue to sin, you and your **k** will be destroyed."
13: 1 Saul was thirty years old when he became **k**,
13:14 The LORD has already chosen him to be **k** over
15: 1 "I anointed you **k** of Israel because the LORD
15: 8 He captured Agag, the Amalekite **k**,
15:11 "I am sorry that I ever made Saul **k**, for he has not
15:17 The LORD has anointed you **k** of Israel.
15:20 I brought back **K** Agag, but I destroyed everyone
15:23 of the LORD, he has rejected you from being **k**."
15:26 he has rejected you from being the **k** of Israel."
15:32 Then Samuel said, "Bring **K** Agag to me."
15:35 was sorry he had ever made Saul **k** of Israel.
16: 1 I have rejected him as **k** of Israel. Now fill your
16: 1 I have selected one of his sons to be my new **k**."
17:25 And have you heard about the huge reward the **k**
17:25 The **k** will give him one of his daughters for a
17:31 Then David's question was reported to **K** Saul, and the **k** sent for him.
17:56 "Well, find out!" the **k** told him.
18: 6 along the way to celebrate and to cheer for **K** Saul,
18: 8 Next they'll be making him their **k**!"
18:22 to David, "The **k** really likes you, and so do we.
18:23 afford the bride price for the daughter of a **k**?"
18:24 When Saul's men reported this back to the **k**,
18:27 and presented all their foreskins to the **k**.
18:28 When the **k** realized how much the LORD was
19: 9 him again. As David played his harp for the **k**,
20:24 the new moon festival began, the **k** sat down to eat.
20:30 know that you want David to be **k** in your place,
20:31 long as that son of Jesse is alive, you'll never be **k**.
21: 2 "The **k** has sent me on a private matter,"
21:10 escaped from Saul and went to **K** Achish of Gath.
21:11 "Isn't this David, the **k** of the land?" they asked.
21:12 and was afraid of what **K** Achish might do to him.
21:14 Finally, **K** Achish said to his men, "Must you
22: 3 where he asked the **k**, "Would you let my father
22: 4 The **k** agreed, and David's parents stayed in Moab
22: 6 the **k** was sitting beneath a tamarisk tree on the hill
22:11 **K** Saul immediately sent for Ahimelech and all his
22:12 "What is it, my **k**?" Ahimelech asked.
22:16 along with your entire family!" the **k** shouted.
22:18 Then the **k** said to Doeg, "You do it." So Doeg
23:17 You are going to be the **k** of Israel, and I will be
23:20 O **k**, and we will catch him and hand him over to
24: 8 came out and shouted after him, "My lord the **k**!"
24:14 Who is the **k** of Israel trying to catch anyway?
24:20 now I realize that you are surely going to be **k**,
25:36 thrown a big party and was celebrating like a **k**.
26:15 So why haven't you guarded your master the **k**
26:17 And David replied, "Yes, my lord the **k**.
26:19 But now let my lord the **k** listen to his servant.
26:20 Why has the **k** of Israel come out to search for a
26:22 "Here is your spear, O **k**," David replied.
27: 2 and went to live at Gath under the protection of **K**
27: 9 and clothing before returning home to see **K**
28: 1 **K** Achish told David, "You and your men will be
28:13 "Don't be afraid!" the **k** told her. "What do you
29: 2 and his men marched at the rear with **K** Achish.
29: 3 the man who ran away from **K** Saul of Israel.
29: 8 can't I fight the enemies of my lord, the **k**?"
31: 5 he fell on his own sword and died beside the **k**.
2Sa 2: 4 and crowned him **k** over the tribe of Judah.
2: 5 so loyal to your **k** and giving him a decent burial.
2: 7 of Judah, who have anointed me as their new **k**."
2: 9 There he proclaimed Ishbosheth **k** over Gilead,
2:10 Ishbosheth was forty years old when he became **k**,
2:11 and he ruled as **k** of Judah for seven and a half
3: 3 was Maacah, the daughter of Talmai, **k** of Geshur.
3:10 I should set him up as **k** over Israel as well as
3:17 "you have wanted to make David your **k**.
3:21 make a covenant with you to make you their **k**.
3:23 told that Abner had just been there visiting the **k**
3:24 he rushed to see the **k**. "What have you done?"
3:31 And **K** David himself walked behind the
3:32 and the **k** and all the people wept at his graveside.
3:33 Then the **k** sang this funeral song for Abner:
3:36 In fact, everything the **k** did pleased them!
3:38 Then **K** David said to the people, "Do you not
3:39 And even though I am the anointed **k**, these two
5: 2 For a long time, even while Saul was our **k**,
5: 3 the LORD. And they anointed him **k** of Israel.
5:11 Then **K** Hiram of Tyre sent messengers to David,
5:12 that the LORD had made him **k** over Israel
5:17 heard that David had been anointed **k** of Israel,
6:12 Then **K** David was told, "The LORD has blessed
6:16 When she saw **K** David leaping and dancing
6:20 "How glorious the **k** of Israel looked today!
7: 1 When the **k** was settled in his palace
7:18 Then **K** David went in and sat before the LORD
8: 3 the forces of Hadadezer son of Rehob, **k** of Zobah,
8: 9 When **K** Toi of Hamath heard that David had
8:11 **K** David dedicated all these gifts to the LORD,
8:12 and from Hadadezer son of Rehob, **k** of Zobah.

9: 2 the **k** asked. "Yes sir, I am," Ziba replied.
9: 3 The **k** then asked him, "Is anyone still alive from
9: 4 the **k** asked. "In Lo-debar," Ziba told him,
9: 8 Mephibosheth fell to the ground before the **k**.
9: 8 "Should the **k** show such kindness to a dead dog
9: 9 Then the **k** summoned Saul's servant Ziba
10: 1 time after this, **K** Nahash of the Ammonites died,
and his son Hanun became **k**.
10: 6 and Zobah, one thousand from the **k** of Maacah,
11:19 "Report all the news of the battle to the **k**.
12: 7 'I anointed you **k** of Israel and saved you from the
13: 4 Why should the son of a **k** look so dejected
13: 6 And when the **k** came to see him, Amnon asked
13:13 Please, just speak to the **k** about it, and he will let
13:21 When **K** David heard what had happened, he was
13:24 He went to the **k** and said, "My sheep-shearers are
13:24 Would the **k** and his servants please come to
13:25 The **k** replied, "No, my son. If we all came,
13:25 Absalom pressed him, but the **k** wouldn't come,
13:26 Amnon instead?" "Why Amnon?" the **k** asked.
13:27 But Absalom kept on pressing the **k** until he finally
13:29 Then the other sons of the **k** jumped on their mules
13:31 The **k** jumped up, tore his robe, and fell prostrate
13:34 He ran to tell the **k**, "I see a crowd of people
13:35 "Look!" Jonadab told the **k**. "There they are
13:36 and the **k** and his officials wept bitterly with them.
13:37 Talmai son of Ammihud, the **k** of Geshur.
14: 1 Joab realized how much the **k** longed to see
14: 3 Then go to the **k** and tell him the story I am about
14: 4 When the woman approached the **k**, she fell with
14: 4 to the floor in front of him and cried out, "O **k**!
14: 5 the **k** asked. "I am a widow," she replied.
14: 8 "Leave it to me," the **k** told her. "Go home,
14:10 the **k** said. "If anyone objects, bring them to me.
14:15 I said to myself, 'Perhaps the **k** will listen to me
14:17 Yes, the **k** will give us peace of mind again.'
14:18 "I want to know one thing," the **k** replied. "Yes,
14:19 woman replied, "My lord the **k**, how can I deny it?
14:21 So the **k** sent for Joab and told him, "All right,
14:22 Joab fell to the ground before the **k** and blessed
14:24 But the **k** gave this order: "Absalom may go to his
14:24 into my presence." So Absalom did not see the **k**.
14:28 for two years without getting to see the **k**.
14:32 "Because I wanted you to ask the **k** why he
14:32 Let me see the **k**; if he finds me guilty of anything,
14:33 So Joab told the **k** what Absalom had said. Then at
14:33 and Absalom came and bowed low before the **k**,
15: 2 When people brought a case to the **k** for judgment,
15: 3 It's too bad the **k** doesn't have anyone to hear it.
15: 7 After four years, Absalom said to the **k**, "Let me
15: 9 "All right," the **k** told him. "Go and fulfill your
15:10 part of Israel to stir up a rebellion against the **k**.
15:10 "you will know that Absalom has been crowned **k**
15:13 A messenger soon arrived in Jerusalem to tell **K**
15:16 So the **k** and his household set out at once. He left
15:17 The **k** and his people set out on foot, and they
15:19 Then the **k** turned to Ittai, the captain of the
15:19 Go on back with your men to **K** Absalom, for you
15:21 But Ittai said to the **k**, "I vow by the LORD
15:23 was deep sadness throughout the land as the **k**
15:27 Then the **k** told Zadok the priest, "Look, here is
16: 2 the **k** asked Ziba. And Ziba replied, "The donkeys
16: 3 the **k** asked him. "He stayed in Jerusalem,"
16: 4 "In that case," the **k** told Ziba, "I give you
16: 6 He threw stones at the **k** and the king's officers
16: 9 "Why should this dead dog curse my lord the **k**?"
16:10 "No!" the **k** said. "What am I going to do with
16:14 The **k** and all who were with him grew weary
16:16 "Long live the **k**!" he exclaimed. "Long live the
k!"
17: 2 everyone will run away. Then I will kill only the **k**,
17:17 them the message they were to take to **K** David.
17:21 crawled out of the well and hurried on to **K** David.
18: 2 The **k** told his troops, "I am going out with you."
18: 4 that's the best plan, I'll do it," the **k** finally agreed.
18: 5 And the **k** gave this command to Joab, Abishai,
18: 5 And all the troops heard the **k** give this order to his
18:12 "We all heard the **k** say to you and Abishai
18:13 And if I had betrayed the **k** by killing his son—
18:13 and the **k** would certainly find out who did it—
18:19 "Let me run to the **k** with the good news that the
18:20 "it wouldn't be good news to the **k** that his son is
18:21 from Cush, "Go tell the **k** what you have seen."
18:25 and the **k** replied, "If he is alone, he has news."
18:26 The **k** replied, "He also will have news."
18:27 and comes with good news," the **k** replied.
18:28 Then Ahimaaz cried out to the **k**, "All is well!"
18:29 the **k** demanded. "Is he all right?"
18:30 "Wait here," the **k** told him. So Ahimaaz stepped
18:31 and said, "I have good news for my lord the **k**.
18:32 the **k** demanded. "Is he all right?"
18:33 The **k** was overcome with emotion. He went up to
19: 1 Word soon reached Joab that the **k** was weeping
19: 4 The **k** covered his face with his hands and kept on
19: 8 So the **k** went out and sat at the city gate, and as
19: 9 "The **k** saved us from our enemies, the Philistines,
19:10 Let's ask David to come back and be our **k** again."
19:11 Then **K** David sent Zadok and Abiathar,
19:11 "Why are you the last ones to reinstate the **k**?
19:14 They sent word to the **k**, "Return to us, and bring
19:15 So the **k** started back to Jerusalem. And when he
19:16 across with the men of Judah to welcome **K** David.
19:17 rushed down to the Jordan to arrive ahead of the **k**.
19:18 As the **k** was about to cross the river, Shimei fell
19:19 "My lord the **k**, please forgive me," he pleaded.
19:21 for he cursed the LORD's anointed **k**!"
19:22 for celebration! I am once again the **k** of Israel!"
19:24 arrived from Jerusalem to meet the **k**.
19:24 his beard since the day the **k** left Jerusalem.
19:25 come with me, Mephibosheth?" the **k** asked him.
19:26 Mephibosheth replied, "My lord the **k**, my servant
19:26 'Saddle my donkey so that I can go with the **k**.'
19:31 from Rogelim to conduct the **k** across the Jordan.
19:32 He was the one who provided food for the **k** during
19:33 and live in Jerusalem," the **k** said to Barzillai.
19:35 I would only be a burden to my lord the **k**.
19:38 "Good," the **k** agreed. "Kimham will go with me,
19:39 So all the people crossed the Jordan with the **k**.
19:40 The **k** then went on to Gilgal, taking Kimham with
19:41 But the men of Israel complained to the **k** that the
19:42 of Judah replied. "The **k** is one of our own tribe.
19:43 "So we have ten times as much right to the **k** as
19:43 to speak of bringing him back to be our **k** again."
20: 2 But the men of Judah stayed with their **k**
20: 3 When the **k** arrived at his palace in Jerusalem,
20: 4 Then the **k** instructed Amasa to mobilize the army
20:21 of Ephraim, who has revolted against **K** David.
20:22 to their homes. Joab returned to the **k** at Jerusalem.
21: 2 So **K** David summoned the Gibeonites. They were
21: 6 "All right," the **k** said, "I will do it."
22:51 You give great victories to your **k**; / you show
24: 2 So the **k** said to Joab, the commander of his army,
24: 3 But Joab replied to the **k**, "May the LORD your
24: 4 But the **k** insisted that they take the census, so Joab
24: 9 Joab reported the number of people to the **k**.
24:20 When Araunah saw the **k** and his men coming
24:20 and bowed before the **k** with his face to the
24:24 But the **k** replied to Araunah, "No, I insist on
1Ki 1: 1 Now **K** David was very old, and no matter how
1: 3 Abishag from Shunem and brought her to the **k**.
1: 4 and she waited on the **k** and took care of him. But
the **k** had no sexual relations with her.
1: 5 decided to make himself **k** in place of his aged
1: 6 Now his father, **K** David, had never disciplined
1: 7 and they agreed to help him become **k**.
1: 9 all his brothers—the other sons of **K** David—
1:11 has made himself **k** and that our lord David doesn't
1:13 Go at once to **K** David and say to him, 'My lord,
1:13 me that my son Solomon would be the next **k**
1:13 your throne? Then why has Adonijah become **k**?'
1:17 God that my son Solomon would be the next **k**
1:18 But instead, Adonijah has become the new **k**,
1:20 And now, my lord the **k**, all Israel is waiting for
1:20 your decision as to who will become **k** after you.
1:22 While she was still speaking with the **k**,
1:23 Nathan went in and bowed low before the **k**.
1:24 have you decided that Adonijah will be the next **k**
1:25 with him and shouting, 'Long live **K** Adonijah!'
1:27 of his servants know who should be the next **k**?"
1:28 So she came back in and stood before the **k**.
1:29 And the **k** vowed, "As surely as the LORD lives,
1:30 I decree that your son Solomon will be the next **k**
1:31 "May my lord **K** David live forever!"
1:32 Then **K** David ordered, "Call Zadok the priest,
1:33 the **k** said to them, "Take Solomon and my
1:34 and Nathan the prophet are to anoint him **k** over
1:34 the trumpets and shout, 'Long live **K** Solomon!'
1:35 He will succeed me as **k**, for I have appointed him
1:36 the God of my lord the **k**, decree it to be so.
1:38 and Solomon rode on **K** David's personal mule.
1:39 all the people shouted, "Long live **K** Solomon!"
1:43 "Our lord **K** David has just declared Solomon **k**!
1:44 The **k** sent him down to Gihon Spring with Zadok
1:45 and Nathan have anointed him as the new **k**.
1:46 Solomon is now sitting on the royal throne as **k**.
1:47 All the royal officials went to **K** David
1:47 Then the **k** bowed his head in worship as he lay in
1:53 So **K** Solomon summoned Adonijah, and they
1:53 He came and bowed low before the **k**,
2: 1 As the time of **K** David's death approached,
2: 7 Make them permanent guests of the **k**, for they
2:12 Solomon succeeded him as **k**, replacing his father,
2:15 was mine; everyone expected me to be the next **k**.
2:17 He replied, "Speak to **K** Solomon on my behalf,
2:18 Bathsheba replied. "I will speak to the **k** for you."
2:19 So Bathsheba went to **K** Solomon to speak on
2:19 The **k** rose from his throne to meet her, and he
2:23 Then **K** Solomon swore solemnly by the LORD:
2:25 So **K** Solomon ordered Benaiah son of Jehoiada to
2:26 Then the **k** said to Abiathar the priest, "Go back to
2:29 When news of this reached **K** Solomon, he sent
2:30 and said to Joab, "The **k** orders you to come out!"
2:30 So Benaiah returned to the **k** and told him what
2:31 "Do as he said," the **k** replied. "Kill him there
2:35 Then the **k** appointed Benaiah to command the
2:36 The **k** then sent for Shimei and told him, "Build a
2:38 I will do whatever my lord the **k** commands."
2:39 two of Shimei's slaves escaped to **K** Achish of
2:44 The **k** also said to Shimei, "You surely remember
2:44 the wicked things you did to my father, **K** David.
3: 1 the **k** of Egypt, and married one of his daughters.
3: 4 so the **k** went there and sacrificed one thousand
3: 7 now you have made me **k** instead of my father,
3:13 No other **k** in all the world will be compared to
3:16 two prostitutes came to the **k** to have an argument
3:22 And so they argued back and forth before the **k**.
3:23 Then the **k** said, "Let's get the facts straight.
3:24 me a sword." So a sword was brought to the **k**.
3:27 Then the **k** said, "Do not kill him, but give the
4: 1 So Solomon was **k** over all Israel,
4: 5 of Nathan, a priest, was a trusted adviser to the **k**.
4:19 including the territories of **K** Sihon of the
Amorites and **K** Og of Bashan.
4:21 **K** Solomon ruled all the kingdoms from the
4:27 governors faithfully provided food for **K** Solomon
5: 1 **K** Hiram of Tyre had always been a loyal friend of
5: 1 that David's son Solomon was the new **k** of Israel,
5: 7 a wise son to be **k** of the great nation of Israel."
5:13 Then **K** Solomon enlisted thirty thousand laborers
6: 2 The Temple that **K** Solomon built for the LORD
7:13 **K** Solomon then asked for a man named Huram to
7:14 from Tyre. So he came to work for **K** Solomon.
7:40 So at last Huram completed everything **K** Solomon
7:46 The **k** had them cast in clay molds in the Jordan
7:51 So **K** Solomon finished all his work on the Temple
8: 2 They all assembled before the **k** at the annual
8: 5 **K** Solomon and the entire community of Israel
8:14 Then the **k** turned around to the entire community
8:16 But now I have chosen David to be **k** over my
8:20 for I have become **k** in my father's place.
8:62 Then the **k** and all Israel with him offered
8:63 And so the **k** and all Israel dedicated the Temple of
8:64 That same day the **k** dedicated the central area of
8:66 They blessed the **k** as they went, and they were all
9:11 to **K** Hiram of Tyre as payment for all the cedar
9:16 (The **k** of Egypt had attacked and captured Gezer,
9:26 Later **K** Solomon built a fleet of ships at
10: 3 nothing was too hard for the **k** to explain to her.
10: 6 She exclaimed to the **k**, "Everything I heard in my
10: 9 he has made you **k** so you can rule with justice
10:10 Then she gave the **k** a gift of nine thousand pounds
10:12 The **k** used the almug wood to make railings for
10:13 **K** Solomon gave the queen of Sheba whatever she
10:16 **K** Solomon made two hundred large shields of
10:17 The **k** placed these shields in the Palace of the
10:18 Then the **k** made a huge ivory throne and overlaid
10:21 All of **K** Solomon's drinking cups were solid gold,
10:22 The **k** had a fleet of trading ships that sailed with
10:23 So **K** Solomon became richer and wiser than any
other **k** in all the earth.
10:27 The **k** made silver as plentiful in Jerusalem as
11: 1 Now **K** Solomon loved many foreign women.
11:13 And even so, I will let him be **k** of one tribe,
11:23 had fled from his master, **K** Hadadezer of Zobah,
11:24 and his men fled to Damascus, where he became **k**.
11:40 but he fled to **K** Shishak of Egypt and stayed there
11:43 Then his son Rehoboam became the next **k**.
12: 1 where all Israel had gathered to make him **k**.
12: 2 for he had fled to Egypt to escape from **K**
12: 6 Then **K** Rehoboam went to discuss the matter with
12:12 Rehoboam's decision, just as the **k** had requested.
12:15 So the **k** paid no attention to the people's demands.
12:16 When all Israel realized that the **k** had rejected
12:18 **K** Rehoboam sent Adoniram, who was in charge of
12:18 When this news reached **K** Rehoboam, he quickly
12:20 called an assembly and made him **k** over all Israel.
12:23 **k** of Judah, and to all the people of Judah
12:27 they will again give their allegiance to **K**
12:27 They will kill me and make him their **k** instead."
12:28 of his counselors, the **k** made two gold calves.
13: 4 **K** Jeroboam was very angry with the man of God
13: 6 The **k** cried out to the man of God, "Please ask the
13: 7 Then the **k** said to the man of God, "Come to the
13: 8 But the man of God said to the **k**, "Even if you
13:11 They also told him what he had said to the **k**.
14: 2 the man who told me I would become **k**.
14:14 And the LORD will raise up a **k** over Israel who
14:20 Jeroboam died, his son Nadab became the next **k**.
14:21 Rehoboam son of Solomon was **k** in Judah.
14:21 He was forty-one years old when he became **k**,
14:25 In the fifth year of **K** Rehoboam's reign,
14:25 **K** Shishak of Egypt came up and attacked
14:28 Whenever the **k** went to the Temple of the
14:31 Then his son Abijam became the next **k**.
15: 8 of David. Then his son Asa became the next **k**.
15:16 There was constant war between **K** Asa of Judah
and **K** Baasha of Israel.
15:17 **K** Baasha of Israel invaded Judah and fortified
15:17 or leaving **K** Asa's territory in Judah.
15:18 and grandson of Hezion, the **k** of Aram,
15:19 Break your treaty with **K** Baasha of Israel so that
15:20 Ben-hadad agreed to **K** Asa's request and sent his
15:22 Then **K** Asa sent an order throughout Judah,
15:24 Then his son Jehoshaphat became the next **k**.
15:25 Israel in the second year of **K** Asa's reign in Judah.
15:28 Baasha killed Nadab in the third year of **K** Asa's
15:28 reign in Judah, and he became the next **k** of Israel.
15:29 He immediately killed all the descendants of **K**
15:32 constant war between Asa and **K** Baasha of Israel.
15:33 Israel in the third year of **K** Asa's reign in Judah.
16: 1 This message from the LORD was delivered to **K**
16: 6 in Tirzah. Then his son Elah became the next **k**.
16: 8 in the twenty-sixth year of **K** Asa's reign in Judah.
16:10 This happened in the twenty-seventh year of **K**
16:10 reign in Judah. Then Zimri became the next **k**.
16:15 the twenty-seventh year of **K** Asa's reign in Judah,
16:16 heard that Zimri had assassinated the **k**, they chose
16:16 commander of the army, as their new **k**.
16:21 people tried to make Tibni son of Ginath their **k**,
16:22 So Tibni was killed, and Omri became the next **k**.
16:23 in the thirty-first year of **K** Asa's reign in Judah.
16:28 in Samaria. Then his son Ahab became the next **k**.
16:29 in the thirty-eighth year of **K** Asa's reign in Judah.
16:31 the daughter of **K** Ethbaal of the Sidonians,
17: 1 told **K** Ahab, "As surely as the LORD, the God
18: 1 to Elijah, "Go and present yourself to **K** Ahab.
18:10 For I swear by the LORD your God that the **k** has
18:10 **K** Ahab forced the **k** of that nation to swear to
19:15 you arrive there, anoint Hazael to be **k** of Aram.
19:16 Then anoint Jehu son of Nimshi to be **k** of Israel,
20: 1 Now **K** Ben-hadad of Aram mobilized his army,

20: 2 the city to relay this message to **K** Ahab of Israel:
20: 9 from Ben-hadad, "Say this to my lord the **k**:
20: 11 The **k** of Israel sent back this answer: "A warrior
20: 13 Then a prophet came to see **K** Ahab and told him,
20: 20 but **K** Ben-hadad and a few others escaped on
20: 22 Afterward the prophet said to **K** Ahab, "Get ready
for another attack by the **k** of Aram
20: 25 So **K** Ben-hadad did as they suggested.
20: 28 Then the man of God went to the **k** of Israel
20: 31 Then perhaps **K** Ahab will let you live."
20: 32 and ropes and went to the **k** of Israel and begged,
20: 32 'Please let me live!' " The **k** of Israel responded,
20: 33 "Go and get him," the **k** of Israel told them.
20: 38 The prophet waited for the **k** beside the road,
20: 39 As the **k** passed by, the prophet called out to him,
20: 40 "Well, it's your own fault," the **k** replied.
20: 41 and the **k** of Israel recognized him as one of the
20: 43 So the **k** of Israel went home to Samaria angry
21: 1 **K** Ahab had a palace in Jezreel, and near the
21: 4 The **k** went to bed with his face to the wall
21: 7 "Are you the **k** of Israel or not?" Jezebel asked.
21: 10 who will accuse him of cursing God and the **k**.
21: 13 him before all the people of cursing God and the **k**.
21: 18 "Go down to meet **K** Ahab, who rules in Samaria.
22: 2 **K** Jehoshaphat of Judah went to visit **K** Ahab of
22: 4 And Jehoshaphat replied to **K** Ahab, "Why,
22: 6 So **K** Ahab summoned his prophets, about four
22: 8 **K** Ahab replied, "There is still one prophet of the
22: 9 So the **k** of Israel called one of his officials
22: 10 **K** Ahab of Israel and **K** Jehoshaphat of Judah,
22: 13 all the prophets are promising victory for the **k**.
22: 15 When Micaiah arrived before the **k**, Ahab asked
22: 15 The LORD will give the **k** a glorious victory!"
22: 16 But the **k** replied sharply, "How many times must
22: 18 I tell you?" the **k** of Israel said to Jehoshaphat.
22: 26 **K** Ahab of Israel then ordered, "Arrest Micaiah
22: 27 Give them this order from the **k**: 'Put this man in
22: 29 So the **k** of Israel and **K** Jehoshaphat of Judah led
their armies
22: 30 Now **K** Ahab said to Jehoshaphat, "As we go into
22: 31 Now the **k** of Aram had issued these orders to his
22: 31 "Attack only the **k** of Israel!"
22: 32 after him. "There is the **k** of Israel!" they shouted.
22: 33 the charioteers realized he was not the **k** of Israel,
22: 34 and the arrow hit the **k** of Israel between the joints
22: 37 So the **k** died, and his body was taken to Samaria
22: 40 Then his son Ahaziah became the next **k**.
22: 41 in the fourth year of **K** Ahab's reign in Israel.
22: 42 He was thirty-five years old when he became **k**,
22: 43 Jehoshaphat was a good **k**, following the example
22: 44 Jehoshaphat also made peace with the **k** of Israel.
22: 47 There was no **k** in Edom at that time, only a
22: 50 of David. Then his son Jehoram became the next **k**.
22: 51 year of **K** Jehoshaphat's reign in Judah.
2Ki 1: 1 After **K** Ahab's death, the nation of Moab declared
1: 2 One day Israel's new **k**, Ahaziah, fell through the
1: 3 and meet the messengers of the **k** of Samaria
1: 3 god of Ekron, to ask whether the **k** will get well?
1: 5 When the messengers returned to the **k**, he asked
1: 6 and told us to go back to the **k** with a message
1: 6 god of Ekron, to ask whether the **k** will get well?
1: 7 "Who was this man?" the **k** demanded.
1: 8 "It was Elijah from Tishbe!" the **k** exclaimed.
1: 9 the **k** has commanded you to come along with us."
1: 11 So the **k** sent another captain with fifty men.
1: 11 the **k** says that you must come down right away."
1: 13 Once more the **k** sent a captain with fifty men.
1: 15 Go with him." So Elijah got up and went to the **k**.
1: 16 And Elijah said to the **k**, "This is what the LORD
1: 17 succeed him, his brother Joram became the next **k**.
1: 17 reign of Jehoram son of Jehoshaphat, **k** of Judah.
3: 1 eighteenth year of **K** Jehoshaphat's reign in Judah.
3: 4 **K** Mesha of Moab and his people were sheep
3: 4 They used to pay the **k** of Israel an annual tribute
3: 5 the **k** of Moab rebelled against the **k** of Israel.
3: 6 So **K** Joram mustered the army of Israel
3: 7 he sent this message to **K** Jehoshaphat of Judah:
3: 7 "The **k** of Moab has rebelled against me. Will you
3: 9 The **k** of Edom and his troops joined them, and all
3: 10 "What should we do?" the **k** of Israel cried out.
3: 10 three of us here to let the **k** of Moab defeat us."
3: 11 But **K** Jehoshaphat of Judah asked, "Is there no
3: 11 One of **K** Joram's officers replied, "Elisha son of
3: 13 want no part of you," Elisha said to the **k** of Israel.
3: 13 your father and mother!" But **K** Joram said, "No!
3: 13 kings here to be destroyed by the **k** of Moab!"
3: 14 except for my respect for **K** Jehoshaphat of Judah.
3: 26 When the **k** of Moab saw that he was losing the
3: 26 break through the enemy lines near the **k** of Edom,
3: 27 his oldest son, who would have been the next **k**,
4: 13 she want me to put in a good word for her to the **k**
5: 1 The **k** of Aram had high admiration for Naaman,
5: 4 So Naaman told the **k** what the young girl from
5: 5 "Go and visit the prophet," the **k** told him. "I will
5: 5 of introduction for you to carry to the **k** of Israel."
5: 6 The letter to the **k** of Israel said: "With this letter I
5: 7 When the **k** of Israel read it, he tore his clothes in
5: 18 When my master the **k** goes into the temple of the
6: 8 When the **k** of Aram was at war with Israel,
6: 9 the man of God, would warn the **k** of Israel,
6: 10 So the **k** of Israel would send word to the place
6: 11 The **k** of Aram became very upset over this.
6: 11 Who has been informing the **k** of Israel of my
6: 12 tells the **k** of Israel even the words you speak in the
6: 13 The **k** commanded, "Go and find out where Elisha
6: 14 So one night the **k** of Aram sent a great army with
6: 21 When the **k** of Israel saw them, he shouted to
6: 23 So the **k** made a great feast for them and then sent
them home to their **k**.
6: 24 **K** Ben-hadad of Aram mobilized his entire army
6: 26 One day as the **k** of Israel was walking along the
6: 26 called to him, "Please help me, my lord the **k**!"
6: 28 But then the **k** asked, "What is the matter?"
6: 30 When the **k** heard this, he tore his clothes in
6: 30 And as the **k** walked along the wall, the people
6: 31 Elisha son of Shaphat this very day," the **k** vowed.
6: 32 when the **k** sent a messenger to summon him.
6: 33 And the **k** said, "It is the LORD who has brought
7: 2 The officer assisting the **k** said to the man of God,
7: 6 "The **k** of Israel has hired the Hittites
7: 12 The **k** got out of bed in the middle of the night
7: 14 and the **k** sent scouts to see what had happened to
7: 15 The scouts returned and told the **k** about it.
7: 17 The **k** appointed his officer to control the traffic at
7: 17 God had predicted when the **k** came to his house.
7: 18 The man of God had said to the **k**, "By this time
8: 3 and she went to see the **k** about getting back her
8: 4 As she came in, the **k** was talking with Gehazi,
8: 4 The **k** had just said, "Tell me some stories about
8: 5 And Gehazi was telling the **k** about the time Elisha
8: 5 of the boy walked in to make her appeal to the **k**.
8: 6 "Is this true?" the **k** asked her. And she told him
8: 7 the capital of Aram, where **K** Ben-hadad lay sick.
8: 7 Someone told the **k** that the man of God had come.
8: 8 When the **k** heard the news, he said to Hazael,
8: 9 "Your servant Ben-hadad, the **k** of Aram,
8: 13 me that you are going to be the **k** of Aram."
8: 14 When Hazael went back, the **k** asked him,
8: 15 he died. Then Hazael became the next **k** of Aram.
8: 16 Jehoram son of **K** Jehoshaphat of Judah began to
8: 16 Judah in the fifth year of **K** Joram's reign in Israel.
8: 17 was thirty-two years old when he became **k**,
8: 18 the kings of Israel and was as wicked as **K** Ahab,
8: 20 revolted against Judah and crowned their own **k**.
8: 24 of David. Then his son Ahaziah became the next **k**.
8: 25 in the twelfth year of **K** Joram's reign in Israel. **K**
Joram was the son of Ahab.
8: 26 was twenty-two years old when he became **k**,
8: 26 was Athaliah, a granddaughter of **K** Omri of Israel.
8: 27 Ahaziah followed the evil example of **K** Ahab's
8: 28 Ahaziah joined **K** Joram of Israel in his war
against **K** Hazael of Aram at Ramoth-gilead.
8: 28 When **K** Joram was wounded in the battle,
8: 29 was there, **K** Ahaziah of Judah went to visit him.
9: 3 I anoint you to be the **k** over Israel.' Then open the
9: 6 I anoint you **k** over the LORD's people, Israel.
9: 12 command he had been anointed **k** over Israel.
9: 13 and blew a trumpet, shouting, "Jehu is **k**!"
9: 14 of Nimshi formed a conspiracy against **K** Joram.
9: 14 defending Israel against the forces of **K** Hazael of
9: 15 the men with him, "Since you want me to be **k**,
9: 16 into a chariot and rode to Jezreel to find **K** Joram,
9: 16 **K** Ahaziah of Judah was there, too, for he had
9: 17 they are coming in peace," **K** Joram shouted back.
9: 18 "The **k** wants to know whether you are coming in
9: 18 The watchman called out to the **k**, "The rider has
9: 19 So the **k** sent out a second rider. He rode up to
9: 19 "The **k** wants to know whether you come in
9: 21 Get my chariot ready!" **K** Joram commanded.
9: 21 Then **K** Joram of Israel and **K** Ahaziah of Judah
rode out in their chariots
9: 22 **K** Joram demanded, "Do you come in peace,
9: 23 Then **K** Joram reined the chariot horses around
and fled, shouting to **K** Ahaziah,
9: 27 When **K** Ahaziah of Judah saw what was
9: 29 in the eleventh year of **K** Joram's reign in Israel.
9: 34 this cursed woman, for she is the daughter of a **k**."
10: 1 the people, and to the guardians of **K** Ahab's sons.
10: 3 the best qualified of **K** Ahab's sons to be your **k**,
10: 5 We will not make anyone **k**; do whatever you think
10: 6 Now the seventy sons of the **k** were being cared
10: 13 he met some relatives of **K** Ahaziah of Judah.
10: 13 And they replied, "We are relatives of **K** Ahaziah.
10: 13 We are going to visit the sons of **K** Ahab
10: 32 **K** Hazael conquered several sections of the
10: 35 Then his son Jehoahaz became the next **k**.
11: 1 When Athaliah, the mother of **K** Ahaziah of Judah,
11: 2 the daughter of **K** Jehoram, took Ahaziah's infant
11: 7 stand guard for the **k** at the LORD's Temple.
11: 8 Form a bodyguard for the **k** and keep your
11: 8 be killed. Stay right beside the **k** at all times."
11: 10 and shields that had once belonged to **K** David
11: 11 The guards stationed themselves around the **k**,
11: 12 a copy of God's covenant and proclaimed him **k**.
11: 12 their hands and shouted, "Long live the **k**!"
11: 14 And she saw the newly crowned **k** standing in his
11: 17 made a covenant between the LORD and the **k**
11: 17 He also made a covenant between the **k**
11: 19 and all the people of the land escorted the **k** from
11: 19 and the **k** took his seat on the royal throne.
11: 21 Joash was seven years old when he became **k**.
12: 1 in the seventh year of **K** Jehu's reign in Israel.
12: 4 One day **K** Joash said to the priests, "Collect all
12: 7 So **K** Joash called for Jehoiada and the other
12: 17 About this time **K** Hazael of Aram went to war
12: 18 **K** Joash collected all the sacred objects that
12: 21 Then his son Amaziah became the next **k**.
13: 1 the twenty-third year of **K** Joash's reign in Judah.
13: 3 and he allowed **K** Hazael of Aram and his son
13: 4 The LORD could see how terribly the **k** of Aram
13: 7 The **k** of Aram had killed the others like they were
13: 9 Then his son Jehoash became the next **k**.
13: 10 the thirty-seventh year of **K** Joash's reign in Judah.
13: 12 his power and his war with **K** Amaziah of Judah,
13: 13 Then his son Jeroboam II became the next **k**.
13: 14 **K** Jehoash of Israel visited him and wept over him.
13: 15 and some arrows." And the **k** did as he was told.
13: 16 Then Elisha told the **k** of Israel to put his hand on
13: 18 So the **k** picked them up and struck the ground
13: 22 **K** Hazael of Aram had oppressed Israel during the
entire reign of **K** Jehoahaz.
13: 24 **K** Hazael of Aram died, and his son Ben-hadad
became the next **k**.
14: 1 the second year of the reign of **K** Jehoash of Israel.
14: 2 was twenty-five years old when he became **k**,
14: 5 When Amaziah was well established as **k**,
14: 8 One day Amaziah sent this challenge to Israel's **k**
14: 9 But **K** Jehoash of Israel replied to **K** Amaziah
14: 11 so **K** Jehoash of Israel mobilized his army against
K Amaziah of Judah.
14: 13 **K** Jehoash of Israel captured **K** Amaziah of
14: 15 his power and his war with **K** Amaziah of Judah,
14: 16 Then his son Jeroboam II became the next **k**.
14: 17 **K** Amaziah of Judah lived on for fifteen years
after the death of **K** Jehoash of Israel.
14: 21 sixteen-year-old son, Uzziah, as their next **k**.
14: 23 began to rule over Israel in the fifteenth year of **K**
14: 29 Then his son Zechariah became the next **k**.
15: 1 year of the reign of **K** Jeroboam II of Israel.
15: 2 He was sixteen years old when he became **k**,
15: 5 The LORD struck the **k** with leprosy,
15: 7 of David. Then his son Jotham became the next **k**.
15: 8 the thirty-eighth year of **K** Uzziah's reign in Judah.
15: 10 assassinated him in public, and became the next **k**.
15: 13 the thirty-ninth year of **K** Uzziah's reign in Judah.
15: 14 and assassinated him, and he became the next **k**.
15: 17 the thirty-ninth year of **K** Uzziah's reign in Judah.
15: 19 Then **K** Tiglath-pileser of Assyria invaded the
15: 20 So the **k** of Assyria turned from attacking Israel
15: 22 his son Pekahiah became the next **k**.
15: 23 in the fiftieth year of **K** Uzziah's reign in Judah.
15: 25 Pekah assassinated the **k**, along with Argob
15: 25 at Samaria. Pekah then became the next **k** of Israel.
15: 27 the fifty-second year of **K** Uzziah's reign in Judah.
15: 29 **K** Tiglath-pileser of Assyria attacked Israel again,
15: 32 in the second year of **K** Pekah's reign in Israel.
15: 33 He was twenty-five years old when he became **k**,
15: 37 In those days the LORD began to send **K** Rezin
15: 37 of Aram and **K** Pekah of Israel to attack Judah.
15: 38 of David. Then his son Ahaz became the next **k**.
16: 1 the seventeenth year of **K** Pekah's reign in Israel.
16: 2 Ahaz was twenty years old when he became **k**,
16: 5 Then **K** Rezin of Aram and **K** Pekah of Israel
declared war on Ahaz.
16: 6 At that time the **k** of Edom recovered the town of
16: 7 **K** Ahaz sent messengers to **K** Tiglath-pileser of
16: 8 and sent it as a gift to the Assyrian **k**.
16: 9 resettling them in Kir. They also killed **K** Rezin.
16: 10 **K** Ahaz then went to Damascus to meet with **K**
16: 11 and it was ready for the **k** when he returned from
16: 12 When the **k** returned, he inspected the altar
16: 13 The **k** presented a burnt offering and a grain
16: 14 Then **K** Ahaz removed the old bronze altar from
16: 16 Uriah the priest did just as **K** Ahaz instructed him.
16: 17 Then the **k** removed the side panels and basins
16: 18 In deference to the **k** of Assyria, he also removed
16: 20 Then his son Hezekiah became the next **k**.
17: 1 in the twelfth year of **K** Ahaz's reign in Judah.
17: 3 **K** Shalmaneser of Assyria attacked and defeated **K**
Hoshea,
17: 4 Then Hoshea conspired against the **k** of Assyria by
17: 4 **K** So of Egypt to help him shake free of Assyria's
17: 4 When the **k** of Assyria discovered this treachery,
17: 5 Then the **k** of Assyria invaded the entire land,
17: 6 Finally, in the ninth year of **K** Hoshea's reign,
17: 21 they chose Jeroboam son of Nebat as their **k**.
17: 24 And the **k** of Assyria transported groups of people
17: 26 So a message was sent to the **k** of Assyria:
17: 27 The **k** of Assyria then commanded, "Send one of
18: 1 in the third year of **K** Hoshea's reign in Israel.
18: 2 He was twenty-five years old when he became **k**,
18: 5 There was never another **k** like him in the land of
18: 7 He revolted against the **k** of Assyria and refused to
18: 9 which was the seventh year of **K** Hoshea's reign in
18: 9 **K** Shalmaneser of Assyria attacked Israel
18: 10 during the sixth year of **K** Hezekiah's reign
18: 10 and the ninth year of **K** Hoshea's reign in Israel,
18: 11 At that time the **k** of Assyria deported the Israelites
18: 13 In the fourteenth year of **K** Hezekiah's reign,
18: 13 **K** Sennacherib of Assyria came to attack the
18: 14 **K** Hezekiah sent this message to the **k** of
18: 14 The **k** of Assyria then demanded a settlement of
18: 15 **K** Hezekiah used all the silver stored in the Temple
18: 16 with gold, and he gave it all to the Assyrian **k**.
18: 17 Nevertheless the **k** of Assyria sent his commander
18: 17 a huge army to confront **K** Hezekiah in Jerusalem.
18: 18 They summoned **K** Hezekiah, but the **k** sent these
officials to meet with them:
18: 19 representative sent this message to **K** Hezekiah:
18: 19 "This is what the great **k** of Assyria says:
18: 22 But isn't he the one who was insulted by **K**
18: 23 My master, the **k** of Assyria, will strike a bargain
18: 28 "Listen to this message from the great **k** of
18: 29 This is what the **k** says: Don't let **K** Hezekiah
deceive you.
18: 30 city will never be handed over to the Assyrian **k**.'
18: 31 These are the terms the **k** of Assyria is offering:
18: 33 ever saved their people from the **k** of Assyria?
18: 37 and they went in to see the **k** and told him what the
19: 1 When **K** Hezekiah heard their report, he tore his
19: 3 They told him, "This is what **K** Hezekiah says:

19: 5 After **K** Hezekiah's officials delivered the king's
19: 7 and the **k** will receive a report from Assyria telling
19: 8 left Jerusalem and went to consult his **k**,
19: 9 Soon afterward **K** Sennacherib received word that
19: 9 **K** Tirhakah of Ethiopia was leading an army to
19:10 "This message is for **K** Hezekiah of Judah.
19:10 Jerusalem will not be captured by the **k** of Assyria.
19:13 What happened to the **k** of Hamath and the **k** of Arpad?
19:20 I have heard your prayer about **K** Sennacherib of
19:29 the LORD will protect this city from Assyria's **k**.
19:32 "And this is what the LORD says about the **k** of
19:33 The **k** will return to his own country by the road on
19:36 Then **K** Sennacherib of Assyria broke camp
19:37 Esarhaddon, became the next **k** of Assyria.
20: 1 He gave the **k** this message: "This is what the
20: 6 will rescue you and this city from the **k** of Assyria.
20:12 **k** of Babylon, sent Hezekiah his best wishes
20:14 Then Isaiah the prophet went to **K** Hezekiah
20:18 who will serve in the palace of Babylon's **k**."
20:19 But the **k** was thinking, "At least there will be
20:21 his son Manasseh became the next **k**.
21: 1 Manasseh was twelve years old when he became **k**,
21: 3 Asherah pole, just as **K** Ahab of Israel had done.
21:11 "**K** Manasseh of Judah has done many detestable
21:18 of Uzza. Then his son Amon became the next **k**.
21:19 was twenty-two years old when he became **k**,
21:24 all those who had conspired against **K** Amon,
21:24 and they made his son Josiah the next **k**.
21:26 of Uzza. Then his son Josiah became the next **k**.
22: 1 Josiah was eight years old when he became **k**,
22: 3 **K** Josiah sent Shaphan son of Azaliah
22: 9 Shaphan returned to the **k** and reported,
22:10 Shaphan also said to the **k**, "Hilkiah the priest has given me a scroll." So Shaphan read it to the **k**.
22:11 When the **k** heard what was written in the Book of
22:18 "But go to the **k** of Judah who sent you to seek the
22:20 place.' " So they took her message back to the **k**.
23: 1 Then the **k** summoned all the leaders of Judah
23: 2 And the **k** went up to the Temple of the LORD
23: 2 There the **k** read to them the entire Book of the
23: 3 The **k** took his place of authority beside the pillar
23: 4 Then the **k** instructed Hilkiah the high priest
23: 4 The **k** had all these things burned outside
23: 6 The **k** removed the Asherah pole from the
23:10 Then the **k** defiled the altar of Topheth in the
23:11 The **k** also burned the chariots dedicated to the
23:12 The **k** destroyed the altars that Manasseh had built
23:13 The **k** also desecrated the pagan shrines east of
23:13 where **K** Solomon of Israel had built shrines for
23:15 The **k** also tore down the altar at Bethel, the pagan
23:21 **K** Josiah then issued this order to all the people:
23:23 during the eighteenth year of **K** Josiah's reign.
23:25 Never before had there been a **k** like Josiah,
23:25 And there has never been a **k** like him since.
23:26 because of all the great evils of **K** Manasseh,
23:29 While Josiah was **k**, Pharaoh Neco, **k** of Egypt, went to the Euphrates River to help the **k** of
23:29 **K** Josiah marched out with his army to fight him,
23:29 but **K** Neco killed him when they met at Megiddo.
23:30 his son Jehoahaz and made him the next **k**.
23:31 was twenty-three years old when he became **k**,
23:36 was twenty-five years old when he became **k**,
24: 1 **K** Nebuchadnezzar of Babylon invaded the land of
24: 6 his son Jehoiachin became the next **k**.
24: 7 The **k** of Egypt never returned after that,
24: 7 for the **k** of Babylon occupied the entire area
24: 8 was eighteen years old when he became **k**,
24:10 the officers of **K** Nebuchadnezzar of Babylon
24:12 Then **K** Jehoiachin, along with his advisers,
24:13 They cut apart all the gold vessels that **K** Solomon
24:14 **K** Nebuchadnezzar took ten thousand captives
24:15 Nebuchadnezzar led **K** Jehoiachin away as a
24:17 Then the **k** of Babylon installed Mattaniah, Jehoiachin's uncle, as the next **k**,
24:18 was twenty-one years old when he became **k**,
24:20 Then Zedekiah rebelled against the **k** of Babylon.
25: 1 **K** Nebuchadnezzar of Babylon led his entire army
25: 2 siege until the eleventh year of **K** Zedekiah's reign.
25: 5 and caught the **k** on the plains of Jericho,
25: 6 They brought him to the **k** of Babylon at Riblah,
25: 7 The **k** of Babylon made Zedekiah watch as all his
25: 8 of the guard, an official of the Babylonian **k**,
25:11 had declared their allegiance to the **k** of Babylon.
25:16 the LORD's Temple in the days of **K** Solomon.
25:20 Nebuzaradan the commander took them all to the **k**
25:21 the **k** of Babylon had them all put to death.
25:22 Then **K** Nebuchadnezzar appointed Gedaliah son
25:23 and their men learned that the **k** of Babylon had
25:24 "Live in the land and serve the **k** of Babylon,
25:27 In the thirty-seventh year of **K** Jehoiachin's exile
25:30 The Babylonian **k** also gave him a regular
1Ch 1:44 Jobab son of Zerah from Bozrah became **k**.
1:45 Husham from the land of the Temanites became **k**.
1:46 Hadad son of Bedad became **k** and ruled from the
1:47 Samlah from the city of Masrekah became **k**.
1:48 city of Rehoboth on the Euphrates River became **k**.
1:49 Shaul died, Baal-hanan son of Acbor became **k**.
1:50 Hadad became **k** and ruled from the city of Pau.
3: 2 was Maacah, the daughter of Talmai, **k** of Geshur.
4:23 in Netaim and Gederah. They all worked for the **k**.
4:31 were under their control until the time of **K** David.
4:41 But during the reign of **K** Hezekiah of Judah,
5: 6 into captivity by **K** Tiglath-pileser of Assyria.
5:17 records during the days of **K** Jotham of Judah and **K** Jeroboam of Israel.
5:26 So the God of Israel caused **K** Pul of Assyria (also
7: 2 At the time of **K** David, the total number of men
11: 2 For a long time, even while Saul was our **k**,
11: 3 They anointed him **k** of Israel, just as the LORD
11:10 all Israel, they determined to make David their **k**,
12:23 They were all eager to see David become **k** instead
12:31 the express purpose of helping David become **k**.
12:38 the single purpose of making David the **k** of Israel.
12:38 all Israel agreed that David should be their **k**.
14: 1 Now **K** Hiram of Tyre sent messengers to David,
14: 2 that the LORD had made him **k** over Israel
14: 8 that David had been anointed **k** over all Israel,
15:29 When she saw **K** David dancing and leaping for
16:31 Tell all the nations that the LORD is **k**.
17:16 Then **K** David went in and sat before the LORD
18: 3 Then David destroyed the forces of **K** Hadadezer
18: 9 When **K** Toi of Hamath heard that David had
18: 9 had destroyed the army of **K** Hadadezer of Zobah,
18:11 **K** David dedicated all these gifts to the LORD,
19: 1 time after this, **K** Nahash of the Ammonites died, and his son Hanun became **k**.
19: 7 and secured the support of the **k** of Maacah and his
21: 4 But the **k** insisted that Joab take the census,
21: 6 so distressed at what the **k** had made him do.
21:21 When Araunah saw the **k** approaching, he left his
21:24 But the **k** replied to Araunah, "No, I insist on
23: 1 he appointed his son Solomon to be **k** over Israel.
24: 6 and assignments in the presence of the **k**,
24:31 It was done in the presence of **K** David, Zadok,
25: 6 Jeduthun, and Heman reported directly to the **k**.
26:26 all the things dedicated to the LORD by **K** David,
26:30 of the LORD and the service of the **k** in that area.
26:32 **K** David sent them to the east side of the Jordan
26:32 to the things of God and the service of the **k**.
27: 1 who served the **k** by supervising the army
27:24 The final total was never recorded in **K** David's
27:31 All these officials were overseers of **K** David's
27:32 David's uncle, was a wise counselor to the **k**,
28: 4 all my father's family to be **k** over Israel forever.
28: 4 the LORD was pleased to make me **k** over all
28:13 The **k** also gave Solomon the instructions
29: 1 Then **K** David turned to the entire assembly
29: 1 whom God has chosen to be the next **k** of Israel,
29: 9 to the LORD, and **K** David was filled with joy.
29:20 bowed low and knelt before the LORD and the **k**.
29:22 they crowned David's son Solomon as their new **k**.
29:24 and the sons of **K** David pledged their loyalty to **K** Solomon.
29:29 All the events of **K** David's reign, from beginning
2Ch 1: 1 Solomon, the son of **K** David, now took firm
1: 8 David, and now you have made me **k** in his place.
1: 9 for you have made me **k** over a people as
1:12 and honor such as no other **k** has ever had before
2: 3 Solomon also sent this message to **K** Hiram at
2:11 **K** Hiram sent this letter of reply to Solomon:
2:11 loves his people that he has made you their **k**!
3: 1 had appeared to Solomon's father, **K** David.
4:11 So at last Huram-abi completed everything **K**
4:16 of the LORD, just as **K** Solomon had requested.
4:17 The **k** had them cast in clay molds in the Jordan
5: 1 **K** David, including all the silver and gold and all
5: 3 They all assembled before the **k** at the annual
5: 6 **K** Solomon and the entire community of Israel
6: 3 Then the **k** turned around to the entire community
6: 5 Nor have I chosen a **k** to lead my people Israel.
6: 6 Jerusalem as that city, and David as that **k**.' "
6:10 for I have become **k** in my father's place.
7: 4 Then the **k** and all the people offered sacrifices to
7: 5 **K** Solomon offered a sacrifice of 22,000 oxen
7: 5 And so the **k** and all the people dedicated the
7: 6 **K** David had made for praising the LORD.
8: 1 now twenty years since Solomon had become **k**,
8: 2 rebuilding the towns that **K** Hiram had given him,
8:10 **K** Solomon also appointed 250 of them to
8:11 "My wife must not live in **K** David's palace,
9: 5 She exclaimed to the **k**, "Everything I heard in my
9: 8 he has made you **k** so you can rule with justice
9: 9 Then she gave the **k** a gift of nine thousand pounds
9:11 The **k** used the almug wood to make steps for the
9:12 **K** Solomon gave the queen of Sheba whatever she
9:15 **K** Solomon made two hundred large shields of
9:16 The **k** placed these shields in the Palace of the
9:17 Then the **k** made a huge ivory throne and overlaid
9:20 All of **K** Solomon's drinking cups were solid gold,
9:21 The **k** had a fleet of trading ships manned by the
9:22 So **K** Solomon became richer and wiser than any other **k** in all the earth.
9:27 The **k** made silver as plentiful in Jerusalem as
9:31 Then his son Rehoboam became the next **k**.
10: 1 where all Israel had gathered to make him **k**.
10: 2 for he had fled to Egypt to escape from **K**
10: 6 Then **K** Rehoboam went to discuss the matter with
10:12 Rehoboam's decision, just as the **k** had requested.
10:15 So the **k** paid no attention to the people's demands.
10:16 When all Israel realized that the **k** had rejected
10:18 **K** Rehoboam sent Adoniram, who was in charge of
10:18 When this news reached **K** Rehoboam, he quickly
11: 3 **k** of Judah, and to all the Israelites in Judah
11:22 making it clear that he would be the next **k**.
12: 2 **K** Shishak of Egypt attacked Jerusalem in the fifth year of **K** Rehoboam's reign.
12: 6 The **k** and the leaders of Israel humbled
12: 9 So **K** Shishak of Egypt came to Jerusalem and took
12:10 **K** Rehoboam later replaced them with bronze
12:11 Whenever the **k** went to the Temple of the
12:13 **K** Rehoboam firmly established himself in
12:13 He was forty-one years old when he became **k**,
12:14 But he was an evil **k**, for he did not seek the
12:16 of David. Then his son Abijah became the next **k**.
13: 3 Judah, led by **K** Abijah, fielded 400,000 seasoned
14: 1 of David. Then his son Asa became the next **k**.
14: 8 **K** Asa had an army of 300,000 warriors from the
15: 2 and he went out to meet **K** Asa as he was returning
15:16 **K** Asa even deposed his grandmother Maacah
16: 1 **K** Baasha of Israel invaded Judah and fortified
16: 1 or leaving **K** Asa's territory in Judah.
16: 2 He sent it to **K** Ben-hadad of Aram, who was
16: 3 Break your treaty with **K** Baasha of Israel so that
16: 4 Ben-hadad agreed to **K** Asa's request and sent his
16: 6 Then **K** Asa called out all the men of Judah to
16: 7 At that time Hanani the seer came to **K** Asa
16: 7 "Because you have put your trust in the **k** of Aram
16: 7 your chance to destroy the army of the **k** of Aram.
17: 1 Then Jehoshaphat, Asa's son, became the next **k**.
17:19 the troops stationed in Jerusalem to serve the **k**,
18: 1 his son to marry the daughter of **K** Ahab of Israel.
18: 5 So **K** Ahab summoned his prophets, four hundred
18: 7 **K** Ahab replied, "There is still one prophet of the
18: 8 So the **k** of Israel called one of his officials
18: 9 **K** Ahab of Israel and **K** Jehoshaphat of Judah,
18:12 all the prophets are promising victory for the **k**.
18:14 When Micaiah arrived before the **k**, Ahab asked
18:15 But the **k** replied sharply, "How many times must
18:17 I tell you?" the **k** of Israel said to Jehoshaphat.
18:19 'Who can entice **K** Ahab of Israel to go into battle
18:25 **K** Ahab of Israel then ordered, "Arrest Micaiah
18:26 Give them this order from the **k**: 'Put this man in
18:28 So the **k** of Israel and **K** Jehoshaphat of Judah led their armies
18:29 Now **K** Ahab said to Jehoshaphat, "As we go into
18:30 Now the **k** of Aram had issued these orders to his charioteers: "Attack only the **k** of Israel!"
18:31 after him. "There is the **k** of Israel!" they shouted.
18:32 the charioteers realized he was not the **k** of Israel,
18:33 and the arrow hit the **k** of Israel between the joints
19: 1 When **K** Jehoshaphat of Judah arrived safely home
19: 2 love those who hate the LORD?" he asked the **k**.
20:15 He said, "Listen, **K** Jehoshaphat! Listen, all you
20:18 Then **K** Jehoshaphat bowed down with his face to
20:21 the **k** appointed singers to walk ahead of the army,
20:25 **K** Jehoshaphat and his men went out to gather the
20:31 He was thirty-five years old when he became **k**,
20:32 Jehoshaphat was a good **k**, following the ways of
20:35 **K** Jehoshaphat of Judah made an alliance with **K** Ahaziah of Israel,
20:37 "Because you have allied yourself with **K**
21: 1 of David. Then his son Jehoram became the next **k**.
21: 3 Jehoram became **k** because he was the oldest.
21: 4 Jehoram had become solidly established as **k**,
21: 5 was thirty-two years old when he became **k**,
21: 6 the kings of Israel and was as wicked as **K** Ahab,
21: 8 revolted against Judah and crowned their own **k**.
21:12 Jehoshaphat, or your grandfather **K** Asa of Judah.
21:13 to worship idols, just as **K** Ahab did in Israel.
21:20 was thirty-two years old when he became **k**,
22: 1 Jehoram's youngest son, their next **k**.
22: 1 So Ahaziah son of Jehoram reigned as **k** of Judah.
22: 2 was twenty-two years old when he became **k**,
22: 2 was Athaliah, a granddaughter of **K** Omri of Israel.
22: 3 Ahaziah also followed the evil example of **K**
22: 5 Ahaziah made an alliance with **K** Joram, the son of **K** Ahab of Israel.
22: 5 They went out to fight **K** Hazael of Aram at
22: 6 and **K** Ahaziah of Judah went to Jezreel to visit
22:10 When Athaliah, the mother of **K** Ahaziah of Judah,
22:11 the daughter of **K** Jehoram, took Ahaziah's infant
23: 3 they made a covenant with Joash, the young **k**.
23: 3 promised that a descendant of David will be our **k**.
23: 7 form a bodyguard for the **k** and keep your weapons
23: 7 be killed. Stay right beside the **k** at all times."
23: 9 and shields that had once belonged to **K** David
23:10 He stationed the guards around the **k**, with their
23:11 with a copy of God's laws and proclaimed him **k**.
23:11 and everyone shouted, "Long live the **k**!"
23:12 people running and the shouts of praise to the **k**,
23:13 And she saw the newly crowned **k** standing in his
23:16 made a covenant between himself and the **k**
23:20 and all the people escorted the **k** from the Temple
23:20 and they seated the **k** on the royal throne.
24: 1 Joash was seven years old when he became **k**,
24: 6 So the **k** called for Jehoiada the high priest
24:12 The **k** and Jehoiada gave the money to the
24:14 they brought the remaining money to the **k**
24:17 leaders of Judah came and bowed before **K** Joash
24:17 and persuaded the **k** to listen to their advice.
24:21 to kill Zechariah, and by order of **K** Joash himself,
24:22 That was how **K** Joash repaid Jehoiada for his love
24:23 Then they sent all the plunder back to their **k** in
24:27 Joash died, his son Amaziah became the next **k**.
25: 1 was twenty-five years old when he became **k**,
25: 3 When Amaziah was well established as **k**,
25: 7 But a man of God came to the **k** and said, "O **k**,
25:14 When **K** Amaziah returned from defeating the
25:16 But the **k** interrupted him and said, "Since when
25:17 **K** Amaziah of Judah sent this challenge to Israel's **k** Jehoash,
25:18 But **K** Jehoash of Israel replied to **K** Amaziah
25:21 So **K** Jehoash of Israel mobilized his army against **K** Amaziah of Judah.
25:23 **K** Jehoash of Israel captured **K** Amaziah of
25:25 **K** Amaziah of Judah lived on for fifteen years after the death of **K** Jehoash of Israel.
26: 1 sixteen-year-old son, Uzziah, as their next **k**.
26: 3 Uzziah was sixteen when he became **k**, and he
26: 5 And as long as the **k** sought the LORD, God gave

26:13 They were prepared to assist the **k** against any
26:18 They confronted **K** Uzziah and said, "It is not for
26:20 And the **k** himself was eager to get out
26:21 So **K** Uzziah had leprosy until the day he died.
26:23 the kings. Then his son Jotham became the next **k**.
27: 1 was twenty-five years old when he became **k**,
27: 6 **K** Jotham became powerful because he was careful
27: 8 He was twenty-five years old when he became **k**,
27: 9 of David, and his son Ahaz became the next **k**.
28: 1 Ahaz was twenty years old when he became **k**,
28: 5 That is why the LORD his God allowed the **k** of
28: 6 Israel's **k**, killed 120,000 of Judah's troops
28:16 About that time **K** Ahaz of Judah asked the **k** of
28:19 was humbling Judah because of **K** Ahaz of Judah,
28:20 So when **K** Tiglath-pileser of Assyria arrived, he oppressed **K** Ahaz instead of helping him.
28:21 and gave them to the **k** of Assyria as tribute.
28:22 And when trouble came to **K** Ahaz, he became
28:24 The **k** took the utensils from the Temple of God
28:27 When **K** Ahaz died, he was buried in Jerusalem
28:27 Then his son Hezekiah became the next **k**.
29: 1 years old when he became the **k** of Judah,
29:15 of the LORD, just as the **k** had commanded.
29:18 Then the Levites went to **K** Hezekiah and gave
29:19 We have also recovered all the utensils taken by **K**
29:20 Early the next morning **K** Hezekiah gathered the
29:21 The **k** commanded the priests, who were
29:23 then brought before the **k** and the assembly of
29:24 The **k** had specifically commanded that this burnt
29:25 **K** Hezekiah then stationed the Levites at the
29:25 the LORD had given to **K** David through Gad,
29:27 and other instruments of David, **k** of Israel.
29:29 Then the **k** and everyone with him bowed down in
29:30 **K** Hezekiah and the officials ordered the Levites to
30: 1 **K** Hezekiah now sent word to all Israel and Judah,
30: 2 The **k**, his officials, and all the community of
30: 4 plan for keeping the Passover seemed right to the **k**
30:12 strong desire to unite in obeying the orders of the **k**
30:18 But **K** Hezekiah prayed for them, and they were
30:24 **K** Hezekiah gave the people one thousand bulls
30:26 this one since the days of Solomon, **K** David's son.
31: 3 The **k** also made a personal contribution of animals
31:13 These appointments were made by **K** Hezekiah
31:20 **K** Hezekiah handled the distribution throughout all
32: 1 **K** Sennacherib of Assyria invaded Judah.
32: 7 Don't be afraid of the **k** of Assyria or his mighty
32: 9 Then **K** Sennacherib of Assyria, while still
32:10 "This is what **K** Sennacherib of Assyria says:
32:11 'The LORD our God will rescue us from the **k** of
32:17 The **k** also sent letters scorning the LORD,
32:20 Then **K** Hezekiah and the prophet Isaiah son of
32:22 and the people of Jerusalem from **K** Sennacherib
32:23 then on **K** Hezekiah became highly respected
32:23 with valuable presents for **K** Hezekiah, too.
32:33 Then his son Manasseh became the next **k**.
33: 1 Manasseh was twelve years old when he became **k**,
33:20 his palace. Then his son Amon became the next **k**.
33:21 was twenty-two years old when he became **k**,
33:25 all those who had conspired against **K** Amon,
33:25 and they made his son Josiah the next **k**.
34: 1 Josiah was eight years old when he became **k**,
34:16 Shaphan took the scroll to the **k** and reported,
34:18 Shaphan also said to the **k**, "Hilkiah the priest has given me a scroll." So Shaphan read it to the **k**.
34:19 When the **k** heard what was written in the law,
34:26 "But go to the **k** of Judah who sent you to seek the
34:28 place.' " So they took her message back to the **k**.
34:29 Then the **k** summoned all the leaders of Judah
34:30 And the **k** went up to the Temple of the LORD
34:30 There the **k** read to them the entire Book of the
34:31 The **k** took his place of authority beside the pillar
35: 4 following the written instructions of **K** David of
35:16 the altar of the LORD, as **K** Josiah had ordered.
35:20 **K** Neco of Egypt led his army up from Egypt to do
35:21 But **K** Neco sent ambassadors to Josiah with this
35:21 "What do you want with me, **k** of Judah? I have
35:23 But the enemy archers hit **K** Josiah with their
36: 1 and made him the next **k** in Jerusalem.
36: 2 was twenty-three years old when he became **k**,
36: 3 Then he was deposed by Neco, the **k** of Egypt,
36: 4 The **k** of Egypt appointed Eliakim, the brother of Jehoahaz, as the next **k** of Judah and Jerusalem,
36: 5 was twenty-five years old when he became **k**,
36: 6 Then **K** Nebuchadnezzar of Babylon came to
36: 8 Then his son Jehoiachin became the next **k**.
36: 9 was eighteen years old when he became **k**,
36:10 Jehoiachin was summoned to Babylon by **K**
36:10 Zedekiah, to be the next **k** in Judah and Jerusalem.
36:11 was twenty-one years old when he became **k**,
36:13 He also rebelled against **K** Nebuchadnezzar,
36:17 So the LORD brought the **k** of Babylon against
36:18 The **k** also took home to Babylon all the utensils,
36:20 and they became servants to the **k** and his sons
36:22 In the first year of **K** Cyrus of Persia, the LORD
36:23 "This is what **K** Cyrus of Persia says:
Ezr 1: 1 In the first year of **K** Cyrus of Persia, the LORD
1: 2 "This is what **K** Cyrus of Persia says:
1: 7 **K** Cyrus himself brought out the valuable items
1: 7 **K** Nebuchadnezzar had taken from the LORD's
2: 1 They had been deported to Babylon by **K**
2:55 The descendants of these servants of **K** Solomon
3: 7 for **K** Cyrus had given permission for this.
3:10 praise the LORD, just as **K** David had prescribed.
4: 2 We have sacrificed to him ever since **K**
4: 3 just as **K** Cyrus of Persia commanded us."
4: 5 This went on during the entire reign of **K** Cyrus of
4: 5 and lasted until **K** Darius of Persia took the throne.
4: 7 And even later during the reign of **K** Artaxerxes of
4: 7 Aramaic language, and it was translated for the **k**.
4: 8 telling **K** Artaxerxes about the situation in
4: 9 They greeted the **k** for all their colleagues—
4:23 When this letter from **K** Artaxerxes was read to
4:24 the second year of the reign of **K** Darius of Persia.
5: 6 west of the Euphrates River sent to **K** Darius:
5: 7 "Greetings to **K** Darius.
5:11 built here many years ago by a great **k** of Israel.
5:12 he abandoned them to **K** Nebuchadnezzar of
5:13 However, **K** Cyrus of Babylon, during the first
5:14 **K** Cyrus returned the gold and silver utensils that
5:14 whom **K** Cyrus appointed as governor of Judah.
5:15 The **k** instructed him to return the utensils to their
5:17 "So now, if it pleases the **k**, we request that you
5:17 **K** Cyrus ever issued a decree to rebuild God's
5:17 then let the **k** send us his decision in this matter."
6: 1 So **K** Darius issued orders that a search be made in
6: 3 "In the first year of **K** Cyrus's reign, a decree was
6: 6 So **K** Darius sent this message: / "To Tattenai,
6:12 as the place to honor his name destroy any **k**
6:13 complied at once with the command of **K** Darius.
6:15 during the sixth year of **K** Darius's reign.
6:22 the attitude of the **k** of Assyria toward them,
7: 1 during the reign of **K** Artaxerxes of Persia,
7: 6 and the **k** gave him everything he asked for,
7: 7 him in the seventh year of **K** Artaxerxes' reign.
7:11 **K** Artaxerxes had presented a copy of this letter to
7:12 from Artaxerxes, the **k** of kings, to Ezra the priest,
7:21 "I, Artaxerxes the **k**, hereby send this decree to all
7:23 bringing God's anger against the realm of the **k**
7:26 and the law of the **k** will be punished immediately
7:27 who made the **k** want to beautify the Temple of the
7:28 unfailing love to me by honoring me before the **k**,
8: 1 from Babylon during the reign of **K** Artaxerxes:
8:20 a group of Temple workers first instituted by **K**
8:22 For I was ashamed to ask the **k** for soldiers
8:22 After all, we had told the **k**, "Our God protects all
8:25 and the other items that the **k**, his council,
Ne 1: 1 In late autumn of the twentieth year of **K**
1:11 Please grant me success now as I go to ask the **k**
2: 1 during the twentieth year of **K** Artaxerxes' reign, I was serving the **k** his wine.
2: 2 So the **k** asked me, "Why are you so sad?
2: 3 but I replied, "Long live the **k**! Why shouldn't I be
2: 4 The **k** asked, "Well, how can I help you?" With a
2: 6 The **k**, with the queen sitting beside him, asked,
2: 6 So the **k** agreed, and I set a date for my departure.
2: 7 I also said to the **k**, "If it please Your Majesty,
2: 8 And the **k** granted these requests,
2: 9 The **k**, I should add, had sent along army officers
2:18 been on me, and about my conversation with the **k**.
2:19 are you doing, rebelling against the **k** like this?"
5:14 thirty-second year of the reign of **K** Artaxerxes—
6: 6 According to his reports, you plan to be their **k**.
6: 7 saying, 'Look! There is a **k** in Judah!'
6: 7 be very sure that this report will get back to the **k**,
7: 6 They had been deported to Babylon by **K**
7:57 "The descendants of these servants of **K** Solomon
9:22 They completely took over the land of **K** Sihon of Heshbon and the land of **K** Og of Bashan.
13: 6 for I had returned to the **k** in the thirty-second year of the reign of **K** Artaxerxes of Babylon,
13:26 "Wasn't this exactly what led **K** Solomon of Israel
13:26 "There was no **k** from any nation who could
13:26 and God loved him and made him **k** over all Israel.
Est 1: 1 This happened in the days of **K** Xerxes,
1: 5 the **k** gave a special banquet for all the palace
1: 7 of royal wine, just as the **k** had commanded.
1: 8 for the **k** had instructed his staff to let everyone
1:10 when **K** Xerxes was half drunk with wine, he told
1:12 This made the **k** furious, and he burned with anger.
1:15 must be done to Queen Vashti?" the **k** demanded.
1:16 Memucan answered the **k** and his princes,
1:16 "Queen Vashti has wronged not only the **k**
1:17 Queen Vashti has refused to appear before the **k**.
1:19 So if it please the **k**, we suggest that you issue a
1:21 The **k** and his princes thought this made good
2: 2 empire to find beautiful young virgins for the **k**.
2: 3 Let the **k** appoint agents in each province to bring
2: 4 This advice was very appealing to the **k**, so he put
2: 6 from Jerusalem to Babylon by **K** Nebuchadnezzar,
2: 6 along with **K** Jehoiachin of Judah and many others.
2:13 When the time came for her to go in to the **k**,
2:14 never going to the **k** again unless he had especially
2:15 When it was Esther's turn to go to the **k**,
2:16 When Esther was taken to **K** Xerxes at the royal
2:17 the **k** loved her more than any of the other young
2:21 became angry at **K** Xerxes and plotted to
2:22 She then told the **k** about it and gave Mordecai
2:23 in *The Book of the History of* **K** *Xerxes' Reign.*
3: 1 **K** Xerxes promoted Haman son of Hammedatha
3: 1 official in the empire next to the **k** himself.
3: 2 he passed by, for so the **k** had commanded.
3: 7 during the twelfth year of **K** Xerxes' reign,
3: 8 Then Haman approached **K** Xerxes and said,
3: 8 and they refuse to obey even the laws of the **k**.
3:10 The **k** agreed, confirming his decision by removing
3:11 the **k** told Haman, "but go ahead and do as you
3:12 These letters were signed in the name of **K** Xerxes,
3:15 Then the **k** and Haman sat down to drink,
4: 8 and to urge her to go to the **k** to beg for mercy
4:11 **k** in his inner court without being invited is
4:11 to die unless the **k** holds out his gold scepter.
4:11 And the **k** has not called for me to come to him in
4:16 it is against the law, I will go in to see the **k**.
5: 1 The **k** was sitting on his royal throne,
5: 3 Then the **k** asked her, "What do you want,
5: 4 let the **k** and Haman come today to a banquet I have prepared for the **k**."
5: 5 The **k** turned to his attendants and said,
5: 5 So the **k** and Haman went to Esther's banquet.
5: 6 they were drinking wine, the **k** said to Esther,
5:11 He bragged about the honors the **k** had given him
5:12 and the **k** himself to the banquet she prepared for
5:12 me to dine with her and the **k** again tomorrow!"
5:14 and in the morning ask the **k** to hang Mordecai on
5:14 go on your merry way to the banquet with the **k**."
6: 1 That night the **k** had trouble sleeping, so he
6: 2 They had plotted to assassinate the **k**.
6: 3 the **k** asked. His attendants replied, "Nothing has
6: 4 the **k** inquired. Now, as it happened, Haman had
6: 4 **k** to hang Mordecai from the gallows he had
6: 5 So the attendants replied to the **k**, "Haman is out there." "Bring him in," the **k** ordered.
6: 6 So Haman came in, and the **k** said, "What should I
6: 6 "Whom would the **k** wish to honor more than
6: 7 So he replied, "If the **k** wishes to honor someone,
6: 9 'This is what happens to those the **k** wishes to
6:10 the **k** said to Haman. "Hurry and get the robe
6:11 "This is what happens to those the **k** wishes to
7: 1 So the **k** and Haman went to Queen Esther's
7: 2 the **k** again asked her, "Tell me what you want,
7: 4 a matter too trivial to warrant disturbing the **k**."
7: 5 **K** Xerxes demanded. "Who would dare touch
7: 6 Haman grew pale with fright before the **k**
7: 7 Then the **k** jumped to his feet in a rage and went
7: 8 just as the **k** returned from the palace garden.
7: 8 in the palace, before my very eyes?" the **k** roared.
7: 8 And as soon as the **k** spoke, his attendants covered
7: 9 the man who saved the **k** from assassination."
7: 9 "Then hang Haman on it!" the **k** ordered.
8: 1 On that same day **K** Xerxes gave the estate of
8: 1 Then Mordecai was brought before the **k**,
8: 1 for Esther had told the **k** how they were related.
8: 2 The **k** took off his signet ring—which he had taken
8: 3 Now once more Esther came before the **k**,
8: 4 Again the **k** held out the gold scepter to Esther.
8: 5 the Jews throughout all the provinces of the **k**.
8: 7 Then **K** Xerxes said to Queen Esther and Mordecai
8:10 Mordecai wrote in the name of **K** Xerxes
8:12 of **K** Xerxes was March 7 of the next year.
9: 1 So on March 7 the two decrees of the **k** were put
9:11 when the **k** was informed of the number of people
9:14 So the **k** agreed, and the decree was announced in
9:25 But when Esther came before the **k**, he issued a
10: 1 **K** Xerxes imposed tribute throughout his empire,
10: 2 greatness of Mordecai, whom the **k** had promoted,
10: 3 with authority next to that of **K** Xerxes himself.
Job 15:24 and anguish, like a **k** preparing for an attack.
18:14 and they are brought down to the **k** of terrors.
29:25 I lived as a **k** among his troops and as one who
41:34 it is the proudest. It is the **k** of beasts."
Ps 2: 6 "I have placed my chosen **k** on the throne
2: 7 The **k** proclaims the LORD's decree:
5: 2 Listen to my cry for help, my **K** and my God,
10:16 The LORD is **k** forever and ever! / Let those who
18:50 You give great victories to your **k**; / you show
20: 6 Now I know that the LORD saves his anointed **k**.
20: 9 Give victory to our **k**, O LORD! / Respond to our
21: 1 How the **k** rejoices in your strength, O LORD!
21: 7 For the **k** trusts in the LORD. / The unfailing love
22:28 For the LORD is **k**! / He rules all the nations.
24: 7 ancient doors, / and let the **K** of glory enter.
24: 8 Who is the **K** of glory? / The LORD, strong
24: 9 ancient doors, / and let the **K** of glory enter.
24:10 Who is the **K** of glory? / The LORD Almighty— / he is the **K** of glory.
28: 8 his people / and gives victory to his anointed **k**.
29:10 the floodwaters. / The LORD reigns as **k** forever.
33:16 The best-equipped army cannot save a **k**, / nor is
44: 4 You are my **K** and my God. / You command
45: 1 I will recite a lovely poem to the **k**,
45:14 In her beautiful robes, she is led to the **k**,
47: 2 is awesome. / He is the great **K** of all the earth.
47: 6 sing praises; / sing praise to our **K**, sing praises!
47: 7 For God is the **K** over all the earth. / Praise him
48: 2 the holy mountain, / is the city of the great **K**!
55:19 God, who is **k** forever, / will hear me and will
61: 6 Add many years to the life of the **k**! / May his
63:11 But the **k** will rejoice in God. / All who trust in
68:24 O God— / the procession of my God and **K**
72: 1 Give justice to the **k**, O God, / and righteousness to
72: 3 hills be fruitful, / because the **k** does what is right.
72:15 Long live the **k**! / May the gold of Sheba be given
74:12 You, O God, are my **k** from ages past,
84: 3 O LORD Almighty, my **K** and my God!
84: 9 O God, look with favor upon the **k**, our protector!
89:18 and he, the Holy One of Israel, has given us our **k**.
89:19 selected him from the common people to be **k**.
89:27 him my firstborn son, / the mightiest **k** on earth.
89:38 are you so angry with the one you chose as **k**?
89:51 O LORD; / they mock the one you anointed as **k**.
93: 1 The LORD is **k**! He is robed in majesty. / Indeed,
95: 3 is a great God, / the great **K** above all gods.
96:10 Tell all the nations that the LORD is **k**.
97: 1 The LORD is **k**! Let the earth rejoice!
98: 6 a joyful symphony before the LORD, the **K**!
99: 1 The LORD is **k**! / Let the nations tremble!
99: 4 Mighty **k**, lover of justice, / you have established
132:10 do not reject the **k** you chose for your people.
132:18 enemies with shame, / but he will be a glorious **k**."
135:11 Sihon **k** of the Amorites, / Og **k** of Bashan,
136:19 Sihon **k** of the Amorites, / His faithful love

136:20 and Og **k** of Bashan. / His faithful love endures
138: 4 Every **k** in all the earth will give you thanks,
145: 1 I will praise you, my God and **K**, / and bless your
146:10 O Jerusalem, your God is **K** in every generation!
149: 2 O people of Jerusalem, exult in your **K**.
Pr 1: 1 the proverbs of Solomon, David's son, **k** of Israel.
14:35 A **k** rejoices in servants who know what they are
16:10 The **k** speaks with divine wisdom; he must never
16:12 A **k** despises wrongdoing, for his rule depends on
16:13 The **k** is pleased with righteous lips; he loves those
16:14 The anger of the **k** is a deadly threat; the wise do
16:15 When the **k** smiles, there is life; his favor refreshes
20: 8 When a **k** judges, he carefully weighs all the
20:26 A wise **k** finds the wicked, lays them out like
20:28 Unfailing love and faithfulness protect the **k**;
24:21 My child, fear the LORD and the **k**, and don't
24:22 punishment from the LORD and the **k** will end?
25: 1 collected by the advisers of **K** Hezekiah of Judah.
25: 6 Don't demand an audience with the **k** or push for a
28:16 but a **k** will have a long reign if he hates
29: 4 A just **k** gives stability to his nation, but one who
29:14 A **k** who is fair to the poor will have a long reign.
30:22 a slave who becomes a **k**, / an overbearing fool
30:27 Locusts—they have no **k**, / but they march like an
30:30 the lion, **k** of animals, who won't turn aside for
30:31 the male goat, / a **k** as he leads his army.
31: 1 These are the sayings of **K** Lemuel, an oracle that
Ecc 1: 1 **K** David's son, who ruled in Jerusalem.
1:12 I, the Teacher, was **k** of Israel, and I lived in
4:13 to be an old and foolish **k** who refuses all advice.
4:14 He might even become **k**, though he was born in
5: 9 Even the **k** milks the land for his own profit!
8: 2 Obey the **k** because you have vowed before God to
8: 3 For the **k** will punish those who disobey him.
9:14 and a great **k** came with his army and besieged it.
9:17 person are better than the shouts of a foolish **k**.
10:16 Destruction is certain for the land whose **k** is a
10:17 Happy is the land whose **k** is a nobleman
10:20 Never make light of the **k**, even in your thoughts.
SS 1: 4 let's run! Bring me into your bedroom, O my **k**."
1:12 "The **k** is lying on his couch, enchanted by the
3: 8 ready to defend the **k** against an attack during the
3: 9 "**K** Solomon has built a carriage for himself from
3:11 "Go out to look upon **K** Solomon, O young
7: 5 A **k** is held captive in your queenly tresses.
Isa 6: 1 In the year **K** Uzziah died, I saw the Lord. He was
6: 5 Yet I have seen the **K**, the LORD Almighty!"
7: 1 Jerusalem was attacked by **K** Rezin of Aram and
K Pekah of Israel,
7: 2 So the hearts of the **k** and his people trembled with
7: 3 "Go out to meet **K** Ahaz, you and your son
7: 3 You will find the **k** at the end of the aqueduct that
7: 4 **K** Rezin of Aram and Pekah son of Remaliah.
7: 6 and install the son of Tabeel as Judah's **k**.'
7: 8 And Damascus is no stronger than its **k**, Rezin.
7: 9 And Samaria is no stronger than its **k**, Pekah son of
7:10 the LORD sent this message to **K** Ahaz:
7:12 But the **k** refused. "No," he said, "I wouldn't test
7:17 The mighty **k** of Assyria will come with his great
8: 4 the **k** of Assyria will invade both Damascus
8: 6 and are rejoicing over what will happen to **K**
Rezin and **K** Pekah.
8: 7 the **k** of Assyria and all his mighty armies.
8:21 fists at heaven and curse their **k** and their God.
10: 7 But the **k** of Assyria will not know that it is I who
10: 8 He will say, 'Each of my princes will soon be a **k**,
10:12 After the Lord has used the **k** of Assyria to
10:12 he will turn against the **k** of Assyria and punish
10:16 Listen now, **k** of Assyria! Because of all your evil
14: 4 you will taunt the **k** of Babylon. You will say,
14:17 Is this the **k** who demolished the world's greatest
14:20 your people. Your son will not succeed you as **k**.
14:28 This message came to me the year **K** Ahaz died:
14:29 that the **k** who attacked you is dead.
16: 1 as a token of alliance with the **k** of Judah.
16: 5 From that throne a faithful **k** will reign, one who
19: 4 cruel master, to a fierce **k**," says the Lord,
19:11 Their best counsel to the **k** of Egypt is stupid
20: 1 In the year when **K** Sargon of Assyria captured the
20: 4 For the **k** of Assyria will take away the Egyptians
20: 6 For we counted on Egypt to protect us from the **k**
30:33 has long been ready for the Assyrian **k**;
32: 1 Look, a righteous **k** is coming! And honest princes
33:17 Your eyes will see the **k** in all his splendor,
33:22 the LORD is our judge, our lawgiver, and our **k**.
36: 1 In the fourteenth year of **K** Hezekiah's reign,
36: 1 **K** Sennacherib of Assyria came to attack the
36: 2 Then the **k** of Assyria sent his personal
36: 2 Lachish to confront **K** Hezekiah in Jerusalem.
36: 4 representative sent this message to **K** Hezekiah:
36: 4 "This is what the great **k** of Assyria says:
36: 7 But isn't he the one who was insulted by **K**
36: 8 My master, the **k** of Assyria, will strike a bargain
36:13 "Listen to this message from the great **k** of
36:14 This is what the **k** says: Don't let **K** Hezekiah
deceive you.
36:15 city will never be handed over to the Assyrian **k**.'
36:16 These are the terms the **k** of Assyria is offering:
36:18 ever saved their people from the **k** of Assyria?
36:22 and they went in to see the **k** and told him what the
37: 1 When **K** Hezekiah heard their report, he tore his
37: 3 They told him, "This is what **K** Hezekiah says:
37: 5 After **K** Hezekiah's officials delivered the king's
37: 7 I myself will make sure that the **k** will receive a
37: 8 left Jerusalem and went to consult his **k**,
37: 9 Soon afterward **K** Sennacherib received word that
K Tirhakah of Ethiopia was leading an army to
37:10 "This message is for **K** Hezekiah of Judah.
37:10 Jerusalem will not be captured by the **k** of Assyria.
37:13 What happened to the **k** of Hamath and the **k** of
Arpad?
37:21 This is my answer to your prayer concerning **K**
37:30 the LORD will protect this city from Assyria's **k**.
37:33 "And this is what the LORD says about the **k** of
37:34 The **k** will return to his own country by the road on
37:37 Then **K** Sennacherib of Assyria broke camp
37:38 Esarhaddon, became the next **k** of Assyria.
38: 1 He gave the **k** this message: "This is what the
38: 6 will rescue you and this city from the **k** of Assyria.
38: 9 When **K** Hezekiah was well again, he wrote this
39: 1 **k** of Babylon, sent Hezekiah his best wishes
39: 3 Then Isaiah the prophet went to **K** Hezekiah
39: 7 who will serve in the palace of Babylon's **k**."
39: 8 But the **k** was thinking, "At least there will be
41: 2 "Who has stirred up this **k** from the east,
41:21 they can do!" says the LORD, the **K** of Israel.
43:15 your Holy One, Israel's Creator and **K**.
44: 6 Israel's **K** and Redeemer, the LORD Almighty,
Jer 1: 2 the thirteenth year of **K** Josiah's reign in Judah.
1: 3 **K** Jehoiakim, until the eleventh year of **K**
Zedekiah's reign in
3: 6 During the reign of **K** Josiah, the LORD said to
4: 9 "the **k** and the officials will tremble in fear.
8:19 "Is her **K** no longer there?" "Oh, why have they
10: 7 Who would not fear you, O **K** of nations? That title
10:10 true God, the living God. He is the everlasting **K**!
13:13 from the **k** sitting on David's throne and from the
13:18 Say to the **k** and his mother, "Come down from
15: 4 son of Hezekiah, **k** of Judah, did in Jerusalem,
17:19 first at the gate where the **k** goes out, and then at
20: 4 I will hand the people of Judah over to the **k** of
21: 1 The LORD spoke through Jeremiah when **K**
21: 2 **K** Nebuchadnezzar of Babylon has begun his
21: 3 "Go back to **K** Zedekiah and tell him,
21: 4 I will make your weapons useless against the **k** of
21: 7 the LORD, even after **K** Zedekiah, his officials,
21: 7 I will hand them over to **K** Nebuchadnezzar of
21:10 It will be captured by the **k** of Babylon, and he will
22: 1 "Go over and speak directly to the **k** of Judah.
22: 2 you **k** of Judah, sitting on David's throne.
22: 4 The **k** will ride through the palace gates in chariots
22:10 Do not weep for the dead **k** or mourn his loss.
22:10 Instead, weep for the captive **k** being led away!
22:11 who succeeded his father, **K** Josiah, and was taken
22:15 "But a beautiful palace does not make a great **k**!
22:18 decree of punishment against **K** Jehoiakim,
22:24 Jehoiachin son of Jehoiakim, **k** of Judah.
22:25 to **K** Nebuchadnezzar of Babylon and the mighty
23: 5 "when I will place a righteous Branch on **K**
23: 5 He will be a **K** who rules with wisdom. He will do
24: 1 After **K** Nebuchadnezzar of Babylon exiled
24: 1 **k** of Judah, to Babylon along with the princes of
24: 8 "represent **K** Zedekiah of Judah, his officials,
25: 1 This was the year when **K** Nebuchadnezzar of
25: 3 of Josiah son of Amon, **k** of Judah, until now—
25: 9 of the north under **K** Nebuchadnezzar of Babylon,
25:11 and her neighboring lands will serve the **k** of
25:12 I will punish the **k** of Babylon and his people for
25:26 the **k** of Babylon himself drank from the cup of the
26: 1 in the reign of Jehoiakim son of Josiah, **k** of Judah.
26:18 during the reign of **K** Hezekiah of Judah.
26:19 But did **K** Hezekiah and the people kill him for
26:21 When **K** Jehoiakim and the army officers
26:21 he was saying, the **k** sent someone to kill him.
26:22 Then **K** Jehoiakim sent Elnathan son of Acbor to
26:23 and brought him back to **K** Jehoiakim.
26:23 The **k** then killed Uriah with a sword and had him
27: 1 in the reign of Zedekiah son of Josiah, **k** of Judah.
27: 3 and Sidon through their ambassadors to **K**
27: 6 Now I will give your countries to **K**
27: 8 So you must submit to Babylon's **k** and serve him;
27: 9 "The **k** of Babylon will not conquer you."
27:11 But the people of any nation that submits to the **k**
27:12 Then I repeated this same message to **K** Zedekiah
27:12 submit to the **k** of Babylon and his people,"
27:13 every nation that refuses to submit to Babylon's **k**?
27:14 'The **k** of Babylon will not conquer you.'
27:17 Surrender to the **k** of Babylon, and you will live.
27:20 **K** Nebuchadnezzar of Babylon left them here
27:20 **k** of Judah, to Babylon, along with all the other
27:21 kept in the Temple and in the palace of Judah's **k**:
28: 1 fourth year of the reign of Zedekiah, **k** of Judah—
28: 2 I will remove the yoke of the **k** of Babylon from
28: 3 I will bring back all the Temple treasures that **K**
28: 4 back Jehoiachin son of Jehoiakim, **k** of Judah,
28: 4 I will surely break the yoke that the **k** of Babylon
28:11 now subject to **K** Nebuchadnezzar of Babylon."
28:14 forcing them into slavery under **K** Nebuchadnezzar
29: 1 had been exiled to Babylon by **K** Nebuchadnezzar.
29: 2 This was after **K** Jehoiachin, the queen mother,
29: 3 when they went to Babylon as **K** Zedekiah's
29:16 But this is what the LORD says about the **k** who
29:22 and Ahab, whom the **k** of Babylon burned alive!'
30: 9 will serve the LORD their God and David their **k**,
32: 1 the tenth year of the reign of Zedekiah, **k** of Judah.
32: 1 This was also the eighteenth year of the reign of **K**
32: 3 **K** Zedekiah had put him there because he
32: 3 I am about to hand this city over to the **k** of
32: 4 **K** Zedekiah will be captured by the Babylonians
32: 4 and taken to the **k** of Babylon to be judged
32:28 **k** of Babylon, and he will capture it.
32:36 'It will fall to the **k** of Babylon through war,
34: 1 **K** Nebuchadnezzar of Babylon came with all the
34: 2 "Go to **K** Zedekiah of Judah, and tell him, 'This is
34: 2 I am about to hand this city over to the **k** of
34: 3 You will stand before the **k** of Babylon to be
34: 4 promise from the LORD, O Zedekiah, **k** of Judah.
34: 5 will weep for you and say, "Alas, our **k** is dead!"
34: 6 delivered the message to **K** Zedekiah of Judah.
34: 8 after **K** Zedekiah made a covenant with the people,
34:21 I will hand over **K** Zedekiah of Judah and his
officials to the army of the **k** of Babylon.
34:21 And though Babylon's **k** has left this city for a
35: 1 when Jehoiakim son of Josiah was **k** of Judah:
35:11 But when **K** Nebuchadnezzar of Babylon arrived
36: 1 year that Jehoiakim son of Josiah was **k** in Judah,
36:16 "We must tell the **k** what we have heard,"
36:20 of Elishama the secretary and went to tell the **k**.
36:21 The **k** sent Jehudi to get the scroll. Jehudi brought
36:21 and read it to the **k** as all his officials stood by.
36:22 and the **k** was in a winterized part of the palace,
36:23 the **k** took his knife and cut off that section of the
36:24 Neither the **k** nor his officials showed any signs of
36:25 and Gemariah begged the **k** not to burn the scroll,
36:26 Then the **k** commanded his son Jerahmeel,
36:27 After the **k** had burned Jeremiah's scroll,
36:28 just as you did on the scroll **K** Jehoiakim burned.
36:29 Then say to the **k**, 'This is what the LORD says:
36:29 because it said the **k** of Babylon would destroy this
36:30 Now this is what the LORD says about **K**
36:32 He wrote everything that had been on the scroll **K**
37: 1 Jehoiachin son of Jehoiakim as the **k** of Judah.
37: 1 He was appointed by **K** Nebuchadnezzar of
37: 2 But neither **K** Zedekiah nor his officials nor the
37: 3 **K** Zedekiah sent Jehucal son of Shelemiah
37: 7 Tell the **k** of Judah, who sent you to ask me what is
37:17 Later **K** Zedekiah secretly requested that Jeremiah
37:17 where the **k** asked him, "Do you have any
37:17 "You will be defeated by the **k** of Babylon."
37:18 Then Jeremiah asked the **k**, "What crime have I
37:19 Where are your prophets now who told you the **k**
37:20 Listen, my lord the **k**, I beg you. Don't send me
37:21 So **K** Zedekiah commanded that Jeremiah not be
37:21 The **k** also commanded that Jeremiah be given a
38: 3 be handed over to the army of the **k** of Babylon,
38: 4 So these officials went to the **k** and said, "Sir,
38: 5 So **K** Zedekiah agreed. "All right," he said.
38: 7 At that time the **k** was holding court at the
38: 9 "My lord the **k**," he said, "these men have done a
38:10 So the **k** told Ebed-melech, "Take along thirty of
38:14 One day **K** Zedekiah sent for Jeremiah to meet him
38:14 "I want to ask you something," the **k** said.
38:16 So **K** Zedekiah secretly promised him, "As surely
38:19 "But I am afraid to surrender," the **k** said,
38:23 You will be seized by the **k** of Babylon, and this
38:25 'Tell us what you and the **k** were talking about.
38:27 and asked him why the **k** had called for him.
38:27 the conversation between Jeremiah and the **k**.
39: 1 It was in January during the ninth year of **K**
Zedekiah's reign that **K** Nebuchadnezzar
39: 4 **K** Zedekiah and his royal guard saw the
39: 5 But the Babylonians chased the **k** and caught him
39: 5 They took him to **K** Nebuchadnezzar of Babylon,
39: 5 There the **k** of Babylon pronounced judgment upon
39:11 **K** Nebuchadnezzar had told Nebuzaradan to find
39:13 and the other officers of Babylon's **k**
40: 5 He has been appointed governor of Judah by the **k**
40: 7 **k** of Babylon had appointed Gedaliah son of
40: 9 "Stay here, and serve the **k** of Babylon," he said,
40:11 and the other nearby countries heard that the **k** of
40:14 to him, "Did you know that Baalis, **k** of Ammon,
41: 2 whom the **k** of Babylon had appointed governor.
41: 9 **K** Asa when he fortified Mizpah to protect himself
against **K** Baasha of Israel.
41:18 the governor appointed by the Babylonian **k**.
42:11 Do not fear the **k** of Babylon anymore,
43:10 **k** of Babylon, here to Egypt.
44:30 I will turn Pharaoh Hophra, **k** of Egypt, over to his
44:30 just as I turned **K** Zedekiah of Judah over to **K**
46: 2 the **k** of Judah, on the occasion of the battle of
Carchemish when Pharaoh Neco, **k** of Egypt,
46: 2 River by **K** Nebuchadnezzar of Babylon.
46:13 about **K** Nebuchadnezzar's plans to attack Egypt.
46:17 There they will say, 'Pharaoh, the **k** of Egypt,
46:18 "As surely as I live," says the **K**, whose name is
46:26 to **K** Nebuchadnezzar of Babylon and his army.
48:15 says the **K**, whose name is the LORD Almighty.
48:45 comes from Heshbon, **K** Sihon's ancestral home,
49:28 which were attacked by **K** Nebuchadnezzar of
49:30 for **K** Nebuchadnezzar of Babylon has plotted
49:34 the beginning of the reign of **K** Zedekiah of Judah.
49:38 the LORD, "and I will destroy its **k** and princes.
50:17 First the **k** of Assyria ate them up. Then **K**
Nebuchadnezzar of Babylon cracked their
50:18 "Now I will punish the **k** of Babylon and his land,
just as I punished the **k** of Assyria.
50:43 The **k** of Babylon has received reports about the
51:31 Messengers from every side come running to the **k**
51:34 "**K** Nebuchadnezzar of Babylon has eaten
51:57 rulers, captains, and warriors," says the **K**,
51:59 when he went to Babylon with **K** Zedekiah of
52: 1 was twenty-one years old when he became **k**,
52: 3 Then Zedekiah rebelled against the **k** of Babylon.
52: 4 **K** Nebuchadnezzar of Babylon led his entire army
52: 5 siege until the eleventh year of **K** Zedekiah's reign.
52: 8 and caught **K** Zedekiah on the plains of Jericho,
52: 9 They brought him to the **k** of Babylon at Riblah,
52:10 the **k** of Babylon made Zedekiah watch as all his
52:12 of the guard, an official of the Babylonian **k**,
52:15 had declared their allegiance to the **k** of Babylon.
52:20 the LORD's Temple in the days of **K** Solomon.

52:26 Nebuzaradan the commander took them all to the **k**
52:27 the **k** of Babylon had them all put to death.
52:31 In the thirty-seventh year of **K** Jehoiachin's exile
52:34 The Babylonian **k** also gave him a regular
La 4:12 Not a **k** in all the earth—no one in all the world—
4:20 Our **k**, the LORD's anointed, the very life of our
Eze 1: 2 This happened during the fifth year of **K**
7:27 The **k** and the prince will stand helpless,
8: 1 during the sixth year of **K** Jehoiachin's captivity,
17:12 The **k** of Babylon came to Jerusalem, took away
her **k** and princes, and brought them to
17:16 the **k** of Israel will die in Babylon,
17:16 the land of the **k** who put him in power and whose
17:17 the **k** of Babylon lays siege to Jerusalem again
17:18 For the **k** of Israel broke his treaty after swearing
19: 9 and brought him before the **k** of Babylon.
20: 1 during the seventh year of **K** Jehoiachin's
21:19 routes on it for the sword of Babylon's **k** to follow.
21:21 The **k** of Babylon now stands at the fork,
21:23 But the **k** of Babylon will remind the people of
24: 1 during the ninth year of **K** Jehoiachin's captivity,
24: 2 because on this very day the **k** of Babylon is
26: 1 during the twelfth year of **K** Jehoiachin's captivity,
26: 7 I will bring **K** Nebuchadnezzar of Babylon—
26: 7 the **k** of kings from the north—against Tyre with
28:12 "Son of man, weep for the **k** of Tyre. Give him
29: 1 during the tenth year of **K** Jehoiachin's captivity,
29: 2 toward Egypt and prophesy against Pharaoh the **k**
29: 3 I am your enemy, O Pharaoh, **k** of Egypt—
29:17 during the twenty-seventh year of **K** Jehoiachin's
29:18 the army of **K** Nebuchadnezzar of Babylon fought
29:19 land of Egypt to Nebuchadnezzar, **k** of Babylon.
30:10 Through **K** Nebuchadnezzar of Babylon, I will
30:20 during the eleventh year of **K** Jehoiachin's
30:21 I have broken the arm of Pharaoh, the **k** of Egypt.
30:22 I am the enemy of Pharaoh, the **k** of Egypt! I will
30:24 I will strengthen the arms of Babylon's **k** and put
30:24 But I will break the arms of Pharaoh, **k** of Egypt,
30:25 I will strengthen the arms of the **k** of Babylon,
30:25 when I put my sword in the hand of Babylon's **k**
31: 1 during the eleventh year of **K** Jehoiachin's
31: 2 message to Pharaoh, **k** of Egypt, and all his people:
32: 1 during the twelfth year of **K** Jehoiachin's captivity,
32: 2 "Son of man, mourn for Pharaoh, **k** of Egypt,
32:11 The sword of the **k** of Babylon will come against
37:22 One **k** will rule them all; no longer will they be
37:24 "My servant David will be their **k**, and they will
Da 1: 1 During the third year of **K** Jehoiakim's reign in
1: 1 **K** Nebuchadnezzar of Babylon came to Jerusalem
1: 2 The Lord gave him victory over **K** Jehoiakim of
1: 3 Then the **k** ordered Ashpenaz, who was in charge
1: 5 The **k** assigned them a daily ration of the best food
1: 8 eating the food and wine given to them by the **k**.
1:10 "My lord the **k** has ordered that you eat this food
1:10 I am afraid the **k** will have me beheaded for
1:15 who had been eating the food assigned by the **k**.
1:18 training period ordered by the **k** was completed,
1:18 the chief official brought all the young men to **K**
1:19 The **k** talked with each of them, and none of them
1:20 the **k** found the advice of these young men to be
1:21 Daniel remained there until the first year of **K**
2: 2 what he had dreamed. As they stood before the **k**,
2: 4 Then the astrologers answered the **k** in Aramaic,
"Long live the **k**!
2: 5 But the **k** said to the astrologers, "I am serious
2: 8 The **k** replied, "I can see through your trick!
2:10 The astrologers replied to the **k**, "There isn't a
2:10 And no **k**, however great and powerful, has ever
2:11 This is an impossible thing the **k** requires. No one
2:12 The **k** was furious when he heard this, and he sent
2:15 "Why has the **k** issued such a harsh decree?"
2:16 Daniel went at once to see the **k** and requested
2:16 so he could tell the **k** what the dream meant.
2:23 of you / and revealed to us what the **k** demanded."
2:24 Take me to the **k**, and I will tell him the meaning
2:25 Then Arioch quickly took Daniel to the **k** and said,
2:26 The **k** said to Daniel (also known as Belteshazzar),
2:27 or fortune-tellers who can tell the **k** such things.
2:28 and he has shown **K** Nebuchadnezzar what will
2:37 Your Majesty, you are a **k** over many kings.
2:46 Then **K** Nebuchadnezzar bowed to the ground
2:47 The **k** said to Daniel, "Truly, your God is the God
2:48 Then the **k** appointed Daniel to a high position
2:49 the **k** appointed Shadrach, Meshach,
3: 1 **K** Nebuchadnezzar made a gold statue ninety feet
3: 3 and were standing before the image **K**
3: 5 bow to the ground to worship **K** Nebuchadnezzar's
3: 7 and worshiped the statue that **K** Nebuchadnezzar
3: 8 But some of the astrologers went to the **k**
3: 9 They said to **K** Nebuchadnezzar, "Long live the **k**!
3:22 And because the **k**, in his anger, had demanded
3:30 Then the **k** promoted Shadrach, Meshach,
4: 1 **K** Nebuchadnezzar sent this message to the people
4:18 that was the dream that I, **K** Nebuchadnezzar, had.
4:19 Finally, the **k** said to him, "Belteshazzar, don't be
4:27 "O **K** Nebuchadnezzar, please listen to me.
4:28 But all these things did happen to **K**
4:31 "O **K** Nebuchadnezzar, this message is for you!
4:37 praise and glorify and honor the **K** of heaven.
5: 1 **K** Belshazzar gave a great feast for a thousand of
5: 3 and the **k** and his nobles, his wives, and his
5: 5 The **k** himself saw the hand as it wrote,
5: 7 The **k** shouted for the enchanters, astrologers,
5: 9 So the **k** grew even more alarmed, and his face
5:10 She said to Belshazzar, "Long live the **k**! Don't be
5:11 Your predecessor, **K** Nebuchadnezzar, made him
5:12 whom the **k** named Belteshazzar, has a sharp mind
5:13 So Daniel was brought in before the **k**. The **k**
asked him, "Are you Daniel,
5:13 Judah by my predecessor, **K** Nebuchadnezzar?
5:17 Daniel answered the **k**, "Keep your gifts or give
5:30 night Belshazzar, the Babylonian **k**, was killed.
6: 2 The **k** also chose Daniel and two others as
6: 3 the **k** made plans to place him over the entire
6: 6 went to the **k** and said, "Long live **K** Darius!
6: 9 So **K** Darius signed the law.
6:12 So they went back to the **k** and reminded him
6:12 "Yes," the **k** replied, "that decision stands;
6:13 Then they told the **k**, "That man Daniel, one of the
6:14 the **k** was very angry with himself for signing the
6:15 In the evening the men went together to the **k**
6:15 no law that the **k** signs can be changed."
6:16 So at last the **k** gave orders for Daniel to be
6:16 The **k** said to him, "May your God, whom you
6:17 The **k** sealed the stone with his own royal seal
6:18 Then the **k** returned to his palace and spent the
6:19 next morning, the **k** hurried out to the lions' den.
6:21 Daniel answered, "Long live the **k**!
6:23 The **k** was overjoyed and ordered that Daniel be
6:24 Then the **k** gave orders to arrest the men who had
6:25 Then **K** Darius sent this message to the people of
7: 1 during the first year of **K** Belshazzar's reign in
7:24 Then another **k** will arise, different from the other
8: 1 During the third year of **K** Belshazzar's reign,
8:21 The shaggy male goat represents the **k** of Greece,
8:21 its eyes represents the first **k** of the Greek Empire.
8:23 a fierce **k**, a master of intrigue, will rise to power.
8:27 I got up and performed my duties for the **k**,
9: 1 of Ahasuerus, who became **k** of the Babylonians.
10: 1 In the third year of the reign of **K** Cyrus of Persia,
11: 3 "Then a mighty **k** will rise to power who will rule
11: 5 "The **k** of the south will increase in power, but one
11: 6 an alliance will be formed between the **k** of the
north and the **k** of the south.
11: 6 The daughter of the **k** of the south will be given in
11: 6 to the **k** of the north to secure the alliance,
11: 7 But when one of her relatives becomes **k** of the
11: 7 and enter the fortress of the **k** of the north
11: 8 For some years afterward he will leave the **k** of the
11: 9 "Later the **k** of the north will invade the realm of
the **k** of the south
11:10 the sons of the **k** of the north will assemble a
11:11 Then the **k** of the south, in great anger, will rally
11:11 the vast forces assembled by the **k** of the north
11:12 the **k** of the south will be filled with pride and will
11:13 the **k** of the north will return with a fully equipped
11:14 be a general uprising against the **k** of the south.
11:15 Then the **k** of the north will come and lay siege to
11:16 "The **k** of the north will march onward
11:17 and will form an alliance with the **k** of the south.
11:20 "His successor will be remembered as the **k** who
11:25 and raise a great army against the **k** of the south.
11:25 The **k** of the south will go to battle with a mighty
11:28 "The **k** of the north will then return home with
11:36 "The **k** will do as he pleases, exalting himself
11:40 time of the end, the **k** of the south will attack him,
11:40 and the **k** of the north will storm out against him
Hos 1: 1 and Jeroboam son of Jehoash was **k** of Israel.
1: 4 for I am about to punish **K** Jehu's dynasty to
3: 4 that Israel will be a long time without a **k**
3: 5 their God and to David's descendant, their **k**.
5:13 Israel turned to Assyria, to the great **k** there,
7: 3 The people make the **k** glad with their wickedness.
7: 5 The **k** makes a fool of himself and drinks with
8:10 they will writhe under the burden of the great **k**!
10: 3 "We have no **k** because we didn't fear the
10: 3 What could a **k** do for us anyway?"
10: 6 go as captives to Assyria, a gift to the great **k** there.
10: 7 and its **k** will disappear like a chip of wood on an
10:15 the **k** of Israel will be completely destroyed.
13:10 Where now is your **k**? Why don't you call on him
Am 1: 1 when Uzziah was **k** of Judah and Jeroboam II, the
son of Jehoash, was **k** of Israel.
1: 4 So I will send down fire on **K** Hazael's palace,
1: 4 and the fortresses of **K** Ben-hadad will be
1: 8 people of Ashdod and destroy the **k** of Ashkelon.
1:15 And their **k** and his princes will go into exile
2: 1 They desecrated the tomb of Edom's **k** and burned
2: 3 And I will destroy their **k** and slaughter all their
5:26 Sakkuth your **k** god and Kaiwan your star god—
6: 5 yourselves to be great musicians, as **K** David was.
7: 9 and I will bring the dynasty of **K** Jeroboam to a
7:10 was saying, he rushed a message to **K** Jeroboam:
Ob 1:21 of Edom. And the LORD himself will be **k**!"
Jnh 3: 6 When the **k** of Nineveh heard what Jonah was
3: 7 Then the **k** and his nobles sent this decree
Mic 2:13 Your **k** will lead you; the LORD himself will
4: 7 will rule from Jerusalem as their **k** forever."
4: 9 Have you no **k** to lead you? He is dead! Have you
6: 5 how **K** Balak of Moab tried to have you cursed
6:16 "The only laws you keep are those of evil **K** Omri;
6:16 the only example you follow is that of wicked **K**
Na 1:11 Who is this **k** of yours who dares to plot evil
2: 5 The **k** shouts to his officers; they stumble in their
3:18 O Assyrian **k**, your princes lie dead in the dust.
Zep 1: 1 when Josiah son of Amon was **k** of Judah.
3:15 the **K** of Israel, will live among you!
Hag 1: 1 On August 29 of the second year of **K** Darius's
1:15 This was on September 21 of the second year of **K**
2:10 On December 18 of the second year of **K** Darius's
Zec 1: 1 In midautumn of the second year of **K** Darius's
1: 7 Then on February 15 of the second year of **K**
6:13 royal honor and will rule as **k** from his throne.
7: 1 On December 7 of the fourth year of **K** Darius's
9: 5 Gaza will be conquered and its **k** killed,
9: 9 Look, your **k** is coming to you. He is righteous
9:10 Your **k** will bring peace to the nations. His realm
11: 6 as well as into the clutches of their **k**.
12: 8 the weakest among them will be as mighty as **K**
14: 5 the earthquake in the days of **K** Uzziah of Judah.
14: 9 And the LORD will be **k** over all the earth.
14:16 go up to Jerusalem each year to worship the **K**,
14:17 that refuses to come to Jerusalem to worship the **K**,
Mal 1:14 For I am a great **k**," says the LORD Almighty,
Mt 1: 1 a descendant of **K** David and of Abraham:
1: 6 Jesse was the father of **K** David. / David was the
1:17 fourteen generations from Abraham to **K** David,
2: 1 Bethlehem in Judea, during the reign of **K** Herod.
2: 2 "Where is the newborn **k** of the Jews? We have
5:35 for Jerusalem is the city of the great **K**.
12: 3 "Haven't you ever read in the Scriptures what **K**
14: 9 The **k** was sorry, but because of his oath and
18:23 the Kingdom of Heaven can be compared to a **k**
18:25 so the **k** ordered that he, his wife, his children,
18:26 But the man fell down before the **k** and begged
18:27 Then the **k** was filled with pity for him, and he
18:28 "But when the man left the **k**, he went to a fellow
18:31 They went to the **k** and told him what had
18:32 Then the **k** called in the man he had forgiven
18:34 Then the angry **k** sent the man to prison until he
21: 5 people of Israel, / 'Look, your **K** is coming to you.
22: 2 a **k** who prepared a great wedding feast for his son.
22: 7 "Then the **k** became furious. He sent out his army
22:11 But when the **k** came in to meet the guests,
22:13 Then the **k** said to his aides, 'Bind him hand
25:34 Then the **K** will say to those on the right, 'Come,
25:40 And the **K** will tell them, 'I assure you, when you
25:41 "Then the **K** will turn to those on the left and say,
27:11 Roman governor. "Are you the **K** of the Jews?"
27:29 him in mockery, yelling, "Hail! **K** of the Jews!"
27:37 It read: "This is Jesus, the **K** of the Jews."
27:42 can't save himself! So he is the **k** of Israel, is he?
Mk 2:25 "Haven't you ever read in the Scriptures what **K**
6:14 Herod Antipas, the **k**, soon heard about Jesus,
6:22 the **k** said to the girl, "and I will give it to you."
6:25 So the girl hurried back to the **k** and told him,
6:26 Then the **k** was very sorry, but he was embarrassed
15: 2 Pilate asked Jesus, "Are you the **K** of the Jews?"
15: 9 "Should I give you the **K** of the Jews?"
15:12 "what should I do with this man you call the **K** of
15:18 Then they saluted, yelling, "Hail! **K** of the Jews!"
15:26 charge against him. It read: "The **K** of the Jews."
15:32 Let this Messiah, this **k** of Israel, come down from
Lk 1: 5 Zechariah, who lived when Herod was **k** of Judea.
1:27 to a man named Joseph, a descendant of **K** David.
2: 4 because Joseph was a descendant of **K** David,
2:38 who had been waiting for the promised **K** to come
6: 3 "Haven't you ever read in the Scriptures what **K**
14:31 "Or what **k** would ever dream of going to war
19:12 called away to a distant empire to be crowned **k**
19:14 him to say they did not want him to be their **k**.
19:15 the **k** called in the servants to whom he had given
19:17 'Well done!' the **k** exclaimed. 'You are a
19:19 'Well done!' the **k** said. 'You can be governor over
19:22 the **k** roared. 'Hard, am I? If you knew so much
19:24 the **k** ordered, 'Take the money from this servant,
19:26 " 'Yes,' the **k** replied, 'but to those who use well
19:27 of mine who didn't want me to be their **k**—
19:38 "Bless the **K** who comes in the name of the Lord!
23: 2 and by claiming he is the Messiah, a **k**."
23: 3 Pilate asked him, "Are you the **K** of the Jews?"
23:37 "If you are the **K** of the Jews, save yourself!"
23:38 with these words: "This is the **K** of the Jews."
Jn 1:49 you are the Son of God—the **K** of Israel!"
6:15 were ready to take him by force and make him **k**,
7:42 the village where **K** David was born."
12:13 in the name of the Lord! / Hail to the **K** of Israel!"
12:15 people of Israel. / Look, your **K** is coming,
18:33 "Are you the **K** of the Jews?" he asked him.
18:36 Then Jesus answered, "I am not an earthly **k**.
18:37 Pilate replied, "You are a **k** then?" "You say that I
am a **k**, and you are right,"
18:39 if you want me to, I'll release the **K** of the Jews."
19: 3 "Hail! **K** of the Jews!" they mocked, and they hit
19:12 Anyone who declares himself a **k** is a rebel against
19:14 And Pilate said to the people, "Here is your **k**!"
19:15 "What? Crucify your **k**?" Pilate asked.
19:15 "We have no **k** but Caesar," the leading priests
19:19 that read, "Jesus of Nazareth, the **K** of the Jews."
19:21 "Change it from 'The **K** of the Jews' to 'He said, I
am **K** of the Jews.' "
Ac 1:16 ago by the Holy Spirit, speaking through **K** David.
2:25 **K** David said this about him: / 'I know the Lord is
4:25 by the Holy Spirit through our ancestor **K** David,
7:10 God gave him favor before Pharaoh, **k** of Egypt.
7:18 then a new **k** came to the throne of Egypt who
7:19 This **k** plotted against our people and forced
7:45 And it was used there until the time of **K** David.
12: 1 About that time **K** Herod Agrippa began to
13: 1 Manaen (the childhood companion of **K** Herod
13:21 Then the people begged for a **k**, and God gave
13:23 "And it is one of **K** David's descendants, Jesus,
17: 7 for they profess allegiance to another **k**, Jesus."
25:13 A few days later **K** Agrippa arrived with his sister,
25:14 Festus discussed Paul's case with the **k**.
25:24 Then Festus said, "**K** Agrippa and all present,
25:26 and especially you, **K** Agrippa, so that after we
26: 2 "I am fortunate, **K** Agrippa, that you are the one
26: 7 Yet, O **k**, they say it is wrong for me to have this
26:19 "And so, O **K** Agrippa, I was not disobedient to
26:26 And **K** Agrippa knows about these things. I speak

26:27 **K** Agrippa, do you believe the prophets? I know
26:30 Then the **k**, the governor, Bernice, and all the
Ro 1: 3 as a man, born into **K** David's royal family line.
4: 6 **K** David spoke of this, describing the happiness of
2Co 11:32 the governor under **K** Aretas kept guards at the city
1Ti 1:17 He is the eternal **K**, the unseen one who never dies;
6:15 almighty God, the **K** of kings and Lord of lords.
2Ti 2: 8 Jesus Christ was a man born into **K** David's family
Heb 7: 1 This Melchizedek was **k** of the city of Salem
7: 2 His name means "**k** of justice." He is also "**k** of
peace" because *Salem* means
11:23 and they were not afraid of what the **k** might do.
11:27 He was not afraid of the **k**. Moses kept right on
1Pe 2:13 accept all authority—the **k** as head of state,
2:14 For the **k** has sent them to punish all who do wrong
2:17 and sisters. Fear God. Show respect for the **k**.
Rev 9:11 Their **k** is the angel from the bottomless pit;
15: 3 and true are your ways, / O **K** of the nations.
17:11 beast that was alive and then died is the eighth **k**.
17:14 he is Lord over all lords and **K** over all kings,
19:16 was written this title: **K** of kings and Lord of lords.

KING'S (199) [KING]

KING'S COMMAND (10) 1Ki 2:46; 5:17; 2Ch 30:6; Est 3:3,15; 8:14; Ecc 8:4; Jer 34:10; Da 3:4,28

KING'S SON (7) 2Sa 13:23; 2Ki 10:2,5,6,7,8; 1Ch 27:32

KING'S SONS (9) Jdg 8:18; 1Sa 18:1; 2Ki 11:4,12; 15:5; 2Ch 23:3,11; 28:7; Ps 72:1

Ge 14:17 him in the valley of Shaveh (that is, the **K** Valley).
39:20 and threw him into the prison where the **k**
41: 9 Then the **k** cup-bearer spoke up. "Today I have
Nu 20:17 We will stay on the **k** road and never leave it until
21:22 We will stay on the **k** road until we have crossed
Jos 2: 7 So the **k** men went looking for the spies along the
2: 7 And as soon as the **k** men had left, the city gate
Jdg 3:21 to his right thigh, and plunged it into the **k** belly.
3:22 so deep that the handle disappeared beneath the **k**
3:22 Ehud left the dagger in, and the **k** bowels emptied.
3:24 the **k** servants returned and found the doors to the
8:18 they replied. "They all had the look of a **k** son."
1Sa 18: 1 talking with Saul, he met Jonathan, the **k** son.
18:18 family in Israel that I should be the **k** son-in-law?"
18:22 Why don't you accept the **k** offer and become his
21: 8 The **k** business was so urgent that I didn't even
26:16 Where are the **k** spear and the jug of water that
2Sa 8:18 Benaiah son of Jehoiada was captain of the **k**
11: 9 palace entrance with some of the **k** other servants.
12:30 David removed the crown from the **k** head, and it
13:18 as was the custom in those days for the **k** virgin
13:23 Absalom invited all the **k** sons to come to a feast.
15:18 David from Gath, along with the **k** bodyguard.
16: 6 He threw stones at the king and the **k** officers
18:18 Absalom had built a monument to himself in the **K**
19: 2 As the troops heard of the **k** deep grief for his son,
19: 5 Then Joab went to the **k** room and said to him,
19:18 and worked hard ferrying the **k** household across
20: 7 guard from Joab's army and the **k** own bodyguard.
20:23 Benaiah son of Jehoiada was commander of the **k**
1Ki 1:10 or Benaiah, or the **k** bodyguard, or his brother
1:15 So Bathsheba went into the **k** bedroom. He was
1:23 The **k** advisers told him, "Nathan the prophet is
1:32 of Jehoiada." When they came into the **k** presence,
1:38 and the **k** bodyguard took Solomon down to Gihon
1:44 son of Jehoiada, protected by the **k** bodyguard.
1:44 They had him ride on the **k** own mule,
2:46 Then, at the **k** command, Benaiah son of Jehoiada
3:28 Word of the **k** decision spread quickly throughout
4: 7 food from the people for the **k** household.
5:17 At the **k** command, the stonecutters quarried
10:28 the **k** traders acquired them from Cilicia at the
13: 4 But instantly the **k** hand became paralyzed in that
13: 6 the LORD, and the **k** hand became normal again.
16:18 he went into the citadel of the **k** house and burned
22:38 and dogs came and licked the **k** blood,
2Ki 5: 8 the man of God, heard about the **k** reaction,
7:19 The **k** officer had replied, "That couldn't happen
8:15 it in water, and held it over the **k** face until he died.
10: 2 "The **k** sons are with you, and you have at your
10: 5 the other leaders and the guardians of the **k** sons,
10: 6 bring the heads of the **k** sons to me at Jezreel at
10: 7 the leaders killed all seventy of the **k** sons.
10: 8 "They have brought the heads of the **k** sons."
11: 2 and stole him away from among the rest of the **k**
11: 4 LORD's Temple; then he showed them the **k** son.
11:12 Then Jehoiada brought out Joash, the **k** son,
11:20 because Athaliah had been killed at the **k** palace.
13:16 and Elisha laid his own hands on the **k** hands.
15: 5 The **k** son Jotham was put in charge of the royal
16:11 Uriah built an altar just like it by following the **k**
16:15 the **k** burnt offering and grain offering,
16:18 as well as the **k** outer entrance to the Temple of the
18:19 Then the Assyrian **k** personal representative sent
18:26 Shebna, and Joah said to the **k** representative,
19: 5 After King Hezekiah's officials delivered the **k**
19: 6 against me from the Assyrian **k** messengers.
22:12 court secretary, and Asaiah the **k** personal adviser:
25: 4 gate between the two walls behind the **k** gardens.
25:19 of the Judean army, five of the **k** personal advisers,
25:29 and allowed him to dine at the **k** table for the rest
1Ch 9:18 they were responsible for the **K** Gate on the east
18:17 Benaiah son of Jehoiada was captain of the **k**
18:17 David's sons served as the **k** chief assistants.
20: 2 at Rabbah, he removed the crown from the **k** head,
25: 2 who proclaimed God's messages by the **k** orders.
25: 5 All these were the sons of Heman, the **k** seer,
27:26 of the field workers who farmed the **k** lands.
27:27 Shimei from Ramah was in charge of the **k**
27:28 Baal-hanan from Geder was in charge of the **k**
27:31 Jaziz the Hagrite was in charge of the **k** sheep.
27:32 the Hacmonite was responsible to teach the **k** sons.
27:33 royal adviser. Hushai the Arkite was the **k** friend.
29: 6 and the **k** administrative officers all gave willingly.
2Ch 1:16 the **k** traders acquired them from Cilicia at the
22:11 and stole him away from among the rest of the **k**
23: 3 "The time has come for the **k** son to reign!
23:11 and his sons brought out Joash, the **k** son,
24:11 became full, the Levites carried it to the **k** officials.
26:11 the direction of Hananiah, one of the **k** officials.
28: 7 warrior from Ephraim, killed Maaseiah, the **k** son;
28: 7 Azrikam, the **k** palace commander; and Elkanah,
the **k** second-in-command.
29:25 through Gad, the **k** seer, and the prophet Nathan.
30: 6 At the **k** command, messengers were sent
34:20 court secretary, and Asaiah the **k** personal adviser:
35: 8 The **k** officials also made willing contributions to
35:10 by their divisions, according to the **k** orders.
35:15 by David, Asaph, Heman, and Jeduthun, the **k** seer.
Ezr 8:36 The **k** decrees were delivered to his lieutenants
Ne 1:11 kind to me." In those days I was the **k** cup-bearer.
2: 8 send a letter to Asaph, the manager of the **k** forest,
2: 9 Euphrates River, I delivered the **k** letters to them.
2:14 I went to the Fountain Gate and to the **K** Pool,
3:15 the wall of the pool of Siloam near the **k** garden,
3:25 from the **k** house beside the court of the guard.
11:24 was the **k** agent in all matters of public
Est 1:12 But when they conveyed the **k** order to Queen
1:15 for a queen who refuses to obey the **k** orders,
2: 8 As a result of the **k** decree, Esther, along with
2: 8 was brought to the **k** harem at the fortress of Susa
2: 9 seven maids specially chosen from the **k** palace,
2:12 Before each young woman was taken to the **k** bed,
2:14 That evening she was taken to the **k** private rooms,
2:14 to the second harem, where the **k** wives lived.
2:14 the care of Shaashgaz, another of the **k** eunuchs.
2:21 two of the **k** eunuchs, Bigthana and Teresh—
2:21 who were guards at the door of the **k** private
3: 2 All the **k** officials would bow down before Haman
3: 3 Then the palace officials at the **k** gate asked
3: 3 "Why are you disobeying the **k** command?"
3: 8 So it is not in the **k** interest to let them live.
3:12 On April 17 Haman called in the **k** secretaries
3:15 At the **k** command, the decree went out by the
4: 3 And as news of the **k** decree reached all the
4: 5 one of the **k** eunuchs who had been appointed as
5: 1 court of the palace, just across from the **k** hall.
6: 2 two of the eunuchs who guarded the door to the **k**
6: 8 he should bring out one of the **k** own royal robes,
6: 8 as well as the **k** own horse with a royal emblem on
6: 9 Instruct one of the **k** most noble princes to dress
the man in the **k** robe
6: 9 and to lead him through the city square on the **k**
6:11 put it on Mordecai, placed him on the **k** own horse,
6:14 the **k** eunuchs arrived to take Haman to the
7: 9 Then Harbona, one of the **k** eunuchs, said,
7:10 set up for Mordecai, and the **k** anger was pacified.
8: 8 and send a message to the Jews in the **k** name,
8: 8 you want, and seal it with the **k** signet ring.
8: 8 But remember that whatever is written in the **k**
8: 9 So on June 25 the **k** secretaries were summoned.
8:10 and sealed the message with the **k** signet ring.
8:10 who rode horses especially bred for the **k** service.
8:11 The **k** decree gave the Jews in every city authority
8:14 So urged on by the **k** command, the messengers
8:14 rode out swiftly on horses bred for the **k** service.
8:17 and province, wherever the **k** decree arrived,
9: 2 **k** provinces to defend themselves against anyone
9: 4 For Mordecai had been promoted in the **k** palace,
9:16 the other Jews throughout the **k** provinces had
9:20 Jews near and far, throughout all the **k** provinces,
Ps 45:15 enthusiastic procession / as they enter the **k** palace!
72: 1 the king, O God, / and righteousness to the **k** son.
72:17 May the **k** name endure forever; / may it continue
105:21 Joseph was put in charge of all the **k** household;
105:21 he became ruler over all the **k** possessions.
105:22 He could instruct the **k** aides as he pleased / and
teach the **k** advisers.
105:30 they were found even in the **k** private rooms.
Pr 14:28 A growing population is a **k** glory; a dwindling
19:12 The **k** anger is like a lion's roar, but his favor is
20: 2 The **k** fury is like a lion's roar; to rouse his anger is
21: 1 The **k** heart is like a stream of water directed by
22:11 a pure heart and gracious speech is the **k** friend.
25: 2 and the **k** privilege to discover them.
25: 3 of the earth, of all that goes on in the **k** mind!
25: 5 Remove the wicked from the **k** court, and his reign
Ecc 8: 4 The **k** command is backed by great power. No one
Isa 23:15 For seventy years, the length of a **k** life, Tyre will
36: 4 Then the Assyrian **k** personal representative sent
36:11 Shebna, and Joah said to the **k** representative,
37: 5 After King Hezekiah's officials delivered the **k**
37: 6 against me from the Assyrian **k** messengers.
Jer 27:18 and in the **k** palace and in the palaces of Jerusalem.
33: 4 and even the **k** palace to get materials to strengthen
34:10 and all the people had obeyed the **k** command,
38:27 it wasn't long before the **k** officials came to
38:27 But Jeremiah followed the **k** instructions, and they
39: 3 the **k** adviser, and many others.
39: 4 a gate between the two walls behind the **k** garden
39:13 a chief officer, and Nergal-sharezer, the **k** adviser,
41:10 Ishmael made captives of the **k** daughters
43: 6 were men, women, and children, the **k** daughters,
52: 7 gate between the two walls behind the **k** gardens.
52:25 the Judean army, seven of the **k** personal advisers,
52:33 and allowed him to dine at the **k** table for the rest
Da 1:13 other young men who are eating the **k** rich food.
2:13 And because of the **k** decree, men were sent to find
2:14 When Arioch, the commander of the **k** guard,
2:49 of Babylon, while Daniel remained in the **k** court.
3: 4 and languages, listen to the **k** command!
3:28 They defied the **k** command and were willing to
5: 5 hand writing on the plaster wall of the **k** palace,
5: 8 But when all the **k** wise men came in, none of
6: 2 the princes and to watch out for the **k** interests.
11: 4 It will not be ruled by the **k** descendants, nor will
11: 5 but one of this **k** own officials will become more
Am 7: 1 This was after the **k** share had been harvested from
Zec 14:10 and from the Tower of Hananel to the **k**

KINGDOM (280) [KING]

KINGDOM OF GOD (67) Mt 6:33; 12:28; 19:24; 21:31,43; Mk 1:15; 4:11,26,30; 9:1,47; 10:14,15,23,24,25; 12:34; 14:25; 15:43; Lk 4:43; 6:20; 7:28; 8:1,10; 9:2,11,27, 60,62; 10:9,11; 11:20; 12:31; 13:18,20,28,29; 14:15; 16:16; 17:20,20,21; 18:16,17,24,25,29; 19:11; 21:31; 22:16,18; 23:51; Jn 3:3,5; Ac 1:3; 8:12; 14:22; 19:8; 28:23,31; Ro 14:17; 1Co 4:20; 6:9,10; 15:50; Gal 5:21; Col 4:11

KINGDOM OF HEAVEN (33) Mt 3:2; 4:17; 5:3,10,19,19,20; 7:21; 8:11; 10:7; 11:11,12; 13:11,24,31,33, 44,45,47,52; 16:19; 18:1,3,4,23; 19:12,14,23; 20:1; 22:2; 23:13; 25:1,14

Ge 20: 9 making me and my **k** guilty of this great sin?
20:15 "Look over my **k**, and choose a place where you
Ex 19: 6 And you will be to me a **k** of priests, my holy
Nu 24: 7 will be greater than Agag; / their **k** will be exalted.
Dt 3: 4 the entire Argob region in his **k** of Bashan.
3: 6 We completely destroyed the **k** of Bashan, just as
3:10 and Edrei, which were part of Og's **k** in Bashan.
3:13 rest of Gilead and all of Bashan—Og's former **k**—
Jos 12: 2 His **k** included Aroer, on the edge of the Arnon
12: 5 His **k** included the northern half of Gilead,
13:21 all the towns of the plain and the entire **k** of Sihon.
13:27 and the rest of the **k** of King Sihon of Heshbon.
13:30 all of Bashan, all the former **k** of King Og,
1Sa 13:13 the LORD would have established your **k** over
15:28 The LORD has torn the **k** of Israel from you
28:17 He has taken the **k** from you and given it to your
2Sa 3:10 just go ahead and give David the rest of Saul's **k**.
5:12 and had made his **k** great for the sake of his people
7:12 of your descendants, and I will make his **k** strong.
7:13 And I will establish the throne of his **k** forever.
7:16 and your **k** will continue for all time before me,
16: 3 'Today I will get back the **k** of my grandfather
24: 3 times as many people in your **k** as there are now!
1Ki 1:47 and may Solomon's **k** be even greater than yours!'
2:15 He replied, "As you know, the **k** was mine;
2:22 might as well be asking me to give him the **k**!
2:46 So the **k** was now firmly in Solomon's grip.
11:11 I will surely tear the **k** away from you and give it
11:12 are still alive. I will take the **k** away from your son.
11:31 'I am about to tear the **k** from the hand of
11:34 " 'But I will not take the entire **k** from Solomon
11:35 But I will take the **k** away from his son and give
12:21 the army of Israel and to restore the **k** to himself.
12:26 the **k** will return to the dynasty of David.
13:34 and resulted in the destruction of Jeroboam's **k**
14: 8 I ripped the **k** away from the family of David
18:10 and **k** on earth from end to end to find you.
2Ki 17:21 For when the LORD tore Israel away from the **k**
20:13 in his palace or **k** that Hezekiah did not show them.
1Ch 10:14 and turned his **k** over to David son of Jesse.
14: 2 and had made his **k** very great for the sake of his
16:20 and forth between nations, / from one **k** to another.
17:11 up one of your sons, and I will make his **k** strong.
17:14 him over my dynasty and my **k** for all time,
22:10 And I will establish the throne of his **k** over Israel
28: 1 the mighty men, and all the other warriors in the **k**.
28: 5 to succeed me on the throne of his **k** of Israel.
28: 7 as he does now, I will make his **k** last forever.'
29:11 on earth is yours, O LORD, and this is your **k**.
2Ch 1: 1 son of King David, now took firm control of the **k**,
9: 8 so much and desires this **k** to last forever,
11: 1 the army of Israel and to restore the **k** to himself.
11:17 This strengthened the **k** of Judah, and for three
13: 8 Do you really think you can stand against the **k** of
14: 5 So Asa's **k** enjoyed a period of peace.
17: 4 instead of following the practices of the **k** of Israel.
17: 5 Jehoshaphat's control over the **k** of Judah.
20:30 So Jehoshaphat's **k** was at peace, for his God had
22: 9 of Ahaziah's family was capable of ruling the **k**.
29:21 and seven male goats as a sin offering for the **k**,
33:13 let Manasseh return to Jerusalem and to his **k**.
36:20 and his sons until the **k** of Persia came to power.
36:22 into writing and to send it throughout his **k**:
Ezr 1: 1 into writing and to send it throughout his **k**:
7:13 "I decree that any of the people of Israel in my **k**,
Ne 9:35 Even while they had their own **k**, they did not
Est 5: 3 I will give it to you, even if it is half the **k**!"
5: 6 I will give it to you, even if it is half the **k**!"
6: 1 an attendant to bring the historical records of his **k**
7: 2 I will give it to you, even if it is half the **k**!"
Ps 103:22 everything he has created, / everywhere in his **k**.
105:13 and forth between nations, / from one **k** to another.
114: 2 became God's sanctuary, / and Israel became his **k**.
145:11 They will talk together about the glory of your **k**;
145:13 For your **k** is an everlasting **k**. / You rule
Isa 10:10 we have finished off many a **k** whose gods were
39: 2 in his palace or **k** that Hezekiah did not show them.

47: 8 "You are a pleasure-crazy **k**, living at ease
Jer 18: 7 that a certain nation or **k** is to be uprooted,
18: 9 that I will build up and plant a certain nation or **k**,
La 2: 2 He has brought to dust the **k** and all its rulers.
Eze 21:27 Destruction! I will surely destroy the **k**.
29:14 But Egypt will remain an unimportant, minor **k**.
Da 1:20 of all the magicians and enchanters in his entire **k**.
2:39 "But after your **k** comes to an end, another great **k**, inferior to yours, will rise to take
2:39 After that **k** has fallen, yet a third great **k**,
2:40 Following that **k**, there will be a fourth great **k**, as
2:40 That **k** will smash and crush all previous empires,
2:41 of iron and clay show that this **k** will be divided.
2:44 the God of heaven will set up a **k** that will never be
4: 3 powerful his wonders! / His **k** will last forever,
4:18 All the wisest men of my **k** have failed me.
4:26 This means that you will receive your **k** back again
4:31 is for you! You are no longer ruler of this **k**.
4:34 His rule is everlasting, / and his **k** is eternal.
4:36 returned to me, so did my honor and glory and **k**.
4:36 me out, and I was reestablished as head of my **k**,
5: 7 He will become the third highest ruler in the **k**!"
5:11 There is a man in your **k** who has within him the
5:16 You will become the third highest ruler in the **k**."
5:28 your **k** has been divided and given to the Medes
5:29 he was proclaimed the third highest ruler in the **k**.
5:31 And Darius the Mede took over the **k** at the age of
6: 1 Darius the Mede decided to divide the **k** into 120
6:26 "I decree that everyone throughout my **k** should
6:26 endure forever. / His **k** will never be destroyed,
7:14 it will never end. His **k** will never be destroyed.
7:18 holy people of the Most High will be given the **k**,
7:22 time arrived for the holy people to take over the **k**.
10:13 But for twenty-one days the spirit prince of the **k**
10:13 and I left him there with the spirit prince of the **k**
10:20 to fight against the spirit prince of the **k** of Persia,
10:20 then against the spirit prince of the **k** of Greece.
11: 2 he will stir up everyone to war against the **k** of
11: 3 king will rise to power who will rule a vast **k**
11: 4 his **k** will be broken apart and divided into four
11: 4 nor will the **k** hold the authority it once had.
11: 5 than he and will rule his **k** with great strength.
11:17 make plans to come with the might of his entire **k**
11:17 marriage in order to overthrow the **k** from within,
11:21 and take over the **k** by flattery and intrigue.
Am 9:11 "In that day I will restore the fallen **k** of David.
Mt 3: 2 turn to God, because the **K** of Heaven is near."
4:17 turn to God, because the **K** of Heaven is near."
4:23 preaching everywhere the Good News about the **K**.
5: 3 for him, / for the **K** of Heaven is given to them.
5:10 they live for God, / for the **K** of Heaven is theirs.
5:19 the same, you will be the least in the **K** of Heaven.
5:19 and teaches them will be great in the **K** of Heaven.
5:20 you can't enter the **K** of Heaven at all!
6:10 May your **k** come soon. / May your will be done
6:33 and make the **K** of God your primary concern.
7:13 "You can enter God's **K** only through the narrow
7:21 but they still won't enter the **K** of Heaven.
8:11 Isaac, and Jacob at the feast in the **K** of Heaven.
8:12 those for whom the **K** was prepared—
9:35 and announcing the Good News about the **K**.
10: 7 and announce to them that the **K** of Heaven is near.
11:11 Yet even the most insignificant person in the **K** of
11:12 the **K** of Heaven has been forcefully advancing,
12:25 and replied, "Any **k** at war with itself is doomed.
12:26 against himself. His own **k** will not survive.
12:28 of God, then the **K** of God has arrived among you.
13:11 to understand the secrets of the **K** of Heaven,
13:19 those who hear the Good News about the **K**
13:24 "The **K** of Heaven is like a farmer who planted
13:31 "The **K** of Heaven is like a mustard seed planted
13:33 "The **K** of Heaven is like yeast used by a woman
13:38 and the good seed represents the people of the **K**.
13:41 and they will remove from my **K** everything that
13:43 godly will shine like the sun in their Father's **K**.
13:44 "The **K** of Heaven is like a treasure that a man
13:45 the **K** of Heaven is like a pearl merchant on the
13:47 the **K** of Heaven is like a fishing net that is thrown
13:52 **K** of Heaven is like a person who brings out of the
16:19 And I will give you the keys of the **K** of Heaven.
16:28 you see me, the Son of Man, coming in my **K**."
18: 1 "Which of us is greatest in the **K** of Heaven?"
18: 3 you will never get into the **K** of Heaven.
18: 4 this little child is the greatest in the **K** of Heaven.
18:23 the **K** of Heaven can be compared to a king who
19:12 and some choose not to marry for the sake of the **K**
19:14 For the **K** of Heaven belongs to such as these."
19:23 it is very hard for a rich person to get into the **K** of
19:24 than for a rich person to enter the **K** of God!"
19:28 Son of Man, sit upon my glorious throne in the **K**,
20: 1 "For the **K** of Heaven is like the owner of an
20:21 She replied, "In your **K**, will you let my two sons
21:31 and prostitutes will get into the **K** of God before
21:43 What I mean is that the **K** of God will be taken
22: 1 told them several other stories to illustrate the **K**.
22: 2 "The **K** of Heaven can be illustrated by the story
23:13 For you won't let others enter the **K** of Heaven,
24:14 And the Good News about the **K** will be preached
25: 1 "The **K** of Heaven can be illustrated by the story
25:14 the **K** of Heaven can be illustrated by the story of a
25:34 inherit the **K** prepared for you from the foundation
26:29 the day I drink it new with you in my Father's **K**."
Mk 1:15 he announced. "The **K** of God is near! Turn from
3:24 A **k** at war with itself will collapse.
4:11 to understand the secret about the **K** of God.
4:26 "Here is another illustration of what the **K** of God
4:30 Jesus asked, "How can I describe the **K** of God?
6:23 give you whatever you ask, up to half of my **k**!"
9: 1 you see the **K** of God arrive in great power!"
9:47 It is better to enter the **K** of God half blind than to
10:14 For the **K** of God belongs to such as these.
10:15 kind of faith will never get into the **K** of God."
10:23 "How hard it is for rich people to get into the **K** of
10:24 it is very hard to get into the **K** of God.
10:25 than for a rich person to enter the **K** of God!"
10:37 "In your glorious **K**, we want to sit in places of
11:10 Bless the coming **k** of our ancestor David!
12:34 said to him, "You are not far from the **K** of God."
14:25 that day when I drink it new in the **K** of God."
15:43 (who was waiting for the **K** of God to come),
Lk 1:33 reign over Israel forever; his **K** will never end!"
4:43 "I must preach the Good News of the **K** of God in
6:20 who are poor, / for the **K** of God is given to you.
7:28 Yet even the most insignificant person in the **K** of
8: 1 the Good News concerning the **K** of God.
8:10 to understand the secrets of the **K** of God.
9: 2 to tell everyone about the coming of the **K** of God
9:11 teaching them about the **K** of God and curing those
9:27 now will not die before you see the **K** of God."
9:60 is to go and preach the coming of the **K** of God."
9:62 then looks back is not fit for the **K** of God."
10: 9 heal them, say, 'The **K** of God is near you now.'
10:11 And don't forget the **K** of God is near!'
11: 2 your name be honored. / May your **K** come soon.
11:17 so he said, "Any **k** at war with itself is doomed.
11:18 me to cast out his demons, how can his **k** survive?
11:20 of God, then the **K** of God has arrived among you.
11:52 You don't enter the **K** yourselves, and you prevent
12:31 if you make the **K** of God your primary concern.
12:32 your Father great happiness to give you the **K**.
13:18 Then Jesus said, "What is the **K** of God like?
13:20 He also asked, "What else is the **K** of God like?
13:28 Jacob, and all the prophets within the **K** of God,
13:29 over the world to take their places in the **K** of God.
14:15 it would be to have a share in the **K** of God!"
16:16 But now the Good News of the **K** of God is
17:20 asked Jesus, "When will the **K** of God come?"
17:20 "The **K** of God isn't ushered in with visible signs.
17:21 'It's over there!' For the **K** of God is among you."
18:16 For the **K** of God belongs to such as these.
18:17 kind of faith will never get into the **K** of God."
18:24 "How hard it is for rich people to get into the **K** of
18:25 than for a rich person to enter the **K** of God!"
18:29 or children, for the sake of the **K** of God,
19:11 he told a story to correct the impression that the **K**
21:31 you can be sure that the **K** of God is near.
22:16 until it comes to fulfillment in the **K** of God."
22:18 For I will not drink wine again until the **K** of God
22:24 as to who would be the greatest in the coming **K**.
22:29 And just as my Father has granted me a **K**, I now
22:30 to eat and drink at my table in that **K**. And you will
23:42 remember me when you come into your **K**."
23:51 and he had been waiting for the **K** of God to come.
Jn 3: 3 are born again, you can never see the **K** of God."
3: 5 no one can enter the **K** of God without being born
18:36 the Jewish leaders. But my **K** is not of this world."
Ac 1: 3 On these occasions he talked to them about the **K**
1: 6 you going to free Israel now and restore our **k**?"
8:12 message of Good News concerning the **K** of God
14:22 reminding them that they must enter into the **K** of
15:16 and I will restore the fallen **k** of David.
19: 8 arguing persuasively about the **K** of God.
20:25 I have preached the **K** will ever see me again.
28:23 He told them about the **K** of God and taught them
28:31 proclaiming the **K** of God with all boldness
Ro 14:17 For the **K** of God is not a matter of what we eat
1Co 4:20 For the **K** of God is not just fancy talk; it is living
6: 9 who do wrong will have no share in the **K** of God?
6:10 none of these will have a share in the **K** of God.
15:24 when he will turn the **K** over to God the Father,
15:50 is that flesh and blood cannot inherit the **K** of God.
Gal 5:21 living that sort of life will not inherit the **K** of God.
Eph 5: 5 or greedy person will inherit the **K** of Christ
Col 1:13 us from the one who rules in the **k** of darkness,
1:13 and he has brought us into the **K** of his dear Son.
4:11 they are working with me here for the **K** of God.
1Th 2:12 For he called you into his **K** to share his glory.
2Th 1: 5 For he will make you worthy of his **K**, for which
2Ti 4: 1 and the dead when he appears to set up his **K**:
4:18 and will bring me safely to his heavenly **K**.
Heb 12:28 Since we are receiving a **k** that cannot be
Jas 2: 5 Aren't they the ones who will inherit the **k** God
1Pe 2: 9 You are a **k** of priests, God's holy nation, his very
2Pe 1:11 for you to enter into the eternal **K** of our Lord
Rev 1: 6 He has made us his **k** and his priests who serve
1: 9 in suffering and in the **K** and in patient endurance.
5:10 And you have caused them to become God's **k**
11:15 "The whole world has now become the **k** of our
12:10 the salvation and power and **k** of our God,
16:10 of the beast, and his **k** was plunged into darkness.

KINGDOMS (54) [KING]

ALL THE...KINGDOMS (19) Dt 3:21; 28:25; 1Ki 4:21,24; 2Ki 19:15,19; 1Ch 29:30; 2Ch 17:10; 20:6; 36:23; Ezr 1:2; Isa 37:16,20; Jer 10:7,7; 15:4; 25:26; Da 7:27; Lk 4:5

KINGDOMS OF THE EARTH (12) Dt 28:25; 2Ki 19:15,19; 2Ch 20:6; 36:23; Ezr 1:2; Ps 68:32; Isa 23:11; 37:16,20; Jer 15:4; Zep 3:8

Dt 3:21 He will do the same to all the **k** on the west side of
28:25 You will be an object of horror to all the **k** of the
Jos 11:10 been the capital of the federation of all these **k**.)
12: 5 and westward to the boundaries of the **k** of Geshur
13:11 the territory of the **k** of Geshur and Maacah,
2Sa 12: 8 and his wives and the **k** of Israel and Judah.
1Ki 4:21 King Solomon ruled all the **k** from the Euphrates
4:24 Solomon's dominion extended over all the **k** west
2Ki 19:15 You alone are God of all the **k** of the earth.
19:19 then all the **k** of the earth will know that you alone,
1Ch 29:30 to him and to Israel and to all the surrounding **k**.
2Ch 17:10 fear of the LORD fell over all the surrounding **k**
20: 6 You are ruler of all the **k** of the earth. You are
20:29 When the surrounding **k** heard that the LORD
36:23 God of heaven, has given me all the **k** of the earth.
Ezr 1: 2 God of heaven, has given me all the **k** of the earth.
Ne 9:22 "Then you helped our ancestors conquer great **k**
Ps 46: 6 The nations are in an uproar, / and **k** crumble!
68:32 Sing to God, you **k** of the earth. / Sing praises to
79: 6 on **k** that do not call upon your name.
102:22 and **k** come to worship the LORD.
Isa 10:14 and gathered up **k** as a farmer gathers eggs.
13:19 Babylon, the most glorious of **k**, the flower of
14:16 one who shook the earth and the **k** of the world?
23:11 He shakes the **k** of the earth. He has spoken out
37:16 You alone are God of all the **k** of the earth.
37:20 then all the **k** of the earth will know that you alone,
47: 5 Never again will you be known as the queen of **k**.
Jer 1:10 I appoint you to stand up against nations and **k**.
1:15 I am calling the armies of the **k** of the north to
10: 7 people of the earth and in all the **k** of the world,
15: 4 people an object of horror to all the **k** of the earth.
25:26 one after the other—all the **k** of the world.
34: 1 came with all the armies from the **k** he ruled,
49:28 was given concerning Kedar and the **k** of Hazor,
51:20 you I will shatter nations and destroy many **k**.
Da 2:43 and clay also shows that these **k** will try to
2:44 It will shatter all these **k** into nothingness, but it
4:17 that the Most High rules over the **k** of the world
4:25 until you learn that the Most High rules over the **k**
4:32 until you learn that the Most High rules over the **k**
5:21 until he learned that the Most High God rules the **k**
7:17 "These four huge beasts represent four **k** that will
7:27 and greatness of all the **k** under heaven will be
Zep 3: 8 For it is my decision to gather together the **k** of the
Hag 2:22 royal thrones, destroying the power of foreign **k**.
Mt 24: 7 and **k** will proclaim war against each other,
Mk 13: 8 and **k** will proclaim war against each other,
Lk 4: 5 and revealed to him all the **k** of the world in a
4: 6 "I will give you the glory of these **k** and authority
21:10 and **k** will proclaim war against each other.
Col 1:16 we can't see—kings, **k**, rulers, and authorities.
Heb 11:33 By faith these people overthrew **k**, ruled with
Rev 17:12 they will be appointed to their **k** for one brief

KINGS (327) [KING]

ALL THE KINGS (9) Jos 9:1; 11:2,17; 1Ki 10:15; 2Ch 9:14,26; Ps 47:9; 135:11; Jer 25:20

BOOK OF THE KINGS (11) 1Ch 9:1; 2Ch 16:11; 20:34; 24:27; 25:26; 27:7; 28:26; 32:32; 33:18; 35:27; 36:8

KING OF KINGS (4) Ezr 7:12; Eze 26:7; 1Ti 6:15; Rev 19:16

KINGS OF ISRAEL (42) 1Ki 14:19; 15:31; 16:5,14,20,27,33; 20:31; 22:39; 2Ki 1:18; 3:12; 8:18; 10:30,34; 13:8,12; 14:15,28,29; 15:11,12,15,21,26,31; 16:3; 17:2,8; 23:19,22; 1Ch 9:1; 2Ch 20:34; 21:6,13; 27:7; 28:2; 33:18; 35:18,27; 36:8; Isa 7:16; Mic 1:14

KINGS OF JUDAH (31) 1Sa 27:6; 1Ki 14:29; 15:7,23; 22:45; 2Ki 8:23; 12:18,19; 14:18; 15:6,36; 16:19; 20:20; 21:17,25; 23:5,11,12,28; 24:5; 2Ch 16:11; 25:26; 28:26; 32:32; 34:11; Isa 1:1; Jer 17:20; 19:3,4; Hos 1:1; Mic 1:1

KINGS OF THE EARTH (11) Ps 2:2; 47:9; 48:4; 68:29; 76:12; 102:15; 148:11; Ac 4:26; Rev 6:15; 17:18; 19:19

Ge 14: 3 The **k** of Sodom, Gomorrah, Admah, Zeboiim,
14: 8 But now the army of the **k** of Sodom, Gomorrah,
14: 9 King Kedorlaomer of Elam and the **k** of Goiim,
14: 9 Babylonia, and Ellasar—four **k** against five.
14:10 And as the army of the **k** of Sodom and Gomorrah
17: 6 represent many nations. **K** will be among them!
17:16 many nations. **K** will be among her descendants!"
35:11 many nations. **K** will be among your descendants!
36:31 These are the **k** who ruled in Edom before there were **k** in Israel:
49:20 "Asher will produce rich foods, / food fit for **k**.
Nu 31: 8 All five of the Midianite **k**—Evi, Rekem, Zur,
Dt 3: 8 of the two Amorite **k** east of the Jordan River—
3:21 that the LORD your God has done to these two **k**.
4:47 of Bashan—the two Amorite **k** east of the Jordan.
7:24 He will put their **k** in your power, and you will
31: 4 he destroyed Sihon and Og, the **k** of the Amorites.
Jos 2:10 the two Amorite **k** east of the Jordan River,
5: 1 When all the Amorite **k** west of the Jordan and all the Canaanite **k** who lived along the
9: 1 Now all the **k** west of the Jordan heard about what
9: 1 (These were the **k** of the Hittites, Amorites,
9: 2 These **k** quickly combined their armies to fight
9:10 did to the two Amorite **k** east of the Jordan River
10: 3 of Jerusalem sent messengers to several other **k**:
10: 5 So these five Amorite **k** combined their armies for
10: 6 For all the Amorite **k** who live in the hill country
10:16 the five **k** escaped and hid in a cave at Makkedah.
10:18 and place guards at the entrance to keep the **k**
10:22 opening of the cave and bring the five **k** to me."
10:23 So they brought the five **k** out of the cave—
10:23 the **k** of Jerusalem, Hebron, Jarmuth, Lachish,
10:26 Then Joshua killed each of the five **k** and hung
10:27 Joshua gave instructions for the bodies of the **k** to
10:40 the **k** and people of the hill country, the Negev,

10:42 In a single campaign Joshua conquered all these **k**
11: 1 he sent urgent messages to the following **k**:
11: 2 all the **k** of the northern hill country; the **k** in the Jordan Valley south of Galilee;
11: 2 the **k** in the western foothills; the **k** of Naphoth-dor
11: 3 the **k** of Canaan, both east and west; the **k** of the Amorites; the **k** of the Hittites; the **k** of the Perizzites; the **k** in the Jebusite hill country;
11: 4 All these **k** responded by mobilizing their warriors
11:12 Joshua slaughtered all the other **k** and their people,
11:17 Joshua killed all the **k** of those territories,
12: 1 These are the **k** east of the Jordan River who had
12: 7 The following is a list of the **k** Joshua
12: 8 and the Jebusites.) These are the **k** Israel defeated:
12:24 In all, thirty-one **k** and their cities were destroyed.
24:12 of you to drive out the two **k** of the Amorites.
Jdg 1: 7 "I once had seventy **k** with thumbs and big toes
5: 3 "Listen, you **k**! / Pay attention, you mighty rulers!
5:19 "The **k** of Canaan fought at Taanach near
5:25 and Jael gave him milk. / In a bowl fit for **k**,
8: 5 chasing Zebah and Zalmunna, the **k** of Midian."
8:12 Zebah and Zalmunna, the two Midianite **k**, fled,
8:26 and pendants, the royal clothing of the **k**,
1Sa 2:35 and his family will be priests to my anointed **k**
14:47 against Moab, Ammon, Edom, the **k** of Zobah,
27: 6 (which still belongs to the **k** of Judah to this day),
2Sa 7:11 that he will build a house for you—a dynasty of **k**!
11: 1 the time of year when **k** go to war, David sent Joab
1Ki 4:34 And **k** from every nation sent their ambassadors to
10:15 from merchants and traders, all the **k** of Arabia,
10:29 resold to the **k** of the Hittites and the **k** of Aram.
14:19 are recorded in *The Book of the History of the K*
14:29 in *The Book of the History of the K of Judah.*
15: 7 *K of Judah.* There was constant war between
15:23 *K of Judah.* In his old age his feet became
15:31 in *The Book of the History of the K of Israel.*
16: 5 in *The Book of the History of the K of Israel.*
16:14 in *The Book of the History of the K of Israel.*
16:20 in *The Book of the History of the K of Israel.*
16:25 even more than any of the **k** before him.
16:27 in *The Book of the History of the K of Israel.*
16:30 even more than any of the **k** before him.
16:33 than any of the other **k** of Israel before him.
20: 1 by the chariots and horses of thirty-two allied **k**.
20:12 and the other **k** as they were drinking in their tents.
20:16 and the thirty-two allied **k** were still in their tents
20:24 Only this time replace the **k** with field
20:31 we have heard that the **k** of Israel are very
22:39 in *The Book of the History of the K of Israel.*
22:45 in *The Book of the History of the K of Judah.*
2Ki 1:18 in *The Book of the History of the K of Israel.*
3:12 So the **k** of Israel, Judah, and Edom went to
3:13 For it was the LORD who called us three **k** here
8:18 But Jehoram followed the example of the **k** of
8:23 in *The Book of the History of the K of Judah.*
10: 4 and said, "Two **k** couldn't stand against this man!
10:30 be the **k** of Israel down to the fourth generation."
10:34 in *The Book of the History of the K of Israel.*
12:18 Jehoram, and Ahaziah, the previous **k** of Judah,
12:19 in *The Book of the History of the K of Judah.*
13: 8 are recorded in *The Book of the History of the K*
13:12 are recorded in *The Book of the History of the K*
14:15 are recorded in *The Book of the History of the K*
14:18 in *The Book of the History of the K of Judah.*
14:28 are recorded in *The Book of the History of the K*
14:29 he was buried with his ancestors, the **k** of Israel.
15: 6 in *The Book of the History of the K of Judah.*
15:11 in *The Book of the History of the K of Israel.*
15:12 "Your descendants will be **k** of Israel down to the
15:15 are recorded in *The Book of the History of the K*
15:21 in *The Book of the History of the K of Israel.*
15:26 in *The Book of the History of the K of Israel.*
15:31 in *The Book of the History of the K of Israel.*
15:36 in *The Book of the History of the K of Judah.*
16: 3 Instead, he followed the example of the **k** of Israel,
16:19 in *The Book of the History of the K of Judah.*
17: 2 but not as much as the **k** of Israel who ruled before
17: 8 as well as the practices the **k** of Israel had
19:11 You know perfectly well what the **k** of Assyria
19:12 The former **k** of Assyria destroyed them all!
19:13 What happened to the **k** of Sepharvaim, Hena,
19:17 that the **k** of Assyria have destroyed all these
20:20 are recorded in *The Book of the History of the K*
21:17 are recorded in *The Book of the History of the K*
21:25 in *The Book of the History of the K of Judah.*
23: 5 who had been appointed by the previous **k** of
23:11 that the former **k** of Judah had dedicated to the sun.
23:12 Josiah tore down the altars that the **k** of Judah had
23:19 They had been built by the various **k** of Israel
23:22 throughout all the years of the **k** of Israel
23:28 in *The Book of the History of the K of Judah.*
24: 5 in *The Book of the History of the K of Judah.*
25:28 treatment over all the other exiled **k** in Babylon.
1Ch 1:43 These are the **k** who ruled in Edom before there **k** in Israel:
9: 1 record in *The Book of the K of Israel.*
16:21 oppress them. / He warned **k** on their behalf:
17:10 will build a house for you—a dynasty of **k**!
19: 9 while the other **k** positioned themselves to fight in
20: 1 the time of year when **k** go to war,
2Ch 1:17 resold to the **k** of the Hittites and the **k** of Aram.
9:14 All the **k** of Arabia and the governors of the land
9:23 **K** from every nation came to visit him and to hear
9:26 He ruled over all the **k** from the Euphrates River to
16:11 are recorded in *The Book of the K of Judah*
20:34 is included in *The Book of the K of Israel.*
21: 6 But Jehoram followed the example of the **k** of
21:13 Instead, you have been as evil as the **k** of Israel.
24:16 He was buried among the **k** in the City of David,
24:27 *on the Book of the K.* When Joash died,
25:26 are recorded in *The Book of the K of Judah*
26:23 buried nearby in a burial field belonging to the **k**.
27: 7 are recorded in *The Book of the K of Israel*
28: 2 he followed the example of the **k** of Israel and cast
28:23 for he said, "These gods helped the **k** of Aram,
28:26 are recorded in *The Book of the K of Judah*
30: 6 who have survived the conquest of the Assyrian **k**.
32: 4 "Why should the **k** of Assyria come here and find
32:13 and the other **k** of Assyria before me have done to
32:32 which is included in *The Book of the K of Judah*
33:18 are recorded in *The Book of the K of Israel.*
34:11 They restored what earlier **k** of Judah had allowed
35:18 None of the **k** of Israel had ever kept a Passover as
35:27 are recorded in *The Book of the K of Israel*
36: 8 are recorded in *The Book of the K of Israel*
Ezr 4:15 because of its long history of sedition against the **k**
4:19 past been a hotbed of insurrection against many **k**.
4:20 Powerful **k** have ruled over Jerusalem
6:14 by Cyrus, Darius, and Artaxerxes, the **k** of Persia.
7:12 from Artaxerxes, the king of **k**, to Ezra the priest,
9: 7 That is why we and our **k** and our priests have been at the mercy of the pagan **k** of the land.
9: 9 he caused the **k** of Persia to treat us favorably.
Ne 9:24 Even the **k** and the Canaanites, who inhabited the
9:32 and upon our **k** and princes and priests
9:32 and ancestors from the days when the **k** of Assyria
9:34 Our **k**, princes, priests, and ancestors did not obey
9:37 in the hands of the **k** whom you have set over us
Est 10: 2 are recorded in *The Book of the History of the K*
Job 3:14 I would rest with the world's **k** and prime
12:18 He removes the royal robe of **k**. With ropes around
12:24 He takes away the understanding of **k**, and he
34:18 For he says to **k** and nobles, 'You are wicked
36: 7 but he establishes and exalts them with **k** forever.
Ps 2: 2 The **k** of the earth prepare for battle; / the rulers
2:10 Now then, you **k**, act wisely! / Be warned,
45:16 Your sons will become **k** like their father.
47: 9 For all the **k** of the earth belong to God. / He is
48: 4 The **k** of the earth joined forces / and advanced
60: 7 my warriors, / and Judah will produce my **k**.
68:12 Enemy **k** and their armies flee, / while the women
68:14 The Almighty scattered the enemy **k** / like a
68:29 The **k** of the earth are bringing tribute / to your
72:10 The western **k** of Tarshish and the islands
72:10 The eastern **k** of Sheba and Seba / will bring him
72:11 All **k** will bow before him, / and all nations will
76:12 of princes / and is feared by the **k** of the earth.
89: 4 'I will establish your descendants as **k** forever;
102:15 The **k** of the earth will tremble before his glory.
105:14 oppress them. / He warned **k** on their behalf:
108: 8 my warriors, / and Judah will produce my **k**.
110: 5 He will strike down many **k** in the day of his
119:46 I will speak to **k** about your decrees, / and I will
135:10 down great nations / and slaughtered mighty **k**—
135:11 Og king of Bashan, / and all the **k** of Canaan.
136:17 Give thanks to him who struck down mighty **k**.
136:18 He killed powerful **k**— / His faithful love endures
136:21 God gave the land of these **k** as an inheritance—
144:10 For you grant victory to **k**! / You are the one who
148:11 **k** of the earth and all people, / rulers and judges of
149: 8 to bind their **k** with shackles / and their leaders
Pr 8:15 Because of me, **k** reign, and rulers make just laws.
22:29 They will serve **k** rather than ordinary people.
31: 3 your strength on women, on those who ruin **k**.
31: 4 And it is not for **k**, O Lemuel, to guzzle wine.
Ecc 1:16 I am wiser than any of the **k** who ruled in
2: 7 more than any of the **k** who lived in Jerusalem
2: 8 and gold, the treasure of many **k** and provinces.
2: 9 So I became greater than any of the **k** who ruled in
10: 5 world go by. **K** and rulers make a grave mistake
Isa 1: 1 Jotham, Ahaz, and Hezekiah—all **k** of Judah.
7: 5 the **k** of Aram and Israel are coming against you.
7:16 two **k** you fear so much—the **k** of Israel and Aram
10:13 destroyed their **k**, and carried off their treasures.
14: 9 and mighty **k** long dead are there to see you.
14:18 "The **k** of the nations lie in stately glory in their
37:11 You know perfectly well what the **k** of Assyria
37:12 The former **k** of Assyria destroyed them all!
37:13 What happened to the **k** of Sepharvaim, Hena,
37:18 that the **k** of Assyria have destroyed all these
41: 2 and permits him to trample their **k** underfoot.
41:25 and I will give him victory over **k** and princes.
45: 1 Before him, mighty **k** will be paralyzed with fear.
49: 7 "**K** will stand at attention when you pass by.
49:23 **K** and queens will serve you. They will care for all
52:15 **K** will stand speechless in his presence.
60: 3 Mighty **k** will come to see your radiance.
60:10 rebuild your cities. **K** and rulers will send you aid.
60:11 The **k** of the world will be led as captives in a
60:16 Powerful **k** and mighty nations will bring the best
62: 2 **K** will be blinded by your glory.
Jer 1:18 None of the **k**, officials, priests, or people of Judah
2:26 **K**, officials, priests, and prophets—all are alike in
8: 1 "the enemy will break open the graves of the **k**
17:20 you **k** of Judah and all you people of Judah
17:25 **K** and their officials will always ride among the
19: 3 you **k** of Judah and citizens of Jerusalem!
19: 4 by their ancestors, or by the **k** of Judah.
19:13 including the palace of Judah's **k**, will become like
20: 5 the precious jewels and gold and silver of your **k**—
25:14 and great **k** will enslave the Babylonians,
25:18 and their **k** and officials drank from the cup.
25:20 the **k** of the land of Uz and the **k** of the Philistine
25:22 the **k** of Tyre and Sidon, and the **k** of the regions
25:24 I went to the **k** of Arabia, the **k** of the nomadic
25:25 and to the **k** of Zimri, Elam, and Media.
25:26 And I went to the **k** of the northern countries,
27: 3 Then send messages to the **k** of Edom, Moab,
27: 7 But then many nations and great **k** will conquer
32:32 the **k**, the officials, the priests, and the prophets—
44: 9 the sins of the **k** and queens of Judah, and the sins
44:17 and as our **k** and princes have always done in the
44:21 that you and your ancestors, your **k** and officials,
50:41 and many **k** are rising against you from far-off
51:11 For the LORD has stirred up the spirit of the **k** of
51:28 Bring against her the armies of the **k** of the Medes
52:32 treatment over all the other exiled **k** in Babylon.
La 2: 6 **K** and priests fall together before his anger.
2: 9 Her **k** and princes have been exiled to distant
Eze 26: 7 the king of **k** from the north—against Tyre with his
27:33 **K** at the ends of the earth / were enriched by your
27:35 Their **k** are filled with horror / and look on with
28:17 the earth and exposed you to the curious gaze of **k**.
32:10 and their **k** will be terrified because of all I do to
32:29 "Edom is there with its **k** and princes. Mighty as
43: 7 and their **k** will not defile my holy name any
43: 7 or by raising monuments in honor of their dead **k**.
43: 9 and the sacred pillars erected to honor their **k**,
Da 2:21 he removes **k** and sets others on the throne.
2:37 Your Majesty, you are a king over many **k**.
2:44 "During the reigns of those **k**, the God of heaven
2:47 of gods, the Lord over **k**, a revealer of mysteries,
7:24 Its ten horns are ten **k** that will rule that empire.
8:20 The two-horned ram represents the **k** of Media
8:22 Empire will break into four sections with four **k**,
9: 6 who spoke your messages to our **k** and princes
9: 8 O LORD, we and our **k**, princes, and ancestors
11: 2 Three more Persian **k** will reign, to be succeeded
11:27 these **k** will plot against each other at the
Hos 1: 1 Jotham, Ahaz, and Hezekiah were **k** of Judah,
7: 7 They kill their **k** one after another, and no one cries
8: 4 The people have appointed **k** and princes, but not
13:11 In my anger I gave you **k**, and in my fury I took
Mic 1: 1 Ahaz, and Hezekiah were **k** of Judah.
1:14 The town of Aczib has deceived the **k** of Israel,
Hab 1:10 They scoff at **k** and princes and scorn all their
Mt 10:18 and **k** because you are my followers.
17:25 Do **k** tax their own people or the foreigners they
20:25 "You know that in this world **k** are tyrants,
Mk 10:42 "You know that in this world **k** are tyrants,
13: 9 before governors and **k** of being my followers.
Lk 10:24 many prophets and **k** have longed to see and hear
21:12 and you will be accused before **k** and governors of
22:25 "In this world the **k** and great men order their
Ac 4:26 The **k** of the earth prepared for battle; / the rulers
9:15 to take my message to the Gentiles and to **k**,
1Co 4: 8 are already rich! Without us you have become **k**!
Col 1:16 we can't see—**k**, kingdoms, rulers, and authorities.
1Ti 2: 2 Pray this way for **k** and all others who are in
6:15 almighty God, the King of **k** and Lord of lords.
Heb 7: 1 home after winning a great battle against many **k**,
Rev 6:15 Then the **k** of the earth, the rulers, the generals,
10:11 about many peoples, nations, languages, and **k**."
16:12 so that the **k** from the east could march their
17: 9 this woman rules. They also represent seven **k**.
17:10 Five **k** have already fallen, the sixth now reigns,
17:12 His ten horns are ten **k** who have not yet risen to
17:14 he is Lord over all lords and King over all **k**,
17:16 which represent ten **k** who will reign with him—
17:18 the great city that rules over the **k** of the earth."
19:16 was written this title: King of **k** and Lord of lords.
19:18 Come and eat the flesh of **k**, captains, and strong
19:19 Then I saw the beast gathering the **k** of the earth

KINGS' (3) [KING]

Jos 10:24 "Come and put your feet on the **k** necks."
Ps 45: 9 **K** daughters are among your concubines. / At your
Pr 30:28 to catch, / but they are found even in **k** palaces.

KINGSHIP (3) [KING]

1Sa 11:14 let us all go to Gilgal to reaffirm Saul's **k**."
Mic 4: 8 The **k** will be restored to my precious Jerusalem.
Ac 13:22 But God removed him from the **k** and replaced him

KINNERETH (2)

Jos 19:35 territory were Ziddim, Zer, Hammath, Rakkath, **K**,
1Ki 15:20 Dan, Abel-beth-maacah, and all **K**, with all the

KINSMAN (1)

Lev 25:25 then a close relative, a **k** redeemer, may buy it

KIOS (1)

Ac 20:15 The next day we passed the island of **K**.

KIR (5) [KIR-HARESETH]

2Ki 16: 9 population away as captives, resettling them in **K**.
Isa 15: 1 night your cities of Ar and **K** will be destroyed.
22: 6 the chariots. The men of **K** hold up the shields.
Am 1: 5 and the people of Aram will return to **K** as slaves.
9: 7 from Crete and led the Arameans out of **K**.

KIR-HARESETH (5) [KIR]

2Ki 3:25 Finally, only **K** was left, but even that came under
Isa 16: 7 people of Moab, mourn for the delicacies of **K**.
16:11 for Moab. My sorrow for **K** will be very great.
Jer 48:31 for Moab; my heart is broken for the men of **K**.
48:36 My heart moans like a flute for Moab and **K**,

KIRIATH-ARBA (8) [HEBRON]
Ge 23: 2 she died at **K** (now called Hebron) in the land of
35:27 which is near **K** (now called Hebron),
Jos 14:15 (Previously Hebron had been called **K**. It had been
15:54 Humtah, **K** (that is, Hebron), and Zior—nine towns
20: 7 and **K** (that is, Hebron), in the hill country of
21:11 **K** (that is, Hebron), in the hill country of Judah,
Jdg 1:10 the Canaanites in Hebron (formerly called **K**),
Ne 11:25 Some of the people of Judah lived in **K** with its

KIRIATH-BAAL (2) [BAAL, KIRIATH-JEARIM]
Jos 15:60 There were also **K** (that is, Kiriath-jearim)
18:14 ending at the village of **K** (that is, Kiriath-jearim),

KIRIATH-HUZOTH (1)
Nu 22:39 Then Balaam accompanied Balak to **K**,

KIRIATH-JEARIM (19) [BAALAH, KIRIATH-BAAL]
Jos 9:17 towns were Gibeon, Kephirah, Beeroth, and **K**.
15: 9 Then it turned toward Baalah (that is, **K**).
15:60 There were also Kiriath-baal (that is, **K**)
18:14 ending at the village of Kiriath-baal (that is, **K**),
18:15 The southern boundary began at the outskirts of **K**.
18:28 Jebus (that is, Jerusalem), Gibeah, and **K**—
Jdg 18:12 They camped at a place west of **K** in Judah,
1Sa 6:21 So they sent messengers to the people at **K**
7: 1 So the men of **K** came to get the Ark of the
7: 2 The Ark remained in **K** for a long time—
1Ch 2:50 wife Ephrathah, were Shobal (the father of **K**),
2:52 The descendants of Shobal (the father of **K**)
2:53 and the families of **K**—the Ithrites, Puthites,
13: 5 to join in bringing the Ark of God from **K**.
13: 6 all Israel went to Baalah of Judah (also called **K**)
2Ch 1: 4 David had already moved the Ark of God from **K**
Ezr 2:25 The peoples of **K**, Kephirah, and Beeroth | 743
Ne 7:29 The peoples of **K**, Kephirah, and Beeroth | 743
Jer 26:20 Uriah son of Shemaiah from **K** was also

KIRIATH-SANNAH (1) [DEBIR]
Jos 15:49 Dannah, **K** (that is, Debir),

KIRIATH-SEPHER (4) [DEBIR]
Jos 15:15 living in the town of Debir (formerly called **K**).
15:16 marriage to the one who attacks and captures **K**."
Jdg 1:11 living in the town of Debir (formerly called **K**).
1:12 marriage to the one who attacks and captures **K**."

KIRIATHAIM (7)
Ge 14: 5 the Zuzites in Ham, the Emites in the plain of **K**,
Nu 32:37 of Reuben built the towns of Heshbon, Elealeh, **K**,
Jos 13:19 **K**, Sibmah, Zereth-shahar on the hill above the
1Ch 6:76 Hammon, and **K**, each with its pasturelands.
Jer 48: 1 The city of **K** will be humiliated and captured;
48:23 and on **K** and Beth-gamul and Beth-meon,
Eze 25: 9 frontier cities—Beth-jeshimoth, Baal-meon, and **K**.

KIRIOTH [KJV] See KERIOTH

KIRJATH [KJV] See KIRIATH-JEARIM

KIRJATH-ARBA [KJV] See KIRIATH-ARBA

KIRJATH-ARIM [KJV] See KIRIATH-JEARIM

KIRJATH-BAAL [KJV] See KIRIATH-BAAL

KIRJATH-HUZOTH [KJV] See KIRIATH-HUZOTH

KIRJATH-JEARIM [KJV] See KIRIATH-JEARIM

KIRJATH-SANNAH [KJV] See KIRIATH-SANNAH

KIRJATH-SEPHER [KJV] See KIRIATH-SEPHER

KIRJATHAIM [KJV] See KIRIATHAIM

KISH (19) [KISH'S]
1Sa 9: 1 **K** was a rich, influential man from the tribe of
10:11 How did the son of **K** become a prophet?"
10:21 And finally Saul son of **K** was chosen from among
14:51 Ner, and Saul's father, **K**, were brothers;
2Sa 21:14 He buried them all in the tomb of **K**, Saul's father,
1Ch 8:30 Jeiel's other sons were Zur, **K**, Baal, Ner, Nadab,
8:33 Ner was the father of **K**. **K** was the father of Saul.
9:36 Jeiel's other sons were Zur, **K**, Baal, Ner, Nadab,
9:39 Ner was the father of **K**. **K** was the father of Saul.
12: 1 at Ziklag while he was hiding from Saul son of **K**.
23:21 and Mushi. The sons of Mahli were Eleazar and **K**.
23:22 His daughters married their cousins, the sons of **K**.
24:29 From the descendants of **K**, the leader was
26:28 Saul son of **K**, Abner son of Ner, and Joab son of
2Ch 29:12 **K** son of Abdi and Azariah son of Jehallelel.
Est 2: 5 and was a descendant of **K** and Shimei.
Ac 13:21 and God gave them Saul son of **K**, a man of the

KISH'S (1) [KISH]
1Sa 9: 3 One day **K** donkeys strayed away, and he told

KISHI (1) [KUSHAIAH]
1Ch 6:44 Ethan's genealogy was traced back through **K**,

KISHION (2)
Jos 19:20 Rabbith, **K**, Ebez,
21:28 From the tribe of Issachar they received **K**,

KISHON (6)
Jdg 4: 7 with his chariots and warriors, to the **K** River.
4:13 marched from Harosheth-haggoyim to the **K** River.
5:21 The **K** River swept them away— / that ancient river, the **K**.
1Ki 18:40 and Elijah took them down to the **K** Valley
Ps 83: 9 or as you did to Sisera and Jabin at the **K** River.

KISLON (1)
Nu 34:21 Benjamin | Elidad son of **K**

KISLOTH-TABOR (1) [KESULLOTH, TABOR]
Jos 19:12 line went east from Sarid to the border of **K**,

KISS (15) [KISSED, KISSES, KISSING]
Ge 27:26 "Come here and **k** me, my son."
31:28 Why didn't you let me **k** my daughters
2Sa 20: 9 the beard with his right hand as though to **k** him.
1Ki 19:20 "First let me go and **k** my father and mother
SS 1: 2 "**K** me again and again, for your love is sweeter
8: 1 Then I could **k** you no matter who was watching,
Isa 60:14 Those who despised you will **k** your feet.
Hos 13: 2 to these," they cry, "and **k** the calf idols!"
Mt 26:48 when I go over and give him the **k** of greeting."
26:49 Teacher!" he exclaimed and gave him the **k**.
Mk 14:44 when I go over and give him the **k** of greeting.
14:45 "Teacher!" he exclaimed, and gave him the **k**.
Lk 7:45 You didn't give me a **k** of greeting, but she has
22:47 walked over to Jesus and greeted him with a **k**.
22:48 can you betray me, the Son of Man, with a **k**?"

KISSED (16) [KISS]
Ge 27:27 So Jacob went over and **k** him. And when Isaac
29:11 Then Jacob **k** Rachel, and tears came to his eyes.
31:55 and he **k** his daughters and grandchildren
33: 4 and embraced him affectionately and **k** him.
45:15 Then Joseph **k** each of his brothers and wept over
48:10 close to him, and Jacob **k** and embraced them.
50: 1 himself on his father and wept over him and **k** him.
Ru 1: 9 Then she **k** them good-bye, and they all broke
1:14 and Orpah **k** her mother-in-law good-bye.
1Sa 10: 1 He **k** Saul on the cheek and said, "I am doing this
2Sa 14:33 and bowed low before the king, and David **k** him.
1Ki 19:18 in Israel who have never bowed to Baal or **k** him!"
Ps 85:10 met together. / Righteousness and peace have **k**!
Pr 7:13 She threw her arms around him and **k** him,
Lk 7:45 but she has **k** my feet again and again from the
15:20 he ran to his son, embraced him, and **k** him.

KISSES (2) [KISS]
Pr 27: 6 Wounds from a friend are better than many **k** from
SS 7: 9 May your **k** be as exciting as the best wine, smooth

KISSING (1) [KISS]
Lk 7:38 Then she kept **k** his feet and putting perfume on

KITCHENS (2)
Eze 46:24 "These are the **k** to be used by the Temple
Da 1: 5 ration of the best food and wine from his own **k**.

KITES (2)
Lev 11:14 the buzzard, **k** of all kinds,
Dt 14:13 the buzzard, **k** of all kinds,

KITLISH (1)
Jos 15:40 Cabbon, Lahmam, **K**,

KITRON (1)
Jdg 1:30 also failed to drive out the Canaanites living in **K**

KITTIM (2)
Ge 10: 4 of Javan were Elishah, Tarshish, **K**, and Rodanim.
1Ch 1: 7 of Javan were Elishah, Tarshish, **K**, and Rodanim.

KNEAD (1) [KNEADED, KNEADING]
Jer 7:18 See how the women **k** dough and make cakes to

KNEADED (1) [KNEAD]
1Sa 28:24 killed it. She **k** dough and baked unleavened bread.

KNEADING (5) [KNEAD]
Ex 8: 3 They will fill even your ovens and your **k** bowls.
12:34 They wrapped their **k** bowls in their spare clothing
Dt 28: 5 with fruit, and with **k** bowls filled with bread.
28:17 empty of fruit, and with **k** bowls empty of bread.
Hos 7: 4 kept hot even while the baker is still **k** the dough.

KNEE (3) [KNEES]
Isa 45:23 Every **k** will bow to me, and every tongue will
Ro 14:11 as I live,' says the Lord, / 'every **k** will bow to me
Php 2:10 so that at the name of Jesus every **k** will bow,

KNEEL (5) [KNEELING, KNELT]
Ge 24:11 There the servant made the camels **k** down beside
41:43 he went the command was shouted, "**K** down!"
Jdg 7: 5 In the other group put all those who **k** down
Ps 95: 6 Let us **k** before the LORD our maker,
Mt 4: 9 "if you will only **k** down and worship me."

KNEELING (3) [KNEEL]
1Ki 8:54 where he had been **k** with his hands raised toward
Lk 7:44 and said to Simon, "Look at this woman **k** here.
10:34 **K** beside him, the Samaritan soothed his wounds

KNEES (22) [KNEE]
Ge 48:12 Joseph took the boys from their grandfather's **k**,
Jdg 7: 6 All the others got down on their **k** and drank with
2Ki 1:13 But this time the captain fell to his **k** before Elijah.
Ezr 9: 5 I fell to my **k**, lifted my hands to the LORD my
Ps 17:13 Stand against them and bring them to their **k**!
59:11 them with your power, and bring them to their **k**,
109:24 My **k** are weak from fasting, / and I am skin
Isa 35: 3 and encourage those who have weak **k**.
45:14 They will fall to their **k** in front of you and say,
La 2:20 little children, those they once bounced on their **k**?
Eze 7:17 will be feeble; their **k** will be as weak as water.
21: 7 strong **k** will tremble and become as weak as
47: 4 This time the water was up to my **k**. After another
Da 5: 6 Such terror gripped him that his **k** knocked
10:10 and lifted me, still trembling, to my hands and **k**.
Na 2:10 of its wealth. Hearts melt in horror, and **k** shake.
Mk 15:19 on him, and dropped to their **k** in mock worship.
Lk 5: 8 he fell to his **k** before Jesus and said, "Oh, Lord,
8:47 she began to tremble and fell to her **k** before him.
Ac 7:60 And he fell to his **k**, shouting, "Lord, don't charge
1Co 14:25 and they will fall down on their **k** and worship
Eph 3:14 of God's plan, I fall to my **k** and pray to the Father,

KNELT (15) [KNEEL]
1Ch 29:20 bowed low and **k** before the LORD and the king.
2Ch 6:13 and then he **k** down and lifted his hands toward
Da 6:10 and **k** down as usual in his upstairs room,
Mt 8: 2 He **k** before him, worshiping. "Lord," the man
9:18 of a synagogue came and **k** down before him.
17:14 for them. A man came and **k** before Jesus and said,
20:20 with her sons. She **k** respectfully to ask a favor.
27:29 Then they **k** before him in mockery, yelling,
Mk 1:40 A man with leprosy came and **k** in front of Jesus,
10:17 up to Jesus, **k** down, and asked, "Good Teacher,
Lk 7:38 Then she **k** behind him at his feet, weeping.
22:41 about a stone's throw, and **k** down and prayed,
Ac 9:40 them all to leave the room; then he **k** and prayed.
20:36 had finished speaking, he **k** and prayed with them.
21: 5 down to the shore with us. There we **k**, prayed,

KNEW (103) [KNOW]
Ge 8:11 Noah now **k** that the water was almost gone.
16: 4 When Hagar **k** she was pregnant, she began to treat
28: 7 He also **k** that Jacob had obeyed his parents
Ex 1: 8 to the throne of Egypt who **k** nothing about Joseph
2:14 because he realized that everyone **k** what he had
21:29 that the owner **k** the bull had gored people in the
Nu 22: 2 **k** what the Israelites had done to the Amorites.
Dt 7:15 suffer from the terrible diseases you **k** in Egypt,
34:10 like Moses, whom the LORD **k** face to face.
Jdg 6:27 He **k** what would happen if they found out who
1Sa 2:22 He **k**, for instance, that his sons were seducing the
3:20 **k** that Samuel was confirmed as a prophet of the
20:39 what Jonathan meant; only Jonathan and David **k**.
22:15 for I **k** nothing of any plot against you."
22:17 They **k** he was running away from me, but they
22:22 David exclaimed, "I **k** it! When I saw Doeg there that day, I **k** he would tell Saul.
26: 3 David was hiding. But David **k** of Saul's arrival,
2Sa 1:10 Amalekite told David, "for I **k** he couldn't live.
3:26 him back with them. But David **k** nothing about it.
3:37 and Israel **k** that David was not responsible for
11:16 he **k** the enemy's strongest men were fighting.
15:11 him as guests, but they **k** nothing of his intentions.
1Ch 12:32 of the times and **k** the best course for Israel to take.
Ne 4:15 When our enemies heard that we **k** of their plans
9:10 for you **k** how arrogantly the Egyptians were
13:30 and Levites, making certain that each **k** his work.
Est 1:13 who **k** all the Persian laws and customs, for he
7: 7 with Queen Esther, for he **k** that he was doomed.
Job 20: 7 Those who **k** him will ask, 'Where is he?'
23: 3 If only I **k** where to find God, I would go to his
Ps 77:19 mighty waters— / a pathway no one **k** was there!
Pr 24:12 keeps watch over your soul, and he knows you **k**!
Ecc 9:15 wise man living there who **k** how to save the town,
12: 9 was wise, he taught the people everything he **k**.
Isa 48: 7 So you cannot say, 'We **k** that all the time!'
Jer 1: 5 "I **k** you before I formed you in your mother's
32: 8 Then I **k** for sure that the message I had heard was
44:15 and all the men who **k** that their wives had burned
Eze 10:20 I was by the Kebar River. I **k** they were cherubim,
28:19 All who **k** you are appalled at your fate. You have
Da 5:22 are his successor, O Belshazzar, and you **k** all this,
11:38 a god his ancestors never **k**—and lavish on him
Jnh 4: 2 I **k** that you were a gracious and compassionate
4: 2 I **k** how easily you could cancel your plans for

Zec 11:11 and they **k** that the LORD was speaking to them
Mt 7:23 But I will reply, 'I never **k** you. Go away;
9: 4 Jesus **k** what they were thinking, so he asked them,
12: 7 aren't guilty if you **k** the meaning of this Scripture:
12:15 But Jesus **k** what they were planning. He left that
12:25 Jesus **k** their thoughts and replied, "Any kingdom
16: 8 Jesus **k** what they were thinking, so he said,
22:18 But Jesus **k** their evil motives. "You hypocrites!"
24:43 A homeowner who **k** exactly when a burglar was
27:18 (He **k** very well that the Jewish leaders had
Mk 1:34 But because they **k** who he was, he refused to
2: 8 Jesus **k** what they were discussing among
8:17 Jesus **k** what they were thinking, so he said,
Lk 2:52 and he was loved by God and by all who **k** him.
4:41 But because they **k** he was the Messiah, he stopped
5:22 Jesus **k** what they were thinking, so he asked them,
6: 8 But Jesus **k** their thoughts. He said to the man with
8:47 When the woman realized that Jesus **k**, she began
8:53 laughed at him because they all **k** she had died.
9:47 But Jesus **k** their thoughts, so he brought a little
11:17 He **k** their thoughts, so he said, "Any kingdom at
12:39 A homeowner who **k** exactly when a burglar was
12:47 for though he **k** his duty, he refused to do it.
19:22 If you **k** so much about me and how tough I am,
Jn 2: 9 of course, the servants **k**), he called the bridegroom
2:24 because he **k** what people were really like.
4:10 "If you only **k** the gift God has for you and who I
5: 6 Jesus saw him and **k** how long he had been ill,
6: 6 for he already **k** what he was going to do.
6:22 For they **k** that he and his disciples had come over
6:61 Jesus **k** within himself that his disciples were
6:64 (For Jesus **k** from the beginning who didn't
believe, and he **k** who would betray him.)
8:19 If you **k** me, then you would know my Father,
9: 8 and others who **k** him as a blind beggar asked each
13: 1 Jesus **k** that his hour had come to leave this world
13: 3 Jesus **k** that the Father had given him authority
13:11 For Jesus **k** who would betray him. That is what he
13:28 None of the others at the table **k** what Jesus meant.
18: 2 Judas, the betrayer, **k** this place, because Jesus had
19:28 Jesus **k** that everything was now finished, and to
Ac 2:30 and he **k** God had promised with an oath that one
7:18 then a new king came to the throne of Egypt who **k**
16: 3 for everyone **k** that his father was a Greek.
18:24 an eloquent speaker who **k** the Scriptures well,
18:25 However, he **k** only about John's baptism.
Ro 1:21 Yes, they **k** God, but they wouldn't worship him as
1:25 Instead of believing what they **k** was the truth
4:19 even though he **k** that he was too old to be a father
8:29 For God **k** his people in advance, and he chose
1Co 13: 2 and if I **k** all the mysteries of the future and **k**
everything about everything,
Gal 1:23 All they **k** was that people were saying, "The one
4: 8 Before you Gentiles **k** God, you were slaves to
Heb 10:34 You **k** you had better things waiting for you in
12: 2 because of the joy he **k** would be his afterward.
12:10 us for a few years, doing the best they **k** how.
Rev 19:12 was written on him, and only he **k** what it meant.

KNIFE (8) [KNIVES]

Ge 22: 6 while he himself carried the **k** and the fire.
22:10 And Abraham took the **k** and lifted it up to kill his
22:12 "Lay down the **k**," the angel said. "Do not hurt
Ex 4:25 his wife, took a flint **k** and circumcised her son.
Jdg 19:29 he took a **k** and cut his concubine's body into
Pr 23: 2 If you are a big eater, put a **k** to your throat,
Jer 36:23 the king took his **k** and cut off that section of the
Heb 4:12 It is sharper than the sharpest **k**, cutting deep into

KNIT (5)

Job 10:11 and you **k** my bones and sinews together.
40:17 The sinews of its thighs are tightly **k** together.
Ps 122: 3 is a well-built city, / **k** together as a single unit.
139:13 and **k** me together in my mother's womb.
Col 2: 2 and **k** together by strong ties of love.

KNIVES (5) [KNIFE]

Jos 5: 2 "Use **k** of flint to make the Israelites a circumcised
5: 3 So Joshua made flint **k** and circumcised the entire
1Ki 18:28 they cut themselves with **k** and swords until the
Pr 30:14 devour the poor with teeth as sharp as swords or **k**.
Eze 40:42 On these tables were placed the butchering **k**

KNOCK (9) [KNOCKED, KNOCKING, KNOCKS]

Ex 21:24 **k** out the tooth of the person who did it.
Isa 28:17 since it is made of lies, a hailstorm will **k** it down.
57:13 so helpless that a breath of wind can **k** them down!
Eze 13:11 great hailstones and mighty winds will **k** it down.
16:39 They will **k** down your pagan shrines and the altars
39: 3 I will **k** your weapons from your hands and leave
Mt 5:38 **k** out the tooth of the person who did it.'
2Co 10: 4 to **k** down the Devil's strongholds.
Rev 3:20 "Look! Here I stand at the door and **k**. If you hear

KNOCKED (21) [KNOCK]

Ge 32:25 Jacob's hip and **k** it out of joint at the socket.
Ex 21:26 If a tooth gets **k** out, knock out the tooth of the
Dt 28:52 the walls you trusted to protect you—are **k** down.
Jdg 6:28 discovered that the altar of Baal had been **k** down
6:31 and destroy the one who **k** down his altar!"
6:32 defend himself," because he **k** down Baal's altar.
7:13 It hit a tent, turned it over, and **k** it flat!"
8:17 He also **k** down the tower of Peniel and killed all
2Ki 7:17 but he was **k** down and trampled to death as the
18: 4 the sacred pillars, and **k** down the Asherah poles.
2Ch 17: 6 He **k** down the pagan shrines and destroyed the
Ps 143: 3 enemy has chased me. / He has **k** me to the ground.
Da 2:35 But the rock that **k** the statue down became a great
5: 6 Such terror gripped him that his knees **k** together
8: 7 and the goat **k** it down and trampled it.
Mt 5:38 If a tooth gets **k** out, knock out the tooth of the
21:12 He **k** over the tables of the money changers
Mk 11:15 He **k** over the tables of the money changers
Lk 9:42 the demon **k** him to the ground and threw him into
Ac 12:13 He **k** at the door in the gate, and a servant girl
2Co 4: 9 We get **k** down, but we get up again and keep

KNOCKING (6) [KNOCK]

SS 5: 2 He was **k** at my bedroom door. 'Open to me,
Mt 7: 7 will find. Keep on **k**, and the door will be opened.
Lk 11: 8 if you keep **k** long enough, he will get up and give
11: 9 will find. Keep on **k**, and the door will be opened.
13:25 Then you will stand outside **k** and pleading,
Ac 12:16 Meanwhile, Peter continued **k**. When they finally

KNOCKS (4) [KNOCK]

Ex 21:27 And if an owner **k** out the tooth of a male
Mt 7: 8 finds. And the door is opened to everyone who **k**.
Lk 11:10 finds. And the door is opened to everyone who **k**.
12:36 and let him in the moment he arrives and **k**.

KNOW (879) [KNEW, KNOWING, KNOWLEDGE, KNOWLEDGEABLE, KNOWN, KNOWS]

Ge 4: 9 Where is Abel?" "I don't **k**!" Cain retorted.
18:21 or not these reports are true. Then I will **k**."
20: 6 "Yes, I **k** you are innocent," God replied.
22:12 in any way, for now I **k** that you truly fear God.
24:14 By this I will **k** that you have shown kindness to
24:49 tell me, then I'll **k** what my next step should be,
29: 5 "Do you **k** a man there named Laban,
30:26 You **k** I have fully paid for them with my service
30:29 "You **k** how faithfully I've served you through
30:33 you will **k** that I have stolen them from you."
31: 6 You **k** how hard I have worked for your father,
31:30 I **k** you feel you must go, and you long intensely
31:32 But Jacob didn't **k** that Rachel had taken them.
31:50 I won't **k** about it if you are harsh to my daughters
40:12 "I **k** what the dream means," Joseph said.
42:16 have a younger brother, then I'll **k** you are spies."
42:20 I will **k** whether or not you are telling me the truth.
42:23 they didn't **k** that Joseph understood them as he
42:34 Then I will **k** that you are honest men and not
43: 7 "He wanted to **k** whether our father was still
44:15 "Didn't you **k** that a man such as I would **k**
44:18 for I **k** you could have me killed in an instant,
44:27 said to us, 'You **k** that my wife had two sons,
46:30 you with my own eyes and **k** you are still alive."
48:19 "I **k** what I'm doing, my son," he said.
Ex 3:19 "But I **k** that the king of Egypt will not let you go
4:18 I don't even **k** whether they are still alive."
5: 2 I don't **k** the LORD, and I will not let Israel go."
6: 7 And you will **k** that I am the LORD your God
8:10 Then you will **k** that no one is as powerful as the
8:22 Then you will **k** that I am the LORD and that I
9:30 I **k** that you still do not fear the LORD God as
10:26 And we won't **k** which sacrifices he will require
11: 7 Then you will **k** that the LORD makes a
14: 4 the Egyptians will **k** that I am the LORD!"
14:18 his army, all Egypt will **k** that I am the LORD!"
16:12 Then you will **k** that I am the LORD your
18:11 I **k** now that the LORD is greater than all other
19: 4 You **k** how I brought you to myself and carried
23: 9 among you. You **k** what it is like to be a foreigner.
29:46 and they will **k** that I am the LORD their God.
32: 1 We don't **k** what has happened to him."
32:22 "You yourself **k** these people and what a wicked
33:16 how will anyone ever **k** that your people and I
33:16 How else will they **k** we are special and distinct
Lev 10:16 When Moses demanded to **k** what had happened to
Nu 10: 3 the people will **k** that they are to gather before you
10:31 "You **k** the places in the wilderness where we
14:13 "They **k** full well the power you displayed in
14:14 They **k**, LORD, that you have appeared in full
14:14 They **k** that you go before them in the pillar of
15:34 because they did not **k** what to do with him.
16:28 "By this you will **k** that the LORD has sent me to
16:30 then you will **k** that these men have despised the
20:14 You **k** all the hardships we have been through,
22: 6 I **k** that blessings fall on the people you bless.
22: 6 I also **k** that the people you curse are doomed."
Dt 18:21 'How will we **k** whether the prophecy is from the
20:20 But you may cut down trees that you **k** are not
21: 1 and you don't **k** who committed the murder.
22: 2 someone nearby or you don't **k** who the owner is,
29: 6 so you would **k** that he is the LORD your God.
31:21 I **k** what these people are like, even before they
31:27 For I **k** how rebellious and stubborn you are.
31:29 I **k** that after my death you will become utterly
32:29 understand this! / Oh, that they might **k** their fate!
Jos 2: 4 here earlier, but I didn't **k** where they were from.
2: 5 were about to close, and I don't **k** where they went.
2: 9 "I **k** the LORD has given you this land," she told
2:10 And we **k** what you did to Sihon and Og, the two
3: 7 Now they will **k** that I am with you, just as I was
3:10 Today you will **k** that the living God is among you.
4:24 so that all the nations of the earth might **k** the
9: 7 "How do we **k** you don't live nearby?
22:16 to **k** why you are betraying the God of Israel.
22:22 But the LORD knows, and let all Israel **k**, too,
22:31 "Today we **k** the LORD is among us because you
23:13 then **k** for certain that the LORD your God will
23:14 Deep in your hearts you **k** that every promise of
Jdg 6:37 then I will **k** that you are going to help me rescue
11:12 demanding to **k** why Israel was being attacked.
17:13 "I **k** the LORD will bless me now," Micah said,
Ru 2:11 "Yes, I **k**," Boaz replied. "But I also **k** about the
love and kindness you
3:14 "No one must **k** that a woman was here at the
4: 3 "You **k** Naomi, who came back from Moab.
4: 4 But if you don't want it, let me **k** right away,
1Sa 3: 7 Samuel did not yet **k** the LORD because he had
6: 3 you will **k** that God didn't send the plague after
6: 9 we will **k** it was the LORD who brought this
6: 9 we will **k** that the plague was simply a coincidence
9:19 In the morning I will tell you what you want to **k**
12:17 You **k** that it does not rain at this time of the year
15:30 Then Saul pleaded again, "I **k** I have sinned.
17:28 I **k** about your pride and dishonesty. You just want
17:46 and the whole world will **k** that there is a God in
17:47 And everyone will **k** that the LORD does not
17:55 whose son is he?" "I really don't **k**," Abner said.
20: 2 I **k** he wouldn't hide something like this from me.
20: 7 If he says, 'Fine!' then you will **k** all is well.
20: 7 then you will **k** he was planning to kill me.
20: 9 "You **k** that if I had the slightest notion my father
20:10 "How will I **k** whether or not your father is
20:12 and let you **k** at once how he feels about you.
20:12 If he speaks favorably about you, I will let you **k**.
20:21 me tell him, 'They're on this side,' then you will **k**,
20:30 "Do you think I don't **k** that you want David to be
22: 3 until I **k** what God is going to do for me?"
23:19 to him. "We **k** where David is hiding," they said.
23:22 has seen him there, for I **k** that he is very crafty.
25:25 I **k** Nabal is a wicked and ill-tempered man;
28: 9 "You **k** that Saul has expelled all the mediums
2Sa 1: 5 "How do you **k** that Saul and Jonathan are dead?"
3:25 You **k** perfectly well that he came to spy on you
7:20 You **k** what I am really like, Sovereign LORD.
11:20 Didn't they **k** there would be shooting from the
13:12 You **k** what a serious crime it is to do such a thing
14:17 I **k** that you are like an angel of God and can
14:18 "I want to **k** one thing," the king replied. "Yes,
14:22 "At last I **k** that I have gained your approval,
15:10 "you will **k** that Absalom has been crowned king
15:20 I don't even **k** where we will go. Go on back
15:28 Let me **k** what happens in Jerusalem before I
16:21 Then all Israel will **k** that you have insulted him
17: 8 You **k** your father and his men; they are mighty
18:29 But I didn't **k** what was happening."
19:20 I **k** how much I sinned. That is why I have come
19:26 I can go with the king.' For as you **k** I am crippled.
19:27 But I **k** that you are like an angel of God, so do
22:44 over nations; / people I don't even **k** now serve me.
24: 2 so that I may **k** how many people there are."
24:13 and let me **k** what answer to give the LORD."
1Ki 1:11 and that our lord David doesn't even **k** about it?
1:18 the new king, and you do not even **k** about it.
1:27 of his servants **k** who should be the next king?"
2: 5 You **k** that Joab son of Zeruiah murdered my two
2: 9 and you will **k** how to arrange a bloody death for
2:15 He replied, "As you **k**, the kingdom was mine;
2:17 my behalf, for I **k** he will do anything you request.
2:20 he asked. "You **k** I won't refuse you."
2:22 You **k** that he is my older brother, and that he has
3: 7 but I am like a little child who doesn't **k** his way
3: 9 and **k** the difference between right and wrong.
5: 3 "You **k** that my father, David, was not able to
5: 6 As you **k**, there is no one among us who can cut
8:39 they deserve, for you alone **k** the human heart.
8:43 Then all the people of the earth will come to **k**
8:43 will **k** that this Temple I have built bears your
8:60 May people all over the earth **k** that the LORD is
17:24 "Now I **k** for sure that you are a man of God,
18:37 Answer me so these people will **k** that you,
20:13 to you. Then you will **k** that I am the LORD."
20:28 vast army. Then you will **k** that I am the LORD."
21:15 "You **k** the vineyard Naboth wouldn't sell you?
2Ki 2: 3 "Did you **k** that the LORD is going to take your
2: 3 "Quiet!" Elisha answered. "Of course I **k** it."
2: 5 "Did you **k** that the LORD is going to take your
2: 5 "Quiet!" he answered again. "Of course I **k** it."
4: 1 you is dead, and you **k** how he feared the LORD.
5:15 "I **k** at last that there is no God in all the world
7:12 and told his officers, "I **k** what has happened.
7:12 The Arameans **k** we are starving, so they have left
8:12 "I **k** the terrible things you will do to the people of
9:11 "You **k** the way such a man babbles on,"
9:18 "The king wants to **k** whether you are coming in
9:18 Jehu replied, "What do you **k** about peace?
9:19 "The king wants to **k** whether you come in
9:19 Jehu answered, "What do you **k** about peace?
17:26 Israel do not **k** how to worship the God of the land.
18:27 He wants them to **k** that if you do not surrender,
19:11 You **k** perfectly well what the kings of Assyria
19:19 then all the kingdoms of the earth will **k** that you
19:27 'But I **k** you well— / your comings and goings
19:27 you do. / I **k** the way you have raged against me.
1Ch 16: 8 Let the whole world **k** what he has done.
17:18 have honored me? You **k** what I am really like.
21: 2 me the totals so I may **k** how many there are."
21:12 and let me **k** what answer to give the LORD."
28: 9 my son, get to **k** the God of your ancestors.
29:17 I **k**, my God, that you examine our hearts
29:17 You **k** I have done all this with good motives,

2Ch 2: 8 for I **k** that your men are without equal at cutting
6:30 they deserve, for you alone **k** the human heart.
6:33 Then all the people of the earth will come to **k**
6:33 will **k** that this Temple I have built bears your
20:12 We do not **k** what to do, but we are looking to you
25:16 "I **k** that God has determined to destroy you
Ezr 4:13 But we wish you to **k** that if this city is rebuilt
7:25 and judges who **k** your God's laws to govern all
Ne 2:16 The city officials did not **k** I had been out there
2:17 to them, "You **k** full well the tragedy of our city.
4:11 were saying, "Before they **k** what's happening,
6: 8 My reply was, "You **k** you are lying. There is no
Job 5: 3 I **k** that fools who turn from God may be
5:24 You will **k** that your home is kept safe. When you
6:30 Don't I **k** the difference between right and wrong?
8: 9 For we were born but yesterday and **k** so little.
9: 2 "Yes, I **k** this is all true in principle. But how can
9:28 For I **k** you will not hold me innocent, O God.
10: 7 Although you **k** I am not guilty, no one can rescue
10:13 your real motive—I **k** this was your intent—
11: 7 Can you discover everything there is to **k** about the
11: 8 what can you **k** in comparison to him?
12: 2 "You really **k** everything, don't you? And when
12: 3 Well, I **k** a few things myself—and you're no
12: 3 Who doesn't **k** these things you've been saying?
12: 9 They all **k** that the LORD has done this.
13: 2 I **k** as much as you do. You are no better than I am.
14: 5 You **k** how many months we will live, and we are
14:21 They never **k** if their sons grow up in honor or sink
15: 9 What do you **k** that we don't? What do you
15:23 saying, 'Where is it?' They **k** their ruin is certain.
19:25 "But as for me, I **k** that my Redeemer lives,
19:29 Then you will **k** that there is judgment."
21:27 "Look, I **k** your thoughts. I **k** the schemes you plot against me.
24:15 me then.' He masks his face so no one will **k** him.
28: 1 "People **k** how to mine silver and refine gold.
28: 2 They **k** how to dig iron from the earth and smelt
28: 3 They **k** how to put light into darkness and explore
28: 6 "People **k** how to find sapphires and gold dust—
28: 9 People **k** how to tear apart flinty rocks
28:12 "But do people **k** where to find wisdom?
28:20 "But do people **k** where to find wisdom?
30:23 And I **k** that you are sending me to my death—
34:32 Or 'I don't **k** what evil I have done; tell me,
37:15 Do you **k** how God controls the storm and causes
37:19 "You think you **k** so much, so teach the rest of us
38: 4 of the earth? Tell me, if you **k** so much.
38: 5 Do you **k** how its dimensions were determined
38:17 Do you **k** where the gates of death are located?
38:18 the extent of the earth? Tell me about it if you **k**!
38:20 you take it to its home? Do you **k** how to get there?
38:21 But of course you **k** all this! For you were born
38:33 Do you **k** the laws of the universe and how God
39: 1 "Do you **k** when the mountain goats give birth?
39: 2 Do you **k** how many months they carry their
42: 2 "I **k** that you can do anything, and no one can stop
Ps 9:10 Those who **k** your name trust in you, / for you,
9:20 O LORD. / Let them **k** they are merely human.
10:17 LORD, you **k** the hopes of the helpless.
12: 7 LORD, we **k** you will protect the oppressed,
16: 8 I **k** the LORD is always with me. / I will not be
17: 2 me innocent, / for you **k** those who do right.
17: 6 I am praying to you because I **k** you will answer,
18:43 over nations; / people I don't even **k** now serve me.
19:12 How can I **k** all the sins lurking in my heart?
20: 6 Now I **k** that the LORD saves his anointed king.
27: 3 army surrounds me, / my heart will **k** no fear.
35:11 They accuse me of things I don't even **k** about.
35:15 I am attacked by people I don't even **k**; / they hurl
35:22 O LORD, you **k** all about this. / Do not stay
37:30 good counsel; / they **k** what is right from wrong.
38: 9 You **k** what I long for, Lord; / you hear my every
40: 9 afraid to speak out, / as you, O LORD, well **k**.
41:11 I **k** that you are pleased with me, / for you have not
46:10 "Be silent, and **k** that I am God! / I will be
54: T and said to Saul, "We **k** where David is hiding."
56: 9 enemies will retreat. / This I **k**: God is on my side.
58: 1 Justice—do you rulers **k** the meaning of the word?
59:13 Then the whole world will **k** / that God reigns in
69: 5 O God, you **k** how foolish I am; / my sins cannot
69: 8 Even my own brothers pretend they don't **k** me;
69:19 You **k** the insults I endure—/ the humiliation
69:19 seen all my enemies / and **k** what they have said.
78: 3 stories we have heard and **k**, / stories our ancestors
78: 6 so the next generation might **k** them—
82: 5 But these oppressors **k** nothing; / they are
87: 4 and Babylon among those who **k** me—
92: 6 Only an ignorant person would not **k** this! / Only a
94:10 doesn't he also **k** what you are doing?
105: 1 Let the whole world **k** what he has done.
119:75 I **k**, O LORD, that your decisions are fair;
119:79 with all who fear you and **k** your decrees.
119:168 and decrees, / because you **k** everything I do.
135: 5 I **k** the greatness of the LORD— / that our Lord is
139: 1 examined my heart / and **k** everything about me.
139: 2 You **k** when I sit down or stand up. / You **k** my every thought when far away.
139: 3 and rest. / Every moment you **k** where I am.
139: 4 You **k** what I am going to say / even before I say
139: 6 is too wonderful for me, / too great for me to **k**!
139:14 workmanship is marvelous—and how well I **k** it.
139:23 Search me, O God, and **k** my heart; / test me and **k** my thoughts.
140:12 But I **k** the LORD will surely help those they
142: 3 and you alone **k** the way I should turn.
147:20 this with any other nation; / they do not **k** his laws.
Pr 2: 9 and you will **k** how to find the right course of
6: 1 or guarantee the debt of someone you hardly **k**—
8:12 I **k** where to discover knowledge and discernment.
9:13 and brash. She is ignorant and doesn't even **k** it.
14:35 A king rejoices in servants who **k** what they are
15:11 How much more does he **k** the human heart!
22:21 you may **k** the truth and bring an accurate report to
23:35 feel it. I didn't even **k** it when they beat me up.
24:12 responsibility by saying you didn't **k** about it.
27: 1 since you don't **k** what the day will bring.
27:23 **K** the state of your flocks, and put your heart into
29: 7 The godly **k** the rights of the poor; the wicked don't care to **k**.
30: 3 mastered human wisdom, nor do I **k** the Holy One.
30: 4 his name—and his son's name? Tell me if you **k**!
Ecc 1:10 How do you **k** it didn't already exist long ago?
3:14 And I **k** that whatever God does is final.
7:10 for you don't **k** whether they were any better than
7:12 but it's important to **k** that only wisdom can save
7:22 For you **k** how often you yourself have laughed at
8: 7 how can people avoid what they don't **k** is going to
8:12 I **k** that those who fear God will be better off.
8:17 Not even the wisest people **k** everything, even if
9: 5 The living at least **k** they will die, but the dead **k** nothing.
10:14 Foolish people claim to **k** all about the future
10:14 But who can really **k** what is going to happen?
11: 2 for you do not **k** what risks might lie ahead.
11: 6 variety of crops, for you never **k** which will grow
SS 1: 8 "If you don't **k**, O most beautiful woman,
Isa 1: 3 **k** their owner and appreciate his care, but not my
5:13 into exile far away because they do not **k** me.
7:15 he will **k** enough to choose what is right and reject
10: 7 But the king of Assyria will not **k** that it is I who
11: 9 so the earth will be filled with people who **k** the
19:21 they will **k** the LORD and will give their
29:12 they will say, "Sorry, we don't **k** how to read."
29:15 to yourselves. "He doesn't **k** what is going on!"
31: 7 I **k** the glorious day will come when every one of
36:12 He wants them to **k** that if you do not surrender,
37:11 You **k** perfectly well what the kings of Assyria
37:20 then all the kingdoms of the earth will **k** that you
37:28 'But I **k** you well— / your comings and goings
37:28 you do. / I **k** the way you have raged against me.
40:28 Don't you **k** that the LORD is the everlasting
43:10 You have been chosen to **k** me, believe in me,
44: 9 that this is so, for their idols neither see nor **k**.
45: 3 I will do this so you may **k** that I am the LORD,
45: 4 I called you by name when you did not **k** me.
45: 5 I have prepared you, even though you do not **k** me,
45: 6 so all the world from east to west will **k** there is no
47:11 will arise so fast that you won't **k** what hit you.
48: 4 "I **k** how stubborn and obstinate you are.
48: 8 entirely new, for I **k** so well what traitors you are.
49:23 your feet. Then you will **k** that I am the LORD.
49:26 All the world will **k** that I, the LORD, am your
50: 4 so that I **k** what to say to all these weary ones.
50: 7 to do his will. And I **k** that I will triumph.
51: 7 you who **k** right from wrong and cherish my law in
52: 6 to my people, and they will come to **k** its power.
52:14 so disfigured one would scarcely **k** he was a
59: 8 They do not **k** what true peace is or what it means
59:12 testify against us. Yes, we **k** what sinners we are.
59:13 We **k** that we have rebelled against the LORD.
59:13 We **k** how unfair and oppressive we have been,
60:16 You will **k** at last that I, the LORD, am your
65:12 very eyes—and chose to do what you **k** I despise."
66: 4 and chose to do what they **k** I despise."
66:18 they are doing, and I **k** what they are thinking.
Jer 4:22 "My people are foolish and do not **k** me,"
5: 4 They don't **k** the ways of the LORD.
5: 5 Surely they will **k** the LORD's ways and what
5:15 a people whose language you do not **k**,
8: 7 They do not **k** what the LORD requires of them.
9:24 that they truly **k** me and understand that I am the
10:23 I **k**, LORD, that a person's life is not his own.
12: 3 But as for me, LORD, you **k** my heart. You see
14:18 but they do not **k** what they are doing.' "
15:15 "LORD, you **k** I am suffering for your sake.
16:21 "At last they will **k** that I am the LORD."
17:10 But I **k**! I, the LORD, search all hearts
18:23 you **k** all about their murderous plots against me.
20:12 You **k** those who are righteous, and you examine
22:16 Isn't that what it means to **k** me?"
29:11 For I **k** the plans I have for you," says the LORD.
31:34 their family, saying, 'You should **k** the LORD.'
31:34 the greatest, will already **k** me," says the LORD.
40:14 to him, "Did you **k** that Baalis, king of Ammon,
42: 2 As you **k**, we are only a tiny remnant compared to
44:21 "Do you think the LORD did not **k** that you
48:29 We **k** of her loftiness, her arrogance, and her
48:30 I **k** about her insolence," says the LORD,
50: 2 so everyone will **k** that Babylon will fall!
La 3:61 You **k** all about the plans they have made—
Eze 2: 5 at least they will **k** they have had a prophet among
5:13 all Israel will **k** that I, the LORD, have spoken to
6: 7 with corpses, you will **k** that I am the LORD.
6:10 They will **k** that I alone am the LORD and that I
6:13 then they will **k** that I alone am the LORD.
6:14 the north. Then they will **k** that I am the LORD."
7: 4 your evil. Then you will **k** that I am the LORD!
7: 9 Then you will **k** that it is I, the LORD, who is
7:27 Then they will **k** that I am the LORD!"
11: 5 Yes, I **k** it is, for I **k** every thought that comes into your minds.
11:10 of Israel, and then you will **k** that I am the LORD.
11:12 and you will **k** that I am the LORD. For you have
12:15 the nations, they will **k** that I am the LORD.
12:16 Then they will **k** that I am the LORD!"
12:20 Then you will **k** that I am the LORD."
13: 9 Then you will **k** that I am the Sovereign LORD!
13:14 crush you. Then you will **k** that I am the LORD!
13:21 Then you will **k** that I am the LORD.
13:23 Then you will **k** that I am the LORD."
14: 8 Then you will **k** that I am the LORD.
15: 7 this happens, you will **k** that I am the LORD.
16:62 with you, and you will **k** that I am the LORD.
17:21 Then you will **k** that I, the LORD, have spoken
17:24 And all the trees will **k** that it is I, the LORD,
20:38 that happens, you will **k** that I am the LORD.
20:42 your ancestors, you will **k** that I am the LORD.
20:44 You will **k** that I am the LORD, O people of
21: 5 All the world will **k** that I am the LORD.
22:16 the nations, you will **k** that I am the LORD."
22:22 Then you will **k** that I, the LORD, have poured
23:49 Then you will **k** that I am the Sovereign LORD."
24:24 time comes, you will **k** that I am the LORD."
24:27 Then they will **k** that I am the LORD."
25: 5 for sheep. Then you will **k** that I am the LORD.
25: 7 Then you will **k** that I am the LORD.
25:11 Then they will **k** that I am the LORD.
25:14 furious vengeance, and Edom will **k** it is from me.
25:17 then they will **k** that I am the LORD."
26: 6 the sword. Then they will **k** that I am the LORD.
28:22 everyone watching will **k** that I am the LORD.
28:23 Then everyone will **k** that I am the LORD.
28:24 then they will **k** that I am the Sovereign LORD.
28:26 they will **k** that I am the LORD their God."
29: 9 and the Egyptians will **k** that I am the LORD.
29:16 Then Israel will **k** that I alone am the Sovereign
29:21 Then they will **k** that I am the LORD."
30: 8 And the people of Egypt will **k** that I am the
30:19 and they will **k** that I am the LORD."
30:25 land of Egypt, Egypt will **k** that I am the LORD.
30:26 Then they will **k** that I am the LORD."
32:15 your people, then you will **k** that I am the LORD.
33:29 then they will **k** that I am the LORD.
33:33 then they will **k** a prophet has been among them."
34:27 then they will **k** that I am the LORD.
34:30 In this way, they will **k** that I, the LORD their
34:30 And they will **k** that they, the people of Israel,
35: 4 and then you will **k** that I am the LORD.
35: 9 be rebuilt. Then you will **k** that I am the LORD.
35:12 Then you will **k** that I, the LORD, have heard
35:15 in Edom! Then you will **k** that I am the LORD!
36:11 Then you will **k** that I am the LORD.
36:23 then the nations will **k** that I am the LORD.
36:36 will **k** that I, the LORD, rebuilt the ruins
36:38 and everyone will **k** that I am the LORD."
37: 3 I replied, "you alone **k** the answer to that."
37: 6 to life. Then you will **k** that I am the LORD.' "
37:13 O my people, you will **k** that I am the LORD.
37:14 own land. Then you will **k** that I am the LORD.
37:28 the nations will **k** that I, the LORD, have set
38:16 Then all the nations will **k** that I am the LORD.
38:23 the world. Then they will **k** that I am the LORD!
39: 6 the coasts. Then they will **k** that I am the LORD.
39: 7 And the nations, too, will **k** that I am the LORD,
39:22 And from that time on the people of Israel will **k**
39:23 then **k** why Israel was sent away to exile—
39:28 Then my people will **k** that I am the LORD their
Da 2: 3 me what I dreamed, for I must **k** what it means."
2: 8 because you **k** I am serious about what I said.
2: 9 then I will **k** that you can tell me what it means."
2:30 because I am wiser than any living person that I **k**
4: 2 "I want you all to **k** about the miraculous signs
4: 9 I **k** that the spirit of the holy gods is in you and that
5:23 gods that neither see nor hear nor **k** anything at all.
7:19 Then I wanted to **k** the true meaning of the fourth
10:20 He replied, "Do you **k** why I have come? Soon I
11:32 But the people who **k** their God will be strong
12:10 Only those who are wise will **k** what it means.
Hos 2:20 you mine, and you will finally **k** me as LORD.
4: 6 are being destroyed because they don't **k** me.
4: 6 you priests, for you yourselves refuse to **k** me.
5: 3 I **k** what you are like, O Israel! You have left me as
5: 4 and through, and you cannot **k** the LORD.
6: 3 Oh, that we might **k** the LORD! Let us press on to **k** him!
6: 6 I want you to **k** God; that's more important than
7: 9 has sapped their strength, but they don't even **k** it.
9: 7 Soon Israel will **k** this all too well. "The prophets
11: 3 But he doesn't **k** or even care that it was I who
14: 4 and faithlessness, and my love will **k** no bounds,
Joel 2:27 Then you will **k** that I am here among my people
3:17 "Then you will **k** that I, the LORD your God,
Am 5:12 For I **k** the vast number of your sins and rebellions.
Ob 1: 7 set traps for you, and you won't even **k** about it.
Jnh 1:12 For I **k** that this terrible storm is all my fault."
Mic 3: 1 of Israel! You are supposed to **k** right from wrong,
4:12 But they do not **k** the LORD's thoughts
4:12 These nations don't **k** that he is gathering them
Zep 3: 5 but no one takes notice—the wicked **k** no shame.
Zec 2: 9 Then you will **k** that the LORD Almighty has
2:11 and you will **k** that the LORD Almighty sent me
4: 5 "Don't you **k**?" the angel asked. "No, my lord,"
4: 9 Then you will **k** that the LORD Almighty has
4:13 "Don't you **k**?" he asked. "No, my lord,"
6:15 you will **k** my messages have been from the
Mal 2: 4 Then at last you will **k** it was I who sent you this
Mt 7:11 If you sinful people **k** how to give good gifts to
8: 9 I **k**, because I am under the authority of my
9:36 so great and they didn't **k** where to go for help.
13:55 and we **k** Mary, his mother, and his brothers—

16:2 He replied, "You **k** the saying, 'Red sky at night
20:22 told them, "You don't **k** what you are asking!
20:25 "You **k** that in this world kings are tyrants,
21:27 So they finally replied, "We don't **k**." And Jesus
22:16 this question: "Teacher, we **k** how honest you are.
22:29 "Your problem is that you don't **k** the Scriptures,
and you don't **k** the power of God.
24:32 you **k** without being told that summer is near.
24:33 you can **k** his return is very near, right at the door.
24:42 because you don't **k** what day your Lord is
24:43 "**K** this: A homeowner who knew exactly when a
25:12 But he called back, 'I don't **k** you!'
25:13 because you do not **k** the day or hour of my return.
25:24 of gold came and said, 'Sir, I **k** you are a hard man,
26:2 "As you **k**, the Passover celebration begins in two
26:48 "You will **k** which one to arrest when I go over
26:70 "I don't **k** what you are talking about," he said.
26:72 with an oath. "I don't even **k** the man," he said.
26:74 Peter said, "I swear by God, I don't **k** the man."
28:5 "I **k** you are looking for Jesus, who was crucified.
Mk 1:24 I **k** who you are—the Holy One sent from God!"
9:6 He didn't really **k** what to say, for they were all
10:19 as for your question, you **k** the commandments:
10:38 "You don't **k** what you are asking!
10:42 "You **k** that in this world kings are tyrants,
11:33 So they finally replied, "We don't **k**." And Jesus
12:14 these men said, "we **k** how honest you are.
12:24 "Your problem is that you don't **k** the Scriptures,
and you don't **k** the power of God.
12:33 And I **k** it is important to love him with all my
13:28 you **k** without being told that summer is near.
13:33 And since you don't **k** when they will happen,
13:35 For you do not **k** when the homeowner will
14:40 their eyes open. And they didn't **k** what to say.
14:44 "You will **k** which one to arrest when I go over
14:68 "I don't **k** what you're talking about," he said,
14:71 by God, I don't **k** this man you're talking about."
Lk 1:18 said to the angel, "How can I **k** this will happen?
2:48 His parents didn't **k** what to think. "Son!"
3:14 and don't accuse people of things you **k** they didn't
3:15 and they were eager to **k** whether John might be
4:34 I **k** who you are—the Holy One sent from God."
7:8 I **k** because I am under the authority of my
7:39 he would **k** what kind of woman is touching him.
9:45 But they didn't **k** what he meant. Its significance
11:13 If you sinful people **k** how to give good gifts to
12:18 So he said, 'I **k**! I'll tear down my barns and build
12:39 "**K** this: A homeowner who knew exactly when a
12:56 You **k** how to interpret the appearance of the earth
13:25 door for us!' But he will reply, 'I do not **k** you.'
13:27 And he will reply, 'I tell you, I don't **k** you.
16:4 I **k** just the thing! And then I'll have plenty of
17:24 Son of Man returns, you will **k** it beyond all doubt.
18:20 as for your question, you **k** the commandments:
18:31 Jesus told them, "As you **k**, we are going to
20:7 Finally they replied, "We don't **k**."
20:13 " 'What will I do?' the owner asked himself. 'I **k**!
20:21 we **k** that you speak and teach what is right and are
21:20 then you will **k** that the time of its destruction has
21:30 you **k** without being told that summer is near.
22:34 you have denied three times that you even **k** me."
22:57 "Woman," he said, "I don't even **k** the man!"
22:60 "Man, I don't **k** what you are talking about."
23:34 because they don't **k** what they are doing."
24:16 But they didn't **k** who he was, because God kept
Jn 1:26 right here in the crowd is someone you do not **k**,
1:31 I didn't **k** he was the one, but I have been baptizing
1:33 I didn't **k** he was the one, but when God sent me to
1:48 "How do you **k** about me?" Nathanael asked.
3:2 "we all **k** that God has sent you to teach us.
3:11 I am telling you what we **k** and have seen,
3:28 You yourselves **k** how plainly I told you that I am
4:22 You Samaritans **k** so little about the one you
worship, while we Jews **k** all about him,
4:25 The woman said, "I **k** the Messiah will come—
4:32 "No," he said, "I have food you don't **k** about."
4:37 You **k** the saying, 'One person plants and someone
5:13 The man didn't **k**, for Jesus had disappeared into
5:42 because I **k** you don't have God's love within you.
6:42 We **k** his father and mother. How can he say,
6:69 and we **k** you are the Holy One of God."
7:15 "How does he **k** so much when he hasn't studied
7:17 Anyone who wants to do the will of God will **k**
7:26 Can it be that our leaders **k** that he really is the
7:27 could he be? For we **k** where this man comes from.
7:27 no one will **k** where he comes from."
7:28 he called out, "Yes, you **k** me, and you **k** where I
come from.
7:28 But I represent one you don't **k**, and he is true.
7:29 I **k** him because I have come from him, and he sent
7:49 ignorant crowds do, but what do they **k** about it?
8:14 For I **k** where I came from and where I am going,
but you don't **k** this about me.
8:19 Jesus answered, "Since you don't **k** who I am, you
don't **k** who my Father is.
8:19 you knew me, then you would **k** my Father, too."
8:32 And you will **k** the truth, and the truth will set you
8:52 "Now we **k** you are possessed by a demon.
8:55 but you do not even **k** him. I **k** him. If I said
otherwise, I would be as great a liar as you! But it
is true—I **k** him and obey him.
9:12 is he now?" they asked. "I don't **k**," he replied.
9:20 "We **k** this is our son and that he was born blind,
9:21 but we don't **k** how he can see or who healed him.
9:24 telling the truth, because we **k** Jesus is a sinner."
9:25 "I don't **k** whether he is a sinner," the man
9:25 "But I **k** this: I was blind, and now I can see!"
9:29 We **k** God spoke to Moses, but as for this man, we
don't **k** anything about him."
9:30 my eyes, and yet you don't **k** anything about him!
10:14 I **k** my own sheep, and they **k** me,
10:15 just as my Father knows me and I **k** the Father.
10:27 recognize my voice; I **k** them, and they follow me.
10:35 And you **k** that the Scriptures cannot be altered.
11:22 But even now I **k** that God will give you whatever
12:50 And I **k** his instructions lead to eternal life; so I say
13:17 You **k** these things—now do them! That is the path
13:18 to all of you; I **k** so well each one of you I chose.
13:38 you will deny three times that you even **k** me.
14:4 And you **k** where I am going and how to get
14:5 "No, we don't **k**, Lord," Thomas said.
14:5 where you are going, so how can we **k** the way?"
14:7 From now on you **k** him and have seen him!"
14:9 "Philip, don't you even yet **k** who I am,
14:20 you will **k** that I am in my Father, and you are in
14:31 so that the world will **k** that I love the Father.
15:21 belong to me, for they don't **k** God who sent me.
16:30 Now we understand that you **k** everything
17:3 to **k** you, the only true God, and Jesus Christ,
17:7 Now they **k** that everything I have is a gift from
17:8 they accepted them and **k** that I came from you,
17:23 Then the world will **k** that you sent me and will
17:25 righteous Father, the world doesn't **k** you, but I do;
and these disciples **k** you sent me.
18:21 Ask those who heard me. They **k** what I said."
20:2 the tomb, and I don't **k** where they have put him!"
20:13 "and I don't **k** where they have put him."
21:15 "Yes, Lord," Peter replied, "you **k** I love you."
21:16 "Yes, Lord," Peter said, "you **k** I love you."
21:17 He said, "Lord, you **k** everything. You **k** I love
you." Jesus said, "Then feed my
21:19 Jesus said this to let him **k** what kind of death he
21:24 And we all **k** that his account of these things is
Ac 1:7 he replied, "and they are not for you to **k**.
1:24 "O Lord," they said, "you **k** every heart.
2:22 wonders, and signs through him, as you well **k**.
2:25 'I **k** the Lord is always with me. / I will not be
3:16 this man—and you **k** how lame he was before.
4:9 Do you want to **k** how he was healed?
4:21 because they didn't **k** how to punish them without
7:40 for we don't **k** what has become of this Moses,
10:28 "You **k** it is against the Jewish laws for me to
10:37 You **k** what happened all through Judea,
10:38 And no doubt you **k** that God anointed Jesus of
15:7 you all **k** that God chose me from among you some
17:20 and we want to **k** what it's all about."
19:2 "No," they replied, "we don't **k** what you mean.
19:15 the spirit replied, "I **k** Jesus, and I **k** Paul.
19:25 you **k** that our wealth comes from this business.
19:32 most of them didn't even **k** why they were there.
19:40 demands an explanation, we won't **k** what to say."
20:18 "You **k** that from the day I set foot in the
20:25 "And now I **k** that none of you to whom I have
20:29 I **k** full well that false teachers, like vicious
20:34 You **k** that these hands of mine have worked to
21:20 But then they said, "You **k**, dear brother,
21:24 Then everyone will **k** that the rumors are all false
21:37 "Do you **k** Greek?" the commander asked,
22:14 'The God of our ancestors has chosen you to **k** his
22:19 'they certainly **k** that I imprisoned and beat those
23:22 "Don't let a soul **k** you told me this,"
24:10 Paul said, "I **k**, sir, that you have been a judge of
25:10 be tried right here. You **k** very well I am not guilty.
26:3 for I **k** you are an expert on Jewish customs
26:5 they **k** that I have been a member of the Pharisees,
26:27 do you believe the prophets? I **k** you do—"
28:22 for the only thing we **k** about these Christians is
Ro 1:13 I want you to **k**, dear friends, that I planned many
2:2 And we **k** that God, in his justice, will punish
2:14 they show that in their hearts they **k** right from
2:18 Yes, you **k** what he wants; you **k** right from wrong
2:27 and **k** so much about God's law but don't obey it.
3:17 They do not **k** what true peace is."
3:20 For the more we **k** God's law, the clearer it
5:3 and trials, for we **k** that they are good for us—
5:5 For we **k** how dearly God loves us, because he has
6:8 with Christ, we **k** we will also share his new life.
7:1 don't you **k** that the law applies only to a person
7:16 I **k** perfectly well that what I am doing is wrong,
7:18 I **k** I am rotten through and through so far as my
8:22 For we **k** that all creation has been groaning as in
8:26 For we don't even **k** what we should pray for,
8:28 And we **k** that God causes everything to work
10:2 I **k** what enthusiasm they have for God, but it is
11:34 For who can **k** what the Lord is thinking?
12:2 Then you will **k** what God wants you to do,
12:2 and you will **k** how good and pleasing and perfect
12:16 of ordinary people. And don't think you **k** it all!
13:11 Another reason for right living is that you **k** how
14:14 I **k** and am perfectly sure on the authority of the
14:16 condemned for doing something you **k** is all right.
14:22 themselves by doing something they **k** is all right.
15:1 We may **k** that these things make no difference,
15:14 You **k** these things so well that you are able to
1Co 1:18 I **k** very well how foolish the message of the cross
2:10 But we **k** these things because God has revealed
2:11 No one can **k** what anyone else is really thinking
2:11 and no one can **k** God's thoughts except God's
2:12 so we can **k** the wonderful things God has freely
2:16 For, / "Who can **k** what the Lord is thinking?
4:18 I **k** that some of you have become arrogant,
6:2 Don't you **k** that someday we Christians are going
6:9 Don't you **k** that those who do wrong will have no
6:16 And don't you **k** that if a man joins himself to a
6:19 Or don't you **k** that your body is the temple of the
8:2 Anyone who claims to **k** all the answers doesn't
really **k** very much.
8:4 we all **k** that an idol is not really a god and that
8:6 But we **k** that there is only one God, the Father,
8:10 You **k** there's nothing wrong with it, but they will
9:13 Don't you **k** that those who work in the Temple get
11:3 But there is one thing I want you to **k**: A man is
12:2 You **k** that when you were still pagans you were
12:3 So I want you to **k** how to discern what is truly
12:10 He gives someone else the ability to **k** whether it is
13:9 Now we **k** only a little, and even the gift of
13:12 All that I **k** now is partial and incomplete, but then
I will **k** everything completely,
14:8 how will the soldiers **k** they are being called to
14:9 don't understand, how will they **k** what you mean?
15:34 shame I say that some of you don't even **k** God.
15:58 for you **k** that nothing you do for the Lord is ever
16:15 You **k** that Stephanas and his household were the
2Co 1:8 I think you ought to **k**, dear friends,
2:3 Surely you **k** that my happiness depends on your
2:4 but I wanted you to **k** how very much I love you.
2:17 And we **k** that the God who sent us is watching us.
4:2 the truth before God, and all who are honest **k** that.
4:14 We **k** that the same God who raised our Lord Jesus
5:1 For we **k** that when this earthly tent we live in is
5:6 even though we **k** that as long as we live in these
5:11 because we **k** this solemn fear of the Lord that we
5:11 knows we are sincere, and I hope you **k** this, too.
7:8 for I **k** that it was painful to you for a little while.
8:9 You **k** how full of love and kindness our Lord
8:21 but we also want everyone else to **k** we are
9:2 For I **k** how eager you are to help, and I have been
11:6 a trained speaker, but I **k** what I am talking about.
11:23 I **k** I sound like a madman, but I have served him
12:3 my body was there or just my spirit, I don't **k**;
12:4 But I do **k** that I was caught up into paradise
12:10 Since I **k** it is all for Christ's good, I am quite
12:19 as Christ's servants, and we **k** that God is listening.
Gal 1:13 You **k** what I was like when I followed the Jewish
1:22 in the churches in Judea didn't **k** me personally.
2:16 And yet we Jewish Christians **k** that we become
4:15 I **k** you would gladly have taken out your own eyes
4:20 But at this distance I frankly don't **k** what else to
4:21 under the law. Do you **k** what the law really says?
Eph 2:12 and you did not **k** the promises God had made to
3:2 As you already **k**, God has given me this special
3:4 you will understand what I **k** about this plan
6:22 He will let you **k** how we are, and he will
Php 1:12 And I want you to **k**, dear friends, that everything
1:16 for they **k** the Lord brought me here to defend the
1:19 For I **k** that as you pray for me and as the Spirit of
1:22 service for Christ. I really don't **k** which is better.
1:27 I will **k** that you are standing side by side,
1:30 and you **k** that I am still in the midst of this great
2:22 But you **k** how Timothy has proved himself.
2:28 for I **k** you will be glad to see him, and that will
3:10 I can really **k** Christ and experience the mighty
4:10 I **k** you have always been concerned for me,
4:12 I **k** how to live on almost nothing or with
4:15 As you **k**, you Philippians were the only ones who
Col 1:10 the while, you will learn to **k** God better and better.
2:1 I want you to **k** how much I have agonized for you
4:8 I have sent him on this special trip to let you **k** how
1Th 1:4 We **k** that God loves you, dear brothers and sisters,
1:5 And you **k** that the way we lived among you was
2:1 You yourselves **k**, dear brothers and sisters,
2:2 You **k** how badly we had been treated at Philippi
2:5 we try to win you with flattery, as you very well **k**.
2:11 And you **k** that we treated each of you as a father
3:3 you **k** that such troubles are going to happen to us
3:4 would soon come—and they did, as you well **k**.
4:13 I want you to **k** what will happen to the Christians
5:2 for you **k** quite well that the day of the Lord will
2Th 1:8 bringing judgment on those who don't **k** God
2:6 And you **k** what is holding him back, for he can be
3:7 For you **k** that you ought to follow our example.
1Ti 1:7 but they don't **k** what they are talking about,
1:8 We **k** these laws are good when they are used as
3:15 you will **k** how people must conduct themselves in
4:3 to be eaten with thanksgiving by people who **k**
4:5 For we **k** it is made holy by the word of God
2Ti 1:5 I **k** that you sincerely trust the Lord, for you have
1:12 not ashamed of it, for I **k** the one in whom I trust,
1:15 As you **k**, all the Christians who came here from
1:18 And you **k** how much he helped me at Ephesus.
3:1 You should also **k** this, Timothy, that in the last
3:10 But you **k** what I teach, Timothy, and how I live,
3:10 You **k** my faith and how long I have suffered.
3:10 You **k** my love and my patient endurance.
3:11 You **k** how much persecution and suffering I have
3:11 You **k** all about how I was persecuted in Antioch,
3:14 You **k** they are true, for you **k** you can trust those
Tit 1:1 and to teach them to **k** the truth that shows them
1:16 Such people claim they **k** God, but they deny him
3:7 And now we **k** that we will inherit eternal life.
Heb 2:16 We all **k** that Jesus came to help the descendants of
4:4 We **k** it is ready because the Scriptures mention the
5:13 and doesn't **k** much about doing what is right.
8:11 their family, / saying, 'You should **k** the Lord.'
8:11 from the least to the greatest, / will already **k** me.
10:30 For we **k** the one who said, / "I will take
13:17 your souls, and they **k** they are accountable to God.
13:23 I want you to **k** that our brother Timothy is now
Jas 1:5 if you want to **k** what God wants you to do—
4:14 How do you **k** what will happen tomorrow?
4:17 it is sin to **k** what you ought to do and then not do

1Pe 1:10 something the prophets wanted to **k** more about.
1:14 ways of doing evil; you didn't **k** any better then.
1:18 For you **k** that God paid a ransom to save you from
2Pe 1: 2 and wonderful peace as you come to **k** Jesus,
1: 3 As we **k** Jesus better, his divine power gives us
1:12 even though you already **k** them and are standing
2:12 They laugh at the terrifying powers they **k** so little
2:21 had never known the right way to live than to **k** it
1Jn 2: 5 That is the way to **k** whether or not we live in him.
2:11 and don't **k** where they are going,
2:13 to you who are mature because you **k** Christ,
2:14 to you who are mature because you **k** Christ,
2:18 From this we **k** that the end of the world has come.
2:20 has come upon you, and all of you **k** the truth.
2:21 to you not because you don't **k** the truth but
because you **k** the difference between truth
2:29 Since we **k** that God is always right, we also **k** that
all who do what is right are his
3: 1 But the people who belong to this world don't **k**
3: 2 But we do **k** that when he comes we will be like
3: 5 And you **k** that Jesus came to take away our sins,
3:15 And you **k** that murderers don't have eternal life
3:16 We **k** what real love is because Christ gave up his
3:19 It is by our actions that we **k** we are living in the
3:24 And we **k** he lives in us because the Holy Spirit
4: 6 to God; that is why those who **k** God listen to us.
4: 6 That is how we **k** if someone has the Spirit of truth
4: 8 But anyone who does not love does not **k** God—
4:16 We **k** how much God loves us, and we have put
5: 2 We **k** we love God's children if we love God
5:10 All who believe in the Son of God **k** that this is
5:13 of God, so that you may **k** you have eternal life.
5:15 And if we **k** he is listening when we make our
5:18 We **k** that those who have become part of God's
5:19 We **k** that we are children of God and that the
5:20 And we **k** that the Son of God has come, and he
5:20 us understanding so that we can **k** the true God.
3Jn 1: 2 and that your body is as healthy as I **k** your soul is.
1:11 and those who do evil prove that they do not **k**
1:12 the same for him, and you **k** we speak the truth.
Jude 1: 5 I must remind you—and you **k** it well—that even
Rev 2: 2 "I **k** all the things you do. I have seen your hard
2: 2 I **k** you don't tolerate evil people.
2: 9 "I **k** about your suffering and your poverty—
2: 9 you are rich! I **k** the slander of those opposing you.
2:13 "I **k** that you live in the city where that great
2:19 "I **k** all the things you do—your love, your faith,
2:23 And all the churches will **k** that I am the one who
3: 1 "I **k** all the things you do, and that you have a
3: 8 "I **k** all the things you do, and I have opened a
3:15 "I **k** all the things you do, that you are neither hot

KNOWING (25) [KNOW]

Ge 3: 5 just like God, **k** everything, both good and evil."
3:22 as we are, **k** everything, both good and evil.
Job 30:13 **k** full well that I have no one to help me.
Ps 119:29 to myself; / give me the privilege of **k** your law.
Pr 7:23 into a snare, little **k** it would cost him his life.
Ecc 6: 8 by being wise and **k** how to act in front of others?
Jer 44:19 without our husbands **k** it and helping us?
Mt 10:29 can fall to the ground without your Father **k** it.
Mk 6:20 **k** that he was a good and holy man,
Lk 9:33 Peter, not even **k** what he was saying, blurted out,
11:44 People walk over them without **k** the corruption
Jn 2: 9 not **k** where it had come from (though, of course,
Ac 5: 7 later his wife came in, not **k** what had happened.
17:23 You have been worshiping him without **k** who he
20:22 by the Holy Spirit, not **k** what awaits me,
Ro 1:20 So they have no excuse whatsoever for not **k** God.
2:13 For it is not merely **k** the law that brings God's
2:23 You are so proud of **k** the law, but you dishonor
15:15 **k** that all you need is this reminder from me.
2Co 10: 5 proud argument that keeps people from **k** God.
Php 3: 8 with the priceless gain of **k** Christ Jesus my Lord.
1Th 3: 8 gives us new life, **k** you remain strong in the Lord.
Heb 11: 8 He went without **k** where he was going.
2Pe 1: 5 A life of moral excellence leads to **k** God better.
1: 6 **K** God leads to self-control. Self-control leads to

KNOWLEDGE (75) [KNOW]

Ge 2: 9 tree of life and the tree of the **k** of good and evil.
2:17 except fruit from the tree of the **k** of good and evil.
Nu 24:16 the words of God, / who has **k** from the Most High,
1Ki 4:29 and understanding, and **k** too vast to be measured.
2Ch 1:10 Give me wisdom and **k** to rule them properly,
1:11 for wisdom and **k** to properly govern my people,
1:12 give you the wisdom and **k** you requested.
Job 11: 8 Such **k** is higher than the heavens—but who are
34: 2 you wise men. Pay attention, you who have **k**.
34:35 'Job speaks without **k**; his words lack insight.'
36: 4 the honest truth, for I am a man of well-rounded **k**.
Ps 119:66 now teach me good judgment and **k**.
139: 6 Such **k** is too wonderful for me, / too great for me
Pr 1: 4 They will give **k** and purpose to young people.
1: 7 Fear of the LORD is the beginning of **k**.
1:29 For they hated **k** and chose not to fear the LORD.
2: 5 to fear the LORD, and you will gain **k** of God.
2: 6 From his mouth come **k** and understanding.
2:10 will enter your heart, and **k** will fill you with joy.
3:20 By his **k** the deep fountains of the earth burst forth,
5: 2 you will learn to be discreet and will store up **k**.
8:10 instruction rather than silver, and **k** over pure gold.
8:12 I know where to discover **k** and discernment.
9:10 **K** of the Holy One results in understanding.
10:14 Wise people treasure **k**, but the babbling of a fool
12:23 Wise people don't make a show of their **k**,
14: 6 but **k** comes easily to those with understanding.
14: 7 Stay away from fools, for you won't find **k** there.
14:18 with folly, but the wise person is crowned with **k**.
19: 2 Zeal without **k** is not good; a person who moves
19:27 my child, you have turned your back on **k**.
22:12 The LORD preserves **k**, but he ruins the plans of
22:20 thirty sayings for you, filled with advice and **k**.
23:12 to instruction; attune your ears to hear words of **k**.
24: 4 Through **k** its rooms are filled with all sorts of
24: 5 and a man of **k** is more powerful than a strong
Ecc 1:16 I have greater wisdom and **k** than any of them."
1:18 my grief. To increase **k** only increases sorrow.
2:21 though I do my work with wisdom, **k**, and skill,
2:26 God gives wisdom, **k**, and joy to those who please
9:10 there will be no work or planning or **k** or wisdom.
Isa 11: 2 the Spirit of **k** and the fear of the LORD.
33: 6 providing a rich store of salvation, wisdom, and **k**.
47:10 and '**k**' have caused you to turn away from me
Jer 3:15 who will guide you with **k** and understanding.
10:14 and have no **k** at all! / They make idols,
51:17 and have no **k** at all! / They make idols,
Da 1: 4 are gifted with **k** and good sense, and have the
2:21 gives wisdom to the wise / and **k** to the scholars.
5:12 has a sharp mind and is filled with divine **k**
12: 4 will rush here and there, and **k** will increase."
Hos 4: 1 no kindness, no **k** of God in your land.
Mal 2: 7 The priests' lips should guard **k**, and people
Mt 13:12 be given, and they will have an abundance of **k**.
Lk 11:52 For you hide the key to **k** from the people.
Ro 1:19 God has put this **k** in their hearts.
2:20 are certain that in God's law you have complete **k**
11:33 How great are his riches and wisdom and **k**!
1Co 1: 5 with the gifts of eloquence and every kind of **k**.
8: 1 that everyone should agree with your perfect **k**.
8: 1 While **k** may make us feel important, it is love that
8:11 So because of your superior **k**, a weak Christian,
12: 8 to another he gives the gift of special **k**.
13: 8 and special **k** will all disappear.
14: 6 or some special **k** or some prophecy or some
14:36 Do you think that the **k** of God's word begins
2Co 8: 7 such gifted speakers, such **k**, such enthusiasm,
Eph 1:17 so that you might grow in your **k** of God.
4:13 and **k** of God's Son that we will be mature and full
Php 1: 9 and that you will keep on growing in your **k**
Col 2: 3 him lie hidden all the treasures of wisdom and **k**.
1Ti 6:20 with those who oppose you with their so-called **k**.
Heb 10:26 sinning after we have received a full **k** of the truth,
2Pe 1: 8 and useful in your **k** of our Lord Jesus Christ.
3:18 and **k** of our Lord and Savior Jesus Christ.

KNOWLEDGEABLE (1) [KNOW]

Pr 28: 2 But with wise and **k** leaders, there is stability.

KNOWN (104) [KNOW]

Ge 17: 5 now you will be **k** as Abraham, for you will be the
19:22 From that time on, that village was **k** as Zoar.
19:37 He became the ancestor of the nation now **k** as the
19:38 He became the ancestor of the nation now **k** as the
21:31 ever since, that place has been **k** as Beersheba—
36: 1 of the descendants of Esau (also **k** as Edom).
36: 8 So Esau (also **k** as Edom) settled in the hill country
36:19 the clans descended from Esau (also **k** as Edom).
43: 7 How could we have **k** he would say, 'Bring me
Ex 16:31 In time, the food became **k** as manna. It was white
21:36 But if the bull was **k** from past experience to gore,
33: 7 It was Moses' custom to set up the tent **k** as the
Nu 11: 3 After that, the area was **k** as Taberah—"the place
13:23 When they came to what is now **k** as the valley of
20:13 This place was **k** as the waters of Meribah,
Dt 3:13 (The Argob region of Bashan used to be **k** as the
3:14 calling it the Towns of Jair, as it is still **k** today.)
9:24 against the LORD as long as I have **k** you.
13: 6 gods that neither you nor your ancestors have **k**.
28:64 gods that neither you nor your ancestors have **k**,
31:13 so that your children who have not **k** these laws
32:17 non-gods, / to gods they had not **k** before,
Jos 19: 8 as Baalath-beer (also **k** as Ramah of the Negev).
Jdg 1:23 They sent spies to Bethel (formerly **k** as Luz),
1:26 the city Luz, and it is **k** by that name to this day.
2Sa 1:18 It is **k** as the Song of the Bow, and it is recorded in
2:16 The place has been **k** ever since as the Field of
18:18 and it is **k** as Absalom's Monument to this day.
1Ki 7: 7 Hall of the Throne, also **k** as the Hall of Judgment,
8: 1 also **k** as Zion, to its new place in the Temple.
9:13 area Cabul—"worthless"—as it is still **k** today.
16:24 Then Omri bought the hill now **k** as Samaria from
1Ch 1:10 who was **k** across the earth as a heroic warrior.
1:27 and Abram, later **k** as Abraham.
5:26 King Pul of Assyria (also **k** as Tiglath-pileser)
17:19 done all these great things and have made them **k**.
27: 6 David's elite military group **k** as the Thirty.
2Ch 5: 2 also **k** as Zion, to its new place in the Temple.
Est 3:14 in every province and made **k** to all the people,
Ps 9:16 The LORD is **k** for his justice. / The wicked have
19: 2 to speak; / night after night they make him **k**.
44:21 God would surely have **k** it, / for he knows the
53: 5 grip them, / terror like they have never **k** before.
67: 2 May your ways be **k** throughout the earth,
76: 1 God is well **k** in Judah; / his name is great in Israel.
119:152 I have **k** from my earliest days / that your decrees
135:13 your fame, O LORD, is **k** to every generation.
Pr 15:11 of Death and Destruction are **k** by the LORD.
16:21 The wise are **k** for their understanding,
20:11 Even children are **k** by the way they act,
31:23 Her husband is well **k**, for he sits in the council
Ecc 6: 5 never have seen the sun or **k** of its existence.
6:10 It was **k** long ago what each person would be.
Isa 7:17 **k** in all the years since Solomon's empire was
8: 2 Zechariah son of Jeberekiah, both **k** as honest men,
12: 5 Make **k** his praise around the world.
19:21 In that day the LORD will make himself **k** to the
38:19 Each generation can make **k** your faithfulness to
45:21 worship pays. Who made these things **k** long ago?
47: 5 Never again will you be **k** as the queen of
58:12 Then you will be **k** as the people who rebuild their
61: 9 Their descendants will be **k** and honored among
62:12 And Jerusalem will be **k** as the Desirable Place
63:19 Why do you act as though we had never been **k** as
Jer 3:17 In that day Jerusalem will be **k** as The Throne of
14: 9 here among us, LORD. We are **k** as your people.
28: 9 Only when his predictions come true can it be **k**
44: 3 nor you nor any of your ancestors have ever **k**.
Eze 23:10 Her name was **k** to every woman in the land as a
38:23 and I will make myself **k** to all the nations of the
39: 7 I will make **k** my holy name among my people of
Da 2:26 The king said to Daniel (also **k** as Belteshazzar),
4:19 Upon hearing this, Daniel (also **k** as Belteshazzar)
10: 1 Cyrus of Persia, Daniel (also **k** as Belteshazzar)
Mal 1: 4 Their country will be **k** as 'The Land of
Lk 2:49 "You should have **k** that I would be in my
3:23 Jesus was **k** as the son of Joseph. / Joseph was the
4:14 Soon he became well **k** throughout the surrounding
Jn 6: 1 the Sea of Galilee, also **k** as the Sea of Tiberias.
8:20 in the section of the Temple **k** as the Treasury.
10:23 walking through the section **k** as Solomon's
14: 7 If you had **k** who I am, then you would have **k**
who my Father is.
16: 3 because they have never **k** the Father or me.
18:20 Jesus replied, "What I teach is widely **k**, because I
Ac 1:23 Joseph called Barsabbas (also **k** as Justus)
2:36 So let it be clearly **k** by everyone in Israel that God
5:12 the Temple in the area **k** as Solomon's Colonnade.
13: 9 Then Saul, also **k** as Paul, filled with the Holy
15:18 he who made these things **k** long ago.'
24: 5 He is a ringleader of the sect **k** as the Nazarenes.
Ro 1: 8 faith in God is becoming **k** throughout the world.
1:19 For the truth about God is **k** to them instinctively.
7: 7 I would never have **k** that coveting is wrong if the
16:26 this message is made **k** to all Gentiles everywhere,
2Co 6: 9 We are well **k**, but we are treated as unknown.
Gal 2: 9 and John, who were **k** as pillars of the church,
Col 2: 1 and for many other friends who have never **k** me
1Ti 1: 7 They want to be **k** as teachers of the law of Moses,
5:25 but there are others whose good deeds won't be **k**
1Pe 3: 4 You should be **k** for the beauty that comes from
2Pe 2:21 It would be better if they had never **k** the right way
1Jn 2:14 to you, children, because you have **k** the Father.
3: 6 But those who keep on sinning have never **k** him

KNOWS (92) [KNOW]

Ge 3: 5 "God **k** that your eyes will be opened when you
Dt 34: 6 in Moab, but to this day no one **k** the exact place.
Jos 22:22 But the LORD **k**, and let all Israel know, too,
Ru 3:11 for everyone in town **k** you are an honorable
1Sa 2: 3 The LORD is a God who **k** your deeds;
20: 3 "Your father **k** perfectly well about our friendship,
24: 6 "The LORD **k** I shouldn't have done it," he said
25:11 a band of outlaws who come from who **k** where?"
2Sa 2:27 "God only **k** what would have happened if you
17:10 For all Israel **k** what a mighty man your father is
1Ki 18:12 the LORD will carry you away to who **k** where.
1Ch 28: 9 and understands and **k** every plan and thought.
2Ch 2:14 He also **k** all about stonework, carpentry,
Est 4:11 "The whole world **k** that anyone who appears
Job 11:11 For he **k** those who are false, and he takes note of
23:10 But he **k** where I am going. And when he has
28:13 No one **k** where to find it, for it is not found among
28:23 "God surely **k** where it can be found,
31: 6 me on the scales of justice, for he **k** my integrity.
34:10 Everyone **k** that God doesn't sin!
Ps 44:21 have known it, / for he **k** the secrets of every heart.
94:10 He **k** everything—doesn't he also know what you
94:11 The LORD **k** people's thoughts, / that they are
103:14 how weak we are; / he **k** we are only dust.
104:19 mark the seasons / and the sun that **k** when to set.
Pr 14:10 Each heart **k** its own bitterness, and no one else
21:12 The Righteous One **k** what is going on in the
24:12 For God **k** all hearts, and he sees you. He keeps
watch over your soul, and he **k** you knew!
24:22 Who **k** where the punishment from the LORD
Ecc 6:12 who **k** how our days can best be spent?
9: 1 no one **k** whether or not God will show them favor
Isa 7:16 But before he **k** right from wrong, the two kings
28:26 The farmer **k** just what to do, for God has given
40:12 Who else **k** the weight of the earth or has weighed
40:13 Who **k** enough to be his teacher or counselor?
Jer 8: 7 The stork **k** the time of her migration, as do the
17: 9 desperately wicked. Who really **k** how bad it is?
23:18 **k** the LORD well enough to hear what he is
26:19 we kill Jeremiah, who **k** what will happen to us?"
38:19 to them. And who **k** what they will do to me?"
Da 2:22 and **k** what lies hidden in darkness,
6:15 "Your Majesty **k** that according to the law of the
9:18 city lies in ruins—for everyone **k** that it is yours.
Joel 2:14 Who **k**? Perhaps even yet he will give you a
Na 1: 7 And he **k** everyone who trusts in him.
Zec 14: 7 Only the LORD **k** how this could happen!
Mt 6: 4 your Father, who **k** all secrets, will reward you.
6: 6 your Father, who **k** all secrets, will reward you.
6: 8 because your Father **k** exactly what you need even
6:18 except your Father, who **k** what you do in secret.
6:18 your Father, who **k** all secrets, will reward you.

6:32 Your heavenly Father already **k** all your needs,
11:27 No one really **k** the Son except the Father, and no one really **k** the Father except the Son
24:36 no one **k** the day or the hour when these things will
24:36 in heaven or the Son himself. Only the Father **k**.
Mk 13:32 no one **k** the day or hour when these things will
13:32 in heaven or the Son himself. Only the Father **k**.
Lk 10:22 No one really **k** the Son except the Father, and no one really **k** the Father except the Son
12:30 most people, but your Father already **k** your needs.
16:15 to look good in public, but God **k** your evil hearts.
Jn 10:15 just as my Father **k** me and I know the Father.
Ac 4:16 and everybody in Jerusalem **k** about it.
15:8 God, who **k** people's hearts, confirmed that he
19:35 "Everyone **k** that Ephesus is the official guardian
26:26 And King Agrippa **k** about these things. I speak
Ro 1:9 God **k** how often I pray for you. Day and night I
8:27 And the Father who **k** all hearts **k** what the
11:34 is thinking? Who **k** enough to be his counselor?
16:19 But everyone **k** that you are obedient to the Lord.
1Co 3:20 And again, / "The Lord **k** the thoughts of the wise,
8:3 But the person who loves God is the one God **k**
13:12 everything completely, just as God **k** me now.
2Co 5:11 God **k** we are sincere, and I hope you know this,
11:11 Why? Because I don't love you? God **k** I do.
11:31 who is to be praised forever, **k** I tell the truth.
12:3 or just my spirit, I don't know; only God **k**.
Php 1:8 God **k** how much I love you and long for you with
1:13 **k** that I am in chains because of Christ.
1Ti 5:24 sinful lives, and everyone **k** they will be judged.
5:25 everyone **k** how much good some people do,
2Ti 2:19 "The Lord **k** those who are his," and "Those who
2Pe 2:9 the Lord **k** how to rescue godly people from their
1Jn 3:20 God is greater than our hearts, and he **k** everything.
4:7 Anyone who loves is born of God and **k** God.
2Jn 1:1 as does everyone else who **k** God's truth—
Rev 2:17 name that no one **k** except the one who receives it.
7:14 And I said to him, "Sir, you are the one who **k**."
12:12 in great anger, and he **k** that he has little time."

KOA (1)
Eze 23:23 all the Chaldeans from Pekod and Shoa and **K**.

KOHATH (27) [KOHATHITE, KOHATHITES]
Ge 46:11 The sons of Levi were Gershon, **K**, and Merari.
Ex 6:16 the first generation were Gershon, **K**, and Merari.
6:18 The descendants of **K** included Amram, Izhar,
6:18 Hebron, and Uzziel. (**K** lived to be 133 years old.)
Nu 3:17 who were named Gershon, **K**, and Merari.
3:19 The clans descended from **K** were named for four
3:27 The descendants of **K** were composed of the clans
16:1 a descendant of **K** son of Levi, conspired with
26:57 The Kohathite clan, named after its ancestor **K**.
26:58 of the Levites. Now **K** was the ancestor of Amram,
1Ch 6:1 The sons of Levi were Gershon, **K**, and Merari.
6:2 The descendants of **K** were Amram, Izhar, Hebron,
6:16 The sons of Levi were Gershon, **K**, and Merari.
6:18 The descendants of **K** included Amram, Izhar,
6:22 The descendants of **K** were Amminadab, Korah,
6:33 Heman the musician was from the clan of **K**.
6:38 Izhar, **K**, Levi, and Israel.
6:54 of Aaron who were from the clan of **K**.
6:61 The remaining descendants of **K** received ten
6:66 The descendants of **K** received from the territory
6:70 The remaining descendants of **K** were assigned
9:32 And some members of the clan of **K** were in
15:5 There were 120 from the clan of **K**, with Uriel as
23:6 the three sons of Levi—Gershon, **K**, and Merari.
23:12 The descendants of **K** included Amram, Izhar,
2Ch 20:19 Then the Levites from the clans of **K** and Korah
29:12 From the clan of **K**: Mahath son of Amasai

KOHATHITE (15) [KOHATH]
Nu 3:28 one month old or older among these **K** clans.
3:30 The leader of the **K** clans was Elizaphan son of
4:2 and families of the **K** division of the Levite tribe.
4:18 "Don't let the **K** clans be destroyed from among
4:34 the community counted the **K** division by its clans
4:37 So this was the total of all those from the **K** clans
7:9 he gave none of the carts or oxen to the **K** division,
10:21 Next came the **K** division of the Levites,
26:57 The **K** clan, named after its ancestor Kohath.
Jos 21:4 who were members of the **K** clan within the tribe
21:5 The other families of the **K** clan were allotted ten
21:10 who were members of the **K** clan within the tribe
21:20 The rest of the **K** clan from the tribe of Levi was
21:26 pasturelands were given to the rest of the **K** clan.
2Ch 34:12 and Meshullam, Levites of the **K** clan.

KOHATHITES (3) [KOHATH]
Nu 4:4 "The duties of the **K** at the Tabernacle will relate
4:15 the **K** will come and carry these things to the next
4:15 the objects of the Tabernacle that the **K** must carry.

KOLAIAH (2)
Ne 11:7 son of Joed, son of Pedaiah, son of **K**, son of
Jer 29:21 Ahab son of **K** and Zedekiah son of Maaseiah—

KORAH (39) [KORAH'S, KORAHITE, KORAHITES]
Ge 36:5 Oholibamah had sons named Jeush, Jalam, and **K**.
36:14 of Zibeon. Their names were Jeush, Jalam, and **K**.
36:16 **K**, Gatam, and Amalek. These clans in the land of
36:18 the leaders of the clans of Jeush, Jalam, and **K**.
Ex 6:21 The descendants of Izhar included **K**, Nepheg,
6:24 The descendants of **K** included Assir, Elkanah,
6:24 Their descendants became the clans of **K**.
Nu 16:1 One day **K** son of Izhar, a descendant of Kohath
16:5 Then he said to **K** and his followers,
16:6 You, **K**, and all your followers must do this:
16:8 Then Moses spoke again to **K**: "Now listen,
16:16 And Moses said to **K**, "Come here tomorrow
16:19 **K** had stirred up the entire community against
16:24 tell all the people to get away from the tents of **K**,
16:27 So all the people stood back from the tents of **K**,
16:40 same thing would happen to him as happened to **K**
16:49 to those who had died in the incident involving **K**.
26:9 leaders who conspired with **K** against Moses
26:10 the earth opened up and swallowed them with **K**,
26:11 However, the sons of **K** did not die that day.
1Ch 1:35 of Esau were Eliphaz, Reuel, Jeush, Jalam, and **K**.
2:43 The sons of Hebron were **K**, Tappuah, Rekem,
6:22 of Kohath were Amminadab, **K**, Assir,
6:37 Tahath, Assir, Abiasaph, **K**,
9:19 a descendant of Abiasaph, from the clan of **K**.
26:19 divisions of the gatekeepers from the clans of **K**
2Ch 20:19 clans of Kohath and **K** stood to praise the LORD,
Ps 42:T choir director: A psalm of the descendants of **K**.
44:T choir director: A psalm of the descendants of **K**.
45:T A psalm of the descendants of **K**, to be sung to the
46:T A psalm of the descendants of **K**, to be sung by
47:T choir director: A psalm of the descendants of **K**.
48:T A psalm of the descendants of **K**. A song.
49:T choir director: A psalm of the descendants of **K**.
84:T A psalm of the descendants of **K**, to be
85:T choir director: A psalm of the descendants of **K**.
87:T A psalm of the descendants of **K**. A song.
88:T A psalm of the descendants of **K**, to be sung to the
Jude 1:11 And like **K**, they will perish because of their

KORAH'S (1) [KORAH]
Nu 27:3 "But he was not among **K** followers, who rebelled

KORAHITE (1) [KORAH]
1Ch 9:31 a Levite and the oldest son of Shallum the **K**,

KORAHITES (4) [KORAH]
Nu 26:58 and the **K** were all subclans of the Levites.
1Ch 9:19 He and his relatives, the **K**, were responsible for
12:6 Azarel, Joezer, and Jashobeam, who were **K**;
26:1 From the **K**, there was Meshelemiah son of Kore,

KORAZIN (2)
Mt 11:21 "What horrors await you, **K** and Bethsaida!
Lk 10:13 "What horrors await you, **K** and Bethsaida!

KORE (3)
1Ch 9:19 Shallum was the son of **K**, a descendant of
26:1 the Korahites, there was Meshelemiah son of **K**,
2Ch 31:14 **K** son of Imnah the Levite, who was the

KOZ (1)
1Ch 4:8 and **K**, who became the ancestor of Anub,

KUSHAIAH (1) [KISHI]
1Ch 15:17 and Ethan son of **K** from the clan of Merari to

L

LAADAH (1)
1Ch 4:21 **L** (the father of Mareshah), the families of linen

LAADEN [KJV] See LADAN

LABAN (51) [LABAN'S]
Ge 24:29 Now Rebekah had a brother named **L**.
24:30 was still standing beside his camels. **L** said to him,
24:32 So the man went home with **L**, and **L** unloaded the camels, gave him straw to bed
24:33 "All right," **L** said, "tell us your mission."
24:50 Then **L** and Bethuel replied, "The LORD has
25:20 Aramean from Paddan-aram and the sister of **L**.
27:43 what you should do. Flee to your uncle **L** in Haran.
28:5 he went to Paddan-aram to stay with his uncle **L**,
29:5 "Do you know a man there named **L**, the grandson
29:12 So Rachel quickly ran and told her father, **L**.
29:13 As soon as **L** heard about Jacob's arrival,
29:13 **L** then brought him home, and Jacob told him his
29:14 my very own flesh and blood!" **L** exclaimed.
29:15 **L** said to him, "You shouldn't work for me
29:16 Now **L** had two daughters: Leah, who was the
29:19 "Agreed!" **L** replied. "I'd rather give her to you
29:21 "I have fulfilled my contract," Jacob said to **L**.
29:22 So **L** invited everyone in the neighborhood to
29:23 when it was dark, **L** took Leah to Jacob,
29:24 And **L** gave Leah a servant, Zilpah, to be her maid.
29:25 "What sort of trick is this?" Jacob raged at **L**.
29:26 daughter ahead of the firstborn," **L** replied.
29:28 Jacob had married Leah, **L** gave him Rachel, too.
29:29 And **L** gave Rachel a servant, Bilhah, to be her
30:25 Jacob said to **L**, "I want to go back home.
30:27 "Please don't leave me," **L** replied, "for I have
30:31 **L** asked again. Jacob replied, "Don't give me
30:34 "All right," **L** replied. "It will be as you have
30:35 But that very day **L** went out and removed all the
30:42 so the weaker lambs belonged to **L**,
31:12 For I have seen all that **L** has done to you.
31:19 **L** was some distance away, shearing his sheep.
31:20 set out secretly and never told **L** they were leaving.
31:22 **L** didn't learn of their flight for three days.
31:24 But the previous night God had appeared to **L** in a
31:25 So when **L** caught up with Jacob as he was camped
31:26 **L** demanded. "Are my daughters prisoners,
31:33 **L** went first into Jacob's tent to search there,
31:34 So although **L** searched all the tents, he couldn't
31:35 So despite his thorough search, **L** didn't find them.
31:36 he demanded of **L**. "What is my crime?
31:43 Then **L** replied to Jacob, "These women are my
31:46 Jacob and **L** then sat down beside the pile of stones
31:48 a witness to remind us of our agreement," **L** said.
31:49 This place was also called Mizpah, for **L** said,
31:55 **L** got up early the next morning, and he kissed his
32:4 I have been living with Uncle **L** until recently,
46:18 the servant given to Leah by her father, **L**.
46:25 the servant given to Rachel by her father, **L**.
Dt 1:1 Paran on one side and Tophel, **L**, Hazeroth,

LABAN'S (9) [LABAN]
Ge 28:2 and marry one of your uncle **L** daughters.
30:36 Meanwhile, Jacob stayed and cared for **L** flock.
30:38 so **L** flocks would see them as they came to drink,
30:40 own flock, thus separating the lambs from **L** flock.
30:40 the streaked and dark-colored rams in **L** flock.
30:40 This is how he built his flock from **L**.
31:1 But Jacob soon learned that **L** sons were beginning
31:2 a considerable cooling in **L** attitude toward him.
31:47 which is Jegar-sahadutha in **L** language

LABEL (1)
Jer 6:30 I will **l** them 'Rejected Silver' because I,

LABOR (38) [LABORERS, LABORS]
Ge 5:29 "He will bring us relief from the painful **l** of
49:15 his shoulder to the task / and submit to forced **l**.
Dt 20:11 then all the people inside will serve you in forced **l**.
1Sa 4:19 were dead, her **l** pains suddenly began.
2Sa 12:31 people of Rabbah and forced them to **l** with saws,
20:24 Adoniram was in charge of the **l** force.
1Ki 4:6 Adoniram son of Abda was in charge of the **l** force.
5:14 at home. Adoniram was in charge of this **l** force.
9:15 This is the account of the forced **l** that Solomon
9:21 So Solomon conscripted them for his **l** force,
9:21 and they serve in the **l** force to this day.
9:22 did not conscript any of the Israelites for forced **l**.
11:28 he put him in charge of the **l** force from the tribes
12:4 "Lighten the harsh **l** demands and heavy taxes that
12:18 who was in charge of the **l** force, to restore order,
1Ch 20:3 people of Rabbah and forced them to **l** with saws,
2Ch 8:8 So Solomon conscripted them for his **l** force,
8:8 and they serve in the **l** force to this day.
8:9 did not conscript any of the Israelites for forced **l**.
10:4 "Lighten the harsh **l** demands and heavy taxes that
10:18 who was in charge of the **l** force, to restore order,
Ps 104:13 and you fill the earth with the fruit of your **l**.
104:23 they **l** until the evening shadows fall again.
107:12 That is why he broke them with hard **l**; / they fell,
128:2 You will enjoy the fruit of your **l**. / How happy you
Pr 5:10 and someone else will enjoy the fruit of your **l**.
6:8 they **l** hard all summer, gathering food for the
Ecc 2:23 Their days of **l** are filled with pain and grief;
3:13 should eat and drink and enjoy the fruits of their **l**,
4:9 as much as one; they get a better return for their **l**.
Jer 22:13 for Jehoiakim, who builds his palace with forced **l**.
Mic 4:9 Pain has gripped you like it does a woman in **l**.
5:3 time when the woman in **l** gives birth to her son.
Hag 2:17 and hail to destroy all the produce of your **l**.
Jn 16:21 It will be like a woman experiencing the pains of **l**.
Gal 4:19 I feel as if I am going through **l** pains for you
2Ti 2:6 farmers are the first to enjoy the fruit of their **l**.
Rev 12:2 and she cried out in the pain of **l** as she awaited her

LABORERS (8) [LABOR]
Dt 24:14 "Never take advantage of poor **l**, whether fellow
1Sa 8:12 of his troops, while others will be slave **l**.
1Ki 5:13 Then King Solomon enlisted thirty thousand **l** from
5:15 Solomon also enlisted seventy thousand common **l**,
2Ch 2:2 He enlisted a force of seventy thousand common **l**,
2:18 He enlisted 70,000 of them as common **l**, 80,000 as
34:13 were put in charge of the **l** of the various trades.
Ne 4:17 The common **l** carried on their work with one hand

LABORS (3) [LABOR]
Job 20:18 His **l** will not be rewarded. His wealth will bring
Ecc 2:10 in hard work, an additional reward for all my **l**.
Heb 4:10 who enter into God's rest will find rest from their **l**,

LACE [KJV] See CORD(S)

LACHISH (19)
Jos 10:3 Hoham of Hebron, Piram of Jarmuth, Japhia of **L**,

10:23 of Jerusalem, Hebron, Jarmuth, **L**, and Eglon.
10:31 Joshua and the Israelites went to **L** and attacked it.
10:33 During the attack on **L**, King Horam of Gezer had
10:35 They captured it in one day, and as at **L**,
12:11 The king of Jarmuth / The king of **L**
15:39 **L**, Bozkath, Eglon,
2Ki 14:19 Amaziah's life in Jerusalem, and he fled to **L**.
18:14 sent this message to the king of Assyria at **L**:
18:17 and his personal representative from **L** with a huge
19: 8 his king, who had left **L** and was attacking Libnah.
2Ch 11: 9 Adoraim, **L**, Azekah,
25:27 against his life in Jerusalem, and he fled to **L**.
32: 9 of Assyria, while still besieging the town of **L**,
Ne 11:30 They were also in **L** and its nearby fields
Isa 36: 2 from **L** to confront King Hezekiah in Jerusalem.
37: 8 his king, who had left **L** and was attacking Libnah.
Jer 34: 7 army was besieging Jerusalem, **L**, and Azekah—
Mic 1:13 your swiftest chariots and flee, you people of **L**.

LACK (21) [LACKED, LACKING, LACKS]

Ge 18:28 Will you destroy the city for **l** of five?"
1Ki 11:22 Pharaoh asked him. "What do you **l** here?
Job 34:35 speaks without knowledge; his words **l** insight.'
36:12 perish in battle and die from **l** of understanding.
Ps 34:10 but those who trust in the LORD will never **l** any
Pr 5:23 He will die for **l** of self-control; he will be lost
10:21 but fools are destroyed by their **l** of common sense.
15:22 Plans go wrong for **l** of advice; many counselors
26:20 Fire goes out for **l** of fuel, and quarrels disappear
28:27 Whoever gives to the poor will **l** nothing. But a
30: 2 too ignorant to be human, and I **l** common sense.
Isa 19: 8 The fishermen will weep for **l** of work. Those who
29:14 and even the most brilliant people **l**
34:16 animals will be missing, and none will **l** a mate,
Jer 14: 4 The ground is parched and cracked for **l** of rain.
Mk 10:21 "You **l** only one thing," he told him. "Go and sell
Lk 8: 6 but soon it withered and died for **l** of moisture.
18:22 "There is still one thing you **l**," Jesus said.
22:35 or extra clothing, did you **l** anything?"
1Co 7: 5 to tempt them because of their **l** of self-control.
2Co 6:12 it is not because of a **l** of love on our part, but

LACKED (3) [LACK]

Dt 2: 7 for your every need so that you **l** nothing." '
Ne 9:21 They **l** nothing in all that time. Their clothes did
Pr 7: 7 and saw a simpleminded young man who **l**

LACKING (4) [LACK]

Dt 8: 9 It is a land where food is plentiful and nothing is **l**.
28:48 be left hungry, thirsty, naked, and **l** in everything.
Jdg 18:10 given us a spacious and fertile land, **l** in nothing!"
Pr 24:30 field of a lazy person, the vineyard of one **l** sense.

LACKS (2) [LACK]

Dt 32:28 "Israel is a nation that **l** sense; / the people are
Pr 11:22 but **l** discretion is like a gold ring in a pig's snout.

LAD [KJV] See ATTENDANT, BOY, HELPER

LADAN (1)

1Ch 7:26 **L**, Ammihud, Elishama,

LADE(D), LADING [KJV] See CARGO, LAID, LOAD, LOADED, LOADS

LADLES (1)

2Ch 24:14 including **l** and other vessels made of gold

LADY (2)

2Jn 1: 1 It is written to the chosen **l** and to her children,
1: 5 And now I want to urge you, dear **l**, that we should

LAEL (1)

Nu 3:24 of the Gershonite clans was Eliasaph son of **L**.

LAGGING (1)

Dt 25:18 and they struck down those who were **l** behind.

LAHAD (1)

1Ch 4: 2 Jahath was the father of Ahumai and **L**.

LAHMAM (1)

Jos 15:40 Cabbon, **L**, Kitlish,

LAHMI (1) [LAHMI'S]

1Ch 20: 5 Elhanan son of Jair killed **L**, the brother of Goliath

LAHMI'S (1) [LAHMI]

1Ch 20: 5 The handle of **L** spear was as thick as a weaver's

LAID (91) [LAY]

Ge 15:10 one down the middle and **l** the halves side by side.
21:17 the boy's cries from the place where you **l** him.
22: 9 tied Isaac up and **l** him on the altar over the wood.
48:17 his father had **l** his right hand on Ephraim's head.
Ex 2: 3 and **l** it among the reeds along the edge of the Nile
15:25 It was there at Marah that the LORD **l** before
Lev 8:14 and Aaron and his sons **l** their hands on its head
8:18 and Aaron and his sons **l** their hands on its head
8:22 Aaron and his sons **l** their hands on its head
24: 8 Every Sabbath day this bread must be **l** out before
Nu 27:23 Moses **l** his hands on him and commissioned him
Dt 34: 9 of wisdom, for Moses had **l** his hands on him.
Jos 2:19 will be killed—not a hand will be **l** on any of them.
7:23 Then they **l** them on the ground in the presence of
2Sa 11: 1 In the process they **l** siege to the city of Rabbah.
18: 7 and twenty thousand men **l** down their lives that
22:16 and the foundations of the earth were **l** bare.
1Ki 3:20 She **l** her dead child in my arms and took mine to
6:37 The foundation of the LORD's Temple was **l** in
13:29 So the prophet **l** the body of the man of God on the
13:30 He **l** the body in his own grave, crying out in grief,
16:34 When he **l** the foundations, his oldest son, Abiram,
17:19 where he lived, and **l** the body on his bed.
18:33 the bull into pieces, and **l** the pieces on the wood.
2Ki 4:31 hurried on ahead and **l** the staff on the child's face,
13:16 and Elisha **l** his own hands on the king's hands.
1Ch 13:10 him dead because he had **l** his hand on the Ark.
20: 1 In the process they **l** siege to the city of Rabbah
2Ch 8:16 from the day its foundation was **l** to the day of its
16:14 He was **l** on a bed perfumed with sweet spices
29:23 the assembly of people, who **l** their hands on them.
32: 1 He **l** siege to the fortified cities, giving orders for
35:22 He **l** aside his royal robes so the enemy would not
Ezr 3:11 the foundation of the LORD's Temple had been **l**.
4:12 They have already **l** the foundation for its walls
5: 8 prepared stones, and timber is being **l** in its walls.
5:16 and **l** the foundations of the Temple of God in
Ne 3: 3 **l** the beams, hung the doors, and put the bolts
3: 6 They **l** the beams, set up the doors, and installed
5:15 governors who had **l** heavy burdens on the people,
Job 21:33 Many pay their respects as the body is **l** to rest
38: 4 "Where were you when I **l** the foundations of the
38: 6 supports its foundations, and who **l** its cornerstone
38:25 of rain? Who **l** out the path for the lightning?
Ps 18:15 and the foundations of the earth were **l** bare.
22:15 You have **l** me in the dust and left me for dead.
24: 2 For he **l** the earth's foundation on the seas
35: 7 I did them no wrong, / they **l** a trap for me.
66:11 your net / and **l** the burden of slavery on our backs.
89:40 and **l** in ruins every fort defending him.
102:25 In ages past you **l** the foundation of the earth,
139:16 Every moment was **l** out / before a single day had
Isa 19:17 for the LORD Almighty has **l** out his plans
48:13 It was my hand that **l** the foundations of the earth.
53: 6 Yet the LORD **l** on him the guilt and sins of us
Jer 17:11 Like a bird that hatches eggs she has not **l**, so are
La 3:60 You have seen the plots my enemies have **l** against
Eze 40:43 on the tables where the sacrificial meat was to be **l**.
Hos 9: 8 yet traps are **l** in front of him wherever he goes.
Hab 3:13 the wicked and **l** bare their bones from head to toe.
Hag 2:18 the foundation of the LORD's Temple was **l**—
Zec 4: 9 "Zerubbabel is the one who **l** the foundation of
8: 9 LORD Almighty ever since the foundation was **l**.
12: 1 out the heavens, **l** the foundations of the earth,
Mt 15:30 physical difficulties, and they **l** them before Jesus.
Mk 6:56 they **l** the sick in the market plazas and streets.
8:23 the man's eyes, he **l** his hands on him and asked,
15:46 and **l** it in a tomb that had been carved out of the
15:47 the mother of Joseph saw where Jesus' body was **l**.
16: 6 from the dead! Look, this is where they **l** his body.
Lk 2: 7 him snugly in strips of cloth and **l** him in a manger,
6:48 on a strong foundation **l** upon the underlying rock.
23:53 and **l** it in a new tomb that had been carved out of
Jn 7:30 but no one **l** a hand on him, because his time had
19:42 the tomb was close at hand, they **l** Jesus there.
Ac 6: 6 who prayed for them as they **l** their hands on them.
7:58 and **l** them at the feet of a young man named Saul.
8:17 and John **l** their hands upon these believers,
9:17 He **l** his hands on him and said, "Brother Saul,
9:37 her for burial and **l** her in an upstairs room.
13: 3 the men **l** their hands on them and sent them on
13:11 And now the Lord has **l** his hand of punishment
19: 6 Then when Paul **l** his hands on them, the Holy
22:20 I kept the coats they **l** aside as they stoned him.'
24: 2 Tertullus **l** charges against Paul in the following
1Co 3:10 I have **l** the foundation like an expert builder.
14:25 As they listen, their secret thoughts will be **l** bare,
1Ti 4:14 when the elders of the church **l** their hands on you.
2Ti 1: 6 gift God gave you when I **l** my hands on you.
Heb 1:10 in the beginning you **l** the foundation of the earth,
Rev 1:17 But he **l** his right hand on me and said, "Don't be

LAISH (7) [DAN]

Jos 19:47 of their land, so they fought against the town of **L**.
Jdg 18: 7 So the five men went on to the town of **L**,
18:14 scouted out the land around **L** said to the others,
18:27 his priest, the men of Dan came to the town of **L**,
18:29 Israel's son, but it had originally been called **L**.
1Sa 25:44 to a man from Gallim named Palti son of **L**.
2Sa 3:15 took Michal away from her husband Palti son of **L**.

LAISHAH (1)

Isa 10:30 Shout out a warning to **L**, for the mighty army

LAKE (33) [LAKESHORE]

Job 14:11 As water evaporates from a **l** and as a river
Mt 8:18 his disciples to cross to the other side of the **l**.
8:23 the boat and started across the **l** with his disciples.
8:28 When Jesus arrived on the other side of the **l** in the
8:32 herd plunged down the steep hillside into the **l**
9: 1 a boat and went back across the **l** to his own town.
14:22 and cross to the other side of the **l** while he sent the
14:34 After they had crossed the **l**, they landed at
16: 5 Later, after they crossed to the other side of the **l**,
17:27 so go down to the **l** and throw in a line.
Mk 3: 7 Jesus and his disciples went out to the **l**,
4:35 "Let's cross to the other side of the **l**."
5: 1 So they arrived at the other side of the **l**, in the land
5:13 pigs plunged down the steep hillside into the **l**,
5:21 Jesus went back across to the other side of the **l**,
6:45 into the boat and head out across the **l** to Bethsaida,
6:47 were in their boat out in the middle of the **l**,
6:53 arrived at Gennesaret on the other side of the **l**,
8:13 left them, and he crossed to the other side of the **l**.
8:15 As they were crossing the **l**, Jesus warned them,
Lk 8:22 "Let's cross over to the other side of the **l**."
8:26 land of the Gerasenes, across the **l** from Galilee.
8:33 herd plunged down the steep hillside into the **l**,
8:37 and left, crossing back to the other side of the **l**.
8:40 On the other side of the **l** the crowds received Jesus
Jn 6:17 and headed out across the **l** toward Capernaum.
6:22 The next morning, back across the **l**, crowds began
Rev 19:20 and his false prophet were thrown alive into the **l**
20:10 was thrown into the **l** of fire that burns with sulfur,
20:14 and the grave were thrown into the **l** of fire. This is
the second death—the **l** of fire.
20:15 in the Book of Life was thrown into the **l** of fire.
21: 8 their doom is in the **l** that burns with fire

LAKESHORE (2) [LAKE, SHORE]

Mk 2:13 Then Jesus went out to the **l** again and taught the
4: 1 Once again Jesus began teaching by the **l**.

LAKKUM (1)

Jos 19:33 Jabneel, and as far as **L**, ending at the Jordan

LAMB (114) [LAMB'S, LAMBS]

Ge 22: 7 said the boy, "but where is the **l** for the sacrifice?"
22: 8 "God will provide a **l**, my son,"
Ex 12: 3 day of this month each family must choose a **l**
12: 4 If a family is too small to eat an entire **l**, let them
share the **l** with another family in the
12: 6 each family in the community must slaughter its **l**.
12: 7 and sides of the doorframe of the house where the **l**
12: 8 That evening everyone must eat roast **l** with bitter
12:21 "Tell each of your families to slaughter the **l** they
12:43 No foreigners are allowed to eat the Passover **l**.
12:46 All who eat the **l** must eat it together in one house.
12:48 male may never eat of the Passover **l**.
13:13 from the LORD by presenting a **l** in its place.
29:41 Offer the other **l** in the evening, along with the
34:20 from the LORD by presenting a **l** in its place.
34:25 And none of the meat of the Passover **l** may be
Lev 9: 3 and a year-old **l** for a whole burnt offering,
12: 6 the woman must bring a year-old **l** for a whole
14:10 and one female year-old **l** with no physical defects,
14:13 then slaughter the **l** there in the sacred area at the
14:21 lambs must bring one male **l** for a guilt offering,
14:24 The priest will take the **l** for the guilt offering,
14:25 Then the priest will slaughter the **l** for the guilt
17: 3 or a **l** or a goat anywhere inside or outside the
22:23 If the bull or **l** is deformed or stunted, it may still
23:12 That same day you must sacrifice a year-old male **l**
Nu 6:12 and each must bring a one-year-old male **l** for a
6:14 a one-year-old male **l** without defect for a burnt
6:14 a one-year-old female **l** without defect for a sin
7:15 and a one-year-old male **l** as a burnt offering;
7:21 and a one-year-old male **l** as a burnt offering;
7:27 and a one-year-old male **l** as a burnt offering;
7:33 and a one-year-old male **l** as a burnt offering;
7:39 and a one-year-old male **l** as a burnt offering;
7:45 and a one-year-old male **l** as a burnt offering;
7:51 and a one-year-old male **l** as a burnt offering;
7:57 and a one-year-old male **l** as a burnt offering;
7:63 and a one-year-old male **l** as a burnt offering;
7:69 and a one-year-old male **l** as a burnt offering;
7:75 and a one-year-old male **l** as a burnt offering;
7:81 and a one-year-old male **l** as a burnt offering;
9:11 They must eat the **l** at that time with bitter herbs
9:12 They must not leave any of the **l** until the next
15: 5 For each **l** offered as a whole burnt offering,
15:11 each sacrificial bull, ram, **l**, or young goat.
28: 4 One **l** will be sacrificed in the morning
28: 5 With each **l** you must offer a grain offering of two
28: 7 of one quart of fermented drink with each **l**,
28: 8 Offer the second **l** in the evening with the same
28:13 and two quarts with each **l**. This burnt offering
28:14 a half pints for the ram, and one quart for each **l**.
Dt 16: 4 And do not let any of the meat of the Passover **l**
16: 7 Roast the **l** and eat it in the place the LORD your
1Sa 7: 9 So Samuel took a young **l** and offered it to the
17:34 a lion or a bear comes to steal a **l** from the flock,
17:35 after it with a club and take the **l** from its mouth.
2Sa 12: 3 but a little **l** he had worked hard to buy.
12: 3 He raised that little **l**, and it grew up with his
12: 4 But instead of killing a **l** from his own flocks for
12: 4 he took the poor man's **l** and killed it and served it
Ezr 6:20 So they slaughtered the Passover **l** for all the
Isa 11: 6 In that day the wolf and the **l** will live together;
53: 7 said a word. He was led as a **l** to the slaughter.
65:25 The wolf and the **l** will feed together. The lion will eat
66: 3 When they sacrifice a **l** or bring an offering of
Jer 11:19 I had been as unaware as a **l** on the way to its
Eze 46: 5 amount of flour he chooses to go with each **l**.
46: 7 And with each **l** he is to bring whatever amount of
46:11 flour as the prince chooses to give with each **l**.
46:13 "Each morning a year-old **l** with no physical
46:14 With the **l**, a grain offering must also be given to
46:15 The **l**, the grain offering, and the olive oil must be

Hos 4:16 and unprotected, like a helpless **l** in an open field.
Jn 1:29 There is the **L** of God who takes away the sin of
1:36 then declared, "Look! There is the **L** of God!"
Ac 8:32 And as a **l** is silent before the shearers, / he did not
1Co 5:7 Christ, our Passover **L**, has been sacrificed for us.
1Pe 1:19 lifeblood of Christ, the sinless, spotless **L** of God.
Rev 5:6 I looked and I saw a **L** that had been killed but was
5:8 and the twenty-four elders fell down before the **L**.
5:12 "The **L** is worthy—the **L** who was killed.
5:13 on the throne / and to the **L** forever and ever."
5:14 elders fell down and worshiped God and the **L**.
6:1 the **L** broke the first of the seven seals on the
6:3 When the **L** broke the second seal, I heard the
6:5 When the **L** broke the third seal, I heard the third
6:7 And when the **L** broke the fourth seal, I heard the
6:9 And when the **L** broke the fifth seal, I saw under
6:12 I watched as the **L** broke the sixth seal, and there
6:16 who sits on the throne and from the wrath of the **L**.
7:9 standing in front of the throne and before the **L**.
7:10 from our God on the throne and from the **L**!"
7:14 They washed their robes in the blood of the **L**
7:17 For the **L** who stands in front of the throne will be
8:1 When the **L** broke the seventh seal, there was
12:11 because of the blood of the **L** and because of their
13:8 which belongs to the **L** who was killed before the
13:11 He had two horns like those of a **l**, and he spoke
14:1 Then I saw the **L** standing on Mount Zion,
14:4 pure as virgins, following the **L** wherever he goes.
14:4 the earth as a special offering to God and to the **L**.
14:10 sulfur in the presence of the holy angels and the **L**.
15:3 the servant of God, and the song of the **L**:
17:14 Together they will wage war against the **L**,
17:14 but the **L** will defeat them because he is Lord over
19:7 the time has come for the wedding feast of the **L**,
19:9 who are invited to the wedding feast of the **L**."
21:9 I will show you the bride, the wife of the **L**."
21:14 written the names of the twelve apostles of the **L**.
21:22 the Lord God Almighty and the **L** are its temple.
21:23 of God illuminates the city, and the **L** is its light.
22:1 flowing from the throne of God and of the **L**,
22:3 For the throne of God and of the **L** will be there,

LAMB'S (4) [LAMB]

Ex 12:7 They are to take some of the **l** blood and smear it
12:22 Drain each **l** blood into a basin. Then take a cluster
12:22 of hyssop branches and dip it into the **l** blood.
Rev 21:27 but only those whose names are written in the **L**

LAMBS (98) [LAMB]

Ge 4:4 while Abel brought several choice **l** from the best
21:28 But when Abraham took seven additional ewe **l**
30:40 thus separating the **l** from Laban's flock.
30:42 so the weaker **l** belonged to Laban,
31:8 the whole flock began to produce speckled **l**.
31:8 the streaked ones, then all the **l** were born streaked.
Ex 12:6 "Take special care of these **l** until the evening of
29:38 on the altar. Offer two one-year-old **l** each day,
Lev 14:10 cured of the skin disease must bring two male **l**
14:12 The priest will take one of the **l** and the olive oil
14:21 "But anyone who cannot afford two **l** must bring
23:18 present seven one-year-old **l** with no physical
23:19 and two one-year-old male **l** as a peace offering.
Nu 7:17 and five one-year-old male **l** for a peace offering.
7:23 and five one-year-old male **l** for a peace offering.
7:29 and five one-year-old male **l** for a peace offering.
7:35 and five one-year-old male **l** for a peace offering.
7:41 and five one-year-old male **l** for a peace offering.
7:47 and five one-year-old male **l** for a peace offering.
7:53 and five one-year-old male **l** for a peace offering.
7:59 and five one-year-old male **l** for a peace offering.
7:65 and five one-year-old male **l** for a peace offering.
7:71 and five one-year-old male **l** for a peace offering.
7:77 and five one-year-old male **l** for a peace offering.
7:83 and five one-year-old male **l** for a peace offering.
7:87 and twelve one-year-old male **l** were donated for
7:88 and sixty one-year-old male **l** were donated for the
9:6 so they could not offer their Passover **l** that day.
28:3 you must offer two one-year-old male **l** with no
28:9 sacrifice two one-year-old male **l** with no physical
28:11 one ram, and seven one-year-old male **l**, all with no
28:19 one ram, and seven one-year-old male **l**, all with no
28:21 and two quarts with each of the seven **l**.
28:27 one ram, and seven one-year-old male **l**.
28:29 and two quarts with each of the seven **l**.
29:2 one ram, and seven one-year-old male **l**, all with no
29:4 and two quarts with each of the seven **l**.
29:8 one ram, and seven one-year-old male **l**, all with no
29:10 two quarts of choice flour with each of the seven **l**.
29:13 two rams, and fourteen one-year-old male **l**,
29:15 and two quarts for each of the fourteen **l**.
29:17 two rams, and fourteen one-year-old male **l**,
29:18 and **l** must be accompanied by the prescribed grain
29:20 two rams, and fourteen one-year-old male **l**,
29:21 and **l** must be accompanied by the prescribed grain
29:23 two rams, and fourteen one-year-old male **l**,
29:24 and **l** must be accompanied by the prescribed grain
29:26 two rams, and fourteen one-year-old male **l**,
29:27 and **l** must be accompanied by the prescribed grain
29:29 two rams, and fourteen one-year-old male **l**,
29:30 and **l** must be accompanied by the prescribed grain
29:32 two rams, and fourteen one-year-old male **l**,
29:33 and **l** must be accompanied by the prescribed grain
29:36 one ram, and seven one-year-old male **l**, all with no
Dt 28:51 you no grain, new wine, olive oil, calves, or **l**,
32:14 the flock, / together with the fat of **l** and goats.
1Sa 15:9 best of the sheep and cattle, the fat calves and **l**—
2Sa 12:6 He must repay four **l** to the poor man for the one
2Ki 3:4 pay the king of Israel an annual tribute of 100,000 **l**
1Ch 15:26 they sacrificed seven bulls and seven **l**.
29:21 and a thousand male **l** as burnt offerings to the
2Ch 29:21 They brought seven bulls, seven rams, seven **l**,
29:22 the altar. And finally, they did the same with the **l**.
29:32 and two hundred **l** for burnt offerings.
30:15 the people slaughtered their Passover **l**.
30:17 the Levites had to slaughter their Passover **l** for
35:1 The Passover **l** were slaughtered at twilight of that
35:6 Slaughter the Passover **l**, purify yourselves,
35:7 from his personal property thirty thousand **l**
35:8 gave the priests twenty-six hundred **l** and young
35:9 gave five thousand **l** and young goats and five
35:11 The Levites then slaughtered the Passover **l**
35:13 Then they roasted the Passover **l** as prescribed;
Ezr 6:9 and **l** for the burnt offerings presented to the God
6:17 hundred rams, and four hundred **l** were sacrificed.
7:17 rams, **l**, and the appropriate grain offerings
8:35 as well as ninety-six rams and seventy-seven **l**.
Job 21:11 Their children skip about like **l** in a flock of sheep.
Ps 78:71 He took David from tending the ewes and **l**
114:4 mountains skipped like rams, / the little hills like **l**!
114:6 did you skip like rams? / Why, little hills, like **l**?
Isa 5:17 feed among the ruins; **l** and kids will pasture there.
16:1 Moab's refugees at Sela send **l** to Jerusalem as a
34:6 with fat as though it had been used for killing **l**
40:11 He will carry the **l** in his arms, holding them close
43:23 You have not brought me **l** for burnt offerings.
Jer 33:12 will once more see shepherds leading sheep and **l**.
51:40 "I will bring them like **l** to the slaughter, like rams
Eze 27:21 and the princes of Kedar brought **l** and rams
39:18 were rams, **l**, goats, and fat young bulls of Bashan!
46:4 will present to the LORD a burnt offering of six **l**
46:6 six **l**, and one ram, all with no physical defects.
Am 6:4 eating the meat of tender **l** and choice calves.
Zec 13:7 will be scattered, and I will turn against the **l**.
Mk 14:12 Bread (the day the Passover **l** were sacrificed),
Lk 10:3 and remember that I am sending you out as **l**
22:7 Bread arrived, when the Passover **l** were sacrificed.
Jn 21:15 I love you." "Then feed my **l**," Jesus told him.

LAME (27)

Lev 21:18 whether he is blind or **l**, stunted or deformed,
Dt 15:21 such as being **l** or blind, or if anything else is
2Sa 5:6 "Even the blind and **l** could keep you out!"
5:8 the city and destroy those '**l**' and 'blind' Jebusites.
5:8 "The blind and the **l** may not enter the house."
Job 29:15 I served as eyes for the blind and feet for the **l**.
Isa 33:23 the people of God. Even the **l** will win their share!
35:6 The **l** will leap like a deer, and those who cannot
Jer 31:8 I will not forget the blind and **l**, the expectant
Mic 4:6 "I will gather together my people who are **l**,
Mt 11:5 the blind see, the **l** walk, the lepers are cured,
15:30 A vast crowd brought him the **l**, blind, crippled,
15:31 were made well, the **l** were walking around,
18:8 or **l** than to be thrown into the unquenchable fire
21:14 The blind and the **l** came to him, and he healed
Lk 7:22 the blind see, the **l** walk, the lepers are cured,
14:13 invite the poor, the crippled, the **l**, and the blind.
14:21 invite the poor, the crippled, the **l**, and the blind.'
Jn 5:3 blind, **l**, or paralyzed—lay on the porches.
Ac 3:2 a man **l** from birth was being carried in.
3:5 The **l** man looked at them eagerly, expecting a gift.
3:7 Then Peter took the **l** man by the right hand
3:10 When they realized he was the **l** beggar they had
3:16 this man—and you know how **l** he was before.
4:22 the healing of a man who had been **l** for more than
8:7 many who had been paralyzed or **l** were healed.
Heb 12:13 though they are weak and **l**, will not stumble

LAMECH (11) [LAMECH'S]

Ge 4:18 of Methushael. / Methushael was the father of **L**.
4:19 **L** married two women—Adah and Zillah.
4:23 One day **L** said to Adah and Zillah, "Listen to me,
5:25 Methuselah was 187 years old, his son **L** was born.
5:26 After the birth of **L**, Methuselah lived another 782
5:28 When **L** was 182 years old, his son Noah was
5:29 **L** named his son Noah, for he said, "He will bring
5:30 **L** lived 595 years, and he had other sons
1Ch 1:3 Enoch, Methuselah, **L**,
Lk 3:36 was the son of Noah. / Noah was the son of **L**.
3:37 **L** was the son of Methuselah. / Methuselah was the

LAMECH'S (1) [LAMECH]

Ge 4:22 To **L** other wife, Zillah, was born Tubal-cain.

LAMENT (6) [LAMENTED, LAMENTS]

Jdg 11:40 days each year to **l** the fate of Jephthah's daughter.
Isa 16:9 So I wail and **l** for Jazer and the vineyards of
Jer 9:20 your daughters to wail; teach one another how to **l**.
47:5 how long will you **l** and mourn?
Am 5:16 and summon professional mourners to wail and **l**.
Mic 1:8 Because of all this, I will mourn and **l**. I will walk

LAMENTATIONS [KJV] See (FUNERAL) SONGS, LAMENTS

LAMENTED (1) [LAMENT]

Ge 37:30 Then he went back to his brothers and **l**, "The boy

LAMENTS (1) [LAMENT]

2Ch 35:25 a tradition and are recorded in *The Book of L*.

LAMP (26) [LAMPS, LAMPSTAND, LAMPSTANDS]

Ex 25:31 the base, center stem, **l** cups, buds, and blossoms.
25:38 The **l** snuffers and trays must also be made of pure
35:14 its accessories; the **l** cups and the oil for lighting;
37:17 Its base, center stem, **l** cups, blossoms, and buds
37:23 the **l** snuffers, and the trays, all of pure gold.
39:37 its accessories; the **l** cups and the oil for lighting;
Nu 4:9 along with its lamps, **l** snuffers, trays, and special
1Sa 3:3 The **l** of God had not yet gone out, and Samuel was
1Ki 7:50 the cups, **l** snuffers, basins, dishes, and firepans,
2Ki 4:10 and furnish it with a bed, a table, a chair, and a **l**.
12:13 **l** snuffers, basins, trumpets, or other articles of
25:14 also took all the pots, shovels, **l** snuffers, dishes,
2Ch 4:22 the **l** snuffers, basins, dishes, and firepans, all of
Job 18:6 The **l** hanging above them will be quenched.
Ps 119:105 Your word is a **l** for my feet / and a light for my
Pr 6:23 and this teaching are a **l** to light the way ahead of
20:20 or mother, the **l** of your life will be snuffed out.
Jer 52:18 took all the pots, shovels, **l** snuffers, basins, dishes,
Mt 6:22 "Your eye is a **l** for your body. A pure eye lets
Mk 4:21 "Would anyone light a **l** and then put it under a
4:21 A **l** is placed on a stand, where its light will shine.
Lk 8:16 "No one would light a **l** and then cover it up
11:33 "No one lights a **l** and then hides it or puts it under
11:34 Your eye is a **l** for your body. A pure eye lets
15:8 Won't she light a **l** and look in every corner of the
Rev 18:23 Her nights will be dark, without a single **l**.

LAMPS (29) [LAMP]

Ex 25:6 olive oil for the **l**; spices for the anointing oil
25:37 Then make the seven **l** for the lampstand, and set
27:21 and his sons will keep the **l** burning in the
30:7 "Every morning when Aaron trims the **l**, he must
30:8 And each evening when he tends to the **l**, he must
35:8 olive oil for the **l**; spices for the anointing oil
37:23 He also made the seven **l**, the lamp snuffers,
40:4 And bring in the lampstand, and set up the **l**.
40:25 Then he set up the **l** in the LORD's presence,
Lev 24:3 and must arrange to have the **l** tended continually,
24:4 The **l** on the pure gold lampstand must be tended
Nu 4:9 along with its **l**, lamp snuffers, trays, and special
8:2 "Tell Aaron that when he sets up the seven **l** in the
8:3 He set up the seven **l** so they reflected their light
1Ki 7:49 flower decorations, **l**, and tongs, all of gold,
1Ch 28:15 of gold needed for the gold lampstands and **l**,
28:15 amount of silver for the silver lampstands and **l**,
2Ch 4:20 and their **l** of pure gold to burn in front of the Most
4:21 flower decorations, **l**, and tongs, all of pure gold;
29:7 to the Temple's foyer, and they snuffed out the **l**.
Zec 4:2 Around the bowl are seven **l**, each one having
4:10 For these seven **l** represent the eyes of the LORD
Mt 25:1 by the story of ten bridesmaids who took their **l**
25:3 The five who were foolish took no oil for their **l**,
25:7 "All the bridesmaids got up and prepared their **l**.
25:8 us some of your oil because our **l** are going out.'
Lk 8:16 No, **l** are mounted in the open, where they can be
Ac 20:8 where we met was lighted with many flickering **l**.
Rev 22:5 there will be no night there—no need for **l** or sun—

LAMPSTAND (34) [LAMP]

Ex 25:31 "Make a **l** of pure, hammered gold. The entire **l**
and its decorations will be one piece—
25:34 The center stem of the **l** will be decorated with four
25:37 Then make the seven lamps for the **l**, and set them
25:39 will need seventy-five pounds of pure gold for the **l**
26:35 and **l** across the room from each other outside the
26:35 The **l** must be placed on the south side,
27:20 of Israel to bring you pure olive oil for the **l**,
27:21 The **l** will be placed outside the inner curtain of the
30:27 the **l** and all its accessories, the incense altar,
31:8 the gold **l** with all its accessories; the incense altar;
35:14 the **l** and its accessories; the lamp cups and the oil
37:17 Then he made the **l**, again using pure,
37:18 The **l** had six branches, three going out from each
37:20 The center stem of the **l** was also decorated with
37:24 The entire **l**, along with its accessories, was made
39:37 the gold **l** and its accessories; the lamp cups
40:4 on it. And bring in the **l**, and set up the lamps.
40:24 He set the **l** in the Tabernacle across from the table
Lev 24:2 Israel to provide you with pure olive oil for the **l**,
24:4 The lamps on the pure gold **l** must be tended
Nu 3:31 the table, the **l**, the altars, the various utensils used
4:9 "Next they must cover the **l** with a dark blue cloth,
4:10 The **l** with its utensils must then be covered with
4:16 the priest will be responsible for the oil of the **l**,
8:2 that when he sets up the seven lamps in the **l**,
8:4 The entire **l**, from its base to its decorative
2Ch 13:11 holy table, and they light the gold **l** every evening.
Da 5:5 on the plaster wall of the king's palace, near the **l**.
Zec 4:2 "I see a solid gold **l** with a bowl of oil on top of it.
4:11 are these two olive trees on each side of the **l**,
Lk 11:33 it is put on a **l** to give light to all who enter the
Heb 9:2 In the first room were a **l**, a table, and loaves of
Rev 2:5 and remove your **l** from its place among the

LAMPSTANDS (13) [LAMP]

1Ki 7:49 the gold **l**, five on the south and five on the north,
1Ch 28:15 Solomon the amount of gold needed for the gold **l**
28:15 and the amount of silver for the silver **l** and lamps,
2Ch 4:7 then cast ten gold **l** according to the specifications
4:20 the **l** and their lamps of pure gold to burn in front
Jer 52:19 the small bowls, firepans, basins, pots, **l**, dishes,
Rev 1:12 to see who was speaking to me, I saw seven gold **l**.

1:13 And standing in the middle of the l was the Son of
1:20 you saw in my right hand and the seven gold l:
1:20 and the seven l are the seven churches.
2: 1 the one who walks among the seven gold l:
4: 5 And in front of the throne were seven l with
11: 4 and the two l that stand before the Lord of all the

LANCETS [KJV] See SWORDS

LAND (1670) [FARMLAND, HIGHLANDS, INLAND, LAND'S, LANDED, LANDING, LANDOWNER, LANDS, LANDSCAPE, LOWLANDS, MAINLAND, PASTURELAND, PASTURELANDS, WASTELAND, WASTELANDS]

ALL THE LAND (35) Ge 2:6; 41:19; 45:9,20,26; 47:20; Ex 9:23; 10:19; Dt 3:8; 7:18; 19:8; 34:2,2; Jos 1:4,6; 11:22; 12:1; 13:4,6; 19:49; 21:43; 23:4; Jdg 11:21; 2Sa 9:7; 1Ki 4:10; 15:20; Job 42:15; Ps 44:2; Isa 7:22; 33:9; Jer 46:7; Eze 25:5; Zec 14:10; Mt 8:10; Lk 7:9

ENTIRE LAND (30) Ge 2:11,13; 41:41,44,45; Ex 8:2,17; 10:22; Lev 18:25; Nu 18:21; Dt 3:2; 34:11; Jos 9:24; 11:23; 1Sa 9:4; 2Sa 24:8; 1Ki 4:24; 2Ki 17:5; 2Ch 34:33; Isa 6:12; 7:24; 16:7; Jer 3:2; 25:11; 48:45; Eze 9:9; 33:24; 48:23; Am 7:4; Zec 5:3

GOOD LAND (16) Dt 1:25,35; 4:21; 6:18; 8:7,10; 9:6; 11:17; Jos 23:13,15,16; 1Ki 14:15; 2Ki 3:19,25; 1Ch 28:8; Eze 20:6

LAND FLOWING WITH MILK AND HONEY (20) Ex 3:8,17; 13:5; 33:3; Lev 20:24; Nu 13:27; 14:8; 16:13,14; Dt 6:3; 11:9; 26:9,15; 27:3; 31:20; Jos 5:6; Jer 11:5; 32:22; Eze 20:6,15

LAND OF CANAAN (48) Ge 11:31; 13:12; 16:3; 17:8; 23:2; 31:18; 36:5,6; 37:1; 42:7,13,29,32; 45:25; 46:6,12,31; 48:3,4,7; 50:5,13; Ex 6:4; 16:35; Lev 25:38; Nu 13:2; 26:19; 32:30; 33:40,51; 34:2,29; 35:10,14; Dt 32:49; Jos 14:7,9; 21:2; 22:9,11,32; 24:3; Jdg 21:12; 1Ch 16:18; Ps 105:11,16; Zep 2:5; Heb 4:8

LAND OF EGYPT (98) Ge 13:10; 41:19,29,41,44,45,55; 45:9,18,20,26; 46:20,27,34; 47:6,11,20,26; 48:5; 50:24; Ex 4:20; 6:26,27; 7:3,21; 8:6,16,17; 9:9,23; 10:12,14,15,19,21; 11:1,3,6,9; 12:1,12,12,13,17,29,30,42; 13:15; 16:6; 22:21; 23:9; 32:11; Lev 11:45; 19:34,36; 23:43; 25:42,55; 26:13; Nu 15:41; 26:59; Dt 6:12; 7:18; 8:14; 10:19; 11:10; 13:5,10; 15:15; 24:22; 29:16,25; 34:11; Jos 24:17; 1Sa 12:6; 1Ki 6:1; 8:9; Ps 78:51; 81:10; Isa 19:14,20; Jer 16:14; 23:7; 31:32; 32:20; 43:11,12; 44:26; Eze 19:4; 29:9,10,19,20; 30:12,25; Na 3:9; Heb 8:9; 11:27

LAND OF GILEAD (15) Nu 32:29; Jos 17:5,6; 22:9,15; Jdg 10:4; 11:29; 20:1; 2Sa 17:26; 1Ki 4:19; 1Ch 2:22; 5:9,16; 26:31; Ob 1:19

LAND OF ISRAEL (42) Nu 18:21; Jos 11:22; Jdg 20:6; 1Sa 13:19; 28:3; 2Sa 21:14; 2Ki 5:2; 6:23; 8:3; 1Ch 12:40; 21:12; 2Ch 2:17; 30:25; 34:7,33; Isa 6:12; 11:11; 33:9; 49:8; Jer 3:14; 24:10; La 2:3; Eze 11:17; 18:2; 20:38; 34:13; 37:12,25; 38:8,18,19; 40:2; 48:1,23; Da 8:9; 11:16,41; Ob 1:13; Na 2:2; Mt 2:20; 8:10; Lk 7:9

LAND OF JUDAH (21) Dt 34:2; Ru 1:2; 1Sa 17:12; 22:5; 30:16; 1Ki 4:19; 2Ki 18:5; 23:24; 24:1; 2Ch 11:23; 12:12; 15:8; 17:2; 20:31; 30:12; 36:23; Ezr 1:2; Ps 114:2; Isa 26:1; Am 7:12; Zec 2:12

LAND OF THE LIVING (4) Ps 27:13; 52:5; Isa 38:11; Eze 26:20

LIVE IN THE LAND (13) Ge 45:10; 47:4; Nu 33:55; Dt 12:1,10; 31:13; 1Ki 8:40; 2Ki 25:24; 2Ch 6:31; Ps 37:27; Pr 2:21; Isa 9:2; Eze 37:25

LIVED IN THE LAND (10) Ge 36:21,30; Dt 4:25; 29:16; Jdg 11:3; 18:1; 2Ki 8:2; 1Ch 5:16; Job 1:1; Mt 4:16

PEOPLE OF THE LAND (22) Ge 23:12; Lev 18:27; Nu 14:9; Dt 1:28; 20:18; 29:25; 2Ki 11:18,19,20; 15:5; 21:24; 2Ch 23:21; 26:21; 33:25; 36:1; Ezr 10:11; Ne 10:28,30,31; 13:25; Est 8:17; Da 9:6

POSSESS(ED) THE LAND (9) Dt 3:8; 11:29; Jos 1:6,15; Ezr 9:11; Ps 37:9,11; Isa 57:13; Am 2:10

WHOLE LAND (22) Ex 8:6; 9:9; Nu 22:11; 32:33; Dt 11:25; 34:1; Jos 2:24; Isa 7:19; 13:5; 15:8; Jer 4:27; 8:16; 12:11; 40:4; 50:38; 51:47; La 2:3; Ob 1:8; Zep 1:18; Mt 27:45; Mk 15:33; Lk 23:44

Ge 1:10 God named the dry ground "l" and the water
1:11 "Let the l burst forth with every sort of grass
1:12 The l was filled with seed-bearing plants and trees,
2: 6 came up out of the ground and watered all the l.
2:10 A river flowed from the l of Eden,
2:11 which flows around the entire l of Havilah,
2:12 The gold of that l is exceptionally pure;
2:13 the Gihon, which flows around the entire l of Cush.
4:14 You have banished me from my l and from your
4:16 the LORD's presence and settled in the l of Nod,
7:22 Everything died that breathed and lived on dry l.
8: 9 But the dove found no place to l because the water
10:10 He built the foundation for his empire in the l of
11: 2 they found a plain in the l of Babylonia and settled
11:31 and left Ur of the Chaldeans to go to the l of
12: 1 father's house, and go to the l that I will show you.
12: 7 "I am going to give this l to your offspring."
12:10 At that time there was a severe famine in the l,
13: 6 But the l could not support both Abram and Lot
13: 7 and Perizzites were also living in the l.
13: 9 Take your choice of any section of the l you want,
13:10 garden of the LORD or the beautiful l of Egypt.
13:11 Lot chose that l for himself—the Jordan Valley to
13:12 So while Abram stayed in the l of Canaan,
13:15 I am going to give all this l to you and your
15: 7 you out of Ur of the Chaldeans to give you this l."
15:13 your descendants will be strangers in a foreign l,
15:16 your descendants will return here to this l,
15:18 and said, "I have given this l to your descendants,
15:19 the l of the Kenites, Kenizzites, Kadmonites,
16: 3 years after Abram first arrived in the l of Canaan.)
17: 8 I will give all this l of Canaan to you and to your
21:32 and they returned home to the l of the Philistines.
22: 2 you love so much—and go to the l of Moriah.
23: 2 (now called Hebron) in the l of Canaan.
23: 4 "Here I am, a stranger in a foreign l, with no place
23: 4 Please let me have a piece of l for a burial plot."
23:12 Abraham bowed again to the people of the l,
23:15 "the l is worth four hundred pieces of silver,
23:17 He bought the plot of l belonging to Ephron at
24: 7 took me from my father's house and my native l,
24: 7 solemnly promised to give this l to my offspring.
24:38 I was to come to his relatives here in this far-off l,
26: 1 Now a severe famine struck the l, as had happened
26: 3 Do as I say, and stay here in this l. If you do,
26: 3 I will give all this l to you and your descendants,
26:27 since you sent me from your l in a most unfriendly
27:39 to him, "You will live off the l and what it yields,
28: 4 May you own this l where we now are foreigners,
28:14 They will cover the l from east to west and from
28:15 I will someday bring you safely back to this l.
29: 1 hurried on, finally arriving in the l of the east.
31: 3 "Return to the l of your father and grandfather
31:13 this country and return to the l you came from.' "
31:18 and set out on his journey to the l of Canaan,
32: 3 to his brother, Esau, in Edom, the l of Seir.
32: 9 you told me to return to my l and to my relatives,
33:19 Jacob bought the l he camped on from the family
34:10 And you may live among us; the l is open to you!
34:21 For the l is large enough to hold them, and we can
34:30 have made me stink among all the people of this l
35:12 And I will pass on to you the l I gave to Abraham
36: 5 All these sons were born to Esau in the l of
36: 6 all the wealth he had gained in the l of Canaan—
36: 7 There was not enough l to support them both
36:16 These clans in the l of Edom were descended from
36:17 These clans in the l of Edom were descended from
36:20 one of the families native to the l of Seir:
36:21 descendants of Seir, who lived in the l of Edom.
36:30 after their clan leaders, who lived in the l of Seir.
36:34 Husham from the l of the Temanites became king.
36:35 destroyed the Midianite army in the l of Moab.
37: 1 So Jacob settled again in the l of Canaan, where his
40:15 the l of the Hebrews, and now I'm here in jail,
41:19 I've never seen such ugly animals in all the l of
41:29 of great prosperity throughout the l of Egypt.
41:30 and wiped out. Famine will destroy the l.
41:34 Let Pharaoh appoint officials over the l, and let
41:36 Otherwise disaster will surely strike the l, and all
41:39 the dreams to you, you are the wisest man in the l!
41:41 "I hereby put you in charge of the entire l of
41:44 or a foot in the entire l of Egypt without your
41:45 So Joseph took charge of the entire l of Egypt.
41:46 he made a tour of inspection throughout the l.
41:52 "God has made me fruitful in this l of my
41:55 Throughout the l of Egypt the people began to
41:56 So with severe famine everywhere in the l,
42: 7 "From the l of Canaan," they replied.
42: 9 You have come to see how vulnerable our l has
42:13 of us brothers, and our father is in the l of Canaan.
42:29 in the l of Canaan and told him all that had
42:30 "The man who is ruler over the l spoke very
42:32 and the youngest is with our father in the l of
42:33 Then the man, the ruler of the l, told us, 'This is
43: 1 no relief from the terrible famine throughout the l.
43:11 Fill your bags with the best products of the l.
45: 9 God has made me master over all the l of Egypt.
45:10 You will live in the l of Goshen so you can be near
45:18 to you the very best territory in the l of Egypt. You will live off the fat of the l!'
45:20 for the best of all the l of Egypt is yours."
45:25 returned to their father, Jacob, in the l of Canaan.
45:26 told him. "And he is ruler over all the l of Egypt!"
46: 6 and all the belongings they had acquired in the l of
46:12 (But Er and Onan had died in the l of Canaan.)
46:20 Joseph's sons, born in the l of Egypt,
46:27 members of Jacob's family in the l of Egypt.
46:28 meet Joseph and get directions to the l of Goshen.
46:31 and tell Pharaoh that you have all come from the l
46:34 he will let you live here in the l of Goshen,
46:34 for shepherds are despised in the l of Egypt."
47: 1 and they are now in the l of Goshen."
47: 4 We request permission to live in the l of Goshen."
47: 6 Give them the best l of Egypt—the l of Goshen will be fine.
47:11 So Joseph assigned the best l of Egypt—the l of Rameses—to his father and brothers,
47:18 We have nothing left but our bodies and l.
47:19 Buy us and our l in exchange for food; we will
47:19 and so the l will not become empty and desolate."
47:20 So Joseph bought all the l of Egypt for Pharaoh.
47:20 so severe, and their l then belonged to Pharaoh.
47:22 The only l he didn't buy was that belonging to the
47:22 food from Pharaoh and didn't need to sell their l.
47:23 "See, I have bought you and your l for Pharaoh.
47:26 then made it a law throughout the l of Egypt—
47:26 receive one-fifth of all the crops grown on his l.
47:26 But since Pharaoh had not taken over the priests' l,
47:27 So the people of Israel settled in the l of Goshen in
48: 3 "God Almighty appeared to me at Luz in the l of
48: 4 and I will give this l of Canaan to you and your
48: 5 who were born here in the l of Egypt before I
48: 6 The l they inherit will be within the territories of
48: 7 from Paddan, Rachel died in the l of Canaan.
48:21 bring you again to Canaan, the l of your ancestors.
49:15 how good the countryside is, / how pleasant the l,
50: 5 take my body back to the l of Canaan, and bury me
50: 8 and flocks and herds in the l of Goshen.
50:13 They carried his body to the l of Canaan
50:24 come for you, to lead you out of this l of Egypt.
50:24 He will bring you back to the l he vowed to give to

Ex 1: 7 so quickly that they soon filled the l.
2:15 fled from Pharaoh and escaped to the l of Midian.
2:22 for he said, "I have been a stranger in a foreign l."
3: 8 out of Egypt into their own good and spacious l.
3: 8 It is a l flowing with milk and honey—the l where the Canaanites, Hittites, Amorites,
3:17 I will lead you to the l now occupied by the
3:17 a l flowing with milk and honey." '
4:20 on a donkey, and headed back to the l of Egypt.
5:12 So the people scattered throughout the l in search
6: 1 rid of them that he will force them to leave his l!"
6: 4 its terms, I swore to give them the l of Canaan,
6: 8 I will bring you into the l I swore to give to
6:26 "Lead all the people of Israel out of the l of Egypt,
6:27 permission to lead the people from the l of Egypt.
7: 3 miraculous signs and wonders in the l of Egypt.
7:21 There was blood everywhere throughout the l of
8: 2 I will send vast hordes of frogs across your entire l
8: 5 so there will be frogs in every corner of the l."
8: 6 did so, and frogs covered the whole l of Egypt!
8: 7 They, too, caused frogs to come up on the l.
8:14 into great heaps, and a terrible stench filled the l.
8:16 into swarms of gnats throughout the l of Egypt."
8:17 Suddenly, gnats infested the entire l,
8:17 All the dust in the l of Egypt turned into gnats.
8:22 But it will be very different in the l of Goshen,
8:22 and that I have power even in the heart of your l.
8:25 to your God," he said. "But do it here in this l.
8:31 to disappear. Not a single fly remained in the l!
9: 9 It will spread like fine dust over the whole l of
9:23 a tremendous hailstorm against all the l of Egypt.
9:26 all Egypt without hail that day was the l of Goshen,
10:12 "Raise your hand over the l of Egypt to bring on
10:12 Let them cover the l and eat all the crops still left
10:14 And the locusts swarmed over the l of Egypt from
10:15 neither tree nor plant, throughout the l of Egypt.
10:19 Not a single locust remained in all the l of Egypt.
10:21 and terrifying darkness will descend on the l of
10:22 and there was deep darkness over the entire l for
11: 1 one more disaster on Pharaoh and the l of Egypt.
11: 3 was considered a very great man in the l of Egypt.
11: 6 Then a loud wail will be heard throughout the l of
11: 9 do even more mighty miracles in the l of Egypt."
12: 1 and Aaron while they were still in the l of Egypt:
12:12 On that night I will pass through the l of Egypt
12:12 and firstborn male animals in the l of Egypt.
12:13 will not touch you when I strike the l of Egypt.
12:17 your forces out of the l of Egypt on this very day.
12:23 For the LORD will pass through the l and strike
12:25 When you arrive in the l the LORD has promised
12:29 killed all the firstborn sons in the l of Egypt,
12:30 and loud wailing was heard throughout the l of
12:33 of Israel to get out of the l as quickly as possible,
12:41 430th year that all the LORD's forces left the l.
12:42 to bring his people out from the l of Egypt,
13: 5 the LORD brings you into the l of the Canaanites,
13: 5 This is the l he swore to give your ancestors—a l flowing with milk and honey.
13: 7 or anywhere within the borders of your l during
13:11 into the l he swore to give your ancestors long ago,
13:11 the l where the Canaanites are now living.
13:15 all the firstborn males throughout the l of Egypt,
13:17 the shortest way from Egypt to the Promised L.
14:21 blew all that night, turning the seabed into dry l.
14:29 had walked through the middle of the sea on dry l,
15:19 the people of Israel had walked through on dry l!
16: 6 the LORD who brought you out of the l of Egypt.
16:35 for forty years until they arrived in the l of Canaan,
18: 3 was born, "I have been a stranger in a foreign l."
18:27 to his father-in-law, who returned to his own l.
20:12 full life in the l the LORD your God will give
22:21 you yourselves were once foreigners in the l of
23: 9 Remember your own experience in the l of Egypt.
23:11 but let the l rest and lie fallow during the seventh
23:20 to lead you safely to the l I have prepared for you.
23:23 and bring you into the l of the Amorites,
23:29 one year because the l would become a wilderness,
23:30 your population has increased enough to fill the l.
23:31 will help you defeat the people now living in the l,
32:11 brought from the l of Egypt with such great power
32:13 I will give them all of this l that I have promised to
33: 1 lead them to the l I solemnly promised Abraham,
33: 1 I told them long ago that I would give this l to their
33: 3 Theirs is a l flowing with milk and honey. But I
33:12 'Take these people up to the Promised L.'
34:12 with the people in the l where you are going.
34:15 treaties of any kind with the people living in the l.
34:24 and conquer your l when you go to appear before

Lev 11:45 am the one who brought you up from the l of
11:46 "These are the instructions regarding the l
14:34 in Canaan, the l I am giving you as an inheritance,
16:22 all the people's sins upon itself into a desolate l.
18:24 from the Promised L have defiled themselves.

18:25 As a result, the entire **l** has become defiled. That is
18:25 who live there, and the **l** will soon vomit them out.
18:27 by the people of the **l** where I am taking you, and
the **l** has become defiled.
18:28 Do not give the **l** a reason to vomit you out for
19:23 "When you enter the **l** and plant fruit trees,
19:29 or the **l** will be filled with promiscuity
19:33 "Do not exploit the foreigners who live in your **l**.
19:34 Remember that you were once foreigners in the **l**
19:36 your God, who brought you out of the **l** of Egypt.
20:22 otherwise the **l** to which I am bringing you will
20:24 But I have promised that you will inherit their **l**, a **l**
flowing with milk and honey.
23:10 "When you arrive in the **l** I am giving you and you
23:22 "When you harvest the crops of your **l**, do not
23:39 after you have harvested all the produce of the **l**,
23:43 shelters when I rescued them from the **l** of Egypt.
25: 2 When you have entered the **l** I am giving you as an
25: 2 the **l** itself must observe a Sabbath to the LORD
25: 4 but during the seventh year the **l** will enjoy a
25: 5 unpruned vines. The **l** is to have a year of total rest.
25: 9 blow the trumpets loud and long throughout the **l**.
25:15 When you buy **l** from your neighbor, the price of
the **l** should be based on the number of
25:16 the person selling the **l** is actually selling you a
25:18 "If you want to live securely in the **l**, keep my
25:19 Then the **l** will yield bumper crops, and you will
25:21 so the **l** will produce a bumper crop, enough to
25:23 the **l** must never be sold on a permanent basis
25:24 "With every sale of **l** there must be a stipulation
that the **l** can be redeemed at any time.
25:25 go bankrupt and are forced to sell some inherited **l**,
25:26 If there is no one to redeem the **l** but the person
25:27 The price of the **l** will be based on the number of
25:27 it back, the original owner may then return to the **l**.
25:28 the **l** will be returned to the original owner.
25:38 who brought you out of Egypt to give you the **l** of
25:42 whom I brought out of the **l** of Egypt, so they must
25:45 including those who have been born in your **l**.
25:55 my servants, whom I brought out of the **l** of Egypt.
26: 1 or shaped stones to be worshiped in your **l**.
26: 4 The **l** will then yield its crops, and the trees will
26: 5 You will eat your fill and live securely in your **l**.
26: 6 "I will give you peace in the **l**, and you will be
26: 6 I will remove the wild animals from your **l**
26:13 who brought you from the **l** of Egypt so you would
26:20 for your **l** will yield no crops, and your trees will
26:32 Yes, I myself will devastate your **l**. Your enemies
26:33 Your **l** will become desolate, and your cities will
26:34 Then at last the **l** will make up for its missed
26:34 during your years of exile in the **l** of your enemies.
26:34 Then the **l** will finally rest and enjoy its Sabbaths.
26:35 As the **l** lies in ruins, it will take the rest you never
26:36 I will demoralize you in the **l** of your enemies far
26:38 and be devoured in the **l** of your enemies.
26:41 and have brought them to the **l** of their enemies,
26:42 and with Abraham, and I will remember the **l**.
26:43 And the **l** will enjoy its years of Sabbath rest as it
26:44 or despise them while they are in exile in the **l** of
27:23 then give the assessed value of the **l** as a sacred
27:30 "A tenth of the produce of the **l**, whether grain
Nu 10: 9 "When you arrive in your own **l** and go to war
10:29 "We are on our way to the Promised **L**.
10:30 will not go. I must return to my own **l** and family."
11:12 a baby—to the **l** you swore to give their ancestors?
13: 2 "Send men to explore the **l** of Canaan, the **l** I am
giving to Israel.
13:16 the names of the men Moses sent to explore the **l**.
13:17 instructions as he sent them out to explore the **l**:
13:18 See what the **l** is like and find out whether the
13:19 What kind of **l** do they live in? Is it good or bad?
13:20 Enter the **l** boldly, and bring back samples of the
13:21 and explored the **l** from the wilderness of Zin as far
13:25 After exploring the **l** for forty days, the men
13:26 showed them the fruit they had taken from the **l**.
13:27 "We arrived in the **l** you sent us to see, and it is
13:27 a **l** flowing with milk and honey.
13:30 "Let's go at once to take the **l**," he said. "We can
13:31 But the other men who had explored the **l** with him
13:32 So they spread discouraging reports about the **l**
13:32 "The **l** we explored will swallow up any who go to
14: 6 Two of the men who had explored the **l**,
14: 7 of Israel, "The **l** we explored is a wonderful **l**!
14: 8 he will bring us safely into that **l** and give it to us.
14: 8 It is a rich **l** flowing with milk and honey, and he
14: 9 and don't be afraid of the people of the **l**.
14:14 They will tell this to the inhabitants of this **l**,
14:16 'The LORD was not able to bring them into the **l**
14:22 not one of these people will ever enter that **l**.
14:23 They will never even see the **l** I swore to give their
14:24 to me, and I will bring him into the **l** he explored.
14:24 descendants will receive their full share of that **l**.
14:25 and don't go on toward the **l** where the Amalekites
14:30 will enter the **l** I swore to give you. The only
14:31 Well, I will bring them safely into the **l**, and they
14:34 " 'Because the men who explored the **l** were there
14:36 by spreading discouraging reports about the **l**
14:38 Of the twelve who had explored the **l**, only Joshua
14:40 but now we are ready to enter the **l** the LORD has
14:42 Do not go into the **l** now. You will only be crushed
15: 2 "When you finally settle in the **l** I am going to
15:18 When you arrive in the **l** where I am taking you,
15:41 you out of the **l** of Egypt that I might be your God.
16:13 a **l** flowing with milk and honey, to kill us here in
16:14 you haven't brought us into the **l** flowing with milk
18:13 All the firstfruits of the **l** that the people present to
18:20 "You priests will receive no inheritance of **l**
18:21 with the tithes from the entire **l** of Israel.
18:23 But the Levites will receive no inheritance of **l**
18:24 receive no inheritance of **l** among the Israelites."
20: 5 This **l** has no grain, figs, grapes, or pomegranates.
20:12 you will not lead them into the **l** I am giving
20:16 camped at Kadesh, a town on the border of your **l**.
20:18 "Stay out of my **l** or I will meet you with an
20:20 "Stay out! You may not pass through our **l**."
20:23 and Aaron at Mount Hor on the border of the **l** of
20:24 He will not enter the **l** I am giving the people of
21: 4 taking the road to the Red Sea to go around the **l** of
21:22 "Let us travel through your **l**. We will stay on the
21:23 But King Sihon refused to let them cross his **l**.
21:24 and occupied their **l** from the Arnon River to the
21:26 and seized all his **l** as far as the Arnon River.
21:34 over Og and his entire army, giving you all his **l**.
21:35 survivor remained. Then Israel occupied their **l**.
22: 5 who was living in his native **l** of Pethor near the
22: 6 be able to conquer them and drive them from the **l**.
22:11 from Egypt and has spread out over the whole **l**.
22:11 to conquer them and drive them from the **l**.' "
22:36 town on the Arnon River at the border of his **l**.
26:19 Er and Onan, who had died in the **l** of Canaan.
26:53 "Divide the **l** among the tribes in proportion to
26:54 the larger tribes more **l** and the smaller tribes less **l**,
26:55 Make sure you assign the **l** by lot, and define the
26:59 of Levi, born among the Levites in the **l** of Egypt.
26:62 because they were not given an inheritance of **l**
27: 7 You must give them an inheritance of **l** along with
27:12 and look out over the **l** I have given the people of
32: 5 please let us have this **l** as our property instead of
giving us **l** across the Jordan River."
32: 7 going across to the **l** the LORD has given them?
32: 8 I sent them from Kadesh-barnea to explore the **l**.
32: 9 went up to the valley of Eshcol and scouted the **l**,
32: 9 from entering the **l** the LORD was giving them.
32:11 or older will ever see the **l** I solemnly promised to
32:18 of Israel have received their inheritance of **l**.
32:19 But we do not want any of the **l** on the other side of
32:22 then you may return when the **l** is finally subdued
32:22 And the **l** on the east side of the Jordan will be
32:29 then when the **l** is conquered, you must give them
the **l** of Gilead as their
32:30 accept **l** with the rest of you in the **l** of Canaan."
32:32 but our inheritance of **l** will be here on this side of
32:33 of the Amorites and the **l** of King Og of Bashan—
32:33 the whole **l** with its towns and surrounding lands.
33:40 of Arad, who lived in the Negev in the **l** of Canaan,
33:40 that the people of Israel were approaching his **l**.
33:51 'When you cross the Jordan River into the **l** of
33:53 Take possession of the **l** and settle in it, because I
33:54 You must distribute the **l** among the clans by
33:54 A larger inheritance of **l** will be allotted to each of
33:54 the **l** will be divided among your ancestral tribes.
33:55 if you fail to drive out the people who live in the **l**,
33:55 They will harass you in the **l** where you live.
34: 2 When you come into the **l** of Canaan, which I am
34:12 the Dead Sea. These are the boundaries of your **l**."
34:13 The LORD commands that the **l** be divided up
34:14 have already received their inheritance of **l**
34:17 "These are the men who are to divide the **l** among
34:29 dividing of the **l** of Canaan among the Israelites."
35:10 'When you cross the Jordan into the **l** of Canaan,
35:14 and three on the west in the **l** of Canaan.
35:33 This will ensure that the **l** where you live will not
be polluted, for murder pollutes the **l**.
35:34 You must not defile the **l** where you are going to
36: 2 the LORD instructed you to divide the **l** by sacred
36: 3 their inheritance of **l** will go with them to the tribe
36: 3 the total area of our tribal **l** will be reduced.
36: 4 their inheritance of **l** will be added to that of the
36: 7 None of the inherited **l** may pass from tribe to
36: 9 Israel must hold on to its allotted inheritance of **l**."
36:12 their inheritance of **l** remained within their
Dt 1: 5 were in the **l** of Moab east of the Jordan River.
1: 7 Go to the **l** of the Canaanites and to Lebanon,
1: 8 I am giving all this **l** to you! Go in and occupy it,
1: 8 for it is the **l** the LORD swore to give to your
1:20 'You have now reached the **l** that the LORD our
1:22 'First, let's send out scouts to explore the **l** for us.
1:25 And they reported that the **l** the LORD our God had
given us was indeed a good **l**.
1:28 They say that the people of the **l** are taller
1:35 to see the good **l** I swore to give your ancestors,
1:36 He will see this **l** because he has followed the
1:36 and his descendants some of the **l** he walked over
1:37 said to me, 'You will never enter the Promised **L**!
1:38 Joshua son of Nun, will lead the people into the **l**.
1:39 I will give the **l** to your innocent children.
1:41 We will go into the **l** and fight for it, as the LORD
2: 5 and I will not give you any of their **l**.
2: 9 and I will not give you any of their **l**.' "
2:12 from the **l** that the LORD had assigned to Israel.)
2:19 and enter the **l** of Ammon. But do not bother the
2:19 I have given the **l** of Ammon to them as their
2:19 and I will not give you any of their **l**.' "
2:20 too, was once considered the **l** of the Rephaites,
2:21 so the Ammonites could occupy their **l**.
2:24 king of Heshbon, and I will give you his **l**. Attack
him and begin to occupy the **l**.
2:27 'Let us pass through your **l**. We will stay on the
2:28 All we want is permission to pass through your **l**.
2:29 into the **l** the LORD our God has given us.'
2:31 begun to hand King Sihon and his **l** over to you.
Begin now to conquer and occupy his **l**.'
3: 1 "Next we headed for the **l** of Bashan, where King
3: 2 over Og and his army, giving you his entire **l**.
3: 8 "We now possessed all the **l** of the two Amorite
3:12 "When we took possession of this **l**, I gave the
3:13 Bashan used to be known as the **l** of the Rephaites.
3:18 your God has given you this **l** as your property,
3:20 and when they occupy the **l** the LORD your God
3:20 then you may return here to the **l** I have given
3:25 the Jordan to see the wonderful **l** on the other side,
3:27 go to Pisgah Peak and view the **l** in every direction,
3:28 He will give them the **l** you now see before you.'
4: 1 so you may enter and occupy the **l** the LORD,
4: 5 and regulations when you arrive in the **l** you are
4:14 and regulations you must obey in the **l** you are
4:21 **l** the LORD your God is giving you as your
4:22 Though you will cross the Jordan to occupy the **l**,
4:25 and have lived in the **l** a long time,
4:26 you will quickly disappear from the **l** you are
4:28 There, in a foreign **l**, you will worship idols made
4:38 you in and give you their **l** as a special possession,
4:40 Then you will enjoy a long life in the **l** the LORD
4:46 (This **l** was formerly occupied by the Amorites
4:47 Israel conquered his **l** and that of King Og of
5:16 full life in the **l** the LORD your God will give
5:21 Do not covet your neighbor's house or **l**, male
5:31 so they can obey them in the **l** I am giving to them
5:33 and prosperous lives in the **l** you are about to enter
6: 1 so you may obey them in the **l** you are about to
6: 3 and you will have many children in the **l** flowing
6:10 the **l** he swore to give your ancestors Abraham,
6:10 It is a **l** filled with large, prosperous cities that you
6:11 not plant. When you have eaten your fill in this **l**,
6:12 who rescued you from slavery in the **l** of Egypt.
6:18 and occupy the good **l** that the LORD solemnly
6:19 You will drive out all the enemies living in your **l**,
6:23 so he could give us this **l** he had solemnly
7: 1 "When the LORD your God brings you into the **l**
7:13 and give fertility to your **l** and your animals.
7:13 When you arrive in the **l** he swore to give your
7:18 your God did to Pharaoh and to all the **l** of Egypt.
8: 1 and occupy the **l** the LORD swore to give your
8: 7 is bringing you into a good **l** of flowing streams
8: 8 It is a **l** of wheat and barley, of grapevines,
8: 9 It is a **l** where food is plentiful and nothing is
8: 9 It is a **l** where iron is as common as stone,
8:10 praise the LORD your God for the good **l** he has
8:14 who rescued you from slavery in the **l** of Egypt.
9: 1 to occupy the **l** belonging to nations much greater
9: 4 'The LORD has given us this **l** because we are
9: 5 upright people that you are about to occupy their **l**.
9: 6 The LORD your God is not giving you this good **l**
9:23 'Go up and take the **l** I have given you.' But you
9:28 because he wasn't able to bring them to the **l** he
10: 7 from there to Jotbathah, a **l** with brooks of water.
10:11 and lead the people into the **l** I swore to give their
10:19 for you yourselves were once foreigners in the **l** of
11: 3 performed in Egypt against Pharaoh and all his **l**.
11: 8 to go in and occupy the **l** you are about to enter.
11: 9 you will enjoy a long life in the **l** the LORD
11: 9 a **l** flowing with milk and honey!
11:10 For the **l** you are about to enter and occupy is not
like the **l** of Egypt from which
11:11 It is a **l** of hills and valleys with plenty of rain—
11:12 a **l** that the LORD your God cares for. He watches
11:17 Then you will quickly die in that good **l** the
11:21 and your children may flourish in the **l** the LORD
11:23 the LORD will drive out all the nations in your **l**,
11:24 Wherever you set your feet, the **l** will be yours.
11:25 he promised you, wherever you go in the whole **l**.
11:29 "When the LORD your God brings you into the **l**
11:30 **l** of the Canaanites who live in the Jordan Valley,
11:31 occupy the **l** the LORD your God is giving you.
When you are living in that **l**,
12: 1 must obey as long as you live in the **l** the LORD,
12:10 and live in the **l** the LORD your God is giving
12:12 for they will have no inheritance of **l** as their own.
12:19 to forget the Levites as long as you live in your **l**.
12:29 and you drive them out and occupy their **l**,
13: 5 who brought you out of slavery in the **l** of Egypt.
13:10 who rescued you from the **l** of Egypt, the place of
15: 4 in the **l** he is giving you as a special possession.
15: 7 arrive in the **l** the LORD your God is giving you,
15:15 Remember that you were slaves in the **l** of Egypt
16: 4 in any house throughout your **l** for seven days.
16:18 They will judge the people fairly throughout the **l**.
16:20 and occupy the **l** that the LORD your God is
17:14 "You will soon arrive in the **l** the LORD your
18: 1 an inheritance of **l** like the other tribes in Israel.
18: 9 "When you arrive in the **l** the LORD your God is
19: 1 soon destroy the nations whose **l** he is giving you,
19: 2 **l** the LORD your God is giving you to occupy.
19: 3 Divide the **l** the LORD your God is giving you
19: 8 and gives you all the **l** he promised them,
19: 9 (He will give you this **l** if you obey all the
19:10 **l** the LORD your God is giving you as a special
19:14 "When you arrive in the **l** the LORD your God is
19:14 never steal someone's **l** by moving the boundary
20:18 This will keep the people of the **l** from teaching
21: 1 a field in the **l** the LORD your God is giving you,
21:23 Do not defile the **l** the LORD your God is giving
22:24 In this way, you will cleanse the **l** of evil.
23:20 in everything you do in the **l** you are about to enter
24: 4 You must not bring guilt upon the **l** the LORD
24:22 Remember that you were slaves in the **l** of Egypt.
25:15 so that you will enjoy a long life in the **l** the
25:19 in the **l** he is giving you as a special possession,
26: 1 "When you arrive in the **l** the LORD your God is
26: 3 me into the **l** he swore to give our ancestors.'
26: 9 and gave us this **l** flowing with milk and honey!

26:15 your people Israel and the l you have given us—a l flowing with milk and honey—
27: 2 and enter the l the LORD your God is giving you,
27: 3 you will soon cross the river to enter the l the
27: 3 a l flowing with milk and honey, just as the
28: 8 The LORD your God will bless you in the l he is
28:11 things in the l he swore to give your ancestors—
28:21 none of you are left in the l you are about to enter
28:40 You will grow olive trees throughout your l,
28:52 to your cities until all the fortified walls in your l—
28:52 They will attack all the towns in the l the LORD
28:63 until you disappear from the l you are about to
29: 1 the Israelites while they were in the l of Moab,
29: 8 We took their l and gave it to the tribes of Reuben
29:16 "Surely you remember how we lived in the l of
29:22 will see the devastation of the l and the diseases
29:24 will ask, 'Why has the LORD done this to his l?
29:25 because the people of the l broke the covenant they
29:25 when he brought them out of the l of Egypt.
29:27 is why the LORD's anger burned against this l,
29:28 fury the LORD uprooted his people from their l and exiled them to another l,
30: 5 He will return you to the l that belonged to your ancestors, and you will possess that l again.
30:16 and the l you are about to enter and occupy.
30:18 good life in the l you are crossing the Jordan to
30:20 Then you will live long in the l the LORD swore
31: 3 living there, and you will take possession of their l.
31: 4 The LORD will destroy the nations living in the l,
31: 7 For you will lead these people into the l that the
31:13 Do this as long as you live in the l you are crossing
31:16 the gods of the l where they are going.
31:20 For I will bring them into the l I swore to give their ancestors—a l flowing with milk and honey.
31:21 even before they have entered the l I swore to give
31:23 You must bring the people of Israel into the l I
32:10 "He found them in a desert l, / in an empty,
32:43 on his enemies / and cleanse his l and his people."
32:47 By obeying them you will enjoy a long life in the l
32:49 Look out across the l of Canaan, the l I am giving to the people of Israel as their
32:52 So you will see the l from a distance, but you may not enter the l I am giving to the
33:13 of Joseph: / "May their l be blessed by the LORD
33:21 The people of Gad took the best l for themselves;
33:28 Jacob in security, / in a l of grain and wine,
34: 1 And the LORD showed him the whole l,
34: 2 all the l of Naphtali; the l of Ephraim and Manasseh; all the l of Judah, extending to the Mediterranean
34: 4 "This is the l I promised on oath to Abraham,
34: 4 allowed you to see it, but you will not enter the l."
34: 5 servant of the LORD, died there in the l of Moab,
34:11 and wonders in the l of Egypt against Pharaoh, all his servants, and his entire l.
Jos 1: 2 across the Jordan River into the l I am giving them.
1: 3 you go, you will be on l I have given you—
1: 4 Sea on the west, and all the l of the Hittites.'
1: 6 for you will lead my people to possess all the l I
1:11 and take possession of the l the LORD your God
1:13 God is giving you rest and has given you this l.'
1:15 possess the l the LORD your God is giving them.
1:15 east side of the Jordan River in the l that Moses,
2: 1 "Spy out the l on the other side of the Jordan
2: 2 Israelites have come here tonight to spy out the l."
2: 9 "I know the LORD has given you this l,"
2:14 our promise when the LORD gives us the l."
2:24 "The LORD will certainly give us the whole l,"
2:24 "for all the people in the l are terrified of us."
5: 6 not let them enter the l he had sworn to give us—a l flowing with milk and honey.
5: 7 been circumcised on the way to the Promised L—
5:11 and roasted grain harvested from the l.
6:27 and his name became famous throughout the l.
7: 9 and all the other people living in the l hear about it,
8: 1 to you the king of Ai, his people, his city, and his l.
9: 6 "We have come from a distant l to ask you to
9:22 Why did you say that you live in a distant l when
9:24 his servant Moses to conquer this entire l
10:40 He completely destroyed everyone in the l,
10:42 Joshua conquered all these kings and their l,
11: 3 the slopes of Mount Hermon, in the l of Mizpah.
11:16 the hill country, the Negev, the l of Goshen,
11:22 Not one was left in all the l of Israel, though some
11:23 So Joshua took control of the entire l, just as the
11:23 special possession, dividing the l among the tribes. So the l finally had rest from war.
12: 1 River who had been killed and whose l was taken.
12: 1 and included all the l east of the Jordan Valley.
12: 6 And Moses gave their l to the tribes of Reuben,
12: 7 (Joshua allotted this l to the tribes of Israel as their
13: 1 growing old, and much l remains to be conquered.
13: 2 The people still need to occupy the l of the
13: 3 This l extends from the stream of Shihor, which is
13: 4 The l of the Avvites in the south also remains to be
13: 4 all the l of the Canaanites, including Mearah
13: 5 the l of the Gebalites and all of the Lebanon
13: 6 including all the l of the Sidonians.
13: 6 "I will drive these people out of the l for the
13: 6 So be sure to give this l to Israel as a special
13: 7 when you divide the l among the nine tribes
13: 8 the LORD, had previously assigned this l to them.
13:14 Moses did not assign any l to the tribe of Levi.
13:21 The l of Reuben also included all the towns of the
13:25 the towns of Gilead, and half of the l of Ammon,
13:33 But Moses gave no l to the tribe of Levi,
14: 1 The remaining tribes of Israel inherited l in Canaan
14: 3 Moses had already given an inheritance of l to the
14: 4 And the Levites were given no l at all, only towns
14: 5 So the distribution of the l was in strict accordance
14: 7 sent me from Kadesh-barnea to explore the l of
14: 8 discouraged them from entering the Promised L.
14: 9 'The l of Canaan on which you were just walking
14:12 I will drive them out of the l, just as the LORD
14:15 hero of the Anakites.) And the l had rest from war.
15: 1 The l assigned to the families of the tribe of Judah
15:19 You have been kind enough to give me l in the
17: 1 The next allotment of l was given to the half-tribe
17: 2 L on the west side of the Jordan was allotted to the
17: 5 Manasseh's inheritance came to ten parcels of l,
17: 5 in addition to the l of Gilead and Bashan across the
17: 6 (The l of Gilead was given to the rest of the male
17: 8 (The l surrounding Tappuah belonged to
17:10 The l south of the ravine belonged to Ephraim,
17:10 and the l north of the ravine belonged to Manasseh,
17:13 as slaves. But they did not drive them out of the l.
17:14 "Why have you given us only one portion of l
17:15 clear out l for yourselves in the forest where the
17:18 Clear as much of the l as you wish and live there.
18: 1 Now that the l was under Israelite control,
18: 3 taking possession of the remaining l the LORD,
18: 5 The scouts will map the l into seven sections,
18: 7 However, the Levites will not receive any l.
18: 7 half-tribe of Manasseh won't receive any more l,
18: 8 As the men who were mapping out the l started on
18: 8 Joshua commanded them, "Go and survey the l.
18: 8 and I will assign the l to the tribes by casting
18:11 The first allotment of l went to the families of the
19: 1 The second allotment of l went to the families of
19:10 The third allotment of l went to the families of the
19:17 The fourth allotment of l went to the families of
19:24 The fifth allotment of l went to the families of the
19:32 The sixth allotment of l went to the families of the
19:40 and last allotment of l went to the families of the
19:47 of Dan had trouble taking possession of their l,
19:49 After all the l was divided among the tribes,
19:49 the Israelites gave a special piece of l to Joshua as
19:51 at Shiloh. So the division of the l was completed.
20: 8 Golan in Bashan, in the l of the tribe of Manasseh.
21: 2 They spoke to them at Shiloh in the l of Canaan,
21:43 So the LORD gave to Israel all the l he had sworn
22: 4 So go home now to the l Moses, the servant of the
22: 7 Now Moses had given the l of Bashan to the
22: 7 The other half of the tribe was given l west of the
22: 9 left the rest of Israel at Shiloh in the l of Canaan.
22: 9 They started the journey back to their own l of
22:11 west of the Jordan River, in the l of Canaan,
22:15 When they arrived in the l of Gilead, they said to
22:19 If you need the altar because your l is defiled,
22:19 in his Tabernacle, and we will share our l with you.
22:32 and returned to the l of Canaan to tell the Israelites
23: 4 I have allotted to you as an inheritance all the l of
23: 4 as well as the l of those we have already
23: 5 This l will be yours, for the LORD your God will
23: 7 with the other people still remaining in the l.
23:13 God will no longer drive them out from your l.
23:13 and you will be wiped out from this good l the
23:15 He will completely wipe you out from this good l
23:16 and you will quickly be wiped out from the good l
24: 3 But I took your ancestor Abraham from the l
24: 3 the Euphrates and led him into the l of Canaan.
24: 8 I brought you into the l of the Amorites on the east
24: 8 over them, and you took possession of their l.
24:13 I gave you l you had not worked for, and I gave
24:15 Or will it be the gods of the Amorites in whose l
24:17 and our ancestors from slavery in the l of Egypt.
24:18 and the other nations living here in the l.
24:30 They buried him in the l he had inherited,
24:32 This l was located in the territory allotted to the
Jdg 1: 2 "Judah, for I have given them victory over the l."
1:15 You have been kind enough to give me l in the
1:26 Later the man moved to the l of the Hittites,
1:28 but they never did drive them out of the l.
1:32 the Canaanites dominated the l where the people of
1:33 the Canaanites dominated the l where they lived.
2: 1 "I brought you out of Egypt into this l that I swore
2: 2 any covenants with the people living in this l;
2: 3 will no longer drive out the people living in your l.
2: 6 each of the tribes left to take possession of the l
2: 9 They buried him in the l he had inherited,
3: 1 The LORD left certain nations in the l to test
3:11 So there was peace in the l for forty years.
3:30 that day, and the l was at peace for eighty years.
4: 6 who lived in Kedesh in the l of Naphtali.
5:14 a l that once belonged to the Amalekites,
5:31 Then there was peace in the l for forty years.
6: 4 camping in the l and destroying crops as far away
6: 5 And they stayed until the l was stripped bare.
6: 9 I drove out your enemies and gave you their l.
6:10 the gods of the Amorites, in whose l you now live.'
6:24 The altar remains in Ophrah in the l of the clan of
8:28 about forty years—the l was at peace.
8:32 Joash, at Ophrah in the l of the clan of Abiezer.
10: 4 and they owned thirty towns in the l of Gilead,
10: 8 of the Jordan River in the l of the Amorites (that is,
11: 2 brothers grew up, they chased Jephthah off the l.
11: 3 fled from his brothers and lived in the l of Tob.
11: 5 the leaders of Gilead sent for Jephthah in the l of
11:13 they stole my l from the Arnon River to the Jabbok
11:13 the Jordan. Now then, give back the l peaceably."
11:15 Israel did not steal any l from Moab or Ammon.
11:17 Edom asking for permission to pass through his l.
11:19 asking for permission to cross through his l to get
11:20 King Sihon didn't trust Israel to pass through his l.
11:21 So Israel took control of all the l of the Amorites,
11:23 who took away the l from the Amorites and gave it
11:25 he try to make a case against Israel for disputed l?
11:26 spread across the l from Heshbon to Aroer and in
11:29 and he went throughout the l of Gilead
15:20 for twenty years, while the Philistines ruled the l.
18: 1 out the people who lived in the l assigned to them.
18: 2 and Eshtaol, to scout out a l for them to settle in.
18: 7 were also wealthy because their l was very fertile.
18: 9 We have seen the l, and it is very good.
18:10 God has given us a spacious and fertile l,
18:14 The five men who had scouted out the l around
19:14 they came to Gibeah, a town in the l of Benjamin,
20: 1 from Dan to Beersheba and from the l of Gilead,
20: 3 (Word soon reached the l of Benjamin that the
20: 4 a town in the l of Benjamin, to spend the night.
20: 6 and sent the pieces throughout the l of Israel,
21:12 them to the camp at Shiloh in the l of Canaan.
21:23 and carried them off to the l of their own
Ru 1: 2 They were Ephrathites from Bethlehem in the l of
2:11 and your own l to live here among complete
4: 3 She is selling the l that belonged to our relative
4: 4 If you want the l, then buy it here in the presence
4: 5 your purchase of the l from Naomi also requires
4: 5 her husband's name and keep the l in the family."
4: 6 my own estate. You redeem the l; I cannot do it."
4: 8 off his sandal as he said to Boaz, "You buy the l."
4:10 And with the l I have acquired Ruth, the Moabite
1Sa 3:20 All the people of Israel from one end of the l to the
6: 2 the LORD? Tell us how to return it to its own l."
6: 4 gold rats, just like those that have ravaged your l.
6: 5 he will stop afflicting you, your gods, and your l.
6: 9 If they cross the border of our l and go to
9: 2 and shoulders taller than anyone else in the l.
9: 4 the l of Shalishah, the Shaalim area, and the entire l of Benjamin,
9:16 I will send you a man from the l of Benjamin.
12: 6 "He brought your ancestors out of the l of Egypt.
12: 8 them from Egypt and to bring them into this l.
13: 2 son Jonathan to Gibeah in the l of Benjamin.
13: 7 and escaped into the l of Gad and Gilead.
13:15 They went up from Gilgal to Gibeah in the l of
13:16 staying at Geba, near Gibeah, in the l of Benjamin.
13:17 One went north toward Ophrah in the l of Shual,
13:19 There were no blacksmiths in the l of Israel in
17:12 an Ephrathite from Bethlehem in the l of Judah.
18:30 name became very famous throughout the l.
21:11 "Isn't this David, the king of the l?" they asked.
22: 5 the stronghold and return to the l of Judah."
28: 3 all mediums and psychics from the l of Israel.
28: 9 expelled all the mediums and psychics from the l.
29:11 So David headed back into the l of the Philistines,
30:14 the territory of Judah, and the l of Caleb, and we
30:16 had taken from the Philistines and the l of Judah.
31: 9 and to the people throughout the l of Philistia.
2Sa 1:13 a foreigner, an Amalekite, who lives in your l."
2: 9 Jezreel, Ephraim, Benjamin, the l of the Ashurites,
7: 1 and the LORD had brought peace to the l,
7:10 It will be their own l where wicked nations won't
8: 2 David also conquered the l of Moab. He made the
9: 7 I will give you all the l that once belonged to your
9:10 and servants are to farm the l for him to produce
10: 2 But when David's ambassadors arrived in the l of
10: 6 of Maacah, and twelve thousand from the l of Tob.
15:23 There was deep sadness throughout the l as the
17:26 and the Israelite army set up camp in the l of
19:29 and Ziba will divide your l equally between you."
21:14 at the town of Zela in the l of Benjamin.
21:14 After that, God ended the famine in the l of Israel.
24: 2 "Take a census of all the people in the l—
24: 6 then to Gilead in the l of Tahtim-hodshi and to
24: 8 Having gone through the entire l, they completed
24:13 you choose three years of famine throughout the l,
24:13 or three days of severe plague throughout your l?
1Ki 4:10 including Socoh and all the l of Hepher.
4:19 Geber son of Uri, in the l of Gilead,
4:19 And there was one governor over the l of Judah.
4:21 from the Euphrates River to the l of the Philistines,
4:24 And there was peace throughout the entire l.
6: 1 were delivered from their slavery in the l of Egypt.
8: 9 of Israel as they were leaving the l of Egypt.
8:34 and return them to this l you gave their ancestors.
8:36 and send rain on your l that you have given to your
8:37 "If there is a famine in the l, or plagues, or crop
8:37 or if your people's enemies are in the l besieging
8:40 and walk in your ways as long as they live in the l
8:46 and take them captive to a foreign l far or near.
8:47 But in that l of exile, they may turn to you again in
8:48 and pray toward the l you gave to their ancestors,
9: 7 then I will uproot the people of Israel from this l I
9: 8 did the LORD do such terrible things to his l
9:11 Solomon gave twenty towns in the l of Galilee to
9:18 Baalath, and Tamar in the desert, within his l.
9:20 There were still some people living in the l who
9:26 a port near Elath in the l of Edom, along the shore
10:13 all her attendants left and returned to their own l.
10:15 all the kings of Arabia, and the governors of the l.
11:18 who gave them a home, food, and some l.
14:15 He will uproot the people of Israel from this good l
14:24 were even shrine prostitutes throughout the l.
14:24 had driven from the l ahead of the Israelites.
15:12 He banished the shrine prostitutes from the l
15:20 and all Kinnereth, with all the l of Naphtali.
17: 7 for there was no rainfall anywhere in the l.
18: 6 So they divided the l between them. Ahab went
20: 7 Then Ahab summoned all the leaders of the l
21:26 the people whom the LORD had driven from the l

22:46 He banished from the l the rest of the shrine
2Ki 2:19 But the water is bad, and the l is unproductive."
3:19 their springs, and ruin all their good l with stones."
3:24 The army of Israel chased them into the l of Moab,
3:25 covered their good l with stones, stopped up the
3:27 so they withdrew and returned to their own l.
4:38 returned to Gilgal, but there was a famine in the l.
5: 2 Now groups of Aramean raiders had invaded the l
6:23 the Aramean raiders stayed away from the l of
8: 2 and lived in the l of the Philistines for seven years.
8: 3 After the famine ended she returned to the l of
8: 3 to see the king about getting back her house and l.
9:10 Jezebel, at the plot of l in Jezreel, and no one will
9:36 'At the plot of l in Jezreel, dogs will eat Jezebel's
11: 3 for six years while Athaliah ruled over the l.
11:14 and people from all over the l were rejoicing
11:18 And all the people of the l went over to the temple
11:19 and all the people of the l escorted the king from
11:20 So all the people of the l rejoiced, and the city was
13:20 Groups of Moabite raiders used to invade the l
15: 5 royal palace, and he governed the people of the l.
15:19 Then King Tiglath-pileser of Assyria invaded the l.
15:20 from attacking Israel and did not stay in the l.
16: 3 had driven from the l ahead of the Israelites.
17: 5 Then the king of Assyria invaded the entire l,
17: 8 the LORD had driven from the l before them,
17:11 the LORD had driven from the l ahead of them.
17:18 Only the tribe of Judah remained in the l.
17:23 So Israel was carried off to the l of Assyria,
17:26 do not know how to worship the God of the l.
17:27 the religious customs of the God of the l."
18: 5 There was never another king like him in the l of
18:25 do you think we have invaded your l without the
18:32 Then I will arrange to take you to another l like
18:32 vineyards, olive trees and honey—a l of plenty.
19: 7 Then I will make him want to return to his l,
19:24 I have dug wells in many a foreign l
19:36 of Assyria broke camp and returned to his own l.
19:37 They then escaped to the l of Ararat, and another
20:14 "They came from the distant l of Babylon."
21: 2 had driven from the l ahead of the Israelites.
21: 8 I will not send them into exile from this l that I
21: 9 had destroyed when the Israelites entered the l.
21:11 than the Amorites, who lived in this l before Israel.
21:24 But the people of the l killed all those who had
22:19 that this l would be cursed and become desolate.
23:24 both in Jerusalem and throughout the l of Judah.
23:33 l of Hamath to prevent him from ruling from
24: 1 King Nebuchadnezzar of Babylon invaded the l of
24:14 So only the poorest people were left in the l.
25:21 And there at Riblah, in the l of Hamath, the king of
25:21 people of Judah were sent into exile from their l.
25:24 "Live in the l and serve the king of Babylon,
1Ch 1:45 Husham from the l of the Temanites became king.
1:46 destroyed the Midianite army in the l of Moab.
2:22 who ruled twenty-three towns in the l of Gilead.
4:40 pastures there, and the l was quiet and peaceful.
4:41 who lived there and took the l for themselves,
5: 9 since they had so many cattle in the l of Gilead,
5:11 Across from the Reubenites in the l of Bashan
5:12 Joel was the leader in the l of Bashan,
5:16 The Gadites lived in the l of Gilead, in Bashan
5:22 So they lived in their l until they were taken away
5:23 The half-tribe of Manasseh spread through the l
5:26 to invade the l and lead away the people of
8: 8 and Baara, he had children in the l of Moab.
10: 9 and to the people throughout the l of Philistia.
11: 4 the Jebusites, original inhabitants of the l, lived.
12:40 There was great joy throughout the l of Israel.
13: 2 send messages to all the Israelites throughout the l,
16:14 our God. / His rule is seen throughout the l.
16:18 "I will give you the l of Canaan / as your special
17: 9 It will be their own l where wicked nations won't
18: 2 David also conquered the l of Moab,
19: 2 But when David's ambassadors arrived in the l of
19: 3 David has sent them to spy out the l so that they
21: 2 "Take a census of all the people in the l—
21:12 brings devastation throughout the l of Israel.
26:31 of Hebron were found at Jazer in the l of Gilead.)
28: 8 so that you may possess this good l and leave it to
29:15 and strangers in the l as our ancestors were before
2Ch 2:17 Solomon took a census of all foreigners in the l of
3: 6 and with pure gold from the l of Parvaim.
6:25 and return them to this l you gave their ancestors.
6:27 and send rain on your l that you have given to your
6:28 "If there is a famine in the l, or plagues, or crop
6:28 or if your people's enemies are in the l besieging
6:31 and walk in your ways as long as they live in the l
6:36 and take them captive to a foreign l far or near.
6:37 But in that l of exile, they may turn to you again in
6:38 and pray toward the l you gave to their ancestors,
7:14 and will forgive their sins and heal their l.
7:20 then I will uproot the people of Israel from this l of
7:21 has the LORD done such terrible things to his l
8: 7 There were still some people living in the l who
8:17 to Ezion-geber and Elath, ports in the l of Edom,
8:18 These ships sailed to the l of Ophir with Solomon's
9:12 all her attendants left and returned to their own l.
9:14 and the governors of the l also brought gold
9:26 from the Euphrates River to the l of the Philistines
11:23 in the fortified cities throughout the l of Judah
12:12 And there was still goodness in the l of Judah.
14: 1 next king. There was peace in the l for ten years,
14: 7 The l is ours because we sought the LORD our
15: 8 and removed all the idols in the l of Judah
17: 2 and he assigned additional garrisons to the l of
19: 3 have removed the Asherah poles throughout the l,
20: 7 did you not drive out those who lived in this l
20: 7 And did you not give this l forever to the
20:11 For they have come to throw us out of your l,
20:31 So Jehoshaphat ruled over the l of Judah. He was
22:12 God for six years while Athaliah ruled over the l.
23:13 and people from all over the l were rejoicing
23:21 So all the people of the l rejoiced, and the city was
26:21 royal palace, and he governed the people of the l.
28: 3 had driven from the l ahead of the Israelites.
28:15 and took all the prisoners back to their own l—
30: 9 and they will be able to return to this l.
30:12 God's hand was on the people in the l of Judah,
30:25 the Levites, all who came from the l of Israel,
32:21 returned home in disgrace to his own l.
32:22 So there was peace at last throughout the l.
32:31 the remarkable events that had taken place in the l,
33: 2 had driven from the l ahead of the Israelites.
33: 8 I will not send them into exile from this l that I
33: 9 had destroyed when the Israelites entered the l.
33:25 But the people of the l killed all those who had
34: 7 He cut down the incense altars throughout the l of
34: 8 after he had purified the l and the Temple,
34:33 all detestable idols from the entire l of Israel
36: 1 Then the people of the l took Josiah's son Jehoahaz
36:21 The l finally enjoyed its Sabbath rest,
36:23 build him a Temple at Jerusalem in the l of Judah.
Ezr 1: 2 build him a Temple at Jerusalem in the l of Judah.
6:21 and by the others in the l who had turned from
6:22 There was great joy throughout the l
9: 1 separate from the other peoples living in the l.
9: 7 have been at the mercy of the pagan kings of the l.
9:11 Your servants the prophets warned us that the l we
9:11 one end to the other, the l is filled with corruption.
9:12 that we would enjoy the good produce of the l
10: 2 for we have married these pagan women of the l.
10:11 Separate yourselves from the people of the l
Ne 4: 4 they themselves become captives in a foreign l!
5:16 working on the wall and refused to acquire any l.
9: 8 and his descendants the l of the Canaanites,
9:11 your people so they could walk through on dry l!
9:15 and take possession of the l you had sworn to give
9:22 you placed your people in every corner of the l.
9:22 They completely took over the l of King Sihon of
Heshbon and the l of King Og of Bashan.
9:23 and brought them into the l you had promised to
9:24 They went in and took possession of the l.
9:24 who inhabited the l, were powerless!
9:25 Our ancestors captured fortified cities and fertile l.
9:30 the pagan inhabitants of the l to conquer them.
9:35 You gave them a large, fertile l, but they refused to
9:36 "So now today we are slaves here in the l of plenty
9:37 The lush produce of this l piles up in the hands of
10:28 the pagan people of the l in order to serve God,
10:30 let our daughters marry the pagan people of the l,
10:31 We further promise that if the people of the l
10:37 to the Levites a tenth of everything our l produces,
12:27 the Levites throughout the l were asked to come to
13:25 children intermarry with the pagan people of the l.
Est 8:17 And many of the people of the l became Jews
Job 1: 1 There was a man named Job who lived in the l of
10:21 before I leave for the l of darkness and utter gloom,
10:22 It is a l as dark as midnight, a l of utter gloom
15:19 those to whom the l was given long before any
22: 8 you think the l belongs to the powerful and that
24: 2 Evil people steal l by moving the boundary
31:38 "If my l accuses me and all its furrows weep
31:40 then let thistles grow on that l instead of wheat
38:26 Who makes the rain fall on barren l, in a desert
42:15 In all the l there were no other women as lovely as
Ps 10:16 those who worship other gods be swept from the l.
12: 8 strut about, / and evil is praised throughout the l.
16: 3 The godly people in the l / are my true heroes!
16: 6 The l you have given me is a pleasant l.
25:13 and their children will inherit the Promised L.
27:13 while I am here in the l of the living.
37: 3 Then you will live safely in the l and prosper.
37: 9 those who trust in the LORD will possess the l.
37:11 Those who are gentle and lowly will possess the l;
37:22 Those blessed by the LORD will inherit the l,
37:27 and do good, / and you will live in the l forever.
37:29 The godly will inherit the l / and will live there
37:34 his path. / He will honor you, giving you the l.
42: 6 source of the Jordan, / from the l of Mount Mizar.
44: 2 and gave all the l to our ancestors; / you crushed
44: 3 They did not conquer the l with their swords;
44:10 our enemies / and allow them to plunder our l.
47: 4 He chose the Promised L as our inheritance,
52: 5 and drag you from the l of the living. / *Interlude*
60: 2 You have shaken our l and split it open.
63: 1 in this parched and weary l / where there is no
68: 9 O God, / to refresh the weary Promised L.
69:35 people will live there / and take possession of the l.
69:36 of those who obey him will inherit the l,
72:16 May there be abundant crops throughout the l,
74:20 for the l is full of darkness and violence!
78:51 the flower of youth throughout the l of Egypt.
78:54 He brought them to the border of his holy l, / to
this l of hills he had won for them.
79: 1 O God, pagan nations have conquered your l,
79: 7 people Israel, / making the l a desolate wilderness.
80: 8 the pagan nations and transplanted us into your l.
80: 9 ground for us, / and we took root and filled the l.
81:10 your God, / who rescued you from the l of Egypt.
85: 1 you have poured out amazing blessings on your l!
85: 9 who honor him; / our l will be filled with his glory.
85:12 his blessings. / Our l will yield its bountiful crops.
88:12 Can anyone in the l of forgetfulness talk about
95: 5 for he made it. / His hands formed the dry l, too.
105: 7 our God. / His rule is seen throughout the l.
105:11 "I will give you the l of Canaan / as your special
105:16 He called for a famine on the l of Canaan,
105:23 Jacob lived as a foreigner in the l of Ham.
105:27 the Egyptians, / and miracles in the l of Ham.
105:30 Then frogs overran the l; / they were found even in
105:32 and flashes of lightning overwhelmed the l.
105:35 They ate up everything green in the l,
105:41 to form a river through the dry and barren l.
106:14 ran wild, / testing God's patience in that dry l.
106:22 such wonderful things in that l, / such awesome
106:24 The people refused to enter the pleasant l,
106:34 Israel failed to destroy the nations in the l,
106:38 idols of Canaan, / they polluted the l with murder.
107:33 rivers into deserts, / and springs of water into dry l.
107:34 He turns the fruitful l into salty wastelands,
107:35 into pools of water, / the dry l into flowing springs.
114: 1 when the family of Jacob left that foreign l—
114: 2 the l of Judah became God's sanctuary, / and Israel
135:12 He gave their l as an inheritance, / a special
136:21 God gave the l of these kings as an inheritance—
137: 4 sing the songs of the LORD / while in a foreign l?
140:11 Don't let liars prosper here in our l.
143: 6 I thirst for you as parched l thirsts for rain.
Pr 2:21 For only the upright will live in the l, and those
2:22 But the wicked will be removed from the l,
3: 9 and with the best part of everything your l
10:30 but the wicked will be removed from the l.
23:10 Don't steal the l of defenseless orphans by moving
26: 2 an unfair curse will not l on its intended victim.
Ecc 5: 8 and justice being miscarried throughout the l,
5: 9 Even the king milks the l for his own profit!
10:16 Destruction is certain for the l whose king is a
10:17 Happy is the l whose king is a nobleman
Isa 2: 8 The l is filled with idols. The people bow down
4: 2 and the fruit of the l will be the pride of its people.
4: 5 and clouds of fire at night, covering the glorious l.
5: 2 He plowed the l, cleared its stones, / and planted it
5: 8 built on great estates so you can be alone in the l.
6:12 distant lands and the entire l of Israel lies deserted.
7:19 come in vast hordes, spreading across the whole l.
7:20 off everything: your l, your crops, and your people.
7:22 The few people still left in the l will live on curds
7:22 wild honey because that is all the l will produce.
7:24 The entire l will be one vast brier patch, a hunting
8: 8 It will submerge Immanuel's l from one end to the
9: 1 The l of Zebulun and Naphtali will soon be
9: 2 a light that will shine on all who live in the l where
9:10 "Our l lies in ruins now, but we will rebuild it
9:19 The l is blackened by the fury of the LORD
10: 3 when I send desolation upon you from a distant l?
10: 8 princes will soon be a king, ruling a conquered l.
11:10 for the l where he lives will be a glorious place.
11:11 returning them to the l of Israel from Assyria,
13: 5 his anger with them and will destroy the whole l.
13: 9 The l will be destroyed and all the sinners with it.
13:20 and go, but the l will never again be lived in.
14: 1 bring them back to settle once again in their own l.
14: 2 and those who come to live in their l will serve
14: 7 But at last the l is at rest and is quiet. Finally it can
14:21 Do not let them rise and conquer the l or rebuild
14:23 I will make Babylon into a desolate l, a place of
14:23 I will sweep the l with the broom of destruction.
15: 8 The whole l of Moab is a l of weeping from
16: 6 the proud l we have heard so much about?
16: 7 The entire l of Moab weeps. Yes, you people of
17: 4 Israel will be very dim, for poverty will stalk the l.
18: 1 Destruction is certain for the l of Ethiopia,
18: 2 Take a message to your l divided by rivers, to your
18: 7 will receive gifts from this l divided by rivers,
19:13 The leaders of Egypt have ruined the l with their
19:14 They cause the l of Egypt to stagger like a sick
19:20 and a witness to the LORD Almighty in the l of
19:25 my people. Blessed be Assyria, the l I have made.
21: 1 This message came to me concerning the l of
22:18 a ball and toss you away into a distant, barren l.
23:13 at the l of Babylonia—the people of that l are gone!
24:11 lowest ebb. Gladness has been banished from the l.
25: 5 You cool the l with the shade of a cloud.
25: 8 all insults and mockery against his l and people.
26: 1 everyone in the l of Judah will sing this song:
27: 8 He has exiled her from her l as though blown away
28:12 God's people could have rest in their own l if they
28:25 barley, and spelt, each in its own section of his l?
32: 2 cool shadow of a large rock in a hot and weary l.
32:13 For your l will be overgrown with thorns
32:17 Quietness and confidence will fill the l forever.
33: 9 All the l of Israel is in trouble. Lebanon has been
33:17 and you will see a l that stretches into the distance.
34: 3 and the stench of rotting bodies will fill the l.
34: 7 The l will be soaked with blood and the soil
34:10 The l will lie deserted from generation to
34:11 For God will bring chaos and destruction to that l.
34:12 It will be called the L of Nothing, and its princes
34:17 He has surveyed and divided the l and deeded it
35: 7 and springs of water will satisfy the thirsty l.
35: 8 a main road will go through that once deserted l.
36:10 do you think we have invaded your l without the
36:17 Then I will arrange to take you to another l like
36:17 and wine, bread and vineyards—a l of plenty.
37: 7 Then I will make him want to return to his l,
37:25 I have dug wells in many a foreign l
37:37 of Assyria broke camp and returned to his own l.
37:38 They then escaped to the l of Ararat, and another
38:11 while still in the l of the living. / Never again will I
39: 3 "They came from the distant l of Babylon."

41:19 myrtle, olive, cypress, fir, and pine—on barren l.
42:15 I will turn the rivers into dry l / and will dry up all
46:11 a leader from a distant l who will come and do my
49: 8 This will prove that I will reestablish the l of Israel
49:19 "Even the most desolate parts of your abandoned l
57:13 But whoever trusts in me will possess the l
60:18 Violence will disappear from your l; the desolation
60:21 They will possess their l forever, for I will plant
62: 4 be called the Godforsaken City or the Desolate L.
62:11 The LORD has sent this message to every l:
65: 9 the people of Israel and of Judah to possess my l.
Jer 1: 1 priests from Anathoth, a town in the l of Benjamin.
1:14 from the north will boil out on the people of this l.
2: 6 a l of deserts and pits, of drought and death,
2: 7 "And when I brought you into a fruitful l to enjoy
2: 7 you defiled my l and corrupted the inheritance I
2:10 west to the l of Cyprus; go east to the l of Kedar.
2:15 The l has been destroyed, and the cities are now in
2:23 you say that? Go and look in any valley in the l!
2:31 Have I been to them a l of darkness? Why then do
3: 1 her back again, for that would surely corrupt the l.
3: 2 Is there anywhere in the entire l where you have
3: 2 You have polluted the l with your prostitution
3: 9 and stone. So now the l has been greatly defiled.
3:14 I will bring you again to the l of Israel—one from
3:16 "And when your l is once more filled with
3:18 They will return to the l I gave their ancestors as an
3:19 nothing more than to give you this beautiful l—
4: 5 Tell them to sound the alarm throughout the l:
4: 7 a destroyer of nations. And it is headed for your l!
4:16 'The enemy is coming from a distant l, raising a
4:20 Waves of destruction roll over the l, until it lies in
4:27 "The whole l will be ruined, but I will not destroy
5:19 and gave yourselves to foreign gods in your own l.
5:19 Now you will serve foreigners in a l that is not
5:30 and shocking thing has happened in this l—
6: 8 Jerusalem! If you do not listen, I will empty the l."
6:12 For I will punish the people of this l,"
7: 3 your evil ways, I will let you stay in your own l.
7: 7 Then I will let you stay in this l that I gave to your
7:34 of Judah. The l will lie in complete desolation.
8:16 be heard all the way from the l of Dan in the north!
8:16 The whole l trembles at the approach of the terrible
8:16 for it is coming to devour the l and everything in
8:19 of my people; it can be heard all across the l.
9:12 Why has the l been ruined so completely that no
9:19 We must leave our l, because our homes have
10:18 I will fling you from this l and pour great troubles
10:25 people Israel, making the l a desolate wilderness.
11: 5 to your ancestors to give you a l flowing with milk
11: 5 the l you live in today.' " Then I replied, "So be
11: 6 Go from town to town throughout the l and say,
12: 4 How long must this l weep? Even the grass in the
12: 4 birds have disappeared because of the evil in the l.
12:11 The whole l is desolate, and no one even cares.
12:12 Destroying armies plunder the l. The sword of the
13:13 I will make everyone in this l so confused that they
14: 8 Why are you like someone passing through the l,
15:14 enemies to take them as captives to a foreign l.
16: 6 Both the great and the lowly will die in this l.
16: 9 an end to the happy singing and laughter in this l.
16:13 So I will throw you out of this l and send you into
a foreign l where you
16:14 who rescued the people of Israel from the l of
16:15 Israel back to their own l from the l of the north
16:15 For I will bring them back to this l that I gave their
16:18 because they have defiled my l with lifeless images
17: 3 to your enemies, for sin runs rampant in your l.
17: 4 and I will send you away as captives to a foreign l.
18:16 Therefore, their l will become desolate,
22:10 For he will never return to see his native l again.
22:12 He will die in a distant l and never again see his
22:26 I will expel you and your mother from this l,
22:27 You will never again return to the l of your desire.
23: 5 He will do what is just and right throughout the l.
23: 7 who rescued the people of Israel from the l of
23: 8 Israel back to their own l from the l of the north
23: 8 exiled them.' Then they will live in their own l."
23:10 For the l is full of adultery, and it lies under a
23:10 The l itself is in mourning—its pastures are dried
23:15 of Jerusalem's prophets that wickedness fills this l.
24: 5 I sent from Judah to the l of the Babylonians.
24:10 and disease until they have vanished from the l of
25: 5 then will I let you live in this l that the LORD
25: 9 I will bring them all against this l and its people
25:11 This entire l will become a desolate wasteland.
25:20 along with all the foreigners living in that l. So did
all the kings of the l of Uz and the kings of
25:30 'The LORD will roar loudly against his own l
25:38 and their l will be made desolate by the sword of
27:10 and I will drive you from your l and send you far
27:11 to stay in their own country to farm the l as usual.
27:15 lies in my name, so I will drive you from this l.
29:14 sent you and bring you home again to your own l."
30: 3 I will bring them home to this l that I gave to their
30:10 and will have peace and quiet in their own l,
31:16 come back to you from the distant l of the enemy.
31:17 "Your children will come again to their own l.
31:32 by the hand and brought them out of the l of Egypt.
32: 8 "Buy my field at Anathoth in the l of Benjamin.
32:15 people will again own property here in this l
32:20 miraculous signs and wonders in the l of Egypt—
32:22 You gave the people of Israel this l that you had
32:22 long before—a l flowing with milk and honey.
32:41 and wholeheartedly replant them in this l.
32:43 and sold in this l about which you now say,
32:43 a l where people and animals have all
32:44 in the l of Benjamin and here in Jerusalem,
33:10 You say, 'This l has been ravaged, and the people
33:11 For I will restore the prosperity of this l to what it
33:12 This l—though it is now desolate and the people
33:13 foothills of Judah, the Negev, the l of Benjamin,
33:15 he will do what is just and right throughout the l.
33:26 I will restore them to their l and have mercy on
35: 7 you will live long, good lives in the l.'
35:15 so that you might live in peace here in the l I gave
36:29 it said the king of Babylon would destroy this l
37: 2 l listened to what the LORD said through
37:12 to leave the city on his way to the l of Benjamin,
39: 5 of Babylon, who was at Riblah in the l of Hamath.
40: 2 your God has brought this disaster on this l,
40: 4 The whole l is before you—go wherever you like.
40: 6 in Judah with the few who were still left in the l.
40:10 Settle in any town you wish, and live off the l.
41:10 with him, he started back toward the l of Ammon.
41:15 men escaped from Johanan into the l of Ammon.
42:10 'Stay here in this l. If you do, I will build you up
42:12 him kind, so he will let you stay here in your l.'
43:11 And when he comes, he will destroy the l of Egypt.
43:12 He will pick clean the l of Egypt as a shepherd
44:22 doing that he made your l an object of cursing—
44:26 be spoken by any of the Judeans in the l of Egypt.
46: 7 the Nile River at floodtime, overflowing all the l?
46:26 But afterward the l will recover from the ravages
47: 2 flood is coming from the north to overflow the l.
47: 2 It will destroy the l and everything in it—cities
47: 2 scream in terror, and everyone in the l will weep.
48:40 "An eagle swoops down on the l of Moab,"
48:45 to devour the entire l with all its rebellious people.
49: 1 Are there no descendants of Israel to inherit the l
49: 2 will come and take back the l you took from her,"
49: 5 "Your neighbors will chase you from your l,
49:10 But I will strip bare the l of Edom, and there will
49:19 I will chase Edom from its l, and I will appoint the
50: 1 concerning Babylon and the l of the Babylonians.
50: 8 flee from Babylon! Leave the l of the Babylonians.
50:12 least of nations—a wilderness, a dry and desolate l.
50:18 "Now I will punish the king of Babylon and his l,
50:19 And I will bring Israel home again to her own l,
50:21 against the l of Merathaim and against the people
50:21 the l of rebels, a l that I will judge!
50:22 "Let the battle cry be heard in the l, a shout of
50:32 O l of pride, you will stumble and fall, and no one
50:38 Because the whole l is filled with idols,
50:44 I will chase Babylon from its l, and I will appoint
50:45 plans against Babylon and the l of the Babylonians.
51: 4 They will fall dead in the l of the Babylonians,
51: 5 even though their l was filled with sin against the
51: 9 Return now to your own l, for her judgment will be
51:47 Her whole l will be disgraced, and her dead will lie
51:50 the LORD, even though you are in a far-off l,
51:52 her wounded people will be heard throughout the l.
51:54 the sound of great destruction from the l of the
52: 9 in the l of Hamath, where sentence was passed
52:27 And there at Riblah in the l of Hamath, the king of
52:27 people of Judah were sent into exile from their l.
La 2: 3 He consumes the whole l of Israel like a raging
4:21 Are you rejoicing in the l of Uz, O people of
Eze 1: 3 there beside the Kebar River in the l of the
5:17 Disease and war will stalk your l, and I will bring
7: 2 east, west, north, or south—your l is finished.
7:22 my eyes as these robbers invade my treasured l
7:23 my people, for the l is bloodied by terrible crimes.
8:12 LORD doesn't see us; he has deserted our l!' "
9: 9 The entire l is full of murder; the city is filled with
9: 9 doesn't see it! The LORD has forsaken the l!'
11:15 the LORD, so now he has given their l to us!'
11:17 and I will give you the l of Israel once again.
12:13 the l of the Babylonians, though he will never see
12:19 because their l will be stripped bare on account of
13: 9 and they will never again see their own l.
14:15 of dangerous wild animals to devastate the l
14:16 would be saved, but the l would be devastated.
14:17 "Or suppose I were to bring war against the l,
14:18 Even if these three men were in the l,
14:19 fury by sending an epidemic of disease into the l,
15: 8 And I will make the l desolate because my people
16:29 by embracing that great merchant l of Babylonia—
17:16 the l of the king who put him in power and whose
18: 2 "Why do you quote this proverb in the l of Israel:
19: 4 They led him away in chains / to the l of Egypt.
19: 7 Everyone in the l trembled in fear / when they
20: 6 and her descendants out of Egypt to a l I had
20: 6 a good l, a l flowing with milk and honey,
20:15 I would not bring them into the l I had given them,
20:15 a l flowing with milk and honey, the most beautiful
20:28 for when I brought them into the l I had promised
20:38 are in exile, but they will never enter the l of Israel.
20:42 Then when I have brought you home to the l I
21: 4 I will make a clean sweep throughout the l from
21:30 you in your own country, the l of your birth.
21:32 and your blood will be spilled in your own l.
22:25 They increase the number of widows in the l.
22:30 rebuild the wall of righteousness that guards the l.
22:30 gap in the wall so I wouldn't have to destroy the l,
23:10 Her name was known to every woman in the l as a
23:15 They were dressed like chariot officers from the l
23:48 I will put an end to lewdness and idolatry in the l,
25: 2 look toward the l of Ammon and prophesy against
25: 4 camps among you and pitch their tents on your l.
25: 5 and all the l of the Ammonites into an enclosure
25:16 I will raise my fist of judgment against the l of the
26:20 a position of respect here in the l of the living.
27: 9 Ships came with goods from every l to barter for
28:25 The people of Israel will again live in their own l,
the l I gave my servant Jacob.
29: 4 and drag you out on the l with fish sticking to your
29: 9 The l of Egypt will become a desolate wasteland,
29:10 I will utterly destroy the l of Egypt, from Migdol to
29:14 and bring its people back to the l of Pathros in
29:19 I will give the l of Egypt to Nebuchadnezzar,
29:20 I have given him the l of Egypt as a reward for his
30: 4 The l of Ethiopia will be ravished.
30:11 the nations—have been sent to demolish the l.
30:12 the Nile River and hand the l over to wicked men.
30:12 I will destroy the l of Egypt and everything in it,
30:13 left in Egypt; anarchy will prevail throughout the l!
30:25 and he brings it against the l of Egypt,
31:12 the mountains and valleys and ravines of the l.
31:14 They will l in the pit along with all the proud
32: 4 I will leave you stranded on the l to die.
32: 4 All the birds of the heavens will l on you,
32: 8 I will bring darkness everywhere across your l.
33: 2 a country, the people of that l choose a watchman.
33:24 and yet he gained possession of the entire l!
33:24 surely the l should be given to us as a possession.'
33:25 Do you really think the l should be yours?
33:26 Idolaters! Adulterers! Should the l belong to you?
33:28 I will destroy the l and demolish her pride.
33:29 When I have ruined the l because of their
34:13 I will bring them back home to their own l of Israel
34:25 and drive away the dangerous animals from the l.
34:29 "And I will give them a l famous for its crops,
36: 5 by gleefully taking my l for themselves as plunder.
36:13 saying, 'Israel is a l that devours her own people!'
36:17 the people of Israel were living in their own l,
36:18 They polluted the l with murder and by worshiping
36:20 and he couldn't keep them safe in his own l!'
36:24 all the nations and bring you home again to your l.
36:28 live in Israel, the l I gave your ancestors long ago.
36:29 you good crops, and I will abolish famine in the l.
36:30 nations be able to scoff at your l for its famines.
36:35 'This godforsaken l is now like Eden's garden!
37:12 Then I will bring you back to the l of Israel.
37:14 and you will live and return home to your own l.
37:21 I will bring them home to their own l from the
37:22 I will unify them into one nation in the l. One king
37:25 They will live in the l of Israel where their
ancestors lived, the l I gave my servant Jacob.
37:26 I will give them their l and multiply them, and I
38: 2 of man, prophesy against Gog of the l of Magog,
38: 8 In the distant future you will swoop down on the l
38: 9 on them like a storm and cover the l like a cloud.
38:11 'Israel is an unprotected l filled with unwalled
38:14 When my people are living in peace in their l,
38:16 and you will cover the l like a cloud. This will
38:16 I will bring you against my l as everyone watches,
38:18 But when Gog invades the l of Israel,
38:19 I promise a mighty shaking in the l of Israel on that
39:12 of Israel to cleanse the l by burying the bodies.
39:14 special crews will be appointed to search the l for
39:14 to bury them, so the l will be made clean again.
39:16 And so the l will finally be cleansed.
39:26 home to live in peace and safety in their own l.
40: 2 In a vision of God he took me to the l of Israel
45: 1 "When you divide the l among the tribes of Israel,
45: 1 This piece of l will be 8-1/3 miles long and 6-2/3
45: 2 A section of this l, measuring 875 feet by 875 feet,
45: 2 An additional strip of l 87-1/2 feet wide is to be
45: 3 measure out a portion of l 8-1/3 miles long
45: 4 This area will be a holy l, set aside for the priests
45: 5 The strip of sacred l next to it, also 8-1/3 miles
45: 6 sacred area will be a section of l 8-1/3 miles long
45: 7 "Two special sections of l will be set apart for the
45: 8 These sections of l will be the prince's allotment.
45: 8 they will assign the rest of the l to the people,
45: 9 Quit robbing and cheating my people out of their l!
46:16 If the prince gives a gift of l to one of his sons,
46:17 But if he gives a gift of l to one of his servants,
46:17 will be set free, and the l will return to the prince.
46:18 property to his sons, it must be from his own l,
47:13 "Follow these instructions for dividing the l for
47:13 The tribe of Joseph will be given two shares of l.
47:14 I swore that I would give this l to your ancestors,
47:21 "Divide the l within these boundaries among the
47:22 Distribute the l as an inheritance for yourselves
47:23 All these immigrants are to be given l within the
48: 1 Dan's territory extends all the way across the l of
48: 3 Naphtali's l lies south of Asher's, also extending
48: 8 "South of Judah is the l set aside for a special
48:10 For the priests there will be a strip of l measuring
48:12 when the l is distributed, the most sacred l of all.
48:12 Next to the priests' territory will lie the l where the
48:13 The l allotted to the Levites will be the same size
48:13 Together these portions of l will measure 8-1/3
48:14 None of this special l will ever be sold or traded
48:15 "An additional strip of l 8-1/3 miles long by 1-2/3
48:22 So the prince's l will include everything between
48:23 and it extends across the entire l of Israel from east
48:24 also extending across the l from east to west.
48:26 which also extends across the l from east to west.
Da 1: 2 the treasure-house of his god in the l of Babylonia.
8: 5 crossing the l so swiftly that it didn't even touch
8: 9 and the east and toward the glorious l of Israel.
9: 6 and ancestors and to all the people of the l.
11: 9 king of the south but will soon return to his own l.
11:16 He will pause in the glorious l of Israel, intent on
11:18 But a commander from another l will put an end to
11:24 warning he will enter the richest areas of the l
11:39 and dividing the l among them as their reward.
11:41 He will enter the glorious l of Israel, and many

Hos 1:11 when God will again plant his people in his **l**.
2:18 I will remove all weapons of war from the **l**,
4:1 no kindness, no knowledge of God in your **l**.
4:3 That is why your **l** is not producing. It is filled with
9:3 You may no longer stay here in this **l** of the
9:15 I will drive them from my **l** because of their evil
12:12 Jacob fled to the **l** of Aram and earned a wife by
13:5 of you in the wilderness, in that dry and thirsty **l**.
13:10 Where are all the leaders of the **l**? You asked for
13:15 against the people of Ephraim, drying up their **l**.
14:7 My people will return again to the safety of their **l**.
Joel 1:6 A vast army of locusts has invaded my **l**. It is a
2:3 Ahead of them the **l** lies as fair as the Garden of
2:18 his people and be indignant for the honor of his **l**!
2:20 stench of their rotting bodies will rise over the **l**."
3:2 among the nations, and for dividing up my **l**.
Am 2:2 So I will send down fire on the **l** of Moab, and all
2:9 the Amorites before my people arrived in the **l**.
2:10 so you could possess the **l** of the Amorites.
5:8 from the oceans and pours it down as rain on the **l**.
5:27 to a **l** east of Damascus," says the LORD,
6:14 "It will oppress you bitterly throughout your **l**—
7:1 to send a vast swarm of locusts over the **l**.
7:4 depths of the sea and was devouring the entire **l**.
7:10 It will lead to rebellion all across the **l**.
7:12 Go on back to the **l** of Judah and do your preaching
7:17 Your **l** will be divided up, and you yourself will
die in a foreign **l**.
8:8 The **l** will rise up like the Nile River at floodtime,
8:11 "when I will send a famine on the **l**—
9:5 the LORD Almighty, touches the **l** and it melts,
9:6 from the oceans and pours it down as rain on the **l**.
9:15 I will firmly plant them there in the **l** I have given
Ob 1:1 revealed to Obadiah concerning the **l** of Edom.
1:7 They will help to chase you from your **l**. They will
1:8 wise person will be left in the whole **l** of Edom!"
1:13 You shouldn't have plundered the **l** of Israel when
1:19 And the people of Benjamin will occupy the **l** of
1:20 The exiles of Israel will return to their **l**
Jnh 1:9 the God of heaven, who made the sea and the **l**."
2:6 out of life and imprisoned in the **l** of the dead.
Mic 2:2 When you want a certain piece of **l**, you find a way
2:4 God has confiscated our **l**, / taking it from us.
2:5 people will have no say in how the **l** is divided.
2:10 This is no longer your **l** and home, for you have
2:12 your **l** will again be filled with noisy crowds!
2:13 of your cities of captivity, back to your own **l**.
5:3 countrymen will return from exile to their own **l**.
5:5 When the Assyrians invade our **l** and break
5:6 and enter the gates of the **l** of Nimrod.
5:6 when they pour over the borders to invade our **l**.
7:13 But the **l** will become empty and desolate
Na 1:15 from Nineveh will never invade your **l** again.
2:2 For the **l** of Israel lies empty and broken after your
3:9 and the **l** of Egypt were the source of her strength,
3:13 The gates of your **l** will be opened wide to the
3:16 of locusts, they strip the **l** and then fly away.
Hab 3:12 You marched across the **l** in awesome anger
Zep 1:2 "I will sweep away everything in all your **l**,"
1:18 For the whole **l** will be devoured by the fire of his
2:5 who live along the coast and in the **l** of Canaan,
2:9 Their **l** will become a place of stinging nettles,
2:9 who are left will plunder them and take their **l**."
2:11 will terrify them as he destroys all the gods in the **l**.
2:11 will worship the LORD, each in their own **l**.
Hag 2:2 and to the remnant of God's people there in the **l**:
2:4 Take courage, all you people still left in the **l**,
2:6 the earth. I will shake the oceans and the dry **l**, too.
Zec 2:12 The **l** of Judah will be the LORD's inheritance in
the holy **l**,
3:9 and I will remove the sins of this **l** in a single day.
5:3 the curse that is going out over the entire **l**.
5:3 that those who steal will be banished from the **l**;
5:3 who swear falsely will be banished from the **l**.
5:6 filled with the sins of everyone throughout the **l**."
5:11 "To the **l** of Babylonia where they will build a
7:14 Their **l** became so desolate that no one even
7:14 The **l** that had been so pleasant became a desert."
9:1 This is the message from the LORD against the **l**
9:8 oppressor will ever again overrun my people's **l**.
9:16 They will sparkle in his **l** like jewels in a crown.
11:6 no longer have pity on the inhabitants of the **l**,"
11:6 They will turn the **l** into a wilderness, and I will
13:2 rid of every trace of idol worship throughout the **l**,
13:2 I will remove from the **l** all false prophets
13:8 Two-thirds of the people in the **l** will be cut off
13:8 says the LORD. But a third will be left in the **l**.
14:10 All the **l** from Geba, north of Judah, to Rimmon,
Mal 1:4 Their country will be known as 'The **L** of
3:12 for your **l** will be such a delight," says the LORD
4:6 I will come and strike the **l** with a curse."
Mt 2:20 take the child and his mother back to the **l** of Israel,
4:15 "In the **l** of Zebulun and of Naphtali,
4:16 And for those who lived in the **l** where death casts
8:10 I haven't seen faith like this in all the **l** of Israel!
8:28 the other side of the lake in the **l** of the Gadarenes,
12:42 because she came from a distant **l** to hear the
14:13 was headed and followed by **l** from many villages.
14:24 the disciples were in trouble far away from **l**,
23:15 For you cross **l** and sea to make one convert,
27:45 darkness fell across the whole **l** until three o'clock.
Mk 5:1 the other side of the lake, in the **l** of the Gerasenes.
6:47 in the middle of the lake, and Jesus was alone on **l**.
15:33 darkness fell across the whole **l** until three o'clock.
Lk 4:25 for three and a half years and hunger stalked the **l**.
4:26 widow of Zarephath—a foreigner in the **l** of Sidon.
7:9 I haven't seen faith like this in all the **l** of Israel!"
8:26 So they arrived in the **l** of the Gerasenes,
11:31 because she came from a distant **l** to hear the
15:13 all his belongings and took a trip to a distant **l**,
15:14 a great famine swept over the **l**, and he began to
21:23 For there will be great distress in the **l** and wrath
23:44 and darkness fell across the whole **l** until three
Jn 1:11 Even in his own **l** and among his own people,
Ac 4:34 because people who owned **l** or houses sold them
5:8 price you and your husband received for your **l**?"
7:3 told him, 'Leave your native **l** and your relatives,
7:3 and come to the **l** that I will show you.'
7:4 So Abraham left the **l** of the Chaldeans and lived in
7:4 Then God brought him here to the **l** where you
7:5 no inheritance here, not even one square foot of **l**.
7:29 and lived as a foreigner in the **l** of Midian,
7:45 the Gentile nations that God drove out of this **l**,
13:19 and gave their **l** to Israel as an inheritance.
20:13 Paul went by **l** to Assos, where he had arranged for
27:27 the Sea of Adria, the sailors sensed **l** was near.
27:43 could swim to jump overboard first and make for **l**,
Ro 13:2 So those who refuse to obey the laws of the **l** are
Heb 4:8 This new place of rest was not the **l** of Canaan,
8:9 by the hand / and led them out of the **l** of Egypt.
11:8 and go to another **l** that God would give him as his
11:9 And even when he reached the **l** God promised
11:27 It was by faith that Moses left the **l** of Egypt.
Jude 1:12 They are like clouds blowing over dry **l** without
Rev 7:2 four angels who had been given power to injure **l**
7:3 Don't hurt the **l** or the sea or the trees until we
10:2 his right foot on the sea and his left foot on the **l**.
10:5 the sea and on the **l** lifted his right hand to heaven.
10:8 the angel who is standing on the sea and on the **l**."

LAND'S (3) [LAND]

Lev 25:7 animals will also be allowed to eat of the **l** bounty.
27:18 the priest must assess the **l** value in proportion to
27:19 you must pay the **l** value as assessed by the priest,

LANDED (9) [LAND]

Jdg 9:53 a woman on the roof threw down a millstone that **l**
Mt 14:34 they had crossed the lake, they **l** at Gennesaret.
Mk 6:33 ran ahead along the shore and met them as they **l**.
Lk 5:11 And as soon as they **l**, they left everything
Jn 6:23 Several boats from Tiberias **l** near the place where
Ac 16:11 of Samothrace, and the next day we **l** at Neapolis.
20:17 But when we **l** at Miletus, he sent a message to the
21:3 it on our left, and **l** at the harbor of Tyre, in Syria,
28:7 Near the shore where we **l** was an estate belonging

LANDING (2) [LAND]

Ac 13:13 by ship for Pamphylia, **l** at the port town of Perga.
27:5 the provinces of Cilicia and Pamphylia, **l** at Myra,

LANDMARK [KJV] See (BOUNDARY) MARKER

LANDOWNER (2) [LAND]

Mt 21:33 A certain **l** planted a vineyard, built a wall around
21:36 So the **l** sent a larger group of his servants to

LANDS (103) [LAND]

Ge 10:5 became the seafaring peoples in various **l**,
26:4 as the stars, and I will give them all these **l**.
41:57 And people from surrounding **l** also came to Egypt
Ex 23:27 "I will send my terror upon all the people whose **l**
Lev 25:10 when each of you returns to the **l** that belonged to
25:13 return to the **l** that belonged to your ancestors.
26:39 Those still left alive will rot away in enemy **l**
Nu 32:1 So when they saw that the **l** of Jazer and Gilead
32:33 the whole land with its towns and surrounding **l**.
35:3 and the surrounding **l** will provide pasture for their
Dt 29:16 and how we traveled through the **l** of enemy
29:22 and the foreigners who come from distant **l**,
32:8 When the Most High assigned **l** to the nations,
2Sa 10:6 Aramean mercenaries from the **l** of Beth-rehob
1Ki 4:21 The conquered peoples of those **l** sent tribute
8:41 and come from distant **l** to worship your great
1Ch 4:10 "Oh, that you would bless me and extend my **l**!
22:9 peace with his enemies in all the surrounding **l**.
26:30 were put in charge of the Israelite **l** west of the
27:26 of the field workers who farmed the king's **l**.
2Ch 6:32 and they come from distant **l** to worship your great
Ezr 4:10 and throughout the neighboring **l** of the province
Ne 5:17 at my table, besides all the visitors from other **l**!
Ps 45:16 You will make them rulers over many **l**.
105:44 He gave his people the **l** of pagan nations,
106:27 among the nations, / exiling them to distant **l**.
107:3 For he has gathered the exiles from many **l**,
111:6 his people / by giving them the **l** of other nations.
Isa 6:12 the LORD has sent everyone away to distant **l**
10:13 By my own strength I have captured many **l**,
11:14 They will occupy all the **l** of Edom, Moab,
13:14 rushing back to their own **l** like hunted deer,
19:23 and Assyrians will move freely between their **l**,
23:1 O ships of Tarshish, returning home from distant **l**!
23:7 Think of all the colonists you sent to distant **l**.
24:15 In eastern **l**, give glory to the LORD.
25:2 Beautiful palaces in distant **l** disappear and will
41:1 "Listen in silence before me, you **l** beyond the sea.
41:5 The **l** beyond the sea watch in fear. Remote **l**
tremble and mobilize for war.
42:4 Even distant **l** beyond the sea will wait for his
49:1 Listen to me, all of you in far-off **l**! The LORD
49:12 from **l** to the north and west, and from as far south
59:18 evil deeds. His fury will fall on his foes in distant **l**.
60:4 Your sons are coming from distant **l**; your little
60:5 to you. They will bring you the wealth of many **l**.
60:11 around the clock to receive the wealth of many **l**.
66:19 and to all the **l** beyond the sea that have not heard
Jer 6:22 A great nation is rising against you from far-off **l**.
9:16 the world, and they will be strangers in distant **l**.
12:14 I will uproot them from their **l** just as Judah will be
12:15 I will bring them home to their own **l** again,
22:28 are he and his children to be exiled to distant **l**?
25:11 and her neighboring **l** will serve the king of
30:10 For I will bring you home again from distant **l**,
46:27 For I will bring you home again from distant **l**,
48:7 his priests and princes, will be exiled to distant **l**!
50:16 sword of the enemy and rush back to their own **l**.
50:26 Yes, come against her from distant **l**. Break open
50:37 her allies from other **l** will become as weak as
50:41 many kings are rising against you from far-off **l**.
51:58 The builders from many **l** have worked in vain,
La 1:5 have been captured and taken away to distant **l**.
1:18 and daughters have been taken captive to distant **l**.
2:9 Her kings and princes have been exiled to distant **l**;
4:15 So they fled to distant **l** and wandered there among
Eze 4:13 Israel will eat defiled bread in the Gentile **l**,
12:4 do when they begin a long march to distant **l**.
20:6 with milk and honey, the best of all **l** anywhere.
20:34 and fury I will bring you out from the **l** where you
23:40 "You sisters sent messengers to distant **l** to get
28:25 For I will gather them from the distant **l** where I
29:12 I will scatter the Egyptians to distant **l**.
30:23 I will scatter the Egyptians to many **l** throughout
32:10 Yes, I will bring terror to many **l**, and their kings
34:21 hungry flock until they are scattered to distant **l**.
35:10 you said, 'The **l** of Israel and Judah will be ours.
36:19 I scattered them to many **l** to punish them for the
38:8 and after the return of her people from many **l**.
39:27 When I bring them home from the **l** of their
45:7 will share a border with the east side of the sacred **l**
45:7 and western borders of the prince's **l** will line up
48:15 homes, pasturelands, and common **l**, with a city at
48:17 Open **l** will surround the city for 150 yards in
48:20 entire area—including the sacred **l** and the city—
48:21 to the east and to the west of the sacred **l**
48:22 except for the areas set aside for the sacred **l**
48:23 territory lies just south of the prince's **l**,
Da 11:40 He will invade various **l** and sweep through them
Hos 8:10 But though they have sold themselves to many **l**,
Am 9:14 my exiled people of Israel back from distant **l**,
Ob 1:12 gloated when they exiled your relatives to distant **l**.
Mic 1:16 for your little ones will be exiled to distant **l**.
7:12 People from many **l** will come and honor you—
Zep 2:13 And the LORD will strike the **l** of the north with
Zec 6:15 Many will come from distant **l** to rebuild the
10:9 still they will remember me in distant **l**.
Mt 2:1 About that time some wise men from eastern **l**
Lk 21:11 and there will be famines and epidemics in many **l**,
Jn 7:35 the country and going to the Jews in other **l**,
Ac 2:8 the languages of the **l** where we were born!
22:11 I even hounded them in distant cities of foreign **l**.
1Pe 1:1 who are living as foreigners in the **l** of Pontus,

LANDSCAPE (2) [LAND]

Jos 11:4 covered the **l** like the sand on the seashore.
Eze 43:2 and the whole **l** shone with his glory.

LANES (1)

Lk 14:23 'Go out into the country **l** and behind the hedges

LANGUAGE (40) [LANGUAGES]

Ge 10:5 peoples in various lands, each tribe with its own **l**.
10:25 of the world were divided into different **l** groups
11:1 At one time the whole world spoke a single **l**
11:6 just begun to take advantage of their common **l**
31:47 which is Jegar-sahadutha in Laban's **l** and Galeed
Dt 28:49 It is a nation whose **l** you do not understand,
1Ch 1:19 of the world were divided into different **l** groups
2Ch 32:18 **l** to the people gathered on the walls of the city,
Ezr 4:7 sent a letter to Artaxerxes in the Aramaic **l**,
Ne 13:24 half their children spoke in the **l** of Ashdod
13:24 and could not speak the **l** of Judah at all.
Est 1:22 the empire, to each province in its own script and **l**,
Isa 19:18 They will even begin to speak the Hebrew **l**.
28:11 foreign oppressors who speak an unknown **l**!
33:19 people with a strange, unknown **l** will disappear.
Jer 5:15 ancient nation, a people whose **l** you do not know,
Eze 3:5 foreign people whose **l** you cannot understand.
Da 1:4 Teach these young men the **l** and literature of the
3:7 all the people, whatever their race or nation or **l**,
3:29 If any people, whatever their race or nation or **l**,
4:1 every race and nation and **l** throughout the world:
6:25 every race and nation and **l** throughout the world:
7:14 of every race and nation and **l** would obey him.
Ac 21:40 and he addressed them in their own **l**, Aramaic.
22:2 When they heard him speaking in their own **l**,
1Co 13:1 If I could speak in any **l** in heaven or on earth
14:6 if I should come to you talking in an unknown **l**,
14:7 are examples of the need for speaking in plain **l**.
14:9 If you talk to people in a **l** they don't understand,
14:19 others than ten thousand words in an unknown **l**.
14:23 and hear everyone talking in an unknown **l**,
14:26 one will speak in an unknown **l**, while another will
14:27 than two or three should speak in an unknown **l**.
Eph 4:29 Don't use foul or abusive **l**. Let everything you say
Col 3:8 rage, malicious behavior, slander, and dirty **l**.
Rev 5:9 from every tribe and **l** and people and nation.

7: 9 from every nation and tribe and people and **l**,
13: 7 rule over every tribe and people and **l** and nation.
14: 6 to this world—to every nation, tribe, **l**, and people.
17:15 represent masses of people of every nation and **l**.

LANGUAGES (24) [LANGUAGE]

Ge 10:20 according to their tribes, **l**, territories, and nations.
10:31 according to their tribes, **l**, territories, and nations.
11: 7 Come, let's go down and give them different **l**.
11: 9 confused the people by giving them many **l**,
Est 3:12 of each province in their own scripts and **l**.
8: 9 in the scripts and **l** of all the peoples of the empire,
Da 3: 4 shouted out, "People of all races and nations and **l**,
5:19 and nations and **l** trembled before him in fear.
Zec 8:23 and **l** around the world will clutch at the hem of
Mk 16:17 out demons in my name, and they will speak new **l**.
Ac 2: 4 with the Holy Spirit and began speaking in other **l**,
2: 6 and they were bewildered to hear their own **l** being
2: 8 and yet we hear them speaking the **l** of the lands
2:11 And we all hear these people speaking in our own **l**
1Co 12:10 person is given the ability to speak in unknown **l**,
12:28 to work together, / those who speak in unknown **l**.
12:30 give all of us the ability to speak in unknown **l**?
12:30 Can everyone interpret unknown **l**? No!
13: 8 but prophecy and speaking in unknown **l**
14:10 There are so many different **l** in the world, and all
14:11 I will not understand people who speak those **l**,
14:21 will speak to my own people / through unknown **l**
Rev 10:11 again about many peoples, nations, **l**, and kings."
11: 9 And for three and a half days all peoples, tribes, **l**,

LANTERNS (2)

Zep 1:12 "I will search with **l** in Jerusalem's darkest corners
Jn 18: 3 Now with blazing torches, **l**, and weapons,

LAODICEA (6)

Col 2: 1 I have agonized for you and for the church at **L**,
4:13 and also for the Christians in **L** and Hierapolis.
4:15 greetings to our Christian brothers and sisters at **L**,
4:16 pass it on to the church at **L** so they can read it,
Rev 1:11 Pergamum, Thyatira, Sardis, Philadelphia, and **L**."
3:14 "Write this letter to the angel of the church in **L**.

LAP (4)

Jdg 7: 5 their hands and **l** it up with their tongues like dogs.
16:19 lulled Samson to sleep with his head in her **l**,
2Ki 4:20 took him home, and his mother held him on her **l**.
Pr 6:27 Can a man scoop fire into his **l** and not be burned?

LAPPIDOTH (1)

Jdg 4: 4 Deborah, the wife of **L**, was a prophet who had

LAPWING [KJV] See HOOPOE

LARGE (131) [ENLARGE, ENLARGED, ENLARGES, LARGER, LARGEST]

Ge 6:20 of bird and each kind of animal, **l** and small alike,
7:14 domestic and wild, **l** and small—along with birds
7:23 people, animals both **l** and small, and birds.
9: 2 **l** and small, and all the birds and fish will be afraid
24:22 for her nose and two **l** gold bracelets for her wrists.
26:14 He acquired **l** flocks of sheep and goats,
34:21 For the land is **l** enough to hold them, and we can
Ex 30:18 "Make a **l** bronze washbasin with a bronze
30:28 its utensils, and the **l** washbasin with its pedestal.
35:16 and utensils; the **l** washbasin with its pedestal;
39:39 and utensils; the **l** washbasin and its pedestal;
40: 7 Set the **l** washbasin between the Tabernacle
40:11 Next anoint the **l** washbasin and its pedestal to
40:30 Next he placed the **l** washbasin between the
Nu 13:23 so **l** that it took two of them to carry it on a pole
13:28 and their cities and towns are fortified and very **l**.
35:17 and kills another person with a **l** stone,
Dt 6:10 It is a land filled with **l**, prosperous cities that you
7:13 you will have **l** crops of grain, grapes, and olives,
8:13 and herds have become very **l** and your silver
17:16 The king must not build up a **l** stable of horses for
27: 2 set up some **l** stones and coat them with plaster.
Jos 10: 2 they heard all this because Gibeon was a **l** city—
10: 2 as **l** as the royal cities and larger than Ai.
10:18 "Cover the opening of the cave with **l** rocks
10:27 Then they covered the opening of the cave with a **l**
17:15 "If the hill country of Ephraim is not **l** enough for
17:17 of Joseph, "Since you are so **l** and strong,
19: 9 because Judah's territory was too **l** for them.
22: 8 Share with them your **l** herds of cattle, your silver
22:10 and the half-tribe of Manasseh built a very **l** altar
Jdg 11: 3 Soon he had a **l** band of rebels following him.
20: 1 came together in one **l** assembly and stood in the
20:38 They sent up a **l** cloud of smoke from the town,
1Sa 6:14 a man named Joshua and stopped beside a **l** rock.
6:15 tumors from the cart and placed them on the **l** rock.
6:18 The **l** rock at Beth-shemesh, where they set the Ark
7:12 Samuel then took a **l** stone and placed it between
14:33 Saul said. "Find a **l** stone and roll it over here.
2Sa 8: 8 along with a **l** amount of bronze from Hadadezer's
1Ki 7:23 Then Huram cast a **l** round tank, 15 feet across
8:65 A **l** crowd had gathered from as far away as
10: 2 She arrived in Jerusalem with a **l** group of
10:16 King Solomon made two hundred **l** shields of
18:32 Then he dug a trench around the altar **l** enough to
18:33 Then he said, "Fill four **l** jars with water, and pour
2Ki 4:38 "Put on a **l** kettle and make some stew for these
12: 9 the priest bored a hole in the lid of a **l** chest
1Ch 4:27 but none of his brothers had **l** families.
4:27 So Simeon's tribe never became as **l** as the tribe of
18: 8 along with a **l** amount of bronze from Hadadezer's
22: 3 David provided **l** amounts of iron for the nails that
2Ch 2: 9 for the Temple I am going to build will be very **l**
4: 2 Then he cast a **l** round tank, 15 feet across from
4: 9 courtyard for the priests and the **l** outer courtyard.
9: 1 She arrived with a **l** group of attendants and a great
9:15 King Solomon made two hundred **l** shields of
14: 8 the tribe of Judah, armed with **l** shields and spears.
24:11 after day, and a **l** amount of money was collected.
28: 5 and to exile **l** numbers of his people to Damascus.
32: 5 and manufactured **l** numbers of weapons
36:18 **l** and small, used in the Temple of God,
Ezr 10: 1 Temple of God, a **l** crowd of people from Israel—
Ne 5: 2 They were saying, "We have such **l** families.
5:18 six fat sheep, and a **l** number of domestic fowl.
5:18 And every ten days we needed a **l** supply of all
7: 4 At that time the city was **l** and spacious,
9:35 You gave them a **l**, fertile land, but they refused to
12:31 the wall and organized two **l** choirs to give thanks.
13: 5 had converted a **l** storage room and placed it at
Ps 107:38 How he blesses them! / They raise **l** families there,
Isa 8: 1 "Make a **l** signboard and clearly write this name
32: 2 and as the cool shadow of a **l** rock in a hot
40:16 fuel to consume a sacrifice **l** enough to honor him.
60:22 The smallest family will multiply into a **l** clan.
Jer 41: 9 **l** one made by King Asa when he fortified Mizpah
43: 9 bury **l** rocks between the pavement stones at the
Eze 4: 1 take a **l** brick and set it down in front of you.
8: 3 where there is a **l** idol that has made the LORD
17: 9 it won't take a strong arm or a **l** army to do it.
23:32 of terror as your sister—a cup that is **l** and deep.
39: 9 will go out and pick up your small and **l** shields,
41: 1 the Holy Place, the **l** main room of the Temple,
41:12 A **l** building stood on the west, facing the Temple
Da 4:10 I dreamed. I saw a **l** tree in the middle of the earth.
8: 5 which had one very **l** horn between its eyes,
8: 8 at the height of its power, its **l** horn was broken off.
8: 8 In the **l** horn's place grew four prominent horns
8:21 and the **l** horn between its eyes represents the first
8:22 The four prominent horns that replaced the one **l**
Jnh 3: 3 a city so **l** that it took three days to see it all.
Hab 2: 2 "Write my answer in **l**, clear letters on a tablet,
Mt 4:25 **L** crowds followed him wherever he went—
8: 1 **L** crowds followed Jesus as he came down the
8:18 When Jesus noticed how **l** the crowd was growing,
8:30 A **l** herd of pigs was feeding in the distance,
13:33 Even though she used a **l** amount of flour, the yeast
15:37 there were seven **l** baskets of food left over!
18: 6 into the sea with a **l** millstone tied around the neck.
Mk 4: 1 There was such a **l** crowd along the shore that he
5:11 There happened to be a **l** herd of pigs feeding on
5:21 a **l** crowd gathered around him on the shore.
8: 8 there were seven **l** baskets of food left over!
8:20 how many **l** baskets of leftovers did you pick up?"
9:42 into the sea with a **l** millstone tied around the neck.
12:41 in their money. Many rich people put in **l** amounts.
14:15 He will take you upstairs to a **l** room that is already
16: 4 looked up and saw that the stone—a very **l** one—
Lk 6:17 the disciples stood with Jesus on a **l**, level area,
6:38 Whatever measure you use in giving—**l** or small—
8: 4 One day Jesus told this story to a **l** crowd that had
8:32 A **l** herd of pigs was feeding on the hillside nearby,
13:21 Even though she used a **l** amount of flour, the yeast
16:10 in small matters, you won't be faithful in **l** ones.
17: 2 It would be better to be thrown into the sea with a **l**
22:12 He will take you upstairs to a **l** room that is already
Jn 14:17 The world at **l** cannot receive him, because it isn't
14:22 yourself only to us and not to the world at **l**?"
21:11 There were 153 **l** fish, and yet the net hadn't torn.
Ac 9:25 some of the other believers let him down in a **l**
10:11 and something like a **l** sheet was let down by its
11: 5 Something like a **l** sheet was let down by its four
11:21 and **l** numbers of these Gentiles believed
11:24 And **l** numbers of people were brought to the Lord.
17: 4 including a **l** number of godly Greek men and also
19:24 a silversmith who had a **l** business manufacturing
28:23 and on that day a **l** number of people came to
Gal 6:11 Notice what **l** letters I use as I write these closing
Jas 3: 3 We can make a **l** horse turn around and go
Rev 12: 3 I saw a **l** red dragon with seven heads and ten
18:21 Then a mighty angel picked up a boulder as **l** as a

LARGER (17) [LARGE]

Lev 13:23 But if the area grows no **l** and does not spread,
Nu 22:15 This time he sent a **l** number of even more
26:54 Give the **l** tribes more land and the smaller tribes
26:56 inheritance must be assigned by lot among the **l**
33:54 A **l** inheritance of land will be allotted to each of
the **l** clans,
35: 5 This area will serve as the **l** pastureland for the
35: 8 The **l** tribes will give more towns to the Levites,
Dt 7: 7 and lavish his love on you because you were **l**
9:14 a nation **l** and more powerful than they are.'
21:16 he may not give the **l** inheritance to his younger
Jos 10: 2 as large as the royal cities and **l** than Ai.
2Ch 24:24 the LORD helped them conquer the much **l** army
Eze 45: 3 Within the **l** sacred area, measure out a portion of
45: 6 "Adjacent to the **l** sacred area will be a section of
Mt 21:36 So the landowner sent a **l** group of his servants to
Lk 7:43 "I suppose the one for whom he canceled the **l**

LARGEST (7) [LARGE]

Ge 43:34 He gave the **l** serving to Benjamin—five times as
2Sa 8: 1 the Philistines by conquering Gath, their **l** city.
2Ki 17: 9 from the smallest outpost to the **l** walled city.
18: 8 from their smallest outpost to their **l** walled city.
Isa 17: 9 Their **l** cities will be as deserted as overgrown
Mt 13:32 but it becomes the **l** of garden plants and grows
Mk 4:32 it grows to become one of the **l** of plants, with long

LASCIVIOUSNESS [KJV] See IMMORAL(ITY), LUSTFUL

LASEA (1)

Ac 27: 8 finally arrived at Fair Havens, near the city of **L**.

LASH (1) [LASHED, LASHES]

Ac 22:25 As they tied Paul down to **l** him, Paul said to the

LASHA (1)

Ge 10:19 Gomorrah, Admah, and Zeboiim, near **L**.

LASHARON (1)

Jos 12:18 The king of Aphek / The king of **L**

LASHED (1) [LASH]

Ac 22:24 and ordered him **l** with whips to make him confess

LASHES (5) [LASH]

Dt 25: 2 and be beaten in his presence with the number of **l**
25: 3 No more than forty **l** may ever be given; more than
forty **l** would publicly humiliate your
Pr 17:10 than a hundred **l** on the back of a fool.
2Co 11:24 Five different times the Jews gave me thirty-nine **l**.

LAST (209) [LASTED, LASTING, LASTS, LATTER]

LAST DAY (7) Ex 12:41; Jn 6:39,40,44,54; 7:37; 1Pe 1:5
LAST DAYS (6) Isa 2:2; Hos 3:5; Mic 4:1; Ac 2:17; 2Ti 3:1; 2Pe 3:3
LAST TIMES (2) 1Ti 4:1; Jude 1:18

Ge 2:23 "At **l**!" Adam exclaimed. "She is part of my own
8:14 more months went by, and at **l** the earth was dry!
19: 3 But Lot insisted, so at **l** they went home with him.
19:34 her younger sister, "I slept with our father **l** night.
24:22 Then at **l**, when the camels had finished drinking,
26:22 he said, "At **l** the LORD has made room for us,
27: 2 Isaac said, "and I expect every day to be my **l**.
31:29 but the God of your father appeared to me **l** night
31:42 That is why he appeared to you **l** night
33: 2 and her children next, and Rachel and Joseph **l**.
35:18 but with her **l** breath she named him Ben-oni;
40: 8 And they replied, "We both had dreams **l** night,
41:15 "I had a dream **l** night," Pharaoh told him,
41:53 At **l** the seven years of plenty came to an end.
47:29 solemnly that you will honor this, my **l** request:
49:33 he lay back in the bed, breathed his **l**, and died.
Ex 3:20 all kinds of miracles. Then at **l** he will let you go.
12:41 it was on the **l** day of the 430th year that all the
26: 4 Put loops of blue yarn along the edge of the **l** sheet
26:10 Put fifty loops along the edge of the **l** sheet in each
36:11 Fifty blue loops were placed along the edge of the **l**
36:17 Then they made fifty loops along the edge of the **l**
39:32 And so at **l** the Tabernacle was finished.
40:33 of the courtyard. So at **l** Moses finished the work.
Lev 19:10 do not strip every **l** bunch of grapes from the vines,
23:34 This festival to the LORD will **l** for seven days.
25:15 be based on the number of years since the **l** jubilee.
26:34 Then at **l** the land will make up for its missed
26:40 "But at **l** my people will confess their sins
26:41 then at **l** their disobedient hearts will be humbled,
26:43 At **l** the people will receive the due punishment for
Nu 10:25 **L** of all, the tribes that camped with Dan set out
14:33 until the **l** of you lies dead in the wilderness.
Dt 2: 2 Then at **l** the LORD said to me,
3:11 King Og of Bashan was the **l** of the giant
28:20 until at **l** you are completely destroyed for doing
Jos 12: 4 the **l** of the Rephaites, lived at Ashtaroth and Edrei.
13:12 King Og was the **l** of the Rephaites, for Moses had
19:40 and **l** allotment of land went to the families of the
Jdg 8: 2 Aren't the **l** grapes of Ephraim's harvest better
14:17 At **l**, on the seventh day, he told her the answer
Ru 4:17 women said, "Now at **l** Naomi has a son again!"
1Sa 14:36 all night and destroy every **l** one of them."
15:16 Listen to what the LORD told me **l** night!"
20:33 So at **l** Jonathan realized that his father was really
20:42 At **l** Jonathan said to David, "Go in peace, for we
23:21 Saul said. "At **l** someone is concerned about me!
2Sa 7:25 Confirm it as a promise that will **l** forever.
11:10 Why didn't you go home **l** night after being away
14:22 "At **l** I know that I have gained your approval,
14:33 Then at **l** David summoned his estranged son,
16: 8 At **l** you will taste some of your own medicine,
19:11 "Why are you the **l** ones to reinstate the king?
19:12 Why are you the **l** ones to welcome me back?"
23: 1 These are the **l** words of David: / "David, the son
1Ki 7:40 So at **l** Huram completed everything King
17:12 I was just gathering a few sticks to cook this **l**
17:13 Go ahead and cook that 'I meal,' but bake me a
20: 9 but this **l** demand of yours I simply cannot
2Ki 5:15 "I know at **l** that there is no God in all the world
8: 1 for a famine on Israel that will **l** for seven years."
13:14 When Elisha was in his **l** illness, King Jehoash of
25: 3 very severe, with the **l** of the food entirely gone.

1Ch 17:23 my family. May it be a promise that will **l** forever.
28: 7 he does now, I will make his kingdom **l** forever.'
2Ch 4:11 So at **l** Huram-abi completed everything King
9: 8 so much and desires this kingdom to **l** forever,
24:22 Zechariah's **l** words as he died were,
32:22 So there was peace at **l** throughout the land.
33:24 At **l** Amon's own officials plotted against him
Ezr 8:32 So at **l** we arrived safely in Jerusalem, where we
Ne 4: 6 At **l** the wall was completed to half its original
13:21 And that was the **l** time they came on the Sabbath.
Job 3: 1 At **l** Job spoke, and he cursed the day of his birth.
5:16 And so at **l** the poor have hope, and the fangs of
8:15 cling to their home for security, but it won't **l**.
14:10 They breathe their **l**, and then where are they?
19:25 and that he will stand upon the earth at **l**.
22:20 The **l** of them have been consumed in the fire.'
22:21 If you agree with him, you will have peace at **l**,
Ps 10:15 Go after them until the **l** one is destroyed!
49:12 They will not **l** long despite their riches—
58:11 Then at **l** everyone will say, / "There truly is a
81:15 before him; / their desolation would **l** forever.
89: 2 Your unfailing love will **l** forever.
104:31 May the glory of the LORD **l** forever!
104:33 as I live. / I will praise my God to my **l** breath!
106:12 Then at **l** his people believed his promises.
Pr 11:18 for the moment, but the reward of the godly will **l**.
27:24 for riches don't **l** forever, and the crown might not
31:30 Charm is deceptive, and beauty does not **l**; but a
Isa 2: 2 In the **l** days, the Temple of the LORD in
5:11 begin long drinking bouts that **l** late into the night.
10:20 Then at **l** those left in Israel and Judah will trust the
10:25 It will not **l** very long. In a little while my anger
11:13 Then at **l** the jealousy between Israel and Judah
14: 7 But at **l** the land is at rest and is quiet. Finally it
17: 7 Then at **l** the people will think of their Creator
20: 3 around naked and barefoot for the **l** three years.
21: 9 Now at **l**—look! Here come the chariots
28: 5 Then at **l** the LORD Almighty will himself be
32:15 until at **l** the Spirit is poured down upon us from
41: 4 It is I, the LORD, the First and the **L**. I alone am
44: 6 I am the First and the **L**; there is no other God.
48:12 chosen one! I alone am God, the First and the **L**.
51: 8 as it eats wool. But my righteousness will **l** forever.
51:17 have drunk the cup of terror, tipping out its **l** drops.
51:22 You will drink no more of my fury. It is gone at **l**!
52: 6 Then at **l** they will recognize that it is I who speaks
59:19 Then at **l** they will respect and glorify the name of
60:16 You will know at **l** that I, the LORD, am your
Jer 2:31 then do my people say, 'At **l** we are free from God!
6: 8 This is your **l** warning, Jerusalem! If you do not
10:18 troubles upon you. At **l** you will feel my anger."
16:21 "At **l** they will know that I am the LORD."
22:22 Surely at **l** you will see your wickedness and be
23:25 'Listen to the dream I had from God **l** night.'
48:13 At **l** Moab will be ashamed of her idol Chemosh,
52: 6 very severe, with the **l** of the food entirely gone.
La 2:16 their teeth and say, "We have destroyed her at **l**!
3:29 down in the dust; then at **l** there is hope for them.
Eze 5: 2 Scatter the **l** third to the wind, for I will scatter my
5:13 Then at **l** my anger will be spent, and I will be
6: 9 Then at **l** they will hate themselves for all their
6:12 by famine. So at **l** I will spend my fury on them.
12:18 Drink your water with fear, as if it were your **l**.
13:15 At **l** my anger against the wall and those who
16:42 "Then at **l** my fury against you will be spent,
29:21 and then at **l** your words will be respected.
39: 9 There will be enough to **l** them seven years!
45:21 the Passover. This festival will **l** for seven days.
Da 4: 3 his wonders! / His kingdom will **l** forever,
4: 8 At **l** Daniel came in before me, and I told him the
6:16 So at **l** the king gave orders for Daniel to be
8:13 "How long will the events of this vision **l**?
11:24 but this will **l** for only a short while.
Hos 3: 5 and they will receive his good gifts in the **l** days.
5: 6 Then at **l**, they will come with their flocks
Am 4: 2 Every **l** one of you will be dragged away like a fish
6:10 he will ask the **l** survivor, "Is there anyone else
Mic 4: 1 In the **l** days, the Temple of the LORD in
5: 3 Then at **l** his fellow countrymen will return from
Hab 2: 6 'You thieves! At **l** justice has caught up with you!
Zep 1: 4 and destroy every **l** trace of their Baal worship.
3:15 At **l** your troubles will be over, and you will fear
Zec 14:11 safe at **l**, never again to be cursed and destroyed.
Mal 2: 4 Then at **l** you will know it was I who sent you this
2:12 the nation of Israel every **l** man who has done this
Mt 5:26 be free again until you have paid the **l** penny.
16:12 Then at **l** they understood that he wasn't speaking
20: 8 and pay them, beginning with the **l** workers first.
20:14 I wanted to pay this **l** worker the same as you.
20:16 so it is, that many who are first now will be **l** then;
and those who are **l** now will be first then."
24:30 And then at **l**, the sign of the coming of the Son of
25:15 of gold to another, and one bag of gold to the **l**—
27:19 because I had a terrible nightmare about him **l**
Mk 1:15 "At **l** the time has come!" he announced.
9:35 "Anyone who wants to be the first must take **l**
12:22 were no children. **L** of all, the woman died, too.
15:37 Jesus uttered another loud cry and breathed his **l**.
Lk 5: 5 "we worked hard all **l** night and didn't catch a
12:59 you won't be free again until you have paid the **l**
22:45 At **l** he stood up again and returned to the disciples,
23:46 And with those words he breathed his **l**.
24:18 things that have happened there the **l** few days."
Jn 6:39 but that I should raise them to eternal life at the **l**
6:40 eternal life—that I should raise them at the **l** day."
6:44 and at the **l** day I will raise them from the dead.
6:54 have eternal life, and I will raise them at the **l** day.
7:37 On the **l** day, the climax of the festival, Jesus stood
15:16 I appointed you to go and produce fruit that will **l**,
16:29 "At **l** you are speaking plainly and not in parables.
Ac 2:17 'In the **l** days, God said, / I will pour out my Spirit
7:21 When at **l** they had to abandon him,
19:35 At **l** the mayor was able to quiet them down
27:20 the sun and the stars, until at **l** all hope was gone.
27:23 For **l** night an angel of the God to whom I belong
Ro 1:10 God willing, to come at **l** to see you.
11:25 but this will **l** only until the complete number of
1Co 13: 8 Love will **l** forever, but prophecy and speaking in
15: 8 **L** of all, I saw him, too, long after the others,
15:26 And the **l** enemy to be destroyed is death.
15:45 But the **l** Adam—that is, Christ—is a life-giving
15:52 blinking of an eye, when the **l** trumpet is blown.
15:54 never die—then at **l** the Scriptures will come true:
2Co 2: 3 That is why I wrote as I did in my **l** letter, so that
4:17 troubles are quite small and won't **l** very long.
4:17 us an immeasurably great glory that will **l** forever!
4:18 soon be over, but the joys to come will **l** forever.
13:11 Dear friends, I close my letter with these **l** words:
Gal 3:19 But this system of law was to **l** only until the
1Th 2:16 But the anger of God has caught up with them at **l**.
1Ti 4: 1 Now the Holy Spirit tells us clearly that in the **l**
2Ti 3: 1 that in the **l** days there will be very difficult times.
1Pe 1: 5 It will be revealed on the **l** day for all to see.
1:23 But this new life will **l** forever because it comes
1:25 But the word of the Lord will **l** forever." And that
2Pe 3: 3 I want to remind you that in the **l** days there will be
1Jn 2:18 Dear children, the **l** hour is here. You have heard
Jude 1:18 that in the **l** times there would be scoffers whose
Rev 1:17 "Don't be afraid! I am the First and the **L**.
2: 8 message from the one who is the First and the **L**,
8:13 because of what will happen when the **l** three
12:10 "It has happened at **l**—the salvation and power
15: 1 Seven angels were holding the seven **l** plagues,
18:20 For at **l** God has judged her on your behalf.
21: 9 seven bowls containing the seven **l** plagues came
22:13 the First and the **L**, the Beginning and the End."

LASTED (8) [LAST]

Jos 22: 3 even though the campaign has **l** for such a long
2Sa 21: 1 There was a famine during David's reign that **l** for
24:15 upon Israel that morning, and it **l** for three days.
2Ki 15: 5 with leprosy, which **l** until the day of his death;
Ezr 4: 5 and **l** until King Darius of Persia took the throne.
Est 1: 4 The celebration **l** six months—a tremendous
1: 5 It **l** for seven days and was held at Susa in the
Job 1: 5 and sometimes they **l** several days—Job would

LASTING (9) [LAST]

1Sa 25:28 The LORD will surely reward you with a **l**
2Sa 7:19 you speak of giving me a **l** dynasty!
1Ch 17:17 you speak of giving me a **l** dynasty!
Ps 19: 9 Reverence for the LORD is pure, / **l** forever.
Pr 10: 2 Ill-gotten gain has no **l** value, but right living can
10:25 wicked away, but the godly have a **l** foundation.
Da 9:15 you brought **l** honor to your name by rescuing your
2Co 3: 5 It is not that we think we can do anything of **l**
Jas 1:27 and **l** religion in the sight of God our Father means

LASTS (6) [LAST]

Lev 13:46 As long as the disease **l**, they will be ceremonially
Ps 30: 5 His anger **l** for a moment, / but his favor **l** a
lifetime!
37:18 and they will receive a reward that **l** forever.
Isa 51: 6 earth will die like flies, but my salvation **l** forever.
Heb 6:11 will keep right on loving others as long as life **l**,

LATCHET [KJV] See THONG

LATE (36) [LATER, LATEST]

Jdg 19: 9 his father-in-law said, "Look, it's getting **l**.
19:11 It was **l** in the day when they reached Jebus,
19:11 servant said to him, "It's getting too **l** to travel;
2Sa 11: 2 **L** one afternoon David got out of bed after taking a
15:14 "Then we must flee at once, or it will be too **l**!"
2Ch 15:10 The people gathered at Jerusalem in **l** spring,
31: 7 The first of these tithes was brought in **l** spring,
Ne 1: 1 In **l** autumn of the twentieth year of King
4:21 We worked early and **l**, from sunrise to sunset.
Est 9:19 celebrate an annual festival and holiday in **l** winter,
Ps 127: 2 so hard / from early morning until **l** at night,
Pr 31:18 for bargains; her lights burn **l** into the night.
Ecc 12: 2 It will be too **l** then to remember him,
Isa 5:11 begin long drinking bouts that last **l** into the night.
Jer 13:16 glory to the LORD your God before it is too **l**.
28: 1 One day in **l** summer of that same year—the fourth
36: 7 and ask the LORD's forgiveness before it is too **l**.
36: 9 on the day of sacred fasting held in **l** autumn,
36:22 It was **l** autumn, and the king was in a winterized
Hos 5: 6 But it will be too **l**! They will not find him,
8: 3 But it is too **l**! The people of Israel have rejected
Na 2: 6 But too **l**! The river gates are open! The enemy has
Mt 5:25 to terms quickly with your enemy before it is too **l**
14:15 "This is a desolate place, and it is getting **l**.
Mk 6:35 **L** in the afternoon his disciples came to him
6:35 "This is a desolate place, and it is getting **l**.
11:11 then he left because it was **l** in the afternoon.
13:35 at evening, midnight, early dawn, or **l** daybreak.
Lk 9:12 **L** in the afternoon the twelve disciples came to him
13:25 of the house has locked the door, it will be too **l**.
19:42 But now it is too **l**, and peace is hidden from you.
23:54 This was done **l** on Friday afternoon, the day of
24:29 to stay the night with them, since it was getting **l**.
Ac 27: 9 long voyages by then because it was so **l** in the fall,
Ro 13:11 reason for right living is that you know how **l** it is;
Heb 12:17 It was too **l** for repentance, even though he wept

LATER (179) [LATE]

Ge 4: 2 **L** she gave birth to a second son and named him
4: 8 **L** Cain suggested to his brother, Abel, "Let's go
7:10 One week **l**, the flood came and covered the earth.
8: 5 Two and a half months **l**, as the waters continued
8:10 Seven days **l**, Noah released the dove again.
8:12 A week **l**, he released the dove again, and this time
11: 6 political unity, just think of what they will do **l**.
14: 5 One year **l**, Kedorlaomer and his allies arrived.
16:14 **L** that well was named Beer-lahairoi, and it can
22: 1 **L** on God tested Abraham's faith and obedience.
26: 8 But some time **l**, Abimelech, king of the
30:21 **L** she gave birth to a daughter and named her
31:23 He caught up with them seven days **l** in the hill
34:25 But three days **l**, when their wounds were still sore,
37:29 Some time **l**, Reuben returned to get Joseph out of
38:24 About three months **l**, word reached Judah that
40: 1 Some time **l**, Pharaoh's chief cup-bearer and chief
40:20 Pharaoh's birthday came three days **l**, and he gave
41: 1 Two years **l**, Pharaoh dreamed that he was standing
41:22 "A little **l** I had another dream. This time there
Ex 2:10 **L**, when he was older, the child's mother brought
2:11 Many years **l**, when Moses had grown up, he went
2:22 **L** they had a baby boy, and Moses named him
16:14 When the dew disappeared **l** in the morning,
16:32 **l** generations will be able to see the bread that the
21:19 If the injured person is **l** able to walk again,
Lev 13:57 If the spot reappears at a **l** time, however,
23:16 fifty days **l**, and bring an offering of new grain to
23:20 the loaves representing the first of your **l** crops.
Nu 9:11 must offer the Passover sacrifice one month **l**,
29: 7 "Ten days **l**, you must call another holy assembly
29:12 "Five days **l**, you must call yet another holy
30: 6 or makes an impulsive pledge and **l** marries.
Dt 24: 1 but **l** discovers something about her that is
Jos 3: 2 Three days **l**, the Israelite leaders went through the
9:16 Three days **l**, the facts came out—these people of
17:13 **L** on, however, when the Israelites became strong
Jdg 1:26 **L** the man moved to the land of the Hittites,
14: 8 **L**, when he returned to Timnah for the wedding,
14:14 Three days **l** they were still trying to figure it out.
15: 1 **L** on, during the wheat harvest, Samson took a
16: 4 **L** Samson fell in love with a woman named
16:31 **L** his brothers and other relatives went down to get
Ru 1: 4 other a woman named Ruth. But about ten years **l**,
1Sa 4:12 and arrived at Shiloh **l** that same day.
10:17 **L** Samuel called all the people of Israel to meet
11: 1 About a month **l**, King Nahash of Ammon led his
21: 2 I am here. I have told my men where to meet me **l**.
22: 3 **L** David went to Mizpeh in Moab, where he asked
25:38 About ten days **l**, the LORD struck him and he
30: 1 Three days **l**, when David and his men arrived
2Sa 1:18 **L** he commanded that it be taught to all the people
13:23 Two years **l**, when Absalom's sheep were being
1Ki 2:39 But three years **l**, two of Shimei's slaves escaped
3:16 Some time **l**, two prostitutes came to the king to
3:18 Three days **l**, she also had a baby. We were alone;
9:26 **L** King Solomon built a fleet of ships at
12:12 Three days **l**, Jeroboam and all the people returned
12:25 **L** he went and built up the town of Peniel.
17:17 Some time **l**, the woman's son became sick.
2Ki 4:14 **L** Elisha asked Gehazi, "What do you think we
6:24 Some time **l**, however, King Ben-hadad of Aram
18:10 Three years **l**, during the sixth year of King
1Ch 1:27 and Abram, **l** known as Abraham.
2: 4 **L** Judah had twin sons through Tamar,
2:23 (**L** Geshur and Aram captured the Towns of Jair
9:21 And **l** Zechariah son of Meshelemiah had been
12:18 who **l** became a leader among the Thirty, and he
18: 8 **L** Solomon melted the bronze and used it for the
2Ch 8:17 **L** Solomon went to Ezion-geber and Elath, ports in
10:12 Three days **l**, Jeroboam and all the people returned
11:20 **L** Rehoboam married another cousin, Maacah,
12:10 King Rehoboam **l** replaced them with bronze
18: 2 A few years **l**, he went to Samaria to visit Ahab,
24: 4 Some time **l**, Joash decided to repair and restore
Ezr 4: 6 Years **l** when Xerxes began his reign, the enemies
4: 7 And even **l** during the reign of King Artaxerxes
7: 1 Many years **l**, during the reign of King Artaxerxes
8:13 From the family of Adonikam, who came **l**:
Ne 6:10 **L** I went to visit Shemaiah son of Delaiah
13: 6 though I **l** received his permission to return.
Est 3: 1 Some time **l**, King Xerxes promoted Haman son of
3: 7 And the day selected was March 7, nearly a year **l**.
3:13 This was scheduled to happen nearly a year **l** on
5: 1 Three days **l**, Esther put on her royal robes
Pr 7:20 and he won't return until **l** in the month."
11:15 is dangerous; it is better to refuse than to suffer **l**.
29:21 A servant who is pampered from childhood will **l**
Ecc 11: 1 Give generously, for your gifts will return to you **l**.
SS 3: 4 A little while **l** I found him and held him. I didn't
Jer 17:11 Sooner or **l** they will lose their riches and,
28:17 Two months **l**, Hananiah died.
34:11 but **l** they changed their minds. They took back the
37:17 **L** King Zedekiah secretly requested that Jeremiah
39: 2 Two and a half years **l**, on July 18, the Babylonians
40:15 **L** Johanan had a private conference with Gedaliah
42: 7 Ten days **l**, the LORD gave his reply to Jeremiah.
Eze 23:17 But **l**, she became disgusted with them and broke
Da 4:29 Twelve months **l**, he was taking a walk on the flat
5: 1 A number of years **l**, King Belshazzar gave a great
8: 3 even though it had begun to grow **l** than the shorter

8:19 "I am here to tell you what will happen l in the
11: 6 "Some years l, an alliance will be formed between
11: 9 "L the king of the north will invade the realm of
11:13 "A few years l, the king of the north will return
Mt 10: 4 (the Zealot), / Judas Iscariot (who l betrayed him).
13: 1 L that same day, Jesus left the house and went
16: 5 L, after they crossed to the other side of the lake,
17: 1 Six days l Jesus took Peter and the two brothers,
17:23 but three days l he will be raised from the dead."
21:29 but l he changed his mind and went anyway.
24: 3 L, Jesus sat on the slopes of the Mount of Olives.
25:11 L, when the other five bridesmaids returned,
26:71 L, out by the gate, another servant girl noticed him
26:73 A little l some other bystanders came over to him
Mk 1:14 L on, after John was arrested by Herod Antipas,
1:36 L Simon and the others went out to find him.
2: 1 Several days l Jesus returned to Capernaum,
3:19 Judas Iscariot (who l betrayed him).
4:10 L, when Jesus was alone with the twelve disciples
8:31 be killed, and three days l he would rise again.
9: 2 Six days l Jesus took Peter, James, and John to the
9:31 but three days l he will rise from the dead."
10:10 L, when he was alone with his disciples in the
10:46 L, as Jesus and his disciples left town, a great
12:35 L, as Jesus was teaching the people in the Temple,
13: 3 L, Jesus sat on the slopes of the Mount of Olives
14:70 A little l some other bystanders began saying to
16:14 Still l he appeared to the eleven disciples as they
Lk 1:39 A few days l Mary hurried to the hill country of
2:21 Eight days l, when the baby was circumcised,
2:46 Three days l they finally discovered him. He was
5:27 L, as Jesus left the town, he saw a tax collector
6:16 of James), / Judas Iscariot (who l betrayed him).
9:22 but three days l I will be raised from the dead."
9:28 About eight days l Jesus took Peter, James,
13:31 A few minutes l some Pharisees said to him,
15:13 "A few days l this younger son packed all his
17:22 L he talked again about this with his disciples.
22:59 About an hour l someone else insisted, "This must
Jn 8:21 L Jesus said to them again, "I am going away.
13:36 can't go with me now, but you will follow me l."
14:17 because he lives with you now and l will be in you.
20:26 Eight days l the disciples were together again,
21: 1 L Jesus appeared again to the disciples beside the
Ac 5: 7 About three hours l his wife came in, not knowing
7:30 "Forty years l, in the desert near Mount Sinai,
7:45 Years l, when Joshua led the battles against the
10:40 but God raised him to life three days l. Then God
17:32 others said, "We want to hear more about this l."
18:21 So he left, saying, "I will come back l,
19: 4 believe in Jesus, the one John said would come l."
20: 6 in Macedonia and five days l arrived in Troas,
20:15 island of Samos. And a day l we arrived at Miletus.
24: 1 Five days l Ananias, the high priest, arrived with
24:24 A few days l Felix came with his wife, Drusilla,
25: 6 Eight or ten days l he returned to Caesarea, and on
25:13 A few days l King Agrippa arrived with his sister,
27:28 A little l they sounded again and found only 90
28:13 A day l a south wind began blowing,
Ro 4:10 accepted him first, and then he was circumcised l!
8:18 is nothing compared to the glory he will give us l.
10:20 And l Isaiah spoke boldly for God: / "I was found
1Co 15: 7 he was seen by James and l by all the apostles.
15:46 the natural body, then the spiritual body comes l.
16:12 He will be seeing you l, when the time is right.
Gal 1:17 into Arabia and l returned to the city of Damascus.
1:18 It was not until three years l that I finally went to
2: 1 Then fourteen years l I went back to Jerusalem
3:17 430 years l when God gave the law to Moses.
1Ti 5:24 are others whose sin will not be revealed until l.
5:25 others whose good deeds won't be known until l.
Heb 3: 5 an illustration of the truths God would reveal l.
4: 7 God announced this through David a long time l in
4: 8 God would not have spoken l about another day of
1Pe 1:12 their lifetime, but many years l, during yours.
2Pe 2: 6 L, he turned the cities of Sodom and Gomorrah
Jude 1: 5 he l destroyed every one of those who did not
Rev 1:19 now happening and the things that will happen l.

LATEST (4) [LATE]

Lev 19: 6 same day you offer it or on the next day at the l.
1Sa 20:12 or the next day at the l, I will talk to my father
Ac 17:21 to spend all their time discussing the l ideas.)
Col 4: 9 He and Tychicus will give you all the l news.

LATIN (1)

Jn 19:20 L, and Greek, so that many people could read it.

LATRINE (3)

Dt 23:12 "Mark off an area outside the camp for a l.
Jdg 3:23 and locked the doors and climbed down the l
3:24 room locked. They thought he might be using the l,

LATTER (2) [LAST]

Jer 48:47 But in the l days I will restore the fortunes of
49:39 But in the l days I will restore the fortunes of

LATTICEWORK (4)

1Ki 7:17 Each capital was decorated with seven sets of l
7:18 the l to decorate the capitals over the pillars.
7:20 beside the rounded surface next to the l.
2Ki 1: 2 fell through the l of an upper room at his palace in

LAUD [KJV] See PRAISE

LAUGH (26) [LAUGHED, LAUGHING, LAUGHINGSTOCK, LAUGHS, LAUGHTER]

Ge 18:13 the LORD said to Abraham, "Why did Sarah l?
18:15 But he said, "That is not true. You did l."
21: 6 All who hear about this will l with me.
2Sa 1:20 of Ashkelon, / or the pagans will l in triumph.
Job 5:22 You will l at destruction and famine; wild animals
12: 4 Yet my friends l at me. I am a man who calls on
12: 4 I am a just and blameless man, yet they l at me.
16:10 People jeer and l at me. They slap my cheek in
22:19 and the innocent will l them to scorn.
Ps 35:24 Don't let my enemies l about me in my troubles.
52: 6 will see it and be amazed. / They will l and say,
59: 8 But LORD, you l at them. / You scoff at all the
Pr 1:26 So I will l when you are in trouble! I will mock
Ecc 3: 4 A time to cry and a time to l. / A time to grieve
Isa 38:11 my friends / or l with those who live in this world.
La 3:14 My own people l at me. All day long they sing
Eze 20: 9 nations wouldn't be able to l at Israel's God,
21:10 it will flash like lightning! Now will you l?
Hos 7: 3 The princes l about the people's many lies.
7:16 Then the people of Egypt will l at them.
Zep 2:15 Everyone passing that way will l in derision
Lk 6:21 for the time will come when you will l with joy.
6:25 What sorrows await you who l carelessly,
14:29 of funds. And then how everyone would l at you!
2Pe 2:12 They l at the terrifying powers they know so little
3: 3 days there will be scoffers who will l at the truth

LAUGHED (14) [LAUGH]

Ge 17:17 down to the ground, but he l to himself in disbelief.
18:12 she l silently to herself. "How could a worn-out
18:15 Sarah was afraid, so she denied that she had l.
2Ch 30:10 But most of the people just l at the messengers
Ecc 7:22 For you know how often you yourself have l at
La 1: 7 Her enemy struck her down and l as she fell.
Eze 25: 3 and l at Judah as she went away into exile,
Hos 10: 6 Israel will be l at and shamed because its people
Mt 9:24 she's only asleep." But the crowd l at him.
Mk 5:40 The crowd l at him, but he told them all to go
Lk 8:53 But the crowd l at him because they all knew she
23:35 The crowd watched, and the leaders l and scoffed.
Ac 17:32 some l, but others said, "We want to hear more
1Co 4:10 You are well thought of, but we are l at.

LAUGHING (3) [LAUGH]

Ecc 2: 2 "It is silly to be l all the time," I said.
7:21 on others—you may hear your servant l at you.
Lk 6:25 for your l will turn to mourning and sorrow.

LAUGHINGSTOCK (1) [LAUGH]

Ge 38:23 We'd be the l of the village if we went back

LAUGHS (7) [LAUGH]

2Ki 19:21 despises you and l at you. / The daughter of
Job 9:23 He l when a plague suddenly kills the innocent.
41:29 do no good, and it l at the swish of the javelins.
Ps 2: 4 But the one who rules in heaven l. / The Lord
37:13 But the Lord just l, / for he sees their day of
Pr 31:25 and dignity, and she l with no fear of the future.
Isa 37:22 despises you and l at you. / The daughter of

LAUGHTER (13) [LAUGH]

Ge 21: 6 And Sarah declared, "God has brought me l!
Job 8:21 He will yet fill your mouth with l and your lips
Ps 126: 2 We were filled with l, / and we sang for joy.
Pr 14:13 L can conceal a heavy heart; when the l ends, the grief remains.
Ecc 7: 3 Sorrow is better than l, for sadness has a refining
7: 6 Indeed, a fool's l is quickly gone, like thorns
10:19 A party gives l, and wine gives happiness,
Jer 7:34 the happy singing and l in the streets of Jerusalem.
16: 9 put an end to the happy singing and l in this land.
25:10 I will take away your happy singing and l.
33:11 the sounds of joy and l. The joyful voices of
Jas 4: 9 Let there be sadness instead of l, and gloom

LAUNCHED (2)

1Sa 11:11 He l a surprise attack against the Ammonites
1Ki 20: 1 the Israelite capital, and l attacks against it.

LAVER [KJV] See BASIN, WASHBASIN

LAVISH (4)

Ex 20: 6 But I l my love on those who love me and obey my
Dt 5:10 But I l my love on those who love me and obey my
7: 7 and l his love on you because you were larger
Da 11:38 and l on him gold, silver, precious stones,

LAW (473) [LAW'S, LAWFUL, LAWGIVER, LAWS, LAWYER]

BOOK OF THE LAW (22) Dt 28:61; 29:21; 30:10; 31:26; Jos 1:8; 8:31,34; 23:6; 24:26; 2Ki 14:6; 22:8,11; 2Ch 17:9; 25:4; 34:14,15; Ne 8:1,3,8,18; 9:3; Gal 3:10

IN THE LAW (24) 1Ki 2:3; 1Ch 16:40; 2Ch 30:5,16; 31:3; 34:19; Ezr 3:2,4; 7:6; Ne 8:15; 10:34; Da 9:11,13; Mt 7:12; 8:4; 12:5; 22:36; Mk 1:44; 12:33; Lk 2:24; 5:14; 14:3; Heb 7:5; 10:1

LAW OF GOD (10) Jos 24:26; Ezr 10:3; Ne 8:8,18; 10:29; Mk 7:13; Ro 7:7; 1Co 9:21; 1Jn 3:4,4

LAW OF MOSES (46) Jos 8:32; 23:6; 1Ki 2:3; 2Ki 14:6; 2Ch 23:18; 25:4; 30:16; Ezr 3:2,4; 7:6; Ne 8:1,18; Da 9:11, 13; Mt 5:17,21,27,31,33,38,43; 8:4; 12:5; 22:36; Mk 1:44; Lk 2:22; 5:14; 10:26; Jn 7:19,22,23; 8:5; Ac 6:13; 15:5; 21:20; 1Co 9:9; Gal 3:5; 5:3; 1Ti 1:7; Heb 7:5,28; 8:4; 9:22; 10:1, 8,28

LAW OF THE LORD (3) Lk 2:23,24,39

LAW OF THE LORD* (16) 2Ki 10:31; 1Ch 16:40; 22:12; 2Ch 12:1; 17:9; 19:8; 31:3,4; 34:14; 35:26; Ezr 7:10; Ne 9:3; Ps 19:7; 119:1; Isa 5:24; Jer 8:8

UNDER THE LAW (2) Gal 4:21; Heb 7:28

Ge 38: 8 as our l requires of the brother of a man who has
47:26 then made it a l throughout the land of Egypt—and it is still the l—
Ex 12:49 This l applies to everyone, whether a native-born
27:21 This is a permanent l for the people of Israel,
28:43 This l is permanent for Aaron and his descendants.
30:21 This is a permanent l for Aaron and his
Lev 3:17 This is a permanent l for you and all your
10: 9 This is a permanent l for you, and it must be kept
16:29 This is a permanent l for you, and it applies to
16:31 the day in fasting. This is a permanent l for you.
16:34 This is a permanent l for you, to make atonement
17: 7 This is a permanent l for them, to be kept
23:14 This is a permanent l for you, and it must be
23:21 This is a permanent l for you, and it must be
23:31 This is a permanent l for you, and it must be
23:41 This is a permanent l for you, and it must be
24: 3 This is a permanent l for you, and it must be kept
Nu 5:29 " 'This is the ritual l for dealing with jealousy.
5:30 and the priest will apply this entire ritual l to her.
6:13 "This is the ritual l of the Nazirites.
6:21 "This is the ritual l of the Nazirites. If any
10: 8 This is a permanent l to be followed from
15:15 to the same laws. This is a permanent l for you.
15:29 This same l applies both to native Israelites
18:23 against it. This is a permanent l among you.
19: 2 "Here is another ritual l required by the LORD:
19:10 This is a permanent l for the people of Israel
19:14 "This is the ritual l that applies when someone
19:21 This is a permanent l. Those who sprinkle the
31:21 LORD has given Moses this requirement of the l:
Dt 1: 5 Jordan River. He began to explain the l as follows:
4:44 This is the l that Moses handed down to the
17:11 After they have interpreted the l and reached a
17:19 He must always keep this copy of the l with him
17:19 LORD his God by obeying all the terms of this l.
27: 3 Then write all the terms of this l on them. I repeat,
27: 8 you must clearly write all the terms of this l."
27:26 not affirm the terms of this l by obeying them.'
28:58 "If you refuse to obey all the terms of this l that
28:61 even those not mentioned in this Book of the L,
29:21 the covenant curses recorded in this Book of the L.
29:29 so that we may obey these words of the l.
30:10 and laws written in this Book of the L,
31: 9 So Moses wrote down this l and gave it to the
31:11 you must read this l to all the people of Israel when
31:12 your God and carefully obey all the terms of this l.
31:24 writing down this entire body of l in a book,
31:26 "Take this Book of the L and place it beside the
32:46 so they will obey every word of this l.
33: 4 Moses charged us with the l, / the special
Jos 1: 8 Study this Book of the L continually. Meditate on
8:31 LORD's servant had written in the Book of the L:
8:32 Joshua copied the l of Moses onto the stones of the
8:34 and curses Moses had written in the Book of the L.
22: 5 all the commands and the l that Moses gave to you.
23: 6 instructions written in the Book of the L of Moses.
24:26 Joshua recorded these things in the Book of the L
1Sa 30:25 From then on David made this a l for all of Israel,
1Ki 2: 3 and stipulations written in the l of Moses so that
2Ki 10:31 But Jehu did not obey the l of the LORD, the God
14: 6 the LORD written in the Book of the L of Moses:
17:13 which are contained in the whole l that I
21: 8 the whole l that was given through my servant
22: 8 "I have found the Book of the L in the LORD's
22:11 king heard what was written in the Book of the L,
1Ch 16:40 obeying everything written in the l of the LORD,
22:12 that you may obey the l of the LORD your God as
2Ch 6:16 their behavior and obey my l as you have done,
12: 1 and strong, he abandoned the l of the LORD,
14: 4 and to obey his l and his commands.
15: 3 without a priest to teach them, and without God's l.
17: 9 They took copies of the Book of the L of the
19: 8 for cases concerning both the l of the LORD
23:18 as prescribed by the l of Moses, and to sing
25: 4 the LORD written in the Book of the L of Moses:
30: 5 it in great numbers as prescribed in the l.
30:16 to the regulations found in the l of Moses,
31: 3 annual festivals as required in the l of the LORD.
31: 4 so they could devote themselves fully to the l of
31:21 and in his efforts to follow the l
34:14 he found the Book of the L of the LORD as it had
34:15 "I have found the Book of the L in the LORD's
34:19 When the king heard what was written in the l,
35:26 done according to the written l of the LORD,
Ezr 3: 2 as instructed in the l of Moses, the man of God.
3: 4 Festival of Shelters as prescribed in the l of Moses,
7: 6 well versed in the l of Moses, which the LORD,
7:10 and obey the l of the LORD and to teach those
7:12 the priest, the teacher of the l of the God of heaven.
7:14 in Judah and Jerusalem, based on your God's l,
7:21 a priest and teacher of the l of the God of heaven.
7:26 Anyone who refuses to obey the l of your God
7:26 and the l of the king will be punished immediately

10: 3 commands of our God. We will obey the **l** of God.
Ne 8: 1 the scribe to bring out the Book of the **L** of Moses,
8: 2 brought the scroll of the **l** before the assembly,
8: 3 people paid close attention to the Book of the **L**.
8: 8 They read from the Book of the **L** of God
8: 9 been weeping as they listened to the words of the **l**.
8: 13 and Levites met with Ezra to go over the **l** in
8: 14 As they studied the **l**, they discovered that the
8: 15 during the festival, as it was prescribed in the **l**.
8: 18 Ezra read from the Book of the **L** of God on each
8: 18 a solemn assembly, as the **l** of Moses required.
9: 3 The Book of the **L** of the LORD their God was
9: 26 They threw away your **l**, they killed the prophets
9: 29 You warned them to return to your **l**, but they
9: 34 and ancestors did not obey your **l** or listen to your
10: 29 obey the **l** of God as issued by his servant Moses.
10: 34 altar of the LORD our God, as required in the **l**.
10: 36 of all our herds and flocks, just as the **l** requires.
12: 44 from the fields as required by the **l** for the priests
13: 3 When this **l** was read, all those of mixed ancestry
Est 1: 15 "What penalty does the **l** provide for a queen who
1: 19 a **l** of the Persians and Medes that cannot be
4: 16 And then, though it is against the **l**, I will go in to
8: 13 A copy of this decree was to be recognized as **l** in
Ps 1: 2 day and night they think about his **l**.
11: 3 The foundations of **l** and order have collapsed.
19: 7 The **l** of the LORD is perfect, / reviving the soul.
37: 31 They fill their hearts with God's **l**, / so they will
40: 8 my God, / for your **l** is written on my heart."
78: 5 issued his decree to Jacob; / he gave his **l** to Israel.
78: 10 God's covenant, / and they refused to live by his **l**.
81: 4 by the laws of Israel; / it is a **l** of the God of Jacob.
89: 30 But if his sons forsake my **l** / and fail to walk in my
94: 12 LORD, / and those whom you teach from your **l**.
119: 1 of integrity, / who follow the **l** of the LORD.
119: 18 my eyes to see / the wonderful truths in your **l**.
119: 29 give me the privilege of knowing your **l**.
119: 34 Give me understanding and I will obey your **l**;
119: 44 I will keep on obeying your **l** / forever and forever.
119: 51 but I do not turn away from your **l**.
119: 53 furious with the wicked, / those who reject your **l**.
119: 55 O LORD, / and I obey your **l** because of this.
119: 61 me into sin, / but I am firmly anchored to your **l**.
119: 70 hearts are dull and stupid, / but I delight in your **l**.
119: 72 Your **l** is more valuable to me / than millions in
119: 77 so I may live, / for your **l** is my delight.
119: 85 These arrogant people who hate your **l** / have dug
119: 92 If your **l** hadn't sustained me with joy, / I would
119: 97 Oh, how I love your **l**! / I think about it all day
119: 109 in the balance, / but I will not stop obeying your **l**.
119: 113 about you, / but my choice is clear—I love your **l**.
119: 126 to act, / for these evil people have broken your **l**.
119: 136 from my eyes / because people disobey your **l**.
119: 142 justice is eternal, / and your **l** is perfectly true.
119: 150 near to attack me; / they live far from your **l**.
119: 153 and rescue me, / for I have not forgotten your **l**.
119: 163 I hate and abhor all falsehood, / but I love your **l**.
119: 165 Those who love your **l** have great peace / and do
119: 174 for your salvation, / and your **l** is my delight.
122: 4 to the name of the LORD / as the **l** requires.
Pr 28: 4 To reject the **l** is to praise the wicked; to obey the **l** is to fight them.
28: 7 Young people who obey the **l** are wise; those who
28: 9 The prayers of a person who ignores the **l** are
29: 18 they run wild. But whoever obeys the **l** is happy.
Ecc 3: 16 Yes, even the courts of **l** are corrupt!
Isa 1: 10 Listen to the **l** of our God, people of Israel.
5: 24 for they have rejected the **l** of the LORD
42: 21 The LORD has magnified his **l** and made it truly
42: 24 go where he sent them, nor would they obey his **l**.
51: 4 Hear me, Israel, for my **l** will be proclaimed,
51: 7 right from wrong and cherish my **l** in your hearts.
Jer 8: 8 are wise because we have the **l** of the LORD,"
9: 13 I gave them; they have refused to obey my **l**.
16: 11 They abandoned me. They did not keep my **l**.
18: 18 We don't need him to teach the **l** and give us
26: 4 not listen to me and obey the **l** I have given you,
32: 7 By **l** you have the right to buy it before it is
32: 8 By **l** you have the right to buy it before it is offered
32: 23 but they refused to obey you or follow your **l**.
44: 10 No one has chosen to follow my **l** and the decrees I
La 2: 9 have been exiled to distant lands; the **l** is no more.
Eze 18: 27 obey the **l**, and do what is just and right, they will
43: 12 And this is the basic **l** of the Temple:
43: 12 is holy. Yes, this is the primary **l** of the Temple.
46: 14 the flour. This will be a permanent **l** for you.
Da 6: 7 should make a **l** that will be strictly enforced.
6: 8 and sign this **l** so it cannot be changed, a **l** of the Medes and Persians,
6: 9 So King Darius signed the **l**.
6: 10 But when Daniel learned that the **l** had been
6: 12 back to the king and reminded him about his **l**.
6: 12 "Did you not sign a **l** that for the next thirty days
6: 12 it is a **l** of the Medes and Persians, which cannot be
6: 13 from Judah, is paying no attention to you or your **l**.
6: 14 king was very angry with himself for signing the **l**,
6: 15 "Your Majesty knows that according to the **l** of the
6: 15 no **l** that the king signs can be changed."
9: 11 All Israel has disobeyed your **l** and turned away,
9: 11 and judgments written in the **l** of Moses,
9: 13 Every curse written against us in the **l** of Moses
Hos 8: 1 broken my covenant and revolted against my **l**.
Mic 6: 2 He will prosecute them to the full extent of the **l**.
Hab 1: 4 The **l** has become paralyzed and useless, and there
Hag 2: 11 Ask the priests this question about the **l**:
Zec 7: 12 so they could not hear the **l** or the messages that
Mal 2: 9 shown partiality in your interpretation of the **l**."
Mt 2: 4 of the leading priests and teachers of religious **l**.
5: 17 I did not come to abolish the **l** of Moses
5: 18 even the smallest detail of God's **l** will remain until
5: 20 you obey God better than the teachers of religious **l**
5: 21 "You have heard that the **l** of Moses says, 'Do not
5: 27 "You have heard that the **l** of Moses says, 'Do not
5: 31 "You have heard that the **l** of Moses says, 'A man
5: 33 "Again, you have heard that the **l** of Moses says,
5: 38 "You have heard that the **l** of Moses says, 'If an
5: 43 "You have heard that the **l** of Moses says,
7: 12 This is a summary of all that is taught in the **l**
7: 29 quite unlike the teachers of religious **l**.
8: 4 Take along the offering required in the **l** of Moses
8: 19 Then one of the teachers of religious **l** said to him,
9: 3 some of the teachers of religious **l** said among
12: 2 It's against the **l** to work by harvesting grain on the
12: 4 for the priests alone. That was breaking the **l**, too.
12: 5 And haven't you ever read in the **l** of Moses that
12: 38 One day some teachers of religious **l** and Pharisees
13: 52 "Every teacher of religious **l** who has become a
15: 1 and teachers of religious **l** now arrived from
16: 21 the leading priests and the teachers of religious **l**.
17: 10 "Why do the teachers of religious **l** insist that
20: 15 Is it against the **l** for me to do what I want with my
20: 18 the leading priests and the teachers of religious **l**.
21: 15 and the teachers of religious **l** saw these wonderful
22: 35 One of them, an expert in religious **l**, tried to trap
22: 36 which is the most important commandment in the **l**
23: 2 "The teachers of religious **l** and the Pharisees are
23: 13 terrible it will be for you teachers of religious **l**
23: 15 terrible it will be for you teachers of religious **l**
23: 23 terrible it will be for you teachers of religious **l**
23: 23 but you ignore the important things of the **l**—
23: 25 terrible it will be for you teachers of religious **l**
23: 27 terrible it will be for you teachers of religious **l**
23: 29 terrible it will be for you teachers of religious **l**
23: 34 and wise men and teachers of religious **l**.
26: 57 where the teachers of religious **l** and other leaders
27: 6 "since it's against the **l** to accept money paid for
27: 41 The leading priests, the teachers of religious **l**,
Mk 1: 22 quite unlike the teachers of religious **l**.
1: 44 Take along the offering required in the **l** of Moses
2: 6 But some of the teachers of religious **l** who were
2: 16 But when some of the teachers of religious **l** who
2: 24 It's against the **l** to work by harvesting grain on the
2: 26 to his companions. That was breaking the **l**, too."
3: 22 But the teachers of religious **l** who had arrived
7: 1 and teachers of religious **l** arrived from Jerusalem
7: 5 the Pharisees and teachers of religious **l** asked him,
7: 10 For instance, Moses gave you this **l** from God:
7: 13 you break the **l** of God in order to protect your own
8: 31 the leading priests, and the teachers of religious **l**.
9: 11 "Why do the teachers of religious **l** insist that
9: 14 as some teachers of religious **l** were arguing with
10: 33 the leading priests and the teachers of religious **l**.
11: 18 and teachers of religious **l** heard what Jesus had
11: 27 the leading priests, the teachers of religious **l**,
12: 19 "Teacher, Moses gave us a **l** that if a man dies,
12: 28 One of the teachers of religious **l** was standing
12: 32 The teacher of religious **l** replied, "Well said,
12: 33 burnt offerings and sacrifices required in the **l**."
12: 35 "Why do the teachers of religious **l** claim that the
12: 38 "Beware of these teachers of religious **l**! For they
14: 1 and the teachers of religious **l** were still looking for
14: 43 the teachers of religious **l**, and the other leaders.
14: 53 and teachers of religious **l** had gathered.
15: 1 other leaders, and teachers of religious **l**—
15: 31 and teachers of religious **l** also mocked Jesus.
Lk 2: 22 as required by the **l** of Moses after the birth of a
2: 23 The **l** of the Lord says, "If a woman's first child is
2: 24 to what was required in the **l** of the Lord—
2: 27 present the baby Jesus to the Lord as the **l** required,
2: 39 fulfilled all the requirements of the **l** of the Lord,
5: 14 Take along the offering required in the **l** of Moses
5: 17 and teachers of religious **l** were sitting nearby.
5: 21 and teachers of religious **l** said to each other.
5: 30 and their teachers of religious **l** complained bitterly
6: 2 It's against the **l** to work by harvesting grain on the
6: 4 some to his friends. That was breaking the **l**, too."
6: 7 The teachers of religious **l** and the Pharisees
7: 30 and experts in religious **l** had rejected God's plan
9: 22 the leading priests, and the teachers of religious **l**.
10: 25 One day an expert in religious **l** stood up to test
10: 26 Jesus replied, "What does the **l** of Moses say?
11: 45 "Teacher," said an expert in religious **l**,
11: 46 terrible it will be for you experts in religious **l**!
11: 52 terrible it will be for you experts in religious **l**!
11: 53 and teachers of religious **l** were furious.
14: 3 Jesus asked the Pharisees and experts in religious **l**,
14: 3 is it permitted in the **l** to heal people on the
15: 2 and teachers of religious **l** complain that he was
16: 17 But that doesn't mean that the **l** has lost its force in
19: 47 but the leading priests, the teachers of religious **l**,
20: 1 the leading priests and teachers of religious **l**
20: 19 When the teachers of religious **l** and the leading
20: 28 "Teacher, Moses gave us a **l** that if a man dies,
20: 39 remarked some of the teachers of religious **l** who
20: 46 "Beware of these teachers of religious **l**! For they
22: 2 and teachers of religious **l** were actively plotting
22: 66 the leading priests and the teachers of religious **l**.
23: 10 and the teachers of religious **l** stood there shouting
23: 56 so they rested all that day as required by the **l**.
Jn 1: 17 For the **l** was given through Moses;
7: 19 None of you obeys the **l** of Moses! In fact, you are
7: 22 too, when you obey Moses' **l** of circumcision.
7: 22 this tradition of circumcision is older than the **l** of
7: 23 and do it, so as not to break the **l** of Moses.
8: 3 the teachers of religious **l** and Pharisees brought a
8: 5 The **l** of Moses says to stone her. What do you
8: 17 Your own **l** says that if two people agree about
10: 34 "It is written in your own **l** that God said to certain
Ac 4: 5 and teachers of religious **l** met in Jerusalem.
5: 34 who was an expert on religious **l** and was very
6: 12 the elders, and the teachers of religious **l**.
6: 13 against the Temple and against the **l** of Moses.
7: 53 You deliberately disobeyed God's **l**, though you
13: 39 with God—something the Jewish **l** could never do.
15: 5 and be required to follow the **l** of Moses.
18: 13 to worship God in ways that are contrary to the **l**."
21: 20 and they all take the **l** of Moses very seriously.
22: 12 He was a godly man in his devotion to the **l**,
23: 3 What kind of judge are you to break the **l** yourself
23: 9 Some of the teachers of religious **l** who were
23: 29 it was something regarding their religious **l**—
24: 14 and I firmly believe the Jewish **l** and everything
25: 16 I quickly pointed out to them that Roman **l** does
Ro 2: 12 even though they never had God's written **l**.
2: 12 the Jews when they sin, for they do have the **l**.
2: 13 For it is not merely knowing the **l** that brings
2: 13 Those who obey the **l** will be declared right in
2: 14 when Gentiles, who do not have God's written **l**, instinctively follow what the **l** says,
2: 15 They demonstrate that God's **l** is written within
2: 17 you are relying on God's **l** for your special
2: 18 from wrong because you have been taught his **l**.
2: 20 For you are certain that in God's **l** you have
2: 23 You are so proud of knowing the **l**, but you
2: 25 is worth something only if you obey God's **l**.
2: 25 But if you don't obey God's **l**, you are no better off
2: 26 And if the Gentiles obey God's **l**, won't God give
2: 27 uncircumcised Gentiles who keep God's **l** will be
2: 27 and know so much about God's **l** but don't obey it.
3: 19 the **l** applies to those to whom it was given,
3: 20 right in God's sight by doing what his **l** commands.
3: 20 For the more we know God's **l**, the clearer it
3: 21 not by obeying the **l** but by the way promised in
3: 28 with God through faith and not by obeying the **l**.
3: 31 does this mean that we can forget about the **l**?
3: 31 only when we have faith do we truly fulfill the **l**.
4: 13 was not based on obedience to God's **l**,
4: 14 that God's promise is for those who obey God's **l**
4: 15 But the **l** brings punishment on those who try to
4: 15 (The only way to avoid breaking the **l** is to have no **l** to break!)
5: 13 Yes, people sinned even before the **l** was given.
5: 13 And though there was no **l** to break, since it had
5: 20 God's **l** was given so that all people could see how
6: 14 for you are no longer subject to the **l**,
6: 15 So since God's grace has set us free from the **l**,
7: 1 dear friends—you who are familiar with the **l**—
7: 1 don't you know that the **l** applies only to a person
7: 2 the **l** binds her to her husband as long as he is alive.
7: 3 she is free from that **l** and does not commit
7: 4 The **l** no longer holds you in its power,
7: 5 and the **l** aroused these evil desires that produced
7: 6 But now we have been released from the **l**, for we
7: 6 not in the old way by obeying the letter of the **l**,
7: 7 am I suggesting that the **l** of God is evil?
7: 7 The **l** is not sinful, but it was the **l** that showed me my sin.
7: 7 known that coveting is wrong if the **l** had not said,
7: 8 But sin took advantage of this **l** and aroused all
7: 8 If there were no **l**, sin would not have that power.
7: 9 I felt fine when I did not understand what the **l**
7: 9 I realized I had broken the **l** and was a sinner,
7: 10 So the good **l**, which was supposed to show me the
7: 11 Sin took advantage of the **l** and fooled me; it took the good **l** and used it to make me guilty of
7: 12 But still, the **l** itself is holy and right and good.
7: 13 Did the **l**, which is good, cause my doom?
7: 14 The **l** is good, then. The trouble is not with the **l** but with me,
7: 16 and my bad conscience shows that I agree that the **l**
7: 22 I love God's **l** with all my heart.
7: 23 But there is another **l** at work within me that is at
7: 23 This **l** wins the fight and makes me a slave to the
7: 25 In my mind I really want to obey God's **l**, but
8: 3 The **l** of Moses could not save us, because of our
8: 4 so that the requirement of the **l** would be fully
9: 4 made covenants with them and gave his **l** to them.
9: 31 so hard to get right with God by keeping the **l**,
9: 32 were trying to get right with God by keeping the **l**
10: 3 of getting right with God by trying to keep the **l**.
10: 4 has accomplished the whole purpose of the **l**.
13: 8 you will fulfill all the requirements of God's **l**.
1Co 9: 8 Doesn't God's **l** say the same thing?
9: 9 For the **l** of Moses says, "Do not keep an ox from
9: 20 do the same, even though I am not subject to the **l**,
9: 21 am with the Gentiles who do not have the Jewish **l**,
9: 21 I do not discard the **l** of God; I obey the **l** of Christ.
14: 34 They should be submissive, just as the **l** says.
15: 56 that results in death, and the **l** gives sin its power.
2Co 3: 7 That old system of **l** etched in stone led to death,
Gal 2: 16 not by doing what the **l** commands, but by faith in
2: 16 in Christ—and not because we have obeyed the **l**.
2: 16 For no one will ever be saved by obeying the **l**."
2: 19 For when I tried to keep the **l**, I realized I could
2: 19 So I died to the **l** so that I might live for God.
2: 21 For if we could be saved by keeping the **l**,
3: 2 Did you receive the Holy Spirit by keeping the **l**?
3: 5 among you because you obey the **l** of Moses?
3: 10 But those who depend on the **l** to make them right
3: 10 that are written in God's Book of the **L**."
3: 11 can ever be right with God by trying to keep the **l**.

3:12 different from this way of faith is the way of l,
3:12 "If you wish to find life by obeying the l,
3:13 has rescued us from the curse pronounced by the l.
3:17 430 years later when God gave the l to Moses.
3:18 could be received only by keeping the l,
3:19 Well then, why was the l given? It was given to
3:19 But this system of l was to last only until the
3:21 is there a conflict between God's l and God's
3:21 If the l could have given us new life, we could
3:23 right with God, we were guarded by the l.
3:24 The l was our guardian and teacher to lead us until
3:25 has come, we no longer need the l as our guardian.
4: 4 sent his Son, born of a woman, subject to the l.
4: 5 to buy freedom for us who were slaves to the l,
4:12 become like you Gentiles were—free from the l.
4:21 Listen to me, you who want to live under the l. Do you know what the l really says?
4:24 Sinai where people first became enslaved to the l.
4:29 are persecuted by those who want us to keep the l,
4:31 not children of the slave woman, obligated to the l.
5: 1 and don't get tied up again in slavery to the l.
5: 3 you must obey all of the regulations in the whole l
5: 4 make yourselves right with God by keeping the l,
5:14 For the whole l can be summed up in this one
5:18 the Holy Spirit, you are no longer subject to the l.
5:23 Here there is no conflict with the l.
6: 2 and problems, and in this way obey the l of Christ.
6:13 circumcision don't really keep the whole l.
Eph 2:15 system of Jewish l that excluded the Gentiles.
Php 3: 5 who demand the strictest obedience to the Jewish l.
3: 6 And I obeyed the Jewish l so carefully that I was
3: 9 on my own goodness or my ability to obey God's l,
1Ti 1: 7 They want to be known as teachers of the l of
Heb 2: 2 people were punished for every violation of the l
7: 5 are commanded in the l of Moses to collect a tithe
7:11 and it was that priesthood on which the l was
7:12 is changed, the l must also be changed to permit it.
7:15 The change in God's l is even more evident from
7:19 For the l made nothing perfect, and now a better
7:28 Those who were high priests under the l of Moses
7:28 But after the l was given, God appointed his Son
8: 4 who offer the gifts required by the l of Moses.
9:22 we can say that according to the l of Moses,
10: 1 The old system in the l of Moses was only a
10: 8 (though they are required by the l of Moses).
10:28 Anyone who refused to obey the l of Moses was
Jas 1:25 if you keep looking steadily into God's perfect l—
1:25 the l that sets you free—and if you do what it says
2: 9 a sin, for you are guilty of breaking that l.
2:11 you murder someone, you have broken the entire l,
2:12 remember that you will be judged by the l of love, the l that set you free.
4:11 then you are criticizing and condemning God's l.
4:11 not a judge who can decide whether the l is right
4:12 God alone, who made the l, can rightly judge
1Jn 3: 4 Those who sin are opposed to the l of God, for all sin opposes the l of God.

LAW'S (1) [LAW]

Ro 10: 5 For Moses wrote that the l way of making a person

LAWFUL (1) [LAW]

Eze 18: 5 a certain man is just and does what is l and right,

LAWGIVER (1) [LAW]

Isa 33:22 For the LORD is our judge, our l, and our king.

LAWLESS (4) [LAWLESSNESS]

Ps 119:150 Those l people are coming near to attack me;
Da 11:14 L ones among your own people will join them in
Ac 2:23 With the help of l Gentiles, you nailed him to the
Heb 10:17 never again remember / their sins and l deeds."

LAWLESSNESS (5) [LAWLESS]

Mt 23:28 inside your hearts are filled with hypocrisy and l.
Ro 6:19 you let yourselves be slaves of impurity and l.
2Th 2: 3 rebellion against God and the man of l is revealed—
2: 7 For this l is already at work secretly, and it will
2: 8 Then the man of l will be revealed, whom the Lord

LAWS (203) [LAW]

Ge 26: 5 my requirements, commands, regulations, and l."
Ex 15:26 is right in his sight, obeying his commands and l,
18:16 and teach them his l and instructions."
18:20 teach them God's l and instructions,
24: 8 LORD has made with you in giving you these l."
Lev 10:11 And you must teach the Israelites all the l that the
18: 4 all my regulations and be careful to keep my l,
18: 5 If you obey my l and regulations, you will find life
18:26 You must strictly obey all of my l and regulations,
18:30 So be careful to obey my l, and do not practice any
19:19 "You must obey all my l. "Do not breed your
19:37 You must be careful to obey all of my l
20: 8 Keep all my l and obey them, for I am the LORD,
20:22 "You must carefully obey all my l and regulations;
25:18 in the land, keep my l and obey my regulations.
26: 3 "If you keep my l and are careful to obey my
26:15 and if you break my covenant by rejecting my l
26:43 for they rejected my regulations and despised my l.
26:46 These are the l, regulations, and instructions that
Nu 9: 3 Be sure to follow all my l and regulations
9:14 they must follow these same l and regulations.
9:14 The same l apply both to you and to the foreigners
15:15 before the LORD and are subject to the same l.
35:29 These are permanent l for you to observe from
Dt 4: 1 listen carefully to these l and regulations that I am
4: 5 "You must obey these l and regulations when you
4: 6 When they hear about these l, they will exclaim,
4: 8 And what great nation has l and regulations as fair as this body of l that I am
4:10 and they will be able to teach my l to their
4:14 time that the LORD commanded me to issue the l
4:40 If you obey all the l and commands that I will give
4:45 These are the stipulations, l, and regulations that
5: 1 "Listen carefully to all the l and regulations I am
5:31 can give you all my commands, l, and regulations.
6: 1 "These are all the commands, l, and regulations
6: 2 If you obey all his l and commands, you will enjoy
6:17 all the stipulations and l he has given you.
6:20 'What is the meaning of these stipulations, l,
6:24 LORD our God commanded us to obey all these l
7:11 Therefore, obey all these commands, l,
8:11 and disobey his commands, regulations, and l.
10:13 and l that I am giving you today for your own
11: 1 all his requirements, l, regulations, and commands.
11:32 you must be careful to obey all the l
12: 1 "These are the l and regulations you must obey as
16:12 slaves in Egypt, so be careful to obey all these l.
17:18 he must copy these l on a scroll for himself in the
26:16 your God has commanded you to obey all these l
26:17 You have promised to obey his l, commands,
27:10 and l that I am giving you today."
28:15 all the commands and l I am giving you today,
28:45 and to obey the commands and l he has given you.
30:10 and l written in this Book of the Law,
30:16 LORD your God and to keep his commands, l,
31:13 so that your children who have not known these l
Jos 1: 7 very courageous. Obey all the l Moses gave you.
2Sa 22:23 For all his l are constantly before me; / I have
1Ki 2: 3 Keep each of the l, commands, regulations,
6:12 if you keep all my l and regulations and obey all
8:58 will in everything and to obey all the commands, l,
8:61 May you always obey his l and commands, just as
9: 4 my commands and keeping my l and regulations,
9: 6 abandon me and disobey my commands and l,
11:11 not kept my covenant and have disobeyed my l,
11:33 He has not obeyed my l and regulations as his
11:34 I chose and who obeyed my commands and l,
11:38 and if you obey my l and commands, as my servant
2Ki 17:13 Obey my commands and l, which are contained in
17:15 They rejected his l and the covenant he had made
17:34 of truly worshiping the LORD and obeying the l,
17:37 Be careful to obey all the l, regulations,
18:12 all the l the LORD had given through his servant
23: 3 regulations, and l with all his heart and soul.
23:24 He did this in obedience to all the l written in the
23:25 and soul and strength, obeying all the l of Moses.
1Ch 22:13 For if you carefully obey the l and regulations that
2Ch 7:17 and obey all my commands, l, and regulations,
7:19 "But if you abandon me and disobey the l
19:10 of God's instructions, commands, l, or regulations,
23:11 They presented Joash with a copy of God's l
30:18 even though this was contrary to God's l.
33: 8 all the instructions, l, and regulations given
34:31 regulations, and l with all his heart and soul.
Ezr 7:10 obey the law of the LORD and to teach those l
7:11 taught the commands and l of the LORD to Israel:
7:25 and judges who know your God's l to govern all
7:25 If the people are not familiar with those l, you must
Ne 1: 7 sinned terribly by not obeying the commands, l,
9:13 that were just, and l and commands that were true.
9:14 You instructed them concerning the l of your holy
9:14 to obey all your commands, l, and instructions.
10:29 l, and regulations of the LORD their Lord.
12:45 as required by the l of David and his son Solomon,
Est 1:13 who knew all the Persian l and customs, for he
3: 8 Their l are different from those of any other nation,
3: 8 and they refuse to obey even the l of the king.
Job 28:26 He made the l of the rain and prepared a path for
38:33 Do you know the l of the universe and how God
Ps 18:22 For all his l are constantly before me; / I have
19: 9 lasting forever. / The l of the LORD are true;
50:16 God says to the wicked: / "Recite my l no longer,
50:17 you refuse my discipline / and treat my l like trash.
81: 4 For this is required by the l of Israel; / it is a law of
94:20 leaders who permit injustice by their l?
105:45 his principles / and obey his l. / Praise the LORD!
119: 7 When I learn your righteous l, / I will thank you by
119:13 I have recited aloud / all the l you have given us.
119:20 overwhelmed continually / with a desire for your l.
119:30 to be faithful; / I have determined to live by your l.
119:39 my shameful ways; / your l are all I want in life.
119:43 of truth from me, / for my only hope is in your l.
119:52 I meditate on your age-old l; / O LORD,
119:62 At midnight I rise to thank you / for your just l.
119:91 Your l remain true today, / for everything serves
119:102 I haven't turned away from your l, / for you have
119:106 I'll promise again: / I will obey your wonderful l.
119:108 accept my grateful thanks / and teach me your l.
119:160 words are true; / all your just l will stand forever.
119:164 you seven times a day / because all your l are just.
119:175 so I can praise you, / and may your l sustain me.
147:19 his words to Jacob, / his principles and l to Israel.
147:20 this with any other nation; / they do not know his l.
Pr 8:15 Because of me, kings reign, and rulers make just l.
Isa 10: 1 for the unjust judges, for those who issue unfair l.
24: 5 violated his l, and broken his everlasting covenant.
26: 8 LORD, we love to obey your l; / our heart's
29:13 to nothing more than human l learned by rote.
43:27 sinned against me—all your leaders broke my l.
58: 2 Temple every day and seem delighted to hear my l.
Jer 17: 1 "My people act as though their evil ways are l to
31:33 "I will put my l in their minds, and I will write
31:36 Israel as I am to do away with the l of nature!
33:25 reject my people than I would change my l of night
44:23 and follow his instructions, l, and stipulations."
Eze 4:14 never eaten any of the animals that our l forbid."
5: 6 She has refused to obey the l I gave her to follow.
5: 7 Since you have refused to obey my l
11:20 so they will obey my l and regulations. Then they
18: 9 and faithfully obeys my l and regulations.
18:17 at interest, and obeys all my regulations and l.
18:19 For if the child does what is right and keeps my l,
18:21 and begin to obey my l and do what is just
20:11 There I gave them my l so they could live by
20:13 and they refused to obey my l there in the
20:16 I told them this because they had rejected my l,
20:19 'Follow my l, pay attention to my instructions,
20:21 They refused to keep my l and follow my
20:24 because they did not obey my l. They scorned my
20:25 worthless customs and l that would not lead to life.
22:26 Your priests have violated my l and defiled my
33:15 and obey my life-giving l, no longer doing what is
36:27 so you will obey my l and do whatever I command.
37:24 They will obey my regulations and keep my l.
44: 8 You have not kept the l I gave you concerning
44:24 my instructions and l at all the sacred festivals,
Da 7:25 He will try to change their sacred festivals and l,
9:10 for we have not followed the l he gave us through
Hos 4: 6 Since you have forgotten the l of your God, I will
8:12 Even though I gave them all my l, they act as if those l don't apply to them.
Am 2: 4 They have rejected the l of the LORD, refusing to
Mic 3:11 can get; you priests teach God's l only for a price;
6:16 "The only l you keep are those of evil King Omri;
Zep 3: 4 Its priests defile the Temple by disobeying God's l.
Mal 3: 7 you have scorned my l and failed to obey them.
4: 4 all the l and regulations that I gave him on Mount
Mt 5:19 But anyone who obeys God's l and teaches them
Mk 7: 8 For you ignore God's specific l and substitute your
7: 9 "You reject God's l in order to hold on to your
Lk 16:16 the l of Moses and the messages of the prophets
Jn 18:31 take him away and judge him by your own l,"
19: 7 "By our l he ought to die because he called
Ac 10:14 my life eaten anything forbidden by our Jewish l."
10:28 "You know it is against the Jewish l for me to
11: 8 never eaten anything forbidden by our Jewish l.'
15:21 For these l of Moses have been preached in Jewish
18:15 a question of words and names and your Jewish l,
21:21 Gentile world to turn their backs on the l of Moses.
21:24 all false and that you yourself observe the Jewish l.
21:28 and tells everybody to disobey the Jewish l.
22: 3 At his feet I learned to follow our Jewish l
25: 8 "I have committed no crime against the Jewish l
Ro 7: 2 if he dies, the l of marriage no longer apply to her.
8: 7 to God. It never did obey God's l, and it never will.
13: 2 So those who refuse to obey the l of the land are
1Co 9:20 When I am with those who follow the Jewish l,
2Co 3: 6 is a covenant, not of written l, but of the Spirit.
Gal 2:14 have discarded the Jewish l and are living like a
2:14 these Gentiles obey the Jewish l you abandoned?
3:19 God gave his l to angels to give to Moses, who was
1Ti 1: 8 We know these l are good when they are used as
1:10 These l are for people who are sexually immoral,
Tit 3: 9 in quarrels and fights about obedience to Jewish l.
Heb 8: 6 to the ministry of those who serve under the old l,
8:10 says the Lord: / I will put my l in their minds
9:19 after Moses had given the people all of God's l,
9:19 and sprinkled both the book of God's l and all the
10:16 says the Lord: / I will put my l in their hearts
12:18 did at Mount Sinai when God gave them his l.
13:11 Under the system of Jewish l, the high priest
Jas 2:10 And the person who keeps all of the l except one is
2:10 guilty as the person who has broken all of God's l.

LAWSUIT (4) [LAWSUITS]

Dt 17: 8 of murder or only of manslaughter, or a difficult l,
Hos 4: 1 The LORD has filed a l against you, saying:
12: 2 Now the LORD is bringing a l against Judah.
1Co 6: 1 why do you file a l and ask a secular court to

LAWSUITS (3) [LAWSUIT]

Dt 21: 5 And they are to decide all l and punishments.
Isa 59: 4 being fair and honest. Their l are based on lies.
1Co 6: 7 To have such l at all is a real defeat for you.

LAWYER (4) [LAW]

Jer 51:36 "I will be your l to plead your case, and I will
La 3:58 Lord, you are my l! Plead my case! For you have
Ac 24: 1 with some of the Jewish leaders and the l Tertullus,
Tit 3:13 Do everything you can to help Zenas the l

LAY (105) [LAID, LAYING, LAYS]

Ge 9:21 on some wine he had made and l naked in his tent.
22:12 "L down the knife," the angel said. "Do not hurt
28:11 found a stone for a pillow and l down to sleep.
34:28 everything they could l their hands on, both inside
48:14 But Jacob crossed his arms as he reached out to l
49:33 he l back in the bed, breathed his last, and died.
Ex 29:10 and his sons will l their hands on its head.
29:15 and his sons must l their hands on the head of one
29:19 have Aaron and his sons l their hands on its head
Lev 1: 4 L your hand on its head so the LORD will accept
1:12 and the priests will l the pieces of the sacrifice,
3: 2 L your hand on the animal's head, and slaughter it

3:13 l your hand on its head, and slaughter it at the
4:4 l his hand on the bull's head, and slaughter it there
4:15 leaders must then l their hands on the bull's head
4:24 He is to l his hand on the goat's head and slaughter
4:29 They are to l a hand on the head of the sin offering
4:33 They are to l a hand on the head of the sin offering
16:21 He is to l both of his hands on the goat's head
16:21 he will l the people's sins on the head of the goat;
24:14 and tell all those who heard him to l their hands on
Nu 8:10 the people of Israel must l their hands on them.
8:12 "Next the Levites will l their hands on the heads
16:46 L incense on it and carry it quickly among the
22:27 the donkey saw the angel, it l down under Balaam.
27:18 who has the Spirit in him, and l your hands on him.
Dt 9:18 and nights I l prostrate before the LORD,
9:25 I fell down and l before the LORD for forty days
28:52 They will l siege to your cities until all the fortified
Jos 6:26 cost of his firstborn son, / he will l its foundation.
8:9 they left that night and l in ambush between Bethel
18:11 It l between the territory previously assigned to the
Jdg 5:27 He sank, he fell, / he l dead at her feet.
19:26 the door of the house and l there until it was light.
Ru 3:7 he l down beside the heap of grain and went to
3:7 Ruth came quietly, uncovered his feet, and l down.
3:14 So Ruth l at Boaz's feet until the morning, but she
1Sa 15:5 to the city of Amalek and l in wait in the valley.
19:24 and l on the ground all day and all night,
25:37 he had a stroke, and he l on his bed paralyzed.
2Sa 4:7 they cut off his head as he l there on his bed.
12:16 without food and l all night on the bare ground.
20:12 But Amasa l in his blood in the middle of the road,
1Ki 1:47 Then the king bowed his head in worship as he l in
13:24 His body l there on the road, with the donkey
13:31 of God is buried. L my bones beside his bones.
18:23 cut it into pieces and l it on the wood of their altar,
18:23 the other bull and l it on the wood on the altar,
19:5 Then he l down and slept under the broom tree.
19:6 jar of water! So he ate and drank and l down again.
2Ki 4:29 Go quickly and l the staff on the child's face."
4:34 Then he l down on the child's body, placing his
8:7 the capital of Aram, where King Ben-hadad l sick.
2Ch 24:25 They assassinated him as he l in bed. Then he was
Ezr 3:6 This was also before they had started to l the
Est 3:6 So he decided it was not enough to l hands on
4:3 and many people l in sackcloth and ashes.
Job 23:4 I would l out my case and present my arguments.
30:12 They send me sprawling; they l traps in my path.
41:8 If you l a hand on it, you will never forget the
Ps 3:5 I l down and slept. / I woke up in safety,
38:12 Meanwhile, my enemies l traps for me;
104:3 you l out the rafters of your home in the rain
Pr 24:16 But one calamity is enough to l the wicked low.
29:5 To flatter people is to l a trap for their feet.
SS 3:1 "One night as I l in bed, I yearned deeply for my
Isa 34:15 There the owl will make her nest and l her eggs.
Jer 4:26 The cities l in ruins, crushed by the LORD's
19:9 I will see to it that your enemies l siege to the city
Eze 6:5 I will l your corpses in front of your idols
16:6 in your own blood. As you l there, I said, 'Live!'
16:22 of the days long ago when you l naked in a field,
19:2 She l down among the young lions / and reared her
31:13 and the wild animals l among its branches.
Da 2:28 and the visions you saw as you l on your bed.
4:5 I saw visions that terrified me as I l in my bed.
4:13 " 'Then as I l there dreaming, I saw a messenger,
7:1 had a dream and saw visions as he l in his bed.
8:18 I fainted and l there with my face to the ground.
8:27 Daniel, was overcome and l sick for several days.
10:9 I fainted and l there with my face to the ground.
11:15 and l siege to a fortified city and capture it.
Hag 2:15 began to l the foundation of the LORD's Temple.
Mt 8:20 home of my own, not even a place to l my head."
9:18 again if you just come and l your hand upon her."
19:13 so he could l his hands on them and pray for them.
25:5 bridegroom was delayed, they all l down and slept.
Mk 7:32 and the people begged Jesus to l his hands on the
9:26 The boy l there motionless, and he appeared to be
Lk 8:23 On the way across, Jesus l down for a nap,
9:58 home of my own, not even a place to l my head."
16:20 At his door l a diseased beggar named Lazarus.
16:21 As Lazarus l there longing for scraps from the rich
Jn 5:3 blind, lame, or paralyzed—l on the porches.
10:15 the Father. And I l down my life for the sheep.
10:17 because I l down my life that I may have it back
10:18 take my life from me. I l down my life voluntarily.
10:18 For I have the right to l it down when I want to
15:13 the greatest love is shown when people l down
Ac 8:19 "so that when I l my hands on people,
15:28 and to us to l no greater burden on you than these
27:19 and anything else they could l their hands on.
Ro 11:13 the apostle to the Gentiles. I l great stress on this,
1Co 3:11 For no one can l any other foundation than the one
Rev 4:10 And they l their crowns before the throne and say,

LAYER (7) [LAYERS]

Ex 26:14 On top of these coverings place a l of tanned ram
26:14 and over them put a l of fine goatskin leather.
1Ki 6:36 so that there was one l of cedar beams after every
7:12 so that there was one l of cedar beams after every
Ezr 6:4 prepared stones will be topped by a l of timber.
Job 41:13 and who can penetrate its double l of armor?
Jer 38:6 but there was a thick l of mud at the bottom,

LAYERS (7) [LAYER]

Ex 36:19 Then they made two more l for the roof covering.
39:34 the l of tanned ram skins and fine goatskin leather;
40:19 the Tabernacle framework and put on the roof l,
Nu 3:25 the tent of the Tabernacle with its l of coverings,
1Ki 6:36 of cedar beams after every three l of hewn stone.
7:12 of cedar beams after every three l of hewn stone,
Ezr 6:4 Every three l of specially prepared stones will be

LAYING (9) [LAY]

Lev 3:8 by l your hand on its head and slaughtering it at the
Jdg 6:26 your God here on this hill, l the stones carefully.
1Ki 15:27 and the Israelite army were l siege to the Philistine
Ps 83:3 your people, / l plans against your precious ones.
Mic 5:1 your troops! The enemy is l siege to Jerusalem.
Ac 9:12 and l his hands on him so that he can see again."
28:3 an armful of sticks and was l them on the fire,
28:8 for him, and l his hands on him, he healed him.
Heb 6:2 the l on of hands, the resurrection of the dead,

LAYPEOPLE (1) [PEOPLE]

Isa 24:2 Priests and l, servants and masters, maids

LAYS (4) [LAY]

Job 39:14 She l her eggs on top of the earth, letting them be
Pr 20:26 wise king finds the wicked, l them out like wheat,
Eze 17:17 the king of Babylon l siege to Jerusalem again
Jn 10:11 The good shepherd l down his life for the sheep.

LAZARUS (21) [LAZARUS'S]

Lk 16:20 At his door lay a diseased beggar named L.
16:21 As L lay there longing for scraps from the rich
16:23 he saw L in the far distance with Abraham.
16:24 Send L over here to dip the tip of his finger in
16:25 had everything you wanted, and L had nothing.
Jn 11:1 A man named L was sick. He lived in Bethany
11:2 wiped them with her hair. Her brother, L, was sick.
11:5 Although Jesus loved Martha, Mary, and L,
11:11 Then he said, "Our friend L has fallen asleep,
11:13 They thought Jesus meant L was having a good night's rest, but Jesus meant L had died.
11:14 Then he told them plainly, "L is dead.
11:17 he was told that L had already been in his grave for
11:37 blind man. Why couldn't he keep L from dying?"
11:43 Then Jesus shouted, "L, come out!"
11:44 And L came out, bound in graveclothes, his face
12:1 Jesus arrived in Bethany, the home of L—
12:2 Martha served, and L sat at the table with him.
12:9 they flocked to see him and also to see L, the man
12:10 Then the leading priests decided to kill L, too,
12:17 Those in the crowd who had seen Jesus call L back

LAZARUS'S (2) [LAZARUS]

Jn 11:4 about it he said, "L sickness will not end in death.
11:31 they assumed she was going to L grave to weep.

LAZINESS (3) [LAZY]

Pr 31:27 and does not have to bear the consequences of l.
Ecc 10:18 L lets the roof leak, and soon the rafters begin to
Eze 16:49 l, and gluttony, while the poor and needy suffered

LAZY (26) [LAZINESS, LAZYBONES]

Ex 5:17 But Pharaoh replied, "You're just l!
Pr 10:4 L people are soon poor; hard workers get rich.
10:26 L people are a pain to their employer. They are
12:24 and become a leader; be l and become a slave.
12:27 L people don't even cook the game they catch,
13:4 L people want much but get little, but those who
15:19 A l person has trouble all through life; the path of
18:9 A l person is as bad as someone who destroys
19:15 A l person sleeps soundly—and goes hungry.
19:24 so l that they won't even lift a finger to feed
20:4 If you are too l to plow in the right season, you will
21:25 The desires of l people will be their ruin, for their
22:13 The l person is full of excuses, saying, "If I go
24:30 I walked by the field of a l person, the vineyard of
26:13 The l person is full of excuses, saying, "I can't go
26:14 on its hinges, so the l person turns over in bed.
26:15 so l that they won't lift a finger to feed themselves.
26:16 L people consider themselves smarter than seven
Ecc 4:6 They feel it is better to be l and barely survive than
Isa 32:9 Listen, you women who lie around in l ease.
Mt 25:26 the master replied, 'You wicked and l servant!
Ro 12:11 Never be l in your work, but serve the Lord
1Th 5:14 and sisters, we urge you to warn those who are l.
2Th 3:7 We were never l when we were with you.
1Ti 5:13 they are likely to become l and spend their time
Tit 1:12 are all liars; they are cruel animals and l gluttons."

LAZYBONES (2) [LAZY]

Pr 6:6 Take a lesson from the ants, you l. Learn from
6:9 But you, l, how long will you sleep? When will

LEAD (148) [LEAD-TIPPED, LEADER, LEADER'S, LEADERS, LEADERSHIP, LEADING, LEADS, LED, RINGLEADER, RINGLEADERS]

Ge 32:16 He told his servants to l them on ahead, each group
33:12 Esau said. "I will stay with you and l the way."
50:24 come for you, to l you out of this land of Egypt.
50:25 he said, "When God comes to l us back to Canaan,
Ex 3:8 and l them out of Egypt into their own good
3:10 You will l my people, the Israelites, out of Egypt."
3:11 "How can you expect me to l the Israelites out of
3:17 I will l you to the land now occupied by the
6:26 "L all the people of Israel out of the land of Egypt,
6:27 permission to l the people from the land of Egypt.
7:4 after which I will l the forces of Israel out with
12:51 And that very day the LORD began to l the
13:17 God did not l them on the road that runs through
15:10 They sank like l / in the mighty waters.
15:13 "With unfailing love you will l / this people whom
23:20 I am sending my angel before you to l you safely
32:1 they said, "make us some gods who can l us.
32:23 They said to me, 'Make us some gods to l us,
32:34 Now go, l the people to the place I told you about.
32:34 Look! My angel will l the way before you!
33:1 l them to the land I solemnly promised Abraham,
Nu 2:9 These three tribes are to l the way whenever the
20:12 you will not l them into the land I am giving
27:17 Give them someone who will l them into battle,
31:22 made of gold, silver, bronze, iron, tin, or l—
32:17 and l our fellow Israelites into battle until we have
Dt 1:38 Joshua son of Nun, will l the people into the land.
3:28 for he will l the people across the Jordan.
7:4 They will l your young people away from me to
10:11 and l the people into the land I swore to give their
13:5 or dreamers who try to l you astray must be put to
17:17 because they will l him away from the LORD.
21:4 They must l it to a valley that is neither plowed nor
29:19 my own stubborn way.' This would l to utter ruin!
31:2 now 120 years old and am no longer able to l you.
31:7 For you will l these people into the land that the
Jos 1:2 you must l my people across the Jordan River into
1:6 for you will l my people to possess all the land I
1:14 must l the other tribes across the Jordan to help
3:6 of the Covenant and l the people across the river."
3:11 the whole earth, will l you across the Jordan River!
6:7 and the armed men will l the way in front of the
Jdg 5:12 Barak! / L your captives away, son of Abinoam!
11:8 "If you will l us in battle against the Ammonites,
20:18 "Which tribe should l the attack against the people
Ru 1:7 and they took the road that would l them back to
1Sa 8:20 Our king will govern us and l us into battle."
30:15 "Will you l me to them?" David asked.
2Sa 7:8 I chose you to l my people Israel when you were
15:18 to let David's troops move past to l the way.
17:11 And I think that you should personally l the troops.
18:1 appointed generals and captains to l his troops.
1Ki 11:2 because the women they married would l them to
1Ch 5:26 invade the land and l away the people of Reuben,
6:31 David assigned the following men to l the music at
16:4 David appointed the following Levites to l the
17:7 I chose you to l my people Israel when you were
2Ch 6:5 Nor have I chosen a king to l my people Israel.
8:14 He also assigned the Levites to l the people in
13:12 blow their trumpets and l us into battle against you.
29:11 and to l the people in worship and make offerings
Ne 12:46 The custom of having choir directors to l the choirs
Est 6:9 and to l him through the city square on the king's
Job 19:24 carved with an iron chisel and filled with l,
40:24 it off guard or put a ring in its nose and l it away.
Ps 5:8 L me in the right path, O LORD, / or my enemies
15:2 Those who l blameless lives / and do what is right,
25:5 L me by your truth and teach me, / for you are the
27:11 O LORD. / L me along the path of honesty,
28:9 your special possession! / L them like a shepherd,
31:3 For the honor of your name, l me out of this peril.
43:3 guide me. / Let them l me to your holy mountain,
44:9 in dishonor. / You no longer l our armies to battle.
61:2 L me to the towering rock of safety,
80:1 Shepherd of Israel, / you who l Israel like a flock.
101:2 I will l a life of integrity / in my own home.
118:20 Those gates l to the presence of the LORD,
139:24 and l me along the path of everlasting life.
143:10 May your gracious Spirit l me forward / on a firm
Pr 4:11 you wisdom's ways and l you in straight paths.
4:13 Guard them, for they will l you to a fulfilled life.
5:5 go down to death; her steps l straight to the grave.
6:22 Wherever you walk, their counsel can l you.
8:16 Rulers l with my help, and nobles make righteous
10:11 The words of the godly l to life; evil people cover
10:17 to life, but those who ignore it will l others astray.
12:26 advice to their friends; the wicked l them astray.
12:28 godly leads to life; their path does not l to death.
21:5 Good planning and hard work l to prosperity, but hasty shortcuts l to poverty.
22:4 True humility and fear of the LORD l to riches,
28:10 Those who l the upright into sin will fall into their
Ecc 9:11 And those who are educated don't always l
10:2 The hearts of the wise l them to do right,
10:2 and the hearts of the foolish l them to do evil.
Isa 11:6 safe among lions, and a little child will l them all.
30:28 will bridle them and l them off to their destruction.
40:11 He will gently l the mother sheep with their young.
42:16 I will l blind Israel down a new path,
49:10 For the LORD in his mercy will l them beside
57:18 I will l them and comfort those who mourn.
58:8 Your godliness will l you forward, and the glory of
Jer 2:17 the LORD your God when he wanted to l you
6:28 cruel as iron. All of them l others into corruption.
23:32 Their imaginary dreams are flagrant lies that l my
31:9 their faces, and I will l them home with great care.
50:8 land of the Babylonians. L my people home again.
50:16 L from Babylon all those who plant crops; send all
Eze 14:3 They have embraced things that l them into sin.
20:14 That way the nations who saw me l my people out
20:25 worthless customs and laws that would not l to life.
22:18 a useless mixture of copper, tin, iron, and l.
22:20 tin, iron, and l are melted down in a furnace.
27:12 your wares in exchange for silver, iron, tin, and l.

38: 4 and put hooks into your jaws to **l** you out to your
Hos 2:14 I will **l** her out into the desert and speak tenderly to
5: 8 **L** on into battle, O warriors of Benjamin!
Am 7:10 It will **l** to rebellion all across the land.
Mic 2:13 Your leader will break out and **l** you out of exile.
2:13 Your king will **l** you; the LORD himself will
4: 9 Have you no king to **l** you? He is dead! Have you
5: 4 And he will stand to **l** his flock with the LORD's
5: 5 seven rulers to watch over us, eight princes to **l** us.
7:14 rule your people; **l** your flock in green pastures.
Zec 5: 7 When the heavy **l** cover was lifted off the basket,
8:16 in your courts that are just and that **l** to peace.
Mt 24: 5 'I am the Messiah.' They will **l** many astray.
24:11 prophets will appear and will **l** many people astray.
Mk 13: 6 to be the Messiah. They will **l** many astray.
Lk 6:39 "What good is it for one blind person to **l** another?
13:15 stalls on the Sabbath and **l** them out for water?
Jn 12:50 And I know his instructions **l** to eternal life;
Ac 7:40 told Aaron, 'Make us some gods who can **l** us,
13:11 begging for someone to take his hand and **l** him.
Ro 6:22 Now you do those things that **l** to holiness
Gal 3:24 our guardian and teacher to **l** us until Christ came.
Eph 4: 1 the Lord, beg you to **l** a life worthy of your calling,
Col 2: 8 Don't let anyone **l** you astray with empty
1Ti 5:24 Remember that some people **l** sinful lives,
2Ti 2:16 foolish discussions that **l** to more and more
Heb 9:14 will purify our hearts from deeds that **l** to death
Jas 1:15 These evil desires **l** to evil actions, and evil actions
l to death.
1Pe 5: 3 to your care, but **l** them by your good example.
1Jn 2:26 need to be aware of those who want to **l** you astray.
5:16 Christian sinning in a way that does not **l** to death,
Rev 2:20 calls herself a prophet—to **l** my servants astray.
7:17 He will **l** them to the springs of life-giving water.

LEAD-TIPPED (3) [LEAD]

Mt 27:26 He ordered Jesus flogged with a **l** whip,
Mk 15:15 He ordered Jesus flogged with a **l** whip,
Jn 19: 1 Then Pilate had Jesus flogged with a **l** whip.

LEADER (159) [LEAD]

Nu 1: 4 assisted by one family **l** from each tribe."
3:24 The **l** of the Gershonite clans was Eliasaph son of
3:30 The **l** of the Kohathite clans was Elizaphan son of
3:35 The **l** of the Merarite clans was Zuriel son of
7: 3 a cart for every two leaders and an ox for each **l**.
7:11 "Let each **l** bring his gift on a different day for the
7:12 **l** of the tribe of Judah, presented his offering.
7:18 **l** of the tribe of Issachar, presented his offering.
7:24 **l** of the tribe of Zebulun, presented his offering.
7:30 **l** of the tribe of Reuben, presented his offering.
7:36 **l** of the tribe of Simeon, presented his offering.
7:42 **l** of the tribe of Gad, presented his offering.
7:48 **l** of the tribe of Ephraim, presented his offering.
7:54 **l** of the tribe of Manasseh, presented his offering.
7:60 **l** of the tribe of Benjamin, presented his offering.
7:66 **l** of the tribe of Dan, presented his offering.
7:72 **l** of the tribe of Asher, presented his offering.
7:78 **l** of the tribe of Naphtali, presented his offering.
13: 2 Send one **l** from each of the twelve ancestral
14: 4 "Let's choose a **l** and go back to Egypt!"
17: 3 for there must be one staff for the **l** of each
25:14 of Salu, the **l** of a family from the tribe of Simeon.
25:15 was the daughter of Zur, the **l** of a Midianite clan.
25:18 because of Cozbi, the daughter of a Midianite **l**,
27:16 please appoint a new **l** for the community.
34:18 Also enlist one **l** from each tribe to help them with
Dt 3:14 Jair, a **l** from the tribe of Manasseh,
31: 3 Joshua is your new **l**, and he will go with you,
Jos 22:14 and each a **l** within the family divisions of Israel.
Jdg 9:30 But when Zebul, the **l** of the city, heard what Gaal
1Sa 9:16 Anoint him to be the **l** of my people, Israel. He will
10: 1 because the LORD has appointed you to be the **l**
12: 2 I have served as your **l** since I was a boy.
15:17 of yourself, are you not the **l** of the tribes of Israel?
22: 2 until David was the **l** of about four hundred men.
25:30 done all he promised and has made you **l** of Israel,
2Sa 3: 6 Abner became a powerful **l** among those who were
3:38 "Do you not realize that a great **l** and a great man
5: 2 of my people Israel. You will be their **l**.' "
6:21 He appointed me as the **l** of Israel, the people of
23:18 the brother of Joab, was the **l** of the Thirty.
1Ki 11:24 and had become the **l** of a gang of rebels.
11:26 Another rebel **l** was Jeroboam son of Nebat,
2Ki 20: 5 "Go back to Hezekiah, the **l** of my people.
1Ch 2:10 was the father of Nahshon, a **l** of Judah.
5: 6 Beerah was the **l** of the Reubenites when they were
5: 7 genealogy by their clans: Jeiel (the **l**), Zechariah,
5:12 Joel was the **l** in the land of Bashan, and Shapham
5:15 son of Abdiel, son of Guni, was the **l** of their clans.
5:24 these men had a great reputation as a warrior and **l**.
7: 2 Each of them was the **l** of an ancestral clan.
11: 2 of my people Israel. You will be their **l**.' "
11:20 the brother of Joab, was the **l** of the Thirty.
11:42 the Reubenite **l** who had thirty men with him;
12: 3 Their **l** was Ahiezer son of Shemaah from Gibeah;
12: 4 a famous warrior and **l** among the Thirty;
12: 9 Ezer was their **l**. / Obadiah was second. / Eliab was
12:18 who later became a **l** among the Thirty, and he
12:27 This included Jehoiada, **l** of the family of Aaron,
15: 5 120 from the clan of Kohath, with Uriel as their **l**.
15: 6 220 from the clan of Merari, with Asaiah as their **l**.
15: 7 130 from the clan of Gershon, with Joel as their **l**.
15: 8 descendants of Elizaphan, with Shemaiah as their **l**.
15: 9 80 descendants of Hebron, with Eliel as their **l**.
15:10 descendants of Uzziel, with Amminadab as their **l**.
15:22 was chosen as the choir **l** because of his skill.
15:27 the Ark, the singers, and Kenaniah the song **l**.
16: 5 Asaph, the **l** of this group, sounded the cymbals.
23: 8 the descendants of Libni were Jehiel (the family **l**),
23:11 Jahath was the family **l**, and Ziza was next. Jeush
23:16 of Gershom included Shebuel, the family **l**.
23:17 Eliezer had only one son, Rehabiah, the family **l**.
23:18 of Izhar included Shelomith, the family **l**.
23:19 of Hebron included Jeriah (the family **l**),
23:20 of Uzziel included Micah (the family **l**)
24:20 the descendants of Amram, the **l** was Shebuel.
24:20 the descendants of Shebuel, the **l** was Jehdeiah.
24:21 the descendants of Rehabiah, the **l** was Isshiah.
24:22 the descendants of Izhar, the **l** was Shelomith.
24:22 the descendants of Shelomith, the **l** was Jahath.
24:23 From the descendants of Hebron, Jeriah was the **l**,
24:24 From the descendants of Uzziel, the **l** was Micah.
24:24 From the descendants of Micah, the **l** was Shamir,
24:25 the descendants of Isshiah, the **l** was Zechariah.
24:26 From the descendants of Jaaziah, the **l** was Beno.
24:28 of Mahli, the **l** was Eleazar, though he had no sons.
24:29 From the descendants of Kish, the **l** was Jerahmeel.
26:10 appointed Shimri as the **l** among his sons,
26:21 of Libni in the clan of Gershon, Jehiel was the **l**.
26:31 who was the **l** of the Hebronites according to the
29:22 They anointed him before the LORD as their **l**,
2Ch 13:12 So you see, God is with us. He is our **l**. His priests
19:11 son of Ishmael, a **l** from the tribe of Judah,
Ezr 1: 8 the **l** of the exiles returning to Judah.
2:69 and each **l** gave as much as he could. The total of
8:17 the **l** of the Levites at Casiphia, to ask him and his
Ne 3: 9 son of Hur, the **l** of half the district of Jerusalem,
3:12 He was the **l** of the other half of the district of
3:14 son of Recab, the **l** of the Beth-hakkerem district.
3:15 son of Col-hozeh, the **l** of the Mizpah district,
3:16 son of Azbuk, the **l** of half the district of Beth-zur.
3:17 came Hashabiah, the **l** of half the district of Keilah,
3:18 the **l** of the other half of the district of Keilah.
3:19 Next to them, Ezer son of Jeshua, the **l** of Mizpah,
9:17 and appointed a **l** to take them back to their slavery
12:12 Meraiah was **l** of the family of Seraiah.
12:12 Hananiah was **l** of the family of Jeremiah.
12:13 Meshullam was **l** of the family of Ezra.
12:13 Jehohanan was **l** of the family of Amariah.
12:14 Jonathan was **l** of the family of Malluch.
12:14 Joseph was **l** of the family of Shecaniah.
12:15 Adna was **l** of the family of Harim.
12:15 Helkai was **l** of the family of Meremoth.
12:16 Zechariah was **l** of the family of Iddo.
12:16 Meshullam was **l** of the family of Ginnethon.
12:17 Zicri was **l** of the family of Abijah.
12:17 There was also a **l** of the family of Miniamin.
12:17 Piltai was **l** of the family of Moadiah.
12:18 Shammua was **l** of the family of Bilgah.
12:18 Jehonathan was **l** of the family of Shemaiah.
12:19 Mattenai was **l** of the family of Joiarib.
12:19 Uzzi was **l** of the family of Jedaiah.
12:20 Kallai was **l** of the family of Sallu.
12:20 Eber was **l** of the family of Amok.
12:21 Hashabiah was **l** of the family of Hilkiah.
12:21 Nethanel was **l** of the family of Jedaiah.
Pr 12:24 Work hard and become a **l**; be lazy and become a
Ecc 4:16 He might become the **l** of millions and be very
Isa 3: 6 his brother, "Since you have a cloak, you be our **l**!
41:25 "But I have stirred up a **l** from the north and east.
46:11 a **l** from a distant land who will come and do my
55: 4 by being my witness and a **l** among the nations.
Jer 49:19 from its land, and I will appoint the **l** of my choice.
50:44 from its land, and I will appoint the **l** of my choice.
51:27 Appoint a **l**, and bring a multitude of horses!
Eze 19: 6 and became a **l** among them. / He learned to catch
22: 6 "Every **l** in Israel who lives within your walls is
Hos 1:11 people of Judah and Israel will unite under one **l**,
Mic 2:13 Your **l** will break out and lead you out of exile.
5: 1 With a rod they will strike the **l** of Israel in the
Hab 1:14 but creeping things that have no **l** to defend them
Mt 9:18 the **l** of a synagogue came and knelt down before
20:26 Whoever wants to be a **l** among you must be your
Mk 5:22 A **l** of the local synagogue, whose name was
5:38 When they came to the home of the synagogue **l**,
10:43 Whoever wants to be a **l** among you must be your
Lk 8:41 a **l** of the local synagogue, came and fell down at
13:14 But the **l** in charge of the synagogue was indignant
14: 1 One Sabbath day Jesus was in the home of a **l** of
18:18 Once a religious **l** asked Jesus this question:
22:26 the lowest rank, and the **l** should be like a servant.
Jn 3: 1 a Jewish religious **l** named Nicodemus, a Pharisee,
7:50 Nicodemus, the **l** who had met with Jesus earlier,
Ac 18: 8 Crispus, the **l** of the synagogue, and all his
18:17 had grabbed Sosthenes, the **l** of the synagogue,
1Co 3:21 So don't take pride in following a particular **l**.
Eph 1:21 or authority or power or **l** or anything else in this
Heb 2:10 the suffering of Jesus, God made him a perfect **l**,
3Jn 1: 9 but Diotrephes, who loves to be the **l**, does not

LEADER'S (3) [LEAD]

Lev 4:26 the priest will make atonement for the **l** sin,
Nu 17: 2 and inscribe each tribal **l** name on his staff.
Dt 33:21 for themselves; / a **l** share was assigned to them.

LEADERS (456) [LEAD]

Ge 34:20 and he appeared with his father before the town **l**
36:15 and grandchildren became the **l** of different clans.
36:15 became the **l** of the clans of Teman, Omar, Zepho,
36:17 The sons of Esau's son Reuel became the **l** of the
36:18 and his wife Oholibamah became the **l** of the clans
36:29 So the **l** of the Horite clans were Lotan, Shobal,
36:30 The Horite clans are named after their clan **l**,
36:40 These are the **l** of the clans of Esau, who lived in
Ex 3:16 "Now go and call together all the **l** of Israel.
3:18 "The **l** of the people of Israel will accept your
4:29 to Egypt and called the **l** of Israel to a meeting.
4:31 The **l** were soon convinced that the LORD had
5: 1 After this presentation to Israel's **l**, Moses
12:21 Then Moses called for the **l** of Israel and said,
15:15 The **l** of Edom will be terrified; / the nobles of
16:22 The **l** of the people came and asked Moses why
17: 5 Then call some of the **l** of Israel and walk on ahead
17: 6 was told; and as the **l** looked on, water gushed out.
18:12 Aaron and the **l** of Israel came out to meet him.
19: 7 the mountain and called together the **l** of the people
24: 1 Nadab, Abihu, and seventy of Israel's **l**.
24: 9 and seventy of the **l** of Israel went up the mountain.
24:11 And though Israel's **l** saw God, he did not destroy
24:14 Moses told the other **l**, "Stay here and wait for us
34:31 asked Aaron and the community **l** to come over
35:27 The **l** brought onyx stones and the other gemstones
Lev 4:14 the **l** of the community must bring a young bull for
4:15 The **l** must then lay their hands on the bull's head
4:22 "If one of Israel's **l** does something forbidden by
9: 1 together Aaron and his sons and the **l** of Israel.
Nu 1: 5 and the names of the **l** chosen for the task:
1:16 These tribal **l**, heads of their own families,
1:17 Now Moses and Aaron and the chosen **l**
1:44 by Moses and Aaron and the twelve **l** of Israel,
2: 3[-4] These are the names of the tribes, their **l**,
2:10[-11] These are the names of the tribes, their **l**,
2:18[-19] These are the names of the tribes, their **l**,
2:25[-26] These are the names of the tribes, their **l**,
4:34 and the other **l** of the community counted the
4:46 and the **l** of Israel counted all the Levites by their
7: 2 Then the **l** of Israel—the tribal **l** who had
organized the census—came
7: 3 There was a cart for every two **l** and an ox for each
7:10 The **l** also presented dedication gifts for the altar at
7:84 brought by the **l** of Israel at the time it was
10: 4 then only the **l** of the tribes of Israel will come to
11:16 "Summon before me seventy of the **l** of Israel.
11:24 Then he gathered the seventy **l** and stationed them
11:25 that was upon Moses and put it upon the seventy **l**.
11:26 They were listed among the **l** but had not gone out
11:30 Then Moses returned to the camp with the **l** of
13: 3 He sent out twelve men, all tribal **l** of Israel,
13: 4 These were the tribes and the names of the **l**:
16: 2 involving 250 other prominent **l**, all members of
16:25 and Abiram, followed closely by the Israelite **l**.
17: 6 and each of the twelve tribal **l**, including Aaron,
21:18 which princes dug, / which great **l** hollowed out
22: 4 The king of Moab said to the **l** of Midian,
26: 3 issued these census instructions to the **l** of Israel:
26: 9 and Abiram are the same community **l** who
27: 2 stood before Moses, Eleazar the priest, the tribal **l**,
30: 1 Now Moses summoned the **l** of the tribes of Israel
31:13 and all the **l** of the people went to meet them
31:26 and the family **l** of each tribe are to make a list of
32: 2 Eleazar the priest, and the other **l** of the people.
32:28 orders to Eleazar, Joshua, and the tribal **l** of Israel.
34:19 These are the tribes and the names of the **l**:
36: 1 to Moses and the family **l** of Israel with a petition.
Dt 1:13 good reputation, and I will appoint them as your **l**.'
5:23 was blazing with fire, all your tribal **l** came to me.
19:12 the **l** of the murderer's hometown must have the
21: 2 your **l** and judges must determine which town is
21: 3 Then the **l** of that town must select a young cow
21: 6 "The **l** of the town nearest the body must wash
21:19 and mother must take the son before the **l** of the
22:15 bring the proof of her virginity to the **l** of the town.
25: 7 she must go to the town gate and say to the **l** there,
25: 8 The **l** of the town will then summon him and try to
25: 9 must walk over to him in the presence of the **l**,
27: 1 and the **l** of Israel charged the people as follows:
29:10 your tribal **l**, your judges, your officers, all the men
31: 9 of the LORD's covenant, and to the **l** of Israel.
31:28 Now summon all the **l** and officials of your tribes
32:42 the captives, / and the heads of the enemy **l**." '
33: 5 in Israel— / when the **l** of the people assembled,
33:21 When the **l** of the people were assembled,
Jos 1:10 Joshua then commanded the **l** of Israel,
3: 2 days later, the Israelite **l** went through the camp
7: 6 and the **l** of Israel tore their clothing in dismay,
8:10 started toward Ai, accompanied by the **l** of Israel.
8:33 along with the **l**, officers, and judges, were divided
9:11 So our **l** and our people instructed us, 'Prepare for
9:14 So the Israelite **l** examined their bread, but they did
9:15 and the **l** of Israel ratified their agreement with a
9:18 for their **l** had made a vow to the LORD, the God
9:18 The people of Israel grumbled against their **l**
9:19 But the **l** replied, "We have sworn an oath in the
9:22 But Joshua called together the Gibeonite **l** and said,
14: 1 the priest, Joshua son of Nun, and the tribal **l**.
17: 4 Joshua son of Nun, and the Israelite **l** and said,
19:51 and the tribal **l** gave as an inheritance to the tribes
20: 4 death will appear before the **l** at the city gate
20: 5 the **l** must not release the accused to them,
21: 1 Then the **l** of the tribe of Levi came to consult with
21: 1 son of Nun, and the **l** of the other tribes of Israel.
23: 2 all the elders, **l**, judges, and officers of Israel.
24: 1 along with their elders, **l**, judges, and officers.
24:31 lifetime of Joshua and of the **l** who outlived him—
Jdg 1: 3 The **l** of Judah said to their relatives from the tribe
2: 7 the lifetime of Joshua and the **l** who outlived him—
5: 2 "When Israel's **l** take charge, / and the people
5: 9 My heart goes out to Israel's **l**, / and to those who

8: 5 reached Succoth, Gideon asked the **l** of the town,
8: 6 But the **l** of Succoth replied, "You haven't caught
8: 14 of all the seventy-seven rulers and **l** in the town.
8: 15 Gideon then returned to Succoth and said to the **l**,
8: 16 Then Gideon took the **l** of the town and taught
10: 18 The **l** of Gilead said to each other,
11: 5 the **l** of Gilead sent for Jephthah in the land of Tob.
11: 10 "The LORD is our witness," the **l** replied.
11: 11 So Jephthah went with the **l** of Gilead, and he
11: 11 Jephthah repeated what he had said to the **l**.
12: 4 The **l** of Ephraim responded, "The men of Gilead
16: 5 The **l** of the Philistines went to her and said,
16: 8 So the Philistine **l** brought Delilah seven new
16: 18 told her the truth, so she sent for the Philistine **l**.
16: 18 So the Philistine **l** returned and brought the money
16: 23 The Philistine **l** held a great festival,
16: 27 All the Philistine **l** were there, and there were
16: 30 And the temple crashed down on the Philistine **l**
20: 2 The **l** of all the people and all the tribes of Israel—
20: 5 That night some of the **l** of Gibeah surrounded the
21: 16 So the Israelite **l** asked, "How can we find wives
Ru 4: 2 Then Boaz called ten **l** from the town and asked
4: 9 Then Boaz said to the **l** and to the crowd standing
4: 11 Then the **l** and all the people standing there replied,
1Sa 4: 3 of Israel retreated to their camp, and their **l** asked,
8: 4 the **l** of Israel met at Ramah to discuss the matter
10: 20 So Samuel called the tribal **l** together before the
11: 3 replied the **l** of Jabesh. "If none of our relatives
14: 38 Then Saul said to the **l**, "Something's wrong!
15: 30 at least honor me before the **l** and before my
16: 4 at Bethlehem, the **l** of the town became afraid.
30: 26 David sent part of the plunder to the **l** of Judah,
30: 27 The gifts were sent to the **l** of the following towns
2Sa 2: 4 Then Judah's **l** came to David and crowned him
3: 17 Abner had consulted with the **l** of Israel.
3: 19 Abner also spoke with the **l** of the tribe of
5: 3 David made a covenant with the **l** of Israel before
7: 7 And I have never once complained to Israel's **l**,
8: 18 David's sons served as priestly **l**.
12: 17 The **l** of the nation pleaded with him to get up
17: 4 good to Absalom and to all the other **l** of Israel.
17: 14 Then Absalom and all the **l** of Israel said,
19: 11 and Abiathar, the priests, to say to the **l** of Judah,
19: 14 Then Amasa convinced all the **l** of Judah, and they
1Ki 8: 1 Solomon then summoned the **l** of all the tribes
8: 3 When all the **l** of Israel arrived, the priests picked
12: 3 The **l** of Israel sent for Jeroboam, and the whole
20: 7 Then Ahab summoned all the **l** of the land and said
20: 8 to any more demands," the **l** and people advised.
21: 8 and other **l** of the city where Naboth lived.
21: 11 and other **l** followed the instructions Jezebel had
2Ki 2: 19 Now the **l** of the town of Jericho visited Elisha.
6: 32 **l** of Israel when the king sent a messenger to
6: 32 before the messenger arrived, Elisha said to the **l**,
10: 1 to the officials of the city, to the **l** of the people,
10: 5 together with the other **l** and the guardians of the
10: 6 the king were being cared for by the **l** of Samaria,
10: 7 the **l** killed all seventy of the king's sons.
23: 1 Then the king summoned all the **l** of Judah
1Ch 1: 51 The clan **l** of Edom were Timna, Alvah, Jetheth,
1: 54 Magdiel, and Iram. These were the clan **l** of Edom.
4: 38 These were the names of some of the **l** of Simeon's
4: 41 the **l** of Simeon invaded it and completely
5: 13 the **l** of seven other clans, were Michael,
5: 24 These were the **l** of their clans: Epher, Ishi, Eliel,
7: 3 and Isshiah. These five became the **l** of clans.
7: 7 and Iri. These five warriors were the **l** of clans.
7: 9 among their descendants, in addition to their clan **l**.
7: 11 They were the **l** of the clans of Jediael, and their
7: 40 They were all skilled warriors and prominent **l**.
8: 6 **l** of the clans living at Geba, were driven out
8: 10 and Mirmah. These sons all became the **l** of clans.
8: 13 They were the **l** of the clans living in Aijalon,
8: 28 These were the **l** of the ancestral clans, and they
9: 9 These men were all **l** of clans, and they were listed
9: 34 and were listed as prominent **l** in their tribal
11: 3 a covenant with the **l** of Israel before the LORD.
11: 10 These are the **l** of David's mighty men.
12: 19 the Philistine **l** refused to let David and his men go
12: 32 there were 200 **l** of the tribe with their relatives.
15: 11 the priests, Zadok and Abiathar, and these Levite **l**:
15: 12 said to them, "You are the **l** of the Levite families.
15: 16 David also ordered the Levite **l** to appoint a choir
15: 25 Then David and the **l** of Israel and the generals of
17: 6 And I never once complained to Israel's **l**,
21: 16 and the **l** of Israel put on sackcloth to show their
22: 17 Then David ordered all the **l** of Israel to assist
23: 2 David summoned all the political **l** of Israel,
23: 9 These were the **l** of the family of Libni. Three of
23: 24 the **l** of their family groups, registered carefully by
24: 4 for there were more family **l** among the
24: 6 and the family **l** of the priests and Levites.
24: 20 These were the other family **l** descended from
24: 26 of Merari, the **l** were Mahli and Mushi.
24: 27 the **l** were Beno, Shoham, Zaccur, and Ibri.
24: 30 of Mushi, the **l** were Mahli, Eder, and Jerimoth.
24: 31 and the family **l** of the priests and the Levites.
26: 12 of the gatekeepers were named for their family **l**,
26: 23 These are the **l** that descended from Amram,
26: 26 the family **l**, and the generals and captains
27: 16 The following were the tribes of Israel and their **l**:
27: 22 Dan | Azarel son of Jeroham These were the **l** of
28: 1 the **l** of the tribes, the commanders of the twelve
28: 21 and the **l** and the entire nation are at your
29: 6 Then the family **l**, the **l** of the tribes of Israel,
2Ch 1: 2 the judges, and all the political and clan **l**.
5: 2 Solomon then summoned the **l** of all the tribes
5: 4 When all the **l** of Israel arrived, the Levites moved
10: 3 The **l** of Israel sent for Jeroboam, and he and all
12: 5 then met with Rehoboam and Judah's **l**,
12: 6 and the **l** of Israel humbled themselves and said,
19: 8 and clan **l** in Israel to serve as judges in Jerusalem
20: 21 After consulting the **l** of the people, the king
21: 4 all his brothers and some of the other **l** of Israel.
23: 2 and clan **l** in Judah's towns to come to Jerusalem.
24: 10 This pleased all the **l** and the people, and they
24: 17 the **l** of Judah came and bowed before King Joash
24: 21 Then the **l** plotted to kill Zechariah, and by order of
24: 23 and Jerusalem and killed all the **l** of the nation.
25: 5 assigning **l** to each clan from Judah and Benjamin.
26: 12 Twenty-six hundred clan **l** commanded these
28: 12 Then some of the **l** of Israel—Azariah son of
28: 14 and handed over the plunder in the sight of all the **l**
34: 29 Then the king summoned all the **l** of Judah
35: 9 The Levite **l**—Conaniah and his brothers Shemaiah
36: 14 All the **l** of the priests and the people became more
Ezr 1: 5 and Levites and the **l** of the tribes of Judah
2: 2 Their **l** were Zerubbabel, Jeshua, Nehemiah,
2: 68 some of the family **l** gave generously toward the
3: 12 Levites, and other **l** remembered the first Temple,
4: 2 approached Zerubbabel and the other **l** and said,
4: 3 Jeshua, and the other **l** of Israel replied,
4: 9 the judges and local **l**, the people of Tarpel,
5: 5 the **l** of the Jews were not prevented from building
5: 9 We asked the **l**, 'Who gave you permission to
5: 10 so that we could tell you who the **l** were.
6: 7 of Judah and the **l** of the Jews in their work.
6: 8 **l** of the Jews as they rebuild this Temple of God.
6: 14 So the Jewish **l** continued their work, and they
7: 28 And I gathered some of the **l** of Israel to return
8: 1 Here is a list of the family **l** and the genealogies of
8: 16 and Meshullam, who were **l** of the people.
8: 24 I appointed twelve **l** of the priests—Sherebiah,
8: 25 and the other items that the king, his council, his **l**,
8: 29 and the **l** of Israel at the storerooms of the
9: 1 But then the Jewish **l** came to me and said,
9: 2 and **l** are some of the worst offenders."
10: 5 and demanded that the **l** of the priests
10: 8 if the **l** and elders so decided, forfeit all their
10: 14 Let our **l** act on behalf of us all. Everyone who has
10: 14 wife will come at the scheduled time with the **l**
10: 16 Ezra selected **l** to represent their families,
10: 16 the **l** sat down to investigate the matter.
Ne 2: 16 I had not yet spoken to the religious and political **l**,
3: 5 people from Tekoa, though their **l** refused to help.
4: 14 I called together the **l** and the people and said to
7: 5 me the idea to call together all the **l** of the city,
7: 7 Their **l** were Zerubbabel, Jeshua, Nehemiah,
7: 70 "Some of the family **l** gave gifts for the work.
7: 71 The other **l** gave to the treasury a total of 20,000
8: 13 On October 9 the family **l** and the priests
9: 5 Then the **l** of the Levites—Jeshua, Kadmiel,
10: 14 The **l** who signed were Parosh, Pahath-moab,
11: 1 Now the **l** of the people were living in Jerusalem,
11: 21 Temple servants, whose **l** were Ziha and Gishpa,
12: 7 These were the **l** of the priests and their associates
12: 12 the family **l** of the priests were as follows:
12: 22 a list was compiled of the family **l** of the Levites
12: 24 These were the family **l** of the Levites: Hashabiah,
12: 31 I led the **l** of Judah to the top of the wall
12: 32 Hoshaiah and half the **l** of Judah followed them,
12: 40 together with the group of **l** who were with me.
13: 11 I immediately confronted the **l** and demanded,
13: 17 So I confronted the **l** of Judah, "Why are you
Est 5: 11 been promoted over all the other officials and **l**.
Job 29: 7 city gate and took my place among the honored **l**.
Ps 94: 20 Can unjust **l** claim that God is on their side— / **l**
who permit injustice by their laws?
107: 32 the congregation / and before the **l** of the nation.
141: 6 When their **l** are thrown down from a cliff,
149: 8 kings with shackles / and their **l** with iron chains,
Pr 24: 7 When the **l** gather, the fool has nothing to say.
28: 2 But with wise and knowledgeable **l**, there is
31: 23 he sits in the council meeting with the other civic **l**.
Ecc 10: 16 king is a child and whose **l** feast in the morning.
10: 17 and whose **l** feast only to gain strength for their
Isa 1: 10 Listen to the LORD, you **l** of Israel! Listen to the
1: 23 Your **l** are rebels, the companions of thieves.
3: 2 He will destroy all the nation's **l**—the heroes,
3: 14 The **l** and the princes will be the first to feel the
9: 15 The **l** of Israel are the head, and the lying prophets
9: 16 For the **l** of the people have led them down the
14: 9 World **l** and mighty kings long dead are there to
19: 13 The **l** of Egypt have ruined the land with their
22: 3 All your **l** flee. They surrender without resistance.
24: 23 in Jerusalem, in the sight of all the **l** of his people.
43: 27 sinned against me—all your **l** broke my laws.
56: 10 For the **l** of my people—the LORD's watchmen,
60: 17 for iron. Peace and righteousness will be your **l**!
Jer 3: 15 And I will give you **l** after my own heart, who will
5: 5 I will go and speak to their **l**. Surely they will
5: 5 But the **l**, too, had utterly rejected their God.
19: 1 Then ask some of the **l** of the people and of the
23: 1 "I will send disaster upon the **l** of my people—
25: 34 evil shepherds! Roll in the dust, you **l** of the flock!
25: 36 to the **l** of the flock shouting in despair,
29: 2 queen mother, the court officials, the **l** of Judah,
40: 7 The **l** of the Judean guerrilla bands in the
40: 8 These are the names of the **l** who came:
40: 13 and the other guerrilla **l** came to Gedaliah at
41: 11 and the rest of the guerrilla **l** heard what Ishmael
51: 46 Then there will be a time of violence as the **l** fight
52: 10 were killed; they also killed all the other **l** of Judah.
La 1: 19 My priests and **l** starved to death in the city,
2: 10 The **l** of Jerusalem sit on the ground in silence,
3: 34 But the **l** of his people trampled prisoners
4: 16 The priests and **l** are no longer honored
Eze 7: 26 from the priests and no counsel from the **l**.
8: 1 while the **l** of Judah were in my home,
8: 11 Seventy **l** of Israel were standing there with
8: 12 have you seen what the **l** of Israel are doing with
9: 6 So they began by killing the seventy **l**.
11: 1 son of Benaiah, who were **l** among the people.
14: 1 Then some of the **l** of Israel visited me, and while
14: 3 of man, these **l** have set up idols in their hearts.
17: 13 He also exiled Israel's most influential **l**,
20: 1 some of the **l** of Israel came to request a message
20: 3 give the **l** of Israel this message from the Sovereign
21: 12 that sword will slaughter my people and their **l**—
22: 27 Your **l** are like wolves, who tear apart their
32: 21 Down in the grave mighty **l** will mockingly
34: 2 prophesy against the shepherds, the **l** of Israel.
Da 8: 24 He will destroy powerful **l** and devastate the holy
Hos 5: 1 "Hear this, you priests and all of Israel's **l**! Listen,
5: 10 "The **l** of Judah have become as bad as thieves.
7: 16 Their **l** will be killed by their enemies because of
9: 15 love them no more because all their **l** are rebels.
13: 10 Where are all the **l** of the land? You asked for
Joel 1: 2 Hear this, you **l** of the people! Everyone listen!
1: 14 Bring the **l** and all the people into the Temple of
Am 3: 9 Announce this to the **l** of Philistia and Egypt:
Mic 1: 15 your town. And the **l** of Israel will go to Adullam.
3: 1 Listen, you **l** of Israel! You are supposed to know
3: 9 Listen to me, you **l** of Israel! You hate justice
Na 3: 10 as servants. All their **l** were bound in chains.
Zep 1: 8 "I will punish the **l** and princes of Judah and all
3: 3 Its **l** are like roaring lions hunting for their
Zec 10: 3 against your shepherds, and I will punish these **l**.
Mt 16: 21 He would suffer at the hands of the **l**
21: 23 the leading priests and other **l** came up to him.
21: 41 The religious **l** replied, "He will put the wicked
26: 3 and other **l** were meeting at the residence of
26: 47 out by the leading priests and other **l** of the people.
26: 57 teachers of religious law and other **l** had gathered.
27: 1 and other **l** met again to discuss how to persuade
27: 3 of silver back to the leading priests and other **l**.
27: 12 and other **l** made their accusations against him,
27: 18 (He knew very well that the Jewish **l** had arrested
27: 20 and other **l** persuaded the crowds to ask for
27: 41 of religious law, and the other **l** also mocked Jesus.
28: 12 A meeting of all the religious **l** was called,
Mk 8: 31 suffer many terrible things and be rejected by the **l**,
11: 27 of religious law, and the other **l** came up to him.
12: 12 The Jewish **l** wanted to arrest him for using this
12: 13 The **l** sent some Pharisees and supporters of Herod
14: 43 the teachers of religious law, and the other **l**.
14: 53 other **l**, and teachers of religious law had gathered.
15: 1 other **l**, and teachers of religious law—
Lk 5: 33 The religious **l** complained that Jesus' disciples
7: 3 he sent some respected Jewish **l** to ask him to come
9: 22 "I will be rejected by the **l**, the leading priests,
19: 47 and the other **l** of the people began planning how
20: 1 of religious law and other **l** came up to him.
20: 20 the **l** sent secret agents pretending to be honest
22: 52 Temple guard and the other **l** who headed the mob.
22: 66 At daybreak all the **l** of the people assembled,
23: 13 together the leading priests and other religious **l**,
23: 35 The crowd watched, and the **l** laughed and scoffed.
23: 51 the decision and actions of the other religious **l**.
24: 20 leading priests and other religious **l** arrested him
Jn 1: 19 This was the testimony of John when the Jewish **l**
2: 18 the Jewish **l** demanded. "If you have this authority
5: 10 So the Jewish **l** objected. They said to the man who
5: 15 Then the man went to find the Jewish **l** and told
5: 16 So the Jewish **l** began harassing Jesus for breaking
5: 18 So the Jewish **l** tried all the more to kill him.
7: 1 He wanted to stay out of Judea where the Jewish **l**
7: 11 The Jewish **l** tried to find him at the festival
7: 13 were afraid of getting in trouble with the Jewish **l**.
7: 15 The Jewish **l** were surprised when they heard him.
7: 26 Can it be that our **l** know that he really is the
7: 30 Then the **l** tried to arrest him; but no one laid a
7: 35 The Jewish **l** were puzzled by this statement.
8: 22 The Jewish **l** asked, "Is he planning to commit
9: 18 The Jewish **l** wouldn't believe he had been blind,
9: 22 said this because they were afraid of the Jewish **l**,
10: 24 The Jewish **l** surrounded him and asked,
10: 31 Once again the Jewish **l** picked up stones to kill
10: 34 own law that God said to certain **l** of the people,
11: 8 "only a few days ago the Jewish **l** in Judea were
11: 53 So from that time on the Jewish **l** began to plot
12: 42 Many people, including some of the Jewish **l**,
13: 33 you cannot come to me—just as I told the Jewish **l**.
18: 14 was the one who had told the other Jewish **l**,
18: 31 to execute someone," the Jewish **l** replied.
18: 36 have fought when I was arrested by the Jewish **l**.
19: 7 The Jewish **l** replied, "By our laws he ought to die
19: 12 but the Jewish **l** told him, "If you release this man,
19: 31 The Jewish **l** didn't want the victims hanging there
19: 38 disciple of Jesus (because he feared the Jewish **l**),
20: 19 because they were afraid of the Jewish **l**.
Ac 3: 17 in ignorance; and the same can be said of your **l**.
4: 8 said to them, "**L** and elders of our nation,
7: 54 The Jewish **l** were infuriated by Stephen's
9: 23 After a while the Jewish **l** decided to kill him.
12: 3 Herod saw how much this pleased the Jewish **l**,
13: 27 and their **l** fulfilled prophecy by condemning Jesus
13: 45 But when the Jewish **l** saw the crowds, they were
13: 50 Then the Jewish **l** stirred up both the influential
religious women and the **l** of the city,
14: 5 A mob of Gentiles and Jews, along with their **l**,

15:22 The men chosen were two of the church l—
17: 5 But the Jewish l were jealous, so they gathered
21:11 of this belt be bound by the Jewish l in Jerusalem
22: 5 and the whole council of l can testify that this is so.
23:14 They went to the leading priests and other l
24: 1 arrived with some of the Jewish l and the lawyer
24:27 Felix wanted to gain favor with the Jewish l,
25: 2 the leading priests and other Jewish l met with him
25: 7 the Jewish l from Jerusalem gathered around
25:15 and other Jewish l pressed charges against him
26: 2 against all these accusations made by the Jewish l,
26: 4 "As the Jewish l are well aware, I was given a
28:17 Paul's arrival, he called together the local Jewish l.
28:19 But when the Jewish l protested the decision,
1Co 4: 6 you won't brag about one of your l at the expense
Gal 2: 2 While I was there I talked privately with the l of
2: 6 And the l of the church who were there had
2: 6 their reputation as great l made no difference to
1Th 5:12 honor those who are your l in the Lord's work.
Heb 13: 7 Remember your l who first taught you the word of
13:17 Obey your spiritual l and do what they say.
13:24 Give my greetings to all your l and to the other

LEADERSHIP (9) [LEAD]

Nu 7: 8 All their work was done under the l of Ithamar son
10:14 under the l of Nahshon son of Amminadab.
10:18 their banner, under the l of Elizur son of Shedeur.
10:22 under the l of Elishama son of Ammihud.
10:25 under the l of Ahiezer son of Ammishaddai.
33: 1 as they marched out of Egypt under the l of Moses
2Ch 34:12 The workers served faithfully under the l of Jahath
Pr 11:14 Without wise l, a nation falls; with many
Ro 12: 8 If God has given you l ability,

LEADING (124) [LEAD]

Ge 32:17 He gave these instructions to the men l the first
Ex 14:19 angel of God, who had been l the people of Israel,
Nu 27:19 him with the responsibility of l the people.
31: 2 "Take vengeance on the Midianites for l the
Jos 2: 7 l to the shallow crossing places of the Jordan
Jdg 16:26 Samson said to the servant who was l him by the
20:31 and along the roads l to Bethel and Gibeah.
1Sa 18:16 he was so successful at l his troops into battle.
29: 2 As the Philistine rulers were l out their troops in
2Sa 16: 1 He was l two donkeys loaded with two hundred
17:24 and was l his troops across the Jordan River.
22:34 as a deer, / l me safely along the mountain heights.
2Ki 18:17 near the road l to the field where cloth is bleached.
19: 2 and the l priests, all dressed in sackcloth,
19: 9 of Ethiopia was l an army to fight against him.
21:16 to commit, l them to do evil in the LORD's sight.
23: 4 instructed Hilkiah the high priest and the l priests
1Ch 26:16 the west gate and the gateway l up to the Temple.
26:18 four to the gateway l up to the Temple, and two to
2Ch 20:27 returned to Jerusalem, with Jehoshaphat l them,
23:13 Singers with musical instruments were l the people
24: 8 and set outside the gate l to the Temple of the
Ezr 8:29 without an ounce lost, to the l priests, the Levites,
Ps 18:33 as a deer, / l me safely along the mountain heights.
42: 4 l a great procession to the house of God,
73:24 me with your counsel, / l me to a glorious destiny.
Pr 16:29 their companions, l them down a harmful path.
Ecc 7:19 A wise person is stronger than the ten l citizens of
SS 1: 7 O my love, where are you l your flock today?
Isa 3:12 They are l you down a pretty garden path to
7: 3 near the road l to the field where cloth is bleached.
36: 2 near the road l to the field where cloth is bleached.
37: 2 and the l priests, all dressed in sackcloth,
37: 9 of Ethiopia was l an army to fight against him.
Jer 23: 2 "Instead of l my flock to safety, you have deserted
33:12 will once more see shepherds l sheep and lambs.
Eze 8:17 l the whole nation into violence, thumbing their
40:22 There were seven steps l up to the gateway
40:23 there was another gateway l to the Temple's inner
40:26 This gateway also had a stairway of seven steps l
40:28 Then the man took me to the south gateway l into
40:30 (The foyers of the gateways l into the inner
40:31 and there were eight steps l to its entrance.
40:32 Then he took me to the east gateway l to the inner
40:34 and there were eight steps l to its entrance.
40:35 Then he took me around to the north gateway l to
40:37 There were eight steps l to its entrance.
40:49 There were ten steps l up to it, with a column on
41:17 The space above the door l into the Most Holy
41:25 The doors l into the Holy Place were decorated
Hos 11: 3 taught Israel how to walk, l him along by the hand.
Mic 3: 5 "You are l my people astray! You promise peace
Mt 2: 4 He called a meeting of the l priests and teachers of
15:14 They are blind guides l the blind, and if one blind
16:21 and the l priests and the teachers of religious law.
20:18 "the Son of Man will be betrayed to the l priests
21:15 The l priests and the teachers of religious law saw
21:23 the l priests and other leaders came up to him.
21:45 When the l priests and Pharisees heard Jesus,
26: 3 At that same time the l priests and other leaders
26:14 one of the twelve disciples, went to the l priests
26:47 They had been sent out by the l priests and other
26:59 the l priests and the entire high council were trying
27: 1 the l priests and other leaders met again to discuss
27: 3 So he took the thirty pieces of silver back to the l
27: 6 The l priests picked up the money. "We can't put
27:12 But when the l priests and other leaders made their
27:20 the l priests and other leaders persuaded the
27:41 The l priests, the teachers of religious law,
27:62 the l priests and Pharisees went to see Pilate.
28:11 had been guarding the tomb went to the l priests
Mk 6:21 army officers, and the l citizens of Galilee.
8:31 and be rejected by the leaders, the l priests,
10:33 "the Son of Man will be betrayed to the l priests
11:18 When the l priests and teachers of religious law
11:27 the l priests, the teachers of religious law,
14: 1 The l priests and the teachers of religious law were
14:10 went to the l priests to arrange to betray Jesus to
14:11 The l priests were delighted when they heard why
14:43 They had been sent out by the l priests,
14:53 Jesus was led to the high priest's home where the l
14:55 the l priests and the entire high council were trying
15: 1 Very early in the morning the l priests,
15: 3 Then the l priests accused him of many crimes,
15:10 (For he realized by now that the l priests had
15:11 But at this point the l priests stirred up the mob to
15:31 The l priests and teachers of religious law also
Lk 9:22 the l priests, and the teachers of religious law.
19:47 but the l priests, the teachers of religious law,
20: 1 the l priests and teachers of religious law and other
20:19 of religious law and the l priests heard this story,
22: 2 The l priests and teachers of religious law were
22: 4 and he went over to the l priests and captains of the
22:52 Then Jesus spoke to the l priests and captains of
22:66 including the l priests and the teachers of religious
23: 2 "This man has been l our people to ruin by telling
23: 4 Pilate turned to the l priests and to the crowd
23:10 the l priests and the teachers of religious law stood
23:13 Then Pilate called together the l priests and other
23:14 brought this man to me, accusing him of l a revolt.
24:20 But our l priests and other religious leaders
Jn 7:32 and the l priests sent Temple guards to arrest Jesus.
7:45 had been sent to arrest him returned to the l priests
11:47 Then the l priests and Pharisees called the high
11:57 the l priests and Pharisees had publicly announced
12:10 Then the l priests decided to kill Lazarus, too,
18: 3 The l priests and Pharisees had given Judas a
18:35 own people and their l priests brought you here.
19: 6 the l priests and Temple guards began shouting,
19:15 no king but Caesar," the l priests shouted back.
19:21 Then the l priests said to Pilate, "Change it from
Ac 4: 1 the l priests, the captain of the Temple guard,
4:23 and told them what the l priests and elders had
5:24 of the Temple guard and the l priests heard this,
9:14 And we hear that he is authorized by the l priests to
9:21 and take them in chains to the l priests."
19:14 Seven sons of Sceva, a l priest, were doing this.
22:30 and ordered the l priests into session with the
23:14 They went to the l priests and other leaders
25: 2 where the l priests and other Jewish leaders met
25:15 the l priests and other Jewish leaders pressed
26:10 Authorized by the l priests, I caused many of the
26:12 with the authority and commission of the l priests.
Gal 5:25 let us follow the Holy Spirit's l in every part of our

LEADS (43) [LEAD]

Dt 27:18 'Cursed is anyone who l a blind person astray on
Jos 11:17 which l up to Seir, to Baal-gad at the foot of Mount
12: 7 of Lebanon to Mount Halak, which l up to Seir.
1Ch 11: 6 "Whoever l the attack against the Jebusites will
Job 12:17 He l counselors away stripped of good judgment;
12:19 He l priests away stripped of status; he overthrows
Ps 1: 6 but the path of the wicked l to destruction.
23: 2 green meadows; / he l me beside peaceful streams.
25: 9 He l the humble in what is right, / teaching them
25:10 The LORD l with unfailing love and faithfulness
37: 8 Do not envy others— / it only l to harm.
68:27 Look, the little tribe of Benjamin l the way.
Pr 2:18 Entering her house l to death; it is the road to hell.
5: 6 a crooked trail and doesn't even realize where it l.
11: 2 Pride l to disgrace, but with humility comes
12:28 The way of the godly l to life; their path does not
13:10 Pride l to arguments; those who take advice are
14:23 Work brings profit, but mere talk l to poverty!
15:24 The path of the wise l to life above; they leave the
16:17 The path of the upright l away from evil;
19:16 and keep your life; despising them l to death.
20: 1 Wine produces mockers; liquor l to brawls.
28:22 tries to get rich quick, but it only l to poverty.
28:25 trusting the LORD l to prosperity.
30:31 the male goat, / a king as he l his army.
Isa 30:29 as when a flutist l a group of pilgrims to
38:16 your discipline is good, / for it l to life and health.
48:17 and l you along the paths you should follow.
Joel 2:11 The LORD l them with a shout! This is his
Jn 8:12 because you will have the light that l to life."
10: 3 He calls his own sheep by name and l them out.
14:17 He is the Holy Spirit, who l into all truth.
Ro 6:16 You can choose sin, which l to death, or you can
8: 2 Christ Jesus from the power of sin that l to death.
2Co 2:14 and l us along in Christ's triumphal procession.
Heb 6:19 It l us through the curtain of heaven into God's
2Pe 1: 5 A life of moral excellence l to knowing God better.
1: 6 Knowing God l to self-control. Self-control l to patient endurance, and patient endurance l to godliness.
1: 7 Godliness l to love for other Christians, and finally
1Jn 5:16 But there is a sin that l to death, and I am not
5:17 Every wrong is sin, but not all sin l to death.

LEAF (6) [LEAFY, LEAVES]

Ge 8:11 the bird returned to him with a fresh olive l in its
Lev 26:36 of a l driven by the wind will send you fleeing.
Job 13:25 Would you terrify a l that is blown by the wind?
Mk 4:28 First a l blade pushes through, then the heads of
11:13 noticed a fig tree a little way off that was in full l,
Rev 7: 1 Not a l rustled in the trees, and the sea became as

LEAFY (3) [LEAF]

Lev 23:40 and collect palm fronds and other l branches
Jnh 4: 6 And the LORD God arranged for a l plant to
Mk 11: 8 and others cut l branches in the fields and spread

LEAGUE [KJV] See ALLIANCE, ALLIED, COVENANT, TREATY

LEAH (26) [LEAH'S]

Ge 29:16 L, who was the oldest, and her younger sister,
29:17 L had pretty eyes, but Rachel was beautiful in
29:23 when it was dark, Laban took L to Jacob,
29:24 And Laban gave L a servant, Zilpah, to be her
29:25 when Jacob woke up in the morning—it was L!
29:28 A week after Jacob had married L, Laban gave
29:30 with Rachel, too, and he loved her more than L.
29:31 But because L was unloved, the LORD let her
29:32 So L became pregnant and had a son. She named
30: 9 L realized that she wasn't getting pregnant
30:11 L named him Gad, for she said, "How fortunate I
30:13 and L named him Asher, for she said, "What joy
30:14 in a field and brought the roots to his mother, L.
30:14 Rachel begged L to give some of them to her.
30:15 But L angrily replied, "Wasn't it enough that you
30:16 home from the fields, L went out to meet him.
31: 4 and L out to the field where he was watching the
31:14 Rachel and L said, "That's fine with us!
33: 2 L and her children next, and Rachel and Joseph
33: 7 Next L came with her children, and they bowed
35:23 The sons of L were Reuben (Jacob's oldest son),
46:15 These are the sons of Jacob who were born to L in
46:15 Jacob's descendants through L numbered
46:18 the servant given to L by her father, Laban.
49:31 Rebekah, are buried. And there I buried L.
Ru 4:11 is now coming into your home like Rachel and L,

LEAH'S (3) [LEAH]

Ge 31:33 then into L, and then he searched the tents of the
34: 1 One day Dinah, L daughter, went to visit some of
35:26 sons of Zilpah, L servant, were Gad and Asher.

LEAK (1) [LEAKING]

Ecc 10:18 Laziness lets the roof l, and soon the rafters begin

LEAKING (1) [LEAK]

Na 2: 8 Nineveh is like a l water reservoir! The people are

LEAN (2) [LEANED, LEANING, LEANS]

2Ki 18:21 If you l on Egypt, you will find it to be a stick that
Isa 36: 6 If you l on Egypt, you will find it to be a stick that

LEANED (4) [LEAN]

Ge 47:31 and Jacob bowed in worship as he l on his staff.
Eze 29: 7 Israel l on you, but like a cracked staff,
Jn 21:20 the one who had l over to Jesus during supper
Heb 11:21 and bowed in worship as he l on his staff.

LEANFLESHED [KJV] See GAUNT

LEANING (4) [LEAN]

2Sa 1: 6 I saw Saul there l on his spear with the enemy
Job 8:14 count on will collapse. They are l on a spiderweb.
SS 8: 5 is this coming up from the desert, l on her lover?"
Jn 13:25 L toward Jesus, he asked, "Lord, who is it?"

LEANS (2) [LEAN]

2Ki 5:18 the god Rimmon to worship there and l on my arm,
Am 5:19 the bear, he l his hand against a wall in his house—

LEAP (7) [LEAPED, LEAPING, LEAPS]

Job 39:20 Did you give it the ability to l forward like a
41:19 Fire and sparks l from its mouth.
Ps 29: 6 a calf / and Mount Hermon to l like a young bull.
Isa 35: 6 The lame will l like a deer, and those who cannot
Joel 2: 5 Look at them as they l along the mountaintops!
Lk 6:23 "When that happens, rejoice! Yes, l for joy!
Rev 16:13 And I saw three evil spirits that looked like frogs l

LEAPED (7) [LEAP]

Jdg 4:15 Then Sisera l down from his chariot and escaped
2Sa 22: 9 from his nostrils; / fierce flames l from his mouth;
Ps 18: 8 from his nostrils; / fierce flames l from his mouth;
Da 3:22 the flames l out and killed the soldiers as they
6:24 The lions l on them and tore them apart before they
Lk 1:41 of Mary's greeting, Elizabeth's child l within her,
Ac 19:16 And he l on them and attacked them with such

LEAPING (8) [LEAP]

Dt 33:22 "Dan is a lion's cub, / l out from Bashan."
2Sa 6:16 When she saw King David l and dancing before
1Ch 15:29 When she saw King David dancing and l for joy,
SS 2: 8 l on the mountains and bounding over the hills.
Jer 49:19 thickets of the Jordan, l on the sheep in the pasture.
50:44 thickets of the Jordan, l on the sheep in the pasture.
Mal 4: 2 go free, l with joy like calves let out to pasture.
Ac 3: 8 Then, walking, l, and praising God, he went into

LEAPS (1) [LEAP]

Job 37: 1 "My heart pounds as I think of this. It l within me.

LEARN (58) [LEARNED, LEARNING, LEARNS]

Ge 31:22 Laban didn't l of their flight for three days.
Lev 26:23 "And if you fail to l a lesson from this
Dt 4:10 they will l to fear me as long as they live,
5:1 you today. L them and be sure to obey them!
17:19 That way he will l to fear the LORD his God by
31:12 they may listen and l to fear the LORD your God
31:13 hear them and will l to fear the LORD your God.
2Ki 5:8 and he will l that there is a true prophet here in
2Ch 12:8 so that they can l how much better it is to serve me
Est 1:17 l that Queen Vashti has refused to appear before
Job 34:4 what is right; let us l together what is good.
Ps 14:4 Will those who do evil never l? / They eat up my
53:4 Will those who do evil never l? / They eat up my
83:18 until they l that you alone are called the LORD,
119:7 When I l your righteous laws, / I will thank you by
130:4 you offer forgiveness, / that we might l to fear you.
Pr 1:9 What you l from them will crown you with grace
4:5 L to be wise, and develop good judgment.
5:2 Then you will l to be discreet and will store up
6:6 you lazybones. L from their ways and be wise!
6:9 will you wake up? I want you to l this lesson:
8:9 with understanding, clear to those who want to l.
9:6 ways behind, and begin to live; l how to be wise."
9:9 be wiser. Teach the righteous, and they will l more.
12:1 To l, you must love discipline; it is stupid to hate
19:25 punish a mocker, the simpleminded will l a lesson;
21:11 A simpleton can l only by seeing mockers
22:25 or you will l to be like them and endanger your
Isa 1:17 L to do good. Seek justice. Help the oppressed.
7:9 want me to protect you, l to believe what I say."
64:2 Then your enemies would l the reason for your
Jer 2:33 The most experienced prostitute could l from you!
12:16 And if these nations quickly l the ways of my
12:16 and if they l to swear by my name, saying,
35:13 'Come and l a lesson about how to obey me.
Eze 14:11 the people of Israel will l not to stray from me,
Da 4:25 until you l that the Most High rules over the
4:32 until you l that the Most High rules over the
Mt 9:13 "Now go and l the meaning of this Scripture:
16:17 to you. You did not l this from any human being.
24:32 "Now l a lesson from the fig tree. When its buds
Mk 8:17 having no food? Won't you ever l or understand?
13:28 "Now, l a lesson from the fig tree. When its buds
Lk 18:6 the Lord said, "L a lesson from this evil judge.
Ac 16:38 the city officials were alarmed to l that Paul
Ro 5:3 that they are good for us—they help us l to endure.
1Co 14:31 so that everyone will l and be encouraged.
Php 3:10 I can l what it means to suffer with him, sharing in
3:17 and l from those who follow our example.
Col 1:10 the while, you will l to know God better and better.
3:10 that is continually being renewed as you l more
1Ti 1:20 to Satan so they would l not to blaspheme God.
2:11 should listen and l quietly and submissively.
4:11 Teach these things and insist that everyone l them.
Tit 3:14 They must l to do good by helping others who
Heb 5:12 basic things a beginner must l about the Scriptures.
Jas 2:20 When will you ever l that faith that does not result
Rev 14:3 And no one could l this song except those 144,000

LEARNED (49) [LEARN]

Ge 9:24 he l what Ham, his youngest son, had done.
14:14 When Abram l that Lot had been captured,
30:27 "for I have l by divination that the LORD has
31:1 But Jacob soon l that Laban's sons were beginning
Jos 10:1 He also l that the Gibeonites had made peace with
Jdg 6:29 they l that it was Gideon, the son of Joash.
1Sa 7:7 The Israelites were badly frightened when they l
23:7 Saul soon l that David was at Keilah. "Good!"
23:9 But David l of Saul's plan and told Abiathar the
2Sa 21:11 When David l what Rizpah, Saul's concubine,
1Ki 2:39 Achish of Gath. When Shimei l where they were,
5:1 so when he l that David's son Solomon was the
12:20 When the people of Israel l of Jeroboam's return
2Ki 11:1 of King Ahaziah of Judah, l that her son was dead,
25:23 and their men l that the king of Babylon had
2Ch 22:10 of King Ahaziah of Judah, l that her son was dead,
Ne 4:1 Sanballat was very angry when he l that we were
13:7 and l the extent of this evil deed of Eliashib—
Est 3:6 Since he had l that Mordecai was a Jew, he decided
4:1 When Mordecai l what had been done, he tore his
Pr 24:32 as I looked and thought about it, I l this lesson:
Isa 29:13 to nothing more than human laws l by rote.
Eze 19:3 He l to catch and devour prey, / and he became a
19:6 He l to catch and devour prey, / and he, too,
Da 4:26 back again when you have l that heaven rules.
5:21 until he l that the Most High God rules the
6:10 But when Daniel l that the law had been signed,
9:2 I l from the word of the LORD, as recorded by
Mt 2:7 At this meeting he l the exact time when they first
2:16 Herod was furious when he l that the wise men had
2:22 But when he l that the new ruler was Herod's son
Jn 4:1 Jesus l that the Pharisees had heard, "Jesus is
Ac 13:12 and was astonished at what he l about the Lord.
14:6 When the apostles l of it, they fled for their lives.
17:13 But when some Jews in Thessalonica l that Paul
22:3 At his feet I l to follow our Jewish laws
23:27 When I l that he was a Roman citizen, I removed
28:1 on shore, we l that we were on the island of Malta.
Ro 7:9 But when I l the truth, I realized I had broken the
2Co 1:9 But as a result, we l not to rely on ourselves,
Eph 4:20 But that isn't what you were taught when you l
4:21 all about him and have l the truth that is in Jesus,
Php 3:16 But we must be sure to obey the truth we have l
4:9 Keep putting into practice all you l from me
4:11 for I have l how to get along happily whether I
4:12 I have l the secret of living in every situation,
2Ti 1:13 Hold on to the pattern of right teaching you l from
Heb 5:8 he l obedience from the things he suffered.
10:32 Don't ever forget those early days when you first l

LEARNING (4) [LEARN]

Pr 15:2 The wise person makes l a joy; fools spout only
Da 1:4 sure they are well versed in every branch of l,
1:17 young men an unusual aptitude for l the literature
2Pe 2:20 the wicked ways of the world by l about our Lord

LEARNS (4) [LEARN]

Nu 30:7 If her husband l of her vow or pledge and raises no
Pr 15:5 whoever l from correction is wise.
21:11 a wise person l from instruction.
Jn 6:45 who hears and l from the Father comes to me.

LEASE (3) [LEASED]

Mt 21:41 and l the vineyard to others who will give him his
Mk 12:9 and kill them all and l the vineyard to others.
Lk 20:16 and kill them all and l the vineyard to others."

LEASED (3) [LEASE]

Mt 21:33 Then he l the vineyard to tenant farmers
Mk 12:1 Then he l the vineyard to tenant farmers
Lk 20:9 man planted a vineyard, l it out to tenant farmers,

LEASING [KJV] See LIES

LEAST (61) [LESS]

Ge 24:55 "But we want Rebekah to stay at l ten days,"
33:15 "at l let me leave some of my men to guide
43:11 to them, "If it can't be avoided, then at l do this.
47:17 But at l they were able to purchase food for that
Ex 16:3 had killed us there! At l there we had plenty to eat.
Nu 23:13 of the nation of Israel. Curse at l that many!"
23:25 aren't going to curse them, at l don't bless them!"
Dt 17:6 There must always be at l two or three witnesses.
Jdg 6:15 of Manasseh, and I am the l in my entire family!"
1Sa 9:8 We can at l offer it to him and see what happens!"
9:21 and my family is the l important of all the families
15:30 at l honor me before the leaders and before my
1Ki 18:5 find enough grass to save at l some of my horses
2Ki 3:2 He at l tore down the sacred pillar of Baal that his
20:19 "At l there will be peace and security during my
23:2 all the people from the l to the greatest.
25:26 all the people of Judah, from the l to the greatest,
2Ch 34:30 all the people from the greatest to the l.
Est 1:5 and officials—from the greatest to the l.
Job 6:10 At l I can take comfort in this: Despite the pain,
21:19 you say, 'at l God will punish their children!'
Ecc 5:18 Even so, I have noticed one thing, at l, that is good.
9:5 The living at l know they will die, but the dead
Isa 39:8 "At l there will be peace and security during my
Jer 6:13 "From the l to the greatest, they trick others to get
8:10 From the l to the greatest, they trick others to get
31:34 For everyone, from the l to the greatest,
42:1 the people, from the l to the greatest, approached
42:8 and for all the people, from the l to the greatest.
44:12 and famine. All will die, from the l to the greatest.
50:12 You will become the l of nations—a wilderness,
Eze 2:5 at l they will know they have had a prophet among
Da 11:21 But he will slip in when l expected and take over
Jnh 3:5 and from the greatest to the l, they decided to go
Hab 3:6 But his power is not diminished in the l!
Mt 5:19 you will be the l in the Kingdom of Heaven.
10:42 a cup of cold water to one of the l of my followers,
19:30 to be important now will be the l important then,
19:30 and those who are considered l here will be the
24:44 For the Son of Man will come when l expected.
25:27 you should at l have put my money into the bank
25:40 when you did it to one of the l of these my brothers
25:45 when you refused to help the l of these my brothers
Mk 6:56 The sick begged him to let them at l touch the
10:31 to be important now will be the l important then,
10:31 and those who are considered l here will be the
Lk 9:48 Whoever is the l among you is the greatest."
12:40 for the Son of Man will come when l expected."
19:23 in the bank so I could at l get some interest on it?'
Jn 14:11 Or at l believe because of what you have seen me
Ac 8:10 The Samaritan people, from the l to the greatest,
26:22 these facts to everyone, from the l to the greatest.
Ro 15:27 they feel the l they can do in return is help them
1Co 12:22 and l important are really the most necessary.
15:9 For I am the l of all the apostles, and I am not
Eph 3:8 and though I am the l deserving Christian there is,
1Ti 5:9 must be a woman who is at l sixty years old
Heb 8:11 For everyone, from the l to the greatest,
2Pe 1:9 these virtues are blind or, at l, very shortsighted.
Rev 11:18 all who fear your name, from the l to the greatest.
19:5 our God, all his servants, from the l to the greatest,

LEATHER (29) [LEATHERWORKER]

Ex 25:5 tanned ram skins and fine goatskin l; acacia wood;
26:14 and over them put a layer of fine goatskin l.
35:7 tanned ram skins and fine goatskin l; acacia wood;
35:23 Some gave tanned ram skins or fine goatskin l.
36:19 and the second was made of fine goatskin l.
39:34 the layers of tanned ram skins and fine goatskin l;
Lev 11:32 the object is made of wood, cloth, l, or sackcloth.
13:48 the hide of an animal, or anything made of l.
13:49 or the l has turned bright green or a reddish color,
13:52 burn the linen or wool clothing or the piece of l
13:53 has not spread in the clothing, the fabric, or the l,
13:56 cut the spot from the clothing, the fabric, or the l.
13:59 linen clothing or fabric, or in anything made of l.
15:17 or l that comes in contact with the semen must be
Nu 4:6 must cover the inner curtain with fine goatskin l,
4:6 and the goatskin l with a dark blue cloth.
4:8 and finally a covering of fine goatskin l on top of
4:10 utensils must then be covered with fine goatskin l,
4:11 cover this cloth with a covering of fine goatskin l.
4:12 covered with fine goatskin l, and placed on the
4:14 and a covering of fine goatskin l must be spread
4:25 its coverings, the outer covering of fine goatskin l,
5:23 the priest will write these curses on a piece of l
31:20 purify all your clothing and everything made of l,
2Ki 1:8 hairy man, and he wore a l belt around his waist."
Jer 27:2 a yoke, and fasten it on your neck with l thongs.
Eze 16:10 and sandals made of fine l.
Mt 3:4 were woven from camel hair, and he wore a l belt;
Mk 1:6 were woven from camel hair, and he wore a l belt;

LEATHERN [KJV] See LEATHER

LEATHERWORKER (3) [LEATHER]

Ac 9:43 stayed a long time in Joppa, living with Simon, a l.
10:6 is staying with Simon, a l who lives near the shore.
10:32 the home of Simon, a l who lives near the shore.'

LEAVE (227) [LEAVES, LEAVING]

Ge 8:16 "L the boat, all of you.
12:1 "L your country, your relatives, and your father's
19:8 Do with them as you wish, but l these men alone,
26:16 And Abimelech asked Isaac to l the country.
30:27 "Please don't l me," Laban replied, "for I have
31:13 Now l this country and return to the land you
33:15 "at least let me l some of my men to guide
42:15 I swear by the life of Pharaoh that you will not l
42:33 L one of your brothers here with me, and take
44:1 When his brothers were ready to l, Joseph gave
44:22 said to you, 'My lord, the boy cannot l his father,
Ex 2:20 "Did you just l him there? Go and invite him
3:21 down with gifts so you will not l empty-handed.
6:1 rid of them that he will force them to l his land!"
6:11 and tell him to let the people of Israel l Egypt."
6:13 and to demand that he let the people of Israel l
7:2 that the people of Israel be allowed to l Egypt.
9:29 "As soon as I l the city, I will lift my hands
9:35 Pharaoh refused to let the people l, just as the
11:1 that he will practically force you to l the country.
11:8 will come running to me, bowing low. 'Please l!'
11:10 so he wouldn't let the Israelites l the country.
12:10 Do not l any of it until the next day. Whatever is
12:22 no one is allowed to l the house until morning.
12:31 "L us!" he cried. "Go away, all of you! Go
12:32 and be gone. Go, but give me a blessing as you l."
14:11 graves for us in Egypt? Why did you make us l?
14:12 Didn't we tell you to l us alone while we were still
20:5 I do not l unpunished the sins of those who hate
21:11 she may l as a free woman without making any
22:30 L the newborn animal with its mother for seven
23:11 L the rest for the animals to eat. The same applies
32:10 Now l me alone so my anger can blaze against
34:7 Even so I do not l sin unpunished, but I punish the
Lev 8:33 Do not l the Tabernacle entrance for seven days,
10:7 But you are not to l the entrance of the Tabernacle,
14:38 he will l the house and lock it up for seven days.
16:23 Most Holy Place, and he must l the garments there.
19:10 L them for the poor and the foreigners who live
19:23 l the fruit unharvested for the first three years
22:30 Don't l any of it until the second day. I am the
23:22 L it for the poor and the foreigners living among
26:30 I will l your corpses piled up beside your lifeless
Nu 9:12 They must not l any of the lamb until the next
10:31 "Please don't l us," Moses pleaded. "You know
11:20 to him, "Why did we ever l Egypt?" '
14:18 Even so he does not l sin unpunished, but he
20:5 Why did you make us l Egypt and bring us here to
20:17 and never l it until we have crossed the opposite
Dt 2:37 the LORD our God had commanded us to l alone.
5:9 I do not l unpunished the sins of those who hate
9:14 L me alone so I may destroy them and erase their
15:16 'I will not l you,' because he loves you and your
23:10 because of a nocturnal emission must l the camp
24:19 L it for the foreigners, orphans, and widows.
24:20 L some of the olives for the foreigners, orphans,
24:21 but l any remaining grapes for the foreigners,
28:51 They will l you no grain, new wine, olive oil,
Jos 2:18 only if you l this scarlet rope hanging from the
Jdg 7:3 'Whoever is timid or afraid may l and go
16:17 If my head were shaved, my strength would l me,
19:5 up early, ready to l, but the woman's father said,
19:7 The man got up to l, but his father-in-law kept
19:8 ready to l, and again the woman's father said,
19:8 to eat; then you can l some time this afternoon."
19:9 and his concubine and servant were preparing to l,
19:10 But this time the man was determined to l. So he
19:27 When her husband opened the door to l, he found
Ru 1:6 and her daughters-in-law got ready to l Moab to
1:16 "Don't ask me to l you and turn back.
1Sa 1:22 and l him there with the LORD permanently."
10:2 When you l me today, you will see two men beside
10:9 As Saul turned and started to l, God changed his
20:22 then it will mean that you must l immediately,
22:5 "L the stronghold and return to the land of
27:9 David didn't l one person alive in the villages he
29:10 and l with your men as soon as it gets light."
2Sa 14:8 "L it to me," the king told her. "Go home,
16:11 L him alone and let him curse, for the LORD has

20:21 hand him over to me, we will l the city in peace."
1Ki 11:32 But I will l him one tribe for the sake of my
15:19 King Baasha of Israel so that he will l me alone."
16:11 of Baasha, and he did not l a single male child.
18:12 But as soon as I l you, the Spirit of the LORD
20:36 a lion will kill you as soon as you l me."
22:24 "When did the Spirit of the LORD l me to speak
2Ki 1:4 You will never l the bed on which you are lying,
1:6 you will never l the bed on which you are lying,
1:16 you will never l the bed on which you are lying,
2:2 and you yourself live, I will never l you!"
2:4 and you yourself live, I will never l you."
2:6 and you yourself live, I will never l you."
4:27 her away, but the man of God said, "L her alone.
7:12 They are expecting us to l the city, and then they
10:8 of the city gate, and l them there until morning."
23:18 Josiah replied, "L it alone. Don't disturb his
1Ch 28:8 and l it to your children as a permanent
2Ch 16:3 King Baasha of Israel so that he will l me alone."
18:23 "When did the Spirit of the LORD l me to speak
35:15 the gates and did not need to l their posts of duty,
Ezr 9:12 and l this prosperity to our children as an
Ne 7:3 "Do not l the gates open during the hottest part of
Job 7:16 Oh, l me alone for these few remaining days.
7:19 Why won't you l me alone—even for a moment?
10:20 I have only a little time left, so l me alone—that I
10:21 before I l for the land of darkness and utter gloom,
11:14 Get rid of your sins and l all iniquity behind you.
13:13 "Be silent now and l me alone. Let me speak—
22:17 For they said to God, 'L us alone! What can the
36:7 His eyes never l the innocent, but he establishes
39:4 open fields, then l their parents and never return.
Ps 16:10 For you will not l my soul among the dead
27:9 Don't l me now; don't abandon me, / O God of my
41:6 and when they l, they spread it everywhere.
49:11 after themselves, / but they l their wealth to others.
119:121 Don't l me to the mercy of my enemies, / for I
Pr 9:6 L your foolish ways behind, and begin to live;
13:22 Good people l an inheritance to their
15:24 wise leads to life above; they l the grave behind.
17:13 repay evil for good, evil will never l your house.
Ecc 2:18 I am disgusted that I must l the fruits of my hard
2:21 I must l everything I gain to people who haven't
Isa 22:4 L me alone to weep; do not try to comfort me.
48:20 L Babylon and the Babylonians, singing as you go!
49:4 Yet I l it all in the LORD's hand; I will trust God
52:11 Go now, l your bonds and slavery. Put Babylon
52:12 You will not l in a hurry, running for your lives.
59:21 "My Spirit will not l them, and neither will these
Jer 5:10 and destroy them, but l a scattered few alive.
9:19 We must l our land, because our homes have been
10:17 "Pack your bag and prepare to l; the siege is about
19:7 The enemy will l the dead bodies as food for the
22:6 But I will destroy you and l you deserted, with no
32:40 hearts to worship me, and they will never l me.
37:12 Jeremiah started to l the city on his way to the land
41:17 where they prepared to l for Egypt.
43:12 from his cloak. And he himself will l unharmed.
46:19 Get ready to l for exile, you citizens of Egypt!
49:9 Those who harvest grapes always l a few for the
50:8 flee from Babylon! L the land of the Babylonians.
50:26 of rubble. Destroy her completely, and l nothing!
Eze 7:15 Any who l the city walls will be killed by enemy
12:3 on your back and l your home to go on a journey.
12:4 as they are watching, l your house in the evening,
12:12 "Even Zedekiah will l Jerusalem at night through
23:8 she did not l her spirit of prostitution behind.
29:5 I will l you and all your fish stranded in the desert
32:4 I will l you stranded on the land to die.
39:3 your weapons from your hands and l you helpless.
39:28 them home. I will l none of my people behind.
42:14 When the priests l the Holy Place, they must not go
44:19 They must l them in the sacred rooms and put on
46:8 the foyer, and he must l the same way he came.
46:9 they must l by the south gateway.
46:9 the south gateway must l by the north gateway.
46:9 They must never l by the same gateway they came
46:10 will enter and l with the people on these occasions.
46:12 Then he will turn and l the way he entered,
Da 4:15 But l the stump and the roots in the ground,
4:23 But l the stump and the roots in the ground,
11:8 For some years afterward he will l the king of the
Hos 2:3 I will l her to die of thirst, as in a desert or a dry
4:17 L her alone because she is married to idolatry.
9:12 be a terrible day when I turn away and l you alone.
Am 4:3 You will l by going straight through the breaks in
Ob 1:5 Those who harvest grapes always l a few for the
Mic 4:10 for you must l this city to live in the open fields.
Mt 2:12 But when it was time to l, they went home another
5:24 l your sacrifice there beside the altar. Go and be
8:16 All the spirits fled when he commanded them to l;
8:34 but they begged him to go away and l them alone.
10:11 and stay in his home until you l for the next town.
10:14 off the dust of that place from your feet as you l.
15:23 "Tell her to l," they said. "She is bothering us
18:12 Won't he l the ninety-nine others and go out into
23:23 but you should not l undone the more important
27:19 "L that innocent man alone, because I had a
27:49 But the rest said, "L him alone. Let's see whether
28:10 Go tell my brothers to l for Galilee, and they will
Mk 5:17 pleading with Jesus to go away and l them alone.
6:11 to you, shake off its dust from your feet as you l.
14:6 But Jesus replied, "L her alone. Why berate her
15:36 to him on a stick so he could drink. "L him alone.
Lk 4:42 finally found him, they begged him not to l them.
5:8 before Jesus and said, "Oh, Lord, please l me—
8:37 region begged Jesus to go away and l them alone,
9:5 enter it, shake off its dust from your feet as you l.
9:33 As Moses and Elijah were starting to l, Peter,
11:42 but you should not l undone the more important
13:8 L it another year, and I'll give it special attention
15:4 wouldn't you l the ninety-nine others to go
16:4 have plenty of friends to take care of me when I l!'
19:44 Your enemies will not l a single stone in place,
Jn 6:67 the Twelve and asked, "Are you going to l, too?"
10:12 He will l the sheep because they aren't his and he
11:31 were at the house trying to console Mary saw her l
11:48 If we l him alone, the whole nation will follow
12:7 Jesus replied, "L her alone. She did it in
13:1 Jesus knew that his hour had come to l this world
13:33 these moments before I must go away and l you!
14:16 give you another Counselor, who will never l you.
16:28 and I will l the world and return to the Father."
Ac 1:4 "Do not l Jerusalem until the Father sends you
2:27 For you will not l my soul among the dead
5:38 "So my advice is, l these men alone. If they are
7:3 told him, 'L your native land and your relatives,
9:40 But Peter asked them all to l the room; then he
16:10 So we decided to l for Macedonia at once, for we
16:36 So the jailer told Paul, "You and Silas are free to l.
16:37 So now they want us to l secretly? Certainly not!
16:39 brought them out and begged them to l the city.
20:29 vicious wolves, will come in among you after I l,
22:18 L Jerusalem, for the people here won't believe you
22:21 "But the Lord said to me, 'L Jerusalem, for I will
23:23 "Get two hundred soldiers ready to l for Caesarea
Ro 12:19 L that to God. For it is written, / "I will take
1Co 1:20 So where does this l the philosophers, the scholars,
5:10 You would have to l this world to avoid people
6:7 Why not just accept the injustice and l it at that?
7:10 but from the Lord. A wife must not l her husband.
7:11 But if she does l him, let her remain single or else
7:11 back to him. And the husband must not l his wife.
7:12 to continue living with him, he must not l her.
7:13 to continue living with her, she must not l him.
2Co 5:1 when we die and l these bodies—we will have a
Heb 11:8 Abraham obeyed when God called him to l home
Rev 3:12 Temple of my God, and they will never have to l it.

LEAVED (GATES) [KJV] FORTRESS (GATES)

LEAVEN [KJV] See YEAST

LEAVES (39) [LEAF, LEAVE]

Ge 2:24 This explains why a man l his father and mother
3:7 So they strung fig l together around their hips to
Nu 35:26 " 'But if the slayer l the city of refuge,
Dt 24:2 If she then l and marries another man
Job 12:24 and he l them wandering in a wasteland without a
30:4 They eat coarse l, and they burn the roots of shrubs
Ps 1:3 Their l never wither, / and in all they do,
Pr 11:28 you go! But the godly flourish like l in spring.
Isa 34:4 the sky, just as withered l and fruit fall from a tree.
64:6 Like autumn l, we wither and fall. And our sins,
Jer 3:20 You have been like a faithless wife who l her
17:8 Their l stay green, and they go right on producing
Eze 17:6 It soon produced strong branches and luxuriant l.
17:8 splendid vine and produce rich l and luscious fruit.
17:9 I will cut off its fruit and let its l wither and die.
47:12 The l of these trees will never turn brown and fall,
47:12 The fruit will be for food and the l for healing."
Da 4:12 It had fresh green l, and it was loaded with fruit for
4:14 its branches! Shake off its l, and scatter its fruit!
4:21 It had fresh green l, and it was loaded with fruit for
Hos 5:3 You have left me as a prostitute l her husband;
Jnh 4:6 and soon it spread its broad l over Jonah's head,
Mic 1:3 He l his throne in heaven and comes to earth,
Mt 12:43 "When an evil spirit l a person, it goes into the
19:5 'This explains why a man l his father and mother
21:19 if there were any figs on it, but there were only l.
24:32 its buds become tender and its l begin to sprout,
Mk 10:7 'This explains why a man l his father and mother
11:13 But there were only l because it was too early in
13:28 its buds become tender and its l begin to sprout,
Lk 9:39 and injuring him. It hardly ever l him alone.
11:24 "When an evil spirit l a person, it goes into the
21:30 When the l come out, you know without being told
Jn 5:22 And the Father l all judgment to his Son,
Gal 4:1 and l great wealth for his young children,
Eph 5:31 "A man l his father and mother and is joined to his
Heb 9:4 some manna, Aaron's staff that sprouted l,
9:16 Now when someone dies and l a will, no one gets
Rev 22:2 The l were used for medicine to heal the nations.

LEAVING (62) [LEAVE]

Ge 23:3 Then, l her body, he went to the Hittite elders
31:20 set out secretly and never told Laban they were l.
35:16 L Bethel, they traveled on toward Ephrath (that is,
39:18 by my screams. He ran out, l his shirt behind!"
Ex 13:20 L Succoth, they camped at Etham on the edge of
15:27 After l Marah, they came to Elim, where there
16:1 They arrived there a month after l Egypt.
Lev 21:12 of his God by l it to attend his parents' funeral,
Nu 10:33 They marched for three days after l the mountain
27:3 "Our father died in the wilderness without l any
33:5 After l Rameses, the Israelites set up camp at
Jos 2:21 l the scarlet rope hanging from the window.
10:36 After l Eglon, they attacked Hebron,
10:39 And they killed everyone in it, l no survivors.
10:40 l no survivors, just as the LORD, the God of
Jdg 7:3 l only ten thousand who were willing to fight.
20:47 l only six hundred men who escaped to the rock of
1Sa 17:20 Israelite army was l for the battlefield with shouts
19:10 escaped into the night, l the spear stuck in the wall.
2Sa 4:7 But before l, they cut off his head as he lay there
17:17 so as not to be seen entering and l the city.
17:18 But a boy saw them l En-rogel to go to David,
1Ki 8:9 people of Israel as they were l the land of Egypt.
11:29 One day as Jeroboam was l Jerusalem, the prophet
15:17 from entering or l King Asa's territory in Judah.
2Ki 19:9 Before l to meet the attack, he sent this message
2Ch 16:1 from entering or l King Asa's territory in Judah.
24:25 Arameans withdrew, l Joash severely wounded.
Ps 49:10 and senseless, / l all their wealth behind.
Isa 37:9 Before l to meet the attack, he sent this message
Jer 11:16 to burn them with fire, l them charred and broken.
37:10 l only a handful of wounded survivors, they would
La 3:11 tore me with his claws, l me helpless and desolate.
Eze 16:39 l you completely naked and ashamed.
23:29 and rob you of all you own, l you naked and bare.
24:7 murders boldly, l blood on the rocks for all to see.
Joel 1:7 their bark and l the branches white and bare.
Ob 1:18 devouring everything and l no survivors in Edom.
Jnh 1:3 port of Joppa, where he found a ship l for Tarshish.
Mt 4:22 followed him, l the boat and their father behind.
9:16 the old cloth, l an even bigger hole than before.
13:36 Then, l the crowds outside, Jesus went into the
24:1 As Jesus was l the Temple grounds, his disciples
Mk 2:21 the old cloth, l an even bigger hole than before.
4:36 l the crowds behind (although other boats
6:33 But many people saw them l, and people from
9:30 L that region, they traveled through Galilee.
11:12 The next morning as they were l Bethany,
12:19 l a wife without children, his brother should marry
13:1 As Jesus was l the Temple that day, one of his
Lk 4:38 After l the synagogue that day, Jesus went to
20:28 l a wife but no children, his brother should marry
20:31 the seven had married her and died, l no children.
Jn 6:22 disciples had gone off in their boat, l him behind.
7:35 "Maybe he is thinking of l the country and going
14:27 "I am l you with a gift—peace of mind and heart.
16:32 each one going his own way, l me alone.
17:11 the world; I am l them behind and coming to you.
Ac 16:40 and encouraged them once more before l town.
20:7 and since he was l the next day, he talked until
21:7 The next stop after l Tyre was Ptolemais, where we
1Co 7:15 or wife who isn't a Christian insists on l,

LEBANAH (2)

Ezr 2:45 L, Hagabah, Akkub,
Ne 7:48 L, Hagabah, Shalmai,

LEBANON (62) [LEBANON'S]

Dt 1:7 Go to the land of the Canaanites and to L, and all
3:25 the beautiful hill country and the L mountains.'
11:24 from the wilderness in the south to L in the north,
Jos 1:4 from the Negev Desert in the south to the L
9:1 Sea as far north as the L mountains.)
11:17 at the foot of Mount Hermon in the valley of L.
12:7 from Baal-gad in the valley of L to Mount Halak,
13:5 and all of the L mountain area to the east,
13:6 and all the hill country from L to
Jdg 3:3 and the Hivites living in the hill country of L from
9:15 fire come out from me and devour the cedars of L.'
1Ki 4:33 from the great cedar of L to the tiny hyssop that
5:6 Now please command that cedars from L be cut
5:9 My servants will bring the logs from the L
5:14 He sent them to L in shifts, ten thousand every
5:14 so that each man would be one month in L and two
7:2 buildings was called the Palace of the Forest of L.
9:19 and L and throughout the entire realm.
10:17 these shields in the Palace of the Forest of L.
10:21 all the utensils in the Palace of the Forest of L.
2Ki 14:9 "Out in the L mountains a thistle sent a message
19:23 highest mountains— / yes, the remotest peaks of L.
2Ch 2:8 send me cedar, cypress, and almug logs from L,
2:16 We will cut whatever timber you need from the L
8:6 and L and throughout the entire realm.
9:16 these shields in the Palace of the Forest of L.
9:20 all the utensils in the Palace of the Forest of L.
25:18 "Out in the L mountains, a thistle sent a message
Ezr 3:7 The logs were brought down from the L mountains
Ps 29:5 the LORD shatters the cedars of L.
72:16 May the fruit trees flourish as they do in L,
92:12 palm trees / and grow strong like the cedars of L.
104:16 well cared for— / the cedars of L that he planted.
SS 4:8 "Come with me from L, my bride. Come down
4:11 is like that of the mountains and the cedars of L.
4:15 as refreshing as the streams from the L
5:15 of the finest gold, strong as the cedars of L.
7:4 Your nose is as fine as the tower of L overlooking
Isa 2:13 He will cut down the tall cedars of L
10:34 the enemy as an ax cuts down the forest trees in L.
14:8 the cypress trees and the cedars of L—sing out this
29:17 the wilderness of L will be a fertile field once
33:9 land of Israel is in trouble. L has been destroyed.
35:2 will become as green as the mountains of L,
37:24 highest mountains— / yes, the remotest peaks of L.
60:13 The glory of L will be yours—the forests of
Jer 18:14 the snow ever melt high up in the mountains of L?
22:6 to me as fruitful Gilead and the green forests of L.
22:20 Search for them in L. Shout for them at Bashan.
22:23 palace lined with lumber from the cedars of L,
Eze 17:3 wings full of many-colored feathers came to L.
27:5 They took a cedar from L to make a mast for you.
31:3 Assyria, too, was once like a cedar of L, full of
31:15 I clothed L in black and caused the trees of the
31:16 trees of Eden, the most beautiful and the best of L,

Hos 14: 5 send roots deep into the soil like the cedars in **L**.
14: 6 olive trees, as fragrant as the cedar forests of **L**.
14: 7 They will be as fragrant as the wines of **L**.
Na 1: 4 and Carmel fade, and the green forests of **L** wilt.
Hab 2:17 You cut down the forests of **L**. Now you will be
Zec 10:10 and Assyria and resettle them in Gilead and **L**.
11: 1 Open your doors, **L**, so that fire may sweep

LEBANON'S (4) [LEBANON]

Ps 29: 6 He makes **L** mountains skip like a calf / and Mount
SS 3: 9 for himself from wood imported from **L** forests.
Isa 40:16 All **L** forests do not contain sufficient fuel to
40:16 All **L** sacrificial animals would not make an

LEBAOTH (1) [BETH-LEBAOTH]

Jos 15:32 **L**, Shilhim, Ain, and Rimmon. In all, there were

LEBBAEUS [KJV] See THADDAEUS

LEBO-HAMATH (11) [HAMATH]

Nu 13:21 from the wilderness of Zin as far as Rehob, near **L**.
34: 8 then to **L**, and on through Zedad
Jos 13: 5 from Baal-gad beneath Mount Hermon to **L**;
Jdg 3: 3 of Lebanon from Mount Baal-hermon to **L**.
1Ki 8:65 A large crowd had gathered from as far away as **L**
2Ki 14:25 II recovered the territories of Israel between **L**
2Ch 7: 8 They came from as far away as **L** in the north,
Eze 47:15 toward Hethlon, then on through **L** to Zedad;
47:20 where the northern border begins, opposite **L**.
48: 1 Its boundary line follows the Hethlon road to **L**
Am 6:14 from **L** in the north to the Arabah Valley in the

LEBONAH (1)

Jdg 21:19 between **L** and Bethel, along the east side of the

LECAH (1)

1Ch 4:21 descendants of Shelah were Er (the father of **L**),

LECTURE (1) [LECTURING]

Ac 19: 9 Then he began preaching daily at the **l** hall of

LECTURING (1) [LECTURE]

Ac 28:23 He began **l** in the morning and went on into the

LED (232) [LEAD]

Ge 24:27 for he has **l** me straight to my master's relatives."
24:48 because he had **l** me along the right path to find a
43:24 The brothers were then **l** into the palace and given
Ex 13:18 So God **l** them along a route through the
13:19 bones with them when God **l** them out of Egypt—
14: 6 called out his troops and **l** the chase in his chariot.
15:20 and **l** all the women in rhythm and dance.
15:22 Then Moses **l** the people of Israel away from the
17:10 He **l** his men out to fight the army of Amalek.
19:17 Moses **l** them out from the camp to meet with God,
32:23 to this man Moses, who **l** us out of Egypt.'
Lev 16:21 into the wilderness, **l** by a man chosen for this task.
24:23 they **l** the blasphemer outside the camp and stoned
Nu 10:15 The tribe of Issachar was **l** by Nethanel son of
10:16 The tribe of Zebulun was **l** by Eliab son of Helon.
10:19 The tribe of Simeon was **l** by Shelumiel son of
10:20 The tribe of Gad was **l** by Eliasaph son of Deuel.
10:23 The tribe of Manasseh was **l** by Gamaliel son of
10:24 The tribe of Benjamin was **l** by Abidan son of
10:26 The tribe of Asher was **l** by Pagiel son of Ocran.
10:27 The tribe of Naphtali was **l** by Ahira son of Enan.
31: 6 and Phinehas son of Eleazar the priest **l** them into
Dt 8: 2 Remember how the LORD your God **l** you
8:15 Do not forget that he **l** you through the great
9:12 because the people you **l** out of Egypt have become
13:13 that some worthless rabble among you have **l** their
28:41 keep them, for they will be **l** away into captivity.
29: 5 For forty years I **l** you through the wilderness,
Jos 4:12 and the half-tribe of Manasseh **l** the Israelites
14: 6 **l** by Caleb son of Jephunneh the Kenizzite, came to
22:13 they sent a delegation **l** by Phinehas son of Eleazar,
24: 3 the Euphrates and **l** him into the land of Canaan.
Jdg 3:27 Then he **l** a band of Israelites down from the hills.
4:14 So Barak **l** his ten thousand warriors down the
9:39 then **l** the men of Shechem into battle against
9:48 so he **l** his forces to Mount Zalmon. He took an ax
11:29 in Gilead, and **l** an army against the Ammonites.
11:32 So Jephthah **l** his army against the Ammonites,
15:13 with two new ropes and **l** him away from the rock.
1Sa 4:18 and very fat. He had **l** Israel for forty years.
11: 1 King Nahash of Ammon **l** his army against the
18:13 but David faithfully **l** his troops into battle.
19: 8 and David **l** his troops against the Philistines.
30:16 So the Egyptian **l** them to the Amalekite
2Sa 2:12 One day Abner **l** some of Ishbosheth's troops from
2:13 Joab son of Zeruiah **l** David's troops from Hebron,
5: 2 was our king, you were the one who really **l** Israel.
5: 6 then **l** his troops to Jerusalem to fight against the
6: 2 He **l** them to Baalah of Judah to bring home the
10: 9 and **l** them out to fight the Arameans in the fields.
10:17 crossed the Jordan River, and **l** the army to Helam.
12:29 So David **l** the rest of his army to Rabbah
15:30 David walked up the road that **l** to the Mount of
22:20 He **l** me to a place of safety; / he rescued me
1Ki 11: 3 they **l** his heart away from the LORD.
15:26 continuing the sins of idolatry that Jeroboam had **l**
15:30 and the sins he had **l** Israel to commit.
15:34 continuing the sins of idolatry that Jeroboam had **l**
16:13 because of all the sins they **l** Israel to commit,
16:17 So Omri **l** the army of Israel away from Gibbethon
16:19 continuing the sins of idolatry that Jeroboam had **l**
16:26 continuing the sins of idolatry that Jeroboam had **l**
20:19 But by now Ahab's provincial commanders had **l**
21:22 him very angry and have **l** all of Israel into sin.
22:29 and King Jehoshaphat of Judah **l** their armies
22:52 of Nebat, who had **l** Israel into the sin of idolatry.
2Ki 3: 3 son of Nebat had **l** the people of Israel to commit.
3:26 he **l** seven hundred of his warriors in a desperate
6:19 you are looking for." And he **l** them to Samaria.
10:29 the great sin that Jeroboam son of Nebat had **l**
10:31 of idolatry that Jeroboam had **l** Israel to commit.
11:16 and **l** her out to the gate where horses enter the
13: 2 that Jeroboam son of Nebat had **l** Israel to commit.
13:11 that Jeroboam son of Nebat had **l** Israel to commit.
14:24 that Jeroboam son of Nebat had **l** Israel to commit.
15: 9 that Jeroboam son of Nebat had **l** Israel to commit.
15:18 that Jeroboam son of Nebat had **l** Israel to commit.
15:24 that Jeroboam son of Nebat had **l** Israel to commit.
15:28 that Jeroboam son of Nebat had **l** Israel to commit.
16: 9 of Damascus and **l** its population away as captives,
21: 9 and Manasseh **l** them to do even more evil than the
21:11 He has **l** the people of Judah into idolatry.
23:15 son of Nebat had made when he **l** Israel into sin.
24:15 Nebuchadnezzar **l** King Jehoiachin away as a
25: 1 King Nebuchadnezzar of Babylon **l** his entire army
25: 7 him in bronze chains, and **l** him away to Babylon.
1Ch 4:42 **l** by Pelatiah, Neariah, Rephaiah, and Uzziel—
8: 7 of Uzza and Ahihud, **l** them when they moved.
11: 2 was our king, you were the one who really **l** Israel.
11: 6 the son of David's sister Zeruiah, **l** the attack,
19:10 and **l** them out to fight the Arameans in the fields.
20: 1 Joab **l** the Israelite army in successful attacks
26:20 Other Levites, **l** by Ahijah, were in charge of the
2Ch 1: 3 Then Solomon **l** the entire assembly to the hill at
13: 3 Judah, **l** by King Abijah, fielded 400,000 seasoned
13: 8 the LORD that is **l** by the descendants of David?
18:28 and King Jehoshaphat of Judah **l** their armies
21:11 and had **l** the people of Jerusalem and Judah to
21:13 You have **l** the people of Jerusalem and Judah to
22: 4 family became his advisers, and they **l** him to ruin.
23:15 and **l** her out to the gate where horses enter the
25:11 his courage and **l** his army to the Valley of Salt,
26:16 he also became proud, which **l** to his downfall.
28:23 they **l** to his ruin and the ruin of all Israel.
33: 9 But Manasseh **l** the people of Judah and Jerusalem
33:11 him in bronze chains, and **l** him away to Babylon.
35:20 King Neco of Egypt **l** his army up from Egypt to
35:22 he **l** his army into battle on the plain of Megiddo.
36: 6 Jehoiakim in chains and **l** him away to Babylon.
Ezr 4: 7 of Judah, **l** by Bishlam, Mithredath, and Tabeel,
Ne 3:13 **l** by Hanun, rebuilt the Valley Gate, hung its doors,
3:18 Next down the line were his countrymen **l** by
9:12 You **l** our ancestors by a pillar of cloud during the
9:19 The pillar of cloud still **l** them forward by day,
12:31 I **l** the leaders of Judah to the top of the wall
12:36 the man of God. Ezra the scribe **l** this procession.
13:26 "Wasn't this exactly what **l** King Solomon of
13:26 But even he was **l** into sin by his foreign wives.
Est 6:11 and **l** him through the city square, shouting,
Job 12:18 With ropes around their waist, they are **l** away.
36:16 "God has **l** you away from danger, giving you
Ps 18:19 He **l** me to a place of safety; / he rescued me
22: 9 and **l** me to trust you when I was a nursing infant.
45:14 In her beautiful robes, she is **l** to the king,
49:14 Like sheep, they are **l** to the grave, / where death
68: 7 O God, when you **l** your people from Egypt,
68:18 to the heights, / you **l** a crowd of captives.
77:19 Your road **l** through the sea, / your pathway
77:20 You **l** your people along that road like a flock of
78:13 he divided the sea before them and **l** them through!
78:14 In the daytime he **l** them by a cloud, / and at night
78:52 But he **l** his own people like a flock of sheep,
78:72 with a true heart / and **l** them with skillful hands.
106: 9 He **l** Israel across the sea bottom that was as dry as
106:36 worshiped their idols, / and this **l** to their downfall.
107: 7 He **l** them straight to safety, / to a city where they
107:14 He **l** them from the darkness and deepest gloom;
136:14 He **l** Israel safely through, / His faithful love
136:16 Give thanks to him who **l** his people through the
Pr 20: 1 Whoever is **l** astray by drink cannot be wise.
Isa 8:21 My people will be **l** away as captives, weary
9:16 For the leaders of the people have **l** them down the
28: 7 Now, however, Israel is being **l** by drunks!
48:21 They were not thirsty when he **l** them through the
53: 7 said a word. He was **l** as a lamb to the slaughter.
53: 8 From prison and trial they **l** him away to his death.
60:11 The kings of the world will be **l** as captives in a
63:11 days of old when Moses **l** his people out of Egypt.
63:13 Where is the one who **l** them through the bottom of
63:14 You **l** your people, LORD, and gained a
Jer 2: 5 "What sin did your ancestors find in me that **l**
2: 6 of Egypt and **l** us through the barren wilderness—
2:37 you will be **l** into exile with your hands on your
7:22 When I **l** your ancestors out of Egypt, it was not
13:17 because the LORD's flock will be **l** away into
22:10 Instead, weep for the captive king being **l** away!
23:13 by Baal and **l** my people of Israel into sin.
38:23 and children will be **l** out to the Babylonians,
41:16 and his officers **l** away all the people they had
50: 6 Their shepherds have **l** them astray and turned
52: 4 King Nebuchadnezzar of Babylon **l** his entire army
52:11 him in bronze chains, and **l** him away to Babylon.
La 1: 3 Judah has been **l** away into captivity, afflicted
5:13 The young men are **l** away to work at millstones,
Eze 19: 4 They **l** him away in chains / to the land of Egypt.
20:10 people out of Egypt and **l** them into the wilderness.
30:18 and its daughters will be **l** away as captives.
35: 5 Your continual hatred for the people of Israel **l** you
37: 2 He **l** me around among the old, dry bones that
40: 7 which **l** to the foyer at the inner end of the gateway
40:27 was another gateway that **l** into the inner courtyard.
40:38 A door **l** from the foyer of the inner gateway on the
41: 7 A stairway **l** up from the bottom level through the
42: 1 Then the man **l** me out of the Temple courtyard by
42:15 he **l** me out through the east gateway to measure
46:19 and **l** me to the sacred rooms assigned to the
46:21 outer courtyard and **l** me to each of its four corners.
47: 2 and **l** me around to the eastern entrance.
47: 3 he **l** me along the stream for 1,750 feet and told me
47: 6 I had seen, then he **l** me back along the riverbank.
Da 7:13 the Ancient One and was **l** into his presence.
Hos 5: 1 For you have **l** the people into a snare by
11: 4 I **l** Israel along with my ropes of kindness and love.
12:13 Then the LORD **l** Jacob's descendants,
Am 2: 4 They have been **l** astray by the same lies that
2:10 and **l** you through the desert for forty years
4: 2 "The time will come when you will be **l** away with
6: 7 you will be the first to be **l** away as captives.
9: 7 from Crete and **l** the Arameans out of Kir.
Mic 1:13 of idol worship, and so you **l** Jerusalem into sin.
Na 3:10 and her people were **l** away as captives.
Mt 4: 1 Then Jesus was **l** out into the wilderness by the
17: 1 James and John, and **l** them up a high mountain.
26:57 Then the people who had arrested Jesus **l** him to
27:31 him again. Then they **l** him away to be crucified.
Mk 7:33 Jesus **l** him to a private place away from the crowd.
8:23 blind man by the hand and **l** him out of the village.
14:53 Jesus was **l** to the high priest's home where the
14:65 And even the guards were hitting him as they **l** him
15:20 him again. Then they **l** him away to be crucified.
Lk 2:27 That day the Spirit **l** him to the Temple. So when
4: 1 He was **l** by the Spirit to go out into the wilderness,
22:47 even as he said this, a mob approached, **l** by Judas,
22:54 and **l** him to the high priest's residence,
22:66 religious law. Jesus was **l** before this high council,
23:26 As they **l** Jesus away, Simon of Cyrene, who was
23:32 both criminals, were **l** out to be executed with him.
24:50 Then Jesus **l** them to Bethany, and lifting his hands
Jn 7:47 "Have you been **l** astray, too?" the Pharisees
19:16 be crucified. / So they took Jesus and **l** him away.
Ac 7:36 and wonders he **l** them out of Egypt,
7:45 when Joshua **l** the battles against the Gentile
8:32 "He was **l** as a sheep to the slaughter. / And as a
9: 9 So his companions **l** him by the hand to Damascus.
12:17 and how the Lord had **l** him out of jail.
13:17 Then he powerfully **l** them out of their slavery.
21:38 "Aren't you the Egyptian who **l** a rebellion some
22:11 and had to be **l** into Damascus by my companions.
23:19 **l** him aside, and asked, "What is it you want to tell
Ro 5:16 For Adam's sin **l** to condemnation, but we have the
8:14 For all who are **l** by the Spirit of God are children
1Co 12: 2 that when you were still pagans you were **l** astray
2Co 3: 7 That old system of law etched in stone **l** to death,
7: 2 wrong to anyone. We have not **l** anyone astray.
11: 3 But I fear that somehow you will be **l** away from
11:29 Who is **l** astray, and I do not burn with anger?
Gal 2:17 Has Christ **l** us into sin? Of course not!
Eph 4: 8 ascended to the heights, / he **l** a crowd of captives
Heb 3:16 Weren't they the ones Moses **l** out of Egypt?
4: 8 was not the land of Canaan, where Joshua **l** them.
8: 9 by the hand / and **l** them out of the land of Egypt.
Rev 9:16 They **l** an army of 200 million mounted troops—

LEDGE (13) [LEDGES]

Ex 27: 5 down into the firebox, resting it on the **l** built there.
38: 4 Next he made a bronze grating that rested on a **l**
Eze 43:14 From the gutter the altar rises 3-1/2 feet to a **l** that
43:14 surrounds the altar; this lower **l** is 21 inches wide.
43:14 From the lower **l** the altar rises 7 feet to the upper
l; this upper **l** is also 21 inches wide.
43:17 The upper **l** also forms a square, measuring 24-1/2
43:20 the four corners of the upper **l**, and the curb that
runs around that **l**.
45:19 the four corners of the upper **l** on the altar,
46:23 Along the inside of these walls was a **l** of stone
46:23 with fireplaces under the **l** all the way around.

LEDGES (2) [LEDGE]

1Ki 6: 6 by beams resting on **l** built out from the wall.
Eze 41: 6 The supports for these rooms rested on **l** in the

LEECH (1)

Pr 30:15 The **l** has two suckers that cry out, "More, more!"

LEEKS (1)

Nu 11: 5 melons, **l**, onions, and garlic that we wanted.

LEES [KJV] See WELL-AGED

LEEWARD (1)

Ac 27: 7 so we sailed down to the **l** side of Crete,

LEFT (576) [LEFT-HANDED, LEFTOVER, LEFTOVERS]

LEFT HAND (12) Ge 48:13,14; Lev 14:15,17,26; Jdg 3:21; 5:26; 2Sa 20:10; 1Ch 12:2; SS 2:6; 8:3; Mt 6:3

Ge 4:16 So Cain **l** the LORD's presence and settled in the
7:23 were all destroyed, and only Noah was **l** alive,

8:18 his wife, and his sons and their wives **l** the boat.
11:31 and **l** Ur of the Chaldeans to go to the land of
12: 4 Abram was seventy-five years old when he **l**
13: 1 So they **l** Egypt and traveled north into the Negev
17:22 That ended the conversation, and God **l** Abraham.
19:30 Afterward Lot **l** Zoar because he was afraid of the
21:15 was gone, she **l** the boy in the shade of a bush.
21:32 Abimelech **l** with Phicol, the commander of his
24:61 mounted the camels and **l** with Abraham's servant.
25: 5 Abraham **l** everything he owned to his son Isaac.
26:22 and the local people finally **l** him alone.
27: 5 So when Esau **l** to hunt for the wild game,
27:30 and almost before Jacob had **l** his father,
27:37 of grain and wine—what is there **l** to give?"
27:38 Esau pleaded, "Not one blessing **l** for me? O my
28:10 Jacob **l** Beersheba and traveled toward Haran.
31:19 At the time they **l**, Laban was some distance away,
32:10 When I **l** home, I owned nothing except a walking
32:24 This **l** Jacob all alone in the camp, and a man came
32:31 The sun rose as he **l** Peniel, and he was limping
38: 1 this time, Judah **l** home and moved to Adullam,
38:13 Someone told Tamar that her father-in-law had **l**
39:12 She was **l** holding it as he ran from the house.
39:15 loud cries, he ran and **l** his shirt behind with me."
41:46 And when Joseph **l** Pharaoh's presence, he made a
42:24 Now he **l** the room and found a place where he
42:38 is dead, and he alone is **l** of his mother's children.
44:20 is dead, and he alone is **l** of his mother's children,
45:24 his brothers off, and as they **l**, he called after them,
45:25 And they **l** Egypt and returned to their father,
46: 5 So Jacob **l** Beersheba, and his sons brought him to
47:10 Then Jacob blessed Pharaoh again before he **l**.
47:18 We have nothing **l** but our bodies and land.
48:13 the boys so Ephraim was at Jacob's **l** hand
48:14 and his **l** hand was on the head of Manasseh,
50: 8 But they **l** their little children and flocks and herds
Ex 4:19 Before Moses **l** Midian, the LORD said to him,
4:26 After that, the LORD **l** him alone.
5:20 As they **l** Pharaoh's court, they met Moses
8:12 So Moses and Aaron **l** Pharaoh, and Moses pleaded
8:30 So Moses **l** Pharaoh and asked the LORD to
9:19 or animal **l** outside will die beneath the hail.' "
9:21 for the word of the LORD **l** them out in the open.
9:25 It **l** all of Egypt in ruins. Everything **l** in the fields
9:33 So Moses **l** Pharaoh and went out of the city.
10:12 and eat all the crops still **l** after the hailstorm."
10:18 So Moses **l** Pharaoh and pleaded with the LORD.
10:26 must go with us; not a hoof can be **l** behind.
11: 8 burning with anger, Moses **l** Pharaoh's presence.
12:37 That night the people of Israel **l** Rameses
12:41 430th year that all the LORD's forces **l** the land.
13: 3 the day you **l** Egypt, the place of your slavery.
13: 8 of what the LORD did for us when we **l** Egypt.'
13:18 and the Israelites **l** Egypt like a marching army.
16: 1 Then they **l** Elim and journeyed into the Sin
16:18 Those who gathered a lot had nothing **l** over,
16:23 want today, and set aside what is **l** for tomorrow."
17: 1 the people of Israel **l** the Sin Desert and moved
19: 1 of Sinai exactly two months after they **l** Egypt.
23:18 And no sacrificial fat may be **l** unoffered until the
25:15 from the rings; they are to be **l** there permanently.
26:12 An extra half sheet of this roof covering will be **l** to
27:15 The curtain on the **l** side will also be 22-1/2 feet
33: 6 So from the time they **l** Mount Sinai, the Israelites
34:18 year in early spring, for that was when you **l** Egypt.
35:20 So all the people **l** Moses and went to their tents to
36: 4 But finally the craftsmen **l** their work to meet with
38:15 The curtain on the **l** side was also 22-1/2 feet long
Lev 4:21 then take what is **l** of the bull outside the camp
6: 9 The burnt offering must be **l** on the altar until the
7:16 and whatever is **l** over may be eaten on the second
7:17 But anything **l** over until the third day must be
8:32 Any meat or bread that is **l** over must then be
10:12 "Take what is **l** of the grain offering after the
14:15 of the olive oil into the palm of his own **l** hand.
14:17 then put some of the oil remaining in his **l** hand on
14:26 of the olive oil into the palm of his own **l** hand.
22:27 is born, it must be **l** with its mother for seven days.
25:15 The seller will charge you only for the crop years **l**
25:50 number of years **l** until the next Year of Jubilee—
26:39 Those still **l** alive will rot away in enemy lands
27:18 to the years **l** until the next Year of Jubilee.
Nu 3: 4 this **l** only Eleazar and Ithamar to serve as priests
12:16 Then they **l** Hazeroth and camped in the wilderness
14:19 just as you have forgiven them ever since they **l**
14:44 nor the Ark of the LORD's covenant **l** the camp.
20:22 The whole community of Israel **l** Kadesh as a
21:18 Then the Israelites **l** the wilderness and proceeded
21:29 of Chemosh! / Chemosh has **l** his sons as refugees,
25: 7 priest saw this, he jumped up and **l** the assembly.
33: 3 The people of Israel **l** defiantly, in full view of all
33: 6 Then they **l** Succoth and camped at Etham on the
33: 7 They **l** Etham and turned back toward Pi-hahiroth,
33: 8 They **l** Pi-hahiroth and crossed the Red Sea into the
33: 9 They **l** Marah and camped at Elim, where there are
33:10 They **l** Elim and camped beside the Red Sea.
33:11 They **l** the Red Sea and camped in the Sin Desert.
33:12 They **l** the Sin Desert and camped at Dophkah.
33:13 They **l** Dophkah and camped at Alush.
33:14 They **l** Alush and camped at Rephidim,
33:15 They **l** Rephidim and camped in the wilderness of
33:16 They **l** the wilderness of Sinai and camped at
33:17 They **l** Kibroth-hattaavah and camped at Hazeroth.
33:18 They **l** Hazeroth and camped at Rithmah.
33:19 They **l** Rithmah and camped at Rimmon-perez.
33:20 They **l** Rimmon-perez and camped at Libnah.
33:21 They **l** Libnah and camped at Rissah.
33:22 They **l** Rissah and camped at Kehelathah.
33:23 They **l** Kehelathah and camped at Mount Shepher.
33:24 They **l** Mount Shepher and camped at Haradah.
33:25 They **l** Haradah and camped at Makheloth.
33:26 They **l** Makheloth and camped at Tahath.
33:27 They **l** Tahath and camped at Terah.
33:28 They **l** Terah and camped at Mithcah.
33:29 They **l** Mithcah and camped at Hashmonah.
33:30 They **l** Hashmonah and camped at Moseroth.
33:31 They **l** Moseroth and camped at Bene-jaakan.
33:32 They **l** Bene-jaakan and camped at Hor-haggidgad.
33:33 They **l** Hor-haggidgad and camped at Jotbathah.
33:34 They **l** Jotbathah and camped at Abronah.
33:35 They **l** Abronah and camped at Ezion-geber.
33:36 They **l** Ezion-geber and camped at Kadesh in the
33:37 They **l** Kadesh and camped at Mount Hor,
33:41 the Israelites **l** Mount Hor and camped at
33:42 Then they **l** Zalmonah and camped at Punon.
33:43 They **l** Punon and camped at Oboth.
33:44 They **l** Oboth and camped at Iye-abarim on the
33:45 They **l** Iye-abarim and camped at Dibon-gad.
33:46 They **l** Dibon-gad and camped at
33:47 They **l** Almon-diblathaim and camped in the
33:48 They **l** the mountains east of the river and camped
Dt 1: 3 But forty years after the Israelites **l** Mount Sinai,
1:19 we **l** Mount Sinai and traveled through the great
4:45 gave to the people of Israel when they **l** Egypt,
9: 7 From the day you **l** Egypt until now, you have
28:21 none of you are **l** in the land you are about to enter
28:48 You will be **l** hungry, thirsty, naked, and lacking in
28:62 few of you will be **l** because you would not listen
29:16 through the lands of enemy nations as we **l**.
32:36 strength is gone / and no one is **l**, slave or free.
Jos 2: 5 They **l** the city at dusk, as the city gates were about
2: 7 And as soon as the king's men had **l**, the city gate
2:10 for you through the Red Sea when you **l** Egypt.
2:17 Before they **l**, the men told her, "We can
3: 1 next morning Joshua and all the Israelites **l** Acacia
5: 4 arms when they **l** Egypt had died in the wilderness.
5: 5 Those who **l** Egypt had all been circumcised,
5: 6 enough to bear arms when they **l** Egypt had died.
8: 6 We will let them chase us until they have all **l** the
8: 9 So they **l** that night and lay in ambush between
8:17 There was not a man **l** in Ai or Bethel who did not
8:17 after the Israelites, and the city was **l** wide open.
8:29 king of Ai on a tree and **l** him there until evening.
9:12 "This bread was hot from the ovens when we **l**.
10: 7 So Joshua and the entire Israelite army **l** Gilgal
10:28 the king. Not one person in the city was **l** alive.
10:30 slaughtered everyone in the city and **l** no survivors.
10:37 the entire population. Not one person was **l** alive.
11: 8 of Mizpah, until not one enemy warrior was **l** alive.
11:22 Not one was **l** in all the land of Israel, though some
22: 9 and the half-tribe of Manasseh **l** the rest of Israel at
22:32 and the ten high officials **l** the tribes of Reuben
24:32 had brought along with them when they **l** Egypt,
Jdg 1:16 When the tribe of Judah **l** Jericho, the Kenites,
2: 6 each of the tribes **l** to take possession of the land
2:21 I will no longer drive out the nations that Joshua **l**
3: 1 The LORD **l** certain nations in the land to test
3: 4 These people were **l** to test the Israelites—to see
3:21 Ehud reached with his **l** hand, pulled out the
3:22 So Ehud **l** the dagger in, and the king's bowels
4:16 of Sisera's warriors. Not a single one was **l** alive.
5: 7 There were few people **l** in the villages of Israel—
5:26 Then with her **l** hand she reached for a tent peg,
6: 4 They **l** the Israelites with nothing to eat, taking all
7:20 They held the blazing torches in their **l** hands
16:19 making his capture certain. And his strength **l** him.
16:20 But he didn't realize the LORD had **l** him.
18:24 all my gods and my priest, and I have nothing **l**!"
19:30 crime has not been committed since Israel **l** Egypt.
20:19 So the Israelites **l** early the next morning
21:15 because the LORD had **l** this gap in the tribes of
Ru 1: 1 a man from Bethlehem in Judah **l** the country
1: 3 and Naomi was **l** with her two sons.
1: 5 This **l** Naomi alone, without her husband or sons.
2:11 I have heard how you **l** your father and mother
2:18 Ruth also gave her the food that was **l** over from
1Sa 2:33 Those who are **l** alive will live in sadness and grief,
5: 4 Only the trunk of his body was **l** intact.
9:26 got ready, and he and Samuel **l** the house together.
11:11 so badly scattered that no two of them were **l**
13:15 Samuel then **l** Gilgal and went on his way,
13:15 were still with him, he found only six hundred **l**!
13:17 Three raiding parties soon **l** the camp of the
14: 3 No one realized that Jonathan had **l** the Israelite
14:13 and his armor bearer killed them right and **l**.
15: 6 up from Egypt." So the Kenites packed up and **l**.
16:14 Now the Spirit of the LORD had **l** Saul,
17:20 So David **l** the sheep with another shepherd and set
17:22 David **l** his things with the keeper of supplies
18:12 and he was jealous because the LORD had **l** him
20:34 Jonathan **l** the table in fierce anger and refused to
20:42 Then David **l**, and Jonathan returned to the city.
22: 1 So David **l** Gath and escaped to the cave of
23:13 **l** Keilah and began roaming the countryside.
24: 7 After Saul had **l** the cave and gone on his way,
27:11 No one was **l** alive to come to Gath and tell where
28:15 and God has **l** me and won't reply by prophets
28:16 "Why ask me if the LORD has **l** you and has
30:13 "My master **l** me behind three days ago because I
2Sa 3:22 But just after Abner **l**, Joab and some of David's
3:26 Joab then **l** David and sent messengers to catch up
10:10 He **l** the rest of the army under the command of his
11: 8 David even sent a gift to Uriah after he had **l** the
13: 9 of here," Amnon told his servants. So they all **l**.
13:30 has killed all your sons; not one is **l** alive!"
14: 7 But if I do that, I will have no one **l**, and my
15:16 He **l** no one behind except ten of his concubines to
16:21 for he has **l** them here to keep the house.
17:12 to the ground, so that not one of his men is **l** alive.
18: 9 His mule kept going and **l** him dangling in the air.
19:19 "Forget the terrible thing I did when you **l**
19:24 his beard since the day the king **l** Jerusalem.
20: 3 he instructed that the ten concubines he had **l** to
20:10 Amasa didn't notice the dagger in his **l** hand,
20:10 Joab and his brother Abishai **l** him lying there
21: 2 but were all that was **l** of the nation of the
1Ki 2:41 Solomon heard that Shimei had **l** Jerusalem
10:13 Then she and all her attendants **l** and returned to
13:10 So he **l** Bethel and went home another way.
15:18 and gold that was **l** in the treasuries of the
15:29 so that not one of the royal family was **l**,
17:12 And I have only a handful of flour **l** in the jar
17:14 and oil **l** in your containers until the time when the
17:16 there was always enough **l** in the containers,
18:22 "I am the only prophet of the LORD who is **l**,
18:45 a terrific rainstorm, and Ahab **l** quickly for Jezreel.
19: 3 a town in Judah, and he **l** his servant there.
19:10 I alone am **l**, and now they are trying to kill me,
19:14 I alone am **l**, and now they are trying to kill me,
19:20 Elisha **l** the oxen standing there, ran after Elijah,
22:19 of heaven around him, on his right and on his **l**.
2Ki 2:16 Perhaps the Spirit of the LORD has **l** him on
2:23 Elisha **l** Jericho and went up to Bethel. As he was
3:25 Finally, only Kir-hareseth was **l**, but even that
4: 7 and there will be enough money **l** over to support
4:21 the man of God, then shut the door and **l** him there.
4:43 be plenty for all. There will even be some **l** over!"
4:44 there was plenty for all and some **l** over,
5:27 When Gehazi **l** the room, he was leprous; his skin
7:12 so they have **l** their camp and have hidden in the
9: 6 So Jehu **l** the others and went into the house.
10:11 So Ahab was **l** without a single survivor.
10:15 When Jehu **l** there, he met Jehonadab son of
10:17 he killed everyone who was **l** there from Ahab's
19: 4 for his words. Oh, pray for those of us who are **l**!"
19: 8 the Assyrian representative **l** Jerusalem and went to
19: 8 who had **l** Lachish and was attacking Libnah.
19:30 And you who are **l** in Judah, who have escaped the
20: 4 But before Isaiah had **l** the middle courtyard,
20:17 off to Babylon. Nothing will be **l**, says the LORD.
21:14 will reject even those few of my people who are **l**,
23: 8 This gate was located to the **l** of the city gate as
24:14 So only the poorest people were **l** in the land.
25:22 of Shaphan as governor over the people **l** in Judah.
1Ch 12: 2 or sling stones with their **l** hand as well as their
19:11 He **l** the rest of the army under the command of his
21:21 he **l** his threshing floor and bowed to the ground
24: 2 and Ithamar were **l** to carry on as priests.
2Ch 5:10 with the people of Israel after they **l** Egypt.
5:11 Then the priests **l** the Holy Place. All the priests
9:12 Then she and all her attendants **l** and returned to
18:18 all the armies of heaven on his right and on his **l**.
20:10 ancestors invade those nations when Israel **l** Egypt,
25:16 you killed!" So the prophet **l** with this warning:
Ezr 7: 9 He had **l** Babylon on April 8 and came to
7:18 Any money that is **l** over may be used in whatever
10: 6 Then Ezra **l** the front of the Temple of God
Ne 3: 8 They **l** out a section of Jerusalem as far as the
8: 4 To his **l** stood Pedaiah, Mishael, Malkijah,
13: 2 been friendly to the Israelites when they **l** Egypt.
Est 5: 9 What a happy man Haman was as he **l** the banquet!
Job 1:12 So Satan **l** the LORD's presence.
2: 7 So Satan **l** the LORD's presence, and he struck
10:20 I have only a little time **l**, so leave me alone—
12: 6 But even robbers are **l** in peace, and those who
20:19 For he oppressed the poor and **l** them destitute.
20:21 Nothing is **l** after he finishes gorging himself;
20:26 will devour his goods, consuming all he has **l**.
Ps 7: 5 Let my honor be **l** in the dust. / *Interlude*
22:15 You have laid me in the dust and **l** me for dead.
79: 2 They have **l** the bodies of your servants / as food
79: 3 all around Jerusalem; / no one is **l** to bury the dead.
88: 4 who is dead, / like a strong man with no strength **l**.
114: 1 when the family of Jacob **l** that foreign land—
Pr 3:16 life in her right hand, and riches and honor in her **l**.
Ecc 5:14 there is nothing **l** to pass on to one's children.
12: 2 and there is no silver lining **l** among the clouds.
SS 2: 6 His **l** hand is under my head, and his right hand
8: 3 Your **l** hand would be under my head and your
Isa 3:24 beauty will be gone. Only shame will be **l** to them.
4: 1 In that day few men will be **l** alive. Seven women
6:11 their cities are destroyed, with no one **l** in them.
7:21 will be fortunate to have a cow and two sheep **l**.
7:22 The few people still **l** in the land will live on curds
10:20 Then at last those **l** in Israel and Judah will trust
13:12 Few will be **l** alive when I have finished my work.
16: 2 The women of Moab are **l** like homeless birds at
16:14 be ended, and few of its people will be **l** alive."
17: 3 The few **l** in Aram will share the fate of Israel's
17: 6 Only a few of its people will be **l**, like the stray
olives **l** on the tree after the harvest.
18: 6 Your mighty army will be **l** dead in the fields for
23: 7 How can this silent ruin be all that is **l** of your once
24: 6 They are **l** desolate, destroyed by fire. Few will be
l alive.
24:12 The city is **l** in ruins, with its gates battered down.
24:13 like the stray olives **l** on the tree or the few grapes **l**
on the vine after harvest, only a remnant is **l**.
24:14 But all who are **l** will shout and sing for joy.
25:10 will be crushed like trampled straw and **l** to rot.
27: 9 be an Asherah pole or incense altar **l** standing.

30: 14 so completely that there won't be a piece **l** that is
30: 17 You will be **l** like a lonely flagpole on a distant
34: 3 Their dead will be **l** unburied, and the stench of
37: 4 for his words. Oh, pray for those of us who are **l**!"
37: 8 the Assyrian representative **l** Jerusalem and went to
37: 8 who had **l** Lachish and was attacking Libnah.
37: 31 And you who are **l** in Judah, who have escaped the
39: 6 off to Babylon. Nothing will be **l**, says the LORD.
44: 17 Then he takes what's **l** and makes his god: a carved
46: 3 "Listen to me, all you who are **l** in Israel. I created
49: 21 I was **l** here all alone. Who bore these children?
51: 18 Not one of your children is **l** alive to help you
51: 19 who is **l** to sympathize? Who is **l** to comfort you?
53: 6 We have **l** God's paths to follow our own.
Jer 3: 8 too, has **l** me and given herself to prostitution.
7: 25 From the day your ancestors **l** Egypt until now,
7: 33 and no one will be **l** to scare them away.
9: 22 after the harvest. No one will be **l** to bury them."
10: 20 home is gone, and no one is **l** to help me rebuild it.
14: 16 and war. There will be no one **l** to bury them.
15: 3 and the wild animals to finish up what is **l**.
15: 9 And those who are **l**, I will hand over to the enemy
22: 20 they are all destroyed. Not one is **l** to help you.
24: 8 his officials, all the people **l** in Jerusalem,
25: 38 He has **l** his den like a lion seeking its prey,
27: 18 gold utensils that are still **l** in the LORD's Temple
27: 20 King Nebuchadnezzar of Babylon **l** them here
28: 11 of Babylon." At that, Jeremiah **l** the Temple area.
30: 14 All your allies have **l** you and do not care about
34: 21 And though Babylon's king has **l** this city for a
34: 22 of Judah are destroyed and **l** completely empty."
36: 20 Then the officials **l** the scroll for safekeeping in the
37: 2 **l** in the land listened to what the LORD said
37: 11 When the Babylonian army **l** Jerusalem because of
37: 21 every day as long as there was any **l** in the city.
38: 4 the morale of the few fighting men we have **l**,
38: 22 All the women **l** in your palace will be brought out
38: 22 your feet sank in the mud, they **l** you to your fate!'
38: 27 and they **l** without finding out the truth.
39: 10 But Nebuzaradan **l** a few of the poorest people in
40: 6 and lived in Judah with the few who were still **l** in
40: 7 over the poor people who were **l** behind in Judah,
40: 11 the king of Babylon had **l** a few people in Judah
40: 15 Why should the few of us who are still **l** be
41: 6 Ishmael **l** Mizpah to meet them, weeping as he
41: 10 and the other people who had been **l** under
43: 6 the captain of the guard, had **l** with Gedaliah.
48: 9 she could fly away, for her cities will be **l** empty,
49: 7 of Teman? Is there no one **l** to give wise counsel?
49: 10 land of Edom, and there will be no place **l** to hide.
51: 29 Babylon will be **l** desolate without a single
La 1: 2 Among all her lovers, there is no one **l** to help her.
5: 8 become our masters; there is no one **l** to rescue us.
Eze 1: 10 on the right side, the face of an ox on the **l** side,
4: 4 "Now lie on your **l** side and place the sins of Israel
9: 8 against Jerusalem wipe out everyone **l** in Israel?"
11: 15 the people still **l** in Jerusalem are talking about
16: 4 Your umbilical cord was **l** uncut, and you were
16: 5 you were dumped in a field and **l** to die, unwanted.
21: 16 O sword, slash to the right, and slash to the **l**,
22: 18 They are the dross that is **l** over—a useless mixture
23: 8 For when she **l** Egypt, she did not leave her spirit
23: 25 as captives, and everything that is **l** will be burned.
30: 13 There will be no rulers **l** in Egypt; anarchy will
31: 12 cut it down and **l** it fallen on the ground.
31: 12 beneath its shadow went away and **l** it lying there.
34: 8 and **l** them to be attacked by every wild animal.
34: 8 took care of yourselves and **l** the sheep to starve.
34: 19 All that is **l** for my flock to eat is what you have
36: 36 all those still **l**—will know that I, the LORD,
41: 9 This **l** an open area between these side rooms
45: 2 land 87-1/2 feet wide is to be **l** empty all around it.
Da 4: 26 But the stump and the roots were **l** in the ground.
7: 4 and it was **l** standing with its two hind feet on the
7: 7 iron teeth and trampled what was **l** beneath its feet.
7: 19 and it trampled what was **l** beneath its feet.
10: 8 So I was **l** there all alone to watch this amazing
10: 8 My strength **l** me, my face grew deathly pale,
10: 13 and I **l** him there with the spirit prince of the
Hos 5: 3 You have **l** me as a prostitute leaves her husband;
5: 14 them off, and there will be no one **l** to rescue them.
Joel 1: 4 the crops, the swarming locusts took what was **l**!
Am 1: 8 and the few Philistines still **l** will be killed.
6: 9 If there are ten men **l** in one house, they will all
9: 12 And Israel will possess what is **l** of Edom and all
Ob 1: 8 At that time not a single wise person will be **l** in
Jnh 4: 2 "Didn't I say before I **l** home that you would do
Mic 2: 12 O Israel, I will gather the few of you who are **l**.
5: 7 Then the few **l** in Israel will go out among the
7: 2 not one fair-minded person is **l** on the earth.
Zep 2: 4 too, will be rooted out and **l** in desolation.
2: 5 LORD will destroy you until not one of you is **l**.
2: 9 Those of my people who are **l** will plunder them
3: 3 who by dawn have **l** no trace of their prey.
3: 12 Those who are **l** will be the lowly and the humble,
Hag 2: 4 Take courage, all you people still **l** in the land,
Zec 6: 7 patrol the earth!" So they **l** at once on their patrol.
10: 8 From the few that are **l**, their population will grow
12: 6 will burn up all the neighboring nations right and **l**,
13: 8 says the LORD. But a third will be **l** in the land.
14: 2 and half will be **l** among the ruins of the city.
Mal 2: 8 But not you! You have **l** God's paths.
Mt 2: 14 That night Joseph **l** for Egypt with the child
4: 12 been arrested, he **l** Judea and returned to Galilee.
4: 20 And they **l** their nets at once and went with him.
6: 3 don't tell your **l** hand what your right hand is
8: 15 But when Jesus touched her hand, the fever **l** her.
9: 27 After Jesus **l** the girl's home, two blind men
9: 32 When they **l**, some people brought to him a man
12: 15 He **l** that area, and many people followed him.
13: 1 Jesus **l** the house and went down to the shore,
13: 53 telling these stories, he **l** that part of the country.
15: 21 Jesus then **l** Galilee and went north to the region of
15: 32 me for three days, and they have nothing **l** to eat.
15: 37 there were seven large baskets of food **l** over!
16: 4 prophet Jonah." Then Jesus **l** them and went away.
16: 9 and the baskets of food that were **l** over?
16: 10 fed with seven loaves, with baskets of food **l** over?
17: 18 Jesus rebuked the demon in the boy, and it **l** him.
18: 28 "But when the man **l** the king, he went to a fellow
19: 1 he **l** Galilee and went southward to the region of
19: 15 hands on their heads and blessed them before he **l**.
20: 21 to you, one at your right and the other at your **l**?"
20: 29 As Jesus and the disciples **l** the city of Jericho,
23: 38 your house is **l** to you, empty and desolate.
24: 2 that not one stone will be **l** on top of another!"
24: 40 together in the field; one will be taken, the other **l**.
24: 41 flour at the mill; one will be taken, the other **l**.
25: 15 proportion to their abilities—and then **l** on his trip.
25: 33 the sheep at his right hand and the goats at his **l**.
25: 41 "Then the King will turn to those on the **l** and say,
26: 42 Again he **l** them and prayed, "My Father! If this
27: 53 They **l** the cemetery, went into the holy city of
27: 60 he rolled a great stone across the entrance as he **l**.
28: 16 Then the eleven disciples **l** for Galilee, going to the
Mk 1: 18 And they **l** their nets at once and went with him.
1: 20 too, and immediately they **l** their father, Zebedee,
1: 26 threw the man into a convulsion, but then he **l** him.
1: 29 After Jesus and his disciples **l** the synagogue,
1: 31 the fever suddenly **l**, and she got up and prepared a
6: 1 Jesus **l** that part of the country and returned with
6: 32 They **l** by boat for a quieter spot.
7: 24 Then Jesus **l** Galilee and went north to the region
7: 31 Jesus **l** Tyre and went to Sidon, then back to the
8: 2 me for three days, and they have nothing **l** to eat.
8: 8 there were seven large baskets of food **l** over!
8: 13 So he got back into the boat and **l** them, and he
8: 27 Jesus and his disciples **l** Galilee and went up to the
9: 26 the boy into another violent convulsion and **l** him.
10: 1 Then Jesus **l** Capernaum and went southward to
10: 28 all that he and the other disciples had **l** behind.
10: 37 "one at your right and the other at your **l**."
10: 46 Later, as Jesus and his disciples **l** town, a great
11: 4 The two disciples **l** and found the colt standing in
11: 11 and then he **l** because it was late in the afternoon.
11: 19 That evening Jesus and the disciples **l** the city.
12: 6 until there was only one **l**—his son whom he loved
12: 12 of the crowds. So they **l** him and went away.
12: 21 the widow, but soon he too died and **l** no children.
13: 2 that not one stone will be **l** on top of another."
13: 34 with that of a man who **l** home to go on a trip.
14: 39 Then Jesus **l** them again and prayed, repeating his
Lk 1: 38 you have said come true." And then the angel **l**.
2: 37 She never **l** the Temple but stayed there day
4: 1 full of the Holy Spirit, **l** the Jordan River.
4: 13 he **l** him until the next opportunity came.
4: 30 but he slipped away through the crowd and **l** them.
4: 35 then it **l** him without hurting him further.
5: 2 for the fishermen had **l** them and were washing
5: 11 they landed, they **l** everything and followed Jesus.
5: 27 Later, as Jesus **l** the town, he saw a tax collector
5: 28 So Levi got up, **l** everything, and followed him.
7: 24 After they **l**, Jesus talked to the crowd about John.
8: 37 So Jesus returned to the boat and **l**, crossing back
10: 30 beat him up, and **l** him half dead beside the road.
13: 35 And now look, your house is **l** to you empty.
14: 9 and will have to take whatever seat is **l** at the foot
17: 29 until the morning Lot **l** Sodom. Then fire
17: 34 one will be taken away, and the other will be **l**.
17: 35 together at the mill; one will be taken, the other **l**."
18: 28 "We have **l** our homes and followed you."
19: 13 Before he **l**, he called together ten servants
21: 6 that not one stone will be **l** on top of another."
22: 39 Jesus **l** the upstairs room and went as usual to the
22: 62 And Peter **l** the courtyard, crying bitterly.
24: 51 he **l** them and was taken up to heaven.
Jn 3: 22 Afterward Jesus and his disciples **l** Jerusalem,
4: 3 So he **l** Judea to return to Galilee.
4: 28 The woman **l** her water jar beside the well
7: 10 But after his brothers had **l** for the festival,
8: 9 until only Jesus was **l** in the middle of the crowd
8: 59 But Jesus hid himself from them and **l** the Temple.
9: 4 because there is little time **l** before the night falls
10: 39 tried to arrest him, but he got away and **l** them.
11: 28 Then she **l** him and returned to Mary. She called
11: 54 public ministry among the people and **l** Jerusalem.
13: 30 So Judas **l** at once, going out into the night.
13: 31 As soon as Judas **l** the room, Jesus said, "The time
Ac 2: 31 He was saying that the Messiah would not be **l**
5: 41 The apostles **l** the high council rejoicing that God
7: 4 So Abraham **l** the land of the Chaldeans and lived
8: 7 were cast out, screaming as they **l** their victims.
12: 9 So Peter **l** the cell, following the angel. But all the
12: 10 down the street, and then the angel suddenly **l** him.
12: 19 Afterward Herod **l** Judea to stay in Caesarea for a
13: 13 and those with him **l** Paphos by ship for
13: 13 There John Mark **l** them and returned to Jerusalem.
13: 42 As Paul and Barnabas **l** the synagogue that day,
14: 17 but he never **l** himself without a witness.
14: 20 The next day he **l** with Barnabas for Derbe.
16: 3 for Timothy to be circumcised before they **l**,
16: 18 to come out of her," he said. And instantly it **l** her.
18: 1 Then Paul **l** Athens and went to Corinth.
18: 19 at the port of Ephesus, Paul **l** the others behind.
18: 21 So he **l**, saying, "I will come back later,
19: 9 so Paul **l** the synagogue and took the believers with
20: 1 Then he said good-bye and **l** for Macedonia.
20: 11 continued talking to them until dawn; then he **l**.
21: 3 We sighted the island of Cyprus, passed it on our **l**,
21: 15 we packed our things and **l** for Jerusalem.
24: 27 favor with the Jewish leaders, he **l** Paul in prison.
25: 1 over his new responsibilities, he **l** for Jerusalem,
25: 14 he told him, "whose case was **l** for me by Felix.
26: 30 Bernice, and all the others stood and **l**.
27: 2 We **l** on a boat whose home port was
27: 21 to me in the first place and not **l** Fair Havens.
27: 40 So they cut off the anchors and **l** them in the sea.
28: 25 they **l** with this final word from Paul:
Ro 11: 3 I alone am **l**, and now they are trying to kill me,
11: 4 God's reply? He said, "You are not the only one **l**.
2Co 8: 15 "Those who gathered a lot had nothing **l** over,
9: 8 you need and plenty **l** over to share with others.
1Th 2: 17 for a little while (though our hearts never **l** you),
1Ti 1: 3 When I **l** for Macedonia, I urged you to stay there
2Ti 2: 18 They have **l** the path of truth, preaching the lie that
4: 13 be sure to bring the coat I **l** with Carpus at Troas.
4: 20 at Corinth, and I **l** Trophimus sick at Miletus.
Tit 1: 5 I **l** you on the island of Crete so you could
Heb 2: 8 it says "all things," it means nothing is **l** out.
11: 22 them to carry his bones with them when they **l**!
11: 27 It was by faith that Moses **l** the land of Egypt.
12: 27 will be shaken, so that only eternal things will be **l**.
1Pe 2: 23 He **l** his case in the hands of God, who always
1Jn 2: 19 These people **l** our churches because they never
2: 19 When they **l** us, it proved that they do not belong
Jude 1: 6 gave them but **l** the place where they belonged.
Rev 3: 2 for even what is **l** is at the point of death.
10: 2 his right foot on the sea and his **l** foot on the land.
16: 2 So the first angel **l** the Temple and poured out his
18: 11 for her, for there is no one **l** to buy their goods.

LEFT-HANDED (2) [HAND, LEFT]

Jdg 3: 15 son of Gera, of the tribe of Benjamin, who was **l**.
20: 16 Seven hundred of Benjamin's warriors were **l**,

LEFTOVER (3) [LEFT]

Ex 16: 24 The next morning the **l** food was wholesome
Ru 2: 2 "Let me go out into the fields to gather **l** grain
Mk 6: 43 and they picked up twelve baskets of **l** bread

LEFTOVERS (7) [LEFT]

Lev 19: 6 Any **l** that remain until the third day must be
26: 10 **l** from the previous year to make room for each
Mt 14: 20 and they picked up twelve baskets of **l**.
Mk 8: 19 How many baskets of **l** did you pick up
8: 20 how many large baskets of **l** did you pick up?"
Lk 9: 17 and they picked up twelve baskets of **l**!
Jn 6: 12 "Now gather the **l**," Jesus told his disciples,

LEG (1) [LEGS]

Pr 26: 7 a fool, a proverb becomes as limp as a paralyzed **l**.

LEGAL (11) [LEGALISTS, LEGALLY]

Nu 27: 11 The Israelites must observe this as a general **l**
1Ki 7: 7 of Judgment, where Solomon sat to hear **l** matters.
Mt 12: 10 "Is it **l** to work by healing on the Sabbath day?"
Mk 3: 4 "Is it **l** to do good deeds on the Sabbath,
Lk 6: 7 because they were eager to find some **l** charge to
6: 9 Is it **l** to do good deeds on the Sabbath, or is it a
Jn 7: 51 "Is it **l** to convict a man before he is given a
Ac 19: 38 the case at once. Let them go through **l** channels.
19: 39 other matters, they can be settled in a **l** assembly.
22: 25 "Is it **l** for you to whip a Roman citizen who hasn't
1Co 6: 4 If you have **l** disputes about such matters, why do

LEGALISTS (1) [LEGAL]

Gal 2: 12 because he was afraid of what these **l** would say.

LEGALLY (1) [LEGAL]

Ge 31: 16 The riches God has given you from our father are **l**

LEGENDS (1)

Ge 6: 4 who became the heroes mentioned in **l** of old.

LEGGINGS (1)

1Sa 17: 6 He also wore bronze **l**, and he slung a bronze

LEGION (2)

Mk 5: 9 And the spirit replied, "**L**, because there are many
Lk 8: 30 "**L**," he replied—for the man was filled with

LEGS (24) [LEG]

Ex 12: 9 roast it all, including the head, **l**, and internal
25: 26 and put the rings at the four corners by the four **l**,
29: 17 the ram and wash off the internal organs and the **l**.
37: 13 rings of gold and attached them to the four table **l**
Lev 1: 9 and **l** must first be washed with water.
1: 13 and **l** must first be washed with water.
4: 11 its hide, meat, head, **l**, internal organs, and dung—
8: 21 washing the internal organs and the **l** with water,
9: 14 Then he washed the internal organs and the **l**
11: 21 These include insects that jump with their hind **l**:
11: 42 as well as those with four **l** and those with many
Ecc 12: 3 with age, and your strong **l** will grow weak.
SS 5: 15 His **l** are like pillars of marble set in sockets of the
Eze 1: 7 Their **l** were straight like human **l**, but their feet

Da 2:33 its l were of iron, and its feet were a combination
5: 6 knocked together and his l gave way beneath him.
Am 3:12 a sheep from a lion's mouth will recover only two l
Hab 3:16 My l gave way beneath me, and I shook in terror.
Lk 14: 2 was a man there whose arms and l were swollen.
Jn 19:31 their deaths by ordering that their l be broken.
19:32 and broke the l of the two men crucified with
19:33 that he was dead already, so they didn't break his l.
Heb 12:12 your tired hands and stand firm on your shaky l.

LEHABITES (2)
Ge 10:13 ancestor of the Ludites, Anamites, L, Naphtuhites,
1Ch 1:11 ancestor of the Ludites, Anamites, L, Naphtuhites,

LEHI (5)
Jdg 15: 9 up camp in Judah and raiding the town of L.
15:14 As Samson arrived at L, the Philistines came
15:19 water to gush out of a hollow in the ground at L,
15:19 Who Cried Out," and it is still in L to this day.
2Sa 23:11 One time the Philistines gathered at L and attacked

LEMA (2)
Mt 27:46 *"Eli, Eli, l sabachthani?"* which means,
Mk 15:34 *"Eloi, Eloi, l sabachthani?"* which means,

LEMUEL (2)
Pr 31: 1 These are the sayings of King L, an oracle that his
31: 4 And it is not for kings, O L, to guzzle wine.

LEND (15) [LENDER, LENDERS, LENDING, LENDS, LENT]
Ex 22:25 "If you l money to a fellow Hebrew in need,
28: 2 beautiful garments that will l dignity to his work.
Lev 25:36 or charge interest on the money you l them.
25:37 your relatives interest on anything you l them,
Dt 15: 6 You will l money to many nations but will never
15: 8 be generous and l them whatever they need.
24:10 "If you l anything to your neighbor, do not enter
28:12 You will l to many nations, but you will never
28:44 They will l money to you, not you to them.
Ps 15: 5 who do not charge interest on the money they l,
112: 5 who l freely and conduct their business fairly.
Eze 18:17 helps the poor, does not l money at interest,
Lk 6:34 And if you l money only to those who can repay
6:34 Even sinners will l to their own kind for a full
6:35 "Love your enemies! Do good to them! L to them!

LENDER (3) [LEND]
Ex 22:25 in need, do not be like a money l, charging interest.
Pr 22: 7 rule the poor, so the borrower is servant to the l.
Jer 15:10 I am neither a l who has threatened to foreclose nor

LENDERS (1) [LEND]
Isa 24: 2 and sellers, l and borrowers, bankers and debtors—

LENDING (2) [LEND]
Ne 5:10 have been l the people money and grain,
Pr 19:17 If you help the poor, you are l to the LORD—

LENDS (1) [LEND]
Eze 18:13 and l money at interest. Should such a sinful

LENGTH (13) [LONG]
Lev 19:35 not use dishonest standards when measuring l,
Dt 33:25 may your strength match the l of your days!"
1Sa 28:20 Saul fell full l on the ground, paralyzed with fright
2Sa 8: 2 and he measured them off in groups with a l of
Job 14: 5 You have decided the l of our lives. You know
Isa 23:15 For seventy years, the l of a king's life, Tyre will
Eze 40:15 The full l of the gateway passage was 87-1/2 feet
41:13 including its walls, was an additional 175 feet in l.
42: 8 This wall added l to the outer block of rooms,
42:11 This complex of rooms was the same l and width
42:18 The south side was the same l,
Ac 15: 2 disagreeing with them, argued forcefully and at l.
Rev 21:16 for its l and width and height were each 1,400

LENGTHENS (2) [LONG]
Pr 10:27 Fear of the LORD l one's life, but the years of the
14:30 A relaxed attitude l life; jealousy rots it away.

LENT (1) [LEND]
Job 22: 6 you must have l money to your friend and

LENTIL (1) [LENTILS]
Ge 25:34 Then Jacob gave Esau some bread and l stew.

LENTILS (3) [LENTIL]
2Sa 17:28 wheat and barley flour, roasted grain, beans, l,
23:11 and attacked the Israelites in a field full of l.
Eze 4: 9 get some wheat, barley, beans, l, millet, and spelt,

LEOPARD (6) [LEOPARDS]
Isa 11: 6 live together; the l and the goat will be at peace.
Jer 5: 6 A l will lurk near their towns, tearing apart any
13:23 Can a l take away its spots? Neither can you start
Da 7: 6 strange beasts appeared, and it looked like a l.
Hos 13: 7 you like a lion, or like a l that lurks along the road.
Rev 13: 2 This beast looked like a l, but it had bear's feet

LEOPARDS (1) [LEOPARD]
Hab 1: 8 Their horses are swifter than l. They are a fierce

LEPER (1) [LEPROSY]
2Ki 5: 7 and said, "This man sends me a l to heal!

LEPERS (5) [LEPROSY]
2Ki 7: 8 When the l arrived at the edge of the camp,
Mt 11: 5 the lame walk, the l are cured, the deaf hear,
Lk 4:27 rather than the many l in Israel who needed help."
7:22 the lame walk, the l are cured, the deaf hear,
17:12 he entered a village there, ten l stood at a distance,

LEPROSY (28) [LEPER, LEPERS, LEPROUS]
Ex 4: 6 it out again, his hand was white as snow with l.
Nu 12:10 Miriam suddenly became white as snow with l.
2Sa 3:29 or l or who walks on crutches or who dies by the
2Ki 5: 1 Naaman was a mighty warrior, he suffered from l.
5: 3 prophet in Samaria. He would heal him of his l."
5: 6 servant Naaman. I want you to heal him of his l."
5:10 skin will be restored, and you will be healed of l."
5:11 "I expected him to wave his hand over the l
5:27 children will suffer from Naaman's l forever."
7: 3 Now there were four men with l sitting at the
15: 5 The LORD struck the king with l, which lasted
2Ch 26:19 l suddenly broke out on his forehead.
26:20 When Azariah and the other priests saw the l,
26:21 So King Uzziah had l until the day he died.
26:23 So Uzziah died, and since he had l, he was buried
Mt 8: 2 Suddenly, a man with l approached Jesus. He knelt
8: 3 "Be healed!" And instantly the l disappeared.
8: 4 law of Moses for those who have been healed of l,
10: 8 Heal the sick, raise the dead, cure those with l,
26: 6 in Bethany at the home of Simon, a man who had l.
Mk 1:40 A man with l came and knelt in front of Jesus,
1:42 Instantly the l disappeared—the man was healed.
1:44 law of Moses for those who have been healed of l,
14: 3 in Bethany at the home of Simon, a man who had l.
Lk 5:12 Jesus met a man with an advanced case of l.
5:13 "Be healed!" And instantly the l disappeared.
5:14 law of Moses for those who have been healed of l,
17:14 the priests." And as they went, their l disappeared.

LEPROUS (1) [LEPROSY]
2Ki 5:27 When Gehazi left the room, he was l; his skin was

LESS (27) [LEAST, LESSER]
Ex 16:17 this food—some getting more, and some getting l.
30:15 must not give more, and the poor must not give l.
Nu 11:32 next day, too. No one gathered l than fifty bushels!
26:54 tribes more land and the smaller tribes l land,
Jos 23: 7 their gods, much l swear by them or worship them.
1Ki 8:27 contain you. How much l this Temple I have built!
2Ch 6:18 contain you. How much l this Temple I have built!
32:15 How much l will your God rescue you from my
Ezr 9:13 But we have actually been punished far l than we
Job 4:19 how much l will he trust those made of clay!
11: 6 God is doubtless punishing you far l than you
15:16 How much l pure is a corrupt and sinful person
25: 6 How much l are mere people, who are but worms
Pr 17: 7 fitting for a fool; even l are lies fitting for a ruler.
Ecc 6:11 The more words you speak, the l they mean.
Isa 40:17 In his eyes they are l than nothing—
41:24 You are l than nothing and can do nothing at all.
Jer 3:11 "Even faithless Israel is l guilty than treacherous
Jn 2:10 doesn't care, he brings out the l expensive wines.
3:30 and greater, and I must become l and l.
1Co 12:15 that does not make it any l a part of the body.
12:16 would that make it any l a part of the body?
12:23 And the parts we regard as l honorable are those
12:24 and care are given to those parts that have l
2Co 12:15 seems that the more I love you, the l you love me.
1Ti 4:12 Don't let anyone think l of you because you are

LESSER (1) [LESS]
Ge 1:16 the l one, the moon, presides through the night.

LESSON (12) [LESSONS]
Lev 26:23 "And if you fail to learn a l from this and continue
Jdg 8:16 took the leaders of the town and taught them a l,
1Sa 14:12 "Come on up here, and we'll teach you a l!"
Job 21:22 "But who can teach a l to God, the supreme
Pr 6: 6 Take a l from the ants, you lazybones. Learn from
6: 9 When will you wake up? I want you to learn this l:
19:25 punish a mocker, the simpleminded will learn a l;
24:32 as I looked and thought about it, I learned this l:
Jer 35:13 'Come and learn a l about how to obey me.
Mt 24:32 "Now learn a l from the fig tree. When its buds
Mk 13:28 "Now, learn a l from the fig tree. When its buds
Lk 18: 6 the Lord said, "Learn a l from this evil judge.

LESSONS (3) [LESSON]
Ps 59:11 Don't kill them, for my people soon forget such l;
78: 2 I will teach you hidden l from our past—
Isa 42:23 Will not even one of you apply these l from the

LEST (1)
Ac 24: 4 But l I bore you, kindly give me your attention for

LET (1048) [LET'S, LETS, LETTING] See Index of Articles, Etc.

LET'S (99) [LET, WE] See Index of Articles, Etc.

LETHAL (1)
Pr 26:18 Just as damaging as a mad man shooting a l

LETS (9) [LET] See Index of Articles, Etc.

LETTER (98) [LETTERS]
Dt 24: 1 So he writes her a l of divorce, gives it to her,
1Sa 17:18 getting along, and bring me back a l from them."
2Sa 11:14 So the next morning David wrote a l to Joab
11:15 The l instructed Joab, "Station Uriah on the front
2Ki 5: 5 "I will send a l of introduction for you to carry to
5: 6 The l to the king of Israel said: "With this l I present my servant Naaman.
10: 1 So Jehu wrote a l and sent copies to Samaria,
10: 1 to the guardians of King Ahab's sons. The l said,
10: 2 and weapons. As soon as you receive this l,
10: 6 Jehu responded with a second l: "If you are on my
10: 7 When the l arrived, the leaders killed all seventy of
19:14 After Hezekiah received the l and read it, he went
2Ch 2:11 King Hiram sent this l of reply to Solomon:
21:12 Then Elijah the prophet wrote Jehoram this l:
Ezr 4: 6 the enemies of Judah wrote him a l of accusation
4: 7 sent a l to Artaxerxes in the Aramaic language,
4: 8 and Shimshai the court secretary wrote the l,
4:11 This is a copy of the l they sent him:
4:18 The l you sent has been translated and read to me.
4:23 When this l from King Artaxerxes was read to
5: 6 This is the l that Tattenai the governor,
7:11 King Artaxerxes had presented a copy of this l to
Ne 2: 8 And please send a l to Asaph, the manager of the
6: 5 Sanballat's servant came with an open l in his
Est 9:26 So because of Mordecai's l and because of what
9:29 wrote another l putting the queen's full authority
9:29 Mordecai's l to establish the Festival of Purim.
Isa 37:14 After Hezekiah received the l and read it, he went
Jer 29: 1 Jeremiah wrote a l from Jerusalem to the elders,
29: 3 He sent the l with Elasah son of Shaphan
29: 3 to Nebuchadnezzar. This is what Jeremiah's l said:
29:25 You wrote a l on your own authority to Zephaniah
29:28 Jeremiah sent a l here to Babylon, predicting that
29:29 when Zephaniah the priest received Shemaiah's l,
29:31 "Send an open l to all the exiles in Babylon.
Mt 5:31 his wife by merely giving her a l of divorce.'
19: 7 a man could merely write an official l of divorce
Mk 10: 4 merely has to write his wife an official l of divorce
Ac 15:23 This is the l they took along with them:
15:23 "This l is from the apostles and elders,
15:30 meeting of the Christians and delivered the l.
21:25 we ask of them is what we already told them in a l:
23:25 Then he wrote this l to the governor:
23:33 they presented Paul and the l to Governor Felix.
Ro 1: 1 This l is from Paul, Jesus Christ's slave, chosen by
7: 6 not in the old way by obeying the l of the law,
16:22 Tertius, the one who is writing this l for Paul,
1Co 1: 1 This l is from Paul, chosen by the will of God to be
7: 1 Now about the questions you asked in your l.
2Co 1: 1 This l is from Paul, appointed by God to be an
2: 3 That is why I wrote as I did in my last l, so that
2: 4 How painful it was to write that l! Heartbroken,
3: 2 But the only l of recommendation we need is you
3: 2 Your lives are a l written in our hearts,
3: 3 Clearly, you are a l from Christ prepared by us.
7: 8 I am no longer sorry that I sent that l to you,
13:11 Dear friends, I close my l with these last words:
Gal 1: 1 This l is from Paul, an apostle. I was not appointed
Eph 1: 1 This l is from Paul, chosen by God to be an apostle
3: 3 As I briefly mentioned earlier in this l,
Php 1: 1 This l is from Paul and Timothy, slaves of Christ
4: 8 let me say one more thing as I close this l.
Col 1: 1 This l is from Paul, chosen by God to be an apostle
4:16 After you have read this l, pass it on to the church
4:16 too. And you should read the l I wrote to them.
1Th 1: 1 This l is from Paul, Silas, and Timothy. It is
5:27 name of the Lord to read this l to all the Christians.
2Th 1: 1 This l is from Paul, Silas, and Timothy. It is
2: 2 a revelation, or a l supposedly from us,
2:15 everything we taught you both in person and by l.
3:14 of those who refuse to obey what we say in this l.
1Ti 1: 1 This l is from Paul, an apostle of Christ Jesus,
2Ti 1: 1 This l is from Paul, an apostle of Christ Jesus by
Tit 1: 1 This l is from Paul, a slave of God and an apostle
1: 4 This l is written to Titus, my true child in the faith
Phm 1: 1 This l is from Paul, in prison for preaching the
1:21 I am confident as I write this l that you will do
Heb 13:22 listen carefully to what I have said in this brief l.
Jas 1: 1 This l is from James, a slave of God and of the
1Pe 1: 1 This l is from Peter, an apostle of Jesus Christ.
5:12 I have written this short l to you with the help of
2Pe 1: 1 This l is from Simon Peter, a slave and apostle of
3: 1 This is my second l to you, dear friends, and in
2Jn 1: 1 This l is from John, the Elder. It is written to the
1:12 more to say to you, but I don't want to say it in a l.
3Jn 1: 1 This l is from John, the Elder. It is written to
1: 9 I sent a brief l to the church about this,
1:13 much to tell you, but I don't want to do it in a l.
Jude 1: 1 This l is from Jude, a slave of Jesus Christ and a
Rev 1: 4 This l is from John to the seven churches in the
2: 1 "Write this l to the angel of the church in Ephesus.
2: 8 "Write this l to the angel of the church in Smyrna.
2:12 "Write this l to the angel of the church in

2:18 "Write this l to the angel of the church in Thyatira.
3:1 "Write this l to the angel of the church in Sardis.
3:7 "Write this l to the angel of the church in
3:14 "Write this l to the angel of the church in

LETTERS (35) [LETTER]

1Ki 21:8 So she wrote l in Ahab's name, sealed them with
21:9 In her l she commanded: "Call the citizens
21:11 the instructions Jezebel had written in the l.
2Ch 30:1 and he wrote l of invitation to Ephraim
30:6 and Judah. They carried l which said:
32:17 The king also sent l scorning the LORD, the God
32:18 The Assyrian officials who brought the l shouted
Ne 2:7 give me l to the governors of the province west of
2:9 Euphrates River, I delivered the king's l to them.
6:17 many l went back and forth between Tobiah
6:19 And Tobiah sent many threatening l to intimidate
Est 1:22 He sent l to all parts of the empire, to each
3:12 the king's secretaries and dictated l to the princes,
3:12 These l were signed in the name of King Xerxes,
3:13 The l decreed that all Jews—young and old,
8:10 He sent the l by swift messengers, who rode horses
9:20 these events and sent l to the Jews near and far,
9:30 l wishing peace and security were sent to the Jews
9:31 These l established the Festival of Purim—
Hab 2:2 clear l on a tablet, so that a runner can read it
Ac 9:2 He requested l addressed to the synagogues in
22:5 For I received l from them to our Jewish brothers
28:21 We have had no l from Judea or reports from
1Co 16:3 When I come I will write l of recommendation for
2Co 1:13 My l have been straightforward, and there is
3:1 Some people need to bring l of recommendation
3:1 or ask you to write l of recommendation for them.
10:1 even though some of you say I am bold in my l
10:9 this is not just an attempt to frighten you by my l.
10:10 His l are demanding and forceful, but in person he
10:11 and forceful in person as we are in our l.
Gal 6:11 Notice what large l I use as I write these closing
2Th 3:17 I do this at the end of all my l to prove that they
2Pe 3:16 speaking of these things in all of his l. Some of his
3:16 and unstable have twisted his l around to mean

LETTING (15) [LET] See Index of Articles, Etc.

LETUSHITES (1)

Ge 25:3 were the Asshurites, L, and Leummites.

LEUMMITES (1)

Ge 25:3 were the Asshurites, Letushites, and L.

LEVEL (16) [LEVELED, LEVELING, LEVELS]

Ps 137:7 "Destroy it!" they yelled. / "L it to the ground!"
Pr 21:22 of the strong and l the fortress in which they trust.
Isa 2:14 He will l the high mountains and hills.
40:4 Fill the valleys and l the hills. Straighten out the
42:15 I will l the mountains and hills / and bring a blight
45:2 "I will go before you, Cyrus, and l the mountains.
49:11 And I will make my mountains into l paths for
Eze 41:6 one above the other, with thirty rooms on each l.
41:7 Each l was wider than the one below it,
41:7 A stairway led up from the bottom l through the middle l to the top l.
42:6 each of the upper levels was set back from the l
Mt 23:8 and all of you are on the same l as brothers
Lk 3:5 Fill in the valleys, / and l the mountains and hills!
6:17 l area, surrounded by many of his followers and by

LEVELED (3) [LEVEL]

Jdg 9:45 He killed the people, l the city, and scattered salt
Jer 51:58 "The wide walls of Babylon will be l to the
Rev 16:20 island disappeared, and all the mountains were l.

LEVELING (1) [LEVEL]

Ps 65:10 with rain, / melting the clods and l the ridges.

LEVELS (8) [LEVEL]

Ps 104:8 and valleys sank / to the l you decreed.
Eze 41:6 These rooms were built in three l, one above the
42:3 The two blocks were built three l high and stood
42:5 Each of the two upper l of rooms was narrower
42:5 because the upper l had to allow space for
42:6 Since there were three l and they did not have
42:6 each of the upper l was set back from the level
Hab 3:6 the everlasting mountains and l the eternal hills.

LEVI (74) [LEVI'S, LEVITE, LEVITE'S, LEVITES, LEVITES', LEVITICAL, MATTHEW]

SONS OF LEVI (4) Ge 46:11; 1Ch 6:1,16; 23:6

TRIBE OF LEVI (30) Ex 2:1; Nu 1:49; 3:6,15; 4:22; 17:3,8; 18:1,2,21; Dt 10:8; 18:1,5; 33:8; Jos 13:14,33; 21:1,4,10,20,27; Jdg 19:1; 1Sa 2:30; 6:15; 1Ki 12:31; 1Ch 12:26; 23:14; Eze 44:10; Ac 4:36; Heb 7:16

Ge 29:34 She named him L, for she said, "Surely now my
34:25 Dinah's brothers, Simeon and L, took their swords,
34:30 Afterward Jacob said to L and Simeon, "You have
35:23 Simeon, L, Judah, Issachar, and Zebulun.
46:11 The sons of L were Gershon, Kohath, and Merari.
49:5 "Simeon and L are two of a kind— / men of
Ex 1:2 Reuben, Simeon, L, Judah,
2:1 and woman from the tribe of L got married.
6:16 These are the descendants of L, listed according to
6:16 (L, their father, lived to be 137 years old.)
Nu 1:49 "Exempt the tribe of L from the census; do not
3:6 "Call forward the tribe of L and present them to
3:15 "Take a census of the tribe of L by its families
3:17 L had three sons, who were named Gershon,
4:22 of the Gershonite division of the tribe of L.
16:1 a descendant of Kohath son of L, conspired with
17:3 Aaron's name on the staff of the tribe of L,
17:8 representing the tribe of L, had sprouted,
18:1 and your relatives from the tribe of L will be held
18:2 "Bring your relatives of the tribe of L to assist you
18:21 As for the tribe of L, your relatives, I will pay
26:59 She also was a descendant of L, born among the
Dt 10:8 At that time the LORD set apart the tribe of L to
18:1 and the rest of the tribe of L will not be given an
18:5 For the LORD your God chose the tribe of L out
27:12 the tribes of Simeon, L, Judah, Issachar, Joseph,
33:8 Moses said this about the tribe of L: / "O LORD,
Jos 13:14 Moses did not assign any land to the tribe of L.
13:33 But Moses gave no land to the tribe of L,
21:1 Then the leaders of the tribe of L came to consult
21:4 of the Kohathite clan within the tribe of L,
21:10 of the Kohathite clan within the tribe of L,
21:20 The rest of the Kohathite clan from the tribe of L
21:27 of Gershon, another clan within the tribe of L,
Jdg 19:1 There was a man from the tribe of L living in a
1Sa 2:30 I had promised that your branch of the tribe of L
6:15 Several men of the tribe of L lifted the Ark of the
1Ki 12:31 those who were not from the priestly tribe of L.
1Ch 2:1 Simeon, L, Judah, Issachar, Zebulun,
6:1 The sons of L were Gershon, Kohath, and Merari.
6:16 The sons of L were Gershon, Kohath, and Merari.
6:38 Izhar, Kohath, L, and Israel.
6:43 Jahath, Gershon, and L.
6:47 Mahli, Mushi, Merari, and L.
12:26 From the tribe of L, there were 4,600 troops.
21:6 But Joab did not include the tribes of L
23:6 the clans descended from the three sons of L—
23:14 of God, his sons were included with the tribe of L.
23:24 These were the descendants of L by clans,
24:20 were the other family leaders descended from L:
24:30 These were the descendants of L in their various
27:17 L | Hashabiah son of Kemuel / Aaron (the priests)
Ezr 8:18 of Mahli, who was a descendant of L son of Israel.
Eze 44:10 And the men of the tribe of L who abandoned me
48:31 the second for Judah, and the third for L.
Zec 12:13 the family of L, and the family of Shimei.
Mk 2:14 he saw L son of Alphaeus sitting at his
2:14 Jesus said to him. So L got up and followed him.
2:15 That night L invited Jesus and his disciples to be
Lk 3:24 Matthat was the son of L. / L was the son of Melki.
3:29 was the son of Matthat. / Matthat was the son of L.
3:30 L was the son of Simeon. / Simeon was the son of
5:27 he saw a tax collector named L sitting at his
5:28 So L got up, left everything, and followed him.
5:29 Soon L held a banquet in his home with Jesus as
Ac 4:36 He was from the tribe of L and came from the
Heb 7:5 Now the priests, who are descendants of L,
7:6 But Melchizedek, who was not even related to L,
7:10 For although L wasn't born yet, the seed from
7:11 if the priesthood of L could have achieved God's
7:11 instead of from the line of L and Aaron?
7:16 the old requirement of belonging to the tribe of L,
Rev 7:7 from L | 12,000 / from Issachar | 12,000

LEVI'S (2) [LEVI]

Lk 5:29 Many of L fellow tax collectors and other guests
Heb 7:9 In addition, we might even say that L descendants,

LEVIATHAN (3)

Ps 74:14 You crushed the heads of L / and let the desert
104:26 and L, which you made to play in the sea.
Isa 27:1 swift sword and punish L, the swiftly moving

LEVIED (1)

2Ch 24:6 l this tax on the community of Israel in order to

LEVITE (34) [LEVI]

Ex 4:14 he said. "What about your brother, Aaron the L?
6:25 These are the ancestors of the L clans,
Nu 3:20 These were the L clans, listed according to their
3:38 or L who came too near the sanctuary was to be
3:39 So among the L clans counted by Moses
4:2 and families of the Kohathite division of the L
4:29 and families of the Merarite division of the L tribe.
18:4 but no one who is not a L may officiate with you.
26:62 The men from the L clans who were one month
Dt 18:6 "Any L who so desires may come from any town
Jdg 17:7 One day a young L from Bethlehem in Judah
17:9 he replied, "I am a L from Bethlehem in Judah,
17:11 The L agreed to this and became like one of
17:12 So Micah ordained the L as his personal priest,
17:13 "because I have a L serving as my priest."
18:15 where the young L lived, and greeted him kindly.
19:25 Then the L took his concubine and pushed her out
20:4 The L, the husband of the woman who had been
1Ch 6:19 The following were the L clans, listed according to
9:31 a L and the oldest son of Shallum the Korahite,
9:34 They were the heads of L families and were listed
15:11 Zadok and Abiathar, and these L leaders:
15:12 to them, "You are the leaders of the L families.
15:16 David also ordered the L leaders to appoint a choir
15:22 Kenaniah, the head L, was chosen as the choir
24:6 a L, acted as secretary and wrote down the names
2Ch 20:14 of Mattaniah, a L who was a descendant of Asaph.
31:12 Conaniah the L was put in charge, assisted by his
31:14 Kore son of Imnah the L, who was the gatekeeper
35:9 The L leaders—Conaniah and his brothers
Ezr 7:24 no priest, L, singer, gatekeeper, Temple servant,
8:15 I found that not one L had volunteered to come
10:15 and Shabbethai the L supported them.
Ne 12:23 The heads of the L families were recorded in *The*

LEVITE'S (1) [LEVI]

Jdg 18:3 Noticing the young L accent, they took him aside

LEVITES (277) [LEVI]

PRIESTS AND (THE) LEVITES (41) Nu 18:22; Dt 18:1; 1Ki 8:4; 1Ch 13:2; 15:4,14; 23:2; 24:6,31; 28:13,21; 2Ch 8:15; 11:13; 13:10; 23:4,6; 24:5; 29:4; 30:15; 31:2,4,9,19; 34:30; 35:10,18; Ezr 1:5; 6:18,20; 7:13; 8:30; 9:1; 10:5; Ne 8:13; 12:1,30,44,44; 13:29,30; Isa 66:21

Ex 6:19 These are the clans of the L, listed according to
32:26 come over here and join me." And all the L came.
32:28 The L obeyed Moses, and about three thousand
32:29 Then Moses told the L, "Today you have been
38:21 Moses directed the L to compile the figures,
Lev 25:32 "The L always have the right to redeem any house
25:33 And any property that can be redeemed by the L—
25:33 the cities reserved for the L are the only property
Nu 1:47 But this total did not include the L.
1:50 You must put the L in charge of the Tabernacle of
1:51 the L will take it down and set it up again.
1:53 But the L will camp around the Tabernacle of the
1:53 The L are responsible to stand guard around the
2:17 "Then the L will set out from the middle of the
2:24 and they will follow the L in the line of march.
2:33 The L were exempted from this census by the
3:9 Assign the L to Aaron and his sons as their
3:12 "I have chosen the L from among the Israelites as
3:12 sons of the people of Israel. The L are mine
3:32 was the chief administrator over all the L,
3:41 The L will be reserved for me as substitutes for the
3:45 "Take the L in place of the firstborn sons of the
3:45 And take the livestock of the L as substitutes for
3:45 of Israel. The L will be mine; I am the LORD.
3:46 of Israel who are in excess of the number of L,
3:49 sons of Israel who exceeded the number of L.
4:18 Kohathite clans be destroyed from among the L!
4:46 and the leaders of Israel counted all the L by their
7:5 Distribute them among the L according to the
7:6 So Moses presented the carts and oxen to the L.
8:6 "Now set the L apart from the rest of the people of
8:9 and present the L at the entrance of the Tabernacle.
8:10 When you bring the L before the LORD,
8:11 Aaron must present the L to the LORD as a
8:12 "Next the L will lay their hands on the heads of
8:12 for a burnt offering, to make atonement for the L.
8:13 Then have the L stand in front of Aaron and his
8:14 you will set the L apart from the rest of the people of Israel, and the L will belong to me.
8:16 all the people of Israel, the L are reserved for me.
8:16 I have taken the L as their substitutes.
8:18 I claim the L in place of all the firstborn sons of
8:19 I have assigned the L to Aaron and his sons.
8:20 the whole community of Israel dedicated the L,
8:21 The L purified themselves and washed their
8:22 then on the L went into the Tabernacle to perform
8:22 that the LORD gave Moses concerning the L.
8:24 "This is the rule the L must follow: They must
8:26 After retirement they may assist their fellow L by
8:26 This is how you will assign duties to the L."
10:17 and Merarite divisions of the L were next in the
10:21 Next came the Kohathite division of the L,
16:7 You L are the ones who have gone too far!"
16:8 Moses spoke again to Korah: "Now listen, you L!
16:10 special ministry only to you and your fellow L,
18:3 But as the L go about their duties under your
18:4 The L must join with you to fulfill their
18:6 I myself have chosen your fellow L from among
18:22 and L are to stay away from the Tabernacle.
18:23 The L must serve at the Tabernacle, and they will
18:23 But the L will receive no inheritance of land
18:26 "Say this to the L: 'When you receive the tithes
18:30 "Also say to the L: 'When you present the best
18:31 You L and your families may eat this food
26:57 This is the census record for the L who were
26:58 and the Korahites were all subclans of the L.
26:59 of Levi, born among the L in the land of Egypt.
26:62 But the L were not included in the total census
31:30 Give this share to the L in charge of maintaining
31:47 and gave them to the L who maintained the
35:2 "Instruct the people of Israel to give to the L from
35:4 The pastureland assigned to the L around these
35:6 "You must give the L six cities of refuge, where a
35:7 the surrounding pastureland will be given to the L.
35:8 The larger tribes will give more towns to the L,
Dt 10:9 That is why the L have no share or inheritance
12:12 And remember the L who live in your towns,
12:18 your servants, and the L who live in your towns,
12:19 Be very careful never to forget the L as long as
14:27 And do not forget the L in your community,
14:29 Give it to the L, who have no inheritance among
16:11 all your servants, the L from your towns,
16:14 your servants, and with the L, foreigners, orphans,
18:1 and L will eat from the offerings given to the
18:7 just like his fellow L who are serving the LORD
26:11 Remember to include the L and the foreigners
26:12 You must give these tithes to the L, foreigners,
26:13 gift from my house and have given it to the L,
27:14 Then the L must shout to all the people of Israel:

31:25 he gave these instructions to the **L** who carried the
33: 8 the sacred lots / to your faithful servants the **L**.
33: 9 The **L** obeyed your word / and guarded your
33:11 Bless the **L**, O LORD, / and accept all their work.
Jos 14: 4 And the **L** were given no land at all, only towns to
18: 7 However, the **L** will not receive any land.
21: 3 So by the command of the LORD the **L** were
21: 8 and pasturelands to the **L** by casting sacred lots.
21:34 The rest of the **L**—the Merari clan—were given
21:41 territory given to the **L** came to forty-eight.
2Sa 15:24 and the **L** took the Ark of the Covenant of God
1Ki 8: 4 Then the priests and **L** took the Ark of the LORD,
1Ch 6:48 Their relatives, also **L**, were appointed to various
6:64 assigned all these towns and pasturelands to the **L**.
9: 2 came some of the priests, **L**, and Temple assistants.
9:14 The **L** who returned were Shemaiah son of
9:18 men served as gatekeepers for the camps of the **L**.
9:26 The four chief gatekeepers, all **L**, were in an office
9:33 The musicians, all prominent **L**, lived at the
13: 2 the priests and **L** in their towns and pasturelands.
15: 2 of God this time, no one except the **L** may carry it.
15: 4 are the priests and **L** who were called together:
15:12 You must purify yourselves and all your fellow **L**,
15:13 Because you **L** did not carry the Ark the first time,
15:14 and the **L** purified themselves in order to bring the
15:15 Then the **L** carried the Ark of God on their
15:16 leaders to appoint a choir of **L** who were singers
15:17 So the **L** appointed Heman son of Joel, Asaph son
15:26 because God was clearly helping the **L** as they
15:27 as were the **L** who carried the Ark, the singers,
16: 4 David appointed the following **L** to lead the people
16: 7 and his fellow **L** this song of thanksgiving to the
16:37 and his fellow **L** to minister regularly before the
16:38 Hosah, and sixty-eight other **L** as gatekeepers.
23: 2 together with the priests and **L**, for the coronation
23: 3 All the **L** who were thirty years old or older were
23: 6 Then David divided the **L** into divisions named
23:26 Now the **L** will no longer need to carry the
23:27 final instructions that all the **L** twenty years old
23:28 The work of the **L** was to assist the priests,
23:31 The proper number of **L** served in the LORD's
23:32 the **L** watched over the Tabernacle and the Temple
24: 6 and the family leaders of the priests and **L**.
24:31 and the family leaders of the priests and the **L**.
26:12 and like the other **L**, they served at the house of the
26:17 Six **L** were assigned each day to the east gate,
26:20 Other **L**, led by Ahijah, were in charge of the
28:13 of priests and **L** in the Temple of the LORD.
28:21 of priests and **L** will serve in the Temple of God.
2Ch 5: 4 the leaders of Israel arrived, the **L** moved the Ark,
5:12 And the **L** who were musicians—Asaph, Heman,
7: 6 and so did the **L** who were singing, "His faithful
7: 6 On the other side of the **L**, the priests blew the
8:14 He also assigned the **L** to lead the people in praise
8:15 concerning the priests and **L** and the treasuries.
11:13 and **L** living among the northern tribes of Israel
11:14 The **L** even abandoned their homes and property
11:16 the God of Israel, followed the **L** to Jerusalem,
13: 9 and the **L** and have appointed your own priests,
13:10 and the **L** alone may help them in their work.
17: 8 He sent **L** along with them, including Shemaiah,
19: 8 Jehoshaphat appointed some of the **L** and priests
19:11 The **L** will assist you in making sure that justice is
20:19 Then the **L** from the clans of Kohath and Korah
23: 2 secretly throughout Judah and summoned the **L**
23: 4 the priests and **L** come on duty on the Sabbath,
23: 6 and **L** on duty may enter the Temple of the
23: 7 You **L**, form a bodyguard for the king and keep
23: 8 So the **L** and the people did everything just as
24: 5 He summoned the priests and **L** and gave them
24: 5 Do not delay!" But the **L** did not act right away.
24: 6 "Why haven't you demanded that the **L** go out
24:11 became full, the **L** carried it to the king's officials.
29: 4 and **L** to meet him at the courtyard east of the
29: 5 He said to them, "Listen to me, you **L**!
29:11 My dear **L**, do not neglect your duties any longer!
29:12 Then these **L** got right to work: / From the clan of
29:15 These men called together their fellow **L**, and they
29:16 From there the **L** carted it all out to the Kidron
29:18 Then the **L** went to King Hezekiah and gave him
29:25 then stationed the **L** at the Temple of the LORD
29:26 The **L** then took their positions around the Temple
29:30 and the officials ordered the **L** to praise the
29:34 so their relatives the **L** helped them until the work
29:34 For the **L** had been more conscientious about
30:15 Then the priests and **L** became ashamed, so they
30:16 The **L** brought the sacrificial blood to the priests,
30:17 the **L** had to slaughter their Passover lambs for
30:21 Each day the **L** and priests sang to the LORD,
30:22 Hezekiah encouraged the **L** for the skill they
30:25 including the priests, the **L**, all who came from the
31: 2 and **L** into divisions to offer the burnt offerings
31: 4 portion of their income to the priests and **L**,
31: 9 come from?" Hezekiah asked the priests and **L**.
31:17 and to the **L** twenty years old or older who were
31:19 and to all the **L** listed in the genealogical records.
34: 9 **L** who served as gatekeepers at the Temple of
34:12 of Jahath and Obadiah, **L** of the Merarite clan,
34:12 and Meshullam, **L** of the Kohathite clan.
34:12 Other **L**, all of whom were skilled musicians,
34:30 of Judah and Jerusalem and the priests and the **L**—
35: 3 He issued this order to the **L**, who had been set
35: 8 willing contributions to the people, priests, and **L**.
35: 9 and five hundred bulls to the **L** for their Passover
35:10 the priests and the **L** took their places,
35:11 The **L** then slaughtered the Passover lambs
35:11 who sprinkled the blood on the altar while the **L**
35:14 Afterward the **L** prepared a meal for themselves
35:14 The **L** took responsibility for all these
35:15 their meals were brought to them by their fellow **L**.
35:18 involving all the priests and **L**, all the people of
Ezr 1: 5 and **L** and the leaders of the tribes of Judah
2:40 These are the **L** who returned from exile:
2:70 So the priests, the **L**, the singers, the gatekeepers,
3: 8 of Jehozadak and his fellow priests, and all the **L**.
3: 8 The **L** who were twenty years old or older were
3: 9 They were helped in this task by the **L** of the
3:10 And the **L**, descendants of Asaph, clashed their
3:12 Many of the older priests, **L**, and other leaders
6:16 great joy by the people of Israel, the priests, the **L**,
6:18 and **L** were divided into their various divisions to
6:20 The priests and **L** had purified themselves
7: 7 **L**, singers, gatekeepers, and Temple servants,
7:13 including the priests and **L**, may volunteer to
8:17 the leader of the **L** at Casiphia, to ask him and his
8:20 The Temple servants were assistants to the **L**—
8:29 without an ounce lost, to the leading priests, the **L**,
8:30 and the **L** accepted the task of transporting these
8:33 Noadiah son of Binnui—both of whom were **L**.
9: 1 of Israel, and even some of the priests and **L**,
10: 5 demanded that the leaders of the priests and the **L**
10:23 These are the **L** who were guilty: Jozabad, Shimei,
Ne 3:17 Next was a group of **L** working under the
7: 1 the gatekeepers, singers, and **L** were appointed.
7:43 "These are the **L** who returned from exile:
7:73 "So the priests, the **L**, the gatekeepers, the singers,
8: 7 Now the **L**—Jeshua, Bani, Sherebiah, Jamin,
8: 9 and the **L** who were interpreting for the people said
8:11 And the **L**, too, quieted the people, telling them,
8:13 and **L** met with Ezra to go over the law in greater
9: 4 Some of the **L** were standing on the stairs,
9: 5 Then the leaders of the **L**—Jeshua, Kadmiel,
9:38 are the names of our princes and **L** and priests."
10: 9 The **L** who signed were Jeshua son of Azaniah,
10:10 and their fellow **L**: Shebaniah, Hodiah, Kelita,
10:28 the priests, **L**, gatekeepers, singers,
10:34 the families of the priests, **L**, and the common
10:37 And we promise to bring to the **L** a tenth of
10:37 for it is the **L** who collect the tithes in all our rural
10:38 will be with the **L** as they receive these tithes.
10:38 be delivered by the **L** to the Temple of our God
10:39 and the **L** must bring these offerings of grain,
11: 3 Most of the people, priests, **L**, Temple servants,
11:15 From the **L**: Shemaiah son of Hasshub, son of
11:18 In all, there were 284 **L** in the holy city.
11:20 The other priests, **L**, and the rest of the Israelites
11:22 The chief officer of the **L** in Jerusalem was Uzzi
11:36 Some of the **L** who lived in Judah were sent to live
12: 1 and **L** who had returned with Zerubbabel son of
12: 8 The **L** who had returned with them were Jeshua,
12:22 a list was compiled of the family leaders of the **L**
12:24 These were the family leaders of the **L**: Hashabiah,
12:27 the **L** throughout the land were asked to come to
12:30 The priests and **L** first dedicated themselves,
12:44 fields as required by the law for the priests and **L**,
12:44 of Judah valued the priests and **L** and their work.
12:47 of food for the singers, the gatekeepers, and the **L**.
12:47 The **L**, in turn, gave a portion of what they
13: 5 had decreed that these offerings belonged to the **L**,
13:10 I also discovered that the **L** had not been given
13:11 Then I called all the **L** back again and restored
13:13 Zadok the scribe, and Pedaiah, one of the **L**,
13:13 job to make honest distributions to their fellow **L**.
13:22 Then I commanded the **L** to purify themselves
13:29 and the promises and vows of the priests and **L**.
13:30 and assigned tasks to the priests and **L**,
Ps 135:20 O **L**, praise the LORD! / All you who fear the
Isa 66:21 some of those who return to be my priests and **L**.
Jer 33:22 my servant, and the **L** who minister before me."
Eze 40:46 for they alone of all the **L** may approach the
45: 5 will be a living area for the **L** who work at the
48:11 when the people of Israel and the rest of the **L** did.
48:12 will lie the land where the other **L** will live.
48:13 The land allotted to the **L** will be the same size
Mal 2: 4 so that my covenant with the **L** may continue,"
2: 5 "The purpose of my covenant with the **L** was to
2: 8 have corrupted the covenant I made with the **L**,"
3: 3 He will purify the **L**, refining them like gold

LEVITES' (2) [LEVI]

Nu 3:41 And the **L** livestock are mine as substitutes for the
18:24 offerings to the LORD. This will be the **L** share.

LEVITICAL (17) [LEVI]

Lev 25:33 all houses within the **L** cities—must be returned in
25:34 The strip of pastureland around each of the **L** cities
Dt 17: 9 where the **L** priests and the judge on duty will hear
17:18 a scroll for himself in the presence of the **L** priests.
18: 1 "Remember that the **L** priests and the rest of the
21: 5 The **L** priests must go there also, for the LORD
24: 8 and follow the instructions of the **L** priests;
27: 9 and the **L** priests addressed all Israel as follows:
Jos 3: 3 "When you see the **L** priests carrying the Ark of
8:33 and between them stood the **L** priests carrying the
2Ch 5: 5 The **L** priests carried them all up to the Temple.
23:18 Jehoiada now put the **L** priests in charge of the
30:27 Then the **L** priests stood and blessed the people,
Jer 33:18 And there will always be **L** priests to offer burnt
33:21 The same is true for my covenant with the **L**
Eze 43:19 At that time, the **L** priests of the family of Zadok,
44:15 the **L** priests of the family of Zadok continued to

LEWD (4) [LEWDNESS]

Eze 16:27 and even they were shocked by your **l** conduct!
16:43 your disgusting sins, you have added these **l** acts.
22: 9 and people who take part in **l** activities.
23: 8 She was still as **l** as in her youth,

LEWDNESS (4) [LEWD]

Eze 23:27 I will put a stop to the **l** and prostitution you
23:35 you must bear the consequences of all your **l**
23:48 I will put an end to **l** and idolatry in the land,
24:13 It is the filth and corruption of your **l** and idolatry.

LIABLE (2)

Ex 21:28 such a case, however, the owner will not be held **l**.
Nu 18: 1 and your sons alone will be held **l** for violations

LIAR (15) [LIE]

Job 34: 6 I am innocent, but they call me a **l**. My suffering is
Ps 52: 4 You love to say things that harm others, / you **l**!
Pr 10:18 To hide hatred is to be a **l**; to slander is to be a fool.
19: 5 witness will not go unpunished, nor will a **l** escape.
19: 9 will not go unpunished, and a **l** will be destroyed.
30: 6 or he may rebuke you, and you will be found a **l**.
Eze 12:22 'Time passes, making a **l** of every prophet'?
Jn 8:44 his character; for he is a **l** and the father of lies.
8:55 If I said otherwise, I would be as great a **l** as you!
Ro 3: 4 Though everyone else in the world is a **l**, God is
1Jn 1:10 we are calling God a **l** and showing that his word
2: 4 that person is a **l** and does not live in the truth.
2:22 And who is the great **l**? The one who says that
4:20 but hates another Christian, that person is a **l**;
5:10 who don't believe this are actually calling God a **l**

LIARS (25) [LIE]

Ex 5: 9 That will teach them to listen to these **l**!"
Ps 26: 4 I do not spend time with **l** / or go along with
43: 1 ungodly people. / Rescue me from these unjust **l**.
55:23 pit of destruction. / Murderers and **l** will die young,
63:11 in him will praise him, / while **l** will be silenced.
101: 7 and **l** will not be allowed to enter my presence.
116:11 I cried out to you, / "These people are all **l**!"
120: 2 Rescue me, O LORD, from **l** / and from all
140:11 Don't let **l** prosper here in our land.
Pr 6:12 and wicked people: They are constant **l**,
17: 4 to wicked talk; **l** pay attention to destructive words.
29:12 If a ruler honors **l**, all his advisers will be wicked.
Isa 44:25 I am the one who exposes the false prophets as **l** by
57: 4 out your tongues? You children of sinners and **l**!
Jer 27:10 They are all **l**, and I will drive you from your land
27:14 king of Babylon will not conquer you.' They are **l**.
Hos 7: 1 Samaria is filled with **l**, thieves, and bandits!
Zep 3: 4 Its prophets are arrogant **l** seeking their own gain.
Mal 3: 5 witness against all sorcerers and adulterers and **l**.
1Ti 1:10 and slave traders, for **l** and oath breakers,
4: 2 These teachers are hypocrites and **l**. They pretend
Tit 1:12 has said about them, "The people of Crete are all **l**;
Rev 2: 2 but are not. You have discovered they are **l**.
3: 9 those **l** who say they are Jews but are not—to come
21: 8 practice witchcraft, and idol worshipers, and all **l**—

LIBERTINES [KJV] See FREED SLAVES

LIBNAH (18) [LIBNITES]

Nu 33:20 They left Rimmon-perez and camped at **L**.
33:21 They left **L** and camped at Rissah.
Jos 10:29 Then Joshua and the Israelites went to **L**
10:30 Then Joshua killed the king of **L** just as he had
10:31 From **L**, Joshua and the Israelites went to Lachish
10:32 the entire population was slaughtered, just as at **L**.
10:39 destroyed Debir just as they had destroyed **L**
12:15 The king of **L** / The king of Adullam
15:42 Besides these, there were **L**, Ether, Ashan,
21:13 for those who accidentally killed someone), **L**,
2Ki 8:22 The town of **L** revolted about that same time.
19: 8 who had left Lachish and was attacking **L**.
23:31 was Hamutal, the daughter of Jeremiah from **L**.
24:18 was Hamutal, the daughter of Jeremiah from **L**.
1Ch 6:57 Hebron (a city of refuge), **L**, Jattir, Eshtemoa,
2Ch 21:10 The town of **L** revolted about that same time,
Isa 37: 8 who had left Lachish and was attacking **L**.
Jer 52: 1 was Hamutal, the daughter of Jeremiah from **L**.

LIBNI (10)

Ex 6:17 The descendants of Gershon included **L**
Nu 3:18 named for two of his descendants, **L** and Shimei.
3:21 were composed of the clans descended from **L**
1Ch 6:17 The descendants of Gershon included **L**
6:20 The descendants of Gershon were **L**, Jahath,
6:29 of Merari were Mahli, **L**, Shimei, Uzzah,
23: 7 units were defined by their lines of descent from **L**
23: 8 Three of the descendants of **L** were Jehiel (the
23: 9 These were the leaders of the family of **L**. Three of
26:21 From the family of **L** in the clan of Gershon,

LIBNITES (1) [LIBNAH]

Nu 26:58 The **L**, the Hebronites, the Mahlites, the Mushites,

LIBYA (6) [LIBYANS]

Jer 46: 9 Come, all you allies from Ethiopia, **L**, and Lydia
Eze 27:10 Lydia, and **L** served in your great army.
30: 5 Ethiopia, **L**, Lydia, and Arabia, with all their other
38: 5 Persia, Ethiopia, and **L** will join you, too, with all

Na 3: 9 The nations of Put and **L** also helped
Ac 2:10 Egypt, and the areas of **L** toward Cyrene,

LIBYANS (4) [LIBYA]
2Ch 12: 3 including **L**, Sukkites, and Ethiopians.
16: 8 to the Ethiopians and **L** and their vast army,
Isa 66:19 to the **L** and Lydians (who are famous as archers),
Da 11:43 and the **L** and Ethiopians will be his servants.

LICE [KJV] See GNAT(S)

LICK (3) [LICKED, LICKING]
1Ki 21:19 dogs will **l** your blood outside the city just as they
Isa 49:23 the earth before you and **l** the dust from your feet.
Lk 16:21 the dogs would come and **l** his open sores.

LICKED (3) [LICK]
1Ki 18:38 and the dust. It even **l** up all the water in the ditch!
21:19 the city just as they **l** the blood of Naboth!' "
22:38 and dogs came and **l** the king's blood,

LICKING (1) [LICK]
Isa 5:14 The grave is **l** its chops in anticipation of

LID (3)
Nu 19:15 tent that was not covered with a **l** is also defiled.
2Ki 12: 9 Then Jehoiada the priest bored a hole in the **l** of a
Zec 5: 8 back into the basket and closed the heavy **l** again.

LIE (141) [LIAR, LIARS, LIED, LIES, LYING]
Ex 23:11 the land rest and **l** fallow during the seventh year.
Lev 6: 3 Or suppose they find a lost item and **l** about it,
19:11 not steal. "Do not cheat one another. "Do not **l**.
26:33 become desolate, and your cities will **l** in ruins.
Nu 23:19 God is not a man, that he should **l**. / He is not a
Dt 25: 2 the judge will command him to **l** down and be
Jos 8:12 That night Joshua sent five thousand men to **l** in
9:22 Gibeonite leaders and said, "Why did you **l** to us?
Jdg 16:10 said to him, "You made fun of me and told me a **l**!
Ru 3: 4 then go and uncover his feet and **l** down there.
3:13 will marry you! Now **l** down here until morning."
1Sa 3: 9 So he said to Samuel, "Go and **l** down again,
15:29 And he who is the Glory of Israel will not **l**,
2Sa 1:27 Stripped of their weapons, they **l** dead.
8: 2 He made the people **l** down on the ground in a row,
1Ki 1: 2 She will **l** in your arms and keep you warm."
2Ki 4:16 "Please don't **l** to me like that, O man of God."
Job 6:28 Look at me! Would I **l** to your face?
7:21 For soon I will **l** down in the dust and die.
11:19 You will **l** down unafraid, and many will look to
14:12 people **l** down and do not rise again.
20:11 just a young man, but his bones will **l** in the dust.
24: 7 All night they **l** naked in the cold, without clothing
33:15 when deep sleep falls on people as they **l** in bed.
38:40 as they **l** in their dens or crouch in the thicket?
Ps 4: 8 I will **l** down in peace and sleep, / for you alone,
12: 2 Neighbors **l** to each other, / speaking with
12: 4 They say, "We will **l** to our hearts' content.
31:17 be disgraced; / let them **l** silent in the grave.
36: 4 They **l** awake at night, hatching sinful plots.
63: 6 I **l** awake thinking of you, / meditating on you
76: 5 They **l** before us in the sleep of death. / No warrior
89:35 an oath to David, / and in my holiness I cannot **l**:
102: 7 I **l** awake, / lonely as a solitary bird on the roof.
119:25 I **l** in the dust, completely discouraged; / revive me
144: 8 full of lies; / they swear to tell the truth, but they **l**.
144:11 full of lies; / they swear to tell the truth, but they **l**.
149: 5 Let them sing for joy as they **l** on their beds.
Pr 3:24 You can **l** down without fear and enjoy pleasant
14: 5 A truthful witness does not **l**; a false witness
24:15 Do not **l** in wait like an outlaw at the home of the
24:28 against innocent neighbors; don't **l** about them.
30: 8 First, help me never to tell a **l**. Second, give me
Ecc 8: 6 even as people's troubles **l** heavily upon them.
11: 2 for you do not know what risks might **l** ahead.
SS 1:16 sight you are, my love, as we **l** here on the grass,
Isa 2:17 Their pride will **l** in the dust. The LORD alone
3: 8 Judah and Jerusalem will **l** in ruins because they
10: 4 stumble along as prisoners or **l** among the dead.
11: 7 Cubs and calves will **l** down together.
14:18 "The kings of the nations **l** in stately glory in their
14:30 poor in my pasture; the needy will **l** down in peace.
17: 2 Sheep will graze in the streets and **l** down unafraid.
21: 4 night is now a faint memory. I **l** awake, trembling.
21: 9 All the idols of Babylon **l** broken on the ground!"
28:20 the bed you have made is too short to **l** on.
29: 4 like a ghost from the earth where you will **l** buried.
32: 9 Listen, you women who **l** around in lazy ease.
34:10 The land will **l** deserted from generation to
41:11 "See, all your angry enemies **l** there, confused
44:20 this idol that I'm holding in my hand, a **l**?"
50:11 from me: You will soon **l** down in great torment.
51:20 For your children have fainted and **l** in the streets,
56:10 They love to **l** around, sleeping and dreaming.
Jer 3:25 Let us now **l** down in shame and dishonor, for we
4: 7 Your towns will **l** in ruins, empty of people.
5:26 "Among my people are wicked men who **l** in wait
6:15 Therefore, they will **l** among the slaughtered.
7: 9 murder, commit adultery, **l**, and worship Baal
7:34 of Judah. The land will **l** in complete desolation.
8:12 Therefore, they will **l** among the slaughtered.
9: 6 They pile **l** upon **l** and utterly refuse to come to
16: 4 and they will **l** scattered on the ground like dung.
26:15 The responsibility for such a deed will **l** on you,
27:16 Temple will be returned from Babylon. It is all a **l**!
36:30 His dead body will be thrown out to **l** unburied—
43: 2 all the other proud men said to Jeremiah, "You **l**!
44: 2 They now **l** in ruins, and no one lives in them.
47: 5 Gaza will be demolished; Ashkelon will **l** in ruins.
48: 1 certain for the city of Nebo; it will soon **l** in ruins.
48:21 All the cities of the plateau **l** in ruins, too.
50:39 will people live there; it will **l** desolate forever.
51:39 And while they **l** inflamed with all their wine,
51:43 Her cities now **l** in ruins; she is a dry wilderness
51:47 will be disgraced, and her dead will **l** in the streets.
51:62 She will **l** empty and abandoned forever.'
La 3:29 Let them **l** face down in the dust; then at last there
4: 1 The sacred gemstones **l** scattered in the streets!
Eze 4: 4 "Now **l** on your left side and place the sins of
4: 4 for the number of days you **l** there on your side.
4: 6 turn over and **l** on your right side for 40 days—
4: 7 **L** there with your arm bared and prophesy her
6:13 When their dead **l** scattered among their idols
13: 8 what you say is false and your visions are a **l**,
26:20 I will send you to the pit to **l** there with those who
26:20 Your city will **l** in ruins, buried beneath the earth,
28:23 and your people will **l** slaughtered within your
29: 5 You will **l** unburied on the open ground, for I have
30:14 Zoan, and Thebes, and they will **l** in ruins,
30:24 of Egypt, and he will **l** there mortally wounded,
31:18 You will **l** there among the outcasts who have died
32:19 go down to the pit and **l** there among the outcasts.'
32:21 they **l** among the outcasts, all victims of the
32:24 but now they **l** in the pit and share the humiliation
32:25 but now they **l** in shame in the pit, all of them
32:28 will **l** crushed and broken among the outcasts,
32:29 they also **l** among those killed by the sword,
32:30 Once a terror, they now **l** there in shame.
32:30 They **l** there as outcasts with all the other dead who
32:32 and his hordes will **l** there among the outcasts who
34:14 There they will **l** down in pleasant places and feed
34:15 tend my sheep and cause them to **l** down in peace,
36:34 The fields that used to **l** empty and desolate—
48:12 Next to the priests' territory will **l** the land where
Da 9: 2 that Jerusalem must **l** desolate for seventy years.
12: 2 Many of those whose bodies **l** dead and buried will
Hos 4: 2 You curse and **l** and kill and steal and commit
8: 8 they **l** among the nations like an old pot that no one
Mic 2: 1 How terrible it will be for you who **l** awake at
Na 3:18 O Assyrian king, your princes **l** dead in the dust.
Hab 3:17 olive crop fails, and the fields **l** empty and barren;
Zep 1:17 and your bodies will **l** there rotting on the
2: 7 They will **l** down to rest in the abandoned houses
2:14 and the cedar paneling will **l** open to the wind
Mal 2: 6 They did not **l** or cheat; they walked with me,
Mt 26:59 trying to find witnesses who would **l** about Jesus,
Mk 14:57 men stood up to testify against him with this **l**:
Ac 6:11 So they persuaded some men to **l** about Stephen,
20:23 me in city after city that jail and suffering **l** ahead.
Ro 9: 1 I do not **l**—and my conscience and the Holy Spirit
Eph 4:14 lied to us and made the **l** sound like the truth.
Col 2: 3 In him **l** hidden all the treasures of wisdom
3: 9 Don't **l** to each other, for you have stripped off
2Ti 2:18 preaching the **l** that the resurrection of the dead has
Tit 1: 2 them before the world began—and he cannot **l**.
Heb 6:18 because it is impossible for God to **l**.
Jas 3:14 brag about being wise. That is the worst kind of **l**.
1Jn 2:27 all things, and what he teaches is true—it is not a **l**.
Rev 11: 8 And their bodies will **l** in the main street of
22:15 the idol worshipers, and all who love to live a **l**.

LIED (11) [LIE]
Jos 7:11 they have also **l** about it and hidden the things
Job 31: 5 "Have I **l** to anyone or deceived anyone?
Ps 58: 3 even from birth they have **l** and gone their own
78:36 with their words; / they **l** to him with their tongues.
119:78 Bring disgrace upon the arrogant people who **l**
Jer 5:12 "They have **l** about the LORD and have said,
29:23 their neighbors' wives and have **l** in my name.
Eze 13: 6 Instead, they have **l** and said, 'My message is from
Mt 5:11 and persecuted and **l** about because you are my
Ac 5: 3 You **l** to the Holy Spirit, and you kept some of the
Eph 4:14 or because someone has cleverly **l** to us and made

LIEN [KJV] See DEFILED, LIVED, TAKEN

LIES (136) [LIE]
Ge 49: 9 Like a lion he crouches and **l** down; / like a
Ex 10: 7 Don't you realize that Egypt **l** in ruins?"
23: 1 Do not cooperate with evil people by telling **l** on
Lev 15: 4 Any bedding on which he **l** and anything on which
15:20 Anything on which she **l** or sits during that time
15:24 and any bed on which he **l** will be defiled.
15:26 Anything on which she **l** or sits during that time
26:34 **l** desolate during your years of exile in the land of
26:35 As the land **l** in ruins, it will take the rest you never
26:43 will enjoy its years of Sabbath rest as it **l** deserted.
Nu 14:33 until the last of you **l** dead in the wilderness.
24: 9 Like a lion, Israel crouches and **l** down; / like a
Jos 12: 2 area of Gilead, which **l** north of the Jabbok River.
Jdg 16:13 have been making fun of me and telling me **l**!
Ru 3: 4 Be sure to notice where he **l** down; then go
1Sa 19:15 Saul ordered, "so I can kill him as he **l** there!"
2Sa 1:19 Your pride and joy, O Israel, **l** dead on the hills!
1:25 fallen in battle! / Jonathan **l** dead upon the hills.
1Ki 22:22 go out and inspire all Ahab's prophets to speak **l**.'
2Ch 18:21 go out and inspire all Ahab's prophets to speak **l**.'
Ne 2:17 It **l** in ruins, and its gates are burned. Let us rebuild
Job 13: 4 For you are smearing me with **l**. As doctors,
13: 7 "Are you defending God by means of **l**
18:10 A snare **l** hidden in the ground. A rope **l** coiled on their path.
27: 4 will speak no evil, and my tongue will speak no **l**.
40:21 It **l** down under the lotus plants, hidden by the
Ps 4: 2 How long will you pursue **l**? / *Interlude*
5: 6 You will destroy those who tell **l**. / The LORD
7:14 they are pregnant with trouble / and give birth to **l**.
10: 7 Their mouths are full of cursing, **l**, and threats.
24: 4 who do not worship idols / and never tell **l**.
34:13 watch your tongue! / Keep your lips from telling **l**!
37:37 for a wonderful future **l** before those who love
50:19 with wickedness, / and your tongues are full of **l**.
52: 2 like a sharp razor; / you're an expert at telling **l**.
52: 3 than good / and **l** more than truth. / *Interlude*
59:12 captured by their pride, / their curses, and their **l**.
62: 4 They delight in telling **l** about me. / They are
69: 4 so without cause. / They attack me with **l**,
88: 7 Your anger **l** heavy on me; / wave after wave
109: 2 while the wicked slander me / and tell **l** about me.
119:69 Arrogant people have made up **l** about me,
144: 8 Their mouths are full of **l**; / they swear to tell the
144:11 Their mouths are full of **l**; / they swear to tell the
Pr 4:25 and fix your eyes on what **l** before you.
6:19 a false witness who pours out **l**, / a person who
12:17 honest witness tells the truth; a false witness tells **l**.
12:19 Truth stands the test of time; **l** are soon exposed.
13: 5 Those who are godly hate **l**; the wicked come to
14: 5 witness does not lie; a false witness breathes **l**.
17: 7 fitting for a fool; even less are **l** fitting for a ruler.
20: 5 Though good advice **l** deep within a person's heart,
25:18 Telling **l** about others is as harmful as hitting them
26:19 is someone who **l** to a friend and then says, "I was
Ecc 11: 3 When a tree falls, whether south or north, there it **l**.
Isa 1: 7 Your country **l** in ruins, and your cities are burned.
6:12 and the entire land of Israel **l** deserted.
9: 1 which **l** along the road that runs between the
9:10 "Our land **l** in ruins now, but we will rebuild it
9:17 they are all hypocrites, speaking wickedness with **l**.
18: 1 of Ethiopia, which **l** at the headwaters of the Nile.
28:15 for we have built a strong refuge made of **l**
28:17 Your refuge looks strong, but since it is made of **l**,
29:21 and tell **l** to tear down the innocent will be no
30:10 tell us the truth. Tell us nice things. Tell us **l**.
30:12 I tell you and trust instead in oppression and **l**,
32: 6 They spread **l** about the LORD; they deprive the
32: 7 including all the **l** they use to oppress the poor in
54:17 And everyone who tells **l** in court will be brought
59: 3 Your mouth is full of **l**, and your lips are tainted
59: 4 and honest. Their lawsuits are based on **l**.
59:13 we have been, carefully planning our deceitful **l**.
Jer 4:20 roll over the land, until it **l** in complete desolation.
5: 2 'As surely as the LORD lives,' they all tell **l**!"
9: 3 people bend their tongues like bows to shoot **l**.
9: 4 of one another and spread their slanderous **l**.
9: 5 With practiced tongues they tell **l**; they wear
9: 8 For their tongues aim **l** like poisoned arrows.
10:15 Idols are worthless; they are **l**! / The time is
14:14 "These prophets are telling **l** in my name.
14:17 a sword and **l** mortally wounded on the ground.
19:11 As this jar **l** shattered, so I will shatter the people
23:10 the land is full of adultery, and it **l** under a curse.
23:25 And then they proceed to tell **l** in my name.
23:32 Their imaginary dreams are flagrant **l** that lead my
27:15 They are telling you **l** in my name, so I will drive
28:15 has not sent you, but the people believe your **l**.
29: 9 because they prophesy **l** in my name. I have not
29:21 of Maaseiah—who are telling you **l** in my name:
29:31 send him and has tricked you into believing his **l**,
48:20 "And the reply comes back, 'Moab **l** in ruins;
50:23 hammer in all the earth, **l** broken and shattered.
51:18 Idols are worthless; they are **l**! / The time is
La 1: 9 Now she **l** in the gutter with no one to lift her out.
2: 1 The fairest of Israel's cities **l** in the dust,
Eze 13:19 By lying to my people who love to listen to **l**,
13:22 You have discouraged the righteous with your **l**,
21:29 have given false visions and told **l** about the sword.
32:22 "Assyria **l** there surrounded by the graves of all its
32:24 "Elam **l** there buried with its hordes who
48: 2 Asher's territory **l** south of Dan's and also extends
48: 3 Naphtali's land **l** south of Asher's, also extending
48:23 Benjamin's territory **l** just south of the prince's
48:24 South of Benjamin's territory **l** that of Simeon,
Da 2: 9 You have conspired to tell me **l** in hopes that
2:22 and knows what **l** hidden in darkness,
9:18 See how your city **l** in ruins—for everyone knows
Hos 7: 3 The princes laugh about the people's many **l**.
7:13 but they have only spoken **l** about me.
10:13 You have eaten the fruit of **l**—trusting in your
11:12 Israel surrounds me with **l** and deceit, but Judah
12: 1 They multiply **l** and violence; they make alliances
Joel 2: 3 Ahead of them the land **l** as fair as the Garden of
Am 2: 4 They have been led astray by the same **l** that
5: 2 never to rise again! / She **l** forsaken on the ground,
Mic 2:11 Suppose a prophet full of **l** were to say to you,
Na 2: 8 For the land of Israel **l** empty and broken after your
3: 1 it will be for Nineveh, the city of murder and **l**!
3: 7 back in horror and say, 'Nineveh **l** in utter ruin.'
Hab 2:18 own hands! What fools you are to believe such **l**!
Zep 3:13 never telling **l** or deceiving one another.
Hag 1: 4 in luxurious houses while my house **l** in ruins?
1: 9 Because my house **l** in ruins, says the LORD
Zec 10: 2 give false advice, fortune-tellers predict only **l**,
13: 3 for you have prophesied **l** in the name of the
Mt 8: 6 "Lord, my young servant **l** in bed, paralyzed
Jn 8:44 When he **l**, it is consistent with his character; for he is a liar and the father of **l**.
12:27 I pray, 'Father, save me from what **l** ahead'?

Ro 1:25 about God, they deliberately chose to believe **l**.
3:13 an open grave. / Their speech is filled with **l**."
Php 3:13 the past and looking forward to what **l** ahead,
2Th 2:11 upon them, and they will believe all these **l**.
1Pe 3:10 speaking evil, / and keep your lips from telling **l**.
2Pe 2:3 In their greed they will make up clever **l** to get hold

LIEUTENANTS (1)

Ezr 8:36 The king's decrees were delivered to his **l**

LIEUTENANTS [KJV] See also OFFICIAL(S)

LIFE (645) [LIVE]

BOOK OF LIFE (8) Ps 69:28; Php 4:3; Rev 3:5; 13:8; 17:8; 20:12,15; 21:27

BREATH OF...LIFE (3) Ge 2:7; Job 33:4; Da 5:23

DAYS OF...LIFE (4) Ps 21:4; 23:6; 27:4; Ecc 9:9

ETERNAL LIFE (57) Mt 19:16,17,29; 25:46; Mk 10:17,30; 16:99; Lk 10:25; 18:18,30; Jn 3:15,16,36,36; 4:14,36; 5:24,29,39,40; 6:27,39,40,47,50,53,54,63,68; 10:28; 11:26; 12:25,50; 17:2,3; Ac 11:18; 13:46,48; Ro 2:7; 5:21; 6:22,23; 2Co 4:12; Gal 1:6; 1Ti 1:16; 6:12; Tit 1:2; 3:7; 1Jn 1:2; 2:25; 3:14,15; 4:9; 5:11,13,20; Jude 1:21

LIFE...DEATH (50) Lev 24:17; Nu 35:31; Dt 30:15,19,19; 1Sa 2:6; 2Sa 1:23; 15:21,21; 1Ki 3:11; 2Ki 18:32; 2Ch 1:11; Ps 22:20; 49:15; 88:3; Pr 1:12; 11:19; 12:28; 19:16; Ecc 3:22; Jer 21:8; Jnh 2:6; Jn 5:24,24; Ac 2:24; Ro 5:10,21; 6:23; 7:10; 8:6,38; 14:8; 1Co 3:22; 2Co 3:6; 4:10,11,12; Gal 6:8; Php 2:30; Col 3:5; 2Ti 1:10; 4:6; Heb 11:35; 1Pe 1:23,23,23; 3:18; 1Jn 3:14; 5:16; Rev 2:10

TREE OF LIFE (8) Ge 2:9; 3:22,24; Pr 3:18; Rev 2:7; 22:2,14,19

WAY OF LIFE (7) Lev 18:3; Ps 16:11; 119:56,104; Ac 2:28; Ro 7:10; Eph 4:22

Ge 1:20 "Let the waters swarm with fish and other **l**.
1:26 They will be masters over all **l**—the fish in the sea,
2:7 of the ground and breathed into it the breath of **l**.
2:9 At the center of the garden he placed the tree of **l**
3:17 All your **l** you will struggle to scratch a living from
3:19 All your **l** you will sweat to produce food,
3:22 and evil. What if they eat the fruit of the tree of **l**?
3:24 and forth, guarding the way to the tree of **l**.
5:24 a close relationship with God throughout his **l**.
9:15 again will there be a flood that will destroy all **l**.
12:13 of their interest in you, and they will spare my **l**."
17:1 serve me faithfully and live a blameless **l**.
19:19 "You have been so kind to me and saved my **l**,
19:20 you see how small it is? Then my **l** will be saved."
19:25 and villages of the plain, eliminating all **l**—
26:35 But Esau's wives made **l** miserable for Isaac
32:30 seen God face to face, yet my **l** has been spared."
38:7 in the LORD's sight, so the LORD took his **l**.
38:10 dead brother. So the LORD took Onan's **l**, too.
42:15 I swear by the **l** of Pharaoh that you will not leave
44:30 the boy. Our father's **l** is bound up in the boy's **l**.
48:15 the God who has been my shepherd all my **l**,
Ex 20:12 full **l** in the land the LORD your God will give
21:30 owner of the bull to compensate for the loss of **l**.
Lev 17:11 for the **l** of any creature is in its blood. I have given
17:11 It is the blood, representing **l**, that brings you
17:14 The **l** of every creature is in the blood. That is why
17:14 for the **l** of any bird or animal is in the blood.
18:3 am taking you. You must not imitate their way of **l**.
18:5 and regulations, you will find **l** through them.
19:16 not try to get ahead at the cost of your neighbor's **l**,
24:17 "Anyone who takes another person's **l** must be put
26:16 causing your eyes to fail and your **l** to ebb away.
Nu 16:22 "O God, the God and source of all **l**,"
23:10 die like the righteous; / let my **l** end like theirs."
35:31 you must never accept a ransom payment for the **l**
Dt 4:40 Then you will enjoy a long **l** in the land the
5:16 full **l** in the land the LORD your God will give
6:2 all his laws and commands, you will enjoy a long **l**.
8:3 you that people need more than bread for their **l**;
8:3 real **l** comes by feeding on every word of the
11:9 you will enjoy a long **l** in the land the LORD
12:23 for the blood is the **l**, and you must not eat the **l** with the meat.
15:17 the door. After that, he will be your servant for **l**.
19:21 Your rule should be **l** for **l**, eye for eye, tooth for
22:7 mother go, so you may prosper and enjoy a long **l**.
25:15 so that you will enjoy a long **l** in the land the
30:15 and disaster, between **l** and death.
30:18 good **l** in the land you are crossing the Jordan to
30:19 "Today I have given you the choice between **l**
30:19 Oh, that you would choose **l**, that you and your
30:20 and commit yourself to him, for he is your **l**.
32:39 I am the one who kills and gives **l**; / I am the one
32:47 instructions are not mere words—they are your **l**!
32:47 By obeying them you will enjoy a long **l** in the
Jos 4:14 and for the rest of his **l** they revered him as much
Jdg 5:18 But Zebulun risked his **l**, / as did Naphtali,
9:17 and risked his **l** when he rescued you from the
12:3 So I risked my **l** and went to battle without you,
13:12 what kind of rules should govern the boy's **l**
Ru 1:20 for the Almighty has made **l** very bitter for me.
1Sa 1:28 and he will belong to the LORD his whole **l**."
2:6 The LORD brings both death and **l**; / he brings
7:15 continued as Israel's judge for the rest of his **l**.
15:9 Saul and his men spared Agag's **l** and kept the best
18:29 he remained David's enemy for the rest of his **l**.
19:5 Have you forgotten about the time he risked his **l**
22:23 with me, and I will protect you with my own **l**,
25:28 you have not done wrong throughout your entire **l**.
25:29 when you are chased by those who seek your **l**,
26:21 longer try to harm you, for you valued my **l** today.
26:24 Now may the LORD value my **l**, even as I have
28:2 "I will make you my personal bodyguard for **l**."
28:21 "Sir, I obeyed your command at the risk of my **l**.
2Sa 1:23 They were together in **l** and in death.
6:23 of Saul, remained childless throughout her **l**.
14:15 because my **l** and my son's **l** have been threatened.
15:21 and by your own **l** that I will go wherever you go,
15:21 what happens—whether it means **l** or death."
17:3 After all, it is only this man's **l** that you seek.
19:5 "We saved your **l** today and the lives of your sons,
19:23 to Shimei, David vowed, "Your **l** will be spared."
1Ki 1:12 If you want to save your own **l** and the **l** of your son Solomon,
3:11 and have not asked for a long **l** or riches for
3:13 will be compared to you for the rest of your **l**!
3:14 your father, David, did, I will give you a long **l**."
11:34 I will let Solomon reign for the rest of his **l**.
15:5 obeyed the LORD's commands throughout his **l**,
15:14 remained faithful to the LORD throughout his **l**.
17:21 my God, please let this child's **l** return to him."
17:22 the **l** of the child returned, and he came back to **l**!
18:12 I have been a true servant of the LORD all my **l**.
19:2 failed to take your **l** like those whom you killed."
19:3 Elijah was afraid and fled for his **l**. He went to
19:4 "Take my **l**, for I am no better than my
2Ki 1:13 of God, please spare my **l** and the lives of these,
1:14 the first two groups. But now please spare my **l**!"
4:31 but nothing happened. There was no sign of **l**.
5:7 leper to heal! Am I God, that I can kill and give **l**?
8:1 the woman whose son he had brought back to **l**,
8:5 about the time Elisha had brought a boy back to **l**.
8:5 is her son—the very one Elisha brought back to **l**!"
9:3 Then open the door and run for your **l**!"
10:24 you will pay for it with your own **l**."
12:2 All his **l** Joash did what was pleasing in the
14:19 There was a conspiracy against Amaziah's **l** in
18:32 a land of plenty. Choose **l** instead of death!
20:6 I will add fifteen years to your **l**, and I will rescue
25:29 him to dine at the king's table for the rest of his **l**.
1Ch 29:28 old age, having enjoyed long **l**, wealth, and honor.
2Ch 1:11 or the death of your enemies or even a long **l**,
15:17 fully committed to the LORD throughout his **l**.
16:12 Even when the disease became **l** threatening,
20:35 But near the end of his **l**, King Jehoshaphat of
25:27 there was a conspiracy against his **l** in Jerusalem,
Ne 6:11 in my position enter the Temple to save his **l**?
9:6 You preserve and give **l** to everything, and all the
9:29 by which people will find **l** if only they obey.
Est 2:14 She would live there for the rest of her **l**,
7:3 my petition is that my **l** and the lives of my people
7:7 But Haman stayed behind to plead for his **l** with
Job 2:4 A man will give up everything he has to save his **l**.
2:6 the LORD said to Satan. "But spare his **l**."
3:20 be given to the weary, and **l** to those in misery?
3:23 Why is **l** given to those with no future,
7:1 A person's **l** is long and hard, like that of a hired
7:7 O God, remember that my **l** is but a breath, and I
7:16 I hate my **l**. I do not want to go on living. Oh,
8:19 That is the end of its **l**, and others spring up from
9:21 but it makes no difference to me—I despise my **l**.
9:25 "My **l** passes more swiftly than a runner. It flees
10:1 "I am disgusted with my **l**. Let me complain
10:5 Is your lifetime merely human? Is your **l** so short
10:12 You gave me **l** and showed me your unfailing love. My **l** was preserved by your care.
11:17 Your **l** will be brighter than the noonday.
12:10 For the **l** of every living thing is in his hand,
13:14 I will take my **l** in my hands and say what I really
14:1 How short is **l**, and how full of trouble!
15:32 They will be cut down in the prime of **l**, and all
21:25 in bitter poverty, never having tasted the good **l**.
22:16 They were snatched away in the prime of **l**,
22:23 If you return to the Almighty and clean up your **l**,
24:22 may rise high, but they have no assurance in **l**.
27:8 when God cuts them off and takes away their **l**?
29:18 die surrounded by my family after a long, good **l**.
31:18 for orphans, and all my **l** I have cared for widows.
33:4 and the breath of the Almighty gives me **l**.
33:24 make him die, for I have found a ransom for his **l**.'
33:28 from the grave, and now my **l** is filled with light.'
34:15 all **l** would cease, and humanity would turn again
35:3 also ask, 'What's the use of living a righteous **l**?
36:21 for it was to prevent you from getting into a **l** of
41:4 work for you? Can you make it be your slave for **l**?
42:12 half of his **l** even more than in the beginning.
42:17 he died, an old man who had lived a long, good **l**.
Ps 16:11 You will show me the way of **l**, / granting me the
18:28 LORD, you have brought light to my **l**; / my God,
19:8 of the LORD are clear, / giving insight to **l**.
21:4 He asked you to preserve his **l**, / and you have
21:4 his request. / The days of his **l** stretch on forever.
22:14 My **l** is poured out like water, / and all my bones
22:20 spare my precious **l** from these dogs.
23:6 unfailing love will pursue me / all the days of my **l**,
25:20 Protect me! Rescue my **l** from them! / Do not let
27:4 in the house of the LORD all the days of my **l**,
31:13 conspire against me, / plotting to take my **l**.
32:8 will guide you along the best pathway for your **l**.
34:12 any of you want to live / a **l** that is long and good?
35:17 their fierce attacks. / Protect my **l** from these lions!
36:9 For you are the fountain of **l**, / the light by which
39:4 days are numbered, / and that my **l** is fleeing away.
39:5 My **l** is no longer than the width of my hand.
39:11 their lives can be crushed like the **l** of a moth.
41:12 You have preserved my **l** because I am innocent;
42:8 I sing his songs, / praying to God who gives me **l**.
49:15 But as for me, God will redeem my **l**. / He will
49:18 In this **l** they consider themselves fortunate,
61:6 Add many years to the **l** of the king! / May his
62:10 don't make it the center of your **l**.
63:3 Your unfailing love is better to me than **l** itself;
68:26 praise the LORD, the source of Israel's **l**.
69:28 Erase their names from the Book of **L**; / don't let
71:7 My **l** is an example to many, / because you have
71:20 much hardship, / but you will restore me to **l** again
73:4 They seem to live such a painless **l**; / their bodies
73:12 enjoying a **l** of ease while their riches multiply.
73:20 Their present **l** is only a dream / that is gone when
73:20 O Lord, / you will make them vanish from this **l**.
84:10 than live the good **l** in the homes of the wicked.
86:4 me happiness, O Lord, / for my **l** depends on you.
87:7 will sing, / "The source of my **l** is in Jerusalem!"
88:3 For my **l** is full of troubles, / and death draws near.
89:47 Remember how short my **l** is, / how empty
91:16 I will satisfy them with a long **l** / and give them my
101:2 I will be careful to live a blameless **l**— / when will
101:2 I will lead a **l** of integrity / in my own home.
102:11 My **l** passes as swiftly as the evening shadows.
102:24 don't take my **l** while I am still so young!
103:5 He fills my **l** with good things. / My youth is
104:25 vast and wide, / teeming with **l** of every kind,
104:30 When you send your Spirit, new **l** is born
109:20 for my accusers / who are plotting against my **l**.
119:6 when I compare my **l** with your commands.
119:37 and give me **l** through your word.
119:39 my shameful ways; / your laws are all I want in **l**.
119:40 Renew my **l** with your goodness.
119:54 Your principles have been the music of my **l**
119:56 This is my happy way of **l**: / obeying your
119:59 I pondered the direction of my **l**, / and I turned to
119:88 In your unfailing love, spare my **l**; / then I can
119:104 no wonder I hate every false way of **l**.
119:107 restore my **l** again, just as you promised.
119:109 My **l** constantly hangs in the balance, / but I will
119:115 Get out of my **l**, you evil-minded people, / for I
119:149 hear my cry; / in your justice, save my **l**.
119:154 take my side! / Protect my **l** as you promised.
119:156 is your mercy; / in your justice, give me back my **l**.
119:159 Give back my **l** because of your unfailing love.
121:7 keeps you from all evil / and preserves your **l**.
128:2 How happy you will be! How rich your **l**!
133:3 has pronounced his blessing, / even **l** forevermore.
138:8 The LORD will work out his plans for my **l**—
139:16 Every day of my **l** was recorded in your book.
139:19 the wicked! / Get out of my **l**, you murderers!
139:24 and lead me along the path of everlasting **l**.
142:5 my place of refuge. / You are all I really want in **l**.
Pr 1:12 Though they are in the prime of **l**, they will go
1:19 are greedy for gain. It ends up robbing them of **l**.
2:19 her is doomed. He will never reach the paths of **l**.
3:2 for they will give you a long and satisfying **l**.
3:16 She offers you **l** in her right hand, and riches
3:18 Wisdom is a tree of **l** to those who embrace her;
3:22 for they fill you with **l** and bring you honor
4:10 and do as I say, and you will have a long, good **l**.
4:12 If you live a **l** guided by wisdom, you won't limp
4:13 Guard them, for they will lead you to a fulfilled **l**.
4:22 for they bring **l** and radiant health to anyone who
5:6 For she does not care about the path to **l**.
5:9 people everything you have achieved in **l**.
6:23 of you. The correction of discipline is the way to **l**.
6:26 with another man's wife may cost you your very **l**.
7:23 into a snare, little knowing it would cost him his **l**.
8:35 For whoever finds me finds **l** and wins approval
9:11 will multiply your days and add years to your **l**.
10:2 no lasting value, but right living can save your **l**.
10:11 The words of the godly lead to **l**; evil people cover
10:17 who accept correction are on the pathway to **l**,
10:27 Fear of the LORD lengthens one's **l**, but the years
11:19 Godly people find **l**; evil people find death.
12:28 The way of the godly leads to **l**; their path does not
13:3 Those who control their tongue will have a long **l**;
13:6 Godliness helps people all through **l**, while the evil
13:9 The **l** of the godly is full of light and joy,
13:12 but when dreams come true, there is **l** and joy.
14:30 A relaxed attitude lengthens **l**; jealousy rots it
15:4 Gentle words bring **l** and health; a deceitful tongue
15:15 for the happy heart, **l** is a continual feast.
15:19 A lazy person has trouble all through **l**; the path of
15:24 The path of the wise leads to **l** above; they leave
16:15 When the king smiles, there is **l**; his favor refreshes
16:31 is a crown of glory; it is gained by living a godly **l**.
18:21 for the tongue can kill or nourish **l**.
19:16 Keep the commandments and keep your **l**;
19:20 instruction you can, and be wise the rest of your **l**.
19:23 Fear of the LORD gives **l**, security,
20:2 a lion's roar; to rouse his anger is to risk your **l**.
20:20 or mother, the lamp of your **l** will be snuffed out.
20:21 An inheritance obtained early in **l** is not a blessing
21:21 pursues godliness and unfailing love will find **l**,
22:4 of the LORD lead to riches, honor, and long **l**.
22:5 treacherous road; whoever values **l** will stay away.
23:22 Listen to your father, who gave you **l**, and don't
31:11 can trust her, and she will greatly enrich his **l**.
31:12 She will not hinder him but help him all her **l**.
Ecc 2:1 Let's look for the 'good things' in **l**." But I found
2:3 most people find during their brief **l** in this world.
2:17 So now I hate **l** because everything done here
2:20 the answer to my search for satisfaction in this **l**.
3:22 No one will bring them back from death to enjoy **l**
5:19 To enjoy your work and accept your lot in **l**—

6: 3 But if he finds no satisfaction in l and in the end
7: 12 to know that only wisdom can save your l.
7: 14 way you will realize that nothing is certain in this l.
7: 15 In this meaningless l, I have seen everything,
8: 14 In this l, good people are often treated as though
8: 15 to do in this world than to eat, drink, and enjoy l.
9: 1 or not God will show them favor in this l.
9: 9 days of l that God has given you in this world.
10: 9 with each stroke of your ax! Such are the risks of l.
11: 8 to be very old, let them rejoice in every day of l.
11: 10 but remember that youth, with a whole l before it,
12: 6 before the silver cord of l snaps and the golden
Isa 23: 15 For seventy years, the length of a king's l,
23: 15 But then the city will come back to l and sing
24: 7 All the joys of l will be gone. The grape harvest
26: 19 sing for joy! / For God's light of l will fall like dew
38: 5 seen your tears. I will add fifteen years to your l,
38: 10 I said, "In the prime of my l, / must I now enter
38: 12 My l has been blown away / like a shepherd's tent
38: 12 cuts cloth from a loom. / Suddenly, my l was over.
38: 13 as though by lions. / Suddenly, my l was over.
38: 16 discipline is good, / for it leads to l and health.
38: 20 every day of my l / in the Temple of the LORD.
42: 5 He gives breath and l to everyone in all the world.
53: 10 Yet when his l is made an offering for sin, he will
53: 10 He will enjoy a long l, and the LORD's plan will
54: 9 again let a flood cover the earth and destroy its l,
55: 3 wide open. Listen, for the l of your soul is at stake.
58: 11 watering your l when you are dry and keeping you
59: 15 and anyone who tries to live a godly l is soon
65: 20 will adults die before they have lived a full l.
Jer 9: 10 For they are desolate and empty of l; the lowing of
10: 14 they are frauds. / They have no l or power in them.
10: 23 I know, LORD, that a person's l is not his own.
20: 18 My entire l has been filled with trouble, sorrow,
21: 8 the LORD says: Take your choice of l or death!
22: 30 to rule in Judah. His l will amount to nothing."
28: 16 Your l will end this very year because you have
31: 12 Their l will be like a watered garden, and all their
38: 20 Your l will be spared, and all will go well for you.
39: 18 I will preserve your l and keep you safe.
48: 2 about Moab again, for there is a plot against her l.
51: 13 but your end has come. The thread of your l is cut.
51: 17 they are frauds. / They have no l or power in them.
52: 11 remained there in prison for the rest of his l.
52: 33 him to dine at the king's table for the rest of his l.
La 2: 12 Their lives ebb away like the l of a warrior
3: 58 Plead my case! For you have redeemed my l.
4: 20 the LORD's anointed, the very l of our nation,
Eze 3: 19 But you will have saved your l because you did
3: 21 and you will have saved your own l, too."
7: 13 Not one person whose l is twisted by sin will
13: 19 and you promise l to those who should not live.
13: 22 have encouraged the wicked by promising them l,
17: 24 green tree wither and gives new l to the dead tree.
18: 14 but decides against that kind of l.
20: 13 even though obedience would have given them l.
20: 21 though obeying them would have given them l.
20: 25 and laws that would not lead to l.
37: 6 I will put breath into you, and you will come to l.
37: 10 They all came to l and stood up on their feet—
Da 5: 23 not honored the God who gives you the breath of l
12: 2 some to everlasting l and some to shame
Jnh 2: 6 I was locked out of l and imprisoned in the land of
Mal 2: 5 of my covenant with the Levites was to bring l
Mt 4: 4 'People need more than bread for their l;
6: 25 "So I tell you, don't worry about everyday l—
6: 25 Doesn't l consist of more than food and clothing?
6: 27 all your worries add a single moment to your l?
7: 14 But the gateway to l is small, and the road is
9: 18 "but you can bring her back to l again if you just
10: 39 If you cling to your l, you will lose it; but if you
11: 5 are cured, the deaf hear, the dead are raised to l,
13: 22 the message is crowded out by the cares of this l
14: 2 "This must be John the Baptist come back to l
16: 25 If you try to keep your l for yourself, you will lose
16: 25 if you give up your l for me, you will find true l.
19: 16 what good things must I do to have eternal l?"
19: 17 you can receive eternal l if you keep the
19: 29 times as much in return and will have eternal l.
20: 28 and to give my l as a ransom for many."
21: 32 the Baptist came and showed you the way to l,
25: 46 but the righteous will go into eternal l."
27: 64 and then telling everyone he came back to l!
Mk 3: 4 Is this a day to save l or to destroy it?"
4: 19 the message is crowded out by the cares of this l,
6: 14 "This must be John the Baptist come back to l
8: 35 If you try to keep your l for yourself, you will lose
8: 35 But if you give up your l for my sake and for the
sake of the Good News, you will find true l.
10: 17 what should I do to get eternal l?"
10: 30 And in the world to come they will have eternal l.
10: 45 and to give my l as a ransom for many."
16: S unfailing message of salvation that gives eternal l.
Lk 4: 4 'People need more than bread for their l.' "
6: 9 Is this a day to save l or to destroy it?"
7: 22 are cured, the deaf hear, the dead are raised to l,
8: 14 out by the cares and riches and pleasures of this l.
8: 55 And at that moment her l returned, and she
9: 7 "This is John the Baptist come back to l again."
9: 24 If you try to keep your l for yourself, you will lose
9: 24 if you give up your l for me, you will find true l.
10: 25 "Teacher, what must I do to receive eternal l?"
11: 36 no dark corners, then your whole l will be radiant,
12: 15 Real l is not measured by how much we own."
12: 22 "So I tell you, don't worry about everyday l—
12: 23 For l consists of far more than food and clothing.
12: 25 all your worries add a single moment to your l?
14: 26 brothers and sisters—yes, more than your own l.
15: 24 son of mine was dead and has now returned to l.
15: 32 For your brother was dead and has come back to l!
17: 33 Whoever clings to this l will lose it, and whoever
loses this l will save it.
18: 18 "Good teacher, what should I do to get eternal l?"
18: 30 will be repaid many times over in this l, as well as
receiving eternal l in the world to
20: 36 They are children of God raised up to new l.
21: 34 and filled with the worries of this l.
Jn 1: 4 L itself was in him, and this l gives light to
everyone.
3: 6 Humans can reproduce only human l, but the Holy
Spirit gives new l from heaven.
3: 15 everyone who believes in me will have eternal l.
3: 16 believes in him will not perish but have eternal l.
3: 36 And all who believe in God's Son have eternal l.
3: 36 don't obey the Son will never experience eternal l,
4: 14 spring within them, giving them eternal l."
4: 36 the fruit they harvest is people brought to eternal l.
5: 24 and believe in God who sent me have eternal l.
5: 24 but they have already passed from death into l.
5: 26 The Father has l in himself, and he has granted his
Son to have l in himself.
5: 29 Those who have done good will rise to eternal l,
5: 39 because you believe they give you eternal l.
5: 40 to come to me so that I can give you this eternal l.
6: 27 Spend your energy seeking the eternal l that I,
6: 33 down from heaven and gives l to the world."
6: 35 Jesus replied, "I am the bread of l. No one who
6: 39 but that I should raise them to eternal l at the last
6: 40 his Son and believe in him should have eternal l—
6: 47 anyone who believes in me already has eternal l.
6: 48 Yes, I am the bread of l!
6: 50 the bread from heaven gives eternal l to everyone
6: 53 his blood, you cannot have eternal l within you.
6: 54 eat my flesh and drink my blood have eternal l,
6: 63 It is the Spirit who gives eternal l. Human effort
6: 63 very words I have spoken to you are spirit and l.
6: 68 You alone have the words that give eternal l.
8: 12 because you will have the light that leads to l."
10: 10 My purpose is to give l in all its fullness.
10: 11 The good shepherd lays down his l for the sheep.
10: 15 the Father. And I lay down my l for the sheep.
10: 17 because I lay down my l that I may have it back
10: 18 No one can take my l from me. I lay down my l
voluntarily.
10: 28 I give them eternal l, and they will never perish.
11: 25 Jesus told her, "I am the resurrection and the l.
11: 26 They are given eternal l for believing in me
12: 17 Lazarus back to l were telling others all about it.
12: 25 Those who love their l in this world will lose it.
12: 25 Those who despise their l in this world will keep it
for eternal l.
12: 50 And I know his instructions lead to eternal l;
14: 6 Jesus told him, "I am the way, the truth, and the l.
14: 20 When I am raised to l again, you will know that I
17: 2 He gives eternal l to each one you have given him.
17: 3 And this is the way to have eternal l—to know you,
20: 31 and that by believing in him you will have l.
Ac 2: 24 the horrors of death and raised him back to l again,
2: 28 You have shown me the way of l, / and you will
3: 15 You killed the author of l, but God raised him to l.
5: 20 the Temple and give the people this message of l!"
8: 33 For his l was taken from the earth."
10: 14 "I have never in all my l eaten anything forbidden
10: 40 but God raised him to l three days later. Then God
11: 18 of turning from sin and receiving eternal l."
13: 46 and judged yourselves unworthy of eternal l—
13: 48 and all who were appointed to eternal l became
17: 25 He himself gives l and breath to everything,
19: 31 begging him not to risk his l by entering the
20: 3 he discovered a plot by some Jews against his l,
20: 24 But my l is worth nothing unless I use it for doing
Ro 1: 17 "It is through faith that a righteous person has l."
2: 7 He will give eternal l to those who persist in doing
2: 16 by Jesus Christ, will judge everyone's secret l.
3: 25 that Jesus shed his blood, sacrificing his l for us.
4: 17 believed in the God who brings the dead back to l
5: 10 be delivered from eternal punishment by his l.
5: 18 all people right in God's sight and gives them l.
5: 21 and resulting in eternal l through Jesus Christ our
6: 8 with Christ, we know we will also share his new l.
6: 13 to God since you have been given new l.
6: 22 things that lead to holiness and result in eternal l.
6: 23 but the free gift of God is eternal l through Christ
7: 10 which was supposed to show me the way of l,
7: 21 It seems to be a fact of l that when I want to do
7: 24 Who will free me from this l that is dominated by
8: 6 Spirit controls your mind, there is l and peace.
8: 11 he will give l to your mortal body by this same
8: 34 is the one who died for us and was raised to l for us
8: 38 Death can't, and l can't. The angels can't,
10: 7 place of the dead" (to bring Christ back to l again).
11: 15 will be. It will be l for those who were dead!
14: 8 So in l and in death, we belong to the Lord.
14: 17 but of living a l of goodness and peace and joy in
1Co 3: 1 or as though you were infants in the Christian l.
3: 22 and Peter; the whole world and l and death;
7: 1 in your letter. Yes, it is good to live a celibate l.
7: 32 I want you to be free from the concerns of this l.
8: 6 and through whom we have been given l.
10: 13 l are no different from what others experience.
15: 19 And if we have hope in Christ only for this l,
15: 20 great harvest of those who will be raised to l again.
15: 22 to Christ, the other man, will be given new l.
2Co 3: 6 in death; in the new way, the Holy Spirit gives l.
3: 8 far greater glory when the Holy Spirit is giving l?
4: 10 so that the l of Jesus may also be seen in our
4: 11 so that the l of Jesus will be obvious in our dying
4: 12 of death, but it has resulted in eternal l for you.
5: 4 dying bodies will be swallowed up by everlasting l.
5: 14 we also believe that we have all died to the old l
5: 15 so that those who receive his new l will no longer
5: 17 for the old l is gone. A new l has begun!
5: 18 All this newness of l is from God, who brought us
12: 6 of me than what they can actually see in my l
Gal 1: 6 and mercy called you to share the eternal l he gives
2: 20 So I live my l in this earthly body by trusting in the
3: 11 "It is through faith that a righteous person has l."
3: 12 "If you wish to find l by obeying the law,
3: 15 Dear friends, here's an example from everyday l.
3: 21 If the law could have given us new l, we could
5: 16 So I advise you to live according to your new l in
5: 21 that anyone living that sort of l will not inherit the
6: 8 the Spirit will harvest everlasting l from the Spirit.
Eph 2: 5 he gave us l when he raised Christ from the dead.
3: 19 Then you will be filled with the fullness of l
4: 1 beg you to lead a l worthy of your calling,
4: 18 they are far away from the l of God because they
4: 22 off your old evil nature and your former way of l,
5: 2 Live a l filled with love for others,
5: 18 be drunk with wine, because that will ruin your l.
5: 23 his body, the church; he gave his l to be her Savior.
5: 25 Christ showed the church. He gave up his l for her
6: 3 your father and mother, "you will live a long l,
Php 1: 11 those good things that are produced in your l by
1: 20 and that my l will always honor Christ, whether I
2: 16 Hold tightly to the word of l, so that when Christ
2: 17 But even if my l is to be poured out like a drink
2: 30 For he risked his l for the work of Christ, and he
3: 19 and all they think about is this l here on earth.
4: 3 whose names are written in the Book of L.
Col 2: 12 And with him you were raised to a new l
3: 1 Since you have been raised to new l with Christ,
3: 3 and your real l is hidden with Christ in God.
3: 4 And when Christ, who is your real l, is revealed to
3: 5 Don't be greedy for the good things of this l,
3: 7 You used to do them when your l was still part of
3: 11 In this new l, it doesn't matter if you are a Jew
1Th 3: 8 It gives us new l, knowing you remain strong in the
4: 11 to live a quiet l, minding your own business
4: 14 believe that Jesus died and was raised to l again,
2Th 1: 11 that our God will make you worthy of the l to
1Ti 1: 4 they don't help people live a l of faith in God.
1: 16 too, can believe in him and receive eternal l.
2: 6 He gave his l to purchase freedom for everyone.
3: 2 For an elder must be a man whose l cannot be
4: 8 for it promises a reward in both this l and the next.
6: 3 and they are the foundation for a godly l.
6: 11 Pursue a godly l, along with faith, love,
6: 12 Hold tightly to the eternal l that God has given
6: 13 who gives l to all, and before Christ Jesus,
6: 19 for the future so that they may take hold of real l.
2Ti 1: 1 sent out to tell others about the l he has promised
1: 9 is God who saved us and chose us to live a holy l.
1: 10 and showed us the way to everlasting l through the
2: 4 let yourself become tied up in the affairs of this l,
2: 21 Your l will be clean, and you will be ready for the
3: 10 and how I live, and what my purpose in l is.
3: 12 and everyone who wants to live a godly l in Christ
4: 6 my l has already been poured out as an offering to
4: 10 deserted me because he loves the things of this l
Tit 1: 2 This truth gives them the confidence of eternal l,
1: 6 An elder must be well thought of for his good l.
1: 7 An elder must live a blameless l because he is
1: 8 be fair. He must live a devout and disciplined l.
2: 14 He gave his l to free us from every kind of sin,
3: 5 and gave us a new l through the Holy Spirit.
3: 7 And now we know that we will inherit eternal l.
Heb 5: 13 living on milk isn't very far along in the Christian l
6: 11 will keep right on loving others as long as l lasts,
7: 3 any of his ancestors—no beginning or end to his l.
7: 16 but by the power of a l that cannot be destroyed.
11: 19 God was able to bring him back to l again.
11: 35 placed their hope in the resurrection to a better l.
12: 1 by such a huge crowd of witnesses to the l of faith,
12: 14 with everyone, and seek to live a clean and holy l,
Jas 1: 12 Afterward they will receive the crown of l that God
3: 6 It is full of wickedness that can ruin your whole l.
3: 6 It can turn the entire course of your l into a blazing
3: 13 live a l of steady goodness so that only good deeds
4: 14 For your l is like the morning fog—it's here a little
1Pe 1: 18 the empty l you inherited from your ancestors.
1: 23 Your new l did not come from your earthly parents
1: 23 because the l they gave you will end in death.
1: 23 But this new l will last forever because it comes
3: 7 but she is your equal partner in God's gift of new l.
3: 10 "If you want a happy l and good days,
3: 15 Instead, you must worship Christ as Lord of your l.
3: 16 they will be ashamed when they see what a good l
3: 18 physical death, but he was raised to l in the Spirit.
4: 2 And you won't spend the rest of your l chasing
2Pe 1: 3 gives us everything we need for living a godly l.
1: 5 to apply the benefits of these promises to your l.
1: 5 Then your faith will produce a l of moral
1: 5 A l of moral excellence leads to knowing God
1: 9 that God has cleansed them from their old l of sin.
3: 14 make every effort to live a pure and blameless l.
1Jn 1: 1 our own hands. He is Jesus Christ, the Word of l.
1: 2 This one who is l from God was shown to us,
1: 2 announce to you that he is the one who is eternal l.
2: 25 And in this fellowship we enjoy the eternal l he

3: 9 family do not sin, because God's **l** is in them.
3: 14 proves that we have passed from death to eternal **l**.
3: 15 And you know that murderers don't have eternal **l**
3: 16 real love is because Christ gave up his **l** for us.
4: 9 so that we might have eternal **l** through him.
5: 11 He has given us eternal **l**, and this **l** is in his Son.
5: 12 So whoever has God's Son has **l**; whoever does not have his Son does not have **l**.
5: 13 of God, so that you may know you have eternal **l**.
5: 16 you should pray, and God will give that person **l**.
5: 20 He is the only true God, and he is eternal **l**.
Jude 1: 18 **l** is to enjoy themselves in every evil way
1: 21 **l** that our Lord Jesus Christ in his mercy is going to
Rev 2: 7 will eat from the tree of **l** in the paradise of God.
2: 10 facing death, and I will give you the crown of **l**.
3: 5 I will never erase their names from the Book of **L**,
11: 11 a half days, the spirit of **l** from God entered them,
13: 8 whose names were not written in the Book of **L**,
13: 14 who was fatally wounded and then came back to **l**.
13: 15 He was permitted to give **l** to this statue so that it
17: 8 whose names were not written in the Book of **L**
20: 4 They came to **l** again, and they reigned with Christ
20: 5 (The rest of the dead did not come back to **l** until
20: 12 the books were opened, including the Book of **L**.
20: 15 in the Book of **L** was thrown into the lake of fire.
21: 6 give the springs of the water of **l** without charge!
21: 27 whose names are written in the Lamb's Book of **L**.
22: 1 angel showed me a pure river with the water of **l**,
22: 2 On each side of the river grew a tree of **l**,
22: 14 gates of the city and eat the fruit from the tree of **l**.
22: 17 them come and drink the water of **l** without charge.
22: 19 God will remove that person's share in the tree of **l**

LIFE-GIVING (14) [GIVE, LIVE]

Ps 56: 13 can walk in your presence, O God, / in your **l** light.
Pr 11: 30 The godly are like trees that bear **l** fruit, and those
13: 14 The advice of the wise is like a **l** fountain;
14: 27 Fear of the LORD is a **l** fountain; it offers escape
16: 22 Discretion is a **l** fountain to those who possess it,
18: 4 A person's words can be **l** water; words of true
Eze 33: 15 and obey my **l** laws, no longer doing what is evil.
Zec 14: 8 On that day **l** waters will flow out from Jerusalem,
Ac 7: 38 and the angel who gave him **l** words on Mount
Ro 8: 2 For the power of the **l** Spirit has freed you through
1Co 15: 45 But the last Adam—that is, Christ—is a **l** Spirit.
2Co 2: 16 But to those who are being saved we are a **l**
Heb 10: 20 **l** way that Christ has opened up for us through the
Rev 7: 17 He will lead them to the springs of **l** water.

LIFEBLOOD (2) [BLOOD, LIVE]

Ge 9: 4 never eat animals that still have their **l** in them.
1Pe 1: 19 He paid for you with the precious **l** of Christ,

LIFEBOAT (2) [BOAT]

Ac 27: 16 where with great difficulty we hoisted aboard the **l**
27: 30 they lowered the **l** as though they were going to put

LIFELESS (5) [LIVE]

Lev 26: 30 I will leave your corpses piled up beside your **l**
Jer 16: 18 because they have defiled my land with **l** images of
Hab 2: 19 How terrible it will be for you who beg **l** wooden
2: 19 overlaid with gold and silver, but they are **l** inside.
1Co 14: 7 like the flute or the harp, though they are **l**,

LIFETIME (32) [LIVE]

Ge 4: 26 It was during his **l** that people first began to
10: 25 for during his **l** the people of the world were
Jos 23: 3 LORD your God has done for you during my **l**.
24: 31 Israel served the LORD throughout the **l** of
Jdg 2: 7 served the LORD throughout the **l** of Joshua
2: 18 people from their enemies throughout the judge's **l**.
8: 28 Throughout the rest of Gideon's **l**—about forty
16: 30 when he died than he had during his entire **l**.
1Sa 1: 11 He will be yours for his entire **l**, and as a sign that
7: 13 And throughout Samuel's **l**, the LORD's
14: 52 constantly with the Philistines throughout Saul's **l**.
2Sa 18: 18 During his **l**, Absalom had built a monument to
1Ki 4: 21 and continued to serve him throughout his **l**.
4: 25 Throughout the **l** of Solomon, all of Judah
21: 29 I will not do what I promised during his **l**.
2Ki 20: 19 least there will be peace and security during my **l**."
1Ch 1: 19 for during his **l** the people of the world were
2Ch 13: 20 Israel never regained his power during Abijah's **l**,
24: 2 sight throughout the **l** of Jehoiada the priest.
24: 14 of the LORD during the **l** of Jehoiada the priest.
32: 26 did not come against them during Hezekiah's **l**.
34: 33 And throughout the rest of his **l**, they did not turn
Job 10: 5 Is your **l** merely human? Is your life so short
Ps 30: 5 anger lasts for a moment, / but his favor lasts a **l**!
39: 5 An entire **l** is just a moment to you;
Ecc 9: 6 Whatever they did in their **l**—loving, hating,
Isa 39: 8 least there will be peace and security during my **l**."
46: 4 I will be your God throughout your **l**—until your
Jer 16: 9 In your own **l**, before your very eyes, I will put an
Eze 12: 25 I will fulfill my threat of destruction in your own **l**,
Lk 16: 25 remember that during your **l** you had everything
1Pe 1: 12 that these things would not happen during their **l**,

LIFT (46) [LIFTED, LIFTING, LIFTS]

Ex 9: 22 said to Moses, "**L** your hand toward the sky,
9: 29 the city, I will **l** my hands and pray to the LORD.
10: 21 "**L** your hand toward heaven, and a deep
14: 14 You won't have to **l** a finger in your defense!"
29: 26 and **l** it up in the LORD's presence as a special
Lev 14: 24 and **l** them up before the LORD as an offering to
23: 11 the priest will **l** it up before the LORD so it may
23: 20 "The priest will **l** up these offerings before the
Nu 5: 25 **l** it up before the LORD, and carry it to the altar.
6: 20 then **l** the gifts up before the LORD in a gesture
Jos 3: 6 "**L** up the Ark of the Covenant and lead the people
Jdg 5: 3 I will **l** up my song to the LORD, the God of
2Sa 23: 10 until his hand was too tired to **l** his sword,
Ezr 9: 6 am utterly ashamed; I blush to **l** up my face to you.
Job 11: 13 your heart and **l** up your hands to him in prayer!
Ps 25: 1 To you, O LORD, I **l** up my soul.
28: 2 as I **l** my hands toward your holy sanctuary.
35: 3 **L** up your spear and javelin / and block the way of
71: 20 and **l** me up from the depths of the earth.
75: 5 Don't **l** your fists in defiance at the heavens
76: 5 of death. / No warrior could **l** a hand against us.
88: 9 I **l** my pleading hands to you for mercy.
116: 13 I will **l** up a cup symbolizing his salvation;
123: 1 I **l** my eyes to you, / O God, enthroned in heaven.
134: 2 **L** your hands in holiness, / and bless the LORD.
Pr 19: 24 so lazy that they won't even **l** a finger to feed
26: 15 so lazy that they won't **l** a finger to feed
Isa 1: 15 From now on, when you **l** up your hands in prayer,
10: 27 the yoke of slavery and **l** it from their shoulders.
Jer 51: 11 Sharpen the arrows! **L** up the shields!
51: 14 and they will **l** their shouts of triumph over you."
La 1: 9 Now she lies in the gutter with no one to **l** her out.
2: 19 to the Lord. **L** up your hands to him in prayer.
3: 41 Let us **l** our hearts and hands to God in heaven
Eze 12: 6 **l** your pack to your shoulders and walk away into
25: 7 I will **l** up my fist against you. I will give you as
Ob 1: 11 refusing to **l** a finger to help when foreign invaders
Na 3: 5 "And now I will **l** your skirts so all the earth will
Zec 12: 3 None of the nations who try to **l** it will escape
Mt 21: 21 'May God **l** you up and throw you into the sea,'
23: 4 and never **l** a finger to help ease the burden.
Mk 11: 23 'May God **l** you up and throw you into the sea,'
Lk 11: 46 and you never **l** a finger to help ease the burden.
18: 13 and dared not even **l** his eyes to heaven as he
Ac 21: 35 so violent the soldiers had to **l** Paul to their
Jas 4: 10 on him, he will **l** you up and give you honor.

LIFTED (54) [LIFT]

Ge 8: 13 the flood began, Noah **l** back the cover to look.
22: 10 and **l** it up to kill his son as a sacrifice to the
48: 17 So he **l** it to place it on Manasseh's head instead.
Ex 9: 23 So Moses **l** his staff toward the sky,
9: 33 As he **l** his hands to the LORD, all at once the
10: 22 So Moses **l** his hand toward heaven, and there was
29: 24 and his sons to be **l** up as a special gift to the
29: 27 and the thigh that were **l** up before the LORD in
40: 36 Now whenever the cloud **l** from the Tabernacle
Lev 8: 29 the breast and **l** it up in the LORD's presence.
9: 21 Aaron then **l** up the breasts and right thighs as an
10: 14 and thigh that were **l** up may be eaten in any place
10: 15 and breast that are **l** up must be **l** up to the
23: 15 the day the bundle of grain was **l** up as an offering,
23: 17 bring two loaves of bread to be **l** up before the
26: 13 I have **l** the yoke of slavery from your neck so you
Nu 6: 20 and thigh pieces that were **l** up before the LORD.
9: 17 When the cloud **l** from over the sacred tent,
9: 21 But day or night, when the cloud **l**, the people
9: 22 But as soon as it **l**, they broke camp and moved on.
10: 11 the cloud **l** from the Tabernacle of the Covenant.
Dt 2: 15 The LORD had **l** his hand against them until all
Jdg 16: 3 and **l** them, bar and all, right out of the ground.
1Sa 6: 15 Several men of the tribe of Levi **l** the Ark of the
1Ki 8: 22 Then Solomon stood with his hands **l** toward
16: 2 "I **l** you out of the dust to make you ruler of my
2Ch 6: 13 then he knelt down and **l** his hands toward heaven.
35: 24 So they **l** Josiah out of his chariot and placed him
Ezr 9: 5 to my knees, **l** my hands to the LORD my God.
Ne 8: 6 Amen!" as they **l** their hands toward heaven.
Ps 40: 2 He **l** me out of the pit of despair, / out of the mud
77: 2 long I pray, with hands **l** toward heaven, pleading.
89: 13 Your right hand is **l** high in glorious strength.
Isa 63: 9 He **l** them up and carried them through all the
63: 12 when Moses **l** up his hand, establishing his
Eze 3: 12 Then the Spirit **l** me up, and I heard a loud
3: 14 The Spirit **l** me up and took me away. I went in
8: 3 Then the Spirit **l** me up into the sky
11: 1 Then the Spirit **l** me and brought me over to the
11: 22 Then the cherubim **l** their wings and rose into the
14: 13 and I **l** my fist to crush them, cutting off their food
Da 6: 23 and ordered that Daniel be **l** from the den.
10: 10 Just then a hand touched me and **l** me,
Hos 11: 4 I **l** the yoke from his neck, and I myself stooped to
Zec 5: 7 When the heavy lead cover was **l** off the basket,
Jn 3: 14 And as Moses **l** up the bronze snake on a pole in
3: 14 so I, the Son of Man, must be **l** up on a pole,
8: 28 "When you have **l** up the Son of Man on the cross,
12: 32 And when I am **l** up on the cross, I will draw
Ac 4: 24 Then all the believers were united as they **l** their
13: 16 So Paul stood, **l** his hand to quiet them, and started
1Ti 2: 8 I want men to pray with holy hands **l** up to God,
Rev 10: 5 the sea and on the land **l** his right hand to heaven.

LIFTING (10) [LIFT]

Ge 7: 17 the ground and **l** the boat high above the earth.
Lev 7: 30 and present it to the LORD by **l** it up before him.
8: 27 and he presented the portions by **l** them up before
14: 12 and offer them as a guilt offering by **l** them up
14: 21 The guilt offering will be presented by **l** it up,
Nu 18: 11 **l** them up before the altar also belong to you as
18: 18 and right thigh that are presented by **l** them up
Ps 63: 4 as long as I live, / **l** up my hands to you in prayer.
Hab 3: 10 mighty deep cried out, **l** its hands to the LORD.
Lk 24: 50 and **l** his hands to heaven, he blessed them.

LIFTS (6) [LIFT]

1Sa 2: 7 he brings one down and **l** another up.
2: 8 He **l** the poor from the dust— / yes, from a pile of
Ps 3: 3 my glory, and the one who **l** my head high.
113: 7 and he **l** the poor from the dirt / and the needy from
145: 14 the fallen / and **l** up those bent beneath their loads.
146: 8 The LORD **l** the burdens of those bent beneath

LIGHT (211) [DAYLIGHT, ENLIGHTENED, FIRELIGHT, FLOODLIGHT, LIGHTED, LIGHTEN, LIGHTENED, LIGHTER, LIGHTING, LIGHTLY, LIGHTS, LIT, SEARCHLIGHT, STARLIGHT, SUNLIGHT, TWILIGHT]

Ge 1: 3 God said, "Let there be **l**," and there was **l**.
1: 4 Then he separated the **l** from the darkness.
1: 5 God called the **l** "day" and the darkness "night."
1: 15 Let their **l** shine down upon the earth." And
1: 17 God set these lights in the heavens to **l** the earth,
1: 18 the night, and to separate the **l** from the darkness.
Ex 10: 23 But there was **l** as usual where the people of Israel
25: 37 and set them so they reflect their **l** forward.
35: 3 Do not even **l** fires in your homes on that day."
35: 28 They also brought spices and olive oil for the **l**,
Nu 8: 2 he is to place them so their **l** shines forward."
8: 3 the seven lamps so they reflected their **l** forward,
Dt 28: 66 reason to believe that you will see the morning **l**.
32: 15 they made **l** of the Rock of their salvation.
Jdg 16: 2 "When the **l** of morning comes, we will kill him."
19: 26 at the door of the house and lay there until it was **l**.
Ru 3: 14 but she got up before it was **l** enough for people to
1Sa 29: 10 and leave with your men as soon as it gets **l**."
2Sa 14: 20 did it to place the matter before you in a different **l**.
21: 17 Why should we risk snuffing out the **l** of Israel?"
22: 29 O LORD, you are my **l**; / yes, LORD, you **l** up my darkness.
23: 4 he is like the **l** of the morning, / like the sunrise
1Ki 3: 21 But when I looked more closely in the morning **l**,
2Ch 13: 11 and they **l** the gold lampstand every evening.
Job 3: 9 Let it hope for **l**, but in vain; may it never see the morning **l**.
3: 16 like a baby who never lives to see the **l**?
3: 20 "Oh, why should **l** be given to the weary, and life
10: 22 and the **l** is as dark as midnight.' "
12: 22 "He floods the darkness with **l**; he brings **l** to the deepest gloom.
12: 25 They grope in the darkness without a **l**. He makes
18: 5 "The truth remains that the **l** of the wicked will be
18: 6 The **l** in their tent will grow dark. The lamp
18: 18 They will be thrust from **l** into darkness,
22: 28 and **l** will shine on the road ahead of you.
24: 13 "Wicked people rebel against the **l**. They refuse to
24: 16 in the daytime. They are not acquainted with the **l**.
25: 3 Does his **l** not shine on all the earth?
28: 3 They know how to put **l** into darkness and explore
28: 11 and bring to **l** the hidden treasures.
30: 26 came instead. I waited for the **l**, but darkness fell.
33: 28 from the grave, and now my life is filled with **l**.'
33: 30 the grave so they may live in the **l** of the living.
38: 14 For the features of the earth take shape as the **l**
38: 15 The **l** disturbs the haunts of the wicked, and it stops
38: 19 "Where does the **l** come from, and where does the
38: 24 Where is the path to the origin of **l**? Where is the
41: 18 "When it sneezes, it flashes **l**! Its eyes are like the
Ps 13: 3 my God! / Restore the **l** to my eyes, or I will die.
18: 28 LORD, you have brought **l** to my life; / my God, you **l** up my darkness.
27: 1 The LORD is my **l** and my salvation— / so why
36: 9 are the fountain of life, / the **l** by which we see.
43: 3 Send out your **l** and your truth; / let them guide me.
49: 19 before them / and never again see the **l** of day.
56: 13 in your presence, O God, / in your life-giving **l**.
84: 11 For the LORD God is our **l** and protector.
89: 15 for they will walk in the **l** of your presence,
97: 11 **L** shines on the godly, / and joy on those who do
104: 2 you are dressed in a robe of **l**. / You stretch out the
105: 39 and gave them a great fire to **l** the darkness.
112: 4 overtakes the godly, **l** will come bursting in.
119: 105 word is a lamp for my feet / and a **l** for my path.
119: 130 As your words are taught, they give **l**;
132: 17 my anointed one will be a **l** for my people.
139: 11 to hide me / and the **l** around me to become night—
139: 12 as day. / Darkness and **l** are both alike to you.
Pr 4: 18 which shines ever brighter until the full **l** of day.
6: 23 and this teaching are a lamp to **l** the way ahead of
13: 9 The life of the godly is full of **l** and joy, but the sinner's **l** is snuffed out.
24: 20 the evil have no future; their **l** will be snuffed out.
26: 21 starts fights as easily as hot embers **l** charcoal
26: 26 by trickery, it will finally come to **l** for all to see.
29: 13 the LORD gives **l** to the eyes of both.
Ecc 2: 13 than foolishness, just as **l** is better than darkness.
10: 20 Never make **l** of the king, even in your thoughts.
11: 7 **L** is sweet; it's wonderful to see the sun!
12: 2 when the **l** of the sun and moon and stars is dim to
Isa 2: 5 people of Israel, let us walk in the **l** of the LORD!
5: 20 and good is evil; that dark is **l** and **l** is dark;
5: 30 hover over Israel. The clouds will blot out the **l**.
8: 20 it is because there is no **l** or truth in them.
9: 2 people who walk in darkness will see a great **l**—
9: 2 a **l** that will shine on all who live in the land where

10:17 The LORD, the L of Israel and the Holy One,
13:10 No l will shine from stars or sun or moon.
26:19 sing for joy! / For God's l of life will fall like dew
28:27 never used on dill; rather, it is beaten with a l stick.
30:26 be seven times brighter—like the l of seven days!
42: 6 And you will be a l to guide all nations to me.
45: 7 I am the one who creates the l and makes the
49: 6 I will make you a l to the Gentiles, and you will
50:10 without a ray of l, trust in the LORD and rely on
50:11 you who live in your own l and warm yourselves
51: 4 and my justice will become a l to the nations.
58:10 Then your l will shine out from the darkness,
59: 9 No wonder we are in darkness when we expected l.
60: 1 Let your l shine for all the nations to see!
60: 3 All nations will come to your l. Mighty kings will
60:19 longer will you need the sun or moon to give you l,
60:19 the LORD your God will be your everlasting l,
60:20 For the LORD will be your everlasting l.
Jer 4:23 I looked at the heavens, and there was no l.
13:16 For then, when you look for l, you will find only
21:14 I will l a fire in your forests that will burn up
31:35 It is the LORD who provides the sun to l the day and the moon and stars to l the night.
50:32 For I will l a fire in the cities of Babylon that will
La 3: 2 brought me into deep darkness, shutting out all l.
Eze 1: 4 flashed with lightning and shone with brilliant l.
32: 7 with a cloud, and the moon will not give you its l.
Da 2:22 in darkness, / though he himself is surrounded by l.
Am 4:13 He turns the l of dawn into darkness and treads the
5:18 That day will not bring l and prosperity,
Mic 7: 8 I sit in darkness, the LORD himself will be my l.
7: 9 will bring me out of my darkness into the l,
Hab 3: 4 Rays of brilliant l flash from his hands. He rejoices
Zec 14: 6 On that day the sources of l will no longer shine,
14: 7 and night, for at evening time it will still be l.
Mt 4:16 people who sat in darkness / have seen a great l.
4:16 where death casts its shadow, / a l has shined."
5:14 You are the l of the world—like a city on a
5:15 Don't hide your l under a basket! Instead, put it on
6:23 But an evil eye shuts out the l and plunges you into
6:23 If the l you think you have is really darkness,
11:30 yoke fits perfectly, and the burden I give you is l."
24:29 sun will be darkened, / the moon will not give l,
Mk 4:21 "Would anyone l a lamp and then put it under a basket or under a bed to shut out the l?
4:21 A lamp is placed on a stand, where its l will shine.
4:22 or secret will eventually be brought to l.
13:24 sun will be darkened, / the moon will not give l,
Lk 1:78 the l from heaven is about to break upon us,
1:79 to give l to those who sit in darkness and in the
2:32 He is a l to reveal God to the nations, / and he is
8:16 "No one would l a lamp and then cover it up
8:17 or secret will eventually be brought to l and made
11:33 it is put on a lampstand to give l to all who enter
11:34 But an evil eye shuts out the l and plunges you into
11:35 Make sure that the l you think you have is not
11:36 If you are filled with l, with no dark corners,
12: 3 you have said in the dark will be heard in the l,
15: 8 Won't she l a lamp and look in every corner of the
23:45 The l from the sun was gone. And suddenly,
Jn 1: 4 itself was in him, and this life gives l to everyone.
1: 5 The l shines through the darkness, and the darkness
1: 7 to tell everyone about the l so that everyone might
1: 8 John himself was not the l; he was only a witness to the l.
1: 9 The one who is the true l, who gives l to everyone,
3:19 The l from heaven came into the world, but they loved the darkness more than the l,
3:20 They hate the l because they want to sin in the
3:20 They stay away from the l for fear their sins will be
3:21 But those who do what is right come to the l
8:12 Jesus said to the people, "I am the l of the world.
8:12 because you will have the l that leads to life."
9: 5 am still here in the world, I am the l of the world."
11: 9 As long as it is l, people can walk safely. They can see because they have the l of this world.
11:10 is there danger of stumbling because there is no l."
12:35 "My l will shine out for you just a little while
12:36 Believe in the l while there is still time; then you will become children of the l."
12:46 I have come as a l to shine in this dark world,
Ac 9: 3 a brilliant l from heaven suddenly beamed down
12: 7 Suddenly, there was a bright l in the cell, and an
13:47 he said, / 'I have made you a l to the Gentiles,
22: 6 about noon a very bright l from heaven suddenly
22: 9 The people with me saw the l but didn't hear the
22:11 "I was blinded by the intense l and had to be led
26:13 a l from heaven brighter than the sun shone down
26:18 their eyes so they may turn from darkness to l,
26:23 and be the first to rise from the dead as a l to Jews
27:13 When a l wind began blowing from the south,
27:33 As the darkness gave way to the early morning l,
Ro 2:19 and a beacon l for people who are lost in darkness
13:12 the armor of right living, as those who live in the l.
1Co 4: 5 he will bring our deepest secrets to l and will
2Co 4: 4 so they are unable to see the glorious l of the Good
4: 6 who said, "Let there be l in the darkness,"
4: 6 has made us understand that this l is the brightness
4: 7 this l and power that now shine within us—
6:14 with wickedness? How can l live with darkness?
11:14 Even Satan can disguise himself as an angel of l.
Eph 1:18 I pray that your hearts will be flooded with l
5: 8 now you are full of l from the Lord, and your
5: 9 For this l within you produces only what is good
5:13 But when the l shines on them, it becomes clear
5:14 And where your l shines, it will expose their evil
5:14 up from the dead, / and Christ will give you l."
Col 1:12 belongs to God's holy people, who live in the l.
1Th 5: 5 For you are all children of the l and of the day;
5: 8 But let us who live in the l think clearly,
1Ti 6:16 and he lives in l so brilliant that no human can
1Pe 2: 9 called you out of the darkness into his wonderful l.
2Pe 1:19 for their words are like a l shining in a dark place
1:19 and his brilliant l shines in your hearts.
1Jn 1: 5 God is l and there is no darkness in him at all.
1: 7 But if we are living in the l of God's presence,
2: 8 is disappearing and the true l is already shining.
2: 9 "I am in the l" but rejects another Christian is still
2:10 who loves other Christians is walking in the l
Rev 21:23 of God illuminates the city, and the Lamb is its l.
21:24 The nations of the earth will walk in its l,

LIGHTED (2) [LIGHT]
Job 29: 3 when he l the way before me and I walked safely
Ac 20: 8 The upstairs room where we met was l with many

LIGHTEN (6) [LIGHT]
1Ki 12: 4 "L the harsh labor demands and heavy taxes that
12: 9 want me to l the burdens imposed by my father?"
2Ch 10: 4 "L the harsh labor demands and heavy taxes that
10: 9 want me to l the burdens imposed by my father?"
Jnh 1: 5 and threw the cargo overboard to l the ship.
Php 2:28 will be glad to see him, and that will l all my cares.

LIGHTENED (1) [LIGHT]
Ac 27:38 the crew l the ship further by throwing the cargo of

LIGHTER (1) [LIGHT]
Ps 62: 9 them on the scales, / they are l than a puff of air.

LIGHTING (3) [LIGHT]
Ex 14:20 turned into a pillar of fire, l the Israelite camp.
35:14 and its accessories; the lamp cups and the oil for l;
39:37 and its accessories; the lamp cups and the oil for l;

LIGHTLY (3) [LIGHT]
Jer 3: 9 Israel treated it all so l—she thought nothing of
Eze 16:59 for you have taken your solemn vows l by breaking
Lk 12:48 that they are doing wrong will be punished only l.

LIGHTNING (42)
Ex 9:23 sent thunder and hail, and l struck the earth.
9:24 like that, with such severe hail and continuous l.
19:16 there was a powerful thunder and l storm,
20:18 and when they saw the l and the smoke billowing
2Sa 22:13 shone before him, / and bolts of l blazed forth.
22:15 his l flashed, and they were confused.
Job 28:26 the laws of the rain and prepared a path for the l.
36:30 See how he spreads the l around him and how it
36:32 He fills his hands with l bolts. He hurls each at its
37: 3 and his l flashes out in every direction.
37:11 the clouds with moisture, and they flash with his l.
37:15 and causes the l to flash forth from his clouds?
38:25 torrents of rain? Who laid out the path for the l?
38:35 Can you make l appear and cause it to strike as you
Ps 18:14 his l flashed, and they were greatly confused.
29: 7 The voice of the LORD strikes with l bolts.
77:17 and crackled in the sky. / Your arrows of l flashed.
77:18 roared from the whirlwind; / the l lit up the world!
78:48 their cattle to the hail, / their livestock to bolts of l.
97: 4 His l flashes out across the world. / The earth sees
105:32 and flashes of l overwhelmed the land.
135: 7 to rise over the earth. / He sends the l with the rain
144: 6 Release your l bolts and scatter your enemies!
Jer 10:13 to rise over the earth. / He sends the l with the rain
51:16 to rise over the earth. / He sends the l with the rain
Eze 1: 4 driving before it a huge cloud that flashed with l
1:13 and it looked as though l was flashing back
1:14 the living beings darted to and fro like flashes of l.
21:10 prepared for terrible slaughter; it will flash like l!
21:15 It flashes like l; it is polished for slaughter!
21:28 it is sharpened to destroy, flashing like l!
Da 10: 6 From his face came flashes like l, and his eyes
Na 2: 4 the squares, swift as l, flickering like torches.
Zec 9:14 appear above his people; his arrows will fly like l!
Mt 24:27 For as the l lights up the entire sky, so it will be
28: 3 His face shone like l, and his clothing was as white
Lk 10:18 "I saw Satan falling from heaven as a flash of l!
17:24 It will be as evident as the l that flashes across the
Rev 4: 5 And from the throne came flashes of l
8: 5 and thunder crashed, l flashed, and there was a
11:19 L flashed, thunder crashed and roared; there was a
16:18 Then the thunder crashed and rolled, and l flashed.

LIGHTS (12) [LIGHT]
Ge 1:14 "Let bright l appear in the sky to separate the day
1:16 For God made two great l, the sun and the moon,
1:17 God set these l in the heavens to light the earth,
Job 36:30 around him and how it l up the depths of the sea.
Ps 136: 7 Give thanks to him who made the heavenly l—
Pr 26:21 easily as hot embers light charcoal or fire l wood.
31:18 watches for bargains; her l burn late into the night.
Ecc 8: 1 Wisdom l up a person's face, softening its
Mt 24:27 For as the lightning l up the entire sky, so it will be
Lk 11:33 "No one l a lamp and then hides it or puts it under
Ac 16:29 the jailer called for l and ran to the dungeon
Jas 1:17 to us from God above, who created all heaven's l.

LIGN [KJV] See ALOES

LIGURE [KJV] See JACINTH

LIKE (1422) [ALIKE, LIKED, LIKELY, LIKENESS, LIKES, LIKEWISE] See Index of Articles, Etc.

LIKED (5) [LIKE]
Ge 25:27 while Jacob was the kind of person who l to stay at
27:14 a delicious meat dish, just the way Isaac l it.
1Sa 16:21 Saul l David very much, and David became one of
Mk 6:20 talked with John, but even so, he l to listen to him.
Jn 21:18 you were able to do as you l and go wherever you

LIKELY (4) [LIKE]
Ex 34:15 them to worship their gods, and you are l to do it.
Jer 31:36 "I am as l to reject my people Israel as I am to do
Ro 5: 7 Now, no one is l to die for a good person,
1Ti 5:13 they are l to become lazy and spend their time

LIKENESS (3) [LIKE]
Ge 5: 1 God created people, he made them in the l of God.
2Co 4: 4 the glory of Christ, who is the exact l of God.
Eph 4:24 because you are a new person, created in God's l—

LIKES (2) [LIKE]
1Sa 18:22 to David, "The king really l you, and so do we.
Joel 2: 2 The l of them have not been seen before and never

LIKEWISE (2) [LIKE]
1Sa 14:22 L, the men who were hiding in the hills joined the
Zec 11: 6 And l, I will no longer have pity on the inhabitants

LIKHI (1)
1Ch 7:19 of Shemida were Ahian, Shechem, L, and Aniam.

LILIES (13) [LILY]
1Ki 7:19 on the columns inside the foyer were shaped like l,
7:22 The capitals on the pillars were shaped like l.
Ps 45: T descendants of Korah, to be sung to the tune "L."
69: T A psalm of David, to be sung to the tune "L."
80: T to be sung to the tune "L of the Covenant."
SS 2:16 lover is mine, and I am his. He feeds among the l!
4: 5 like twin fawns of a gazelle, feeding among the l.
5:13 His lips are like perfumed l. His breath is like
6: 2 to his spice beds, to graze and to gather the l.
6: 3 and my lover is mine. He grazes among the l!"
7: 2 is lovely, like a heap of wheat set about with l.
Mt 6:28 Look at the l and how they grow. They don't work
Lk 12:27 "Look at the l and how they grow. They don't

LILY (6) [LILIES]
1Ki 7:26 flared out like a cup and resembled a l blossom.
2Ch 4: 5 flared out like a cup and resembled a l blossom.
Ps 60: T To be sung to the tune "L of the Testimony."
SS 2: 1 "I am the rose of Sharon, the l of the valley."
2: 2 my beloved is like a l among thorns."
Hos 14: 5 It will blossom like the l; it will send roots deep

LIMB (4) [LIMBS]
Da 2: 5 and what it means, you will be torn l from l,
3:29 and Abednego, they will be torn l from l,

LIMBS (7) [LIMB]
Job 18:13 Disease eats their skin; death devours their l.
40:18 Its bones are tubes of bronze. Its l are bars of iron.
41:12 the tremendous strength in the crocodile's l
Ps 80:11 our l east to the Euphrates River.
Ecc 12: 3 Your l will tremble with age, and your strong legs
Isa 17: 6 four or five out on the tips of the l.
Eze 19:14 and devoured its fruit. / None of the remaining l

LIMIT (8) [LIMITATIONS, LIMITED, LIMITING, LIMITS]
Nu 11:23 said to Moses, "Is there any l to my power?
1Sa 18:26 to accept the offer. So before the time l expired,
Ne 5: 4 "We have already borrowed to the l on our fields
Job 22: 5 because of your wickedness! Your guilt has no l!
Ps 119:96 has its limits, / but your commands have no l.
Jer 5:28 and there is no l to their wicked deeds.
Na 3: 9 the source of her strength, which seemed without l.
Jn 3:34 for God's Spirit is upon him without measure or l.

LIMITATIONS (2) [LIMIT]
Jn 8:15 You judge me with all your human l, but I am not
Heb 9:10 that are in effect only until their l can be corrected.

LIMITED (4) [LIMIT]
Jn 3:31 and my understanding is l to the things of earth,
1Co 7: 5 and wife to refrain from sexual intimacy for a l
10:29 why should my freedom be l by what someone else
Heb 7:28 the law of Moses were l by human weakness.

LIMITING (1) [LIMIT]
Job 38:10 For I locked it behind barred gates, l its shores.

LIMITS (5) [LIMIT]
Ex 19:23 around the mountain and to declare it off l."
Nu 35:27 victim's nearest relative finds him outside the city l
Ps 119:96 Even perfection has its l, / but your commands

Pr 8:29 I was there when he set the l of the seas, so they
Jude 1:6 not stay within the l of authority God gave them

LIMP (2) [LIMPING]

Pr 4:12 by wisdom, you won't l or stumble as you run.
26:7 a fool, a proverb becomes as l as a paralyzed leg.

LIMPING (1) [LIMP]

Ge 32:31 as he left Peniel, and he was l because of his hip.

LINE (56) [LINED, LINES, LINING]

Ge 19:32 That way we will preserve our family l through our
19:34 That way our family l will be preserved."
31:52 I will not cross this l to harm you, and you will not
31:53 God of his father, Isaac, to respect the boundary l.
44:12 going on down the l to the youngest.
Nu 2:16 These three tribes will be second in l whenever the
2:24 and they will follow the Levites in the l of march.
3:1 This is the family l of Aaron and Moses as it was
10:17 of the Levites were next in the l of march,
21:13 The Arnon is the boundary l between the Moabites
36:8 l to inherit property must marry within their tribe,
Jos 15:11 The boundary l then proceeded to the slope of the
19:12 the boundary l went east from Sarid to the border
Ru 4:4 because I am next in l to redeem it after you."
4:18 This is their family l beginning with their ancestor
1Sa 24:21 kill my family and destroy my l of descendants!"
2Ki 11:11 They formed a l from the south side of the Temple
1Ch 1:24 So this is the family l descended from Shem:
7:25 Ephraim's l of descent was Rephah, Resheph,
2Ch 23:10 They formed a l from the south side of the Temple
Ezr 2:36 The family of Jedaiah (through the l of Jeshua)
Ne 3:18 Next down the l were his countrymen led by
7:39 The family of Jedaiah (through the l of Jeshua)
Ps 110:4 "You are a priest forever in the l of
132:12 I teach them, / then your royal l will never end."
Pr 25:7 for an invitation than to be sent to the end of the l,
Ecc 7:13 Notice the way God does things; then fall into l.
Isa 19:11 Will they dare tell Pharaoh about their long l of
28:10 us everything over and over again, a l at a time,
28:13 repeating it over and over, a l at a time, in very
28:17 "I will take the measuring l of justice
28:17 and the plumb l of righteousness to check the
Jer 31:39 A measuring l will be stretched out over the hill of
Eze 45:7 and western borders of the prince's lands will l up
48:1 Its boundary l follows the Hethlon road to
Da 11:21 man who is not directly in l for royal succession.
Am 7:7 beside a wall that had been built using a plumb l.
7:7 He was checking it with a plumb l to see if it was
7:8 what do you see?" I answered, "A plumb l."
7:8 "I will test my people with this plumb l.
Jnh 1:8 "Who are you? What is your l of work?
Zec 2:1 I saw a man with a measuring l in his hand.
4:10 to see the plumb l in Zerubbabel's hand.
12:7 and the royal l of David will not have greater
Mt 17:27 so go down to the lake and throw in a l.
Lk 1:5 Elizabeth, was also from the priestly l of Aaron.
1:69 from the royal l of his servant David,
Jn 7:42 the Messiah will be born of the royal l of David,
Ro 1:3 as a man, born into King David's royal family l.
Heb 5:6 are a priest forever / in the l of Melchizedek."
5:10 him to be a High Priest in the l of Melchizedek.
6:20 He has become our eternal High Priest in the l of
7:11 send a different priest from the l of Melchizedek,
7:11 instead of from the l of Levi and Aaron?
7:17 are a priest forever / in the l of Melchizedek."
1Jn 5:14 we ask him for anything in l with his will.

LINEAGE [KJV] See ANCIENT (HOME)

LINED (3) [LINE]

Ex 18:13 They were l up in front of him from morning till
Jer 22:23 It may be nice to live in a beautiful palace l with
Hos 12:11 their altars are l up like the heaps of stone along

LINEN (92) [LINENS]

FINE LINEN (37) Ex 25:4; 26:1,31,36; 27:9,16,18; 28:5,6,8,15,39; 35:6,23,25,35; 36:8,35,37; 38:9,16,18,23; 39:2,5,8,27,28,29; 1Ch 15:27; 2Ch 3:14; 5:12; Est 8:15; Eze 16:13; 27:16; Rev 18:12; 19:8

Ex 25:4 blue, purple, and scarlet yarn; fine l; goat hair for
26:1 "Make the Tabernacle from ten sheets of fine l.
26:31 Tabernacle hang a special curtain made of fine l,
26:36 "Make another curtain from fine l for the entrance
27:9 enclosed with curtains made from fine l.
27:16 Fashion it from fine l, and decorate it with
27:18 curtain walls 7-1/2 feet high, made from fine l.
28:5 These items must be made of fine l cloth
28:6 "The ephod must be made of fine l cloth
28:8 fine l cloth embroidered with gold thread and blue,
28:15 fine l cloth embroidered with gold thread and blue,
28:39 "Weave Aaron's patterned tunic from fine l cloth.
28:39 Fashion the turban out of this l as well. Also make
28:42 Also make l underclothes for them, to be worn
35:6 blue, purple, and scarlet yarn; fine l; goat hair for
35:23 brought blue, purple, and scarlet yarn, fine l,
35:25 purple, and scarlet yarn, and fine l cloth, and they
35:35 in blue, purple, and scarlet yarn on fine l cloth.
36:8 skilled weavers first made ten sheets from fine l.
36:35 The inner curtain was made of fine l cloth,
36:37 It was made of fine l cloth and embroidered with
38:9 feet long. It consisted of curtains made of fine l.
38:16 used in the courtyard walls were made of fine l.
38:18 entrance to the courtyard was made of fine l cloth
38:23 purple, and scarlet yarn on fine l cloth.
39:2 The ephod was made from fine l cloth
39:3 He then embroidered it into the l with the blue,
39:5 fine l cloth; blue, purple, and scarlet yarn; and gold
39:8 crafted from fine l cloth and embroidered with
39:27 then made for Aaron and his sons from fine l cloth.
39:28 and the underclothes were all made of this fine l.
39:29 The sashes were made of fine l cloth
Lev 6:10 after dressing in his special l clothing
13:47 mildew contaminates some woolen or l clothing,
13:48 some woolen or l fabric, the hide of an animal,
13:52 The priest must burn the l or wool clothing
13:59 infectious mildew in woolen or l clothing or fabric,
16:4 he must wash his entire body and put on his l tunic
16:4 He must tie the l sash around his waist and put the l turban on his head.
16:23 he must take off the l garments he wore when he
16:32 ancestor Aaron. He will put on the holy l garments
Dt 22:11 wear clothing made of wool and l woven together.
Jdg 14:12 I will give you thirty plain l robes and thirty fancy
14:13 then you must give me thirty l robes and thirty
1Sa 2:18 He wore a l tunic just like that of a priest.
14:3 Ahijah the priest, who was wearing the l ephod.
1Ch 4:21 the families of l workers at Beth-ashbea,
15:27 David was dressed in a robe of fine l, as were the
2Ch 2:14 blue, and scarlet cloth and in working with l.
3:14 Solomon hung a curtain made of fine l and blue,
5:12 were dressed in fine l robes and stood at the east
Est 1:6 with beautifully woven white and blue l hangings,
8:15 and he wore an outer cloak of fine l and purple.
Pr 7:16 My bed is spread with colored sheets of finest l
31:24 She makes belted l garments and sashes to sell to
Isa 3:23 their mirrors, l garments, head ornaments,
Jer 13:1 "Go and buy a l belt and put it around your waist,
13:4 "Take the l belt you are wearing, and go to the
13:6 and get the l belt that I told you to hide there."
13:10 Therefore, they will become like this l belt—
Eze 9:2 One of them was dressed in l and carried a writer's
9:3 And the LORD called to the man dressed in l who
9:11 Then the man in l clothing, who carried the
10:2 Then the LORD spoke to the man in l clothing
10:6 The LORD said to the man in l clothing,
10:7 He put the coals into the hands of the man in l
16:10 I gave you expensive clothing of l and silk,
16:13 Your clothes were made of fine l and were
27:7 Your sails were made of Egypt's finest l, and they
27:16 purple dyes, embroidery, fine l, and jewelry of
44:17 the inner courtyard, they must wear only l clothing.
44:18 They must wear l turbans and l undergarments.
Da 10:5 I looked up and saw a man dressed in l clothing,
12:6 One of them asked the man dressed in l, who was
12:7 The man dressed in l, who was standing above the
Hos 2:5 them for food and drink, for clothing of wool and l,
2:9 I will take away the l and wool clothing I gave her
Mt 27:59 took the body and wrapped it in a long l cloth.
Mk 14:51 along behind, clothed only in a l nightshirt.
15:46 Joseph bought a long sheet of l cloth, and taking
Lk 23:53 from the cross and wrapped it in a long l cloth
24:12 he peered in and saw the empty l wrappings;
Jn 19:40 Together they wrapped Jesus' body in a long l
20:5 and looked in and saw the l cloth lying there,
20:6 He also noticed the l wrappings lying there,
Rev 15:6 clothed in spotless white l with gold belts across
18:12 silver, jewels, pearls, fine l, purple dye, silk,
19:8 She is permitted to wear the finest white l."
19:8 (Fine l represents the good deeds done by the
19:14 The armies of heaven, dressed in pure white l,

LINENS (1) [LINEN]

Rev 18:16 like a woman clothed in finest purple and scarlet l,

LINES (14) [LINE]

Ge 10:32 listed nation by nation according to their l of
Ex 19:12 Set boundary l that the people may not pass.
2Sa 10:8 The Ammonite troops drew up their battle l at the
11:15 "Station Uriah on the front l where the battle is
23:16 So the Three broke through the Philistine l,
1Ki 20:27 Israel then mustered its army, set up supply l,
2Ki 3:26 break through the enemy l near the king of Edom,
14:11 The two armies drew up their battle l at
1Ch 11:18 So the Three broke through the Philistine l,
19:9 The Ammonite troops drew up their battle l at the
23:7 The Gershonite family units were defined by their l
2Ch 25:21 The two armies drew up their battle l at
SS 6:13 so gracefully between two l of dancers?"
2Co 1:13 and there is nothing written between the l

LINGERING (2)

Ps 119:60 I will hurry, without l, / to obey your commands.
SS 8:13 "O my beloved, l in the gardens, how wonderful

LINING (2) [LINE]

Ecc 12:2 and there is no silver l left among the clouds.
Jer 5:7 committing adultery and l up at the city's brothels.

LINTEL [KJV] See TOP

LINUS (1)

2Ti 4:21 and so do Pudens, L, Claudia, and all the brothers

LION (72) [LION'S, LIONESS, LIONS, LIONS']

Ge 49:9 Judah is a young l / that has finished eating its
49:9 Like a l he crouches and lies down; / like a
Nu 23:24 rise up like a lioness; / like a majestic l they stand.
24:9 Like a l, Israel crouches and lies down; / like a
Dt 33:20 Gad is poised there like a l / to tear off an arm
Jdg 14:5 a young l attacked Samson near the vineyards of
14:8 he turned off the path to look at the carcass of the l.
14:9 he had taken the honey from the carcass of the l.
14:18 What is stronger than a l?" / Samson replied,
1Sa 17:34 "When a l or a bear comes to steal a lamb from the
17:37 The LORD who saved me from the claws of the l
2Sa 17:10 though they have the heart of a l, will be paralyzed
23:20 Another time he chased a l down into a pit. Then,
23:20 and slippery ground, he caught the l and killed it.
1Ki 10:19 with the figure of a l standing on each side of the
10:20 Solomon made twelve other l figures, one standing
13:24 was traveling along, a l came out and killed him.
13:24 with the donkey and the l standing beside it.
13:25 body lying in the road and the l standing beside it,
13:26 The LORD has fulfilled his word by causing the l
13:28 and l were still standing there beside it,
13:28 for the l had not eaten the body nor attacked the
20:36 a l will kill you as soon as you leave me."
20:36 when he had gone, a l attacked and killed him.
1Ch 11:22 Another time he chased a l down into a pit. Then,
11:22 and slippery ground, he caught the l and killed it.
2Ch 9:18 with the figure of a l standing on each side of the
9:19 Solomon made twelve other l figures, one standing
Job 4:11 The fierce l will starve, and the cubs of the lioness
10:16 you hunt me like a l and display your awesome
28:8 upon those treasures; no l has set his paw there.
Ps 7:2 If you don't, they will maul me like a l,
Pr 22:13 I might meet a l in the street and be killed!"
26:13 go outside because there might be a l on the road! Yes, I'm sure there's a l out there!"
28:15 A wicked ruler is as dangerous to the poor as a l
30:30 the l, king of animals, who won't turn aside for
Ecc 9:4 "It is better to be a live dog than a dead l!"
Isa 31:4 "When a l, even a young one, kills a sheep,
65:25 will feed together. The l will eat straw like the ox.
Jer 2:30 You yourselves have killed your prophets as a l
4:7 A l stalks from its den, a destroyer of nations.
5:6 So now a l from the forest will attack them; a wolf
12:8 My chosen people have roared at me like a l of the
25:38 He has left his den like a l seeking its prey,
49:19 I will come like a l from the thickets of the Jordan,
50:44 "I will come like a l from the thickets of the
La 3:10 He hid like a bear or a l, waiting to attack me.
Eze 1:10 the face of a l on the right side, the face of an ox on
10:14 was a human face, the third was the face of a l,
19:3 to become a strong young l. / He learned to catch
19:5 'When the mother l saw / that all her hopes for him
19:5 of her cubs / and taught him to be a strong l.
32:2 You think of yourself as a strong young l among
41:19 The other face—that of a young l—looked toward
Da 7:4 The first beast was like a l with eagles' wings.
Hos 5:14 tear at Israel and Judah as a l rips apart its prey.
11:10 I will roar like a l, and my people will return
13:7 So now I will attack you like a l, or like a leopard
13:8 will tear you apart and devour you like a hungry l.
Am 3:4 Does a l ever roar in a thicket without first finding
3:4 Does a young l growl in its den without first
3:8 The l has roared—tremble in fear! The Sovereign
5:19 day you will be like a man who runs from a l—
Mic 5:8 go out among the nations and be as strong as a l.
Na 2:11 l of the nations, full of fight and boldness,
2:12 O Nineveh, you were once a mighty l!
1Pe 5:8 He prowls around like a roaring l, looking for
Rev 4:7 The first of these living beings had the form of a l;
5:5 Look, the L of the tribe of Judah, the heir to
9:8 a woman, and their teeth were like the teeth of a l.
10:3 And he gave a great shout, like the roar of a l.

LION'S (6) [LION]

Dt 33:22 "Dan is a l cub, / leaping out from Bashan."
Jdg 14:6 and he ripped the l jaws apart with his bare hands.
Pr 19:12 The king's anger is like a l roar, but his favor is
20:2 The king's fury is like a l roar; to rouse his anger is
Am 3:12 "A shepherd who tries to rescue a sheep from a l
Rev 13:2 like a leopard, but it had bear's feet and a l mouth!

LIONESS (6) [LION]

Ge 49:9 lies down; / like a l—who will dare to rouse him?
Nu 23:24 These people rise up like a l; / like a majestic lion
24:9 and lies down; / like a l, who dares to arouse her?
Job 4:11 will starve, and the cubs of the l will be scattered.
38:39 "Can you stalk prey for a l and satisfy the young
Eze 19:2 'What is your mother? / A l among lions! / She lay

LIONLIKE [KJV] See (MIGHTIEST) WARRIORS

LIONS (48) [LION]

1Sa 17:36 I have done this to both l and bears, and I'll do it to
2Sa 1:23 swifter than eagles; / they were stronger than l.
1Ki 7:29 and the crossbars were decorated with carved l,
7:29 Above and below the l and oxen were wreath
7:36 Carvings of cherubim, l, and palm trees decorated
2Ki 17:25 the LORD sent l among them to kill some of
17:26 He has sent l among them to destroy them
1Ch 12:8 as fierce as l and as swift as deer on the mountains.
Job 4:10 Though they are fierce young l, they will all be
Ps 10:9 Like l they crouch silently, / waiting to pounce on
17:12 They are like hungry l, eager to tear me apart—
17:12 like young l in hiding, waiting for their chance.
22:13 Like roaring l attacking their prey, / they come at
34:10 Even strong young l sometimes go hungry,
35:17 their fierce attacks. / Protect my life from these l!

57: 4 I am surrounded by fierce l / who greedily devour
58: 6 O God! / Smash the jaws of these l, O LORD!
91: 13 You will trample down l and poisonous snakes;
91: 13 you will crush fierce l and serpents under your
104: 21 Then the young l roar for their food, / but they are
Pr 28: 1 one is chasing them, but the godly are as bold as l.
SS 4: 8 where l have their dens and panthers prowl.
Isa 5: 29 Roaring like l, they will pounce on their prey.
11: 6 Calves and yearlings will be safe among l, and a
11: 7 And l will eat grass as the livestock do.
15: 9 L will hunt down the survivors, both those who try
30: 6 they go, where l and poisonous snakes live.
35: 9 L will not lurk along its course, and there will be
38: 13 all night, / but I was torn apart as though by l.
Jer 2: 15 L have roared against her. The land has been
50: 17 are like sheep that have been scattered by l.
51: 38 drunken feasts, the people of Babylon roar like l.
Eze 19: 2 'What is your mother? / A lioness among l!
19: 2 She lay down among the young l / and reared her
19: 6 He prowled among the other l / and became a
22: 25 Your princes plot conspiracies just as l stalk their
Da 6: 7 except to Your Majesty—will be thrown to the l.
6: 12 except to Your Majesty—will be thrown to the l?"
6: 16 Daniel to be arrested and thrown into the den of l.
6: 17 so that no one could rescue Daniel from the l.
6: 20 able to rescue you from the l?"
6: 24 The l leaped on them and tore them apart before
6: 27 He has rescued Daniel / from the power of the l."
Joel 1: 6 to count! Its teeth are as sharp as the teeth of l!
Zep 3: 3 Its leaders are like roaring l hunting for their
Zec 11: 3 Hear the young l roaring, for their thickets in the
Heb 11: 33 had promised them. They shut the mouths of l,
Rev 9: 17 The horses' heads were like the heads of l, and fire

LIONS' (5) [LION]

Job 38: 39 prey for a lioness and satisfy the young l appetites
Ps 22: 21 Snatch me from the l jaws, / and from the horns of
Da 6: 19 the next morning, the king hurried out to the l den.
6: 22 My God sent his angel to shut the l mouths so that
6: 24 He had them thrown into the l den, along with their

LIPS (50)

Ex 13: 9 LORD's instructions in your minds and on your l.
Dt 30: 14 it is on your l and in your heart so that you can
1Sa 1: 13 Seeing her l moving but hearing no sound,
Job 8: 21 mouth with laughter and your l with shouts of joy.
27: 4 my l will speak no evil, and my tongue will speak
Ps 12: 2 speaking with flattering l and insincere hearts.
12: 4 Our l are our own—who can stop us?"
31: 18 May their lying l be silenced— / those proud and
arrogant l that accuse the godly.
34: 13 watch your tongue! / Keep your l from telling lies!
45: 2 of all. / Gracious words stream from your l.
51: 15 Unseal my l, O Lord, / that I may praise you.
59: 7 the piercing swords that fly from their l.
59: 12 they say, / because of the evil that is on their l,
119: 171 Let my l burst forth with praise, / for you have
140: 3 a snake; / the poison of a viper drips from their l.
141: 3 of what I say, O LORD, / and keep my l sealed.
Pr 5: 3 The l of an immoral woman are as sweet as honey,
10: 13 Wise words come from the l of people with
16: 13 The king is pleased with righteous l; he loves those
18: 7 of fools are their ruin; their l get them into trouble.
18: 20 the right words on a person's l bring satisfaction.
22: 18 deep within yourself, always ready on your l.
Ecc 12: 4 are gone, keep your l tightly closed when you eat!
SS 4: 3 Your l are like a ribbon of scarlet. Oh,
4: 11 Your l, my bride, are as sweet as honey. Yes,
5: 13 His l are like perfumed lilies. His breath is like
7: 9 and sweet, flowing gently over l and teeth."
Isa 6: 7 He touched my l with it and said, "See, this coal
has touched your l.
29: 13 They honor me with their l, but their hearts are far
30: 27 His l are filled with fury; his words consume like
57: 19 Then words of praise will be on their l. May they
59: 3 full of lies, and your l are tainted with corruption.
59: 21 They will be on your l and on the l of your children
60: 18 and praise will be on the l of all who enter there.
Jer 7: 28 from among them; it is no longer heard on their l.
12: 2 Your name is on their l, but in their hearts they
Da 10: 16 Then the one who looked like a man touched my l,
Hab 3: 16 when I heard all this; my l quivered with fear.
Zep 3: 9 "On that day I will purify the l of all people,
Mal 2: 7 The priests' l should guard knowledge, and people
Mk 7: 7 'These people honor me with their l, / but their
Lk 4: 22 amazed by the gracious words that fell from his l.
Jn 19: 29 put it on a hyssop branch, and held it up to his l.
Ro 3: 13 "The poison of a deadly snake drips from their l."
10: 8 is close at hand; it is on your l and in your heart."
1Co 14: 21 and through the l of foreigners. / But even then,
1Pe 3: 10 speaking evil, / and keep your l from telling lies.

LIQUID (1) [LIQUIDS]

Eze 45: 10 volume measures, and honest l volume measures.

LIQUIDS (1) [LIQUID]

Lev 19: 36 for measuring dry goods or l must be accurate.

LIQUOR (5)

Pr 20: 1 Wine produces mockers; l leads to brawls.
31: 4 to guzzle wine. Rulers should not crave l.
31: 6 L is for the dying, and wine for those in deep
Isa 5: 22 who boast about all the l they can hold.
Lk 1: 15 He must never touch wine or hard l, and he will be

LIQUOR [KJV] See also JUICE, WINE

LIST (26) [LISTED, LISTING, LISTINGS, LISTS]

Ge 25: 13 Here is a l, by their names and clans, of Ishmael's
36: 9 This is a l of Esau's descendants, the Edomites,
49: 3 You are first on the l in rank and honor.
Ex 6: 26 and Moses named in this l are the same Aaron
25: 3 Here is a l of items you may accept on my behalf:
Nu 1: 2 and families. L the names of all the men
31: 26 and the family leaders of each tribe are to make a l
Jos 12: 7 The following is a l of the kings Joshua
1Ch 12: 20 Here is a l of the men from Manasseh who
25: 1 Here is a l of their names and their work:
27: 1 This is the l of Israelite generals and captains,
2Ch 33: 19 a l of the locations where he built pagan shrines
Ezr 2: 1 Here is the l of the Jewish exiles of the provinces
5: 4 They also asked for a l of the names of all the
8: 1 Here is a l of the family leaders
Ne 7: 6 "Here is the l of the Jewish exiles of the provinces
11: 3 Here is a l of the names of the provincial officials
12: 1 Here is the l of the priests and Levites who had
12: 22 a l was compiled of the family leaders of the
Ps 40: 5 for us. / Your plans for us are too numerous to l.
106: 2 Who can l the glorious miracles of the LORD?
Eze 48: 1 "Here is the l of the tribes of Israel
Ac 1: 13 Here is the l of those who were present: / Peter,
1Co 12: 28 Here is a l of some of the members that God has
1Ti 5: 9 A widow who is put on the l for support must be a
5: 11 The younger widows should not be on the l,

LISTED (29) [LIST]

Ge 10: 32 l nation by nation according to their lines of
25: 16 l according to the places they settled and camped.
Ex 6: 16 of Levi, l according to their family groups.
6: 19 of the Levites, l according to their genealogies.
6: 25 the Levite clans, l according to their family groups.
Nu 1: 20[-21] each l according to his own clan and family:
1: 44 of Israel, all l according to their ancestral descent.
2: 32 the troops of Israel l by their families totaled
3: 20 the Levite clans, l according to their family groups.
11: 26 They were l among the leaders but had not gone
Dt 30: 1 to you—the blessings and the curses I have l—
1Ch 5: 1 Reuben is not l in the genealogy as the firstborn
5: 7 Beerah's relatives are l in their genealogy by their
5: 17 All of these were l in the genealogical records
6: 19 Levite clans, l according to their ancestral descent:
7: 5 All of them were l in their tribal genealogy.
7: 7 All of them were l in their family genealogy.
7: 40 among the descendants l in their tribal genealogy.
8: 28 and they were l in their tribal genealogy.
9: 1 All Israel was l in the genealogical record in *The*
9: 9 of clans, and they were l in their tribal genealogy.
9: 22 and they were l by genealogies in their villages.
9: 34 and were l as prominent leaders in their tribal
2Ch 31: 17 And they distributed gifts to the priests who were l
31: 17 or older who were l according to their jobs
31: 18 to all the families l in the genealogical records,
31: 19 and to all the Levites l in the genealogical records.
Ezr 8: 20 instituted by King David. They were all l by name.
Mt 1: 17 All those l above include fourteen generations

LISTEN (529) [LISTENED, LISTENERS, LISTENING, LISTENS]

Ge 4: 10 L—your brother's blood cries out to me from the
4: 23 said to Adah and Zillah, "L to me, my wives.
23: 11 "No, sir," he said to Abraham, "please l to me.
23: 13 "No, l to me," he insisted. "I will buy it from
37: 6 "L to this dream," he announced.
37: 9 "L to this dream," he said. "The sun, moon,
42: 21 and heard his pleadings, but we wouldn't l.
42: 22 Reuben asked. "But you wouldn't l. And now we
49: 2 "Come and l, O sons of Jacob; / l to Israel, your
father.
Ex 5: 2 "And who is the LORD that I should l to him
5: 9 That will teach them to l to these liars!"
6: 9 the LORD had said, but they wouldn't l anymore.
6: 12 "My own people won't l to me anymore.
6: 12 How can I expect Pharaoh to l? I'm no orator!"
6: 30 I'm no orator. Why should Pharaoh l to me?"
7: 4 Even then Pharaoh will refuse to l to you. So I will
7: 13 He still refused to l, just as the LORD had
7: 16 Until now, you have refused to l to him.
7: 22 He refused to l to Moses and Aaron, just as the
8: 2 If you refuse, then l carefully to this: I will send
8: 15 He refused to l to Moses and Aaron, just as the
8: 19 He wouldn't l to them, just as the LORD had
9: 12 and he refused to l, just as the LORD had
11: 9 had told Moses, "Pharaoh will not l to you.
15: 26 "If you will l carefully to the voice of the LORD
16: 20 some of them didn't l and kept some of it until
20: 19 "You tell us what God says, and we will l.
Lev 26: 14 if you do not l to me or obey my commands,
26: 27 "If after this you still refuse to l and still remain
Nu 12: 6 And the LORD said to them, "Now l to me!
14: 22 but again and again they tested me by refusing to l.
16: 8 Moses spoke again to Korah: "Now l, you Levites!
20: 10 gather at the rock. "L, you rebels!" he shouted.
23: 18 "Rise up, Balak, and l! / Hear me, son of Zippor.
Dt 1: 43 This is what I told you, but you would not l.
1: 45 and wept before the LORD, but he refused to l.
3: 26 with me because of you, and he would not l to me.
4: 1 l carefully to these laws and regulations that I am
4: 30 to the LORD your God and l to what he tells you.
5: 1 "L carefully to all the laws and regulations I am
5: 27 You go and l to what the LORD our God says.
5: 27 us everything he tells you, and we will l and obey.'
6: 3 L closely, Israel, to everything I say. Be careful to
7: 12 "If you l to these regulations and obey them
11: 2 L! I am not talking now to your children, who have
13: 3 do not l to them. The LORD your God is testing
13: 4 his commands, l to his voice, and cling to him.
13: 8 If they do this, do not give in or l, and have no
18: 15 fellow Israelites, and you must l to that prophet.
18: 16 You begged that you might never again have to l to
18: 19 I will personally deal with anyone who will not l to
20: 3 He will say, 'L to me, all you men of Israel!
23: 5 (But the LORD your God would not l to Balaam.
27: 9 all Israel as follows: "O Israel, be quiet and l!
28: 13 If you l to these commands of the LORD your
28: 15 "But if you refuse to l to the LORD your God
28: 45 "If you refuse to l to the LORD your God and to
28: 62 because you would not l to the LORD your God.
30: 15 "Now l! Today I am giving you a choice between
30: 17 But if your heart turns away and you refuse to l,
31: 12 so they may l and learn to fear the LORD your
32: 1 "L, O heavens, and I will speak! / Hear, O earth,
Jos 3: 9 "Come and l to what the LORD your God says.
24: 10 but I would not l to him. Instead, I made Balaam
Jdg 2: 17 Yet Israel did not l to the judges but prostituted
5: 3 "L, you kings! / Pay attention, you mighty rulers!
5: 10 and sit on fancy saddle blankets, l! / And you who
must walk along the road, l!
5: 11 L to the village musicians gathered at the watering
7: 11 L to what the Midianites are saying, and you will
9: 7 the top of Mount Gerizim and shouted, "L to me,
9: 7 L to me if you want God to l to you!
19: 25 But they wouldn't l to him. Then the Levite took
20: 13 this evil." But the people of Benjamin would not l.
Ru 2: 8 went over and said to Ruth, "L, my daughter.
1Sa 2: 25 But Eli's sons wouldn't l to their father,
8: 19 But the people refused to l to Samuel's warning.
12: 14 and worship the LORD and l to his voice,
12: 15 the LORD's commands and refuse to l to him,
15: 1 me to. Now l to this message from the LORD!
15: 16 "Stop! L to what the LORD told me last night!"
22: 7 "L here, you men of Benjamin!" Saul shouted
22: 12 When they arrived, Saul shouted at him, "L to me,
24: 9 "Why do you l to the people who say I am trying
25: 24 this matter, my lord. Please l to what I have to say.
26: 19 But now let my lord the king l to his servant.
30: 24 Do you think anyone will l to you when you talk
2Sa 13: 14 But Amnon wouldn't l to her, and since he was
13: 16 done to me." But Amnon wouldn't l to her.
14: 15 I said to myself, 'Perhaps the king will l to me
20: 16 in the city called out to Joab, "L to me, Joab.
20: 17 So she said, "L carefully to your servant."
1Ki 4: 34 their ambassadors to l to the wisdom of Solomon.
8: 28 L to my prayer and my request, O LORD my
11: 10 but Solomon did not l to the LORD's command.
11: 38 If you l to what I tell you and follow my ways
22: 19 Micaiah continued, "L to what the LORD says!
2Ki 14: 11 But Amaziah refused to l, so King Jehoash of
17: 14 But the Israelites would not l. They were as
17: 40 But the people would not l and continued to follow
18: 12 For they had refused to l to the LORD their God.
18: 28 "L to this message from the great king of Assyria!
18: 31 "Don't l to Hezekiah! These are the terms the king
18: 32 "Don't l to Hezekiah when he tries to mislead you
19: 7 L! I myself will move against him, and the king
19: 16 L to me, O LORD, and hear! Open your eyes,
19: 16 L to Sennacherib's words of defiance against the
20: 16 to Hezekiah, "L to this message from the LORD:
21: 9 But the people refused to l, and Manasseh led them
2Ch 6: 19 L to my prayer and my request, O LORD my
7: 15 I will l to every prayer made in this place,
13: 4 to Jeroboam and the Israelite army: "L to me!
15: 2 "L to me, Asa!" he shouted. "L, all you people of
Judah and Benjamin!
18: 18 Micaiah continued, "L to what the LORD says!
20: 15 He said, "L, King Jehoshaphat! L, all you people
of Judah and Jerusalem!
20: 20 the way Jehoshaphat stopped and said, "L to me,
24: 17 and persuaded the king to l to their advice.
24: 19 bring them back to him, but the people would not l.
25: 20 But Amaziah would not l, for God was arranging
28: 11 L to me and return these captives you have taken,
29: 5 He said to them, "L to me, you Levites!
35: 22 But Josiah refused to l to Neco, to whom God had
Ne 1: 6 l to my prayer! Look down and see me praying
1: 11 L to the prayers of those of us who delight in
9: 17 "They refused to l and did not remember the
9: 29 turned their backs on you and refused to l.
9: 30 them about their sins. But still they wouldn't l!
9: 34 or l to your commands and solemn warnings.
Job 5: 27 is true. L to my counsel, and apply it to yourself."
9: 16 and he responded, he would never l to me.
11: 6 for true wisdom is not a simple matter. L!
13: 6 L to my charge; pay attention to my arguments.
13: 17 "L closely to what I am about to say. Hear me out.
15: 17 "If you will l, I will answer you from my own
21: 2 "L closely to what I am saying. You can console
22: 22 L to his instructions, and store them in your heart.
23: 5 Then I would l to his reply and understand what he
27: 9 Will God l to their cry when trouble comes upon
31: 35 "If only I had someone who would l to me and try
32: 10 So l to me and let me express my opinion.
33: 1 "L, Job, to what I have to say.
33: 31 Mark this well, Job. L to me, and let me say more.
33: 33 But if not, then l to me. Keep silent and I will teach
34: 2 "L to me, you wise men. Pay attention, you who
34: 10 "L to me, you who have understanding.
34: 16 "L now and try to understand.

35:13 But it is wrong to say God doesn't l, to say the
36:11 "If they l and obey God, then they will be blessed
36:12 But if they refuse to l to him, they will perish in
37: 2 L carefully to the thunder of God's voice as it rolls
37:14 "L, Job; stop and consider the wonderful miracles
42: 4 "You said, 'L and I will speak! I have some
Ps 5: 2 L to my cry for help, my King and my God,
5: 3 L to my voice in the morning, LORD.
10:17 Surely you will l to their cries and comfort them.
17: 1 hear my plea for justice. / L to my cry for help.
17: 6 will answer, O God. / Bend down and l as I pray.
17:10 They are without pity. / L to their boasting.
27: 7 L to my pleading, O LORD. / Be merciful
28: 2 L to my prayer for mercy / as I cry out to you for
31: 2 Bend down and l to me; / rescue me quickly.
34:11 Come, my children, and l to me, / and I will teach
39:12 my prayer, O LORD! / L to my cries for help!
40: 6 Now that you have made me l, I finally
45:10 L to me, O royal daughter; take to heart what I say.
49: 1 L to this, all you people! / Pay attention,
49: 2 High and low, / rich and poor—l!
49: 4 I l carefully to many proverbs / and solve riddles
50: 7 "O my people, l as I speak. / Here are my charges
54: 2 O God, l to my prayer. / Pay attention to my plea.
55: 1 L to my prayer, O God. / Do not ignore my cry for
55: 2 Please l and answer me, / for I am overwhelmed by
58: 4 they are like cobras that refuse to l,
59: 7 L to the filth that comes from their mouths,
61: 1 O God, l to my cry! / Hear my prayer!
64: 1 O God, l to my complaint. / Do not let my
66:16 Come and l, all you who fear God, / and I will tell
66:19 But God did l! / He paid attention to my prayer.
71: 2 you are just. / Turn your ear to l and set me free.
77: 1 holding back. / Oh, that God would l to me!
78: 1 O my people, l to my teaching. / Open your ears to
79:11 L to the moaning of the prisoners.
80: 1 Please l, O Shepherd of Israel, / you who lead
81: 8 "L to me, O my people, while I give you stern
warnings. / O Israel, if you would only l!
81:11 "But no, my people wouldn't l. / Israel did not
81:13 But oh, that my people would l to me! / Oh,
84: 8 hear my prayer. / L, O God of Israel. / *Interlude*
85: 8 I l carefully to what God the LORD is saying,
86: 6 L closely to my prayer, O LORD; / hear my
88: 2 Now hear my prayer; / l to my cry.
95: 7 his care. / Oh, that you would l to his voice today!
102: 1 LORD, hear my prayer! / L to my plea!
102:17 He will l to the prayers of the destitute. / He will
119:169 O LORD, l to my cry; / give me the discerning
119:170 L to my prayer; / rescue me as you promised.
140: 6 my God!" / L, O LORD, to my cries for mercy!
141: 1 Please hurry! / L when I cry to you for help!
141: 6 they will l to my words and find them pleasing.
143: 1 Hear my prayer, O LORD; / l to my plea!
Pr 1: 5 Let those who are wise l to these proverbs
1: 8 L, my child, to what your father teaches you.
1:23 Come here and l to me! I'll pour out the spirit of
1:33 But all who l to me will live in peace and safety,
2: 1 My child, l to me and treasure my instructions.
4: 1 My children, l to me. L to your father's instruction.
4:10 My child, l to me and do as I say, and you will
4:20 Pay attention, my child, to what I say. L carefully.
5: 1 to my wisdom; l carefully to my wise counsel.
5: 7 So now, my sons, l to me. Never stray from what I
5:13 Oh, why didn't I l to my teachers? Why didn't I
7:24 L to me, my sons, and pay attention to my words.
8: 1 L as wisdom calls out! Hear as understanding
8: 6 L to me! For I have excellent things to tell you.
8:32 "And so, my children, l to me, for happy are all
8:33 L to my counsel and be wise. Don't ignore it.
8:34 "Happy are those who l to me, watching for me
12:15 think they need no advice, but the wise l to others.
13: 1 a parent's discipline; a young mocker refuses to l.
15:31 If you l to constructive criticism, you will be at
15:32 but if you l to correction, you grow in
16:20 Those who l to instruction will prosper; those who
17: 4 Wrongdoers l to wicked talk; liars pay attention to
22:17 L to the words of the wise; apply your heart to my
23:19 My child, l and be wise. Keep your heart on the
23:22 L to your father, who gave you life, and don't
Ecc 10:12 It is pleasant to l to wise words, but the speech of
SS 8:13 how wonderful that your companions can l to your
Isa 1: 2 Hear, O heavens! L, O earth! This is what the
1:10 L to the LORD, you leaders of Israel! L to the law
1:15 Even though you offer many prayers, I will not l.
1:20 But if you keep turning away and refusing to l,
7:13 Then Isaiah said, "L well, you royal family of
8: 9 L all you nations. Prepare for battle—and die!
8:19 Do not l to their whisperings and mutterings.
10:16 L now, king of Assyria! Because of all your evil
13: 4 L, as the armies march! It is the noise
18: 3 the world take notice. When I blow the trumpet, l!
19:22 and he will l to their pleas and heal them.
24:16 L to them as they sing to the LORD from the
26:11 O LORD, they do not l when you threaten.
28:11 Since they refuse to l, God will speak to them
28:12 if they would only obey him, but they will not l.
28:14 Therefore, l to this message from the LORD,
28:23 L to me; l as I plead!
32: 3 for God, and those who can hear will l to his voice.
32: 9 L, you women who lie around in lazy ease.
32: 9 L to me, and I will tell you of your reward.
33:13 L to what I have done, you nations far away!
33:15 who refuse to l to those who plot murder,
34: 1 Come here and l, O nations of the earth.
36:13 "L to this message from the great king of Assyria!
36:16 "Don't l to Hezekiah! These are the terms the king
37: 7 L! I myself will make sure that the king will
37:17 L to me, O LORD, and hear! Open your eyes,
37:17 L to Sennacherib's words of defiance against the
39: 5 "L to this message from the LORD Almighty:
40: 3 L! I hear the voice of someone shouting, "Make a
41: 1 "L in silence before me, you lands beyond the sea.
42:18 Why won't you l? Why do you refuse to see?
42:20 to act on it. You hear, but you don't really l."
44: 1 "But now, l to me, Jacob my servant, Israel my
46: 3 "L to me, all you who are left in Israel. I created
46:12 L to me, you stubborn, evil people!
48: 1 "L to me, O family of Jacob, who are called by the
48: 1 L, you who take oaths in the name of the LORD
48:12 "L to me, O family of Jacob, Israel my chosen
48:14 Come, all of you, and l: 'The LORD has chosen
48:16 Come closer and l. I have always told you plainly
49: 1 L to me, all of you in far-off lands! The LORD
51: 1 "L to me, all who hope for deliverance—all who
51: 4 "L to me, my people. Hear me, Israel, for my law
51: 7 "L to me, you who know right from wrong
51:21 But now l to this, you afflicted ones, who sit in a
55: 2 L, and I will tell you where to get food that is good
55: 3 wide open. L, for the life of your soul is at stake.
59: 1 L! The LORD is not too weak to save you,
59: 2 he has turned away and will not l anymore.
65:12 you did not answer. When I spoke, you did not l.
66: 4 they did not answer. When I spoke, they did not l.
Jer 1:15 L! I am calling the armies of the kingdoms of the
2: 4 L to the word of the LORD, people of Jacob—
2:31 "O my people, l to the words of the LORD!
5:21 L, you foolish and senseless people—who have
6: 8 Jerusalem! If you do not l, I will empty the land."
6:10 Who will l when I speak? Their ears are closed,
6:10 word of the LORD. They don't want to l at all.
6:17 you who said, 'L for the sound of the trumpet!'
6:18 "Therefore, l to this, all you nations. Take note of
6:19 L, all the earth! I will bring disaster upon my
6:19 of their own sin because they refuse to l to me.
7: 2 'O Judah, l to this message from the LORD! L to it,
all of you who worship here!
7:13 to you about it repeatedly, but you would not l.
7:16 don't beg me to help them, for I will not l to you.
7:24 "But my people would not l to me. They kept on
7:27 "Tell them all this, but do not expect them to l.
8: 6 I l to their conversations, and what do I hear?
8:19 L to the weeping of my people; it can be heard all
9:15 So now, l to what the LORD Almighty, the God
9:20 L, you women, to the words of the LORD;
10:22 L! Hear the terrifying roar of great armies as they
11: 8 did not pay any attention; they would not even l.
11:10 They have refused to l to me and are worshiping
11:11 they beg for mercy, I will not l to their cries.
11:14 for I will not l to them when they cry out to me in
13:10 These wicked people refuse to l to me.
13:11 an honor to my name. But they would not l to me.
13:15 L! Do not be proud, for the LORD has spoken.
13:17 And if you still refuse to l, I will weep alone
16:12 follow your own evil desires and refuse to l to me.
17:20 'L to this message from the LORD, you kings of
17:21 what the LORD says: L to my warning and live!
17:23 but they did not l or obey. They stubbornly refused
17:27 " 'But if you do not l to me and refuse to keep the
18:19 help me! L to what they are planning to do to me!
19: 3 Say to them, 'L to this message from the LORD,
19:15 because you have stubbornly refused to l to me."
21:11 of Judah, 'L to this message from the LORD!
22: 2 'L to this message from the LORD, you king of
22: 2 Let your officials and your people l, too.
22:21 you have been that way—you simply will not l!
22:29 earth, earth! L to this message from the LORD!
23:16 "Do not l to these prophets when they prophesy to
23:18 is saying? Has even one of them cared enough to l?
23:25 'L to the dream I had from God last night.'
25: 7 "But you would not l to me," says the LORD.
25:36 L to the frantic cries of the shepherds,
26: 3 Perhaps they will l and turn from their evil ways.
26: 4 If you will not l to me and obey the law I have
26: 5 and if you will not l to my servants, the prophets—
26: 5 again to warn you, but you would not l to them—
27: 9 " 'Do not l to your false prophets, fortune-tellers,
27:14 Do not l to the false prophets who keep telling you,
27:16 Do not l to your prophets who claim that soon the
27:17 Do not l to them. Surrender to the king of Babylon,
28: 7 But l now to the solemn words I speak to you in
28:15 the prophet said to Hananiah, "L, Hananiah!
29: 8 in Babylon trick you. Do not l to their dreams
29:12 In those days when you pray, I will l.
29:19 For they refuse to l to me, though I have spoken to
29:20 Therefore, l to this message from the LORD,
31:10 "L to this message from the LORD, you nations
32:33 right from wrong, but they would not l or obey.
34: 4 "But l to this promise from the LORD,
35:14 to you again and again, and you refuse to l or obey.
35:15 your ancestors. But you would not l to me or obey.
35:16 but you have refused to l to me.'
35:17 Because you refuse to l or answer when I call,
36:25 the king not to burn the scroll, he wouldn't l.
36:31 for they would not l to my warnings.' "
37:14 But Irijah wouldn't l, and he took Jeremiah before
37:20 L, my lord the king, I beg you. Don't send me
38:15 if I give you advice, you won't l to me anyway."
42:19 "L, you remnant of Judah. The LORD has told
44: 5 But my people would not l or turn back from their
44:16 "We will not l to your messages from the LORD!
44:24 the women, "L to this message from the LORD,
44:26 "But l to this message from the LORD, all you
49:20 L to the LORD's plans for Edom and the people
50:24 L, Babylon, for I have set a trap for you. You are
50:28 L to the people who have escaped from Babylon,
50:45 L to the LORD's plans against Babylon
51:45 "L, my people, flee from Babylon.
51:54 L! Hear the cry of Babylon, the sound of great
La 1:18 L, people everywhere; look upon my anguish
Eze 2: 5 And whether they l or not—for remember, they are
2: 7 You must give them my messages whether they l
2: 7 But they won't l, for they are completely
2: 8 Son of man, l to what I say to you. Do not join
3: 6 and difficult speech. If I did, they would l!
3: 7 but they won't l to you any more than they l to
3:10 own heart first. L to them carefully for yourself.
3:11 Do this whether they l to you or not."
3:20 If good people turn bad and don't l to my warning,
3:27 Some of them will l, but some will ignore you,
8:18 And though they scream for mercy, I will not l."
12: 2 They could hear me if they would l, but they won't
l because they are rebellious.
13: 2 Tell them to l to the word of the LORD.
13:19 By lying to my people who love to l to lies,
16:35 you prostitute, l to this message from the LORD!
18:25 Lord isn't being just!' L to me, O people of Israel.
20: 8 "But they rebelled against me and would not l.
20:31 Should I l to you or help you, O people of Israel?
33: 5 They heard the warning but wouldn't l,
33: 7 Therefore, l to what I say and warn them for me.
37: 4 and say, 'Dry bones, l to the word of the LORD!
40: 4 He said to me, "Son of man, watch and l.
44: 5 L to everything I tell you about the regulations
Da 3: 4 and languages, l to the king's command!
4:27 "O King Nebuchadnezzar, please l to me.
9: 6 We have refused to l to your servants the prophets,
9:11 and turned away, refusing to l to your voice.
9:17 L as I plead. For your own sake, Lord, smile again
9:18 "O my God, l to me and hear my request.
9:19 "O Lord, hear. O Lord, forgive. O Lord, l and act!
9:23 Now l, so you can understand the meaning of your
9:25 Now l and understand! Seven sets of seven plus
10:11 of God, l carefully to what I have to say to you.
Hos 5: 1 Israel's leaders! L, all you men of the royal family!
9:17 the people of Israel because they will not l or obey.
14: 9 Let those who are discerning l carefully. The paths
Joel 1: 2 Everyone l! In all your history, has anything like
1: 9 L to the weeping of these ministers of the LORD!
2: 5 L to the noise they make—like the rumbling of
Am 3: 1 L to this message that the LORD has spoken
3:13 Now l to this, and announce it throughout all
4: 1 L to me, you "fat cows" of Samaria, you women
5: 1 L, you people of Israel! L to this funeral song I am
5:23 I will not l to your music, no matter how lovely it
7:16 "Now then, l to this message from the LORD!
7:17 Because you have refused to l, your wife will
8: 4 L to this, you who rob the poor and trample the
Mic 1: 2 Attention! Let all the people of the world l!
3: 1 L, you leaders of Israel! You are supposed to know
3: 4 Do you really expect him to l? After all the evil
3: 9 L to me, you leaders of Israel! You hate justice
6: 1 L to what the LORD is saying: "Stand up
6: 2 O mountains, l to the LORD's complaint!
6: 9 L! Fear the LORD if you are wise! His voice is
Na 2: 7 L to them moan like doves; watch them beat their
3: 2 L! Hear the crack of the whips as the chariots rush
Hab 1: 2 But you do not l! "Violence!" I cry, but you do
Zep 3: 2 It proudly refuses to l even to the voice of the
3: 7 Surely they will l to my warnings, so I won't need
Zec 1: 4 Do not be like your ancestors who would not l
3: 8 L to me, O Jeshua the high priest, and all you other
7:11 "Your ancestors would not l to this message.
7:13 "Since they refused to l when I called to them,
7:13 I would not l when they called to me,
11: 3 L to the wailing of the shepherds, for their wealth
Mal 2: 1 "L, you priests; this command is for you!
2: 2 L to me and take it to heart. Honor my name,"
Mt 10:14 If a village doesn't welcome you or l to you,
11:15 Anyone who is willing to hear should l
12:42 than Solomon is here—and you refuse to l to him.
13: 9 Anyone who is willing to hear should l
13:43 Anyone who is willing to hear should l
15:10 and said, "L to what I say and try to understand.
17: 5 and I am fully pleased with him. L to him."
18:17 If that person still refuses to l, take your case to the
21:33 "Now l to this story. A certain landowner planted
Mk 4: 3 "L! A farmer went out to plant some seed.
4: 9 "Anyone who is willing to hear should l
4:23 Anyone who is willing to hear should l
6:11 "And if a village won't welcome you or l to you,
6:20 talked with John, but even so, he liked to l to him.
7:14 "All of you l," he said, "and try to understand.
8:34 his disciples and the crowds to come over and l.
9: 7 cloud said, "This is my beloved Son. L to him."
11:24 L to me! You can pray for anything, and if you
Lk 5: 1 great crowds pressed in on him to l to the word of
6:27 "But if you are willing to l, I say, love your
8: 8 "Anyone who is willing to hear should l
9:35 "This is my Son, my Chosen One. L to him."
9:44 "L to me and remember what I say. The Son of
11:31 than Solomon is here—and you refuse to l to him.
14:35 Anyone who is willing to hear should l
15: 1 and other notorious sinners often came to l to Jesus
16:31 'If they won't l to Moses and the prophets,
16:31 they won't l even if someone rises from the
Jn 5:24 those who l to my message and believe in God
5:25 voice of the Son of God. And those who l will live.
5:33 you sent messengers to l to John the Baptist,
9:27 the man exclaimed. "I told you once. Didn't you l?
9:31 Well, God doesn't l to sinners, but he is ready to

10: 8 and robbers. But the true sheep did not l to them.
10:16 I must bring them also, and they will l to my voice;
10:20 a demon, or he's crazy. Why l to a man like that?"
15:20 if they had listened to me, they would l to you!
Ac 2:14 "L carefully, all of you, fellow Jews and residents
2:22 "People of Israel, l! God publicly endorsed Jesus
3:22 L carefully to everything he tells you.'
3:23 'Anyone who will not l to that Prophet will be cut
7: 2 "Brothers and honorable fathers, l to me.
13:16 Gentiles who fear the God of Israel, l to me.
13:38 "Brothers, l! In this man Jesus there is forgiveness
15:13 James stood and said, "Brothers, l to me.
18:14 Gallio turned to Paul's accusers and said, "L,
18:14 or a serious crime, I would be obliged to l to you.
22: 1 Paul said, "l to me as I offer my defense."
26: 3 and controversies. Now please l to me patiently!
Ro 2: 5 But no, you won't l. So you are storing up terrible
9:18 and he chooses to make some people refuse to l.
1Co 14:21 But even then, they will not l to me,"
14:25 As they l, their secret thoughts will be laid bare,
2Co 11:16 But even if you do, l to me, as you would to a
Gal 2: 5 But we refused to l to them for a single moment.
4:21 L to me, you who want to live under the law.
5: 2 L! I, Paul, tell you this: If you are counting on
1Ti 2:11 Women should l and learn quietly
2:12 or have authority over them. Let them l quietly.
5:19 Do not l to complaints against an elder unless there
2Ti 4: 3 For a time is coming when people will no longer l
Heb 2: 1 So we must l very carefully to the truth we have
3: 7 Holy Spirit says, / "Today you must l to his voice.
3:15 the warning: / "Today you must l to his voice.
4: 7 "Today you must l to his voice. / Don't harden
5:11 But you don't seem to l, so it's hard to make you
12:25 did not escape when they refused to l to Moses,
13:22 please l carefully to what I have said in this brief
Jas 1:19 Dear friends, be quick to l, slow to speak, and slow
1:22 it is a message to obey, not just to l to.
1:23 For if you just l and don't obey, it is like looking at
2: 5 L to me, dear brothers and sisters. Hasn't God
5: 4 For l! Hear the cries of the field workers whom
1Pe 2: 8 because they do not l to God's word or obey it,
1Jn 4: 6 to God; that is why those who know God l to us.
4: 6 If they do not belong to God, they do not l to us.
5:14 And we can be confident that he will l to us
Rev 1: 3 and he blesses all who l to it and obey what it says.
2: 7 "Anyone who is willing to hear should l to the
2:11 "Anyone who is willing to hear should l to the
2:17 "Anyone who is willing to hear should l to the
2:29 Anyone who is willing to hear should l to the Spirit
3: 6 Anyone who is willing to hear should l to the Spirit
3:13 Anyone who is willing to hear should l to the Spirit
3:22 Anyone who is willing to hear should l to the Spirit
13: 9 Anyone who is willing to hear should l

LISTENED (47) [LISTEN]

Ge 3:17 "Because you l to your wife and ate the fruit I told
19:29 But God had l to Abraham's request and kept Lot
23:10 and he answered Abraham as the others l,
23:13 and he replied to Ephron as everyone l. "No,
26: 5 I will do this because Abraham l to me and obeyed
Ex 18:24 Moses l to his father-in-law's advice and followed
Dt 9:19 was ready to destroy you. But again he l to me.
Jdg 6:10 land you now live.' But you have not l to me."
1Sa 19: 6 So Saul l to Jonathan and vowed, "As surely as the
2Ch 30:20 And the LORD l to Hezekiah's prayer and healed
33:13 the LORD l to him and was moved by his request
Ne 8: 9 All the people had been weeping as they l to the
9:28 you again for help, you l once more from heaven.
Job 29:21 "Everyone l to me and valued my advice.
32:12 I have l, but not one of you has refuted Job
Ps 22:24 and walked away. / He has l to their cries for help.
66:18 the sin in my heart, / my Lord would not have l.
106:44 he pitied them in their distress / and l to their cries.
Isa 48:18 Oh, that you had l to my commands! Then you
50: 5 Sovereign LORD has spoken to me, and I have l.
Jer 7:26 But my people have not l to me or even tried to
23:22 If they had l to me, they would have spoken my
25: 3 passed them on to you, but you have not l.
25: 4 but you have not l or even tried to hear.
25: 8 Almighty says: Because you have not l to me,
26: 7 and all the people l to Jeremiah as he spoke in front
28: 1 in the Temple while all the priests and people l.
29:19 And you who are in exile have not l either,"
32:13 Then I said to Baruch as they all l,
37: 2 land l to what the LORD said through Jeremiah.
La 3:56 You l to my pleading; you heard my weeping!
Eze 2: 2 and set me on my feet. I l carefully to his words.
33: 5 If they had l to the warning, they could have saved
Mal 3:16 each other, and the LORD l to what they said.
Mt 13: 2 he sat and taught as the people l on the shore.
Mk 12:37 And the crowd l to him with great interest.
Jn 15:20 And if they had l to me, they would listen to you!
Ac 8: 6 Crowds l intently to what he had to say because of
15:12 and everyone l as Barnabas and Paul told about the
16:14 As she l to us, the Lord opened her heart, and she
17: 4 Some who l were persuaded and became converts,
17:11 and they l eagerly to Paul's message.
22:22 The crowd l until Paul came to that word,
24:24 they l as he told them about faith in Christ Jesus.
27:11 But the officer in charge of the prisoners l more to
27:21 you should have l to me in the first place and not
2Co 7:15 than ever when he remembers the way you l to him

LISTENERS (2) [LISTEN]

Lk 20:16 such a thing should ever happen," his l protested.
Ac 2:40 preaching for a long time, strongly urging all his l,

LISTENING (36) [LISTEN]

Ge 18:10 Now Sarah was l to this conversation from the tent
22:11 Abraham!" "Yes," he answered. "I'm l."
31:11 said to me, 'Jacob!' And I replied, 'Yes, I'm l!'
Jdg 9: 3 And after l to their proposal, they decided in favor
1Sa 3: 9 your servant is l.' " So Samuel went back to bed.
3:10 And Samuel replied, "Yes, your servant is l."
15:22 L to him is much better than offering the fat of
2Sa 20:17 carefully to your servant." "I'm l," he said.
1Ki 10: 8 to stand here day after day, l to your wisdom!
2Ch 9: 7 to stand here day after day, l to your wisdom!
Job 15: 8 Were you l at God's secret council? Do you have a
21: 2 what I am saying. You can console me by l to me.
32:11 all this time, l very carefully to your arguments, l
to you grope for words.
Ps 103:20 carry out his plans, / l for each of his commands.
Pr 7: 5 from l to the flattery of an adulterous woman.
18:13 what folly, to give advice before l to the facts!
19:27 If you stop l to instruction, my child, you have
Isa 30:11 of Israel.' We are tired of l to what he has to say."
Eze 33:31 come pretending to be sincere and sit before you l.
Mt 13:12 But to those who are not l, even what they have
Mk 4:25 But to those who are not l, even what they have
12:28 religious law was standing there l to the discussion.
Lk 8:18 But to those who are not l, even what they think
10:39 Mary, sat at the Lord's feet, l to what he taught.
19:11 The crowd was l to everything Jesus said. And
20:45 Then, with the crowds l, he turned to his disciples
Ac 14: 9 He was l as Paul preached, and Paul noticed him
14:11 When the l crowd saw what Paul had done,
16:25 hymns to God, and the other prisoners were l.
Ro 9:19 "Why does God blame people for not l?
10:17 Yet faith comes from l to this message of Good
2Co 11:19 you, who think you are so wise, enjoy l to fools!
12:19 as Christ's servants, and we know that God is l.
Tit 1:14 They must stop l to Jewish myths
1Jn 5:15 And if we know he is l when we make our

LISTENS (9) [LISTEN]

Job 5: 1 "You may cry for help, but no one l. You may turn
Ps 116: 2 Because he bends down and l, / I will pray as long
Eze 7:14 but no one l, for my fury is against them all.
Mt 7:24 "Anyone who l to my teaching and obeys me is
18:15 If the other person l and confesses it, you have won
Lk 6:47 comes to me, l to my teaching, and then obeys me.
6:49 But anyone who l and doesn't obey is like a person
Jn 8:47 Anyone whose Father is God l gladly to the words
1Jn 4: 5 the world's viewpoint, and the world l to them.

LISTING (2) [LIST]

Jos 18: 9 into seven sections, l the towns in each section.
Ps 50:21 I will rebuke you, / l all my charges against you.

LISTINGS (1) [LIST]

Nu 26:55 of each ancestral tribe by means of the census l.

LISTS (1) [LIST]

Ezr 8:15 for three days while I went over the l of the people

LIT (3) [LIGHT]

Jdg 15: 5 Then he l the torches and let the foxes run through
Ps 77:18 from the whirlwind; / the lightning l up the world!
Lk 22:55 The guards l a fire in the courtyard and sat around

LITERATURE (2)

Da 1: 4 men the language and l of the Babylonians."
1:17 young men an unusual aptitude for learning the l

LITTERED (1)

Eze 6: 7 Then when the place is l with corpses, you will

LITTLE (200)

LITTLE CHILD (9) 1Ki 3:7; Isa 11:6,8; Mt 18:4,5; Mk 9:36,37; Lk 9:47,48

LITTLE CHILDREN (13) Ge 50:8; Isa 13:16; 28:9; Jer 49:20; 50:45; La 2:11,20; Eze 9:6; 20:31; Mt 18:3; 21:15; Lk 18:15; 2Co 12:14

LITTLE FAITH (4) Mt 6:30; 8:26; 16:8; Lk 12:28

Ge 19:21 grant your request. I will not destroy that l village.
22: 5 "The boy and I will travel a l farther. We will
30:30 You had l indeed before I came, and your wealth
41:22 "A l later I had another dream. This time there
43: 2 said to his sons, "Go again and buy us a l food."
43: 8 and not only we, but you and our l ones.
44:25 when he said, 'Go back again and buy us a l food,'
45:19 and l ones and to bring your father here.
46: 5 They carried their l ones and wives in the wagons
47:24 your households, and your l ones."
50: 8 But they left their l children and flocks and herds
Ex 2: 3 she got a l basket made of papyrus reeds
2: 5 When the princess saw the l basket among the
10:10 to be with you if you try to take your l ones along!
16:18 and those who gathered only a l had enough.
23:30 I will drive them out a l at a time until your
Lev 11:17 the l owl, the cormorant, the great owl,
Nu 14: 3 Our wives and l ones will be carried off as slaves!
16:27 their tents with their wives and children and l ones.
Dt 7:22 will drive those nations out ahead of you l by l.
14:16 the l owl, the great owl, the white owl,
28:38 "You will plant much but harvest l, for locusts
29:11 With you are your l ones, your wives,

Jdg 8: 2 better than the entire crop of my l clan of Abiezer?
21:13 l remnant of Benjamin who were living at the rock
1Sa 14:29 I feel now that I have eaten this l bit of honey.
14:43 "I tasted a l honey," Jonathan admitted.
14:43 "It was only a l bit on the end of a stick.
15:17 told him, "Although you may think l of yourself,
20: 2 me everything he's going to do, even the l things.
2Sa 12: 3 but a l lamb he had worked hard to buy.
12: 3 He raised that l lamb, and it grew up with his
1Ki 3: 7 but I am like a l child who doesn't know his way
10:21 because silver was considered of l value in
12:10 'My l finger is thicker than my father's waist—
17:12 the jar and a l cooking oil in the bottom of the jug.
17:13 that 'last meal,' but bake me a l loaf of bread first.
18:44 "I saw a l cloud about the size of a hand rising
20:27 But the Israelite army looked like two l flocks of
2Ki 4:10 Let's make a l room for him on the roof
19:26 That is why their people have so l power / and are
2Ch 9:20 because silver was considered of l value in
10:10 'My l finger is thicker than my father's waist—
20:13 of Judah stood before the LORD with their l ones,
31:18 including the l babies, the wives, and the sons
Ezr 9:14 Surely your anger will destroy us until even this l
Job 8: 7 And though you started with l, you will end with
8: 9 For we were born but yesterday and know so l.
10:20 I have only a l time left, so leave me alone—that I
may have a l moment of comfort
14: 6 So give us a l rest, won't you? Turn away your
15:11 "Is God's comfort too l for you? Is his gentle word
41: 5 like a bird, or give it to your l girls to play with?
Ps 8: 5 For you made us only a l lower than God,
37:10 In a l while, the wicked will disappear.
37:16 It is better to be godly and have l / than to be evil
68:27 Look, the l tribe of Benjamin leads the way.
114: 4 skipped like rams, / the l hills like lambs!
114: 6 did you skip like rams? / Why, l hills, like lambs?
Pr 6:10 A l extra sleep, a l more slumber, a l folding of the
hands to rest—
7:23 into a snare, l knowing it would cost him his life.
13: 4 Lazy people want much but get l, but those who
15:16 It is better to have l with fear for the LORD than
24:33 A l extra sleep, a l more slumber, a l folding of the
hands to rest—
Ecc 5:12 work hard sleep well, whether they eat l or much.
10:15 so exhausted by a l work that they have no strength
10:20 either. A l bird may tell them what you have said.
SS 2:15 Catch all the l foxes before they ruin the vineyard
3: 4 A l while later I found him and held him. I didn't
8: 8 "We have a l sister too young for breasts.
Isa 9: 4 the army of Midian with Gideon's l band.
10:25 In a l while my anger against you will end, and
11: 6 safe among lions, and a l child will lead them all.
11: 8 a l child will put its hand in a nest of deadly snakes
13:16 Their l children will be dashed to death right
27: 8 but he has punished Israel only a l. He has exiled
28: 9 Are we l children, barely old enough to talk?
30: 5 your shame. He will not help you even one l bit."
30:14 coals from a fireplace or a l water from the well."
32:10 In a short time—in just a l more than a year—
37:27 That is why their people have so l power / and are
49:22 They will carry your l sons back to you in their
54: 8 In a moment of anger I turned my face away for a l
60: 4 your l daughters will be carried home.
Jer 3: 5 Surely you won't be angry about such a l thing!
7:31 where they sacrifice their l sons and daughters in
11:22 die in battle, and their l boys and girls will starve.
48: 4 Moab is being destroyed. Her l ones will cry out.
49:20 Even the l children will be dragged off, and their
50:45 Even l children will be dragged off, and their
51:33 In just a l while her harvest will begin."
La 2:11 L children and tiny babies are fainting and dying in
2:20 Should mothers eat their l children, those they once
4: 4 The parched tongues of their l ones stick with thirst
Eze 9: 6 old and young, girls and women and l children.
20:31 and give your l children to be burned as sacrifices,
Da 7: 8 This l horn had eyes like human eyes and a mouth
7:11 because I could hear the l horn's boastful speech.
7:20 and the l horn that came up afterward
11:34 persecutions are going on, a l help will arrive,
Hos 13:16 their l ones dashed to death against the ground,
Joel 3: 3 and l girls for enough wine to get drunk.
Am 5:11 and steal what l they have through taxes and unfair
Mic 1:16 for your l ones will be exiled to distant lands.
6:14 You will save a l, but I will give it to those who
Hag 1: 6 You have planted much but harvested l. You have
2: 6 In just a l while I will again shake the heavens
Zec 1:15 I was only a l angry with my people,
Mt 4:21 A l farther up the shore he saw two other brothers,
6:30 he more surely care for you? You have so l faith!
8:26 You have so l faith!" Then he stood up
16: 8 were thinking, so he said, "You have so l faith!
18: 3 you turn from your sins and become as l children,
18: 4 anyone who becomes as humble as this l child is
18: 5 And anyone who welcomes a l child like this on
18: 6 But if anyone causes one of these l ones who trusts
18:10 that you don't despise a single one of these l ones.
18:14 will that even one of these l ones should perish.
18:29 fell down before him and begged for a l more time.
21:15 and heard even the l children in the Temple
25:29 even what l they have will be taken away.
26:39 He went on a l farther and fell face down on the
26:73 A l later some other bystanders came over to him
Mk 1:19 A l farther up the shore Jesus saw Zebedee's sons,
5:23 pleading with him to heal his l daughter. "She is
5:41 Holding her hand, he said to her, "Get up, l girl!"
7:25 Right away a woman came to him whose l girl was
7:30 her l girl was lying quietly in bed, and the demon

9:36 Then he put a **l** child among them. Taking the child
9:37 "Anyone who welcomes a **l** child like this on my
9:42 "But if anyone causes one of these **l** ones who
11:13 He noticed a fig tree a **l** way off that was in full
14:35 He went on a **l** farther and fell face down on the
14:70 A **l** later some other bystanders began saying to
Lk 1:76 "And you, my **l** son, / will be called the prophet of
7:47 But a person who is forgiven **l** shows only **l**
8:42 His only child was dying, a **l** girl twelve years old.
8:49 home with the message, "Your **l** girl is dead.
8:51 James, John, and the **l** girl's father and mother.
9:47 their thoughts, so he brought a **l** child to his side.
9:48 "Anyone who welcomes a **l** child like this on my
12:26 And if worry can't do **l** things like that,
12:28 he more surely care for you? You have so **l** faith!
12:32 "So don't be afraid, **l** flock. For it gives your
16:10 If you cheat even a **l**, you won't be honest with
17:2 in store for harming one of these **l** ones.
18:15 One day some parents brought their **l** children to
19:17 You have been faithful with the **l** I entrusted to
19:26 even what **l** they have will be taken away.
Jn 4:22 Samaritans know so **l** about the one you worship,
4:49 "Lord, please come now before my **l** boy dies."
7:33 But Jesus told them, "I will be here a **l** longer.
9:4 because there is **l** time left before the night falls
12:35 "My light will shine out for you just a **l** while
14:19 In just a **l** while the world will not see me again,
16:16 "In just a **l** while I will be gone, and you won't see
16:16 Then, just a **l** while after that, you will see me
16:18 And what does he mean by 'a **l** while'? We don't
16:19 I said in just a **l** while I will be gone, and you
16:19 Then, just a **l** while after that, you will see me
Ac 12:12 After a **l** thought, he went to the home of Mary,
16:13 On the Sabbath we went a **l** way outside the city to
27:28 A **l** later they sounded again and found only 90
Ro 15:24 And after I have enjoyed your fellowship for a **l**
1Co 4:3 it matters very **l** what you or anyone else thinks.
6:2 can't you decide these **l** things among yourselves?
13:9 Now we know only a **l**, and even the gift of prophecy reveals **l**!
15:37 but only a dry **l** seed of wheat or whatever it is you
2Co 7:8 for I know that it was painful to you for a **l** while.
8:13 so much that you suffer from having too **l**.
8:15 and those who gathered only a **l** had enough."
11:16 would to a foolish person, while I also boast a **l**.
12:14 **l** children don't pay for their parents' food.
Gal 5:9 a **l** yeast spreads quickly through the whole batch
5:20 is wrong except those in your own **l** group,
Php 4:11 how to get along happily whether I have much or **l**.
4:12 it is with a full stomach or empty, with plenty or **l**.
1Th 2:17 after we were separated from you for a **l** while
1Ti 5:23 You ought to drink a **l** wine for the sake of your
Phm 1:15 Onesimus ran away for a **l** while so you could have
Heb 2:7 For a **l** while you made him lower than the angels,
2:9 who "for a **l** while was made lower than the
10:37 "For in just a **l** while, / the Coming One will come
Jas 4:14 the morning fog—it's here a **l** while, then it's gone.
1Pe 5:10 After you have suffered a **l** while, he will restore,
2Pe 2:12 at the terrifying powers they know so **l** about,
Rev 3:2 Strengthen what **l** remains, for even what is left is
3:8 You have **l** strength, yet you obeyed my word
6:11 And they were told to rest a **l** longer until the full
10:9 and asked him to give me the **l** scroll.
10:10 So I took the **l** scroll from the hands of the angel,
12:12 in great anger, and he knows that he has **l** time."
20:3 Afterward he would be released again for a **l** while.

LIVE (749) [ALIVE, EVER-LIVING, LIFE, LIFE-GIVING, LIFEBLOOD, LIFELESS, LIFETIME, LIVED, LIVES, LIVING, MIDLIFE, OUTLIVED, SHORT-LIVED, THOUGHT-LIFE, WILDLIFE]

AS I LIVE (30) Nu 14:21,28; Dt 32:40; 1Sa 20:14; Job 27:3,6; Ps 63:4; 104:33; 116:9; 146:2; Isa 49:18; Jer 22:24; 46:18; Eze 5:11; 16:48; 17:16,19; 18:3; 20:3,31,33; 33:11,27; 34:8; 35:6,11; Zep 2:9; Ro 14:11; 1Co 8:13; 2Pe 1:13

LIVE FOREVER (15) Ge 3:22; 1Ki 1:31; 8:13; 2Ch 6:2; Ps 49:9; 61:4; 68:16; 89:48; 132:14; Jn 6:51,58; 12:34; 1Co 15:50; Heb 12:9; 1Jn 2:17

LIVE IN THE LAND (13) Ge 45:10; 47:4; Nu 33:55; Dt 12:1,10; 31:13; 1Ki 8:40; 2Ki 25:24; 2Ch 6:31; Ps 37:27; Pr 2:21; Isa 9:2; Eze 37:25

Ge 3:14 You will grovel in the dust as long as you **l**,
3:22 fruit of the tree of life? Then they will **l** forever!"
4:20 He became the first of the herdsmen who **l** in tents.
6:3 In the future, they will **l** no more than 120 years."
16:12 he will **l** at odds with the rest of his brothers."
17:1 serve me faithfully and **l** a blameless life.
19:30 and he went to **l** in a cave in the mountains with his
20:7 pray for you, for he is a prophet. Then you will **l**.
20:15 and choose a place where you would like to **l**,"
24:5 then take Isaac there to **l** among your relatives?"
27:39 to him, "You will **l** off the land and what it yields,
27:40 and you will **l** by your sword. You will serve your
29:4 the shepherds and asked them, "Where do you **l**?"
31:44 you and I, and we will **l** by its terms."
34:10 And you may **l** among us; the land is open to you!
34:16 we will intermarry with you and **l** here and unite
34:21 "Let's invite them to **l** here among us and ply their
36:9 the Edomites, who **l** in the hill country of Seir.
42:18 a God-fearing man. If you do as I say, you will **l**.
45:10 You will **l** in the land of Goshen so you can be
45:18 all of their families, and to come here to Egypt to **l**.
45:18 land of Egypt. You will **l** off the fat of the land!'
46:34 he will let you **l** here in the land of Goshen,
47:4 We have come to **l** here in Egypt, for there is no
47:4 We request permission to **l** in the land of Goshen."
47:6 choose any place you like for them to **l**. Give them
50:22 and their families continued to **l** in Egypt.
Ex 1:16 as they are born. Allow only the baby girls to **l**."
1:17 refused to obey the king and allowed the boys to **l**,
1:18 "Why have you allowed the boys to **l**?"
2:21 the invitation, and he settled down to **l** with them.
3:8 Amorites, Perizzites, Hivites, and Jebusites **l**.
8:22 in the land of Goshen, where the Israelites **l**.
9:16 But I have let you **l** for this reason—that you might
12:20 Wherever you **l**, eat only bread that has no yeast in
18:2 Zipporah, and his two sons to **l** with Jethro,
20:12 Then you will **l** a long, full life in the land the
21:35 then the two owners must sell the **l** bull and divide
22:18 "A sorceress must not be allowed to **l**.
23:23 Hivites, and Jebusites, so you may **l** there.
23:33 Do not even let them **l** among you! If you do,
25:8 me a sacred residence where I can **l** among them.
29:45 I will **l** among the people of Israel and be their
29:46 them out of Egypt so that I could **l** among them.
32:8 turned from the way I commanded them to **l**.
33:20 directly at my face, for no one may see me and **l**."
Lev 3:17 and all your descendants, wherever they may **l**."
13:46 and must **l** in isolation outside the camp.
14:8 and may return to **l** inside the camp.
17:12 and the foreigners who **l** among you must never eat
18:3 where you used to **l**, or like the people of Canaan,
18:25 That is why I am punishing the people who **l** there,
18:28 as it will vomit out the people who **l** there now.
19:10 for the poor and the foreigners who **l** among you,
19:33 "Do not exploit the foreigners who **l** in your land.
20:23 Do not **l** by the customs of the people whom I will
22:13 and she returns to **l** in her father's home,
23:3 for worship. It must be observed wherever you **l**.
23:14 for you, and it must be observed wherever you **l**.
23:17 From wherever you **l**, bring two loaves of bread to
23:21 for you, and it must be observed wherever you **l**.
23:31 for you, and it must be observed wherever you **l**.
23:42 all of you who are Israelites by birth must **l** in
23:43 **l** in shelters when I rescued them from the land of
24:18 in full—a **l** animal for the animal that was killed.
24:22 Israelites by birth and foreigners who **l** among you.
25:6 and any foreigners who **l** with you may eat the
25:10 a time to proclaim release for all who **l** there.
25:18 "If you want to **l** securely in the land, keep my
25:19 and you will eat your fill and **l** securely in it.
25:35 a resident foreigner and allow them to **l** with you.
25:36 show your fear of God by letting them **l** with you
25:40 or as resident foreigners who **l** with you,
25:44 or female slaves from among the foreigners who **l**
26:5 You will eat your fill and **l** securely in your land.
26:11 I will **l** among you, and I will not despise you.
26:36 You will **l** there in such constant fear that the
Nu 4:19 This is what you must do so they will **l** and not die
5:3 will not defile the camp, where I **l** among you."
13:19 What kind of land do they **l** in? Is it good or bad?
13:29 The Amalekites **l** in the Negev, and the Hittites,
13:29 Jebusites, and Amorites **l** in the hill country.
13:29 The Canaanites **l** along the coast of the
13:32 we explored will swallow up any who go to **l** there.
14:21 But as surely as I **l**, and as surely as the earth is
14:25 the land where the Amalekites and Canaanites **l**.
14:28 'As surely as I **l**, I will do to you the very things I
19:10 of Israel and any foreigners who **l** among them.
21:8 Those who are bitten will **l** if they simply look at
23:9 from the hills. / I see a people who **l** by themselves,
31:15 "Why have you let all the women **l**?"
31:18 Only the young girls who are virgins may **l**;
32:19 We would rather **l** here on the east side where we
33:55 But if you fail to drive out the people who **l** in the
33:55 They will harass you in the land where you **l**.
35:2 Levites from their property certain towns to **l** in,
35:25 and they must send the slayer back to **l** in a city of
35:29 generation to generation, wherever you may **l**.
35:33 This will ensure that the land where you **l** will not
35:34 must not defile the land where you are going to **l**, for I **l** there myself.
Dt 1:35 **l** to see the good land I swore to give your
2:4 the descendants of Esau, who **l** in Seir.
2:8 the descendants of Esau, who **l** in Seir,
2:22 The descendants of Esau **l** there to this day.
2:29 their country, and so did the Moabites, who **l** in Ar.
3:18 command to the tribes that will **l** east of the Jordan:
4:1 Obey them so that you may **l**, so you may enter
4:9 things escape from your mind as long as you **l**!
4:10 they will learn to fear me as long as they **l**,
4:26 You will **l** there only a short time; then you will be
5:16 Then you will **l** a long, full life in the land the
5:24 have seen God speaking to humans, and yet we **l**!
5:33 Then you will **l** long and prosperous lives in the
6:2 might fear the LORD your God as long as you **l**.
8:1 Then you will **l** and multiply, and you will enter
8:12 and prosperous and have built fine homes to **l** in,
9:1 They **l** in cities with walls that reach to the sky!
9:12 turned from the way I commanded them to **l**
10:12 to **l** according to his will, to love and worship him
11:30 land of the Canaanites who **l** in the Jordan Valley,
12:1 and regulations you must obey as long as you **l** in
12:2 "When you drive out the nations that **l** there,
12:10 and **l** in the land the LORD your God is giving
12:12 And remember the Levites who **l** in your towns,
12:18 your servants, and the Levites who **l** in your towns,
12:19 to forget the Levites as long as you **l** in your land.
13:7 that you worship the gods of peoples who **l** nearby
16:3 the day you departed from Egypt as long as you **l**.
16:11 orphans, and widows who **l** among you.
16:20 so you may **l** and occupy the land that the LORD
23:6 You must never, as long as you **l**, try to help the
23:16 Let them **l** among you in whatever town they
26:5 was a wandering Aramean who went to **l** in Egypt.
28:30 will build a house, but someone else will **l** in it.
28:66 You will **l** night and day in fear, with no reason to
29:28 them to another land, where they still **l** today!'
30:6 him with all your heart and soul, and so you may **l**!
30:16 you do this, you will **l** and become a great nation,
30:18 You will not **l** a long, good life in the land you are
30:19 choose life, that you and your descendants might **l**!
30:20 Then you will **l** long in the land the LORD swore
31:5 will hand over to you the people who **l** there,
31:13 Do this as long as you **l** in the land you are
32:40 my hand to heaven / and declare, "As surely as I **l**,
33:6 "Let the tribe of Reuben **l** and not die out,
33:12 and **l** in safety beside him. / He surrounds them
33:28 So Israel will **l** in safety, / prosperous Jacob in
Jos 1:5 to stand their ground against you as long as you **l**.
2:13 you will let me **l**, along with my father and mother,
9:7 "How do we know you don't **l** nearby?
9:20 We must let them **l**, for God would be angry with
9:21 Let them **l**. But we will make them chop the wood
9:22 Why did you say that you **l** in a distant land when you **l** right here among us?
10:6 For all the Amorite kings who **l** in the hill country
13:13 so they continue to **l** among the Israelites to this
14:4 only towns to **l** in and the surrounding pasturelands
15:63 so the Jebusites **l** there among the people of Judah
16:10 so the people of Gezer **l** as slaves among the
17:12 drive out the Canaanites who continued to **l** there.
17:15 in the forest where the Perizzites and Rephaites **l**."
17:18 Clear as much of the land as you wish and **l** there.
20:4 accused to enter the city and **l** there among them.
20:6 **l** in that city until the death of the high priest who
21:2 LORD instructed Moses to give us towns to **l** in
23:5 You will **l** there instead of them, just as the
24:15 the gods of the Amorites in whose land you now **l**?
Jdg 1:21 So to this day the Jebusites **l** in Jerusalem among
1:29 so the Canaanites continued to **l** there among them.
1:30 and Nahalol, who continued to **l** among them.
5:24 May she be blessed above all women who **l** in
6:10 gods of the Amorites, in whose land you now **l**.'
9:31 and his brothers have come to **l** in Shechem,
14:19 and he went back home to **l** with his father
15:8 Then he went to **l** in a cave in the rock of Etam.
17:8 that area of Ephraim, looking for a good place to **l**.
17:9 in Judah, and I am looking for a place to **l**."
Ru 1:1 and two sons and went to **l** in the country of Moab.
1:16 I will go wherever you go and **l** wherever you **l**.
2:11 and your own land to **l** here among complete
4:13 married Ruth and took her home to **l** with him.
1Sa 2:31 die before their time. None will **l** to a ripe old age.
2:32 But no members of your family will ever **l** out their
2:33 Those who are left alive will **l** in sadness and grief,
10:24 And all the people shouted, "Long **l** the king!"
15:6 "Move away from where the Amalekites **l** or else
17:58 "His name is Jesse, and we **l** in Bethlehem."
19:18 Then Samuel took David with him to **l** at Naioth.
20:13 kill me if I don't warn you so you can escape and **l**.
20:14 with the faithful love of the LORD as long as I **l**.
22:3 and mother **l** here under royal protection until I
23:29 then went to **l** in the strongholds of En-gedi.
25:26 as surely as the LORD lives and you yourself **l**,
26:19 so I can no longer **l** among the LORD's people
27:2 and went to **l** at Gath under the protection of King
27:5 we would rather **l** in one of the country towns
2Sa 1:10 Amalekite told David, "for I knew he couldn't **l**.
4:3 fled to Gittaim, where they still **l** as foreigners.
7:5 Are you the one to build me a temple to **l** in?
9:7 and you may **l** here with me at the palace!"
9:10 But Mephibosheth will **l** here at the palace with
9:13 in both feet, moved to Jerusalem to **l** at the palace.
12:22 LORD will be gracious to me and let the child **l**.'
16:16 "Long **l** the king!" he exclaimed. "Long **l** the king!"
19:33 "Come across with me and **l** in Jerusalem,"
24:3 "May the LORD your God let you **l** until there
1Ki 1:25 with him and shouting, 'Long **l** King Adonijah!'
1:31 "May my lord King David **l** forever!"
1:34 the trumpets and shout, 'Long **l** King Solomon!'
1:39 all the people shouted, "Long **l** King Solomon!"
2:4 'If your descendants **l** as they should and follow
2:36 "Build a house here in Jerusalem and **l** there.
3:1 He brought her to **l** in the City of David until he
3:17 "this woman and I **l** in the same house.
3:27 give the baby to the woman who wants him to **l**,
6:13 I will **l** among the people of Israel and never
8:12 you have said that you would **l** in thick darkness.
8:13 Temple for you, where you can **l** forever!"
8:27 "But will God really **l** on earth? Why,
8:30 Yes, hear us from heaven where you **l**, and when
8:39 then hear from heaven where you **l**, and forgive.
8:40 and walk in your ways as long as they **l** in the land
8:43 then hear from heaven where you **l**, and grant what
8:49 then hear their prayers from heaven where you **l**.
16:31 And as though it were not enough to **l** like
17:9 "Go and **l** in the village of Zarephath, near the city
20:31 Then perhaps King Ahab will let you **l**."
20:32 'Please let me **l**!' " The king of Israel responded,
2Ki 2:2 "As surely as the LORD lives and you yourself **l**,
2:4 "As surely as the LORD lives and you yourself **l**,
2:6 "As surely as the LORD lives and you yourself **l**,
4:30 "As surely as the LORD lives and you yourself **l**,
7:4 If they let us **l**, so much the better. But if they kill
11:12 their hands and shouted, "Long **l** the king!"

16: 6 the people of Judah and sent Edomites to l there,
25: 24 "L in the land and serve the king of Babylon,
1Ch 17: 4 You are not the one to build me a temple to l in.
23: 25 given us peace, and he will always l in Jerusalem.
2Ch 6: 1 you have said that you would l in thick darkness.
6: 2 Temple for you, where you can l forever!"
6: 18 "But will God really l on earth among people?
6: 21 Yes, hear us from heaven where you l, and when
6: 30 then hear from heaven where you l, and forgive.
6: 31 and walk in your ways as long as they l in the land
6: 33 then hear from heaven where you l, and grant what
6: 39 then hear their prayers from heaven where you l.
8: 11 "My wife must not l in King David's palace,
23: 11 and everyone shouted, "Long l the king!"
27: 6 because he was careful to l in obedience to the
Ezr 1: 4 Those who l in any place where Jewish survivors
Ne 2: 3 but I replied, "Long l the king! Why shouldn't I be
5: 5 children into slavery just to get enough money to l.
8: 14 l in shelters during the festival to be held that
8: 15 shelters in which they would l during the festival,
11: 1 and Benjamin were chosen by sacred lots to l
11: 3 l in their own homes in the various towns of Judah,
11: 36 in Judah were sent to l with the tribe of Benjamin.
Est 2: 14 She would l there for the rest of her life,
3: 8 So it is not in the king's interest to let them l.
Job 3: 12 Why did my mother let me l? Why did she nurse
3: 23 no future, those destined by God to l in distress?
5: 26 You will l to a good old age. You will not be
8: 6 if you are pure and l with complete integrity,
9: 34 and I would no longer l in terror of his punishment.
12: 6 and God has them in his power—l in safety!
14: 5 You know how many months we will l, and we are
14: 14 If mortals die, can they l again? This thought
15: 24 They l in distress and anguish, like a king
15: 28 They will l in abandoned houses that are ready to
21: 7 "The truth is that the wicked l to a good old age.
21: 8 They l to see their children grow to maturity,
24: 23 They may be allowed to l in security, but God is
27: 3 As long as I l, while I have breath from God,
27: 6 My conscience is clear for as long as I l.
30: 6 So now they l in frightening ravines and in caves
30: 15 I l in terror now. They hold me in contempt,
30: 23 me to my death—the destination of all who l.
33: 30 the grave so they may l in the light of the living.
34: 21 "For God carefully watches the way people l;
36: 6 He does not let the wicked l but gives justice to the
Ps 23: 6 of my life, / and I will l in the house of the LORD
25: 13 They will l in prosperity, / and their children will
27: 4 is to l in the house of the LORD all the days of
27: 11 Teach me how to l, O LORD. / Lead me along the
33: 14 his throne he observes / all who l on the earth.
34: 12 Do any of you want to l / a life that is long
37: 3 Then you will l safely in the land and prosper.
37: 11 the land; / they will l in prosperous security.
37: 27 and do good, / and you will l in the land forever.
37: 29 godly will inherit the land / and will l there forever.
43: 3 to your holy mountain, / to the place where you l.
49: 9 to l forever / and never see the grave.
58: 11 "There truly is a reward for those who l for God;
61: 4 Let me l forever in your sanctuary, / safe beneath
63: 4 I will honor you as long as I l, / lifting up my
65: 4 to bring near, / those who l in your holy courts.
65: 8 Those who l at the ends of the earth / stand in awe
68: 16 at Mount Zion, where God has chosen to l, / where
the LORD himself will l forever?
68: 18 Now the LORD God will l among us here.
69: 32 and be glad. / Let all who seek God's help l in joy.
69: 35 rebuild the towns of Judah. / His people will l there
69: 36 and those who love him will l there in safety.
72: 5 May he l as long as the sun shines, / as long as the
72: 15 Long l the king! / May the gold of Sheba be given
73: 4 They seem to l such a painless life; / their bodies
75: 3 When the earth quakes and its people l in turmoil,
78: 10 God's covenant, / and they refused to l by his law.
84: 4 How happy are those who can l in your house,
84: 10 than l the good life in the homes of the wicked.
86: 11 O LORD, / that I may l according to your truth!
89: 48 No one can l forever; all will die. / No one can
90: 9 We l our lives beneath your wrath. / We end our
91: 1 Those who l in the shelter of the Most High
101: 2 I will be careful to l a blameless life— / when will
102: 28 will l in security. / Their children's children
104: 33 I will sing to the LORD as long as I l. / I will
107: 7 straight to safety, / to a city where they could l.
107: 34 because of the wickedness of those who l there.
116: 9 in the LORD's presence / as I l here on earth!
118: 17 I will not die, but I will l / to tell what the LORD
119: 17 to your servant, / that I may l and obey your word.
119: 30 be faithful; / I have determined to l by your laws.
119: 77 Surround me with your tender mercies so I may l,
119: 116 LORD, sustain me as you promised, that I may l!
119: 144 help me to understand them, that I may l.
119: 150 near to attack me; / they l far from your law.
119: 175 Let me l so I can praise you, / and may your laws
120: 5 It pains me to l with these people from Kedar!
128: 5 May you see Jerusalem prosper as long as you l.
128: 6 May you l to enjoy your grandchildren. / And may
132: 14 "This is my home where I will l forever," he said.
132: 14 "I will l here, for this is the place I desired.
133: 1 when brothers l together in harmony!
140: 13 your name, / for they will l in your presence.
143: 3 He forces me to l in darkness like those in the
146: 2 I will praise the LORD as long as I l. / I will sing
Pr 1: 33 But all who listen to me will l in peace and safety,
2: 21 For only the upright will l in the land, and those
4: 4 to heart. Follow my instructions and you will l.
4: 12 If you l a life guided by wisdom, you won't limp
7: 2 Obey them and l! Guard my teachings as your
8: 12 "I, Wisdom, l together with good judgment.
9: 6 Leave your foolish ways behind, and begin to l;
15: 27 the whole family, but those who hate bribes will l.
16: 7 he makes even their enemies l at peace with them.
16: 19 It is better to l humbly with the poor than to share
19: 10 It isn't right for a fool to l in luxury or for a slave
21: 9 It is better to l alone in the corner of an attic than
21: 19 It is better to l alone in the desert than with a
24: 15 And don't raid the house where the godly l.
25: 24 It is better to l alone in the corner of an attic than
29: 16 But the godly will l to see the tyrant's downfall.
Ecc 5: 15 People who l only for wealth come to the end of
5: 17 Throughout their lives, they l under a cloud—
5: 18 under the sun—for however long God lets them l.
6: 3 might have a hundred children and l to be very old.
6: 6 He might l a thousand years twice over but not find
7: 15 die young and some wicked people l on and on.
8: 13 The wicked will never l long, good lives, for they
9: 4 "It is better to be a l dog than a dead lion!"
9: 9 L happily with the woman you love through all the
11: 8 When people l to be very old, let them rejoice in
Isa 5: 8 who buy up property so others have no place to l.
7: 22 The few people still left in the land will l on curds
9: 2 a light that will shine on all who l in the land
11: 6 In that day the wolf and the lamb will l together;
13: 21 Ostriches will l among the ruins, and wild goats
14: 2 and those who come to l in their land will serve
23: 6 to Tarshish! Wail, you people who l by the sea!
26: 19 Those who belong to God will l; / their bodies will
30: 6 they go, where lions and poisonous snakes l.
30: 19 O people of Zion, who l in Jerusalem, you will
32: 18 My people will l in safety, quietly at home.
33: 14 "can l here in the presence of this all-consuming
33: 15 The ones who can l here are those who are honest
34: 10 to generation. No one will l there anymore.
38: 11 or laugh with those who l in this world.
38: 16 restored my health / and have allowed me to l!
42: 10 sail the seas, / all you who l in distant coastlands.
43: 4 Others died that you might l. I traded their lives for
45: 12 who made the earth and created people to l on it.
49: 18 As surely as I l," says the LORD, "they will be
50: 11 you who l in your own light and warm yourselves
52: 4 "Long ago my people went to l as resident
54: 3 will take over other nations and l in their cities.
54: 4 "Fear not; you will no longer l in shame.
54: 14 You will l under a government that is just and fair.
54: 14 enemies will stay far away; you will l in peace.
55: 12 You will l in joy and peace. The mountains
57: 15 "I l in that high and holy place with those whose
59: 15 and anyone who tries to l a godly life is soon
65: 21 people will l in the houses they build and eat the
65: 22 For my people will l as long as trees and will have
Jer 4: 2 and begin to l good, honest lives and uphold
5: 24 'Let us l in awe of the LORD our God, for he
8: 3 wish to die rather than l where I will send them.
9: 2 and forget them and l in a shack in the desert,
9: 26 the people who l in distant places, and yes,
11: 5 the land you l in today.' " Then I replied, "So be
17: 6 They will l in the barren wilderness, on the salty
17: 21 what the LORD says: Listen to my warning and l!
18: 12 We will continue to l as we want to, following our
21: 9 who go out and surrender to the Babylonians will l.
22: 23 It may be nice to l in a beautiful palace lined with
22: 24 "And as surely as I l," says the LORD, "I will
23: 6 day Judah will be saved, and Israel will l in safety.
23: 8 exiled them.' Then they will l in their own land."
24: 8 people left in Jerusalem, and those who l in Egypt.
25: 5 then will I let you l in this land that the LORD
25: 23 and Buz, and to the people who l in distant places.
27: 12 "If you want to l, submit to the king of Babylon
27: 17 Surrender to the king of Babylon, and you will l.
30: 3 and they will possess it and l here again.
31: 24 and shepherds alike will l together in peace
32: 37 to this very city and let them l in peace and safety.
33: 16 Judah will be saved, and Jerusalem will l in safety.
35: 2 settlement where the families of the Recabites l,
35: 7 or plant crops or vineyards, but always l in tents.
35: 7 you will l long, good lives in the land.'
35: 15 so that you might l in peace here in the land I gave
38: 2 but those who surrender to the Babylonians will l.
38: 17 surrender to Babylon, you and your family will l,
40: 10 Settle in any town you wish, and l off the land.
42: 14 and if you insist on going to l in Egypt where you
42: 17 one of you who insists on going to l in Egypt.
44: 24 all you citizens of Judah who l in Egypt.
46: 18 "As surely as I l," says the King, whose name is
48: 28 L in the caves like doves that nest in the clefts of
49: 16 And you are proud because you l in a rock fortress
49: 16 Though you l among the peaks with the eagles,
49: 18 says the LORD. "No one will l there anymore.
49: 31 "They l alone in the desert without walls or gates.
49: 32 I will scatter to the winds these people who l in
49: 33 be desolate forever. No one will l there anymore."
50: 3 and bring such destruction that no one will l in her
50: 39 Never again will people l there; it will lie desolate
50: 40 says the LORD. "No one will l there anymore.
Eze 3: 21 But if you warn them and they repent, they will l,
5: 11 "As surely as I l, says the Sovereign LORD,
6: 6 Wherever you l there will be desolation. I will
10: 7 and took some l coals from the fire burning among
12: 2 you l among rebels who could see the truth if they
13: 19 and you promise life to those who should not l.
16: 6 in your own blood. As you lay there, I said, 'L!'
16: 48 As surely as I l, says the Sovereign LORD,
17: 16 For as surely as I l, says the Sovereign LORD,
17: 19 As surely as I l, I will punish him for breaking my
18: 3 As surely as I l, says the Sovereign LORD,
18: 9 who does these things is just and will surely l,
18: 13 Should such a sinful person l? No! He must die
18: 17 because of his father's sins; he will surely l.
18: 19 is right and keeps my laws, that child will surely l.
18: 21 what is just and right, they will surely l and not die.
18: 22 and they will l because of the righteous things they
18: 23 want them to turn from their wicked ways and l.
18: 24 like other sinners, should they be allowed to l?
18: 28 They will l, because after thinking it over,
18: 32 says the Sovereign LORD. Turn back and l!
20: 3 my help? As surely as I l, I will tell you nothing.
20: 11 them my laws so they could l by keeping them.
Yes, all those who keep them will l!
20: 31 As surely as I l, says the Sovereign LORD,
20: 33 As surely as I l, says the Sovereign LORD,
22: 11 Within your walls l men who commit adultery with
25: 16 and utterly destroy the people who l by the sea.
27: 35 All who l along the coastlands / are appalled at
28: 25 The people of Israel will again l in their own land,
28: 26 They will l safely in Israel and build their homes
30: 16 be torn apart; Memphis will l in constant terror.
33: 11 As surely as I l, says the Sovereign LORD,
33: 11 them to turn from their wicked ways so they can l.
33: 13 When I tell righteous people that they will l,
33: 15 If they do this, then they will surely l and not die.
33: 16 done what is just and right, and they will surely l.
33: 19 and do what is just and right, they will l.
33: 27 As surely as I l, those living in the ruins will die by
34: 8 As surely as I l, says the Sovereign LORD,
34: 13 and by the rivers in all the places where people l.
34: 27 yield bumper crops, and everyone will l in safety.
34: 28 They will l in safety, and no one will make them
35: 6 As surely as I l, says the Sovereign LORD,
35: 11 Therefore, as surely as I l, says the Sovereign
35: 15 you people of Mount Seir and all who l in Edom!
36: 11 of Israel, I will bring people to l on you once again.
36: 28 "And you will l in Israel, the land I gave your
36: 33 I will bring people to l in your cities, and the ruins
37: 5 going to breathe into you and make you l again!
37: 9 these dead bodies so that they may l again.' "
37: 14 and you will l and return home to your own land.
37: 25 They will l in the land of Israel where their
37: 25 and their grandchildren after them will l there
38: 11 and destroy these people who l in such confidence!
39: 6 and on all your allies who l safely on the coasts.
39: 26 and treachery against me after they come home to l
43: 9 honor their kings, and I will l among them forever.
44: 9 including those who l among the people of Israel,
45: 6 to be a city where anyone in Israel can come and l.
47: 9 that touches the water of this river will l.
47: 9 Wherever this water flows, everything will l.
47: 23 the territory of the tribe with whom they now l.
48: 12 will lie the land where the other Levites will l.
Da 2: 4 answered the king in Aramaic, "Long l the king!
2: 11 you your dream, and they do not l among people."
3: 9 said to King Nebuchadnezzar, "Long l the king!
4: 15 and let him l like an animal among the plants of the
4: 25 and you will l in the fields with the wild animals.
4: 25 Seven periods of time will pass while you l this
4: 32 You will l in the fields with the wild animals,
4: 32 Seven periods of time will pass while you l this
4: 35 and with those who l on earth. / No one can stop
5: 10 She said to Belshazzar, "Long l the king! Don't be
6: 6 went to the king and said, "Long l King Darius!
6: 21 Daniel answered, "Long l the king!
7: 12 but they were allowed to l for a while longer.
Hos 2: 18 so you can l unafraid in peace and safety.
3: 3 "You must l in my house for many days and stop
6: 2 he will restore us so we can l in his presence.
9: 3 where you will l on food that is ceremonially
12: 6 and always l in confident dependence on your God.
12: 9 And I will make you l in tents again, as you do
14: 9 and righteous people l by walking in them.
Joel 3: 17 LORD your God, l in Zion, my holy mountain.
Am 5: 4 to the family of Israel: "Come back to me and l!
5: 6 Come back to the LORD and l! If you don't,
5: 11 you will never l in the beautiful stone houses you
5: 14 what is good and run from evil—that you may l!
9: 14 will rebuild their ruined cities and l in them again.
Ob 1: 3 You are proud because you l in a rock fortress
Mic 4: 4 Everyone will l quietly in their own homes in
4: 10 for you must leave this city to l in the open fields.
5: 4 Then his people will l there undisturbed, for he
7: 13 because of the wickedness of those who l there.
7: 14 Help them to l in peace and prosperity.
Na 1: 14 you are despicable and don't deserve to l!"
Hab 2: 4 are crooked; but the righteous will l by their faith.
Zep 1: 11 all you who l in the market area, for all who buy
1: 13 They will never have a chance to l in the new
2: 5 it will be for you Philistines who l along the coast
2: 9 Now, as surely as I l," says the LORD Almighty,
2: 14 Owls of many kinds will l among the ruins of its
2: 15 has become an utter ruin, a place where animals l!
3: 10 My scattered people who l beyond the rivers of
3: 13 They will l peaceful lives, lying down to sleep in
3: 15 the King of Israel, will l among you!
3: 17 For the LORD your God has arrived to l among
Zec 2: 4 Many will l outside the city walls, with all their
2: 10 O Jerusalem, for I am coming to l among you.
2: 11 I will l among you, and you will know that the
8: 3 returning to Mount Zion, and I will l in Jerusalem.
8: 8 I will bring them home again to l safely in
Mt 3: 8 Prove by the way you l that you have really turned
4: 15 in Galilee where so many Gentiles l—
5: 10 those who are persecuted because they l for God,
6: 33 you all you need from day to day if you l for him

8:20 But Jesus said, "Foxes have dens to **l** in, and birds
11: 8 Those who dress like that **l** in palaces, not out in
12:45 than itself, and they all enter the person and **l** there.
13:56 All his sisters **l** right here among us. What makes
Mk 5:23 place your hands on her; heal her so she can **l**."
6: 3 and Simon. And his sisters **l** right here among us."
9:50 among yourselves and **l** in peace with each other."
Lk 3: 8 Prove by the way you **l** that you have really turned
7:25 and **l** in luxury are found in palaces,
9:58 But Jesus replied, "Foxes have dens to **l** in,
10: 6 If those who **l** there are worthy, the blessing will
10:28 Jesus told him. "Do this and you will **l**!"
11:26 than itself, and they all enter the person and **l** there.
13:31 "Get out of here if you want to **l**, because Herod
20: 9 and moved to another country to **l** for several
Jn 4:50 Jesus told him, "Go back home. Your son will **l**!"
4:53 time that Jesus had told him, "Your son will **l**."
5:25 of the Son of God. And those who listen will **l**.
6:51 Anyone who eats this bread will **l** forever;
6:51 this bread is my flesh, offered so the world may **l**."
6:57 I **l** by the power of the living Father who sent me;
6:57 those who partake of me will **l** because of me.
6:58 Anyone who eats this bread will **l** forever and not
11:25 though they die like everyone else, will **l** again.
12:34 from Scripture that the Messiah would **l** forever.
14:19 but you will. For I will **l** again, and you will, too.
14:23 and we will come to them and **l** with them.
Ac 7: 4 God brought him here to the land where you now **l**.
7: 6 But God also told him that his descendants would **l**
7:48 the Most High doesn't **l** in temples made by human
17:24 and earth, he doesn't **l** in man-made temples,
17:28 For in him we **l** and move and exist. As one of
22:22 with such a fellow! Kill him! He isn't fit to **l**!"
28: 4 escaped the sea, justice will not permit him to **l**."
Ro 2: 8 his anger and wrath on those who **l** for themselves,
5:17 gracious gift of righteousness will **l** in triumph
6: 2 we have died to sin, how can we continue to **l** in it?
6: 4 power of the Father, now we also may **l** new lives.
6:11 and able to **l** for the glory of God through Christ
6:12 Do not let sin control the way you **l**; do not give in
8:13 Spirit you turn from it and its evil deeds, you will **l**.
12:16 **L** in harmony with each other. Don't try to act
12:18 Do your part to **l** in peace with everyone, as much
13:12 So don't **l** in darkness. Get rid of your evil deeds.
13:12 armor of right living, as those who **l** in the light.
14: 7 For we are not our own masters when we **l** or when
14: 8 While we **l**, we **l** to please the Lord. And when
14:11 " 'As surely as I **l**,' says the Lord,
14:13 Decide instead to **l** in such a way that you will not
15: 5 help you **l** in complete harmony with each other—
1Co 7: 1 in your letter. Yes, it is good to **l** a celibate life.
7:15 for God wants his children to **l** in peace.)
8:13 I will never eat meat again as long as I **l**—
9: 4 Don't we have the right to **l** in your homes
10:11 who **l** at the time when this age is drawing to a
15:50 These perishable bodies of ours are not able to **l**
2Co 1: 8 and we thought we would never **l** through it.
4:11 we **l** under constant danger of death because we
4:12 So we **l** in the face of death, but it has resulted in
5: 1 For we know that when this earthly tent we **l** in is
5: 6 even though we know that as long as we **l** in these
5: 7 That is why we **l** by believing and not by seeing.
5:14 that we have all died to the old life we used to **l**.
5:15 his new life will no longer **l** to please themselves.
5:15 Instead, they will **l** to please Christ, who died
6: 3 We try to **l** in such a way that no one will be
6: 9 We **l** close to death, but here we are, still alive.
6:14 with wickedness? How can light **l** with darkness?
6:16 As God said: / "I will **l** in them / and walk among
7: 3 our hearts forever. We **l** or die together with you.
11: 9 I was with you and didn't have enough to **l** on,
13: 4 are weak, but we **l** in him and have God's power—
13:11 **L** in harmony and peace. Then the God of love
Gal 1: 4 to rescue us from this evil world in which we **l**.
2:19 So I died to the law so that I might **l** for God.
2:20 I myself no longer **l**, but Christ lives in me. So I **l**
my life in this earthly body by trusting in the
4:12 I plead with you to **l** as I do in freedom from these
4:21 Listen to me, you who want to **l** under the law.
4:25 because she and her children **l** in slavery.
5: 5 But we who **l** by the Spirit eagerly wait to receive
5:13 dear friends, have been called to **l** in freedom—
5:16 So I advise you to **l** according to your new life in
6: 8 Those who **l** only to satisfy their own sinful desires
6: 8 But those who **l** to please the Spirit will harvest
6:16 and peace be upon all those who **l** by this principle.
Eph 2: 2 You used to **l** just like the rest of the world, full of
2: 3 All of us used to **l** that way, following the passions
4: 9 first came down to the lowly world in which we **l**.
4:17 **L** no longer as the ungodly do, for they are
4:30 sorrow to God's Holy Spirit by the way you **l**.
5: 2 **L** a life filled with love for others,
5:15 So be careful how you **l**, not as fools but as those
6: 3 your father and mother, "you will **l** a long life,
Php 1:10 so that you may **l** pure and blameless lives until
1:20 For I **l** in eager expectation and hope that I will
1:20 life will always honor Christ, whether I **l** or I die.
1:22 Yet if I **l**, that means fruitful service for Christ.
1:23 Sometimes I want to **l**, and sometimes I long to go
1:24 but it is better for you that I **l**.
1:27 you must **l** in a manner worthy of the Good News
2: 3 don't **l** to make a good impression on others.
2:15 You are to **l** clean, innocent lives as children of
4: 7 your hearts and minds as you **l** in Christ Jesus.
4:12 I know how to **l** on almost nothing or with
Col 1:10 Then the way you **l** will always honor and please
1:12 belongs to God's holy people, who **l** in the light.
1:19 For God in all his fullness was pleased to **l** in
2: 6 you must continue to **l** in obedience to him.
3:15 For as members of one body you are all called to **l**
3:16 their richness, **l** in your hearts and make you wise.
4: 5 **L** wisely among those who are not Christians,
1Th 2:12 and urged you to **l** your lives in a way that God
4: 1 we urge you in the name of the Lord Jesus to **l** in a
4: 4 control your body and **l** in holiness and honor—
4: 7 God has called us to be holy, not to **l** impure lives.
4: 8 Anyone who refuses to **l** by these rules is not
4:11 to **l** a quiet life, minding your own business
4:12 who are not Christians will respect the way you **l**,
5: 8 But let us who **l** in the light think clearly,
5:10 He died for us so that we can **l** with him forever,
5:13 And remember to **l** peaceably with each other.
1Ti 1: 4 they don't help people **l** a life of faith in God.
2: 2 so that we can **l** in peace and quietness,
2:15 and by continuing to **l** in faith,
3: 2 **l** wisely, and have a good reputation.
3: 9 Christian faith and must **l** with a clear conscience.
4:12 in the way you **l**, in your love, your faith, and your
2Ti 1: 9 is God who saved us and chose us to **l** a holy life.
1:13 And remember to **l** in the faith and love that you
2:11 If we die with him, / we will also **l** with him.
3:10 But you know what I teach, Timothy, and how I **l**,
3:12 and everyone who wants to **l** a godly life in Christ
Tit 1: 1 the truth that shows them how to **l** godly lives.
1: 7 An elder must **l** a blameless life because he is
1: 8 He must **l** wisely and be fair. He must **l** a devout
and disciplined life.
1:16 know God, but they deny him by the way they **l**.
2: 2 to be worthy of respect, and to **l** wisely.
2: 3 teach the older women to **l** in a way that is
2: 5 to **l** wisely and be pure, to take care of their homes,
2: 6 encourage the young men to **l** wisely in all they do.
2:12 We should **l** in this evil world with self-control,
Heb 10:38 And a righteous person will **l** by faith. / But I will
12: 9 the discipline of our heavenly Father and **l** forever?
12:14 Try to **l** in peace with everyone, and seek to **l** a
clean and holy life,
13:18 and we want to **l** honorably in everything we do.
Jas 3:13 **l** a life of steady goodness so that only good deeds
4:15 the Lord wants us to, we will **l** and do this or that."
1Pe 1: 3 Now we **l** with a wonderful expectation
1:17 So you must **l** in reverent fear of him during your
2:12 Be careful how you **l** among your unbelieving
2:16 excuse to do evil. You are free to **l** as God's slaves.
2:24 so we can be dead to sin and **l** for what is right.
3: 7 Treat her with understanding as you **l** together.
3:16 be ashamed when they see what a good life you **l**
4: 6 they could still **l** in the spirit as God does.
2Pe 1:13 on reminding you of these things as long as I **l**.
2:21 had never known the right way to **l** than to know it
3:14 make every effort to **l** a pure and blameless life.
1Jn 2: 4 that person is a liar and does not **l** in the truth.
2: 5 is the way to know whether or not we **l** in him.
2: 6 Those who say they **l** in God should **l** their lives
2:17 But if you do the will of God, you will **l** forever.
2:24 you will continue to **l** in fellowship with the Son
2:27 what he has taught you, and continue to **l** in Christ.
2:28 continue to **l** in fellowship with Christ so that when
3: 6 So if we continue to **l** in him, we won't sin either.
3:17 But if one of you has money enough to **l** well
3:24 Those who obey God's commandments **l** in
4:13 And God has given us his Spirit as proof that we **l**
4:15 of God have God living in them, and they **l** in God.
4:16 God is love, and all who **l** in love **l** in God,
4:17 And as we **l** in God, our love grows more perfect.
2Jn 1: 3 Christ his Son, be with us who **l** in truth and love.
3Jn 1: 4 joy than to hear that my children **l** in the truth.
Jude 1: 1 I am writing to all who are called to **l** in the love of
1: 4 saying that God's forgiveness allows us to **l**
1: 8 from their dreams, **l** immoral lives, defy authority,
1:19 They **l** by natural instinct because they do not have
1:21 **L** in such a way that God's love can bless you as
Rev 2:13 "I know that you **l** in the city where that great
7:15 And he who sits on the throne will **l** among them
12:12 O heavens! And you who **l** in the heavens, rejoice!
13: 6 slandering his name and all who **l** in heaven,
21: 3 He will **l** with them, and they will be his people.
22:15 the idol worshipers, and all who love to **l** a lie.

LIVED (246) [LIVE]

LIVED IN THE LAND (10) Ge 36:21,30; Dt 4:25; 29:16; Jdg 11:3; 18:1; 2Ki 8:2; 1Ch 5:16; Job 1:1; Mt 4:16

Ge 5: 4 Adam **l** another 800 years, and he had other sons
5: 7 Seth **l** another 807 years, and he had other sons
5:10 Enosh **l** another 815 years, and he had other sons
5:13 Kenan **l** another 840 years, and he had other sons
5:16 Mahalalel **l** 830 years, and he had other sons
5:19 Jared **l** another 800 years, and he had other sons
5:22 Enoch **l** another 300 years in close fellowship with
5:23 Enoch **l** 365 years in all.
5:26 Methuselah **l** another 782 years, and he had other
5:30 Lamech **l** 595 years, and he had other sons
6: 4 and even afterward, giants **l** on the earth,
7:22 Everything died that breathed and **l** on dry land.
9:28 Noah **l** another 350 years after the Flood.
10:30 The descendants of Joktan **l** in the area extending
11:11 Shem **l** another 500 years and had other sons
11:13 Arphaxad **l** another 403 years and had other sons
11:15 Shelah **l** another 403 years and had other sons
11:17 Eber **l** another 430 years and had other sons
11:19 Peleg **l** another 209 years and had other sons
11:21 Reu **l** another 207 years and had other sons
11:23 Serug **l** another 200 years and had other sons
11:25 Nahor **l** another 119 years and had other sons
11:32 Terah **l** for 205 years and died while still at Haran.
14:12 captured Lot—Abram's nephew who **l** in Sodom—
21:34 And Abraham **l** in Philistine country for a long
22:19 where Abraham **l** for quite some time.
25: 7 Abraham **l** for 175 years,
26: 1 where Abimelech, king of the Philistines, **l**.
26:17 moved to the Gerar Valley and **l** there instead.
31:18 to the land of Canaan, where his father, Isaac, **l**.
34: 1 went to visit some of the young women who **l** in
35:27 (now called Hebron), where Abraham had also **l**.
35:28 Isaac **l** for 180 years,
36:21 the descendants of Seir, who **l** in the land of Edom.
36:30 after their clan leaders, who **l** in the land of Seir.
36:40 clans of Esau, who **l** in the places named for them:
37: 1 again in the land of Canaan, where his father had **l**.
38:21 So he asked the men who **l** there, "Where can I
47: 9 Jacob replied, "I have **l** for 130 hard years, but I
47:28 Jacob **l** for seventeen years after his arrival in
50:23 He **l** to see three generations of descendants of his
Ex 6:16 (Levi, their father, **l** to be 137 years old.)
6:18 Hebron, and Uzziel. (Kohath **l** to be 133 years old.)
6:20 and Moses. (Amram **l** to be 137 years old.)
9:26 the land of Goshen, where the people of Israel **l**.
10:23 was light as usual where the people of Israel **l**.
12:40 The people of Israel had **l** in Egypt for 430 years.
Lev 26:35 it to take every seventh year while you **l** in it.
Nu 13:22 Sheshai, and Talmai—all descendants of Anak—**l**.
14:45 and the Canaanites who **l** in those hills came down
20:15 We **l** there a long time and suffered as slaves to the
21: 1 The Canaanite king of Arad, who **l** in the Negev,
21:32 the region and drove out the Amorites who **l** there.
31:10 the towns and villages where the Midianites had **l**.
32:40 descendants of Manasseh, and they **l** there.
33:40 of Arad, who **l** in the Negev in the land of Canaan,
Dt 1:44 But the Amorites who **l** there came out against you
2:10 called the Emites had once **l** in the area of Ar.
2:12 In earlier times the Horites had **l** at Mount Seir,
2:23 who had **l** in villages in the area of Gaza.)
4:25 and have **l** in the land a long time,
23: 7 and you **l** as foreigners among the Egyptians.
29:16 "Surely you remember how we **l** in the land of
32:12 guided them; / they **l** without any foreign gods.
Jos 5: 1 and all the Canaanite kings who **l** along the
8:26 who had **l** in Ai was completely destroyed.
8:35 and the foreigners who **l** among the Israelites.
9: 1 Hivites, and Jebusites, who **l** in the hill country,
9:10 and King Og of Bashan (who **l** in Ashtaroth).
9:16 facts came out—these people of Gibeon **l** nearby!
11:21 who **l** in the hill country of Hebron, Debir, Anab,
12: 2 of the Amorites, who **l** in Heshbon, was defeated.
12: 4 the last of the Rephaites, **l** at Ashtaroth and Edrei.
12: 8 The people who **l** in this region were the Hittites,
15:63 out the Jebusites, who **l** in the city of Jerusalem,
18:16 crossing south of the slope where the Jebusites **l**,
19:50 of Ephraim. He rebuilt the town and **l** there.
24: 2 and Nahor, **l** beyond the Euphrates River,
24: 7 Then you **l** in the wilderness for many years.
24:14 worshiped when they **l** beyond the Euphrates River
Jdg 1:32 dominated the land where the people of Asher **l**.
1:33 the Canaanites dominated the land where they **l**.
2:19 behaving worse than those who had **l** before them.
3: 5 So Israel **l** among the Canaanites, Hittites,
4: 2 army was Sisera, who **l** in Harosheth-haggoyim.
4: 6 who **l** in Kedesh in the land of Naphtali.
9:21 Then Jotham escaped and **l** in Beer because he was
9:46 When the people who **l** in the tower of Shechem
9:49 So all the people who had **l** in the tower of
10: 1 but **l** in the town of Shamir in the hill country of
11: 3 fled from his brothers and **l** in the land of Tob.
11:21 all the land of the Amorites, who **l** in that region,
12: 8 Ibzan became Israel's judge. He **l** in Bethlehem,
13: 2 a man named Manoah from the tribe of Dan **l** in
16: 4 named Delilah, who **l** in the valley of Sorek.
17: 1 A man named Micah **l** in the hill country of
17:12 as his personal priest, and he **l** in Micah's house.
18: 1 for they had not yet driven out the people who **l** in
18: 2 who **l** in the towns of Zorah and Eshtaol, to scout
18: 7 And they **l** a great distance from Sidon and had no
18:15 where the young Levite **l**, and greeted him kindly.
18:28 for they **l** a great distance from Sidon and had no
18:28 of the tribe of Dan rebuilt the town and **l** there.
20:15 to join the seven hundred warriors who **l** there.
20:47 the rock of Rimmon, where they **l** for four months.
21:23 Then they rebuilt their towns and **l** in them.
Ru 2:23 But all the while she **l** with her mother-in-law.
1Sa 1: 1 There was a man named Elkanah who **l** in Ramah
12:11 and Samuel to save you, and you **l** in safety.
27: 7 and they **l** there among the Philistines for a year
27: 8 people who had **l** near Shur, along the road to
2Sa 7: 6 I have never **l** in a temple, from the day I brought
13:20 So Tamar **l** as a desolate woman in Absalom's
14:28 Absalom **l** in Jerusalem for two years without
15:12 one of David's counselors who **l** in Giloh.
19: 6 If Absalom had **l** and all of us had died, you would
20: 3 So each of them **l** like a widow until she died.
1Ki 2:38 So Shimei **l** in Jerusalem for a long time.
4:25 all of Judah and Israel **l** in peace and safety.
12:17 rule over the Israelites who **l** in the towns of Judah.
13:25 and reported it in Bethel, where the old prophet **l**.
14: 9 You have done more evil than all who **l** before
17:19 where he **l**, and laid the body on his bed.
21: 8 and other leaders of the city where Naboth **l**.
2Ki 4: 8 A wealthy woman **l** there, and she invited him to
8: 2 and **l** in the land of the Philistines for seven years.
13: 5 Then Israel **l** in safety again as they had in former
14:17 King Amaziah of Judah **l** on for fifteen years after

15: 5 the day of his death; he l in a house by himself.
17:29 In town after town where they l, they placed their
21:11 than the Amorites, who l in this land before Israel.
1Ch 4:14 so called because many craftsmen l there.
4:23 They were the potters who l in Netaim
4:28 They l in Beersheba, Moladah, Hazar-shual,
4:32 Their descendants also l in Etam, Ain, Rimmon,
4:41 They killed everyone who l there and took the land
4:43 who had survived, and they have l there ever since.
5: 8 These Reubenites l in the area that stretches from
5:11 Across from the Reubenites in the land of Bashan l
5:16 The Gadites l in the land of Gilead, in Bashan
5:22 So they l in their land until they were taken away
7:28 The descendants of Ephraim l in the territory that
7:29 The descendants of Joseph son of Israel l in these
8:28 in their tribal genealogy. They all l in Jerusalem.
8:29 Jeiel (the father of Gibeon) l in Gibeon. His wife's
8:32 All these families l near each other in Jerusalem.
9:16 son of Elkanah, who l in the area of Netophah.
9:33 all prominent Levites, l at the Temple.
9:34 All these men l in Jerusalem. They were the heads
9:35 Jeiel (the father of Gibeon) l in Gibeon. His wife's
9:38 All these families l near each other in Jerusalem.
11: 4 the Jebusites, original inhabitants of the land, l.
12:37 and Gad and the half-tribe of Manasseh l—
17: 5 I have never l in a temple, from the day I brought
2Ch 10:17 rule over the Israelites who l in the towns of Judah.
19: 4 So Jehoshaphat l in Jerusalem, but he went out
20: 7 did you not drive out those who l in this land when
21:16 and the Arabs, who l near the Ethiopians,
24:15 Jehoiada l to a very old age, finally dying at 130.
25:25 King Amaziah of Judah l on for fifteen years after
26:21 He l in isolation, excluded from the Temple of the
30:25 came to the festival, and all those who l in Judah.
Ne 4:12 The Jews who l near the enemy came and told us
8:17 So everyone who had returned from captivity l in
11: 6 There were also 468 descendants of Perez who l in
11:20 and the rest of the Israelites l wherever their family
11:21 were Ziha and Gishpa, all l on the hill of Ophel.
11:25 Some of the people of Judah l in Kiriath-arba with
11:26 They also l in Jeshua, Moladah, Beth-pelet,
11:31 Some of the people of Benjamin l at Geba,
11:36 Some of the Levites who l in Judah were sent to
Est 2:14 to the second harem, where the king's wives l.
Job 1: 1 There was a man named Job who l in the land of
12:12 and understanding to those who have l many years.
29:25 I l as a king among his troops and as one who
42:16 Job l 140 years after that, living to see four
42:17 he died, an old man who had l a long, good life.
Ps 26: 3 and I have l according to your truth.
32: 2 of sin, / whose lives are l in complete honesty!
68:13 Though they l among the sheepfolds, / now they
78:60 the Tabernacle where he had l among the people.
105:23 Jacob l as a foreigner in the land of Ham.
Ecc 1:12 was king of Israel, and I l in Jerusalem.
2: 7 more than any of the kings who l in Jerusalem
Isa 13:20 and go, but the land will never again be l in.
35: 7 rushes will flourish where desert jackals once l.
44:26 and the towns of Judah will be l in once again,
45:18 He made the world to be l in, not to be a place of
65:20 No longer will adults die before they have l a full
Jer 32:23 Our ancestors came and conquered it and l in it,
35:10 We have l in tents and have fully obeyed all the
40: 6 and l in Judah with the few who were still left in
48:11 "From her earliest history, Moab has l in peace.
La 4: 5 Those who once l in palaces now search the
Eze 16:46 who l with her daughters in the north.
16:46 was Sodom, who l with her daughters in the south.
31: 6 All the great nations of the world l in its shadow.
31:12 All those who l beneath its shadow went away
31:17 the grave—all those nations that had l in its shade.
32:24 They terrorized the nations while they l, but now
32:25 Yes, they terrorized the nations while they l,
36:19 lands to punish them for the evil way they had l.
37:25 live in the land of Israel where their ancestors l,
Da 4:12 Wild animals l in its shade, and birds nested in its
4:21 Wild animals l in its shade, and birds nested in its
4:33 He l this way until his hair was as long as eagles'
5:21 of an animal, and he l among the wild donkeys.
11:12 his enemies killed. But his success will be short l.
Jnh 4:10 to put it there. And a plant is only, at best, short l.
Na 1: 1 came as a vision to Nahum, who l in Elkosh.
2:11 and the young and tender l with nothing to fear?
Zec 7:14 the distant nations where they l as strangers.
Mt 2:23 So they went and l in a town called Nazareth.
4:16 And for those who l in the land where death casts
8:28 They l in a cemetery and were so dangerous that
11:11 "I assure you, of all who have ever l, none is
15:22 A Gentile woman who l there came to him,
Mk 1: 4 He l in the wilderness and was preaching that
5: 3 This man l among the tombs and could not be
Lk 1: 5 Zechariah, who l when Herod was king of Judea.
1:40 where Zechariah l. She entered the house
1:80 Then he l out in the wilderness until he began his
2:25 Now there was a man named Simeon who l in
7:28 I tell you, of all who have ever l, none is greater
8:27 and naked, he had l in a cemetery for a long time.
16:19 splendidly clothed and who l each day in luxury.
Jn 1:14 became human and l here on earth among us.
7:25 Some of the people who l there in Jerusalem said
11: 1 He l in Bethany with his sisters, Mary and Martha.
Ac 7: 4 the Chaldeans and l in Haran until his father died.
7:29 and l as a foreigner in the land of Midian,
10: 1 In Caesarea there l a Roman army officer named
16:32 the Lord with him and all who l in his household.
18: 3 Paul l and worked with them, for they were
18: 7 worshiped God and l next door to the synagogue.
22:12 A man named Ananias l there. He was a godly man
23: 1 I have always l before God in all good
28:30 the next two years, Paul l in his own rented house.
Ro 15:18 by my message and by the way I l before them.
2Co 11:27 I have l with weariness and pain and sleepless
Eph 2:12 You l in this world without God and without hope.
1Th 1: 5 And you know that the way we l among you was
Heb 2:15 Only in this way could he deliver those who have l
11: 9 the land God promised him, he l there by faith—
Jude 1:14 Now Enoch, who l seven generations after Adam,
Rev 18: 7 She has l in luxury and pleasure, so match it now

LIVELIHOOD (1)

Zec 13: 5 The soil has been my means of l from my earliest

LIVELY [KJV] See LIFE-GIVING, LIVING, MANY, STRONG, WONDERFUL

LIVER (11) [LIVERS]

Ex 29:13 also the long lobe of the l and the two kidneys with
29:22 Also, take the long lobe of the l, the two kidneys
Lev 3: 4 and the lobe of the l, which is to be removed with
3:10 and the lobe of the l, which is to be removed with
3:15 and the lobe of the l, which is to be removed with
4: 9 around them near the loins, and the lobe of the l.
7: 4 and the lobe of the l, which is to be removed with
8:16 the lobe of the l, and the two kidneys and their fat,
8:25 the fat around the internal organs, the lobe of the l,
9:10 and the lobe of the l from the sin offering,
9:19 along with the kidneys and the lobe of the l.

LIVERS (1) [LIVER]

Eze 21:21 They will inspect the l of their animal sacrifices.

LIVES (258) [LIVE]

AS THE LORD* LIVES (26) Jdg 8:19; Ru 3:13; 1Sa 14:45; 19:6; 20:21; 25:26; 28:10; 2Sa 4:9; 12:5; 14:11; 1Ki 1:29; 2:24; 22:14; 2Ki 2:2,4,6; 4:30; 5:16,20; 2Ch 18:13; Jer 5:2; 12:16; 16:14,15; 23:7,8

WHO LIVES FOREVER (8) Ps 41:13; 102:24; Da 4:34; 12:7; Rev 4:9,10; 10:6; 15:7

Ge 9:15 my covenant with you and with everything that l.
19:17 "Run for your l!" the angels warned. "Do not
45: 5 He sent me here ahead of you to preserve your l.
47:19 Just give us grain so that our l may be saved and
47:25 "You have saved our l!" they exclaimed. "May it
50:20 I have today so I could save the l of many people.
Ex 18:20 and show them how to conduct their l.
23:26 among your people, and I will give you long, full l.
30:16 and it will make atonement for your l."
Lev 22:10 even if the person l in a priest's home or is one of
Nu 16:38 of these men who have sinned at the cost of their l.
30:16 a father and a young daughter who still l at home.
31:50 This will make atonement for our l before the
35:34 the LORD, who l among the people of Israel.' "
Dt 5:33 and prosperous l in the land you are about to enter
6:15 your God, who l among you, is a jealous God.
17:19 the law with him and read it daily as long as he l.
28:66 Your l will hang in doubt. You will live night
Jos 2:14 "We offer our own l as a guarantee for your
6:25 And she l among the Israelites to this day.
9:24 So we feared for our l because of you. That is why
22:19 where the LORD l among us in his Tabernacle,
22:22 If we have done so, do not spare our l this day.
Jdg 8:19 "As surely as the LORD l, I wouldn't kill you if
18: 7 where they noticed the people living carefree l,
18:10 get there, you will find the people living carefree l.
Ru 3:13 then as surely as the LORD l, I will marry you!
1Sa 9: 6 There is a man of God who l here in this town.
14:45 As surely as the LORD l, not one hair on his head
16: 1 Find a man named Jesse who l there, for I have
19: 6 and vowed, "As surely as the LORD l,
20:21 as surely as the LORD l, that all is well,
25:26 as surely as the LORD l and you yourself live,
25:29 But the l of your enemies will disappear like stones
28:10 and promised, "As surely as the LORD l,
2Sa 1:13 am a foreigner, an Amalekite, who l in your land."
3:14 for I bought her with the l of one hundred
4: 9 to Recab and Baanah, "As surely as the LORD l,
4:11 own bed? Should I not also demand your very l?"
12: 5 "As surely as the LORD l," he vowed,
14:11 "As surely as the LORD l," he replied, "not a
14:14 Our l are like water spilled out on the ground,
14:14 He does not sweep away the l of those he cares
18: 7 and twenty thousand men laid down their l that
19: 5 "We saved your life today and the l of your sons,
22:47 "The LORD l! Blessed be my rock! / May God,
23:17 of these men who risked their l to bring it to me."
1Ki 1:29 And the king vowed, "As surely as the LORD l,
2:24 So as surely as the LORD l, Adonijah will die this
17: 1 "As surely as the LORD, the God of Israel, l—
22:14 But Micaiah replied, "As surely as the LORD l,
2Ki 1:13 man of God, please spare my life and the l of these,
2: 2 "As surely as the LORD l and you yourself live,
2: 4 "As surely as the LORD l and you yourself live,
2: 6 "As surely as the LORD l and you yourself live,
3:14 "As surely as the LORD Almighty l, whom I
4:30 "As surely as the LORD l and you yourself live,
5:16 "As surely as the LORD l, whom I serve,
5:20 As surely as the LORD l, I will chase after him
7: 7 and everything else, and they fled for their l.
1Ch 11:19 of these men who risked their l to bring it to me."
12:19 "It will cost us our l if David switches loyalties to
2Ch 18:13 But Micaiah replied, "As surely as the LORD l,
Ezr 1: 3 the LORD, the God of Israel, who l in Jerusalem.
7:15 an offering to the God of Israel who l in Jerusalem.
Ne 9: 5 for he l from everlasting to everlasting!"
Est 7: 3 that my life and the l of my people will be spared.
8:11 in every city authority to unite to defend their l.
9:16 provinces had gathered together to defend their l.
Job 3:16 like a baby who never l to see the light?
14: 5 You have decided the length of our l. You know
15:20 "Wicked people are in pain throughout their l.
19:25 "But as for me, I know that my Redeemer l,
22:16 and the foundations of their l were washed away
28: 4 a mine shaft into the earth far from where anyone l.
36:11 will be blessed with prosperity throughout their l.
36:14 They die young after wasting their l in immoral
38:26 rain fall on barren land, in a desert where no one l?
39:28 It l on the cliffs, making its home on a distant,
Ps 15: 2 Those who lead blameless l / and do what is right,
18:46 The LORD l! Blessed be my rock! / May the God
19: 4 The sun l in the heavens / where God placed it.
32: 2 of sin, / whose l are lived in complete honesty!
37:23 the LORD. / He delights in every detail of their l.
39:11 their l can be crushed like the life of a moth.
41:13 of Israel, / who l forever from eternal ages past.
46: 5 God himself l in that city; it cannot be destroyed.
66: 9 Our l are in his hands, / and he keeps our feet from
68: 1 Let those who hate God run for their l.
72:14 and from violence, / for their l are precious to him.
76: 2 Jerusalem is where he l; / Mount Zion is his home.
78:33 So he ended their l in failure / and gave them years
78:50 against them; / he did not spare the Egyptians' l
90: 9 We live our l beneath your wrath. / We end our l with a groan.
90:14 so we may sing for joy to the end of our l.
97:10 hate evil! / He protects the l of his godly people
102:24 But I cried to him, "My God, who l forever,
124: 5 of their fury / would have overwhelmed our very l.
135:21 be praised from Zion, / for he l here in Jerusalem.
150: 6 Let everything that l sing praises to the LORD!
Pr 1:18 for themselves; they booby-trap their own l!
10:16 The earnings of the godly enhance their l, but evil
11:30 life-giving fruit, and those who save l are wise.
12: 6 but the words of the godly save l.
14:25 A truthful witness saves l, but a false witness is a
19: 3 People ruin their l by their own foolishness and
19:18 there is hope. If you don't, you will ruin their l.
27:10 go to a neighbor than to a relative who l far away.
Ecc 5:15 only for wealth come to the end of their l as naked
5:17 Throughout their l, they live under a cloud—
6: 7 All people spend their l scratching for food,
6:12 In the few days of our empty l, who knows how
8:12 person sins a hundred times and still l a long time,
8:13 never live long, good l, for they do not fear God.
9:11 who are educated don't always lead successful l.
Isa 10:29 the city of Saul—are running for their l.
11:10 for the land where he l will be a glorious place.
12: 6 For great is the Holy One of Israel who l among
33: 5 Though the LORD is very great and l in heaven,
43: 4 I traded their l for yours because you are precious
43:17 their l snuffed out like a smoldering candlewick.
52:12 You will not leave in a hurry, running for your l.
56: 4 to do what pleases me and commit their l to me:
Jer 2: 6 and death, where no one l or even travels?'
2:15 cities are now in ruins. No one l in them anymore.
4: 2 and begin to live good, honest l and uphold justice,
4: 5 'Run for your l! Flee to the fortified cities!'
5: 2 saying, 'As surely as the LORD l,' they all tell
6: 1 "Run for your l, you people of Benjamin!
12:16 'As surely as the LORD l' (just as they taught my
16:14 will no longer say, 'As surely as the LORD l,
16:15 Instead, they will say, 'As surely as the LORD l,
17: 6 barren wilderness, on the salty flats where no one l.
17:11 at the end of their l, will become poor old fools.
20: 3 you are to be called 'The Man Who L in Terror.'
20:10 They call me "The Man Who L in Terror."
23: 7 will no longer say, 'As surely as the LORD l,
23: 8 Instead, they will say, 'As surely as the LORD l,
35: 7 you will live long, good l in the land.'
38:16 "As surely as the LORD our Creator l, I will not
44: 2 They now lie in ruins, and no one l in them.
44:26 this oath: 'As surely as the Sovereign LORD l!'
48: 6 Flee for your l! Hide in the wilderness!
49:30 Flee for your l," says the LORD.
51:43 she is a dry wilderness where no one l or even
La 1: 3 She l among foreign nations and has no place of
1:19 even as they searched for food to save their l.
2:12 Their l ebb away like the life of a warrior wounded
4:18 couldn't go into the streets without danger to our l.
5: 9 hunt for food in the wilderness at the risk of our l.
Eze 17:17 to Jerusalem again and destroys the l of many.
18:27 and do what is just and right, they will save their l.
22: 6 "Every leader in Israel who l within your walls is
22:27 They actually destroy people's l for profit!
32:10 They will shudder in fear for their l as I brandish
33: 5 to the warning, they could have saved their l.
Da 4:34 the Most High and honored the one who l forever.
12: 7 and took this solemn oath by the one who l
Am 2:16 men will drop their weapons and run for their l.
Jnh 1: 5 Fearing for their l, the desperate sailors shouted to
1: 6 Maybe he will have mercy on us and spare our l."
Hab 2: 4 They trust in themselves, and their l are crooked;
2:10 you have shamed your name and forfeited your l.
Zep 3:13 They will live peaceful l, lying down to sleep in
Mal 2: 6 they walked with me, living good and righteous l, and they turned many from l of sin.
Mt 23:21 you are swearing by it and by God, who l in it.
Lk 7:35 But wisdom is shown to be right by the l of those
Jn 6:34 they said, "give us that bread every day of our l."

12:24 many new kernels—a plentiful harvest of new **l**.
14:10 but my Father who **l** in me does his work through
14:17 because he **l** with you now and later will be in you.
15:13 when people lay down their **l** for their friends.
Ac 10: 6 with Simon, a leatherworker who **l** near the shore.
10:32 of Simon, a leatherworker who **l** near the shore.'
14: 6 the apostles learned of it, they fled for their **l**.
15:26 who have risked their **l** for the sake of our Lord
27:10 loss of cargo, injuries, and danger to our **l**."
27:22 None of you will lose your **l**, even though the ship
Ro 1:29 Their **l** became full of every kind of wickedness,
6: 4 power of the Father, now we also may live new **l**.
6: 6 with Christ so that sin might lose its power in our **l**.
6:10 to defeat sin, and now he **l** for the glory of God.
8:10 Since Christ **l** within you, even though your body
8:11 of God, who raised Jesus from the dead, **l** in you.
16: 4 In fact, they risked their **l** for me. I am not the only
1Co 3:16 temple of God and that the Spirit of God **l** in you?
6:19 who **l** in you and was given to you by God?
7:39 A wife is married to her husband as long as he **l**.
12: 6 There are different ways God works in our **l**,
15:30 should we ourselves be continually risking our **l**,
16:15 and they are spending their **l** in service to other
2Co 2:15 Our **l** are a fragrance presented by Christ to God.
3: 2 Your **l** are a letter written in our hearts,
6: 9 We have been beaten within an inch of our **l**.
7:10 For God can use sorrow in our **l** to help us turn
13: 4 he now **l** by the mighty power of God.
Gal 2:20 I myself no longer live, but Christ **l** in me. So I live
3: 3 After starting your Christian **l** in the Spirit, why are
4:19 continue until Christ is fully developed in your **l**.
5:19 sinful nature, your **l** will produce these evil results:
5:22 But when the Holy Spirit controls our **l**, he will
5:25 the Holy Spirit's leading in every part of our **l**.
Eph 2:22 as part of this dwelling where God **l** by his Spirit.
4:19 Their **l** are filled with all kinds of impurity
Php 1:10 may live pure and blameless **l** until Christ returns.
2:12 to put into action God's saving work in your **l**,
2:15 innocent **l** as children of God in a dark world full
2:15 Let your **l** shine brightly before them.
3:17 Dear friends, pattern your **l** after mine, and learn
3:20 citizens of heaven, where the Lord Jesus Christ **l**.
Col 1: 6 It is changing **l** everywhere, just as it changed
1: 9 understanding of what he wants to do in your **l**,
1:27 Christ **l** in you, and this is your assurance that you
2: 7 Let your **l** overflow with thanksgiving for all he
2: 9 For in Christ the fullness of God **l** in a human
3:11 Christ is all that matters, and he **l** in all of us.
1Th 2: 8 you not only God's Good News but our own **l**,
2:12 and urged you to live your **l** in a way that God
4: 7 God has called us to be holy, not to live impure **l**.
2Th 3: 6 Stay away from any Christian who **l** in idleness
3:11 Yet we hear that some of you are living idle **l**,
1Ti 5: 6 But the widow who **l** only for pleasure is
5:24 Remember that some people lead sinful **l**,
6:16 and he **l** in light so brilliant that no human can
2Ti 1:14 With the help of the Holy Spirit who **l** within us,
3:16 and to make us realize what is wrong in our **l**.
Tit 1: 1 the truth that shows them how to live godly **l**.
3: 3 Our **l** were full of evil and envy. We hated others,
3:14 For our people should not have unproductive **l**.
Heb 2:15 have lived all their **l** as slaves to the fear of dying.
7: 8 than they are, because we are told that he **l** on.
7:25 He **l** forever to plead with God on their behalf.
12: 4 you have not yet given your **l** in your struggle
13: 7 Think of all the good that has come from their **l**,
Jas 1:21 So get rid of all the filth and evil in your **l**,
1Pe 2:15 It is God's will that your good **l** should silence
3: 1 Your godly **l** will speak to them better than any
2Pe 3:11 what holy, godly **l** you should be living!
1Jn 2: 6 Those who say they live in God should live their **l**
2:27 have received the Holy Spirit, and he **l** within you,
3:16 so we also ought to give up our **l** for our Christian
3:24 we know he **l** in us because the Holy Spirit **l** in us.
4: 4 because the Spirit who **l** in you is greater than the
spirit who **l** in the world.
4:12 But if we love each other, God **l** in us, and his love
4:16 all who live in love live in God, and God **l** in them.
2Jn 1: 2 the truth that **l** in us and will be in our hearts
Jude 1: 4 that God's forgiveness allows us to live immoral **l**.
1: 8 from their dreams, live immoral **l**, defy authority,
1:20 must continue to build your **l** on the foundation of
Rev 4: 9 on the throne, the one who **l** forever and ever,
4:10 and worship the one who **l** forever and ever.
10: 6 And he swore an oath in the name of the one who **l**
15: 7 terrible wrath of God, who **l** forever and forever.
18:13 and slaves—yes, she even traded in human **l**.

LIVESTOCK (57)

Ge 1:24 kind of animal—**l**, small animals, and wildlife."
1:25 all sorts of wild animals, **l**, and small animals,
1:26 the birds in the sky, and all the **l**, wild animals,
2:20 He gave names to all the **l**, birds, and wild animals.
9:10 with you—all these birds and **l** and wild animals.
12: 5 his **l** and all the people who had joined his
13: 2 for Abram was very rich in **l**, silver, and gold.
31:18 all the **l** he had acquired at Paddan-aram—
36: 7 support them both because of all their cattle and **l**.
39: 5 to run smoothly, and his crops and **l** flourished.
46: 6 They brought their **l**, too, and all the belongings
46:32 tell him, 'These men are shepherds and **l** breeders.
46:34 tell him, 'We have been **l** breeders from our youth,
47: 6 special skills, put them in charge of my **l**, too."
47:16 "since your money is gone, give me your **l**.
47:17 So they gave their **l** to Joseph in exchange for food.
47:18 and said, "Our money is gone, and our **l** are yours.
Ex 9: 4 Not a single one of Israel's **l** will die!' "
9: 6 The next morning all the **l** of the Egyptians began
9:19 Order your **l** and servants to come in from the
9:20 They immediately brought their **l** and servants in
12:29 Even the firstborn of their **l** were killed.
17: 3 us here? We, our children, and our **l** will all die!"
20:10 your male and female servants, your **l**,
Lev 25: 7 And your **l** and the wild animals will also be
Nu 3:41 And the Levites' **l** are mine as substitutes for the
3:41 for the firstborn **l** of the whole nation of Israel."
3:45 And take the **l** of the Levites as substitutes for the
firstborn **l** of the people of Israel.
20: 4 into this wilderness to die, along with all our **l**?
20: 8 from the rock to satisfy all the people and their **l**."
20:11 So all the people and their **l** drank their fill.
20:19 If any of our **l** drinks your water, we will pay for it.
32: 1 tribes of Reuben and Gad owned vast numbers of **l**.
35: 3 provide pasture for their cattle, flocks, and other **l**.
Dt 2:35 We took all the **l** as plunder for ourselves,
3: 7 But we kept all the **l** for ourselves and took plunder
3:19 Your wives, children, and numerous **l**, however,
5:14 your oxen and donkeys and other **l**,
7:14 will be childless, and all your **l** will bear young.
13:15 destroy all its inhabitants, as well as all the **l**.
20:14 all the women, children, **l**, and other plunder.
28:11 many children, numerous **l**, and abundant crops.
28:51 Its armies will devour your **l** and crops, and you
30: 9 He will give you many children and numerous **l**,
Jdg 18:21 started on their way again, placing their children, **l**,
1Sa 23: 5 They slaughtered the Philistines and took all their **l**
1Ch 7:21 and Elead were killed trying to steal **l** from the
28: 1 the overseers of the royal property and **l**,
2Ch 26:10 because he kept great herds of **l** in the foothills of
Ezr 1: 4 and gold, supplies for the journey, and **l**,
1: 6 of silver and gold, supplies for the journey, and **l**.
Ps 78:48 their cattle to the hail, / their **l** to bolts of lightning.
148:10 wild animals and all **l**, / reptiles and birds,
Isa 11: 7 down together. And lions will eat grass as the **l** do.
Eze 25: 4 They will harvest all your fruit and steal your **l**.
Zec 2: 4 will live outside the city walls, with all their **l**—

LIVING (380) [LIVE]

LAND OF THE LIVING (4) Ps 27:13; 52:5; Isa 38:11; Eze 26:20
LIVING BEING (6) Ge 9:6; Eze 1:9,23; Rev 6:3,5,7
LIVING BEINGS (30) Eze 1:5,9,11,13,14,19,20,20, 21,21,21,21; 3:13; 10:15,17,20; Rev 4:6,7,8,9; 5:6,8,11,14; 6:1,6; 7:11; 14:3; 15:7; 19:4
LIVING GOD (31) Dt 5:26; Jos 3:10; 1Sa 17:26,36; 2Ki 19:4,16; Job 27:2; Ps 42:2; 84:2; Isa 37:4,17; Jer 10:10; 23:36; Da 6:20,26; Hos 1:10; Mt 16:16; 26:63; Ac 14:15; Ro 9:26; 2Co 3:3; 6:16; 1Th 1:9; 1Ti 3:15; 4:10; 6:17; Heb 3:12; 9:14; 10:31; 12:22; Rev 7:2
LIVING THING (10) Ge 6:17; 7:23; Dt 5:26; 11:6; 20:16; Jos 11:11; Jdg 20:48; Job 12:10; Ps 136:25; 145:16
LIVING WATER (7) SS 4:15; Jer 2:13; 17:13; Jn 4:10,11; 7:38,39

Ge 2: 7 the breath of life. And the man became a **l** person.
3:17 All your life you will struggle to scratch a **l** from it.
6: 9 the only blameless man **l** on earth at the time.
6:13 to Noah, "I have decided to destroy all **l** creatures,
6:17 earth with a flood that will destroy every **l** thing.
7: 3 that every kind of **l** creature will survive the flood.
7: 4 And I will wipe from the earth all the **l** things I
7:21 All the **l** things on earth died—birds,
7:23 Every **l** thing on the earth was wiped out—people,
8:21 destroying all **l** things, even though people's
9: 6 for to kill a person is to kill a **l** being made in
9:11 never to send another flood to kill all **l** creatures
9:12 of my eternal covenant with you and all **l** creatures.
9:16 between God and every **l** creature on earth."
13: 6 with all their flocks and herds **l** so close together.
13: 7 and Perizzites were also **l** in the land.
14: 7 and also the Amorites **l** in Hazazon-tamar.
21:23 to me and to this country in which you are **l**."
32: 4 I have been **l** with Uncle Laban until recently,
38: 5 At the time of Shelah's birth, they were **l** at Kezib.
43: 7 "He wanted to know whether our father was still **l**,
Ex 6: 4 give them the land of Canaan, where they were **l**.
12:19 These same regulations apply to the foreigners **l**
12:48 "If there are foreigners **l** among you who want to
13:11 long ago, the land where the Canaanites are now **l**.
20:10 your livestock, and any foreigners **l** among you.
21:36 The owner of the **l** bull must pay in full for the
23: 9 "Do not oppress the foreigners **l** among you.
23:31 I will help you defeat the people now **l** in the land,
34:15 treaties of any kind with the people **l** in the land.
Lev 11:46 and all the **l** things that move through the water
14: 6 He will then dip the **l** bird, along with the
14: 7 the priest will set the **l** bird free so it can fly away
14:51 and the **l** bird into the blood of the slaughtered
14:53 he will release the **l** bird in the open fields outside
16:20 and the altar, he must bring the **l** goat forward.
16:29 by birth, as well as to the foreigners **l** among you.
17: 8 to Israelites and to the foreigners **l** among you.
17:10 whether an Israelite or a foreigner **l** among you,
17:13 to Israelites and to the foreigners **l** among you.
17:15 both to Israelites and the foreigners **l** among you.
18:26 by birth and to the foreigners **l** among you.
20: 2 by birth as well as to the foreigners **l** among you.
22:18 by birth as well as to the foreigners **l** among you.
23:22 it for the poor and the foreigners **l** among you.
25:23 You are only foreigners and tenants **l** with me.
Nu 9:14 And if foreigners **l** among you want to celebrate
9:14 both to you and to the foreigners **l** among you.' "
13:18 and find out whether the people **l** there are strong
13:28 But the people **l** there are powerful, and their cities
13:28 We also saw the descendants of Anak who are **l**
15:14 And if any foreigners **l** among you want to present
15:16 both to you and to the foreigners **l** among you."
15:26 including the foreigners **l** among you, for the entire
15:29 to native Israelites and the foreigners **l** among you.
16:48 He stood between the **l** and the dead until the
22: 5 who was **l** in his native land of Pethor near the
27:16 "O LORD, the God of the spirits of all **l** things,
30: 3 or a pledge under oath while she is still **l** at her
30:10 and **l** in her husband's home when she makes a
32:39 and they drove out the Amorites, who were **l** there.
33:52 you must drive out all the people **l** there. You must
Dt 1:16 but also to the foreigners **l** among you.
5:14 other livestock, and any foreigners **l** among you.
5:26 Can any **l** thing hear the voice of the **l** God
6:19 You will drive out all the enemies **l** in your land,
10:18 He shows love to the foreigners **l** among you
11: 6 and tents and every **l** thing that belonged to them.
11:31 God is giving you. When you are **l** in that land,
14:21 You may give it to a foreigner **l** among you,
14:29 as well as to the foreigners **l** among you,
15: 3 not to the foreigners **l** among you.
18: 6 from wherever he is **l**, to the place the LORD
18: 9 the detestable customs of the nations **l** there.
20:16 a special possession, destroy every **l** thing in them.
22:21 being promiscuous while **l** in her parents' home.
24: 6 as a pledge, for the owner uses it to make a **l**.
24:14 fellow Israelites or foreigners **l** in your towns.
24:17 "True justice must be given to foreigners **l** among
25: 5 "If two brothers are **l** together on the same
26:11 and the foreigners **l** among you in the celebration.
28:43 The foreigners **l** among you will become stronger
29:11 and the foreigners **l** among you who chop your
30: 1 and you meditate on them as you are **l** among the
31: 3 He will destroy the nations **l** there, and you will
31: 4 The LORD will destroy the nations **l** in the land,
31:12 children, and the foreigners **l** in your towns—
Jos 2: 9 "We are all afraid of you. Everyone is **l** in terror.
3:10 Today you will know that the **l** God is among you.
7: 9 and all the other people **l** in the land hear about it,
9:24 this entire land and destroy all the people **l** in it.
11:11 The Israelites completely destroyed every **l** thing in
13:21 princes **l** in the region who were allied with Sihon.
14:12 as scouts we found the Anakites **l** there in great,
15:15 Then he fought against the people **l** in the town of
17: 7 to the people **l** near the spring of Tappuah.
20: 9 Israelites as well as the foreigners **l** among them.
23: 5 your God will drive out all the people **l** there now.
24:13 did not build—the cities in which you are now **l**.
24:18 and the other nations **l** here in the land.
Jdg 1: 3 "Join with us to fight against the Canaanites **l** in
1: 9 Then they turned south to fight the Canaanites **l** in
1:11 From there they marched against the people **l** in the
1:17 to fight against the Canaanites **l** in Zephath,
1:19 But they failed to drive out the people **l** in the
1:20 And Caleb drove out the people **l** there, who were
1:21 to drive out the Jebusites, who were **l** in Jerusalem.
1:27 failed to drive out the people **l** in Beth-shan,
1:29 also failed to drive out the Canaanites **l** in Gezer,
1:30 also failed to drive out the Canaanites **l** in Kitron
2: 2 make any covenants with the people **l** in this land;
2: 3 I will no longer drive out the people **l** in your land.
3: 3 the Philistines (those **l** under the five Philistine
3: 3 and the Hivites **l** in the hill country of Lebanon
11:26 Israel has been **l** here all this time, spread across
18: 7 where they noticed the people **l** carefree lives,
18:10 get there, you will find the people **l** carefree lives.
19: 1 There was a man from the tribe of Levi **l** in a
19:16 but he was **l** in Gibeah in the territory of Benjamin.
20:48 and slaughtered every **l** thing in all the towns—
21:13 of Benjamin who were **l** at the rock of Rimmon.
Ru 1: 7 she set out from the place where she had been **l**,
1Sa 17:26 that he is allowed to defy the armies of the **l**
17:36 too, for he has defied the armies of the **l** God!
22: 4 in Moab while David was **l** in his stronghold.
27:11 and again while he was **l** among the Philistines.
2Sa 7: 2 "Here I am **l** in this beautiful cedar palace,
11:11 and the armies of Israel and Judah are **l** in tents,
12:21 "While the baby was still **l**, you wept and refused
1Ki 3:22 certainly was your son, and the **l** child is mine."
3:22 "the dead one is yours, and the **l** one is mine."
3:23 Both of you claim the **l** child is yours, and each
3:25 "Cut the **l** child in two and give half to each of
3:26 woman who really was the mother of the **l** child,
7: 8 Solomon's **l** quarters surrounded a courtyard
7: 8 He also built similar **l** quarters for Pharaoh's
9:20 There were still some people **l** in the land who
13:11 it happened, there was an old prophet **l** in Bethel,
2Ki 10: 1 Now Ahab had seventy sons **l** in the city of
10:11 Then Jehu killed all of Ahab's relatives **l** in Jezreel
19: 4 the Assyrian representative defying the **l** God
19:16 Sennacherib's words of defiance against the **l** God.
23: 8 the LORD, who were **l** in other towns of Judah.
25:30 to cover his **l** expenses until the day of his death.
1Ch 2:55 and the families of scribes **l** at Jabez—
4:40 Some of Ham's descendants had been **l** in the
8: 6 leaders of the clans **l** at Geba, were driven out
8:13 They were the leaders of the clans **l** in Aijalon,
12:15 and drove out all the people **l** in the lowlands on
17: 1 "Here I am **l** in this beautiful cedar palace,
22: 2 orders to call together the foreigners **l** in Israel,
2Ch 8: 7 There were still some people **l** in the land who
11:13 and Levites **l** among the northern tribes of Israel
31:19 who were **l** in the open villages around the towns,

Ezr 4:17 and their colleagues **l** in Samaria and throughout
9:1 separate from the other peoples **l** in the land.
9:11 by the detestable practices of the people **l** there.
Ne 3:26 and the Temple servants **l** on the hill of Ophel,
4:22 I also told everyone **l** outside the walls to move
11:1 Now the leaders of the people were **l** in Jerusalem,
11:30 So the people of Judah were **l** all the way from
Est 2:20 just as she did when she was **l** in his home.
9:19 rural Jews **l** in unwalled villages celebrate an
Job 7:16 I do not want to go on **l**. Oh, leave me alone for
12:10 For the life of every **l** thing is in his hand,
16:12 "I was **l** quietly until he broke me apart. He took
27:2 "I make this vow by the **l** God, who has taken
28:13 where to find it, for it is not found among the **l**.
33:30 the grave so they may live in the light of the **l**.
35:3 you also ask, 'What's the use of **l** a righteous life?
36:14 die young after wasting their lives in immoral **l**.
42:16 **l** to see four generations of his children
Ps 16:11 and the pleasures of **l** with you forever.
27:13 while I am here in the land of the **l**.
34:14 and do good. / Work hard at **l** in peace with others.
42:2 I thirst for God, the **l** God. / When can I come
52:5 and drag you from the land of the **l**. / *Interlude*
81:12 stubborn way, / **l** according to their own desires.
84:2 and soul, / I will shout joyfully to the **l** God.
98:7 his praise! / Let the earth and all **l** things join in.
104:30 new life is born / to replenish all the **l** of the earth.
119:7 righteous laws, / I will thank you by **l** as I should!
120:6 I am tired of **l** here / among people who hate peace.
136:25 He gives food to every **l** thing. / His faithful love
145:16 you satisfy the hunger and thirst of every **l** thing.
Pr 1:31 That is why they must eat the bitter fruit of **l** their
10:2 has no lasting value, but right **l** can save your life.
11:4 but right **l** is a safeguard against death.
16:31 is a crown of glory; it is gained by **l** a godly life.
22:14 those **l** under the LORD's displeasure will fall
Ecc 4:2 I concluded that the dead are better off than the **l**.
9:4 There is hope only for the **l**. For as they say,
9:5 The **l** at least know they will die, but the dead
9:14 There was a small town with only a few people **l** in
9:15 wise man **l** there who knew how to save the town,
12:1 youth before you grow old and no longer enjoy **l**.
SS 4:15 You are a garden fountain, a well of **l** water,
Isa 8:19 Can the **l** find out the future from the dead?
37:4 the Assyrian representative defying the **l** God
37:17 Sennacherib's words of defiance against the **l** God.
38:11 while still in the land of the **l**. / Never again will I
38:19 Only the **l** can praise you as I do today.
47:8 **l** at ease and feeling secure,
58:3 because you are **l** for yourselves even while you
Jer 2:13 They have forsaken me—the fountain of **l** water.
9:11 Judah will be ghost towns, with no one **l** in them."
10:10 But the LORD is the only true God, the **l** God.
17:13 have forsaken the LORD, the fountain of **l** water.
17:20 you people of Judah and everyone **l** in Jerusalem.
22:6 you deserted, with no one **l** within your walls.
23:36 of our God, the **l** God, the LORD Almighty.
25:20 along with all the foreigners **l** in that land. So did
26:15 lie on you, on this city, and on every person **l** in it.
29:16 and all those still **l** here in Jerusalem—
44:1 Judeans **l** in northern Egypt in the cities of Migdol,
44:15 a great crowd of all the Judeans **l** in Pathros,
44:26 from the LORD, all you Judeans now **l** in Egypt:
46:19 will be destroyed, without a single person **l** there.
47:7 and the people **l** along the sea must be destroyed."
48:9 her cities will be left empty, with no one **l** in them.
49:1 Why are you, who worship Molech, **l** in its towns?
51:37 and contempt, without a single person **l** there.
52:34 to cover his **l** expenses until the day of his death.
Eze 1:5 From the center of the cloud came four **l** beings
1:9 The wings of each **l** being touched the wings of the
1:9 The **l** beings were able to fly in any direction
1:11 one pair stretched out to touch the wings of the **l**
1:13 The **l** beings looked like bright coals of fire
1:14 And the **l** beings darted to and fro like flashes of
1:19 When the four **l** beings moved, the wheels moved
1:20 The spirit of the four **l** beings was in the wheels.
1:20 spirit went, the wheels and the **l** beings went, too.
1:21 When the **l** beings moved, the wheels moved.
1:21 When the **l** beings stopped, the wheels stopped.
1:21 When the **l** beings flew into the air, the wheels rose
1:21 For the spirit of the **l** beings was in the wheels.
1:23 Beneath this surface the wings of each **l** being
3:13 It was the sound of the wings of the **l** beings as
10:15 These were the same **l** beings I had seen beside the
10:17 for the spirit of the **l** beings was in the wheels.
10:20 These were the same **l** beings I had seen beneath
12:19 the Sovereign LORD concerning those **l** in Israel
14:20 Even if Noah, Daniel, and Job were **l** there,
26:20 given a position of respect here in the land of the **l**.
32:32 For I have caused my terror to fall upon all the **l**.
33:24 the scattered remnants of Judah **l** among the ruined
33:27 as I live, those **l** in the ruins will die by the sword.
33:27 Those **l** in the open fields will be eaten by wild
36:17 when the people of Israel were **l** in their own land,
37:3 of man, can these bones become **l** people again?"
38:14 When my people are **l** in peace in their land,
38:20 All **l** things—all the fish, birds, animals,
43:7 remain here forever, **l** among the people of Israel.
45:5 will be a **l** area for the Levites who work at the
Da 2:30 because I am wiser than any **l** person that I know
4:4 was **l** in my palace in comfort and prosperity.
6:20 out in anguish, "Daniel, servant of the **l** God!
6:26 For he is the **l** God, / and he will endure forever.
Hos 1:10 it will be said, 'You are children of the **l** God.'
4:3 and all **l** things are becoming sick and dying.
11:9 I am the Holy One **l** among you, and I will not
Am 5:24 a river of righteous **l** that will never run dry.
Ob 1:19 "Then my people **l** in the Negev will occupy the
1:19 Those **l** in the foothills of Judah will possess the
Jnh 4:11 But Nineveh has more than 120,000 people **l** in
Hag 1:4 "Why are you **l** in luxurious houses while my
Zec 12:6 while the people **l** in Jerusalem remain secure.
Mal 2:6 they walked with me, **l** good and righteous lives,
3:5 or who deprive the foreigners **l** among you of
Mt 16:16 "You are the Messiah, the Son of the **l** God."
22:32 of Jacob.' So he is the God of the **l**, not the dead."
26:63 "I demand in the name of the **l** God that you tell us
Mk 12:27 So he is the God of the **l**, not the dead. You have
Lk 3:2 son of Zechariah, who was **l** out in the wilderness.
15:13 and there he wasted all his money on wild **l**.
20:38 So he is the God of the **l**, not the dead. They are all
21:34 Don't let me find you **l** in careless ease
21:35 For that day will come upon everyone **l** on the
Jn 4:10 you would ask me, and I would give you **l** water."
4:11 very deep well. Where would you get this **l** water?
4:18 and you aren't even married to the man you're **l**
6:51 I am the **l** bread that came down out of heaven.
6:57 I live by the power of the **l** Father who sent me;
7:38 For the Scriptures declare that rivers of **l** water will
7:39 (When he said "**l** water," he was speaking of the
Ac 1:20 his home become desolate, with no one **l** in it.'
2:5 Godly Jews from many nations were **l** in Jerusalem
9:43 long time in Joppa, **l** with Simon, a leatherworker.
10:42 of God to be the judge of all—the **l** and the dead.
14:15 turn from these worthless things to the **l** God,
21:21 **l** in the Gentile world to turn their backs on the
Ro 7:1 that the law applies only to a person who is still **l**?
8:9 by the Spirit if you have the Spirit of God **l** in you.
8:9 Spirit of Christ **l** in them are not Christians at all.)
8:11 your mortal body by this same Spirit **l** within you.
9:26 he will say, / 'You are children of the **l** God.' "
12:1 Let them be a **l** and holy sacrifice—the kind he will
13:11 Another reason for right **l** is that you know how
13:12 Clothe yourselves with the armor of right **l**,
13:13 or in adultery and immoral **l**, or in fighting
14:17 but of **l** a life of goodness and peace and joy in the
1Co 4:12 worked wearily with our own hands to earn our **l**.
4:20 God is not just fancy talk; it is **l** by God's power.
5:1 your church who is **l** in sin with his father's wife.
7:12 and she is willing to continue **l** with him,
7:13 and he is willing to continue **l** with her, she must
9:2 for you are **l** proof that I am the Lord's apostle.
15:45 "The first man, Adam, became a **l** person."
15:52 And then we who are **l** will be transformed so that
2Co 3:3 with pen and ink, but with the Spirit of the **l** God.
6:16 and idols? For we are the temple of the **l** God.
Gal 2:14 discarded the Jewish laws and are **l** like a Gentile,
5:21 that anyone **l** that sort of life will not inherit the
5:25 If we are **l** now by the Holy Spirit, let us follow the
Eph 2:12 In those days you were **l** apart from Christ.
4:6 who is over us all and **l** through us all.
Php 1:21 For to me, **l** is for Christ, and dying is even better.
4:12 I have learned the secret of **l** in every situation,
Col 2:5 am very happy because you are **l** as you should and
1Th 1:9 turned away from idols to serve the true and **l** God.
2:9 Night and day we toiled to earn a **l** so that our
4:15 We who are still **l** when the Lord returns will not
2Th 3:11 Yet we hear that some of you are **l** idle lives,
3:12 Settle down and get to work. Earn your own **l**.
1Ti 3:15 This is the church of the **l** God, which is the pillar
4:10 for our hope is in the **l** God, who is the Savior of
5:8 especially those **l** in the same household,
6:17 But their trust should be in the **l** God, who richly
2Ti 4:1 who will someday judge the **l** and the dead when
4:19 and those **l** at the household of Onesiphorus.
Tit 2:1 promote the kind of **l** that reflects right teaching.
2:12 And we are instructed to turn from godless **l**
Heb 3:12 and unbelieving, turning you away from the **l** God.
4:12 For the word of God is full of **l** power. It is sharper
5:13 And a person who is **l** on milk isn't very far along
9:14 that lead to death so that we can worship the **l** God.
10:31 It is a terrible thing to fall into the hands of the **l**
11:9 by faith—for he was like a foreigner, **l** in a tent.
12:11 of right **l** for those who are trained in this way.
12:22 to the city of the **l** God, the heavenly Jerusalem,
1Pe 1:1 I am writing to God's chosen people who are **l** as
1:23 because it comes from the eternal, **l** word of God.
2:4 to Christ, who is the **l** cornerstone of God's temple.
2:5 building you, as **l** stones, into his spiritual temple.
3:11 and do good. / Work hard at **l** in peace with others.
4:5 who will judge everyone, both the **l** and the dead.
2Pe 1:3 his divine power gives us everything we need for **l**
2:18 those who have just escaped from such wicked **l**.
3:11 melt away, what holy, godly lives you should be **l**!
1Jn 1:6 with God but go on **l** in spiritual darkness. We are
not **l** in the truth.
1:7 But if we are **l** in the light of God's presence,
2:14 because you are strong with God's word **l** in your
3:19 It is by our actions that we know we are **l** in the
4:15 that Jesus is the Son of God have God **l** in them,
2Jn 1:4 some of your children and find them **l** in the truth,
3Jn 1:3 your faithfulness and that you are **l** in the truth.
Jude 1:19 because they do not have God's Spirit **l** in them.
Rev 1:18 I am the **l** one who died. Look, I am alive forever
4:6 and around the throne were four **l** beings,
4:7 The first of these **l** beings had the form of a lion;
4:8 Each of these **l** beings had six wings, and their
4:9 Whenever the **l** beings give glory and honor
5:6 and the four **l** beings and among the twenty-four
5:8 the four **l** beings and the twenty-four elders fell
5:11 around the throne and the **l** beings and the elders.
5:14 And the four **l** beings said, "Amen!"
6:1 Then one of the four **l** beings called out with a
6:3 I heard the second **l** being say, "Come!"
6:5 third seal, I heard the third **l** being say, "Come!"
6:6 And a voice from among the four **l** beings said,
6:7 I heard the fourth **l** being say, "Come!"
7:2 from the east, carrying the seal of the **l** God.
7:11 and around the elders and the four **l** beings.
8:9 And one-third of all things **l** in the sea died.
14:3 and before the four **l** beings and the twenty-four
15:7 And one of the four **l** beings handed each of the
18:3 have grown rich as a result of her luxurious **l**."
19:4 and the four **l** beings fell down and worshiped

LIZARD (4) [LIZARDS]

Lev 11:29 the mole, the mouse, the great **l** of all varieties,
11:30 the monitor **l**, the common **l**, the sand **l**, and the

LIZARDS (2) [LIZARD]

Pr 30:28 **L**—they are easy to catch, / but they are found
Eze 8:10 with all kinds of snakes, **l**, and hideous creatures.

LO-AMMI (1)

Hos 1:9 And the LORD said, "Name him **L**—'Not my

LO-DEBAR (4)

Jos 13:26 and Betonim, and from Mahanaim to **L**.
2Sa 9:4 "In **L**," Ziba told him, "at the home of Makir son
17:27 an Ammonite, and by Makir son of Ammiel of **L**,
Am 6:13 as stupid is this bragging about your conquest of **L**.

LO-RUHAMAH (2)

Hos 1:6 LORD said to Hosea, "Name your daughter **L**—
1:8 After Gomer had weaned **L**, she again became

LOAD (12) [LOADED, LOADING, LOADS]

Ge 45:17 "Tell your brothers to **l** their pack animals
Ex 3:21 They will **l** you down with gifts so you will not
5:9 **L** them down with more work. Make them sweat!
18:22 They will help you carry the **l**, making the task
23:5 who hates you struggling beneath a heavy **l**,
Nu 4:19 and assign a specific duty or **l** to each person.
11:14 all these people by myself! The **l** is far too heavy!
2Ki 5:17 but please allow me to **l** two of my mules with
Ne 4:17 on their work with one hand supporting their **l**.
Pr 11:5 their honesty; the wicked fall beneath their **l** of sin.
Isa 17:11 Your only harvest will be a **l** of grief and incurable
Hos 5:5 against her; she will stumble under her **l** of guilt.

LOADED (25) [LOAD]

Ge 24:10 He **l** ten of Abraham's camels with gifts and set
42:26 So they **l** up their donkeys with the grain
44:3 and set out on their journey with their **l** donkeys.
44:13 **l** the donkeys again, and returned to the city.
45:23 He sent his father ten donkeys **l** with the good
45:23 and ten donkeys **l** with grain and all kinds of other
45:27 and when he saw the wagons **l** with the food sent
1Sa 16:20 and a donkey **l** down with food and wine.
2Sa 16:1 He was leading two donkeys **l** with two hundred
1Ki 10:2 and a great caravan of camels **l** with spices,
10:22 **l** down with gold, silver, ivory, apes, and peacocks.
2Ki 8:9 So Hazael **l** down forty camels with the finest
2Ch 9:1 and a great caravan of camels **l** with spices,
9:21 **l** down with gold, silver, ivory, apes, and peacocks.
Ps 105:37 people safely out of Egypt, **l** with silver and gold;
144:14 and may our oxen be **l** down with produce.
Isa 1:4 They are **l** down with a burden of guilt. They are
22:24 He will be **l** down with responsibility, and he will
30:6 and camels **l** with treasure to pay for Egypt's aid.
Da 4:12 green leaves, and it was **l** with fruit for all to eat.
4:21 green leaves, and it was **l** with fruit for all to eat.
Hos 10:1 prosperous Israel is—a luxuriant vine **l** with fruit!
Am 2:13 as a wagon groans when it is **l** down with grain.
Jn 21:8 with the boat and pulled the **l** net to the shore,
Rev 14:19 and **l** the grapes into the great winepress of God's

LOADING (2) [LOAD]

Jos 9:4 **l** their donkeys with weathered saddlebags and old
Ne 13:15 in bundles of grain and **l** them on their donkeys.

LOADS (9) [LOAD]

Nu 4:24 be in the areas of general service and carrying **l**.
4:27 They must assign the Gershonites the **l** they are to
4:31 duties at the Tabernacle will consist of carrying **l**.
4:32 You must assign the various **l** to each man by
Job 37:11 He **l** the clouds with moisture, and they flash with
Ps 145:14 the fallen / and lifts up those bent beneath their **l**.
146:8 lifts the burdens of those bent beneath their **l**.
Jer 17:27 and if on the Sabbath day you bring **l** of
La 5:13 and the children stagger under heavy **l** of wood.

LOAF (19) [LOAVES]

Ex 29:23 Then take one **l** of bread, one cake mixed with
Lev 8:26 On top of these he placed a **l** of unleavened bread,
24:5 choice flour, using three quarts of flour for each **l**.
Jdg 7:13 and in my dream a **l** of barley bread came tumbling
2Sa 6:19 a **l** of bread, a cake of dates, and a cake of raisins.
1Ki 17:13 that 'last meal,' but bake me a little **l** of bread first.
1Ch 16:3 a **l** of bread, a cake of dates, and a cake of raisins.
Jer 37:21 **l** of fresh bread every day as long as there was any
Mt 7:9 if your children ask for a **l** of bread, do you give
26:26 Jesus took a **l** of bread and asked God's blessing
Mk 8:14 so there was only one **l** of bread with them in the
14:22 Jesus took a **l** of bread and asked God's blessing

Lk 4: 3 Son of God, change this stone into a **l** of bread."
22: 19 Then he took a **l** of bread; and when he had
24: 30 As they sat down to eat, he took a small **l** of bread,
1Co 10: 16 And when we break the **l** of bread, aren't we
10: 17 And we all eat from one **l**, showing that we are one
11: 23 he was betrayed, the Lord Jesus took a **l** of bread,
Rev 6: 6 "A **l** of wheat bread or three loaves of barley for a

LOAN (8) [LOANED, LOANS]

Dt 15: 9 Do not be mean-spirited and refuse someone a **l**
15: 9 If you refuse to make the **l** and the needy person
Job 24: 3 must surrender her valuable ox as collateral for a **l**.
24: 9 her breast; they take the baby as a pledge for a **l**.
Pr 6: 1 if you co-sign a **l** for a friend or guarantee the debt
11: 15 Guaranteeing a **l** for a stranger is dangerous;
22: 26 or put up a guarantee for someone else's **l**.
Eze 22: 12 There are hired murderers, **l** racketeers,

LOANED (2) [LOAN]

Dt 23: 19 food, or anything else that may be **l** with interest.
Lk 7: 41 "A man **l** money to two people—five hundred

LOANS (5) [LOAN]

Dt 15: 2 Creditors must cancel the **l** they have made to their
23: 19 "Do not charge interest on the **l** you make to a
Ne 5: 10 and grain, but now let us stop this business of **l**.
Ps 37: 26 The godly always give generous **l** to others,
Eze 18: 8 And suppose he grants **l** without interest,

LOATHE (2) [LOATHED, LOATHES, LOATHING, LOATHSOME]

Ps 88: 8 You have caused my friends to **l** me; / you have
Eze 23: 28 hand you over to your enemies, to those you **l**.

LOATHED (1) [LOATHE]

Eze 16: 45 For your mother **l** her husband and her children,

LOATHES (1) [LOATHE]

Pr 21: 27 God **l** the sacrifice of an evil person,

LOATHING (1) [LOATHE]

Dt 32: 19 "The LORD saw this and was filled with **l**.

LOATHSOME (8) [LOATHE]

Job 19: 17 is repulsive to my wife. I am **l** to my own family.
Eze 14: 6 away from your idols, and stop all your **l** practices.
16: 2 "Son of man, confront Jerusalem with her **l** sins.
16: 22 In all your years of adultery and **l** sin, you have not
16: 50 She was proud and did **l** things, so I wiped her out,
16: 51 You have done far more **l** things than your sisters
18: 12 worships idols and takes part in **l** practices,
20: 4 Make them realize how **l** the actions of their

LOAVES (44) [LOAF]

Ex 29: 2 fine wheat flour and no yeast, make **l** of bread,
Lev 7: 12 **l**, wafers, and cakes—all made without yeast
7: 13 must also be accompanied by **l** of yeast bread.
23: 17 bring two **l** of bread to be lifted up before the
23: 17 These **l** must be baked from three quarts of choice
23: 20 together with the **l** representing the first of your
24: 5 "You must bake twelve **l** of bread from choice
24: 6 and arrange the **l** in two rows, with six in each row.
24: 9 The **l** of bread belong to Aaron and his male
1Sa 10: 3 young goats, another will have three **l** of bread,
10: 4 They will greet you and offer you two of the **l**,
17: 17 and these ten **l** of bread to your brothers.
21: 3 Give me five **l** of bread or anything else you
25: 18 She quickly gathered two hundred **l** of bread,
2Sa 16: 1 two donkeys loaded with two hundred **l** of bread,
1Ki 14: 3 Take him a gift of ten **l** of bread, some cakes,
2Ki 4: 42 and twenty **l** of barley bread made from the first
Mt 4: 3 Son of God, change these stones into **l** of bread."
14: 17 "We have only five **l** of bread and two fish!"
14: 19 And he took the five **l** and two fish, looked up
14: 19 Breaking the **l** into pieces, he gave some of the
14: 21 five thousand men had eaten from those five **l**,
15: 34 Jesus asked, "How many **l** of bread do you have?"
15: 36 Then he took the seven **l** and the fish, thanked God
16: 9 you remember the five thousand I fed with five **l**,
16: 10 you remember the four thousand I fed with seven **l**,
Mk 6: 38 "We have five **l** of bread and two fish."
6: 41 Jesus took the five **l** and two fish, looked up
6: 41 Breaking the **l** into pieces, he kept giving the bread
6: 44 Five thousand men had eaten from those five **l**!
6: 52 the significance of the miracle of the multiplied **l**,
8: 5 "How many **l** of bread do you have?" he asked.
8: 6 Then he took the seven **l**, thanked God for them,
8: 19 What about the five thousand men I fed with five **l**
8: 20 "And when I fed the four thousand with seven **l**,
Lk 9: 13 "We have only five **l** of bread and two fish.
9: 16 Jesus took the five **l** and two fish, looked up
9: 16 Breaking the **l** into pieces, he kept giving the bread
11: 5 at midnight, wanting to borrow three **l** of bread.
Jn 6: 9 "There's a young boy here with five barley **l**
6: 11 Then Jesus took the **l**, gave thanks to God,
6: 13 There were only five barley **l** to start with,
Heb 9: 2 a table, and **l** of holy bread on the table.
Rev 6: 6 of wheat bread or three **l** of barley for a day's pay.

LOBE (14)

Ex 29: 13 also the long **l** of the liver and the two kidneys with
29: 22 Also, take the long **l** of the liver, the two kidneys
Lev 3: 4 and the **l** of the liver, which is to be removed with
3: 10 and the **l** of the liver, which is to be removed with
3: 15 and the **l** of the liver, which is to be removed with
4: 9 around them near the loins, and the **l** of the liver.
7: 4 and the **l** of the liver, which is to be removed with
8: 16 the **l** of the liver, and the two kidneys and their fat,
8: 23 of its blood and put it on the **l** of Aaron's right ear,
8: 24 and put some of the blood on the **l** of their right
8: 25 the fat around the internal organs, the **l** of the liver,
9: 10 and the **l** of the liver from the sin offering,
9: 19 along with the kidneys and the **l** of the liver.
14: 28 oil from his hand on the **l** of the person's right ear,

LOCAL (29)

Ge 24: 3 that you will not let my son marry one of these **l**
24: 37 not let Isaac marry one of the **l** Canaanite women.
26: 20 But then the **l** shepherds came and claimed the
26: 22 and the **l** people finally left him alone.
27: 46 "I'm sick and tired of these **l** Hittite women.
28: 8 that his father despised the **l** Canaanite women.
34: 2 But when the **l** prince, Shechem son of Hamor the
50: 11 The **l** residents, the Canaanites, renamed the place
Nu 25: 1 themselves by sleeping with the **l** Moabite women.
32: 17 so they will be safe from any attacks by the **l**
Dt 17: 8 "Suppose a case arises in a **l** court that is too hard
Jdg 9: 27 held in the temple of the **l** god, the wine flowed
1Ki 3: 2 people of Israel sacrificed their offerings at **l** altars,
3: 3 offered sacrifices and burned incense at the **l** altars.
1Ch 7: 21 to steal livestock from the **l** farmers near Gath.
Ezr 3: 3 Even though the people were afraid of the **l**
4: 4 Then the **l** residents tried to discourage
4: 9 the judges and **l** leaders, the people of Tarpel,
Est 3: 12 and the **l** officials of each province in their own
8: 9 and **l** officials of all the 127 provinces stretching
Mk 5: 22 A leader of the **l** synagogue, whose name was
Lk 8: 41 a leader of the **l** synagogue, came and fell down at
15: 15 He persuaded a **l** farmer to hire him to feed his
Ac 14: 11 they shouted in their **l** dialect, "These men are
15: 2 accompanied by some **l** believers, to talk to the
21: 4 We went ashore, found the **l** believers, and stayed
21: 12 were traveling with him, as well as the **l** believers,
25: 24 man whose death is demanded both by the **l** Jews
28: 17 he called together the **l** Jewish leaders.

LOCATED (20) [LOCATION, LOCATIONS, RELOCATED]

Ge 10: 12 city of the empire, **l** between Nineveh and Calah.
Nu 2: 2 The Tabernacle will be **l** at the center of these
Dt 11: 30 They are **l** toward the west, not far from the oaks
Jos 15: 8 of the Jebusites, where the city of Jerusalem is **l**.
24: 32 This land was **l** in the territory allotted to the tribes
Jdg 13: 25 which is **l** between the towns of Zorah and Eshtaol,
1Sa 10: 5 of God, where the garrison of the Philistines is **l**,
2Ki 2: 19 "This town is **l** in beautiful natural surroundings,
23: 8 This gate was **l** to the left of the city gate as one
1Ch 21: 29 made in the wilderness were **l** at the hill of Gibeon.
2Ch 1: 3 the hill at Gibeon where God's Tabernacle was **l**.
28: 18 And the Philistines had raided towns **l** in the
Ne 11: 20 inheritance was **l** in any of the towns of Judah.
Job 38: 17 Do you know where the gates of death are **l**?
Jer 26: 6 the place where the Tabernacle was **l**.
35: 4 This room was **l** next to the one used by the palace
Eze 45: 3 it the sanctuary of the Most Holy Place will be **l**.
45: 4 for their homes, and my Temple will be **l** within it.
Ac 14: 13 The temple of Zeus was **l** on the outskirts of the
Rev 2: 13 live in the city where that great throne of Satan is **l**,

LOCATION (4) [LOCATED]

Nu 10: 21 the Tabernacle would already be set up at its new **l**.
1Ki 8: 1 LORD's covenant from its **l** in the City of David,
1Ch 22: 1 "This will be the **l** for the Temple of the LORD
2Ch 5: 2 LORD's covenant from its **l** in the City of David,

LOCATIONS (1) [LOCATED]

2Ch 33: 19 includes a list of the **l** where he built pagan shrines

LOCK (5) [LOCKED, LOCKS]

Lev 14: 38 he will leave the house and **l** it up for seven days.
2Sa 13: 17 this woman out, and **l** the door behind her!"
Job 41: 17 They **l** together so nothing can penetrate them.
Isa 26: 20 Go home, my people, and **l** your doors! Hide until
Mt 16: 19 Whatever you **l** on earth will be locked in heaven,

LOCKED (15) [LOCK]

Jdg 3: 23 Then Ehud closed and **l** the doors and climbed
3: 24 and found the doors to the upstairs room **l**.
Job 38: 10 For I **l** it behind barred gates, limiting its shores.
Ps 33: 7 its boundaries / and **l** the oceans in vast reservoirs.
Pr 18: 19 Arguments separate friends like a gate **l** with iron
Isa 24: 10 in chaos; every home is **l** to keep out looters.
Jnh 2: 6 I was **l** out of life and imprisoned in the land of the
Mt 16: 19 Whatever you lock on earth will be **l** in heaven,
25: 10 with him to the marriage feast, and the door was **l**.
Lk 11: 7 The door is **l** for the night, and we are all in bed.
13: 25 but when the head of the house has **l** the door,
Jn 20: 19 the disciples were meeting behind **l** doors
20: 26 The doors were **l**; but suddenly, as before,
Ac 5: 23 "The jail was **l**, with the guards standing outside,
Rev 20: 3 which he then shut and **l** so Satan could not

LOCKS (1) [LOCK]

La 2: 9 All their **l** and bars are destroyed, for he has

LOCUST (3) [LOCUSTS]

Ex 10: 14 It was the worst **l** plague in Egyptian history,
10: 19 Not a single **l** remained in all the land of Egypt.
Job 39: 20 Did you give it the ability to leap forward like a **l**?

LOCUSTS (40) [LOCUST]

Ex 10: 4 tomorrow I will cover the whole country with **l**.
10: 12 your hand over the land of Egypt to bring on the **l**.
10: 13 morning arrived, the east wind had brought the **l**.
10: 14 And the **l** swarmed over the land of Egypt from
10: 15 For the **l** covered the surface of the whole country,
10: 19 west wind that blew the **l** out into the Red Sea.
Lev 11: 22 **l** of all varieties, crickets, bald **l**, and grasshoppers.
Dt 28: 38 but harvest little, for **l** will eat your crops.
Jdg 6: 5 coming with their cattle and tents as thick as **l**,
7: 12 the east had settled in the valley like a swarm of **l**.
1Ki 8: 37 or crop disease, or attacks of **l** or caterpillars,
2Ch 6: 28 or crop disease, or attacks of **l** or caterpillars,
7: 13 or I might command **l** to devour your crops,
Ps 78: 46 to caterpillars; / their harvest was consumed by **l**.
105: 34 He spoke, and hordes of **l** came— / **l** beyond number.
Pr 30: 27 **L**—they have no king, / but they march like an
Isa 33: 4 Just as **l** strip the fields and vines, so Jerusalem
Jer 51: 14 will be filled with enemies, like fields filled with **l**,
Joel 1: 4 After the cutting **l** finished eating the crops, the swarming **l** took what was left!
1: 4 After them came the hopping **l**, and then the stripping **l**, too!
1: 6 A vast army of **l** has invaded my land. It is a
2: 25 will give you back what you lost to the stripping **l**, the cutting **l**, the swarming **l**, and the hopping **l**.
Am 4: 9 **L** devoured all your fig and olive trees.
7: 1 I saw him preparing to send a vast swarm of **l** over
7: 2 In my vision the **l** ate everything in sight that was
Na 3: 15 The enemy will consume you like **l**,
3: 16 But like a swarm of **l**, they strip the land and
3: 17 Your princes and officials are also like **l**,
3: 17 But like **l** that fly away when the sun comes up to
Mt 3: 4 wore a leather belt; his food was **l** and wild honey.
Mk 1: 6 wore a leather belt; his food was **l** and wild honey.
Rev 9: 3 Then **l** came from the smoke and descended on the
9: 7 The **l** looked like horses armed for battle. They had

LOD (4)

1Ch 8: 12 Shemed (who built Ono and **L** and their villages),
Ezr 2: 33 The citizens of **L**, Hadid, and Ono | 725
Ne 7: 37 The citizens of **L**, Hadid, and Ono | 721
11: 35 **L**, Ono, and the Valley of Craftsmen.

LODGING (3) [LODGE]

Lk 9: 12 and farms, so they can find food and **l** for the night.
Ac 28: 16 Paul was permitted to have his own private **l**,
Ro 12: 13 home for dinner or, if they need **l**, for the night.

LOFT [KJV] STORIES, UPPER ROOM

LOFTINESS (1) [LOFTY]

Jer 48: 29 We know of her **l**, her arrogance, and her haughty

LOFTY (4) [LOFTINESS]

Isa 6: 1 He was sitting on a **l** throne, and the train of his
57: 15 The high and **l** one who inhabits eternity, the Holy
Hab 3: 11 The **l** sun and moon began to fade, obscured by
1Co 2: 1 when I first came to you I didn't use **l** words

LOG (6) [LOGS]

Mt 7: 3 your friend's eye when you have a **l** in your own?
7: 4 when you can't see past the **l** in your own eye?
7: 5 First get rid of the **l** from your own eye,
Lk 6: 41 your friend's eye when you have a **l** in your own?
6: 42 when you can't see past the **l** in your own eye?
6: 42 First get rid of the **l** from your own eye;

LOGIC (2)

Job 32: 14 with me, I would not answer with that kind of **l**!
Gal 1: 11 preach is not based on mere human reasoning or **l**.

LOGS (11) [LOG]

2Sa 5: 11 a palace. Hiram also sent many cedar **l** for lumber.
1Ki 5: 9 My servants will bring the **l** from the Lebanon
2Ki 6: 2 to the Jordan River, where there are plenty of **l**.
1Ch 14: 1 a palace. Hiram also sent many cedar **l** for lumber.
22: 4 He also provided innumerable cedar **l**, for the men
2Ch 2: 3 "Send me cedar **l** like the ones that were supplied
2: 8 me cedar, cypress, and almug **l** from Lebanon,
2: 16 and will float the **l** in rafts down the coast of the
2: 16 From there you can transport the **l** up to
Ezr 3: 7 and bought cedar **l** from the people of Tyre
3: 7 The **l** were brought down from the Lebanon

LOINS (8)

Lev 3: 4 two kidneys with the fat around them near the **l**,
3: 10 two kidneys with the fat around them near the **l**,
3: 15 two kidneys with the fat around them near the **l**,
4: 9 two kidneys with the fat around them near the **l**,
7: 4 two kidneys with the fat around them near the **l**,
Dt 33: 11 Crush the **l** of their enemies; / strike down their
Job 40: 16 See its powerful **l** and the muscles of its belly.
Heb 7: 10 the seed from which he came was in Abraham's **l**

LOIS (1)
2Ti 1: 5 of your mother, Eunice, and your grandmother, **L.**

LONE (1) [ALONE]
2Sa 18: 24 he looked, he saw a **l** man running toward them.

LONELY (4) [ALONE]
Ps 68: 6 God places the **l** in families; / he sets the prisoners
102: 6 in the desert, / like a **l** owl in a far-off wilderness.
102: 7 I lie awake, / **l** as a solitary bird on the roof.
Isa 30: 17 You will be left like a **l** flagpole on a distant

LONG (520) [LENGTH, LENGTHENS, LONG-DESERTED, LONG-STANDING, LONGED, LONGER, LONGING, LONGINGLY, LONGS]
Ge 3: 14 You will grovel in the dust as **l** as you live,
6: 3 will not put up with humans for such a **l** time,
6: 15 Make it 450 feet **l**, 75 feet wide, and 45 feet high.
8: 22 As **l** as the earth remains, there will be springtime
13: 10 Lot took a **l** look at the fertile plains of the Jordan
14: 11 and Gomorrah and began their **l** journey home,
18: 11 and Sarah was **l** past the age of having children,
21: 34 And Abraham lived in Philistine country for a **l**
31: 30 and you **l** intensely for your childhood home,
39: 22 Before **l**, the jailer put Joseph in charge of all the
42: 21 because of what we did to Joseph **l** ago.
46: 29 his father and wept on his shoulder for a **l** time.
47: 27 And before **l**, they began to prosper there, and their
48: 1 One day not **l** after this, word came to Joseph that
Ex 1: 14 and mortar and to work **l** hours in the fields.
10: 3 says: How **l** will you refuse to submit to me?
10: 7 to him. "How **l** will you let these disasters go on?
12: 11 eat this meal, as though prepared for a **l** journey.
13: 11 into the land he swore to give your ancestors **l** ago,
16: 28 "How **l** will these people refuse to obey my
17: 11 As **l** as Moses held up the staff with his hands,
19: 13 until they hear one **l** blast from the ram's horn.
19: 16 There was a **l**, loud blast from a ram's horn,
20: 12 Then you will live a **l**, full life in the land the
23: 26 among your people, and I will give you **l**, full lives.
25: 10 a sacred chest 3-3/4 feet **l**, 2-1/4 feet wide,
25: 17 It must be 3-3/4 feet **l** and 2-1/4 feet wide.
25: 23 3 feet **l**, 1-1/2 feet wide, and 2-1/4 feet high.
26: 2 Each sheet must be forty-two feet **l** and six feet
26: 8 each forty-five feet **l** and six feet wide. All eleven
27: 1 7-1/2 feet wide, 7-1/2 feet **l**, and 4-1/2 feet high.
27: 12 on the west end of the courtyard will be 75 feet **l**,
27: 13 The east end will also be 75 feet **l**.
27: 14 The curtain on the right side will be 22-1/2 feet **l**,
27: 15 curtain on the left side will also be 22-1/2 feet **l**,
27: 16 to the courtyard, make a curtain that is 30 feet **l**.
27: 18 So the entire courtyard will be 150 feet **l** and 75
29: 13 also the **l** lobe of the liver and the two kidneys with
29: 22 Also, take the **l** lobe of the liver, the two kidneys
33: 1 I told them **l** ago that I would give this land to their
36: 9 the same size—forty-two feet **l** and six feet wide.
36: 15 the same size—forty-five feet **l** and six feet wide.
37: 1 It was 3-3/4 feet **l**, 2-1/4 feet wide, and 2-1/4 feet
37: 6 It was 3-3/4 feet **l** and 2-1/4 feet wide.
37: 10 3 feet **l**, 1-1/2 feet wide, and 2-1/4 feet high.
38: 9 the courtyard. The south wall was 150 feet **l**.
38: 11 The north wall was also 150 feet **l**, with twenty
38: 14 The curtain on the right side was 22-1/2 feet **l**
38: 15 The curtain on the left side was also 22-1/2 feet **l**
38: 18 It was 30 feet **l** and 7-1/2 feet high, just like the
Lev 13: 46 As **l** as the disease lasts, they will be ceremonially
15: 25 the woman will be ceremonially unclean as **l** as the
25: 9 blow the trumpets loud and **l** throughout the land.
Nu 6: 4 As **l** as they are bound by their Nazirite vow,
6: 5 That is why they must let their hair grow **l**.
6: 8 This applies as **l** as they are set apart to the
9: 18 Then they remained where they were as **l** as the
9: 19 If the cloud remained over the Tabernacle for a **l**
9: 19 the Israelites stayed for a **l** time, just as the LORD
14: 11 said to Moses, "How **l** will these people reject me?
14: 27 "How **l** will this wicked nation complain about
20: 15 We lived there a **l** time and suffered as slaves to
25: 3 Before **l** Israel was joining in the worship of Baal
36: 6 as **l** as it is within their own ancestral tribe.
Dt 1: 6 'You have stayed at this mountain **l** enough.
1: 46 So you stayed there at Kadesh for a **l** time.
2: 1 and we wandered around Mount Seir for a **l** time.
2: 3 wandering around in this hill country **l** enough;
3: 11 His iron bed was more than thirteen feet **l** and six
4: 9 Do not let these things escape from your mind as **l**
4: 10 they will learn to fear me as **l** as they live,
4: 25 and have lived in the land a **l** time,
4: 40 Then you will enjoy a **l** life in the land the LORD
5: 3 The LORD did not make this covenant **l** ago with
5: 16 Then you will live a **l**, full life in the land the
5: 33 Then you will live **l** and prosperous lives in the
6: 2 might fear the LORD your God as **l** as you live.
6: 2 all his laws and commands, you will enjoy a **l** life.
9: 24 you have been rebelling against the LORD as **l** as
11: 9 you will enjoy a **l** life in the land the LORD
11: 21 so that as **l** as the sky remains above the earth,
12: 1 and regulations you must obey as **l** as you live in
12: 19 Be very careful never to forget the Levites as **l** as
12: 21 his name to be honored is a **l** way from your home.
14: 24 to be honored might be a **l** way from your home.
16: 3 the day you departed from Egypt as **l** as you live.
17: 19 the law with him and read it daily as **l** as he lives.
22: 7 mother go, so you may prosper and enjoy a **l** life.
23: 6 You must never, as **l** as you live, try to help the
25: 15 so that you will enjoy a **l** life in the land the
28: 32 Your heart will break as you **l** for them,
30: 18 You will not live a **l**, good life in the land you are
30: 20 Then you will live **l** in the land the LORD swore
31: 13 Do this as **l** as you live in the land you are crossing
32: 7 Remember the days of **l** ago; / think about the
32: 47 By obeying them you will enjoy a **l** life in the land
Jos 1: 5 to stand their ground against you as **l** as you live.
6: 5 When you hear the priests give one **l** blast on the
6: 16 as the priests sounded the **l** blast on their horns,
9: 11 our people instructed us, 'Prepare for a **l** journey.
9: 13 our clothing and sandals are worn out from our **l**,
11: 18 waging war for a **l** time to accomplish this.
18: 3 "How **l** are you going to wait before taking
22: 3 even though the campaign has lasted for such a **l**
Jdg 3: 16 a double-edged dagger that was eighteen inches **l**,
3: 25 But when the king didn't come out after a **l** delay,
5: 28 saying, / 'Why is his chariot so **l** in coming?
16: 22 But before **l** his hair began to grow back.
18: 31 as **l** as the Tabernacle of God remained at Shiloh.
1Sa 7: 2 The Ark remained in Kiriath-jearim for a **l** time—
7: 13 and didn't invade Israel again for a **l** time.
10: 24 And all the people shouted, "**L** live the king!"
16: 1 to Samuel, "You have mourned **l** enough for Saul.
20: 14 with the faithful love of the LORD as **l** as I live.
20: 31 As **l** as that son of Jesse is alive, you'll never be
30: 12 and nights. It wasn't **l** before his strength returned.
2Sa 3: 1 That was the beginning of a **l** war between those
5: 2 For a **l** time, even while Saul was our king,
8: 10 Hadadezer and Toi had **l** been enemies, and there
11: 10 you go home last night after being away for so **l**?"
13: 18 She was wearing a **l**, beautiful robe, as was the
14: 2 a woman who has been in deep sorrow for a **l** time.
16: 16 "**L** live the king!" he exclaimed. "**L** live the king!"
17: 29 and thirsty after your **l** march through the
1Ki 1: 25 with him and shouting, '**L** live King Adonijah!'
1: 34 the trumpets and shout, '**L** live King Solomon!'
1: 39 all the people shouted, "**L** live King Solomon!"
2: 38 So Shimei lived in Jerusalem for a **l** time.
3: 11 and have not asked for a **l** life or riches for yourself
3: 14 as your father, David, did, I will give you a **l** life."
6: 2 King Solomon built for the LORD was 90 feet **l**,
6: 17 outside the Most Holy Place, was 60 feet **l**.
6: 20 This inner sanctuary was 30 feet **l**, 30 feet wide,
6: 24 cherubim was 15 feet, each wing being 7-1/2 feet **l**.
7: 2 It was 150 feet **l**, 75 feet wide, and 45 feet high.
7: 6 of Pillars, which was 75 feet **l** and 45 feet wide.
7: 10 Some of the huge foundation stones were 15 feet **l**, and some were 12 feet **l**.
7: 27 each 6 feet **l**, 6 feet wide, and 4-1/2 feet tall.
8: 8 so **l** that their ends could be seen from the front
8: 40 and walk in your ways as **l** as they live in the land
18: 21 "How **l** are you going to waver between two
19: 7 some more, for there is a **l** journey ahead of you."
2Ki 9: 22 "How can there be peace as **l** as the idolatry
11: 12 their hands and shouted, "**L** live the king!"
19: 25 It was I, the LORD, who decided this **l** ago.
19: 25 **L** ago I planned what I am now causing to happen,
1Ch 7: 22 Their father, Ephraim, mourned for them a **l** time,
11: 2 For a **l** time, even while Saul was our king,
18: 10 Hadadezer and Toi had **l** been enemies, and there
29: 28 old age, having enjoyed **l** life, wealth, and honor.
2Ch 1: 11 or the death of your enemies or even a **l** life,
3: 3 foundation for the Temple of God was ninety feet **l**
3: 11 One wing of the first figure was 7-1/2 feet **l**,
3: 11 The other wing, also 7-1/2 feet **l**, touched one of
3: 12 the second figure had one wing 7-1/2 feet **l** that
3: 12 The other wing, also 7-1/2 feet **l**, touched the wing
4: 1 Solomon also made a bronze altar 30 feet **l**, 30 feet
5: 9 so **l** that their ends could be seen from the front
6: 13 He had made a bronze platform 7-1/2 feet **l**,
6: 31 and walk in your ways as **l** as they live in the land
15: 2 The LORD will stay with you as **l** as you stay
15: 3 For a **l** time, Israel was without the true God,
23: 11 and everyone shouted, "**L** live the king!"
26: 5 And as **l** as the king sought the LORD, God gave
Ezr 4: 15 because of its **l** history of sedition against the kings
Ne 2: 3 but I replied, "**L** live the king! Why shouldn't I be
2: 6 beside him, asked, "How **l** will you be gone?
12: 46 and thanks to God began **l** ago in the days of David
Est 5: 13 "But all this is meaningless as **l** as I see Mordecai
Job 3: 21 They **l** for death, and it won't come. They search
7: 1 A person's life is **l** and hard, like that of a hired
7: 3 months of futility, **l** and weary nights of misery.
7: 8 You see me now, but not for **l**. Your eyes will be
8: 2 "How **l** will you go on like this? Your words are a
13: 3 Oh, how I **l** to speak directly to the Almighty.
15: 19 those to whom the land was given **l** before any
18: 2 "How **l** before you stop talking? Speak sense if
19: 2 "How **l** will you torture me? How **l** will you try to break me with your words?
20: 13 He savored it, holding it **l** in his mouth.
27: 3 As **l** as I live, while I have breath from God,
27: 6 My conscience is clear for as **l** as I live.
29: 2 "I **l** for the years gone by when God took care of
29: 18 I will die surrounded by my family after a **l**,
36: 20 Do not **l** for the cover of night, for that is when
42: 17 he died, an old man who had lived a **l**, good life.
Ps 4: 2 How **l** will you people ruin my reputation?
4: 2 How **l** will you make these groundless
4: 2 How **l** will you pursue lies? / *Interlude*
6: 3 at heart. / How **l**, O LORD, until you restore me?
13: 1 O LORD, how **l** will you forget me? Forever? / How **l** will you look the other way?
13: 2 How **l** must I struggle with anguish in my soul,
13: 2 How **l** will my enemy have the upper hand?
25: 5 who saves me. / All day **l** I put my hope in you.
25: 6 which you have shown from **l** ages past.
32: 3 I was weak and miserable, / and I groaned all day **l**.
34: 12 any of you want to live / a life that is **l** and good?
35: 17 How **l**, O Lord, will you look on and do nothing?
35: 28 and goodness, / and I will praise you all day **l**.
38: 9 You know what I **l** for, Lord; / you hear my every
38: 12 They think up treacherous deeds all day **l**.
42: 1 pants for streams of water, / so I **l** for you, O God.
44: 1 of all you did in other days, / in days **l** ago:
44: 8 O God, we give glory to you all day **l**
49: 12 They will not last **l** despite their riches—
52: 2 All day **l** you plot destruction. / Your tongue cuts
56: 1 press in on me. / My foes attack me all day **l**.
63: 4 I will honor you as **l** as I live, / lifting up my hands
71: 8 stop praising you; / I declare your glory all day **l**.
71: 15 All day **l** I will proclaim your saving power,
71: 24 all day **l**, / for everyone who tried to hurt me
72: 5 May he live as **l** as the sun shines, / as **l** as the moon continues in the skies.
72: 15 **L** live the king! / May the gold of Sheba be given
72: 15 always pray for him / and bless him all day **l**.
72: 17 may it continue as **l** as the sun shines.
73: 14 All I get is trouble all day **l**; / every morning brings
74: 10 How **l**, O God, will you allow our enemies to mock
74: 22 Remember how these fools insult you all day **l**.
77: 2 All night **l** I pray, with hands lifted toward heaven,
77: 5 I think of the good old days, **l** since ended,
77: 11 I remember your wonderful deeds of **l** ago.
79: 5 O LORD, how **l** will you be angry with us? Forever? / How **l** will your jealousy burn like fire?
80: 4 how **l** will you be angry and reject our prayers?
82: 2 "How **l** will you judges hand down unjust
82: 2 How **l** will you shower special favors on the
84: 2 I **l**, yes, I faint with longing / to enter the courts of
88: 17 They swirl around me like floodwaters all day **l**.
89: 16 They rejoice all day **l** in your wonderful reputation.
89: 46 O LORD, how **l** will this go on? / Will you hide
89: 46 How **l** will your anger burn like fire?
90: 13 come back to us! / How **l** will you delay?
91: 16 I will satisfy them with a **l** life / and give them my
94: 3 How **l**, O LORD? / How **l** will the wicked be allowed to gloat?
104: 33 I will sing to the LORD as **l** as I live. / I will
112: 6 Those who are righteous will be **l** remembered.
116: 2 and listens, / I will pray as **l** as I have breath!
119: 40 I **l** to obey your commandments! / Renew my life
119: 84 How **l** must I wait? / When will you punish those
119: 97 how I love your law! / I think about it all day **l**.
119: 166 I **l** for your salvation, LORD, / so I have obeyed
128: 5 May you see Jerusalem prosper as **l** as you live.
129: 3 with cuts, / as if a farmer had plowed **l** furrows.
130: 6 I **l** for the Lord / more than sentries **l** for the dawn, / yes, more than sentries **l** for the dawn.
140: 2 evil in their hearts / and stir up trouble all day **l**.
146: 2 I will praise the LORD as **l** as I live. / I will sing
Pr 1: 22 "How **l** will you go on being simpleminded?
1: 22 How **l** will you mockers relish your mocking?
1: 22 How **l** will you fools fight the facts?
3: 2 for they will give you a **l** and satisfying life.
4: 10 and do as I say, and you will have a **l**, good life.
6: 9 But you, lazybones, how **l** will you sleep?
7: 19 for my husband is not home. He's away on a **l** trip.
13: 3 Those who control their tongue will have a **l** life;
22: 4 fear of the LORD lead to riches, honor, and **l** life.
23: 30 It is the one who spends **l** hours in the taverns,
28: 16 but a king will have a **l** reign if he hates dishonesty
29: 14 A king who is fair to the poor will have a **l** reign.
Ecc 1: 10 How do you know it didn't already exist **l** ago?
3: 12 be happy and to enjoy themselves as **l** as they can.
4: 6 especially when in the **l** run everything is so futile.
5: 18 under the sun—for however **l** God lets them live.
6: 10 It was known **l** ago what each person would be.
7: 10 Don't **l** for "the good old days," for you don't
8: 12 person sins a hundred times and still lives a **l** time,
8: 13 The wicked will never live **l**, good lives, for they
8: 13 Their days will never grow **l** like the evening
9: 6 loving, hating, envying—is all **l** gone.
9: 16 What they say will not be appreciated for **l**.
SS 1: 10 is your neck, accented with a **l** string of jewels.
Isa 5: 11 begin **l** drinking bouts that last late into the night.
6: 11 Then I said, "Lord, how **l** must I do this?" And he
7: 10 Not **l** after this, the LORD sent this message to
10: 24 they oppress you just as the Egyptians did **l** ago.
10: 25 It will not last very **l**. In a little while my anger
11: 16 just as he did for Israel **l** ago when they returned
14: 9 and mighty kings **l** dead are there to see you.
17: 9 abandoned when the Israelites came here so **l** ago.
19: 11 Will they dare tell Pharaoh about their **l** line of
22: 11 God for help. He is the one who planned this **l** ago.
23: 16 **L** absent from her lovers, she will take a harp,
25: 1 You planned them **l** ago, and now you have
26: 9 All night **l** I search for you; / earnestly I seek for
26: 14 and destroyed them, / and they are **l** forgotten.
29: 17 Soon—and it will not be very **l**—the wilderness of
30: 33 burning—has **l** been ready for the Assyrian king;
37: 26 It was I, the LORD, who decided this **l** ago.
37: 26 **L** ago I planned what I am now causing to happen,
41: 22 "Let them try to tell us what happened **l** ago
42: 14 He will say, "I have **l** been silent; / yes, I have
45: 21 Who made these things known **l** ago?
51: 5 They will wait for me and **l** for my power.
52: 4 "**L** ago my people went to live as resident
52: 5 My name is being blasphemed all day **l**.
53: 10 He will enjoy a **l** life, and the LORD's plan will
61: 4 the ancient ruins, repairing cities **l** ago destroyed.

64: 3 When you came down l ago, you did awesome
65: 2 "I opened my arms to my own people all day l,
65: 3 All day l they insult me to my face by worshiping
65:22 For my people will live as l as trees and will have
Jer 2: 2 you were to please me as a young bride l ago,
2:20 L ago I broke your yoke and tore away the chains
4:14 How l will you harbor your evil thoughts?
4:21 How l must this go on? How l must I be
surrounded by war and death?
12: 4 How l must this land weep? Even the grass in the
13: 6 A l time afterward, the LORD said to me,
13:27 Jerusalem! How l will it be before you are pure?"
17: 8 by the heat or worried by l months of drought.
20:16 Terrify him all day l with battle shouts,
22:15 Why did your father, Josiah, reign so l? Because he
23:26 How l will this go on? If they are prophets,
29:28 predicting that our captivity will be a l one.
30:20 Their children will prosper as they did l ago.
31: 3 L ago the LORD said to Israel: "I have loved
31:20 I l for him and surely will have mercy on him.
31:22 How l will you wander, my wayward daughter?
32:14 into a pottery jar to preserve them for a l time.
32:22 that you had promised their ancestors l before—
34:13 I made a covenant with your ancestors l ago when
35: 7 you will live l, good lives in the land.'
37:21 every day as l as there was any left in the city.
38:27 it wasn't l before the king's officials came to
47: 5 how l will you lament and mourn?
La 1:13 made me desolate, racked with sickness all day l.
2:16 L have we awaited this day, and it is finally here!"
2:17 He has fulfilled the promises of disaster he made l
3: 6 has buried me in a dark place, like a person l dead.
3:14 at me. All day l they sing their mocking songs.
3:62 enemies whisper and mutter against me all day l.
5:20 to forget us? Why have you forsaken us for so l?
Eze 6: 9 and lustful eyes that l for other gods.
11:21 But as for those who l for idols, I will repay them
12: 4 just as captives do when they begin a l march to
12:27 'His visions won't come true for a l, l time.'
16:22 you have not once thought of the days l ago when
26:20 to lie there with those who descended there l ago.
31: 5 It prospered and grew l thick branches because of
36:28 live in Israel, the land I gave your ancestors l ago.
38: 8 A l time from now you will be called into action.
38:17 You are the one I was talking about l ago, when I
40: 5 man took a measuring rod that was 10-1/2 feet l
40:21 The gateway passage was 87-1/2 feet l and 43-3/4
40:25 the gateway passage was 87-1/2 feet l and 43-3/4
40:29 the gateway passage was 87-1/2 feet l and 43-3/4
40:33 The gateway passage measured 87-1/2 feet l
40:36 The gateway passage measured 87-1/2 feet l
40:43 There were hooks, each three inches l, fastened to
41: 2 The Holy Place itself was 70 feet l and 35 feet
41:12 It was 122-1/2 feet wide and 157-1/2 feet l, and its
41:13 the Temple, and he found it to be 175 feet l.
42: 2 the north, was 175 feet l and 87-1/2 feet wide.
42: 7 from the outer courtyard; it was 87-1/2 feet l.
42:16 He measured the east side; it was 875 feet l.
44:20 "They must neither let their hair grow too l nor
45: 1 This piece of land will be 8-1/3 miles l and 6-2/3
45: 3 measure out a portion of land 8-1/3 miles l
45: 5 next to it, also 8-1/3 miles l and 3-1/3 miles wide,
45: 6 sacred area will be a section of land 8-1/3 miles l
46:22 Each of these enclosures was 70 feet l and 52-1/2
48: 9 for the LORD's Temple will be 8-1/3 miles l
48:10 land measuring 8-1/3 miles l by 3-1/3 miles wide,
48:13 to the priests—8-1/3 miles l and 3-1/3 miles wide.
48:13 will measure 8-1/3 miles l by 6-2/3 miles wide.
48:15 "An additional strip of land 8-1/3 miles l by 1-2/3
48:30 the city: On the north wall, which is 1-1/2 miles l,
48:32 On the east wall, also 1-1/2 miles l, the gates will
48:33 The south wall, also 1-1/2 miles l, will have gates
48:34 And on the west wall, also 1-1/2 miles l, the gates
Da 2: 4 answered the king in Aramaic, "L live the king!
3: 9 said to King Nebuchadnezzar, "L live the king!
4:33 He lived this way until his hair was as l as eagles'
5:10 She said to Belshazzar, "L live the king! Don't be
6: 6 went to the king and said, "L live King Darius!
6:21 Daniel answered, "L live the king!
8: 3 I saw in front of me a ram with two l horns
8:13 "How l will the events of this vision last?
8:13 How l will the rebellion that causes desecration
8:13 How l will the Temple and heaven's armies be
8:26 But none of these things will happen for a l time,
12: 6 "How l will it be until these shocking events
Hos 2:15 to me there, as she did l ago when she was young,
3: 4 This illustrates that Israel will be a l time without a
8: 5 How l will you be incapable of innocence?
9: 9 are as depraved as what they did in Gibeah l ago.
12: 1 the wind; they chase after the east wind all day l.
Am 4:10 you like the plagues I sent against Egypt l ago.
Mic 7:14 pastures of Bashan and Gilead as they did l ago.
7:20 an oath to our ancestors Abraham and Jacob l ago.
Hab 1: 2 How l, O LORD, must I call for help? But you do
Zec 1: 5 "Your ancestors and their prophets are now l dead.
1:12 How l will it be until you again show mercy to
2: 2 to see how wide and how l it is."
5: 2 "It appears to be about thirty feet l and fifteen feet
Mt 11:21 their people would have sat in deep repentance l
17:17 How l must I be with you until you believe?
17:17 How l must I put up with you? Bring the boy to
22:31 L after Abraham, Isaac, and Jacob had died,
23: 5 and they wear extra l tassels on their robes.
25:19 "After a l time their master returned from his trip
26:24 of Man, must die, as the Scriptures declared l ago.
27:29 They made a crown of l, sharp thorns and put it on
27:59 took the body and wrapped it in a l linen cloth.
Mk 1:35 The next morning Jesus awoke l before daybreak
4:32 with l branches where birds can come and find
5: 5 All day l and throughout the night he would
8: 3 For some of them have come a l distance."
9:19 How l must I be with you until you believe?
9:19 How l must I put up with you? Bring the boy to
9:21 "How l has this been happening?" Jesus asked the
12:26 L after Abraham, Isaac, and Jacob had died,
12:40 they really are, they make l prayers in public.
14:21 of Man, must die, as the Scriptures declared l ago.
15:17 him in a purple robe and made a crown of l,
15:46 Joseph bought a l sheet of linen cloth, and taking
Lk 1:21 to come out, wondering why he was taking so l.
1:70 as he promised / through his holy prophets l ago.
8: 1 Not l afterward Jesus began a tour of the nearby
8:27 and naked, he had lived in a cemetery for a l time.
9:36 They didn't tell anyone what they had seen until l
9:41 "how l must I be with you and put up with you?
10:13 their people would have sat in deep repentance l
11: 8 if you keep knocking l enough, he will get up
11:47 for the very prophets your ancestors killed l ago.
15:20 And while he was still a l distance away, his father
17:22 "The time is coming when you will l to share in
19:43 Before l your enemies will build ramparts against
20:37 L after Abraham, Isaac, and Jacob had died,
20:47 they really are, they make l prayers in public.
23: 8 and had been hoping for a l time to see him
23:53 from the cross and wrapped it in a l linen cloth
24:46 it was written l ago that the Messiah must suffer
Jn 1:15 greater than I am, for he existed l before I did.' "
1:30 far greater than I am, for he existed l before I did.'
4: 6 and Jesus, tired from the l walk, sat wearily beside
4:41 l enough for many of them to hear his message
5: 6 Jesus saw him and knew how l he had been ill,
10:24 "How l are you going to keep us in suspense?
11: 9 As l as it is light, people can walk safely. They can
19: 2 The soldiers made a crown of l, sharp thorns
19:40 Together they wrapped Jesus' body in a l linen
Ac 1: 9 It was not l after he said this that he was taken up
1:16 This was predicted l ago by the Holy Spirit,
2:40 Then Peter continued preaching for a l time,
3:21 as God promised l ago through his prophets.
4:25 you spoke l ago by the Holy Spirit through our
9:43 And Peter stayed a l time in Joppa, living with
14: 3 The apostles stayed there a l time, preaching boldly
14:28 there with the believers in Antioch for a l time.
15: 7 after a l discussion, Peter stood and addressed them
15:18 he who made these things known l ago.'
27: 9 The weather was becoming dangerous for l
27:21 No one had eaten for a l time. Finally, Paul called
28: 6 But when they had waited a l time and saw no
Ro 1: 2 This Good News was promised l ago by God
1:11 For I l to visit you so I can share a spiritual
3:21 but by the way promised in the Scriptures l ago.
7: 2 the law binds her to her husband as l as he is alive.
10:21 God said, / "All day l I opened my arms to them,
15: 4 Such things were written in the Scriptures l ago to
15:22 my visit to you has been delayed so l because I
15:23 and after all these l years of waiting, I am eager to
1Co 7:39 A wife is married to her husband as l as he lives.
8:13 I will never eat meat again as l as I live—
10: 1 what happened to our ancestors in the wilderness l
11:14 that it's disgraceful for a man to have l hair?
11:15 And isn't it obvious that l hair is a woman's pride
15: 8 Last of all, I saw him, too, l after the others,
2Co 4:17 troubles are quite small and won't last very l.
5: 2 and we l for the day when we will put on our
5: 6 even though we know that as l as we live in these
Gal 3: 8 God promised this good news to Abraham l ago
6:14 of that cross, my interest in this world died l ago,
6:14 and the world's interest in me is also l dead.
Eph 1: 4 L ago, even before he made the world, God loved
1: 9 designed l ago according to his good pleasure.
1:11 and all things happen just as he decided l ago.
1:13 you the Holy Spirit, whom he promised l ago.
2:10 we can do the good things he planned for us l ago.
3:18 God's people should, how wide, how l, how high,
6: 3 your father and mother, "you will live a l life,
Php 1: 8 and l for you with the tender compassion of Christ
1:23 to live, and sometimes I l to go and be with Christ.
4: 1 and sisters, I love you and l to see you,
1Ti 6: 9 But people who l to be rich fall into temptation
2Ti 1: 4 I l to see you again, for I remember your tears as
1: 9 because that was his plan l before the world
3: 9 But they won't get away with this for l.
3:10 You know my faith and how l I have suffered.
Heb 1: 1 L ago God spoke many times and in many ways to
3:13 each other every day, as l as it is called "today,"
4: 7 God announced this through David a l time later in
5:12 You have been Christians a l time now, and you
6:11 will keep right on loving others as l as life lasts,
9: 8 was not open to the people as l as the first room
11: 4 And although Abel is l dead, he still speaks to us
11:32 It would take too l to recount the stories of the faith
1Pe 1: 2 God the Father chose you l ago, and the Spirit has
1:20 God chose him for this purpose l before the world
3:20 those who disobeyed God l ago when God waited
2Pe 1:13 on reminding you of these things as l as I live.
1:15 I want you to remember them l after I am gone.
2: 3 But God condemned them l ago, and their
3: 2 and understand what the holy prophets said l ago
Jude 1: 4 The fate of such people was determined l ago,
Rev 1:13 He was wearing a l robe with a gold sash across his
6:10 how l will it be before you judge the people who
9: 6 find it. They will l to die, but death will flee away!
9: 8 Their hair was l like the hair of a woman, and their
11: 6 so that no rain will fall for as l as they prophesy.
14:20 from the winepress in a stream about 180 miles l
21:16 he found it was a square, as wide as it was l.

LONG-DESERTED (1) [DESERT, LONG]

Eze 36: 4 ruined wastes and l cities that have been destroyed

LONG-STANDING (1) [LONG]

Eze 25:15 acted against Judah out of revenge and l contempt.

LONGED (9) [LONG]

2Sa 13:39 l to be reunited with his son Absalom.
14: 1 Joab realized how much the king l to see Absalom.
Job 29:23 They l for me to speak as they l for rain.
Ps 12: 5 up to rescue them, / as they have l for me to do."
119:174 O LORD, I have l for your salvation, / and your
Eze 23:16 saw these paintings, she l to give herself to them,
Mt 13:17 many prophets and godly people have l to see
Lk 10:24 many prophets and kings have l to see and hear

LONGER (204) [LONG]

Ge 4:12 No l will it yield abundant crops for you, no matter
17: 5 It will no l be Abram; now you will be known as
17:15 your wife—her name will no l be Sarai;
32:28 "Your name will no l be Jacob," the man told
35:10 and said, "Your name is no l Jacob; you will now
37:17 "Yes," the man told him, "but they are no l here.
42:13 our father, and one of our brothers is no l with us."
45: 1 Joseph could stand it no l. "Out, all of you!"
49: 4 as the waves of the sea, / and you will be first no l.
Ex 2: 3 But when she could no l hide him, she got a little
17:12 finally became too tired to hold up the staff any l.
21: 9 he may no l treat her as a slave girl, but he must
40:35 Moses was no l able to enter the Tabernacle
Lev 17: 7 The people must no l be unfaithful to the LORD
22:12 she may no l eat the sacred offerings.
25:41 and their children will no l be obligated to you,
26:13 the land of Egypt so you would no l be slaves.
Nu 6:12 were completed before their defilement no l count.
Dt 31: 2 now 120 years old and am no l able to lead you.
31:17 have come because God is no l among us!'
Jos 7:12 I will not remain with you any l unless you destroy
7:26 Trouble ever since. So the LORD was no l angry.
23:13 your God will no l drive them out from your land.
Jdg 2: 3 I will no l drive out the people living in your land.
2:14 all around, and they were no l able to resist them.
2:21 I will no l drive out the nations that Joshua left
8: 3 heard Gideon's answer, they were no l angry.
10: 6 abandoned the LORD and no l served him at all.
16:16 day she nagged him until he couldn't stand it any l.
1Sa 1:18 and began to eat again, and she was no l sad.
2:31 to your family, so it will no l serve as my priests.
5: 7 can't keep the Ark of the God of Israel here any l!
8: 7 not you. They don't want me to be their king any l.
26:19 so I can no l live among the LORD's people
26:21 back home, my son, and I will no l try to harm you,
2Sa 1:21 the shield of Saul will no l be anointed with oil.
19:35 years old today, and I can no l enjoy anything.
19:35 Food and wine are no l tasty, and I cannot hear the
20: 3 he said, but he would no l sleep with them.
20: 5 but it took him l than the three days he had been
1Ki 14: 4 He was an old man now and could no l see.
2Ki 2:21 It will no l cause death or infertility."
6:33 on us! Why should I wait any l for the LORD?"
1Ch 19:19 the Arameans were no l willing to help the
23:26 Now the Levites will no l need to carry the
2Ch 29:11 My dear Levites, do not neglect your duties any l!
36:16 until the LORD's anger could no l be restrained
Ezr 9:14 us until even this little remnant no l survives.
10:13 rainy season, so we cannot stay out here much l.
Job 9:34 and I would no l live in terror of his punishment.
14: 5 we will live, and we are not given a minute l.
15:29 and their possessions will no l spread across the
15:31 Let them no l trust in empty riches. They are only
Ps 10:18 the oppressed, / so people can no l terrify them.
39: 5 My life is no l than the width of my hand.
44: 9 in dishonor. / You no l lead our armies to battle.
50:16 God says to the wicked: / "Recite my laws no l,
60:10 O God? / Will you no l march with our armies?
108:11 O God? / Will you no l march with our armies?
Ecc 9: 6 They no l have a part in anything here on earth.
12: 1 youth before you grow old and no l enjoy living.
Isa 1:16 and be clean! Let me no l see your evil deeds.
9: 5 In that day of peace, battle gear will no l be issued.
10:20 They will no l depend on the Assyrians,
14:25 my mountains. My people will no l be their slaves.
17: 8 They will no l ask their idols for help or worship
21:11 to me, "Watchman, how much l until morning?
26:21 The earth will no l hide those who have been
29:22 "My people will no l pale with fear or be ashamed.
33:24 The people of Israel will no l say, "We are sick
38:18 to destruction / can no l hope in your faithfulness.
52: 1 and godless people will no l enter your gates.
54: 4 "Fear not; you will no l live in shame. The shame
60:19 "No l will you need the sun or moon to give you
62:12 as the Desirable Place and the City No L Forsaken.
63:17 you given us stubborn hearts so we no l fear you?
65:20 "No l will babies die when only a few days old.
65:20 No l will adults die before they have lived a full
65:20 No l will people be considered old at one hundred!
Jer 3:16 "you will no l wish for 'the good old days' when
3:17 They will no l stubbornly follow their own evil
7:28 from among them; it is no l heard on their lips.
7:32 "when that place will no l be called Topheth
7:34 and brides will no l be heard in the towns of Judah.
8:19 "Is her King no l there?" "Oh, why have they

9:21 Children no **l** play in the streets, and young men no **l** gather in the squares.
10:21 They no **l** follow the LORD or ask what he wants
14:10 my paths. Now I will no **l** accept you as my people.
16:9 of bridegrooms and brides will no **l** be heard.
16:14 "when people who are taking an oath will no **l** say,
19:6 when this place will no **l** be called Topheth
23:7 they will no **l** say, 'As surely as the LORD lives,
25:10 of bridegrooms and brides will no **l** be heard.
30:8 their chains. Foreigners will no **l** be their masters.
31:16 "Do not weep any **l**, for I will reward you.
31:29 "The people will no **l** quote this proverb:
33:21 then will he no **l** have a descendant to reign on his
44:22 because the LORD could no **l** bear all the evil
44:26 that my name will no **l** be spoken by any of the
48:42 Moab will no **l** be a nation, for she has boasted
51:30 Her mightiest warriors no **l** fight. They stay in their
51:44 The nations will no **l** come and worship him.
La 1:4 no **l** filled with crowds on their way to celebrate
2:11 I have cried until the tears no **l** come. My heart is
4:16 himself has scattered them, and he no **l** helps them.
4:16 The priests and leaders are no **l** honored
5:14 The old men no **l** sit in the city gates; the young men no **l** dance and sing.
Eze 13:21 from your grasp. They will no **l** be your victims.
13:23 But you will no **l** talk of seeing visions that you
25:10 the Ammonites will no **l** be counted among the
28:24 No **l** will Israel's scornful neighbors prick and tear
29:16 "Then Israel will no **l** be tempted to trust in Egypt
33:15 obey my life-giving laws, no **l** doing what is evil.
34:10 their mouths; the sheep will no **l** be their prey.
34:22 and they will no **l** be abused and destroyed.
34:28 They will no **l** be prey for other nations, and wild animals will no **l** attack them.
36:15 and you will no **l** be shamed by them or cause your
36:25 be washed away, and you will no **l** worship idols.
37:22 them all; no **l** will they be divided into two nations.
43:7 and their kings will not defile my holy name any **l**
45:8 "My princes will no **l** oppress and rob my people;
Da 4:31 is for you! You are no **l** ruler of this kingdom.
7:12 but they were allowed to live for a while **l**.
8:3 One of the horns was **l** than the other, even though
Hos 1:6 for I will no **l** show love to the people of Israel
2:2 call Israel to account, for she is no **l** my wife, and I am no **l** her husband.
2:17 of Baal; even their names will no **l** be spoken.
9:3 You may no **l** stay here in this land of the LORD.
Joel 2:10 and moon grow dark, and the stars no **l** shine.
2:19 You will no **l** be an object of mockery among the
3:15 moon will grow dark, and the stars will no **l** shine.
Am 1:3 forget it. I will not let them go unpunished any **l**!
1:6 forget it. I will not let them go unpunished any **l**!
1:9 forget it. I will not let them go unpunished any **l**!
1:11 forget it. I will not let them go unpunished any **l**!
1:13 forget it. I will not let them go unpunished any **l**!
2:1 forget it. I will not let them go unpunished any **l**!
2:4 forget it. I will not let them go unpunished any **l**!
2:6 forget it. I will not let them go unpunished any **l**!
7:8 this plumb line. I will no **l** ignore all their sins.
Mic 2:10 This is no **l** your land and home, for you have
6:12 so used to lying that their tongues can no **l** tell the
Na 3:18 There is no **l** a shepherd to gather them together.
Zep 1:6 those who used to worship me but now no **l** do.
1:6 They no **l** ask for the LORD's guidance or seek
3:11 then you will no **l** need to be ashamed of
3:11 for you will no **l** be rebels against me.
Zec 8:13 But no **l**! Now I will rescue you and make you both
9:7 They will no **l** eat meat with blood in it or feed on
11:6 I will no **l** have pity on the inhabitants of the
11:9 So I told them, "I won't be your shepherd any **l**.
14:6 On that day the sources of light will no **l** shine,
14:21 And on that day there will no **l** be traders in the
Mt 19:6 Since they are no **l** two but one, let no one separate
26:11 among you, but I will not be here with you much **l**.
Mk 10:8 united into one.' Since they are no **l** two but one,
14:7 want to. But I will not be here with you much **l**.
Lk 15:19 and I am no **l** worthy of being called your son.
15:21 and I am no **l** worthy of being called your son.'
Jn 4:21 the time is coming when it will no **l** matter whether
7:33 But Jesus told them, "I will be here a little **l**.
12:8 but I will not be here with you much **l**."
12:35 light will shine out for you just a little while **l**.
12:46 so that all who put their trust in me will no **l**
15:15 I no **l** call you servants, because a master doesn't
16:4 because I was going to be with you for a while **l**.
20:27 in my side. Don't be faithless any **l**. Believe!"
Ac 18:20 They asked him to stay **l**, but he declined.
19:22 on ahead to Macedonia while he stayed awhile **l** in
Ro 4:8 whose sin is no **l** counted against them by the
6:6 its power in our lives. We are no **l** slaves to sin.
6:9 die again. Death no **l** has any power over him.
6:14 Sin is no **l** your master, for you are no **l** subject to the law, which enslaves
7:2 if he dies, the laws of marriage no **l** apply to her.
7:4 The law no **l** holds you in its power, because you
7:6 with Christ, and we are no **l** captive to its power.
8:4 for us who no **l** follow our sinful nature
8:35 Does it mean he no **l** loves us if we have trouble
1Co 7:34 a woman who is no **l** married or has never been
2Co 5:15 so that those who receive his new life will no **l** live
5:19 no **l** counting people's sins against them.
7:8 I am no **l** sorry that I sent that letter to you,
Gal 2:20 I myself no **l** live, but Christ lives in me. So I live
3:25 has come, we no **l** need the law as our guardian.
3:28 There is no **l** Jew or Gentile, slave or free, male
4:7 Now you are no **l** a slave but God's own child.
5:18 by the Holy Spirit, you are no **l** subject to the law.
Eph 2:19 So now you Gentiles are no **l** strangers
4:14 Then we will no **l** be like children,
4:17 Live no **l** as the ungodly do, for they are hopelessly
Php 3:9 I no **l** count on my own goodness or my ability to
1Th 3:1 Finally, when we could stand it no **l**, we decided
3:5 That is why, when I could bear it no **l**, I sent
2Ti 4:3 For a time is coming when people will no **l** listen
Phm 1:16 He is no **l** just a slave; he is a beloved brother,
1Pe 4:4 you no **l** join them in the wicked things they do,
Rev 6:11 And they were told to rest a little **l** until the full
10:6 and everything in it. He said, "God will wait no **l**.
22:3 No **l** will anything be cursed. For the throne of God

LONGING (14) [LONG]

Ps 77:3 and I moan, / overwhelmed with **l** for his help.
84:2 I long, yes, I faint with **l** / to enter the courts of the
119:81 I faint with **l** for your salvation; / but I have put my
119:131 panting expectantly, / **l** for your commands.
Isa 28:6 He will give a **l** for justice to their judges. He will
Eze 20:24 Sabbath days and **l** for the idols of their ancestors.
23:27 You will never again cast **l** eyes on those things
Hos 4:12 **L** after idols has made them foolish. They have
Lk 16:21 As Lazarus lay there **l** for scraps from the rich
22:15 "I have looked forward to this hour with deep **l**,
Ro 10:1 the **l** of my heart and my prayer to God is that the
2Co 7:11 such alarm, such **l** to see me, such zeal,
Php 2:26 him home again, for he has been **l** to see you,
1Th 2:17 because of our intense **l** to see you again.

LONGINGLY (2) [LONG]

2Sa 23:15 David remarked **l** to his men, "Oh, how I would
1Ch 11:17 David remarked **l** to his men, "Oh, how I would

LONGS (4) [LONG]

Ge 34:8 with your daughter, and he **l** for her to be his wife.
Job 7:2 like a worker who **l** for the day to end, like a
Ps 63:1 My soul thirsts for you; / my whole body **l** for you
Jas 4:5 placed within us, jealously **l** for us to be faithful?

LONGSUFFERING [KJV] See also PATIENCE, SLOW (TO ANGER)

LOOK (367) [FINE-LOOKING, GOOD-LOOKING, HEALTHY-LOOKING, LOOKED, LOOKING, LOOKOUT, LOOKOUTS, LOOKS, ONLOOKERS]

Ge 1:29 And God said, "**L**! I have given you the
4:6 LORD asked him. "Why do you **l** so dejected?
6:17 "**L**! I am about to cover the earth with a flood that
8:13 the flood began, Noah lifted back the cover to **l**.
11:6 "**L**!" he said. "If they can accomplish this when
13:10 Lot took a long **l** at the fertile plains of the Jordan
13:14 "**L** as far as you can see in every direction.
15:5 "**L** up into the heavens and count the stars if you
19:8 **L**—I have two virgin daughters. Do with them as
19:17 And don't **l** back! Escape to the mountains, or you
20:15 "**L** over my kingdom, and choose a place where
20:16 "**L**," he said, "I am giving your 'brother' a
25:32 "**L**, I'm dying of starvation!" said Esau.
26:29 And now **l** how the LORD has blessed you!"
29:6 **L**, here comes his daughter Rachel with the
31:12 The angel said, '**L**, and you will see that only the
39:8 "**L**," he told her, "my master trusts me with
40:6 The next morning Joseph noticed the dejected **l** on
40:7 "Why do you **l** so worried today?" he asked.
42:28 "**L**!" he exclaimed to his brothers. "My money is
Ex 3:6 face in his hands because he was afraid to **l** at God.
4:1 Moses protested again, "**L**, they won't believe me!
4:14 Aaron the Levite? He is a good speaker. And **l**!
5:5 **L**, there are many people here in Egypt, and you
7:17 **L**! I will hit the water of the Nile with this staff,
10:15 of the whole country, making the ground **l** black.
11:3 (Now the LORD had caused the Egyptians to **l**
12:36 The LORD caused the Egyptians to **l** favorably
16:4 Then the LORD said to Moses, "**L**, I'm going to
20:26 someone might **l** up under the skirts of your
31:2 "**L**, I have chosen Bezalel son of Uri, grandson of
32:1 "**L**," they said, "make us some gods who can lead
32:34 **L**! My angel will lead the way before you!
33:20 But you may not **l** directly at my face, for no one
Lev 26:9 "I will **l** favorably upon you and multiply your
Nu 4:20 and **l** at the sacred objects for even a moment,
21:8 Those who are bitten will live if they simply **l** at
22:29 "Because you have made me **l** like a fool!"
27:12 and **l** out over the land I have given the people of
Dt 1:21 **L**! He has placed it in front of you. Go and occupy
2:24 **L**, I will help you defeat Sihon the Amorite,
2:31 "Then the LORD said to me, '**L**, I have begun to
4:19 And when you **l** up into the sky and see the sun,
22:4 or donkey lying on the road, do not **l** the other way.
26:15 **L** down from your holy dwelling place in heaven
32:39 **L** now; I myself am he! / There is no god other
32:49 **L** out across the land of Canaan, the land I am
Jos 22:28 '**L** at this copy of the LORD's altar that our
Jdg 8:18 they replied. "They all had the **l** of a king's son."
9:36 When Gaal saw them, he said to Zebul, "**L**,
9:36 "It's just the shadows of the hills that **l** like men."
13:6 He was like one of God's angels, terrifying to **l** at.
14:8 he turned off the path to **l** at the carcass of the lion.
15:2 But **l**, her sister is more beautiful than she is.
19:9 his father-in-law said, "**L**, it's getting late.
1Sa 1:11 if you will **l** down upon my sorrow and answer my
8:5 "**L**," they told him, "you are now old, and your
9:3 "Take a servant with you, and go **l** for them."
10:14 "We went to **l** for the donkeys," Saul replied,
12:13 **L** him over. You asked for him, and the LORD
14:11 Philistines saw them coming, they shouted, "**L**!
14:33 Someone reported to Saul, "**L**, the men are sinning
16:6 Samuel took one **l** at Eliab and thought,
24:11 **L**, my father, at what I have in my hand. It is a
26:5 David slipped over to Saul's camp one night to **l**
26:16 your master, the LORD's anointed! **L** around!
28:14 "What does he **l** like?" Saul asked. "He is an old
2Sa 4:8 "**L**!" they exclaimed. "Here is the head of
6:22 and I am willing to **l** even more foolish than this,
7:2 summoned Nathan the prophet. "**L**!" David said.
13:4 Why should the son of a king **l** so dejected
13:35 "**L**!" Jonadab told the king. "There they are now!
15:27 the king told Zadok the priest, "**L**, here is my plan.
22:31 He is a shield for all who **l** to him for protection.
23:5 He will constantly **l** after my safety and success.
1Ki 12:16 Israel! **L** out for your own house, O David!"
17:23 him to his mother. "**L**, your son is alive!" he said.
18:43 said to his servant, "Go and **l** out toward the sea."
18:43 Seven times Elijah told him to go and **l**, and seven
20:7 to them, "**L** how this man is stirring up trouble!
22:13 "**L**, all the prophets are promising victory for the
2Ki 1:7 the king demanded. "What did he **l** like?"
3:22 across the water, making it **l** as red as blood.
4:25 He said to Gehazi, "**L**, the woman from Shunem is
8:5 "**L**, my lord!" Gehazi exclaimed. "Here is the
19:22 At whom did you **l** in such proud condescension?
2Ch 10:16 Israel! **L** out for your own house, O David!"
18:12 "**L**, all the prophets are promising victory for the
Ne 1:6 **L** down and see me praying night and day for your
2:2 are you? You **l** like a man with deep troubles."
4:2 **L** at those charred stones they are pulling out of
6:7 to prophesy about you in Jerusalem, saying, '**L**!
Job 1:10 in everything he does. **L** how rich he is!
6:7 My appetite disappears when I **l** at it; I gag at the
6:28 **L** at me! Would I lie to your face?
7:21 and die. When you **l** for me, I will be gone."
8:20 "But **l**! God will not reject a person of integrity,
11:19 lie down unafraid, and many will **l** to you for help.
13:1 "**L**, I have seen many instances such as you
21:5 **L** at me and be stunned. Put your hand over your
21:27 "**L**, I know your thoughts. I know the schemes you
22:26 delight yourself in the Almighty and **l** up to God.
29:24 at them. My **l** of approval was precious to them.
30:20 I stand before you, and you don't bother to **l**.
31:1 "I made a covenant with my eyes not to **l** with lust
31:35 see my side! **L**, I will sign my name to my defense.
33:6 "**L**, you and I are the same before God. I, too,
35:5 **L** up into the sky and see the clouds high above
36:22 "**L**, God is all-powerful. Who is a teacher like
36:26 "**L**, God is exalted beyond what we can
37:21 We cannot **l** at the sun, for it shines brightly in the
40:15 "Take a **l** at the mighty hippopotamus. I made it,
Ps 7:9 For you **l** deep within the mind and heart,
8:3 When I **l** at the night sky and see the work of your
13:1 Forever? / How long will you **l** the other way?
18:30 He is a shield for all who **l** to him for protection.
20:3 and **l** favorably on your burnt offerings.
25:7 **l** instead through the eyes of your unfailing love,
34:5 Those who **l** to him for help will be radiant with
35:17 How long, O Lord, will you **l** on and do nothing?
35:25 Don't let them say, "**L**! We have what we wanted!
36:12 **L**! They have fallen! / They have been thrown
37:10 Though you **l** for them, they will be gone.
37:37 **L** at those who are honest and good, / for a
40:7 Then I said, "**L**, I have come. / And this has been
44:24 Why do you **l** the other way? / Why do you ignore
51:18 **L** with favor on Zion and help her;
52:7 "**L** what happens to mighty warriors / who do not
57:1 O God, have mercy! / I **l** to you for protection.
59:4 to kill me. / Rise up and help me! **L** on my plight!
59:10 He will let me **l** down in triumph on all my
68:16 Why do you **l** with envy, O rugged mountains,
68:27 **L**, the little tribe of Benjamin leads the way.
73:12 **L** at these arrogant people— / enjoying a life of
80:14 **L** down from heaven and see our plight.
84:9 O God, **l** with favor upon the king, our protector!
86:16 **L** down and have mercy on me. / Give strength to
101:3 I will refuse to **l** at / anything vile and vulgar.
113:6 him are the heavens and the earth. / He stoops to **l**,
118:7 help me. / I will **l** in triumph at those who hate me.
119:135 **L** down on me with love; / teach me all your
119:153 **L** down upon my sorrows and rescue me, / for I
121:1 I **l** up to the mountains— / does my help come
123:2 We **l** to the LORD our God for his mercy,
128:3 within your home. / And **l** at all those children!
141:8 I **l** to you for help, O Sovereign LORD. / You are
142:4 I **l** for someone to come and help me, / but no one
145:15 All eyes **l** to you for help; / you give them their
Pr 4:25 **L** straight ahead, and fix your eyes on what lies
7:13 and kissed him, and with a brazen **l** she said,
11:23 The godly can **l** forward to happiness,
14:8 The wise **l** ahead to see what is coming, but fools
15:30 A cheerful **l** brings joy to the heart; good news
18:15 always open to new ideas. In fact, they **l** for them.
Ecc 1:16 I said to myself, "**L**, I am wiser than any of the
2:1 Let's **l** for the 'good things' in life." But I found
5:20 People who do this rarely **l** with sorrow on the
SS 1:6 "Don't **l** down on me, you fair city girls, just
2:9 or a young deer. **L**, there he is behind the wall!
3:7 **L**, it is Solomon's carriage, with sixty of Israel's
3:11 "Go out to **l** upon King Solomon, O young women
6:5 **L** away, for your eyes overcome me! Your hair,
Isa 1:15 you lift up your hands in prayer, I will refuse to **l**.
3:9 The very **l** on their faces gives them away

7:14 **L**! The virgin will conceive a child! She will give
8:22 Wherever they **l**, there will be trouble and anguish
10:28 **L**, the mighty armies of Assyria are coming!
10:33 But **l**! The Lord, the LORD Almighty, will chop
13:8 They **l** helplessly at one another as the flames of
17:1 "**L**, Damascus will disappear! It will become a
17:12 **L**! The armies rush forward like waves thundering
19:1 **L**! The LORD is advancing against Egypt,
21:5 **L**! They are preparing a great feast. They are
21:9 Now at last—**l**! Here come the chariots
23:13 **L** at the land of Babylonia—the people of that land
24:1 **L**! The LORD is about to destroy the earth
26:21 **L**! The LORD is coming from heaven to punish
28:16 this is what the Sovereign LORD says: "**L**!
30:6 **L** at the animals moving slowly across the terrible
30:27 **L**! The LORD is coming from far away,
31:1 Destruction is certain for those who **l** to Egypt for
32:1 **L**, a righteous king is coming! And honest princes
37:23 At whom did you **l** in such proud condescension?
40:26 **L** up into the heavens. Who created all the stars?
41:12 You will **l** for them in vain. They will all be gone!
41:27 I was the first to tell Jerusalem, '**L**! Help is on the
42:1 "**L** at my servant, whom I strengthen. He is my
45:22 Let all the world **l** to me for salvation! For I am
46:1 are being hauled away on ox carts. But **l**!
49:18 **L** and see, for all your children will come back to
51:6 **L** up to the skies above, and gaze down on the
59:11 We **l** for justice, but it is nowhere to be found.
59:11 We **l** to be rescued, but it is far away from us.
60:4 "**L** and see, for everyone is coming home!
62:11 the people of Israel, '**L**, your Savior is coming.
63:15 **l** down from heaven and see us from your holy,
64:9 **L** at us, we pray, and see that we are all your
65:6 "**L**, my decree is written out in front of me:
65:17 "**L**! I am creating new heavens and a new earth—
65:18 Be glad; rejoice forever in my creation! And **l**!
Jer 1:11 Then the LORD said to me, "**L**, Jeremiah!
1:17 or I will make you **l** foolish in front of them.
2:23 you say that? Go and **l** in any valley in the land!
3:2 "**L** all around you. Is there anywhere in the entire
5:1 "**L** high and low; search throughout the city!
6:16 **L** for the old, godly way, and walk in it. Travel its
9:15 the LORD Almighty, the God of Israel, says: **L**!
11:13 **L** now, people of Judah, you have as many gods as
13:16 For then, when you **l** for light, you will find only
23:19 **L**! The LORD's anger bursts out like a storm,
25:32 This is what the LORD Almighty says: "**L**!
29:13 If you **l** for me in earnest, you will find me when
30:23 **L**! The LORD's anger bursts out like a storm,
39:12 "**L** after him well, and give him anything he
46:5 But **l**! The Egyptian army flees in terror.
49:5 But **l**! I will bring terror upon you," says the Lord,
50:9 For **l**, I am raising up an army of great nations
50:15 **L**! She surrenders! Her walls have fallen.
50:41 "**L**! A great army is marching from the north!
51:25 "**L**, O mighty mountain, destroyer of the earth!
La 1:11 "O LORD, **l**," she mourns, "and see how I am
1:12 **L** around and see if there is any suffering like
1:18 **l** upon my anguish and despair, for my sons
1:22 "**L** at all their evil deeds, LORD. Punish them,
3:63 **L** at them! In all their activities, they constantly
Eze 3:8 But **l**, I have made you as hard and stubborn as
4:17 so scarce that the people will **l** at one another in
6:2 **l** over toward the mountains of Israel and prophesy
7:2 Wherever you **l**—east, west, north, or south—
7:25 They will **l** for peace but will not find it.
7:26 They will **l** in vain for a vision from the prophets.
8:5 said to me, "Son of man, **l** toward the north."
12:6 into the night. Cover your face and don't **l** around.
20:43 You will **l** back at all your sins and hate yourselves
20:46 of man, **l** toward the south and speak out against it;
21:2 **l** toward Jerusalem and prophesy against Israel
25:2 **l** toward the land of Ammon and prophesy against
27:26 "But **l**! Your oarsmen are rowing your ship of
27:35 are filled with horror / and **l** on with twisted faces.
28:21 **l** toward the city of Sidon and prophesy against it.
37:5 **L**! I am going to breathe into you and make you
Da 1:11 appointed by the chief official to **l** after Daniel,
1:13 see how we **l** compared to the other young men
3:25 "**L**!" Nebuchadnezzar shouted. "I see four men,
4:30 he said, "Just **l** at this great city of Babylon!
Hos 2:10 strip her naked in public, while all her lovers **l** on.
4:4 **L**, you priests, my complaint is with you!
5:15 until they admit their guilt and **l** to me for help.
7:16 They **l** everywhere except to heaven, to the Most
Joel 2:4 They **l** like tiny horses, and they run as fast.
2:5 **L** at them as they leap along the mountaintops!
2:19 He will reply, "**L**! I am sending you grain
Am 6:2 than they were, and **l** at how they were destroyed.
Mic 1:3 **L**! The LORD is coming! He leaves his throne in
3:4 all the evil you have done, he won't even **l** at you!
7:7 As for me, I **l** to the LORD for his help. I wait
Na 1:15 **L**! A messenger is coming over the mountains with
Hab 1:3 Wherever I **l**, I see destruction and violence.
1:5 LORD replied, "**L** at the nations and be amazed!
2:4 "**L** at the proud! They trust in themselves,
Zep 2:15 But now, **l** how it has become an utter ruin, a place
Hag 2:3 In comparison, how does it **l** to you now?
Zec 3:9 Now **l** at the jewel I have set before Jeshua,
5:5 talking with me came forward and said, "**L** up!
9:9 **L**, your king is coming to you. He is righteous
10:3 For the LORD Almighty has arrived to **l** after his
11:16 nor **l** after the young, nor heal the injured, nor feed
12:10 They will **l** on me whom they have pierced
Mal 3:1 "**L**! I am sending my messenger, and he will
3:1 whom you **l** for so eagerly, is surely coming,"
4:5 "**L**, I am sending you the prophet Elijah before the
Mt 1:23 "**L**! The virgin will conceive a child! / She will
6:16 who try to **l** pale and disheveled so people will
6:26 **L** at the birds. They don't need to plant or harvest
6:28 **L** at the lilies and how they grow. They don't work
10:16 "**L**, I am sending you out as sheep among wolves.
11:10 '**L**, I am sending my messenger before you,
12:18 "**L** at my Servant, / whom I have chosen. / He is
21:5 people of Israel, / '**L**, your King is coming to you.
23:28 You try to **l** like upright people outwardly,
23:38 And now **l**, your house is left to you, empty
24:23 '**L**, here is the Messiah,' or 'There he is,' don't pay
24:26 "So if someone tells you, '**L**, the Messiah is out in the desert,' don't bother to go and **l**.
24:26 Or, '**L**, he is hiding here,' don't believe it!
25:6 roused by the shout, '**L**, the bridegroom is coming!
26:45 **L**, the time has come. I, the Son of Man,
Mk 1:2 "**L**, I am sending my messenger before you,
8:24 very clearly. They **l** like trees walking around."
11:21 on the previous day and exclaimed, "**L**, Teacher!
13:1 "Teacher, **l** at these tremendous buildings!
13:1 **L** at the massive stones in the walls!"
13:21 '**L**, here is the Messiah,' or, 'There he is,'
15:29 "Ha! **L** at you now!" they yelled at him.
16:6 from the dead! **L**, this is where they laid his body.
Lk 2:44 they started to **l** for him among their relatives
7:27 '**L**, I am sending my messenger before you,
7:44 said to Simon, "**L** at this woman kneeling here.
9:38 "Teacher, **l** at my boy, who is my only son.
12:24 **L** at the ravens. They don't need to plant or harvest
12:27 "**L** at the lilies and how they grow. They don't
13:35 And now **l**, your house is left to you empty.
15:8 and **l** in every corner of the house and sweep every
15:31 said to him, '**L**, dear son, you and I are very close,
16:15 he said to them, "You like to **l** good in public,
17:23 Don't believe such reports or go out to **l** for him.
19:3 He tried to get a **l** at Jesus, but he was too short to
21:28 stand straight and **l** up, for your salvation is near!"
24:12 However, Peter ran to the tomb to **l**. Stooping,
24:39 **L** at my hands. **L** at my feet. You can see that
Jn 1:29 John saw Jesus coming toward him and said, "**L**!
1:36 John looked at him and then declared, "**L**!
1:45 Philip went off to **l** for Nathanael and told him,
4:35 **L** around you! Vast fields are ripening all around
6:24 and went across to Capernaum to **l** for him.
9:27 "**L**!" the man exclaimed. "I told you once.
12:15 people of Israel. / **L**, your King is coming,
12:19 **L**, the whole world has gone after him!"
19:37 and "They will **l** on him whom they pierced."
Ac 3:4 looked at him intently and Peter said, "**L** at us!"
3:12 And why **l** at us as though we had made this man
6:3 "Now **l** around among yourselves, friends,
7:32 Moses shook with terror and dared not **l**.
7:56 And he told them, "**L**, I see the heavens opened
8:36 they came to some water, and the eunuch said, "**L**!
13:41 '**L** you mockers, / be amazed and die! / For I am
Ro 1:23 they worshiped idols made to **l** like mere people,
5:2 and joyfully **l** forward to sharing God's glory.
8:24 we are saved, we eagerly **l** forward to this freedom.
8:25 But if we **l** forward to something we don't have
14:3 eat anything must not **l** down on those who won't.
14:10 Why do you **l** down on another Christian?
1Co 1:20 God has made them all **l** foolish and has shown
4:1 So **l** at Apollos and me as mere servants of Christ
4:10 Our dedication to Christ makes us **l** like fools,
2Co 3:7 people of Israel could not bear to **l** at Moses' face.
4:18 So we don't **l** at the troubles we can see right now;
4:18 rather, we **l** forward to what we have not yet seen.
2Ti 4:3 and will **l** for teachers who will tell them whatever
4:8 but for all who eagerly **l** forward to his glorious
Tit 2:13 while we **l** forward to that wonderful event when
Heb 10:7 Then I said, '**L**, I have come to do your will,
10:9 Then he added, "**L**, I have come to do your will."
10:27 There will be nothing to **l** forward to
12:15 **L** after each other so that none of you will miss out
Jas 1:24 walk away, and forget what you **l** like.
4:13 **L** here, you people who say, "Today or tomorrow
5:1 **L** here, you rich people, weep and groan with
5:7 Consider the farmers who eagerly **l** for the rains in
5:9 and sisters, or God will judge you. For **l**!
5:10 **l** at the prophets who spoke in the name of the
1Pe 1:13 **L** forward to the special blessings that will come to
2Pe 3:12 You should **l** forward to that day and hurry it
Jude 1:14 these people. He said, / "**L**, the Lord is coming
Rev 1:7 **L**! He comes with the clouds of heaven.
1:18 **L**, I am alive forever and ever! And I hold the keys
2:5 **L** how far you have fallen from your first love!
3:9 **L**! I will force those who belong to Satan—
3:11 **L**, I am coming quickly. Hold on to what you have,
3:20 "**L**! Here I stand at the door and knock. If you
5:5 **L**, the Lion of the tribe of Judah, the heir to
9:12 The first terror is past, but **l**, two more terrors are
11:14 The second terror is past, but **l**, now the third terror
21:3 I heard a loud shout from the throne, saying, "**L**,
21:5 the throne said, "**L**, I am making all things new!"
22:7 "**L**, I am coming soon! Blessed are those who

LOOKED (168) [LOOK]

Ge 1:31 Then God **l** over all he had made, and he saw that
3:6 The fruit **l** so fresh and delicious, and it would
9:23 they **l** the other way so they wouldn't see him
19:26 But Lot's wife **l** back as she was following along
19:28 He **l** out across the plain to Sodom and Gomorrah
22:13 Then Abraham **l** up and saw a ram caught by its
24:63 meditating, he **l** up and saw the camels coming.
24:64 When Rebekah **l** up and saw Isaac, she quickly
26:8 **l** out a window and saw Isaac fondling Rebekah.
33:5 Then Esau **l** at the women and children and asked,
48:8 Then Jacob **l** over at the two boys. "Are these your
Ex 2:25 He **l** down on the Israelites and felt deep concern
14:24 the LORD **l** down on the Egyptian army from the
16:10 spoke to the people, they **l** out toward the desert.
17:6 was told; and as the leaders **l** on, water gushed out.
24:17 LORD on the mountaintop **l** like a devouring fire.
37:9 The cherubim faced each other as they **l** down on
Nu 11:7 The manna **l** like small coriander seeds,
13:33 next to them, and that's what we **l** like to them!"
21:9 Whenever those who were bitten **l** at the bronze
24:1 Instead, he turned and **l** out toward the wilderness,
24:20 Then Balaam **l** over at the people of Amalek
24:21 Then he **l** over at the Kenites and prophesied:
Jos 5:13 he **l** up and saw a man facing him with sword in
8:20 When the men of Ai **l** behind them, smoke from
Jdg 5:28 "From the window Sisera's mother **l** out.
20:40 But when the warriors of Benjamin **l** behind them
1Sa 6:19 because they **l** into the Ark of the LORD.
9:16 for I have **l** down on my people in mercy and have
10:21 But when they **l** for him, he had disappeared!
24:8 And when Saul **l** around, David bowed low before
2Sa 2:20 When Abner **l** back and saw him coming, he called
6:16 the daughter of Saul, **l** down from her window.
6:20 "How glorious the king of Israel **l** today!
11:2 As he **l** out over the city, he noticed a woman of
17:20 Absalom's men **l** for them without success
18:24 As he **l**, he saw a lone man running toward them.
1Ki 3:21 But when I **l** more closely in the morning light,
18:43 The servant went and **l**, but he returned to Elijah
19:6 He **l** around and saw some bread baked on hot
20:27 But the Israelite army **l** like two little flocks of
2Ki 2:24 Elisha turned around and **l** at them, and he cursed
6:17 opened his servant's eyes, and when he **l** up,
9:32 Jehu **l** up and saw her at the window and shouted,
9:32 my side?" And two or three eunuchs **l** out at him.
23:16 and **l** up at the tomb of the man of God who had
1Ch 15:29 the daughter of Saul, **l** down from her window.
21:16 David **l** up and saw the angel of the LORD
Ne 4:14 Then as I **l** over the situation, I called together the
Job 30:26 So I **l** for good, but evil came instead. I waited for
31:16 or crushed the hopes of widows who **l** to me for
31:26 Have I **l** at the sun shining in the skies, or the moon
Ps 37:36 But when I **l** again, they were gone! / Though I
77:16 Sea saw you, O God, / its waters **l** and trembled!
102:19 Tell them the LORD **l** down / from his heavenly
102:19 He **l** to the earth from heaven
Pr 24:32 Then, as I **l** and thought about it, I learned this
Ecc 2:11 But as I **l** at everything I had worked so hard to
Isa 53:3 backs on him and **l** the other way when he went by.
59:15 The LORD **l** and was displeased to find that there
63:5 I **l**, but no one came to help my people. I was
Jer 3:19 I **l** forward to your calling me 'Father,' and I
4:23 I **l** at the earth, and it was empty and formless.
4:23 I **l** at the heavens, and there was no light.
4:24 I **l** at the mountains and hills, and they trembled
4:25 I **l**, and all the people were gone. All the birds of
4:26 I **l**, and the fertile fields had become a wilderness.
31:26 At this, I woke up and **l** around. My sleep had been
La 4:17 We **l** in vain for our allies to come and save us,
Eze 1:4 As I **l**, I saw a great storm coming toward me from
1:5 of the cloud came four living beings that **l** human,
1:13 The living beings **l** like bright coals of fire
1:13 and it **l** as though lightning was flashing back
1:15 As I **l** at these beings, I saw four wheels on the
1:16 All four wheels **l** the same; each wheel had a
1:26 Above the surface over their heads was what **l** like
1:27 From his waist up, he **l** like gleaming amber,
1:27 he **l** like a burning flame, shining with splendor.
2:9 Then I **l** and saw a hand reaching out to me,
8:2 From the waist down he **l** like a burning flame.
8:2 From the waist up he **l** like gleaming amber.
8:5 So I **l**, and there to the north, beside the entrance to
10:1 As I **l**, I saw what appeared to be a throne of blue
10:8 (All the cherubim had what **l** like human hands
10:10 All four wheels **l** the same; each wheel had a
10:21 and what **l** like human hands under their wings.
12:7 Then in the evening while the people **l** on, I dug
16:13 than ever. You **l** like a queen, and so you were!
22:30 "I **l** for someone who might rebuild the wall of
26:21 You will be **l** for, but you will never be found.
29:6 for you collapsed like a reed when Israel **l** to you
41:19 that of a man—**l** toward the palm tree on one side.
41:19 **l** toward the palm tree on the other side.
42:3 Another block of rooms **l** out onto the pavement of
44:4 I **l** and saw that the glory of the LORD filled the
Da 1:15 Daniel and his three friends **l** healthier and better
4:30 As he **l** out across the city, he said, "Just look at
4:34 had passed, I, Nebuchadnezzar, **l** up to heaven.
7:5 Then I saw a second beast, and it **l** like a bear.
7:6 strange beasts appeared, and it **l** like a leopard.
7:13 I saw someone who **l** like a man coming with the
8:3 As I **l** up, I saw in front of me a ram with two long
8:15 someone who **l** like a man suddenly stood in front
10:5 I **l** up and saw a man dressed in linen clothing,
10:6 His body **l** like a dazzling gem. From his face came
10:15 I **l** down at the ground, unable to say a word.
10:16 Then the one who **l** like a man touched my lips,
10:18 Then the one who **l** like a man touched me again,
12:5 **l** and saw two others standing on opposite banks of
Hos 13:1 because the other Israelite tribes **l** up to them.
Zec 1:18 Then I **l** up and saw four animal horns.
2:1 When I **l** around me again, I saw a man with a
5:1 I **l** up again and saw a scroll flying through the air.
5:9 Then I **l** up and saw two women flying toward us,
6:1 Then I **l** up again and saw four chariots coming
Mt 11:13 all the teachings of the Scriptures **l** forward to this

14:19 the five loaves and two fish, l up toward heaven,
14:30 But when he l around at the high waves, he was
17:8 And when they l, they saw only Jesus with them.
19:26 Jesus l at them intently and said,
Mk 3:5 He l around at them angrily, because he was
3:34 Then he l at those around him and said, "These are
6:41 the five loaves and two fish, l up toward heaven,
8:24 The man l around. "Yes," he said, "I see people,
8:33 Jesus turned and l at his disciples and then said to
9:8 Suddenly they l around, and Moses and Elijah
10:21 Jesus felt genuine love for this man as he l at him.
10:23 Jesus l around and said to his disciples, "How hard
10:27 Jesus l at them intently and said,
11:11 He l around carefully at everything, and then he
14:67 She l at him closely and then said, "You were one
16:4 they arrived, they l up and saw that the stone—
Lk 6:10 He l around at them one by one and then said to
9:16 the five loaves and two fish, l up toward heaven,
10:32 assistant walked over and l at him lying there,
15:16 the pods he was feeding the pigs l good to him.
17:14 He l at them and said, "Go show yourselves to the
19:5 he l up at Zacchaeus and called him by name.
20:17 Jesus l at them and said, "Then what do the
22:15 "I have l forward to this hour with deep longing,
22:58 After a while someone else l at him and said,
22:61 At that moment the Lord turned and l at Peter.
Jn 1:36 John l at him and then declared, "Look!
1:38 Jesus l around and saw them following. "What do
8:56 Your ancestor Abraham rejoiced as he l forward to
11:41 Then Jesus l up to heaven and said, "Father,
13:22 The disciples l at each other, wondering whom he
17:1 he l up to heaven and said, "Father, the time has
20:5 He stooped and l in and saw the linen cloth lying
20:11 tomb crying, and as she wept, she stooped and l in.
Ac 2:3 what l like flames or tongues of fire appeared
3:4 Peter and John l at him intently and Peter said,
3:5 The lame man l at them eagerly, expecting a gift.
11:6 When I l inside the sheet, I saw all sorts of small
13:9 the Holy Spirit, l the sorcerer in the eye and said,
Gal 3:8 the Scriptures l forward to this time when God
Rev 4:1 Then as I l, I saw a door standing open in heaven,
4:7 the second l like an ox; the third had a human face;
5:6 I l and I saw a Lamb that had been killed but was
5:11 Then I l again, and I heard the singing of thousands
6:2 I l up and saw a white horse. Its rider carried a
6:5 And I l up and saw a black horse, and its rider was
6:8 And I l up and saw a horse whose color was pale
8:13 Then I l up. And I heard a single eagle crying
9:7 The locusts l like horses armed for battle. They had
13:2 This beast l like a leopard, but it had bear's feet
15:5 Then I l and saw that the Temple in heaven,
16:13 And I saw three evil spirits that l like frogs leap

LOOKING (83) [LOOK]

Ge 37:15 the countryside. "What are you l for?" he asked.
42:1 "Why are you standing around l at one another?
43:29 L at his brother Benjamin, Joseph asked, "Is this
Ex 2:12 After l around to make sure no one was watching,
25:20 l down on the atonement cover with their wings
Dt 1:33 who goes before you l for the best places to camp,
22:2 the owner is, keep it until the owner comes l for it;
Jos 2:7 So the king's men went l for the spies along the
Jdg 4:22 When Barak came l for Sisera, Jael went out to
4:22 and I will show you the man you are l for."
17:8 in that area of Ephraim, l for a good place to live.
17:9 in Judah, and I am l for a place to live."
2Sa 18:3 to Absalom's troops; they will be l only for you.
2Ki 6:19 and I will take you to the man you are l for."
23:16 Then as Josiah was l around, he noticed several
2Ch 20:12 not know what to do, but we are l to you for help."
Ps 25:15 My eyes are always l to the LORD for help,
51:9 Don't keep l at my sins. / Remove the stain of my
94:7 "The LORD isn't l," they say, / "and besides,
Pr 7:6 I was l out the window of my house one day
7:15 It's you I was l for! I came out to find you,
23:28 l for another victim who will be unfaithful to his
Ecc 7:27 "I came to this result after l into the matter from
SS 2:9 Now he is l in through the window, gazing into the
Isa 31:1 and chariots instead of l to the LORD,
32:3 Then everyone who can see will be l for God,
38:14 My eyes grew tired of l to heaven for help.
65:1 I am being found by people who were not l for me.
Jer 14:6 They strain their eyes l for grass to eat, but there is
La 4:17 but we were l to nations that could offer no help at
Eze 34:4 You have not gone l for those who have wandered
34:12 I will be like a shepherd l for his scattered flock.
Da 6:14 He spent the rest of the day l for a way to get
7:8 As I was l at the horns, suddenly another small
Hos 2:13 and jewels, and went out l for her lovers,"
8:9 Like a wild donkey l for a mate, they have gone up
Mt 7:7 Keep on l, and you will find. Keep on knocking,
11:3 or should we keep l for someone else?"
11:9 Were you l for a prophet? Yes, and he is more than
26:16 Judas began l for the right time and place to betray
28:5 "I know you are l for Jesus, who was crucified.
Mk 5:32 But he kept on l around to see who had done it.
7:34 And l up to heaven, he sighed and commanded,
14:1 and the teachers of religious law were still l for an
14:11 So he began l for the right time and place to betray
16:6 You are l for Jesus, the Nazarene, who was
Lk 7:19 or should we keep l for someone else?"
7:20 or should we keep l for someone else?' "
7:26 Were you l for a prophet? Yes, and he is more than
11:9 Keep on l, and you will find. Keep on knocking,
22:6 So he began l for an opportunity to betray Jesus
24:5 "Why are you l in a tomb for someone who is
Jn 1:33 resting upon someone, he is the one you are l for.
1:42 L intently at Simon, Jesus said, "You are Simon,
4:23 The Father is l for anyone who will worship him
6:5 a great crowd of people climbing the hill, l for him.
7:18 Those who present their own ideas are l for praise
14:17 because it isn't l for him and doesn't recognize
18:4 to meet them, he asked, "Whom are you l for?"
20:15 Jesus asked her. "Who are you l for?"
Ac 2:31 David was l into the future and predicting the
5:42 "The Messiah you are l for is Jesus."
10:19 said to him, "Three men have come l for you.
10:21 went down and said, "I'm the man you are l for.
18:5 telling them, "The Messiah you are l for is Jesus."
18:28 to them, "The Messiah you are l for is Jesus."
26:6 because I am l forward to the fulfillment of God's
Ro 10:20 "I was found by people / who were not l for me.
11:7 Jews have not found the favor of God they are l for
1Co 16:11 I am l forward to seeing him soon, along with the
2Co 7:7 When he told me how much you were l forward to
Php 3:13 the past and l forward to what lies ahead,
Col 1:5 because you are l forward to the joys of heaven—
1Th 1:10 And they speak of how you are l forward to the
Heb 11:10 because he was confidently l forward to a city with
11:14 And obviously people who talk like that are l
11:16 But they were l for a better place, a heavenly
11:26 for he was l ahead to the great reward that God
13:14 we are l forward to our city in heaven, which is yet
Jas 1:23 it is like l at your face in a mirror but doing
1:25 But if you keep l steadily into God's perfect law—
1Pe 5:8 like a roaring lion, l for some victim to devour.
2Pe 3:13 But we are l forward to the new heavens and new

LOOKINGGLASSES [KJV] See MIRRORS

LOOKOUT (5) [LOOK]

2Ch 20:24 So when the army of Judah arrived at the l point in
Mt 13:45 is like a pearl merchant on the l for choice pearls.
21:33 for pressing out the grape juice, and built a l tower.
Mk 12:1 for pressing out the grape juice, and built a l tower.
13:35 So keep a sharp l! For you do not know when the

LOOKOUTS (1) [LOOK]

1Sa 14:16 Saul's l in Gibeah saw a strange sight—the vast

LOOKS (17) [LOOK]

Lev 14:35 'It l like my house has some kind of disease.'
1Sa 16:7 but the LORD l at a person's thoughts
Job 28:24 for he l throughout the whole earth, under all the
Ps 14:2 The LORD l down from heaven / on the entire
14:2 he l to see if there is even one with real
33:13 The LORD l down from heaven / and sees the
53:2 God l down from heaven / on the entire human
53:2 he l to see if there is even one with real
Isa 28:17 Your refuge l strong, but since it is made of lies,
La 3:50 until the LORD l down from heaven and sees.
Eze 3:9 So don't be afraid of them or fear their angry l,
Da 3:25 the flames! And the fourth l like a divine being!"
Hos 14:8 I am the one who l after you and cares for you.
Hab 3:6 the earth shakes. When he l, the nations tremble.
Mt 5:28 anyone who even l at a woman with lust in his eye
Lk 9:62 then l back is not fit for the Kingdom of God."
Jn 9:9 and others said, "No, but he surely l like him!"

LOOM (6)

Jdg 16:13 the seven braids of my hair into the fabric on your
l and tighten it with the l shuttle,
16:14 and tightened it with the l shuttle. Again she cried
16:14 But Samson woke up, pulled back the l shuttle,
16:14 and yanked his hair away from the l and the fabric.
Isa 38:12 cut short, / as when a weaver cuts cloth from a l.

LOOPS (11)

Ex 26:4 Put l of blue yarn along the edge of the last sheet in
26:5 The fifty l along the edge of one set are to match
the fifty l along the edge of the other.
26:6 Then make fifty gold clasps to fasten the l of the
26:10 Put fifty l along the edge of the last sheet in each
36:11 Fifty blue l were placed along the edge of the last
36:12 The fifty l along the edge of the first set of sheets
36:12 matched the l along the edge of the second set.
36:13 Then fifty gold clasps were made to connect the l
36:17 Then they made fifty l along the edge of the last
36:18 also made fifty small bronze clasps to couple the l,

LOOSE (10) [LOOSED, LOOSEN]

Ge 27:40 but then you will shake l from him and be free."
49:21 "Naphtali is a deer let l, / producing magnificent
Lev 10:6 "Do not mourn by letting your hair hang l or by
13:45 tear their clothing and allow their hair to hang l.
21:10 must never let his hair hang l or tear his clothing.
1Ki 19:11 was such a terrible blast that the rocks were torn l,
Isa 5:27 Not a belt will be l, not a sandal thong broken.
33:23 The enemies' sails hang l on broken masts with
Jer 50:6 led them astray and turned them l in the mountains.
Rev 9:15 and year were turned l to kill one-third of all the

LOOSED (1) [LOOSE]

Ps 78:49 He l on them his fierce anger— / all his fury,

LOOSEN (1) [LOOSE]

Eze 3:27 a message, I will l your tongue and let you speak.

LOOT (5) [LOOTED, LOOTERS, LOOTING]

Pr 1:13 And the l we'll get! We'll fill our houses with all
1:14 in your lot with us; we'll split our l with you."
12:12 Thieves are jealous of each other's l,
Na 2:9 L the silver! Plunder the gold! There seems no end
Zep 1:9 and kill to fill their masters' homes with l.

LOOTED (2) [LOOT]

Isa 24:3 The earth will be completely emptied and l.
Ob 1:6 and cranny of Edom will be searched and l.

LOOTERS (1) [LOOT]

Isa 24:10 in chaos; every home is locked to keep out l.

LOOTING (1) [LOOT]

Ob 1:13 l their homes and making yourselves rich at their

LOP (1)

Da 4:14 "Cut down the tree; l off its branches!

LORD (852) [LORD'S, LORDING, LORDS]

ANGEL OF THE LORD (11) Mt 1:20,24; 2:13,19; 28:2; Lk 1:11; 2:9; Ac 5:19; 8:26; 12:7,23

BEFORE THE LORD (10) Jos 7:16,17; Ps 97:5; La 2:18; Zec 6:5; 1Co 4:5; 2Co 8:21; Jas 4:10; 1Jn 3:19; Rev 11:4

DAY OF THE LORD (6) Jer 46:10; Ac 2:20; 1Th 5:2,4; 2Th 2:2; 2Pe 3:10

FEAR OF THE LORD (4) Job 28:28; Ac 9:31; 2Co 5:11; Col 3:22

LORD ALMIGHTY (3) Ro 9:29; 2Co 6:18; Jas 5:4

LORD GOD (11) Da 9:3; Lk 1:32; Rev 1:8; 4:8; 11:17; 15:3; 16:7; 18:8; 21:22; 22:5,6

LORD GOD ALMIGHTY (5) Rev 4:8; 11:17; 15:3; 16:7; 21:22

LORD HIS/MY/OUR/THEIR/YOUR GOD (11) Ps 38:15; 86:12; 90:17; Da 9:9,15; Mk 12:29; Lk 1:16; Jn 20:28; Ac 2:39; Rev 4:11; 19:6

LORD JESUS (102) Mk 16:19; Lk 24:3; Ac 1:21; 4:33; 7:59; 8:16; 9:17; 11:17,20; 15:11,26; 16:31; 19:5,13,17; 20:21,24,35; 21:13; 28:31; Ro 1:7; 5:11; 13:14; 14:14; 15:6, 30; 16:20; 1Co 1:3,7,8,10; 5:4,4; 6:11; 8:6; 11:23; 15:31; 16:23; 2Co 1:2,3,14; 4:14; 8:9; 11:31; 13:13; Gal 1:3; 6:14, 18; Eph 1:3,15,17; 5:20; 6:23,24; Php 1:2; 2:19; 3:20; 4:23; Col 1:3; 3:17; 1Th 1:1,3; 2:15,19; 3:11,13; 4:1,2; 5:9,23,28; 2Th 1:1,2,7,8,12,12; 2:1,8,14,16; 3:6,12,18; 1Ti 6:3,14; Phm 1:3,5,25; Heb 2:3; 13:20; Jas 1:1; 2:1; 1Pe 1:3; 2Pe 1:8,14,16; Jude 1:4,17,21; Rev 22:20,21

LORD JESUS CHRIST (59) Ac 11:17; 15:26; 28:31; Ro 1:7; 5:11; 13:14; 15:6,30; 16:20; 1Co 1:3,7,8,10; 8:6; 15:31; 2Co 1:2,3; 8:9; 13:13; Gal 1:3; 6:14,18; Eph 1:3,17; 5:20; 6:23,24; Php 1:2; 3:20; 4:23; Col 1:3; 1Th 1:1,3; 5:9,23, 28; 2Th 1:1,2,12; 2:1,14,16; 3:6,12,18; 1Ti 6:3,14; Phm 1:3, 25; Jas 1:1; 2:1; 1Pe 1:3; 2Pe 1:8,14,16; Jude 1:4,17,21

LORD OF HEAVEN (4) Da 5:23; Mt 11:25; Lk 10:21; Ac 17:24

LOVE THE LORD (4) Mt 22:37; Mk 12:30; Lk 10:27; 1Co 16:22

MY LORD THE KING (18) 1Sa 24:8; 26:17,19; 29:8; 2Sa 14:19; 16:9; 18:31; 19:19,26,35; 1Ki 1:20,36; 2:38; 20:9; 2Ki 6:26; Jer 37:20; 38:9; Da 1:10

NAME OF THE LORD (21) Mt 21:9; 23:39; Mk 11:9; Lk 13:35; 19:38; Jn 12:13; Ac 2:21; 8:16; 9:28; 19:5,13,17; 22:16; Ro 10:13; 1Co 5:4; 1Th 4:1,2; 5:27; 2Th 3:12; Jas 5:10,14

SAYS THE LORD (15) Isa 19:4; 21:16; Jer 49:5; 50:31; Am 3:13; Ro 12:19; 14:11; 1Co 14:21; 2Co 6:17,18; Heb 8:8,9,10; 10:16; Rev 1:8

SOVEREIGN LORD (2) Ac 4:24; Rev 6:10

SPIRIT OF THE LORD (5) Lk 4:18; Ac 5:9; 8:39; 2Co 3:17,18

WORD OF THE LORD (8) Mt 8:17; Ac 8:25; 13:44; 15:35,36; 16:32; 1Th 1:8; 1Pe 1:25

Ge 18:3 "My l," he said, "if it pleases you, stop here for a
18:27 let me go on and speak further to my L,
18:30 "Please don't be angry, my L," Abraham pleaded.
18:31 "Since I have dared to speak to the L, let me
18:32 Finally, Abraham said, "L, please do not get
20:4 so he said, "L, will you kill an innocent man?
33:8 Jacob replied, "They are gifts, my l, to ensure your
33:13 But Jacob replied, "You can see, my l, that some
42:10 "No, my l!" they exclaimed. "We have come to
44:16 And Judah said, "Oh, my l, what can we say to
44:16 My l, we have all returned to be your slaves—
44:18 Then Judah stepped forward and said, "My l,
44:19 "You asked us, my l, if we had a father or a
44:22 But we said to you, 'My l, the boy cannot leave his
44:30 "And now, my l, I cannot go back to my father
44:32 My l, I made a pledge to my father that I would
44:33 Please, my l, let me stay here as a slave instead of
Ex 4:10 the LORD, "O L, I'm just not a good speaker.
4:13 But Moses again pleaded, "L, please!
5:22 have you mistreated your own people like this, L?
15:17 the sanctuary, O L, that your hands have made.
34:9 favor in your sight, O L, then please go with us.
Nu 12:11 he cried out to Moses, "Oh, my l! Please don't
14:17 "Please, L, prove that your power is as great as
Dt 10:17 your God is the God of gods and L of lords.

Jos 3:11 which belongs to the **L** of the whole earth,
3:13 the Ark of the LORD, the **L** of all the earth.
7: 8 **L**, what am I to say, now that Israel has fled from
Jdg 6:15 "But **L**," Gideon replied, "how can I rescue
13: 8 He said, "**L**, please let the man of God come back
1Sa 24: 8 came out and shouted after him, "My **l** the king!"
25:24 and said, "I accept all blame in this matter, my **l**.
25:26 "Now, my **l**, as surely as the LORD lives and you
26:17 And David replied, "Yes, my **l** the king.
26:19 But now let my **l** the king listen to his servant.
29: 8 "Why can't I fight the enemies of my **l**, the king?"
2Sa 1:10 his bracelets so I could bring them to you, my **l**."
5:20 (which means "the **L** who bursts through").
9:11 "Yes, my **l**; I will do all that you have
14: 9 "Oh, thank you, my **l**," she replied. "And I'll take
14:18 the king replied. "Yes, my **l**?" she asked.
14:19 woman replied, "My **l** the king, how can I deny it?
16: 9 "Why should this dead dog curse my **l** the king?"
18:31 and said, "I have good news for my **l** the king.
19:19 "My **l** the king, please forgive me," he pleaded.
19:26 Mephibosheth replied, "My **l** the king, my servant
19:28 and I could expect only death from you, my **l**,
19:30 "I am content just to have you back again, my **l**!"
19:35 I would only be a burden to my **l** the king.
24:21 "Why have you come, my **l**?" Araunah asked.
24:22 "Take it, my **l**, and use it as you wish,"
1Ki 1:11 and that our **l** David doesn't even know about it?
1:13 Go at once to King David and say to him, 'My **l**,
1:17 She replied, "My **l**, you vowed to me by the
1:20 And now, my **l** the king, all Israel is waiting for
1:24 He asked, "My **l**, have you decided that Adonijah
1:27 Has my **l** really done this without letting any of his
1:31 "May my **l** King David live forever!"
1:36 the God of my **l** the king, decree it to be so.
1:43 "Our **l** King David has just declared Solomon
2:38 I will do whatever my **l** the king commands."
3:10 The **L** was pleased with Solomon's reply and was
3:17 "Please, my **l**," one of them began, "this woman
3:26 loved him very much, cried out, "Oh no, my **l**!
18: 7 "Is it really you, my **l** Elijah?" he asked.
18:13 Has no one told you, my **l**, about the time when
20: 4 "All right, my **l**," Ahab replied. "All that I have is
20: 9 from Ben-hadad, "Say this to my **l** the king:
22: 6 The **L** will give you a glorious victory!"
2Ki 2:19 "We have a problem, my **l**," they told him.
4:16 "No, my **l**!" she protested. "Please don't lie to me
4:28 Then she said, "It was you, my **l**, who said I would
6: 5 "Ah, my **l**!" he cried. "It was a borrowed ax!"
6:12 "It's not us, my **l**," one of the officers replied.
6:15 "Ah, my **l**, what will we do now?" he cried out to
6:26 called to him, "Please help me, my **l** the king!"
7: 6 For the **L** had caused the whole army of Aram to
8: 5 "Look, my **l**!" Gehazi exclaimed. "Here is the
8:12 "What's the matter, my **l**?" Hazael asked him.
19:23 By your messengers you have mocked the **L**.
1Ch 14:11 (which means "the **L** who bursts through").
21: 3 But why, my **l**, do you want to do this? Are they
21:23 "Take it, my **l**, and use it as you wish,"
2Ch 2:14 your craftsmen and those appointed by my **l** David,
Ne 1:11 O **L**, please hear my prayer! Listen to the prayers
4:14 Remember the **L**, who is great and glorious,
8:10 This is a sacred day before our **L**. Don't be
10:29 laws, and regulations of the LORD their **L**.
Job 28:28 'The fear of the **L** is true wisdom; to forsake evil
Ps 2: 4 who rules in heaven laughs. / The **L** scoffs at them.
8: 1 O LORD, our **L**, the majesty of your name fills
8: 9 O LORD, our **L**, the majesty of your name fills
22:30 Our children will hear about the wonders of the **L**.
30: 8 O LORD. / I begged the **L** for mercy, saying,
35:17 How long, O **L**, will you look on and do nothing?
35:22 Do not stay silent. / Don't abandon me now, O **L**.
35:23 my defense! / Take up my case, my God and my **L**.
37:13 But the **L** just laughs, / for he sees their day of
38: 9 You know what I long for, **L**; / you hear my every
38:15 You must answer for me, O **L** my God.
38:22 Come quickly to help me, O **L** my savior.
39: 7 And so, **L**, where do I put my hope? / My only
40:17 but the **L** is thinking about me right now.
44:23 Wake up, O **L**! Why do you sleep? / Get up!
45:11 in your beauty; / honor him, for he is your **l**.
51:15 Unseal my lips, O **L**, / that I may praise you.
54: 4 my helper. / The **L** is the one who keeps me alive!
55: 9 Destroy them, **L**, and confuse their speech,
57: 9 I will thank you, **L**, in front of all the people.
59:11 and bring them to their knees, / O **L** our shield.
62:12 unfailing love, O **L**, is yours. / Surely you judge all
66:18 sin in my heart, / my **L** would not have listened.
68:11 The **L** announces victory, / and throngs of women
68:17 the **L** came from Mount Sinai into his sanctuary.
68:19 Praise the **L**; praise God our savior! / For each day
68:22 The **L** says, "I will bring my enemies down from
68:32 of the earth. / Sing praises to the **L**. / *Interlude*
71: 5 O **L**, you alone are my hope. / I've trusted you,
73:20 is gone when they awake. / When you arise, O **L**,
77: 2 When I was in deep trouble, / I searched for the **L**.
77: 7 Has the **L** rejected me forever? / Will he never
78:65 Then the **L** rose up as though waking from sleep,
79:12 O **L**, take sevenfold vengeance on our neighbors
86: 3 Be merciful, O **L**, / for I am calling on you
86: 4 Give me happiness, O **L**, / for my life depends on
86: 5 O **L**, you are so good, so ready to forgive, / so full
86: 8 among the pagan gods is there a god like you, O **L**.
86: 9 each one— / will come and bow before you, **L**;
86:12 With all my heart I will praise you, O **L** my God.
86:15 But you, O **L**, are a merciful and gracious God,
89:49 **L**, where is your unfailing love? / You promised it
89:50 Consider, **L**, how your servants are disgraced!
90: 1 **L**, through all the generations / you have been our
90:17 And may the **L** our God show us his approval
97: 5 before the LORD, / before the **L** of all the earth.
110: 1 The LORD said to my **L**, / "Sit in honor at my
110: 5 The **L** stands at your right hand to protect you.
114: 7 Tremble, O earth, at the presence of the **L**,
130: 2 Hear my cry, O **L**. / Pay attention to my prayer.
130: 3 record of our sins, / who, O **L**, could ever survive?
130: 6 I long for the **L** / more than sentries long for the
135: 5 that our **L** is greater than any other god.
136: 3 Give thanks to the **L** of lords. / His faithful love
147: 5 How great is our **L**! His power is absolute!
Isa 1:24 Therefore, the **L**, the LORD Almighty,
3: 1 The **L**, the LORD Almighty, will cut off the
3:15 like that!" demands the **L**, the LORD Almighty.
3:17 The **L** will send a plague of scabs to ornament
3:18 The **L** will strip away their artful beauty—
4: 4 The **L** will wash the moral filth from the women of
6: 1 In the year King Uzziah died, I saw the **L**. He was
6: 8 Then I heard the **L** asking, "Whom should I send
6: 8 go for us?" And I said, "**L**, I'll go! Send me."
6:11 Then I said, "**L**, how long must I do this?" And he
7:14 All right then, the **L** himself will choose the sign.
7:20 In that day the **L** will take this "razor"—
8: 7 the **L** will overwhelm them with a mighty flood
9: 8 The **L** has spoken out against that braggart Israel,
9:17 That is why the **L** has no joy in the young men
10:12 After the **L** has used the king of Assyria to
10:16 your evil boasting, the **L**, the LORD Almighty,
10:23 Yes, the **L**, the LORD Almighty, has already
10:24 So this is what the **L**, the LORD Almighty,
10:33 The **L**, the LORD Almighty, will chop down the
11:11 In that day the **L** will bring back a remnant of his
19: 4 cruel master, to a fierce king," says the **L**,
21: 6 Meanwhile, the **L** said to me, "Put a watchman on
21: 8 after day I have stood on the watchtower, my **l**.
21:16 "But within a year," says the **L**, "all the glory of
22: 5 What a day of confusion and terror the **L**,
22:12 The **L**, the LORD Almighty, called you to weep
22:14 That is the judgment of the **L**, the LORD
22:15 Furthermore, the **L**, the LORD Almighty, told me
28: 2 For the **L** will send the mighty Assyrian army
28:22 For the **L**, the LORD Almighty, has plainly told
29:13 And so the **L** says, "These people say they are
30:20 Though the **L** gave you adversity for food
37:24 By your messengers you have mocked the **L**.
38:14 to heaven for help. / I am in trouble, **L**. Help me!"
38:16 **L**, your discipline is good, / for it leads to life
49:14 LORD has deserted us; the **L** has forgotten us."
Jer 2:19 I, the **L**, the LORD Almighty, have spoken!
37:20 Listen, my **l** the king, I beg you. Don't send me
38: 9 "My **l** the king," he said, "these men have done a
46:10 For this is the day of the **L**, the LORD Almighty,
46:10 The **L**, the LORD Almighty, will receive a
49: 5 upon you," says the **L**, the LORD Almighty.
50:31 I am your enemy, O proud people," says the **L**,
La 1:14 The **L** sapped my strength and gave me to my
1:15 "The **L** has treated my mighty men with contempt.
1:15 The **L** has trampled his beloved city as grapes are
2: 1 The **L** in his anger has cast a dark shadow over
2: 1 the **L** has shown no mercy even to his Temple.
2: 2 Without mercy the **L** has destroyed every home in
2: 3 The **L** has withdrawn his protection as the enemy
2: 5 Yes, the **L** has vanquished Israel like an enemy.
2: 7 The **L** has rejected his own altar; he despises his
2:18 Cry aloud before the **L**, O walls of Jerusalem!
2:19 cry out. Pour out your hearts like water to the **L**.
3:31 For the **L** does not abandon anyone forever.
3:36 in the courts. Do they think the **L** didn't see it?
3:58 **L**, you are my lawyer! Plead my case! For you
Eze 18:25 "Yet you say, 'The **L** isn't being just!' Listen to
18:29 the people of Israel keep saying, 'The **L** is unjust!'
33:17 "Your people are saying, 'The **L** is not just,'
33:20 people of Israel, you are saying, 'The **L** is not just.'
Da 1: 2 The **L** gave him victory over King Jehoiakim of
1:10 "My **l** the king has ordered that you eat this food
2:47 of gods, the **L** over kings, a revealer of mysteries,
4:19 happen to your enemies, my **l**, and not to you!
5:23 For you have defied the **L** of heaven and have had
9: 3 So I turned to the **L** God and pleaded with him in
9: 4 "O **L**, you are a great and awesome God!
9: 7 "**L**, you are in the right; but our faces are covered
9: 9 But the **L** our God is merciful and forgiving,
9:15 "O **L** our God, you brought lasting honor to your
9:16 In view of all your faithful mercies, **L**, please turn
9:17 For your own sake, **L**, smile again on your desolate
9:19 "O **L**, hear. O **L**, forgive. O **L**, listen and act!
10:16 the vision I have seen, my **l**, and I am very weak.
10:17 someone like me, your servant, talk to you, my **l**?
10:19 and said to him, "Now you may speak, my **l**,
12: 8 So I asked, "How will all this finally end, my **l**?"
Hos 12:14 so their **L** will now sentence them to death in
Am 3:13 all Israel," says the **L**, the LORD God Almighty.
5:16 Therefore, this is what the **L**, the LORD God
7: 7 I saw the **L** standing beside a wall that had been
7: 8 And the **L** replied, "I will test my people with this
9: 1 Then I saw a vision of the **L** standing beside the
9: 5 The **L**, the LORD Almighty, touches the land
Mic 1: 2 against you; the **L** speaks from his holy Temple.
4:13 acquired as offerings to me, the **L** of all the earth."
Zec 1: 9 with me, "My **l**, what are all those horses for?"
4: 4 Then I asked the angel, "What are these, my **l**?
4: 5 the angel asked. "No, my **l**," I replied.
4:13 you know?" he asked. "No, my **l**," I replied.
4:14 anointed ones who assist the **L** of all the earth."
6: 4 "And what are these, my **l**?" I asked the angel
6: 5 of heaven who stand before the **L** of all the earth.
9: 4 But now the **L** will strip away Tyre's possessions
Mal 1:14 but then sacrifices a defective one to the **L**.
3: 1 Then the **L** you are seeking will suddenly come to
Mt 1:20 and an angel of the **L** appeared to him in a dream.
1:24 he did what the angel of the **L** commanded.
2:13 an angel of the **L** appeared to Joseph in a dream.
2:15 This fulfilled what the **L** had spoken through the
2:19 an angel of the **L** appeared in a dream to Joseph in
4: 7 also say, 'Do not test the **L** your God.' "
4:10 'You must worship the **L** your God;
5:33 must carry out the vows you have made to the **L**.'
7:21 They may refer to me as '**L**,' but they still won't
7:22 '**L**, **L**, we prophesied in your name and cast out
8: 2 "**L**," the man said, "if you want to, you can
8: 6 "**L**, my young servant lies in bed, paralyzed
8: 8 Then the officer said, "**L**, I am not worthy to have
8:17 This fulfilled the word of the **L** through Isaiah,
8:21 "**L**, first let me return home and bury my father."
8:25 to him and woke him up, shouting, "**L**, save us!
9:28 you see?" "Yes, **L**," they told him, "we do."
9:38 So pray to the **L** who is in charge of the harvest;
11:25 "O Father, **L** of heaven and earth, thank you for
14:28 Then Peter called to him, "**L**, if it's really you,
14:30 and began to sink. "Save me, **L**!" he shouted.
15:22 pleading, "Have mercy on me, O **L**, Son of David!
15:25 worshiped him and pleaded again, "**L**, help me!"
15:27 "Yes, **L**," she replied, "but even dogs are
16:22 and corrected him. "Heaven forbid, **L**," he said.
17: 4 Peter blurted out, "**L**, this is wonderful! If you
17:15 "**L**, have mercy on my son, because he has
18:21 Then Peter came to him and asked, "**L**, how often
20:25 and officials **l** it over the people beneath them.
20:30 "**L**, Son of David, have mercy on us!"
20:31 "**L**, Son of David, have mercy on us!"
20:33 "**L**," they said, "we want to see!"
21: 3 what you are doing, just say, 'The **L** needs them,'
21: 9 Bless the one who comes in the name of the **L**!
22:37 " 'You must love the **L** your God with all your
22:43 the inspiration of the Holy Spirit, call him **L**?
22:44 'The LORD said to my **L**, / Sit in honor at my
22:45 Since David called him **L**, how can he be his son at
23:39 the one who comes in the name of the **L**!' "
24:42 because you don't know what day your **L** is
25:37 '**L**, when did we ever see you hungry and feed
25:44 "Then they will reply, '**L**, when did we ever see
26:22 began to ask him, "I'm not the one, am I, **L**?"
27:10 purchased the potter's field, / as the **L** directed."
28: 2 because an angel of the **L** came down from heaven
Mk 5:19 and tell them what wonderful things the **L** has
7:28 She replied, "That's true, **L**, but even the dogs
10:42 and officials **l** it over the people beneath them.
11: 3 'The **L** needs it and will return it soon.' "
11: 9 Bless the one who comes in the name of the **L**!
12:29 O Israel! The **L** our God is the one and only **L**.
12:30 And you must love the **L** your God with all your
12:36 the Holy Spirit, said, / 'The LORD said to my **L**,
12:37 Since David himself called him **L**, how can he be
13:20 In fact, unless the **L** shortens that time of calamity,
16:19 When the **L** Jesus had finished talking with them,
16:20 and preached, and the **L** worked with them,
Lk 1:11 in the sanctuary when an angel of the **L** appeared,
1:15 for he will be great in the eyes of the **L**. He must
1:16 persuade many Israelites to turn to the **L** their God.
1:17 He will precede the coming of the **L**,
1:25 "How kind the **L** is!" she exclaimed. "He has
1:28 "Greetings, favored woman! The **L** is with you!"
1:32 And the **L** God will give him the throne of his
1:43 this is, that the mother of my **L** should visit me!
1:45 because you believed that the **L** would do what he
1:46 Mary responded, / "Oh, how I praise the **L**.
1:58 and relatives that the **L** had been very kind to her,
1:66 For the hand of the **L** is surely upon him in a
1:68 "Praise the **L**, the God of Israel, / because he has
1:76 because you will prepare the way for the **L**.
2: 9 Suddenly, an angel of the **L** appeared among them,
2:11 The Savior—yes, the Messiah, the **L**—has been
2:15 that has happened, which the **L** has told us about."
2:22 took him to Jerusalem to present him to the **L**.
2:23 The law of the **L** says, "If a woman's first child is
a boy, he must be dedicated to the **L**."
2:24 to what was required in the law of the **L**—
2:27 and Joseph came to present the baby Jesus to the **L**
2:29 "**L**, now I can die in peace! / As you promised me,
2:39 fulfilled all the requirements of the law of the **L**,
4: 8 'You must worship the **L** your God;
4:12 also say, 'Do not test the **L** your God.' "
4:18 "The Spirit of the **L** is upon me, / for he has
5: 8 he fell to his knees before Jesus and said, "Oh, **L**,
5:12 "**L**," he said, "if you want to, you can make me
6:46 "So why do you call me '**L**,' when you won't
7: 6 the house, the officer sent some friends to say, "**L**,
7:13 When the **L** saw her, his heart overflowed with
7:19 and he sent them to the **L** to ask him, "Are you the
9:54 and John heard about it, they said to Jesus, "**L**,
9:59 The man agreed, but he said, "**L**, first let me return
9:61 Another said, "Yes, **L**, I will follow you, but first
10: 1 The **L** now chose seventy-two other disciples
10: 2 Pray to the **L** who is in charge of the harvest,
10:17 they joyfully reported to him, "**L**,
10:21 and said, "O Father, **L** of heaven and earth,
10:27 " 'You must love the **L** your God with all your
10:40 She came to Jesus and said, "**L**, doesn't it seem
10:41 But the **L** said to her, "My dear Martha, you are
11: 1 disciples came to him as he finished and said, "**L**,
11:39 Then the **L** said to him, "You Pharisees are
12:41 Peter asked, "**L**, is this illustration just for us
12:42 And the **L** replied, "I'm talking to any faithful,

13:15 But the L replied, "You hypocrite! You work on
13:23 Someone asked him, "L, will only a few be
13:25 you will stand outside knocking and pleading, 'L,
13:35 the one who comes in the name of the L!' "
17: 5 One day the apostles said to the L, "We need more
17: 6 the L answered, "you could say to this mulberry
17:37 "L, where will this happen?" the disciples asked.
18: 6 Then the L said, "Learn a lesson from this evil
18:41 do for you?" "L," he pleaded, "I want to see!"
19: 8 Zacchaeus stood there and said to the L,
19: 8 "I will give half my wealth to the poor, L,
19:31 what you are doing, just say, 'The L needs it.' "
19:34 the disciples simply replied, "The L needs it."
19:38 "Bless the King who comes in the name of the L!
20:37 he referred to the L as 'the God of Abraham,
20:42 'The LORD said to my L, / Sit in honor at my
20:44 Since David called him L, how can he be his son at
22:33 Peter said, "L, I am ready to go to prison with
22:38 "L," they replied, "we have two swords among
22:49 to happen, they exclaimed, "L, should we fight?
22:61 At that moment the L turned and looked at Peter.
22:61 Then Peter remembered that the L had said,
24: 3 but they couldn't find the body of the L Jesus.
24:34 "The L has really risen! He appeared to Peter!"
Jn 4:49 The official pleaded, "L, please come now before
6:23 near the place where the L had blessed the bread
6:68 Simon Peter replied, "L, to whom would we go?
8:11 "No, L," she said. And Jesus said, "Neither do I.
9:38 "Yes, L," the man said, "I believe!" And he
11: 3 telling him, "L, the one you love is very sick."
11:12 The disciples said, "L, if he is sleeping,
11:21 Martha said to Jesus, "L, if you had been here,
11:27 "Yes, L," she told him. "I have always believed
11:32 saw Jesus, she fell down at his feet and said, "L,
11:34 he asked them. They told him, "L, come and see."
11:39 But Martha, the dead man's sister, said, "L,
12:13 Bless the one who comes in the name of the L!
12:38 "L, who has believed our message? / To whom
will the L reveal his saving power?"
12:40 "The L has blinded their eyes / and hardened their
13: 6 he came to Simon Peter, Peter said to him, "L,
13: 9 "Then wash my hands and head as well, L,
13:13 You call me 'Teacher' and 'L,' and you are right,
13:14 And since I, the L and Teacher, have washed your
13:25 Leaning toward Jesus, he asked, "L, who is it?"
13:36 Simon Peter said, "L, where are you going?"
13:37 "But why can't I come now, L?" he asked.
14: 5 "No, we don't know, L," Thomas said.
14: 8 Philip said, "L, show us the Father and we will be
14:22 said to him, "L, why are you going to reveal
20:13 "Because they have taken away my L,"
20:18 the disciples and told them, "I have seen the L!"
20:20 They were filled with joy when they saw their L!
20:25 They told him, "We have seen the L!" But he
20:28 "My L and my God!" Thomas exclaimed.
21: 7 whom Jesus loved said to Peter, "It is the L!"
21: 7 When Simon Peter heard that it was the L, he put
21:12 And no one dared ask him if he really was the L
21:15 "Yes, L," Peter replied, "you know I love you."
21:16 "Yes, L," Peter said, "you know I love you."
21:17 He said, "L, you know everything. You know I
21:20 leaned over to Jesus during supper and asked, "L,
21:21 Peter asked Jesus, "What about him, L?"
Ac 1: 6 they kept asking him, "L, are you going to free
1:21 with us all the time that we were with the L Jesus
1:24 "O L," they said, "you know every heart.
2:20 before that great and glorious day of the L arrives.
2:21 And anyone who calls on the name of the L
2:25 'I know the L is always with me. / I will not be
2:34 yet he said, / 'The LORD said to my L,
2:36 made this Jesus whom you crucified to be both L
2:39 all who have been called by the L our God."
2:47 And each day the L added to their group those who
3:20 refreshment will come from the presence of the L,
3:22 'The L your God will raise up a Prophet like me
4:24 "O Sovereign L, Creator of heaven and earth,
4:26 against the L / and against his Messiah.'
4:29 And now, O L, hear their threats, and give your
4:33 powerful witness to the resurrection of the L Jesus,
5: 9 conspiring together to test the Spirit of the L?
5:14 more people believed and were brought to the L—
5:19 But an angel of the L came at night,
7:31 he went to see, the voice of the L called out to him,
7:33 "And the L said to him, 'Take off your sandals,
7:49 asks the L. / 'Could you build a dwelling place for
7:59 Stephen prayed, "L Jesus, receive my spirit."
7:60 And he fell to his knees, shouting, "L,
8:16 had only been baptized in the name of the L Jesus.
8:22 Turn from your wickedness and pray to the L.
8:24 "Pray to the L for me," Simon exclaimed,
8:25 and preaching the word of the L in Samaria,
8:26 As for Philip, an angel of the L said to him,
8:39 the water, the Spirit of the L caught Philip away.
9:10 The L spoke to him in a vision, calling,
"Ananias!" "Yes, L!" he replied.
9:11 The L said, "Go over to Straight Street,
9:13 "But L," exclaimed Ananias, "I've heard about
9:15 But the L said, "Go and do what I say. For Saul is
9:17 hands on him and said, "Brother Saul, the L Jesus,
9:27 and told them how Saul had seen the L on the way
9:27 Barnabas also told them what the L had said to
9:28 preaching boldly in the name of the L.
9:31 The believers were walking in the fear of the L
9:35 and Sharon turned to the L when they saw Aeneas
9:42 the whole town, and many believed in the L.
10:14 "Never, L," Peter declared. "I have never in all
10:33 waiting before God to hear the message the L has
10:36 with God through Jesus Christ, who is L of all.
11: 8 " 'Never, L,' I replied. 'I have never eaten
11:17 he gave us when we believed in the L Jesus Christ,
11:20 began preaching to Gentiles about the L Jesus.
11:21 The power of the L was upon them, and large
11:21 of these Gentiles believed and turned to the L.
11:23 he encouraged the believers to stay true to the L.
11:24 large numbers of people were brought to the L.
12: 7 the cell, and an angel of the L stood before Peter.
12:11 "The L has sent his angel and saved me from
12:17 and how the L had led him out of jail.
12:23 an angel of the L struck Herod with a sickness,
13: 2 One day as these men were worshiping the L
13:10 you never stop perverting the true ways of the L?
13:11 And now the L has laid his hand of punishment
13:12 and was astonished at what he learned about the L.
13:44 turned out to hear them preach the word of the L.
13:47 For this is as the L commanded us when he said,
13:48 were very glad and thanked the L for his message;
14: 3 preaching boldly about the grace of the L.
14: 3 The L proved their message was true by giving
14:23 turning them over to the care of the L, in whom
15:11 the same way, by the special favor of the L Jesus."
15:17 so that the rest of humanity might find the L,
15:17 I have called to be mine. / This is what the L says,
15:26 who have risked their lives for the sake of our L
15:35 and preaching the word of the L there.
15:36 where we previously preached the word of the L,
16:14 As she listened to us, the L opened her heart,
16:15 "If you agree that I am faithful to the L," she said,
16:31 "Believe on the L Jesus and you will be saved,
16:32 Then they shared the word of the L with him
17:24 Since he is L of heaven and earth, he doesn't live
18: 8 and all his household believed in the L.
18: 9 One night the L spoke to Paul in a vision and told
18:23 and helping them to grow in the L.
18:25 He had been taught the way of the L and talked to
19: 5 they were baptized in the name of the L Jesus.
19:13 out evil spirits tried to use the name of the L Jesus.
19:17 and the name of the L Jesus was greatly honored.
19:20 So the message about the L spread widely and had
20:21 and turning to God, and of faith in our L Jesus.
20:24 it for doing the work assigned me by the L Jesus—
20:35 You should remember the words of the L Jesus:
21:13 but also to die for the sake of the L Jesus."
21:14 we gave up and said, "The will of the L be done."
22:10 "I said, 'What shall I do, L?' And the L told me,
'Get up and go into Damascus,
22:16 sins washed away, calling on the name of the L.'
22:19 " 'But L,' I argued, 'they certainly know that I
22:21 "But the L said to me, 'Leave Jerusalem, for I
23:11 That night the L appeared to Paul and said,
26:15 "And the L replied, 'I am Jesus, the one you are
28:31 all boldness and teaching about the L Jesus Christ.
Ro 1: 4 And Jesus Christ our L was shown to be the Son of
1: 7 yours from God our Father and the L Jesus Christ.
1:11 with you that will help you grow strong in the L.
4: 8 sin is no longer counted against them by the L."
4:24 who brought Jesus our L back from the dead.
5: 1 because of what Jesus Christ our L has done for us.
5:11 because of what our L Jesus Christ has done for us
5:21 resulting in eternal life through Jesus Christ our L.
6:23 of God is eternal life through Christ Jesus our L.
7:25 Thank God! The answer is in Jesus Christ our L.
8:39 love of God that is revealed in Christ Jesus our L.
9:28 For the L will carry out his sentence upon the earth
9:29 Isaiah said in another place, / "If the L Almighty
10: 9 For if you confess with your mouth that Jesus is L
10:12 They all have the same L, who generously gives
10:13 For "Anyone who calls on the name of the L will
10:16 for Isaiah the prophet said, "L, who has believed
11: 3 "L, they have killed your prophets and torn down
11:34 For who can know what the L is thinking?
12:11 lazy in your work, but serve the L enthusiastically.
12:19 I will repay those who deserve it," / says the L.
13:14 But let the L Jesus Christ take control of you,
14: 4 They are responsible to the L, so let him tell them
14: 6 Those who have a special day for worshiping the L
14: 6 who eat all kinds of food do so to honor the L,
14: 6 who won't eat everything also want to please the L
14: 8 While we live, we live to please the L. And when
we die, we go to be with the L. So in life and in
death, we belong to the L.
14: 9 so that he might be L of those who are alive
14:11 Scriptures say, / " 'As surely as I live,' says the L,
14:14 and am perfectly sure on the authority of the L
15: 2 what helps them, we will build them up in the L.
15: 6 and glory to God, the Father of our L Jesus Christ.
15:11 And yet again, / "Praise the L, all you Gentiles;
15:30 I urge you in the name of our L Jesus Christ to join
16: 2 Receive her in the L, as one who is worthy of high
16:12 to dear Persis, who has worked so hard for the L.
16:13 whom the L picked out to be his very own;
16:18 Such people are not serving Christ our L; they are
16:19 But everyone knows that you are obedient to the L.
16:20 May the grace of our L Jesus Christ be with you.
1Co 1: 2 upon the name of Jesus Christ, our L and theirs.
1: 3 and the L Jesus Christ give you his grace
1: 7 eagerly wait for the return of our L Jesus Christ.
1: 8 on the great day when our L Jesus Christ returns.
1: 9 friendship with his Son, Jesus Christ our L.
1:10 I appeal to you by the authority of the L Jesus
1:31 should boast only of what the L has done."
2: 8 they would never have crucified our glorious L.
2:16 For, / "Who can know what the L is thinking?
3: 3 are acting like people who don't belong to the L.
3: 5 to believe. Each of us did the work the L gave us.
3:20 "The L knows the thoughts of the wise,
4: 4 It is the L himself who will examine me
4: 5 to conclusions before the L returns as to whether
4: 5 When the L comes, he will bring our deepest
4:17 he is my beloved and trustworthy child in the L.
4:19 if the L will let me, and then I'll find out whether
5: 4 in the name of the L Jesus. You are to call a
5: 4 and the power of the L Jesus will be with you as
5: 5 and he himself will be saved when the L returns.
6:11 right with God because of what the L Jesus Christ
6:13 made for the L, and the L cares about our bodies.
6:14 just as he raised our L from the dead.
6:17 But the person who is joined to the L becomes one
7:10 command that comes not from me, but from the L.
7:12 though I do not have a direct command from the L.
7:17 You must accept whatever situation the L has put
7:22 if you were a slave when the L called you,
7:22 the L has now set you free from the awful power
7:22 And if you were free when the L called you,
7:25 I do not have a command from the L for them.
7:25 But the L in his kindness has given me wisdom
7:34 been married can be more devoted to the L in body
7:35 you to do whatever will help you serve the L best,
7:39 but this must be a marriage acceptable to the L.
8: 6 And there is only one L, Jesus Christ,
9: 1 Haven't I seen Jesus our L with my own eyes?
9: 1 because of my hard work that you are in the L?
9:14 the L gave orders that those who preach the Good
10:21 You cannot drink from the cup of the L and from
11:23 For this is what the L himself said, and I pass it on
11:23 he was betrayed, the L Jesus took a loaf of bread,
11:27 this bread or drinks this cup of the L unworthily,
11:27 of sinning against the body and the blood of the L.
11:32 But when we are judged and disciplined by the L,
12: 3 and no one is able to say, "Jesus is L," except by
12: 5 in the church, but it is the same L we are serving.
14: 3 who prophesies is helping others grow in the L,
14: 4 in tongues is strengthened personally in the L,
14:21 even then, they will not listen to me," / says the L.
14:26 must be useful to all and build them up in the L.
14:30 another person receives a revelation from the L,
14:37 I am saying is a command from the L himself.
15:31 This is as certain as my pride in what the L Jesus
15:57 over sin and death through Jesus Christ our L!
15:58 for you know that nothing you do for the L is ever
16: 7 want to come and stay awhile, if the L will let me.
16:19 in the province of Asia greet you heartily in the L,
16:22 If anyone does not love the L, that person is
cursed. Our L, come!
16:23 May the grace of the L Jesus be with you.
2Co 1: 2 and the L Jesus Christ give you his grace
1: 3 praise to the God and Father of our L Jesus Christ.
1:14 Then on the day when our L Jesus comes back
2:12 of Christ, the L gave me tremendous opportunities.
2:14 we go he uses us to tell others about the L
3:16 But whenever anyone turns to the L, then the veil
3:17 Now, the L is the Spirit, and wherever the Spirit of
the L is, he gives
3:18 be mirrors that brightly reflect the glory of the L.
3:18 And as the Spirit of the L works within us,
4: 5 about ourselves; we preach Christ Jesus, the L.
4:14 We know that the same God who raised our L
5: 6 live in these bodies we are not at home with the L.
5: 8 for then we will be at home with the L.
5:11 because we know this solemn fear of the L that we
6: 3 be hindered from finding the L by the way we act,
6:17 and separate yourselves from them, says the L.
6:18 be my sons and daughters, / says the L Almighty."
8: 5 first action was to dedicate themselves to the L
8: 9 full of love and kindness our L Jesus Christ was.
8:19 a service that glorifies the L and shows our
8:21 We are careful to be honorable before the L,
10: 8 too much about the authority given to us by the L.
10:17 should boast only of what the L has done."
10:18 But when the L commends someone,
11:17 Such bragging is not something the L wants,
11:31 God, the Father of our L Jesus, who is to be
12: 1 the visions and revelations I received from the L.
12: 8 Three different times I begged the L to take it
13:10 For I want to use the authority the L has given me
13:13 May the grace of our L Jesus Christ, the love of
Gal 1: 3 from God our Father and from the L Jesus Christ.
5:10 I am trusting the L to bring you back to believing
6:14 anything except the cross of our L Jesus Christ.
6:18 may the grace of our L Jesus Christ be with you
Eph 1: 2 to you from God our Father and Jesus Christ our L.
1: 3 we praise God, the Father of our L Jesus Christ,
1:15 Ever since I first heard of your strong faith in the L
1:17 the glorious Father of our L Jesus Christ,
2:21 joined together, becoming a holy temple for the L.
3:11 now been carried out through Christ Jesus our L.
4: 1 Therefore I, a prisoner for serving the L, beg you
4: 5 There is only one L, one faith, one baptism,
4:13 Son that we will be mature and full grown in the L,
5: 8 now you are full of light from the L, and your
5:10 Try to find out what is pleasing to the L.
5:17 but try to understand what the L wants you to do.
5:19 making music to the L in your hearts.
5:20 God the Father in the name of our L Jesus Christ.
5:22 will submit to your husbands as you do to the L.
6: 1 obey your parents because you belong to the L,
6: 4 the discipline and instruction approved by the L.
6: 7 as though you were working for the L rather than
6: 8 Remember that the L will reward each one of us
6:23 from God the Father and the L Jesus Christ.
6:24 May God's grace be upon all who love our L Jesus
Php 1: 2 and the L Jesus Christ give you grace and peace.

1:16 for they know the L brought me here to defend the
2:11 every tongue will confess that Jesus Christ is L,
2:19 If the L Jesus is willing, I hope to send Timothy to
2:24 And I have confidence from the L that I myself
3: 1 dear friends, may the L give you joy.
3: 8 the priceless gain of knowing Christ Jesus my L.
3:20 citizens of heaven, where the L Jesus Christ lives.
4: 1 So please stay true to the L, my dear friends.
4: 2 Please, because you belong to the L, settle your
4: 4 Always be full of joy in the L. I say it again—
4: 5 in all you do. Remember, the L is coming soon.
4:10 and how I praise the L that you are concerned
4:23 May the grace of the L Jesus Christ be with your
Col 1: 3 and we give thanks to God the Father of our L
1:10 way you live will always honor and please the L,
2: 6 just as you accepted Christ Jesus as your L,
2:10 He is the L over every ruler and authority in the
3:13 Remember, the L forgave you, so you must forgive
3:17 or say, let it be as a representative of the L Jesus,
3:18 as is fitting for those who belong to the L.
3:20 obey your parents, for this is what pleases the L.
3:22 because of your reverent fear of the L.
3:23 as though you were working for the L rather than
3:24 Remember that the L will give you an inheritance
4: 7 He is a faithful helper who serves the L with me.
4:17 "Be sure to carry out the work the L gave you."
1Th 1: 1 belong to God the Father and the L Jesus Christ.
1: 3 anticipation of the return of our L Jesus Christ.
1: 6 In this way, you imitated both us and the L.
1: 8 And now the word of the L is ringing out from you
2:15 own prophets, and some even killed the L Jesus.
2:19 before our L Jesus when he comes back again.
3: 8 us new life, knowing you remain strong in the L.
3:11 and our L Jesus make it possible for us to come to
3:12 And may the L make your love grow and overflow
3:13 L Jesus comes with all those who belong to him.
4: 1 we urge you in the name of the L Jesus to live in a
4: 2 what we taught you in the name of the L Jesus.
4: 6 for the L avenges all such sins, as we have
4:15 I can tell you this directly from the L: We who are
still living when the L returns will not
4:16 For the L himself will come down from heaven
4:17 be caught up in the clouds to meet the L in the air
5: 2 for you know quite well that the day of the L will
5: 4 and you won't be surprised when the day of the L
5: 9 For God decided to save us through our L Jesus
5:23 that day when our L Jesus Christ comes again.
5:27 I command you in the name of the L to read this
5:28 And may the grace of our L Jesus Christ be with
2Th 1: 1 belong to God our Father and the L Jesus Christ.
1: 2 and the L Jesus Christ give you grace and peace.
1: 7 and also for us when the L Jesus appears from
1: 8 who refuse to obey the Good News of our L Jesus.
1: 9 forever separated from the L and from his glorious
1:12 will give honor to the name of our L Jesus
1:12 because of the undeserved favor of our God and L,
2: 1 let us tell you about the coming again of our L
2: 2 and troubled by those who say that the day of the L
2: 8 whom the L Jesus will consume with the breath of
2:13 for you, dear brothers and sisters loved by the L.
2:14 now you can share in the glory of our L Jesus
2:16 May our L Jesus Christ and God our Father,
3: 2 and evil people, for not everyone believes in the L.
3: 3 But the L is faithful; he will make you strong
3: 4 And we are confident in the L that you are
3: 5 May the L bring you into an ever deeper
3: 6 command with the authority of our L Jesus Christ:
3:12 In the name of the L Jesus Christ we appeal to
3:16 May the L of peace himself always give you his
3:16 no matter what happens. The L be with you all.
3:18 May the grace of our L Jesus Christ be with you
1Ti 1: 2 our Father and Christ Jesus our L give you grace,
1:12 How thankful I am to Christ Jesus our L for
1:14 Oh, how kind and gracious the L was! He filled me
6: 3 wholesome teachings of the L Jesus Christ,
6:14 you from now until our L Jesus Christ returns.
6:15 almighty God, the King of kings and L of lords.
2Ti 1: 2 our Father and Christ Jesus our L give you grace,
1: 5 I know that you sincerely trust the L, for you have
1: 8 must never be ashamed to tell others about our L.
1:16 May the L show special kindness to Onesiphorus
1:18 May the L show him special kindness on the day
2: 7 The L will give you understanding in all these
2:19 "The L knows those who are his," and "Those who
claim they belong to the L must
2:22 of those who call on the L with pure hearts.
3:11 and Lystra—but the L delivered me from all of it.
4: 5 Don't be afraid of suffering for the L. Work at
4: 8 the crown of righteousness that the L, the righteous
4:14 but the L will judge him for what he has done.
4:17 But the L stood with me and gave me strength,
4:18 and the L will deliver me from every evil attack
4:22 May the L be with your spirit. Grace be with you
Tit 2: 3 way that is appropriate for someone serving the L.
Phm 1: 3 and the L Jesus Christ give you grace and peace.
1: 5 because I keep hearing of your trust in the L Jesus
1:16 to you, both as a slave and as a brother in the L.
1:25 The grace of the L Jesus Christ be with your spirit.
Heb 1:10 "L, in the beginning you laid the foundation of the
2: 3 that was announced by the L Jesus himself?
7:14 I mean is, our L came from the tribe of Judah,
7:21 to Jesus did he say, / "The L has taken an oath
8: 2 the true place of worship that was built by the L
8: 8 "The day will come, says the L, / when I will
8: 9 so I turned my back on them, says the L.
8:10 with the people of Israel on that day, says the L:
8:11 their family, / saying, 'You should know the L.'
10:16 with my people on that day, says the L: / I will put
10:30 He also said, / "The L will judge his own people."
10:35 Do not throw away this confident trust in the L,
12: 5 don't ignore it when the L disciplines you,
12: 6 For the L disciplines those he loves, / and he
12:14 for those who are not holy will not see the L.
13: 6 can say with confidence, / "The L is my helper,
13: 7 come from their lives, and trust the L as they do.
13:20[-21] brought again from the dead our L Jesus,
Jas 1: 1 a slave of God and of the L Jesus Christ.
1: 7 should not expect to receive anything from the L.
2: 1 L Jesus Christ if you favor some people more than
3: 9 Sometimes it praises our L and Father,
4:10 When you bow down before the L and admit your
4:15 "If the L wants us to, we will live and do this
5: 4 reapers have reached the ears of the L Almighty.
5: 8 And take courage, for the coming of the L is near.
5:10 at the prophets who spoke in the name of the L.
5:13 thankful should continually sing praises to the L.
5:14 anointing them with oil in the name of the L.
5:15 will heal the sick, and the L will make them well.
1Pe 1: 3 honor to the God and Father of our L Jesus Christ,
1:25 But the word of the L will last forever." And that
3:12 The eyes of the L watch over those who do right,
3:12 But the L turns his face / against those who do
3:15 Instead, you must worship Christ as L of your life.
5: 3 Don't l it over the people assigned to your care,
2Pe 1: 2 to know Jesus, our God and L, better and better.
1: 8 and useful in your knowledge of our L Jesus
1:11 for you to enter into the eternal Kingdom of our L
1:14 But the L Jesus Christ has shown me that my days
1:16 we told you about the power of our L Jesus Christ
2: 9 the L knows how to rescue godly people from their
2:20 wicked ways of the world by learning about our L
3: 2 and what our L and Savior commanded through
3: 8 that a day is like a thousand years to the L,
3: 9 The L isn't really being slow about his promise to
3:10 But the day of the L will come as unexpectedly as
3:15 the L is waiting so that people have time to be
3:18 and knowledge of our L and Savior Jesus Christ.
1Jn 3:19 we will be confident when we stand before the L,
3Jn 1: 7 For they are traveling for the L and accept nothing
Jude 1: 4 they have turned against our only Master and L,
1: 5 that even though the L rescued the whole nation of
1: 9 but simply said, "The L rebuke you."
1:12 in fellowship meals celebrating the love of the L,
1:14 these people. He said, / "Look, the L is coming
1:17 must remember what the apostles of our L Jesus
1:21 L Jesus Christ in his mercy is going to give you.
1:25 is God our Savior, through Jesus Christ our L.
Rev 1: 8 the beginning and the end," says the L God.
4: 8 "Holy, holy, holy is the L God Almighty—
4:11 "You are worthy, O L our God, / to receive glory
6:10 They called loudly to the L and said, "O Sovereign
L, holy and true,
11: 4 and the two lampstands that stand before the L of
11: 8 and "Egypt," the city where their L was crucified.
11:15 world has now become the kingdom of our L
11:17 "We give thanks to you, L God Almighty,
14:13 Blessed are those who die in the L from now on.
15: 3 and marvelous are your actions, / L God Almighty.
15: 4 Who will not fear, O L, and glorify your name?
16: 7 "Yes, L God Almighty, your punishments are true
16:14 the L on that great judgment day of God Almighty.
17:14 because he is L over all lords and King over all
18: 8 by fire, for the L God who judges her is mighty."
19: 6 For the L our God, the Almighty, reigns.
19:16 was written this title: King of kings and L of lords.
21:22 for the L God Almighty and the Lamb are its
22: 5 or sun—for the L God will shine on them.
22: 6 'The L God, who tells his prophets what the future
22:20 I am coming soon!" Amen! Come, L Jesus!
22:21 The grace of the L Jesus be with you all.

LORD'S (65) [LORD]

LORD'S DAY (2) 1Co 16:2; Rev 1:10

LORD'S SUPPER (6) Ac 2:42,46; 20:7,11; 1Co 11:20,33

LORD'S TABLE (3) Mal 1:12; 1Co 10:16,21

1Ki 3:15 and stood before the Ark of the L covenant,
La 2:20 and prophets die within the L Temple?
3:37 Can anything happen without the L permission?
Mal 1:12 you are saying it's all right to defile the L table.
Mt 1:22 All of this happened to fulfill the L message
3: 3 'Prepare a pathway for the L coming! / Make a
21:42 This is the L doing, / and it is marvelous to see.'
Mk 1: 3 'Prepare a pathway for the L coming! / Make a
12:11 This is the L doing, / and it is marvelous to
Lk 1: 6 careful to obey all of the L commandments
1: 9 the sanctuary and burn incense in the L presence.
1:38 Mary responded, "I am the L servant, and I am
2: 9 and the radiance of the L glory surrounded them.
2:26 he would not die until he had seen the L Messiah.
3: 4 'Prepare a pathway for the L coming! / Make a
4:19 and that the time of the L favor has come."
5:17 And the L healing power was strongly with Jesus.
10:39 Her sister, Mary, sat at the L feet, listening to what
Jn 1:23 'Prepare a straight pathway for the L coming!' "
11: 2 who poured the expensive perfume on the L feet
20: 2 "They have taken the L body out of the tomb,
Ac 2:42 sharing in the L Supper and in prayer.
2:46 met in homes for the L Supper, and shared their
9: 1 He was eager to destroy the L followers, so he
9:32 and in his travels he came to the L people in the
11:16 Then I thought of the L words when he said,
13:49 So the L message spread throughout that region.
15:40 sent them off, entrusting them to the L grace.
19:10 both Jews and Greeks—heard the L message.
20: 7 of the week, we gathered to observe the L Supper.
20:11 went back upstairs and ate the L Supper together.
20:19 I have done the L work humbly—yes, and with
Ro 14: 4 The L power will help them do as they should.
16: 8 whom I love as one of the L own children,
16:12 hello to Tryphena and Tryphosa, the L workers,
1Co 7:32 An unmarried man can spend his time doing the L
9: 2 for you are living proof that I am the L apostle.
9: 5 the other disciples and the L brothers and Peter do?
10:16 When we bless the cup at the L Table, aren't we
10:21 You cannot eat at the L Table and at the table of
10:22 Do you dare to rouse the L jealousy as Israel did?
10:26 For "the earth is the L, and everything in it."
11:11 But in relationships among the L people,
11:20 It's not the L Supper you are concerned about
11:26 you are announcing the L death until he comes
11:33 and sisters, when you gather for the L Supper,
15:58 and steady, always enthusiastic about the L work,
16: 2 On every L Day, each of you should put aside
16:10 with respect. He is doing the L work, just as I am.
Gal 1:19 apostle I met at that time was James, our L brother.
Eph 4:17 With the L authority let me say this: Live no
6:10 A final word: Be strong with the L mighty power.
6:21 loved brother and faithful helper in the L work,
1Th 5:12 honor those who are your leaders in the L work.
2Th 3: 1 Pray first that the L message will spread rapidly
1Ti 1:18 you the confidence to fight well in the L battles.
2Ti 2: 5 Follow the L rules for doing his work, just as an
2:24 The L servants must not quarrel but must be kind
Phm 1:20 please do me this favor for the L sake.
Jas 2: 8 it is good when you truly obey our L royal
5: 7 you must be patient as you wait for the L return.
5:11 From his experience we see how the L plan finally
1Pe 2: 3 now that you have had a taste of the L kindness.
2:13 For the L sake, accept all authority—the king as
Rev 1:10 It was the L Day, and I was worshiping in the

LORD* (6375) [LORD'S* (YAHWEH'S)]

ANGEL OF THE LORD* (52) Ge 16:7,9; 22:11,15; Ex 3:2; Nu 22:22,23,24,25,26,31,32,34,35; Jdg 2:1,4; 5:23; 6:11,12,21,21,22,22; 13:3,13,15,16,16,17,18,20,21; 2Sa 24:16; 1Ki 19:7; 2Ki 1:3,15; 19:35; 1Ch 21:12,15,16,18,30; Ps 34:7; 35:5,6; Isa 37:36; Zec 1:11,12; 3:1,5,6; 12:8

ARK OF THE LORD* (34) Jos 3:13; 4:5,11; 6:7,11,12,13, 13; 7:6; 1Sa 4:6; 5:3,4; 6:1,2,8,11,15,18,19,21; 7:1; 2Sa 6:9, 10,11,15,16,17; 1Ki 8:4; 1Ch 15:2,3,12,14; 16:4; 2Ch 8:11

AS THE LORD* LIVES (26) Jdg 8:19; Ru 3:13; 1Sa 14:45; 19:6; 20:21; 25:26; 28:10; 2Sa 4:9; 12:5; 14:11; 1Ki 1:29; 2:24; 22:14; 2Ki 2:2,4,6; 4:30; 5:16,20; 2Ch 18:13; Jer 5:2; 12:16; 16:14,15; 23:7,8

BEFORE THE LORD* (128) Ge 13:10; Ex 28:12,30; 29:23,27; 30:20; 34:24; 40:23; Lev 4:6,15,17,24; 6:6,7; 8:27; 10:2,17; 14:11,12,16,18,24,27,31; 15:15,30; 16:12,18; 19:22; 23:11,17,20,28,40; 24:3,8; Nu 3:4; 5:16,18,25,30; 6:16,20,20; 8:10; 14:37; 15:15,28; 16:7,16,17; 20:9; 25:4; 26:61; 27:5; 31:50; 32:22; 33:4; Dt 1:45; 4:10; 9:18,25; 10:8; 16:8,11,16; 18:13; 19:17; 26:10; 27:7; 29:10; 31:11; 1Sa 7:6; 10:17,19,20, 21,25; 11:15; 12:3,7; 15:33; 20:8; 21:6; 23:18; 2Sa 5:3; 6:5, 14,16,21; 7:18; 21:6,7,9; 23:16; 1Ki 1:30; 2Ki 19:14,15; 22:19; 1Ch 11:3,18; 16:33,39; 17:16; 23:30; 25:7; 29:20,22; 2Ch 20:13; 33:23; Ne 8:9; Job 1:6; 2:1; Ps 69:10; 95:6; 96:13; 97:5; 98:6,9; 102:T,15; 109:15; 132:2; Isa 37:14,15; 44:11; Jer 4:4; Zec 2:13

BLESS THE LORD* (8) Jdg 5:2,9; Ps 16:7; 41:13; 72:18; 134:1,2; 144:1

BLESSED BE THE LORD* (9) 2Sa 18:28; 1Ki 1:48; 8:15; 1Ch 16:36; 2Ch 2:12; 6:4; Ps 89:52; 106:48; 124:6

COVENANT OF THE LORD* (7) Dt 31:26; Jos 3:3; 7:15; 23:16; 1Sa 4:3,4,5

DAY OF THE LORD* (13) Isa 13:9; Eze 13:5; 30:3; Joel 1:15; 2:1,11,31; 3:14; Am 5:18,20; Zep 1:14; Zec 14:1; Mal 4:5

EVIL IN THE SIGHT OF THE LORD* (5) Dt 4:25; 17:2; 2Ch 29:6; 36:5,12

FEAR OF THE LORD* (12) 2Ch 17:10; 19:9; Pr 1:7; 9:10; 10:27; 14:27; 15:33; 16:6; 19:23; 22:4; Isa 11:2; 33:6

FEAR THE LORD* (30) Ex 9:30; Dt 6:2,13; 10:20; 14:23; 17:19; 31:12,13; Jos 4:24; 1Sa 12:24; 2Ch 19:7; Ps 25:12; 33:8; 34:11; 112:1; 115:11,13; 118:4; 128:1; 135:20; Pr 1:29; 2:5; 3:7; 8:13; 14:2,26; 23:17; 24:21; Hos 10:3; Mic 6:9

GLORY OF THE LORD* (20) Ex 16:10; 24:17; 40:35; Ps 104:31; 138:5; Isa 40:5; 58:8; 60:1,2; Eze 1:28; 3:12,23; 10:4,4,18; 11:23; 43:4,5; 44:4; Hab 2:14

HAND OF THE LORD* (5) 1Ch 28:19; Ezr 7:6,28; Isa 66:14; Eze 1:3

HOUSE OF THE LORD* (23) Ex 34:26; Dt 23:18; 1Ch 6:31; 9:23; 23:24,28,32; 24:19; 25:6; 26:12,22,27; 29:8; Ps 23:6; 27:4; 116:19; 118:26; 122:1,9; 134:1; 135:2; Jer 29:26; Hag 1:14

I AM THE LORD* (137) Ge 15:7; 28:13; Ex 6:2,6,7,8,29; 7:5,17; 8:22; 10:2; 12:12; 14:4,18; 15:26; 16:12; 20:2; 29:46, 46; 31:13; 34:6,6; Lev 18:5,6,21; 19:12,14,16,18,28,30,32,37; 20:8; 21:12,23; 22:2,3,8,9,16,30,31,33; 26:2; Nu 3:13,41,45; 10:10; 15:41,41; 35:34; Dt 5:6; Jdg 6:10; 1Ki 20:13,28; 2Ki 10:16; Isa 41:14; 42:8; 43:3,11,15,16; 44:24; 45:3,5,6,18; 48:17; 49:23; 51:15; Jer 9:24; 16:21; 32:27; Eze 6:7,14; 7:4, 27; 11:10,12; 12:15,16,20,25; 13:14,21,23; 14:8; 15:7; 16:62; 20:7,19,20,38,42,44; 21:5; 22:16; 24:24,27; 25:5,7,11,17; 26:6; 28:22,23,26; 29:6,9,21; 30:8,19,25,26; 32:15; 33:29;

34:27; 35:4,9,15; 36:11,23,38; 37:6,13,14; 38:16,23; 39:6,7, 22,28; Hos 12:9; 13:4; Zec 10:6; Mal 3:6

LAW OF THE LORD* (16) 2Ki 10:31; 1Ch 16:40; 22:12; 2Ch 12:1; 17:9; 19:8; 31:3,4; 34:14; 35:26; Ezr 7:10; Ne 9:3; Ps 19:7; 119:1; Isa 5:24; Jer 8:8

LORD* ALMIGHTY (260) 1Sa 1:3,11; 4:4; 15:2; 17:45; 2Sa 6:2,18; 7:8,26,27; 1Ki 18:15; 2Ki 3:14; 19:31; 1Ch 11:9; 17:7,24; Ps 24:10; 46:7,11; 48:8; 69:6; 84:1,3,12; Isa 1:9,24; 2:12; 3:1,15; 5:7,9,16,24; 6:3,5; 8:13,18; 9:7,13,19; 10:16,23, 24,26,33; 13:4,13; 14:22,23,24,27; 17:3; 18:7,7; 19:4,12,16, 17,18,20,25; 21:10; 22:5,12,14,14,15,25; 23:9; 24:23; 25:6; 28:5,22,29; 29:6; 31:4,5; 37:16,32; 39:5; 44:6; 45:13; 47:4; 48:2; 51:15; 54:5; Jer 2:19; 6:6,9; 7:3,21; 8:3; 9:7,15,17; 10:16; 11:17,20,22; 16:9; 19:3,11,15; 20:12; 23:15,16,36; 25:8,27,28,29,32; 26:18; 27:4,18,19,21; 28:2,14; 29:4,8,17, 21,25; 30:8; 31:23,35; 32:14,15,18; 33:11,12; 35:13,18,19; 39:16; 42:15,18; 43:10; 44:2,11,25; 46:10,10,18,25; 48:1,15; 49:5,7,26,35; 50:18,25,31,33,34; 51:5,14,19,33,57,58; Am 9:5; Mic 4:4; Na 2:13; 3:5; Hab 2:13; Zep 2:9,10; Hag 1:2,5,7, 9,14; 2:4,6,7,8,9,9,11,23,23; Zec 1:3,3,4,6,12,14,16,17; 2:8,9, 11; 3:7,9,10; 4:6,9; 5:4; 6:12,15; 7:3,4,9,12,12,13; 8:1,2,3,4,6, 6,7,9,9,11,14,14, 18,19,20,21,22,23; 9:15; 10:3; 12:5; 13:2,7; 14:16,17,21,21; Mal 1:4,6,8,9,10,11,13,14; 2:2,4,7,8,12,16; 3:1,5,7,10,11,12,14,17; 4:1,3

LORD*...APPEARED (21) Ge 12:7; 17:1; 18:1; 26:2,24; Ex 3:2; 4:1; Lev 9:23; Nu 14:10; 16:19,42; 20:6; Dt 31:15; Jdg 6:12; 13:3; 1Ki 3:5; 9:2; 11:9; 2Ch 3:1; 7:12; Eze 1:28

LORD* BLESS (11) Nu 6:24; Jdg 17:2; Ru 1:9; 2:4,19,20; 3:10; 1Sa 15:13; 23:21; 2Sa 2:5; Jer 31:23

LORD* BLESSED (6) Ge 26:12; Ex 20:11; Jdg 13:24; 2Sa 6:11; 1Ch 13:14; Job 42:12

LORD* GOD (61) Ge 2:4,5,7,8,9,15,16,18,19,21,22; 3:1, 8,9,11,13,14,21,22,23,24; Ex 9:30; 2Sa 5:10; 7:25; 1Ki 19:10, 14; 1Ch 17:16,17; 22:1,19; 28:20; 29:1; 2Ch 1:9; 6:41,41,42; 26:18; 32:16; Ne 9:7; Ps 59:5; 68:18; 72:18; 80:4,19; 84:8,11; 89:8; Jer 5:14; 15:16; 35:17; 38:17; 44:7; Hos 12:5; Am 3:13; 4:13; 5:14,15,16; 6:8,14; Jnh 4:6

LORD* GOD ALMIGHTY (21) 2Sa 5:10; 1Ki 19:10,14; Ps 59:5; 80:4,19; 84:8; 89:8; Jer 5:14; 15:16; 35:17; 38:17; 44:7; Hos 12:5; Am 3:13; 4:13; 5:14,15,16; 6:8,14

LORD* MY/HIS/OUR/THEIR/YOUR GOD (195) Ge 9:26; 28:21; Ex 3:18; 5:3; 8:10,26,27; 10:7,25,26; 29:46, 46; 32:11; Lev 4:22; Nu 22:18; 23:21; Dt 1:6,19,20,25,41; 2:29,33,36,37; 3:3; 4:5,7; 5:2,24,25,27; 6:4,20,24,25; 17:19; 18:7; 26:14; 29:18,29; Jos 14:8,9; 18:6; 22:19,29,34; 24:17, 24; Jdg 3:7; 8:34; 11:24; 1Sa 7:8; 12:9; 30:6; 2Sa 24:24; 1Ki 3:7; 5:3,4,5; 8:28,57,59,61,65; 9:9; 11:4; 15:3,4; 17:20,21; 2Ki 5:11; 16:2; 17:7,9,14,16,19; 18:12,22; 19:19; 1Ch 13:2; 15:13; 16:14; 21:17; 22:7; 29:16; 2Ch 1:1; 2:4,4; 6:19; 13:10, 11; 14:2,7,11,11; 15:9; 19:7; 26:16; 27:6; 28:5; 29:6; 31:6,20; 32:8,11; 33:12,17; 34:8,33; 36:5,12; Ezr 7:6,28; 9:5,8; Ne 9:3, 3,4; 10:34; Ps 7:1,3; 13:3; 20:7; 30:2,12; 35:24; 40:5; 94:23; 99:5,8,9,9; 104:1; 105:7; 106:47; 109:26; 113:5; 122:9; 123:2; 146:5; Isa 26:13; 36:7; 37:20; 61:10; Jer 3:21,22,23,25; 5:19, 24; 7:28; 8:14; 14:22; 16:10; 22:9; 26:16; 30:9; 31:6,18; 37:3; 42:6,20; 43:1,2; 50:4,28; 51:10; Eze 28:26; 34:30; 39:22,28; Da 9:4,10,13, 14,20; Hos 1:7; 3:5; 7:10; Jnh 2:1,6; Mic 4:5; 5:4; 7:17; Hab 1:12; Zep 2:7; Hag 1:12,12; Zec 9:16; 10:6; 11:4; 13:9; 14:5

LOVE THE LORD* (12) Dt 6:5; 11:1,13; 19:9; 30:16,20; Jos 22:5; 23:11; Ps 31:23; 97:10; 116:1; Eze 44:9

NAME OF THE LORD* (50) Ex 20:7; Dt 5:11; 18:7; 28:58; 32:3; 1Sa 14:39; 17:45; 28:10; 2Sa 6:2,18; 1Ki 3:2; 5:3,5; 8:17,20; 10:1; 18:24; 2Ki 2:24; 5:11; 1Ch 13:6; 16:2; 22:7; 2Ch 2:4; 6:7,10; 33:18; Job 1:21; Ps 7:17; 113:1,2,3; 116:4,17; 118:10,11,12,26; 122:4; 135:1; 148:13; Pr 18:10; Isa 24:15; 48:1; 59:19; Jer 26:16; Joel 2:32; Am 6:10; Mic 5:4; Zep 3:12; Zec 13:3

PEOPLE OF THE LORD* (10) Nu 16:3; 27:17; Dt 14:1; 27:9; Jdg 5:11,13; 2Sa 6:21; Eze 36:20; Hos 8:1; Zep 2:10

PRAISE (TO) THE LORD* (80) Ge 29:35; Dt 8:10; Ru 4:14; 1Sa 25:32,39; 1Ki 5:7; 8:56; 1Ch 16:4; 23:5; 25:3; 29:20; 2Ch 20:19; 29:27,30; 31:2; Ezr 3:10; 7:27; Ne 9:5; Ps 22:23; 26:12; 28:6; 31:21; 33:2; 34:1; 68:26; 98:5; 102:18; 103:1,2,20,21,22,22; 104:1,35,35; 105:45; 106:1,48; 107:8, 15,21,31; 111:1; 112:1; 113:1,9; 115:18,18; 116:19; 117:1,2; 135:1,3,19,19,20,21; 145:21; 146:1,1,2,10; 147:1,12,20; 148:1,1,5,7,14; 149:1,9; 150:1,6; Isa 12:1; 63:7; Jer 20:13; Joel 2:26; Zec 11:5

SAYS THE LORD* (240) 2Ki 3:17; 9:26; 19:33; 20:17; 22:19; 2Ch 34:27; Isa 1:11,18; 8:20; 17:3,6; 22:19; 30:1; 31:9; 37:34; 39:6; 41:21; 43:10,12; 48:22; 49:14,18; 54:1,8, 10; 55:8; 56:1; 57:19; 59:20,21; 65:7,8; 66:12,17,20,22; Jer 2:12,29; 3:1,10,14,16,20,22; 4:1,9,17,22; 5:1,11,15,18; 6:12, 15; 7:11,13,30,32; 8:1,12,17; 9:3,6,11,25; 10:18; 11:11; 13:11,14,25; 14:15; 15:3,6,9; 16:5,14,16,21; 17:24; 19:6,12; 21:7,10,14; 22:5,24; 23:1,4,5,7,11,16,30,32; 25:7,12; 27:8,22; 29:9,11,14,19,23; 30:8,10,11,17,21; 31:1,17,27,28,31,32,33, 34,38; 32:30; 33:11,14; 34:5; 42:11; 44:26,29; 46:5,23,28; 48:12,25,30,35,40,43,44,47; 49:2,2,6,13,16,18,26,30,31,32, 37,38,39; 50:4,10,20,21,30,35,40; 51:20,24,25,26,39,48,52, 53; Eze 16:58; Hos 2:13,16,21; 11:11; Joel 3:1; Am 3:10; 4:6,8,9,10,11; 5:27; 6:14; 9:8,13,15; Ob 1:8; Mic 4:6,13; 5:10; 7:15; Na 2:13; Zep 1:2,3,8,10; 2:9,12; Hag 1:8,9,13; 2:4,4,4,7, 8,9,14,17,23,23; Zec 1:3,16; 2:5; 3:9,10; 4:6; 7:13; 8:11,14, 17; 11:6; 12:4; 13:2,7,8; Mal 1:2,8,10,11,13,14; 2:2,4,8,16,16; 3:1,5,7,10,11,12,13,17; 4:3

SERVANT OF THE LORD* (18) Dt 34:5; Jos 1:13,15; 8:33; 11:12; 12:6; 13:8; 14:7; 18:7; 22:2,4; 24:29; Jdg 2:8; 1Ki 18:12; 2Ch 24:6; Ps 18:T; 36:T; Isa 42:19

SOVEREIGN LORD* (290) Ge 15:2,8; Ex 23:17; 34:23; Dt 3:24; 9:26; Jos 7:7; Jdg 6:22; 16:28; 2Sa 7:18,19,19,20, 22,28,29; 1Ki 2:26; 8:53; Ps 68:20; 69:6; 71:16; 73:28; 109:21; 140:7; 141:8; Isa 7:7; 25:8; 28:16; 30:15; 40:10; 48:16; 49:22; 50:4,5,7,9; 51:22; 52:4; 56:8; 61:1,11; 65:13,15; Jer 1:6; 2:22; 4:10; 7:20; 14:13; 32:17,25; 44:26; 50:25; Eze 2:4; 3:11,27; 4:14; 5:5,7,8,11; 6:3,3,11; 7:2,5; 8:1; 9:8; 11:7,8, 13,16,17,21; 12:10,19,23,25,28,28; 13:3,8,8,9,13,16,18,20; 14:4,6,11,14,16,18,20,21,23; 15:6,8; 16:3,8,14,19,23,30,36, 43,48,59,63; 17:3,9,12,16,19,22; 18:3,9,23,30,32; 20:3,3,5, 27,30,31,33,36,39,40,44,47,49; 21:7,13,24,26,28; 22:3,12,19, 28,31; 23:22,28,32,34,35,46,49; 24:3,6,9,14,21; 25:3,3,6,8,12, 13,14,15,16; 26:3,5,7,14,15,19,21; 27:3; 28:2,6,10,12,22,24, 25; 29:3,8,13,16,19,20; 30:2,6,10,13,22; 31:10,15,18; 32:3,8, 11,14,16,31,32; 33:11,25,27; 34:2,8,10,11,15,17,20,30,31; 35:3,6,11,14; 36:2,3,4,5,6,7,13,14,15,22,23,32,33,37; 37:3,5, 9,12,19,21; 38:3,10,14,17,18,21; 39:1,5,8,10,13,17,20,25,29; 43:18,19,27; 44:6,9,12,15,27; 45:9,15,18; 46:1,16; 47:13,23; 48:29; Am 1:8; 3:7,8,11; 4:2,5; 5:3; 6:8; 7:1,2,4,5,6; 8:1,3,9, 11; 9:8; Ob 1:1; Mic 1:2; Hab 3:19; Zep 1:7; Zec 9:14

SPIRIT OF THE LORD* (22) Jdg 3:10; 6:34; 11:29; 13:25; 14:6,19; 15:14; 1Sa 10:6; 16:13,14; 2Sa 23:2; 1Ki 18:12; 22:24; 2Ki 2:16; 2Ch 18:23; 20:14; Isa 11:2; 40:13; 63:14; Eze 11:5; 37:1; Mic 3:8

TEMPLE OF THE LORD* (120) 1Ki 3:1; 6:1; 7:40,45, 48,51; 8:10,63; 9:1,10; 10:5,12; 12:27; 14:26,28; 15:15; 2Ki 11:3,4,10,15,18,19; 12:9,13; 14:14; 15:35; 16:8,18; 18:15; 19:1; 20:5,8; 21:4; 22:3,5,9; 23:2,7; 25:9; 1Ch 6:32; 22:1,5, 11,14; 23:4; 28:13,20; 2Ch 3:1; 4:16; 5:1,13; 7:2,11; 8:16; 9:4,11; 12:9,11; 20:5,28; 23:6,14,18,20; 24:4,7,8,12,14,14,18; 26:21; 27:2; 29:3,5,15,16,17,18,20,25,31,35; 30:1,15; 31:11; 33:4; 34:8,17,30; 35:2; 36:7,10,14; Ezr 1:3,5; 2:68; 7:27; Isa 2:2; 37:1; 38:20,22; Jer 7:4; 19:14; 20:1; 26:2; 41:5; 52:13; Eze 44:4; Joel 1:9,14; Mic 4:1; Zec 6:12,14,15; 7:3; 8:9; 11:13; 14:20,21

VOICE OF THE LORD* (12) Ex 15:26; Dt 18:16; 1Ki 20:36; Ps 29:3,4,4,5,7,8,9; Isa 66:6; Zep 3:2

WORD OF THE LORD* (21) Ex 9:21; Dt 8:3; 1Sa 15:23; 2Sa 12:9; 24:11; 2Ch 30:12; 34:21; Ps 33:4; Jer 2:4; 6:10; 8:9; 10:1; Eze 13:2; 20:47; 34:7,9; 36:1; 37:4; Da 9:2; Hos 4:1; Am 8:12

Ge 2: 4 When the **L** God made the heavens and the earth,
2: 5 on the earth, for the **L** God had not sent any rain.
2: 7 And the **L** God formed a man's body from the dust
2: 8 Then the **L** God planted a garden in Eden,
2: 9 And the **L** God planted all sorts of trees in the
2:15 The **L** God placed the man in the Garden of Eden
2:16 But the **L** God gave him this warning: "You may
2:18 And the **L** God said, "It is not good for the man to
2:19 So the **L** God formed from the soil every kind of
2:21 So the **L** God caused Adam to fall into a deep
2:22 Then the **L** God made a woman from the rib
3: 1 shrewdest of all the creatures the **L** God had made.
3: 8 Toward evening they heard the **L** God walking
3: 9 The **L** God called to Adam, "Where are you?"
3:11 told you that you were naked?" the **L** God asked.
3:13 Then the **L** God asked the woman, "How could
3:14 So the **L** God said to the serpent, "Because you
3:21 And the **L** God made clothing from animal skins
3:22 Then the **L** God said, "The people have become as
3:23 So the **L** God banished Adam and his wife from
3:24 the **L** God stationed mighty angelic beings to the
4: 3 At harvest time Cain brought to the **L** a gift of his
4: 4 best of his flock. The **L** accepted Abel's offering,
4: 6 "Why are you so angry?" the **L** asked him.
4: 9 Afterward the **L** asked Cain, "Where is your
4:10 But the **L** said, "What have you done? Listen—
4:13 Cain replied to the **L**, "My punishment is too great
4:15 The **L** replied, "They will not kill you, for I will
4:15 Then the **L** put a mark on Cain to warn anyone
4:26 lifetime that people first began to worship the **L**.
5:29 of farming this ground that the **L** has cursed."
6: 3 Then the **L** said, "My Spirit will not put up with
6: 5 Now the **L** observed the extent of the people's
6: 6 So the **L** was sorry he had ever made them.
6: 7 And the **L** said, "I will completely wipe out this
6: 8 But Noah found favor with the **L**.
7: 1 Finally, the day came when the **L** said to Noah,
7: 5 So Noah did exactly as the **L** had commanded him.
7:16 as God had commanded. Then the **L** shut them in.
8:20 Then Noah built an altar to the **L** and sacrificed on
8:21 And the **L** was pleased with the sacrifice and said
9:26 "May Shem be blessed by the **L** my God;
11: 5 But the **L** came down to see the city and the tower
11: 8 In that way, the **L** scattered them all over the earth;
11: 9 because it was there that the **L** confused the people
12: 1 Then the **L** told Abram, "Leave your country,
12: 4 So Abram departed as the **L** had instructed him,
12: 7 Then the **L** appeared to Abram and said, "I am
12: 8 There he built an altar and worshiped the **L**.
12:17 But the **L** sent a terrible plague upon Pharaoh's
13: 4 built the altar, and there he again worshiped the **L**.
13:10 like the garden of the **L** or the beautiful land of
13:10 (This was before the **L** had destroyed Sodom
13:13 unusually wicked and sinned greatly against the **L**.
13:14 After Lot was gone, the **L** said to Abram,
13:18 which is at Hebron. There he built an altar to the **L**.
14:22 Abram replied, "I have solemnly promised the **L**,
15: 1 Afterward the **L** spoke to Abram in a vision
15: 2 But Abram replied, "O Sovereign **L**, what good
15: 4 Then the **L** said to him, "No, your servant will not
15: 5 Then the **L** brought Abram outside beneath the
15: 6 And Abram believed the **L**, and the **L** declared
him righteous because of his
15: 7 Then the **L** told him, "I am the **L** who brought you
15: 8 But Abram replied, "O Sovereign **L**, how can I be
15: 9 Then the **L** told him, "Bring me a three-year-old
15:13 Then the **L** told Abram, "You can be sure that
15:18 So the **L** made a covenant with Abram that day
16: 2 "The **L** has kept me from having any children,"
16: 5 The **L** will make you pay for doing this to me!"
16: 7 The angel of the **L** found Hagar beside a desert
16: 9 Then the angel of the **L** said, "Return to your
16:11 for the **L** has heard about your misery.
16:13 Thereafter, Hagar referred to the **L**, who had
17: 1 the **L** appeared to him and said, "I am God
18: 1 The **L** appeared again to Abraham while he was
18:13 Then the **L** said to Abraham, "Why did Sarah
18:14 Is anything too hard for the **L**? About a year from
18:17 I hide my plan from Abraham?" the **L** asked.
18:19 and their families to keep the way of the **L** and do
18:20 So the **L** told Abraham, "I have heard that the
18:22 but the **L** remained with Abraham for a while.
18:26 And the **L** replied, "If I find fifty innocent people
18:28 And the **L** said, "I will not destroy it if I find
18:29 And the **L** replied, "I will not destroy it if there are
18:30 And the **L** replied, "I will not destroy it if there are
18:31 And the **L** said, "Then I will not destroy it for the
18:32 And the **L** said, "Then, for the sake of the ten,
18:33 The **L** went on his way when he had finished his
19:13 The stench of the place has reached the **L**, and he
19:14 get out of the city! The **L** is going to destroy it."
19:16 to safety outside the city, for the **L** was merciful.
19:24 Then the **L** rained down fire and burning sulfur
20:18 For the **L** had stricken all the women with
21: 1 Then the **L** did exactly what he had promised.
21:33 and he worshiped the **L**, the Eternal God, at that
22:10 lifted it up to kill his son as a sacrifice to the **L**.
22:11 At that moment the angel of the **L** shouted to him
22:14 Abraham named the place "The **L** Will Provide."
22:14 "On the mountain of the **L** it will be provided."
22:15 Then the angel of the **L** called again to Abraham
22:16 "This is what the **L** says: Because you have
24: 1 old man, and the **L** had blessed him in every way.
24: 3 "Swear by the **L**, the God of heaven and earth,
24: 7 For the **L**, the God of heaven, who took me from
24:12 "O **L**, God of my master," he prayed. "Give me
24:21 or not she was the one the **L** intended him to meet.
24:26 man fell down to the ground and worshiped the **L**.
24:27 "Praise be to the **L**, the God of my master,
24:27 "The **L** has been so kind and faithful to Abraham,
24:31 and stay with us, you who are blessed by the **L**.
24:35 "And the **L** has blessed my master richly; he has
24:35 The **L** has given him flocks of sheep and herds of
24:40 'You will,' he told me, 'for the **L**, in whose
24:42 'O **L**, the God of my master, Abraham, if you are
24:44 **L**, let her be the one you have selected to be the
24:48 "Then I bowed my head and worshiped the **L**.
24:48 I praised the **L**, the God of my master, Abraham,
24:50 "The **L** has obviously brought you here,
24:51 wife of your master's son, as the **L** has directed."
24:52 servant bowed to the ground and worshiped the **L**.
24:56 The **L** has made my mission successful, and I want
25:21 Isaac pleaded with the **L** to give Rebekah a child
25:21 So the **L** answered Isaac's prayer, and his wife
25:22 So she went to ask the **L** about it. "Why is this
25:23 And the **L** told her, "The sons in your womb will
26: 2 The **L** appeared to him there and said, "Do not go
26:12 more grain than he planted, for the **L** blessed him.
26:22 for he said, "At last the **L** has made room for us,
26:24 where the **L** appeared to him on the night of his
26:25 Isaac built an altar there and worshiped the **L**.
26:28 "We can plainly see that the **L** is with you.
26:29 And now look how the **L** has blessed you!"
27:20 "Because the **L** your God put it in my path!"
27:27 smell of the open fields that the **L** has blessed.
28:13 At the top of the stairway stood the **L**, and he said,
"I am the **L**, the God of your
28:16 woke up and said, "Surely the **L** is in this place,
28:21 to my father, then I will make the **L** my God.
29:31 Leah was unloved, the **L** let her have a child,
29:32 for she said, "The **L** has noticed my misery,
29:33 "The **L** heard that I was unloved and has given me
29:35 for she said, "Now I will praise the **L**!"
30:24 she said, "May the **L** give me yet another son."
30:27 "for I have learned by divination that the **L** has
30:30 The **L** has blessed you from everything I do!
31: 3 Then the **L** said to Jacob, "Return to the land of
31:49 "May the **L** keep watch between us to make sure
32: 9 O **L**, you told me to return to my land and to my
32:11 O **L**, please rescue me from my brother, Esau.
38: 7 man in the LORD's sight, so the **L** took his life.
38:10 But the **L** considered it a wicked thing for Onan to
38:10 to his dead brother. So the **L** took Onan's life, too.
39: 2 The **L** was with Joseph and blessed him greatly as
39: 3 and realized that the **L** was with Joseph,
39: 5 the **L** began to bless Potiphar for Joseph's sake.
39:21 But the **L** was with Joseph there, too, and he
39:23 The **L** was with him, making everything run
49:18 I trust in you for salvation, O **L**!

Ex 3: 2 the angel of the **L** appeared to him as a blazing fire
3: 4 When the **L** saw that he had caught Moses'
3: 7 Then the **L** told him, "You can be sure I have seen
3:15 God also said, "Tell them, 'The **L**, the God of
3:16 Tell them, 'The **L**, the God of your ancestors—
3:18 straight to the king of Egypt and tell him, 'The **L**,
3:18 the wilderness to offer sacrifices to the **L** our God.'
4: 1 just say, 'The **L** never appeared to you.' "
4: 2 Then the **L** asked him, "What do you have there in
4: 3 "Throw it down on the ground," the **L** told him.
4: 4 Then the **L** told him, "Take hold of its tail."
4: 5 and they will believe you," the **L** told him.

4: 5 "Then they will realize that the **L**, the God of their
4: 6 Then the **L** said to Moses, "Put your hand inside
4: 7 your hand back into your robe again," the **L** said.
4: 8 they will believe the second," the **L** said.
4:10 But Moses pleaded with the **L**, "O Lord, I'm just
4:11 the **L** asked him. "Who makes people so they can
4:11 or not hear, see or not see? Is it not I, the **L**?
4:14 Then the **L** became angry with Moses.
4:19 Before Moses left Midian, the **L** said to him,
4:21 Then the **L** reminded him, "When you arrive back
4:22 Then you will tell him, 'This is what the **L** says:
4:24 the **L** confronted Moses and was about to kill him.
4:26 the circumcision.) After that, the **L** left him alone.
4:27 Now the **L** had said to Aaron, "Go out into the
4:28 then told Aaron everything the **L** had commanded
4:30 Aaron told them everything the **L** had told Moses,
4:31 The leaders were soon convinced that the **L** had
4:31 And when they realized that the **L** had seen their
5: 1 They told him, "This is what the **L**, the God of
5: 2 "And who is the **L** that I should listen to him
5: 2 I don't know the **L**, and I will not let Israel go."
5: 3 so we can offer sacrifices to the **L** our God.
5:17 'Let us go, so we can offer sacrifices to the **L**.'
5:21 "May the **L** judge you for getting us into this
5:22 So Moses went back to the **L** and protested,
6: 1 see what I will do to Pharaoh," the **L** told Moses.
6: 2 And God continued, "I am the **L**.
6: 3 though I did not reveal my name, the **L**, to them.
6: 6 'I am the **L**, and I will free you from your slavery
6: 7 And you will know that I am the **L** your God who
6: 8 It will be your very own property. I am the **L**!' "
6: 9 So Moses told the people what the **L** had said,
6:10 Then the **L** said to Moses,
6:12 "But **L**!" Moses objected. "My own people won't
6:13 But the **L** ordered Moses and Aaron to return to
6:26 are the same Aaron and Moses to whom the **L** said,
6:28 At that time, the **L** had said to them,
6:29 "I am the **L**! Give Pharaoh the message I have
6:30 is the same Moses who had argued with the **L**,
7: 1 Then the **L** said to Moses, "Pay close attention to
7: 5 the Israelites go, they will realize that I am the **L**."
7: 6 and Aaron did just as the **L** had commanded them.
7: 8 Then the **L** said to Moses and Aaron,
7:10 and they performed the miracle just as the **L** had
7:13 still refused to listen, just as the **L** had predicted.
7:14 Then the **L** said to Moses, "Pharaoh is very
7:16 Say to him, 'The **L**, the God of the Hebrews,
7:17 Now the **L** says, "You are going to find out that I
am the **L**."
7:19 Then the **L** said to Moses: "Tell Aaron to point his
7:20 and Aaron did just as the **L** had commanded them.
7:22 to Moses and Aaron, just as the **L** had predicted.
7:25 An entire week passed from the time the **L** turned
8: 1 Then the **L** said to Moses, "Go to Pharaoh once
again and tell him, 'This is what the **L** says:
8: 5 Then the **L** said to Moses, "Tell Aaron to point his
8: 8 "Plead with the **L** to take the frogs away from me
8: 8 people go, so they can offer sacrifices to the **L**."
8:10 know that no one is as powerful as the **L** our God.
8:12 and Moses pleaded with the **L** about the frogs he
8:13 And the **L** did as Moses had promised. The frogs
8:15 to Moses and Aaron, just as the **L** had predicted.
8:16 So the **L** said to Moses, "Tell Aaron to strike the
8:17 and Aaron did just as the **L** had commanded them.
8:19 listen to them, just as the **L** had predicted.
8:20 Next the **L** told Moses, "Get up early in the
8:20 Say to him, 'This is what the **L** says: Let my
8:22 Then you will know that I am the **L** and that I have
8:24 And the **L** did just as he had said. There were
8:26 detest the sacrifices that we offer to the **L** our God.
8:27 the wilderness to offer sacrifices to the **L** our God,
8:28 "I will let you go to offer sacrifices to the **L** your
8:29 "I will ask the **L** to cause the swarms of flies to
8:29 refuse to let the people go to sacrifice to the **L**."
8:30 and asked the **L** to remove all the flies.
8:31 And the **L** did as Moses asked and caused the
9: 1 "Go back to Pharaoh," the **L** commanded Moses.
9: 1 "Tell him, 'This is what the **L**, the God of the
9: 3 the **L** will send a deadly plague to destroy your
9: 4 But the **L** will again make a distinction between
9: 5 The **L** announced that he would send the plague
9: 8 Then the **L** said to Moses and Aaron, "Take soot
9:12 But the **L** made Pharaoh even more stubborn,
9:12 he refused to listen, just as the **L** had predicted.
9:13 Then the **L** said to Moses, "Get up early in the
9:13 Go to Pharaoh and tell him, 'The **L**, the God of the
9:20 Some of Pharaoh's officials believed what the **L**
9:21 But those who had no respect for the word of the **L**
9:22 Then the **L** said to Moses, "Lift your hand toward
9:23 and the **L** sent thunder and hail, and lightning
9:23 The **L** sent a tremendous hailstorm against all the
9:27 "The **L** is right, and my people and I are wrong.
9:28 Please beg the **L** to end this terrifying thunder
9:29 the city, I will lift my hands and pray to the **L**.
9:29 will prove to you that the earth belongs to the **L**.
9:30 I know that you still do not fear the **L** God as you
9:33 As he lifted his hands to the **L**, all at once the
9:35 to let the people leave, just as the **L** had predicted.
10: 1 Then the **L** said to Moses, "Return to Pharaoh
10: 2 among the Egyptians to prove that I am the **L**."
10: 3 went to Pharaoh and said, "This is what the **L**,
10: 7 Please let the Israelites go to serve the **L** their God!
10: 8 "All right, go and serve the **L** your God," he said.
10: 9 We must all join together in a festival to the **L**."
10:10 "The **L** will certainly need to be with you if you
10:11 Only the men may go and serve the **L**, for that is
10:12 Then the **L** said to Moses, "Raise your hand over
10:13 and the **L** caused an east wind to blow all that day
10:16 "I confess my sin against the **L** your God
10:17 and plead with the **L** your God to take away this
10:18 So Moses left Pharaoh and pleaded with the **L**.
10:19 The **L** responded by sending a strong west wind
10:20 But the **L** made Pharaoh stubborn once again,
10:21 Then the **L** said to Moses, "Lift your hand toward
10:24 "Go and worship the **L**," he said. "But let your
10:25 for sacrifices and burnt offerings to the **L** our God.
10:26 We will have to choose our sacrifices for the **L** our
10:27 So the **L** hardened Pharaoh's heart once more,
11: 1 Then the **L** said to Moses, "I will send just one
11: 3 (Now the **L** had caused the Egyptians to look
11: 4 announced to Pharaoh, "This is what the **L** says:
11: 7 Then you will know that the **L** makes a distinction
11: 9 Now the **L** had told Moses, "Pharaoh will not
11:10 the **L** hardened his heart so he wouldn't let the
12: 1 Now the **L** gave the following instructions to
12:12 against all the gods of Egypt, for I am the **L**!
12:14 you will celebrate it as a special festival to the **L**.
12:23 For the **L** will pass through the land and strike
12:23 of the doorframe, the **L** will pass over your home.
12:25 When you arrive in the land the **L** has promised to
12:28 So the people of Israel did just as the **L** had
12:29 And at midnight the **L** killed all the firstborn sons
12:31 of you! Go and serve the **L** as you have requested.
12:36 The **L** caused the Egyptians to look favorably on
12:42 This night had been reserved by the **L** to bring his
12:43 Then the **L** said to Moses and Aaron, "These are
12:51 And that very day the **L** began to lead the people
13: 1 Then the **L** said to Moses,
13: 3 For the **L** has brought you out by his mighty
13: 5 You must celebrate this day when the **L** brings you
13: 6 you will celebrate a great feast to the **L**.
13: 8 'This is a celebration of what the **L** did for us when
13: 9 it was the **L** who rescued you from Egypt with
13:11 And remember these instructions when the **L**
13:12 firstborn male animals must be presented to the **L**.
13:13 from the **L** by presenting a lamb in its place.
13:14 'With mighty power the **L** brought us out of Egypt
13:15 so the **L** killed all the firstborn males throughout
13:15 we now offer all the firstborn males to the **L**—
13:16 It is a visible reminder that it was the **L** who
13:21 The **L** guided them by a pillar of cloud during the
13:22 And the **L** did not remove the pillar of cloud
14: 1 Then the **L** gave these instructions to Moses:
14: 4 the Egyptians will know that I am the **L**!"
14: 8 The **L** continued to strengthen Pharaoh's resolve,
14:10 began to panic, and they cried out to the **L** for help.
14:13 stand where you are and watch the **L** rescue you.
14:14 The **L** himself will fight for you. You won't have
14:15 Then the **L** said to Moses, "Why are you crying
14:18 his army, all Egypt will know that I am the **L**!"
14:21 and the **L** opened up a path through the water with
14:24 the **L** looked down on the Egyptian army from the
14:25 "The **L** is fighting for Israel against us!"
14:26 the **L** said to Moses, "Raise your hand over the sea
14:27 and the **L** swept the terrified Egyptians into the
14:30 This was how the **L** rescued Israel from the
14:31 that the **L** had displayed against the Egyptians,
14:31 they feared the **L** and put their faith in him and his
15: 1 and the people of Israel sang this song to the **L**:
15: 1 "I will sing to the **L**, for he has triumphed
15: 2 The **L** is my strength and my song; / he has
15: 3 The **L** is a warrior; / yes, the **L** is his name!
15: 6 "Your right hand, O **L**, / is glorious in power. /
Your right hand, O **L**,
15:11 "Who else among the gods is like you, O **L**?
15:16 silent like a stone, / until your people pass by, O **L**,
15:17 the place you have made as your home, O **L**,
15:18 The **L** will reign forever and ever!"
15:19 the **L** brought the water crashing down on them.
15:21 "I will sing to the **L**, for he has triumphed
15:25 So Moses cried out to the **L** for help, and the **L**
showed him a branch.
15:25 It was there at Marah that the **L** laid before them
15:26 "If you will listen carefully to the voice of the **L**
15:26 on the Egyptians; for I am the **L** who heals you."
16: 3 "It would have been better if the **L** had killed us
16: 4 Then the **L** said to Moses, "Look, I'm going to
16: 6 "In the evening you will realize that it was the **L**
16: 7 you will see the glorious presence of the **L**.
16: 7 which are against the **L** and not against us.
16: 8 The **L** will give you meat to eat in the evening
16: 8 Yes, your complaints are against the **L**, not against
16:10 they could see the awesome glory of the **L**.
16:11 And the **L** said to Moses,
16:12 Then you will know that I am the **L** your God.' "
16:15 told them, "It is the food the **L** has given you.
16:16 The **L** says that each household should gather as
16:23 "The **L** has appointed tomorrow as a day of rest, a
holy Sabbath to the **L**.
16:25 food for today, for today is a Sabbath to the **L**.
16:28 and instructions?" the **L** asked Moses.
16:32 Then Moses gave them this command from the **L**:
16:32 **L** provided in the wilderness when he brought you
16:34 did this, just as the **L** had commanded Moses.
17: 2 arguing with me? And why are you testing the **L**?"
17: 4 Then Moses pleaded with the **L**, "What should I
17: 5 The **L** said to Moses, "Take your shepherd's staff,
17: 7 argued with Moses and tested the **L** by saying,
17: 7 "Is the **L** going to take care of us or not?"
17:14 Then the **L** instructed Moses, "Write this down as
17:15 an altar there and called it "The **L** Is My Banner."
17:16 so now the **L** will be at war with Amalek
18: 1 He had heard about how the **L** had brought them
18: 8 the **L** had done to rescue Israel from Pharaoh
18: 8 and how the **L** had delivered his people from all
18: 9 **L** had done for Israel as he brought them out of
18:10 "Praise be to the **L**," Jethro said, "for he has
18:11 I know now that the **L** is greater than all other
19: 3 The **L** called out to him from the mountain
19: 7 of the people and told them what the **L** had said.
19: 8 "We will certainly do everything the **L** asks of
19: 8 Moses brought the people's answer back to the **L**.
19: 9 Then the **L** said to Moses, "I am going to come to
19: 9 Moses told the **L** what the people had said.
19:10 Then the **L** told Moses, "Go down and prepare the
19:18 because the **L** had descended on it in the form of
19:20 The **L** came down on the top of Mount Sinai
19:21 Then the **L** told Moses, "Go back down and warn
19:21 They must not come up here to see the **L**, for those
19:22 Even the priests who regularly come near to the **L**
19:23 "But **L**, the people cannot come up on the
19:24 But the **L** said, "Go down anyway and bring
19:25 to the people and told them what the **L** had said.
20: 2 "I am the **L** your God, who rescued you from
20: 5 or bow down to them, for I, the **L** your God,
20: 7 "Do not misuse the name of the **L** your God.
20: 7 The **L** will not let you go unpunished if you misuse
20:10 day is a day of rest dedicated to the **L** your God.
20:11 For in six days the **L** made the heavens, the earth,
20:11 That is why the **L** blessed the Sabbath day and set
20:12 full life in the land the **L** your God will give you.
20:22 And the **L** said to Moses, "Say this to the people
22:11 take an oath of innocence in the presence of the **L**.
22:20 to any god other than the **L** must be destroyed.
23:17 man in Israel must appear before the Sovereign **L**.
23:19 It must be offered to the **L** your God.
23:25 "You must serve only the **L** your God. If you do,
24: 1 Then the **L** instructed Moses: "Come up here to
24: 2 Moses, are allowed to come near to the **L**.
24: 3 the teachings and regulations the **L** had given him,
24: 3 "We will do everything the **L** has told us to do."
24: 5 as burnt offerings and peace offerings to the **L**.
24: 7 "We will do everything the **L** has commanded.
24: 8 "This blood confirms the covenant the **L** has made
24:12 And the **L** said to Moses, "Come up to me on the
24:16 And the glorious presence of the **L** rested upon
24:16 On the seventh day the **L** called to Moses from the
24:17 The awesome glory of the **L** on the mountaintop
25: 1 The **L** said to Moses,
28:12 Aaron will carry these names before the **L** as a
28:29 goes into the presence of the **L** in the Holy Place.
28:29 the **L** will be reminded of his people continually.
28:30 for his people whenever he goes in before the **L**.
28:35 he enters the Holy Place to minister to the **L**,
28:36 these words: SET APART AS HOLY TO THE **L**.
28:38 always wear it so the **L** will accept the people.
29:18 This is a burnt offering to the **L**, which is very
29:21 and their clothing will be set apart as holy to the **L**.
29:23 of yeastless bread that was placed before the **L**.
29:24 his sons to be lifted up as a special gift to the **L**.
29:25 as a burnt offering that will be pleasing to the **L**.
29:27 and the thigh that were lifted up before the **L** in the
29:28 peace offerings or thanksgiving offerings to the **L**,
29:41 It will be a fragrant offering to the **L**, an offering
29:46 and they will know that I am the **L** their God.
29:46 that I could live among them. I am the **L** their God.
30:11 And the **L** said to Moses,
30:12 is counted must pay a ransom for himself to the **L**.
30:13 His payment to the **L** will be one-fifth of an ounce
30:14 twentieth birthday must give this offering to the **L**.
30:15 When this offering is given to the **L** to make
30:17 And the **L** said to Moses,
30:20 they go into the Tabernacle to appear before the **L**
30:20 they approach the altar to burn offerings to the **L**.
30:22 Then the **L** said to Moses,
30:37 It is reserved for the **L**, and you must treat it as
31: 1 The **L** also said to Moses,
31:12 The **L** then gave these further instructions to
31:13 It helps you to remember that I am the **L**,
31:15 Because the **L** considers it a holy day, anyone who
31:17 For in six days the **L** made heaven and earth,
31:18 Then as the **L** finished speaking with Moses on
32: 5 "Tomorrow there will be a festival to the **L**!"
32: 7 Then the **L** told Moses, "Quick! Go down the
32: 9 Then the **L** said, "I have seen how stubborn
32:11 But Moses pleaded with the **L** his God not to do it.
32:11 "O **L**!" he exclaimed. "Why are you so angry
32:14 So the **L** withdrew his threat and didn't bring
32:27 He told them, "This is what the **L**, the God of
32:29 you have been ordained for the service of the **L**,
32:30 but I will return to the **L** on the mountain.
32:31 So Moses returned to the **L** and said, "Alas,
32:33 The **L** replied to Moses, "I will blot out whoever
32:35 And the **L** sent a great plague upon the people
33: 1 The **L** said to Moses, "Now that you have brought
33: 5 For the **L** had told Moses to tell them, "You are an
33: 7 Everyone who wanted to consult with the **L** would
33: 9 and hover at the entrance while the **L** spoke with
33:11 the **L** would speak to Moses face to face,
33:12 Moses said to the **L**, "You have been telling me,
33:14 And the **L** replied, "I will personally go with you,
33:17 And the **L** replied to Moses, "I will indeed do
33:19 The **L** replied, "I will make all my goodness pass
33:19 and I will call out my name, 'the **L**,' to you.
33:21 The **L** continued, "Stand here on this rock beside
34: 1 The **L** told Moses, "Prepare two stone tablets like
34: 4 he climbed Mount Sinai as the **L** had told him,
34: 5 Then the **L** came down in a pillar of cloud
34: 5 of cloud and called out his own name, "the **L**,"
34: 6 He passed in front of Moses and said, "I am the **L**,
I am the **L**, the merciful and gracious God.

34:10 The **L** replied, "All right. This is the covenant I
34:10 people around you will see the power of the **L**—
34:14 You must worship no other gods, but only the **L**,
34:20 from the **L** by presenting a lamb in its place.
34:23 men of Israel must appear before the Sovereign **L**,
34:24 before the **L** your God those three times each year.
34:26 of each year's crop to the house of the **L** your God.
34:27 And the **L** said to Moses, "Write down all these
34:28 Moses was up on the mountain with the **L** forty
34:29 because he had spoken to the **L** face to face.
34:32 and Moses gave them the instructions the **L** had
34:34 went into the Tent of Meeting to speak with the **L**,
34:34 people whatever instructions the **L** had given him,
34:35 veil on again until he returned to speak with the **L**.
35: 1 "You must obey these instructions from the **L**.
35: 2 a day of total rest, a holy day that belongs to the **L**.
35: 4 the people, "This is what the **L** has commanded.
35: 5 is invited to bring these offerings to the **L**:
35:10 Construct everything that the **L** has commanded:
35:21 they brought to the **L** their offerings of materials
35:22 Some brought to the **L** their offerings of gold—
35:22 They presented gold objects of every kind to the **L**.
35:24 and bronze objects as their offering to the **L**.
35:29 and woman who wanted to help in the work the **L**
35:29 through Moses—brought their offerings to the **L**.
35:30 "The **L** has chosen Bezalel son of Uri, grandson of
35:31 The **L** has filled Bezalel with the Spirit of God,
35:34 And the **L** has given both him and Oholiab son of
35:35 The **L** has given them special skills as jewelers,
36: 1 and the other craftsmen whom the **L** has gifted
36: 1 the Tabernacle, just as the **L** has commanded."
36: 2 with all those who were specially gifted by the **L**.
36: 5 now to complete the job the **L** has given us to do!"
38:22 just as the **L** had commanded Moses.
39: 1 just as the **L** had commanded Moses.
39: 5 gold thread, just as the **L** had commanded Moses.
39: 7 These stones served as reminders to the **L**
39: 7 All this was done just as the **L** had commanded
39:21 All this was done just as the **L** had commanded
39:26 was to be worn when Aaron ministered to the **L**, just as the **L** had commanded Moses.
39:29 scarlet yarn, just as the **L** had commanded Moses.
39:30 these words: SET APART AS HOLY TO THE **L**.
39:31 a blue cord, just as the **L** had commanded Moses.
39:32 The Israelites had done everything just as the **L**
39:43 because it had been done as the **L** had commanded
40: 1 The **L** now said to Moses,
40:16 Moses proceeded to do everything as the **L** had
40:19 the roof layers, just as the **L** had commanded him.
40:21 shield it from view, just as the **L** had commanded.
40:23 the Presence on the table that stands before the **L**, just as the **L** had commanded.
40:25 LORD's presence, just as the **L** had commanded.
40:27 from sweet spices, just as the **L** had commanded.
40:29 and a grain offering, just as the **L** had commanded.
40:32 and wash, just as the **L** had commanded Moses.
40:34 and the glorious presence of the **L** filled it.
40:35 was filled with the awesome glory of the **L**.
40:38 The cloud of the **L** rested on the Tabernacle during
Lev 1: 1 The **L** called to Moses from the Tabernacle
1: 2 Whenever you present offerings to the **L**, you must
1: 3 of the Tabernacle so it will be accepted by the **L**.
1: 4 its head so the **L** will accept it as your substitute,
1: 9 burnt offering made by fire, very pleasing to the **L**.
1:13 burnt offering made by fire, very pleasing to the **L**.
1:14 "If you bring a bird as a burnt offering to the **L**,
1:17 burnt offering made by fire, very pleasing to the **L**.
2: 1 "When you bring a grain offering to the **L**,
2: 2 is an offering made by fire, very pleasing to the **L**.
2: 3 holy part of the offerings given to the **L** by fire.
2: 8 has been prepared before being offered to the **L**,
2: 9 made by fire, and it will be very pleasing to the **L**.
2:10 holy part of the offerings given to the **L** by fire.
2:11 in any of the grain offerings you present to the **L**,
2:11 or honey may be burned as an offering to the **L** by
2:12 burned on the altar as an offering pleasing to the **L**.
2:14 "If you present a grain offering to the **L** from the
2:16 and burn it as an offering given to the **L** by fire.
3: 1 The animal you offer to the **L** must have no
3: 3 be presented to the **L** as an offering made by fire.
3: 5 is an offering made by fire, very pleasing to the **L**.
3: 6 "If you present a peace offering to the **L** from the
3: 7 you bring a sheep as your gift, present it to the **L**
3: 9 be presented to the **L** as an offering made by fire.
3:11 the altar as food, an offering given to the **L** by fire.
3:12 "If you bring a goat as your offering to the **L**,
3:14 Part of this offering must be presented to the **L** as
3:16 made by fire; these will be very pleasing to the **L**.
3:16 Remember, all the fat belongs to the **L**.
4: 1 Then the **L** said to Moses,
4: 3 he must bring to the **L** a young bull with no
4: 4 He must present the bull to the **L** at the entrance of
4: 6 and sprinkle it seven times before the **L** in front of
4:13 community does something forbidden by the **L**
4:15 the bull's head and slaughter it there before the **L**.
4:17 and sprinkle it seven times before the **L** in front of
4:22 does something forbidden by the **L** his God,
4:24 and slaughter it before the **L** at the place where
4:27 citizens of Israel do something forbidden by the **L**,
4:31 on the altar, and it will be very pleasing to the **L**.
4:35 altar on top of the offerings given to the **L** by fire.
5: 6 and bring to the **L** as their penalty a female from
5: 7 they must bring to the **L** two young turtledoves
5:12 just like any other offering given to the **L** by fire.
5:14 Then the **L** said to Moses,
5:15 they must bring to the **L** a ram from the flock as
5:17 them sin by doing something forbidden by the **L**,
5:19 they have been guilty of an offense against the **L**."
6: 1 And the **L** said to Moses,
6: 2 "Suppose some of the people sin against the **L** by
6: 6 to the priest, who will present it before the **L**.
6: 7 then make atonement for them before the **L**,
6: 8 Then the **L** said to Moses,
6:14 Aaron's sons must present this offering to the **L** in
6:15 on the altar, and it will be very pleasing to the **L**.
6:18 share of the offerings given to the **L** by fire.
6:19 And the **L** said to Moses,
6:20 they must bring to the **L** a grain offering of two
6:21 grain offering, and it will be very pleasing to the **L**.
6:24 Then the **L** said to Moses,
7: 5 on the altar as an offering to the **L** made by fire.
7:11 of peace offerings that may be presented to the **L**.
7:14 kind of bread must be presented as a gift to the **L**.
7:18 on the third day, it will not be accepted by the **L**.
7:20 to the **L** must be cut off from the community.
7:22 Then the **L** said to Moses,
7:25 the **L** by fire must be cut off from the community.
7:28 Then the **L** said to Moses,
7:29 When you present a peace offering to the **L**,
7:29 bring part of it as a special gift to the **L**.
7:30 own hands as an offering given to the **L** by fire.
7:30 and present it to the **L** by lifting it up before him.
7:35 **L** by fire from the time they were appointed to serve the **L** as priests.
7:36 The **L** commanded that the Israelites were to give
7:38 The **L** gave these instructions to Moses on Mount
7:38 their offerings to the **L** in the wilderness of Sinai.
8: 1 The **L** said to Moses,
8: 5 "The **L** has commanded what I am now going to
8: 9 at its front, just as the **L** had commanded him.
8:13 their turbans, just as the **L** had commanded him.
8:17 the camp, just as the **L** had commanded Moses.
8:18 Then Moses presented the ram to the **L** for the
8:21 It was an offering given to the **L** by fire, very pleasing to the **L**.
8:21 All this was done just as the **L** had commanded
8:27 the portions by lifting them up before the **L**.
8:28 It was an offering given to the **L** by fire, very pleasing to the **L**.
8:29 of ordination, just as the **L** had commanded him.
8:34 by the **L** in order to make atonement for you.
8:35 for seven days, doing everything the **L** requires.
8:35 in this, you will die. This is what the **L** has said."
8:36 and his sons did everything the **L** had commanded
9: 2 no physical defects, and present them to the **L**.
9: 4 Tell them to present all these offerings to the **L**
9: 4 because the **L** will appear to them today."
9: 6 you have followed these instructions from the **L**,
9: 6 the glorious presence of the **L** will appear to you."
9: 7 for the people, just as the **L** has commanded."
9:10 sin offering, just as the **L** had commanded Moses.
9:21 the breasts and right thighs as an offering to the **L**,
9:23 and the glorious presence of the **L** appeared to the
10: 1 they disobeyed the **L** by burning before him a
10: 2 burned them up, and they died there before the **L**.
10: 3 to Aaron, "This is what the **L** meant when he said,
10: 6 and the **L** will be angry with the whole community
10: 6 and Abihu, whom the **L** has destroyed by fire.
10: 7 for the anointing oil of the **L** is upon you."
10: 8 Then the **L** said to Aaron,
10:11 all the laws that the **L** has given through Moses."
10:12 the handful has been presented to the **L** by fire.
10:13 share of the offerings given to the **L** by fire.
10:15 **L** along with the fat of the offerings given by fire.
10:15 just as the **L** has commanded."
10:17 for making atonement for the people before the **L**.
10:19 sin offering and their burnt offering to the **L**,"
10:19 Would the **L** have approved if I had eaten the sin
11: 1 Then the **L** said to Moses and Aaron,
11:44 After all, I, the **L**, am your God. You must be holy
11:45 I, the **L**, am the one who brought you up from the
12: 1 The **L** said to Moses, "Give these instructions to
12: 7 The priest will then present them to the **L**
13: 1 The **L** said to Moses and Aaron,
14: 1 And the **L** said to Moses,
14:11 before the **L** at the entrance of the Tabernacle.
14:12 as a guilt offering by lifting them up before the **L**.
14:16 the oil and sprinkle it seven times before the **L**.
14:18 the priest will make atonement before the **L** for the
14:24 and lift them up before the **L** as an offering to him.
14:27 and sprinkle some of it seven times before the **L**.
14:31 the priest will make atonement before the **L** for the
14:33 Then the **L** said to Moses and Aaron,
15: 1 The **L** said to Moses and Aaron,
15:14 and present himself to the **L** at the entrance of the
15:15 for the man before the **L** for his discharge.
15:30 the priest will make atonement for her before the **L**
16: 1 The **L** spoke to Moses after the death of Aaron's
16: 1 a different kind of fire than the **L** had commanded.
16: 2 The **L** said to Moses, "Warn your brother Aaron
16: 7 and present them to the **L** at the entrance of the
16: 8 to determine which goat will be sacrificed to the **L**
16: 9 The goat chosen to be sacrificed to the **L** will be
16:10 to be the scapegoat will be presented to the **L** alive.
16:12 coals from the altar that stands before the **L**.
16:18 the **L** by smearing some of the blood from the bull
16:34 Moses followed all these instructions that the **L**
17: 1 Then the **L** said to Moses,
17: 2 and all the Israelites these commands from the **L**:
17: 4 the Tabernacle to present it as an offering to the **L**,
17: 5 so he can present them to the **L** as peace offerings.
17: 6 and it will be very pleasing to the **L**.
17: 7 The people must no longer be unfaithful to the **L**
17: 9 the entrance of the Tabernacle to offer it to the **L**,
18: 1 Then the **L** said to Moses,
18: 2 your people, the Israelites: I, the **L**, am your God.
18: 4 careful to keep my laws, for I, the **L**, am your God.
18: 5 you will find life through them. I am the **L**.
18: 6 intercourse with a close relative, for I am the **L**.
18:21 not profane the name of your God. I am the **L**.
18:30 by doing any of them, for I, the **L**, am your God."
19: 1 The **L** also said to Moses,
19: 2 must be holy because I, the **L** your God, am holy.
19: 3 my Sabbath days of rest, for I, the **L**, am your God.
19: 4 of metal for yourselves. I, the **L**, am your God.
19: 5 "When you sacrifice a peace offering to the **L**,
19: 8 for the sin of profaning what is holy to the **L**
19:10 who live among you, for I, the **L**, am your God.
19:12 so profane the name of your God. I am the **L**.
19:14 by not taking advantage of the blind. I am the **L**.
19:16 at the cost of your neighbor's life, for I am the **L**.
19:18 but love your neighbor as yourself. I am the **L**.
19:21 and present it to the **L** at the entrance of the
19:22 then make atonement for him before the **L** with the
19:24 will be devoted to the **L** as an outburst of praise.
19:25 its yield will be increased. I, the **L**, am your God.
19:28 or mark your skin with tattoos, for I am the **L**.
19:30 reverence toward my sanctuary, for I am the **L**.
19:31 you will be defiled by them. I, the **L**, am your God.
19:32 and showing respect for the aged. I am the **L**.
19:34 in the land of Egypt. I, the **L**, am your God.
19:36 I, the **L**, am your God, who brought you out of the
19:37 all of my laws and regulations, for I am the **L**."
20: 1 The **L** said to Moses,
20: 7 apart to be holy, for I, the **L**, am your God.
20: 8 Keep all my laws and obey them, for I am the **L**,
20:24 I, the **L**, am your God, who has set you apart from
20:26 You must be holy because I, the **L**, am holy.
21: 1 The **L** said to Moses, "Tell the priests to avoid
21: 6 the ones who present the offerings to the **L** by fire,
21: 8 must consider them holy because I, the **L**, am holy,
21:12 holy by the anointing oil of his God. I am the **L**.
21:15 his clan, because I, the **L**, have made him holy."
21:16 Then the **L** said to Moses,
21:21 him from presenting offerings to the **L** by fire.
21:23 holy places. I am the **L** who makes them holy."
22: 1 The **L** said to Moses,
22: 2 so they do not profane my holy name. I am the **L**.
22: 3 they must be cut off from my presence. I am the **L**!
22: 8 for this would defile them. I am the **L**.
22: 9 violating them. I am the **L** who makes them holy.
22:15 sacred offerings brought to the **L** by the Israelites
22:16 I am the **L**, who makes them holy."
22:17 And the **L** said to Moses,
22:18 If you offer a whole burnt offering to the **L**,
22:21 "If you bring a peace offering to the **L** from the
22:22 or a scab must never be offered to the **L** by fire on
22:24 or is castrated, it may never be offered to the **L**.
22:26 And the **L** said to Moses,
22:27 it will be acceptable as an offering given to the **L**
22:29 When you bring a thanksgiving offering to the **L**,
22:30 leave any of it until the second day. I am the **L**.
22:31 all my commands by obeying them, for I am the **L**.
22:32 people of Israel. It is I, the **L**, who makes you holy.
22:33 that I might be your very own God. I am the **L**."
23: 1 The **L** said to Moses,
23: 4 to the Sabbath, the **L** has established festivals,
23: 6 This festival to the **L** continues for seven days,
23: 8 the people must present an offering to the **L** by
23: 9 Then the **L** told Moses
23:11 the priest will lift it up before the **L** so it may be
23:12 physical defects as a whole burnt offering to the **L**.
23:13 It will be an offering given to the **L** by fire, and it
23:16 and bring an offering of new grain to the **L**.
23:17 of bread to be lifted up before the **L** as an offering.
23:17 They will be an offering to the **L** from the first of
23:18 one bull, and two rams as burnt offerings to the **L**.
23:18 will be given to the **L** by fire and will be pleasing
23:20 priest will lift up these offerings before the **L**,
23:20 These offerings are holy to the **L** and will belong
23:22 living among you. I, the **L**, am your God."
23:23 The **L** told Moses
23:25 you are to present offerings to the **L** by fire."
23:26 Then the **L** said to Moses,
23:27 and present offerings to the **L** by fire.
23:28 when atonement will be made for you before the **L**
23:33 And the **L** said to Moses,
23:34 This festival to the **L** will last for seven days.
23:36 you must present offerings to the **L** by fire.
23:36 and present another offering to the **L** by fire.
23:37 present all the various offerings to the **L** by fire—
23:38 any freewill offerings that you present to the **L**.
23:39 begin to celebrate this seven-day festival to the **L**.
23:40 Then rejoice before the **L** your God for seven days.
23:41 You must observe this seven-day festival to the **L**
23:43 from the land of Egypt. I, the **L**, am your God."
23:44 the annual festivals of the **L** to the Israelites.
24: 1 The **L** said to Moses,
24: 3 from evening until morning, before the **L**.
24: 7 of the bread as an offering given to the **L** by fire.
24: 8 **L** on behalf of the Israelites as a continual part of
24: 9 portion of the offerings given to the **L** by fire."
24:13 Then the **L** said to Moses,
24:22 who live among you. I, the **L**, am your God."
24:23 him to death, just as the **L** had commanded Moses.
25: 1 Moses was on Mount Sinai, the **L** said to him,
25: 2 the land itself must observe a Sabbath to the **L**
25: 4 the land will enjoy a Sabbath year of rest to the **L**.
25:17 advantage of each other. I, the **L**, am your God.
25:38 I, the **L**, am your God, who brought you out of
25:55 out of the land of Egypt. I, the **L**, am your God.

26: 1 be worshiped in your land. I, the **L**, am your God.
26: 2 and show reverence for my sanctuary. I am the **L**.
26:13 I, the **L**, am your God, who brought you from the
26:44 them by wiping them out. I, the **L**, am their God.
26:45 all the nations watched. I, the **L**, am their God."
26:46 and instructions that the **L** gave to the Israelites
27: 1 The **L** said to Moses,
27: 2 to the **L** by paying the value of that person,
27: 9 one that is acceptable as an offering to the **L**—
27: 9 then your gift to the **L** will be considered holy.
27:11 one that is not acceptable as an offering to the **L**—
27:14 "If you dedicate a house to the **L**, the priest must
27:16 "If you dedicate to the **L** a piece of your ancestral
27:17 If the field is dedicated to the **L** in the Year of
27:21 it will be holy, a field specially set apart for the **L**.
27:22 "If you dedicate to the **L** a field that you have
27:23 value of the land as a sacred donation to the **L**.
27:26 "You may not dedicate to the **L** the firstborn of
27:28 "However, anything specially set apart by the **L**—
27:28 in this way has been set apart for the **L** as holy.
27:29 A person specially set apart by the **L** for
27:30 belongs to the **L** and must be set apart to him as
27:32 The **L** also owns every tenth animal counted off
27:34 These are the commands that the **L** gave to the
Nu 1: 1 the **L** spoke to Moses in the Tabernacle in the
1:19 just as the **L** had commanded Moses. So Moses
1:48 For the **L** had said to Moses,
1:54 So the Israelites did everything just as the **L** had
2: 1 Then the **L** gave these instructions to Moses
2:34 So the people of Israel did everything just as the **L**
2:34 and marched under their banners exactly as the **L**
3: 1 and Moses as it was recorded when the **L** spoke to
3: 4 **L** a different kind of fire than he had commanded.
3: 5 Then the **L** said to Moses,
3:11 And the **L** said to Moses,
3:13 and animals. They are mine; I am the **L**."
3:14 The **L** spoke again to Moses, there in the
3:16 counted them, just as the **L** had commanded.
3:40 Then the **L** said to Moses, "Now count all the
3:41 for the firstborn sons of Israel; I am the **L**.
3:42 the people of Israel, just as the **L** had commanded.
3:44 Now the **L** said to Moses,
3:45 of Israel. The Levites will be mine; I am the **L**.
3:51 to Aaron and his sons as the **L** had commanded.
4: 1 Then the **L** said to Moses and Aaron,
4:17 Then the **L** said to Moses and Aaron,
4:21 And the **L** said to Moses,
4:37 just as the **L** had commanded through Moses.
4:41 counted them, just as the **L** had commanded.
4:45 just as the **L** had commanded through Moses.
4:49 just as the **L** had commanded through Moses.
4:49 just as the **L** had commanded Moses.
5: 1 The **L** gave these instructions to Moses:
5: 4 So the Israelites did just as the **L** had commanded
5: 5 Then the **L** said to Moses,
5: 6 betray the **L** by doing wrong to another person,
5: 8 it belongs to the **L** and must be given to the priest,
5:11 And the **L** said to Moses,
5:16 " 'The priest must then present her before the **L**.
5:18 When he has presented her before the **L**, he must
5:25 lift it up before the **L**, and carry it to the altar.
5:30 the husband must present his wife before the **L**,
6: 1 Then the **L** said to Moses, "Speak to the people of
6: 2 setting themselves apart to the **L** in a special way,
6: 5 their vow, for they are holy and set apart to the **L**.
6: 6 body during the entire period of their vow to the **L**,
6: 8 This applies as long as they are set apart to the **L**.
6:12 They must rededicate themselves to the **L** for the
6:14 and offer these sacrifices to the **L**: a one-year-old
6:16 priest will present these offerings before the **L**:
6:20 then lift the gifts up before the **L** in a gesture of
6:20 and thigh pieces that were lifted up before the **L**.
6:21 If any Nazirites have vowed to give the **L** anything
6:22 Then the **L** said to Moses,
6:24 'May the **L** bless you / and protect you.
6:25 May the **L** smile on you / and be gracious to you.
6:26 May the **L** show you his favor / and give you his
7: 3 They presented these to the **L** in front of the
7: 4 Then the **L** said to Moses,
7:11 The **L** said to Moses, "Let each leader bring his
7:89 went into the Tabernacle to speak with the **L**,
7:89 of the Covenant. The **L** spoke to him from there.
8: 1 The **L** said to Moses,
8: 3 just as the **L** had commanded Moses.
8: 4 It was built according to the exact design the **L** had
8: 5 Then the **L** said to Moses,
8:10 When you bring the Levites before the **L**,
8:11 Aaron must present the Levites to the **L** as a
8:12 heads of the young bulls and present them to the **L**.
8:13 and present them as a special offering to the **L**.
8:21 and Aaron presented them to the **L** as a special
8:22 So they carried out all the commands that the **L**
8:23 The **L** also instructed Moses,
9: 1 The **L** gave these instructions to Moses in early
9: 5 festival there, just as the **L** had commanded Moses.
9: 8 I have received instructions for you from the **L**."
9:14 among you want to celebrate the Passover to the **L**,
9:19 stayed for a long time, just as the **L** commanded.
9:23 and they did whatever the **L** told them through
10: 1 Now the **L** said to Moses,
10: 9 so the **L** your God will remember you and rescue
10:10 The trumpets will remind the **L** your God of his
covenant with you. I am the **L** your God."
10:13 move arrived, the **L** gave the order through Moses.
10:29 for the **L** has given wonderful promises to Israel!"
10:32 you all the good things that the **L** does for us."
10:33 for three days after leaving the mountain of the **L**,
10:34 on each day, the cloud of the **L** hovered over them.
10:35 the Ark set out, Moses would cry, "Arise, O **L**,
10:36 Ark was set down, he would say, "Return, O **L**,
11: 1 The people soon began to complain to the **L** about
11: 1 and when the **L** heard them, his anger blazed
11: 1 Fire from the **L** raged among them and destroyed
11: 2 and when he prayed to the **L**, the fire stopped.
11: 3 because fire from the **L** had burned among them
11:10 tents weeping, and the **L** became extremely angry.
11:11 And Moses said to the **L**, "Why are you treating
11:16 Then the **L** said to Moses, "Summon before me
11:18 'The **L** has heard your whining and complaints:
11:18 Now the **L** will give you meat, and you will have
11:20 For you have rejected the **L**, who is here among
11:23 Then the **L** said to Moses, "Is there any limit to
11:25 And the **L** came down in the cloud and spoke to
11:29 and that the **L** would put his Spirit upon them all!"
11:31 Now the **L** sent a wind that brought quail from the
11:33 the anger of the **L** blazed against the people,
12: 2 "Has the **L** spoken only through Moses?
12: 2 he spoken through us, too?" But the **L** heard them.
12: 4 So immediately the **L** called to Moses, Aaron,
12: 5 Then the **L** descended in the pillar of cloud
12: 6 And the **L** said to them, "Now listen to me!
12: 6 I the **L** communicate by visions and dreams.
12: 8 directly and not in riddles! He sees the **L** as he is.
12: 9 The **L** was furious with them, and he departed.
12:13 So Moses cried out to the **L**, "Heal her, O God,
12:14 And the **L** said to Moses, "If her father had spit in
13: 1 The **L** now said to Moses,
13: 3 So Moses did as the **L** commanded him. He sent
14: 3 "Why is the **L** taking us to this country only to
14: 8 And if the **L** is pleased with us, he will bring us
14: 9 Do not rebel against the **L**, and don't be afraid of
14: 9 They have no protection, but the **L** is with us!
14:10 Then the glorious presence of the **L** appeared to all
14:11 And the **L** said to Moses, "How long will these
14:13 they hear about it?" Moses pleaded with the **L**.
14:14 They know, **L**, that you have appeared in full view
14:16 'The **L** was not able to bring them into the land he
14:18 'The **L** is slow to anger and rich in unfailing love,
14:20 Then the **L** said, "I will pardon them as you have
14:26 Then the **L** said to Moses and Aaron,
14:28 very things I heard you say. I, the **L**, have spoken!
14:35 I, the **L**, have spoken! I will do these things to
14:36 **L** by spreading discouraging reports about the
14:37 were struck dead with a plague before the **L**.
14:40 but now we are ready to enter the land the **L** has
14:42 by your enemies because the **L** is not with you.
14:43 The **L** will abandon you because you have
abandoned the **L**."
15: 1 The **L** told Moses to give these instructions to the
15: 3 and you want to please the **L** with a burnt offering
15: 4 whoever brings it must also give to the **L** a grain
15: 7 This sacrifice will be very pleasing to the **L**.
15: 8 of a special vow or as a peace offering to the **L**,
15:10 be an offering made by fire, very pleasing to the **L**.
15:13 present an offering by fire that is pleasing to the **L**,
15:14 pleasing to the **L**, they must follow the same
15:15 and foreigners are the same before the **L**
15:17 The **L** also said to Moses at this time,
15:19 But you must set some aside as a gift to the **L**.
15:21 you are to present this offering to the **L** each year
15:22 that the **L** has given you through Moses.
15:23 everything the **L** has commanded through Moses.
15:24 It will be pleasing to the **L**, and it must be offered
15:25 it with their offering given to the **L** by fire
15:28 make atonement for the guilty person before the **L**,
15:30 native Israelites or foreigners, blaspheme the **L**,
15:35 Then the **L** said to Moses, "The man must be put
15:36 him to death, just as the **L** had commanded Moses.
15:37 And the **L** said to Moses,
15:39 tassels will remind you of the commands of the **L**,
15:41 I am the **L** your God who brought you out of the
15:41 I might be your God. I am the **L** your God!' "
16: 3 Everyone in Israel has been set apart by the **L**,
16: 3 anyone else among all these people of the **L**?"
16: 5 "Tomorrow morning the **L** will show us who
16: 5 The **L** will allow those who are chosen to enter his
16: 7 and burn incense in them tomorrow before the **L**.
16: 7 Then we will see whom the **L** chooses as his holy
16:11 The one you are really revolting against is the **L**!
16:15 Then Moses became very angry and said to the **L**,
16:16 and present yourself before the **L** with all your
16:17 on it, so you can present them before the **L**.
16:19 Then the glorious presence of the **L** appeared to
16:20 and the **L** said to Moses and Aaron,
16:23 And the **L** said to Moses,
16:28 "By this you will know that the **L** has sent me to
16:29 die a natural death, then the **L** has not sent me.
16:30 But if the **L** performs a miracle and the ground
16:30 will know that these men have despised the **L**."
16:35 Then fire blazed forth from the **L** and burned up
16:36 And the **L** said to Moses,
16:42 and the glorious presence of the **L** appeared.
16:44 and the **L** said to Moses,
17: 1 Then the **L** said to Moses,
17:10 And the **L** said to Moses: "Place Aaron's staff
17:11 So Moses did as the **L** commanded him.
17:13 even comes close to the Tabernacle of the **L** dies.
18: 1 The **L** now said to Aaron: "You, your sons,
18: 6 They are dedicated to the **L** for service in the
18: 8 The **L** gave these further instructions to Aaron:
18:12 gifts brought by the people as offerings to the **L**—
18:13 land that the people present to the **L** belong to you.
18:14 "Whatever is specially set apart for the **L** also
18:15 or animal, that is offered to the **L** will be yours.
18:17 They are holy and have been set apart for the **L**.
18:17 as an offering given by fire, very pleasing to the **L**.
18:19 offerings that the people of Israel bring to the **L**.
18:19 This is an unbreakable covenant between the **L**
18:20 And the **L** said to Aaron, "You priests will receive
18:24 which have been set apart as offerings to the **L**.
18:25 The **L** also told Moses,
18:26 you receive—a tithe of the tithe—to the **L** as a gift.
18:27 The **L** will consider this to be your harvest
18:28 tithe received from the Israelites as a gift to the **L**.
18:29 of the gifts given to you as your gifts to the **L**.'
19: 1 The **L** said to Moses and Aaron,
19: 2 "Here is another ritual law required by the **L**:
19:20 for they have defiled the sanctuary of the **L**.
20: 6 Then the glorious presence of the **L** appeared to
20: 7 and the **L** said to Moses,
20: 9 staff from the place where it was kept before the **L**.
20:12 But the **L** said to Moses and Aaron, "Because you
20:13 was where the people of Israel argued with the **L**,
20:16 But when we cried out to the **L**, he heard us
20:23 Then the **L** said to Moses and Aaron at Mount Hor
20:27 So Moses did as the **L** commanded. The three of
21: 2 Then the people of Israel made this vow to the **L**:
21: 3 The **L** heard their request and gave them victory
21: 6 So the **L** sent poisonous snakes among them,
21: 7 "We have sinned by speaking against the **L**
21: 7 Pray that the **L** will take away the snakes."
21: 8 Then the **L** told him, "Make a replica of a
21:14 For this reason *The Book of the Wars of the L*
21:16 which is the well where the **L** said to Moses,
21:34 The **L** said to Moses, "Do not be afraid of him,
22: 8 "In the morning I will tell you whatever the **L**
22:13 on home! The **L** will not let me go with you."
22:18 to do anything against the will of the **L** my God.
22:19 But stay here one more night to see if the **L** has
22:22 so he sent the angel of the **L** to stand in the road to
22:23 Balaam's donkey suddenly saw the angel of the **L**
22:24 Then the angel of the **L** stood at a place where the
22:25 When the donkey saw the angel of the **L** standing
22:26 Then the angel of the **L** moved farther down the
22:28 Then the **L** caused the donkey to speak.
22:31 Then the **L** opened Balaam's eyes, and he saw the
angel of the **L** standing in the
22:32 the angel of the **L** demanded. "I have come to
22:34 Then Balaam confessed to the angel of the **L**,
22:35 But the angel of the **L** told him, "Go with these
23: 3 and I will go to see if the **L** will respond to me.
23: 5 Then the **L** gave Balaam a message for King Balak
23: 8 those whom the **L** has not condemned?
23:12 "Can I say anything except what the **L** tells me?"
23:15 by your burnt offering while I go to meet the **L**."
23:16 So the **L** met Balaam and gave him a message.
23:17 "What did the **L** say?" Balak asked eagerly.
23:21 store for Israel. / For the **L** their God is with them;
23:26 "Didn't I tell you that I must do whatever the **L**
24: 1 By now Balaam realized that the **L** intended to
24: 6 They are like aloes planted by the **L**, / like cedars
24:11 but the **L** has kept you from your reward."
24:13 powerless to do anything against the will of the **L**.'
24:13 I told you that I could say only what the **L** says!
25: 4 The **L** issued the following command to Moses:
25: 4 and execute them before the **L** in broad daylight,
25:10 Then the **L** said to Moses,
25:16 Then the **L** said to Moses,
26: 1 the **L** said to Moses and to Eleazar son of Aaron,
26: 4 and older, just as the **L** commanded Moses."
26: 9 Korah against Moses and Aaron, defying the **L**.
26:10 were destroyed that day by fire from the **L**.
26:52 Then the **L** said to Moses,
26:61 and Abihu died when they burned before the **L** a
26:65 For the **L** had said of them, "They will all die in
27: 3 Korah's followers, who rebelled against the **L**.
27: 5 So Moses brought their case before the **L**.
27: 6 And the **L** replied to Moses,
27:11 just as the **L** commanded Moses.' "
27:12 One day the **L** said to Moses, "Climb to the top of
27:15 Then Moses said to the **L**,
27:16 "O **L**, the God of the spirits of all living things,
27:17 so the people of the **L** will not be like sheep
27:18 The **L** replied, "Take Joshua son of Nun, who has
27:21 When direction from the **L** is needed, Joshua will
27:22 So Moses did as the **L** commanded and presented
27:23 just as the **L** had commanded through Moses.
28: 1 The **L** said to Moses, "Give these instructions to
28: 3 present your daily whole burnt offerings to the **L**,
28: 6 an offering made by fire, very pleasing to the **L**.
28: 7 out in the Holy Place as an offering to the **L**.
28: 8 is an offering made by fire, very pleasing to the **L**.
28:11 present an extra burnt offering to the **L** of two
28:13 by fire, and it will be very pleasing to the **L**.
28:15 offer one male goat for a sin offering to the **L**.
28:19 You must present as a burnt offering to the **L** two
28:24 to be presented by fire, very pleasing to the **L**.
28:26 you present the first of your new grain to the **L**,
28:27 will be offered that day, very pleasing to the **L**.
29: 2 present a burnt offering, very pleasing to the **L**.
29: 6 These offerings are given to the **L** by fire and are
29: 8 present a burnt offering, very pleasing to the **L**.
29:12 Festival of Shelters, a seven-day festival to the **L**.
29:13 burnt offering by fire, very pleasing to the **L**.
29:36 present a burnt offering, very pleasing to the **L**.
29:39 "You must present these offerings to the **L** at your
29:40 people of Israel, just as the **L** had commanded him.
30: 1 told them, "This is what the **L** has commanded:
30: 2 A man who makes a vow to the **L** or makes a
30: 3 "If a young woman makes a vow to the **L** or a
30: 5 The **L** will forgive her because her father would

30:8 her commitments, and the L will forgive her.
30:12 pledge will be nullified, and the L will forgive her.
30:16 These are the regulations the L gave Moses
31:1 Then the L said to Moses,
31:7 They attacked Midian just as the L had
31:16 of Israel to rebel against the L at Mount Peor.
31:21 "The L has given Moses this requirement of the
31:25 And the L said to Moses,
31:28 But first give the L his share of the captives,
31:29 half to Eleazar the priest as an offering to the L.
31:31 and Eleazar the priest did as the L commanded
31:41 Eleazar the priest, just as the L had directed him.
31:47 All this was done just as the L had commanded
31:50 offering to the L from our share of the plunder—
31:50 will make atonement for our lives before the L."
31:52 as a gift to the L weighed about 420 pounds.
31:54 to the L that the people of Israel belong to him.
32:4 the L has conquered this whole area for the people
32:7 going across to the land the L has given them?
32:9 from entering the land the L was giving them.
32:10 Then the L was furious with them, and he vowed,
32:12 for they have wholeheartedly followed the L.'
32:13 "The L was furious with Israel and made them
32:14 You are making the L even angrier with Israel.
32:21 and if your troops cross the Jordan until the L has
32:22 when the land is finally subdued before the L.
32:22 You will have discharged your duty to the L
32:22 of the Jordan will be your inheritance from the L.
32:23 then you will have sinned against the L,
32:27 able to bear arms will cross over to fight for the L,
32:31 "Sir, we will do as the L has commanded!
32:32 Jordan into Canaan fully armed to fight for the L,
33:4 whom the L had killed the night before.
33:4 The L had defeated the gods of Egypt that night
33:38 Aaron the priest was directed by the L to go up the
33:50 of Moab opposite Jericho, the L said to Moses,
34:1 Then the L said to Moses,
34:13 The L commands that the land be divided up
34:16 And the L said to Moses,
34:29 These are the men the L has appointed to oversee
35:1 of Moab, across from Jericho, the L said to Moses,
35:9 And the L said to Moses,
35:34 I am the L, who lives among the people of
36:2 the L instructed you to divide the land by sacred
36:2 You were told by the L to give the inheritance of
36:5 gave the Israelites this command from the L:
36:6 This is what the L commands concerning the
36:10 The daughters of Zelophehad did as the L
36:13 and regulations that the L gave to the people of
Dt 1:3 telling them everything the L had commanded him
1:6 we were at Mount Sinai, the L our God said to us,
1:8 for it is the land the L swore to give to your
1:10 The L your God has made you as numerous as the
1:11 And may the L, the God of your ancestors,
1:19 'Then, just as the L our God directed us, we left
1:20 'You have now reached the land that the L our
1:21 Go and occupy it as the L, the God of your
1:25 And they reported that the land the L our God had
1:26 "But you rebelled against the command of the L
1:27 in your tents and said, 'The L must hate us,
1:30 The L your God is going before you. He will fight
1:31 And you saw how the L your God cared for you
1:32 all he did, you refused to trust the L your God,
1:34 "When the L heard your complaining, he became
1:36 because he has followed the L completely.
1:37 "And the L was also angry with me because of
1:41 you confessed, 'We have sinned against the L!
1:41 and fight for it, as the L our God has told us.'
1:42 "But the L said to me, 'Tell them not to attack,
1:45 Then you returned and wept before the L, but he
2:1 just as the L had instructed me, and we wandered
2:2 Then at last the L said to me,
2:7 The L your God has blessed everything you have
2:7 the L your God has been with you and provided
2:9 the L warned us, 'Do not bother the Moabites,
2:12 from the land that the L had assigned to Israel.)
2:13 "Then the L told us to cross Zered Brook, and we
2:14 For the L had vowed that this could not happen
2:15 The L had lifted his hand against them until all of
2:17 the L said to me,
2:21 But the L destroyed them so the Ammonites could
2:24 Moses continued, "Then the L said, 'Now cross
2:29 Jordan into the land the L our God has given us.'
2:30 because the L your God made Sihon stubborn
2:31 "Then the L said to me, 'Look, I have begun to
2:33 But the L our God handed him over to us, and we
2:36 "The L our God helped us conquer Aroer on the
2:37 all the places the L our God had commanded us to
3:2 But the L told me, 'Do not be afraid of him,
3:3 So the L our God handed King Og and all his
3:18 'Although the L your God has given you this land
3:20 When the L has given security to the rest of the
3:20 and when they occupy the land the L your God is
3:21 'You have seen all that the L your God has done to
3:22 for the L your God will fight for you.'
3:23 "At that time I pleaded with the L and said,
3:24 'O Sovereign L, I am your servant. You have only
3:26 "But the L was angry with me because of you,
4:1 so you may enter and occupy the land the L,
4:2 commands I am giving you from the L your God.
4:3 You saw what the L did to you at Baal-peor,
4:3 where the L your God destroyed everyone who
4:4 But all of you who were faithful to the L your God
4:5 The L my God gave them to me and commanded
4:7 L our God is near to us whenever we call on him?
4:9 to forget what you have seen the L do for you.
4:10 you stood before the L your God at Mount Sinai,
4:12 And the L spoke to you from the fire. You heard
4:14 It was at that time that the L commanded me to
4:19 The L your God designated these heavenly bodies
4:20 Remember that the L rescued you from the
4:21 "But the L was very angry with me because of
4:21 L your God is giving you as your special
4:23 So be careful not to break the covenant the L your
4:23 for the L your God has absolutely forbidden this.
4:24 The L your God is a devouring fire, a jealous God.
4:25 This is evil in the sight of the L your God and will
4:27 For the L will scatter you among the nations,
4:29 From there you will search again for the L your
4:30 you will finally return to the L your God and listen
4:31 For the L your God is merciful—he will not
4:34 Yet that is what the L your God did for you in
4:35 these things so you would realize that the L is God
4:39 The L is God both in heaven and on earth,
4:40 Then you will enjoy a long life in the land the L
5:2 the L our God made a covenant with us.
5:3 The L did not make this covenant long ago with
5:4 The L spoke to you face to face from the heart of
5:5 I stood as an intermediary between you and the L,
5:6 " 'I am the L your God, who rescued you from
5:9 or bow down to them, for I, the L your God,
5:11 " 'Do not misuse the name of the L your God.
5:11 The L will not let you go unpunished if you misuse
5:12 it holy, as the L your God has commanded you.
5:14 day is a day of rest dedicated to the L your God.
5:15 and that the L your God brought you out with
5:15 That is why the L your God has commanded you
5:16 and mother, as the L your God commanded you.
5:16 full life in the land the L your God will give you.
5:22 "The L spoke these words with a loud voice to all
5:24 'The L our God has shown us his glory
5:25 If the L our God speaks to us again, we will
5:27 You go and listen to what the L our God says.
5:28 "The L heard your request and said to me, 'I have
5:32 "You must obey all the commands of the L your
5:33 Stay on the path that the L your God has
6:1 and regulations that the L your God told me to
6:2 and grandchildren might fear the L your God as
6:3 land flowing with milk and honey, just as the L,
6:4 O Israel! The L is our God, the L alone.
6:5 And you must love the L your God with all your
6:10 "The L your God will soon bring you into the land
6:12 be careful not to forget the L, who rescued you
6:13 You must fear the L your God and serve him.
6:15 for the L your God, who lives among you, is a
6:16 Do not test the L your God as you did when you
6:17 You must diligently obey the commands of the L
6:18 and occupy the good land that the L solemnly
6:19 living in your land, just as the L said you would.
6:20 and regulations that the L our God has given us?'
6:21 but the L brought us out of Egypt with amazing
6:22 Before our eyes the L did miraculous signs
6:24 And the L our God commanded us to obey all
6:25 all the commands the L our God has given us.'
7:1 "When the L your God brings you into the land
7:2 When the L your God hands these nations over to
7:4 Then the anger of the L will burn against you,
7:6 are a holy people, who belong to the L your God.
7:6 the L your God has chosen you to be his own
7:7 "The L did not choose you and lavish his love on
7:8 It was simply because the L loves you, and
7:8 That is why the L rescued you with such amazing
7:9 therefore, that the L your God is indeed God.
7:12 the L your God will keep his covenant of unfailing
7:15 And the L will protect you from all sickness.
7:16 "You must destroy all the nations the L your God
7:18 Just remember what the L your God did to Pharaoh
7:19 Remember the great terrors the L your God sent
7:19 The L your God will use this same power against
7:20 then the L your God will send hornets to drive out
7:21 for the L your God is among you, and he is a great
7:22 The L your God will drive those nations out ahead
7:23 But the L your God will hand them over to you.
7:25 snare to you, for it is detestable to the L your God.
8:1 and occupy the land the L swore to give your
8:2 Remember how the L your God led you through
8:3 real life comes by feeding on every word of the L.
8:5 the L your God disciplines you to help you.
8:6 "So obey the commands of the L your God by
8:7 For the L your God is bringing you into a good
8:10 praise the L your God for the good land he has
8:11 Beware that in your plenty you do not forget the L
8:14 proud at that time and forget the L your God,
8:18 Always remember that it is the L your God who
8:19 If you ever forget the L your God and follow other
8:20 Just as the L has destroyed other nations in your
8:20 you also will be destroyed for not obeying the L
9:3 But the L your God will cross over ahead of you
9:3 and drive them out, just as the L has promised.
9:4 "After the L your God has done this for you,
9:4 'The L has given us this land because we are
9:5 The L your God will drive these nations out ahead
9:6 The L your God is not giving you this good land
9:7 "Remember how angry you made the L your God
9:8 Remember how angry you made the L at Mount
9:9 with the covenant that the L had made with you.
9:10 The L gave me the covenant, the tablets on which
9:11 the L handed me the two stone tablets with the
9:12 Then the L said to me, 'Go down immediately
9:13 "The L said to me, 'I have been watching this
9:16 made in your terrible sin against the L your God.
9:16 How quickly you had turned from the path the L
9:18 forty days and nights I lay prostrate before the L,
9:18 because you had sinned by doing what the L hated,
9:19 feared for you, for the L was ready to destroy you.
9:20 The L was so angry with Aaron that he wanted to
9:20 But I prayed for Aaron, and the L spared him.
9:22 "You also made the L angry at Taberah, Massah,
9:23 And at Kadesh-barnea the L sent you out with this
9:23 But you rebelled against the command of the L
9:24 you have been rebelling against the L as long as I
9:25 why I fell down and lay before the L for forty days
9:26 I prayed to the L and said, 'O Sovereign L,
9:28 "The L destroyed them because he wasn't able to
10:1 "At that time the L said to me, 'Prepare two stone
10:4 The L again wrote the terms of the covenant—
10:4 They were the same words the L had spoken to
10:5 which I had made, just as the L commanded me.
10:8 At that time the L set apart the tribe of Levi to
10:8 to minister before the L, and to pronounce
10:9 The L himself is their inheritance, as the L your God told them.
10:10 And once again the L yielded to my pleas
10:11 But the L said to me, 'Get up and lead the people
10:12 Israel, what does the L your God require of you?
10:14 and everything in it all belong to the L your God.
10:15 Yet the L chose your ancestors as the objects of his
10:17 "The L your God is the God of gods and Lord of
10:20 You must fear the L your God and worship him
10:22 But now the L your God has made you as
11:1 "You must love the L your God and obey all his
11:2 who have never experienced the discipline of the L
11:4 They didn't see what the L did to the armies of
11:5 They didn't see how the L cared for you in the
11:9 you will enjoy a long life in the land the L swore
11:12 a land that the L your God cares for. He watches
11:13 and if you love the L your God with all your heart
11:16 "But do not let your heart turn away from the L to
11:17 Then you will quickly die in that good land the L
11:21 and your children may flourish in the land the L
11:22 show love to the L your God by walking in his
11:23 Then the L will drive out all the nations in your
11:25 for the L your God will send fear and dread ahead
11:27 of the L your God that I am giving you today.
11:28 if you reject the commands of the L your God
11:29 "When the L your God brings you into the land to
11:31 to occupy the land the L your God is giving you.
12:1 must obey as long as you live in the land the L,
12:4 "Do not worship the L your God in the way these
12:5 you must seek the L your God at the place he
12:6 There you will bring to the L your burnt offerings,
12:7 will feast in the presence of the L your God,
12:7 because the L your God has blessed you.
12:9 when you arrive in the place of rest the L your God
12:10 and live in the land the L your God is giving you
12:11 to the place the L your God will choose for his
12:12 and all your servants in the presence of the L your
12:14 so only at the place the L will choose within one of
12:15 You may eat as many animals as the L your God
12:18 You must eat these in the presence of the L your
12:18 celebrating in the presence of the L your God in all
12:20 "When the L your God enlarges your territory as
12:21 It might happen that the place the L your God
12:21 any of the cattle or sheep the L has given you,
12:25 because you will be doing what pleases the L.
12:26 to fulfill a vow to the place the L chooses to dwell.
12:27 your burnt offerings on the altar of the L your God.
12:27 be poured out beside the altar of the L your God,
12:28 because you will be doing what pleases the L your
12:29 "When the L your God destroys the nations
12:31 You must not do this to the L your God.
12:31 committed many detestable acts that the L hates,
13:3 The L your God is testing you to see if you love
13:4 Serve only the L your God and fear him alone.
13:5 for they encourage rebellion against the L your
13:5 Since they try to keep you from following the L
13:10 have tried to draw you away from the L your God,
13:12 "Suppose you hear in one of the towns the L your
13:16 to the torch as a burnt offering to the L your God.
13:17 Then the L will turn from his fierce anger and be
13:18 "The L your God will be merciful only if you
14:1 "Since you are the people of the L your God,
14:2 You have been set apart as holy to the L your God,
14:21 for you are set apart as holy to the L your God.
14:23 Bring this tithe to the place the L your God
14:23 is to teach you always to fear the L your God.
14:24 Now the place the L your God chooses for his
14:25 and take the money to the place the L your God
14:26 Then feast there in the presence of the L your God
14:29 Then the L your God will bless you in all your
15:4 for the L your God will greatly bless you in the
15:5 of the L your God that I am giving you today.
15:6 The L your God will bless you as he has promised.
15:7 arrive in the land the L your God is giving you,
15:9 the loan and the needy person cries out to the L,
15:10 and the L your God will bless you in everything
15:14 with which the L your God has blessed you.
15:15 land of Egypt and the L your God redeemed you!
15:18 and the L your God will bless you in all you do.
15:19 "You must set aside for the L your God all the
15:20 the L your God each year at the place he chooses.
15:21 with it, you must not sacrifice it to the L your God.
16:1 "In honor of the L your God, always celebrate the
16:1 for that was when the L your God brought you out
16:2 and it must be sacrificed to the L your God at the
16:5 in the towns that the L your God is giving you.
16:6 It must be offered at the place the L your God will
16:7 and eat it in the place the L your God chooses.
16:8 the people must assemble before the L your God,
16:10 the Festival of Harvest to honor the L your God.
16:11 It is a time to celebrate before the L your God at

16:15 to honor the L your God at the place he chooses,
16:15 for it is the L your God who gives you bountiful
16:16 They must appear before the L your God at the
16:16 and they must bring a gift to the L.
16:17 according to the blessings given to them by the L
16:18 in all the towns the L your God is giving you.
16:20 and occupy the land that the L your God is giving
16:21 an Asherah pole beside the altar of the L your God.
16:22 pillars for worship, for the L your God hates them.
17: 1 a sick or defective ox or sheep to the L your God,
17: 2 in one of your towns that the L your God is giving
17: 2 has done evil in the sight of the L your God
17: 8 Take such cases to the place the L your God will
17:10 The decision they make at the place the L chooses
17:12 or of the priest who represents the L your God
17:14 "You will soon arrive in the land the L your God
17:15 be sure that you select as king the man the L your
17:16 for the L has told you, 'You must never return to
17:17 because they will lead him away from the L.
17:19 That way he will learn to fear the L his God by
18: 1 will eat from the offerings given to the L by fire,
18: 2 The L himself is their inheritance, just as he
18: 5 For the L your God chose the tribe of Levi out of
18: 6 wherever he is living, to the place the L chooses.
18: 7 He may minister there in the name of the L his
18: 7 just like his fellow Levites who are serving the L
18: 9 "When you arrive in the land the L your God is
18:12 things is an object of horror and disgust to the L.
18:12 the L your God will drive them out ahead of you.
18:13 You must be blameless before the L your God.
18:14 but the L your God forbids you to do such things.
18:15 "The L your God will raise up for you a prophet
18:16 For this is what you yourselves requested of the L
18:16 again have to listen to the voice of the L your God
18:17 "Then the L said to me, 'Fine, I will do as they
18:21 will we know whether the prophecy is from the L
18:22 it does not happen, the L did not give the message.
19: 1 "The L your God will soon destroy the nations
19: 2 in the land the L your God is giving you to occupy.
19: 3 Divide the land the L your God is giving you into
19: 8 "If the L your God enlarges your territory, as he
19: 9 if you always love the L your God and walk in his
19:10 L your God is giving you as a special possession,
19:14 "When you arrive in the land the L your God is
19:17 and judges who are on duty before the L.
20: 1 The L your God, who brought you safely out of
20: 4 For the L your God is going with you! He will
20:13 When the L your God hands it over to you,
20:14 your enemies that the L your God has given you.
20:16 "As for the towns of the nations the L your God is
20:17 just as the L your God has commanded you.
20:18 which would cause you to sin deeply against the L
21: 1 in a field in the land the L your God is giving you,
21: 5 for the L your God has chosen them to minister
21: 8 O L, forgive your people Israel whom you have
21:10 and the L your God hands them over to you
21:23 Do not defile the land the L your God is giving
22: 5 The L your God detests people who do this.
23: 1 he may not be included in the assembly of the L.
23: 2 may not be included in the assembly of the L.
23: 3 may be included in the assembly of the L.
23: 5 (But the L your God would not listen to Balaam.
23: 5 into a blessing because the L your God loves you.)
23: 8 you from Egypt may enter the assembly of the L.
23:14 for the L your God moves around in your camp to
23:18 Do not bring to the house of the L your God any
23:18 for both are detestable to the L your God.
23:20 so the L your God may bless you in everything
23:21 "When you make a vow to the L your God,
23:21 For the L your God demands that you promptly
23:23 for you have made a vow to the L your God.
24: 4 been defiled. That would be detestable to the L.
24: 4 You must not bring guilt upon the land the L your
24: 9 Remember what the L your God did to Miriam as
24:13 And the L your God will count it as a righteous
24:15 Otherwise they might cry out to the L against you,
24:18 in Egypt and that the L your God redeemed you.
24:19 Then the L your God will bless you in all you do.
25:15 so that you will enjoy a long life in the land the L
25:16 and measures are detestable to the L your God.
25:19 when the L your God has given you rest from all
26: 1 "When you arrive in the land the L your God is
26: 2 and bring it to the place the L your God chooses
26: 3 'With this gift I acknowledge that the L your God
26: 4 and set it before the altar of the L your God.
26: 5 then say in the presence of the L your God,
26: 7 we cried out to the L, the God of our ancestors.
26: 8 So the L brought us out of Egypt with amazing
26:10 And now, O L, I have brought you a token of the
26:10 Then place the produce before the L your God
26:11 because of all the good things the L your God has
26:13 Then you must declare in the presence of the L
26:14 I have obeyed the L my God and have done
26:16 "Today the L your God has commanded you to
26:17 You have declared today that the L is your God.
26:18 The L has declared today that you are his people,
26:19 You will be a nation that is holy to the L your God,
27: 2 and enter the land the L your God is giving you,
27: 3 you will soon cross the river to enter the land the L
27: 3 a land flowing with milk and honey, just as the L,
27: 5 Then build an altar there to the L your God,
27: 6 On the altar you must offer burnt offerings to the L
27: 7 and feast there with great joy before the L your
27: 9 Today you have become the people of the L your
27:10 So obey the L your God by keeping all these
27:15 the work of craftsmen, are detestable to the L.'
28: 1 "If you fully obey the L your God by keeping all
28: 1 the L your God will exalt you above all the nations
28: 2 all these blessings if you obey the L your God:
28: 7 "The L will conquer your enemies when they
28: 8 "The L will bless everything you do and will fill
28: 8 The L your God will bless you in the land he is
28: 9 "If you obey the commands of the L your God
28: 9 the L will establish you as his holy people as he
28:10 will see that you are a people claimed by the L,
28:11 "The L will give you an abundance of good things
28:12 The L will send rain at the proper time from his
28:13 If you listen to these commands of the L your God
28:13 the L will make you the head and not the tail,
28:15 "But if you refuse to listen to the L your God
28:20 "The L himself will send against you curses,
28:21 The L will send diseases among you until none of
28:22 The L will strike you with wasting disease, fever,
28:24 The L will turn your rain into sand and dust,
28:25 "The L will cause you to be defeated by your
28:27 "The L will afflict you with the boils of Egypt
28:28 The L will strike you with madness, blindness,
28:35 The L will cover you from head to foot with
28:36 "The L will exile you and the king you crowned to
28:37 among all the nations to which the L sends you.
28:45 "If you refuse to listen to the L your God and to
28:47 Because you have not served the L your God with
28:48 you will serve your enemies whom the L will send
28:49 "The L will bring a distant nation against you
28:52 They will attack all the towns in the land the L
28:53 whom the L your God has given you.
28:58 and awesome name of the L your God,
28:59 then the L will overwhelm both you and your
28:61 The L will bring against you every sickness
28:62 because you would not listen to the L your God.
28:63 "Just as the L has found great pleasure in helping
28:63 the L will find pleasure in destroying you,
28:64 For the L will scatter you among all the nations
28:65 And the L will cause your heart to tremble,
28:68 Then the L will send you back to Egypt in ships,
29: 1 These are the terms of the covenant the L
29: 2 own eyes everything the L did in Egypt to Pharaoh
29: 4 But to this day the L has not given you minds that
29: 6 so you would know that he is the L your God.
29:10 are standing today before the L your God.
29:12 today to enter into a covenant with the L your God.
29:12 The L is making this covenant with you today,
29:14 But you are not the only ones with whom the L is
29:15 The L your God is making this covenant with you
29:18 The L made this covenant with you so that no man,
29:18 or tribe among you would turn away from the L
29:20 The L will not pardon such people. His anger
29:20 and the L will erase their names from under
29:21 The L will separate them from all the tribes of
29:22 the land and the diseases the L will send against it.
29:23 and Zeboiim, which the L destroyed in his anger.
29:24 will ask, 'Why has the L done this to his land?
29:25 the land broke the covenant they made with the L,
29:26 gods that the L had not designated for them.
29:28 and fury the L uprooted his people from their land
29:29 "There are secret things that belong to the L our
30: 1 nations to which the L your God has exiled you.
30: 2 If at that time you return to the L your God,
30: 3 then the L your God will restore your fortunes.
30: 4 the L your God will go and find you and bring you
30: 6 "The L your God will cleanse your heart
30: 7 The L your God will inflict all these curses on
30: 8 Then you will again obey the L and keep all the
30: 9 The L your God will make you successful in
30: 9 for the L will delight in being good to you as he
30:10 The L your God will delight in you if you obey his
30:10 and if you turn to the L your God with all your
30:16 I have commanded you today to love the L your
30:16 and the L your God will bless you and the land you
30:20 Choose to love the L your God and to obey him
30:20 Then you will live long in the land the L swore to
31: 2 The L has told me that I will not cross the Jordan
31: 3 But the L your God himself will cross over ahead
31: 3 and he will go with you, just as the L promised.
31: 4 The L will destroy the nations living in the land,
31: 5 The L will hand over to you the people who live
31: 6 of them! The L your God will go ahead of you.
31: 7 the land that the L swore to give their ancestors.
31: 8 for the L is the one who goes before you.
31:11 before the L your God at the place he chooses.
31:12 so they may listen and learn to fear the L your God
31:13 hear them and will learn to fear the L your God.
31:14 Then the L said to Moses, "The time has come for
31:15 And the L appeared to them in a pillar of cloud at
31:16 The L said to Moses, "You are about to die
31:23 Then the L commissioned Joshua son of Nun with
31:26 beside the Ark of the Covenant of the L your God,
31:27 am still with you, you have rebelled against the L.
31:29 for you will make the L very angry by doing what
32: 3 I will proclaim the name of the L; / how glorious is
32: 6 Is this the way you repay the L, / you foolish
32: 9 For the people of Israel belong to the L; / Jacob is
32:12 The L alone guided them; / they lived without any
32:19 "The L saw this and was filled with loathing.
32:27 has triumphed! / It was not the L who did this!" '
32:30 had sold them, / unless the L had given them up?
32:36 "Indeed, the L will judge his people, / and he will
32:48 That same day the L said to Moses,
33: 2 "The L came from Mount Sinai / and dawned
33: 5 The L became king in Israel— / when the leaders
33: 7 "O L, hear the cry of Judah / and bring them again
33: 8 "O L, you have given the sacred lots / to your
33:11 Bless the Levites, O L, / and accept all their work.
33:12 "The people of Benjamin are loved by the L
33:13 of Joseph: / "May their land be blessed by the L
33:29 Who else is like you, a people saved by the L?
34: 1 And the L showed him the whole land,
34: 4 Then the L said to Moses, "This is the land I
34: 5 So Moses, the servant of the L, died there in the
land of Moab, just as the L had said.
34: 9 and did everything just as the L had commanded
34:10 prophet like Moses, whom the L knew face to face.
34:11 The L sent Moses to perform all the miraculous
34:12 And it was through Moses that the L demonstrated
Jos 1: 1 the L spoke to Joshua son of Nun,
1: 9 For the L your God is with you wherever you go."
1:11 and take possession of the land the L your God has
1:13 what Moses, the servant of the L, commanded you:
1:13 'The L your God is giving you rest and has given
1:15 until the L gives rest to them as he has given rest
1:15 possess the land the L your God is giving them.
1:15 land that Moses, the servant of the L, gave you."
1:17 And may the L your God be with you as he was
2: 9 "I know the L has given you this land," she told
2:10 For we have heard how the L made a dry path for
2:11 For the L your God is the supreme God of the
2:12 Now swear to me by the L that you will be kind to
2:14 we will keep our promise when the L gives us the
2:24 "The L will certainly give us the whole land,"
3: 3 the Ark of the Covenant of the L your God,
3: 5 for tomorrow the L will do great wonders among
3: 7 The L told Joshua, "Today I will begin to make
3: 9 "Come and listen to what the L your God says.
3:13 The priests will be carrying the Ark of the L,
4: 1 were safely across the river, the L said to Joshua,
4: 5 the Jordan, in front of the Ark of the L your God.
4: 8 each tribe, just as the L had commanded Joshua.
4:11 the priests crossed over with the Ark of the L.
4:14 That day the L made Joshua great in the eyes of all
4:15 The L had said to Joshua,
4:23 For the L your God dried up the river right before
4:24 of the earth might know the power of the L,
4:24 and that you might fear the L your God forever."
5: 1 heard how the L had dried up the Jordan River
5: 2 At that time the L told Joshua, "Use knives of flint
5: 6 For they had disobeyed the L, and the L vowed he
would not let them enter the
5: 9 Then the L said to Joshua, "Today I have rolled
6: 2 But the L said to Joshua, "I have given you
6: 7 will lead the way in front of the Ark of the L."
6: 8 horns started marching in the presence of the L,
6:11 So the Ark of the L was carried around the city
6:12 and the priests again carried the Ark of the L.
6:13 rams' horns marched in front of the Ark of the L,
6:13 priests with the horns and behind the Ark of the L.
6:16 "Shout! For the L has given you the city!
6:17 be completely destroyed as an offering to the L.
6:19 or iron is sacred to the L and must be brought into
6:26 "May the curse of the L fall on anyone / who tries
6:27 So the L was with Joshua, and his name became
7: 1 unfaithful concerning the things set apart for the L.
7: 1 so the L was very angry with the Israelites.
7: 6 and bowed down facing the Ark of the L until
7: 7 Then Joshua cried out, "Sovereign L, why did you
7:10 But the L said to Joshua, "Get up! Why are you
7:13 For this is what the L, the God of Israel, says:
7:13 among you, O Israel, are things set apart for the L.
7:14 and the L will point out the tribe to which the
7:14 its clans, and the L will point out the guilty clan.
7:14 and the L will point out the guilty family.
7:15 for he has broken the covenant of the L and has
7:16 Joshua brought the tribes of Israel before the L,
7:17 Then the families of Zerah came before the L,
7:19 "My son, give glory to the L, the God of Israel,
7:20 Achan replied, "I have sinned against the L,
7:23 laid them on the ground in the presence of the L.
7:25 The L will now bring trouble on you." And all the
7:26 Trouble ever since. So the L was no longer angry.
8: 1 Then the L said to Joshua, "Do not be afraid
8: 7 of the city, for the L your God will give it to you.
8: 8 Set the city on fire, as the L has commanded.
8:18 Then the L said to Joshua, "Point your spear
8:27 for themselves, as the L had commanded Joshua.
8:30 Then Joshua built an altar to the L, the God of
8:31 burnt offerings and peace offerings to the L.
8:33 the servant of the L, had given for blessing the
9: 9 We have heard of the might of the L your God
9:14 their bread, but they did not consult the L.
9:18 for their leaders had made a vow to the L, the God
9:19 "We have sworn an oath in the presence of the L,
9:24 because we were told that the L your God
9:27 for the people of Israel and for the altar of the L—
9:27 wherever the L would choose to build it.
10: 8 "Do not be afraid of them," the L said to Joshua,
10:10 The L threw them into a panic, and the Israelites
10:11 the L destroyed them with a terrible hailstorm that
10:12 On the day the L gave the Israelites victory over
10:12 Joshua prayed to the L in front of all the people of
10:14 The L fought for Israel that day. Never before
10:14 when the L answered such a request from a human
10:19 for the L your God has given you victory over
10:25 for the L is going to do this to all of your
10:30 There, too, the L gave them the city and its king.
10:32 And the L gave it to them on the second day.
10:40 just as the L, the God of Israel, had commanded.
10:42 conquered all these kings and their land, for the L,
11: 6 Then the L said to Joshua, "Do not be afraid of
11: 8 And the L gave them victory over their enemies.
11: 9 and burned all the chariots, as the L had instructed.
11:12 just as Moses, the servant of the L,
11:15 As the L had commanded his servant Moses,

11:20 For the **L** hardened their hearts and caused them to
11:20 as the **L** had commanded Moses.
11:23 the entire land, just as the **L** had instructed Moses.
12: 6 Moses, the servant of the **L**, and the Israelites had
13: 1 old man, the **L** said to him, "You are growing old,
13: 8 for Moses, the servant of the **L**, had previously
13:14 Instead, as the **L** had promised them,
13:14 from the offerings burned on the altar to the **L**,
13:33 for the **L**, the God of Israel, had promised to be
14: 6 "Remember what the **L** said to Moses, the man of
14: 7 forty years old when Moses, the servant of the **L**,
14: 8 For my part, I followed the **L** my God completely.
14: 9 because you wholeheartedly followed the **L** my
14:10 the **L** has kept me alive and well as he promised
14:12 to give me the hill country that the **L** promised me.
14:12 But if the **L** is with me, I will drive them out of the
land, just as the **L** said."
14:14 because he wholeheartedly followed the **L**,
15:13 The **L** instructed Joshua to assign some of Judah's
17: 4 "The **L** commanded Moses to give us an
17: 4 along with their uncles, as the **L** had commanded.
17:14 only one portion of land when the **L** has given us
18: 3 taking possession of the remaining land the **L**,
18: 6 Then I will cast sacred lots in the presence of the **L**
18: 7 Their role as priests of the **L** is their inheritance.
18: 7 which Moses, the servant of the **L**,
18: 8 lots in the presence of the **L** here at Shiloh."
18:10 Joshua cast sacred lots in the presence of the **L** to
19:50 For the **L** had said he could have any town he
19:51 the **L** at the entrance of the Tabernacle at Shiloh.
20: 1 The **L** said to Joshua,
21: 2 "The **L** instructed Moses to give us towns to live
21: 3 So by the command of the **L** the Levites were
21:43 So the **L** gave to Israel all the land he had sworn to
21:44 And the **L** gave them rest on every side, just as he
21:44 for the **L** helped them conquer all their enemies.
21:45 All of the good promises that the **L** had given
22: 2 as Moses, the servant of the **L**, commanded you,
22: 3 of the **L** your God up to the present day.
22: 4 And now the **L** your God has given the other tribes
22: 4 home now to the land Moses, the servant of the **L**,
22: 5 Love the **L** your God, walk in all his ways,
22:16 "The whole community of the **L** demands to know
22:16 How could you turn away from the **L** and build an
22:17 the plague that struck the entire assembly of the **L**.
22:18 today you are turning away from following the **L**.
22:18 If you rebel against the **L** today, he will be angry
22:19 where the **L** lives among us in his Tabernacle,
22:19 But do not rebel against the **L** or draw us into your
22:19 There is only one true altar of the **L** our God.
22:20 sinned by stealing the things set apart for the **L**?
22:22 "The **L** alone is God! The **L** alone is God!
22:22 have not built the altar in rebellion against the **L**.
22:22 But the **L** knows, and let all Israel know, too,
22:23 built an altar for ourselves to turn away from the **L**.
22:23 it for this purpose, may the **L** himself punish us.
22:24 'What right do you have to worship the **L**, the God
22:25 The **L** has placed the Jordan River as a barrier
22:25 and your people. You have no claim to the **L**.'
22:25 may make our descendants stop worshiping the **L**.
22:27 have the right to worship the **L** at his sanctuary
22:27 able to say to ours, 'You have no claim to the **L**.'
22:28 of the relationship both of us have with the **L**.'
22:29 Far be it from us to rebel against the **L** or turn
22:29 Only the altar of the **L** our God that stands in front
22:31 "Today we know the **L** is among us because you
have not sinned against the **L** as we
22:31 rescued Israel from being destroyed by the **L**."
22:34 witness between us and them that the **L** is our God,
23: 1 and the **L** had given the people of Israel rest from
23: 3 You have seen everything the **L** your God has
23: 3 The **L** your God has fought for you against your
23: 5 for the **L** your God will drive out all the people
23: 5 of them, just as the **L** your God promised you.
23: 8 But be faithful to the **L** your God as you have done
23: 9 "For the **L** has driven out great and powerful
23:10 for the **L** your God fights for you, just as he has
23:11 So be very careful to love the **L** your God.
23:13 then know for certain that the **L** your God will no
23:13 from this good land the **L** your God has given you.
23:14 every promise of the **L** your God has come true.
23:15 But as surely as the **L** your God has given you the
23:16 If you break the covenant of the **L** your God by
24: 2 "This is what the **L**, the God of Israel, says:
24: 7 When you cried out to the **L**, I put darkness
24:14 "So honor the **L** and serve him wholeheartedly.
24:14 Euphrates River and in Egypt. Serve the **L** alone.
24:15 But if you are unwilling to serve the **L**,
24:15 as for me and my family, we will serve the **L**."
24:16 "We would never forsake the **L** and worship other
24:17 For the **L** our God is the one who rescued us
24:18 It was the **L** who drove out the Amorites
24:18 So we, too, will serve the **L**, for he alone is our
24:19 "You are not able to serve the **L**, for he is a holy
24:20 If you forsake the **L** and serve other gods, he will
24:21 saying, "No, we are determined to serve the **L**!"
24:22 "You have chosen to serve the **L**." "Yes,"
24:23 and turn your hearts to the **L**, the God of Israel."
24:24 said to Joshua, "We will serve the **L** our God.
24:25 binding contract between themselves and the **L**.
24:26 the oak tree beside the Tabernacle of the **L**.
24:27 "This stone has heard everything the **L** said to us.
24:29 after this, Joshua son of Nun, the servant of the **L**,
24:31 Israel served the **L** throughout the lifetime of
24:31 experienced all that the **L** had done for Israel.
Jdg 1: 1 After Joshua died, the Israelites asked the **L**,
1: 2 The **L** answered, "Judah, for I have given them
1: 4 the **L** gave them victory over the Canaanites
1:19 The **L** was with the people of Judah, and they took
1:22 the town of Bethel, and the **L** was with them.
2: 1 The angel of the **L** went up from Gilgal to Bokim
2: 4 When the angel of the **L** finished speaking,
2: 5 and they offered sacrifices to the **L**.
2: 7 And the Israelites served the **L** throughout the
2: 7 those who had seen all the great things the **L** had
2: 8 of Nun, the servant of the **L**, died at the age of 110.
2:10 grew up who did not acknowledge the **L**
2:12 They abandoned the **L**, the God of their ancestors,
2:12 the people around them. And they angered the **L**.
2:13 They abandoned the **L** to serve Baal
2:14 This made the **L** burn with anger against Israel,
2:15 the **L** fought against them, bringing them defeat,
2:16 Then the **L** raised up judges to rescue the Israelites
2:18 Whenever the **L** placed a judge over Israel, he was
2:18 For the **L** took pity on his people, who were
2:20 So the **L** burned with anger against Israel. He said,
2:22 or not they would obey the **L** as their ancestors
2:23 That is why the **L** did not quickly drive the nations
3: 1 The **L** left certain nations in the land to test those
3: 4 the **L** had given to their ancestors through Moses.
3: 7 They forgot about the **L** their God, and they
3: 8 Then the **L** burned with anger against Israel,
3: 9 But when Israel cried out to the **L** for help, the **L**
raised up a man to rescue them.
3:10 The Spirit of the **L** came upon him, and he became
3:10 of Aram, and the **L** gave Othniel victory over him.
3:12 so the **L** gave King Eglon of Moab control over
3:15 But when Israel cried out to the **L** for help, the **L**
raised up a man to rescue them.
3:28 "for the **L** has given you victory over Moab your
4: 2 So the **L** handed them over to King Jabin of Hazor,
4: 3 Then the Israelites cried out to the **L** for help.
4: 6 She said to him, "This is what the **L**, the God of
4:14 Today the **L** will give you victory over Sisera, for
the **L** is marching ahead of you."
4:15 the **L** threw Sisera and all his charioteers
5: 2 and the people gladly follow— / bless the **L**!
5: 3 you mighty rulers! / For I will sing to the **L**.
5: 3 I will lift up my song to the **L**, the God of Israel.
5: 4 "**L**, when you set out from Seir / and marched
5: 5 The mountains quaked at the coming of the **L**.
5: 5 Even Mount Sinai shook in the presence of the **L**,
5: 9 and to those who gladly followed. / Bless the **L**!
5:11 They recount the righteous victories of the **L**,
5:11 Then the people of the **L** / marched down to the
5:13 The people of the **L** marched down against mighty
5:23 of Meroz be cursed,' said the angel of the **L**.
5:23 because they did not come to help the **L**,
5:23 to help the **L** against the mighty warriors.'
5:31 "**L**, may all your enemies die as Sisera did!
6: 1 So the **L** handed them over to the Midianites for
6: 6 Then the Israelites cried out to the **L** for help.
6: 7 When they cried out to the **L** because of Midian,
6: 8 the **L** sent a prophet to the Israelites. He said,
"This is what the **L**, the God of Israel,
6:10 I told you, 'I am the **L** your God. You must not
6:11 Then the angel of the **L** came and sat beneath the
6:12 The angel of the **L** appeared to him and said,
"Mighty hero, the **L** is with you!"
6:13 "Sir," Gideon replied, "if the **L** is with us,
6:13 they say, 'The **L** brought us up out of Egypt'?
6:13 But now the **L** has abandoned us and handed us
6:14 Then the **L** turned to him and said, "Go with the
6:16 The **L** said to him, "I will be with you. And you
6:17 show me a sign to prove that it is really the **L**
6:18 The **L** answered, "I will stay here until you
6:21 Then the angel of the **L** touched the meat
6:21 had brought. And the angel of the **L** disappeared.
6:22 Gideon realized that it was the angel of the **L**,
6:22 he cried out, "Sovereign **L**, I have seen the angel
of the **L** face to face!"
6:23 "It is all right," the **L** replied. "Do not be afraid.
6:24 And Gideon built an altar to the **L** there and named
it "The **L** Is Peace."
6:25 That night the **L** said to Gideon, "Take the second
6:26 Then build an altar to the **L** your God here on this
6:27 of his servants and did as the **L** had commanded.
6:34 Then the Spirit of the **L** took possession of Gideon.
7: 2 The **L** said to Gideon, "You have too many
7: 4 But the **L** told Gideon, "There are still too many!
7: 5 the **L** told him, "Divide the men into two groups.
7: 7 The **L** told Gideon, "With these three hundred
7: 9 During the night, the **L** said, "Get up! Go down
7:15 For the **L** has given you victory over the
7:18 and shout, 'For the **L** and for Gideon!' "
7:20 and shouted, "A sword for the **L** and for Gideon!"
7:22 the **L** caused the warriors in the camp to fight
8: 7 "After the **L** gives me victory over Zebah
8:19 "As surely as the **L** lives, I wouldn't kill you if
8:23 nor will my son. The **L** will rule over you!
8:34 They forgot the **L** their God, who had rescued
10: 6 but they abandoned the **L** and no longer served
10: 7 So the **L** burned with anger against Israel, and he
10:10 Finally, they cried out to the **L**, saying, "We have
10:11 The **L** replied, "Did I not rescue you from the
10:15 But the Israelites pleaded with the **L** and said,
10:16 put aside their foreign gods and served the **L**.
11: 9 and if the **L** gives me victory over the Ammonites,
11:10 "The **L** is our witness," the leaders replied.
11:11 At Mizpah, in the presence of the **L**,
11:21 But the **L**, the God of Israel, gave his people
11:23 "So you see, it was the **L**, the God of Israel,
11:24 and we will keep whatever the **L** our God gives us.
11:27 Let the **L**, who is judge, decide today which of us
11:29 At that time the Spirit of the **L** came upon
11:30 And Jephthah made a vow to the **L**. He said,
11:31 I will give to the **L** the first thing coming out of my
11:32 the Ammonites, and the **L** gave him victory.
11:35 For I have made a vow to the **L** and cannot take it
11:36 "Father, you have made a promise to the **L**.
11:36 for the **L** has given you a great victory over your
12: 3 and the **L** gave me victory over the Ammonites.
13: 1 so the **L** handed them over to the Philistines,
13: 3 The angel of the **L** appeared to Manoah's wife
13: 8 Then Manoah prayed to the **L**. He said, "Lord,
13:13 The angel of the **L** replied, "Be sure your wife
13:15 Then Manoah said to the angel of the **L**,
13:16 "I will stay," the angel of the **L** replied, "but I
13:16 prepare a burnt offering as a sacrifice to the **L**."
13:16 (Manoah didn't realize it was the angel of the **L**.)
13:17 Then Manoah asked the angel of the **L**, "What is
13:18 do you ask my name?" the angel of the **L** replied.
13:19 and offered it on a rock as a sacrifice to the **L**.
13:19 and his wife watched, the **L** did an amazing thing.
13:20 the sky, the angel of the **L** ascended in the fire.
13:21 Manoah finally realized it was the angel of the **L**,
13:23 But his wife said, "If the **L** were going to kill us,
13:24 And the **L** blessed him as he grew up.
13:25 the Spirit of the **L** began to take hold of him.
14: 4 and mother didn't realize the **L** was at work in this,
14: 6 At that moment the Spirit of the **L** powerfully took
14:19 Then the Spirit of the **L** powerfully took control of
15:14 But the Spirit of the **L** powerfully took control of
15:18 Samson was very thirsty, and he cried out to the **L**,
16:20 But he didn't realize the **L** had left him.
16:28 Then Samson prayed to the **L**, "Sovereign **L**,
remember me again.
17: 2 "The **L** bless you for admitting it," his mother
17: 3 "I now dedicate these silver coins to the **L**.
17:13 "I know the **L** will bless me now," Micah said,
18: 6 "For the **L** will go ahead of you on your journey."
19:18 and we're going to the Tabernacle of the **L**.
20: 1 and stood in the presence of the **L** at Mizpah.
20:18 The **L** answered, "Judah is to go first."
20:23 and wept in the presence of the **L** until evening.
20:23 Then they asked the **L**, "Should we fight against
20:23 And the **L** said, "Go out and fight against them.")
20:26 and wept in the presence of the **L** and fasted until
20:26 burnt offerings and peace offerings to the **L**.
20:27 the Israelites went up seeking direction from the **L**.
20:28 The Israelites asked the **L**, "Should we fight
20:28 or should we stop?" The **L** said, "Go!
20:35 So the **L** helped Israel defeat Benjamin, and that
21: 3 "O **L**, God of Israel," they cried out, "why has
21: 5 our council in the presence of the **L** at Mizpah?"
21: 7 since we have sworn by the **L** not to give them our
21: 8 when we presented ourselves to the **L** at Mizpah?"
21:15 because the **L** had left this gap in the tribes of
21:19 Then they thought of the annual festival of the **L**
Ru 1: 6 Then Naomi heard in Moab that the **L** had blessed
1: 8 And may the **L** reward you for your kindness to
1: 9 May the **L** bless you with the security of another
1:13 because the **L** himself has caused me to suffer."
1:17 May the **L** punish me severely if I allow anything
1:21 away full, but the **L** has brought me home empty.
1:21 Why should you call me Naomi when the **L** has
2: 4 the harvesters. "The **L** be with you!" he said. "The
L bless you!" the harvesters replied.
2:12 May the **L**, the God of Israel, under whose wings
2:19 May the **L** bless the one who helped you!"
2:20 "May the **L** bless him!" Naomi told her
3:10 "The **L** bless you, my daughter!" Boaz exclaimed.
3:13 then as surely as the **L** lives, I will marry you!
4:11 May the **L** make the woman who is now coming
4:12 And may the **L** give you descendants by this young
4:13 with her, the **L** enabled her to become pregnant,
4:14 "Praise the **L** who has given you a family
1Sa 1: 3 and sacrifice to the **L** Almighty at the Tabernacle.
1: 3 The priests of the **L** at that time were the two sons
1: 5 even though the **L** had given her no children.
1: 6 of Hannah because the **L** had closed her womb.
1: 9 to the Tabernacle after supper to pray to the **L**.
1:10 crying bitterly as she prayed to the **L**.
1:11 "O **L** Almighty, if you will look down upon my
1:11 and as a sign that he has been dedicated to the **L**,
1:12 As she was praying to the **L**, Eli watched her.
1:15 very sad, and I was pouring out my heart to the **L**.
1:19 and went to worship the **L** once more.
1:19 slept with Hannah, the **L** remembered her request,
1:20 him Samuel, for she said, "I asked the **L** for him."
1:21 on their annual trip to offer a sacrifice to the **L**.
1:22 and leave him there with the **L** permanently."
1:23 and may the **L** help you keep your promise."
1:26 who stood here several years ago praying to the **L**.
1:27 I asked the **L** to give me this child, and he has
1:28 I am giving him to the **L**, and he will belong to the
L his whole life." And they worshiped the **L** there.
2: 1 "My heart rejoices in the **L**! / Oh, how the **L** has
blessed me!
2: 2 No one is holy like the **L**! / There is no one besides
2: 3 The **L** is a God who knows your deeds;
2: 6 The **L** brings both death and life; / he brings some
2: 7 The **L** makes one poor and another rich; / he brings
2:10 Those who fight against the **L** will be broken.
2:10 from heaven; / the **L** judges throughout the earth.
2:12 Eli were scoundrels who had no respect for the **L**
2:20 "May the **L** give you other children to take the
place of this one she gave to the **L**."
2:21 And the **L** gave Hannah three sons and two
2:21 Samuel grew up in the presence of the **L**.
2:25 But if someone sins against the **L**, who can

2:25 for the **L** was already planning to put them to
2:26 he also continued to gain favor with the **L** and with
2:27 came to Eli and gave him this message from the **L**:
2:30 "Therefore, the **L**, the God of Israel, says:
3: 1 the boy Samuel was serving the **L** by assisting Eli.
3: 1 Now in those days messages from the **L** were very
3: 4 Suddenly, the **L** called out, "Samuel! Samuel!"
3: 6 Then the **L** called out again, "Samuel!"
3: 7 Samuel did not yet know the **L** because he had
never had a message from the **L**
3: 8 So now the **L** called a third time, and once more
3: 8 Then Eli realized it was the **L** who was calling the
3: 9 and if someone calls again, say, 'Yes, **L**,
3:10 And the **L** came and called as before, "Samuel!
3:11 Then the **L** said to Samuel, "I am about to do a
3:15 He was afraid to tell Eli what the **L** had said to
3:17 "What did the **L** say to you? Tell me everything.
3:19 As Samuel grew up, the **L** was with him,
3:20 that Samuel was confirmed as a prophet of the **L**.
3:21 The **L** continued to appear at Shiloh and gave
4: 3 "Why did the **L** allow us to be defeated by the
4: 3 "Let's bring the Ark of the Covenant of the **L**
4: 4 back the Ark of the Covenant of the **L** Almighty,
4: 5 of the Covenant of the **L** coming into the camp,
4: 6 told it was because the Ark of the **L** had arrived,
5: 3 his face to the ground in front of the Ark of the **L**!
5: 4 had fallen face down before the Ark of the **L** again.
5: 6 Then the **L** began to afflict the people of Ashdod
5: 9 the **L** began afflicting its people, young and old,
6: 1 The Ark of the **L** remained in Philistine territory
6: 2 "What should we do about the Ark of the **L**?
6: 8 Put the Ark of the **L** on the cart, and beside it place
6: 9 we will know it was the **L** who brought this great
6: 9 a coincidence and was not sent by the **L** at all."
6:11 Then the Ark of the **L** and the chest containing the
6:14 and sacrificed them to the **L** as a burnt offering.
6:15 men of the tribe of Levi lifted the Ark of the **L**
6:15 and sacrifices were offered to the **L** that day by the
6:17 to the **L** were gifts from the rulers of Ashdod,
6:18 at Beth-shemesh, where they set the Ark of the **L**,
6:19 But the **L** killed seventy men from Beth-shemesh
6:19 because they looked into the Ark of the **L**.
6:19 mourned greatly because of what the **L** had done.
6:20 "Who is able to stand in the presence of the **L**,
6:21 "The Philistines have returned the Ark of the **L**.
7: 1 of Kiriath-jearim came to get the Ark of the **L**.
7: 2 because it seemed that the **L** had abandoned them.
7: 3 are really serious about wanting to return to the **L**,
7: 3 Determine to obey only the **L**; then he will rescue
7: 4 of Baal and Ashtoreth and worshiped only the **L**.
7: 5 to Mizpah, all of you. I will pray to the **L** for you."
7: 6 water from a well and poured it out before the **L**.
7: 6 and confessed that they had sinned against the **L**.
7: 8 "Plead with the **L** our God to save us from the
7: 9 and offered it to the **L** as a whole burnt offering.
7: 9 He pleaded with the **L** to help Israel, and the **L**
answered.
7:10 But the **L** spoke with a mighty voice of thunder
7:12 he said, "Up to this point the **L** has helped us!"
7:17 And Samuel built an altar to the **L** at Ramah.
8: 6 with their request and went to the **L** for advice.
8: 7 "Do as they say," the **L** replied, "for it is me they
8:18 you are demanding, but the **L** will not help you."
8:21 So Samuel told the **L** what the people had said,
8:22 and the **L** replied, "Do as they say, and give them
9:15 Now the **L** had told Samuel the previous day,
9:17 When Samuel noticed Saul, the **L** said,
10: 1 because the **L** has appointed you to be the leader of
10: 6 At that time the Spirit of the **L** will come upon you
10:17 people of Israel to meet before the **L** at Mizpah.
10:18 And he gave them this message from the **L**,
10:19 present yourselves before the **L** by tribes
10:20 called the tribal leaders together before the **L**,
10:21 each family of the tribe of Benjamin before the **L**,
10:22 So they asked the **L**, "Where is he?"
10:22 And the **L** replied, "He is hiding among the
10:24 "This is the man the **L** has chosen as your king.
10:25 them down on a scroll and placed it before the **L**.
11: 7 And the **L** made the people afraid of Saul's anger,
11:13 for today the **L** has rescued Israel!"
11:15 and in a solemn ceremony before the **L** they
11:15 Then they offered peace offerings to the **L**,
12: 3 Now tell me as I stand before the **L** and before his
12: 5 "The **L** and his anointed one are my witnesses,"
12: 6 "It was the **L** who appointed Moses and Aaron,"
12: 7 Now stand here quietly before the **L** as I remind
12: 7 you of all the great things the **L** has done for you
12: 8 the Israelites were in Egypt and cried out to the **L**,
12: 9 But the people soon forgot about the **L** their God,
12:10 "Then they cried to the **L** again and confessed,
12:10 'We have sinned by turning away from the **L**
12:11 Then the **L** sent Gideon, Barak, Jephthah,
12:12 even though the **L** your God was already your
12:13 asked for him, and the **L** has granted your request.
12:14 "Now if you will fear and worship the **L** and listen
12:14 and if you and your king follow the **L** your God,
12:16 and see the great thing the **L** is about to do.
12:17 I will ask the **L** to send thunder and rain today.
12:17 wicked you have been in asking the **L** for a king!"
12:18 So Samuel called to the **L**, and the **L** sent thunder
12:18 And all the people were terrified of the **L** and of
12:19 "Pray to the **L** your God for us, or we will die!"
12:20 but make sure now that you worship the **L** with all
12:22 The **L** will not abandon his chosen people, for that
12:23 I will certainly not sin against the **L** by ending my
12:24 But be sure to fear the **L** and sincerely worship
13:13 "You have disobeyed the command of the **L** your
13:13 the **L** would have established your kingdom over
13:14 for the **L** has sought out a man after his own heart.
13:14 The **L** has already chosen him to be king over his
14: 3 the priest of the **L** who had served at Shiloh.)
14: 6 "Perhaps the **L** will help us, for nothing can hinder
the **L**.
14:12 "for the **L** will help us defeat them!"
14:23 So the **L** saved Israel that day, and the battle
14:33 the men are sinning against the **L** by eating meat
14:34 Do not sin against the **L** by eating meat with the
14:35 And Saul built an altar to the **L**, the first one he
14:39 I vow by the name of the **L** who rescued Israel that
14:41 Then Saul prayed, "O **L**, God of Israel,
14:45 As surely as the **L** lives, not one hair on his head
15: 1 you king of Israel because the **L** told me to. Now
listen to this message from the **L**!
15: 2 This is what the **L** Almighty says: 'I have decided
15:10 Then the **L** said to Samuel,
15:11 he heard this that he cried out to the **L** all night.
15:13 him cheerfully. "May the **L** bless you," he said.
15:15 "But they are going to sacrifice them to the **L** your
15:16 "Stop! Listen to what the **L** told me last night!"
15:17 of Israel? The **L** has anointed you king of Israel.
15:18 And the **L** sent you on a mission and told you,
15:19 Why haven't you obeyed the **L**? Why did you rush
15:19 and do exactly what the **L** said not to do?"
15:20 "But I did obey the **L**," Saul insisted. "I carried
15:21 and plunder to sacrifice to the **L** your God in
15:22 Samuel replied, "What is more pleasing to the **L**:
15:23 because you have rejected the word of the **L**,
15:25 my sin now and go with me to worship the **L**."
15:28 The **L** has torn the kingdom of Israel from you
15:30 by going with me to worship the **L** your God."
15:31 and went with him, and Saul worshiped the **L**.
15:33 And Samuel cut Agag to pieces before the **L** at
15:35 And the **L** was sorry he had ever made Saul king
16: 1 Finally, the **L** said to Samuel, "You have mourned
16: 2 "Take a heifer with you," the **L** replied, "and say
16: 2 that you have come to make a sacrifice to the **L**.
16: 4 So Samuel did as the **L** instructed him. When he
16: 5 Samuel replied. "I have come to sacrifice to the **L**.
16: 7 But the **L** said to Samuel, "Don't judge by his
16: 7 The **L** doesn't make decisions the way you do!
16: 7 but the **L** looks at a person's thoughts
16: 8 "This is not the one the **L** has chosen."
16: 9 "Neither is this the one the **L** has chosen."
16:10 to Jesse, "The **L** has not chosen any of these."
16:12 And the **L** said, "This is the one; anoint him."
16:13 And the Spirit of the **L** came mightily upon him
16:14 Now the Spirit of the **L** had left Saul,
16:14 and the **L** sent a tormenting spirit that filled him
16:18 a fine-looking young man, and the **L** is with him."
17:37 The **L** who saved me from the claws of the lion
17:37 he said. "And may the **L** be with you!"
17:45 but I come to you in the name of the **L** Almighty—
17:46 Today the **L** will conquer you, and I will kill you
17:47 And everyone will know that the **L** does not need
17:47 is his battle, not ours. The **L** will give you to us!"
18:12 and he was jealous because the **L** had left him
18:14 in everything he did, for the **L** was with him.
18:28 When the king realized how much the **L** was with
19: 5 and how the **L** brought a great victory to Israel as a
19: 6 to Jonathan and vowed, "As surely as the **L** lives,
19: 9 the tormenting spirit from the **L** suddenly came
20: 3 I swear it by the **L** and by your own soul!"
20: 8 for we made a covenant together before the **L**—
20:12 told David, "I promise by the **L**, the God of Israel,
20:13 may the **L** kill me if I don't warn you so you can
20:13 May the **L** be with you as he used to be with my
20:14 me with the faithful love of the **L** as long as I live.
20:15 even when the **L** destroys all your enemies."
20:16 saying, "May the **L** destroy all your enemies!"
20:21 will know, as surely as the **L** lives, that all is well,
20:22 leave immediately, for the **L** is sending you away.
20:23 And may the **L** make us keep our promises to each
21: 6 that was placed before the **L** in the Tabernacle.
22:10 Ahimelech consulted the **L** to find out what David
22:17 "Kill these priests of the **L**, for they are allies
22:21 told David that Saul had killed the priests of the **L**,
23: 2 David asked the **L**, "Should I go and attack
23: 2 "Yes, go and save Keilah," the **L** told him.
23: 4 So David asked the **L** again, and again the **L**
replied, "Go down to Keilah,
23: 6 with him to get answers for David from the **L**.
23: 9 bring the ephod and ask the **L** what he should do.
23:10 And David prayed, "O **L**, God of Israel, I have
23:11 O **L**, God of Israel, please tell me." And the **L**
said, "He will come."
23:12 And the **L** replied, "Yes, they will betray you."
23:18 renewed their covenant of friendship before the **L**.
23:21 "The **L** bless you," Saul said. "At last someone is
24: 4 "Today is the day the **L** was talking about when
24: 6 "The **L** knows I shouldn't have done it," he said
24: 6 anointed one, for the **L** himself has chosen him."
24:10 For the **L** placed you at my mercy back there in the
24:12 The **L** will decide between us. Perhaps the **L** will
punish you for what you are
24:15 May the **L** judge which of us is right and punish
24:18 for when the **L** put me in a place where you could
24:19 May the **L** reward you well for the kindness you
24:21 swear to me by the **L** that when that happens you
25:26 as surely as the **L** lives and you yourself live,
25:26 since the **L** has kept you from murdering
25:28 The **L** will surely reward you with a lasting
25:29 you are safe in the care of the **L** your God,
25:30 When the **L** has done all he promised and has
25:31 And when the **L** has done these great things for
25:32 replied to Abigail, "Praise the **L**, the God of Israel,
25:34 For I swear by the **L**, the God of Israel, who has
25:38 About ten days later, the **L** struck him and he died.
25:39 he said, "Praise the **L**, who has paid back Nabal
26:10 Surely the **L** will strike Saul down someday,
26:11 But the **L** forbid that I should kill the one he has
26:12 because the **L** had put Saul's men into a deep
26:16 I swear by the **L** that you and your men deserve to
26:19 If the **L** has stirred you up against me, then let him
26:19 then may those involved be cursed by the **L**.
26:20 die on foreign soil, far from the presence of the **L**?
26:23 The **L** gives his own reward for doing good and for
26:23 and I refused to kill you even when the **L** placed
26:24 Now may the **L** value my life, even as I have
28: 6 He asked the **L** what he should do, but the **L**
refused to answer him, either by dreams
28:10 But Saul took an oath in the name of the **L**
28:10 and promised, "As surely as the **L** lives,
28:16 "Why ask me if the **L** has left you and has become
28:17 The **L** has done just as he said he would. He has
28:18 The **L** has done this because you did not obey his
28:19 the **L** will hand you and the army of Israel over to
28:19 The **L** will bring the entire army of Israel down in
29: 6 "I swear by the **L**," he told them, "you are some
30: 6 But David found strength in the **L** his God.
30: 8 Then David asked the **L**, "Should I chase them?
30: 8 And the **L** told him, "Yes, go after them.
30:23 Don't be selfish with what the **L** has given us.
2Sa 2: 1 After this, David asked the **L**, "Should I move
2: 1 And the **L** replied, "Yes." Then David asked,
2: 1 should I go to?" And the **L** replied, "Hebron."
2: 5 "May the **L** bless you for being so loyal to your
2: 6 May the **L** be loyal to you in return and reward you
3: 9 help David get all that the **L** has promised him!
3:18 For the **L** has said, 'I have chosen David to save
3:28 "I vow by the **L** that I and my people are innocent
3:39 So may the **L** repay these wicked men for their
4: 8 Today the **L** has given you revenge on Saul and his
4: 9 to Recab and Baanah, "As surely as the **L** lives,
5: 2 And the **L** has told you, 'You will be the shepherd
5: 3 a covenant with the leaders of Israel before the **L**.
5:10 because the **L** God Almighty was with him.
5:12 And David realized that the **L** had made him king
5:19 So David asked the **L**, "Should I go out to fight
5:19 them over to me?" The **L** replied, "Yes, go ahead.
5:20 "The **L** has done it!" David exclaimed.
5:23 And once again David asked the **L** what to do.
5:23 "Do not attack them straight on," the **L** replied.
5:24 That will be the signal that the **L** is moving ahead
5:25 So David did what the **L** commanded, and he
6: 2 which bears the name of the **L** Almighty, who is
6: 5 were celebrating before the **L** with all their might,
6: 9 David was now afraid of the **L** and asked,
6: 9 "How can I ever bring the Ark of the **L** back into
6:10 So David decided not to move the Ark of the **L**
6:11 The Ark of the **L** remained there with the family of
6:11 and the **L** blessed him and his entire household.
6:12 "The **L** has blessed Obed-edom's home
6:14 And David danced before the **L** with all his might,
6:15 and all Israel brought up the Ark of the **L** with
6:16 But as the Ark of the **L** entered the City of David,
6:16 saw King David leaping and dancing before the **L**,
6:17 The Ark of the **L** was placed inside the special tent
6:17 burnt offerings and peace offerings to the **L**.
6:18 David blessed the people in the name of the **L**
6:21 retorted to Michal, "I was dancing before the **L**,
6:21 me as the leader of Israel, the people of the **L**.
6:21 to act like a fool in order to show my joy in the **L**.
7: 1 his palace and the **L** had brought peace to the land,
7: 3 do what you have in mind, for the **L** is with you."
7: 4 But that same night the **L** said to Nathan,
7: 5 tell my servant David, 'This is what the **L** says:
7: 8 servant David, 'This is what the **L** Almighty says:
7:11 " 'And now the **L** declares that he will build a
7:17 to David and told him everything the **L** had said.
7:18 David went in and sat before the **L** and prayed,
"Who am I, O Sovereign **L**,
7:19 And now, Sovereign **L**, in addition to everything
7:19 you deal with everyone this way, O Sovereign **L**?
7:20 You know what I am really like, Sovereign **L**.
7:22 "How great you are, O Sovereign **L**! There is no
7:24 people forever, and you, O **L**, became their God.
7:25 "And now, O **L** God, do as you have promised
7:26 will say, 'The **L** Almighty is God over Israel!'
7:27 "O **L** Almighty, God of Israel, I have been bold
7:28 For you are God, O Sovereign **L**. Your words are
7:29 O Sovereign **L**, it is an eternal blessing!"
8: 6 So the **L** gave David victory wherever he went.
8:11 King David dedicated all these gifts to the **L**,
8:14 This was another example of how the **L** made
11:27 But the **L** was very displeased with what David
12: 1 So the **L** sent Nathan the prophet to tell David this
12: 5 "As surely as the **L** lives," he vowed, "any man
12: 7 The **L**, the God of Israel, says, 'I anointed you king
12: 9 have you despised the word of the **L** and done this
12:11 " 'Because of what you have done, I, the **L**,
12:13 to Nathan, "I have sinned against the **L**."
12:13 Nathan replied, "Yes, but the **L** has forgiven you,
12:14 But you have given the enemies of the **L** great
12:15 his home, the **L** made Bathsheba's baby deathly ill.
12:20 he went to the Tabernacle and worshiped the **L**.
12:22 'Perhaps the **L** will be gracious to me and let the
12:24 they named him Solomon. The **L** loved the child
12:25 "beloved of the **L**"—because the **L** loved him.
14:11 "Please swear to me by the **L** your God that you
14:11 "As surely as the **L** lives," he replied, "not a hair
14:17 from evil. May the **L** your God be with you."

15: 7 "Let me go to Hebron to offer a sacrifice to the L
15:20 and may the L show you his unfailing love
15:21 "I vow by the L and by your own life that I will go
15:25 "If the L sees fit," David said, "he will bring me
15:31 David prayed, "O L, let Ahithophel give Absalom
16: 8 "The L is paying you back for murdering Saul
16: 8 and now the L has given it to your son Absalom.
16:10 If the L has told him to curse me, who am I to stop
16:11 and let him curse, for the L has told him to do it.
16:12 And perhaps the L will see that I am being
16:18 because I work for the man who is chosen by the L
17:14 For the L had arranged to defeat the counsel of
18:19 the L has saved him from his enemy Absalom."
18:28 the ground and said, "Blessed be the L your God,
18:31 Today the L has rescued you from all those who
19: 7 the troops, for I swear by the L that if you don't,
20:19 do you want to destroy what belongs to the L?"
21: 1 for three years, so David asked the L about it.
21: 1 And the L said, "The famine has come
21: 3 Tell me so that the L will bless his people again."
21: 6 and we will execute them before the L at Gibeon,
on the mountain of the L."
21: 7 oath David and Jonathan had sworn before the L.
21: 9 executed them on the mountain before the L.
22: 1 David sang this song to the L after the L had
22: 2 "The L is my rock, my fortress, and my savior;
22: 4 I will call on the L, who is worthy of praise,
22: 7 But in my distress I cried out to the L; / yes,
22:14 The L thundered from heaven; / the Most High
22:16 Then at the command of the L, / at the blast of his
22:19 when I was weakest, / but the L upheld me.
22:21 The L rewarded me for doing right;
22:22 For I have kept the ways of the L; / I have not
22:25 The L rewarded me for doing right, / because of
22:29 O L, you are my light; / yes, L, you light up my
darkness.
22:32 For who is God except the L? / Who but our God
22:42 They cried to the L, but he refused to answer them.
22:47 "The L lives! Blessed be my rock! / May God,
22:50 For this, O L, I will praise you among the nations;
23: 2 "The Spirit of the L speaks through me;
23:10 and the L gave him a great victory that day.
23:12 So the L brought about a great victory.
23:16 to drink it. Instead, he poured it out before the L.
23:17 "The L forbid that I should drink this!"
24: 1 Once again the anger of the L burned against
24: 1 the people of Israel and Judah," the L told him.
24: 3 "May the L your God let you live until there are a
24:10 And he said to the L, "I have sinned greatly
24:10 Please forgive me, L, for doing this foolish thing."
24:11 The next morning the word of the L came to the
24:12 "Go and say to David, 'This is what the L says:
24:13 and let me know what answer to give the L."
24:14 "But let us fall into the hands of the L, for his
24:15 So the L sent a plague upon Israel that morning,
24:16 the L relented and said to the angel, "Stop!
24:16 At that moment the angel of the L was by the
24:17 When David saw the angel, he said to the L,
24:18 and build an altar to the L on the threshing floor of
24:19 So David went to do what the L had commanded
24:21 threshing floor and to build an altar to the L there,
so that the L will stop the plague."
24:23 and may the L your God accept your sacrifice."
24:24 for I cannot present burnt offerings to the L my
24:25 David built an altar there to the L and offered
24:25 And the L answered his prayer, and the plague was
1Ki 1:17 you vowed to me by the L your God that my son
1:29 And the king vowed, "As surely as the L lives,
1:30 just as I swore to you before the L, the God of
1:36 "May the L, the God of my lord the king, decree it
1:37 And may the L be with Solomon as he has been
1:48 'Blessed be the L, the God of Israel, who today
2: 3 Observe the requirements of the L your God
2: 4 then the L will keep the promise he made to me:
2: 8 I swore by the L that I would not kill him.
2:15 brother instead; for that is the way the L wanted it.
2:23 Then King Solomon swore solemnly by the L:
2:24 The L has confirmed me and placed me on the
2:24 So as surely as the L lives, Adonijah will die this
2:26 because you carried the Ark of the Sovereign L for
2:27 Abiathar from his position as priest of the L,
2:27 thereby fulfilling the decree the L had made at
2:28 he ran to the sacred tent of the L and caught hold
2:30 Benaiah went into the sacred tent of the L and said
2:32 Then the L will repay him for the murders of two
2:33 and may the L grant peace to David and his
2:42 "Didn't I make you swear by the L and warn you
2:43 Then why haven't you kept your oath to the L
2:44 King David. May the L punish you for them.
3: 1 and the Temple of the L and the wall around the
3: 2 for a temple honoring the name of the L had not
3: 3 Solomon loved the L and followed all the
3: 5 That night the L appeared to Solomon in a dream,
3: 7 O L my God, now you have made me king instead
5: 3 build a Temple to honor the name of the L his God
5: 3 He could not build until the L gave him victory
5: 4 But now the L my God has given me peace on
5: 5 a Temple to honor the name of the L my God,
5: 5 For the L told him, 'Your son, whom I will place
5: 7 "Praise the L for giving David a wise son to be
5:12 So the L gave great wisdom to Solomon just as he
6: 1 he began the construction of the Temple of the L.
6: 2 The Temple that King Solomon built for the L was
6:11 Then the L gave this message to Solomon:
7:40 had assigned him to make for the Temple of the L:
7:45 All these utensils for the Temple of the L that
7:48 made all the furnishings of the Temple of the L:
7:51 finished all his work on the Temple of the L.
8: 4 Then the priests and Levites took the Ark of the L,
8: 9 where the L made a covenant with the people of
8:10 inner sanctuary, a cloud filled the Temple of the L.
8:11 because the glorious presence of the L filled the
8:12 Then Solomon prayed, "O L, you have said that
8:15 "Blessed be the L, the God of Israel, who has kept
8:17 to build this Temple to honor the name of the L,
8:18 But the L told him, 'It is right for you to want to
8:20 "And now the L has done what he promised,
8:20 have built this Temple to honor the name of the L,
8:21 which contains the covenant that the L made with
8:22 of the L in front of the entire community of Israel.
8:23 He prayed, "O L, God of Israel, there is no God
8:25 And now, O L, God of Israel, carry out your
8:28 Listen to my prayer and my request, O L my God.
8:44 and if they pray to the L toward this city that you
8:53 our ancestors out of Egypt, O Sovereign L,
8:54 making these prayers and requests to the L,
8:54 he stood up in front of the altar of the L,
8:56 "Praise the L who has given rest to his people
8:57 May the L our God be with us as he was with our
8:59 in the presence of the L be before him constantly,
8:59 so that the L our God may uphold my cause
8:60 May people all over the earth know that the L is
8:61 his people, always be faithful to the L our God.
8:62 and all Israel with him offered sacrifices to the L.
8:63 Solomon sacrificed peace offerings to the L
8:63 and all Israel dedicated the Temple of the L.
8:65 of Shelters in the presence of the L their God.
8:66 because the L had been good to his servant David
9: 1 So Solomon finished building the Temple of the L,
9: 2 Then the L appeared to Solomon a second time,
9: 3 The L said to him, "I have heard your prayer
9: 8 'Why did the L do such terrible things to his land
9: 9 'Because his people forgot the L their God,
9: 9 That is why the L has brought all these disasters
9:10 during which Solomon built the Temple of the L
9:25 and peace offerings to the L on the altar he had
9:25 He also burned incense to the L. And so he
10: 1 which brought honor to the name of the L,
10: 5 offerings Solomon made at the Temple of the L.
10: 9 The L your God is great indeed! He delights in you
10: 9 Because the L loves Israel with an eternal love,
10:12 wood to make railings for the Temple of the L
11: 2 The L had clearly instructed his people not to
11: 3 sure enough, they led his heart away from the L.
11: 4 their gods instead of trusting only in the L his God,
11: 6 he refused to follow the L completely, as his
11: 9 The L was very angry with Solomon, for his heart
had turned away from the L, the God
11:11 So now the L said to him, "Since you have not
11:14 Then the L raised up Hadad the Edomite,
11:31 for this is what the L, the God of Israel, says:
12:15 This turn of events was the will of the L, for it
12:24 'This is what the L says: Do not fight against your
12:24 doing!' " So they obeyed the message of the L
12:24 and went home, as the L had commanded.
12:27 to offer sacrifices at the Temple of the L,
13: 2 "O altar, altar! This is what the L says:
13: 3 and he said, "The L has promised to give this sign:
13: 5 of God had predicted in his message from the L.
13: 6 "Please ask the L your God to restore my hand
13: 6 So the man of God prayed to the L, and the king's
13: 9 For the L gave me this command: 'You must not
13:17 For the L gave me this command: 'You must not
13:18 And an angel gave me this message from the L:
13:20 a message from the L came to the old prophet.
13:21 man of God from Judah, "This is what the L says:
13:21 and have disobeyed the command the L your God
13:26 The L has fulfilled his word by causing the lion to
13:32 For the message the L told him to proclaim against
14: 5 But the L had told Ahijah, "Jeroboam's wife will
14: 7 Jeroboam, this message from the L, the God of
14:11 I, the L, vow that the members of your family who
14:13 for this child is the only good thing that the L,
14:14 And the L will raise up a king over Israel who will
14:15 Then the L will shake Israel like a reed whipped
14:15 for they have angered the L by worshiping
14:18 as the L had promised through the prophet Ahijah.
14:21 the city the L had chosen from among all the tribes
14:24 L had driven from the land ahead of the Israelites.
14:26 He ransacked the Temple of the L and the royal
14:28 Whenever the king went to the Temple of the L,
15: 3 and his heart was not right with the L his God,
15: 4 the L his God allowed his dynasty to continue,
15:14 Asa remained faithful to the L throughout his life.
15:15 He brought into the Temple of the L the silver
15:29 just as the L had promised concerning Jeroboam
15:30 because Jeroboam had aroused the anger of the L,
16: 1 This message from the L was delivered to King
16: 7 This message from the L had been spoken against
16:12 So Zimri destroyed the dynasty of Baasha as the L
16:13 arousing the anger of the L, the God of Israel,
16:26 Thus, he aroused the anger of the L, the God of
16:33 He did more to arouse the anger of the L, the God
16:34 L concerning Jericho spoken by Joshua son of
17: 1 told King Ahab, "As surely as the L, the God of
17: 2 Then the L said to Elijah,
17: 5 So Elijah did as the L had told him and camped
17: 8 Then the L said to Elijah,
17:12 "I swear by the L your God that I don't have a
17:14 For this is what the L, the God of Israel, says:
17:14 containers until the time when the L sends rain
17:16 just as the L had promised through Elijah.
17:20 Then Elijah cried out to the L, "O L my God,
17:21 three times and cried out to the L, "O L my God,
17:22 The L heard Elijah's prayer, and the life of the
17:24 of God, and that the L truly speaks through you."
18: 1 the L said to Elijah, "Go and present yourself to
18: 3 (Now Obadiah was a devoted follower of the L.
18:10 For I swear by the L your God that the king has
18:12 the Spirit of the L will carry you away to who
18:12 Yet I have been a true servant of the L all my life.
18:15 But Elijah said, "I swear by the L Almighty,
18:18 you have refused to obey the commands of the L
18:21 If the L is God, follow him! But if Baal is God,
18:22 "I am the only prophet of the L who is left,
18:24 of your god, and I will call on the name of the L.
18:30 repaired the altar of the L that had been torn down.
18:36 prophet walked up to the altar and prayed, "O L,
18:37 O L, answer me! Answer me so these people will
18:37 O L, are God and that you have brought them back
18:38 Immediately the fire of the L flashed down from
18:39 fell on their faces and cried out, "The L is God!
The L is God!"
18:46 Now the L gave special strength to Elijah.
19: 4 "I have had enough, L," he said. "Take my life,
19: 7 Then the angel of the L came again and touched
19: 9 But the L said to him, "What are you doing here,
19:10 "I have zealously served the L God Almighty.
19:11 stand before me on the mountain," the L told him.
19:11 And as Elijah stood there, the L passed by, and a
19:11 were torn loose, but the L was not in the wind.
19:11 an earthquake, but the L was not in the earthquake.
19:12 there was a fire, but the L was not in the fire.
19:14 "I have zealously served the L God Almighty.
19:15 Then the L told him, "Go back the way you came,
20:13 King Ahab and told him, "This is what the L says:
20:13 over to you. Then you will know that I am the L."
20:14 And the prophet replied, "This is what the L says:
20:28 king of Israel and said, "This is what the L says:
20:28 The Arameans have said that the L is a god of the
20:28 vast army. Then you will know that I am the L."
20:35 the L instructed one of the group of prophets to say
20:36 "Because you have not obeyed the voice of the L,
20:42 the prophet told him, "This is what the L says:
21: 3 "The L forbid that I should give you the
21:17 But the L said to Elijah, who was from Tishbe,
21:19 Give him this message: 'This is what the L says:
21:21 The L is going to bring disaster to you and sweep
21:23 The L has also told me that the dogs of Jezreel will
21:26 the people whom the L had driven from the land
21:28 Then another message from the L came to Elijah,
22: 5 "But first let's find out what the L says."
22: 7 "Isn't there a prophet of the L around, too?
22: 8 "There is still one prophet of the L, but I hate him.
22:11 and proclaimed, "This is what the L says:
22:12 and be victorious, for the L will give you victory!"
22:14 But Micaiah replied, "As surely as the L lives,
22:14 I will say only what the L tells me to say."
22:15 The L will give the king a glorious victory!"
22:16 speak only the truth when you speak for the L?"
22:17 And the L said, 'Their master has been killed.
22:19 Micaiah continued, "Listen to what the L says!
22:19 I saw the L sitting on his throne with all the armies
22:20 And the L said, 'Who can entice Ahab to go into
22:21 until finally a spirit approached the L and said,
22:22 the L asked. "And the spirit replied, 'I will go out
22:22 " 'You will succeed,' said the L. 'Go ahead
22:23 the L has put a lying spirit in the mouths of your
22:23 For the L has determined disaster for you."
22:24 "When did the Spirit of the L leave me to speak to
22:28 return safely, the L has not spoken through me!"
22:38 licked the king's blood, just as the L had promised.
22:53 arousing the anger of the L, the God of Israel,
2Ki 1: 3 But the angel of the L told Elijah, who was from
1: 4 Now, therefore, this is what the L says: You will
1: 6 to go back to the king with a message from the L.
1:15 Then the angel of the L said to Elijah, "Don't be
1:16 Elijah said to the king, "This is what the L says:
1:17 just as the L had promised through Elijah.
2: 1 When the L was about to take Elijah up to heaven
2: 2 "Stay here, for the L has told me to go to Bethel."
2: 2 "As surely as the L lives and you yourself live,
2: 3 "Did you know that the L is going to take your
2: 4 for the L has told me to go to Jericho."
2: 4 "As surely as the L lives and you yourself live,
2: 5 "Did you know that the L is going to take your
2: 6 for the L has told me to go to the Jordan River."
2: 6 "As surely as the L lives and you yourself live,
2:14 with the cloak and cried out, "Where is the L,
2:16 Perhaps the Spirit of the L has left him on some
2:21 salt into it. And he said, "This is what the L says:
2:24 at them, and he cursed them in the name of the L.
3:10 "The L has brought the three of us here to let the
3:11 "Is there no prophet of the L with us?
3:11 If there is, we can ask the L what to do." One of
3:12 "Then the L will speak through him."
3:13 For it was the L who called us three kings here to
3:14 "As surely as the L Almighty lives, whom I serve,
3:15 the power of the L came upon Elisha,
3:16 and he said, "This is what the L says: This dry
3:17 You will see neither wind nor rain, says the L,
3:18 But this is only a simple thing for the L, for he will
4: 1 you is dead, and you know how he feared the L.
4:27 her deeply, and the L has not told me what it is."
4:30 "As surely as the L lives and you yourself live,
4:33 and shut the door behind him and prayed to the L.
4:43 can eat, for the L says there will be plenty for all.
4:44 and some left over, just as the L had promised.
5: 1 because through him the L had given Aram great
5:11 and call on the name of the L his God and heal me!
5:16 "As surely as the L lives, whom I serve,

5:17 or sacrifices to any other god except the **L**.
5:18 However, may the **L** pardon me in this one thing.
5:18 my arm, may the **L** pardon me when I bow, too."
5:20 As surely as the **L** lives, I will chase after him
6:17 "O **L**, open his eyes and let him see!"
6:17 The **L** opened his servant's eyes, and when he
6:18 Elisha prayed, "O **L**, please make them blind."
And the **L** did as Elisha asked.
6:20 Elisha prayed, "O **L**, now open their eyes and let
6:20 And the **L** did, and they discovered that they were
6:27 "If the **L** doesn't help you, what can I do?"
6:33 "It is the **L** who has brought this trouble on us!
Why should I wait any longer for the **L**?"
7:1 Elisha replied, "Hear this message from the **L**!
This is what the **L** says:
7:2 "That couldn't happen even if the **L** opened the
7:16 half an ounce of silver, just as the **L** had promised.
7:19 "That couldn't happen even if the **L** opened the
8:1 for the **L** has called for a famine on Israel that will
8:8 Then tell him to ask the **L** if I will get well again."
8:10 But the **L** has shown me that he will actually die!"
8:13 "The **L** has shown me that you are going to be the
8:19 But the **L** was not willing to destroy Judah, for he
9:3 over his head. Say to him, 'This is what the **L** says:
9:6 oil over Jehu's head and said, "This is what the **L**,
9:25 The **L** pronounced this message against him:
9:26 says the **L**, for the murder of Naboth and his sons
9:26 him out on Naboth's field, just as the **L** said."
9:36 he stated, "This fulfills the message from the **L**,
10:10 You can be sure that the message of the **L** that was
10:10 The **L** declared through his servant Elijah that this
10:16 with me, and see how devoted I am to the **L**."
10:17 just as the **L** had promised through Elijah.
10:23 Don't let anyone in who worships the **L**!"
10:30 Nonetheless the **L** said to Jehu, "You have done
10:31 But Jehu did not obey the law of the **L**, the God of
10:32 At about that time the **L** began to reduce the size of
11:3 **L** for six years while Athaliah ruled over the land.
11:4 and the guards to come to the Temple of the **L**.
11:10 and were stored in the Temple of the **L**.
11:15 Do not kill her here in the Temple of the **L**."
11:17 Then Jehoiada made a covenant between the **L**
11:18 the priest stationed guards at the Temple of the **L**.
11:19 land escorted the king from the Temple of the **L**.
12:9 of the altar at the entrance of the Temple of the **L**.
12:13 articles of gold or silver for the Temple of the **L**.
13:3 So the **L** was very angry with Israel, and he
13:4 for the LORD's help, and the **L** heard his prayer.
13:4 The **L** could see how terribly the king of Aram was
13:5 So the **L** raised up a deliverer to rescue the
13:23 But the **L** was gracious to the people of Israel,
14:6 for he obeyed the command of the **L** written in the
14:14 and all the utensils from the Temple of the **L**,
14:25 and the Dead Sea, just as the **L**, the God of Israel,
14:26 For the **L** saw the bitter suffering of everyone in
14:27 because the **L** had not said he would blot out the
15:5 The **L** struck the king with leprosy, which lasted
15:35 who rebuilt the upper gate of the Temple of the **L**.
15:37 In those days the **L** began to send King Rezin of
16:2 do what was pleasing in the sight of the **L** his God,
16:3 **L** had driven from the land ahead of the Israelites.
16:8 and gold from the Temple of the **L** and the palace
16:18 as the king's outer entrance to the Temple of the **L**.
17:7 other gods, sinning against the **L** their God,
17:8 the **L** had driven from the land before them,
17:9 things that were not pleasing to the **L** their God.
17:11 just like the nations the **L** had driven from the land
17:13 Again and again the **L** had sent his prophets
17:14 and refused to believe in the **L** their God.
17:16 They defied all the commands of the **L** their God
17:18 And because the **L** was angry, he swept them from
17:19 refused to obey the commands of the **L** their God.
17:20 So the **L** rejected all the descendants of Israel.
17:21 For when the **L** tore Israel away from the kingdom
17:21 Jeroboam drew Israel away from following the **L**
17:23 until the **L** finally swept them away, just as all his
17:25 did not worship the **L** when they first arrived,
17:25 the **L** sent lions among them to kill some of them.
17:28 and taught the new residents how to worship the **L**.
17:32 These new residents worshiped the **L**, but they
17:33 And though they worshiped the **L**, they continued
17:34 former practices instead of truly worshiping the **L**
17:35 For the **L** had made a covenant with the
17:36 Worship only the **L**, who brought you out of Egypt
17:39 You must worship only the **L** your God. He is the
17:41 So while these new residents worshiped the **L**,
18:5 Hezekiah trusted in the **L**, the God of Israel.
18:6 He remained faithful to the **L** in everything,
18:6 and he carefully obeyed all the commands the **L**
18:7 So the **L** was with him, and Hezekiah was
18:12 For they had refused to listen to the **L** their God.
18:12 all the laws the **L** had given through his servant
18:15 used all the silver stored in the Temple of the **L**
18:22 you will say, 'We are trusting in the **L** our God!'
18:25 The **L** himself told us, 'Go and destroy it!' "
18:30 Don't let him fool you into trusting in the **L** by
saying, 'The **L** will rescue us!
18:32 to mislead you by saying, 'The **L** will rescue us!'
18:35 So what makes you think that the **L** can rescue
19:1 and went into the Temple of the **L** to pray.
19:4 But perhaps the **L** your God has heard the Assyrian
19:6 "Say to your master, 'This is what the **L** says:
19:14 LORD's Temple and spread it out before the **L**.
19:15 And Hezekiah prayed this prayer before the **L**:
19:15 "O **L**, God of Israel, you are enthroned between
19:16 Listen to me, O **L**, and hear! Open your eyes, O **L**,
and see!
19:17 "It is true, **L**, that the kings of Assyria have
19:19 Now, O **L** our God, rescue us from his power;
19:19 the earth will know that you alone, O **L**, are God."
19:20 "This is what the **L**, the God of Israel, says:
19:21 This is the message that the **L** has spoken against
19:25 It was I, the **L**, who decided this long ago.
19:29 "Here is the proof that the **L** will protect this city
19:31 The passion of the **L** Almighty will make this
19:32 "And this is what the **L** says about the king of
19:33 he came. He will not enter this city, says the **L**.
19:35 That night the angel of the **L** went out to the
20:1 "This is what the **L** says: Set your affairs in order,
20:2 he turned his face to the wall and prayed to the **L**,
20:3 "Remember, O **L**, how I have always tried to be
20:4 this message came to him from the **L**:
20:5 Tell him, 'This is what the **L**, the God of your
20:5 will get out of bed and go to the Temple of the **L**.
20:8 "What sign will the **L** give to prove that he will
20:8 and that I will go to the Temple of the **L** three days
20:9 "This is the sign that the **L** will give you to prove
20:11 So Isaiah asked the **L** to do this, and he caused the
20:16 to Hezekiah, "Listen to this message from the **L**:
20:17 off to Babylon. Nothing will be left, says the **L**.
20:19 "This message you have given me from the **L** is
21:2 **L** had driven from the land ahead of the Israelites.
21:4 He even built pagan altars in the Temple of the **L**,
21:4 the place where the **L** had said his name should be
21:7 the very place where the **L** had told David and his
21:9 **L** had destroyed when the Israelites entered the
21:10 Then the **L** said through his servants the prophets:
21:12 So this is what the **L**, the God of Israel, says:
21:22 He abandoned the **L**, the God of his ancestors,
22:3 the court secretary, to the Temple of the **L**.
22:5 use it to pay workers to repair the Temple of the **L**.
22:9 collected at the Temple of the **L** to the workers
22:13 and speak to the **L** for me and for the people
22:15 She said to them, "The **L**, the God of Israel,
22:16 'This is what the **L** says: I will destroy this city
22:18 go to the king of Judah who sent you to seek the **L**
22:18 'This is what the **L**, the God of Israel,
22:19 and humbled yourself before the **L** when you heard
22:19 So I have indeed heard you, says the **L**.
23:2 And the king went up to the Temple of the **L** with
23:3 He pledged to obey the **L** by keeping all his
23:7 prostitutes that were inside the Temple of the **L**,
23:8 brought back to Jerusalem all the priests of the **L**,
23:16 This happened just as the **L** had promised through
23:19 kings of Israel and had made the **L** very angry.
23:21 "You must celebrate the Passover to the **L** your
23:23 This Passover was celebrated to the **L** in Jerusalem
23:25 who turned to the **L** with all his heart and soul
23:27 For the **L** had said, "I will destroy Judah just as I
24:2 Then the **L** sent bands of Babylonian, Aramean,
24:2 just as the **L** had promised through his prophets.
24:4 innocent blood, and the **L** would not forgive this.
24:13 As the **L** had said beforehand,
24:20 So the **L**, in his anger, finally banished the people
25:9 He burned down the Temple of the **L**, the royal
1Ch 2:3 Er, was a wicked man, so the **L** killed him.
2:7 by taking plunder that had been set apart for the **L**.
6:15 who went into exile when the **L** sent the people of
6:31 at the house of the **L** after he put the Ark there.
6:32 Solomon built the Temple of the **L** in Jerusalem.
9:1 to Babylon because they were unfaithful to the **L**.
9:19 had guarded the Tabernacle in the camp of the **L**.
9:20 in earlier times, and the **L** had been with him.
9:23 for guarding the entrance to the house of the **L**,
10:13 So Saul died because he was unfaithful to the **L**.
10:14 instead of asking the **L** for guidance.
10:14 So the **L** killed him and turned his kingdom over to
11:2 And the **L** your God has told you, 'You will be the
11:3 a covenant with the leaders of Israel before the **L**.
11:3 just as the **L** had promised through Samuel.
11:9 because the **L** Almighty was with him.
11:10 just as the **L** had promised concerning Israel.
11:14 So the **L** saved them by giving them a great
11:18 to drink it. Instead, he poured it out before the **L**.
12:23 king instead of Saul, just as the **L** had promised.
13:2 you approve and if it is the will of the **L** our God,
13:6 which bears the name of the **L** who is enthroned
13:14 and the **L** blessed him and his entire household.
14:2 And David realized that the **L** had made him king
14:10 The **L** replied, "Yes, go ahead. I will give you the
14:17 and the **L** caused all the nations to fear David.
15:2 The **L** has chosen them to carry the Ark of the **L**
15:3 the Ark of the **L** to the place he had prepared for it.
15:12 so you can bring the Ark of the **L**, the God of
15:13 the anger of the **L** our God burst out against us.
15:14 themselves in order to bring the Ark of the **L**,
15:15 carrying poles, just as the **L** had instructed Moses.
16:2 David blessed the people in the name of the **L**.
16:4 before the Ark of the **L** by asking for his blessings
and giving thanks and praise to the **L**,
16:7 fellow Levites this song of thanksgiving to the **L**:
16:8 Give thanks to the **L** and proclaim his greatness.
16:10 in his holy name; / O worshipers of the **L**, rejoice!
16:11 Search for the **L** and for his strength, / and keep on
16:14 He is the **L** our God. / His rule is seen throughout
16:23 Let the whole earth sing to the **L**! / Each day
16:25 Great is the **L**! He is most worthy of praise!
16:26 are merely idols, / but the **L** made the heavens!
16:28 O nations of the world, recognize the **L**,
16:28 recognize that the **L** is glorious and strong.
16:29 Give to the **L** the glory he deserves! / Bring your
16:29 Worship the **L** in all his holy splendor.
16:31 Tell all the nations that the **L** is king.
16:33 trees of the forest rustle with praise before the **L**!
16:34 Give thanks to the **L**, for he is good! / His faithful
16:36 Blessed be the **L**, the God of Israel,
16:36 all the people shouted "Amen!" and praised the **L**.
16:39 and his fellow priests at the Tabernacle of the **L** on
16:39 where they continued to minister before the **L**.
16:40 They sacrificed the regular burnt offerings to the **L**
16:40 obeying everything written in the law of the **L**,
16:41 the others chosen by name to give thanks to the **L**,
17:4 tell my servant David, 'This is what the **L** says:
17:7 servant David, 'This is what the **L** Almighty says:
17:10 " 'And now I declare that the **L** will build a house
17:15 to David and told him everything the **L** had said.
17:16 David went in and sat before the **L** and prayed,
"Who am I, O **L** God,
17:17 as though I were someone very great, O **L** God!
17:19 For my sake, O **L**, and according to your will,
17:20 "O **L**, there is no one like you—there is no other
17:22 and you, O **L**, have become their God.
17:23 "And now, O **L**, do as you have promised
17:24 will say, 'The **L** Almighty is God over Israel!'
17:26 For you are God, O **L**. And you have promised
17:27 grant a blessing, O **L**, it is an eternal blessing!"
18:6 So the **L** gave David victory wherever he went.
18:11 King David dedicated all these gifts to the **L**,
18:13 This was another example of how the **L** made
21:3 "May the **L** increase the number of his people a
21:9 Then the **L** spoke to Gad, David's seer. This was
21:10 "Go and say to David, 'This is what the **L** says:
21:11 "These are the choices the **L** has given you.
21:12 or three days of severe plague as the angel of the **L**
21:12 and let me know what answer to give the **L**."
21:13 "But let me fall into the hands of the **L**, for his
21:14 So the **L** sent a plague upon Israel, and seventy
21:15 the **L** relented and said to the death angel, "Stop!
21:15 At that moment the angel of the **L** was standing by
21:16 and saw the angel of the **L** standing between
21:17 O **L** my God, let your anger fall against me and my
21:18 Then the angel of the **L** told Gad to instruct David
21:18 **L** at the threshing floor of Araunah the Jebusite.
21:19 So David obeyed the instructions the **L** had given
21:22 Then I will build an altar to the **L** there, so that he
21:24 I cannot take what is yours and give it to the **L**.
21:26 David built an altar there to the **L** and sacrificed
21:26 the **L** answered him by sending fire from heaven to
21:27 Then the **L** spoke to the angel, who put the sword
21:28 When David saw that the **L** had answered his
21:29 the Tabernacle of the **L** and the altar that Moses
21:30 terrified by the drawn sword of the angel of the **L**.
22:1 "This will be the location for the Temple of the **L**
22:5 and the Temple of the **L** must be a magnificent
22:6 and instructed him to build a Temple for the **L**,
22:7 a Temple to honor the name of the **L** my God,"
22:8 "But the **L** said to me, 'You have killed many men
22:11 may the **L** be with you and give you success as you
22:11 in building the Temple of the **L** your God.
22:12 And may the **L** give you wisdom
22:12 that you may obey the law of the **L** your God as
22:13 and regulations that the **L** gave to Israel through
22:14 materials for building the Temple of the **L**—
22:16 Now begin the work, and may the **L** be with you!"
22:18 "The **L** your God is with you," he declared.
22:18 and they are now subject to the **L** and his people.
22:19 Now seek the **L** your God with all your heart.
22:19 Build the sanctuary of the **L** God so that you can
23:4 will supervise the work at the Temple of the **L**.
23:5 and another four thousand will praise the **L** with
23:13 sacrifices in the LORD's presence, to serve the **L**,
23:24 or older to qualify for service in the house of the **L**.
23:25 For David said, "The **L**, the God of Israel,
23:28 of Aaron, as they served at the house of the **L**.
23:30 and evening they stood before the **L** to sing songs
23:31 that were presented to the **L** on Sabbath days,
23:32 out their duties of service at the house of the **L**.
24:19 **L** according to the procedures established by their
24:19 Aaron in obedience to the commands of the **L**,
25:3 of the harp, offering thanks and praise to the **L**.
25:6 fathers as they made music at the house of the **L**.
25:7 were all trained in making music before the **L**,
26:12 the other Levites, they served at the house of the **L**.
26:22 in charge of the treasuries of the house of the **L**.
26:26 all the things dedicated to the **L** by King David,
26:27 had gained in battle to maintain the house of the **L**.
26:28 the items dedicated to the **L** by Samuel the seer,
26:30 for all matters related to the things of the **L**
27:23 because the **L** had promised to make the Israelites
28:4 "Yet the **L**, the God of Israel, has chosen me from
28:4 the **L** was pleased to make me king over all Israel.
28:5 my sons—for the **L** has given me many children—
28:8 Be careful to obey all the commands of the **L** your
28:9 For the **L** sees every heart and understands
28:10 The **L** has chosen you to build a Temple as his
28:13 of priests and Levites in the Temple of the **L**.
28:19 given to me in writing from the hand of the **L**."
28:20 of the task, for the **L** God, my God, is with you.
28:20 related to the Temple of the **L** is finished correctly.
29:1 just another building—it is for the **L** God himself!
29:5 Who is willing to give offerings to the **L** today?"
29:8 of the house of the **L** under the care of Jehiel,
29:9 they had given freely and wholeheartedly to the **L**,
29:10 Then David praised the **L** in the presence of the
29:10 "O **L**, the God of our ancestor Israel, may you be
29:11 Yours, O **L**, is the greatness, the power, the glory,
29:11 in the heavens and on earth is yours, O **L**,
29:16 "O **L** our God, even these materials that we have
29:18 "O **L**, the God of our ancestors Abraham, Isaac,
29:20 "Give praise to the **L** your God!"
29:20 And the entire assembly praised the **L**, the God of

29:20 bowed low and knelt before the L and the king.
29:21 a thousand male lambs as burnt offerings to the L.
29:22 They anointed him before the L as their leader,
29:23 So Solomon took the throne of the L in place of his
29:25 And the L exalted Solomon so the entire nation of
2Ch 1: 1 for the L his God was with him and made him very
1: 5 still at Gibeon in front of the Tabernacle of the L.
1: 5 the people gathered in front of it to consult the L.
1: 9 Now, L God, please keep your promise to David
2: 1 that the time had come to build a Temple for the L
2: 4 a Temple to honor the name of the L my God.
2: 4 and at the other appointed festivals of the L our
2:11 because the L loves his people that he has made
2:12 Blessed be the L, the God of Israel, who made the
2:12 who will build a Temple for the L and a royal
3: 1 So Solomon began to build the Temple of the L in
3: 1 where the L had appeared to Solomon's father,
4:16 out of burnished bronze for the Temple of the L.
5: 1 the work related to building the Temple of the L,
5:10 when the L made a covenant with the people of
5:13 in unison to praise and give thanks to the L.
5:13 their voices and praised the L with these words:
5:13 At that moment a cloud filled the Temple of the L.
5:14 because the glorious presence of the L filled the
6: 1 Then Solomon prayed, "O L, you have said that
6: 4 "Blessed be the L, the God of Israel, who has kept
6: 7 to build this Temple to honor the name of the L,
6: 8 But the L told him, 'It is right for you to want to
6:10 "And now the L has done what he promised,
6:10 have built this Temple to honor the name of the L,
6:11 and in the Ark is the covenant that the L made with
6:12 of the L in front of the entire community of Israel.
6:14 He prayed, "O L, God of Israel, there is no God
6:16 And now, O L, God of Israel, carry out your
6:17 Now, O L, God of Israel, fulfill this promise to
6:19 Listen to my prayer and my request, O L my God.
6:41 O L God, arise and enter this resting place of
6:41 May your priests, O L God, be clothed with
6:42 O L God, do not reject your anointed one.
7: 1 and the glorious presence of the L filled the
7: 2 priests could not even enter the Temple of the L
7: 2 because the glorious presence of the L filled it.
7: 3 and the glorious presence of the L filling the
7: 3 on the ground and worshiped and praised the L,
7: 4 and all the people offered sacrifices to the L.
7: 6 King David had made for praising the L.
7:10 and happy because the L had been so good to
7:11 So Solomon finished building the Temple of the L,
7:12 Then one night the L appeared to Solomon
7:21 'Why has the L done such terrible things to his
7:22 will be, 'Because his people abandoned the L,
8:11 for the Ark of the L has been there, and it is holy
8:12 Then Solomon sacrificed burnt offerings to the L
8:16 to building the Temple of the L was carried out,
9: 4 offerings Solomon made at the Temple of the L.
9: 8 The L your God is great indeed! He delights in you
9:11 almug wood to make steps for the Temple of the L
10:15 for it fulfilled the prophecy of the L spoken to
11: 2 But the L said to Shemaiah, the man of God,
11: 4 'This is what the L says: Do not fight against your
11: 4 doing!' " So they obeyed the message of the L
11:14 and his sons would not allow them to serve the L
11:16 those who sincerely wanted to worship the L,
11:16 where they could offer sacrifices to the L, the God
11:17 and earnestly sought to obey the L as they had
12: 1 and strong, he abandoned the law of the L,
12: 2 Because they were unfaithful to the L,
12: 5 Shemaiah told them, "This is what the L says:
12: 6 and said, "The L is right in doing this to us!"
12: 7 When the L saw their change of heart, he gave this
12: 9 took away all the treasures of the Temple of the L
12:11 Whenever the king went to the Temple of the L,
12:13 the city the L had chosen from among all the tribes
12:14 for he did not seek the L with all his heart.
13: 5 Don't you realize that the L, the God of Israel,
13: 8 of the L that is led by the descendants of David?
13: 9 And you have chased away the priests of the L
13:10 "But as for us, the L is our God, and we have not
13:10 Only the descendants of Aaron serve the L as
13:11 and fragrant incense to the L every morning
13:11 We are following the instructions of the L our
13:12 O people of Israel, do not fight against the L,
13:14 and the rear, they cried out to the L for help.
13:18 Judah defeated Israel because they trusted in the L,
13:20 and finally the L struck him down and he died.
14: 2 and good in the sight of the L his God.
14: 4 He commanded the people of Judah to seek the L,
14: 6 for the L was giving him rest from his enemies.
14: 7 The land is ours because we sought the L our God,
14:11 Then Asa cried out to the L his God, "O L, no one
but you can help the powerless
14:11 Help us, O L our God, for we trust in you alone.
14:11 O L, you are our God; do not let mere men prevail
14:12 So the L defeated the Ethiopians in the presence of
14:13 They were destroyed by the L and his army,
14:14 and terror from the L came upon the people there.
15: 2 The L will stay with you as long as you stay with
15: 4 whenever you were in distress and turned to the L,
15: 8 And he repaired the altar of the L, which stood in
15: 9 when they saw that the L his God was with him.
15:11 On that day they sacrificed to the L some of the
15:12 Then they entered into a covenant to seek the L,
15:13 agreed that anyone who refused to seek the L,
15:14 They shouted out their oath of loyalty to the L with
15:15 And the L gave them rest from their enemies on
15:17 Asa remained fully committed to the L throughout
16: 7 in the king of Aram instead of in the L your God,
16: 8 At that time you relied on the L, and he handed
16: 9 The eyes of the L search the whole earth in order
17: 3 The L was with Jehoshaphat because he followed
17: 5 So the L established Jehoshaphat's control over the
17: 6 He was committed to the ways of the L.
17: 9 They took copies of the Book of the Law of the L
17:10 Then the fear of the L fell over all the surrounding
18: 4 "But first let's find out what the L says."
18: 6 "Isn't there a prophet of the L around, too?
18: 7 "There is still one prophet of the L, but I hate him.
18:10 and proclaimed, "This is what the L says:
18:11 The L will give you a glorious victory!"
18:13 But Micaiah replied, "As surely as the L lives,
18:15 speak only the truth when you speak for the L?"
18:16 And the L said, 'Their master has been killed.
18:18 Micaiah continued, "Listen to what the L says!
18:18 I saw the L sitting on his throne with all the armies
18:19 And the L said, 'Who can entice King Ahab of
18:20 until finally a spirit approached the L and said,
18:20 can do it!' " 'How will you do this?' the L asked.
18:21 " 'You will succeed,' said the L. 'Go ahead
18:22 the L has put a lying spirit in the mouths of your
18:22 For the L has determined disaster for you."
18:23 "When did the Spirit of the L leave me to speak to
18:27 return safely, the L has not spoken through me!"
18:31 But Jehoshaphat cried out to the L to save him,
19: 2 help the wicked and love those who hate the L?"
19: 4 encouraging the people to return to the L, the God
19: 6 do not judge to please people but to please the L.
19: 7 Fear the L and judge with care, for the L our God
does not tolerate perverted
19: 8 for cases concerning both the law of the L
19: 9 "You must always act in the fear of the L,
19:10 you must warn them not to sin against the L,
19:11 will have final say in all cases concerning the L.
19:11 and may the L be with those who do what is
20: 3 by this news and sought the L for guidance.
20: 4 towns of Judah came to Jerusalem to seek the L.
20: 5 front of the new courtyard at the Temple of the L.
20: 6 He prayed, "O L, God of our ancestors, you alone
20:13 As all the men of Judah stood before the L with
20:14 the Spirit of the L came upon one of the men
20:15 of Judah and Jerusalem! This is what the L says:
20:17 Go out there tomorrow, for the L is with you!"
20:18 and Jerusalem did the same, worshiping the L.
20:19 clans of Kohath and Korah stood to praise the L,
20:20 Believe in the L your God, and you will be able to
20:21 singing to the L and praising him for his holy
20:21 This is what they sang: / "Give thanks to the L;
20:22 the L caused the armies of Ammon, Moab,
20:26 the people praised and thanked the L there.
20:27 full of joy that the L had given them victory over
20:28 and proceeded to the Temple of the L.
20:29 When the surrounding kingdoms heard that the L
20:37 with King Ahaziah, the L will destroy your work."
21: 7 But the L was not willing to destroy David's
21:10 because Jehoram had abandoned the L, the God of
21:12 "This is what the L, the God of your ancestor
21:14 So now the L is about to strike you, your people,
21:16 Then the L stirred up the Philistines and the Arabs,
21:18 It was after this that the L struck Jehoram with the
22: 7 whom the L had appointed to end the dynasty of
22: 9 a man who sought the L with all his heart."
23: 3 The L has promised that a descendant of David
23: 6 Levites on duty may enter the Temple of the L,
23:14 Do not kill her here in the Temple of the L."
23:18 Levitical priests in charge of the Temple of the L,
23:18 them to present burnt offerings to the L,
23:20 people escorted the king from the Temple of the L.
24: 4 decided to repair and restore the Temple of the L.
24: 6 Moses, the servant of the L, levied this tax on the
24: 7 the Temple of the L to worship the images of Baal.
24: 8 set outside the gate leading to the Temple of the L.
24: 9 telling the people to bring to the L the tax that
24:12 and carpenters to restore the Temple of the L.
24:14 used to make utensils for the Temple of the L—
24:14 of the L during the lifetime of Jehoiada the priest.
24:18 They decided to abandon the Temple of the L,
24:19 The L sent prophets to bring them back to him,
24:20 You have abandoned the L, and now he has
24:22 "May the L see what they are doing and hold them
24:24 the L helped them conquer the much larger army
24:24 The people of Judah had abandoned the L, the God
25: 4 for he obeyed the command of the L written in the
25: 7 hire troops from Israel, for the L is not with Israel.
25: 9 "The L is able to give you much more than this!"
25:15 This made the L very angry, and he sent a prophet
25:27 After Amaziah turned away from the L, there was
26: 5 And as long as the king sought the L, God gave
26:15 for the L helped him wonderfully until he became
26:16 He sinned against the L his God by entering the
26:17 went in after him with eighty other priests of the L,
26:18 "It is not for you, Uzziah, to burn incense to the L.
26:18 The L God will not honor you for this!"
26:20 was eager to get out because the L had struck him.
26:21 in isolation, excluded from the Temple of the L.
27: 2 Jotham did not enter the Temple of the L.
27: 6 was careful to live in obedience to the L his God.
28: 1 did not do what was pleasing in the sight of the L,
28: 3 L had driven from the land ahead of the Israelites.
28: 5 That is why the L his God allowed the king of
28: 6 Judah's troops because they had abandoned the L,
28: 9 But a prophet of the L named Oded was there in
28: 9 He went out to meet them and said, "The L,
28:10 What about your own sins against the L your God?
28:19 The L was humbling Judah because of King Ahaz
28:19 to sin and had been utterly unfaithful to the L.
28:22 he became even more unfaithful to the L.
28:25 In this way, he aroused the anger of the L, the God
29: 3 reopened the doors of the Temple of the L
29: 5 Purify yourselves, and purify the Temple of the L,
29: 6 and did what was evil in the sight of the L our
29: 6 They abandoned the L and his Temple; they turned
29:10 But now I will make a covenant with the L,
29:11 The L has chosen you to stand in his presence,
29:15 Then they began to purify the Temple of the L,
29:16 the sanctuary of the Temple of the L to cleanse it,
29:17 Then they purified the Temple of the L itself,
29:18 "We have purified the Temple of the L, the altar
29:19 They are now in front of the altar of the L, purified
29:20 the city officials and went to the Temple of the L.
29:21 to sacrifice the animals on the altar of the L.
29:25 then stationed the Levites at the Temple of the L
29:25 He obeyed all the commands that the L had given
29:27 songs of praise to the L were begun,
29:28 The entire assembly worshiped the L as the singers
29:30 and the officials ordered the Levites to praise the L
29:31 thanksgiving offerings to the Temple of the L."
29:32 The people brought to the L seventy bulls,
29:35 So the Temple of the L was restored to service.
30: 1 He asked everyone to come to the Temple of the L
30: 1 at Jerusalem to celebrate the Passover of the L,
30: 5 to Jerusalem to celebrate the Passover of the L,
30: 6 "O people of Israel, return to the L, the God of
30: 7 your ancestors and relatives who abandoned the L,
30: 8 as they were, but submit yourselves to the L.
30: 8 Worship the L your God so that his fierce anger
30: 9 For if you return to the L, your relatives and your
30: 9 For the L your God is gracious and merciful.
30:12 who were following the word of the L.
30:15 and brought burnt offerings to the Temple of the L.
30:17 lambs for them, to set them apart for the L.
30:18 "May the L, who is good, pardon those
30:19 who decide to follow the L, the God of their
30:20 And the L listened to Hezekiah's prayer
30:21 Each day the Levites and priests sang to the L,
30:22 for the skill they displayed as they served the L.
30:22 and the people confessed their sins to the L,
31: 2 and praise to the L at the gates of the Temple.
31: 3 annual festivals as required in the law of the L.
31: 4 could devote themselves fully to the law of the L.
31: 6 things that had been dedicated to the L their God,
31: 8 they thanked the L and his people Israel!
31:10 plenty to spare, for the L has blessed his people."
31:11 have storerooms prepared in the Temple of the L,
31:14 and the things that had been dedicated to the L.
31:20 and good in the sight of the L his God.
32: 8 We have the L our God to help us and to fight our
32:11 'The L our God will rescue us from the king of
32:16 And Sennacherib's officials further mocked the L
32:17 The king also sent letters scorning the L, the God
32:21 And the L sent an angel who destroyed the
32:22 That is how the L rescued Hezekiah and the people
32:23 and many gifts for the L arrived at Jerusalem,
32:24 He prayed to the L, who healed him and gave him
33: 2 L had driven from the land ahead of the Israelites.
33: 4 He even built pagan altars in the Temple of the L,
33: 4 the place where the L had said his name should be
33: 9 L had destroyed when the Israelites entered the
33:10 The L spoke to Manasseh and his people, but they
33:11 So the L sent the Assyrian armies, and they took
33:12 Manasseh sought the L his God and cried out
33:13 the L listened to him and was moved by his
33:13 So the L let Manasseh return to Jerusalem and to
33:13 Manasseh had finally realized that the L alone is
33:16 Then he restored the altar of the L and sacrificed
33:16 encouraged the people of Judah to worship the L,
33:17 at the pagan shrines, but only to the L their God.
33:18 words the seers spoke to him in the name of the L,
33:23 his father, he did not humble himself before the L.
34: 8 to repair the Temple of the L his God.
34:14 he found the Book of the Law of the L as it had
34:17 Temple of the L has been given to the supervisors
34:21 "Go to the Temple and speak to the L for me
34:21 our ancestors have not obeyed the word of the L.
34:23 She said to them, "The L, the God of Israel,
34:24 'This is what the L says: I will certainly destroy
34:26 go to the king of Judah who sent you to seek the L
34:26 'This is what the L, the God of Israel,
34:27 So I have indeed heard you, says the L.
34:30 And the king went up to the Temple of the L with
34:31 He pledged to obey the L by keeping all his
34:33 and required everyone to worship the L their God.
34:33 they did not turn away from the L, the God of their
35: 1 Then Josiah announced that the Passover of the L
35: 2 them in their work at the Temple of the L.
35: 3 who had been set apart to serve the L and were
35: 3 spend your time serving the L your God and his
35: 6 Follow all the instructions that the L gave through
35:12 so they could offer them to the L according to the
35:16 offerings were sacrificed on the altar of the L,
35:26 done according to the written law of the L,
36: 5 But he did what was evil in the sight of the L his
36: 7 some of the treasures from the Temple of the L,
36:10 Many treasures from the Temple of the L were
36:12 He did what was evil in the sight of the L his God,
36:12 of the prophet Jeremiah, who spoke for the L.
36:13 refusing to turn to the L, the God of Israel.
36:14 desecrating the Temple of the L in Jerusalem.
36:15 The L, the God of their ancestors, repeatedly sent
36:17 So the L brought the king of Babylon against
36:21 So the message of the L spoken through Jeremiah
36:22 the L fulfilled Jeremiah's prophecy by stirring the
36:23 The L, the God of heaven, has given me all the

36:23 for this task. May the **L** your God be with you!"
Ezr 1: 1 the **L** fulfilled Jeremiah's prophecy by stirring the
1: 2 The **L**, the God of heaven, has given me all the
1: 3 Jerusalem in Judah to rebuild this Temple of the **L**,
1: 5 return to Jerusalem to rebuild the Temple of the **L**.
2:63 the **L** about the matter by means of sacred lots.
2:68 When they arrived at the Temple of the **L** in
3: 3 to sacrifice burnt offerings on the altar to the **L**.
3: 5 and the other annual festivals to the **L**.
3: 5 Freewill offerings were also sacrificed to the **L** by
3: 6 had begun to sacrifice burnt offerings to the **L**.
3:10 of Asaph, clashed their cymbals to praise the **L**,
3:11 and thanks, they sang this song to the **L**:
3:11 praising the **L** because the foundation of the
4: 1 that the exiles were rebuilding a Temple to the **L**,
4: 3 We alone will build the Temple for the **L**, the God
6:21 from their immoral customs to worship the **L**,
6:22 because the **L** had changed the attitude of the king
7: 6 the law of Moses, which the **L**, the God of Israel,
7: 6 because the gracious hand of the **L** his God was on
7:10 and obey the law of the **L** and to teach those laws
7:11 taught the commands and laws of the **L** to Israel:
7:27 Praise the **L**, the God of our ancestors, who made
7:27 want to beautify the Temple of the **L** in Jerusalem!
7:28 because the gracious hand of the **L** my God was on
8:28 these treasures have been set apart as holy to the **L**.
8:28 This silver and gold is a freewill offering to the **L**,
8:35 All this was given as a burnt offering to the **L**.
9: 5 fell to my knees, lifted my hands to the **L** my God.
9: 8 for the **L** our God has allowed a few of us to
9:15 O **L**, God of Israel, you are just. We stand before
10:11 Confess your sin to the **L**, the God of your
Ne 1: 5 Then I said, "O **L**, God of heaven, the great
5:13 "Amen," and they praised the **L**.
7:65 the **L** about the matter by means of sacred lots.
8: 1 of Moses, which the **L** had given for Israel to obey.
8: 6 Then Ezra praised the **L**, the great God, and all the
8: 6 and worshiped the **L** with their faces to the ground.
8: 9 For today is a sacred day before the **L** your God."
8:10 and sad, for the joy of the **L** is your strength!"
8:14 they discovered that the **L** had commanded
9: 3 The Book of the Law of the **L** their God was read
9: 3 their sins and worshiping the **L** their God.
9: 4 on the stairs, crying out to the **L** their God.
9: 5 "Stand up and praise the **L** your God, for he lives
9: 6 You alone are the **L**. You made the skies
9: 7 "You are the **L** God, who chose Abram
10:29 laws, and regulations of the **L** their Lord.
10:34 Temple to be burned on the altar of the **L** our God,
Job 1: 6 angels came to present themselves before the **L**,
1: 7 "Where have you come from?" the **L** asked Satan.
1: 7 And Satan answered the **L**, "I have been going
1: 8 Then the **L** asked Satan, "Have you noticed my
1: 9 Satan replied to the **L**, "Yes, Job fears God,
1:12 "All right, you may test him," the **L** said to Satan.
1:21 The **L** gave me everything I had, / and the **L** has taken it away. / Praise the name of the **L**!"
2: 1 came again to present themselves before the **L**,
2: 2 "Where have you come from?" the **L** asked Satan.
2: 2 And Satan answered the **L**, "I have been going
2: 3 Then the **L** asked Satan, "Have you noticed my
2: 4 Satan replied to the **L**, "Skin for skin—he blesses
2: 6 do with him as you please," the **L** said to Satan.
12: 9 They all know that the **L** has done this.
38: 1 Then the **L** answered Job from the whirlwind:
40: 1 Then the **L** said to Job,
40: 3 Then Job replied to the **L**,
40: 6 Then the **L** answered Job from the whirlwind:
42: 1 Then Job replied to the **L**:
42: 7 After the **L** had finished speaking to Job, he said to
42: 9 and Zophar the Naamathite did as the **L**
42: 9 and the **L** accepted Job's prayer.
42:10 prayed for his friends, the **L** restored his fortunes.
42:10 In fact, the **L** gave him twice as much as before!
42:11 because of all the trials the **L** had brought against
42:12 So the **L** blessed Job in the second half of his life
Ps 1: 2 But they delight in doing everything the **L** wants;
1: 6 For the **L** watches over the path of the godly,
2: 2 for battle; / the rulers plot together / against the **L**
2: 6 For the **L** declares, "I have placed my chosen king
2: 7 "The **L** said to me, 'You are my son. / Today I
2:11 Serve the **L** with reverent fear, / and rejoice with
3: 1 O **L**, I have so many enemies; / so many are
3: 3 But you, O **L**, are a shield around me, / my glory,
3: 4 I cried out to the **L**, / and he answered me from his
3: 5 up in safety, / for the **L** was watching over me.
3: 7 Arise, O **L**! / Rescue me, my God! / Slap all my
3: 8 Victory comes from you, O **L**. / May your
4: 3 The **L** has set apart the godly for himself. / The **L** will answer when I call to him.
4: 5 Offer proper sacrifices, / and trust in the **L**.
4: 6 Let the smile of your face shine on us, **L**.
4: 8 and sleep, / for you alone, O **L**, will keep me safe.
5: 1 O **L**, hear me as I pray; / pay attention to my
5: 3 Listen to my voice in the morning, **L**.
5: 6 tell lies. / The **L** detests murderers and deceivers.
5: 8 Lead me in the right path, O **L**, / or my enemies
5:12 For you bless the godly, O **L**, / surrounding them
6: 1 O **L**, do not rebuke me in your anger / or discipline
6: 2 Have compassion on me, **L**, for I am weak. / Heal me, **L**, for my body is in agony.
6: 3 at heart. / How long, O **L**, until you restore me?
6: 4 Return, O **L**, and rescue me. / Save me because of
6: 8 you who do evil, / for the **L** has heard my crying.
6: 9 The **L** has heard my plea; / the **L** will answer my prayer.
7: T which he sang to the **L** concerning Cush of the
7: 1 I come to you for protection, O **L** my God.
7: 3 O **L** my God, if I have done wrong / or am guilty
7: 6 Arise, O **L**, in anger! / Stand up against the fury of
7: 8 The **L** passes judgment on the nations.
7: 8 Declare me righteous, O **L**, / for I am innocent,
7:17 I will thank the **L** because he is just; / I will sing praise to the name of the **L** Most High.
8: 1 O **L**, our Lord, the majesty of your name fills the
8: 9 O **L**, our Lord, the majesty of your name fills the
9: 1 I will thank you, **L**, with all my heart; / I will tell
9: 7 But the **L** reigns forever, / executing judgment
9: 9 The **L** is a shelter for the oppressed, / a refuge in
9:10 for you, O **L**, have never abandoned anyone who
9:11 Sing praises to the **L** who reigns in Jerusalem.
9:13 **L**, have mercy on me. / See how I suffer at the
9:16 The **L** is known for his justice. / The wicked have
9:19 Arise, O **L**! / Do not let mere mortals defy you!
9:20 Make them tremble in fear, O **L**. / Let them know
10: 1 O **L**, why do you stand so far away? / Why do you
10: 3 they praise the greedy and curse the **L**.
10:12 Arise, O **L**! / Punish the wicked, O God! / Do not
10:16 The **L** is king forever and ever! / Let those who
10:17 **L**, you know the hopes of the helpless.
11: 1 I trust in the **L** for protection. / So why do you say
11: 4 But the **L** is in his holy Temple; / the **L** still rules from heaven.
11: 5 The **L** examines both the righteous and the wicked.
11: 7 For the **L** is righteous, and he loves justice.
12: 1 Help, O **L**, for the godly are fast disappearing!
12: 3 May the **L** bring their flattery to an end
12: 5 The **L** replies, "I have seen violence done to the
12: 7 Therefore, **L**, we know you will protect the
13: 1 O **L**, how long will you forget me? Forever?
13: 3 Turn and answer me, O **L** my God!
13: 6 I will sing to the **L** / because he has been so good
14: 2 The **L** looks down from heaven / on the entire
14: 4 they wouldn't think of praying to the **L**.
14: 6 the oppressed, / but the **L** will protect his people.
14: 7 For when the **L** restores his people, / Jacob will
15: 1 Who may worship in your sanctuary, **L**?
15: 4 and honor the faithful followers of the **L**
16: 2 I said to the **L**, "You are my Master!
16: 5 **L**, you alone are my inheritance, my cup of
16: 7 I will bless the **L** who guides me; / even at night
16: 8 I know the **L** is always with me. / I will not be
17: 1 O **L**, hear my plea for justice. / Listen to my cry
17:13 Arise, O **L**! / Stand against them and bring them to
17:14 Save me by your mighty hand, O **L**, / from those
18: T A psalm of David, the servant of the **L**.
18: T He sang this song to the **L** on the day the **L**
18: 1 I love you, **L**; you are my strength.
18: 2 The **L** is my rock, my fortress, and my savior;
18: 3 I will call on the **L**, who is worthy of praise,
18: 6 But in my distress I cried out to the **L**; / yes,
18:13 The **L** thundered from heaven; / the Most High
18:15 Then at your command, O **L**, / at the blast of your
18:18 when I was weakest, / but the **L** upheld me.
18:20 The **L** rewarded me for doing right;
18:21 For I have kept the ways of the **L**; / I have not
18:24 The **L** rewarded me for doing right, / because of
18:28 **L**, you have brought light to my life; / my God,
18:31 For who is God except the **L**? / Who but our God
18:41 They cried to the **L**, but he refused to answer them.
18:46 The **L** lives! Blessed be my rock! / May the God of
18:49 For this, O **L**, I will praise you among the nations;
19: 7 The law of the **L** is perfect, / reviving the soul. / The decrees of the **L** are trustworthy,
19: 8 The commandments of the **L** are right,
19: 8 The commands of the **L** are clear, / giving insight
19: 9 Reverence for the **L** is pure, / lasting forever. / The laws of the **L** are true;
19:14 pleasing to you, / O **L**, my rock and my redeemer.
20: 1 In times of trouble, may the **L** respond to your cry.
20: 5 our God. / May the **L** answer all your prayers.
20: 6 Now I know that the **L** saves his anointed king.
20: 7 and weapons, / but we boast in the **L** our God.
20: 9 Give victory to our king, O **L**! / Respond to our cry
21: 1 How the king rejoices in your strength, O **L**!
21: 7 For the king trusts in the **L**. / The unfailing love of
21: 9 The **L** will consume them in his anger;
21:13 We praise you, **L**, for all your glorious power.
22: 8 "Is this the one who relies on the **L**? / Then let the **L** save him! / If the **L** loves him so much, / let the **L** rescue him!"
22:19 O **L**, do not stay away! / You are my strength;
22:23 Praise the **L**, all you who fear him! / Honor him,
22:26 be satisfied. / All who seek the **L** will praise him.
22:27 The whole earth will acknowledge the **L** and return
22:28 For the **L** is king! / He rules all the nations.
23: 1 The **L** is my shepherd; / I have everything I need.
23: 6 of my life, / and I will live in the house of the **L**
24: 3 Who may climb the mountain of the **L**? / Who may
24: 8 The **L**, strong and mighty, / the **L**, invincible in battle.
24:10 The **L** Almighty— / he is the King of glory.
25: 1 To you, O **L**, I lift up my soul.
25: 4 Show me the path where I should walk, O **L**;
25: 6 Remember, O **L**, your unfailing love
25: 7 of your unfailing love, / for you are merciful, O **L**.
25: 8 The **L** is good and does what is right; / he shows
25:10 The **L** leads with unfailing love and faithfulness
25:11 For the honor of your name, O **L**, / forgive my
25:12 Who are those who fear the **L**? / He will show
25:14 Friendship with the **L** is reserved for those who
25:15 My eyes are always looking to the **L** for help,
26: 1 Declare me innocent, O **L**, / for I have acted with
26: 1 I have trusted in the **L** without wavering.
26: 2 Put me on trial, **L**, and cross-examine me.
26: 6 declare my innocence. / I come to your altar, O **L**,
26: 8 I love your sanctuary, **L**, / the place where your
26:12 taken a stand, / and I will publicly praise the **L**.
27: 1 The **L** is my light and my salvation— / so why
27: 1 The **L** protects me from danger— / so why should
27: 4 The one thing I ask of the **L**— / the thing I seek
27: 4 is to live in the house of the **L** all the days of my
27: 6 of joy, / singing and praising the **L** with music.
27: 7 Listen to my pleading, O **L**. / Be merciful
27: 8 And my heart responds, "**L**, I am coming."
27:10 mother abandon me, / the **L** will hold me close.
27:11 Teach me how to live, O **L**. / Lead me along the
27:14 Wait patiently for the **L**. / Be brave and courageous. / Yes, wait patiently for the **L**.
28: 1 O **L**, you are my rock of safety. / Please help me;
28: 5 They care nothing for what the **L** has done
28: 6 Praise the **L**! / For he has heard my cry for mercy.
28: 7 The **L** is my strength, my shield from every
28: 8 The **L** protects his people / and gives victory to his
29: 1 Give honor to the **L**, you angels; / give honor to the **L** for his glory and strength.
29: 2 Give honor to the **L** for the glory of his name.
29: 2 Worship the **L** in the splendor of his holiness.
29: 3 The voice of the **L** echoes above the sea.
29: 3 The **L** thunders over the mighty sea.
29: 4 The voice of the **L** is powerful; / the voice of the **L** is full of majesty.
29: 5 The voice of the **L** splits the mighty cedars;
29: 5 the **L** shatters the cedars of Lebanon.
29: 7 The voice of the **L** strikes with lightning bolts.
29: 8 The voice of the **L** makes the desert quake; / the **L** shakes the desert of Kadesh.
29: 9 The voice of the **L** twists mighty oaks / and strips
29:10 The **L** rules over the floodwaters. / The **L** reigns as king forever.
29:11 The **L** gives his people strength. / The **L** blesses them with peace.
30: 1 I will praise you, **L**, for you have rescued me.
30: 2 O **L** my God, I cried out to you for help, / and you
30: 3 You brought me up from the grave, O **L**.
30: 4 Sing to the **L**, all you godly ones! / Praise his holy
30: 7 Your favor, O **L**, made me as secure as a
30: 8 I cried out to you, O **L**. / I begged the Lord for
30:10 Hear me, **L**, and have mercy on me. / Help me, O **L**."
30:12 O **L** my God, I will give you thanks forever!
31: 1 O **L**, I have come to you for protection; / don't let
31: 5 Rescue me, **L**, for you are a faithful God.
31: 6 who worship worthless idols. / I trust in the **L**.
31: 9 Have mercy on me, **L**, for I am in distress.
31:14 But I am trusting you, O **L**, / saying, "You are my
31:17 Don't let me be disgraced, O **L**, / for I call out to
31:21 Praise the **L**, / for he has shown me his unfailing
31:22 I had cried out, / "I have been cut off from the **L**!"
31:23 Love the **L**, all you faithful ones! / For the **L** protects those who are loyal to him,
31:24 take courage, / all you who put your hope in the **L**!
32: 2 for those / whose record the **L** has cleared of sin,
32: 5 to myself, "I will confess my rebellion to the **L**."
32: 8 The **L** says, "I will guide you along the best
32:10 but unfailing love surrounds those who trust the **L**.
32:11 So rejoice in the **L** and be glad, all you who obey
33: 1 Let the godly sing with joy to the **L**, / for it is
33: 2 Praise the **L** with melodies on the lyre;
33: 4 For the word of the **L** holds true, / and everything
33: 6 The **L** merely spoke, / and the heavens were
33: 8 Let everyone in the world fear the **L**, / and let
33:10 The **L** shatters the plans of the nations
33:12 What joy for the nation whose God is the **L**,
33:13 The **L** looks down from heaven / and sees the
33:18 But the **L** watches over those who fear him,
33:20 We depend on the **L** alone to save us. / Only he
33:22 Let your unfailing love surround us, **L**, / for our
34: 1 I will praise the **L** at all times. / I will constantly
34: 2 I will boast only in the **L**; / let all who are
34: 4 I prayed to the **L**, and he answered me,
34: 6 I cried out to the **L** in my suffering, and he heard
34: 7 For the angel of the **L** guards all who fear him,
34: 8 Taste and see that the **L** is good. / Oh, the joys of
34:10 but those who trust in the **L** will never lack any
34:11 listen to me, / and I will teach you to fear the **L**.
34:15 The eyes of the **L** watch over those who do right;
34:16 But the **L** turns his face against those who do evil;
34:17 The **L** hears his people when they call to him for
34:18 The **L** is close to the brokenhearted; / he rescues
34:19 but the **L** rescues them from each and every one.
34:20 For the **L** protects them from harm— / not one of
34:22 But the **L** will redeem those who serve him.
35: 1 O **L**, oppose those who oppose me. / Declare war
35: 5 in the wind— / a wind sent by the angel of the **L**.
35: 6 with the angel of the **L** pursuing them.
35: 9 Then I will rejoice in the **L**. / I will be glad
35:10 "**L**, who can compare with you? / Who else
35:22 O **L**, you know all about this. / Do not stay silent.
35:24 "not guilty," O **L** my God, for you give justice.
35:27 Let them continually say, "Great is the **L**,
36: T A psalm of David, the servant of the **L**.
36: 5 Your unfailing love, O **L**, is as vast as the heavens;
36: 6 You care for people and animals alike, O **L**.
37: 3 Trust in the **L** and do good. / Then you will live
37: 4 Take delight in the **L**, / and he will give you your
37: 5 Commit everything you do to the **L**. / Trust him,
37: 7 Be still in the presence of the **L**, / and wait
37: 9 but those who trust in the **L** will possess the land.
37:17 be shattered, / but the **L** takes care of the godly.
37:18 Day by day the **L** takes care of the innocent,

37:22 Those blessed by the **L** will inherit the land,
37:23 The steps of the godly are directed by the **L**.
37:24 will not fall, / for the **L** holds them by the hand.
37:28 For the **L** loves justice, / and he will never abandon
37:33 But the **L** will not let the wicked succeed / or let
37:34 Don't be impatient for the **L** to act!
37:39 The **L** saves the godly; / he is their fortress in times
37:40 The **L** helps them, / rescuing them from the
38: 1 O **L**, don't rebuke me in your anger!
38:15 For I am waiting for you, O **L**. / You must answer
38:21 Do not abandon me, **L**. / Do not stand at a
39: 4 "**L**, remind me how brief my time on earth will be.
39:12 Hear my prayer, O **L**! / Listen to my cries for help!
40: 1 I waited patiently for the **L** to help me, / and he
40: 3 be astounded. / They will put their trust in the **L**.
40: 4 Oh, the joys of those who trust the **L**, / who have
40: 5 O **L** my God, you have done many miracles for us.
40: 9 been afraid to speak out, / as you, O **L**, well know.
40:11 **L**, don't hold back your tender mercies from me.
40:13 Please, **L**, rescue me! / Come quickly, **L**, and help me.
40:16 repeatedly shout, "The **L** is great!"
41: 1 the poor. / The **L** rescues them in times of trouble.
41: 2 The **L** protects them / and keeps them alive.
41: 3 The **L** nurses them when they are sick / and eases
41: 4 "O **L**," I prayed, "have mercy on me. / Heal me,
41:10 **L**, have mercy on me. / Make me well again,
41:13 Bless the **L**, the God of Israel, / who lives forever
42: 8 Through each day the **L** pours his unfailing love
46: 7 The **L** Almighty is here among us; / the God of
46: 8 Come, see the glorious works of the **L**: / See how
46:11 The **L** Almighty is here among us; / the God of
47: 2 For the **L** Most High is awesome. / He is the great
47: 5 The **L** has ascended with trumpets blaring.
48: 1 How great is the **L**, / and how much we should
48: 8 seen it ourselves— / the city of the **L** Almighty.
50: 1 The mighty God, the **L**, has spoken; / he has
54: 6 offering to you; / I will praise your name, O **L**,
55:16 But I will call on God, / and the **L** will rescue me.
55:17 aloud in my distress, / and the **L** hears my voice.
55:22 Give your burdens to the **L**, / and he will take care
56:10 I praise your word. / Yes, **L**, I praise your word.
58: 6 O God! / Smash the jaws of these lions, O **L**!
59: 3 though I have done them no wrong, O **L**.
59: 5 O **L** God Almighty, the God of Israel, / rise up to
59: 8 But **L**, you laugh at them. / You scoff at all the
64:10 The godly will rejoice in the **L** / and find shelter in
68: 4 His name is the **L**— / rejoice in his presence!
68:16 to live, / where the **L** himself will live forever?
68:18 Now the **L** God will live among us here.
68:20 The Sovereign **L** rescues us from death.
68:26 of Israel; / praise the **L**, the source of Israel's life.
69: 6 because of me, / O Sovereign **L** Almighty.
69:10 When I weep and fast before the **L**, / they scoff at
69:13 But I keep right on praying to you, **L**, / hoping this
69:16 Answer my prayers, O **L**, / for your unfailing love
69:31 For this will please the **L** more than sacrificing an
69:33 For the **L** hears the cries of his needy ones;
70: 1 rescue me! / Come quickly, **L**, and help me.
70: 5 are my helper and my savior; / O **L**, do not delay!
71: 1 O **L**, you are my refuge; / never let me be
71: 5 my hope. / I've trusted you, O **L**, from childhood.
71:16 I will praise your mighty deeds, O Sovereign **L**.
72:18 Bless the **L** God, the God of Israel, / who alone
73:28 I have made the Sovereign **L** my shelter,
74:18 See how these enemies scoff at you, **L**. / A foolish
75: 8 For the **L** holds a cup in his hand; / it is full of
76:11 Make vows to the **L** your God, and fulfill them.
77:11 I recall all you have done, O **L**; / I remember your
78: 4 next generation about the glorious deeds of the **L**.
78:21 When the **L** heard them, he was angry. / The fire of
79: 5 O **L**, how long will you be angry with us? Forever?
80: 4 O **L** God Almighty, / how long will you be angry
80:19 Turn us again to yourself, O **L** God Almighty.
81:10 For it was I, the **L** your God, / who rescued you
81:15 Those who hate the **L** would cringe before him;
83:16 until they submit to your name, O **L**.
83:18 until they learn that you alone are called the **L**,
84: 1 lovely is your dwelling place, / O **L** Almighty.
84: 2 I faint with longing / to enter the courts of the **L**.
84: 3 your altar, / O **L** Almighty, my King and my God!
84: 5 Happy are those who are strong in the **L**, / who set
84: 8 O **L** God Almighty, hear my prayer. / Listen,
84:11 For the **L** God is our light and protector. / He gives
84:11 and glory. / No good thing will the **L** withhold
84:12 O **L** Almighty, / happy are those who trust in you.
85: 1 **L**, you have poured out amazing blessings on your
85: 7 Show us your unfailing love, O **L**, / and grant us
85: 8 I listen carefully to what God the **L** is saying,
85:12 Yes, the **L** pours down his blessings. / Our land
86: 1 Bend down, O **L**, and hear my prayer; / answer me,
86: 6 Listen closely to my prayer, O **L**; / hear my urgent
86:11 Teach me your ways, O **L**, / that I may live
86:17 put to shame, / for you, O **L**, help and comfort me.
87: 1 holy mountain stands the city founded by the **L**.
87: 6 When the **L** registers the nations, / he will say,
88: 1 O **L**, God of my salvation, / I have cried out to you
88: 9 by my tears. / Each day I beg for your help, O **L**;
88:13 O **L**, I cry out to you. / I will keep on pleading day
88:14 O **L**, why do you reject me? / Why do you turn
89: 1 I will sing of the tender mercies of the **L** forever!
89: 3 The **L** said, "I have made a solemn agreement
89: 5 All heaven will praise your miracles, **L**;
89: 6 For who in all of heaven can compare with the **L**?
89: 6 What mightiest angel is anything like the **L**?
89: 8 O **L** God Almighty! / Where is there anyone as mighty as you, **L**?
89:15 for they will walk in the light of your presence, **L**.
89:18 Yes, our protection comes from the **L**, / and he,
89:46 O **L**, how long will this go on? / Will you hide
89:51 Your enemies have mocked me, O **L**; / they mock
89:52 Blessed be the **L** forever! / Amen and amen!
90:13 O **L**, come back to us! / How long will you delay?
91: 2 This I declare of the **L**: / He alone is my refuge,
91: 9 If you make the **L** your refuge, / if you make the
91:14 The **L** says, "I will rescue those who love me.
92: 1 It is good to give thanks to the **L**, / to sing praises
92: 4 You thrill me, **L**, with all you have done for me!
92: 5 O **L**, what great miracles you do! / And how deep
92: 8 in the heavens. / You, O **L**, continue forever.
92: 9 Your enemies, **L**, will surely perish; / all evildoers
92:15 They will declare, "The **L** is just! / He is my rock!
93: 1 The **L** is king! He is robed in majesty. / Indeed,
93: 1 the **L** is robed in majesty and armed with strength.
93: 2 Your throne, O **L**, has been established from time
93: 3 The mighty oceans have roared, O **L**. / The mighty
93: 4 on the shore— / the **L** above is mightier than these!
93: 5 The nature of your reign, O **L**, is holiness forever.
94: 1 O **L**, the God to whom vengeance belongs,
94: 3 How long, O **L**? / How long will the wicked be
94: 5 They oppress your people, **L**, / hurting those you
94: 7 "The **L** isn't looking," they say, / "and besides,
94:11 The **L** knows people's thoughts, / that they are
94:12 Happy are those whom you discipline, **L**,
94:14 The **L** will not reject his people; / he will not
94:17 Unless the **L** had helped me, / I would soon have
94:18 and your unfailing love, O **L**, supported me.
94:22 But the **L** is my fortress; / my God is a mighty rock
94:23 for their sins. / The **L** our God will destroy them.
95: 1 Come, let us sing to the **L**! / Let us give a joyous
95: 3 For the **L** is a great God, / the great King above all
95: 6 bow down. / Let us kneel before the **L** our maker,
95: 8 The **L** says, "Don't harden your hearts as Israel
96: 1 Sing a new song to the **L**! / Let the whole earth sing to the **L**!
96: 2 Sing to the **L**; bless his name. / Each day proclaim
96: 4 Great is the **L**! He is most worthy of praise!
96: 5 are merely idols, / but the **L** made the heavens!
96: 7 O nations of the world, recognize the **L**;
96: 7 recognize that the **L** is glorious and strong.
96: 8 Give to the **L** the glory he deserves! / Bring your
96: 9 Worship the **L** in all his holy splendor. / Let all the
96:10 Tell all the nations that the **L** is king. / The world
96:13 before the **L**! / For the **L** is coming!
97: 1 The **L** is king! Let the earth rejoice!
97: 5 The mountains melt like wax before the **L**,
97: 8 of Judah are glad / because of your justice, **L**!
97: 9 For you, O **L**, are most high over all the earth;
97:10 You who love the **L**, hate evil! / He protects the
97:12 May all who are godly be happy in the **L**
98: 1 Sing a new song to the **L**, / for he has done
98: 2 The **L** has announced his victory / and has revealed
98: 4 Shout to the **L**, all the earth; / break out in praise
98: 5 Sing your praise to the **L** with the harp,
98: 6 Make a joyful symphony before the **L**, the King!
98: 9 before the **L**. / For the **L** is coming to judge the earth.
99: 1 The **L** is king! / Let the nations tremble! / He sits
99: 2 The **L** sits in majesty in Jerusalem,
99: 5 Exalt the **L** our God! / Bow low before his feet,
99: 6 They cried to the **L** for help, / and he answered
99: 8 O **L** our God, you answered them. / You were a
99: 9 Exalt the **L** our God / and worship at his holy mountain in Jerusalem, / for the **L** our God is holy!
100: 1 Shout with joy to the **L**, O earth!
100: 2 Worship the **L** with gladness. / Come before him,
100: 3 Acknowledge that the **L** is God! / He made us,
100: 5 For the **L** is good. / His unfailing love continues
101: 1 and justice. / I will praise you, **L**, with songs.
101: 8 and free the city of the **L** from their grip.
102: T with trouble, pouring out problems before the **L**.
102: 1 **L**, hear my prayer! / Listen to my plea!
102:12 But you, O **L**, will rule forever. / Your fame will
102:15 And the nations will tremble before the **L**.
102:16 For the **L** will rebuild Jerusalem. / He will appear
102:18 so that a nation yet to be created will praise the **L**.
102:19 Tell them the **L** looked down / from his heavenly
102:22 and kingdoms come to worship the **L**.
103: 1 Praise the **L**, I tell myself; / with my whole heart,
103: 2 Praise the **L**, I tell myself, / and never forget the
103: 6 The **L** gives righteousness / and justice to all who
103: 8 The **L** is merciful and gracious; / he is slow to get
103:13 The **L** is like a father to his children, / tender
103:17 But the love of the **L** remains forever / with those
103:19 The **L** has made the heavens his throne;
103:20 Praise the **L**, you angels of his, / you mighty
103:21 Yes, praise the **L**, you armies of angels / who serve
103:22 Praise the **L**, everything he has created,
103:22 his kingdom. / As for me—I, too, will praise the **L**.
104: 1 Praise the **L**, I tell myself; / O **L** my God, how great you are!
104:16 The trees of the **L** are well cared for— / the cedars
104:24 O **L**, what a variety of things you have made!
104:31 May the glory of the **L** last forever! / The **L** rejoices in all he has made!
104:33 I will sing to the **L** as long as I live. / I will praise
104:34 these thoughts about him, / for I rejoice in the **L**.
104:35 As for me—I will praise the **L**! / Praise the **L**!
105: 1 Give thanks to the **L** and proclaim his greatness.
105: 3 in his holy name; / O worshipers of the **L**, rejoice!
105: 4 Search for the **L** and for his strength, / and keep on
105: 7 He is the **L** our God. / His rule is seen throughout
105:19 fulfill his word, / the **L** tested Joseph's character.
105:24 And the **L** multiplied the people of Israel
105:26 But the **L** sent Moses his servant, / along with
105:28 The **L** blanketed Egypt in darkness, / for they had
105:39 The **L** spread out a cloud above them as a covering
105:45 his principles / and obey his laws. / Praise the **L**!
106: 1 Praise the **L**! / Give thanks to the **L**, for he is good!
106: 2 Who can list the glorious miracles of the **L**?
106: 4 Remember me, too, **L**, when you show favor to
106:23 chosen one, stepped between the **L** and the people.
106:25 grumbled in their tents / and refused to obey the **L**.
106:29 They angered the **L** with all these things, / so a
106:32 At Meribah, too, they angered the **L**,
106:34 the nations in the land, / as the **L** had told them to.
106:47 O **L** our God, save us! / Gather us back from
106:48 Blessed be the **L**, the God of Israel,
106:48 Let all the people say, "Amen!" / Praise the **L**!
107: 1 Give thanks to the **L**, for he is good! / His faithful
107: 2 Has the **L** redeemed you? Then speak out!
107: 6 "**L**, help!" they cried in their trouble, / and he
107: 8 Let them praise the **L** for his great love / and for all
107:13 "**L**, help!" they cried in their trouble, / and he
107:15 Let them praise the **L** for his great love / and for all
107:19 "**L**, help!" they cried in their trouble, / and he
107:21 Let them praise the **L** for his great love / and for all
107:28 "**L**, help!" they cried in their trouble, / and he
107:31 Let them praise the **L** for his great love / and for all
107:40 the **L** pours contempt on their princes,
107:43 will see in our history the faithful love of the **L**.
108: 3 I will thank you, **L**, in front of all the people.
109:14 May the **L** never forget the sins of his ancestors;
109:15 May these sins always remain before the **L**,
109:21 But deal well with me, O Sovereign **L**,
109:26 Help me, O **L** my God! / Save me because of your
109:27 is your doing, / that you yourself have done it, **L**.
109:30 But I will give repeated thanks to the **L**,
110: 1 The **L** said to my Lord, / "Sit in honor at my right
110: 2 The **L** will extend your powerful dominion from
110: 4 The **L** has taken an oath and will not break his
111: 1 Praise the **L**! / I will thank the **L** with all my heart
111: 2 How amazing are the deeds of our **L**! / All who
111: 4 How gracious and merciful is our **L**!
111:10 Reverence for the **L** is the foundation of true
112: 1 Praise the **L**! / Happy are those who fear the **L**. / Yes, happy are
112: 7 they confidently trust the **L** to care for them.
113: 1 Praise the **L**! / Yes, give praise, O servants of the **L**. / Praise the name of the **L**!
113: 2 Blessed be the name of the **L** / forever and ever.
113: 3 from east to west— / praise the name of the **L**.
113: 4 For the **L** is high above the nations; / his glory is
113: 5 Who can be compared with the **L** our God,
113: 9 that she becomes a happy mother. / Praise the **L**!
115: 1 Not to us, O **L**, but to you goes all the glory
115: 9 O Israel, trust the **L**! / He is your helper; he is your
115:10 O priests of Aaron, trust the **L**! / He is your helper;
115:11 All you who fear the **L**, trust the **L**!
115:12 The **L** remembers us, / and he will surely bless us.
115:13 He will bless those who fear the **L**, / both great
115:14 May the **L** richly bless / both you and your
115:15 May you be blessed by the **L**, / who made heaven
115:16 The heavens belong to the **L**, / but he has given the
115:17 The dead cannot sing praises to the **L**, / for they
115:18 But we can praise the **L** / both now and forever! / Praise the **L**!
116: 1 I love the **L** because he hears / and answers my
116: 4 Then I called on the name of the **L**: / "Please, **L**, save me!"
116: 5 How kind the **L** is! How good he is! / So merciful,
116: 6 The **L** protects those of childlike faith; / I was
116: 7 I can rest again, / for the **L** has been so good to me.
116:10 in you, so I prayed, / "I am deeply troubled, **L**."
116:12 What can I offer the **L** / for all he has done for me?
116:14 I will keep my promises to the **L** / in the presence
116:16 O **L**, I am your servant; / yes, I am your servant,
116:17 of thanksgiving / and call on the name of the **L**.
116:18 I will keep my promises to the **L** / in the presence
116:19 in the house of the **L**, / in the heart of Jerusalem. / Praise the **L**!
117: 1 Praise the **L**, all you nations. / Praise him, all you
117: 2 the faithfulness of the **L** endures forever. / Praise the **L**!
118: 1 Give thanks to the **L**, for he is good! / His faithful
118: 4 Let all who fear the **L** repeat: / "His faithful love
118: 5 In my distress I prayed to the **L**, / and the **L** answered me and rescued me.
118: 6 The **L** is for me, so I will not be afraid. / What can
118: 7 Yes, the **L** is for me; he will help me. / I will look
118: 8 It is better to trust the **L** / than to put confidence in
118: 9 It is better to trust the **L** / than to put confidence in
118:10 I destroyed them all in the name of the **L**.
118:11 but I destroyed them all in the name of the **L**.
118:12 But I destroyed them all in the name of the **L**.
118:13 to kill me, O my enemy, / but the **L** helped me.
118:14 The **L** is my strength and my song; / he has
118:15 The strong right arm of the **L** has done glorious
118:16 The strong right arm of the **L** is raised in triumph.
118:16 The strong right arm of the **L** has done glorious
118:17 not die, but I will live / to tell what the **L** has done.
118:18 The **L** has punished me severely, / but he has not
118:19 righteous enter, / and I will go in and thank the **L**.
118:20 Those gates lead to the presence of the **L**,
118:24 This is the day the **L** has made. / We will rejoice
118:25 Please, **L**, please save us. / Please, **L**, please give us success.
118:26 Bless the one who comes in the name of the **L**.
118:26 We bless you from the house of the **L**.
118:27 The **L** is God, shining upon us. / Bring forward the
118:29 Give thanks to the **L**, for he is good! / His faithful

119: 1 people of integrity, / who follow the law of the **L**.
119:12 Blessed are you, O **L**; / teach me your principles.
119:31 to your decrees. / **L**, don't let me be put to shame!
119:33 Teach me, O **L**, / to follow every one of your
119:41 **L**, give to me your unfailing love, / the salvation
119:52 on your age-old laws; / O **L**, they comfort me.
119:55 I reflect at night on who you are, O **L**, / and I obey
119:57 **L**, you are mine! / I promise to obey your words!
119:64 O **L**, the earth is full of your unfailing love;
119:65 You have done many good things for me, **L**,
119:75 I know, O **L**, that your decisions are fair;
119:89 Forever, O **L**, / your word stands firm in heaven.
119:107 I have suffered much, O **L**; / restore my life again,
119:108 **L**, accept my grateful thanks / and teach me your
119:116 **L**, sustain me as you promised, that I may live!
119:126 **L**, it is time for you to act, / for these evil people
119:137 O **L**, you are righteous, / and your decisions are
119:145 I pray with all my heart; answer me, **L**! / I will
119:149 In your faithful love, O **L**, hear my cry; / in your
119:151 But you are near, O **L**, / and all your commands
119:156 **L**, how great is your mercy; / in your justice,
119:159 See how I love your commandments, **L**.
119:166 I long for your salvation, **L**, / so I have obeyed
119:169 O **L**, listen to my cry; / give me the discerning
119:174 O **L**, I have longed for your salvation, / and your
120: 1 I took my troubles to the **L**; / I cried out to him,
120: 2 Rescue me, O **L**, from liars / and from all deceitful
121: 2 My help comes from the **L**, / who made the
121: 5 The **L** himself watches over you! / The **L** stands
beside you as your protective shade.
121: 7 The **L** keeps you from all evil / and preserves your
121: 8 The **L** keeps watch over you as you come and go,
122: 1 said to me, / "Let us go to the house of the **L**."
122: 4 They come to give thanks to the name of the **L**
122: 9 For the sake of the house of the **L** our God,
123: 2 We look to the **L** our God for his mercy, / just as
123: 3 Have mercy on us, **L**, have mercy, / for we have
124: 1 If the **L** had not been on our side— / let Israel now
124: 2 if the **L** had not been on our side / when people
124: 6 Blessed be the **L**, / who did not let their teeth tear
124: 8 Our help is from the **L**, / who made the heavens
125: 1 Those who trust in the **L** are as secure as Mount
125: 2 so the **L** surrounds and protects his people,
125: 4 O **L**, do good to those who are good,
125: 5 But banish those who turn to crooked ways, O **L**.
126: 1 When the **L** restored his exiles to Jerusalem,
126: 2 "What amazing things the **L** has done for them."
126: 3 Yes, the **L** has done amazing things for us!
126: 4 Restore our fortunes, **L**, / as streams renew the
127: 1 Unless the **L** builds a house, / the work of the
builders is useless. / Unless the **L** protects a city,
127: 3 Children are a gift from the **L**; / they are a reward
128: 1 How happy are those who fear the **L**— / all who
128: 5 May the **L** continually bless you from Zion.
129: 4 But the **L** is good; / he has cut the cords used by
130: 1 From the depths of despair, O **L**, / I call for your
130: 3 **L**, if you kept a record of our sins, / who, O Lord,
130: 5 I am counting on the **L**; / yes, I am counting on
130: 7 O Israel, hope in the **L**; / for with the **L** there is
unfailing love
131: 1 **L**, my heart is not proud; / my eyes are not
131: 3 O Israel, put your hope in the **L**— / now
132: 1 **L**, remember David / and all that he suffered.
132: 2 He took an oath before the **L**. / He vowed to the
132: 5 until I find a place to build a house for the **L**,
132: 7 Let us go to the dwelling place of the **L**; / let us
132: 8 Arise, O **L**, and enter your sanctuary, / along with
132:11 The **L** swore to David / a promise he will never
132:13 For the **L** has chosen Jerusalem; / he has desired it
133: 3 And the **L** has pronounced his blessing, / even life
134: 1 Oh, bless the **L**, all you servants of the **L**,
134: 1 serve as night watchmen in the house of the **L**.
134: 2 Lift your hands in holiness, / and bless the **L**.
134: 3 May the **L**, who made heaven and earth,
135: 1 Praise the **L**! / Praise the name of the **L**! / Praise
him, you who serve the **L**,
135: 2 you who serve in the house of the **L**, / in the courts
135: 3 Praise the **L**, for the **L** is good;
135: 4 For the **L** has chosen Jacob for himself, / Israel for
135: 5 I know the greatness of the **L**— / that our Lord is
135: 6 The **L** does whatever pleases him / throughout all
135:13 Your name, O **L**, endures forever; / your fame, O
L, is known to every generation.
135:14 For the **L** will vindicate his people / and have
135:19 O Israel, praise the **L**! / O priests of Aaron, praise
the **L**!
135:20 O Levites, praise the **L**! / All you who fear the **L**,
praise the **L**!
135:21 The **L** be praised from Zion, / for he lives here in
Jerusalem. / Praise the **L**!
136: 1 Give thanks to the **L**, for he is good! / His faithful
137: 4 But how can we sing the songs of the **L** / while in a
137: 7 O **L**, remember what the Edomites did / on the day
138: 1 I give you thanks, O **L**, with all my heart; / I will
138: 4 king in all the earth will give you thanks, O **L**,
138: 5 for the glory of the **L** is very great.
138: 6 Though the **L** is great, he cares for the humble,
138: 8 The **L** will work out his plans for my life—
138: 8 for your faithful love, O **L**, endures forever.
139: 1 O **L**, you have examined my heart / and know
139: 4 what I am going to say, / even before I say it, **L**.
139:21 O **L**, shouldn't I hate those who hate you?
140: 1 O **L**, rescue me from evil people. / Preserve me
140: 4 O **L**, keep me out of the hands of the wicked.
140: 6 I said to the **L**, "You are my God!" / Listen, O **L**,
to my cries for mercy!
140: 7 O Sovereign **L**, my strong savior, / you protected
140: 8 **L**, do not give in to their evil desires. / Do not let
140:12 But I know the **L** will surely help those they
141: 1 O **L**, I am calling to you. Please hurry!
141: 3 Take control of what I say, O **L**, / and keep my lips
141: 8 I look to you for help, O Sovereign **L**. / You are
142: 1 I cry out to the **L**; / I plead for the LORD's
142: 5 Then I pray to you, O **L**. / I say, "You are my
143: 1 Hear my prayer, O **L**; / listen to my plea!
143: 7 Come quickly, **L**, and answer me, / for my
143: 9 Save me from my enemies, **L**; / I run to you to hide
143:11 For the glory of your name, O **L**, save me.
144: 1 Bless the **L**, who is my rock. / He gives me
144: 3 O **L**, what are mortals that you should notice us,
144: 5 Bend down the heavens, **L**, and come down.
144:15 Happy indeed are those whose God is the **L**.
145: 3 Great is the **L**! He is most worthy of praise!
145: 8 The **L** is kind and merciful, / slow to get angry,
145: 9 The **L** is good to everyone. / He showers
145:10 All of your works will thank you, **L**, / and your
145:13 The **L** is faithful in all he says; / he is gracious in
145:14 The **L** helps the fallen / and lifts up those bent
145:17 The **L** is righteous in everything he does; / he is
145:18 The **L** is close to all who call on him, / yes, to all
145:20 The **L** protects all those who love him, / but he
145:21 I will praise the **L**, / and everyone on earth will
146: 1 Praise the **L**! / Praise the **L**, I tell myself.
146: 2 I will praise the **L** as long as I live. / I will sing
146: 5 as their helper, / whose hope is in the **L** their God.
146: 7 and food to the hungry. / The **L** frees the prisoners.
146: 8 The **L** opens the eyes of the blind. / The **L** lifts the
burdens of those bent beneath their loads. / The **L**
loves the righteous.
146: 9 The **L** protects the foreigners among us. / He cares
146:10 The **L** will reign forever. / O Jerusalem, your God
is King in every generation! / Praise the **L**!
147: 1 Praise the **L**! / How good it is to sing praises to our
147: 2 The **L** is rebuilding Jerusalem / and bringing the
147: 6 The **L** supports the humble, / but he brings the
147: 7 Sing out your thanks to the **L**; / sing praises to our
147:12 Praise the **L**, O Jerusalem! / Praise your God,
147:20 they do not know his laws. / Praise the **L**!
148: 1 Praise the **L**! / Praise the **L** from the heavens!
148: 5 Let every created thing give praise to the **L**,
148: 7 Praise the **L** from the earth, / you creatures of the
148:13 Let them all praise the name of the **L**. / For his
148:14 of Israel who are close to him. / Praise the **L**!
149: 1 Praise the **L**! / Sing to the **L** a new song.
149: 4 For the **L** delights in his people; / he crowns the
149: 9 This is the glory of his faithful ones. / Praise the **L**!
150: 1 Praise the **L**! / Praise God in his heavenly
150: 6 Let everything that lives sing praises to the **L**! /
Praise the **L**!
Pr 1: 7 Fear of the **L** is the beginning of knowledge.
1:29 they hated knowledge and chose not to fear the **L**.
2: 5 you will understand what it means to fear the **L**,
2: 6 For the **L** grants wisdom! From his mouth come
3: 5 Trust in the **L** with all your heart; do not depend on
3: 7 Instead, fear the **L** and turn your back on evil.
3: 9 Honor the **L** with your wealth and with the best
3:11 don't ignore it when the **L** disciplines you,
3:12 For the **L** corrects those he loves, just as a father
3:19 By wisdom the **L** founded the earth;
3:26 for the **L** is your security. He will keep your foot
3:32 Such wicked people are an abomination to the **L**,
3:33 The curse of the **L** is on the house of the wicked,
3:34 The **L** mocks at mockers, but he shows favor to the
5:21 For the **L** sees clearly what a man does,
6:16 There are six things the **L** hates—no, seven things
8:13 All who fear the **L** will hate evil. That is why I
8:22 "The **L** formed me from the beginning, before he
8:35 finds me finds life and wins approval from the **L**.
9:10 Fear of the **L** is the beginning of wisdom.
10: 3 The **L** will not let the godly starve to death, but he
10:22 The blessing of the **L** makes a person rich, and he
10:27 Fear of the **L** lengthens one's life, but the years of
10:29 The **L** protects the upright but destroys the wicked.
11: 1 The **L** hates cheating, but he delights in honesty.
11:20 The **L** hates people with twisted hearts, but he
12: 2 The **L** approves of those who are good, but he
12:22 The **L** hates those who don't keep their word,
14: 2 Those who follow the right path fear the **L**;
14:26 Those who fear the **L** are secure; he will be a place
14:27 Fear of the **L** is a life-giving fountain; it offers
15: 3 The **L** is watching everywhere, keeping his eye on
15: 8 The **L** hates the sacrifice of the wicked, but he
15: 9 The **L** despises the way of the wicked, but he loves
15:11 of Death and Destruction are known by the **L**.
15:16 It is better to have little with fear for the **L** than to
15:25 The **L** destroys the house of the proud, but he
15:26 The **L** despises the thoughts of the wicked, but he
15:29 The **L** is far from the wicked, but he hears the
15:33 Fear of the **L** teaches a person to be wise;
16: 1 our thoughts, but the **L** gives the right answer.
16: 2 their own eyes, but the **L** examines their motives.
16: 3 Commit your work to the **L**, and then your plans
16: 4 The **L** has made everything for his own purposes,
16: 5 The **L** despises pride; be assured that the proud
16: 6 cover sin; evil is avoided by fear of the **L**.
16: 7 When the ways of people please the **L**, he makes
16: 9 make our plans, but the **L** determines our steps.
16:11 The **L** demands fairness in every business deal;
16:20 will prosper; those who trust the **L** will be happy.
16:33 throw the dice, but the **L** determines how they fall.
17: 3 purity of silver and gold, but the **L** tests the heart.
17:15 The **L** despises those who acquit the guilty
18:10 The name of the **L** is a strong fortress; the godly
18:22 wife finds a treasure and receives favor from the **L**.
19: 3 their own foolishness and then are angry at the **L**.
19:14 but only the **L** can give an understanding wife.
19:17 If you help the poor, you are lending to the **L**—
19:23 Fear of the **L** gives life, security, and protection
20:10 The **L** despises double standards of every kind.
20:12 to hear and eyes to see—both are gifts from the **L**.
20:22 this wrong." Wait for the **L** to handle the matter.
20:23 The **L** despises double standards; he is not pleased
20:24 road we travel? It is the **L** who directs our steps.
21: 1 heart is like a stream of water directed by the **L**;
21: 2 doing what is right, but the **L** examines the heart.
21: 3 The **L** is more pleased when we do what is just
21:30 or well advised, cannot stand against the **L**.
21:31 for battle, but the victory belongs to the **L**.
22: 2 poor have this in common: The **L** made them both.
22: 4 True humility and fear of the **L** lead to riches,
22:12 The **L** preserves knowledge, but he ruins the plans
22:19 you today—yes, you—so you will trust in the **L**.
22:23 For the **L** is their defender. He will injure anyone
23:17 envy sinners, but always continue to fear the **L**.
24:18 For the **L** will be displeased with you and will turn
24:21 My child, fear the **L** and the king, and don't
24:22 Who knows where the punishment from the **L**
25:22 coals on their heads, and the **L** will reward you.
28: 5 but those who follow the **L** understand completely.
28:25 causes fighting; trusting the **L** leads to prosperity.
29:13 in common—the **L** gives light to the eyes of both.
29:25 is a dangerous trap, but to trust the **L** means safety.
29:26 the ruler's favor, but justice comes from the **L**.
30: 9 I may deny you and say, "Who is the **L**?"
31:30 but a woman who fears the **L** will be greatly
Isa 1: 2 Listen, O earth! This is what the **L** says:
1: 4 corrupt children who have turned away from the **L**.
1: 9 If the **L** Almighty had not spared a few of us,
1:10 Listen to the **L**, you leaders of Israel! Listen to the
1:11 "I am sick of your sacrifices," says the **L**.
1:18 "Come now, let us argue this out," says the **L**.
1:20 by your enemies. I, the **L**, have spoken!"
1:24 Therefore, the Lord, the **L** Almighty, the Mighty
1:27 Because the **L** is just and righteous, the repentant
1:28 for they refuse to come to the **L**.
2: 2 the Temple of the **L** in Jerusalem will become the
2: 3 "Come, let us go up to the mountain of the **L**,
2: 4 The **L** will settle international disputes.
2: 5 people of Israel, let us walk in the light of the **L**!
2: 6 The **L** has rejected the people of Israel
2: 9 The **L** cannot simply ignore their sins!
2:10 Hide from the terror of the **L** and the glory of his
2:11 be brought low and the **L** alone will be exalted.
2:12 In that day the **L** Almighty will punish the proud,
2:17 will lie in the dust. The **L** alone will be exalted!
2:19 When the **L** rises to shake the earth, his enemies
2:19 hide in caves in the rocks from the terror of the **L**
2:21 they will try to escape the terror of the **L**
3: 1 The Lord, the **L** Almighty, will cut off the supplies
3: 8 because they speak out against the **L** and refuse to
3:13 The **L** takes his place in court. He is the great
3:15 like that!" demands the Lord, the **L** Almighty.
3:16 Next the **L** will judge the women of Jerusalem,
3:17 Yes, the **L** will make them bald for all to see!
4: 2 But in the future, Israel—the branch of the **L**—
4: 5 Then the **L** will provide shade for Jerusalem
5: 7 They are the vineyard of the **L** Almighty.
5: 9 But the **L** Almighty has sealed your awful fate.
5:12 But you never think about the **L** or notice what he
5:16 But the **L** Almighty is exalted by his justice.
5:24 for they have rejected the law of the **L** Almighty.
5:25 That is why the anger of the **L** burns against his
6: 3 they sang, "Holy, holy, holy is the **L** Almighty!
6: 5 Yet I have seen the King, the **L** Almighty!"
6:12 Do not stop until the **L** has sent everyone away to
7: 3 Then the **L** said to Isaiah, "Go out to meet King
7: 7 "But this is what the Sovereign **L** says:
7:10 after this, the **L** sent this message to King Ahaz:
7:12 "No," he said, "I wouldn't test the **L** like that."
7:17 "The **L** will bring a terrible curse on you,
7:18 In that day the **L** will whistle for the army of
8: 1 Again the **L** said to me, "Make a large signboard
8: 3 And the **L** said, "Call him Maher-shalal-hash-baz.
8: 5 Then the **L** spoke to me again and said,
8:11 The **L** has said to me in the strongest terms:
8:13 Do not fear anything except the **L** Almighty.
8:16 these things as a testimony of what the **L** will do.
8:17 I will wait for the **L** to help us, though he has
8:18 and the children the **L** has given me have names
8:18 reveal the plans the **L** Almighty has for his people.
8:20 predictions against my testimony," says the **L**.
9: 7 The passionate commitment of the **L** Almighty
9:11 The **L** will reply to their bragging by bringing
9:13 will still not repent and turn to the **L** Almighty.
9:14 the **L** will destroy both the head and the tail,
9:19 The land is blackened by the fury of the **L**
10:16 of all your evil boasting, the Lord, the **L** Almighty,
10:17 The **L**, the Light of Israel and the Holy One,
10:18 The **L** will completely destroy Assyria's warriors,
10:20 at last those left in Israel and Judah will trust the **L**,
10:22 The **L** has rightly decided to destroy his people.
10:23 Yes, the Lord, the **L** Almighty, has already decided
10:24 So this is what the Lord, the **L** Almighty, says:
10:26 The **L** Almighty will beat them with his whip,
10:27 In that day the **L** will end the bondage of his
10:33 The Lord, the **L** Almighty, will chop down the
11: 2 And the Spirit of the **L** will rest on him—the Spirit
of knowledge and the fear of the **L**.
11: 3 He will delight in obeying the **L**. He will never
11: 9 earth will be filled with people who know the **L**.
11:15 The **L** will make a dry path through the Red Sea.

12: 1 "Praise the **L**! / He was angry with me, / but now
12: 2 The **L** GOD is my strength and my song;
12: 4 "Thank the **L**! / Praise his name! / Tell the world
12: 5 Sing to the **L**, / for he has done wonderful things.
13: 3 I, the **L**, have assigned this task to these armies,
13: 4 The **L** Almighty has brought them here to form an
13: 9 For see, the day of the **L** is coming—the terrible
13: 11 "I, the **L**, will punish the world for its evil
13: 13 I, the **L** Almighty, will show my fury and fierce
14: 1 But the **L** will have mercy on the descendants of
14: 3 In that wonderful day when the **L** gives his people
14: 5 For the **L** has crushed your wicked power
14: 22 This is what the **L** Almighty says: "I, myself,
14: 23 of destruction. I, the **L** Almighty, have spoken!"
14: 24 The **L** Almighty has sworn this oath: "It will all
14: 27 The **L** Almighty has spoken—who can change his
14: 32 Tell them that the **L** has built Jerusalem, and that
16: 13 The **L** has already said this about Moab in the past.
16: 14 But now the **L** says, "Within three years,
17: 3 of Israel's departed glory," says the **L** Almighty.
17: 6 bare of people," says the **L**, the God of Israel.
18: 4 For the **L** has told me this: "I will watch quietly
18: 5 the **L** will cut you off as though with pruning
18: 7 But the time will come when the **L** Almighty will
18: 7 They will bring the gifts to the **L** Almighty in
19: 1 The **L** is advancing against Egypt, riding on a swift
19: 4 to a fierce king," says the Lord, the **L** Almighty.
19: 12 let them tell you what the **L** Almighty is going to
19: 14 The **L** has sent a spirit of foolishness on them,
19: 16 in fear beneath the upraised fist of the **L** Almighty.
19: 17 for the **L** Almighty has laid out his plans against
19: 18 In that day five of Egypt's cities will follow the **L**
19: 19 In that day there will be an altar to the **L** in the
19: 19 and there will be a monument to the **L** at its
19: 20 and a witness to the **L** Almighty in the land of
19: 20 When the people cry to the **L** for help against those
19: 21 In that day the **L** will make himself known to the
19: 21 they will know the **L** and will give their sacrifices
19: 21 They will make promises to the **L** and keep them.
19: 22 The **L** will strike Egypt in a way that will bring
19: 22 For the Egyptians will turn to the **L**, and he will
19: 25 For the **L** Almighty will say, "Blessed be Egypt,
20: 2 the **L** told Isaiah son of Amoz, "Take off all your
20: 3 Then the **L** said, "My servant Isaiah has been
21: 10 I have told you everything the **L** Almighty,
21: 17 I, the **L**, the God of Israel, have spoken!"
22: 5 of confusion and terror the Lord, the **L** Almighty,
22: 12 The Lord, the **L** Almighty, called you to weep
22: 14 The **L** Almighty has revealed to me that this sin
22: 14 That is the judgment of the Lord, the **L** Almighty.
22: 15 Furthermore, the Lord, the **L** Almighty, told me to
22: 17 For the **L** is about to seize you and hurl you away.
22: 19 "Yes, I will drive you out of office," says the **L**.
22: 25 The **L** Almighty says: "When that time comes,
22: 25 it supports will fall with it. I, the **L**, have spoken!"
23: 9 The **L** Almighty has done it to destroy your pride
23: 11 The **L** holds out his hand over the seas. He shakes
23: 17 Yes, after seventy years the **L** will revive Tyre.
23: 18 end her businesses will give their profits to the **L**.
24: 1 The **L** is about to destroy the earth and make it a
24: 3 completely emptied and looted. The **L** has spoken!
24: 15 In eastern lands, give glory to the **L**.
24: 15 the sea, praise the name of the **L**, the God of Israel.
24: 16 Listen to them as they sing to the **L** from the ends
24: 21 In that day the **L** will punish the fallen angels in
24: 23 Then the **L** Almighty will mount his throne on
25: 1 O **L**, I will honor and praise your name, for you are
25: 4 But to the poor, O **L**, you are a refuge from the
25: 6 the **L** Almighty will spread a wonderful feast for
25: 8 The Sovereign **L** will wipe away all tears. He will
25: 8 against his land and people. The **L** has spoken!
25: 9 and he saved us. This is the **L**, in whom we trusted.
26: 4 Trust in the **L** always, / for the **L** GOD is the
eternal Rock.
26: 8 **L**, we love to obey your laws; / our heart's desire
26: 11 O **L**, they do not listen when you threaten.
26: 12 **L**, you will grant us peace, / for all we have
26: 13 O **L** our God, others have ruled us, / but we
26: 15 We praise you, **L**! / You have made our nation
26: 16 **L**, in distress we searched for you. / We were
26: 17 out in pain. / When we are in your presence, **L**,
26: 21 The **L** is coming from heaven to punish the people
27: 1 In that day the **L** will take his terrible, swift sword
27: 3 I, the **L**, will watch over it and tend its fruitful
27: 7 Has the **L** punished Israel in the same way he has
27: 9 The **L** did this to purge away Israel's sin. When he
27: 12 Yet the time will come when the **L** will gather
27: 13 Jerusalem to worship the **L** on his holy mountain.
28: 5 Then at last the **L** Almighty will himself be Israel's
28: 9 They say, "Who does the **L** think we are?
28: 13 So the **L** will spell out his message for them again,
28: 14 Therefore, listen to this message from the **L**,
28: 16 Therefore, this is what the Sovereign **L** says:
28: 21 The **L** will come suddenly and in anger, as he did
28: 22 For the Lord, the **L** Almighty, has plainly told me
28: 29 The **L** Almighty is a wonderful teacher, and he
29: 6 In an instant, I, the **L** Almighty, will come against
29: 10 For the **L** has poured out on you a spirit of deep
29: 15 for those who try to hide their plans from the **L**,
29: 15 "The **L** can't see us," you say to yourselves.
29: 19 humble will be filled with fresh joy from the **L**.
29: 22 That is why the **L**, who redeemed Abraham,
30: 1 is certain for my rebellious children," says the **L**.
30: 15 The Sovereign **L**, the Holy One of Israel, says,
30: 18 But the **L** still waits for you to come to him so he
30: 18 and compassion. For the **L** is a faithful God.
30: 23 Then the **L** will bless you with rain at planting
30: 26 So it will be when the **L** begins to heal his people
30: 27 The **L** is coming from far away, burning with
30: 29 the mountain of the **L**—to the Rock of Israel.
30: 30 And the **L** will make his majestic voice heard.
30: 32 And as the **L** strikes them, his people will keep
30: 33 The breath of the **L**, like fire from a volcano,
31: 1 and chariots instead of looking to the **L**,
31: 2 In his wisdom, the **L** will send great disaster;
31: 3 When the **L** clenches his fist against them,
31: 4 But the **L** has told me this: "When a lion, even a
31: 4 the **L** Almighty will come and fight on Mount
31: 5 The **L** Almighty will hover over Jerusalem as a
31: 6 are such wicked rebels, come and return to the **L**.
31: 9 flee when they see the battle flags," says the **L**,
32: 6 They spread lies about the **L**; they deprive the
33: 2 But **L**, be merciful to us, for we have waited for
33: 5 Though the **L** is very great and lives in heaven,
33: 6 The fear of the **L** is the key to this treasure.
33: 10 But the **L** says: "I will stand up and show my
33: 21 The **L** will be our Mighty One. He will be like a
33: 22 For the **L** is our judge, our lawgiver, and our king.
33: 24 and helpless," for the **L** will forgive their sins.
34: 2 For the **L** is enraged against the nations. His fury is
34: 6 The sword of the **L** is drenched with blood. It is
34: 6 the **L** will offer a great sacrifice in the rich city of
34: 16 Search the book of the **L**, and see what he will do.
34: 16 none will lack a mate, for the **L** has promised this.
35: 2 There the **L** will display his glory, the splendor of
35: 10 Those who have been ransomed by the **L** will
36: 7 you will say, 'We are trusting in the **L** our God!'
36: 10 The **L** himself told us, 'Go and destroy it!' "
36: 15 Don't let him fool you into trusting in the **L** by
saying, 'The **L** will rescue us!
36: 18 mislead you by saying, 'The **L** will rescue us!'
36: 20 So what makes you think that the **L** can rescue
37: 1 and went into the Temple of the **L** to pray.
37: 4 But perhaps the **L** your God has heard the Assyrian
37: 6 "Say to your master, 'This is what the **L** says:
37: 14 LORD's Temple and spread it out before the **L**.
37: 15 And Hezekiah prayed this prayer before the **L**:
37: 16 "O **L** Almighty, God of Israel, you are enthroned
37: 17 Listen to me, O **L**, and hear! Open your eyes, O **L**,
37: 18 "It is true, **L**, that the kings of Assyria have
37: 20 Now, O **L** our God, rescue us from his power;
37: 20 the earth will know that you alone, O **L**, are God."
37: 21 "This is what the **L**, the God of Israel, says:
37: 22 This is the message that the **L** has spoken against
37: 26 It was I, the **L**, who decided this long ago.
37: 30 "Here is the proof that the **L** will protect this city
37: 32 The passion of the **L** Almighty will make this
37: 33 "And this is what the **L** says about the king of
37: 34 he came. He will not enter this city, says the **L**.
37: 36 That night the angel of the **L** went out to the
38: 1 "This is what the **L** says: Set your affairs in order,
38: 2 he turned his face to the wall and prayed to the **L**,
38: 3 "Remember, O **L**, how I have always tried to be
38: 4 Then this message came to Isaiah from the **L**:
38: 5 back to Hezekiah and tell him, 'This is what the **L**,
38: 7 " 'And this is the sign that the **L** will give you to
38: 11 I said, "Never again will I see the **L** GOD
38: 20 Think of it—the **L** has healed me! / I will sing his
38: 20 every day of my life / in the Temple of the **L**.
38: 22 go to the Temple of the **L** three days from now?"
39: 5 "Listen to this message from the **L** Almighty:
39: 6 off to Babylon. Nothing will be left, says the **L**.
39: 8 "This message you have given me from the **L** is
40: 2 the **L** has punished her in full for all her sins."
40: 3 "Make a highway for the **L** through the
40: 5 Then the glory of the **L** will be revealed, and all
people will see it together. The **L** has spoken!"
40: 7 and the flowers fade beneath the breath of the **L**.
40: 10 the Sovereign **L** is coming in all his glorious
40: 13 Who is able to advise the Spirit of the **L**?
40: 14 Has the **L** ever needed anyone's advice? Does he
40: 27 how can you say the **L** does not see your troubles?
40: 28 Don't you know that the **L** is the everlasting God,
40: 31 But those who wait on the **L** will find new
41: 2 victory at every step? Who, indeed, but the **L**?
41: 4 It is I, the **L**, the First and the Last. I alone am he."
41: 13 you by your right hand—I, the **L** your God.
41: 14 for I will help you. I am the **L**, your Redeemer.
41: 16 And the joy of the **L** will fill you to overflowing.
41: 17 from thirst, then I, the **L**, will answer them.
41: 20 will see this miracle and understand that it is the **L**,
41: 21 what they can do!" says the **L**, the King of Israel.
42: 5 God, the **L**, created the heavens and stretched them
42: 6 "I, the **L**, have called you to demonstrate my
42: 8 "I am the **L**; that is my name! I will not give my
42: 10 Sing a new song to the **L**! / Sing his praises from
42: 12 Let the coastlands glorify the **L**; / let them sing his
42: 13 The **L** will march forth like a mighty man;
42: 19 as blind as my chosen people, the servant of the **L**?
42: 21 The **L** has magnified his law and made it truly
42: 24 Israel to be robbed and hurt? Was it not the **L**?
42: 24 It was the **L** whom we sinned against,
43: 1 But now, O Israel, the **L** who created you says:
43: 3 For I am the **L**, your God, the Holy One of Israel,
43: 10 "But you are my witnesses, O Israel!" says the **L**.
43: 11 I am the **L**, and there is no other Savior.
43: 12 are witnesses that I am the only God," says the **L**.
43: 14 The **L** your Redeemer, the Holy One of Israel,
43: 15 I am the **L**, your Holy One, Israel's Creator
43: 16 I am the **L**, who opened a way through the waters,
44: 2 The **L** who made you and helps you says: O Jacob,
44: 5 Some will proudly claim, 'I belong to the **L**.'
44: 6 "This is what the **L**, Israel's King and Redeemer,
the **L** Almighty, says:
44: 11 All who worship idols will stand before the **L** in
44: 21 I, the **L**, made you, and I will not forget to help
44: 23 O heavens, for the **L** has done this wondrous thing.
44: 23 For the **L** has redeemed Jacob and is glorified in
44: 24 The **L**, your Redeemer and Creator, says: "I am
the **L**, who made all things.
45: 1 This is what the **L** says to Cyrus, his anointed one,
45: 2 This is what the **L** says: "I will go before you,
45: 3 I will do this so you may know that I am the **L**,
45: 5 I am the **L**; there is no other God. I have prepared
45: 6 is no other God. I am the **L**, and there is no other.
45: 7 I, the **L**, am the one who does these things.
45: 8 can sprout up together. I, the **L**, created them.
45: 11 This is what the **L**, the Creator and Holy One of
45: 13 not for a reward! I, the **L** Almighty, have spoken!"
45: 14 This is what the **L** says: "The Egyptians,
45: 17 But the **L** will save the people of Israel with
45: 18 For the **L** is God, and he created the heavens
45: 18 "I am the **L**," he says, "and there is no other.
45: 19 to give. I, the **L**, speak only what is true and right.
45: 21 Was it not I, the **L**? For there is no other God
45: 24 "The **L** is the source of all my righteousness
45: 25 In the **L** all the generations of Israel will be
47: 4 Our Redeemer, whose name is the **L** Almighty,
48: 1 you who take oaths in the name of the **L** and call
48: 2 the God of Israel, whose name is the **L** Almighty.
48: 14 and listen: 'The **L** has chosen Cyrus as his ally.
48: 16 And now the Sovereign **L** and his Spirit have sent
48: 17 "The **L**, your Redeemer, the Holy One of Israel,
48: 17 I am the **L** your God, who teaches you what is
48: 20 Shout to the ends of the earth that the **L** has
48: 22 there is no peace for the wicked," says the **L**.
49: 1 The **L** called me before my birth; from within the
49: 5 And now the **L** speaks—he who formed me in my
49: 5 The **L** has honored me, and my God has given me
49: 7 The **L**, the Redeemer and Holy One of Israel,
49: 7 will bow low because the **L** has chosen you.
49: 7 He, the faithful **L**, the Holy One of Israel,
49: 8 This is what the **L** says: "At just the right time,
49: 10 For the **L** in his mercy will lead them beside cool
49: 13 For the **L** has comforted his people and will have
49: 14 Yet Jerusalem says, "The **L** has deserted us;
49: 18 As surely as I live," says the **L**, "they will be like
49: 22 This is what the Sovereign **L** says: "See, I will
49: 23 your feet. Then you will know that I am the **L**.
49: 25 But the **L** says, "The captives of warriors will be
49: 26 the **L**, am your Savior and Redeemer, the Mighty
50: 1 The **L** asks, "Did I sell you as slaves to my
50: 4 The Sovereign **L** has given me his words of
50: 5 The Sovereign **L** has spoken to me, and I have
50: 7 Because the Sovereign **L** helps me, I will not be
50: 9 See, the Sovereign **L** is on my side! Who will
50: 10 Who among you fears the **L** and obeys his servant?
50: 10 a ray of light, trust in the **L** and rely on your God.
51: 1 all who hope for deliverance—all who seek the **L**!
51: 3 The **L** will comfort Israel again and make her
51: 3 become as beautiful as Eden—the garden of the **L**.
51: 9 Wake up, **L**! Robe yourself with strength!
51: 11 Those who have been ransomed by the **L** will
51: 13 Yet you have forgotten the **L**, your Creator,
51: 15 For I am the **L** your God, who stirs up the sea,
51: 15 its waves to roar. My name is the **L** Almighty.
51: 20 The **L** has poured out his fury; God has rebuked
51: 22 This is what the Sovereign **L**, your God
52: 3 For this is what the **L** says: "When I sold you into
52: 4 This is what the Sovereign **L** says: "Long ago my
52: 5 And now, what is this?" asks the **L**. "Why are my
52: 8 for before their very eyes they see the **L** bringing
52: 9 joyful song, for the **L** has comforted his people.
52: 10 The **L** will demonstrate his holy power before the
52: 11 you who carry home the vessels of the **L**.
52: 12 For the **L** will go ahead of you, and the God of
53: 1 To whom will the **L** reveal his saving power?
53: 6 Yet the **L** laid on him the guilt and sins of us all.
54: 1 has more than all the other women," says the **L**.
54: 5 The **L** Almighty is his name! He is your
54: 6 For the **L** has called you back from your grief—
54: 8 compassion on you," says the **L**, your Redeemer.
54: 10 be broken," says the **L**, who has mercy on you.
54: 17 benefits are enjoyed by the servants of the **L**;
54: 17 will come from me. I, the **L**, have spoken!
55: 5 because I, the **L** your God, the Holy One of Israel,
55: 6 Seek the **L** while you can find him. Call on him
55: 7 Let them turn to the **L** that he may have mercy on
55: 8 are completely different from yours," says the **L**.
56: 1 "Be just and fair to all," says the **L**. "Do what is
56: 3 too, when they commit themselves to the **L**.
56: 6 bless the Gentiles who commit themselves to the **L**
56: 8 For the Sovereign **L**, who brings back the outcasts
57: 19 and far, for I will heal them all," says the **L**.
58: 5 Do you really think this will please the **L**?
58: 8 and the glory of the **L** will protect you from
58: 9 Then when you call, the **L** will answer. 'Yes,
58: 11 The **L** will guide you continually, watering your
58: 13 Honor the **L** in everything you do, and don't
58: 14 the **L** will be your delight. I will give you great
58: 14 to Jacob, your ancestor. I, the **L**, have spoken!"
59: 1 The **L** is not too weak to save you, and he is not
59: 13 We know that we have rebelled against the **L**.
59: 15 The **L** looked and was displeased to find that there
59: 19 and glorify the name of the **L** throughout the
59: 19 like a flood tide driven by the breath of the **L**.
59: 20 Redeemer will come to Jerusalem," says the **L**,
59: 21 And this is my covenant with them," says the **L**.
59: 21 children's children forever. I, the **L**, have spoken!
60: 1 to see! For the glory of the **L** is shining upon you.
60: 2 but the glory of the **L** will shine over you.

60: 6 bring gold and incense for the worship of the **L**.
60: 9 and it will bring great honor to the **L** your God,
60: 14 They will call you the City of the **L**, and Zion of
60: 16 the **L**, am your Savior and Redeemer, the Mighty
60: 19 for the **L** your God will be your everlasting light,
60: 20 go down. For the **L** will be your everlasting light.
60: 22 I, the **L**, will bring it all to pass at the right time."
61: 1 The Spirit of the Sovereign **L** is upon me,
61: 1 because the **L** has appointed me to bring good
61: 3 For the **L** has planted them like strong and graceful
61: 6 You will be called priests of the **L**, ministers of our
61: 8 "For I, the **L**, love justice. I hate robbery
61: 9 Everyone will realize that they are a people the **L**
61: 10 I am overwhelmed with joy in the **L** my God!
61: 11 The Sovereign **L** will show his justice to the
62: 2 your glory. And the **L** will give you a new name.
62: 3 The **L** will hold you in his hands for all to see—
62: 4 for the **L** delights in you and will claim you as his
62: 6 they will pray to the **L** day and night for the
62: 7 Give the **L** no rest until he makes Jerusalem the
62: 8 The **L** has sworn to Jerusalem by his own strength:
62: 9 You raised it, and you will keep it, praising the **L**.
62: 11 The **L** has sent this message to every land:
62: 12 Holy People and the People Redeemed by the **L**.
63: 1 "It is I, the **L**, announcing your salvation! It is I,
the **L**, who is mighty to save!"
63: 7 I will praise the **L** for all he has done.
63: 14 peaceful valley, the Spirit of the **L** gave them rest.
63: 14 You led your people, **L**, and gained a magnificent
63: 15 **L**, look down from heaven and see us from your
63: 16 Even if Abraham and Jacob would disown us, **L**,
63: 17 **L**, why have you allowed us to turn from your
63: 19 **L**, why do you treat us as though we never
64: 8 And yet, **L**, you are our Father. We are the clay,
64: 9 Oh, don't be so angry with us, **L**. Please don't
64: 12 After all this, **L**, must you still refuse to help us?
65: 1 The **L** says, "People who never before inquired
65: 7 and for those of their ancestors," says the **L**.
65: 8 "But I will not destroy them all," says the **L**.
65: 11 "But because the rest of you have forsaken the **L**
65: 13 Therefore, this is what the Sovereign **L** says:
65: 15 for the Sovereign **L** will destroy you and call his
65: 23 For they are people blessed by the **L**, and their
65: 25 on my holy mountain. I, the **L**, have spoken!"
66: 1 This is what the **L** says: "Heaven is my throne,
66: 2 and they are mine. I, the **L**, have spoken!
66: 5 Hear this message from the **L**, and tremble at his
66: 5 'Let the **L** be honored!' they scoff. 'Be joyful in
66: 6 It is the voice of the **L** taking vengeance against
66: 9 of birth and then not deliver it?" asks the **L**. "No!
66: 12 will overflow Jerusalem like a river," says the **L**.
66: 14 Everyone will see the good hand of the **L** on his
66: 15 See, the **L** is coming with fire, and his swift
66: 16 The **L** will punish the world by fire and by his
sword, and many will be killed by the **L**.
66: 17 will come to a terrible end," says the **L**.
66: 20 holy mountain in Jerusalem as an offering to the **L**.
66: 20 and on mules and camels," says the **L**.
66: 21 to be my priests and Levites. I, the **L**, have spoken!
66: 22 with a name that will never disappear," says the **L**.
Jer 1: 2 The **L** first gave messages to Jeremiah during the
1: 4 The **L** gave me a message. He said,
1: 6 "O Sovereign **L**," I said, "I can't speak for you!
1: 7 "Don't say that," the **L** replied, "for you must go
1: 8 and take care of you. I, the **L**, have spoken!"
1: 9 Then the **L** touched my mouth and said, "See,
1: 11 Then the **L** said to me, "Look, Jeremiah! What do
1: 12 And the **L** said, "That's right, and it means that I
1: 13 Then the **L** spoke to me again and asked,
1: 14 "Yes," the **L** said, "for terror from the north will
1: 19 and I will take care of you. I, the **L**, have spoken!"
2: 1 The **L** gave me another message. He said,
2: 2 in Jerusalem's streets: 'This is what the **L** says:
2: 3 In those days Israel was holy to the **L**, the first of
2: 3 disaster fell upon them. I, the **L**, have spoken!' "
2: 4 Listen to the word of the **L**, people of Jacob—
2: 5 This is what the **L** says: "What sin did your
2: 6 'Where is the **L** who brought us safely out of
2: 8 The priests did not ask, 'Where is the **L**?'
2: 9 in the years to come. I, the **L**, have spoken!
2: 12 and shrink back in horror and dismay, says the **L**.
2: 17 the **L** your God when he wanted to lead you
2: 19 bitter thing it is to forsake the **L** your God,
2: 19 of him. I, the Lord, the **L** Almighty, have spoken!
2: 22 be washed away. I, the Sovereign **L**, have spoken!
2: 29 You are the ones who have rebelled, says the **L**.
2: 31 "O my people, listen to the words of the **L**!
2: 37 for the **L** has rejected the nations you trust.
3: 1 prostituted yourself with many lovers, says the **L**.
3: 6 During the reign of King Josiah, the **L** said to me,
3: 10 She has only pretended to be sorry," says the **L**.
3: 11 Then the **L** said to me, "Even faithless Israel is
3: 12 say these words to Israel, 'This is what the **L** says:
3: 13 Admit that you rebelled against the **L** your God
3: 13 refused to follow me. I, the **L**, have spoken!' "
3: 14 says the **L**, "for I am your husband.
3: 16 land is once more filled with people," says the **L**,
3: 17 Jerusalem will be known as The Throne of the **L**.
3: 17 All nations will come there to honor the **L**.
3: 20 wife who leaves her husband," says the **L**.
3: 21 For they have forgotten the **L** their God
3: 22 says the **L**, "come back to me,
3: 22 the people reply, "for you are the **L** our God.
3: 23 Only in the **L** our God will Israel ever find
3: 25 and our ancestors have always sinned against the **L**
4: 1 "O Israel, come back to me," says the **L**. "If you
4: 3 This is what the **L** says to the people of Judah
4: 4 Cleanse your minds and hearts before the **L**,
4: 8 for the fierce anger of the **L** is still upon us.
4: 9 says the **L**, "the king and the officials will tremble
4: 10 Then I said, "O Sovereign **L**, the people have been
4: 11 The time is coming when the **L** will say to the
4: 17 people have rebelled against me,' " says the **L**.
4: 22 are foolish and do not know me," says the **L**.
4: 27 This is what the **L** says: "The whole land will be
5: 1 and down every street in Jerusalem," says the **L**.
5: 2 saying, 'As surely as the **L** lives,' they all tell
5: 3 **L**, you are searching for honesty. You struck your
5: 4 and ignorant? They don't know the ways of the **L**.
5: 9 Should I not punish them for this?" asks the **L**.
5: 10 from the vine, for they do not belong to the **L**.
5: 11 Judah are full of treachery against me," says the **L**.
5: 12 "They have lied about the **L** and have said,
5: 14 Therefore, this is what the **L** God Almighty says:
5: 15 bring a distant nation against you," says the **L**.
5: 18 I will not blot you out completely," says the **L**.
5: 19 'Why is the **L** our God doing this to us?'
5: 22 I, the **L**, am the one who defines the ocean's sandy
5: 24 'Let us live in awe of the **L** our God, for he gives
5: 29 Should I not punish them for this?" asks the **L**.
6: 6 This is what the **L** Almighty says: "Cut down the
6: 9 This is what the **L** Almighty says: "Disaster will
6: 10 they cannot hear. They scorn the word of the **L**.
6: 12 I will punish the people of this land," says the **L**.
6: 15 humbled beneath my punishing anger," says the **L**.
6: 16 So now the **L** says, "Stop right where you are!
6: 21 Therefore, this is what the **L** says: "I will put
6: 22 This is what the **L** says: "See a great army
6: 30 I will label them 'Rejected Silver' because I, the **L**,
7: 1 The **L** gave another message to Jeremiah. He said,
7: 2 'O Judah, listen to this message from the **L**!
7: 3 The **L** Almighty, the God of Israel, says:
7: 4 your safety because the Temple of the **L** is here.
7: 11 I see all the evil going on there, says the **L**.
7: 13 says the **L**, I spoke to you about it repeatedly,
7: 19 asks the **L**. "Most of all, they hurt themselves,
7: 20 So the Sovereign **L** says: "I will pour out my
7: 21 This is what the **L** Almighty, the God of Israel,
7: 28 nation whose people will not obey the **L** their God
7: 29 For the **L** has rejected and forsaken this generation
7: 30 have sinned before my very eyes," says the **L**.
7: 32 So beware, for the time is coming," says the **L**,
8: 1 "In that day," says the **L**, "the enemy will break
8: 3 I will send them. I, the **L** Almighty, have spoken!
8: 4 say to the people, 'This is what the **L** says:
8: 7 They do not know what the **L** requires of them.
8: 8 "We are wise because we have the law of the **L**,"
8: 9 their sin, for they have rejected the word of the **L**.
8: 12 be humbled when they are punished, says the **L**.
8: 13 for them will soon be gone. I, the **L**, have spoken!'
8: 14 For the **L** our God has decreed our destruction
8: 14 of poison to drink because we sinned against the **L**.
8: 17 poisonous snakes you cannot charm," says the **L**.
8: 19 "Has the **L** abandoned Jerusalem?" the people
8: 19 their carved idols and worthless gods?" asks the **L**.
9: 3 to worse! They care nothing for me," says the **L**.
9: 6 and utterly refuse to come to me," says the **L**.
9: 7 Therefore, the **L** Almighty says, "See, I will melt
9: 9 Should I not punish them for this?" asks the **L**.
9: 11 make Jerusalem into a heap of ruins," says the **L**.
9: 12 Who has been instructed by the **L** and can explain
9: 13 The **L** replies, "This has happened because my
9: 15 So now, listen to what the **L** Almighty, the God of
9: 17 This is what the **L** Almighty says: "Think about
9: 20 Listen, you women, to the words of the **L**;
9: 22 And the **L** says, "Bodies will be scattered across
9: 23 This is what the **L** says: "Let not the wise man
9: 24 and understand that I am the **L** who is just
9: 24 that I delight in these things. I, the **L**, have spoken!
9: 25 "A time is coming," says the **L**, "when I will
10: 1 Hear the word of the **L**, O Israel!
10: 2 This is what the **L** says: "Do not act like other
10: 6 **L**, there is no one like you! For you are great,
10: 10 But the **L** is the only true God, the living God.
10: 16 special possession. / The **L** Almighty is his name!
10: 18 says the **L**. "For suddenly, I will fling you from
10: 21 They no longer follow the **L** or ask what he wants
10: 23 I know, **L**, that a person's life is not his own.
10: 24 So correct me, **L**, but please be gentle. Do not
11: 1 The **L** gave another message to Jeremiah. He said,
11: 3 Say to them, 'This is what the **L**, the God of Israel,
11: 5 live in today.' " Then I replied, "So be it, **L**!"
11: 6 Then the **L** said, "Broadcast this message in the
11: 9 Again the **L** spoke to me and said, "I have
11: 11 Therefore, says the **L**, I am going to bring calamity
11: 16 "I, the **L**, once called them a thriving olive tree,
11: 17 I, the **L** Almighty, who planted this olive tree,
11: 18 Then the **L** told me about the plots my enemies
11: 20 O **L** Almighty, you are just, and you examine the
11: 22 So this is what the **L** Almighty says about them:
12: 1 **L**, you always give me justice when I bring a case
12: 3 But as for me, **L**, you know my heart. You see me
12: 4 Yet the people say, "The **L** won't do anything!"
12: 5 Then the **L** replied to me, "If racing against mere
12: 12 The sword of the **L** kills people from one end of
12: 13 for the fierce anger of the **L** is upon them."
12: 14 Now this is what the **L** says: "As for all the evil
12: 16 'As surely as the **L** lives' (just as they taught my
12: 17 be uprooted and destroyed. I, the **L**, have spoken!"
13: 1 This is what the **L** said to me: "Go and buy a linen
13: 2 So I bought the belt as the **L** directed me and put it
13: 3 Then the **L** gave me another message:
13: 5 and hid it at the Euphrates as the **L** had instructed
13: 6 A long time afterward, the **L** said to me, "Go back
13: 8 Then I received this message from the **L**:
13: 9 "The **L** says: This illustrates how I will rot away
13: 11 and Israel to cling to me," says the **L**.
13: 12 "So tell them, 'The **L**, the God of Israel, says:
13: 13 Then tell them, 'No, this is what the **L** means:
13: 14 the other, even parents against children, says the **L**.
13: 15 Listen! Do not be proud, for the **L** has spoken.
13: 16 Give glory to the **L** your God before it is too late.
13: 21 How will you feel when the **L** sets your foreign
13: 25 your allotment, that which is due you," says the **L**.
14: 1 This message came to Jeremiah from the **L**,
14: 7 The people say, "**L**, our wickedness has caught up
14: 9 to save us? You are right here among us, **L**.
14: 10 So the **L** replies to his people, "You love to
14: 11 Then the **L** said to me, "Do not pray for these
14: 13 Then I said, "O Sovereign **L**, their prophets are
14: 13 will come. The **L** will surely send you peace.' "
14: 14 Then the **L** said, "These prophets are telling lies in
14: 15 Therefore, says the **L**, I will punish these lying
14: 19 **L**, have you completely rejected Judah? Do you
14: 20 **L**, we confess our wickedness and that of our
14: 21 the sake of your own name, **L**, do not abandon us.
14: 22 No, it comes from you, the **L** our God! Only you
15: 1 Then the **L** said to me, "Even if Moses
15: 2 can we go?' tell them, 'This is what the **L** says:
15: 3 four kinds of destroyers against them," says the **L**.
15: 6 and turned your back on me," says the **L**.
15: 9 hand over to the enemy to be killed," says the **L**.
15: 11 The **L** replied, "All will be well with you,
15: 15 Then I said, "**L**, you know I am suffering for your
15: 16 for I bear your name, O **L** God Almighty.
15: 19 The **L** replied, "If you return to me, I will restore
15: 20 will protect and deliver you. I, the **L**, have spoken!
16: 1 The **L** gave me another message. He said,
16: 3 For this is what the **L** says about the children born
16: 5 and show sympathy for them," says the **L**,
16: 9 For the **L** Almighty, the God of Israel, says:
16: 10 'Why has the **L** decreed such terrible things
16: 10 What is our sin against the **L** our God?'
16: 14 "But the time is coming," says the **L**,
16: 14 oath will no longer say, 'As surely as the **L** lives,
16: 15 Instead, they will say, 'As surely as the **L** lives,
16: 16 many fishermen who will catch them," says the **L**.
16: 19 **L**, you are my strength and fortress, my refuge in
16: 21 will show them my power and might," says the **L**.
16: 21 "At last they will know that I am the **L**."
17: 1 The **L** says, "My people act as though their evil
17: 5 This is what the **L** says: "Cursed are those who
17: 5 and turn their hearts away from the **L**.
17: 7 "But blessed are those who trust in the **L** and have
made the **L** their hope and confidence.
17: 10 I, the **L**, search all hearts and examine secret
17: 13 O **L**, the hope of Israel, all who turn away from
17: 13 and dusty grave, for they have forsaken the **L**,
17: 14 O **L**, you alone can heal me; you alone can save.
17: 15 "What is this 'message from the **L**' you keep
17: 16 **L**, I have not abandoned my job as a shepherd for
17: 17 **L**, do not desert me now! You alone are my hope
17: 19 Then the **L** said to me, "Go and stand in the gates
17: 20 'Listen to this message from the **L**, you kings of
17: 21 This is what the **L** says: Listen to my warning
17: 24 " 'But if you obey me, says the **L**, and do not
18: 1 The **L** gave another message to Jeremiah. He said,
18: 5 Then the **L** gave me this message:
18: 11 Say to them, 'This is what the **L** says:
18: 13 Then the **L** said, "Has anyone ever heard of such a
18: 19 **L**, help me! Listen to what they are planning to do
18: 23 **L**, you know all about their murderous plots
19: 1 The **L** said to me, "Go and buy a clay jar.
19: 3 Say to them, 'Listen to this message from the **L**,
19: 3 This is what the **L** Almighty, the God of Israel,
19: 6 So beware, for the time is coming, says the **L**,
19: 11 say to them, 'This is what the **L** Almighty says:
19: 12 I will do to this place and its people, says the **L**.
19: 14 and he stopped in front of the Temple of the **L**.
19: 15 "This is what the **L** Almighty, the God of Israel,
20: 1 the priest in charge of the Temple of the **L**,
20: 3 "Pashhur, the **L** has changed your name.
20: 4 For this is what the **L** says: I will send terror upon
20: 7 O **L**, you persuaded me, and I allowed myself to be
20: 8 So these messages from the **L** have made me a
20: 9 If I say I'll never mention the **L** or speak in his
20: 11 But the **L** stands beside me like a great warrior.
20: 12 O **L** Almighty! You know those who are righteous,
20: 13 Now I will sing out my thanks to the **L**!
20: 13 Praise the **L**! For though I was poor and needy,
20: 16 cities of old that the **L** overthrew without mercy.
21: 1 The **L** spoke through Jeremiah when King
21: 2 "Please ask the **L** to help us.
21: 2 Perhaps the **L** will be gracious and do a mighty
21: 4 'This is what the **L**, the God of Israel, says: I will
21: 7 And then, says the **L**, even after King Zedekiah,
21: 8 "Tell all the people, 'This is what the **L** says:
21: 10 and not good upon this city, says the **L**.
21: 11 of Judah, 'Listen to this message from the **L**!
21: 12 This is what the **L** says to the dynasty of David:
21: 14 will punish you for your sinfulness, says the **L**.
22: 1 Then the **L** said to me, "Go over and speak
22: 2 'Listen to this message from the **L**, you king of
22: 3 This is what the **L** says: Be fair-minded and just.
22: 5 I swear by my own name, says the **L**, that this
22: 6 Now this is what the **L** says concerning the royal
22: 8 'Why did the **L** destroy such a great city?'
22: 9 'Because they violated their covenant with the **L**
22: 11 For this is what the **L** says about Jehoahaz,
22: 13 And the **L** says, "Destruction is certain for
22: 16 Isn't that what it means to know me?" asks the **L**.

22:24 surely as I live," says the **L**, "I will abandon you,
22:29 earth, earth! Listen to this message from the **L**!
22:30 This is what the **L** says: Let the record show that
23: 1 ones they were expected to care for," says the **L**.
23: 2 This is what the **L**, the God of Israel, says to these
23: 4 one of them will be lost or missing," says the **L**.
23: 5 "For the time is coming," says the **L**, "when I
23: 6 this is his name: 'The **L** Is Our Righteousness.'
23: 7 "In that day," says the **L**, "when people are
23: 7 they will no longer say, 'As surely as the **L** lives,
23: 8 Instead, they will say, 'As surely as the **L** lives,
23: 9 because of the holy words the **L** has spoken against
23:11 acts right here in my own Temple," says the **L**.
23:12 time of punishment comes. I, the **L**, have spoken!
23:15 this is what the **L** Almighty says concerning the
23:16 my warning to my people," says the **L** Almighty.
23:16 everything they say. They do not speak for the **L**!
23:17 'Don't worry! The **L** says you will have peace!'
23:18 the **L** well enough to hear what he is saying?
23:20 The anger of the **L** will not diminish until it has
23:23 Am I a God who is only in one place?" asks the **L**.
23:24 in all the heavens and earth?" asks the **L**.
23:29 Does not my word burn like fire?" asks the **L**.
23:30 "Therefore," says the **L**, "I stand against these
23:31 prophets who say, 'This prophecy is from the **L**!'
23:32 have no message at all for my people," says the **L**.
23:33 'What prophecy has the **L** burdened you with
23:33 are the burden! The **L** says he will abandon you!'
23:34 anyone else says, 'I have a prophecy from the **L**,'
23:35 the LORD's answer?' or 'What is the **L** saying?'
23:36 But stop using this phrase, 'prophecy from the **L**.'
23:36 words of our God, the living God, the **L** Almighty.
23:37 the LORD's answer?' or 'What is the **L** saying?'
23:38 they respond, 'This is a prophecy from the **L**!'
23:38 Then you should say, 'This is what the **L** says:
23:38 have used this phrase, "prophecy from the **L**,"
24: 1 all the skilled craftsmen, the **L** gave me this vision.
24: 3 Then the **L** said to me, "What do you see,
24: 4 Then the **L** gave me this message:
24: 5 "This is what the **L**, the God of Israel, says:
24: 7 give them hearts that will recognize me as the **L**.
24: 8 "But the rotten figs," the **L** said, "represent King
25: 1 **L** during the fourth year of Jehoiakim's reign over
25: 3 until now—the **L** has been giving me his messages.
25: 4 "Again and again, the **L** has sent you his prophets,
25: 5 then will I let you live in this land that the **L** gave
25: 7 "But you would not listen to me," says the **L**.
25: 8 And now the **L** Almighty says: Because you have
25:12 and his people for their sins, says the **L**.
25:15 Then the **L**, the God of Israel, said to me,
25:17 So I took the cup of anger from the **L** and made all
25:17 drink from it—every nation the **L** sent me to.
25:27 Then the **L** said to me, "Now tell them, 'The **L** Almighty, the God of
25:28 to accept the cup, tell them, 'The **L** Almighty says:
25:29 of the earth. I, the **L** Almighty, have spoken!'
25:30 'The **L** will roar loudly against his own land from
25:31 for the **L** will bring his case against all the nations.
25:31 the wicked with his sword. The **L** has spoken!' "
25:32 This is what the **L** Almighty says: "Look!
25:33 In that day those the **L** has slaughtered will fill the
25:36 in despair, for the **L** is spoiling their pastures.
26: 1 This message came to Jeremiah from the **L** early in
26: 2 The **L** said, "Stand out in front of the Temple of the **L**,
26: 4 "Say to them, 'This is what the **L** says: If you will
26: 8 saying everything the **L** had told him to say,
26:12 "The **L** sent me to prophesy against this Temple
26:12 "The **L** gave me every word that I have spoken.
26:13 your sinning and begin to obey the **L** your God,
26:15 For it is absolutely true that the **L** sent me to speak
26:16 for he has spoken to us in the name of the **L** our
26:18 of Judah, 'This is what the **L** Almighty says:
26:19 they turned from their sins and worshiped the **L**.
26:19 Then the **L** held back the terrible disaster he had
26:20 Kiriath-jearim was also prophesying for the **L**.
27: 1 This message came to Jeremiah from the **L** early in
27: 2 The **L** said to me, "Make a yoke, and fasten it on
27: 4 'This is what the **L** Almighty, the God of Israel,
27: 8 any nation that refuses to be his slave, says the **L**.
27:11 farm the land as usual. I, the **L**, have spoken!' "
27:13 which the **L** will bring against every nation that
27:15 This is what the **L** says: I have not sent these
27:16 and the people and said, "This is what the **L** says:
27:18 let them pray to the **L** Almighty about the gold
27:19 "For this is what the **L** Almighty says about the
27:21 Yes, this is what the **L** Almighty, the God of Israel,
27:22 will stay there until I send for them, says the **L**.
28: 2 "The **L** Almighty, the God of Israel, says: I will
28: 4 has put on your necks. I, the **L**, have spoken!"
28: 6 come true! I hope the **L** does everything you say.
28: 9 true can it be known that he is really from the **L**."
28:11 "The **L** has promised that within two years he will
28:12 Soon afterward the **L** gave this message to
28:13 "Go and tell Hananiah, 'This is what the **L** says:
28:14 The **L** Almighty, the God of Israel, says: I have put
28:15 The **L** has not sent you, but the people believe your
28:16 Therefore, the **L** says you must die. Your life will
28:16 because you have rebelled against the **L**."
29: 4 The **L** Almighty, the God of Israel, sends this
29: 7 Pray to the **L** for that city where you are held
29: 8 The **L** Almighty, the God of Israel, says, "Do not
29: 9 lies in my name. I have not sent them," says the **L**.
29:11 For I know the plans I have for you," says the **L**.
29:14 I will be found by you," says the **L**. "I will end
29:15 You may claim that the **L** has raised up prophets
29:16 But this is what the **L** says about the king who sits
29:17 This is what the **L** Almighty says: "I will send
29:19 are in exile have not listened either," says the **L**.
29:20 Therefore, listen to this message from the **L**,
29:21 This is what the **L** Almighty, the God of Israel,
29:22 'May the **L** make you like Zedekiah and Ahab,
29:23 in my name. I am a witness to this," says the **L**.
29:24 The **L** sent this message to Shemaiah the
29:25 "This is what the **L** Almighty, the God of Israel,
29:26 'The **L** has appointed you to replace Jehoiada as
29:26 as the priest in charge of the house of the **L**.
29:30 Then the **L** gave this message to Jeremiah:
29:31 'This is what the **L** says concerning Shemaiah the
29:32 you to rebel against me. I, the **L**, have spoken!' "
30: 1 The **L** gave another message to Jeremiah. He said,
30: 2 "This is what the **L**, the God of Israel, says:
30: 3 and live here again. I, the **L**, have spoken!"
30: 4 This is the message the **L** gave concerning Israel
30: 5 "This is what the **L** says: I have heard the people
30: 8 "For in that day, says the **L** Almighty, I will break
30: 9 For my people will serve the **L** their God
30:10 my servant; do not be dismayed, Israel, says the **L**.
30:11 For I am with you and will save you, says the **L**.
30:12 "This is what the **L** says: Yours is an incurable
30:17 back your health and heal your wounds, says the **L**.
30:18 But the **L** says this: When I bring you home again
30:21 I will invite him to approach me, says the **L**,
30:24 The fierce anger of the **L** will not diminish until it
31: 1 "In that day," says the **L**, "I will be the God of all
31: 3 Long ago the **L** said to Israel: "I have loved you,
31: 6 let us go up to Jerusalem to worship the **L** our
31: 7 Now this is what the **L** says: "Sing with joy for
31: 7 'Save your people, O **L**, the remnant of Israel!'
31:10 "Listen to this message from the **L**, you nations of
31:10 The **L**, who scattered his people, will gather them
31:11 For the **L** has redeemed Israel from those too
31:12 because of the many gifts the **L** has given them—
31:14 people with my bounty. I, the **L**, have spoken!"
31:15 This is what the **L** says: "A cry of anguish is heard
31:16 But now the **L** says, "Do not weep any longer,
31:17 There is hope for your future," says the **L**.
31:18 and restore me, for you alone are the **L** my God.
31:20 Israel still my son, my darling child?" asks the **L**.
31:22 For the **L** will cause something new and different
31:23 This is what the **L** Almighty, the God of Israel,
31:23 and its cities will again say, 'The **L** bless you—
31:27 "The time will come," says the **L**, "when I will
31:28 future I will plant it and build it up," says the **L**.
31:31 "The day will come," says the **L**, "when I will
31:32 them as a husband loves his wife," says the **L**.
31:33 with the people of Israel on that day," says the **L**.
31:34 their family, saying, 'You should know the **L**.'
31:34 to the greatest, will already know me," says the **L**.
31:35 It is the **L** who provides the sun to light the day
31:35 His name is the **L** Almighty, and this is what he
31:37 away forever for their sins. I, the **L**, have spoken!
31:38 "The time is coming," says the **L**, "when all
31:40 as far as the Horse Gate—will be holy to the **L**.
32: 1 the **L** in the tenth year of the reign of Zedekiah,
32: 3 to give this prophecy: "This is what the **L** says:
32: 6 At that time the **L** sent me a message. He said,
32: 8 Then, just as the **L** had said he would,
32: 8 sure that the message I had heard was from the **L**.
32:14 "The **L** Almighty, the God of Israel, says:
32:15 For the **L** Almighty, the God of Israel, says:
32:16 I had given the papers to Baruch, I prayed to the **L**:
32:17 "O Sovereign **L**! You have made the heavens
32:18 are the great and powerful God, the **L** Almighty.
32:25 And yet, O Sovereign **L**, you have told me to buy
32:26 Then this message came to Jeremiah from the **L**:
32:27 "I am the **L**, the God of all the peoples of the
32:30 infuriated me with all their evil deeds," says the **L**.
32:36 But this is what the **L**, the God of Israel, says:
32:42 good I have promised them. I, the **L**, have spoken!
32:44 restore prosperity to them. I, the **L**, have spoken!"
33: 1 of the guard, the **L** gave him this second message:
33: 2 "The **L**, the Maker of the heavens and earth—the **L** is his name—says this:
33: 4 For this is what the **L**, the God of Israel, says:
33:10 "This is what the **L** says: You say, 'This land has
33:11 of people bringing thanksgiving offerings to the **L**.
33:11 'Give thanks to the **L** Almighty, for the **L** is good.
33:11 of this land to what it was in the past, says the **L**.
33:12 "This is what the **L** Almighty says: This land—
33:13 and all the towns of Judah. I, the **L**, have spoken!
33:14 "The day will come, says the **L**, when I will do for
33:16 And their motto will be 'The **L** is our
33:17 For this is what the **L** says: David will forever
33:19 Then this message came to Jeremiah from the **L**:
33:23 The **L** gave another message to Jeremiah. He said,
33:24 'The **L** chose Judah and Israel and then abandoned
34: 1 time this message came to Jeremiah from the **L**:
34: 2 and tell him, 'This is what the **L**, the God of Israel,
34: 4 "But listen to this promise from the **L**,
34: 4 king of Judah. This is what the **L** says:
34: 5 king is dead!" This I have decreed, says the **L**.' "
34: 8 This message came to Jeremiah from the **L** after
34:12 So the **L** gave them this message through
34:13 "This is what the **L**, the God of Israel, says:
34:17 "Therefore, this is what the **L** says: Since you
35: 1 This is the message the **L** gave Jeremiah when
35:12 Then the **L** gave this message to Jeremiah:
35:13 "The **L** Almighty, the God of Israel, says: Go
35:17 "Therefore, the **L** God Almighty, the God of
35:18 and said, "This is what the **L** Almighty,
35:19 I, the **L** Almighty, the God of Israel,
36: 1 in Judah, the **L** gave this message to Jeremiah:
36: 4 Baruch wrote down all the prophecies that the **L**
36: 6 and read the messages from the **L** that are on this
36: 8 and read these messages from the **L** to the people
36:11 of Shaphan heard the messages from the **L**,
36:26 and Jeremiah. But the **L** had hidden them.
36:27 the **L** gave Jeremiah another message.
36:29 Then say to the king, 'This is what the **L** says:
36:30 Now this is what the **L** says about King Jehoiakim
37: 2 land listened to what the **L** said through Jeremiah.
37: 3 "Please pray to the **L** our God for us."
37: 6 Then the **L** gave this message to Jeremiah:
37: 7 "This is what the **L**, the God of Israel, says:
37: 9 The **L** says: Do not fool yourselves that the
37:17 "Do you have any messages from the **L**?"
38: 2 "This is what the **L** says: Everyone who stays in
38: 3 The **L** also says: The city of Jerusalem will surely
38:16 "As surely as the **L** our Creator lives, I will not
38:17 "The **L** God Almighty, the God of Israel, says:
38:20 handed over to them if you choose to obey the **L**.
38:21 to surrender, this is what the **L** has revealed to me:
39:15 The **L** had given the following message to
39:16 'The **L** Almighty, the God of Israel, says:
39:18 and keep you safe. I, the **L**, have spoken!' "
40: 1 The **L** gave a message to Jeremiah after
40: 2 "The **L** your God has brought this disaster on this
40: 3 For these people have sinned against the **L**
41: 5 They had come to worship at the Temple of the **L**.
42: 2 They said, "Please pray to the **L** your God for us.
42: 3 Beg the **L** your God to show us what to do
42: 4 "I will pray to the **L** your God, and I will tell you
42: 5 "May the **L** your God be a faithful witness against
42: 6 we will obey the **L** our God to whom we send you
42: 7 Ten days later, the **L** gave his reply to Jeremiah.
42: 9 He said to them, "You sent me to the **L**, the God
42:11 not fear the king of Babylon anymore, says the **L**.
42:13 "But if you refuse to obey the **L** your God
42:15 then this is what the **L** says to the remnant of
42:15 The **L** Almighty, the God of Israel, says: 'If you
42:18 "For the **L** Almighty, the God of Israel, says:
42:19 The **L** has told you: 'Do not go to Egypt!'
42:20 you sent me to pray to the **L** your God for you,
42:20 saying, 'Just tell us what the **L** our God says,
42:21 but you will not obey the **L** your God any better
43: 1 message from the **L** their God to all the people,
43: 2 The **L** our God hasn't forbidden us to go to Egypt!
43: 7 The people refused to obey the **L** and went to
43: 8 the **L** gave another message to Jeremiah.
43:10 of Judah, 'The **L** Almighty, the God of Israel, says:
44: 2 "This is what the **L** Almighty, the God of Israel,
44: 7 "And now the **L** God Almighty, the God of Israel,
44:11 "Therefore, the **L** Almighty, the God of Israel,
44:16 "We will not listen to your messages from the **L**!
44:21 "Do you think the **L** did not know that you
44:22 because the **L** could no longer bear all the evil
44:23 burned incense to idols and sinned against the **L**,
44:24 the women, "Listen to this message from the **L**,
44:25 The **L** Almighty, the God of Israel, says: You
44:26 "But listen to this message from the **L**, all you
44:26 I have sworn by my great name, says the **L**,
44:26 use this oath: 'As surely as the Sovereign **L** lives!'
44:29 And this is the proof I give you, says the **L**, that all
44:30 of Babylon. I, the **L**, have spoken!"
45: 2 "This is what **L**, the God of Israel, says to you,
45: 3 And now the **L** has added more! I am weary of my
45: 4 "Baruch, this is what the **L** says: I will destroy this
45: 5 you wherever you go. I, the **L**, have spoken!"
46: 1 the prophet from the **L** concerning foreign nations.
46: 5 They are terrorized at every turn, says the **L**.
46:10 For this is the day of the Lord, the **L** Almighty,
46:10 The Lord, the **L** Almighty, will receive a sacrifice
46:13 Then the **L** gave the prophet Jeremiah this message
46:15 cannot stand because the **L** has driven them away.
46:18 says the King, whose name is the **L** Almighty,
46:23 will cut down her people like trees," says the **L**,
46:25 The **L** Almighty, the God of Israel, says: "I will
46:26 from the ravages of war. I, the **L**, have spoken!
46:28 Fear not, Jacob, my servant," says the **L**, "for I
47: 2 This is what the **L** says: "A flood is coming from
47: 4 Yes, the **L** is destroying the Philistines,
47: 6 "Now, O sword of the **L**, when will you be at rest
47: 7 But how can it be still when the **L** has sent it on an
48: 1 This is what the **L** Almighty, the God of Israel,
48: 8 and in the valleys, for the **L** has spoken.
48:10 Cursed be those who refuse to do the work the **L**
48:12 But the time is coming soon," says the **L**, "when I
48:15 says the King, whose name is the **L** Almighty.
48:25 and her arms have been broken," says the **L**.
48:26 like a drunkard, for she has rebelled against the **L**.
48:30 says the **L**, "but her boasts are false;
48:35 "I will put an end to Moab," says the **L**, "for they
48:40 swoops down on the land of Moab," says the **L**.
48:42 be a nation, for she has boasted against the **L**.
48:43 and snares will be your lot, O Moab," says the **L**.
48:44 the time of your judgment has come," says the **L**.
48:47 I will restore the fortunes of Moab," says the **L**.
49: 1 This is what the **L** says: "What are you doing?
49: 2 I will punish you for this," says the **L**,
49: 2 take back the land you took from her," says the **L**.
49: 5 terror upon you," says the Lord, the **L** Almighty.
49: 6 the fortunes of the Ammonites," says the **L**.
49: 7 This is what the **L** Almighty says: "Where are all
49:12 And this is what the **L** says: "If the innocent must
49:13 For I have sworn by my own name," says the **L**,
49:14 I have heard a message from the **L** that an
49:15 This is what the **L** says: "I will cut you down to
49:16 I will bring you crashing down," says the **L**.
49:18 and their neighboring towns," says the **L**.
49:23 This is what the **L** says: "The towns of Hamath

49:26 warriors will all be killed," says the **L** Almighty.
49:28 This is what the **L** says: "Advance against Kedar!
49:30 Flee for your lives," says the **L**. "Hide yourselves
49:31 those self-sufficient nomadic tribes," says the **L**.
49:32 upon them from every direction," says the **L**.
49:34 **L** at the beginning of the reign of King Zedekiah
49:35 This is what the **L** Almighty says: "I will destroy
49:37 disaster upon the people of Elam," says the **L**.
49:38 says the **L**, "and I will destroy its king
49:39 I will restore the fortunes of Elam," says the **L**.
50: 1 The **L** gave Jeremiah the prophet this message
50: 2 This is what the **L** says: "Tell the whole world,
50: 4 says the **L**, "weeping and seeking the **L** their God.
50: 5 They will bind themselves to the **L** with an eternal
50: 7 for they have sinned against the **L**, their place of
50:10 the attackers are glutted with plunder," says the **L**.
50:14 Spare no arrows, for she has sinned against the **L**.
50:15 The **L** has taken vengeance, so do not spare her.
50:18 Therefore, the **L** Almighty, the God of Israel,
50:20 In those days," says the **L**, "no sin will be found
50:21 as I have commanded you," says the **L**.
50:24 You are caught, for you have fought against the **L**.
50:25 "The **L** has opened his armory and brought out
50:25 will be the work of the Sovereign **L** Almighty.
50:28 as they declare in Jerusalem how the **L** our God
50:29 for she has defied the **L**, the Holy One of Israel.
50:30 Her warriors will all be killed," says the **L**.
50:31 O proud people," says the Lord, the **L** Almighty.
50:33 And now the **L** Almighty says this: "The people of
50:34 His name is the **L** Almighty. He will defend them
50:35 will strike the Babylonians," says the **L**.
50:40 and their neighboring towns," says the **L**.
51: 1 This is what the **L** says: "I will stir up a destroyer
51: 5 For the **L** Almighty has not forsaken Israel
51:10 The **L** has vindicated us. Come, let us announce in
Jerusalem everything the **L** our
51:11 For the **L** has stirred up the spirit of the kings of
51:12 for the **L** will fulfill all his plans against Babylon.
51:14 The **L** Almighty has taken this vow and has sworn
51:19 special possession. / The **L** Almighty is his name!
51:20 "You are my battle-ax and sword," says the **L**.
51:24 have done to my people in Jerusalem," says the **L**.
51:25 of the earth! I am your enemy," says the **L**.
51:26 You will be completely wiped out," says the **L**.
51:29 for everything the **L** has planned against her stands
51:33 For the **L** Almighty, the God of Israel, says:
51:36 The **L** says to Jerusalem, "I will be your lawyer to
51:39 fall asleep, never again to waken," says the **L**.
51:48 destroying armies against Babylon," says the **L**.
51:50 Remember the **L**, even though you are in a far-off
51:52 "Yes," says the **L**, "but the time is coming when
51:53 I will send enemies to plunder her," says the **L**.
51:55 For the **L** is destroying Babylon. He will silence
51:56 For the **L** is a God who gives just punishment,
51:57 says the King, whose name is the **L** Almighty.
51:58 This is what the **L** Almighty says: "The wide
51:62 Then say, '**L**, you have said that you will destroy
52: 3 So the **L**, in his anger, finally banished the people
52:13 He burned down the Temple of the **L**, the royal
La 1: 5 for the **L** has punished Jerusalem for her many
1: 9 "**L**, see my deep misery," she cries. "The enemy
1:10 the place the **L** had forbidden them to enter.
1:11 "O **L**, look," she mourns, "and see how I am
1:12 which the **L** brought on me in the day of his fierce
1:17 Regarding his people, the **L** has said, "Let their
1:18 "And the **L** is right," she groans, "for I rebelled
1:20 "**L**, see my anguish! My heart is broken and my
1:22 "Look at all their evil deeds, **L**. Punish them,
2: 6 The **L** has blotted out all memory of the holy
2: 8 The **L** was determined to destroy the walls of
2: 9 Her prophets receive no more visions from the **L**.
2:17 But it is the **L** who did it just as he warned. He has
2:20 "O **L**, think about this!" Jerusalem cries.
3:18 Everything I had hoped for from the **L** is lost!"
3:22 The unfailing love of the **L** never ends! By his
3:24 I say to myself, "The **L** is my inheritance;
3:25 The **L** is wonderfully good to those who wait for
3:26 it is good to wait quietly for salvation from the **L**.
3:40 our ways. Let us turn again in repentance to the **L**.
3:50 until the **L** looks down from heaven and sees.
3:55 called on your name, **L**, from deep within the well,
3:59 You have seen the wrong they have done to me, **L**.
3:61 **L**, you have heard the vile names they call me.
3:64 Pay them back, **L**, for all the evil they have done.
4:11 But now the anger of the **L** is satisfied. His fiercest
4:16 The **L** himself has scattered them, and he no longer
5: 1 **L**, remember everything that has happened to us.
5:19 But **L**, you remain the same forever! Your throne
5:21 Restore us, O **L**, and bring us back to you again!
Eze 1: 3 The **L** gave a message to me, Ezekiel son of Buzi,
1: 3 and I felt the hand of the **L** take hold of me.
1:28 This was the way the glory of the **L** appeared to
2: 4 say to them, 'This is what the Sovereign **L** says!'
3:11 say to them, 'This is what the Sovereign **L** says!'
3:12 (May the glory of the **L** be praised in his place!)
3:16 end of the seven days, the **L** gave me a message.
3:22 Then the **L** took hold of me, and he said to me,
3:23 and went, and there I saw the glory of the **L**,
3:27 say to them, 'This is what the Sovereign **L** says!'
4:13 For this is what the **L** says: Israel will eat defiled
4:14 Then I said, "O Sovereign **L**, must I be defiled by
4:15 "All right," the **L** said. "You may bake your
5: 5 "This is what the Sovereign **L** says: This is an
5: 7 So this is what the Sovereign **L** says: Since you
5: 8 I myself, the Sovereign **L**, am now your enemy.
5:11 "As surely as I live, says the Sovereign **L**, I will
5:13 all Israel will know that I, the **L**, have spoken to
5:15 They will see what happens when the **L** turns
5:15 a nation in furious rebuke. I, the **L**, have spoken!
5:17 of the enemy against you. I, the **L**, have spoken!"
6: 1 Again a message came to me from the **L**:
6: 3 of Israel this message from the Sovereign **L**.
6: 3 This is what the Sovereign **L** says to the mountains
6: 7 with corpses, you will know that I am the **L**.
6:10 They will know that I alone am the **L** and that I
6:11 "This is what the Sovereign **L** says: Clap your
6:13 then they will know that I alone am the **L**.
6:14 in the north. Then they will know that I am the **L**."
7: 1 Then this message came to me from the **L**:
7: 2 of man, this is what the Sovereign **L** says to Israel:
7: 4 all your evil. Then you will know that I am the **L**!
7: 5 "This is what the Sovereign **L** says: With one
7: 9 know that it is I, the **L**, who is striking the blow.
7:27 Then they will know that I am the **L**!"
8: 1 in my home, the Sovereign **L** took hold of me.
8: 3 where there is a large idol that has made the **L** very
8: 5 Then the **L** said to me, "Son of man, look toward
8: 5 stood the idol that had made the **L** so angry.
8:12 Then the **L** said to me, "Son of man, have you
8:12 They are saying, 'The **L** doesn't see us; he has
9: 1 Then the **L** thundered, "Bring on the men
9: 3 And the **L** called to the man dressed in linen who
9: 5 Then I heard the **L** say to the other men,
9: 7 "Defile the Temple!" the **L** commanded. "Fill its
9: 8 down in the dust and cried out, "O Sovereign **L**!
9: 9 They are saying, 'The **L** doesn't see it! The **L** has
forsaken the land!'
10: 2 Then the **L** spoke to the man in linen clothing
10: 4 Then the glory of the **L** rose up from above the
10: 4 courtyard glowed brightly with the glory of the **L**.
10: 6 The **L** said to the man in linen clothing,
10:18 Then the glory of the **L** moved from the door of
11: 5 Then the Spirit of the **L** came upon me, and he told
11: 5 "This is what the **L** says to the people of Israel:
11: 7 "Therefore, this is what the Sovereign **L** says:
11: 8 the war you so greatly fear, says the Sovereign **L**.
11:10 of Israel, and then you will know that I am the **L**.
11:12 and you will know that I am the **L**. For you have
11:13 down in the dust and cried out, "O Sovereign **L**,
11:14 Then this message came to me from the **L**:
11:15 saying, 'They are far away from the **L**, so now he
11:16 give the exiles this message from the Sovereign **L**:
11:17 I, the Sovereign **L**, will gather you back from the
11:21 them fully for their sins, says the Sovereign **L**."
11:23 Then the glory of the **L** went up from the city
11:25 And I told the exiles everything the **L** had shown
12: 1 Again a message came to me from the **L**:
12: 8 next morning this message came to me from the **L**:
12:10 Say to them, 'This is what the Sovereign **L** says:
12:15 among the nations, they will know that I am the **L**.
12:16 have been. Then they will know that I am the **L**!"
12:17 Then this message came to me from the **L**:
12:19 Give the people this message from the Sovereign **L**
12:20 Then you will know that I am the **L**."
12:21 Again a message came to me from the **L**:
12:23 the people this message from the Sovereign **L**:
12:25 For I am the **L**! What I threaten always happens.
12:25 in your own lifetime, says the Sovereign **L**."
12:26 Then this message came to me from the **L**:
12:28 give them this message from the Sovereign **L**:
12:28 I, the Sovereign **L**, have spoken!"
13: 1 Then this message came to me from the **L**:
13: 2 Tell them to listen to the word of the **L**.
13: 3 This is what the Sovereign **L** says: Destruction is
13: 5 helped it to stand firm in battle on the day of the **L**.
13: 6 have lied and said, 'My message is from the **L**,'
even though the **L** never sent them.
13: 7 false if you claim, 'This message is from the **L**,'
13: 8 "Therefore, this is what the Sovereign **L** says:
13: 8 I will stand against you, says the Sovereign **L**.
13: 9 Then you will know that I am the Sovereign **L**!
13:13 "Therefore, this is what the Sovereign **L** says:
13:14 crush you. Then you will know that I am the **L**!
13:16 was no peace. I, the Sovereign **L**, have spoken!'
13:18 This is what the Sovereign **L** says: Destruction is
13:20 "And so the Sovereign **L** says: I am against all
13:21 your victims. Then you will know that I am the **L**.
13:23 your grasp. Then you will know that I am the **L**."
14: 2 this message came to me from the **L**:
14: 4 Give them this message from the Sovereign **L**:
14: 4 I, the **L**, will punish the people of Israel who set up
14: 6 of Israel this message from the Sovereign **L**:
14: 7 I, the **L**, will punish all those, both Israelites
14: 8 Then you will know that I am the **L**.
14: 9 it is because I, the **L**, have deceived that prophet.
14:11 and I will be their God, says the Sovereign **L**."
14:12 Then this message came to me from the **L**:
14:14 no one but themselves, declares the Sovereign **L**.
14:16 the Sovereign **L** swears that it would do no good—
14:18 the Sovereign **L** swears that they could not save
14:20 the Sovereign **L** swears that they could not save
14:21 "Now this is what the Sovereign **L** says:
14:23 to Israel without cause, says the Sovereign **L**."
15: 1 Then this message came to me from the **L**:
15: 6 "And this is what the Sovereign **L** says:
15: 7 When this happens, you will know that I am the **L**.
15: 8 have been unfaithful to me, says the Sovereign **L**."
16: 1 Then another message came to me from the **L**:
16: 3 Give her this message from the Sovereign **L**:
16: 8 says the Sovereign **L**, and you became mine.
16:14 you perfected your beauty, says the Sovereign **L**.
16:19 and honey I had given you, says the Sovereign **L**.
16:23 "Your destruction is certain, says the Sovereign **L**.
16:30 says the Sovereign **L**, to do such things as these,
16:35 you prostitute, listen to this message from the **L**!
16:36 This is what the Sovereign **L** says: Because you
16:43 you for all of your sins, says the Sovereign **L**.
16:48 says the Sovereign **L**, Sodom and her daughters
16:58 punishment for all your disgusting sins, says the **L**.
16:59 "Now this is what the Sovereign **L** says: I will
16:62 with you, and you will know that I am the **L**.
16:63 of all that you have done, says the Sovereign **L**."
17: 1 Then this message came to me from the **L**:
17: 3 Give them this message from the Sovereign **L**:
17: 9 "So now the Sovereign **L** asks: Should I let this
17:11 Then this message came to me from the **L**:
17:12 I will tell you, says the Sovereign **L**. The king of
17:16 For as surely as I live, says the Sovereign **L**,
17:19 "So this is what the Sovereign **L** says: As surely
17:21 will know that I, the **L**, have spoken these words.
17:22 "And the Sovereign **L** says: I will take a tender
17:24 the **L**, who cuts down the tall tree and helps the
17:24 I, the **L**, have spoken! I will do what I have said."
18: 1 Then another message came to me from the **L**:
18: 3 As surely as I live, says the Sovereign **L**, you will
18: 9 is just and will surely live, says the Sovereign **L**.
18:23 "Do you think, asks the Sovereign **L**, that I like to
18:30 according to your actions, says the Sovereign **L**.
18:32 I don't want you to die, says the Sovereign **L**.
20: 1 of Israel came to request a message from the **L**.
20: 2 Then this message came to me from the **L**:
20: 3 of Israel this message from the Sovereign **L**:
20: 3 you nothing. This is the word of the Sovereign **L**!
20: 5 Give them this message from the Sovereign **L**:
20: 5 in Egypt, I swore that I, the **L**, would be her God.
20: 7 with the Egyptian gods, for I am the **L** your God.'
20:12 It was to remind them that I, the **L**, had set them
20:19 'I am the **L** your God,' I told them. 'Follow my
20:20 for they are a sign to remind you that I am the **L**
20:26 and show them that I alone am the **L**.
20:27 of Israel this message from the Sovereign **L**:
20:30 of Israel this message from the Sovereign **L**:
20:31 As surely as I live, says the Sovereign **L**, I will not
20:33 As surely as I live, says the Sovereign **L**, I will rule
20:36 bringing them out of Egypt, says the Sovereign **L**.
20:38 when that happens, you will know that I am the **L**.
20:39 people of Israel, this is what the Sovereign **L** says:
20:40 For on my holy mountain, says the Sovereign **L**,
20:42 your ancestors, you will know that I am the **L**.
20:44 You will know that I am the **L**, O people of Israel,
20:44 spite of your wickedness, says the Sovereign **L**."
20:45 Then this message came to me from the **L**:
20:47 wilderness this message from the Sovereign **L**:
20:47 Hear the word of the **L**! I will set you on fire,
20:48 the world will see that I, the **L**, have set this fire.
20:49 Then I said, "O Sovereign **L**, they are saying of
21: 1 Then this message came to me from the **L**:
21: 3 Give her this message from the **L**: I am your
21: 5 All the world will know that I am the **L**. My sword
21: 7 And the Sovereign **L** says: It is coming! It's on its
21: 8 Then the **L** said to me,
21: 9 of man, give the people this message from the **L**:
21:13 So now the Sovereign **L** asks: What chance do
21:17 and I will satisfy my fury. I, the **L**, have spoken!"
21:18 Then this message came to me from the **L**:
21:24 "Therefore, this is what the Sovereign **L** says:
21:26 off your jeweled crown, says the Sovereign **L**.
21:28 Give them this message from the Sovereign **L**:
21:32 memory lost to history. I, the **L**, have spoken!"
22: 1 Now this message came to me from the **L**:
22: 3 and give her this message from the Sovereign **L**:
22:12 of me and my commands, says the Sovereign **L**.
22:14 I, the **L**, have spoken! I will do what I have said.
22:16 the nations, you will know that I am the **L**."
22:17 Then this message came to me from the **L**:
22:19 So give them this message from the Sovereign **L**:
22:22 Then you will know that I, the **L**, have poured out
22:23 Again a message came to me from the **L**:
22:28 They say, 'My message is from the Sovereign **L**,'
22:28 when the **L** hasn't spoken a single word to them.
22:31 penalty for all their sins, says the Sovereign **L**."
23: 1 This message came to me from the **L**:
23:22 Oholibah, this is what the Sovereign **L** says:
23:28 "For this is what the Sovereign **L** says: I will
23:32 "Yes, this is what the Sovereign **L** says: You will
23:34 in anguish. For I, the Sovereign **L**, have spoken!
23:35 and turned your back on me, says the Sovereign **L**,
23:36 The **L** said to me, "Son of man, you must accuse
23:46 "Now this is what the Sovereign **L** says: Bring an
23:49 Then you will know that I am the Sovereign **L**."
24: 1 this message came to me from the **L**:
24: 3 give them a message from the Sovereign **L**.
24: 6 "Now this is what the Sovereign **L** says:
24: 9 "This is what the Sovereign **L** says: Destruction is
24:14 I, the **L**, have spoken! The time has come and I
24:14 of all your wicked actions, says the Sovereign **L**."
24:15 Then this message came to me from the **L**:
24:20 said to them, "A message came to me from the **L**,
24:21 This is what the Sovereign **L** says: I will desecrate
24:24 that time comes, you will know that I am the **L**."
24:25 Then the **L** said to me, "Son of man, on the day I
24:27 Then they will know that I am the **L**."
25: 1 Then this message came to me from the **L**:
25: 3 Ammonites this message from the Sovereign **L**:
25: 3 Hear the word of the Sovereign **L**! Because you
25: 5 for sheep. Then you will know that I am the **L**.
25: 6 "And the Sovereign **L** says: Because you clapped
25: 7 Then you will know that I am the **L**.
25: 8 "And the Sovereign **L** says: Because the people of
25:11 the Moabites. Then they will know that I am the **L**.
25:12 "And the Sovereign **L** says: The people of Edom

25:13 Therefore, says the Sovereign **L**, I will raise my
25:14 it is from me. I, the Sovereign **L**, have spoken!
25:15 "And the Sovereign **L** says: The people of
25:16 Therefore, says the Sovereign **L**, I will raise my
25:17 my revenge, then they will know that I am the **L**."
26: 1 this message came to me from the **L**:
26: 3 "Therefore, this is what the Sovereign **L** says:
26: 5 their nets, for I have spoken, says the Sovereign **L**.
26: 6 by the sword. Then they will know that I am the **L**.
26: 7 "For the Sovereign **L** says: I will bring King
26:14 will never be rebuilt, for I, the **L**, have spoken! This is the word of the Sovereign **L**.
26:15 "This is what the Sovereign **L** says to Tyre:
26:19 "For the Sovereign **L** says: I will make Tyre an
26:21 never be found. I, the Sovereign **L**, have spoken!"
27: 1 Then this message came to me from the **L**:
27: 3 Give Tyre this message from the Sovereign **L**:
28: 1 Then this message came to me from the **L**:
28: 2 prince of Tyre this message from the Sovereign **L**:
28: 6 "Therefore, this is what the Sovereign **L** says:
28:10 of foreigners. I, the Sovereign **L**, have spoken!"
28:11 Then this further message came to me from the **L**:
28:12 Give him this message from the Sovereign **L**:
28:20 Then another message came to me from the **L**:
28:22 of Sidon this message from the Sovereign **L**:
28:22 everyone watching will know that I am the **L**.
28:23 Then everyone will know that I am the **L**.
28:24 then they will know that I am the Sovereign **L**.
28:25 "This is what the Sovereign **L** says: The people of
28:26 they will know that I am the **L** their God."
29: 1 this message came to me from the **L**:
29: 3 Give them this message from the Sovereign **L**:
29: 6 the people of Egypt will discover that I am the **L**,
29: 8 So now the Sovereign **L** says: I will bring an army
29: 9 and the Egyptians will know that I am the **L**.
29:13 "But the Sovereign **L** also says: At the end of the
29:16 Israel will know that I alone am the Sovereign **L**."
29:17 this message came to me from the **L**:
29:19 Therefore, this is what the Sovereign **L** says:
29:20 says the Sovereign **L**, because he was working for
29:21 Then they will know that I am the **L**."
30: 1 is another message that came to me from the **L**:
30: 2 and give this message from the Sovereign **L**:
30: 3 the terrible day is almost here—the day of the **L**!
30: 6 "For this is what the **L** says: All of Egypt's allies
30: 6 be slaughtered by the sword, says the Sovereign **L**.
30: 8 And the people of Egypt will know that I am the **L**
30:10 "For this is what the Sovereign **L** says:
30:12 using foreigners to do it. I, the **L**, have spoken!
30:13 "This is what the Sovereign **L** says: I will smash
30:19 and they will know that I am the **L**."
30:20 this message came to me from the **L**:
30:22 Therefore, this is what the Sovereign **L** says:
30:25 the land of Egypt, Egypt will know that I am the **L**.
30:26 the nations. Then they will know that I am the **L**."
31: 1 this message came to me from the **L**:
31:10 "Therefore, this is what the Sovereign **L** says:
31:15 "This is what the Sovereign **L** says: When Assyria
31:18 teeming hordes. I, the Sovereign **L**, have spoken!"
32: 1 this message came to me from the **L**:
32: 3 "Therefore, this is what the Sovereign **L** says:
32: 8 dark above you. I, the Sovereign **L**, have spoken!
32:11 "For this is what the Sovereign **L** says: The sword
32:14 as smoothly as olive oil, says the Sovereign **L**.
32:15 your people, then you will know that I am the **L**.
32:16 and its hordes. I, the Sovereign **L**, have spoken!"
32:17 another message came to me from the **L**:
32:31 his entire army killed, says the Sovereign **L**.
32:32 by the sword. I, the Sovereign **L**, have spoken!"
33: 1 Once again a message came to me from the **L**:
33:11 As surely as I live, says the Sovereign **L**, I take no
33:22 The previous evening the **L** had taken hold of me
33:23 Then this message came to me from the **L**:
33:25 these people this message from the Sovereign **L**:
33:27 "Give them this message from the Sovereign **L**:
33:29 then they will know that I am the **L**.
33:30 Let's go hear the prophet tell us what the **L** is
34: 1 Then this message came to me from the **L**:
34: 2 Give them this message from the Sovereign **L**:
34: 7 you shepherds, hear the word of the **L**:
34: 8 As surely as I live, says the Sovereign **L**,
34: 9 Therefore, you shepherds, hear the word of the **L**.
34:10 This is what the Sovereign **L** says: I now consider
34:11 "For this is what the Sovereign **L** says: I myself
34:15 them to lie down in peace, says the Sovereign **L**.
34:17 my people, this is what the Sovereign **L** says:
34:20 "Therefore, this is what the Sovereign **L** says:
34:24 And I, the **L**, will be their God, and my servant
34:24 a prince among my people. I, the **L**, have spoken!
34:27 then they will know that I am the **L**.
34:30 will know that I, the **L** their God, am with them.
34:30 of Israel, are my people, says the Sovereign **L**.
34:31 and I am your God, says the Sovereign **L**."
35: 1 Again a message came to me from the **L**:
35: 3 Give them this message from the Sovereign **L**:
35: 4 and then you will know that I am the **L**.
35: 6 As surely as I live, says the Sovereign **L**, since you
35: 9 be rebuilt. Then you will know that I am the **L**.
35:10 of them. What do we care that the **L** is there!'
35:11 Therefore, as surely as I live, says the Sovereign **L**,
35:12 Then you will know that I, the **L**, have heard every
35:14 "This is what the Sovereign **L** says: The whole
35:15 live in Edom! Then you will know that I am the **L**!
36: 1 O mountains of Israel, hear the word of the **L**!
36: 2 This is what the Sovereign **L** says: Your enemies
36: 3 of Israel this message from the Sovereign **L**:
36: 4 of Israel, hear the word of the Sovereign **L**.
36: 5 This is what the Sovereign **L** says: My jealous
36: 6 Give them this message from the Sovereign **L**:
36: 7 Therefore, says the Sovereign **L**, I have raised my
36:11 were before. Then you will know that I am the **L**.
36:13 "This is what the Sovereign **L** says: Now the other
36:14 or bereave your nation, says the Sovereign **L**.
36:15 or cause your nation to fall, says the Sovereign **L**."
36:16 Then this further message came to me from the **L**:
36:20 the nations said, 'These are the people of the **L**,
36:22 of Israel this message from the Sovereign **L**:
36:23 says the Sovereign **L**, then the nations will know that I am the **L**.
36:32 But remember, says the Sovereign **L**, I am not
36:33 "This is what the Sovereign **L** says: When I
36:36 the **L**, rebuilt the ruins and planted lush crops in
36:36 For I, the **L**, have promised this, and I will do it.
36:37 "This is what the Sovereign **L** says: I am ready to
36:38 and everyone will know that I am the **L**."
37: 1 The **L** took hold of me, and I was carried away by the Spirit of the **L** to a
37: 3 "O Sovereign **L**," I replied, "you alone know the
37: 4 and say, 'Dry bones, listen to the word of the **L**!
37: 5 This is what the Sovereign **L** says: Look! I am
37: 6 to life. Then you will know that I am the **L**.' "
37: 9 'This is what the Sovereign **L** says: Come,
37:12 give them this message from the Sovereign **L**:
37:13 O my people, you will know that I am the **L**.
37:14 own land. Then you will know that I am the **L**.
37:14 just as I promised. I, the **L**, have spoken!"
37:15 Again a message came to me from the **L**:
37:19 say to them, 'This is what the Sovereign **L** says:
37:21 And give them this message from the Sovereign **L**:
37:28 the nations will know that I, the **L**, have set Israel
38: 1 is another message that came to me from the **L**:
38: 3 Give him this message from the Sovereign **L**:
38:10 "This is what the Sovereign **L** says: At that time
38:14 Give him this message from the Sovereign **L**:
38:16 Then all the nations will know that I am the **L**.
38:17 "This is what the Sovereign **L** says: You are the
38:18 of Israel, says the Sovereign **L**, my fury will rise!
38:21 you throughout Israel, says the Sovereign **L**.
38:23 of the world. Then they will know that I am the **L**!
39: 1 Give him this message from the Sovereign **L**:
39: 5 for I have spoken, says the Sovereign **L**.
39: 6 on the coasts. Then they will know that I am the **L**.
39: 7 And the nations, too, will know that I am the **L**,
39: 8 day of judgment will come, says the Sovereign **L**.
39:10 planned to plunder them, says the Sovereign **L**.
39:13 my glory on that day, says the Sovereign **L**.
39:17 the birds and wild animals, says the Sovereign **L**.
39:20 riders, and valiant warriors, says the Sovereign **L**.
39:22 of Israel will know that I am the **L** their God.
39:25 "So now the Sovereign **L** says: I will end the
39:28 Then my people will know that I am the **L** their
39:29 out my Spirit upon them, says the Sovereign **L**."
40: 1 after the fall of Jerusalem—the **L** took hold of me.
40:46 Levites may approach the **L** to minister to him."
42:13 sacrifices to the **L** will eat the most holy offerings.
43: 4 And the glory of the **L** came into the Temple
43: 5 and the glory of the **L** filled the Temple.
43: 7 And the **L** said to me, "Son of man, this is the
43:18 "Son of man, this is what the Sovereign **L** says:
43:19 young bull for a sin offering, says the Sovereign **L**.
43:24 You are to present them to the **L**, and the priests
43:24 and offer them as a burnt offering to the **L**.
43:27 Then I will accept you, says the Sovereign **L**."
44: 2 And the **L** said to me, "This gate must remain
44: 2 for the **L**, the God of Israel, entered here.
44: 4 the glory of the **L** filled the Temple of the **L**,
44: 5 And the **L** said to me, "Son of man, take careful
44: 6 of Israel, this message from the Sovereign **L**:
44: 9 "So this is what the Sovereign **L** says:
44: 9 have not been circumcised and do not love the **L**.
44:12 consequences for their sins, says the Sovereign **L**.
44:15 and blood of the sacrifices, says the Sovereign **L**.
44:27 a sin offering for himself, says the Sovereign **L**.
44:29 Whatever anyone sets apart for the **L** will belong
44:30 and all the gifts brought to the **L** will go to the
44:30 given to the priests so the **L** will bless your homes.
45: 1 you must set aside a section of it for the **L** as his
45: 4 set aside for the priests who minister to the **L** in the
45: 9 For this is what the Sovereign **L** says: Enough,
45:15 the people who bring them, says the Sovereign **L**.
45:18 "This is what the Sovereign **L** says: In early
45:23 the feast he will prepare a burnt offering to the **L**.
46: 1 "This is what the Sovereign **L** says: The east
46: 3 The common people will worship the **L** in front of
46: 4 "Each Sabbath day the prince will present to the **L**
46: 9 to worship the **L** during the religious festivals,
46:12 voluntary burnt offering or peace offering to the **L**,
46:13 must be sacrificed as a burnt offering to the **L**.
46:14 a grain offering must also be given to the **L**—
46:16 "This is what the Sovereign **L** says: If the prince
47:13 This is what the Sovereign **L** says: "Follow these
47:23 they now live. I, the Sovereign **L**, have spoken!
48:14 or traded or used by others, for it belongs to the **L**;
48:29 for each tribe's inheritance, says the Sovereign **L**.
48:35 the name of the city will be 'The **L** Is There.' "
Da 9: 2 I learned from the word of the **L**, as recorded by
9: 4 I prayed to the **L** my God and confessed: "O Lord,
9: 8 O **L**, we and our kings, princes, and ancestors are
9:10 We have not obeyed the **L** our God, for we have
9:13 But we have refused to seek mercy from the **L** our
9:14 The **L** has brought against us the disaster he
9:14 and the **L** our God is just in everything he does.
9:20 pleading with the **L** my God for Jerusalem,
Hos 1: 1 The **L** gave these messages to Hosea son of Beeri
1: 2 When the **L** first began speaking to Israel through
1: 2 openly committing adultery against the **L** by
1: 4 And the **L** said, "Name the child Jezreel, for I am
1: 6 And the **L** said to Hosea, "Name your daughter
1: 7 But I, the **L** their God, will show love to the people
1: 9 And the **L** said, "Name him Lo-ammi—'Not my
2:13 and went out looking for her lovers," says the **L**.
2:16 "In that coming day," says the **L**, "you will call
2:20 you mine, and you will finally know me as **L**.
2:21 "In that day," says the **L**, "I will answer the
3: 1 Then the **L** said to me, "Go and get your wife
3: 1 For the **L** still loves Israel even though the people
3: 5 But afterward the people will return to the **L** their
3: 5 They will come trembling in awe to the **L**,
4: 1 Hear the word of the **L**, O people of Israel!
4: 1 The **L** has filed a lawsuit against you, saying:
4:10 for they have deserted the **L** to worship other gods.
4:16 as a heifer, so the **L** will put her out to pasture.
5: 4 and through, and you cannot know the **L**.
5: 6 their flocks and herds to offer sacrifices to the **L**.
5: 7 For they have betrayed the honor of the **L**,
6: 1 "Come, let us return to the **L**! He has torn us in
6: 3 Oh, that we might know the **L**! Let us press on to
6: 4 what should I do with you?" asks the **L**.
7:10 yet he doesn't return to the **L** his God or even try
8: 1 descends like an eagle on the people of the **L**,
9: 3 You may no longer stay here in this land of the **L**.
9: 4 be allowed to pour out wine as a sacrifice to the **L**.
9: 4 feed themselves, but they may not offer it to the **L**.
9:10 The **L** says, "O Israel, when I first found you,
9:14 O **L**, what should I request for your people?
9:15 The **L** says, "All their wickedness began at Gilgal;
10: 2 The **L** will break down their foreign altars
10: 3 "We have no king because we didn't fear the **L**.
10: 9 The **L** says, "O Israel, ever since that awful night
10:12 for now is the time to seek the **L**, that he may come
11:10 "For someday the people will follow the **L**.
11:11 And I will bring them home again," says the **L**.
12: 2 Now the **L** is bringing a lawsuit against Judah.
12: 5 the **L** God Almighty, the **L** is his name!
12: 9 "I am the **L** your God, who rescued you from your
12:13 Then the **L** led Jacob's descendants, the Israelites,
12:14 the people of Israel have bitterly provoked the **L**,
13: 4 "I am the **L** your God, who rescued you from your
13:15 but the east wind—a blast from the **L**—
14: 1 Return, O Israel, to the **L** your God, for your sins
14: 2 Bring your petitions, and return to the **L**. Say to
14: 4 The **L** says, "Then I will heal you of your idolatry
14: 9 The paths of the **L** are true and right, and righteous
Joel 1: 1 The **L** gave this message to Joel son of Pethuel.
1: 9 is no grain or wine to offer at the Temple of the **L**.
1: 9 Listen to the weeping of these ministers of the **L**!
1:14 and all the people into the Temple of the **L** your
1:15 The day of the **L** is on the way, the day when
1:19 **L**, help us! The fire has consumed the pastures
2: 1 tremble in fear because the day of the **L** is upon us.
2:11 The **L** leads them with a shout! This is his mighty
2:11 The day of the **L** is an awesome, terrible thing.
2:12 That is why the **L** says, "Turn to me now,
2:13 Return to the **L** your God, for he is gracious
2:14 offer grain and wine to the **L** your God as before!
2:17 weeping. Let them pray, "Spare your people, **L**!
2:18 Then the **L** will pity his people and be indignant
2:20 over the land." Surely the **L** has done great things!
2:21 and rejoice because the **L** has done great things.
2:23 people of Jerusalem! Rejoice in the **L** your God!
2:25 The **L** says, "I will give you back what you lost to
2:26 and you will praise the **L** your God, who does
2:27 of Israel and that I alone am the **L** your God.
2:31 before that great and terrible day of the **L** arrives.
2:32 And anyone who calls on the name of the **L** will be
2:32 in Jerusalem who escape, just as the **L** has said.
2:32 These will be among the survivors whom the **L** has
3: 1 prosperity of Judah and Jerusalem," says the **L**,
3: 8 a nation far away. I, the **L**, have spoken!"
3:11 the valley." And now, O **L**, call out your warriors!
3:12 There I, the **L**, will sit to pronounce judgment on
3:14 It is there that the day of the **L** will soon arrive.
3:16 the **L** will be a welcoming refuge and a strong
3:17 the **L** your God, live in Zion, my holy mountain.
3:21 and I, the **L**, will make my home in Jerusalem with
Am 1: 3 This is what the **L** says: "The people of Damascus
1: 5 will return to Kir as slaves. I, the **L**, have spoken!"
1: 6 This is what the **L** says: "The people of Gaza have
1: 8 will be killed. I, the Sovereign **L**, have spoken!"
1: 9 This is what the **L** says: "The people of Tyre have
1:11 This is what the **L** says: "The people of Edom
1:13 This is what the **L** says: "The people of Ammon
1:15 will go into exile together. I, the **L**, have spoken!"
2: 1 This is what the **L** says: "The people of Moab
2: 3 slaughter all their princes. I, the **L**, have spoken!"
2: 4 This is what the **L** says: "The people of Judah
2: 4 They have rejected the laws of the **L**, refusing to
2: 6 This is what the **L** says: "The people of Israel
2:11 you deny this, my people of Israel?" asks the **L**.
2:16 and run for their lives. I, the **L**, have spoken!"
3: 1 Listen to this message that the **L** has spoken
3: 6 comes to a city, isn't it because the **L** planned it?
3: 7 I, the Sovereign **L**, have now done this."
3: 8 The Sovereign **L** has spoken—I dare not refuse to
3:10 forgotten what it means to do right," says the **L**.
3:11 Therefore," says the Sovereign **L**, "an enemy is
3:12 This is what the **L** says: "A shepherd who tries to
3:13 all Israel," says the Lord, the **L** God Almighty.
3:15 palaces filled with ivory. I, the **L**, have spoken!"
4: 2 The Sovereign **L** has sworn this by his holiness:
4: 3 thrown from your fortresses. I, the **L**, have spoken!

4: 5 you Israelites love to do," says the Sovereign **L**.
4: 6 But still you wouldn't return to me," says the **L**.
4: 8 But still you wouldn't return to me," says the **L**.
4: 9 But still you wouldn't return to me," says the **L**.
4:10 But still you wouldn't return to me," says the **L**.
4:11 But still you wouldn't return to me," says the **L**.
4:13 For the **L** is the one who shaped the mountains,
4:13 under his feet. The **L** God Almighty is his name!
5: 3 The Sovereign **L** says: "When one of your cities
5: 4 Now this is what the **L** says to the family of Israel:
5: 6 Come back to the **L** and live! If you don't, he will
5: 8 It is the **L** who created the stars, the Pleiades
5: 8 it down as rain on the land. The **L** is his name!
5:14 Then the **L** God Almighty will truly be your
5:15 Perhaps even yet the **L** God Almighty will have
5:16 this is what the Lord, the **L** God Almighty, says:
5:17 and destroy them all. I, the **L**, have spoken!"
5:18 you who say, "If only the day of the **L** were here!
5:18 then the **L** would rescue us from all our enemies."
5:20 the day of the **L** will be a dark and hopeless day,
5:27 into exile, to a land east of Damascus," says the **L**,
6: 8 The Sovereign **L** has sworn by his own name,
6: 8 and this is what he, the **L** God Almighty, says:
6:10 "Hush! Don't even whisper the name of the **L**.
6:11 When the **L** gives the command, homes both great
6:14 nation against you," says the **L** God Almighty.
7: 1 The Sovereign **L** showed me a vision. I saw him
7: 2 Then I said, "O Sovereign **L**, please forgive your
7: 3 So the **L** relented and did not fulfill the vision.
7: 4 Then the Sovereign **L** showed me another vision.
7: 5 Then I said, "O Sovereign **L**, please don't do it.
7: 6 Then the **L** turned from this plan, too. "I won't do
that either," said the Sovereign **L**.
7: 8 And the **L** said to me, "Amos, what do you see?"
7:15 But the **L** called me away from my flock and told
7:16 "Now then, listen to this message from the **L**!
7:17 But this is what the **L** says: Because you have
8: 1 Then the Sovereign **L** showed me another vision.
8: 2 Then the **L** said, "This fruit represents my people
8: 3 city in silence. I, the Sovereign **L**, have spoken!"
8: 7 Now the **L** has sworn this oath by his own name,
8: 9 At that time," says the Sovereign **L**, "I will make
8:11 time is surely coming," says the Sovereign **L**,
8:11 or water but of hearing the words of the **L**.
8:12 searching for the word of the **L**, running here
9: 5 The Lord, the **L** Almighty, touches the land and it
9: 6 it down as rain on the land. The **L** is his name!
9: 7 asks the **L**. "I brought you out of Egypt, but have I
9: 8 "I, the Sovereign **L**, am watching this sinful nation
9: 8 destroy the family of Israel," says the **L**.
9:12 I, the **L**, have spoken, and I will do these things.
9:13 says the **L**, "when the grain and grapes will grow
9:15 the land I have given them," says the **L** your God.
Ob 1: 1 This is the vision that the Sovereign **L** revealed to
1: 1 We have heard a message from the **L** that an
1: 2 The **L** says, "I will cut you down to size among
1: 4 bring you crashing down. I, the **L**, have spoken!
1: 8 says the **L**. "For on the mountains of Edom I will
1:15 "The day is near when I, the **L**, will judge the
1:18 no survivors in Edom. I, the **L**, have spoken!
1:21 of Edom. And the **L** himself will be king!"
Jnh 1: 1 The **L** gave this message to Jonah son of Amittai:
1: 3 opposite direction in order to get away from the **L**.
1: 3 away to the west he could escape from the **L**.
1: 4 suddenly the **L** flung a powerful wind over the sea,
1: 9 "I am a Hebrew, and I worship the **L**, the God of
1:10 he told them that he was running away from the **L**.
1:14 Then they cried out to the **L**, Jonah's God.
1:14 "O **L**," they pleaded, "don't make us die for this
1:14 O **L**, you have sent this storm upon him for your
1:17 Now the **L** had arranged for a great fish to swallow
2: 1 Then Jonah prayed to the **L** his God from inside
2: 2 He said, "I cried out to the **L** in my great trouble,
2: 2 from the world of the dead, and **L**, you heard me!
2: 4 Then I said, 'O **L**, you have driven me from your
2: 6 But you, O **L** my God, have snatched me from the
2: 7 all hope, I turned my thoughts once more to the **L**.
2: 9 For my salvation comes from the **L** alone."
2:10 Then the **L** ordered the fish to spit up Jonah on the
3: 1 Then the **L** spoke to Jonah a second time:
4: 2 So he complained to the **L** about it: "Didn't I say
before I left home that you would do this, **L**?
4: 3 Just kill me now, **L**! I'd rather be dead than alive
4: 4 The **L** replied, "Is it right for you to be angry
4: 6 And the **L** God arranged for a leafy plant to grow
4:10 Then the **L** said, "You feel sorry about the plant,
Mic 1: 1 The **L** gave these messages to Micah of Moresheth
1: 2 The Sovereign **L** has made accusations against
1: 3 Look! The **L** is coming! He leaves his throne in
1: 6 "So I, the **L**, will make the city of Samaria a heap
2: 3 But this is what the **L** says: "I will reward your
2: 7 Will the **L** have patience with such behavior?
2:13 king will lead you; the **L** himself will guide you."
3: 4 Then you beg the **L** for help in times of trouble!
3: 5 This is what the **L** says to you false prophets:
3: 8 I am filled with power and the Spirit of the **L**.
3:11 Yet all of you claim you are depending on the **L**.
3:11 to us," you say, "for the **L** is here among us."
4: 1 the Temple of the **L** in Jerusalem will become the
4: 2 "Come, let us go up to the mountain of the **L**,
4: 3 The **L** will settle international disputes.
4: 4 nothing to fear. The **L** Almighty has promised this!
4: 5 we will follow the **L** our God forever and ever.
4: 6 "In that coming day," says the **L**, "I will gather
4: 7 Then I, the **L**, will rule from Jerusalem as their
4:10 But the **L** will rescue you there; he will redeem
4:13 and destroy the nations, O Jerusalem!" says the **L**.
5: 4 in the majesty of the name of the **L** his God.
5: 7 They will be like dew sent by the **L** or like rain
5:10 "At that same time," says the **L**, "I will destroy
6: 1 Listen to what the **L** is saying: "Stand up and state
6: 5 your journey from Acacia to Gilgal, when I, the **L**,
6: 6 What can we bring to the **L** to make up for what
6: 7 of rivers of olive oil? Would that please the **L**?
6: 8 O people, the **L** has already told you what is good,
6: 9 Listen! Fear the **L** if you are wise! His voice is
6: 9 of destruction are coming; the **L** is sending them.
7: 7 As for me, I look to the **L** for his help. I wait
7: 8 I sit in darkness, the **L** himself will be my light.
7: 9 I will be patient as the **L** punishes me, for I have
7: 9 The **L** will bring me out of my darkness into the
7:10 Then my enemies will see that the **L** is on my side.
7:10 that they taunted me, saying, "Where is the **L**—
7:14 O **L**, come and rule your people; lead your flock in
7:15 "Yes," says the **L**, "I will do mighty miracles for
7:16 will stand amazed at what the **L** will do for you.
7:17 they will come out to meet the **L** our God.
Na 1: 2 The **L** is a jealous God, filled with vengeance
1: 3 The **L** is slow to get angry, but his power is great,
1: 7 The **L** is good. When trouble comes, he is a strong
1: 9 Why are you scheming against the **L**? He will
1:11 king of yours who dares to plot evil against the **L**?
1:12 This is what the **L** says: "Even though the
1:14 And this is what the **L** says concerning the
2: 2 but the **L** will restore its honor and power again.
2:13 "I am your enemy!" says the **L** Almighty.
3: 5 declares the **L** Almighty. "And now I will lift your
Hab 1: 1 prophet Habakkuk received from the **L** in a vision.
1: 2 How long, O **L**, must I call for help? But you do
1: 5 The **L** replied, "Look at the nations and be
1:12 O **L** my God, my Holy One, you who are eternal—
1:12 O **L** our Rock, you have decreed the rise of these
2: 1 and wait to see what the **L** will say to me and how
2: 2 Then the **L** said to me, "Write my answer in large,
2:13 Has not the **L** Almighty promised that the wealth
2:14 the sea, with an awareness of the glory of the **L**.
2:20 But the **L** is in his holy Temple. Let all the earth be
3: 2 I have heard all about you, **L**, and I am filled with
3: 8 Was it in anger, **L**, that you struck the rivers
3:10 mighty deep cried out, lifting its hands to the **L**.
3:18 yet I will rejoice in the **L**! I will be joyful in the
3:19 The Sovereign **L** is my strength! He will make me
Zep 1: 1 The **L** gave these messages to Zephaniah when
1: 2 away everything in all your land," says the **L**.
1: 3 along with the rest of humanity," says the **L**.
1: 5 They claim to follow the **L**, but then they worship
1: 7 in silence in the presence of the Sovereign **L**,
1: 7 The **L** has prepared his people for a great slaughter
1: 8 says the **L**, "I will punish the leaders and princes
1:10 "On that day," says the **L**, "a cry of alarm will
1:12 indifferent to the **L**, thinking he will do nothing at
1:14 "That terrible day of the **L** is near. Swiftly it
1:17 "Because you have sinned against the **L**, I will
2: 2 before the fierce fury of the **L** falls and the terrible
2: 3 Beg the **L** to save you—all you who are humble,
2: 3 Perhaps even yet the **L** will protect you from his
2: 5 The **L** will destroy you until not one of you is left.
2: 7 For the **L** their God will visit his people in
2: 9 says the **L** Almighty, the God of Israel, "Moab
2:10 for they have scoffed at the people of the **L**
2:11 The **L** will terrify them as he destroys all the gods
2:11 from nations around the world will worship the **L**,
2:12 will also be slaughtered by my sword," says the **L**.
2:13 And the **L** will strike the lands of the north with his
3: 2 proudly refuses to listen even to the voice of the **L**.
3: 2 It does not trust in the **L** or draw near to its God.
3: 5 But the **L** is still there in the city, and he does no
3: 8 So now the **L** says: "Be patient; the time is
3: 9 so that everyone will be able to worship the **L**
3:12 for it is they who trust in the name of the **L**.
3:15 For the **L** will remove his hand of judgment
3:15 And the **L** himself, the King of Israel, will live
3:17 For the **L** your God has arrived to live among you.
3:20 before their very eyes. I, the **L**, have spoken!"
Hag 1: 1 the **L** gave a message through the prophet Haggai
1: 2 "This is what the **L** Almighty says: The people are
1: 3 So the **L** sent this message through the prophet
1: 5 This is what the **L** Almighty says: Consider how
1: 7 "This is what the **L** Almighty says: Consider how
1: 8 will take pleasure in it and be honored, says the **L**.
1: 9 my house lies in ruins, says the **L** Almighty,
1:12 people obeyed the message from the **L** their God.
1:12 prophet Haggai, whom the **L** their God had sent,
1:12 and the people worshiped the **L** in earnest.
1:13 message from the **L**: "I am with you, says the **L**!"
1:14 So the **L** sparked the enthusiasm of Zerubbabel son
1:14 and began their work on the house of the **L**
2: 1 the **L** sent another message through the prophet
2: 4 But now take courage, Zerubbabel, says the **L**.
2: 4 all you people still left in the land, says the **L**.
2: 4 and work, for I am with you, says the **L** Almighty.
2: 6 "For this is what the **L** Almighty says: In just a
2: 7 will fill this place with glory, says the **L** Almighty.
2: 8 is mine, and the gold is mine, says the **L** Almighty.
2: 9 be greater than its past glory, says the **L** Almighty.
2: 9 will bring peace. I, the **L** Almighty, have spoken!"
2:10 the **L** sent this message to the prophet Haggai:
2:11 "This is what the **L** Almighty says! Ask the priests
2:14 it is with this people and this nation, says the **L**.
2:17 even so, you refused to return to me, says the **L**.
2:20 The **L** sent this second message to Haggai on
2:23 says the **L** Almighty, I will honor you,
2:23 says the **L**, for I have specially chosen you. I, the
L Almighty, have spoken!"
Zec 1: 1 the **L** gave this message to the prophet Zechariah
1: 2 "I, the **L**, was very angry with your ancestors.
1: 3 to the people, 'This is what the **L** Almighty says:
1: 3 and I will return to you, says the **L** Almighty.'
1: 4 said to them, 'This is what the **L** Almighty says:
1: 6 'We have received what we deserved from the **L**
1: 7 the **L** sent another message to the prophet
1:10 "They are the ones the **L** has sent out to patrol the
1:11 Then the other riders reported to the angel of the **L**,
1:12 hearing this, the angel of the **L** prayed this prayer:
1:12 "O **L** Almighty, for seventy years now you have
1:13 And the **L** spoke kind and comforting words to the
1:14 'This is what the **L** Almighty says: My love for
1:16 " 'Therefore, this is what the **L** says: I have
1:16 My Temple will be rebuilt, says the **L** Almighty,
1:17 Say this also: 'This is what the **L** Almighty says:
1:17 and the **L** will again comfort Zion and choose
1:20 Then the **L** showed me four blacksmiths.
2: 5 will be a wall of fire around Jerusalem, says the **L**.
2: 6 The **L** says, "Come away! Flee from the north,
2: 8 the **L** Almighty sent me against the nations who
2: 9 Then you will know that the **L** Almighty has sent
2:10 The **L** says, "Shout and rejoice, O Jerusalem,
2:11 Many nations will join themselves to the **L** on that
2:11 and you will know that the **L** Almighty sent me to
2:13 Be silent before the **L**, all humanity, for he is
3: 1 the high priest standing before the angel of the **L**.
3: 2 And the **L** said to Satan, "I, the **L**, reject your
accusations, Satan.
3: 2 Yes, the **L**, who has chosen Jerusalem,
3: 5 in new clothes while the angel of the **L** stood by.
3: 6 Then the angel of the **L** spoke very solemnly to
3: 7 "This is what the **L** Almighty says: If you follow
3: 9 engrave an inscription on it, says the **L** Almighty,
3:10 And on that day, says the **L** Almighty, each of you
4: 6 to me, "This is what the **L** says to Zerubbabel:
4: 6 by strength, but by my Spirit, says the **L** Almighty.
4: 8 Then another message came to me from the **L**:
4: 9 Then you will know that the **L** Almighty has sent
4:10 for the **L** rejoices to see the work begin,
4:10 For these seven lamps represent the eyes of the **L**
5: 4 And this is what the **L** Almighty says: I am
6: 7 And the **L** said, "Go and patrol the earth!"
6: 8 Then the **L** summoned me and said, "Those who
6: 9 Then I received another message from the **L**:
6:12 Tell him that the **L** Almighty says: Here is the man
6:12 out where he is and build the Temple of the **L**.
6:14 the Temple of the **L** to honor those who gave it—
6:15 from distant lands to rebuild the Temple of the **L**.
6:15 you will know my messages have been from the **L**
6:15 carefully obey the commands of the **L** your God.
7: 1 another message came to Zechariah from the **L**.
7: 3 and of the priests at the Temple of the **L** Almighty:
7: 4 The **L** Almighty sent me this message:
7: 7 Isn't this the same message the **L** proclaimed
7: 8 Then this message came to Zechariah from the **L**:
7: 9 "This is what the **L** Almighty says: Judge fairly
7:12 or the messages that the **L** Almighty had sent them
7:12 That is why the **L** Almighty was so angry with
7:13 when they called to me, says the **L** Almighty.
8: 1 Then another message came to me from the **L**
8: 2 "This is what the **L** Almighty says: My love for
8: 3 And now the **L** says: I am returning to Mount
8: 3 the mountain of the **L** Almighty will be called the
8: 4 This is what the **L** Almighty says: Once again old
8: 6 "This is what the **L** Almighty says: All this may
8: 6 think this is impossible for me, the **L** Almighty?
8: 7 This is what the **L** Almighty says: You can be sure
8: 9 "This is what the **L** Almighty says: Take heart
8: 9 the **L** Almighty ever since the foundation was laid.
8:11 as I treated them before, says the **L** Almighty.
8:14 "For this is what the **L** Almighty says: I did not
8:14 I promised to punish them, says the **L** Almighty.
8:17 that are false. I hate all these things, says the **L**."
8:18 message that came to me from the **L** Almighty.
8:19 "This is what the **L** Almighty says: The traditional
8:20 "This is what the **L** Almighty says: People from
8:21 'Let us go to Jerusalem to ask the **L** to bless us and
to seek the **L** Almighty.
8:22 will come to Jerusalem to seek the **L** Almighty and
to ask the **L** to bless them.
8:23 "This is what the **L** Almighty says: In those days
9: 1 This is the message from the **L** against the land of
9: 1 including the people of Israel, are on the **L**.
9:14 The **L** will appear above his people; his arrows
9:14 The Sovereign **L** will sound the trumpet; he will go
9:15 The **L** Almighty will protect his people, and they
9:16 day arrives, the **L** their God will rescue his people,
10: 1 Ask the **L** for rain in the spring, and he will give it.
10: 1 It is the **L** who makes storm clouds that drop
10: 3 For the **L** Almighty has arrived to look after his
10: 5 Since the **L** is with them as they fight, they will
10: 6 for I am the **L** their God, who will hear their cries.
10: 7 and be glad; their hearts will rejoice in the **L**.
10:12 they wish by my authority. I, the **L**, have spoken!"
11: 4 This is what the **L** my God says: "Go and care for
11: 5 The sellers will say, 'Praise the **L**, I am now rich!'
11: 6 pity on the inhabitants of the land," says the **L**.
11:11 and they knew that the **L** was speaking to them
11:13 And the **L** said to me, "Throw it to the potters"—
11:13 threw them to the potters in the Temple of the **L**.
11:15 Then the **L** said to me, "Go again and play the part
12: 1 concerning the fate of Israel came from the **L**:
12: 1 "This message is from the **L**, who stretched out
12: 4 "On that day, says the **L**, I will cause every horse
12: 5 Jerusalem have found strength in the **L** Almighty,
12: 7 The **L** will give victory to the rest of Judah first,

12: 8 On that day the L will defend the people of
12: 8 like the angel of the L who goes before them!
13: 2 "And on that day, says the L Almighty, I will get
13: 3 for you have prophesied lies in the name of the L.'
13: 7 the man who is my partner, says the L Almighty.
13: 8 in the land will be cut off and die, says the L.
13: 9 and they will say, 'The L is our God.' "
14: 1 for the day of the L is coming when your
14: 3 Then the L will go out to fight against those
14: 5 Then the L my God will come, and all his holy
14: 7 Only the L knows how this could happen!
14: 9 And the L will be king over all the earth. On that
day there will be one L—his name alone
14:12 And the L will send a plague on all the nations that
14:13 will be terrified, stricken by the L with great panic.
14:16 the L Almighty, and to celebrate the Festival of
14:17 the King, the L Almighty, will have no rain.
14:18 the L will punish them with the same plague that
14:20 these words: SET APART AS HOLY TO THE L.
14:20 And the cooking pots in the Temple of the L will
14:21 and Judah will be set apart as holy to the L
14:21 longer be traders in the Temple of the L Almighty.
Mal 1: 1 This is the message that the L gave to Israel
1: 2 "I have loved you deeply," says the L. But you
1: 2 And the L replies, "I showed my love for you by
1: 4 But this is what the L Almighty says: "They may
1: 4 'The People with Whom the L Is Forever Angry.'
1: 6 The L Almighty says to the priests: "A son honors
1: 7 "You defile them by saying the altar of the L
1: 8 and see how pleased he is!" says the L Almighty.
1: 9 show you any favor at all?" asks the L Almighty.
1:10 not at all pleased with you," says the L Almighty,
1:11 is great among the nations," says the L Almighty.
1:13 You say, 'It's too hard to serve the L,' and you
1:13 noses at his commands," says the L Almighty.
1:13 from you such offerings as these?" asks the L.
1:14 For I am a great king," says the L Almighty,
2: 2 Honor my name," says the L Almighty, "or I will
2: 4 the Levites may continue," says the L Almighty.
2: 7 for the priests are the messengers of the L
2: 8 I made with the Levites," says the L Almighty.
2:12 May the L cut off from the nation of Israel every
2:12 and yet brings an offering to the L Almighty.
2:14 You cry out, "Why has the L abandoned us?"
2:14 Because the L witnessed the vows you and your
2:15 Didn't the L make you one with your wife?
2:16 I hate divorce!" says the L, the God of Israel.
2:16 victim's bloodstained coat," says the L Almighty.
2:17 You have wearied the L with your words.
2:17 You have wearied him by suggesting that the L
3: 1 is surely coming," says the L Almighty.
3: 3 once again offer acceptable sacrifices to the L.
3: 4 Then once more the L will accept the offerings
3: 5 people do not fear me," says the L Almighty.
3: 6 "I am the L, and I do not change. That is why you
3: 7 and I will return to you," says the L Almighty.
3:10 If you do," says the L Almighty, "I will open the
3:11 shrivel before they are ripe," says the L Almighty.
3:12 land will be such a delight," says the L Almighty.
3:13 have said terrible things about me," says the L.
3:14 or by trying to show the L Almighty that we are
3:16 Then those who feared the L spoke with each
other, and the L listened to what they said.
3:17 "They will be my people," says the L Almighty.
4: 1 The L Almighty says, "The day of judgment is
4: 3 were dust under your feet," says the L Almighty.
4: 5 before the great and dreadful day of the L arrives.
Mt 22:44 'The L said to my Lord, / Sit in honor at my right
Mk 12:36 of the Holy Spirit, said, / 'The L said to my Lord,
Lk 20:42 'The L said to my Lord, / Sit in honor at my right
Ac 2:34 into heaven, yet he said, / 'The L said to my Lord,

LORD'S* (557) [GOD*, LORD* (YAHWEH)]

LORD'S* ANOINTED (10) 1Sa 16:6; 24:6,10; 26:9,16, 23; 2Sa 1:14,16; 19:21; La 4:20

LORD'S* COMMAND (25) Ex 17:1; Nu 2:33; 3:39; 9:18,20,23; Dt 1:43; Jos 14:2; 21:8; 22:9; 1Sa 13:14; 15:13, 24,26; 1Ki 11:10; 13:1,2,26; 2Ki 9:12; 17:15; 24:3; 1Ch 10:13; Isa 30:31; Jer 43:4; Jnh 3:3

LORD'S* HOUSE (2) Jos 6:24; Hag 1:2

LORD'S* PEOPLE (15) Nu 11:29; 16:41; 20:4; 31:16; 1Sa 2:24; 26:19; 2Ki 9:6; 11:17; 2Ch 23:16; 36:23; Ps 34:9; 122:4; Isa 5:7; 14:2; Mic 2:5

LORD'S* PRESENCE (52) Ge 4:16; 19:27; 27:7; Ex 16:9; 27:21; 28:30,35; 29:11,26,42; 30:8; 40:25; Lev 1:5,11; 4:4,7, 18; 6:25; 8:26,29; 9:5,24; 10:2; 14:23; 16:13,30; 24:4,6; Nu 3:4; 16:38,40; 17:7,9; 20:3; Dt 10:10; Jos 4:13; Jdg 21:5; 1Ki 8:64; 2Ki 23:3; 1Ch 23:13,31; 29:22; 2Ch 1:6; 34:31; Job 1:12; 2:7; Ps 116:9; Isa 53:2; Eze 41:22; 44:3; Hos 9:5; Joel 2:17

LORD'S* TEMPLE (88) 1Ki 6:37; 7:12,51; 8:64; 9:15; 15:18; 2Ki 11:4,7,13; 12:4,10,11,12,16,18; 16:14; 18:16; 19:14; 21:5; 22:4,8; 23:2,4,6,11,12,24; 24:13; 25:13,16; 1Ch 28:12,13; 2Ch 7:7; 8:1; 15:8; 16:2; 23:5,12,19; 24:12,21; 26:16,19; 27:3; 28:21,24; 29:17; 31:10,16; 33:5,15; 34:10,14, 15,30; 36:18; Ezr 1:7; 3:6,8,10,11; 8:29; Ne 10:35; Isa 37:14; Jer 7:2; 17:26; 20:2; 24:1; 26:7; 27:18; 35:2; 38:14; 51:51; 52:17,20; La 2:7; Eze 8:14,16,16; 10:19; 11:1; 44:5; 48:9,10; Joel 3:18; Hag 2:15,18; Zec 6:13

Ge 4: 1 gave birth to Cain, and she said, "With the L help,
4:16 So Cain left the L presence and settled in the land
10: 9 He was a mighty hunter in the L sight. His name
10: 9 "like Nimrod, a mighty hunter in the L sight."
12: 7 built an altar there to commemorate the L visit.
19:27 to the place where he had stood in the L presence.
27: 7 He wants to bless Esau in the L presence before he
38: 7 But Er was a wicked man in the L sight,
Ex 12:11 Eat the food quickly, for this is the L Passover.
12:27 will reply, 'It is the celebration of the L Passover,
12:41 of the 430th year that all the L forces left the land.
12:42 to generation, to remember the L deliverance.
12:48 among you who want to celebrate the L Passover,
12:50 So the people of Israel followed all the L
13: 9 Let it remind you always to keep the L instructions
16: 9 'Come into the L presence, and hear his reply to
16:32 forever as a treasured memorial of the L provision.
17: 1 At the L command, the people of Israel left the Sin
17:16 "They have dared to raise their fist against the L
24: 4 Then Moses carefully wrote down all the L
27:21 and his sons will keep the lamps burning in the L
28:30 Aaron's heart when he goes into the L presence.
28:30 L will for his people whenever he goes in before
28:35 will tinkle as he goes in and out of the L presence.
29:11 then slaughter it in the L presence at the entrance
29:26 and lift it up in the L presence as a special gift to
29:42 Offer it in the L presence at the Tabernacle
30: 8 he must again burn incense in the L presence.
30:10 for this is the L supremely holy altar."
30:16 It will bring you, the Israelites, to the L attention,
30:34 These were the L instructions to Moses concerning
32:26 and shouted, "All of you who are on the L side,
39:42 So the people of Israel followed all of the L
40:25 Then he set up the lamps in the L presence, just as
Lev 1: 5 Then slaughter the animal in the L presence,
1:11 on the north side of the altar in the L presence.
4: 2 by doing anything forbidden by the L commands.
4: 4 and slaughter it there in the L presence.
4: 7 that stands in the L presence in the Tabernacle.
4:18 that stands in the L presence in the Tabernacle.
5:15 by unintentionally defiling the L sacred property,
6:22 It is the L regular share, and it must be completely
6:25 and must be slaughtered in the L presence at the
7:21 and then eats meat from the L sacrifices,
8: 4 So Moses followed the L instructions, and all the
8:26 without yeast that was placed in the L presence.
8:29 took the breast and lifted it up in the L presence.
9: 5 and stood there in the L presence.
9:24 Fire blazed forth from the L presence
10: 2 So fire blazed forth from the L presence
14:23 in the L presence at the Tabernacle entrance.
16:13 There in the L presence, he will put the incense on
16:30 be cleansed from all your sins in the L presence.
17: 6 and burn the fat on the L altar at the entrance of
23: 2 "Give the Israelites instructions regarding the L
23: 3 It is the L Sabbath day of complete rest, a holy day
23: 5 "First comes the L Passover, which begins at
23:37 "These are the L appointed annual festivals.
23:38 observed in addition to the L regular Sabbath days.
24: 4 must be tended continually in the L presence.
24: 6 Place the bread in the L presence on the pure gold
24:11 this son of an Israelite woman blasphemed the L
24:12 They put the man in custody until the L will in the
24:16 Anyone who blasphemes the L name must be
24:16 or foreigner among you who blasphemes the L
27:31 If you want to redeem the L tenth of the fruit
Nu 1:53 people of Israel protection from the L fierce anger.
2:33 from this census by the L command to Moses.
3: 4 and Abihu died in the L presence in the wilderness
3:39 counted by Moses and Aaron at the L command,
5:21 "then may the people see that the L curse is upon
8:11 of Israel, thus dedicating them to the L service.
8:20 carefully following all the L instructions to Moses.
9: 7 L offering at the proper time with the rest of the
9: 9 This was the L reply:
9:10 they may still celebrate the L Passover.
9:13 failing to present the L offering at the proper time.
9:18 they traveled at the L command and stopped
9:20 Then at the L command they would break camp.
9:23 So they camped or traveled at the L command,
10:33 with the Ark of the L covenant moving ahead of
11:24 went out and reported the L words to the people.
11:29 I wish that all the L people were prophets, and that
14:21 and as surely as the earth is filled with the L glory,
14:39 When Moses reported the L words to the Israelites,
14:41 "Why are you now disobeying the L orders to
14:44 Moses nor the Ark of the L covenant left the camp.
15:30 "But those who brazenly violate the L will,
15:31 Since they have treated the L word with contempt
16: 9 to be near him as you serve in the L Tabernacle
16:38 because they were used in the L presence.
16:40 should ever enter the L presence to burn incense.
16:40 the L instructions to Moses were carried out.
16:41 saying, "You two have killed the L people!"
16:46 The L anger is blazing among them—the plague
17: 7 Moses put the staffs in the L presence in the
17: 9 When Moses brought all the staffs out from the L
18: 5 the L anger will never again blaze against the
18:28 From this you must present the L portion to Aaron
18:32 L tithes if you give the best portion to the priests.
19:13 in the proper way defile the L Tabernacle
20: 3 "We wish we had died in the L presence with our
20: 4 Did you bring the L people into this wilderness to
25: 3 causing the L anger to blaze against his people.
27:21 who will determine the L will by means of sacred
28:16 in early spring, you must celebrate the L Passover.
31: 3 "Choose some men to fight the L war of
31:16 ones who caused the plague to strike the L people.
31:28 Set apart one out of every five hundred as the L
31:30 in charge of maintaining the L Tabernacle."
31:37 of which 675 were the L share;
31:38 36,000 cattle, of which 72 were the L share;
31:39 30,500 donkeys, of which 61 were the L share;
31:40 16,000 young girls, of whom 32 were the L share.
31:41 Moses gave all the L share to Eleazar the priest,
31:47 and gave them to the Levites who maintained the L
32:20 your word and arm yourselves for the L battles,
32:29 and Reuben who are able to fight the L battles
33: 2 At the L direction, Moses kept a written record of
Dt 1:43 you again rebelled against the L command
4:15 You did not see the L form on the day he spoke to
6:18 Do what is right and good in the L sight, so all will
10: 8 tribe of Levi to carry the Ark of the L covenant,
10:10 I stayed on the mountain in the L presence for
10:13 and to obey the L commands and laws that I am
11: 7 But you have seen all the L mighty deeds with
11:17 If you do, the L anger will burn against you.
15: 2 or relatives, for the L time of release has arrived.
18: 5 of all your tribes to minister in the L name forever.
18:22 If the prophet predicts something in the L name
21: 5 and to pronounce blessings in the L name.
21: 9 and doing what is right in the L sight,
29:27 That is why the L anger burned against this land,
31: 9 the priests, who carried the Ark of the L covenant,
31:25 the Levites who carried the Ark of the L covenant:
33:21 were assembled, / they carried out the L justice
33:23 you are rich in favor / and full of the L blessings;
Jos 1: 1 After the death of Moses the L servant,
3:17 the priests who were carrying the Ark of the L
4: 7 when the Ark of the L covenant went across.'
4:10 middle of the river until all of the L instructions,
4:13 over to the plains of Jericho in the L presence.
4:18 Ark of the L covenant came up out of the riverbed,
5:14 "I am commander of the L army." At this,
5:15 The commander of the L army replied, "Take off
6: 8 And the priests carrying the Ark of the L covenant
6:24 or iron were kept for the treasury of the L house.
8:31 He followed the instructions that Moses the L
8:33 priests carrying the Ark of the L covenant.
11:15 carefully obeying all of the L instructions to
14: 2 in accordance with the L command through
14: 5 strict accordance with the L instructions to Moses.
21: 8 So the Israelites obeyed the L command to Moses
22: 9 them according to the L command through Moses.
22:28 'Look at this copy of the L altar that our ancestors
Jdg 2:11 Then the Israelites did what was evil in the L sight
2:17 who had walked in obedience to the L commands.
3: 7 The Israelites did what was evil in the L sight.
3:12 Once again the Israelites did what was evil in the L
4: 1 the Israelites again did what was evil in the L
4: 9 For the L victory over Sisera will be at the hands
6: 1 Again the Israelites did what was evil in the L
10: 6 Again the Israelites did evil in the L sight.
13: 1 Again the Israelites did what was evil in the L
21: 5 At that time they had taken a solemn oath in the L
1Sa 2: 8 them in seats of honor. / "For all the earth is the L,
2:11 And the boy became the L helper, for he assisted
2:17 these young men was very serious in the L sight,
2:17 for they treated the L offerings with contempt.
2:18 Now Samuel, though only a boy, was the L helper.
2:24 The reports I hear among the L people are not
3:18 hold anything back. "It is the L will," Eli replied.
7:13 the L powerful hand was raised against the
8:10 So Samuel passed on the L warning to the people.
12:14 and if you do not rebel against the L commands,
12:15 But if you rebel against the L commands
13:12 and I haven't even asked for the L help!'
13:14 for you have not obeyed the L command."
14:10 That will be the L sign that he will help us defeat
15:13 he said. "I have carried out the L command!"
15:24 disobeyed your instructions and the L command,
15:26 Since you have rejected the L command, he has
16: 6 and thought, "Surely this is the L anointed!"
18:17 to be a real warrior by fighting the L battles."
20:42 in peace, for we have made a pact in the L name.
20:42 and each other's children into the L hands
22:17 But Saul's men refused to kill the L priests.
24: 6 "It is a serious thing to attack the L anointed one,
24:10 'I will never harm him—he is the L anointed one.'
25:28 a lasting dynasty, for you are fighting the L battles.
26: 9 For who can remain innocent after attacking the L
26:16 you failed to protect your master, the L anointed!
26:19 so I can no longer live among the L people
26:23 you in my power, for you are the L anointed one.
30:26 for you, taken from the L enemies," he said.
2Sa 1:12 and for the L army and the nation of Israel,
1:14 "Were you not afraid to kill the L anointed one?"
1:16 "for you yourself confessed that you killed the L
6: 7 Then the L anger blazed out against Uzzah for
6: 8 because the L anger had blazed out against Uzzah.
10:12 the cities of our God. May the L will be done."
19:21 should die, for he cursed the L anointed king!"
22:31 his way is perfect. / All the L promises prove true.
1Ki 2:45 But may I receive the L rich blessings, and may
6:19 where the Ark of the L covenant would be placed.
6:37 The foundation of the L Temple was laid in
7:12 just like the walls of the inner courtyard of the L
7:51 and he stored them in the treasuries of the L
8: 1 They were to bring the Ark of the L covenant from
8: 6 Then the priests carried the Ark of the L covenant
8:64 area of the courtyard in front of the L Temple.
8:64 because the bronze altar in the L presence was too
9:15 that Solomon conscripted to build the L Temple,
11: 6 Thus, Solomon did what was evil in the L sight;
11:10 but Solomon did not listen to the L command.
12:15 for it fulfilled the L message to Jeroboam son of
13: 1 At the L command, a man of God from Judah went
13: 2 Then at the L command, he shouted, "O altar,
13:21 You have defied the L message and have

13:26 "It is the man of God who disobeyed the L
14:22 the people of Judah did what was evil in the L
15: 5 For David had done what was pleasing in the L
15: 5 and had obeyed the L commands throughout his
15:11 Asa did what was pleasing in the L sight, as his
15:18 and gold that was left in the treasuries of the L
15:26 But he did what was evil in the L sight
15:34 But he did what was evil in the L sight
16: 7 because Baasha had done what was evil in the L
16:19 had done what was evil in the L sight and followed
16:25 But Omri did what was evil in the L sight,
16:30 But Ahab did what was evil in the L sight,
18: 4 Once when Jezebel had tried to kill all the L
18:13 when Jezebel was trying to kill the L prophets?
18:32 and he used the stones to rebuild the L altar.
21:20 have sold yourself to what is evil in the L sight.
21:25 to what was evil in the L sight as did Ahab,
22:43 Asa. He did what was pleasing in the L sight.
22:52 But he did what was evil in the L sight,
2Ki 3: 2 He did what was evil in the L sight, but he was not
8:18 So Jehoram did what was evil in the L sight.
8:27 doing what was evil in the L sight, because he was
9: 6 says: I anoint you king over the L people, Israel.
9: 7 and all the L servants who were killed by Jezebel.
9:12 and that at the L command he had been anointed
11: 4 swear an oath of loyalty there in the L Temple;
11: 7 must stand guard for the king at the L Temple.
11:13 she hurried to the L Temple to see what was
11:17 and the people that they would be the L people.
12: 2 All his life Joash did what was pleasing in the L
12: 4 brought as a sacred offering to the L Temple,
12:10 the money that had been brought to the L Temple
12:11 who used it to pay the people working on the L
12:12 and cut stone for repairing the L Temple,
12:16 and sin offerings was not brought into the L
12:18 along with all the gold in the treasuries of the L
13: 2 But he did what was evil in the L sight.
13: 4 Then Jehoahaz prayed for the L help,
13:11 But he did what was evil in the L sight. He refused
13:17 Then Elisha proclaimed, "This is the L arrow,
14: 3 Amaziah did what was pleasing in the L sight,
14:24 He did what was evil in the L sight. He refused to
15: 3 He did what was pleasing in the L sight, just as his
15: 9 Zechariah did what was evil in the L sight, as his
15:12 So the L message to Jehu came true:
15:18 But Menahem did what was evil in the L sight.
15:24 But Pekahiah did what was evil in the L sight.
15:28 But Pekah did what was evil in the L sight.
15:34 Jotham did what was pleasing in the L sight,
16:14 old bronze altar from the front of the L Temple,
17: 2 He did what was evil in the L sight, but not as
17:11 had done many evil things, arousing the L anger.
17:12 despite the L specific and repeated warnings.
17:15 disobeying the L command not to imitate them.
17:17 and sold themselves to evil, arousing the L anger.
18: 3 He did what was pleasing in the L sight, just as his
18:16 stripped the gold from the doors of the L Temple
18:25 have invaded your land without the L direction?
19:14 he went up to the L Temple and spread it out
21: 2 He did what was evil in the L sight,
21: 5 of heaven in both courtyards of the L Temple.
21: 6 He did much that was evil in the L sight,
21:16 to commit, leading them to do evil in the L sight.
21:20 He did what was evil in the L sight, just as his
21:22 his ancestors, and he refused to follow the L ways.
22: 2 He did what was pleasing in the L sight
22: 4 have collected from the people at the L Temple.
22: 8 "I have found the Book of the Law in the L
22:13 The L anger is burning against us because our
23: 2 the Covenant that had been found in the L Temple.
23: 3 and renewed the covenant in the L presence.
23: 4 and the Temple gatekeepers to remove from the L
23: 6 The king removed the Asherah pole from the L
23: 9 not allowed to serve at the L altar in Jerusalem,
23:11 He removed from the entrance of the L Temple the
23:12 had built in the two courtyards of the L Temple.
23:24 that Hilkiah the priest had found in the L Temple.
23:26 the L anger burned against Judah because of all the
23:32 He did what was evil in the L sight, just as his
23:37 He did what was evil in the L sight, just as his
24: 3 happened to Judah according to the L command.
24: 9 Jehoiachin did what was evil in the L sight, just as
24:13 carried away all the treasures from the L Temple
24:19 But Zedekiah did what was evil in the L sight,
25:13 and the bronze Sea that were at the L Temple,
25:16 These things had been made for the L Temple in
1Ch 10:13 He failed to obey the L command, and he even
13:10 Then the L anger blazed out against Uzzah, and he
13:11 because the L anger had blazed out against Uzzah.
15:25 L covenant up to Jerusalem with a great
15:26 Levites as they carried the Ark of the L covenant,
15:28 So all Israel brought up the Ark of the L covenant
15:29 But as the Ark of the L covenant entered the City
16:37 regularly before the Ark of the L covenant,
17: 1 but the Ark of the L covenant is out in a tent!"
19:13 the cities of our God. May the L will be done."
22:19 so that you can bring the Ark of the L covenant
22:19 God into the Temple built to honor the L name."
23:13 to offer sacrifices in the L presence, to serve the
23:31 The proper number of Levites served in the L
28: 2 to build a temple where the Ark of the L covenant,
28: 8 give you this charge for all Israel, the L assembly:
28:12 he had in mind for the courtyards of the L Temple,
28:13 And he gave specifications for the items in the L
28:18 were stretched out over the Ark of the L covenant.
29:22 and drank in the L presence with great joy that
2Ch 1: 3 the L servant, had constructed in the wilderness.
1: 6 Solomon went up to the bronze altar in the L
5: 2 They were to bring the Ark of the L covenant from
5: 7 Then the priests carried the Ark of the L covenant
7: 7 area of the courtyard in front of the L Temple
8: 1 and the great building projects of the L Temple
12:12 humbled himself, the L anger was turned aside,
15: 8 which stood in front of the foyer of the L Temple.
16: 2 and gold from the treasuries of the L Temple
16:12 he did not seek the L help but sought help only
17:16 son of Zicri, who volunteered for the L service,
19: 2 "What you have done has brought the L anger
20:17 then stand still and watch the L victory.
20:32 Asa. He did what was pleasing in the L sight.
21: 6 So Jehoram did what was evil in the L sight.
22: 4 He did what was evil in the L sight, just as Ahab
23: 5 else should stay in the courtyards of the L Temple.
23: 6 The rest of the people must obey the L instructions
23:12 she hurried to the L Temple to see what was
23:16 and the people that they would be the L people.
23:19 He stationed gatekeepers at the gates of the L
24: 2 Joash did what was pleasing in the L sight
24:12 made articles of iron and bronze for the L Temple.
24:20 Why do you disobey the L commands so that you
24:21 they stoned him to death in the courtyard of the L
25: 2 Amaziah did what was pleasing in the L sight,
26: 4 He did what was pleasing in the L sight, just as his
26:16 his God by entering the sanctuary of the L Temple
26:19 priests before the incense altar in the L Temple,
27: 2 He did what was pleasing in the L sight, just as his
27: 3 Jotham rebuilt the Upper Gate to the L Temple
28:11 because now the L fierce anger has been turned
28:13 and the L fierce anger is already turned against
28:21 Ahaz took valuable items from the L Temple,
28:24 He shut the doors of the L Temple so that no one
29: 2 He did what was pleasing in the L sight, just as his
29: 8 That is why the L anger has fallen upon Judah
29:15 They were careful to follow all the L instructions
29:17 days they had reached the foyer of the L Temple.
31:10 people began bringing their gifts to the L Temple,
31:16 who came daily to the L Temple to perform their
32:12 is the very person who destroyed all the L shrines
32:25 So the L anger came against him and against Judah
32:26 So the L anger did not come against them during
33: 2 He did what was evil in the L sight,
33: 5 stars of heaven in both courtyards of the L Temple.
33: 6 He did much that was evil in the L sight,
33:15 from the hills and the idol from the L Temple.
33:22 He did what was evil in the L sight, just as his
34: 2 He did what was pleasing in the L sight
34:10 to supervise the restoration of the L Temple.
34:14 recording the money collected at the L Temple,
34:15 "I have found the Book of the Law in the L
34:21 The L anger has been poured out against us
34:30 the Covenant that had been found in the L Temple.
34:31 and renewed the covenant in the L presence.
35:16 The entire ceremony for the L Passover was
36: 9 Jehoiachin did what was evil in the L sight.
36:16 They scoffed at the prophets until the L anger
36:18 and the treasures from both the L Temple
36:23 All of you who are the L people may return to
Ezr 1: 7 had taken from the L Temple in Jerusalem
3: 6 had started to lay the foundation of the L Temple.
3: 8 or older were put in charge of rebuilding the L
3:10 completed the foundation of the L Temple,
3:11 because the foundation of the L Temple had been
8:29 and the leaders of Israel at the storerooms of the L
Ne 10:35 the first part of every harvest to the L Temple—
Job 1:12 him physically." So Satan left the L presence.
2: 7 So Satan left the L presence, and he struck Job
Ps 2: 7 The king proclaims the L decree: / "The LORD
12: 6 The L promises are pure, / like silver refined in a
18:30 his way is perfect. / All the L promises prove true.
24: 1 The earth is the L, and everything in it. / The world
24: 5 They will receive the L blessing / and have right
27: 4 days of my life, / delighting in the L perfections
27:13 Yet I am confident that I will see the L goodness
33:11 But the L plans stand firm forever; / his intentions
34: 3 Come, let us tell of the L greatness; / let us exalt
34: 9 Let the L people show him reverence, / for those
37:20 The L enemies are like flowers in a field—
38: T psalm of David, to bring us to the L remembrance.
70: T psalm of David, to bring us to the L remembrance.
92: T A psalm to be sung on the L Day. A song.
92:13 For they are transplanted into the L own house.
102:21 And so the L fame will be celebrated in Zion,
105:25 and they plotted against the L servants.
106: 7 in Egypt / were not impressed by the L miracles.
106:16 of Moses / and envious of Aaron, the L holy priest.
106:39 and their love of idols was adultery in the L sight.
106:40 That is why the L anger burned against his people,
107:24 They, too, observed the L power in action,
109:20 May those curses become the L punishment for my
116: 9 And so I walk in the L presence / as I live here on
116:13 I will praise the L name for saving me.
116:15 The L loved ones are precious to him; / it grieves
118:23 This is the L doing, / and it is marvelous to see.
122: 4 All the people of Israel—the L people—
128: 4 That is the L reward / for those who fear him.
129: 8 "The L blessings be upon you; / we bless you in
the L name."
138: 5 Yes, they will sing about the L ways,
142: 1 I cry out to the LORD; / I plead for the L mercy.
147:11 Rather, the L delight is in those who honor him,
Pr 19:21 make many plans, but the L purpose will prevail.
20:27 The L searchlight penetrates the human spirit,
22:14 those living under the L displeasure will fall into
Isa 2: 3 For in those days the L teaching and his word will
3:14 and the princes will be the first to feel the L
5: 7 This is the story of the L people. / They are the
5:25 But even then the L anger will not be satisfied.
9:12 But even then the L anger will not be satisfied.
9:17 But even then the L anger will not be satisfied.
9:21 But even then the L anger will not be satisfied.
10: 4 But even then the L anger will not be satisfied.
10:26 or when the L staff was raised to drown the
13: 5 They are the L weapons; they carry his anger with
13: 6 Scream in terror, for the L time has arrived—
14: 2 The nations of the world will help the L people to
23:18 good food and fine clothing for the L priests.
24:14 Those in the west will praise the L majesty.
25:10 For the L good hand will rest on Jerusalem.
26:10 doing wrong and take no notice of the L majesty.
26:20 Hide until the L anger against your enemies has
30: 9 refuse to pay any attention to the L instructions.
30:31 At the L command, the Assyrians will be
34: 8 For it is the day of the L vengeance, the year when
36:10 have invaded your land without the L direction?
37:14 he went up to the L Temple and spread it out
44: 5 Some will write the L name on their hands
49: 4 Yet I leave it all in the L hand; I will trust God for
51:17 You have drunk enough from the cup of the L
52:11 You are the L holy people. Purify yourselves,
53: 2 My servant grew up in the L presence like a tender
53:10 But it was the L good plan to crush him and fill
53:10 long life, and the L plan will prosper in his hands.
55:13 This miracle will bring great honor to the L name;
56:10 the L watchmen, his shepherds—are blind to every
58:13 and speak of it with delight as the L holy day.
61: 2 who mourn that the time of the L favor has come,
63: 7 I will tell of the L unfailing love. I will praise the
Jer 3:16 when you possessed the Ark of the L covenant.
4:26 cities lay in ruins, crushed by the L fierce anger.
5: 5 Surely they will know the L ways and what God
6:11 So now I am filled with the L fury. Yes, I am
7: 2 "Go to the entrance of the L Temple, and give this
11:21 kill me if I did not stop speaking in the L name.
13:17 because the L flock will be led away into exile.
16:11 Tell them that this is the L reply: It is because your
17:26 and thanksgiving offerings to the L Temple.
20: 2 and put in stocks at the Benjamin Gate of the L
22:18 this is the L decree of punishment against King
23:19 The L anger bursts out like a storm, a whirlwind
23:35 keep asking each other, 'What is the L answer?'
23:37 'What is the L answer?' or 'What is the LORD
24: 1 I saw two baskets of figs placed in front of the L
25:26 himself drank from the cup of the L anger.
25:37 be turned into a wasteland by the L fierce anger.
25:38 by the sword of the enemy and the L fierce anger.
26: 7 to Jeremiah as he spoke in front of the L Temple.
26: 9 "What right do you have to prophesy in the L
27:18 If they really are the L prophets, let them pray to
27:18 the gold utensils that are still left in the L Temple
30:23 The L anger bursts out like a storm, a driving wind
33:25 But this is the L reply: I would no more reject my
35: 2 Recabites live, and invite them to the L Temple.
36: 7 and ask the L forgiveness before it is too late.
36: 7 For the L terrible anger has been pronounced
38:14 to meet him at the third entrance of the L Temple.
43: 4 and all the people refused to obey the L command
47: 1 This is the L message to the prophet Jeremiah
49:20 Listen to the L plans for Edom and the people of
50:13 Because of the L anger, Babylon will become a
50:45 Listen to the L plans against Babylon and the land
51: 6 It is the L time for vengeance; he will fully repay
51: 7 Babylon has been like a golden cup in the L hands,
51:45 Save yourselves! Run from the L fierce anger.
51:51 because the L Temple has been defiled by
52: 2 But Zedekiah did what was evil in the L sight,
52:17 and the bronze Sea that were at the L Temple,
52:20 These things had been made for the L Temple in
La 2: 7 They shout in the L Temple as though it were a
2:22 In the day of the L anger, no one has escaped
3: 1 afflictions that come from the rod of the L anger.
3:28 Let them sit alone in silence beneath the L
3:66 destroying them from beneath the L heavens.
4:20 Our king, the L anointed, the very life of our
4:21 too, must drink from the cup of the L anger.
Eze 3:14 and turmoil, but the L hold on me was strong.
7:19 It won't buy their deliverance in that day of the L
8:14 He brought me to the north gate of the L Temple,
8:16 me into the inner courtyard of the L Temple.
8:16 were standing with their backs to the L Temple.
10:19 with their wheels to the east gate of the L Temple.
11: 1 and brought me over to the east gateway of the L
41:22 "is the table that stands in the L presence."
44: 3 sit inside this gateway to feast in the L presence.
44: 5 about the regulations concerning the L Temple.
48: 9 "The area set aside for the L Temple will be 8-1/3
48:10 3-1/3 miles wide, with the L Temple at the center.
Hos 4:15 is mere pretense as they take oaths in the L name.
9: 5 What will you do on days of feasting in the L
Joel 2:17 The priests, who minister in the L presence,
3:16 The L voice will roar from Zion and thunder from
3:18 and a fountain will burst forth from the L Temple,
Am 1: 2 "The L voice roars from his Temple on Mount
8:13 will grow faint and weary, thirsting for the L word.
9: 6 The upper stories of the L home are in the heavens,
Jnh 1:16 The sailors were awestruck by the L great power,
3: 3 This time Jonah obeyed the L command and went
Mic 1:12 but only bitterness awaits them as the L judgment
2: 5 and the L people will have no say in how the land
4: 2 For in those days the L teaching and his word will
4:12 But they do not know the L thoughts or understand
5: 4 And he will stand to lead his flock with the L

6: 2 O mountains, listen to the **L** complaint!
Hab 2: 16 Drink from the cup of the **L** judgment, and all your
Zep 1: 6 They no longer ask for the **L** guidance or seek my
1: 7 for the awesome day of the **L** judgment has come.
1: 15 It is a day when the **L** anger will be poured out.
1: 18 will be of no use to you on that day of the **L** anger.
2: 2 and the terrible day of the **L** anger begins.
Hag 1: 2 'The time has not yet come to rebuild the **L**
1: 13 Then Haggai, the **L** messenger, gave the people
2: 15 you began to lay the foundation of the **L** Temple.
2: 18 the day when the foundation of the **L** Temple was
Zec 2: 12 The land of Judah will be the **L** inheritance in the
6: 13 He will build the **L** Temple, and he will receive
7: 2 along with their men, to seek the **L** favor.
Mal 1: 5 the **L** great power reaches far beyond our
2: 11 for the men of Judah have defiled the **L** beloved
2: 13 You cover the **L** altar with tears, weeping

LORDING (1) [LORD]

Ex 9: 17 But you are still **l** it over my people, and you

LORDS (8) [LORD]

Ge 19: 2 "My **l**," he said, "come to my home to wash your
19: 18 "Oh no, my **l**, please," Lot begged.
Dt 10: 17 your God is the God of gods and Lord of **l**.
Ps 136: 3 Give thanks to the Lord of **l**. / His faithful love
1Co 8: 5 there are many so-called gods and many **l**, both in
1Ti 6: 15 almighty God, the King of kings and Lord of **l**.
Rev 17: 14 because he is Lord over all **l** and King over all
19: 16 was written this title: King of kings and Lord of **l**.

LORDSHIP [KJV] See LORD (IT OVER)

LOSE (45) [LOSES, LOSING, LOSS, LOSSES, LOST]

Ge 27: 45 for you. Why should I **l** both of you in one day?"
Ex 9: 6 but the Israelites didn't **l** a single animal from their
Dt 20: 3 you go out to fight today! Do not **l** heart or panic.
2Sa 22: 46 They all **l** their courage / and come trembling from
1Ch 22: 13 and courageous; do not be afraid or **l** heart!
Job 11: 20 But the wicked will **l** hope. They have no escape.
14: 10 "But when people die, they **l** all strength.
33: 20 They **l** their appetite and do not care for even the
Ps 18: 45 They all **l** their courage / and come trembling from
Pr 3: 21 don't **l** sight of good planning and insight.
4: 21 Don't **l** sight of my words. Let them penetrate deep
5: 9 you will **l** your honor and hand over to merciless
11: 24 but those who are stingy will **l** everything.
28: 8 who makes money by charging interest will **l** it.
Ecc 3: 6 A time to search and a time to **l**. / A time to keep
Isa 19: 3 The Egyptians will **l** heart, and I will confuse their
47: 8 I will never be a widow or **l** my children.'
Jer 17: 11 Sooner or later they will **l** their riches and,
Da 11: 6 but she will **l** her influence over him, and so will
Hos 2: 6 I will block the road to make her **l** her way.
Zec 12: 4 every horse to panic and every rider to **l** his nerve.
Mt 5: 29 It is better for you to **l** one part of your body than
5: 30 It is better for you to **l** one part of your body than
6: 1 then you will **l** the reward from your Father in
10: 39 If you cling to your life, you will **l** it; but if you
16: 25 you try to keep your life for yourself, you will **l** it.
16: 26 whole world but **l** your own soul in the process?
18: 6 one of these little ones who trusts in me to **l** faith,
25: 25 I was afraid I would **l** your money, so I hid it in the
Mk 8: 35 you try to keep your life for yourself, you will **l** it.
8: 36 whole world but **l** your own soul in the process?
9: 42 one of these little ones who trusts in me to **l** faith,
Lk 9: 24 you try to keep your life for yourself, you will **l** it.
9: 25 but **l** or forfeit your own soul in the process?
17: 33 Whoever clings to this life will **l** it, and whoever
Jn 6: 39 that I should not **l** even one of all those he has
12: 25 Those who love their life in this world will **l** it.
Ac 19: 27 of the great goddess Artemis will **l** its influence
27: 22 None of you will **l** your lives, even though the ship
Ro 6: 6 so that sin might **l** its power in our lives.
1Co 1: 17 for fear that the cross of Christ would **l** its power.
9: 15 I would rather die than **l** my distinction of
Php 2: 16 I will be proud that I did not **l** the race and that my
2Pe 3: 17 I don't want you to **l** your own secure footing.
2Jn 1: 8 so that you do not **l** the prize for which we have

LOSES (9) [LOSE]

Lev 13: 40 "If a man **l** his hair and his head becomes bald,
13: 41 And if he **l** hair on his forehead, he simply has a
Dt 22: 3 clothing, or anything else your neighbor **l**.
1Sa 20: 7 But if he is angry and **l** his temper, then you will
Mk 9: 50 But if it **l** its flavor, how do you make it salty
Lk 14: 34 But if it **l** its flavor, how do you make it salty
15: 8 a woman has ten valuable silver coins and **l** one.
17: 33 life will lose it, and whoever **l** this life will save it.
1Co 13: 7 never gives up, never **l** faith, is always hopeful,

LOSING (3) [LOSE]

1Sa 30: 6 because his men were very bitter about **l** their
2Ki 3: 26 When the king of Moab saw that he was **l** the
Ps 143: 4 I am **l** all hope; / I am paralyzed with fear.

LOSS (17) [LOSE]

Ge 31: 39 to reduce the count of your flock? No, I took the **l**!
31: 39 from the flocks, whether the **l** was my fault or not.
Ex 21: 30 owner of the bull to compensate for the **l** of life.
22: 15 because this **l** was covered by the rental fee.
Lev 5: 16 holy things they have defiled by paying for the **l**,
Jdg 16: 28 so that I may pay back the Philistines for the **l** of
2Ki 7: 13 it won't be a greater **l** than if they stay here and die
1Ch 9: 28 They checked them in and out to avoid any **l**.
Isa 47: 9 widowhood and the **l** of your children. Yes,
Jer 6: 26 and weep bitterly, as for the **l** of an only son.
22: 10 Do not weep for the dead king or mourn his **l**.
La 3: 20 never forget this awful time, as I grieve over my **l**.
Jn 11: 19 and console Martha and Mary on their **l**.
Ac 19: 27 I'm not just talking about the **l** of public respect for
27: 10 shipwreck, **l** of cargo, injuries, and danger to our
27: 21 You would have avoided all this injury and **l**.
1Co 3: 15 work is burned up, the builder will suffer great **l**.

LOSSES (2) [LOSE]

2Ch 13: 17 Abijah and his army inflicted heavy **l** on them;
Eze 7: 12 they find or for sellers to grieve over their **l**,

LOST (79) [LOSE]

Ge 34: 19 and Shechem **l** no time in acting on this request,
Ex 21: 19 the assailant must pay for time **l** because of the
22: 6 then the one who started the fire must pay for the **l**
Lev 6: 2 an item entrusted to their safekeeping has been **l**
6: 3 Or suppose they find a **l** item and lie about it,
6: 4 or a **l** object that they claimed as their own,
Nu 36: 4 causing it to be **l** forever to our ancestral tribe."
Jos 5: 1 they **l** heart and were paralyzed with fear.
Jdg 20: 46 So the tribe of Benjamin **l** twenty-five thousand
21: 6 "Today we have **l** one of the tribes from our
21: 17 so that an entire tribe of Israel will not be **l** forever.
1Sa 9: 20 And don't worry about those donkeys that were **l**
13: 6 they **l** their nerve entirely and tried to hide in
25: 18 Abigail **l** no time. She quickly gathered two
25: 21 and nothing he owned was **l** or stolen.
2Sa 4: 1 he **l** all courage, and his people were paralyzed
1Ki 20: 25 Recruit another army like the one you **l**. Give us
2Ki 8: 6 to it that everything she had **l** was restored to her,
Ezr 2: 62 But they had **l** their genealogical records, so they
4: 16 the province west of the Euphrates River will be **l**
8: 29 without an ounce **l**, to the leading priests,
Ne 7: 64 But they had **l** their genealogical records, so they
Job 3: 4 Let it be **l** even to God on high, and let it be
20: 26 "His treasures will be **l** in deepest darkness.
29: 13 I helped those who had **l** hope, and they blessed
Ps 9: 6 Even the memory of their uprooted cities is **l**.
40: 12 the hairs on my head. / I have **l** all my courage.
102: 4 withered like grass, / and I have **l** my appetite.
107: 4 Some wandered in the desert, / **l** and homeless.
119: 176 I have wandered away like a **l** sheep; / come
Pr 2: 4 Search for them as you would for **l** money
5: 23 he will be **l** because of his incredible folly.
14: 22 If you plot evil, you will be **l**; but if you plan good,
Ecc 5: 8 and matters of justice only get **l** in red tape
5: 14 investments that turn sour, and everything is **l**.
Isa 24: 19 Everything is **l**, abandoned, and confused.
40: 26 And he counts them to see that none are **l** or have
Jer 10: 21 The shepherds of my people have **l** their senses.
23: 4 Not a single one of them will be **l** or missing,"
40: 15 the few of us who are still left be scattered and **l**?"
50: 6 "My people have been **l** sheep. Their shepherds
50: 6 They have **l** their way and cannot remember how
51: 31 side come running to the king to tell him all is **l**!
La 3: 18 Everything I had hoped for from the LORD is **l**!"
4: 1 How the gold has **l** its luster! Even the finest gold
Eze 21: 32 will be utterly wiped out, your memory **l** to history.
27: 27 Everything is **l**—your riches and wares,
34: 4 for those who have wandered away and are **l**.
34: 8 you didn't search for my sheep when they were **l**.
34: 16 I will search for my **l** ones who strayed away,
Da 11: 13 a fully equipped army far greater than the one he **l**.
Joel 2: 25 "I will give you back what you **l** to the stripping
Am 9: 9 is sifted in a sieve, yet not one true kernel will be **l**.
Jnh 1: 7 terrible storm. When they did this, Jonah **l** the toss.
2: 7 "When I had **l** all hope, I turned my thoughts once
Zec 10: 2 So my people are wandering like **l** sheep, without a
Mt 5: 13 the earth. But what good is salt if it has **l** its flavor?
10: 6 but only to the people of Israel—God's **l** sheep.
15: 24 of Israel—God's **l** sheep—not the Gentiles."
18: 12 and one wanders away and is **l**, what will he do?
18: 12 and go out into the hills to search for the **l** one?
Lk 15: 4 of them strayed away and was **l** in the wilderness,
15: 4 to go and search for the **l** one until you found it?
15: 6 rejoice with you because your **l** sheep was found.
15: 7 heaven will be happier over one **l** sinner who
15: 9 rejoice with her because she has found her **l** coin.
15: 24 He was **l**, but now he is found.' So the party began.
15: 32 back to life! He was **l**, but now he is found!' "
16: 17 But that doesn't mean that the law has **l** its force in
19: 10 come to seek and save those like him who are **l**."
Jn 12: 19 Then the Pharisees said to each other, "We've **l**.
17: 12 I guarded them so that not one was **l**,
18: 9 "I have not **l** a single one of those you gave me."
Ac 27: 9 We had **l** a lot of time. The weather was becoming
Ro 2: 19 and a beacon light for people who are **l** in darkness
2Co 11: 16 don't think that I have **l** my wits to talk like this.
Gal 3: 3 Have you **l** your senses? After starting your
1Pe 2: 25 Once you were wandering like **l** sheep. But now
Rev 12: 8 And the dragon **l** the battle and was forced out of

LOT (109) [LOT'S, LOTS]

Ge 11: 27 Nahor, and Haran; and Haran had a son named **L**.
11: 31 and his grandson **L** (his son Haran's child)
12: 4 LORD had instructed him, and **L** went with him.
12: 5 He took his wife, Sarai, his nephew **L**, and all his
13: 1 Abram with his wife and **L** and all that they
13: 5 Now **L**, who was traveling with Abram, was also
13: 6 and **L** with all their flocks and herds living so close
13: 7 broke out between the herdsmen of Abram and **L**.
13: 8 Then Abram talked it over with **L**. "This arguing
13: 10 **L** took a long look at the fertile plains of the
13: 11 **L** chose that land for himself—the Jordan Valley to
13: 12 **L** moved his tents to a place near Sodom,
13: 14 After **L** was gone, the LORD said to Abram,
14: 12 They also captured **L**—Abram's nephew who lived
14: 14 When Abram learned that **L** had been captured,
14: 16 Abram's nephew **L** with his possessions, and all
19: 1 of Sodom, and **L** was sitting there as they arrived.
19: 3 But **L** insisted, so at last they went home with him.
19: 5 They shouted to **L**, "Where are the men who came
19: 6 **L** stepped outside to talk to them, shutting the door
19: 9 And they lunged at **L** and began breaking down the
19: 10 reached out and pulled **L** in and bolted the door.
19: 14 So **L** rushed out to tell his daughters' fiancés,
19: 15 "Hurry," they said to **L**. "Take your wife
19: 16 When **L** still hesitated, the angels seized his hand
19: 18 "Oh no, my lords, please," **L** begged.
19: 23 The sun was rising as **L** reached the village.
19: 29 had listened to Abraham's request and kept **L** safe,
19: 30 Afterward **L** left Zoar because he was afraid of the
Ex 16: 18 Those who gathered a **l** had nothing left over,
Nu 26: 55 Make sure you assign the land by **l**, and define the
26: 56 Each inheritance must be assigned by **l** among the
33: 54 distribute the land among the clans by sacred **l**
33: 54 The decision of the sacred **l** is final. In this way,
34: 13 you are to divide among yourselves by sacred **l**.
36: 2 the land by sacred **l** among the people of Israel.
Dt 2: 9 the descendants of **L**, or start a war with them.
2: 19 the descendants of **L**, or start a war with them.
Jos 21: 10 tribe of Levi, since the sacred **l** fell to them first:
1Sa 25: 21 been saying, "A **l** of good it did to help this fellow.
2Sa 18: 29 Joab told me to come, there was a **l** of commotion.
1Ch 24: 7 The first **l** fell to Jehoiarib. / The second **l** fell to Jedaiah.
24: 8 third **l** fell to Harim. / The fourth **l** fell to Seorim.
24: 9 The fifth **l** fell to Malkijah. / The sixth **l** fell to Mijamin.
24: 10 The seventh **l** fell to Hakkoz. / The eighth **l** fell to Abijah.
24: 11 ninth **l** fell to Jeshua. / The tenth **l** fell to Shecaniah.
24: 12 The eleventh **l** fell to Eliashib. / The twelfth **l** fell to Jakim.
24: 13 The thirteenth **l** fell to Huppah. / The fourteenth **l** fell to Jeshebeab.
24: 14 The fifteenth **l** fell to Bilgah. / The sixteenth **l** fell to Immer.
24: 15 The seventeenth **l** fell to Hezir. / The eighteenth **l** fell to Happizzez.
24: 16 The nineteenth **l** fell to Pethahiah. / The twentieth **l** fell to Jehezkel.
24: 17 The twenty-first **l** fell to Jakin. / The twenty-second **l** fell to Gamul.
24: 18 The twenty-third **l** fell to Delaiah. / The twenty-fourth **l** fell to Maaziah.
25: 9 The first **l** fell to Joseph of the Asaph clan
25: 9 The second **l** fell to Gedaliah and twelve of his
25: 10 The third **l** fell to Zaccur and twelve of his sons
25: 11 The fourth **l** fell to Zeri and twelve of his sons
25: 12 The fifth **l** fell to Nethaniah and twelve of his sons
25: 13 The sixth **l** fell to Bukkiah and twelve of his sons
25: 14 The seventh **l** fell to Asarelah and twelve of his
25: 15 The eighth **l** fell to Jeshaiah and twelve of his sons
25: 16 The ninth **l** fell to Mattaniah and twelve of his sons
25: 17 The tenth **l** fell to Shimei and twelve of his sons
25: 18 The eleventh **l** fell to Uzziel and twelve of his sons
25: 19 The twelfth **l** fell to Hashabiah and twelve of his
25: 20 The thirteenth **l** fell to Shubael and twelve of his
25: 21 The fourteenth **l** fell to Mattithiah and twelve of his
25: 22 The fifteenth **l** fell to Jerimoth and twelve of his
25: 23 The sixteenth **l** fell to Hananiah and twelve of his
25: 24 The seventeenth **l** fell to Joshbekashah and twelve
25: 25 The eighteenth **l** fell to Hanani and twelve of his
25: 26 The nineteenth **l** fell to Mallothi and twelve of his
25: 27 The twentieth **l** fell to Eliathah and twelve of his
25: 28 The twenty-first **l** fell to Hothir and twelve of his
25: 29 The twenty-second **l** fell to Geddalti and twelve of
25: 30 The twenty-third **l** fell to Mahazioth and twelve of
25: 31 The twenty-fourth **l** fell to Romamti-ezer
Ne 9: 16 But our ancestors were a proud and stubborn **l**,
Job 11: 2 Is a person proved innocent just by talking a **l**?
30: 2 A **l** of good they are to me—those worn-out
Ps 78: 55 before them; / he gave them their inheritance by **l**.
83: 8 too, / and is allied with the descendants of **L**.
Pr 1: 14 Come on, throw in your **l** with us; we'll split our
6: 33 Wounds and constant disgrace are his **l**. His shame
Ecc 5: 19 To enjoy your work and accept your **l** in life—
Isa 24: 17 Terror and traps and snares will be your **l**,
51: 19 These two things have been your **l**: desolation
Jer 48: 43 "Terror and traps and snares will be your **l**,
Eze 3: 7 For the whole **l** of them are hard-hearted
Lk 1: 9 he was chosen by **l** to enter the sanctuary and burn
17: 28 "And the world will be as it was in the days of **L**.
17: 29 until the morning **L** left Sodom. Then fire
Jn 7: 12 There was a **l** of discussion about him among the
Ac 16: 16 She was a fortune-teller who earned a **l** of money
27: 9 We had lost a **l** of time. The weather was becoming
2Co 8: 15 "Those who gathered a **l** had nothing left over,
2Pe 2: 7 God rescued **L** out of Sodom because he was a

LOT'S (3) [LOT]

Ge 19: 26 But **L** wife looked back as she was following along
19: 36 So both of **L** daughters became pregnant by their
Lk 17: 32 Remember what happened to **L** wife!

LOTAN (5) [LOTAN'S]
Ge 36:20 native to the land of Seir: L, Shobal, Zibeon, Anah,
36:22 The sons of L were Hori and Heman.
36:29 So the leaders of the Horite clans were L, Shobal,
1Ch 1:38 The sons of Seir were L, Shobal, Zibeon, Anah,
1:39 The sons of L were Hori and Heman.

LOTAN'S (2) [LOTAN]
Ge 36:22 were Hori and Heman. L sister was named Timna.
1Ch 1:39 were Hori and Heman. L sister was named Timna.

LOTHE [KJV] HATE

LOTION (2) [LOTIONS]
Ps 55:21 in his heart is war. / His words are as soothing as l,
104:15 to make them glad, / olive oil as l for their skin,

LOTIONS (1) [LOTION]
2Sa 12:20 washed himself, put on l, and changed his clothes.

LOTS (38) [LOT]
Lev 16: 8 He is to cast sacred l to determine which goat will
Nu 27:21 determine the LORD's will by means of sacred l.
Dt 33: 8 "O LORD, you have given the sacred l / to your
Jos 14: 2 received their inheritance by means of sacred l,
18: 6 Then I will cast sacred l in the presence of the
18: 8 l in the presence of the LORD here at Shiloh."
18:10 Joshua cast sacred l in the presence of the LORD
19:51 l in the presence of the LORD at the entrance of
21: 8 and pasturelands to the Levites by casting sacred l.
Jdg 20: 9 we will draw l to decide who will attack Gibeah.
1Sa 25:10 There are l of servants these days who run away
28: 6 either by dreams or by sacred l or by the prophets.
1Ch 6:54 and territory assigned by means of sacred l to the
6:61 of the half-tribe of Manasseh by means of sacred l.
6:62 The descendants of Gershon received by sacred l
6:63 The descendants of Merari received by sacred l
6:65 were also assigned by means of sacred l.
24: 5 assigned to the various groups by means of sacred l
24: 6 of Eleazar and Ithamar took turns casting l.
24:31 were assigned to their duties by means of sacred l,
25: 8 particular term of service by means of sacred l,
26:13 for it was all decided by means of sacred l.
Ezr 2:63 the LORD about the matter by means of sacred l.
Ne 7:65 the LORD about the matter by means of sacred l.
10:34 "We have cast sacred l to determine when—
11: 1 and Benjamin were chosen by sacred l to live
Est 3: 7 l were cast (the l were called *purim*)
9:24 and month determined by casting l (the l were
9:26 because it is the ancient word for casting l.)
Pr 18:18 Casting l can end arguments and settle disputes
Eze 21:21 They will cast l by shaking arrows from the quiver.
Joel 3: 3 They cast l to decide which of my people would be
Ob 1:11 off their wealth and cast l to divide up Jerusalem.
Jnh 1: 7 Then the crew cast l to see which of them had
Na 3:10 Soldiers cast l to see who would get the Egyptian
Ac 1:26 Then they cast l, and in this way Matthias was

LOTUS (2)
Job 40:21 It lies down under the l plants, hidden by the reeds.
40:22 The l plants give it shade among the willows

LOUD (41) [ALOUD, LOUDER, LOUDLY, LOUDMOUTH, LOUDMOUTHED]
Ge 27:34 When Esau understood, he let out a l and bitter cry.
39:15 When he heard my l cries, he ran and left his shirt
Ex 11: 6 Then a l wail will be heard throughout the land of
12:30 and l wailing was heard throughout the land of
19:16 There was a long, l blast from a ram's horn,
20:18 heard the thunder and the l blast of the horn,
Lev 23:24 Festival of Trumpets—with l blasts from a trumpet.
25: 9 blow the trumpets l and long throughout the land.
Dt 5:22 "The LORD spoke these words with a l voice to
Jos 6:20 sound of the horns, they shouted as l as they could.
1Sa 4: 5 of joy was so l that it made the ground shake!
1Ch 15:28 of cymbals, and l playing on harps and lyres.
2Ch 20:19 the LORD, the God of Israel, with a very l shout.
30:21 sang to the LORD, accompanied by l instruments.
Ezr 3:13 and weeping mingled together in a l commotion
Est 4: 1 out into the city, crying with a l and bitter wail.
Ps 55: 3 shout at me, / making l and wicked threats.
68: 4 Sing l praises to him who rides the clouds.
150: 5 of cymbals; / praise him with l clanging cymbals.
Pr 9:13 The woman named Folly is l and brash. She is
Isa 54: 1 Break forth into l and joyful song, O Jerusalem,
Eze 3:12 me up, and I heard a l rumbling sound behind me.
Mt 12:23 Son of David, the Messiah?" they wondered out l.
27:46 Jesus called out with a l voice, "*Eli, Eli,*
Mk 15:34 Then, at that time Jesus called out with a l voice,
15:37 Then Jesus uttered another l cry and breathed his
Lk 8:54 Jesus took her by the hand and said in a l voice,
Jn 11:42 but I said it out l for the sake of all these people
Ac 8: 2 people came and buried Stephen with l weeping.)
14:10 So Paul called to him in a l voice, "Stand up!"
1Co 13: 1 I would only be making meaningless noise like a l
Gal 4:27 Break forth into l and joyful song,
Heb 5: 7 and pleadings, with a l cry and tears,
Rev 1:10 Suddenly, I heard a l voice behind me, a voice that
5: 2 I saw a strong angel, who shouted with a l voice:
11:12 Then a l voice shouted from heaven, "Come up
11:15 and there were l voices shouting in heaven:
12:10 Then I heard a l voice shouting across the heavens,
14:15 and called out in a l voice to the one sitting on the
19: 6 of mighty ocean waves, or the crash of l thunder:
21: 3 I heard a l shout from the throne, saying, "Look,

LOUDER (17) [LOUD]
Ex 19:19 As the horn blast grew l and l, Moses spoke,
1Sa 14:19 confusion in the Philistine camp grew l and l.
1Ki 18:27 "You'll have to shout l," he scoffed, "for surely
18:28 So they shouted l, and following their normal
Ps 74:23 have said. / Their uproar of rebellion grows ever l.
Isa 40: 9 Shout l to Jerusalem—do not be afraid.
Mt 20:31 but they only shouted l, "Lord, Son of David,
27:23 But the crowd only roared the l, "Crucify him!"
Mk 10:48 But he only shouted l, "Son of David, have mercy
15:14 But the crowd only roared the l, "Crucify him!"
Lk 18:39 but he only shouted l, "Son of David, have mercy
23:23 But the crowd shouted l and l for Jesus' death,
Ac 23:10 The shouting grew l and l, and the men were

LOUDLY (8) [LOUD]
Jdg 2: 4 the LORD finished speaking, the Israelites wept l.
Ne 12:42 They played and sang l and clearly under the
Job 2:12 Wailing l, they tore their robes and threw dust into
Ps 49:18 and the world l applauds their success.
Jer 25:30 'The LORD will roar l against his own land from
Eze 11: 4 son of man, prophesy against them l and clearly."
Rev 6:10 They called l to the Lord and said, "O Sovereign
8:13 And I heard a single eagle crying l as it flew

LOUDMOUTH (1) [LOUD, MOUTH]
Jer 46:17 king of Egypt, is a l who missed his opportunity!'

LOUDMOUTHED (1) [LOUD, MOUTH]
Jude 1:16 They are l braggarts, and they flatter others to get

LOUNGE (2)
Am 2: 8 they l around in clothing stolen from their debtors.
6: 1 How terrible it will be for you who l in luxury

LOVE (651) [BELOVED, LOVED, LOVER, LOVER'S, LOVERS, LOVES, LOVESICK, LOVING, LOVINGLY]
FAITHFUL LOVE ENDURES FOREVER (40) 1Ch 16:34,41; 2Ch 5:13; 7:3,6; 20:21; Ps 106:1; 107:1; 118:1,2,3, 4,29; 136:1,2,3,4,5,6,7,8,9,10,11,12,13,14,15,16, 17,18,19,20, 21,22,23,24,25,26; Jer 33:11

LOVE OF CHRIST (2) Eph 3:19; 1Ti 1:14

LOVE OF GOD (5) Lk 11:42; Ro 8:39; 2Co 13:13; 2Th 3:5; Jude 1:1

LOVE ONE ANOTHER (7) 1Th 4:9; 1Jn 2:7; 3:11,23; 4:7; 2Jn 1:5,6

LOVE THE LORD (4) Mt 22:37; Mk 12:30; Lk 10:27; 1Co 16:22

LOVE THE LORD* (12) Dt 6:5; 11:1,13; 19:9; 30:16,20; Jos 22:5; 23:11; Ps 31:23; 97:10; 116:1; Eze 44:9

LOVE YOUR NEIGHBOR (10) Lev 19:18; Mt 5:43; 19:19; 22:39; Mk 12:31; Lk 10:27; Ro 13:8,9; Gal 5:14; Jas 2:8

UNFAILING LOVE (111) Ge 32:10; Ex 15:13; 34:6,7; Nu 14:18,19; Dt 7:12; 2Sa 2:6; 7:15; 15:20; 22:51; 1Ki 8:23; 1Ch 17:13; 2Ch 6:14,42; Ezr 7:28; 9:9; Ne 1:5; 9:17,32; 13:22; Job 10:12; 37:13; Ps 5:7; 6:4; 13:5; 17:7; 18:50; 21:7; 23:6; 25:6,7,10; 26:3; 31:7,16,21; 32:10; 33:5,18,22; 36:5,7,10; 40:10,11; 42:8; 44:26; 48:9; 51:1; 52:8; 57:3,10; 59:10,16,17; 61:7; 62:12; 63:3; 66:20; 69:13,16; 77:8; 85:7,10; 86:5,15; 88:11; 89:2,14,24,49; 90:14; 92:2; 94:18; 100:5; 103:8,11; 106:45; 108:4; 109:26; 115:1; 117:2; 119:41,64,76,88,124, 159; 130:7; 138:2; 143:8,12; 145:8; 147:11; Pr 14:22; 16:6; 20:28; 21:21; Isa 55:3; 63:7; Jer 16:5; 31:3; La 3:22,32; Da 9:4; Hos 2:19; Jnh 4:2; Mic 7:20; Jn 1:14,17

UNFAILING LOVE AND FAITHFULNESS (14) Ex 34:6; 2Sa 15:20; Ps 25:10; 40:10,11; 57:3; 61:7; 115:1; 138:2; Pr 14:22; 16:6; 20:28; Jn 1:14,17

Ge 22: 2 your only son—yes, Isaac, whom you l so much—
29:18 Since Jacob was in l with Rachel, he told her
29:20 But his l for her was so strong that it seemed to
29:32 my misery, and now my husband will l me."
32:10 and unfailing l you have shown to me,
34: 3 But Shechem's l for Dinah was strong, and he tried
34: 8 "My son Shechem is truly in l with your daughter,
Ex 15:13 "With unfailing l you will lead / this people whom
20: 6 But I lavish my l on those who l me and obey
21: 5 'I l my master, my wife, and my children.
34: 6 to anger and rich in unfailing l and faithfulness.
34: 7 I show this unfailing l to many thousands by
Lev 19:18 against anyone, but l your neighbor as yourself.
19:34 and you must l them as you l yourself.
Nu 14:18 LORD is slow to anger and rich in unfailing l,
14:19 because of your magnificent, unfailing l,
Dt 5:10 But I lavish my l on those who l me and obey
6: 5 And you must l the LORD your God with all your
7: 7 and lavish his l on you because you were larger
7: 9 and constantly loves those who l him and obey his
7:12 God will keep his covenant of unfailing l with you,
7:13 He will l you and bless you and make you into a
10:12 to l and worship him with all your heart and soul,
10:15 chose your ancestors as the objects of his l.
10:18 He shows l to the foreigners living among you
10:19 You, too, must show l to foreigners, for you
11: 1 "You must l the LORD your God and obey all
11:13 and if you l the LORD your God with all your
11:22 show l to the LORD your God by walking in his
13: 3 The LORD your God is testing you to see if you l
19: 9 if you always l the LORD your God and walk in
21:15 firstborn son is the son of the wife he does not l.
21:17 he is the son of the wife his father does not l.
30: 6 so that you will l him with all your heart and soul,
30:16 I have commanded you today to l the LORD your
30:20 Choose to l the LORD your God and to obey him
33: 3 Indeed, you l the people; / all your holy ones are in
Jos 22: 5 L the LORD your God, walk in all his ways,
23:11 So be very careful to l the LORD your God.
Jdg 5:31 But may those who l you rise like the sun at full
14:16 came to him in tears and said, "You don't l me;
16: 4 Later Samson fell in l with a woman named
16:15 "How can you say you l me when you don't
Ru 2:11 "But I also know about the l and kindness you
1Sa 18: 1 There was an immediate bond of l between them,
18:20 Saul's daughter Michal had fallen in l with David,
20:14 And may you treat me with the faithful l of the
20:15 treat my family with this faithful l, even when the
2Sa 1:26 And your l for me was deep, / deeper than the l of women!
2: 6 you in return and reward you with his unfailing l!
7:15 But my unfailing l will not be taken from him as I
13: 1 her half brother, fell desperately in l with her.
13: 2 impossible that he could ever fulfill his l for her.
13: 4 "I am in l with Tamar, Absalom's sister."
13:15 Then suddenly Amnon's l turned to hate, and he
15:20 and may the LORD show you his unfailing l
19: 6 You seem to l those who hate you and hate those who l you.
22:51 your king; / you show unfailing l to your anointed,
23:15 how I would l some of that good water from the
1Ki 8:23 and show unfailing l to all who obey you
10: 9 Because the LORD loves Israel with an eternal l,
1Ch 11:17 how I would l some of that good water from the
16:34 for he is good! / His faithful l endures forever.
16:41 the LORD, "for his faithful l endures forever."
17:13 I will not take my unfailing l from him as I took it
29:18 See to it that their l for you never changes.
2Ch 5:13 "He is so good! / His faithful l endures forever!"
6:14 and show unfailing l to all who obey you
6:42 Remember your unfailing l for your servant
7: 3 "He is so good! / His faithful l endures forever!"
7: 6 were singing, "His faithful l endures forever!"
19: 2 the wicked and l those who hate the LORD?"
20:21 to the LORD; / his faithful l endures forever!"
24:22 That was how King Joash repaid Jehoiada for his l
Ezr 3:11 His faithful l for Israel endures forever!"
7:28 And praise him for demonstrating such unfailing l
9: 9 but in his unfailing l our God did not abandon us in
Ne 1: 5 covenant of unfailing l with those who l him
9:17 to become angry, and full of unfailing l and mercy.
9:30 In your l, you were patient with them for many
9:32 who keeps his covenant of unfailing l,
13:22 on me according to your great and unfailing l.
Job 10:12 You gave me life and showed me your unfailing l.
37:13 as a punishment or as a sign of his unfailing l.
Ps 5: 7 Because of your unfailing l, I can enter your house;
5:11 so all who l your name may be filled with joy.
5:12 surrounding them with your shield of l.
6: 4 rescue me. / Save me because of your unfailing l.
13: 5 But I trust in your unfailing l. / I will rejoice
17: 7 Show me your unfailing l in wonderful ways.
18: 1 I l you, LORD; you are my strength.
18:50 your king; / you show unfailing l to your anointed,
21: 7 The unfailing l of the Most High will keep him
23: 6 your goodness and unfailing l will pursue me
25: 6 O LORD, your unfailing l and compassion,
25: 7 look instead through the eyes of your unfailing l,
25:10 The LORD leads with unfailing l and faithfulness
26: 3 For I am constantly aware of your unfailing l,
26: 8 I l your sanctuary, LORD, / the place where your
31: 7 am overcome with joy because of your unfailing l,
31:16 on your servant. / In your unfailing l, save me.
31:21 the LORD, / for he has shown me his unfailing l.
31:23 L the LORD, all you faithful ones!
32:10 but unfailing l surrounds those who trust the
33: 5 and good, / and his unfailing l fills the earth.
33:18 who fear him, / those who rely on his unfailing l.
33:22 Let your unfailing l surround us, LORD, / for our
36: 5 Your unfailing l, O LORD, is as vast as the
36: 7 How precious is your unfailing l, O God!
36:10 Pour out your unfailing l on those who l you;
37:37 for a wonderful future lies before those who l
40:10 of your unfailing l and faithfulness.
40:11 My only hope is in your unfailing l
40:16 and gladness. / May those who l your salvation
42: 8 Through each day the LORD pours his unfailing l
44:26 and help us! / Save us because of your unfailing l.
45: T to be sung to the tune "Lilies." A l song.
45: 7 You l what is right and hate what is wrong.
48: 9 O God, we meditate on your unfailing l / as we
51: 1 mercy on me, O God, / because of your unfailing l.
52: 3 You l evil more than good / and lies more than
52: 4 You l to say things that harm others, / you liar!
52: 8 I trust in God's unfailing l / forever and ever.
57: 3 My God will send forth his unfailing l
57:10 For your unfailing l is as high as the heavens.
59:10 In his unfailing l, my God will come and help me.
59:16 with joy each morning because of your unfailing l.
59:17 my refuge, / the God who shows me unfailing l.
61: 7 Appoint your unfailing l and faithfulness to watch
62:12 unfailing l, O Lord, is yours. / Surely you judge all
63: 3 Your unfailing l is better to me than life itself;
66:20 and did not withdraw his unfailing l from me.
68:21 crushing the skulls of those who l their guilty

69:13 In your unfailing l, O God, / answer my prayer
69:16 O LORD, / for your unfailing l is wonderful.
69:36 and those who l him will live there in safety.
70: 4 and gladness. / May those who l your salvation
77: 8 Is his unfailing l gone forever? / Have his promises
80:17 Strengthen the man you l, / the son of your choice.
85: 7 Show us your unfailing l, O LORD, / and grant us
85:10 Unfailing l and truth have met together.
86: 5 so full of unfailing l for all who ask your aid.
86:13 for your l for me is very great. / You have rescued
86:15 slow to get angry, / full of unfailing l and truth.
88:11 Can those in the grave declare your unfailing l?
89: 2 Your unfailing l will last forever.
89:14 Unfailing l and truth walk before you as attendants.
89:24 My faithfulness and unfailing l will be with him,
89:28 I will l him and be kind to him forever;
89:49 Lord, where is your unfailing l? / You promised it
90:14 Satisfy us in the morning with your unfailing l,
91:14 The LORD says, "I will rescue those who l me.
92: 2 It is good to proclaim your unfailing l in the
94: 5 oppress your people, LORD, / hurting those you l.
94:18 and your unfailing l, O LORD, supported me.
97:10 You who l the LORD, hate evil! / He protects the
98: 3 He has remembered his promise to l and be faithful
100: 5 is good. / His unfailing l continues forever,
101: 1 I will sing of your l and justice. / I will praise you,
102:14 For your people l every stone in her walls
103: 4 and surrounds me with l and tender mercies.
103: 8 he is slow to get angry and full of unfailing l.
103:11 For his unfailing l toward those who fear him
103:17 But the l of the LORD remains forever
106: 1 for he is good! / His faithful l endures forever.
106:39 and their l of idols was adultery in the LORD's
106:45 with them / and relented because of his unfailing l.
107: 1 for he is good! / His faithful l endures forever.
107: 8 Let them praise the LORD for his great l / and for
107:15 Let them praise the LORD for his great l / and for
107:21 Let them praise the LORD for his great l / and for
107:31 Let them praise the LORD for his great l / and for
107:43 they will see in our history the faithful l of the
108: 4 For your unfailing l is higher than the heavens.
109: 4 I l them, but they try to destroy me— / even as I
109: 5 They return evil for good, / and hatred for my l.
109:26 my God! / Save me because of your unfailing l.
115: 1 all the glory / for your unfailing l and faithfulness.
116: 1 I l the LORD because he hears / and answers my
117: 2 For he loves us with unfailing l; / the faithfulness
118: 1 for he is good! / His faithful l endures forever.
118: 2 of Israel repeat: / "His faithful l endures forever."
118: 3 repeat: / "His faithful l endures forever."
118: 4 LORD repeat: / "His faithful l endures forever."
118:29 for he is good! / His faithful l endures forever.
119:36 your decrees; / do not inflict me with l for money!
119:41 LORD, give to me your unfailing l, / the salvation
119:47 How I delight in your commands! / How I l them!
119:48 I honor and l your commands. / I meditate on your
119:64 O LORD, the earth is full of your unfailing l;
119:76 Now let your unfailing l comfort me, / just as you
119:88 In your unfailing l, spare my life; / then I can
119:97 Oh, how I l your law! / I think about it all day long.
119:113 about you, / but my choice is clear—I l your law.
119:119 you skim off; / no wonder I l to obey your decrees!
119:124 I am your servant; / deal with me in unfailing l,
119:127 Truly, I l your commands / more than gold,
119:132 your mercy, / as you do for all who l your name.
119:135 Look down on me with l; / teach me all your
119:140 thoroughly tested; / that is why I l them so much.
119:149 In your faithful l, O LORD, hear my cry; / in your
119:159 See how I l your commandments, LORD.
119:159 Give back my life because of your unfailing l.
119:163 I hate and abhor all falsehood, / but I l your law.
119:165 Those who l your law have great peace / and do
119:167 obeyed your decrees, / and I l them very much.
122: 6 of Jerusalem. / May all who l this city prosper.
130: 7 for with the LORD there is unfailing l
136: 1 for he is good! / His faithful l endures forever.
136: 2 to the God of gods. / His faithful l endures forever.
136: 3 the Lord of lords. / His faithful l endures forever.
136: 4 mighty miracles. / His faithful l endures forever.
136: 5 so skillfully. / His faithful l endures forever.
136: 6 earth on the water. / His faithful l endures forever.
136: 7 heavenly lights— / His faithful l endures forever.
136: 8 sun to rule the day, / His faithful l endures forever.
136: 9 to rule the night. / His faithful l endures forever.
136:10 firstborn of Egypt. / His faithful l endures forever.
136:11 Israel out of Egypt. / His faithful l endures forever.
136:12 and powerful arm. / His faithful l endures forever.
136:13 parted the Red Sea. / His faithful l endures forever.
136:14 safely through, / His faithful l endures forever.
136:15 army into the sea. / His faithful l endures forever.
136:16 the wilderness. / His faithful l endures forever.
136:17 mighty kings. / His faithful l endures forever.
136:18 powerful kings— / His faithful l endures forever.
136:19 of the Amorites, / His faithful l endures forever.
136:20 Og king of Bashan. / His faithful l endures forever.
136:21 as an inheritance— / His faithful l endures forever.
136:22 his servant Israel. / His faithful l endures forever.
136:23 our utter weakness. / His faithful l endures forever.
136:24 from our enemies. / His faithful l endures forever.
136:25 every living thing. / His faithful l endures forever.
136:26 the God of heaven. / His faithful l endures forever.
138: 2 to your name / for your unfailing l and faithfulness,
138: 8 for your faithful l, O LORD, endures forever.
143: 8 Let me hear of your unfailing l to me in the
143:12 In your unfailing l, cut off all my enemies
145: 8 slow to get angry, full of unfailing l.
145:20 The LORD protects all those who l him, / but he
147:11 those who put their hope in his unfailing l.
Pr 4: 6 she will protect you. L her, and she will guard you.
5:15 your own well—share your l only with your wife.
5:19 May you always be captivated by her l.
7: 4 L wisdom like a sister; make insight a beloved
7:18 Come, let's drink our fill of l until morning.
8:17 "I l all who l me. Those who search for me
8:21 Those who l me inherit wealth, for I fill their
8:36 injured themselves. All who hate me l death."
9: 8 the wise, when rebuked, will l you all the more.
10:12 Hatred stirs up quarrels, but l covers all offenses.
12: 1 To learn, you must l discipline; it is stupid to hate
13:24 your children, it proves you don't l them;
13:24 if you l your children, you will be prompt to
14:22 you will be granted unfailing l and faithfulness.
15:12 Mockers don't l those who rebuke them, so they
15:17 A bowl of soup with someone you l is better than
16: 6 Unfailing l and faithfulness cover sin; evil is
17: 9 Disregarding another person's faults preserves l;
18:21 Those who l to talk will experience the
19: 8 To acquire wisdom is to l oneself; people who
20:13 If you l sleep, you will end in poverty. Keep your
20:28 Unfailing l and faithfulness protect the king; his
throne is made secure through l.
21:10 Evil people l to harm others; their neighbors get no
21:17 Those who l pleasure become poor; wine
21:21 pursues godliness and unfailing l will find life,
21:26 always greedy for more, while the godly l to give!
27: 5 An open rebuke is better than hidden l!
Ecc 3: 8 A time to l and a time to hate. / A time for war
5:10 Those who l money will never have enough.
9: 9 Live happily with the woman you l through all the
SS 1: 2 and again, for your l is sweeter than wine.
1: 3 your name! No wonder all the young women l you!
1: 4 are for him! We praise his l even more than wine."
1: 7 "Tell me, O my l, where are you leading your
1:16 "What a lovely, pleasant sight you are, my l,
2: 5 Oh, feed me with your l—your 'raisins' and your
2: 7 of the wild, not to awaken l until the time is right.
2:15 little foxes before they ruin the vineyard of your l,
2:17 and the shadows flee away, come back to me, my l.
3: 3 you seen him anywhere, this one I l so much?'
3: 5 of the wild, not to awaken l until the time is right."
3:10 Its interior was a gift of l from the young women
4:10 How sweet is your l, my treasure, my bride!
5: 1 eat and drink! Yes, drink deeply of this l!"
5: 8 my beloved one, tell him that I am sick with l."
7:11 Come, my l, let us go out into the fields and spend
7:12 are in flower. And there I will give you my l.
8: 4 not to awaken l until the time is right."
8: 6 For l is as strong as death, and its jealousy is as
8: 6 L flashes like fire, the brightest kind of flame.
8: 7 Many waters cannot quench l; neither can rivers
8: 7 If a man tried to buy l with everything he owned,
8:14 "Come quickly, my l! Move like a swift gazelle
Isa 5: 1 Now I will sing a song for the one I l about his
16: 5 then David's throne will be established by l.
26: 8 LORD, we l to obey your laws; / our heart's
30:18 to him so he can show you his l and compassion.
43: 4 are precious to me. You are honored, and I l you.
49:15 Can she feel no l for a child she has borne?
54: 8 But with everlasting l I will have compassion on
55: 3 and unfailing l that I promised to David.
55:13 it will be an everlasting sign of his power and l.
56: 6 to the LORD and serve him and l his name,
56:10 They l to lie around, sleeping and dreaming.
57: 9 into the world of the dead, to find new gods to l.
58: 2 They l to make a show of coming to me and asking
61: 8 "For I, the LORD, l justice. I hate robbery
62: 1 Because I l Zion, because my heart yearns for
63: 7 I will tell of the LORD's unfailing l. I will praise
63: 7 which he has granted according to his mercy and l.
63: 9 In his l and mercy he redeemed them. He lifted
66:10 glad with her, all you who l her and mourn for her.
66:12 her breasts, carried in her arms, and treated with l.
Jer 2:25 I have fallen in l with these foreign gods, and I
3:19 'I would l to treat you as my own children!'
9:24 who is just and righteous, whose l is unfailing,
14:10 "You l to wander far from me and do not follow in
16: 5 I have taken away my unfailing l and my mercy.
23:14 They commit adultery, and they l dishonesty.
31: 3 have loved you, my people, with an everlasting l.
31: 3 With unfailing l I have drawn you to myself.
31:20 "I had to punish him, but I still l him. I long for
33:11 LORD is good. / His faithful l endures forever!'
50:38 and the people are madly in l with them.
La 3:22 The unfailing l of the LORD never ends! By his
3:32 according to the greatness of his unfailing l.
Eze 7:19 for their l of money made them stumble into sin.
13:19 By lying to my people who l to listen to lies,
16:31 you have not even demanded payment for your l!
23: 5 and she gave her l to the Assyrians, her neighbors.
23:14 She fell in l with pictures that were painted on a
23:17 adultery with her, defiling her in the bed of l.
33:31 They express l with their mouths, but their hearts
33:32 like someone who sings l songs with a beautiful
44: 9 not been circumcised and do not l the LORD.
Da 9: 4 You always fulfill your promises of unfailing l to
those who l you
Hos 1: 6 for I will no longer show l to the people of Israel
1: 7 their God, will show l to the people of Judah.
2: 1 you will call your sisters Ruhamah—'The ones I l.'
2: 4 And I will not l her children as I would my own
2:19 and justice, unfailing l and compassion.
2:23 I will show l to those I called 'Not loved.'
3: 1 Bring her back to you and l her, even though she
4:18 Their l for shame is greater than their l for
6: 4 "For your l vanishes like the morning mist
8:13 The people of Israel l their rituals of sacrifice,
9: 7 and shows only hatred for those who l God.
9:15 I will l them no more because all their leaders are
10: 6 This idol they l so much will be carted away with
10:12 and you will harvest a crop of my l.
11: 4 I led Israel along with my ropes of kindness and l.
12: 6 Act on the principles of l and justice, and always
12: 7 selling from dishonest scales—they l to cheat.
14: 4 and faithlessness, and my l will know no bounds,
Am 4: 5 This is the kind of thing you Israelites l to do,"
5:15 Hate evil and l what is good; remodel your courts
Jnh 4: 2 slow to get angry and filled with unfailing l.
Mic 1:16 for the children you l will be snatched away,
3: 2 but you are the very ones who hate good and l evil.
6: 8 to do what is right, to l mercy, and to walk humbly
7:20 and unfailing l as you promised with an oath to our
Hab 1: 3 I am surrounded by people who l to argue
Zep 3:17 With his l, he will calm all your fears.
Zec 1:14 My l for Jerusalem and Mount Zion is passionate
8: 2 My l for Mount Zion is passionate and strong;
8:19 for the people of Judah. So l truth and peace.
10: 6 I will reestablish them because I l them.
Mal 1: 2 "I showed my l for you by loving your ancestor
Mt 5:43 'L your neighbor' and hate your enemy.
5:44 But I say, l your enemies! Pray for those who
5:46 If you l only those who l you, what good is
6: 5 don't be like the hypocrites who l to pray publicly
6:24 For you will hate one and l the other, or be devoted
10:37 If you l your father or mother more than you l me,
10:37 or if you l your son or daughter more than me,
19:19 and mother. L your neighbor as yourself.' "
22:37 " 'You must l the Lord your God with all your
22:39 equally important: 'L your neighbor as yourself.'
23: 6 And how they l to sit at the head table at banquets
24:12 and the l of many will grow cold.
Mk 10:21 Jesus felt genuine l for this man as he looked at
12:30 And you must l the Lord your God with all your
12:31 equally important: 'L your neighbor as yourself.'
12:33 And I know it is important to l him with all my
12:33 all my strength, and to l my neighbors as myself.
12:38 For they l to parade in flowing robes and to have
12:39 And how they l the seats of honor in the
Lk 6:27 if you are willing to listen, I say, l your enemies.
6:32 deserve credit merely for loving those who l you?
6:35 "L your enemies! Do good to them! Lend to them!
7:47 have been forgiven, so she has shown me much l.
7:47 a person who is forgiven little shows only little l."
10:27 " 'You must l the Lord your God with all your
10:27 And, 'L your neighbor as yourself.' "
11:42 completely forget about justice and the l of God.
11:43 For how you l the seats of honor in the synagogues
14:26 "If you want to be my follower you must l me
15:20 Filled with l and compassion, he ran to his son,
16:13 For you will hate one and l the other, or be devoted
20:46 For they l to parade in flowing robes and to have
20:46 And how they l the seats of honor in the
Jn 1:14 He was full of unfailing l and faithfulness. And we
1:17 God's unfailing l and faithfulness came through
5:42 because I know you don't have God's l within you.
8:42 "If God were your Father, you would l me,
8:44 the Devil, and you l to do the evil things he does.
11: 3 telling him, "Lord, the one you l is very sick."
12:25 Those who l their life in this world will lose it.
13: 1 now showed the disciples the full extent of his l.
13:34 L each other. Just as I have loved you, you should
l each other.
13:35 Your l for one another will prove to the world that
14:15 "If you l me, obey my commandments.
14:21 obey my commandments are the ones who l me.
14:21 And because they l me, my Father will l them, and
I will l them.
14:23 "All those who l me will do what I say.
14:23 My Father will l them, and we will come to them
14:24 Anyone who doesn't l me will not do what I say.
14:28 If you really l me, you will be very happy for me,
14:31 so that the world will know that I l the Father.
15: 9 even as the Father has loved me. Remain in my l.
15:10 When you obey me, you remain in my l, just as I
obey my Father and remain in his l.
15:12 I command you to l each other in the same way
that I l you.
15:13 the greatest l is shown when people lay down their
15:17 I command you to l each other.
15:19 The world would l you if you belonged to it,
16:27 because you l me and believe that I came from
17:23 understand that you l them as much as you l me.
17:26 I will do this so that your l for me may be in them
18:37 All who l the truth recognize that what I say is
21:15 son of John, do you l me more than these?"
21:15 "Yes, Lord," Peter replied, "you know I l you."
21:16 "Simon son of John, do you l me?" "Yes, Lord,"
Peter said, "you know I l you."
21:17 he asked him, "Simon son of John, do you l me?"
21:17 You know I l you." Jesus said, "Then feed my
Ac 20:24 Good News about God's wonderful kindness and l.
Ro 5: 5 given us the Holy Spirit to fill our hearts with his l.
5: 8 But God showed his great l for us by sending
7:22 I l God's law with all my heart.
8:28 to work together for the good of those who l God
8:35 Can anything ever separate us from Christ's l?
8:38 that nothing can ever separate us from his l.
8:38 and even the powers of hell can't keep God's l
8:39 l of God that is revealed in Christ Jesus our Lord.
9:25 And I will l those / whom I did not l before."
12: 9 Don't just pretend that you l others. Really l them.
12:10 L each other with genuine affection, and take

13: 8 Pay all your debts, except the debt of l for others.
13: 8 If you l your neighbor, you will fulfill all the
13: 9 "L your neighbor as yourself."
13:10 L does no wrong to anyone, so l satisfies all of God's requirements.
14:15 what you eat, you are not acting in l if you eat it.
15:30 Do this because of your l for me, given to you by
16: 8 whom I l as one of the Lord's own children,
16:16 Greet each other in Christian l. All the churches of
1Co 2: 9 what God has prepared / for those who l him."
4:21 or should I come with quiet l and gentleness?
8: 1 it is l that really builds up the church.
13: 1 language in heaven or on earth but didn't l others,
13: 2 but didn't l others, what good would I be?
13: 2 it move, without l I would be no good to anybody.
13: 3 but if I didn't l others, I would be of no value
13: 4 L is patient and kind. L is not jealous or boastful
13: 5 or rude. L does not demand its own way. L is not irritable, and it keeps no record of when it
13: 7 L never gives up, never loses faith, is always
13: 8 L will last forever, but prophecy and speaking in
13:13 faith, hope, and l—and the greatest of these is l.
14: 1 Let l be your highest goal, but also desire the
16:14 And everything you do must be done with l.
16:20 greet you for them. Greet each other in Christian l.
16:22 If anyone does not l the Lord, that person is cursed.
16:24 My l to all of you in Christ Jesus.
2Co 2: 4 but I wanted you to know how very much I l you.
2: 8 Now show him that you still l him.
5:14 we do, it is because Christ's l controls us.
6: 6 our patience, our kindness, our sincere l,
6:12 it is not because of a lack of l on our part, but because you have withheld your l from us.
7: 7 and how loyal your l is for me, I was filled with
8: 7 such enthusiasm, and such l for us—
8: 8 to do it. This is one way to prove your l is real.
8: 9 You know how full of l and kindness our Lord
8:24 So show them your l, and prove to all the churches
11:11 Why? Because I don't l you? God knows I do.
12:15 it seems that the more I l you, the less you l me.
13:11 Then the God of l and peace will be with you.
13:12 Greet each other in Christian l. All the Christians
13:13 the grace of our Lord Jesus Christ, the l of God,
Gal 1: 6 who in his l and mercy called you to share the
5: 6 What is important is faith expressing itself in l.
5:13 sinful nature, but freedom to serve one another in l.
5:14 one command: "L your neighbor as yourself."
5:15 But if instead of showing l among yourselves you
5:22 l, joy, peace, patience, kindness, goodness,
Eph 1:15 Lord Jesus and your l for Christians everywhere,
3:17 go down deep into the soil of God's marvelous l.
3:18 how long, how high, and how deep his l really is.
3:19 May you experience the l of Christ, though it is
4: 2 allowance for each other's faults because of your l.
4:15 Instead, we will hold to the truth in l,
4:16 whole body is healthy and growing and full of l.
5: 2 Live a life filled with l for others,
5:25 And you husbands must l your wives with the same l Christ showed the church.
5:28 husbands ought to l their wives as they l their
5:33 each man must l his wife as he loves himself,
6:23 dear friends, and l with faith, from God the Father
6:24 May God's grace be upon all who l our Lord Jesus Christ with an undying l.
Php 1: 8 God knows how much I l you and long for you
1: 9 I pray that your l for each other will overflow more
1:16 They preach because they l me, for they know the
2: 1 Any comfort from his l? Any fellowship together
2:29 Welcome him with Christian l and with great joy,
4: 1 and sisters, I l you and long to see you,
Col 1: 4 in Christ Jesus and that you l all of God's people.
1: 8 He is the one who told us about the great l for
2: 2 be encouraged and knit together by strong ties of l.
3:14 important piece of clothing you must wear is l.
3:14 L is what binds us all together in perfect harmony.
3:19 And you husbands must l your wives and never
1Th 3: 6 news that your faith and l are as strong as ever.
3:12 And may the Lord make your l grow and overflow
3:12 everyone else, just as our l overflows toward you.
4: 9 l that should be shown among God's people.
4: 9 For God himself has taught you to l one another.
4:10 your l is already strong toward all the Christians in
4:10 dear friends, we beg you to l them more and more.
5: 8 protected by the body armor of faith and l,
5:13 highly of them and give them your wholehearted l
5:26 Greet each other in Christian l.
2Th 1: 3 and you are all growing in l for each other.
3: 5 into an ever deeper understanding of the l of God
1Ti 1: 5 would be filled with l that comes from a pure heart,
1:14 me completely with faith and the l of Christ Jesus.
2:15 continuing to live in faith, l, holiness, and modesty.
4:12 way you live, in your l, your faith, and your purity.
6:10 For the l of money is at the root of all kinds of evil.
6:11 along with faith, l, perseverance, and gentleness.
2Ti 1: 7 us a spirit of fear and timidity, but of power, l,
1: 9 to show his l and kindness to us through Christ
1:13 live in the faith and l that you have in Christ Jesus.
2:22 Pursue faith and l and peace, and enjoy the
3: 2 For people will l only themselves and their money.
3: 4 up with pride, and l pleasure rather than God.
3:10 You know my l and my patient endurance.
Tit 1: 8 guests in his home and must l all that is good.
2: 2 have strong faith and be filled with l and patience.
2: 4 must train the younger women to l their husbands
3: 4 then God our Savior showed us his kindness and l.
3:15 give my greetings to all of the believers who l us.
Phm 1: 5 the Lord Jesus and your l for all of God's people.
1: 7 have gained much joy and comfort from your l,
1: 9 but because of our l, I prefer just to ask you.
Heb 1: 9 You l what is right and hate what is wrong.
6:10 and how you have shown your l to him by caring
10:24 of ways to encourage one another to outbursts of l
13: 1 Continue to l each other with true Christian l.
13: 5 Stay away from the l of money; be satisfied with
Jas 1:12 of life that God has promised to those who l him.
2: 5 the kingdom God promised to those who l him?
2: 8 in the Scriptures: "L your neighbor as yourself."
2:12 remember that you will be judged by the law of l,
1Pe 1: 8 You l him even though you have never seen him.
1:22 Now you can have sincere l for each other as
1:22 So see to it that you really do l each other intensely
2:17 L your Christian brothers and sisters. Fear God.
4: 8 continue to show deep l for each other, for l covers a multitude of sins.
5:14 Greet each other in Christian l. Peace be to all of
2Pe 1: 7 Godliness leads to l for other Christians,
1: 7 and finally you will grow to have genuine l for
2:13 They l to indulge in evil pleasures in broad
1Jn 2: 5 But those who obey God's word really do l him.
2: 7 This commandment—to l one another—is the
2:15 and all that it offers you, for when you l the world,
2:15 you show that you do not have the l of the Father
3:10 and does not l other Christians does not belong to
3:11 from the beginning: We should l one another.
3:14 If we l other Christians, it proves that we have
3:14 But a person who doesn't l them is still dead.
3:16 We know what real l is because Christ gave up his
3:17 to help—how can God's l be in that person?
3:18 let us stop just saying we l each other;
3:23 Jesus Christ, and l one another, just as he
4: 7 continue to l one another, for l comes from God.
4: 8 But anyone who does not l does not know God—for God is l.
4:10 This is real l. It is not that we loved God, but that
4:11 us that much, we surely ought to l each other.
4:12 But if we l each other, God lives in us, and his l has been brought to full expression
4:16 God is l, and all who live in l live in God,
4:17 And as we live in God, our l grows more perfect.
4:18 Such l has no fear because perfect l expels all fear.
4:18 and this shows that his l has not been perfected in
4:19 We l each other as a result of his loving us first.
4:20 If someone says, "I l God," but hates another
4:20 for if we don't l people we can see, how can we l God, whom we have not seen?
4:21 And God himself has commanded that we must l
5: 2 We know we l God's children if we l God
2Jn 1: 1 and to her children, whom I l in the truth,
1: 3 Christ his Son, be with us who live in truth and l.
1: 5 urge you, dear lady, that we should l one another.
1: 6 L means doing what God has commanded us,
1: 6 and he has commanded us to l one another, just as
3Jn 1: 1 to Gaius, my dear friend, whom I l in the truth.
Jude 1: 1 I am writing to all who are called to live in the l of
1: 2 and more of God's mercy, peace, and l.
1:12 in fellowship meals celebrating the l of the Lord,
1:21 Live in such a way that God's l can bless you as
Rev 2: 4 You don't l me or each other as you did at first!
2: 5 Look how far you have fallen from your first l!
2:19 your l, your faith, your service, and your patient
3: 9 They will acknowledge that you are the ones I l.
3:19 the one who corrects and disciplines everyone I l.
22:15 the idol worshipers, and all who l to live a lie.

LOVED (86) [LOVE]

Ge 24:67 He l her very much, and she was a special comfort
25:28 Isaac l Esau in particular because of the wild game
29:30 with Rachel, too, and he l her more than Leah.
37: 3 Now Jacob l Joseph more than any of his other
Dt 4:37 Because he l your ancestors, he chose to bless their
33:12 "The people of Benjamin are l by the LORD
1Sa 1: 5 a special portion because he l her very much,
18:16 But all Israel and Judah l David because he was
18:28 was with David and how much Michal l him,
20:17 for Jonathan l David as much as he l himself.
2Sa 1:26 my brother Jonathan! / Oh, how much I l you!
12:24 they named him Solomon. The LORD l the child
12:25 of the LORD"—because the LORD l him.
13:15 and he hated her even more than he had l her.
1Ki 3: 3 Solomon l the LORD and followed all the
3:26 and who l him very much, cried out, "Oh no,
11: 1 Now King Solomon l many foreign women.
2Ch 11:21 Rehoboam l Maacah more than any of his other
26:10 on the plains. He was also a man who l the soil.
Ne 13:26 and God l him and made him king over all Israel.
Est 2:17 the king l her more than any of the other young
Job 19:19 friends abhor me. Those I l have turned against me.
Ps 38:11 My l ones and friends stay away, fearing my
78:68 the tribe of Judah, / Mount Zion, which he l.
88:18 You have taken away my companions and l ones;
109:17 He l to curse others; / now you curse him.
116:15 The LORD's l ones are precious to him;
127: 2 for food to eat; / for God gives rest to his l ones.
Pr 4: 3 tenderly l by my mother as an only child.
SS 5: 9 what is it about your l one that brings you to tell us
Jer 2: 2 how you l me and followed me even through the
8: 2 the gods my people have l, served, and worshiped.
28: 6 the treasures of this Temple and all our l ones.
31: 3 "I have l you, my people, with an everlasting love.
31:32 though I l them as a husband loves his wife,"
Eze 16:37 sinned, both those you l and those you hated—
Da 10:11 the man said to me, "O Daniel, greatly l of God,
10:19 be afraid," he said, "for you are deeply l by God.
Hos 1: 6 "Name your daughter Lo-ruhamah—'Not l'—
2:23 I will show love to those I called 'Not l.'
11: 1 "When Israel was a child, I l him as a son, and I
Mal 1: 2 "I have l you deeply," says the LORD. But you retort, "Really? How have you l us?"
3:16 of those who feared him and l to think about him.
Mk 12: 6 there was only one left—his son whom he l dearly.
Lk 2:52 and he was l by God and by all who knew him.
7:42 Who do you suppose l him more after that?"
16:14 The Pharisees, who dearly l their money,
Jn 3:16 "For God so l the world that he gave his only Son,
3:19 but they l the darkness more than the light, for their
11: 5 Although Jesus l Martha, Mary, and Lazarus,
11:36 standing nearby said, "See how much he l him."
12:43 For they l human praise more than the praise of
13:23 One of Jesus' disciples, the one Jesus l, was sitting
13:34 Just as I have l you, you should love each other.
15: 9 "I have l you even as the Father has l me.
17:24 because you l me even before the world began!
19:26 his mother standing there beside the disciple he l,
20: 2 and the other disciple, the one whom Jesus l.
21: 7 Then the disciple whom Jesus l said to Peter,
21:20 and saw the disciple Jesus l following them—
Ro 8:37 victory is ours through Christ, who l us.
9:13 of the Scriptures, "I l Jacob, but I rejected Esau."
Gal 2:20 the Son of God, who l me and gave himself for me.
Eph 1: 4 God l us and chose us in Christ to be holy
1: 6 out on us because we belong to his dearly l Son.
2: 4 God is so rich in mercy, and he l us so very much,
5: 2 who l you and gave himself as a sacrifice to take
6:21 a much l brother and faithful helper in the Lord's
Col 1: 7 Epaphras, our much l co-worker, was the one who
4: 7 Tychicus, a much l brother, will tell you how I am
4: 9 a faithful and much l brother, one of your own
1Th 2: 8 We l you so much that we gave you not only God's
2Th 2:13 for you, dear brothers and sisters l by the Lord.
2:16 who l us and in his special favor gave us
Phm 1: 1 It is written to Philemon, our much l co-worker,
Heb 11:35 Women received their l ones back again from
2Pe 2:15 son of Beor, who l to earn money by doing wrong.
1Jn 4: 9 God showed how much he l us by sending his only
4:10 It is not that we l God, but that he l us
4:11 Dear friends, since God l us that much, we surely
Jude 1: 3 Dearly l friends, I had been eagerly planning to
Rev 18:14 "All the fancy things you l so much are gone,"

LOVELIER (1) [LOVELY]

Eze 32:19 to them, 'O Egypt, are you l than the other nations?

LOVELY (38) [LOVELIER]

Ge 24:53 and gold jewelry and l clothing for Rebekah.
29:17 in every way, with a l face and shapely figure.
Nu 24: 5 O Jacob; / how l are your homes, O Israel!
Est 2: 7 This man had a beautiful and l young cousin,
Job 42:15 In all the land there were no other women as l as
Ps 45: 1 I will recite a l poem to the king,
84: 1 How l is your dwelling place, / O LORD
Pr 4: 9 She will place a l wreath on your head; she will
21: 9 of an attic than with a contentious wife in a l home.
25:11 Timely advice is as l as golden apples in a silver
25:24 of an attic than with a contentious wife in a l home.
SS 1: 9 What a l filly you are, my beloved one!
1:10 How l are your cheeks, with your earrings setting
1:16 "What a l, pleasant sight you are, my love, as we
2:14 For your voice is pleasant, and you are l."
4: 3 veil are like pomegranate halves—l and delicious.
4:13 You are like a l orchard bearing precious fruit,
4:14 from every incense tree, and every other l spice.
4:16 on my garden and waft its l perfume to my lover.
5: 2 my darling, my treasure, my l dove,' he said,
5: 5 my fingers with l myrrh, as I pulled back the bolt.
5:16 His mouth is altogether sweet; he is l in every way.
6: 4 you are as beautiful as the l town of Tirzah.
6: 7 veil are like pomegranate halves—l and delicious.
7: 2 Your belly is l, like a heap of wheat set about with
Isa 5:12 You furnish l music and wine at your grand
23:12 Once you were a l city, but you will never again be
35: 2 as l as Mount Carmel's pastures and the plain of
47: 1 never again will you be the l princess, tender
51: 3 L songs of thanksgiving will fill the air.
Jer 22:14 throughout with fragrant cedar and painted a l red.'
Eze 16:11 I gave you l jewelry, bracelets, and beautiful
16:12 earrings for your ears, and a l crown for your head.
16:16 You used the l things I gave you to make shrines
16:19 You set before them as a l sacrifice the fine flour
26:12 They will destroy your l homes and dump your
Am 5:23 will not listen to your music, no matter how l it is.
Php 4: 8 about things that are pure and l and admirable.

LOVER (20) [LOVE]

Ps 99: 4 Mighty king, l of justice, / you have established
SS 1:13 My l is like a sachet of myrrh lying between my
2: 3 my l is like the finest apple tree in the orchard.
2: 8 "Ah, I hear him—my l! Here he comes, leaping on
2: 9 My l is like a swift gazelle or a young deer. Look,
2:10 "My l said to me, 'Rise up, my beloved, my fair
2:16 "My l is mine, and I am his. He feeds among the
3: 1 I yearned deeply for my l, but he did not come.
4:16 on my garden and waft its lovely perfume to my l.
5: 1 "Oh, l and beloved, eat and drink! Yes,
5: 2 awakened in a dream. I heard the voice of my l.
5: 4 "My l tried to unlatch the door, and my heart
5: 6 I opened to my l, but he was gone. I yearned for
5:10 "My l is dark and dazzling, better than ten
5:16 O women of Jerusalem, is my l, my friend."

6: 1 rarest of beautiful women, where has your **l** gone?
6: 3 I am my lover's, and my **l** is mine. He grazes
7: 13 as old, for I have stored them up for you, my **l**."
8: 5 this coming up from the desert, leaning on her **l**?"
8: 10 am now full breasted. And my **l** is content with me.

LOVER'S (2) [LOVE]

SS 6: 3 I am my **l**, and my lover is mine. He grazes among
7: 10 "I am my **l**, the one he desires.

LOVERS (22) [LOVE]

Isa 23: 16 Long absent from her **l**, she will take a harp,
Jer 2: 33 "How you plot and scheme to win your **l**.
3: 1 But you have prostituted yourself with many **l**,
La 1: 2 Among all her **l**, there is no one left to help her.
Eze 16: 26 Then you added lustful Egypt to your **l**,
16: 28 too. It seems you can never find enough new **l**!
16: 29 You added to your **l** by embracing that great
16: 33 You give gifts to your **l**, bribing them to come to
16: 36 have exposed yourself in prostitution to all your **l**,
16: 37 these **l** of yours with whom you have sinned,
16: 39 Then I will give you to your **l**—these many
16: 41 and end your payments to your many **l**.
23: 5 "Then Oholah lusted after other **l** instead of me,
23: 9 And so I handed her over to her Assyrian **l**,
23: 20 She lusted after **l** whose attentions were gross
23: 22 I will send your **l** against you—those very nations
Hos 2: 5 'I'll run after other **l** and sell myself to them for
2: 7 When she runs after her **l**, she won't be able to
2: 10 strip her naked in public, while all her **l** look on.
2: 12 and orchards, things she claims her **l** gave her.
2: 13 and jewels, and went out looking for her **l**,"
8: 9 people of Israel have sold themselves to many **l**.

LOVES (61) [LOVE]

Ge 44: 20 mother's children, and his father **l** him very much.'
Dt 7: 8 It was simply because the LORD **l** you, and
7: 9 and constantly **l** those who love him and obey his
15: 16 not leave you,' because he **l** you and your family,
21: 15 but he **l** one and not the other, and both have given
21: 16 to his younger son, the son of the wife he **l**.
23: 5 a blessing because the LORD your God **l** you.)
28: 56 will be cruel to the husband she **l** and to her own
Ru 4: 15 For he is the son of your daughter-in-law who **l**
1Ki 10: 9 Because the LORD **l** Israel with an eternal love,
2Ch 2: 11 because the LORD **l** his people that he has made
9: 8 Because God **l** Israel so much and desires this
Ps 11: 5 the wicked. / He hates everyone who **l** violence.
11: 7 For the LORD is righteous, and he **l** justice.
22: 8 If the LORD **l** him so much, / let the LORD
33: 5 He **l** whatever is just and good, / and his unfailing
37: 28 For the LORD **l** justice, / and he will never
47: 4 possession of Jacob's descendants, whom he **l**.
87: 2 He **l** the city of Jerusalem / more than any other
117: 2 For he **l** us with unfailing love; / the faithfulness of
146: 8 beneath their loads. / The LORD **l** the righteous.
Pr 3: 12 For the LORD corrects those he **l**, just as a father
15: 9 of the wicked, but he **l** those who pursue godliness.
16: 13 with righteous lips; he **l** those who speak honestly.
17: 19 Anyone who **l** to quarrel **l** sin; anyone who
22: 11 Anyone who **l** a pure heart and gracious speech is
29: 3 The man who **l** wisdom brings joy to his father,
30: 19 a ship navigates the ocean, / how a man **l** a woman.
SS 2: 4 so everyone can see how much he **l** me.
Jer 31: 32 though I loved them as a husband **l** his wife,"
Da 9: 23 to tell you what it was, for God **l** you very much.
Hos 3: 1 to you and love her, even though she **l** adultery.
3: 1 For the LORD still **l** Israel even though the
10: 11 to treading out the grain—an easy job that she **l**.
Lk 7: 5 "for he **l** the Jews and even built a synagogue for
Jn 3: 35 The Father **l** his Son, and he has given him
5: 20 For the Father **l** the Son and tells him everything
10: 17 "The Father **l** me because I lay down my life that I
16: 27 for the Father himself **l** you dearly because you
Ro 1: 7 God **l** you dearly, and he has called you to be his
5: 5 For we know how dearly God **l** us, because he has
8: 35 Does it mean he no longer **l** us if we have trouble
1Co 8: 3 But the person who **l** God is the one God knows
2Co 9: 7 For God **l** the person who gives cheerfully.
Gal 5: 17 The old sinful nature **l** to do evil, which is just
Eph 5: 28 For a man is actually loving himself when he **l** his
5: 33 each man must love his wife as he **l** himself,
Col 3: 12 God chose you to be the holy people whom he **l**,
1Th 1: 4 We know that God **l** you, dear brothers and sisters,
1Ti 3: 3 be gentle, peace loving, and not one who **l** money.
2Ti 4: 10 has deserted me because he **l** the things of this life
Heb 12: 6 For the Lord disciplines those he **l**, / and he
1Jn 2: 10 But anyone who **l** other Christians is walking in the
3: 1 See how very much our heavenly Father **l** us,
4: 7 Anyone who **l** is born of God and knows God.
4: 16 We know how much God **l** us, and we have put our
5: 1 And everyone who **l** the Father **l** his children,
3Jn 1: 9 but Diotrephes, who **l** to be the leader, does not
Rev 1: 5 All praise to him who **l** us and has freed us from

LOVESICK (1) [LOVE]

SS 2: 5 your 'raisins' and your 'apples'—for I am utterly **l**!

LOVING (23) [LOVE]

2Sa 20: 19 I am one who is peace **l** and faithful in Israel.
1Ki 11: 2 Yet Solomon insisted on **l** them anyway.
Ps 89: 33 But I will never stop **l** him, / nor let my promise to
144: 2 He is my **l** ally and my fortress, / my tower of
Pr 5: 19 She is a **l** doe, a graceful deer. Let her breasts
Ecc 9: 6 their lifetime—**l**, hating, envying—is all long gone.
Isa 57: 8 for you are **l** these idols instead of **l** me.
Jer 2: 25 these foreign gods, and I can't stop **l** them now!'
32: 18 You are **l** and kind to thousands, though children
Mal 1: 2 "I showed my love for you by **l** your ancestor
Lk 6: 32 "Do you think you deserve credit merely for **l**
Eph 5: 28 For a man is actually **l** himself when he loves his
Php 2: 2 **l** one another, and working together with one heart
1Th 1: 3 we think of your faithful work, your **l** deeds,
1Ti 3: 3 He must be gentle, peace **l**, and not one who loves
Heb 6: 11 Our great desire is that you will keep right on **l**
Jas 3: 17 It is also peace **l**, gentle at all times, and willing to
1Pe 3: 8 **l** one another with tender hearts and humble minds.
1Jn 2: 15 Stop **l** this evil world and all that it offers you,
4: 19 We love each other as a result of his **l** us first.
5: 3 **L** God means keeping his commandments,
3Jn 1: 6 church here of your friendship and your **l** deeds.

LOVINGKINDNESS [KJV] See (FAITHFUL) LOVE

LOVINGLY (1) [LOVE]

Eph 5: 29 No one hates his own body but **l** cares for it,

LOW (43) [BELOW, LOWER, LOWERED, LOWEST, LOWING, LOWLANDS, LOWLIEST, LOWLY]

Ge 18: 2 welcoming them by bowing **l** to the ground.
19: 1 he welcomed them and bowed **l** to the ground.
23: 7 Then Abraham bowed **l** before them and said,
27: 29 May all your mother's sons bow **l** before you.
33: 3 his brother, he bowed **l** seven times before him.
33: 6 with their children and bowed **l** before him.
37: 7 all gathered around and bowed **l** before it!"
37: 9 moon, and eleven stars bowed **l** before me!"
42: 6 They bowed **l** before him, with their faces to the
43: 26 they gave him their gifts and bowed **l** before him.
48: 12 their grandfather's knees, and he bowed **l** to him.
50: 18 Then his brothers came and bowed **l** before him.
Ex 11: 8 of Egypt will come running to me, bowing **l**.
33: 10 would stand and bow **l** at their tent entrances.
Dt 33: 29 Your enemies will bow **l** before you,
1Sa 24: 8 Saul looked around, David bowed **l** before him.
25: 23 got off her donkey and bowed **l** before him.
25: 41 She bowed **l** to the ground and responded, "Yes,
2Sa 9: 6 he bowed **l** in great fear and said, "I am your
14: 33 and Absalom came and bowed **l** before the king,
18: 28 He bowed **l** with his face to the ground and said,
1Ki 1: 16 Bathsheba bowed **l** before him. "What can I do for
1: 23 Nathan went in and bowed **l** before the king.
1: 31 Then Bathsheba bowed **l** before him again
1: 53 He came and bowed **l** before the king,
1Ch 29: 20 and they bowed **l** and knelt before the LORD
Job 6: 5 no green grass, and oxen **l** when they have no food.
22: 29 If someone is brought **l** and you say, 'Help him
Ps 49: 2 High and **l**, / rich and poor—listen!
79: 8 meet our needs, / for we are brought **l** to the dust.
99: 5 our God! / Bow **l** before his feet, for he is holy!
132: 7 place of the LORD; / let us bow **l** before him.
142: 6 Hear my cry, / for I am very **l**. / Rescue me from
Pr 24: 16 But one calamity is enough to lay the wicked **l**.
Isa 2: 9 So now everyone will be humbled and brought **l**.
2: 11 day is coming when your pride will be brought **l**
2: 17 The arrogance of all people will be brought **l**.
28: 1 that city—the pride of a people brought **l** by wine.
49: 7 Princes will bow **l** because the LORD has chosen
Jer 5: 1 "Look high and **l**; search throughout the city!
Eze 17: 6 It took root there and grew into a **l**, spreading vine.
21: 26 the lowly are exalted, and the mighty are brought **l**.
Lk 24: 5 women were terrified and bowed **l** before them.

LOWER (18) [LOW]

Ex 28: 26 and attach them to the two **l** inside corners of the
39: 19 Two more gold rings were attached to the **l** inside
Lev 25: 16 the price; the fewer the years, the **l** the price.
Jos 15: 19 So Caleb gave her the upper and **l** springs.
16: 3 territory of the Japhletites as far as **L** Beth-horon,
18: 13 to the top of the hill south of **L** Beth-horon.
Jdg 1: 15 So Caleb gave her the upper and **l** springs.
1Ki 9: 17 He also built up the towns of **L** Beth-horon,
1Ch 7: 24 She built the towns of **L** and Upper Beth-horon
2Ch 8: 5 the cities of Upper Beth-horon and **L** Beth-horon,
Ps 8: 5 For you made us only a little **l** than God, / and you
Isa 11: 11 **L** Egypt, Upper Egypt, Ethiopia, Elam, Babylonia,
22: 9 to be repaired. You store up water in the **l** pool.
Eze 40: 18 as the gateway entrance. This was the **l** pavement.
43: 14 surrounds the altar; this **l** ledge is 21 inches wide.
43: 14 From the **l** ledge the altar rises 7 feet to the upper
Heb 2: 7 For a little while you made him **l** than the angels,
2: 9 who "for a little while was made **l** than the

LOWERED (12) [LOW]

Ge 24: 18 she said, and she quickly **l** the jug for him to drink.
24: 46 She quickly **l** the jug from her shoulder so I could
Ex 17: 11 But whenever he **l** his hands, the Amalekites
Jer 38: 6 and **l** him by ropes into an empty cistern in the
38: 11 to the cistern and **l** them to Jeremiah on a rope.
Eze 1: 25 As they stood with their wings **l**, a voice spoke
Mk 2: 4 Then they **l** the sick man on his mat, right down in
Lk 5: 19 and **l** the sick man down into the crowd, still on his
Ac 27: 17 so they **l** the sea anchor and were thus driven
27: 30 they **l** the lifeboat as though they were going to put
27: 40 Then they **l** the rudders, raised the foresail,
2Co 11: 33 But I was **l** in a basket through a window in the

LOWEST (6) [LOW]

Ge 9: 25 May they be the **l** of servants / to the descendants
Ne 4: 13 So I placed armed guards behind the **l** parts of the
Ps 88: 6 You have thrust me down to the **l** pit,
Isa 14: 15 down to the place of the dead, down to its **l** depths.
24: 11 crying out for wine. Joy has reached its **l** ebb.
Lk 22: 26 those who are the greatest should take the **l** rank,

LOWING (3) [LOW]

1Sa 6: 12 the road toward Beth-shemesh, **l** as they went.
15: 14 is all the bleating of sheep and **l** of cattle I hear?"
Jer 9: 10 the **l** of cattle is heard no more; the birds and wild

LOWLANDS (3) [LOW]

Jos 11: 16 Jordan Valley, and the mountains and **l** of Israel.
17: 16 and the Canaanites in the **l** around Beth-shan
1Ch 12: 15 and drove out all the people living in the **l** on both

LOWLIEST (5) [LOW]

Ex 11: 5 sits on the throne, to the oldest son of his **l** slave.
Ps 62: 9 From the greatest to the **l**— / all are nothing in his
Isa 22: 24 and he will bring honor to even the **l** members of
Eze 29: 15 It will be the **l** of all the nations, never again great
Da 4: 17 to anyone he chooses—even to the **l** of humans."

LOWLY (14) [LOW]

Dt 1: 17 those who are rich; be fair to **l** and great alike.
Ps 37: 11 Those who are gentle and **l** will possess the land;
60: 8 Moab will become my **l** servant, / and Edom will
108: 9 Moab will become my **l** servant, / and Edom will
Isa 5: 14 Her great and **l** will be swallowed up, with all her
Jer 16: 6 Both the great and the **l** will die in this land.
Eze 21: 26 now the **l** are exalted, and the mighty are brought
Mic 7: 17 They will come to realize what **l** creatures they
Zep 3: 12 Those who are left will be the **l** and the humble,
Mt 2: 6 of Judah, / you are not just a **l** village in Judah,
5: 5 God blesses those who are gentle and **l**,
Lk 1: 48 For he took notice of his **l** servant girl, / and now
1: 52 taken princes from their thrones / and exalted the **l**.
Eph 4: 9 This means that Christ first came down to the **l**

LOWRING [KJV] (FOUL) WEATHER

LOYAL (41) [LOYALTIES, LOYALTY]

Ge 21: 23 I have been **l** to you, so now swear that you will be **l** to me and to this
Nu 14: 24 He has remained **l** to me, and I will bring him into
Dt 33: 9 They were more **l** to you / than to their parents,
1Sa 15: 11 for he has not been **l** to me and has again refused to
26: 23 his own reward for doing good and for being **l**,
2Sa 2: 5 so **l** to your king and giving him a decent burial.
2: 6 May the LORD be **l** to you in return and reward
2: 7 my strong and **l** subjects like the people of Judah,
2: 10 Meanwhile, the tribe of Judah remained **l** to David.
3: 1 a long war between those who had been **l** to Saul and those who were **l** to David.
3: 6 leader among those who were **l** to Saul's dynasty.
10: 2 Nahash, was always completely **l** to me."
20: 19 faithful in Israel. But you are destroying a **l** city.
1Ki 1: 8 But among those who remained **l** to David
1: 52 Solomon replied, "If he proves himself to be **l**,
5: 1 King Hiram of Tyre had always been a **l** friend of
12: 4 imposed on us. Then we will be your **l** subjects."
12: 7 they will always be your **l** subjects."
12: 20 So only the tribe of Judah remained **l** to the family
2Ki 10: 15 said to him, "Are you as **l** to me as I am to you?"
1Ch 12: 29 Most of the Benjaminites had remained **l** to Saul
12: 33 and prepared for battle and completely **l** to David.
19: 2 Nahash, was always completely **l** to me."
2Ch 10: 4 imposed on us. Then we will be your **l** subjects."
10: 7 please them, they will always be your **l** subjects."
Ezr 4: 11 from your **l** subjects in the province west of the
4: 14 "Since we are **l** to you as your subjects and we do
Ps 31: 23 For the LORD protects those who are **l** to him,
78: 37 Their hearts were not **l** to him. / They did not keep
132: 9 of salvation; / may your **l** servants sing for joy.
Pr 17: 17 A friend is always **l**, and a brother is born to help
20: 6 Many will say they are **l** friends, but who can find
Isa 54: 10 but even then I will remain **l** to you.
66: 5 and throw you out for being **l** to my name.
Mal 2: 15 guard yourself; remain **l** to the wife of your youth.
2: 16 guard yourself; always remain **l** to your wife."
2Co 7: 7 and how **l** your love is for me, I was filled with
10: 6 remained disobedient after the rest of you became **l**
Rev 2: 13 is located, and yet you have remained **l** to me.

LOYALTIES (1) [LOYAL]

1Ch 12: 19 "It will cost us our lives if David switches **l** to

LOYALTY (13) [LOYAL]

Jdg 8: 35 Nor did they show any **l** to the family of Jerubbaal
Ru 3: 10 "You are showing more family **l** now than ever by
2Sa 10: 2 "I am going to show complete **l** to Hanun
2Ki 11: 4 and made them swear an oath of **l** there in the
1Ch 19: 2 "I am going to show complete **l** to Hanun
29: 24 and the sons of King David pledged their **l** to King
2Ch 15: 14 They shouted out their oath of **l** to the LORD
24: 22 King Joash repaid Jehoiada for his love and **l**—
36: 13 even though he had taken an oath of **l** in God's
Ps 44: 17 All this has happened despite our **l** to you.
Pr 3: 3 Never let **l** and kindness get away from you!
19: 22 **L** makes a person attractive. And it is better to be
Eze 17: 13 of the royal family and made him take an oath of **l**.

LUBIM(S) [KJV] See LIBYA, LIBYANS

LUCAS [KJV] See LUKE

LUCIFER [KJV] See (SHINING) STAR

LUCIUS (2)

Ac 13: 1 (called "the black man"), **L** (from Cyrene),
Ro 16:21 and **L**, Jason, and Sosipater, my relatives,

LUCRE [KJV] See MONEY

LUD (2) [LUDITES]

Ge 10:22 Shem were Elam, Asshur, Arphaxad, **L**, and Aram.
1Ch 1:17 Shem were Elam, Asshur, Arphaxad, **L**, and Aram.

LUDITES (2) [LUD]

Ge 10:13 Mizraim was the ancestor of the **L**, Anamites,
1Ch 1:11 Mizraim was the ancestor of the **L**, Anamites,

LUHITH (2)

Isa 15: 5 Weeping, they climb the road to **L**.
Jer 48: 5 Her refugees will climb the hills of **L**,

LUKE (3)

Col 4:14 Dear Doctor **L** sends his greetings, and so does
2Ti 4:11 Only **L** is with me. Bring Mark with you when you
Phm 1:24 So do Mark, Aristarchus, Demas, and **L**,

LUKEWARM (1) [WARM]

Rev 3:16 But since you are like **l** water, I will spit you out of

LULLED (1)

Jdg 16:19 Delilah **l** Samson to sleep with his head in her lap,

LUMBER (5)

2Sa 5:11 a palace. Hiram also sent many cedar logs for **l**.
1Ki 9:11 and cypress **l** and gold he had furnished for the
1Ch 14: 1 a palace. Hiram also sent many cedar logs for **l**.
22:14 I have also gathered **l** and stone for the walls,
Jer 22:23 palace lined with **l** from the cedars of Lebanon,

LUMP (2)

Jer 18: 4 so the potter squashed the jar into a **l** of clay
Ro 9:21 doesn't he have a right to use the same **l** of clay to

LUNATICK [KJV] EPILEPTICS, SEIZURES

LUNCH (2) [LUNCHEON, LUNCHTIME]

Ru 2:18 also gave her the food that was left over from her **l**.
Ac 10:10 But while **l** was being prepared, he fell into a

LUNCHEON (1) [LUNCH]

Lk 14:12 "When you put on a **l** or a dinner," he said,

LUNCHTIME (1) [LUNCH]

Ru 2:14 At **l** Boaz called to her, "Come over here and help

LUNGE (1) [LUNGED]

Joel 2: 8 They **l** through the gaps, and no weapon can stop

LUNGED (1) [LUNGE]

Ge 19: 9 And they **l** at Lot and began breaking down the

LURE (5) [LURED, LURING]

Jdg 4: 7 I will **l** Sisera, commander of Jabin's army,
Mt 13:22 out by the cares of this life and the **l** of wealth,
Mk 4:19 the **l** of wealth, and the desire for nice things,
Jas 1:14 Temptation comes from the **l** of our own evil
2Pe 2:18 they **l** back into sin those who have just escaped

LURED (1) [LURE]

Jos 8:16 In this way, they were **l** away from the city.

LURING (1) [LURE]

2Pe 2:14 They make a game of **l** unstable people into sin.

LURK (3) [LURKING, LURKS]

Ps 10: 8 They **l** in dark alleys, / murdering the innocent who
Isa 35: 9 Lions will not **l** along its course, and there will be
Jer 5: 6 A leopard will **l** near their towns, tearing apart any

LURKING (4) [LURK]

Ps 19:12 How can I know all the sins **l** in my heart?
68:30 these wild animals **l** in the reeds,
Eze 29: 3 you great monster, **l** in the streams of the Nile.
Col 3: 5 put to death the sinful, earthly things **l** within you.

LURKS (1) [LURK]

Hos 13: 7 like a lion, or like a leopard that **l** along the road.

LUSCIOUS (2)

Eze 17: 8 a splendid vine and produce rich leaves and **l** fruit.
Joel 2:22 The trees will again be filled with **l** fruit; fig trees

LUSH (17)

Dt 11:15 He will give you **l** pastureland for your cattle to
1Ch 4:40 They found **l** pastures there, and the land was quiet
Ne 9:37 The **l** produce of this land piles up in the hands of
Job 8:16 so strong, like a **l** plant growing in the sunshine,
Ps 65:12 The wilderness becomes a **l** pasture,
Isa 4: 2 will be **l** and beautiful, and the fruit of the land will
7:23 In that day the **l** vineyards, now worth as much as a
29:17 And the fertile fields will become a **l** and fertile
32:15 and the fertile field will become a **l** and fertile
Eze 19:10 by the water's edge. / It had **l**, green foliage
19:11 of its height / and because of its many **l** branches.
34:14 in pleasant places and feed in **l** mountain pastures.
36:36 the ruins and planted **l** crops in the wilderness.
Am 1: 2 Suddenly, the **l** pastures of the shepherds dry up.
5:11 You will never drink wine from the **l** vineyards
Na 1: 4 dry up, the **l** pastures of Bashan and Carmel fade,
Zec 10: 1 of rain so that every field becomes a **l** pasture.

LUST (20) [LUSTED, LUSTFUL, LUSTS, LUSTY]

Job 22:24 Give up your **l** for money, and throw your precious
31: 1 my eyes not to look with **l** upon a young woman.
31:11 For **l** is a shameful sin, a crime that should be
Ps 141: 4 Don't let me **l** for evil things; / don't let me
Pr 6:25 Don't **l** for her beauty. Don't let her coyness
Jer 2:24 the wind at mating time. Who can restrain your **l**?
13:27 I am keenly aware of your adultery and **l**, and your
Eze 23:11 abandoning herself to her **l** and prostitution.
Hos 7: 4 They are all adulterers, always aflame with **l**.
Mt 5:28 anyone who even looks at a woman with **l** in his
5:29 causes you to **l**, gouge it out and throw it away.
Ro 1:27 with women, burned with **l** for each other.
1Co 7: 9 and marry. It's better to marry than to burn with **l**.
Eph 4:22 rotten through and through, full of **l** and deception.
Col 3: 5 with sexual sin, impurity, **l**, and shameful desires.
2Ti 2:22 Run from anything that stimulates youthful **l**.
1Pe 4: 3 their immorality and **l**, their feasting
2Pe 2:14 with their eyes, and their **l** is never satisfied.
1Jn 2:16 For the world offers only the **l** for physical
2:16 the **l** for everything we see, and pride in our

LUSTED (4) [LUST]

Job 31: 7 or if my heart has **l** for what my eyes have seen,
31: 9 by a woman, or if I have **l** for my neighbor's wife,
Eze 23: 5 "Then Oholah **l** after other lovers instead of me,
23:20 She **l** after lovers whose attentions were gross

LUSTER (1)

La 4: 1 How the gold has lost its **l**! Even the finest gold

LUSTFUL (11) [LUST]

Eze 6: 9 and **l** eyes that long for other gods.
16:26 Then you added **l** Egypt to your lovers,
23:42 They were **l** men and drunkards from the
23:44 with all the zest of **l** young men.
Mk 7:22 deceit, eagerness for **l** pleasure, envy, slander,
Ro 6:12 the way you live; do not give in to its **l** desires.
2Co 12:21 sexual immorality, and eagerness for **l** pleasure.
Gal 5:19 impure thoughts, eagerness for **l** pleasure,
1Th 4: 5 not in **l** passion as the pagans do, in their ignorance
2Pe 2:10 their own evil, **l** desires and who despise authority.
2:18 With **l** desire as their bait, they lure back into sin

LUSTS (2) [LUST]

Eze 23: 8 when the Egyptians satisfied their **l** with her
23:18 before them and gave herself to satisfy their **l**.

LUSTY (1) [LUST]

Jer 5: 8 They are well-fed, **l** stallions, each neighing for his

LUTE (1)

Ps 92: 3 accompanied by the harp and **l** / and the harmony

LUXURIANT (3)

Eze 17: 6 It soon produced strong branches and **l** leaves.
31: 4 springs watered it and helped it to grow tall and **l**.
Hos 10: 1 prosperous Israel is—a **l** vine loaded with fruit!

LUXURIES (1) [LUXURY]

Rev 18:14 "The **l** and splendor that you prized so much will

LUXURIOUS (2) [LUXURY]

Hag 1: 4 "Why are you living in **l** houses while my house
Rev 18: 3 world have grown rich as a result of her **l** living."

LUXURY (10) [LUXURIES, LUXURIOUS]

Pr 19:10 It isn't right for a fool to live in **l** or for a slave to
21:17 become poor; wine and **l** are not the way to riches.
21:20 The wise have wealth and **l**, but fools spend
Am 6: 1 How terrible it will be for you who lounge in **l**
6: 4 you who sprawl on ivory beds surrounded with **l**,
Lk 7:25 beautiful clothes and live in **l** are found in palaces,
16:19 splendidly clothed and who lived each day in **l**.
Jas 5: 5 You have spent your years on earth in **l**,
Rev 18: 7 She has lived in **l** and pleasure, so match it now
18: 9 and enjoyed her great **l** will mourn for her as they

LUZ (7) [BETHEL]

Ge 28:19 though the name of the nearby village was **L**.
35: 6 Finally, they arrived at **L** (now called Bethel)
48: 3 "God Almighty appeared to me at **L** in the land of
Jos 16: 2 From Bethel (that is, **L**) it ran over to Ataroth in
18:13 From there the boundary went south to **L** (that is,
Jdg 1:23 They sent spies to Bethel (formerly known as **L**),
1:26 He named the city **L**, and it is known by that name

LYCAONIA (1)

Ac 14: 6 They went to the region of **L**, to the cities of Lystra

LYCIA (1)

Ac 27: 5 landing at Myra, in the province of **L**.

LYDDA (3)

Ac 9:32 he came to the Lord's people in the town of **L**.
9:35 Then the whole population of **L** and Sharon turned
9:38 But they had heard that Peter was nearby at **L**,

LYDIA (5) [LYDIANS]

Jer 46: 9 and **L** who are skilled with the shield and bow!
Eze 27:10 Men from distant Persia, **L**, and Libya served in
30: 5 Ethiopia, Libya, **L**, and Arabia, with all their other
Ac 16:14 One of them was **L** from Thyatira, a merchant of
16:40 Paul and Silas then returned to the home of **L**,

LYDIANS (1) [LYDIA]

Isa 66:19 to the Libyans and **L** (who are famous as archers),

LYE (2)

Job 9:30 and cleanse my hands with **l** to make them
Jer 2:22 No amount of soap or **l** can make you clean.

LYING (79) [LIE]

Ge 19:33 He was unaware of her **l** down or getting up again.
19:35 he was unaware of her **l** down or getting up again.
28:13 Isaac. The ground you are **l** on belongs to you.
29: 2 He saw in the distance three flocks of sheep **l** in an
Dt 6: 7 when you are **l** down and when you are getting up
11:19 when you are **l** down and when you are getting up
19:18 and if the accuser is found to be **l**,
22: 4 see your neighbor's ox or donkey **l** on the road,
Jos 7:10 "Get up! Why are you **l** on your face like this?
Jdg 4:22 her into the tent and found Sisera **l** there dead,
15:15 Then he picked up a donkey's jawbone that was **l**
19:27 She was **l** face down, with her hands on the
Ru 3: 8 He was surprised to find a woman **l** at his feet!
1Sa 5: 4 hands had broken off and were **l** in the doorway.
26: 7 Abner and the warriors were **l** asleep around him.
2Sa 2:23 and stood still when they saw Asahel **l** there.
13: 8 she went to the room where he was **l** down so he
20:10 Joab and his brother Abishai left him **l** there
1Ki 13:18 and water to drink.' " But the old man was **l** to
13:25 People came by and saw the body **l** in the road
13:28 and he went out and found the body **l** in the road.
22:23 the LORD has put a **l** spirit in the mouths of your
2Ki 1: 4 You will never leave the bed on which you are **l**,
1: 6 you will never leave the bed on which you are **l**,
1:16 you will never leave the bed on which you are **l**,
4:32 child was indeed dead, **l** there on the prophet's bed.
9:12 "You're **l**," they said. "Tell us." So Jehu told
9:16 to find King Joram, who was **l** there wounded.
2Ch 18:22 the LORD has put a **l** spirit in the mouths of your
20:24 there were dead bodies **l** on the ground for as far as
36:21 **l** desolate for seventy years, just as the prophet had
Ne 6: 8 My reply was, "You know you are **l**. There is no
Job 6:30 Do you think I am **l**? Don't I know the difference
Ps 12: 7 preserving them forever from this **l** generation,
31:18 May their **l** lips be silenced— / those proud
44:25 We collapse in the dust, / **l** face down in the dirt.
45: 5 nations fall before you, / **l** down beneath your feet.
119:29 Keep me from **l** to myself; / give me the privilege
Pr 6:17 haughty eyes, / a **l** tongue, / hands that kill the
21: 6 Wealth created by **l** is a vanishing mist and a
26:28 A **l** tongue hates its victims, and flattery causes
SS 1:12 "The king is **l** on his couch, enchanted by the
1:13 My lover is like a sachet of myrrh **l** between my
Isa 9:15 Israel are the head, and the **l** prophets are the tail.
22: 2 Bodies are **l** everywhere, killed by famine
Jer 14:14 They speak foolishness made up in their own **l**
14:15 says the LORD, I will punish these **l** prophets,
40:16 to do any such thing, for you are **l** about Ishmael."
La 2:21 "See them **l** in the streets—young and old, boys
Eze 4: 9 during the 390 days you will be **l** on your side.
13: 9 I will raise my fist against all the **l** prophets,
13:16 They were **l** prophets who claimed peace would
13:19 By **l** to my people who love to listen to lies,
31:12 beneath its shadow went away and left it **l** there.
38: 8 which will be **l** in peace after her recovery from
Da 4:10 " 'While I was **l** in my bed, this is what I
Hos 6: 9 are bands of robbers, **l** in ambush for their victims.
Mic 6:12 so used to **l** that their tongues can no longer tell the
Na 3: 3 The dead are **l** in the streets—dead bodies, heaps of
Zep 3:13 will live peaceful lives, **l** down to sleep in safety;
Mt 15:19 all other sexual immorality, theft, **l**, and slander.
28: 6 would happen. Come, see where his body was **l**.
Mk 5:40 three disciples into the room where the girl was **l**.
7:30 her little girl was **l** quietly in bed, and the demon
Lk 2:12 You will find a baby **l** in a manger,
2:16 And there was the baby, **l** in the manger.
10:31 but when he saw the man **l** there, he crossed to the
10:32 assistant walked over and looked at him **l** there,
Jn 5: 5 One of the men **l** there had been sick for
20: 5 and looked in and saw the linen cloth **l** there,

20: 6 He also noticed the linen wrappings **l** there,
20: 7 Jesus' head was folded up and **l** to the side.
20:12 of the place where the body of Jesus had been **l**.
Ac 5: 4 a thing like this? You weren't **l** to us but to God."
6:13 The **l** witnesses said, "This man is always
1Co 15:15 And we apostles would all be **l** about God, for we
Gal 1:20 am saying, for I declare before God that I am not **l**.
1Ti 4: 1 they will follow **l** spirits and teachings that come
1Jn 1: 6 So we are **l** if we say we have fellowship with God

LYRE (9) [LYRES]
1Sa 10: 5 be playing a harp, a tambourine, a flute, and a **l**,
Ps 33: 2 Praise the LORD with melodies on the **l**;
57: 8 Wake up, my soul! / Wake up, O harp and **l**!
71:22 O God. / I will sing for you with a **l**,
81: 2 the tambourine. / Play the sweet **l** and the harp.
92: 3 by the harp and lute / and the harmony of the **l**.
108: 2 Wake up, O harp and **l**! / I will waken the dawn
150: 3 of the trumpet; / praise him with the **l** and harp!
Da 3: 5 flute, zither, **l**, harp, pipes, and other instruments,

LYRES (16) [LYRE]
2Sa 6: 5 **l**, harps, tambourines, castanets, and cymbals.
1Ki 10:12 and to construct harps and **l** for the musicians.
1Ch 13: 8 **l**, harps, tambourines, cymbals, and trumpets.
15:16 to sing joyful songs to the accompaniment of **l**,
15:20 Maaseiah, and Benaiah were chosen to play the **l**.
15:28 of cymbals, and loud playing on harps and **l**.
16: 5 Obed-edom, and Jeiel. They played the harps and **l**.
25: 1 to the accompaniment of harps, **l**, and cymbals.
25: 6 of cymbals, **l**, and harps at the house of God.
2Ch 5:12 east side of the altar playing cymbals, harps, and **l**.
9:11 and to construct harps and **l** for the musicians.
20:28 **l**, and trumpets and proceeded to the Temple of the
29:25 Temple of the LORD with cymbals, harps, and **l**.
Ne 12:27 and with the music of cymbals, **l**, and harps.
Ps 137: 2 We put away our **l**, / hanging them on the branches
Isa 5:12 the harps, **l**, tambourines, and flutes are superb!

LYSANIAS (1)
Lk 3: 1 and Traconitis; **L** was ruler over Abilene.

LYSIAS (2)
Ac 23:26 "From Claudius **L**, to his Excellency,
24:22 adjourned the hearing and said, "Wait until **L**,

LYSTRA (6)
Ac 14: 6 to the cities of **L** and Derbe and the surrounding
14: 8 While they were at **L**, Paul and Barnabas came
14:21 Paul and Barnabas returned again to **L**, Iconium,
16: 1 and Silas went first to Derbe and then on to **L**.
16: 2 Timothy was well thought of by the believers in **L**
2Ti 3:11 I was persecuted in Antioch, Iconium, and **L**—

M

MAACAH (25) [ABEL-BETH-MAACAH, ARAM-MAACAH, MAACAH'S, MAACATHITE, MAACATHITES]
Ge 22:24 Their names were Tebah, Gaham, Tahash, and **M**.
Jos 12: 5 the boundaries of the kingdoms of Geshur and **M**.
13:11 the territory of the kingdoms of Geshur and **M**,
13:13 failed to drive out the people of Geshur and **M**,
2Sa 3: 3 whose mother was **M**, the daughter of Talmai,
10: 6 and Zobah, one thousand from the king of **M**,
10: 8 and **M** positioned themselves to fight in the open
23:34 Eliphelet son of Ahasbai from **M**; / Eliam son of
1Ki 15: 2 His mother was **M**, the daughter of Absalom.
15:10 His grandmother was **M**, the daughter of Absalom.
15:13 He even deposed his grandmother **M** from her
1Ch 2:48 **M**, gave birth to Sheber and Tirhanah.
3: 2 whose mother was **M**, the daughter of Talmai,
7:15 and Shuppim. Makir's sister was named **M**.
7:16 Makir's wife, **M**, gave birth to a son whom she
8:29 lived in Gibeon. His wife's name was **M**,
9:35 lived in Gibeon. His wife's name was **M**,
11:43 Hanan son of **M**; / Joshaphat from Mithna;
19: 7 and secured the support of the king of **M** and his
27:16 son of Zicri / Simeon | Shephatiah son of **M**
2Ch 11:20 another cousin, **M**, the daughter of Absalom.
11:20 **M** gave birth to Abijah, Attai, Ziza, and Shelomith.
11:21 Rehoboam loved **M** more than any of his other
13: 2 His mother was **M**, a daughter of Uriel from
15:16 King Asa even deposed his grandmother **M** from

MAACAH'S (1) [MAACAH]
2Ch 11:22 Rehoboam made **M** son Abijah chief among the

MAACATHITE (3) [MAACAH]
2Ki 25:23 and Jaazaniah son of the **M**, and all their men.
1Ch 4:19 and another was the father of Eshtemoa the **M**.
Jer 40: 8 Jaazaniah son of the **M**, and all their men.

MAACATHITES (1) [MAACAH]
Dt 3:14 all the way to the borders of the Geshurites and **M**.

MAADAI (1)
Ezr 10:34 From the family of Bani: **M**, Amram, Uel,

MAAI (1)
Ne 12:36 Azarel, Milalai, Gilalai, **M**, Nethanel, Judah,

MAALEH-ACRABBIM [KJV] See SCORPION PASS

MAARATH (1)
Jos 15:59 **M**, Beth-anoth, and Eltekon—six towns with their

MAASAI (1)
1Ch 9:12 of Malkijah, and **M** son of Adiel, son of Jahzerah,

MAASEIAH (23)
1Ch 15:18 Jehiel, Unni, Eliab, Benaiah, **M**, Mattithiah,
15:20 Aziel, Shemiramoth, Jehiel, Unni, Eliab, **M**,
2Ch 23: 1 Azariah son of Obed, **M** son of Adaiah,
26:11 the secretary of the army, and his assistant, **M**.
28: 7 a warrior from Ephraim, killed **M**, the king's son;
34: 8 **M** the governor of Jerusalem, and Joah son of
Ezr 10:18 and his brothers: **M**, Eliezer, Jarib, and Gedaliah.
10:21 of Harim: **M**, Elijah, Shemaiah, Jehiel, and Uzziah.
10:22 Elioenai, **M**, Ishmael, Nethanel, Jozabad,
10:30 Adna, Kelal, Benaiah, **M**, Mattaniah, Bezalel,
Ne 3:23 and Azariah son of **M** and grandson of Ananiah
8: 4 Shema, Anaiah, Uriah, Hilkiah, and **M**.
8: 7 Hodiah, **M**, Kelita, Azariah, Jozabad, Hanan,
10:25 Rehum, Hashabnah, **M**,
11: 5 and **M** son of Baruch, son of Col-hozeh, son of
11: 7 of Pedaiah, son of Kolaiah, son of **M**, son of Ithiel,
12:41 Eliakim, **M**, Miniamin, Micaiah, Elioenai,
12:42 **M**, Shemaiah, Eleazar, Uzzi, Jehohanan, Malkijah,
Jer 21: 1 Pashhur son of Malkijah and Zephaniah son of **M**,
29:21 Ahab son of Kolaiah and Zedekiah son of **M**—
29:25 on your own authority to Zephaniah son of **M**,
35: 4 directly above the room of **M** son of Shallum,
37: 3 Zephaniah the priest, son of **M**, to ask Jeremiah,

MAATH (2)
Lk 3:26 Naggai was the son of **M**. / **M** was the son of Mattathias.

MAAZ (1)
1Ch 2:27 oldest son of Jerahmeel, were **M**, Jamin, and Eker.

MAAZIAH (2)
1Ch 24:18 fell to Delaiah. / The twenty-fourth lot fell to **M**.
Ne 10: 8 **M**, Bilgai, and Shemaiah. These were the priests.

MACBANNAI (1)
1Ch 12:13 Jeremiah was tenth. / **M** was eleventh.

MACBENAH (1)
1Ch 2:49 and Sheva (the father of **M** and Gibea).

MACEDONIA (21) [MACEDONIAN]
Ac 16: 9 He saw a man from **M** in northern Greece,
16:10 So we decided to leave for **M** at once, for we could
16:12 a major city of the district of **M** and a Roman
18: 5 And after Silas and Timothy came down from **M**,
19:21 felt impelled by the Holy Spirit to go over to **M**
19:22 on ahead to **M** while he stayed awhile longer in the
19:29 who were Paul's traveling companions from **M**.
20: 1 Then he said good-bye and left for **M**.
20: 3 against his life, so he decided to return through **M**.
20: 6 we boarded a ship at Philippi in **M** and five days
1Co 16: 5 I am coming to visit you after I have been to **M**,
16: 5 for I am planning to travel through **M**.
2Co 1:16 I wanted to stop and see you on my way to **M**
2:13 So I said good-bye and went on to **M** to find him.
7: 5 When we arrived in **M** there was no rest for us.
8: 1 in his kindness has done for the churches in **M**.
9: 2 and I have been boasting to our friends in **M** that
11: 9 For the brothers who came from **M** brought me
Php 4:15 you the Good News and then traveled on from **M**.
1Th 4:10 already strong toward all the Christians in all of **M**.
1Ti 1: 3 When I left for **M**, I urged you to stay there in

MACEDONIAN (2) [MACEDONIA]
Ac 27: 2 And Aristarchus, a **M** from Thessalonica, was also
2Co 9: 4 if some **M** Christians came with me, only to find

MACHINES (1)
2Ch 26:15 And he produced **m** mounted on the walls of

MACHPELAH (6)
Ge 23: 9 to let me have the cave of **M**, down at the end of
23:17 bought the plot of land belonging to Ephron at **M**,
23:19 in the cave of **M**, near Mamre, which is at Hebron.
25: 9 and Ishmael buried him in the cave of **M**,
49:30 This is the cave in the field of **M**, near Mamre in
50:13 of Canaan and buried it there in the cave of **M**.

MACNADEBAI (1)
Ezr 10:40 **M**, Shashai, Sharai,

MAD (7) [MADLY, MADMAN, MADNESS]
Dt 28:34 You will go **m** because of all the tragedy around
2Ki 7:15 had thrown away in their **m** rush to escape.
Pr 26:18 Just as damaging as a **m** man shooting a lethal
Ecc 9: 3 Instead, they choose their own **m** course, for they
Jer 51: 7 which he made the whole earth drink and go **m**.
Hos 9: 7 "The inspired men are **m**!" So they taunt,
2Pe 2:16 But Balaam was stopped from his **m** course when

MADAI (2)
Ge 10: 2 Magog, **M**, Javan, Tubal, Meshech, and Tiras.
1Ch 1: 5 Magog, **M**, Javan, Tubal, Meshech, and Tiras.

MADE (975) [MAKE]
Ge 1: 5 darkness "night." Together these **m** up one day.
1: 7 God **m** this space to separate the waters above
1:16 For God **m** two great lights, the sun and the moon,
1:16 presides through the night. He also **m** the stars.
1:25 God **m** all sorts of wild animals, livestock,
1:31 Then God looked over all he had **m**, and he saw
2: 4 When the LORD God **m** the heavens
2:22 Then the LORD God **m** a woman from the rib
3: 1 of all the creatures the LORD God had **m**.
3:19 For you were **m** from dust, and to the dust you will
3:21 And the LORD God **m** clothing from animal
3:23 to cultivate the ground from which he had been **m**.
4: 5 This **m** Cain very angry and dejected.
4:14 you have **m** me a wandering fugitive.
5: 1 created people, he **m** them in the likeness of God.
6: 6 So the LORD was sorry he had ever **m** them.
6: 7 and birds, too. I am sorry I ever **m** them."
8: 6 Noah opened the window he had **m** in the boat
9: 6 for to kill a person is to kill a living being **m** in
9:21 One day he became drunk on some wine he had **m**
14:23 you might say, 'I am the one who **m** Abram rich!'
15:18 So the LORD **m** a covenant with Abram that day
19: 3 complete with fresh bread **m** without yeast.
21:27 and oxen to Abimelech, and they **m** a treaty.
23:18 **m** in the presence of the Hittite elders at the city
24:11 There the servant **m** the camels kneel down beside
24:37 And my master **m** me swear that I would not let
24:56 The LORD has **m** my mission successful, and I
25:30 Give me some of that red stew you've **m**."
26:10 and you would have **m** us guilty of great sin."
26:11 Then Abimelech **m** a public proclamation:
26:22 he said, "At last the LORD has **m** room for us,
26:35 But Esau's wives **m** life miserable for Isaac
27:16 She **m** him a pair of gloves from the hairy skin of
27:37 "I have **m** Jacob your master and have declared
28:20 Then Jacob **m** this vow: "If God will be with me
31: 9 God has **m** me wealthy at your father's expense.
31:13 the pillar of stone and **m** a vow to serve me.
31:39 You **m** me pay for every animal stolen from the
33: 7 Rachel and Joseph came and **m** their bows.
33:17 a house and **m** shelters for his flocks and herds.
34:30 "You have **m** me stink among all the people of
37:18 him in the distance and **m** plans to kill him.
41:46 he **m** a tour of inspection throughout the land.
41:51 "God has **m** me forget all my troubles
41:52 "God has **m** me fruitful in this land of my
42:12 to discover how vulnerable the famine has **m** us."
43:30 Then Joseph **m** a hasty exit because he was
44:32 I **m** a pledge to my father that I would take care of
45: 8 And he has **m** me a counselor to Pharaoh—
45: 9 God has **m** me master over all the land of Egypt.
47:26 then **m** it a law throughout the land of Egypt—
50: 5 "Tell Pharaoh that my father **m** me swear an oath.
50:25 Then Joseph **m** the sons of Israel swear an oath,
Ex 1:11 So the Egyptians **m** the Israelites their slaves
2: 3 she got a little basket **m** of papyrus reeds
7: 7 and Aaron was eighty-three at the time they **m**
9:12 But the LORD **m** Pharaoh even more stubborn,
10: 1 I have **m** him and his officials stubborn so I can
10:20 But the LORD **m** Pharaoh stubborn once again,
12: 8 lamb with bitter herbs and bread **m** without yeast.
12:15 you may eat only bread **m** without yeast.
12:15 Anyone who eats bread **m** with yeast at any time
12:19 Anyone who eats anything **m** with yeast during
12:20 during those days you must not eat anything **m**
12:34 The Israelites took with them their bread dough **m**
12:39 It was **m** without yeast because the people were
13:19 for Joseph had **m** the sons of Israel swear that they
15:17 the place you have **m** as your home, O LORD,
15:17 the sanctuary, O Lord, that your hands have **m**.
15:25 it into the water. This **m** the water good to drink.
18:25 all over Israel and **m** them judges over the people.
20:11 For in six days the LORD **m** the heavens,
22: 3 If payment is not **m**, the thief must be sold as a
22:12 was stolen, payment must be **m** to the owner.
23:15 For seven days you are to eat bread **m** without
24: 8 LORD has **m** with you in giving you these laws."
25:38 and trays must also be **m** of pure gold.
26:15 will consist of frames **m** of acacia wood.
26:17 the next frame. All the frames must be **m** this way.
26:24 Both of these corner frames will be **m** the same
26:31 Tabernacle hang a special curtain **m** of fine linen,
26:32 gold hooks set into four posts **m** from acacia wood
26:37 gold hooks set into five posts **m** from acacia wood
27: 3 meat hooks, and firepans will all be **m** of bronze.
27: 8 The altar must be hollow, **m** from planks.
27: 9 enclosed with curtains **m** from fine linen.
27:18 curtain walls 7-1/2 feet high, **m** from fine linen.

27:18 The bases supporting its walls will be **m** of bronze.
27:19 and the courtyard curtains, must be **m** of bronze.
28: 5 These items must be **m** of fine linen cloth
28: 6 "The ephod must be **m** of fine linen cloth
28: 8 And the sash will be **m** of the same materials:
28:13 The settings are to be **m** of gold filigree,
28:14 and two cords **m** of pure gold will be attached to
28:16 This chestpiece will be **m** of two folds of cloth,
29:41 offering to the LORD, an offering **m** by fire.
30: 5 The poles are to be **m** of acacia wood and overlaid
30:10 blood from the offering **m** for the atonement of sin.
31:17 For in six days the LORD **m** heaven and earth,
32: 8 They have **m** an idol shaped like a calf, and they
32:20 He took the calf they had **m** and melted it in the
32:20 mixed it with water. Then he **m** the people drink it.
32:31 They have **m** gods of gold for themselves.
32:35 because they had worshiped the calf Aaron had **m**.
34:25 "You must not offer bread **m** with yeast as a
36: 8 The skilled weavers first **m** ten sheets from fine
36:10 one set, and a second set was **m** of the other five.
36:13 Then fifty gold clasps were **m** to connect the loops
36:14 a roof covering was **m** from eleven sheets of cloth
m from goat hair.
36:17 Then they **m** fifty loops along the edge of the last
36:18 They also **m** fifty small bronze clasps to couple the
36:19 Then they **m** two more layers for the roof
36:19 The first was **m** of tanned ram skins,
36:19 and the second was **m** of fine goatskin leather.
36:20 they **m** frames of acacia wood standing on end.
36:22 to the next frame. All the frames were **m** this way.
36:23 They **m** twenty frames to support the south side,
36:25 They also **m** twenty frames for the north side of
36:27 which was its rear, was **m** from six frames,
36:29 They **m** two of these, one for each rear corner.
36:30 So for the west side they **m** a total of eight frames,
36:31 Then they **m** five crossbars from acacia wood to tie
36:32 They **m** another five for the north side and five for
36:34 The rings used to hold the crossbars were **m** of
36:35 The inner curtain was **m** of fine linen cloth,
36:37 Then they **m** another curtain for the entrance to the
36:37 It was **m** of fine linen cloth and embroidered with
37: 1 Next Bezalel **m** the Ark out of acacia wood.
37: 4 Then he **m** poles from acacia wood and overlaid
37: 6 Then, from pure gold, he **m** the Ark's cover—
37: 7 He **m** two figures of cherubim out of hammered
37: 8 They were **m** so they were actually a part of the
37:10 Then he **m** a table out of acacia wood, 3 feet long,
37:14 These were **m** to hold the carrying poles in place.
37:15 He **m** the carrying poles of acacia wood
37:16 using pure gold, he **m** the plates, dishes, bowls,
37:17 Then he **m** the lampstand, again using pure,
37:23 He also **m** the seven lamps, the lamp snuffers,
37:24 was **m** from seventy-five pounds of pure gold.
37:25 The incense altar was **m** of acacia wood. It was
37:25 with its corner horns **m** from the same piece of
37:28 The carrying poles were **m** of acacia wood
37:29 Then he **m** the sacred oil for anointing the priests
38: 3 Then he **m** all the bronze utensils to be used with
38: 4 Next he **m** a bronze grating that rested on a ledge
38: 6 The carrying poles themselves were **m** of acacia
38: 7 The altar was hollow and was **m** from planks.
38: 9 feet long. It consisted of curtains **m** of fine linen.
38:12 The walls were **m** from curtains supported by ten
38:16 All the curtains used in the courtyard walls were **m**
38:18 entrance to the courtyard was **m** of fine linen cloth
38:19 and the hooks and rods were also **m** of silver.
38:20 in the Tabernacle and courtyard were **m** of bronze.
39: 1 the craftsmen **m** beautiful garments of blue,
39: 2 The ephod was **m** from fine linen cloth
39: 3 A skilled craftsman **m** gold thread by beating gold
39: 4 They **m** two shoulder-pieces for the ephod,
39: 5 They also **m** an elaborate woven sash of the same
39: 8 The chestpiece was **m** in the same style as the
39:15 to the ephod, they **m** braided cords of pure gold.
39:16 They also **m** two gold rings and attached them to
39:27 Tunics were then **m** for Aaron and his sons from
39:28 and the underclothes were all **m** of this fine linen.
39:29 The sashes were **m** of fine linen cloth
39:30 they **m** the sacred medallion of pure gold to be
40: 5 Set up the curtain **m** for the entrance of the
40:27 On it he burned the fragrant incense **m** from sweet
Lev 1: 9 It is a whole burnt offering **m** by fire, very pleasing
1:13 It is a whole burnt offering **m** by fire, very pleasing
1:17 It is a whole burnt offering **m** by fire, very pleasing
2: 2 It is an offering **m** by fire, very pleasing to the
2: 4 it must be **m** of choice flour mixed with olive oil
2: 5 it must be **m** of choice flour and olive oil, and it
2: 7 it also must be **m** of choice flour and olive oil.
2: 9 and burn it on the altar as an offering **m** by fire,
3: 3 presented to the LORD as an offering **m** by fire.
3: 5 It is an offering **m** by fire, very pleasing to the
3: 9 presented to the LORD as an offering **m** by fire.
3:14 presented to the LORD as an offering **m** by fire.
3:16 them on the altar as food, an offering **m** by fire;
7: 5 on the altar as an offering to the LORD **m** by fire.
7:12 all **m** without yeast and soaked with olive oil.
8:15 set the altar apart as holy and **m** atonement for it.
8:26 All these were taken from the basket of bread **m**
8:30 he **m** Aaron and his sons and their clothing holy.
11:32 This is true whether the object is **m** of wood,
13:48 the hide of an animal, or anything **m** of leather.
13:59 or fabric, or in anything **m** of leather.
16:30 On this day, atonement will be **m** for you, and you
21:12 because he has been **m** holy by the anointing oil of
21:15 because I, the LORD, have **m** him holy."
23: 6 time all the bread you eat must be **m** without yeast.
23:28 when atonement will be **m** for you before the
23:28 your God, and payment will be **m** for your sins.
27:10 But if such an exchange is in fact **m**, then both the
27:33 If any exchange is in fact **m**, then both the original
Nu 5: 8 are no near relatives to whom restitution can be **m**,
6: 3 They must not use vinegar **m** from wine, they must
6:15 a basket of bread **m** without yeast—cakes of choice
6:17 along with the basket of bread **m** without yeast.
6:19 one cake **m** without yeast, and one wafer **m**
without yeast,
8: 4 to its decorative blossoms, was **m** of beaten gold.
9:11 time with bitter herbs and bread **m** without yeast.
11: 8 and **m** flour by grinding it with hand mills
11: 8 Then they boiled it in a pot and **m** it into flat cakes.
15:10 This will be an offering **m** by fire, very pleasing to
16:47 burned the incense and **m** atonement for them.
21: 2 Then the people of Israel **m** this vow to the
21: 9 So Moses **m** a snake out of bronze and attached it
22:29 "Because you have **m** me look like a fool!"
25:13 and **m** atonement for the people of Israel."
28: 6 an offering **m** by fire, very pleasing to the LORD.
28: 8 It, too, is an offering **m** by fire, very pleasing to the
28:17 but no bread **m** with yeast may be eaten.
31:20 all your clothing and everything **m** of leather,
31:22 Anything **m** of gold, silver, bronze, iron, tin,
31:23 must be passed through fire in order to be **m**
32:13 and **m** them wander in the wilderness for forty
35:33 And no atonement can be **m** for murder except by
Dt 1:10 The LORD your God has **m** you as numerous as
2:30 because the LORD your God **m** Sihon stubborn
4:23 covenant the LORD your God has **m** with you.
4:28 you will worship idols **m** from wood and stone,
4:31 or forget the solemn covenant he **m** with your
5: 2 the LORD our God **m** a covenant with us.
7:25 not desire the silver or gold with which they are **m**.
8:17 your own strength and energy that **m** you wealthy.
8:18 and he does it to fulfill the covenant he **m** with
9: 7 "Remember how angry you **m** the LORD your
9: 8 Remember how angry you **m** the LORD at Mount
9: 9 the covenant that the LORD had **m** with you.
9:16 **m** in your terrible sin against the LORD your
9:21 I took your sin—the calf you had **m**—and I melted
9:22 "You also **m** the LORD angry at Taberah,
10: 3 "So I **m** a chest of acacia wood and cut two stone
10: 5 which I had **m**, just as the LORD commanded
10:22 But now the LORD your God has **m** you as
15: 2 Creditors must cancel the loans they have **m** to
16: 3 Eat it with bread **m** without yeast. For seven days
eat only bread **m** without yeast,
16: 8 For the next six days you may not eat bread **m** with
22:11 "Do not wear clothing **m** of wool and linen woven
22:19 The payment will be **m** to the woman's father.
23:23 But once you have voluntarily **m** a vow, be careful
23:23 for you have **m** a vow to the LORD your God.
28:64 ancestors have known, gods **m** of wood and stone!
29: 1 in addition to the covenant he had **m** with them at
29:17 You have seen their detestable idols **m** of wood,
29:18 The LORD **m** this covenant with you so that no
29:25 land broke the covenant they **m** with the LORD,
31:16 and break the covenant I have **m** with them.
32: 6 Has he not **m** you and established you?
32:13 He **m** them ride over the highlands; / he let them
32:14 drank the finest wine, / **m** from the juice of grapes.
32:15 Then they abandoned the God who had **m** them;
32:15 they **m** light of the Rock of their salvation.
Jos 2:10 For we have heard how the LORD **m** a dry path
4:14 That day the LORD **m** Joshua great in the eyes of
5: 3 So Joshua **m** flint knives and circumcised the
6:19 Everything **m** from silver, gold, bronze, or iron is
6:24 Only the things **m** from silver, gold, bronze,
9:18 for their leaders had **m** a vow to the LORD,
9:27 But that day he **m** the Gibeonites the
10: 1 He also learned that the Gibeonites had **m** peace
10: 4 "for they have **m** peace with Joshua
11:19 No one in this region **m** peace with the Israelites
13:32 These are the allotments Moses had **m** while he
14:10 forty-five years since Moses **m** this promise—
22:28 copy of the LORD's altar that our ancestors **m**.
24:10 I **m** Balaam bless you, and so I rescued you from
24:25 So Joshua **m** a covenant with the people that day at
Jdg 2:14 This **m** the LORD burn with anger against Israel,
2:20 have violated the covenant I **m** with their ancestors
3:16 So Ehud **m** himself a double-edged dagger that
4: 9 But since you have **m** this choice, you will receive
6: 2 where they **m** hiding places for themselves in
8:27 Gideon **m** a sacred ephod from the gold and put it
9: 6 the pillar at Shechem and **m** Abimelech their king.
11:26 Why have you **m** no effort to recover it before
11:30 And Jephthah **m** a vow to the LORD. He said,
11:35 For I have **m** a vow to the LORD and cannot take
11:36 "Father, you have **m** a promise to the LORD.
14: 8 And he found that a swarm of bees had **m** some
15:16 the jawbone of a donkey, / I've **m** heaps on heaps!
16:10 said to him, "You **m** fun of me and told me a lie!
16:15 You've **m** fun of me three times now, and you still
16:21 bronze chains and **m** to grind grain in the prison.
16:25 and **m** to stand at the center of the temple,
17: 4 who **m** them into an image and an idol.
17: 5 and he **m** a sacred ephod and some household
Ru 1:18 So when Naomi saw that Ruth had **m** up her mind
1:20 for the Almighty has **m** life very bitter for me.
1Sa 1: 6 But Peninnah **m** fun of Hannah
1:11 And she **m** this vow: "O LORD Almighty,
2:19 Each year his mother **m** a small coat for him
4: 5 of joy was so loud that it **m** the ground shake!
11: 7 And the LORD **m** the people afraid of Saul's
12:22 great name. He **m** you a special nation for himself.
14:24 because Saul had **m** them take an oath, saying,
14:28 "Your father **m** the army take a strict oath that
14:29 "My father has **m** trouble for us all!"
14:37 us defeat them?" But God **m** no reply that day.
15:11 "I am sorry that I ever **m** Saul king, for he has not
15:35 And the LORD was sorry he had ever **m** Saul
18: 3 And Jonathan **m** a special vow to be David's
18: 5 So Saul **m** him a commander in his army,
18: 8 This **m** Saul very angry. "What's this?" he said.
20: 8 for we **m** a covenant together before the LORD—
20:16 So Jonathan **m** a covenant with David, saying,
20:17 And Jonathan **m** David reaffirm his vow of
20:26 "Something must have **m** David ceremonially
20:42 for we have **m** a pact in the LORD's name.
25:30 all he promised and has **m** you leader of Israel,
30: 1 they found that the Amalekites had **m** a raid into
30:25 From then on David **m** this a law for all of Israel,
2Sa 2:11 David **m** Hebron his capital, and he ruled as king
3:35 But David had **m** a vow, saying, "May God kill
5: 3 David **m** a covenant with the leaders of Israel
5: 9 So David **m** the fortress his home, and he called it
5:12 And David realized that the LORD had **m** him
5:12 and had **m** his kingdom great for the sake of his
7:23 You **m** a great name for yourself when you rescued
7:24 You **m** Israel your people forever, and you,
8: 2 He **m** the people lie down on the ground in a row,
8:14 This was another example of how the LORD **m**
12:15 the LORD **m** Bathsheba's baby deathly ill.
12:30 The crown was **m** of gold and set with gems,
12:31 He also **m** slaves of the people of Rabbah
15: 7 to the LORD in fulfillment of a vow I **m** to him.
15:35 Tell them the plans that are being **m** to capture me,
17: 7 "this time I think Ahithophel has **m** a mistake.
17:17 Arrangements had been **m** for a servant girl to
19: 6 You have **m** it clear today that we mean nothing to
22:33 God is my strong fortress; / he has **m** my way safe.
22:36 of your salvation; / your help has **m** me great.
22:37 You have **m** a wide path for my feet / to keep them
22:41 You **m** them turn and run; / I have destroyed all
23: 5 Yes, he has **m** an everlasting covenant with me.
23:22 These are some of the deeds that **m** Benaiah almost
23:23 And David **m** him commander of his bodyguard.
1Ki 1:11 has **m** himself king and that our lord David doesn't
2: 4 then the LORD will keep the promise he **m** to
2:27 thereby fulfilling the decree the LORD had **m** at
3: 1 Solomon **m** an alliance with Pharaoh, the king of
3: 7 now you have **m** me king instead of my father,
5:12 and Solomon **m** a formal alliance of peace.
6: 4 Solomon also **m** narrow, recessed windows
6: 9 Solomon put in a ceiling **m** of beams and planks of
6:12 I will fulfill through you the promise I **m** to your
6:20 pure gold. He also overlaid the altar **m** of cedar.
6:21 and he **m** gold chains to protect the entrance to the
6:23 Solomon placed two cherubim **m** of olive wood,
6:31 Solomon **m** double doors of olive wood with
6:33 Then he **m** four-sided doorposts of olive wood for
7:16 For the tops of the pillars he **m** capitals of molded
7:18 He also **m** two rows of pomegranates that
7:27 Huram also **m** ten bronze water carts, each 6 feet
7:37 water carts were the same size and were **m** alike,
7:38 Huram also **m** ten bronze basins, one for each cart.
7:40 He also **m** the necessary pots, shovels, and basins.
7:45 **m** for Solomon were **m** of burnished bronze.
7:48 So Solomon **m** all the furnishings of the Temple of
8: 9 where the LORD **m** a covenant with the people of
8:15 who has kept the promise he **m** to my father,
8:21 which contains the covenant that the LORD **m**
8:24 You **m** that promise with your own mouth,
9: 5 For I **m** this promise to your father, David:
10: 5 and the burnt offerings Solomon **m** at the Temple
10: 9 he has **m** you king so you can rule with justice
10:16 King Solomon **m** two hundred large shields of
10:17 He also **m** three hundred smaller shields of
10:18 Then the king **m** a huge ivory throne and overlaid
10:20 Solomon **m** twelve other lion figures, one standing
10:21 They were not **m** of silver because silver was
10:27 The king **m** silver as plentiful in Jerusalem as
11:25 and he **m** trouble, just as Hadad did.
12:20 called an assembly and **m** him king over all Israel.
12:28 of his counselors, the king **m** two gold calves.
12:32 himself offered sacrifices to the calves he had **m**.
12:32 appointed priests for the pagan shrines he had **m**.
14: 7 and **m** you ruler over my people Israel.
14: 9 You have **m** other gods and have **m** me furious
14:16 and **m** all of Israel sin along with him."
14:26 including all the gold shields Solomon had **m**.
14:27 Afterward Rehoboam **m** bronze shields as
15:12 and removed all the idols his ancestors had **m**.
15:13 because she had **m** an obscene Asherah pole.
16: 9 half of the royal chariots, **m** plans to kill him.
18:18 "I have **m** no trouble for Israel," Elijah replied.
18:26 they danced wildly around the altar they had **m**.
20:34 So they **m** a treaty, and Ben-hadad was set free.
21: 5 "What has **m** you so upset that you are not
21:22 for you have **m** him very angry and have led all of
22:11 of Kenaanah, **m** some iron horns and proclaimed,
22:44 Jehoshaphat also **m** peace with the king of Israel.
2Ki 2:21 I have **m** this water wholesome. It will no longer
4:42 and twenty loaves of barley bread **m** from the first
6:23 So the king **m** a great feast for them and then sent
8:19 for he had **m** a covenant with David and promised
11: 4 He **m** a pact with them and **m** them swear an oath
11:13 When Athaliah heard all the noise **m** by the guards
11:17 Then Jehoiada **m** a covenant between the LORD
11:17 He also **m** a covenant between the king
16:12 he inspected the altar and **m** offerings on it.
17:15 and the covenant he had **m** with their ancestors,
17:16 LORD their God and **m** two calves from metal.

17:21 the LORD and **m** them commit a great sin.
17:35 For the LORD had **m** a covenant with the
17:38 Do not forget the covenant I **m** with you, and do
18: 4 He broke up the bronze serpent that Moses had **m**,
21: 7 Manasseh even took an Asherah pole he had **m**
21:24 and they **m** his son Josiah the next king.
23:15 the pagan shrine that Jeroboam son of Nebat had **m**
23:19 kings of Israel and had **m** the LORD very angry.
23:30 his son Jehoahaz and **m** him the next king.
25: 4 and all the soldiers **m** plans to escape from the city.
25: 4 They **m** a dash across the fields, in the direction of
25: 7 The king of Babylon **m** Zedekiah watch as all his
25:15 and all the other utensils **m** of pure gold or silver.
25:16 These things had been **m** for the LORD's Temple
1Ch 6:49 They **m** atonement for Israel by following all the
11: 3 So there at Hebron David **m** a covenant with the
11: 7 David **m** the fortress his home, and that is why it is
11:24 These are some of the deeds that **m** Benaiah as
11:25 And David **m** him commander of his bodyguard.
12:18 join him, and he **m** them officers over his troops.
12:39 for preparations had been **m** by their relatives for
14: 2 And David realized that the LORD had **m** him
14: 2 and had **m** his kingdom very great for the sake of
16:15 the commitment he **m** to a thousand generations.
16:16 This is the covenant he **m** with Abraham
16:26 are merely idols, / but the LORD **m** the heavens!
17:19 all these great things and have **m** them known.
17:21 You **m** a great name for yourself when you rescued
18:13 This was another example of how the LORD **m**
20: 2 The crown was **m** of gold and set with gems,
20: 3 He also **m** slaves of the people of Rabbah
21: 6 so distressed at what the king had **m** him do.
21:29 and the altar that Moses **m** in the wilderness were
23: 5 LORD with the musical instruments I have **m**."
23:29 the wafers **m** without yeast, the cakes cooked in
25: 6 as they **m** music at the house of the LORD.
26:31 of David's reign, a search was **m** in the records,
28: 2 I **m** the necessary preparations for building it,
29:12 and it is at your discretion that people are **m** great
29:19 for which I have **m** all these preparations."
2Ch 1: 1 his God was with him and **m** him very powerful.
1: 5 But the bronze altar **m** by Bezalel son of Uri
1: 8 David, and now you have **m** me king in his place.
1: 9 for you have **m** me king over a people as numerous
2:11 because the LORD loves his people that he has **m**
2:12 God of Israel, who **m** the heavens and the earth!
3:10 Solomon **m** two figures shaped like cherubim
3:14 Solomon hung a curtain **m** of fine linen and blue,
3:15 Solomon **m** two pillars that were 27 feet tall,
3:16 He **m** a network of interwoven chains and used
3:16 He also **m** one hundred decorative pomegranates
4: 1 Solomon also **m** a bronze altar 30 feet long,
4: 6 He also **m** ten basins for water to wash the
4: 9 He **m** doors for the courtyard entrances
4:11 Huram-abi also **m** the necessary pots, shovels,
4:16 Huram-abi **m** all these things out of burnished
4:19 So Solomon **m** all the furnishings for the Temple
5:10 when the LORD **m** a covenant with the people of
6: 4 who has kept the promise he **m** to my father,
6:11 and in the Ark is the covenant that the LORD **m**
6:13 He had **m** a bronze platform 7-1/2 feet long,
6:15 You **m** that promise with your own mouth,
6:40 be attentive to all the prayers **m** to you in this
7: 6 King David had **m** for praising the LORD.
7:15 I will listen to every prayer **m** in this place,
8:16 So Solomon **m** sure that all the work related to
9: 4 and the burnt offerings Solomon **m** at the Temple
9: 8 he has **m** you king so you can rule with justice
9:15 King Solomon **m** two hundred large shields of
9:16 He also **m** three hundred smaller shields of
9:17 Then the king **m** a huge ivory throne and overlaid
9:19 Solomon **m** twelve other lion figures, one standing
9:20 They were not **m** of silver because silver was
9:27 The king **m** silver as plentiful in Jerusalem as
11:15 they worshiped the goat and calf idols he had **m**.
11:22 Rehoboam **m** Maacah's son Abijah chief among
13: 5 **m** an unbreakable covenant with David,
13: 8 those gold calves that Jeroboam **m** as your gods!
15:16 because she had **m** an obscene Asherah pole.
18:10 of Kenaanah, **m** some iron horns and proclaimed,
20:35 King Jehoshaphat of Judah **m** an alliance with
21: 7 for he had **m** a covenant with David and promised
22: 1 Then the people of Jerusalem **m** Ahaziah,
22: 5 Ahaziah **m** an alliance with King Joram,
23: 1 and **m** a pact with five army commanders:
23: 3 where they **m** a covenant with Joash, the young
23:16 Then Jehoiada **m** a covenant between himself
24: 8 So now Joash gave instructions for a chest to be **m**
24:12 who **m** articles of iron and bronze for the
24:13 worked hard, and they **m** steady progress.
24:14 and other vessels **m** of gold and silver.
25:10 This **m** them angry with Judah, and they returned
25:15 This **m** the LORD very angry, and he sent a
28:25 He **m** pagan shrines in all the towns of Judah for
29: 8 He has **m** us an object of dread, horror,
29:24 and sin offering should be **m** for all Israel.
30:10 just laughed at the messengers and **m** fun of them.
31: 3 The king also **m** a personal contribution of animals
31:13 These appointments were **m** by King Hezekiah
32:19 he were one of the pagan gods, **m** by human hands.
32:28 and he **m** many stalls for his cattle and folds for his
33: 7 Manasseh even took a carved idol he had **m**
33:22 and sacrificed to all the idols his father had **m**.
33:25 and they **m** his son Josiah the next king.
34: 4 He also **m** sure that the Asherah poles, the carved
35: 8 The king's officials also **m** willing contributions to
36: 1 and **m** him the next king in Jerusalem.

Ezr 3: 8 The work force was **m** up of everyone who had
4:17 Then Artaxerxes **m** this reply: / "To Rehum the
4:19 I have ordered a search to be **m** of the records
6: 1 So King Darius issued orders that a search be **m** in
7:27 who **m** the king want to beautify the Temple of the
10: 1 While Ezra prayed and **m** this confession, weeping
10: 7 Then a proclamation was **m** throughout Judah
Ne 4: 8 They all **m** plans to come and fight against
5:12 Then I called the priests and **m** the nobles
8: 4 wooden platform that had been **m** for the occasion.
8:15 He had said that a proclamation should be **m**
9: 6 You **m** the skies and the heavens and all the stars.
9: 6 You **m** the earth and the seas and everything in
9: 8 you **m** a covenant with him to give him and his
9:18 even though they **m** an idol shaped like a calf
9:23 You **m** their descendants as numerous as the stars
13:25 I **m** them swear before God that they would not let
13:26 and God loved him and **m** him king over all Israel.
13:31 I also **m** sure that the supply of wood for the altar
Est 1:12 This **m** the king furious, and he burned with anger.
1:21 and his princes thought this **m** good sense,
2: 1 and what she had done and the decree he had **m**.
2: 4 the young woman who pleases you most will be **m**
2:23 When an investigation was **m** and Mordecai's
3:14 in every province and **m** known to all the people,
Job 1:10 You have **m** him prosperous in everything he does.
4:19 how much less will he trust those **m** of clay!
6:12 strength as hard as stone? Is my body **m** of bronze?
7:20 Why have you **m** me your target? Am I a burden to
9: 9 He **m** all the stars—the Bear, Orion, the Pleiades,
10: 8 you **m** me, and yet you completely destroy me.
10: 9 Remember that I am **m** of dust—will you turn me
15: 7 ever born? Were you born before the hills were **m**?
17: 6 "God has **m** a mockery of me among the people;
23:16 God has **m** my heart faint; the Almighty has
26:13 His Spirit **m** the heavens beautiful, and his power
27:18 a spiderweb, as flimsy as a shelter **m** of branches.
28:25 He **m** the winds blow and determined how much
28:26 He **m** the laws of the rain and prepared a path for
29:16 and **m** sure that even strangers received a fair trial.
29:17 and **m** them release their victims.
31: 1 "I **m** a covenant with my eyes not to look with lust
33: 4 For the Spirit of God has **m** me, and the breath of
34:19 to the rich than to the poor. He **m** them all.
38:22 Have you seen where the hail is **m** and stored?
40:15 I **m** it, just as I **m** you. It eats grass like an ox.
Ps 8: 5 For you **m** us only a little lower than God,
8: 6 You put us in charge of everything you **m**,
18:32 arms me with strength; / he has **m** my way safe.
18:35 supports me; / your gentleness has **m** me great.
18:36 You have **m** a wide path for my feet / to keep them
18:40 You **m** them turn and run; / I have destroyed all
28: 5 or for what his hands have **m**. / So he will tear
30: 7 O LORD, **m** me as secure as a mountain.
33:15 He **m** their hearts, / so he understands everything
40: 6 Now that you have **m** me listen, I finally
44:14 You have **m** us the butt of their jokes; / we are
50: 5 those who **m** a covenant with me by giving
66: 6 He **m** a dry path through the Red Sea, / and his
66:13 burnt offerings / to fulfill the vows I **m** to you—
73:28 I have **m** the Sovereign LORD my shelter,
74:16 belong to you; / you **m** the starlight and the sun.
78:16 He **m** streams pour from the rock,
78:58 They **m** God angry by building altars to other
gods; / they **m** him jealous with their idols.
78:71 and **m** him the shepherd of Jacob's descendants—
79: 1 holy Temple / and **m** Jerusalem a heap of ruins.
80: 5 and **m** us drink tears by the bucketful.
80: 6 You have **m** us the scorn of neighboring nations.
81: 5 He **m** it a decree for Israel / when he attacked
86: 9 All the nations—and you **m** each one—
89: 3 "I have **m** a solemn agreement with David,
89:42 his enemies against him / and **m** them all rejoice.
89:43 You have **m** his sword useless / and have refused
89:45 You have **m** him old before his time / and publicly
90: 2 before you **m** the earth and the world,
92:10 But you have **m** me as strong as a wild bull.
94: 9 Is the one who **m** your ears deaf? / Is the one who
95: 5 The sea belongs to him, for he **m** it. / His hands
95:11 So in my anger I **m** a vow: / 'They will never
96: 5 are merely idols, / but the LORD **m** the heavens!
100: 3 He **m** us, and we are his. / We are his people,
103:19 The LORD has **m** the heavens his throne;
104:19 You **m** the moon to mark the seasons / and the sun
104:24 O LORD, what a variety of things you have **m**!
104:24 In wisdom you have **m** them all. / The earth is full
104:26 and Leviathan, which you **m** to play in the sea.
104:31 last forever! / The LORD rejoices in all he has **m**!
105: 8 the commitment he **m** to a thousand generations.
105: 9 This is the covenant he **m** with Abraham
106:19 The people **m** a calf at Mount Sinai; / they bowed
before an image **m** of gold.
106:33 They **m** Moses angry, / and he spoke foolishly.
114: 5 Red Sea, that **m** you hurry out of their way?
115:15 blessed by the LORD, / who **m** heaven and earth.
118:24 This is the day the LORD has **m**. / We will
119:69 Arrogant people have **m** up lies about me, / but in
119:73 You **m** me; you created me. / Now give me the
121: 2 the LORD, / who **m** the heavens and the earth!
124: 8 the LORD, / who **m** the heavens and the earth.
134: 3 May the LORD, who **m** heaven and earth,
136: 5 Give thanks to him who **m** the heavens
136: 7 Give thanks to him who **m** the heavenly lights—
138: 8 Don't abandon me, for you **m** me.
139:13 You **m** all the delicate, inner parts of my body
146: 6 He is the one who **m** heaven and earth, / the sea,
148:14 He has **m** his people strong, / honoring his godly

Pr 2:17 and ignores the covenant she **m** before God.
8:26 before he had **m** the earth and fields and the first
16: 4 The LORD has **m** everything for his own
20:28 the king; his throne is **m** secure through love.
22: 2 have this in common: The LORD **m** them both.
25: 5 and his reign will be **m** secure by justice.
25:12 the one who heeds it as jewelry **m** from finest gold.
Ecc 2: 5 I **m** gardens and parks, filling them with all kinds
3:11 God has **m** everything beautiful for its own time.
5: 6 messenger that the promise you **m** was a mistake.
7:13 for who can straighten out what he has **m** crooked?
SS 3: 3 The watchmen stopped me as they **m** their rounds,
Isa 2: 6 because they have **m** alliances with foreigners
2: 8 bow down and worship these things they have **m**.
14:17 destroyed the world and **m** it into a wilderness?
17: 8 for help or worship what their own hands have **m**.
19:25 my people. Blessed be Assyria, the land I have **m**.
26:15 LORD! / You have **m** our nation great;
27:11 the one who **m** them will show them no pity
28:15 avoid death and have **m** a deal to dodge the grave.
28:15 for we have built a strong refuge **m** of lies
28:17 Your refuge looks strong, but since it is **m** of lies,
28:17 Since it is **m** of deception, the enemy will come
28:18 I will cancel the bargain you **m** to avoid death,
28:20 the bed you have **m** is too short to lie on.
29:16 the thing that was created say to the one who **m** it,
29:16 a jar ever say, "The potter who **m** me is stupid"?
31: 7 and silver images that your sinful hands have **m**.
33: 8 and care nothing for the promises they **m** before
42:21 has magnified his law and **m** it truly glorious.
43: 7 God will come, for I have **m** them for my glory.
43:21 I have **m** Israel for myself, and they will someday
44: 2 The LORD who **m** you and helps you says:
44:19 The person who **m** the idol never stops to reflect,
44:21 I, the LORD, **m** you, and I will not forget to help
44:24 says: "I am the LORD, who **m** all things.
44:24 By myself I **m** the earth and everything in it.
45:12 I am the one who **m** the earth and created people to
45:18 He **m** the world to be lived in, not to be a place of
45:21 Who **m** these things known long ago?
46: 4 I **m** you, and I will care for you. I will carry you
49: 2 He **m** my words of judgment as sharp as a sword.
53:10 Yet when his life is **m** an offering for sin, he will
55: 5 the Holy One of Israel, have **m** you glorious."
57:16 people would pass away—all the souls I have **m**.
63: 6 and **m** them stagger and fall to the ground."
66: 2 My hands have **m** both heaven and earth, and they
Jer 1:16 they worship idols that they themselves have **m**!
1:18 today I have **m** you immune to their attacks.
2:28 Why don't you call on these gods you have **m**?
3: 9 adultery by worshiping idols **m** of wood
4:28 I have **m** up my mind and will not change it."
6:27 "Jeremiah, I have **m** you a tester of metals,
10: 8 The things they worship are **m** of wood!
10: 9 Then they dress these gods in royal purple robes **m**
10:12 But God **m** the earth by his power, / and he
11: 6 'Remember the covenant your ancestors **m**,
11:10 and Judah have both broken the covenant I **m** with
12:11 They have **m** it an empty wasteland; I hear its
14:14 They speak foolishness **m** up in their own lying
17: 7 and have **m** the LORD their hope and confidence.
18: 2 down to the shop where clay pots and jars are **m**.
20: 8 So these messages from the LORD have **m** me a
21: 5 for I am very angry. You have **m** me furious!
22:16 He **m** sure that justice and help were given to the
25: 6 me angry by worshiping the idols you have **m**.
25: 7 "You **m** me furious by worshiping your idols,
25:17 the LORD and **m** all the nations drink from it—
25:38 and their land will be **m** desolate by the sword of
27: 5 By my great power I have **m** the earth and all its
31:32 This covenant will not be like the one I **m** with
32:17 You have **m** the heavens and earth by your great
32:20 You have **m** your name very great, as it is today.
34: 8 after King Zedekiah **m** a covenant with the people,
34:13 I **m** a covenant with your ancestors long ago when
34:15 and **m** a solemn covenant with me in my Temple.
39: 6 He **m** Zedekiah watch as they killed his sons
41: 9 **m** by King Asa when he fortified Mizpah to
41:10 Ishmael **m** captives of the king's daughters
44: 8 incense to the idols you have **m** here in Egypt?
44:11 I have **m** up my mind to destroy every one of you!
44:22 doing that he **m** your land an object of cursing—
48:37 their hands and put on clothes **m** of sackcloth.
51: 7 a cup from which he **m** the whole earth drink
51:15 He **m** the earth by his power, / and he preserves it
52: 7 and all the soldiers **m** plans to escape from the city.
52: 7 They **m** a dash across the fields, in the direction of
52:10 the king of Babylon **m** Zedekiah watch as all his
52:19 and all the other utensils **m** of pure gold or silver.
52:20 These things had been **m** for the LORD's Temple
La 1:13 He has **m** me desolate, racked with sickness all day
2: 8 He **m** careful plans for their destruction, then he
2:17 He has fulfilled the promises of disaster he **m** long
3: 4 He has **m** my skin and flesh grow old. He has
3:16 He has **m** me grind my teeth on gravel. He has
3:61 You know all about the plans they have **m**—
Eze 1:16 The wheels sparkled as if **m** of chrysolite. All four
1:26 was what looked like a throne **m** of blue sapphire.
3: 8 I have **m** you as hard and stubborn as they are.
3: 9 I have **m** you as hard as rock! So don't be afraid of
6: 6 and all the other religious objects you have **m**.
7:19 for their love of money **m** them stumble into sin.
8: 3 where there is a large idol that has **m** the LORD
8: 5 stood the idol that had **m** the LORD so angry.
16: 8 I **m** a covenant with you, says the Sovereign
16:10 and sandals **m** of fine leather.
16:13 And so you were **m** beautiful with gold and silver.

16:13 Your clothes were **m** of fine linen and were
16:17 and **m** statues of men and worshiped them,
16:60 Yet I will keep the covenant I **m** with you when
17:13 He **m** a treaty with a member of the royal family
and **m** him take an oath of loyalty.
17:19 and despising the solemn oath he **m** in my name.
20:13 and I **m** plans to utterly consume them in the
27: 4 into the sea. Your builders **m** you glorious!
27: 6 They **m** your deck of pine wood, brought from the
27: 7 Your sails were **m** of Egypt's finest linen, and they
27: 7 and purple awnings **m** bright with dyes from the
27:24 carpets bound with cords and **m** secure.
28: 5 Yes, your wisdom has **m** you very rich, and your
riches have **m** you very proud.
29: 3 'The Nile River is mine; I **m** it for myself!'
29: 9 you said, 'The Nile River is mine; I **m** it,'
31:15 I **m** the deep places mourn, and I restrained the
31:16 I **m** the nations shake with fear at the sound of its
39:14 to bury them, so the land will be **m** clean again.
41:22 There was an altar **m** of wood, 3-1/2 feet square
41:22 Its corners, base, and sides were all **m** of wood.
Da 1: 5 then some of them would be **m** his advisers in the
1: 8 But Daniel **m** up his mind not to defile himself by
2:32 The head of the statue was **m** of fine gold, its chest
2:38 He has **m** you the ruler over all the inhabited world
2:48 He **m** Daniel ruler over the whole province of
3: 1 King Nebuchadnezzar **m** a gold statue ninety feet
3:15 and worship the statue I have **m** when you hear the
5: 4 They drank toasts from them to honor their idols **m**
5:11 **m** him chief over all the magicians, enchanters,
5:19 He **m** him so great that people of all races
6: 3 the king **m** plans to place him over the entire
11:35 and cleansed and **m** pure until the time of the end,
Hos 4:12 Longing after idols has **m** them foolish. They have
7:15 "I trained them and **m** them strong, yet now they
8: 5 I reject this calf—this idol you have **m**.
10: 9 more sin! You have **m** no progress whatsoever.
14: 3 Never again will we call the idols we have **m** 'our
Am 4: 5 Present your bread **m** with yeast as an offering of
5:26 your star god—the images you yourselves **m**.
Jnh 1: 9 the God of heaven, who **m** the sea and the land."
4: 5 and **m** a shelter to sit under as he waited to see if
Mic 1: 2 The Sovereign LORD has **m** accusations against
Hab 1:16 "These nets are the gods who have **m** us rich!"
2:18 How foolish to trust in something **m** by your own
Zec 1:16 and plans will be **m** for the reconstruction of
7:12 They **m** their hearts as hard as stone, so they could
9:11 Because of the covenant I **m** with you, sealed with
11:10 showing that I had revoked the covenant I had **m**
Mal 2: 8 You have corrupted the covenant I **m** with the
2: 9 "So I have **m** you despised and humiliated in the
2:14 and your wife **m** to each other on your wedding
Mt 5:33 you must carry out the vows you have **m** to the
9:22 be encouraged! Your faith has **m** you well."
10:26 will be revealed; all that is secret will be **m** public.
14:22 Jesus **m** his disciples get back into the boat
15:31 the crippled were **m** well, the lame were walking
19: 4 "They record that from the beginning 'God **m**
19:12 as eunuchs, some have been **m** that way by others,
27: 7 and they **m** it into a cemetery for foreigners.
27:12 and other leaders **m** their accusations against him,
27:29 They **m** a crown of long, sharp thorns and put it on
Mk 2:27 to them, "The Sabbath was **m** to benefit people,
5:34 said to her, "Daughter, your faith has **m** you well.
6:45 Jesus **m** his disciples get back into the boat
7:17 him what he meant by the statement he had **m**.
10: 6 of creation, for 'He **m** them male and female.'
12:27 not the dead. You have **m** a serious error."
14:58 'I will destroy this Temple **m** with human hands,
14:58 I will build another, **m** without human hands.' "
14:61 Jesus **m** no reply. Then the high priest asked him,
15:17 him in a purple robe and **m** a crown of long,
Lk 8:17 eventually be brought to light and **m** plain to all.
8:48 he said to her, "your faith has **m** you well.
12: 2 will be revealed; all that is secret will be **m** public.
12:14 who **m** me a judge over you to decide such things
15: 2 This **m** the Pharisees and teachers of religious law
17:19 "Stand up and go. Your faith has **m** you well."
19: 1 entered Jericho and **m** his way through the town.
Jn 1:10 But although the world was **m** through him,
2:15 Jesus **m** a whip from some ropes and chased them
8:20 Jesus **m** these statements while he was teaching in
9: 6 Then he spit on the ground, **m** mud with the saliva,
9:11 "The man they call Jesus **m** mud and smoothed it
10:33 because you, a mere man, have **m** yourself God."
12: 3 jar of expensive perfume **m** from essence of nard,
12:41 Isaiah was referring to Jesus when he **m** this
18:18 were standing around a charcoal fire they had **m**
19: 2 The soldiers **m** a crown of long, sharp thorns
19:39 pounds of embalming ointment **m** from myrrh
Ac 2:36 **m** this Jesus whom you crucified to be both Lord
3:12 And why look at us as though we had **m** this man
7:27 'Who **m** you a ruler and judge over us?' he asked.
7:35 'Who **m** you a ruler and judge over us?'
7:41 So they **m** an idol shaped like a calf, and they
7:41 to it and rejoiced in this thing they had **m**.
7:43 and the images you **m** to worship them.
7:48 the Most High doesn't live in temples **m** by human
9:39 and other garments Dorcas had **m** for them.
12:20 They **m** friends with Blastus, Herod's personal
12:21 sat on his throne, and **m** a speech to them.
13:17 chose our ancestors and **m** them prosper in Egypt.
13:47 he said, / 'I have **m** you a light to the Gentiles,
14:15 who **m** heaven and earth, the sea, and everything in
15: 9 He **m** no distinction between us and them, for he
15:18 he who **m** these things known long ago.'
16:38 When the police **m** their report, the city officials
17:24 "He is the God who **m** the world and everything in
25: 2 met with him and **m** their accusations against Paul.
25: 7 and **m** many serious accusations they couldn't
25:18 But the accusations **m** against him weren't at all
26: 2 all these accusations **m** by the Jewish leaders,
26: 6 fulfillment of God's promise **m** to our ancestors.
26:24 are insane. Too much study has **m** you crazy!"
27: 4 we encountered headwinds that **m** it difficult to
Ro 1:20 have seen the earth and sky and all that God **m**.
1:23 they worshiped idols **m** to look like mere people,
1:25 So they worshiped the things God **m** but not the
3:20 For no one can ever be **m** right in God's sight by
3:22 We are **m** right in God's sight when we trust in
3:25 We are **m** right with God when we believe that
3:28 So we are **m** right with God through faith and not
4:11 They are **m** right with God by faith.
4:17 "I have **m** you the father of many nations."
5: 1 since we have been **m** right in God's sight by faith,
5: 9 And since we have been **m** right in God's sight by
5:19 many people will be **m** right in God's sight.
8:10 is alive because you have been **m** right with God.
9: 4 He **m** covenants with them and gave his law to
9:19 Haven't they simply done what he **m** them do?"
9:20 the thing that was created say to the one who **m** it,
"Why have you **m** me like this?"
9:30 The Gentiles have been **m** right with God by faith,
10: 4 All who believe in him are **m** right with God.
10:10 For it is by believing in your heart that you are **m**
11: 7 has chosen—but the rest were **m** unresponsive.
15: 8 God is true to the promises he **m** to their ancestors.
16:26 this message is **m** known to all Gentiles
1Co 1: 2 He **m** you holy by means of Christ Jesus, just as he
1:20 God has **m** them all look foolish and has shown
1:30 God alone **m** it possible for you to be in Christ
1:30 For our benefit God **m** Christ to be wisdom itself.
1:30 He is the one who **m** us acceptable to God.
1:30 He **m** us pure and holy, and he gave himself to
2: 7 though he **m** it for our benefit before the world
3: 6 watered it, but it was God, not we, who **m** it grow.
6:11 You have been **m** right with God because of what
6:13 But our bodies were not **m** for sexual immorality.
6:13 They were **m** for the Lord, and the Lord cares
8: 6 through whom God **m** everything and through
11: 7 for man is God's glory, **m** in God's own image,
11: 9 And man was not **m** for woman's benefit, but
woman was **m** for man.
12:18 But God **m** our bodies with many parts, and he has
15:47 was **m** from the dust of the earth, while Christ,
2Co 1:17 I changed my plan. Hadn't I **m** up my mind yet?
2: 3 I will not be **m** sad by the very ones who ought to
2:14 who **m** us his captives and leads us along in
4: 6 has **m** us understand that this light is the brightness
5: 1 an eternal body **m** for us by God himself and not
5:21 For God **m** Christ, who never sinned, to be the
5:21 so that we could be **m** right with God through
7: 4 you have **m** me happy despite all our troubles.
12:11 You have **m** me act like a fool—boasting like this.
Gal 2: 6 their reputation as great leaders **m** no difference to
2:17 But what if we seek to be **m** right with God
3:17 The agreement God **m** with Abraham could not be
3:19 of the child to whom God's promise was **m**.
3:20 but God acted on his own when he **m** his promise
3:21 we could have been **m** right with God by obeying
3:24 through faith in Christ, we are **m** right with God.
3:27 with Christ in baptism have been **m** like him.
Eph 1: 4 Long ago, even before he **m** the world, God loved
2:12 and you did not know the promises God had **m** to
2:14 For Christ himself has **m** peace between us Jews
4:14 lied to us and **m** the lie sound like the truth.
6:12 For we are not fighting against people **m** of flesh
Php 2: 7 He **m** himself nothing; he took the humble position
Col 1:15 He existed before God **m** anything at all and is
1:16 He **m** the things we can see and the things we can't
1:20 He **m** peace with everything in heaven and on
2:13 Then God **m** you alive with Christ. He forgave all
2:18 but their sinful minds have **m** them proud.
2Th 1:12 This is all **m** possible because of the undeserved
1Ti 1: 9 But they were not **m** for people who do what is
2:13 For God **m** Adam first, and afterward he **m** Eve.
4: 5 For we know it is **m** holy by the word of God
2Ti 1:10 And now he has **m** all of this plain to us by the
2:20 In a wealthy home some utensils are **m** of gold and
silver, and some are **m** of wood and clay.
Heb 1: 2 and through the Son he **m** the universe
1: 7 as the wind, / and servants **m** of flaming fire."
2: 7 For a little while you **m** him lower than the angels,
2: 9 who "for a little while was **m** lower than the
2:10 who **m** everything and for whom everything was **m**
2:10 the suffering of Jesus, God **m** him a perfect leader,
2:14 **m** of flesh and blood—Jesus also became flesh
3: 4 a builder, but God is the one who **m** everything.
3:11 So in my anger I **m** a vow: / 'They will never
3:17 And who **m** God angry for forty years? Wasn't it
4: 3 God said, / "In my anger I **m** a vow:
4: 3 place of rest has been ready since he **m** the world.
7:19 For the law **m** nothing perfect, and now a better
7:28 an oath, and his Son has been **m** perfect forever.
8: 9 I **m** with their ancestors / when I took them by the
8:13 it means he has **m** the first one obsolete.
9:11 not **m** by human hands and not part of this created
9:20 "This blood confirms the covenant God has **m**
10:10 And what God wants is for us to be **m** holy by the
11: 7 rest of the world and was **m** right in God's sight.
12:23 redeemed in heaven who have now been **m** perfect.
Jas 2:22 His faith was **m** complete by what he did—by his
2:24 you see, we are **m** right with God by what we do,
2:25 She was **m** right with God by her actions—
3: 9 those who have been **m** in the image of God.
4:12 God alone, who **m** the law, can rightly judge
1Pe 1: 2 chose you long ago, and the Spirit has **m** you holy.
3: 5 That is the way the holy women of old **m**
4:19 and trust yourself to the God who **m** you, for he
2Pe 2: 6 He **m** them an example of what will happen to
3: 5 They deliberately forget that God **m** the heavens
1Jn 2:11 they are going, for the darkness has **m** them blind.
3Jn 1: 3 and **m** me very happy by telling me about your
Rev 1: 6 He has **m** us his kingdom and his priests who serve
7:14 robes in the blood of the Lamb and **m** them white.
8:11 It **m** one-third of the water bitter, and many people
9: 9 They wore armor **m** of iron, and their wings roared
9:20 continued to worship demons and idols **m** of gold,
10:10 was sweet in my mouth, but it **m** my stomach sour.
13: 8 the Lamb who was killed before the world was **m**.
14: 7 Worship him who **m** heaven and earth, the sea,
14: 8 and **m** them drink the wine of her passionate
16:19 and he **m** her drink the cup that was filled with the
17: 2 been **m** drunk by the wine of her immorality."
17: 4 and beautiful jewelry **m** of gold and precious gems
18:12 objects **m** of expensive wood, bronze, iron,
18:19 great city! She **m** us all rich from her great wealth.
21:18 The wall was **m** of jasper, and the city was pure
21:21 The twelve gates were **m** of pearls—each gate

MADIAN [KJV] See MIDIAN

MADLY (2) [MAD]

Jer 47: 3 Terrified fathers run **m**, without a backward glance
50:38 with idols, and the people are **m** in love with them.

MADMAN (3) [MAD]

1Sa 18:10 overwhelmed Saul, and he began to rave like a **m**.
21:14 Achish said to his men, "Must you bring me a **m**?
2Co 11:23 I know I sound like a **m**, but I have served him far

MADMANNAH (2)

Jos 15:31 Ziklag, **M**, Sansannah,
1Ch 2:49 She also gave birth to Shaaph (the father of **M**)

MADMEN (1)

Jer 48: 2 The city of **M**, too, will be silenced; the sword will

MADMENAH (1)

Isa 10:31 There go the people of **M**, all fleeing.

MADNESS (4) [MAD]

Dt 28:28 The LORD will strike you with **m**, blindness,
Job 12:17 stripped of good judgment; he drives judges to **m**.
Ecc 7:25 that wickedness is stupid and that foolishness is **m**.
10:13 their conclusions will be wicked **m**.

MADON (2)

Jos 11: 1 King Jobab of **M**; the king of Shimron; the king of
12:19 The king of **M** / The king of Hazor

MAGADAN (1)

Mt 15:39 got into a boat and crossed over to the region of **M**.

MAGBISH (1)

Ezr 2:30 The citizens of **M** | 156

MAGDALA [KJV] See MAGADAN

MAGDALENE (12)

Mt 27:56 Among them were Mary **M**, Mary (the mother of
27:61 Both Mary **M** and the other Mary were sitting
28: 1 Mary **M** and the other Mary went out to see the
Mk 15:40 watching from a distance, including Mary **M**,
15:47 Mary **M** and Mary the mother of Joseph saw where
16: 1 Mary **M** and Salome and Mary the mother of
16: 9 and the first person who saw him was Mary **M**,
Lk 8: 2 Among them were Mary **M**, from whom he had
24:10 The women who went to the tomb were Mary **M**,
Jn 19:25 Mary (the wife of Clopas), and Mary **M**.
20: 1 Mary **M** came to the tomb and found that the stone
20:18 Mary **M** found the disciples and told them, "I have

MAGDIEL (2)

Ge 36:43 **M**, and Iram. These are the names of the clans of
1Ch 1:54 **M**, and Iram. These were the clan leaders of Edom.

MAGGOTS (3)

Ex 16:20 By then it was full of **m** and had a terrible smell.
16:24 food was wholesome and good, without **m** or odor.
Isa 14:11 Now **m** are your sheet and worms your blanket.'

MAGIC (10) [MAGICIAN, MAGICIANS]

Pr 17: 8 A bribe seems to work like **m** for those who give
Isa 2: 6 with foreigners from the East who practice **m**
47: 9 come upon you, despite all your witchcraft and **m**.
Eze 13:18 You tie **m** charms on their wrists and furnish them
with **m** veils.
13:20 I am against all your **m** charms, which you use to
13:21 I will tear off the **m** veils and save my people from
13:23 that you never saw, nor will you practice your **m**.
Ac 8:11 very influential because of the **m** he performed.
19:19 A number of them who had been practicing **m**

MAGICIAN (4) [MAGIC]
Jos 13:22 The Israelites also killed Balaam the **m**, the son of
Da 2:10 has ever asked such a thing of any **m**, enchanter,
4: 9 "I said to him, 'O Belteshazzar, master **m**, I know
Gal 3: 1 What **m** has cast an evil spell on you?

MAGICIANS (16) [MAGIC]
Ge 41: 8 So he called for all the **m** and wise men of Egypt
41:24 I told these dreams to my **m**, but not one of them
Ex 7:11 Then Pharaoh called in his wise men and **m**,
7:22 But again the **m** of Egypt used their secret arts,
8: 7 But the **m** were able to do the same thing with their
8:18 Pharaoh's **m** tried to do the same thing with their
8:19 is the finger of God!" the **m** exclaimed to Pharaoh.
9:11 Even the **m** were unable to stand before Moses,
Isa 3: 3 honorable citizens, advisers, skilled **m**,
Eze 21:21 or Rabbah. He will call his **m** to use divination.
21:29 Your **m** and false prophets have given false visions
Da 1:20 men to be ten times better than that of all the **m**
2: 2 He called in his **m**, enchanters, sorcerers,
2:27 "There are no wise men, enchanters, **m**,
4: 7 When all the **m**, enchanters, astrologers,
5:11 made him chief over all the **m**, enchanters,

MAGISTRATES (2)
Ezr 7:25 to use the wisdom God has given you to appoint **m**
Da 3: 2 governors, advisers, counselors, judges, **m**,

MAGNIFICENCE (1) [MAGNIFICENT, MAGNIFIED]
Eze 31: 9 Because of the **m** I gave this tree, it was the envy

MAGNIFICENT (13) [MAGNIFICENCE]
Ge 49:21 "Naphtali is a deer let loose, / producing **m** fawns.
Nu 13:27 you sent us to see, and it is indeed a **m** country—
14:19 pardon the sins of this people because of your **m**,
1Ch 22: 5 and the Temple of the LORD must be a **m**
2Ch 2: 5 "This will be a **m** Temple because our God is an
2: 9 I am going to build will be very large and **m**.
6:41 place of yours, where your **m** Ark has been placed.
Ps 48: 2 It is **m** in elevation— / the whole earth rejoices to
Isa 63:14 your people, LORD, and gained a **m** reputation."
Jer 22:14 'I will build a **m** palace with huge rooms and many
Zec 11:13 the potters"—this **m** sum at which they valued me!
Mk 13: 2 "These **m** buildings will be so completely
Ac 19:27 this **m** goddess worshiped throughout the province

MAGNIFIED (1) [MAGNIFICENCE]
Isa 42:21 The LORD has **m** his law and made it truly

MAGOG (5)
Ge 10: 2 **M**, Madai, Javan, Tubal, Meshech, and Tiras.
1Ch 1: 5 **M**, Madai, Javan, Tubal, Meshech, and Tiras.
Eze 38: 2 of man, prophesy against Gog of the land of **M**,
39: 6 And I will rain down fire on **M** and on all your
Rev 20: 8 corner of the earth, which are called Gog and **M**.

MAGPIASH (1)
Ne 10:20 **M**, Meshullam, Hezir,

MAHALALEL (8)
Ge 5:12 Kenan was 70 years old, his son **M** was born.
5:13 After the birth of **M**, Kenan lived another 840
5:15 When **M** was 65 years old, his son Jared was born.
5:16 **M** lived 830 years, and he had other sons
1Ch 1: 2 Kenan, **M**, Jared,
Ne 11: 4 son of Amariah, son of Shephatiah, son of **M**,
Lk 3:37 Jared was the son of **M**. / **M** was the son of Kenan.

MAHALATH (3)
Ge 28: 9 His new wife's name was **M**. She was the sister of
2Ch 11:18 Rehoboam married his cousin **M**, the daughter of
11:19 **M** had three sons—Jeush, Shemariah, and Zaham.

MAHALI [KJV] See MAHLI

MAHANAIM (15)
Ge 32: 2 "This is God's camp!" So he named the place **M**.
Jos 13:26 and Betonim, and from **M** to Lo-debar.
13:30 Their territory extended from **M**, including all of
21:38 received Ramoth in Gilead (a city of refuge), **M**,
2Sa 2: 8 had already gone to **M** with Saul's son Ishbosheth.
2:10 became king, and he ruled from **M** for two years.
2:12 led some of Ishbosheth's troops from **M** to Gibeon.
2:29 and they did not stop until they arrived at **M**.
17:24 David soon arrived at **M**. By now, Absalom had
17:27 When David arrived at **M**, he was warmly greeted
18:23 and got to **M** ahead of the man from Cush.
19:32 provided food for the king during his stay in **M**.
1Ki 2: 8 me with a terrible curse as I was fleeing to **M**.
4:14 Ahinadab son of Iddo, in **M**.
1Ch 6:80 of Gad, they received Ramoth in Gilead, **M**,

MAHANEH-DAN (2) [DAN]
Jdg 13:25 And in **M**, which is located between the towns of
18:12 in Judah, which is called **M** to this day.

MAHARAI (3)
2Sa 23:28 Zalmon from Ahoah; / **M** from Netophah;
1Ch 11:30 **M** from Netophah; / Heled son of Baanah from
27:13 **M**, a descendant of Zerah from Netophah,

MAHATH (3)
1Ch 6:35 Zuph, Elkanah, **M**, Amasai,
2Ch 29:12 **M** son of Amasai and Joel son of Azariah.
31:13 Asahel, Jerimoth, Jozabad, Eliel, Ismakiah, **M**,

MAHAVAH (1)
1Ch 11:46 Eliel from **M**; / Jeribai and Joshaviah, the sons of

MAHAZIOTH (2)
1Ch 25: 4 Joshbekashah, Mallothi, Hothir, and **M**.
25:30 The twenty-third lot fell to **M** and twelve of his

MAHER-SHALAL-HASH-BAZ (2)
Isa 8: 1 and clearly write this name on it: **M**."
8: 3 and had a son. And the LORD said, "Call him **M**.

MAHLAH (5)
Nu 26:33 but his daughters' names were **M**, Noah, Hoglah,
27: 1 **M**, Noah, Hoglah, Milcah, and Tirzah.
36:11 **M**, Tirzah, Hoglah, Milcah, and Noah all married
Jos 17: 3 Their names were **M**, Noah, Hoglah, Milcah,
1Ch 7:18 gave birth to Ishhod, Abiezer, and **M**.

MAHLI (13) [MAHLITES]
Ex 6:19 The descendants of Merari included **M** and Mushi.
Nu 3:20 named for two of his descendants, **M** and Mushi.
3:33 were composed of the clans descended from **M**
1Ch 6:19 The descendants of Merari included **M** and Mushi.
6:29 The descendants of Merari were **M**, Libni, Shimei,
6:47 **M**, Mushi, Merari, and Levi.
23:21 The descendants of Merari included **M** and Mushi. The sons of **M** were Eleazar and Kish.
23:23 The three sons of Mushi were **M**, Eder,
24:26 of Merari, the leaders were **M** and Mushi.
24:28 From the descendants of **M**, the leader was
24:30 of Mushi, the leaders were **M**, Eder, and Jerimoth.
Ezr 8:18 He was a very astute man and a descendant of **M**,

MAHLITES (1) [MAHLI]
Nu 26:58 The Libnites, the Hebronites, the **M**, the Mushites,

MAHLON (4)
Ru 1: 2 was Naomi. Their two sons were **M** and Kilion.
1: 5 both **M** and Kilion died. This left Naomi alone,
4: 9 all the property of Elimelech, Kilion, and **M**.
4:10 the Moabite widow of **M**, to be my wife.

MAHOL (1)
1Ki 4:31 and Heman, Calcol, and Darda—the sons of **M**.

MAHSEIAH (2)
Jer 32:12 them to Baruch son of Neriah and grandson of **M**.
51:59 Seraiah son of Neriah and grandson of **M**, when he

MAID (4) [HANDMAID, MAIDEN, MAIDENS, MAIDS]
Ge 29:24 Laban gave Leah a servant, Zilpah, to be her **m**.
29:29 Laban gave Rachel a servant, Bilhah, to be her **m**.
2Ki 5: 2 girl who had been given to Naaman's wife as a **m**.
SS 6:13 "Return, return to us, O **m** of Shulam. Come back,

MAIDEN (1) [MAID]
SS 7: 1 beautiful are your sandaled feet, O queenly **m**.

MAIDENS (2) [MAID]
Ps 148:12 young men and **m**, / old men and children.
Jer 51:22 old people and children, young men and **m**.

MAIDS (6) [MAID]
Est 2: 9 He also assigned her seven **m** specially chosen
2: 9 and her **m** into the best place in the harem.
4: 4 When Queen Esther's **m** and eunuchs came
4:16 night or day. My **m** and I will do the same.
Isa 4: 1 by your name so we won't be mocked as old **m**."
24: 2 **m** and mistresses, buyers and sellers, lenders

MAIL (4)
1Sa 17: 5 and a coat of **m** that weighed 125 pounds.
17:38 his own armor—a bronze helmet and a coat of **m**.
2Ch 26:14 spears, helmets, coats of **m**, bows, and sling stones.
Ne 4:16 guard with spears, shields, bows, and coats of **m**.

MAIN (24)
Ge 10:12 the **m** city of the empire, located between Nineveh
Nu 20:19 Israelites answered, "We will stay on the **m** road.
Dt 2:27 We will stay on the **m** road and won't turn off into
Jos 8: 5 When our **m** army attacks, the men of Ai will
8:13 So they stationed the **m** army north of the city
Jdg 5: 6 in the days of Jael, / people avoided the **m** roads,
20:33 When the **m** group of Israelite warriors reached
1Ki 6:17 The **m** room of the Temple, outside the Most Holy
6:29 and the **m** room were decorated with carvings of
7:50 Most Holy Place and the **m** room of the Temple,
8: 8 from the front entrance of the Temple's **m** room—
2Ch 3: 5 The **m** room of the Temple was paneled with
3:13 and faced out toward the **m** room of the Temple.
4:22 Most Holy Place and the **m** room of the Temple,
5: 9 from the front entrance of the Temple's **m** room—
Pr 1:21 She calls out to the crowds along the **m** street,
Isa 35: 8 And a **m** road will go through that once deserted
Eze 41: 1 the Holy Place, the large **m** room of the Temple,
Am 7: 1 from the fields and as the **m** crop was coming up.
Jn 12:18 That was the **m** reason so many went out to meet
Heb 8: 1 Here is the **m** point: Our High Priest sat down in
Rev 11: 8 And their bodies will lie in the **m** street of
21:21 And the **m** street was pure gold, as clear as glass.
22: 2 coursing down the center of the **m** street. On each

MAINLAND (3) [LAND]
Eze 26: 6 and its **m** villages will be destroyed by the sword.
26: 8 First he will destroy your **m** villages. Then he will
Ac 27: 4 north of Cyprus between the island and the **m**.

MAINSAIL [KJV] See FORESAIL

MAINTAIN (9) [MAINTAINED, MAINTAINING, MAINTENANCE]
Nu 3: 8 They will also **m** all the furnishings of the sacred
1Ch 26:27 had gained in battle to **m** the house of the LORD.
2Ch 24: 6 in order to **m** the Tabernacle of the Covenant."
Job 2: 9 to him, "Are you still trying to **m** your integrity?
27: 6 I will **m** my innocence without wavering.
Ps 140:12 they persecute; / he will **m** the rights of the poor.
Eze 17:14 with Babylon could Israel **m** her national identity.
Da 11:20 who sent a tax collector to **m** the royal splendor,
Ac 24:16 I always try to **m** a clear conscience before God

MAINTAINED (2) [MAINTAIN]
Nu 31:47 and gave them to the Levites who **m** the LORD's
Job 2: 3 And he has **m** his integrity, even though you

MAINTAINING (1) [MAINTAIN]
Nu 31:30 Give this share to the Levites in charge of **m** the

MAINTENANCE (3) [MAINTAIN]
Nu 18: 4 for the care and **m** of the Tabernacle,
Eze 40:45 gate is for the priests who supervise the Temple **m**.
44:14 and are relegated to doing **m** work and helping the

MAJESTIC (15) [MAJESTY]
Nu 23:24 rise up like a lioness; / like a **m** lion they stand.
Dt 33:26 to help you, / across the skies in **m** splendor.
Job 39:20 like a locust? Its **m** snorting is something to hear!
Ps 45: 3 O mighty warrior! / You are so glorious, so **m**!
68:15 The **m** mountains of Bashan / stretch high into the
76: 4 You are glorious and more **m** / than the everlasting
145: 5 I will meditate on your **m**, glorious splendor
SS 6: 4 You are as **m** as an army with banners!
6:10 bright as the sun, as **m** as an army with banners?'
7: 5 Your head is as **m** as Mount Carmel, and the sheen
Isa 30:30 And the LORD will make his **m** voice heard.
53: 2 was nothing beautiful or **m** about his appearance,
Heb 1: 3 of honor at the right hand of the **m** God of heaven.
2Pe 1:16 We have seen his **m** splendor with our own eyes.
1:17 **m** voice called down from heaven, "This is my

MAJESTY (60) [MAJESTIC]
Ex 15: 7 In the greatness of your **m**, / you overthrew those
Dt 33:17 Joseph has the strength and **m** of a young bull;
1Ch 16:27 Honor and **m** surround him; / strength and beauty
29:11 the power, the glory, the victory, and the **m**.
Ne 2: 5 "If it please Your **M** and if you are pleased with
2: 7 I also said to the king, "If it please Your **M**,
Est 3: 9 If it please Your **M**, issue a decree that they be
5: 4 "If it please Your **M**, let the king and Haman
5: 8 If Your **M** is pleased with me and wants to grant
7: 3 "If Your **M** is pleased with me and wants to grant
8: 5 "If Your **M** is pleased with me and if he thinks it
9:13 And Esther said, "If it please Your **M**,
Job 13:11 Doesn't his **m** strike terror into your heart?
31:23 For if the **m** of God opposes me, what hope is
37: 4 of the thunder—the tremendous voice of his **m**.
40:10 put on your robes of state, your **m** and splendor.
Ps 8: 1 our Lord, the **m** of your name fills the earth!
8: 9 our Lord, the **m** of your name fills the earth!
21: 5 and you have clothed him with splendor and **m**.
29: 4 is powerful; / the voice of the LORD is full of **m**.
45: 4 In your **m**, ride out to victory, / defending truth,
68:34 about God's power. / His **m** shines down on Israel;
93: 1 He is robed in **m**. / Indeed, the LORD is robed in **m** and armed with strength.
96: 6 Honor and **m** surround him; / strength and beauty
99: 2 The LORD sits in **m** in Jerusalem,
104: 1 you are! / You are robed with honor and with **m**;
111: 3 Everything he does reveals his glory and **m**.
145:12 and about the **m** and glory of your reign.
Isa 2:10 the terror of the LORD and the glory of his **m**.
2:19 the terror of the LORD and the glory of his **m**.
2:21 and the glory of his **m** as he rises to shake the
24:14 Those in the west will praise the LORD's **m**.
26:10 and take no notice of the LORD's **m**.
La 1: 6 All the beauty and **m** of Jerusalem are gone.
Da 2: 7 They said again, "Please, Your **M**. Tell us the
2:10 "There isn't a man alive who can tell Your **M** his
2:25 will tell Your **M** the meaning of your dream!"
2:29 "While Your **M** was sleeping, you dreamed about
2:31 "Your **M**, in your vision you saw in front of you a
2:36 the dream; now I will tell Your **M** what it means.
2:37 Your **M**, you are a king over many kings. The God
2:45 "The great God has shown Your **M** what will

3:12 They have defied Your **M** by refusing to serve
3:17 He will rescue us from your power, Your **M**.
3:18 Your **M** can be sure that we will never serve your
3:24 "Yes," they said, "we did indeed, Your **M**."
4:22 That tree, Your **M**, is you. For you have grown
4:24 "This is what the dream means, Your **M**, and what
5:18 Your **M**, the Most High God gave sovereignty,
5:18 **m**, glory, and honor to your predecessor,
6: 7 **M** should make a law that will be strictly enforced.
6: 7 to anyone, divine or human—except to Your **M**—
6: 8 And let Your **M** issue and sign this law so it cannot
6:12 to anyone, divine or human—except to Your **M**—
6:15 "Your **M** knows that according to the law of the
6:22 his sight. And I have not wronged you, Your **M**."
Mic 5: 4 in the **m** of the name of the LORD his God.
Ac 26:13 About noon, Your **M**, a light from heaven brighter
Jude 1:25 Yes, glory, **m**, power, and authority belong to him,

MAJOR (2) [MAJORITY]

Ac 16:12 a **m** city of the district of Macedonia and a Roman
1Co 7:29 so husbands should not let marriage be their **m**

MAJORITY (1) [MAJOR]

Ex 23: 2 swayed in your testimony by the opinion of the **m**.

MAKAZ (1)

1Ki 4: 9 Ben-deker, in **M**, Shaalbim, Beth-shemesh,

MAKE (791) [HANDMADE, MADE, MAKER, MAKERS, MAKES, MAKING, MAN-MADE, PEACEMAKER, PEACEMAKERS]

Ge 1:26 Then God said, "Let us **m** people in our image,
2:18 I will **m** a companion who will help him."
3: 6 so fresh and delicious, and it would **m** her so wise!
6:14 "**M** a boat from resinous wood and seal it with tar,
6:15 **M** it 450 feet long, 75 feet wide, and 45 feet high.
11: 3 "let's **m** great piles of burnt brick and collect
12: 2 I will bless you and **m** you famous, and I will **m**
you a blessing to others.
16: 5 The LORD will **m** you pay for doing this to me!"
17: 2 I will **m** a covenant with you, by which I will
guarantee to **m** you into a mighty
17: 4 I will **m** you the father of not just one nation,
21:13 But I will **m** a nation of the descendants of Hagar's
21:18 for I will **m** a great nation from his descendants."
24:40 angel with you and will **m** your mission successful.
24:42 if you are planning to **m** my mission a success,
27:21 I want to touch you to **m** sure you really are
28:21 to my father, then I will **m** the LORD my God.
30:33 This will **m** it easy for you to see whether or not I
30:37 and peeled off strips of the bark to **m** white streaks
31:44 and we will **m** a peace treaty, you and I,
31:49 "May the LORD keep watch between us to **m**
39:17 you've had around here tried to **m** a fool of me,"
41:32 and that he will **m** these events happen soon.
48: 4 He said to me, 'I will **m** you a multitude of nations,
48:20 'May God **m** you as prosperous as Ephraim
Ex 1:13 and decided to **m** their slavery more bitter still.
1:14 forcing them to **m** bricks and mortar and to work
2:12 After looking around to **m** sure no one was
4:21 But I will **m** him stubborn so he will not let the
5: 9 Load them down with more work. **M** them sweat!
5:16 but we are still told to **m** as many bricks as before.
6: 7 I will **m** you my own special people, and I will be
7: 1 I will **m** you seem like God to Pharaoh.
8:23 I will **m** a clear distinction between your people
9: 4 But the LORD will again **m** a distinction between
10: 1 "Return to Pharaoh and again **m** your demands.
13:13 But if you decide not to **m** the exchange,
14:11 graves for us in Egypt? Why did you **m** us leave?
15:26 then I will not **m** you suffer the diseases I sent on
20: 4 "Do not **m** idols of any kind, whether in the shape
20:23 you must not **m** or worship idols of silver or gold.
20:24 "The altars you **m** for me must be simple altars of
20:25 a tool, for that would **m** them unfit for holy use.
22:29 "You must **m** the necessary payment for
23:32 "**M** no treaties with them and have nothing to do
25: 9 You must **m** this Tabernacle and its furnishings
25:10 "**M** an Ark of acacia wood—a sacred chest 3-3/4
25:13 **M** poles from acacia wood, and overlay them with
25:17 "Then **m** the Ark's cover—the place of
25:18 Then use hammered gold to **m** two cherubim,
25:23 "Then **m** a table of acacia wood, 3 feet long,
25:26 **M** four gold rings, and put the rings at the four
25:28 **M** these poles from acacia wood and overlay them
25:29 And **m** gold plates and dishes, as well as pitchers
25:31 "**M** a lampstand of pure, hammered gold.
25:37 Then **m** the seven lamps for the lampstand, and set
25:40 "Be sure that you **m** everything according to the
26: 1 "**M** the Tabernacle from ten sheets of fine linen.
26: 6 Then **m** fifty gold clasps to fasten the loops of the
26: 7 "**M** heavy sheets of cloth from goat hair to cover
26:26 "**M** crossbars of acacia wood to run across the
26:27 Also **m** five crossbars for the rear of the
26:29 and **m** gold rings to support the crossbars.
26:36 "**M** another curtain from fine linen for the
27: 1 **m** a square altar 7-1/2 feet wide, 7-1/2 feet long,
27: 2 **M** a horn at each of the four corners of the altar
27: 4 **M** a bronze grating, with a metal ring at each
27: 6 For moving the altar, **m** poles from acacia wood,
27: 9 "Then **m** a courtyard for the Tabernacle,
27:16 to the courtyard, **m** a curtain that is 30 feet long.
28: 2 **M** special clothing for Aaron to show his
28: 3 **m** the garments that will set Aaron apart from
28: 4 They are to **m** a chestpiece, an ephod, a robe,
28: 4 They will also **m** special garments for Aaron's
28:15 **m** a chestpiece that will be used to determine
28:22 to the ephod, **m** braided cords of pure gold.
28:23 Then **m** two gold rings and attach them to the top
28:26 Then **m** two more gold rings, and attach them to
28:27 And **m** two more gold rings and attach them to the
28:31 "**M** the robe of the ephod entirely of blue cloth,
28:33 **M** pomegranates out of blue, purple, and scarlet
28:36 "Next **m** a medallion of pure gold.
28:39 linen as well. Also **m** him an embroidered sash.
28:40 "Then for Aaron's sons, **m** tunics, sashes,
28:42 Also **m** linen underclothes for them, to be worn
29: 2 fine wheat flour and no yeast, **m** loaves of bread,
29:36 Afterward **m** an offering to cleanse the altar.
29:36 atonement for it; **m** it holy by anointing it with oil.
29:37 **M** atonement for the altar every day for seven
29:44 I will **m** the Tabernacle and the altar most holy,
30: 1 "Then **m** a small altar out of acacia wood for
30:15 When this offering is given to the LORD to **m**
30:16 and it will **m** atonement for your lives."
30:18 "**M** a large bronze washbasin with a bronze
30:29 Sanctify them to **m** them entirely holy. After this,
30:32 and you must never **m** any of it for yourselves.
30:37 Never **m** this incense for yourselves. It is reserved
30:38 Those who **m** it for their own enjoyment will be
31: 6 can **m** all the things I have instructed you to **m**:
32: 1 they said, "**m** us some gods who can lead us.
32:10 Then I will **m** you, Moses, into a great nation
32:13 'I will **m** your descendants as numerous as the
32:21 "How did they ever **m** you bring such terrible sin
32:23 They said to me, '**M** us some gods to lead us,
33:19 "I will **m** all my goodness pass before you,
34:10 This is the covenant I am going to **m** with you.
34:12 "Be very careful never to **m** treaties with the
34:15 "Do not **m** treaties of any kind with the people
34:15 If you **m** peace with them, they will invite you to
34:17 You must **m** no gods for yourselves at all.
34:20 But if you decide not to **m** the exchange, you must
36:10 Five of these sheets were joined together to **m** one
36:16 joined five of these sheets together to **m** one set,
36:16 and the six remaining sheets were joined to **m** a
38:28 was used to **m** the rods and hooks and to overlay
38:31 Bronze was also used to **m** the bases for the posts
40: 9 and on all its furnishings to **m** them holy.
40:11 large washbasin and its pedestal to **m** them holy.
Lev 4:20 the priest will **m** atonement for the people,
4:26 the priest will **m** atonement for the leader's sin,
4:31 In this way, the priest will **m** atonement for them,
4:35 In this way, the priest will **m** atonement for them,
5: 4 "Or if they **m** a rash vow of any kind, whether its
5: 6 their sin, and the priest will **m** atonement for them.
5:10 the priest will **m** atonement for those who are
5:13 the priest will **m** atonement for those who are
5:16 then **m** restitution for whatever holy things they
5:16 he will **m** atonement for them with the ram
5:18 the priest will **m** atonement for those who are
6: 7 then **m** atonement for them before the LORD,
6:30 **m** atonement in the Holy Place for the people's
8:34 by the LORD in order to **m** atonement for you.
9: 7 and your whole burnt offering to **m** atonement for
9: 7 Then present the offerings to **m** atonement for the
10:12 **M** sure there is no yeast in it, and eat it beside the
11:24 "The following creatures **m** you ceremonially
12: 7 them to the LORD and **m** atonement for her.
13: 5 On the seventh day the priest will **m** another
13:15 The priest must **m** this pronouncement as soon as
14:18 the priest will **m** atonement before the LORD for
14:20 the priest will **m** atonement for the person being
14:29 the priest will **m** atonement for the person being
14:31 the priest will **m** atonement before the LORD for
14:53 this way, the priest will **m** atonement for the house,
15:15 the priest will **m** atonement for the man before the
15:30 the priest will **m** atonement for her before the
16: 6 to **m** atonement for himself and his family.
16:10 the wilderness, it will **m** atonement for the people.
16:16 he will **m** atonement for the Most Holy Place,
16:17 goes in to **m** atonement for the Most Holy Place.
16:18 "Then Aaron will go out to **m** atonement for the
16:24 he will **m** atonement for himself and for the
16:27 the Most Holy Place to **m** atonement for Israel,
16:33 and **m** atonement for the Most Holy Place,
16:34 to **m** atonement for the Israelites once each year."
17:11 the blood so you can **m** atonement for your sins.
19: 4 trust in idols or **m** gods of metal for yourselves.
19:22 then **m** atonement for him before the LORD with
20:25 therefore **m** a distinction between ceremonially
21: 8 because I, the LORD, am holy, and I **m** you holy.
23:38 the offerings you **m** to accompany your vows,
24:21 "Whoever kills an animal must **m** full restitution,
25:14 "When you **m** an agreement with a neighbor to
26: 1 "Do not **m** idols or set up carved images,
26:10 the previous year to **m** room for each new harvest.
26:31 I will **m** your cities desolate and destroy your
26:34 Then at last the land will **m** up for its missed
27: 2 If you **m** a special vow to dedicate someone to the
27: 8 If you desire to **m** such a vow but cannot afford to
Nu 5: 7 and **m** full restitution for what they have done,
5:22 the curse enter your body and **m** you infertile."
5:24 He will then **m** the woman drink the bitter water,
6:11 he will **m** atonement for the guilt they incurred
6:17 The priest must also **m** the prescribed grain
8: 6 people of Israel and **m** them ceremonially clean.
8:12 a burnt offering, to **m** atonement for the Levites.
8:19 behalf of the Israelites and **m** atonement for them
10: 2 "**M** two trumpets of beaten silver to be used for
11:28 protested, "Moses, my master, **m** them stop!"
14:12 Then I will **m** you into a nation far greater
15:25 With it the priest will **m** atonement for the whole
15:28 The priest will **m** atonement for the guilty person
15:38 'Throughout the generations to come you must **m**
16:46 and carry it quickly among the people to **m**
20: 5 Why did you **m** us leave Egypt and bring us here
21: 8 "**M** a replica of a poisonous snake and attach it to
26:55 **M** sure you assign the land by lot, and define the
28:22 as a sin offering, to **m** atonement for yourselves.
28:30 offer one male goat to **m** atonement for yourselves.
29: 5 as a sin offering, to **m** atonement for yourselves.
31:26 and the family leaders of each tribe are to **m** a list
31:50 This will **m** atonement for our lives before the
Dt 1:17 When you **m** decisions, never favor those who are
2:25 Beginning today I will **m** all people throughout the
4:23 You will break it if you **m** idols of any shape
5: 3 The LORD did not **m** this covenant long ago with
5: 8 " 'Do not **m** idols of any kind, whether in the
7: 2 **M** no treaties with them and show them no mercy.
7:13 and bless you and **m** you into a great nation.
9:14 Then I will **m** a mighty nation of your descendants,
10: 1 and **m** a sacred chest of wood to keep them in.
13:17 have compassion on you and **m** you a great nation,
15: 9 If you refuse to **m** the loan and the needy person
17:10 The decision they **m** at the place the LORD
20:12 But if they refuse to **m** peace and prepare to fight,
20:20 Use them to **m** the equipment you need to besiege
23:19 "Do not charge interest on the loans you **m** to a
23:21 "When you **m** a vow to the LORD your God,
24: 6 as a pledge, for the owner uses it to **m** a living.
26:19 he will **m** you greater than any other nation.
28:13 the LORD will **m** you the head and not the tail,
28:68 a journey I promised you would never again **m**.
29: 1 **m** with the Israelites while they were in the land of
30: 5 He will **m** you even more prosperous
30: 9 The LORD your God will **m** you successful in
30:19 on heaven and earth to witness the choice you **m**.
31:29 for you will **m** the LORD very angry by doing
32:42 I will **m** my arrows drunk with blood, / and my
Jos 3: 4 and the Ark. **M** sure you don't come any closer."
3: 7 "Today I will begin to **m** you great in the eyes of
5: 2 "Use knives of flint to **m** the Israelites a
7:19 **M** your confession and tell me what you have
7:22 So Joshua sent some men to **m** a search. They ran
8:31 "**M** me an altar from stones that are uncut
9: 6 land to ask you to **m** a peace treaty with us."
9: 7 For if you do, we cannot **m** a treaty with you."
9:21 But we will **m** them chop the wood and carry the
22:25 And your descendants may **m** our descendants stop
23: 7 **M** sure you do not associate with the other people
Jdg 2: 2 you were not to **m** any covenants with the people
6:39 be angry with me, but let me **m** one more request.
9:15 'If you truly want to **m** me your king, come
9:16 "Now **m** sure you have acted honorably and in
11: 8 we will **m** you ruler over all the people of Gilead."
11: 9 will you really **m** me ruler over all the people?"
11:25 Did he try to **m** a case against Israel for disputed
11:26 But now after three hundred years you **m** an issue
14:15 Did you invite us to this party just to **m** us poor?"
Ru 4:11 May the LORD **m** the woman who is now
1Sa 6: 4 five rulers, **m** five gold tumors and five gold rats,
6: 5 **M** these things to show honor to the God of Israel.
6: 7 **M** sure the cows have never been yoked to a cart.
8:11 into his army and **m** them run before his chariots.
8:12 while others will **m** his weapons and chariot
8:13 them to cook and bake and **m** perfumes for him.
11: 1 "**M** a treaty with us, and we will be your
12: 3 and I will **m** right whatever I have done wrong."
12:20 but **m** sure now that you worship the LORD with
13:19 wouldn't allow them for fear they would **m** swords
16: 2 "and say that you have come to **m** a sacrifice to
16: 7 The LORD doesn't **m** decisions the way you do!
20:23 And may the LORD **m** us keep our promises to
22: 7 Has he promised to **m** you commanders in his
27:10 "Where did you **m** your raid today?"
28: 2 "I will **m** you my personal bodyguard for life."
2Sa 3:12 to David, saying, "Let's **m** an agreement,
3:17 "you have wanted to **m** David your king.
3:21 They will **m** a covenant with you to **m** you their
7: 9 Now I will **m** your name famous throughout the
7:12 your descendants, and I will **m** his kingdom strong.
18: 3 it will **m** no difference to Absalom's troops;
19:42 Why should this **m** you angry? We have charged
21: 3 asked them, "What can I do for you to **m** amends?
1Ki 1: 5 decided to **m** himself king in place of his aged
1:37 and may he **m** Solomon's reign even greater than
1:47 'May your God **m** Solomon's fame even greater
2: 7 **M** them permanent guests of the king, for they
2: 9 But that oath does not **m** him innocent. You are a
2:13 "Have you come to **m** trouble?" she asked him.
2:20 "I have one small request to **m** of you," she said.
2:42 "Didn't I **m** you swear by the LORD and warn
7:40 assigned him to **m** for the Temple of the LORD:
8:29 May you always hear the prayers I **m** toward this
8:50 against you. **M** their captors merciful to them,
9: 7 I will **m** Israel an object of mockery and ridicule
10:12 The king used the almug wood to **m** railings for
12: 1 where all Israel had gathered to **m** him king.
12:27 They will kill me and **m** him their king instead."
16: 2 "I lifted you out of the dust to **m** you ruler of my
16:21 Half the people tried to **m** Tibni son of Ginath their
2Ki 3:18 for he will **m** you victorious over the army of
4:10 Let's **m** a little room for him on the roof
4:38 on a large kettle and **m** some stew for these men."
6:18 Elisha prayed, "O LORD, please **m** them blind."
8: 5 the mother of the boy walked in to **m** her appeal to
10: 5 We will not **m** anyone king; do whatever you think

10:23 "**M** sure that only those who worship Baal are
18:22 and **m** everyone in Judah worship only at the altar
18:31 **M** peace with me—open the gates and come out.
19: 7 Then I will **m** him want to return to his land,
19:28 and my bridle in your mouth. / I will **m** you return
19:31 The passion of the LORD Almighty will **m** this
20: 7 "**M** an ointment from figs and spread it over the
20:10 Hezekiah replied. "**M** it go backward instead."
1Ch 11:10 all Israel, they determined to **m** David their king,
17: 8 Now I will **m** your name famous throughout the
17:11 one of your sons, and I will **m** his kingdom strong.
27:23 because the LORD had promised to **m** the
28: 4 the LORD was pleased to **m** me king over all
28: 7 as he does now, I will **m** his kingdom last forever.'
28:14 and silver should be used to **m** the necessary items.
29:18 **m** your people always want to obey you.
2Ch 4:11 had assigned him to **m** for the Temple of God:
6:20 May you always hear the prayers I **m** toward this
7:20 I will **m** it a spectacle of contempt among the
9:11 The king used the almug wood to **m** steps for the
10: 1 where all Israel had gathered to **m** him king.
14: 6 No one tried to **m** war against him at this time,
24:14 It was used to **m** utensils for the Temple of the
28:10 And now you are planning to **m** slaves of these
29:10 But now I will **m** a covenant with the LORD,
29:11 the people in worship and **m** offerings to him."
29:24 and sprinkled their blood on the altar to **m**
32:12 altar at the Temple and to **m** sacrifices on it alone.
34:32 and the people of Benjamin to **m** a similar pledge.
Ezr 9: 2 To **m** matters worse, the officials and leaders are
10: 3 Let us now **m** a covenant with our God to divorce
Ne 2: 8 I will need it to **m** beams for the gates of the
6:13 and **m** me sin by following his suggestion.
8:15 They were to use these branches to **m** shelters in
10:33 and for the sin offerings to **m** atonement for Israel.
13:13 and it was their job to **m** honest distributions to
Est 9: 2 But no one could **m** a stand against them,
Job 7:17 mere mortals, that you should **m** so much of us?
8:20 of integrity, nor will he **m** evildoers prosper.
9:30 and cleanse my hands with lye to **m** them
9:34 The mediator could **m** God stop beating me,
11: 3 mock God, shouldn't someone **m** you ashamed?
17:13 I might go to the grave and **m** my bed in darkness.
18: 4 to be abandoned? Will it **m** rocks fall from a cliff?
21:12 and harp. They **m** merry to the sound of the flute.
27: 2 "I **m** this vow by the living God, who has taken
33: 5 if you can; **m** your case and take your stand.
33: 7 I am not some great person to **m** you nervous
33:11 feet in the stocks and watches every move I **m**.'
33:24 Do not **m** him die, for I have found a ransom for
34:29 When he is quiet, who can **m** trouble? But when he
37:19 We are too ignorant to **m** our own arguments.
38:34 "Can you shout to the clouds and **m** it rain?
38:35 Can you **m** lightning appear and cause it to strike
39:27 that the eagle rises to the heights to **m** its nest?
41: 4 work for you? Can you **m** it be your slave for life?
41: 5 Can you **m** it a pet like a bird, or give it to your
41:15 The overlapping scales on its back **m** a shield.
41:28 Arrows cannot **m** it flee. Stones shot from a sling
Ps 4: 2 How long will you **m** these groundless
7:16 They **m** trouble, / but it backfires on them.
9:20 **M** them tremble in fear, O LORD. / Let them
19: 2 to speak; / night after night they **m** him known.
33: 2 **m** music for him on the ten-stringed harp.
35: 6 **M** their path dark and slippery, / with the angel of
36: 4 never good. / They **m** no attempt to turn from evil.
37: 6 He will **m** your innocence as clear as the dawn,
38:12 lay traps for me; / they **m** plans to ruin me.
38:14 I choose to hear nothing, / and I **m** no reply.
41:10 on me. / **M** me well again, so I can pay them back!
44:10 You **m** us retreat from our enemies / and allow
45:16 You will **m** them rulers over many lands.
48: 8 It is the city of our God; / he will **m** it safe forever.
51:12 of your salvation, / and **m** me willing to obey you.
58: 7 **M** their weapons useless in their hands.
62:10 don't **m** it the center of your life.
66:14 yes, the sacred vows you heard me **m** / when I was
69:11 in sackcloth to show sorrow, / they **m** fun of me.
73:20 O Lord, / you will **m** them vanish from this life.
74:17 of the earth, / and you **m** both summer and winter.
76:11 **M** vows to the LORD your God, and fulfill them.
80: 3 **M** your face shine down upon us. / Only then will
80: 7 **M** your face shine down upon us. / Only then will
80:19 **M** your face shine down upon us. / Only then will
83:17 **M** them failures in everything they do,
89:21 I will steady him, / and I will **m** him strong.
89:27 I will **m** him my firstborn son, / the mightiest king
90:12 Teach us to **m** the most of our time, / so that we
90:17 and **m** our efforts successful. / Yes, **m** our efforts
91: 9 If you **m** the LORD your refuge, / if you **m** the Most High your shelter,
94:23 God will **m** the sins of evil people fall back upon
98: 6 **M** a joyful symphony before the LORD,
104: 3 You **m** the clouds your chariots; / you ride upon
104:10 You **m** the springs pour water into ravines,
104:15 wine to **m** them glad, / olive oil as lotion for their
104:17 There the birds **m** their nests, / and the storks **m** their homes in the firs.
109:29 **M** their humiliation obvious to all; / clothe my
115: 8 And those who **m** them are just like them, / as are
119:35 **M** me walk along the path of your commands,
119:98 Your commands **m** me wiser than my enemies,
122: 4 the LORD's people— / **m** their pilgrimage here.
132:15 I will **m** this city prosperous / and satisfy its poor
132:16 I will **m** its priests the agents of salvation;
135:18 And those who **m** them are just like them, / as are
137: 6 if I don't **m** Jerusalem my highest joy.

Pr 1: 4 These proverbs will **m** the simpleminded clever.
1:23 out the spirit of wisdom upon you and **m** you wise.
3:30 Don't **m** accusations against someone who hasn't
6: 7 have no prince, governor, or ruler to **m** them work,
7: 4 **m** insight a beloved member of your family.
8:15 Because of me, kings reign, and rulers **m** just laws.
8:16 with my help, and nobles **m** righteous judgments.
11:11 Upright citizens bless a city and **m** it prosper,
12:18 Some people **m** cutting remarks, but the words of
12:23 Wise people don't **m** a show of their knowledge,
12:27 but the diligent **m** use of everything they find.
14: 9 Fools **m** fun of guilt, but the godly acknowledge it
14:29 those with a hasty temper will **m** mistakes.
16: 9 We can **m** our plans, but the LORD determines
18:19 It's harder to **m** amends with an offended friend
19:21 You can **m** many plans, but the LORD's purpose
20:25 It is dangerous to **m** a rash promise to God before
25:16 Don't eat too much of it, or it will **m** you sick!
30:21 There are three things that **m** the earth tremble—
30:26 but they **m** their homes among the rocky cliffs.
Ecc 5: 2 And don't **m** rash promises to God, for he is in
5: 4 So when you **m** a promise to God, don't delay in
5: 4 in fools. Keep all the promises you **m** to him.
5: 6 That would **m** God angry, and he might wipe out
10: 5 world go by. Kings and rulers **m** a grave mistake
10:20 Never **m** light of the king, even in your thoughts.
10:20 And don't **m** fun of a rich man, either.
SS 1:11 We will **m** earrings of gold for you and beads of
5: 8 "**M** this promise to me, O women of Jerusalem!
Isa 1:18 I can **m** you as clean as freshly fallen snow.
1:18 as red as crimson, I can **m** you as white as wool.
3:17 Yes, the LORD will **m** them bald for all to see!
5: 6 I will **m** it a wild place. / I will not prune the vines
7:11 you like, and **m** it as difficult as you want."
8: 1 "**M** a large signboard and clearly write this name
11:15 The LORD will **m** a dry path through the Red
11:16 He will **m** a highway from Assyria for the remnant
12: 5 **M** known his praise around the world.
13:22 and jackals will **m** their dens in its palaces.
14:23 I will **m** Babylon into a desolate land, a place of
16: 8 The wine from those vineyards used to **m** the
19: 2 "I will **m** the Egyptians fight against each other—
19:21 In that day the LORD will **m** himself known to
19:21 They will **m** promises to the LORD and keep
20: 4 He will **m** them walk naked and barefoot,
24: 1 to destroy the earth and **m** it a vast wasteland.
26:10 Your kindness to the wicked does not **m** them do
28: 7 They **m** stupid mistakes as they carry out their
29:16 say to the one who made it, "He didn't **m** us"?
29:21 Those who **m** the innocent guilty by their false
30: 1 "You **m** plans that are contrary to my will.
30:17 of you. Five of them will **m** all of you flee.
30:30 And the LORD will **m** his majestic voice heard.
33: 5 he will **m** Jerusalem his home of justice
34: 6 of Bozrah. He will **m** a mighty slaughter in Edom.
34:15 There the owl will **m** her nest and lay her eggs.
34:16 promised this. His Spirit will **m** it all come true.
36: 7 and **m** everyone in Judah worship only at the altar
36:16 **M** peace with me—open the gates and come out.
37: 7 I myself will **m** sure that the king will receive a
37: 7 Then I will **m** him want to return to his land,
37:29 and my bridle in your mouth. / I will **m** you return
37:32 The passion of the LORD Almighty will **m** this
38:19 Each generation can **m** known your faithfulness to
38:21 "**M** an ointment from figs and spread it over the
40: 3 "**M** a highway for the LORD through the
40: 3 **M** a straight, smooth road through the desert for
40:16 All Lebanon's sacrificial animals would not **m** an
41: 7 The craftsmen rush to **m** new idols. The carver
41:21 "Can your idols **m** such claims as these? Let them
42:16 I will **m** the darkness bright before them
43:19 I will **m** a pathway through the wilderness for my
43:20 Yes, I will **m** springs in the desert, so that my
44:10 Who but a fool would **m** his own god—an idol that
44:11 mere humans—who claim they can **m** a god.
44:12 The blacksmith stands at his forge to **m** a sharp
44:15 he uses part of the wood to **m** a fire to warm
45:10 was I born? Why did you **m** me this way?' "
45:16 All who **m** idols will be humiliated and disgraced.
46: 6 and gold and hire a craftsman to **m** a god from it.
49: 6 I will **m** you a light to the Gentiles, and you will
49:11 And I will **m** my mountains into level paths for
50: 2 the reason! For I can speak to the sea and **m** it dry!
51: 3 comfort Israel again and **m** her deserts blossom.
53:11 my righteous servant will **m** it possible for many to
54:11 and **m** the walls of your houses from precious
54:12 I will **m** your towers of sparkling rubies and your
55: 3 I am ready to **m** an everlasting covenant with you.
57: 6 are your inheritance. Does all this **m** me happy?
58: 2 They love to **m** a show of coming to me and asking
60: 7 my altars. In that day I will **m** my Temple glorious.
60:15 will be a joy to all generations, for I will **m** you so.
61: 8 and **m** an everlasting covenant with them.
64: 2 to boil, your coming would **m** the nations tremble.
Jer 1:17 or I will **m** you look foolish in front of them.
2:22 No amount of soap or lye can **m** you clean.
5:20 "**M** this announcement to Israel and to Judah:
7:18 and **m** cakes to offer to the Queen of Heaven.
9:11 "I will **m** Jerusalem into a heap of ruins,"
10: 9 materials to skillful craftsmen who **m** their idols.
10:11 who did not **m** the heavens and earth,
10:14 They **m** idols, but the idols will disgrace their
13:13 I will **m** everyone in this land so confused that they
15: 4 I will **m** my people an object of horror to all the
15:20 but I will **m** you as secure as a fortified wall.
16:20 Can people **m** their own god? The gods they **m** are not real gods at all!"

17:22 do your work on the Sabbath, but **m** it a holy day.
21: 4 I will **m** your weapons useless against the king of
22:15 "But a beautiful palace does not **m** a great king!
23:40 And I will **m** you an object of ridicule, and your
24: 9 I will **m** them an object of horror and evil to every
25: 6 Do not **m** me angry by worshiping the idols you
25: 9 and **m** you an object of horror and contempt
25:12 I will **m** the country of the Babylonians an
25:15 and **m** all the nations to whom I send you drink
26: 2 and **m** an announcement to the people who have
26: 6 And I will **m** Jerusalem an object of cursing in
27: 2 The LORD said to me, "**M** a yoke, and fasten it
29:17 disease upon them and **m** them like rotting figs—
29:18 I will **m** them an object of damnation, horror,
29:22 'May the LORD **m** you like Zedekiah and Ahab,
30:10 in their own land, and no one will **m** them afraid.
30:19 and **m** of them a great and honored nation.
31:31 "when I will **m** a new covenant with the people of
31:33 "But this is the new covenant I will **m** with the
32:40 "And I will **m** an everlasting covenant with them,
44: 8 and **m** yourselves an object of cursing
46:27 and quiet, and nothing will **m** them afraid.
48:27 Did you not **m** Israel the object of your ridicule?
51:17 They **m** idols, but the idols will disgrace their
51:39 I will **m** them drink until they fall asleep,
51:57 "I will **m** drunk her officials, wise men, rulers,
Eze 3:26 And I will **m** your tongue stick to the roof of your
4: 9 Use this food to **m** bread for yourself during the
6:14 and **m** their cities desolate from the wilderness in
7:20 and used it to **m** vile and detestable idols.
7:20 That is why I will **m** all their wealth disgusting to
12: 3 **M** your preparations in broad daylight
14: 8 such people and **m** a terrible example of them,
15: 8 And I will **m** the land desolate because my people
16:16 You used the lovely things I gave you to **m** shrines
16:52 In comparison, you **m** your sisters seem innocent!
16:54 for your sins **m** them feel good in comparison.
16:61 I will **m** your sisters, Samaria and Sodom, to be
20: 4 **M** them realize how loathsome the actions of their
21: 4 I will **m** a clean sweep throughout the land from
21:19 **m** a map and trace two routes on it for the sword of
22: 4 I will **m** you an object of mockery throughout the
24:10 on the wood! Let the fire roar to **m** the pot boil.
25:13 I will **m** a wasteland of everything from Teman to
26: 4 I will scrape away its soil and **m** it a bare rock!
26:14 I will **m** your island a bare rock, a place for
26:19 LORD says: I will **m** Tyre an uninhabited ruin.
27: 5 They took a cedar from Lebanon to **m** a mast for
29:12 I will **m** Egypt desolate, and it will be surrounded
30:11 They will **m** war against Egypt until slaughtered
30:21 Neither has it been bound up with a splint to **m** it
30:22 and I will **m** his sword clatter to the ground.
34:25 "I will **m** a covenant of peace with them and drive
34:28 will live in safety, and no one will **m** them afraid.
35: 4 I will demolish your cities and **m** you desolate,
35: 7 I will **m** Mount Seir utterly desolate, killing off all
35: 9 I will **m** you desolate forever. Your cities will
35:14 The whole world will rejoice when I **m** you
36:11 I will **m** you even more prosperous than you were
37: 5 am going to breathe into you and **m** you live again!
37:19 to Judah. I will **m** them one stick in my hand.'
37:26 And I will **m** a covenant of peace with them,
37:27 I will **m** my home among them. I will be their God,
38: 4 and cavalry and **m** you a vast and mighty horde,
38:13 and seize their goods and **m** them poor?'
38:23 and I will **m** myself known to all the nations of the
39: 7 I will **m** known my holy name among my people
39:11 "And I will **m** a vast graveyard for Gog and his
39:26 then no one will bother them or **m** them afraid.
43:20 This will cleanse and **m** atonement for the altar.
43:22 Then cleanse and **m** atonement for the altar again,
43:26 days to cleanse and **m** atonement for the altar,
45:15 and peace offerings that will **m** atonement for the
45:17 and peace offerings to **m** reconciliation for the
45:20 In that way, you will **m** atonement for the Temple.
47: 8 waters of the Dead Sea and **m** them fresh and pure.
Da 1: 4 "**M** sure they are well versed in every branch of
3:29 Therefore, I **m** this decree: If any people,
6: 7 should **m** a law that will be strictly enforced.
7: 8 were wrenched out, roots and all, to **m** room for it.
9:27 He will **m** a treaty with the people for a period of
11:17 He will **m** plans to come with the might of his
11:23 deceitful promises, he will **m** various alliances.
11:27 But it will **m** no difference, for an end will still
Hos 2: 6 I will block the road to **m** her lose her way.
2:18 At that time I will **m** a covenant with all the wild
2:19 I will **m** you my wife forever, showing you
2:20 I will be faithful to you and **m** you mine, and you
7: 3 The people **m** the king glad with their wickedness.
10: 4 and **m** promises they don't intend to keep.
10:13 believing that great armies could **m** your nation
12: 1 they **m** alliances with Assyria and cut deals with
12: 9 And I will **m** you live in tents again, as you do
Joel 2: 5 Listen to the noise they **m**—like the rumbling of
3:21 will **m** my home in Jerusalem with my people."
Am 2:13 "So I will **m** you groan as a wagon groans when it
6:12 and **m** bitter the sweet fruit of righteousness.
8: 9 "I will **m** the sun go down at noon and darken the
Ob 1: 3 and **m** your home high in the mountains.
Jnh 1:13 was too violent for them, and they couldn't **m** it.
1:14 they pleaded, "don't **m** us die for this man's sin.
Mic 1: 6 will **m** the city of Samaria a heap of rubble.
1:16 **M** yourselves as bald as an eagle, for your little
2: 4 In that day your enemies will **m** fun of you by
4: 7 but I will **m** them strong again, a mighty nation.
6: 3 what have I done to **m** you turn from me?
6: 6 What can we bring to the LORD to **m** up for what

6: 7 for the sins of our souls? Would that **m** him glad?
6: 15 trample the grapes but get no juice to **m** your wine.
6: 16 Therefore, I will **m** an example of you,
Na 3: 14 the defenses! **M** bricks to repair the walls!
Hab 2: 15 "How terrible it will be for you who **m** your
3: 19 He will **m** me as surefooted as a deer and bring me
Zep 1: 17 I will **m** you as helpless as a blind man searching
1: 18 He will **m** a terrifying end of all the people on
2: 13 He will destroy Assyria and **m** its great capital,
3: 13 in safety; there will be no one to **m** them afraid."
Zec 6: 11 their gifts and **m** a crown from the silver and gold.
7: 10 And do not **m** evil plans to harm each other.
8: 12 Once more I will **m** the remnant in Judah
8: 13 Now I will rescue you and **m** you both a symbol
8: 17 Do not **m** evil plots to harm each other. And stop
10: 3 he will **m** them strong and glorious, like a proud
10: 12 I will **m** my people strong in my power, and they
12: 2 I will **m** Jerusalem and Judah like an intoxicating
12: 3 On that day I will **m** Jerusalem a heavy stone,
12: 6 "On that day I will **m** the clans of Judah like a
13: 9 bring that group through the fire and **m** them pure,
Mal 2: 15 Didn't the LORD **m** you one with your wife?
Mt 3: 3 Lord's coming! / **M** a straight road for him!' "
5: 13 Can you **m** it useful again? It will be thrown out
5: 34 But I say, don't **m** any vows! If you say,
6: 16 don't **m** it obvious, as the hypocrites do, who try to
6: 28 they grow. They don't work or **m** their clothing,
6: 33 and **m** the Kingdom of God your primary concern.
8: 2 "if you want to, you can **m** me well again."
9: 28 asked them, "Do you believe I can **m** you see?"
12: 33 **M** a tree good, and its fruit will be good. **M** a tree
bad, and its fruit will be bad.
15: 20 never defile you and **m** you unacceptable to God!"
17: 4 I'll **m** three shrines, one for you, one for Moses,
23: 15 For you cross land and sea to **m** one convert,
28: 19 Therefore, go and **m** disciples of all the nations,
Mk 1: 3 Lord's coming! / **M** a straight road for him!' "
1: 40 you want to, you can **m** me well again," he said.
7: 23 what defile you and **m** you unacceptable to God."
9: 3 far whiter than any earthly process could ever **m** it.
9: 5 "We will **m** three shrines—one for you, one for
9: 50 if it loses its flavor, how do you **m** it salty again?
12: 40 they really are, they **m** long prayers in public.
14: 13 So Jesus sent two of them into Jerusalem to **m** the
Lk 3: 4 for the Lord's coming! / **M** a straight road for him!
3: 13 "**M** sure you collect no more taxes than the
5: 12 "if you want to, you can **m** me well again."
6: 38 shaken together to **m** room for more,
9: 33 We will **m** three shrines—one for you, one for
11: 35 **M** sure that the light you think you have is not
11: 40 Didn't God **m** the inside as well as the outside?
12: 27 They don't work or **m** their clothing, yet Solomon
12: 31 you **m** the Kingdom of God your primary concern.
14: 34 if it loses its flavor, how do you **m** it salty again?
16: 9 worldly resources to benefit others and **m** friends.
20: 47 they really are, they **m** long prayers in public.
24: 39 Touch me and **m** sure that I am not a ghost,
Jn 1: 3 there is. Nothing exists that he didn't **m**.
6: 15 were ready to take him by force and **m** him king,
7: 6 you can go anytime, and it will **m** no difference.
8: 14 "These claims are valid even though I **m** them
17: 17 **M** them pure and holy by teaching them your
Ac 2: 14 residents of Jerusalem! **M** no mistake about this.
7: 40 told Aaron, '**M** us some gods who can lead us,
7: 50 Didn't I **m** everything in heaven and earth?'
9: 34 Jesus Christ heals you! Get up and **m** your bed!"
12: 20 So they sent a delegation to **m** peace with him
16: 23 The jailer was ordered to **m** sure they didn't
18: 14 But just as Paul started to **m** his defense,
22: 24 and ordered him lashed with whips to **m** him
24: 10 and this gives me confidence as I **m** my defense.
25: 5 anything wrong, you can **m** your accusations."
26: 28 "Do you think you can **m** me a Christian
27: 2 it was scheduled to **m** several stops at ports along
27: 13 from the south, the sailors thought they could **m** it.
27: 42 The soldiers wanted to kill the prisoners to **m** sure
27: 43 could swim to jump overboard first and **m** for land,
Ro 4: 25 and he was raised from the dead to **m** us right with
7: 11 the good law and used it to **m** me guilty of death.
7: 18 matter which way I turn, I can't **m** myself do right.
9: 7 doesn't **m** them truly Abraham's children.
9: 18 and he chooses to **m** some people refuse to listen.
9: 21 the same lump of clay to **m** one jar for decoration
10: 19 I will **m** you angry by blessing the foolish
11: 11 His purpose was to **m** his salvation available to the
11: 14 for I want to find a way to **m** the Jews want what
11: 19 "those branches were broken off to **m** room for
15: 1 We may know that these things **m** no difference,
16: 17 And now I **m** one more appeal, my dear brothers
16: 25 God is able to **m** you strong, just as the Good
1Co 7: 31 **m** good use of them without becoming attached to
8: 1 While knowledge may **m** us feel important, it is
8: 13 If what I eat is going to **m** another Christian sin,
8: 13 for I don't want to **m** another Christian stumble.
12: 12 but the many parts **m** up only one body.
12: 15 that does not **m** it any less a part of the body.
12: 16 would that **m** it any less a part of the body?
13: 2 so that I could speak to a mountain and **m** it move,
16: 7 This time I don't want to **m** just a short visit
2Co 2: 1 I won't **m** them unhappy with another painful
2: 2 For if I cause you pain and **m** you sad, who is
going to **m** me glad?
2: 17 are many of them—who preach just to **m** money.
5: 4 Our dying bodies **m** us groan and sigh, but it's not
7: 11 have done everything you could to **m** things right.
8: 9 so that by his poverty he could **m** you rich.
9: 5 of me to **m** sure the gift you promised is ready.
9: 7 You must each **m** up your own mind as to how
10: 7 The trouble with you is that you **m** your decisions
11: 20 You put up with it when they **m** you their slaves,
Gal 2: 2 I wanted to **m** sure they did not disagree, or my
2: 14 why are you trying to **m** these Gentiles obey the
2: 18 I **m** myself guilty if I rebuild the old system I
3: 10 But those who depend on the law to **m** them right
5: 1 Now **m** sure that you stay free, and don't get tied
5: 2 If you are counting on circumcision to **m** you right
5: 4 For if you are trying to **m** yourselves right with
6: 15 It doesn't **m** any difference now whether we have
Eph 2: 15 His purpose was to **m** peace between Jews
5: 16 **M** the most of every opportunity for doing good in
5: 26 to **m** her holy and clean, washed by baptism
6: 4 Don't **m** your children angry by the way you treat
Php 1: 4 and I **m** my requests with a heart full of joy
1: 17 intending to **m** my chains more painful to me.
2: 2 Then **m** me truly happy by agreeing
2: 3 don't live to **m** a good impression on others.
3: 15 on some point, I believe God will **m** it plain to you.
Col 1: 9 and we ask him to **m** you wise with spiritual
3: 13 You must **m** allowance for each other's faults
3: 16 their richness, live in your hearts and **m** you wise.
4: 5 and **m** the most of every opportunity.
4: 10 **m** Mark welcome if he comes your way.
4: 12 for you, asking God to **m** you strong and perfect,
1Th 2: 7 As apostles of Christ we certainly had a right to **m**
3: 11 and our Lord Jesus **m** it possible for us to come to
3: 12 And may the Lord **m** your love grow and overflow
3: 13 Christ will **m** your hearts strong, blameless,
5: 23 Now may the God of peace **m** you holy in every
2Th 1: 5 For he will **m** you worthy of his Kingdom,
1: 11 that our God will **m** you worthy of the life to
3: 3 he will **m** you strong and guard you from the evil
1Ti 2: 1 As you **m** your requests, plead for God's mercy
2: 10 **m** themselves attractive by the good things they
3: 6 and the Devil will use that pride to **m** him fall.
2Ti 3: 5 but they will reject the power that could **m** them
3: 16 and to **m** us realize what is wrong in our lives.
Tit 1: 13 So rebuke them as sternly as necessary to **m** them
2: 10 Then they will **m** the teaching about God our
2: 14 to cleanse us, and to **m** us his very own people,
Heb 3: 12 **M** sure that your own hearts are not evil
5: 11 seem to listen, so it's hard to **m** you understand.
6: 11 in order to **m** certain that what you hope for will
8: 3 our High Priest must **m** an offering, too.
8: 5 "Be sure that you **m** everything according to the
8: 8 says the Lord, / when I will **m** a new covenant
8: 10 But this is the new covenant I will **m**
10: 16 "This is the new covenant I will **m** / with my
10: 22 been sprinkled with Christ's blood to **m** us clean,
12: 16 **M** sure that no one is immoral or godless like
13: 12 and died outside the city gates in order to **m** his
Jas 1: 8 They can't **m** up their minds. They waver back
1: 18 In his goodness he chose to **m** us his own children
1: 20 Your anger can never **m** things right in God's
3: 2 We all **m** many mistakes, but those who control
3: 3 We can **m** a large horse turn around and go
4: 13 a year. We will do business there and **m** a profit."
5: 15 will heal the sick, and the Lord will **m** them well.
1Pe 2: 8 people stumble, / the rock that will **m** them fall."
2: 15 those who **m** foolish accusations against you.
4: 13 because these trials will **m** you partners with Christ
2Pe 1: 5 So **m** every effort to apply the benefits of these
1: 15 So I will work hard to **m** these things clear to you.
2: 3 In their greed they will **m** up clever lies to get hold
2: 14 They **m** a game of luring unstable people into sin.
2: 22 They **m** these proverbs come true: "A dog returns
3: 14 **m** every effort to live a pure and blameless life.
1Jn 5: 15 And if we know he is listening when we **m** our
5: 18 of God's family do not **m** a practice of sinning,
Rev 10: 9 you swallow it, it will **m** your stomach sour!"
13: 14 He ordered the people of the world to **m** a great

MAKER (9) [MAKE]

Ex 30: 35 Using the usual techniques of the incense **m**,
37: 29 using the techniques of the most skilled incense **m**.
Ps 95: 6 Let us kneel before the LORD our **m**,
149: 2 O Israel, rejoice in your **M**. / O people of
Pr 14: 31 Those who oppress the poor insult their **M**,
17: 5 Those who mock the poor insult their **M**;
Isa 45: 9 Does a clay pot ever argue with its **m**?
Jer 33: 2 "The LORD, the **M** of the heavens and earth—
Hos 8: 14 But they have both forgotten their **M**. Therefore,

MAKERS (2) [MAKE]

Jer 10: 14 make idols, but the idols will disgrace their **m**,
51: 17 make idols, but the idols will disgrace their **m**,

MAKES (106) [MAKE]

Ex 4: 11 "Who **m** mouths?" the LORD asked him.
4: 11 "Who **m** people so they can speak or not speak,
7: 9 When he **m** this demand, say to Aaron,
11: 7 Then you will know that the LORD **m** a
23: 8 for a bribe **m** you ignore something that you
31: 13 remember that I am the LORD, who **m** you holy.
Lev 20: 8 obey them, for I am the LORD, who **m** you holy.
21: 23 holy places. I am the LORD who **m** them holy."
22: 4 or any kind of discharge that **m** them ceremonially
22: 9 I am the LORD who **m** them holy.
22: 16 I am the LORD, who **m** them holy."
22: 32 of Israel. It is I, the LORD, who **m** you holy.
Nu 5: 21 curse is upon you when he **m** you infertile.
30: 2 A man who **m** a vow to the LORD or **m** a pledge
under oath must never break it.
30: 3 "If a young woman **m** a vow to the LORD
30: 6 a vow or **m** an impulsive pledge and later marries.
30: 10 and living in her husband's home when she **m** a
30: 13 nullify any vows or pledges she **m** to deny herself.
Jdg 16: 5 "Find out from Samson what **m** him so strong
16: 6 "Please tell me what **m** you so strong and what it
16: 15 and you still haven't told me what **m** you
1Sa 2: 7 The LORD **m** one poor and another rich;
2Sa 22: 34 He **m** me as surefooted as a deer, / leading me
2Ki 18: 19 What are you trusting in that **m** you so confident?
18: 35 So what **m** you think that the LORD can rescue
2Ch 32: 10 What are you trusting in that **m** you think you can
32: 14 What **m** you think your God can do any better?
Job 9: 21 "I am innocent, but it **m** no difference to me—
12: 23 He **m** nations expand, and he abandons them.
12: 25 without a light. He **m** them stagger like drunkards.
16: 3 What have I said that **m** you speak so endlessly?
32: 8 the Almighty within them, that **m** them intelligent.
35: 11 Where is the one who **m** us wiser than the animals
37: 18 he **m** the skies reflect the heat like a giant mirror.
38: 26 Who **m** the rain fall on barren land, in a desert
38: 27 parched ground and **m** the tender grass spring up?
39: 5 "Who **m** the wild donkey wild?
39: 26 "Are you the one who **m** the hawk soar and spread
41: 31 "The crocodile **m** the water boil with its
Ps 18: 33 He **m** me as surefooted as a deer, / leading me
29: 6 He **m** Lebanon's mountains skip like a calf
29: 8 The voice of the LORD **m** the desert quake;
55: 15 them alive, / for evil **m** its home within them.
147: 8 and **m** the green grass grow in mountain pastures.
Pr 10: 22 The blessing of the LORD **m** a person rich,
13: 12 Hope deferred **m** the heart sick, but when dreams
15: 2 The wise person **m** learning a joy; fools spout only
15: 13 A glad heart **m** a happy face; a broken heart
15: 30 joy to the heart; good news **m** for good health.
16: 7 he **m** even their enemies live at peace with them.
19: 4 Wealth **m** many "friends"; poverty drives them
19: 22 Loyalty **m** a person attractive. And it is better to be
19: 28 A corrupt witness **m** a mockery of justice;
28: 8 A person who **m** money by charging interest will
31: 24 She **m** belted linen garments and sashes to sell to
Ecc 5: 3 being a fool **m** you a blabbermouth.
Isa 8: 14 people to stumble and a rock that **m** them fall.
29: 16 greater than you. You are only the jars he **m**!
36: 4 What are you trusting in that **m** you so confident?
37: 20 So what **m** you think that the LORD can rescue
40: 22 heavens like a curtain and **m** his tent from them.
44: 12 His work **m** him hungry and thirsty, weak
44: 15 of it and **m** himself a god for people to worship!
44: 15 He **m** an idol and bows down and praises it!
44: 17 Then he takes what's left and **m** his god: a carved
45: 7 the one who creates the light and **m** the darkness.
54: 16 the forge and **m** the weapons of destruction.
62: 7 Give the LORD no rest until he **m** Jerusalem the
Jer 12: 5 to me, "If racing against mere men **m** you tired,
Eze 16: 44 Everyone who **m** up proverbs will say of you,
17: 24 It is I who **m** the green tree wither and gives new
Hos 7: 5 The king **m** a fool of himself and drinks with those
Zec 10: 1 It is the LORD who **m** storm clouds that drop
Mt 13: 56 live right here among us. What **m** him so great?"
23: 17 the gold, or the Temple that **m** the gold sacred?
23: 19 gift on the altar, or the altar that **m** the gift sacred?
Mk 9: 18 and **m** him foam at the mouth and grind his teeth
9: 22 The evil spirit often **m** him fall into the fire or into
Ro 1: 17 This Good News tells us how God **m** us right in his
3: 30 He **m** people right with himself only by faith,
5: 18 but Christ's one act of righteousness **m** all people
7: 17 because it is sin inside me that **m** me do these evil
7: 23 and **m** me a slave to the sin that is still within me.
9: 21 When a potter **m** jars out of clay, doesn't he have a
9: 33 people to stumble, / and a rock that **m** them fall.
11: 9 a snare, / a trap that **m** them think all is well.
14: 20 But it is wrong to eat anything if it **m** another
16: 19 This **m** me very happy. I want you to see clearly
1Co 3: 7 because he is the one who **m** the seed grow.
4: 7 What **m** you better than anyone else? What do you
4: 10 Our dedication to Christ **m** us look like fools,
7: 19 For it **m** no difference whether or not a man has
12: 25 This **m** for harmony among the members, so that
15: 11 So it **m** no difference whether I preach or they
2Co 3: 9 is the new covenant, which **m** us right with God!
Gal 5: 6 it **m** no difference to God whether we are
2Th 2: 13 a salvation that came through the Spirit who **m** you
2Ti 2: 22 Follow anything that **m** you want to do right.
Heb 2: 3 What **m** us think that we can escape if we are
2: 11 and the ones he **m** holy have the same Father.
12: 26 shook the earth, but now he **m** another promise:
Jas 3: 4 And a tiny rudder **m** a huge ship turn wherever the
4: 4 Don't you realize that friendship with this world **m**
1Pe 2: 8 also say, / "He is the stone that **m** people stumble,
2Pe 1: 1 our God and Savior, who **m** us right with God.

MAKEUP (1)

Hos 2: 2 Tell her to take off her garish **m** and suggestive

MAKHELOTH (2)

Nu 33: 25 They left Haradah and camped at **M**.
33: 26 They left **M** and camped at Tahath.

MAKI (1)

Nu 13: 15 Gad | Geuel son of **M**

MAKING (139) [MAKE]

Ge 9: 9 "I am **m** a covenant with you and your
20: 9 **m** me and my kingdom guilty of this great sin?

21: 9 and her Egyptian servant Hagar—**m** fun of Isaac.
21:32 After **m** their covenant, Abimelech left with
39:23 **m** everything run smoothly and successfully.
Ex 5: 7 the people with any more straw for **m** bricks.
5:16 It is the fault of your slave drivers for **m** such
10:15 of the whole country, **m** the ground look black.
14:25 to come off, **m** their chariots impossible to drive.
18:22 help you carry the load, **m** the task easier for you.
21:11 she may leave as a free woman without **m** any
25:19 end of the atonement cover, **m** it all one piece.
26: 6 of sheets together, **m** the Tabernacle a single unit.
29:36 Purify the altar by **m** atonement for it; make it holy
Lev 1: 4 it as your substitute, thus **m** atonement for you.
8:10 and everything in it, thus **m** them holy.
8:11 and the washbasin and its pedestal, **m** them holy.
8:12 thus anointing him and **m** him holy for his work.
10:17 and for **m** atonement for the people before the
12: 8 will sacrifice them, thus **m** atonement for her,
14:21 thus **m** atonement for the person being cleansed.
16:17 No one may enter until he comes out again after **m**
16:20 "When Aaron has finished **m** atonement for the
19:29 "Do not defile your daughter by **m** her a
21: 1 "Tell the priests to avoid **m** themselves
26:19 I will break down your arrogant spirit by **m** the
Nu 25:12 So tell him that I am **m** my special covenant of
32:14 You are **m** the LORD even angrier with Israel.
35:24 the assembly must follow these regulations in **m** a
Dt 4:16 So do not corrupt yourselves by **m** a physical
4:25 do not corrupt yourselves by **m** idols of any kind.
9:18 what the LORD hated, thus **m** him very angry.
23:22 However, it is not a sin to refrain from **m** a vow.
26: 6 and humiliated us by **m** us their slaves,
28:59 **m** you miserable and unbearably sick.
29:12 The LORD is **m** this covenant with you today,
29:14 the LORD is **m** this covenant with its obligations.
29:15 The LORD your God is **m** this covenant with you
Jdg 6:29 And after asking around and **m** a careful search,
8:33 the images of Baal, **m** Baal-berith their god.
9:16 and in good faith by **m** Abimelech your king,
14:10 As his father was **m** final arrangements for the
16:13 "You have been **m** fun of me and telling me lies!
16:19 a man to shave off his hair, **m** his capture certain.
16:27 who were watching Samson and **m** fun of him.
1Sa 18: 8 only thousands. Next they'll be **m** him their king!"
25:43 Ahinoam from Jezreel, **m** both of them his wives.
2Sa 14:13 You have convicted yourself in **m** this decision,
19: 5 Yet you act like this, **m** us feel ashamed, as though
1Ki 8:28 and the prayer that your servant is **m** to you today.
8:54 When Solomon finished **m** these prayers
2Ki 2:23 from the town began mocking and **m** fun of him.
3:22 shining across the water, **m** it look as red as blood.
12:13 to the Temple was not used for **m** silver cups,
25:14 and all the other bronze utensils used for **m**
1Ch 12:38 the single purpose of **m** David the king of Israel.
22: 5 So I will begin **m** preparations for it now."
25: 7 and their families were all trained in **m** music
2Ch 2:14 He is skillful at **m** things from gold, silver, bronze,
6:19 and the prayer that your servant is **m** to you.
7:12 and have chosen this Temple as the place for **m**
11:22 **m** it clear that he would be the next king.
19:11 The Levites will assist you in **m** sure that justice is
Ne 9:38 we are **m** a solemn promise and putting it in
13:30 and Levites, **m** certain that each knew his work.
Est 3: 1 **m** him the most powerful official in the empire
9:18 third day, **m** that their day of feasting and gladness.
Job 39:28 on the cliffs, **m** its home on a distant, rocky crag.
Ps 19: 7 the LORD are trustworthy, / **m** wise the simple.
55: 3 enemies shout at me, / **m** loud and wicked threats.
60: 3 hard on us, / **m** us drink wine that sent us reeling.
65: 9 care of the earth and water it, / **m** it rich and fertile.
78:16 the rock, / **m** the waters flow down like a river!
79: 7 people Israel, / **m** the land a desolate wilderness.
110: 1 **m** them a footstool under your feet."
139:14 Thank you for **m** me so wonderfully complex!
Pr 6:13 signaling their true intentions to their friends by **m**
Ecc 5: 6 In such cases, your mouth is **m** you sin. And don't
SS 5: 7 The watchmen found me as they were **m** their
Isa 33:15 are honest and fair, who reject **m** a profit by fraud,
41:15 tear all your enemies apart, **m** chaff of mountains.
41:26 else predicted this, **m** you admit that he was right?
43:16 through the waters, **m** a dry path through the sea.
51:10 **m** a path of escape when you saved your people?
57: 4 you mock, **m** faces and sticking out your tongues?
58: 9 the helpless and stop **m** false accusations
Jer 10:25 people Israel, **m** the land a desolate wilderness.
11:18 me about the plots my enemies were **m** against me.
18: 4 But the jar he was **m** did not turn out as he had
18: 9 a certain nation or kingdom, **m** it strong and great,
19: 8 of the earth, **m** it a monument to their stupidity.
23:16 futile hopes. They are **m** up everything they say.
34:11 the people they had freed, **m** them slaves again.
34:16 women you had freed, **m** them slaves once again.
37:13 The sentry **m** the arrest was Irijah son of
42:12 I will be merciful to you by **m** him kind, so he will
44:19 and **m** cakes marked with her image, without our
52:18 and all the other bronze utensils used for **m**
Eze 12:22 in Israel: 'Time passes, **m** a liar of every prophet'?
15: 3 Can its wood be used for **m** things, like pegs to
20:12 them apart to be holy, **m** them my special people.
33: 7 I am **m** you a watchman for the people of Israel.
Da 11:23 By **m** deceitful promises, he will make various
Hos 7: 5 and drinks with those who are **m** fun of him.
8: 4 By **m** idols for themselves from their silver
13: 2 Now they keep on sinning by **m** silver idols to
Am 2:12 "But you caused the Nazirites to sin by **m** them
5: 7 **m** it a bitter pill for the poor and oppressed.
Ob 1:13 their homes and **m** yourselves rich at their expense.
Mic 2: 8 **m** them as ragged as men who have just come
3: 6 **m** it impossible for you to predict the future.
Zec 14: 4 **m** a wide valley running from east to west,
Mt 13:33 of Heaven is like yeast used by a woman **m** bread.
Lk 1:62 communicating to him by **m** gestures.
9:39 An evil spirit keeps seizing him, **m** him scream.
13:21 It is like yeast used by a woman **m** bread.
14:18 But they all began **m** excuses. One said he had just
20:43 **m** them a footstool under your feet.'
Jn 4: 1 is baptizing and **m** more disciples than John"
5:18 as his Father, thereby **m** himself equal with God.
7:23 So why should I be condemned for **m** a man
8:13 "You are **m** false claims about yourself!"
Ac 2:35 **m** them a footstool under your feet.'
14:21 the Good News in Derbe and **m** many disciples,
Ro 5:11 Christ has done for us in **m** us friends of God.
10: 3 For they don't understand God's way of **m** people
10: 5 For Moses wrote that the law's way of **m** a person
1Co 13: 1 I would only be **m** meaningless noise like a loud
16:17 They have been **m** up for the help you weren't here
Eph 2:14 us Jews and you Gentiles by **m** us all one people.
4: 2 **m** allowance for each other's faults because of
5:19 **m** music to the Lord in your hearts.
Php 3: 9 For God's way of **m** us right with himself depends
Heb 1:13 **m** them a footstool under your feet."
10:14 he perfected forever all those whom he is **m** holy.
1Pe 4:15 it must not be for murder, stealing, **m** trouble,
2Pe 1:16 For we were not **m** up clever stories when we told
Rev 13:13 such as **m** fire flash down to earth from heaven
21: 5 the throne said, "Look, I am **m** all things new!"

MAKIR (19) [MAKIR'S, MAKIRITE, MAKIRITES]

Ge 50:23 and the children of Manasseh's son **M**,
Nu 26:29 The Makirite clan, named after its ancestor **M**.
27: 1 son of Gilead, son of **M**, son of Manasseh, son of
32:39 Then the descendants of **M** of the tribe of
36: 1 descendants of **M**, son of Manasseh, son of
Dt 3:15 I gave Gilead to the clan of **M**.
Jos 13:31 All this was given to the descendants of **M**,
17: 1 Jordan had already been given to the family of **M**
17: 1 (**M** was Manasseh's oldest son and was the father
17: 3 of Manasseh, **M**, and Gilead, had no sons.
Jdg 5:14 From **M** the commanders marched down;
2Sa 9: 4 told him, "at the home of **M** son of Ammiel."
17:27 and by **M** son of Ammiel of Lo-debar,
1Ch 2:21 he married Gilead's sister, the daughter of **M**.
2:23 All these were descendants of **M**, the father of
7:14 to his Aramean concubine, were Asriel and **M**. **M** was the father of Gilead.
7:15 **M** found wives for Huppim and Shuppim.
7:17 descendants of **M** son of Manasseh.

MAKIR'S (5) [MAKIR]

Nu 26:29 named after its ancestor Gilead, **M** son.
2Sa 9: 5 David sent for him and brought him from **M** home.
1Ch 7:15 and Shuppim. **M** sister was named Maacah.
7:16 **M** wife, Maacah, gave birth to a son whom she
7:18 **M** sister Hammoleketh gave birth to Ishhod,

MAKIRITE (1) [MAKIR]

Nu 26:29 The **M** clan, named after its ancestor Makir.

MAKIRITES (1) [MAKIR]

Nu 32:40 So Moses gave Gilead to the **M**, descendants of

MAKKEDAH (7)

Jos 10:10 to Beth-horon and attacked them at Azekah and **M**,
10:16 the five kings escaped and hid in a cave at **M**.
10:21 the Israelites returned safely to their camp at **M**.
10:28 day Joshua completely destroyed the city of **M**,
10:28 He killed the king of **M** as he had killed the king of
12:16 The king of **M** / The king of Bethel
15:41 Gederoth, Beth-dagon, Naamah, and **M**—

MAKTESH [KJV] See MARKET

MALACHI (1)

Mal 1: 1 the LORD gave to Israel through the prophet **M**.

MALCAM (1)

1Ch 8: 9 new wife, gave birth to Jobab, Zibia, Mesha, **M**,

MALCHAM [KJV] See MALCAM, MOLECH

MALCHI-SHUA [KJV] See MALKISHUA

MALCHIAH [KJV] See MALKIJAH

MALCHUS (1)

Jn 18:10 drew a sword and slashed off the right ear of **M**,

MALE (163) [MALES]

Ge 1:27 after himself; / **m** and female he created them.
5: 2 He created them **m** and female, and he blessed
6:19 a pair of every kind of animal—a **m** and a female
7: 3 There must be a **m** and a female in each pair to
7: 9 They came into the boat in pairs, **m** and female,
7:16 **m** and female, just as God had commanded.
12:16 sheep, cattle, donkeys, **m** and female servants,
17:10 Each **m** among you must be circumcised;
17:12 Every **m** child must be circumcised on the eighth
17:23 and every other **m** in his household
30:35 and removed all the **m** goats that were speckled
31:10 and saw that the **m** goats mating with the flock
32:14 twenty **m** goats, two hundred ewes, twenty rams,
32:15 twenty female donkeys, and ten **m** donkeys.
Ex 12: 5 This animal must be a one-year-old **m**, either a
12:12 and firstborn **m** animals in the land of Egypt.
12:48 But an uncircumcised **m** may never eat of the
13: 2 sons of Israel and every firstborn **m** animal.
13:12 and firstborn **m** animals must be presented to the
13:13 A firstborn **m** donkey may be redeemed from the
20:10 and daughters, your **m** and female servants,
20:17 **m** or female servant, ox or donkey,
21:20 "If a **m** or female slave is beaten and dies,
21:26 "If an owner hits a **m** or female slave in the eye
21:27 And if an owner knocks out the tooth of a **m**
21:32 But if the bull gores a slave, either **m** or female,
34:19 "Every firstborn **m** belongs to me—of both cattle
34:20 A firstborn **m** donkey may be redeemed from the
Lev 1:10 bring a **m** sheep or goat with no physical defects.
3: 6 It may be either **m** or female, and it must have no
4:23 he must bring as his offering a **m** goat with no
6:18 Any of Aaron's **m** descendants, from generation to
9: 3 Then tell the Israelites to take a **m** goat for a sin
14:10 cured of the skin disease must bring two **m** lambs
14:21 lambs must bring one **m** lamb for a guilt offering,
16: 5 then bring him two **m** goats for a sin offering
16: 7 Then he must bring the two **m** goats and present
18:23 and a woman must never present herself to a **m**
20:16 If a woman approaches a **m** animal to have
22:19 it will be accepted only if it is a **m** animal with no
22:19 It may be either a bull, a ram, or a **m** goat.
22:27 "When a bull or a ram or a **m** goat is born, it must
23:12 That same day you must sacrifice a year-old **m**
23:19 Then you must offer one **m** goat as a sin offering
23:19 and two one-year-old **m** lambs as a peace offering.
24: 9 of bread belong to Aaron and his **m** descendants,
25: 6 But you, your **m** and female slaves, your hired
25:44 you may purchase **m** or female slaves from among
Nu 3:15 Count every **m** who is one month old or older."
6:12 and each must bring a one-year-old **m** lamb for a
6:14 a one-year-old **m** lamb without defect for a burnt
7:15 and a one-year-old **m** lamb as a burnt offering;
7:16 a **m** goat for a sin offering;
7:17 and two oxen, five rams, five **m** goats, and five
7:17 and five one-year-old **m** lambs for a peace
7:21 and a one-year-old **m** lamb as a burnt offering;
7:22 a **m** goat for a sin offering;
7:23 and two oxen, five rams, five **m** goats, and five
7:23 and five one-year-old **m** lambs for a peace
7:27 and a one-year-old **m** lamb as a burnt offering;
7:28 a **m** goat for a sin offering;
7:29 and two oxen, five rams, five **m** goats, and five
7:29 and five one-year-old **m** lambs for a peace
7:33 and a one-year-old **m** lamb as a burnt offering;
7:34 a **m** goat for a sin offering;
7:35 and two oxen, five rams, five **m** goats, and five
7:35 and five one-year-old **m** lambs for a peace
7:39 and a one-year-old **m** lamb as a burnt offering;
7:40 a **m** goat for a sin offering;
7:41 and two oxen, five rams, five **m** goats, and five
7:41 and five one-year-old **m** lambs for a peace
7:45 and a one-year-old **m** lamb as a burnt offering;
7:46 a **m** goat for a sin offering;
7:47 and two oxen, five rams, five **m** goats, and five
7:47 and five one-year-old **m** lambs for a peace
7:51 and a one-year-old **m** lamb as a burnt offering;
7:52 a **m** goat for a sin offering;
7:53 and two oxen, five rams, five **m** goats, and five
7:53 and five one-year-old **m** lambs for a peace
7:57 and a one-year-old **m** lamb as a burnt offering;
7:58 a **m** goat for a sin offering;
7:59 and two oxen, five rams, five **m** goats, and five
7:59 and five one-year-old **m** lambs for a peace
7:63 and a one-year-old **m** lamb as a burnt offering;
7:64 a **m** goat for a sin offering;
7:65 and two oxen, five rams, five **m** goats, and five
7:65 and five one-year-old **m** lambs for a peace
7:69 and a one-year-old **m** lamb as a burnt offering;
7:70 a **m** goat for a sin offering;
7:71 and two oxen, five rams, five **m** goats, and five
7:71 and five one-year-old **m** lambs for a peace
7:75 and a one-year-old **m** lamb as a burnt offering;
7:76 a **m** goat for a sin offering;
7:77 and two oxen, five rams, five **m** goats, and five
7:77 and five one-year-old **m** lambs for a peace
7:81 and a one-year-old **m** lamb as a burnt offering;
7:82 a **m** goat for a sin offering;
7:83 and two oxen, five rams, five **m** goats, and five
7:83 and five one-year-old **m** lambs for a peace
7:87 and twelve one-year-old **m** lambs were donated for
7:87 Twelve **m** goats were brought for the sin offerings.
7:88 young bulls, sixty rams, sixty **m** goats,
7:88 and sixty one-year-old **m** lambs were donated for
15:24 and with one **m** goat for a sin offering.
18:11 **m** and female alike, may eat of these offerings.
28: 3 you must offer two one-year-old **m** lambs with no
28: 9 sacrifice two one-year-old **m** lambs with no
28:11 one ram, and seven one-year-old **m** lambs, all with
28:15 offer one **m** goat for a sin offering to the LORD.
28:19 one ram, and seven one-year-old **m** lambs, all with
28:22 You must also offer a **m** goat as a sin offering,
28:27 one ram, and seven one-year-old **m** lambs.
28:30 offer one **m** goat to make atonement for
29: 2 one ram, and seven one-year-old **m** lambs, all with
29: 5 you must sacrifice a **m** goat as a sin offering,
29: 8 one ram, and seven one-year-old **m** lambs, all with
29:11 You must also sacrifice one **m** goat for a sin

29:13 two rams, and fourteen one-year-old **m** lambs,
29:16 You must also sacrifice a **m** goat as a sin offering,
29:17 two rams, and fourteen one-year-old **m** lambs,
29:19 You must also sacrifice a **m** goat as a sin offering,
29:20 two rams, and fourteen one-year-old **m** lambs,
29:22 You must also sacrifice a **m** goat as a sin offering,
29:23 two rams, and fourteen one-year-old **m** lambs,
29:25 You must also sacrifice a **m** goat as a sin offering,
29:26 two rams, and fourteen one-year-old **m** lambs,
29:28 You must also sacrifice a **m** goat as a sin offering,
29:29 two rams, and fourteen one-year-old **m** lambs,
29:31 You must also sacrifice a **m** goat as a sin offering,
29:32 two rams, and fourteen one-year-old **m** lambs,
29:34 You must also sacrifice one **m** goat as a sin
29:36 one ram, and seven one-year-old **m** lambs, all with
29:38 You must also sacrifice one **m** goat as a sin
Dt 5:14 your **m** and female servants, your oxen
5:14 All your **m** and female servants must rest as you
5:21 or land, **m** or female servant, ox or donkey,
15:13 "When you release a **m** servant, do not send him
Jos 5:3 and circumcised the entire **m** population of Israel
17:6 an inheritance along with the **m** descendants.
17:6 (The land of Gilead was given to the rest of the **m**
1Sa 8:16 He will want your **m** and female slaves
1Ki 11:15 the Israelite army had killed nearly every **m** in
16:11 of Baasha, and he did not leave a single **m** child.
21:21 He will not let a single one of your **m** descendants,
2Ki 9:8 wiped out—every **m**, slave and free alike, in Israel.
1Ch 29:21 and a thousand **m** lambs as burnt offerings to the
2Ch 17:11 hundred rams and seventy-seven hundred **m** goats.
29:21 and seven **m** goats as a sin offering for the
29:23 The **m** goats for the sin offering were then brought
31:19 to distribute portions to every **m** among the priests
Ezr 6:17 And twelve **m** goats were presented as a sin
Job 31:13 "If I have been unfair to my **m** or female servants,
Pr 30:31 the strutting rooster, / the **m** goat, / a king as he
Jer 2:23 are like a restless female camel, desperate for a **m**!
Eze 43:22 sacrifice as a sin offering a young **m** goat that has
43:25 "Every day for seven days a **m** goat, a young bull,
45:23 A **m** goat will also be given each day for a sin
Da 8:5 suddenly a **m** goat appeared from the west,
8:21 The shaggy **m** goat represents the king of Greece,
Mt 19:4 record that from the beginning 'God made them **m**
Mk 10:6 of creation, for 'He made them **m** and female.'
1Co 6:9 adulterers, **m** prostitutes, homosexuals,
Gal 3:28 longer Jew or Gentile, slave or free, **m** or female.

MALEFACTOR(S) [KJV] See CRIMINAL(S)

MALES (18) [MALE]

Ge 31:12 and spotted **m** are mating with the females of your
Ex 12:48 LORD's Passover, let all the **m** be circumcised.
13:15 so the LORD killed all the firstborn **m** throughout
13:15 That is why we now offer all the firstborn **m** to the
Lev 6:29 Only **m** from a priest's family may eat of this
7:6 All **m** from a priest's family may eat the meat,
Nu 3:22 There were 7,500 **m** one month old or older among
3:28 There were 8,600 **m** one month old or older among
3:34 There were 6,200 **m** one month old or older among
3:39 there were 22,000 **m** one month old or older.
8:17 For all the firstborn **m** among the people of Israel
18:10 All the **m** may eat of it, and you must treat it as
18:15 and the firstborn **m** of ritually unclean animals.
Dt 14:23 and the firstborn **m** of your flocks and herds.
15:19 your God all the firstborn **m** from your flocks
Jos 5:8 After all the **m** had been circumcised, they rested
Jdg 21:11 "Completely destroy all the **m** and every woman
2Ch 31:16 They also distributed the gifts to all **m** three years

MALICIOUS (6) [MALICIOUSLY]

Dt 19:16 If a **m** witness comes forward and accuses
Ps 35:11 **M** witnesses testify against me. / They accuse me
Ro 1:29 envy, murder, fighting, deception, **m** behavior,
Eph 4:31 and slander, as well as all types of **m** behavior.
Col 3:8 rage, **m** behavior, slander, and dirty language.
1Pe 2:1 So get rid of all **m** behavior and deceit. Don't just

MALICIOUSLY (1) [MALICIOUS]

Da 6:24 to arrest the men who had **m** accused Daniel.

MALIGNANT (1)

Rev 16:2 **m** sores broke out on everyone who had the mark

MALIGNITY [KJV] See MALICIOUS (BEHAVIOR)

MALKIEL (3) [MALKIELITES]

Ge 46:17 named Serah. Beriah's sons were Heber and **M**.
Nu 26:45 The Malkielites, named after their ancestor **M**.
1Ch 7:31 Beriah were Heber and **M** (the father of Birzaith).

MALKIELITES (1) [MALKIEL]

Nu 26:45 The **M**, named after their ancestor Malkiel.

MALKIJAH (15)

1Ch 6:40 Michael, Baaseiah, **M**,
9:12 son of Pashhur, son of **M**, and Maasai son of
24:9 The fifth lot fell to **M**. / The sixth lot fell to
Ezr 10:25 Ramiah, Izziah, **M**, Mijamin, Eleazar, Hashabiah,
10:31 of Harim: Eliezer, Ishijah, **M**, Shemaiah, Shimeon,
Ne 3:11 Then came **M** son of Harim and Hasshub son of
3:14 The Dung Gate was repaired by **M** son of Recab,
3:31 **M**, one of the goldsmiths, repaired the wall as far
8:4 Mishael, **M**, Hashum, Hashbaddanah, Zechariah,
10:3 Pashhur, Amariah, **M**,
11:12 son of Zechariah, son of Pashhur, son of **M**;
12:42 Eleazar, Uzzi, Jehohanan, **M**, Elam, and Ezer.
Jer 21:1 when King Zedekiah sent Pashhur son of **M**
38:1 and Pashhur son of **M** heard what Jeremiah had
38:6 It belonged to **M**, a member of the royal family.

MALKIRAM (1)

1Ch 3:18 **M**, Pedaiah, Shenazzar, Jekamiah, Hoshama,

MALKISHUA (5)

1Sa 14:49 Saul's sons included Jonathan, Ishbosheth, and **M**.
31:2 three of his sons—Jonathan, Abinadab, and **M**.
1Ch 8:33 the father of Jonathan, **M**, Abinadab, and Eshbaal.
9:39 the father of Jonathan, **M**, Abinadab, and Eshbaal.
10:2 three of his sons—Jonathan, Abinadab, and **M**.

MALLOTHI (2)

1Ch 25:4 Geddalti, Romamti-ezer, Joshbekashah, **M**, Hothir,
25:26 The nineteenth lot fell to **M** and twelve of his sons

MALLOWS [KJV] See (COARSE) LEAVES

MALLUCH (7)

1Ch 6:44 was traced back through Kishi, Abdi, **M**,
Ezr 10:29 Meshullam, **M**, Adaiah, Jashub, Sheal,
10:32 Benjamin, **M**, and Shemariah.
Ne 10:4 Hattush, Shebaniah, **M**,
10:27 **M**, Harim, and Baanah.
12:2 Amariah, **M**, Hattush,
12:14 Jonathan was leader of the family of **M**.

MALTA (1)

Ac 28:1 we learned that we were on the island of **M**.

MAMA (2) [MOTHER]

Isa 8:4 this child is old enough to say 'Papa' or '**M**,'
La 2:12 "**M**, we want food," they cry, and then collapse in

MAMMON [KJV] See MONEY, RESOURCES, WEALTH

MAMRE (11)

Ge 13:18 moved his camp to the oak grove owned by **M**,
14:13 who was camped at the oak grove belonging to **M**
14:13 **M** and his relatives, Eshcol and Aner,
14:24 of the goods to my allies—Aner, Eshcol, and **M**."
18:1 he was camped near the oak grove belonging to **M**.
23:17 land belonging to Ephron at Machpelah, near **M**.
23:19 cave of Machpelah, near **M**, which is at Hebron.
25:9 near **M**, in the field of Ephron son of Zohar the
35:27 So Jacob came home to his father Isaac in **M**,
49:30 cave in the field of Machpelah, near **M** in Canaan,
50:13 place in the field of Ephron the Hittite, near **M**.

MAN (1197) [COUNTRYMEN, FOOTMEN, FOREMAN, FOREMEN, GATEMEN, HORSEMEN, MAN'S, MAN-EATER, MAN-MADE, MANHOOD, MANKIND, MANNED, MEN, MEN'S, SPOKESMAN, WOODSMEN, WORKMAN'S, WORKMEN]

EVERY MAN (12) Ge 34:15,25; Ex 23:17; 35:29; Dt 16:16; 20:13; Jdg 5:30; 2Sa 6:19; 2Ki 3:21; 1Ch 16:3; Est 1:22; Eze 16:15

MAN OF GOD (77) Dt 33:1; Jos 14:6; Jdg 13:6,8; 1Sa 9:6,10; 1Ki 12:22; 13:1,3,4,5,6,6,7,8,11,12,14,14,15,19,21, 23,24,26,29,31; 17:18,24; 20:28; 2Ki 1:9,10,11,12,13; 4:7,9, 16,21,22,25,27,27,40,42; 5:8,14,15; 6:6,9,10,15; 7:2,17,18, 19; 8:2,4,7,8,11; 13:19; 23:16,16,17; 1Ch 23:14; 2Ch 8:14; 11:2; 25:7,9,9; 30:16; Ezr 3:2; Ne 12:24,36; Ps 90:T; Jer 35:4

OLD MAN (23) Ge 24:1; 27:2; 43:27; 44:20; Jos 13:1; 23:2; Jdg 19:16,20,22,23; 1Sa 17:12; 28:14; 1Ki 13:11,18; 14:4; 2Ki 4:14; 1Ch 23:1; 2Ch 15:13; Job 42:17; Hos 7:9; Lk 1:18; Jn 3:4; Phm 1:9

RIGHTEOUS MAN (6) Ge 6:9; Ps 106:31; Lk 2:25; 23:50; Heb 11:4; 2Pe 2:8

SON OF MAN (176) Eze 2:1,3,6,8; 3:1,4,10,17; 4:1,16; 5:1; 6:2; 7:2; 8:5,6,8,12,17; 11:2,4,15; 12:2,9,18,22,27; 13:2, 17; 14:3,13; 15:2; 16:2; 17:2; 20:3,4,27,46; 21:2,6,9,12,14,19, 28; 22:2,18,24; 23:2,36; 24:2,16,25; 25:2; 26:2; 27:2; 28:2,12, 21; 29:2,18; 30:2,21; 31:2; 32:2,18; 33:2,7,10,12,24,30; 34:2; 35:2; 36:1,3,17; 37:3,11,16; 38:2,14; 39:1,17; 40:4; 43:7,10, 18; 44:5; Da 8:17; Mt 8:20; 9:6; 10:23; 11:19; 12:8,32,40; 13:37,41; 16:13,27,28; 17:9,12,22; 19:28; 20:18,28; 24:27,30, 30,37,39,44; 25:31; 26:2,24,45,64; Mk 2:10,28; 8:31,38; 9:9, 12,31; 10:33,45; 13:26,34; 14:21,41,62; Lk 5:24; 6:5,22; 7:34; 9:22,26,44,58; 11:30; 12:8,10,40; 17:22,23,24,25,26,30; 18:8,31; 19:10; 21:27,36; 22:22,48,69; 24:7; Jn 1:51; 3:13,14; 5:27; 6:27,53,62; 8:28; 9:35; 12:23,34,34; 13:31; Ac 7:56; Heb 2:6; Rev 1:13; 14:14

YOUNG MAN (31) Ge 39:6; Ex 33:11; Nu 11:27; Jdg 8:14; 9:54; 1Sa 14:1,52; 16:18; 30:15; 2Sa 1:6,13; 14:21; 18:32; 1Ki 11:28; Job 20:11; Ps 127:4; Pr 7:7; Ecc 11:9; Isa 62:5; Zec 2:4; Mt 19:20,22; Mk 14:51; 16:5; Lk 7:14; Ac 7:58; 20:9,12; 23:17,18,22

Ge 2:7 breath of life. And the **m** became a living person.
2:8 the east, and there he placed the **m** he had created.
2:15 The LORD God placed the **m** in the Garden of
2:18 God said, "It is not good for the **m** to be alone.
2:23 because she was taken out of a **m**."
2:24 This explains why a **m** leaves his father
4:1 the LORD's help, I have brought forth a **m**!"
6:9 Noah was a righteous **m**, the only blameless **m** living on earth at the time.
19:31 "There isn't a **m** anywhere in this entire area for
20:3 in a dream and told him, "You are a dead **m**,
20:4 so he said, "Lord, will you kill an innocent **m**?
24:1 Abraham was now a very old **m**, and the LORD
24:2 One day Abraham said to the **m** in charge of his
24:16 and she was a virgin; no **m** had ever slept with her.
24:26 The **m** fell down to the ground and worshiped the
24:30 where the **m** was still standing beside his camels.
24:32 So the **m** went home with Laban, and Laban
24:35 my master richly; he has become a great **m**.
24:58 "Are you willing to go with this **m**?" they asked
24:65 "Who is that **m** walking through the fields to meet
25:27 became a skillful hunter, a **m** of the open fields,
26:11 "Anyone who harms this **m** or his wife will die!"
26:13 He became a rich **m**, and his wealth only continued
27:2 "I am an old **m** now," Isaac said, "and I expect
29:5 "Do you know a **m** there named Laban,
32:24 and a **m** came and wrestled with him until dawn.
32:25 When the **m** saw that he couldn't win the match,
32:26 Then the **m** said, "Let me go, for it is dawn."
32:27 is your name?" the **m** asked. He replied, "Jacob."
32:28 name will no longer be Jacob," the **m** told him.
32:29 asked him. "Why do you ask?" the **m** replied.
34:14 It would be a disgrace for her to marry a **m** like
34:15 If every **m** among you will be circumcised like we
34:25 without opposition, and slaughtered every **m** there,
37:15 a **m** noticed him wandering around the
37:17 "Yes," the **m** told him, "but they are no longer
38:1 to Adullam, where he visited a **m** named Hirah.
38:7 But Er was a wicked **m** in the LORD's sight,
38:8 as our law requires of the brother of a **m** who has
38:25 "The **m** who owns this identification seal
39:6 was a very handsome and well-built young **m**.
41:12 We told the dreams to a young Hebrew **m** who was
41:33 "My suggestion is that you find the wisest **m** in
41:38 For he is a **m** who is obviously filled with the spirit
41:39 dreams to you, you are the wisest **m** in the land!
42:18 day Joseph said to them, "I am a God-fearing **m**.
42:30 "The **m** who is ruler over the land spoke very
42:33 Then the **m**, the ruler of the land, told us, 'This is
43:3 "The **m** wasn't joking when he warned that we
43:5 Remember that the **m** said, 'You won't be allowed
43:7 "But the **m** specifically asked us about our
43:11 Take them to the **m** as gifts—balm, honey, spices,
43:13 Then take your brother and go back to the **m**.
43:14 Almighty give you mercy as you go before the **m**,
43:17 So the **m** did as he was told and took them to
43:19 they went over to the **m** in charge of Joseph's
43:27 "How is your father—the old **m** you spoke about?
44:1 Joseph gave these instructions to the **m** in charge
44:6 So the **m** caught up with them and spoke to them
44:10 "Fair enough," the **m** replied, "except that only
44:15 "Didn't you know that a **m** such as I would know
44:17 "Only the **m** who stole the cup will be my slave.
44:20 We said, 'Yes, we have a father, an old **m**, and a
44:26 We won't be allowed to see the **m** in charge of the
Ex 2:1 a **m** and woman from the tribe of Levi got married.
2:14 "Who do you think you are?" the **m** replied.
11:3 and Moses was considered a very great **m** in the
21:4 then the **m** will be free in the seventh year, but his
21:7 "When a **m** sells his daughter as a slave, she will
21:8 If she does not please the **m** who bought her,
21:28 "If a bull gores a **m** or woman to death, the bull
22:16 "If a **m** seduces a virgin who is not engaged to
22:17 the **m** must still pay the money for her dowry.
23:17 every **m** in Israel must appear before the Sovereign
30:12 each **m** who is counted must pay a ransom for
32:1 This **m** Moses, who brought us here from Egypt,
32:23 for something has happened to this **m** Moses,
33:11 to Moses face to face, as a **m** speaks to his friend.
33:11 but the young **m** who assisted him, Joshua son of
35:29 every **m** and woman who wanted to help in the
Lev 13:29 "If anyone, whether a **m** or woman, has an open
13:38 "If anyone, whether a **m** or woman, has shiny
13:40 "If a **m** loses his hair and his head becomes bald,
13:44 the **m** is infected with a contagious skin disease
15:2 Any **m** who has a genital discharge is ceremonially
15:3 or is stopped up. In either case the **m** is unclean.
15:6 If you sit where the **m** with the discharge has sat,
15:7 The same instructions apply if you touch the **m**
15:9 Any blanket on which the **m** rides will be defiled.
15:11 If the **m** touches you without first rinsing his
15:12 Any clay pot touched by the **m** with the discharge
15:15 the priest will make atonement for the **m** before the
15:16 "Whenever a **m** has an emission of semen,
15:18 both the **m** and the woman must bathe,
15:24 If a **m** has sexual intercourse with her during this
15:32 These are the instructions for dealing with a **m**
15:33 for dealing with anyone, **m** or woman, who has
15:33 and for dealing with a **m** who has had intercourse
16:21 into the wilderness, led by a **m** chosen for this task.
16:22 After the **m** sets it free in the wilderness, the goat
16:26 "The **m** chosen to send the goat out into the
16:28 The **m** who does the burning must wash his clothes
18:23 "A **m** must never defile himself by having sexual
19:20 "If a **m** has sexual intercourse with a slave girl
19:21 The **m**, however, must bring a ram as a guilt
19:22 of the guilt offering, and the **m** will be forgiven.
20:10 "If a **m** commits adultery with another man's wife,
20:10 both the **m** and the woman must be put to death.

20:11 If a **m** has intercourse with his father's wife,
20:11 both the **m** and the woman must die, for they are
20:12 If a **m** has intercourse with his daughter-in-law,
20:14 If a **m** has intercourse with both a woman and her
20:15 "If a **m** has sexual intercourse with an animal,
20:17 "If a **m** has sexual intercourse with his sister,
20:17 Since the **m** has had intercourse with his sister,
20:18 If a **m** has intercourse with a woman suffering
20:19 "If a **m** has sexual intercourse with his aunt,
20:20 If a **m** has intercourse with his uncle's wife,
20:20 Both the **m** and woman involved are guilty of a
20:21 If a **m** marries his brother's wife, it is an act of
24:10 One day a **m** who had an Israelite mother and an
24:11 So the **m** was brought to Moses for judgment.
24:12 They put the **m** in custody until the LORD's will
27: 3 A **m** between the ages of twenty and sixty is
27: 7 A **m** older than sixty is valued at fifteen pieces of
Nu 4:32 You must assign the various loads to each **m** by
4:49 Each **m** was assigned his task and told what to
5:13 Suppose she sleeps with another **m**, but there is no
5:19 and say to her, "If no other **m** has slept with you,
5:20 and defiled yourself by sleeping with another **m**"—
5:30 or if a **m** is overcome with jealousy and suspicion
11:27 A young **m** ran and reported to Moses, "Eldad
15:32 they caught a **m** gathering wood on the Sabbath
15:35 said to Moses, "The **m** must be put to death!
15:36 So the whole community took the **m** outside the
16:22 angry with all the people when only one **m** sins?"
16:40 would warn the Israelites that no unauthorized **m**—
17: 5 Buds will sprout on the staff belonging to the **m** I
17: 9 them to the people. Each **m** claimed his own staff.
19: 8 The **m** who burns the animal must also wash his
19:10 The **m** who gathers up the ashes of the heifer must
23:19 God is not a **m**, that he should lie. / He is not a
24: 3 the prophecy of the **m** whose eyes see clearly,
24:15 the prophecy of the **m** whose eyes see clearly,
25: 8 and rushed after the **m** into his tent.
25:14 The Israelite **m** killed with the Midianite woman
27: 8 'If a **m** dies and has no sons, then give his
30: 2 A **m** who makes a vow to the LORD or makes a
30:16 gave Moses concerning relationships between a **m**
31:17 and all the women who have slept with a **m**.
32:42 a **m** named Nobah captured the town of Kenath
36: 3 But if any of them marries a **m** from another tribe,
Dt 4:16 image in any form—whether of a **m** or a woman,
15:12 "If an Israelite **m** or woman voluntarily becomes
16:16 "Each year every **m** in Israel must celebrate these
17: 2 "Suppose a **m** or woman among you, in one of
17: 5 then that **m** or woman must be taken to the gates of
17:15 be sure that you select as king the **m** the LORD
20:13 God hands it over to you, kill every **m** in the town.
21:15 "Suppose a **m** has two wives, but he loves one
21:16 When the **m** divides the inheritance, he may not
21:18 "Suppose a **m** has a stubborn, rebellious son who
22: 5 and a **m** must not wear women's clothing.
22:13 "Suppose a **m** marries a woman and, after sleeping
22:14 falsely accuses her of having slept with another **m**.
22:15 If the **m** does this, the woman's father and mother
22:16 'I gave my daughter to this **m** to be his wife,
22:18 The judges must then punish the **m**.
22:22 "If a **m** is discovered committing adultery, both he
22:23 "Suppose a **m** meets a young woman, a virgin
22:24 The **m** must die because he violated another man's
22:25 "But if the **m** meets the engaged woman out in the
22:25 and he rapes her, then only the **m** should die.
22:27 Since the **m** raped her out in the country, it must be
22:28 "If a **m** is caught in the act of raping a young
22:30 "A **m** must not have intercourse with his father's
23:10 "Any **m** who becomes ceremonially defiled
23:17 "No Israelite **m** or woman may ever become a
23:18 whether a **m** or a woman, for both are detestable to
24: 1 "Suppose a **m** marries a woman but later discovers
24: 2 If she then leaves and marries another **m**
24: 5 "A newly married **m** must not be drafted into the
25: 9 'This is what happens to a **m** who refuses to raise
25:10 'the family of the **m** whose sandal was pulled off'!
25:11 husband by grabbing the testicles of the other **m**,
28:30 to a woman, but another **m** will ravish her.
28:54 The most tenderhearted **m** among you will have no
29:18 LORD made this covenant with you so that no **m**,
33: 1 This is the blessing that Moses, the **m** of God,
Jos 5:13 and saw a **m** facing him with sword in hand.
7: 1 A **m** named Achan had stolen some of these
7:14 point out the tribe to which the guilty **m** belongs.
8:17 There was not a **m** left in Ai or Bethel who did not
13: 1 When Joshua was an old **m**, the LORD said to
14: 6 the **m** of God, about you and me when we were at
23: 2 of Israel. He said to them, "I am an old **m** now.
Jdg 1:24 who confronted a **m** coming out of the city.
1:25 they killed everyone in the city except for this **m**
1:26 Later the **m** moved to the land of the Hittites,
3: 9 for help, the LORD raised up a **m** to rescue them.
3:15 for help, the LORD raised up a **m** to rescue them.
4:22 and I will show you the **m** you are looking for."
5:30 goods they found— / a woman or two for every **m**.
6:16 Midianites as if you were fighting against one **m**."
7:13 Gideon crept up just as a **m** was telling his friend
7:13 The **m** said, "I had this dream, and in my dream a
7:16 and gave each **m** a ram's horn and a clay jar with a
7:21 Each **m** stood at his position around the camp
8:14 There he captured a young **m** from Succoth
9: 2 ruled by all seventy of Gideon's sons or by one **m**.
9:54 So the young **m** stabbed him with his sword,
10: 3 a **m** from Gilead named Jair judged Israel for
12: 5 they would ask. If the **m** said, "No, I'm not,"
13: 2 a **m** named Manoah from the tribe of Dan lived in
13: 6 told her husband, "A **m** of God appeared to me!
13: 8 please let the **m** of God come back to us again
13:10 "The **m** who appeared to me the other day is here
13:11 "Are you the **m** who talked to my wife the other
14:20 So his wife was given in marriage to the **m** who
14:20 who had been Samson's best **m** at the wedding.
15: 2 "so I gave her in marriage to your best **m**.
15: 6 gave Samson's wife to be married to his best **m**."
16:19 and she called in a **m** to shave off his hair,
17: 1 A **m** named Micah lived in the hill country of
18:19 of Israel than just for the household of one **m**?"
19: 1 There was a **m** from the tribe of Levi living in a
19: 5 On the fourth day the **m** was up early, ready to
19: 7 The **m** got up to leave, but his father-in-law kept
19:10 But this time the **m** was determined to leave.
19:16 That evening an old **m** came home from his work
19:18 have been in Bethlehem in Judah," the **m** replied.
19:20 are welcome to stay with me," the old **m** said.
19:22 beating at the door and shouting to the old **m**,
19:22 "Bring out the **m** who is staying with you so we
19:23 The old **m** stepped outside to talk to them. "No,
19:23 For this **m** is my guest, and such a thing would be
19:24 But don't do such a shameful thing to this **m**."
21: 1 in marriage to a **m** from the tribe of Benjamin.
21:12 young virgins who had never slept with a **m**,
Ru 1: 1 a **m** from Bethlehem in Judah left the country
2: 1 and influential **m** in Bethlehem named Boaz,
2:19 So Ruth told her mother-in-law about the **m** in
2:19 "The **m** I worked with today is named Boaz."
2:20 That **m** is one of our closest relatives, one of our
3:10 now than ever by not running after a younger **m**,
3:12 there is another **m** who is more closely related to
3:18 The **m** won't rest until he has followed through on
4: 4 The **m** replied, "All right, I'll redeem it."
1Sa 1: 1 There was a **m** named Elkanah who lived in
2:16 The **m** offering the sacrifice might reply, "Take as
4:12 A **m** from the tribe of Benjamin ran from the
6:14 The cart came into the field of a **m** named Joshua
9: 1 a rich, influential **m** from the tribe of Benjamin.
9: 2 His son Saul was the most handsome **m** in Israel—
9: 6 There is a **m** of God who lives here in this town.
9:10 So they started into the town where the **m** of God
9:16 "About this time tomorrow I will send you a **m**
9:17 the LORD said, "That's the **m** I told you about!
10:24 "This is the **m** the LORD has chosen as your
10:27 men who complained, "How can this **m** save us?"
12: 2 own sons, and I stand here, an old, gray-haired **m**.
13:14 for the LORD has sought out a **m** after his own
14: 1 One day Jonathan said to the young **m** who carried
14:52 So whenever Saul saw a young **m** who was brave
16: 1 Find a **m** named Jesse who lives there, for I have
16:18 He is also a fine-looking young **m**, and the LORD
17: 4 He was a giant of a **m**, measuring over nine feet
17: 9 If your **m** is able to kill me, then we will be your
17:10 of Israel! Send me a **m** who will fight with me!"
17:12 Now David was the son of a **m** named Jesse,
17:12 Jesse was an old **m** at that time, and he had eight
17:26 "What will a **m** get for killing this Philistine
18:19 Merab in marriage to Adriel, a **m** from Meholah.
18:23 "How can a poor **m** from a humble family afford
19: 5 Why should you murder an innocent **m** like
24:17 he said to David, "You are a better **m** than I am,
25: 2 There was a wealthy **m** from Maon who owned
25:22 May God deal with me severely if even one **m** of
25:25 I know Nabal is a wicked and ill-tempered **m**;
25:33 Bless you for keeping me from murdering the **m**
25:44 to a **m** from Gallim named Palti son of Laish.
26:15 "Well, Abner, you're a great **m**, aren't you?"
28: 8 "I have to talk to a **m** who has died," he said.
28:14 "He is an old **m** wrapped in a robe," she replied.
29: 3 the **m** who ran away from King Saul of Israel.
30:11 Some of David's troops found an Egyptian **m** in a
30:15 The young **m** replied, "If you swear by God's
2Sa 1: 2 a **m** arrived from the Israelite battlefront.
1: 3 escaped from the Israelite camp," the **m** replied.
1: 4 The **m** replied, "Our entire army fled. Many men
1: 6 The young **m** answered, "I happened to be on
1:13 Then David said to the young **m** who had brought
1:15 So the **m** thrust his sword into the Amalekite
3:29 generation be cursed with a **m** who has open sores
3:38 and a great **m** has fallen today in Israel?
4:11 who have killed an innocent **m** in his own house
6:19 Then he gave a gift of food to every **m** and woman
9: 2 He summoned a **m** named Ziba, who had been one
12: 2 The rich **m** owned many sheep and cattle.
12: 3 The poor **m** owned nothing but a little lamb he had
12: 4 One day a guest arrived at the home of the rich **m**.
12: 5 "any **m** who would do such a thing deserves to
12: 6 He must repay four lambs to the poor **m** for the
12: 7 Then Nathan said to David, "You are that **m**!
12:11 I will give your wives to another **m**, and he will go
14:21 go and bring back the young **m** Absalom."
14:25 head to foot, he was the perfect specimen of a **m**.
16: 5 a **m** came out of the village cursing them.
16:18 because I work for the **m** who is chosen by the
17:10 For all Israel knows what a mighty **m** your father
17:18 where a **m** hid them inside a well in his courtyard.
18:12 it for a thousand pieces of silver," the **m** replied.
18:21 Then Joab said to a **m** from Cush, "Go tell the
18:21 what you have seen." The **m** bowed and ran off.
18:23 and got to Mahanaim ahead of the **m** from Cush.
18:24 he looked, he saw a lone **m** running toward them.
18:26 the watchman saw another **m** running toward
18:27 "The first **m** runs like Ahimaaz son of Zadok,"
18:27 "He is a good **m** and comes with good news,"
18:31 Then the **m** from Cush arrived and said, "I have
18:32 and in the future, be as that young **m** is!"
19:16 son of Gera the Benjaminite, the **m** from Bahurim,
20:21 All I want is a **m** named Sheba son of Bicri from
21:20 a huge **m** with six fingers on each hand and six
23: 1 the **m** to whom God gave such wonderful success,
23: 1 David, the **m** anointed by the God of Jacob,
1Ki 1: 6 Adonijah was a very handsome **m** and had been
1:42 Adonijah said to him, "for you are a good **m**.
2: 2 earth must someday go. Take courage and be a **m**.
2: 9 You are a wise **m**, and you will know how to
5:14 so that each **m** would be one month in Lebanon
7:13 then asked for a **m** named Huram to come from
11:28 Jeroboam was a very capable young **m**, and when
12:22 But God said to Shemaiah, the **m** of God,
13: 1 a **m** of God from Judah went to Bethel,
13: 3 That same day the **m** of God gave a sign to prove
13: 4 King Jeroboam was very angry with the **m** of God
13: 4 pointed at the **m** and shouted, "Seize that **m**!"
13: 5 just as the **m** of God had predicted in his message
13: 6 The king cried out to the **m** of God, "Please ask
13: 6 So the **m** of God prayed to the LORD,
13: 7 Then the king said to the **m** of God, "Come to the
13: 8 But the **m** of God said to the king, "Even if you
13:11 and told him what the **m** of God had done in
13:12 So they told their father which road the **m** of God
13:13 "Quick, saddle the donkey," the old **m** said.
13:14 he rode after the **m** of God and found him sitting
13:14 "Are you the **m** of God who came from Judah?"
13:15 Then he said to the **m** of God, "Come home with
13:18 and water to drink.' " But the old **m** was lying to
13:19 and the **m** of God ate some food and drank some
13:21 He cried out to the **m** of God from Judah, "This is
13:23 Now after the **m** of God had finished eating
13:24 and the **m** of God started off again. But as he was
13:26 "It is the **m** of God who disobeyed the LORD's
13:29 So the prophet laid the body of the **m** of God on
13:31 bury me in the grave where the **m** of God is buried.
14: 2 the **m** who told me I would become king.
14: 4 He was an old **m** now and could no longer see.
16:34 reign that Hiel, a **m** from Bethel, rebuilt Jericho.
17:18 She then said to Elijah, "O **m** of God, what have
17:24 "Now I know for sure that you are a **m** of God,
20: 7 to them, "Look how this **m** is stirring up trouble!
20:28 Then the **m** of God went to the king of Israel
20:35 one of the group of prophets to say to another **m**,
20:35 But the **m** refused to strike the prophet.
20:37 Then the prophet turned to another **m** and said,
20:39 I was in the battle, and a **m** brought me a prisoner.
20:39 He said, 'Guard this **m**; if for any reason he gets
20:42 Because you have spared the **m** I said must be
21: 1 and near the palace was a vineyard owned by a **m**
22:27 'Put this **m** in prison, and feed him nothing
2Ki 1: 6 "A **m** came up to us and told us to go back to the
1: 7 "Who was this **m**?" the king demanded.
1: 8 They replied, "He was a hairy **m**, and he wore a
1: 9 The captain said to him, "**M** of God, the king has
1:10 "If I am a **m** of God, let fire come down from
1:11 The captain said to him, "**M** of God, the king says
1:12 Elijah replied, "If I am a **m** of God, let fire come
1:13 "O **m** of God, please spare my life and the lives of
3:21 they mobilized every **m** who could fight, young
4: 7 When she told the **m** of God what had happened,
4: 9 "I am sure this **m** who stops in from time to time is
a holy **m** of God.
4:14 doesn't have a son, and her husband is an old **m**."
4:16 "Please don't lie to me like that, O **m** of God."
4:21 She carried him up to the bed of the **m** of God,
4:22 and a donkey so that I can hurry to the **m** of God
4:25 As she approached the **m** of God at Mount Carmel,
4:27 But when she came to the **m** of God at the
4:27 but the **m** of God said, "Leave her alone.
4:40 had eaten a bite or two they cried out, "**M** of God,
4:42 One day a **m** from Baal-shalishah brought the **m**
5: 7 and said, "This **m** sends me a leper to heal!
5: 8 But when Elisha, the **m** of God, heard about the
5:14 seven times, as the **m** of God had instructed him.
5:15 and his entire party went back to find the **m** of
6: 6 "Where did it fall?" the **m** of God asked. When he
6: 7 said to him. And the **m** reached out and grabbed it.
6: 9 But immediately Elisha, the **m** of God, would warn
6:10 send word to the place indicated by the **m** of God,
6:15 When the servant of the **m** of God got up early the
6:19 and I will take you to the **m** you are looking for."
6:32 the leaders, "A murderer has sent a **m** to kill me.
7: 2 The officer assisting the king said to the **m** of God,
7:17 So everything happened exactly as the **m** of God
7:18 The **m** of God had said to the king, "By this time
7:19 And the **m** of God had said, "You will see it
8: 2 So the woman did as the **m** of God instructed.
8: 4 talking with Gehazi, the servant of the **m** of God.
8: 7 Someone told the king that the **m** of God had
8: 8 he said to Hazael, "Take a gift to the **m** of God.
8:11 Then the **m** of God started weeping.
9:11 "You know the way such a **m** babbles on,"
9:12 So Jehu told them what the **m** had said and that at
10: 4 "Two kings couldn't stand against this **m**!
13:19 But the **m** of God was angry with him.
13:21 Once when some Israelites were burying a **m**,
13:21 the dead **m** revived and jumped to his feet!
22:15 has spoken! Go and tell the **m** who sent you,
23:16 **m** of God as Jeroboam stood beside the altar at the
23:16 and looked up at the tomb of the **m** of God who
23:17 "It is the tomb of the **m** of God who came from
1Ch 2: 3 But the oldest son, Er, was a wicked **m**,
2:17 Abigail married a **m** named Jether, an Ishmaelite,
4: 9 There was a **m** named Jabez who was more
16: 3 Then he gave a gift of food to every **m** and woman
20: 6 a huge **m** with six fingers on each hand and six
23: 1 When David was an old **m**, he appointed his son

23:14 As for Moses, the **m** of God, his sons were
26:14 to his son Zechariah, a **m** of unusual wisdom.
27:32 to the king, a **m** of great insight, and a scribe.
2Ch 2:13 craftsman named Huram-abi. He is a brilliant **m**,
8:14 following the commands of David, the **m** of God.
11:2 But the LORD said to Shemaiah, the **m** of God,
15:13 put to death—whether young or old, **m** or woman.
18:26 'Put this **m** in prison, and feed him nothing
20:35 King Ahaziah of Israel, who was a very wicked **m**.
22:9 a **m** who sought the LORD with all his heart."
25:7 But a **m** of God came to the king and said,
25:9 Amaziah asked the **m** of God, "But what should I
25:9 The **m** of God replied, "The LORD is able to
26:10 on the plains. He was also a **m** who loved the soil.
30:16 found in the law of Moses, the **m** of God.
34:23 has spoken! Go and tell the **m** who sent you,
36:13 Zedekiah was a hard and stubborn **m**, refusing to
Ezr 3:2 as instructed in the law of Moses, the **m** of God.
5:14 and delivered into the safekeeping of a **m** named
7:1 Artaxerxes of Persia, there was a **m** named Ezra.
8:18 they sent us a **m** named Sherebiah, along with
8:18 He was a very astute **m** and a descendant of Mahli,
Ne 2:2 are you? You look like a **m** with deep troubles."
6:19 They kept telling me what a wonderful **m** Tobiah
7:2 for he was a faithful **m** who feared God more than
12:24 just as commanded by David, the **m** of God.
12:36 instruments prescribed by David, the **m** of God.
Est 1:22 proclaiming that every **m** should be the ruler of his
2:7 This **m** had a beautiful and lovely young cousin,
5:9 What a happy **m** Haman was as he left the
6:6 "What should I do to honor a **m** who truly pleases
6:9 noble princes to dress the **m** in the king's robe
6:13 this **m** who has humiliated you—is a Jew, you will
7:9 the **m** who saved the king from assassination."
Job 1:1 There was a **m** named Job who lived in the land of
1:1 He was blameless, a **m** of complete integrity.
1:8 He is the finest **m** in all the earth—a **m** of complete integrity.
2:3 He is the finest **m** in all the earth—a **m** of complete integrity.
2:4 A **m** will give up everything he has to save his life.
12:4 I am a **m** who calls on God and receives an
12:4 I am a just and blameless **m**, yet they laugh at me.
15:2 "You are supposed to be a wise **m**, and yet you
17:10 try again! But I will not find a wise **m** among you.
20:11 He was just a young **m**, but his bones will lie in the
31:10 then may my wife belong to another **m**; may other
34:7 "Has there ever been a **m** as arrogant as Job,
36:4 for I am a **m** of well-rounded knowledge.
42:17 he died, an old **m** who had lived a long, good life.
Ps 22:6 But I am a worm and not a **m**. / I am scorned
62:3 So many enemies against one **m**— / all of them
78:65 like a mighty **m** aroused from a drunken stupor.
80:17 Strengthen the **m** you love, / the son of your
88:4 who is dead, / like a strong **m** with no strength left.
90:T A prayer of Moses, the **m** of God.
106:31 So he has been regarded as a righteous **m**
127:4 Children born to a young **m** / are like sharp arrows
127:5 How happy is the **m** whose quiver is full of them!
147:10 how puny in his sight is the strength of a **m**.
Pr 2:19 The **m** who visits her is doomed. He will never
5:21 For the LORD sees clearly what a **m** does,
5:22 An evil **m** is held captive by his own sins; they are
6:27 Can a **m** scoop fire into his lap and not be burned?
6:29 So it is with the **m** who sleeps with another man's
6:32 But the **m** who commits adultery is an utter fool,
7:7 and saw a simpleminded young **m** who lacked
18:22 The **m** who finds a wife finds a treasure
24:5 A wise **m** is mightier than a strong **m**, and a **m** of knowledge is more powerful than a strong **m**.
26:18 Just as damaging as a mad **m** shooting a lethal
29:3 The **m** who loves wisdom brings joy to his father,
30:19 navigates the ocean, / how a **m** loves a woman.
Ecc 2:8 I had everything a **m** could desire!
4:8 This is the case of a **m** who is all alone, without a
6:3 A **m** might have a hundred children and live to be
6:5 than he has in growing up to be an unhappy **m**.
9:15 wise **m** living there who knew how to save the
10:20 And don't make fun of a rich **m**, either.
11:9 Young **m**, it's wonderful to be young! Enjoy every
SS 8:7 If a **m** tried to buy love with everything he owned,
Isa 3:5 **m** against **m**, neighbor fighting neighbor.
3:6 In those days a **m** will say to his brother,
6:5 for I am a sinful **m** and a member of a sinful race.
14:4 You will say, "The mighty **m** has been destroyed.
22:17 is going to send you into captivity, you strong **m**!
42:13 The LORD will march forth like a mighty **m**;
44:13 takes the tool, and carves the figure of a **m**.
53:3 a **m** of sorrows, acquainted with bitterest grief.
62:5 O Jerusalem, just as a young **m** cares for his bride.
Jer 3:1 "If a **m** divorces a woman and she marries
9:23 "Let not the wise **m** gloat in his wisdom, or the mighty **m** in his might, or the rich **m** in his riches.
11:19 "Let's destroy this **m** and all his words,"
15:12 Can a **m** break a bar of iron from the north, or a
20:3 From now on you are to be called 'The **M** Who
20:10 They call me "The **M** Who Lives in Terror."
22:28 "Why is this **m** Jehoiachin like a discarded,
22:30 Let the record show that this **m** Jehoiachin was
26:11 and the people. "This **m** should die!" they said.
26:15 rest assured that you will be killing an innocent **m**!
26:16 "This **m** does not deserve the death sentence,
35:4 to the sons of Hanan son of Igdaliah, a **m** of God.
38:4 went to the king and said, "Sir, this **m** must die!
38:4 as that of all the people, too. This **m** is a traitor!"
44:7 not a **m**, woman, or child among you who has
Eze 1:26 a figure whose appearance was like that of a **m**.
2:1 "Stand up, son of **m**," said the voice. "I want to
2:3 "Son of **m**," he said, "I am sending you to the
2:6 "Son of **m**, do not fear them. Don't be afraid even
2:8 Son of **m**, listen to what I say to you. Do not join
3:1 The voice said to me, "Son of **m**, eat what I am
3:4 Then he said, "Son of **m**, go to the people of Israel
3:10 Then he added, "Son of **m**, let all my words sink
3:17 "Son of **m**, I have appointed you as a watchman
4:1 "And now, son of **m**, take a large brick and set it
4:16 Then he told me, "Son of **m**, I will cause food to
5:1 "Son of **m**, take a sharp sword and use it as a razor
6:2 "Son of **m**, look over toward the mountains of
7:2 "Son of **m**, this is what the Sovereign LORD
8:2 I saw a figure that appeared to be a **m**.
8:5 said to me, "Son of **m**, look toward the north."
8:6 "Son of **m**," he said, "do you see what they are
8:8 He said to me, "Now, son of **m**, dig into the
8:12 Then the LORD said to me, "Son of **m**, have you
8:17 "Have you seen this, son of **m**?" he asked. "Is it
9:3 And the LORD called to the **m** dressed in linen
9:11 Then the **m** in linen clothing, who carried the
10:2 Then the LORD spoke to the **m** in linen clothing
10:3 the south end of the Temple when the **m** went in,
10:6 The LORD said to the **m** in linen clothing,
10:6 So the **m** went in and stood beside one of the
10:7 He put the coals into the hands of the **m** in linen clothing, and the **m** took them and went out.
11:2 Then the Spirit said to me, "Son of **m**, these are
11:4 Therefore, son of **m**, prophesy against them loudly
11:15 "Son of **m**, the people still left in Jerusalem are
12:2 "Son of **m**, you live among rebels who could see
12:9 "Son of **m**, these rebels, the people of Israel,
12:18 "Son of **m**, tremble as you eat your food.
12:22 "Son of **m**, what is that proverb they quote in
12:27 "Son of **m**, the people of Israel are saying,
13:2 "Son of **m**, speak against the false prophets of
13:17 "Now, son of **m**, also speak out against the women
14:3 "Son of **m**, these leaders have set up idols in their
14:13 "Son of **m**, suppose the people of a country were
15:2 "Son of **m**, how does a grapevine compare to a
16:2 "Son of **m**, confront Jerusalem with her loathsome
16:15 You gave yourself as a prostitute to every **m** who
17:2 "Son of **m**, tell this story to the people of Israel.
17:15 this **m** of Israel's royal family rebelled against
18:5 "Suppose a certain **m** is just and does what is
18:10 "But suppose that **m** has a son who grows up to be
20:3 "Son of **m**, give the leaders of Israel this message
20:4 "Son of **m**, bring judgment against them
20:27 "Therefore, son of **m**, give the people of Israel this
20:46 "Son of **m**, look toward the south and speak out
21:2 "Son of **m**, look toward Jerusalem and prophesy
21:6 "Son of **m**, groan before the people! Groan before
21:9 "Son of **m**, give the people this message from the
21:12 "Son of **m**, cry out and wail; pound your thighs in
21:14 "Son of **m**, prophesy to them and clap your hands
21:19 "Son of **m**, make a map and trace two routes on it
21:28 "And now, son of **m**, prophesy concerning the
22:2 "Son of **m**, are you ready to judge Jerusalem?
22:18 "Son of **m**, the people of Israel are the worthless
22:24 "Son of **m**, give the people of Israel this message:
23:2 "Son of **m**, once there were two sisters who were
23:36 The LORD said to me, "Son of **m**, you must
24:2 "Son of **m**, write down today's date, because on
24:16 "Son of **m**, I am going to take away your dearest
24:25 Then the LORD said to me, "Son of **m**,
25:2 "Son of **m**, look toward the land of Ammon
26:2 "Son of **m**, Tyre has rejoiced over the fall of
27:2 "Son of **m**, sing a funeral song for Tyre,
28:2 "Son of **m**, give the prince of Tyre this message
28:2 But you are only a **m** and not a god, though you
28:9 To them you will be no god but merely a **m**!
28:12 "Son of **m**, weep for the king of Tyre. Give him
28:21 "Son of **m**, look toward the city of Sidon
29:2 "Son of **m**, turn toward Egypt and prophesy
29:18 "Son of **m**, the army of King Nebuchadnezzar of
30:2 "Son of **m**, prophesy and give this message from
30:21 "Son of **m**, I have broken the arm of Pharaoh,
31:2 "Son of **m**, give this message to Pharaoh, king of
32:2 "Son of **m**, mourn for Pharaoh, king of Egypt,
32:18 "Son of **m**, weep for the hordes of Egypt and for
33:2 "Son of **m**, give your people this message: When I
33:7 "Now, son of **m**, I am making you a watchman for
33:10 "Son of **m**, give the people of Israel this message:
33:12 "Son of **m**, give your people this message:
33:21 a **m** who had escaped from Jerusalem came to me
33:22 so I would be able to speak when this **m** arrived
33:24 "Son of **m**, the scattered remnants of Judah living
33:24 'Abraham was only one **m**, and yet he gained
33:30 "Son of **m**, your people are whispering behind
34:2 "Son of **m**, prophesy against the shepherds,
35:2 "Son of **m**, turn toward Mount Seir, and prophesy
36:1 "Son of **m**, prophesy to Israel's mountains.
36:3 Therefore, son of **m**, give the mountains of Israel
36:17 "Son of **m**, when the people of Israel were living
37:3 Then he asked me, "Son of **m**, can these bones
37:11 Then he said to me, "Son of **m**, these bones
37:16 "Son of **m**, take a stick and carve on it these
38:2 "Son of **m**, prophesy against Gog of the land of
38:14 "Therefore, son of **m**, prophesy against Gog.
39:1 "Son of **m**, prophesy against Gog. Give him this
39:17 "And now, son of **m**, call all the birds and wild
40:3 I saw a **m** whose face shone like bronze standing
40:4 He said to me, "Son of **m**, watch and listen.
40:5 The **m** took a measuring rod that was 10-1/2 feet
40:11 The **m** measured the gateway entrance, which was
40:17 Then the **m** brought me through the gateway into
40:19 Then the **m** measured across the Temple's outer
40:20 just like the one on the east, and the **m** measured it.
40:24 Then the **m** took me around to the south gateway
40:28 Then the **m** took me to the south gateway leading
40:45 And the **m** said to me, "The building beside the
40:47 Then the **m** measured the inner courtyard
41:1 After that, the **m** brought me into the Holy Place,
41:13 Then the **m** measured the Temple, and he found it
41:19 One face—that of a **m**—looked toward the palm
41:22 "This," the **m** told me, "is the table that stands in
42:1 Then the **m** led me out of the Temple courtyard by
42:13 Then the **m** told me, "These rooms that overlook
42:15 When the **m** had finished taking these
43:1 the **m** brought me back around to the east gateway.
43:6 (The **m** who had been measuring was still standing
43:7 And the LORD said to me, "Son of **m**, this is the
43:10 "Son of **m**, describe to the people of Israel the
43:18 Then he said to me, "Son of **m**, this is what the
44:1 Then the **m** brought me back to the east gateway in
44:2 No **m** will ever pass through it, for the LORD,
44:4 Then the **m** brought me through the north gateway
44:5 said to me, "Son of **m**, take careful notice;
46:19 Then the **m** brought me through the entrance
46:24 The **m** said to me, "These are the kitchens to be
47:1 Then the **m** brought me back to the entrance of the
47:2 The **m** brought me outside the wall through the
Da 2:10 "There isn't a **m** alive who can tell Your Majesty
2:31 in front of you a huge and powerful statue of a **m**,
5:11 There is a **m** in your kingdom who has within him
5:11 this **m** was found to have insight, understanding,
5:12 This **m** Daniel, whom the king named
6:13 Then they told the king, "That **m** Daniel, one of
7:13 I saw someone who looked like a **m** coming with
8:15 someone who looked like a **m** suddenly stood in
8:16 "Gabriel, tell this **m** the meaning of his vision."
8:17 "Son of **m**," he said, "you must understand that
10:5 I looked up and saw a **m** dressed in linen clothing,
10:11 And the **m** said to me, "O Daniel, greatly loved of
10:16 Then the one who looked like a **m** touched my lips,
10:18 Then the one who looked like a **m** touched me
11:21 **m** who is not directly in line for royal succession.
12:6 One of them asked the **m** dressed in linen,
12:7 The **m** dressed in linen, who was standing above
Hos 7:9 Israel is like an old **m** with graying hair,
12:3 when he became a **m**, he even fought with God.
Am 5:19 In that day you will be like a **m** who runs from a
Na 2:1 Sound the alarm! **M** the ramparts! Muster your
Zep 1:17 I will make you as helpless as a blind **m** searching
Zec 1:8 I saw a **m** sitting on a red horse that was standing
1:10 So the **m** standing among the myrtle trees
2:1 I saw a **m** with a measuring line in his hand.
2:4 other angel said, "Hurry, and say to that young **m**,
3:2 This **m** is like a burning stick that has been
6:12 Here is the **m** called the Branch. He will branch
13:7 against my shepherd, the **m** who is my partner,
Mal 2:12 the nation of Israel every last **m** who has done this
Mt 1:19 Joseph, her fiancé, being a just **m**, decided to break
5:31 'A **m** can divorce his wife by merely giving her a
5:32 But I say that a **m** who divorces his wife,
8:2 Suddenly, a **m** with leprosy approached Jesus.
8:2 "Lord," the **m** said, "if you want to, you can
8:20 and birds have nests, but I, the Son of **M**, have no
9:2 Some people brought to him a paralyzed **m** on a
9:2 Jesus said to the paralyzed **m**, "Take heart, son!
9:3 "Blasphemy! This **m** talks like he is God!"
9:6 I will prove that I, the Son of **M**, have the authority
9:6 Then Jesus turned to the paralyzed **m** and said,
9:7 And the **m** jumped up and went home!
9:8 They praised God for sending a **m** with such great
9:32 some people brought to him a **m** who couldn't
9:33 cast out the demon, and instantly the **m** could talk.
10:11 search for a worthy **m** and stay in his home until
10:23 I assure you that I, the Son of **M**, will return before
10:35 I have come to set a **m** against his father, and a
11:7 "Who is this **m** in the wilderness that you went out
11:8 Or were you expecting to see a **m** dressed in
11:10 John is the **m** to whom the Scriptures refer when
11:19 And I, the Son of **M**, feast and drink, and you say,
12:8 For I, the Son of **M**, am master even of the
12:10 where he noticed a **m** with a deformed hand.
12:13 Then he said to the **m**, "Reach out your hand."
12:13 The **m** reached out his hand, and it became normal,
12:22 Then a demon-possessed **m**, who was both blind
12:22 He healed the **m** so that he could both speak
12:32 against me, the Son of **M**, can be forgiven,
12:40 for three days and three nights, so I, the Son of **M**,
13:37 "I, the Son of **M**, am the farmer who plants the
13:41 I, the Son of **M**, will send my angels, and they will
13:44 a treasure that a **m** discovered hidden in a field.
16:13 "Who do people say that the Son of **M** is?"
16:27 For I, the Son of **M**, will come in the glory of my
16:28 see me, the Son of **M**, coming in my Kingdom."
17:9 the Son of **M**, have been raised from the dead."
17:12 And soon the Son of **M** will also suffer at their
17:14 A **m** came and knelt before Jesus and said,
17:22 told them, "The Son of **M** is going to be betrayed.
18:26 But the **m** fell down before the king and begged
18:28 "But when the **m** left the king, he went to a fellow
18:30 He had the **m** arrested and jailed until the debt
18:32 Then the king called in the **m** he had forgiven
18:34 Then the angry king sent the **m** to prison until he
19:3 "Should a **m** be allowed to divorce his wife for
19:5 'This explains why a **m** leaves his father
19:7 "Then why did Moses say a **m** could merely write
19:9 a **m** who divorces his wife and marries another
19:18 "Which ones?" the **m** asked. And Jesus replied:
19:20 all these commandments," the young **m** replied.
19:22 But when the young **m** heard this, he went sadly

19:28 “I assure you that when I, the Son of **M**,
20:18 “the Son of **M** will be betrayed to the leading
20:28 For even I, the Son of **M**, came here not to be
21:28 A **m** with two sons told the older boy, ‘Son,
22:11 he noticed a **m** who wasn’t wearing the proper
22:12 wedding clothes?’ And the **m** had no reply.
22:24 Moses said, ‘If a **m** dies without children,
24:27 entire sky, so it will be when the Son of **M** comes.
24:30 the sign of the coming of the Son of **M** will appear
24:30 And they will see the Son of **M** arrive on the
24:37 “When the Son of **M** returns, it will be like it was
24:39 That is the way it will be when the Son of **M**
24:44 For the Son of **M** will come when least expected.
25:14 be illustrated by the story of a **m** going on a trip.
25:24 gold came and said, ‘Sir, I know you are a hard **m**,
25:26 You think I’m a hard **m**, do you, harvesting crops I
25:31 “But when the Son of **M** comes in his glory,
26: 2 and I, the Son of **M**, will be betrayed
26: 6 at the home of Simon, a **m** who had leprosy.
26:18 the city,” he told them, “you will see a certain **m**.
26:24 For I, the Son of **M**, must die, as the Scriptures
26:45 I, the Son of **M**, am betrayed into the hands of
26:61 who declared, “This **m** said, ‘I am able to destroy
26:64 And in the future you will see me, the Son of **M**,
26:71 “This **m** was with Jesus of Nazareth.”
26:72 with an oath. “I don’t even know the **m**,” he said.
26:74 Peter said, “I swear by God, I don’t know the **m**.”
27: 4 he declared, “for I have betrayed an innocent **m**.”
27:16 notorious criminal in prison, a **m** named Barabbas.
27:19 “Leave that innocent **m** alone, because I had a
27:24 saying, “I am innocent of the blood of this **m**.
27:32 they came across a **m** named Simon, who was
27:57 a rich **m** from Arimathea who was one of Jesus’
Mk 1:23 A **m** possessed by an evil spirit was in the
1:25 cut him short. “Be silent! Come out of the **m**.”
1:26 spirit screamed and threw the **m** into a convulsion,
1:40 A **m** with leprosy came and knelt in front of Jesus,
1:42 the leprosy disappeared—the **m** was healed.
1:45 But as the **m** went on his way, he spread the news,
2: 3 Four men arrived carrying a paralyzed **m** on a mat.
2: 4 Then they lowered the sick **m** on his mat,
2: 5 their faith, Jesus said to the paralyzed **m**, “My son,
2: 9 Is it easier to say to the paralyzed **m**, ‘Your sins
2:10 I will prove that I, the Son of **M**, have the authority
2:10 Then Jesus turned to the paralyzed **m** and said,
2:12 The **m** jumped up, took the mat, and pushed his
2:28 And I, the Son of **M**, am master even of the
3: 1 and noticed a **m** with a deformed hand.
3: 3 Jesus said to the **m**, “Come and stand in front of
3: 5 Then he said to the **m**, “Reach out your hand.”
3: 5 The **m** reached out his hand, and it became normal
4:41 “Who is this **m**, that even the wind and waves
5: 2 a **m** possessed by an evil spirit ran out from a
5: 3 This **m** lived among the tombs and could not be
5: 6 Jesus was still some distance away, the **m** saw him.
5: 8 to the spirit, “Come out of the **m**, you evil spirit.”
5: 9 because there are many of us here inside this **m**.”
5:13 So the evil spirits came out of the **m** and entered
5:15 but they were frightened when they saw the **m** who
5:16 Those who had seen what happened to the **m**
5:18 the **m** who had been demon possessed begged to
5:20 So the **m** started off to visit the Ten Towns of that
6:16 “John, the **m** I beheaded, has come back from the
6:20 knowing that he was a good and holy **m**,
7:32 A deaf **m** with a speech impediment was brought
7:32 begged Jesus to lay his hands on the **m** to heal him.
7:35 Instantly the **m** could hear perfectly and speak
8:22 some people brought a blind **m** to Jesus, and they
begged him to touch and heal the **m**.
8:23 Jesus took the blind **m** by the hand and led him out
8:24 The **m** looked around. “Yes,” he said, “I see
8:25 As the **m** stared intently, his sight was completely
8:31 the Son of **M**, would suffer many terrible things
8:38 these adulterous and sinful days, I, the Son of **M**,
9: 9 until he, the Son of **M**, had risen from the dead.
9:12 in the Scriptures that the Son of **M** must suffer
9:31 to them, “The Son of **M** is going to be betrayed.
9:38 we saw a **m** using your name to cast out demons,
10: 2 “Should a **m** be allowed to divorce his wife?”
10: 4 “He said a **m** merely has to write his wife an
10: 7 ‘This explains why a **m** leaves his father
10:17 a **m** came running up to Jesus, knelt down,
10:20 “Teacher,” the **m** replied, “I’ve obeyed all these
10:21 Jesus felt genuine love for this **m** as he looked at
10:33 “the Son of **M** will be betrayed to the leading
10:45 For even I, the Son of **M**, came here not to be
10:49 So they called the blind **m**. “Cheer up,” they said.
10:51 “Teacher,” the blind **m** said, “I want to see!”
10:52 healed you.” And instantly the blind **m** could see!
12: 1 “A **m** planted a vineyard, built a wall around it,
12:19 “Teacher, Moses gave us a law that if a **m** dies,
13:26 Then everyone will see the Son of **M** arrive on the
13:34 “The coming of the Son of **M** can be compared
with that of a **m** who left home to go on a trip.
14: 3 at the home of Simon, a **m** who had leprosy.
14:13 “a **m** carrying a pitcher of water will meet you.
14:21 For I, the Son of **M**, must die, as the Scriptures
14:41 I, the Son of **M**, am betrayed into the hands of
14:51 There was a young **m** following along behind,
14:62 “I am, and you will see me, the Son of **M**,
14:69 the others, “That **m** is definitely one of them!”
14:71 I don’t know this **m** you’re talking about.”
15:12 “what should I do with this **m** you call the King of
15:21 A **m** named Simon, who was from Cyrene,
16: 5 and there on the right sat a young **m** clothed in a
Lk 1:17 He will be a **m** with the spirit and power of Elijah,
1:18 I’m an old **m** now, and my wife is also well along
1:27 She was engaged to be married to a **m** named
2:25 Now there was a **m** named Simeon who lived in
2:25 He was a righteous **m** and very devout. He was
4:33 a **m** possessed by a demon began shouting at Jesus,
4:35 he told the demon. “Come out of the **m**!”
4:35 The demon threw the **m** to the floor as the crowd
5:12 Jesus met a **m** with an advanced case of leprosy.
5:12 When the **m** saw Jesus, he fell to the ground,
5:13 Jesus reached out and touched the **m**. “I want to,”
5:18 Some men came carrying a paralyzed **m** on a
5:19 and lowered the sick **m** down into the crowd,
5:20 Seeing their faith, Jesus said to the **m**, “Son,
5:21 “Who does this **m** think he is?” the Pharisees
5:24 I will prove that I, the Son of **M**, have the authority
5:24 Then Jesus turned to the paralyzed **m** and said,
5:25 the **m** jumped to his feet, picked up his mat,
6: 5 And Jesus added, “I, the Son of **M**, am master
6: 6 a **m** with a deformed right hand was in the
6: 7 whether Jesus would heal the **m** on the Sabbath,
6: 8 He said to the **m** with the deformed hand, “Come
6: 8 where everyone can see.” So the **m** came forward.
6:10 around at them one by one and then said to the **m**,
6:10 The **m** reached out his hand, and it became normal
6:22 because you are identified with me, the Son of **M**.
7: 4 begged Jesus to come with them and help the **m**.
7:14 bearers stopped. “Young **m**,” he said, “get up.”
7:24 “Who is this **m** in the wilderness that you went out
7:25 Or were you expecting to see a **m** dressed in
7:27 John is the **m** to whom the Scriptures refer when
7:34 And I, the Son of **M**, feast and drink, and you say,
7:41 “A **m** loaned money to two people—five hundred
7:49 “Who does this **m** think he is, going around
8:25 “Who is this **m**, that even the winds and waves
8:27 a **m** who was possessed by demons came out to
8:29 This spirit had often taken control of the **m**.
8:30 for the **m** was filled with many demons.
8:33 So the demons came out of the **m** and entered the
8:35 And they saw the **m** who had been possessed by
8:36 how the demon-possessed **m** had been healed.
8:38 The **m** who had been demon possessed begged to
8:41 And now a **m** named Jairus, a leader of the local
9: 9 “so who is this **m** about whom I hear such strange
9:22 “For I, the Son of **M**, must suffer many terrible
9:26 ashamed of me and my message, I, the Son of **M**,
9:38 A **m** in the crowd called out to him, “Teacher,
9:44 what I say. The Son of **M** is going to be betrayed.”
9:58 and birds have nests, but I, the Son of **M**, have no
9:59 The **m** agreed, but he said, “Lord, first let me
10:27 The **m** answered, “ ‘You must love the Lord your
10:29 The **m** wanted to justify his actions, so he asked
10:30 “A Jewish **m** was traveling on a trip from
10:31 but when he saw the **m** lying there, he crossed to
10:33 and when he saw the **m**, he felt deep pity.
10:34 Then he put the **m** on his own donkey and took
10:35 pieces of silver and told him to take care of the **m**.
10:36 neighbor to the **m** who was attacked by bandits?”
10:37 The **m** replied, “The one who showed him
11:14 One day Jesus cast a demon out of a **m** who
11:30 God has sent me, the Son of **M**, to these people.
12: 8 me publicly here on earth, I, the Son of **M**,
12:10 Yet those who speak against the Son of **M** may be
12:16 “A rich **m** had a fertile farm that produced fine
12:40 for the Son of **M** will come when least expected.”
13: 6 “A **m** planted a fig tree in his garden and came
14: 2 because there was a **m** there whose arms and legs
14: 4 Jesus touched the sick **m** and healed him and sent
14:15 a **m** sitting at the table with Jesus exclaimed,
14:16 “A **m** prepared a great feast and sent out many
15:11 Jesus told them this story: “A **m** had two sons.
15:19 your son. Please take me on as a hired **m**.” ’
16: 1 “A rich **m** hired a manager to handle his affairs,
16: 6 The **m** replied, ‘I owe him eight hundred gallons of
16: 7 he asked the next **m**. ‘A thousand bushels of
16: 8 “The rich **m** had to admire the dishonest rascal for
16:19 “There was a certain rich **m** who was splendidly
16:22 The rich **m** also died and was buried,
16:24 “The rich **m** shouted, ‘Father Abraham, have some
16:27 “Then the rich **m** said, ‘Please, Father Abraham,
16:30 “The rich **m** replied, ‘No, Father Abraham!
17:16 for what he had done. This **m** was a Samaritan.
17:19 And Jesus said to the **m**, “Stand up and go.
17:22 you will long to share in the days of the Son of **M**,
17:23 “Reports will reach you that the Son of **M** has
17:24 For when the Son of **M** returns, you will know it
17:25 But first the Son of **M** must suffer terribly and be
17:26 “When the Son of **M** returns, the world will be
17:30 right up to the hour when the Son of **M** returns.
18: 2 “who was a godless **m** with great contempt for
18: 4 ‘I fear neither God nor **m**,’ he said to himself,
18: 8 But when I, the Son of **M**, return, how many will I
18:21 The **m** replied, “I’ve obeyed all these
18:23 But when the **m** heard this, he became sad
18:31 prophets concerning the Son of **M** will come true.
18:39 The crowds ahead of Jesus tried to hush the **m**,
18:40 and ordered that the **m** be brought to him.
18:41 Then Jesus asked the **m**, “What do you want me to
18:43 Instantly the **m** could see, and he followed Jesus,
19: 2 There was a **m** there named Zacchaeus. He was
19: 9 for this **m** has shown himself to be a son of
19:10 And I, the Son of **M**, have come to seek and save
19:21 I was afraid because you are a hard **m** to deal with,
20: 9 “A **m** planted a vineyard, leased it out to tenant
20:12 A third **m** was sent and the same thing happened.
20:28 “Teacher, Moses gave us a law that if a **m** dies,
21:27 Then everyone will see the Son of **M** arrive on the
21:36 these horrors and stand before the Son of **M**.”
22:10 a **m** carrying a pitcher of water will meet you.
22:21 among us as a friend, is the **m** who will betray me.
22:22 For I, the Son of **M**, must die since it is part of
22:48 can you betray me, the Son of **M**, with a kiss?”
22:56 she said, “This **m** was one of Jesus’ followers!”
22:57 “Woman,” he said, “I don’t even know the **m**!”
22:58 be one of them!” “No, **m**, I’m not!” Peter replied.
22:60 But Peter said, “**M**, I don’t know what you are
22:69 But the time is soon coming when I, the Son of **M**,
23: 2 “This **m** has been leading our people to ruin by
23: 4 and said, “I find nothing wrong with this **m**!”
23:14 “You brought this **m** to me, accusing him of
23:15 Nothing this **m** has done calls for the death
23:25 the **m** in prison for insurrection and murder.
23:41 but this **m** hasn’t done anything wrong.”
23:47 and said, “Surely this **m** was innocent.”
23:50 there was a good and righteous **m** named Joseph.
24: 7 that the Son of **M** must be betrayed into the hands
24:19 to Jesus, the **m** from Nazareth,” they said.
Jn 1:30 ‘Soon a **m** is coming who is far greater than I am,
1:47 Jesus said, “Here comes an honest **m**—
1:51 of God going up and down upon the Son of **M**.”
3: 4 “How can an old **m** go back into his mother’s
3:13 For only I, the Son of **M**, have come to earth
3:14 so I, the Son of **M**, must be lifted up on a pole,
3:26 the **m** you met on the other side of the Jordan
4:18 and you aren’t even married to the **m** you’re living
4:29 and meet a **m** who told me everything I ever did!
4:50 And the **m** believed Jesus’ word and started home.
5: 7 “I can’t, sir,” the sick **m** said, “for I have no one
5: 9 Instantly, the **m** was healed! He rolled up the mat
5:10 They said to the **m** who was cured, “You can’t
5:11 He replied, “The **m** who healed me said to me,
5:13 The **m** didn’t know, for Jesus had disappeared into
5:15 Then the **m** went to find the Jewish leaders
5:20 Son will do far greater things than healing this **m**.
5:27 to judge all mankind because he is the Son of **M**.
5:34 But the best testimony about me is not from a **m**,
6:27 the eternal life that I, the Son of **M**, can give you.
6:52 “How can this **m** give us his flesh to eat?”
6:53 unless you eat the flesh of the Son of **M** and drink
6:62 you see me, the Son of **M**, return to heaven again?
7:12 Some said, “He’s a wonderful **m**,” while others
7:21 “I worked on the Sabbath by healing a **m**,
7:23 So why should I be condemned for making a **m**
7:25 “Isn’t this the **m** they are trying to kill?
7:27 he be? For we know where this **m** comes from.
7:31 do more miraculous signs than this **m** has done?”
7:40 of them declared, “This **m** surely is the Prophet.”
7:51 “Is it legal to convict a **m** before he is given a
8:28 “When you have lifted up the Son of **M** on the
9: 1 he saw a **m** who had been blind from birth.
9: 2 disciples asked him, “why was this **m** born blind?
9: 7 So the **m** went and washed, and came back seeing!
9: 8 beggar asked each other, “Is this the same **m**—
9: 9 And the beggar kept saying, “I am the same **m**!”
9:11 “The **m** they call Jesus made mud and smoothed it
9:13 Then they took the **m** to the Pharisees.
9:14 it happened, Jesus had healed the **m** on a Sabbath.
9:15 The Pharisees asked the **m** all about it. So he told
9:16 the Pharisees said, “This **m** Jesus is not from God,
9:17 Then the Pharisees once again questioned the **m**
9:17 and demanded, “This **m** who opened your eyes—
9:17 The **m** replied, “I think he must be a prophet.”
9:24 So for the second time they called in the **m** who
9:25 don’t know whether he is a sinner,” the **m** replied.
9:27 “Look!” the **m** exclaimed. “I told you once.
9:29 We know God spoke to Moses, but as for this **m**,
9:30 “Why, that’s very strange!” the **m** replied.
9:33 If this **m** were not from God, he couldn’t do it.”
9:35 he found the **m** and said, “Do you believe in the
Son of **M**?”
9:36 The **m** answered, “Who is he, sir, because I would
9:38 “Yes, Lord,” the **m** said, “I believe!” And he
10:20 or he’s crazy. Why listen to a **m** like that?”
10:21 “This doesn’t sound like a **m** possessed by a
10:33 but for blasphemy, because you, a mere **m**,
10:41 “but all his predictions about this **m** have come
11: 1 A **m** named Lazarus was sick. He lived in Bethany
11:37 But some said, “This **m** healed a blind **m**.
11:47 “This **m** certainly performs many miraculous
11:50 be destroyed? Let this one **m** die for the people.”
12: 1 of Lazarus—the **m** he had raised from the dead.
12: 9 see Lazarus, the **m** Jesus had raised from the dead.
12:23 “The time has come for the Son of **M** to enter into
12:34 Why are you saying the Son of **M** will die? Who is
this Son of **M** you are talking about?”
13:31 the Son of **M**, to enter into my glory, and God will
18:23 for it. Should you hit a **m** for telling the truth?”
18:26 a relative of the **m** whose ear Peter had cut off,
18:29 and asked, “What is your charge against this **m**?”
18:40 shouted back, “No! Not this **m**, but Barabbas!”
19: 5 the purple robe. And Pilate said, “Here is the **m**!”
19:12 “If you release this **m**, you are not a friend of
19:39 the **m** who had come to Jesus at night, also came,
Ac 1:24 Then they all prayed for the right **m** to be chosen.
3: 2 a **m** lame from birth was being carried in.
3: 5 The lame **m** looked at them eagerly, expecting a
3: 7 Then Peter took the lame **m** by the right hand
3:12 And why look at us as though we had made this **m**
3:16 “The name of Jesus has healed this **m**—and you
4: 9 because we’ve done a good deed for a crippled **m**?
4:10 the **m** you crucified, but whom God raised from
4:14 But since the **m** who had been healed was standing
4:22 the healing of a **m** who had been lame for more
5: 1 There was also a **m** named Ananias who, with his
6: 5 Stephen (a **m** full of faith and the Holy Spirit),
6: 8 Stephen, a **m** full of God’s grace and power,

6:13 "This **m** is always speaking against the Temple
7:24 he saw an Egyptian mistreating a **m** of Israel.
7:27 "But the **m** in the wrong pushed Moses aside
7:35 so God sent back the same **m** his people had
7:56 and the Son of **M** standing in the place of honor at
7:58 and laid them at the feet of a young **m** named Saul.
8:9 A **m** named Simon had been a sorcerer there for
8:30 and heard the **m** reading from the prophet Isaiah;
8:31 The **m** replied, "How can I, when there is no one
9:12 I have shown him a vision of a **m** named Ananias
9:13 "I've heard about the terrible things this **m** has
9:21 "Isn't this the same **m** who persecuted Jesus'
9:33 There he met a **m** named Aeneas, who had been
10:2 He was a devout **m** who feared the God of Israel,
10:2 and was a **m** who regularly prayed to God.
10:5 Now send some men down to Joppa to find a **m**
10:21 and said, "I'm the **m** you are looking for.
10:22 He is a devout **m** who fears the God of Israel
10:30 a **m** in dazzling clothes was standing in front of
11:12 and we soon arrived at the home of the **m** who had
11:24 Barnabas was a good **m**, full of the Holy Spirit
12:22 shouting, "It is the voice of a god, not of a **m**!"
13:1 Simeon (called "the black **m**"), Lucius (from
13:7 a **m** of considerable insight and understanding.
13:21 a **m** of the tribe of Benjamin, who reigned for forty
13:22 him with David, a **m** about whom God said,
13:22 'David son of Jesse is a **m** after my own heart,
13:38 In this **m** Jesus there is forgiveness for your sins.
14:8 and Barnabas came upon a **m** with crippled feet.
14:10 And the **m** jumped to his feet and started walking.
16:9 He saw a **m** from Macedonia in northern Greece,
17:26 From one **m** he created all the nations throughout
17:31 the world with justice by the **m** he has appointed,
19:15 But when they tried it on a **m** possessed by an evil
19:26 this **m** Paul has persuaded many people that
20:9 Paul spoke on and on, a young **m** named Eutychus,
20:12 Meanwhile, the young **m** was taken home unhurt,
21:10 our stay of several days, a **m** named Agabus,
21:16 a **m** originally from Cyprus and one of the early
21:28 This is the **m** who teaches against our people
22:12 A **m** named Ananias lived there. He was a godly
m in his devotion to the law,
22:26 are you doing? This **m** is a Roman citizen!"
23:17 and said, "Take this young **m** to the commander.
23:18 and asked me to bring this young **m** to you
23:22 the commander warned the young **m** as he sent
23:27 This **m** was seized by some Jews, and they were
24:4 moment as I briefly outline our case against this **m**.
24:5 a **m** who is constantly inciting the Jews throughout
25:22 "I'd like to hear the **m** myself," Agrippa said.
25:24 this is the **m** whose death is demanded both by the
26:31 "This **m** hasn't done anything worthy of death
Ro 1:3 News about his Son, Jesus, who came as a **m**,
5:15 For this one **m**, Adam, brought death to many
5:15 But this other **m**, Jesus Christ, brought forgiveness
5:17 The sin of this one **m**, Adam, caused death to rule
5:17 in triumph over sin and death through this one **m**,
7:3 be committing adultery if she married another **m**.
16:10 to Apelles, a good **m** whom Christ approves.
1Co 5:1 I am told that you have a **m** in your church who is
5:2 And why haven't you removed this **m** from your
5:5 Then you must cast this **m** out of the church
6:15 Should a **m** take his body, which belongs to Christ,
6:16 And don't you know that if a **m** joins himself to a
7:2 each **m** should have his own wife,
7:12 If a Christian **m** has a wife who is an unbeliever
7:18 a **m** who was circumcised before he became a
7:18 And the **m** who was uncircumcised when he
7:19 or not a **m** has been circumcised.
7:32 An unmarried **m** can spend his time doing the
7:33 But a married **m** can't do that so well. He has to
7:36 But if a **m** thinks he ought to marry his fiancée
11:3 A **m** is responsible to Christ, a woman is
11:4 A **m** dishonors Christ if he covers his head while
11:7 A **m** should not wear anything on his head when
11:7 for **m** is God's glory, made in God's own image,
but woman is the glory of **m**.
11:8 For the first **m** didn't come from woman, but the
first woman came from **m**.
11:9 And **m** was not made for woman's benefit, but
woman was made for **m**.
11:12 For although the first woman came from **m**,
11:14 Isn't it obvious that it's disgraceful for a **m** to have
15:21 just as death came into the world through a **m**,
15:21 from the dead has begun through another **m**,
15:22 because all of us are related to Adam, the first **m**.
15:22 to Christ, the other **m**, will be given new life.
15:45 The Scriptures tell us, "The first **m**, Adam,
15:47 Adam, the first **m**, was made from the dust of the
15:47 while Christ, the second **m**, came from heaven.
15:49 Just as we are now like Adam, the **m** of the earth,
15:49 will someday be like Christ, the **m** from heaven.
2Co 2:5 I am not overstating it when I say that the **m** who
2:10 When you forgive this **m**, I forgive him, too.
Eph 5:28 For a **m** is actually loving himself when he loves
5:31 "A **m** leaves his father and mother and is joined to
5:33 each **m** must love his wife as he loves himself,
2Th 2:3 against God and the **m** of lawlessness is revealed—
2:8 Then the **m** of lawlessness will be revealed,
2:9 This evil **m** will come to do the work of Satan with
1Ti 2:5 and people. He is the **m** Christ Jesus.
3:2 For an elder must be a **m** whose life cannot be
3:5 For if a **m** cannot manage his own household,
5:1 Never speak harshly to an older **m**, but appeal to
2Ti 2:8 Never forget that Jesus Christ was a **m** born into
Phm 1:9 an old **m**, now in prison for the sake of Christ
Heb 2:6 "What is **m** that you should think of him,
2:6 and the son of **m** that you should care for him?
5:1 Now a high priest is a **m** chosen to represent other
11:4 Abel's offering to show that he was a righteous **m**.
11:12 And so a whole nation came from this one **m**,
Jas 2:6 And yet, you insult the poor **m**! Isn't it the rich
5:11 Job is an example of a **m** who endured patiently.
2Pe 2:7 because he was a good **m** who was sick of all the
2:8 he was a righteous **m** who was distressed by the
Rev 1:13 in the middle of the lampstands was the Son of **M**.
13:18 number of the beast, for it is the number of a **m**.
14:14 Then I saw the Son of **M** sitting on a white cloud.

MAN'S (46) [MAN]

Ge 2:7 And the LORD God formed a **m** body from the
44:1 and put each **m** money back into his sack.
Lev 15:5 "So if you touch the **m** bedding, you will be
15:13 "When the **m** discharge heals, he must count off a
20:10 "If a man commits adultery with another **m** wife,
Nu 5:12 'Suppose a **m** wife goes astray and is unfaithful to
25:8 Phinehas thrust the spear all the way through the **m**
Dt 22:19 The woman will then remain the **m** wife, and he
22:20 "But suppose the **m** accusations are true, and her
22:22 both he and the other **m** wife must be killed.
22:24 man must die because he violated another **m** wife.
23:1 "If a **m** testicles are crushed or his penis is cut off,
25:7 But if the dead **m** brother refuses to marry the
Jdg 8:21 said to Gideon, "Don't ask a boy to do a **m** job!
19:11 and the **m** servant said to him, "It's getting too late
19:24 take my virgin daughter and this **m** concubine.
Ru 1:2 The **m** name was Elimelech, and his wife was
1Sa 25:3 This **m** name was Nabal, and his wife, Abigail,
2Sa 10:4 and shaved off half of each **m** beard,
12:3 It ate from the **m** own plate and drank from his
12:4 he took the poor **m** lamb and killed it and served it
17:3 After all, it is only this **m** life that you seek.
17:19 The **m** wife put a cloth over the top of the well
Job 20:6 Though the godless **m** pride reaches to the heavens
Pr 6:26 and sleeping with another **m** wife may cost you
6:29 So it is with the man who sleeps with another **m**
Isa 53:9 like a criminal; he was put in a rich **m** grave.
Jnh 1:14 they pleaded, "don't make us die for this **m** sin.
Mt 12:29 You can't enter a strong **m** house and rob him
Mk 3:2 Would he heal the **m** hand on the Sabbath? If he
3:27 You can't enter a strong **m** house and rob him
7:33 He put his fingers into the **m** ears. Then,
7:33 he touched the **m** tongue with the spittle.
8:23 Then, spitting on the **m** eyes, he laid his hands on
8:25 Then Jesus placed his hands over the **m** eyes again.
10:22 At this, the **m** face fell, and he went sadly away
12:34 Realizing this **m** understanding, Jesus said to him,
Lk 4:36 "What authority and power this **m** words possess!
11:14 couldn't speak, and the **m** voice returned to him.
16:21 lay there longing for scraps from the rich **m** table,
22:51 And he touched the place where the **m** ear had
Jn 9:6 and smoothed the mud over the blind **m** eyes.
11:39 But Martha, the dead **m** sister, said, "Lord, by now
Ac 3:7 the **m** feet and anklebones were healed
5:28 "Didn't we tell you never again to teach in this **m**
Ro 5:16 is very different from the result of that one **m** sin.

MAN-EATER (2) [EAT, MAN]

Eze 19:3 to catch and devour prey, / and he became a **m**.
19:6 and devour prey, / and he, too, became a **m**.

MAN-MADE (4) [MAN, MAKE]

Hab 2:18 "What have you gained by worshiping all your **m**
Mt 15:9 God's commands with their own **m** teachings.' "
Mk 7:7 God's commands with their own **m** teachings.'
Ac 17:24 of heaven and earth, he doesn't live in **m** temples,

MANAEN (1)

Ac 13:1 **M** (the childhood companion of King Herod

MANAGE (5) [MANAGED, MANAGER, MANAGES, MANAGING]

Ge 41:40 You will **m** my household and organize all my
1Ti 3:4 He must **m** his own family well, with children who
3:5 For if a man cannot **m** his own household, how can
3:12 and he must **m** his children and household well.
1Pe 4:10 **M** them well so that God's generosity can flow

MANAGED (1) [MANAGE]

Jos 10:20 a tiny remnant that **m** to reach their fortified cities.

MANAGER (14) [MANAGE]

Ge 43:16 he said to the **m** of his household, "These men will
43:23 Don't worry about it," the household **m** told them.
44:2 So the household **m** did as he was told.
44:4 Joseph said to his household **m**, "Chase after them
45:8 **m** of his entire household and ruler over all Egypt.
1Ki 4:6 Ahishar was **m** of palace affairs. / Adoniram son of
Ne 2:8 send a letter to Asaph, the **m** of the king's forest,
Lk 8:3 Joanna, the wife of Chuza, Herod's business **m**;
16:1 "A rich man hired a **m** to handle his affairs,
16:1 but soon a rumor went around that the **m** was
16:3 "The **m** thought to himself, 'Now what?
16:6 So the **m** told him, 'Tear up that bill and write
16:7 'Here,' the **m** said, 'take your bill and replace it
1Co 4:2 a person who is put in charge as a **m** must be

MANAGES (1) [MANAGE]

Lev 25:26 but the person who sold it **m** to get enough money

MANAGING (2) [MANAGE]

Mt 24:45 can give the responsibility of **m** his household
Lk 12:42 master gives the responsibility of **m** his household

MANAHATH (3) [MANAHATHITES]

Ge 36:23 Shobal were Alvan, **M**, Ebal, Shepho, and Onam.
1Ch 1:40 Shobal were Alvan, **M**, Ebal, Shepho, and Onam.
8:6 living at Geba, were driven out and moved to **M**.

MANAHATHITES (2) [MANAHATH]

1Ch 2:52 father of Kiriath-jearim) were Haroeh, half the **M**,
2:54 the other half of the **M**, the Zorites,

MANASSEH (149) [MANASSEH'S]

Ge 41:51 Joseph named his older son **M**, for he said,
46:20 born in the land of Egypt, were **M** and Ephraim.
48:1 he took with him his two sons, **M** and Ephraim.
48:5 Ephraim and **M**, who were born here in the land of
48:6 will be within the territories of Ephraim and **M**.
48:13 at Jacob's left hand and **M** was at his right hand.
48:14 and his left hand was on the head of **M**, the older.
48:19 "**M**, too, will become a great people, but his
48:20 as prosperous as Ephraim and **M**.' " In this way,
Jacob put Ephraim ahead of **M**.
Nu 1:10 **M** son of Joseph | Gamaliel son of Pedahzur
1:34[-35] **M** son of Joseph | 32,200
2:18[-19] "The divisions of Ephraim, **M**, and Benjamin
2:20[-21] **M** | Gamaliel son of Pedahzur | 32,200
7:54 leader of the tribe of **M**, presented his offering.
10:23 The tribe of **M** was led by Gamaliel son of
13:11 **M** son of Joseph | Gaddi son of Susi
26:28 Two clans were descended from Joseph through **M**
26:29 These were the clans descended from **M**:
26:34 The men from all the clans of **M** numbered 52,700.
26:37 These clans of **M** and Ephraim were all
27:1 son of Gilead, son of Makir, son of **M**, son of
32:33 and half the tribe of **M** son of Joseph the territory
32:39 Then the descendants of Makir of the tribe of **M**
32:40 descendants of **M**, and they lived there.
32:41 The people of Jair, another clan of the tribe of **M**,
34:14 and half the tribe of **M** have already received their
34:23 **M** son of Joseph | Hanniel son of Ephod
36:1 descendants of Makir, son of **M**, son of Joseph—
36:12 They married into the clans of **M** son of Joseph.
Dt 3:13 Og's former kingdom—to the half-tribe of **M**.
3:14 Jair, a leader from the tribe of **M**,
4:43 tribe of Gad; Golan in Bashan for the tribe of **M**.
29:8 and to the half-tribe of **M** as their inheritance.
33:17 multitudes of Ephraim / and the thousands of **M**."
34:2 the land of Ephraim and **M**; all the land of Judah,
Jos 1:12 the tribes of Reuben, Gad, and the half-tribe of **M**.
4:12 and the half-tribe of **M** led the Israelites across the
12:6 the tribes of Reuben, Gad, and the half-tribe of **M**.
13:7 among the nine tribes and the half-tribe of **M**."
13:8 Half the tribe of **M** and the tribes of Reuben
13:29 area to the families of the half-tribe of **M**.
14:4 had become two separate tribes—**M** and Ephraim.
16:4 **M** and Ephraim, received their inheritance.
16:9 villages in the territory of the half-tribe of **M**.
17:1 allotment of land was given to the half-tribe of **M**,
17:2 to the remaining families within the tribe of **M**:
17:3 who was a descendant of **M**, Makir, and Gilead,
17:6 because the female descendants of **M** received an
17:6 given to the rest of the male descendants of **M**.)
17:7 The boundary of the tribe of **M** extended from the
17:8 (The land surrounding Tappuah belonged to **M**,
17:9 the border of **M** followed the northern side of the
17:10 and the land north of the ravine belonged to **M**,
17:10 North of **M** was the territory of Asher, and to the
17:11 territory of Issachar and Asher were given to **M**:
17:12 But the descendants of **M** were unable to occupy
17:17 Then Joshua said to the tribes of Ephraim and **M**,
18:7 and the half-tribe of **M** won't receive any more
20:8 and Golan in Bashan, in the land of the tribe of **M**.
21:5 of Ephraim, Dan, and the half-tribe of **M**.
21:6 Naphtali, and the half-tribe of **M** in Bashan.
21:25 The half-tribe of **M** allotted the following towns
21:27 with their pasturelands from the half-tribe of **M**:
22:1 the tribes of Reuben, Gad, and the half-tribe of **M**.
22:7 of Bashan to the half-tribe of **M** east of the Jordan.
22:9 and the half-tribe of **M** left the rest of Israel at
22:10 and the half-tribe of **M** built a very large altar near
22:13 the tribes of Reuben, Gad, and the half-tribe of **M**.
22:15 the tribes of Reuben, Gad, and the half-tribe of **M**,
22:21 and the half-tribe of **M** answered these high
22:30 Gad, and the half-tribe of **M**, they were satisfied.
24:32 territory allotted to the tribes of Ephraim and **M**,
Jdg 1:27 The tribe of **M** failed to drive out the people living
6:15 My clan is the weakest in the whole tribe of **M**,
6:35 He also sent messengers throughout **M**, Asher,
7:23 sent for the warriors of Naphtali, Asher, and **M**,
11:29 and he went throughout the land of Gilead and **M**,
12:4 nothing more than rejects from Ephraim and **M**."
1Ki 4:13 the Towns of Jair (named for Jair son of **M**)
11:28 the labor force from the tribes of Ephraim and **M**.
2Ki 10:33 including all of Gilead, Gad, Reuben, and **M**.
20:21 Hezekiah died, his son **M** became the next king.
21:1 **M** was twelve years old when he became king,
21:6 **M** even sacrificed his own son in the fire.
21:7 **M** even took an Asherah pole he had made and set
21:9 and **M** led them to do even more evil than the
21:11 "King **M** of Judah has done many detestable
21:16 **M** also murdered many innocent people until
21:18 When **M** died, he was buried in the palace garden,
21:20 the LORD's sight, just as his father, **M**, had done.

23:12 The king destroyed the altars that **M** had built in
23:26 because of all the great evils of King **M**,
24: 3 from his presence because of the many sins of **M**.
1Ch 3:13 Ahaz, Hezekiah, **M**,
5:18 armies of Reuben, Gad, and the half-tribe of **M**.
5:23 The half-tribe of **M** spread through the land from
5:26 Gad, and the half-tribe of **M** as captives.
6:61 of the half-tribe of **M** by means of sacred lots.
6:62 Asher, Naphtali, and from the Bashan area of **M**,
6:70 towns from the territory of the half-tribe of **M**:
6:71 **M** the town of Golan in Bashan with its
7:14 The sons of **M**, born to his Aramean concubine,
7:17 descendants of Makir son of **M**.
7:29 Along the border of **M** were the towns of
9: 3 Ephraim, and **M** came and settled in Jerusalem.
12:19 Some men from **M** defected from the Israelite
12:20 Here is a list of the men from **M** who defected to
12:20 commanded a thousand troops from the tribe of **M**.
12:31 From the half-tribe of **M** west of the Jordan,
12:37 of Reuben and Gad and the half-tribe of **M** lived—
26:32 tribes of Reuben and Gad and the half-tribe of **M**.
27:20 son of Azaziah / **M** (west) | Joel son of Pedaiah
27:21 **M** (east) | Iddo son of Zechariah / Benjamin
2Ch 15: 9 along with the people of Ephraim, **M**,
30: 1 he wrote letters of invitation to Ephraim and **M**.
30:10 and **M** and as far as the territory of Zebulun.
30:11 However, some from Asher, **M**, and Zebulun
30:18 of those who came from Ephraim, **M**, Issachar,
31: 1 Benjamin, Ephraim, and **M**, and they smashed the
32:33 at his death. Then his son **M** became the next king.
33: 1 **M** was twelve years old when he became king,
33: 6 **M** even sacrificed his own sons in the fire in the
33: 7 **M** even took a carved idol he had made and set it
33: 9 But **M** led the people of Judah and Jerusalem to do
33:10 The LORD spoke to **M** and his people, but they
33:11 the Assyrian armies, and they took **M** prisoner.
33:12 **M** sought the LORD his God and cried out
33:13 So the LORD let **M** return to Jerusalem and to his
33:13 **M** had finally realized that the LORD alone is
33:14 It was after this that **M** rebuilt the outer wall of the
33:15 **M** also removed the foreign gods from the hills
33:20 When **M** died, he was buried at his palace.
33:22 the LORD's sight, just as his father **M** had done.
34: 6 He did the same thing in the towns of **M**, Ephraim,
34: 9 The gifts were brought by people from **M**,
Ezr 10:30 Maaseiah, Mattaniah, Bezalel, Binnui, and **M**.
10:33 Mattenai, Mattattah, Zabad, Eliphelet, Jeremai, **M**,
Ps 60: 7 Gilead is mine, / and **M** is mine. / Ephraim will
80: 2 to Ephraim, Benjamin, and **M**. / Show us your
108: 8 Gilead is mine, / and **M** is mine. / Ephraim will
Isa 9:21 **M** will feed on Ephraim, Ephraim will feed on **M**,
Jer 15: 4 Because of the wicked things **M** son of Hezekiah,
Eze 48: 4 Then comes **M** south of Naphtali, and its territory
48: 5 South of **M** is Ephraim,
Mt 1:10 Hezekiah was the father of **M**. / **M** was the father
Rev 7: 6 from Naphtali | 12,000 / from **M** | 12,000

MANASSEH'S (11) [MANASSEH]

Ge 48:17 So he lifted it to place it on **M** head instead.
50:23 his son Ephraim and the children of **M** son Makir,
Jos 13:31 to the descendants of Makir, who was **M** son.
17: 1 (Makir was **M** oldest son and was the father of
17: 5 a result, **M** inheritance came to ten parcels of land,
17: 8 the town of Tappuah, on the border of **M** territory,
17: 9 (Several towns in **M** territory belonged to the tribe
17:10 with the Mediterranean Sea forming **M** western
2Ki 21:17 The rest of the events in **M** reign and all his deeds,
2Ch 33:18 The rest of the events of **M** reign, his prayer to
33:19 **M** prayer, the account of the way God answered

MANASSES [KJV] See MANASSEH

MANDRAKE (3) [MANDRAKES]

Ge 30:15 Now will you steal my son's **m** roots, too?"
30:15 with you tonight in exchange for the **m** roots."
30:16 "I have paid for you with some **m** roots my son

MANDRAKES (2) [MANDRAKE]

Ge 30:14 Reuben found some **m** growing in a field
SS 7:13 There the **m** give forth their fragrance,

MANE (1)

Job 39:19 its strength or clothed its neck with a flowing **m**?

MANEH [KJV] See MINA

MANEUVER (1)

Jdg 20:36 to give those hiding in ambush more room to **m**.

MANGER (3)

Lk 2: 7 him snugly in strips of cloth and laid him in a **m**,
2:12 You will find a baby lying in a **m**, wrapped snugly
2:16 And there was the baby, lying in the **m**.

MANHOOD (1) [MAN]

Dt 21:17 who represents the strength of his father's **m**

MANKIND (1) [MAN]

Jn 5:27 And he has given him authority to judge all **m**

MANNA (19)

Ex 16:31 In time, the food became known as **m**. It was white
16:32 "Take two quarts of **m** and keep it forever as a
16:33 "Get a container and put two quarts of **m** into it.
16:35 So the people of Israel ate **m** for forty years until
16:36 (The container used to measure the **m** was an
Nu 11: 6 day after day we have nothing to eat but this **m**!"
11: 7 The **m** looked like small coriander seeds,
11: 9 The **m** came down on the camp with the dew
21: 5 nothing to drink. And we hate this wretched **m**!"
Dt 8: 3 you go hungry and then feeding you with **m**,
8:16 He fed you with **m** in the wilderness, a food
Jos 5:12 No **m** appeared that day, and it was never seen
Ps 78:24 and rained down **m** for them to eat. / He gave them
105:40 them quail; / he gave them **m**—bread from heaven.
Jn 6:31 our ancestors ate **m** while they journeyed through
6:49 Your ancestors ate **m** in the wilderness, but they all
6:58 your ancestors did, even though they ate the **m**."
Heb 9: 4 Inside the Ark were a gold jar containing some **m**,
Rev 2:17 Everyone who is victorious will eat of the **m** that

MANNED (3) [MAN]

2Ch 8:18 and **m** by experienced crews of sailors.
9:21 The king had a fleet of trading ships **m** by the
Eze 27:11 Your towers were **m** by men from Gammad.

MANNER (2)

Php 1:27 you must live in a **m** worthy of the Good News
3Jn 1: 6 You do well to send them on their way in a **m** that

MANOAH (14) [MANOAH'S]

Jdg 13: 2 a man named **M** from the tribe of Dan lived in the
13: 8 Then **M** prayed to the LORD. He said, "Lord,
13: 9 in the field. But her husband, **M**, was not with her.
13:11 **M** ran back with his wife and asked, "Are you the
13:12 So **M** asked him, "When your words come true,
13:15 Then **M** said to the angel of the LORD,
13:16 (**M** didn't realize it was the angel of the LORD.)
13:17 Then **M** asked the angel of the LORD, "What is
13:19 Then **M** took a young goat and a grain offering
13:19 And as **M** and his wife watched, the LORD did
13:20 When **M** and his wife saw this, they fell with their
13:21 The angel did not appear again to **M** and his wife.
13:21 **M** finally realized it was the angel of the LORD,
16:31 and Eshtaol, where his father, **M**, was buried.

MANOAH'S (1) [MANOAH]

Jdg 13: 3 The angel of the LORD appeared to **M** wife

MANSIONS (2)

Jer 9:21 in through our windows and has entered our **m**.
Am 3:15 their winter **m** and their summer houses, too—

MANSLAUGHTER (1) [MAN, SLAUGHTER]

Dt 17: 8 whether someone is guilty of murder or only of **m**,

MANSLAYER(S) [KJV] See MURDER, SLAYER

MANUFACTURE (1) [MANUFACTURED, MANUFACTURER, MANUFACTURING]

Isa 44: 9 How foolish are those who **m** idols to be their

MANUFACTURED (2) [MANUFACTURE]

2Ch 32: 5 and **m** large numbers of weapons and shields.
Eze 27:14 All these things were exchanged for your **m** goods.

MANUFACTURER (1) [MANUFACTURE]

Ne 3: 8 Beyond him was Hananiah, a **m** of perfumes.

MANUFACTURING (1) [MANUFACTURE]

Ac 19:24 a silversmith who had a large business **m** silver

MANY (624) [MANY-COLORED]

Ge 9: 7 Now you must have **m** children and repopulate the
10: 1 **M** children were born to them after the Flood.
11: 9 confused the people by giving them **m** languages,
12:16 Then Pharaoh gave Abram **m** gifts because of her
13: 5 also very wealthy with sheep, cattle, and **m** tents.
13: 6 There were too **m** animals for the available
13:16 And I am going to give you so **m** descendants that,
15: 5 descendants will be like that—too **m** to count!"
17: 5 for you will be the father of **m** nations.
17: 6 of descendants who will represent **m** nations.
17:16 and she will become the mother of **m** nations.
24:35 and gold, and **m** servants and camels and donkeys.
24:60 may you become / the mother of **m** millions!
26:14 and goats, great herds of cattle, and **m** servants.
26:24 I will give you **m** descendants, and they will
27:29 May **m** nations become your servants. May you be
28: 3 God Almighty bless you and give you **m** children.
30:29 faithfully I've served you through these **m** years,
30:43 with **m** servants, camels, and donkeys.
32: 5 donkeys, sheep, goats, and **m** servants, both men
32:12 as the sands along the seashore—too **m** to count."
35:11 the earth! Become a great nation, even **m** nations.
37:34 He mourned deeply for his son for **m** days.
42: 9 And he remembered the dreams he had had **m**
46:34 as our ancestors have been for **m** generations.'
47: 9 but I am still not nearly as old as **m** of my
50:20 I have today so I could save the lives of **m** people.
Ex 1: 7 But their descendants had **m** children
1: 9 a threat to us because there are so **m** of them.
2:11 **M** years later, when Moses had grown up, he went
5: 5 Look, there are **m** people here in Egypt, and you
5:11 But you must produce just as **m** bricks as before!"
5:16 but we are still told to make as **m** bricks as before.
10: 5 so **m** that you won't be able to see the ground.
12:38 **M** people who were not Israelites went with them,
along with the **m** flocks and herds.
23:29 and the wild animals would become too **m** to
34: 7 I show this unfailing love to **m** thousands by
Lev 11:42 well as those with four legs and those with **m** feet.
15:25 "If the menstrual flow of blood continues for **m**
25:51 If **m** years still remain, they will repay most of
Nu 11:31 For **m** miles in every direction from the camp there
13:18 people living there are strong or weak, few or **m**.
13:20 is the soil? Is it fertile or poor? Are there **m** trees?
21: 6 among them, and **m** of them were bitten and died.
22: 3 And when they saw how **m** Israelites there were,
23:13 of the nation of Israel. Curse at least that **m**!"
26: 2 to find out how **m** of each family are of military
32:41 captured **m** of the towns in Gilead and changed the
Dt 3: 5 We also took **m** unwalled villages at the same
6: 3 and you will have **m** children in the land flowing
7: 1 he will clear away **m** nations ahead of you:
7:13 He will give you **m** children and give fertility to
12:15 You may eat as **m** animals as the LORD your
12:31 These nations have committed **m** detestable acts
15: 6 You will lend money to **m** nations but will never
15: 6 You will rule **m** nations, but they will not rule over
17:17 The king must not take **m** wives for himself,
17:20 and his descendants will reign for **m** generations in
28: 4 You will be blessed with **m** children
28:11 **m** children, numerous livestock, and abundant
28:12 You will lend to **m** nations, but you will never
30: 9 He will give you **m** children and numerous
Jos 17:14 land when the LORD has given us so **m** people?"
24: 3 I gave him **m** descendants through his son Isaac.
24: 7 Then you lived in the wilderness for **m** years.
24:11 There were also **m** others who fought you,
Jdg 7: 2 to Gideon, "You have too **m** warriors with you.
7: 4 the LORD told Gideon, "There are still too **m**!
7:12 grains of sand on the seashore—too **m** to count!
8:30 He had seventy sons, for he had **m** wives.
9:40 **M** of Shechem's warriors were killed,
15: 8 Philistines with great fury and killed **m** of them.
16:24 one who killed so **m** of us is now in our power!"
18:26 When Micah saw that there were too **m** of them for
1Sa 2: 5 but the woman with **m** children will have no more.
6:15 **M** burnt offerings and sacrifices were offered to
13: 5 and as **m** warriors as the grains of sand along the
14: 6 He can win a battle whether he has **m** warriors
14:30 think how **m** more we could have killed!"
15:33 "As your sword has killed the sons of **m** mothers,
19: 4 about David, saying **m** good things about him.
31: 1 **M** were slaughtered on the slopes of Mount
2Sa 1: 4 **M** men are dead and wounded on the battlefield,
1:12 nation of Israel, because so **m** had died that day.
5:11 a palace. Hiram also sent **m** cedar logs for lumber.
5:13 and concubines, and he had **m** sons and daughters.
8:10 and there had been **m** wars between them.
8:10 Joram presented David with **m** gifts of silver,
12: 2 The rich man owned **m** sheep and cattle.
13:37 And David mourned **m** days for his son Amnon.
15:12 Soon **m** others also joined Absalom,
23:20 He did **m** heroic deeds, which included killing two
24: 2 so that I may know how **m** people there are."
24: 3 as **m** people in your kingdom as there are now!
1Ki 1: 1 and no matter how **m** blankets covered him,
1:19 He has sacrificed **m** oxen, fattened calves,
1:25 Today he has sacrificed **m** oxen, fattened calves,
5: 3 because of the **m** wars he waged with surrounding
7:47 not weigh all the utensils because there were so **m**;
8:64 presence was too small to handle so **m** offerings.
10:10 so **m** spices brought in as those the queen of Sheba
10:26 He stationed **m** of them in the chariot cities,
10:29 **M** of these were then resold to the kings of the
11: 1 Now King Solomon loved **m** foreign women.
17:15 to eat from her supply of flour and oil for **m** days.
18: 1 After **m** months passed, in the third year of the
18:25 of Baal, "You go first, for there are **m** of you.
22:16 "How **m** times must I demand that you speak only
22:20 he can be killed there?' There were **m** suggestions,
2Ki 4: 3 "Borrow as **m** empty jars as you can from your
4: 5 Her sons brought **m** jars to her, and she filled one
6:14 the king of Aram sent a great army with **m** chariots
17: 9 The people of Israel had also secretly done **m**
17:11 So the people of Israel had done **m** evil things,
19:23 You have said, "With my **m** chariots / I have
19:24 I have dug wells in **m** a foreign land
21:11 "King Manasseh of Judah has done **m** detestable
21:16 Manasseh also murdered **m** innocent people until
24: 3 his presence because of the **m** sins of Manasseh.
1Ch 4:14 so called because **m** craftsmen lived there.
5: 9 since they had so **m** cattle in the land of Gilead,
5:22 **M** of the Hagrites were killed in the battle
7: 4 for all five of them had **m** wives and **m** sons.
8:40 They had **m** sons and grandsons—150 in all.
10: 1 **M** were slaughtered on the slopes of Mount
11:22 He did **m** heroic deeds, which included killing two
14: 1 a palace. Hiram also sent **m** cedar logs for lumber.
14: 3 in Jerusalem, and they had **m** sons and daughters.
18:10 and there had been **m** wars between them.
18:10 Joram presented David with **m** gifts of gold,
21: 2 me the totals so I may know how **m** there are."
22: 8 'You have killed **m** men in the great battles you
22:15 You have **m** skilled stonemasons and carpenters
23:11 as a single family because neither had **m** sons.
23:28 and served in **m** other ways in the house of God.
24: 5 for there were **m** qualified officials serving God in

28: 5 for the LORD has given me **m** children—
29:21 and **m** other sacrifices on behalf of Israel.
2Ch 1:14 He stationed **m** of them in the chariot cities,
1:17 **M** of these were then resold to the kings of the
9:25 He stationed **m** of them in the chariot cities,
9:28 were imported from Egypt and **m** other countries.
14:13 so **m** Ethiopians fell that they were unable to rally.
14:15 the camps of herdsmen and captured **m** sheep
15: 9 **M** had moved to Judah during Asa's reign when
18:15 "How **m** times must I demand that you speak only
18:19 he can be killed there?' There were **m** suggestions,
26:10 forts in the wilderness and dug **m** water cisterns,
26:10 He had **m** workers who cared for his farms
28: 5 and inflicted **m** casualties on his army.
29:35 and a great deal of fat from the **m** peace offerings.
30:17 Since **m** of the people there had not purified
30:24 Meanwhile, **m** more priests purified themselves.
32:23 and **m** gifts for the LORD arrived at Jerusalem,
32:28 He also constructed **m** storehouses for his grain,
32:28 and he made **m** stalls for his cattle and folds for his
32:29 He built **m** towns and acquired vast flocks
36:10 **M** treasures from the Temple of the LORD were
Ezr 1: 6 They gave them **m** choice gifts in addition to all
3:12 **M** of the older priests, Levites, and other leaders
4:19 past been a hotbed of insurrection against **m** kings.
5:11 built here **m** years ago by a great king of Israel.
7: 1 **M** years later, during the reign of King Artaxerxes
9: 1 came to me and said, "**M** of the people of Israel,
10:13 for **m** of us are involved in this extremely sinful
Ne 6:17 **m** letters went back and forth between Tobiah
6:18 For **m** in Judah had sworn allegiance to him
6:19 And Tobiah sent **m** threatening letters to intimidate
9:22 ancestors conquer great kingdoms and **m** nations,
9:30 your love, you were patient with them for **m** years.
12:43 **M** sacrifices were offered on that joyous day,
Est 1: 7 Drinks were served in gold goblets of **m** designs,
2: 6 along with King Jehoiachin of Judah and **m** others.
2: 8 Esther, along with **m** other young women,
4: 3 and **m** people lay in sackcloth and ashes.
5:11 to them about his great wealth and his **m** children.
8:17 And **m** of the people of the land became Jews
Job 1: 3 female donkeys, and he employed **m** servants.
4: 3 "In the past you have encouraged **m** a troubled
5: 5 and their wealth satisfies the thirst of **m** others,
5:25 Your children will be **m**; your descendants will be
11:19 lie down unafraid, and **m** will look to you for help.
12:12 and understanding to those who have lived **m**
13: 1 I have seen **m** instances such as you describe.
14: 5 You know how **m** months we will live, and we are
21:33 **M** pay their respects as the body is laid to rest
36: 3 I will give you **m** illustrations of the righteousness
39: 2 Do you know how **m** months they carry their
Ps 3: 1 LORD, I have so **m** enemies; / so **m** are against me.
3: 2 So **m** are saying, / "God will never rescue him!"
4: 6 **M** people say, "Who will show us better times?"
5:10 Drive them away because of their **m** sins,
25:11 your name, O LORD, / forgive my **m**, **m** sins.
25:19 See how **m** enemies I have, / and how viciously
31:13 I have heard the **m** rumors about me, / and I am
32:10 **M** sorrows come to the wicked, / but unfailing love
34:19 The righteous face **m** troubles, / but the LORD
38:19 My enemies are **m**; / they hate me though I have
40: 3 **M** will see what he has done and be astounded.
40: 5 LORD my God, you have done **m** miracles for us.
40:12 For troubles surround me— / too **m** to count!
45:16 You will make them rulers over **m** lands.
48:12 Walk around and count the **m** towers.
49: 4 I listen carefully to **m** proverbs / and solve riddles
55:18 against me, / even though **m** still oppose me.
56: 2 me constantly, / and **m** are boldly attacking me.
61: 6 Add **m** years to the life of the king! / May his years
62: 3 So **m** enemies against one man— / all of them
62:11 has spoken plainly, / and I have heard it **m** times:
71: 7 My life is an example to **m**, / because you have
78:38 destroy them all. / **M** a time he held back his anger
89:50 I carry in my heart the insults of so **m** people.
95: 9 they courted my wrath though they had seen my **m**
106: 7 They soon forgot his **m** acts of kindness to them.
107: 3 For he has gathered the exiles from **m** lands,
110: 5 He will strike down **m** kings in the day of his
119:65 You have done **m** good things for me, LORD,
119:157 **M** persecute and trouble me, / yet I have not
Pr 7:26 For she has been the ruin of **m**; numerous men
11:14 a nation falls; with **m** counselors, there is safety.
12:14 People can get **m** good things by the words they
12:14 the work of their hands also gives them **m** benefits.
14:20 their neighbors, while the rich have **m** "friends."
15:22 for lack of advice; **m** counselors bring success.
19: 4 Wealth makes **m** "friends"; poverty drives them
19: 6 **M** beg favors from a prince; everyone is the friend
19:21 You can make **m** plans, but the LORD's purpose
20: 6 **M** will say they are loyal friends, but who can find
24: 6 victory depends on having **m** counselors.
24:24 will be cursed by **m** people and denounced by the
27: 6 Wounds from a friend are better than **m** kisses
29:26 **M** seek the ruler's favor, but justice comes from
31:29 "There are **m** virtuous and capable women in the
Ecc 2: 6 the water to irrigate my **m** flourishing groves.
2: 8 and gold, the treasure of **m** kings and provinces.
2: 8 and women, and had **m** beautiful concubines.
11: 2 Divide your gifts among **m**, for you do not know
11: 8 them also remember that the dark days will be **m**.
SS 8: 7 **M** waters cannot quench love; neither can rivers
Isa 1:15 Even though you offer **m** prayers, I will not listen.
2: 3 **M** nations will come and say, "Come, let us go up
2: 7 of silver and gold and **m** horses and chariots.
5: 9 "**M** beautiful homes will stand deserted,

8:15 **M** of them will stumble and fall, never to rise
again. **M** will be captured."
10:10 we have finished off **m** a kingdom whose gods
10:13 By my own strength I have captured **m** lands,
13: 4 It is the noise and the shout of **m** nations.
14: 1 And people from **m** different nations will come
27:13 **M** who were dying in exile in Assyria and Egypt
29: 1 Year after year you offer your **m** sacrifices.
29:23 For when they see their **m** children and material
37:24 You have said, "With my **m** chariots / I have
37:25 I have dug wells in **m** a foreign land
41: 2 He gives him victory over **m** nations and permits
41:15 You will be a new threshing instrument with **m**
48:19 as the sands along the seashore—too **m** to count!
52:14 **M** were amazed when they saw him—beaten
52:15 And he will again startle **m** nations. Kings will
53:10 he will have a multitude of children, **m** heirs.
53:11 my righteous servant will make it possible for **m** to
53:12 He bore the sins of **m** and interceded for sinners.
60: 5 to you. They will bring you the wealth of **m** lands.
60:11 around the clock to receive the wealth of **m** lands.
61: 4 though they have been empty for **m** generations.
66:16 by his sword, and **m** will be killed by the LORD.
Jer 2:28 For you have as **m** gods as there are cities
3: 1 But you have prostituted yourself with **m** lovers,
5: 6 For their rebellion is great, and their sins are **m**.
7:32 so **m** bodies in Topheth that there won't be room
11:13 you have as **m** gods as there are cities and towns.
11:15 where they have done so **m** immoral things?
12:10 "**M** rulers have ravaged my vineyard,
13:22 It is because of your **m** sins! That is why you have
16:16 "But now I am sending for **m** fishermen who will
20:10 I have heard the **m** rumors about me. They call me
22: 8 People from **m** nations will pass by the ruins of
22:14 palace with huge rooms and **m** windows,
25:14 **M** nations and great kings will enslave the
27: 7 But then **m** nations and great kings will conquer
28: 8 preceded you and me spoke against **m** nations,
29: 6 find spouses for them, and have **m** grandchildren.
29:28 should build homes and plan to stay for **m** years.
29:28 because we will be here to eat the fruit for **m** years
30:14 For your sins are **m**, and your guilt is great.
30:15 because your sins are **m** and your guilt is great.
31:12 because of the **m** gifts the LORD has given
37:16 into a dungeon cell, where he remained for **m** days.
39: 3 the king's adviser, and **m** others.
46:11 But your **m** medicines will bring you no healing.
50:41 and **m** kings are rising against you from far-off
51:20 you I will shatter nations and destroy **m** kingdoms.
51:27 Signal **m** nations to mobilize for war against
51:58 The builders from **m** lands have worked in vain,
La 1: 5 for the LORD has punished Jerusalem for her **m**
1:22 my sins. My groans are **m**, and my heart is faint."
2:14 Your "prophets" have said so **m** foolish things,
3: 9 He has twisted the road before me with **m** detours.
4:22 just beginning; soon your **m** sins will be revealed.
Eze 16:39 these **m** nations—and they will destroy you.
16:41 your homes and punish you in front of **m** women.
16:41 and end your payments to your **m** lovers.
17:15 to Egypt to request a great army and **m** horses.
17:17 to Jerusalem again and destroys the lives of **m**.
18:18 But the father will die for the **m** sins he
19:11 of its height / and because of its **m** lush branches.
23:42 From your room came the sound of **m** men
24:10 Cook the meat well with **m** spices. Then empty the
25: 7 I will give you as plunder to **m** nations.
26: 3 O Tyre, and I will bring **m** nations against you,
26: 5 Tyre will become the prey of **m** nations,
27:33 you traded / satisfied the needs of **m** nations.
28: 8 in the heart of the sea, pierced with **m** wounds.
28:18 You defiled your sanctuaries with your **m** sins
30:23 I will scatter the Egyptians to **m** lands throughout
32: 3 I will send **m** people to catch you in my net
32: 9 that you have never seen, I will disturb **m** hearts.
32:10 Yes, I will bring terror to **m** lands, and their kings
32:20 The Egyptians will fall with the **m** who have died
33:24 We are **m**; surely the land should be given to us as
36: 3 and now you are possessed by **m** nations.
36:19 I scattered them to **m** lands to punish them for the
38: 6 from the distant north and **m** others.
38: 8 and after the return of her people from **m** lands.
38:12 people who have returned from exile in **m** nations.
38:12 capture vast amounts of plunder and take **m** slaves,
40: 4 been brought here so I can show you **m** things.
47: 7 **m** trees were now growing on both sides of the
Da 2: 6 I will give you **m** wonderful gifts and honors.
2:37 Your Majesty, you are a king over **m** kings.
2:48 to a high position and gave him **m** valuable gifts.
7: 5 a voice saying to it, "Get up! Devour **m** people!"
8:25 defeating **m** by catching them off guard.
11:12 and will have **m** thousands of his enemies killed.
11:18 his attention to the coastal cities and conquer **m**.
11:26 His army will be swept away, and **m** will be killed.
11:33 "Those who are wise will give instruction to **m**.
11:33 But for a time **m** of these teachers will die by fire
11:34 though **m** who join them will not be sincere.
11:41 of Israel, and **m** nations will fall, but Moab, Edom,
11:42 He will conquer **m** countries, and Egypt will not
11:44 and he will set out in great anger to destroy **m** as
12: 2 **M** of those whose bodies lie dead and buried will
12: 3 and those who turn **m** to righteousness will shine
12: 4 **M** will rush here and there, and knowledge will
12:10 **M** will be purified, cleansed, and refined by these
Hos 1:10 be like the sands of the seashore—too **m** to count!
3: 3 "You must live in my house for **m** days and stop
7: 3 The princes laugh about the people's **m** lies.
8: 9 The people of Israel have sold themselves to **m**

8:10 But though they have sold themselves to **m** lands,
8:11 "Israel has built **m** altars to take away sin,
10: 2 down their foreign altars and smash their **m** idols.
12:10 I sent my prophets to warn you with **m** visions
Mic 4: 2 **M** nations will come and say, "Come, let us go up
4:11 **m** nations have gathered together against you,
4:13 so you can trample **m** nations to pieces.
7:12 People from **m** lands will come and honor you—
7:12 and from **m** distant seas and mountains.
Na 1:12 "Even though the Assyrians have **m** allies,
2: 9 There seems no end to Nineveh's **m** treasures—
Hab 2: 5 In their greed they have gathered up **m** nations
2: 8 You have plundered **m** nations; now they will
Zep 2:14 Owls of **m** kinds will live among the ruins of its
3: 6 "I have wiped out **m** nations, devastating their
Zec 2: 4 **M** will live outside the city walls, with all their
2:11 **M** nations will join themselves to the LORD on
3: 1 angel's right hand, accusing Jeshua of **m** things.
6:15 **M** will come from distant lands to rebuild the
7: 3 as we have done for so **m** years?"
8:22 People from **m** nations, even powerful nations,
Mal 2: 6 and they turned **m** from lives of sin.
2: 8 Your 'guidance' has caused **m** to stumble into sin.
Mt 3: 7 But when he saw **m** Pharisees and Sadducees
4:15 in Galilee where so **m** Gentiles live—
7:13 and its gate is wide for the **m** who choose the easy
7:22 On judgment day **m** will tell me, 'Lord, Lord,
7:22 and performed **m** miracles in your name.'
8:11 that **m** Gentiles will come from all over the world
8:12 But **m** Israelites—those for whom the Kingdom
8:16 That evening **m** demon-possessed people were
9:10 tax collectors and **m** other notorious sinners.
12:15 He left that area, and **m** people followed him.
13: 3 He told **m** stories such as this one: "A farmer went
13:17 **m** prophets and godly people have longed to see
14:13 was headed and followed by land from **m** villages.
15:30 mute, and **m** others with physical difficulties,
15:34 "How **m** loaves of bread do you have?"
19:22 he went sadly away because he had **m** possessions.
19:30 But **m** who seem to be important now will be the
20:16 so it is, that **m** who are first now will be last then;
20:28 and to give my life as a ransom for **m**."
22: 3 **M** guests were invited, and when the banquet was
22:14 For **m** are called, but few are chosen."
24: 5 For **m** will come in my name, saying, 'I am the
Messiah.' They will lead **m** astray.
24: 7 and earthquakes in **m** parts of the world.
24:10 And **m** will turn away from me and betray and hate
24:11 And **m** false prophets will appear and will lead **m**
people astray.
24:12 and the love of **m** will grow cold.
25:21 so now I will give you **m** more responsibilities.
25:23 so now I will give you **m** more responsibilities.
26:28 his people. It is poured out to forgive the sins of **m**.
26:60 But even though they found **m** who agreed to give
27:13 "Don't you hear their **m** charges against you?"
27:52 The bodies of **m** godly men and women who had
27:53 holy city of Jerusalem, and appeared to **m** people.
27:55 And **m** women who had come from Galilee with
Mk 1:32 **m** sick and demon-possessed people were brought
1:34 sick people who had **m** different kinds of diseases,
1:34 and he ordered **m** demons to come out of their
1:39 and expelling demons from **m** people.
2:15 tax collectors and **m** other notorious sinners.
2:15 (There were **m** people of this kind among the
3:10 There had been **m** healings that day. As a result, **m**
sick people were crowding around him,
4: 2 He began to teach the people by telling **m** stories
4:33 He used **m** such stories and illustrations to teach
5: 9 because there are **m** of us here inside this man."
5:26 She had suffered a great deal from **m** doctors
6: 2 and **m** who heard him were astonished.
6:13 they cast out **m** demons and healed **m** sick people,
6:31 There were so **m** people coming and going that
6:33 But **m** people saw them leaving, and people from
m towns ran ahead along the
6:34 without a shepherd. So he taught them **m** things.
7: 4 This is but one of **m** traditions they have clung to
7:13 is only one example. There are **m**, **m** others."
8: 5 "How **m** loaves of bread do you have?" he asked.
8:19 How **m** baskets of leftovers did you pick up
8:20 how **m** large baskets of leftovers did you pick
8:31 would suffer **m** terrible things and be rejected by
10:22 he went sadly away because he had **m** possessions.
10:31 But **m** who seem to be important now will be the
10:45 and to give my life as a ransom for **m**."
11: 8 **M** in the crowd spread their coats on the road
12:41 their money. **M** rich people put in large amounts.
13: 6 because **m** will come in my name, claiming to be
the Messiah. They will lead **m** astray.
13: 8 and there will be earthquakes in **m** parts of the
14:24 said to them, "This is my blood, poured out for **m**,
14:56 **M** false witnesses spoke against him, but they
15: 3 Then the leading priests accused him of **m** crimes,
15:41 and **m** other women had come with him to
16:20 confirming what they said by **m** miraculous signs.
Lk 1: 1 **M** people have written accounts about the events
1:14 and **m** will rejoice with you at his birth,
1:16 And he will persuade **m** Israelites to turn to the
2:34 "This child will be rejected by **m** in Israel,
2:34 But he will be the greatest joy to **m** others.
2:35 the deepest thoughts of **m** hearts will be revealed.
3:18 John used **m** such warnings as he announced the
3:19 and for **m** other wrongs he had done.
3:20 put John in prison, adding this sin to his **m** others.
4:25 "Certainly there were **m** widows in Israel who
4:27 rather than the **m** lepers in Israel who needed

5: 4 let down your nets, and you will catch **m** fish."
5:29 **M** of Levi's fellow tax collectors and other guests
6:17 surrounded by **m** of his followers and by the
6:18 and to be healed, and Jesus cast out **m** evil spirits.
7:12 and **m** mourners from the village were with her.
7:21 he cured **m** people of their various diseases,
7:47 I tell you, her sins—and they are **m**—have been
8: 3 and **m** others who were contributing from their
8: 4 that had gathered from **m** towns to hear him:
8:30 he replied—for the man was filled with **m** demons.
9:22 of Man, must suffer **m** terrible things," he said.
10:24 **m** prophets and kings have longed to see and hear
11:53 From that time on they grilled him with **m** hostile
13:24 Work hard to get in, because **m** will try to enter,
14:16 prepared a great feast and sent out **m** invitations.
18: 8 return, how **m** will I find who have faith?"
18:30 will be repaid **m** times over in this life, as well as
21: 8 For **m** will come in my name, claiming to be the
21:11 there will be famines and epidemics in **m** lands,
21:26 The courage of **m** people will falter because of the
23:27 along behind, including **m** grief-stricken women.
24:45 Then he opened their minds to understand these **m**
Jn 2:23 **m** people were convinced that he was indeed the
4:39 **M** Samaritans from the village believed in Jesus
4:41 long enough for **m** of them to hear his message
6:66 At this point **m** of his disciples turned away
7:31 **M** among the crowds at the Temple believed in
8:30 Then **m** who heard him say these things believed
10:32 "At my Father's direction I have done **m** things to
10:41 And **m** followed him. "John didn't do miracles,"
10:42 And **m** believed in him there.
11:19 and **m** of the people had come to pay their respects
11:45 **M** of the people who were with Mary believed in
11:47 "This man certainly performs **m** miraculous signs.
11:55 and **m** people from the country arrived in
12:11 because of him that **m** of the people had deserted
12:18 was the main reason so **m** went out to meet him—
12:24 But its death will produce **m** new kernels—
12:42 **M** people, including some of the Jewish leaders,
14: 2 There are **m** rooms in my Father's home, and I am
16:33 Here on earth you will have **m** trials and sorrows.
17:13 I have told them **m** things while I was with them
18: 2 because Jesus had gone there **m** times with his
19:20 Latin, and Greek, so that **m** people could read it.
20:30 Jesus' disciples saw him do **m** other miraculous
21: 6 draw in the net because there were so **m** fish in it.
Ac 1: 3 and proved to them in **m** ways that he was actually
2: 5 Godly Jews from **m** nations were living in
2:43 and the apostles performed **m** miraculous signs
4: 4 But **m** of the people who heard their message
5:12 the apostles were performing **m** miraculous signs
6: 7 and **m** of the Jewish priests were converted,
7:36 And by means of **m** miraculous signs and wonders
8: 7 **M** evil spirits were cast out, screaming as they left
8: 7 And **m** who had been paralyzed or lame were
8: 9 Simon had been a sorcerer there for **m** years,
8:12 As a result, **m** men and women were baptized.
8:25 And they stopped in **m** Samaritan villages along
8:35 then used **m** others to tell him the Good News
9:42 the whole town, and **m** believed in the Lord.
12:12 of John Mark, where **m** were gathered for prayer.
12:24 spreading rapidly, and there were **m** new believers.
13:31 And he appeared over a period of **m** days to those
13:43 **M** Jews and godly converts to Judaism who
14:21 the Good News in Derbe and making **m** disciples,
14:22 into the Kingdom of God through **m** tribulations.
15:21 in every city on every Sabbath for **m** generations."
15:35 and Barnabas stayed in Antioch to assist **m** others
17: 4 and also **m** important women of the city.
17:12 As a result, **m** Jews believed, as did some of the prominent Greek women and **m** men.
17:23 for as I was walking along I saw your **m** altars.
18: 8 **M** others in Corinth also became believers
18:10 because **m** people here in this city belong to me."
19:18 **M** who became believers confessed their sinful
19:24 goddess Artemis. He kept **m** craftsmen busy.
19:26 this man Paul has persuaded **m** people that
20: 8 where we met was lighted with **m** flickering lamps.
20:31 over you night and day, and my **m** tears for you.
21:20 how **m** thousands of Jews have also believed,
24:10 that you have been a judge of Jewish affairs for **m**
25: 7 and made **m** serious accusations they couldn't
26:10 I caused **m** of the believers in Jerusalem to be sent
26:11 **M** times I had them whipped in the synagogues to
27:20 The terrible storm raged unabated for **m** days,
Ro 1:13 dear friends, that I planned **m** times to visit you,
3: 2 Yes, being a Jew has **m** advantages. First of all,
4:17 "I have made you the father of **m** nations."
4:18 that he would become the father of **m** nations,
5:15 Adam, brought death to **m** through his sin.
5:15 brought forgiveness to **m** through God's bountiful
5:16 by God, even though we are guilty of **m** sins.
5:19 person disobeyed God, **m** people became sinners.
5:19 **m** people will be made right in God's sight.
8:29 would be the firstborn, with **m** brothers and sisters.
11:28 **M** of the Jews are now enemies of the Good News.
12: 4 Just as our bodies have **m** parts and each part has a
16: 2 for she has helped **m** in their needs, including me.
1Co 4:11 We have endured **m** beatings, and we have no
8: 5 there are **m** so-called gods and **m** lords, both in
11:30 That is why **m** of you are weak and sick and some
12:12 The human body has **m** parts, but the **m** parts make up only one body.
12:14 Yes, the body has **m** different parts, not just one
12:18 But God made our bodies with **m** parts, and he has
12:20 Yes, there are **m** parts, but only one body.
14:10 There are so **m** different languages in the world,
16: 9 a great work here, and **m** people are responding. But there are **m** who oppose me.
2Co 1:11 **m** will give thanks to God because so **m** people's prayers for our safety have been
2:17 not like those hucksters—and there are **m** of them
8: 7 Since you excel in so **m** ways—you have so much
8:22 and has shown how earnest he is on **m** occasions.
9: 2 it was your enthusiasm that stirred up **m** of them to
9:10 he will give you **m** opportunities to do good,
11:26 I have traveled **m** weary miles. I have faced danger
12:12 For I patiently did **m** signs and wonders
12:21 because **m** of you who sinned earlier have not
Gal 3:16 was to his children, as if it meant **m** descendants.
Eph 2: 1 doomed forever because of your **m** sins.
Php 1:14 **m** of the Christians here have gained confidence
3:18 that there are **m** whose conduct shows they are
Col 2: 1 and for **m** other friends who have never known me
4: 3 that God will give us **m** opportunities to preach
1Th 2: 2 even though we were surrounded by **m** who
1Ti 6: 9 and are trapped by **m** foolish and harmful desires
6:10 the faith and pierced themselves with **m** sorrows.
6:12 you have confessed so well before **m** witnesses.
2Ti 2: 2 You have heard me teach **m** things that have been confirmed by **m** reliable witnesses.
3: 6 with the guilt of sin and controlled by **m** desires.
Tit 1:10 For there are **m** who rebel against right teaching;
3: 3 and became slaves to **m** wicked desires and evil
Heb 1: 1 Long ago God spoke **m** times and in **m** ways to our ancestors through the
2:10 was made—should bring his **m** children into glory.
7: 1 home after winning a great battle against **m** kings,
7:23 Another difference is that there were **m** priests
9:28 as a sacrifice to take away the sins of **m** people.
11:12 a nation with so **m** people that, like the stars of the
12:15 it springs up, **m** are corrupted by its poison.
Jas 3: 1 not **m** of you should become teachers in the
3: 2 We all make **m** mistakes, but those who control
5:20 and bring about the forgiveness of **m** sins.
1Pe 1: 6 even though it is necessary for you to endure **m**
1:10 even though they had **m** questions as to what it all
1:12 their lifetime, but **m** years later, during yours.
2Pe 2: 2 **M** will follow their evil teaching and shameful
1Jn 2:18 and already **m** such antichrists have appeared.
4: 1 For there are **m** false prophets in the world.
2Jn 1: 7 **M** deceivers have gone out into the world. They do
Rev 6: 2 He rode out to win **m** battles and gain the victory.
7: 4 And I heard how **m** were marked with the seal of
8:11 and **m** people died because the water was so bitter.
9:16 I heard an announcement of how **m** there were.
10:11 "You must prophesy again about **m** peoples,
14: 2 It was like the sound of **m** harpists playing
17: 1 come on the great prostitute, who sits on **m** waters.
19:12 like flames of fire, and on his head were **m** crowns.

MANY-COLORED (2) [COLOR, MANY]

Eze 17: 3 A great eagle with broad wings full of **m** feathers
27:24 and **m** carpets bound with cords and made secure.

MAON (7) [MAONITES]

Jos 15:55 Besides these, there were **M**, Carmel, Ziph, Juttah,
1Sa 23:24 and his men had moved into the wilderness of **M**
23:25 and he remained there in the wilderness of **M**.
25: 1 Then David moved down to the wilderness of **M**.
25: 2 There was a wealthy man from **M** who owned
1Ch 2:45 The son of Shammai was **M**. **M** was the father of Beth-zur.

MAONITES (1) [MAON]

Jdg 10:12 the Sidonians, the Amalekites, and the **M**?

MAP (5) [MAPPED, MAPPING]

Jos 18: 5 The scouts will **m** the land into seven sections,
Eze 4: 1 Then draw a **m** of the city of Jerusalem on it.
5: 2 Place a third of it at the center of your **m** of
5: 2 Scatter another third across your **m** and slash at it
21:19 make a **m** and trace two routes on it for the sword

MAPPED (1) [MAP]

Jos 18: 9 and **m** the entire territory into seven sections,

MAPPING (1) [MAP]

Jos 18: 8 As the men who were **m** out the land started on

MAR [KJV] See BLOCK, CLIP, ENDANGER, ROT, RUIN

MARA (1)

Ru 1:20 "Instead, call me **M**, for the Almighty has made

MARAH (6)

Ex 15:23 When they came to **M**, they finally found water.
15:23 (That is why the place was called **M**, which means
15:25 It was there at **M** that the LORD laid before them
15:27 After leaving **M**, they came to Elim, where there
Nu 33: 8 days into the Etham wilderness and camped at **M**.
33: 9 They left **M** and camped at Elim, where there are

MARALAH (1)

Jos 19:11 it went west, going past **M**, touching Dabbesheth,

MARANATHA [KJV] See LORD (COME!)

MARAUDERS (2) [MARAUDING]

Jdg 2:14 so he handed them over to **m** who stole their
6: 3 planted their crops, **m** from Midian, Amalek,

MARAUDING (2) [MARAUDERS]

Ge 49:19 "Gad will be plundered by **m** bands, / but he will
2Ch 22: 1 The **m** bands of Arabs had killed all the older sons.

MARBLE (5)

1Ch 29: 2 costly jewels, and all kinds of fine stone and **m**.
Est 1: 6 ribbons to silver rings embedded in **m** pillars.
1: 6 **m**, mother-of-pearl, and other costly stones.
SS 5:15 His legs are like pillars of **m** set in sockets of the
Rev 18:12 made of expensive wood, bronze, iron, and **m**.

MARCH (45) [MARCHED, MARCHES, MARCHING]

Ex 14: 2 "Tell the people to **m** toward Pi-hahiroth between
Nu 2:24 and they will follow the Levites in the line of **m**.
10:14 The tribes that camped with Judah headed the **m**
10:17 divisions of the Levites were next in the line of **m**,
32:30 if they refuse to cross over and **m** ahead of you,
33: 2 These are the stages of their **m**, identified by the
Jos 6: 3 Your entire army is to **m** around the city once a
6: 4 On the seventh day you are to **m** around the city
6: 7 "**M** around the city, and the armed men will lead
Jdg 5:21 the Kishon. / **M** on, my soul, with courage!
1Sa 13:12 I said, 'The Philistines are ready to **m** against us,
23: 8 So Saul mobilized his entire army to **m** to Keilah
2Sa 17:29 and thirsty after your long **m** through the
2Ki 19:32 They will not **m** outside its gates with their shields
2Ch 20:16 Tomorrow, **m** out against them. You will find
26:11 ready to **m** into battle, unit by unit.
Ezr 6:15 The Temple was completed on **M** 12,
10:17 By **M** 27 of the next year they had finished dealing
Est 3: 7 And the day selected was **M** 7, nearly a year later.
3:13 scheduled to happen nearly a year later on **M** 7.
8:12 of King Xerxes was **M** 7 of the next year.
9: 1 So on **M** 7 the two decrees of the king were put
9:15 Then the Jews at Susa gathered together on **M** 8
9:17 Throughout the provinces this was done on **M** 7.
Ps 60:10 O God? / Will you no longer **m** with our armies?
108:11 O God? / Will you no longer **m** with our armies?
Pr 30:27 have no king, / but they **m** like an army in ranks.
Isa 13: 2 Wave to them as they **m** against Babylon to
13: 4 Listen, as the armies **m**! It is the noise
37:33 They will not **m** outside its gates with their shields
42:13 The LORD will **m** forth like a mighty man;
Jer 50:21 Yes, **m** against Babylon, the land of rebels, a land
51:11 of the kings of the Medes to **m** against Babylon
52:31 and released him from prison on **M** 31 of that year.
La 4:12 would have believed an enemy could **m** through
Eze 12: 4 just as captives do when they begin a long **m** to
32: 1 On **M** 3, during the twelfth year of King
32:17 On **M** 17, during the twelfth year, another message
38:11 I will **m** against her and destroy these people who
Da 11:16 "The king of the north will **m** onward unopposed;
Joel 2: 7 The attackers **m** like warriors and scale city walls
2: 7 Straight forward they **m**, never breaking rank.
3:12 Let them **m** to the valley of Jehoshaphat. There I,
Hab 1: 6 and violent nation who will **m** across the world
Rev 16:12 so that the kings from the east could **m** their armies

MARCHED (39) [MARCH]

Nu 2:34 and **m** under their banners exactly as the LORD
10:28 This was the order in which the tribes **m**,
10:33 They **m** for three days after leaving the mountain
20:20 and **m** out to meet them with an imposing force.
21:33 Then they turned and **m** toward Bashan, but King
33: 1 they **m** out of Egypt under the leadership of Moses
Jos 6: 8 of the LORD, blowing the horns as they **m**.
6: 9 Armed guards **m** both in front of the priests
6:13 The seven priests with the rams' horns **m** in front
6:13 Armed guards **m** both in front of the priests with
6:14 On the second day they **m** around the city once
6:15 and **m** around the city as they had done before.
Jdg 1:10 Judah **m** against the Canaanites in Hebron
1:11 From there they **m** against the people living in the
4:10 and ten thousand warriors **m** up with him. Deborah also **m** with them.
4:13 and they **m** from Harosheth-haggoyim to the
5: 4 and **m** across the fields of Edom, / the earth
5:11 people of the LORD / **m** down to the city gates.
5:13 "Down from Tabor **m** the remnant against the
5:13 The people of the LORD **m** down against mighty
5:14 From Makir the commanders **m** down;
1Sa 29: 2 and his men **m** at the rear with King Achish.
2Sa 8: 3 when Hadadezer **m** out to strengthen his control
1Ki 20:17 the troops of the provincial commanders **m** out of
20:26 up the Aramean army and **m** out against Israel,
2Ki 3: 6 mustered the army of Israel and **m** from Samaria.
14:13 of Judah at Beth-shemesh and **m** on to Jerusalem.
23:29 King Josiah **m** out with his army to fight him,
1Ch 14: 8 so he and his men **m** out to meet them.
15:24 were chosen to blow the trumpets as they **m** in
18: 3 when Hadadezer **m** out to strengthen his control
2Ch 20:28 They **m** into Jerusalem to the music of harps,
21:17 They **m** against Judah, broke down its defenses,
24:23 of the year, the Aramean army **m** against Joash.
35:20 and Josiah and his army **m** out to fight him.
Ps 68: 7 from Egypt, / when you **m** through the wilderness,
Hab 3:12 You **m** across the land in awesome anger
Heb 11:30 It was by faith that the people of Israel **m** around

MARCHES (4) [MARCH]
Job 9: 8 out the heavens and **m** on the waves of the sea.
Isa 41: 4 of the human race as each new generation **m** by?
Jer 46:22 The invading army **m** in; they come against her
Hab 3: 5 Pestilence **m** before him; plague follows close

MARCHING (17) [MARCH]
Ex 13:18 and the Israelites left Egypt like a **m** army.
14:10 could see them in the distance, **m** toward them.
Jos 6: 8 the seven priests with the rams' horns started **m** in
Jdg 4:14 over Sisera, for the LORD is **m** ahead of you."
2Sa 5:24 When you hear a sound like **m** feet in the tops of
2Ki 3:21 Moab heard about the three armies **m** against them,
1Ch 14:15 When you hear a sound like **m** feet in the tops of
2Ch 20: 2 "A vast army from Edom is **m** against you from
Isa 63: 1 in royal robes, **m** in the greatness of his strength?
Jer 2:16 **m** from their cities of Memphis and Tahpanhes,
4:29 At the noise of **m** armies, the people flee in terror
6:22 LORD says: "See a great army **m** from the north!
6:23 They are **m** in battle formation to destroy you,
13:20 See the armies **m** down from the north! Where is
50:41 "Look! A great army is **m** from the north! A great
50:42 They are **m** in battle formation to destroy you,
Lk 14:31 twenty thousand soldiers who are **m** against him?

MARCUS [KJV] See MARK

MARDUK (1)
Jer 50: 2 Her gods Bel and **M** will be utterly disgraced.

MARESHAH (8)
Jos 15:44 Keilah, Aczib, and **M**—nine towns with their
1Ch 2:42 Caleb's second son was **M**, the father of Hebron.
4:21 Laadah (the father of **M**), the families of linen
2Ch 11: 8 Gath, **M**, Ziph,
14: 9 hundred chariots. They advanced to the city of **M**,
14:10 his armies for battle in the valley north of **M**.
20:37 Then Eliezer son of Dodavahu from **M** prophesied
Mic 1:15 You people of **M**, I will bring a conqueror to

MARINE (5)
Lev 11: 9 "As for **m** animals, you may eat whatever has both
11:10 eat **m** animals that do not have both fins
11:12 any **m** animal that does not have both fins
Dt 14: 9 "As for **m** animals, you may eat whatever has both
14:10 eat **m** animals that do not have both fins

MARISHES [KJV] See MARSHES

MARK (39) [MARKED, MARKER, MARKERS, MARKS]
Ge 1:14 They will be signs to **m** off the seasons, the days,
4:15 Then the LORD put a **m** on Cain to warn anyone
17:13 Your bodies will thus bear the **m** of my everlasting
35:14 Jacob set up a stone pillar to **m** the place where
Ex 13: 9 like a **m** branded on your hands or your forehead.
13:16 this ceremony will be like a **m** branded on your
Lev 19:28 mourning for the dead or **m** your skin with tattoos,
Dt 19:14 markers your ancestors set up to **m** their property.
23:12 "**M** off an area outside the camp for a latrine.
Job 14:13 But **m** your calendar to think of me again!
33:31 **M** this well, Job. Listen to me, and let me say
Ps 104:19 You made the moon to **m** the seasons / and the sun
Pr 4:26 **M** out a straight path for your feet; then stick to the
20: 3 Avoiding a fight is a **m** of honor; only fools insist
Jer 31:21 **M** well the path by which you came. Come back
50: 9 The enemies' arrows will go straight to the **m**;
Eze 9: 4 and put a **m** on the foreheads of all those who
9: 6 little children. But do not touch anyone with the **m**.
Mt 26:29 **M** my words—I will not drink wine again until the
Ac 12:12 went to the home of Mary, the mother of John **M**,
12:25 returned to Antioch, taking John **M** with them.
13: 5 of God. (John **M** went with them as their assistant.)
13:13 There John **M** left them and returned to Jerusalem.
15:37 Barnabas agreed and wanted to take along John **M**.
15:38 since John **M** had deserted them in Pamphylia
15:39 Barnabas took John **M** with him and sailed for
Col 4:10 his greetings, and so does **M**, Barnabas's cousin.
4:10 make **M** welcome if he comes your way.
2Ti 4:11 Bring **M** with you when you come, for he will be
Phm 1:24 So do **M**, Aristarchus, Demas, and Luke,
Heb 12:13 **M** out a straight path for your feet. Then those who
1Pe 5:13 Rome sends you greetings, and so does my son **M**.
Rev 13:16 to be given a **m** on the right hand or on the
13:17 no one could buy or sell anything without that **m**,
14: 9 or who accepts his **m** on the forehead or the hand
14:11 his statue and have accepted the **m** of his name.
16: 2 broke out on everyone who had the **m** of the beast
19:20 miracles that deceived all who had accepted the **m**
20: 4 nor accepted his **m** on their forehead or their

MARKED (7) [MARK]
Jos 4:19 the month that **m** their exodus from Egypt.
5:10 the month that **m** their exodus from Egypt.
13:23 The Jordan River **m** the western boundary for the
Pr 8:29 And when he **m** off the earth's foundations,
Jer 44:19 and making cakes **m** with her image, without our
Eze 9: 5 the city and kill everyone whose forehead is not **m**.
Rev 7: 4 And I heard how many were **m** with the seal of

MARKER (2) [MARK]
Dt 27:17 from a neighbor by moving a boundary **m**.'
Eze 39:15 a **m** will be set up beside them so the burial crews

MARKERS (4) [MARK]
Dt 19:14 **m** your ancestors set up to mark their property.
Job 24: 2 Evil people steal land by moving the boundary **m**.
Pr 22:28 the ancient boundary **m** set up by your ancestors.
23:10 orphans by moving the ancient boundary **m**,

MARKET (3) [MARKETPLACE, MARKETPLACES, MARKETS]
Zep 1:11 all you who live in the **m** area, for all who buy
Mk 6:56 they laid the sick in the **m** plazas and streets.
7: 4 they eat nothing bought from the **m** unless they

MARKETPLACE (4) [MARKET]
Mt 20: 3 in the morning he was passing through the **m**
Jn 2:16 of here. Don't turn my Father's house into a **m**!"
Ac 16:19 and dragged them before the authorities at the **m**.
1Co 10:25 You may eat any meat that is sold in the **m**.

MARKETPLACES (2) [MARKET]
Mk 12:38 have everyone bow to them as they walk in the **m**.
Lk 20:46 have everyone bow to them as they walk in the **m**.

MARKETS (5) [MARKET]
2Ki 7: 1 By this time tomorrow in the **m** of Samaria,
7:18 "By this time tomorrow in the **m** of Samaria,
Pr 7:12 She is often seen in the streets and **m**, soliciting at
Eze 27:15 Numerous coastlands were your captive **m**;
Lk 11:43 from everyone as you walk through the **m**!

MARKS (1) [MARK]
Isa 44:13 wood-carver measures and **m** out a block of wood,

MARKSMEN (1)
Jer 49:35 destroy the archers of Elam—the best of their **m**.

MAROTH (1)
Mic 1:12 The people of **M** anxiously wait for relief, but only

MARRIAGE (34) [MARRY]
Ge 21:21 and his mother arranged a **m** for him with a young
38: 6 Judah arranged his **m** to a young woman named
Jos 15:16 "I will give my daughter Acsah in **m** to the one
Jdg 1:12 "I will give my daughter Acsah in **m** to the one
3: 6 and Israelite daughters were given in **m** to their
14:10 father was making final arrangements for the **m**,
14:20 So his wife was given in **m** to the man who had
15: 2 "so I gave her in **m** to your best man.
21: 1 in **m** to a man from the tribe of Benjamin.
21: 7 the LORD not to give them our daughters in **m**?"
21:18 But we cannot give them our own daughters in **m**
21:22 you did not give your daughters in **m** to them.' "
Ru 1: 9 LORD bless you with the security of another **m**."
1Sa 18:19 Saul gave Merab in **m** to Adriel, a man from
2Ki 8:27 because he was related by **m** to the family of Ahab.
14: 9 'Give your daughter in **m** to my son.' But just
2Ch 25:18 'Give your daughter in **m** to my son.' But just
Eze 16: 8 to cover your nakedness and declared my **m** vows.
Da 11: 6 in **m** to the king of the north to secure the alliance,
11:17 He will give him a daughter in **m** in order to
Mal 2:14 your faithful companion, the wife of your **m** vows.
Mt 1:20 "do not be afraid to go ahead with your **m** to
25:10 who were ready went in with him to the **m** feast,
Lk 20:34 Jesus replied, "**M** is for people here on earth.
Ro 7: 2 if he dies, the laws of **m** no longer apply to her.
1Co 7: 7 God gives some the gift of **m**, and to others he
7:14 For the Christian wife brings holiness to her **m**,
7:14 and the Christian husband brings holiness to his **m**.
7:27 If you have a wife, do not end the **m**. If you do not
7:28 to spare you the extra problems that come with **m**.
7:29 so husbands should not let **m** be their major
7:39 but this must be a **m** acceptable to the Lord.
Heb 13: 4 Give honor to **m**, and remain faithful to one another in **m**.

MARRIAGES (1) [MARRY]
Ezr 9: 2 holy race has become polluted by these mixed **m**.

MARRIED (111) [MARRY]
Ge 4:19 Lamech **m** two women—Adah and Zillah.
11:29 Abram **m** Sarai, and his brother Nahor **m** Milcah,
20: 3 are a dead man, for that woman you took is **m**."
20:12 though different mothers—and I **m** her.
25: 1 Now Abraham **m** again. Keturah was his new wife,
25:20 When Isaac was forty years old, he **m** Rebekah,
26:34 of forty, Esau **m** a young woman named Judith,
26:34 He also **m** Basemath, the daughter of Elon the
28: 9 and **m** one of Ishmael's daughters,
29:21 "Now give me my wife so we can be **m**."
29:28 A week after Jacob had **m** Leah, Laban gave him
36: 2 Esau **m** two young women from Canaan: Adah,
36: 3 He also **m** his cousin Basemath, who was the
38: 2 the daughter of Shua, and he **m** her.
Ex 2: 1 a man and woman from the tribe of Levi got **m**.
6:20 Amram **m** his father's sister Jochebed, and she
6:23 Aaron **m** Elisheba, the daughter of Amminadab
6:25 Eleazar son of Aaron **m** one of the daughters of
21: 3 when he became your slave and then **m** afterward,
21: 3 But if he was **m** before he became a slave, then his
Nu 12: 1 because he had **m** a Cushite woman.
30:10 "Suppose a woman is **m** and living in her
36:11 and Noah all **m** cousins on their father's side.
36:12 They **m** into the clans of Manasseh son of Joseph.
Dt 20: 7 Well, go home and get **m**! You might die in the
22:14 'I discovered she was not a virgin when I **m** her.'
22:17 claiming that she was not a virgin when he **m** her.
22:23 a virgin who is engaged to be **m**, and he has sexual
24: 5 "A newly **m** man must not be drafted into the
24: 5 one year, bringing happiness to the wife he has **m**.
Jos 15:18 When Acsah **m** Othniel, she urged him to ask her
Jdg 1:14 When Acsah **m** Othniel, she urged him to ask her
3: 6 Israelite sons **m** their daughters, and Israelite
12: 9 He **m** his daughters to men outside his clan
15: 6 gave Samson's wife to be **m** to his best man."
Ru 1: 4 The two sons **m** Moabite women. One **m** a woman
1:12 and I were to get **m** tonight and bear sons,
4:13 So Boaz **m** Ruth and took her home to live with
1Sa 25:43 David also **m** Ahinoam from Jezreel, making both
2Sa 5:13 David **m** more wives and concubines, and he had
1Ki 3: 1 the king of Egypt, and **m** one of his daughters.
4:11 (He was **m** to Taphath, one of Solomon's
4:15 (He was **m** to Basemath, another of Solomon's
9:16 daughter as a wedding gift when she **m** Solomon.
11: 1 he **m** women from Moab, Ammon, Edom, Sidon,
11: 2 because the women they **m** would lead them to
16:31 he **m** Jezebel, the daughter of King Ethbaal of the
2Ki 8:18 King Ahab, for he had **m** one of Ahab's daughters.
1Ch 2:17 Abigail **m** a man named Jether, an Ishmaelite,
2:19 After Azubah died, Caleb **m** Ephrathah, and they
2:21 he **m** Gilead's sister, the daughter of Makir.
4:17 Mered **m** an Egyptian woman, who became the
4:18 Mered also **m** a woman of Judah, who became the
14: 3 Then David **m** more wives in Jerusalem, and they
23:22 His daughters **m** their cousins, the sons of Kish.
2Ch 11:18 Rehoboam **m** his cousin Mahalath, the daughter of
11:20 Later Rehoboam **m** another cousin, Maacah,
13:21 He **m** fourteen wives and had twenty-two sons
21: 6 King Ahab, for he had **m** one of Ahab's daughters.
Ezr 2:61 (This Barzillai had **m** one of the daughters of
9: 2 For the men of Israel have **m** women from these
10: 2 for we have **m** these pagan women of the land.
10:10 "You have sinned, for you have **m** pagan women.
10:17 dealing with all the men who had **m** pagan wives.
10:18 These are the priests who had **m** pagan wives:
Ne 6:18 because his son Jehohanan was **m** to the daughter
7:63 (This Barzillai had **m** one of the daughters of
13:23 of the men of Judah had **m** women from Ashdod,
13:28 priest had **m** a daughter of Sanballat the Horonite,
Eze 16: 8 and saw you again, you were old enough to be **m**.
23: 4 I **m** them, and they bore me sons and daughters.
Hos 1: 3 So Hosea **m** Gomer, the daughter of Diblaim,
4:17 Leave her alone because she is **m** to idolatry.
Mt 1:18 His mother, Mary, was engaged to be **m** to Joseph.
22:25 The oldest **m** and then died without children,
22:25 so the second brother **m** the widow.
22:26 and the wife was **m** to the next brother, and so on
22:30 For when the dead rise, they won't be **m**. They will
Mk 6:17 his brother Philip's wife, but Herod had **m** her.
12:20 The oldest of them **m** and then died without
12:21 So the second brother **m** the widow, but soon he
12:21 Then the next brother **m** her and died without
12:22 This continued until all the brothers had **m** her
12:23 in the resurrection? For all seven were **m** to her."
12:25 For when the dead rise, they won't be **m**. They will
Lk 1:27 She was engaged to be **m** to a man named Joseph,
2:36 for her husband had died when they had been **m**
14:20 Another had just been **m**, so he said he couldn't
20:29 The oldest **m** and then died without children.
20:30 His brother **m** the widow, but he also died. Still no
20:31 until each of the seven had **m** her and died,
20:33 in the resurrection? For all seven were **m** to her!"
20:35 of being raised from the dead won't be **m** then.
Jn 4:18 and you aren't even **m** to the man you're living
Ro 7: 3 she would be committing adultery if she **m** another
9:10 When he grew up, he **m** Rebekah, who gave birth
1Co 7: 3 which is her right as a **m** woman, nor should the
7: 8 Now I say to those who aren't **m** and to widows—
7:10 for those who are **m** I have a command that comes
7:25 Now, about the young women who are not yet **m**.
7:27 If you do not have a wife, do not get **m**.
7:28 But if you do get **m**, it is not a sin. And if a young woman gets **m**, it is not a sin.
7:33 But a **m** man can't do that so well. He has to think
7:34 a woman who is no longer **m** or has never been **m** can be more devoted to the
7:34 while the **m** woman must be concerned about her
7:39 A wife is **m** to her husband as long as he lives.
1Ti 4: 3 They will say it is wrong to be **m** and wrong to eat

MARRIES (16) [MARRY]
Ex 21:10 If he himself **m** her and then takes another wife,
Lev 20:21 If a man **m** his brother's wife, it is an act of
22:12 If a priest's daughter **m** someone outside the
Nu 30: 6 a vow or makes an impulsive pledge and later **m**.
36: 3 But if any of them **m** a man from another tribe,
Dt 22:13 "Suppose a man **m** a woman and, after sleeping
24: 1 "Suppose a man **m** a woman but later discovers
24: 2 If she then leaves and **m** another man
Jer 3: 1 a man divorces a woman and she **m** someone else,
Mt 5:32 And anyone who **m** a divorced woman commits
19: 9 his wife and **m** another commits adultery—
Mk 10:11 and **m** someone else commits adultery against her.
Lk 16:18 his wife and **m** someone else commits adultery,
16:18 and anyone who **m** a divorced woman commits
Ro 7: 2 When a woman **m**, the law binds her to her
1Co 7:38 So the person who **m** does well, and the person

MARRY (83) [INTERMARRIAGE, INTERMARRIED, INTERMARRY, INTERMARRYING, MARRIAGE, MARRIAGES, MARRIED, MARRIES, MARRYING, REMARRIES, REMARRY]

Ge 12:19 Why were you willing to let me **m** her, saying she
19:31 a man anywhere in this entire area for us to **m**.
24: 3 that you will not let my son **m** one of these local
24:37 not let Isaac **m** one of the local Canaanite women.
24:38 bring back a young woman from here to **m** his son.
27:46 I'd rather die than see Jacob **m** one of them."
28: 1 "Do not **m** any of these Canaanite women.
28: 2 and **m** one of your uncle Laban's daughters.
28: 6 and that he had warned Jacob not to **m** a Canaanite
29:21 Finally, the time came for him to **m** her. "I have
29:26 "It's not our custom to **m** off a younger daughter
34: 4 girl for me," he demanded. "I want to **m** her."
34: 8 longs for her to be his wife. Please let him **m** her.
34: 9 We invite you to let your daughters **m** our sons,
34:14 It would be a disgrace for her to **m** a man like you!
38: 8 said to Er's brother Onan, "You must **m** Tamar,
38:11 not to **m** again at that time but to return to her
38:11 his youngest son, Shelah, was old enough to **m** her.
38:14 but they had not called her to come and **m** him.
38:26 because I didn't keep my promise to let her **m** my
Ex 21: 9 And if the slave girl's owner arranges for her to **m**
22:17 But if her father refuses to let her **m** him, the man
Lev 18:17 and her daughter or **m** both a woman and her
18:18 "Do not **m** a woman and her sister because they
18:18 if your wife dies, then it is all right to **m** her sister.
21: 7 "The priests must not **m** women defiled by
21:13 "The high priest must **m** a virgin.
21:14 He must not **m** a widow, a divorced woman,
Nu 36: 3 will go with them to the tribe into which they **m**.
36: 6 Let them **m** anyone they like, as long as it is within
36: 8 in line to inherit property must **m** within their tribe,
Dt 7: 3 and sons **m** their sons and daughters.
20: 7 battle, and someone else would **m** your fiancée.'
21:11 and you are attracted to her and want to **m** her.
21:13 her father and mother. After that you may **m** her.
21:14 But if you **m** her and then decide you do not like
22:29 Then he must **m** the young woman because he
24: 4 the former husband may not **m** her again, for she
25: 5 a son, his widow must not **m** outside the family.
25: 5 her husband's brother must **m** her and fulfill the
25: 7 But if the dead man's brother refuses to **m** the
25: 7 his brother's name in Israel—he refuses to **m** me.'
25: 8 If he still insists that he doesn't want to **m** her,
Jdg 12: 9 young women from outside his clan to **m** his sons.
14: 2 "I want to **m** a young Philistine woman I saw in
14: 3 our tribe or among all the Israelites you could **m**?
15: 2 sister is more beautiful than she is. **M** her instead."
Ru 1:12 your parents' homes, for I am too old to **m** again.
1:13 for them to grow up and refuse to **m** someone else?
3:13 If he is willing to redeem you, then let him **m** you.
3:13 then as surely as the LORD lives, I will **m** you!
4: 5 land from Naomi also requires that you **m** Ruth,
1Sa 25:40 "David has sent us to ask if you will **m** him."
2Sa 13:13 to the king about it, and he will let you **m** me."
1Ki 2:21 "Then let your brother Adonijah **m** Abishag,
2Ch 18: 1 and he arranged for his son to **m** the daughter of
Ezr 9:12 You told us not to let our daughters **m** their sons,
9:12 and not to let our sons **m** their daughters, and not
Ne 10:30 "We promise not to let our daughters **m** the pagan
10:30 of the land, nor to let our sons **m** their daughters.
SS 8: 8 What will we do if someone asks to **m** her?
Isa 4: 1 over each of them and say, "Let us all **m** you!
Jer 16: 2 "Do not **m** or have children in this place.
29: 6 **M**, and have children. Then find spouses for them,
Eze 44:22 They may not **m** other widows or divorced women.
Hos 1: 2 he said to him, "Go and **m** a prostitute, so some of
Mt 14: 4 kept telling Herod, "It is illegal for you to **m** her."
19:10 then said to him, "Then it is better not to **m**!"
19:12 and some choose not to **m** for the sake of the
22:24 his brother should **m** the widow and have a child
Mk 6:18 "It is illegal for you to **m** your brother's wife."
12:19 his brother should **m** the widow and have a child
Lk 20:28 his brother should **m** the widow and have a child
1Co 7: 9 control themselves, they should go ahead and **m**.
It's better to **m** than to burn with lust.
7:36 But if a man thinks he ought to **m** his fiancée
7:36 is passing, it is all right; it is not a sin. Let them **m**.
7:37 But if he has decided firmly not to **m** and there is
7:37 he can control his passion, he does well not to **m**.
7:38 and the person who doesn't **m** does even better.
7:39 she is free to **m** whomever she wishes,
7:40 it will be better for her if she doesn't **m** again,
1Ti 5:14 So I advise these younger widows to **m** again,

MARRYING (4) [MARRY]

Ne 13:27 and acting unfaithfully toward God by **m** foreign
Mal 2:11 sanctuary by **m** women who worship idols.
Lk 3:19 ruler of Galilee, for **m** Herodias, his brother's wife,
1Co 7: 7 I wish everyone could get along without **m**, just as

MARS [KJV] See COUNCIL (OF PHILOSOPHERS)

MARSENA (1)

Est 1:14 Shethar, Admatha, Tarshish, Meres, **M**,

MARSH (2) [MARSHES]

Job 8:11 "Can papyrus reeds grow where there is no **m**?
Isa 35: 7 **M** grass and reeds and rushes will flourish where

MARSHAL (1)

Mic 5: 1 Mobilize! **M** your troops! The enemy is laying

MARSHES (4) [MARSH]

Ex 7:19 of Egypt—all its rivers, canals, **m**, and reservoirs.
8: 5 and **m** of Egypt so there will be frogs in every
Isa 14:23 a place of porcupines, filled with swamps and **m**.
Eze 47:11 But the **m** and swamps will not be purified;

MART (1)

Isa 23: 3 You were the merchandise **m** of the world.

MARTHA (13)

Lk 10:38 they came to a village where a woman named **M**
10:40 But **M** was worrying over the big dinner she was
10:41 "My dear **M**, you are so upset over all these
Jn 11: 1 He lived in Bethany with his sisters, Mary and **M**.
11: 5 Although Jesus loved **M**, Mary, and Lazarus,
11:19 and console **M** and Mary on their loss.
11:20 When **M** got word that Jesus was coming,
11:21 **M** said to Jesus, "Lord, if you had been here,
11:24 "Yes," **M** said, "when everyone else rises,
11:26 and will never perish. Do you believe this, **M**?"
11:30 outside the village, at the place where **M** met him.
11:39 But **M**, the dead man's sister, said, "Lord, by now
12: 2 **M** served, and Lazarus sat at the table with him.

MARTYRED (3)

Rev 2:13 was **m** among you by Satan's followers.
6: 9 souls of all who had been **m** for the word of God
6:11 full number of the servants of Jesus had been **m**.

MARVELED (2) [MARVELOUS]

Mt 9:33 and instantly the man could talk. The crowds **m**.
Rev 13: 3 All the world **m** at this miracle and followed the

MARVELING (1) [MARVELOUS]

Lk 9:43 While everyone was **m** over all the wonderful

MARVELOUS (15) [MARVELED, MARVELING]

Ex 10: 2 and grandchildren about the **m** things I am doing
Job 5: 9 For he does great works too **m** to understand.
9:10 His great works are too **m** to understand.
Ps 9: 1 I will tell of all the **m** things you have done.
19: 1 of God. / The skies display his **m** craftsmanship.
118:23 This is the LORD's doing, / and it is **m** to see.
139:14 Your workmanship is **m**—and how well I know it.
Eze 28: 7 draw their swords against your **m** wisdom
Mt 21:42 This is the Lord's doing, / and it is **m** to see.'
Mk 12:11 This is the Lord's doing, / and it is **m** to see.' "
1Co 6:14 raise our bodies from the dead by his **m** power,
2Co 6: 1 we beg you not to reject this **m** message of God's
Eph 3:17 roots go down deep into the soil of God's **m** love.
Rev 15: 1 another significant event, and it was great and **m**.
15: 3 "Great and **m** are your actions, / Lord God

MARY (64) [MARY'S]

Mt 1:16 Jacob was the father of Joseph, the husband of **M**.
1:16 **M** was the mother of Jesus, who is called the
1:18 His mother, **M**, was engaged to be married to
1:20 not be afraid to go ahead with your marriage to **M**.
1:24 He brought **M** home to be his wife,
2:11 the house where the child and his mother, **M**, were,
2:14 night Joseph left for Egypt with the child and **M**,
13:55 and we know **M**, his mother, and his brothers—
27:56 were **M** Magdalene, **M** (the mother of James and
27:61 Both **M** Magdalene and the other **M** were sitting
28: 1 **M** Magdalene and the other **M** went out to see the
Mk 6: 3 the son of **M** and brother of James, Joseph, Judas,
15:40 from a distance, including **M** Magdalene, **M** (the
mother of James the younger and of
15:47 **M** Magdalene and **M** the mother of Joseph saw
16: 1 **M** Magdalene and Salome and **M** the mother of
16: 9 and the first person who saw him was **M**
Lk 1:27 to a virgin named **M**. She was engaged to be
1:29 **M** tried to think what the angel could mean.
1:30 "Don't be frightened, **M**," the angel told her,
1:34 **M** asked the angel, "But how can I have a baby?
1:38 **M** responded, "I am the Lord's servant, and I am
1:39 A few days later **M** hurried to the hill country of
1:42 Elizabeth gave a glad cry and exclaimed to **M**,
1:46 **M** responded, / "Oh, how I praise the Lord.
1:56 **M** stayed with Elizabeth about three months
2: 5 He took with him **M**, his fiancée, who was
2:16 They ran to the village and found **M** and Joseph.
2:19 but **M** quietly treasured these things in her heart
2:27 So when **M** and Joseph came to present the baby
2:33 and **M** were amazed at what was being said about
2:34 Then Simeon blessed them, and he said to **M**,
2:38 She came along just as Simeon was talking with **M**
8: 2 Among them were **M** Magdalene, from whom he
10:39 Her sister, **M**, sat at the Lord's feet, listening to
10:42 **M** has discovered it—and I won't take it away
24:10 The women who went to the tomb were **M**
24:10 Joanna, **M** the mother of James, and several others.
Jn 11: 1 lived in Bethany with his sisters, **M** and Martha.
11: 2 This is the **M** who poured the expensive perfume
11: 5 Although Jesus loved Martha, **M**, and Lazarus,
11:19 and console Martha and **M** on their loss.
11:20 she went to meet him. But **M** stayed at home.
11:28 she left him and returned to **M**. She called **M** aside
11:29 So **M** immediately went to him.
11:31 at the house trying to console **M** saw her leave
11:32 When **M** arrived and saw Jesus, she fell down at
11:45 Many of the people who were with **M** believed in
12: 3 Then **M** took a twelve-ounce jar of expensive
19:25 **M** (the wife of Clopas), and **M** Magdalene.
20: 1 **M** Magdalene came to the tomb and found that the
20:11 **M** was standing outside the tomb crying, and as
20:16 "**M**!" Jesus said. She turned toward him
20:18 **M** Magdalene found the disciples and told them,
Ac 1:14 along with **M** the mother of Jesus, several other
12:12 After a little thought, he went to the home of **M**,
Ro 16: 6 Give my greetings to **M**, who has worked so hard

MARY'S (1) [MARY]

Lk 1:41 At the sound of **M** greeting, Elizabeth's child

MASCARA (1)

Jer 4:30 Why do you brighten your eyes with **m**?

MASH (2)

Ge 10:23 of Aram were Uz, Hul, Gether, and **M**.
1Ch 1:17 of Aram were Uz, Hul, Gether, and **M**.

MASHAL (1) [MISHAL]

1Ch 6:74 the territory of Asher, they received **M**, Abdon,

MASKS (1)

Job 24:15 me then.' He **m** his face so no one will know him.

MASONS (5) [STONEMASONS]

2Ki 12:12 the **m**, and the stonecutters. They also used the
22: 6 They will need to hire carpenters, builders, and **m**.
2Ch 24:12 who hired **m** and carpenters to restore the Temple
34:11 they hired carpenters and **m** and purchased cut
Ezr 3: 7 Then they hired **m** and carpenters and bought

MASREKAH (2)

Ge 36:36 Samlah from the city of **M** became king.
1Ch 1:47 Samlah from the city of **M** became king.

MASS (2) [MASSES, MASSIVE]

Ge 1: 2 was empty, a formless **m** cloaked in darkness.
Isa 14:19 you will be dumped into a **m** grave with those

MASSA (2)

Ge 25:14 Mishma, Dumah, **M**,
1Ch 1:30 Mishma, Dumah, **M**, Hadad, Tema,

MASSACRE (1)

Eze 21:14 to symbolize the great **m** they will face!

MASSAH (5) [MERIBAH]

Ex 17: 7 Moses named the place **M**—"the place of
Dt 6:16 your God as you did when you complained at **M**.
9:22 angry at Taberah, **M**, and Kibroth-hattaavah.
33: 8 the Levites. / You put them to the test at **M**
Ps 95: 8 at Meribah, / as they did at **M** in the wilderness.

MASSES (1) [MASS]

Rev 17:15 is sitting represent **m** of people of every nation

MASSIVE (1) [MASS]

Mk 13: 1 Look at the **m** stones in the walls!"

MAST (2) [MASTS]

Pr 23:34 like a sailor tossed at sea, clinging to a swaying **m**.
Eze 27: 5 They took a cedar from Lebanon to make a **m** for

MASTER (135) [MASTER'S, MASTERED, MASTERPIECE, MASTERS, MASTERS']

Ge 3:16 will be for your husband, he will be your **m**."
18:12 "And when my **m**—my husband—is also so old?"
24:10 taking with him the best of everything his **m**
24:12 "O LORD, God of my **m**," he prayed. "Give me
success and show kindness to my **m**,
24:14 know that you have shown kindness to my **m**."
24:27 the LORD, the God of my **m**, Abraham," he said.
24:35 "And the LORD has blessed my **m** richly;
24:36 and my **m** has given him everything he owns.
24:37 And my **m** made me swear that I would not let
24:42 'O LORD, the God of my **m**, Abraham, if you are
24:48 I praised the LORD, the God of my **m**, Abraham,
24:49 or won't you show true kindness to my **m**?
24:54 next morning, he said, "Send me back to my **m**."
24:56 and I want to report back to my **m**."
24:65 asked the servant. And he replied, "It is my **m**."
27:29 your servants. May you be the **m** of your brothers.
27:37 "I have made Jacob your **m** and have declared that
32: 4 He told them, "Give this message to my **m** Esau:
32:18 They are a present for his **m** Esau! He is coming
39: 2 greatly as he served in the home of his Egyptian **m**.
39: 8 "my **m** trusts me with everything in his entire
45: 9 God has made me **m** over all the land of Egypt.
Ex 21: 4 "If his **m** gave him a wife while he was a slave,
21: 4 but his wife and children will still belong to his **m**.
21: 5 'I love my **m**, my wife, and my children.

21: 6 If he does this, his **m** must present him before God.
21: 6 Then his **m** must take him to the door and publicly
21: 6 After that, the slave will belong to his **m** forever.
31: 5 and in carving wood. Yes, he is a **m** at every craft!
Nu 11:28 protested, "Moses, my **m**, make them stop!"
Jdg 3:25 the door, they found their **m** dead on the floor.
19:12 "No," his **m** said, "we can't stay in this foreign
1Sa 20:38 gathered up the arrows and ran back to his **m**.
25:14 sent men from the wilderness to talk to our **m**,
25:17 for there is going to be trouble for our **m** and his
26:15 So why haven't you guarded your **m** the king when
26:16 because you failed to protect your **m**, the LORD's
29: 4 himself with his **m** than by turning on us in battle?
30:13 "My **m** left me behind three days ago because I
30:15 that you will not kill me or give me back to my **m**,
2Sa 10: 3 Hanun's advisers said to their **m**, "Do you really
1Ki 11:23 Rezon had fled from his **m**, King Hadadezer of
12: 4 "Your father was a hard **m**," they said.
18: 8 "Now go and tell your **m** I am here."
18:11 you say, 'Go and tell your **m** that Elijah is here'!
18:14 you say, 'Go and tell your **m** that Elijah is here'!
22:17 And the LORD said, 'Their **m** has been killed.
2Ki 2: 3 is going to take your **m** away from you today?"
2: 5 is going to take your **m** away from you today?"
2:16 men will search the wilderness for your **m**.
5: 3 "I wish my **m** would go to see the prophet in
5:18 When my **m** the king goes into the temple of the
5:20 "My **m** should not have let this Aramean get away
5:22 "but my **m** has sent me to tell you that two young
5:25 When he went in to his **m**, Elisha asked him,
6:22 and drink and send them home again to their **m**."
6:32 and keep him out. His **m** will soon follow him."
9: 7 You are to destroy the family of Ahab, your **m**.
9:31 You are just like Zimri, who murdered his **m**!"
10: 9 "I am the one who conspired against my **m**
18:23 My **m**, the king of Assyria, will strike a bargain
18:27 "My **m** wants everyone in Jerusalem to hear this,
19: 6 the prophet replied, "Say to your **m**, 'This is what
2Ch 2: 7 "So send me a **m** craftsman who can work with
2:13 "I am sending you a **m** craftsman named
10: 4 "Your father was a hard **m**," they said.
13: 6 of David's son Solomon, became a traitor to his **m**.
18:16 And the LORD said, 'Their **m** has been killed.
Job 3:19 are there alike, and the slave is free from his **m**.
Ps 16: 2 I said to the LORD, "You are my **M**!
123: 2 just as servants keep their eyes on their **m**,
Isa 19: 4 cruel **m**, to a fierce king," says the Lord,
22:18 broken and useless. You are a disgrace to your **m**.
36: 8 My **m**, the king of Assyria, will strike a bargain
36:12 "My **m** wants everyone in Jerusalem to hear this,
37: 6 the prophet replied, "Say to your **m**, 'This is what
Da 4: 9 "I said to him, 'O Belteshazzar, **m** magician,
8:23 a fierce king, a **m** of intrigue, will rise to power.
8:25 He will be a **m** of deception, defeating many by
Hos 2:16 will call me 'my husband' instead of 'my **m**.'
Mal 1: 6 son honors his father, and a servant respects his **m**.
1: 6 I am your father and **m**, but where are the honor
Mt 10:24 the teacher. A servant is not greater than the **m**.
10:25 And since I, the **m** of the household, have been
12: 8 the Son of Man, am **m** even of the Sabbath."
23:10 And don't let anyone call you '**M**,' for there is
only one **m**, the Messiah.
24:45 to whom the **m** can give the responsibility of
24:46 If the **m** returns and finds that the servant has done
24:47 the **m** will put that servant in charge of all he
24:48 and thinks, 'My **m** won't be back for a while,'
24:50 the **m** will return unannounced and unexpected.
25:19 "After a long time their **m** returned from his trip
25:21 The **m** was full of praise. 'Well done, my good
25:23 The **m** said, 'Well done, my good and faithful
25:26 "But the **m** replied, 'You wicked and lazy servant!
Mk 2:28 the Son of Man, am **m** even of the Sabbath!"
Lk 5: 5 "**M**," Simon replied, "we worked hard all last
6: 5 the Son of Man, am **m** even of the Sabbath."
8:24 shouting, "**M**, **M**, we're going to drown!"
8:45 Everyone denied it, and Peter said, "**M**, this whole
9:33 he was saying, blurted out, "**M**, this is wonderful!
9:49 John said to Jesus, "**M**, we saw someone using
12:36 as though you were waiting for your **m** to return
12:42 sensible servant to whom the **m** gives the
12:43 If the **m** returns and finds that the servant has done
12:44 the **m** will put that servant in charge of all he
12:45 servant thinks, 'My **m** won't be back for a while,'
12:46 the **m** will return unannounced and unexpected.
14:21 servant returned and told his **m** what they had said.
14:21 His **m** was angry and said, 'Go quickly into the
14:23 So his **m** said, 'Go out into the country lanes
17:13 crying out, "Jesus, **M**, have mercy on us!"
19:25 " 'But, **m**,' they said, 'that servant has enough
22:27 Normally the **m** sits at the table and is served by
Jn 2: 8 some out and take it to the **m** of ceremonies."
2: 9 When the **m** of ceremonies tasted the water that
13:16 true it is that a servant is not greater than the **m**.
15:15 because a **m** doesn't confide in his servants.
15:20 'A servant is not greater than the **m**.' Since they
Ro 6:14 Sin is no longer your **m**, for you are no longer
6:16 whatever you choose to obey becomes your **m**?
6:18 Now you are free from sin, your old **m**, and you
have become slaves to your new **m**,
7:14 because I am sold into slavery, with sin as my **m**.
Eph 6: 9 remember, you both have the same **M** in heaven,
Col 3:24 your reward, and the **M** you are serving is Christ.
4: 1 Remember that you also have a **M**—in heaven.
1Ti 6: 2 If your **m** is a Christian, that is no excuse for being
2Ti 2:21 and you will be ready for the **M** to use you for
1Pe 3: 6 Abraham, when she called him her **m**.
2Pe 2: 1 and even turn against their **M** who bought them.
Jude 1: 4 for they have turned against our only **M** and Lord,

MASTER'S (17) [MASTER]

Ge 24:27 for he has led me straight to my **m** relatives."
24:36 When Sarah, my **m** wife, was very old, she gave
birth to my **m** son,
24:44 one you have selected to be the wife of my **m** son.'
24:48 to find a wife from the family of my **m** relatives.
24:51 Yes, let her be the wife of your **m** son,
44: 5 What do you mean by stealing my **m** personal
44: 8 would we steal silver or gold from your **m** house?
44: 9 And all the rest of us will be your **m** slaves
2Sa 9: 9 "I have given your **m** grandson everything that
2Ki 18:24 even the weakest contingent of my **m** troops,
Pr 17: 2 A wise slave will rule over the **m** shameful sons
Isa 36: 9 even the weakest contingent of my **m** troops,
Mt 10:25 The servant shares the **m** fate. And since I,
15:27 to eat crumbs that fall beneath their **m** table."
25:18 the ground and hid the **m** money for safekeeping.
Lk 17: 8 He must first prepare his **m** meal and serve him his

MASTERBUILDER [KJV] See (EXPERT) BUILDER

MASTERED (1) [MASTER]

Pr 30: 3 I have not **m** human wisdom, nor do I know the

MASTERPIECE (1) [MASTER]

Eph 2:10 For we are God's **m**. He has created us anew in

MASTERS (21) [MASTER]

Ge 1:26 They will be **m** over all life—the fish in the sea,
1:28 Be **m** over the fish and birds and all the animals."
Dt 23:15 "If slaves should escape from their **m** and take
1Sa 25:10 of servants these days who run away from their **m**.
Isa 24: 2 servants and **m**, maids and mistresses, buyers
Jer 27: 4 Give them this message for their **m**: 'This is what
30: 8 their chains. Foreigners will no longer be their **m**.
La 1: 5 Her oppressors have become her **m**, and her
5: 8 Slaves have now become our **m**; there is no one
Mt 6:24 "No one can serve two **m**. For you will hate one
Lk 16:13 "No one can serve two **m**. For you will hate one
Ac 16:16 fortune-teller who earned a lot of money for her **m**.
Ro 6:19 this way, using the illustration of slaves and **m**,
14: 7 For we are not our own **m** when we live or when
Eph 6: 5 obey your earthly **m** with deep respect and fear.
6: 6 but not just to please your **m** when they are
6: 9 the same way, you **m** must treat your slaves right.
Col 3:22 You slaves must obey your earthly **m** in everything
1Ti 6: 1 Christians who are slaves should give their **m** full
Tit 2: 9 Slaves must obey their **m** and do their best to
1Pe 2:18 are slaves must accept the authority of your **m**.

MASTERS' (2) [MASTER]

Zep 1: 9 who steal and kill to fill their **m** homes with loot.
Ac 16:19 Her **m** hopes of wealth were now shattered, so they

MASTS (1) [MAST]

Isa 33:23 The enemies' sails hang loose on broken **m** with

MAT (15) [MATS]

Mt 9: 2 people brought to him a paralyzed man on a **m**.
9: 6 paralyzed man and said, "Stand up, take your **m**,
Mk 2: 3 men arrived carrying a paralyzed man on a **m**.
2: 4 Then they lowered the sick man on his **m**,
2: 9 sins are forgiven' or 'Get up, pick up your **m**,
2:11 "Stand up, take your **m**, and go on home,
2:12 The man jumped up, took the **m**, and pushed his
Lk 5:18 came carrying a paralyzed man on a sleeping **m**.
5:19 the crowd, still on his **m**, right in front of Jesus.
5:24 paralyzed man and said, "Stand up, take your **m**,
5:25 the man jumped to his feet, picked up his **m**,
Jn 5: 8 "Stand up, pick up your sleeping **m**, and walk!"
5: 9 He rolled up the **m** and began walking!
5:10 the Sabbath! It's illegal to carry that sleeping **m**!"
5:11 to me, 'Pick up your sleeping **m** and walk.' "

MATCH (8) [MATCHED]

Ge 32:25 When the man saw that he couldn't win the **m**,
Ex 26: 5 The fifty loops along the edge of one set are to **m**
Dt 33:25 may your strength **m** the length of your days!"
2Sa 10:15 The Arameans now realized that they were no **m**
1Ch 19:16 The Arameans now realized that they were no **m**
Job 39:13 but they are no **m** for the feathers of the stork.
Lk 5:36 and the patch wouldn't even **m** the old garment.
Rev 18: 7 so **m** it now with torments and sorrows.

MATCHED (4) [MATCH]

Ex 36:12 **m** the loops along the edge of the second set.
SS 4: 2 They are perfectly **m**; not one is missing.
6: 6 washed ewes, perfectly **m** and not one missing.
Eze 40:21 All the measurements **m** those of the east gateway.

MATE (5) [MATED, MATING]

Ge 30:41 Whenever the stronger females were ready to **m**,
Isa 34:15 And the vultures will come, each one with its **m**.
34:16 animals will be missing, and none will lack a **m**,
Hos 8: 9 Like a wild donkey looking for a **m**, they have
Na 2:12 your enemies to feed your cubs and your **m**.

MATED (2) [MATE]

Ge 30:38 as they came to drink, for that was when they **m**.
30:39 So when the flocks **m** in front of the

MATERIAL (4) [MATERIALS]

Lev 13:51 the **m** is clearly contaminated by an infectious
14:40 The contaminated **m** will then be thrown into an
Isa 29:23 they see their many children and **m** blessings,
Lk 1: 2 They used as their source **m** the reports circulating

MATERIALS (16) [MATERIAL]

Ex 28: 8 And the sash will be made of the same **m**:
28:15 Use the same **m** as you did for the ephod:
35:21 they brought to the LORD their offerings of **m** for
36: 3 Moses gave them the **m** donated by the people for
36: 5 "We have more than enough **m** on hand now to
36: 6 "Bring no more **m**! You have already given more
38:21 Here is an inventory of the **m** used in building the
39: 5 also made an elaborate woven sash of the same **m**:
1Ki 15:22 Asa used these **m** to fortify the town of Geba in
1Ch 22: 5 So David collected vast amounts of building **m**
22:14 "I have worked hard to provide **m** for building the
29: 3 This is in addition to the building **m** I have already
29:16 even these **m** that we have gathered to build a
2Ch 16: 6 Asa used these **m** to fortify the towns of Geba
Jer 10: 9 and they give these **m** to skillful craftsmen who
33: 4 and even the king's palace to get **m** to strengthen

MATHUSALA [KJV] See METHUSELAH

MATING (5) [MATE]

Ge 30:40 Then at **m** time, he turned the flocks toward the
31:10 During the **m** season, I had a dream and saw that
the male goats **m** with the flock were
31:12 and spotted males are **m** with the females of your
Jer 2:24 are like a wild donkey, sniffing the wind at **m** time.

MATRED (2)

Ge 36:39 the daughter of **M** and granddaughter of Mezahab.
1Ch 1:50 the daughter of **M** and granddaughter of Me-zahab.

MATRITES (1)

1Sa 10:21 the LORD, and the family of the **M** was chosen.

MATS (3) [MAT]

2Sa 17:28 They brought sleeping **m**, cooking pots,
Mk 6:55 and began carrying sick people to him on **m**.
Ac 5:15 were brought out into the streets on beds and **m**

MATTAN (3)

2Ki 11:18 and they killed **M** the priest of Baal in front of the
2Ch 23:17 and they killed **M** the priest of Baal in front of the
Jer 38: 1 Now Shephatiah son of **M**, Gedaliah son of

MATTANAH (1)

Nu 21:18 left the wilderness and proceeded on through **M**,

MATTANIAH (16) [MATTANIAH'S]

2Ki 24:17 Then the king of Babylon installed **M**,
1Ch 9:15 Galal; **M** son of Mica, son of Zicri, son of Asaph;
25: 4 **M**, Uzziel, Shubael, Jerimoth, Hananiah, Hanani,
25:16 The ninth lot fell to **M** and twelve of his sons
2Ch 20:14 son of Benaiah, son of Jeiel, son of **M**,
29:13 From the family of Asaph: Zechariah and **M**.
Ezr 10:26 **M**, Zechariah, Jehiel, Abdi, Jeremoth, and Elijah.
10:27 Elioenai, Eliashib, **M**, Jeremoth, Zabad, and Aziza.
10:30 Kelal, Benaiah, Maaseiah, **M**, Bezalel, Binnui,
10:37 **M**, Mattenai, and Jaasu.
Ne 11:17 **M** son of Mica, son of Zabdi, a descendant of
11:22 son of Hashabiah, son of **M**, son of Mica,
12: 8 Binnui, Kadmiel, Sherebiah, Judah, and **M**,
12:25 This included **M**, Bakbukiah, and Obadiah.
12:35 son of **M**, son of Micaiah, son of Zaccur,
13:13 son of Zaccur and grandson of **M** as their assistant.

MATTANIAH'S (2) [MATTANIAH]

2Ki 24:17 next king, and he changed **M** name to Zedekiah.
Ne 11:17 Bakbukiah, who was **M** assistant; and Abda son of

MATTATHA (2)

Lk 3:31 Menna was the son of **M**. / **M** was the son of
Nathan.

MATTATHIAS (4)

Lk 3:25 Joseph was the son of **M**. / **M** was the son of Amos.
3:26 Maath was the son of **M**. / **M** was the son of
Semein.

MATTATTAH (1)

Ezr 10:33 Mattenai, **M**, Zabad, Eliphelet, Jeremai, Manasseh,

MATTENAI (3)

Ezr 10:33 **M**, Mattattah, Zabad, Eliphelet, Jeremai,
10:37 Mattaniah, **M**, and Jaasu.
Ne 12:19 **M** was leader of the family of Joiarib. / Uzzi was

MATTER (71) [MATTERS]

Ge 4:12 abundant crops for you, no **m** how hard you work!
20:16 This will settle any claim against me in this **m**."

34: 6 came out to discuss the **m** with Jacob.
34: 12 No **m** what dowry or gift you demand, I will pay
41: 32 it means that the **m** has been decreed by God
Lev 2: 8 "No **m** how a grain offering has been prepared
4: 13 and the **m** escapes the community's notice,
24: 12 the LORD's will in the **m** should become clear.
Nu 5: 31 husband will be innocent of any guilt in this **m**,
30: 9 must fulfill all her vows and pledges no **m** what.
Dt 17: 4 you hear about it, investigate the **m** thoroughly.
1Sa 1: 8 "What's the **m**, Hannah?" Elkanah would ask.
8: 4 the leaders of Israel met at Ramah to discuss the **m**
10: 12 "It doesn't **m** who his father is;
11: 5 he returned to town, he asked, "What's the **m**?
21: 2 "The king has sent me on a private **m**,"
22: 15 Please don't accuse me and my family in this **m**,
25: 24 and said, "I accept all blame in this **m**, my lord.
2Sa 11: 10 and asked, "What's the **m** with you?
14: 20 He did it to place the **m** before you in a different
15: 21 I will go wherever you go, no **m** what happens—
1Ki 1: 1 and no **m** how many blankets covered him,
12: 6 Then King Rehoboam went to discuss the **m** with
17: 16 For no **m** how much they used, there was always
21: 5 "What in the world is the **m**?" his wife, Jezebel,
2Ki 6: 28 But then the king asked, "What is the **m**?"
8: 12 "What's the **m**, my lord?" Hazael asked him.
2Ch 10: 6 Then King Rehoboam went to discuss the **m** with
25: 8 you will be defeated no **m** how well you fight.
Ezr 2: 63 the LORD about the **m** by means of sacred lots.
5: 17 then let the king send us his decision in this **m**."
10: 9 because of the seriousness of the **m** and because it
10: 16 the leaders sat down to investigate the **m**.
Ne 7: 65 the LORD about the **m** by means of sacred lots.
Est 1: 8 his staff to let everyone decide this **m** for himself.
7: 4 for that would have been a **m** too trivial to warrant
Job 11: 6 of wisdom, for true wisdom is not a simple **m**.
16: 6 my grief remains no **m** how I defend myself.
Ps 58: 5 snake charmers, / no **m** how skillfully they play.
Pr 17: 14 so drop the **m** before a dispute breaks out.
20: 22 this wrong." Wait for the LORD to handle the **m**.
21: 30 Human plans, no **m** how wise or well advised,
25: 9 So discuss the **m** with them privately. Don't tell
Ecc 1: 8 No **m** how much we see, we are never satisfied.
1: 8 No **m** how much we hear, we are not content.
7: 27 "I came to this result after looking into the **m** from
8: 17 in our world, no **m** how hard they work at it.
SS 8: 1 Then I could kiss you no **m** who was watching,
Isa 1: 3 No **m** what I do for them, they still do not
1: 18 "No **m** how deep the stain of your sins, I can
Jer 8: 17 "No **m** what you do, they will bite you, and you
12: 6 not trust them, no **m** how pleasantly they speak.
Am 5: 23 will not listen to your music, no **m** how lovely it is.
Mt 8: 19 "Teacher, I will follow you no **m** where you go!"
Lk 4: 40 No **m** what their diseases were, the touch of his
9: 57 to Jesus, "I will follow you no **m** where you go."
12: 58 try to settle the **m** before it reaches the judge,
Jn 4: 21 the time is coming when it will no longer **m**
Ac 19: 36 you shouldn't be disturbed, no **m** what is said.
Ro 3: 22 no **m** who we are or what we have done.
7: 18 No **m** which way I turn, I can't make myself do
14: 5 should have a personal conviction about this **m**.
14: 17 For the Kingdom of God is not a **m** of what we eat
1Co 6: 1 a lawsuit and ask a secular court to decide the **m**,
10: 29 It might not be a **m** of conscience for you, but it is
Col 3: 11 it doesn't **m** if you are a Jew or a Gentile,
1Th 4: 6 Never cheat another Christian in this **m** by taking
5: 18 No **m** what happens, always be thankful, for this is
2Th 3: 16 always give you his peace no **m** what happens.
Heb 10: 35 confident trust in the Lord, no **m** what happens.
1Pe 5: 12 the grace of God is with you no **m** what happens.

MATTERS (23) [MATTER]

Ex 18: 22 But they can take care of the smaller **m**
18: 26 but they judged the smaller **m** themselves.
1Ki 7: 7 of Judgment, where Solomon sat to hear legal **m**.
1Ch 26: 30 They were responsible for all **m** related to the
26: 32 They were responsible for all **m** related to the
Ezr 9: 2 To make **m** worse, the officials and leaders are
Ne 11: 24 was the king's agent in all **m** of public
Ps 131: 1 I don't concern myself with **m** too great
Ecc 5: 8 and **m** of justice only get lost in red tape
Da 1: 20 In all **m** requiring wisdom and balanced judgment,
Lk 16: 10 "Unless you are faithful in small **m**, you won't be
Jn 16: 25 "I have spoken of these **m** in parables, but the time
Ac 18: 15 you take care of it. I refuse to judge such **m**."
19: 39 And if there are complaints about other **m**,
1Co 4: 3 it **m** very little what you or anyone else thinks.
4: 4 My conscience is clear, but that isn't what **m**.
6: 4 If you have legal disputes about such **m**, why do
11: 34 I'll give you instructions about the other **m** after I
14: 20 and wise in understanding **m** of this kind.
Php 1: 10 For I want you to understand what really **m**,
2: 21 for themselves and not for what **m** to Jesus Christ.
Col 3: 11 Christ is all that **m**, and he lives in all of us.
1Ti 4: 15 Give your complete attention to these **m**.

MATTHAN (2)

Mt 1: 15 Eleazar was the father of **M**. / **M** was the father of Jacob.

MATTHAT (4)

Lk 3: 24 Heli was the son of **M**. / **M** was the son of Levi.
3: 29 Jorim was the son of **M**. / **M** was the son of Levi.

MATTHEW (7) [LEVI]

Mt 9: 9 he saw **M** sitting at his tax-collection booth.
9: 9 Jesus said to him. So **M** got up and followed him.
9: 10 That night **M** invited Jesus and his disciples to be
10: 3 Bartholomew, / Thomas, / **M** (the tax collector),
Mk 3: 18 Andrew, / Philip, / Bartholomew, / **M**, / Thomas,
Lk 6: 15 **M**, / Thomas, / James (son of Alphaeus),
Ac 1: 13 Andrew, / Philip, / Thomas, / Bartholomew, / **M**,

MATTHIAS (2)

Ac 1: 23 called Barsabbas (also known as Justus) and **M**.
1: 26 and in this way **M** was chosen and became an

MATTITHIAH (8)

1Ch 9: 31 **M**, a Levite and the oldest son of Shallum the
15: 18 Jehiel, Unni, Eliab, Benaiah, Maaseiah, **M**,
15: 21 **M**, Eliphelehu, Mikneiah, Obed-edom, Jeiel,
16: 5 Jehiel, **M**, Eliab, Benaiah, Obed-edom, and Jeiel.
25: 3 Zeri, Jeshaiah, Shimei, Hashabiah, and **M**.
25: 21 The fourteenth lot fell to **M** and twelve of his sons
Ezr 10: 43 Jeiel, **M**, Zabad, Zebina, Jaddai, Joel, and Benaiah.
Ne 8: 4 To his right stood **M**, Shema, Anaiah, Uriah,

MATURE (9) [MATURITY]

1Co 2: 6 Yet when I am among **m** Christians, I do speak
3: 1 I couldn't talk to you as I would to **m** Christians.
14: 20 but be **m** and wise in understanding matters of this
Eph 4: 13 and knowledge of God's Son that we will be **m**
Php 3: 15 I hope all of you who are **m** Christians will agree
Heb 5: 14 Solid food is for those who are **m**, who have
6: 1 go on instead and become **m** in our understanding.
1Jn 2: 13 I am writing to you who are **m** because you know
2: 14 I have written to you who are **m** because you know

MATURITY (3) [MATURE]

Job 21: 8 They live to see their children grow to **m**, and they
Lk 8: 14 of this life. And so they never grow into **m**.
2Co 13: 9 What we pray for is your restoration to **m**.

MAUL (1) [MAULED]

Ps 7: 2 If you don't, they will **m** me like a lion,

MAULED (1) [MAUL]

2Ki 2: 24 came out of the woods and **m** forty-two of them.

MAW [KJV] See BELLY, STOMACH

MAXIMUM (1)

Job 34: 36 you deserve the **m** penalty for the wicked way you

MAY (827) See Index of Articles, Etc.

MAYBE (4)

1Ki 18: 27 Or **m** he is away on a trip, or he is asleep
Jnh 1: 6 **M** he will have mercy on us and spare our lives."
Jn 7: 35 "**M** he is thinking of leaving the country and going
7: 35 the Jews in other lands, or **m** even to the Gentiles!

MAYOR (1)

Ac 19: 35 At last the **m** was able to quiet them down enough

ME (4054) [I] See Index of Articles, Etc.

ME-JARKON (1)

Jos 19: 46 and **M**, also Rakkon along with the territory across

ME-ZAHAB (1)

1Ch 1: 50 the daughter of Matred and granddaughter of **M**.

MEADOW (1) [MEADOWS]

Jer 50: 11 You frisk about like a calf in a **m** and neigh like a

MEADOWS (3) [MEADOW]

Ps 23: 2 He lets me rest in green **m**; / he leads me beside
65: 13 The **m** are clothed with flocks of sheep,
Jer 25: 37 Peaceful **m** will be turned into a wasteland by the

MEAH [KJV] See HUNDRED

MEAL (38) [MEALS]

Ge 18: 16 Then the men got up from their **m** and started on
19: 3 with fresh bread made without yeast. After the **m**,
27: 7 to prepare him a delicious **m** of wild game.
31: 46 sat down beside the pile of stones to share a **m**.
Ex 2: 20 him there? Go and invite him home for a **m**!"
12: 11 "Wear your traveling clothes as you eat this **m**,
18: 12 They all joined him in a sacrificial **m** in God's
24: 11 they shared a **m** together in God's presence!
Ru 3: 3 don't let Boaz see you until he has finished his **m**.
3: 7 After Boaz had finished his **m** and was in good
1Sa 28: 25 She brought the **m** to Saul and his men, and they
1Ki 4: 22 150 bushels of choice flour and 300 bushels of **m**,
17: 12 was just gathering a few sticks to cook this last **m**,
17: 13 Go ahead and cook that 'last **m**,' but bake me a
18: 41 Elijah said to Ahab, "Go and enjoy a good **m**!
2Ch 30: 18 and they were allowed to eat the Passover **m**
35: 14 Afterward the Levites prepared a **m** for themselves
Ezr 6: 21 The Passover **m** was eaten by the people of Israel
6: 22 They ate the Passover **m** and celebrated the
Ne 8: 12 people went away to eat and drink at a festive **m**,
Jer 16: 7 No one will offer a **m** to comfort those who mourn
Mt 8: 15 left her. Then she got up and prepared a **m** for him.
26: 18 and I will eat the Passover **m** with my disciples at
Mk 1: 31 and she got up and prepared a **m** for them.
14: 14 where I can eat the Passover **m** with my disciples?'
Lk 4: 39 She got up at once and prepared a **m** for them.
7: 36 Pharisees asked Jesus to come to his home for a **m**,
11: 37 one of the Pharisees invited him home for a **m**.
17: 8 He must first prepare his master's **m** and serve him
22: 8 and said, "Go and prepare the Passover **m**,
22: 11 where I can eat the Passover **m** with my disciples?'
22: 15 anxious to eat this Passover **m** with you before my
Ac 1: 4 In one of these meetings as he was eating a **m** with
16: 34 them into his house and set a **m** before them.
1Co 11: 21 to eat your own **m** without sharing with others.
Heb 12: 16 his birthright as the oldest son for a single **m**.
1Pe 4: 9 share your home with those who need a **m**
Rev 3: 20 I will come in, and we will share a **m** as friends.

MEALS (6) [MEAL]

Lev 23: 37 grain offerings, sacrificial **m** and drink offerings—
2Ch 35: 15 for their **m** were brought to them by their fellow
Ac 2: 46 and shared their **m** with great joy and generosity—
1Co 9: 4 the right to live in your homes and share your **m**?
9: 13 **m** from the food brought to the Temple as
Jude 1: 12 When these people join you in fellowship **m**

MEAN (73) [MEAN-SPIRITED, MEANING, MEANINGLESS, MEANINGLESSNESS, MEANINGS, MEANNESS, MEANS, MEANT]

Ge 29: 25 for Rachel. What do you **m** by this trickery?"
31: 26 "What do you **m** by sneaking off like this?"
37: 10 "What do you **m**?" his father asked. "Will your
40: 8 but there is no one here to tell us what they **m**."
40: 12 Joseph said. "The three branches **m** three days.
40: 18 Joseph told him. "The three baskets **m** three days.
41: 8 very concerned as to what the dreams might **m**.
41: 24 but not one of them could tell me what they **m**."
41: 25 "Both dreams **m** the same thing," Joseph told
44: 5 What do you **m** by stealing my master's personal
Ex 12: 26 your children will ask, 'What does all this **m**?
13: 14 your children will ask you, 'What does all this **m**?'
Nu 32: 6 "Do you **m** you want to stay back here while your
Jos 4: 6 will ask, 'What do these stones **m** to you?'
4: 21 your children will ask, 'What do these stones **m**?'
Jdg 7: 14 friend said, "Your dream can **m** only one thing—
18: 24 "What do you **m**, What do I want?"
1Sa 20: 22 then it will **m** that you must leave immediately,
25: 3 of Caleb, was **m** and dishonest in all his dealings.
2Sa 3: 24 "What do you **m** by letting Abner get away?
19: 6 You have made it clear today that we **m** nothing to
Job 31: 28 for it would **m** I had denied the God of heaven.
Ps 86: 14 are trying to kill me. / And you **m** nothing to them.
Pr 23: 7 "Eat and drink," they say, but they don't **m** it.
Ecc 6: 11 The more words you speak, the less they **m**.
Isa 45: 19 dark corner so no one can understand what I **m**.
Jer 26: 9 What do you **m**, saying that Jerusalem will be
Eze 24: 19 Then the people asked, "What does all this **m**?
37: 18 When your people ask you what your actions **m**,
Da 4: 35 saying, 'What do you **m** by doing these things?'
5: 26 This is what these words **m**: / *Mene* means
Zec 4: 4 "What are these, my lord? What do they **m**?"
Mal 3: 8 have cheated me! "But you ask, 'What do you **m**?
3: 13 says the LORD. "But you say, 'What do you **m**?
Mt 21: 43 What I **m** is that the Kingdom of God will be taken
Mk 4: 10 they asked him, "What do your stories **m**?"
9: 23 "What do you **m**, 'If I can'?" Jesus asked.
Lk 1: 29 Mary tried to think what the angel could **m**.
16: 17 But that doesn't **m** that the law has lost its force in
20: 17 at them and said, "Then what do the Scriptures **m**?
Jn 3: 4 "What do you **m**?" exclaimed Nicodemus.
3: 9 "What do you **m**?" Nicodemus asked.
7: 36 What does he **m** when he says, 'You will search
8: 22 What does he **m**, 'You cannot come where I am
8: 33 to anyone on earth. What do you **m**, 'set free'?"
13: 22 at each other, wondering whom he could **m**.
14: 26 and by the Counselor I **m** the Holy Spirit—he will
16: 15 this is what I **m** when I say that the Spirit will
16: 17 "What does he **m** when he says, 'You won't see
16: 17 And what does he **m** when he says, 'I am going to
16: 18 And what does he **m** by 'a little while'? We don't
Ac 2: 12 there amazed and perplexed. "What can this **m**?"
10: 17 What could the vision **m**? Just then the men sent
19: 2 "No," they replied, "we don't know what you **m**.
Ro 3: 3 does that **m** God will break his promises?
3: 31 does this **m** that we can forget about the law?
4: 17 That is what the Scriptures **m** when God told him,
6: 15 from the law, does this **m** we can go on sinning?
8: 35 Does it **m** he no longer loves us if we have trouble
10: 15 That is what the Scriptures **m** when they say,
1Co 2: 9 That is what the Scriptures **m** when they say,
14: 9 how will they know what you **m**?
14: 11 but to me they **m** nothing. I will not understand
2Co 1: 17 of the world who say yes when they really **m** no?
1: 24 But that does not **m** we want to tell you exactly
8: 13 I don't **m** you should give so much that you suffer
8: 13 I only **m** that there should be some equality.
Php 3: 12 I don't **m** to say that I have already achieved these
Phm 1: 16 Now he will **m** much more to you, both as a slave
Heb 7: 14 What I **m** is, our Lord came from the tribe of
Jas 4: 5 What do you think the Scriptures **m** when they say
1Pe 1: 10 they had many questions as to what it all could **m**.
2Pe 3: 16 and unstable have twisted his letters around to **m**

MEAN-SPIRITED (1) [MEAN, SPIRIT]

Dt 15: 9 Do not be **m** and refuse someone a loan

MEANING (36) [MEAN]

Ge 40: 5 each had a dream, and each dream had its own m.
40:16 baker saw that the first dream had such a good m,
41:11 and I each had a dream, and each dream had a m.
41:39 "Since God has revealed the m of the dreams to
Dt 6:20 ask you, 'What is the m of these stipulations, laws,
Ne 8: 8 and clearly explained the m of what was being
Ps 58: 1 Justice—do you rulers know the m of the word?
119:27 Help me understand the m of your
Pr 1: 6 by exploring the depth of m in these proverbs,
4:22 radiant health to anyone who discovers their m.
Ecc 2: 4 I also tried to find m by building huge homes for
Isa 6: 9 will see what I do, but you will not perceive its m.'
Eze 17:12 Don't you understand the m of this riddle of the
Da 2:24 the king, and I will tell him the m of his dream."
2:25 who will tell Your Majesty the m of your dream!"
2:45 That is the m of the rock cut from the mountain by
2:45 the future. The dream is true, and its m is certain."
4:19 overcome for a time, aghast at the m of the dream.
5:16 If you can read these words and tell me their m,
7:19 Then I wanted to know the true m of the fourth
8:15 was trying to understand the m of this vision,
8:16 "Gabriel, tell this man the m of his vision."
9:23 so you can understand the m of your vision.
Mt 1:23 he will be called Immanuel / (m, God is with us)."
9:13 "Now go and learn the m of this Scripture:
12: 7 aren't guilty if you knew the m of this Scripture:
13:14 see what I do, / but you will not perceive its m.
21:31 of course." Then Jesus explained his m:
Mk 4:12 see what I do, / but they don't perceive its m.
4:34 with his disciples, he explained the m to them.
Lk 4:23 m, 'Why don't you do miracles here in your
8:11 "This is the m of the story: The seed is God's
Ac 28:26 see what I do, / but you will not perceive its m.
Gal 3: 1 For you used to see the m of Jesus Christ's death
1Ti 6: 4 unhealthy desire to quibble over the m of words.
Rev 1:20 This is the m of the seven stars you saw in my

MEANINGLESS (31) [MEAN]

Est 5:13 "But all this is m as long as I see Mordecai the
Ecc 1: 2 "Everything is m," says the Teacher, "utterly m!"
1:14 Everything under the sun is m, like chasing the
2: 1 things' in life." But I found that this, too, was m.
2:11 had worked so hard to accomplish, it was all so m.
2:15 Then I said to myself, "This is all so m!"
2:17 Everything is m, like chasing the wind.
2:19 I have gained by my skill and hard work. How m!
2:23 even at night they cannot rest. It is all utterly m.
2:26 Even this, however, is m, like chasing the wind.
3:19 have no real advantage over the animals. How m!
4: 4 But this, too, is m, like chasing the wind.
4: 8 pleasure now?" It is all so m and depressing.
4:16 So again, it is all m, like chasing the wind.
6: 2 others get it all! This is m—a sickening tragedy.
6: 4 I realize that his birth would have been m
6: 9 Just dreaming about nice things is m; it is like
7: 6 like thorns crackling in a fire. This also is m.
7:15 In this m life, I have seen everything,
8:14 And this is not all that is m in our world. In this
8:14 treated as though they were good. This is so m!
9: 9 m days of life that God has given you in this
11: 8 days will be many. Everything still to come is m.
12: 8 "All is m," says the Teacher, "utterly m."
Hos 8:13 of sacrifice, but to me their sacrifices are all m!
Am 5: 7 Righteousness and fair play are m fictions to you.
Ro 4:14 is useless. And in that case, the promise is also m.
1Co 13: 1 I would only be making m noise like a loud gong
Gal 2:21 not one of those who treats the grace of God as m.

MEANINGLESSNESS (2) [MEAN]

Ecc 4: 7 I observed yet another example of m in our world.
11:10 a whole life before it, still faces the threat of m.

MEANINGS (1) [MEAN]

Da 1:17 special ability in understanding the m of visions

MEANNESS (1) [MEAN]

Pr 24:29 "Now I can pay them back for all their m to me!

MEANS (114) [MEAN]

Ge 40:12 "I know what the dream m," Joseph said.
40:18 "I'll tell you what it m," Joseph told him.
41:15 "and none of these men can tell me what it m.
41:16 "But God will tell you what it m and will set you
41:32 it m that the matter has been decreed by God
Ex 15:23 the place was called Marah, which m "bitter.")
28:37 to the front of Aaron's turban by m of a blue cord.
Nu 26:55 of each ancestral tribe by m of the census listings.
27:21 who will determine the LORD's will by m of
Dt 4:34 himself by rescuing it from another by m of trials,
Jos 14: 2 and a half tribes received their inheritance by m of
Jdg 6:32 which m "Let Baal defend himself,"
2Sa 5:20 So David named that place Baal-perazim (which m
6: 8 He named that place Perez-uzzah (which m
15:21 matter what happens—whether it m life or death."
2Ki 5:23 "By all m, take 150 pounds of silver,"
1Ch 6:54 and territory assigned by m of sacred lots to the
6:61 of the half-tribe of Manasseh by m of sacred lots.
6:65 were also assigned by m of sacred lots.
13:11 He named that place Perez-uzzah (which m
14:11 So that place was named Baal-perazim (which m
24: 5 All tasks were assigned to the various groups by m
24:31 they were assigned to their duties by m of sacred
25: 8 their particular term of service by m of sacred lots,
26:13 for it was all decided by m of sacred lots.
Ezr 2:63 the LORD about the matter by m of sacred lots.
Ne 7:65 the LORD about the matter by m of sacred lots.
Job 13: 7 "Are you defending God by m of lies
36:15 But by m of their suffering, he rescues those who
Pr 2: 5 Then you will understand what it m to fear the
6:31 even if it m selling everything in his house to pay
12:11 Hard work m prosperity; only fools idle away their
29:25 a dangerous trap, but to trust the LORD m safety.
Isa 29: 2 For Jerusalem will become as her name Ariel m—
59: 8 what true peace is or what it m to be just and good.
Jer 1:12 "That's right, and it m that I am watching,
13:13 Then tell them, 'No, this is what the LORD m:
17:11 so are those who get their wealth by unjust m.
22:16 Isn't that what it m to know me?"
Eze 12: 3 perhaps they will even yet consider what this m,
12: 9 people of Israel, have asked you what all this m.
39:16 which m 'horde.') And so the land will finally be
Da 2: 3 me what I dreamed, for I must know what it m."
2: 4 Tell us the dream, and we will tell you what it m."
2: 5 don't tell me what my dream was and what it m,
2: 6 you tell me what I dreamed and what the dream m,
2: 6 and honors. Just tell me the dream and what it m!"
2: 7 Tell us the dream, and we will tell you what it m."
2: 9 then I will know that you can tell me what it m."
2:26 you tell me what my dream was and what it m?"
2:34 a rock was cut from a mountain by supernatural m.
2:36 the dream; now I will tell Your Majesty what it m.
2:45 the rock cut from the mountain by supernatural m,
4: 9 for you to solve. Now tell me what my dream m.
4:18 Now tell me what it m, for no one else can help
4:19 don't be alarmed by the dream and what it m."
4:24 "This is what the dream m, Your Majesty,
4:26 This m that you will receive your kingdom back
5: 7 and tell me what it m will be dressed in purple
5:12 and he will tell you what the writing m."
5:17 but I will tell you what the writing m.
5:26 *Mene* m 'numbered'—God has numbered the
5:27 *Tekel* m 'weighed'—you have been weighed on
5:28 *Parsin* m 'divided'—your kingdom has been
12:10 Only those who are wise will know what it m.
Am 3:10 "My people have forgotten what it m to do right,"
Hab 2: 9 terrible it will be for you who get rich by unjust m!
Zec 8:13 and Israel had become symbols of what it m to be
13: 5 The soil has been my m of livelihood from my
Mt 16: 2 'Red sky at night m fair weather tomorrow,
16: 3 red sky in the morning m foul weather all day.'
23:16 For you say that it m nothing to swear 'by God's
27:33 to a place called Golgotha (which m Skull Hill).
27:46 "*Eli, Eli, lema sabachthani?*" which m,
Mk 15:22 to a place called Golgotha (which m Skull Hill).
15:34 "*Eloi, Eloi, lema sabachthani?*" which m,
Jn 1:38 They replied, "Rabbi" (which m Teacher),
1:41 "We have found the Messiah" (which m the
1:42 but you will be called Cephas" (which m Peter).
5:41 "Your approval or disapproval m nothing to me,
9: 7 and wash in the pool of Siloam" (Siloam m Sent).
11:12 if he is sleeping, that m he is getting better!"
Ac 1:19 name *Akeldama,* which m "Field of Blood.")
4:36 the one the apostles nicknamed Barnabas (which m
7:36 And by m of many miraculous signs and wonders
13: 8 the sorcerer (as his name m in Greek), interfered
Ro 1: 4 raised him from the dead by m of the Holy Spirit.
9: 8 This m that Abraham's physical descendants are
1Co 1: 2 He made you holy by m of Christ Jesus, just as he
2:14 have the Spirit can understand what the Spirit m.
9:19 This m I am not bound to obey people just
12: 7 A spiritual gift is given to each of us as a m of
2Co 1:18 is true, I am not that sort of person. My yes m yes
5:17 What this m is that those who become Christians
13: 5 Christ is among you, it m you have failed the test.
Gal 3:16 was to his child—and that, of course, m Christ.
Eph 2:16 Christ reconciled both groups to God by m of his
4: 9 This m that Christ first came down to the lowly
Php 1:22 Yet if I live, that m fruitful service for Christ.
3:10 I can learn what it m to suffer with him, sharing in
Col 1:20 and on earth by m of his blood on the cross.
Heb 2: 8 when it says "all things," it m nothing is left out.
7: 2 His name m "king of justice." He is also "king of
peace" because *Salem* m "peace."
8:13 it m he has made the first one obsolete.
10:20 the sacred curtain, by m of his death for us.
12: 8 it m that you are illegitimate and are not really his
12:10 for us because it m we will share in his holiness.
12:27 This m that the things on earth will be shaken,
Jas 1:27 of God our Father m that we must care for orphans
3: 3 and go wherever we want by m of a small bit in its
1Pe 5:10 you to his eternal glory by m of Jesus Christ.
1Jn 5: 3 Loving God m keeping his commandments,
2Jn 1: 6 Love m doing what God has commanded us,

MEANT (43) [MEAN]

Ge 37:11 gave it some thought and wondered what it all m.
41: 8 but not one of them could suggest what they m.
41:12 the guard. He told us what each of our dreams m,
50:20 God turned into good what you m for evil.
Ex 32:29 for you obeyed him even though it m killing your
Lev 10: 3 "This is what the LORD m when he said,
1Sa 20:39 of course, didn't understand what Jonathan m;
2Ki 25:24 that the Babylonian officials m them no harm.
Job 19: 3 Ten times now you have m to insult me.
Da 2:16 so he could tell the king what the dream m.
4: 6 so they could tell me what my dream m.
4: 7 the dream, but they could not tell me what it m.
5: 8 them could read the writing or tell him what it m.
7:16 beside the throne and asked him what it all m.
10: 1 and Daniel understood what the vision m.
12: 8 what he said, but I did not understand what he m.
Mt 15:15 "Explain what you m when you said people aren't
Mk 7:17 and his disciples asked him what he m by the
9:10 but they often asked each other what he m by
9:32 and they were afraid to ask him what he m.
Lk 2:50 But they didn't understand what he m.
8: 9 His disciples asked him what the story m.
9:45 But they didn't know what he m. Its significance
Jn 2:21 But by "this temple," Jesus m his body.
6:52 began arguing with each other about what he m.
6:65 "That is what I m when I said that people can't
10: 6 use this illustration didn't understand what he m,
11:13 They thought Jesus m Lazarus was having a good
night's rest, but Jesus m Lazarus had died.
13:11 That is what he m when he said, "Not all of you
13:28 None of the others at the table knew what Jesus m.
16:19 so he said, "Are you asking yourselves what I m?
Ro 11:15 For since the Jews' rejection m that God offered
15: 9 That is what the psalmist m when he wrote:
1Co 5:11 What I m was that you are not to associate with
7: 6 my suggestion. It's not m to be an absolute rule.
Gal 3:16 was to his children, as if it m many descendants.
4:27 That is what Isaiah m when he prophesied,
Heb 6: 9 We are confident that you are m for better things,
10:32 faithful even though it m terrible suffering.
11:15 If they had m the country they came from,
2Pe 3:16 to mean something quite different from what he m,
Rev 19:12 was written on him, and only he knew what it m.

MEANTIME (3) [TIME]

Ex 19:24 In the m, do not let the priests or the people cross
1Sa 18:20 In the m, Saul's daughter Michal had fallen in love
1Co 16: 8 In the m, I will be staying here at Ephesus until the

MEANWHILE (87) [WHILE]

Ge 11:29 M, Abram married Sarai, and his brother Nahor
24:62 M, Isaac, whose home was in the Negev,
28:10 M, Jacob left Beersheba and traveled toward
30: 9 M, Leah realized that she wasn't getting pregnant
30:36 M, Jacob stayed and cared for Laban's flock.
33:17 M, Jacob and his household traveled on to
34: 6 M, Hamor, Shechem's father, came out to discuss
37:36 M, in Egypt, the traders sold Joseph to Potiphar,
47:13 M, the famine became worse and worse,
Ex 17:10 M Moses, Aaron, and Hur went to the top of a
Lev 6:12 M, the fire on the altar must be kept burning;
Nu 16:19 M, Korah had stirred up the entire community
32:17 M, our families will stay in the fortified cities we
32:42 M, a man named Nobah captured the town of
33: 4 M, the Egyptians were burying all their firstborn
33:41 M, the Israelites left Mount Hor and camped at
Jos 3:17 M, the priests who were carrying the Ark of the
4:10 M, the people hurried across the riverbed.
Jdg 4:17 M, Sisera ran to the tent of Jael, the wife of Heber
1Sa 2:21 M, Samuel grew up in the presence of the LORD.
2:26 M, as young Samuel grew taller, he also continued
3: 1 M, the boy Samuel was serving the LORD by
13: 7 M, Saul stayed at Gilgal, and his men were
13:23 The pass at Micmash had m been secured by a
14: 2 M, Saul and his six hundred men were camped on
23:24 M, David and his men had moved into the
25:14 M, one of Nabal's servants went to Abigail
25:44 Saul, m, had given his daughter Michal,
28: 3 M, Samuel had died, and all Israel had mourned
2Sa 2:10 M, the tribe of Judah remained loyal to David.
2:30 M, Joab and his men also returned home.
3:17 M, Abner had consulted with the leaders of Israel.
12:26 M, Joab and the Israelite army were successfully
13:34 M Absalom escaped. Then the watchman on the
16:15 M, Absalom and his men arrived at Jerusalem,
17:18 M, they escaped to Bahurim, where a man hid
17:23 M, Ahithophel was publicly disgraced when
19: 8 M, the Israelites who supported Absalom had fled
20:14 M, Sheba had traveled across Israel to mobilize his
1Ki 14:21 M, Rehoboam son of Solomon was king in Judah.
18: 2 M, the famine had become very severe in Samaria.
20:35 M, the LORD instructed one of the group of
22:13 M, the messenger who went to get Micaiah said to
2Ki 3:21 M, when the people of Moab heard about the three
9: 1 M, Elisha the prophet had summoned a member of
19: 8 M, the Assyrian representative left Jerusalem
20: 8 M, Hezekiah had said to Isaiah, "What sign will
1Ch 16:39 M, David stationed Zadok the priest and his fellow
2Ch 13:13 M, Jeroboam had secretly sent part of his army
18:12 M, the messenger who went to get Micaiah said to
25:13 M, the hired troops that Amaziah had sent home
30:24 M, many more priests purified themselves.
Ne 4:11 M, our enemies were saying, "Before they know
Est 9:16 M, the other Jews throughout the king's provinces
Ps 38:12 M, my enemies lay traps for me; / they make plans
119:78 m, I will concentrate on your commandments.
Isa 21: 6 M, the Lord said to me, "Put a watchman on the
37: 8 M, the Assyrian representative left Jerusalem
Jer 39: 8 M, the Babylonians burned Jerusalem,
41:15 M, Ishmael and eight of his men escaped from
Eze 4: 7 "M, continue your demonstration of the siege of
Mt 14:24 M, the disciples were in trouble far away from
26: 6 M, Jesus was in Bethany at the home of Simon,
26:58 M, Peter was following far behind and eventually
26:69 M, as Peter was sitting outside in the courtyard,
27:20 M, the leading priests and other leaders persuaded
Mk 14: 3 M, Jesus was in Bethany at the home of Simon,
14:50 M, all his disciples deserted him and ran away.
14:54 M, Peter followed far behind and then slipped
14:66 M, Peter was below in the courtyard. One of the

Lk 1:21 **M**, the people were waiting for Zechariah to come
12:1 **M**, the crowds grew until thousands were milling
15:25 "**M**, the older son was in the fields working.
19:8 **M**, Zacchaeus stood there and said to the Lord,
23:10 **M**, the leading priests and the teachers of religious
Jn 4:31 **M**, the disciples were urging Jesus to eat.
11:57 **M**, the leading priests and Pharisees had publicly
18:25 **M**, as Simon Peter was standing by the fire,
Ac 5:12 **M**, the apostles were performing many miraculous
8:40 **M**, Philip found himself farther north at the city of
9:1 **M**, Saul was uttering threats with every breath.
10:19 **M**, as Peter was puzzling over the vision, the Holy
11:19 **M**, the believers who had fled from Jerusalem
12:16 **M**, Peter continued knocking. When they finally
18:24 **M**, a Jew named Apollos, an eloquent speaker who
20:12 **M**, the young man was taken home unhurt,
Php 2:25 **M**, I thought I should send Epaphroditus back to

MEARAH (1)

Jos 13:4 including **M** (which belongs to the Sidonians),

MEASURE (31) [MEASURED, MEASUREMENT, MEASUREMENTS, MEASURES, MEASURING]

Ex 16:36 (The container used to **m** the manna was an omer,
Nu 35:5 **M** off 3,000 feet outside the town walls in every
1Ki 7:9 of stone, cut and trimmed to exact **m** on all sides.
7:11 of stone used in the walls were also cut to **m**,
2Ki 21:13 and by the same **m** I used for the family of Ahab.
2Ch 11:12 and spears in these towns as a further safety **m**.
Ps 28:4 **M** it out in proportion to their wickedness.
60:6 with joy. / I will **m** out the valley of Succoth.
108:7 with joy. / I will **m** out the valley of Succoth.
Isa 5:10 Ten measures of seed will yield only one **m** of
40:28 No one can **m** the depths of his understanding.
Eze 4:11 Then **m** out a jar of water for each day, and drink it
42:15 he led me out through the east gateway to **m** the
45:3 **m** out a portion of land 8-1/3 miles long and 3-1/3
45:11 and the bath will each **m** one-tenth of a homer.
48:13 Together these portions of land will **m** 8-1/3 miles
48:16 The city will **m** 1-1/2 miles on each side.
Hos 3:2 and about five bushels of barley and a **m** of wine.
Am 8:5 You **m** out your grain in false measures and weigh
Zec 2:2 He replied, "I am going to **m** Jerusalem, to see
Mt 7:2 Whatever **m** you use in judging others, it will be
used to **m** how you are judged.
Lk 6:38 Your gift will return to you in full **m**,
6:38 Whatever **m** you use in giving—large or small—
6:38 it will be used to **m** what is given back to you."
Jn 3:34 for God's Spirit is upon him without **m** or limit.
15:13 And here is how to **m** it—the greatest love is
Rev 11:1 "Go and **m** the Temple of God and the altar,
11:2 But do not **m** the outer courtyard, for it has been
21:15 in his hand a gold measuring stick to **m** the city,
21:17 feet thick (the angel used a standard human **m**).

MEASURED (42) [MEASURE]

Lev 5:15 and it must be of the proper value in silver as **m** by
27:25 All the value assessments must be **m** in terms of
Ru 3:15 He **m** out six scoops of barley into the cloak
2Sa 8:2 and he **m** them off in groups with a length of rope.
8:2 He **m** off two groups to be executed for every one
1Ki 4:29 and knowledge too vast to be **m**.
7:47 so many; the weight of the bronze could not be **m**.
Job 28:27 he had done all this, he saw wisdom and **m** it.
Isa 40:12 Who has **m** off the heavens with his fingers?
Jer 13:25 "I have **m** it out especially for you, because you
31:37 Just as the heavens cannot be **m** and the foundation
33:22 and the sand on the seashores cannot be **m**,
51:9 for her judgment will be so great it cannot be **m**.
52:20 the twelve bulls beneath it was too great to be **m**.
Eze 40:5 rod that was 10-1/2 feet long and **m** the wall,
40:6 the steps and **m** the threshold of the gateway;
40:8 He also **m** the foyer of the gateway
40:11 The man **m** the gateway entrance, which was
40:13 Then he **m** the entire width of the gateway,
40:14 He **m** the dividing walls all along the inside of the
40:19 Then the man **m** across the Temple's outer
40:20 just like the one on the east, and the man **m** it.
40:24 to the south gateway and **m** its various parts,
40:28 He **m** it and found that it had the same
40:32 He **m** it and found that it had the same
40:33 The gateway passage **m** 87-1/2 feet long
40:35 He **m** it and found that it had the same
40:36 The gateway passage **m** 87-1/2 feet long
40:47 Then the man **m** the inner courtyard and found it to
40:48 He **m** its supporting columns and found them to be
41:1 and he **m** the columns that framed its doorway.
41:3 He **m** the columns at the entrance and found them
41:5 Then he **m** the wall of the Temple and found that it
41:10 This open area **m** 35 feet in width, and it went all
41:13 Then the man **m** the Temple, and he found it to be
42:16 He **m** the east side; it was 875 feet long.
42:17 He also **m** the north side and got the same
47:4 He **m** off another 1,750 feet and told me to go
47:5 Then he **m** another 1,750 feet, and the river was
Lk 12:15 Real life is not **m** by how much we own."
Rev 21:16 When he **m** it, he found it was a square, as wide as
21:17 Then he **m** the walls and found them to be 216 feet

MEASUREMENT (1) [MEASURE]

Eze 42:17 also measured the north side and got the same **m**.

MEASUREMENTS (8) [MEASURE]

Eze 40:10 Each had the same **m**, and the dividing walls
40:21 All the **m** matched those of the east gateway.
40:28 and found that it had the same **m** as the other
40:32 and found that it had the same **m** as the other
40:35 and found that it had the same **m** as the other
40:36 and foyer of this gateway had the same **m** as in the
42:15 When the man had finished taking these **m**, he led
43:13 "These are the **m** of the altar: There is a gutter all

MEASURES (12) [MEASURE]

Ge 18:6 Get three **m** of your best flour, and bake some
Dt 25:14 and you must use full and honest **m**.
25:15 Yes, use honest weights and **m**, so that you will
25:16 and **m** are detestable to the LORD your God.
1Ch 23:29 also responsible to check all the weights and **m**.
Isa 5:10 Ten **m** of seed will yield only one measure of
44:13 Then the wood-carver **m** and marks out a block of
Eze 45:10 honest weights and scales, honest dry volume **m**,
and honest liquid volume **m**.
48:20 is a square that **m** 8-1/3 miles on each side.
Am 8:5 You measure out your grain in false **m** and weigh
Mic 6:10 by dishonestly measuring out grain in short **m**.

MEASURING (24) [MEASURE]

Lev 19:35 "Do not use dishonest standards when **m** length,
19:36 Your containers for **m** dry goods or liquids must be
1Sa 17:4 He was a giant of a man, **m** over nine feet tall!
Isa 28:17 "I will take the **m** line of justice and the plumb
Jer 31:39 A **m** line will be stretched out over the hill of
Eze 40:3 holding in his hand a **m** tape and a **m** rod.
40:5 The man took a **m** rod that was 10-1/2 feet long
40:13 **m** the distance between the back walls of facing
43:6 (The man who had been **m** was still standing
43:16 The top of the altar is square, **m** 21 feet by 21 feet.
43:17 **m** 24-1/2 feet on each side, with a 21-inch gutter
45:2 A section of this land, **m** 875 feet by 875 feet,
45:11 The homer will be your standard unit for **m**
47:3 **M** as he went, he led me along the stream for 1,750
48:10 For the priests there will be a strip of land **m** 8-1/3
Mic 6:10 by dishonestly **m** out grain in short measures.
Zec 2:1 me again, I saw a man with a **m** line in his hand.
5:6 He replied, "It is a basket for **m** grain, and it is
Ro 12:3 **m** your value by how much faith God has given
2Co 10:12 with each other, and **m** themselves by themselves.
Eph 4:13 in the Lord, **m** up to the full stature of Christ.
Rev 11:1 Then I was given a **m** stick, and I was told, "Go
21:15 held in his hand a gold **m** stick to measure the city,

MEAT (109) [MEATS]

Ge 18:8 some cheese curds and milk and the roasted **m**,
27:14 She took them and cooked a delicious **m** dish,
27:17 Then she gave him the **m** dish, with its rich aroma,
27:25 Then Isaac said, "Now, my son, bring me the **m**.
27:31 Esau prepared his father's favorite **m** dish
32:32 the people of Israel don't eat **m** from near the hip,
Ex 12:9 The **m** must never be eaten raw or boiled; roast it
12:46 You must not carry any of its **m** outside, and you
16:8 The LORD will give you **m** to eat in the evening
16:12 tell them, 'In the evening you will have **m** to eat,
27:3 The ash buckets, shovels, basins, **m** hooks,
29:31 and boil its **m** in a sacred place.
29:32 Aaron and his sons are to eat this **m**, along with the
29:33 They alone may eat the **m** and bread used for their
29:34 If any of the ordination **m** or bread remains until
34:25 And none of the **m** of the Passover lamb may be
38:3 shovels, basins, **m** hooks, and firepans.
Lev 4:11 its hide, **m**, head, legs, internal organs, and dung—
6:27 or anyone who touches the sacrificial **m** will
6:28 If a clay pot is used to boil the sacrificial **m**,
6:30 none of that animal's **m** may be eaten.
7:6 All males from a priest's family may eat the **m**,
7:7 the **m** of the sacrificed animal belongs to the priest
7:15 The animal's **m** must be eaten on the same day it is
7:16 the **m** may be eaten on that same day,
7:18 If any of the **m** from this peace offering is eaten on
7:18 By then, the **m** will be contaminated; if you eat it,
7:19 "**M** that touches anything ceremonially unclean
7:19 And as for **m** that may be eaten, it may only be
7:20 but eats **m** from a peace offering that was
7:21 and then eats **m** from the LORD's sacrifices,
8:17 rest of the bull, including its hide, **m**, and dung,
8:31 "Boil the rest of the **m** at the Tabernacle entrance,
8:32 Any **m** or bread that is left over must then be
9:11 The **m** and the hide, however, he burned outside
10:18 you should have eaten the **m** in the sanctuary area
11:8 You may not eat the **m** of these animals or touch
11:11 You must never eat their **m** or even touch their
11:40 If you eat any of its **m** or carry away its carcass,
19:26 "Never eat **m** that has not been drained of its
Nu 11:4 to complain. "Oh, for some **m**!" they exclaimed.
11:13 Where am I supposed to get **m** for all these
11:13 They keep complaining and saying, 'Give us **m**!'
11:18 for tomorrow they will have **m** to eat.
11:18 and complaints: "If only we had **m** to eat!
11:18 Now the LORD will give you **m**, and you will
11:21 and yet you promise them **m** for a whole month!
11:33 But while they were still eating the **m**, the anger of
11:34 the people there who had craved **m** from Egypt.
18:18 The **m** of these animals will be yours, just like the
19:5 must be burned—its hide, **m**, blood, and dung.
22:40 He sent portions of the **m** to Balaam
Dt 12:15 "But you may butcher animals for **m** in any town,
12:15 ceremonially clean or unclean, may eat that **m**.
12:20 has promised, you may eat **m** whenever you want.
12:21 and you may eat the **m** at your home as I have
12:22 ceremonially clean or unclean, may eat that **m**,
12:23 is the life, and you must not eat the life with the **m**.
12:27 You must offer the **m** and blood of your burnt
12:27 of the LORD your God, but you may eat the **m**.
16:4 And do not let any of the **m** of the Passover lamb
28:31 your eyes, but you won't get a single bite of the **m**.
Jdg 6:19 carrying the **m** in a basket and the broth in a pot,
6:20 "Place the **m** and the unleavened bread on this
6:21 Then the angel of the LORD touched the **m**
1Sa 2:13 While the **m** of the sacrificed animal was still
2:15 He would demand raw **m** before it had been boiled
9:23 the cook to bring Saul the finest cut of **m**,
14:33 the LORD by eating **m** that still has blood in it."
14:34 Do not sin against the LORD by eating **m** with
25:11 and the **m** I've slaughtered for my shearers
1Ki 17:6 him bread and **m** each morning and evening,
19:21 He passed around the **m** to the other plowmen,
1Ch 28:17 gold **m** hooks used to handle the sacrificial **m**
2Ch 4:16 the pots, the shovels, the **m** hooks, and all the
Ps 78:20 but he can't give his people bread and **m**."
78:27 He rained down **m** as thick as dust— / birds as
78:30 had craved, / while the **m** was yet in their mouths,
105:40 They asked for **m**, and he sent them quail;
Isa 22:13 sacrificial animals, feast on **m**, and drink wine.
44:16 He burns part of the tree to roast his **m** and to keep
44:19 and used it to bake my bread and roast my **m**.
Eze 11:3 Inside it we will be like **m**—safe from all harm.'
11:7 the victims of your injustice are the pieces of **m**.
11:11 pot for you, and you will not be the **m**, safe inside.
24:4 Fill it with choice **m**—the rump and the shoulder
24:5 pot to a boil, and cook the bones along with the **m**.
24:6 So take the **m** out chunk by chunk in whatever
24:10 Cook the **m** well with many spices. Then empty
33:25 You eat **m** with blood in it, you worship idols,
40:38 **m** for sacrifices was washed before being taken to
40:43 and set on the tables where the sacrificial **m** was to
44:31 The priests may never eat **m** from any bird
46:20 "This is where the priests will cook the **m** from
Da 10:3 All that time I had eaten no rich food or **m**,
Am 6:4 eating the **m** of tender lambs and choice calves.
Mic 3:3 You chop them up like **m** for the cooking pot.
Zec 9:7 They will no longer eat **m** with blood in it or feed
11:16 this shepherd will eat the **m** of the fattest sheep
Ac 15:20 and tell them to abstain from eating **m** sacrificed to
15:20 or eating the **m** of strangled animals.
15:29 or eating the **m** of strangled animals,
21:25 consume blood, nor eat **m** from strangled animals,
Ro 14:21 Don't eat **m** or drink wine or do anything else if it
1Co 8:4 Should we eat **m** that has been sacrificed to idols?
8:13 I will never eat **m** again as long as I live—
10:25 You may eat any **m** that is sold in the marketplace.
10:28 But suppose someone warns you that this **m** has

MEATS (2) [MEAT]

Isa 66:17 feasting on pork and rats and other forbidden **m**,
Mt 22:4 been prepared, and choice **m** have been cooked.

MECONAH (1)

Ne 11:28 Ziklag, and **M** with its villages.

MEDAD (2)

Nu 11:26 Two men, Eldad and **M**, were still in the camp
11:27 "Eldad and **M** are prophesying in the camp!"

MEDALLION (6) [MEDALLIONS]

Ex 28:36 "Next make a **m** of pure gold.
28:37 This **m** will be attached to the front of Aaron's
29:6 And place on his head the turban with the gold **m**.
39:30 they made the sacred **m** of pure gold to be worn on
39:31 This **m** was tied to the turban with a blue cord,
Lev 8:9 head the turban with the gold **m** at its front,

MEDALLIONS (1) [MEDALLION]

Ex 35:22 **m**, earrings, rings from their fingers,

MEDAN (2)

Ge 25:2 Jokshan, **M**, Midian, Ishbak, and Shuah.
1Ch 1:32 Jokshan, **M**, Midian, Ishbak, and Shuah.

MEDDLING (1)

2Th 3:11 and wasting time **m** in other people's business.

MEDE (4) [MEDIA]

Da 5:31 And Darius the **M** took over the kingdom at the
6:1 Darius the **M** decided to divide the kingdom into
9:1 It was the first year of the reign of Darius the **M**,
11:1 since the first year of the reign of Darius the **M**.)

MEDEBA (5)

Nu 21:30 wiped them out / as far away as Nophah and **M**."
Jos 13:9 the gorge) to the plain beyond **M**, as far as Dibon.
13:16 in the middle of the gorge) to the plain beyond **M**.
1Ch 19:7 These forces camped at **M**, where they were joined
Isa 15:2 and shrines, weeping for the fate of Nebo and **M**.

MEDES (12) [MEDIA]

2Ki 17:6 River in Gozan, and among the cities of the **M**.
18:11 River in Gozan, and among the cities of the **M**.
Est 1:19 law of the Persians and **M** that cannot be revoked.
Isa 13:17 For I will stir up the **M** against Babylon, and no
21:2 Go ahead, you Elamites and **M**, take part in the

Jer 51:11 of the kings of the **M** to march against Babylon
51:28 Bring against her the armies of the kings of the **M**
Da 5:28 been divided and given to the **M** and Persians."
6: 8 it cannot be changed, a law of the **M** and Persians,
6:12 it is a law of the **M** and Persians, which cannot be
6:15 Majesty knows that according to the law of the **M**
Ac 2: 9 Parthians, **M**, Elamites, people from Mesopotamia,

MEDIA (6) [MEDE, MEDES]

Ezr 6: 2 in the province of **M** that a scroll was found.
Est 1: 3 He invited all the military officers of **M** and Persia,
1:14 seven high officials of Persia and **M**.
10: 2 in *The Book of the History of the Kings of* **M**
Jer 25:25 and to the kings of Zimri, Elam, and **M**.
Da 8:20 The two-horned ram represents the kings of **M**

MEDIATE (2) [MEDIATOR]

1Sa 2:25 another person, God can **m** for the guilty party.
Job 16:21 that someone would **m** between God and me,

MEDIATES (3) [MEDIATE]

Job 16:21 and me, as a person **m** between friends.
Heb 9:15 That is why he is the one who **m** the new covenant
12:24 the one who **m** the new covenant between God

MEDIATOR (6) [MEDIATE, MEDIATES]

Job 9:33 If only there were a **m** who could bring us
9:34 The **m** could make God stop beating me, and I
Ac 7:38 He was the **m** between the people of Israel
Gal 3:19 who was the **m** between God and the people.
3:20 Now a **m** is needed if two people enter into an
1Ti 2: 5 and one **M** who can reconcile God and people.

MEDICAL (1) [MEDICINE]

Ex 21:19 of the injury and must pay for the **m** expenses.

MEDICINE (9) [MEDICAL, MEDICINES]

2Sa 16: 8 At last you will taste some of your own **m**,
Ps 141: 5 a kindness! / If they reprove me, it is soothing **m**.
Pr 17:22 A cheerful heart is good **m**, but a broken spirit saps
Jer 4:18 This punishment is a bitter dose of your own **m**.
8:22 Is there no **m** in Gilead? Is there no physician
30:13 up your injury. You are beyond the help of any **m**.
51: 8 too, has fallen. Weep for her, and give her **m**.
Lk 10:34 the Samaritan soothed his wounds with **m**
Rev 22: 2 The leaves were used for **m** to heal the nations.

MEDICINES (1) [MEDICINE]

Jer 46:11 But your many **m** will bring you no healing.

MEDITATE (9) [MEDITATING, MEDITATION]

Dt 30: 1 and you **m** on them as you are living among the
Jos 1: 8 **M** on it day and night so you may be sure to obey
Ps 48: 9 O God, we **m** on your unfailing love / as we
119:23 speak against me, / but I will **m** on your principles.
119:27 and I will **m** on your wonderful miracles.
119:48 and love your commands. / I **m** on your principles.
119:52 I **m** on your age-old laws; / O LORD,
119:117 then I will **m** on your principles continually.
145: 5 I will **m** on your majestic, glorious splendor

MEDITATING (3) [MEDITATE]

Ge 24:63 **m**, he looked up and saw the camels coming.
Ps 27: 4 in the LORD's perfections / and **m** in his Temple.
63: 6 thinking of you, / **m** on you through the night.

MEDITATION (2) [MEDITATE]

Ps 53: T For the choir director: A **m** of David.
54: T A **m** of David, regarding the time the Ziphites

MEDITERRANEAN (37)

Ex 23:31 your boundaries from the Red Sea to the **M** Sea,
Nu 13:29 The Canaanites live along the coast of the **M** Sea
34: 5 toward the brook of Egypt and end at the **M** Sea.
34: 6 boundary will be the coastline of the **M** Sea.
34: 7 "Your northern boundary will begin at the **M** Sea
Dt 11:24 and from the Euphrates River in the east to the **M**
34: 2 all the land of Judah, extending to the **M** Sea;
Jos 1: 4 from the Euphrates River on the east to the **M** Sea
5: 1 and all the Canaanite kings who lived along the **M**
9: 1 and along the coast of the **M** Sea as far north as the
15: 4 brook of Egypt, which it followed to the **M** Sea.
15:11 It passed Jabneel and ended at the **M** Sea.
15:12 The western boundary was the shoreline of the **M**
15:47 brook of Egypt and along the coast of the **M** Sea.
16: 3 then to Gezer and on over to the **M** Sea.
16: 6 then on to the **M** Sea. The northern boundary began at the **M**, ran east
16: 8 following the Kanah Ravine to the **M** Sea.
17: 9 northern side of the Kanah Ravine to the **M** Sea.
17:10 with the **M** Sea forming Manasseh's western
19:29 city of Tyre and came to the **M** Sea at Hosah.
23: 4 from the Jordan River to the **M** Sea in the west.
1Ki 5: 9 the logs from the Lebanon mountains to the **M** Sea
2Ch 2:16 logs in rafts down the coast of the **M** Sea to Joppa.
Ezr 3: 7 and floated along the coast of the **M** Sea to Joppa,
Ps 80:11 We spread our branches west to the **M** Sea,
89:25 I will extend his rule from the **M** Sea in the west
Jer 47: 5 You remnant of the **M** plain, how long will you
Eze 47:10 kind will fill the Dead Sea, just as they fill the **M**!
47:15 "The northern border will run from the **M** toward
47:17 So the northern border will run from the **M** to
47:19 follow the course of the brook of Egypt to the **M**.
47:20 "On the west side the **M** itself will be your border
48:28 and then follows the brook of Egypt to the **M**.
Joel 2:20 the Dead Sea; those at the front will go into the **M**.
Zec 9: 4 and hurl its fortifications into the **M** Sea.
14: 8 half toward the Dead Sea and half toward the **M**,

MEDIUM (3) [MEDIUMS]

1Sa 28: 7 "Find a woman who is a **m**, so I can go and ask
28: 7 His advisers replied, "There is a **m** at Endor."
1Ch 10:13 LORD's command, and he even consulted a **m**

MEDIUMS (13) [MEDIUM]

Lev 19:31 "Do not rely on **m** and psychics, for you will be
20: 6 by consulting and following **m** or psychics,
20:27 "Men and women among you who act as **m**
Dt 18:11 or cast spells, or function as **m** or psychics, or call
1Sa 28: 3 And Saul had banned all **m** and psychics from the
28: 9 "You know that Saul has expelled all the **m**
2Ki 21: 6 and he consulted with **m** and psychics.
23:24 Josiah also exterminated the **m** and psychics,
2Ch 33: 6 and he consulted with **m** and psychics.
Isa 8:19 you trying to find out the future by consulting **m**
19: 3 They will call on spirits, **m**, and psychics to show
Jer 27: 9 fortune-tellers, interpreters of dreams, **m**,
29: 8 and **m** who are there in Babylon trick you.

MEET (144) [MEETING, MEETINGS, MEETS, MET]

Ge 14:17 the king of Sodom came out to **m** him in the valley
18: 2 He got up and ran to **m** them, welcoming them by
19: 1 When he saw them, he stood up to **m** them.
24:21 she was the one the LORD intended him to **m**.
24:65 "Who is that man walking through the fields to **m**
29:13 he rushed out to **m** him and greeted him warmly.
30:16 home from the fields, Leah went out to **m** him.
32: 1 on their way again, angels of God came to **m** him.
32: 6 the news that Esau was on his way to **m** Jacob—
32:17 "When you **m** Esau, he will ask, 'Where are you
33: 4 Then Esau ran to **m** him and embraced him
33:14 will follow at our own pace and **m** you at Seir."
46:28 Jacob sent Judah on ahead to **m** Joseph and get
46:29 his chariot and traveled to Goshen to **m** his father.
Ex 4:14 And look! He is on his way to **m** you now.
4:27 "Go out into the wilderness to **m** Moses."
5:13 "**M** your daily quota of bricks, just as you did
7:15 the river. Stand on the riverbank and **m** him there.
8:20 and **m** Pharaoh as he goes down to the river.
17: 6 I will **m** you by the rock at Mount Sinai.
18: 7 So Moses went out to **m** his father-in-law.
18:12 and the leaders of Israel came out to **m** him.
19:17 Moses led them out from the camp to **m** with God,
25:22 I will **m** with you there and talk to you from above
29:42 where I will **m** you and speak with you.
29:43 I will **m** the people of Israel there,
30: 6 the Ark of the Covenant. I will **m** with you there.
30:36 where I will **m** with you in the Tabernacle.
36: 4 But finally the craftsmen left their work to **m** with
Lev 8: 3 Then call the entire community of Israel to **m** you
Nu 17: 4 of the Ark of the Covenant, where I **m** with you.
20:18 out of my land or I will **m** you with an army!"
20:20 and marched out to **m** them with an imposing
22:36 he went out to **m** him at a Moabite town on the
23:15 "Stand here by your burnt offering while I go to **m**
31:13 and all the leaders of the people went to **m** them
35:19 When they **m**, the avenger must execute the
35:21 relative must execute the murderer when they **m**.
Jos 9:11 Go **m** with the people of Israel and declare our
Jdg 4:18 Jael went out to **m** Sisera and said to him,
4:22 came looking for Sisera, Jael went out to **m** him.
11:34 ran out to **m** him, playing on a tambourine
1Sa 10: 5 you will **m** a band of prophets coming down from
10:17 Later Samuel called all the people of Israel to **m**
13:10 Saul went out to **m** and welcome him,
13:15 but the rest of the troops went with Saul to **m** the
15:35 Samuel never went to **m** with Saul again, but he
17:48 closer to attack, David quickly ran out to **m** him.
21: 2 am here. I have told my men where to **m** me later.
25:32 the God of Israel, who has sent you to **m** me today!
25:34 that if you had not hurried out to **m** me,
2Sa 6:20 Michal came out to **m** him and said in disgust,
19:15 the people of Judah came to Gilgal to **m** him
19:24 arrived from Jerusalem to **m** the king.
23:13 David's fighting men) went down to **m** him there.
1Ki 2: 8 When he came down to **m** me at the Jordan River,
2:19 The king rose from his throne to **m** her, and he
18:16 that Elijah had come, and Ahab went out to **m** him.
20: 9 **m**.' " So the messengers returned to Ben-hadad
21:18 "Go down to **m** King Ahab, who rules in Samaria.
2Ki 1: 3 and **m** the messengers of the king of Samaria
2:15 And they went to **m** him and bowed down before
4:26 Run out to **m** her and ask her, 'Is everything all
4:31 He returned to **m** Elisha and told him, "The child
5:11 "I thought he would surely come out to **m** me!"
5:21 climbed down from his chariot and went to **m** him.
5:26 Naaman stepped down from his chariot to **m** you?
6: 1 this place where we **m** with you is too small.
6: 2 There we can build a new place for us to **m**."
9:18 So a rider went out to **m** Jehu and said, "The king
9:21 of Judah rode out in their chariots to **m** Jehu.
10:15 son of Recab, who was coming to **m** him.
14: 8 grandson of Jehu: "Come and **m** me in battle!"
16:10 then went to Damascus to **m** with King
18:18 but the king sent these officials to **m** with them:
19: 9 Before leaving to **m** the attack, he sent this
1Ch 11:15 David's fighting men) went down to **m** him there.
12:17 David went out to **m** them and said, "If you have
14: 8 so he and his men marched out to **m** them.
2Ch 15: 2 and he went out to **m** King Asa as he was returning
19: 2 Jehu son of Hanani the seer went out to **m** him.
22: 7 went out with Joram to **m** Jehu son of Nimshi,
22: 8 he happened to **m** some of Judah's officials
25:17 grandson of Jehu: "Come and **m** me in battle!"
28: 9 He went out to **m** them and said, "The LORD,
29: 4 and Levites to **m** him at the courtyard east of the
Ne 6: 2 and Geshem sent me a message asking me to **m**
6: 3 I cannot stop to come and **m** with you."
6:10 "Let us **m** together inside the Temple of God
12:38 went northward around the other way to **m** them.
Ps 79: 8 Let your tenderhearted mercies quickly **m** our
111: 1 with all my heart / as I **m** with his godly people.
Pr 17:12 It is safer to **m** a bear robbed of her cubs than to
22:13 I might **m** a lion in the street and be killed!"
28:28 When the wicked **m** disaster, the godly multiply.
Isa 7: 3 "Go out to **m** King Ahaz, you and your son
36: 3 These are the officials who went out to **m** with
37: 9 Before leaving to **m** the attack, he sent this
Jer 38:14 One day King Zedekiah sent for Jeremiah to **m**
40:10 before the Babylonians who come to **m** with us.
41: 6 Ishmael left Mizpah to **m** them, weeping as he
Eze 14:23 When you **m** them and see their behavior, you will
Am 4:12 Prepare to **m** your God as he comes in judgment,
5:19 like a man who runs from a lion—only to **m** a bear.
Mic 7:17 they will come out to **m** the LORD our God.
Zec 2: 3 Then the angel who was with me went to **m** a
6:10 **m** them at the home of Josiah son of Zephaniah.
Mt 8:34 The entire town came out to **m** Jesus, but they
22:11 But when the king came in to **m** the guests,
25: 1 took their lamps and went to **m** the bridegroom.
26:32 will go ahead of you to Galilee and **m** you there."
Mk 5: 2 by an evil spirit ran out from a cemetery to **m** him.
5: 6 He ran to **m** Jesus and fell down before him.
14:13 "a man carrying a pitcher of water will **m** you.
14:28 will go ahead of you to Galilee and **m** you there."
Lk 7: 7 I am not even worthy to come and **m** you. Just say
8:27 who was possessed by demons came out to **m** him.
12:58 are on the way to court and you **m** your accuser,
22:10 a man carrying a pitcher of water will **m** you.
Jn 1:42 Then Andrew brought Simon to **m** Jesus.
4:29 and **m** a man who told me everything I ever did!
11:20 word that Jesus was coming, she went to **m** him.
12:13 palm branches and went down the road to **m** him.
12:18 was the main reason so many went out to **m** him—
12:21 in Galilee. They said, "Sir, we want to **m** Jesus."
18: 4 Stepping forward to **m** them, he asked,
Ac 9:26 he tried to **m** with the believers, but they were all
10:24 together his relatives and close friends to **m** Peter.
20:17 at Ephesus, asking them to come down to **m** him.
21:18 The next day Paul went in with us to **m** with
28:15 and they came to **m** us at the Forum on the Appian
1Co 5: 4 power of the Lord Jesus will be with you as you **m**.
11:17 harm than good is done when you **m** together.
11:18 are divisions among you when you **m** as a church,
11:34 judgment upon yourselves when you **m** together.
14:26 When you **m**, one will sing, another will teach,
Col 4:15 and to Nympha and those who **m** in her house.
1Th 4:12 and you will not need to depend on others to **m**
4:15 to **m** him ahead of those who are in their graves.
4:17 be caught up in the clouds to **m** the Lord in the air
2Th 2: 1 and how we will be gathered together to **m** him.
Tit 3:12 do your best to **m** me at Nicopolis as quickly as
1Pe 2: 8 so they **m** the fate that has been planned for them.
2Jn 1: 4 How happy I was to **m** some of your children

MEETING (44) [MEET]

Ge 20: 8 and hastily called a **m** of all his servants.
32:20 Esau with the presents before **m** him face to face.
Ex 4:29 to Egypt and called the leaders of Israel to a **m**.
16: 6 and Aaron called a **m** of all the people of Israel
33: 7 tent known as the Tent of **M** far outside the camp.
33: 8 Whenever Moses went out to the Tent of **M**,
33:11 Inside the Tent of **M**, the LORD would speak to
33:11 Joshua son of Nun, stayed behind in the Tent of **M**.
34:34 But whenever he went into the Tent of **M** to speak
35: 1 Now Moses called a **m** of all the people and told
Jdg 9: 6 and Beth-millo called a **m** under the oak beside the
1Sa 25:36 so she didn't tell him anything about her **m** with
2Ki 6:32 Elisha was sitting in his house at a **m** with the
9: 5 he found Jehu sitting in a **m** with the other army
10:18 Then Jehu called a **m** of all the people of the city
Ne 5: 7 Then I called a public **m** to deal with the problem.
5: 8 At the **m** I said to them, "The rest of us are doing
Pr 31:23 for he sits in the council **m** with the other civic
Jer 36:12 palace where the administrative officials were **m**.
Joel 1:14 of fasting; call the people together for a solemn **m**.
2:15 of fasting; call the people together for a solemn **m**.
Mt 2: 4 He called a **m** of the leading priests and teachers of
2: 7 At this **m** he learned the exact time when they first
12:14 Then the Pharisees called a **m** and discussed plans
26: 3 and other leaders were **m** at the residence of
28:12 A **m** of all the religious leaders was called,
Jn 7:53 Then the **m** broke up and everybody went home.
20:19 the disciples were **m** behind locked doors
Ac 2: 1 the believers were **m** together in one place.
2: 2 and it filled the house where they were **m**.
4:31 this prayer, the building where they were **m** shook,
5:12 And the believers were **m** regularly at the Temple
6: 2 So the Twelve called a **m** of all the believers.
15: 7 At the **m**, after a long discussion, Peter stood
15:30 where they called a general **m** of the Christians
1Co 5: 4 You are to call a **m** of the church, and I will be

14:19 But in a church **m** I would much rather speak five
14:23 don't understand these things come into your **m**
14:24 don't understand these things come into your **m**,
14:28 they must be silent in your church **m** and speak in
Heb 7:16 not by **m** the old requirement of belonging to the
10:25 And let us not neglect our **m** together, as some
Jas 2:2 suppose someone comes into your **m** dressed in
2Jn 1:10 If someone comes to your **m** and does not teach

MEETINGS (6) [MEET]

Isa 1:13 even your most pious **m**—are all sinful and false.
Ac 1:4 In one of these **m** as he was eating a meal with
11:28 **m** to predict by the Spirit that a great famine was
1Co 14:34 Women should be silent during the church **m**.
14:35 for it is improper for women to speak in church **m**.
16:19 the others who gather in their home for church **m**.

MEETS (6) [MEET]

Dt 22:23 "Suppose a man **m** a young woman, a virgin who
22:25 "But if the man **m** the engaged woman out in the
Isa 41:2 king from the east, who **m** victory at every step?
Ro 16:5 Please give my greetings to the church that **m** in
16:23 I am his guest, and the church **m** here in his home.
Phm 1:2 I am also writing to the church that **m** in your

MEGIDDO (11) [MEGIDDO'S]

Jos 12:21 The king of Taanach / The king of **M**
17:11 (that is, Naphoth-dor), Endor, Taanach, and **M**,
Jdg 1:27 Taanach, Dor, Ibleam, **M**, and their surrounding
1Ki 4:12 Baana son of Ahilud, in Taanach and **M**, all of
9:15 and the cities of Hazor, **M**, and Gezer.
2Ki 9:27 He was able to go on as far as **M**, but he died there.
23:29 but King Neco killed him when they met at **M**.
23:30 his body back in a chariot from **M** to Jerusalem
1Ch 7:29 Taanach, **M**, Dor, and their surrounding villages.
2Ch 35:22 he led his army into battle on the plain of **M**.
Zec 12:11 mourning of Hadad-rimmon in the valley of **M**.

MEGIDDO'S (1) [MEGIDDO]

Jdg 5:19 "The kings of Canaan fought at Taanach near **M**

MEHEBEL (1)

Jos 19:29 at Hosah. The territory also included **M**, Aczib,

MEHETABEL (3)

Ge 36:39 Hadad's wife was **M**, the daughter of Matred
1Ch 1:50 His wife was **M**, the daughter of Matred
Ne 6:10 visit Shemaiah son of Delaiah and grandson of **M**,

MEHIDA (2)

Ezr 2:52 Bazluth, **M**, Harsha,
Ne 7:54 Bazluth, **M**, Harsha,

MEHIR (2)

1Ch 4:11 was the father of **M**. **M** was the father of Eshton.

MEHOLAH (2)

1Sa 18:19 gave Merab in marriage to Adriel, a man from **M**.
2Sa 21:8 the wife of Adriel son of Barzillai from **M**.

MEHUJAEL (2)

Ge 4:18 Irad was the father of **M**. / **M** was the father of

MEHUMAN (1)

Est 1:10 he told **M**, Biztha, Harbona, Bigtha, Abagtha,

MEHUNIM [KJV] See MEUNIM

MEHUNIMS [KJV] See MEUNITES

MEKERAH (1)

1Ch 11:36 Hepher from **M**; / Ahijah from Pelon;

MELATIAH (1)

Ne 3:7 Next to them were **M** from Gibeon, Jadon from

MELCHI-SHUA [KJV] See MALKISHUA

MELCHIZEDEK (20)

Ge 14:18 Then **M**, the king of Salem and a priest of God
14:19 **M** blessed Abram with this blessing: / "Blessed be
14:20 Then Abram gave **M** a tenth of all the goods he
Ps 110:4 "You are a priest forever in the line of **M**."
Heb 5:6 "You are a priest forever / in the line of **M**."
5:10 designated him to be a High Priest in the line of **M**.
6:20 become our eternal High Priest in the line of **M**.
7:1 This **M** was king of the city of Salem and also a
7:1 against many kings, **M** met him and blessed him.
7:2 of all he had won in the battle and gave it to **M**.
7:4 Consider then how great this **M** was.
7:4 recognized how great **M** was by giving him a tenth
7:6 But **M**, who was not even related to Levi,
7:6 And **M** placed a blessing upon Abraham, the one
7:8 But **M** is greater than they are, because we are told
7:9 paid a tithe to **M** through their ancestor Abraham.
7:10 loins when **M** collected the tithe from him.
7:11 need to send a different priest from the line of **M**,
7:15 a different priest, who is like **M**, has now come.
7:17 "You are a priest forever / in the line of **M**."

MELEA (2)

Lk 3:31 Eliakim was the son of **M**. / **M** was the son of

MELECH (2)

1Ch 8:35 was the father of Pithon, **M**, Tahrea, and Ahaz.
9:41 sons of Micah were Pithon, **M**, Tahrea, and Ahaz.

MELICU [KJV] See MALLUCH

MELITA [KJV] See MALTA

MELKI (4)

Lk 3:24 Levi was the son of **M**. / **M** was the son of Jannai.
3:28 Neri was the son of **M**. / **M** was the son of Addi.

MELODIES (1) [MELODY]

Ps 33:2 Praise the LORD with **m** on the lyre;

MELODIOUS (2) [MELODY]

Ps 98:5 LORD with the harp, / with the harp and **m** song,
Isa 24:8 no more. The **m** chords of the harp will be silent.

MELODY (1) [MELODIES, MELODIOUS]

1Co 14:7 For no one will recognize the **m** unless the notes

MELONS (1)

Nu 11:5 **m**, leeks, onions, and garlic that we wanted.

MELT (21) [MELTED, MELTING, MELTS]

Ex 15:15 All the people of Canaan will **m** with fear;
1Sa 14:16 the vast army of Philistines began to **m** away in
Job 20:12 of his wickedness, letting it **m** under his tongue.
Ps 68:2 **M** them like wax in fire. / Let the wicked perish in
97:5 The mountains **m** like wax before the LORD,
Isa 1:25 I will **m** you down and skim off your slag.
13:7 is paralyzed with fear. Even the strongest hearts **m**
14:31 **M** in fear, for everyone will be destroyed.
19:1 The hearts of the Egyptians **m** with fear.
34:4 The heavens above will **m** away and disappear like
Jer 9:7 I will **m** them in a crucible and test them like
18:14 Does the snow ever **m** high up in the mountains of
Eze 21:7 it comes true, the boldest heart will **m** with fear;
21:15 Let their hearts **m** with terror, for the sword glitters
22:20 I will **m** you down in the heat of my fury, just as
22:22 and you will **m** like silver in fierce heat. Then you
Mic 1:4 They **m** beneath his feet and flow into the valleys
Na 1:5 the mountains quake, and the hills **m** away;
2:10 of its wealth. Hearts **m** in horror, and knees shake.
2Pe 3:11 Since everything around us is going to **m** away,
3:12 and the elements will **m** away in the flames.

MELTED (10) [MELT]

Ex 16:21 the food they had not picked up **m**
32:4 **m** it down, and molded and tooled it into the shape
32:20 He took the calf they had made and **m** it in the fire.
Dt 9:21 and I **m** it in the fire and ground it into fine dust.
Jos 2:11 No wonder our hearts have **m** in fear! No one has
7:5 at this turn of events, and their courage **m** away.
1Ch 18:8 Later Solomon **m** the bronze and used it for the
Job 28:5 but below the surface the earth is **m** as by fire.
Ps 66:10 you have purified us like silver **m** in a crucible.
Eze 22:20 tin, iron, and lead are **m** down in a furnace.

MELTING (3) [MELT]

Job 6:16 when it is swollen with ice and **m** snow.
Ps 22:14 out of joint. / My heart is like wax, / **m** within me.
65:10 with rain, / **m** the clods and leveling the ridges.

MELTS (3) [MELT]

Ps 46:6 God thunders, / and the earth **m**!
147:18 Then, at his command, it all **m**. / He sends his
Am 9:5 the LORD Almighty, touches the land and it **m**,

MELZAR [KJV] See ATTENDANT

MEMBER (28) [MEMBERS]

Ge 34:19 Shechem was a highly respected **m** of his family,
39:1 a **m** of the personal staff of Pharaoh, the king of
Nu 14:35 I will do these things to every **m** of the community
18:11 Any **m** of your family who is ceremonially clean,
18:13 Any **m** of your family who is ceremonially clean
Jos 7:14 each **m** of the guilty family must come one by one.
7:18 Every **m** of Zimri's family was brought forward
22:20 a **m** of the clan of Zerah, sinned by stealing the
Jdg 12:5 "Are you a **m** of the tribe of Ephraim?"
1Sa 22:14 and a highly honored **m** of your household!
2Sa 16:5 It was Shimei son of Gera, a **m** of Saul's family.
1Ki 11:14 a **m** of Edom's royal family, to be an enemy
14:13 He is the only **m** of your family who will have a
2Ki 9:1 Elisha the prophet had summoned a **m** of the group
Pr 7:4 a sister; make insight a beloved **m** of your family.
Isa 6:5 for I am a sinful man and a **m** of a sinful race.
Jer 38:6 It belonged to Malkijah, a **m** of the royal family.
41:1 of Elishama, who was a **m** of the royal family,
Eze 17:13 He made a treaty with a **m** of the royal family
Mk 15:43 an honored **m** of the high council, Joseph from
Lk 1:5 Zechariah was a **m** of the priestly order of Abijah.
23:50 He was a **m** of the Jewish high council,
Jn 8:35 A slave is not a permanent **m** of the family, but a
Ac 5:34 But one **m** had a different perspective. He was a
17:34 a **m** of the Council, a woman named Damaris,
26:5 they know that I have been a **m** of the Pharisees,
Ro 11:1 of Abraham and a **m** of the tribe of Benjamin.
Php 3:5 What's more, I was a **m** of the Pharisees,

MEMBERS (41) [MEMBER]

Ge 17:12 This applies not only to **m** of your family, but also
46:27 there were seventy **m** of Jacob's family in the land
Lev 21:15 dishonor his descendants among the **m** of his clan,
22:13 only **m** of the priests' families are allowed to eat
Nu 16:2 other prominent leaders, all **m** of the assembly.
Jos 2:18 And all your family **m**—your father, mother,
21:4 who were **m** of the Kohathite clan within the tribe
21:10 who were **m** of the Kohathite clan within the tribe
Jdg 4:11 had moved away from the other **m** of his tribe
6:27 because he was afraid of the other **m** of his father's
1Sa 2:31 All the **m** of your family will die before their time.
2:32 But no **m** of your family will ever live out their
2Sa 5:1 and told him, "We are all **m** of your family.
9:12 all the **m** of Ziba's household were
23:23 He was more honored than the other **m** of the
23:24 Other **m** of the Thirty included: / Asahel,
1Ki 14:11 vow that the **m** of your family who die in the city
21:24 The **m** of your family who die in the city will be
1Ch 9:32 And some **m** of the clan of Kohath were in charge
11:1 and told him, "We are all **m** of your family.
11:25 He was more honored than the other **m** of the
12:28 with twenty-two **m** of his family who were all
2Ch 22:4 **m** of Ahab's family became his advisers, and they
22:9 None of the surviving **m** of Ahaziah's family was
Job 19:15 The **m** of my household have forgotten me.
Isa 22:24 and he will bring honor to even the lowliest **m** of
Jer 12:6 **m** of your own family, have turned on you.
Mt 10:25 will it happen to you, the **m** of the household!
Lk 4:40 the village brought sick family **m** to Jesus.
Ac 4:13 The **m** of the council were amazed when they saw
16:15 She was baptized along with other **m** of her
21:38 and took four thousand **m** of the Assassins out into
23:6 Paul realized that some **m** of the high council were
Ro 16:10 And give my best regards to the **m** of the
1Co 1:11 For some **m** of Chloe's household have told me
12:25 This makes for harmony among the **m**, so that all
the **m** care for each other equally.
12:28 Here is a list of some of the **m** that God has placed
Eph 2:19 of God's holy people. You are **m** of God's family.
Col 3:15 For as **m** of one body you are all called to live in
Heb 7:13 a different tribe, whose **m** do not serve at the altar.

MEMOIRS (1) [MEMORY]

Ne 1:1 These are the **m** of Nehemiah son of Hacaliah.

MEMORANDUM (1) [MEMORY]

Ezr 6:3 "**M**: / "In the first year of King Cyrus's reign,

MEMORIAL (13) [MEMORY]

Ge 28:18 had used as a pillow and set it upright as a **m** pillar.
28:22 This **m** pillar will become a place for worshiping
Ex 16:32 and keep it forever as a treasured **m** of the
28:12 of the ephod as **m** stones for the people of Israel.
Jos 4:6 We will use these stones to build a **m**.
4:7 These stones will stand as a permanent **m** among
4:8 camped for the night and constructed the **m** there.
4:9 Joshua also built another **m** of twelve stones in the
4:9 were standing. The **m** remains there to this day.
22:27 but as a **m**. It will remind our descendants and your
Isa 56:5 a **m** and a name far greater than the honor they
Zec 6:14 "The crown will be a **m** in the Temple of the
Lk 21:5 of the Temple and the **m** decorations on the walls.

MEMORIES (1) [MEMORY]

Pr 10:7 We all have happy **m** of the godly, but the name of

MEMORY (18) [MEMOIRS, MEMORANDUM, MEMORIAL, MEMORIES]

Ge 32:32 near the hip, in **m** of what happened that night.
41:31 so terrible that even the **m** of the good years will
Dt 25:19 and erase their **m** from under heaven.
32:26 so even the **m** of them would disappear.
Est 9:28 nor would the **m** of what happened ever die out
Job 18:17 All **m** of their existence will perish from the earth.
Ps 9:6 Even the **m** of their uprooted cities is lost.
34:16 who do evil; / he will erase their **m** from the earth.
83:4 We will destroy the very **m** of its existence."
109:15 but may his name be cut off from human **m**.
Isa 21:4 The sleep I once enjoyed at night is now a faint **m**.
Jer 34:5 They will burn incense in your **m**, just as they did
La 2:6 The LORD has blotted out all **m** of the holy
Eze 21:32 will be utterly wiped out, your **m** lost to history.
Zep 1:4 so that even the **m** of them will disappear.
Mt 26:13 this woman's deed will be talked about in her **m**."
Mk 14:9 this woman's deed will be talked about in her **m**."
2Pe 3:1 your wholesome thinking and refresh your **m**.

MEMPHIS (8)

Isa 19:13 Zoan are fools, and those from **M** are deluded.
Jer 2:16 marching from their cities of **M** and Tahpanhes,
44:1 Tahpanhes, and **M**, and throughout southern Egypt
46:14 it in the cities of Migdol, **M**, and Tahpanhes!
46:19 The city of **M** will be destroyed, without a single
Eze 30:13 will smash the idols of Egypt and the images at **M**.
30:16 will be torn apart; **M** will live in constant terror.
Hos 9:6 you will be conquered by Egypt. **M** will bury you.

MEMUCAN (2) [MEMUCAN'S]

Est 1:14 Admatha, Tarshish, Meres, Marsena, and **M**—
1:16 **M** answered the king and his princes,

MEMUCAN'S (1) [MEMUCAN]

Est 1:21 this made good sense, so he followed **M** counsel.

MEN (922) [MAN]

ALL THE MEN (34) Ge 19:4; 34:24; 39:14; Ex 34:23; 38:26; Nu 1:2,45; 4:3,23,30,35,39,43,47; 26:2,4; 31:7,49; 32:29; Dt 2:14,16; 21:21; 29:10; Jos 5:4,6; 8:16,24; Jdg 8:17; 2Ch 16:6; 20:13; Ezr 10:17; Est 1:11; Jer 32:12; 44:15

MEN AND WOMEN (29) Ge 20:14; 32:5; Ex 11:2; 35:22; Lev 20:27; Nu 5:3; Jos 6:21; Jdg 9:49; 1Sa 22:19; 2Ch 36:17; Ezr 2:65; Ne 7:67; 8:2; Ecc 2:7,8; Jer 34:9,16; 44:20; 51:22; Joel 2:29; Zec 8:4; 9:17; Mt 27:52; Ac 2:18; 5:14; 8:3,12; 9:2; 22:4

MEN OF ISRAEL (23) Ex 34:23; Nu 1:18,45; 26:2,4; Dt 20:3; 29:10; Jos 9:6; 1Sa 7:11; 11:8; 13:6; 14:24; 2Sa 2:17; 19:41; 20:1,2; Ezr 2:2; 9:2; Ne 7:7; Hos 4:18; Ac 5:35; 7:26; 21:28

OLD MEN (8) Ps 148:12; Jer 18:21; 26:17; La 5:12,14; Joel 2:28; Zec 8:4; Ac 2:17

WISE MEN (23) Ge 41:8; Ex 7:11; 1Ki 4:30,30; Ezr 8:16; Job 15:18; 34:2; Isa 19:13; Jer 18:18; 49:7; 50:35; 51:57; Da 2:12,18,24,24,27,48; 4:6; 5:7,8,15; Mt 23:34

YOUNG MEN (68) Ge 14:24; 19:14; 22:5,19; 34:9; Ex 24:5; Dt 32:25; Jos 6:23; Jdg 14:11,17; Ru 2:9,15; 1Sa 2:17; 21:4; 25:5,9,27; 26:22; 30:17; 2Sa 4:12; 16:2; 1Ki 12:8,10; 2Ki 4:39; 8:12; 2Ch 10:8,10; 36:17; Job 30:1; Ps 78:31,63; 148:12; Isa 9:17; 34:7; 40:30; 59:10; Jer 6:11; 9:21; 11:22; 15:8; 18:21; 49:26; 50:30; 51:22; La 5:13,14; Eze 23:6,12,44; 30:17; Da 1:3,4,4,6,13,15,17,18,20; Joel 2:28; Am 4:10; 8:13; Zec 9:17; Ac 2:17; 5:6,9,10; Tit 2:6

Ge 14:13 One of the **m** who escaped came and told Abram
14:14 he called together the **m** born into his household,
14:15 There he divided his **m** and attacked during the
14:24 All I'll accept is what these young **m** of mine have
17:27 along with all the other **m** and boys of the
18: 2 he suddenly noticed three **m** standing nearby.
18: 8 and the roasted meat, and he served it to the **m**.
18:16 Then the **m** got up from their meal and started on
18:22 The two other **m** went on toward Sodom,
19: 4 all the **m** of Sodom, young and old, came from all
19: 5 "Where are the **m** who came to spend the night
19: 8 with them as you wish, but leave these **m** alone,
19: 9 We'll treat you far worse than those other **m**!"
19:11 Then they blinded the **m** of Sodom so they
19:14 But the young **m** thought he was only joking.
20:14 and oxen and servants—both **m** and women—
22: 5 with the donkey," Abraham told the young **m**.
22:19 Then they returned to Abraham's young **m**
24:54 and the **m** with him stayed there overnight.
24:59 sent her away with Abraham's servant and his **m**.
26: 7 And when the **m** there asked him about Rebekah,
26:21 Isaac's **m** then dug another well, but again there
31:46 He also told his **m** to gather stones and pile them
32: 5 goats, and many servants, both **m** and women.
32: 6 to meet Jacob—with an army of four hundred **m**!
32:17 He gave these instructions to the **m** leading the
32:28 struggled with both God and **m** and have won."
33: 1 Jacob saw Esau coming with his four hundred **m**.
33:15 "at least let me leave some of my **m** to guide
34: 9 will give our daughters as wives for your young **m**.
34:21 "Those **m** are our friends," they said.
34:22 Every one of us **m** must be circumcised, just as
34:24 So all the **m** agreed and were circumcised.
38:21 So he asked the **m** who lived there, "Where can I
38:22 and that the **m** of the village had claimed they
39:14 Soon all the **m** around the place came running.
41: 8 and wise **m** of Egypt and told them about his
41:15 "and none of these **m** can tell me what it means.
42:11 We are all brothers and honest **m**, sir! We are not
42:31 But we said, 'We are honest **m**, not spies.
42:33 'This is the way I will find out if you are honest **m**.
42:34 Then I will know that you are honest **m** and not
43:16 "These **m** will eat with me this noon.
46:32 'These **m** are shepherds and livestock breeders.
49: 5 and Levi are two of a kind— / **m** of violence.
49: 6 For in their anger they murdered **m**, / and they
Ex 2:13 his people again, he saw two Hebrew **m** fighting.
7:11 Then Pharaoh called in his wise **m** and magicians,
10:11 Only the **m** may go and serve the LORD, for that
11: 2 Tell all the Israelite **m** and women to ask their
12:37 There were about 600,000 **m**, plus all the women
17:10 He led his **m** out to fight the army of Amalek.
18:21 honest **m** who fear God and hate bribes.
18:22 These **m** can serve the people, resolving all the
18:25 He chose capable **m** from all over Israel and made
18:26 These **m** were constantly available to administer
21: 7 not be freed at the end of six years as the **m** are.
24: 5 Then he sent some of the young **m** to sacrifice
34:23 Three times each year all the **m** of Israel must
35:22 Both **m** and women came, all whose hearts were
38:26 This included all the **m** who were twenty years
Lev 20:27 "**M** and women among you who act as mediums
24:10 father got into a fight with one of the Israelite **m**.
Nu 1: 2 and families. List the names of all the **m**
1:18 The **m** of Israel twenty years old or older were
1:20[-21] This is the number of **m** twenty years old
1:44 These were the **m** counted by Moses and Aaron
1:45 all the **m** of Israel who were twenty years old
3:13 apart for myself all the firstborn in Israel of both **m**
4: 3 Count all the **m** between the ages of thirty and fifty
4:23 Count all the **m** between the ages of thirty and fifty
4:30 Count all the **m** between the ages of thirty and fifty
4:35 The count included all the **m** between thirty
4:39 The count included all the **m** between thirty
4:43 The count included all the **m** between thirty
4:47 All the **m** between thirty and fifty years of age who
5: 3 This applies to **m** and women alike. Remove them
5: 6 If any of the people—**m** or women—
6: 2 If some of the people, either **m** or women,
9: 6 But some of the **m** had been ceremonially defiled
11:26 Two **m**, Eldad and Medad, were still in the camp
13: 2 "Send **m** to explore the land of Canaan, the land I
13: 3 He sent out twelve **m**, all tribal leaders of Israel,
13:16 These are the names of the **m** Moses sent to
13:17 Moses gave the **m** these instructions as he sent
13:25 exploring the land for forty days, the **m** returned
13:31 But the other **m** who had explored the land with
14: 6 Two of the **m** who had explored the land,
14:34 " 'Because the **m** who explored the land were
16:18 So these **m** came with their incense burners,
16:26 "Get away from the tents of these wicked **m**,
16:29 If these **m** die a natural death, then the LORD has
16:30 then you will know that these **m** have despised the
16:32 The earth opened up and swallowed the **m**,
16:35 and burned up the 250 **m** who were offering
16:38 from the burners of these **m** who have sinned at the
16:39 that had been used by the **m** who died in the fire,
21:32 After Moses sent **m** to explore the Jazer area,
22: 9 and asked him, "Who are these **m** with you?"
22:20 "Since these **m** have come for you, get up and go
22:35 angel of the LORD told him, "Go with these **m**,
25: 1 some of the **m** defiled themselves by sleeping with
25: 6 then one of the Israelite **m** brought a Midianite
26: 2 "Take a census of all the **m** of Israel who are
26: 4 "Count all the **m** of Israel twenty years old
26: 7 The **m** from all the clans of Reuben numbered
26:14 The **m** from all the clans of Simeon numbered
26:18 The **m** from all the clans of Gad numbered 40,500.
26:22 The **m** from all the clans of Judah numbered
26:25 The **m** from all the clans of Issachar numbered
26:27 The **m** from all the clans of Zebulun numbered
26:34 The **m** from all the clans of Manasseh numbered
26:37 The **m** from all the clans of Ephraim numbered
26:41 The **m** from all the clans of Benjamin numbered
26:43 and the **m** from these clans numbered 64,400.
26:47 The **m** from all the clans of Asher numbered
26:50 The **m** from all the clans of Naphtali numbered
26:51 So the total number of Israelite **m** counted in the
26:62 The **m** from the Levite clans who were one month
31: 3 "Choose some **m** to fight the LORD's war of
31: 4 tribe of Israel, send one thousand **m** into battle."
31: 5 So they chose one thousand **m** from each tribe of
31: 5 a total of twelve thousand **m** armed for battle.
31: 6 sent them out, a thousand **m** from each tribe,
31: 7 had commanded Moses, and they killed all the **m**.
31:21 Then Eleazar the priest said to the **m** who were in
31:27 and give half to the **m** who fought the battle
31:32 the fighting **m** had taken totaled 675,000 sheep,
31:36 So the half of the plunder given to the fighting **m**
31:42 from the half belonging to the fighting **m**,
31:49 we have accounted for all the **m** who went out to
31:53 All the fighting **m** had taken some of the plunder
32:29 "If all the **m** of Gad and Reuben who are able to
34:17 "These are the **m** who are to divide the land
34:29 These are the **m** the LORD has appointed to
36: 5 "The **m** of the tribe of Joseph are right.
Dt 1:13 Choose some **m** from each tribe who have wisdom,
1:15 and respected **m** you had selected from your tribes
1:41 So your **m** strapped on their weapons, thinking it
2:14 **m** old enough to fight in battle had died in the
2:16 "When all the **m** of fighting age had died,
2:34 destroyed everyone—**m**, women, and children.
3: 6 we conquered—**m**, women, and children alike.
3:18 all your fighting **m** must cross the Jordan, armed
7:14 None of your **m** or women will be childless,
20: 3 He will say, 'Listen to me, all you **m** of Israel!
21:21 Then all the **m** of the town must stone him to
22:21 and the **m** of the town will stone her to death.
25:11 "If two Israelite **m** are fighting and the wife of one
29:10 your judges, your officers, all the **m** of Israel—
31:12 **m**, women, children, and the foreigners living in
32:25 both young **m** and young women, / both infants
Jos 2: 1 So the two **m** set out and came to the house of a
2: 3 "Bring out the **m** who have come into your house.
2: 4 Rahab, who had hidden the two **m**, replied, "The **m** were here earlier,
2: 7 So the king's **m** went looking for the spies along
2: 7 And as soon as the king's **m** had left, the city gate
2:14 lives as a guarantee for your safety," the **m** agreed.
2:16 "Hide there for three days until the **m** who are
2:17 Before they left, the **m** told her, "We can
2:22 The **m** who were chasing them had searched
3:12 Now choose twelve **m**, one from each tribe.
4: 2 "Now choose twelve **m**, one from each tribe.
4: 3 Tell the **m** to take twelve stones from where the
4: 4 So Joshua called together the twelve **m**
4: 8 So the **m** did as Joshua told them. They took
5: 4 because all the **m** who were old enough to bear
5: 6 **m** who were old enough to bear arms when they
6: 7 and the armed **m** will lead the way in front of the
6:21 **m** and women, young and old, cattle, sheep,
6:23 The young **m** went in and brought out Rahab,
7: 2 Joshua sent some of his **m** from Jericho to spy out
7: 4 but they were soundly defeated. The **m** of Ai
7:22 So Joshua sent some **m** to make a search. They ran
8: 3 Joshua chose thirty thousand fighting **m** and sent
8: 5 the **m** of Ai will come out to fight as they did
8:10 Early the next morning Joshua roused his **m**
8:12 That night Joshua sent five thousand **m** to lie in
8:16 and all the **m** in the city were called out to chase
8:19 the **m** in ambush jumped up and poured into the
8:20 When the **m** of Ai looked behind them,
8:21 the city, they turned and attacked the **m** of Ai.
8:22 So the **m** of Ai were caught in a trap, and all of
8:24 When the Israelite army finished killing all the **m**
9: 6 at Gilgal, they told Joshua and the **m** of Israel,
10: 2 And the Gibeonite **m** were mighty warriors.
10: 6 The **m** of Gibeon quickly sent messengers to
10:25 ever be afraid or discouraged," Joshua told his **m**.
10:33 But Joshua's **m** killed him and destroyed his entire
17: 4 us an inheritance along with the **m** of our tribe."
18: 4 Select three **m** from each tribe, and I will send
18: 8 As the **m** who were mapping out the land started
18: 9 The **m** did as they were told and mapped the entire
22: 9 So the **m** of Reuben, Gad, and the half-tribe of
24:11 to Jericho, the **m** of Jericho fought against you.
Jdg 1: 3 So the **m** of Simeon went with Judah.
1: 4 When the **m** of Judah attacked, the LORD gave
1: 8 The **m** of Judah attacked Jerusalem and captured it,
6:34 and the **m** of the clan of Abiezer came to him.
7: 5 LORD told him, "Divide the **m** into two groups.
7: 6 Only three hundred of the **m** drank from their
7: 7 "With these three hundred **m** I will rescue you
7: 8 But he kept the three hundred **m** with him.
7:16 He divided the three hundred **m** into three groups
7:19 and the one hundred **m** with him reached the outer
7:24 And the **m** of Ephraim did as they were told.
8: 3 When the **m** of Ephraim heard Gideon's answer,
8: 4 crossed the Jordan River with his three hundred **m**,
8:17 tower of Peniel and killed all the **m** in the town.
8:18 and Zalmunna, "The **m** you killed at Tabor—
9:24 and the **m** of Shechem for murdering Gideon's
9:28 Serve the **m** of Hamor, who are Shechem's true
9:34 So Abimelech and his **m** went by night and split
9:36 just the shadows of the hills that look like **m**."
9:38 The **m** you mocked are right outside the city!
9:39 then led the **m** of Shechem into battle against
9:43 he divided his **m** into three groups and set an
9:43 and his **m** jumped up from their hiding places
9:44 and his group stormed the city gate to keep the **m**
9:48 "Quick, do as I have done!" he told his **m**.
9:49 of Shechem died, about a thousand **m** and women.
9:55 When Abimelech's **m** saw that he was dead,
9:57 God also punished the **m** of Shechem for all their
12: 4 "The **m** of Gilead are nothing more than rejects
12: 4 and attacked the **m** of Ephraim and defeated them.
12: 5 back across, the **m** of Gilead would challenge him.
12: 9 He married his daughters to **m** outside his clan
14:11 Thirty young **m** from the town were invited to be
14:17 Then she gave the answer to the young **m**.
14:18 the **m** of the town came to Samson with their
14:19 of Ashkelon, killed thirty **m**, took their belongings,
14:19 and gave their clothing to the **m** who had answered
15:10 The **m** of Judah asked the Philistines, "Why have
15:11 So three thousand **m** of Judah went down to get
15:12 But the **m** of Judah told him, "We have come to
15:16 jawbone of a donkey, / I've killed a thousand **m**!"
16: 2 so the **m** of Gaza gathered together and waited all
16: 9 She had hidden some **m** in one of the rooms of her
16:12 The **m** were hiding in the room as before,
18: 2 So the **m** of Dan chose five warriors from among
18: 7 So the five **m** went on to the town of Laish,
18: 8 When the **m** returned to Zorah and Eshtaol,
18: 9 The **m** replied, "Let's attack! We have seen the
18:14 The five **m** who had scouted out the land around
18:15 So the five **m** went over to Micah's house,
18:18 When the priest saw the **m** carrying all the sacred
18:23 The **m** of Dan turned around and said, "What do
18:23 Why have you called these **m** together and chased
18:25 The **m** of Dan said, "Watch what you say!
18:26 So the **m** of Dan went on their way. When Micah
18:27 his priest, the **m** of Dan came to the town of Laish,
19:22 some of the wicked **m** in the town surrounded the
19:25 The **m** of the town abused her all night,
20: 6 for these **m** have committed this terrible
20:10 One tenth of the **m** from each tribe will be chosen
20:13 Give up these evil **m** from Gibeah so we can
20:20 Then they advanced toward Gibeah to attack the **m**
20:25 but the **m** of Benjamin killed another eighteen
20:32 so that the **m** of Benjamin would chase them along
20:47 leaving only six hundred **m** who escaped to the
21:14 Then the **m** of Benjamin returned to their homes,
21:20 They told the **m** of Benjamin who still needed
21:23 So the **m** of Benjamin did as they were told.
Ru 2: 9 I have warned the young **m** not to bother you.
2:15 back to work again, Boaz ordered his young **m**,
1Sa 2:17 So the sin of these young **m** was very serious in the
4: 2 the army of Israel, killing four thousand **m**.
4: 4 So they sent **m** to Shiloh to bring back the Ark of
4:10 was great; thirty thousand Israelite **m** died that day.
6:15 Several **m** of the tribe of Levi lifted the Ark of the
6:19 But the LORD killed seventy **m** from
7: 1 So the **m** of Kiriath-jearim came to get the Ark of
7:11 The **m** of Israel chased them from Mizpah to
10: 2 you will see two **m** beside Rachel's tomb at
10: 3 you will see three **m** coming toward you who are
10:26 a band of **m** whose hearts God had touched
10:27 But there were some wicked **m** who complained,
11: 8 he found that there were 300,000 **m** of Israel,
11:10 The **m** of Jabesh then told their enemies,
11:12 "Now where are those **m** who said Saul shouldn't
13: 2 the army of Israel and sent the rest of the **m** home.
13: 2 He took two thousand of the chosen **m** with him to

13: 6 When the **m** of Israel saw the vast number of
13: 7 at Gilgal, and his **m** were trembling with fear.
13:11 Saul replied, "I saw my **m** scattering from me,
13:15 When Saul counted the **m** who were still with him,
14: 2 and his six hundred **m** were camped on the
14: 3 (Among Saul's **m** was Ahijah the priest, who was
14:14 They killed about twenty **m** in all, and their bodies
14:20 and his six hundred **m** rushed out to the battle
14:22 the **m** who were hiding in the hills joined the chase
14:24 Now the **m** of Israel were worn out that day,
14:28 But one of the **m** saw him and said, "Your father
14:30 If the **m** had been allowed to eat freely from the
14:33 the **m** are sinning against the LORD by eating
14:36 His **m** replied, "We'll do whatever you think is
15: 3 **m**, women, children, babies, cattle, sheep, camels,
15: 4 There were 200,000 troops in addition to 10,000 **m**
15: 9 Saul and his **m** spared Agag's life and kept the best
17:25 "Have you seen the giant?" the **m** were asking.
17:28 Eliab, heard David talking to the **m**, he was angry.
17:46 then I will give the dead bodies of your **m** to the
18: 5 appointment that was applauded by the fighting **m**
18:13 him commander over only a thousand **m**,
18:22 Then Saul told his **m** to say confidentially to
18:23 When Saul's **m** said these things to David,
18:24 When Saul's **m** reported this back to the king,
18:27 he and his **m** went out and killed two hundred
19:20 the Spirit of God came upon Saul's **m**, and they
21: 2 am here. I have told my **m** where to meet me later.
21: 4 which I guess you can have if your young **m** have
21: 5 "I never allow my **m** to be with women when they
21:14 Finally, King Achish said to his **m**, "Must you
22: 2 **m** who were in trouble or in debt or who were just
22: 2 David was the leader of about four hundred **m**.
22: 7 "Listen here, you **m** of Benjamin!" Saul shouted
22: 9 who was standing there with Saul's **m**, spoke up.
22:17 But Saul's **m** refused to kill the LORD's priests.
22:19 **m** and women, children and babies, and all the
23: 3 But David's **m** said, "We're afraid even here in
23: 5 So David and his **m** went to Keilah.
23: 8 to march to Keilah and attack David and his **m**.
23:11 Will the **m** of Keilah surrender me to him?
23:12 "Will these **m** of Keilah really betray me and my **m** to Saul?"
23:13 So David and his **m**—about six hundred of them
23:19 But now the **m** of Ziph went to Saul in Gibeah
23:24 So the **m** of Ziph returned home ahead of Saul.
23:24 and his **m** had moved into the wilderness of Maon
23:25 heard that Saul and his **m** were searching for him,
23:26 Just as Saul and his **m** began to close in on David and his **m**,
24: 2 and his **m** near the rocks of the wild goats.
24: 3 David and his **m** were hiding in that very cave!
24: 4 your opportunity!" David's **m** whispered to him.
24: 6 knows I shouldn't have done it," he said to his **m**.
24: 7 So David sharply rebuked his **m** and did not let
24:10 and some of my **m** told me to kill you, but I spared
24:22 But David and his **m** went back to their stronghold.
25: 5 he sent ten of his young **m** to Carmel. He told them
25: 9 David's young **m** gave this message to Nabal
25:13 Four hundred **m** started off with David, and two
25:14 "David sent **m** from the wilderness to talk to our
25:15 But David's **m** were very good to us, and we never
25:20 she saw David and his **m** coming toward her.
25:27 a present I have brought to you and your young **m**.
25:34 not one of Nabal's **m** would be alive tomorrow
26:12 because the LORD had put Saul's **m** into a deep
26:16 by the LORD that you and your **m** deserve to die,
26:22 "Let one of your young **m** come over and get it.
27: 2 So David took his six hundred **m** and their families
27: 8 and his **m** spent their time raiding the Geshurites,
28: 1 and your **m** will be expected to join me in battle."
28: 8 home at night, accompanied by two of his **m**.
28:23 The **m** who were with him also urged him to eat,
28:25 She brought the meal to Saul and his **m**, and they
29: 2 and his **m** marched at the rear with King Achish.
29: 6 So Achish finally summoned David and his **m**.
29: 6 "you are some of the finest **m** I've ever met.
29:10 and leave with your **m** as soon as it gets light."
30: 1 and his **m** arrived home at their town of Ziklag,
30: 3 When David and his **m** saw the ruins and realized
30: 6 because his **m** were very bitter about losing their
30: 9 So David and his six hundred **m** set out, and they
30:10 But two hundred of the **m** were too exhausted to
30:16 When David and his **m** arrived, the Amalekites
30:17 David and his **m** rushed in among them
30:17 except four hundred young **m** who fled on camels.
30:21 and met the two hundred **m** who had been too tired
30:22 But some troublemakers among David's **m** said,
30:27 following towns where David and his **m** had been:
2Sa 1: 4 Many **m** are dead and wounded on the battlefield,
1:11 and his **m** tore their clothes in sorrow when they
1:15 Then David said to one of his **m**, "Kill him!"
2: 3 and his **m** and their families all moved to Judah,
2: 4 When David heard that the **m** of Jabesh-gilead had
2:15 So twelve **m** were chosen from each side to fight
2:17 and the **m** of Israel had been defeated by the forces
2:21 "Take on one of the younger **m** and strip him of
2:26 When will you call off your **m** from chasing their
2:28 and his **m** stopped chasing the troops of Israel.
2:29 and his **m** retreated through the Jordan Valley.
2:30 Meanwhile, Joab and his **m** also returned home.
2:30 he discovered that only nineteen **m** were missing,
2:31 But three hundred and sixty of Abner's **m**, all from
2:32 and his **m** took Asahel's body to Bethlehem
3:20 When Abner came to Hebron with his twenty **m**,
3:39 So may the LORD repay these wicked **m** for their
4:11 Now what reward should I give the wicked **m** who
4:12 So David ordered his young **m** to kill them,
6:13 After the **m** who were carrying it had gone six
10: 3 "Do you really think these **m** are coming here to
10: 5 he sent messengers to tell the **m** to stay at Jericho
10: 8 from Zobah and Rehob and the **m** from Tob
11:16 he knew the enemy's strongest **m** were fighting.
11:24 Some of our **m** were killed, including Uriah the
12: 1 "There were two **m** in a certain town. One was
13:28 Absalom told his **m**, "Wait until Amnon gets
15:11 He took two hundred **m** from Jerusalem with him
15:14 or it will be too late!" David urged his **m**. "Hurry!
15:19 Go on back with your **m** to King Absalom, for you
15:22 So Ittai and his six hundred **m** and their families
16: 2 and summer fruit are for the young **m** to eat.
16:13 So David and his **m** continued on, and Shimei kept
16:15 Absalom and his **m** arrived at Jerusalem.
17: 1 "Let me choose twelve thousand **m** to start out
17: 8 You know your father and his **m**; they are mighty
17: 9 he comes out and attacks and a few of your **m** fall,
17: 9 and everyone will start shouting that your **m** are
17:12 to the ground, so that not one of his **m** is left alive.
17:20 When Absalom's **m** arrived, they asked her,
17:20 Absalom's **m** looked for them without success
17:21 Then the two **m** crawled out of the well
18: 3 But his **m** objected strongly. "You must not go,"
18: 7 Israelite troops were beaten back by David's **m**.
18: 7 and twenty thousand **m** laid down their lives that
18: 8 and more **m** died because of the forest than were
18: 9 came unexpectedly upon some of David's **m**.
18:10 One of David's **m** saw what had happened and told
18:16 and his **m** returned from chasing the army of
19:16 hurried across with the **m** of Judah to welcome
19:17 A thousand **m** from the tribe of Benjamin were
19:41 But the **m** of Israel complained to the king that the
19:41 **m** of Judah had gotten to do most of the work in
19:42 "Why not?" the **m** of Judah replied. "The king is
19:43 and the **m** of Judah were very harsh in their replies.
20: 1 Come on, you **m** of Israel, let's all go home!"
20: 2 So the **m** of Israel deserted David and followed
20: 2 But the **m** of Judah stayed with their king
21: 9 The **m** of Gibeon executed them on the mountain
21:10 Then Rizpah, the mother of two of the **m**,
21:13 as well as the bones of the **m** the Gibeonites had
21:15 when David and his **m** were in the thick of battle,
21:17 After that, David's **m** declared, "You are not
23: 8 These are the names of David's mightiest **m**.
23: 8 the three greatest warriors among David's **m**.
23:13 an elite group among David's fighting **m**)
23:15 David remarked longingly to his **m**, "Oh, how I
23:17 "This water is as precious as the blood of these **m**
24: 9 There were 800,000 **m** of military age in Israel
24:20 saw the king and his **m** coming toward him,
1Ki 1: 5 and recruited fifty **m** to run in front of him.
2:32 for the murders of two **m** who were more righteous
4:30 his wisdom exceeded that of all the wise **m** of the East and the wise **m** of Egypt.
5: 6 Let my **m** work alongside yours, and I will pay your **m** whatever wages you ask.
5:18 **M** from the city of Gebal helped Solomon's
9:22 Instead, he assigned them to serve as fighting **m**,
9:27 of sailors to sail the ships with Solomon's **m**.
11:24 Rezon and his **m** fled to Damascus, where he
12: 6 with the older **m** who had counseled his father,
12: 8 and instead asked the opinion of the young **m** who
12:10 The young **m** replied, "This is what you should
20:15 out the rest of his army of seven thousand **m**.
20:25 us the same number of horses, chariots, and **m**,
20:33 The **m** were quick to grasp at this straw of hope,
22:49 "Let my **m** sail an expedition with your **m**."
2Ki 1:10 from heaven and destroy you and your fifty **m**!"
1:11 So the king sent another captain with fifty **m**.
1:12 from heaven and destroy you and your fifty **m**!"
1:13 Once more the king sent a captain with fifty **m**.
2: 7 Fifty **m** from the group of prophets also went
2:16 and fifty of our strongest **m** will search the
2:17 So fifty **m** searched for three days but did not find
3: 9 But there was no water for the **m** or their pack
4:38 a large kettle and make some stew for these **m**."
4:39 One of the young **m** went out into the field to
4:40 But after the **m** had eaten a bite or two they cried
5:24 the gifts from the servants and sent the **m** back.
7: 3 Now there were four **m** with leprosy sitting at the
8:12 kill their young **m**, dash their children to the
9:15 So Jehu told the **m** with him, "Since you want me
10:14 "Take them alive!" Jehu shouted to his **m**.
10:24 had surrounded the building with eighty of his **m**
10:25 Then Jehu's **m** went into the fortress of the temple
11: 9 The commanders took charge of the **m** reporting
14: 5 he executed the **m** who had assassinated his father.
15:25 With fifty **m** from Gilead, Pekah assassinated the
20:14 and asked him, "What did those **m** want?
22: 5 Entrust this money to the **m** assigned to supervise
25: 5 for by then his **m** had all abandoned him.
25:23 and their **m** learned that the king of Babylon had
25:23 Jaazaniah son of the Maacathite, and all their **m**.
25:25 went to Mizpah with ten **m** and assassinated
1Ch 5:24 Each of these **m** had a great reputation as a warrior
6:31 David assigned the following **m** to lead the music
6:33 These are the **m** who served, along with their sons:
7: 2 the total number of **m** available for military service
7: 4 The total number of **m** available for military
7: 5 The total number of **m** available for military
7: 7 The total number of **m** available for military
7: 9 there were 20,200 **m** available for military service
7:11 and their descendants included 17,200 **m** available
7:40 There were 26,000 **m** available for military service
9: 9 These **m** were all leaders of clans, and they were
9:13 They were heads of clans and very able **m**.
9:18 These **m** served as gatekeepers for the camps of
9:22 their ancestors because they were reliable **m**.
9:34 All these **m** lived in Jerusalem. They were the
11:10 These are the leaders of David's mighty **m**.
11:11 Here is the record of David's mightiest **m**:
11:11 the three greatest warriors among David's **m**.
11:15 an elite group among David's fighting **m**)
11:17 David remarked longingly to his **m**, "Oh, how I
11:19 "This water is as precious as the blood of these **m**
11:26 were also included among David's mighty **m**:
11:42 the Reubenite leader who had thirty **m** with him;
12: 1 The following **m** joined David at Ziklag while he
12:19 Some **m** from Manasseh defected from the Israelite
12:19 refused to let David and his **m** go with them.
12:20 Here is a list of the **m** from Manasseh who
12:22 Day after day more **m** joined David until he had a
12:31 18,000 **m** were sent for the express purpose of
12:32 All these **m** understood the temper of the times
12:38 All these **m** came in battle array to Hebron with
14: 8 so he and his **m** marched out to meet them.
15:18 The following **m** were chosen as their assistants:
19: 3 "Do you really think these **m** are coming here to
19: 5 he sent messengers to tell the **m** to stay at Jericho
21: 5 There were 1,100,000 **m** of military age in Israel,
22: 4 for the **m** of Tyre and Sidon had brought vast
22: 8 'You have killed many **m** in the great battles you
25: 1 then appointed **m** from the families of Asaph,
25: 6 All these **m** were under the direction of their
26: 7 Elihu and Semakiah, were also very capable **m**.
26: 8 were very capable **m**, well qualified for their work.
26: 9 and relatives were also very capable **m**.
26:27 These **m** had dedicated some of the plunder they
26:30 and his relatives—seventeen hundred capable **m**—
26:31 and capable **m** from the clan of Hebron were found
26:32 There were twenty-seven hundred capable **m**
28: 1 and livestock, the palace officials, the mighty **m**,
2Ch 2: 8 for I know that your **m** are without equal at cutting timber. I will send my **m** to help them.
2:10 I will pay your **m** 100,000 bushels of crushed
8: 9 Instead, he assigned them to serve as fighting **m**,
8:18 ships sailed to the land of Ophir with Solomon's **m**
10: 6 with the older **m** who had counseled his father,
10: 8 and instead asked the opinion of the young **m** who
10:10 The young **m** replied, "This is what you should
13: 3 while Jeroboam mustered 800,000 courageous **m**
13:13 around behind the **m** of Judah to ambush them.
13:15 and the **m** of Judah began to shout. At the sound of
14: 8 armies were composed of courageous fighting **m**.
14: 9 Zerah attacked Judah with an army of a million **m**
14:11 our God; do not let mere **m** prevail against you!"
15: 7 you **m** of Judah, be strong and courageous,
16: 6 Then King Asa called out all the **m** of Judah to
17:18 who commanded 180,000 armed **m**.
20:13 As all the **m** of Judah stood before the LORD
20:14 the Spirit of the LORD came upon one of the **m**
20:25 and his **m** went out to gather the plunder.
21:13 your own brothers, **m** who were better than you.
22: 9 Then Jehu's **m** searched for Ahaziah, and they
23: 2 These **m** traveled secretly throughout Judah
23: 8 The commanders took charge of the **m** reporting
24:13 So the **m** in charge of the renovation worked hard,
25: 3 he executed the **m** who had assassinated his father.
25: 5 and found that he had an army of 300,000 **m**
25: 6 to hire 100,000 experienced fighting **m** from Israel.
26:11 This great army of fighting **m** had been mustered
26:13 The army consisted of 307,500 **m**, all elite troops.
26:15 designed by brilliant **m** to shoot arrows and hurl
26:17 eighty other priests of the LORD, all brave **m**.
28:12 and confronted the **m** returning from battle.
28:15 Then the four **m** mentioned by name came forward
29:15 These **m** called together their fellow Levites,
31:19 **m** were appointed to distribute portions to every
32: 8 He may have a great army, but they are just **m**.
34:10 He entrusted the money to the **m** assigned to
34:22 and the other **m** went to the newer Mishneh section
35:23 He cried out to his **m**, "Take me from the battle,
36:17 The Babylonians killed Judah's young **m**,
36:17 and old, **m** and women, healthy and sick.
Ezr 2: 2 This is the number of the **m** of Israel who returned
2:65 and 200 singers, both **m** and women.
8: 3 the family of Parosh: Zechariah and 150 other **m**.
8: 4 Eliehoenai son of Zerahiah and 200 other **m**.
8: 5 Shecaniah son of Jahaziel and 300 other **m**.
8: 6 of Adin: Ebed son of Jonathan and 50 other **m**.
8: 7 of Elam: Jeshaiah son of Athaliah and 70 other **m**.
8: 8 Zebadiah son of Michael and 80 other **m**.
8: 9 of Joab: Obadiah son of Jehiel and 218 other **m**.
8:10 Shelomith son of Josiphiah and 160 other **m**.
8:11 of Bebai: Zechariah son of Bebai and 28 other **m**.
8:12 Johanan son of Hakkatan and 110 other **m**.
8:13 Eliphelet, Jeuel, Shemaiah, and 60 other **m**.
8:14 family of Bigvai: Uthai, Zaccur, and 70 other **m**.
8:16 for Joiarib and Elnathan, who were very wise **m**.
9: 2 For the **m** of Israel have married women from
10: 1 **m**, women, and children—gathered and wept
10:17 with all the **m** who had married pagan wives.
10:44 Each of these **m** had a pagan wife, and some even
Ne 1: 2 came to visit me with some other **m** who had just
4:16 only half my **m** worked while the other half stood
4:21 to sunset. And half the **m** were always on guard.
5: 1 About this time some of the **m** and their wives
7: 7 This is the number of **m** of Israel who returned
7:67 and 245 singers, both **m** and women.
8: 2 which included the **m** and women and all the
11: 6 Perez who lived in Jerusalem—all outstanding **m**.
12:44 On that day **m** were appointed to be in charge of

13: 13 These **m** had an excellent reputation, and it was
13: 15 One Sabbath day I saw some **m** of Judah treading
13: 16 There were also some **m** from Tyre bringing in fish
13: 23 About the same time I realized that some of the **m**
Est 1: 11 He wanted all the **m** to gaze on her beauty, for she
1: 14 The names of these **m** were Carshena, Shethar,
2: 23 to be true, the two **m** were hanged on a gallows.
Job 15: 10 gray-haired **m** much older than your father!
15: 18 And it is confirmed by the experience of wise **m**
27: 7 like the wicked, my adversary like evil **m**.
30: 1 by young **m** whose fathers are not worthy to run
31: 10 to another man; may other **m** sleep with her.
34: 2 "Listen to me, you wise **m**. Pay attention, you who
34: 8 of evil people. He spends his time with wicked **m**.
Ps 54: 3 are attacking me; / violent **m** are trying to kill me.
78: 31 rose against them, / and he killed their strongest **m**;
78: 31 he struck down the finest of Israel's young **m**.
78: 63 Their young **m** were killed by fire; / their young
82: 7 But in death you are mere **m**. / You will fall as any
148: 12 young **m** and maidens, / old **m** and children.
Pr 2: 20 Follow the steps of good **m** instead, and stay on the
7: 26 ruin of many; numerous **m** have been her victims.
9: 15 She calls out to **m** going by who are minding their
9: 18 But the **m** don't realize that her former guests are
11: 16 women obtain wealth, and violent **m** get rich.
Ecc 2: 7 I bought slaves, both **m** and women, and others
2: 8 I hired wonderful singers, both **m** and women,
7: 28 Just one out of every thousand **m** I interviewed can
SS 3: 7 with sixty of Israel's mightiest **m** surrounding it.
8: 9 she is promiscuous, we will shut her off from **m**."
Isa 3: 16 eyes rove among the crowds, flirting with the **m**.
3: 25 The **m** of the city will die in battle.
4: 1 In that day few **m** will be left alive. Seven women
8: 2 son of Jeberekiah, both known as honest **m**,
9: 17 That is why the Lord has no joy in the young **m**
19: 13 The wise **m** from Zoan are fools, and those from
22: 6 the chariots. The **m** of Kir hold up the shields.
31: 8 will be destroyed, but not by the swords of **m**.
34: 7 The strongest will die—veterans and young **m**, too.
39: 3 and asked him, "What did those **m** want?
40: 30 will become exhausted, and young **m** will give up.
59: 10 like corpses when compared to vigorous young **m**!
Jer 5: 26 "Among my people are wicked **m** who lie in wait
6: 11 on gatherings of young **m**, and on husbands
9: 21 and young **m** no longer gather in the squares.
11: 21 The **m** of Anathoth wanted me dead. They said
11: 22 Their young **m** will die in battle, and their little
12: 5 to me, "If racing against mere **m** makes you tired,
15: 8 bring a destroyer against the mothers of young **m**.
15: 21 will certainly keep you safe from these wicked **m**.
18: 18 We have our own priests and wise **m** and prophets.
18: 21 Let their old **m** die in a plague, and let their young **m** be killed in battle!
19: 10 "As these **m** watch, Jeremiah, smash the jar you
23: 11 are like the prophets, all ungodly, wicked **m**.
26: 17 Then some of the wise old **m** stood and spoke to
26: 22 Egypt along with several other **m** to capture Uriah.
29: 23 For these **m** have done terrible things among my
30: 6 Do **m** give birth to babies? Then why do they stand
31: 13 The young women will dance for joy, and the **m**—
32: 12 the deed, and all the **m** of Judah who were there.
33: 5 The **m** of this city are already as good as dead,
34: 9 to free their Hebrew slaves—both **m** and women.
34: 16 and defiled my name by taking back the **m**
38: 4 the morale of the few fighting **m** we have left,
38: 9 "these **m** have done a very evil thing in putting
38: 10 told Ebed-melech, "Take along thirty of my **m**,
38: 11 So Ebed-melech took the **m** with him and went to
38: 16 or hand you over to the **m** who want you dead."
40: 8 Jaazaniah son of the Maacathite, and all their **m**.
41: 1 arrived in Mizpah accompanied by ten **m**.
41: 2 Ishmael and his ten **m** suddenly drew their swords
41: 5 eighty **m** arrived from Shechem, Shiloh,
41: 7 Ishmael and his **m** killed all but ten of them
41: 9 **m** he murdered was the large one made by King
41: 12 they took all their **m** and set out to stop him.
41: 13 shouted for joy when they saw Johanan and his **m**.
41: 15 and eight of his **m** escaped from Johanan into the
43: 2 and all the other proud **m** said to Jeremiah,
43: 6 In the crowd were **m**, women, and children,
44: 15 and all the **m** who knew that their wives had
44: 20 **m** and women alike, who had given him that
46: 5 The bravest of its fighting **m** run without a
46: 24 she will be handed over to **m** from the north."
48: 14 used to boast, 'We are heroes, mighty **m** of war.'
48: 31 my heart is broken for the **m** of Kir-hareseth.
49: 7 "Where are all the wise **m** of Teman?
49: 26 Her young **m** will fall in the streets and die.
50: 30 Her young **m** will fall in the streets and die.
50: 35 people of Babylon—her princes and wise **m**, too.
51: 22 With you I will shatter **m** and women, old people and children, young **m** and maidens.
51: 56 Her mighty **m** are captured, and their weapons
51: 57 wise **m**, rulers, captains, and warriors,"
52: 8 for by then his **m** had all abandoned him.
La 1: 15 "The Lord has treated my mighty **m** with
5: 12 and the old **m** are treated with contempt.
5: 13 The young **m** are led away to work at millstones,
5: 14 The old **m** no longer sit in the city gates; the young **m** no longer dance and sing.
Eze 8: 16 about twenty-five **m** were standing with their
9: 1 "Bring on the **m** appointed to punish the city!
9: 2 Six **m** soon appeared from the upper gate that faces
9: 5 Then I heard the LORD say to the other **m**,
11: 1 where I saw twenty-five prominent **m** of the city.
11: 2 these are the **m** who are responsible for the wicked
14: 16 Even if these three **m** were there, the Sovereign
14: 18 Even if these three **m** were in the land,
16: 17 and made statues of **m** and worshiped them,
21: 31 I will hand you over to cruel **m** who are skilled in
22: 10 **M** sleep with their fathers' wives and have
22: 11 Within your walls live **m** who commit adultery
23: 6 They were all attractive young **m**, captains
23: 7 herself with the most desirable **m** of Assyria,
23: 12 those handsome young **m** on fine horses,
23: 24 surrounding you with **m** armed for battle.
23: 40 sisters sent messengers to distant lands to get **m**.
23: 42 From your room came the sound of many **m**
23: 42 They were lustful **m** and drunkards from the
23: 44 with all the zest of lustful young **m**.
27: 8 your helmsmen were skilled **m** from Tyre itself.
27: 10 **M** from distant Persia, Lydia, and Libya served in
27: 11 **M** from Arvad and from Helech stood on your
27: 11 Your towers were manned by **m** from Gammad.
30: 12 the Nile River and hand the land over to wicked **m**.
30: 17 The young **m** of Heliopolis and Bubastis will die in
32: 23 These mighty **m** who once struck terror in the
38: 21 Your **m** will turn against each other in mortal
39: 18 Eat the flesh of mighty **m** and drink the blood of
44: 10 And the **m** of the tribe of Levi who abandoned me
44: 15 These **m** will serve as my ministers. They will
Da 1: 3 to bring to the palace some of the young **m** of
1: 4 healthy, and good-looking young **m**," he said.
1: 4 Teach these young **m** the language and literature of
1: 6 and Azariah were four of the young **m** chosen,
1: 13 see how we look compared to the other young **m**
1: 15 and better nourished than the young **m** who had
1: 17 God gave these four young **m** an unusual aptitude
1: 18 the chief official brought all the young **m** to King
1: 20 the king found the advice of these young **m** to be
2: 12 and he sent out orders to execute all the wise **m** of
2: 13 **m** were sent to find and kill Daniel and his friends.
2: 18 executed along with the other wise **m** of Babylon.
2: 24 who had been ordered to execute the wise **m** of
2: 24 Daniel said to him, "Don't kill the wise **m**.
2: 27 "There are no wise **m**, enchanters, magicians,
2: 48 of Babylon, as well as chief over all his wise **m**.
3: 20 Then he ordered some of the strongest **m** of his
3: 22 and killed the soldiers as they threw the three **m** in!
3: 24 "Didn't we tie up three **m** and throw them into the
3: 25 "I see four **m**, unbound, walking around in the
4: 6 So I issued an order calling in all the wise **m** of
4: 18 All the wisest **m** of my kingdom have failed me.
5: 7 He said to these wise **m** of Babylon,
5: 8 But when all the king's wise **m** came in, none of
5: 15 My wise **m** and enchanters have tried to read this
6: 15 In the evening the **m** went together to the king
6: 24 Then the king gave orders to arrest the **m** who had
10: 7 The **m** with me saw nothing, but they were
Hos 1: 2 of her children will be born to you from other **m**.
4: 14 For you **m** are doing the same thing, sinning with
4: 18 The **m** of Israel finish up their drinking bouts
5: 1 Listen, all you **m** of the royal family!
9: 7 "The inspired **m** are mad!" So they taunt,
10: 9 Was it not right that the wicked **m** of Gibeah were
Joel 2: 28 old **m** will dream dreams. Your young **m** will see
2: 29 my Spirit even on servants, **m** and women alike.
3: 9 Let all your fighting **m** advance for the attack!
Am 2: 16 the most courageous of your fighting **m** will drop
4: 10 I killed your young **m** in war and slaughtered all
5: 3 "When one of your cities sends a thousand **m** to
6: 9 If there are ten **m** left in one house, they will all
8: 13 and fine young **m** will grow faint and weary,
Mic 2: 8 making them as ragged as **m** who have just come
Zep 1: 14 it comes—a day when strong **m** will cry bitterly.
Zec 1: 21 "What are these **m** coming to do?" I asked.
7: 2 and Regemmelech, along with their **m**,
8: 4 Once again old **m** and women will walk
9: 17 The young **m** and women will thrive on the
Mal 2: 11 for the **m** of Judah have defiled the LORD's
Mt 2: 1 About that time some wise **m** from eastern lands
2: 7 Then Herod sent a private message to the wise **m**,
2: 9 After this interview the wise **m** went their way.
2: 13 After the wise **m** were gone, an angel of the Lord
2: 16 Herod was furious when he learned that the wise **m**
2: 16 because the wise **m** had told him the star first
8: 28 two **m** who were possessed by demons met him.
8: 32 So the demons came out of the **m** and entered the
8: 33 what happened to the demon-possessed **m**.
9: 27 two blind **m** followed along behind him, shouting,
12: 34 How could evil **m** like you speak what is good
14: 21 About five thousand **m** had eaten from those five
15: 38 There were four thousand **m** who were fed that
17: 2 As the **m** watched, Jesus' appearance changed
20: 30 Two blind **m** were sitting beside the road.
21: 41 "He will put the wicked **m** to a horrible death
23: 34 I will send you prophets and wise **m** and teachers
24: 40 "Two **m** will be working together in the field;
26: 51 One of the **m** with Jesus pulled out a sword
26: 60 they could use. Finally, two **m** were found
27: 52 The bodies of many godly **m** and women who had
28: 11 some of the **m** who had been guarding the tomb
Mk 1: 20 in the boat with the hired **m** and went with him.
2: 3 Four **m** arrived carrying a paralyzed man on a mat.
6: 44 Five thousand **m** had eaten from those five loaves!
8: 19 What about the five thousand **m** I fed with five
9: 2 As the **m** watched, Jesus' appearance changed,
9: 17 One of the **m** in the crowd spoke up and said,
12: 14 "Teacher," these **m** said, "we know how honest
14: 57 some **m** stood up to testify against him with this
Lk 5: 17 (It seemed that these **m** showed up from every
5: 18 Some **m** came carrying a paralyzed man on a
7: 49 The **m** at the table said among themselves,
9: 14 For there were about five thousand **m** there.
9: 30 Then two **m**, Moses and Elijah, appeared
9: 32 saw Jesus' glory and the two **m** standing with him.
13: 4 And what about the eighteen **m** who died when the
15: 17 'At home even the hired **m** have food enough to
17: 17 Jesus asked, "Didn't I heal ten **m**? Where are the
18: 10 "Two **m** went to the Temple to pray. One was a
20: 20 sent secret agents pretending to be honest **m**.
22: 25 the kings and great **m** order their people around,
24: 4 Suddenly, two **m** appeared to them, clothed in
24: 5 Then the **m** asked, "Why are you looking in a
24: 7 of Man must be betrayed into the hands of sinful **m**
24: 24 Some of our **m** ran out to see, and sure enough,
Jn 1: 40 was one of these **m** who had heard what John said
5: 5 One of the **m** lying there had been sick for
6: 10 all of them—the **m** alone numbered five thousand
17: 6 "I have told these **m** about you. They were in the
19: 32 and broke the legs of the two **m** crucified with
Ac 1: 10 two white-robed **m** suddenly stood there among
1: 11 They said, "**M** of Galilee, why are you standing
1: 23 So they nominated two **m**: Joseph called Barsabbas
1: 24 Show us which of these **m** you have chosen
2: 17 young **m** will see visions, / and your old **m** will
2: 18 upon all my servants, **m** and women alike,
4: 4 number of believers totaled about five thousand **m**,
4: 13 for they could see that they were ordinary **m** who
4: 13 They also recognized them as **m** who had been
4: 16 "What should we do with these **m**?" they asked
5: 6 Then some young **m** wrapped him in a sheet
5: 9 Just outside that door are the young **m** who buried
5: 10 When the young **m** came in and saw that she was
5: 14 to the Lord—crowds of both **m** and women.
5: 22 Temple guards went to the jail, the **m** were gone.
5: 25 Then someone arrived with the news that the **m**
5: 35 "**M** of Israel, take care what you are planning to do to these **m**!
5: 38 "So my advice is, leave these **m** alone. If they are
6: 3 and select seven **m** who are well respected and are
6: 9 But one day some **m** from the Synagogue of Freed
6: 11 So they persuaded some **m** to lie about Stephen,
7: 26 them again and saw two **m** of Israel fighting.
7: 26 be a peacemaker. '**M**,' he said, 'you are brothers.
8: 3 dragging out both **m** and women to throw them
8: 12 As a result, many **m** and women were baptized.
9: 2 He wanted to bring them—both **m** and women—
9: 7 The **m** with Saul stood speechless with surprise,
9: 38 so they sent two **m** to beg him, "Please come as
10: 5 Now send some **m** down to Joppa to find a man
10: 17 then the **m** sent by Cornelius found the house
10: 19 said to him, "Three **m** have come looking for you.
10: 23 So Peter invited the **m** to be his guests for the
10: 32 Now send some **m** to Joppa and summon Simon
11: 11 then three **m** who had been sent from Caesarea
13: 2 One day as these **m** were worshiping the Lord
13: 3 the **m** laid their hands on them and sent them on
13: 43 and Barnabas, and the two **m** urged them,
14: 11 "These **m** are gods in human bodies!"
15: 1 some **m** from Judea arrived and began to teach the
15: 5 then some of the **m** who had been Pharisees before
15: 22 The **m** chosen were two of the church leaders—
15: 24 "We understand that some **m** from here have
16: 17 "These **m** are servants of the Most High God,
16: 35 sent the police to tell the jailer, "Let those **m** go!"
17: 4 including a large number of godly Greek **m**
17: 12 some of the prominent Greek women and many **m**.
17: 22 "**M** of Athens, I notice that you are very religious,
19: 7 There were about twelve **m** in all.
19: 37 You have brought these **m** here, but they have
20: 4 Several **m** were traveling with him. They were
21: 8 one of the seven **m** who had been chosen to
21: 23 We have four **m** here who have taken a vow
21: 26 he went through the purification ritual with the **m**
21: 28 yelling, "**M** of Israel! Help! This is the man who
22: 4 binding and delivering both **m** and women to
23: 10 and the **m** were tugging at Paul from both sides,
23: 21 There are more than forty **m** hiding along the way
24: 13 These **m** certainly cannot prove the things they
24: 15 I have hope in God, just as these **m** do, that he will
24: 20 Ask these **m** here what wrongdoing the Jewish
25: 11 has a right to turn me over to these **m** to kill me.
25: 23 by military officers and prominent **m** of the city.
27: 21 Paul called the crew together and said, "**M**,
Ro 1: 27 And the **m**, instead of having normal sexual
1: 27 **M** did shameful things with other **m** and, as a
1Co 11: 11 women are not independent of **m**, and **m** are not independent of women.
11: 12 all **m** have been born from women ever since,
15: 32 those **m** of Ephesus—if there will be no
2Co 10: 12 these other **m** who tell you how important they are!
11: 26 And I have faced danger from **m** who claim to be
12: 17 Did any of the **m** I sent to you take advantage of
Php 3: 2 those dogs, those wicked **m** and their evil deeds,
1Ti 2: 8 I want **m** to pray with holy hands lifted up to God,
2: 12 I do not let women teach **m** or have authority over
5: 1 Talk to the younger **m** as you would to your own
Tit 1: 12 One of their own **m**, a prophet from Crete, has said
2: 2 Teach the older **m** to exercise self-control, to be
2: 6 encourage the young **m** to live wisely in all they
Heb 7: 8 of Jewish priests, tithes are paid to **m** who will die.
1Pe 5: 5 You younger **m**, accept the authority of the elders.

MEN'S (2) [MAN]

Ge 42: 25 then ordered his servants to fill the **m** sacks with
Dt 22: 5 "A woman must not wear **m** clothing, and a man

MENAHEM (8) [MENAHEM'S]

2Ki 15: 14 Then **M** son of Gadi went to Samaria from Tirzah

15:16 At that time **M** destroyed the town of Tappuah
15:17 **M** son of Gadi began to rule over Israel in the
15:18 But **M** did what was evil in the LORD's sight.
15:19 But **M** paid him thirty-seven tons of silver to gain
15:20 **M** extorted the money from the rich of Israel,
15:22 When **M** died, his son Pekahiah became the next
15:23 Pekahiah son of **M** began to rule over Israel in the

MENAHEM'S (1) [MENAHEM]
2Ki 15:21 The rest of the events in **M** reign and all his deeds

MENAN [KJV] See MENNA

MENCHILDREN [KJV] See MALES

MEND (1) [MENDING]
Ecc 3: 7 A time to tear and a time to **m**. / A time to be quiet

MENDING (2) [MEND]
Mt 4:21 in a boat with their father, Zebedee, **m** their nets.
Mk 1:19 James and John, in a boat **m** their nets.

MENE (3)
Da 5:25 that was written: M, M, TEKEL, PARSIN.
5:26 *M* means 'numbered'—God has numbered the

MENNA (2)
Lk 3:31 Melea was the son of **M**. / **M** was the son of Mattatha.

MENPLEASERS [KJV] See PLEASE

MENSTEALERS [KJV] See (SLAVE) TRADERS

MENSTRUAL (12) [MENSTRUATION]
Lev 12: 2 just as she is defiled during her **m** period.
12: 5 just as she is defiled during her **m** period.
15:19 "Whenever a woman has her **m** period, she will be
15:24 her **m** impurity will be transmitted to him.
15:25 "If the **m** flow of blood continues for many days
15:26 just as it would be during her normal **m** period.
15:28 "When the woman's **m** discharge stops, she must
15:30 for her before the LORD for her **m** discharge.
15:33 for dealing with a woman during her monthly **m**
18:19 with her during her period of **m** impurity.
2Sa 11: 4 the purification rites after having her **m** period.)
Eze 18: 6 or have intercourse with a woman during her **m**

MENSTRUATING (1) [MENSTRUATION]
Eze 22:10 and have intercourse with women who are **m**.

MENSTRUATION (1) [MENSTRUAL, MENSTRUATING]
Lev 15:25 or if she discharges blood unrelated to her **m**,

MENTION (11) [MENTIONED]
Ge 40:14 **M** me to Pharaoh, and ask him to let me out of
Ex 23:13 by any other gods. Do not even **m** their names.
Jos 23: 7 Do not even **m** the names of their gods, much less
Ne 5:14 I would like to **m** that for the entire twelve years
Ps 50:12 If I were hungry, I would not **m** it to you, / for all
Jer 20: 9 If I say I'll never **m** the LORD or speak in his
Jnh 4:11 in spiritual darkness, not to **m** all the animals.
Mk 10:28 Then Peter began to **m** all that he and the other
1Co 11:17 But now when I **m** this next issue, I cannot praise
Phm 1:19 And I won't **m** that you owe me your very soul!
Heb 4: 4 is ready because the Scriptures **m** the seventh day,

MENTIONED (12) [MENTION]
Ge 6: 4 who became the heroes **m** in legends of old.
Dt 28:61 there is, even those not **m** in this Book of the Law,
Ru 4: 1 When the family redeemer he had **m** came by,
1Sa 4:18 When the messenger **m** what had happened to the
1Ch 6:65 of Judah, Simeon, and Benjamin, **m** above,
2Ch 2:15 the wheat, barley, olive oil, and wine that you **m**.
28:15 Then the four men **m** by name came forward
Isa 48: 6 Now I will tell you new things I have not **m**
Hag 2:13 and then brushes against any of the things **m**,
Eph 3: 3 As I briefly **m** earlier in this letter, God himself
Heb 7:14 and Moses never **m** Judah in connection with the
11:39 All of these people we have **m** received God's

MENU (1)
Est 2: 9 He quickly ordered a special **m** for her

MEONENIM [KJV] See DIVINER'S (OAK)

MEONOTHAI (2)
1Ch 4:13 and Seraiah. Othniel's sons were Hathath and **M**.
4:14 **M** was the father of Ophrah. Seraiah was the father

MEPHAATH (4)
Jos 13:18 Jahaz, Kedemoth, **M**,
21:37 Kedemoth, and **M**—four towns with their
1Ch 6:79 Kedemoth, and **M**, each with its pasturelands.
Jer 48:21 out on them all—on Holon and Jahaz and **M**,

MEPHIBOSHETH (16) [MEPHIBOSHETH'S, MERIBBAAL]
2Sa 4: 4 (Saul's son Jonathan had a son named **M**, who was
9: 6 His name was **M**; he was Jonathan's son
9: 8 **M** fell to the ground before the king.
9:10 But **M** will live here at the palace with me."
9:11 from that time on, **M** ate regularly with David,
9:12 **M** had a young son named Mica. And from
9:13 And **M**, who was crippled in both feet, moved to
16: 1 when Ziba, the servant of **M**, caught up with him.
16: 3 "And where is **M**?" the king asked him.
16: 4 king told Ziba, "I give you everything **M** owns."
19:24 Now **M**, Saul's grandson, arrived from Jerusalem
19:25 "Why didn't you come with me, **M**?" the king
19:26 **M** replied, "My lord the king, my servant Ziba
19:30 "Give him all of it," **M** said. "I am content just to
21: 7 David spared Jonathan's son **M**, who was Saul's
21: 8 But he gave them Saul's two sons Armoni and **M**,

MEPHIBOSHETH'S (1) [MEPHIBOSHETH]
2Sa 9:12 all the members of Ziba's household were **M**

MERAB (4)
1Sa 14:49 had two daughters: **M**, who was older, and Michal.
18:17 to give you my older daughter, **M**, as your wife.
18:19 Saul gave **M** in marriage to Adriel, a man from
2Sa 21: 8 also gave them the five sons of Saul's daughter **M**,

MERAIAH (1)
Ne 12:12 **M** was leader of the family of Seraiah.

MERAIOTH (6)
1Ch 6: 6 father of Zerahiah. / Zerahiah was the father of **M**.
6: 7 **M** was the father of Amariah. / Amariah was the
6:52 **M**, Amariah, Ahitub,
9:11 son of Zadok, son of **M**, son of Ahitub.
Ezr 7: 3 son of Amariah, son of Azariah, son of **M**,
Ne 11:11 son of Zadok, son of **M**, son of Ahitub,

MERARI (29) [MERARITE, MERARITES]
Ge 46:11 The sons of Levi were Gershon, Kohath, and **M**.
Ex 6:16 the first generation were Gershon, Kohath, and **M**.
6:19 The descendants of **M** included Mahli and Mushi.
Nu 3:17 who were named Gershon, Kohath, and **M**.
3:20 The clans descended from **M** were named for two
3:33 The descendants of **M** were composed of the clans
26:57 The Merarite clan, named after its ancestor **M**.
Jos 21: 7 The clan of **M** received twelve cities from the
21:34 The rest of the Levites—the **M** clan—were given
21:40 So twelve towns were allotted to the clan of **M**.
1Ch 6: 1 The sons of Levi were Gershon, Kohath, and **M**.
6:16 The sons of Levi were Gershon, Kohath, and **M**.
6:19 The descendants of **M** included Mahli and Mushi.
6:29 The descendants of **M** were Mahli, Libni, Shimei,
6:44 second assistant was Ethan from the clan of **M**.
6:47 Mahli, Mushi, **M**, and Levi.
6:63 The descendants of **M** received by sacred lots
6:77 The remaining descendants of **M** received from the
9:14 of Azrikam, son of Hashabiah, a descendant of **M**;
15: 6 There were 220 from the clan of **M**, with Asaiah as
15:17 and Ethan son of Kushaiah from the clan of **M** to
23: 6 the three sons of Levi—Gershon, Kohath, and **M**.
23:21 The descendants of **M** included Mahli and Mushi.
24:26 From the descendants of **M**, the leaders were
24:27 From the descendants of **M** through Jaaziah,
26:10 Hosah, of the **M** clan, appointed Shimri as the
26:19 of the gatekeepers from the clans of Korah and **M**.
2Ch 29:12 From the clan of **M**: Kish son of Abdi and Azariah
Ezr 8:19 together with Jeshaiah from the descendants of **M**,

MERARITE (9) [MERARI]
Nu 3:34 one month old or older among these **M** clans.
3:35 The leader of the **M** clans was Zuriel son of
4:29 and families of the **M** division of the Levite tribe.
4:42 The **M** division was also counted by its clans
4:45 So this was the total of all those from the **M** clans
7: 8 and eight oxen to the **M** division for their work.
10:17 and **M** divisions of the Levites were next in the
26:57 The **M** clan, named after its ancestor Merari.
2Ch 34:12 of Jahath and Obadiah, Levites of the **M** clan,

MERARITES (1) [MERARI]
Nu 4:33 So these are the duties of the **M** at the Tabernacle.

MERATHAIM (1)
Jer 50:21 against the land of **M** and against the people of

MERCENARIES (4)
2Sa 10: 6 so they hired twenty thousand Aramean **m** from
2Ki 11: 4 priest summoned the commanders, the Carite **m**,
11:19 Then the commanders, the Carite **m**, the guards,
Jer 46:21 Egypt's famed **m** have become like fattened

MERCHANDISE (13) [MERCHANT]
Dt 25:13 must use accurate scales when you weigh out **m**,
Ne 10:31 that if the people of the land should bring any **m**
13:16 men from Tyre bringing in fish and all kinds of **m**.
13:19 so that no **m** could be brought in on the Sabbath
Isa 23: 3 along the Nile. You were the **m** mart of the world.
45:14 They will come to you with all their **m**, and it will
Jer 17:27 and if on the Sabbath day you bring loads of **m**
Eze 26:12 all your riches and **m** and break down your walls.
27:19 Greeks from Uzal came to trade for your **m**.
27:23 Asshur, and Kilmad came with their **m**, too.
27:33 The **m** you traded / satisfied the needs of many
27:34 All your **m** and your crew / have passed away with
Mk 11:16 and he stopped everyone from bringing in **m**.

MERCHANT (4) [MERCHANDISE, MERCHANT'S, MERCHANTS]
Eze 16:29 by embracing that great **m** land of Babylonia—
Mt 13:45 the Kingdom of Heaven is like a pearl **m** on the
Ac 16:14 from Thyatira, a **m** of expensive purple cloth.
Rev 18:17 And all the shipowners and captains of the **m** ships

MERCHANT'S (1) [MERCHANT]
Pr 31:14 She is like a **m** ship; she brings her food from afar.

MERCHANTMEN [KJV] See MERCHANTS, TRADERS

MERCHANTS (33) [MERCHANT]
Nu 35:15 of Israelites, resident foreigners, and traveling **m**.
1Ki 10:15 include the additional revenue he received from **m**
2Ch 9:14 include the additional revenue he received from **m**
Ne 3:31 far as the housing for the Temple servants and **m**,
3:32 and **m** repaired the wall from that corner to the
13:20 The **m** and tradesmen with a variety of wares
Job 41: 6 Will **m** try to buy it? Will they sell it in their
Pr 31:24 belted linen garments and sashes to sell to the **m**.
Isa 23: 2 you people of the coast and you **m** of Sidon.
60: 5 for **m** from around the world will come to you.
Eze 7:13 And if any **m** should survive, they will never
17: 4 Then he carried it away to a city filled with **m**,
27:13 **M** from Greece, Tubal, and Meshech brought
27:15 **M** came to you from Dedan. Numerous coastlands
27:16 "Aram sent **m** to buy your wares. They traded
27:22 The **m** of Sheba and Raamah came with all kinds
27:27 your ship builders, **m**, and warriors.
27:36 The **m** of the nations / shake their heads at the
38:13 and Dedan and the **m** of Tarshish will ask,
Hos 12: 7 the people are like crafty **m** selling from dishonest
Mic 6:11 And how can I tolerate all your **m** who use
Na 3:16 **M**, as numerous as the stars, have filled your city
Mt 21:12 and began to drive out the **m** and their customers.
21:23 "By whose authority did you drive out the **m** from
Mk 11:15 and began to drive out the **m** and their customers.
11:28 "By whose authority did you drive out the **m** from
Lk 19:45 and began to drive out the **m** from their stalls.
20: 2 "By whose authority did you drive out the **m** from
Jn 2:14 In the Temple area he saw **m** selling cattle, sheep,
Rev 18: 3 and **m** throughout the world have grown rich as a
18:11 The **m** of the world will weep and mourn for her,
18:15 The **m** who became wealthy by selling her these
18:23 This will happen because her **m**, who were the

MERCIES (13) [MERCY]
Ps 40:11 LORD, don't hold back your tender **m** from me.
52: 9 for what you have done. / I will wait for your **m**
79: 8 Let your tenderhearted **m** quickly meet our needs,
89: 1 I will sing of the tender **m** of the LORD forever!
103: 4 and surrounds me with love and tender **m**.
119:77 Surround me with your tender **m** so I may live,
Isa 55: 3 I will give you all the **m** and unfailing love that I
La 3:22 By his **m** we have been kept from complete
3:23 is his faithfulness; his **m** begin afresh each day.
Da 9:16 In view of all your faithful **m**, Lord, please turn
Jnh 2: 8 worship false gods turn their backs on all God's **m**.
Zec 9:12 I promise this very day that I will repay you two **m**
Ro 15: 9 might also give glory to God for his **m** to them.

MERCIFUL (47) [MERCY]
Ge 19:16 to safety outside the city, for the LORD was **m**.
Ex 22:27 to me for help, then I will hear, for I am very **m**.
34: 6 I am the LORD, the **m** and gracious God.
Dt 4:31 For the LORD your God is **m**—he will not
13:17 will turn from his fierce anger and be **m** to you.
13:18 "The LORD your God will be **m** only if you
1Ki 8:50 sinned against you. Make their captors **m** to them,
20:31 we have heard that the kings of Israel are very **m**.
2Ch 30: 9 For the LORD your God is gracious and **m**.
Ne 9:17 gracious and **m**, slow to become angry, and full of
9:31 them forever. What a gracious and **m** God you are!
Job 37:23 yet he is so just and **m** that he does not oppress us.
Ps 25: 7 of your unfailing love, / for you are **m**, O LORD.
27: 7 to my pleading, O LORD. / Be **m** and answer me!
67: 1 May God be **m** and bless us. / May his face shine
78:38 Yet he was **m** and forgave their sins / and didn't
86: 3 Be **m**, O Lord, / for I am calling on you constantly.
86:15 But you, O Lord, are a **m** and gracious God,
103: 8 The LORD is **m** and gracious; / he is slow to get
111: 4 How gracious and **m** is our LORD!
116: 5 How good he is! / So **m**, this God of ours!
119:58 I want your blessings. / Be **m** just as you promised.
145: 8 The LORD is kind and **m**, / slow to get angry,
Isa 33: 2 But LORD, be **m** to us, for we have waited for
Jer 3:12 come home to me again, for I am **m**.
7: 5 I will be **m** only if you stop your wicked thoughts
15:15 Be **m** to me and give them what they deserve!
42:12 I will be **m** to you by making him kind, so he will
Eze 18: 7 Suppose he is a **m** creditor, not keeping the items
Da 4:27 Break from your wicked past by being **m** to the
9: 9 But the Lord our God is **m** and forgiving,
9:18 we deserve help, but because you are so **m**.

Hos 6: 6 I want you to be **m**; I don't want your sacrifices.
Joel 2:13 to the LORD your God, for he is gracious and **m**.
Mal 1: 9 "Go ahead, beg God to be **m** to you! But when
Mt 5: 7 God blesses those who are **m**, / for they will be
9:13 'I want you to be **m**; I don't want your sacrifices.'
12: 7 'I want you to be **m**; I don't want your sacrifices.'
Mk 5:19 Lord has done for you and how **m** he has been."
Lk 1:54 He has not forgotten his promise to be **m**.
1:55 and his children— / to be **m** to them forever."
1:72 He has been **m** to our ancestors / by remembering
18:13 saying, 'O God, be **m** to me, for I am a sinner.'
Ro 11:30 Jews refused his mercy, God was **m** to you instead.
Heb 2:17 so that he could be our **m** and faithful High Priest
Jas 2:13 no mercy for you if you have not been **m** to others.
2:13 But if you have been **m**, then God's mercy toward

MERCIFULLY (2) [MERCY]

2Ch 30: 9 and your children will be treated **m** by their
Eze 20:44 when I have honored my name by treating you **m**

MERCILESS (1) [MERCY]

Pr 5: 9 and hand over to **m** people everything you have

MERCILESSLY (1) [MERCY]

Jos 11:20 So they were completely and **m** destroyed,

MERCURIUS [KJV] See HERMES

MERCY (162) [MERCIES, MERCIFUL, MERCIFULLY, MERCILESS, MERCILESSLY]

Ge 19:19 saved my life, and you have granted me such **m**.
43:14 May God Almighty give you **m** as you go before
Ex 33:19 I choose, and I will show **m** to anyone I choose.
Dt 7: 2 Make no treaties with them and show them no **m**.
7:16 Show them no **m** and do not worship their gods.
30: 3 He will have **m** on you and gather you back from
Jos 9:25 Now we are at your **m**—do whatever you think is
Jdg 1:24 a way into the city, and we will have **m** on you."
1Sa 9:16 for I have looked down on my people in **m**
24:10 For the LORD placed you at my **m** back there in
2Sa 24:14 into the hands of the LORD, for his **m** is great.
1Ch 21:13 the hands of the LORD, for his **m** is very great.
2Ch 28: 9 But you have gone too far, killing them without **m**,
Ezr 9: 7 and our priests have been at the **m** of the pagan
Ne 9:17 to become angry, and full of unfailing love and **m**.
9:19 But in your great **m** you did not abandon them to
9:27 In great **m**, you sent them deliverers who rescued
9:28 In your wonderful **m**, you rescued them
9:31 But in your great **m**, you did not destroy them
Est 4: 8 and to urge her to go to the king to beg for **m**
Job 9:15 I would have no defense. I could only plead for **m**.
16:13 and his arrows pierced me without **m**.
19:21 "Have **m** on me, my friends, have **m**,
27:22 It whirls down on them without **m**. They struggle
41: 3 Will it beg you for **m** or implore you for pity?
Ps 4: 1 my distress. / Have **m** on me and hear my prayer.
9:13 LORD, have **m** on me. / See how I suffer at the
25:16 Turn to me and have **m** on me, / for I am alone
26:11 I do what is right. / So in your **m**, save me.
28: 2 Listen to my prayer for **m** / as I cry out to you for
28: 6 the LORD! / For he has heard my cry for **m**.
30: 8 O LORD. / I begged the Lord for **m**, saying,
30:10 Hear me, LORD, and have **m** on me. / Help me,
31: 9 Have **m** on me, LORD, for I am in distress.
31:22 But you heard my cry for **m** / and answered my
41: 4 "O LORD," I prayed, "have **m** on me.
41:10 LORD, have **m** on me. / Make me well again,
51: 1 Have **m** on me, O God, / because of your unfailing
56: 1 O God, have **m** on me. / The enemy troops press in
57: 1 Have **m** on me, O God, have **m**! / I look to you
59: 5 Show no **m** to wicked traitors. / *Interlude*
69:16 and take care of me, / for your **m** is so plentiful.
84: 9 Have **m** on the one you have anointed.
86:16 Look down and have **m** on me. / Give strength to
88: 9 O LORD; / I lift my pleading hands to you for **m**.
102:13 You will arise and have **m** on Jerusalem—
119:121 Don't leave me to the **m** of my enemies, / for I
119:132 Come and show me your **m**, / as you do for all who
119:156 LORD, how great is your **m**; / in your justice,
123: 2 We look to the LORD our God for his **m**,
123: 3 Have **m** on us, LORD, have **m**, / for we have
140: 6 my God!" / Listen, O LORD, to my cries for **m**!
142: 1 out to the LORD; / I plead for the LORD's **m**.
Pr 6: 3 You have placed yourself at your friend's **m**.
6:34 and he will have no **m** in his day of vengeance.
18:23 The poor plead for **m**; the rich answer with insults.
21:10 harm others; their neighbors get no **m** from them.
28:13 and forsake them, they will receive **m**.
Isa 9:17 and no **m** on even the widows and orphans.
13:18 They will have no **m** on helpless babies and will
14: 1 But the LORD will have **m** on the descendants of
14:17 greatest cities and had no **m** on his prisoners?'
27:11 one who made them will show them no pity or **m**.
47: 6 But you, Babylon, showed them no **m**. You have
49:10 For the LORD in his **m** will lead them beside
51: 5 My **m** and justice are coming soon. Your salvation
54:10 be broken," says the LORD, who has **m** on you.
55: 7 Let them turn to the LORD that he may have **m**
60:10 my anger, I will have **m** on you through my grace.
63: 7 which he has granted according to his **m** and love.
63: 9 In his love and **m** he redeemed them. He lifted
63:15 Where are your **m** and compassion now?
64: 7 one calls on your name or pleads with you for **m**.
Jer 6:23 They are cruel and show no **m**. As they ride
11:11 Though they beg for **m**, I will not listen to their
13:14 I will not let my pity or **m** or compassion keep me
16: 5 I have taken away my unfailing love and my **m**.
20:16 cities of old that the LORD overthrew without **m**.
21: 7 He will slaughter them all without **m**, pity,
26:19 the LORD. They begged him to have **m** on them.
31:20 I long for him and surely will have **m** on him.
33:26 restore them to their land and have **m** on them."
50:42 They are cruel and show no **m**. As they ride
La 2: 1 the Lord has shown no **m** even to his Temple.
2: 2 Without **m** the Lord has destroyed every home in
2:17 He has destroyed Jerusalem without **m** and caused
2:21 them in your anger, slaughtering them without **m**.
3:43 chased us down, and slaughtered us without **m**.
Eze 8:18 And though they scream for **m**, I will not listen."
9: 5 forehead is not marked. Show no **m**; have no pity!
39:25 I will have **m** on Israel, for I am jealous for my
Da 2:18 to show them his **m** by telling them the secret,
9:13 But we have refused to seek **m** from the LORD
Hos 14: 3 No, in you alone do the orphans find **m**."
Am 1:11 They showed them no **m** and were unrelenting in
5:15 Almighty will have **m** on his people who remain.
Jnh 1: 6 Maybe he will have **m** on us and spare our lives."
3:10 he had **m** on them and didn't carry out the
Mic 6: 8 to do what is right, to love **m**, and to walk humbly
7:18 people forever, because you delight in showing **m**.
Hab 3: 2 to save us. And in your anger, remember your **m**.
Zec 1:12 How long will it be until you again show **m** to
1:16 I have returned to show **m** to Jerusalem.
7: 9 and show **m** and kindness to one another.
Mt 5: 7 those who are merciful, / for they will be shown **m**.
9:27 shouting, "Son of David, have **m** on us!"
15:22 pleading, "Have **m** on me, O Lord, Son of David!
17:15 "Lord, have **m** on my son, because he has seizures
18:33 Shouldn't you have **m** on your fellow servant, just
as I had **m** on you?'
20:30 "Lord, Son of David, have **m** on us!"
20:31 "Lord, Son of David, have **m** on us!"
23:23 important things of the law—justice, **m**, and faith.
Mk 9:22 trying to kill him. Have **m** on us and help us.
10:47 shout out, "Jesus, Son of David, have **m** on me!"
10:48 shouted louder, "Son of David, have **m** on me!"
Lk 1:50 His **m** goes on from generation to generation,
1:78 Because of God's tender **m**, / the light from heaven
10:37 The man replied, "The one who showed him **m**."
17:13 crying out, "Jesus, Master, have **m** on us!"
18:38 "Jesus, Son of David, have **m** on me!"
18:39 shouted louder, "Son of David, have **m** on me!"
Ro 9:15 to Moses, / "I will show **m** to anyone I choose,
9:16 hard for it. God will show **m** to anyone he chooses.
9:18 God shows **m** to some just because he wants to,
9:23 upon those he prepared to be the objects of his **m**
11:30 but when the Jews refused his **m**, God was
11:31 Jews are the rebels, and God's **m** has come to you.
11:31 But someday they too will share in God's **m**.
11:32 so he could have **m** on everyone.
2Co 1: 3 He is the source of every **m** and the God who
4: 1 since God in his **m** has given us this wonderful
Gal 1: 6 and **m** called you to share the eternal life he gives
1:15 even before I was born! What undeserved **m**!
6:16 May God's **m** and peace be upon all those who
Eph 2: 4 But God is so rich in **m**, and he loved us so very
Php 2:27 But God had **m** on him—and also on me, so that I
Col 3:12 you must clothe yourselves with tenderhearted **m**,
1Ti 1: 2 Jesus our Lord give you grace, **m**, and peace.
1:13 But God had **m** on me because I did it in ignorance
1:16 But that is why God had **m** on me, so that Christ
2: 1 plead for God's **m** upon them, and give thanks.
2Ti 1: 2 Jesus our Lord give you grace, **m**, and peace.
Tit 3: 5 of the good things we did, but because of his **m**.
Heb 4:16 There we will receive his **m**, and we will find
10:28 put to death without **m** on the testimony of two
10:29 and enraged the Holy Spirit who brings God's **m** to
Jas 2:13 For there will be no **m** for you if you have not been
2:13 then God's **m** toward you will win out over his
3:17 It is full of **m** and good deeds. It shows no
5:11 ended in good, for he is full of tenderness and **m**.
1Pe 1: 3 for it is by his boundless **m** that God has given us
2:10 Once you received none of God's **m**; / now you
have received his **m**."
2Jn 1: 3 May grace, **m**, and peace, which come from God
Jude 1: 2 May you receive more and more of God's **m**,
1:21 our Lord Jesus Christ in his **m** is going to give you.
1:22 Show **m** to those whose faith is wavering.
1:23 are still others to whom you need to show **m**,

MERCYSEAT [KJV] See ARK'S (COVER)

MERE (40) [MERELY]

Dt 32:47 These instructions are not **m** words—they are your
2Ki 18:20 Do you think that **m** words can substitute for
2Ch 13: 6 who was a **m** servant of David's son Solomon,
14:11 our God; do not let **m** men prevail against you!"
Job 7:17 "What are **m** mortals, that you should make
25: 4 How can a **m** mortal stand before God and claim to
25: 6 How much less are **m** people, who are but worms
Ps 8: 4 of us, / **m** humans that you should care for us?
9:19 O LORD! / Do not let **m** mortals defy you!
56: 4 should I be afraid? / What can **m** mortals do to me?
56:11 should I be afraid? / What can **m** mortals do to me?
82: 7 But in death you are **m** men. / You will fall as any
118: 6 will not be afraid. / What can **m** mortals do to me?
144: 3 notice us, / **m** humans that you should care for us?
Pr 14:23 Work brings profit, but **m** talk leads to poverty!
29:19 For a servant, **m** words are not enough—
Isa 2:22 Stop putting your trust in **m** humans. They are as
31: 3 For these Egyptians are **m** humans, not God!
36: 5 Do you think that **m** words can substitute for
40:17 they are less than nothing—**m** emptiness and froth.
44:11 along with all these craftsmen—**m** humans—
51:12 So why are you afraid of **m** humans, who wither
66: 8 Has a country ever come forth in a **m** moment?
Jer 12: 5 to me, "If racing against **m** men makes you tired,
17: 5 "Cursed are those who put their trust in **m** humans
La 3:39 Then why should we, **m** humans, complain when
Da 11:23 With a **m** handful of followers, he will become
Hos 4:15 Their worship is **m** pretense as they take oaths in
11: 9 destroy Israel, for I am God and not a **m** mortal.
Jn 10:33 but for blasphemy, because you, a **m** man,
Ro 1:23 they worshiped idols made to look like **m** people,
9:20 Who are you, a **m** human being, to criticize God?
1Co 4: 1 and me as **m** servants of Christ who have been put
9:11 much to ask, in return, for **m** food and clothing?
2Co 10: 4 God's mighty weapons, not **m** worldly weapons,
Gal 1:11 which I preach is not based on **m** human reasoning
Col 2:22 Such rules are **m** human teaching about things that
Heb 13: 6 not be afraid. / What can **m** mortals do to me?"
1Pe 1: 7 and your faith is far more precious to God than **m**
1:18 And the ransom he paid was not **m** gold or silver.

MERED (3) [MERED'S]

1Ch 4:17 sons of Ezrah were Jether, **M**, Epher, and Jalon.
4:17 **M** married an Egyptian woman, who became the
4:18 **M** also married a woman of Judah, who became

MERED'S (1) [MERED]

1Ch 4:18 **M** Egyptian wife was named Bithiah, and she was

MERELY (42) [MERE]

Lev 13:23 and does not spread, it is **m** the scar from the boil,
Jdg 9:28 He's **m** the son of Gideon, and Zebul is his
1Ch 16:26 The gods of other nations are **m** idols,
Job 10: 5 Is your lifetime **m** human? Is your life so short
23: 6 Would he **m** argue with me in his greatness?
26:14 minor things he does, **m** a whisper of his power.
Ps 9:20 O LORD. / Let them know they are **m** human.
33: 6 The LORD **m** spoke, / and the heavens were
39: 6 We are **m** moving shadows, / and all our busy
78:39 For he remembered that they were **m** mortal,
96: 5 The gods of other nations are **m** idols,
115: 4 Their idols are **m** things of silver and gold,
135:15 Their idols are **m** things of silver and gold,
Ecc 1: 9 History **m** repeats itself. It has all been done
Isa 10: 7 He will **m** think he is attacking my people as part
La 2: 6 his Temple as though it were **m** a garden shelter.
Eze 16:47 But you have not **m** sinned as they did—no,
28: 9 kill you? To them you will be no god but **m** a man!
Mt 5:31 'A man can divorce his wife by **m** giving her a
16:23 You are seeing things **m** from a human point of
19: 7 "Then why did Moses say a man could **m** write an
21:25 baptism come from heaven or was it **m** human?"
21:26 But if we say it was **m** human, we'll be mobbed,
Mk 8:33 You are seeing things **m** from a human point of
10: 4 "He said a man **m** has to write his wife an official
11:30 baptism come from heaven or was it **m** human?
11:32 But do we dare say it was **m** human?" For they
Lk 6:32 "Do you think you deserve credit **m** for loving
17: 9 because he is **m** doing what he is supposed to do.
20: 4 baptism come from heaven, or was it **m** human?"
20: 6 But if we say it was **m** human, the people will
Jn 5:30 the will of God who sent me; it is not **m** my own.
7:17 whether my teaching is from God or is **m** my own.
8:54 Jesus answered, "If I am **m** boasting about myself,
10:13 The hired hand runs away because he is **m** hired
Ac 5:38 and doing these things **m** on their own,
14:15 We are **m** human beings like yourselves!
18:15 But since it is **m** a question of words and names
Ro 2:13 For it is not **m** knowing the law that brings God's
1Co 9: 8 And this isn't **m** human opinion. Doesn't God's
2Co 5:16 that way, as though he were **m** a human being.
Heb 9:24 for that was **m** a copy of the real Temple in

MEREMOTH (7)

Ezr 8:33 and entrusted to **M** son of Uriah the priest and to
10:36 Vaniah, **M**, Eliashib,
Ne 3: 4 **M** son of Uriah and grandson of Hakkoz repaired
3:21 **M** son of Uriah and grandson of Hakkoz rebuilt
10: 5 Harim, **M**, Obadiah,
12: 3 Shecaniah, Harim, **M**,
12:15 of Harim. / Helkai was leader of the family of **M**.

MERES (1)

Est 1:14 Shethar, Admatha, Tarshish, **M**, Marsena,

MERIBAH (11) [MASSAH, MERIBAH-KADESH]

Ex 17: 7 "the place of testing"—and **M**—"the place of
Nu 20:13 This place was known as the waters of **M**,
20:24 my instructions concerning the waters of **M**.
27:14 (These are the waters of **M** at Kadesh in the
Dt 32:51 the waters of **M** at Kadesh in the wilderness of Zin.
33: 8 and contended with them at the waters of **M**.
Ps 81: 7 out of the thundercloud. / I tested your faith at **M**,
95: 8 "Don't harden your hearts as Israel did at **M**,
106:32 At **M**, too, they angered the LORD,
Eze 47:19 go west from Tamar to the waters of **M** at Kadesh
48:28 Gad runs from Tamar to the waters of **M** at Kadesh

MERIBAH-KADESH (1) [KADESH, MERIBAH]
Dt 33: 2 and came from **M** / with flaming fire at his right

MERIBBAAL (4) [MEPHIBOSHETH]
1Ch 8:34 Jonathan was the father of **M**. **M** was the father of
9:40 Jonathan was the father of **M**. **M** was the father of

MERODACH-BALADAN (2)
2Ki 20:12 Soon after this, **M** son of Baladan, king of
Isa 39: 1 Soon after this, **M** son of Baladan, king of

MEROM (2)
Jos 11: 5 around the water near **M** to fight against Israel.
11: 7 and his warriors traveled to the water near **M**

MERONOTH (2)
1Ch 27:30 Jehdeiah from **M** was in charge of the donkeys.
Ne 3: 7 Jadon from **M**, and people from Gibeon

MEROZ (1)
Jdg 5:23 'Let the people of **M** be cursed,' said the angel of

MERRILY (1) [MERRY]
Jer 31: 4 again be happy and dance **m** with tambourines.

MERRY (5) [MERRILY, MERRYMAKERS]
Est 5:14 you can go on your **m** way to the banquet with the
Job 21:12 and harp. They make **m** to the sound of the flute.
Isa 22:13 drink wine. "Let's eat, drink, and be **m**," you say.
Jer 15:17 I never joined the people in their **m** feasts. I sat
Lk 12:19 to come. Now take it easy! Eat, drink, and be **m**!'

MERRYMAKERS (1) [MERRY]
Isa 24: 7 there will be no wine. The **m** will sigh and mourn.

MESHA (4)
Ge 10:30 from **M** toward the eastern hills of Sephar.
2Ki 3: 4 King **M** of Moab and his people were sheep
1Ch 2:42 brother of Jerahmeel, was **M**, the father of Ziph.
8: 9 new wife, gave birth to Jobab, Zibia, **M**, Malcam,

MESHACH (14) [MISHAEL]
Da 1: 7 Mishael was called **M**. / Azariah was called
2:49 Daniel's request, the king appointed Shadrach, **M**,
3:12 are some Jews—Shadrach, **M**, and Abednego—
3:13 flew into a rage and ordered Shadrach, **M**,
3:14 to them, "Is it true, Shadrach, **M**, and Abednego,
3:16 Shadrach, **M**, and Abednego replied,
3:19 Nebuchadnezzar was so furious with Shadrach, **M**,
3:20 **M**, and Abednego and throw them into the blazing
3:23 So Shadrach, **M**, and Abednego, securely tied,
3:26 "Shadrach, **M**, and Abednego, servants of the
3:26 So Shadrach, **M**, and Abednego stepped out of the
3:28 to the God of Shadrach, **M**, and Abednego!
3:29 **M**, and Abednego, they will be torn limb from
3:30 Then the king promoted Shadrach, **M**,

MESHECH (7)
Ge 10: 2 Magog, Madai, Javan, Tubal, **M**, and Tiras.
1Ch 1: 5 Magog, Madai, Javan, Tubal, **M**, and Tiras.
Ps 120: 5 How I suffer among these scoundrels of **M**!
Eze 27:13 Tubal, and **M** brought slaves and bronze dishes.
32:26 "**M** and Tubal are there, surrounded by the graves
38: 2 the prince who rules over the nations of **M**
39: 1 O Gog, ruler of the nations of **M** and Tubal.

MESHELEMIAH (4) [MESHELEMIAH'S]
1Ch 9:21 And later Zechariah son of **M** had been responsible
26: 1 From the Korahites, there was **M** son of Kore,
26: 2 The sons of **M** were Zechariah (the oldest),
26:14 The responsibility for the east gate went to **M**

MESHELEMIAH'S (1) [MESHELEMIAH]
1Ch 26: 9 **M** eighteen sons and relatives were also very

MESHEZABEL (3)
Ne 3: 4 Meshullam son of Berekiah and grandson of **M**,
10:21 **M**, Zadok, Jaddua,
11:24 Pethahiah son of **M**, a descendant of Zerah son of

MESHILLEMITH (1) [MESHILLEMOTH]
1Ch 9:12 son of Meshullam, son of **M**, son of Immer.

MESHILLEMOTH (2) [MESHILLEMITH]
2Ch 28:12 Berekiah son of **M**, Jehizkiah son of Shallum,
Ne 11:13 of Azarel, son of Ahzai, son of **M**, son of Immer;

MESHOBAB (1)
1Ch 4:34 Other descendants of Simeon included **M**,

MESHULLAM (25)
2Ki 22: 3 sent Shaphan son of Azaliah and grandson of **M**,
1Ch 3:19 The sons of Zerubbabel were **M** and Hananiah.
5:13 **M**, Sheba, Jorai, Jacan, Zia, and Eber.
8:17 Zebadiah, **M**, Hizki, Heber,
9: 7 From the tribe of Benjamin came Sallu son of **M**,
9: 8 **M** son of Shephatiah, son of Reuel, son of Ibnijah.
9:11 son of **M**, son of Zadok, son of Meraioth, son of
9:12 son of Jahzerah, son of **M**, son of Meshillemith,
2Ch 34:12 Levites of the Merarite clan, and Zechariah and **M**,
Ezr 8:16 Jarib, Elnathan, Nathan, Zechariah, and **M**,
10:15 and **M** and Shabbethai the Levite supported them.
10:29 **M**, Malluch, Adaiah, Jashub, Sheal, and Jeremoth.
Ne 3: 4 Beside him were **M** son of Berekiah and grandson
3: 6 by Joiada son of Paseah and **M** son of Besodeiah.
3:30 while **M** son of Berekiah rebuilt the wall next to
6:18 was married to the daughter of **M** son of Berekiah.
8: 4 Hashum, Hashbaddanah, Zechariah, and **M**.
10: 7 **M**, Abijah, Mijamin,
10:20 Magpiash, **M**, Hezir,
11: 7 Sallu son of **M**, son of Joed, son of Pedaiah,
11:11 son of **M**, son of Zadok, son of Meraioth, son of
12:13 **M** was leader of the family of Ezra.
12:16 **M** was leader of the family of Ginnethon.
12:25 **M**, Talmon, and Akkub were the gatekeepers in
12:33 along with Azariah, Ezra, **M**,

MESHULLEMETH (1)
2Ki 21:19 His mother was **M**, the daughter of Haruz from

MESOPOTAMIA (2)
Ac 2: 9 Parthians, Medes, Elamites, people from **M**, Judea,
7: 2 ancestor Abraham in **M** before he moved to Haran.

MESS [KJV] See GIFT, SERVING

MESSAGE (514) [MESSAGES, MESSENGER, MESSENGERS]
Ge 32: 4 He told them, "Give this **m** to my master Esau:
38:25 out to kill her, she sent this **m** to her father-in-law:
50:16 So they sent this **m** to Joseph: "Before your father
50:17 When Joseph received the **m**, he broke down
Ex 3:18 leaders of the people of Israel will accept your **m**.
5:23 Since I gave Pharaoh your **m**, he has been even
6:29 Give Pharaoh the **m** I have given you."
19: 6 my holy nation.' Give this **m** to the Israelites."
36: 6 and this **m** was sent throughout the camp:
Nu 20:14 sent ambassadors to the king of Edom with this **m**:
20:14 "This **m** is from your relatives, the people of
21:21 to King Sihon of the Amorites with this **m**:
22: 5 He sent this **m** to request that Balaam come to help
22:10 son of Zippor, king of Moab, has sent me this **m**:
22:16 They went to Balaam and gave him this **m**:
23: 5 Then the LORD gave Balaam a **m** for King Balak
23:16 So the LORD met Balaam and gave him a **m**.
23:16 he said, "Go back to Balak and give him this **m**."
24:15 "This is the **m** of Balaam son of Beor,
Dt 18:20 But any prophet who claims to give a **m** from
18:22 it does not happen, the LORD did not give the **m**.
30:14 The **m** is very close at hand; it is on your lips
Jdg 2: 1 from Gilgal to Bokim with a **m** for the Israelites.
3:19 to Eglon and said, "I have a secret **m** for you."
3:20 and said, "I have a **m** for you from God!"
11:14 Jephthah sent this **m** back to the Ammonite king:
11:28 king of Ammon paid no attention to Jephthah's **m**.
12: 1 over to Zaphon. They sent this **m** to Jephthah:
1Sa 2:27 came to Eli and gave him this **m** from the LORD:
3: 7 because he had never had a **m** from the LORD
9: 9 (In those days if people wanted a **m** from God,
9:27 for I have received a special **m** for you from God."
10:18 And he gave them this **m** from the LORD,
11: 5 So they told him about the **m** from Jabesh.
11: 7 to carry them throughout Israel with this **m**:
11: 9 there was throughout the city when that **m** arrived!
15: 1 told me to. Now listen to this **m** from the LORD!
15: 6 Saul sent this **m** to the Kenites: "Move away from
23:27 an urgent **m** reached Saul that the Philistines were
25: 5 men to Carmel. He told them to deliver this **m**:
25: 9 David's young men gave this **m** to Nabal
2Sa 2: 5 he sent them this **m**: "May the LORD bless you
3:14 David then sent this **m** to Ishbosheth, Saul's son:
5: 8 When the insulting **m** from the defenders of the
11: 5 she was pregnant, she sent a **m** to inform David.
15:10 "As soon as you hear the trumpets," his **m** read,
15:28 the Jordan River and wait there for a **m** from you.
17:17 bring them the **m** they were to take to King David.
24:11 who was David's seer. This was the **m**:
1Ki 5: 2 Then Solomon sent this **m** back to Hiram:
5: 7 When Hiram received Solomon's **m**, he was very
5: 8 "I have received your **m**, and I will do as you have
6:11 Then the LORD gave this **m** to Solomon:
12:15 for it fulfilled the LORD's **m** to Jeroboam son of
12:24 doing!' " So they obeyed the **m** of the LORD
13: 3 day the man of God gave a sign to prove his **m**,
13: 5 just as the man of God had predicted in his **m** from
13:18 And an angel gave me this **m** from the LORD:
13:20 a **m** from the LORD came to the old prophet.
13:21 You have defied the LORD's **m** and have
13:32 For the **m** the LORD told him to proclaim against
14: 7 Jeroboam, this **m** from the LORD, the God of
15:18 who was ruling in Damascus, along with this **m**:
16: 1 This **m** from the LORD was delivered to King
16: 7 This **m** from the LORD had been spoken against
16:34 This all happened according to the **m** from the
19: 2 So Jezebel sent this **m** to Elijah: "May the gods
20: 2 into the city to relay this **m** to King Ahab of Israel:
20: 7 I already agreed when he sent the **m** demanding
20:10 Then Ben-hadad sent this **m** to Ahab:
21:19 Give him this **m**: 'This is what the LORD says:
21:27 When Ahab heard this **m**, he tore his clothing,
21:28 Then another **m** from the LORD came to Elijah,
2Ki 1: 4 will surely die.' " So Elijah went to deliver the **m**.
1: 6 and told us to go back to the king with a **m** from
3: 7 he sent this **m** to King Jehoshaphat of Judah:
4:22 She sent a **m** to her husband: "Send one of the
5: 8 about the king's reaction, he sent this **m** to him:
5:10 Elisha sent a messenger out to him with this **m**:
7: 1 Elisha replied, "Hear this **m** from the LORD!
9: 5 "I have a **m** for you, Commander," he said.
9:25 The LORD pronounced this **m** against him:
9:36 he stated, "This fulfills the **m** from the LORD,
10: 5 guardians of the king's sons, sent this **m** to Jehu:
10:10 You can be sure that the **m** of the LORD that was
14: 9 "Out in the Lebanon mountains a thistle sent a **m**
15:12 So the LORD's **m** to Jehu came true:
16: 7 to King Tiglath-pileser of Assyria with this **m**:
17:26 So a **m** was sent to the king of Assyria:
18:14 King Hezekiah sent this **m** to the king of Assyria at
18:19 representative sent this **m** to King Hezekiah:
18:28 "Listen to this **m** from the great king of Assyria!
19: 5 officials delivered the king's **m** to Isaiah,
19: 9 he sent this **m** back to Hezekiah in Jerusalem:
19:10 "This **m** is for King Hezekiah of Judah. Don't let
19:17 have destroyed all these nations, just as the **m** says.
19:20 Then Isaiah son of Amoz sent this **m** to Hezekiah:
19:21 This is the **m** that the LORD has spoken against
20: 1 He gave the king this **m**: "This is what the
20: 4 this **m** came to him from the LORD:
20:16 to Hezekiah, "Listen to this **m** from the LORD:
20:19 "This **m** you have given me from the LORD is
22:18 says concerning the **m** you have just heard:
22:20 this place.' " So they took her **m** back to the king.
1Ch 21: 9 spoke to Gad, David's seer. This was the **m**:
2Ch 2: 3 Solomon also sent this **m** to King Hiram at Tyre:
11: 4 doing!' " So they obeyed the **m** of the LORD
12: 7 their change of heart, he gave this **m** to Shemaiah:
15: 8 When Asa heard this **m** from Azariah the prophet,
16: 2 who was ruling in Damascus, along with this **m**:
25:18 a thistle sent a **m** to a mighty cedar tree:
32: 9 sent officials to Jerusalem with this **m** for
34:26 says concerning the **m** you have just heard:
34:28 this place.' " So they took her **m** back to the king.
35:21 King Neco sent ambassadors to Josiah with this **m**:
36:21 So the **m** of the LORD spoken through Jeremiah
Ezr 6: 6 So King Darius sent this **m**: / "To Tattenai,
Ne 6: 2 and Geshem sent me a **m** asking me to meet them
6: 3 so I replied by sending this **m** to them: "I am
6: 4 Four times they sent the same **m**, and each time I
Est 4: 9 So Hathach returned to Esther with Mordecai's **m**.
4:10 Hathach to go back and relay this **m** to Mordecai,
4:12 So Hathach gave Esther's **m** to Mordecai.
8: 8 and send a **m** to the Jews in the king's name,
8:10 and sealed the **m** with the king's signet ring.
Ps 19: 4 yet their **m** has gone out to all the earth, / and their
Pr 26: 6 Trusting a fool to convey a **m** is as foolish as
30: 1 The **m** of Agur son of Jakeh. An oracle. I am
Isa 7:10 after this, the LORD sent this **m** to King Ahaz:
13: 1 Isaiah son of Amoz received this **m** concerning the
14:28 This **m** came to me the year King Ahaz died:
15: 1 This **m** came to me concerning Moab: In one night
17: 1 This **m** came to me concerning Damascus: "Look,
18: 2 Take a **m** to your land divided by rivers, to your
19: 1 This **m** came to me concerning Egypt: Look!
21: 1 This **m** came to me concerning the land of
21:11 This **m** came to me concerning Edom:
21:13 This **m** came to me concerning Arabia: O caravans
22: 1 This **m** came to me concerning Jerusalem: What is
22:15 the palace administrator, and to give him this **m**:
23: 1 This **m** came to me concerning Tyre: Weep,
28:13 So the LORD will spell out his **m** for them again,
28:13 will stumble over this simple, straightforward **m**.
28:14 Therefore, listen to this **m** from the LORD,
28:19 This **m** will bring terror to your people.
36: 4 representative sent this **m** to King Hezekiah:
36:13 "Listen to this **m** from the great king of Assyria!
37: 5 officials delivered the king's **m** to Isaiah,
37: 9 he sent this **m** back to Hezekiah in Jerusalem:
37:10 "This **m** is for King Hezekiah of Judah. Don't let
37:18 have destroyed all these nations, just as the **m** says.
37:21 Then Isaiah son of Amoz sent this **m** to Hezekiah:
37:22 This is the **m** that the LORD has spoken against
38: 1 He gave the king this **m**: "This is what the
38: 4 Then this **m** came to Isaiah from the LORD:
39: 5 "Listen to this **m** from the LORD Almighty:
39: 8 "This **m** you have given me from the LORD is
48:16 and his Spirit have sent me with this **m**:
53: 1 Who has believed our **m**? To whom will the
62:11 The LORD has sent this **m** to every land:
66: 5 Hear this **m** from the LORD, and tremble at his
Jer 1: 4 The LORD gave me a **m**. He said,
2: 1 The LORD gave me another **m**. He said,
7: 1 The LORD gave another **m** to Jeremiah. He said,
7: 2 LORD's Temple, and give this **m** to the people:
7: 2 'O Judah, listen to this **m** from the LORD!
11: 1 The LORD gave another **m** to Jeremiah. He said,
11: 6 "Broadcast this **m** in the streets of Jerusalem.
13: 3 Then the LORD gave me another **m**:
13: 8 Then I received this **m** from the LORD:
14: 1 This **m** came to Jeremiah from the LORD,
16: 1 The LORD gave me another **m**. He said,
17:15 "What is this '**m** from the LORD' you keep
17:16 It is your **m** I have given them, not my own.
17:20 'Listen to this **m** from the LORD, you kings of
18: 1 The LORD gave another **m** to Jeremiah. He said,
18: 5 Then the LORD gave me this **m**:
19: 3 Say to them, 'Listen to this **m** from the LORD,
19:14 from Topheth where he had delivered this **m**,
21:11 of Judah, 'Listen to this **m** from the LORD!

22: 2 'Listen to this **m** from the LORD, you king of
22:29 earth, earth! Listen to this **m** from the LORD!
23:21 for me. I have given them no **m**, yet they prophesy.
23:32 and they have no **m** at all for my people,"
24: 4 Then the LORD gave me this **m**:
25: 1 This **m** for all the people of Judah came to
25: 5 Each time the **m** was this: 'Turn from the evil road
26: 1 This **m** came to Jeremiah from the LORD early in
26: 2 Give them my entire **m**; include every word.
26: 8 But when Jeremiah had finished his **m**,
27: 1 This **m** came to Jeremiah from the LORD early in
27: 4 Give them this **m** for their masters: 'This is what
27:12 Then I repeated this same **m** to King Zedekiah of
28:12 Soon afterward the LORD gave this **m** to
29: 4 sends this **m** to all the captives he has exiled to
29:20 Therefore, listen to this **m** from the LORD,
29:24 The LORD sent this **m** to Shemaiah the
29:30 Then the LORD gave this **m** to Jeremiah:
30: 1 The LORD gave another **m** to Jeremiah. He said,
30: 4 This is the **m** the LORD gave concerning Israel
31:10 "Listen to this **m** from the LORD, you nations of
32: 1 The following **m** came to Jeremiah from the
32: 6 At that time the LORD sent me a **m**. He said,
32: 8 Then I knew for sure that the **m** I had heard was
32:26 Then this **m** came to Jeremiah from the LORD:
33: 1 of the guard, the LORD gave him this second **m**:
33:19 Then this **m** came to Jeremiah from the LORD:
33:23 The LORD gave another **m** to Jeremiah. He said,
34: 1 At that time this **m** came to Jeremiah from the
34: 6 So Jeremiah the prophet delivered the **m** to King
34: 8 This **m** came to Jeremiah from the LORD after
34:12 So the LORD gave them this **m** through
35: 1 This is the **m** the LORD gave Jeremiah when
35:12 Then the LORD gave this **m** to Jeremiah:
36: 1 in Judah, the LORD gave this **m** to Jeremiah:
36: 2 Begin with the first **m** back in the days of Josiah,
36: 2 and write down every **m** you have given, right up
36:27 the LORD gave Jeremiah another **m**.
37: 6 Then the LORD gave this **m** to Jeremiah:
39:15 The LORD had given the following **m** to
40: 1 The LORD gave a **m** to Jeremiah after
43: 1 When Jeremiah had finished giving this **m** from
43: 8 the LORD gave another **m** to Jeremiah.
44: 1 This is the **m** Jeremiah received concerning the
44:24 the women, "Listen to this **m** from the LORD,
44:26 "But listen to this **m** from the LORD, all you
45: 1 The prophet Jeremiah gave a **m** to Baruch son of
46: 2 This **m** concerning Egypt was given in the fourth
46:13 Then the LORD gave the prophet Jeremiah this **m**
47: 1 This is the LORD's **m** to the prophet Jeremiah
48: 1 This **m** was given concerning Moab. This is what
49: 1 This **m** was given concerning the Ammonites.
49: 7 This **m** was given concerning Edom. This is what
49:14 I have heard a **m** from the LORD that an
49:23 This **m** was given concerning Damascus. This is
49:28 This **m** was given concerning Kedar
49:34 This **m** concerning Elam came to the prophet
50: 1 The LORD gave Jeremiah the prophet this **m**
51:59 The prophet Jeremiah gave this **m** to Zedekiah's
Eze 1: 3 The LORD gave a **m** to me, Ezekiel son of Buzi,
3: 1 Then go and give its **m** to the people of Israel."
3:16 end of the seven days, the LORD gave me a **m**.
3:17 Whenever you receive a **m** from me, pass it on to
3:27 But whenever I give you a **m**, I will loosen your
6: 1 Again a **m** came to me from the LORD:
6: 3 Give the mountains of Israel this **m** from the
7: 1 Then this **m** came to me from the LORD:
11:14 Then this **m** came to me from the LORD:
11:16 give the exiles this **m** from the Sovereign LORD:
12: 1 Again a **m** came to me from the LORD:
12: 8 The next morning this **m** came to me from the
12:10 These actions contain a **m** for Zedekiah in
12:17 Then this **m** came to me from the LORD:
12:19 Give the people this **m** from the Sovereign LORD
12:21 Again a **m** came to me from the LORD:
12:23 Give the people this **m** from the Sovereign
12:26 Then this **m** came to me from the LORD:
12:28 give them this **m** from the Sovereign LORD:
13: 1 Then this **m** came to me from the LORD:
13: 6 have lied and said, 'My **m** is from the LORD,'
13: 7 false if you claim, 'This **m** is from the LORD,'
14: 2 this **m** came to me from the LORD:
14: 4 Give them this **m** from the Sovereign LORD:
14: 6 give the people of Israel this **m** from the Sovereign
14: 9 if a prophet is deceived and gives a **m** anyway,
14:12 Then this **m** came to me from the LORD:
15: 1 Then this **m** came to me from the LORD:
16: 1 Then another **m** came to me from the LORD:
16: 3 Give her this **m** from the Sovereign LORD:
16:35 you prostitute, listen to this **m** from the LORD!
17: 1 Then this **m** came to me from the LORD:
17: 3 Give them this **m** from the Sovereign LORD:
17:11 Then this **m** came to me from the LORD:
18: 1 Then another **m** came to me from the LORD:
20: 1 some of the leaders of Israel came to request a **m**
20: 2 Then this **m** came to me from the LORD:
20: 3 give the leaders of Israel this **m** from the Sovereign
20: 5 Give them this **m** from the Sovereign LORD:
20:27 give the people of Israel this **m** from the Sovereign
20:30 give the people of Israel this **m** from the Sovereign
20:31 I will not give you a **m** even though you have
20:45 Then this **m** came to me from the LORD:
20:47 Give the southern wilderness this **m** from the
21: 1 Then this **m** came to me from the LORD:
21: 3 Give her this **m** from the LORD: I am your
21: 9 of man, give the people this **m** from the LORD:
21:18 Then this **m** came to me from the LORD:
21:28 Give them this **m** from the Sovereign LORD:
22: 1 Now this **m** came to me from the LORD:
22: 3 and give her this **m** from the Sovereign LORD:
22:17 Then this **m** came to me from the LORD:
22:19 So give them this **m** from the Sovereign LORD:
22:23 Again a **m** came to me from the LORD:
22:24 "Son of man, give the people of Israel this **m**:
22:28 They say, 'My **m** is from the Sovereign LORD,'
23: 1 This **m** came to me from the LORD:
24: 1 this **m** came to me from the LORD:
24: 3 give them a **m** from the Sovereign LORD.
24:15 Then this **m** came to me from the LORD:
24:20 said to them, "A **m** came to me from the LORD,
24:21 and I was told to give this **m** to the people of
25: 1 Then this **m** came to me from the LORD:
25: 3 Give the Ammonites this **m** from the Sovereign
26: 1 this **m** came to me from the LORD:
27: 1 Then this **m** came to me from the LORD:
27: 3 Give Tyre this **m** from the Sovereign LORD:
28: 1 Then this **m** came to me from the LORD:
28: 2 give the prince of Tyre this **m** from the Sovereign
28:11 Then this further **m** came to me from the LORD:
28:12 Give him this **m** from the Sovereign LORD:
28:20 Then another **m** came to me from the LORD:
28:22 Give the people of Sidon this **m** from the
29: 1 this **m** came to me from the LORD:
29: 3 Give them this **m** from the Sovereign LORD:
29:17 this **m** came to me from the LORD:
30: 1 This is another **m** that came to me from the
30: 2 and give this **m** from the Sovereign LORD:
30:20 this **m** came to me from the LORD:
31: 1 this **m** came to me from the LORD:
31: 2 "Son of man, give this **m** to Pharaoh, king of
32: 1 this **m** came to me from the LORD:
32: 2 for Pharaoh, king of Egypt, and give him this **m**:
32:17 another **m** came to me from the LORD:
33: 1 Once again a **m** came to me from the LORD:
33: 2 "Son of man, give your people this **m**: When I
33:10 "Son of man, give the people of Israel this **m**:
33:12 "Son of man, give your people this **m**: The good
33:23 Then this **m** came to me from the LORD:
33:25 Now give these people this **m** from the Sovereign
33:27 "Give them this **m** from the Sovereign LORD:
34: 1 Then this **m** came to me from the LORD:
34: 2 Give them this **m** from the Sovereign LORD:
35: 1 Again a **m** came to me from the LORD:
35: 3 Give them this **m** from the Sovereign LORD:
36: 1 Give them this **m**: O mountains of Israel,
36: 3 give the mountains of Israel this **m** from the
36: 6 Give them this **m** from the Sovereign LORD:
36:16 Then this further **m** came to me from the LORD:
36:22 give the people of Israel this **m** from the Sovereign
37:12 Now give them this **m** from the Sovereign
37:15 Again a **m** came to me from the LORD:
37:21 And give them this **m** from the Sovereign LORD:
38: 1 This is another **m** that came to me from the
38: 3 Give him this **m** from the Sovereign LORD:
38:14 Give him this **m** from the Sovereign LORD:
39: 1 Give him this **m** from the Sovereign LORD:
44: 6 of Israel, this **m** from the Sovereign LORD:
Da 4: 1 King Nebuchadnezzar sent this **m** to the people of
4:31 "O King Nebuchadnezzar, this **m** is for you!
5:24 So God has sent this hand to write a **m**.
5:25 "This is the **m** that was written: MENE, MENE,
6:25 Then King Darius sent this **m** to the people of
Joel 1: 1 The LORD gave this **m** to Joel son of Pethuel.
Am 1: 1 This **m** was given to Amos, a shepherd from the
1: 1 He received this **m** in visions two years before the
3: 1 Listen to this **m** that the LORD has spoken
3: 8 has spoken—I dare not refuse to proclaim his **m**!
7:10 was saying, he rushed a **m** to King Jeroboam:
7:16 "Now then, listen to this **m** from the LORD!
Ob 1: 1 We have heard a **m** from the LORD that an
Jnh 1: 1 The LORD gave this **m** to Jonah son of Amittai:
3: 2 and deliver the **m** of judgment I have given you."
3: 5 The people of Nineveh believed God's **m**,
Na 1: 1 This **m** concerning Nineveh came as a vision to
1:15 He is bringing a **m** of peace. Celebrate your
Hab 1: 1 This is the **m** that the prophet Habakkuk received
Hag 1: 1 the LORD gave a **m** through the prophet Haggai
1: 3 So the LORD sent this **m** through the prophet
1:12 people obeyed the **m** from the LORD their God.
1:13 gave the people this **m** from the LORD:
2: 1 the LORD sent another **m** through the prophet
2:10 the LORD sent this **m** to the prophet Haggai:
2:20 The LORD sent this second **m** to Haggai on
Zec 1: 1 the LORD gave this **m** to the prophet Zechariah
1: 7 the LORD sent another **m** to the prophet
1:14 the angel said to me, "Shout this **m** for all to hear:
4: 8 Then another **m** came to me from the LORD:
6: 9 Then I received another **m** from the LORD:
7: 1 another **m** came to Zechariah from the LORD.
7: 4 The LORD Almighty sent me this **m**:
7: 7 Isn't this the same **m** the LORD proclaimed
7: 8 Then this **m** came to Zechariah from the LORD:
7:11 "Your ancestors would not listen to this **m**.
8: 1 Then another **m** came to me from the LORD
8:18 Here is another **m** that came to me from the
9: 1 This is the **m** from the LORD against the land of
12: 1 This **m** concerning the fate of Israel came from the
12: 1 "This **m** is from the LORD, who stretched out
Mal 1: 1 This is the **m** that the LORD gave to Israel
Mt 1:22 All of this happened to fulfill the Lord's **m** through
2: 7 Then Herod sent a private **m** to the wise men,
3: 1 preaching in the Judean wilderness. His **m** was,
13:20 The rocky soil represents those who hear the **m**
13:22 but all too quickly the **m** is crowded out by the
13:23 the hearts of those who truly accept God's **m**
27:19 on the judgment seat, his wife sent him this **m**:
28: 8 to find the disciples to give them the angel's **m**.
Mk 4:14 about is the one who brings God's **m** to others.
4:15 on the hard path represents those who hear the **m**,
4:16 The rocky soil represents those who hear the **m**
4:19 but all too quickly the **m** is crowded out by the
4:20 and accept God's **m** and produce a huge harvest—
5:35 messengers arrived from Jairus' home with the **m**,
8:38 and my **m** in these adulterous and sinful days,
16: 7 Now go and give this **m** to his disciples,
16: S and unfailing **m** of salvation that gives eternal life.
Lk 3: 2 At this time a **m** from God came to John son of
8:11 is the meaning of the story: The seed is God's **m**.
8:12 on the hard path represents those who hear the **m**,
8:13 The rocky soil represents those who hear the **m**
8:14 represents those who hear and accept the **m**,
8:14 but all too quickly the **m** is crowded out by the
8:15 good-hearted people who hear God's **m**, cling to it,
8:21 and my brothers are all those who hear the **m** of
8:49 a messenger arrived from Jairus' home with the **m**,
9: 5 If the people of the village won't receive your **m**
9:26 If a person is ashamed of me and my **m**, I, the Son
10:16 "Anyone who accepts your **m** is also accepting
24:47 take this **m** of repentance to all the nations,
Jn 4:41 long enough for many of them to hear his **m**
5:24 those who listen to my **m** and believe in God who
5:38 and you do not have his **m** in your hearts,
8:37 because my **m** does not find a place in your hearts.
10:35 So if those people, who received God's **m**,
11: 3 So the two sisters sent a **m** to Jesus telling him,
12:38 "Lord, who has believed our **m**? / To whom will
12:48 and my **m** will be judged at the day of judgment by
14:24 my own. This **m** is from the Father who sent me.
15: 3 for greater fruitfulness by the **m** I have given you.
20:18 have seen the Lord!" Then she gave them his **m**.
Ac 4: 4 But many of the people who heard their **m**
4:31 And they preached God's **m** with boldness.
5:20 to the Temple and give the people this **m** of life!"
5:42 they continued to teach and preach this **m**:
6: 7 God's **m** was preached in ever-widening circles.
8:12 But now the people believed Philip's **m** of Good
8:14 that the people of Samaria had accepted God's **m**,
9:15 For Saul is my chosen instrument to take my **m** to
10:22 so you can go to his house and give him a **m**."
10:33 waiting before God to hear the **m** the Lord has
10:44 the Holy Spirit fell upon all who had heard the **m**.
13:15 those in charge of the service sent them this **m**:
13:48 were very glad and thanked the Lord for his **m**;
13:49 So the Lord's **m** spread throughout that region.
14: 2 But the Jews who spurned God's **m** stirred up
14: 3 The Lord proved their **m** was true by giving them
15:31 church that day as they read this encouraging **m**.
17:11 and they listened eagerly to Paul's **m**.
17:15 then they returned to Berea with a **m** for Silas
19: 9 But some rejected his **m** and publicly spoke
19:10 both Jews and Greeks—heard the Lord's **m**.
19:20 So the **m** about the Lord spread widely and had a
19:31 the province, friends of Paul, also sent a **m** to him,
20:17 he sent a **m** to the elders of the church at Ephesus,
20:21 I have had one **m** for Jews and Gentiles alike—
20:32 his **m** that is able to build you up and give you an
22:15 You are to take his **m** everywhere,
Ro 2:16 will judge everyone's secret life. This is my **m**.
9:11 anything good or bad, she received a **m** from God.
9:11 (This **m** proves that God chooses according to his
10: 8 which is the **m** we preach—is already within easy
10: 8 the Scriptures say, "The **m** is close at hand;
10:16 prophet said, "Lord, who has believed our **m**?"
10:17 Yet faith comes from listening to this **m** of Good
10:18 Have they actually heard the **m**? Yes, they have:
10:18 "The **m** of God's creation has gone out to
15:18 I have brought the Gentiles to God by my **m**
16:25 It is the **m** about Jesus Christ and his plan for you
16:26 this **m** is made known to all Gentiles everywhere,
1Co 1:18 I know very well how foolish the **m** of the cross
1:18 But we who are being saved recognize this **m** as
2: 1 lofty words and brilliant ideas to tell you God's **m**.
2: 4 And my **m** and my preaching were very plain.
15: 1 do now, for your faith is built on this wonderful **m**.
2Co 2:17 We preach God's **m** with sincerity and with
4: 4 They don't understand the **m** we preach about the
5:19 This is the wonderful **m** he has given us to tell
6: 1 we beg you not to reject this marvelous **m** of
12: 6 what they can actually see in my life and my **m**,
Gal 1: 8 who preaches any other **m** than the one we told
1: 8 comes from heaven and preaches any other **m**,
1:12 For my **m** came by a direct revelation from Jesus
3: 2 after you believed the **m** you heard about Christ.
3: 5 because you believe the **m** you heard about Christ.
Eph 6:20 I am in chains now for preaching this **m** as God's
Php 1:18 the fact remains that the **m** about Christ is being
Col 1:25 his **m** in all its fullness to you Gentiles.
1:26 This **m** was kept secret for centuries
4: 4 Pray that I will proclaim this **m** as clearly as I
1Th 1: 5 among you was further proof of the truth of our **m**.
1: 6 So you received the **m** with joy from the Holy
2:13 thanking God that when we preached his **m** to you,
2Th 3: 1 Pray first that the Lord's **m** will spread rapidly
1Ti 2: 6 This is the **m** that God gave to the world at the
4: 6 one who is fed by the **m** of faith and the true
Tit 1: 9 and steadfast belief in the trustworthy **m** he was
Heb 2: 2 The **m** God delivered through angels has always
2: 4 and God verified the **m** by signs and wonders
12:19 an awesome trumpet blast and a voice with a **m**
Jas 1:21 and humbly accept the **m** God has planted in your
1:22 And remember, it is a **m** to obey, not just to listen

2Pe 1:19 we have even greater confidence in the **m**
1Jn 1: 5 This is the **m** he has given us to announce to you:
2: 7 love one another—is the same **m** you heard before.
3:11 This is the **m** we have heard from the beginning:
Rev 2: 1 This is the **m** from the one who holds the seven
2: 8 This is the **m** from the one who is the First
2:12 This is the **m** from the one who has a sharp
2:18 This is the **m** from the Son of God, whose eyes are
2:24 But I also have a **m** for the rest of you in Thyatira
3: 1 This is the **m** from the one who has the sevenfold
3: 7 This is the **m** from the one who is holy and true.
3:14 This is the **m** from the one who is the Amen—
22:16 have sent my angel to give you this **m** for the

MESSAGES (43) [MESSAGE]

Ge 45:27 But when they had given him Joseph's **m**,
Nu 22:38 I will speak only the **m** that God gives me."
Dt 18:19 listen to the **m** the prophet proclaims on my behalf.
Jos 11: 1 he sent urgent **m** to the following kings:
1Sa 3: 1 Now in those days **m** from the LORD were very
3:21 and gave **m** to Samuel there at the Tabernacle.
1Ch 13: 2 let us send **m** to all the Israelites throughout the
25: 1 and Jeduthun to proclaim God's **m** to the
25: 2 who proclaimed God's **m** by the king's orders.
25: 3 who proclaimed God's **m** to the accompaniment of
Jer 1: 2 The LORD first gave **m** to Jeremiah during the
1: 3 He continued to give **m** throughout the reign of
5:14 I will give you **m** that will burn them up as if they
14:14 or tell them to speak. I did not give them any **m**.
20: 8 So these **m** from the LORD have made me a
23:30 "I stand against these prophets who get their **m**
25: 3 until now—the LORD has been giving me his **m**.
27: 3 Then send **m** to the kings of Edom, Moab,
36: 2 and write down all my **m** against Israel, Judah,
36: 6 and read the **m** from the LORD that are on this
36: 8 and read these **m** from the LORD to the people at
36:11 and grandson of Shaphan heard the **m** from the
36:13 When Micaiah told them about the **m** Baruch was
36:14 to ask Baruch to come and read the **m** to them,
36:17 "But first, tell us how you got these **m**. Did they
37:17 "Do you have any **m** from the LORD?"
44:16 "We will not listen to your **m** from the LORD!
46: 1 The following **m** were given to Jeremiah the
51:64 upon her.' " This is the end of Jeremiah's **m**.
Eze 2: 7 You must give them my **m** whether they listen
3: 4 of man, go to the people of Israel with my **m**.
22:28 prophets announce false visions and speak false **m**.
Da 3: 2 Then he sent **m** to the princes, prefects, governors,
9: 6 who spoke your **m** to our kings and princes
Hos 1: 1 The LORD gave these **m** to Hosea son of Beeri
Mic 1: 1 The LORD gave these **m** to Micah of Moresheth
1: 1 The **m** concerned both Samaria and Jerusalem,
3: 7 And you will admit that your **m** were not from
Zep 1: 1 The LORD gave these **m** to Zephaniah when
Zec 6:15 you will know my **m** have been from the LORD
7:12 or the **m** that the LORD Almighty had sent them
Lk 4:17 The scroll containing the **m** of Isaiah the prophet
16:16 and the **m** of the prophets were your guides.

MESSENGER (46) [MESSAGE]

1Sa 4:13 When the **m** arrived and told what had happened,
4:14 noise about?" Eli asked. The **m** rushed over to Eli,
4:17 "Israel has been defeated," the **m** replied.
4:18 When the **m** mentioned what had happened to the
2Sa 11:19 He told his **m**, "Report all the news of the battle to
11:22 So the **m** went to Jerusalem and gave a complete
15:13 A **m** soon arrived in Jerusalem to tell King David,
18:20 You can be my **m** some other time, but not today."
18:25 he is alone, he has news." As the **m** came closer,
1Ki 22:13 the **m** who went to get Micaiah said to him,
2Ki 5:10 But Elisha sent a **m** out to him with this message:
6:32 of Israel when the king sent a **m** to summon him.
6:32 But before the **m** arrived, Elisha said to the leaders,
6:33 While Elisha was still saying this, the **m** arrived.
10: 8 A **m** went to Jehu and said, "They have brought
2Ch 18:12 the **m** who went to get Micaiah said to him,
Job 1:14 a **m** arrived at Job's home with this news:
1:16 still speaking, another **m** arrived with this news:
1:17 still speaking, a third **m** arrived with this news:
1:18 still speaking, another **m** arrived with this news:
33:23 "But if a special **m** from heaven is there to
Pr 13:17 An unreliable **m** stumbles into trouble, but a
reliable **m** brings healing.
Ecc 5: 6 And don't defend yourself by telling the Temple **m**
Isa 6: 8 "Whom should I send as a **m** to my people?
40: 9 **M** of good news, shout to Zion from the
Jer 20:15 I curse the **m** who told my father, "Good news—
Da 4:13 I saw a **m**, a holy one, coming down from heaven.
4:14 The **m** shouted, "Cut down the tree; lop off its
4:23 "Then you saw a **m**, a holy one, coming down
Na 1:15 A **m** is coming over the mountains with good
Hag 1:13 Then Haggai, the LORD's **m**, gave the people
Mal 3: 1 I am sending my **m**, and he will prepare the way
3: 1 The **m** of the covenant, whom you look for
Mt 11:10 they say, / 'Look, I am sending my **m** before you,
Mk 1: 2 God said, / "Look, I am sending my **m** before you,
1: 4 This **m** was John the Baptist. He lived in the
Lk 7:27 they say, / 'Look, I am sending my **m** before you,
8:49 a **m** arrived from Jairus' home with the message,
Jn 13:20 anyone who welcomes my **m** is welcoming me,
Ro 12: 3 As God's **m**, I give each of you this warning:
15:16 a special **m** from Christ Jesus to you Gentiles.
2Co 12: 7 a **m** from Satan to torment me and keep me from
Php 2:25 And he was your **m** to help me in my need.
Heb 3: 1 about this Jesus whom we declare to be God's **M**
12:25 the earthly **m**, how terrible our danger if we reject

MESSENGERS (88) [MESSAGE]

Ge 32: 3 Jacob now sent **m** to his brother, Esau, in Edom,
32: 5 I have sent these **m** to inform you of my coming,
32: 6 The **m** returned with the news that Esau was on his
Nu 22: 5 sent **m** to Balaam son of Beor, who was living in
22: 7 Balak's **m**, officials of both Moab and Midian,
24:12 "Don't you remember what I told your **m**?
Jos 10: 3 So King Adoni-zedek of Jerusalem sent **m** to
10: 6 The men of Gibeon quickly sent **m** to Joshua at
Jdg 6:35 He also sent **m** throughout Manasseh, Asher,
7:24 Gideon also sent **m** throughout the hill country of
9:31 He sent **m** to Abimelech in Arumah, telling him,
11:12 Then Jephthah sent **m** to the king of Ammon,
11:13 The king of Ammon answered Jephthah's **m**,
11:17 they sent **m** to the king of Edom asking for
11:19 "Then Israel sent **m** to King Sihon of the
20:12 The Israelites sent **m** to the tribe of Benjamin,
1Sa 6:21 So they sent **m** to the people at Kiriath-jearim
11: 3 "Give us seven days to send **m** throughout
11: 4 When the **m** came to Gibeah, Saul's hometown,
11: 7 and sent the **m** to carry them throughout Israel with
11: 9 So Saul sent the **m** back to Jabesh-gilead to say,
16:19 So Saul sent **m** to Jesse to say, "Send me your son
25:12 So David's **m** returned and told him what Nabal
25:25 But I never even saw the **m** you sent.
25:39 Then David wasted no time in sending **m** to
25:40 When the **m** arrived at Carmel, they told Abigail,
25:42 mounted her donkey, and went with David's **m**.
26: 1 Now some **m** from Ziph came back to Saul at
2Sa 3:12 Then Abner sent **m** to David, saying, "Let's make
3:26 then left David and sent **m** to catch up with Abner.
5:11 Then King Hiram of Tyre sent **m** to David,
10: 5 he sent **m** to tell the men to stay at Jericho until
12:27 Joab sent **m** to tell David, "I have fought against
15:10 he sent secret **m** to every part of Israel to stir up a
1Ki 20: 2 Ben-hadad sent **m** into the city to relay this
20: 5 Soon Ben-hadad's **m** returned again and said,
20: 9 So Ahab told the **m** from Ben-hadad, "Say this to
20: 9 So the **m** returned to Ben-hadad with the response.
2Ki 1: 2 So he sent **m** to the temple of Baal-zebub, the god
1: 3 "Go and meet the **m** of the king of Samaria
1: 5 When the **m** returned to the king, he asked them,
1:16 Why did you send **m** to Baal-zebub, the god of
10:21 He sent **m** throughout all Israel summoning those
16: 7 King Ahaz sent **m** to King Tiglath-pileser of
19: 6 speech against me from the Assyrian king's **m**.
19:23 By your **m** you have mocked the Lord. / You have
1Ch 14: 1 Now King Hiram of Tyre sent **m** to David,
19: 5 he sent **m** to tell the men to stay at Jericho until
2Ch 20: 2 **M** came and told Jehoshaphat, "A vast army from
30: 6 **m** were sent throughout Israel and Judah.
30:10 The **m** went from town to town throughout
30:10 But most of the people just laughed at the **m**
36:16 But the people mocked these **m** of God
Est 3:13 and sent by **m** into all the provinces of the empire.
3:15 the decree went out by the swiftest **m**,
8:10 He sent the letters by swift **m**, who rode horses
8:14 the **m** rode out swiftly on horses bred for the
Ps 104: 4 The winds are your **m**; / flames of fire are your
Pr 25:13 Faithful **m** are as refreshing as snow in the heat of
Isa 14:32 What should we tell the enemy **m**? Tell them that
18: 2 Go home, swift **m**! Take a message to your land
37: 6 speech against me from the Assyrian king's **m**.
37:24 By your **m** you have mocked the Lord. / You have
42:19 own people, my servant? Who is as deaf as my **m**?
66:19 And I will send those who survive to be **m** to the
Jer 23:28 but let my true **m** faithfully proclaim my every
39:14 sent **m** to bring Jeremiah out of the prison.
51:31 **M** from every side come running to the king to tell
Eze 23:16 so she sent **m** to Babylonia to invite them to come
23:40 "You sisters sent **m** to distant lands to get men.
30: 9 At that time I will send swift **m** in ships to terrify
Da 4:17 For this has been decreed by the **m**; it is
Na 2:13 Never again will the voices of your proud **m** be
Mal 2: 7 for the priests are the **m** of the LORD Almighty.
Mt 22: 6 Others seized his **m** and treated them shamefully,
23:37 the city that kills the prophets and stones God's **m**!
Mk 5:35 **m** arrived from Jairus' home with the message,
Lk 9:52 He sent **m** ahead to a Samaritan village to prepare
13:34 the city that kills the prophets and stones God's **m**!
Jn 5:33 In fact, you sent **m** to listen to John the Baptist,
13:16 Nor are **m** more important than the one who sends
Ac 10: 9 The next day as Cornelius' **m** were nearing the
11:13 told him, 'Send **m** to Joppa to find Simon Peter.
15:30 The four **m** went at once to Antioch, where they
1Co 16: 3 the **m** you choose to deliver your gift to Jerusalem.
1Th 2: 4 For we speak as **m** who have been approved by
Heb 1: 7 God calls his angels / "**m** swift as the wind,
Jas 2:25 when she hid those **m** and sent them safely away

MESSIAH (88) [CHRIST, MESSIAH'S, MESSIAHS]

Mt 1: 1 This is a record of the ancestors of Jesus the **M**,
1:16 was the mother of Jesus, who is called the **M**.
1:17 and fourteen from the Babylonian exile to the **M**.
1:18 Now this is how Jesus the **M** was born.
2: 4 "Where did the prophets say the **M** would be
2:23 was spoken by the prophets concerning the **M**:
11: 2 heard about all the things the **M** was doing.
11: 3 "Are you really the **M** we've been waiting for,
12:23 it be that Jesus is the Son of David, the **M**?"
16:16 Simon Peter answered, "You are the **M**, the Son of
16:20 warned them not to tell anyone that he was the **M**.
17:10 that Elijah must return before the **M** comes?"
22:42 "What do you think about the **M**? Whose son is
23:10 you 'Master,' for there is only one master, the **M**.
24: 5 many will come in my name, saying, 'I am the **M**.'
24:23 'Look, here is the **M**,' or 'There he is,' don't pay
24:26 'Look, the **M** is out in the desert,' don't bother to
26:63 living God that you tell us whether you are the **M**,
26:68 saying, "Prophesy to us, you **M**! Who hit you that
27:17 to you—Barabbas, or Jesus who is called the **M**?"
27:22 should I do with Jesus who is called the **M**?"
Mk 1: 1 Here begins the Good News about Jesus the **M**,
8:29 you say I am?" Peter replied, "You are the **M**."
9:11 that Elijah must return before the **M** comes?"
9:41 even a cup of water because you belong to the **M**,
12:35 law claim that the **M** will be the son of David?
13: 6 many will come in my name, claiming to be the **M**.
13:21 'Look, here is the **M**,' or, 'There he is,' don't pay
14:61 "Are you the **M**, the Son of the blessed God?"
15:32 Let this **M**, this king of Israel, come down from the
Lk 2:11 The Savior—yes, the **M**, the Lord—has been born
2:25 and he eagerly expected the **M** to come and rescue
2:26 he would not die until he had seen the Lord's **M**.
3:15 Everyone was expecting the **M** to come soon,
3:15 were eager to know whether John might be the **M**.
4:41 But because they knew he was the **M**, he stopped
7:19 to ask him, "Are you the **M** we've been expecting,
7:20 us to ask, 'Are you the **M** we've been expecting,
9:20 Peter replied, "You are the **M** sent from God!"
20:41 "that the **M** is said to be the son of David?
21: 8 claiming to be the **M** and saying, 'The time has
22:67 and they said, "Tell us if you are the **M**." But he
23: 2 Roman government and by claiming he is the **M**,
23:35 himself if he is really God's Chosen One, the **M**."
23:39 beside him scoffed, "So you're the **M**, are you?
24:21 We had thought he was the **M** who had come to
24:26 **M** would have to suffer all these things before
24:46 it was written long ago that the **M** must suffer
Jn 1:19 to ask John whether he claimed to be the **M**.
1:20 He flatly denied it. "I am not the **M**," he said.
1:25 "If you aren't the **M** or Elijah or the Prophet,
1:41 "We have found the **M**" (which means the
2:23 people were convinced that he was indeed the **M**.
3:26 the one you said was the **M**, is also baptizing
3:28 know how plainly I told you that I am not the **M**.
4:25 The woman said, "I know the **M** will come—
4:26 Then Jesus told her, "I am the **M**!"
4:29 told me everything I ever did! Can this be the **M**?"
7:26 it be that our leaders know that he really is the **M**?
7:27 When the **M** comes, he will simply appear; no one
7:31 "would you expect the **M** to do more miraculous
7:41 Others said, "He is the **M**." Still others said,
7:41 "But he can't be! Will the **M** come from Galilee?
7:42 For the Scriptures clearly state that the **M** will be
9:22 was the **M** would be expelled from the synagogue.
10:24 us in suspense? If you are the **M**, tell us plainly."
11:27 "I have always believed you are the **M**, the Son of
12:34 "We understood from Scripture that the **M** would
13:19 that when it happens you will believe I am the **M**.
20:31 so that you may believe that Jesus is the **M**,
Ac 2:30 descendants would sit on David's throne as the **M**.
2:31 He was saying that the **M** would not be left among
2:36 whom you crucified to be both Lord and **M**!"
3:18 prophets had declared about the **M** beforehand—
3:20 and he will send Jesus your **M** to you again.
4:26 against the Lord / and against his **M**.'
5:42 "The **M** you are looking for is Jesus."
7:52 the **M** whom you betrayed and murdered.
8: 5 of Samaria and told the people there about the **M**.
9:22 refute his proofs that Jesus was indeed the **M**.
13:25 his ministry he asked, 'Do you think I am the **M**?
17: 3 the prophecies about the sufferings of the **M**
17: 3 "This Jesus I'm telling you about is the **M**."
18: 5 "The **M** you are looking for is Jesus."
18:28 to them, "The **M** you are looking for is Jesus."
26:23 that the **M** would suffer and be the first to rise
28:20 the hope of Israel—the **M**—has already come."
Heb 11:26 sake of the **M** than to own the treasures of Egypt,

MESSIAH'S (2) [MESSIAH]

Jn 12:41 because he was given a vision of the **M** glory.
Ac 2:31 into the future and predicting the **M** resurrection.

MESSIAHS (2) [MESSIAH]

Mt 24:24 For false **m** and false prophets will rise up
Mk 13:22 For false **m** and false prophets will rise up

MET (63) [MEET]

Ge 31:13 I am the God you **m** at Bethel, the place where you
33: 8 what were all the flocks and herds I **m** as I came?"
38: 2 There he **m** a Canaanite woman, the daughter of
Ex 3:18 the God of the Hebrews, has **m** with us.
5: 3 "The God of the Hebrews has **m** with us,"
5:14 "Why haven't you **m** your quotas either yesterday
5:20 left Pharaoh's court, they **m** Moses and Aaron,
Nu 23: 4 and God **m** him there. Balaam said to him, "I have
23:16 So the LORD **m** Balaam and gave him a
1Sa 8: 4 the leaders of Israel **m** at Ramah to discuss the
9:11 they **m** some young women coming out to draw
13: 4 army mobilized again and **m** Saul at Gilgal.
18: 1 talking with Saul, he **m** Jonathan, the king's son.
29: 6 "you are some of the finest men I've ever **m**.
30:21 and **m** the two hundred men who had been too
2Sa 2:13 and they **m** Abner at the pool of Gibeon.
20: 8 Amasa **m** them, coming from the opposite
1Ki 10: 2 When she **m** with Solomon, they talked about
11:29 the prophet Ahijah from Shiloh **m** him on the road,
2Ki 9:18 "The rider has **m** them, but he is not returning."

9:20 The watchman exclaimed, "The rider has **m** them,
9:21 They **m** him at the field that had belonged to
10:13 he **m** some relatives of King Ahaziah of Judah.
10:15 Jehu left there, he **m** Jehonadab son of Recab,
23:29 but King Neco killed him when they **m** at
2Ch 9:2 When she **m** with Solomon, they talked about
12:5 then **m** with Rehoboam and Judah's leaders,
20:37 So the ships **m** with disaster and never put out to
Ne 8:13 and Levites **m** with Ezra to go over the law in
Ps 9:6 My enemies have **m** their doom; / their cities are
85:10 Unfailing love and truth have **m** together.
Hos 12:4 There at Bethel he **m** God face to face, and God
Mt 8:28 two men who were possessed by demons **m** him.
22:15 Then the Pharisees **m** together to think of a way to
27:1 and other leaders **m** again to discuss how to
28:9 And as they went, Jesus **m** them. "Greetings!"
Mk 3:6 and **m** with the supporters of Herod to discuss
6:12 went out, telling all they **m** to turn from their sins.
6:33 ahead along the shore and **m** them as they landed.
15:1 entire high council—**m** to discuss their next step.
Lk 5:12 Jesus **m** a man with an advanced case of leprosy.
9:37 come down the mountain, a huge crowd **m** Jesus.
Jn 3:26 the man you **m** on the other side of the Jordan
4:51 some of his servants **m** him with the news that his
7:50 the leader who had **m** with Jesus earlier,
11:30 the village, at the place where Martha **m** him.
Ac 1:14 They all **m** together continually for prayer,
2:44 And all the believers **m** together constantly
2:46 **m** in homes for the Lord's Supper, and shared their
4:5 and teachers of religious law **m** in Jerusalem.
8:27 So he did, and he **m** the treasurer of Ethiopia,
9:33 There he **m** a man named Aeneas, who had been
13:6 where they **m** a Jewish sorcerer, a false prophet
16:1 There they **m** Timothy, a young disciple whose
16:13 where we supposed that some people **m** for prayer,
16:16 of prayer, we **m** a demon-possessed slave girl.
16:40 where they **m** with the believers and encouraged
20:8 The upstairs room where we **m** was lighted with
25:2 and other Jewish leaders **m** with him
2Co 8:14 need it. In this way, everyone's needs will be **m**.
9:12 the needs of the Christians in Jerusalem will be **m**,
Gal 1:19 And the only other apostle I **m** at that time was
Heb 7:1 many kings, Melchizedek **m** him and blessed him.

METAL (11) [METALS, METALWORKERS]

Ge 4:22 He was the first to work with **m**,
Ex 27:4 a bronze grating, with a **m** ring at each corner.
32:20 And when the **m** had cooled, he ground it into
Lev 19:4 trust in idols or make gods of **m** for yourselves.
Nu 16:38 then hammer the **m** of the incense burners into a
16:39 and they were hammered out into a sheet of **m** to
31:23 These **m** objects must then be further purified with
2Ki 17:16 LORD their God and made two calves from **m**.
Isa 48:5 and **m** god commanded it to happen!'
Jer 9:7 I will melt them in a crucible and test them like **m**.
Mal 3:2 For he will be like a blazing fire that refines **m**

METALS (3) [METAL]

Nu 31:23 that is, **m** that do not burn—must be passed
Ps 68:31 Let Egypt come with gifts of precious **m**;
Jer 6:27 "Jeremiah, I have made you a tester of **m**, that you

METALWORKERS (1) [METAL]

2Ch 24:12 They also hired **m**, who made articles of iron

METEYARD [KJV] See MEASURING

METHODS (3)

Ro 11:33 it is for us to understand his decisions and his **m**!
2Co 4:2 We reject all shameful and underhanded **m**. We do
10:3 but we don't wage war with human plans and **m**.

METHUSELAH (7)

Ge 5:21 Enoch was 65 years old, his son **M** was born.
5:22 After the birth of **M**, Enoch lived another 300
5:25 When **M** was 187 years old, his son Lamech was
5:26 **M** lived another 782 years, and he had other sons
1Ch 1:3 Enoch, **M**, Lamech,
Lk 3:37 Lamech was the son of **M**. / **M** was the son of Enoch.

METHUSHAEL (2)

Ge 4:18 Mehujael was the father of **M**. / **M** was the father

MEUNIM (2)

Ezr 2:50 Asnah, **M**, Nephusim,
Ne 7:52 Besai, **M**, Nephusim,

MEUNITES (4)

1Ch 4:41 homes of the descendants of Ham and of the **M**.
2Ch 20:1 and some of the **M** declared war on Jehoshaphat.
26:7 with the Arabs of Gur and in his wars with the **M**.
26:8 The **M** paid annual tribute to him, and his fame

MEZAHAB (1)

Ge 36:39 the daughter of Matred and granddaughter of **M**.

MIAMIN [KJV] See MIJAMIN

MIBHAR (1)

1Ch 11:38 Joel, the brother of Nathan; / **M** son of Hagri;

MIBSAM (3)

Ge 25:13 was Nebaioth, followed by Kedar, Abdeel, **M**,
1Ch 1:29 were Nebaioth (the oldest), Kedar, Adbeel, **M**,
4:25 of Shaul were Shallum, **M**, and Mishma.

MIBZAR (2)

Ge 36:42 Kenaz, Teman, **M**,
1Ch 1:53 Kenaz, Teman, **M**,

MICA (5)

2Sa 9:12 Mephibosheth had a young son named **M**.
1Ch 9:15 Mattaniah son of **M**, son of Zicri, son of Asaph;
Ne 10:11 **M**, Rehob, Hashabiah,
11:17 Mattaniah son of **M**, son of Zabdi, a descendant of
11:22 son of Hashabiah, son of Mattaniah, son of **M**,

MICAH (23) [MICAH'S]

Jdg 17:1 A man named **M** lived in the hill country of
17:5 **M** set up a shrine, and he made a sacred ephod
17:9 **M** asked him. And he replied, "I am a Levite from
17:10 "Stay here with me," **M** said, "and you can be a
17:12 So **M** ordained the Levite as his personal priest,
17:13 "I know the LORD will bless me now," **M** said,
18:4 He told them about his agreement with **M** and that
18:13 country of Ephraim and came to the house of **M**.
18:22 **M** and some of his neighbors came chasing after
18:24 "What do you mean, What do I want?" **M** replied.
18:26 When **M** saw that there were too many of them for
1Ch 5:5 **M**, Reaiah, Baal,
8:34 of Meribbaal. Meribbaal was the father of **M**.
8:35 **M** was the father of Pithon, Melech, Tahrea,
9:40 of Meribbaal. Meribbaal was the father of **M**.
9:41 The sons of **M** were Pithon, Melech, Tahrea,
23:20 The descendants of Uzziel included **M** (the family
24:24 From the descendants of Uzziel, the leader was **M**.
24:24 From the descendants of **M**, the leader was
24:25 along with Isshiah, the brother of **M**.
Jer 26:18 "Think back to the days when **M** of Moresheth
Mic 1:1 The LORD gave these messages to **M** of
1:1 and they came to **M** in the form of visions.

MICAH'S (11) [MICAH]

Jdg 17:4 and an idol. And these were placed in **M** house.
17:8 He happened to stop at **M** house as he was
17:11 agreed to this and became like one of **M** sons.
17:12 as his personal priest, and he lived in **M** house.
18:2 they came to **M** home and spent the night there.
18:4 with Micah and that he was **M** personal priest.
18:15 So the five men went over to **M** house,
18:18 carrying all the sacred objects out of **M** shrine,
18:22 tribe of Dan were quite a distance from **M** home,
18:27 Then, with **M** idols and his priest, the men of Dan
18:31 So **M** carved image was worshiped by the tribe of

MICAIAH (33)

1Ki 22:8 bad news for me! His name is **M** son of Imlah."
22:9 and said, "Quick! Go and get **M** son of Imlah."
22:13 the messenger who went to get **M** said to him,
22:14 But **M** replied, "As surely as the LORD lives,
22:15 When **M** arrived before the king, Ahab asked him, "**M**,
22:15 And **M** replied, "Go right ahead!
22:17 So **M** told him, "In a vision I saw all Israel
22:19 Then **M** continued, "Listen to what the LORD
22:24 Then Zedekiah son of Kenaanah walked up to **M**
22:25 And **M** replied, "You will find out soon enough
22:26 "Arrest **M** and take him back to Amon,
22:28 But **M** replied, "If you return safely, the LORD
2Ki 22:12 Ahikam son of Shaphan, Acbor son of **M**,
2Ch 17:7 Obadiah, Zechariah, Nethanel, and **M**.
18:7 bad news for me! His name is **M** son of Imlah."
18:8 and said, "Quick! Go and get **M** son of Imlah."
18:12 the messenger who went to get **M** said to him,
18:13 But **M** replied, "As surely as the LORD lives,
18:14 When **M** arrived before the king, Ahab asked him, "**M**,
18:14 And **M** replied, "Go right ahead!
18:16 So **M** told him, "In a vision I saw all Israel
18:18 Then **M** continued, "Listen to what the LORD
18:23 Then Zedekiah son of Kenaanah walked up to **M**
18:24 And **M** replied, "You will find out soon enough,
18:25 "Arrest **M** and take him back to Amon,
18:27 But **M** replied, "If you return safely, the LORD
34:20 Ahikam son of Shaphan, Acbor son of **M**,
Ne 12:35 son of Mattaniah, son of **M**, son of Zaccur,
12:41 Eliakim, Maaseiah, Miniamin, **M**, Elioenai,
Jer 36:11 When **M** son of Gemariah and grandson of
36:13 When **M** told them about the messages Baruch was

MICHA [KJV] See MICA

MICHAEL (17)

Nu 13:13 Asher | Sethur son of **M**
1Ch 5:13 were **M**, Meshullam, Sheba, Jorai, Jacan, Zia,
5:14 son of Jaroah, son of Gilead, son of **M**, son of
6:40 **M**, Baaseiah, Malkijah,
7:3 The sons of Izrahiah were **M**, Obadiah, Joel,
8:16 **M**, Ishpah, and Joha were the sons of Beriah.
12:20 Adnah, Jozabad, Jediael, **M**, Jozabad, Elihu,
27:18 (a brother of David) / Issachar | Omri son of **M**
2Ch 21:2 were Azariah, Jehiel, Zechariah, Azariahu, **M**,
Ezr 8:8 Zebadiah son of **M** and 80 other men.
Da 10:13 Then **M**, one of the archangels, came to help me,
10:21 to help me against these spirit princes except **M**,
11:1 I have been standing beside **M** as his support
12:1 "At that time **M**, the archangel who stands guard
Jude 1:9 But even **M**, one of the mightiest of the angels,
1:9 (This took place when **M** was arguing with Satan
Rev 12:7 **M** and the angels under his command fought the

MICHAIAH [KJV] See MICAIAH

MICHAL (16)

1Sa 14:49 had two daughters: Merab, who was older, and **M**.
18:20 Saul's daughter **M** had fallen in love with David,
18:27 the king. So Saul gave **M** to David to be his wife.
18:28 was with David and how much **M** loved him,
19:11 But **M**, David's wife, warned him, "If you don't
19:17 Saul demanded of **M**. "I had to," **M** replied.
25:44 Saul, meanwhile, had given his daughter **M**,
2Sa 3:13 with you unless you bring back my wife **M**,
3:14 "Give me back my wife **M**, for I bought her with
3:15 So Ishbosheth took **M** away from her husband
6:16 **M**, the daughter of Saul, looked down from her
6:20 **M** came out to meet him and said in disgust,
6:21 David retorted to **M**, "I was dancing before the
6:23 So **M**, the daughter of Saul, remained childless
1Ch 15:29 **M**, the daughter of Saul, looked down from her

MICMASH (11)

1Sa 13:2 two thousand of the chosen men with him to **M**
13:5 the seashore! They camped at **M** east of Beth-aven.
13:11 and the Philistines are at **M** ready for battle.
13:16 The Philistines set up their camp at **M**.
13:23 The pass at **M** had meanwhile been secured by a
14:5 The cliff on the north was in front of **M**,
14:31 and killed the Philistines all day from **M** to
Ezr 2:27 The people of **M** | 122
Ne 7:31 The people of **M** | 122
11:31 **M**, Aija, and Bethel with its surrounding villages.
Isa 10:28 They are storing some of their equipment at **M**.

MICMETHATH (3)

Jos 16:6 began at the Mediterranean, ran east past **M**,
17:7 Manasseh extended from the border of Asher to **M**,
17:7 Then the boundary went south from **M** to the

MICRI (1)

1Ch 9:8 son of Jeroham; Elah son of Uzzi, son of **M**;

MIDAUTUMN (7)

1Ki 6:38 every detail by **m** of the eleventh year of his reign.
12:32 held on a day in **m**, similar to the annual Festival
12:33 So on the appointed day in **m**, a day that he
2Ki 25:25 But in **m** of that year, Ishmael son of Nethaniah
Ne 7:73 Now in **m**, when the Israelites had settled in their
Jer 41:1 But in **m**, Ishmael son of Nethaniah and grandson
Zec 1:1 In **m** of the second year of King Darius's reign,

MIDDAY (1) [DAY]

Ps 91:6 in darkness, / nor the disaster that strikes at **m**.

MIDDIN (1)

Jos 15:61 there were the towns of Beth-arabah, **M**, Secacah,

MIDDLE (37) [MIDST]

Ge 6:16 bottom, **m**, and upper—and put a door in the side.
15:10 He cut each one down the **m** and laid the halves
Ex 14:29 The people of Israel had walked through the **m** of
15:8 in the **m** of the sea the waters became hard.
26:28 The **m** crossbar, halfway up the frames, will run all
28:32 with an opening for Aaron's head in the **m** of it.
36:33 The **m** crossbar of the five was halfway up the
39:23 with an opening for Aaron's head in the **m** of it.
Nu 2:17 "Then the Levites will set out from the **m** of the
Dt 3:16 from Gilead to the **m** of the Arnon Gorge,
13:16 Then you must pile all the plunder in the **m** of the
Jos 3:17 the **m** of the riverbed as the people passed by them.
4:3 the priests are standing in the **m** of the Jordan
4:5 and told them, "Go into the **m** of the Jordan,
4:8 They took twelve stones from the **m** of the Jordan
4:9 memorial of twelve stones in the **m** of the Jordan,
4:10 **m** of the river until all of the LORD's
10:13 The sun stopped in the **m** of the sky, and it did not
12:2 and extended from the **m** of the Arnon Gorge to
13:9 Gorge (including the town in the **m** of the gorge)
13:16 Gorge (including the town in the **m** of the gorge)
2Sa 20:12 But Amasa lay in his blood in the **m** of the road,
23:12 but Shammah held his ground in the **m** of the field
2Ki 7:12 The king got out of bed in the **m** of the night
20:4 But before Isaiah had left the **m** courtyard,
1Ch 11:14 and David held their ground in the **m** of the field
Ecc 7:18 try to walk a **m** course—but those who fear God
Isa 5:2 with choice vines. / In the **m** he built a watchtower
Jer 39:3 army came in and sat in triumph at the **M** Gate:
Eze 8:11 there with Jaazaniah son of Shaphan in the **m**.
41:7 bottom level through the **m** level to the top level.
Da 4:10 I dreamed. I saw a large tree in the **m** of the earth.
Na 3:15 But in the **m** of your preparations, the fire will
Mk 6:47 the disciples were in their boat out in the **m** of the
Lk 12:38 He may come in the **m** of the night or just before
Jn 8:9 until only Jesus was left in the **m** of the crowd with
Rev 1:13 And standing in the **m** of the lampstands was the

MIDIAN (29) [MIDIAN'S, MIDIANITE, MIDIANITES]

Ge 25: 2 Jokshan, Medan, **M**, Ishbak, and Shuah.
Ex 2:15 fled from Pharaoh and escaped to the land of **M**.
2:15 When Moses arrived in **M**, he sat down beside a
2:16 Now it happened that the priest of **M** had seven
3: 1 Jethro, the priest of **M**, and he went deep into the
4:19 Before Moses left **M**, the LORD said to him,
18: 1 the priest of **M** and Moses' father-in-law,
Nu 22: 4 The king of Moab said to the leaders of **M**,
22: 7 officials of both Moab and **M**, set out and took
31: 3 to fight the LORD's war of vengeance against **M**.
31: 7 They attacked **M** just as the LORD had
Jos 13:21 was killed by Moses along with the chiefs of **M**—
Jdg 6: 3 planted their crops, marauders from **M**, Amalek,
6: 7 When they cried out to the LORD because of **M**,
6:33 Soon afterward the armies of **M**, Amalek,
7: 1 The armies of **M** were camped north of them in the
7:12 The armies of **M**, Amalek, and the people of the
7:14 victory over all the armies united with **M**!"
7:23 joined in the chase after the fleeing army of **M**.
8: 5 chasing Zebah and Zalmunna, the kings of **M**."
8:22 be our rulers, for you have rescued us from **M**."
8:28 That is the story of how Israel subdued **M**,
1Ki 11:18 They escaped from **M** and went to Paran,
1Ch 1:32 Jokshan, Medan, **M**, Ishbak, and Shuah.
1:33 The sons of **M** were Ephah, Epher, Hanoch,
Isa 9: 4 just as he did when he destroyed the army of **M**
60: 6 will converge on you, the camels of **M** and Ephah.
Hab 3: 7 the peoples of Cushan and **M** trembling in terror.
Ac 7:29 and lived as a foreigner in the land of **M**,

MIDIAN'S (1) [MIDIAN]

Ge 25: 4 **M** sons were Ephah, Epher, Hanoch, Abida,

MIDIANITE (17) [MIDIAN]

Ge 36:35 He was the one who destroyed the **M** army in the
Nu 10:29 to his brother-in-law, Hobab son of Reuel the **M**,
25: 6 then one of the Israelite men brought a **M** woman
25:14 The Israelite man killed with the **M** woman was
25:15 was the daughter of Zur, the leader of a **M** clan.
25:18 because of Cozbi, the daughter of a **M** leader,
31: 8 All five of the **M** kings—Evi, Rekem, Zur, Hur,
31: 9 Then the Israelite army captured the **M** women
Jdg 7: 8 Now the **M** camp was in the valley just below
7: 9 Go down into the **M** camp, for I have given you
7:13 bread came tumbling down into the **M** camp.
7:19 with him reached the outer edge of the **M** camp.
7:25 They captured Oreb and Zeeb, the two **M** generals,
8: 3 over Oreb and Zeeb, the generals of the **M** army.
8:11 and Jogbehah, taking the **M** army by surprise.
8:12 Zebah and Zalmunna, the two **M** kings, fled,
1Ch 1:46 He was the one who destroyed the **M** army in the

MIDIANITES (21) [MIDIAN]

Nu 25:17 "Attack the **M** and destroy them,
31: 2 "Take vengeance on the **M** for leading the
31:10 all the towns and villages where the **M** had lived.
Jdg 6: 1 So the LORD handed them over to the **M** for
6: 2 The **M** were so cruel that the Israelites fled to the
6: 6 So Israel was reduced to starvation by the **M**.
6:11 of a winepress to hide the grain from the **M**.
6:13 has abandoned us and handed us over to the **M**."
6:14 strength you have and rescue Israel from the **M**.
6:16 And you will destroy the **M** as if you were fighting
7: 2 If I let all of you fight the **M**, the Israelites will
7: 7 I will rescue you and give you victory over the **M**.
7:11 Listen to what the **M** are saying, and you will be
7:15 the LORD has given you victory over the **M**!"
7:21 and watched as all the **M** rushed around in a panic,
7:24 of Ephraim, saying, "Come down to attack the **M**.
7:25 of Zeeb. And they continued to chase the **M**.
8: 1 for us when you first went out to fight the **M**?"
9:17 risked his life when he rescued you from the **M**.
Ps 83: 9 Do to them as you did to the **M** / or as you did to
Isa 10:26 as he did when Gideon triumphed over the **M** at

MIDLIFE (1) [LIVE]

Ps 102:23 He has cut me down in **m**, / shortening my days.

MIDNIGHT (15) [NIGHT]

Ex 11: 4 LORD says: About **m** I will pass through Egypt.
12:29 And at **m** the LORD killed all the firstborn sons
Jdg 7:19 It was just after **m**, after the changing of the guard,
16: 3 But Samson stayed in bed only until **m**. Then he
Ru 3: 8 Around **m**, Boaz suddenly woke up and turned
Job 10:22 It is a land as dark as **m**, a land of utter gloom
10:22 confusion reigns and the light is as dark as **m**.' "
34:20 At **m** they all pass away; the mighty are removed
Ps 119:62 At **m** I rise to thank you / for your just laws.
Mt 25: 6 At **m** they were roused by the shout, 'Look,
Mk 13:35 at evening, **m**, early dawn, or late daybreak.
Lk 11: 5 "Suppose you went to a friend's house at **m**,
Ac 16:25 Around **m**, Paul and Silas were praying
20: 7 he was leaving the next day, he talked until **m**.
27:27 About **m** on the fourteenth night of the storm,

MIDSPRING (9) [SPRING]

Nu 1: 1 One day in **m**, during the second year after Israel's
10:11 One day in **m**, during the second year after Israel's
1Ki 6: 1 It was in **m**, during the fourth year of Solomon's
6:37 laid in **m** of the fourth year of Solomon's reign.
2Ch 3: 2 The construction began in **m**, during the fourth
30: 2 of Jerusalem decided to celebrate Passover in **m**.
30:13 so a huge crowd assembled at Jerusalem in **m** to
30:15 On the appointed day in **m**, the people slaughtered
Ezr 3: 8 construction of the Temple of God began in **m**,

MIDST (4) [MIDDLE]

Job 20:22 "In the **m** of plenty, he will run into trouble,
Ps 2:12 and you will be destroyed in the **m** of your
La 1: 7 And now in the **m** of her sadness and wandering,
Php 1:30 and you know that I am still in the **m** of this great

MIDSUMMER (2) [SUMMER]

Nu 33:38 This happened on a day in **m**, during the fortieth
Zec 8:19 **m**, autumn, and winter are now ended.

MIDWAY (1) [WAY]

Jn 7:14 Then, **m** through the festival, Jesus went up to the

MIDWIFE (3) [MIDWIVES]

Ge 35:17 the **m** finally exclaimed, "Don't be afraid—
38:28 and the **m** tied a scarlet thread around the wrist of
38:29 "What!" the **m** exclaimed. "How did you break

MIDWINTER (1) [WINTER]

Dt 1: 3 on a day in **m**, Moses gave these speeches to the

MIDWIVES (6) [MIDWIFE]

Ex 1:15 gave this order to the Hebrew **m**, Shiphrah
1:17 But because the **m** feared God, they refused to
1:18 Then the king called for the **m**. "Why have you
1:20 So God blessed the **m**, and the Israelites continued
1:21 And because the **m** feared God, he gave them
1Sa 4:20 but before she passed away the **m** tried to

MIGDAL-EL (1)

Jos 19:38 Yiron, **M**, Horem, Beth-anath, and Beth-shemesh

MIGDAL-GAD (1)

Jos 15:37 Also included were Zenan, Hadashah, **M**,

MIGDOL (6)

Ex 14: 2 the people to march toward Pi-hahiroth between **M**
Nu 33: 7 opposite Baal-zephon, and camped near **M**.
Jer 44: 1 Judeans living in northern Egypt in the cities of **M**,
46:14 Publish it in the cities of **M**, Memphis,
Eze 29:10 from **M** to Aswan, as far south as the border of
30: 6 From **M** to Aswan they will be slaughtered by the

MIGHT (166) [ALMIGHTY, MIGHTIER, MIGHTIEST, MIGHTILY, MIGHTY]

Ge 4:15 on Cain to warn anyone who **m** try to kill him.
14:23 Otherwise you **m** say, 'I am the one who made
26:10 "Someone **m** have taken your wife and slept with
41: 8 very concerned as to what the dreams **m** mean.
42: 4 however, for fear some harm **m** come to him.
43:14 that he **m** release Simeon and return Benjamin.
Ex 9:16 that you **m** see my power and that my fame **m** spread throughout the earth.
13:17 they **m** change their minds and return to Egypt."
20:26 someone **m** look up under the skirts of your
Lev 22:33 you from Egypt, that I **m** be your very own God.
25:20 But you **m** ask, 'What will we eat during the
Nu 15:41 you out of the land of Egypt that I **m** be your God.
Dt 5:29 that they **m** fear me and obey all my commands!
6: 2 and grandchildren **m** fear the LORD your God as
9:28 Or they **m** say, "He destroyed them because he
12:21 It **m** happen that the place the LORD your God
13: 7 They **m** suggest that you worship the gods of
14:24 to be honored **m** be a long way from your home.
18:16 You begged that you **m** never again have to listen
19: 6 an enraged avenger **m** be able to chase down
20: 5 You **m** be killed in the battle, and someone else
20: 6 You **m** die in battle, and someone else would eat
20: 7 You **m** die in the battle, and someone else would
22:14 He **m** say, 'I discovered she was not a virgin when
23:14 thing among you, or he **m** turn away from you.
24:15 Otherwise they **m** cry out to the LORD against
30:19 choose life, that you and your descendants **m** live!
32:27 that their adversaries **m** misunderstand and say,
32:29 understand this! / Oh, that they **m** know their fate!
Jos 4:24 so that all the nations of the earth **m** know the
4:24 and that you **m** fear the LORD your God
9: 9 We have heard of the **m** of the LORD your God
Jdg 3:24 They thought he **m** be using the latrine,
16:29 the temple and pushed against them with all his **m**.
18:25 and they **m** get angry and kill you and your
19:20 man said. "I will give you anything you **m** need.
Ru 4: 6 "because this **m** endanger my own estate.
1Sa 2:10 his king; / he increases the **m** of his anointed one."
2:16 The man offering the sacrifice **m** reply, "Take as
21:12 and was afraid of what King Achish **m** do to him.
25: 8 Please give us any provisions you **m** have on
2Sa 3:11 because he was afraid of what Abner **m** do.
6: 5 celebrating before the LORD with all their **m**,
6:14 David danced before the LORD with all his **m**,
6:20 the servant girls like any indecent person **m** do!"
11:20 But he **m** get angry and ask, 'Why did the troops
14:32 I **m** as well have stayed there. Let me see the king;
1Ki 2:22 "You **m** as well be asking me to give him the
19: 4 a solitary broom tree and prayed that he **m** die.
2Ki 7: 4 So we **m** as well go out and surrender to the
1Ch 13: 8 Israel were celebrating before God with all their **m**,
29:12 Power and **m** are in your hand, and it is at your
2Ch 7:13 At times I **m** shut up the heavens so that no rain
7:13 or I **m** command locusts to devour your crops, or I **m** send plagues among you.
Ne 1:10 the people you rescued by your great power and **m**.
Est 8:11 or province who **m** attack them or their children
8:17 for they feared what the Jews **m** do to them.
9: 2 against anyone who **m** try to harm them.
Job 6: 8 "Oh, that I **m** have my request, that God would
13:15 God **m** kill me, but I cannot wait. I am going to
17:13 I **m** go to the grave and make my bed in darkness.
17:14 And I **m** call the grave my father, and the worm
39:15 She doesn't worry that a foot **m** crush them or that wild animals **m** destroy them.
Ps 28: 1 For if you are silent, / I **m** as well give up and die.
30:12 that I **m** sing praises to you and not be silent.
54: 1 O God, and rescue me! / Defend me with your **m**.
68:28 Summon your **m**, O God. / Display your power,
77:15 the descendants of Jacob and of Joseph by your **m**.
78: 6 so the next generation **m** know them—
78: 6 that they in turn **m** teach their children.
78:61 He allowed the Ark of his **m** to be captured;
119:11 word in my heart, / that I **m** not sin against you.
125: 3 for then the godly **m** be forced to do wrong.
130: 4 offer forgiveness, / that we **m** learn to fear you.
Pr 6:30 Excuses **m** be found for a thief who steals
22:13 I **m** meet a lion in the street and be killed!"
25: 7 You **m** go down before your neighbors in shameful
26:13 go outside because there **m** be a lion on the road!
27:24 and the crown **m** not be secure for the next
Ecc 4:14 He **m** even become king, though he was born in
4:16 He **m** become the leader of millions and be very
5: 6 and he **m** wipe out everything you have achieved.
6: 3 A man **m** have a hundred children and live to be
6: 6 He **m** live a thousand years twice over but not find
9:12 People can never predict when hard times **m** come.
10: 9 you work in a quarry, stones **m** fall and crush you!
11: 2 for you do not know what risks **m** lie ahead.
Isa 11: 2 and understanding, the Spirit of counsel and **m**,
14:11 Your **m** and power are gone; they were buried with
33:10 "I will stand up and show my power and **m**.
33:13 And you that are near, acknowledge my **m**!"
40:18 What image **m** we find to resemble him?
43: 4 Others died that you **m** live. I traded their lives for
44:12 sharp tool, pounding and shaping it with all his **m**.
53: 5 He was beaten that we **m** have peace. He was
63:15 and the **m** you used to show on our behalf?
Jer 9:23 or the mighty man in his **m**, or the rich man in his
16:21 "So now I will show them my power and **m**,"
35:15 so that you **m** live in peace here in the land I gave
La 1:16 any who **m** encourage me are far away.
Eze 12: 7 filled with the things I **m** carry into exile.
20:26 so I **m** devastate them and show them that I alone
20:34 With **m** and fury I will bring you out from the
22:30 "I looked for someone who **m** rebuild the wall of
33:15 they **m** give back a borrower's pledge,
Da 5: 2 his wives, and his concubines **m** drink from them.
11:17 He will make plans to come with the **m** of his
Hos 2: 7 'I **m** as well return to my husband because I was
4: 5 just as you **m** at night, and so will your false
6: 3 Oh, that we **m** know the LORD! Let us press on
10:13 trusting in your military **m**, believing that great
Am 6:10 whisper the name of the LORD. He **m** hear you!"
Mic 3: 8 I am filled with justice and **m**, fearlessly pointing
4: 8 your royal **m** and power will come back to you
Mk 4:12 so that the Scriptures **m** be fulfilled: / 'They see
14:35 the awful hour awaiting him **m** pass him by.
Lk 3:15 and they were eager to know whether John **m** be
6:35 And don't be concerned that they **m** not repay.
8:10 so that the Scriptures **m** be fulfilled:
14:29 you **m** complete only the foundation before
Jn 1: 7 so that everyone **m** believe because of his
5:34 you about John's testimony so you **m** be saved.
17:19 entirely to you so they also **m** be entirely yours.
Ac 5:15 so that Peter's shadow **m** fall across some of them
15:17 so that the rest of humanity **m** find the Lord,
25:26 we examine him, I **m** have something to write.
26:29 and everyone here in this audience **m** become the
Ro 3: 7 "But," some **m** still argue, "how can God judge
3: 8 you **m** as well say that the more we sin the better it
5: 7 though someone **m** be willing to die for a person
6: 6 so that sin **m** lose its power in our lives.
9:17 so that my fame **m** spread throughout the earth."
9:19 Well then, you **m** say, "Why does God blame
10: 1 and my prayer to God is that the Jewish people **m**
11:14 and in that way I **m** save some of them.
14: 9 so that he **m** be Lord of those who are alive and of
14:21 or do anything else if it **m** cause another Christian
15: 9 so the Gentiles **m** also give glory to God for his
15:16 so that you **m** be pure and pleasing to him by the
16:26 so that they **m** believe and obey Christ.
1Co 2: 5 so that you **m** trust the power of God rather than
7:16 You wives must remember that your husbands **m**
7:16 must remember that your wives **m** be converted
9:22 their oppression so that I **m** bring them to Christ.
9:22 with everyone so that I **m** bring them to Christ.
9:27 I fear that after preaching to others I myself **m** be
10:29 It **m** not be a matter of conscience for you, but it is
14: 9 You **m** as well be talking to an empty room.
2Co 8: 5 and to us for whatever directions God **m** give
Gal 2:16 that we **m** be accepted by God because of our faith
2:19 So I died to the law so that I **m** live for God.
Eph 1:17 so that you **m** grow in your knowledge of God.
4:10 so that his rule **m** fill the entire universe.
1Th 2:16 News to the Gentiles, for fear some **m** be saved.
1Ti 3: 6 because he **m** be proud of being chosen so soon,
2Ti 4:17 that I **m** preach the Good News in all its fullness

Heb 4: 1 with fear that some of you **m** fail to get there.
7: 9 we **m** even say that Levi's descendants,
11:23 and they were not afraid of what the king **m** do.
1Pe 3: 6 is right without fear of what your husbands **m** do.
3:18 but he died for sinners that he **m** bring us safely
1Jn 4: 9 so that we **m** have eternal life through him.
5:21 keep away from anything that **m** take God's place

MIGHTIER (5) [MIGHT]

Nu 14:12 you into a nation far greater and **m** than they are!"
Ps 93: 4 But **m** than the violent raging of the seas, / **m** than the breakers on the shore— / the LORD above is **m** than these!
Pr 24: 5 A wise man is **m** than a strong man, and a man of

MIGHTIEST (20) [MIGHT]

2Sa 23: 8 These are the names of David's **m** men. The first
23:20 which included killing two of Moab's **m** warriors.
1Ch 11:11 Here is the record of David's **m** men: The first was
11:22 which included killing two of Moab's **m** warriors.
Job 9:13 The **m** forces against him are crushed beneath his
Ps 76: 5 The **m** of our enemies have been plundered.
89: 6 What **m** angel is anything like the LORD?
89:27 make him my firstborn son, / the **m** king on earth.
95: 4 of the earth, / and even the **m** mountains are his.
SS 3: 7 with sixty of Israel's **m** men surrounding it.
Jer 46: 6 swiftest cannot flee; the **m** warriors cannot escape.
46:12 Your **m** warriors will stumble across each other
48:41 Even the **m** warriors will be as frightened as a
49:22 Even the **m** warriors will be as frightened as a
50:23 Babylon, the **m** hammer in all the earth,
50:36 When it strikes her **m** warriors, panic will seize
51:30 Her **m** warriors no longer fight. They stay in their
Am 2:14 Even the **m** warriors will be unable to save
Ob 1: 9 The **m** warriors of Teman will be terrified,
Jude 1: 9 But even Michael, one of the **m** of the angels,

MIGHTILY (2) [MIGHT]

1Sa 11: 6 Then the Spirit of God came **m** upon Saul, and he
16:13 And the Spirit of the LORD came **m** upon him

MIGHTY (289) [MIGHT]

MIGHTY DEEDS (6) Dt 5:15; 11:7; 1Ch 29:30; Ps 71:16; 145:12; Isa 41:4

MIGHTY ONE (9) Ge 49:24; Ps 132:2,5; Isa 1:24; 10:34; 33:21; 49:26; 60:16; Lk 1:49

MIGHTY WARRIOR(S) (11) Jos 6:2; 10:2; Jdg 5:13,23; 2Sa 16:6; 17:8; 2Ki 5:1; Ps 45:3; 52:7; Jer 46:9; Eze 32:12; Zec 10:5,7

Ge 3:24 the LORD God stationed **m** angelic beings to the
7:11 and the rain fell in **m** torrents from the sky.
10: 9 He was a **m** hunter in the LORD's sight.
10: 9 "like Nimrod, a **m** hunter in the LORD's sight."
17: 2 by which I will guarantee to make you into a **m**
18:18 "For Abraham will become a great and **m** nation,
48:16 Isaac. And may they become a **m** nation."
49:24 by the **M** One of Jacob, / the Shepherd, the Rock
Ex 6: 6 I will redeem you with **m** power and great acts of
11: 9 to do even more **m** miracles in the land of Egypt."
13: 3 For the LORD has brought you out by his **m**
13:14 'With **m** power the LORD brought us out of
14:31 When the people of Israel saw the **m** power that
15:10 They sank like lead / in the **m** waters.
32:11 land of Egypt with such great power and **m** acts?
Dt 5:15 brought you out with amazing power and **m** deeds.
9:14 Then I will make a **m** nation of your descendants,
9:26 redeemed from Egypt by your **m** power
9:29 whom you brought from Egypt by your **m** power
10:17 He is the great God, **m** and awesome, who shows
10:21 the one who has done **m** miracles that you
11: 7 But you have seen all the LORD's **m** deeds with
26: 5 but in Egypt they became a **m** and numerous
34:12 Moses that the LORD demonstrated his **m** power
Jos 6: 2 given you Jericho, its king, and all its **m** warriors.
6: 5 on the horns, have all the people give a **m** shout.
10: 2 than Ai. And the Gibeonite men were **m** warriors.
24:17 He performed **m** miracles before our very eyes.
Jdg 2:10 or remember the **m** things he had done for Israel.
5: 3 "Listen, you kings! / Pay attention, you **m** rulers!
5:13 from Tabor marched the remnant against the **m**.
5:13 of the LORD marched down against **m** warriors.
5:22 the galloping, galloping of Sisera's **m** steeds.
5:23 to help the LORD against the **m** warriors.'
6:12 of the LORD appeared to him and said, "**M** hero,
1Sa 2: 4 Those who were **m** are **m** no more;
2:10 the earth. / He gives **m** strength to his king;
4: 8 Who can save us from these **m** gods of Israel?
7:10 But the LORD spoke with a **m** voice of thunder
13: 5 The Philistines mustered a **m** army of three
14:45 for he has been used of God to do a **m** miracle
26:15 "Where in all Israel is there anyone as **m**?
2Sa 1:19 dead on the hills! / How the **m** heroes have fallen!
1:21 For there the shield of the **m** was defiled;
1:25 How the **m** heroes have fallen in battle!
1:27 How the **m** heroes have fallen! / Stripped of their
16: 6 and all the **m** warriors who surrounded them.
17: 8 your father and his men; they are **m** warriors.
17:10 For all Israel knows what a **m** man your father is
22:11 Mounted on a **m** angel, he flew, / soaring on the
22:14 from heaven; / the Most High gave a **m** shout.
1Ki 8:42 of you and of your **m** miracles and your power—
18:41 a good meal! For I hear a **m** rainstorm coming!"
19:11 passed by, and a **m** windstorm hit the mountain.
2Ki 5: 1 But though Naaman was a **m** warrior, he suffered
14: 9 a thistle sent a message to a **m** cedar tree:
17:36 who brought you out of Egypt with such **m**
19:15 you are enthroned between the **m** cherubim!
1Ch 11:10 These are the leaders of David's **m** men.
11:26 These were also included among David's **m** men:
28: 1 and livestock, the palace officials, the **m** men,
29:30 These accounts include the **m** deeds of his reign
2Ch 6:32 when foreigners hear of you and your **m** miracles,
14:11 but you can help the powerless against the **m**!
20: 6 You are powerful and **m**; no one can stand against
20:12 We are powerless against this **m** army that is about
20:15 Don't be discouraged by this **m** army, for the battle
25:18 a thistle sent a message to a **m** cedar tree:
32: 7 be afraid of the king of Assyria or his **m** army,
Ezr 7:28 before the king, his council, and all his **m** princes!
Ne 9:11 They sank like stones beneath the **m** waters.
9:32 our God, the great and **m** and awesome God,
Job 9: 4 For God is so wise and so **m**. Who has ever
12:19 away stripped of status; he overthrows the **m**.
34:20 the **m** are removed without human hand.
34:24 He brings the **m** to ruin without asking anyone,
35: 9 to them. They groan beneath the power of the **m**.
36: 5 "God is **m**, yet he does not despise anyone!
36: 5 He is **m** in both power and understanding.
36:19 your wealth and **m** efforts keep you from distress?
36:24 Instead, glorify his **m** works, singing songs of
36:31 By his **m** acts he governs the people, giving them
40:15 "Take a look at the **m** hippopotamus. I made it,
41:25 When it rises, the **m** are afraid, gripped by terror.
Ps 17:14 Save me by your **m** hand, O LORD, / from those
18:10 Mounted on a **m** angel, he flew, / soaring on the
18:13 from heaven; / the Most High gave a **m** shout.
21:13 With music and singing we celebrate your **m** acts.
24: 8 The LORD, strong and **m**, / the LORD,
27: 3 Though a **m** army surrounds me, / my heart will
29: 3 The LORD thunders over the **m** sea.
29: 5 The voice of the LORD splits the **m** cedars;
29: 9 The voice of the LORD twists **m** oaks / and strips
36: 6 Your righteousness is like the **m** mountains,
37:35 proud and evil people thriving like **m** trees.
44: 3 It was by your **m** power that they succeeded;
45: 3 Put on your sword, O **m** warrior! / You are
47: 5 God has ascended with a **m** shout. / The LORD
48: 7 or like the **m** ships of Tarshish / being shattered by
50: 1 The **m** God, the LORD, has spoken; / he has
52: 7 "Look what happens to **m** warriors / who do not
60:12 With God's help we will do **m** things, / for he will
64: 9 will stand in awe, / proclaiming the **m** acts of God,
65: 1 What **m** praise, O God, / belongs to you in Zion.
65: 6 your power / and armed yourself with **m** strength.
66: 3 Your enemies cringe before your **m** power.
68:33 his **m** voice thundering from the sky.
68:34 down on Israel; / his strength is **m** in the heavens.
71:16 I will praise your **m** deeds, O Sovereign LORD.
71:18 your **m** miracles to all who come after me.
75: 1 People everywhere tell of your **m** miracles.
77:13 your ways are holy. / Is there any god as **m** as you?
77:19 the sea, / your pathway through the **m** waters—
78: 4 will tell of his power and the **m** miracles he did.
78:26 and guided the south wind by his **m** power.
78:65 like a **m** man aroused from a drunken stupor.
80: 2 and Manasseh. / Show us your **m** power.
80:10 the **m** cedars were covered with our branches.
83:11 Let their **m** nobles die as Oreb and Zeeb did.
89: 8 Where is there anyone as **m** as you, LORD?
89:10 You scattered your enemies with your **m** arm.
93: 3 The **m** oceans have roared, O LORD. / The **m** oceans roar like thunder;
93: 3 the **m** oceans roar as they pound the shore.
94:22 my God is a **m** rock where I can hide.
98: 1 He has won a **m** victory / by his power
99: 4 **M** king, lover of justice, / you have established
103:20 of his, / you **m** creatures who carry out his plans,
105:24 until they became too **m** for their enemies.
106: 8 of his name / and to demonstrate his **m** power.
108:13 With God's help we will do **m** things, / for he will
132: 2 the LORD. / He vowed to the **M** One of Israel,
132: 5 a sanctuary for the **M** One of Israel."
135:10 down great nations / and slaughtered **m** kings—
136: 4 Give thanks to him who alone does **m** miracles.
136:17 Give thanks to him who struck down **m** kings.
145: 4 each generation tell its children / of your **m** acts.
145:12 They will tell about your **m** deeds / and about the
150: 1 heavenly dwelling; / praise him in his **m** heaven!
150: 2 Praise him for his **m** works; / praise his unequaled
Isa 1:24 the LORD Almighty, the **M** One of Israel, says,
2:13 tall cedars of Lebanon and the **m** oaks of Bashan.
6: 2 Hovering around him were **m** seraphim, each with
7:17 The **m** king of Assyria will come with his great
8: 7 the Lord will overwhelm them with a **m** flood from
8: 7 the king of Assyria and all his **m** armies.
9: 6 **M** God, Everlasting Father, Prince of Peace.
10:19 Only a few from all that **m** army will survive—
10:21 A remnant of them will return to the **M** God.
10:28 Look, the **m** armies of Assyria are coming!
10:30 out a warning to Laishah, for the **m** army comes.
10:33 the LORD Almighty, will chop down the **m** tree!
10:34 The **M** One will cut down the enemy as an ax cuts
11:15 sending a **m** wind to divide it into seven streams
12: 4 the world what he has done. / Oh, how **m** he is!
13: 2 Babylon to destroy the palaces of the high and **m**.
13:11 of the proud and the haughtiness of the **m**.
14: 4 You will say, "The **m** man has been destroyed.
14: 9 and **m** kings long dead are there to see you.
14:26 for my **m** power reaches throughout the world.
18: 6 Your **m** army will be left dead in the fields for the
25: 2 You turn **m** cities into heaps of ruins. Cities with
28: 2 For the Lord will send the **m** Assyrian army
28: 2 Like a **m** hailstorm and a torrential rain, they will
30:30 With angry indignation he will bring down his **m**
31: 3 Their horses are puny flesh, not **m** spirits!
33:21 The LORD will be our **M** One. He will be like a
34: 6 of Bozrah. He will make a **m** slaughter in Edom.
37:16 you are enthroned between the **m** cherubim!
41: 4 Who has done such **m** deeds, directing the affairs
41:23 Or perform a **m** miracle that will fill us with
42:13 The LORD will march forth like a **m** man;
43:17 I called forth the **m** army of Egypt with all its
45: 1 Before him, **m** kings will be paralyzed with fear.
49:26 your Savior and Redeemer, the **M** One of Israel."
53:12 I will give him the honors of one who is **m**
59:16 So he himself stepped in to save them with his **m**
60: 3 your light. **M** kings will come to see your radiance.
60:16 and **m** nations will bring the best of their goods to
60:16 your Savior and Redeemer, the **M** One of Israel.
60:22 The tiniest group will become a **m** nation. I,
63: 1 It is I, the LORD, who is **m** to save!"
Jer 5:15 "It is a **m** nation, an ancient nation, a people
5:16 Their weapons are deadly; their warriors are **m**.
9:23 or the **m** man in his might, or the rich man in his
21: 2 and do a **m** miracle as he has done in the past.
22:25 of Babylon and the **m** Babylonian army.
23:29 "Is it not like a **m** hammer that smashes rock to
32:19 You have all wisdom and do great and **m** miracles.
32:21 "You brought Israel out of Egypt with **m** signs
46: 9 you horses and chariots and **m** warriors of Egypt!
48:14 used to boast, 'We are heroes, **m** men of war.'
51:25 "Look, O **m** mountain, destroyer of the earth!
51:56 Her **m** men are captured, and their weapons break
La 1:15 "The Lord has treated my **m** men with contempt.
Eze 1:24 of the Almighty, or like the shouting of a **m** army.
13:11 great hailstones and **m** winds will knock it down.
17:17 and all his **m** army will fail to help Israel when the
21:26 the lowly are exalted, and the **m** are brought low.
27: 3 that **m** gateway to the sea, the trading center of the
27:26 Your **m** vessel flounders in the heavy eastern gale.
28:14 and anointed you as the **m** angelic guardian.
28:16 I expelled you, O **m** guardian, from your place
31: 3 You are as Assyria was—a great and **m** nation.
31:11 I handed it over to a **m** nation that destroyed it as
31:15 deep places mourn, and I restrained the **m** waters.
32:12 I will destroy you with the swords of **m** warriors—
32:18 the hordes of Egypt and for the other **m** nations.
32:21 Down in the grave **m** leaders will mockingly
32:23 These **m** men who once struck terror in the hearts
32:29 **M** as they were, they also lie among those killed
38: 4 and cavalry and make you a vast and **m** horde,
38:15 north with your vast cavalry and your **m** army,
38:19 I promise a **m** shaking in the land of Israel on that
39:18 Eat the flesh of **m** men and drink the blood of
Da 4:30 I, by my own **m** power, have built this beautiful
11: 3 "Then a **m** king will rise to power who will rule a
11:10 the sons of the king of the north will assemble a **m**
11:25 The king of the south will go to battle with a **m**
Hos 4:19 So a **m** wind will sweep them away. They will die
Joel 2: 2 spreading across the mountains, a **m** army appears!
2: 5 across a field, or like a **m** army moving into battle.
2:11 This is his **m** army, and they follow his orders.
Am 1:14 the battle, swirling like a whirlwind in a **m** storm.
5:24 Instead, I want to see a **m** flood of justice, a river
Mic 4: 7 But I will make them strong again, a **m** nation.
7:15 says the LORD, "I will do **m** miracles for you,
Na 2:12 O Nineveh, you were once a **m** lion! You crushed
Hab 3:10 The **m** deep cried out, lifting its hands to the
3:15 sea with your horses, and the **m** waters piled high.
Zep 3:17 He is a **m** savior. He will rejoice over you with
Zec 4: 7 Nothing, not even a **m** mountain, will stand in
10: 5 They will be like **m** warriors in battle,
10: 7 The people of Israel will become like **m** warriors,
12: 8 the weakest among them will be as **m** as King
Mt 7:27 against that house, it will fall with a **m** crash."
24:31 his angels with the sound of a **m** trumpet blast,
Mk 6: 5 he couldn't do any **m** miracles among them except
Lk 1:49 For he, the **M** One, is holy, / and he has done great
1:51 His **m** arm does tremendous things! / How he
1:69 He has sent us a **m** Savior / from the royal line of
7:16 saying, "A **m** prophet has risen among us,"
23:18 Then a **m** roar rose from the crowd, and with one
24:19 He was a **m** teacher, highly regarded by both God
Jn 12:18 because they had heard about this **m** miracle.
Ac 2: 2 roaring of a **m** windstorm in the skies above them,
7:22 and he became **m** in both speech and action.
1Co 1:24 Christ is the **m** power of God and the wonderful
2Co 10: 4 We use God's **m** weapons, not mere worldly
13: 3 his dealings with you; he is a **m** power among you.
13: 4 in weakness, he now lives by the **m** power of God.
Eph 1:19 for us who believe him. This is the same **m** power
2: 2 the **m** prince of the power of the air.
3: 7 By God's special favor and **m** power, I have been
3:16 unlimited resources he will give you **m** inner
3:20 By his **m** power at work within us, he is able to
4:27 for anger gives a **m** foothold to the Devil.
6:10 A final word: Be strong with the Lord's **m** power.
6:12 against those **m** powers of darkness who rule this
Php 3:10 and experience the **m** power that raised him from
3:21 using the same **m** power that he will use to
Col 1:29 as I depend on Christ's **m** power that works within
2:12 new life because you trusted the **m** power of God,
2Th 1: 7 from heaven. He will come with his **m** angels,
Heb 1: 3 He sustains the universe by the **m** power of his
1Pe 1: 5 And God, in his **m** power, will protect you until
5: 6 So humble yourselves under the **m** power of God,
2Pe 1: 4 And by that same **m** power, he has given us all of
3: 6 used the water to destroy the world with a **m** flood.

Rev 1:15 and his voice thundered like **m** ocean waves.
4:1 spoke to me with the sound of a **m** trumpet blast.
5:12 And they sang in a **m** chorus: / "The Lamb is
6:4 Its rider was given a **m** sword and the authority to
6:13 green figs falling from trees shaken by **m** winds.
7:10 And they were shouting with a **m** shout,
8:6 the seven trumpets prepared to blow their **m** blasts.
10:1 Then I saw another **m** angel coming down from
10:5 Then the **m** angel standing on the sea and on the
11:19 and the world was shaken by a **m** earthquake.
14:2 of a great waterfall or the rolling of **m** thunder.
16:1 Then I heard a **m** voice shouting from the Temple
16:17 And a **m** shout came from the throne of the
18:2 He gave a **m** shout, "Babylon is fallen—that great
18:8 by fire, for the Lord God who judges her is **m**."
18:21 Then a **m** angel picked up a boulder as large as a
19:6 or the roar of **m** ocean waves, or the crash of loud
19:20 and with him the false prophet who did **m** miracles
20:8 a **m** host, as numberless as sand along the shore.

MIGRATED (1) [MIGRATION]

Ge 11:2 As the people **m** eastward, they found a plain in

MIGRATION (1) [MIGRATED]

Jer 8:7 The stork knows the time of her **m**, as do the

MIGRON (2)

1Sa 14:2 of Gibeah, around the pomegranate tree at **M**.
Isa 10:28 are coming! They are now at Aiath, now at **M**.

MIJAMIN (3)

1Ch 24:9 fifth lot fell to Malkijah. / The sixth lot fell to **M**.
Ezr 10:25 Ramiah, Izziah, Malkijah, **M**, Eleazar, Hashabiah,
Ne 10:7 Meshullam, Abijah, **M**,

MIKLOTH (4)

1Ch 8:32 and **M**, who was the father of Shimeam. All these
9:37 Gedor, Ahio, Zechariah, and **M**.
9:38 **M** was the father of Shimeam. All these families
27:4 troops in his division, and **M** was his chief officer.

MIKNEIAH (2)

1Ch 15:18 Benaiah, Maaseiah, Mattithiah, Eliphelehu, **M**,
15:21 Mattithiah, Eliphelehu, **M**, Obed-edom, Jeiel,

MILALAI (1)

Ne 12:36 Azarel, **M**, Gilalai, Maai, Nethanel, Judah,

MILCAH (11)

Ge 11:29 married Sarai, and his brother Nahor married **M**,
11:29 their brother Haran. (**M** had a sister named Iscah.)
22:20 Soon after this, Abraham heard that **M**, his brother
22:24 In addition to his eight sons from **M**, Nahor had
24:15 son of Abraham's brother Nahor and his wife, **M**.
24:24 she replied. "My grandparents are Nahor and **M**.
24:47 is Bethuel, the son of Nahor and his wife, **M**.'
Nu 26:33 were Mahlah, Noah, Hoglah, **M**, and Tirzah.
27:1 Mahlah, Noah, Hoglah, **M**, and Tirzah.
36:11 Mahlah, Tirzah, Hoglah, **M**, and Noah all married
Jos 17:3 were Mahlah, Noah, Hoglah, **M**, and Tirzah.

MILDEW (16) [MILDEWED]

Lev 13:47 "Now suppose an infectious **m** contaminates some
13:49 it is contaminated with an infectious **m** and must
13:51 material is clearly contaminated by an infectious **m**
13:52 it has been contaminated by an infectious **m**.
13:57 at a later time, however, the **m** is clearly spreading,
13:59 for dealing with infectious **m** in woolen
14:34 some of your houses with an infectious **m**.
14:39 If the **m** on the walls of the house has spread,
14:43 "But if the **m** reappears after all these things have
14:44 are clearly contaminated with an infectious **m**,
14:48 because the infectious **m** is clearly gone.
14:54 kinds of contagious skin disease and infectious **m**,
14:57 with any contagious skin disease or infectious **m**,
Dt 28:22 scorching heat and drought, and with blight and **m**.
Am 4:9 struck your farms and vineyards with blight and **m**.
Hag 2:17 I sent blight and **m** and hail to destroy all the

MILDEWED (1) [MILDEW]

Jer 13:7 But now it was **m** and falling apart. The belt was

MILE (3) [MILES]

Jos 3:4 Stay about a half **m** behind them, keeping a clear
Mt 5:41 a soldier demands that you carry his gear for a **m**,
Ac 1:12 so they walked the half **m** back to Jerusalem.

MILES (37) [MILE]

Nu 11:31 For many **m** in every direction from the camp there
Eze 45:1 land will be 8-1/3 **m** long and 6-2/3 **m** wide.
45:3 portion of land 8-1/3 **m** long and 3-1/3 **m** wide.
45:5 next to it, also 8-1/3 **m** long and 3-1/3 **m** wide,
45:6 a section of land 8-1/3 **m** long and 1-2/3 **m** wide.
48:8 It will be 8-1/3 **m** wide and will extend as far east
48:9 for the LORD's Temple will be 8-1/3 **m** long and 6-2/3 **m** wide.
48:10 land measuring 8-1/3 **m** long by 3-1/3 **m** wide,
48:13 to the priests—8-1/3 **m** long and 3-1/3 **m** wide.
48:13 will measure 8-1/3 **m** long by 6-2/3 **m** wide.
48:15 strip of land 8-1/3 **m** long by 1-2/3 **m** wide,
48:16 The city will measure 1-1/2 **m** on each side.
48:18 be a farming area that stretches 3-1/3 **m** to the east
48:18 and 3-1/3 **m** to the west along the border of the
48:20 is a square that measures 8-1/3 **m** on each side.
48:21 Each of these areas will be 8-1/3 **m** wide,
48:30 the city: On the north wall, which is 1-1/2 **m** long,
48:32 On the east wall, also 1-1/2 **m** long, the gates will
48:33 The south wall, also 1-1/2 **m** long, will have gates
48:34 And on the west wall, also 1-1/2 **m** long, the gates
48:35 "The distance around the entire city will be six **m**.
Mt 5:41 that you carry his gear for a mile, carry it two **m**.
Lk 24:13 the village of Emmaus, seven **m** out of Jerusalem.
Jn 6:19 or four **m** out when suddenly they saw Jesus
11:18 Bethany was only a few **m** down the road from
2Co 11:26 I have traveled many weary **m**. I have faced danger
Rev 14:20 from the winepress in a stream about 180 **m** long
21:16 its length and width and height were each 1,400 **m**.

MILETUS (3)

Ac 20:15 island of Samos. And a day later we arrived at **M**.
20:17 But when we landed at **M**, he sent a message to the
2Ti 4:20 stayed at Corinth, and I left Trophimus sick at **M**.

MILITARY (32)

Nu 26:2 to find out how many of each family are of **m**
31:14 But Moses was furious with all the **m** commanders
31:48 Then all the **m** commanders came to Moses
31:51 received the gold from all the **m** commanders,
31:54 priest accepted the gifts from the **m** commanders
2Sa 24:9 There were 800,000 men of **m** age in Israel
2Ki 18:20 Do you think that mere words can substitute for **m**
18:20 Which of your allies will give you any **m** backing
1Ch 7:2 the total number of men available for **m** service
7:4 The total number of men available for **m** service
7:5 The total number of men available for **m** service
7:7 The total number of men available for **m** service
7:9 there were 20,200 men available for **m** service
7:11 included 17,200 men available for **m** service.
7:40 There were 26,000 men available for **m** service
21:5 There were 1,100,000 men of **m** age in Israel,
27:6 David's elite **m** group known as the Thirty.
2Ch 1:14 Solomon built up a huge **m** force, which included
32:3 he consulted with his officials and **m** advisers,
32:6 He appointed **m** officers over the people and asked
33:14 And he stationed his **m** officers in all of the
Est 1:3 He invited all the **m** officers of Media and Persia,
Isa 2:4 wars will stop, and **m** training will come to an end.
10:5 of my anger. Its **m** power is a club in my hand.
36:5 Do you think that mere words can substitute for **m**
36:5 Which of your allies will give you any **m** backing
Eze 23:14 pictures of Babylonian **m** officers, outfitted in
Hos 1:5 by breaking its **m** power in the Jezreel Valley."
10:13 trusting in your **m** might, believing that great
Mic 4:3 wars will stop, and **m** training will come to an end.
Mk 15:44 so he called for the Roman **m** officer in charge
Ac 25:23 accompanied by **m** officers and prominent men of

MILK (42) [MILKS]

MILK AND HONEY (21) Ex 3:8,17; 13:5; 33:3; Lev 20:24; Nu 13:27; 14:8; 16:13,14; Dt 6:3; 11:9; 26:9,15; 27:3; 31:20; Jos 5:6; Job 20:17; Jer 11:5; 32:22; Eze 20:6,15

Ge 18:8 some cheese curds and **m** and the roasted meat,
49:12 darker than wine, / and his teeth are whiter than **m**.
Ex 3:8 It is a land flowing with **m** and honey—the land
3:17 a land flowing with **m** and honey." '
13:5 your ancestors—a land flowing with **m** and honey.
23:19 must not cook a young goat in its mother's **m**.
33:3 Theirs is a land flowing with **m** and honey. But I
34:26 must not cook a young goat in its mother's **m**."
Lev 20:24 their land, a land flowing with **m** and honey.
Nu 13:27 a land flowing with **m** and honey.
14:8 It is a rich land flowing with **m** and honey, and he
16:13 a land flowing with **m** and honey, to kill us here in
16:14 haven't brought us into the land flowing with **m**
Dt 6:3 have many children in the land flowing with **m**
11:9 a land flowing with **m** and honey!
14:21 "Do not boil a young goat in its mother's **m**.
26:9 and gave us this land flowing with **m** and honey!
26:15 given us—a land flowing with **m** and honey—
27:3 a land flowing with **m** and honey, just as the
31:20 their ancestors—a land flowing with **m** and honey.
32:14 them curds from the herd and **m** from the flock,
Jos 5:6 to give us—a land flowing with **m** and honey.
Jdg 4:19 So she gave him some **m** to drink and covered him
5:25 Sisera asked for water, / and Jael gave him **m**.
Job 20:17 streams of olive oil or rivers of **m** and honey.
29:6 In those days my cows produced **m** in abundance,
Pr 27:27 And you will have enough goats' **m** for you,
SS 5:1 I drink my wine with my **m**." / "Oh, lover
Isa 55:1 Come, take your choice of wine or **m**—it's all free!
Jer 11:5 your ancestors to give you a land flowing with **m**
32:22 long before—a land flowing with **m** and honey.
Eze 20:6 a good land, a land flowing with **m** and honey,
20:15 a land flowing with **m** and honey, the most
34:3 You drink the **m**, wear the wool, and butcher the
Hos 9:14 that don't give birth and breasts that give no **m**.
Joel 3:18 with sweet wine, and the hills will flow with **m**.
1Co 3:2 I had to feed you with **m** and not with solid food,
9:7 of sheep and isn't allowed to drink some of the **m**?
Heb 5:12 You are like babies who drink only **m** and cannot
5:13 And a person who is living on **m** isn't very far
1Pe 2:2 You must crave pure spiritual **m** so that you can
2:2 Cry out for this nourishment as a baby cries for **m**,

MILKS (1) [MILK]

Ecc 5:9 Even the king **m** the land for his own profit!

MILL (2) [MILLING, MILLS, MILLSTONE, MILLSTONES]

Mt 24:41 Two women will be grinding flour at the **m**;
Lk 17:35 women will be grinding flour together at the **m**;

MILLET (1)

Eze 4:9 some wheat, barley, beans, lentils, **m**, and spelt,

MILLING (2) [MILL]

Lk 12:1 the crowds grew until thousands were **m** about
Rev 18:22 no industry of any kind, and no more **m** of grain.

MILLION (4) [MILLIONS]

2Ch 14:9 Zerah attacked Judah with an army of a **m** men
Da 7:10 to him, and a hundred **m** stood to attend him.
Ac 19:19 The value of the books was several **m** dollars.
Rev 9:16 They led an army of 200 **m** mounted troops—

MILLIONS (10) [MILLION]

Ge 17:6 I will give you **m** of descendants who will
22:17 I will multiply your descendants into countless **m**,
24:60 may you become / the mother of many **m**!
Ps 119:72 is more valuable to me / than **m** in gold and silver!
Ecc 4:16 He might become the leader of **m** and be very
Isa 45:12 All the **m** of stars are at my command.
Da 7:10 **M** of angels ministered to him, and a hundred
Mt 18:24 was brought in who owed him **m** of dollars.
Heb 6:14 will multiply your descendants into countless **m**."
Rev 5:11 and **m** of angels around the throne and the living

MILLO (6) [BETH-MILLO]

2Sa 5:9 the city, starting at the **M** and working inward.
1Ki 9:15 the royal palace, the **M**, the wall of Jerusalem,
9:24 palace he had built for her, he constructed the **M**.
11:27 Solomon was rebuilding the **M** and repairing the
1Ch 11:8 He extended the city from the **M** to the
2Ch 32:5 He also reinforced the **M** in the City of David

MILLS (1) [MILL]

Nu 11:8 and made flour by grinding it with hand **m**

MILLSTONE (8) [MILL, STONE]

Dt 24:6 or even just the upper **m**, as a pledge, for the owner
Jdg 9:53 a woman on the roof threw down a **m** that landed
2Sa 11:21 by a woman who threw a **m** down on him?'
Job 41:24 Its heart is as hard as rock, as hard as a **m**.
Mt 18:6 into the sea with a large **m** tied around the neck.
Mk 9:42 into the sea with a large **m** tied around the neck.
Lk 17:2 **m** tied around the neck than to face the punishment
Rev 18:21 angel picked up a boulder as large as a great **m**.

MILLSTONES (3) [MILL, STONE]

Dt 24:6 "It is wrong to take a pair of **m**, or even just the
Isa 47:2 Take heavy **m** and grind the corn. Remove your
La 5:13 The young men are led away to work at **m**,

MINA (1)

Eze 45:12 and sixty shekels are equal to one **m**.

MIND (82) [EVIL-MINDED, FAIR-MINDED, MINDING, MINDLESS, MINDS, OPEN-MINDED, SIMPLEMINDED, SINGLE-MINDED]

Ge 31:8 And when he changed his **m** and said I could have
Ex 7:23 to his palace and put the whole thing out of his **m**.
8:29 don't change your **m** again and refuse to let the
32:12 Change your **m** about this terrible disaster you are
Nu 23:19 He is not a human, that he should change his **m**.
Dt 4:9 Do not let these things escape from your **m** as long
4:39 So remember this and keep it firmly in **m**:
22:13 after sleeping with her, changes his **m** about her
32:36 and he will change his **m** about his servants,
Ru 1:18 So when Naomi saw that Ruth had made up her **m**
1Sa 14:19 So Saul said to Ahijah, "Never **m**; let's get
15:29 of Israel will not lie, nor will he change his **m**,
15:29 for he is not human that he should change his **m**!"
18:25 But what Saul had in **m** was that David would be
2Sa 7:3 "Go ahead and do what you have in **m**,
14:17 Yes, the king will give us peace of **m** again.'
1Ki 3:9 Give me an understanding **m** so that I can govern
3:12 and understanding **m** such as no one else has ever
10:2 they talked about everything she had on her **m**.
1Ch 17:2 "Go ahead with what you have in **m**,
28:9 him with your whole heart and with a willing **m**.
28:12 David also gave Solomon all the plans he had in **m**
2Ch 9:2 they talked about everything she had on her **m**.
Job 23:13 his **m** concerning me remains unchanged,
32:17 will say my piece. I will speak my **m**. I surely will.
Ps 7:9 For you look deep within the **m** and heart,
64:6 Yes, the human heart and **m** are cunning.
94:19 When doubts filled my **m**, / your comfort gave me
119:95 kill me, / I will quietly keep my **m** on your decrees.
119:169 my cry; / give me the discerning **m** you promised.
Pr 12:8 with good sense, but a warped **m** is despised.
16:23 From a wise **m** comes wise speech; the words of
25:3 of the earth, or all that goes on in the king's **m**!

29:17 and they will give you happiness and peace of **m**.
Isa 21: 4 My **m** reels; my heart races. The sleep I once
31: 2 will send great disaster; he will not change his **m**.
Jer 4:28 I have made up my **m** and will not change it."
7:31 it never even crossed my **m** to command such a
19: 5 it never even crossed my **m** to command such a
32:35 it never even crossed my **m** to command such a
32:39 give them one heart and **m** to worship me forever,
44:11 I have made up my **m** to destroy every one of you!
Eze 20:32 But what you have in **m** will never happen.
24:14 and I won't hold back; I will not change my **m**.
38:10 At that time evil thoughts will come to your **m**,
47: 6 He told me to keep in **m** what I had seen, then he
Da 1: 8 But Daniel made up his **m** not to defile himself by
4:16 let him have the **m** of an animal instead of a
5:12 has a sharp **m** and is filled with divine knowledge
5:20 when his heart and **m** were hardened with pride,
5:21 He was given the **m** of an animal, and he lived
7: 4 a human being. And a human **m** was given to it.
Zec 8:14 I did not change my **m** when your ancestors
Mt 21:29 but later he changed his **m** and went anyway.
22:37 with all your heart, all your soul, and all your **m**.'
26:75 Suddenly, Jesus' words flashed through Peter's **m**:
Mk 3:21 home with them. "He's out of his **m**," they said.
12:30 all your soul, all your **m**, and all your strength.'
14:72 Suddenly, Jesus' words flashed through Peter's **m**:
Lk 10:27 all your soul, all your strength, and all your **m**.'
Jn 14:27 am leaving you with a gift—peace of **m** and heart.
Ac 4:32 All the believers were of one heart and **m**, and they
7:27 Moses aside and told him to **m** his own business.
12:15 "You're out of your **m**," they said. When she
Ro 7:23 law at work within me that is at war with my **m**.
7:25 In my **m** I really want to obey God's law, but
8: 6 If your sinful nature controls your **m**, there is
8: 6 But if the Holy Spirit controls your **m**, there is life
1Co 1:10 I plead with you to be of one **m**, united in thought
2: 9 no ear has heard, / and no **m** has imagined
2:16 these things, for we have the **m** of Christ.
2Co 1:17 I changed my plan. Hadn't I made up my **m** yet?
7:13 the way you welcomed him and set his **m** at ease.
9: 7 You must each make up your own **m** as to how
Php 4: 7 which is far more wonderful than the human **m** can
Col 4: 2 Devote yourselves to prayer with an alert **m**
2Th 2:15 With all these things in **m**, dear brothers
2Ti 4: 5 But you should keep a clear **m** in every situation.
Heb 6:17 perfectly sure that he would never change his **m**.
11:40 For God had far better things in **m** for us that
Jas 1: 6 for a doubtful **m** is as unsettled as a wave of the
1Pe 3: 8 Finally, all of you should be of one **m**, full of

MINDING (3) [MIND]

Ps 35:20 innocent people / who are **m** their own business.
Pr 9:15 She calls out to men going by who are **m** their own
1Th 4:11 **m** your own business and working with your

MINDLESS (1) [MIND]

Ecc 5: 1 Don't be a fool who doesn't realize that **m**

MINDS (38) [MIND]

Ex 13: 9 to keep the LORD's instructions in your **m**
13:17 they might change their **m** and return to Egypt."
14: 5 Pharaoh and his officials changed their **m**.
Dt 29: 4 But to this day the LORD has not given you **m**
Job 17: 4 You have closed their **m** to understanding, but do
33:17 He causes them to change their **m**; he keeps them
Ps 84: 5 who set their **m** on a pilgrimage to Jerusalem.
Isa 44:18 Their **m** are shut, and they cannot think.
55: 7 Let them banish from their **m** the very thought of
Jer 4: 4 Cleanse your **m** and hearts before the LORD,
11:20 you examine the deepest thoughts of hearts and **m**.
20:12 you examine the deepest thoughts of hearts and **m**.
31:33 "I will put my laws in their **m**, and I will write
34:11 but later they changed their **m**. They took back the
Eze 11: 5 for I know every thought that comes into your **m**.
14: 5 I will do this to capture the **m** and hearts of all my
Lk 1:17 and he will change disobedient **m** to accept godly
24:45 Then he opened their **m** to understand these many
Ac 28: 6 they changed their **m** and decided he was a god.
Ro 1:21 The result was that their **m** became dark
1:28 he abandoned them to their evil **m** and let them do
2Co 3:14 But the people's **m** were hardened, and even to this
3:14 a veil covers their **m** so they cannot understand the
4: 4 has blinded the **m** of those who don't believe,
5:13 And if we are in our right **m**, it is for your benefit.
Eph 4:14 forever changing our **m** about what we believe
4:18 Their closed **m** are full of darkness; they are far
4:18 the life of God because they have shut their **m**
Php 4: 7 your hearts and **m** as you live in Christ Jesus.
Col 2:18 but their sinful **m** have made them proud.
1Ti 6: 5 Their **m** are corrupt, and they don't tell the truth.
2Ti 3: 8 Their **m** are depraved, and their faith is counterfeit.
Tit 1:15 because their **m** and consciences are defiled.
Heb 8:10 says the Lord: / I will put my laws in their **m**
10:16 understand them, / and I will write them on their **m**
Jas 1: 8 They can't make up their **m**. They waver back
1Pe 3: 8 one another with tender hearts and humble **m**.
Rev 17:17 For God has put a plan into their **m**, a plan that will

MINE (81) [I, MINED, MINES] See also Index of Articles, Etc.

Job 28: 1 "People know how to **m** silver and refine gold.
28: 4 They sink a **m** shaft into the earth far from where

MINED (1) [MINE]

Isa 51: 1 Consider the quarry from which you were **m**,

MINES (1) [MINE]

Job 28: 8 for they are deep within the **m**. No wild animal has

MINGLE (2) [MINGLED]

Isa 34:14 Wild animals of the desert will **m** there with
Hos 7: 8 "My people of Israel **m** with godless foreigners,

MINGLED (2) [MINGLE]

Ezr 3:13 and weeping **m** together in a loud commotion that
Ps 106:35 Instead, they **m** among the pagans / and adopted

MINIAMIN (4)

2Ch 31:15 **M**, Jeshua, Shemaiah, Amariah, and Shecaniah.
Ne 12: 5 **M**, Moadiah, Bilgah,
12:17 There was also a leader of the family of **M**.
12:41 Eliakim, Maaseiah, **M**, Micaiah, Elioenai,

MINISH(ED) [KJV] See DECREASE

MINISTER (27) [MINISTERED, MINISTERING, MINISTERS, MINISTRY]

Ex 28: 1 They will be my priests and will **m** to me.
28:35 he enters the Holy Place to **m** in the LORD,
29:30 days before beginning to **m** in the Tabernacle
30:30 so they can **m** before me as priests.
31:10 and the garments for his sons to wear as they **m** as
Nu 3: 3 They were anointed and set apart to **m** as priests.
16: 9 and to stand before the people to **m** to them?
Dt 10: 8 to **m** before the LORD, and to pronounce
18: 5 all your tribes to **m** in the LORD's name forever.
18: 7 He may **m** there in the name of the LORD his
21: 5 for the LORD your God has chosen them to **m**
1Ch 15: 2 Ark of the LORD and to **m** before him forever."
16:37 and his fellow Levites to **m** regularly before the
16:39 where they continued to **m** before the LORD.
2Ch 29:11 to **m** to him, and to lead the people in worship
Ne 10:36 We will present them to the priests who **m** in the
Est 3: 1 son of Hammedatha the Agagite to prime **m**,
10: 3 Mordecai the Jew became the prime **m**,
Jer 33:21 with the Levitical priests who **m** before me.
33:22 my servant, and the Levites who **m** before me."
Eze 40:46 Levites may approach the LORD to **m** to him."
43:19 priests of the family of Zadok, who **m** before me,
44:13 They may not approach me to **m** as priests.
44:15 **m** faithfully in the Temple when Israel abandoned
45: 4 set aside for the priests who **m** to the LORD in
Joel 2:17 The priests, who **m** in the LORD's presence,
Tit 1: 7 must live a blameless life because he is God's **m**.

MINISTERED (3) [MINISTER]

Ex 39:26 This robe was to be worn when Aaron **m** to the
1Ch 6:32 They **m** with music there at the Tabernacle until
Da 7:10 Millions of angels **m** to him, and a hundred million

MINISTERING (8) [MINISTER]

Ex 30:20 They must always wash before **m** in these ways,
35:19 for the priests to wear while **m** in the Holy Place;
39: 1 clothing to be worn while **m** in the Holy Place.
39:41 garments to be worn while **m** in the Holy Place—
1Ch 9:13 They were responsible for **m** at the house of God.
Ne 10:39 and place them in the sacred containers near the **m**
Eze 42:14 must first take off the clothes they wore while **m**
44:19 they must take off the clothes they wear while **m** to

MINISTERS (9) [MINISTER]

Ezr 8:17 and the Temple servants to send us **m** for the
Job 3:14 I would rest with the world's kings and prime **m**,
Isa 61: 6 will be called priests of the LORD, **m** of our God.
Eze 44:15 These men will serve as my **m**. They will stand in
Joel 1: 9 Listen to the weeping of these **m** of the LORD!
1:13 spend the night in sackcloth, you **m** of my God!
2Co 6: 4 we do we try to show that we are true **m** of God.
11:15 can also do it by pretending to be godly **m**.
Heb 8: 2 There he **m** in the sacred tent, the true place of

MINISTRATION [KJV] See DISTRIBUTION, SERVICE

MINISTRY (24) [MINISTER]

Nu 16:10 He has given this special **m** only to you and your
Mk 6:30 The apostles returned to Jesus from their **m** tour
Lk 1:80 wilderness until he began his public **m** to Israel.
3:23 about thirty years old when he began his public **m**.
Jn 1:27 who will soon begin his **m**. I am not even worthy
11:54 Jesus stopped his public **m** among the people
Ac 1:17 was one of us, chosen to share in the **m** with us."
1:25 as an apostle to replace Judas the traitor in this **m**,
13:25 As John was finishing his **m** he asked, 'Do you
15: 4 on what God had been doing through their **m**.
21:19 accomplished among the Gentiles through his **m**.
Ro 16: 3 They have been co-workers in my **m** for Christ
2Co 4: 1 God in his mercy has given us this wonderful **m**,
5:12 **m** rather than having a sincere heart before God.
6: 3 we act, and so no one can find fault with our **m**.
8: 6 you to complete your share in this **m** of giving.
8: 7 now I want you to excel also in this gracious **m** of
13: 7 not to show that our **m** to you has been successful,
Gal 2: 2 not disagree, or my **m** would have been useless.
Eph 3: 2 God has given me this special **m** of announcing his
2Ti 4: 5 to Christ. Complete the **m** God has given you.
Phm 1:10 because he became a believer as a result of my **m**
Heb 8: 6 But our High Priest has been given a **m** that is far
8: 6 to the **m** of those who serve under the old laws,

MINNI (1)

Jer 51:27 Bring out the armies of Ararat, **M**, and Ashkenaz.

MINNITH (2)

Jdg 11:33 the Ammonites from Aroer to an area near **M**—
Eze 27:17 offering wheat from **M**, early figs, honey, oil,

MINOR (2)

Job 26:14 "These are some of the **m** things he does, merely a
Eze 29:14 Egypt will remain an unimportant, **m** kingdom.

MINSTREL [KJV] See PLAYS (WELL)

MINUTE (2) [MINUTES, MINUTES']

Job 14: 5 we will live, and we are not given a **m** longer.
Ecc 11: 9 it's wonderful to be young! Enjoy every **m** of it.

MINUTES (1) [MINUTE]

Lk 13:31 A few **m** later some Pharisees said to him,

MINUTES' (1) [MINUTE]

Ru 2: 7 except for a few **m** rest over there in the shelter."

MIPHKAD [KJV] See INSPECTION (GATE)

MIRACLE (15) [MIRACLE-WORKING, MIRACLES, MIRACULOUS]

Ex 7: 9 "Pharaoh will demand that you show him a **m** to
7:10 and they performed the **m** just as the LORD had
Nu 16:30 But if the LORD performs a **m** and the ground
1Sa 14:45 for he has been used of God to do a mighty **m**
Isa 41:20 Everyone will see this **m** and understand that it is
41:23 Or perform a mighty **m** that will fill us with
55:13 This **m** will bring great honor to the LORD's
Jer 21: 2 and do a mighty **m** as he has done in the past.
Mt 9:26 The report of this **m** swept through the entire
12:24 But when the Pharisees heard about the **m**,
Mk 6:52 the significance of the **m** of the multiplied loaves,
Lk 23: 8 hoping for a long time to see him perform a **m**.
Jn 5: 9 But this **m** happened on the Sabbath day.
12:18 because they had heard about this mighty **m**.
Rev 13: 3 All the world marveled at this **m** and followed the

MIRACLE-WORKING (1) [MIRACLE, WORK]

Rev 16:14 These **m** demons caused all the rulers of the world

MIRACLES (93) [MIRACLE]

Ex 3:20 and strike at the heart of Egypt with all kinds of **m**.
4:21 and perform the **m** I have empowered you to do.
11: 9 to do even more mighty **m** in the land of Egypt."
11:10 and Aaron did these **m** in Pharaoh's presence,
Dt 10:21 the one who has done mighty **m** that you
13: 1 about the future, and they promise you signs or **m**,
13: 2 and the predicted signs or **m** take place.
Jos 24:17 He performed mighty **m** before our very eyes.
Jdg 6:13 And where are all the **m** our ancestors told us
13:23 told us this wonderful thing and done these **m**."
2Sa 7:23 You performed awesome **m** and drove out the
1Ki 8:42 of you and of your mighty **m** and your power—
2Ki 17:36 who brought you out of Egypt with such mighty **m**
1Ch 16: 9 sing his praises. / Tell everyone about his **m**.
16:12 the **m**, and the judgments he handed down,
17:21 You performed awesome **m** and drove out the
2Ch 6:32 when foreigners hear of you and your mighty **m**,
Ne 9:17 and did not remember the **m** you had done for
Job 5: 9 to understand. He performs **m** without number.
9:10 to understand. He performs **m** without number.
37:14 Job; stop and consider the wonderful **m** of God!
Ps 26: 7 a song of thanksgiving / and telling of all your **m**.
40: 5 O LORD my God, you have done many **m** for us.
66: 5 what awesome **m** he does for his people!
71:18 your mighty **m** to all who come after me.
75: 1 People everywhere tell of your mighty **m**.
77:14 You are the God of **m** and wonders!
78: 4 We will tell of his power and the mighty **m** he did.
78: 7 hope anew on God, / remembering his glorious **m**
78:11 had done— / the wonderful **m** he had shown them,
78:12 the **m** he did for their ancestors in Egypt,
78:32 kept on sinning. / They refused to believe in his **m**.
86: 8 O Lord. / There are no other **m** like yours.
86:10 For you are great and perform great **m**. / You alone
88:10 Of what use to the dead are your **m**? / Do the dead
88:12 Can the darkness speak of your **m**? / Can anyone
89: 5 All heaven will praise your **m**, LORD;
90:16 Let us see your **m** again; / let our children see your
92: 5 O LORD, what great **m** you do! / And how deep
95: 9 my wrath though they had seen my many **m**.
105: 2 sing his praises. / Tell everyone about his **m**.
105: 5 the **m** and the judgments he handed down,
105:27 among the Egyptians, / and **m** in the land of Ham.
106: 2 Who can list the glorious **m** of the LORD?
106: 7 in Egypt / were not impressed by the LORD's **m**.
119:27 and I will meditate on your wonderful **m**.
136: 4 Give thanks to him who alone does mighty **m**.

145: 5 glorious splendor / and your wonderful **m**.
Jer 32:19 You have all wisdom and do great and mighty **m**.
32:20 And you have continued to do great **m** in Israel
Joel 2:26 the LORD your God, who does these **m** for you.
Mic 7:15 says the LORD, "I will do mighty **m** for you,
Mt 7:22 your name and performed many **m** in your name.'
11:20 the cities where he had done most of his **m**,
11:21 For if the **m** I did in you had been done in wicked
11:23 For if the **m** I did for you had been done in Sodom,
13:54 "Where does he get his wisdom and his **m**?
13:58 And so he did only a few **m** there because of their
14: 2 back to life again! That is why he can do such **m**."
21:15 teachers of religious law saw these wonderful **m**
Mk 3: 8 The news about his **m** had spread far and wide,
6: 2 all his wisdom and the power to perform such **m**?
6: 5 he couldn't do any mighty **m** among them except
6:14 back to life again. That is why he can do such **m**."
9:39 "No one who performs **m** in my name will soon
Lk 4:23 'Why don't you do **m** here in your hometown like
9: 7 When reports of Jesus' **m** reached Herod Antipas,
10:13 For if the **m** I did in you had been done in wicked
13:32 and doing **m** of healing today and tomorrow;
19:37 praising God for all the wonderful **m** they had
24:19 "He was a prophet who did wonderful **m**.
Jn 5:36 witness than John—my teachings and my **m**.
6: 2 because they saw his **m** as he healed the sick.
7: 3 "Go where your followers can see your **m**!"
10:41 "John didn't do **m**," they remarked to one
Ac 2:22 endorsed Jesus of Nazareth by doing wonderful **m**,
6: 8 performed amazing **m** and signs among the people.
8: 6 to what he had to say because of the **m** he did.
8:13 and he was amazed by the great **m** and signs Philip
19:11 God gave Paul the power to do unusual **m**,
Ro 15:19 I have won them over by the **m** done through me
1Co 12:10 He gives one person the power to perform **m**,
12:28 third are teachers, / then those who do **m**,
12:29 Does everyone have the power to do **m**?
2Co 12:12 did many signs and wonders and **m** among you.
Gal 3: 5 give you the Holy Spirit and work **m** among you
2Th 2: 9 of Satan with counterfeit power and signs and **m**.
Heb 2: 4 the message by signs and wonders and various **m**
3: 9 even though they saw my **m** for forty years.
Rev 13:13 He did astounding **m**, such as making fire flash
13:14 And with all the **m** he was allowed to perform on
19:20 and with him the false prophet who did mighty **m**
19:20 **m** that deceived all who had accepted the mark of

MIRACULOUS (64) [MIRACLE]

Ex 4: 8 "If they do not believe the first **m** sign, they will
4:17 so you can perform the **m** signs I have shown
4:28 And he told him about the **m** signs they were to
4:30 and Moses performed the **m** signs as they watched.
7: 3 so I can multiply my **m** signs and wonders in the
8:23 This **m** sign will happen tomorrow.' "
10: 1 my power by performing **m** signs among them.
Nu 14:11 even after all the **m** signs I have done among
14:22 and the **m** signs I performed both in Egypt and in
Dt 4:34 **m** signs, wonders, war, awesome power,
6:22 Before our eyes the LORD did **m** signs
7:19 And remember the **m** signs and wonders,
11: 3 They weren't there to see the **m** signs and wonders
26: 8 overwhelming terror, and **m** signs and wonders.
29: 3 of strength, the **m** signs, and the amazing wonders.
34:11 The LORD sent Moses to perform all the **m** signs
2Ch 32:24 who healed him and gave him a **m** sign.
Ne 9:10 You displayed **m** signs and wonders against
Ps 74: 9 We see no **m** signs / as evidence that you will save
78:43 They forgot his **m** signs in Egypt, / his wonders on
105:27 They performed **m** signs among the Egyptians,
135: 9 He performed **m** signs and wonders in Egypt;
Jer 32:20 You performed **m** signs and wonders in the land of
Da 4: 2 "I want you all to know about the **m** signs
6:27 his people; / he performs **m** signs and wonders
Mt 12:38 we want you to show us a **m** sign to prove that you
12:39 faithless generation would ask for a **m** sign;
16: 1 by asking him to show them a **m** sign from heaven.
16: 4 faithless generation would ask for a **m** sign,
24:24 and perform great **m** signs and wonders so as to
Mk 8:11 "Give us a **m** sign from heaven to prove
8:12 "Why do you people keep demanding a **m** sign?
13:22 and perform **m** signs and wonders so as to deceive,
16:20 confirming what they said by many **m** signs.
Lk 11:16 others asked for a **m** sign from heaven to see if he
11:29 keeps asking me to show them a **m** sign.
21:11 terrifying things and great **m** signs in the heavens.
Jn 2:11 This **m** sign at Cana in Galilee was Jesus' first
2:18 authority from God, show us a **m** sign to prove it."
2:23 Because of the **m** signs he did in Jerusalem at the
3: 2 Your **m** signs are proof enough that God is with
4:45 Passover celebration and had seen all his **m** signs.
4:48 "Must I do **m** signs and wonders before you
4:54 This was Jesus' second **m** sign in Galilee after
6:14 When the people saw this **m** sign, they exclaimed,
6:26 because I fed you, not because you saw the **m** sign.
6:30 "You must show us a **m** sign if you want us to
7:31 "would you expect the Messiah to do more **m**
9:16 "But how could an ordinary sinner do such **m**
11:47 "This man certainly performs many **m** signs.
12:37 But despite all the **m** signs he had done, most of
15:24 If I hadn't done such **m** signs among them that no
20:30 Jesus' disciples saw him do many other **m** signs
Ac 2:43 and the apostles performed many **m** signs
4:16 "We can't deny they have done a **m** sign,
4:22 for this **m** sign—the healing of a man who had
4:30 may **m** signs and wonders be done through the
5:12 the apostles were performing many **m** signs
7:36 And by means of many **m** signs and wonders he
14: 3 was true by giving them power to do **m** signs
15:12 as Barnabas and Paul told about the **m** signs
1Co 10: 3 And all of them ate the same **m** food,
10: 4 and all of them drank the same **m** water. For they all drank from the **m** rock that traveled

MIRE (3)

Ps 40: 2 of the pit of despair, / out of the mud and the **m**.
69: 2 Deeper and deeper I sink into the **m**; / I can't find a
Isa 57:20 is never still but continually churns up **m** and dirt.

MIRIAM (13)

Ex 15:20 Then **M** the prophet, Aaron's sister, took a
15:21 And **M** sang this song: / "I will sing to the
Nu 12: 1 **M** and Aaron criticized Moses because he had
12: 4 Aaron, and **M** and said, "Go out to the Tabernacle,
12: 5 "Aaron and **M**!" he called, and they stepped
12:10 **M** suddenly became white as snow with leprosy.
12:15 So **M** was excluded from the camp for seven days,
20: 1 While they were there, **M** died and was buried.
26:59 the parents of Aaron, Moses, and their sister, **M**.
Dt 24: 9 Remember what the LORD your God did to **M** as
1Ch 4:17 who became the mother of **M**, Shammai,
6: 3 children of Amram were Aaron, Moses, and **M**.
Mic 6: 4 I sent Moses, Aaron, and **M** to help you.

MIRMAH (1)

1Ch 8:10 Jeuz, Sakia, and **M**. These sons all became the

MIRROR (3) [MIRRORS]

Job 37:18 he makes the skies reflect the heat like a giant **m**.
1Co 13:12 Now we see things imperfectly as in a poor **m**,
Jas 1:23 it is like looking at your face in a **m** but doing

MIRRORS (3) [MIRROR]

Ex 38: 8 and its bronze pedestal were cast from bronze **m**
Isa 3:23 their **m**, linen garments, head ornaments,
2Co 3:18 so that we can be **m** that brightly reflect the glory

MISCARRIAGE (1) [MISCARRIAGES, MISCARRIED]

Job 21:10 fail to breed. Their cows bear calves without **m**.

MISCARRIAGES (1) [MISCARRIAGE]

Ex 23:26 There will be no **m** or infertility among your

MISCARRIED (1) [MISCARRIAGE]

Ecc 5: 8 and justice being **m** throughout the land,

MISCHIEF (1)

Pr 16:30 they plot evil; without a word, they plan their **m**.

MISCHIEF(S) [KJV] See CALAMITY, DESTRUCTION, DISASTER, EVIL, WRONG

MISDIRECTED (1)

Ro 10: 2 enthusiasm they have for God, but it is **m** zeal.

MISERABLE (9) [MISERY]

Ge 26:35 But Esau's wives made life **m** for Isaac
Dt 28:59 without relief, making you **m** and unbearably sick.
Job 10:19 Then I would have been spared this **m** existence.
16: 2 heard all this before. What **m** comforters you are!
Ps 32: 3 I refused to confess my sin, / I was weak and **m**,
107:10 and deepest gloom, / **m** prisoners in chains.
Ro 7:24 Oh, what a **m** person I am! Who will free me from
1Co 15:19 for this life, we are the most **m** people in the world.
Rev 3:17 are wretched and **m** and poor and blind and naked.

MISERABLY (1) [MISERY]

Nu 11:11 "Why are you treating me, your servant, so **m**?

MISERIES (1) [MISERY]

Da 9:26 and its **m** are decreed from that time to the very

MISERY (24) [MISERABLE, MISERABLY, MISERIES]

Ge 16:11 for the LORD has heard about your **m**.
29:32 for she said, "The LORD has noticed my **m**,
Ex 3: 7 "You can be sure I have seen the **m** of my people
4:31 they realized that the LORD had seen their **m**
Nu 11:15 than treat me like this. Please spare me this **m**!"
Jdg 10:16 the LORD. And he was grieved by their **m**.
2Sa 1: 9 'Come over here and put me out of my **m**,
Ne 9:37 serve them at their pleasure, and we are in great **m**.
Job 3:20 light be given to the weary, and life to those in **m**?
7: 3 months of futility, long and weary nights of **m**.
7:13 and I will try to forget my **m** with sleep,'
10:15 I am filled with shame and **m** so that I can't hold
11:16 You will forget your **m**. It will all be gone like
Ps 31:10 **M** has drained my strength; / I am wasting away
90:15 Give us gladness in proportion to our former **m**!
119:92 me with joy, / I would have died in my **m**.
Isa 59: 7 Wherever they go, **m** and destruction follow them.
La 1: 9 "LORD, see my deep **m**," she cries.
Joel 1:18 there is no pasture for them. The sheep bleat in **m**.
Mic 7: 1 What **m** is mine! I feel like the fruit picker after the
Hab 1: 3 Must I forever see this sin and **m** all around me?
Ac 7:11 There was great **m** for our ancestors, as they ran
7:34 You can be sure that I have seen the **m** of my
Ro 3:16 Wherever they go, destruction and **m** follow them.

MISFORTUNE (5)

Nu 23:21 No **m** is in sight for Jacob; / no trouble is in store
Job 31: 3 calamity for the wicked, **m** for those who do evil.
Pr 17: 5 those who rejoice at the **m** of others will be
Isa 65:23 and their children will not be doomed to **m**.
Ob 1:12 have rejoiced because they were suffering such **m**.

MISHAEL (8) [MESHACH]

Ex 6:22 The descendants of Uzziel included **M**, Elzaphan,
Lev 10: 4 Then Moses called for **M** and Elzaphan,
Ne 8: 4 **M**, Malkijah, Hashum, Hashbaddanah, Zechariah,
Da 1: 6 Daniel, Hananiah, **M**, and Azariah were four of the
1: 7 **M** was called Meshach. / Azariah was called
1:11 to look after Daniel, Hananiah, **M**, and Azariah.
1:19 him as much as Daniel, Hananiah, **M**, and Azariah.
2:17 went home and told his friends Hananiah, **M**,

MISHAL (2) [MASHAL]

Jos 19:26 Allammelech, Amad, and **M**. The boundary on the
21:30 From the tribe of Asher they received **M**, Abdon,

MISHAM (1)

1Ch 8:12 **M**, Shemed (who built Ono and Lod and their

MISHMA (4)

Ge 25:14 **M**, Dumah, Massa,
1Ch 1:30 **M**, Dumah, Massa, Hadad, Tema,
4:25 of Shaul were Shallum, Mibsam, and **M**.
4:26 The descendants of **M** were Hammuel, Zaccur,

MISHMANNAH (1)

1Ch 12:10 **M** was fourth. / Jeremiah was fifth.

MISHNEH (3)

2Ki 22:14 and Asaiah went to the newer **M** section of
2Ch 34:22 and the other men went to the newer **M** section of
Zep 1:10 and echo throughout the newer **M** section of the

MISHRAITES (1)

1Ch 2:53 the Ithrites, Puthites, Shumathites, and **M**,

MISLEAD (5) [MISLEADING, MISLED]

2Ki 18:32 "Don't listen to Hezekiah when he tries to **m** you
Isa 36:18 "Don't let Hezekiah **m** you by saying,
Mt 24: 4 Jesus told them, "Don't let anyone **m** you.
Mk 13: 5 Jesus replied, "Don't let anyone **m** you,
Lk 21: 8 He replied, "Don't let anyone **m** you. For many

MISLEADING (2) [MISLEAD]

2Ch 32:11 Surely Hezekiah is **m** you, sentencing you to death
Eze 12:24 and **m** predictions about peace in Israel.

MISLED (4) [MISLEAD]

Jer 38:22 friends you have! They have betrayed and **m** you.
Gal 6: 7 Don't be **m**. Remember that you can't ignore God
Tit 3: 3 We were **m** by others and became slaves to many
Jas 1:16 So don't be **m**, my dear brothers and sisters.

MISPAR (2)

Ezr 2: 2 Reelaiah, Mordecai, Bilshan, **M**, Bigvai, Rehum,
Ne 7: 7 Nahamani, Mordecai, Bilshan, **M**, Bigvai, Rehum,

MISREPHOTH-MAIM (2)

Jos 11: 8 Israelites chased them as far as Great Sidon and **M**,
13: 6 and all the hill country from Lebanon to **M**,

MISS (6) [MISSED, MISSES, MISSING]

Pr 8:36 But those who **m** me have injured themselves.
Isa 34:16 He will not **m** a single detail. Not one of these
Jer 50: 9 will go straight to the mark; they will not **m**!
Lk 2:43 in Jerusalem. His parents didn't **m** him at first,
1Co 8: 8 We don't **m** out on anything if we don't eat it,
Heb 12:15 so that none of you will **m** out on the special favor

MISSED (8) [MISS]

Lev 26:34 Then at last the land will make up for its **m**
1Sa 20:18 You will be **m** when your place at the table is
2Ch 16: 7 you **m** your chance to destroy the army of the king
Job 8:18 But when it is uprooted, it isn't even **m**!
Jer 3:16 Those days will not be **m** or even thought about,
6: 9 a second time to pick the grapes that were **m**."
46:17 of Egypt, is a loudmouth who **m** his opportunity!'
1Ti 1: 6 But some teachers have **m** this whole point.

MISSES (2) [MISS]

Hos 7:16 They are like a crooked bow that always **m** its
1Co 9:26 I am not like a boxer who **m** his punches.

MISSING (14) [MISS]

Ge 37:29 When he discovered that Joseph was **m**, he tore his
Nu 31:49 to battle under our command; not one of us is **m**!
Jdg 20:16 and hit a target within a hairsbreadth, without **m**.
21: 3 has this happened? Now one of our tribes is **m**!"
1Sa 30:19 Nothing was **m**: small or great, son or daughter,
2Sa 2:30 he discovered that only nineteen men were **m**,

Job 5:24 When you visit your pastures, nothing will be **m**.
Ecc 1:15 cannot be righted. What is **m** cannot be recovered.
SS 4: 2 They are perfectly matched; not one is **m**.
6: 6 washed ewes, perfectly matched and not one **m**.
Isa 34:16 Not one of these birds and animals will be **m**,
Jer 23: 4 Not a single one of them will be lost or **m**,"
Lk 24:23 They said his body was **m**, and they had seen
1Th 3:10 to fill up anything that may still be **m** in your faith.

MISSION (10)

Ge 24:33 "All right," Laban said, "tell us your **m**."
24:40 angel with you and will make your **m** successful.
24:42 if you are planning to make my **m** a success,
24:56 The LORD has made my **m** successful, and I
Dt 1:36 of the land he walked over during his scouting **m**.'
1Sa 15:18 And the LORD sent you on a **m** and told you,
15:20 Saul insisted. "I carried out the **m** he gave me.
Ac 9: 3 As he was nearing Damascus on this **m**, a brilliant
12:25 and Saul had finished their **m** in Jerusalem,
26:12 "One day I was on such a **m** to Damascus,

MIST (4) [MISTS]

Pr 21: 6 Wealth created by lying is a vanishing **m** and a
Hos 6: 4 "For your love vanishes like the morning **m**
13: 3 Therefore, they will disappear like the morning **m**,
Ac 13:11 Instantly **m** and darkness fell upon him, and he

MISTAKE (9) [MISTAKEN, MISTAKENLY, MISTAKES]

Ge 43:12 in your sacks, as it was probably someone's **m**.
Nu 15:24 If the **m** was done unintentionally,
2Sa 17: 7 "this time I think Ahithophel has made a **m**.
2Ch 22: 7 But this turned out to be a fatal **m**, for God had
Ecc 5: 6 messenger that the promise you made was a **m**.
10: 5 the world go by. Kings and rulers make a grave **m**
Jer 8: 4 start down the wrong road and discover their **m**,
Eze 21:23 The people of Jerusalem will think it is a **m**,
Ac 2:14 and residents of Jerusalem! Make no **m** about this.

MISTAKEN (1) [MISTAKE]

1Co 14:36 and ends with you Corinthians? Well, you are **m**!

MISTAKENLY (1) [MISTAKE]

2Co 5:16 Once I **m** thought of Christ that way, as though he

MISTAKES (4) [MISTAKE]

Pr 14:29 those with a hasty temper will make **m**.
Ecc 10: 4 A quiet spirit can overcome even great **m**.
Isa 28: 7 They make stupid **m** as they carry out their
Jas 3: 2 We all make many **m**, but those who control their

MISTREAT (3) [MISTREATED, MISTREATING]

Pr 19:26 Children who **m** their father or chase away their
Jer 22: 3 Do not **m** foreigners, orphans, and widows.
Gal 4:12 You did not **m** me when I first preached to you.

MISTREATED (7) [MISTREAT]

Ex 5:22 "Why have you **m** your own people like this,
Dt 26: 6 When the Egyptians **m** and humiliated us by
Mt 17:12 but he wasn't recognized, and he was badly **m**.
Mk 9:13 Elijah has already come, and he was badly **m**,
Ac 7: 6 they would be **m** as slaves for four hundred years.
Heb 11:37 of sheep and goats, hungry and oppressed and **m**.
13: 3 Share the sorrow of those being **m**, as though you

MISTREATING (1) [MISTREAT]

Ac 7:24 this visit, he saw an Egyptian **m** a man of Israel.

MISTRESS (7) [MISTRESSES]

Ge 16: 4 she began to treat her **m** Sarai with contempt.
16: 8 "I am running away from my **m**," she replied.
16: 9 "Return to your **m** and submit to her authority."
2Ki 5: 3 One day the girl said to her **m**, "I wish my master
Ps 123: 2 as a slave girl watches her **m** for the slightest
Pr 30:23 a husband, / a servant girl who supplants her **m**.
Na 3: 4 and faithless city, **m** of deadly charms,

MISTRESSES (1) [MISTRESS]

Isa 24: 2 maids and **m**, buyers and sellers, lenders

MISTS (1) [MIST]

Isa 44:22 I have swept away your sins like the morning **m**.

MISUNDERSTAND (2) [MISUNDERSTANDINGS, MISUNDERSTOOD]

Dt 32:27 that their adversaries might **m** and say,
Mt 5:17 "Don't **m** why I have come. I did not come to

MISUNDERSTANDINGS (1) [MISUNDERSTAND]

1Co 12: 1 each of us, for I must correct your **m** about them.

MISUNDERSTOOD (2) [MISUNDERSTAND]

Mt 27:47 Some of the bystanders **m** and thought he was
Mk 15:35 Some of the bystanders **m** and thought he was

MISUSE (4)

Ex 20: 7 "Do not **m** the name of the LORD your God.
20: 7 will not let you go unpunished if you **m** his name.
Dt 5:11 " 'Do not **m** the name of the LORD your God.
5:11 will not let you go unpunished if you **m** his name.

MITE(S) [KJV] See PENNY

MITHCAH (2)

Nu 33:28 They left Terah and camped at **M**.
33:29 They left **M** and camped at Hashmonah.

MITHNA (1)

1Ch 11:43 Hanan son of Maacah; / Joshaphat from **M**;

MITHREDATH (2)

Ezr 1: 8 Cyrus directed **M**, the treasurer of Persia, to count
4: 7 enemies of Judah, led by Bishlam, **M**, and Tabeel,

MITRE [KJV] See TURBAN

MITYLENE (1)

Ac 20:14 He joined us there and we sailed together to **M**.

MIX (9) [MIXED, MIXTURE]

Ex 29:21 the altar and **m** it with some of the anointing oil.
Lev 5:11 they must not **m** it with olive oil or put any incense
Nu 5:15 Do not **m** it with olive oil or frankincense, for it is
5:17 and **m** it with dust from the Tabernacle floor.
2Sa 13: 8 lying down so he could watch her **m** some dough.
Eze 4: 9 and spelt, and **m** them together in a storage jar.
Da 2:43 will not succeed, just as iron and clay do not **m**.
Am 8: 6 And you **m** the wheat you sell with chaff swept
Rev 8: 3 to him to **m** with the prayers of God's people,

MIXED (50) [MIX]

Ex 29: 2 make loaves of bread, thin cakes **m** with olive oil,
29:23 take one loaf of bread, one cake **m** with olive oil,
29:40 offer two quarts of fine flour **m** with one quart of
32:20 he ground it into powder and **m** it with water.
Lev 2: 2 and he will take a handful of the flour **m** with olive
2: 4 it must be made of choice flour **m** with olive oil
2: 4 It may be presented in the form of cakes **m** with
2:16 token portion of the roasted grain **m** with olive oil,
6:15 of the choice flour that has been **m** with olive oil
6:21 and it must be well **m** and broken into pieces.
7:10 whether flour **m** with olive oil or dry flour,
9: 4 and flour **m** with olive oil for a grain offering.
14:10 along with five quarts of choice flour **m** with olive
14:21 along with two quarts of choice flour **m** with olive
23:13 of three quarts of choice flour **m** with olive oil.
Nu 6:15 cakes of choice flour **m** with olive oil and wafers
7:13 grain offerings of choice flour **m** with olive oil.
7:19 grain offerings of choice flour **m** with olive oil.
7:25 grain offerings of choice flour **m** with olive oil.
7:31 grain offerings of choice flour **m** with olive oil.
7:37 grain offerings of choice flour **m** with olive oil.
7:43 grain offerings of choice flour **m** with olive oil.
7:49 grain offerings of choice flour **m** with olive oil.
7:55 grain offerings of choice flour **m** with olive oil.
7:61 grain offerings of choice flour **m** with olive oil.
7:67 grain offerings of choice flour **m** with olive oil.
7:73 grain offerings of choice flour **m** with olive oil.
7:79 grain offerings of choice flour **m** with olive oil.
8: 8 and a grain offering of choice flour **m** with olive
15: 4 quarts of choice flour **m** with one quart of olive oil.
15: 6 give three quarts of choice flour **m** with two
15: 9 of choice flour **m** with two quarts of olive oil,
28: 5 quarts of choice flour **m** with one quart of olive oil.
28: 9 of three quarts of choice flour **m** with olive oil,
28:12 grain offerings of choice flour **m** with olive oil—
28:20 grain offerings of choice flour **m** with olive oil—
28:28 grain offerings of choice flour **m** with olive oil—
29: 3 grain offerings of choice flour **m** with olive oil—
29: 9 grain offerings of choice flour **m** with olive oil—
29:14 a grain offering of choice flour **m** with olive oil—
1Ch 23:29 cakes cooked in olive oil, and the other **m** breads.
Ezr 9: 2 So the holy race has become polluted by these **m**
Ne 13: 3 all those of **m** ancestry were immediately expelled
Ps 75: 8 his hand; / it is full of foaming wine **m** with spices.
Pr 9: 2 a great banquet, **m** the wines, and set the table.
9: 5 "Come, eat my food, and drink the wine I have **m**.
Mt 27:34 The soldiers gave him wine **m** with bitter gall,
Rev 8: 4 of the incense, **m** with the prayers of the saints,
8: 7 and fire **m** with blood were thrown down upon the
15: 2 I saw before me what seemed to be a crystal sea **m**

MIXTURE (2) [MIX]

Eze 22:18 a useless **m** of copper, tin, iron, and lead.
Da 2:43 This **m** of iron and clay also shows that these

MIZAR (1)

Ps 42: 6 source of the Jordan, / from the land of Mount **M**.

MIZPAH (38)

Ge 31:49 This place was also called **M**, for Laban said,
Jos 11: 3 on the slopes of Mount Hermon, in the land of **M**.
11: 8 and eastward into the valley of **M**,
Jdg 10:17 in Gilead, preparing to attack Israel's army at **M**.
11:11 At **M**, in the presence of the LORD,
11:29 of Gilead and Manasseh, including **M** in Gilead,
11:34 When Jephthah returned home to **M**, his daughter
20: 1 and stood in the presence of the LORD at **M**.
20: 3 Benjamin that the other tribes had gone up to **M**.)
21: 1 The Israelites had vowed at **M** never to give their
21: 5 our council in the presence of the LORD at **M**?"
21: 8 we presented ourselves to the LORD at **M**?"
1Sa 7: 5 Then Samuel told them, "Come to **M**, all of you.
7: 6 So it was at **M** that Samuel became Israel's judge.
7: 7 rulers heard that all Israel had gathered at **M**,
7:11 The men of Israel chased them from **M** to
7:12 and placed it between the towns of **M**
7:16 court first at Bethel, then at Gilgal, and then at **M**.
10:17 people of Israel to meet before the LORD at **M**.
1Ki 15:22 the town of Geba in Benjamin and the town of **M**.
2Ki 25:23 Gedaliah as governor, they joined him at **M**.
25:25 went to **M** with ten men and assassinated Gedaliah
2Ch 16: 6 these materials to fortify the towns of Geba and **M**.
Ne 3: 7 from Meronoth, and people from Gibeon and **M**,
3:15 son of Col-hozeh, the leader of the **M** district,
3:19 Next to them, Ezer son of Jeshua, the leader of **M**,
Jer 40: 6 Jeremiah returned to Gedaliah son of Ahikam at **M**
40: 8 So they came to see Gedaliah at **M**. These are the
40:10 I will stay at **M** to represent you before the
40:12 They stopped at **M** to discuss their plans with
40:13 the other guerrilla leaders came to Gedaliah at **M**.
41: 1 arrived in **M** accompanied by ten men.
41: 3 Babylonian soldiers who were with Gedaliah at **M**.
41: 6 Ishmael left **M** to meet them, weeping as he went.
41: 9 **M** to protect himself against King Baasha of Israel.
41:10 left under Gedaliah's care in **M** by Nebuzaradan,
41:14 And all the captives from **M** escaped and began to
Hos 5: 1 people into a snare by worshiping the idols at **M**

MIZPAR [KJV] See MISPAR

MIZPEH (3)

Jos 15:38 Dilean, **M**, Joktheel,
18:26 **M**, Kephirah, Mozah,
1Sa 22: 3 Later David went to **M** in Moab, where he asked

MIZRAIM (4) [ABEL-MIZRAIM]

Ge 10: 6 of Ham were Cush, **M**, Put, and Canaan.
10:13 **M** was the ancestor of the Ludites, Anamites,
1Ch 1: 8 of Ham were Cush, **M**, Put, and Canaan.
1:11 **M** was the ancestor of the Ludites, Anamites,

MIZZAH (3)

Ge 36:13 of Reuel were Nahath, Zerah, Shammah, and **M**.
36:17 of the clans of Nahath, Zerah, Shammah, and **M**.
1Ch 1:37 of Reuel were Nahath, Zerah, Shammah, and **M**.

MNASON (1)

Ac 21:16 and they took us to the home of **M**, a man

MOAB (145) [MOAB'S, MOABITE, MOABITES]

Ge 19:37 daughter gave birth to a son, she named him **M**.
36:35 destroyed the Midianite army in the land of **M**.
Ex 15:15 will be terrified; / the nobles of **M** will tremble.
Nu 21:11 in the wilderness on the eastern border of **M**.
21:15 as far as the settlement of Ar on the border of **M**."
21:20 Then they went to the valley in **M** where Pisgah
21:28 the city of Sihon. / It burned the city of Ar in **M**;
21:29 Your destruction is certain, O people of **M**!
22: 1 the people of Israel traveled to the plains of **M**
22: 4 The king of **M** said to the leaders of Midian,
22: 4 like an ox devours grass!" So Balak, king of **M**,
22: 7 officials of both **M** and Midian, set out and took
22: 8 So the officials from **M** stayed there with Balaam.
22:10 said to God, "Balak son of Zippor, king of **M**,
23: 6 his burnt offerings with all the officials of **M**.
23: 7 the king of **M** brought me from the eastern hills.
23:17 and the officials of **M** were standing beside
25: 2 feasting with them and worshiping the gods of **M**.
26: 3 on the plains of **M** beside the Jordan River,
26:63 and Eleazar the priest on the plains of **M** beside the
31:12 which was camped on the plains of **M** beside the
33:44 and camped at Iye-abarim on the border of **M**.
33:48 and camped on the plains of **M** beside the Jordan
33:49 as far as Abel-shittim on the plains of **M**.
33:50 Jordan River on the plains of **M** opposite Jericho,
35: 1 was camped beside the Jordan on the plains of **M**,
36:13 on the plains of **M** beside the Jordan River,
Dt 1: 5 were in the land of **M** east of the Jordan River.
2: 8 northward along the desert route through **M**,
2:18 'Today you will cross the border of **M** at Ar
29: 1 the Israelites while they were in the land of **M**,
32:49 "Go to **M**, to the mountains east of the river,
34: 1 Moses went to Mount Nebo from the plains of **M**
34: 5 servant of the LORD, died there in the land of **M**,
34: 6 He was buried in a valley near Beth-peor in **M**,
34: 8 mourned thirty days for Moses on the plains of **M**,
Jos 13:32 Moses had made while he was on the plains of **M**,
24: 9 Then Balak son of Zippor, king of **M**, started a war
Jdg 3:12 so the LORD gave King Eglon of **M** control over
3:14 And the Israelites were subject to Eglon of **M** for
3:15 to deliver their tax money to King Eglon of **M**.
3:28 "for the LORD has given you victory over **M**
3:28 of the shallows of the Jordan River across from **M**,
3:30 So **M** was conquered by Israel that day,
10: 6 gods of Aram, Sidon, **M**, Ammon, and Philistia.
11:15 Israel did not steal any land from **M** or Ammon.
11:17 Then they asked the king of **M** for similar
11:18 went around Edom and **M** through the wilderness.
11:18 they never once crossed the Arnon River into **M**.

11:25 any better than Balak son of Zippor, king of **M**?
Ru 1: 1 and two sons and went to live in the country of **M**.
1: 2 in the land of Judah. During their stay in **M**,
1: 6 Then Naomi heard in **M** that the LORD had
1: 6 and her daughters-in-law got ready to leave **M** to
1:22 So Naomi returned from **M**, accompanied by her
2: 6 "She is the young woman from **M** who came back
4: 3 "You know Naomi, who came back from **M**.
1Sa 12: 9 and by the Philistines and the king of **M**.
14:47 against **M**, Ammon, Edom, the kings of Zobah,
22: 3 Later David went to Mizpeh in **M**, where he asked
22: 4 and David's parents stayed in **M** while David was
2Sa 8: 2 David also conquered the land of **M**. He made the
8:12 Edom, **M**, Ammon, Philistia, and Amalek—
1Ki 11: 1 he married women from **M**, Ammon, Edom,
11: 7 the detestable god of **M**, and another for Molech,
11:33 Chemosh, the god of **M**; and Molech, the god of
2Ki 1: 1 the nation of **M** declared its independence from
3: 4 King Mesha of **M** and his people were sheep
3: 5 the king of **M** rebelled against the king of Israel.
3: 7 "The king of **M** has rebelled against me. Will you
3:10 the three of us here to let the king of **M** defeat us."
3:13 kings here to be destroyed by the king of **M**!"
3:18 he will make you victorious over the army of **M**!
3:21 when the people of **M** heard about the three armies
3:24 The army of Israel chased them into the land of **M**,
3:26 When the king of **M** saw that he was losing the
1Ch 1:46 destroyed the Midianite army in the land of **M**.
4:22 and Saraph, who ruled over **M** and Jashubi-lehem.
8: 8 and Baara, he had children in the land of **M**.
11:46 the sons of Elnaam; / Ithmah from **M**;
18: 2 David also conquered the land of **M**,
18:11 Edom, **M**, Ammon, Philistia, and Amalek.
2Ch 20:10 armies of Ammon, **M**, and Mount Seir are doing.
20:22 the LORD caused the armies of Ammon, **M**,
20:23 The armies of **M** and Ammon turned against their
Ne 13:23 married women from Ashdod, Ammon, and **M**.
Ps 60: 8 **M** will become my lowly servant, / and Edom will
108: 9 **M** will become my lowly servant, / and Edom will
Isa 11:14 occupy all the lands of Edom, **M**, and Ammon.
15: 1 This message came to me concerning **M**: In one
15: 4 The bravest warriors of **M** will cry out in utter
15: 5 My heart weeps for **M**. Its people flee to Zoar
15: 8 The whole land of **M** is a land of weeping from
16: 2 The women of **M** are left like homeless birds at the
16: 6 Is this **M**, the proud land we have heard so much
16: 7 land of **M** weeps. Yes, you people of **M**, mourn for
16: 8 **M** was once like a spreading grapevine.
16:11 I will weep for **M**. My sorrow for Kir-hareseth will
16:12 On the hilltops the people of **M** will pray in
16:13 The LORD has already said this about **M** in the
16:14 without fail, the glory of **M** will be ended,
25:10 **M** will be crushed like trampled straw and left to
25:12 The high walls of **M** will be demolished
Jer 25:21 I went to the nations of Edom, **M**, and Ammon,
27: 3 messages to the kings of Edom, **M**, Ammon, Tyre,
40:11 When the Judeans in **M**, Ammon, Edom,
48: 1 This message was given concerning **M**. This is
48: 2 No one will ever brag about **M** again, for there is a
48: 4 for all **M** is being destroyed. Her little ones will
48: 9 Oh, that **M** had wings so she could fly away,
48:11 "From her earliest history, **M** has lived in peace.
48:13 At last **M** will be ashamed of her idol Chemosh,
48:15 But now **M** and her towns will be destroyed.
48:16 "Calamity is coming fast to **M**; it threatens
48:17 "You friends of **M**, weep for her and cry! See how
48:18 for those who destroy **M** will shatter Dibon,
48:19 They shout to those who flee from **M**, 'What has
48:20 "And the reply comes back, '**M** lies in ruins;
48:20 banks of the Arnon River: **M** has been destroyed!'
48:24 and Bozrah—all the cities of **M**, far and near.
48:25 "The strength of **M** has ended. Her horns have
48:26 **M** will wallow in her own vomit, ridiculed by all.
48:28 "You people of **M**, flee from your cities
48:29 We have heard of the pride of **M**, for it is very
48:31 Yes, I wail for **M**; my heart is broken for the men
48:33 Joy and gladness are gone from fruitful **M**.
48:35 "I will put an end to **M**," says the LORD,
48:36 My heart moans like a flute for **M**
48:38 For I have smashed **M** like an old,
48:39 is broken! Hear the wailing! See the shame of **M**!
48:40 "An eagle swoops down on the land of **M**,"
48:42 **M** will no longer be a nation, for she has boasted
48:43 snares will be your lot, O **M**," says the LORD.
48:46 "O **M**, your destruction is sure! The people of the
48:47 in the latter days I will restore the fortunes of **M**,"
48:47 is the end of Jeremiah's prophecy concerning **M**.
Eze 25: 8 Because the people of **M** have said that Judah is
25:10 And I will hand **M** over to nomads from the
Da 11:41 of Israel, and many nations will fall, but **M**, Edom,
Am 2: 1 "The people of **M** have sinned again and again,
2: 2 So I will send down fire on the land of **M**, and all
Mic 6: 5 how King Balak of **M** tried to have you cursed
Zep 2: 8 "I have heard the taunts of the people of **M**
2: 9 "**M** and Ammon will be destroyed as completely

MOAB'S (6) [MOAB]

Nu 24:17 It will crush the foreheads of **M** people,
Jdg 11:18 They traveled along **M** eastern border and camped
2Sa 23:20 which included killing two of **M** mightiest
1Ch 11:22 which included killing two of **M** mightiest
Isa 16: 1 **M** refugees at Sela send lambs to Jerusalem as a
25:11 God will push down **M** people as a swimmer

MOABITE (15) [MOAB]

Nu 21:26 He had conquered a former **M** king and seized all
22: 2 Balak son of Zippor, the **M** king, knew what the
22:14 So the **M** officials returned to King Balak
22:21 his donkey and started off with the **M** officials.
22:36 he went out to meet him at a **M** town on the Arnon
25: 1 themselves by sleeping with the local **M** women.
Ru 1: 4 The two sons married **M** women. One married a
1:22 by her daughter-in-law Ruth, the young **M** woman.
4: 5 also requires that you marry Ruth, the **M** widow.
4:10 the **M** widow of Mahlon, to be my wife.
2Ki 13:20 Groups of **M** raiders used to invade the land each
24: 2 LORD sent bands of Babylonian, Aramean, **M**,
2Ch 24:26 the son of a **M** woman named Shomer.
Ne 13: 1 or **M** should ever be permitted to enter the
Jer 48:38 Crying and sorrow will be in every **M** home

MOABITES (18) [MOAB]

Ge 19:37 the ancestor of the nation now known as the **M**.
Nu 21:13 The Arnon is the boundary line between the **M**
Dt 2: 9 'Do not bother the **M**, the descendants of Lot,
2:11 to as the Rephaites, but the **M** called them Emites.
2:29 their country, and so did the **M**, who live in Ar.
23: 3 "No Ammonites or **M**, or any of their descendants
23: 6 try to help the Ammonites or the **M** in any way.
Jdg 3:29 They attacked the **M** and killed about ten thousand
2Sa 8: 2 The **M** who were spared became David's servants
2Ki 3:23 "It's blood!" the **M** exclaimed. "The three armies
3:24 the army of Israel rushed out and attacked the **M**,
23:13 and for Chemosh, the detestable god of the **M**;
1Ch 18: 2 and the **M** became David's subjects and brought
2Ch 20: 1 After this, the armies of the **M**, Ammonites,
Ezr 9: 1 Perizzites, Jebusites, Ammonites, **M**, Egyptians,
Ps 83: 6 these Edomites and Ishmaelites, / **M** and Hagrites,
Jer 9:26 the Egyptians, Edomites, Ammonites, **M**,
Eze 25:11 I will bring my judgment down on the **M**.

MOADIAH (2)

Ne 12: 5 Miniamin, **M**, Bilgah,
12:17 Piltai was leader of the family of **M**.

MOAN (6) [MOANED, MOANING, MOANS]

Ps 77: 3 I think of God, and I **m**, / overwhelmed with
Isa 59:11 like hungry bears; we **m** like mournful doves.
Jer 25:34 Weep and **m**, you evil shepherds! Roll in the dust,
Eze 7:16 and escape to the mountains will **m** like doves,
Joel 1:18 How the animals **m** with hunger! The cattle
Na 2: 7 Listen to them **m** like doves; watch them beat their

MOANED (3) [MOAN]

Ge 43: 6 Jacob **m**. "Why did you have to treat me with such
Ex 16: 3 "Oh, that we were back in Egypt," they **m**.
Isa 38:14 or a crane, / and then I **m** like a mourning dove.

MOANING (2) [MOAN]

Job 24:12 cry for help, yet God does not respond to their **m**.
Ps 79:11 Listen to the **m** of the prisoners.

MOANS (1) [MOAN]

Jer 48:36 My heart **m** like a flute for Moab and Kir-hareseth,

MOB (21) [MOBBED. MOBS]

Nu 22: 4 "This **m** will devour everything in sight, like an ox
Jdg 6:31 But Joash shouted to the **m**, "Why are you
Job 16:10 my cheek in contempt. A **m** gathers against me.
Jer 26:24 the court not to turn him over to the **m** to be killed.
Eze 16:40 They will band together in a **m** to stone you
Mt 26:47 arrived with a **m** that was armed with swords
Mk 14:43 arrived with a **m** that was armed with swords
14:51 in a linen nightshirt. When the **m** tried to grab him,
15: 8 The **m** began to crowd in toward Pilate, asking him
15:11 But at this point the leading priests stirred up the **m**
Lk 22:47 even as he said this, a **m** approached, led by Judas,
22:52 and the other leaders who headed the **m**.
Ac 13:50 and they incited a **m** against Paul and Barnabas
14: 5 A **m** of Gentiles and Jews, along with their leaders,
14:19 and turned the crowds into a murderous **m**.
16:22 A **m** quickly formed against Paul and Silas,
17: 5 worthless fellows from the streets to form a **m**
18:17 The **m** had grabbed Sosthenes, the leader of the
21:27 Paul in the Temple and roused a **m** against him.
21:32 When the **m** saw the commander and the troops
21:35 the **m** grew so violent the soldiers had to lift Paul

MOBBED (3) [MOB]

Jer 26: 8 and all the people at the Temple **m** him.
Mt 21:26 But if we say it was merely human, we'll be **m**,
Lk 4:29 they **m** him and took him to the edge of the hill on

MOBILIZE (11) [MOBILIZED, MOBILIZING]

2Sa 17:11 "I suggest that you **m** the entire army of Israel,
20: 4 Then the king instructed Amasa to **m** the army of
20:14 Sheba had traveled across Israel to **m** his own clan
2Ki 6: 8 "We will **m** our forces at such and such a place."
6: 9 for the Arameans are planning to **m** their troops
Isa 41: 5 in fear. Remote lands tremble and **m** for war.
Jer 46:14 **M** for battle, for the sword of destruction will
51:27 Signal many nations to **m** for war against Babylon.
Eze 7:14 "The trumpets call Israel's army to **m**, but no one
38: 4 I will **m** your troops and cavalry and make you a
Mic 5: 1 **M**! Marshal your troops! The enemy is laying

MOBILIZED (26) [MOBILIZE]

Ge 14: 3 and **m** their armies in Siddim Valley (that is,
Nu 20:20 With that he **m** his army and marched out to meet
21:23 he **m** his entire army and attacked Israel in the
Dt 2:32 declared war on us and **m** his forces at Jahaz.
Jdg 11:20 Instead, he **m** his army at Jahaz and attacked them.
12: 1 Then the tribe of Ephraim **m** its army and crossed
1Sa 7: 7 at Mizpah, they **m** their army and advanced.
11: 8 When Saul **m** them at Bezek, he found that there
13: 4 So the entire Israelite army **m** again and met Saul
15: 4 So Saul **m** his army at Telaim. There were 200,000
23: 8 So Saul **m** his entire army to march to Keilah
29: 1 The entire Philistine army now **m** at Aphek,
2Sa 5:17 of Israel, they **m** all their forces to capture him.
6: 1 Then David **m** thirty thousand special troops.
10:17 he **m** all Israel, crossed the Jordan River, and led
17:24 Absalom had **m** the entire army of Israel and was
1Ki 12:21 he **m** the armies of Judah and Benjamin—
20: 1 Now King Ben-hadad of Aram **m** his army,
2Ki 3:21 they **m** every man who could fight, young and old,
6:24 King Ben-hadad of Aram **m** his entire army
14:11 so King Jehoash of Israel **m** his army against King
1Ch 14: 8 all Israel, they **m** all their forces to capture him.
19:17 he **m** all Israel, crossed the Jordan River,
2Ch 11: 1 he **m** the armies of Judah and Benjamin—
25:21 So King Jehoash of Israel **m** his army against King
Eze 38: 7 Keep all the armies around you **m**, and take

MOBILIZING (1) [MOBILIZE]

Jos 11: 4 All these kings responded by **m** their warriors

MOBS (2) [MOB]

Isa 24:11 **M** gather in the streets, crying out for wine.
2Co 6: 5 have been beaten, been put in jail, faced angry **m**,

MOCK (22) [MOCKED, MOCKER, MOCKERS, MOCKERY, MOCKING, MOCKINGLY, MOCKS]

Job 11: 3 When you **m** God, shouldn't someone make you
12: 5 People who are at ease **m** those in trouble.
21: 3 let me speak. After I have spoken, you may **m** me.
30: 9 "And now their sons **m** me with their vulgar song!
Ps 35:16 They **m** me with the worst kind of profanity,
39: 8 my rebellion, / for even fools **m** me when I rebel.
44:13 You have caused all our neighbors to **m** us.
74:10 O God, will you allow our enemies to **m** you?
89:41 along has robbed him / while his neighbors **m**.
89:51 O LORD; / they **m** the one you anointed as king.
102: 8 taunt me day after day. / They **m** and curse me.
Pr 1:26 I will **m** you when disaster overtakes you—
17: 5 Those who **m** the poor insult their Maker;
Isa 5:19 They even **m** the Holy One of Israel and say,
50: 6 from shame, for they **m** me and spit in my face.
57: 4 Whom do you **m**, making faces and sticking out
La 3:63 they constantly **m** me with their songs.
Eze 23:32 And all the world will **m** and scorn you in your
Da 9:16 All the neighboring nations **m** Jerusalem and your
Mk 10:34 They will **m** him, spit on him, beat him with their
15:19 on him, and dropped to their knees in **m** worship.
Jude 1:10 But these people **m** and curse the things they do

MOCKED (31) [MOCK]

Jdg 9:38 The men you **m** are right outside the city! Go out
2Ki 19:23 By your messengers you have **m** the Lord.
2Ch 32:16 And Sennacherib's officials further **m** the LORD
36:16 But the people **m** these messengers of God
Ne 4: 1 the wall. He flew into a rage and **m** the Jews,
4: 4 "Hear us, O our God, for we are being **m**.
5: 9 God in order to avoid being **m** by enemy nations?
Job 30: 1 "But now I am **m** by those who are younger than
Ps 69: 7 For I am **m** and shamed for your sake;
79: 4 We are **m** by our neighbors, / an object of scorn
89:51 Your enemies have **m** me, O LORD; / they mock
Isa 4: 1 by your name so we won't be **m** as old maids."
37:24 By your messengers you have **m** the Lord.
Jer 20: 7 Now I am **m** by everyone in the city.
24: 9 They will be disgraced and **m**, taunted and cursed,
49:13 and a heap of rubble; it will be **m** and cursed.
Eze 22: 5 you will be **m** by people both far and near.
25: 3 **m** Israel in her desolation, and laughed at Judah as
36: 4 and **m** by foreign nations everywhere.
Mic 6:16 be treated with contempt, **m** by all who see you."
Zep 3:19 my former exiles, who have been **m** and shamed.
Mt 5:11 "God blesses you when you are **m** and persecuted
20:19 they will hand him over to the Romans to be **m**,
27:41 religious law, and the other leaders also **m** Jesus.
Mk 15:31 and teachers of religious law also **m** Jesus.
Lk 6:22 you who are hated and excluded and **m** and cursed
18:32 He will be handed over to the Romans to be **m**,
23:36 The soldiers **m** him, too, by offering him a drink of
Jn 7:47 "Have you been led astray, too?" the Pharisees **m**.
19: 3 they **m**, and they hit him with their fists.
Heb 11:36 Some were **m**, and their backs were cut open with

MOCKER (6) [MOCK]

Pr 9: 7 Anyone who rebukes a **m** will get a smart retort.
13: 1 a parent's discipline; a young **m** refuses to listen.
14: 6 A **m** seeks wisdom and never finds it,
19:25 If you punish a **m**, the simpleminded will learn a
22:10 Throw out the **m**, and fighting, quarrels,
24: 9 of a fool are sinful; everyone despises a **m**.

MOCKERS (12) [MOCK]

Job 17: 2 I am surrounded by **m**. I watch how bitterly they
Ps 44:16 All we hear are the taunts of our **m**. / All we see

Pr 1:22 How long will you **m** relish your mocking?
3:34 The LORD mocks at **m**, but he shows favor to the
9: 8 So don't bother rebuking **m**; they will only hate
15:12 **M** don't love those who rebuke them, so they stay
19:29 **M** will be punished, and the backs of fools will be
20: 1 Wine produces **m**; liquor leads to brawls.
21:11 A simpleton can learn only by seeing **m** punished;
21:24 **M** are proud and haughty; they act with boundless
29: 8 **M** can get a whole town agitated, but those who
Ac 13:41 'Look you **m**, / be amazed and die! / For I am

MOCKERY (19) [MOCK]

Dt 28:37 and a **m** among all the nations to which the
1Ki 9: 7 I will make Israel an object of **m** and ridicule
Job 17: 6 "God has made a **m** of me among the people;
Ps 109:25 I am an object of **m** to people everywhere;
Pr 19:28 A corrupt witness makes a **m** of justice; the mouth
Isa 25: 8 all insults and **m** against his land and people.
Jer 29:18 an object of damnation, horror, contempt, and **m**.
42:18 an object of damnation, horror, cursing, and **m**.
44: 8 of cursing and **m** for all the nations of the earth.
44:12 be an object of damnation, horror, cursing, and **m**.
Eze 5:14 a **m** in the eyes of the surrounding nations and to
5:15 You will become an object of **m** and taunting
21:28 prophesy concerning the Ammonites and their **m**.
22: 4 I will make you an object of **m** throughout the
Joel 2:17 to you, so don't let them become an object of **m**.
2:19 You will no longer be an object of **m** among the
Mt 27:29 Then they knelt before him in **m**, yelling, "Hail!
27:39 by shouted abuse, shaking their heads in **m**.
Mk 15:29 by shouted abuse, shaking their heads in **m**.

MOCKING (11) [MOCK]

1Ki 18:27 About noontime Elijah began **m** them.
2Ki 2:23 a group of boys from the town began **m**
Pr 1:22 How long will you mockers relish your **m**?
La 3:14 laugh at me. All day long they sing their **m** songs.
Eze 36: 3 You are the object of much **m** and slander.
Zep 2: 8 **m** my people and invading their borders.
Mt 27:31 When they were finally tired of **m** him, they took
Mk 15:20 When they were finally tired of **m** him, they took
Lk 22:63 Now the guards in charge of Jesus began **m**
23:11 Now Herod and his soldiers began **m**
Ac 2:13 But others in the crowd were **m**. "They're drunk,

MOCKINGLY (1) [MOCK]

Eze 32:21 Down in the grave mighty leaders will **m** welcome

MOCKS (4) [MOCK]

Job 27:23 But everyone jeers at them and **m** them.
Ps 22: 7 Everyone who sees me **m** me. / They sneer
Pr 3:34 The LORD **m** at mockers, but he shows favor to
30:17 The eye that **m** a father and despises a mother will

MODEL (1)

2Ki 16:10 So he sent a **m** of the altar to Uriah the priest,

MODERATION [KJV] See CONSIDERATE

MODEST (1) [MODESTY]

1Ti 2: 9 And I want women to be **m** in their appearance.

MODESTY (1) [MODEST]

1Ti 2:15 continuing to live in faith, love, holiness, and **m**.

MODIFY (1)

Dt 17:11 must be fully executed; do not **m** it in any way.

MOISTEN (2) [MOISTURE]

Isa 44: 3 to quench your thirst and to **m** your parched fields.
Eze 46:14 with a third of a gallon of olive oil to **m** the flour.

MOISTURE (3) [MOISTEN]

Job 37:11 He loads the clouds with **m**, and they flash with his
Hos 2:22 of the grain, the grapes, and the olive trees for **m**.
Lk 8: 6 but soon it withered and died for lack of **m**.

MOLADAH (4)

Jos 15:26 Amam, Shema, **M**,
19: 2 inheritance included Beersheba, Sheba, **M**,
1Ch 4:28 They lived in Beersheba, **M**, Hazar-shual,
Ne 11:26 They also lived in Jeshua, **M**, Beth-pelet,

MOLD (2) [MOLDED, MOLDER, MOLDING, MOLDS]

1Ki 7:37 made alike, for each was cast from the same **m**.
Isa 40:19 Can he be compared to an idol formed in a **m**,

MOLDED (5) [MOLD]

Ex 32: 4 and **m** and tooled it into the shape of a calf.
36:38 with gold. The five bases were **m** from bronze.
1Ki 7:16 For the tops of the pillars he made capitals of **m**
1Ch 18: 8 He **m** it into the bronze Sea, the pillars,
2Ch 4: 8 north wall. Then he **m** one hundred gold basins.

MOLDER (1) [MOLD]

Isa 41: 7 hurries the goldsmith, and the **m** helps at the anvil.

MOLDING (10) [MOLD]

Ex 25:11 with pure gold, and put a **m** of gold all around it.
25:24 it with pure gold and run a **m** of gold around it.
25:25 the top edge, and put a gold **m** all around the rim.
30: 3 pure gold, and run a gold **m** around the entire altar.
30: 4 Beneath the **m**, on opposite sides of the altar,
37: 2 and out, and it had a **m** of gold all the way around.
37:11 with pure gold, with a gold **m** all around the edge.
37:12 of the table, and a gold **m** ran around the rim.
37:26 with pure gold and ran a gold **m** around the edge.
37:27 beneath the **m**, to hold the carrying poles.

MOLDS (3) [MOLD]

1Ki 7:46 The king had them cast in clay **m** in the Jordan
2Ch 4:17 The king had them cast in clay **m** in the Jordan
Na 3:14 Go into the pits to trample clay, and pack it into **m**!

MOLDY (2)

Jos 9: 5 And they took along dry, **m** bread for provisions.
9:12 we left. But now, as you can see, it is dry and **m**.

MOLE (1) [MOLES]

Lev 11:29 the **m**, the mouse, the great lizard of all varieties,

MOLE [KJV] See CHAMELEON

MOLECH (16)

Lev 18:21 not give any of your children as a sacrifice to **M**,
20: 2 them devote their children as burnt offerings to **M**,
20: 3 my holy name by giving their children to **M**.
20: 4 community ignore this offering of children to **M**
20: 5 those who commit prostitution by worshiping **M**.
1Ki 11: 5 the goddess of the Sidonians, and **M**,
11: 7 the detestable god of Moab, and another for **M**,
11:33 god of Moab; and **M**, the god of the Ammonites.
2Ki 23:10 a son or daughter in the fire as an offering to **M**.
23:13 and for **M**, the detestable god of the Ammonites.
Isa 57: 9 have given olive oil and perfume to **M** as your gift.
Jer 32:35 there they sacrifice their sons and daughters to **M**.
49: 1 Why are you, who worship **M**, living in its towns?
49: 3 for your god **M** will be exiled along with his
Zep 1: 5 follow the LORD, but then they worship **M**, too.
Ac 7:43 interest was in your pagan gods— / the shrine of **M**

MOLES (1) [MOLE]

Isa 2:20 their gold and silver idols to the **m** and bats.

MOLID (1)

1Ch 2:29 and his wife Abihail were Ahban and **M**.

MOLLUSK (1)

Ex 30:34 resin droplets, **m** scent, galbanum, and pure

MOLOCH [KJV] See MOLECH, SAKKUTH

MOLTEN (2)

Nu 33:52 You must destroy all their carved and **m** images
1Ki 7:33 rims, and hubs were all cast from **m** bronze.

MOLTEN [KJV] See also CAST, MOLD, SMELT(ED)

MOMENT (60) [MOMENT'S, MOMENTS]

Ge 3: 7 At that **m**, their eyes were opened, and they
22:11 At that **m** the angel of the LORD shouted to him
44:18 Be patient with me for a **m**, for I know you could
Ex 33: 5 If I were there among you for even a **m**, I would
Nu 4:20 and look at the sacred objects for even a **m**,
Jdg 13: 7 the **m** of his birth until the day of his death.' "
14: 6 At that **m** the Spirit of the LORD powerfully took
2Sa 22:19 They attacked me at a **m** when I was weakest,
24:16 At that **m** the angel of the LORD was by the
2Ki 8: 5 At that very **m**, the mother of the boy walked in to
1Ch 21:15 At that **m** the angel of the LORD was standing by
29:15 We are here for only a **m**, visitors and strangers in
2Ch 5:13 At that **m** a cloud filled the Temple of the LORD.
20:22 At the **m** they began to sing and give praise,
Ezr 9: 8 "But now we have been given a brief **m** of grace,
Est 4:13 "Don't think for a **m** that you will escape there in
Job 5: 3 who turn from God may be successful for the **m**,
7:18 examine us every morning and test us every **m**.
7:19 Why won't you leave me alone—even for a **m**?
10:20 me alone—that I may have a little **m** of comfort
14: 2 Like a flower, we blossom for a **m** and then wither.
24:24 in a **m** they will be gone like all others,
34:20 In a **m** they die. At midnight they all pass away;
Ps 18:18 They attacked me at a **m** when I was weakest,
22:10 You have been my God from the **m** I was born.
30: 5 His anger lasts for a **m**, / but his favor lasts a
39: 5 An entire lifetime is just a **m** to you;
51: 5 yes, from the **m** my mother conceived me.
78:39 gone in a **m** like a breath of wind, never to return.
139: 3 to stop and rest. / Every **m** you know where I am.
139:16 Every **m** was laid out / before a single day had
146: 4 and in a **m** all their plans come to an end.
Pr 11:18 Evil people get rich for the **m**, but the reward of
Isa 47: 9 those two things will come upon you in a **m**:
54: 7 "For a brief **m** I abandoned you, but with great
54: 8 In a **m** of anger I turned my face away for a little
66: 8 Has a country ever come forth in a mere **m**?
Jer 4:20 tent is destroyed; in a **m**, every shelter is crushed.
La 4: 6 where utter disaster struck in a **m** with no one to
Da 5: 5 At that very **m** they saw the fingers of a human
9:23 The **m** you began praying, a command was given.
Mt 6:27 Can all your worries add a single **m** to your life?
9:22 you well." And the woman was healed at that **m**.
17:18 and it left him. From that **m** the boy was well.
27:51 At that **m** the curtain in the Temple was torn in
Lk 4: 5 him all the kingdoms of the world in a **m** of time.
8:55 And at that **m** her life returned, and she
12:25 Can all your worries add a single **m** to your life?
12:36 and let him in the **m** he arrives and knocks.
22:53 But this is your **m**, the time when the power of
22:61 At that **m** the Lord turned and looked at Peter.
24:31 recognized him. And at that **m** he disappeared!
Ac 24: 4 kindly give me your attention for only a **m** as I
1Co 4:13 like everybody's trash—right up to the present **m**.
15:52 It will happen in a **m**, in the blinking of an eye,
Gal 2: 5 But we refused to listen to them for a single **m**.
Php 4:18 At the **m** I have all I need—more than I need!
Rev 17:12 kingdoms for one brief **m** to reign with the beast.
18:10 In one single **m** God's judgment came on her."
18:17 And in one single **m** all the wealth of the city is

MOMENT'S (1) [MOMENT]

Isa 59: 8 and those who follow them cannot experience a **m**

MOMENTS (1) [MOMENT]

Jn 13:33 how brief are these **m** before I must go away

MOMENTUM (1)

2Sa 15:12 also joined Absalom, and the conspiracy gained **m**.

MONARCHS (1)

Pr 30:29 There are three stately **m** on the earth—no, four:

MONEY (207)

Ge 42:27 to feed the donkeys, he found his **m** in the sack.
42:28 "My **m** is here in my sack!" They were filled with
42:35 there at the top of each one was the bag of **m** paid
43:12 Take double the **m** that you found in your sacks,
43:15 and the gifts and double the **m** and hurried to
43:18 because of the **m** returned to us in our sacks,"
43:21 The **m** we had used to pay for the grain was there
43:22 We also have additional **m** to buy more grain.
43:22 We have no idea how the **m** got into our sacks."
43:23 have put it there. We collected your **m** all right."
44: 1 and put each man's **m** back into his sack.
44: 2 youngest brother's sack, along with his grain **m**."
44: 8 Didn't we bring back the **m** we found in our sacks?
47:14 Joseph collected all the **m** in Egypt and Canaan in
47:14 and he brought the **m** to Pharaoh's treasure-house.
47:15 the people of Egypt and Canaan ran out of **m**,
47:15 "Our **m** is gone," they said, "but give us bread.
47:16 then," Joseph replied, "since your **m** is gone,
47:18 year they came again and said, "Our **m** is gone,
Ex 21:35 sell the live bull and divide the **m** between them.
21:36 to keep it under control, the **m** will not be divided.
22: 7 "Suppose someone entrusts **m** or goods to a
22:17 the man must still pay the **m** for her dowry.
22:25 "If you lend **m** to a fellow Hebrew in need, do not be like a **m** lender, charging interest.
30:16 Use this **m** for the care of the Tabernacle. It will
Lev 22:11 However, if the priest buys slaves with his own **m**,
25:26 sold it manages to get enough **m** to buy it back,
25:36 or charge interest on the **m** you lend them.
25:37 on anything you lend them, whether **m** or food.
25:49 may also redeem themselves if they can get the **m**.
Nu 3:49 So Moses collected redemption **m** for the firstborn
3:51 And Moses gave the redemption **m** to Aaron
22: 7 and took **m** with them to pay Balaam to curse
Dt 14:25 and take the **m** to the place the LORD your God
14:26 you arrive, use the **m** to buy anything you want—
15: 6 You will lend **m** to many nations but will never
23:19 whether it is **m**, food, or anything else that may be
28:44 They will lend **m** to you, not you to them.
Jdg 3:15 The Israelites sent Ehud to deliver their tax **m** to
3:17 He brought the tax **m** to Eglon, who was very fat.
3:18 Ehud sent home those who had carried the tax **m**.
16:18 leaders returned and brought the **m** with them.
17: 3 He returned the **m** to her, and she said, "I now
1Sa 2:36 before his descendants, begging for **m** and food.
8: 3 not like their father, for they were greedy for **m**.
2Sa 8: 2 David's servants and brought him tribute **m**.
8: 6 David's subjects and brought him tribute **m**.
21: 4 "Well, **m** won't do it," the Gibeonites replied.
1Ki 4:21 peoples of those lands sent tribute **m** to Solomon
2Ki 4: 7 and there will be enough **m** left over to support
5:23 him two sets of clothing, tied up the **m** in two bags,
5:26 Is this the time to receive **m** and clothing and olive
12: 4 "Collect all the **m** brought as a sacred offering to
12: 5 Let the priests take some of that **m** to pay for
12: 8 So the priests agreed not to collect any more **m**
12:10 and the high priest counted the **m** that had been
12:11 Then they gave the **m** to the construction
12:12 They also used the **m** to buy timber and cut stone
12:13 The **m** brought to the Temple was not used for
12:16 the **m** that was contributed for guilt offerings
15:20 Menahem extorted the **m** from the rich of Israel,
18:14 I will pay whatever tribute **m** you demand if you
22: 4 and have him count the **m** the gatekeepers have
22: 5 Entrust this **m** to the men assigned to supervise the
22: 7 supervisors to keep account of the **m** they receive,
22: 9 "Your officials have given the **m** collected at the
1Ch 18: 2 David's subjects and brought him tribute **m**.

18: 6 David's subjects and brought him tribute **m**.
2Ch 24:10 and they gladly brought their **m** and filled the chest
24:11 and an officer of the high priest counted the **m**
24:11 after day, and a large amount of **m** was collected.
24:12 and Jehoiada gave the **m** to the construction
24:14 they brought the remaining **m** to the king
34: 9 They gave Hilkiah the high priest the **m** that had
34:10 He entrusted the **m** to the men assigned to
34:14 As Hilkiah the high priest was recording the **m**
34:17 The **m** that was collected at the Temple of the
Ezr 7:18 Any **m** that is left over may be used in whatever
7:20 If you run short of **m** for anything necessary for
Ne 5: 2 We need more **m** just so we can buy the food we
5: 5 children into slavery just to get enough **m** to live.
5: 7 by charging them interest when they borrow **m**!"
5:10 have been lending the people **m** and grain,
5:11 Repay the interest you charged on their **m**, grain,
10:32 so that there will be enough **m** to care for the
Est 3:11 "Keep the **m**," the king told Haman, "but go
4: 7 and told him how much **m** Haman had promised to
Job 22: 6 you must have lent **m** to your friend and then kept
22:24 Give up your lust for **m**, and throw your precious
27:16 "Evil people may have all the **m** in the world,
27:17 and the innocent will divide all that **m**.
31:24 "Have I put my trust in **m** or felt secure because of
42:11 And each of them brought him a gift of **m** and a
Ps 15: 5 Those who do not charge interest on the **m** they
119:36 your decrees; / do not inflict me with love for **m**!
Pr 2: 4 Search for them as you would for lost **m** or hidden
7:20 He has taken a wallet full of **m** with him, and he
10:16 their lives, but evil people squander their **m** on sin.
11:28 Trust in your **m** and down you go! But the godly
15:27 Dishonest **m** brings grief to the whole family,
28: 8 A person who makes **m** by charging interest will
Ecc 5:10 Those who love **m** will never have enough.
7:12 Wisdom or **m** can get you almost anything, but it's
10:19 and wine gives happiness, and **m** gives everything!
Isa 55: 1 Come and drink—even if you have no **m**! Come,
55: 2 Why spend your **m** on food that does not give you
Jer 32:25 paying good **m** for it before these witnesses—
40: 5 gave Jeremiah some food and **m** and let him go.
Eze 7:19 "They will throw away their **m**, tossing it out like
7:19 for their love of **m** made them stumble into sin.
18:13 and lends **m** at interest. Should such a sinful
18:17 helps the poor, does not lend **m** at interest,
33:31 their mouths, but their hearts seek only after **m**.
Am 2: 8 present offerings of wine purchased with stolen **m**.
Mic 1: 7 These things were bought with the **m** earned by her
6:14 And though you try to save your **m**, it will come to
7: 3 The people with **m** and influence pay them off,
Hab 2:12 for you who build cities with **m** gained by murder
Mt 6:24 the other. You cannot serve both God and **m**.
10: 9 "Don't take any **m** with you.
13:44 and sold everything he owned to get enough **m** to
15: 5 for their needs if you give the **m** to God instead.'
18:23 date with servants who had borrowed **m** from him.
19:21 and sell all you have and give the **m** to the poor,
20:15 the law for me to do what I want with my **m**?
21:12 He knocked over the tables of the **m** changers
25:14 and gave them **m** to invest for him while he was
25:16 bags of gold began immediately to invest the **m**
25:17 of gold also went right to work and doubled the **m**.
25:18 the ground and hid the master's **m** for safekeeping.
25:19 to give an account of how they had used his **m**.
25:25 I was afraid I would lose your **m**, so I hid it in the
25:27 you should at least have put my **m** into the bank
25:28 Take the **m** from this servant and give it to the one
26: 8 they saw this. "What a waste of **m**," they said.
26: 9 sold it for a fortune and given the **m** to the poor."
27: 5 Then Judas threw the **m** onto the floor of the
27: 6 The leading priests picked up the **m**. "We can't
27: 6 "since it's against the law to accept **m** paid for
Mk 6: 8 a walking stick—no food, no traveler's bag, no **m**.
10:21 and sell all you have and give the **m** to the poor,
11:15 He knocked over the tables of the **m** changers
12:41 and watched as the crowds dropped in their **m**.
14: 5 it for a small fortune and given the **m** to the poor!"
Lk 3:14 John replied, "Don't extort **m**, and don't accuse
6:34 And if you lend **m** only to those who can repay
7:41 "A man loaned **m** to two people—five hundred
9: 3 "nor a traveler's bag, nor food, nor **m**.
10: 4 Don't take along any **m**, or a traveler's bag,
10:30 They stripped him of his clothes and **m**, beat him
14:28 then checking to see if there is enough **m** to pay
14:30 and ran out of **m** before it was finished!'
15:13 and there he wasted all his **m** on wild living.
15:14 About the time his **m** ran out, a great famine swept
15:30 back after squandering your **m** on prostitutes,
16: 5 "So he invited each person who owed **m** to his
16:12 And if you are not faithful with other people's **m**,
16:12 why should you be trusted with **m** of your own?
16:13 the other. You cannot serve both God and **m**."
16:14 The Pharisees, who dearly loved their **m**,
18:22 "Sell all you have and give the **m** to the poor,
19:15 called in the servants to whom he had given the **m**.
19:15 wanted to find out what they had done with the **m**
19:20 brought back only the original amount of **m**
19:23 why didn't you deposit the **m** in the bank so I
19:24 the king ordered, 'Take the **m** from this servant,
22:35 to preach the Good News and you did not have **m**,
22:36 he said, "take your **m** and a traveler's bag.
Jn 2:14 and he saw **m** changers behind their counters.
2:15 scattered the **m** changers' coins over the floor,
12: 5 have been sold and the **m** given to the poor."
13:29 and pay for the food or to give some **m** to the poor.
Ac 1:18 (Judas bought a field with the **m** he received for
3: 3 John about to enter, he asked them for some **m**.
3: 6 But Peter said, "I don't have any **m** for you.
4:35 and brought the **m** to the apostles to give to others
4:37 and brought the **m** to the apostles for those in need.
5: 2 He brought part of the **m** to the apostles, but he
5: 3 and you kept some of the **m** for yourself.
5: 4 And after selling it, the **m** was yours to give away.
8:18 people's heads, he offered **m** to buy this power.
8:20 "May your **m** perish with you for thinking God's
16:16 She was a fortune-teller who earned a lot of **m** for
20:33 "I have never coveted anyone's **m** or fine clothing.
24:17 I returned to Jerusalem with **m** to aid my people
Ro 12: 8 do it! If you have **m**, share it generously.
15:28 As soon as I have delivered this **m** and completed
1Co 16: 1 Now about the **m** being collected for the Christians
16: 2 each of you should put aside some amount of **m** in
2Co 2:17 are many of them—who preach just to make **m**.
9: 3 told them you would be, with your **m** all collected.
1Th 2: 5 to be your friends so you would give us **m**!
1Ti 3: 3 be gentle, peace loving, and not one who loves **m**.
3: 8 be heavy drinkers and must not be greedy for **m**.
6:10 For the love of **m** is at the root of all kinds of evil.
6:10 And some people, craving **m**, have wandered from
6:17 world not to be proud and not to trust in their **m**,
6:18 Tell them to use their **m** to do good. They should
2Ti 3: 2 For people will love only themselves and their **m**.
Tit 1: 7 not be a heavy drinker, violent, or greedy for **m**.
1:11 from the truth. Such teachers only want your **m**.
Heb 13: 5 Stay away from the love of **m**; be satisfied with
2Pe 2: 3 they will make up clever lies to get hold of your **m**.
2:15 son of Beor, who loved to earn **m** by doing wrong.
1Jn 3:17 But if one of you has **m** enough to live well
Jude 1:11 Like Balaam, they will do anything for **m**.

MONITOR (1)

Lev 11:30 the gecko, the **m** lizard, the common lizard,

MONOPOLY (1)

Job 15: 8 secret council? Do you have a **m** on wisdom?

MONSTER (7) [MONSTER'S]

Job 3: 8 those who are ready to rouse the sea **m**—curse that
7:12 Am I a sea **m** that you place a guard on me?
26:12 grew calm. By his skill he crushed the great sea **m**.
Ps 89:10 You are the one who crushed the great sea **m**.
Jer 51:34 He has swallowed us like a great **m** and filled his
Eze 29: 3 you great **m**, lurking in the streams of the Nile.
32: 2 but you are really just a sea **m**, heaving around in

MONSTER'S (1) [MONSTER]

Ps 74:13 by your strength / and smashed the sea **m** heads.

MONSTERS [KJV] See JACKALS

MONTH (70) [MONTHLY, MONTHS]

FIRST MONTH (7) Ex 12:2,6; Jos 4:19; 5:10; 1Ch 27:2,3; 2Ch 29:3

Ge 7:11 years old, on the seventeenth day of the second **m**,
29:14 After Jacob had been there about a **m**,
Ex 12: 2 this **m** will be the first **m** of the year for you.
12: 3 day of this **m** each family must choose a lamb
12: 6 the evening of the fourteenth day of this first **m**.
12:18 **m** until the evening of the twenty-first day of the **m**.
16: 1 They arrived there a **m** after leaving Egypt.
Lev 27: 6 A boy between the ages of one **m** and five years is
Nu 3:15 Count every male who is one **m** old or older."
3:22 There were 7,500 males one **m** old or older among
3:28 There were 8,600 males one **m** old or older among
3:34 There were 6,200 males one **m** old or older among
3:39 there were 22,000 males one **m** old or older.
3:40 all the firstborn sons in Israel who are one **m** old
3:43 total number of firstborn sons who were one **m** old
9:11 They must offer the Passover sacrifice one **m** later,
9:22 a **m**, or a year, the people of Israel stayed in camp
10:10 and at the beginning of each **m** to rejoice over your
11:20 You will eat it for a whole **m** until you gag and are
11:21 and yet you promise them meat for a whole **m**!
18:16 Redeem them when they are one **m** old.
26:62 The men from the Levite clans who were one **m**
28:11 "On the first day of each **m**, present an extra burnt
28:14 on the first day of each **m** throughout the year.
28:15 on the first day of each **m** you must offer one male
Dt 21:13 Then she must remain in your home for a full **m**,
33:14 grow in the sun, / and the bounty produced each **m**;
Jos 4:19 crossed the Jordan on the tenth day of the first **m**—
4:19 the **m** that marked their exodus from Egypt.
5:10 the evening of the fourteenth day of the first **m**—
5:10 the **m** that marked their exodus from Egypt.
1Sa 11: 1 About a **m** later, King Nahash of Ammon led his
1Ki 4: 7 Each of them arranged provisions for one **m** of the
4:27 and his court, each during his assigned **m**.
5:14 them to Lebanon in shifts, ten thousand every **m**,
5:14 so that each man would be one **m** in Lebanon
2Ki 15:13 in Judah. Shallum reigned in Samaria only one **m**.
1Ch 27: 1 divisions that were on duty each **m** of the year.
27: 1 Each division served for one **m** and had
27: 2 which was on duty during the first **m**.
27: 3 in charge of all the army officers for the first **m**.
27: 4 which was on duty during the second **m**.
27: 5 which was on duty during the third **m**.
27: 7 which was on duty during the fourth **m**.
27: 8 which was on duty during the fifth **m**.
27: 9 which was on duty during the sixth **m**.
27:10 which was on duty during the seventh **m**.
27:11 which was on duty during the eighth **m**.
27:12 which was on duty during the ninth **m**.
27:13 which was on duty during the tenth **m**.
27:14 which was on duty during the eleventh **m**.
27:15 which was on duty during the twelfth **m**.
2Ch 29: 3 In the very first **m** of the first year of his reign,
30: 3 Passover was normally celebrated one **m** earlier,
Ne 8:14 in shelters during the festival to be held that **m**.
Est 3: 7 So in the **m** of April, during the twelfth year of
3: 7 to determine the best day and **m** to take action.
4:11 called for me to come to him in more than a **m**."
9:24 and **m** determined by casting lots (the lots were
Pr 7:20 with him, and he won't return until later in the **m**."
Isa 66:23 me from week to week and from **m** to **m**.
Eze 47:12 There will be a new crop every **m**, without fail!
Zec 11: 8 I got rid of their three evil shepherds in a single **m**.
Lk 1:26 In the sixth **m** of Elizabeth's pregnancy, God sent
1:36 she was barren, but she's already in her sixth **m**.
Rev 9:15 had been prepared for this hour and day and **m**
22: 2 twelve crops of fruit, with a fresh crop each **m**.

MONTHLY (5) [MONTH]

Ge 31:35 Rachel explained. "I'm having my **m** period."
Lev 15:33 for dealing with a woman during her **m** menstrual
Nu 28:14 Present this **m** burnt offering on the first day of
29: 6 special sacrifices are in addition to your regular **m**
2Ch 31: 3 Sabbath festivals and **m** new moon festivals,

MONTHS (53) [MONTH]

SEVEN MONTHS (3) 1Sa 6:1; Eze 39:12,14

THREE MONTHS (16) Ge 38:24; Ex 2:2; 2Sa 6:11; 24:13; 2Ki 23:31; 24:8; 1Ch 13:14; 21:12; 2Ch 36:2,9; Lk 1:56; Ac 7:20; 19:8; 20:3; 28:11; Heb 11:23

Ge 8: 4 exactly five **m** from the time the flood began,
8: 5 Two and a half **m** later, as the waters continued to
8:13 years old, ten and a half **m** after the flood began,
8:14 Two more **m** went by, and at last the earth was
38:24 About three **m** later, word reached Judah that
Ex 2: 2 baby he was and kept him hidden for three **m**.
19: 1 of Sinai exactly two **m** after they left Egypt.
Jdg 11:37 in the hills and weep with my friends for two **m**,
11:38 And he let her go away for two **m**. She and her
19: 2 father's home in Bethlehem. After about four **m**,
20:47 the rock of Rimmon, where they lived for four **m**.
1Sa 6: 1 remained in Philistine territory seven **m** in all.
27: 7 there among the Philistines for a year and four **m**.
2Sa 5: 5 over Judah from Hebron for seven years and six **m**,
6:11 there with the family of Obed-edom for three **m**,
24: 8 they completed their task in nine **m** and twenty
24:13 three **m** of fleeing from your enemies, or three
1Ki 5:14 be one month in Lebanon and two **m** at home.
11:16 Joab and the army had stayed there for six **m**,
18: 1 After many **m** passed, in the third year of the
2Ki 15: 8 reign in Judah. He reigned in Samaria six **m**.
23:31 became king, and he reigned in Jerusalem three **m**.
24: 8 became king, and he reigned in Jerusalem three **m**.
1Ch 13:14 there with the family of Obed-edom for three **m**,
21:12 of famine, three **m** of destruction by your enemies,
2Ch 36: 2 when he became king, but he reigned only three **m**.
36: 9 but he reigned in Jerusalem only three **m** and ten
Est 1: 4 The celebration lasted six **m**—a tremendous
2:12 she was given the prescribed twelve **m** of beauty
2:12 six **m** with oil of myrrh, followed by six **m** with special perfumes
Job 3: 6 of the year, never again to appear among the **m**.
7: 3 I, too, have been assigned **m** of futility, long
14: 5 You know how many **m** we will live, and we are
39: 2 Do you know how many **m** they carry their young?
Jer 17: 8 by the heat or worried by long **m** of drought.
28:17 Two **m** later, Hananiah died.
Eze 39:12 It will take seven **m** for the people of Israel to
39:14 At the end of the seven **m**, special crews will be
Da 4:29 Twelve **m** later, he was taking a walk on the flat
Lk 1:24 and went into seclusion for five **m**.
1:56 Mary stayed with Elizabeth about three **m** and
Jn 4:35 not begin until the summer ends four **m** from now?
Ac 7:20 His parents cared for him at home for three **m**.
19: 8 and preached boldly for the next three **m**,
20: 3 where he stayed for three **m**. He was preparing to
28:11 It was three **m** after the shipwreck that we set sail
Gal 4:10 don't do on certain days or **m** or seasons or years.
Heb 11:23 by faith that Moses' parents hid him for three **m**.
Rev 9: 5 but to torture them for five **m** with agony like the
9:10 This power was given to them for five **m**.
11: 2 They will trample the holy city for 42 **m**.
13: 5 authority to do what he wanted for forty-two **m**.

MONUMENT (12) [MONUMENTS]

Ge 11: 4 that reaches to the skies—a **m** to our greatness!
31:45 So Jacob took a stone and set it up as a **m**.
35:20 Jacob set up a stone **m** over her grave, and it can
1Sa 15:12 "Saul went to Carmel to set up a **m** to himself;
2Sa 18:18 Absalom had built a **m** to himself in the King's
18:18 He named the **m** after himself, and it is known as Absalom's **M** to this day.
2Ki 23:17 "What is that **m** over there?" Josiah asked.
Job 19:23 be written. Oh, that they could be inscribed on a **m**,
Isa 19:19 and there will be a **m** to the LORD at its border.
Jer 18:16 land will become desolate, a **m** to their stupidity.
19: 8 face of the earth, making it a **m** to their stupidity.

MONUMENTS (1) [MONUMENT]

Eze 43: 7 or by raising **m** in honor of their dead kings.

MOON (60) [NEW-MOON]

NEW MOON (16) 1Sa 20:5,18,24; 2Ki 4:23; 1Ch 23:31; 2Ch 2:4; 8:13; 31:3; Ezr 3:5; Ne 10:33; Isa 1:13; Eze 45:17; 46:1,3,6; Hos 2:11

Ge 1:16 the sun and the **m**, to shine down upon the earth.
1:16 the lesser one, the **m**, presides through the night.
37: 9 "The sun, **m**, and eleven stars bowed low before
Dt 4:19 look up into the sky and see the sun, **m**, and stars—
17: 3 other gods or by worshiping the sun, the **m**,
Jos 10:12 and the **m** over the valley of Aijalon."
10:13 and **m** stood still until the Israelites had defeated
1Sa 20: 5 "Tomorrow we celebrate the new **m** festival.
20:18 "Tomorrow we celebrate the new **m** festival.
20:24 and when the new **m** festival began, the king sat
2Ki 4:23 "It is neither a new **m** festival nor a Sabbath."
23: 5 and to the sun, the **m**, the constellations, and to all
1Ch 23:31 at new **m** celebrations, and at all the appointed
2Ch 2: 4 on the Sabbaths, at new **m** celebrations,
8:13 on new **m** festivals, and at the three annual
31: 3 Sabbath festivals and monthly new **m** festivals,
Ezr 3: 5 and the offerings required for the new **m**
Ne 10:33 the new **m** celebrations, and the annual festivals;
Job 25: 5 God is so glorious that even the **m** and stars
31:26 or the **m** walking down its silver pathway,
Ps 8: 3 the **m** and the stars you have set in place—
72: 5 as long as the **m** continues in the skies.
81: 3 when the **m** is new, / when the **m** is full.
89:37 as eternal as the **m**, / my faithful witness in the
104:19 You made the **m** to mark the seasons / and the sun
121: 6 sun will not hurt you by day, / nor the **m** at night.
136: 9 and the **m** and stars to rule the night. / His faithful
148: 3 Praise him, sun and **m**! / Praise him, all you
Ecc 12: 2 when the light of the sun and **m** and stars is dim to
SS 6:10 like the dawn, as fair as the **m**, as bright as the sun,
Isa 1:13 Your celebrations of the new **m** and the Sabbath
13:10 No light will shine from stars or sun or **m**.
24:23 of the sun and **m** will seem to fade away.
30:26 The **m** will be as bright as the sun, and the sun will
60:19 will you need the sun or **m** to give you light,
60:20 The sun will never set; the **m** will not go down.
Jer 8: 2 out on the ground before the sun, **m**, and stars—
31:35 light the day and the **m** and stars to light the night.
Eze 32: 7 with a cloud, and the **m** will not give you its light.
45:17 the new **m** celebrations, the Sabbath days, and all
46: 1 Sabbath days and the days of new **m** celebrations.
46: 3 Sabbath days and the days of new **m** celebrations.
46: 6 At the new **m** celebrations, he will bring one
Hos 2:11 her new **m** celebrations, and her Sabbath days—
Joel 2:10 The sun and **m** grow dark, and the stars no longer
2:31 and the **m** will turn bloodred before that great
3:15 The sun and **m** will grow dark, and the stars will
Hab 3:11 The lofty sun and **m** began to fade, obscured by
Zep 1: 5 up to their roofs and bow to the sun, **m**, and stars.
Mt 24:29 sun will be darkened, / the **m** will not give light,
Mk 13:24 sun will be darkened, / the **m** will not give light,
Lk 21:25 events in the skies—signs in the sun, **m**, and stars.
Ac 2:20 into darkness, / and the **m** will turn bloodred
7:42 up to serve the sun, **m**, and stars as their gods!
1Co 15:41 while the **m** and stars each have another kind.
Rev 6:12 as black cloth, and the **m** became as red as blood.
8:12 and one-third of the **m**, and one-third of the stars,
12: 1 clothed with the sun, with the **m** beneath her feet,
21:23 And the city has no need of sun or **m**, for the glory

MOONSTONE (3) [STONE]

Ex 28:18 will contain a turquoise, a sapphire, and a white **m**.
39:11 row were a turquoise, a sapphire, and a white **m**.
Eze 28:13 white **m**, beryl, onyx, jasper, sapphire, turquoise,

MORAL (4)

Pr 28: 2 When there is **m** rot within a nation,
Isa 4: 4 The Lord will wash the **m** filth from the women of
2Pe 1: 5 Then your faith will produce a life of **m**
1: 5 A life of **m** excellence leads to knowing God

MORALE (1)

Jer 38: 4 That kind of talk will undermine the **m** of the few

MORASTHITE [KJV] See MORESHETH

MORDECAI (53) [MORDECAI'S]

Ezr 2: 2 Reelaiah, **M**, Bilshan, Mispar, Bigvai, Rehum,
Ne 7: 7 Nahamani, **M**, Bilshan, Mispar, Bigvai, Rehum,
Est 2: 5 Susa there was a certain Jew named **M** son of Jair.
2: 7 **M** adopted her into his family and raised her as his
2:10 and family background, for **M** had told her not to.
2:11 Every day **M** would take a walk near the courtyard
2:19 second harem and **M** had become a palace official,
2:21 One day as **M** was on duty at the palace, two of the
2:22 But **M** heard about the plot and passed the
2:22 the king about it and gave **M** credit for the report.
3: 2 But **M** refused to bow down or show him respect.
3: 3 the palace officials at the king's gate asked **M**,
3: 4 since **M** had told them he was a Jew.
3: 5 When Haman saw that **M** would not bow down
3: 6 So he decided it was not enough to lay hands on **M**
3: 6 Since he had learned that **M** was a Jew, he decided
4: 1 When **M** learned what had been done, he tore his
4: 4 and eunuchs came and told her about **M**,
4: 5 She ordered him to go to **M** and find out what was
4: 6 So Hathach went out to **M** in the square in front of
4: 7 **M** told him the whole story and told him how
4: 8 **M** gave Hathach a copy of the decree issued in
4:10 Hathach to go back and relay this message to **M**,
4:12 So Hathach gave Esther's message to **M**.
4:13 **M** sent back this reply to Esther: "Don't think for
4:15 Then Esther sent this reply to **M**:
4:17 So **M** went away and did as Esther told him.
5: 9 But when he saw **M** sitting at the gate, not standing
5:13 "But all this is meaningless as long as I see **M** the
5:14 and in the morning ask the king to hang **M** on it.
6: 2 of how **M** had exposed the plot of Bigthana
6: 3 or recognition did we ever give **M** for this?"
6: 4 king to hang **M** from the gallows he had prepared.
6:10 and do just as you have said for **M** the Jew,
6:11 So Haman took the robe and put it on **M**,
6:12 Afterward **M** returned to the palace gate,
6:13 friends what had happened, they said, "Since **M**—
7: 9 He intended to use it to hang **M**, the man who
7:10 hanged Haman on the gallows he had set up for **M**,
8: 1 Then **M** was brought before the king, for Esther
8: 2 he had taken back from Haman—and gave it to **M**.
8: 2 And Esther appointed **M** to be in charge of
8: 7 King Xerxes said to Queen Esther and **M** the Jew,
8: 9 As **M** dictated, they wrote a decree to the Jews
8:10 **M** wrote in the name of King Xerxes and sealed
8:15 Then **M** put on the royal robe of blue and white
9: 3 the royal officials helped the Jews for fear of **M**.
9: 4 For **M** had been promoted in the king's palace,
9:20 **M** recorded these events and sent letters to the
9:29 the daughter of Abihail, along with **M** the Jew,
9:31 decreed by both **M** the Jew and Queen Esther.
10: 2 and the full account of the greatness of **M**,
10: 3 **M** the Jew became the prime minister,

MORDECAI'S (7) [MORDECAI]

Est 2:20 She was still following **M** orders, just as she did
2:23 was made and **M** story was found to be true,
3: 4 about this to see if he would tolerate **M** conduct,
4: 9 So Hathach returned to Esther with **M** message.
9:23 So the Jews adopted **M** suggestion and began this
9:26 So because of **M** letter and because of what they
9:29 behind **M** letter to establish the Festival of Purim.

MORE (593)

Ge 1:25 each able to reproduce **m** of its own kind.
6: 3 In the future, they will live no **m** than 120 years."
7:20 standing **m** than twenty-two feet above the highest
8:14 Two **m** months went by, and at last the earth was
16:10 "I will give you **m** descendants than you can
17: 5 What's **m**, I am changing your name. It will no
18:32 please do not get angry; I will speak but once **m**!
26:12 He harvested a hundred times **m** grain than he
28:15 What's **m**, I will be with you, and I will protect
29:28 So Jacob agreed to work seven **m** years. A week
29:30 with Rachel, too, and he loved her **m** than Leah.
33:11 I have **m** than enough." Jacob continued to insist,
37: 3 Now Jacob loved Joseph **m** than any of his other
37: 5 to his brothers, causing them to hate him even **m**.
37: 8 And they hated him all the **m** for his dream
38:26 were his and said, "She is **m** in the right than I am,
39: 9 No one here has **m** authority than I do! He has held
39:23 The chief jailer had no **m** worries after that,
41: 6 seven **m** heads appeared on the stalk,
42:24 Returning, he talked some **m** with them. He
43:22 We also have additional money to buy **m** grain.
Ex 1:12 But the **m** the Egyptians oppressed them, the **m**
quickly the Israelites multiplied!
1:13 and decided to make their slavery **m** bitter still.
1:20 to multiply, growing **m** and **m** powerful.
5: 7 "Do not supply the people with any **m** straw for
5: 9 Load them down with **m** work. Make them sweat!
5:23 he has been even **m** brutal to your people.
9:12 But the LORD made Pharaoh even **m** stubborn,
10:27 So the LORD hardened Pharaoh's heart once **m**,
11: 1 "I will send just one **m** disaster on Pharaoh
11: 9 But this will give me the opportunity to do even **m**
16:17 this food—some getting **m**, and some getting less.
17: 2 So once **m** the people grumbled and complained to
28:26 Then make two **m** gold rings, and attach them to
28:27 And make two **m** gold rings and attach them to the
30:15 the rich must not give **m**, and the poor must not
33: 6 left Mount Sinai, the Israelites wore no **m** jewelry.
33:13 your intentions so I will understand you **m** fully
33:18 Then Moses had one **m** request. "Please let me see
36: 5 "We have **m** than enough materials on hand now
36: 6 "Bring no **m** materials! You have already given **m**
than enough."
36: 7 Their contributions were **m** than enough to
36:19 Then they made two **m** layers for the roof
39:19 Two **m** gold rings were attached to the lower
Lev 13: 3 turned white and appears to be **m** than skin-deep,
13: 4 but does not appear to be **m** than skin-deep,
13: 5 will put the person in quarantine for seven **m** days.
13:20 If the priest finds the disease to be **m** than
13:21 and if it doesn't appear to be **m** than skin-deep
13:25 and the problem appears to be **m** than skin-deep,
13:26 and the problem appears to be no **m** than skin-deep
13:30 If it appears to be **m** than skin-deep and fine
13:32 and if the infection does not appear to be **m** than
13:34 not spread and appears to be no **m** than skin-deep,
13:54 to be washed and then isolated for seven **m** days.
25:16 The **m** the years, the higher the price; the fewer the
26:21 I will inflict you with seven **m** disasters for your
Nu 12: 3 Now Moses was **m** humble than any other person
16:14 What's **m**, you haven't brought us into the land
22:15 This time he sent a larger number of even **m**
22:19 But stay here one **m** night to see if the LORD has
26:54 Give the larger tribes **m** land and the smaller tribes
30:15 If he waits **m** than a day and then tries to nullify a
35: 8 The larger tribes will give **m** towns to the Levites,
35:30 but only if there is **m** than one witness.
Dt 1:11 multiply you a thousand times **m** and bless you as
1:28 of the land are taller and **m** powerful than we are,
3:11 His iron bed was **m** than thirteen feet long and six
3:26 'That's enough!' he ordered. 'Speak of it no **m**.
7: 1 These seven nations are all **m** powerful than you.
7:17 nations that are so much **m** powerful than we are?'
8: 3 He did it to teach you that people need **m** than
9: 1 to nations much greater and **m** powerful than you.
9:14 a nation larger and **m** powerful than they are.'
25: 3 No **m** than forty lashes may ever be given;
25: 3 **m** than forty lashes would publicly humiliate your
30: 5 He will make you even **m** prosperous
31:27 How much **m** rebellious will you be after my
33: 9 They were **m** loyal to you / than to their parents,
Jos 7: 3 and it won't take **m** than two or three thousand of
7:21 and a bar of gold weighing **m** than a pound.
10:11 The hail killed **m** of the enemy than the Israelites
17:17 and strong, you will be given **m** than one portion.
18: 7 half-tribe of Manasseh won't receive any **m** land,
22:33 and spoke no **m** of war against Reuben and Gad.
Jdg 6:39 be angry with me, but let me make one **m** request.
9:29 'Get some **m** soldiers, and come out and fight!' "
12: 4 "The men of Gilead are nothing **m** than rejects
13: 8 and give us **m** instructions about this son who is to
15: 2 But look, her sister is **m** beautiful than she is.
16:18 "Come back one **m** time," she said, "for he has
16:28 please strengthen me one **m** time so that I may pay
16:30 So he killed **m** people when he died than he had
20:36 give those hiding in ambush **m** room to maneuver.
Ru 1:13 Things are far **m** bitter for me than for you,
2:14 and Boaz gave her food—**m** than she could eat.
2:21 Then Ruth said, "What's **m**, Boaz even told me to
3:10 "You are showing **m** family loyalty now than ever
3:12 there is another man who is **m** closely related to
1Sa 1:19 and went to worship the LORD once **m**.
2: 4 Those who were mighty are mighty no **m**;
2: 5 but the woman with many children will have no **m**.
2:29 Why do you honor your sons **m** than me—for you
3: 8 and once **m** Samuel jumped up and ran to Eli.
9: 5 By now my father will be **m** worried about us than
13: 4 Philistines now hated the Israelites **m** than ever.
14:30 think how many **m** we could have killed!"
14:31 Micmash to Aijalon, growing **m** and **m** faint.
15:22 "What is **m** pleasing to the LORD:
18:15 recognized this, he became even **m** afraid of him.
18:29 he became even **m** afraid of him, and he remained
18:30 David was **m** successful against them than all the
21: 5 even on ordinary trips, how much **m** on this one!"
23:23 and come back with a **m** definite report.
28:19 What's **m**, the LORD will hand you and the army
30: 4 they wept until they could weep no **m**.
2Sa 5:10 And David became **m** and **m** powerful,
5:13 David married **m** wives and concubines, and he
6:22 and I am willing to look even **m** foolish than this,
7:20 What **m** can I say? You know what I am really
12: 8 I would have given you much, much **m**.
13:15 and he hated her even **m** than he had loved her.
14:11 I want no **m** bloodshed." "As surely as the
14:12 "Please let me ask one **m** thing of you!" she said.
16:11 Shouldn't this relative of Saul have even **m** reason
18: 8 and **m** men died because of the forest than were
20: 6 "That troublemaker Sheba is going to hurt us **m**
21:16 his bronze spearhead weighed **m** than seven
23:23 He was **m** honored than the other members of the
1Ki 2:32 for the murders of two men who were **m** righteous
3:21 But when I looked **m** closely in the morning light,
14: 9 You have done **m** evil than all who lived before
16:25 even **m** than any of the kings before him.
16:30 even **m** than any of the kings before him.
16:33 He did **m** to arouse the anger of the LORD,
19: 7 touched him and said, "Get up and eat some **m**,
20: 8 "Don't give in to any **m** demands," the leaders
20:10 provide **m** than a handful for each of my soldiers."
2Ki 1:13 Once **m** the king sent a captain with fifty men.
4: 6 "There aren't any **m**!" he told her. And
6:16 "For there are **m** on our side than on theirs!"
12: 7 Don't use any **m** gifts for your own needs.
12: 8 So the priests agreed not to collect any **m** money
18:14 then demanded a settlement of **m** than eleven tons
18:25 What's **m**, do you think we have invaded your land
21: 9 and Manasseh led them to do even **m** evil than the
21:11 He is even **m** wicked than the Amorites, who lived
1Ch 4: 9 There was a man named Jabez who was **m**
11: 9 And David became **m** and **m** powerful,
11:25 He was **m** honored than the other members of the
12:22 Day after day **m** men joined David until he had a
14: 3 Then David married **m** wives in Jerusalem,
17:18 What **m** can I say about the way you have honored
22: 3 and **m** bronze than they could ever weigh.
22:14 stone for the walls, though you may need to add **m**.
24: 4 for there were **m** family leaders among the
29: 4 I am donating **m** than 112 tons of gold from Ophir
2Ch 11:21 Rehoboam loved Maacah **m** than any of his other
13:21 Abijah of Judah grew **m** and **m** powerful.
15:19 So there was no **m** war until the thirty-fifth year of
17:12 So Jehoshaphat became **m** and **m** powerful
20:25 and other valuables—**m** than they could carry.
25: 9 "The LORD is able to give you much **m** than
28:22 he became even **m** unfaithful to the LORD.
29:34 was finished and until **m** priests had been purified.
29:34 For the Levites had been **m** conscientious about
30:24 Meanwhile, many **m** priests purified themselves.
33: 9 and Jerusalem to do even **m** evil than the pagan
33:23 before the LORD. Instead, Amon sinned even **m**.
36:14 and the people became **m** and **m** unfaithful.

Ezr 10:10 Now we are even **m** deeply under condemnation
Ne 5:2 We need **m** money just so we can buy the food we
5:12 and demand nothing **m** from the people.
7:2 for he was a faithful man who feared God **m** than
9:3 Then for three **m** hours they took turns confessing
9:28 and once **m** you let their enemies conquer them.
9:28 again for help, you listened once **m** from heaven.
13:12 And once **m** all the people of Judah began bringing
13:18 Now you are bringing even **m** wrath upon the
Est 1:8 one should be compelled to take **m** than he wanted.
1:19 and that you choose another queen **m** worthy than
2:17 the king loved her **m** than any of the other young
4:11 called for me to come to him in **m** than a month."
4:14 What's **m**, who can say but that you have been
6:6 "Whom would the king wish to honor **m** than
8:3 Now once **m** Esther came before the king,
9:4 throughout all the provinces as he became **m** and
m powerful.
9:12 But now, what **m** do you want? It will be granted
9:15 on March 8 and killed three hundred **m** people,
Job 3:21 They search for death **m** eagerly than for hidden
9:25 "My life passes **m** swiftly than a runner. It flees
11:12 **m** than a wild donkey can bear human offspring!
14:12 Until the heavens are no **m**, they will not wake up
28:17 Wisdom is far **m** valuable than gold and crystal.
33:31 this well, Job. Listen to me, and let me say **m**.
34:19 and he doesn't pay any **m** attention to the rich than
34:31 say to God, 'I have sinned, but I will sin no **m**'?
35:14 And it is even **m** false to say he doesn't see what is
40:5 said too much already. I have nothing **m** to say."
42:12 half of his life even **m** than in the beginning.
42:13 gave Job seven **m** sons and three **m** daughters.
Ps 17:14 May their children inherit **m** of the same,
19:10 They are **m** desirable than gold, / even the finest
37:19 even in famine they will have **m** than enough.
39:13 can smile again / before I am gone and exist no **m**.
40:12 They are **m** numerous than the hairs on my head.
45:7 pouring out the oil of joy on you **m** than on anyone
49:16 and their homes become ever **m** splendid.
50:9 But I want no **m** bulls from your barns; / I want no
m goats from your pens.
52:3 You love evil **m** than good / and lies **m** than truth.
52:7 and grow **m** and **m** bold in their wickedness."
63:5 You satisfy me **m** than the richest of foods.
69:4 are **m** numerous than the hairs on my head.
69:31 For this will please the LORD **m** than sacrificing
71:14 for you to help me; / I will praise you **m** and **m**.
73:25 but you? / I desire you **m** than anything on earth.
76:4 You are glorious and **m** majestic
80:18 Revive us so we can call on your name once **m**.
87:2 city of Jerusalem / **m** than any other city in Israel.
89:7 He is far **m** awesome than those who surround his
119:72 Your law is **m** valuable to me / than millions in
119:99 Yes, I have **m** insight than my teachers, / for I am
119:127 **m** than gold, even the finest gold.
130:6 **m** than sentries long for the dawn, / yes, **m** than
sentries long for the dawn.
Pr 3:15 Wisdom is **m** precious than rubies; nothing you
6:10 A little extra sleep, a little **m** slumber, a little
8:11 For wisdom is far **m** valuable than rubies.
9:8 the wise, when rebuked, will love you all the **m**.
9:9 Teach the righteous, and they will learn **m**.
11:24 It is possible to give freely and become **m** wealthy,
11:31 how much **m** true that the wicked and the sinner
15:11 How much **m** does he know the human heart!
17:10 A single rebuke does **m** for a person of
19:7 how much **m** will their friends avoid them.
20:15 is rarer and **m** valuable than gold and rubies.
21:3 The LORD is **m** pleased when we do what is just
21:26 They are always greedy for **m**, while the godly
24:5 and a man of knowledge is **m** powerful than a
24:33 A little extra sleep, a little **m** slumber, a little
25:1 These are **m** proverbs of Solomon, collected by the
26:1 Honor doesn't go with fools any **m** than snow with
26:12 There is **m** hope for fools than for people who
28:23 people appreciate frankness **m** than flattery.
29:20 There is **m** hope for a fool than for someone who
30:15 leech has two suckers that cry out, "**M, m**!"
31:7 their poverty and remember their troubles no **m**.
31:10 capable wife? She is worth **m** than precious rubies.
Ecc 2:7 **m** than any of the kings who lived in Jerusalem
2:13 Wisdom is of **m** value than foolishness, just as
4:9 Two people can accomplish **m** than twice as much
5:11 The **m** you have, the **m** people come to help you
6:5 Yet he would have had **m** peace than he has in
6:11 The **m** words you speak, the less they mean.
7:1 A good reputation is **m** valuable than the most
7:26 I discovered that a seductive woman is **m** bitter
9:3 That is why people are not **m** careful to be good.
9:15 But afterward no one thought any **m** about him.
SS 1:1 song of songs, **m** wonderful than any other.
1:4 for him! We praise his love even **m** than wine."
4:10 Your perfume is **m** fragrant than the richest of
Isa 1:11 "Don't bring me any **m** burnt offerings!
1:13 and false. I want nothing **m** to do with them.
5:4 What **m** could I have done / to cultivate a rich
5:6 command the clouds / to drop no **m** rain on it."
13:12 as scarce as gold—**m** rare than the gold of Ophir.
16:10 happy singing in the vineyards will be heard no **m**.
24:8 the happy cries of celebration will be heard no **m**.
28:22 So scoff no **m**, or your punishment will be even
29:13 And their worship of me amounts to nothing **m**
29:21 tell lies to tear down the innocent will be no **m**.
30:10 We don't want any **m** of your reports." They say,
30:11 We have heard **m** than enough about your 'Holy
30:19 who live in Jerusalem, you will weep no **m**.
32:10 In a short time—in just a little **m** than a year—
36:10 What's **m**, do you think we have invaded your land
47:13 You have **m** than enough advisers, astrologers,
49:6 "You will do **m** than restore the people of Israel to
49:20 in exile will return and say, 'We need **m** room!
51:22 You will drink no **m** of my fury. It is gone at last!
54:1 no children now has **m** than all the other women,"
54:4 sorrows of widowhood will be remembered no **m**,
57:11 Why were you **m** afraid of them than of me?
65:19 sound of weeping and crying will be heard no **m**.
65:25 Poisonous snakes will strike no **m**. In those days,
66:3 it is no **m** acceptable than a human sacrifice.
Jer 3:16 "And when your land is once **m** filled with
3:19 I wanted nothing **m** than to give you this beautiful
4:1 away your detestable idols and go astray no **m**,
7:16 "Pray no **m** for these people, Jeremiah. Do not
9:10 the lowing of cattle is heard no **m**; the birds
11:14 "Pray no **m** for these people, Jeremiah. Do not
15:8 "There will be **m** widows than the grains of sand
19:11 the bodies in Topheth until there is no **m** room.
25:27 and vomit, and you will fall to rise no **m**,
32:36 "Now I want to say something **m** about this city.
33:10 Judah's other towns, there will be heard once **m**
33:12 will once **m** see shepherds leading sheep
33:25 I would no **m** reject my people than I would
36:32 in the fire. Only this time, he added much **m**!
45:3 And now the LORD has added **m**! I am weary of
46:23 "for they are **m** numerous than grasshoppers.
48:32 I will weep for you even **m** than I did for Jazer.
49:10 will be destroyed—and Edom itself will be no **m**.
49:12 the innocent must suffer, how much **m** must you!
50:19 and to be satisfied once **m** on the hill country of
52:29 Nebuchadnezzar's eighteenth year he took 832 **m**.
52:30 his captain of the guard, who took 745 **m**—
La 2:9 have been exiled to distant lands; the law is no **m**.
2:9 Her prophets receive no **m** visions from the
Eze 3:7 but they won't listen to you any **m** than they listen
5:6 and has been even **m** wicked than the surrounding
5:9 I will punish you **m** severely than I have punished
5:16 The famine will become **m** and **m** severe until
every crumb of food is gone.
12:25 There will be no **m** delays, you rebels of Israel!
12:28 No **m** delay! I will now do everything I have
16:13 and olive oil—and became **m** beautiful than ever.
16:51 You have done far **m** loathsome things than your
23:11 And she was even **m** depraved, abandoning herself
26:13 No **m** will the sound of harps be heard among your
26:21 bring you to a terrible end, and you will be no **m**.
27:36 come to a horrible end / and will be no **m**.' "
28:19 have come to a terrible end, and you are no **m**."
36:11 I will make you even **m** prosperous than you were
36:38 ruined cities will be crowded with people once **m**,
40:40 up to the north entrance, there were two **m** tables.
Da 2:16 went at once to see the king and requested **m** time
3:15 I will give you one **m** chance. If you bow down
5:9 So the king grew even **m** alarmed, and his face
6:3 Daniel soon proved himself **m** capable than all the
11:2 Three **m** Persian kings will reign, to be succeeded
11:5 but one of this king's own officials will become **m**
11:19 but will stumble and fall, and he will be seen no **m**.
Hos 4:7 The **m** priests there are, the **m** they sin against me.
6:6 that's **m** important than burnt offerings.
9:15 I will love them no **m** because all their leaders are
9:16 Their roots are dried up; they will bear no **m** fruit.
10:1 But the **m** wealth the people got, the **m** they
poured it on the altars of their foreign
10:1 the **m** beautiful the statues and idols they built.
10:9 night in Gibeah, there has been only sin and **m** sin!
11:2 But the **m** I called to him, the **m** he rebelled,
Joel 2:22 fig trees and grapevines will flourish once **m**.
2:23 Once **m** the autumn rains will come, as well as the
Am 9:7 "Do you Israelites think you are **m** important to
Jnh 2:7 I turned my thoughts once **m** to the LORD.
4:11 But Nineveh has **m** than 120,000 people living in
Mic 5:12 there will be no **m** fortune-tellers to consult.
7:4 the straightest is **m** crooked than a hedge of thorns.
Na 1:14 "You will have no **m** children to carry on your
Hab 1:8 are a fierce people, **m** fierce than wolves at dusk.
1:13 destroy people who are **m** righteous than they?
Zep 3:5 Day by day his justice is **m** evident, but no one
3:15 will be over, and you will fear disaster no **m**.
3:18 appointed festivals; you will be disgraced no **m**.
Zec 8:12 Once **m** I will make the remnant in Judah
Mal 3:4 Then once **m** the LORD will accept the offerings
Mt 4:4 'People need **m** than bread for their life;
6:25 Doesn't life consist of **m** than food and clothing?
6:26 And you are far **m** valuable to him than they are.
6:30 gone tomorrow, won't he **m** surely care for you?
7:11 how much **m** will your heavenly Father give good
9:38 ask him to send out **m** workers for his fields."
10:25 how much **m** will it happen to you, the members of
10:31 you are **m** valuable to him than a whole flock of
10:37 love your father or mother **m** than you love me,
10:37 or if you love your son or daughter **m** than me,
11:9 for a prophet? Yes, and he is **m** than a prophet.
12:12 And how much **m** valuable is a person than a
12:45 Then the spirit finds seven other spirits **m** evil than
13:12 to my teaching, **m** understanding will be given,
16:26 the process? Is anything worth **m** than your soul?
18:13 he will surely rejoice over it **m** than over the
18:29 down before him and begged for a little **m** time.
20:6 and saw some **m** people standing around.
20:10 get their pay, they assumed they would receive **m**.
21:21 you can do things like this and much **m**.
22:46 no one dared to ask him any **m** questions.
23:23 but you should not leave undone the **m** important
25:21 so now I will give you many **m** responsibilities.
25:23 so now I will give you many **m** responsibilities.
25:29 even **m** will be given, and they will have an
Mk 2:2 visitors that there wasn't room for one **m** person,
4:24 The **m** you do this, the **m** you will
understand—and even **m**, besides.
4:25 to my teaching, **m** understanding will be given.
7:36 but the **m** he told them not to, the **m** they spread
the news,
8:37 Is anything worth **m** than your soul?
9:31 in order to spend **m** time with his disciples
10:32 Jesus once **m** began to describe everything that
12:33 This is **m** important than to offer all of the burnt
12:34 no one dared to ask him any **m** questions.
12:43 this poor widow has given **m** than all the others
Lk 1:36 What's **m**, your relative Elizabeth has become
3:13 "Make sure you collect no **m** taxes than the
4:4 'People need **m** than bread for their life.' "
6:38 shaken together to make room for **m**,
7:26 for a prophet? Yes, and he is **m** than a prophet.
7:42 Who do you suppose loved him **m** after that?"
8:18 to my teaching, **m** understanding will be given.
10:2 and ask him to send out **m** workers for his fields.
11:5 Then, teaching them **m** about prayer, he used this
11:13 how much **m** will your heavenly Father give the
11:26 Then the spirit finds seven other spirits **m** evil than
11:28 "But even **m** blessed are all who hear the word of
11:42 but you should not leave undone the **m** important
12:4 only kill the body; they cannot do any **m** to you.
12:7 you are **m** valuable to him than a whole flock of
12:23 For life consists of far **m** than food and clothing.
12:24 And you are far **m** valuable to him than any birds!
12:28 gone tomorrow, won't he **m** surely care for you?
12:48 and much **m** is required from those to whom much
m is given.
13:8 "The gardener answered, 'Give it one **m** chance.
14:8 What if someone **m** respected than you has also
14:22 done this, he reported, 'There is still room for **m**.'
14:26 follower you must love me **m** than your own father
14:26 brothers and sisters—yes, **m** than your own life.
16:8 And it is true that the citizens of this world are **m**
16:17 and **m** permanent than heaven and earth.
17:5 the apostles said to the Lord, "We need **m** faith;
19:26 well what they are given, even **m** will be given.
20:40 ended their questions; no one dared to ask any **m**.
21:3 "this poor widow has given **m** than all the rest of
22:44 He prayed **m** fervently, and he was in such agony
Jn 2:3 "They have no **m** wine," she told him.
3:19 but they loved the darkness **m** than the light,
4:1 is baptizing and making **m** disciples than John"
5:18 So the Jewish leaders tried all the **m** to kill him.
7:31 "would you expect the Messiah to do **m**
8:11 And Jesus said, "Neither do I. Go and sin no **m**."
10:29 to me, and he is **m** powerful than anyone else.
12:43 For they loved human praise **m** than the praise of
13:16 Nor are messengers **m** important than the one who
14:30 "I don't have much **m** time to talk to you,
15:2 that do bear fruit so they will produce even **m**.
16:10 I go to the Father, and you will see me no **m**.
16:12 "Oh, there is so much **m** I want to tell you,
17:16 They are not part of this world any **m** than I am.
18:7 Once **m** he asked them, "Whom are you searching
19:8 Pilate heard this, he was **m** frightened than ever.
21:15 son of John, do you love me **m** than these?"
21:17 Once **m** he asked him, "Simon son of John,
Ac 4:22 the healing of a man who had been lame for **m**
5:14 And **m** and **m** people believed and were
9:22 Saul's preaching became **m** and **m** powerful,
13:3 So after **m** fasting and prayer, the men laid their
13:35 Another psalm explains **m** fully, saying, 'You will
16:40 and encouraged them once **m** before leaving town.
17:11 And the people of Berea were **m** open-minded than
17:19 "Come and tell us **m** about this new religion,"
17:32 others said, "We want to hear **m** about this later."
18:26 and explained the way of God **m** accurately.
20:35 'It is **m** blessed to give than to receive.' "
23:13 There were **m** than forty of them.
23:15 "Pretend you want to examine his case **m** fully.
23:20 pretending they want to get some **m** information.
23:21 There are **m** than forty men hiding along the way
24:11 You can quickly discover that it was no **m** than
24:25 "When it is **m** convenient, I'll call for you again."
27:11 of the prisoners listened **m** to the ship's captain
27:24 What's **m**, God in his goodness has granted safety
Ro 3:7 his truthfulness and brings him **m** glory?"
3:8 you might as well say that the **m** we sin the better
3:20 For the **m** we know God's law, the clearer it
5:20 But as people sinned **m** and **m**,
5:20 God's wonderful kindness became **m** abundant.
6:1 so that God can show us **m** and **m** kindness and
forgiveness?
11:15 how much **m** wonderful their acceptance will be.
11:24 he will be far **m** eager to graft the Jews back into
14:5 some think one day is **m** holy than another day,
16:17 And now I make one **m** appeal, my dear brothers
1Co 7:5 so they can give themselves **m** completely to
7:34 or has never been married can be **m** devoted to the
11:17 For it sounds as if **m** harm than good is done when
14:5 but even **m** I wish you were all able to prophesy.
14:5 and **m** useful gift than speaking in tongues,
14:18 I thank God that I speak in tongues **m** than all of
14:27 No **m** than two or three should speak in an
15:6 he was seen by **m** than five hundred of his
2Co 1:5 You can be sure that the **m** we suffer for Christ,
1:5 the **m** God will shower us with his comfort through
2:5 trouble hurt your entire church **m** than he hurt me.
3:9 how much **m** glorious is the new covenant,
3:18 we become **m** and **m** like him and reflect his glory
even **m**.

4:15 as God's grace brings **m** and **m** people to Christ,
4:15 and God will receive **m** and **m** glory.
7:15 Now he cares for you **m** than ever when he
8: 3 gave not only what they could afford but far **m**.
8:22 He is now even **m** enthusiastic because of his
9:11 so that you can give even **m** generously.
11:23 sound like a madman, but I have served him far **m**!
11:23 I have worked harder, been put in jail **m** often,
12: 6 I don't want anyone to think **m** highly of me than
12:15 even though it seems that the **m** I love you, the less
Gal 3: 8 What's **m**, the Scriptures looked forward to this
4: 9 back again and become slaves once **m** to the weak
4:17 from me so that you will pay **m** attention to them.
4:20 right now, so that I could be **m** gentle with you.
4:27 now has **m** than all the other women!"
Eph 1:14 This is just one **m** reason for us to praise our
3:17 that Christ will be **m** and **m** at home in your hearts
3:20 he is able to accomplish infinitely **m** than we
4:15 becoming **m** and **m** in every way like Christ,
Php 1: 9 your love for each other will overflow **m** and **m**,
1:14 and become **m** bold in telling others about Christ.
1:17 intending to make my chains **m** painful to me.
1:26 you will have even **m** reason to boast about what
2:12 And now that I am away you must be even **m**
2:28 So I am all the **m** anxious to send him back to you,
3: 4 for confidence in their own efforts, I have even **m**!
3: 5 What's **m**, I was a member of the Pharisees,
4: 7 which is far **m** wonderful than the human mind can
4: 8 let me say one **m** thing as I close this letter.
4:16 Even when I was in Thessalonica you sent help **m**
4:18 At the moment I have all I need—**m** than I need!
Col 3:10 being renewed as you learn **m** and **m** about Christ,
1Th 4: 1 and we encourage you to do so **m** and **m**.
4:10 dear friends, we beg you to love them **m** and **m**.
1Ti 4: 8 but spiritual exercise is much **m** important,
2Ti 2:16 discussions that lead to **m** and **m** ungodliness.
Tit 3:10 After that, have nothing **m** to do with that person.
Phm 1:16 Now he will mean much **m** to you, both as a slave
1:21 this letter that you will do what I ask and even **m**!
Heb 1: 9 pouring out the oil of joy on you **m** than on anyone
3: 3 But Jesus deserves far **m** glory than Moses, just as
3: 3 fine house deserves **m** praise than the house itself.
5:11 so much **m** we would like to say about this.
7:15 The change in God's law is even **m** evident from
9:14 Just think how much **m** the blood of Christ will
10:18 there is no need to offer any **m** sacrifices.
10:29 Think how much **m** terrible the punishment will be
11: 4 It was by faith that Abel brought a **m** acceptable
11:13 They agreed that they were no **m** than foreigners
11:32 Well, how much **m** do I need to say? It would take
12: 9 should we not all the **m** cheerfully submit to the
Jas 2: 1 Christ if you favor some people **m** than others?
4: 6 He gives us **m** and **m** strength to stand against
1Pe 1: 2 May you have **m** and **m** of God's special favor
1: 7 and your faith is far **m** precious to God than mere
1:10 something the prophets wanted to know **m** about.
2: 5 What's **m**, you are God's holy priests, who offer
2Pe 1: 8 The **m** you grow like this, the **m** you will become
3: 9 so he is giving **m** time for everyone to repent.
1Jn 4:17 And as we live in God, our love grows **m** perfect.
2Jn 1:12 Well, I have much **m** to say to you, but I don't
Jude 1: 2 May you receive **m** and **m** of God's mercy,
Rev 2:24 of Satan, really). I will ask nothing **m** of you
9:12 terror is past, but look, two **m** terrors are coming!
18:22 no **m** harps, songs, flutes, or trumpets.
18:22 no industry of any kind, and no **m** milling of grain.
21: 4 and there will be no **m** death or sorrow or crying

MOREH (3)

Ge 12: 6 and set up camp beside the oak at **M**.
Dt 11:30 toward the west, not far from the oaks of **M**.)
Jdg 7: 1 north of them in the valley near the hill of **M**.

MOREOVER (6)

Ex 31: 6 **M**, I have given special skill to all the naturally
Nu 27: 8 **M** announce this to the people of Israel: 'If a man
1Ki 1:46 **M**, Solomon is now sitting on the royal throne as
Ezr 6: 8 **M** I hereby decree that you are to help these
7:16 "**M** you are to take any silver and gold which you
Ac 24: 6 **M** he was trying to defile the Temple when we

MORESHETH (2) [MORESHETH-GATH]

Jer 26:18 "Think back to the days when Micah of **M**
Mic 1: 1 The LORD gave these messages to Micah of **M**

MORESHETH-GATH (1) [GATH, MORESHETH]

Mic 1:14 Send a farewell gift to **M**; there is no hope of

MORIAH (2)

Ge 22: 2 whom you love so much—and go to the land of **M**.
2Ch 3: 1 Temple of the LORD in Jerusalem on Mount **M**,

MORNING (244) [MORNINGS]

EVERY MORNING (7) Ex 30:7; 2Sa 15:2; 1Ch 9:27; 2Ch 13:11; Job 7:18; Ps 73:14; Eze 46:15

IN THE MORNING (56) Ge 19:2; 29:25; 49:27; Ex 7:15; 8:20; 9:13; 14:24; 16:7,8,12,14; 29:39,41; 34:2,4; Lev 6:20; Nu 22:8; 28:4; Dt 28:67; Jos 3:6; 7:14; Jdg 6:37,40; 9:33; Ru 3:13; 1Sa 9:19; 29:10; 1Ki 3:21,21; 2Ki 10:9; Est 5:14; Job 1:5; 4:20; Ps 5:3; 49:14; 90:5,6,14; 92:2; 139:18; 143:8; Pr 6:22; 27:14; Ecc 10:16; Hos 7:6; 13:3; Mt 14:25; 16:3; 20:3; 21:18; 27:1; Mk 6:48; 15:1,25; Ac 2:15; 28:23

MORNING...EVENING; EVENING...MORNING (31) Ge 49:27; Ex 16:8,12,13; 18:13; 29:39,41; Lev 6:20; 24:3; Nu 9:15; 28:4; Dt 28:67,67; 1Sa 17:16; 1Ki 17:6; 2Ki 16:15; 1Ch 16:40; 23:30; 2Ch 2:4; 13:11; 31:3; Ezr 3:3; Est 2:14; Job 4:20; Ps 90:6; 92:2; Eze 24:18,18; 33:22; Ac 4:3; 28:23

UNTIL (THE) MORNING (15) Ex 12:22; 16:20; 29:34; Lev 24:3; Nu 9:15; Jdg 19:25; Ru 3:13,14; 1Sa 3:15; 2Ki 7:9; 10:8; Pr 7:18; Isa 21:11; Lk 17:29; Ac 4:3

Ge 19: 2 You may then get up in the **m** as early as you like
19:15 At dawn the next **m** the angels became insistent.
19:27 The next **m** Abraham was up early and hurried out
19:34 The next **m** the older daughter said to her younger
20: 8 Abimelech got up early the next **m** and hastily
21:14 So Abraham got up early the next **m**,
22: 3 The next **m** Abraham got up early. He saddled his
24:54 But early the next **m**, he said, "Send me back to
26:31 Early the next **m**, they each took a solemn oath of
28:18 The next **m** he got up very early. He took the stone
29:25 But when Jacob woke up in the **m**—it was Leah!
31:55 Laban got up early the next **m**, and he kissed his
40: 6 The next **m** Joseph noticed the dejected look on
41: 8 The next **m**, as he thought about it,
49:27 that prowls. / He devours his enemies in the **m**,
Ex 7:15 So go to Pharaoh in the **m** as he goes down to the
8:20 "Get up early in the **m** and meet Pharaoh as he
9: 6 The next **m** all the livestock of the Egyptians
9:13 the LORD said to Moses, "Get up early in the **m**.
10:13 When **m** arrived, the east wind had brought the
12:10 is not eaten that night must be burned before **m**.
12:22 no one is allowed to leave the house until **m**.
14:24 But early in the **m**, the LORD looked down on
16: 7 In the **m** you will see the glorious presence of the
16: 8 you meat to eat in the evening and bread in the **m**,
16:12 to eat, and in the **m** you will be filled with bread.
16:13 The next **m** the desert all around the camp was wet
16:14 When the dew disappeared later in the **m**,
16:20 of them didn't listen and kept some of it until **m**.
16:21 The people gathered the food **m** by **m**,
16:24 The next **m** the leftover food was wholesome
18:13 They were lined up in front of him from **m** till
19:16 On the **m** of the third day, there was a powerful
23:18 fat may be left unoffered until the next **m**.
24: 4 Early the next **m** he built an altar at the foot of the
29:34 the ordination meat or bread remains until the **m**,
29:39 one in the **m** and the other in the evening.
29:41 the same offerings of flour and wine as in the **m**.
30: 7 "Every **m** when Aaron trims the lamps, he must
32: 6 So the people got up early the next **m** to sacrifice
34: 2 Be ready in the **m** to come up Mount Sinai
34: 4 Early in the **m** he climbed Mount Sinai as the
34:25 lamb may be kept over until the following **m**.
36: 3 Additional gifts were brought each **m**.
Lev 6: 9 offering must be left on the altar until the next **m**,
6:10 The next **m**, after dressing in his special linen
6:12 Each **m** the priest will add fresh wood to the fire
6:20 half to be offered in the **m** and half to be offered in
7:15 is offered. None of it may be saved for the next **m**.
9:17 in addition to the regular **m** burnt offering.
24: 3 from evening until **m**, before the LORD.
Nu 9:12 must not leave any of the lamb until the next **m**,
9:15 Then from evening until **m** the cloud over the
9:21 stayed only overnight and moved on the next **m**.
14:40 So they got up early the next **m** and set out for the
16: 5 "Tomorrow **m** the LORD will show us who
16:41 But the very next **m** the whole community began
22: 8 "In the **m** I will tell you whatever the LORD
22:13 The next **m** Balaam got up and told Balak's
22:21 So the next **m** Balaam saddled his donkey
22:41 The next **m** Balak took Balaam up to Bamoth-baal.
28: 4 One lamb will be sacrificed in the **m** and the other
28:23 offerings in addition to your regular **m** sacrifices.
33: 3 They set out from the city of Rameses on the **m**
Dt 16: 4 meat of the Passover lamb remain until the next **m**.
16: 7 Then go back to your tents the next **m**.
28:66 with no reason to believe that you will see the **m**
28:67 In the **m** you will say, 'If only it were night!'
28:67 in the evening you will say, 'If only it were **m**!'
Jos 3: 1 Early the next **m** Joshua and all the Israelites left
3: 6 In the **m** Joshua said to the priests, "Lift up the
6:12 Joshua got up early the next **m**, and the priests
7:14 In the **m** you must present yourselves by tribes,
7:16 Early the next **m** Joshua brought the tribes of Israel
8:10 Early the next **m** Joshua roused his men and started
8:14 all his army hurriedly went out early the next **m**
Jdg 6:28 Early the next **m**, as the people of the town began
6:31 Whoever pleads his case will be put to death by **m**!
6:37 If the fleece is wet with dew in the **m**
6:38 When Gideon got up the next **m**, he squeezed the
6:40 The fleece was dry in the **m**, but the ground was
9:33 In the **m**, as soon as it is daylight, storm the city.
16: 2 "When the light of **m** comes, we will kill him."
19: 8 On the **m** of the fifth day he was up early again,
19:25 her all night, taking turns raping her until **m**.
20:19 So the Israelites left early the next **m** and camped
21: 4 Early the next **m** the people built an altar
Ru 2: 7 She asked me this **m** if she could gather grain
3:13 Stay here tonight, and in the **m** I will talk to him.
3:13 I will marry you! Now lie down here until **m**."
3:14 So Ruth lay at Boaz's feet until the **m**, but she got
1Sa 1:19 The entire family got up early the next **m** and went
3:15 Samuel stayed in bed until **m**, then got up
5: 3 the citizens of Ashdod went to see it the next **m**,
5: 4 But the next **m** the same thing happened—the idol
9:19 In the **m** I will tell you what you want to know
9:26 At daybreak the next **m**, Samuel called up to Saul,
11:11 But before dawn the next **m**, Saul arrived,
11:11 the Ammonites and slaughtered them the whole **m**.
15:12 Early the next **m** Samuel went to find Saul.
17:16 For forty days, twice a day, **m** and evening,
17:20 and set out early the next **m** with the gifts.
19: 2 "Tomorrow **m**," he warned him, "you must find a
19: 4 The next **m** Jonathan spoke with his father about
19:11 told to kill David when he came out the next **m**.
19:11 don't get away tonight, you will be dead by **m**."
20:35 The next **m**, as agreed, Jonathan went out into the
25:22 man of his household is still alive tomorrow **m**!"
25:34 one of Nabal's men would be alive tomorrow **m**."
25:36 about her meeting with David until the next **m**.
25:37 The next **m** when he was sober, she told him what
29:10 Now get up early in the **m**, and leave with your
2Sa 2:29 the Jordan River, traveling all through the **m**,
11:14 So the next **m** David wrote a letter to Joab
13: 4 son of a king look so dejected **m** after **m**?"
15: 2 He got up early every **m** and went out to the gate
23: 4 he is like the light of the **m**, / like the sunrise
24:11 The next **m** the word of the LORD came to the
24:15 So the LORD sent a plague upon Israel that **m**,
1Ki 3:21 And in the **m** when I tried to nurse my son, he was
3:21 But when I looked more closely in the **m** light,
17: 6 brought him bread and meat each **m** and evening,
18:26 Then they called on the name of Baal all **m**,
2Ki 3:20 the next day at about the time when the **m** sacrifice
3:22 But when they got up the next **m**, the sun was
6:15 servant of the man of God got up early the next **m**
7: 9 If we wait until **m**, some terrible calamity will
10: 8 of the city gate, and leave them there until **m**."
10: 9 In the **m** he went out and spoke to the crowd that
16:15 "Use the new altar for the **m** sacrifices of burnt
19:35 When the surviving Assyrians woke up the next **m**,
1Ch 9:27 It was also their job to open the gates every **m**.
16:40 the regular burnt offerings to the LORD each **m**
23:30 And each **m** and evening they stood before the
2Ch 2: 4 and to sacrifice burnt offerings each **m**
13:11 and fragrant incense to the LORD every **m**
20:20 Early the next **m** the army of Judah went out into
29:20 Early the next **m** King Hezekiah gathered the city
31: 3 a personal contribution of animals for the daily **m**
35:14 because the priests had been busy from **m** till night
Ezr 3: 3 to the LORD. They did this each **m** and evening.
Ne 8: 3 just inside the Water Gate from early **m** until noon
Est 2:14 and the next **m** she was brought to the second
5:14 and in the **m** ask the king to hang Mordecai on it.
Job 1: 5 He would get up early in the **m** and offer a burnt
3: 9 Let its **m** stars remain dark. Let it hope for light,
but in vain; may it never see the **m** light.
4:20 They are alive in the **m**, but by evening they are
7: 4 When I go to bed, I think, 'When will it be **m**?'
7:18 For you examine us every **m** and test us every
11:17 the noonday. Any darkness will be as bright as **m**.
24:17 The black night is their **m**. They ally themselves
38: 7 as the **m** stars sang together and all the angels
38:12 "Have you ever commanded the **m** to appear
Ps 5: 3 Listen to my voice in the **m**, LORD.
5: 3 Each **m** I bring my requests to you and wait
30: 5 may go on all night, / but joy comes with the **m**.
49:14 In the **m** the godly will rule over them.
55:17 **M**, noon, and night / I plead aloud in my distress,
59:16 I will shout with joy each **m** because of your
73:14 is trouble all day long; / every **m** brings me pain.
90: 5 or like grass that springs up in the **m**.
90: 6 In the **m** it blooms and flourishes, / but by evening
90:14 Satisfy us in the **m** with your unfailing love,
92: 2 It is good to proclaim your unfailing love in the **m**,
110: 3 your vigor will be renewed each day like the **m**
127: 2 to work so hard / from early **m** until late at night,
139: 9 If I ride the wings of the **m**, / if I dwell by the
139:18 And when I wake up in the **m**, / you are still with
143: 8 Let me hear of your unfailing love to me in the **m**,
Pr 6:22 When you wake up in the **m**, they will advise you.
7:18 Come, let's drink our fill of love until **m**.
27:14 greeting to your neighbor too early in the **m**,
Ecc 10:16 king is a child and whose leaders feast in the **m**.
Isa 14:12 fallen from heaven, O shining star, son of the **m**!
17:11 so well that they blossom on the very **m** you plant
18: 4 or as the dew forms on an autumn **m** during the
21:11 to me, "Watchman, how much longer until **m**?
21:12 The watchman replies, "**M** is coming, but night
28:19 **m** after **m**, day and night, until you are
29: 8 but is still faint from thirst when **m** comes.
37:36 When the surviving Assyrians woke up the next **m**,
44:22 I have swept away your sins like the **m** mists.
50: 4 **M** by **m** he wakens me and opens my
51:13 fear the anger of your enemies from **m** till night?
Eze 12: 8 The next **m** this message came to me from the
24:18 So I proclaimed this to the people the next **m**,
24:18 The next **m** I did everything I had been told to do.
33:22 be able to speak when this man arrived the next **m**.
46:13 "Each **m** a year-old lamb with no physical defects
46:15 be given as a daily sacrifice every **m** without fail.
Da 6:19 Very early the next **m**, the king hurried out to the
Hos 6: 4 "For your love vanishes like the **m** mist
7: 6 and in the **m** it flames forth like a raging fire.
13: 3 Therefore, they will disappear like the **m** mist,
13: 3 like dew in the **m** sun, like chaff blown by the
Am 4: 4 Offer sacrifices each **m** and bring your tithes every
5: 8 He is he who turns darkness into **m** and day into
Jnh 4: 7 The next **m** at dawn the worm ate through the stem
Mal 1:11 by people of other nations from **m** till night.
Mt 14:25 About three o'clock in the **m** Jesus came to them,
16: 3 red sky in the **m** means foul weather all day.'
20: 1 out early one **m** to hire workers for his vineyard.
20: 3 "At nine o'clock in the **m** he was passing through

21:18 In the **m**, as Jesus was returning to Jerusalem,
27: 1 Very early in the **m**, the leading priests and other
27:17 the crowds gathered before Pilate's house that **m**,
28: 1 Early on Sunday **m**, as the new day was dawning,
Mk 1:35 The next **m** Jesus awoke long before daybreak
6:48 About three o'clock in the **m** he came to them,
11:12 The next **m** as they were leaving Bethany,
11:20 The next **m** as they passed by the fig tree he had
15: 1 Very early in the **m** the leading priests,
15:25 It was nine o'clock in the **m** when the crucifixion
16: 2 Very early on Sunday **m**, just at sunrise, they came
16: 9 It was early on Sunday **m** when Jesus rose from
Lk 4:42 Early the next **m** Jesus went out into the
17:29 until the **m** Lot left Sodom. Then fire and burning
21:38 The crowds gathered early each **m** to hear him.
22:34 The rooster will not crow tomorrow **m** until you
22:61 "Before the rooster crows tomorrow **m**, you will
24: 1 But very early on Sunday **m** the women came to
24:22 of his followers were at his tomb early this **m**,
Jn 6:22 The next **m**, back across the lake, crowds began
8: 2 but early the next **m** he was back again at the
13:38 No, before the rooster crows tomorrow **m**, you will
18:28 before Caiaphas ended in the early hours of the **m**.
20: 1 Early Sunday **m**, while it was still dark,
Ac 2:15 People don't get drunk by nine o'clock in the **m**.
2:16 what you see this **m** was predicted centuries ago by
4: 3 since it was already evening, jailed them until **m**.
16:35 The next **m** the city officials sent the police to tell
23:12 The next **m** a group of Jews got together
23:32 They returned to the fortress the next **m**,
27:33 As the darkness gave way to the early **m** light,
27:39 When **m** dawned, they didn't recognize the
28:23 He began lecturing in the **m** and went on into the
Jas 4:14 For your life is like the **m** fog—it's here a little
Rev 2:28 my Father, and I will also give them the **m** star!
22:16 and the heir to his throne. I am the bright **m** star."

MORNINGS (2) [MORNING]
Da 8:14 will take twenty-three hundred evenings and **m**;
8:26 the twenty-three hundred evenings and **m** is true.

MORROW [KJV] See also DAY (AFTER, FOLLOWING, NEXT), MORNING, TOMORROW

MORSEL (1) [MORSELS]
Isa 5:14 in anticipation of Jerusalem, this delicious **m**.

MORSELS (2) [MORSEL]
Pr 18: 8 What dainty **m** rumors are—but they sink deep into
26:22 What dainty **m** rumors are—but they sink deep into

MORTAL (13) [MORTALLY, MORTALS]
Ge 6: 3 for such a long time, for they are only **m** flesh.
Job 4:17 'Can a **m** be just and upright before God? Can a
9:32 "God is not a **m** like me, so I cannot argue with
15:14 Can a **m** be pure? Can a human be just?
25: 4 How can a mere **m** stand before God and claim to
Ps 78:39 For he remembered that they were merely **m**,
Jer 6:14 superficial treatments for my people's **m** wound.
8:11 superficial treatments for my people's **m** wound.
Eze 38:21 Your men will turn against each other in **m**
Hos 11: 9 destroy Israel, for I am God and not a mere **m**.
Ro 8:11 he will give life to your **m** body by this same Spirit
2Co 1:10 And he did deliver us from **m** danger. And we are
Php 3:21 He will take these weak **m** bodies of ours

MORTALITY [KJV] See DYING

MORTALLY (2) [MORTAL]
Jer 14:17 with a sword and lies **m** wounded on the ground.
Eze 30:24 king of Egypt, and he will lie there **m** wounded,

MORTALS (11) [MORTAL]
Job 7:17 "What are mere **m**, that you should make so much
14:14 If **m** die, can they live again? This thought would
34:23 For it is not up to **m** to decide when to come before
Ps 8: 4 what are **m** that you should think of us,
9:19 Arise, O LORD! / Do not let mere **m** defy you!
22:29 Let all **m**—those born to die—bow down in his
56: 4 should I be afraid? / What can mere **m** do to me?
56:11 should I be afraid? / What can mere **m** do to me?
118: 6 I will not be afraid. / What can mere **m** do to me?
144: 3 O LORD, what are **m** that you should notice us,
Heb 13: 6 I will not be afraid. / What can mere **m** do to me?"

MORTAR (3) [MORTARS]
Ge 11: 3 burnt brick and collect natural asphalt to use as **m**.
Ex 1:14 forcing them to make bricks and **m** and to work
Pr 27:22 even though you grind them like grain with **m**

MORTARS (1) [MORTAR]
Nu 11: 8 by grinding it with hand mills or pounding it in **m**.

MORTER [KJV] See also MORTAR, PLASTER, WHITEWASH

MORTGAGED (2)
Ne 5: 3 Others said, "We have **m** our fields, vineyards,
5: 5 our fields and vineyards are already **m** to others."

MORTICIANS (1)
Ge 50: 2 Then Joseph told his **m** to embalm the body.

MORTIFY [KJV] See TURN

MOSAIC (1)
Est 1: 6 and silver couches stood on a **m** pavement of

MOSERAH (1) [MOSEROTH]
Dt 10: 6 wells of the people of Jaakan and traveled to **M**,

MOSEROTH (2) [MOSERAH]
Nu 33:30 They left Hashmonah and camped at **M**.
33:31 They left **M** and camped at Bene-jaakan.

MOSES (888) [MOSES']
BOOK OF MOSES (3) 2Ch 35:12; Ezr 6:18; Ne 13:1

LAW OF MOSES (46) Jos 8:32; 23:6; 1Ki 2:3; 2Ki 14:6; 2Ch 23:18; 25:4; 30:16; Ezr 3:2,4; 7:6; Ne 8:1,18; Da 9:11, 13; Mt 5:17,21,27,31,33,38,43; 8:4; 12:5; 22:36; Mk 1:44; Lk 2:22; 5:14; 10:26; Jn 7:19,22,23; 8:5; Ac 6:13; 15:5; 21:20; 1Co 9:9; Gal 3:5; 5:3; 1Ti 1:7; Heb 7:5,28; 8:4; 9:22; 10:1, 8,28

MOSES, THE SERVANT (16) Dt 34:5; Jos 1:13,15; 8:33; 11:12; 12:6; 13:8; 14:7; 18:7; 22:2,4; 1Ch 6:49; 2Ch 24:6,9; Da 9:11; Rev 15:3

SERVANT MOSES (13) Ex 14:31; Nu 12:7; Jos 1:2; 9:24; 11:15; 1Ki 8:53,56; 2Ki 18:12; 21:8; Ne 1:7,8; 10:29; Mal 4:4

Ex 2:10 The princess named him **M**, for she said, "I drew
2:11 Many years later, when **M** had grown up, he went
2:12 **M** killed the Egyptian and buried him in the sand.
2:13 next day, as **M** was out visiting his people again,
2:13 like that?" **M** said to the one in the wrong.
2:14 **M** was badly frightened because he realized that
2:15 he gave orders to have **M** arrested and killed.
2:15 But **M** fled from Pharaoh and escaped to the land
2:15 When **M** arrived in Midian, he sat down beside a
2:17 This time, however, **M** came to their aid,
2:21 **M** was happy to accept the invitation, and he
2:21 In time, Reuel gave **M** one of his daughters,
2:22 baby boy, and **M** named him Gershom, for he said,
3: 1 One day **M** was tending the flock of his
3: 2 **M** was amazed because the bush was engulfed in
3: 3 "Amazing!" **M** said to himself. "Why isn't that
3: 4 God called to him from the bush, "**M**! **M**!" "Here I am!" **M** replied.
3: 6 When **M** heard this, he hid his face in his hands
3:11 am I to appear before Pharaoh?" **M** asked God.
3:13 But **M** protested, "If I go to the people of Israel
4: 1 But **M** protested again, "Look, they won't believe
4: 2 in your hand?" "A shepherd's staff," **M** replied.
4: 3 So **M** threw it down, and it became a snake!
4: 3 **M** was terrified, so he turned and ran away.
4: 4 So **M** reached out and grabbed it, and it became a
4: 6 Then the LORD said to **M**, "Put your hand inside
4: 6 **M** did so, and when he took it out again, his hand
4: 7 **M** did, and when he took it out this time, it was as
4:10 But **M** pleaded with the LORD, "O Lord,
4:13 But **M** again pleaded, "Lord, please!
4:14 Then the LORD became angry with **M**.
4:18 Then **M** went back home and talked it over with
4:18 "With your permission," **M** said, "I would like to
4:19 Before **M** left Midian, the LORD said to him,
4:20 So **M** took his wife and sons, put them on a
4:24 when **M** and his family had stopped for the night,
4:24 the LORD confronted **M** and was about to kill
4:26 (When she called **M** a "blood-smeared
4:27 to Aaron, "Go out into the wilderness to meet **M**."
4:27 where he found **M** and greeted him warmly.
4:28 **M** then told Aaron everything the LORD had
4:29 So **M** and Aaron returned to Egypt and called the
4:30 told them everything the LORD had told **M**,
4:30 and **M** performed the miraculous signs as they
4:31 were soon convinced that the LORD had sent **M**
5: 1 Israel's leaders, **M** and Aaron went to see Pharaoh.
5: 3 But Aaron and **M** persisted. "The God of the
5:20 they left Pharaoh's court, they met **M** and Aaron,
5:22 So **M** went back to the LORD and protested,
6: 1 what I will do to Pharaoh," the LORD told **M**.
6: 9 So **M** told the people what the LORD had said,
6:10 Then the LORD said to **M**,
6:12 "But LORD!" **M** objected. "My own people
6:13 But the LORD ordered **M** and Aaron to return to
6:20 sister Jochebed, and she bore him Aaron and **M**.
6:26 and **M** named in this list are the same Aaron and **M** to whom the LORD said,
6:30 This is the same **M** who had argued with the
7: 1 Then the LORD said to **M**, "Pay close attention
7: 6 So **M** and Aaron did just as the LORD had
7: 7 **M** was eighty years old, and Aaron was
7: 8 Then the LORD said to **M** and Aaron,
7:10 So **M** and Aaron went to see Pharaoh, and they
7:14 Then the LORD said to **M**, "Pharaoh is very
7:19 Then the LORD said to **M**: "Tell Aaron to point
7:20 So **M** and Aaron did just as the LORD had
7:20 **M** raised his staff and hit the water of the Nile.
7:22 He refused to listen to **M** and Aaron, just as the
8: 1 Then the LORD said to **M**, "Go to Pharaoh once
8: 5 Then the LORD said to **M**, "Tell Aaron to point
8: 8 Then Pharaoh summoned **M** and Aaron
8: 9 "You set the time!" **M** replied. "Tell me when
8:10 "All right," **M** replied, "it will be as you have
8:12 So **M** and Aaron left Pharaoh, and **M** pleaded with
8:13 And the LORD did as **M** had promised. The frogs
8:15 He refused to listen to **M** and Aaron, just as the
8:16 So the LORD said to **M**, "Tell Aaron to strike the
8:17 So **M** and Aaron did just as the LORD had
8:20 Next the LORD told **M**, "Get up early in the
8:25 Pharaoh hastily called for **M** and Aaron.
8:26 But **M** replied, "That won't do! The Egyptians
8:29 "As soon as I go," **M** said, "I will ask the
8:30 So **M** left Pharaoh and asked the LORD to
8:31 And the LORD did as **M** asked and caused the
9: 1 back to Pharaoh," the LORD commanded **M**.
9: 8 Then the LORD said to **M** and Aaron,
9: 8 and have **M** toss it into the sky while Pharaoh
9:10 Pharaoh watched, **M** tossed the soot into the air,
9:11 Even the magicians were unable to stand before **M**,
9:13 Then the LORD said to **M**, "Get up early in the
9:22 Then the LORD said to **M**, "Lift your hand
9:23 So **M** lifted his staff toward the sky,
9:27 Then Pharaoh urgently sent for **M** and Aaron.
9:29 "All right," **M** replied. "As soon as I leave the
9:33 So **M** left Pharaoh and went out of the city. As he
10: 1 Then the LORD said to **M**, "Return to Pharaoh
10: 3 So **M** and Aaron went to Pharaoh and said,
10: 6 And with that, **M** turned and walked out.
10: 8 So **M** and Aaron were brought back to Pharaoh.
10: 9 "Young and old, all of us will go," **M** replied.
10:12 Then the LORD said to **M**, "Raise your hand
10:13 So **M** raised his staff, and the LORD caused an
10:16 Pharaoh quickly sent for **M** and Aaron. "I confess
10:18 So **M** left Pharaoh and pleaded with the LORD.
10:21 Then the LORD said to **M**, "Lift your hand
10:22 So **M** lifted his hand toward heaven, and there was
10:24 Then Pharaoh called for **M**. "Go and worship the
10:25 "No," **M** said, "we must take our flocks
10:28 "Get out of here!" Pharaoh shouted at **M**.
10:29 "Very well," **M** replied. "I will never see you
11: 1 Then the LORD said to **M**, "I will send just one
11: 3 and **M** was considered a very great man in the land
11: 4 So **M** announced to Pharaoh, "This is what the
11: 8 burning with anger, **M** left Pharaoh's presence.
11: 9 Now the LORD had told **M**, "Pharaoh will not
11:10 Although **M** and Aaron did these miracles in
12: 1 the LORD gave the following instructions to **M**
12:21 Then **M** called for the leaders of Israel and said,
12:28 did just as the LORD had commanded through **M**
12:31 Pharaoh sent for **M** and Aaron during the night.
12:35 And the people of Israel did as **M** had instructed
12:43 Then the LORD said to **M** and Aaron, "These are
12:50 Israel followed all the LORD's instructions to **M**
13: 1 Then the LORD said to **M**,
13: 3 So **M** said to the people, "This is a day to
13:19 **M** took the bones of Joseph with him, for Joseph
14: 1 Then the LORD gave these instructions to **M**:
14:11 Then they turned against **M** and complained,
14:13 But **M** told the people, "Don't be afraid. Just stand
14:15 Then the LORD said to **M**, "Why are you crying
14:21 Then **M** raised his hand over the sea,
14:26 the LORD said to **M**, "Raise your hand over the
14:27 sun began to rise, **M** raised his hand over the sea.
14:31 and put their faith in him and his servant **M**.
15: 1 Then **M** and the people of Israel sang this song to
15:22 Then **M** led the people of Israel away from the Red
15:24 Then the people turned against **M**. "What are we
15:25 So **M** cried out to the LORD for help,
15:25 **M** took the branch and threw it into the water.
16: 2 community of Israel spoke bitterly against **M**
16: 4 Then the LORD said to **M**, "Look, I'm going to
16: 6 Then **M** and Aaron called a meeting of all the
16: 9 Then **M** said to Aaron, "Say this to the entire
16:11 And the LORD said to **M**,
16:15 And **M** told them, "It is the food the LORD has
16:19 Then **M** told them, "Do not keep any of it
16:20 a terrible smell. And **M** was very angry with them.
16:22 people came and asked **M** why this had happened.
16:25 **M** said, "This is your food for today, for today is a
16:28 and instructions?" the LORD asked **M**.
16:32 Then **M** gave them this command from the
16:33 **M** said to Aaron, "Get a container and put two
16:34 did this, just as the LORD had commanded **M**.
17: 2 more the people grumbled and complained to **M**.
17: 2 to drink!" they demanded. "Quiet!" **M** replied.
17: 4 Then **M** pleaded with the LORD, "What should I
17: 5 The LORD said to **M**, "Take your shepherd's
17: 6 **M** did just as he was told; and as the leaders
17: 7 **M** named the place Massah—"the place of
17: 7 because the people of Israel argued with **M**
17: 9 **M** commanded Joshua, "Call the Israelites to
17:10 So Joshua did what **M** had commanded. He led his
17:10 Meanwhile **M**, Aaron, and Hur went to the top of a
17:11 As long as **M** held up the staff with his hands,
17:14 Then the LORD instructed **M**, "Write this down
17:15 **M** built an altar there and called it "The LORD Is
18: 1 about all the wonderful things God had done for **M**
18: 2 time before this, **M** had sent his wife, Zipporah,
18: 3 for **M** had said when the boy was born, "I have
18: 4 for **M** had said at his birth, "The God of my
18: 5 Jethro now came to visit **M**, and he brought
18: 5 They arrived while **M** and the people were camped
18: 6 **M** was told, "Jethro, your father-in-law, has come
18: 7 So **M** went out to meet his father-in-law.
18: 8 **M** told his father-in-law about everything the
18:13 **M** sat as usual to hear the people's complaints
18:14 When Moses' father-in-law saw all that **M** was
18:15 **M** replied, "Well, the people come to me to seek
18:24 **M** listened to his father-in-law's advice
18:26 They brought the hard cases to **M**, but they judged

18:27 after this, **M** said good-bye to his father-in-law,
19: 3 Then **M** climbed the mountain to appear before
19: 7 **M** returned from the mountain and called together
19: 8 So **M** brought the people's answer back to the
19: 9 Then the LORD said to **M**, "I am going to come
19: 9 **M** told the LORD what the people had said.
19:10 Then the LORD told **M**, "Go down and prepare
19:14 So **M** went down to the people. He purified them
19:17 **M** led them out from the camp to meet with God,
19:19 the horn blast grew louder and louder, **M** spoke,
19:20 and called **M** to the top of the mountain. So **M** climbed the mountain.
19:21 Then the LORD told **M**, "Go back down
19:23 **M** protested. "You already told them not to.
19:25 So **M** went down to the people and told them what
20:19 And they said to **M**, "You tell us what God says,
20:20 "Don't be afraid," **M** said, "for God has come in
20:21 **M** entered into the deep darkness where God was.
20:22 And the LORD said to **M**, "Say this to the people
24: 1 Then the LORD instructed **M**: "Come up here to
24: 2 You alone, **M**, are allowed to come near to the
24: 3 When **M** had announced to the people all the
24: 4 Then **M** carefully wrote down all the LORD's
24: 6 **M** took half the blood from these animals and drew
24: 8 Then **M** sprinkled the blood from the basins over
24: 9 Then **M**, Aaron, Nadab, Abihu, and seventy of the
24:12 And the LORD said to **M**, "Come up to me on
24:13 So **M** and his assistant Joshua climbed up the
24:14 **M** told the other leaders, "Stay here and wait for
24:15 Then **M** went up the mountain, and the cloud
24:16 On the seventh day the LORD called to **M** from
24:18 Then **M** disappeared into the cloud as he climbed
25: 1 The LORD said to **M**,
30:11 And the LORD said to **M**,
30:17 And the LORD said to **M**,
30:22 Then the LORD said to **M**,
30:34 These were the LORD's instructions to **M**
31: 1 The LORD also said to **M**,
31:12 then gave these further instructions to **M**:
31:18 Then as the LORD finished speaking with **M** on
32: 1 When **M** failed to come back down the mountain
32: 1 This man **M**, who brought us here from Egypt,
32: 7 Then the LORD told **M**, "Quick! Go down the
32:10 Then I will make you, **M**, into a great nation
32:11 But **M** pleaded with the LORD his God not to do
32:15 Then **M** turned and went down the mountain.
32:17 he exclaimed to **M**, "It sounds as if there is a war
32:18 But **M** replied, "No, it's neither a cry of victory
32:19 near the camp, **M** saw the calf and the dancing.
32:23 for something has happened to this man **M**,
32:25 When **M** saw that Aaron had let the people get
32:28 The Levites obeyed **M**, and about three thousand
32:29 Then **M** told the Levites, "Today you have been
32:30 The next day **M** said to the people, "You have
32:31 So **M** returned to the LORD and said, "Alas,
32:33 The LORD replied to **M**, "I will blot out
33: 1 The LORD said to **M**, "Now that you have
33: 5 For the LORD had told **M** to tell them, "You are
33: 8 Whenever **M** went out to the Tent of Meeting,
33: 8 They would all watch **M** until he disappeared
33: 9 at the entrance while the LORD spoke with **M**.
33:11 the LORD would speak to **M** face to face,
33:11 Afterward **M** would return to the camp,
33:12 **M** said to the LORD, "You have been telling me,
33:14 "I will personally go with you, **M**.
33:15 Then **M** said, "If you don't go with us personally,
33:17 And the LORD replied to **M**, "I will indeed do
33:18 Then **M** had one more request. "Please let me see
34: 1 The LORD told **M**, "Prepare two stone tablets
34: 4 So **M** cut two tablets of stone like the first ones.
34: 5 "the LORD," as **M** stood there in his presence.
34: 6 He passed in front of **M** and said, "I am the
34: 8 **M** immediately fell to the ground and worshiped.
34:27 And the LORD said to **M**, "Write down all these
34:28 **M** was up on the mountain with the LORD forty
34:29 When **M** came down the mountain carrying the
34:31 But **M** called to them and asked Aaron
34:32 and **M** gave them the instructions the LORD had
34:33 When **M** had finished speaking with them, he put a
35: 1 Now **M** called a meeting of all the people and told
35: 4 Then **M** said to all the people, "This is what the
35:20 So all the people left **M** and went to their tents to
35:29 the work the LORD had given them through **M**—
35:30 And **M** told them, "The LORD has chosen
36: 2 So **M** told Bezalel and Oholiab to begin the work,
36: 3 **M** gave them the materials donated by the people
36: 4 the craftsmen left their work to meet with **M**.
36: 6 So **M** gave the command, and this message was
38:21 **M** directed the Levites to compile the figures,
38:22 just as the LORD had commanded **M**.
39: 1 just as the LORD had commanded **M**.
39: 5 just as the LORD had commanded **M**.
39: 7 was done just as the LORD had commanded **M**.
39:21 was done just as the LORD had commanded **M**.
39:26 just as the LORD had commanded **M**.
39:29 just as the LORD had commanded **M**.
39:31 blue cord, just as the LORD had commanded **M**.
39:32 everything just as the LORD had commanded **M**.
39:33 And they brought the entire Tabernacle to **M**:
39:42 followed all of the LORD's instructions to **M**.
39:43 **M** inspected all their work and blessed them
40: 1 The LORD now said to **M**,
40:16 **M** proceeded to do everything as the LORD had
40:18 **M** put it together by setting its frames into their
40:31 **M** and Aaron and Aaron's sons washed their hands
40:32 and wash, just as the LORD had commanded **M**.
40:33 of the courtyard. So at last **M** finished the work.
40:35 **M** was no longer able to enter the Tabernacle
Lev 1: 1 The LORD called to **M** from the Tabernacle
4: 1 Then the LORD said to **M**,
5:14 Then the LORD said to **M**,
6: 1 And the LORD said to **M**,
6: 8 Then the LORD said to **M**,
6:19 And the LORD said to **M**,
6:24 Then the LORD said to **M**,
7:22 Then the LORD said to **M**,
7:28 Then the LORD said to **M**,
7:38 The LORD gave these instructions to **M** on
8: 1 The LORD said to **M**,
8: 4 So **M** followed the LORD's instructions, and all
8: 5 **M** announced to them, "The LORD has
8: 8 Then **M** placed the chestpiece on Aaron and put
8:10 Then **M** took the anointing oil and anointed the
8:13 Next **M** presented Aaron's sons and clothed them
8:14 Then **M** brought in the bull for the sin offering,
8:15 as **M** slaughtered it. **M** took some of the blood,
8:17 the camp, just as the LORD had commanded **M**.
8:18 Then **M** presented the ram to the LORD for the
8:19 as **M** slaughtered it. Then **M** took the ram's blood
8:21 **M** burned the entire ram on the altar as a whole
8:21 was done just as the LORD had commanded **M**.
8:22 Next **M** presented the second ram, which was the
8:23 as **M** slaughtered it. Then **M** took some of its blood
8:28 **M** then took all the offerings back and burned
8:29 Then **M** took the breast and lifted it up in the
8:30 Next **M** took some of the anointing oil and some of
8:31 Then **M** said to Aaron and his sons, "Boil the rest
8:36 the LORD had commanded through **M**.
9: 1 **M** called together Aaron and his sons
9: 5 just as **M** had commanded, and the whole
9: 6 Then **M** told them, "When you have followed
9: 7 Then **M** said to Aaron, "Approach the altar
9:10 just as the LORD had commanded **M**.
9:21 offering to the LORD, just as **M** had commanded.
9:23 Next **M** and Aaron went into the Tabernacle,
10: 3 Then **M** said to Aaron, "This is what the LORD
10: 4 Then **M** called for Mishael and Elzaphan,
10: 5 of the camp by their tunics as **M** had commanded.
10: 6 Then **M** said to Aaron and his sons Eleazar
10: 7 is upon you." So they did as **M** commanded.
10:11 the laws that the LORD has given through **M**."
10:12 Then **M** said to Aaron and his remaining sons,
10:16 When **M** demanded to know what had happened to
10:19 Then Aaron answered **M** on behalf of his sons.
10:20 And when **M** heard this, he approved.
11: 1 Then the LORD said to **M** and Aaron,
12: 1 The LORD said to **M**, "Give these instructions to
13: 1 The LORD said to **M** and Aaron,
14: 1 And the LORD said to **M**,
14:33 Then the LORD said to **M** and Aaron,
15: 1 The LORD said to **M** and Aaron,
16: 1 The LORD spoke to **M** after the death of Aaron's
16: 2 The LORD said to **M**, "Warn your brother Aaron
16:34 **M** followed all these instructions that the LORD
17: 1 Then the LORD said to **M**,
18: 1 Then the LORD said to **M**,
19: 1 The LORD also said to **M**,
20: 1 The LORD said to **M**,
21: 1 The LORD said to **M**, "Tell the priests to avoid
21:16 Then the LORD said to **M**,
21:24 So **M** gave these instructions to Aaron and his sons
22: 1 The LORD said to **M**,
22:17 And the LORD said to **M**,
22:26 And the LORD said to **M**,
23: 1 The LORD said to **M**,
23: 9 Then the LORD told **M**
23:23 The LORD told **M**
23:26 Then the LORD said to **M**,
23:33 And the LORD said to **M**,
23:44 So **M** gave these instructions regarding the annual
24: 1 The LORD said to **M**,
24:11 So the man was brought to **M** for judgment.
24:13 Then the LORD said to **M**,
24:23 After **M** gave all these instructions to the Israelites,
24:23 to death, just as the LORD had commanded **M**.
25: 1 While **M** was on Mount Sinai, the LORD said to
26:46 gave to the Israelites through **M** on Mount Sinai.
27: 1 The LORD said to **M**,
27:34 gave to the Israelites through **M** on Mount Sinai.
Nu 1: 1 the LORD spoke to **M** in the Tabernacle in the
1:17 Now **M** and Aaron and the chosen leaders
1:19 as the LORD had commanded **M**. So **M** counted
1:44 These were the men counted by **M** and Aaron
1:48 For the LORD had said to **M**,
1:54 everything just as the LORD had commanded **M**.
2: 1 Then the LORD gave these instructions to **M**
2:33 from this census by the LORD's command to **M**.
2:34 everything just as the LORD had commanded **M**.
3: 1 and **M** as it was recorded when the LORD spoke to **M** on Mount Sinai:
3: 5 Then the LORD said to **M**,
3:11 And the LORD said to **M**,
3:14 The LORD spoke again to **M**, there in the
3:16 So **M** counted them, just as the LORD had
3:38 toward the sunrise was reserved for the tents of **M**
3:39 So among the Levite clans counted by **M**
3:40 Then the LORD said to **M**, "Now count all the
3:42 So **M** counted the firstborn sons of the people of
3:44 Now the LORD said to **M**,
3:49 So **M** collected redemption money for the firstborn
3:51 And **M** gave the redemption money to Aaron
4: 1 Then the LORD said to **M** and Aaron,
4:17 Then the LORD said to **M** and Aaron,
4:21 And the LORD said to **M**,
4:34 So **M**, Aaron, and the other leaders of the
4:37 **M** and Aaron counted them, just as the LORD had commanded through **M**.
4:41 **M** and Aaron counted them, just as the LORD
4:45 **M** and Aaron counted them, just as the LORD had commanded through **M**.
4:46 So **M**, Aaron, and the leaders of Israel counted all
4:49 just as the LORD had commanded through **M**.
4:49 just as the LORD had commanded **M**.
5: 1 The LORD gave these instructions to **M**:
5: 4 did just as the LORD had commanded **M**
5: 5 Then the LORD said to **M**,
5:11 And the LORD said to **M**,
6: 1 Then the LORD said to **M**, "Speak to the people
6:22 Then the LORD said to **M**,
7: 1 On the day **M** set up the Tabernacle, he anointed it
7: 4 Then the LORD said to **M**,
7: 6 So **M** presented the carts and oxen to the Levites.
7:11 The LORD said to **M**, "Let each leader bring his
7:89 Whenever **M** went into the Tabernacle to speak
8: 1 The LORD said to **M**,
8: 3 just as the LORD had commanded **M**.
8: 4 to the exact design the LORD had shown **M**.
8: 5 Then the LORD said to **M**,
8:20 So **M**, Aaron, and the whole community of Israel
8:20 following all the LORD's instructions to **M**.
8:22 that the LORD gave **M** concerning the Levites.
8:23 The LORD also instructed **M**,
9: 1 The LORD gave these instructions to **M** in early
9: 4 So **M** told the people to celebrate the Passover
9: 5 just as the LORD had commanded **M**.
9: 6 that day. So they came to **M** and Aaron that day
9: 8 **M** answered, "Wait here until I have received
9:23 did whatever the LORD told them through **M**.
10: 1 Now the LORD said to **M**,
10:13 the LORD gave the order through **M**.
10:29 One day **M** said to his brother-in-law, Hobab son
10:31 "Please don't leave us," **M** pleaded. "You know
10:35 the Ark set out, **M** would cry, "Arise, O LORD,
11: 2 The people screamed to **M** for help; and when he
11:10 **M** heard all the families standing in front of their
11:10 extremely angry. **M** was also very aggravated.
11:11 And **M** said to the LORD, "Why are you treating
11:16 Then the LORD said to **M**, "Summon before me
11:21 But **M** said, "There are 600,000 foot soldiers here
11:23 Then the LORD said to **M**, "Is there any limit to
11:24 So **M** went out and reported the LORD's words
11:25 LORD came down in the cloud and spoke to **M**.
11:25 He took some of the Spirit that was upon **M**
11:27 A young man ran and reported to **M**, "Eldad
11:28 protested, "**M**, my master, make them stop!"
11:29 But **M** replied, "Are you jealous for my sake?
11:30 Then **M** returned to the camp with the leaders of
12: 1 Miriam and Aaron criticized **M** because he had
12: 2 "Has the LORD spoken only through **M**?
12: 3 Now **M** was more humble than any other person
12: 4 So immediately the LORD called to **M**, Aaron,
12: 7 that is not how I communicate with my servant **M**.
12:11 he cried out to **M**, "Oh, my lord! Please don't
12:13 So **M** cried out to the LORD, "Heal her, O God,
12:14 And the LORD said to **M**, "If her father had spit
13: 1 The LORD now said to **M**,
13: 3 So **M** did as the LORD commanded him. He sent
13:16 These are the names of the men **M** sent to explore
13:16 By this time **M** had changed Hoshea's name to
13:17 **M** gave the men these instructions as he sent them
13:26 to **M**, Aaron, and the people of Israel at Kadesh in
13:27 This was their report to **M**: "We arrived in the
13:30 to encourage the people as they stood before **M**.
14: 2 rose in a great chorus of complaint against **M**
14: 5 Then **M** and Aaron fell face down on the ground
14:11 And the LORD said to **M**, "How long will these
14:13 they hear about it?" **M** pleaded with the LORD.
14:26 Then the LORD said to **M** and Aaron,
14:39 When **M** reported the LORD's words to the
14:41 But **M** said, "Why are you now disobeying the
14:44 despite the fact that neither **M** nor the Ark of the
15: 1 The LORD told **M** to give these instructions to
15:17 The LORD also said to **M** at this time,
15:22 that the LORD has given you through **M**.
15:23 the LORD has commanded through **M**.
15:33 He was apprehended and taken before **M**, Aaron,
15:35 Then the LORD said to **M**, "The man must be
15:36 to death, just as the LORD had commanded **M**.
15:37 And the LORD said to **M**,
16: 2 They incited a rebellion against **M**, involving 250
16: 3 They went to **M** and Aaron and said, "You have
16: 4 When **M** heard what they were saying, he threw
16: 8 Then **M** spoke again to Korah: "Now listen,
16:12 Then **M** summoned Dathan and Abiram, the sons
16:15 Then **M** became very angry and said to the
16:16 And **M** said to Korah, "Come here tomorrow
16:18 and stood at the entrance of the Tabernacle with **M**
16:19 had stirred up the entire community against **M**
16:20 and the LORD said to **M** and Aaron,
16:22 But **M** and Aaron fell face down on the ground.
16:23 And the LORD said to **M**,
16:25 So **M** got up and rushed over to the tents of Dathan
16:28 And **M** said, "By this you will know that the
16:36 And the LORD said to **M**,
16:40 the LORD's instructions to **M** were carried out.
16:41 community began muttering again against **M**
16:42 As the people gathered to protest to **M** and Aaron,
16:43 **M** and Aaron came and stood at the entrance of the
16:44 and the LORD said to **M**,
16:45 But **M** and Aaron fell face down on the ground.
16:46 And **M** said to Aaron, "Quick, take an incense

16:47 Aaron did as **M** told him and ran out among the
16:50 Aaron returned to **M** at the entrance of the
17: 1 Then the LORD said to **M**,
17: 6 So **M** gave the instructions to the people of Israel,
17: 6 tribal leaders, including Aaron, brought **M** a staff.
17: 7 **M** put the staffs in the LORD's presence in the
17: 9 When **M** brought all the staffs out from the
17:10 And the LORD said to **M**: "Place Aaron's staff
17:11 So **M** did as the LORD commanded him.
17:12 Then the people of Israel said to **M**, "We are as
18:25 The LORD also told **M**,
19: 1 The LORD said to **M** and Aaron,
20: 2 that place, so they rebelled against **M** and Aaron.
20: 3 The people blamed **M** and said, "We wish we had
20: 6 **M** and Aaron turned away from the people
20: 7 and the LORD said to **M**,
20: 9 So **M** did as he was told. He took the staff from the
20:11 Then **M** raised his hand and struck the rock twice
20:12 But the LORD said to **M** and Aaron,
20:14 While **M** was at Kadesh, he sent ambassadors to
20:23 Then the LORD said to **M** and Aaron at Mount
20:27 So **M** did as the LORD commanded. The three of
20:28 **M** removed the priestly garments from Aaron
20:28 the mountain, and **M** and Eleazar went back down.
21: 5 and they began to murmur against God and **M**.
21: 7 Then the people came to **M** and cried out,
21: 7 away the snakes." So **M** prayed for the people.
21: 9 So **M** made a snake out of bronze and attached it to
21:16 which is the well where the LORD said to **M**,
21:32 After **M** sent men to explore the Jazer area,
21:34 The LORD said to **M**, "Do not be afraid of him,
25: 4 The LORD issued the following command to **M**:
25: 5 So **M** ordered Israel's judges to execute everyone
25: 6 right before the eyes of **M** and all the people,
25:10 Then the LORD said to **M**,
25:16 Then the LORD said to **M**,
26: 1 the LORD said to **M** and to Eleazar son of Aaron,
26: 3 So **M** and Eleazar the priest issued these census
26: 4 and older, just as the LORD commanded **M**."
26: 9 leaders who conspired with Korah against **M**
26:52 Then the LORD said to **M**,
26:59 the parents of Aaron, **M**, and their sister, Miriam.
26:63 figures of the people of Israel as prepared by **M**
26:64 Not one person that **M** and Aaron counted in this
27: 2 These women went and stood before **M**,
27: 5 So **M** brought their case before the LORD.
27: 6 And the LORD replied to **M**,
27:11 just as the LORD commanded **M**.' "
27:12 One day the LORD said to **M**, "Climb to the top
27:15 Then **M** said to the LORD,
27:22 So **M** did as the LORD commanded
27:23 **M** laid his hands on him and commissioned him to
27:23 just as the LORD had commanded through **M**.
28: 1 The LORD said to **M**, "Give these instructions to
29:40 So **M** gave all of these instructions to the people of
30: 1 Now **M** summoned the leaders of the tribes of
30:16 These are the regulations the LORD gave **M**
31: 1 Then the LORD said to **M**,
31: 3 So **M** said to the people, "Choose some men to
31: 6 Then **M** sent them out, a thousand men from each
31: 7 Midian just as the LORD had commanded **M**,
31:12 they brought them all to **M** and Eleazar the priest,
31:13 **M**, Eleazar the priest, and all the leaders of the
31:14 But **M** was furious with all the military
31:21 "The LORD has given **M** this requirement of the
31:25 And the LORD said to **M**,
31:31 So **M** and Eleazar the priest did as the LORD commanded **M**.
31:41 **M** gave all the LORD's share to Eleazar the
31:42 which **M** had separated from the half belonging to
31:47 **M** took one of every fifty prisoners and animals
31:47 was done just as the LORD had commanded **M**.
31:48 Then all the military commanders came to **M**
31:51 So **M** and Eleazar the priest received the gold from
31:54 So **M** and Eleazar the priest accepted the gifts from
32: 2 they came to **M**, Eleazar the priest, and the other
32: 6 **M** asked the Reubenites and Gadites,
32:16 But they responded to **M**, "We simply want to
32:20 Then **M** said, "If you keep your word and arm
32:28 So **M** gave orders to Eleazar, Joshua, and the tribal
32:33 So **M** assigned to the tribes of Gad, Reuben,
32:40 So **M** gave Gilead to the Makirites, descendants of
33: 1 marched out of Egypt under the leadership of **M**
33: 2 **M** kept a written record of their progress.
33:50 of Moab opposite Jericho, the LORD said to **M**,
34: 1 Then the LORD said to **M**,
34:13 Then **M** told the Israelites, "This is the territory
34:16 And the LORD said to **M**,
35: 1 across from Jericho, the LORD said to **M**,
35: 9 And the LORD said to **M**,
36: 1 came to **M** and the family leaders of Israel with a
36: 5 So **M** gave the Israelites this command from the
36:10 of Zelophehad did as the LORD commanded **M**.
36:13 **M** while they were camped on the plains of Moab
Dt 1: 1 This book records the words that **M** spoke to all
1: 3 **M** gave these speeches to the Israelites,
1: 5 So **M** addressed the people of Israel while they
2:13 **M** continued, "Then the LORD told us to cross
2:24 **M** continued, "Then the LORD said, 'Now cross
4:41 Then **M** set apart three cities of refuge east of the
4:44 This is the law that **M** handed down to the
4:45 and regulations that **M** gave to the people of Israel
4:46 He and his people had been destroyed by **M**
5: 1 **M** called all the people of Israel together and said,
5:32 So **M** told the people, "You must obey all the
27: 1 Then **M** and the leaders of Israel charged the
27: 9 Then **M** and the Levitical priests addressed all
27:11 That same day **M** gave this charge to the people:
29: 1 **M** to make with the Israelites while they were in
29: 2 **M** summoned all the Israelites and said to them,
31: 1 When **M** had finished saying these things to all the
31: 7 Then **M** called for Joshua, and as all Israel
31: 9 So **M** wrote down this law and gave it to the
31:10 Then **M** gave them this command: "At the end of
31:14 Then the LORD said to **M**, "The time has come
31:14 So **M** and Joshua went and presented themselves at
31:16 The LORD said to **M**, "You are about to die
31:22 So that very day **M** wrote down the words of the
31:24 When **M** had finished writing down this entire
31:30 So **M** recited this entire song to the assembly of
32:44 So **M** came with Joshua son of Nun and recited all
32:45 When **M** had finished reciting these words to
32:48 That same day the LORD said to **M**,
33: 1 This is the blessing that **M**, the man of God,
33: 4 **M** charged us with the law, / the special possession
33: 6 **M** said this about the tribe of Reuben:
33: 7 **M** said this about the tribe of Judah: / "O LORD,
33: 8 **M** said this about the tribe of Levi: / "O LORD,
33:12 **M** said this about the tribe of Benjamin:
33:13 **M** said this about the tribes of Joseph:
33:18 **M** said this about the tribes of Zebulun
33:20 **M** said this about the tribe of Gad: / "Blessed is
33:22 **M** said this about the tribe of Dan: / "Dan is a
33:23 **M** said this about the tribe of Naphtali:
33:24 **M** said this about the tribe of Asher: / "May Asher
34: 1 Then **M** went to Mount Nebo from the plains of
34: 4 Then the LORD said to **M**, "This is the land I
34: 5 So **M**, the servant of the LORD, died there in the
34: 7 **M** was 120 years old when he died, yet his
34: 8 The people of Israel mourned thirty days for **M** on
34: 9 spirit of wisdom, for **M** had laid his hands on him.
34: 9 everything just as the LORD had commanded **M**.
34:10 There has never been another prophet like **M**,
34:11 The LORD sent **M** to perform all the miraculous
34:12 And it was through **M** that the LORD
Jos 1: 1 After the death of **M** the LORD's servant,
1: 2 "Now that my servant **M** is dead, you must lead
1: 3 I promise you what I promised **M**:
1: 5 For I will be with you as I was with **M**. I will not
1: 7 very courageous. Obey all the laws **M** gave you.
1:13 "Remember what **M**, the servant of the LORD,
1:15 the east side of the Jordan River in the land that **M**,
1:17 We will obey you just as we obeyed **M**. And may
1:17 LORD your God be with you as he was with **M**.
3: 7 will know that I am with you, just as I was with **M**.
4:10 which **M** had given to Joshua, were carried out.
4:12 Israelites across the Jordan, just as **M** had directed.
4:14 they revered him as much as they had revered **M**.
8:31 He followed the instructions that **M** the LORD's
8:32 Joshua copied the law of **M** onto the stones of the
8:33 This was all done according to the instructions **M**,
8:34 and curses **M** had written in the Book of the Law.
8:35 Every command **M** had ever given was read to the
9:24 instructed his servant **M** to conquer this entire land
11:12 just as **M**, the servant of the LORD,
11:15 As the LORD had commanded his servant **M**, so **M** commanded Joshua.
11:15 obeying all of the LORD's instructions to **M**.
11:20 as the LORD had commanded **M**.
11:23 entire land, just as the LORD had instructed **M**.
12: 6 **M**, the servant of the LORD, and the Israelites
12: 6 And **M** gave their land to the tribes of Reuben,
13: 8 for **M**, the servant of the LORD, had previously
13:12 for **M** had attacked them and driven them out.
13:14 **M** did not assign any land to the tribe of Levi.
13:15 **M** had assigned the following area to the families
13:21 and was killed by **M** along with the chiefs of
13:24 **M** had assigned the following area to the families
13:29 **M** had assigned the following area to the families
13:32 These are the allotments **M** had made while he was
13:33 But **M** gave no land to the tribe of Levi,
14: 2 with the LORD's command through **M**.
14: 3 **M** had already given an inheritance of land to the
14: 5 accordance with the LORD's instructions to **M**.
14: 6 "Remember what the LORD said to **M**, the man
14: 7 I was forty years old when **M**, the servant of the
14: 9 So that day **M** promised me, 'The land of Canaan
14:10 these forty-five years since **M** made this promise—
14:11 I am as strong now as I was when **M** sent me on
17: 4 "The LORD commanded **M** to give us an
18: 7 which **M**, the servant of the LORD,
20: 2 to designate the cities of refuge, as I instructed **M**.
21: 2 "The LORD instructed **M** to give us towns to
21: 8 the Israelites obeyed the LORD's command to **M**
22: 2 He told them, "You have done as **M**, the servant
22: 4 So go home now to the land **M**, the servant of the
22: 5 all the commands and the law that **M** gave to you.
22: 7 Now **M** had given the land of Bashan to the
22: 9 according to the LORD's command through **M**.
23: 6 instructions written in the Book of the Law of **M**.
24: 5 "Then I sent **M** and Aaron, and I brought terrible
Jdg 1:20 The city of Hebron was given to Caleb as **M** had
3: 4 LORD had given to their ancestors through **M**.
18:30 son of Gershom, a descendant of **M**, as their priest.
1Sa 12: 6 "It was the LORD who appointed **M**
12: 8 he sent **M** and Aaron to rescue them from Egypt
1Ki 2: 3 and stipulations written in the law of **M** so that you
8: 9 tablets that **M** had placed there at Mount Sinai,
8:53 you told your servant **M** that you had separated
8:56 promises he gave through his servant **M**.
2Ki 14: 6 the LORD written in the Book of the Law of **M**:
18: 4 He broke up the bronze serpent that **M** had made,
18: 6 all the commands the LORD had given **M**.
18:12 laws the LORD had given through his servant **M**.
21: 8 whole law that was given through my servant **M**—
23:25 and soul and strength, obeying all the laws of **M**.
1Ch 6: 3 children of Amram were Aaron, **M**, and Miriam.
6:49 for Israel by following all the commands that **M**,
15:15 just as the LORD had instructed **M**.
21:29 and the altar that **M** made in the wilderness were
22:13 that the LORD gave to Israel through **M**,
23:13 The sons of Amram were Aaron and **M**. Aaron
23:14 As for **M**, the man of God, his sons were included
23:15 The sons of **M** were Gershom and Eliezer.
26:24 Shebuel was a descendant of Gershom son of **M**.
2Ch 1: 3 This was the Tabernacle that **M**, the LORD's
5:10 tablets that **M** had placed there at Mount Sinai,
8:13 to day according to the commands **M** had given.
23:18 as prescribed by the law of **M**, and to sing
24: 6 **M**, the servant of the LORD, levied this tax on
24: 9 the people to bring to the LORD the tax that **M**,
25: 4 the LORD written in the Book of the Law of **M**:
30:16 according to the regulations found in the law of **M**,
33: 8 laws, and regulations given through **M**—
34:14 of the LORD as it had been given through **M**.
35: 6 the instructions that the LORD gave through **M**."
35:12 to the instructions recorded in the Book of **M**.
Ezr 3: 2 as instructed in the law of **M**, the man of God.
3: 4 Festival of Shelters as prescribed in the law of **M**,
6:18 all the instructions recorded in the Book of **M**.
7: 6 well versed in the law of **M**, which the LORD,
Ne 1: 7 that you gave us through your servant **M**.
1: 8 "Please remember what you told your servant **M**:
8: 1 the scribe to bring out the Book of the Law of **M**,
8:14 **M** that the Israelites should live in shelters during
8:18 held a solemn assembly, as the law of **M** required.
9:14 you commanded them, through **M** your servant,
10:29 to obey the law of God as issued by his servant **M**.
13: 1 that same day, as the Book of **M** was being read,
13: 5 **M** had decreed that these offerings belonged to the
Ps 77:20 of sheep, / with **M** and Aaron as their shepherds.
90: T A prayer of **M**, the man of God.
99: 6 **M** and Aaron were among his priests;
103: 7 He revealed his character to **M** / and his deeds to
105:26 But the LORD sent **M** his servant, / along with
106:16 The people in the camp were jealous of **M**
106:23 But **M**, his chosen one, stepped between the
106:32 angered the LORD, / causing **M** serious trouble.
106:33 They made **M** angry, / and he spoke foolishly.
Isa 63:11 Then they remembered those days of old when **M**
63:11 Israel through the sea, with **M** as their shepherd?
63:12 when **M** lifted up his hand, establishing his
Jer 15: 1 "Even if **M** and Samuel stood before me pleading
Da 9:11 and judgments written in the law of **M**,
9:13 Every curse written against us in the law of **M** has
Mic 6: 4 I sent **M**, Aaron, and Miriam to help you.
Mal 4: 4 to obey the instructions of my servant **M**,
Mt 5:17 I did not come to abolish the law of **M**
5:21 "You have heard that the law of **M** says, 'Do not
5:27 "You have heard that the law of **M** says, 'Do not
5:31 "You have heard that the law of **M** says, 'A man
5:33 "Again, you have heard that the law of **M** says,
5:38 "You have heard that the law of **M** says, 'If an eye
5:43 "You have heard that the law of **M** says,
8: 4 Take along the offering required in the law of **M**
12: 5 And haven't you ever read in the law of **M** that the
17: 3 **M** and Elijah appeared and began talking with
17: 4 one for you, one for **M**, and one for Elijah."
19: 7 "Then why did **M** say a man could merely write
19: 8 "**M** permitted divorce as a concession to your
22:24 "Teacher, **M** said, 'If a man dies without children,
22:36 most important commandment in the law of **M**?"
Mk 1:44 Take along the offering required in the law of **M**
7:10 For instance, **M** gave you this law from God:
9: 4 Then Elijah and **M** appeared and began talking
9: 5 one for you, one for **M**, and one for Elijah."
9: 8 they looked around, and **M** and Elijah were gone,
10: 3 "What did **M** say about divorce?" Jesus asked
12:19 "Teacher, **M** gave us a law that if a man dies,
12:26 you ever read about this in the writings of **M**,
12:26 Isaac, and Jacob had died, God said to **M**,
Lk 2:22 as required by the law of **M** after the birth of a
5:14 Take along the offering required in the law of **M**
9:30 **M** and Elijah, appeared and began talking with
9:33 As **M** and Elijah were starting to leave, Peter,
9:33 one for you, one for **M**, and one for Elijah."
10:26 Jesus replied, "What does the law of **M** say?
16:16 the laws of **M** and the messages of the prophets
16:29 '**M** and the prophets have warned them.
16:31 'If they won't listen to **M** and the prophets,
20:28 "Teacher, **M** gave us a law that if a man dies,
20:37 even **M** proved this when he wrote about the
24:27 Jesus quoted passages from the writings of **M**
24:44 I told you that everything written about me by **M**
Jn 1:17 For the law was given through **M**; God's unfailing
1:45 "We have found the very person **M**
3:14 And as **M** lifted up the bronze snake on a pole in
5:45 **M** will accuse you! Yes, **M**, on whom you set your
5:46 But if you had believed **M**, you would have
6:31 '**M** gave them bread from heaven to eat.' "
6:32 assure you, **M** didn't give them bread from heaven.
7:19 None of you obeys the law of **M**! In fact, you are
7:22 of circumcision is older than the law of **M**;
7:23 go ahead and do it, so as not to break the law of **M**.
8: 5 The law of **M** says to stone her. What do you
9:28 "You are his disciple, but we are disciples of **M**.
9:29 We know God spoke to **M**, but as for this man,
Ac 3:22 **M** said, 'The Lord your God will raise up a
3:23 Then **M** said, 'Anyone who will not listen to that
6:11 saying, "We heard him blaspheme **M**, and even
6:13 against the Temple and against the law of **M**.

6:14 and change the customs **M** handed down to us."
7:20 "At that time **M** was born—a beautiful child in
7:22 **M** was taught all the wisdom of the Egyptians,
7:24 So **M** came to his defense and avenged him,
7:25 **M** assumed his brothers would realize that God
7:27 "But the man in the wrong pushed **M** aside
7:29 When **M** heard that, he fled the country and lived
7:30 an angel appeared to **M** in the flame of a burning
7:31 **M** saw it and wondered what it was. As he went to
7:32 **M** shook with terror and dared not look.
7:35 **M** was sent to be their ruler and savior.
7:37 "**M** himself told the people of Israel, 'God will
7:38 **M** was with the assembly of God's people in the
7:39 "But our ancestors rejected **M** and wanted to
7:40 for we don't know what has become of this **M**,
7:44 accordance with the plan shown to **M** by God.
13:15 After the usual readings from the books of **M**
15: 1 Jewish custom of circumcision taught by **M**,
15: 5 and be required to follow the law of **M**.
15:21 For these laws of **M** have been preached in Jewish
21:20 and they all take the law of **M** very seriously.
21:21 Gentile world to turn their backs on the laws of **M**.
26:22 what the prophets and **M** said would happen—
28:23 from the five books of **M** and the books of the
Ro 8: 3 The law of **M** could not save us, because of our
9:15 For God said to **M**, / "I will show mercy to anyone
10: 5 For **M** wrote that the law's way of making a
10:19 Yes, they did, for even in the time of **M**, God had
1Co 9: 9 For the law of **M** says, "Do not keep an ox from
10: 2 As followers of **M**, they were all baptized in the
2Co 3:13 We are not like **M**, who put a veil over his face
Gal 3: 5 among you because you obey the law of **M**?
3:17 430 years later when God gave the law to **M**.
3:19 God gave his laws to angels to give to **M**, who was
5: 3 obey all of the regulations in the whole law of **M**.
1Ti 1: 7 want to be known as teachers of the law of **M**,
2Ti 3: 8 truth just as Jannes and Jambres fought against **M**.
Heb 3: 2 just as **M** served faithfully and was entrusted with
3: 3 But Jesus deserves far more glory than **M**, just as a
3: 5 **M** was certainly faithful in God's house, but only
3:16 Weren't they the ones **M** led out of Egypt?
7: 5 are commanded in the law of **M** to collect a tithe
7:14 and **M** never mentioned Judah in connection with
7:28 Those who were high priests under the law of **M**
8: 4 who offer the gifts required by the law of **M**.
8: 5 For when **M** was getting ready to build the
9:19 For after **M** had given the people all of God's laws,
9:22 In fact, we can say that according to the law of **M**,
10: 1 The old system in the law of **M** was only a shadow
10: 8 them" (though they are required by the law of **M**).
10:28 Anyone who refused to obey the law of **M** was put
11:24 It was by faith that **M**, when he grew up, refused to
11:27 It was by faith that **M** left the land of Egypt.
11:27 **M** kept right on going because he kept his eyes on
11:28 It was by faith that **M** commanded the people of
12:21 **M** himself was so frightened at the sight that he
12:25 did not escape when they refused to listen to **M**,
Rev 15: 3 And they were singing the song of **M**, the servant

MOSES' (20) [MOSES]

Ex 3: 4 When the LORD saw that he had caught **M**
4:25 She threw the foreskin at **M** feet and said, "What a
17:12 **M** arms finally became too tired to hold up the
18: 1 the priest of Midian and **M** father-in-law,
18: 3 The name of **M** first son was Gershom, for Moses
18: 5 and he brought **M** wife and two sons with him.
18: 7 and then went to **M** tent to talk further.
18:14 When **M** father-in-law saw all that Moses was
33: 7 It was **M** custom to set up the tent known as the
34:30 and the people of Israel saw the radiance of **M**
Lev 8:29 This was **M** share of the ram of ordination, just as
Nu 11:28 who had been **M** personal assistant since his youth,
Jos 1: 1 LORD spoke to Joshua son of Nun, **M** assistant.
Jdg 1:16 who were descendants of **M** father-in-law,
4:11 a descendant of **M** brother-in-law Hobab,
Jn 7:22 too, when you obey **M** law of circumcision.
2Co 3: 7 people of Israel could not bear to look at **M** face.
3:15 Yes, even today when they read **M** writings,
Heb 11:23 It was by faith that **M** parents hid him for three
Jude 1: 9 Michael was arguing with Satan about **M** body.)

MOST (218) [INMOST, INNERMOST, SOUTHERNMOST, TOPMOST]

GOD MOST HIGH (6) Ge 14:18,19,20,22; Ps 57:2; Heb 7:1

MOST HIGH (57) Ge 14:18,19,20,22; Nu 24:16; Dt 32:8; 2Sa 22:14; Ps 7:8,17; 9:2; 18:13; 21:7; 46:4; 47:2; 50:14; 57:2; 73:11; 77:10; 78:17,35,56; 82:6; 83:18; 87:5; 91:1,9; 92:1; 97:9; 107:11; Isa 14:14; La 3:35,38; Da 3:26; 4:2,17,24, 25,32,34; 5:18,21; 7:18,22,25,25,27; Hos 7:16; 11:7; Mk 5:7; Lk 1:32,35,76; 6:35; 8:28; Ac 7:48; 16:17; Heb 7:1

MOST HIGH GOD (7) Da 3:26; 4:2; 5:18,21; Mk 5:7; Lk 8:28; Ac 16:17

MOST HOLY (62) Ex 26:33,34; 27:21; 29:44; 30:36; 35:12; 39:34; 40:3,10; Lev 2:3,10; 4:6; 6:17,25,29; 7:1,6; 10:12; 14:13; 16:2,16,17,20,23,27,33; 21:22; 24:3,9; Nu 18:9,9,10,10; 1Ki 6:16,17,21,22; 7:49,50; 8:6; 1Ch 6:49; 23:13; 2Ch 3:8,10,14; 4:20,22; 5:7; Eze 41:4,15,17,21,23; 42:13; 45:3; Da 9:24; Heb 9:3,7,8,12,25; 10:19

MOST HOLY PLACE (42) Ex 26:33,34; 27:21; 35:12; 39:34; 40:3; Lev 4:6; 16:2,16,17,20,23,27,33; 24:3; 1Ki 6:16,17,21,22; 7:49,50; 8:6; 1Ch 6:49; 2Ch 3:8,10,14; 4:20,22; 5:7; Eze 41:4,15,17,21,23; 45:3; Da 9:24; Heb 9:3,7,8,12,25; 10:19

Ge 14:18 the king of Salem and a priest of God **M** High,
14:19 "Blessed be Abram by God **M** High, / Creator of
14:20 And blessed be God **M** High, / who has helped you
14:22 God **M** High, Creator of heaven and earth,
26:27 since you sent me from your land in a **m**
47:29 swear **m** solemnly that you will honor this, my last
Ex 26:33 separate the Holy Place from the **M** Holy Place.
26:34 on top of the Ark of the Covenant inside the **M**
27:21 curtain of the **M** Holy Place in the Tabernacle.
28:15 "Then, with the **m** careful workmanship, make a
29:44 I will make the Tabernacle and the altar **m** holy,
30:36 with you in the Tabernacle. This incense is **m** holy.
35:12 the inner curtain to enclose the Ark in the **M** Holy
37:29 using the techniques of the **m** skilled incense
39:34 the inner curtain that enclosed the **M** Holy Place;
40: 3 to enclose the Ark within the **M** Holy Place.
40:10 Then the altar will become **m** holy.
Lev 2: 3 It will be considered a **m** holy part of the offerings
2:10 It will be considered a **m** holy part of the offerings
4: 6 in front of the inner curtain of the **M** Holy Place.
6:17 the sin offering and the guilt offering, it is **m** holy.
6:25 The animal given as a sin offering is **m** holy
6:29 family may eat of this offering, for it is **m** holy.
7: 1 instructions for the guilt offering, which is **m** holy.
7: 6 it must be eaten in a sacred place, for it is **m** holy.
10:12 in it, and eat it beside the altar, for it is **m** holy.
14:13 will be given to the priest. It is a **m** holy offering.
16: 2 "Warn your brother Aaron not to enter the **M** Holy
16:16 he will make atonement for the **M** Holy Place,
16:17 goes in to make atonement for the **M** Holy Place.
16:20 finished making atonement for the **M** Holy Place,
16:23 he wore when he entered the **M** Holy Place,
16:27 whose blood Aaron brought into the **M** Holy Place
16:33 and make atonement for the **M** Holy Place,
21:22 the holy offerings and the **m** holy offerings.
24: 3 curtain of the **M** Holy Place in the Tabernacle
24: 9 for they represent a **m** holy portion of the offerings
25:51 they will repay **m** of what they received when they
Nu 4: 4 the Tabernacle will relate to the **m** sacred objects.
4:19 and not die when they approach the **m** sacred
18: 9 You are allotted the portion of the **m** holy offerings
18: 9 From all the **m** holy offerings—including the grain
18:10 You must eat it as a **m** holy offering. All the males
18:10 may eat of it, and you must treat it as **m** holy.
24:16 of God, / who has knowledge from the **M** High,
Dt 28:54 The **m** tenderhearted man among you will have no
28:56 The **m** tender and delicate woman among you—
32: 8 When the **M** High assigned lands to the nations,
32:10 he guarded them as his **m** precious possession.
Jdg 5:24 "**M** blessed is Jael, / the wife of Heber the Kenite.
1Sa 9: 2 His son Saul was the **m** handsome man in Israel—
2Sa 19:41 do **m** of the work in helping him cross the Jordan.
22:14 from heaven; / the **M** High gave a mighty shout.
23:19 Abishai was the **m** famous of the Thirty and was
1Ki 3: 4 The **m** important of these altars was at Gibeon,
6:16 the **M** Holy Place—at the far end of the Temple.
6:17 outside the **M** Holy Place, was 60 feet long.
6:21 chains to protect the entrance to the **M** Holy Place.
6:22 including the altar that belonged to the **M** Holy
7:49 in front of the **M** Holy Place, the flower
7:50 the doors for the entrances to the **M** Holy Place
8: 6 the **M** Holy Place—and placed it beneath the
1Ch 5: 2 It was the descendants of Judah that became the **m**
6:49 all the other duties related to the **M** Holy Place.
11:21 Abishai was the **m** famous of the Thirty and was
12:29 **M** of the Benjaminites had remained loyal to Saul
16:25 Great is the LORD! He is **m** worthy of praise!
23:13 were set apart to dedicate the **m** holy things,
2Ch 3: 8 The **M** Holy Place was thirty feet wide,
3:10 with gold. These were placed in the **M** Holy Place.
3:14 Across the entrance of the **M** Holy Place,
4:20 to burn in front of the **M** Holy Place as prescribed;
4:22 the doors for the entrances to the **M** Holy Place
5: 7 the **M** Holy Place—and placed it beneath the
30:10 But **m** of the people just laughed at the messengers
30:18 **M** of those who came from Ephraim, Manasseh,
Ne 7: 2 was a faithful man who feared God more than **m**.
11: 3 **M** of the people, priests, Levites, Temple servants,
Est 2: 4 the young woman who pleases you **m** will be made
3: 1 making him the **m** powerful official in the empire
6: 9 Instruct one of the king's **m** noble princes to dress
Job 33:20 and do not care for even the **m** delicious food.
Ps 7: 8 O LORD, / for I am innocent, O **M** High!
7:17 I will sing praise to the name of the LORD **M**
9: 2 I will sing praises to your name, O **M** High.
10: 1 Why do you hide when I need you the **m**?
18:13 from heaven; / the **M** High gave a mighty shout.
21: 7 The unfailing love of the **M** High will keep him
27: 4 thing I ask of the LORD— / the thing I seek **m**—
45: 2 You are the **m** handsome of all. / Gracious words
46: 4 city of our God, / the sacred home of the **M** High.
47: 2 For the LORD **M** High is awesome. / He is the
50:14 I want you to fulfill your vows to the **M** High.
57: 2 I cry out to God **M** High, / to God who will fulfill
73:11 "Is the **M** High even aware of what is
77:10 that the blessings of the **M** High have changed to
78:17 rebelling against the **M** High in the desert.
78:35 their rock, / that their redeemer was the **M** High.
78:56 They rebelled against the **M** High / and refused to
82: 6 'You are gods / and children of the **M** High.
83:18 that you alone are the **M** High, supreme over all
87: 5 And the **M** High will personally bless this city.
90:12 Teach us to make the **m** of our time, / so that we
91: 1 Those who live in the shelter of the **M** High
91: 9 if you make the **M** High your shelter,
92: 1 to the LORD, / to sing praises to the **M** High.
96: 4 Great is the LORD! He is **m** worthy of praise!

97: 9 For you, O LORD, are **m** high over all the earth;
107:11 of God, / scorning the counsel of the **M** High.
145: 3 Great is the LORD! He is **m** worthy of praise!
Pr 4: 7 Getting wisdom is the **m** important thing you can
7: 2 Guard my teachings as your **m** precious
Ecc 2: 3 I hoped to experience the only happiness **m** people
4: 3 And **m** fortunate of all are those who were never
4: 4 Then I observed that **m** people are motivated to
7: 1 A good reputation is more valuable than the **m**
SS 1: 8 "If you don't know, O **m** beautiful woman,
Isa 1:13 even your **m** pious meetings—are all sinful
2: 2 will become the **m** important place on earth.
13:19 Babylon, the **m** glorious of kingdoms, the flower
14:14 to the highest heavens and be like the **M** High.'
29:14 and even the **m** brilliant people lack
49:19 "Even the **m** desolate parts of your abandoned
49:21 For **m** of my children were killed, and the rest
Jer 2:33 The **m** experienced prostitute could learn from
4:30 Why do you dress up in your **m** beautiful clothing
7:19 "**M** of all, they hurt themselves, to their own
17: 9 "The human heart is **m** deceitful and desperately
25:32 A great whirlwind of fury is rising from the **m**
48:15 Her **m** promising youth are doomed to slaughter,"
La 2:15 "Is this the city called '**M** Beautiful in All the
3:35 their God-given rights in defiance of the **M** High.
3:38 Is it not the **M** High who helps one and harms
Eze 7:21 I will give it as plunder to foreigners from the **m**
7:24 I will bring the **m** ruthless of nations to occupy
17:13 He also exiled Israel's **m** influential leaders,
20:15 and honey, the **m** beautiful place on earth.
23: 7 so she prostituted herself with the **m** desirable men
24: 4 and the shoulder and all the **m** tender cuts.
31:16 of Eden, the **m** beautiful and the best of Lebanon,
41: 4 "This," he told me, "is the **M** Holy Place."
41:15 The Holy Place, the **M** Holy Place, and the foyer
41:17 The space above the door leading into the **M** Holy
41:21 and the ones at the entrance of the **M** Holy Place
41:23 and the **M** Holy Place had double doorways,
42:13 to the LORD will eat the **m** holy offerings.
45: 3 Within it the sanctuary of the **M** Holy Place will be
48:12 the land is distributed, the **m** sacred land of all.
Da 3:26 servants of the **M** High God, come out!
4: 2 and wonders the **M** High God has performed for
4:17 the **M** High rules over the kingdoms of the world
4:24 and what the **M** High has declared will happen to
4:25 until you learn that the **M** High rules over the
4:32 until you learn that the **M** High rules over the
4:34 and I praised and worshiped the **M** High
5:18 the **M** High God gave sovereignty, majesty,
5:21 until he learned that the **M** High God rules the
7:18 the holy people of the **M** High will be given the
7:22 and judged in favor of the holy people of the **M**
7:25 He will defy the **M** High and wear down the holy
people of the **M** High.
7:27 will be given to the holy people of the **M** High.
9:24 prophetic vision, and to anoint the **M** Holy Place.
Hos 7:16 look everywhere except to heaven, to the **M** High.
11: 7 They call me the **M** High, but they don't truly
13:15 Ephraim was the **m** fruitful of all his brothers,
Am 2:16 the **m** courageous of your fighting men will drop
4: 7 the rain from falling when you needed it the **m**,
Mic 4: 1 will become the **m** important place on earth.
Zec 2: 8 'Anyone who harms you harms my **m** precious
11: 2 the tallest and **m** beautiful of them are fallen.
Mt 11:11 Yet even the **m** insignificant person in the
11:20 the cities where he had done **m** of his miracles,
21: 8 **M** of the crowd spread their coats on the road
22:36 which is the **m** important commandment in the law
23: 6 and in the **m** prominent seats in the synagogue!
Mk 5: 7 you bothering me, Jesus, Son of the **M** High God?
12:28 the commandments, which is the **m** important?"
12:29 "The **m** important commandment is this:
Lk 1: 1 **M** honorable Theophilus: Many people have
1:32 and will be called the Son of the **M** High.
1:35 and the power of the **M** High will overshadow you.
1:76 will be called the prophet of the **M** High,
6:35 and you will truly be acting as children of the **M**
7:28 Yet even the **m** insignificant person in the
8:28 you bothering me, Jesus, Son of the **M** High God?
12:30 These things dominate the thoughts of **m** people,
19: 2 He was one of the **m** influential Jews in the Roman
19:24 and give it to the one who earned the **m**.'
Jn 12:37 had done, **m** of the people did not believe in him.
Ac 7:48 the **M** High doesn't live in temples made by
16:17 "These men are servants of the **M** High God,
19:32 **m** of them didn't even know why they were there.
20:38 sad **m** of all because he had said that they would
26:25 "I am not insane, **M** Excellent Festus.
27:12 **m** of the crew wanted to go to Phoenix, farther up
Ro 11: 7 **M** of the Jews have not found the favor of God
1Co 1:19 and discard their **m** brilliant ideas."
10: 5 after all this, God was not pleased with **m** of them,
12:22 and least important are really the **m** necessary.
12:31 in any event, you should desire the **m** helpful gifts.
15: 3 I passed on to you what was **m** important and what
15: 6 **m** of whom are still alive, though some have died
15:19 we are the **m** miserable people in the world.
2Co 2: 6 He was punished enough when **m** of you were
Gal 1:14 I was one of the **m** religious Jews of my own age,
Eph 5:16 Make the **m** of every opportunity for doing good in
Col 3:14 And the **m** important piece of clothing you must
4: 5 and make the **m** of every opportunity.
Heb 7: 1 the city of Salem and also a priest of God **M** High.
9: 3 was the second room called the **M** Holy Place.
9: 7 But only the high priest goes into the **M** Holy
9: 8 **M** Holy Place was not open to the people as long
9:12 Once for all time he took blood into that **M** Holy

9:25 like the earthly high priest who enters the **M** Holy
10:19 we can boldly enter heaven's **M** Holy Place
Jas 5:12 But **m** of all, dear brothers and sisters, never take
1Pe 4:8 **M** important of all, continue to show deep love for

MOTE [KJV] See SPECK

MOTH (4) [MOTH-EATEN, MOTHS]

Ps 39:11 their lives can be crushed like the life of a **m**.
Isa 51:8 For the **m** will destroy them as it destroys clothing.
Hos 5:12 I will destroy Israel as a **m** consumes wool. I will
Lk 12:33 no thief can steal it and no **m** can destroy it.

MOTH-EATEN (3) [EAT, MOTH]

Job 13:28 I waste away like rotting wood, like a **m** coat.
Mt 6:20 where they will never become **m** or rusty
Jas 5:2 is rotting away, and your fine clothes are **m** rags.

MOTHER (279) [GRANDMOTHER, MOTHER'S, MOTHER-IN-LAW, MOTHERS, MOTHERS']

FATHER AND MOTHER (38) Ge 2:24; Ex 20:12; Dt 5:16; 21:13,19; 22:15; Jos 2:13; Jdg 14:2,3,4,9,19; Ru 2:11; 1Sa 22:3; 2Sa 19:37; 1Ki 19:20; 22:52; 2Ki 3:2,13; Est 2:7; Ps 27:10; Isa 45:10; Zec 13:3,3; Mt 15:4; 19:5,19; Mk 5:40; 7:10; 10:7,19; Lk 8:51; 14:26; 18:20; Jn 6:42; Eph 5:31; 6:2,3

MOTHER AND FATHER (1) Lev 19:3

Ge 2:24 leaves his father and **m** and is joined to his wife,
3:20 because she would be the **m** of all people
17:16 and she will become the **m** of many nations.
21:21 and his **m** arranged a marriage for him with a
24:53 He also gave valuable presents to her **m**
24:55 to stay at least ten days," her brother and **m** said.
24:60 may you become / the **m** of many millions!
24:67 a special comfort to him after the death of his **m**.
27:11 "But **M**!" Jacob replied. "He won't be fooled that
30:14 growing in a field and brought the roots to his **m**,
37:10 "Will your **m**, your brothers, and I actually come
46:10 and Shaul. (Shaul's **m** was a Canaanite woman.)
46:20 Their **m** was Asenath, daughter of Potiphera,
Ex 2:8 So the girl rushed home and called the baby's **m**.
2:9 So the baby's **m** took her baby home and nursed
2:10 the child's **m** brought him back to the princess,
6:15 Zohar, and Shaul (whose **m** was a Canaanite).
20:12 "Honor your father and **m**. Then you will live a
21:15 who strikes father or **m** must be put to death.
21:17 who curses father or **m** must be put to death.
22:30 Leave the newborn animal with its **m** for seven
Lev 18:7 father by having sexual intercourse with your **m**.
18:7 She is your **m**; you must never have intercourse
19:3 Each of you must show respect for your **m**
20:9 who curse their father or **m** must be put to death.
20:14 man has intercourse with both a woman and her **m**,
20:17 the daughter of either his father or his **m**, it is a
21:2 **m** or father, son or daughter, brother
21:11 near a dead person, even if it is his father or **m**.
22:27 is born, it must be left with its **m** for seven days.
22:28 But you must never slaughter a **m** animal and her
24:10 One day a man who had an Israelite **m** and an
Nu 6:7 if their own father, **m**, brother, or sister has died.
18:15 "The firstborn of every **m**, whether human
Dt 5:16 " 'Honor your father and **m**, as the LORD your
21:13 for a full month, mourning for her father and **m**.
21:18 rebellious son who will not obey his father or **m**,
21:19 and **m** must take the son before the leaders of the
22:6 or eggs in it with the **m** sitting in the nest, do not
take the **m** with the young.
22:7 but let the **m** go, so you may prosper and enjoy a
22:15 and **m** must bring the proof of her virginity to the
27:16 'Cursed is anyone who despises father or **m**.'
27:22 whether she is the daughter of his father or his **m**.'
Jos 2:13 along with my father and **m**, my brothers
2:18 your father, **m**, brothers, and all your relatives—
6:23 and brought out Rahab, her father, **m**, brothers,
Jdg 5:7 of Israel— / until Deborah arose as a **m** for Israel.
5:28 "From the window Sisera's **m** looked out.
11:1 was the son of Gilead, but his **m** was a prostitute.
14:2 When he returned home, he told his father and **m**,
14:3 His father and **m** objected strenuously, "Isn't there
14:4 and **m** didn't realize the LORD was at work in
14:6 But he didn't tell his father or **m** about it.
14:9 He also gave some to his father and **m**, and they
14:16 haven't even given the answer to my father or **m**,"
14:19 he went back home to live with his father and **m**.
17:2 One day he said to his **m**, "I heard you curse the
17:2 LORD bless you for admitting it," his **m** replied.
17:4 So his **m** took two hundred of the silver coins to a
Ru 2:11 I have heard how you left your father and **m**
1Sa 2:19 Each year his **m** made a small coat for him
15:33 of many mothers, now your **m** will be childless."
20:30 king in your place, shaming yourself and your **m**?
22:3 and **m** live here under royal protection until I know
2Sa 3:2 was Amnon, whose **m** was Ahinoam of Jezreel.
3:3 The second was Kileab, whose **m** was Abigail,
3:3 whose **m** was Maacah, the daughter of Talmai,
3:4 The fourth was Adonijah, whose **m** was Haggith.
3:4 The fifth was Shephatiah, whose **m** was Abital.
3:5 was Ithream, whose **m** was David's wife Eglah.
17:8 Right now they are probably as enraged as a **m**
17:25 His **m**, Abigail daughter of Nahash, was the sister
of Joab's **m**, Zeruiah.)
19:37 my own town, where my father and **m** are buried.
21:8 whose **m** was Rizpah daughter of Aiah.
21:10 Then Rizpah, the **m** of two of the men,
1Ki 1:5 time David's son Adonijah, whose **m** was Haggith,
1:11 Solomon's **m**, and asked her, "Did you realize that
2:13 One day Adonijah, whose **m** was Haggith, came to
see Bathsheba, Solomon's **m**.
2:19 he ordered that a throne be brought for his **m**,
2:20 "What is it, my **m**?" he asked. "You know I
3:26 Then the woman who really was the **m** of the
3:27 woman who wants him to live, for she is his **m**!"
7:14 since his **m** was a widow from the tribe of
11:26 in Ephraim, and his **m** was Zeruah, a widow.
14:21 Rehoboam's **m** was Naamah, an Ammonite
14:31 His **m** was Naamah, an Ammonite woman.
15:2 His **m** was Maacah, the daughter of Absalom.
15:13 grandmother Maacah from her position as queen **m**
17:23 down from the upper room and gave him to his **m**.
19:20 let me go and kiss my father and **m** good-bye,
22:42 His **m** was Azubah, the daughter of Shilhi.
22:52 following the example of his father and **m**
2Ki 3:2 but he was not as wicked as his father and **m**.
3:13 "Go to the pagan prophets of your father and **m**!"
4:19 one of the servants, "Carry him home to his **m**."
4:20 took him home, and his **m** held him on her lap.
4:30 But the boy's **m** said, "As surely as the LORD
4:36 "Call the child's **m**!" he said. And when she came
8:5 the **m** of the boy walked in to make her appeal to
8:26 His **m** was Athaliah, a granddaughter of King
9:22 as long as the idolatry and witchcraft of your **m**,
9:30 When Jezebel, the queen **m**, heard that Jehu had
10:13 to visit the sons of King Ahab and the queen **m**."
11:1 When Athaliah, the **m** of King Ahaziah of Judah,
12:1 forty years. His **m** was Zibiah, from Beersheba.
14:2 His **m** was Jehoaddin, from Jerusalem.
15:2 His **m** was Jecoliah, from Jerusalem.
15:33 His **m** was Jerusha, the daughter of Zadok.
18:2 His **m** was Abijah, the daughter of Zechariah.
19:3 to be born, but the **m** has no strength to deliver it.
21:1 Jerusalem fifty-five years. His **m** was Hephzibah.
21:19 His **m** was Meshullemeth, the daughter of Haruz
22:1 His **m** was Jedidah, the daughter of Adaiah from
23:31 His **m** was Hamutal, the daughter of Jeremiah from
23:36 His **m** was Zebidah, the daughter of Pedaiah from
24:8 His **m** was Nehushta, the daughter of Elnathan
24:12 nobles, and officials, and the queen **m**,
24:15 along with his wives and officials, the queen **m**,
24:18 His **m** was Hamutal, the daughter of Jeremiah from
1Ch 2:26 wife named Atarah. She was the **m** of Onam.
3:1 was Amnon, whose **m** was Ahinoam of Jezreel.
3:1 was Kileab, whose **m** was Abigail from Carmel.
3:2 whose **m** was Maacah, the daughter of Talmai,
3:2 The fourth was Adonijah, whose **m** was Haggith.
3:3 The fifth was Shephatiah, whose **m** was Abital.
3:3 The sixth was Ithream, whose **m** was Eglah.
3:5 the daughter of Ammiel, was the **m** of these sons.
4:9 His **m** named him Jabez because his birth had been
4:17 who became the **m** of Miriam, Shammai,
4:18 who became the **m** of Jered (the father of Gedor),
2Ch 12:13 Rehoboam's **m** was Naamah, a woman from
13:2 His **m** was Maacah, a daughter of Uriel from
15:16 grandmother Maacah from her position as queen **m**
20:31 His **m** was Azubah, the daughter of Shilhi.
22:2 His **m** was Athaliah, a granddaughter of King
22:3 for his **m** encouraged him in doing wrong.
22:10 When Athaliah, the **m** of King Ahaziah of Judah,
24:1 forty years. His **m** was Zibiah, from Beersheba.
25:1 His **m** was Jehoaddin, from Jerusalem.
26:3 His **m** was Jecoliah, from Jerusalem.
27:1 His **m** was Jerusha, the daughter of Zadok.
29:1 His **m** was Abijah, the daughter of Zechariah.
Est 2:7 When her father and **m** had died,
Job 3:12 Why did my **m** let me live? Why did she nurse me
17:14 my father, and the worm my **m** and my sister.
24:20 Even the sinner's own **m** will forget him.
38:29 Who is the **m** of the ice? Who gives birth to the
Ps 27:10 Even if my father and **m** abandon me,
35:14 or family, / as if I were grieving for my own **m**.
51:5 yes, from the moment my **m** conceived me.
113:9 woman a home, / so that she becomes a happy **m**.
131:2 just as a small child is quiet with its **m**.
Pr 4:3 tenderly loved by my **m** as an only child.
10:1 joy to a father; a foolish child brings grief to a **m**.
15:20 joy to their father; foolish children despise their **m**.
17:25 child brings grief to a father and bitterness to a **m**.
19:26 or chase away their **m** are a public disgrace and an
20:20 If you curse your father or **m**, the lamp of your life
29:15 but a **m** is disgraced by an undisciplined child.
30:11 people curse their father and do not thank their **m**.
30:17 and despises a **m** will be plucked out by ravens of
31:1 of King Lemuel, an oracle that his **m** taught him.
SS 3:11 See the crown with which his **m** crowned him on
6:9 perfect one, the only beloved daughter of her **m**!
8:5 under the apple tree, where your **m** gave you birth,
Isa 23:10 sweep over your **m** Tyre like the flooding Nile,
37:3 to be born, but the **m** has no strength to deliver it.
40:11 He will gently lead the **m** sheep with their young.
45:10 be if a newborn baby said to its father and **m**,
49:15 "Never! Can a **m** forget her nursing child?
50:1 Is your **m** gone because I divorced her and sent her
50:1 And your **m**, too, was taken because of your sins.
66:13 you there as a child is comforted by its **m**."
Jer 2:27 chiseled out of stone they say, 'You are my **m**.'
13:18 Say to the king and his **m**, "Come down from your
15:9 The **m** of seven grows faint and gasps for breath;
15:10 Then I said, "What sadness is mine, my **m**. Oh,
16:7 the dead—not even for the death of a **m** or a father.
22:26 I will expel you and your **m** from this land,
29:2 the queen **m**, the court officials, the leaders of
Eze 16:3 Your father was an Amorite and your **m** a Hittite!
16:44 proverbs will say of you, 'Like **m**, like daughter.'
16:45 For your **m** loathed her husband and her children,
16:45 Truly your **m** must have been a Hittite and your
19:2 'What is your **m**? / A lioness among lions!
19:5 'When the **m** lion saw / that all her hopes for him
19:10 'Your **m** was like a vine / planted by the water's
23:2 two sisters who were daughters of the same **m**.
44:25 is his father, **m**, child, brother, or unmarried sister.
Da 5:10 But when the queen **m** heard what was happening,
Hos 2:5 For their **m** is a shameless prostitute and became
4:5 false prophets. And I will destroy your **m**, Israel.
Mic 7:6 son despises his father. The daughter defies her **m**.
Zec 13:3 his own father and **m** will tell him, 'You must die,
13:3 Then his own father and **m** will stab him.
Mt 1:3 the father of Perez and Zerah (their **m** was Tamar).
1:5 Salmon was the father of Boaz (his **m** was Rahab).
1:5 Boaz was the father of Obed (his **m** was Ruth).
1:6 David was the father of Solomon (his **m** was
1:16 Mary was the **m** of Jesus, who is called the
1:18 His **m**, Mary, was engaged to be married to
2:11 They entered the house where the child and his **m**,
2:13 and flee to Egypt with the child and his **m**,"
2:14 left for Egypt with the child and Mary, his **m**,
2:20 take the child and his **m** back to the land of Israel,
2:21 immediately to Israel with Jesus and his **m**.
10:35 against his father, and a daughter against her **m**,
10:37 you love your father or **m** more than you love me,
12:46 his **m** and brothers were outside, wanting to talk
12:47 told Jesus, "Your **m** and your brothers are outside,
12:48 Jesus asked, "Who is my **m**? Who are my
12:49 and said, "These are my **m** and brothers.
12:50 Father in heaven is my brother and sister and **m**!"
13:55 and we know Mary, his **m**, and his brothers—
14:11 a tray and given to the girl, who took it to her **m**.
15:4 For instance, God says, 'Honor your father and **m**,'
15:4 speaks evil of father or **m** must be put to death.'
19:5 leaves his father and **m** and is joined to his wife,
19:19 Honor your father and **m**. Love your neighbor as
19:29 or brothers or sisters or father or **m** or children
20:20 Then the **m** of James and John, the sons of
27:56 Mary (the **m** of James and Joseph), and Zebedee's
wife, the **m** of James and John.
Mk 3:31 Jesus' **m** and brothers arrived at the house where
3:32 "Your **m** and your brothers and sisters are outside,
3:33 Jesus replied, "Who is my **m**? Who are my
3:34 and said, "These are my **m** and brothers.
3:35 does God's will is my brother and sister and **m**."
5:40 Then he took the girl's father and **m** and his three
6:24 She went out and asked her **m**, "What should I ask
6:24 Her **m** told her, "Ask for John the Baptist's
6:28 a tray, and gave it to the girl, who took it to her **m**.
7:10 'Honor your father and **m**,' and 'Anyone who
speaks evil of father or **m** must be put to death.'
10:7 leaves his father and **m** and is joined to his wife,
10:19 Do not cheat. Honor your father and **m**.' "
10:29 or brothers or sisters or **m** or father or children
15:40 Mary (the **m** of James the younger and of Joseph),
15:47 and Mary the **m** of Joseph saw where Jesus' body
16:1 and Salome and Mary the **m** of James went out
Lk 1:43 this is, that the **m** of my Lord should visit me!
2:48 "Son!" his **m** said to him. "Why have you done
2:51 and his **m** stored all these things in her heart.
7:15 around him! And Jesus gave him back to his **m**.
8:19 Once when Jesus' **m** and brothers came to see
8:20 told Jesus, "Your **m** and your brothers are outside,
8:21 "My **m** and my brothers are all those who hear the
8:51 James, John, and the little girl's father and **m**.
11:27 in the crowd called out, "God bless your **m**—
12:53 a division between father and son, **m** and daughter,
14:26 must love me more than your own father and **m**,
18:20 not testify falsely. Honor your father and **m**.' "
24:10 Joanna, Mary the **m** of James, and several others.
Jn 2:1 The next day Jesus' **m** was a guest at a wedding
2:3 so Jesus' **m** spoke to him about the problem.
2:5 But his **m** told the servants, "Do whatever he tells
2:12 he went to Capernaum for a few days with his **m**,
6:42 We know his father and **m**. How can he say,
19:25 Standing near the cross were Jesus' **m**, and his
19:26 When Jesus saw his **m** standing there beside the
19:27 And he said to this disciple, "She is your **m**."
Ac 1:14 along with Mary the **m** of Jesus, several other
12:12 he went to the home of Mary, the **m** of John Mark,
16:1 a young disciple whose **m** was a Jewish believer,
Ro 16:13 and also his dear **m**, who has been a **m** to me.
Gal 4:26 the heavenly Jerusalem. And she is our **m**.
Eph 5:31 leaves his father and **m** and is joined to his wife,
6:2 "Honor your father and **m**." This is the first of the
6:3 If you honor your father and **m**, "you will live a
1Th 2:7 but we were as gentle among you as a **m** feeding
1Ti 1:9 who murder their father or **m** or other people.
5:2 Treat the older women as you would your **m**,
2Ti 1:5 for you have the faith of your **m**, Eunice, and your
Heb 7:3 record of his father or **m** or any of his ancestors—
Rev 17:5 **M** of All Prostitutes and Obscenities in the

MOTHER'S (39) [MOTHER]

Ge 24:67 And Isaac brought Rebekah into his **m** tent,
27:14 So Jacob followed his **m** instructions, bringing her
27:29 May all your **m** sons bow low before you. All who
28:5 his **m** brother, the son of Bethuel the Aramean.
29:10 the daughter of his **m** brother, and
42:38 is dead, and he alone is left of his **m** children.
44:20 is dead, and he alone is left of his **m** children,
Ex 23:19 "You must not cook a young goat in its **m** milk.
34:26 "You must not cook a young goat in its **m** milk."
Lev 18:9 she is your father's daughter or your **m** daughter,

18:13 your **m** sister, because she is your **m** close relative.
20:19 whether his **m** sister or his father's sister, he has
24:11 Moses for judgment. His **m** name was Shelomith.
Dt 14:21 your God. "Do not boil a young goat in its **m** milk.
Jdg 9: 1 went to Shechem to visit his **m** brothers.
9: 1 He said to them and to the rest of his **m** family,
Job 1:21 He said, / "I came naked from my **m** womb,
3:10 Curse it for its failure to shut my **m** womb,
10:18 then, did you bring me out of my **m** womb?
Ps 22: 9 Yet you brought me safely from my **m** womb
50:20 and slander a brother— / your own **m** son.
71: 6 from my **m** womb you have cared for me.
109:14 may his **m** sins never be erased from the record.
139:13 of my body / and knit me together in my **m** womb.
Pr 1: 8 father teaches you. Don't neglect your **m** teaching.
6:20 and don't neglect your **m** teaching.
23:22 and don't despise your **m** experience when she is
Ecc 11: 5 as a tiny baby being formed in a **m** womb.
SS 3: 4 into my **m** bedroom, where I had been conceived.
8: 1 you were my brother, who nursed at my **m** breast.
Isa 49: 5 he who formed me in my **m** womb to be his
66:11 even as an infant drinks at its **m** generous breasts.
Jer 1: 5 "I knew you before I formed you in your **m**
20:17 Oh, that I had died in my **m** womb, that her body
52: 1 His **m** name was Hamutal, the daughter of
Mt 14: 8 At her **m** urging, the girl asked, "I want the head
Jn 3: 4 "How can an old man go back into his **m** womb
19:25 and his **m** sister, Mary (the wife of Clopas),

MOTHER-IN-LAW (15) [MOTHER]

Dt 27:23 is anyone who has sexual intercourse with his **m**.'
Ru 1:14 wept together, and Orpah kissed her **m** good-bye.
2:11 and kindness you have shown your **m** since the
2:18 carried it back into town and showed it to her **m**.
2:19 So Ruth told her **m** about the man in whose field
2:23 too. But all the while she lived with her **m**.
3: 6 that night and followed the instructions of her **m**.
3:16 When Ruth went back to her **m**, Naomi asked,
3:17 'Don't go back to your **m** empty-handed.' "
Mic 7: 6 her mother. The daughter-in-law defies her **m**.
Mt 8:14 Peter's **m** was in bed with a high fever.
10:35 her mother, and a daughter-in-law against her **m**.
Mk 1:30 Simon's **m** was sick in bed with a high fever.
Lk 4:38 where he found Simon's **m** very sick with a high
12:53 mother and daughter, **m** and daughter-in-law."

MOTHER-OF-PEARL (1) [PEARL]

Est 1: 6 of porphyry, marble, **m**, and other costly stones.

MOTHERS (13) [MOTHER]

Ge 20:12 we both have the same father, though different **m**
1Sa 15:33 "As your sword has killed the sons of many **m**,
Jer 15: 8 At noontime I will bring a destroyer against the **m**
16: 3 born here in this city and about their **m** and fathers:
31: 8 the expectant **m** and women about to give birth.
La 2:20 Should **m** eat their little children, those they once
5: 3 are orphaned and fatherless. Our **m** are widowed.
Eze 22: 7 Fathers and **m** are contemptuously ignored.
Hos 10:14 Even **m** and children were dashed to death there.
Mt 24:19 and for **m** nursing their babies in those days.
Mk 10:30 houses, brothers, sisters, **m**, children,
13:17 and for **m** nursing their babies in those days.
Lk 21:23 pregnant women and for **m** nursing their babies.

MOTHERS' (2) [MOTHER]

Ru 1: 8 "Go back to your **m** homes instead of coming with
La 2:12 they cry, and then collapse in their **m** arms.

MOTHS (3) [MOTH]

Job 4:19 is dust, and they are crushed as easily as **m**.
Isa 50: 9 like old clothes that have been eaten by **m**!
Mt 6:19 where they can be eaten by **m** and get rusty,

MOTIONED (6) [MOTIONS]

Lk 1:63 He **m** for a writing tablet, and to everyone's
Jn 13:24 Simon Peter **m** to him to ask who would do this
Ac 12:17 He **m** for them to quiet down and told them what
19:33 He **m** for silence and tried to speak in defense.
21:40 stood on the stairs and **m** to the people to be quiet.
24:10 The governor **m** for him to rise and speak.

MOTIONLESS (1) [MOTIONS]

Mk 9:26 The boy lay there **m**, and he appeared to be dead.

MOTIONS (1) [MOTIONED, MOTIONLESS]

Isa 58: 5 You humble yourselves by going through the **m** of

MOTIVATED (2)

Ecc 4: 4 Then I observed that most people are **m** to success
Jas 3:15 things are earthly, unspiritual, and **m** by the Devil.

MOTIVE (3) [MOTIVES]

Job 10:13 " 'Yet your real **m**—I know this was your intent—
Pr 20:27 the human spirit, exposing every hidden **m**.
Jas 4: 3 you don't get it because your whole **m** is wrong—

MOTIVES (13) [MOTIVE]

1Ch 29:17 You know I have done all this with good **m**,
Ps 26: 2 and cross-examine me. / Test my **m** and affections.
Pr 16: 2 their own eyes, but the LORD examines their **m**.
21:27 especially when it is brought with ulterior **m**.
Jer 17:10 search all hearts and examine secret **m**.
Mt 22:18 But Jesus knew their evil **m**. "You hypocrites!"
1Co 4: 5 secrets to light and will reveal our private **m**.
2Co 10: 2 with those who think we act from purely human **m**.
Php 1:15 But others preach about Christ with pure **m**.
1:17 Those others do not have pure **m** as they preach
1:18 But whether or not their **m** are pure, the fact
1Th 2: 4 He is the one who examines the **m** of our hearts.
Jas 2: 4 show that you are guided by wrong **m**?

MOTTO (1)

Jer 33:16 And their **m** will be 'The LORD is our

MOULDY [KJV] See MOLDY

MOUND (1) [MOUNDS]

Jos 8:28 So Ai became a permanent **m** of ruins, desolate to

MOUNDS (2) [MOUND]

Jos 11:13 Joshua did not burn any of the cities built on **m**
Job 27:16 the world, and they may store away **m** of clothing.

MOUNT (189) [MOUNTAIN, MOUNTAINS, MOUNTAINSIDE, MOUNTAINSIDES, MOUNTAINTOP, MOUNTAINTOPS, MOUNTED, MOUNTING]

MOUNT HOR (11) Nu 20:22,23,25,27; 21:4; 33:37,38, 39,41; 34:7; Dt 32:50

MOUNT SEIR (17) Ge 14:6; Dt 1:2; 2:1,5,12,22,29; 33:2; Jos 15:10; 1Ch 4:42; 2Ch 20:10,22,23; Eze 35:2,3,7,15

MOUNT SINAI (43) Ex 16:1; 17:6; 19:2,11,18,20; 24:16; 31:18; 33:6; 34:2,4,32; Lev 7:38; 25:1; 26:46; 27:34; Nu 3:1; 28:6; Dt 1:2,3,6,19; 4:10,15; 5:2; 9:8; 18:16; 29:1; 33:2; Jdg 5:5; 1Ki 8:9; 19:8; 2Ch 5:10; Ne 9:13; Ps 68:17; 106:19; Mal 4:4; Ac 7:30,38; Gal 4:24,25; Heb 12:18,26

MOUNT ZION (24) 2Ki 19:31; Ps 14:7; 48:2,11; 50:2; 53:6; 68:16; 76:2; 78:68; 125:1; Isa 10:32; 24:23; 31:4; 37:32; Jer 26:18; Joel 2:32; Am 1:2; Ob 1:21; Mic 3:12; Zec 1:14; 8:2,3; Heb 12:22; Rev 14:1

Ge 14: 6 and the Horites in **M** Seir, as far as El-paran at the
Ex 16: 1 into the Sin Desert, between Elim and **M** Sinai.
17: 6 I will meet you by the rock at **M** Sinai.
19: 2 they came to the base of **M** Sinai and set up camp
19:11 for I will come down upon **M** Sinai as all the
19:18 All **M** Sinai was covered with smoke
19:20 The LORD came down on the top of **M** Sinai
24:16 presence of the LORD rested upon **M** Sinai,
28:11 engraves a seal. **M** the stones in gold settings.
31:18 LORD finished speaking with Moses on **M** Sinai,
33: 6 So from the time they left **M** Sinai, the Israelites
34: 2 Be ready in the morning to come up **M** Sinai
34: 4 Early in the morning he climbed **M** Sinai as the
34:32 instructions the LORD had given him on **M** Sinai.
Lev 7:38 **M** Sinai when he commanded the Israelites to
25: 1 While Moses was on **M** Sinai, the LORD said to
26:46 gave to the Israelites through Moses on **M** Sinai.
27:34 gave to the Israelites through Moses on **M** Sinai.
Nu 3: 1 when the LORD spoke to Moses on **M** Sinai:
20:22 Israel left Kadesh as a group and arrived at **M** Hor.
20:23 and Aaron at **M** Hor on the border of the land of
20:25 Now take Aaron and his son Eleazar up **M** Hor.
20:27 The three of them went up **M** Hor together as the
21: 4 Then the people of Israel set out from **M** Hor,
23:28 So Balak took Balaam to the top of **M** Peor,
28: 6 This is the regular burnt offering ordained at **M**
31:16 of Israel to rebel against the LORD at **M** Peor.
33:23 They left Kehelathah and camped at **M** Shepher.
33:24 They left **M** Shepher and camped at Haradah.
33:37 They left Kadesh and camped at **M** Hor,
33:38 While they were at the foot of **M** Hor,
33:39 Aaron was 123 years old when he died there on **M**
33:41 the Israelites left **M** Hor and camped at Zalmonah.
33:47 in the mountains east of the river, near **M** Nebo.
34: 7 the Mediterranean Sea and run eastward to **M** Hor,
Dt 1: 2 days to travel from **M** Sinai to Kadesh-barnea, going by way of **M** Seir.
1: 3 But forty years after the Israelites left **M** Sinai,
1: 6 "When we were at **M** Sinai, the LORD our God
1:19 we left **M** Sinai and traveled through the great
2: 1 and we wandered around **M** Seir for a long time.
2: 5 for I have given them all the hill country around **M**
2:12 In earlier times the Horites had lived at **M** Seir,
2:22 similarly helped the descendants of Esau at **M** Seir,
2:29 The descendants of Esau at **M** Seir allowed us to
3: 8 from the Arnon Gorge to **M** Hermon.
3: 9 (**M** Hermon is called Sirion by the Sidonians;
4:10 you stood before the LORD your God at **M** Sinai,
4:15 the day he spoke to you from the fire at **M** Sinai.
4:48 Arnon Gorge to **M** Sirion, also called **M** Hermon.
5: 2 "While we were at **M** Sinai, the LORD our God
9: 8 Remember how angry you made the LORD at **M**
11:29 you must pronounce a blessing from **M** Gerizim and a curse from **M** Ebal.
18:16 your God when you were assembled at **M** Sinai.
27: 4 set up these stones at **M** Ebal and coat them with
27:12 and Benjamin must stand on **M** Gerizim to
27:13 and Naphtali must stand on **M** Ebal to proclaim a
29: 1 to the covenant he had made with them at **M** Sinai.
32:49 and climb **M** Nebo, which is across from Jericho.
32:50 died on **M** Hor and joined his ancestors.
33: 2 The LORD came from **M** Sinai / and dawned upon us from **M** Seir; / he shone forth from **M** Paran
34: 1 Then Moses went to **M** Nebo from the plains of
Jos 8:30 altar to the LORD, the God of Israel, on **M** Ebal.
8:33 One group stood at the foot of **M** Gerizim, the other at the foot of **M** Ebal.
11: 3 and the Hivites in the towns on the slopes of **M**
11:17 territory now extended all the way from **M** Halak,
11:17 to Baal-gad at the foot of **M** Hermon in the valley
12: 1 extended from the Arnon Gorge to **M** Hermon
12: 5 He ruled a territory stretching from **M** Hermon to
12: 7 from Baal-gad in the valley of Lebanon to **M**
13: 5 from Baal-gad beneath **M** Hermon to
13:11 of Geshur and Maacah, all of **M** Hermon,
15: 9 and from there to the towns on **M** Ephron.
15:10 The border circled west of Baalah to **M** Seir,
15:10 of Kesalon on the northern slope of **M** Jearim,
15:11 where it turned toward Shikkeron and **M** Baalah.
24:30 in the hill country of Ephraim, north of **M** Gaash.
Jdg 1:35 The Amorites were determined to stay in **M** Heres,
2: 9 in the hill country of Ephraim, north of **M** Gaash.
3: 3 of Lebanon from **M** Baal-hermon to Lebo-hamath.
4: 6 the tribes of Naphtali and Zebulun at **M** Tabor.
4:12 Barak son of Abinoam had gone up to **M** Tabor,
4:14 warriors down the slopes of **M** Tabor into battle.
5: 5 Even **M** Sinai shook in the presence of the
9: 7 he climbed to the top of **M** Gerizim and shouted,
9:48 so he led his forces to **M** Zalmon. He took an ax
1Sa 31: 1 Many were slaughtered on the slopes of **M** Gilboa.
31: 8 the bodies of Saul and his three sons on **M** Gilboa.
2Sa 1: 6 man answered, "I happened to be on **M** Gilboa.
15:30 David walked up the road that led to the **M** of
15:32 As they reached the spot at the top of the **M** of
1Ki 8: 9 tablets that Moses had placed there at **M** Sinai,
11: 7 On the **M** of Olives, east of Jerusalem, he even
18:19 Now bring all the people of Israel to **M** Carmel,
18:20 all the people and the prophets to **M** Carmel.
18:42 But Elijah climbed to the top of **M** Carmel and fell
19: 8 to travel forty days and forty nights to **M** Sinai,
2Ki 2:25 From there Elisha went to **M** Carmel and finally
4:25 As she approached the man of God at **M** Carmel,
19:31 from Jerusalem, a group of survivors from **M** Zion.
23:13 of Jerusalem and south of the **M** of Corruption,
1Ch 4:42 invaders from the tribe of Simeon went to **M** Seir,
5:23 Bashan to Baal-hermon, Senir, and **M** Hermon.
10: 1 Many were slaughtered on the slopes of **M** Gilboa.
10: 8 found the bodies of Saul and his sons on **M** Gilboa.
2Ch 3: 1 Temple of the LORD in Jerusalem on **M** Moriah,
5:10 tablets that Moses had placed there at **M** Sinai,
13: 4 Abijah stood on **M** Zemaraim and shouted to
20:10 armies of Ammon, Moab, and **M** Seir are doing.
20:22 and **M** Seir to start fighting among themselves.
20:23 and Ammon turned against their allies from **M** Seir
Ne 9:13 "You came down on **M** Sinai and spoke to them
Ps 14: 7 that salvation would come from **M** Zion to rescue
29: 6 a calf / and **M** Hermon to leap like a young bull.
42: 6 from **M** Hermon, the source of the Jordan, / from the land of **M** Mizar.
48: 2 **M** Zion, the holy mountain, / is the city of the great
48:11 Let the people on **M** Zion rejoice. / Let the towns
50: 2 From **M** Zion, the perfection of beauty,
53: 6 that salvation would come from **M** Zion to rescue
68:14 like a blowing snowstorm on **M** Zalmon.
68:16 at **M** Zion, where God has chosen to live,
68:17 the Lord came from **M** Sinai into his sanctuary.
76: 2 Jerusalem is where he lives; / **M** Zion is his home.
78:68 the tribe of Judah, / **M** Zion, which he loved.
89:12 **M** Tabor and **M** Hermon praise your name.
106:19 The people made a calf at **M** Sinai; / they bowed
125: 1 Those who trust in the LORD are as secure as **M**
133: 3 Harmony is as refreshing as the dew from **M**
SS 4: 8 Come down from the top of **M** Amana,
4: 8 from **M** Senir and **M** Hermon, where lions
7: 5 Your head is as majestic as **M** Carmel,
Isa 10:32 that day. He shakes his fist at **M** Zion in Jerusalem.
24:23 the LORD Almighty will **m** his throne on **M** Zion.
28:21 as he did against the Philistines at **M** Perazim
31: 4 LORD Almighty will come and fight on **M** Zion.
35: 2 as lovely as **M** Carmel's pastures and the plain of
37:32 from Jerusalem, a group of survivors from **M** Zion.
Jer 18:14 flowing streams from the crags of **M** Hermon ever
26:18 **M** Zion will be plowed like an open field;
46: 4 Harness the horses, and prepare to **m** them. Put on
46:18 "one is coming against Egypt who is as tall as **M** Tabor or **M** Carmel by the sea!
Eze 35: 2 "Son of man, turn toward **M** Seir, and prophesy
35: 3 I am your enemy, O **M** Seir, and I will raise my
35: 7 I will make **M** Seir utterly desolate, killing off all
35:15 you people of **M** Seir and all who live in Edom!
Joel 2:32 There will be people on **M** Zion in Jerusalem who
Am 1: 2 "The LORD's voice roars from his Temple on **M**
1: 2 All the grass on **M** Carmel withers and dies."
9: 3 Even if they hide at the very top of **M** Carmel,
Ob 1:21 Deliverers will go up to **M** Zion in Jerusalem to
Mic 3:12 of you, **M** Zion will be plowed like an open field;
Hab 3: 3 across the deserts from Edom and **M** Paran.
Zec 1:14 for Jerusalem and **M** Zion is passionate and strong.
8: 2 My love for **M** Zion is passionate and strong;
8: 3 I am returning to **M** Zion, and I will live in
14: 4 On that day his feet will stand on the **M** of Olives,
14: 4 And the **M** of Olives will split apart, making a
Mal 4: 4 and regulations that I gave him on **M** Sinai for all
Mt 21: 1 they came to the town of Bethphage on the **M** of
24: 3 Later, Jesus sat on the slopes of the **M** of Olives.
26:30 they sang a hymn and went out to the **M** of Olives.
Mk 11: 1 of Bethphage and Bethany, on the **M** of Olives.
13: 3 Jesus sat on the slopes of the **M** of Olives across
14:26 they sang a hymn and went out to the **M** of Olives.
Lk 19:29 of Bethphage and Bethany, on the **M** of Olives,
19:37 where the road started down from the **M** of Olives,

21:37 he returned to spend the night on the **M** of Olives.
22:39 and went as usual to the **M** of Olives.
Jn 4:20 while we Samaritans claim it is here at **M** Gerizim,
8:1 Jesus returned to the **M** of Olives,
Ac 1:12 The apostles were at the **M** of Olives when this
7:30 "Forty years later, in the desert near **M** Sinai,
7:38 him life-giving words on **M** Sinai to pass on to us.
Gal 4:24 represents **M** Sinai where people first became
4:25 And now Jerusalem is just like **M** Sinai in Arabia,
Heb 12:18 as the Israelites did at **M** Sinai when God gave
12:22 No, you have come to **M** Zion, to the city of the
12:26 When God spoke from **M** Sinai his voice shook the
Rev 14:1 Then I saw the Lamb standing on **M** Zion,

MOUNTAIN (156) [MOUNT]

HOLY MOUNTAIN (24) Ps 3:4; 43:3; 48:1,2; 87:1; 99:9; Isa 11:9; 27:13; 56:7; 57:13; 65:25; 66:20; Jer 31:23; Eze 20:40; 28:14; Da 9:16,20; 11:45; Joel 2:1; 3:17; Ob 1:16; Zep 3:11; Zec 8:3; 2Pe 1:18

Ge 8:5 to go down, other **m** peaks began to appear.
22:14 "On the **m** of the LORD it will be provided."
Ex 3:1 deep into the wilderness near Sinai, the **m** of God.
3:12 will return here to worship God at this very **m**."
4:27 So Aaron traveled to the **m** of God, where he
15:17 bring them in and plant them on your own **m**—
18:5 and the people were camped near the **m** of God.
19:3 Then Moses climbed the **m** to appear before God.
19:3 The LORD called out to him from the **m** and said,
19:7 Moses returned from the **m** and called together the
19:12 Do not go up on the **m** or even touch its
19:13 The people must stay away from the **m** until they
19:13 Then they must gather at the foot of the **m**."
19:16 and a dense cloud came down upon the **m**.
19:17 meet with God, and they stood at the foot of the **m**.
19:18 and the whole **m** shook with a violent earthquake.
19:20 to the top of the **m**. So Moses climbed the **m**.
19:23 the people cannot come up on the **m**!"
19:23 You told me to set boundaries around the **m**
20:18 the lightning and the smoke billowing from the **m**,
24:2 other people are allowed to climb on the **m** at all."
24:4 next morning he built an altar at the foot of the **m**.
24:9 and seventy of the leaders of Israel went up the **m**.
24:12 LORD said to Moses, "Come up to me on the **m**.
24:13 and his assistant Joshua climbed up the **m** of God.
24:15 Then Moses went up the **m**, and the cloud covered
24:17 The Israelites at the foot of the **m** saw an awesome
24:18 into the cloud as he climbed higher up the **m**.
24:18 He stayed on the **m** forty days and forty nights.
25:40 to the pattern I have shown you here on the **m**.
26:30 according to the design you were shown on the **m**.
27:8 careful to build it just as you were shown on the **m**.
32:1 When Moses failed to come back down the **m** right
32:7 the LORD told Moses, "Quick! Go down the **m**!
32:15 Then Moses turned and went down the **m**. He held
32:19 to the ground, smashing them at the foot of the **m**.
32:30 but I will return to the LORD on the **m**.
34:2 present yourself to me there on the top of the **m**.
34:3 In fact, no one is allowed anywhere on the **m**.
34:3 not even let the flocks or herds graze near the **m**."
34:28 Moses was up on the **m** with the LORD forty
34:29 When Moses came down the **m** carrying the stone
Nu 10:33 They marched for three days after leaving the **m** of
20:28 Then Aaron died there on top of the **m**, and Moses
33:38 priest was directed by the LORD to go up the **m**,
Dt 1:6 said to us, 'You have stayed at this **m** long enough.
4:11 You came near and stood at the foot of the **m**,
while the **m** was burning with fire.
5:4 you face to face from the heart of the fire on the **m**.
5:5 you were afraid of the fire and did not climb the **m**.
5:23 while the **m** was blazing with fire, all your tribal
9:9 That was when I was on the **m** receiving the tablets
9:10 words he had spoken to you from the fire on the **m**.
9:15 "So I came down from the fiery **m**, holding in my
9:21 the dust into the stream that cascades down the **m**.
10:1 of wood to keep them in. Return to me on the **m**,
10:3 like the first two, and I took the tablets up the **m**.
10:4 of the fire on the **m** as you were assembled below.
10:10 I stayed on the **m** in the LORD's presence for
14:5 wild goat, the ibex, the antelope, and the **m** sheep.
32:50 Then you must die there on the **m** and join your
33:19 They summon the people to the **m** / to offer proper
Jos 10:40 the Negev, the western foothills, and the **m** slopes.
12:8 western foothills, the Jordan Valley, the **m** slopes,
13:5 and all of the Lebanon **m** area to the east,
15:8 Then it went west to the top of the **m** above the
15:9 of the **m** to the spring at the waters of Nephtoah,
18:16 and down to the base of the **m** beside the valley of
1Sa 23:26 and David were now on opposite sides of a **m**.
25:20 As she was riding her donkey into a **m** ravine,
2Sa 15:30 their heads and wept as they climbed the **m**.
21:6 the LORD at Gibeon, on the **m** of the LORD."
21:9 The men of Gibeon executed them on the **m** before
22:34 as a deer, / leading me safely along the **m** heights.
1Ki 19:8 and forty nights to Mount Sinai, the **m** of God.
19:11 "Go out and stand before me on the **m**,"
19:11 passed by, and a mighty windstorm hit the **m**.
2Ki 2:16 the Spirit of the LORD has left him on some **m**
4:27 But when she came to the man of God at the **m**,
Job 24:8 They are soaked by **m** showers, and they huddle
37:22 Golden splendor comes from the **m** of God.
39:1 "Do you know when the **m** goats give birth?
Ps 3:4 and he answered me from his holy **m**.
18:33 as a deer, / leading me safely along the **m** heights.
24:3 Who may climb the **m** of the LORD? / Who may
30:7 Your favor, O LORD, made me as secure as a **m**.
43:3 them guide me. / Let them lead me to your holy **m**,
48:1 in the city of our God, / which is on his holy **m**!
48:2 Mount Zion, the holy **m**, / is the city of the great
87:1 On the holy **m** stands the city founded by the
99:9 our God / and worship at his holy **m** in Jerusalem,
147:8 and makes the green grass grow in **m** pastures.
Pr 27:25 crop appears, and the **m** grasses are gathered in,
SS 4:6 I will go to the **m** of myrrh and to the hill of
Isa 2:3 "Come, let us go up to the **m** of the LORD,
11:9 Nothing will hurt or destroy in all my holy **m**.
14:13 I will preside on the **m** of the gods far away in the
18:3 When I raise my battle flag on the **m**, let all the
18:6 army will be left dead in the fields for the **m** birds
27:13 to Jerusalem to worship the LORD on his holy **m**.
30:25 will be streams of water flowing down every **m**
30:29 the **m** of the LORD—to the Rock of Israel.
56:7 I will bring them also to my holy **m** of Jerusalem
57:13 in me will possess the land and inherit my holy **m**.
65:25 no one will be hurt or destroyed on my holy **m**.
66:20 They will bring them to my holy **m** in Jerusalem as
Jer 21:13 of Jerusalem that boasts, "We are safe on our **m**!
31:23 LORD bless you—O righteous home, O holy **m**!'
51:25 "Look, O mighty **m**, destroyer of the earth!
Eze 6:13 on every hill and **m** and under every green tree
11:23 from the city and stopped above the **m** to the east.
17:22 and I will plant it on the top of Israel's highest **m**.
20:40 For on my holy **m**, says the Sovereign LORD,
28:14 You had access to the holy **m** of God and walked
28:16 So I banished you from the **m** of God. I expelled
34:14 in pleasant places and feed in lush **m** pastures.
40:2 land of Israel and set me down on a very high **m**.
Da 2:34 a rock was cut from a **m** by supernatural means.
2:35 became a great **m** that covered the whole earth.
2:45 That is the meaning of the rock cut from the **m** by
9:16 away from your city of Jerusalem, your holy **m**.
9:20 the LORD my God for Jerusalem, his holy **m**.
11:45 He will halt between the glorious holy **m**
Joel 2:1 Sound the alarm on my holy **m**! Let everyone
3:17 the LORD your God, live in Zion, my holy **m**.
Ob 1:16 as you swallowed up my people on my holy **m**,
Mic 4:2 "Come, let us go up to the **m** of the LORD,
Zep 3:11 among you. There will be no pride on my holy **m**.
Zec 4:7 Nothing, not even a mighty **m**, will stand in
8:3 the **m** of the LORD Almighty will be called the
Holy **M**.
14:4 for half the **m** will move toward the north and half
Mt 4:8 the Devil took him to the peak of a very high **m**
5:14 like a city on a **m**, glowing in the night for all to
17:1 James and John, and led them up a high **m**.
17:9 As they descended the **m**, Jesus commanded them,
17:14 When they arrived at the foot of the **m**, a huge
17:20 as small as a mustard seed you could say to this **m**,
21:21 You can even say to this **m**, 'May God lift you up
28:16 going to the **m** where Jesus had told them to go.
Mk 3:13 Afterward Jesus went up on a **m** and called the
9:2 took Peter, James, and John to the top of a **m**.
9:14 At the foot of the **m** they found a great crowd
11:23 I assure you that you can say to this **m**, 'May God
Lk 6:12 One day soon afterward Jesus went to a **m** to pray,
6:17 When they came down the slopes of the **m**,
9:28 Jesus took Peter, James, and John to a **m** to pray.
9:37 The next day, after they had come down the **m**,
1Co 13:2 so that I could speak to a **m** and make it move,
Heb 8:5 to the design I have shown you here on the **m**."
12:18 You have not come to a physical **m**, to a place of
12:20 "If even an animal touches the **m**, it must be
2Pe 1:18 voice when we were there with him on the holy **m**.
Rev 8:8 and a great **m** of fire was thrown into the sea.
21:10 high **m**, and he showed me the holy city,

MOUNTAINS (164) [MOUNT]

MOUNTAINS OF ISRAEL (13) Eze 6:2,3; 19:9; 33:28; 34:13; 35:12; 36:1,3,4,8,11; 39:2,17

Ge 7:19 the water covered even the highest **m** on the earth,
8:4 the boat came to rest on the **m** of Ararat.
14:10 into the tar pits, while the rest escaped into the **m**.
19:17 don't look back! Escape to the **m**, or you will die."
19:19 But I cannot go to the **m**. Disaster would catch up
19:30 and he went to live in a cave in the **m** with his two
22:2 him there as a burnt offering on one of the **m**,
49:26 be greater than the blessings of the eternal **m**,
Ex 32:12 'God tricked them into coming to the **m** so he
Nu 27:12 "Climb to the top of the **m** east of the river,
33:47 and camped in the **m** east of the river,
33:48 They left the **m** east of the river and camped on the
Dt 3:25 the beautiful hill country and the Lebanon **m**.'
11:30 (These two **m** are west of the Jordan River in the
12:2 high on the **m**, up on the hills, and under every
32:22 all its crops / and ignites the foundations of the **m**.
32:49 "Go to Moab, to the **m** east of the river, and climb
33:15 with the finest crops of the ancient **m**,
Jos 1:4 Desert in the south to the Lebanon **m** in the north,
9:1 Mediterranean Sea as far north as the Lebanon **m**.)
11:16 Jordan Valley, and the **m** and lowlands of Israel.
Jdg 5:5 The **m** quaked at the coming of the LORD.
6:2 so cruel that the Israelites fled to the **m**,
1Sa 26:20 does he hunt me down like a partridge on the **m**?"
2Sa 1:21 O **m** of Gilboa, / let there be no dew or rain upon
1Ki 5:9 logs from the Lebanon **m** to the Mediterranean Sea
22:17 "In a vision I saw all Israel scattered on the **m**,
2Ki 14:9 "Out in the Lebanon **m** a thistle sent a message to
19:23 I have conquered the highest **m**— / yes,
1Ch 12:8 as fierce as lions and as swift as deer on the **m**.
2Ch 2:16 cut whatever timber you need from the Lebanon **m**
18:16 "In a vision I saw all Israel scattered on the **m**,
25:18 "Out in the Lebanon **m**, a thistle sent a message to
Ezr 3:7 The logs were brought down from the Lebanon **m**
Job 9:5 "Without warning, he moves the **m**,
14:18 "But as **m** fall and crumble and as rocks fall from
28:9 tear apart flinty rocks and overturn the roots of **m**.
39:8 The **m** are its pastureland, where it searches for
40:20 The **m** offer it their best food, where all the wild
Ps 11:1 why do you say to me, / "Fly to the **m** for safety!
18:7 and trembled; / the foundations of the **m** shook;
29:6 He makes Lebanon's **m** skip like a calf
36:6 Your righteousness is like the mighty **m**,
46:2 earthquakes come / and the **m** crumble into the sea.
46:3 and foam. / Let the **m** tremble as the waters surge!
50:11 Every bird of the **m** / and all the animals of the
65:6 You formed the **m** by your power / and armed
68:15 The majestic **m** of Bashan / stretch high into the
68:16 Why do you look with envy, O rugged **m**,
72:3 May the **m** yield prosperity for all, / and may the
76:4 and more majestic / than the everlasting **m**.
80:10 The **m** were covered with our shade; / the mighty
83:14 through a forest / and as a flame sets **m** ablaze,
90:2 Before the **m** were created, / before you made the
95:4 of the earth, / and even the mightiest **m** are his.
97:5 The **m** melt like wax before the LORD,
104:6 floods of water, / water that covered even the **m**.
104:8 **M** rose and valleys sank / to the levels you
104:10 into ravines, / so streams gush down from the **m**.
104:13 You send rain on the **m** from your heavenly home,
104:18 High in the **m** are pastures for the wild goats,
104:32 at his glance; / the **m** burst into flame at his touch.
114:4 The **m** skipped like rams, / the little hills like
114:6 Why, **m**, did you skip like rams? / Why, little hills,
121:1 I look up to the **m**— / does my help come from
125:2 Just as the **m** surround and protect Jerusalem,
133:3 that falls on the **m** of Zion. / And the LORD has
144:5 come down. / Touch the **m** so they billow smoke.
148:9 **m** and all hills, / fruit trees and all cedars,
Pr 8:25 Before the **m** and the hills were formed, I was
SS 2:8 leaping on the **m** and bounding over the hills.
2:17 like a gazelle or a young stag on the rugged **m**."
4:11 The scent of your clothing is like that of the **m**
4:15 as refreshing as the streams from the Lebanon **m**."
8:14 swift gazelle or a young deer on the **m** of spices."
Isa 2:14 He will level the high **m** and hills.
13:4 Hear the noise on the **m**! Listen, as the armies
14:25 they are in Israel; I will trample them on my **m**.
33:16 The rocks of the **m** will be their fortress of safety.
34:3 will fill the land. The **m** will flow with their blood.
35:2 The deserts will become as green as the **m** of
37:24 I have conquered the highest **m**— / yes,
40:12 of the earth or has weighed out the **m** and the hills?
41:15 tear all your enemies apart, making chaff of **m**.
42:15 I will level the **m** and hills / and bring a blight on
44:23 forth into song, O **m** and forests and every tree!
45:2 "I will go before you, Cyrus, and level the **m**.
49:11 And I will make my **m** into level paths for them.
49:13 Rejoice, O earth! Burst into song, O **m**!
52:7 How beautiful on the **m** are the feet of those who
54:10 For the **m** may depart and the hills disappear,
55:12 The **m** and hills will burst into song, and the trees
64:1 How the **m** would quake in your presence!
64:3 highest expectations. And oh, how the **m** quaked!
65:7 "For they also burned incense on the **m**
Jer 3:21 Voices are heard high on the windswept **m**,
3:23 orgies on the hills and **m** are completely false.
4:24 I looked at the **m** and hills, and they trembled
4:29 They hide in the bushes and run for the **m**.
7:29 your head in mourning, and weep alone on the **m**.
9:10 I will weep for the **m** and wail for the desert
13:16 causing you to stumble and fall on the dark **m**.
18:14 Does the snow ever melt high up in the **m** of
31:5 Again you will plant your vineyards on the **m** of
49:16 you live in a rock fortress and hide high in the **m**.
50:6 led them astray and turned them loose in the **m**.
La 4:19 If we fled to the **m**, they found us. If we hid in the
Eze 6:2 look over toward the **m** of Israel and prophesy
6:3 Give the **m** of Israel this message from the
6:3 This is what the Sovereign LORD says to the **m**
7:16 and escape to the **m** will moan like doves,
18:6 and he has not feasted in the **m** before Israel's
18:11 worships idols on the **m**, commits adultery,
18:15 Suppose this son refuses to worship idols on the **m**,
19:9 could never again be heard / on the **m** of Israel.
31:12 Its branches were scattered across the **m**
32:6 earth with your gushing blood all the way to the **m**,
33:28 The **m** of Israel will be so ruined that no one will
34:6 They have wandered through the **m** and hills,
34:13 I will feed them on the **m** of Israel and by the
35:8 I will fill your **m** with the dead. Your hills,
35:12 word you spoke against the **m** of Israel.
36:1 "Son of man, prophesy to Israel's **m**. Give them
36:1 O **m** of Israel, hear the word of the LORD!
36:3 give the **m** of Israel this message from the
36:4 Therefore, O **m** of Israel, hear the word of the
36:4 He speaks to the hills and **m**, ravines and valleys,
36:6 prophesy to the hills and **m**, the ravines and valleys
36:8 But the **m** of Israel will produce heavy crops of
36:11 O **m** of Israel, I will bring people to live on you
38:20 **M** will be thrown down; cliffs will crumble;
39:2 will turn you and drive you toward the **m** of Israel,
39:4 You and all your vast hordes will die on the **m**.
39:17 Come from far and near to the **m** of Israel,
Hos 4:13 They offer sacrifices to idols on the tops of **m**.
10:8 They will beg the **m** to bury them and the hills to
Joel 2:2 Suddenly, like dawn spreading across the **m**,
3:18 In that day the **m** will drip with sweet wine,
Am 4:13 For the LORD is the one who shaped the **m**,
4:13 dawn into darkness and treads the **m** under his feet.
Ob 1:3 a rock fortress and make your home high in the **m**.

1: 8 "For on the **m** of Edom I will destroy everyone
1: 9 and everyone on the **m** of Edom will be cut down
1:19 living in the Negev will occupy the **m** of Edom.
1:21 Zion in Jerusalem to rule over the **m** of Edom.
Jnh 2: 6 I sank down to the very roots of the **m**. I was
Mic 6: 1 Let the **m** and hills be called to witness your
6: 2 "And now, O **m**, listen to the LORD's
7:12 and from many distant seas and **m**.
Na 1: 5 In his presence the **m** quake, and the hills melt
1: 6 like fire, and the **m** crumble to dust in his presence.
1:15 A messenger is coming over the **m** with good
3:18 in the dust. Your people are scattered across the **m**.
Hab 3: 6 He shatters the everlasting **m** and levels the eternal
3:10 The **m** watched and trembled. Onward swept the
3:19 as a deer and bring me safely over the **m**.
Zec 6: 1 four chariots coming from between two bronze **m**.
Lk 3: 5 Fill in the valleys, / and level the **m** and hills!
23:30 People will beg the **m** to fall on them and the hills
Heb 11:38 They wandered over deserts and **m**, hiding in caves
Rev 6:14 And all of the **m** and all of the islands disappeared.
6:15 in the caves and among the rocks of the **m**.
6:16 And they cried to the **m** and the rocks, "Fall on us
16:20 island disappeared, and all the **m** were leveled.

MOUNTAINSIDE (3) [MOUNT]

Mt 5: 1 Jesus went up the **m** with his disciples and sat
8: 1 crowds followed Jesus as he came down the **m**.
Mk 9: 9 As they descended the **m**, he told them not to tell

MOUNTAINSIDES (1) [MOUNT]

Isa 22: 5 been broken, and cries of death echo from the **m**.

MOUNTAINTOP (2) [MOUNT]

Ex 24:17 The awesome glory of the LORD on the **m**
Isa 30:17 will be left like a lonely flagpole on a distant **m**."

MOUNTAINTOPS (5) [MOUNT]

Ps 72:16 throughout the land, / flourishing even on the **m**.
Isa 40: 9 of good news, shout to Zion from the **m**!
42:11 of Sela sing for joy; / shout praises from the **m**!
57: 7 You have committed adultery on the **m** by
Joel 2: 5 Look at them as they leap along the **m**! Listen to

MOUNTED (10) [MOUNT]

Ge 24:61 Then Rebekah and her servants **m** the camels
1Sa 25:42 **m** her donkey, and went with David's messengers.
2Sa 22:11 **M** on a mighty angel, he flew, / soaring on the
2Ki 13: 7 Jehoahaz's army was reduced to fifty **m** troops,
2Ch 26:15 And he produced machines **m** on the walls of
Job 28:17 It cannot be purchased with jewels **m** in fine gold.
Ps 18:10 **M** on a mighty angel, he flew, / soaring on the
Isa 21: 7 and warriors **m** on donkeys and camels."
Lk 8:16 No, lamps are **m** in the open, where they can be
Rev 9:16 They led an army of 200 million **m** troops—

MOUNTING (1) [MOUNT]

Am 4: 4 Keep on disobeying—your sins are **m** up!

MOURN (49) [MOURNED, MOURNERS, MOURNFUL, MOURNING, MOURNS]

Lev 10: 6 "Do not **m** by letting your hair hang loose or by
10: 6 your relatives, may **m** for Nadab and Abihu,
1Ki 13:29 and took it back to the city to **m** over him and bury
14:13 All Israel will **m** for him and bury him. He is the
Job 27:15 with no one to **m** them, not even their wives.
29:25 his troops and as one who comforts those who **m**.
Ps 78:64 and their widows could not **m** their deaths.
Isa 3:26 The gates of Jerusalem will weep and **m**. The city
15: 2 Your people in Dibon will **m** at their temples
16: 7 of Moab, **m** for the delicacies of Kir-hareseth.
22:12 the LORD Almighty, called you to weep and **m**.
23: 2 **M** in silence, you people of the coast and you
24: 7 will be no wine. The merrymakers will sigh and **m**.
57:18 I will lead them and comfort those who **m**.
61: 2 He has sent me to tell those who **m** that the time of
61: 3 To all who **m** in Israel, he will give beauty for
66:10 glad with her, all you who love her and **m** for her.
Jer 4:28 The earth will **m**, the heavens will be draped in
6:26 **M** and weep bitterly, as for the loss of an only son.
16: 4 No one will **m** for them or bury them, and they
16: 5 "Do not go to their funerals to **m** and show
16: 6 in this land. No one will bury them or **m** for them.
16: 7 No one will offer a meal to comfort those who **m**
22:10 Do not weep for the dead king or **m** his loss.
25:33 No one will **m** for them or gather up their bodies to
47: 5 how long will you lament and **m**?
Eze 24:22 You will not **m** in public or console yourselves by
24:23 You will not **m** or weep, but you will waste away
24:23 You will **m** privately for all the evil you have
27:32 As they wail and **m**, they sing this sad funeral
31:15 I made the deep places **m**, and I restrained the
32: 2 "Son of man, **m** for Pharaoh, king of Egypt,
32:16 Let all the nations **m** for Egypt and its hordes.
Hos 10: 5 The people **m** over it, and the priests wail for it,
Am 8: 8 will tremble for your deeds, and everyone will **m**.
9: 5 touches the land and it melts, and all its people **m**.
Mic 1: 8 Because of all this, I will **m** and lament. I will walk
1:11 The people of Beth-ezel **m** because the very
Na 2: 7 and all the servant girls **m** its capture.
Zep 3:18 "I will gather you who **m** for the appointed
Zec 7: 3 "Should we continue to **m** and fast each summer
12:10 have pierced and **m** for him as for an only son.
12:12 The family of David will **m**, along with the family
12:14 Each of the surviving families from Judah will **m**
Mt 5: 4 God blesses those who **m**, / for they will be
9:15 "Should the wedding guests **m** while celebrating
Jn 16:20 and **m** over what is going to happen to me,
Rev 18: 9 and enjoyed her great luxury will **m** for her as they
18:11 merchants of the world will weep and **m** for her,

MOURNED (17) [MOURN]

Ge 23: 2 of Canaan. There Abraham **m** and wept for her.
37:34 He **m** deeply for his son for many days.
Nu 20:29 Aaron had died, all Israel **m** for him thirty days.
Dt 34: 8 The people of Israel **m** thirty days for Moses on
1Sa 6:19 And the people **m** greatly because of what the
7: 2 all Israel **m** because it seemed that the LORD had
15:35 meet with Saul again, but he **m** constantly for him.
16: 1 to Samuel, "You have **m** long enough for Saul.
28: 3 Samuel had died, and all Israel had **m** for him.
2Sa 1:12 They **m** and wept and fasted all day for Saul
11:26 heard that her husband was dead, she **m** for him.
13:37 And David **m** many days for his son Amnon.
1Ki 14:18 the people of Israel buried him, they **m** for him,
1Ch 7:22 Their father, Ephraim, **m** for them a long time,
2Ch 35:24 And all Judah and Jerusalem **m** for him.
Ne 1: 4 In fact, for days I **m**, fasted, and prayed to the God
Zec 7: 5 when you fasted and **m** in the summer and at the

MOURNERS (5) [MOURN]

Ecc 12: 5 the **m** will walk along the streets.
Jer 9:17 about what is going on! Call for the **m** to come.
Am 5:16 and summon professional **m** to wail and lament.
Lk 7:12 and many **m** from the village were with her.
Jn 11:28 She called Mary aside from the **m** and told her,

MOURNFUL (2) [MOURN]

Isa 59:11 growl like hungry bears; we moan like **m** doves.
Jer 12:11 have made it an empty wasteland; I hear its **m** cry.

MOURNING (62) [MOURN]

Ge 37:35 "I will die in **m** for my son," he would say,
38:12 After the time of **m** was over, Judah and his friend
50: 3 and there was a period of national **m** for seventy
50: 4 When the period of **m** was over,
50:10 with a seven-day period of **m** for Joseph's father.
50:11 "This is a place of very deep **m** for these
Ex 33: 4 they went into **m** and refused to wear their jewelry
Lev 19:28 "Never cut your bodies in **m** for the dead or mark
Dt 21:13 for a full month, in **m** for her father and mother.
26:14 I have not eaten any of it while in **m**; I have not
34: 8 until the customary period of **m** was over.
2Sa 1: 2 and put dirt on his head to show that he was in **m**.
3:31 and put on sackcloth. Go into deep **m** for Abner."
11:27 When the period of **m** was over, David sent for her
12:21 you have stopped your **m** and are eating again."
14: 2 He said to her, "Pretend you are in **m**;
14: 2 wear **m** clothes and don't bathe or wear any
15:30 was covered and his feet were bare as a sign of **m**.
15:32 his clothing and put dirt on his head as a sign of **m**.
19: 1 that the king was weeping and **m** for Absalom.
1Ki 21:27 even slept in sackcloth and went about in deep **m**.
Ezr 9: 5 I stood up from where I had sat in **m** with my
10: 6 He was still in **m** because of the unfaithfulness of
Est 4: 2 was allowed to enter while wearing clothes of **m**.
4: 3 the provinces, there was great **m** among the Jews.
4: 5 out what was troubling him and why he was in **m**.
9:22 was turned into gladness and their **m** into joy.
9:31 to establish the times of fasting and **m**.)
Ps 30:11 You have turned my **m** into joyful dancing.
30:11 You have taken away my clothes of **m** and clothed
Isa 35:10 Sorrow and **m** will disappear, and they will be
38:14 or a crane, / and then I moaned like a **m** dove.
50: 3 out across the skies, bringing it to a state of **m**."
51:11 Sorrow and **m** will disappear, and they will be
60:20 Your days of **m** will come to an end.
61: 3 joy instead of **m**, praise instead of despair.
Jer 4: 8 So put on clothes of **m** and weep with broken
7:29 O Jerusalem, shave your head in **m**, and weep
14: 2 All the people sit on the ground in **m**, and a great
23:10 The land itself is in **m**—its pastures are dried up.
31:13 I will turn their **m** into joy. I will comfort them
31:15 is heard in Ramah—**m** and weeping unrestrained.
48:37 They shave their heads and beards in **m**.
49: 3 Put on your clothes of **m**. Weep and wail, hiding in
La 1: 1 a widow broken with grief, she sits alone in her **m**.
1: 4 The roads to Jerusalem are in **m**, no longer filled
5:15 our hearts has ended; our dancing has turned to **m**.
Eze 24:17 Do not perform the rituals of **m** or accept any food
27:31 They weep for you with bitter anguish and deep **m**.
Da 10: 2 to me, I, Daniel, had been in **m** for three weeks.
Hos 9: 4 just as food touched by a person in **m** is unclean.
Joel 1: 9 The priests are **m** because there are no offerings.
2:12 your hearts. Come with fasting, weeping, and **m**.
Am 8:10 I will turn your celebrations into times of **m**,
Zec 8:19 and times of **m** you have kept in early summer,
12:11 and **m** in Jerusalem on that day will be like the
12:11 **m** of Hadad-rimmon in the valley of Megiddo.
Mt 2:18 is heard in Ramah— / weeping and **m** unrestrained.
24:30 and there will be deep **m** among all the nations of
Lk 6:25 for your laughing will turn to **m** and sorrow.
1Co 5: 2 Why aren't you **m** in sorrow and shame?
Rev 18: 8 the sorrows of death and **m** and famine will

MOURNS (1) [MOURN]

La 1:11 "O LORD, look," she **m**, "and see how I am

MOUSE (1)

Lev 11:29 the mole, the **m**, the great lizard of all varieties,

MOUTH (88) [BLABBERMOUTH, LOUDMOUTH, LOUDMOUTHED, MOUTHS]

Ge 29: 2 But a heavy stone covered the **m** of the well.
29: 3 the stone would be rolled back over the **m** of the
Lev 13:45 they must cover their **m** and call out, 'Unclean!
Jos 15: 5 along the Dead Sea to the **m** of the Jordan River.
Jdg 9:38 "Now where is that big **m** of yours?"
1Sa 17:35 after it with a club and take the lamb from its **m**.
2Sa 16:23 as though it had come directly from the **m** of God.
22: 9 his nostrils; / fierce flames leaped from his **m**;
1Ki 8:24 You made that promise with your own **m**,
2Ki 4:34 placing his **m** on the child's **m**, his eyes on the
19:28 and my bridle in your **m**. / I will make you return
2Ch 6:15 You made that promise with your own **m**,
Job 8:21 He will yet fill your **m** with laughter and your lips
9:20 my own **m** would pronounce me guilty.
12:11 Just as the **m** tastes good food, so the ear tests the
15: 5 Your sins are telling your **m** what to say.
15: 6 why should I condemn you? Your own **m** does!
20:13 He savored it, holding it long in his **m**.
21: 5 be stunned. Put your hand over your **m** in shock.
34: 3 'Just as the **m** tastes good food, the ear tests the
37: 2 the thunder of God's voice as it rolls from his **m**.
40: 4 I will put my hand over my **m** in silence.
41:19 Fire and sparks leap from its **m**.
41:21 would kindle coals, for flames shoot from its **m**.
Ps 16: 9 is filled with joy, / and my **m** shouts his praises!
18: 8 his nostrils; / fierce flames leaped from his **m**;
19:14 May the words of my **m** and the thoughts of my
22:15 My tongue sticks to the roof of my **m**. / You have
81:10 Open your **m** wide, and I will fill it with good
119:131 I open my **m**, panting expectantly, / longing for
137: 6 May my tongue stick to the roof of my **m** / if I fail
Pr 2: 6 From his **m** come knowledge and understanding.
5: 3 as sweet as honey, and her **m** is smoother than oil.
19:28 of justice; the **m** of the wicked gulps down evil.
20:17 bread tastes sweet, but it turns to gravel in the **m**.
21:23 If you keep your **m** shut, you will stay out of
22:14 The **m** of an immoral woman is a deep pit;
26: 7 In the **m** of a fool, a proverb becomes as limp as a
26: 9 A proverb in a fool's **m** is as dangerous as a
30:32 about it—cover your **m** with your hand in shame.
Ecc 5: 1 of God, keep your ears open and your **m** shut!
5: 6 In such cases, your **m** is making you sin.
SS 4: 3 like a ribbon of scarlet. Oh, how beautiful your **m**!
5:16 His **m** is altogether sweet; he is lovely in every
Isa 11: 4 and destroy them with the breath of his **m**.
24: 9 and song; strong drink now turns bitter in the **m**.
37:29 and my bridle in your **m**. / I will make you return
51:16 And I have put my words in your **m** and hidden
53: 7 is silent before the shearers, he did not open his **m**.
59: 3 Your **m** is full of lies, and your lips are tainted
Jer 1: 9 Then the LORD touched my **m** and said, "See, I have put my words in your **m**!
51:44 of Babylon, and pull from his **m** what he has taken.
Eze 2: 8 a rebel. Open your **m**, and eat what I give you."
3: 2 So I opened my **m**, and he fed me the scroll.
3:26 I will make your tongue stick to the roof of your **m**
16:63 remember your sins and cover your **m** in silence
33:22 LORD had taken hold of me and opened my **m**,
Da 6:17 was brought and placed over the **m** of the den.
7: 5 and it had three ribs in its **m** between its teeth.
7: 8 human eyes and a **m** that was boasting arrogantly.
7:20 human eyes and a **m** that was boasting arrogantly.
10:16 my lips, and I opened my **m** and began to speak.
Am 3:12 a sheep from a lion's **m** will recover only two legs
Mt 17:27 Open the **m** of the first fish you catch, and you will
Mk 9:18 and makes him foam at the **m** and grind his teeth
9:20 fell to the ground, writhing and foaming at the **m**.
Lk 9:39 him into convulsions so that he foams at the **m**.
Ac 2:26 is filled with joy, / and my **m** shouts his praises!
8:32 silent before the shearers, / he did not open his **m**.
23: 2 those close to Paul to slap him on the **m**.
Ro 10: 9 For if you confess with your **m** that Jesus is Lord
10:10 and it is by confessing with your **m** that you are
2Th 2: 8 Lord Jesus will consume with the breath of his **m**
Jas 3: 3 wherever we want by means of a small bit in its **m**.
3:10 and cursing come pouring out of the same **m**.
Rev 1:16 and a sharp two-edged sword came from his **m**.
2:16 and fight against them with the sword of my **m**.
3:16 like lukewarm water, I will spit you out of my **m**!
10:10 It was sweet in my **m**, but it made my stomach
12:15 with a flood of water that flowed from its **m**.
12:16 But the earth helped her by opening its **m**
12:16 the river that gushed out from the **m** of the dragon.
13: 2 like a leopard, but it had bear's feet and a lion's **m**!
16:13 looked like frogs leap from the **m** of the dragon,
19:15 From his **m** came a sharp sword, and with it he
19:21 out of the **m** of the one riding the white horse.

MOUTHS (34) [MOUTH]

Ex 4:11 "Who makes **m**?" the LORD asked him.
Jdg 7: 5 kneel down and drink with their **m** in the stream."
7: 6 their knees and drank with their **m** in the stream.
1Ki 22:23 the LORD has put a lying spirit in the **m** of your
2Ch 18:22 the LORD has put a lying spirit in the **m** of your
Job 29: 9 stood in silence and put their hands over their **m**.
Ps 10: 7 Their **m** are full of cursing, lies, and threats.
22:13 their prey, / they come at me with open **m**.
50:19 Your **m** are filled with wickedness, / and your

59: 7 Listen to the filth that comes from their **m**,
78: 30 had craved, / while the meat was yet in their **m**,
115: 5 They cannot talk, though they have **m**, / or see,
135: 16 They cannot talk, though they have **m**, / or see,
144: 8 Their **m** are full of lies; / they swear to tell the
144: 11 Their **m** are full of lies; / they swear to tell the
149: 6 Let the praises of God be in their **m**, / and a sharp
Pr 17: 28 when they keep their **m** shut, they seem intelligent.
18: 7 The **m** of fools are their ruin; their lips get them
Jer 31: 29 but their children's **m** pucker at the taste.'
31: 30 sour grapes will be the ones whose **m** will pucker.
La 4: 4 little ones stick with thirst to the roofs of their **m**.
Eze 18: 2 but their children's **m** pucker at the taste'?
33: 31 They express love with their **m**, but their hearts
34: 10 I will rescue my flock from their **m**; the sheep will
Da 6: 22 My God sent his angel to shut the lions' **m** so that
Na 3: 12 that fall into the **m** of those who shake the trees.
Hab 2: 5 and wide, with their **m** opened as wide as death,
Zec 14: 12 and their tongues will decay in their **m**.
Ro 3: 14 "Their **m** are full of cursing and bitterness."
Heb 11: 33 God had promised them. They shut the **m** of lions,
Rev 9: 17 and burning sulfur billowed from their **m**.
9: 18 and burning sulfur that came from the **m** of the
9: 19 Their power was in their **m**, but also in their tails.
11: 5 fire flashes from the **m** of the prophets

MOVE (46) [MOVED, MOVEMENT, MOVEMENTS, MOVES, MOVING]

Ge 13: 9 stay in this area, then I'll **m** on to another place."
24: 49 step should be, whether to **m** this way or that."
35: 1 to Jacob, "Now **m** on to Bethel and settle there.
41: 44 but no one will **m** a hand or a foot in the entire
Ex 33: 15 us personally, don't let us **m** a step from this place.
Lev 11: 25 If you **m** the dead body of an unclean animal,
11: 28 If you pick up and **m** its carcass, you must
11: 46 and all the living things that **m** through the water
Nu 2: 31 rear whenever the Israelites **m** to a new campsite."
9: 22 people of Israel stayed in camp and did not **m** on.
10: 5 "When you sound the signal to **m** on, the tribes on
10: 5 of the Tabernacle will break camp and **m** forward.
10: 13 When the time to **m** arrived, the LORD gave the
Dt 1: 7 It is time to break camp and **m** on. Go to the hill
1Sa 5: 8 and replied, "**M** it to the city of Gath."
15: 6 "**M** away from where the Amalekites live or else
2Sa 2: 1 asked the LORD, "Should I **m** back to Judah?"
6: 10 So David decided not to **m** the Ark of the LORD
15: 18 to let David's troops **m** past to lead the way.
2Ki 8: 1 "Take your family and **m** to some other place,
19: 7 I myself will **m** against him, and the king will
20: 11 and he caused the shadow to **m** ten steps backward
1Ch 13: 13 So David decided not to **m** the Ark into the City of
15: 13 We failed to ask God how to **m** it in the proper
Ne 4: 22 I also told everyone living outside the walls to **m**
Job 17: 9 The righteous will **m** onward and forward,
33: 11 my feet in the stocks and watches every **m** I make.'
Ps 69: 34 and earth, / the seas and all that **m** in them.
SS 8: 14 **M** like a swift gazelle or a young deer on the
Isa 13: 13 the heavens, and the earth will **m** from its place.
13: 21 Wild animals of the desert will **m** into the ruined
19: 23 and Assyrians will **m** freely between their lands,
38: 8 I will cause the sun's shadow to **m** ten steps
44: 13 Now he has a wonderful idol that cannot even **m**
46: 7 they set it down, it stays there. It cannot even **m**!
Jer 35: 11 Aramean armies. So we decided to **m** to Jerusalem.
Eze 1: 17 The beings could **m** forward in any of the four
10: 11 The cherubim could **m** forward in any of the four
Na 2: 3 Watch as their glittering chariots **m** into position,
Zec 14: 4 for half the mountain will **m** toward the north
Mt 17: 20 '**M** from here to there,' and it would **m**.
Lk 10: 7 enter a town, don't **m** around from home to home.
Ac 17: 28 For in him we live and **m** and exist. As one of your
1Co 13: 2 so that I could speak to a mountain and make it **m**,
Heb 6: 3 we will **m** forward to further understanding.

MOVEABLE [KJV] See STAGGERS

MOVED (76) [MOVE]

Ge 13: 12 Lot **m** his tents to a place near Sodom,
13: 18 Then Abram **m** his camp to the oak grove owned
20: 1 Now Abraham **m** south to the Negev and settled
26: 1 So Isaac **m** to Gerar, where Abimelech, king of the
26: 17 So Isaac **m** to the Gerar Valley and lived there
26: 23 From there Isaac **m** to Beersheba,
36: 6 of Canaan—and **m** away from his brother, Jacob.
38: 1 this time, Judah left home and **m** to Adullam,
Ex 10: 23 During all that time the people scarcely **m**, for they
14: 19 the people of Israel, **m** to a position behind them,
14: 19 and the pillar of cloud also **m** around behind them.
15: 22 the Red Sea, and they **m** out into the Shur Desert.
17: 1 left the Sin Desert and **m** from place to place.
40: 36 the cloud lifted from the Tabernacle and **m**,
40: 37 the cloud stayed, they would stay until it **m** again.
Lev 13: 28 But if the affected area has not **m** or spread on the
Nu 1: 51 Whenever the Tabernacle is **m**, the Levites will
9: 21 stayed only overnight and **m** on the next morning.
9: 22 But as soon as it lifted, they broke camp and **m** on.
10: 34 As they **m** on each day, the cloud of the LORD
12: 10 As the cloud **m** from above the Tabernacle,
21: 13 Then they **m** to the far side of the Arnon River,
22: 26 Then the angel of the LORD **m** farther down the
Jos 6: 23 They **m** her whole family to a safe place near the
10: 5 They **m** all their troops into place and attacked
Jdg 1: 26 Later the man **m** to the land of the Hittites,
4: 11 had **m** away from the other members of his tribe
9: 26 At that time Gaal son of Ebed **m** to Shechem with
1Sa 5: 8 So they **m** the Ark of the God of Israel to Gath.
13: 18 and the third **m** toward the border above the valley
15: 11 so deeply **m** when he heard this that he cried out to
17: 48 As Goliath **m** closer to attack, David quickly ran
23: 24 and his men had **m** into the wilderness of Maon in
25: 1 Then David **m** down to the wilderness of Maon.
31: 7 So the Philistines **m** in and occupied their towns.
2Sa 2: 3 and his men and their families all **m** to Judah,
9: 13 in both feet, **m** to Jerusalem to live at the palace.
1Ki 9: 24 After Solomon **m** his wife, Pharaoh's daughter,
20: 27 its army, set up supply lines, and **m** into the battle.
1Ch 3: 4 Then David **m** the capital to Jerusalem, where he
5: 10 Then they **m** into the Hagrite settlements all along
8: 6 at Geba, were driven out and **m** to Manahath.
8: 7 father of Uzza and Ahihud, led them when they **m**.
10: 7 So the Philistines **m** in and occupied their towns.
2Ch 1: 4 David had already **m** the Ark of God from
5: 4 the leaders of Israel arrived, the Levites **m** the Ark,
8: 11 Solomon **m** his wife, Pharaoh's daughter,
11: 14 and property and **m** to Judah and Jerusalem,
15: 9 Many had **m** to Judah during Asa's reign when
31: 6 The people who had **m** to Judah from Israel,
33: 13 listened to him and was **m** by his request for help.
Ne 4: 10 so much rubble to be **m** that we could never get it
Est 2: 9 and he **m** her and her maids into the best place in
Ps 104: 5 world on its foundation / so it would never be **m**.
Isa 38: 8 the shadow on the sundial **m** backward ten steps.
Eze 1: 12 and they **m** straight forward in all directions
1: 17 directions they faced, without turning as they **m**.
1: 19 When the four living beings **m**, the wheels **m** with them.
1: 21 When the living beings **m**, the wheels **m**.
9: 3 it had rested, and **m** to the entrance of the Temple.
10: 11 directions they faced, without turning as they **m**.
10: 16 When the cherubim **m**, the wheels **m** with them.
10: 18 Then the glory of the LORD **m** from the door of
Mt 11: 7 him weak as a reed, **m** by every breath of wind?
21: 33 to tenant farmers and **m** to another country.
Mk 1: 41 **M** with pity, Jesus touched him. "I want to,"
12: 1 to tenant farmers and **m** to another country.
Lk 7: 24 him weak as a reed, **m** by every breath of wind?
20: 9 and **m** to another country to live for several years.
Jn 11: 33 he was **m** with indignation and was deeply
Ac 7: 2 Abraham in Mesopotamia before he **m** to Haran.
1Co 10: 1 God guided all of them by sending a cloud that **m**
2Pe 1: 21 It was the Holy Spirit who **m** the prophets to speak

MOVEMENT (2) [MOVE]

Ps 66: 7 He watches every **m** of the nations; / let no rebel
Ac 5: 36 their various ways. The whole **m** came to nothing.

MOVEMENTS (3) [MOVE]

1Sa 26: 4 so he sent out spies to watch his **m**.
Job 38: 31 "Can you hold back the **m** of the stars? Are you
Zec 9: 8 invading armies. I am closely watching their **m**.

MOVER [KJV] See INCITING

MOVES (9) [MOVE]

Nu 4: 5 When the camp **m**, Aaron and his sons must enter
Dt 23: 14 for the LORD your God **m** around in your camp
2Ki 20: 10 "The shadow always **m** forward,"
Job 9: 5 "Without warning, he **m** the mountains,
9: 11 see him. When he **m** on, I do not see him go.
Pr 19: 2 a person who **m** too quickly may go the wrong
SS 6: 13 as she **m** so gracefully between two lines of
Isa 14: 27 his plans? When his hand **m**, who can stop him?"
Joel 2: 8 jostle each other; each **m** in exactly the right place.

MOVING (23) [MOVE]

Ex 14: 15 are you crying out to me? Tell the people to get **m**!
27: 6 For **m** the altar, make poles from acacia wood,
Nu 4: 27 whether it involves **m** or doing other work.
10: 6 You must sound short blasts to signal **m** on.
10: 33 with the Ark of the LORD's covenant **m** ahead of
Dt 19: 14 never steal someone's land by **m** the boundary
27: 17 from a neighbor by **m** a boundary marker.'
1Sa 1: 13 Seeing her lips **m** but hearing no sound, he thought
2Sa 5: 13 After **m** from Hebron to Jerusalem, David married
5: 24 That will be the signal that the LORD is **m** ahead
7: 6 always been a tent, **m** from one place to another.
1Ch 14: 15 That will be the signal that God is **m** ahead of you
17: 5 always been a tent, **m** from one place to another.
Job 24: 2 Evil people steal land by **m** the boundary markers.
Ps 39: 6 We are merely **m** shadows, / and all our busy
Pr 22: 28 Do not steal your neighbor's property by **m** the
23: 10 Don't steal the land of defenseless orphans by **m**
Isa 10: 15 Can a whip strike unless a hand is **m** it? Can a cane
27: 1 the swiftly **m** serpent, the coiling, writhing serpent,
30: 6 Look at the animals **m** slowly across the terrible
Eze 10: 5 The **m** wings of the cherubim sounded like the
Joel 2: 5 across a field, or like a mighty army **m** into battle.
Hab 3: 3 **m** across the deserts from Edom and Mount Paran.

MOZA (5)

1Ch 2: 46 Ephah gave birth to Haran, **M**, and Gazez.
8: 36 Azmaveth, and Zimri. / Zimri was the father of **M**.
8: 37 **M** was the father of Binea. / Binea was the father
9: 42 Azmaveth, and Zimri. / Zimri was the father of **M**.
9: 43 **M** was the father of Binea. / Binea's son was

MOZAH (1)

Jos 18: 26 Mizpeh, Kephirah, **M**,

MUCH (298)

Ge 14: 23 that I will not take so **m** as a single thread
21: 11 This upset Abraham very **m** because Ishmael was
22: 2 your only son—yes, Isaac, whom you love so **m**—
24: 67 He loved her very **m**, and she was a special
25: 25 so **m** hair that one would think he was wearing a
29: 15 because we are relatives. How **m** do you want?"
30: 28 How **m** do I owe you? Whatever it is, I'll pay it."
38: 16 "How **m** will you pay me?" Tamar asked.
39: 10 and he kept out of her way as **m** as possible.
41: 49 There was so **m** grain, like sand on the seashore,
43: 34 five times as **m** as to any of the others.
44: 1 "Fill each of their sacks with as **m** grain as they
44: 20 and his father loves him very **m**.'
Ex 12: 4 on the size of each family and how **m** they can eat.
16: 4 and pick up as **m** food as they need for that day.
16: 5 Tell them to pick up twice as **m** as usual on the
16: 16 that each household should gather as **m** as it needs.
16: 22 there was twice as **m** as usual on the ground—
16: 23 So bake or boil as **m** as you want today, and set
16: 29 That is why I give you twice as **m** food on the
32: 25 and **m** to the amusement of their enemies—
Lev 20: 23 do these terrible things that I detest them so **m**.
Nu 14: 39 there was **m** sorrow among the people.
16: 15 I have not taken so **m** as a donkey from them,
Dt 7: 17 nations that are so **m** more powerful than we are?'
9: 1 to occupy the land belonging to nations **m** greater
11: 23 though they are **m** greater and stronger than you.
28: 38 "You will plant **m** but harvest little, for locusts
28: 56 would not so **m** as touch her feet to the ground—
28: 60 you all the diseases of Egypt that you feared so **m**,
31: 27 How **m** more rebellious will you be after my
Jos 4: 14 and for the rest of his life they revered him as **m** as
7: 21 than a pound. I wanted them so **m** that I took them.
13: 1 growing old, and **m** land remains to be conquered.
17: 18 Clear as **m** of the land as you wish and live there.
23: 7 their gods, **m** less swear by them or worship them.
Ru 2: 19 "So **m**!" Naomi exclaimed. "Where did you
4: 15 so **m** and who has been better to you than seven
1Sa 1: 5 a special portion because he loved her very **m**,
2: 16 "Take as **m** as you want, but the fat must first be
10: 19 But though I have done so **m** for you, you have
14: 27 the honey. After he had eaten it, he felt **m** better.
14: 29 See how **m** better I feel now that I have eaten this
15: 22 Listening to him is **m** better than offering the fat of
16: 21 Saul liked David very **m**, and David became one of
18: 28 When the king realized how **m** the LORD was
18: 28 was with David and how **m** Michal loved him,
20: 17 for Jonathan loved David as **m** as he loved himself.
21: 5 even on ordinary trips, how **m** more on this one!"
2Sa 1: 26 my brother Jonathan! / Oh, how **m** I loved you!
3: 22 from a raid, bringing **m** plunder with them.
3: 36 This pleased the people very **m**. In fact,
6: 15 brought up the Ark of the LORD with **m** shouting
12: 8 I would have given you **m**, **m** more.
13: 25 all came, we would be too **m** of a burden on you."
14: 1 Joab realized how **m** the king longed to see
14: 13 "Why don't you do as **m** for all the people of God
19: 9 And throughout the tribes of Israel there was **m**
19: 20 I know how **m** I sinned. That is why I have come
19: 43 "So we have ten times as **m** right to the king as
1Ki 3: 26 and who loved him very **m**, cried out, "Oh no,
5: 10 So Hiram produced for Solomon as **m** cedar
8: 27 contain you. How **m** less this Temple I have built!
12: 28 "It is too **m** trouble for you to worship in
17: 16 For no matter how **m** they used, there was always
2Ki 7: 4 If they let us live, so **m** the better. But if they kill
17: 2 but not as **m** as the kings of Israel who ruled before
21: 6 He did **m** that was evil in the LORD's sight,
1Ch 12: 19 After **m** discussion, they sent them back, for they
22: 8 And since you have shed so **m** blood before me,
22: 14 and so **m** iron and bronze that it cannot be
28: 3 for you are a warrior and have shed **m** blood.'
28: 14 David gave instructions regarding how **m** gold
29: 2 I have gathered as **m** as I could for building the
2Ch 6: 18 contain you. How **m** less this Temple I have built!
9: 8 Because God loves Israel so **m** and desires this
12: 8 so that they can learn how **m** better it is to serve
20: 25 so **m** plunder that it took them three days just to
24: 16 so **m** good in Israel for God and his Temple.
24: 24 the LORD helped them conquer the **m** larger
25: 9 "The LORD is able to give you **m** more than
32: 15 How **m** less will your God rescue you from my
33: 6 He did **m** that was evil in the LORD's sight,
Ezr 2: 69 and each leader gave as **m** as he could. The total of
4: 13 it will be **m** to your disadvantage, for the Jews will
10: 13 rainy season, so we cannot stay out here **m** longer.
Ne 4: 10 so **m** rubble to be moved that we could never get it
Est 1: 8 But those who wished could have as **m** as they
4: 7 and told him how **m** money Haman had promised
Job 4: 19 how **m** less will he trust those made of clay!
7: 17 mere mortals, that you should make so **m** of us?
8: 7 though you started with little, you will end with **m**.
13: 2 I know as **m** as you do. You are no better than I
13: 12 Your statements have about as **m** value as ashes.
15: 10 gray-haired men **m** older than your father!
15: 16 How **m** less pure is a corrupt and sinful person
25: 6 How **m** less are mere people, who are but worms
28: 25 and determined how **m** rain should fall.
37: 19 "You think you know so **m**, so teach the rest of us
38: 4 of the earth? Tell me, if you know so **m**.
40: 5 I have said too **m** already. I have nothing more to
42: 10 In fact, the LORD gave him twice as **m** as before!
Ps 22: 8 If the LORD loves him so **m**, / let the LORD
31: 19 so **m** for those who come to you for protection,
37: 16 and have little / than to be evil and possess **m**.

48: 1 is the LORD, / and how **m** we should praise him
63: 7 I think how **m** you have helped me; / I sing for joy
71:15 for I am overwhelmed by how **m** you have done
71:20 You have allowed me to suffer **m** hardship,
109:18 Cursing is as **m** a part of him as his clothing,
119:14 I have rejoiced in your decrees / as **m** as in riches.
119:107 I have suffered **m**, O LORD; / restore my life
119:140 thoroughly tested; / that is why I love them so **m**.
119:167 obeyed your decrees, / and I love them very **m**.
Pr 6:31 he will be fined seven times as **m** as he stole,
10:19 Don't talk too **m**, for it fosters sin. Be sensible
11:31 how **m** more true that the wicked and the sinner
13: 4 Lazy people want **m** but get little, but those who
13:23 A poor person's farm may produce **m** food,
15:11 How **m** more does he know the human heart!
16:16 How **m** better to get wisdom than gold,
19: 7 how **m** more will their friends avoid them.
20:19 don't hang around with someone who talks too **m**.
23: 7 They are always thinking about how **m** it costs.
23:21 to poverty. Too **m** sleep clothes a person with rags.
24: 7 Wisdom is too **m** for a fool. When the leaders
25:16 Don't eat too **m** of it, or it will make you sick!
25:27 Just as it is not good to eat too **m** honey, it is not
Ecc 1: 8 No matter how **m** we see, we are never satisfied.
1: 8 No matter how **m** we hear, we are not content.
2: 3 After **m** thought, I decided to cheer myself with
4: 8 yet who works hard to gain as **m** wealth as he can.
4: 8 Why am I giving up so **m** pleasure now?" It is all
4: 9 Two people can accomplish more than twice as **m**
5:12 work hard sleep well, whether they eat little or **m**.
7: 4 A wise person thinks **m** about death, while the fool
9:18 of war, but one sinner can destroy **m** that is good.
SS 2: 4 so everyone can see how **m** he loves me.
3: 3 you seen him anywhere, this one I love so **m**?'
4:10 my bride! How **m** better it is than wine!
Isa 7:16 right from wrong, the two kings you fear so **m**—
7:23 now worth as **m** as a thousand pieces of silver,
16: 6 the proud land we have heard so **m** about?
21:11 to me, "Watchman, how **m** longer until morning?
29: 2 and there will be **m** weeping and sorrow.
33:18 and estimated how **m** plunder they would get from
56: 3 the eunuchs. They are as **m** mine as anyone else.
58: 3 We have done **m** penance, and you don't even
Jer 36:32 in the fire. Only this time, he added **m** more!
39:17 but I will rescue you from those you fear so **m**.
44: 4 'Don't do these horrible things that I hate so **m**.'
44:17 and sacrifice to her just as **m** as we like—
49:12 the innocent must suffer, how **m** more must you!
Eze 23: 9 to her Assyrian lovers, whom she desired so **m**.
36: 3 You are the object of **m** mocking and slander.
46:11 and as **m** flour as the prince chooses to give with
Da 1:19 and none of them impressed him as **m** as Daniel,
2: 1 that disturbed him so **m** that he couldn't sleep.
9:23 to tell you what it was, for God loves you very **m**.
11:28 doing **m** damage before continuing his journey.
Hos 6:11 I wanted so **m** to restore the fortunes of my people!
10: 6 so **m** will be carted away with them when they go
11: 9 I will not punish you as **m** as my burning anger
Joel 2:14 give you so **m** that you will be able to offer grain
Am 9: 7 but have I not done as **m** for other nations, too?
Zep 3: 7 however **m** I punish them, they continue their evil
Hag 1: 6 You have planted **m** but harvested little. You have
Zec 9: 3 built a strong fortress and has piled up so **m** silver
Mt 3:11 so **m** greater that I am not even worthy to be his
5:46 good is that? Even corrupt tax collectors do that **m**.
7:11 how **m** more will your heavenly Father give good
10:25 how **m** more will it happen to you, the members of
12:12 And how **m** more valuable is a person than a
13: 8 and even a hundred times as **m** as had been
13:23 or even a hundred times as **m** as had been
14:20 They all ate as **m** as they wanted, and they picked
14:31 "You don't have **m** faith," Jesus said.
19:29 will receive a hundred times as **m** in return
20:12 and yet you've paid them just as **m** as you paid us
21:21 you can do things like this and **m** more.
26:11 but I will not be here with you **m** longer.
26:15 "How **m** will you pay me to betray Jesus to you?"
27:14 said nothing, **m** to the governor's great surprise.
Mk 1: 7 so **m** greater that I am not even worthy to be his
4: 8 and even a hundred times as **m** as had been
4:20 or even a hundred times as **m** as had been
4:33 and illustrations to teach the people as **m** as they
6:38 "How **m** food do you have?" he asked. "Go
6:42 They all ate as **m** as they wanted,
14: 7 want to. But I will not be here with you **m** longer.
15: 5 But Jesus said nothing, **m** to Pilate's surprise.
Lk 3:16 so **m** greater that I am not even worthy to be his
5: 8 I'm too **m** of a sinner to be around you."
6:33 is that so wonderful? Even sinners do that **m**!
7:47 have been forgiven, so she has shown me **m** love.
8: 8 and produced a crop one hundred times as **m** as
9:17 They all ate as **m** as they wanted, and they picked
11:13 how **m** more will your heavenly Father give the
12:15 Real life is not measured by how **m** we own."
12:48 **M** is required from those to whom **m** is given,
12:48 and **m** more is required from those to whom **m**
16: 5 He asked the first one, 'How **m** do you owe him?'
16: 7 " 'And how **m** do you owe my employer?'
19: 8 I will give them back four times as **m**!"
19:16 ten times as **m** as the original amount!
19:22 If you knew so **m** about me and how tough I am,
Jn 7:15 so **m** when he hasn't studied everything we've
8:26 I have **m** to say about you and **m** to condemn,
11:36 standing nearby said, "See how **m** he loved him."
12: 8 but I will not be here with you **m** longer."
14:30 "I don't have **m** more time to talk to you,
15: 5 remain in me, and I in them, will produce **m** fruit.
15: 8 My true disciples produce **m** fruit. This brings
16:12 "Oh, there is so **m** more I want to tell you, but you
17:23 and will understand that you love them as **m** as
Ac 2:15 are drunk. It isn't true! It's **m** too early for that.
9:16 And I will show him how **m** he must suffer for
11:29 in Judea, everyone giving as **m** as they could.
12: 3 When Herod saw how **m** this pleased the Jewish
15: 3 They told them—**m** to everyone's joy—
26:24 you are insane. Too **m** study has made you crazy!"
Ro 2:27 be **m** better off than you Jews who are circumcised
2:27 and know so **m** about God's law but don't obey it.
11:12 think how **m** greater a blessing the world will share
11:15 how **m** more wonderful their acceptance will be.
11:35 give him so **m** that he would have to pay it back?
12: 1 of what he has done for you, is this too **m** to ask?
12: 3 measuring your value by how **m** faith God has
12:18 to live in peace with everyone, as **m** as possible.
1Co 7: 2 But because there is so **m** sexual immorality,
8: 2 know all the answers doesn't really know very **m**.
9: 1 Do I not have as **m** freedom as anyone else?
9:11 Is it too **m** to ask, in return, for mere food
9:21 the Jewish law, I fit in with them as **m** as I can.
14:19 But in a church meeting I would **m** rather speak
2Co 2: 4 but I wanted you to know how very **m** I love you.
3: 9 how **m** more glorious is the new covenant,
7: 7 When he told me how **m** you were looking forward
7:12 so that in the sight of God you could show how **m**
8: 2 Though they have been going through **m** trouble
8: 7 you have so **m** faith, such gifted speakers,
8:12 it isn't important how **m** you are able to give.
8:13 so **m** that you suffer from having too little.
9: 7 up your own mind as to how **m** you should give.
10: 7 **m** as those who proudly declare that they belong to
10: 8 I may seem to be boasting too **m** about the
10:18 boast about themselves, it doesn't count for **m**.
Gal 3: 4 You have suffered so **m** for the Good News.
4: 1 those children are not **m** better off than slaves until
Eph 2: 4 so rich in mercy, and he loved us so very **m**,
6:21 a **m** loved brother and faithful helper in the Lord's
Php 1: 8 God knows how **m** I love you and long for you
1:11 for this will bring **m** glory and praise to God.
4:11 learned how to get along happily whether I have **m**
Col 1: 7 Epaphras, our **m** loved co-worker, was the one
2: 1 I want you to know how **m** I have agonized for you
4: 7 Tychicus, a **m** loved brother, will tell you how I
4: 9 a faithful and **m** loved brother, one of your own
1Th 2: 2 we came to you and how **m** we suffered there.
2: 8 so **m** that we gave you not only God's Good News
2:18 We wanted very **m** to come, and I, Paul,
2:19 you will bring us **m** joy as we stand together
3: 6 and that you want to see us just as **m** as we want to
1Ti 4: 8 but spiritual exercise is **m** more important,
4:10 and suffer **m** in order that people will believe the
5: 4 This is something that pleases God very **m**.
5: 5 she asks God for help and spends **m** time in prayer.
5:25 everyone knows how **m** good some people do,
2Ti 1:18 And you know how **m** he helped me at Ephesus.
3:11 You know how **m** persecution and suffering I have
4:14 Alexander the coppersmith has done me **m** harm,
Phm 1: 1 It is written to Philemon, our **m** loved co-worker,
1: 7 I myself have gained **m** joy and comfort from your
1:11 Onesimus hasn't been of **m** use to you in the past,
1:16 Now he will mean **m** more to you, both as a slave
Heb 5:11 so **m** more we would like to say about this.
5:13 and doesn't know **m** about doing what is right.
9:14 Just think how **m** more the blood of Christ will
10:29 Think how **m** more terrible the punishment will be
11:32 Well, how **m** more do I need to say? It would take
Jas 2:22 so **m** that he was willing to do whatever God told
1Pe 1: 7 it will bring you **m** praise and glory and honor on
2Pe 2:10 at the glorious ones without so **m** as trembling.
2:17 by the wind—promising **m** and delivering nothing.
1Jn 3: 1 See how very **m** our heavenly Father loves us,
4: 9 God showed how **m** he loved us by sending his
4:11 Dear friends, since God loved us that **m**, we surely
4:16 We know how **m** God loves us, and we have put
2Jn 1:12 Well, I have **m** more to say to you, but I don't
3Jn 1:13 I have **m** to tell you, but I don't want to do it in a
Jude 1:12 giving rain, promising **m** but producing nothing.
Rev 18: 6 for others, so give her twice as **m** as she gave out.
18:14 "All the fancy things you loved so **m** are gone,"
18:14 that you prized so **m** will never be yours again.

MUD (16) [MUDDY, MUDDYING]

Job 30:19 He has thrown me into the **m**. I have become as
38:38 turning the dry dust to clumps of **m**?
41:30 They tear up the ground as it drags through the **m**.
Ps 40: 2 of the pit of despair, / out of the **m** and the mire.
69:14 Pull me out of the **m**; / don't let me sink any
Jer 38: 6 but there was a thick layer of **m** at the bottom,
38:22 When your feet sank in the **m**, they left you to your
Eze 32: 2 in your own rivers, stirring up **m** with your feet.
Mic 7:10 I will see them trampled down like **m** in the streets.
Zec 10: 5 trampling their enemies in the **m** under their feet.
Jn 9: 6 he spit on the ground, made **m** with the saliva,
9: 6 and smoothed the **m** over the blind man's eyes.
9:11 "The man they call Jesus made **m** and smoothed it
9:11 'Go to the pool of Siloam and wash off the **m**.'
9:15 he told them, "He smoothed the **m** over my eyes,
2Pe 2:22 its vomit," and "A washed pig returns to the **m**."

MUDDY (3) [MUD]

Job 9:31 you would plunge me into a **m** ditch, and I would
Jer 18:15 of good, and they walk the **m** paths of sin.
Eze 34:18 Must you also **m** the rest with your feet?

MUDDYING (1) [MUD]

Pr 25:26 it is like polluting a fountain or **m** a spring.

MUFFLERS [KJV] See VEILS

MULBERRY (1)

Lk 17: 6 the Lord answered, "you could say to this **m** tree,

MULE (6) [MULES]

2Sa 18: 9 He tried to escape on his **m**, but as he rode beneath
18: 9 His **m** kept going and left him dangling in the air.
1Ki 1:33 Solomon is to ride on my personal **m**.
1:38 and Solomon rode on King David's personal **m**.
1:44 They had him ride on the king's own **m**,
Ps 32: 9 Do not be like a senseless horse or **m** / that needs a

MULES (11) [MULE]

2Sa 13:29 Then the other sons of the king jumped on their **m**
1Ki 10:25 and gold, clothing, weapons, spices, horses, and **m**.
18: 5 grass to save at least some of my horses and **m**."
2Ki 5:17 but please allow me to load two of my **m** with
1Ch 12:40 brought food on donkeys, camels, **m**, and oxen.
2Ch 9:24 and gold, clothing, weapons, spices, horses, and **m**.
Ezr 2:66 They took with them 736 horses, 245 **m**,
Ne 7:68 They took with them 736 horses, 245 **m**,
Isa 66:20 in chariots and wagons, and on **m** and camels,"
Eze 27:14 came riding horses, chariot horses, and **m**.
Zec 14:15 plague will strike the horses, **m**, camels, donkeys,

MULTIPLIED (7) [MULTIPLY]

Ex 1: 7 they **m** so quickly that they soon filled the land.
1:12 oppressed them, the more quickly the Israelites **m**!
Dt 8:13 and gold have **m** along with everything else,
Ps 105:24 And the LORD **m** the people of Israel / until they
Hos 10:10 of the nations to punish you for your **m** sins.
Mk 6:52 the significance of the miracle of the **m** loaves,
Ac 6: 1 But as the believers rapidly **m**, there were

MULTIPLIES (1) [MULTIPLY]

Job 9:17 and he **m** my wounds without cause.

MULTIPLY (32) [MULTIPLIED, MULTIPLIES, MULTIPLYING]

Ge 1:22 saying, "Let the fish **m** and fill the oceans.
1:28 and told them, "**M** and fill the earth and subdue it.
9: 1 and his sons and told them, "**M** and fill the earth.
9: 7 repopulate the earth. Yes, **m** and fill the earth!"
17:20 I will cause him to **m** and become a great nation.
22:17 I will **m** your descendants into countless millions,
32:12 and to **m** my descendants until they become as
35:11 "I am God Almighty. **M** and fill the earth!
Ex 1:20 and the Israelites continued to **m**, growing more
7: 3 so I can **m** my miraculous signs and wonders in the
Lev 26: 9 will look favorably upon you and **m** your people
Dt 1:11 **m** you a thousand times more and bless you as he
7:22 the wild animals would **m** too quickly for you.
8: 1 Then you will live and **m**, and you will enter
28:63 great pleasure in helping you to prosper and **m**,
2Ki 19:30 in your own soil, and you will flourish and **m**.
Ps 73:12 enjoying a life of ease while their riches **m**.
144:13 May the flocks in our fields **m** by the thousands,
Pr 9:11 Wisdom will **m** your days and add years to your
28:28 When the wicked meet disaster, the godly **m**.
Isa 37:31 in your own soil, and you will flourish and **m**.
60:22 The smallest family will **m** into a large clan.
Jer 29: 6 many grandchildren. **M**! Do not dwindle away!
30:19 and I will **m** my people and make of them a great
31:27 and **m** the number of cattle here in Israel
33:22 so I will **m** the descendants of David, my servant,
Eze 36:11 but your flocks and herds will also greatly **m**.
36:38 I will **m** them like the sacred flocks that fill
37:26 I will give them their land and **m** them, and I will
Hos 12: 1 They **m** lies and violence; they make alliances with
Na 3:15 will be no escape, even if you **m** like grasshoppers.
Heb 6:14 and I will **m** your descendants into countless

MULTITUDE (8) [MULTITUDES]

Ge 17: 4 father of not just one nation, but a **m** of nations!
48: 4 He said to me, 'I will make you a **m** of nations,
48:19 His descendants will become a **m** of nations!"
Job 27:14 If they have a **m** of children, their children will die
Isa 53:10 for sin, he will have a **m** of children, many heirs.
Jer 51:27 Appoint a leader, and bring a **m** of horses!
Da 10: 6 and his voice was like the roaring of a vast **m** of
1Pe 4: 8 love for each other, for love covers a **m** of sins.

MULTITUDES (3) [MULTITUDE]

Dt 33:17 This is my blessing for the **m** of Ephraim
Ps 102:22 when **m** gather together / and kingdoms come to
Lk 16:16 is preached, and eager **m** are forcing their way in.

MUNITION [KJV] See WALLS, RAMPARTS

MUPPIM (1) [SHUPHAM]

Ge 46:21 Gera, Naaman, Ehi, Rosh, **M**, Huppim, and Ard.

MURDER (74) [MURDERED, MURDERER, MURDERER'S, MURDERERS, MURDERING, MURDEROUS, MURDERS]

Ge 9: 5 And **m** is forbidden. Animals that kill people must

Ex 20:13 "Do not **m**.
22: 3 the one who killed the thief is guilty of **m**.
Nu 35:16 it must be presumed to be **m**, and the murderer
35:17 it is **m**, and the murderer must be executed.
35:18 It must be presumed to be **m**, and the murderer
35:20 a dangerous object and the person dies, it is **m**.
35:21 person with a fist and the person dies, it is **m**.
35:27 and kills him, it will not be considered **m**.
35:31 payment for the life of someone judged guilty of **m**
35:33 live will not be polluted, for **m** pollutes the land.
35:33 And no atonement can be made for **m** except by
Dt 5:17 " 'Do not **m**.
17: 8 whether someone is guilty of **m** or only of
19:10 and you will not be held responsible for **m**.
19:13 Purge the guilt of **m** from Israel so all may go well
21: 1 and you don't know who committed the **m**.
21: 9 you will cleanse the guilt of **m** from your
1Sa 19: 5 Why should you **m** an innocent man like David?
2Ki 9: 7 I will avenge the **m** of my prophets and all the
9:26 for the **m** of Naboth and his sons that I saw
2Ch 19:10 whether a **m** case or some other violation of God's
22:11 hid the child so that Athaliah could not **m** him.
Ps 9:12 For he who avenges **m** cares for the helpless.
55:11 **M** and robbery are everywhere there; / threats
94: 6 They kill widows and foreigners / and **m** orphans.
106:38 idols of Canaan, / they polluted the land with **m**.
Pr 1:16 rush to commit crimes. They hurry to commit **m**.
28:24 wrong with that?" is as serious as committing **m**.
Isa 33:15 who refuse to listen to those who plot **m**,
59: 7 feet run to do evil, and they rush to commit **m**.
Jer 7: 9 **m**, commit adultery, lie, and worship Baal and all
22:17 You **m** the innocent, oppress the poor, and reign
40:15 "Why should we let him come and **m** you?"
41: 4 before anyone had heard about Gedaliah's **m**,
Eze 9: 9 The entire land is full of **m**; the city is filled with
16:38 I will punish you for your **m** and adultery. I will
22: 4 you are guilty of both **m** and idolatry. Your day of
22: 6 in Israel who lives within your walls is bent on **m**.
23:37 They have committed both adultery and **m**—
23:37 and **m** by burning their children as sacrifices on
33:25 in it, you worship idols, and you **m** the innocent.
36:18 They polluted the land with **m** and by worshiping
Hos 4: 2 is violence everywhere, with one **m** after another.
6: 9 Gangs of priests **m** travelers along the road to
Mic 3:10 You are building Jerusalem on a foundation of **m**
Na 3: 1 it will be for Nineveh, the city of **m** and lies!
Hab 2:12 for you who build cities with money gained by **m**
2:17 Now terror will strike you because of your **m**
Mt 5:21 have heard that the law of Moses says, 'Do not **m**.
5:21 If you commit **m**, you are subject to judgment.'
15:19 **m**, adultery, all other sexual immorality, theft,
19:18 the man asked. And Jesus replied: " 'Do not **m**.
27: 6 it's against the law to accept money paid for **m**."
Mk 7:21 come evil thoughts, sexual immorality, theft, **m**,
10:19 'Do not **m**. Do not commit adultery. Do not steal.
15: 7 convicted along with others for **m** during an
Lk 11:50 **m** of all God's prophets from the creation of the
11:51 from the **m** of Abel to the **m** of Zechariah,
18:20 Do not **m**. Do not steal. Do not testify falsely.
22: 2 of religious law were actively plotting Jesus' **m**.
23:19 (Barabbas was in prison for **m** and for taking part
23:25 the man in prison for insurrection and **m**.
Ac 9:24 and night at the city gate so they could **m** him.
9:29 Greek-speaking Jews, but they plotted to **m** him.
Ro 1:29 sin, greed, hate, envy, **m**, fighting, deception,
3:15 "They are quick to commit **m**.
13: 9 against adultery and **m** and stealing and coveting—
1Ti 1: 9 who **m** their father or mother or other people.
Jas 2:11 not commit adultery," also said, "Do not **m**."
2:11 So if you **m** someone, you have broken the entire
1Pe 4:15 you suffer, however, it must not be for **m**, stealing,
Rev 19: 2 and he has avenged the **m** of his servants."

MURDERED (25) [MURDER]

Ge 42:22 And now we are going to die because we **m** him."
49: 6 For in their anger they **m** men, / and they crippled
Dt 21: 1 "Suppose someone is found **m** in a field in the
Jdg 20: 4 the husband of the woman who had been **m**,
2Sa 3:34 your feet were not chained. / No, you were **m**—
12: 9 For you have **m** Uriah and stolen his wife.
13:29 So at Absalom's signal they **m** Amnon.
1Ki 2: 5 You know that Joab son of Zeruiah **m** my two
2Ki 9:31 You are just like Zimri, who **m** his master!"
11: 2 to hide him from Athaliah, so the child was not **m**.
21:16 Manasseh also **m** many innocent people until
Job 15:22 go out into the darkness for fear they will be **m**.
31:39 or if I have stolen its crops or **m** its owners,
Isa 26:21 earth will no longer hide those who have been **m**.
Jer 41: 9 **m** was the large one made by King Asa when he
Eze 11: 6 You have **m** endlessly and filled your streets with
23:39 On the very day that they **m** their children in front
Mt 21:39 took him out of the vineyard, and **m** him.
23:31 the descendants of those who **m** the prophets.
23:35 whom you **m** in the Temple between the altar
Mk 12: 8 So they grabbed him and **m** him and threw his
Lk 13: 1 **m** some people from Galilee as they were
20:15 they dragged him out of the vineyard and **m** him.
Ac 2:23 you nailed him to the cross and **m** him.
7:52 the Messiah whom you betrayed and **m**.

MURDERER (19) [MURDER]

Nu 35:16 to be murder, and the **m** must be executed.
35:17 it is murder, and the **m** must be executed.
35:18 to be murder, and the **m** must be executed.
35:19 relative is responsible for putting the **m** to death.
35:19 When they meet, the avenger must execute the **m**.
35:21 the victim's nearest relative must execute the **m**
35:33 made for murder except by the execution of the **m**.
Dt 19:12 have the **m** brought back from the city of refuge
19:13 Do not feel sorry for that **m**! Purge the guilt of
2Sa 16: 7 "Get out of here, you **m**, you scoundrel!"
16: 8 will taste some of your own medicine, you **m**!"
2Ki 6:32 to the leaders, "A **m** has sent a man to kill me.
9:31 shouted at him, "Have you come in peace, you **m**?
Job 24:14 The **m** rises in the early dawn to kill the poor
Eze 18:10 to be a robber or **m** and refuses to do what is right.
Jn 8:44 He was a **m** from the beginning and has always
Ac 3:14 and instead demanded the release of a **m**.
28: 4 and said to each other, "A **m**, no doubt!
1Jn 3:15 Anyone who hates another Christian is really a **m**

MURDERER'S (2) [MURDER]

Dt 19:12 the leaders of the **m** hometown must have the
Pr 28:17 A **m** tormented conscience will drive him into the

MURDERERS (25) [MURDER]

Nu 35:30 " 'All **m** must be executed, but only if there is
35:31 to execution; **m** must always be put to death.
Ps 5: 6 tell lies. / The LORD detests **m** and deceivers.
26: 9 fate of sinners. / Don't condemn me along with **m**.
55:23 the pit of destruction. / **M** and liars will die young,
59: 2 me from these criminals; / save me from these **m**.
139:19 destroy the wicked! / Get out of my life, you **m**!
Isa 1:21 and righteousness, she is now filled with **m**.
59: 3 Your hands are the hands of **m**, and your fingers
Jer 4:31 pleading for help, prostrate before their **m**.
Eze 22: 2 Are you ready to judge this city of **m**?
22: 3 O city of **m**, doomed and damned—city of idols,
22:12 There are hired **m**, loan racketeers,
23:45 cities for what they really are—adulteresses and **m**.
24: 6 Destruction is certain for Jerusalem, the city of **m**!
24: 9 Destruction is certain for Jerusalem, the city of **m**!
33:26 **M**! Idolaters! Adulterers! Should the land belong
Mic 7: 2 They are all **m**, even setting traps for their own
Hab 2: 8 many nations; now they will plunder you. You **m**!
Mt 22: 7 He sent out his army to destroy the **m** and burn
Lk 11:48 **M**! You agree with your ancestors that what they
1Jn 3:15 And you know that **m** don't have eternal life
Rev 16: 6 So you have given their **m** blood to drink. It is
21: 8 and unbelievers, and the corrupt, and **m**,
22:15 the sexually immoral, the **m**, the idol worshipers,

MURDERING (13) [MURDER]

Dt 21: 8 Israel with the guilt of **m** an innocent person.'
Jdg 9:24 and the men of Shechem for **m** Gideon's seventy
9:56 done against his father by **m** his seventy brothers.
1Sa 25:26 since the LORD has kept you from **m** and taking
25:33 Bless you for keeping me from **m** the man
2Sa 14: 7 your son. We will execute him for **m** his brother.
16: 8 "The LORD is paying you back for **m** Saul
21: 1 and his family are guilty of **m** the Gibeonites."
2Ch 24:25 But his own officials decided to kill him for **m** the
Ps 10: 8 lurk in dark alleys, / **m** the innocent who pass by.
Jer 7: 6 orphans, and widows; and if you stop your **m**;
22: 3 orphans, and widows. Stop **m** the innocent!
Mt 23:35 you will become guilty of **m** all the godly people

MURDEROUS (5) [MURDER]

Ps 17: 9 attack me, / from **m** enemies who surround me.
105:32 Instead of rain, he sent **m** hail, / and flashes of
Pr 12: 6 The words of the wicked are like a **m** ambush,
Jer 18:23 you know all about their **m** plots against me.
Ac 14:19 and Iconium and turned the crowds into a **m** mob.

MURDERS (11) [MURDER]

Ge 9: 5 must die, and any person who **m** must be killed.
9: 6 you must execute anyone who **m** another person,
Dt 19:11 deliberately ambushes and **m** that neighbor and
22:26 to that of someone who attacks and **m** a neighbor.
1Ki 2:31 This will remove the guilt of his senseless **m** from
2:32 Then the LORD will repay him for the **m** of two
2:33 and his descendants be forever guilty of these **m**,
Eze 24: 7 She **m** boldly, leaving blood on the rocks for all to
Hos 1: 4 dynasty to avenge the **m** he committed at Jezreel.
Hab 2:10 But by the **m** you committed, you have shamed
Rev 9:21 And they did not repent of their **m** or their

MURMUR (3) [MURMURED, MURMURING]

Nu 21: 5 and they began to **m** against God and Moses.
Mk 9:26 A **m** ran through the crowd, "He's dead."
Jn 6:41 Then the people began to **m** in disagreement

MURMUR(ED, -S, -INGS) [KJV] See COMPLAIN, COMPLAINED, COMPLAINING, COMPLAINTS, GRUMBLE, GRUMBLED, GRUMBLERS, MUTTERING, REBELLED, SCOLDED

MURMURED (1) [MURMUR]

Dt 1:27 You **m** and complained in your tents and said,

MURMURING (3) [MURMUR]

Nu 17: 5 Then I will finally put an end to this **m**
1Sa 4:21 is the glory?"—**m**, "Israel's glory is gone."
Jn 7:32 When the Pharisees heard that the crowds were **m**

MURRAIN [KJV] (DEADLY) PLAGUE

MUSCLES (3)

Job 40:16 See its powerful loins and the **m** of its belly.
Eze 37: 6 I will put flesh and **m** on you and cover you with
37: 8 as I watched, **m** and flesh formed over the bones.

MUSHI (9) [MUSHITES]

Ex 6:19 The descendants of Merari included Mahli and **M**.
Nu 3:20 named for two of his descendants, Mahli and **M**.
3:33 of the clans descended from Mahli and **M**.
1Ch 6:19 The descendants of Merari included Mahli and **M**.
6:47 Mahli, **M**, Merari, and Levi.
23:21 The descendants of Merari included Mahli and **M**.
23:23 The three sons of **M** were Mahli, Eder,
24:26 of Merari, the leaders were Mahli and **M**.
24:30 From the descendants of **M**, the leaders were

MUSHITES (1) [MUSHI]

Nu 26:58 The Libnites, the Hebronites, the Mahlites, the **M**,

MUSIC (26) [MUSICAL, MUSICIAN, MUSICIANS]

1Sa 16:16 The harp **m** will quiet you, and you will soon be
1Ch 6:31 David assigned the following men to lead the **m** at
6:32 They ministered with **m** there at the Tabernacle
25: 6 fathers as they made **m** at the house of the LORD.
25: 7 and their families were all trained in making **m**
2Ch 7: 6 They accompanied the singing with **m** from the
20:28 They marched into Jerusalem to the **m** of harps,
Ne 12:27 songs of thanksgiving and with the **m** of cymbals,
Job 30:31 My harp plays sad **m**, and my flute accompanies
Ps 21:13 With **m** and singing we celebrate your mighty acts.
27: 6 of joy, / singing and praising the LORD with **m**.
33: 2 the lyre; / make **m** for him on the ten-stringed harp.
45: 8 with ivory, / you are entertained by the **m** of harps.
71:22 Then I will praise you with **m** on the harp,
119:54 Your principles have been the **m** of my life
135: 3 is good; / celebrate his wonderful name with **m**.
Isa 5:12 You furnish lovely **m** and wine at your grand
14:11 All the pleasant **m** in your palace has ceased.
30:32 his people will keep time with the **m** of
Eze 26:13 I will stop the **m** of your songs. No more will the
33:32 a beautiful voice or plays fine **m** on an instrument.
Am 5:23 I will not listen to your **m**, no matter how lovely it
Mt 9:23 noticed the noisy crowds and heard the funeral **m**.
Lk 15:25 he heard **m** and dancing in the house,
Eph 5:19 making **m** to the Lord in your hearts.
Rev 18:22 Never again will the sound of **m** be heard there—

MUSICAL (9) [MUSIC]

2Sa 6: 5 and playing all kinds of **m** instruments—
1Ch 13: 8 singing and playing all kinds of **m** instruments—
23: 5 the LORD with the **m** instruments I have made."
2Ch 23:13 Singers with **m** instruments were leading the
Ne 12:36 They used the **m** instruments prescribed by David,
Da 3: 7 So at the sound of the **m** instruments,
3:10 when they hear the sound of the **m** instruments.
3:15 when you hear the sound of the **m** instruments,
1Co 14: 7 Even **m** instruments like the flute or the harp,

MUSICIAN (4) [MUSIC]

Ge 4:21 His brother's name was Jubal, the first **m**—
1Sa 16:16 "Let us find a good **m** to play the harp for you
1Ch 6:33 Heman the **m** was from the clan of Kohath.
25: 7 of them—288 in all—was an accomplished **m**.

MUSICIANS (13) [MUSIC]

Jdg 5:11 Listen to the village **m** gathered at the watering
2Sa 19:35 longer tasty, and I cannot hear the **m** as they play.
1Ki 10:12 and to construct harps and lyres for the **m**.
1Ch 9:33 The **m**, all prominent Levites, lived at the Temple.
15:16 and **m** to sing joyful songs to the accompaniment
15:17 Kushaiah from the clan of Merari to direct the **m**.
25: 8 The **m** were appointed to their particular term of
2Ch 5:12 And the Levites who were **m**—Asaph, Heman,
9:11 and to construct harps and lyres for the **m**.
34:12 Other Levites, all of whom were skilled **m**,
35:15 The **m**, descendants of Asaph, were in their
Ps 68:25 Singers are in front, **m** are behind; / with them are
Am 6: 5 and you fancy yourselves to be great **m**, as King

MUST (1443) See Index of Articles, Etc.

MUSTARD (5)

Mt 13:31 "The Kingdom of Heaven is like a **m** seed planted
17:20 even if you had faith as small as a **m** seed you
Mk 4:31 It is like a tiny **m** seed. Though this is one of the
Lk 13:19 It is like a tiny **m** seed planted in a garden; it grows
17: 6 "Even if you had faith as small as a **m** seed,"

MUSTER (1) [MUSTERED]

Na 2: 1 **M** your defenses, and keep a sharp watch for the

MUSTERED (8) [MUSTER]

1Sa 13: 5 The Philistines **m** a mighty army of three thousand
17: 1 The Philistines now **m** their army for battle
28: 1 About that time the Philistines **m** their armies for
1Ki 20:15 So Ahab **m** the troops of the 232 provincial
20:27 Israel then **m** its army, set up supply lines,
2Ki 3: 6 So King Joram **m** the army of Israel and marched
2Ch 13: 3 while Jeroboam **m** 800,000 courageous men from
26:11 This great army of fighting men had been **m**

MUTE (3) [MUTENESS]
Jer 8:21 my people. I am stunned and silent, **m** with grief.
Mt 15:30 crowd brought him the lame, blind, crippled, **m**,
Mk 7:37 He even heals those who are deaf and **m**."

MUTENESS (1) [MUTE]
Mk 9:25 "Spirit of deafness and **m**," he said, "I command

MUTILATE (2) [MUTILATED, MUTILATORS]
Gal 5:12 **m** you by circumcision would **m** themselves.

MUTILATED (3) [MUTILATE]
Lev 22:22 injured, **m**, or that has a growth, an open sore,
22:25 You must never accept **m** or defective animals
Mal 1:13 Animals that are stolen and **m**, crippled and sick—

MUTILATORS (1) [MUTILATE]
Php 3: 2 those **m** who say you must be circumcised to be

MUTTER (1) [MUTTERED, MUTTERING, MUTTERINGS]
La 3:62 enemies whisper and **m** against me all day long.

MUTTERED (1) [MUTTER]
Ac 22:28 "I am too," the commander **m**, "and it cost me

MUTTERING (1) [MUTTER]
Nu 16:41 whole community began **m** again against Moses

MUTTERINGS (1) [MUTTER]
Isa 8:19 Do not listen to their whisperings and **m**.

MUTUALLY (1)
Rev 17:17 They will **m** agree to give their authority to the

MY (4300) [I] See Index of Articles, Etc.

MYRA (1)
Ac 27: 5 provinces of Cilicia and Pamphylia, landing at **M**,

MYRIADS (1)
Ps 89: 5 **m** of angels will praise you for your faithfulness.

MYRRH (17)
Ge 37:25 taking spices, balm, and **m** from Gilead to Egypt.
43:11 balm, honey, spices, **m**, pistachio nuts,
Ex 30:23 12-1/2 pounds of pure **m**, 6-1/4 pounds each of
Est 2:12 six months with oil of **m**, followed by six months
Ps 45: 8 Your robes are perfumed with **m**, aloes, and cassia.
Pr 7:17 I've perfumed my bed with **m**, aloes,
SS 1:13 My lover is like a sachet of **m** lying between my
3: 6 Who is it that smells of **m** and frankincense
4: 6 I will go to the mountain of **m** and to the hill of
4:14 and saffron, calamus and cinnamon, **m** and aloes,
5: 1 I gather my **m** with my spices and eat my
5: 5 my fingers with lovely **m**, as I pulled back the bolt.
5:13 lips are like perfumed lilies. His breath is like **m**.
Mt 2:11 and gave him gifts of gold, frankincense, and **m**.
Mk 15:23 They offered him wine drugged with **m**, but he
Jn 19:39 pounds of embalming ointment made from **m**
Rev 18:13 spice, incense, **m**, frankincense, wine, olive oil,

MYRTLE (5) [MYRTLES]
Ne 8:15 from olive, wild olive, **m**, palm, and fig trees.
Isa 41:19 cedar, acacia, **m**, olive, cypress, fir, and pine—
Zec 1: 8 standing among some **m** trees in a small valley.
1:10 So the man standing among the **m** trees explained,
1:11 who was standing among the **m** trees, "We have

MYRTLES (1) [MYRTLE]
Isa 55:13 will grow. Where briers grew, **m** will sprout up.

MYSELF (135) [I, SELF] See Index of Articles, Etc.

MYSIA (2)
Ac 16: 7 Then coming to the borders of **M**, they headed for
16: 8 they went on through **M** to the city of Troas.

MYSTERIES (5) [MYSTERY]
Job 11: 7 "Can you solve the **m** of God? Can you discover
Da 2:29 The revealer of **m** has shown you what is going to
2:47 God of gods, the Lord over kings, a revealer of **m**,
Mt 13:35 I will explain **m** hidden since the creation of the
1Co 13: 2 and if I knew all the **m** of the future and knew

MYSTERIOUS (6) [MYSTERY]
Ecc 11: 5 and as **m** as a tiny baby being formed in a mother's
Isa 45:15 our Savior, you work in strange and **m** ways.
Da 2:22 He reveals deep and **m** things / and knows what
1Co 14: 2 by the power of the Spirit, but it will all be **m**.
Rev 10: 7 blows his trumpet, God's **m** plan will be fulfilled.
17: 5 A **m** name was written on her forehead:

MYSTERY (5) [MYSTERIES, MYSTERIOUS]
Da 4: 9 in you and that no **m** is too great for you to solve.
Ro 11:25 I want you to understand this **m**, dear friends,
Eph 5:32 This is a great **m**, but it is an illustration of the way
1Ti 3:16 Without question, this is the great **m** of our faith:
Rev 17: 7 "I will tell you the **m** of this woman and of the

MYTHS (3)
1Ti 1: 4 people waste time in endless speculation over **m**
2Ti 4: 4 They will reject the truth and follow strange **m**.
Tit 1:14 They must stop listening to Jewish **m**

N

NAAM (1)
1Ch 4:15 of Caleb son of Jephunneh were Iru, Elah, and **N**.

NAAMAH (5)
Ge 4:22 and iron. Tubal-cain had a sister named **N**.
Jos 15:41 Gederoth, Beth-dagon, **N**, and Makkedah—
1Ki 14:21 Rehoboam's mother was **N**, an Ammonite woman.
14:31 His mother was **N**, an Ammonite woman. Then his
2Ch 12:13 Rehoboam's mother was **N**, a woman from

NAAMAN (24) [NAAMAN'S, NAAMITES]
Ge 46:21 Beker, Ashbel, Gera, **N**, Ehi, Rosh, Muppim,
Nu 26:40 The Naamites, named after their ancestor **N**.
2Ki 5: 1 The king of Aram had high admiration for **N**,
5: 1 But though **N** was a mighty warrior, he suffered
5: 4 So **N** told the king what the young girl from Israel
5: 5 So **N** started out, taking as gifts 750 pounds of
5: 6 "With this letter I present my servant **N**.
5: 8 Send **N** to me, and he will learn that there is a true
5: 9 So **N** went with his horses and chariots and waited
5:11 But **N** became angry and stalked away. "I thought
5:12 be healed?" So **N** turned and went away in a rage.
5:14 So **N** went down to the Jordan River and dipped
5:15 Then **N** and his entire party went back to find the
5:15 They stood before him, and **N** said, "I know at last
5:16 And though **N** urged him to take the gifts,
5:17 Then **N** said, "All right, but please allow me to
5:19 in peace," Elisha said. So **N** started home again.
5:21 When **N** saw him running after him, he climbed
5:21 to meet him. "Is everything all right?" **N** asked.
5:23 all means, take 150 pounds of silver," **N** insisted.
5:26 **N** stepped down from his chariot to meet you?
1Ch 8: 4 Abishua, **N**, Ahoah,
8: 7 Ehud's sons were **N**, Ahijah, and Gera. Gera,
Lk 4:27 of the prophet Elisha, who healed **N**, a Syrian,

NAAMAN'S (2) [NAAMAN]
2Ki 5: 2 girl who had been given to **N** wife as a maid.
5:27 and your children's children will suffer from **N**

NAAMATHITE (4)
Job 2:11 Bildad the Shuhite, and Zophar the **N**.
11: 1 Then Zophar the **N** replied to Job:
20: 1 Then Zophar the **N** replied:
42: 9 and Zophar the **N** did as the LORD commanded

NAAMITES (1) [NAAMAN]
Nu 26:40 The **N**, named after their ancestor Naaman.

NAARAH (3) [NAARAN]
Jos 16: 7 From Janoah it turned southward to Ataroth and **N**,
1Ch 4: 5 of Tekoa) had two wives, named Helah and **N**.
4: 6 **N** gave birth to Ahuzzam, Hepher, Temeni,

NAARAN (1) [NAARAH]
1Ch 7:28 **N** to the east, Gezer and its villages to the west,

NABAL (15) [NABAL'S]
1Sa 25: 3 This man's name was **N**, and his wife, Abigail,
25: 3 But **N**, a descendant of Caleb, was mean
25: 4 When David heard that **N** was shearing his sheep,
25: 9 David's young men gave this message to **N**
25:10 "Who is this fellow David?" **N** sneered.
25:12 messengers returned and told him what **N** had said.
25:25 I know **N** is a wicked and ill-tempered man;
25:26 let all your enemies be as cursed as **N** is.
25:36 she found that **N** had thrown a big party and was
25:39 When David heard that **N** was dead, he said,
25:39 who has paid back **N** and kept me from doing it
25:39 **N** has received the punishment for his sin."
30: 5 of Jezreel and Abigail, the widow of **N** of Carmel,
2Sa 2: 2 and Abigail, the widow of **N** from Carmel.
3: 3 mother was Abigail, the widow of **N** from Carmel.

NABAL'S (3) [NABAL]
1Sa 25:14 one of **N** servants went to Abigail and told her,
25:34 not one of **N** men would be alive tomorrow
27: 3 of Jezreel and Abigail of Carmel, **N** widow.

NABOTH (14) [NABOTH'S]
1Ki 21: 1 palace was a vineyard owned by a man named **N**.
21: 2 One day Ahab said to **N**, "Since your vineyard is
21: 3 But **N** replied, "The LORD forbid that I should
21: 6 "I asked **N** to sell me his vineyard or to trade it,
21: 8 and other leaders of the city where **N** lived.
21: 9 for fasting and prayer and give **N** a place of honor.
21:12 and put **N** at a prominent place before the people.
21:14 word to Jezebel, "**N** has been stoned to death."
21:15 "You know the vineyard **N** wouldn't sell you?
21:19 Isn't killing **N** bad enough? Must you rob him,
21:19 the city just as they licked the blood of **N**!' "
2Ki 9:21 They met him at the field that had belonged to **N** of
9:25 "Throw him into the field of **N** of Jezreel.
9:26 for the murder of **N** and his sons that I saw

NABOTH'S (5) [NABOTH]
1Ki 21: 4 went home angry and sullen because of **N** answer.
21: 7 and don't worry about it. I'll get you **N** vineyard!"
21:18 He will be at **N** vineyard in Jezreel,
2Ki 9:26 'I solemnly swear that I will repay him here on **N**
9:26 So throw him out on **N** field, just as the LORD

NACHOR [KJV] See NAHOR

NACON (2)
2Sa 6: 6 But when they arrived at the threshing floor of **N**,
1Ch 13: 9 But when they arrived at the threshing floor of **N**,

NADAB (21) [NADAB'S]
Ex 6:23 and she bore him **N**, Abihu, Eleazar, and Ithamar.
24: 1 up here to me, and bring along Aaron, **N**, Abihu,
24: 9 Then Moses, Aaron, **N**, Abihu, and seventy of the
28: 1 and his sons, **N**, Abihu, Eleazar, and Ithamar,
Lev 10: 1 Aaron's sons **N** and Abihu put coals of fire in their
10: 6 your relatives, may mourn for **N** and Abihu,
Nu 3: 2 Aaron's sons were **N** (the firstborn), Abihu,
3: 4 But **N** and Abihu died in the LORD's presence in
26:60 To Aaron were born **N**, Abihu, Eleazar,
26:61 But **N** and Abihu died when they burned before the
1Ki 14:20 Jeroboam died, his son **N** became the next king.
15:25 **N** son of Jeroboam began to rule over Israel in the
15:27 plotted against **N** and assassinated him while he
15:28 Baasha killed **N** in the third year of King Asa's
1Ch 2:28 The sons of Shammai were **N** and Abishur.
2:30 The sons of **N** were Seled and Appaim. Seled died
6: 3 The sons of Aaron were **N**, Abihu, Eleazar,
8:30 Jeiel's other sons were Zur, Kish, Baal, Ner, **N**,
9:36 Jeiel's other sons were Zur, Kish, Baal, Ner, **N**,
24: 1 The sons of Aaron were **N**, Abihu, Eleazar,
24: 2 But **N** and Abihu died before their father did,

NADAB'S (1) [NADAB]
1Ki 15:31 The rest of the events in **N** reign and all his deeds

NAGGAI (2)
Lk 3:25 Nahum was the son of Esli. / Esli was the son of **N**.
3:26 **N** was the son of Maath. / Maath was the son of

NAGGED (1) [NAGGING]
Jdg 16:16 So day after day she **n** him until he couldn't stand

NAGGING (3) [NAGGED]
Jdg 14:17 he told her the answer because of her persistent **n**.
Pr 19:13 a father; a **n** wife annoys like a constant dripping.
27:15 A **n** wife is as annoying as the constant dripping on

NAHALAL (2) [NAHALOL]
Jos 19:15 **N**, Shimron, Idalah, and Bethlehem—
21:35 Dimnah, and **N**—four towns with their

NAHALE-GAASH (2)
2Sa 23:30 Benaiah from Pirathon; / Hurai from **N**;
1Ch 11:32 Hurai from near **N**; / Abi-albon the Arbathite;

NAHALIEL (1)
Nu 21:19 **N**, and Bamoth.

NAHALOL (1) [NAHALAL]
Jdg 1:30 to drive out the Canaanites living in Kitron and **N**,

NAHAM (1)
1Ch 4:19 Hodiah's wife was the sister of **N**. One of her sons

NAHAMANI (1)
Ne 7: 7 Seraiah, Reelaiah, **N**, Mordecai, Bilshan, Mispar,

NAHARAI (2)
2Sa 23:37 **N** from Beeroth (Joab's armor bearer);
1Ch 11:39 **N** from Beeroth (Joab's armor bearer);

NAHASH (9)
1Sa 11: 1 King **N** of Ammon led his army against the
11: 2 "All right," **N** said, "but only on one condition.
12:12 "But when you were afraid of **N**, the king of
2Sa 10: 1 time after this, King **N** of the Ammonites died,
10: 2 complete loyalty to Hanun because his father, **N**,
17:25 His mother, Abigail daughter of **N**, was the sister
17:27 he was warmly greeted by Shobi son of **N** of

1Ch 19: 1 time after this, King **N** of the Ammonites died,
19: 2 complete loyalty to Hanun because his father, **N**,

NAHATH (5)

Ge 36:13 The sons of Reuel were **N**, Zerah, Shammah,
36:17 son Reuel became the leaders of the clans of **N**,
1Ch 1:37 The sons of Reuel were **N**, Zerah, Shammah,
6:26 Elkanah, Zophai, **N**,
2Ch 31:13 Azaziah, **N**, Asahel, Jerimoth, Jozabad, Eliel,

NAHBI (1)

Nu 13:14 Naphtali | **N** son of Vophsi

NAHOR (19) [NAHOR'S]

Ge 11:22 When Serug was 30 years old, his son **N** was born.
11:23 After the birth of **N**, Serug lived another 200 years
11:24 When **N** was 29 years old, his son Terah was born.
11:25 **N** lived another 119 years and had other sons
11:26 he became the father of Abram, **N**, and Haran.
11:27 Terah was the father of Abram, **N**, and Haran;
11:29 married Sarai, and his brother **N** married Milcah,
22:20 his brother Nahor's wife, had borne **N** eight sons.
22:24 **N** had four other children from his concubine
24:10 the village where Abraham's brother **N** had settled.
24:15 who was the son of Abraham's brother **N** and his
24:24 she replied. "My grandparents are **N** and Milcah.
24:47 is Bethuel, the son of **N** and his wife, Milcah.'
29: 5 a man there named Laban, the grandson of **N**?"
31:53 and the God of my grandfather **N**—
Jos 24: 2 including Terah, the father of Abraham and **N**,
1Ch 1:26 Serug, **N**, Terah,
Lk 3:34 was the son of Terah. / Terah was the son of **N**.
3:35 **N** was the son of Serug. / Serug was the son of

NAHOR'S (1) [NAHOR]

Ge 22:20 his brother **N** wife, had borne Nahor eight sons.

NAHSHON (14)

Ex 6:23 the daughter of Amminadab and sister of **N**,
Nu 1: 7 Judah | **N** son of Amminadab
2: 3[-4] Judah | **N** son of Amminadab | 74,600
7:12 On the first day **N** son of Amminadab, leader of
7:17 This was the offering brought by **N** son of
10:14 under the leadership of **N** son of Amminadab.
Ru 4:20 Amminadab was the father of **N**. / **N** was the father
1Ch 2:10 Amminadab was the father of **N**, a leader of Judah.
2:11 **N** was the father of Salmon. / Salmon was the
Mt 1: 4 Amminadab was the father of **N**. / **N** was the father
Lk 3:32 was the son of Salmon. / Salmon was the son of **N**.
3:33 **N** was the son of Amminadab. / Amminadab was

NAHUM (3)

Na 1: 1 concerning Nineveh came as a vision to **N**,
Lk 3:25 Amos was the son of **N**. / **N** was the son of Esli.

NAIL (1) [NAILED, NAILING, NAILS]

Jn 20:25 "I won't believe it unless I see the **n** wounds in his

NAILED (5) [NAIL]

Mt 27:35 After they had **n** him to the cross, the soldiers
Mk 15:24 Then they **n** him to the cross. They gambled for his
Lk 23:38 A signboard was **n** to the cross above him with
Ac 2:23 you **n** him to the cross and murdered him.
Gal 5:24 Those who belong to Christ Jesus have **n** the

NAILING (2) [NAIL]

Col 2:14 He took it and destroyed it by **n** it to Christ's cross.
Heb 6: 6 because they are **n** the Son of God to the cross

NAILS (4) [NAIL]

1Ch 22: 3 David provided large amounts of iron for the **n** that
2Ch 3: 9 They used gold **n** that weighed about twenty
Jer 10: 4 it securely with hammer and **n** so it won't fall over.
Da 4:33 eagles' feathers and his **n** were like birds' claws.

NAIN (1)

Lk 7:11 Jesus went with his disciples to the village of **N**,

NAIOTH (5)

1Sa 19:18 Then Samuel took David with him to live at **N**.
19:19 When the report reached Saul that David was at **N**
19:22 "They are at **N** in Ramah," someone told him.
19:23 But on the way to **N** the Spirit of God came upon
20: 1 David now fled from **N** in Ramah and found

NAIVE (1)

Pr 8: 5 How **n** you are! Let me give you common sense.

NAKED (40) [NAKEDNESS]

Ge 2:25 Now, although Adam and his wife were both **n**,
3:10 heard you, so I hid. I was afraid because I was **n**."
3:11 "Who told you that you were **n**?" the LORD
9:21 on some wine he had made and lay **n** in his tent.
9:22 saw that his father was **n** and went outside and told
9:23 into the tent, and covered their father's **n** body.
9:23 looked the other way so they wouldn't see him **n**.
Dt 28:48 You will be left hungry, thirsty, **n**, and lacking in
2Ch 28:15 from the plunder to the prisoners who were **n**.
Job 1:21 He said, / "I came **n** from my mother's womb,
24: 7 All night they lie **n** in the cold, without clothing
24:10 The poor must go about **n**, without any clothing.
26: 6 The underworld is **n** in God's presence. There is
Ecc 5:15 only for wealth come to the end of their lives as **n**
Isa 20: 2 as he was told and walked around **n** and barefoot.
20: 3 "My servant Isaiah has been walking around **n**
20: 4 He will make them walk **n** and barefoot,
47: 3 You will be **n** and burdened with shame. I will take
La 1: 8 for they have seen her stripped **n** and humiliated.
4:21 You, too, will be stripped **n** in your drunkenness.
Eze 16: 7 and your hair grew, though you were still **n**.
16:22 of the days long ago when you lay **n** in a field,
16:37 and I will strip you **n** in front of them so they can
16:39 leaving you completely **n** and ashamed.
23:29 rob you of all you own, leaving you **n** and bare.
Hos 2: 3 I will strip her as **n** as she was on the day she was
2:10 I will strip her **n** in public, while all her lovers look
Mic 1: 8 I will walk around **n** and barefoot in sorrow
1:11 go as captives into exile—**n** and ashamed.
Mt 25:36 I was **n**, and you gave me clothing. I was sick,
25:38 show you hospitality? Or **n** and give you clothing?
25:43 I was **n**, and you gave me no clothing. I was sick
25:44 or thirsty or a stranger or **n** or sick or in prison,
Mk 14:52 tore off his clothes, but he escaped and ran away **n**.
Lk 8:27 Homeless and **n**, he had lived in a cemetery for a
Ac 19:16 that they fled from the house, **n** and badly injured.
Heb 4:13 Everything is **n** and exposed before his eyes.
Rev 3:17 and miserable and poor and blind and **n**.
16:15 so they will not need to walk **n** and ashamed."
17:16 They will strip her **n**, eat her flesh, and burn her

NAKEDNESS (7) [NAKED]

Ge 3: 7 and they suddenly felt shame at their **n**.
Ex 20:26 up under the skirts of your clothing and see your **n**.
Eze 16: 8 So I wrapped my cloak around you to cover your **n**
Hos 2: 9 and wool clothing I gave her to cover her **n**.
Na 3: 5 so all the earth will see your **n** and shame.
Hab 2:15 so that you can gloat over their **n** and shame.
Rev 3:18 so you will not be shamed by your **n**.

NAME (588) [NAMED, NAMELESS, NAMELY, NAMES, NAMING, NICKNAMED, RENAMED]

GLORIOUS NAME (3) 1Ch 29:13; Ne 9:5; Ps 72:19

HOLY NAME (25) Lev 20:3; 22:2,32; 1Ch 16:10,35; 29:16; Ps 30:4; 33:21; 74:7; 86:9; 97:12; 103:1; 105:3; 106:47; 145:21; Pr 30:9; Eze 20:39; 22:26; 36:20,21,22; 39:7; 43:7,8; Am 2:7

NAME FOREVER (9) Ex 3:15; Dt 18:5; 1Ch 23:13; Ps 72:19; 74:10; 86:12; 111:10; 145:1,21

NAME OF JESUS (11) Ac 2:38; 3:6,16; 5:40,41; 8:12; 9:27; 10:48; 16:18; 1Co 1:2; Php 2:10

NAME OF THE LORD (21) Mt 21:9; 23:39; Mk 11:9; Lk 13:35; 19:38; Jn 12:13; Ac 2:21; 8:16; 9:28; 19:5,13,17; 22:16; Ro 10:13; 1Co 5:4; 1Th 4:1,2; 5:27; 2Th 3:12; Jas 5:10,14

NAME OF THE LORD* (50) Ex 20:7; Dt 5:11; 18:7; 28:58; 32:3; 1Sa 14:39; 17:45; 28:10; 2Sa 6:2,18; 1Ki 3:2; 5:3,5; 8:17,20; 10:1; 18:24; 2Ki 2:24; 5:11; 1Ch 13:6; 16:2; 22:7; 2Ch 2:4; 6:7,10; 33:18; Job 1:21; Ps 7:17; 113:1,2,3; 116:4,17; 118:10,11,12,26; 122:4; 135:1; 148:13; Pr 18:10; Isa 24:15; 48:1; 59:19; Jer 26:16; Joel 2:32; Am 6:10; Mic 5:4; Zep 3:12; Zec 13:3

Ge 2:19 would call them, and Adam chose a **n** for each one.
4:21 His brother's **n** was Jubal, the first musician—
10: 9 His **n** became proverbial, and people would speak
10:25 and dispersed. His brother's **n** was Joktan.
16:11 You are to **n** him Ishmael, for the LORD has
17: 5 What's more, I am changing your **n**. It will no
17:15 your wife—her **n** will no longer be Sarai;
17:19 You will **n** him Isaac, and I will confirm my
21:23 "Swear to me in God's **n** that you won't deceive
22:14 This **n** has now become a proverb:
25:30 (This was how Esau got his other **n**, Edom—
27:36 Esau said bitterly, "No wonder his **n** is Jacob,
28: 9 His new wife's **n** was Mahalath. She was the sister
28:19 though the **n** of the nearby village was Luz.
31:42 would have sent me off without a penny to my **n**.
32:27 "What is your **n**?" the man asked. He replied,
32:28 "Your **n** will no longer be Jacob," the man told
32:29 "What is your **n**?" Jacob asked him. "Why do
35:10 and said, "Your **n** is no longer Jacob; you will
36:43 each clan giving its **n** to the area it occupied.
48:16 May they preserve my **n** and the names of my
Ex 3:13 What is his **n**?' Then what should I tell them?"
3:15 This will be my **n** forever; it has always been my **n**, and it will be used
6: 3 though I did not reveal my **n**, the LORD, to them.
15: 3 LORD is a warrior; / yes, the LORD is his **n**!
18: 3 The **n** of Moses' first son was Gershom, for Moses
18: 4 The **n** of his second son was Eliezer, for Moses
20: 7 "Do not misuse the **n** of the LORD your God.
20: 7 will not let you go unpunished if you misuse his **n**.
23:21 your sins. He is my representative—he bears my **n**.
28:21 and the **n** of that tribe will be engraved on it as
33:12 You call me by **n** and tell me I have found favor
33:19 and I will call out my **n**, 'the LORD,' to you.
34: 5 down in a pillar of cloud and called out his own **n**,
39:14 each with the **n** of one of the twelve tribes of
Lev 18:21 for you must not profane the **n** of your God.
19:12 "Do not use my **n** to swear a falsehood and so profane the **n** of your God.
20: 3 and profaned my holy **n** by giving their children to
21: 6 to God as holy and must never dishonor his **n**.
22: 2 with great care, so they do not profane my holy **n**.
22:32 Do not treat my holy **n** as common and ordinary.
24:11 of an Israelite woman blasphemed the LORD's **n**.
24:11 for judgment. His mother's **n** was Shelomith.
24:16 Anyone who blasphemes the LORD's **n** must be
24:16 who blasphemes the LORD's **n** will surely die.
Nu 3:40 are one month old or older, and register each **n**.
4:32 must assign the various loads to each man by **n**.
5:27 and her **n** will become a curse word among her
13:16 By this time Moses had changed Hoshea's **n** to
17: 2 and inscribe each tribal leader's **n** on his staff.
17: 3 Inscribe Aaron's **n** on the staff of the tribe of Levi,
25:15 The woman's **n** was Cozbi; she was the daughter
27: 4 Why should the **n** of our father disappear just
32:41 and changed the **n** of that region to the Towns of
Dt 5:11 " 'Do not misuse the **n** of the LORD your God.
5:11 will not let you go unpunished if you misuse his **n**.
6:13 When you take an oath, you must use only his **n**.
9:14 destroy them and erase their **n** from under heaven.
10: 8 the LORD, and to pronounce blessings in his **n**.
10:20 cling to him. Your oaths must be in his **n** alone.
12: 5 from among all the tribes for his **n** to be honored.
12:11 your God will choose for his **n** to be honored.
12:21 his **n** to be honored is a long way from your home.
12:31 that the LORD hates, all in the **n** of their gods.
14:23 LORD your God chooses for his **n** to be honored,
14:24 **n** to be honored might be a long way from your
16: 2 at the place he chooses for his **n** to be honored.
16: 6 your God will choose for his **n** to be honored.
16:11 at the place he chooses for his **n** to be honored.
18: 5 your tribes to minister in the LORD's **n** forever.
18: 7 He may minister there in the **n** of the LORD his
18:22 the prophet predicts something in the LORD's **n**
21: 5 and to pronounce blessings in the LORD's **n**.
25: 6 so that his **n** will not be forgotten in Israel.
25: 7 refuses to preserve his brother's **n** in Israel—
26: 2 LORD your God chooses for his **n** to be honored.
28:58 and awesome **n** of the LORD your God,
32: 3 I will proclaim the **n** of the LORD; / how glorious
Jos 6:27 and his **n** became famous throughout the land.
7: 9 what will happen to the honor of your great **n**?"
Jdg 1:26 the city Luz, and it is known by that **n** to this day.
3: 9 His **n** was Othniel, the son of Caleb's younger
3:15 His **n** was Ehud son of Gera, of the tribe of
13: 6 ask where he was from, and he didn't tell me his **n**.
13:17 asked the angel of the LORD, "What is your **n**?
13:18 "Why do you ask my **n**?" the angel of the LORD
Ru 1: 2 The man's **n** was Elimelech, and his wife was
4: 5 have children who will carry on her husband's **n**
4:10 a son to carry on the family **n** of her dead husband
1Sa 12:22 chosen people, for that would dishonor his great **n**.
14:39 I vow by the **n** of the LORD who rescued Israel
17:45 but I come to you in the **n** of the LORD
17:58 And David replied, "His **n** is Jesse, and we live in
18:30 So David's **n** became very famous throughout the
20:42 for we have made a pact in the LORD's **n**.
25: 3 This man's **n** was Nabal, and his wife, Abigail,
25:25 to him. He is a fool, just as his **n** suggests.
28:10 But Saul took an oath in the **n** of the LORD
30:15 "If you swear by God's **n** that you will not kill me
2Sa 6: 2 which bears the **n** of the LORD Almighty, who is
6:18 David blessed the people in the **n** of the LORD
7: 9 Now I will make your **n** famous throughout the
7:13 one who will build a house—a temple—for my **n**.
7:23 You made a great **n** for yourself when you rescued
7:26 And may your **n** be honored forever so that all the
9: 6 His **n** was Mephibosheth; he was Jonathan's son
12:25 Nathan the prophet that his **n** should be Jedidiah—
14: 7 and my husband's **n** and family will disappear
14:27 His daughter's **n** was Tamar, and she was very
18:18 for he had said, "I have no son to carry on my **n**."
22:50 among the nations; / I will sing joyfully to your **n**.
1Ki 3: 2 for a temple honoring the **n** of the LORD had not
5: 3 was not able to build a Temple to honor the **n** of
5: 5 So I am planning to build a Temple to honor the **n**
5: 5 your throne, will build the Temple to honor my **n**.'
8:16 where a temple should be built to honor my **n**.
8:17 wanted to build this Temple to honor the **n** of the
8:18 for you to want to build the Temple to honor my **n**,
8:20 I have built this Temple to honor the **n** of the
8:29 place where you have said you would put your **n**.
8:33 and if they turn to you and call on your **n** and pray
8:35 and confess your **n** and turn from their sins
8:41 come from distant lands to worship your great **n**—
8:43 know that this Temple I have built bears your **n**.
8:44 and toward this Temple that I have built for your **n**,
8:48 toward this Temple I have built to honor your **n**,
9: 3 so that my **n** will be honored there forever.
9: 7 this Temple that I have set apart to honor my **n**.
10: 1 which brought honor to the **n** of the LORD,
11:36 the city I have chosen to be the place for my **n**.
14:21 all the tribes of Israel as the place to honor his **n**.
18:24 Then call on the **n** of your god, and I will call on the **n** of the LORD.
18:25 and prepare it and call on the **n** of your god.
18:26 Then they called on the **n** of Baal all morning,
21: 8 So she wrote letters in Ahab's **n**, sealed them with
22: 8 bad news for me! His **n** is Micaiah son of Imlah."
2Ki 2:24 and he cursed them in the **n** of the LORD.
5:11 and call on the **n** of the LORD his God and heal
14: 7 also conquered Sela and changed its **n** to Joktheel.
14:27 said he would blot out the **n** of Israel completely,
17:34 of Jacob, whose **n** he changed to Israel.
18:35 **N** just one! So what makes you think that the
21: 4 the place where the LORD had said his **n** should
21: 7 "My **n** will be honored here forever in this Temple
23:27 and the Temple where my **n** was to be honored."

23:34 and he changed Eliakim's **n** to Jehoiakim.
24:17 and he changed Mattaniah's **n** to Zedekiah.
1Ch 1:19 and dispersed. His brother's **n** was Joktan.
7:16 His brother's **n** was Sheresh. The sons of Peresh
8:29 lived in Gibeon. His wife's **n** was Maacah,
9:35 lived in Gibeon. His wife's **n** was Maacah,
13: 6 which bears the **n** of the LORD who is enthroned
16: 2 David blessed the people in the **n** of the LORD.
16:10 Exult in his holy **n**; / O worshipers of the LORD,
16:35 among the nations, / so we can thank your holy **n**
16:41 and the others chosen by **n** to give thanks to the
17: 8 Now I will make your **n** famous throughout the
17:21 You made a great **n** for yourself when you rescued
17:24 And may your **n** be established and honored
22: 7 "I wanted to build a Temple to honor the **n** of the
22: 8 not be the one to build a Temple to honor my **n**.
22: 9 His **n** will be Solomon, and I will give peace
22:10 is the one who will build a Temple to honor my **n**.
22:19 into the Temple built to honor the LORD's **n**."
23:13 and to pronounce blessings in his **n** forever.
23:24 of their family groups, registered carefully by **n**.
28: 3 'You must not build a temple to honor my **n**,
29:13 our God, we thank you and praise your glorious **n**!
29:16 a Temple to honor your holy **n** come from you!
2Ch 2: 4 I am about to build a Temple to honor the **n** of the
6: 5 where a temple should be built to honor my **n**.
6: 7 wanted to build this Temple to honor the **n** of the
6: 8 for you to want to build the Temple to honor my **n**,
6:10 I have built this Temple to honor the **n** of the
6:20 place where you have said you would put your **n**.
6:24 and if they turn to you and call on your **n** and pray
6:26 and confess your **n** and turn from their sins
6:32 come from distant lands to worship your great **n**
6:33 know that this Temple I have built bears your **n**.
6:34 and toward this Temple that I have built for your **n**,
6:38 toward this Temple I have built to honor your **n**,
7:14 Then if my people who are called by my **n** will
7:20 this Temple that I have set apart to honor my **n**.
12:13 all the tribes of Israel as the place to honor his **n**.
14:11 It is in your **n** that we have come against this vast
18: 7 bad news for me! His **n** is Micaiah son of Imlah."
20: 2 (This was another **n** for En-gedi.)
20: 9 before this Temple where your **n** is honored.
20:14 His **n** was Jahaziel son of Zechariah, son of
20:26 which got its **n** that day because the people praised
28:15 Then the four men mentioned by **n** came forward
32:14 **N** just one time when any god, anywhere, was able
33: 4 the place where the LORD had said his **n** should
33: 7 "My **n** will be honored here forever in this Temple
33:18 and the words the seers spoke to him in the **n** of
36: 4 and he changed Eliakim's **n** to Jehoiakim.
36:13 though he had taken an oath of loyalty in God's **n**.
Ezr 2:61 Barzillai from Gilead and had taken her family **n**.)
5: 1 and Zechariah son of Iddo prophesied in the **n** of
6:12 as the place to honor his **n** destroy any king
8:20 by King David. They were all listed by **n**.
10:16 designating each of the representatives by **n**.
Ne 1: 9 to the place I have chosen for my **n** to be honored.'
7:63 Barzillai from Gilead and had taken her family **n**.)
9: 5 Then they continued, "Praise his glorious **n**!
Est 2:14 had especially enjoyed her and requested her by **n**.
3:12 These letters were signed in the **n** of King Xerxes,
8: 8 and send a message to the Jews in the king's **n**,
8: 8 remember that whatever is written in the king's **n**
8:10 Mordecai wrote in the **n** of King Xerxes and sealed
Job 1:21 has taken it away. / Praise the **n** of the LORD!"
31:35 see my side! Look, I will sign my **n** to my defense.
Ps 5:11 so all who love your **n** may be filled with joy.
7:17 I will sing praise to the **n** of the LORD Most
8: 1 our Lord, the majesty of your **n** fills the earth!
8: 9 our Lord, the majesty of your **n** fills the earth!
9: 2 I will sing praises to your **n**, O Most High.
9:10 Those who know your **n** trust in you, / for you,
18:49 among the nations; / I will sing joyfully to your **n**.
22:22 Then I will declare the wonder of your **n** to my
23: 3 me along right paths, / bringing honor to his **n**.
25:11 For the honor of your **n**, O LORD, / forgive my
29: 2 Give honor to the LORD for the glory of his **n**.
30: 4 all you godly ones! / Praise his holy **n**.
31: 3 For the honor of your **n**, lead me out of this peril.
33:21 hearts rejoice, / for we are trusting in his holy **n**.
34: 3 LORD's greatness; / let us exalt his **n** together.
44: 5 only in your **n** can we trample our foes.
44: 8 and constantly praise your **n**. / *Interlude*
45:17 I will bring honor to your **n** in every generation.
48:10 As your **n** deserves, O God, / you will be praised to
49:11 They may **n** their estates after themselves,
54: 6 offering to you; / I will praise your **n**, O LORD,
61: 5 an inheritance reserved for those who fear your **n**.
61: 8 Then I will always sing praises to your **n** / as I
66: 2 Sing about the glory of his **n**! / Tell the world how
66: 4 your praises, / shouting your **n** in glorious songs."
68: 4 Sing praises to God and to his **n**! / Sing loud
68: 4 His **n** is the LORD— / rejoice in his presence!
69:30 Then I will praise God's **n** with singing, / and I
72:17 May the king's **n** endure forever; / may it continue
72:19 Bless his glorious **n** forever! / Let the whole earth
74: 7 utterly defiled the place that bears your holy **n**.
74:10 Will you let them dishonor your **n** forever?
74:18 LORD. / A foolish nation has dishonored your **n**.
74:21 let these poor and needy ones give praise to your **n**.
76: 1 is well known in Judah; / his **n** is great in Israel.
79: 6 on kingdoms that do not call upon your **n**.
79: 9 Help us for the honor of your **n**. / Oh, save us
79: 9 and forgive our sins / for the sake of your **n**.
80:18 Revive us so we can call on your **n** once more.
83:16 until they submit to your **n**, O LORD.
86: 9 Lord; / they will praise your great and holy **n**.
86:12 Lord my God. / I will give glory to your **n** forever,
89:12 Mount Tabor and Mount Hermon praise your **n**.
91:14 love me. / I will protect those who trust in my **n**.
96: 2 Sing to the LORD; bless his **n**. / Each day
97:12 be happy in the LORD / and praise his holy **n**!
99: 3 praise your great and awesome **n**. / Your **n** is holy!
99: 6 among his priests; / Samuel also called on his **n**.
100: 4 with praise. / Give thanks to him and bless his **n**.
103: 1 with my whole heart, I will praise his holy **n**.
105: 3 Exult in his holy **n**; / O worshipers of the LORD,
106: 8 he saved them— / to defend the honor of his **n**
106:47 among the nations, / so we can thank your holy **n**
109:13 May his family **n** be blotted out in a single
109:15 but may his **n** be cut off from human memory.
111: 9 What a holy, awe-inspiring **n** he has!
111:10 come to all who obey him. / Praise his **n** forever!
113: 1 of the LORD. / Praise the **n** of the LORD!
113: 2 Blessed be the **n** of the LORD / forever and ever.
113: 3 from east to west— / praise the **n** of the LORD.
116: 4 Then I called on the **n** of the LORD: / "Please,
116:13 I will praise the LORD's **n** for saving me.
116:17 of thanksgiving / and call on the **n** of the LORD.
118:10 I destroyed them all in the **n** of the LORD.
118:11 but I destroyed them all in the **n** of the LORD.
118:12 But I destroyed them all in the **n** of the LORD.
118:26 Bless the one who comes in the **n** of the LORD.
119:132 your mercy, / as you do for all who love your **n**.
122: 4 They come to give thanks to the **n** of the LORD
129: 8 be upon you; / we bless you in the LORD's **n**."
135: 1 Praise the **n** of the LORD! / Praise him, you who
135: 3 is good; / celebrate his wonderful **n** with music.
135:13 Your **n**, O LORD, endures forever; / your fame,
138: 2 I will give thanks to your **n** / for your unfailing
138: 2 promises are backed / by all the honor of your **n**.
139:20 blaspheme you; / your enemies take your **n** in vain.
140:13 Surely the godly are praising your **n**, / for they will
143:11 For the glory of your **n**, O LORD, save me.
145: 1 and King, / and bless your **n** forever and ever.
145:21 and everyone on earth will bless his holy **n**
147: 4 He counts the stars / and calls them all by **n**.
148:13 Let them all praise the **n** of the LORD. / For his **n** is very great; / his glory towers over the
149: 3 Praise his **n** with dancing, / accompanied by
Pr 6: 3 your pride; go and beg to have your **n** erased.
10: 7 the godly, but the **n** of a wicked person rots away.
18:10 The **n** of the LORD is a strong fortress; the godly
30: 4 What is his **n**—and his son's **n**? Tell me if you
30: 9 too poor, I may steal and thus insult God's holy **n**.
Ecc 6: 4 ended in darkness. He wouldn't even have had a **n**,
SS 1: 3 fragrant your cologne, and how pleasing your **n**!
Isa 4: 1 Only let us be called by your **n** so we won't be
8: 1 a large signboard and clearly write this **n** on it:
8: 4 This **n** prophesies that within a couple of years,
12: 4 "Thank the LORD! / Praise his **n**!
18: 7 in Jerusalem, the place where his **n** dwells.
19:17 Just to speak the **n** of Israel will strike deep terror
22:23 He will bring honor to his family **n**, for I will drive
24:15 praise the **n** of the LORD, the God of Israel.
25: 1 O LORD, I will honor and praise your **n**, for you
26: 8 your laws; / our heart's desire is to glorify your **n**.
29: 2 For Jerusalem will become as her **n** Ariel means—
36:20 **N** just one! So what makes you think that the
40:26 them out one after another, calling each by its **n**.
41:25 He will come against the nations and call on my **n**,
42: 8 "I am the LORD; that is my **n**! I will not give my
43: 1 I have called you by **n**; you are mine.
44: 5 Some will write the LORD's **n** on their hands
44: 5 and will take the honored **n** of Israel as their own.
45: 3 the God of Israel, the one who calls you by **n**.
45: 4 I called you by **n** when you did not know me.
45:23 I have sworn by my own **n**, and I will never go
45:23 and every tongue will confess allegiance to my **n**."
47: 4 Our Redeemer, whose **n** is the LORD Almighty,
48: 1 who are called by the **n** of Israel and born into the
48: 1 you who take oaths in the **n** of the LORD and call
48: 2 God of Israel, whose **n** is the LORD Almighty.
48: 9 Yet for my own sake and for the honor of my **n**,
49: 1 my birth; from within the womb he called me by **n**.
49:16 See, I have written your **n** on my hand. Ever before
51:15 its waves to roar. My **n** is the LORD Almighty.
52: 5 My **n** is being blasphemed all day long.
52: 6 But I will reveal my **n** to my people, and they will
54: 5 The LORD Almighty is his **n**! He is your
55:13 miracle will bring great honor to the LORD's **n**;
56: 5 and a **n** far greater than the honor they would have
56: 5 For the **n** I give them is an everlasting one.
56: 6 to the LORD and serve him and love his **n**,
59:19 and glorify the **n** of the LORD throughout the
62: 2 your glory. And the LORD will give you a new **n**.
62: 4 Your new **n** will be the City of God's Delight
64: 7 Yet no one calls on your **n** or pleads with you for
65:15 Your **n** will be a curse word among my people,
65:15 destroy you and call his true servants by another **n**.
66: 5 and throw you out for being loyal to my **n**.
66:22 with a **n** that will never disappear,"
Jer 2: 8 and the prophets spoke in the **n** of Baal,
4: 2 and if you will swear by my **n** alone, and begin to
4: 2 and all people will come and praise my **n**."
7:11 which honors my **n**, is a den of thieves?
7:12 where I once put the Tabernacle to honor my **n**.
7:14 destroy this Temple that was built to honor my **n**,
10: 6 For you are great, and your **n** is full of power.
10:16 The LORD Almighty is his **n**!
10:25 on nations that do not call upon your **n**.
11:19 kill him, so his **n** will be forgotten forever."
11:21 me if I did not stop speaking in the LORD's **n**.
12: 2 Your **n** is on their lips, but in their hearts they give
12:16 and if they learn to swear by my **n**, saying,
12:16 they taught my people to swear by the **n** of Baal),
13:11 my people, my pride, my glory—an honor to my **n**.
14:14 "These prophets are telling lies in my **n**.
14:15 for they have spoken in my **n** even though I never
14:21 For the sake of your own **n**, LORD, do not
15:16 for I bear your **n**, O LORD God Almighty.
20: 3 "Pashhur, the LORD has changed your **n**.
20: 9 I'll never mention the LORD or speak in his **n**,
22: 5 I swear by my own **n**, says the LORD, that this
23: 6 And this is his **n**: 'The LORD Is Our
23:18 "But can you **n** even one of these prophets who
23:25 And then they proceed to tell lies in my **n**.
23:40 and your **n** will be infamous throughout the
25:29 the city where my own **n** is honored.
26: 9 **n** that this Temple will be destroyed like Shiloh?
26:16 for he has spoken to us in the **n** of the LORD our
27:15 They are telling you lies in my **n**, so I will drive
29: 9 because they prophesy lies in my **n**. I have not sent
29:21 son of Maaseiah—who are telling you lies in my **n**:
29:23 with their neighbors' wives and have lied in my **n**.
31:35 His **n** is the LORD Almighty, and this is what he
32:20 You have made your **n** very great, as it is today.
33: 2 and earth—the LORD is his **n**—says this:
34:16 and defiled my **n** by taking back the men
44:26 I have sworn by my great **n**, says the LORD,
44:26 that my **n** will no longer be spoken by any of the
44:26 None of you may invoke my **n** or use this oath:
46:18 says the King, whose **n** is the LORD Almighty,
48:15 says the King, whose **n** is the LORD Almighty.
49:13 For I have sworn by my own **n**," says the LORD,
50:34 His **n** is the LORD Almighty. He will defend
51:14 taken this vow and has sworn to it by his own **n**:
51:19 The LORD Almighty is his **n**!
51:57 says the King, whose **n** is the LORD Almighty.
52: 1 His mother's **n** was Hamutal, the daughter of
La 3:55 But I called on your **n**, LORD, from deep within
Eze 17:19 and despising the solemn oath he made in my **n**.
20: 9 do it, for I acted to protect the honor of my **n**.
20:14 I held back in order to protect the honor of my **n**.
20:22 **n** among the nations who had seen my power in
20:39 to me. Such desecration of my holy **n** must stop!
20:44 when I have honored my **n** by treating you
22:26 so that my holy **n** is greatly dishonored among
23:10 Her **n** was known to every woman in the land as a
35:11 And I will bring honor to my **n** by what I do to
36:20 the nations, they brought dishonor to my holy **n**.
36:21 Then I was concerned for my holy **n**, which had
36:22 I am doing it to protect my holy **n**, which you
36:23 I will show how holy my great **n** is—the **n** you dishonored among the nations.
39: 7 I will make known my holy **n** among my people of
39:11 and they will change the **n** of the place to the
43: 7 and their kings will not defile my holy **n** any
43: 8 They defiled my holy **n** by such wickedness,
48:35 And from that day the **n** of the city will be 'The
Da 2:20 saying, / "Praise the **n** of God forever and ever,
9:15 you brought lasting honor to your **n** by rescuing
9:19 for your people and your city bear your **n**."
12: 1 But at that time every one of your people whose **n**
Hos 1: 4 And the LORD said, "**N** the child Jezreel, for I
1: 6 said to Hosea, "**N** your daughter Lo-ruhamah—
1: 9 And the LORD said, "**N** him Lo-ammi—'Not my
4:15 pretense as they take oaths in the LORD's **n**.
12: 5 the LORD God Almighty, the LORD is his **n**!
Joel 2:17 Don't let their **n** become a proverb of unbelieving
2:32 And anyone who calls on the **n** of the LORD will
Am 2: 7 sleep with the same woman, corrupting my holy **n**.
4:13 under his feet. The LORD God Almighty is his **n**!
5: 8 it down as rain on the land. The LORD is his **n**!
5:27 says the LORD, whose **n** is God Almighty.
6: 8 The Sovereign LORD has sworn by his own **n**,
6:10 "Hush! Don't even whisper the **n** of the LORD.
8: 7 Now the LORD has sworn this oath by his own **n**,
9: 6 it down as rain on the land. The LORD is his **n**!
Mic 5: 4 in the majesty of the **n** of the LORD his God.
Na 1:14 will have no more children to carry on your **n**.
Hab 2:10 you have shamed your **n** and forfeited your lives.
Zep 3:12 for it is they who trust in the **n** of the LORD.
3:20 I will give you a good **n**, a **n** of distinction among all the nations of the
Zec 5: 4 the house of everyone who swears falsely by my **n**.
5: 8 The angel said, "The woman's **n** is Wickedness,"
13: 3 for you have prophesied lies in the **n** of the
13: 9 They will call on my **n**, and I will answer them.
14: 9 be one LORD—his **n** alone will be worshiped.
Mal 1: 6 You have despised my **n**! "But you ask, 'How have we ever despised your **n**?'
1: 7 "You have despised my **n** by offering defiled
1:11 But my **n** is honored by people of other nations
1:11 sweet incense and pure offerings in honor of my **n**.
1:11 For my **n** is great among the nations,"
1:12 "But you dishonor my **n** with your actions.
1:14 "and my **n** is feared among the nations!
2: 2 Honor my **n**," says the LORD Almighty, "or I
2: 5 they greatly revered me and stood in awe of my **n**.
4: 2 "But for you who fear my **n**, the Sun of
Mt 1:21 she will have a son, and you are to **n** him Jesus,
6: 9 Our Father in heaven, / may your **n** be honored.
7:22 we prophesied in your **n** and cast out demons in your **n**
7:22 and performed many miracles in your **n**.'
12:21 And his **n** will be the hope / of all the world."
21: 9 Bless the one who comes in the **n** of the Lord!
23:39 'Bless the one who comes in the **n** of the Lord!' "
24: 5 For many will come in my **n**, saying, 'I am the

26:63 “I demand in the **n** of the living God that you tell
28:19 baptizing them in the **n** of the Father and the Son
Mk 5: 9 Then Jesus asked, “What is your **n**?”
5:22 whose **n** was Jairus, came and fell down before
9:38 we saw a man using your **n** to cast out demons,
9:39 “No one who performs miracles in my **n** will soon
11: 9 Bless the one who comes in the **n** of the Lord!
13: 6 because many will come in my **n**, claiming to be
16:17 They will cast out demons in my **n**, and they will
Lk 1:13 will bear you a son! And you are to **n** him John.
1:31 and have a son, and you are to **n** him Jesus.
1:59 They wanted to **n** him Zechariah, after his father.
1:60 But Elizabeth said, “No! His **n** is John!”
1:61 “There is no one in all your family by that **n**.”
1:63 to everyone’s surprise he wrote, “His **n** is John!”
2:21 the **n** given him by the angel even before he was
8:30 “What is your **n**?” Jesus asked. “Legion,”
9:49 we saw someone using your **n** to cast out demons.
10:17 even the demons obey us when we use your **n**!”
11: 2 should pray: / “Father, may your **n** be honored.
13:35 ‘Bless the one who comes in the **n** of the Lord!’ ”
19: 5 he looked up at Zacchaeus and called him by **n**.
19:38 “Bless the King who comes in the **n** of the Lord!
21: 8 For many will come in my **n**, claiming to be the
Jn 1:45 His **n** is Jesus, the son of Joseph from Nazareth.”
10: 3 He calls his own sheep by **n** and leads them out.
10:25 The proof is what I do in the **n** of my Father.
12:13 Bless the one who comes in the **n** of the Lord!
12:28 Father, bring glory to your **n**.” Then a voice spoke
14:13 You can ask for anything in my **n**, and I will do it,
14:14 Yes, ask anything in my **n**, and I will do it!
14:22 Judas Iscariot, but the other disciple with that **n**)
15:16 will give you whatever you ask for, using my **n**.
16:23 he will grant your request because you use my **n**.
16:24 Ask, using my **n**, and you will receive, and you
16:26 Then you will ask in my **n**. I’m not saying I will
Ac 1:19 and they gave the place the Aramaic **n**
2:21 And anyone who calls on the **n** of the Lord
2:38 and be baptized in the **n** of Jesus Christ for the
3: 6 In the **n** of Jesus Christ of Nazareth, get up
3:16 “The **n** of Jesus has healed this man—and you
3:16 Faith in Jesus’ **n** has caused this healing before
4: 7 and demanded, “By what power, or in whose **n**,
4:10 all the people of Israel that he was healed in the **n**
4:12 There is no other **n** in all of heaven for people to
4:17 them not to speak to anyone in Jesus’ **n** again.”
4:30 and wonders be done through the **n** of your holy
5:28 we tell you never again to teach in this man’s **n**?”
5:40 them never again to speak in the **n** of Jesus,
5:41 them worthy to suffer dishonor for the **n** of Jesus.
7:52 **N** one prophet your ancestors didn’t persecute!
8:12 the Kingdom of God and the **n** of Jesus Christ.
8:16 for they had only been baptized in the **n** of the
9:27 and how he boldly preached in the **n** of Jesus in
9:28 in Jerusalem, preaching boldly in the **n** of the Lord.
10:43 in him will have their sins forgiven through his **n**.”
10:48 So he gave orders for them to be baptized in the **n**
13: 8 the sorcerer (as his **n** means in Greek), interfered
16:18 “I command you in the **n** of Jesus Christ to come
19: 5 they were baptized in the **n** of the Lord Jesus.
19:13 out evil spirits tried to use the **n** of the Lord Jesus.
19:17 and the **n** of the Lord Jesus was greatly honored.
22:16 sins washed away, calling on the **n** of the Lord.’
Ro 1: 5 will believe and obey him, bringing glory to his **n**.
2:24 “The world blasphemes the **n** of God because of
10:13 For “Anyone who calls on the **n** of the Lord will
15: 9 the Gentiles; / I will sing praises to your **n**.”
15:20 News where the **n** of Christ has never been heard,
15:30 I urge you in the **n** of our Lord Jesus Christ to join
1Co 1: 2 whoever calls upon the **n** of Jesus Christ, our Lord
1:13 Were any of you baptized in the **n** of Paul?
1:15 now no one can say they were baptized in my **n**.
5: 4 in the **n** of the Lord Jesus. You are to call a
Eph 5:20 to God the Father in the **n** of our Lord Jesus Christ.
Php 2: 9 and gave him a **n** that is above every other **n**,
2:10 so that at the **n** of Jesus every knee will bow,
1Th 4: 1 we urge you in the **n** of the Lord Jesus to live in a
4: 2 For you remember what we taught you in the **n** of
5:27 I command you in the **n** of the Lord to read this
2Th 1:12 Then everyone will give honor to the **n** of our Lord
3:12 In the **n** of the Lord Jesus Christ we appeal to such
1Ti 1:13 even though I used to scoff at the **n** of Christ.
6: 1 so that the **n** of God and his teaching will not be
2Ti 2:14 and command them in God’s **n** to stop fighting
Phm 1: 8 I could demand it in the **n** of Christ because it is
Heb 1: 4 just as the **n** God gave him is far greater than their
2:12 “I will declare the wonder of your **n** to my
6:13 swear by, God took an oath in his own **n**, saying:
7: 2 His **n** means “king of justice.” He is also “king of
13:15 of praise to God by proclaiming the glory of his **n**.
Jas 2: 7 who slander Jesus Christ, whose noble **n** you bear?
5:10 look at the prophets who spoke in the **n** of the
5:14 anointing them with oil in the **n** of the Lord.
1Pe 4:16 the privilege of being called by his wonderful **n**!
1Jn 3:23 We must believe in the **n** of his Son, Jesus Christ,
Rev 2:17 and on the stone will be engraved a new **n** that no
3:12 And I will write my God’s **n** on them, and they
3:12 And they will have my new **n** inscribed upon them.
6: 8 And Death was the **n** of its rider, who was
8:11 The **n** of the star was Bitterness. It made one-third
9:11 his **n** in Hebrew is *Abaddon,* and in Greek,
10: 6 And he swore an oath in the **n** of the one who lives
11:18 all who fear your **n**, from the least to the greatest.
13: 6 slandering his **n** and all who live in heaven,
13:17 which was either the **n** of the beast or the number
representing his **n**.
14: 1 his **n** and his Father’s **n** written on their foreheads.
14:11 and his statue and have accepted the mark of his **n**.
15: 2 and his statue and the number representing his **n**.
15: 4 Who will not fear, O Lord, and glorify your **n**?
16: 9 and they cursed the **n** of God, who sent all of these
17: 5 A mysterious **n** was written on her forehead:
19:12 A **n** was written on him, and only he knew what it
20:15 And anyone whose **n** was not found recorded in
22: 4 and his **n** will be written on their foreheads.

NAMED (284) [NAME]

Ge 1:10 God **n** the dry ground “land” and the water
3:20 Then Adam **n** his wife Eve, because she would be
4: 2 she gave birth to a second son and **n** him Abel.
4:17 and gave birth to a son, and they **n** him Enoch.
4:17 Cain founded a city, he **n** it Enoch after his son.
4:20 Adah gave birth to a baby **n** Jabal. He became the
4:22 and iron. Tubal-cain had a sister **n** Naamah.
4:25 She **n** him Seth, for she said, “God has granted me
4:26 Seth grew up, he had a son and **n** him Enosh.
5:29 Lamech **n** his son Noah, for he said, “He will
10:25 The first was **n** Peleg—“division”—for during his
11:27 Nahor, and Haran; and Haran had a son **n** Lot.
11:29 their brother Haran. (Milcah had a sister **n** Iscah.)
16: 1 took her servant, an Egyptian woman **n** Hagar,
16:14 Later that well was **n** Beer-lahairoi, and it can still
16:15 gave Abram a son, and Abram **n** him Ishmael.
19:37 daughter gave birth to a son, she **n** him Moab.
19:38 daughter gave birth to a son, she **n** him Ben-ammi.
21: 3 And Abraham **n** his son Isaac.
22:14 Abraham **n** the place “The LORD Will
22:21 The oldest was **n** Uz, the next oldest was Buz,
24:15 a young woman **n** Rebekah arrived with a water
24:29 Now Rebekah had a brother **n** Laban.
26:20 So Isaac **n** the well “Argument,” because they had
26:21 was a fight over it. So Isaac **n** it “Opposition.”
26:33 So Isaac **n** the well “Oath,” and from that time to
26:34 of forty, Esau married a young woman **n** Judith,
28:19 He **n** the place Bethel—“house of God”—
29: 5 “Do you know a man there **n** Laban, the grandson
29:32 She **n** him Reuben, for she said, “The LORD has
29:33 She **n** him Simeon, for she said, “The LORD
29:34 She **n** him Levi, for she said, “Surely now my
29:35 She **n** him Judah, for she said, “Now I will praise
30: 6 Rachel **n** him Dan, for she said, “God has
30: 8 Rachel **n** him Naphtali, for she said, “I have had
30:11 Leah **n** him Gad, for she said, “How fortunate I
30:13 and Leah **n** him Asher, for she said, “What joy is
30:18 She **n** him Issachar, for she said, “God has
30:20 She **n** him Zebulun, for she said, “God has given
30:21 Later she gave birth to a daughter and **n** her Dinah.
30:24 And she **n** him Joseph, for she said,
31:47 They **n** it “Witness Pile,” which is
32: 2 is God’s camp!” So he **n** the place Mahanaim.
32:30 Jacob **n** the place Peniel—“face of God”—for he
33:17 and herds. That is why the place was **n** Succoth.
35: 7 Jacob built an altar there and **n** it El-bethel,
35:18 to die, but with her last breath she **n** him Ben-oni;
36: 4 Esau and Adah had a son **n** Eliphaz. Esau and
Basemath had a son **n** Reuel.
36: 5 Esau and Oholibamah had sons **n** Jeush, Jalam,
36:12 Eliphaz had another son **n** Amalek, born to Timna,
36:22 were Hori and Heman. Lotan’s sister was **n** Timna.
36:30 The Horite clans are **n** after their clan leaders,
36:40 clans of Esau, who lived in the places **n** for them:
38: 1 to Adullam, where he visited a man **n** Hirah.
38: 3 and had a son, and Judah **n** the boy Er.
38: 4 Judah’s wife had another son, and she **n** him Onan.
38: 5 And when she had a third son, she **n** him Shelah.
38: 6 Judah arranged his marriage to a young woman **n**
38:30 thread on his wrist was born, and he was **n** Zerah.
41:45 a young woman **n** Asenath, the daughter of
41:51 Joseph **n** his older son Manasseh, for he said,
41:52 Joseph **n** his second son Ephraim, for he said,
46:17 Ishvah, Ishvi, and Beriah. Their sister was **n** Serah.
Ex 2:10 The princess **n** him Moses, for she said, “I drew
2:22 baby boy, and Moses **n** him Gershom, for he said,
6:26 and Moses **n** in this list are the same Aaron
17: 7 Moses **n** the place Massah—“the place of
Lev 11: 4 eat the animals **n** here because they either have
Nu 3:17 who were **n** Gershon, Kohath, and Merari.
3:18 The clans descended from Gershon were **n** for two
3:19 The clans descended from Kohath were **n** for four
3:20 The clans descended from Merari were **n** for two
25:14 the Midianite woman was **n** Zimri son of Salu,
26: 5 The Hanochite clan, **n** after its ancestor Hanoch.
26: 5 The Palluite clan, **n** after its ancestor Pallu.
26: 6 The Hezronite clan, **n** after its ancestor Hezron.
26: 6 The Carmite clan, **n** after its ancestor Carmi.
26:12 The Nemuelite clan, **n** after its ancestor Nemuel.
26:12 The Jaminite clan, **n** after its ancestor Jamin.
26:12 The Jakinite clan, **n** after its ancestor Jakin.
26:13 The Zerahite clan, **n** after its ancestor Zerah.
26:13 The Shaulite clan, **n** after its ancestor Shaul.
26:15 The Zephonite clan, **n** after its ancestor Zephon.
26:15 The Haggite clan, **n** after its ancestor Haggi.
26:15 The Shunite clan, **n** after its ancestor Shuni.
26:16 The Oznite clan, **n** after its ancestor Ozni.
26:16 The Erite clan, **n** after its ancestor Eri.
26:17 The Arodite clan, **n** after its ancestor Arodi.
26:17 The Arelite clan, **n** after its ancestor Areli.
26:20 The Shelanite clan, **n** after its ancestor Shelah.
26:20 The Perezite clan, **n** after its ancestor Perez.
26:20 The Zerahite clan, **n** after its ancestor Zerah.
26:21 The Hezronites, **n** after their ancestor Hezron.
26:21 The Hamulites, **n** after their ancestor Hamul.
26:23 The Tolaite clan, **n** after its ancestor Tola.
26:23 The Puite clan, **n** after its ancestor Puah.
26:24 The Jashubite clan, **n** after its ancestor Jashub.
26:24 The Shimronite clan, **n** after its ancestor Shimron.
26:26 The Seredite clan, **n** after its ancestor Sered.
26:26 The Elonite clan, **n** after its ancestor Elon.
26:26 The Jahleelite clan, **n** after its ancestor Jahleel.
26:29 The Makirite clan, **n** after its ancestor Makir.
26:29 **n** after its ancestor Gilead, Makir’s son.
26:30 The Iezerites, **n** after their ancestor Iezer.
26:30 The Helekites, **n** after their ancestor Helek.
26:31 The Asrielites, **n** after their ancestor Asriel.
26:31 The Shechemites, **n** after their ancestor Shechem.
26:32 The Shemidaites, **n** after their ancestor Shemida.
26:32 The Hepherites, **n** after their ancestor Hepher.
26:35 Shuthelahite clan, **n** after its ancestor Shuthelah.
26:35 The Bekerite clan, **n** after its ancestor Beker.
26:35 The Tahanite clan, **n** after its ancestor Tahan.
26:36 The Eranites, **n** after their ancestor Eran.
26:38 The Belaite clan, **n** after its ancestor Bela.
26:38 The Ashbelite clan, **n** after its ancestor Ashbel.
26:38 The Ahiramite clan, **n** after its ancestor Ahiram.
26:39 Shuphamite clan, **n** after its ancestor Shupham.
26:39 The Huphamite clan, **n** after its ancestor Hupham.
26:40 The Ardites, **n** after their ancestor Ard.
26:40 The Naamites, **n** after their ancestor Naaman.
26:42 The Shuhamite clan, **n** after its ancestor Shuham.
26:44 The Imnite clan, **n** after its ancestor Imnah.
26:44 The Ishvite clan, **n** after its ancestor Ishvi.
26:44 The Beriite clan, **n** after its ancestor Beriah.
26:45 The Heberites, **n** after their ancestor Heber.
26:45 The Malkielites, **n** after their ancestor Malkiel.
26:46 Asher also had a daughter **n** Serah.
26:48 The Jahzeelite clan, **n** after its ancestor Jahzeel.
26:48 The Gunite clan, **n** after its ancestor Guni.
26:49 The Jezerite clan, **n** after its ancestor Jezer.
26:49 The Shillemite clan, **n** after its ancestor Shillem.
26:57 The Gershonite clan, **n** after its ancestor Gershon.
26:57 The Kohathite clan, **n** after its ancestor Kohath.
26:57 The Merarite clan, **n** after its ancestor Merari.
26:59 and Amram’s wife was **n** Jochebed. She also was a
32:42 a man **n** Nobah captured the town of Kenath
Jos 2: 1 and came to the house of a prostitute **n** Rahab
7: 1 A man **n** Achan had stolen some of these things,
14:15 It had been **n** after Arba, a great hero of the
15:13 Hebron), which had been **n** after Anak’s ancestor.
22:34 people of Reuben and Gad **n** the altar “Witness,”
Jdg 1:17 destroyed the town. So the town was **n** Hormah.
1:26 He **n** the city Luz, and it is known by that name to
6:24 LORD there and **n** it “The LORD Is Peace.”
8:31 in Shechem, who bore him a son **n** Abimelech.
10: 3 a man from Gilead **n** Jair judged Israel for
13: 2 a man **n** Manoah from the tribe of Dan lived in the
13:24 When her son was born, they **n** him Samson.
15:17 the jawbone; and the place was **n** Jawbone Hill.
15:19 Then he **n** that place “The Spring of the One Who
16: 4 Later Samson fell in love with a woman **n** Delilah,
17: 1 A man **n** Micah lived in the hill country of
Ru 1: 4 One married a woman **n** Orpah, and the other a
woman **n** Ruth.
2: 1 and influential man in Bethlehem **n** Boaz,
2:19 “The man I worked with today is **n** Boaz.”
4:17 And they **n** him Obed. He became the father of
1Sa 1: 1 There was a man **n** Elkanah who lived in Ramah in
1:20 She **n** him Samuel, for she said, “I asked the
4:21 She **n** the child Ichabod—“Where is the glory?”—
4:21 She **n** him this because the Ark of God had been
6:14 The cart came into the field of a man **n** Joshua
7:12 He **n** it Ebenezer—“the stone of help”—for he
16: 1 Find a man **n** Jesse who lives there, for I have
17:12 Now David was the son of a man **n** Jesse,
25:44 to a man from Gallim **n** Palti son of Laish.
2Sa 3: 7 one of his father’s concubines, a woman **n** Rizpah.
4: 4 (Saul’s son Jonathan had a son **n** Mephibosheth,
5:20 So David **n** that place Baal-perazim (which means
6: 8 He **n** that place Perez-uzzah (which means
9: 2 He summoned a man **n** Ziba, who had been one of
9:12 Mephibosheth had a young son **n** Mica. And from
12:24 and gave birth to a son, and they **n** him Solomon.
13: 1 David’s son Absalom had a beautiful sister **n**
18:18 He **n** the monument after himself, and it is known
20: 1 Then a troublemaker **n** Sheba son of Bicri,
20:21 All I want is a man **n** Sheba son of Bicri from the
1Ki 4:13 including the Towns of Jair (**n** for Jair son of
7:13 then asked for a man **n** Huram to come from Tyre,
7:21 He **n** the one on the south Jakin, and the one on the
13: 2 A child **n** Josiah will be born into the dynasty of
21: 1 palace was a vineyard owned by a man **n** Naboth.
1Ch 1:19 The first was **n** Peleg—“division”—for during his
1:39 were Hori and Heman. Lotan’s sister was **n** Timna.
2:16 Their sisters were **n** Zeruiah and Abigail.
2:16 Zeruiah had three sons **n** Abishai, Joab,
2:17 Abigail married a man **n** Jether, an Ishmaelite, and
they had a son **n** Amasa.
2:18 Hezron’s son Caleb had two wives **n** Azubah
2:18 Azubah’s sons were **n** Jesher, Shobab, and Ardon.
2:19 married Ephrathah, and they had a son **n** Hur.
2:21 the daughter of Makir. They had a son **n** Segub.
2:24 his wife Abijah gave birth to a son **n** Ashhur (the
2:26 Jerahmeel had a second wife **n** Atarah. She was the
2:31 but Appaim had a son **n** Ishi. The son of Ishi was
Sheshan. Sheshan had a descendant **n** Ahlai.
2:32 Jada, had two sons **n** Jether and Jonathan.
2:33 but Jonathan had two sons **n** Peleth and Zaza.
2:34 He also had an Egyptian servant **n** Jarha.
2:35 to be the wife of Jarha, and they had a son **n** Attai.
2:49 and Gibea). Caleb also had a daughter **n** Acsah.
3: 9 David also had a daughter **n** Tamar.

3:19 He also had a daughter n Shelomith.
4: 5 of Tekoa) had two wives, n Helah and Naarah.
4: 9 There was a man n Jabez who was more
4: 9 His mother n him Jabez because his birth had been
4:18 Mered's Egyptian wife was n Bithiah, and she was
7:15 and Shuppim. Makir's sister was n Maacah.
7:16 Maacah, gave birth to a son whom she n Peresh.
7:23 Ephraim n him Beriah because of the tragedy his
7:24 Ephraim had a daughter n Sheerah. She built the
7:30 Ishvi, and Beriah. They had a sister n Serah.
7:32 Shomer, and Hotham. They had a sister n Shua.
8:30 and his oldest son was n Abdon. Jeiel's other sons
9:36 and his oldest son was n Abdon. Jeiel's other sons
13:11 He n that place Perez-uzzah (which means
14:11 So that place was n Baal-perazim (which means
23: 6 Then David divided the Levites into divisions n
26:12 These divisions of the gatekeepers were n for their
2Ch 2:13 "I am sending you a master craftsman n
3:17 He n the one on the south Jakin, and the one on the
14: 9 Once an Ethiopian n Zerah attacked Judah with an
24:26 the son of an Ammonite woman n Shimeath,
24:26 the son of a Moabite woman n Shomer.
28: 9 But a prophet of the LORD n Oded was there in
Ezr 5:14 and delivered into the safekeeping of a man n
7: 1 King Artaxerxes of Persia, there was a man n Ezra.
8:18 they sent us a man n Sherebiah, along with
Est 2: 5 there was a certain Jew n Mordecai son of Jair.
Job 1: 1 There was a man n Job who lived in the land of
42:14 He n his first daughter Jemimah, the second
Pr 9:13 The woman n Folly is loud and brash. She is
Isa 35: 8 It will be n the Highway of Holiness.
Eze 23: 4 The older girl was n Oholah, and her sister was
39:16 (There will be a town there n Hamonah—
48:31 be three gates, each one n after a tribe of Israel.
48:31 The first will be n for Reuben, the second for
48:32 the gates will be n for Joseph, Benjamin, and Dan.
48:33 will have gates n for Simeon, Issachar,
48:34 the gates will be n for Gad, Asher, and Naphtali.
Da 4: 8 (He was n Belteshazzar after my god, and the spirit
5:12 whom the king n Belteshazzar, has a sharp mind
Zec 11: 7 and n one Favor and the other Union.
Mt 1:25 until her son was born. And Joseph n him Jesus.
27:16 a notorious criminal in prison, a man n Barabbas.
27:32 they came across a man n Simon, who was from
Mk 6:22 also n Herodias, came in and performed a dance
10:46 A blind beggar n Bartimaeus (son of Timaeus)
15:21 A man n Simon, who was from Cyrene,
Lk 1:27 to a virgin n Mary. She was engaged to be married to a man n Joseph,
2:21 when the baby was circumcised, he was n Jesus,
2:25 Now there was a man n Simeon who lived in
5:27 he saw a tax collector n Levi sitting at his
8:41 And now a man n Jairus, a leader of the local
10:38 they came to a village where a woman n Martha
16:20 At his door lay a diseased beggar n Lazarus.
19: 2 There was a man there n Zacchaeus. He was one of
23:50 there was a good and righteous man n Joseph.
Jn 3: 1 a Jewish religious leader n Nicodemus, a Pharisee,
11: 1 A man n Lazarus was sick. He lived in Bethany
Ac 5: 1 There was also a man n Ananias who, with his
5:34 He was a Pharisee n Gamaliel, who was an expert
7:58 and laid them at the feet of a young man n Saul.
8: 9 A man n Simon had been a sorcerer there for many
9:10 Now there was a believer in Damascus n Ananias.
9:12 I have shown him a vision of a man n Ananias
9:33 There he met a man n Aeneas, who had been
9:36 There was a believer in Joppa n Tabitha (which in
10: 1 In Caesarea there lived a Roman army officer n
10: 5 men down to Joppa to find a man n Simon Peter.
11:28 One of them n Agabus stood up in one of the
12:13 and a servant girl n Rhoda came to open it.
13: 6 met a Jewish sorcerer, a false prophet n Bar-Jesus.
17:34 of the Council, a woman n Damaris, and others.
18: 2 There he became acquainted with a Jew n Aquila,
18:24 Meanwhile, a Jew n Apollos, an eloquent speaker
20: 9 Paul spoke on and on, a young man n Eutychus,
21:10 During our stay of several days, a man n Agabus,
22:12 A man n Ananias lived there. He was a godly man
27: 1 placed in the custody of an army officer n Julius,
27:16 We sailed behind a small island n Cauda,
Rev 19:11 And the one sitting on the horse was n Faithful

NAMELESS (1) [NAME]

Job 30: 8 They are n fools, outcasts of civilization.

NAMES (87) [NAME]

Ge 2:20 He gave n to all the livestock, birds, and wild
22:24 Their n were Tebah, Gaham, Tahash, and Maacah.
25:13 Here is a list, by their n and clans, of Ishmael's
25:16 the founders of twelve tribes that bore their n,
26:18 using the n Abraham had given them.
35:22 These are the n of the twelve sons of Jacob:
36:14 of Zibeon. Their n were Jeush, Jalam, and Korah.
36:20 These are the n of the tribes that descended from
36:43 These are the n of the clans of Esau, the ancestor
46: 8 These are the n of the Israelites, the descendants of
48:16 and the n of my grandfather Abraham and my
48:20 "The people of Israel will use your n to bless each
Ex 23:13 by any other gods. Do not even mention their n.
28: 9 and engrave on them the n of the tribes of Israel.
28:10 Six n will be on each stone, naming all the tribes in
28:11 Engrave these n in the same way a gemcutter
28:12 Aaron will carry these n before the LORD as a
28:29 Aaron will carry the n of the tribes of Israel on the
39: 6 The stones were engraved with the n of the tribes
Nu 1: 2 their clans and families. List the n of all the men
1: 5 and the n of the leaders chosen for the task:
2: 3[-4] These are the n of the tribes, their leaders,
2:10[-11] These are the n of the tribes, their leaders,
2:18[-19] These are the n of the tribes, their leaders,
2:25[-26] These are the n of the tribes, their leaders,
13: 4 These were the tribes and the n of the leaders:
13:16 These are the n of the men Moses sent to explore
26:33 but his daughters' n were Mahlah, Noah, Hoglah,
32:38 They changed the n of some of the towns they
34:19 These are the tribes and the n of the leaders:
Dt 7:24 and you will erase their n from the face of the
12: 3 Erase the n of their gods from those places!
20: 9 they will announce the n of the unit commanders.
29:20 and the LORD will erase their n from under
Jos 9:17 The n of these towns were Gibeon, Kephirah,
17: 3 Their n were Mahlah, Noah, Hoglah, Milcah,
23: 7 Do not even mention the n of their gods, much less
Jdg 8:14 and demanded that he write down the n of all the
1Sa 17:43 And he cursed David by the n of his gods.
2Sa 5:14 These are the n of David's sons who were born in
23: 8 These are the n of David's mightiest men. The first
1Ki 4: 8 These are the n of the twelve governors: / Ben-hur,
15:23 and the n of the cities he built are recorded in *The*
1Ch 2: 3 Their n were Er, Onan, and Shelah. But the oldest
2: 4 Their n were Perez and Zerah. So Judah had five
4:22 These n all come from ancient records.
4:33 and these n are recorded in their family genealogy.
4:38 These were the n of some of the leaders of
9:44 and their n were Azrikam, Bokeru, Ishmael,
14: 4 These are the n of David's sons who were born in
24: 6 acted as secretary and wrote down the n
25: 1 Here is a list of their n and their work:
26: 7 Their n were Othni, Rephael, Obed, and Elzabad.
Ezr 5: 4 They also asked for a list of the n of all the people
5:10 And we demanded their n so that we could tell you
Ne 9: 4 Their n were Jeshua, Bani, Kadmiel, Shebaniah,
9:38 On this sealed document are the n of our princes
10: 1 was ratified and sealed with the following n:
11: 3 Here is a list of the n of the provincial officials
Est 1:14 The n of these men were Carshena, Shethar,
Ps 9: 5 the wicked; / you have wiped out their n forever.
16: 4 their sacrifices / or even speak the n of their gods.
69:28 Erase their n from the Book of Life; / don't let
Isa 4: 3 All those whose n are written down, who have
8:18 and the children the LORD has given me have n
Jer 40: 8 These are the n of the leaders who came:
La 3:61 LORD, you have heard the vile n they call me.
Eze 13: 9 I will blot their n from Israel's record books,
Da 1: 7 official renamed them with these Babylonian n:
Hos 2:17 of Baal; even their n will no longer be spoken.
Zec 13: 2 so that even the n of the idols will be forgotten.
Mal 3:16 written to record the n of those who feared him
Mt 10: 2 Here are the n of the twelve apostles: / first Simon
Mk 3:16 These are the n of the twelve he chose: / Simon (he
Lk 6:13 twelve of them to be apostles. Here are their n:
10:20 because your n are registered as citizens of
Ac 18:15 a question of words and n and your Jewish laws,
Php 4: 3 whose n are written in the Book of Life.
Heb 1: 4 the name God gave him is far greater than their n.
12:23 firstborn children, whose n are written in heaven.
Rev 3: 5 I will never erase their n from the Book of Life,
13: 1 And written on each head were n that blasphemed
13: 8 They are the ones whose n were not written in the
17: 8 whose n were not written in the Book of Life from
21:12 And the n of the twelve tribes of Israel were
21:14 and on them were written the n of the twelve
21:27 but only those whose n are written in the Lamb's

NAMING (1) [NAME]

Ex 28:10 n all the tribes in the order of their ancestors'

NAOMI (30) [NAOMI'S]

Ru 1: 2 man's name was Elimelech, and his wife was N.
1: 3 Elimelech died and N was left with her two sons.
1: 5 This left N alone, without her husband or sons.
1: 6 Then N heard in Moab that the LORD had
1: 6 So N and her daughters-in-law got ready to leave
1: 8 on the way, N said to her two daughters-in-law,
1:11 But N replied, "Why should you go on with me?
1:14 But Ruth insisted on staying with N.
1:15 "See," N said to her, "your sister-in-law has gone
1:18 So when N saw that Ruth had made up her mind to
1:19 their arrival. "Is it really N?" the women asked.
1:20 "Don't call me N," she told them. "Instead,
1:21 Why should you call me N when the LORD has
1:22 So N returned from Moab, accompanied by her
2: 2 One day Ruth said to N, "Let me go out into the
2: 2 And N said, "All right, my daughter, go ahead."
2: 6 young woman from Moab who came back with N.
2:19 "So much!" N exclaimed. "Where did you gather
2:20 LORD bless him!" N told her daughter-in-law.
2:22 is wonderful!" N exclaimed. "Do as he said.
3: 1 One day N said to Ruth, "My daughter, it's time
3:16 N asked, "What happened, my daughter?"
3:16 Ruth told N everything Boaz had done for her,
3:18 Then N said to her, "Just be patient, my daughter,
4: 3 "You know N, who came back from Moab.
4: 5 your purchase of the land from N also requires that
4: 9 have bought from N all the property of Elimelech,
4:14 And the women of the town said to N,
4:16 N took care of the baby and cared for him as if he
4:17 women said, "Now at last N has a son again!"

NAOMI'S (1) [NAOMI]

Ru 2: 1 who was a relative of N husband, Elimelech.

NAP (3)

2Sa 4: 5 home around noon as he was taking a n.
11: 2 one afternoon David got out of bed after taking a n
Lk 8:23 On the way across, Jesus lay down for a n,

NAPHISH (2) [NAPHISHITES]

Ge 25:15 Hadad, Tema, Jetur, N, and Kedemah.
1Ch 1:31 Jetur, N, and Kedemah. These were the sons of

NAPHISHITES (1) [NAPHISH]

1Ch 5:19 the Jeturites, the N, and the Nodabites.

NAPHOTH-DOR (4) [DOR]

Jos 11: 2 in the western foothills; the kings of N on the west;
12:23 The king of Dor in the city of N / The king of
17:11 Ibleam, Dor (that is, N), Endor, Taanach,
1Ki 4:11 Ben-abinadab, in N. (He was married to Taphath,

NAPHTALI (52) [NAPHTALI'S]

Ge 30: 8 Rachel named him N, for she said, "I have had an
35:25 sons of Bilhah, Rachel's servant, were Dan and N.
46:24 The sons of N were Jahzeel, Guni, Jezer,
49:21 "N is a deer let loose, / producing magnificent
Ex 1: 4 Dan, N, Gad, and Asher.
Nu 1:15 N | Ahira son of Enan
1:42[-43] N | 53,400
2:25[-26] and N are to camp on the north side of the
2:29[-30] N | Ahira son of Enan | 53,400
7:78 leader of the tribe of N, presented his offering.
10:27 The tribe of N was led by Ahira son of Enan.
13:14 N | Nahbi son of Vophsi
26:48 were the clans descended from the sons of N:
26:50 The men from all the clans of N numbered 45,400.
34:28 N | Pedahel son of Ammihud
Dt 27:13 and N must stand on Mount Ebal to proclaim a
33:23 Moses said this about the tribe of N:
33:23 "O N, you are rich in favor / and full of the
34: 2 all the land of N; the land of Ephraim
Jos 19:32 of land went to the families of the tribe of N.
19:39 the inheritance of the families of the tribe of N.
20: 7 Kedesh of Galilee, in the hill country of N;
21: 6 Asher, N, and the half-tribe of Manasseh in
21:32 From the tribe of N they received Kedesh in
Jdg 1:33 The tribe of N also failed to drive out the residents
1:33 forced to work as slaves for the people of N.
4: 6 of Abinoam, who lived in Kedesh in the land of N.
4: 6 ten thousand warriors from the tribes of N
4:10 Barak called together the tribes of Zebulun and N,
5:18 risked his life, / as did N, on the battlefield.
6:35 Asher, Zebulun, and N, summoning their warriors,
7:23 Then Gideon sent for the warriors of N, Asher,
1Ki 4:15 Ahimaaz, in N. (He was married to Basemath,
7:14 since his mother was a widow from the tribe of N,
15:20 and all Kinnereth, with all the land of N.
2Ki 15:29 conquered the regions of Gilead, Galilee, and N,
1Ch 2: 2 Dan, Joseph, Benjamin, N, Gad, and Asher.
6:62 Asher, N, and from the Bashan area of Manasseh,
6:76 From the territory of N, they were given Kedesh in
7:13 The sons of N were Jahzeel, Guni, Jezer,
12:34 From the tribe of N, there were 1,000 officers
12:40 and N brought food on donkeys, camels, mules,
27:19 son of Obadiah / N | Jeremoth son of Azriel
2Ch 16: 4 Abel-beth-maacah, and all the store cities in N.
34: 6 Ephraim, and Simeon, even as far as N.
Ps 68:27 from Judah / and all the rulers of Zebulun and N.
Isa 9: 1 The land of Zebulun and N will soon be humbled,
Eze 48: 4 Then comes Manasseh south of N, and its territory
48:34 the gates will be named for Gad, Asher, and N.
Mt 4:13 the Sea of Galilee, in the region of Zebulun and N.
4:15 "In the land of Zebulun and of N, / beside the sea,
Rev 7: 6 from Asher | 12,000 / from N | 12,000

NAPHTALI'S (1) [NAPHTALI]

Eze 48: 3 N land lies south of Asher's, also extending from

NAPHTUHITES (2)

Ge 10:13 ancestor of the Ludites, Anamites, Lehabites, N,
1Ch 1:11 ancestor of the Ludites, Anamites, Lehabites, N,

NAPKIN [KJV] See CLOTH, HEADCLOTH

NARCISSUS (1)

Ro 16:11 Greet the Christians in the household of N.

NARD (2)

SS 4:14 n and saffron, calamus and cinnamon, myrrh
Jn 12: 3 jar of expensive perfume made from essence of n,

NARROW (6) [NARROWED, NARROWER, NARROWING]

Nu 22:26 a place so n that the donkey could not get by at all.
1Ki 6: 4 Solomon also made n, recessed windows
Isa 28:20 short to lie on. The blankets are too n to cover you.
Mt 7:13 can enter God's Kingdom only through the n gate.
7:14 and the road is n, and only a few ever find it.
Lk 13:24 "The door to heaven is n. Work hard to get in,

NARROWED (3) [NARROW]

Nu 22:24 where the road n between two vineyard walls.
Pr 16:30 With n eyes, they plot evil; without a word,
Eze 40:16 There were recessed windows that n inward

NARROWER (1) [NARROW]
Eze 42: 5 Each of the two upper levels of rooms was **n** than

NARROWING (1) [NARROW]
Eze 41: 7 corresponding to the **n** of the Temple wall as it

NATHAN (43)
2Sa 5:14 born in Jerusalem: Shimea, Shobab, **N**, Solomon,
7: 2 David summoned **N** the prophet. "Look!"
7: 3 **N** replied, "Go ahead and do what you have in
7: 4 But that same night the LORD said to **N**,
7:17 So **N** went back to David and told him everything
12: 1 So the LORD sent **N** the prophet to tell David this
12: 7 Then **N** said to David, "You are that man!
12:13 Then David confessed to **N**, "I have sinned against
12:13 **N** replied, "Yes, but the LORD has forgiven you,
12:15 After **N** returned to his home, the LORD made
12:25 and sent word through **N** the prophet that his name
23:36 Igal son of **N** from Zobah; / Bani from Gad;
1Ki 1: 8 son of Jehoiada, **N** the prophet, Shimei, Rei,
1:10 But he did not invite **N** the prophet, or Benaiah,
1:11 Then **N** the prophet went to Bathsheba,
1:22 still speaking with the king, **N** the prophet arrived.
1:23 told him, "**N** the prophet is here to see you."
1:23 **N** went in and bowed low before the king.
1:32 "Call Zadok the priest, **N** the prophet,
1:34 and **N** the prophet are to anoint him king over
1:38 So Zadok the priest, **N** the prophet, Benaiah son of
1:44 **N** the prophet, and Benaiah son of Jehoiada,
1:45 and **N** have anointed him as the new king.
4: 5 Azariah son of **N** presided over the district
4: 5 Zabud son of **N**, a priest, was a trusted adviser to
1Ch 2:36 Attai was the father of **N**. / **N** was the father of Zabad.
3: 5 included Shimea, Shobab, **N**, and Solomon.
11:38 Joel, the brother of **N**; / Mibhar son of Hagri;
14: 4 born in Jerusalem: Shimea, Shobab, **N**, Solomon,
17: 1 was settled in his palace, he said to **N** the prophet,
17: 2 **N** replied, "Go ahead with what you have in mind,
17: 3 But that same night God said to **N**,
17:15 So **N** went back to David and told him everything
29:29 *The Record of* **N** *the Prophet,* and *The Record of*
2Ch 9:29 are recorded in *The Record of* **N** *the Prophet*
29:25 through Gad, the king's seer, and the prophet **N**.
Ezr 8:16 Ariel, Shemaiah, Elnathan, Jarib, Elnathan, **N**,
10:39 Shelemiah, **N**, Adaiah,
Ps 51: T regarding the time **N** the prophet came to him after
Zec 12:12 of David will mourn, along with the family of **N**,
Lk 3:31 Mattatha was the son of **N**. / **N** was the son of David.

NATHAN-MELECH (1)
2Ki 23:11 They were near the quarters of **N** the eunuch,

NATHANAEL (5)
Jn 1:45 Philip went off to look for **N** and told him,
1:46 "Nazareth!" exclaimed **N**. "Can anything good
1:48 **N** asked. And Jesus replied, "I could see you
1:49 **N** replied, "Teacher, you are the Son of God—
21: 2 **N** from Cana in Galilee, the sons of Zebedee,

NATION (225) [INTERNATIONAL, NATION'S, NATIONAL, NATIONALITY, NATIONS, NATIONWIDE]
ENTIRE NATION (7) Nu 26:3,10; 32:15; 2Sa 3:12; 1Ch 28:21; 29:25; Jn 11:51

EVERY NATION (19) 1Ki 4:34; 10:24; 18:10; 2Ch 9:23; Ps 22:27; 46:10; 97:6; 98:2; Isa 66:20; Jer 24:9; 25:17; 26:6; 27:13; 29:18; Mk 13:10; Ac 10:35; Rev 7:9; 14:6; 17:15

WHOLE NATION (7) Nu 3:41; Eze 8:17; Mal 3:9; Jn 11:48,50; Heb 11:12; Jude 1:5

Ge 10:32 listed **n** by **n** according to their lines of
12: 2 I will cause you to become the father of a great **n**.
15:14 But I will punish the **n** that enslaves them, and in
17: 2 I will guarantee to make you into a mighty **n**."
17: 4 I will make you the father of not just one **n**, but a
17:20 I will cause him to multiply and become a great **n**.
18:18 "For Abraham will become a great and mighty **n**,
19:37 He became the ancestor of the **n** now known as the
19:38 He became the ancestor of the **n** now known as the
21:13 But I will make a **n** of the descendants of Hagar's
21:18 for I will make a great **n** from his descendants."
25:23 One **n** will be stronger than the other;
26:24 many descendants, and they will become a great **n**.
35:11 the earth! Become a great **n**, even many nations.
45: 7 families alive so that you will become a great **n**.
46: 3 for I will see to it that you become a great **n** there.
48:16 Isaac. And may they become a mighty **n**."
49: 7 their descendants / throughout the **n** of Israel.
Ex 19: 6 will be to me a kingdom of priests, my holy **n**.'
32:10 make you, Moses, into a great **n** instead of them."
33:13 don't forget that this **n** is your very own people."
34:10 done before anywhere in all the earth or in any **n**.
Nu 3:41 the firstborn livestock of the whole **n** of Israel."
14:12 Then I will make you into a **n** far greater
14:27 "How long will this wicked **n** complain about me?
23:13 There you will see only a portion of the **n** of Israel.
26: 3 At that time the entire **n** of Israel was camped on
26:10 This served as a warning to the entire **n** of Israel.
32:15 will be responsible for destroying this entire **n**!"
Dt 4: 6 'What other **n** is as wise and prudent as this!'
4: 7 For what great **n** has a god as near to them as the
4: 8 And what great **n** has laws and regulations as fair
4:33 Has any **n** ever heard the voice of God speaking
4:34 Has any other god taken one **n** for himself by
7:13 and bless you and make you into a great **n**.
9:14 Then I will make a mighty **n** of your descendants,
9:14 a **n** larger and more powerful than they are.'
10:15 chose you, their descendants, above every other **n**.
13:17 have compassion on you and make you a great **n**,
26: 5 in Egypt they became a mighty and numerous **n**.
26:19 you do, he will make you greater than any other **n**.
26:19 You will be a **n** that is holy to the LORD your
28:33 A foreign **n** you have never heard about will eat
28:36 and the king you crowned to a **n** unknown to you
28:49 "The LORD will bring a distant **n** against you
28:49 It is a **n** whose language you do not understand,
28:50 and heartless **n** that shows no respect for the old
30:16 If you do this, you will live and become a great **n**,
32:28 "Israel is a **n** that lacks sense; / the people are
Ru 4:11 from whom all the **n** of Israel descended!
1Sa 12:22 great name. He made you a special **n** for himself.
15: 2 'I have decided to settle accounts with the **n** of
15: 3 and completely destroy the entire Amalekite **n**—
2Sa 1:12 and for the LORD's army and the **n** of Israel,
3:12 and I will help turn the entire **n** of Israel over to
7:23 What other **n** on earth is like Israel? What other **n**, O God, have you redeemed from
12:17 The leaders of the **n** pleaded with him to get up
21: 2 but were all that was left of the **n** of the Amorites.
24:15 Seventy thousand people died throughout the **n**.
1Ki 3: 8 a **n** so great they are too numerous to count!
3: 9 For who by himself is able to govern this great **n** of
4:34 And kings from every **n** sent their ambassadors to
5: 7 a wise son to be king of the great **n** of Israel."
10:24 People from every **n** came to visit him and to hear
18:10 your God that the king has searched every **n**
18:10 King Ahab forced the king of that **n** to swear to the
2Ki 1: 1 the **n** of Moab declared its independence from
17: 7 This disaster came upon the **n** of Israel
18:35 What god of any **n** has ever been able to save its
1Ch 5: 2 most powerful tribe and provided a ruler for the **n**,
17:21 What other **n** on earth is like Israel? What other **n**, O God, have you redeemed from
28:21 the leaders and the entire **n** are at your command."
29:25 so the entire **n** of Israel stood in awe of him,
2Ch 1:10 for who is able to govern this great **n** of yours?"
9:23 Kings from every **n** came to visit him and to hear
15: 5 to travel. Problems troubled the **n** on every hand.
15: 6 **N** fought against **n**, and city against city,
19: 5 He appointed judges throughout the **n** in all the
24:23 and Jerusalem and killed all the leaders of the **n**.
32:15 no god of any **n** has ever yet been able to rescue
35:21 I only want to fight the **n** with which I am at war.
Ezr 6:12 or **n** that violates this command and destroys this
9:12 these things, we would become a prosperous **n**.
Ne 13:26 "There was no king from any **n** who could
Est 3: 8 Their laws are different from those of any other **n**,
Ps 22:27 People from every **n** will bow down before him.
33:12 What joy for the **n** whose God is the LORD,
46:10 that I am God! / I will be honored by every **n**.
74:18 LORD. / A foolish **n** has dishonored your name.
83: 4 "Come," they say, "let us wipe out Israel as a **n**.
97: 6 declare his righteousness; / every **n** sees his glory.
98: 2 and has revealed his righteousness to every **n**!
102:18 so that a **n** yet to be created will praise the
105:20 the ruler of the **n** opened his prison door.
107:32 the congregation / and before the leaders of the **n**.
147:14 He sends peace across your **n** / and satisfies you
147:20 He has not done this with any other **n**; / they do not
Pr 11:14 Without wise leadership, a **n** falls; with many
14:28 is a king's glory; a dwindling **n** is his doom.
14:34 Godliness exalts a **n**, but sin is a disgrace to any
28: 2 When there is moral rot within a **n**, its government
29: 4 A just king gives stability to his **n**, but one who
Isa 1: 4 Oh, what a sinful **n** they are! They are loaded
7:17 a terrible curse on you, your **n**, and your family.
10: 6 will enslave my people, who are a godless **n**.
14:20 for you have destroyed your **n** and slaughtered
26:15 praise you, LORD! / You have made our **n** great;
27:11 Israel is a foolish and stupid **n**, for its people have
34: 5 fall upon Edom, the **n** I have completely destroyed.
36:20 What god of any **n** has ever been able to save its
49: 7 to the one who is despised and rejected by a **n**,
51: 2 But when I blessed him, he became a great **n**."
54:15 If any **n** comes to fight you, it will not be because I
58: 2 You would almost think this was a righteous **n** that
60:22 The tiniest group will become a mighty **n**. I,
66: 8 as this? Has a **n** ever been born in a single day?
66: 8 the baby will be born; the **n** will come forth.
66: 9 Would I ever bring this **n** to the point of birth
66: 9 I would never keep this **n** from being born,"
66:20 the remnant of your people back from every **n**.
Jer 2:11 Has any **n** ever exchanged its gods for another god,
2:14 "Why has Israel become a **n** of slaves? Why has
5: 9 "Should I not avenge myself against a **n** such as
5:15 O Israel, I will bring a distant **n** against you,"
5:15 "It is a mighty **n**, an ancient **n**, a people
5:29 "Should I not avenge myself against a **n** such as
6: 1 army is coming from the north to destroy this **n**.
6:22 A great **n** is rising against you from far-off lands.
7:28 'This is the **n** whose people will not obey the
8: 3 And the people of this evil **n** who survive will wish
9: 9 "Should I not avenge myself against a **n** such as
12:12 kills people from one end of the **n** to the other.
12:15 own lands again, each **n** to its own inheritance.
12:17 But any **n** who refuses to obey me will be uprooted
17:25 then this **n** will continue forever. There will always
18: 7 If I announce that a certain **n** or kingdom is to be
18: 8 but then that **n** renounces its evil ways, I will not
18: 9 I will build up and plant a certain **n** or kingdom,
18:10 but then that **n** turns to evil and refuses to obey me,
18:10 I will not bless that **n** as I had said I would.
24: 9 an object of horror and evil to every **n** on earth.
25:17 drink from it—every **n** the LORD sent me to.
25:32 "Look! Disaster will fall upon **n** after **n**!
26: 6 an object of cursing in every **n** on earth.' "
26:20 disaster against the city and **n** as Jeremiah did.
27: 8 I will punish any **n** that refuses to be his slave,
27: 8 and disease upon that **n** until Babylon has
27:11 But the people of any **n** that submits to the king of
27:13 which the LORD will bring against every **n** that
29:18 In every **n** where I send them, I will make them an
30:19 and make of them a great and honored **n**.
30:20 I will establish them as a **n** before me, and I will
31:28 In the past I uprooted and tore down this **n**.
33:24 that Israel is not worthy to be counted as a **n**.
45: 4 I will destroy this **n** that I built. I will uproot what I
48: 2 they say, 'we will cut her off from being a **n**.'
48:42 Moab will no longer be a **n**, for she has boasted
50: 3 For a **n** will attack her from the north and bring
50:41 A great **n** and many kings are rising against you
La 4:20 the LORD's anointed, the very life of our **n**,
4:20 we could hold our own against any **n** on earth!
Eze 2: 3 he said, "I am sending you to the **n** of Israel, a **n** that is rebelling against me.
5:15 the LORD turns against a **n** in furious rebuke.
8:17 leading the whole **n** into violence, thumbing their
13: 5 to strengthen the breaks in the walls around the **n**.
25: 7 I will cut you off from being a **n** and destroy you
31: 3 You are as Assyria was—a great and mighty **n**.
31:11 I handed it over to a mighty **n** that destroyed it as
31:14 Let no other **n** proudly exult in its own prosperity,
36:14 never again devour your people or bereave your **n**,
36:15 longer be shamed by them or cause your **n** to fall,
37:22 I will unify them into one **n** in the land. One king
Da 3: 7 the people, whatever their race or **n** or language,
3:29 If any people, whatever their race or **n** or language,
4: 1 and **n** and language throughout the world:
6:25 and **n** and language throughout the world:
7:14 so that people of every race and **n** and language
12: 1 the archangel who stands guard over your **n**,
Hos 1:10 when Israel will prosper and become a great **n**.
9: 7 for the **n** is burdened with sin and shows only
10:13 believing that great armies could make your **n**
Joel 3: 8 sell them to the peoples of Arabia, a **n** far away.
Am 6: 6 caring nothing at all that your **n** is going to ruin.
6:14 I am about to bring an enemy **n** against you,"
7: 2 Israel will not survive, for we are only a small **n**."
7: 5 Israel will not survive, for we are only a small **n**."
9: 8 am watching this sinful **n** of Israel, and I will
Mic 4: 7 but I will make them strong again, a mighty **n**.
Hab 1: 6 and violent **n** who will march across the world
Zep 2: 1 Gather together and pray, you shameless **n**.
Hag 2:14 "That is how it is with this people and this **n**,
Zec 11: 8 with these sheep—this **n**—and they hated me, too.
11:16 This will illustrate how I will give this **n** a
14:17 And any **n** anywhere in the world that refuses to
Mal 2:12 May the LORD cut off from the **n** of Israel every
3: 9 a curse, for your whole **n** has been cheating me.
Mt 21:43 and given to a **n** that will produce the proper fruit.
Mk 13:10 the Good News must first be preached to every **n**.
Jn 11:48 the whole **n** will follow him, and then the Roman
11:48 and destroy both our Temple and our **n**."
11:50 Why should the whole **n** be destroyed? Let this one
11:51 This prophecy that Jesus should die for the entire **n**
Ac 4: 8 said to them, "Leaders and elders of our **n**,
7: 7 'But I will punish the **n** that enslaves them,'
7: 8 the father of the twelve patriarchs of the Jewish **n**.
10:35 In every **n** he accepts those who fear him and do
13:17 "The God of this **n** of Israel chose our ancestors
Ro 4: 1 humanly speaking, the founder of our Jewish **n**.
1Co 10:18 And think about the **n** of Israel; all who eat the
Heb 11:12 And so a whole **n** came from this one man,
11:12 a **n** with so many people that, like the stars of the
1Pe 2: 9 of priests, God's holy **n**, his very own possession.
Jude 1: 5 that even though the Lord rescued the whole **n** of
Rev 5: 9 from every tribe and language and people and **n**.
7: 9 from every **n** and tribe and people and language,
13: 7 over every tribe and people and language and **n**.
14: 6 this world—to every **n**, tribe, language, and people.
17:15 is sitting represent masses of people of every **n**

NATION'S (2) [NATION]
Ps 105:29 He turned the **n** water into blood, / poisoning all
Isa 3: 2 He will destroy all the **n** leaders—the heroes,

NATIONAL (2) [NATION]
Ge 50: 3 and there was a period of **n** mourning for seventy
Eze 17:14 with Babylon could Israel maintain her **n** identity.

NATIONALITY (4) [NATION]
Est 2:10 Esther had not told anyone of her **n** and family
2:20 Esther continued to keep her **n** and family
8:11 and annihilate anyone of any **n** or province who
Jnh 1: 8 What country are you from? What is your **n**?"

NATIONS (557) [NATION]
ALL NATIONS (15) Ge 49:10; Dt 7:7; Ps 72:11,17; Isa 42:6; 56:7; 60:3; 66:18; Jer 3:17; Mal 3:12; Mt 24:14; Mk 11:17; Gal 3:8; Rev 12:5; 15:4

OTHER NATIONS (42) Ex 23:24; Nu 23:9; Dt 7:7; 8:20; 9:4; 17:14; 18:12; 29:18; 32:21; Jos 24:18; 1Sa 8:5; 2Sa 7:14;

8:11; 2Ki 18:33; 19:12; 1Ch 16:26; 18:11; 2Ch 32:17; Ps 96:5; 111:6; 126:2; Isa 36:18; 37:12; 54:3; Jer 10:2,2; 25:9; 36:2; Eze 23:30; 25:8; 31:18; 32:19; 34:28; 36:13; Am 9:7,9; Mic 5:8; Zec 1:15; 14:18,19; Mal 1:11; Ro 10:19

Ge 10:20 to their tribes, languages, territories, and **n**.
10:31 to their tribes, languages, territories, and **n**.
10:32 The earth was populated with the people of these **n**
17: 4 father of not just one nation, but a multitude of **n**!
17: 5 as Abraham, for you will be the father of many **n**.
17: 6 of descendants who will represent many **n**.
17:16 and she will become the mother of many **n**.
18:18 and all the **n** of the earth will be blessed through
22:18 all the **n** of the earth will be blessed—
25:23 "The sons in your womb will become two rival **n**.
26: 4 And through your descendants all the **n** of the earth
27:29 May many **n** become your servants. May you be
28: 3 your descendants become a great assembly of **n**!
35:11 fill the earth! Become a great nation, even many **n**.
48: 4 He said to me, 'I will make you a multitude of **n**,
48:19 His descendants will become a multitude of **n**!"
49:10 whom it belongs, / the one whom all **n** will obey.
Ex 15:14 The **n** will hear and tremble; / anguish will grip the
19: 5 special treasure from among all the **n** of the earth;
23:24 Do not worship the gods of these other **n** or serve
34:24 I will drive out the **n** that stand in your way
Lev 26:33 I will scatter you among the **n** and attack you with
26:38 You will die among the foreign **n** and be devoured
26:45 whom I brought out of Egypt while all the **n**
Nu 14:15 the **n** that have heard of your fame will say,
23: 9 who live by themselves, / set apart from other **n**.
24: 8 He devours all the **n** that oppose him,
24:20 this prophecy: / "Amalek was the greatest of **n**,
Dt 3:22 Do not be afraid of the **n** there, for the LORD
4: 6 your wisdom and intelligence to the surrounding **n**.
4:27 For the LORD will scatter you among the **n**,
4:38 He drove out **n** far greater than you, so he could
6:14 must not worship any of the gods of neighboring **n**,
7: 1 he will clear away many **n** ahead of you:
7: 1 These seven **n** are all more powerful than you.
7: 2 When the LORD your God hands these **n** over to
7: 7 because you were larger or greater than other **n**,
for you were the smallest of all **n**!
7:14 You will be blessed above all the **n** of the earth.
7:16 "You must destroy all the **n** the LORD your God
7:17 'How can we ever conquer these **n** that are
7:21 "No, do not be afraid of those **n**, for the LORD
7:22 The LORD your God will drive those **n** out ahead
8:20 Just as the LORD has destroyed other **n** in your
9: 1 to occupy the land belonging to **n** much greater
9: 4 because of the wickedness of the other **n** that he is
9: 5 The LORD your God will drive these **n** out ahead
11:23 Then the LORD will drive out all the **n** in your
12: 2 "When you drive out the **n** that live there,
12:29 "When the LORD your God destroys the **n**
12:30 Do not say, 'How do these **n** worship their gods?
12:31 These **n** have committed many detestable acts that
13: 2 'Come, let us worship the gods of foreign **n**,'
14: 2 his own special treasure from all the **n** of the earth.
15: 6 You will lend money to many **n** but will never
15: 6 You will rule many **n**, but they will not rule over
17:14 'We ought to have a king like the other **n** around
18: 9 imitate the detestable customs of the **n** living there.
18:12 because the other **n** have done these things that the
19: 1 "The LORD your God will soon destroy the **n**
20:15 only to distant towns, not to the towns of **n** nearby.
20:16 "As for the towns of the **n** the LORD your God is
23: 4 These **n** did not welcome you with food and water
28: 1 God will exalt you above all the **n** of the world.
28:10 Then all the **n** of the world will see that you are a
28:12 You will lend to many **n**, but you will never need
28:37 and a mockery among all the **n** to which the
28:64 For the LORD will scatter you among all the **n**
28:65 There among those **n** you will find no place of
29:16 and how we traveled through the lands of enemy **n**
29:18 LORD our God to worship these gods of other **n**,
29:24 The surrounding **n** will ask, 'Why has the LORD
30: 1 **n** to which the LORD your God has exiled you.
30: 3 and gather you back from all the **n** where he has
31: 3 He will destroy the **n** living there, and you will
31: 4 The LORD will destroy the **n** living in the land,
32: 8 When the Most High assigned lands to the **n**,
32:21 Now I will rouse their jealousy by blessing other **n**;
33:17 He will gore distant **n**, / driving them to the ends of
Jos 4:24 so that all the **n** of the earth might know the power
23: 4 inheritance all the land of the **n** yet unconquered,
23: 9 has driven out great and powerful **n** for you,
23:12 and intermarry with the survivors of these **n**
24:18 and the other **n** living here in the land.
Jdg 2:21 I will no longer drive out the **n** that Joshua left
2:23 That is why the LORD did not quickly drive the **n**
3: 1 The LORD left certain **n** in the land to test those
3: 3 These were the **n**: the Philistines (those living
1Sa 8: 5 like you. Give us a king like all the other **n** have."
8:20 "We want to be like the **n** around us. Our king will
10:18 and from all of the **n** that were oppressing you.
2Sa 7:10 It will be their own land where wicked **n** won't
7:14 my son. If he sins, I will use other **n** to punish him.
7:23 and drove out the **n** and gods that stood in their
8:11 and gold he had set apart from the other **n** he had
22:44 You preserved me as the ruler over **n**; / people I
22:48 those who harm me; / he subdues the **n** under me
22:50 For this, O LORD, I will praise you among the **n**;
1Ki 4:31 His fame spread throughout all the surrounding **n**.
5: 3 of the many wars he waged with surrounding **n**.
8:53 **n** of the earth to be your own special possession."
9: 7 an object of mockery and ridicule among the **n**.
9:21 These were descendants of the **n** that Israel had not
11: 2 his people not to intermarry with those **n**,
14:24 **n** the LORD had driven from the land ahead of
2Ki 16: 3 He imitated the detestable practices of the pagan **n**
17: 8 They had imitated the practices of the pagan **n** the
17:11 just like the **n** the LORD had driven from the land
17:15 They followed the example of the **n** around them,
17:33 religious customs of the **n** from which they came.
18:33 Have the gods of any other **n** ever saved their
19:12 Have the gods of other **n** rescued them—
19:12 such **n** as Gozan, Haran, Rezeph, and the people of
19:17 the kings of Assyria have destroyed all these **n**,
19:18 And they have thrown the gods of these **n** into the
21: 2 imitating the detestable practices of the pagan **n**
21: 9 **n** whom the LORD had destroyed when the
1Ch 5:25 They worshiped the gods of the **n** that God had
14:17 and the LORD caused all the **n** to fear David.
16:20 They wandered back and forth between **n**,
16:24 Publish his glorious deeds among the **n**.
16:26 The gods of other **n** are merely idols,
16:28 O **n** of the world, recognize the LORD,
16:31 Tell all the **n** that the LORD is king.
16:35 Gather and rescue us from among the **n**,
17: 9 It will be their own land where wicked **n** won't
17:21 and drove out the **n** that stood in their way.
18:11 and gold he had taken from the other **n** he had
22:18 "He has given you peace with the surrounding **n**.
2Ch 7:20 I will make it a spectacle of contempt among the **n**.
8: 8 These were descendants of the **n** that Israel had not
13: 9 appointed your own priests, just like the pagan **n**.
20:10 You would not let our ancestors invade those **n**
28: 3 He imitated the detestable practices of the pagan **n**
32:13 Were any of the gods of those **n** able to rescue
32:17 "Just as the gods of all the other **n** failed to rescue
32:23 became highly respected among the surrounding **n**,
33: 2 imitating the detestable practices of the pagan **n**
33: 9 **n** whom the LORD had destroyed when the
36:14 followed the pagan practices of the surrounding **n**,
Ezr 9:12 their daughters, and not to help those **n** in any way.
Ne 1: 8 'If you sin, I will scatter you among the **n**.
5: 9 God in order to avoid being mocked by enemy **n**?
6:16 our enemies and the surrounding **n** heard about it,
9:22 our ancestors conquer great kingdoms and many **n**,
9:24 You subdued whole **n** before them. Even the kings
Job 12:23 He raises up **n**, and he destroys them. He makes **n**
expand, and he abandons them.
Ps 2: 1 Why do the **n** rage? / Why do the people waste
2: 8 and I will give you the **n** as your inheritance,
7: 7 Gather the **n** before you. / Sit on your throne high
7: 8 The LORD passes judgment on the **n**.
9: 5 You have rebuked the **n** and destroyed the wicked;
9: 8 world with justice / and rule the **n** with fairness.
9:15 The **n** have fallen into the pit they dug for others.
9:17 This is the fate of all the **n** who ignore God.
9:19 defy you! / Let the **n** be judged in your presence!
18:43 You appointed me as the ruler over **n**;
18:47 those who harm me; / he subdues the **n** under me
18:49 For this, O LORD, I will praise you among the **n**;
20: 7 Some **n** boast of their armies and weapons,
20: 8 Those **n** will fall down and collapse, / but we will
22:28 For the LORD is king! / He rules all the **n**.
33:10 The LORD shatters the plans of the **n**
44: 2 You drove out the pagan **n** / and gave all the land
44:11 you have scattered us among the **n**.
44:13 an object of scorn and derision to the **n** around us.
45: 5 The **n** fall before you, / lying down beneath your
45:17 Therefore, the **n** will praise you forever and ever.
46: 6 The **n** are in an uproar, / and kingdoms crumble!
47: 3 He subdues the **n** before us, / putting our enemies
47: 8 God reigns above the **n**, / sitting on his holy
57: 9 the people. / I will sing your praises among the **n**.
59: 5 the God of Israel, / rise up to punish hostile **n**.
59: 8 you laugh at them. / You scoff at all the hostile **n**.
65: 7 and silenced the shouting of the **n**.
66: 7 He watches every movement of the **n**; / let no rebel
67: 3 May the **n** praise you, O God. / Yes, may all the **n**
praise you.
67: 4 How glad the **n** will be, singing for joy,
67: 5 May the **n** praise you, O God. / Yes, may all the **n**
praise you.
68:30 Rebuke these enemy **n**— / these wild animals
68:30 tribute from us. / Scatter the **n** that delight in war.
72:11 will bow before him, / and all **n** will serve him.
72:17 May all **n** be blessed through him / and bring him
77:14 demonstrate your awesome power among the **n**.
78:55 He drove out the **n** before them; / he gave them
79: 1 O God, pagan **n** have conquered your land,
79: 6 Pour out your wrath on the **n** that refuse to
79:10 Why should pagan **n** be allowed to scoff, / asking,
79:10 Show us your vengeance against the **n**,
80: 6 You have made us the scorn of neighboring **n**.
80: 8 you drove away the pagan **n** and transplanted us
82: 8 and judge the earth, / for all the **n** belong to you.
86: 9 All the **n**—and you made each one— / will come
87: 6 When the LORD registers the **n**, / he will say,
94:10 He punishes the **n**—won't he also punish you?
96: 3 Publish his glorious deeds among the **n**.
96: 5 The gods of other **n** are merely idols,
96: 7 O **n** of the world, recognize the LORD;
96:10 Tell all the **n** that the LORD is king. / The world
96:13 with righteousness / and all the **n** with his truth.
98: 9 the world with justice, / and the **n** with fairness.
99: 1 The LORD is king! / Let the **n** tremble! / He sits
99: 2 in majesty in Jerusalem, / supreme above all the **n**.
102:15 And the **n** will tremble before the LORD.
105:13 They wandered back and forth between **n**,
105:44 He gave his people the lands of pagan **n**, / and they
106:27 he would scatter their descendants among the **n**,
106:34 Israel failed to destroy the **n** in the land,
106:41 He handed them over to pagan **n**, / and those who
106:47 save us! / Gather us back from among the **n**,
108: 3 the people. / I will sing your praises among the **n**.
110: 6 He will punish the **n** / and fill them with their dead;
111: 6 to his people / by giving them the lands of other **n**.
113: 4 For the LORD is high above the **n**; / his glory is
115: 2 Why let the **n** say, / "Where is their God?"
117: 1 Praise the LORD, all you **n**. / Praise him, all you
118:10 Though hostile **n** surrounded me, / I destroyed
126: 2 and we sang for joy. / And the other **n** said,
135:10 He struck down great **n** / and slaughtered mighty
144: 2 I take refuge in him. / He subdues the **n** under me.
149: 7 to execute vengeance on the **n** / and punishment on
Pr 24:24 be cursed by many people and denounced by the **n**.
Isa 2: 3 Many **n** will come and say, "Come, let us go up to
2: 4 All the **n** will beat their swords into plowshares
5:26 He will send a signal to the **n** far away. He will
5:30 The enemy **n** will growl over their victims like the
8: 9 Listen all you **n**. Prepare for battle—and die!
11:10 The **n** will rally to him, for the land where he lives
11:12 He will raise a flag among the **n** for Israel to rally
11:14 they will attack and plunder the **n** to the east.
13: 4 It is the noise and the shout of many **n**.
14: 1 And people from many different **n** will come
14: 2 The **n** of the world will help the LORD's people
14: 6 blows of rage and held the **n** in your angry grip.
14:12 to the earth, you who destroyed the **n** of the world.
14:18 "The kings of the **n** lie in stately glory in their
16: 8 vineyards used to make the rulers of the **n** drunk.
21: 2 and the groaning of all the **n** she enslaved will end.
24:21 the heavens and the proud rulers of the **n** on earth.
25: 3 Therefore, strong **n** will declare your glory;
ruthless **n** will revere you.
25: 5 of the desert. But you silence the roar of foreign **n**.
29: 7 All the **n** fighting against Jerusalem will vanish
30:28 He will sift out the proud **n**. He will bridle them
33: 3 of your voice. When you stand up, the **n** flee!
33:13 Listen to what I have done, you **n** far away!
34: 1 Come here and listen, O **n** of the earth.
34: 2 For the LORD is enraged against the **n**. His fury
36:18 Have the gods of any other **n** ever saved their
37:12 Have the gods of other **n** rescued them—
37:12 such **n** as Gozan, Haran, Rezeph, and the people of
37:18 the kings of Assyria have destroyed all these **n**,
37:19 And they have thrown the gods of these **n** into the
40:15 for all the **n** of the world are nothing in comparison
40:17 The **n** of the world are as nothing to him. In his
41: 2 He gives him victory over many **n** and permits him
41:25 He will come against the **n** and call on my name,
42: 1 my Spirit upon him. He will reveal justice to the **n**.
42: 6 And you will be a light to guide all **n** to me.
43: 9 Gather the **n** together! Which of their idols has
45:20 and come, you fugitives from surrounding **n**.
48:11 the pagan **n** will not be able to claim that their gods
49:22 "See, I will give a signal to the godless **n**.
51: 4 and my justice will become a light to the **n**.
51: 5 I will rule the **n**. They will wait for me and long for
52:10 his holy power before the eyes of all the **n**.
52:15 And he will again startle many **n**. Kings will stand
54: 3 Your descendants will take over other **n** and live in
55: 4 by being my witness and a leader among the **n**.
55: 5 You also will command the **n**, and they will come
56: 7 Temple will be called a house of prayer for all **n**.
60: 1 Jerusalem! Let your light shine for all the **n** to see!
60: 2 Darkness as black as night will cover all the **n** of
60: 3 All **n** will come to your light. Mighty kings will
60:12 For the **n** that refuse to be your allies will be
60:16 and mighty **n** will bring the best of their goods to
61: 6 You will be fed with the treasures of the **n** and will
61: 9 will be known and honored among the **n**.
61:11 LORD will show his justice to the **n** of the world.
62: 2 The **n** will see your righteousness. Kings will be
62:10 out the boulders; raise a flag for all the **n** to see.
63: 6 I crushed the **n** in my anger and made them stagger
64: 2 to boil, your coming would make the **n** tremble.
66:12 the LORD. "The wealth of the **n** will flow to her.
66:18 So I will gather all **n** and peoples together,
66:19 send those who survive to be messengers to the **n**
66:19 There they will declare my glory to the **n**.
Jer 1:10 Today I appoint you to stand up against **n**
2:37 for the LORD has rejected the **n** you trust.
3:17 All **n** will come there to honor the LORD.
4: 2 then you will be a blessing to the **n** of the world,
4: 7 A lion stalks from its den, a destroyer of **n**. And it
4:16 "Warn the surrounding **n** and announce to
6:18 "Therefore, listen to this, all you **n**. Take note of
9:26 Like all these pagan **n**, the people of Israel also
10: 2 "Do not act like other **n** who try to read their
10: 2 even though other **n** are terrified by them.
10: 7 Who would not fear you, O King of **n**? That title
10:10 trembles at his anger. The **n** hide before his wrath.
10:25 Pour out your wrath on the **n** that refuse to
10:25 on **n** that do not call upon your name.
12:14 "As for all the evil **n** reaching out for the
12:16 And if these **n** quickly learn the ways of my
16:19 **N** from around the world will come to you and say,
18:13 heard of such a thing, even among the pagan **n**?
22: 8 People from many **n** will pass by the ruins of this
25: 9 and its people and against the other **n** near you.
25:13 the penalties announced by Jeremiah against the **n**.
25:14 Many **n** and great kings will enslave the
25:15 and make all the **n** to whom I send you drink from
25:17 from the LORD and made all the **n** drink from it—
25:21 Then I went to the **n** of Edom, Moab, and Ammon,
25:29 I will call for war against all the **n** of the earth.

25:31 for the LORD will bring his case against all the **n**.
27: 7 All the **n** will serve him and his son and his
27: 7 But then many **n** and great kings will conquer
28: 8 who preceded you and me spoke against many **n**,
28:11 **n** now subject to King Nebuchadnezzar of
28:14 have put a yoke of iron on the necks of all these **n**,
29:14 I will gather you out of the **n** where I sent you
30:11 I will completely destroy the **n** where I have
31: 7 Shout for the greatest of **n**! Shout out with praise
31:10 this message from the LORD, you **n** of the world;
33: 9 glory, and honor before all the **n** of the earth!
34:17 You will be considered a disgrace by all the **n** of
36: 2 my messages against Israel, Judah, and the other **n**.
44: 8 of cursing and mockery for all the **n** of the earth.
46: 1 the prophet from the LORD concerning foreign **n**.
46:12 The **n** have heard of your shame. The earth is filled
46:28 I will destroy the **n** to which I have exiled you,
49:14 that an ambassador was sent to the **n** to say,
49:15 "I will cut you down to size among the **n**, Edom.
50: 9 I am raising up an army of great **n** from the north.
50:12 You will become the least of **n**—a wilderness,
50:14 prepare to attack Babylon, all you **n** round about.
50:23 and shattered. Babylon is desolate among the **n**!
51:20 "With you I will shatter **n** and destroy many
51:27 Signal many **n** to mobilize for war against
51:44 The **n** will no longer come and worship him.
La 1: 1 Once the queen of **n**, she is now a slave.
1: 3 She lives among foreign **n** and has no place of rest.
3:45 discarded us as refuse and garbage among the **n**.
4:15 distant lands and wandered there among foreign **n**,
4:17 but we were looking to **n** that could offer no help
Eze 5: 5 to Jerusalem. I placed her at the center of the **n**,
5: 6 been even more wicked than the surrounding **n**.
5: 8 I will punish you publicly while all the **n** watch.
5:14 a mockery in the eyes of the surrounding **n** and to
5:15 You will be a warning to all the **n** around you.
6: 8 and they will be scattered among the **n** of the
6: 9 Then when they are exiled among the **n**, they will
7:21 plunder to foreigners from the most wicked of **n**,
7:24 I will bring the most ruthless of **n** to occupy their
11:12 you have copied the sins of the **n** around you."
11:17 will gather you back from the **n** where you are
12:15 And when I scatter them among the **n**, they will
16:39 these many **n**—and they will destroy you.
19: 4 Then the **n** heard about him, / and he was trapped
19: 7 He demolished fortresses in nearby **n**
19: 8 Then the armies of the **n** attacked him,
20: 9 That way the surrounding **n** wouldn't be able to
20:14 That way the **n** who saw me lead my people out of
20:22 **n** who had seen my power in bringing them out of
20:23 I vowed I would scatter them among all the **n**
20:32 "You say, 'We want to be like the **n** all around us,
20:35 I will bring you into the wilderness of the **n**,
20:41 And I will display my holiness in you as all the **n**
22:15 I will scatter you among the **n** and purge you of
22:16 And when you have been dishonored among the **n**,
23:22 those very **n** from which you turned away in
23:30 this on yourself by prostituting yourself to other **n**,
25: 7 against you. I will give you as plunder to many **n**.
25: 8 have said that Judah is just like all the other **n**,
25:10 will no longer be counted among the **n**.
26: 3 O Tyre, and I will bring many **n** against you,
26: 5 Tyre will become the prey of many **n**,
27:33 you traded / satisfied the needs of many **n**.
27:36 The merchants of the **n** / shake their heads at the
28: 7 against you an enemy army, the terror of the **n**.
28:25 I will reveal to the **n** of the world my holiness
28:26 And when I punish the neighboring **n** that treated
29:12 and it will be surrounded by other desolate **n**.
29:13 from the **n** to which they have been scattered.
29:15 It will be the lowliest of all the **n**, never again great
30: 3 of clouds and gloom, a day of despair for the **n**!
30: 7 Egypt will be desolate, surrounded by desolate **n**,
30:11 He and his armies—ruthless among the **n**—
30:26 I will scatter the Egyptians among the **n**. Then they
31: 6 All the great **n** of the world lived in its shadow.
31:12 the terror of the **n**—cut it down and left it fallen on
31:16 I made the **n** shake with fear at the sound of its fall,
31:17 to the grave—all those **n** that had lived in its shade.
31:18 be brought down to the pit with all these other **n**.
32: 2 of yourself as a strong young lion among the **n**,
32: 9 remains to distant **n** that you have never seen,
32:12 the swords of mighty warriors—the terror of the **n**.
32:16 Let all the **n** mourn for Egypt and its hordes.
32:18 for the hordes of Egypt and for the other mighty **n**.
32:19 'O Egypt, are you lovelier than the other **n**?
32:24 They terrorized the **n** while they lived, but now
32:25 Yes, they terrorized the **n** while they lived,
34:13 own land of Israel from among the peoples and **n**.
34:28 They will no longer be prey for other **n**, and wild
34:29 go hungry or be shamed by the scorn of foreign **n**.
36: 3 and now you are possessed by many **n**.
36: 4 and mocked by foreign **n** everywhere.
36: 5 My jealous anger is on fire against these **n**,
36: 6 you have suffered shame before the surrounding **n**.
36: 7 and sworn an oath that those **n** will soon have their
36:13 Now the other **n** taunt you, saying, 'Israel is a land
36:15 I will not allow those foreign **n** to sneer at you,
36:20 But when they were scattered among the **n**,
36:20 For the **n** said, 'These are the people of the
36:22 dishonored while you were scattered among the **n**.
36:23 name is—the name you dishonored among the **n**.
36:23 then the **n** will know that I am the LORD.
36:24 For I will gather you up from all the **n** and bring
36:30 and never again will the surrounding **n** be able to
36:36 Then the **n** all around—all those still left—
37:21 I will gather the people of Israel from among the **n**.
37:22 them all; no longer will they be divided into two **n**.
37:28 the **n** will know that I, the LORD, have set Israel
38: 2 the prince who rules over the **n** of Meshech
38:12 people who have returned from exile in many **n**.
38:16 Then all the **n** will know that I am the LORD.
38:23 and I will make myself known to all the **n** of the
39: 1 O Gog, ruler of the **n** of Meshech and Tubal.
39: 7 And the **n**, too, will know that I am the LORD,
39:21 "Thus, I will demonstrate my glory among the **n**.
39:23 The **n** will then know why Israel was sent away to
39:27 my holiness will be displayed to the **n**.
Da 3: 4 "People of all races and **n** and languages,
5:19 He made him so great that people of all races and **n**
7:14 honor, and royal power over all the **n** of the world,
9:16 All the neighboring **n** mock Jerusalem and your
11:41 of Israel, and many **n** will fall, but Moab, Edom,
12: 1 greater than any since **n** first came into existence.
Hos 8: 8 they lie among the **n** like an old pot that no one
9:17 They will be wanderers, homeless among the **n**.
10:10 I will call out the armies of the **n** to punish you for
Joel 2:19 be an object of mockery among the surrounding **n**.
3: 2 for scattering my inheritance among the **n**, and for
3: 9 Say to the **n** far and wide: "Get ready for war!
3:11 Come quickly, all you **n** everywhere!
3:12 "Let the **n** be called to arms. Let them march to
Am 9: 7 but have I not done as much for other **n**, too?
9: 9 by the other **n** as grain is sifted in a sieve,
9:12 left of Edom and all the **n** I have called to be mine.
Ob 1: 1 that an ambassador was sent to the **n** to say,
1: 2 "I will cut you down to size among the **n**, Edom;
1:15 near when I, the LORD, will judge the godless **n**!
1:16 and the surrounding **n** will swallow the punishment
1:16 you **n** will drink and stagger and disappear from
Mic 4: 2 Many **n** will come and say, "Come, let us go up to
4: 3 All the **n** will beat their swords into plowshares
4: 5 Even though the **n** around us worship idols,
4:11 True, many **n** have gathered together against you,
4:12 These **n** don't know that he is gathering them
4:13 "Rise up and destroy the **n**, O Jerusalem!"
4:13 so you can trample many **n** to pieces.
5: 7 Then the few left in Israel will go out among the **n**.
5: 8 The remnant of Israel will go out among the **n**
5: 8 And the other **n** will be like helpless sheep, with no
5:15 I will pour out my vengeance on all the **n** that
7:16 All the **n** of the world will stand amazed at what
Na 2:11 lion of the **n**, full of fight and boldness,
2:13 will you bring back plunder from conquered **n**.
3: 4 of deadly charms, enticed the **n** with her beauty.
3: 9 The **n** of Put and Libya also helped and supported
Hab 1: 5 LORD replied, "Look at the **n** and be amazed!
2: 5 In their greed they have gathered up many **n**
2: 8 You have plundered many **n**; now they will
2:13 promised that the wealth of **n** will turn to ashes?
3: 6 the earth shakes. When he looks, the **n** tremble.
3:12 in awesome anger and trampled the **n** in your fury.
Zep 2:11 Then people from **n** around the world will worship
3: 6 "I have wiped out many **n**, devastating their
3: 8 soon when I will stand up and accuse these evil **n**.
3:20 a name of distinction among all the **n** of the earth.
Hag 2: 7 I will shake all the **n**, and the treasures of all the **n** will come to this
Zec 1:15 But I am very angry with the other **n** that enjoy
1:15 but the **n** punished them far beyond my intentions.
2: 8 the LORD Almighty sent me against the **n** who
2:11 Many **n** will join themselves to the LORD on that
7:14 among the distant **n** where they lived as strangers.
8:13 Among the **n**, Judah and Israel had become
8:20 People from **n** and cities around the world will
8:22 People from many **n**, even powerful **n**,
8:23 In those days ten people from **n** and languages
9:10 Your king will bring peace to the **n**. His realm will
10: 9 I have scattered them like seeds among the **n**,
11:10 revoked the covenant I had made with all the **n**.
12: 2 **n** that send their armies to besiege Jerusalem.
12: 3 None of the **n** who try to lift it will escape
12: 6 They will burn up all the neighboring **n** right
12: 9 For my plan is to destroy all the **n** that come
14: 2 On that day I will gather all the **n** to fight against
14: 3 the LORD will go out to fight against those **n**,
14:12 And the LORD will send a plague on all the **n**
14:14 The wealth of all the neighboring **n** will be
14:18 that he sends on the other **n** who refuse to go.
14:19 and the other **n** will all be punished if they don't go
Mal 1:11 But my name is honored by people of other **n** from
1:11 For my name is great among the **n**,"
1:14 "and my name is feared among the **n**!
3:12 "Then all **n** will call you blessed, for your land
Mt 4: 8 and showed him the **n** of the world and all their
12:18 upon him, / and he will proclaim justice to the **n**.
24: 7 The **n** and kingdoms will proclaim war against
24:14 the whole world, so that all **n** will hear it;
24:30 and there will be deep mourning among all the **n** of
25:32 All the **n** will be gathered in his presence, and he
28:19 Therefore, go and make disciples of all the **n**,
Mk 11:17 Temple will be called a place of prayer for all **n**,'
13: 8 **N** and kingdoms will proclaim war against each
Lk 2:32 He is a light to reveal God to the **n**, / and he is the
21:10 "**N** and kingdoms will proclaim war against each
21:24 or sent away as captives to all the **n** of the world.
21:25 And down here on earth the **n** will be in turmoil,
24:47 take this message of repentance to all the **n**,
Ac 2: 5 Godly Jews from many **n** were living in Jerusalem
4:25 your servant, saying, / 'Why did the **n** rage?
7:45 when Joshua led the battles against the Gentile **n**
13:19 Then he destroyed seven **n** in Canaan and gave
14:16 In earlier days he permitted all the **n** to go their
17:26 From one man he created all the **n** throughout the
17:27 "His purpose in all of this was that the **n** should
Ro 4:17 told him, "I have made you the father of many **n**."
4:18 that he would become the father of many **n**,
10:19 "I will rouse your jealousy by blessing other **n**.
Gal 3: 8 he said, "All **n** will be blessed through you."
1Ti 3:16 was seen by angels / and was announced to the **n**.
Jas 1: 1 written to Jewish Christians scattered among the **n**.
Rev 1: 7 And all the **n** of the earth will weep because of
2:26 to the very end, I will give authority over all the **n**.
2:27 They will rule the **n** with an iron rod and smash
10:11 about many peoples, **n**, languages, and kings."
11: 2 for it has been turned over to the **n**.
11: 9 languages, and **n** will come to stare at their bodies.
11:18 The **n** were angry with you, / but now the time of
12: 5 She gave birth to a boy who was to rule all **n** with
14: 8 because she seduced the **n** of the world and made
15: 3 Just and true are your ways, / O King of the **n**.
15: 4 are holy. / All **n** will come and worship before you,
18: 3 For all the **n** have drunk the wine of her passionate
18:23 in the world, deceived the **n** with her sorceries.
19:15 a sharp sword, and with it he struck down the **n**.
20: 3 so Satan could not deceive the **n** anymore until the
20: 8 He will go out to deceive the **n** from every corner
21:24 The **n** of the earth will walk in its light,
21:26 And all the **n** will bring their glory and honor into
22: 2 The leaves were used for medicine to heal the **n**.

NATIONWIDE (1) [NATION]

Ge 41:33 in Egypt and put him in charge of a **n** program.

NATIVE (9) [NATIVE-BORN]

Ge 24: 7 took me from my father's house and my **n** land,
36:20 the Horite, one of the families **n** to the land of Seir:
Nu 15:13 If you **n** Israelites want to present an offering by
15:15 **N** Israelites and foreigners are the same before the
15:29 This same law applies both to **n** Israelites
15:30 whether **n** Israelites or foreigners,
22: 5 who was living in his **n** land of Pethor near the
Jer 22:10 For he will never return to see his **n** land again.
Ac 7: 3 told him, 'Leave your **n** land and your relatives,

NATIVE-BORN (2) [BEAR, NATIVE]

Ex 12:49 whether a **n** Israelite or a foreigner who has settled
Eze 47:22 They will be just like **n** Israelites to you, and they

NATIVITY [KJV] See BIRTH, BORN, OWN

NATURAL (14) [NATURE]

Ge 11: 3 burnt brick and collect **n** asphalt to use as mortar.
Lev 17:15 from the carcass of an animal that died a **n** death
22: 8 may never eat an animal that has died a **n** death
Nu 16:29 If these men die a **n** death, then the LORD has
19:16 was killed with a sword or who died a **n** death,
Dt 14:21 "Do not eat anything that has died a **n** death.
27: 5 altar there to the LORD your God, using **n** stones.
2Ki 2:19 "This town is located in beautiful **n** surroundings,
Eze 44:31 meat from any bird or animal that dies a **n** death
Ro 1:26 Even the women turned against the **n** way to have
1Co 15:44 They are **n** human bodies now, but when they are
15:44 For just as there are **n** bodies, so also there are
15:46 What came first was the **n** body, then the spiritual
Jude 1:19 They live by **n** instinct because they do not have

NATURALLY (11) [NATURE]

Ge 39: 4 So Joseph **n** became quite a favorite with him.
Ex 31: 6 I have given special skill to all the **n** talented
Lev 25: 5 And don't store away the crops that grow **n**
25: 6 the produce that grows **n** during the Sabbath year.
25:11 or store away any of the crops that grow **n**,
25:12 eat the produce that grows **n** in the fields that year.
Nu 19:18 touched a person who was killed or who died **n**,
Lk 16:14 who dearly loved their money, **n** scoffed at all this.
Jn 8:45 when I tell the truth, you just **n** don't believe me!
15:20 they persecuted me, **n** they will persecute you.
Ac 6:12 **N**, this roused the crowds, the elders,

NATURE (35) [NATURAL, NATURALLY, SUPERNATURAL]

Lev 20:12 They have acted contrary to **n** and are guilty of a
Ps 93: 5 The **n** of your reign, O LORD, is holiness
Jer 31:36 Israel as I am to do away with the laws of **n**!
Jn 2:25 No one needed to tell him about human **n**.
Ro 1:20 invisible qualities—his eternal power and divine **n**.
7: 5 When we were controlled by our old **n**,
7:18 and through so far as my old sinful **n** is concerned.
7:25 but because of my sinful **n** I am a slave to sin.
8: 3 Moses could not save us, because of our sinful **n**.
8: 4 for us who no longer follow our sinful **n**
8: 5 Those who are dominated by the sinful **n** think
8: 6 If your sinful **n** controls your mind, there is death.
8: 7 For the sinful **n** is always hostile to God. It never
8: 8 the control of their sinful **n** can never please God.
8: 9 But you are not controlled by your sinful **n**.
8:12 to do what your sinful **n** urges you to do.
9: 5 and Christ himself was a Jew as far as his human **n**
11:24 by **n**, branches from a wild olive tree and graft you
1Co 5: 5 so that his sinful **n** will be destroyed and he
Gal 5:13 not freedom to satisfy your sinful **n**, but freedom to
5:16 Then you won't be doing what your sinful **n**
5:17 The old sinful **n** loves to do evil, which is just
5:17 that are opposite from what the sinful **n** desires.
5:19 When you follow the desires of your sinful **n**,
5:24 and desires of their sinful **n** to his cross

Eph 2: 3 following the passions and desires of our evil **n**.
2: 3 We were born with an evil **n**, and we were under
4:22 throw off your old evil **n** and your former way of
4:24 You must display a new **n** because you are a new
Col 2:11 the cutting away of your sinful **n**.
2:13 and because your sinful **n** was not yet cut away.
3: 9 for you have stripped off your old evil **n** and all its
3:10 **n** that is continually being renewed as you learn
3:10 about Christ, who created this new **n** within you.
2Pe 1: 4 evil desires and that you will share in his divine **n**.

NAUGHTINESS, NAUGHTY [KJV] See BAD, EVIL, SCHEMES, SCOUNDREL, WICKEDNESS

NAUM [KJV] See NAHUM

NAVAL (1) [NAVY]

Eze 26:17 been destroyed! / Your people, with their **n** power,

NAVEL (1)

SS 7: 2 Your **n** is as delicious as a goblet filled with wine.

NAVES [KJV] See HUBS

NAVIGATES (1)

Pr 30:19 a snake slithers on a rock, / how a ship **n** the ocean,

NAVY (1) [NAVAL]

Da 11:40 against him with chariots, cavalry, and a vast **n**.

NAVY [KJV] See also FLEET

NAY [KJV] See DENY, NO, NOT

NAZARITE [KJV] See NAZIRITE

NAZARENE (3) [NAZARETH]

Mt 2:23 concerning the Messiah: "He will be called a **N**."
Mk 14:67 "You were one of those with Jesus, the **N**."
16: 6 are looking for Jesus, the **N**, who was crucified.

NAZARENES (1) [NAZARETH]

Ac 24: 5 He is a ringleader of the sect known as the **N**.

NAZARETH (30) [NAZARENE, NAZARENES]

JESUS OF NAZARETH (12) Mt 26:71; Mk 1:24; Lk 4:34; 18:37; Jn 18:5,7; 19:19; Ac 2:22; 6:14; 10:38; 22:8; 26:9

Mt 2:23 So they went and lived in a town called **N**.
4:13 But instead of going to **N**, he went to Capernaum,
13:54 He returned to **N**, his hometown. When he taught
21:11 "It's Jesus, the prophet from **N** in Galilee."
26:71 standing around, "This man was with Jesus of **N**."
Mk 1: 9 One day Jesus came from **N** in Galilee, and he was
1:24 "Why are you bothering us, Jesus of **N**?
6: 1 of the country and returned with his disciples to **N**,
10:47 When Bartimaeus heard that Jesus from **N** was
Lk 1:26 God sent the angel Gabriel to **N**, a village in
2: 4 He traveled there from the village of **N** in Galilee.
2:39 of the Lord, they returned home to **N** in Galilee.
2:43 the celebration was over, they started home to **N**,
2:51 Then he returned to **N** with them and was obedient
4:16 When he came to the village of **N**, his boyhood
4:34 "Go away! Why are you bothering us, Jesus of **N**?
18:37 They told him that Jesus of **N** was going by.
24:19 happened to Jesus, the man from **N**," they said.
Jn 1:45 His name is Jesus, the son of Joseph from **N**."
1:46 "**N**!" exclaimed Nathanael. "Can anything good
18: 5 "Jesus of **N**," they replied. "I am he," Jesus said.
18: 7 And again they replied, "Jesus of **N**."
19:19 him that read, "Jesus of **N**, the King of the Jews."
Ac 2:22 God publicly endorsed Jesus of **N** by doing
3: 6 In the name of Jesus Christ of **N**, get up
4:10 in the name and power of Jesus Christ from **N**,
6:14 We have heard him say that this Jesus of **N** will
10:38 that God anointed Jesus of **N** with the Holy Spirit
22: 8 And he replied, 'I am Jesus of **N**, the one you are
26: 9 I could to oppose the followers of Jesus of **N**.

NAZIRITE (6) [NAZIRITE'S, NAZIRITES]

Nu 6: 2 either men or women, take the special vow of a **N**,
6: 4 As long as they are bound by their **N** vow, they are
6:21 beyond what is required by their normal **N** vow,
Jdg 13: 5 For he will be dedicated to God as a **N** from birth.
13: 7 For your son will be dedicated to God as a **N** from
16:17 "for I was dedicated to God as a **N** from birth.

NAZIRITE'S (2) [NAZIRITE]

Nu 6:19 After each **N** head has been shaved, the priest will
6:19 without yeast, and put them all into the **N** hands.

NAZIRITES (8) [NAZIRITE]

Nu 6:13 "This is the ritual law of the **N**. At the conclusion of their time of separation as **N**,
6:18 "Then the **N** will shave their hair at the entrance of
6:20 After this ceremony the **N** may again drink wine.
6:21 "This is the ritual law of the **N**. If any **N** have vowed to give the LORD anything
Am 2:11 of your sons to be prophets and others to be **N**.
2:12 "But you caused the **N** to sin by making them

NEAH (1)

Jos 19:13 Eth-kazin, and Rimmon and turned toward **N**.

NEAPOLIS (1)

Ac 16:11 of Samothrace, and the next day we landed at **N**.

NEAR (229) [NEARBY, NEARED, NEARER, NEAREST, NEARING, NEARLY]

Ge 10:19 **n** Gaza, and to Sodom, Gomorrah, Admah, and Zeboiim, **n** Lasha.
12: 6 they came to a place **n** Shechem and set up camp
13:12 Lot moved his tents to a place **n** Sodom,
18: 1 was camped **n** the oak grove belonging to Mamre.
23:17 land belonging to Ephron at Machpelah, **n** Mamre.
23:19 cave of Machpelah, **n** Mamre, which is at Hebron.
25: 9 **n** Mamre, in the field of Ephron son of Zohar the
25:11 on Isaac, who settled **n** Beer-lahairoi in the Negev.
32:32 the people of Israel don't eat meat from **n** the hip,
35: 4 and he buried them beneath the tree **n** Shechem.
35:27 which is **n** Kiriath-arba (now called Hebron),
45:10 so you can be **n** me with all your children
47:29 As the time of his death drew **n**, he called for his
49:30 in the field of Machpelah, **n** Mamre in Canaan,
50:10 **n** the Jordan River, they held a very great
50:13 place in the field of Ephron the Hittite, **n** Mamre.
Ex 3: 1 and he went deep into the wilderness **n** Sinai,
14: 9 they were camped beside the shore **n** Pi-hahiroth,
18: 5 and the people were camped **n** the mountain of
19:22 Even the priests who regularly come **n** to the
24: 2 Moses, are allowed to come **n** to the LORD.
28:27 gold rings and attach them to the ephod **n** the sash.
32:19 When they came **n** the camp, Moses saw the calf
34: 3 even let the flocks or herds graze **n** the mountain."
34:30 of Moses' face, they were afraid to come **n** him.
39:20 Then two gold rings were attached to the ephod **n**
40:29 and he placed the altar of burnt offering **n** the
Lev 3: 4 the two kidneys with the fat around them **n** the
3: 9 This includes the fat of the entire tail cut off **n** the
3:10 the two kidneys with the fat around them **n** the
3:15 the two kidneys with the fat around them **n** the
4: 9 the two kidneys with the fat around them **n** the
7: 4 the two kidneys with the fat around them **n** the
10: 3 among those who are **n** me. / I will be glorified
21:11 He must never defile himself by going **n** a dead
21:18 No one who has a defect may come **n** to me,
21:23 go behind the inner curtain or come **n** the altar,
24: 7 Sprinkle some pure frankincense **n** each row.
Nu 1:51 Anyone else who goes too **n** the Tabernacle will be
3:10 Anyone else who comes too **n** the sanctuary must
3:38 or Levite who came too **n** the sanctuary was to be
5: 8 and there are no **n** relatives to whom restitution can
6: 6 And they may not go **n** a dead body during the
13:21 wilderness of Zin as far as Rehob, **n** Lebo-hamath.
16: 9 be **n** him as you serve in the LORD's Tabernacle
18: 7 Any other person who comes too **n** the sanctuary
18:22 If they come too **n**, they will be judged guilty
22: 5 who was living in his native land of Pethor **n** the
33: 7 opposite Baal-zephon, and camped **n** Migdol.
33:47 in the mountains east of the river, **n** Mount Nebo.
33:50 While they were camped **n** the Jordan River on the
Dt 1: 1 They were camped in the Jordan Valley **n** Suph,
3:29 So we stayed in the valley **n** Beth-peor.
4: 7 For what great nation has a god as **n** to them as the
4: 7 our God is **n** to us whenever we call on him?
4:11 You came **n** and stood at the foot of the mountain,
4:46 and as they camped in the valley **n** Beth-peor east
11:30 live in the Jordan Valley, **n** the town of Gilgal.
34: 6 He was buried in a valley **n** Beth-peor in Moab,
Jos 3:16 town upstream called Adam, which is **n** Zarethan.
3:16 Then all the people crossed over **n** the city of
6:23 They moved her whole family to a safe place **n** the
7: 2 spy out the city of Ai, east of Bethel, **n** Beth-aven.
11: 5 They established their camp around the water **n**
11: 7 and his warriors traveled to the water **n** Merom
12: 9 The king of Jericho / The king of Ai, **n** Bethel
15:46 and included the towns **n** Ashdod with their
16: 1 Joseph extended from the Jordan River **n** Jericho,
17: 7 to the people living **n** the spring of Tappuah.
22:10 altar **n** the Jordan River at a place called Geliloth.
Jdg 1:16 the people there, **n** the town of Arad in the Negev.
3:19 But when Ehud reached the stone carvings **n**
4:11 his tent by the Oak of Zaanannim, **n** Kedesh.
5:19 "The kings of Canaan fought at Taanach **n**
7: 1 north of them in the valley **n** the hill of Moreh.
7:22 fled to places as far away as Beth-shittah **n** Zererah
7:22 and to the border of Abel-meholah **n** Tabbath.
11:33 the Ammonites from Aroer to an area **n** Minnith—
14: 5 a young lion attacked Samson **n** the vineyards of
18:28 This happened in the valley **n** Beth-rehob.
20:19 left early the next morning and camped **n** Gibeah.
20:41 point Benjamin's warriors realized disaster was **n**
20:45 they had killed another two thousand **n** Gidom.
1Sa 3: 3 and Samuel was sleeping in the Tabernacle **n** the
4: 1 The Israelite army was camped **n** Ebenezer,
4:19 was pregnant and **n** her time of delivery.
7:14 The Israelite towns **n** Ekron and Gath that the
13:16 at Geba, **n** Gibeah, in the land of Benjamin.
13:18 above the valley of Zeboim **n** the wilderness.
17: 2 Saul countered by gathering his troops **n** the valley
20:41 David came out from where he had been hiding **n**
23:15 One day **n** Horesh, David received the news that
24: 2 and his men **n** the rocks of the wild goats.
25: 1 his funeral. They buried him **n** his home at Ramah.
25: 2 who owned property **n** the village of Carmel.
25: 7 While your shepherds stayed among us **n** Carmel,
26: 3 of Hakilah, **n** Jeshimon, where David was hiding.
26:12 the spear and jug of water that were **n** Saul's head.
27: 8 people who had lived **n** Shur, along the road to
2Sa 2: 3 to Judah, and they settled **n** the town of Hebron.
2:24 down as they arrived at the hill of Ammah **n** Giah,
5:23 behind them and attack them **n** the balsam trees.
13:23 were being sheared at Baal-hazor **n** Ephraim,
1Ki 1: 9 Adonijah went to the stone of Zoheleth **n** the
4:12 all of Beth-shan **n** Zarethan below Jezreel,
8:46 and take them captive to a foreign land far or **n**.
9:26 a port **n** Elath in the land of Edom, along the shore
10:26 in the chariot cities, and some **n** him in Jerusalem.
17: 9 live in the village of Zarephath, **n** the city of Sidon.
21: 1 and **n** the palace was a vineyard owned by a man
22:10 were sitting on thrones at the threshing floor **n** the
2Ki 3:26 break through the enemy lines **n** the king of Edom,
6: 9 warn the king of Israel, "Do not go **n** that place,
9:27 in his chariot at the Ascent of Gur, **n** Ibleam.
15: 7 he was buried **n** his ancestors in the City of David.
18:17 **n** the road leading to the field where cloth is
23:11 They were **n** the quarters of Nathan-melech the
1Ch 7:21 to steal livestock from the local farmers **n** Gath.
8:32 All these families lived **n** each other in Jerusalem.
9:38 All these families lived **n** each other in Jerusalem.
11:15 Once when David was at the rock **n** the cave of
11:32 Hurai from **n** Nahale-gaash;
14:14 behind them and attack them **n** the balsam trees.
2Ch 1:14 in the chariot cities, and some **n** him in Jerusalem.
4:10 The Sea was placed **n** the southeast corner of the
6:36 and take them captive to a foreign land far or **n**.
9:25 in the chariot cities, and some **n** him in Jerusalem.
18: 9 were sitting on thrones at the threshing floor **n** the
20:35 But **n** the end of his life, King Jehoshaphat of
21:16 and the Arabs, who lived **n** the Ethiopians,
Ezr 2:70 the common people settled in villages **n** Jerusalem.
Ne 3:15 Then he repaired the wall of the pool of Siloam **n**
4:12 The Jews who lived **n** the enemy came and told us
10:39 and place them in the sacred containers **n** the
Est 2:11 Every day Mordecai would take a walk **n** the
9:20 these events and sent letters to the Jews **n** and far,
Job 9:11 Yet when he comes **n**, I cannot see him. When he
17: 1 "My spirit is crushed, and I am **n** death. The grave
30:10 They despise me and won't come **n** me, except to
Ps 22:11 Do not stay so far from me, / for trouble is **n**,
31:11 even my friends are afraid to come **n** me.
65: 4 What joy for those you choose to bring **n**,
73:28 But as for me, how good it is to be **n** God! / I have
75: 1 O God! / We give thanks because you are **n**.
84: 3 and raises her young— / at a place **n** your altar,
85: 9 Surely his salvation is **n** to those who honor him;
88: 3 For my life is full of troubles, / and death draws **n**.
91:10 no plague will come **n** your dwelling.
107:18 Their appetites were gone, / and death was **n**.
119:150 Those lawless people are coming **n** to attack me;
119:151 But you are **n**, O LORD, / and all your commands
Pr 5: 8 Run from her! Don't go **n** the door of her house!
7: 8 He was crossing the street **n** the house of an
Ecc 12: 5 And as you **n** your everlasting home, the mourners
Isa 7: 3 **n** the road leading to the field where cloth is
15: 9 The stream **n** Dibon runs red with blood, but I am
33:13 And you that are **n**, acknowledge my might!"
36: 2 **n** the road leading to the field where cloth is
50: 8 He who gives me justice is **n**. Who will dare to
54:14 you will live in peace. Terror will not come **n**.
55: 6 you can find him. Call on him now while he is **n**.
57:19 May they have peace, both **n** and far, for I will heal
Jer 5: 6 A leopard will lurk **n** their towns, tearing apart any
12: 5 what will you do in the thickets **n** the Jordan?
25: 9 and its people and against the other nations **n** you.
25:26 northern countries, far and **n**, one after the other—
36:10 courtyard of the Temple, **n** the New Gate entrance.
41:12 They caught up with him at the pool **n** Gibeon.
41:17 all to the village of Geruth-kimham **n** Bethlehem,
48:24 and Bozrah—all the cities of Moab, far and **n**.
La 4:18 Our end was **n**; our days were numbered. We were
Eze 7: 7 The time has come; the day of trouble is **n**. It will
22: 5 you will be mocked by people both far and **n**.
39:17 Come from far and **n** to the mountains of Israel,
Da 5: 5 plaster wall of the king's palace, **n** the lampstand.
9: 7 and Jerusalem and all Israel, scattered **n** and far,
Ob 1:15 "The day is **n** when I, the LORD, will judge the
Jnh 2: 5 "I sank beneath the waves, and death was very **n**.
Zep 1:14 "That terrible day of the LORD is **n**. Swiftly it
3: 2 does not trust in the LORD or draw **n** to its God.
Zec 9: 2 **n** Damascus, and for the cities of Tyre and Sidon,
Mt 3: 2 to God, because the Kingdom of Heaven is **n**."
4:17 to God, because the Kingdom of Heaven is **n**."
10: 7 to them that the Kingdom of Heaven is **n**.
24: 6 And wars will break out **n** and far, but don't panic.
24:28 so these signs indicate that the end is **n**.
24:32 you know without being told that summer is **n**.
24:33 you can know his return is very **n**, right at the door.
Mk 1:15 he announced. "The Kingdom of God is **n**!
13: 7 And wars will break out **n** and far, but don't panic.
13:28 you know without being told that summer is **n**.
13:29 you can be sure that his return is very **n**, right at
Lk 7: 2 slave of a Roman officer was sick and **n** death.
9:51 As the time drew **n** for his return to heaven,
10: 9 say, 'The Kingdom of God is **n** you now.'
10:11 And don't forget the Kingdom of God is **n**!'
14: 7 the dinner were trying to sit **n** the head of the table,
17:37 so these signs indicate that the end is **n**."
21:28 and look up, for your salvation is **n**!"
21:30 you know without being told that summer is **n**.
21:31 you can be sure that the Kingdom of God is **n**.
22: 1 with the Passover celebration, was drawing **n**.
Jn 1:18 who is himself God, is **n** to the Father's heart;

3:23 **n** Salim, because there was plenty of water there
4: 5 **n** the parcel of ground that Jacob gave to his son
5: 2 Inside the city, **n** the Sheep Gate, was the pool of
6:23 Several boats from Tiberias landed **n** the place
10:40 He went beyond the Jordan River to stay **n** the
11:54 He went to a place **n** the wilderness, to the village
19:20 The place where Jesus was crucified was **n** the
19:25 Standing **n** the cross were Jesus' mother, and his
19:41 The place of crucifixion was **n** a garden,
Ac 7:17 "As the time drew **n** when God would fulfill his
7:30 "Forty years later, in the desert **n** Mount Sinai,
10: 6 with Simon, a leatherworker who lives **n** the shore.
10:32 of Simon, a leatherworker who lives **n** the shore.'
23: 4 Those standing **n** Paul said to him, "Is that the
27: 8 finally arrived at Fair Havens, **n** the city of Lasea.
27:27 the Sea of Adria, the sailors sensed land was **n**.
28: 7 **N** the shore where we landed was an estate
Eph 2:13 now you have been brought **n** to him because of
2:17 far away from him, and to us Jews who were **n**.
2Ti 4: 6 as an offering to God. The time of my death is **n**.
Heb 7:19 taken its place. And that is how we draw **n** to God.
10:25 that the day of his coming back again is drawing **n**.
Jas 5: 8 And take courage, for the coming of the Lord is **n**.
Rev 1: 3 For the time is **n** when these things will happen.
22:10 prophetic words you have written, for the time is **n**.

NEARBY (41) [NEAR]

Ge 18: 2 he suddenly noticed three men standing **n**. He got
18:10 was listening to this conversation from the tent **n**.
19:20 See, there is a small village **n**. Please let me go
23:17 the field, the cave that was in it, and all the trees **n**.
28:19 though the name of the **n** village was Luz.
41:48 and stored them for the government in **n** cities.
Ex 17:10 Aaron, and Hur went to the top of a **n** hill.
Dt 13: 7 that you worship the gods of peoples who live **n**
20:15 only to distant towns, not to the towns of nations **n**.
22: 2 If it does not belong to someone **n** or you don't
Jos 9: 7 these Hivites, "How do we know you don't live **n**?
9:16 facts came out—these people of Gibeon lived **n**!
Jdg 18: 7 a great distance from Sidon and had no allies **n**.
18:28 a great distance from Sidon and had no allies **n**.
1Sa 5: 6 and the **n** villages with a plague of tumors.
2Sa 16:13 and Shimei kept pace with them on a **n** hillside,
2Ch 26:23 he was buried **n** in a burial field belonging to the
Ne 11:30 They were also in Lachish and its **n** fields
Isa 5: 2 and carved a winepress in the **n** rocks.
Jer 40:11 and the other **n** countries heard that the king of
43: 5 from the **n** countries to which they had fled.
Eze 6:12 War will destroy those who are **n**. And anyone
19: 7 He demolished fortresses in **n** nations
31: 4 abundant that there was enough for all the trees **n**.
Zec 12: 2 and Judah like an intoxicating drink to all the **n**
Mt 8:33 The herdsmen fled to the **n** city, telling everyone
24:28 gathering of vultures shows there is a carcass **n**,
27:61 and the other Mary were sitting **n** watching.
Mk 5:11 to be a large herd of pigs feeding on the hillside **n**.
5:14 The herdsmen fled to the **n** city
6:36 so they can go to the **n** farms and villages
10:47 Bartimaeus heard that Jesus from Nazareth was **n**,
Lk 5:17 and teachers of religious law were sitting **n**.
8: 1 Not long afterward Jesus began a tour of the **n**
8:32 A large herd of pigs was feeding on the hillside **n**,
8:34 they fled to the **n** city and the surrounding
9:12 "Send the crowds away to the **n** villages
17:37 gathering of vultures shows there is a carcass **n**,
23:49 Then turning to the others standing **n**, the king
Jn 11:36 The people who were standing **n** said, "See how
Ac 9:38 But they had heard that Peter was **n** at Lydda,

NEARED (1) [NEAR]

Ac 27: 7 and after great difficulty we finally **n** Cnidus.

NEARER (2) [NEAR]

Eze 40: 3 As he brought me **n**, I saw a man whose face shone
Ro 13:11 for the coming of our salvation is **n** now than when

NEAREST (10) [NEAR]

Nu 27:11 pass on his inheritance to the **n** relative in his clan.
35:19 The victim's **n** relative is responsible for putting
35:21 the victim's **n** relative must execute the murderer
35:24 the slayer and the avenger, the victim's **n** relative.
35:27 and the victim's **n** relative finds him outside the
Dt 14:28 the tithe of all your crops and store it in the **n** town.
19: 6 If the distance to the **n** city of refuge was too far,
21: 2 and judges must determine which town is **n** the
21: 6 "The leaders of the town **n** the body must wash
2Sa 17:13 and drag the walls of the city into the **n** valley until

NEARIAH (3)

1Ch 3:22 and his sons, Hattush, Igal, Bariah, **N**,
3:23 The sons of **N** were Elioenai, Hizkiah,
4:42 led by Pelatiah, **N**, Rephaiah, and Uzziel—

NEARING (5) [NEAR]

Lk 19:11 And because he was **n** Jerusalem, he told a story to
24:28 By this time they were **n** Emmaus and the end of
Ac 9: 3 As he was **n** Damascus on this mission, a brilliant
10: 9 The next day as Cornelius' messengers were **n** the
22: 6 "As I was on the road, **n** Damascus, about noon a

NEARLY (13) [NEAR]

Ge 47: 9 but I am still not **n** as old as many of my
Jdg 21: 6 one of the tribes from our family; it is **n** wiped out.
1Sa 25:18 five dressed sheep, **n** a bushel of roasted grain,
1Ki 10:17 each containing **n** four pounds of gold.
11:15 the Israelite army had killed **n** every male in
1Ch 22:14 **n** four thousand tons of gold, **n** forty thousand tons of silver, and so much iron
Est 3: 7 And the day selected was March 7, **n** a year later.
3:13 This was scheduled to happen **n** a year later on
Ps 107: 5 Hungry and thirsty, / they **n** died.
Mk 4:37 to break into the boat until it was **n** full of water.
Jn 6: 4 (It was **n** time for the annual Passover celebration.)
Heb 9:22 **n** everything was purified by sprinkling with

NEBAI (1)

Ne 10:19 Hariph, Anathoth, **N**,

NEBAIOTH (5)

Ge 25:13 The oldest was **N**, followed by Kedar, Abdeel,
28: 9 She was the sister of **N** and the daughter of
36: 3 was the daughter of Ishmael and the sister of **N**.
1Ch 1:29 The sons of Ishmael were **N** (the oldest), Kedar,
Isa 60: 7 and the rams of **N** will be brought for my altars.

NEBALLAT (1)

Ne 11:34 Hadid, Zeboim, **N**,

NEBAT (23)

1Ki 11:26 Another rebel leader was Jeroboam son of **N**,
12: 2 When Jeroboam son of **N** heard of Solomon's
12:15 son of **N** through the prophet Ahijah from Shiloh.
16: 3 I destroyed the descendants of Jeroboam son of **N**.
21:22 family as he did the family of Jeroboam son of **N**
22:52 and mother and the example of Jeroboam son of **N**,
2Ki 3: 3 son of **N** had led the people of Israel to commit.
9: 9 as I destroyed the families of Jeroboam son of **N**
10:29 the great sin that Jeroboam son of **N** had led Israel
13: 2 He followed the example of Jeroboam son of **N**,
13: 2 that Jeroboam son of **N** had led Israel to commit.
13:11 that Jeroboam son of **N** had led Israel to commit.
14:24 that Jeroboam son of **N** had led Israel to commit.
15: 9 that Jeroboam son of **N** had led Israel to commit.
15:18 that Jeroboam son of **N** had led Israel to commit.
15:24 that Jeroboam son of **N** had led Israel to commit.
15:28 that Jeroboam son of **N** had led Israel to commit.
17:21 they chose Jeroboam son of **N** as their king.
23:15 the pagan shrine that Jeroboam son of **N** had made
2Ch 9:29 *of Iddo the Seer,* concerning Jeroboam son of **N**.
10: 2 When Jeroboam son of **N** heard of Solomon's
10:15 son of **N** by the prophet Ahijah from Shiloh.
13: 6 Yet Jeroboam son of **N**, who was a mere servant of

NEBO (13) [NEBO-SARSEKIM]

Nu 32: 3 Jazer, Nimrah, Heshbon, Elealeh, Sebam, **N**,
32:38 **N**, Baal-meon, and Sibmah. They changed the
33:47 in the mountains east of the river, near Mount **N**.
Dt 32:49 and climb Mount **N**, which is across from Jericho.
34: 1 Then Moses went to Mount **N** from the plains of
1Ch 5: 8 lived in the area that stretches from Aroer to **N**
Ezr 2:29 The citizens of **N** | 52
10:43 From the family of **N**: Jeiel, Mattithiah, Zabad,
Ne 7:33 The people of **N** | 52
Isa 15: 2 and shrines, weeping for the fate of **N** and Medeba.
46: 1 The idols of Babylon, Bel and **N**, are being hauled
Jer 48: 1 "Destruction is certain for the city of **N**; it will
48:22 and on Dibon and **N** and Beth-diblathaim,

NEBO-SARSEKIM (1) [NEBO]

Jer 39: 3 and **N**, a chief officer, and Nergal-sharezer,

NEBUCHADNEZZAR (90) [NEBUCHADNEZZAR'S]

2Ki 24: 1 King **N** of Babylon invaded the land of Judah.
24:10 the officers of King **N** of Babylon came up against
24:11 **N** himself arrived at the city during the siege.
24:13 **N** carried away all the treasures from the LORD's
24:14 King **N** took ten thousand captives from Jerusalem,
24:15 **N** led King Jehoiachin away as a captive to
25: 1 King **N** of Babylon led his entire army against
25:22 Then King **N** appointed Gedaliah son of Ahikam
1Ch 6:15 of Judah and Jerusalem into captivity under **N**.
2Ch 36: 6 Then King **N** of Babylon came to Jerusalem
36: 7 **N** also took some of the treasures from the Temple
36:10 Jehoiachin was summoned to Babylon by King **N**.
36:10 And **N** appointed Jehoiachin's uncle, Zedekiah,
36:13 He also rebelled against King **N**, even though he
36:17 healthy and sick. God handed them all over to **N**.
Ezr 1: 7 **N** had taken from the LORD's Temple in
2: 1 They had been deported to Babylon by King **N**.
5:12 he abandoned them to King **N** of Babylon,
5:14 and silver utensils that **N** had taken from the
6: 5 which were taken to Babylon by **N** from the
Ne 7: 6 They had been deported to Babylon by King **N**.
Est 2: 6 been exiled from Jerusalem to Babylon by King **N**,
Jer 21: 2 King **N** of Babylon has begun his attack on Judah.
21: 2 Perhaps he will force **N** to withdraw his armies."
21: 7 I will hand them over to King **N** of Babylon.
22:25 to King **N** of Babylon and the mighty Babylonian
24: 1 After King **N** of Babylon exiled Jehoiachin son of
25: 1 This was the year when King **N** of Babylon began
25: 9 the armies of the north under King **N** of Babylon,
27: 6 Now I will give your countries to King **N** of
27:20 King **N** of Babylon left them here when he exiled
28: 3 treasures that King **N** carried off to Babylon.
28:11 all the nations now subject to King **N** of Babylon."
28:14 forcing them into slavery under King **N** of
29: 1 people who had been exiled to Babylon by King **N**.
29: 3 to Babylon as King Zedekiah's ambassadors to **N**.
29:21 "I will turn them over to **N** for a public execution.
32: 1 also the eighteenth year of the reign of King **N**.
32:28 hand this city over to the Babylonians and to **N**,
34: 1 King **N** of Babylon came with all the armies from
35:11 But when King **N** of Babylon arrived in this
37: 1 of Judah. He was appointed by King **N** of Babylon.
39: 1 ninth year of King Zedekiah's reign that King **N**
39: 5 They took him to King **N** of Babylon, who was at
39:11 King **N** had told Nebuzaradan to find Jeremiah.
43:10 I will surely bring my servant **N**, king of Babylon,
44:30 Zedekiah of Judah over to King **N** of Babylon.
46: 2 beside the Euphrates River by King **N** of Babylon.
46:26 them killed—to King **N** of Babylon and his army.
49:28 which were attacked by King **N** of Babylon.
49:30 for King **N** of Babylon has plotted against you
50:17 Then King **N** of Babylon cracked their bones."
51:34 "King **N** of Babylon has eaten and crushed us
52: 4 King **N** of Babylon led his entire army against
Eze 26: 7 I will bring King **N** of Babylon—the king of kings
29:18 the army of King **N** of Babylon fought so hard
29:18 Yet **N** and his army won no plunder to compensate
29:19 I will give the land of Egypt to **N**, king of Babylon.
30:10 Through King **N** of Babylon, I will destroy the
Da 1: 1 King **N** of Babylon came to Jerusalem
1: 2 When **N** returned to Babylon, he took with him
1:18 chief official brought all the young men to King **N**.
2: 1 **N** had a dream that disturbed him so much that he
2:28 and he has shown King **N** what will happen in the
2:46 Then King **N** bowed to the ground before Daniel
3: 1 King **N** made a gold statue ninety feet tall and nine
3: 3 and were standing before the image King **N** had set
3: 7 and worshiped the statue that King **N** had set up.
3: 9 They said to King **N**, "Long live the king!
3:13 Then **N** flew into a rage and ordered Shadrach,
3:14 **N** said to them, "Is it true, Shadrach, Meshach,
3:16 Shadrach, Meshach, and Abednego replied, "O **N**,
3:19 **N** was so furious with Shadrach, Meshach,
3:24 **N** jumped up in amazement and exclaimed to his
3:25 "Look!" **N** shouted. "I see four men, unbound,
3:26 Then **N** came as close as he could to the door of
3:28 Then **N** said, "Praise to the God of Shadrach,
4: 1 King **N** sent this message to the people of every
4: 4 "I, **N**, was living in my palace in comfort
4:18 that was the dream that I, King **N**, had.
4:27 "O King **N**, please listen to me. Stop sinning
4:28 But all these things did happen to King **N**.
4:31 from heaven, "O King **N**, this message is for you!
4:33 and **N** was driven from human society.
4:34 this time had passed, I, **N**, looked up to heaven.
4:37 **N**, praise and glorify and honor the King of
5: 2 in the gold and silver cups that his predecessor, **N**,
5:11 Your predecessor, King **N**, made him chief over all
5:13 exiled from Judah by my predecessor, King **N**?
5:18 majesty, glory, and honor to your predecessor, **N**.

NEBUCHADNEZZAR'S (8) [NEBUCHADNEZZAR]

2Ki 24:12 In the eighth year of **N** reign, he took Jehoiachin
25: 8 which was the nineteenth year of **N** reign,
Jer 46:13 this message about King **N** plans to attack Egypt.
52:12 which was the nineteenth year of **N** reign,
52:28 Babylon in the seventh year of **N** reign was 3,023.
52:29 Then in **N** eighteenth year he took 832 more.
Da 3: 5 bow to the ground to worship King **N** gold statue.
5:11 During **N** reign, this man was found to have

NEBUSHAZBAN (1)

Jer 39:13 and **N**, a chief officer, and Nergal-sharezer,

NEBUZARADAN (18)

2Ki 25: 8 **N**, captain of the guard, an official of the
25:11 **N**, captain of the guard, then took as exiles those
25:15 **N**, captain of the guard, also took the firepans
25:20 **N** the commander took them all to the king of
Jer 39: 9 Then **N**, the captain of the guard, sent to Babylon
39:10 But **N** left a few of the poorest people in Judah,
39:11 King Nebuchadnezzar had told **N** to find Jeremiah.
39:13 So **N**, the captain of the guard, and Nebushazban,
40: 1 The LORD gave a message to Jeremiah after **N**,
40: 5 Then **N** gave Jeremiah some food and money
41:10 been left under Gedaliah's care in Mizpah by **N**,
43: 6 the king's daughters, and all those whom **N**,
52:12 **N**, captain of the guard, an official of the
52:15 **N**, captain of the guard, then took as exiles some of
52:16 But **N** allowed some of the poorest people to stay
52:19 **N**, captain of the guard, also took the small bowls,
52:26 **N** the commander took them all to the king of
52:30 In his twenty-third year he sent **N**, his captain of

NECESSARILY (2) [NECESSARY]

Ecc 9:11 are often poor, and the skillful are not **n** wealthy.
Ro 9: 8 physical descendants are not **n** children of God.

NECESSARY (27) [NECESSARILY, NECESSITY]

Ex 22:29 "You must make the **n** payment for redemption of
35:33 and in carving wood. In fact, he has every **n** skill.
Nu 4:26 the **n** cords, and all the altar's accessories.
Ru 3:11 I will do what is **n**, for everyone in town knows
2Sa 2:27 for we would have chased you all night if **n**."
1Ki 4:28 They also brought the **n** barley and straw for the
7:40 He also made the **n** pots, shovels, and basins.

1Ch 28: 2 I made the **n** preparations for building it,
28:14 and silver should be used to make the **n** items.
2Ch 4:11 Huram-abi also made the **n** pots, shovels,
Ezr 7:20 If you run short of money for anything **n** for your
Ne 10:33 It will also provide for the other items **n** for the
Mt 14: 9 down in front of his guests, he issued the **n** orders.
14:16 But Jesus replied, "That isn't **n**—you feed them."
Lk 13:16 Wasn't it **n** for me, even on the Sabbath day,
Jn 16:25 but the time will come when this will not be **n**,
Ac 1:16 it was **n** for the Scriptures to be fulfilled
13:46 "It was **n** that this Good News from God be given
28:19 the decision, I felt it **n** to appeal to Caesar,
1Co 12:22 and least important are really the most **n**.
12:27 and each one of you is a separate and **n** part of it.
2Co 10: 2 I hope it won't be **n**, but when I come I may have
Tit 1:13 So rebuke them as sternly as **n** to make them
2:15 your people to do them, correcting them when **n**.
Heb 2:17 it was **n** for Jesus to be in every respect like us,
9:26 If that had been **n**, he would have had to die again
1Pe 1: 6 even though it is **n** for you to endure many trials

NECESSITY (1) [NECESSARY]

Ac 20:21 the **n** of turning from sin and turning to God,

NECHO [KJV] See NECO

NECK (31) [NECKS]

Ge 27:16 she fastened a strip of the goat's skin around his **n**.
41:42 and placed the royal gold chain about his **n**.
Ex 13:13 the donkey must be killed by breaking its **n**.
34:20 you must kill the donkey by breaking its **n**.
Lev 5: 8 The priest will wring its **n** but without severing its
26:13 I have lifted the yoke of slavery from your **n**
Dt 21: 4 through it. There they must break the cow's **n**.
21: 6 hands over the young cow whose **n** was broken.
1Sa 4:18 He broke his **n** and died, for he was old and very
Job 16:12 He took me by the **n** and dashed me to pieces.
39:19 its strength or clothed its **n** with a flowing mane?
41:22 "The tremendous strength in its **n** strikes terror
Ps 69: 1 O God, / for the floodwaters are up to my **n**.
105:18 feet with fetters / and placed his **n** in an iron collar.
Pr 6:21 always in your heart. Tie them around your **n**.
SS 1:10 How stately is your **n**, accented with a long string
4: 4 Your **n** is as stately as the tower of David,
7: 4 Your **n** is as stately as an ivory tower. Your eyes
Isa 52: 2 Remove the slave bands from your **n**, O captive
Jer 27: 2 a yoke, and fasten it on your **n** with leather thongs.
27: 8 and serve him; put your **n** under Babylon's yoke!
28:10 the prophet took the yoke off Jeremiah's **n**
29:26 claims to be a prophet in the stocks and **n** irons.
Da 5: 7 and will wear a gold chain around his **n**.
5:16 and you will wear a gold chain around your **n**.
5:29 purple robes, a gold chain was hung around his **n**,
Hos 10:11 Now I will put a heavy yoke on her tender **n**.
11: 4 I lifted the yoke from his **n**, and I myself stooped
Mt 18: 6 the sea with a large millstone tied around the **n**.
Mk 9:42 the sea with a large millstone tied around the **n**.
Lk 17: 2 **n** than to face the punishment in store for harming

NECKLACE (3) [NECKLACES]

Ps 73: 6 They wear pride like a jeweled **n**, / and their
Pr 3: 3 Wear them like a **n**; write them deep within your
SS 4: 9 glance of your eyes, by a single bead of your **n**.

NECKLACES (4) [NECKLACE]

Ex 35:22 earrings, rings from their fingers, and **n**.
Nu 31:50 armbands, bracelets, rings, earrings, and **n**.
Isa 3:18 their ornaments, headbands, and crescent **n**;
Eze 16:11 gave you lovely jewelry, bracelets, and beautiful **n**,

NECKS (8) [NECK]

Jos 10:24 "Come and put your feet on the kings' **n**."
Jdg 8:21 and took the royal ornaments from the **n** of their
8:26 or the chains around the **n** of their camels.
Isa 48: 4 obstinate you are. Your **n** are as unbending as iron.
Jer 28: 2 the yoke of the king of Babylon from your **n**.
28: 4 yoke that the king of Babylon has put on your **n**.
28:14 I have put a yoke of iron on the **n** of all these
30: 8 I will break the yoke from their **n** and snap their

NECO (11)

2Ki 23:29 While Josiah was king, Pharaoh **N**, king of Egypt,
23:29 but King **N** killed him when they met at Megiddo.
23:33 Pharaoh **N** put Jehoahaz in prison at Riblah in the
23:34 Pharaoh **N** then installed Eliakim, another of
23:35 and gold demanded as tribute by Pharaoh **N**,
2Ch 35:20 King **N** of Egypt led his army up from Egypt to do
35:21 But King **N** sent ambassadors to Josiah with this
35:22 But Josiah refused to listen to **N**, to whom God had
36: 3 Then he was deposed by **N**, the king of Egypt,
36: 4 Then **N** took Jehoahaz to Egypt as a prisoner.
Jer 46: 2 of the battle of Carchemish when Pharaoh **N**,

NECROMANCER [KJV] See CALL (...SPIRITS)

NEDABIAH (1)

1Ch 3:18 Pedaiah, Shenazzar, Jekamiah, Hoshama, and **N**.

NEED (195) [NEEDED, NEEDLESS, NEEDS, NEEDY]

Ge 47:22 food from Pharaoh and didn't **n** to sell their land.
50: 5 Now I **n** to go and bury my father. After his burial
Ex 10:10 "The LORD will certainly **n** to be with you if
16: 4 and pick up as much food as they **n** for that day.
16:21 by morning, each family according to its **n**.
22:25 "If you lend money to a fellow Hebrew in **n**,
22:27 Your neighbor will **n** it to stay warm during the
25:39 You will **n** seventy-five pounds of pure gold for
Lev 13:11 the person **n** not be quarantined for further
14:49 To purify the house the priest will **n** two birds,
26:10 **n** to get rid of the leftovers from the previous year
Nu 24: 7 their offspring are supplied with all they **n**.
Dt 2: 7 and provided for your every **n** so that you lacked
8: 3 He did it to teach you that people **n** more than
15: 6 money to many nations but will never **n** to borrow!
15: 8 be generous and lend them whatever they **n**.
15:11 freely with the poor and with other Israelites in **n**.
18:22 prophet has spoken on his own and **n** not be feared.
20:19 They are not enemies that **n** to be attacked!
20:20 Use them to make the equipment you **n** to besiege
28:12 but you will never **n** to borrow from them.
Jos 7: 3 destroy it. There's no **n** for all of us to go there."
13: 2 The people still **n** to occupy the land of the
22:19 If you **n** the altar because your land is defiled,
Jdg 11: 8 "Because we **n** you," they replied. "If you will
19:19 even though we have everything we **n**. We have
19:20 man said. "I will give you anything you might **n**.
1Sa 3: 5 and ran to Eli. "Here I am. What do you **n**?"
3: 6 to Eli. "Here I am," he said. "What do you **n**?"
3: 8 to Eli. "Here I am," he said. "What do you **n**?"
17: 8 "Do you **n** a whole army to settle this?
17:47 LORD does not **n** weapons to rescue his people.
26: 8 him to the ground, and I won't **n** to strike twice!"
2Sa 18: 3 stay here in the city and send us help if we **n** it."
19:36 to go across the river with you is all the honor I **n**!
20:10 Joab did not **n** to strike again, and Amasa soon
2Ki 22: 6 They will **n** to hire carpenters, builders,
22: 7 But there will be no **n** for the construction
1Ch 22:14 stone for the walls, though you may **n** to add more.
23:26 Now the Levites will no longer **n** to carry the
2Ch 2:16 We will cut whatever timber you **n** from the
20:17 But you will not even **n** to fight. Take your
35: 3 and you do not **n** to carry it back and forth on your
35:15 the gates and did not **n** to leave their posts of duty,
Ezr 6: 9 salt, wine, and olive oil that they **n** each day.
Ne 2: 8 I will **n** it to make beams for the gates of the
5: 2 We **n** more money just so we can buy the food we
n to survive."
Job 27:12 But I don't **n** to, for you yourselves have seen all
29:12 For I helped the poor in their **n** and the orphans
33: 7 So you don't **n** to be afraid of me. I am not some
Ps 10: 1 Why do you hide when I **n** you the most?
23: 1 LORD is my shepherd; / I have everything I **n**.
34: 9 for those who honor him will have all they **n**.
49: 5 There is no **n** to fear when times of trouble come,
50:13 I don't **n** the bulls you sacrifice; / I don't **n** the
blood of goats.
86: 1 and hear my prayer; / answer me, for I **n** your help.
104:27 on you / to give them their food as they **n** it.
112: 9 They give generously to those in **n**. / Their good
119:19 on earth; / I **n** the guidance of your commands.
138: 3 you encourage me by giving me the strength I **n**.
145:15 for help; / you give them their food as they **n** it.
Pr 3:25 You **n** not be afraid of disaster or the destruction
11:26 bless the one who sells to them in their time of **n**.
12:15 Fools think they **n** no advice, but the wise listen to
17:17 and a brother is born to help in time of **n**.
21:13 of the poor will be ignored in their own time of **n**.
27:10 Then in your time of **n**, you won't have to ask your
Isa 7: 4 Tell him he doesn't **n** to fear the fierce anger of
8:13 Holy One. If you fear him, you **n** fear nothing else.
28:16 Whoever believes **n** never run away again.
40:14 Does he **n** instruction about what is good or what
48:19 There would have been no **n** for your destruction."
49:20 in exile will return and say, 'We **n** more room!
58: 7 Give clothes to those who **n** them, and do not hide
from relatives who **n** your help.
60:16 the best of their goods to satisfy your every **n**.
60:19 "No longer will you **n** the sun or moon to give you
Jer 2:24 Those who desire you do not even **n** to search,
3:16 and there will be no **n** to rebuild the Ark.
13:12 you don't **n** to tell us how prosperous we will be!'
18:18 We don't **n** him to teach the law and give us advice
31:34 And they will not **n** to teach their neighbors,
31:34 nor will they **n** to teach their family, saying,
Eze 18: 7 to the hungry and provides clothes for people in **n**.
39:10 They will **n** nothing else for their fires. They won't
n to cut wood from the fields
39:10 for these weapons will give them all they **n**.
Da 3:16 we do not **n** to defend ourselves before you.
Ob 1:11 relatives in Israel during their time of greatest **n**.
Na 1: 9 you with one blow; he won't **n** to strike twice!
Hab 3: 2 In this time of our deep **n**, begin again to help us,
Zep 3: 7 listen to my warnings, so I won't **n** to strike again.'
3:11 then you will no longer **n** to be ashamed of
Mt 4: 4 'People **n** more than bread for their life;
5: 3 "God blesses those who realize their **n** for him,
6: 2 When you give a gift to someone in **n**, don't shout
6: 8 because your Father knows exactly what you **n**
6:26 They don't **n** to plant or harvest or put food in
6:33 and he will give you all you **n** from day to day if
8: 9 I only **n** to say, 'Go,' and they go, or 'Come,'
9:12 Jesus replied, "Healthy people don't **n** a doctor—
15: 5 'You don't **n** to honor your parents by caring for
26:65 "Blasphemy! Why do we **n** other witnesses?
Mk 2:17 he told them, "Healthy people don't **n** a doctor—
14:63 and said, "Why do we **n** other witnesses?
Lk 2:49 "But why did you **n** to search?" he asked.
4: 4 'People **n** more than bread for their life.' "
5:31 "Healthy people don't **n** a doctor—
7: 8 I only **n** to say, 'Go,' and they go, or 'Come,'
12:24 They don't **n** to plant or harvest or put food in
12:31 He will give you all you **n** from day to day if you
12:33 "Sell what you have and give to those in **n**.
17: 5 the apostles said to the Lord, "We **n** more faith;
18: 1 a story to illustrate their **n** for constant prayer
22:71 "What **n** do we have for other witnesses?"
Jn 13:10 "A person who has bathed all over does not **n** to
16:23 At that time you won't **n** to ask me for anything.
16:30 and don't **n** anyone to tell you anything.
Ac 2:45 and shared the proceeds with those in **n**.
4:35 the money to the apostles to give to others in **n**.
4:37 brought the money to the apostles for those in **n**.
13:24 John the Baptist preached the **n** for everyone in
17:25 to everything, and he satisfies every **n** there is.
28:10 people put on board all sorts of things we would **n**
Ro 8:24 already have something, you don't **n** to hope for it.
10: 6 "You don't **n** to go to heaven" (to find Christ
10: 7 "You don't **n** to go to the place of the dead" (to
12:13 When God's children are in **n**, be the one to help
12:13 home for dinner or, if they **n** lodging, for the night.
13: 6 For government workers **n** to be paid so they can
15:15 knowing that all you **n** is this reminder from me.
1Co 1: 7 Now you have every spiritual gift you **n** as you
4: 8 You think you already have everything you **n**!
12:21 eye can never say to the hand, "I don't **n** you."
12:21 The head can't say to the feet, "I don't **n** you."
14: 7 are examples of the **n** for speaking in plain
2Co 3: 1 Some people **n** to bring letters of recommendation
3: 2 But the only letter of recommendation we **n** is you
8:14 other time they can share with you when you **n** it.
9: 1 I really don't **n** to write to you about this gift for
9: 8 And God will generously provide all you **n**.
9: 8 Then you will always have everything you **n**
9:11 And when we take your gifts to those who **n** them,
12: 9 time he said, "My gracious favor is all you **n**.
13:10 hoping that I won't **n** to deal harshly with you
Gal 2:21 the law, then there was no **n** for Christ to die.
3:25 has come, we no longer **n** the law as our guardian.
6: 3 think you are too important to help someone in **n**,
6: 4 and you won't **n** to compare yourself to anyone
Eph 4:28 and then give generously to others in **n**.
6:16 In every battle you will **n** faith as your shield to
Php 2:25 And he was your messenger to help me in my **n**.
4: 6 Tell God what you **n**, and thank him for all he has
4:11 Not that I was ever in **n**, for I have learned how to
4:13 the help of Christ who gives me the strength I **n**.
4:18 At the moment I have all I **n**—more than I **n**!
Col 1:11 will have all the patience and endurance you **n**.
1Th 1: 8 your faith in God. We don't **n** to tell them about it,
4: 9 But I don't **n** to write to you about the Christian
4:12 and you will not **n** to depend on others to meet
5: 1 I really don't **n** to write to you about how
1Ti 6:17 who richly gives us all we **n** for our enjoyment.
6:18 and should give generously to those in **n**,
2Ti 2:15 one who does not **n** to be ashamed and who
Tit 3:13 See that they are given everything they **n**.
Heb 4:16 and we will find grace to help us when we **n** it.
5:12 you **n** someone to teach you again the basic things
6: 1 Surely we don't **n** to start all over again with the
6: 2 You don't **n** further instruction about baptisms,
7:11 why did God **n** to send a different priest from the
7:26 He is the kind of high priest we **n** because he is
7:27 He does not **n** to offer sacrifices every day like the
8: 7 there would have been no **n** for a second covenant
8:11 And they will not **n** to teach their neighbors,
8:11 nor will they **n** to teach their family,
10:18 there is no **n** to offer any more sacrifices.
10:36 Patient endurance is what you **n** now, so you will
11:32 Well, how much more do I **n** to say? It would take
13:16 and to share what you have with those in **n**,
13:19 I especially **n** your prayers right now so that I can
13:20[-21] equip you with all you **n** for doing his will.
Jas 1: 5 If you **n** wisdom—if you want to know what God
1Pe 4: 9 Cheerfully share your home with those who **n** a
2Pe 1: 3 his divine power gives us everything we **n** for
1Jn 2:26 because you **n** to be aware of those who want to
2:27 so you don't **n** anyone to teach you what is true.
3:17 and sees a brother or sister in **n** and refuses to
Jude 1:23 There are still others to whom you **n** to show
Rev 3:17 I have everything I want. I don't **n** a thing!'
16:15 so they will not **n** to walk naked and ashamed."
21:23 And the city has no **n** of sun or moon, for the glory
22: 5 will be no night there—no **n** for lamps or sun—

NEEDED (27) [NEED]

Ex 16:18 a little had enough. Each family had just what it **n**.
35:35 They excel in all the crafts **n** for the work.
Nu 27:21 When direction from the LORD is **n**, Joshua will
Jdg 21:20 They told the men of Benjamin who still **n** wives,
1Sa 13:20 So whenever the Israelites **n** to sharpen their
2Ki 12: 5 to pay for whatever repairs are **n** at the Temple."
19: 7 from Assyria telling him that he is **n** at home.
22: 6 the timber and the cut stone **n** to repair the Temple.
1Ch 16:37 doing whatever **n** to be done each day.
22: 3 the nails that would be **n** for the doors in the gates
28:15 He told Solomon the amount of gold **n** for the gold
2Ch 2: 9 An immense amount of timber will be **n**,
Ezr 6: 9 Give the priests in Jerusalem whatever is **n** in the
Ne 5:18 And every ten days we **n** a large supply of all kinds
Ps 119:75 are fair; / you disciplined me because I **n** it.
Pr 29:19 mere words are not enough—discipline is **n**.
Isa 37: 7 from Assyria telling him that he is **n** at home.
40:14 Has the LORD ever **n** anyone's advice? Does he
Jer 31:18 I was like a calf that **n** to be trained for the yoke

Eze 34:26 of blessings, which will come just when they are **n**.
Da 1: 4 and have the poise **n** to serve in the royal palace.
Am 4: 7 "I kept the rain from falling when you **n** it the
Lk 4:25 many widows in Israel who **n** help in Elijah's time,
4:27 rather than the many lepers in Israel who **n** help."
Jn 2:25 No one **n** to tell him about human nature.
Gal 3:20 Now a mediator is **n** if two people enter into an
Rev 13:18 Wisdom is **n** to understand this. Let the one who

NEEDLE (3)

Mt 19:24 it is easier for a camel to go through the eye of a **n**
Mk 10:25 It is easier for a camel to go through the eye of a **n**
Lk 18:25 It is easier for a camel to go through the eye of a **n**

NEEDLESS (1) [NEED]

1Sa 25:31 conscience the staggering burden of **n** bloodshed

NEEDS (40) [NEED]

Ex 16:16 that each household should gather as much as it **n**.
2Sa 20: 3 Their **n** were to be cared for, he said, but he would
1Ki 8:59 the cause of his people Israel, fulfilling our daily **n**.
18:27 on a trip, or he is asleep and **n** to be wakened!"
2Ki 12: 7 Don't use any more gifts for your own **n**.
Ezr 7:20 for your God's Temple or for any similar **n**,
Ps 32: 9 that **n** a bit and bridle to keep it under control."
79: 8 Let your tenderhearted mercies quickly meet our **n**,
Pr 30: 8 nor riches! Give me just enough to satisfy my **n**.
Isa 22: 9 You inspect the walls of Jerusalem to see what **n** to
49:23 will serve you. They will care for all your **n**.
65:24 While they are still talking to me about their **n**,
Jer 10: 5 and it **n** to be carried because it cannot walk.
Eze 27:33 you traded / satisfied the **n** of many nations.
Joel 2:19 and wine and olive oil, enough to satisfy your **n**.
Mt 3:14 "I am the one who **n** to be baptized by you,"
6:32 Your heavenly Father already knows all your **n**,
15: 5 for their **n** if you give the money to God instead.'
21: 3 what you are doing, just say, 'The Lord **n** them,'
Mk 2:22 ruining the skins. New wine **n** new wineskins."
11: 3 just say, 'The Lord **n** it and will return it soon.' "
Lk 12:12 for the Holy Spirit will teach you what **n** to be said
12:30 but your Father already knows your **n**.
19:31 what you are doing, just say, 'The Lord **n** it.' "
19:34 And the disciples simply replied, "The Lord **n** it."
Ac 17:25 human hands can't serve his **n**—for he has no **n**.
20:34 and I have even supplied the **n** of those who were
24:23 allow his friends to visit him and take care of his **n**.
27: 3 to visit with friends so they could provide for his **n**.
Ro 1: 9 and night I bring you and your **n** in prayer to God,
12: 5 to each other, and each of us **n** all the others.
16: 2 for she has helped many in their **n**, including me.
2Co 8:14 you need it. In this way, everyone's **n** will be met.
9:12 the **n** of the Christians in Jerusalem will be met,
Php 4:19 me will supply all your **n** from his glorious riches,
1Th 4:12 need to depend on others to meet your financial **n**.
2Th 3:15 as you would to a Christian who **n** to be warned.
Tit 3:14 to do good by helping others who have urgent **n**.
Jas 2:15 you see a brother or sister who **n** food or clothing,

NEEDY (36) [NEED]

Dt 15: 9 the loan and the **n** person cries out to the LORD,
Job 24: 4 kicked aside; the **n** must hide together for safety.
24:14 rises in the early dawn to kill the poor and **n**;
24:21 protecting sons. They refuse to help the **n** widows.
30:24 "Surely no one would turn against the **n** when they
30:25 in trouble? Was I not deeply grieved for the **n**?
34:28 God's attention. Yes, he hears the cries of the **n**.
Ps 9:18 For the **n** will not be forgotten forever; / the hopes
22:24 For he has not ignored the suffering of the **n**.
35:10 the poor and **n** from those who want to rob them?"
40:17 As for me, I am poor and **n**, / but the Lord is
68:10 O God, / you provided for your **n** people.
69:33 For the LORD hears the cries of his **n** ones;
70: 5 But I am poor and **n**; / please hurry to my aid,
72: 4 to defend the poor, / to rescue the children of the **n**,
72:13 He feels pity for the weak and the **n**, / and he will
74:21 let these poor and **n** ones give praise to your name.
109:16 kindness to others; / he persecuted the poor and **n**,
109:22 For I am poor and **n**, / and my heart is full of pain.
109:31 For he stands beside the **n**, / ready to save them
113: 7 from the dirt / and the **n** from the garbage dump.
Pr 22:22 because they are poor or exploit the **n** in court.
30:14 They destroy the **n** from the face of the earth.
31:20 hand to the poor and opens her arms to the **n**.
Isa 14:30 poor in my pasture; the **n** will lie down in peace.
25: 4 To the **n** in distress, you are a shelter from the rain
41:17 "When the poor and **n** search for water and there
Jer 20:13 For though I was poor and **n**, he delivered me from
22:16 that justice and help were given to the poor and **n**,
Eze 16:49 while the poor and **n** suffered outside her door.
18:16 son feeds the hungry, provides clothes for the **n**,
22:29 rob the **n**, and deprive foreigners of justice.
Am 4: 1 you women who oppress the poor and crush the **n**
8: 4 to this, you who rob the poor and trample the **n**!
Mk 7:12 You let them disregard their **n** parents.
Lk 11:41 So give to the **n** what you greedily possess,

NEESINGS [KJV] See SNEEZES

NEGEV (33) [RAMOTH-NEGEV]

Ge 12: 9 Abram traveled south by stages toward the **N**.
13: 1 So they left Egypt and traveled north into the **N**—
20: 1 Now Abraham moved south to the **N** and settled
24:62 Meanwhile, Isaac, whose home was in the **N**,
25:11 on Isaac, who settled near Beer-lahairoi in the **N**.
Nu 13:17 "Go northward through the **N** into the hill country.
13:22 they passed first through the **N** and arrived at
13:29 The Amalekites live in the **N**, and the Hittites,
21: 1 The Canaanite king of Arad, who lived in the **N**,
33:40 of Arad, who lived in the **N** in the land of Canaan,
Dt 1: 7 the hill country, the western foothills, the **N**,
34: 3 the **N**; the Jordan Valley with Jericho—the city of
Jos 1: 4 from the **N** Desert in the south to the Lebanon
10:40 the **N**, the western foothills, and the mountain
11:16 the hill country, the **N**, the land of Goshen,
12: 8 mountain slopes, the Judean wilderness, and the **N**.
15:19 have been kind enough to give me land in the **N**;
19: 8 as Baalath-beer (also known as Ramah of the **N**).
Jdg 1: 9 in the hill country, the **N**, and the western foothills.
1:15 have been kind enough to give me land in the **N**;
1:16 the people there, near the town of Arad in the **N**.
1Sa 30: 1 that the Amalekites had made a raid into the **N**
30:14 our way back from raiding the Kerethites in the **N**,
2Ch 28:18 located in the foothills of Judah and in the **N**.
Isa 21: 1 like a whirlwind sweeping in from the **N**.
Jer 13:19 The towns of the **N** will close their gates, and no
17:26 western foothills and the hill country and the **N**,
32:44 in the foothills of Judah and in the **N**, too.
33:13 the foothills of Judah, the **N**, the land of Benjamin,
Eze 20:46 out against it; prophesy against the fields of the **N**.
Ob 1:19 "Then my people living in the **N** will occupy the
1:20 to their homeland and resettle the villages of the **N**.
Zec 7: 7 and the **N** and the foothills of Judah were

NEGLECT (6) [NEGLECTED, NEGLECTING, NEGLIGENT]

2Ch 29:11 My dear Levites, do not **n** your duties any longer!
Ne 10:39 "So we promise together not to **n** the Temple of
Pr 1: 8 teaches you. Don't **n** your mother's teaching.
6:20 and don't **n** your mother's teaching.
1Ti 4:14 Do not **n** the spiritual gift you received through the
Heb 10:25 And let us not **n** our meeting together, as some

NEGLECTED (4) [NEGLECT]

Dt 32:18 You **n** the Rock who had fathered you; / you forgot
1Ch 13: 3 of our God, for we **n** it during the reign of Saul."
Ne 13:11 "Why has the Temple of God been **n**?"
Lk 7:46 You **n** the courtesy of olive oil to anoint my head,

NEGLECTING (1) [NEGLECT]

Da 1:10 I am afraid the king will have me beheaded for **n**

NEGLIGENT (1) [NEGLECT]

Lev 22:16 The **n** priest would bring guilt upon the people

NEGOTIATE (2)

2Sa 3:13 "but I will not **n** with you unless you bring back
Isa 47: 3 I will take vengeance against you and will not **n**."

NEHELAMITE (2)

Jer 29:24 The LORD sent this message to Shemaiah the **N**
29:31 what the LORD says concerning Shemaiah the **N**:

NEHEMIAH (9)

Ezr 2: 2 Jeshua, **N**, Seraiah, Reelaiah, Mordecai, Bilshan,
Ne 1: 1 These are the memoirs of **N** son of Hacaliah.
3:16 Next to him was **N** son of Azbuk, the leader of half
7: 7 Jeshua, **N**, Seraiah, Reelaiah, Nahamani, Mordecai,
8: 9 Then **N** the governor, Ezra the priest and scribe,
8:10 And **N** continued, "Go and celebrate with a feast
10: 1 **N** the governor, the son of Hacaliah.
12:26 and in the days of **N** the governor and of Ezra the
12:47 So now, in the days of Zerubbabel and of **N**,

NEHUSHTA (1)

2Ki 24: 8 His mother was **N**, the daughter of Elnathan from

NEHUSHTAN (1)

2Ki 18: 4 incense to it. The bronze serpent was called **N**.

NEIEL (1)

Jos 19:27 of Iphtah-el, running north to Beth-emek and **N**.

NEIGH (1) [NEIGHING]

Jer 50:11 about like a calf in a meadow and **n** like a stallion.

NEIGHBOR (52) [NEIGHBOR'S, NEIGHBORHOOD, NEIGHBORING, NEIGHBORS, NEIGHBORS']

LOVE YOUR NEIGHBOR (10) Lev 19:18; Mt 5:43; 19:19; 22:39; Mk 12:31; Lk 10:27; Ro 13:8,9; Gal 5:14; Jas 2:8

Ex 2:13 "What are you doing, hitting your **n** like that?"
20:16 "Do not testify falsely against your **n**.
20:17 ox or donkey, or anything else your **n** owns."
22: 7 someone entrusts money or goods to a **n**,
22: 8 or not it was the **n** who stole the property.
22:10 "Now suppose someone asks a **n** to care for a
22:11 The **n** must then take an oath of innocence in the
22:14 "If someone borrows an animal from a **n** and it is
22:27 Your **n** will need it to stay warm during the night.
22:27 do not return it and your **n** cries out to me for help,
Lev 6: 2 **n** that an item entrusted to their safekeeping has
19:18 grudge against anyone, but love your **n** as yourself.
25:14 "When you make an agreement with a **n** to buy
25:15 When you buy land from your **n**, the price of the
Dt 5:20 " 'Do not testify falsely against your **n**.
5:21 ox or donkey, or anything else your **n** owns.'
19: 4 "If someone accidentally kills a **n** without
19: 5 suppose someone goes into the forest with a **n** to
19:11 "But suppose someone hates a **n** and deliberately ambushes and murders that **n** and
22: 3 clothing, or anything else your **n** loses.
22: 4 the other way. Go and help your **n** get it to its feet!
22:26 to that of someone who attacks and murders a **n**.
24:10 "If you lend anything to your **n**, do not enter your
24:12 If your **n** is poor and has only a cloak to give as
24:13 by sunset so your **n** can sleep in it and bless you.
25: 3 than forty lashes would publicly humiliate your **n**.
27:17 'Cursed is anyone who steals property from a **n** by
Ru 4:17 The **n** women said, "Now at last Naomi has a son
Pr 3:28 If you can help your **n** now, don't say,
11:12 It is foolish to belittle a **n**; a person with good
27:10 It is better to go to a **n** than to a relative who lives
27:14 If you shout a pleasant greeting to your **n** too early
Isa 3: 5 each other—man against man, **n** fighting **n**.
19: 2 **n** against **n**, city against city,
Jer 9: 4 "Beware of your **n**! Beware of your brother!
Zec 3:10 each of you will invite your **n** into your home to
Mt 5:43 Moses says, 'Love your **n**' and hate your enemy.
19:19 and mother. Love your **n** as yourself.' "
22:39 is equally important: 'Love your **n** as yourself.'
Mk 12:31 is equally important: 'Love your **n** as yourself.'
Lk 10:27 all your mind.' And, 'Love your **n** as yourself.' "
10:29 so he asked Jesus, "And who is my **n**?"
10:36 "Now which of these three would you say was a **n**
Ro 13: 8 If you love your **n**, you will fulfill all the
13: 9 one commandment: "Love your **n** as yourself."
Gal 5:14 in this one command: "Love your **n** as yourself."
Eph 4:25 put away all falsehood and "tell your **n** the truth"
Jas 2: 8 in the Scriptures: "Love your **n** as yourself."
4:12 So what right do you have to condemn your **n**?

NEIGHBOR'S (20) [NEIGHBOR]

Ex 20:17 "Do not covet your **n** house. Do not covet your **n** wife, male or female servant,
21:35 "If someone's bull injures a **n** bull and the injured
22: 7 a neighbor, and they are stolen from the **n** house.
22:11 The owner must accept the **n** word, and no
22:26 If you take your **n** cloak as a pledge of repayment,
Lev 18:20 by having sexual intercourse with your **n** wife.
19:16 "Do not try to get ahead at the cost of your **n** life,
Dt 5:21 " 'Do not covet your **n** wife. Do not covet your **n** house or land, male or female
22: 1 "If you see your **n** ox or sheep wandering away,
22: 3 Do the same if you find your **n** donkey, clothing,
22: 4 "If you see your **n** ox or donkey lying on the road,
23:24 "You may eat your fill of grapes from your **n**
23:25 And you may pluck a few heads of your **n** grain by
24:10 do not enter your **n** house to claim the security.
Job 31: 9 by a woman, or if I have lusted for my **n** wife,
Pr 17:18 friend's note, to become responsible for a **n** debts.
22:28 Do not steal your **n** property by moving the ancient
Jer 5: 8 lusty stallions, each neighing for his **n** wife.

NEIGHBORHOOD (3) [NEIGHBOR]

Ge 29:22 So Laban invited everyone in the **n** to celebrate
Ex 12: 4 them share the lamb with another family in the **n**.
Lk 1:65 Wonder fell upon the whole **n**, and the news of

NEIGHBORING (13) [NEIGHBOR]

Dt 1: 7 country of the Amorites and to all the **n** regions—
6:14 "You must not worship any of the gods of **n**
Ezr 4:10 and throughout the **n** lands of the province west of
Ps 80: 6 You have made us the scorn of **n** nations.
Jer 25:11 and her **n** lands will serve the king of Babylon for
49: 2 a desolate heap, and the **n** towns will be burned.
49:18 of Sodom and Gomorrah and their **n** towns,"
50:40 and Gomorrah and their **n** towns,"
Eze 28:26 And when I punish the **n** nations that treated them
Da 9:16 All the **n** nations mock Jerusalem and your people
Zec 12: 6 They will burn up all the **n** nations right and left,
14:14 The wealth of all the **n** nations will be captured—
Jude 1: 7 cities of Sodom and Gomorrah and their **n** towns,

NEIGHBORS (51) [NEIGHBOR]

Ex 3:22 and fine clothing from their Egyptian **n**
11: 2 and women to ask their Egyptian **n** for articles of
32:27 killing even your brothers, friends, and **n**."
Lev 19:15 "Always judge your **n** fairly, neither favoring the
19:17 "Confront your **n** directly so you will not be held
Dt 15: 2 They must not demand payment from their **n**
Jdg 18:22 Micah and some of his **n** came chasing after them.
1Sa 10:12 But one of the **n** responded, "It doesn't matter
2Ki 4: 3 empty jars as you can from your friends and **n**.
Ezr 1: 6 And all their **n** assisted by giving them vessels of
Job 19:14 My **n** and my close friends are all gone.
Ps 12: 2 **N** lie to each other, / speaking with flattering lips
15: 3 or harm their **n** / or speak evil of their friends.
28: 3 those who speak friendly words to their **n**
31:11 by all my enemies / and despised by my **n**—
44:13 You have caused all our **n** to mock us. / We are an
79: 4 We are mocked by our **n**, / an object of scorn
79:12 O Lord, take sevenfold vengeance on our **n**
89:41 comes along has robbed him / while his **n** mock.
101: 5 I will not tolerate people who slander their **n**.
Pr 3:29 Do not plot against your **n**, for they trust you.
14:20 The poor are despised even by their **n**,
14:21 It is sin to despise one's **n**; blessed are those who
21:10 to harm others; their **n** get no mercy from them.

24:28 Do not testify spitefully against innocent **n**;
25:8 You might go down before your **n** in shameful
25:17 Don't visit your **n** too often, or you will wear out
Ecc 4:4 are motivated to success by their envy of their **n**.
Isa 9:20 They fight against their own **n** to steal food,
Jer 6:21 over them. **N** and friends will collapse together."
9:8 They promise peace to their **n** while planning to
31:34 And they will not need to teach their **n**, nor will
48:39 object of ridicule, an example of ruin to all her **n**.
49:5 "Your **n** will chase you from your land, and no
49:10 Its children, its brothers, and its **n**—all will be
La 1:17 LORD has said, "Let their **n** be their enemies!
Eze 5:7 and have behaved even worse than your **n**,
16:57 is scorned—by Edom and all her **n** and by Philistia.
23:5 and she gave her love to the Assyrians, her **n**.
23:12 She fawned over her Assyrian **n**, those handsome
28:24 No longer will Israel's scornful **n** prick and tear at
29:15 never again great enough to rise above its **n**.
Hab 2:15 "How terrible it will be for you who make your **n**
Mk 12:33 and all my strength, and to love my **n** as myself.
Lk 1:58 The word spread quickly to her **n** and relatives that
14:12 invite your friends, brothers, relatives, and rich **n**.
15:6 and **n** to rejoice with you because your lost sheep
15:9 she will call in her friends and **n** to rejoice with her
Jn 9:8 His **n** and others who knew him as a blind beggar
Heb 8:11 And they will not need to teach their **n**, / nor will
1Pe 2:12 careful how you live among your unbelieving **n**.

NEIGHBORS' (3) [NEIGHBOR]

Ex 3:22 from their Egyptian neighbors and their **n** guests.
Jer 29:23 They have committed adultery with their **n** wives
Eze 22:11 live men who commit adultery with their **n** wives,

NEIGHING (1) [NEIGH]

Jer 5:8 lusty stallions, each **n** for his neighbor's wife.

NEITHER (61) [NOR]

Ge 2:25 wife were both naked, **n** of them felt any shame.
45:6 during which there will be **n** plowing nor harvest.
Ex 10:15 **n** tree nor plant, throughout the land of Egypt.
32:18 "No, it's **n** a cry of victory nor a cry of defeat.
34:28 and forty nights. In all that time he **n** ate nor drank.
Lev 19:15 **n** favoring the poor nor showing deference to the
27:10 **n** a good animal for a bad one nor a bad animal for
Nu 14:44 despite the fact that **n** Moses nor the Ark of the
Dt 4:28 gods that **n** see nor hear nor eat nor smell.
9:18 the LORD, **n** eating bread nor drinking water.
12:17 **n** the tithe of your grain and new wine and olive
13:6 gods that **n** you nor your ancestors have known.
21:4 They must lead it to a valley that is **n** plowed nor
28:64 There you will worship foreign gods that **n** you nor
31:6 ahead of you. He will **n** fail you nor forsake you."
31:8 be with you; he will **n** fail you nor forsake you."
Jos 5:14 "**N** one," he replied. "I am commander of the
1Sa 5:5 That is why to this day **n** the priests of Dagon nor
16:9 "**N** is this the one the LORD has chosen."
2Sa 14:14 lives of those he cares about—and **n** should you!
1Ki 1:26 **n** were Zadok the priest, Benaiah son of Jehoiada,
3:26 "All right, he will be **n** yours nor mine;
2Ki 3:17 You will see **n** wind nor rain, says the LORD,
4:23 "It is **n** a new moon festival nor a Sabbath."
6:27 he retorted. "I have **n** food nor wine to give you."
1Ch 23:11 as a single family because **n** had many sons.
Ne 5:14 **n** I nor my officials drew on our official food
Job 18:19 They will have **n** children nor grandchildren,
20:9 **N** his friends nor his family will ever see him
Pr 30:8 to tell a lie. Second, give me **n** poverty nor riches!
SS 8:7 waters cannot quench love; **n** can rivers drown it.
Isa 44:9 that this is so, for their idols **n** see nor know.
49:10 They will **n** hunger nor thirst. The searing sun
59:21 and **n** will these words I have given you.
Jer 10:5 for they can **n** harm you nor do you any good."
13:23 **N** can you start doing good, for you always do evil.
15:10 I am **n** a lender who has threatened to foreclose nor
36:24 **N** the king nor his officials showed any signs of
37:2 But **n** King Zedekiah nor his officials nor the
44:3 gods that **n** they nor you nor any of your ancestors
51:62 so that **n** people nor animals will remain here.
Eze 7:9 I will **n** spare nor pity you. I will repay you for all
7:19 It will **n** satisfy nor feed them, for their love of
8:18 deal with them in fury. I will **n** pity nor spare them.
29:11 not a soul will pass that way, **n** people nor animals.
30:21 **N** has it been bound up with a splint to make it
44:20 "They must **n** let their hair grow too long nor
Da 5:23 gods that **n** see nor hear nor know anything at all.
11:20 he will die, though **n** in battle nor open conflict.
Hos 5:13 great king there, but he could **n** help nor cure them.
Zec 8:15 **N** will I change my decision to bless Jerusalem
Lk 7:42 But **n** of them could repay him, so he kindly
14:35 Flavorless salt is good **n** for the soil nor for
18:4 him out. 'I fear **n** God nor man,' he said to himself,
Jn 8:11 And Jesus said, "**N** do I. Go and sin no more."
Ac 15:10 that **n** we nor our ancestors were able to bear?
23:12 and bound themselves with an oath to **n** eat nor
23:14 "We have bound ourselves under oath to **n** eat nor
25:11 **n** you nor anyone else has a right to turn me over
Rev 3:15 all the things you do, that you are **n** hot nor cold.
9:20 and wood—idols that **n** see nor hear nor walk!

NEKODA (4)

Ezr 2:48 Rezin, **N**, Gazzam,
2:60 of the families of Delaiah, Tobiah, and **N**—
Ne 7:50 Reaiah, Rezin, **N**,
7:62 included the families of Delaiah, Tobiah, and **N**—

NEMUEL (3) [JEMUEL, NEMUELITE]

Nu 26:9 and Eliab was the father of **N**, Dathan,
26:12 The Nemuelite clan, named after its ancestor **N**.
1Ch 4:24 The sons of Simeon were **N**, Jamin, Jarib, Zerah,

NEMUELITE (1) [NEMUEL]

Nu 26:12 The **N** clan, named after its ancestor Nemuel.

NEPHEG (4)

Ex 6:21 descendants of Izhar included Korah, **N**, and Zicri.
2Sa 5:15 Ibhar, Elishua, **N**, Japhia,
1Ch 3:7 Nogah, **N**, Japhia,
14:6 Nogah, **N**, Japhia,

NEPHEW (7)

Ge 12:5 He took his wife, Sarai, his **n** Lot, and all his
14:12 captured Lot—Abram's **n** who lived in Sodom—
14:16 Abram's **n** Lot with his possessions, and all the
Lev 25:49 an uncle, a **n**, or anyone else who is closely related.
2Sa 19:13 told them to tell Amasa, "Since you are my **n**,
Ac 23:16 But Paul's **n** heard of their plan and went to the
23:20 Paul's **n** told him, "Some Jews are going to ask you

NEPHTHALIM [KJV] See NAPHTALI

NEPHTOAH (2)

Jos 15:9 of the mountain to the spring at the waters of **N**,
18:15 it ran westward to the spring at the waters of **N**,

NEPHUSIM (2)

Ezr 2:50 Asnah, Meunim, **N**,
Ne 7:52 Besai, Meunim, **N**,

NER (10) [NER'S]

1Sa 14:51 Abner's father, **N**, and Saul's father, Kish,
26:5 Saul and his general, Abner son of **N**,
2Sa 2:8 But Abner son of **N**, the commander of Saul's
1Ki 2:5 Abner son of **N** and Amasa son of Jether.
2:32 was no party to the deaths of Abner son of **N**,
1Ch 8:30 Jeiel's other sons were Zur, Kish, Baal, **N**, Nadab,
8:33 **N** was the father of Kish. Kish was the father of
9:36 Jeiel's other sons were Zur, Kish, Baal, **N**, Nadab,
9:39 **N** was the father of Kish. Kish was the father of
26:28 Saul son of Kish, Abner son of **N**, and Joab son of

NER'S (1) [NER]

1Sa 14:50 Saul's army was his cousin Abner, his uncle **N** son.

NEREUS (1)

Ro 16:15 Julia, **N** and his sister, and to Olympas and all the

NERGAL (1) [NERGAL-SHAREZER]

2Ki 17:30 Those from Cuthah worshiped their god **N**.

NERGAL-SHAREZER (3) [NERGAL]

Jer 39:3 **N** of Samgar, and Nebo-sarsekim, a chief officer,
and **N**, the king's adviser, and many
39:13 and Nebushazban, a chief officer, and **N**, the king's

NERI (2)

Lk 3:27 the son of Shealtiel. / Shealtiel was the son of **N**.
3:28 **N** was the son of Melki. / Melki was the son of

NERIAH (5)

Jer 32:12 and I handed them to Baruch son of **N**
36:4 So Jeremiah sent for Baruch son of **N**, and as
43:3 Baruch son of **N** has convinced you to say this,
45:1 **N** in the fourth year of the reign of Jehoiakim son
51:59 Seraiah son of **N** and grandson of Mahseiah,

NERVE (2) [NERVOUS, NERVOUSLY]

1Sa 13:6 they lost their **n** entirely and tried to hide in caves,
Zec 12:4 every horse to panic and every rider to lose his **n**.

NERVOUS (1) [NERVE]

Job 33:7 I am not some great person to make you **n**

NERVOUSLY (1) [NERVE]

Est 5:9 not standing up or trembling **n** before him, he was

NEST (14) [NESTED, NESTLINGS, NESTS]

Nu 24:21 are strongly situated; / your **n** is set in the rocks.
Dt 22:6 "If you find a bird's **n** on the ground or in a tree
22:6 or eggs in it with the mother sitting in the **n**,
Job 39:27 that the eagle rises to the heights to make its **n**?
Ps 84:3 finds a home there, / and the swallow builds her **n**
104:12 The birds **n** beside the streams / and sing among
Pr 27:8 from home is like a bird that strays from its **n**.
Isa 11:8 a little child will put its hand in a **n** of deadly
31:5 hover over Jerusalem as a bird hovers around its **n**.
34:15 There the owl will make her **n** and lay her eggs.
Jer 48:28 Live in the caves like doves that **n** in the clefts of
Eze 17:23 Birds of every sort will **n** in it, finding shelter
Ob 1:4 as high as eagles and build your **n** among the stars,
Rev 18:2 of demons and evil spirits, a **n** for filthy buzzards,

NESTED (3) [NEST]

Eze 31:6 The birds **n** in its branches, and in its shade all the
Da 4:12 lived in its shade, and birds **n** in its branches.
4:21 lived in its shade, and birds **n** in its branches.

NESTLINGS (1) [NEST]

Job 39:30 Its **n** gulp down blood, for it feeds on the carcass

NESTS (5) [NEST]

Ps 104:17 There the birds make their **n**, / and the storks make
Isa 10:14 By my greatness I have robbed their **n** of riches
60:8 flying like clouds to Israel, like doves to their **n**?
Mt 8:20 and birds have **n**, but I, the Son of Man, have no
Lk 9:58 and birds have **n**, but I, the Son of Man, have no

NET (19) [NETS]

Job 18:8 "The wicked walk into a **n**. They fall into a pit
Ps 66:11 You captured us in your **n** / and laid the burden of
140:5 set a trap to catch me; / they have stretched out a **n**;
Pr 6:5 from a hunter, like a bird fleeing from a **n**.
Ecc 9:12 Like fish in a **n** or birds in a snare, people are often
Isa 51:20 in the streets, helpless as antelopes caught in a **n**.
Eze 12:13 Then I will spread out my **n** and capture him in my
17:20 I will throw my **n** over him and capture him in my
32:3 I will send many people to catch you in my **n**
Hos 7:12 I will throw my **n** over them and bring them down
Mt 4:18 fishing with a **n**, for they were commercial
13:47 the Kingdom of Heaven is like a fishing **n** that is
13:48 When the **n** is full, they drag it up onto the shore,
Mk 1:16 and his brother, Andrew, fishing with a **n**,
Jn 21:6 "Throw out your **n** on the right-hand side of the
21:6 and they couldn't draw in the **n** because there were
21:8 with the boat and pulled the loaded **n** to the shore,
21:11 Peter went aboard and dragged the **n** to the shore.
21:11 were 153 large fish, and yet the **n** hadn't torn.

NETAIM (1)

1Ch 4:23 They were the potters who lived in **N** and Gederah.

NETHANEL (14)

Nu 1:8 Issachar | **N** son of Zuar
2:5[-6] Issachar | **N** son of Zuar | 54,400
7:18 On the second day **N** son of Zuar, leader of the
7:23 This was the offering brought by **N** son of Zuar.
10:15 The tribe of Issachar was led by **N** son of Zuar.
1Ch 2:14 his fourth was **N**, his fifth was Raddai,
15:24 Joshaphat, **N**, Amasai, Zechariah, Benaiah,
24:6 Shemaiah son of **N**, a Levite, acted as secretary
26:4 Joah (the third), Sacar (the fourth), **N** (the fifth),
2Ch 17:7 Obadiah, Zechariah, **N**, and Micaiah.
35:9 Conaniah and his brothers Shemaiah and **N**,
Ezr 10:22 Elioenai, Maaseiah, Ishmael, **N**, Jozabad,
Ne 12:21 of Hilkiah. / **N** was leader of the family of Jedaiah.
12:36 Azarel, Milalai, Gilalai, Maai, **N**, Judah,

NETHANIAH (10)

2Ki 25:23 These included Ishmael son of **N**, Johanan son of
25:25 Ishmael son of **N** and grandson of Elishama,
1Ch 25:2 there were Zaccur, Joseph, **N**, and Asarelah.
25:12 The fifth lot fell to **N** and twelve of his sons
2Ch 17:8 **N**, Zebadiah, Asahel, Shemiramoth, Jehonathan,
Jer 36:14 the officials sent Jehudi son of **N**, grandson of
40:8 Ishmael son of **N**, Johanan and Jonathan, sons of
40:14 has sent Ishmael son of **N** to assassinate you?"
41:1 Ishmael son of **N** and grandson of Elishama,
41:9 of Israel. Ishmael son of **N** filled it with corpses.

NETHER(MOST) [KJV] See also BELOW, LOWER, LOWEST

NETHINIMS [KJV] See (TEMPLE) SERVANTS

NETOPHAH (9)

2Sa 23:28 Zalmon from Ahoah; / Maharai from **N**;
23:29 Heled son of Baanah from **N**; / Ithai son of Ribai
1Ch 9:16 of Asa, son of Elkanah, who lived in the area of **N**.
11:30 Maharai from **N**; / Heled son of Baanah from **N**;
27:13 Maharai, a descendant of Zerah from **N**,
27:15 Heled, a descendant of Othniel from **N**,
Ezr 2:22 The people of **N** | 56
Ne 7:26 The peoples of Bethlehem and **N** | 188

NETOPHATHITE (2) [NETOPHATHITES]

2Ki 25:23 son of Kareah, Seraiah son of Tanhumeth the **N**,
Jer 40:8 son of Tanhumeth, the sons of Ephai the **N**,

NETOPHATHITES (2) [NETOPHATHITE]

1Ch 2:54 the **N**, Atroth-beth-joab, the other half of the
Ne 12:28 and from the villages of the **N**.

NETS (16) [NET]

Ps 10:9 capture their victims / and drag them away in **n**.
Isa 19:8 and those who use **n** will all be unemployed.
Eze 19:8 They spread out their **n** for him / and captured him
26:5 It will be a place for fishermen to spread their **n**,
26:14 a bare rock, a place for fishermen to spread their **n**.
47:10 The shores will be covered with **n** drying in the
Hab 1:15 and dragged out in their **n** while they rejoice?
1:16 Then they will worship their **n** and burn incense in
1:16 "These **n** are the gods who have made us rich!"
Mt 4:20 And they left their **n** at once and went with him.
4:21 a boat with their father, Zebedee, mending their **n**.
Mk 1:18 And they left their **n** at once and went with him.

1:19 James and John, in a boat mending their **n**.
Lk 5: 2 fishermen had left them and were washing their **n**.
5: 4 go out where it is deeper and let down your **n**,
5: 6 And this time their **n** were so full they began to

NETTLES (3)

Job 30: 7 they huddle together for shelter beneath the **n**.
Isa 34:13 will overrun its palaces; **n** will grow in its forts.
Zep 2: 9 Their land will become a place of stinging **n**,

NETWORK (4) [NETWORKS]

2Ki 25:17 and was decorated with a **n** of bronze
2Ch 3:16 He made a **n** of interwoven chains and used them
Jer 52:22 and was decorated with a **n** of bronze
52:23 and a total of one hundred on the **n** around the top.

NETWORKS (4) [NETWORK]

1Ki 7:41 two **n** of chains that decorated the capitals,
7:42 **n** that were hung around the capitals on top of the
2Ch 4:12 two **n** of chains that decorated the capitals,
4:13 **n** that were hung around the capitals on top of the

NEVER (767) [NEVER-ENDING, NEVERTHELESS]

Ge 8:21 and said to himself, "I will **n** again curse the earth,
9: 4 But you must **n** eat animals that still have their
9:11 I solemnly promise **n** to send another flood to kill
9:15 **N** again will there be a flood that will destroy all
24: 6 "Be careful **n** to take my son there.
31:20 out secretly and **n** told Laban they were leaving.
31:38 In all those years I **n** touched a single ram of yours
34: 7 a thing that should **n** have been done.
38:21 "We've **n** had a prostitute here," they replied.
38:26 son Shelah." But Judah **n** slept with Tamar again.
40:23 all about Joseph, **n** giving him another thought.
41:19 I've **n** seen such ugly animals in all the land of
44:28 and that one of them went away and **n** returned—
44:28 by some wild animal. I have **n** seen him since.
48:11 said to Joseph, "I **n** thought I would see you again,
49: 6 May I **n** be a party to their wicked plans.
Ex 4: 1 just say, 'The LORD **n** appeared to you.' "
4:10 I **n** have been, and I'm not now, even after you
9:24 **N** in all the history of Egypt had there been a storm
10: 6 **N** in the history of Egypt has there been a plague
10:11 **N**! Only the men may go and serve the LORD,
10:14 and there has **n** again been one like it.
10:29 Moses replied. "I will **n** see you again."
11: 6 there has **n** been such wailing before and there **n** will be again.
12: 9 The meat must **n** be eaten raw or boiled; roast it
12:48 But an uncircumcised male may **n** eat of the
14:13 The Egyptians that you see today will **n** be seen
20: 5 You must **n** worship or bow down to them, for I,
23: 7 **N** put an innocent or honest person to death.
23:13 **n** pray to or swear by any other gods.
23:18 "Sacrificial blood must **n** be offered together with
23:24 them in any way, and **n** follow their evil example.
25:15 These carrying poles must **n** be taken from the
30:32 It must **n** be poured on the body of an ordinary
30:32 and you must **n** make any of it for yourselves.
30:37 **N** make this incense for yourselves. It is reserved
34:10 I will perform wonders that have **n** been done
34:12 "Be very careful **n** to make treaties with the
Lev 2:12 but these must **n** be burned on the altar as an
2:13 **N** forget to add salt to your grain offerings.
3:17 "You must **n** eat any fat or blood. This is a
6:12 on the altar must be kept burning; it must **n** go out.
6:13 burning on the altar at all times. It must **n** go out.
6:17 this flour may **n** be prepared with yeast.
7:23 You must **n** eat fat, whether from oxen or sheep
7:24 or killed by a wild animal may **n** be eaten,
7:26 you must **n** eat the blood of any bird or animal.
10: 9 "You and your descendants must **n** drink wine
11: 6 and the hare, so they also may **n** be eaten.
11:11 You must **n** eat their meat or even touch their dead
11:13 "These are the birds you must **n** eat because they
11:41 along the ground; such animals may **n** be eaten.
11:43 **N** defile yourselves by touching such animals.
17:12 and the foreigners who live among you must **n** eat
17:14 That is why I have told the people of Israel **n** to eat
18: 6 "You must **n** have sexual intercourse with a close
18: 7 your mother; you must **n** have intercourse with her.
18:23 "A man must **n** defile himself by having sexual
18:23 and a woman must **n** present herself to a male
19:18 "**N** seek revenge or bear a grudge against anyone,
19:26 "**N** eat meat that has not been drained of its blood.
19:28 "**N** cut your bodies in mourning for the dead
21: 5 "The priests must **n** shave their heads,
21: 6 to God as holy and must **n** dishonor his name.
21:10 must **n** let his hair hang loose or tear his clothing.
21:11 He must **n** defile himself by going near a dead
21:23 he must **n** go behind the inner curtain or come near
22: 8 The priests may **n** eat an animal that has died a
22:22 or a scab must **n** be offered to the LORD by fire
22:24 or is castrated, it may **n** be offered to the LORD.
22:25 You must **n** accept mutilated or defective animals
22:28 But you must **n** slaughter a mother animal and her
25:14 you must **n** take advantage of each other.
25:23 the land must **n** be sold on a permanent basis
25:34 around each of the Levitical cities may **n** be sold.
25:42 the land of Egypt, so they must **n** be sold as slaves.
25:43 **n** exercise your power over them in a ruthless way.
25:46 of Israel, your relatives, must **n** be treated this way.
26:35 it will take the rest you **n** allowed it to take every
27:10 The animal should **n** be exchanged or substituted
27:20 someone else by the priests, it can **n** be redeemed.
27:28 or an inherited field—must **n** be sold or redeemed.
Nu 6: 5 "They must **n** cut their hair throughout the time of
14:11 Will they **n** believe me, even after all the
14:23 They will **n** even see the land I swore to give their
16:15 and I have **n** hurt a single one of them."
18: 5 the LORD's anger will **n** again blaze against the
19: 2 physical defects and has **n** been yoked to a plow.
20:17 and **n** leave it until we have crossed the opposite
30: 2 or makes a pledge under oath must **n** break it.
35:31 you must **n** accept a ransom payment for the life of
35:32 And **n** accept a ransom payment from someone
Dt 1:17 you make decisions, **n** favor those who are rich;
1:37 said to me, 'You will **n** enter the Promised Land!
4: 9 Be very careful **n** to forget what you have seen the
4:21 He vowed that I would **n** cross the Jordan River
5: 9 You must **n** worship or bow down to them, for I,
8:17 so you would **n** think that it was your own strength
11: 2 who have **n** experienced the discipline of the
12:19 Be very careful **n** to forget the Levites as long as
12:23 The only restriction is **n** to eat the blood,
13:11 and such wickedness will **n** again be done among
13:16 must remain a ruin forever; it may **n** be rebuilt.
14: 1 **n** cut yourselves or shave the hair above your
15: 6 money to many nations but will **n** need to borrow!
16:19 You must **n** twist justice or show partiality.
16:19 **N** accept a bribe, for bribes blind the eyes of the
16:21 "You must **n** set up an Asherah pole beside the
16:22 And **n** set up sacred pillars for worship,
17: 1 "**N** sacrifice a sick or defective ox or sheep to the
17: 6 But **n** put a person to death on the testimony of
17:16 and he must **n** send his people to Egypt to buy
17:16 has told you, 'You must **n** return to Egypt.'
18:10 **n** sacrifice your son or daughter as a burnt
18:16 You begged that you might **n** again have to listen
19:14 **n** steal someone's land by moving the boundary
19:15 "**N** convict anyone of a crime on the testimony of
19:21 You must **n** show pity! Your rule should be life for
21: 3 must select a young cow that has **n** been trained
21:23 the body must **n** remain on the tree overnight.
22:19 remain the man's wife, and he may **n** divorce her.
22:29 and he will **n** be allowed to divorce her.
23: 6 You must **n**, as long as you live, try to help the
24:14 "**N** take advantage of poor laborers,
24:17 and you must **n** accept a widow's garment in
25:17 "**N** forget what the Amalekites did to you as you
25:19 their memory from under heaven. **N** forget this!
28:12 but you will **n** need to borrow from them.
28:30 will plant a vineyard, but you will **n** enjoy its fruit.
28:31 Your donkey will be driven away, **n** to be returned.
28:33 A foreign nation you have **n** heard about will eat
28:40 but you will **n** use the olive oil, for the trees will
28:68 a journey I promised you would **n** again make.
31:21 for it will **n** be forgotten by their descendants.
32:17 to gods their ancestors had **n** feared.
33:11 strike down their foes so they **n** rise again."
34:10 There has **n** been another prophet like Moses,
Jos 3: 4 Since you have **n** traveled this way before,
5:12 manna appeared that day, and it was **n** seen again.
7:13 You will **n** defeat your enemies until you remove
10:14 **N** before or since has there been a day like that
24:16 "We would **n** forsake the LORD and worship
Jdg 1:28 as slaves, but they **n** did drive them out of the land.
2: 1 and I said I would **n** break my covenant with you.
8:28 of how Israel subdued Midian, which **n** recovered.
11:18 But they **n** once crossed the Arnon River into
11:38 and wept because she would **n** have children.
13: 5 and give birth to a son, and his hair must **n** be cut.
16:11 "If I am tied up with brand-new ropes that have **n**
16:17 "My hair has **n** been cut," he confessed, "for I
21: 1 The Israelites had vowed at Mizpah **n** to give their
21:12 young virgins who had **n** slept with a man,
1Sa 1:11 dedicated to the LORD, his hair will **n** be cut."
3: 7 because he had **n** had a message from the LORD
3:14 and his sons will **n** be forgiven by sacrifices
4: 7 We have **n** had to face anything like this before!
4: 9 Fight as you **n** have before, Philistines! If you
6: 7 Make sure the cows have **n** been yoked to a cart.
12: 4 "you have **n** cheated or oppressed us in any way,
12: 4 and you have **n** taken even a single bribe."
12: 5 "that you can **n** accuse me of robbing you."
14:19 So Saul said to Ahijah, "**N** mind; let's get going!"
15:35 Samuel **n** went to meet with Saul again, but he
17:39 it was like, for he had **n** worn such things before.
19: 4 "He's **n** done anything to harm you.
20: 9 "**N**!" Jonathan exclaimed. "You know that if I
20:31 long as that son of Jesse is alive, you'll **n** be king.
21: 5 "I **n** allow my men to be with women when they
23:17 reassured him. "My father will **n** find you!
24:10 For I said, 'I will **n** harm him—he is the LORD's
24:12 you are trying to do to me, but I will **n** harm you.
24:13 evil deeds.' So you can be sure I will **n** harm you.
25: 7 we **n** harmed them, and nothing was ever stolen
25:15 good to us, and we **n** suffered any harm from them.
25:25 But I **n** even saw the messengers you sent.
29: 3 and I've **n** found a single fault in him since he
2Sa 2:22 I will **n** be able to face your brother Joab if I have
5: 6 "You'll **n** get in here," the Jebusites taunted.
7: 6 I have **n** lived in a temple, from the day I brought
7: 7 And I have **n** once complained to Israel's leaders,
7: 7 I have **n** asked them, "Why haven't you built me
7:10 a secure place where they will **n** be disturbed.
7:22 We have **n** even heard of another god like you!
11:11 I swear that I will **n** be guilty of acting like that."
13:22 And though Absalom **n** spoke to Amnon about it,
14:10 I can assure you they will **n** complain again!"
14:24 but he must **n** come into my presence."
22:23 before me; / I have **n** abandoned his principles.
1Ki 1: 6 King David, had **n** disciplined him at any time,
6:13 the people of Israel and **n** forsake my people."
8:16 I have **n** chosen a city among the tribes of Israel as
8:46 "If they sin against you—and who has **n** sinned?—
8:57 as he was with our ancestors; may he **n** forsake us.
9: 5 'You will **n** fail to have a successor on the throne
10:10 **N** again were so many spices brought in as those
10:12 **N** before or since has there been such a supply of
19:18 others in Israel who have **n** bowed to Baal
22: 8 He **n** prophesies anything but bad news for me!
22:18 He **n** prophesies anything but bad news for me."
22:48 But the ships **n** set sail, for they were wrecked at
2Ki 1: 4 You will **n** leave the bed on which you are lying,
1: 6 you will **n** leave the bed on which you are lying,
1:16 you will **n** leave the bed on which you are lying,
2: 2 and you yourself live, I will **n** leave you!"
2: 4 and you yourself live, I will **n** leave you."
2: 6 and you yourself live, I will **n** leave you."
5:17 From now on I will **n** again offer any burnt
18: 5 There was **n** another king like him in the land of
18:29 He will **n** be able to rescue you from my power.
18:30 This city will **n** be handed over to the Assyrian
23:25 **N** before had there been a king like Josiah,
23:25 And there has **n** been a king like him since.
24: 7 The king of Egypt **n** returned after that,
1Ch 4:27 So Simeon's tribe **n** became as large as the tribe of
11: 5 of Jebus said to David, "You will **n** get in here!"
17: 5 I have **n** lived in a temple, from the day I brought
17: 6 And I **n** once complained to Israel's leaders,
17: 6 I have **n** asked them, "Why haven't you built me
17: 9 a secure place where they will **n** be disturbed.
17:20 We have **n** even heard of another god like you!
27:24 Joab began the census but **n** finished it
27:24 The final total was **n** recorded in King David's
29:18 See to it that their love for you **n** changes.
2Ch 6: 5 I have **n** chosen a city among the tribes of Israel as
6:36 "If they sin against you—and who has **n** sinned?—
7:18 'You will **n** fail to have a successor who rules over
9: 9 **N** before had there been spices as fine as those the
9:11 **N** before had there been such beautiful instruments
13:20 So Jeroboam of Israel **n** regained his power during
18: 7 He **n** prophesies anything but bad news for me!
18:17 He **n** prophesies anything but bad news for me."
20:33 and the people **n** fully committed themselves to
20:37 So the ships met with disaster and **n** put out to sea.
35:18 **N** since the time of the prophet Samuel had there
Ne 2: 1 I had **n** appeared sad in his presence before this
4:10 so much rubble to be moved that we could **n** get it
9:10 You have a glorious reputation that has **n** been
Est 2:14 **n** going to the king again unless he had especially
6:13 you will **n** succeed in your plans against him.
8: 8 and sealed with his ring can **n** be revoked."
9:27 They declared they would **n** fail to celebrate these
9:28 These days would **n** cease to be celebrated among
Job 2:10 things from the hand of God and **n** anything bad?"
3: 6 **n** again to be counted among the days of the year, **n** again to appear among the months.
3: 9 but in vain; may it **n** see the morning light.
3:16 like a baby who **n** lives to see the light?
7: 7 a breath, and I will **n** again experience pleasure.
7:10 gone forever from their home—**n** to be seen again.
9:16 and he responded, he would **n** listen to me.
10:21 the land of darkness and utter gloom, **n** to return.
14:21 They **n** know if their sons grow up in honor or sink
16:22 must go down that road from which I will **n** return.
20:17 He will **n** again enjoy abundant streams of olive oil
20:20 He was always greedy but **n** satisfied. Of all the
21:10 Their bulls **n** fail to breed. Their cows bear calves
21:25 dies in bitter poverty, **n** having tasted the good life.
27: 5 I will **n** concede that you are right; until I die,
31:30 I have **n** cursed anyone or asked for revenge.
31:31 My servants have **n** let others go hungry.
31:32 I have **n** turned away a stranger but have opened
36: 7 His eyes **n** leave the innocent, but he establishes
39: 4 open fields, then leave their parents and **n** return.
41: 8 hand on it, you will **n** forget the battle that follows, and you will **n** try it again!
Ps 1: 3 Their leaves **n** wither, / and in all they do,
3: 2 So many are saying, / "God will **n** rescue him!"
5: 2 and my God, / for I will **n** pray to anyone but you.
9:10 have **n** abandoned anyone who searches for you.
10:11 "God isn't watching! / He will **n** notice!"
10:13 can they think, "God will **n** call us to account"?
14: 4 Will those who do evil **n** learn? / They eat up my
18:22 before me; / I have **n** abandoned his principles.
21:10 face of the earth; / they will **n** have descendants.
21:11 against you, / their evil schemes will **n** succeed.
22: 5 put their trust in you and were **n** disappointed.
24: 4 who do not worship idols / and **n** tell lies.
27:12 For they accuse me of things I've **n** done
28: 5 like old buildings, / and they will **n** be rebuilt!
33:11 stand firm forever; / his intentions can **n** be shaken.
34:10 but those who trust in the LORD will **n** lack any
36: 4 sinful plots. / Their course of action is **n** good.
36:12 They have been thrown down, **n** to rise again.
37:21 The wicked borrow and **n** repay, / but the godly are
37:25 I am old. / Yet I have **n** seen the godly forsaken,
37:28 loves justice, / and he will **n** abandon the godly.
37:31 with God's law, / so they will **n** slip from his path.
40: 5 I would **n** come to the end of them.
41: 8 they say. / "He will **n** get out of that bed!"
49: 9 to live forever / and **n** see the grave.
49:19 before them / and **n** again see the light of day.
53: 4 Will those who do evil **n** learn? / They eat up my
53: 5 grip them, / terror like they have **n** known before.

58: 8 like a stillborn child who will **n** see the sun.
62: 2 my fortress where I will **n** be shaken.
71: 1 you are my refuge; / **n** let me be disgraced.
71: 8 That is why I can **n** stop praising you; / I declare
74:15 gush forth, / and you dried up rivers that **n** run dry.
77: 7 me forever? / Will he **n** again show me favor?
78:39 in a moment like a breath of wind, **n** to return.
80:18 Then we will **n** forsake you again. / Revive us
81: 9 You must **n** have a foreign god; / you must not
89:28 to him forever; / my covenant with him will **n** end.
89:33 But I will **n** stop loving him, / nor let my promise
95:11 a vow: / 'They will **n** enter my place of rest.' "
102:27 But you are always the same; / your years **n** end.
103: 2 and **n** forget the good things he does for me.
103:16 and we are gone— / as though we had **n** been here.
104: 5 world on its foundation / so it would **n** be moved.
104: 9 the seas, / so they would **n** again cover the earth.
109:14 May the LORD **n** forget the sins of his ancestors;
109:14 may his mother's sins **n** be erased from the record.
109:17 now you curse him. / He **n** blessed others;
111: 3 his glory and majesty. / His righteousness **n** fails.
112: 3 and their good deeds will **n** be forgotten.
112: 9 Their good deeds will **n** be forgotten. / They will
119:80 your principles; / then I will **n** have to be ashamed.
119:93 I will **n** forget your commandments, / for you have
119:152 from my earliest days / that your decrees **n** change.
121: 4 who watches over Israel / **n** tires and **n** sleeps.
129: 2 but they have **n** been able to finish me off.
132:11 swore to David / a promise he will **n** take back:
132:12 I teach them, / then your royal line will **n** end."
139: 7 I can **n** escape from your spirit! / I can **n** get away from your presence!
148: 6 and forever. / His orders will **n** be revoked.
Pr 2:19 her is doomed. He will **n** reach the paths of life.
3: 1 My child, **n** forget the things I have taught you.
3: 3 **N** let loyalty and kindness get away from you!
5: 7 listen to me. **N** stray from what I am about to say:
6:33 disgrace are his lot. His shame will **n** be erased.
7:11 was the brash, rebellious type who **n** stays at home.
10:30 The godly will **n** be disturbed, but the wicked will
12: 3 Wickedness **n** brings stability; only the godly have
14: 6 A mocker seeks wisdom and **n** finds it,
16:10 with divine wisdom; he must **n** judge unfairly.
17:13 repay evil for good, evil will **n** leave your house.
25:10 Then you will **n** regain your good reputation.
27:10 **N** abandon a friend—either yours or your father's.
27:20 Just as Death and Destruction are **n** satisfied, so human desire is **n** satisfied.
28:21 Showing partiality is **n** good, yet some will do
30: 8 First, help me **n** to tell a lie. Second, give me
30:10 **N** slander a person to his employer. If you do,
30:15 three other things—no, four!—that are **n** satisfied:
Ecc 1: 7 The rivers run into the sea, but the sea is **n** full.
1: 8 No matter how much we see, we are **n** satisfied.
4: 3 And most fortunate of all are those who were **n**
4: 3 For they have **n** seen all the evil that is done in our
5:10 Those who love money will **n** have enough.
6: 5 and he would **n** have seen the sun or known of its
6: 7 for food, but they **n** seem to have enough.
7:20 in all the earth who is always good and **n** sins.
8:13 The wicked will **n** live long, good lives, for they
8:13 Their days will **n** grow long like the evening
9:12 People can **n** predict when hard times might come.
10:20 **N** make light of the king, even in your thoughts.
11: 4 perfect conditions, you will **n** get anything done.
11: 6 of crops, for you **n** know which will grow—
Isa 5:12 But you **n** think about the LORD or notice what
7: 7 LORD says: This invasion will **n** happen,
8:15 of them will stumble and fall, **n** to rise again.
9: 5 **N** again will uniforms be bloodstained by war.
9: 7 ever expanding, peaceful government will **n** end.
11: 3 He will **n** judge by appearance, false evidence,
13:20 Babylon will **n** rise again. Generation after
13:20 and go, but the land will **n** again be lived in.
14:22 children's children, so they will **n** sit on his throne.
17: 8 They will **n** again bow down to their Asherah poles
17:11 but you will **n** pick any grapes from them.
22:11 are to no avail because you **n** ask God for help.
22:14 sin will **n** be forgiven you until the day you die.
23:12 He says, "**N** again will you rejoice, O daughter of
23:12 were a lovely city, but you will **n** again be strong.
25: 2 in distant lands disappear and will **n** be rebuilt.
26:14 are dead and gone. / **N** again will they return!
28:15 You say, "The Assyrians can **n** touch us, for we
28:16 build on. Whoever believes need **n** run away again.
28:24 Does a farmer always plow and **n** sow? Is he forever cultivating the soil and **n** planting it?
28:27 A heavy sledge is **n** used on dill; rather, it is beaten
28:27 A threshing wheel is **n** rolled on cummin; instead,
32:10 crop will fail, and the harvest will **n** take place.
33: 1 around you but have **n** felt destruction yourselves.
34:10 This judgment on Edom will **n** end; the smoke of
35: 8 of Holiness. Evil-hearted people will **n** travel on it.
35: 8 who walk in God's ways; fools will **n** walk there.
36:14 deceive you. He will **n** be able to rescue you.
36:15 This city will **n** be handed over to the Assyrian
38:11 I said, "**N** again will I see the LORD GOD
38:11 land of the living. / **N** again will I see my friends
40:21 Have you **n** heard or understood? Are you deaf to
40:28 Have you **n** heard or understood? Don't you know
40:28 Creator of all the earth? He **n** grows faint or weary.
41:17 I, the God of Israel, will **n** forsake them.
43:10 no other God; there **n** has been and **n** will be.
43:25 for my own sake and will **n** think of them again.
44:19 The person who made the idol **n** stops to reflect,
45: 1 gates will be opened, **n** again to shut against him.
45:17 They will **n** again be humiliated and disgraced
45:23 my own name, and I will **n** go back on my word:
47: 1 **n** again will you be the lovely princess, tender
47: 5 **N** again will you be known as the queen of
47: 8 I will **n** be a widow or lose my children.'
48: 5 That way, you could **n** say, 'My idols did it.
49:15 "**N**! Can a mother forget her nursing child?
49:23 Those who wait for me will **n** be put to shame."
51: 6 lasts forever. My righteous rule will **n** end!
53: 7 and treated harshly, yet he **n** said a word.
53: 9 He had done no wrong, and he **n** deceived anyone.
54: 1 even though you **n** gave birth to a child.
54: 9 "Just as I swore in the time of Noah that I would **n**
54: 9 so now I swear that I will **n** again pour out my
54:10 My covenant of blessing will **n** be broken,"
56: 5 give them is an everlasting one. It will **n** disappear!
56:11 And they are as greedy as dogs, **n** satisfied.
57:10 You grew weary in your search, but you **n** gave up.
57:20 It is **n** still but continually churns up mire and dirt.
58: 2 a righteous nation that would **n** abandon its God.
58: 4 This kind of fasting will **n** get you anywhere with
60:20 The sun will **n** set; the moon will not go down.
62: 4 **N** again will you be called the Godforsaken City
62: 8 "I will **n** again hand you over to your enemies.
62: 8 **N** again will foreign warriors come and take away
63:13 stallions racing through the desert, **n** stumbling.
63:19 why do you treat us as though we **n** belonged to
63:19 Why do you act as though we had **n** been known as
65: 1 "People who **n** before inquired about me are now
65: 5 in my nostrils, an acrid smell that **n** goes away.
66: 9 I would **n** keep this nation from being born,"
66:22 with a name that will **n** disappear,"
66:24 For the worms that devour them will **n** die,
66:24 and the fire that burns them will **n** go out.
Jer 3:10 her faithless sister Judah has **n** sincerely returned
3:19 and I thought you would **n** turn away from me
3:25 the LORD our God. We have **n** obeyed him."
5:22 and roar, but they can **n** pass the bounds I set.
6:29 But it will **n** purify and cleanse them because there
7: 8 because the Temple is here you will **n** suffer?
7:31 I have **n** commanded such a horrible deed; it **n** even crossed my mind to command such a
10:20 have been taken away, and I will **n** see them again.
14:14 and revelations they have **n** seen or heard.
14:15 for they have spoken in my name even though I **n**
15:17 I **n** joined the people in their merry feasts. I sat
16:13 land where you and your ancestors have **n** been.
19: 4 idols **n** before worshiped by this generation,
19: 5 I have **n** commanded such a horrible deed; it **n** even crossed my mind to command such a
20: 9 If I say I'll **n** mention the LORD or speak in his
20:11 Their dishonor will **n** be forgotten.
22:10 For he will **n** return to see his native land again.
22:11 was taken away as a captive: "He will **n** return.
22:12 in a distant land and **n** again see his own country."
22:27 You will **n** again return to the land of your desire.
23: 4 to care for them, and they will **n** be afraid again.
30: 7 In all history there has **n** been such a time of terror.
31:34 and will **n** again remember their sins."
31:40 The city will **n** again be captured or destroyed."
32: 5 against the Babylonians, you will **n** succeed."
32:35 I have **n** commanded such a horrible deed; it **n** even crossed my mind to command such a
32:40 hearts to worship me, and they will **n** leave me.
33:26 I will **n** abandon the descendants of Jacob
34:14 freed after serving six years. But this was **n** done.
35: 6 'You and your descendants must **n** drink wine.
35: 8 We have **n** had a drink of wine since then,
42:18 And you will **n** see your homeland again.'
44:25 and your wives have said that you will **n** give up
50: 5 an eternal covenant that will **n** again be broken.
50:39 **N** again will people live there; it will lie desolate
51:26 Even your stones will **n** again be used for building.
51:39 fall asleep, **n** again to waken," says the LORD.
51:57 "They will fall asleep and **n** wake up again!"
51:64 and her people will sink, **n** again to rise,
La 3:20 I will **n** forget this awful time, as I grieve over my
3:22 The unfailing love of the LORD **n** ends! By his
3:52 My enemies, whom I have **n** harmed, chased me
Eze 4:14 human dung? For I have **n** been defiled before.
4:14 From the time I was a child until now I have **n**
4:14 And I have **n** eaten any of the animals that our
7:13 should survive, they will **n** return to their business.
10:11 in which their heads were turned, **n** turning aside.
12:12 and his eyes will **n** see his homeland again.
12:13 though he will **n** see it, and he will die there.
13: 6 the LORD,' even though the LORD **n** sent them.
13: 9 and they will **n** again see their own land.
13:23 no longer talk of seeing visions that you **n** saw,
16: 4 and you were **n** washed, rubbed with salt,
16:28 It seems you can **n** find enough new lovers!
16:48 Sodom and her daughters were **n** as wicked as you
18:11 son does all the evil things his father would **n** do—
19: 9 in captivity, / so his voice could **n** again be heard
20:32 But what you have in mind will **n** happen.
20:38 are in exile, but they will **n** enter the land of Israel.
22:12 They **n** even think of me and my commands,
23:27 You will **n** again cast longing eyes on those things
26:14 You will **n** be rebuilt, for I, the LORD,
26:20 **N** again will you be given a position of respect
26:21 You will be looked for, but you will **n** be found.
29:15 **n** again great enough to rise above its neighbors.
32: 9 remains to distant nations that you have **n** seen,
32:13 **N** again will people or animals disturb those waters
34:29 so my people will **n** again go hungry or be shamed
35: 9 you desolate forever. Your cities will **n** be rebuilt.
36:12 You will **n** again devour their children.
36:14 But you will **n** again devour your people
36:30 and **n** again will the surrounding nations be able to
39:29 And I will **n** again turn my back on them, for I will
44: 2 gate must remain closed; it will **n** again be opened.
44:21 The priests must **n** drink wine before entering the
44:25 A priest must **n** defile himself by being in the
44:31 The priests may **n** eat meat from any bird
46: 9 They must **n** leave by the same gateway they came
46:18 And the prince may **n** take anyone's property by
47:12 The leaves of these trees will **n** turn brown
Da 2:44 will set up a kingdom that will **n** be destroyed;
3:18 Your Majesty can be sure that we will **n** serve your
6:26 His kingdom will **n** be destroyed, / and his rule will **n** end.
7:14 His rule is eternal—it will **n** end. His kingdom will **n** be destroyed.
9:12 **N** in all history has there been a disaster like the
11:38 a god his ancestors **n** knew—and lavish on him
Hos 5: 2 But **n** forget—I will settle with all of you for what
9:11 or perish in the womb or **n** even be conceived.
14: 3 **N** again will we call the idols we have made 'our
Joel 2: 2 have not been seen before and **n** will be seen again.
2: 7 Straight forward they march, **n** breaking rank.
2: 8 They **n** jostle each other; each moves in exactly the
2:26 **N** again will my people be disgraced like this.
2:27 My people will **n** again be disgraced like this.
3:17 and foreign armies will **n** conquer her again.
Am 4: 8 for a drink of water, but there was **n** enough.
5: 2 "The virgin Israel has fallen, / **n** to rise again!
5:11 you will **n** live in the beautiful stone houses you
5:11 You will **n** drink wine from the lush vineyards you
5:24 a river of righteous living that will **n** run dry.
7:14 I certainly **n** trained to be one. I'm just a shepherd,
8: 7 "I will **n** forget the wicked things you have done!
8:14 and Beersheba will fall down, **n** to rise again."
9: 8 Yet I have promised that I will **n** completely
9:15 your God. "Then they will **n** be uprooted again."
Ob 1:16 from history, as though you had **n** even existed.
Mic 1:16 be snatched away, and you will **n** see them again.
2: 6 like that. Such disasters will **n** come our way!"
5:13 so you will **n** again worship the work of your own
6:14 You will eat but **n** have enough. Your hunger
Na 1: 3 is great, and he **n** lets the guilty go unpunished.
1:15 for your enemies from Nineveh will **n** invade your
2:13 **N** again will you bring back plunder from
2:13 **N** again will the voices of your proud messengers
Hab 2: 5 is treacherous, and the arrogant are **n** at rest.
2: 5 opened as wide as death, but they are **n** satisfied.
Zep 1:13 They will **n** have a chance to live in the new homes
1:13 They will **n** drink wine from the vineyards they
3:13 each other, **n** telling lies or deceiving one another.
Zec 10: 6 It will be as though I had **n** rejected them, for I am
14:11 safe at last, **n** again to be cursed and destroyed.
Mal 3: 7 'How can we return when we have **n** gone away?'
Mt 6:20 where they will **n** become moth-eaten or rusty
7:23 But I will reply, 'I **n** knew you. Go away;
12:31 against the Holy Spirit, which can **n** be forgiven.
12:32 but blasphemy against the Holy Spirit will **n** be
13:34 he **n** spoke to them without using such parables.
15:20 Eating with unwashed hands could **n** defile you
16:22 Lord," he said. "This will **n** happen to you!"
18: 3 you will **n** get into the Kingdom of Heaven.
21:19 Then he said to it, "May you **n** bear fruit again!"
23: 4 and **n** lift a finger to help ease the burden.
23:30 'We **n** would have joined them in killing the
23:39 tell you this, you will **n** see me again until you say,
26:24 Far better for him if he had **n** been born!"
26:33 "Even if everyone else deserts you, I **n** will."
26:35 even if I have to die with you! I will **n** deny you!"
Mk 2:12 "We've **n** seen anything like this before!"
3:26 how can he stand? He would **n** survive.
3:29 against the Holy Spirit will **n** be forgiven.
9:25 to come out of this child and **n** enter him again!"
9:48 'where the worm **n** dies and the fire **n** goes out.'
10:15 anyone who doesn't have their kind of faith will **n**
11: 2 you will see a colt tied there that has **n** been
13:19 God created the world. And it will **n** happen again.
14:21 Far better for him if he had **n** been born!"
14:29 "Even if everyone else deserts you, I **n** will."
14:31 I will **n** deny you!" And all the others vowed the
Lk 1:15 He must **n** touch wine or hard liquor, and he will
1:33 over Israel forever; his Kingdom will **n** end!"
2:37 She **n** left the Temple but stayed there day
6:44 Figs **n** grow on thornbushes or grapes on bramble
8:14 of this life. And so they **n** grow into maturity.
11:46 and you **n** lift a finger to help ease the burden.
12:10 against the Holy Spirit will **n** be forgiven.
13:35 And you will **n** see me again until you say,
15:29 and **n** once refused to do a single thing you told me
15:29 And in all that time you **n** gave me even one young
18: 1 and to show them that they must **n** give up.
18:11 For I **n** cheat, I don't sin, I don't commit adultery,
18:17 anyone who doesn't have their kind of faith will **n**
19:30 you will see a colt tied there that has **n** been
20:36 And they will **n** die again. In these respects they
23:29 borne a child and the breasts that have **n** nursed.'
Jn 1: 5 the darkness, and the darkness can **n** extinguish it.
3: 3 born again, you can **n** see the Kingdom of God."
3:36 Those who don't obey the Son will **n** experience
4:15 Then I'll **n** be thirsty again, and I won't have to
5:17 But Jesus replied, "My Father **n** stops working,
5:24 They will **n** be condemned for their sins, but they
5:37 You have **n** heard his voice or seen him face to
6:35 Those who believe in me will **n** thirst.
6:37 given me will come to me, and I will **n** reject them.
7:46 "We have **n** heard anyone talk like this!"
8: 7 But let those who have **n** sinned throw the first
8:33 "We have **n** been slaves to anyone on earth.

8:51 anyone who obeys my teaching will n die!"
8:52 say that those who obey your teaching will n die!
9:32 N since the world began has anyone been able to
10:28 I give them eternal life, and they will n perish.
11:26 eternal life for believing in me and will n perish.
13: 8 Peter protested, "you will n wash my feet!"
14:16 give you another Counselor, who will n leave you.
16: 3 because they have n known the Father or me.
19:41 where there was a new tomb, n used before.
Ac 2:34 For David himself n ascended into heaven, yet he
4:18 and told them n again to speak or teach about
5:28 "Didn't we tell you n again to teach in this man's
5:40 Then they ordered them n again to speak in the
8:39 The eunuch n saw him again but went on his way
10:14 "N, Lord," Peter declared. "I have n in all my life eaten anything forbidden
10:28 But God has shown me that I should n think of
11: 8 " 'N, Lord,' I replied. 'I have n eaten anything forbidden by our Jewish
13:10 will you n stop perverting the true ways of the
13:34 to raise him from the dead, n again to die.
13:39 with God—something the Jewish law could n do.
14: 8 had been that way from birth, so he had n walked.
14:17 but he n left himself without a witness. There were
20:20 Yet I n shrank from telling you the truth,
20:33 "I have n coveted anyone's money or fine
20:38 because he had said that they would n see him
Ro 1:28 and let them do things that should n be done.
2:12 even though they n had God's written law.
4:19 his wife, had n been able to have children.
4:20 Abraham n wavered in believing God's promise.
6: 9 Christ rose from the dead, and he will n die again.
7: 7 I would n have known that coveting is wrong if the
8: 7 to God. It n did obey God's laws, and it n will.
8: 8 the control of their sinful nature can n please God.
9:31 right with God by keeping the law, n succeeded.
10:14 And how can they believe in him if they have n
11: 4 I have seven thousand others who have n bowed
11:29 For God's gifts and his call can n be withdrawn.
12:11 N be lazy in your work, but serve the Lord
12:17 N pay back evil for evil to anyone. Do things in
12:19 Dear friends, n avenge yourselves. Leave that to
13: 8 You can n finish paying that! If you love your
15:20 News where the name of Christ has n been heard,
15:21 "Those who have n been told about him will see,
15:21 and those who have n heard of him will
1Co 1: 4 I can n stop thanking God for all the generous gifts
1:21 world would n find him through human wisdom,
2: 8 they would n have crucified our glorious Lord.
4:18 become arrogant, thinking I will n visit you again.
6:15 belongs to Christ, and join it to a prostitute? N!
7:34 or has n been married can be more devoted to the
8:13 I will n eat meat again as long as I live—
9:12 to be supported? Yet we have n used this right.
9:15 Yet I have n used any of these rights. And I am not
9:18 to anyone, n demanding my rights as a preacher.
12:21 The eye can n say to the hand, "I don't need you."
13: 6 It is n glad about injustice but rejoices whenever
13: 7 Love n gives up, n loses faith, is always hopeful,
15: 2 you believed something that was n true in the first
15:42 when they are resurrected, for they will n die.
15:52 are living will be transformed so that we will n die.
15:53 transformed into heavenly bodies that will n die.
15:54 transformed into heavenly bodies that will n die—
2Co 1: 8 and we thought we would n live through it.
1:19 the Son of God, n wavers between yes and no.
4: 1 has given us this wonderful ministry, we n give up.
4: 9 We are hunted down, but God n abandons us.
4:16 That is why we n give up. Though our bodies are
5:21 For God made Christ, who n sinned, to be the
7:10 We will n regret that kind of sorrow.
9: 9 the poor. / Their good deeds will n be forgotten."
11: 9 I have n yet asked you for any support, and I n will.
11:10 I will n stop boasting about this all over Greece.
13: 8 Our responsibility is n to oppose the truth, but to
Gal 2:19 the law, I realized I could n earn God's approval.
4:27 even though you n gave birth to a child.
5:17 and your choices are n free from this conflict.
Eph 1:16 I have n stopped thanking God for you. I pray for
3:19 though it is so great you will n fully understand it.
Php 1:20 and hope that I will n do anything that causes me
3: 1 Lord give you joy. I n get tired of telling you this.
3: 6 so carefully that I was n accused of any fault.
Col 2: 1 and for many other friends who have n known me
3:19 must love your wives and n treat them harshly.
1Th 2: 5 N once did we try to win you with flattery, as you
2: 6 we have n asked for it from you or anyone else.
2:13 And we will n stop thanking God that when we
2:17 you for a little while (though our hearts n left you),
4: 6 N cheat another Christian in this matter by taking
2Th 3: 7 We were n lazy when we were with you.
3: 8 We n accepted food from anyone without paying
3:13 dear brothers and sisters, n get tired of doing good.
1Ti 1:17 He is the eternal King, the unseen one who n dies;
5: 1 N speak harshly to an older man, but appeal to him
5:22 N be in a hurry about appointing an elder. Do not
6:16 He alone can n die, and he lives in light so brilliant
2Ti 1: 8 So you must n be ashamed to tell others about our
1:16 He was n ashamed of me because I was in prison.
2: 8 N forget that Jesus Christ was a man born into
3: 7 new teachings, but they n understand the truth.
Heb 1: 5 For God n said to any angel what he said to Jesus:
1:12 you are always the same; / you will n grow old."
1:13 And God n said to an angel, as he did to his Son,
3:11 a vow: / 'They will n enter my place of rest.' "
3:15 But n forget the warning: / "Today you must listen
3:18 he vowed that they would n enter his place of rest?
4: 3 'They will n enter my place of rest,' " even
4: 5 God said, "They will n enter my place of rest."
4:14 Let us cling to him and n stop trusting him.
6:17 be perfectly sure that he would n change his mind.
7:14 and Moses n mentioned Judah in connection with
7:20 be a priest, but he n did this for any other priest.
7:24 remains a priest forever; his priesthood will n end.
8:12 and I will n again remember their sins."
10: 1 but they were n able to provide perfect cleansing
10:11 offering sacrifices that can n take away sins.
10:17 Then he adds, / "I will n again remember
11: 7 who warned him about something that had n
12: 7 Whoever heard of a child who was n disciplined?
13: 5 For God has said, / "I will n fail you. / I will n forsake you."
Jas 1:13 God is n tempted to do wrong, and he n tempts anyone else either.
1:17 he n changes or casts shifting shadows.
1:20 Your anger can n make things right in God's sight.
5:12 n take an oath, by heaven or earth or anything else.
1Pe 1: 8 You love him even though you have n seen him.
2: 6 who believes in him / will n be disappointed."
2:22 He n sinned, and he n deceived anyone.
3:18 He n sinned, but he died for sinners that he might
4:17 what terrible fate awaits those who have n believed
4:19 to the God who made you, for he will n fail you.
2Pe 1:10 Doing this, you will n stumble or fall away.
2:11 n speak out disrespectfully against the glorious
2:14 with their eyes, and their lust is n satisfied.
2:21 It would be better if they had n known the right
1Jn 2:19 because they n really belonged with us;
3: 6 But those who keep on sinning have n known him
Rev 3: 5 I will n erase their names from the Book of Life,
3:12 of my God, and they will n have to leave it.
7:16 They will n again be hungry or thirsty, and they
18:14 that you prized so much will n be yours again.
18:22 N again will the sound of music be heard there—
21:25 Its gates n close at the end of day because there is

NEVER-ENDING (5) [END, NEVER]

1Ch 16:17 as a decree, / to the people of Israel as a n treaty:
Ps 105:10 as a decree, / to the people of Israel as a n treaty:
Mt 3:12 grain in his barn but burning the chaff with n fire."
Lk 3:17 grain in his barn but burning the chaff with n fire."
1Pe 5: 4 your reward will be a n share in his glory

NEVERTHELESS (11) [NEVER]

Jdg 1:33 N, the people of Beth-shemesh and Beth-anath
2Ki 3: 3 N he continued in the sins of idolatry that
18:17 N the king of Assyria sent his commander in chief,
2Ch 27: 2 N, the people continued in their corrupt ways.
Job 23:13 N, his mind concerning me remains unchanged,
Isa 9: 1 N, that time of darkness and despair will not go on
Jer 33: 6 "N, the time will come when I will heal
37: 3 N, King Zedekiah sent Jehucal son of Shelemiah
Eze 17:15 "N, this man of Israel's royal family rebelled
20:17 N, I pitied them and held back from destroying
20:22 N, I withdrew my judgment against them to protect

NEW (267) [ANEW, BRAND-NEW, NEW-MOON, NEWBORN, NEWER, NEWLY, NEWNESS]

NEW COVENANT (15) Jer 31:31,33; Lk 22:20; 1Co 11:25; 2Co 3:6,9,10,11,12; Heb 8:8,10,13; 9:15; 10:16; 12:24

NEW MOON (16) 1Sa 20:5,18,24; 2Ki 4:23; 1Ch 23:31; 2Ch 2:4; 8:13; 31:3; Ezr 3:5; Ne 10:33; Isa 1:13; Eze 45:17; 46:1,3,6; Hos 2:11

NEW SONG (8) Ps 40:3; 96:1; 98:1; 144:9; 149:1; Isa 42:10; Rev 5:9; 14:3

NEW WINE (19) Dt 12:17; 14:23; 18:4; 28:51; 2Ch 31:5; 32:28; Ne 10:37,39; 13:5,12; Joel 1:5; Zec 9:17; Mt 9:17,17; Mk 2:22,22; Lk 5:37,37,38

Ge 13:17 and explore the n possessions I am giving you."
25: 1 Abraham married again. Keturah was his n wife,
28: 9 His n wife's name was Mahalath. She was the
45:22 And he gave each of them n clothes—but to
Ex 1: 8 Then a n king came to the throne of Egypt who
40: 2 "Set up the Tabernacle on the first day of the n
40:17 was set up on the first day of the n year.
Lev 2:14 bring kernels of n grain that have been roasted on a
23:16 and bring an offering of n grain to the LORD.
23:43 This will remind each n generation of Israelites
25:22 you will eat from the old crop until the n harvest
25:28 then it will belong to the n owner until the next
26:10 the previous year to make room for each n harvest.
Nu 2: 9 way whenever the Israelites travel to a n campsite.
2:31 whenever the Israelites move to a n campsite."
10:21 the Tabernacle would already be set up at its n
27:16 please appoint a n leader for the community
28:26 when you present the first of your n grain to the
36: 4 of land will be added to that of the n tribe,
Dt 12:17 the tithe of your grain and n wine and olive oil,
14:23 applies to your tithes of grain, n wine, olive oil,
18: 4 the n wine, the olive oil, and the wool at shearing
20: 5 'Has anyone just built a n house but not yet
22: 8 "Every n house you build must have a barrier
28:51 you no grain, n wine, olive oil, calves, or lambs,
28:57 them the afterbirth and the n baby she has borne,
31: 3 Joshua is your n leader, and he will go with you,
Jos 9:13 These wineskins were n when we filled them,
Jdg 5: 8 When Israel chose n gods, / war erupted at the city
6:28 In their place a n altar had been built, and it had
15:13 So they tied him up with two n ropes and led him
16: 7 "If I am tied up with seven n bowstrings that have
16: 8 So the Philistine leaders brought Delilah seven n
16:12 So Delilah took n ropes and tied him up with them.
1Sa 6: 7 Now build a n cart, and find two cows that have
16: 1 for I have selected one of his sons to be my n
20: 5 "Tomorrow we celebrate the n moon festival.
20:18 "Tomorrow we celebrate the n moon festival.
20:24 and when the n moon festival began, the king sat
2Sa 2: 7 of Judah, who have anointed me as their n king."
6: 3 They placed the Ark of God on a n cart
21:16 seven pounds, and he was armed with a n sword.
1Ki 1:18 But instead, Adonijah has become the n king,
1:45 and Nathan have anointed him as the n king.
5: 1 that David's son Solomon was the n king of Israel,
8: 1 also known as Zion, to its n place in the Temple.
9:24 from the City of David to the n palace he had built
11:29 Shiloh met him on the road, wearing a n cloak.
11:30 and Ahijah took the n cloak he was wearing
16:16 commander of the army, as their n king.
2Ki 1: 2 One day Israel's n king, Ahaziah, fell through the
2:20 Elisha said, "Bring me a n bowl with salt in it."
4:23 "It is neither a n moon festival nor a Sabbath."
6: 2 There we can build a n place for us to meet."
16:14 had stood between the entrance and the n altar,
16:14 and placed it on the north side of the n altar.
16:15 "Use the n altar for the morning sacrifices of burnt
16:15 and sacrifices should be sprinkled over the n altar.
17:27 Let him teach the n residents the religious customs
17:28 and taught the n residents how to worship the
17:32 These n residents worshiped the LORD, but they
17:41 So while these n residents worshiped the LORD,
25:29 He supplied Jehoiachin with n clothes to replace
1Ch 8: 9 Hodesh, his n wife, gave birth to Jobab, Zibia,
13: 7 of God from the house of Abinadab on a n cart,
23:31 at n moon celebrations, and at all the appointed
29:22 they crowned David's son Solomon as their n king.
2Ch 2: 4 on the Sabbaths, at n moon celebrations,
5: 2 also known as Zion, to its n place in the Temple.
8:11 from the City of David to the n palace he had built
8:13 on n moon festivals, and at the three annual
20: 5 and Jerusalem in front of the n courtyard at the
26: 6 Then he built n towns in the Ashdod area and in
31: 3 Sabbath festivals and monthly n moon festivals,
31: 5 of their crops and grain, n wine, olive oil, honey,
32:28 storehouses for his grain, n wine, and olive oil;
Ezr 3: 5 and the offerings required for the n moon
3:12 and they wept aloud when they saw the n Temple's
Ne 10:33 the n moon celebrations, and the annual festivals;
10:37 our fruit, and the best of our n wine and olive oil.
10:39 n wine, and olive oil to the Temple and place them
12:27 During the dedication of the n wall of Jerusalem,
13: 5 and tithes of grain, n wine, olive oil,
13:12 n wine, and olive oil to the Temple storerooms.
Est 8:15 And the people of Susa celebrated the n decree.
Job 14: 7 hope that it will sprout again and grow n branches.
14: 9 it may bud and sprout again like a n seedling.
29:20 N honors are constantly bestowed on me, and my
Ps 33: 3 Sing n songs of praise to him; / play skillfully on
40: 3 He has given me a n song to sing, / a hymn of
71:18 Let me proclaim your power to this n generation,
81: 3 when the moon is n, / when the moon is full.
96: 1 Sing a n song to the LORD! / Let the whole earth
98: 1 Sing a n song to the LORD, / for he has done
104:30 When you send your Spirit, n life is born
144: 9 I will sing a n song to you, O God! / I will sing
149: 1 Praise the LORD! / Sing to the LORD a n song.
Pr 18:15 Intelligent people are always open to n ideas.
23:30 long hours in the taverns, trying out n drinks.
27:25 After the hay is harvested, the n crop appears,
Ecc 1: 9 been done before. Nothing under the sun is truly n.
1:10 What can you point to that is n? How do you know
SS 6:11 and out to the valley to see the n growth brought
7:13 the n as well as old, for I have stored them up for
Isa 1:13 Your celebrations of the n moon and the Sabbath
11: 1 yes, a n Branch bearing fruit from the old root.
40:31 But those who wait on the LORD will find n
41: 4 directing the affairs of the human race as each n
41: 7 The craftsmen rush to make n idols. The carver
41:15 You will be a n threshing instrument with many
42:10 Sing a n song to the LORD! / Sing his praises
42:16 I will lead blind Israel down a n path,
48: 6 Now I will tell you n things I have not mentioned
48: 7 They are brand n, not things from the past. So you
48: 8 "Yes, I will tell you of things that are entirely n,
57: 9 into the world of the dead, to find n gods to love.
57:15 and give n courage to those with repentant hearts.
62: 2 And the LORD will give you a n name.
62: 4 Your n name will be the City of God's Delight
65:17 I am creating n heavens and a n earth—
66:22 "As surely as my n heavens and earth will remain,
Jer 2:36 But your n friends in Egypt will let you down,
7: 9 worship Baal and all those other n gods of yours,
26:10 and sat down at the N Gate of the Temple to hold
31:22 For the LORD will cause something n
31:31 "when I will make a n covenant with the people of
31:33 "But this is the n covenant I will make with the
36:10 courtyard of the Temple, near the N Gate entrance.
52:33 He supplied Jehoiachin with n clothes to replace
Eze 11:19 singleness of heart and put a n spirit within them.
12:23 Now give them this n proverb to replace the old
16:28 It seems you can never find enough n lovers!
17:24 green tree wither and gives n life to the dead tree.
18:31 and get for yourselves a n heart and a n spirit.
36:26 And I will give you a n heart with n and right desires, and I will put a n spirit in you.
36:26 take out your stony heart of sin and give you a n,
45:17 the n moon celebrations, the Sabbath days, and all

45:18 In early spring, on the first day of each **n** year,
45:20 Do this also on the seventh day of the **n** year for
45:21 "On the fourteenth day of the **n** year, you must
46: 1 Sabbath days and the days of **n** moon celebrations.
46: 3 Sabbath days and the days of **n** moon celebrations.
46: 6 At the **n** moon celebrations, he will bring one
47:12 There will be a **n** crop every month, without fail!
Hos 2:11 her **n** moon celebrations, and her Sabbath days—
13:13 The people have been offered **n** birth, but they are
Joel 1: 5 the grapes are ruined, and all your **n** wine is gone!
Hab 1: 6 I am raising up the Babylonians to be a **n** power on
Zep 1:13 They will never have a chance to live in the **n**
Zec 3: 4 and now I am giving you these fine **n** clothes."
3: 5 and dressed him in **n** clothes while the angel of the
9: 7 our God and be adopted as a **n** clan in Judah.
9:17 will thrive on the abundance of grain and **n** wine.
Mt 2:22 But when he learned that the **n** ruler was Herod's
9:17 And no one puts **n** wine into old wineskins.
9:17 the skins. **N** wine must be stored in **n** wineskins.
13:52 the storehouse the **n** teachings as well as the old."
26:29 I will not drink wine again until the day I drink it **n**
27:60 He placed it in his own **n** tomb, which had been
28: 1 as the **n** day was dawning, Mary Magdalene
28:20 Teach these **n** disciples to obey all the commands I
Mk 1:27 "What sort of **n** teaching is this?" they asked
2:21 For the **n** patch shrinks and pulls away from the
2:22 And no one puts **n** wine into old wineskins.
2:22 ruining the skins. **N** wine needs **n** wineskins."
14:25 day when I drink it **n** in the Kingdom of God."
16:17 in my name, and they will speak **n** languages.
Lk 5:36 "No one tears a piece of cloth from a **n** garment
5:36 For then the **n** garment would be torn,
5:37 And no one puts **n** wine into old wineskins.
5:37 The **n** wine would burst the old skins,
5:38 **N** wine must be put into **n** wineskins.
5:39 the old wine seems to want the fresh and the **n**.
20:36 They are children of God raised up to **n** life.
22:20 "This wine is the token of God's **n** covenant to
23:53 and laid it in a **n** tomb that had been carved out of
Jn 3: 6 but the Holy Spirit gives **n** life from heaven.
12:24 But its death will produce many **n** kernels—a plentiful harvest of **n** lives.
13:34 So now I am giving you a **n** commandment:
16:21 because she has brought a **n** person into the world.
19:41 where there was a **n** tomb, never used before.
Ac 7:18 then a **n** king came to the throne of Egypt who
7:45 the Tabernacle was taken with them into their **n**
8:15 they prayed for these **n** Christians to receive the
12:24 and there were many **n** believers.
15:36 to see how the **n** believers are getting along."
17:19 "Come and tell us more about this **n** religion,"
25: 1 in Caesarea to take over his **n** responsibilities,
Ro 1:30 They are forever inventing **n** ways of sinning
4:13 but on the **n** relationship with God that comes by
5:11 So now we can rejoice in our wonderful **n**
6: 4 power of the Father, now we also may live **n** lives.
6: 8 with Christ, we know we will also share his **n** life.
6:13 to God since you have been given **n** life.
6:17 but now you have obeyed with all your heart the **n**
6:18 and you have become slaves to your **n** master,
7: 6 the letter of the law, but in the **n** way, by the Spirit.
8:23 including the **n** bodies he has promised us.
12: 2 but let God transform you into a **n** person by
1Co 5: 8 but by eating the **n** bread of purity and truth.
7:24 stay there in your **n** relationship with God.
11:25 "This cup is the **n** covenant between God and you,
15:22 to Christ, the other man, will be given **n** life.
15:38 God gives it a **n** body—just the kind he wants
2Co 3: 6 He is the one who has enabled us to represent his **n**
3: 6 in death; in the **n** way, the Holy Spirit gives life.
3: 9 how much more glorious is the **n** covenant,
3:10 with the overwhelming glory of the **n** covenant.
3:11 was full of glory, then the **n** covenant,
3:12 Since this **n** covenant gives us such confidence,
5: 2 we will put on our heavenly bodies like **n** clothing.
5: 3 but we will put on **n** heavenly bodies.
5: 4 We want to slip into our **n** bodies so that these
5:15 so that those who receive his **n** life will no longer
5:17 those who become Christians become **n** persons.
5:17 for the old life is gone. A **n** life has begun!
Gal 3:21 If the law could have given us **n** life, we could
5:16 So I advise you to live according to your **n** life in
6:15 is whether we really have been changed into **n**
6:16 by this principle. They are the **n** people of God.
Eph 2:15 and Gentiles by creating in himself one **n** person
4:24 You must display a **n** nature because you are a **n** person,
Col 2:12 And with him you were raised to a **n** life
3: 1 Since you have been raised to **n** life with Christ,
3:10 about Christ, who created this **n** nature within you.
3:11 In this **n** life, it doesn't matter if you are a Jew
1Th 3: 8 It gives us **n** life, knowing you remain strong in the
1Ti 3: 6 An elder must not be a **n** Christian, because he
2Ti 3: 7 Such women are forever following **n** teachings,
Tit 3: 5 and gave us a **n** life through the Holy Spirit.
Heb 4: 8 This **n** place of rest was not the land of Canaan,
6:18 we who have fled to him for refuge can take **n**
8: 8 says the Lord, / when I will make a **n** covenant
8:10 But this is the **n** covenant I will make
8:13 When God speaks of a **n** covenant, it means he has
9:15 That is why he is the one who mediates the **n**
10:16 "This is the **n** covenant I will make / with my
10:20 This is the **n**, life-giving way that Christ has
12:12 So take a **n** grip with your tired hands and stand
12:24 the one who mediates the **n** covenant between God
13: 9 So do not be attracted by strange, **n** ideas.
1Pe 1:23 Your **n** life did not come from your earthly parents
1:23 But this **n** life will last forever because it comes
3: 7 but she is your equal partner in God's gift of **n** life.
2Pe 3:13 looking forward to the **n** heavens and **n** earth
1Jn 2: 7 Dear friends, I am not writing a **n** commandment,
2: 8 Yet it is also **n**. This commandment is true in
2Jn 1: 5 This is not a **n** commandment, but one we had
Rev 2:17 and on the stone will be engraved a **n** name that no
3:12 the **n** Jerusalem that comes down from heaven
3:12 And they will have my **n** name inscribed upon
5: 9 And they sang a **n** song with these words:
14: 3 This great choir sang a wonderful **n** song in front
21: 1 Then I saw a **n** heaven and a **n** earth, for the old
21: 2 And I saw the holy city, the **n** Jerusalem,
21: 5 the throne said, "Look, I am making all things **n**!"

NEW-MOON (1) [MOON, NEW]

Col 2:16 certain holy days or **n** ceremonies or Sabbaths.

NEWBORN (7) [BEAR, NEW]

Ex 1:22 "Throw all the **n** Israelite boys into the Nile River.
22:30 Leave the **n** animal with its mother for seven days;
1Sa 6:10 Two cows with **n** calves were hitched to the cart,
Isa 45:10 How terrible it would be if a **n** baby said to its
Jer 14: 5 The deer abandons her **n** fawn because there is no
Mt 2: 2 "Where is the **n** king of the Jews? We have seen
Ac 7:19 and forced parents to abandon their **n** babies

NEWER (3) [NEW]

2Ki 22:14 and Asaiah went to the **n** Mishneh section of
2Ch 34:22 and the other men went to the **n** Mishneh section
Zep 1:10 and echo throughout the **n** Mishneh section of the

NEWLY (4) [NEW]

Dt 24: 5 "A **n** married man must not be drafted into the
2Ki 11:14 And she saw the **n** crowned king standing in his
2Ch 23:13 And she saw the **n** crowned king standing in his
SS 4: 2 teeth are as white as sheep, **n** shorn and washed.

NEWNESS (1) [NEW]

2Co 5:18 All this **n** of life is from God, who brought us back

NEWS (227)

GOOD NEWS (156) 2Sa 4:10; 18:19,20,27,31; 1Ki 1:42; 1Ch 16:23; Ps 40:10; 96:2; Pr 15:30; 25:25; Isa 40:9; 52:7; 61:1; Jer 20:15; Na 1:15; Mt 4:23; 9:35; 11:5; 13:19,22; 24:14; 26:13; Mk 1:1,14,15; 4:18; 8:35; 10:29; 13:10; 14:9; 16:15; Lk 1:19; 2:10; 3:18; 4:18,43; 7:22; 8:1; 9:6; 16:16; 20:1; 22:35; Ac 8:4,12,25,35,40; 10:36; 11:15,19; 12:24; 13:32,46; 14:7,15,21; 15:7; 16:10; 20:24; 23:11; Ro 1:1,2,3,9, 15,16,17; 10:15,16,17,17; 11:28; 15:16,19,20,27; 16:25; 1Co 1:17; 4:15; 9:12,14,16,18,23; 15:1,2; 2Co 2:12,14; 4:3,4; 8:18; 9:13; 10:14,16; 11:7; Gal 1:7,7,11,16; 2:5,7,14; 3:4,8; 4:13; Eph 1:13; 2:17; 3:6,7; 6:15,19; Php 1:5,7,12,16,27,27; 2:22; 4:3,15; Col 1:5,6,7,23,23; 1Th 1:5; 2:2,4,8,9,16; 3:2,6; 2Th 1:8; 2:14; 1Ti 1:11; 2Ti 1:8,10,11; 2:8,9; 4:17; Tit 1:3; Phm 1:1,13; Heb 4:2,6; 1Pe 1:12,22,25; 3:1; 4:6,17; Jude 1:3; Rev 14:6

Ge 32: 6 The messengers returned with the **n** that Esau was
32: 7 Jacob was terrified at the **n**. He divided his
45: 2 and the **n** was quickly carried to Pharaoh's palace.
45:16 The **n** soon reached Pharaoh: "Joseph's brothers
45:26 Jacob was stunned at the **n**—he couldn't believe it.
1Sa 4:13 Eli was waiting beside the road to hear the **n** of the
13: 3 The **n** spread quickly among the Philistines that
22: 6 The **n** of his arrival in Judah soon reached Saul.
22: 7 of Benjamin!" Saul shouted when he heard the **n**.
23: 1 One day **n** came to David that the Philistines were
23:15 David received the **n** that Saul was on the way to
31: 9 Then they proclaimed the **n** of Saul's death in their
2Sa 1:11 tore their clothes in sorrow when they heard the **n**.
1:13 said to the young man who had brought the **n**,
1:20 Don't announce the **n** in Gath, / or the Philistines
4: 4 When **n** of the battle reached the capital,
4:10 is dead,' thinking he was bringing me good **n**.
4:10 at Ziklag. That's the reward I gave him for his **n**!
11:19 "Report all the **n** of the battle to the king.
18:19 "Let me run to the king with the good **n** that the
18:20 "it wouldn't be good **n** to the king that his son is
18:25 He shouted the **n** down to David, and the king replied, "If he is alone, he has **n**."
18:26 The king replied, "He also will have **n**."
18:27 "He is a good man and comes with good **n**,"
18:31 and said, "I have good **n** for my lord the king.
19: 8 and as the **n** spread throughout the city that he was
1Ki 1:42 "for you are a good man. You must have good **n**."
2:29 When **n** of this reached King Solomon, he sent
11:21 When the **n** reached Hadad in Egypt that David
12:18 When this **n** reached King Rehoboam, he quickly
14: 6 Then he told her, "I have bad **n** for you.
21:15 When Jezebel heard the **n**, she said to Ahab,
22: 8 He never prophesies anything but bad **n** for me!
22:18 He never prophesies anything but bad **n** for me."
2Ki 7: 9 This is wonderful **n**, and we aren't sharing it with
7:11 Then the gatekeepers shouted the **n** to the people in
8: 8 When the king heard the **n**, he said to Hazael,
1Ch 10: 9 Then they proclaimed the **n** of Saul's death before
16:23 Each day proclaim the good **n** that he saves.
2Ch 10:18 When this **n** reached King Rehoboam, he quickly
18: 7 He never prophesies anything but bad **n** for me!
18:17 He never prophesies anything but bad **n** for me."
20: 3 Jehoshaphat was alarmed by this **n** and sought the
Est 4: 3 And as **n** of the king's decree reached all the
Job 1:14 a messenger arrived at Job's home with this **n**:
1:16 another messenger arrived with this **n**:
1:17 a third messenger arrived with this **n**:
1:18 another messenger arrived with this **n**:
Ps 40:10 I have not kept this good **n** hidden in my heart;
68:11 and throngs of women shout the happy **n**.
96: 2 Each day proclaim the good **n** that he saves.
112: 7 They do not fear bad **n**; / they confidently trust the
Pr 15:30 joy to the heart; good **n** makes for good health.
25:25 Good **n** from far away is like cold water to the
Isa 7: 2 The **n** had come to the royal court: "Aram is allied
23: 5 When Egypt hears the **n** about Tyre, there will be
35: 3 With this **n**, strengthen those who have tired hands,
40: 9 Messenger of good **n**, shout to Zion from the
52: 7 are the feet of those who bring good **n** of peace
52: 7 and salvation, the **n** that the God of Israel reigns!
61: 1 has appointed me to bring good **n** to the poor.
Jer 20:15 the messenger who told my father, "Good **n**—
49:23 for they have heard the **n** of their destruction.
Eze 21: 7 'I groan because of the terrifying **n** I have heard.
Da 11:44 "But then **n** from the east and the north will alarm
Na 1:15 is coming over the mountains with good **n**!
Mt 4:23 preaching everywhere the Good **N** about the
4:24 **N** about him spread far beyond the borders of
9:35 and announcing the Good **N** about the Kingdom.
11: 5 and the Good **N** is being preached to the poor.
13:19 those who hear the Good **N** about the Kingdom
13:22 represents those who hear and accept the Good **N**,
14:13 As soon as Jesus heard the **n**, he went off by
14:35 The **n** of their arrival spread quickly throughout
24:14 And the Good **N** about the Kingdom will be
26:13 wherever the Good **N** is preached throughout the
Mk 1: 1 Here begins the Good **N** about Jesus the Messiah,
1:14 Jesus went to Galilee to preach God's Good **N**.
1:15 Turn from your sins and believe this Good **N**!"
1:28 The **n** of what he had done spread quickly through
1:45 But as the man went on his way, he spread the **n**,
2: 1 and the **n** of his arrival spread quickly through the
3: 8 The **n** about his miracles had spread far and wide,
4:18 represents those who hear and accept the Good **N**,
5:14 spreading the **n** as they ran.
7:24 As usual, the **n** of his arrival spread fast.
7:36 he told them not to, the more they spread the **n**,
8:35 life for my sake and for the sake of the Good **N**,
10:29 or property, for my sake and for the Good **N**,
13:10 And the Good **N** must first be preached to every
14: 9 wherever the Good **N** is preached throughout the
16:15 all the world and preach the Good **N** to everyone,
Lk 1:19 It was he who sent me to bring you this good **n**!
1:65 and the **n** of what had happened spread throughout
2:10 "I bring you good **n** of great joy for everyone!
3:18 as he announced the Good **N** to the people.
4:18 for he has appointed me to preach Good **N** to the
4:43 "I must preach the Good **N** of the Kingdom of
7:22 and the Good **N** is being preached to the poor.
8: 1 and villages to announce the Good **N** concerning
8:34 spreading the **n** as they ran.
9: 6 preaching the Good **N** and healing the sick.
16:16 But now the Good **N** of the Kingdom of God is
20: 1 and preaching the Good **N** in the Temple,
22:35 "When I sent you out to preach the Good **N**
Jn 4:51 some of his servants met him with the **n** that his
12:12 the **n** that Jesus was on the way to Jerusalem swept
Ac 1:19 The **n** of his death spread rapidly among all the
5:25 Then someone arrived with the **n** that the men they
8: 4 everywhere preaching the Good **N** about Jesus.
8:12 of Good **N** concerning the Kingdom of God
8:25 along the way to preach the Good **N** to them,
8:35 then used many others to tell him the Good **N**
8:40 He preached the Good **N** there and in every city
9:42 The **n** raced through the whole town, and many
10:36 I'm sure you have heard about the Good **N** for the
11: 1 Soon the **n** reached the apostles and other believers
11:15 "Well, I began telling them the Good **N**, but just
11:19 They preached the Good **N**, but only to Jews.
12:24 But God's Good **N** was spreading rapidly,
13:32 and I are here to bring you this Good **N**.
13:46 "It was necessary that this Good **N** from God be
14: 7 and they preached the Good **N** there.
14:15 We have come to bring you the Good **N** that you
14:21 After preaching the Good **N** in Derbe and making
15: 7 so that they could hear the Good **N** and believe.
16:10 God was calling us to preach the Good **N** there.
20:24 the work of telling others the Good **N** about God's
23:11 you must preach the Good **N** in Rome."
Ro 1: 1 to be an apostle and sent out to preach his Good **N**.
1: 2 This Good **N** was promised long ago by God
1: 3 It is the Good **N** about his Son, Jesus, who came as
1: 9 heart by telling others the Good **N** about his Son.
1:15 to you in Rome, too, to preach God's Good **N**.
1:16 For I am not ashamed of this Good **N** about Christ.
1:17 This Good **N** tells us how God makes us right in
10:15 beautiful are the feet of those who bring good **n**!"
10:16 But not everyone welcomes the Good **N**, for Isaiah
10:17 comes from listening to this message of Good **N**—the Good **N** about Christ.
11:28 Many of the Jews are now enemies of the Good **N**.
15:16 I bring you the Good **N** and offer you up as a
15:19 I have fully presented the Good **N** of Christ all the
15:20 **N** where the name of Christ has never been heard,
15:27 of the Good **N** from the Jewish Christians,
16:25 able to make you strong, just as the Good **N** says.
1Co 1:17 send me to baptize, but to preach the Good **N**—
4:15 Christ Jesus when I preached the Good **N** to you.
9:12 an obstacle in the way of the Good **N** about Christ.
9:14 **N** should be supported by those who benefit from
9:16 For preaching the Good **N** is not something I can
9:18 preaching the Good **N** without expense to anyone,
9:23 I do all this to spread the Good **N**, and in doing

15: 1 of the Good **N** I preached to you before.
15: 2 And it is this Good **N** that saves you if you firmly
2Co 2:12 to the city of Troas to preach the Good **N** of Christ,
2:14 and to spread the Good **N** like a sweet perfume.
4: 3 If the Good **N** we preach is veiled from anyone,
4: 4 light of the Good **N** that is shining upon them.
7: 7 so was the **n** he brought of the encouragement he
8:18 in all the churches as a preacher of the Good **N**.
9:13 that you are obedient to the Good **N** of Christ.
10:14 all the way to you with the Good **N** of Christ.
10:16 and preach the Good **N** in other places that are far
11: 7 and honored you by preaching God's Good **N** to
Gal 1: 7 that pretends to be the Good **N** but is not the Good **N** at all.
1:11 I solemnly assure you that the Good **N** of salvation
1:16 so that I could proclaim the Good **N** about Jesus to
2: 5 We wanted to preserve the truth of the Good **N** for
2: 7 of preaching the Good **N** to the Gentiles,
2:14 they were not following the truth of the Good **N**,
3: 4 You have suffered so much for the Good **N**.
3: 8 God promised this good **n** to Abraham long ago
4:13 sick when I first brought you the Good **N** of Christ.
Eph 1:13 heard the truth, the Good **N** that God saves you.
2:17 He has brought this Good **N** of peace to you
3: 6 Both groups have believed the Good **N**, and both
3: 7 privilege of serving him by spreading this Good **N**.
6:15 put on the peace that comes from the Good **N**,
6:19 secret plan that the Good **N** is for the Gentiles,
Php 1: 5 **N** about Christ from the time you first heard it until
1: 7 defending the truth and telling others the Good **N**.
1:12 to me here has helped to spread the Good **N**.
1:16 the Lord brought me here to defend the Good **N**.
1:27 you must live in a manner worthy of the Good **N**
1:27 side by side, fighting together for the Good **N**.
2:22 he has helped me in preaching the Good **N**.
4: 3 worked hard with me in telling others the Good **N**.
4:15 me financial help when I brought you the Good **N**
Col 1: 5 ever since you first heard the truth of the Good **N**.
1: 6 This same Good **N** that came to you is going out
1: 7 was the one who brought you the Good **N**.
1:23 you received when you heard the Good **N**.
1:23 The Good **N** has been preached all over the world,
4: 9 He and Tychicus will give you all the latest **n**.
1Th 1: 5 For when we brought you the Good **N**, it was not
2: 2 the courage to declare his Good **N** to you boldly,
2: 4 approved by God to be entrusted with the Good **N**.
2: 8 so much that we gave you not only God's Good **N**
2: 9 there as we preached God's Good **N** among you.
2:16 by trying to keep us from preaching the Good **N** to
3: 2 and our brother in proclaiming the Good **N** of
3: 6 bringing the good **n** that your faith and love are as
2Th 1: 8 and on those who refuse to obey the Good **N** of our
2:14 you to salvation when we told you the Good **N**;
1Ti 1:11 that comes from the glorious Good **N** entrusted to
2Ti 1: 8 suffer with me for the proclamation of the Good **N**.
1:10 us the way to everlasting life through the Good **N**.
1:11 an apostle, and a teacher of this Good **N**.
2: 8 raised from the dead. This is the Good **N** I preach.
2: 9 And because I preach this Good **N**, I am suffering
4:17 that I might preach the Good **N** in all its fullness
Tit 1: 3 now at the right time he has revealed this Good **N**,
Phm 1: 1 in prison for preaching the Good **N** about Christ
1:13 I am in these chains for preaching the Good **N**,
Heb 4: 2 For this Good **N**—that God has prepared a place of
4: 6 But those who formerly heard the Good **N** failed to
1Pe 1:12 And now this Good **N** has been announced by
1:22 sins when you accepted the truth of the Good **N**.
1:25 And that word is the Good **N** that was preached to
3: 1 even those who refuse to accept the Good **N**.
4: 6 That is why the Good **N** was preached even to
4:17 those who have never believed God's Good **N**?
Jude 1: 3 urging you to defend the truth of the Good **N**.
Rev 14: 6 carrying the everlasting Good **N** to preach to the

NEXT (353)

Ge 17:21 be born to you and Sarah about this time **n** year."
18:10 of them said, "About this time **n** year I will return,
19:15 At dawn the **n** morning the angels became
19:27 The **n** morning Abraham was up early and hurried
19:34 The **n** morning the older daughter said to her
20: 8 Abimelech got up early the **n** morning and hastily
21:14 So Abraham got up early the **n** morning,
22: 3 The **n** morning Abraham got up early. He saddled
22:21 The oldest was named Uz, the **n** oldest was Buz,
24:49 tell me, then I'll know what my **n** step should be,
24:54 But early the **n** morning, he said, "Send me back
26:31 Early the **n** morning, they each took a solemn oath
28:18 The **n** morning he got up very early. He took the
29:20 So Jacob spent the **n** seven years working to pay
31:55 Laban got up early the **n** morning, and he kissed
33: 2 Leah and her children **n**, and Rachel and Joseph
33: 7 **N** Leah came with her children, and they bowed
40: 6 The **n** morning Joseph noticed the dejected look on
41: 8 The **n** morning, as he thought about it,
41:29 The **n** seven years will be a period of great
41:47 for the **n** seven years there were bumper crops
47:18 The **n** year they came again and said, "Our money
47:24 and use it to plant the **n** year's crop and to feed
Ex 2:13 The **n** day, as Moses was out visiting his people
8:20 **N** the LORD told Moses, "Get up early in the
9: 5 that he would send the plague the very **n** day,
9: 6 The **n** morning all the livestock of the Egyptians
12:10 Do not leave any of it until the **n** day. Whatever is
16:13 The **n** morning the desert all around the camp was
16:24 The **n** morning the leftover food was wholesome
18:13 The **n** day, Moses sat as usual to hear the people's
23:18 fat may be left unoffered until the **n** morning.
24: 4 Early the **n** morning he built an altar at the foot of
26:17 on each frame so they can be joined to the **n** frame.
28:26 inside corners of the chestpiece **n** to the ephod.
28:36 "**N** make a medallion of pure gold.
28:42 to be worn **n** to their bodies, reaching from waist to
29: 8 **N** present his sons, and dress them in their tunics
29:15 "**N** Aaron and his sons must lay their hands on the
29:30 Whoever is the **n** high priest after Aaron will wear
32: 6 So the people got up early the **n** morning to
32:30 The **n** day Moses said to the people, "You have
36:22 each frame so they could be joined to the **n** frame.
37: 1 **N** Bezalel made the Ark out of acacia wood.
37:14 **n** to the rim. These were made to hold the carrying
37:16 **N**, using pure gold, he made the plates, dishes,
38: 4 **N** he made a bronze grating that rested on a ledge
39:19 inside corners of the chestpiece **n** to the ephod.
40:11 **N** anoint the large washbasin and its pedestal to
40:22 **N** he placed the table in the Tabernacle,
40:30 **N** he placed the large washbasin between the
Lev 6: 9 must be left on the altar until the **n** morning,
6:10 The **n** morning, after dressing in his special linen
7:15 None of it may be saved for the **n** morning.
8:13 **N** Moses presented Aaron's sons and clothed them
8:20 **N** he cut the ram into pieces and burned the head,
8:22 **N** Moses presented the second ram, which was the
8:24 **N** he presented Aaron's sons and put some of the
8:25 **N** he took the fat, including the fat from the tail,
8:30 **N** Moses took some of the anointing oil and some
9:12 **N** Aaron slaughtered the animal for the whole
9:15 **N** Aaron presented the sacrifices for the people.
9:23 **N** Moses and Aaron went into the Tabernacle,
14:10 "On the **n** day, the eighth day, each person cured
14:41 **N** the inside walls of the entire house must be
16: 4 and the undergarments worn **n** to his body.
19: 6 same day you offer it or on the **n** day at the latest.
23: 8 On each of the **n** seven days, the people must
25:15 for the crop years left until the **n** Year of Jubilee.
25:27 on the number of years until the **n** Year of Jubilee.
25:28 then it will belong to the new owner until the **n**
25:50 number of years left until the **n** Year of Jubilee—
27:18 to the years left until the **n** Year of Jubilee.
27:23 based on the years until the **n** Year of Jubilee.
Nu 4: 7 "**N** they must spread a blue cloth over the table,
4: 9 "**N** they must cover the lampstand with a dark blue
4:15 and carry these things to the **n** destination.
8:12 "**N** the Levites will lay their hands on the heads of
9:12 They must not leave any of the lamb until the **n**
9:21 only overnight and moved on the **n** morning.
10:17 and Merarite divisions of the Levites were **n** in the
10:21 **N** came the Kohathite division of the Levites,
10:21 When they arrived at the **n** camp, the Tabernacle
11:32 that day and throughout the night and all the **n** day,
13:33 We felt like grasshoppers **n** to them, and that's
14:40 So they got up early the **n** morning and set out for
16:41 But the very **n** morning the whole community
17: 8 into the Tabernacle of the Covenant the **n** day,
21:10 The Israelites traveled **n** to Oboth and camped
22:13 The **n** morning Balaam got up and told Balak's
22:21 So the **n** morning Balaam saddled his donkey
22:41 The **n** morning Balak took Balaam up to
Dt 3: 1 "**N** we headed for the land of Bashan, where King
16: 4 of the Passover lamb remain until the **n** morning.
16: 7 Then go back to your tents the **n** morning.
16: 8 For the **n** six days you may not eat bread made
Jos 3: 1 Early the **n** morning Joshua and all the Israelites
5:11 The very **n** day they began to eat unleavened bread
6:12 Joshua got up early the **n** morning, and the priests
7:16 Early the **n** morning Joshua brought the tribes of
8:10 Early the **n** morning Joshua roused his men
8:14 and all his army hurriedly went out early the **n**
17: 1 The **n** allotment of land was given to the half-tribe
Jdg 6:28 Early the **n** morning, as the people of the town
6:38 When Gideon got up the **n** morning, he squeezed
9:42 The **n** day the people of Shechem went out into the
20:19 So the Israelites left early the **n** morning
21: 4 Early the **n** morning the people built an altar
Ru 4: 4 because I am **n** in line to redeem it after you."
1Sa 1:19 The entire family got up early the **n** morning
1:21 The **n** year Elkanah, Peninnah, and their children
5: 3 citizens of Ashdod went to see it the **n** morning,
5: 4 But the **n** morning the same thing happened—
9:26 At daybreak the **n** morning, Samuel called up to
11:11 But before dawn the **n** morning, Saul arrived,
15:12 Early the **n** morning Samuel went to find Saul.
16: 9 **N** Jesse summoned Shammah, but Samuel said,
17:20 and set out early the **n** morning with the gifts.
18: 8 **N** they'll be making him their king!"
18:10 The very **n** day, in fact, a tormenting spirit from
19: 4 The **n** morning Jonathan spoke with his father
19:11 told to kill David when he came out the **n** morning.
20:12 or the **n** day at the latest, I will talk to my father
20:27 But when David's place was empty again the **n**
20:35 The **n** morning, as agreed, Jonathan went out into
23:17 and I will be **n** to you, as my father is well aware."
25:36 about her meeting with David until the **n** morning.
25:37 The **n** morning when he was sober, she told him
30:17 that night and the entire **n** day until evening.
31: 8 The **n** day, when the Philistines went out to strip
2Sa 11:12 So Uriah stayed in Jerusalem that day and the **n**.
11:14 So the **n** morning David wrote a letter to Joab
11:25 Fight harder **n** time, and conquer the city!"
14:30 set fire to Joab's barley field, the field **n** to mine."
16:20 and asked him, "What should I do **n**?"
23: 9 **N** in rank among the Three was Eleazar son of
23:11 **N** in rank was Shammah son of Agee from Harar.
24:11 The **n** morning the word of the LORD came to
1Ki 1: 6 and had been born **n** after Absalom.
1:13 me that my son Solomon would be the **n** king
1:17 God that my son Solomon would be the **n** king
1:24 have you decided that Adonijah will be the **n** king
1:27 of his servants know who should be the **n** king?"
1:30 today I decree that your son Solomon will be the **n**
2:15 was mine; everyone expected me to be the **n** king.
7:20 beside the rounded surface **n** to the latticework.
11:43 Then his son Rehoboam became the **n** king.
14:20 Jeroboam died, his son Nadab became the **n** king.
14:31 Then his son Abijam became the **n** king.
15: 8 of David. Then his son Asa became the **n** king.
15:24 Then his son Jehoshaphat became the **n** king.
15:28 reign in Judah, and he became the **n** king of Israel.
16: 6 in Tirzah. Then his son Elah became the **n** king.
16:10 reign in Judah. Then Zimri became the **n** king.
16:22 So Tibni was killed, and Omri became the **n** king.
16:28 in Samaria. Then his son Ahab became the **n** king.
17: 1 or rain during the **n** few years unless I give the
20:22 for another attack by the king of Aram **n** spring."
22:40 Then his son Ahaziah became the **n** king.
22:50 Then his son Jehoram became the **n** king.
2Ki 1:17 succeed him, his brother Joram became the **n** king.
3:20 the **n** day at about the time when the morning
3:22 But when they got up the **n** morning, the sun was
3:27 his oldest son, who would have been the **n** king,
4:16 "**N** year at about this time you will be holding a
6:15 of the man of God got up early the **n** morning
6:28 that we eat my son one day and her son the **n**.
6:29 Then the **n** day I said, 'Kill your son so we can eat
6:30 he was wearing sackcloth underneath **n** to his skin.
8:15 But the **n** day Hazael took a blanket, soaked it in
8:15 he died. Then Hazael became the **n** king of Aram.
8:24 of David. Then his son Ahaziah became the **n** king.
10:35 Then his son Jehoahaz became the **n** king.
12:21 Then his son Amaziah became the **n** king.
13: 9 Then his son Jehoash became the **n** king.
13:13 Then his son Jeroboam II became the **n** king.
13:24 and his son Ben-hadad became the **n** king.
14:16 Then his son Jeroboam II became the **n** king.
14:21 sixteen-year-old son, Uzziah, as their **n** king.
14:29 Then his son Zechariah became the **n** king.
15: 7 of David. Then his son Jotham became the **n** king.
15:10 assassinated him in public, and became the **n** king.
15:14 and assassinated him, and he became the **n** king.
15:22 his son Pekahiah became the **n** king.
15:25 at Samaria. Pekah then became the **n** king of Israel.
15:38 of David. Then his son Ahaz became the **n** king.
16:20 Then his son Hezekiah became the **n** king.
19:29 and **n** year you will eat what springs up from that.
19:35 When the surviving Assyrians woke up the **n**
19:37 Esarhaddon, became the **n** king of Assyria.
20:21 his son Manasseh became the **n** king.
21:18 of Uzza. Then his son Amon became the **n** king.
21:24 and they made his son Josiah the **n** king.
21:26 of Uzza. Then his son Josiah became the **n** king.
23:30 his son Jehoahaz and made him the **n** king.
24: 6 his son Jehoiachin became the **n** king.
24:17 Jehoiachin's uncle, as the **n** king,
1Ch 10: 8 The **n** day when the Philistines went out to strip
11:12 **N** in rank among the Three was Eleazar son of
23:11 Jahath was the family leader, and Ziza was **n**.
29: 1 whom God has chosen to be the **n** king of Israel,
29:21 The **n** day they brought a thousand bulls,
2Ch 7: 8 For the **n** seven days they celebrated the Festival of
9:31 Then his son Rehoboam became the **n** king.
11:22 making it clear that he would be the **n** king.
12:16 of David. Then his son Abijah became the **n** king.
14: 1 of David. Then his son Asa became the **n** king.
17: 1 Then Jehoshaphat, Asa's son, became the **n** king.
17:15 **N** in command was Jehohanan, who commanded
17:16 **N** was Amasiah son of Zicri, who volunteered for
17:18 **N** in command was Jehozabad, who commanded
20:20 Early the **n** morning the army of Judah went out
21: 1 Then his son Jehoram became the **n** king.
22: 1 Jehoram's youngest son, their **n** king.
24:27 Joash died, his son Amaziah became the **n** king.
26: 1 sixteen-year-old son, Uzziah, as their **n** king.
26:23 the kings. Then his son Jotham became the **n** king.
27: 5 For the **n** three years, he received from them an
27: 9 of David, and his son Ahaz became the **n** king.
28:27 Then his son Hezekiah became the **n** king.
29:20 Early the **n** morning King Hezekiah gathered the
29:22 **N** they killed the rams and sprinkled their blood on
32:33 Then his son Manasseh became the **n** king.
33:20 his palace. Then his son Amon became the **n** king.
33:25 and they made his son Josiah the **n** king.
36: 1 and made him the **n** king in Jerusalem.
36: 4 of Jehoahaz, as the **n** king of Judah and Jerusalem.
36: 8 *and Judah.* Then his son Jehoiachin became the **n**
36:10 Zedekiah, to be the **n** king in Judah and Jerusalem.
Ezr 10:17 By March 27 of the **n** year they had finished
Ne 3: 2 People from the city of Jericho worked **n** to them,
3: 4 and grandson of Hakkoz repaired the **n** section of
3: 5 **N** were the people from Tekoa, though their
3: 7 **N** to them were Melatiah from Gibeon, Jadon from
3: 8 **N** was Uzziel son of Harhaiah, a goldsmith by
3: 9 district of Jerusalem, was **n** to them on the wall.
3:10 **N** Jedaiah son of Harumaph repaired the wall
3:10 and **n** to him was Hattush son of Hashabneiah.
3:12 and his daughters repaired the **n** section.
3:16 **N** to him was Nehemiah son of Azbuk, the leader
3:17 **N** was a group of Levites working under the
3:18 **N** down the line were his countrymen led by
3:19 **N** to them, Ezer son of Jeshua, the leader of
3:20 **N** to him was Baruch son of Zabbai, who repaired
3:23 and grandson of Ananiah repaired the sections **n** to

3:24 **N** was Binnui son of Henadad, who rebuilt another
3:25 of the guard. **N** to him were Pedaiah son of Parosh
3:29 **N** Zadok son of Immer also rebuilt the wall **n** to
3:30 **N** Hananiah son of Shelemiah and Hanun, the sixth
3:30 of Berekiah rebuilt the wall **n** to his own house.
Est 2:14 and the **n** morning she was brought to the second
3:1 official in the empire **n** to the king himself.
8:12 of King Xerxes was March 7 of the **n** year.
10:3 with authority **n** to that of King Xerxes himself.
Ps 78:4 but will tell the **n** generation about the glorious
78:6 so the **n** generation might know them—
Pr 27:24 and the crown might not be secure for the **n**
Ecc 4:16 But then the **n** generation grows up and rejects
Isa 3:16 **N** the LORD will judge the women of Jerusalem,
37:30 and **n** year you will eat what springs up from that.
37:36 When the surviving Assyrians woke up the **n**
37:38 Esarhaddon, became the **n** king of Assyria.
38:19 can make known your faithfulness to the **n**.
Jer 20:3 The **n** day, when Pashhur finally released him,
35:4 This room was located **n** to the one used by the
36:6 So you go to the Temple on the **n** day of fasting,
41:4 The **n** day, before anyone had heard about
Eze 12:8 The **n** morning this message came to me from the
24:18 So I proclaimed this to the people the **n** morning,
24:18 The **n** morning I did everything I had been told to
33:22 able to speak when this man arrived the **n** morning.
43:8 They put their idol altars right **n** to mine with only
45:5 The strip of sacred land **n** to it, also 8-1/3 miles
48:12 **N** to the priests' territory will lie the land where
48:25 **N** is the territory of Issachar with the same eastern
Da 6:7 Give orders that for the **n** thirty days anyone who
6:12 "Did you not sign a law that for the **n** thirty days
6:19 Very early the **n** morning, the king hurried out to
11:21 "The **n** to come to power will be a despicable man
Jnh 4:7 The **n** morning at dawn the worm ate through the
Mt 4:8 **N** the Devil took him to the peak of a very high
10:11 and stay in his home until you leave for the **n**
10:23 you are persecuted in one town, flee to the **n**.
20:21 will you let my two sons sit in places of honor **n** to
20:23 right to say who will sit on the thrones **n** to mine.
22:26 and the wife was married to the **n** brother, and
25:22 "**N** came the servant who had received the two
27:62 The **n** day—on the first day of the Passover
Mk 1:35 The **n** morning Jesus awoke long before daybreak
6:2 The **n** Sabbath he began teaching in the synagogue,
10:37 we want to sit in places of honor **n** to you,"
10:40 right to say who will sit on the thrones **n** to mine.
11:12 The **n** morning as they were leaving Bethany,
11:20 The **n** morning as they passed by the fig tree he
12:5 The **n** servant he sent was killed. Others who were
12:21 Then the **n** brother married her and died without
15:1 the entire high council—met to discuss their **n** step.
16:1 The **n** evening, when the Sabbath ended,
Lk 4:13 he left him until the **n** opportunity came.
4:42 Early the **n** morning Jesus went out into the
9:37 The **n** day, after they had come down the
10:35 The **n** day he handed the innkeeper two pieces of
10:35 'I'll pay the difference the **n** time I am here.'
13:9 If we get figs **n** year, fine. If not, you can cut it
13:33 and the **n** day I must proceed on my way.
16:7 he asked the **n** man. 'A thousand bushels of
19:18 "The **n** servant also reported a good gain—
Jn 1:29 The **n** day John saw Jesus coming toward him
1:43 The **n** day Jesus decided to go to Galilee. He found
2:1 The **n** day Jesus' mother was a guest at a wedding
6:22 The **n** morning, back across the lake, crowds began
8:2 but early the **n** morning he was back again at the
11:6 he stayed where he was for the **n** two days and did
12:12 The **n** day, the news that Jesus was on the way to
13:23 one Jesus loved, was sitting **n** to Jesus at the table.
19:31 didn't want the victims hanging there the **n** day,
Ac 4:5 The **n** day the council of all the rulers and elders
7:26 "The **n** day he visited them again and saw two
10:9 The **n** day as Cornelius' messengers were nearing
10:23 The **n** day he went with them, accompanied by
13:42 and speak about these things the **n** week.
14:20 The **n** day he left with Barnabas for Derbe.
16:6 **N** Paul and Silas traveled through the area of
16:11 and the **n** day we landed at Neapolis.
16:35 The **n** morning the city officials sent the police to
18:7 worshiped God and lived **n** door to the synagogue.
18:11 So Paul stayed there for the **n** year and a half,
18:22 The **n** stop was at the port of Caesarea. From there
19:8 and preached boldly for the **n** three months,
19:10 This went on for the **n** two years, so that people
20:7 and since he was leaving the **n** day, he talked until
20:15 The **n** day we passed the island of Kios.
21:1 The **n** day we reached Rhodes and then went to
21:7 The **n** stop after leaving Tyre was Ptolemais,
21:18 The **n** day Paul went in with us to meet with
21:26 and the **n** day he went through the purification
22:30 The **n** day the commander freed Paul from his
23:12 The **n** morning a group of Jews got together
23:32 They returned to the fortress the **n** morning,
25:17 I called the case the very **n** day and ordered Paul
25:23 So the **n** day Agrippa and Bernice arrived at the
27:3 The **n** day when we docked at Sidon, Julius was
27:18 The **n** day, as gale-force winds continued to batter
28:30 For the **n** two years, Paul lived in his own rented
Ro 8:34 and is sitting at the place of highest honor **n** to
9:9 For God had promised, "**N** year I will return,
1Co 11:17 But now when I mention this **n** issue, I cannot
16:6 then you can send me on my way to the **n**
2Co 13:2 I did before, that this **n** time I will not spare them.
1Ti 4:8 for it promises a reward in both this life and the **n**.
Jas 5:17 none fell for the **n** three and a half years!
1Pe 3:22 He is seated in the place of honor **n** to God, and all

NEZIAH (2)

Ezr 2:54 **N**, and Hatipha.
Ne 7:56 **N**, and Hatipha.

NEZIB (1)

Jos 15:43 Iphtah, Ashnah, **N**,

NIBHAZ (1)

2Ki 17:31 The Avvites worshiped their gods **N** and Tartak.

NIBSHAN (1)

Jos 15:62 **N**, the City of Salt, and En-gedi—six towns with

NICANOR (1)

Ac 6:5 Philip, Procorus, **N**, Timon, Parmenas,

NICE (5) [NICELY, NICEST]

Ecc 6:9 Just dreaming about **n** things is meaningless;
Isa 30:10 tell us the truth. Tell us **n** things. Tell us lies.
Jer 22:23 It may be **n** to live in a beautiful palace lined with
Mk 4:19 the lure of wealth, and the desire for **n** things,
Jas 5:5 Now your hearts are **n** and fat, ready for the

NICELY (1) [NICE]

1Co 14:17 You will be giving thanks very **n**, no doubt,

NICEST (1) [NICE]

Ru 3:3 and put on perfume and dress in your **n** clothes.

NICKNAMED (5) [NAME]

Mk 3:17 of Zebedee, but Jesus **n** them "Sons of Thunder"),
Jn 11:16 Thomas, **n** the Twin, said to his fellow disciples,
20:24 One of the disciples, Thomas (**n** the Twin), was not
21:2 Simon Peter, Thomas (**n** the Twin),
Ac 4:36 the one the apostles **n** Barnabas (which means

NICODEMUS (5)

Jn 3:1 a Jewish religious leader named **N**, a Pharisee,
3:4 "What do you mean?" exclaimed **N**. "How can
3:9 "What do you mean?" **N** asked.
7:50 **N**, the leader who had met with Jesus earlier,
19:39 **N**, the man who had come to Jesus at night,

NICOLAITANS (2)

Rev 2:6 You hate the deeds of the immoral **N**, just as I do.
2:15 In the same way, you have some **N** among you—

NICOLAS (1)

Ac 6:5 and **N** of Antioch (a Gentile convert to the Jewish

NICOPOLIS (1)

Tit 3:12 do your best to meet me at **N** as quickly as you

NIGH [KJV] See ADVANCED, ALONG, APPROACH, APPROACHED, APPROACHES, CLOSE, FORWARD, NEAR, NEARBY, NEARER, NEARLY, NEIGHBORS

NIGHT (343) [MIDNIGHT, NIGHT'S, NIGHTFALL, NIGHTS, NOCTURNAL, OVERNIGHT, TONIGHT]

Ge 1:5 God called the light "day" and the darkness "**n**."
1:14 appear in the sky to separate the day from the **n**.
1:16 the lesser one, the moon, presides through the **n**.
1:18 to govern the day and the **n**, and to separate the
8:22 cold and heat, winter and summer, day and **n**."
14:15 and attacked during the **n** from several directions.
15:5 LORD brought Abram outside beneath the **n** sky
19:2 to wash your feet, and be my guests for the **n**.
19:2 "we'll just spend the **n** out here in the city
19:4 as they were preparing to retire for the **n**,
19:5 "Where are the men who came to spend the **n** with
19:33 So that **n** they got him drunk, and the older
19:34 her younger sister, "I slept with our father last **n**.
19:35 So that **n** they got him drunk again,
20:3 But one **n** God came to Abimelech in a dream
24:23 your father have any room to put us up for the **n**?"
26:24 where the LORD appeared to him on the **n** of his
28:11 place to set up camp and stopped there for the **n**.
29:23 That **n**, when it was dark, Laban took Leah to
31:24 But the previous **n** God had appeared to Laban in a
31:29 but the God of your father appeared to me last **n**
31:42 That is why he appeared to you last **n**
31:54 Afterward they spent the **n** there in the hills.
32:13 Jacob stayed where he was for the **n** and prepared
32:21 sent on ahead, and Jacob spent that **n** in the camp.
32:22 But during the **n** Jacob got up and sent his two
32:32 near the hip, in memory of what happened that **n**.
37:5 One **n** Joseph had a dream and promptly reported
39:16 with her, and when her husband came home that **n**,
40:5 One **n** the cup-bearer and the baker each had a
40:8 And they replied, "We both had dreams last **n**,
41:11 One **n** the chief baker and I each had a dream,
41:15 "I had a dream last **n**," Pharaoh told him,
42:27 But when they stopped for the **n** and one of them
43:21 we stopped for the **n** and opened our sacks.
46:2 During the **n** God spoke to him in a vision.
Ex 4:24 when Moses and his family had stopped for the **n**,
10:13 an east wind to blow all that day and through the **n**.
12:10 Whatever is not eaten that **n** must be burned before
12:12 On that **n** I will pass through the land of Egypt
12:30 and all the people of Egypt woke up during the **n**,
12:31 Pharaoh sent for Moses and Aaron during the **n**.
12:37 That **n** the people of Israel left Rameses and started
12:42 This **n** had been reserved by the LORD to bring
12:42 land of Egypt, so this same **n** now belongs to him.
13:21 of cloud during the day and a pillar of fire at **n**.
13:21 way they could travel whether it was day or **n**.
14:20 As **n** came, the pillar of cloud turned into a pillar
14:21 The wind blew all that **n**, turning the seabed into
22:27 neighbor will need it to stay warm during the **n**.
27:21 burning in the LORD's presence day and **n**.
40:38 and at **n** there was fire in the cloud so all the
Lev 6:9 and the altar fire must be kept burning all **n**.
8:35 of the Tabernacle day and **n** for seven days,
Nu 8:17 I set them apart for myself on the **n** I killed all the
9:16 at **n** the cloud changed to the appearance of fire.
9:21 But day or **n**, when the cloud lifted, the people
11:9 came down on the camp with the dew during the **n**.
11:32 that day and throughout the **n** and all the next day,
14:1 people began weeping aloud, and they cried all **n**.
14:14 pillar of cloud by day and the pillar of fire by **n**.
22:9 That **n** God came to Balaam and asked him,
22:19 But stay here one more **n** to see if the LORD has
22:20 That **n** God came to Balaam and told him,
33:4 whom the LORD had killed the **n** before.
33:4 The LORD had defeated the gods of Egypt that **n**
Dt 1:33 guiding you by a pillar of fire at **n** and a pillar of
16:1 LORD your God brought you out of Egypt by **n**.
28:66 You will live **n** and day in fear, with no reason to
28:67 In the morning you will say, 'If only it were **n**!'
Jos 1:8 Meditate on it day and **n** so you may be sure to
2:1 a prostitute named Rahab and stayed there that **n**.
2:8 Before the spies went to sleep that **n**, Rahab went
4:8 them to the place where they camped for the **n**
6:11 then everyone returned to spend the **n** in the camp.
8:3 thousand fighting men and sent them out at **n**
8:9 So they left that **n** and lay in ambush between
8:9 remained among the people in the camp that **n**.
8:12 That **n** Joshua sent five thousand men to lie in
8:13 the city. Joshua himself spent that **n** in the valley.
10:9 Joshua traveled all **n** from Gilgal and took the
Jdg 6:25 That **n** the LORD said to Gideon,
6:27 But he did it at **n** because he was afraid of the
6:40 So that **n** God did as Gideon asked. The fleece was
7:9 During the **n**, the LORD said, "Get up! Go down
9:32 Come by **n** with an army and hide out in the fields.
9:34 So Abimelech and his men went by **n** and split into
16:1 city of Gaza and spent the **n** with a prostitute.
16:2 gathered together and waited all **n** at the city gates.
16:2 They kept quiet during the **n**, saying to themselves,
18:2 they came to Micah's home and spent the **n** there.
19:6 "Please stay the **n** and enjoy yourself."
19:7 him to stay, so he finally gave in and stayed the **n**.
19:9 it's getting late. Stay the **n** and enjoy yourself.
19:13 We will find a place to spend the **n** in either
19:15 so they stopped there to spend the **n**. They rested in
19:15 the town square, but no one took them in for the **n**.
19:18 the LORD. But no one has taken us in for the **n**,
19:20 whatever you do, don't spend the **n** in the square."
19:25 The men of the town abused her all **n**, taking turns
20:4 a town in the land of Benjamin, to spend the **n**.
20:5 That **n** some of the leaders of Gibeah surrounded
Ru 3:6 So she went down to the threshing floor that **n**
1Sa 3:2 One **n** Eli, who was almost blind by now, had just
14:34 it.' " So that **n** all the troops brought their animals
14:36 "Let's chase the Philistines all **n** and destroy every
15:11 he heard this that he cried out to the LORD all **n**.
15:16 "Stop! Listen to what the LORD told me last **n**!"
19:10 dodged out of the way and escaped into the **n**,
19:24 his clothes and lay on the ground all day and all **n**,
25:16 and **n** they were like a wall of protection to us
26:5 David slipped over to Saul's camp one **n** to look
28:8 Then he went to the woman's home at **n**,
28:20 for he had eaten nothing all day and all **n**.
28:25 and they ate it. Then they went out into the **n**.
30:17 and slaughtered them throughout that **n**
31:12 their warriors traveled all **n** to Beth-shan and took
2Sa 2:27 for we would have chased you all **n** if necessary."
2:29 All that **n** Abner and his men retreated through the
2:32 Then they traveled all **n** and reached Hebron at
4:7 they fled across the Jordan Valley through the **n**.
7:4 But that same **n** the LORD said to Nathan,
11:9 He stayed that **n** at the palace entrance with some
11:10 Why didn't you go home last **n** after being away
12:16 went without food and lay all **n** on the bare ground.
17:8 He won't be spending the **n** among the troops.
17:22 him went across the Jordan River during the **n**,
21:10 and stopped wild animals from eating them at **n**.
1Ki 3:5 That **n** the LORD appeared to Solomon in a
3:19 But her baby died during the **n** when she rolled
3:20 Then she got up in the **n** and took my son from
8:29 May you watch over this Temple both day and **n**,
8:59 day and **n**, so that the LORD our God may uphold
19:9 There he came to a cave, where he spent the **n**.
2Ki 6:14 So one **n** the king of Aram sent a great army with
7:7 So they panicked and fled into the **n**,
7:12 The king got out of bed in the middle of the **n**
8:21 but he escaped at **n** under cover of darkness.
19:35 That **n** the angel of the LORD went out to the
1Ch 9:27 They would spend the **n** around the house of God,
17:3 But that same **n** God said to Nathan,
2Ch 1:7 That **n** God appeared to Solomon in a dream
6:20 May you watch over this Temple both day and **n**,
7:12 Then one **n** the LORD appeared to Solomon

21: 9 but he escaped at **n** under cover of darkness.
35:14 from morning till **n** offering the burnt offerings
Ezr 10: 6 He spent the **n** there, but he did not eat any food
Ne 1: 6 Look down and see me praying **n** and day for your
2:12 I slipped out during the **n**, taking only a few others
4: 9 guarded the city day and **n** to protect ourselves.
4:22 and their servants could go on guard duty at **n** as
9:12 and a pillar of fire at **n** so that they could find their
9:19 pillar of fire showed them the way through the **n**.
Est 4:16 Do not eat or drink for three days, **n** or day.
6: 1 That **n** the king had trouble sleeping, so he ordered
Job 3: 3 and cursed be the **n** when I was conceived.
3: 6 Let that **n** be blotted off the calendar, never again
3: 7 Let that **n** be barren. Let it have no joy.
4:13 It came in a vision at **n** as others slept.
5:14 they see no better in the daytime than at **n**.
7: 4 But the **n** drags on, and I toss till dawn.
17:12 They say that **n** is day and day is **n**; how they
20: 8 not be found. He will vanish like a vision in the **n**.
24: 7 All **n** they lie naked in the cold, without clothing
24:14 dawn to kill the poor and needy; at **n** he is a thief.
24:16 They break into houses at **n** and sleep in the
24:17 The black **n** is their morning. They ally themselves
26:10 the waters; he set the boundaries for day and **n**.
27:20 and they are blown away in the storms of the **n**.
33:15 in visions of the **n** when deep sleep falls on people
34:25 and in the **n** he overturns them, destroying them.
35:10 God my Creator, the one who gives songs in the **n**?
36:20 Do not long for the cover of **n**, for that is when
Ps 1: 2 day and **n** they think about his law.
6: 6 out from sobbing. / Every **n** tears drench my bed;
8: 3 When I look at the **n** sky and see the work of your
16: 7 who guides me; / even at **n** my heart instructs me.
17: 3 my thoughts and examined my heart in the **n**.
19: 2 to speak; / **n** after **n** they make him known.
22: 2 Every **n** you hear my voice, but I find no relief.
30: 5 favor lasts a lifetime! / Weeping may go on all **n**,
32: 4 and **n** your hand of discipline was heavy on me.
36: 4 They lie awake at **n**, hatching sinful plots.
42: 3 Day and **n**, I have only tears for food, / while my
42: 8 upon me, / and through each **n** I sing his songs,
51: 3 my shameful deeds— / they haunt me day and **n**.
55:10 Its walls are patrolled day and **n** against invaders,
55:17 Morning, noon, and **n** / I plead aloud in my
59: 6 They come at **n**, / snarling like vicious dogs
59:14 My enemies come out at **n**, / snarling like vicious
63: 6 thinking of you, / meditating on you through the **n**.
74:16 Both day and **n** belong to you; / you made the
77: 2 All **n** long I pray, with hands lifted toward heaven,
78:14 led them by a cloud, / and at **n** by a pillar of fire.
88: 1 my salvation, / I have cried out to you day and **n**.
91: 5 Do not be afraid of the terrors of the **n**, / nor fear
104:20 You send the darkness, and it becomes **n**,
119:55 I reflect at **n** on who you are, O LORD, / and I
119:148 I stay awake through the **n**, / thinking about your
121: 6 sun will not hurt you by day, / nor the moon at **n**.
127: 2 so hard / from early morning until late at **n**,
134: 1 you who serve as **n** watchmen in the house of the
136: 9 and the moon and stars to rule the **n**. / His faithful
139:11 hide me / and the light around me to become **n**—
139:12 To you the **n** shines as bright as day. / Darkness
Pr 7: 9 as the day was fading, as the dark of **n** set in.
31:18 for bargains; her lights burn late into the **n**.
Ecc 2:23 with pain and grief; even at **n** they cannot rest.
4:11 And on a cold **n**, two under the same blanket can
8:16 that there is ceaseless activity, day and **n**.
SS 3: 1 "One **n** as I lay in bed, I yearned deeply for my
3: 8 to defend the king against an attack during the **n**.
5: 2 "One **n** as I was sleeping, my heart awakened in a
5: 2 lovely dove,' he said, 'for I have been out in the **n**.
5: 2 with dew, my hair with the wetness of the **n**.'
7:11 the fields and spend the **n** among the wildflowers.
Isa 4: 5 cloud throughout the day and clouds of fire at **n**,
5:11 begin long drinking bouts that last late into the **n**.
10:17 In a single **n** he will burn those thorns and briers,
15: 1 In one **n** your cities of Ar and Kir will be
21: 4 The sleep I once enjoyed at **n** is now a faint
21: 8 my lord. **N** after **n** I have remained at my post.
21:11 longer until morning? When will the **n** be over?"
21:12 "Morning is coming, but **n** will soon follow.
26: 9 All **n** long I search for you; / earnestly I seek for
27: 3 day and **n** I will watch to keep enemies away.
28:19 morning after morning, day and **n**, until you are
29: 7 her walls will vanish like a vision in the **n**.
34:14 mingle there with hyenas, their howls filling the **n**.
34:14 the ruins, and **n** creatures will come there to rest.
37:36 That **n** the angel of the LORD went out to the
38:13 I waited patiently all **n**, / but I was torn apart as
51:13 the anger of your enemies from morning till **n**?
60: 2 Darkness as black as **n** will cover all the nations of
62: 6 and **n** for the fulfillment of his promises.
65: 4 At **n** they go out among the graves and secret
Jer 6: 5 So let us attack by **n** and destroy her palaces!' "
9: 1 and **n** for all my people who have been
14: 8 passing through the land, stopping only for the **n**?
14:17 to them: '**N** and day my eyes overflow with tears.
23:25 'Listen to the dream I had from God last **n**.'
31:35 light the day and the moon and stars to light the **n**.
33:20 you can break my covenant with the day and the **n**
33:25 reject my people than I would change my laws of **n**
39: 4 so they fled when the darkness of **n** arrived.
49: 9 If thieves came at **n**, even they would not take
La 1: 2 She sobs through the **n**; tears stream down her
2:18 Give yourselves no rest from weeping day or **n**.
2:19 Rise during the **n** and cry out. Pour out your hearts
3: 3 against me. Day and **n** his hand is heavy upon me.
Eze 12: 6 pack to your shoulders and walk away into the **n**.
12:12 "Even Zedekiah will leave Jerusalem at **n** through
Da 2: 1 One **n** during the second year of his reign,
2:19 That **n** the secret was revealed to Daniel in a
4: 5 But one **n** I had a dream that greatly frightened me;
5:30 That very **n** Belshazzar, the Babylonian king,
6:18 king returned to his palace and spent the **n** fasting.
6:18 usual entertainment and couldn't sleep at all that **n**.
7: 2 In my vision that **n**, I, Daniel, saw a great storm
7: 7 Then in my vision that **n**, I saw a fourth beast,
7:13 As my vision continued that **n**, I saw someone who
Hos 4: 5 just as you might at **n**, and so will your false
6: 5 will strike you as surely as day follows **n**.
7: 6 Their plot smolders through the **n**, and in the
10: 9 "O Israel, ever since that awful **n** in Gibeah,
Joel 1:13 Come, spend the **n** in sackcloth, you ministers of
Am 5: 8 who turns darkness into morning and day into **n**.
Ob 1: 5 "If thieves came at **n** and robbed you, they would
Mic 2: 1 How terrible it will be for you who lie awake at **n**,
3: 6 Now the **n** will close around you, cutting off all
Na 1: 8 He pursues his foes into the darkness of **n**.
Zec 1: 8 In a vision during the **n**, I saw a man sitting on a
14: 7 There will be no normal day and **n**, for at evening
Mal 1:11 by people of other nations from morning till **n**.
Mt 2:14 That **n** Joseph left for Egypt with the child
5:14 city on a mountain, glowing in the **n** for all to see.
9:10 That **n** Matthew invited Jesus and his disciples to
13:25 But that **n** as everyone slept, his enemy came
14:23 by himself to pray. **N** fell while he was there alone.
16: 2 'Red sky at **n** means fair weather tomorrow,
26:34 "Peter," Jesus replied, "the truth is, this very **n**,
27:19 I had a terrible nightmare about him last **n**."
28:13 'Jesus' disciples came during the **n** while we were
Mk 2:15 That **n** Levi invited Jesus and his disciples to be
5: 5 and throughout the **n** he would wander among the
6:47 During the **n**, the disciples were in their boat out in
14:30 "Peter," Jesus replied, "the truth is, this very **n**,
Lk 2: 8 That **n** some shepherds were in the fields outside
2:37 never left the Temple but stayed there day and **n**,
5: 5 "we worked hard all last **n** and didn't catch a
6:12 to a mountain to pray, and he prayed to God all **n**.
9:12 so they can find food and lodging for the **n**.
11: 7 The door is locked for the **n**, and we are all in bed.
12:20 said to him, 'You fool! You will die this very **n**.
12:38 He may come in the middle of the **n** or just before
17:34 That **n** two people will be asleep in one bed;
18: 7 his chosen people who plead with him day and **n**?
21:37 and each evening he returned to spend the **n** on the
24:29 but they begged him to stay the **n** with them,
Jn 9: 4 because there is little time left before the **n** falls
11:10 Only at **n** is there danger of stumbling
13:30 So Judas left at once, going out into the **n**.
19:39 the man who had come to Jesus at **n**, also came,
21: 3 went out in the boat, but they caught nothing all **n**.
Ac 5:19 But an angel of the Lord came at **n**,
9:24 and **n** at the city gate so they could murder him.
9:25 So during the **n**, some of the other believers let him
10:23 So Peter invited the men to be his guests for the **n**.
12: 6 The **n** before Peter was to be placed on trial,
16: 9 That **n** Paul had a vision. He saw a man from
17:10 That very **n** the believers sent Paul and Silas to
18: 9 One **n** the Lord spoke to Paul in a vision and told
20:31 my constant watch and care over you **n** and day,
23:11 That **n** the Lord appeared to Paul and said,
23:31 So that **n**, as ordered, the soldiers took Paul as far
26: 7 is why the twelve tribes of Israel worship God **n**
27:23 For last **n** an angel of the God to whom I belong
27:27 About midnight on the fourteenth **n** of the storm,
Ro 1: 9 Day and **n** I bring you and your needs in prayer to
12:13 home for dinner or, if they need lodging, for the **n**.
13:12 The **n** is almost gone; the day of salvation will
1Co 11:23 On the **n** when he was betrayed, the Lord Jesus
2Co 11:25 Once I spent a whole **n** and a day adrift at sea.
1Th 2: 9 **N** and day we toiled to earn a living so that our
3:10 **N** and day we pray earnestly for you, asking God
5: 2 Lord will come unexpectedly, like a thief in the **n**.
5: 5 and of the day; we don't belong to darkness and **n**.
5: 7 **N** is the time for sleep and the time when people
2Th 3: 8 We worked hard day and **n** so that we would not
1Ti 5: 5 **N** and day she asks God for help and spends much
2Ti 1: 3 **N** and day I constantly remember you in my
Rev 4: 8 after day and **n** after **n** they keep on saying,
7:15 of God, serving him day and **n** in his Temple.
8:12 of the day was dark and one-third of the **n** also.
12:10 our brothers and sisters before our God day and **n**.
14:11 and ever, and they will have no relief day or **n**,
20:10 they will be tormented day and **n** forever and ever.
21:25 never close at the end of day because there is no **n**.
22: 5 And there will be no **n** there—no need for lamps

NIGHT'S (3) [NIGHT]

Job 38:13 of the earth, to bring an end to the **n** wickedness?
Ecc 5:12 always worrying and seldom get a good **n** sleep.
Jn 11:13 Jesus meant Lazarus was having a good **n** rest,

NIGHTFALL (3) [NIGHT]

Ex 22:26 as a pledge of repayment, you must return it by **n**.
2Ki 25: 4 they waited for **n** and fled through the gate
Jer 52: 7 they waited for **n** and fled through the gate

NIGHTHAWK (2) [HAWK]

Lev 11:16 the ostrich, the **n**, the seagull, hawks of all kinds,
Dt 14:15 the ostrich, the **n**, the seagull, hawks of all kinds,

NIGHTMARE (1) [NIGHTMARES]

Mt 27:19 because I had a terrible **n** about him last night."

NIGHTMARES (1) [NIGHTMARE]

Ecc 5: 3 Just as being too busy gives you **n**, being a fool

NIGHTS (24) [NIGHT]

FORTY NIGHTS (7) Ge 7:4,12; Ex 24:18; 34:28; Dt 9:9; 1Ki 19:8; Mt 4:2

Ge 7: 4 today I will begin forty days and forty **n** of rain.
7:12 rain continued to fall for forty days and forty **n**.
31:40 heat of the day and through cold and sleepless **n**.
Ex 24:18 He stayed on the mountain forty days and forty **n**.
34:28 mountain with the LORD forty days and forty **n**.
Dt 9: 9 I was there for forty days and forty **n**, and all that
9:11 "At the end of the forty days and **n**, the LORD
9:18 forty days and **n** I lay prostrate before the LORD,
9:25 and **n** when he was ready to destroy you.
10:10 in the LORD's presence for forty days and **n**,
1Sa 30:12 had anything to eat or drink for three days and **n**.
1Ki 19: 8 to travel forty days and forty **n** to Mount Sinai,
Job 2:13 sat on the ground with him for seven days and **n**.
7: 3 months of futility, long and weary **n** of misery.
30:17 My weary **n** are filled with pain as though
Ps 77: 6 when my **n** were filled with joyful songs. / I search
Jer 36:30 to lie unburied—exposed to hot days and frosty **n**.
Jnh 1:17 was inside the fish for three days and three **n**.
Mt 4: 2 For forty days and forty **n** he ate nothing
12:40 belly of the great fish for three days and three **n**,
12:40 in the heart of the earth for three days and three **n**.
2Co 6: 5 worked to exhaustion, endured sleepless **n**,
11:27 have lived with weariness and pain and sleepless **n**.
Rev 18:23 Her **n** will be dark, without a single lamp.

NIGHTSHIRT (1) [SHIRT]

Mk 14:51 following along behind, clothed only in a linen **n**.

NILE (28)

Ge 41: 1 that he was standing on the bank of the **N** River.
41:17 "I was standing on the bank of the **N** River,"
Ex 1:22 "Throw all the newborn Israelite boys into the **N**
2: 3 and laid it among the reeds along the edge of the **N**
4: 9 then take some water from the **N** River and pour it
7:17 I will hit the water of the **N** with this staff,
7:18 will not be able to drink any water from the **N**.' "
7:20 Moses raised his staff and hit the water of the **N**.
7:25 the LORD turned the water of the **N** to blood.
8: 3 The **N** River will swarm with them. They will
8: 9 Then only the frogs in the **N** River will remain
17: 5 one you used when you struck the water of the **N**.
Isa 18: 1 of Ethiopia, which lies at the headwaters of the **N**.
18: 2 and ambassadors are sent in fast boats down the **N**.
19: 5 The waters of the **N** will fail to rise and flood the
19: 6 The canals of the **N** will dry up, and the streams of
23: 3 grain from Egypt and harvests from along the **N**.
23:10 sweep over your mother Tyre like the flooding **N**,
51: 9 of old when you slew Egypt, the dragon of the **N**.
Jer 2:18 What good to you are the waters of the **N**
46: 7 "Who is this, rising like the **N** River at floodtime,
Eze 29: 3 you great monster, lurking in the streams of the **N**.
29: 3 For you have said, 'The **N** River is mine; I made it
29: 9 "Because you said, 'The **N** River is mine; I made
30:12 I will dry up the **N** River and hand the land over to
Am 8: 8 The land will rise up like the **N** River at floodtime,
9: 5 The ground rises like the **N** River at floodtime,
Zec 10:11 And the waters of the **N** will become dry.

NIMRAH (1) [BETH-NIMRAH]

Nu 32: 3 Dibon, Jazer, **N**, Heshbon, Elealeh, Sebam, Nebo,

NIMRIM (2)

Isa 15: 6 Even the waters of **N** are dried up! The grassy
Jer 48:34 Even the waters of **N** are dried up now.

NIMROD (4)

Ge 10: 8 One of Cush's descendants was **N**, who became a
10: 9 people would speak of someone as being "like **N**,
1Ch 1:10 Cush was also the ancestor of **N**, who was known
Mic 5: 6 drawn swords and enter the gates of the land of **N**.

NIMSHI (5)

1Ki 19:16 Then anoint Jehu son of **N** to be king of Israel,
2Ki 9: 2 find Jehu son of Jehoshaphat and grandson of **N**.
9:14 and grandson of **N** formed a conspiracy against
9:20 It must be Jehu son of **N**, for he is driving
2Ch 22: 7 went out with Joram to meet Jehu son of **N**,

NINE (24) [NINTH, 9]

Ex 28:16 folds of cloth, forming a pouch **n** inches square.
39: 9 doubled over to form a pouch, **n** inches square.
Nu 29:26 of the festival, sacrifice **n** young bulls, two rams,
34:13 commands that the land be divided up among the **n**
Jos 13: 7 when you divide the land among the **n** tribes
14: 2 These **n** and a half tribes received their inheritance
15:44 **n** towns with their surrounding villages.
15:54 and Zior—**n** towns with their surrounding villages.
21:16 and Beth-shemesh—**n** towns from these two tribes.
Jdg 4: 3 Sisera, who had **n** hundred iron chariots,
4:13 he called for all **n** hundred of his iron chariots
1Sa 17: 4 was a giant of a man, measuring over **n** feet tall!
2Sa 24: 8 they completed their task in **n** months and twenty
1Ki 9:14 Hiram had sent Solomon **n** thousand pounds of
10:10 Then she gave the king a gift of **n** thousand pounds
2Ki 17: 1 reign in Judah. He reigned in Samaria **n** years.
1Ch 3: 6 David also had **n** other sons: Ibhar, Elishua,

2Ch 9: 9 Then she gave the king a gift of **n** thousand pounds
Da 3: 1 made a gold statue ninety feet tall and **n** feet wide
Mt 20: 3 "At **n** o'clock in the morning he was passing
Mk 15:25 It was **n** o'clock in the morning when the
Lk 17:17 "Didn't I heal ten men? Where are the other **n**?
Ac 2:15 People don't get drunk by **n** o'clock in the
23:23 ready to leave for Caesarea at **n** o'clock tonight.

NINETEEN (2) [NINETEENTH, 19]
Jos 19:38 **n** cities with their surrounding villages.
2Sa 2:30 he discovered that only **n** men were missing,

NINETEENTH (4) [NINETEEN]
2Ki 25: 8 which was the **n** year of Nebuchadnezzar's reign,
1Ch 24:16 The **n** lot fell to Pethahiah. / The twentieth lot fell
25:26 The **n** lot fell to Mallothi and twelve of his sons
Jer 52:12 which was the **n** year of Nebuchadnezzar's reign,

NINETY (5) [90]
Ge 17:17 "Besides, Sarah is **n**; how could she have a
2Ch 3: 3 The foundation for the Temple of God was **n** feet
Ezr 6: 3 Its height will be **n** feet, and its width will be **n** feet.
Da 3: 1 King Nebuchadnezzar made a gold statue **n** feet

NINETY-EIGHT (1) [98]
1Sa 4:15 who was **n** years old and blind.

NINETY-NINE (6)
Ge 17: 1 When Abram was **n** years old, the LORD
17:24 Abraham was **n** years old at that time,
Mt 18:12 Won't he leave the **n** others and go out into the
18:13 he will surely rejoice over it more than over the **n**
Lk 15: 4 wouldn't you leave the **n** others to go and search
15: 7 to God than over **n** others who are righteous

NINETY-SIX (2)
Ezr 8:35 as well as **n** rams and seventy-seven lambs.
Jer 52:23 There were **n** pomegranates on the sides, and a

NINEVEH (26) [NINEVEH'S]
Ge 10:11 to Assyria, where he built **N**, Rehoboth-ir, Calah,
10:12 city of the empire, located between **N** and Calah.
2Ki 19:36 He went home to his capital of **N** and stayed there.
Isa 37:37 He went home to his capital of **N** and stayed there.
Jnh 1: 2 "Get up and go to the great city of **N**!
3: 2 "Get up and go to the great city of **N**, and deliver
3: 3 obeyed the LORD's command and went to **N**,
3: 4 "Forty days from now **N** will be destroyed!"
3: 5 The people of **N** believed God's message,
3: 6 When the king of **N** heard what Jonah was saying,
4:11 But **N** has more than 120,000 people living in
Na 1: 1 This message concerning **N** came as a vision to
1:14 the LORD says concerning the Assyrians in **N**:
1:15 for your enemies from **N** will never invade your
2: 1 **N**, you are already surrounded by enemy armies!
2: 8 **N** is like a leaking water reservoir! The people are
2:11 Where now is that great **N**, lion of the nations,
2:12 O **N**, you were once a mighty lion! You crushed
3: 1 How terrible it will be for **N**, the city of murder
3: 4 All this because **N**, the beautiful and faithless city,
3: 7 shrink back in horror and say, '**N** lies in utter ruin.'
3:11 And you, **N**, will also stagger like a drunkard.
Zep 2:13 **N**, a desolate wasteland, parched like a desert.
Mt 12:41 The people of **N** will rise up against this generation
Lk 11:30 a sign to the people of **N** that God had sent him.
11:32 The people of **N**, too, will rise up against this

NINEVEH'S (2) [NINEVEH]
Na 2: 7 **N** exile has been decreed, and all the servant girls
2: 9 There seems no end to **N** many treasures—its vast,

NINTH (15) [NINE]
Lev 23:27 on the **n** day after the Festival of Trumpets.
25:22 old crop until the new harvest comes in the **n** year.'
Nu 7:60 On the **n** day Abidan son of Gideoni, leader of the
2Ki 17: 6 Finally, in the **n** year of King Hoshea's reign,
18:10 and the **n** year of King Hoshea's reign in Israel,
25: 1 January 15, during the **n** year of Zedekiah's reign,
1Ch 12:12 Johanan was eighth. / Elzabad was **n**.
24:11 The **n** lot fell to Jeshua. / The tenth lot fell to
25:16 The **n** lot fell to Mattaniah and twelve of his sons
27:12 of Benjamin was commander of the **n** division,
27:12 which was on duty during the **n** month.
Jer 39: 1 It was in January during the **n** year of King
52: 4 January 15, during the **n** year of Zedekiah's reign,
Eze 24: 1 during the **n** year of King Jehoiachin's captivity,
Rev 21:20 the eighth beryl, the **n** topaz, the tenth chrysoprase,

NISROCH (2)
2Ki 19:37 he was worshiping in the temple of his god **N**,
Isa 37:38 he was worshiping in the temple of his god **N**,

NITRE [KJV] See LYE, SALT (IN A WOUND)

NO (1730) [NAUGHT, NONE, NOR, NOT, NOTHING, NOTHINGNESS] See Index of Articles, Etc.

NO [THE CITY] [KJV] See THEBES

NOADIAH (2)
Ezr 8:33 with Jozabad son of Jeshua and **N** son of Binnui—
Ne 6:14 And remember **N** the prophet and all the prophets

NOAH (53) [NOAH'S]
Ge 5:28 Lamech was 182 years old, his son **N** was born.
5:29 Lamech named his son **N**, for he said, "He will
5:30 After the birth of **N**, Lamech lived 595 years,
5:32 By the time **N** was 500 years old, he had three
6: 8 But **N** found favor with the LORD.
6: 9 This is the history of **N** and his family. **N** was a righteous man, the only blameless man
6:10 **N** had three sons: Shem, Ham, and Japheth.
6:13 So God said to **N**, "I have decided to destroy all
6:22 So **N** did everything exactly as God had
7: 1 Finally, the day came when the LORD said to **N**,
7: 5 So **N** did exactly as the LORD had commanded
7: 9 male and female, just as God had commanded **N**.
7:11 When **N** was 600 years old, on the seventeenth day
7:13 But **N** had gone into the boat that very day with his
7:23 They were all destroyed, and only **N** was left alive,
8: 1 But God remembered **N** and all the animals in the
8: 6 **N** opened the window he had made in the boat
8: 9 and **N** held out his hand and drew the dove back
8:10 Seven days later, **N** released the dove again.
8:11 **N** now knew that the water was almost gone.
8:13 when **N** was 601 years old, ten and a half months
8:13 the flood began, **N** lifted back the cover to look.
8:15 Then God said to **N**,
8:18 So **N**, his wife, and his sons and their wives left the
8:20 Then **N** built an altar to the LORD and sacrificed
9: 1 God blessed **N** and his sons and told them,
9: 8 Then God told **N** and his sons,
9:17 Then God said to **N**, "Yes, this is the sign of my
9:18 Shem, Ham, and Japheth, the three sons of **N**,
9:19 From these three sons of **N** came all the people
9:20 **N** became a farmer and planted a vineyard.
9:24 When **N** woke up from his drunken stupor,
9:26 Then **N** said, / "May Shem be blessed by the
9:28 **N** lived another 350 years after the Flood.
10: 1 of Shem, Ham, and Japheth, the three sons of **N**.
Nu 26:33 were Mahlah, **N**, Hoglah, Milcah, and Tirzah.
27: 1 Mahlah, **N**, Hoglah, Milcah, and Tirzah.
36:11 and **N** all married cousins on their father's side.
Jos 17: 3 were Mahlah, **N**, Hoglah, Milcah, and Tirzah.
1Ch 1: 4 and **N**. The sons of **N** were Shem, Ham, and
Isa 54: 9 "Just as I swore in the time of **N** that I would
Eze 14:14 Even if **N**, Daniel, and Job were there,
14:20 Even if **N**, Daniel, and Job were living there,
Mt 24:38 and weddings right up to the time **N** entered his
Lk 3:36 Shem was the son of **N**. / **N** was the son of Lamech.
17:27 and weddings right up to the time **N** entered his
Heb 11: 7 It was by faith that **N** built an ark to save his
1Pe 3:20 waited patiently while **N** was building his boat.
2Pe 2: 5 except for **N** and his family of seven.
2: 5 **N** warned the world of God's righteous judgment.

NOAH'S (3) [NOAH]
Ge 10:32 These are the families that came from **N** sons,
Mt 24:37 Son of Man returns, it will be like it was in **N** day.
Lk 17:26 the world will be like the people were in **N** day.

NOB (6)
1Sa 21: 1 David went to the city of **N** to see Ahimelech the
22: 9 "When I was at **N**," he said, "I saw David talking
22:11 and all his family, who served as priests at **N**.
22:19 Then he went to **N**, the city of the priests,
Ne 11:32 They were also in Anathoth, **N**, Ananiah,
Isa 10:32 But the enemy stops at **N** for the rest of that day.

NOBAH (3) [KENATH]
Nu 32:42 a man named **N** captured the town of Kenath
32:42 and he renamed that area **N** after himself.
Jdg 8:11 circled around by the caravan route east of **N**

NOBLE (5) [NOBLEMAN, NOBLEMEN, NOBLES]
Ezr 4:10 and **n** Ashurbanipal had deported and relocated in
Est 6: 9 Instruct one of the king's most **n** princes to dress
Eze 17:23 It will become a **n** cedar, sending forth its branches
Da 1: 3 men of Judah's royal family and other **n** families,
Jas 2: 7 who slander Jesus Christ, whose **n** name you bear?

NOBLEMAN (2) [NOBLE]
Ecc 10:17 Happy is the land whose king is a **n** and whose
Lk 19:12 "A **n** was called away to a distant empire to be

NOBLEMEN (1) [NOBLE]
Est 1: 3 and Persia, as well as the **n** and provincial officials.

NOBLES (19) [NOBLE]
Ex 15:15 will be terrified; / the **n** of Moab will tremble.
2Ki 24:12 **n**, and officials, and the queen mother,
2Ch 23:20 Then the commanders, **n**, rulers, and all the people
Ne 4:19 Then I explained to the **n** and officials and all the
5: 7 I spoke out against these **n** and officials.
5:12 Then I called the priests and made the **n**
Job 34:18 For he says to kings and **n**, 'You are wicked
Ps 83:11 Let their mighty **n** die as Oreb and Zeeb did.
Pr 8:16 with my help, and **n** make righteous judgments.
17:26 for being good or to punish **n** for being honest!
Jer 14: 3 The **n** send servants to get water, but all the wells
39: 6 watch as they killed his sons and all the **n** of Judah.
Da 5: 1 gave a great feast for a thousand of his **n**
5: 2 in Jerusalem, so that he and his **n**, his wives,
5: 3 and the king and his **n**, his wives, and his
5: 9 face turned ashen white. His **n**, too, were shaken.
5:23 You and your **n** and your wives and concubines
6:17 stone with his own royal seal and the seals of his **n**,
Jnh 3: 7 and his **n** sent this decree throughout the city:

NOBODIES (1) [NOBODY]
Isa 3: 5 and **n** will sneer at honorable people.

NOBODY (6) [NOBODIES]
2Sa 14:19 **N** can hide anything from you. Yes, Joab sent me
2Ki 8:13 "How could a **n** like me ever accomplish such a
Pr 12: 9 It is better to be a **n** with a servant than to be
Isa 19:15 **N** in Egypt, whether rich or poor, important
Jer 30:17 called an outcast—'Jerusalem for whom **n** cares.'
Gal 6: 3 you are only fooling yourself. You are really a **n**.

NOCTURNAL (1) [NIGHT]
Dt 23:10 because of a **n** emission must leave the camp

NOD (1)
Ge 4:16 the LORD's presence and settled in the land of **N**,

NODABITES (1)
1Ch 5:19 the Jeturites, the Naphishites, and the **N**.

NOE [KJV] See NOAH

NOGAH (2)
1Ch 3: 7 **N**, Nepheg, Japhia,
14: 6 **N**, Nepheg, Japhia,

NOHAH (1)
1Ch 8: 2 **N**, and Rapha.

NOISE (26) [NOISY]
Ex 32:17 When Joshua heard the **n** of the people shouting
1Sa 4:14 "What is all the **n** about?" Eli asked.
1Ki 1:45 and rejoicing. That's what all the **n** is about.
2Ki 11:13 When Athaliah heard all the **n** made by the guards
2Ch 23:12 When Athaliah heard the **n** of the people running
Job 39: 7 It hates the **n** of the city, and it has no driver to
39:25 It quivers at the **n** of battle and the shout of the
Ps 50: 3 Our God approaches with the **n** of thunder.
Isa 13: 4 Hear the **n** on the mountains! Listen, as the armies
13: 4 It is the **n** and the shout of many nations.
29: 6 them with thunder and earthquake and great **n**,
31: 4 it pays no attention to the shepherd's shouts and **n**.
66: 6 the city? What is that terrible **n** from the Temple?
Jer 4:29 At the **n** of marching armies, the people flee in
6:23 the **n** of their army is like a roaring sea.
49:21 The earth will shake with the **n** of Edom's fall,
50:42 the **n** of their army is like a roaring sea.
50:46 The earth will shake with the **n** of Babylon's fall,
51:55 against her; the **n** of battle rings through the city.
Eze 37: 7 I spoke, there was a rattling **n** all across the valley.
Joel 2: 5 Listen to the **n** they make—like the rumbling of
Am 2: 2 The people will fall in the **n** of battle,
5:23 They are only **n** to my ears. I will not listen to your
Lk 18:36 When he heard the **n** of a crowd going past,
1Co 13: 1 I would only be making meaningless **n** like a loud
2Pe 3:10 Then the heavens will pass away with a terrible **n**,

NOISED [KJV] See NEWS, HEARD

NOISOME [KJV] See DANGEROUS, DESTROYING, FATAL, MALIGNANT

NOISY (3) [NOISE]
1Ki 1:40 and **n** that the earth shook with the sound.
Mic 2:12 your land will again be filled with **n** crowds!
Mt 9:23 he noticed the **n** crowds and heard the funeral

NOMAD (1) [NOMADIC, NOMADS]
Jer 3: 2 You sit alone like a **n** in the desert. You have

NOMADIC (2) [NOMAD]
Jer 25:24 of Arabia, the kings of the **n** tribes of the desert,
49:31 "Go up and attack those self-sufficient **n** tribes,"

NOMADS (5) [NOMAD]
Ps 72: 9 Desert **n** will bow before him; / his enemies will
Isa 13:20 **N** will refuse to camp there, and shepherds will not
Eze 25: 4 I will allow **n** from the eastern deserts to overrun
25:10 And I will hand Moab over to **n** from the eastern
Heb 11:13 were no more than foreigners and **n** here on earth.

NOMINATED (1)
Ac 1:23 So they **n** two men: Joseph called Barsabbas (also

NON [KJV] See NUN

NON-GODS (2) [GOD]
Dt 32:17 They offered sacrifices to demons, **n**, / to gods they
32:21 They have roused my jealousy by worshiping **n**;

NONAGGRESSION (1)
Ge 26:31 next morning, they each took a solemn oath of **n**.

NONE (91) [NO]
Ge 28:17 It is **n** other than the house of God—the gateway to
31:14 **n** of our father's wealth will come to us anyway.
41:15 "and **n** of these men can tell me what it means.
Ex 9:7 true that **n** of the Israelites' animals were dead.
16:27 was the Sabbath day. But there was **n** to be found.
24:2 **n** of the other people are allowed to climb on the
34:25 And **n** of the meat of the Passover lamb may be
Lev 6:23 entirely burned up. **N** of the flour may be eaten."
6:30 **n** of that animal's meat may be eaten.
7:15 **N** of it may be saved for the next morning.
Nu 7:9 But he gave **n** of the carts or oxen to the Kohathite
14:23 **N** of those who have treated me with contempt will
14:29 **n** of you who are twenty years old or older
28:18 **N** of your regular work may be done on that day.
28:25 **N** of your regular work may be done on that day.
28:26 **N** of your regular work may be done on that day.
36:7 **N** of the inherited land may pass from tribe to
Dt 7:14 **N** of your men or women will be childless, and all
13:17 Keep **n** of the plunder that has been set apart for
28:21 The LORD will send diseases among you until **n**
29:19 Let **n** of those who hear the warnings of this curse
Jos 5:5 but **n** of those born after the Exodus,
21:44 **N** of their enemies could stand against them,
1Sa 2:31 die before their time. **N** will live to a ripe old age.
11:3 "If **n** of our relatives will come to save us, we will
13:22 So **n** of the people of Israel had a sword or spear,
30:17 **N** of the Amalekites escaped except four hundred
2Ki 10:14 them at the well of Beth-eked. **N** of them escaped.
1Ch 4:27 but **n** of his brothers had large families.
2Ch 17:10 so that **n** of them declared war on Jehoshaphat.
22:9 **N** of the surviving members of Ahaziah's family
35:18 **N** of the kings of Israel had ever kept a Passover as
Ezr 9:15 though in such a condition **n** of us can stand in
Ne 4:23 During this time, **n** of us—not I, nor my relatives,
Job 6:20 but finding **n**, their hopes are dashed.
9:33 who could bring us together, but there is **n**.
Ecc 8:8 **N** of us can hold back our spirit from departing.
8:8 **N** of us has the power to prevent the day of our
SS 5:15 strong as the cedars of Lebanon. **N** can rival him.
Isa 24:2 bankers and debtors—**n** will be spared.
30:15 is your strength. But you would have **n** of it.
34:16 animals will be missing, and **n** will lack a mate,
40:26 And he counts them to see that **n** are lost or have
41:17 the poor and needy search for water and there is **n**,
57:12 so righteous. **N** of them will benefit or save you.
Jer 1:18 **N** of the kings, officials, priests, or people of Judah
14:6 for grass to eat, but there is **n** to be found."
22:30 for **n** of his children will ever sit on the throne of
29:32 **N** of his descendants will see the good things I will
42:17 **N** of you will escape from the disaster I will bring
44:26 **N** of you may invoke my name or use this oath:
50:29 Surround the city so **n** can escape. Do to her as she
La 4:15 among foreign nations, but **n** would let them stay.
Eze 7:11 **N** of these proud and wicked people will survive.
19:14 and devoured its fruit. / **N** of the remaining limbs
33:13 then **n** of their good deeds will be remembered.
33:16 **N** of their past sins will be brought up again,
39:28 them home. I will leave **n** of my people behind.
43:25 **N** of these animals may have physical defects of
48:14 **N** of this special land will ever be sold or traded
Da 1:19 and **n** of them impressed him as much as Daniel,
5:8 **n** of them could read the writing or tell him what it
8:22 with four kings, **n** of them as great as the first.
8:26 But **n** of these things will happen for a long time,
11:16 onward unopposed; **n** will be able to stop him.
11:24 and do something that **n** of his predecessors ever
12:10 in their wickedness, and **n** of them will understand.
Hos 9:4 **N** of the sacrifices you offer there will please him.
Am 5:2 forsaken on the ground, / with **n** to raise her up."
Mic 2:3 **n** of you will ever again walk proudly in the
Zec 12:3 **N** of the nations who try to lift it will escape
Mt 11:11 have ever lived, **n** is greater than John the Baptist.
12:43 it goes into the desert, seeking rest but finding **n**.
Lk 7:28 of all who have ever lived, **n** is greater than John.
11:24 But when it finds **n**, it says, 'I will return to the
14:24 For **n** of those I invited first will get even the
21:15 and such wisdom that **n** of your opponents will be
Jn 4:27 but **n** of them asked him why he was doing it
7:19 **N** of you obeys the law of Moses! In fact, you are
13:28 **N** of the others at the table knew what Jesus meant.
16:5 and **n** of you has asked me where I am going.
Ac 6:10 **N** of them was able to stand against the wisdom
20:25 "And now I know that **n** of you to whom I have
27:22 **N** of you will lose your lives, even though the ship
1Co 6:10 **n** of these will have a share in the Kingdom of
Eph 2:9 things we have done, so **n** of us can boast about it.
Heb 3:13 so that **n** of you will be deceived by sin
11:39 yet **n** of them received all that God had promised.
12:15 so that **n** of you will miss out on the special favor
Jas 5:17 **n** fell for the next three and a half years!
1Pe 2:10 of God. / Once you received **n** of God's mercy;

NONETHELESS (2)
Ex 21:19 **N**, the assailant must pay for time lost because of
2Ki 10:30 **N** the LORD said to Jehu, "You have done well

NONSENSE (6)
2Sa 18:14 "Enough of this **n**," Joab said. Then he took three
Jer 2:8 spoke in the name of Baal, wasting their time on **n**.
Lk 24:11 but the story sounded like **n**, so they didn't believe
1Co 1:20 and has shown their wisdom to be useless **n**.
1:23 Jews are offended, and the Gentiles say it's all **n**.
Col 2:8 and high-sounding **n** that come from human

NOOK (2)
Ob 1:6 Every **n** and cranny of Edom will be searched
Lk 15:8 and sweep every **n** and cranny until she finds it?

NOON (17) [AFTERNOON, NOONDAY, NOONTIME]
Ge 18:1 One day about **n**, as Abraham was sitting at the
43:16 his household, "These men will eat with me this **n**.
43:25 they prepared their gifts for Joseph's arrival at **n**.
2Sa 4:5 went to Ishbosheth's home around **n** as he was
Ne 8:3 inside the Water Gate from early morning until **n**
Ps 55:17 Morning, **n**, and night / I plead aloud in my
SS 1:7 flock today? Where will you rest your sheep at **n**?
Jer 6:4 They shout, 'Prepare for battle and attack at **n**!
Am 8:9 "I will make the sun go down at **n** and darken the
Mt 20:5 At **n** and again around three o'clock he did the
27:45 At **n**, darkness fell across the whole land until
Mk 15:33 At **n**, darkness fell across the whole land until
Lk 23:44 By this time it was **n**, and darkness fell across the
Jn 19:14 It was now about **n** of the day of preparation for
Ac 10:9 went up to the flat roof to pray. It was about **n**,
22:6 about **n** a very bright light from heaven suddenly
26:13 About **n**, Your Majesty, a light from heaven

NOONDAY (2) [NOON]
Job 11:17 Your life will be brighter than the **n**. Any darkness
Ps 37:6 and the justice of your cause will shine like the **n**

NOONTIME (8) [NOON]
1Sa 11:9 to say, "We will rescue you by **n** tomorrow!"
1Ki 18:27 About **n** Elijah began mocking them. "You'll have
20:16 About **n**, as Ben-hadad and the thirty-two allied
2Ki 4:20 mother held him on her lap. But around **n** he died.
Isa 59:10 Even at brightest **n**, we fall down as though it were
Jer 15:8 At **n** I will bring a destroyer against the mothers of
Jn 4:6 the long walk, sat wearily beside the well about **n**.
Rev 7:16 will be fully protected from the scorching **n** heat.

NOOSE (2)
Job 18:9 grabs them by the heel. A **n** tightens around them.
41:1 a crocodile with a hook or put a **n** around its jaw?

NOPHAH (1)
Nu 21:30 wiped them out / as far away as **N** and Medeba."

NOR (129) [NEITHER, NO] See Index of Articles, Etc.

NORMAL (18) [NORMALLY]
Ex 16:23 On this day we will rest from our **n** daily tasks.
Lev 6:11 Then he must change back into his **n** clothing
15:25 continues for many days beyond the **n** period,
15:26 just as it would be during her **n** menstrual period.
Nu 6:21 beyond what is required by their **n** Nazirite vow,
9:12 They must follow all the **n** regulations concerning
Jos 10:13 middle of the sky, and it did not set as on a **n** day.
1Ki 13:6 the LORD, and the king's hand became **n** again.
18:28 they shouted louder, and following their **n** custom,
Ezr 4:19 In fact, rebellion and sedition are **n** there!
Isa 38:10 of the dead? / Am I to be robbed of my **n** years?"
Zec 14:7 There will be no **n** day and night, for at evening
Mt 12:13 his hand, and it became **n**, just like the other one.
20:2 He agreed to pay the **n** daily wage and sent them
Mk 3:5 man reached out his hand, and it became **n** again!
Lk 4:39 and immediately her temperature returned to **n**.
6:10 man reached out his hand, and it became **n** again!
Ro 1:27 instead of having **n** sexual relationships with

NORMALLY (6) [NORMAL]
Ge 37:24 This pit was **n** used to store water, but it was
Lev 14:32 but who cannot afford to bring the sacrifices **n**
Dt 1:2 **N** it takes only eleven days to travel from Mount
2Ch 30:3 Passover was **n** celebrated one month earlier,
Job 31:33 Have I tried to hide my sins as people **n** do,
Lk 22:27 **N** the master sits at the table and is served by his

NORTH (177) [NORTHEAST, NORTHEASTER, NORTHERN, NORTHWARD, NORTHWEST]
Ge 13:1 So they left Egypt and traveled **n** into the Negev—
14:15 but Abram chased them to Hobah, **n** of Damascus.
28:14 the land from east to west and from **n** to south.
Ex 26:20 On the **n** side there will also be twenty of these
26:26 five crossbars for the **n** side of the Tabernacle
26:35 south side, and the table must be set toward the **n**.
27:11 It will be the same on the **n** side of the courtyard—
36:25 They also made twenty frames for the **n** side of the
36:32 They made another five for the **n** side and five for
38:11 The **n** wall was also 150 feet long, with twenty
40:22 along the **n** side of the Holy Place, just outside the
Lev 1:11 Slaughter the animal on the **n** side of the altar in
Nu 2:25[-26] and Naphtali are to camp on the **n** side of the
3:35 They were assigned the area **n** of the Tabernacle
35:5 east, south, west, **n**—with the town at the center.
Dt 11:24 the wilderness in the south to Lebanon in the **n**,
Jos 1:4 in the south to the Lebanon mountains in the **n**,
8:11 They camped on the **n** side of Ai, with a valley
8:13 So they stationed the main army **n** of the city
9:1 Sea as far **n** as the Lebanon mountains.)
12:2 area of Gilead, which lies **n** of the Jabbok River.
12:3 Sihon also controlled the Jordan Valley as far **n** as
12:5 stretching from Mount Hermon to Salecah in the **n**
13:4 In the **n**, this area has not yet been conquered:
13:27 extending as far **n** as the Sea of Galilee.
15:6 then proceeded **n** of Beth-arabah to the stone of
15:7 valley of Achor to Debir, turning **n** toward Gilgal,
15:11 then proceeded to the slope of the hill **n** of Ekron,
17:10 and the land **n** of the ravine belonged to Manasseh,
17:10 **N** of Manasseh was the territory of Asher, and to
18:5 in the south and Joseph's territory in the **n**.
18:12 went **n** of the slope of Jericho, then west through
18:18 From there it passed along the **n** side of the slope
18:19 ran past the **n** slope of Beth-hoglah, and ended at the **n** bay of the Dead Sea,
19:27 of Iphtah-el, running **n** to Beth-emek and Neiel. It then continued **n** to Cabul,
24:30 in the hill country of Ephraim, **n** of Mount Gaash.
Jdg 2:9 in the hill country of Ephraim, **n** of Mount Gaash.
7:1 The armies of Midian were camped **n** of them in
1Sa 13:17 One went **n** toward Ophrah in the land of Shual,
14:5 The cliff on the **n** was in front of Micmash,
2Sa 24:2 from Dan in the **n** to Beersheba in the south—
1Ki 7:21 one toward the south and one toward the **n**.
7:21 one on the south Jakin, and the one on the **n** Boaz.
7:25 Three faced **n**, three faced west, three faced south,
7:39 the south side of the Temple and five on the **n** side.
7:49 five on the south and five on the **n**,
8:65 in the **n** to the brook of Egypt in the south.
2Ki 10:33 of Aroer by the Arnon Gorge to as far **n** as Gilead
11:11 the south side of the Temple around to the **n** side
16:14 and placed it on the **n** side of the new altar.
1Ch 7:28 and its surrounding villages to the **n** as far as
9:24 on all four sides—east, west, **n**, and south.
21:2 from Beersheba in the south to Dan in the **n**—
26:14 The **n** gate was assigned to his son Zechariah,
26:17 four to the **n** gate, four to the south gate, and two
2Ch 3:17 to the south of the entrance and the other to the **n**.
3:17 one on the south Jakin, and the one on the **n** Boaz.
4:4 Three faced **n**, three faced west, three faced south,
4:6 five to the south of the Sea and five to the **n**.
4:7 south wall, and five were placed against the **n** wall.
4:8 five along the south wall and five along the **n** wall.
7:8 came from as far away as Lebo-hamath in the **n**,
14:10 his armies for battle in the valley **n** of Mareshah.
23:10 the south side of the Temple around to the **n** side
30:5 from Beersheba in the south to Dan in the **n**,
Job 23:9 I do not see him in the **n**, for he is hidden. I turn to
Ps 89:12 You created **n** and south. / Mount Tabor
107:3 from east and west, from **n** and south.
Pr 25:23 As surely as a wind from the **n** brings rain, so a
Ecc 1:6 The wind blows south and **n**, here and there,
11:3 When a tree falls, whether south or **n**, there it lies.
SS 4:16 "Awake, **n** wind! Come, south wind! Blow on my
Isa 14:13 on the mountain of the gods far away in the **n**.
14:31 A powerful army is coming out of the **n**.
41:25 "But I have stirred up a leader from the **n** and east.
43:6 and from **n** and south. I will bring my sons
49:12 from lands to the **n** and west, and from as far south
Jer 1:13 "I see a pot of boiling water, tipping from the **n**."
1:14 "for terror from the **n** will boil out on the people
1:15 I am calling the armies of the kingdoms of the **n** to
3:18 and Israel will return together from exile in the **n**.
4:6 terrible destruction upon you from the **n**."
6:1 army is coming from the **n** to destroy this nation.
6:22 "See a great army marching from the **n**!
8:16 be heard all the way from the land of Dan in the **n**!
10:22 roar of great armies as they roll down from the **n**.
13:20 See the armies marching down from the **n**!
15:12 Can a man break a bar of iron from the **n**, or a bar
16:15 Israel back to their own land from the land of the **n**
23:8 Israel back to their own land from the land of the **n**
25:9 I will gather together all the armies of the **n** under
31:8 For I will bring them from the **n** and from the
46:6 By the Euphrates River to the **n** they stumble
46:10 will receive a sacrifice today in the **n** country
46:20 a young cow, but a gadfly from the **n** is on its way!
46:24 she will be handed over to men from the **n**."
47:2 "A flood is coming from the **n** to overflow the
50:3 For a nation will attack her from the **n** and bring
50:9 am raising up an army of great nations from the **n**.
50:41 "Look! A great army is marching from the **n**!
51:48 for out of the **n** will come destroying armies
Eze 1:4 I saw a great storm coming toward me from the **n**,
6:14 from the wilderness in the south to Riblah in the **n**.
7:2 Wherever you look—east, west, **n**, or south—
8:3 I was taken to the **n** gate of the inner courtyard of
8:5 said to me, "Son of man, look toward the **n**."
8:5 So I looked, and there to the **n**, beside the entrance
8:14 He brought me to the **n** gate of the LORD's
9:2 soon appeared from the upper gate that faces **n**,
16:46 who lived with her daughters in the **n**.
20:47 they will scorch everything from south to **n**.
21:4 a clean sweep throughout the land from south to **n**.
23:24 They will all come against you from the **n** with
26:7 the king of kings from the **n**—against Tyre with his
32:30 All the princes of the **n** and the Sidonians are there,
38:6 the armies of Beth-togarmah from the distant **n**
38:15 homeland in the distant **n** with your vast cavalry
39:2 of Israel, bringing you from the distant **n**.
40:20 There was a gateway on the **n** just like the one on
40:23 Here on the **n** side, just as on the east, there was
40:35 Then he took me around to the **n** gateway leading
40:38 **n** side into a side room where the meat for
40:40 on each side of the stairs going up to the **n**
40:44 one beside the **n** gateway, facing south,

40:44 and the other beside the south gateway, facing **n**.
40:45 "The building beside the **n** inner gate is for the
41:11 feet wide. One door faced **n** and the other south.
42: 1 of the Temple courtyard by way of the **n** gateway.
42: 1 and came to a group of rooms against the **n** wall of
42: 2 whose entrance opened toward the **n**, was 175 feet
42: 4 the complex, and all the doors faced toward the **n**.
42:10 rooms were arranged just like the rooms on the **n**.
42:11 just like the complex on the **n** side of the Temple.
42:13 rooms that overlook the Temple from the **n**
42:17 He also measured the **n** side and got the same
44: 4 Then the man brought me through the **n** gateway to
46: 9 But when the people come in through the **n**
46: 9 the south gateway must leave by the **n** gateway.
46:19 assigned to the priests, which faced toward the **n**.
47: 2 The man brought me outside the wall through the **n**
47:17 on the border between Hamath to the **n**
48: 1 to receive. The territory of Dan is in the extreme **n**.
48: 1 on the border of Damascus, with Hamath to the **n**.
48:30 the city: On the **n** wall, which is 1-1/2 miles long,
Da 8: 4 to the **n**, and to the south, and no one could stand
11: 6 alliance will be formed between the king of the **n**
11: 6 marriage to the king of the **n** to secure the alliance,
11: 7 and enter the fortress of the king of the **n**
11: 8 afterward he will leave the king of the **n** alone.
11: 9 "Later the king of the **n** will invade the realm of
11:10 the sons of the king of the **n** will assemble a
11:11 the vast forces assembled by the king of the **n**
11:13 the king of the **n** will return with a fully equipped
11:15 Then the king of the **n** will come and lay siege to a
11:16 "The king of the **n** will march onward unopposed;
11:28 "The king of the **n** will then return home with
11:40 and the king of the **n** will storm out against him
11:44 then news from the east and the **n** will alarm him,
Joel 2:20 I will remove these armies from the **n** and send
Am 6:14 from Lebo-hamath in the **n** to the Arabah Valley in
Ob 1:20 and occupy the Phoenician coast as far **n** as
1:20 The captives from Jerusalem exiled in the **n** will
Zep 2:13 And the LORD will strike the lands of the **n** with
Zec 2: 6 Flee from the **n**, for I have scattered you to the four
6: 6 The chariot with black horses is going **n**,
6: 8 "Those who went **n** have vented the anger of my
14: 4 for half the mountain will move toward the **n**
14:10 **n** of Judah, to Rimmon, south of Jerusalem,
Mt 15:21 and went **n** to the region of Tyre and Sidon.
Mk 7:24 Jesus left Galilee and went **n** to the region of Tyre.
Lk 6:17 and from as far **n** as the seacoasts of Tyre
Ac 8:40 Philip found himself farther **n** at the city of
27: 4 so we sailed **n** of Cyprus between the island
Gal 1:21 I went **n** into the provinces of Syria and Cilicia.
Rev 21:13 three gates on each side—east, **n**, south, and west.

NORTHEAST (1) [EAST, NORTH]

Jos 18:17 From En-rogel the boundary proceeded **n** to

NORTHEASTER (1) [EAST, NORTH]

Ac 27:14 and a wind of typhoon strength (a "**n**," they called

NORTHERN (25) [NORTH]

Nu 34: 7 "Your **n** boundary will begin at the Mediterranean
34: 9 to Hazar-enan. This will be your **n** boundary.
Jos 11: 2 all the kings of the **n** hill country; the kings in the
12: 5 His kingdom included the **n** half of Gilead,
15: 5 The **n** boundary began at the bay where the Jordan
15: 8 and on up to the **n** end of the valley of Rephaim.
15:10 passed along to the town of Kesalon on the **n** slope
16: 6 The **n** boundary began at the Mediterranean,
17: 9 the border of Manasseh followed the **n** side of the
18:12 The **n** boundary began at the Jordan River,
18:16 of Hinnom, at the **n** end of the valley of Rephaim.
19:14 The **n** boundary of Zebulun passed Hannathon
1Ki 12:19 The **n** tribes of Israel have refused to be ruled by a
12:29 calf idols at the southern and **n** ends of Israel—
2Ch 10:19 The **n** tribes of Israel have refused to be ruled by a
11:13 and Levites living among the **n** tribes of Israel
Job 26: 7 God stretches the **n** sky over empty space
Jer 25:26 And I went to the kings of the **n** countries, far
44: 1 Judeans living in **n** Egypt in the cities of Migdol,
Eze 37:16 on it: 'This stick represents the **n** tribes of Israel.'
37:19 I will take the **n** tribes and join them to Judah.
47:15 "The **n** border will run from the Mediterranean
47:17 So the **n** border will run from the Mediterranean to
47:20 border to the point where the **n** border begins,
Ac 16: 9 He saw a man from Macedonia in **n** Greece,

NORTHWARD (7) [NORTH]

Nu 13:17 "Go **n** through the Negev into the hill country.
13:22 Going **n**, they passed first through the Negev
Dt 2: 3 around in this hill country long enough; turn **n**.
2: 8 "Then as we traveled **n** along the desert route
Jos 13: 3 the boundary of Egypt, **n** to the boundary of Ekron,
13: 4 stretching **n** to Aphek on the border of the
Ne 12:38 The second choir went **n** around the other way to

NORTHWEST (1) [NORTH, WEST]

Ac 27:12 good harbor with only a southwest and **n** exposure.

NOSE (10) [NOSE-RING, NOSES]

Ge 24:22 he gave her a gold ring for her **n** and two large
2Ki 19:28 heard for myself, / I will put my hook in your **n**
2Ch 33:11 They put a ring through his **n**, bound him in bronze
Job 40:24 it off guard or put a ring in its **n** and lead it away.
41: 2 Can you tie it with a rope through the **n** or pierce
Pr 30:33 and a blow to the **n** causes bleeding, so anger
SS 7: 4 Your **n** is as fine as the tower of Lebanon
Isa 37:29 heard for myself, / I will put my hook in your **n**
Eze 16:12 a ring for your **n** and earrings for your ears, and a
23:25 They will cut off your **n** and ears, and any

NOSE-RING (1) [NOSE, RING]

Ge 24:30 When he saw the **n** and the bracelets on his sister's

NOSES (6) [NOSE]

Ps 115: 6 cannot hear with their ears, / or smell with their **n**,
135:17 cannot hear with their ears / or smell with their **n**.
Isa 3:16 who walk around with their **n** in the air,
Eze 8:17 thumbing their **n** at me, and rousing my fury
Am 4: 2 when you will be led away with hooks in your **n**.
Mal 1:13 and you turn up your **n** at his commands,"

NOSTRILS (5)

2Sa 22: 9 Smoke poured from his **n**; / fierce flames leaped
Job 41:20 Smoke streams from its **n** like steam from a boiling
Ps 18: 8 Smoke poured from his **n**; / fierce flames leaped
Isa 1:13 The incense you bring me is a stench in my **n**!
65: 5 They are a stench in my **n**, an acrid smell that

NOT (3435) [AREN'T, CAN'T, CANNOT, COULDN'T, DIDN'T, DOESN'T, DON'T, HADN'T, HASN'T, HAVEN'T, ISN'T, NO, SHOULDN'T, WASN'T, WEREN'T, WON'T, WOULDN'T] See Index of Articles, Etc.

NOTE (12) [NOTES]

1Ki 22:28 standing around, "Take **n** of what I have said."
2Ch 18:27 standing around, "Take **n** of what I have said."
Job 11:11 those who are false, and he takes **n** of all their sins.
Ps 10:14 they cause. / You take **n** of it and punish them.
48:13 Take **n** of the fortified walls, / and tour all the
Pr 17:18 It is poor judgment to co-sign a friend's **n**,
22:26 Do not co-sign another person's **n** or put up a
Jer 6:18 all you nations. Take **n** of my people's condition.
Eze 44: 5 Take careful **n** of who may be admitted to the
Lk 13:30 And **n** this: Some who are despised now will be
2Th 3:14 Take **n** of those who refuse to obey what we say in
Rev 16:15 "Take **n**: I will come as unexpectedly as a thief!

NOTES (1) [NOTE]

1Co 14: 7 For no one will recognize the melody unless the **n**

NOTHING (281) [NO, THING]

Ge 11: 6 they will do later. **N** will be impossible for them!
19:22 But hurry! For I can do **n** until you are there."
31:14 There's **n** for us here—none of our father's wealth
32:10 I left home, I owned **n** except a walking stick,
34: 5 fields herding cattle so he did **n** until they returned.
39: 9 He has held back **n** from me except you,
40:15 and now I'm here in jail, but I did **n** to deserve it."
47:18 are yours. We have **n** left but our bodies and land.
Ex 1: 8 to the throne of Egypt who knew **n** about Joseph
16:18 Those who gathered a lot had **n** left over, and those
21: 2 and he will owe you **n** for his freedom.
23:32 treaties with them and have **n** to do with their gods.
Lev 26:20 All your work will be for **n**, for your land will
Nu 11: 6 and day after day we have **n** to eat but this
20:19 want to pass through your country and **n** else."
21: 5 "There is **n** to eat here and **n** to drink.
30: 4 her father hears of the vow or pledge but says **n**,
30:11 If her husband hears of it and does **n** to stop her,
30:14 But if he says **n** on the day he hears of it, then he is
Dt 2: 7 for your every need so that you lacked **n**." '
8: 9 It is a land where food is plentiful and **n** is lacking.
9: 9 and all that time I ate **n** and drank no water.
22:26 Do **n** to the young woman; she has committed no
28:32 break as you long for them, but **n** you do will help.
28:55 because he has **n** else to eat during the siege that
28:57 She will have **n** else to eat during the siege
29:23 and salt, with **n** planted and **n** growing,
Jdg 6: 4 They left the Israelites with **n** to eat, taking all the
12: 4 "The men of Gilead are **n** more than rejects from
18:10 given us a spacious and fertile land, lacking in **n**!"
18:24 all my gods and my priest, and I have **n** left!"
1Sa 14: 6 LORD will help us, for **n** can hinder the LORD.
18:18 David exclaimed. "My father's family is **n**!"
21: 9 Take that if you want it, for there is **n** else here."
21: 9 "There is **n** like it!" David replied. "Give it to
22:15 this matter, for I knew **n** of any plot against you."
25: 7 harmed them, and **n** was ever stolen from them.
25:15 **N** was stolen from us the whole time they were
25:21 the wilderness, and **n** he owned was lost or stolen.
28:10 **n** bad will happen to you for doing this."
28:20 for he had eaten **n** all day and all night.
30:19 **N** was missing: small or great, son or daughter,
2Sa 3:26 him back with them. But David knew **n** about it.
12: 3 The poor man owned **n** but a little lamb he had
15:11 him as guests, but they knew **n** of his intentions.
19: 6 You have made it clear today that we mean **n** to
19:42 We have charged him **n**. And he hasn't fed us
20: 1 and shouted, "We have **n** to do with David.
24:24 to the LORD my God that have cost me **n**."
1Ki 8: 9 **N** was in the Ark except the two stone tablets that
10: 3 **n** was too hard for the king to explain to her.
11:22 "**N** is wrong," he replied. "But even so, I must
22:27 and feed him **n** but bread and water until I return
2Ki 4: 2 "**N** at all, except a flask of olive oil," she replied.
4:31 laid the staff on the child's face, but **n** happened.
20:13 There was **n** in his palace or kingdom that
20:17 off to Babylon. **N** will be left, says the LORD.
1Ch 21:24 will not offer a burnt offering that has cost me **n**!"
2Ch 5:10 **N** was in the Ark except the two stone tablets that
9: 2 **n** was too hard for him to explain to her.
18:26 and feed him **n** but bread and water until I return
34:25 out against this place, and **n** will be able to stop it.'
Ezr 4: 3 no part in this work, for we have **n** in common.
9:15 We stand before you in our guilt as **n** but an
Ne 5: 8 And they had **n** to say in their defense.
5:12 and demand **n** more from the people.
5:17 I asked for **n**, even though I regularly fed 150
8:10 and share gifts of food with people who have **n**
9:21 They lacked **n** in all that time. Their clothes did not
9:32 all the hardships we have suffered be as **n** to you.
Est 2:15 She asked for **n** except what he suggested, and she
6: 3 His attendants replied, "**N** has been done."
Job 1: 8 He fears God and will have **n** to do with evil."
2: 3 He fears God and will have **n** to do with evil.
2:10 anything bad?" So in all this, Job said **n** wrong.
5:24 When you visit your pastures, **n** will be missing.
6:18 but there is **n** there to drink, and so they perish in
8:13 forget God. The hope of the godless comes to **n**.
15: 2 us all this foolish talk. You are **n** but a windbag.
20:20 Of all the things he dreamed about, **n** remains.
20:21 **N** is left after he finishes gorging himself;
21:16 so I will have **n** to do with that kind of thinking.
22:18 so I will have **n** to do with that kind of thinking.
26: 7 sky over empty space and hangs the earth on **n**.
29:22 And after I spoke, they had **n** to add, for my
40: 4 "I am **n**—how could I ever find the answers?
40: 5 have said too much already. I have **n** more to say."
41:17 They lock together so **n** can penetrate them.
41:27 To the crocodile, iron is **n** but straw, and bronze is
41:33 There is **n** else so fearless anywhere on earth.
Ps 10: 6 say to themselves, "**N** bad will ever happen to us!
17: 3 You have scrutinized me and found **n** amiss,
19: 6 course to the other end. / **N** can hide from its heat.
21: 2 you have held back **n** that he requested.
28: 5 They care **n** for what the LORD has done
30: 6 I was prosperous I said, / "**N** can stop me now!"
35:17 How long, O Lord, will you look on and do **n**?
38:14 I choose to hear **n**, / and I make no reply.
38:19 they hate me though I have done **n** against them.
39: 6 and all our busy rushing ends in **n**.
41: 5 But my enemies say **n** but evil about me.
44:12 for a pittance. / You valued us at **n** at all.
49:17 For when they die, they carry **n** with them.
54: 3 to kill me. / They care **n** for God. / *Interlude*
62: 9 the greatest to the lowliest— / all are **n** in his sight.
73:13 Was it for **n** that I kept my heart pure / and kept
82: 5 But these oppressors know **n**; / they are
86:14 are trying to kill me. / And you mean **n** to them.
92:15 He is my rock! / There is **n** but goodness in him!"
101: 3 crooked dealings; / I will have **n** to do with them.
119:158 these traitors / because they care **n** for your word.
Pr 3:15 than rubies; **n** you desire can compare with her.
8: 8 and good. There is **n** crooked or twisted in it.
8:11 than rubies. **N** you desire can be compared with it.
24: 7 When the leaders gather, the fool has **n** to say.
28:27 Whoever gives to the poor will lack **n**. But a curse
Ecc 1: 4 Generations come and go, but **n** really changes.
1: 9 all been done before. **N** under the sun is truly new.
2:11 There was **n** really worthwhile anywhere.
2:24 So I decided there is **n** better than to enjoy food
3:12 So I concluded that there is **n** better for people than
3:14 does is final. **N** can be added to it or taken from it.
3:22 So I saw that there is **n** better for people than to be
5: 5 It is better to say **n** than to promise something that
5:14 the end, there is **n** left to pass on to one's children.
5:16 so they depart. All their hard work is for **n**.
7:14 That way you will realize that **n** is certain in this
8:15 because there is **n** better for people to do in this
9: 3 have no hope. There is **n** ahead but death anyway.
9: 5 at least know they will die, but the dead know **n**.
Isa 1:13 all sinful and false. I want **n** more to do with them.
8:13 Holy One. If you fear him, you need fear **n** else.
11: 9 **N** will hurt or destroy in all my holy mountain.
26:18 writhe in agony, / but **n** comes of our suffering.
26:18 We have done **n** to rescue the world;
29:13 And their worship of me amounts to **n** more than
30: 6 All this, and Egypt will give you **n** in return.
33: 8 and care **n** for the promises they made before
33:11 You Assyrians will gain **n** by all your efforts.
34:12 It will be called the Land of **N**, and its princes soon
39: 2 There was **n** in his palace or kingdom that
39: 6 off to Babylon. **N** will be left, says the LORD.
40:15 for all the nations of the world are **n** in comparison
40:17 The nations of the world are as **n** to him. In his
eyes they are less than **n**—mere emptiness
40:23 great people of the world and brings them all to **n**.
41:24 You are less than **n** and can do **n** at all.
43:18 all that—it is **n** compared to what I am going to do.
49: 4 I have spent my strength for **n** and to no purpose at
53: 2 There was **n** beautiful or majestic about his
appearance, **n** to attract us to him.
59: 6 **N** they do is productive; all their activity is filled
Jer 2:11 gods for another god, even though its gods are **n**?
3: 9 she thought **n** of committing adultery by
3:19 I wanted **n** more than to give you this beautiful
9: 3 to worse! They care **n** for me," says the LORD.
13:10 they will become like this linen belt—good for **n**!
22:30 David to rule in Judah. His life will amount to **n**."
29:27 So why have you done **n** to stop Jeremiah from
32:17 earth by your great power. **N** is too hard for you!
32:30 Israel and Judah have done **n** but wrong since their

32: 31 it has done **n** but anger me, so I am determined to
38: 5 he said. "Do as you like. I will do **n** to stop you."
42: 4 you everything he says. I will hide **n** from you."
46: 27 have peace and quiet, and **n** will make them afraid.
48: 30 "but her boasts are false; they accomplish **n**.
50: 2 "Tell the whole world, and keep **n** back! Raise a
50: 26 of rubble. Destroy her completely, and leave **n**!
51: 9 helped her if we could, but **n** can save her now.
51: 25 I am finished, you will be **n** but a heap of rubble.
La 1: 12 "Is it **n** to you, all you who pass by? Look around
Eze 8: 17 "Is it **n** to the people of Judah that they commit
13: 3 their own imaginations and have seen **n** at all!
13: 5 They have done **n** to strengthen the breaks in the
16: 3 You are **n** but a Canaanite! Your father was an
16: 47 merely sinned as they did—no, that was **n** to you.
20: 3 for my help? As surely as I live, I will tell you **n**.
39: 10 They will need **n** else for their fires. They won't
Da 4: 35 All the people of the earth / are **n** compared to him.
9: 26 will be killed, appearing to have accomplished **n**,
10: 7 The men with me saw **n**, but they were suddenly
11: 27 Seeking **n** but each other's harm, these kings will
Joel 2: 3 Behind them is **n** but desolation; not one thing
Am 3: 5 Does a trap ever spring shut when there's **n** there
5: 5 and the people of Bethel will come to **n**."
6: 6 caring **n** at all that your nation is going to ruin.
9: 10 all those who say, 'N bad will happen to us.'
Jnh 4: 3 because **n** I predicted is going to happen."
4: 10 about the plant, though you did **n** to put it there.
Mic 4: 4 in peace and prosperity, for there will be **n** to fear.
6: 14 to save your money, it will come to **n** in the end.
7: 1 fruit picker after the harvest who can find **n** to eat.
Na 2: 11 and the young and tender lived with **n** to fear?
Zep 1: 12 to the LORD, thinking he will do **n** at all to them.
Hag 2: 3 does it look to you now? It must seem like **n** at all!
Zec 4: 7 **N**, not even a mighty mountain, will stand in
Mt 3: 9 we're the descendants of Abraham.' That proves **n**.
4: 2 For forty days and forty nights he ate **n**
9: 33 "**N** like this has ever happened in Israel!"
15: 32 with me for three days, and they have **n** left to eat.
17: 20 and it would move. **N** would be impossible."
20: 3 and saw some people standing around doing **n**.
23: 16 For you say that it means **n** to swear 'by God's
27: 14 But Jesus said **n**, much to the governor's great
Mk 6: 8 He told them to take **n** with them except a walking
7: 4 they eat **n** bought from the market unless they have
8: 2 with me for three days, and they have **n** left to eat.
15: 5 But Jesus said **n**, much to Pilate's surprise.
16: 8 saying **n** to anyone because they were too
Lk 1: 37 For **n** is impossible with God."
3: 8 we're the descendants of Abraham.' That proves **n**.
4: 2 He ate **n** all that time and was very hungry.
9: 12 There is **n** to eat here in this deserted place."
10: 19 and scorpions and crush them. **N** will injure you.
11: 6 just arrived for a visit, and I have **n** for him to eat.'
16: 25 had everything you wanted, and Lazarus had **n**.
19: 48 But they could think of **n**, because all the people
23: 4 and said, "I find **n** wrong with this man!"
23: 15 **N** this man has done calls for the death penalty.
Jn 1: 3 everything there is. **N** exists that he didn't make.
5: 19 "I assure you, the Son can do **n** by himself.
5: 30 But I do **n** without consulting the Father. I judge as
5: 41 "Your approval or disapproval means **n** to me,
6: 12 Jesus told his disciples, "so that **n** is wasted."
6: 63 gives eternal life. Human effort accomplishes **n**.
7: 12 while others said, "He's **n** but a fraud,
7: 26 he is, speaking in public, and they say **n** to him.
8: 28 will realize that I am he and that I do **n** on my own,
15: 5 much fruit. For apart from me you can do **n**.
18: 20 and I teach **n** in private that I have not said in
21: 3 went out in the boat, but they caught **n** all night.
Ac 4: 14 right there among them, the council had **n** to say.
5: 36 various ways. The whole movement came to **n**.
7: 18 to the throne of Egypt who knew **n** about Joseph.
19: 37 but they have stolen **n** from the temple and have
20: 24 But my life is worth **n** unless I use it for doing the
23: 9 "We see **n** wrong with him," they shouted.
23: 29 certainly **n** worthy of imprisonment or death.
25: 25 But in my opinion he has done **n** worthy of death.
26: 22 I teach **n** except what the prophets and Moses said
28: 17 even though I had done **n** against our people
28: 21 They replied, "We have heard **n** against you.
Ro 8: 18 Yet what we suffer now is **n** compared to the glory
8: 38 And I am convinced that **n** can ever separate us
8: 39 **n** in all creation will ever be able to separate us
14: 20 there is **n** wrong with these things in themselves.
14: 22 You may have the faith to believe that there is **n**
1Co 1: 28 despised by the world, things counted as **n** at all,
1: 28 and used them to bring to **n** what the world
2: 6 rulers of this world, who are being brought to **n**.
8: 10 You know there's **n** wrong with it, but they will be
14: 11 but to me they mean **n**. I will not understand
15: 58 for you know that **n** you do for the Lord is ever
2Co 1: 13 there is **n** written between the lines and **n** you can't
6: 10 to others. We own **n**, and yet we have everything.
8: 15 "Those who gathered a lot had **n** left over,
12: 11 these "super apostles," even though I am **n** at all.
Gal 2: 6 were there had **n** to add to what I was preaching.
4: 11 afraid that all my hard work for you was worth **n**.
Eph 3: 8 Though I did **n** to deserve it, and though I am the
Php 2: 7 He made himself **n**; he took the humble position of
4: 12 I know how to live on almost **n** or with everything.
Col 3: 5 Have **n** to do with sexual sin, impurity, lust,
1Ti 1: 9 who consider **n** sacred and defile what is holy,
2Ti 3: 2 and ungrateful. They will consider **n** sacred.
Tit 1: 15 But **n** is pure to those who are corrupt
3: 10 After that, have **n** more to do with that person.
Heb 2: 8 when it says "all things," it means **n** is left out.
4: 13 **N** in all creation can hide from him. Everything is
7: 19 For the law made **n** perfect, and now a better hope
10: 27 There will be **n** to look forward to but the terrible
Jas 1: 23 a mirror but doing **n** to improve your appearance.
2Pe 2: 17 by the wind—promising much and delivering **n**.
3Jn 1: 7 and accept **n** from those who are not Christians.
Jude 1: 12 giving rain, promising much but producing **n**.
Rev 2: 24 depths of Satan, really). I will ask **n** more of you
21: 27 **N** evil will be allowed to enter—no one who

NOTHINGNESS (1) [NO, THING]
Da 2: 44 It will shatter all these kingdoms into **n**, but it will

NOTICE (24) [NOTICED, NOTICES, NOTICING]
Ge 31: 2 And Jacob began to **n** a considerable cooling in
Lev 4: 13 and the matter escapes the community's **n**,
13: 2 "If some of the people **n** a swelling or a rash
Ru 3: 4 Be sure to **n** where he lies down; then go
2Sa 20: 10 Amasa didn't **n** the dagger in his left hand,
Ps 10: 11 "God isn't watching! / He will never **n**!"
64: 5 to set their traps. / "Who will ever **n**?" they ask.
144: 3 O LORD, what are mortals that you should **n** us,
Ecc 7: 13 **N** the way God does things; then fall into line.
Isa 5: 12 think about the LORD or **n** what he is doing.
18: 3 battle flag on the mountain, let all the world take **n**.
26: 10 and take no **n** of the LORD's majesty.
58: 3 have done much penance, and you don't even **n** it!'
Jer 18: 17 my back on them and refuse to **n** their distress."
Eze 44: 5 LORD said to me, "Son of man, take careful **n**;
Am 5: 22 I won't even **n** all your choice peace offerings.
Zep 3: 5 his justice is more evident, but no one takes **n**—
Lk 1: 48 For he took **n** of his lowly servant girl, / and now
21: 29 this illustration: "**N** the fig tree, or any other tree.
Ac 17: 22 "Men of Athens, I **n** that you are very religious,
Ro 11: 22 **N** how God is both kind and severe. He is severe to
Gal 3: 17 And **n** that it doesn't say the promise was to his
6: 11 **N** what large letters I use as I write these closing
Eph 4: 9 **N** that it says "he ascended." This means that

NOTICED (35) [NOTICE]
Ge 18: 2 he suddenly **n** three men standing nearby. He got
29: 32 for she said, "The LORD has **n** my misery,
37: 15 a man **n** him wandering around the countryside.
37: 25 they **n** a caravan of camels in the distance coming
38: 15 Judah **n** her as he went by and thought she was a
39: 3 Potiphar **n** this and realized that the LORD was
40: 6 The next morning Joseph **n** the dejected look on
Jdg 14: 1 was in Timnah, he **n** a certain Philistine woman.
18: 7 where they **n** the people living carefree lives,
1Sa 9: 17 When Samuel **n** Saul, the LORD said,
2Sa 11: 2 he **n** a woman of unusual beauty taking a bath.
2Ki 16: 10 While he was there, he **n** an unusual altar. So he
23: 16 he **n** several tombs in the side of the hill.
Job 1: 8 asked Satan, "Have you **n** my servant Job?
2: 3 asked Satan, "Have you **n** my servant Job?
Ecc 3: 16 I also **n** that throughout the world there is evil in
5: 18 Even so, I have **n** one thing, at least, that is good.
Eze 41: 8 I **n** that the Temple was built on a terrace,
Mt 8: 18 When Jesus **n** how large the crowd was growing,
9: 23 he **n** the noisy crowds and heard the funeral music.
12: 10 where he **n** a man with a deformed hand.
21: 19 and he **n** a fig tree beside the road. He went over to
22: 11 he **n** a man who wasn't wearing the proper clothes
26: 71 another servant girl **n** him and said to those
Mk 3: 1 and **n** a man with a deformed hand.
7: 2 They **n** that some of Jesus' disciples failed to
11: 13 He **n** a fig tree a little way off that was in full leaf,
11: 20 the disciples **n** it was withered from the roots.
14: 67 **n** Peter warming himself at the fire. She looked at
Lk 5: 2 He **n** two empty boats at the water's edge,
14: 7 When Jesus **n** that all who had come to the dinner
22: 56 A servant girl **n** him in the firelight and began
Jn 20: 6 He also **n** the linen wrappings lying there,
Ac 10: 31 and your gifts to the poor have been **n** by God!
14: 9 and Paul **n** him and realized he had faith to be

NOTICES (1) [NOTICE]
Lev 13: 8 If the priest **n** that the rash has spread, then he

NOTICING (1) [NOTICE]
Jdg 18: 3 **N** the young Levite's accent, they took him aside

NOTIFY (3)
2Sa 20: 5 So Amasa went out to **n** the troops, but it took him
Mt 22: 3 he sent his servants to **n** everyone that it was time
Lk 14: 17 he sent his servant around to **n** the guests that it

NOTION (1)
1Sa 20: 9 "You know that if I had the slightest **n** my father

NOTORIOUS (6)
Hab 1: 7 They are **n** for their cruelty. They do as they like,
Mt 9: 10 his fellow tax collectors and many other **n** sinners.
27: 16 This year there was a **n** criminal in prison, a man
Mk 2: 15 his fellow tax collectors and many other **n** sinners.
Lk 15: 1 and other **n** sinners often came to listen to Jesus
19: 7 "He has gone to be the guest of a **n** sinner,"

NOTWITHSTANDING [KJV] See BUT, HOWEVER, NEVERTHELESS, STILL, THEN, YET

NOUGHT [KJV] See ANYTHING, BAD, CONTEMPT, CRUMBLE, DESPISE, DISAPPEAR, FAIL, FRUSTRATED, IGNORED, VAIN, NOTHING, PERISH, REJECTED, RIDICULED, RUIN, WITHOUT

NOURISH (1) [NOURISHED, NOURISHMENT]
Pr 18: 21 the consequences, for the tongue can kill or **n** life.

NOURISHED (5) [NOURISH]
Dt 31: 20 will eat all the food they want and become well **n**.
32: 13 He **n** them with honey from the cliffs, / with olive
Pr 11: 17 Your own soul is **n** when you are kind, but you
Isa 44: 14 he plants the cedar in the forest to be **n** by the rain.
Da 1: 15 and better **n** than the young men who had been

NOURISHMENT (7) [NOURISH]
Mt 13: 6 because the roots had no **n** in the shallow soil.
Mk 4: 6 because the roots had no **n** in the shallow soil.
Jn 4: 34 "My **n** comes from doing the will of God,
Ro 11: 17 sharing in God's rich **n** of his special olive tree.
Col 2: 7 grow down into him and draw up **n** from him,
2: 19 and we grow only as we get our **n** and strength
1Pe 2: 2 Cry out for this **n** as a baby cries for milk,

NOVICE [KJV] See NEW (CHRISTIAN)

NOW (1437) [NOW'S] See Index of Articles, Etc.

NOW'S (1) [NOW] See Index of Articles, Etc.
1Sa 24: 4 "**N** your opportunity!" David's men whispered to

NOWHERE (6)
Jos 8: 20 the city was filling the sky, and they had **n** to go.
Ps 86: 8 **N** among the pagan gods is there a god like you,
Ecc 1: 6 and there, twisting back and forth, getting **n**.
Isa 59: 11 We look for justice, but it is **n** to be found.
59: 14 who are righteous, and justice is **n** to be found.
La 1: 3 have chased her down, and she has **n** to turn.

NULLIFIED (1) [NULLIFY]
Nu 30: 12 her vow or pledge will be **n**, and the LORD will

NULLIFIES (1) [NULLIFY]
Nu 30: 8 he **n** her commitments, and the LORD will

NULLIFY (3) [NULLIFIED, NULLIFIES]
Nu 30: 13 So her husband may either confirm or **n** any vows
30: 15 than a day and then tries to **n** a vow or pledge,
Mt 15: 6 you **n** the direct commandment of God.

NUMBER (76) [NUMBERED, NUMBERING, NUMBERLESS, NUMBERS, NUMEROUS]
Ge 46: 26 So the total **n** of Jacob's direct descendants who
47: 12 and brothers in amounts appropriate to the **n** of
50: 7 with a great **n** of Pharaoh's counselors
50: 9 So a great **n** of chariots, cavalry, and people
Lev 25: 15 the price of the land should be based on the **n** of
25: 16 land is actually selling you a certain **n** of harvests.
25: 27 The price of the land will be based on the **n** of
25: 50 The price of their freedom will be based on the **n**
25: 50 whatever it would cost to hire a servant for that **n**
Nu 1: 20[-21] This is the **n** of men twenty years old or older
1: 46 The total **n** was 603,550.
2: 3[-4] leaders, and the **n** of their available troops:
2: 10[-11] leaders, and the **n** of their available troops:
2: 18[-19] leaders, and the **n** of their available troops:
2: 25[-26] leaders, and the **n** of their available troops:
3: 43 The total **n** of firstborn sons who were one month
3: 46 sons of Israel who are in excess of the **n** of Levites,
3: 49 sons of Israel who exceeded the **n** of Levites.
4: 36 and the total **n** came to 2,750.
4: 40 and the total **n** came to 2,630.
4: 44 and the total **n** came to 3,200.
22: 15 This time he sent a larger **n** of even more
26: 51 So the total **n** of Israelite men counted in the
Dt 25: 2 and be beaten in his presence with the **n** of lashes
26: 5 His family was few in **n**, but in Egypt they became
32: 8 the peoples / according to the **n** of angelic beings.
Jos 21: 41 The total **n** of towns and pasturelands within
1Sa 13: 6 When the men of Israel saw the vast **n** of enemy
2Sa 24: 9 Joab reported the **n** of people to the king.
1Ki 20: 25 Give us the same **n** of horses, chariots, and men,
1Ch 7: 2 the total **n** of men available for military service
7: 4 The total **n** of men available for military service
7: 5 The total **n** of men available for military service
7: 7 The total **n** of men available for military service
16: 19 He said this when they were few in **n**, / a tiny
21: 3 "May the LORD increase the **n** of his people a
21: 5 and reported the **n** of people to David. There were
23: 31 The proper **n** of Levites served in the LORD's
2Ch 8: 13 The **n** of sacrifices varied from day to day
Ezr 2: 2 This is the **n** of the men of Israel who returned
8: 34 Everything was accounted for by **n** and weight,
Ne 5: 18 six fat sheep, and a large **n** of domestic fowl.
7: 7 This is the **n** of Israel who returned from
Est 9: 11 when the king was informed of the **n** of people

Job 5: 9 to understand. He performs miracles without **n**.
9: 10 to understand. He performs miracles without **n**.
36: 26 what we can understand. His years are without **n**.
Ps 105: 12 He said this when they were few in **n**, / a tiny
105: 34 and hordes of locusts came— / locusts beyond **n**.
107: 39 When they decrease in **n** and become
Jer 23: 3 and they will be fruitful and increase in **n**.
31: 27 and multiply the **n** of cattle here in Israel
44: 28 "Only a small **n** will escape death and return to
52: 28 The **n** of captives taken to Babylon in the seventh
Eze 4: 4 You are to bear their sins for the **n** of days you lie
22: 25 They increase the **n** of widows in the land.
Da 5: 1 A **n** of years later, King Belshazzar gave a great
Am 5: 12 For I know the vast **n** of your sins and rebellions.
Ac 4: 4 so that the **n** of believers totaled about five
6: 7 The **n** of believers greatly increased in Jerusalem,
7: 17 the **n** of our people in Egypt greatly increased.
14: 1 and preached with such power that a great **n** of
17: 4 including a large **n** of godly Greek men and also
19: 19 A **n** of them who had been practicing magic
27: 37 us began eating—for that is the **n** we had aboard.
28: 23 and on that day a large **n** of people came to Paul's
Ro 9: 27 on the seashore, / only a small **n** will be saved.
11: 25 but this will last only until the complete **n** of
2Co 11: 23 been whipped times without **n**, and faced death
Rev 6: 11 full **n** of the servants of Jesus had been martyred.
11: 1 and the altar, and count the **n** of worshipers.
13: 17 name of the beast or the **n** representing his name.
13: 18 Let the one who has understanding solve the **n** of the beast, for it is the **n** of a man. His **n** is 666.
15: 2 and his statue and the **n** representing his name.

NUMBERED (28) [NUMBER]

Ge 46: 15 Jacob's descendants through Leah **n** thirty-three.
Nu 4: 48 **n** 8,580.
26: 7 The men from all the clans of Reuben **n** 43,730.
26: 14 The men from all the clans of Simeon **n** 22,200.
26: 18 The men from all the clans of Gad **n** 40,500.
26: 22 The men from all the clans of Judah **n** 76,500.
26: 25 The men from all the clans of Issachar **n** 64,300.
26: 27 The men from all the clans of Zebulun **n** 60,500.
26: 34 The men from all the clans of Manasseh **n** 52,700.
26: 37 The men from all the clans of Ephraim **n** 32,500.
26: 41 The men from all the clans of Benjamin **n** 45,600.
26: 43 and the men from these clans **n** 64,400.
26: 47 The men from all the clans of Asher **n** 53,400.
26: 50 The men from all the clans of Naphtali **n** 45,400.
26: 51 of Israelite men counted in the census **n** 601,730.
26: 62 clans who were one month old or older **n** 23,000.
1Ch 26: 11 who served as gatekeepers, **n** thirteen in all.
Ezr 2: 58 and the descendants of Solomon's servants **n** 392.
Ne 7: 60 and the descendants of Solomon's servants **n** 392.
Ps 39: 4 Remind me that my days are **n**, / and that my life is
Isa 13: 22 Babylon's days are **n**; its time of destruction will
La 4: 18 Our end was near; our days were **n**. We were
Da 5: 26 *Mene* means '**n**'—God has **n** the days of your reign and has brought it
Mt 10: 30 And the very hairs on your head are all **n**.
Lk 12: 7 And the very hairs on your head are all **n**. So don't
Jn 6: 10 So all of them—the men alone **n** five thousand—
2Pe 1: 14 has shown me that my days here on earth are **n**

NUMBERING (1) [NUMBER]

1Ki 8: 63 peace offerings to the LORD **n** 22,000 oxen

NUMBERLESS (1) [NUMBER]

Rev 20: 8 a mighty host, as **n** as sand along the shore.

NUMBERS (19) [NUMBER]

Ge 8: 17 so they can breed and reproduce in great **n**."
Ex 16: 13 That evening vast **n** of quail arrived and covered
Lev 26: 22 so your **n** will dwindle and your roads will be
Nu 32: 1 of Reuben and Gad owned vast **n** of livestock.
Jos 10: 10 and the Israelites slaughtered them in great **n** at
1Ki 8: 5 and oxen before the Ark in such **n** that no one
1Ch 12: 23 These are the **n** of armed warriors who joined
2Ch 5: 6 and oxen before the Ark in such **n** that no one
18: 2 They butchered great **n** of sheep and oxen for the
28: 5 and to exile large **n** of his people to Damascus.
30: 5 The people had not been celebrating it in great **n** as
32: 5 and manufactured large **n** of weapons and shields.
Mk 1: 34 So Jesus healed great **n** of sick people who had
3: 8 and vast **n** of people came to see him for
Ac 9: 31 and Samaria, and it grew in strength and **n**.
11: 21 and large **n** of these Gentiles believed and turned
11: 24 And large **n** of people were brought to the Lord.
11: 26 church for a full year, teaching great **n** of people.
16: 5 strengthened in their faith and grew daily in **n**.

NUMEROUS (39) [NUMBER]

Ge 26: 4 I will cause your descendants to become as **n** as
28: 14 Your descendants will be as **n** as the dust of the
32: 12 they become as **n** as the sands along the seashore—
Ex 32: 13 'I will make your descendants as **n** as the stars of
Nu 22: 6 and curse them for me because they are so **n**.
23: 10 Who can count Jacob's descendants, as **n** as dust?
Dt 1: 10 The LORD your God has made you as **n** as the
2: 10 (A **n** and powerful race of giants called the Emites
2: 21 They were a **n** and powerful race, as tall as the
3: 19 Your wives, children, and **n** livestock, however,
10: 22 But now the LORD your God has made you as **n**
26: 5 but in Egypt they became a mighty and **n** nation.
28: 11 many children, **n** livestock, and abundant crops.
28: 62 Though you are as **n** as the stars in the sky, few of
30: 5 even more prosperous and **n** than your ancestors!
30: 9 He will give you many children and **n** livestock,
Jdg 6: 5 arrived on droves of camels too **n** to count.
2Sa 17: 11 That way you will have an army as **n** as the sand
1Ki 3: 8 a nation so great they are too **n** to count!
4: 20 and Israel were as **n** as the sand on the seashore.
1Ch 5: 23 Senir, and Mount Hermon. They were very **n**.
23: 17 the family leader. Rehabiah had **n** descendants.
27: 23 to make the Israelites as **n** as the stars in heaven.
29: 8 They also contributed **n** precious stones,
2Ch 1: 9 for you have made me king over a people as **n** as
17: 13 He stored **n** supplies in Judah's towns
Ne 9: 23 You made their descendants as **n** as the stars in the
Ps 40: 5 miracles for us. / Your plans for us are too **n** to list.
40: 12 They are more **n** than the hairs on my head.
69: 4 are more **n** than the hairs on my head.
Pr 7: 26 the ruin of many; **n** men have been her victims.
Isa 10: 22 But though the people of Israel are as **n** as the sand
48: 19 Then you would have become as **n** as the sands
Jer 46: 23 "for they are more **n** than grasshoppers.
Eze 27: 15 **N** coastlands were your captive markets;
Joel 1: 6 It is a terrible army, too **n** to count! Its teeth are as
Na 3: 16 Merchants, as **n** as the stars, have filled your city
Ro 4: 18 "Your descendants will be as **n** as the stars,"
9: 27 "Though the people of Israel are as **n** as the sand

NUN (23)

Ex 33: 11 the young man who assisted him, Joshua son of **N**,
Nu 11: 28 Joshua son of **N**, who had been Moses' personal
13: 8 Ephraim | Hoshea son of **N**
14: 6 Joshua son of **N** and Caleb son of Jephunneh,
14: 30 be Caleb son of Jephunneh and Joshua son of **N**.
26: 65 were Caleb son of Jephunneh and Joshua son of **N**.
27: 18 The LORD replied, "Take Joshua son of **N**,
32: 12 of Jephunneh the Kenizzite and Joshua son of **N**,
34: 17 the people: Eleazar the priest and Joshua son of **N**.
Dt 1: 38 Instead, your assistant, Joshua son of **N**, will lead
31: 23 Then the LORD commissioned Joshua son of **N**
32: 44 So Moses came with Joshua son of **N** and recited
34: 9 Now Joshua son of **N** was full of the spirit of
Jos 1: 1 the LORD spoke to Joshua son of **N**,
14: 1 the priest, Joshua son of **N**, and the tribal leaders.
17: 4 Joshua son of **N**, and the Israelite leaders and said,
19: 51 territories that Eleazar the priest, Joshua son of **N**,
21: 1 Joshua son of **N**, and the leaders of the other tribes
24: 29 Soon after this, Joshua son of **N**, the servant of the
Jdg 2: 8 Then Joshua son of **N**, the servant of the LORD,
1Ki 16: 34 concerning Jericho spoken by Joshua son of **N**.
1Ch 7: 27 **N**, and Joshua.
Ne 8: 17 this way since the days of Joshua son of **N**.

NURSE (13) [NURSED, NURSES, NURSING]

Ge 24: 59 The woman who had been Rebekah's childhood **n**
35: 8 Soon after this, Rebekah's old **n**, Deborah, died.
Ex 2: 7 and find one of the Hebrew women to **n** the baby
2: 9 "Take this child home and **n** him for me,"
Lev 19: 17 "Do not **n** hatred in your heart for any of your
Nu 11: 12 like a **n** carries a baby—to the land you swore to
2Sa 4: 4 the capital, the child's **n** grabbed him and fled.
1Ki 1: 2 young virgin who will wait on you and be your **n**.
3: 21 And in the morning when I tried to **n** my son,
2Ki 11: 2 and his **n** in a bedroom to hide him from Athaliah,
11: 3 and his **n** remained hidden in the Temple of the
2Ch 22: 11 She put Joash and his **n** in a bedroom. In this way,
Job 3: 12 let me live? Why did she **n** me at her breasts?

NURSED (6) [NURSE]

Ex 2: 9 the baby's mother took her baby home and **n** him.
1Sa 1: 23 So she stayed home and **n** the baby.
SS 8: 1 you were my brother, who **n** at my mother's breast.
Isa 66: 12 Her children will be **n** at her breasts, carried in her
Lk 11: 27 from which you came, and the breasts that **n** you!"
23: 29 borne a child and the breasts that have never **n**.'

NURSES (1) [NURSE]

Ps 41: 3 The LORD **n** them when they are sick / and eases

NURSING (6) [NURSE]

Ps 8: 2 You have taught children and **n** infants / to give
22: 9 and led me to trust you when I was a **n** infant.
Isa 49: 15 "Never! Can a mother forget her **n** child? Can she
Mt 24: 19 and for mothers **n** their babies in those days.
Mk 13: 17 and for mothers **n** their babies in those days.
Lk 21: 23 pregnant women and for mothers **n** their babies.

NUT (1) [NUTS]

SS 6: 11 "I went down into the grove of **n** trees and out to

NUTS (1) [NUT]

Ge 43: 11 balm, honey, spices, myrrh, pistachio **n**,

NYMPHA (1)

Col 4: 15 and to **N** and those who meet in her house.

O

O (754) [OH] See Index of Articles, Etc.

O'CLOCK (18)

Mt 14: 25 About three **o** in the morning Jesus came to them,
20: 3 "At nine **o** in the morning he was passing through
20: 5 and again around three **o** he did the same thing.
20: 6 At five **o** that evening he was in town again
20: 9 When those hired at five **o** were paid,
27: 45 darkness fell across the whole land until three **o**.
27: 46 At about three **o**, Jesus called out with a loud
Mk 6: 48 About three **o** in the morning he came to them,
15: 25 It was nine **o** in the morning when the crucifixion
15: 33 darkness fell across the whole land until three **o**.
Lk 23: 44 darkness fell across the whole land until three **o**.
Jn 1: 39 It was about four **o** in the afternoon when they
4: 52 "Yesterday afternoon at one **o** his fever suddenly
Ac 2: 15 People don't get drunk by nine **o** in the morning.
3: 1 afternoon to take part in the three **o** prayer service.
10: 3 One afternoon about three **o**, he had a vision in
10: 30 praying in my house at three **o** in the afternoon.
23: 23 ready to leave for Caesarea at nine **o** tonight.

OAK (21) [OAKS]

Ge 12: 6 and set up camp beside the **o** at Moreh.
13: 18 Then Abram moved his camp to the **o** grove owned
14: 13 who was camped at the **o** grove belonging to
18: 1 was camped near the **o** grove belonging to Mamre.
35: 8 She was buried beneath the **o** tree in the valley
35: 8 the tree has been called the "**O** of Weeping."
Jos 19: 33 ran from Heleph, from the **o** at Zaanannim,
24: 26 and rolled it beneath the **o** tree beside the
Jdg 4: 11 and pitched his tent by the **O** of Zaanannim,
6: 11 LORD came and sat beneath the **o** tree at Ophrah,
6: 19 them to the angel, who was under the **o** tree.
9: 6 and Beth-millo called a meeting under the **o** beside
9: 37 is coming down the road past the Diviners' **O**."
1Sa 10: 3 "When you get to the **o** of Tabor, you will see
2Sa 18: 9 as he rode beneath the thick branches of a great **o**,
18: 14 heart as he dangled from the **o** still alive.
1Ki 13: 14 man of God and found him sitting under an **o** tree.
1Ch 10: 12 Then they buried their remains beneath the **o** tree
Isa 1: 30 You will wither away like an **o** or garden without
44: 14 cuts down cedars; he selects the cypress and the **o**;
Eze 6: 13 and great **o** where they offered incense to their

OAKS (10) [OAK]

Dt 11: 30 toward the west, not far from the **o** of Moreh.)
Ps 29: 9 The voice of the LORD twists mighty **o**
56: T To be sung to the tune "Dove on Distant **O**."
Isa 1: 29 sacrifices to idols in your groves of sacred **o**.
2: 13 tall cedars of Lebanon and the mighty **o** of Bashan.
61: 3 them like strong and graceful **o** for his own glory.
Eze 27: 6 They carved oars for you from the **o** of Bashan.
Hos 4: 13 the hills to burn incense in the pleasant shade of **o**,
Am 2: 9 were as tall as cedar trees and strong as **o**,
Zec 11: 2 Weep, you **o** of Bashan, as you watch the thickest

OARS (1) [OARSMEN]

Eze 27: 6 They carved **o** for you from the oaks of Bashan.

OARSMEN (3) [OARS]

Eze 27: 8 "Your **o** came from Sidon and Arvad;
27: 26 Your **o** are rowing your ship of state into a
27: 29 All the **o** abandon their ships; the sailors

OATH (89) [OATHS]

Ge 21: 31 has been known as Beersheba—"well of the **o**"—because that was where they had sworn an **o**.
24: 8 come back with you, then you are free from this **o**.
24: 9 So the servant took a solemn **o** that he would
24: 41 to let her come, you will be free from your **o**.'
25: 33 So Esau swore an **o**, thereby selling all his rights as
26: 31 they each took a solemn **o** of nonaggression.
26: 33 So Isaac named the well "**O**," and from that time
26: 33 there has been called Beersheba—"well of the **o**."
31: 53 So Jacob took an **o** before the awesome God of his
47: 31 So Joseph gave his **o**, and Jacob bowed in worship
50: 5 "Tell Pharaoh that my father made me swear an **o**.
50: 25 Then Joseph made the sons of Israel swear an **o**,
Ex 22: 11 then take an **o** of innocence in the presence of the
Lev 6: 3 lie about it, or they deny something while under **o**,
Nu 5: 19 The priest will put the woman under **o** and say to
5: 21 point the priest must put the woman under this **o**—
30: 2 or makes a pledge under **o** must never break it.
30: 3 or a pledge under **o** while she is still living at her
Dt 6: 13 When you take an **o**, you must use only his name.
7: 8 because he was keeping the **o** he had sworn to your
9: 5 and to fulfill the **o** he had sworn to your ancestors
29: 12 with you today, and he has sealed it with an **o**.
34: 4 "This is the land I promised on **o** to Abraham,
Jos 2: 19 they will be killed, and we cannot be held to our **o**.
2: 20 however, we are not bound by this **o** in any way."
9: 15 of Israel ratified their agreement with a binding **o**.
9: 19 "We have sworn an **o** in the presence of the

9:20 for God would be angry with us if we broke our **o**.
Jdg 21:5 At that time they had taken a solemn **o** in the
21:18 because we have sworn with a solemn **o** that
1Sa 14:24 because Saul had made them take an **o**, saying,
14:26 because they all feared the **o** they had taken.
14:28 "Your father made the army take a strict **o** that
20:3 Then David took an **o** before Jonathan and said,
28:10 But Saul took an **o** in the name of the LORD
2Sa 21:7 because of the **o** David and Jonathan had sworn
1Ki 2:9 But that **o** does not make him innocent. You are a
2:43 Then why haven't you kept your **o** to the LORD
8:31 and is required to take an **o** of innocence in front of
2Ki 11:4 and made them swear an **o** of loyalty there in the
1Ch 16:16 made with Abraham / and the **o** he swore to Isaac.
2Ch 6:22 and is required to take an **o** of innocence in front of
15:14 They shouted out their **o** of loyalty to the LORD
36:13 even though he had taken an **o** of loyalty in God's
Ezr 10:5 Shecaniah had said. And they all swore a solemn **o**.
Ne 10:29 now all heartily bound themselves with an **o**.
Ps 89:3 my chosen servant. / I have sworn this **o** to him:
89:35 I have sworn an **o** to David, / and in my holiness I
105:9 made with Abraham / and the **o** he swore to Isaac.
110:4 The LORD has taken an **o** and will not break his
132:2 He took an **o** before the LORD. / He vowed to the
Isa 14:24 The LORD Almighty has sworn this **o**: "It will
65:16 or take an **o** will do so by the God of truth.
Jer 5:2 Even when they are under **o**, saying, 'As surely as
16:14 "when people who are taking an **o** will no longer
23:7 says the LORD, "when people are taking an **o**,
34:16 But now you have shrugged off your **o** and defiled
34:19 or common people—for you have broken your **o**.
44:26 None of you may invoke my name or use this **o**:
Eze 17:13 the royal family and made him take an **o** of loyalty.
17:19 and despising the solemn **o** he made in my name.
20:23 But I took a solemn **o** against them while they
36:7 and sworn an **o** that those nations will soon have
44:12 and taken an **o** that they must bear the
Da 12:7 and took this solemn **o** by the one who lives
Am 8:7 Now the LORD has sworn this **o** by his own
Mic 7:20 and unfailing love as you promised with an **o** to
Mt 14:7 so he promised with an **o** to give her anything she
14:9 but because of his **o** and because he didn't want to
23:16 to swear 'by God's Temple'—you can break that **o**.
23:18 And you say that to take an **o** 'by the altar' can be
26:72 Again Peter denied it, this time with an **o**. "I don't
Mk 6:26 but he was embarrassed to break his **o** in front of
Ac 2:30 and he knew God had promised with an **o** that one
23:12 and bound themselves with an **o** to neither eat nor
23:14 "We have bound ourselves under **o** to neither eat
1Ti 1:10 and slave traders, for liars and **o** breakers,
Heb 6:13 swear by, God took an **o** in his own name, saying:
6:16 When people take an **o**, they call on someone
6:16 to it. And without any question that **o** is binding.
6:17 God also bound himself with an **o**, so that those
6:18 So God has given us both his promise and his **o**.
7:20 God took an **o** that Christ would always be a priest,
7:21 to Jesus did he say, / "The Lord has taken an **o**
7:22 Because of God's **o**, it is Jesus who guarantees the
7:28 law was given, God appointed his Son with an **o**,
Jas 5:12 never take an **o**, by heaven or earth or anything
Rev 10:6 And he swore an **o** in the name of the one who

OATHS (4) [OATH]

Dt 10:20 cling to him. Your **o** must be in his name alone.
Ecc 9:2 and people who take **o** are treated like people who
Isa 48:1 you who take **o** in the name of the LORD and call
Hos 4:15 Their worship is mere pretense as they take **o** in

OBADIAH (22) [OBADIAH'S]

1Ki 18:3 So Ahab summoned **O**, who was in charge of the
18:3 (Now **O** was a devoted follower of the LORD.
18:4 **O** had hidden one hundred of them in two caves.
18:5 Ahab said to **O**, "We must check every spring
18:6 by himself, and **O** went another way by himself.
18:7 As **O** was walking along, he saw Elijah coming
18:7 **O** recognized him at once and fell to the ground
18:9 "Oh, sir," **O** protested, "what harm have I done
18:16 So **O** went to tell Ahab that Elijah had come,
1Ch 3:21 Rephaiah's son was Arnan. Arnan's son was **O**.
7:3 of Izrahiah were Michael, **O**, Joel, and Isshiah.
8:38 Azrikam, Bokeru, Ishmael, Sheariah, **O**,
9:16 **O** son of Shemaiah, son of Galal, son of Jeduthun;
9:44 Bokeru, Ishmael, Sheariah, **O**, and Hanan.
12:9 was their leader. / **O** was second. / Eliab was third.
27:19 Zebulun | Ishmaiah son of **O** / Naphtali
2Ch 17:7 **O**, Zechariah, Nethanel, and Micaiah.
34:12 faithfully under the leadership of Jahath and **O**,
Ezr 8:9 family of Joab: **O** son of Jehiel and 218 other men.
Ne 10:5 Harim, Meremoth, **O**,
12:25 This included Mattaniah, Bakbukiah, and **O**.
Ob 1:1 revealed to **O** concerning the land of Edom.

OBADIAH'S (1) [OBADIAH]

1Ch 3:21 Arnan's son was Obadiah. **O** son was Shecaniah.

OBAL (2)

Ge 10:28 **O**, Abimael, Sheba,
1Ch 1:22 **O**, Abimael, Sheba,

OBED (14)

Ru 4:17 And they named him **O**. He became the father of
4:21 was the father of Boaz. / Boaz was the father of **O**.
4:22 **O** was the father of Jesse. / Jesse was the father of
1Ch 2:12 Boaz was the father of **O**. / **O** was the father of Jesse.
2:37 the father of Ephlal. / Ephlal was the father of **O**.
2:38 **O** was the father of Jehu. / Jehu was the father of
11:47 Eliel and **O**; / Jaasiel from Zobah.
26:7 Their names were Othni, Rephael, **O**, and Elzabad.
2Ch 23:1 Azariah son of **O**, Maaseiah son of Adaiah,
Mt 1:5 Boaz was the father of **O** (his mother was Ruth). / **O** was the father of Jesse.
Lk 3:32 Jesse was the son of **O**. / **O** was the son of Boaz.

OBED-EDOM (15) [OBED-EDOM'S]

2Sa 6:10 He took it instead to the home of **O** of Gath.
6:11 there with the family of **O** for three months,
1Ch 13:13 He took it instead to the home of **O** of Gath.
13:14 there with the family of **O** for three months,
15:18 Mikneiah, and the gatekeepers, **O** and Jeiel.
15:21 Mattithiah, Eliphelehu, Mikneiah, **O**, Jeiel,
15:24 **O** and Jehiah were chosen to guard the Ark.
15:25 **O** to bring the Ark of the LORD's covenant up to
16:5 Jehiel, Mattithiah, Eliab, Benaiah, **O**, and Jeiel.
16:38 This group included **O** (son of Jeduthun), Hosah,
26:4 The sons of **O**, also gatekeepers, were Shemaiah
26:5 Peullethai (the eighth). God had richly blessed **O**.
26:8 All of these descendants of **O**, including their sons
26:15 The south gate went to **O**, and his sons were put in
2Ch 25:24 the Temple of God that had been in the care of **O**.

OBED-EDOM'S (2) [OBED-EDOM]

2Sa 6:12 "The LORD has blessed **O** home and everything
1Ch 26:6 **O** son Shemaiah had sons with great ability who

OBEDIENCE (14) [OBEY]

Ge 22:1 Later on God tested Abraham's faith and **o**.
Jdg 2:17 who had walked in **o** to the LORD's commands.
1Sa 15:22 and sacrifices or your **o** to his voice? **O** is far better than sacrifice.
2Ki 23:24 He did this in **o** to all the laws written in the scroll
1Ch 24:19 Aaron in **o** to the commands of the LORD,
2Ch 27:6 because he was careful to live in **o** to the LORD
Eze 20:13 They wouldn't obey my instructions even though **o**
Ro 4:13 and his descendants was not based on **o** to God's
10:5 right with God requires **o** to all of its commands.
Php 3:5 who demand the strictest **o** to the Jewish law.
Col 2:6 your Lord, you must continue to live in **o** to him.
Tit 3:9 or in quarrels and fights about **o** to Jewish laws.
Heb 5:8 he learned **o** from the things he suffered.

OBEDIENT (8) [OBEY]

Ps 119:101 path of evil, / that I may remain **o** to your word.
Eze 36:26 your stony heart of sin and give you a new, **o** heart.
Mal 3:17 I will spare them as a father spares an **o** and dutiful
Lk 2:51 returned to Nazareth with them and was **o** to them;
Ro 16:19 But everyone knows that you are **o** to the Lord.
2Co 9:13 prove that you are **o** to the Good News of Christ.
10:6 after the rest of you became loyal and **o**.
Tit 3:1 They should be **o**, always ready to do what is good.

OBEDIENTLY (1) [OBEY]

Php 2:8 And in human form he **o** humbled himself even

OBEISANCE [KJV] See BOW, BOWED, BOWING

OBEY (360) [OBEDIENCE, OBEDIENT, OBEDIENTLY, OBEYED, OBEYING, OBEYS]

Ge 17:9 told Abraham, "is to **o** the terms of the covenant.
49:10 whom it belongs, / the one whom all nations will **o**.
Ex 1:17 they refused to **o** the king and allowed the boys to
16:28 "How long will these people refuse to **o** my
19:5 Now if you will **o** me and keep my covenant,
20:6 love on those who love me and **o** my commands,
23:13 "Be sure to **o** all my instructions. And remember,
23:21 Pay attention to him, and **o** all of his instructions.
23:22 But if you are careful to **o** him, following all my
24:7 the LORD has commanded. We will **o**."
34:11 Your responsibility is to **o** all the commands I am
35:1 "You must **o** these instructions from the LORD.
Lev 18:4 You must **o** all my regulations and be careful to
18:5 If you **o** my laws and regulations, you will find life
18:26 You must strictly **o** all of my laws and regulations,
18:30 So be careful to **o** my laws, and do not practice any
19:19 "You must **o** all my laws. "Do not breed your
19:37 You must be careful to **o** all of my laws
20:8 Keep all my laws and **o** them, for I am the LORD,
20:22 "You must carefully **o** all my laws
25:18 in the land, keep my laws and **o** my regulations.
26:3 keep my laws and are careful to **o** my commands,
26:14 if you do not listen to me or **o** my commands,
26:21 then you remain hostile toward me and refuse to **o**,
Nu 15:39 and that you are to **o** his commands instead of
15:40 you remember that you must **o** all my commands
27:20 so the whole community of Israel will **o** him.
Dt 4:1 **O** them so that you may live, so you may enter
4:2 you from the LORD your God. Just **o** them.
4:5 "You must **o** these laws and regulations when you
4:6 If you **o** them carefully, you will display your
4:14 and regulations you must **o** in the land you are
4:40 If you **o** all the laws and commands that I will give
5:1 you today. Learn them and be sure to **o** them!
5:10 love on those who love me and **o** my commands,
5:27 everything he tells you, and we will listen and **o**.'
5:29 that they might fear me and **o** all my commands!
5:31 so they can **o** them in the land I am giving to them
5:32 "You must **o** all the commands of the LORD
6:1 so you may **o** them in the land you are about to
6:2 If you **o** all his laws and commands, you will enjoy
6:3 Israel, to everything I say. Be careful to **o**.
6:17 You must diligently **o** the commands of the
6:24 And the LORD our God commanded us to **o** all
6:25 For we are righteous when we **o** all the commands
7:9 loves those who love him and **o** his commands.
7:11 Therefore, **o** all these commands, laws,
7:12 listen to these regulations and **o** them faithfully,
8:1 "Be careful to **o** all the commands I am giving you
8:2 or not you would really **o** his commands.
8:6 "So **o** the commands of the LORD your God by
9:23 your God and refused to trust him or **o** him.
10:13 and to **o** the LORD's commands and laws that I
11:1 the LORD your God and **o** all his requirements,
11:8 be careful to **o** every command I am giving you
11:9 If you **o**, you will enjoy a long life in the land the
11:13 "If you carefully **o** all the commands I am giving
11:22 "Be careful to **o** all the commands I give you;
11:27 You will be blessed if you **o** the commands of the
11:32 you must be careful to **o** all the laws
12:1 and regulations you must **o** as long as you live in
12:28 Be careful to **o** all my commands so that all will go
12:32 Carefully **o** all the commands I give you. Do not
13:4 **O** his commands, listen to his voice, and cling to
13:18 your God will be merciful only if you **o** him
15:5 You will receive this blessing if you carefully **o** the
16:12 slaves in Egypt, so be careful to **o** all these laws.
19:9 (He will give you this land if you **o** all the
21:18 rebellious son who will not **o** his father or mother,
21:20 of ours is stubborn and rebellious and refuses to **o**.
24:8 **o** the commands I have given them.
26:16 your God has commanded you to **o** all these laws
26:17 You have promised to **o** his laws, commands,
26:18 and that you must **o** all his commands.
27:10 So **o** the LORD your God by keeping all these
28:1 "If you fully **o** the LORD your God by keeping
28:2 You will experience all these blessings if you **o** the
28:9 "If you **o** the commands of the LORD your God
28:13 of the LORD your God and carefully **o** them,
28:15 and do not **o** all the commands and laws I am
28:45 and to **o** the commands and laws he has given you,
28:58 "If you refuse to **o** all the terms of this law that are
29:9 **o** the terms of this covenant so that you will
29:29 so that we may **o** these words of the law.
30:2 and your children begin wholeheartedly to **o** all the
30:8 Then you will again **o** the LORD and keep all the
30:10 The LORD your God will delight in you if you **o**
30:12 and bring it down so we can hear and **o** it?'
30:13 the sea to bring it to us so we can hear and **o** it?'
30:14 on your lips and in your heart so that you can **o** it.
30:20 and to **o** him and commit yourself to him,
31:12 your God and carefully **o** all the terms of this law.
32:46 your children so they will **o** every word of this law.
Jos 1:7 very courageous. **O** all the laws Moses gave you.
1:8 so you may be sure to **o** all that is written in it.
1:17 We will **o** you just as we obeyed Moses. And may
1:18 and does not **o** your every command will be put to
22:3 You have been careful to **o** the commands of the
22:5 But be very careful to **o** all the commands
22:5 in all his ways, **o** his commands, be faithful to him,
24:24 serve the LORD our God. We will **o** him alone."
Jdg 2:22 or not they would **o** the LORD as their ancestors
3:4 to see whether they would **o** the commands the
1Sa 7:3 Determine to **o** only the LORD; then he will
15:11 been loyal to me and has again refused to **o** me."
15:20 "But I did **o** the LORD," Saul insisted.
28:18 because you did not **o** his instructions concerning
1Ki 3:14 you follow me and **o** my commands as your father,
6:12 my laws and regulations and **o** all my commands,
8:23 and show unfailing love to all who **o** you
8:58 his will in everything and to **o** all the commands,
8:61 May you always **o** his laws and commands, just as
11:38 and if you **o** my laws and commands, as my
18:18 for you have refused to **o** the commands of the
2Ki 5:13 So you should certainly **o** him when he says simply
10:6 "If you are on my side and are going to **o** me,
10:31 But Jehu did not **o** the law of the LORD, the God
17:13 **O** my commands and laws, which are contained in
17:19 But even the people of Judah refused to **o** the
17:37 Be careful to **o** all the laws, regulations,
21:8 If the Israelites will **o** my commands—the whole
23:3 He pledged to **o** the LORD by keeping all his
1Ch 10:13 He failed to **o** the LORD's command, and he
22:12 that you may **o** the law of the LORD your God as
22:13 For if you carefully **o** the laws and regulations that
28:7 And if he continues to **o** my commands
28:8 Be careful to **o** all the commands of the LORD
29:18 and Israel, make your people always want to **o** you.
29:19 Give my son Solomon the wholehearted desire to **o**
2Ch 6:14 and show unfailing love to all who **o** you
6:16 their behavior and **o** my law as you have done,
7:17 David, did and **o** all my commands, laws,
11:17 and earnestly sought to **o** the LORD as they had
14:4 their ancestors, and to **o** his law and his commands.
23:6 The rest of the people must **o** the LORD's
33:8 If the Israelites will **o** my commands—
34:31 He pledged to **o** the LORD by keeping all his
34:31 He promised to **o** all the terms of the covenant that
Ezr 7:10 and **o** the law of the LORD and to teach those
7:26 Anyone who refuses to **o** the law of your God
10:3 commands of our God. We will **o** the law of God.
Ne 1:5 love with those who love him and **o** his commands,
1:9 But if you return to me and **o** my commands,
8:1 which the LORD had given for Israel to **o**.

9:14 to **o** all your commands, laws, and instructions.
9:16 and they refused to **o** your commands.
9:29 by which people will find life if only they **o**.
9:34 and ancestors did not **o** your law or listen to your
10:29 to **o** the law of God as issued by his servant Moses.
10:32 we promise to **o** the command to pay the annual
Est 1:15 for a queen who refuses to **o** the king's orders,
3:8 and they refuse to **o** even the laws of the king.
Job 21:15 Who is the Almighty, and why should we **o** him?
36:11 "If they listen and **o** God, then they will be blessed
Ps 7:9 of the ungodly, / but help all those who **o** you.
14:5 will grip them, / for God is with those who **o** him.
19:11 there is great reward for those who **o** them.
25:10 all those who keep his covenant and **o** his decrees.
32:11 in the LORD and be glad, all you who **o** him!
50:16 laws no longer, / and don't pretend that you **o** me.
51:12 of your salvation, / and make me willing to **o** you.
69:36 The descendants of those who **o** him will inherit
89:31 if they do not **o** my decrees / and fail to keep my
103:18 his covenant, / of those who **o** his commandments!
105:45 his principles / and **o** his laws. / Praise the LORD!
106:25 in their tents / and refused to **o** the LORD.
111:10 The rewards of wisdom come to all who **o** him.
119:2 Happy are those who **o** his decrees / and search for
119:8 I will **o** your principles. / Please don't give up on
119:17 to your servant, / that I may live and **o** your word.
119:34 Give me understanding and I will **o** your law;
119:40 I long to **o** your commandments! / Renew my life
119:55 O LORD, / and I **o** your law because of this.
119:57 you are mine! / I promise to **o** your words!
119:60 without lingering, / to **o** your commands.
119:69 but in truth I **o** your commandments with all my
119:83 But I cling to your principles and **o** them.
119:88 my life; / then I can continue to **o** your decrees.
119:94 For I have applied myself to **o** your
119:106 I'll promise again: / I will **o** your wonderful laws.
119:115 for I intend to **o** the commands of my God.
119:119 you skim off; / no wonder I love to **o** your decrees!
119:129 Your decrees are wonderful. / No wonder I **o** them!
119:134 of evil people; / then I can **o** your commandments.
119:145 answer me, LORD! / I will **o** your principles.
119:146 out to you; save me, / that I may **o** your decrees.
119:168 Yes, I **o** your commandments and decrees,
132:12 If your descendants **o** the terms of my covenant
148:8 snow and storm, / wind and weather that **o** him,
Pr 6:20 My son, **o** your father's commands, and don't
7:2 **O** them and live! Guard my teachings as your most
28:4 to praise the wicked; to **o** the law is to fight them.
28:7 Young people who **o** the law are wise; those who
Ecc 8:2 **O** the king because you have vowed before God to
8:5 Those who **o** him will not be punished. Those who
12:13 Fear God and **o** his commands, for this is the duty
Isa 1:19 If you will only **o** me and let me help you, then you
2:3 he will teach us his ways, so that we may **o** him."
3:8 speak out against the LORD and refuse to **o** him.
26:8 LORD, we love to **o** your laws; / our heart's
28:12 rest in their own land if they would only **o** him,
42:24 go where he sent them, nor would they **o** his law.
55:5 and they will come running to **o**, because I,
Jer 2:20 of your slavery, but still you would not **o** me.
2:30 but it did them no good. They still refuse to **o**.
7:23 '**O** me, and I will be your God, and you will be my
7:28 'This is the nation whose people will not **o** the
9:13 I gave them; they have refused to **o** my law.
11:3 Cursed is anyone who does not **o** the terms of my
11:4 "If you **o** me and do whatever I command you,
11:7 and over again to this day: "**O** me!"
11:8 And because they refused to **o**, I brought upon
12:17 But any nation who refuses to **o** me will be
17:23 but they did not listen or **o**. They stubbornly
17:24 " 'But if you **o** me, says the LORD, and do not
18:10 then that nation turns to evil and refuses to **o** me,
22:4 If you **o** me, there will always be a descendant of
26:4 not listen to me and **o** the law I have given you,
26:13 your sinning and begin to **o** the LORD your God,
32:23 but they refused to **o** you or follow your law.
32:33 right from wrong, but they would not listen or **o**.
35:13 'Come and learn a lesson about how to **o** me.
35:14 you again and again, and you refuse to listen or **o**.
35:15 But you would not listen to me or **o**.
38:20 over to them if you choose to **o** the LORD.
42:5 us if we refuse to **o** whatever he tells us to do!
42:6 we will **o** the LORD our God to whom we send
42:6 For if we **o** him, everything will turn out well for
42:13 "But if you refuse to **o** the LORD your God
42:21 but you will not **o** the LORD your God any better
43:4 and all the people refused to **o** the LORD's
43:7 The people refused to **o** the LORD and went to
44:23 refusing to **o** him and follow his instructions,
Eze 5:6 She has refused to **o** the laws I gave her to follow.
5:7 Since you have refused to **o** my laws
11:12 For you have refused to **o** me; instead, you have
11:20 so they will **o** my laws and regulations. Then they
17:18 king of Israel broke his treaty after swearing to **o**;
18:21 and begin to **o** my laws and do what is just
18:27 **o** the law, and do what is just and right, they will
20:13 and they refused to **o** my laws there in the
20:13 They wouldn't **o** my instructions even though
20:24 because they did not **o** my laws. They scorned my
33:15 and **o** my life-giving laws, no longer doing what is
36:27 so you will **o** my laws and do whatever I
37:24 They will **o** my regulations and keep my laws.
44:24 And the priests themselves must **o** my instructions
Da 3:6 Anyone who refuses to **o** will immediately be
3:11 That decree also states that those who refuse to **o**
7:14 every race and nation and language would **o** him.
7:27 rule forever, and all rulers will serve and **o** them."

9:14 for we did not **o** him, and the LORD our God is
Hos 9:17 people of Israel because they will not listen or **o**.
Am 2:4 rejected the laws of the LORD, refusing to **o** him.
Mic 4:2 he will teach us his ways, so that we may **o** him."
5:15 vengeance on all the nations that refuse to **o** me."
Zec 3:7 If you follow my ways and **o** my requirements,
6:15 All this will happen if you carefully **o** the
Mal 3:7 you have scorned my laws and failed to **o** them.
4:4 "Remember to **o** the instructions of my servant
Mt 5:20 unless you **o** God better than the teachers of
7:21 The decisive issue is whether they **o** my Father in
8:27 "Even the wind and waves **o** him!"
23:3 So practice and **o** whatever they say to you,
28:20 Teach these new disciples to **o** all the commands I
Mk 1:27 has such authority! Even evil spirits **o** his orders!"
4:41 is this man, that even the wind and waves **o** him?"
Lk 1:6 careful to **o** all of the Lord's commandments
4:36 Even evil spirits **o** him and flee at his command!"
6:46 why do you call me 'Lord,' when you won't **o** me?
6:49 and doesn't **o** is like a person who builds a house
8:21 all those who hear the message of God and **o** it."
8:25 this man, that even the winds and waves **o** him?"
10:17 even the demons **o** us when we use your name!"
10:20 But don't rejoice just because evil spirits **o** you;
17:6 and throw you into the sea,' and it would **o** you!
17:10 In the same way, when you **o** me you should say,
Jn 3:36 Those who don't **o** the Son will never experience
7:22 too, when you **o** Moses' law of circumcision.
8:52 but you say that those who **o** your teaching will
8:55 a liar as you! But it is true—I know him and **o** him.
12:47 If anyone hears me and doesn't **o** me, I am not his
14:15 "If you love me, **o** my commandments.
14:21 Those who **o** my commandments are the ones who
15:10 When you **o** me, you remain in my love, just as I **o**
my Father and remain in his love.
15:14 You are my friends if you **o** me.
Ac 4:19 "Do you think God wants us to **o** you rather than
5:29 "We must **o** God rather than human authority.
5:32 who is given by God to those who **o** him."
Ro 1:5 so that they will believe and **o** him, bringing glory
2:8 who refuse to **o** the truth and practice evil deeds.
2:13 Those who **o** the law will be declared right in
2:25 is worth something only if you **o** God's law.
2:25 But if you don't **o** God's law, you are no better off
2:26 And if the Gentiles **o** God's law, won't God give
2:27 and know so much about God's law but don't **o** it.
4:14 that God's promise is for those who **o** God's law
4:15 the law brings punishment on those who try to **o** it.
6:16 Don't you realize that whatever you choose to **o**
6:16 or you can choose to **o** God and receive his
7:25 In my mind I really want to **o** God's law, but
8:7 It never did **o** God's laws, and it never will.
13:1 **O** the government, for God is the one who put it
13:2 So those who refuse to **o** the laws of the land are
refusing to **o** God,
13:5 So you must **o** the government for two reasons:
15:31 rescued from those in Judea who refuse to **o** God.
16:26 so that they might believe and **o** Christ.
1Co 9:19 This means I am not bound to **o** people just
9:21 not discard the law of God; I **o** the law of Christ.
2Co 10:5 rebellious ideas, and we teach them to **o** Christ.
Gal 2:14 why are you trying to make these Gentiles **o** the
3:5 among you because you **o** the law of Moses?
3:10 and **o** all these commands that are written in God's
3:12 obeying the law, you must **o** all of its commands."
4:2 They have to **o** their guardians until they reach
5:3 you must **o** all of the regulations in the whole law
6:2 and problems, and in this way **o** the law of Christ.
Eph 2:2 at work in the hearts of those who refuse to **o** God.
6:1 **o** your parents because you belong to the Lord,
6:5 **o** your earthly masters with deep respect and fear.
Php 2:13 giving you the desire to **o** him and the power to do
3:9 on my own goodness or my ability to **o** God's law,
3:16 But we must be sure to **o** the truth we have learned
Col 3:20 You children must always **o** your parents, for this
3:22 You slaves must **o** your earthly masters in
3:22 **O** them willingly because of your reverent fear of
2Th 1:8 and on those who refuse to **o** the Good News of
3:14 Take note of those who refuse to **o** what we say in
1Ti 3:4 family well, with children who respect and **o** him.
5:21 and the holy angels to **o** these instructions without
6:2 Timothy, and encourage everyone to **o** them.
6:14 that you **o** his commands with all purity. Then no
Tit 2:9 Slaves must **o** their masters and do their best to
Heb 5:9 source of eternal salvation for all those who **o** him.
8:10 so they will **o** them. / I will be their God, / and they
10:5 But you have given me a body so that I may **o** you.
10:16 write them on their minds / so they will **o** them."
10:28 Anyone who refused to **o** the law of Moses was put
11:31 all the others in her city who refused to **o** God.
12:25 See to it that you **o** God, the one who is speaking
13:17 **O** your spiritual leaders and do what they say.
Jas 1:22 And remember, it is a message to **o**, not just to
1:22 If you don't **o**, you are only fooling yourself.
1:23 For if you just listen and don't **o**, it is like looking
2:8 it is good when you truly **o** our Lord's royal
4:11 the law is right or wrong. Your job is to **o** it.
1Pe 1:14 **O** God because you are his children. Don't slip
2:8 because they do not listen to God's word or **o** it,
1Jn 2:4 but doesn't **o** God's commandments, that person is
2:5 But those who **o** God's word really do love him.
3:10 Anyone who does not **o** God's commands and does
3:22 because we **o** him and do the things that please
3:24 Those who **o** God's commandments live in
5:2 children if we love God and **o** his commandments.
Rev 1:3 he blesses all who listen to it and **o** what it says.
2:26 all who are victorious, who **o** me to the very end,

22:7 Blessed are those who **o** the prophecy written in
22:9 as well as all who **o** what is written in this scroll.

OBEYED (69) [OBEY]

Ge 22:16 Because you have **o** me and have not withheld
22:18 earth will be blessed—all because you have **o** me."
26:5 Abraham listened to me and **o** all my requirements,
28:7 He also knew that Jacob had **o** his parents
Ex 32:3 All the people **o** Aaron and brought him their gold
32:28 The Levites **o** Moses, and about three thousand
32:29 for you **o** him even though it meant killing your
Nu 32:11 and Jacob, for they have not **o** me completely.
Dt 26:14 I have **o** the LORD my God and have done
33:9 The Levites **o** your word / and guarded your
33:21 and **o** his regulations for Israel."
34:9 So the people of Israel **o** him and did everything
Jos 1:17 We will obey you just as we **o** Moses. And may
21:8 So the Israelites **o** the LORD's command to
22:2 and you have **o** every order I have given you.
1Sa 13:13 Had you **o**, the LORD would have established
13:14 for you have not **o** the LORD's command."
15:19 Why haven't you **o** the LORD? Why did you rush
28:21 "Sir, I **o** your command at the risk of my life.
1Ki 2:43 your oath to the LORD and **o** my command?"
11:33 He has not **o** my laws and regulations as his father,
11:34 whom I chose and who **o** my commands and laws,
12:24 for what has happened is my doing!' " So they **o**
14:8 who **o** my commands and followed me with all his
15:5 and had **o** the LORD's commands throughout his
20:36 "Because you have not **o** the voice of the LORD,
2Ki 14:6 for he **o** the command of the LORD written in the
18:6 and he carefully **o** all the commands the LORD
22:13 because our ancestors have not **o** the words in this
1Ch 21:19 So David **o** the instructions the LORD had given
29:23 and he prospered greatly, and all Israel **o** him.
2Ch 11:4 for what has happened is my doing!' " So they **o**
17:4 and **o** his commands instead of following the
25:4 for he **o** the command of the LORD written in the
29:25 He **o** all the commands that the LORD had given
34:21 because our ancestors have not **o** the word of the
Ezr 6:12 issued this decree. Let it be **o** with all diligence."
Ps 111:8 forever true, / to be **o** faithfully and with integrity.
119:22 and insult me, / for I have **o** your decrees.
119:166 LORD, / so I have **o** your commands.
119:167 I have **o** your decrees, / and I love them very much.
Jer 3:25 the LORD our God. We have never **o** him."
17:1 act as though their evil ways are laws to be **o**,
34:10 and all the people had **o** the king's command,
34:17 Since you have not **o** me by setting your
35:8 So we have **o** him in all these things. We have
35:10 and have fully **o** all the commands of Jehonadab,
35:16 The families of Recab have **o** their ancestor
35:18 You have **o** your ancestor Jehonadab in every
Eze 48:11 the descendants of Zadok who **o** me and did not go
Da 9:10 We have not **o** the LORD our God, for we have
Jnh 3:3 This time Jonah **o** the LORD's command
Hag 1:12 and the whole remnant of God's people **o** the
Mal 2:9 For you have not **o** me but have shown partiality in
Mt 19:20 "I've **o** all these commandments," the young man
Mk 10:20 "I've **o** all these commandments since I was a
11:23 you into the sea,' and your command will be **o**.
Lk 18:21 "I've **o** all these commandments since I was a
Ac 16:4 regarding the commandments that were to be **o**,
Ro 5:19 But because one other person **o** God, many people
6:17 but now you have **o** with all your heart the new
Gal 2:16 in Christ—and not because we have **o** the law.
Php 3:6 And I **o** the Jewish law so carefully that I was
Heb 11:7 He **o** God, who warned him about something that
11:8 It was by faith that Abraham **o** when God called
1Pe 1:2 you have **o** Jesus Christ and are cleansed by his
3:6 For instance, Sarah **o** her husband, Abraham,
Rev 3:8 yet you **o** my word and did not deny me.
3:10 "Because you have **o** my command to persevere,

OBEYING (36) [OBEY]

Ex 15:26 is right in his sight, **o** his commands and laws,
Lev 22:31 "You must faithfully keep all my commands by **o**
Dt 8:20 you also will be destroyed for not **o** the LORD
17:19 the LORD his God by **o** all the terms of this law.
27:26 does not affirm the terms of this law by **o** them.'
32:47 By **o** them you will enjoy a long life in the land
Jos 11:15 carefully **o** all of the LORD's instructions to
1Ki 9:4 always **o** my commands and keeping my laws
2Ki 17:34 of truly worshiping the LORD and **o** the laws,
23:25 and soul and strength, **o** all the laws of Moses.
1Ch 16:40 **o** everything written in the law of the LORD,
2Ch 30:12 giving them a strong desire to unite in **o** the orders
Ne 1:7 We have sinned terribly by not **o** the commands,
Ps 78:7 his glorious miracles / and **o** his commands.
119:9 By **o** your word and following its rules.
119:44 I will keep on **o** your law / forever and forever.
119:56 is my happy way of life: / **o** your commandments.
119:109 in the balance, / but I will not stop **o** your law.
Isa 11:3 He will delight in **o** the LORD. He will never
Eze 20:21 even though **o** them would have given them life.
Mal 3:14 What have we gained by **o** his commands or by
Mt 21:31 Which of the two was **o** his father?" They replied,
Jn 8:31 "You are truly my disciples if you keep **o** my
8:41 you are **o** your real father when you act that way."
Ro 3:20 the clearer it becomes that we aren't **o** it.
3:21 not by **o** the law but by the way promised in the
3:28 right with God through faith and not by **o** the law.
7:6 not in the old way by **o** the letter of the law,
2Co 2:9 as I did to find out how far you would go in **o** me.
Gal 2:16 For no one will ever be saved by **o** the law."
3:12 which says, "If you wish to find life by **o** the law,

3:21 we could have been made right with God by o it.
Eph 2:2 full of sin, o Satan, the mighty prince of the power
Php 2:12 in your lives, o God with deep reverence and fear.
1Jn 2:3 that we belong to him? By o his commandments.
Rev 14:12 to the end, o his commands and trusting in Jesus."

OBEYS (10) [OBEY]

Ps 119:63 my friend— / anyone who o your commandments.
Pr 29:18 they run wild. But whoever o the law is happy.
Isa 50:10 among you fears the LORD and o his servant?
Eze 18:9 and faithfully o my laws and regulations.
18:17 at interest, and o all my regulations and laws.
Mt 5:19 But anyone who o God's laws and teaches them
7:24 who listens to my teaching and o me is wise,
Lk 6:47 to me, listens to my teaching, and then o me.
Jn 7:19 None of you o the law of Moses! In fact, you are
8:51 anyone who o my teaching will never die!"

OBIL (1)

1Ch 27:30 O the Ishmaelite was in charge of the camels.

OBJECT (50) [OBJECTED, OBJECTIONS, OBJECTS]

Lev 6:4 to them, or a lost o that they claimed as their own,
11:32 that o, whatever its use, will be unclean.
11:32 This is true whether the o is made of wood, cloth,
11:34 If the water used to cleanse an unclean o touches
11:35 Any o on which the dead body of such an animal
13:54 the priest will order the contaminated o to be
13:55 Then the priest must inspect the o again. If he sees
13:55 even if it did not spread, the o is defiled.
13:57 and the contaminated o must be burned up.
13:58 But if the spot disappears after the o is washed,
15:22 The same applies if you touch an o on which she
Nu 35:20 or throws a dangerous o and the person dies,
Dt 18:12 Anyone who does these things is an o of horror
28:25 You will be an o of horror to all the kingdoms of
28:37 You will become an o of horror, a proverb and a
1Ki 9:7 I will make Israel an o of mockery and ridicule
2Ch 29:8 He has made us an o of dread, horror, and ridicule,
30:7 and became an o of derision, as you yourselves can
Ps 44:13 We are an o of scorn and derision to the nations
79:4 an o of scorn and derision to those around us.
109:25 I am an o of mockery to people everywhere;
Isa 62:7 Jerusalem the o of praise throughout the earth.
Jer 15:4 I will make my people an o of horror to all the
23:40 And I will make you an o of ridicule, and your
24:9 I will make them an o of horror and evil to every
25:9 and make you an o of horror and contempt and a
25:18 an o of horror, contempt, and cursing.
26:6 And I will make Jerusalem an o of cursing in
29:18 I will make them an o of damnation, horror,
42:18 You will become an o of damnation, horror,
44:8 and make yourselves an o of cursing
44:12 They will be an o of damnation, horror, cursing,
44:22 doing that he made your land an o of cursing—
48:27 Did you not make Israel the o of your ridicule?
48:39 She has become an o of ridicule, an example of
49:13 "that Bozrah will become an o of horror and a
49:17 "Edom will be an o of horror. All who pass by
51:37 It will be an o of horror and contempt, without a
Eze 5:15 You will become an o of mockery and taunting
22:4 I will make you an o of mockery throughout the
36:3 You are the o of much mocking and slander.
Da 9:27 he will set up a sacrilegious o that causes
11:31 and setting up the sacrilegious o that causes
12:11 and the sacrilegious o that causes desecration is set
Joel 2:17 to you, so don't let them become an o of mockery.
2:19 You will no longer be an o of mockery among the
Mt 24:15 the sacrilegious o that causes desecration standing
Mk 13:14 o that causes desecration standing where it should
Ac 10:47 "Can anyone o to their being baptized, now that
2Th 2:4 and tear down every o of adoration and worship.

OBJECTED (5) [OBJECT]

Ex 6:12 "But LORD!" Moses o. "My own people won't
Jdg 14:3 His father and mother o strenuously, "Isn't there
2Sa 18:3 But his men o strongly. "You must not go,"
Jn 5:10 So the Jewish leaders o. They said to the man who
11:8 But his disciples o. "Teacher," they said, "only a

OBJECTIONS (2) [OBJECT]

Nu 30:7 or pledge and raises no o on the day he hears of it,
Ac 11:18 all their o were answered and they began praising

OBJECTS (28) [OBJECT]

Ex 28:30 Aaron will always carry the o used to determine
31:4 He is able to create beautiful o from gold, silver,
35:22 They presented gold o of every kind to the
35:24 and bronze o as their offering to the LORD.
35:32 He is able to create beautiful o from gold, silver,
Nu 4:4 at the Tabernacle will relate to the most sacred o.
4:15 But they must not touch the sacred o, or they will
4:15 So these are the o of the Tabernacle that the
4:19 and not die when they approach the most sacred o.
4:20 and look at the sacred o for even a moment,
7:9 since they were required to carry the sacred o of
7:85 In all, the silver o weighed about 60 pounds,
10:21 carrying the sacred o from the Tabernacle.
18:3 must be careful not to touch any of the sacred o
31:6 They carried along the holy o of the sanctuary
31:23 These metal o must then be further purified with
31:51 all kinds of jewelry and crafted o.
Dt 7:26 Do not bring any detestable o into your home,
10:15 Yet the LORD chose your ancestors as the o of
Jdg 18:18 carrying all the sacred o out of Micah's shrine,
2Sa 14:10 the king said. "If anyone o, bring them to me.
2Ki 12:18 King Joash collected all the sacred o that
Isa 44:9 These highly valued o are really worthless.
Eze 6:6 and all the other religious o you have made.
Da 1:2 he took with him some of the sacred o from the
Ro 9:22 patient with those who are the o of his judgment
9:23 upon those he prepared to be the o of his mercy—
Rev 18:12 o made of expensive wood, bronze, iron,

OBLATION(S) [KJV] See GIFT, OFFERING(S), PORTION(S), SACRIFICE

OBLIGATED (2) [OBLIGATION]

Lev 25:41 and their children will no longer be o to you,
Gal 4:31 are not children of the slave woman, o to the law.

OBLIGATION (3) [OBLIGATED, OBLIGATIONS, OBLIGED]

Ecc 8:8 There is no escaping that o, that dark battle.
Ro 1:14 For I have a great sense of o to people in our
8:12 you have no o whatsoever to do what your sinful

OBLIGATIONS (1) [OBLIGATION]

Dt 29:14 the LORD is making this covenant with its o.

OBLIGED (2) [OBLIGATION]

1Sa 13:12 So I felt o to offer the burnt offering myself before
Ac 18:14 or a serious crime, I would be o to listen to you.

OBOTH (3)

Nu 21:10 The Israelites traveled next to O and camped there.
33:43 They left Punon and camped at O.
33:44 They left O and camped at Iye-abarim on the

OBSCENE (3) [OBSCENITIES]

1Ki 15:13 because she had made an o Asherah pole.
2Ch 15:16 because she had made an o Asherah pole.
Eph 5:4 O stories, foolish talk, and coarse jokes—these are

OBSCENITIES (2) [OBSCENE]

Rev 17:4 She held in her hand a gold goblet full of o
17:5 Mother of All Prostitutes and O in the World."

OBSCURED (1) [OBSCURITIES]

Hab 3:11 o by brilliance from your arrows and the flashing

OBSCURITIES (1) [OBSCURED]

Isa 45:19 I do not whisper o in some dark corner so no one

OBSERVANCE (1) [OBSERVE]

Ne 9:1 On October 31 the people returned for another o.

OBSERVATION (1) [OBSERVE]

Lev 13:11 the person need not be quarantined for further o

OBSERVE (17) [OBSERVANCE, OBSERVATION, OBSERVED, OBSERVES]

Ex 20:8 "Remember to o the Sabbath day by keeping it
Lev 19:3 and you must always o my Sabbath days of rest,
23:41 You must o this seven-day festival to the LORD
25:2 the land itself must o a Sabbath to the LORD
25:12 and you must o it as a special and holy time.
Nu 27:11 The Israelites must o this as a general legal
35:29 These are permanent laws for you to o from
Dt 5:12 " 'O the Sabbath day by keeping it holy,
5:15 God has commanded you to o the Sabbath day.
1Ki 2:3 O the requirements of the LORD your God
2Ch 20:3 that everyone throughout Judah should o a fast.
Est 9:31 (The people decided to o this festival, just as they
Job 28:7 that no bird of prey can see, no falcon's eye o—
Ecc 8:16 I tried to o everything that goes on all across the
Ac 20:7 of the week, we gathered to o the Lord's Supper.
21:24 all false and that you yourself o the Jewish laws.
Gal 3:10 "Cursed is everyone who does not o and obey all

OBSERVED (15) [OBSERVE]

Ge 6:5 Now the LORD o the extent of the people's
6:12 God o all this corruption in the world, and he saw
Ex 12:24 and must be o by you and your descendants
Lev 23:3 for worship. It must be o wherever you live.
23:4 the holy occasions to be o at the proper time each
23:14 law for you, and it must be o wherever you live.
23:21 law for you, and it must be o wherever you live.
23:31 law for you, and it must be o wherever you live.
23:38 These festivals must be o in addition to the
Dt 16:13 must be o for seven days at the end of the harvest
Ps 107:24 They, too, o the LORD's power in action,
Ecc 4:1 Again I o all the oppression that takes place in our
4:4 Then I o that most people are motivated to success
4:7 I o yet another example of meaninglessness in our
9:11 I have o something else in this world of ours.

OBSERVES (1) [OBSERVE]

Ps 33:14 From his throne he o / all who live on the earth.

OBSESSED (2)

2Sa 13:2 so o with Tamar that he became ill.
Job 36:17 But you are too o with judgment on the godless.

OBSOLETE (1)

Heb 8:13 it means he has made the first one o.

OBSTACLE (2) [OBSTACLES]

Ro 14:13 you will not put an o in another Christian's path.
1Co 9:12 an o in the way of the Good News about Christ.

OBSTACLES (1) [OBSTACLE]

Jer 6:21 "I will put o in my people's path. Fathers and sons

OBSTINATE (2)

Ne 9:29 but they became proud and o and disobeyed your
Isa 48:4 "I know how stubborn and o you are. Your necks

OBTAIN (4) [OBTAINED]

Ex 32:30 Perhaps I will be able to o forgiveness for you."
Ezr 7:16 and gold which you may o from the province of
Pr 5:10 Strangers will o your wealth, and someone else
11:16 Beautiful women o wealth, and violent men get

OBTAINED (1) [OBTAIN]

Pr 20:21 An inheritance o early in life is not a blessing in

OBVIOUS (7) [OBVIOUSLY]

Jdg 18:14 and a cast idol. It's o what we ought to do."
Ps 109:29 Make their humiliation o to all; / clothe my
Mt 6:16 don't make it o, as the hypocrites do, who try to
16:3 the sky, but you can't read the o signs of the times!
1Co 11:14 Isn't it o that it's disgraceful for a man to have
11:15 And isn't it o that long hair is a woman's pride
2Co 4:11 so that the life of Jesus will be o in our dying

OBVIOUSLY (11) [OBVIOUS]

Ge 24:50 "The LORD has o brought you here,
26:9 for Isaac and exclaimed, "She is o your wife!
26:27 "This is o no friendly visit, since you sent me from
41:38 For he is a man who is o filled with the spirit of
Ex 5:8 They o don't have enough to do. If they did,
5:17 You o don't have enough to do. If you did,
Job 8:4 Your children o sinned against him, so their
Lk 2:5 his fiancée, who was o pregnant by this time.
Ro 3:19 O, the law applies to those to whom it was given,
Gal 1:10 O, I'm not trying to be a people pleaser! No,
Heb 11:14 And o people who talk like that are looking

OCCASION (8) [OCCASIONS]

Ge 21:8 Abraham gave a big party to celebrate the happy o.
1Sa 20:5 I've always eaten with your father on this o,
2Sa 13:24 and his servants please come to celebrate the o
Ne 8:4 wooden platform that had been made for the o.
12:27 They were to take part in the joyous o with their
Est 2:18 To celebrate the o, he gave a banquet in Esther's
Jer 46:2 on the o of the battle of Carchemish when Pharaoh
Eph 6:18 and on every o in the power of the Holy Spirit.

OCCASIONED [KJV] See CAUSED

OCCASIONS (9) [OCCASION]

Lev 23:4 the holy o to be observed at the proper time each
Dt 16:16 God at the place he chooses on each of these o,
2Ki 13:25 Jehoash defeated Ben-hadad on three o, and
Job 1:4 On these o they would get together to eat
Eze 45:17 the Sabbath days, and all other similar o.
46:10 will enter and leave with the people on these o.
Ac 1:3 On these o he talked to them about the Kingdom of
2Co 8:22 and has shown how earnest he is on many o.
2Ti 2:20 The expensive utensils are used for special o,

OCCUPATION (2)

Ge 46:33 Pharaoh calls for you and asks you about your o,
47:3 Pharaoh asked them, "What is your o?" And they

OCCUPIED (12) [OCCUPY]

Ge 36:43 each clan giving its name to the area it o.
Ex 3:17 I will lead you to the land now o by the
Nu 21:24 and o their land from the Arnon River to the
21:31 So the people of Israel o the territory of the
21:35 single survivor remained. Then Israel o their land.
Dt 4:46 (This land was formerly o by the Amorites under
1Sa 31:7 So the Philistines moved in and o their towns.
2Sa 23:14 and a Philistine detachment had o the town of
2Ki 24:7 for the king of Babylon o the entire area formerly
1Ch 10:7 So the Philistines moved in and o their towns.
11:16 and a Philistine detachment had o the town of
2Ch 28:18 its villages, and the Philistines had o these towns.

OCCUPY (42) [OCCUPIED, OCCUPYING]

Lev 26:32 Your enemies who come to o it will be utterly
Nu 33:53 and settle in it, because I have given it to you to o.
Dt 1:8 Go in and o it, for it is the land the LORD swore
1:21 Go and o it as the LORD, the God of your
1:39 be captured, but they will be the ones who o it.
2:21 so the Ammonites could o their land.
2:24 you his land. Attack him and begin to o the land.
2:31 over to you. Begin now to conquer and o his land.'
3:20 and when they o the land the LORD your God is

4: 1 so you may enter and **o** the land the LORD,
4: 5 you arrive in the land you are about to enter and **o**.
4: 14 must obey in the land you are about to enter and **o**.
4: 22 Though you will cross the Jordan to **o** the land,
4: 26 from the land you are crossing the Jordan to **o**.
5: 33 lives in the land you are about to enter and **o**.
6: 1 obey them in the land you are about to enter and **o**,
6: 18 and **o** the good land that the LORD solemnly
7: 1 you into the land you are about to enter and **o**,
8: 1 and **o** the land the LORD swore to give your
9: 1 Today you are about to cross the Jordan River to **o**
9: 5 upright people that you are about to **o** their land.
11: 8 to go in and **o** the land you are about to enter.
11: 10 and **o** is not like the land of Egypt from which you
11: 31 For you are about to cross the Jordan to **o** the land
12: 29 and you drive them out and **o** their land,
16: 20 and **o** the land that the LORD your God is giving
19: 2 the land the LORD your God is giving you to **o**.
23: 20 you do in the land you are about to enter and **o**.
28: 21 are left in the land you are about to enter and **o**.
28: 63 from the land you are about to enter and **o**.
30: 16 bless you and the land you are about to enter and **o**.
30: 18 life in the land you are crossing the Jordan to **o**.
31: 13 live in the land you are crossing the Jordan to **o**."
32: 47 in the land you are crossing the Jordan River to **o**."
Jos 13: 2 The people still need to **o** the land of the Philistines
17: 12 But the descendants of Manasseh were unable to **o**
Isa 11: 14 They will **o** all the lands of Edom, Moab,
Eze 7: 24 I will bring the most ruthless of nations to **o** their
Ob 1: 19 "Then my people living in the Negev will **o** the
1: 19 And the people of Benjamin will **o** the land of
1: 20 and **o** the Phoenician coast as far north as
Zec 9: 6 Foreigners will **o** the city of Ashdod. Thus, I will

OCCUPYING (1) [OCCUPY]

1Ki 22: 3 "Do you realize that the Arameans are still **o** our

OCCUR (1) [OCCURRED, OCCURS]

Isa 41: 23 If you are gods, tell what will **o** in the days ahead.

OCCURRED (4) [OCCUR]

Nu 19: 14 and those who were inside when the death **o**,
Dt 13: 14 and can prove that such a detestable act has **o**
Ac 4: 28 everything they did **o** according to your eternal
2Ti 2: 18 lie that the resurrection of the dead has already **o**;

OCCURS (2) [OCCUR]

Eze 45: 25 of Shelters, which **o** every year in early autumn,
Lk 21: 12 "But before all this **o**, there will be a time of great

OCEAN (16) [OCEAN'S, OCEANS]

Job 28: 14 'It is not here,' says the **o**. 'Nor is it here,'
Ps 8: 8 the sea, / and everything that swims the **o** currents.
24: 2 on the seas / and built it on the **o** depths.
36: 6 mighty mountains, / your justice like the **o** depths.
104: 25 Here is the **o**, vast and wide, / teeming with life of
148: 7 from the earth, / you creatures of the **o** depths,
Pr 30: 19 slithers on a rock, / how a ship navigates the **o**,
Eze 27: 25 The ships of Tarshish were your **o** caravans.
Hos 10: 7 will disappear like a chip of wood on an **o** wave.
Am 9: 3 Even if they hide at the bottom of the **o**, I will send
Jnh 2: 3 You threw me into the **o** depths, and I sank down
Mic 7: 19 your feet and throw them into the depths of the **o**!
Ro 8: 39 we are high above the sky or in the deepest **o**,
Rev 1: 15 and his voice thundered like mighty **o** waves.
18: 21 He threw it into the **o** and shouted, "Babylon,
19: 6 or the roar of mighty **o** waves, or the crash of loud

OCEAN'S (1) [OCEAN]

Jer 5: 22 am the one who defines the **o** sandy shoreline,

OCEANS (18) [OCEAN]

Ge 1: 22 saying, "Let the fish multiply and fill the **o**.
Ps 33: 7 its boundaries / and locked the **o** in vast reservoirs.
46: 3 Let the **o** roar and foam. / Let the mountains
65: 7 You quieted the raging **o** / with their pounding
89: 9 You are the one who rules the **o**. / When their
93: 3 The mighty **o** have roared, O LORD. / The mighty **o** roar like thunder;
93: 3 the mighty **o** roar as they pound the shore.
139: 9 wings of the morning, / if I dwell by the farthest **o**,
Pr 8: 24 I was born before the **o** were created,
8: 27 the heavens, when he drew the horizon on the **o**.
30: 4 wind in his fists? Who wraps up the **o** in his cloak?
Isa 40: 12 Who else has held the **o** in his hand? Who has
Am 5: 8 It is he who draws up water from the **o** and pours it
9: 6 He draws up water from the **o** and pours it down as
Na 1: 4 At his command the **o** and rivers dry up, the lush
Hag 2: 6 the earth. I will shake the **o** and the dry land, too.
Rev 11: 6 have the power to turn the rivers and **o** into blood,

OCRAN (5)

Nu 1: 13 Asher | Pagiel son of **O**
2: 27[-28] Asher | Pagiel son of **O** | 41,500
7: 72 On the eleventh day Pagiel son of **O**, leader of the
7: 77 This was the offering brought by Pagiel son of **O**.
10: 26 The tribe of Asher was led by Pagiel son of **O**.

OCTOBER (6)

Ne 6: 15 So on **O** 2 the wall was finally finished—
8: 2 So on **O** 8 Ezra the priest brought the scroll of the
8: 13 On **O** 9 the family leaders and the priests
8: 18 Then on **O** 15 they held a solemn assembly,
9: 1 On **O** 31 the people returned for another
Hag 2: 1 Then on **O** 17 of that same year, the LORD sent

ODD [KJV] See EXTRA

ODDS (1)

Ge 16: 12 he will live at **o** with the rest of his brothers."

ODED (2)

2Ch 15: 1 the Spirit of God came upon Azariah son of **O**,
28: 9 But a prophet of the LORD named **O** was there in

ODOR (1)

Ex 16: 24 was wholesome and good, without maggots or **o**.

ODOUR [KJV] See FRAGRANCE

OF (23057) See Index of Articles, Etc.

OFF (345) [OFFSPRING]

Ge 1: 14 They will be signs to mark **o** the seasons, the days,
17: 11 the flesh of his foreskin must be cut **o**. This will be
17: 14 **o** from the covenant family for violating the
17: 23 and circumcised them, cutting **o** their foreskins,
21: 28 ewe lambs and set them **o** by themselves,
25: 6 sons of his concubines and sent them **o** to the east,
27: 39 "You will live **o** the land and what it yields,
29: 26 "It's not our custom to marry **o** a younger
30: 37 and peeled **o** strips of the bark to make white
31: 26 "What do you mean by sneaking **o** like this?"
31: 42 you would have sent me **o** without a penny to my
37: 23 Joseph arrived, they pulled **o** his beautiful robe
38: 19 Afterward she went home, took **o** her veil, and put
39: 12 tore himself away, but as he did, his shirt came **o**.
40: 19 Three days from now Pharaoh will cut **o** your head
45: 18 land of Egypt. You will live **o** the fat of the land!'
45: 24 So he sent his brothers **o**, and as they left, he called
49: 17 bites the horse's heels / so the rider is thrown **o**.
Ex 3: 5 "Take **o** your sandals, for you are standing on holy
12: 15 festival will be cut **o** from the community of Israel.
12: 19 week will be cut **o** from the community of Israel.
14: 25 Their chariot wheels began to come **o**,
19: 23 around the mountain and to declare it **o** limits."
24: 6 blood from these animals and drew it **o** into basins.
29: 17 and wash **o** the internal organs and the legs.
30: 33 not a priest will be cut **o** from the community.' "
30: 38 enjoyment will be cut **o** from the community."
31: 14 anyone who works on that day will be cut **o** from
32: 2 and daughters to take **o** their gold earrings,
Lev 1: 15 twist **o** its head, and burn the head on the altar.
3: 9 This includes the fat of the entire tail cut **o** near the
6: 27 it must be washed **o** in a sacred place.
7: 20 to the LORD must be cut **o** from the community.
7: 21 that person must be cut **o** from the community."
7: 25 LORD by fire must be cut **o** from the community.
7: 27 Anyone who eats blood must be cut **o** from the
13: 33 the infected person must shave **o** all hair except the
14: 8 shaving **o** all their hair, and bathing themselves in
14: 9 seventh day, they must again shave **o** all their hair,
15: 13 he must count **o** a period of seven days.
15: 28 she must count **o** a period of seven days.
16: 23 he must take **o** the linen garments he wore when he
17: 4 shed blood and must be cut **o** from the community.
17: 9 you will be cut **o** from the community.
17: 10 I will cut **o** such a person from the community,
17: 14 So whoever eats or drinks blood must be cut **o**.
18: 29 things will be cut **o** from the community of Israel.
19: 8 and must be cut **o** from the community.
19: 27 "Do not trim **o** the hair on your temples or clip the
20: 3 against them and cut them **o** from the community,
20: 5 against them and cut them **o** from the community,
20: 6 against them and cut them **o** from the community.
20: 17 Both of them must be publicly cut **o** from the
20: 18 both of them must be cut **o** from the community,
22: 3 they must be cut **o** from my presence.
23: 15 was lifted up as an offering, count **o** seven weeks.
23: 29 day in humility will be cut **o** from the community.
25: 8 you must count **o** seven Sabbath years,
27: 32 every tenth animal counted **o** from your herds
Nu 5: 23 of leather and wash them **o** into the bitter water.
9: 13 will be cut **o** from the community of Israel for
11: 18 meat to eat! Surely we were better **o** in Egypt!"
14: 3 and little ones will be carried **o** as slaves!
15: 30 and they must be cut **o** from the community.
15: 31 they must be completely cut **o** and suffer the
19: 13 and will be cut **o** from the community of Israel.
19: 20 and do not purify themselves will be cut **o** from the
22: 21 his donkey and started **o** with the Moabite officials.
22: 23 The donkey bolted **o** the road into a field,
35: 5 Measure **o** 3,000 feet outside the town walls in
Dt 2: 27 and won't turn **o** into the fields on either side.
15: 16 and your family, and he is well **o** with you.
16: 9 "Count **o** seven weeks from the beginning of your
19: 5 swings an ax and the ax head flies **o** the handle,
23: 1 a man's testicles are crushed or his penis is cut **o**,
23: 12 "Mark **o** an area outside the camp for a latrine.
25: 10 'the family of the man whose sandal was pulled **o**'!
25: 12 her hand must be cut **o** without pity.
33: 20 poised there like a lion / to tear **o** an arm or a head.
Jos 3: 13 the water, the flow of water will be cut **o** upstream,
5: 15 "Take **o** your sandals, for this is holy ground."
7: 9 surround us and wipe us **o** the face of the earth.
8: 24 they went back and finished **o** everyone inside.
15: 18 As she got down **o** her donkey, Caleb asked her,
Jdg 1: 6 captured him and cut **o** his thumbs and big toes.
1: 7 had seventy kings with thumbs and big toes cut **o**,
1: 14 As she got down **o** her donkey, Caleb asked her,
5: 19 but they carried **o** no treasures of battle.
7: 24 Cut them **o** at the shallows of the Jordan River at
11: 2 brothers grew up, they chased Jephthah **o** the land.
14: 8 he turned **o** the path to look at the carcass of the
16: 19 and she called in a man to shave **o** his hair,
21: 23 and carried them **o** to the land of their own
Ru 4: 8 So the other family redeemer drew **o** his sandal as
1Sa 5: 4 This time his head and hands had broken **o**
17: 39 "I'm not used to them." So he took them **o** again.
17: 46 and I will kill you and cut **o** your head.
17: 51 David used it to kill the giant and cut **o** his head.
19: 24 He tore **o** his clothes and lay on the ground all day
24: 4 crept forward and cut **o** a piece of Saul's robe.
24: 11 a piece of your robe! I cut it **o**, but I didn't kill you.
25: 13 Four hundred men started **o** with David, and two
25: 23 she quickly got **o** her donkey and bowed low
30: 2 They had carried **o** the women and children
31: 9 So they cut **o** Saul's head and stripped **o** his armor.
2Sa 2: 26 When will you call **o** your men from chasing their
4: 7 they cut **o** his head as he lay there on his bed.
4: 12 They cut **o** their hands and feet and hung their
8: 2 and he measured them **o** in groups with a length of
8: 2 He measured **o** two groups to be executed for
10: 4 and shaved **o** half of each man's beard,
10: 4 cut **o** their robes at the buttocks, and sent them
14: 16 and rescue us from those who would cut us **o** from
16: 9 "Let me go over and cut **o** his head!"
18: 21 what you have seen." The man bowed and ran **o**.
19: 7 Then you will be worse **o** than you have ever
20: 12 So he pulled him **o** the road into a field and threw a
20: 22 and they cut **o** Sheba's head and threw it out to
1Ki 6: 16 He partitioned **o** an inner sanctuary—the Most
13: 24 and the man of God started **o** again. But as he was
2Ki 5: 21 So Gehazi set **o** after him. When Naaman saw him
11: 7 The other two units who are **o** duty on the Sabbath
11: 9 as well as those who were going **o** duty.
12: 18 So Hazael called **o** his attack on Jerusalem.
14: 14 He carried **o** all the gold and silver and all the
17: 23 So Israel was carried **o** to the land of Assyria,
20: 17 by your ancestors—will be carried **o** to Babylon.
1Ch 10: 9 So they stripped **o** Saul's armor and cut **o** his head.
19: 4 their beards, cut **o** their robes at the buttocks,
2Ch 14: 13 and the army of Judah carried **o** vast quantities of
20: 23 After they had finished **o** the army of Seir,
23: 8 as well as those who were going **o** duty.
25: 12 took them to the top of a cliff and threw them **o**,
25: 13 and carrying **o** great quantities of plunder.
25: 24 He carried **o** all the gold and silver and all the
32: 4 cutting **o** the brook that ran through the fields.
Ezr 8: 31 Canal on April 19 and started **o** to Jerusalem.
Ne 4: 23 who were with me—ever took **o** our clothes.
Est 8: 2 The king took **o** his signet ring—which he had
Job 3: 6 Let that night be blotted **o** the calendar,
16: 4 I could spout **o** my criticisms against you
27: 8 hope do the godless have when God cuts them **o**
30: 11 humbled me, so they have thrown **o** all restraint.
40: 24 No one can catch it **o** guard or put a ring in its nose
41: 13 Who can strip **o** its hide, and who can penetrate its
Ps 31: 22 cried out, / "I have been cut **o** from the LORD!"
58: 6 Break **o** their fangs, O God! / Smash the jaws of
68: 2 Drive them **o** like smoke blown by the wind.
75: 10 God says, "I will cut **o** the strength of the wicked,
88: 5 as dead. / I am forgotten, / cut **o** from your care.
88: 16 has overwhelmed me. / Your terrors have cut me **o**.
104: 23 Then people go **o** to their work; / they labor until
105: 16 on the land of Canaan, / cutting **o** its food supply.
107: 23 Some went **o** in ships, / plying the trade routes of
109: 15 but may his name be cut **o** from human memory.
119: 67 I used to wander **o** until you disciplined me;
119: 87 They almost finished me **o**, / but I refused to
119: 119 the wicked of the earth are the scum you skim **o**;
129: 2 but they have never been able to finish me **o**.
143: 12 In your unfailing love, cut **o** all my enemies
Pr 6: 4 Don't put it **o**. Do it now! Don't rest until you do.
8: 29 And when he marked **o** the earth's foundations,
10: 19 for it fosters sin. Be sensible and turn **o** the flow!
10: 31 but the tongue that deceives will be cut **o**.
21: 28 A false witness will be cut **o**, but an attentive
26: 6 a message is as foolish as cutting **o** one's feet
Ecc 4: 2 So I concluded that the dead are better **o** than the
6: 3 I say he would have been better **o** born dead.
8: 12 I know that those who fear God will be better **o**.
SS 5: 3 "But I said, 'I have taken **o** my robe. Should I get
5: 7 The watchman on the wall tore **o** my veil.
8: 9 she is promiscuous, we will shut her **o** from men."
Isa 1: 4 One of Israel, cutting themselves **o** from his help.
1: 25 I will melt you down and skim **o** your slag.
3: 1 will cut **o** the supplies of food and water from
5: 29 seize my people and carry them **o** into captivity,
7: 20 to protect you—and use it to shave **o** everything:
10: 10 we have finished **o** many a kingdom whose gods
10: 13 destroyed their kings, and carried **o** their treasures.
13: 17 and no amount of silver or gold will buy them **o**.
15: 2 shave their heads in sorrow and cut **o** their beards.
18: 5 the LORD will cut you **o** as though with pruning
20: 2 "Take **o** all your clothes, including your sandals."
27: 11 broken **o** and used for kindling beneath the
30: 28 bridle them and lead them **o** to their destruction.
32: 11 you women of ease; throw **o** your unconcern.
32: 11 Strip **o** your pretty clothes, and wear sackcloth in
39: 6 by your ancestors—will be carried **o** to Babylon.
40: 4 out the curves and smooth **o** the rough spots.
40: 12 Who has measured **o** the heavens with his fingers?
40: 24 work withers. The wind carries them **o** like straw.

46: 2 protect the gods. They go **o** into captivity together.
47: 2 the corn. Remove your veil and strip **o** your robe.
59: 2 is a problem—your sins have cut you **o** from God.
Jer 9:21 It has killed **o** the flower of our youth:
18:15 They have stumbled **o** the ancient highways of
20: 5 silver of your kings—will be carried **o** to Babylon.
22:24 signet ring on my right hand, I would pull you **o**.
28: 3 that King Nebuchadnezzar carried **o** to Babylon.
28:10 Then Hananiah the prophet took the yoke **o**
34:16 But now you have shrugged **o** your oath
36:10 This room was just **o** the upper courtyard of the
36:23 took his knife and cut **o** that section of the scroll.
40: 4 Now I am going to take **o** your chains and let you
40:10 Settle in any town you wish, and live **o** the land.
41: 5 They had shaved **o** their beards, torn their clothes,
43: 3 by the Babylonians or be carried **o** into exile."
44:17 to eat, and we were well **o** and had no troubles!
48: 2 they say, 'we will cut her **o** from being a nation.'
48:25 Her horns have been cut **o**, and her arms have been
49:20 Even the little children will be dragged **o**, and their
50:45 Even little children will be dragged **o**, and their
La 3:11 He dragged me **o** the path and tore me with his
4: 9 Those killed by the sword are far better **o** than
Eze 5:11 the Sovereign LORD, I will cut you **o** completely.
12: 3 to show them what it will be like to go **o** into exile.
13:21 I will tear **o** the magic veils and save my people
14: 9 and cut them **o** from the community of Israel.
14:13 cutting **o** their food supply and sending a famine to
16: 9 "Then I bathed you and washed **o** your blood,
17: 4 and plucked **o** its topmost shoot. Then he carried it
17: 9 I will cut **o** its fruit and let its leaves wither
19:12 and tore **o** its branches. / Its stem was destroyed by
21:26 Take **o** your jeweled crown, says the Sovereign
23:17 disgusted with them and broke **o** their relationship.
23:25 They will cut **o** your nose and ears, and any
24:17 Do not uncover your head or take **o** your sandals.
24:23 and your sandals must not be taken **o**.
25: 7 I will cut you **o** from being a nation and destroy
26:16 and take **o** their royal robes and beautiful clothing.
29:19 He will carry **o** their wealth, plundering everything
35: 7 killing **o** all who try to escape and any who return.
42:14 They must first take **o** the clothes they wore while
44:19 they must take **o** the clothes they wear while
44:20 their hair grow too long nor shave it **o** completely.
47: 4 He measured **o** another 1,750 feet and told me to
Da 4:14 "Cut down the tree; lop **o** its branches!
4:14 Shake **o** its leaves, and scatter its fruit!
7: 4 As I watched, its wings were pulled **o**, and it was
8: 7 at the ram and struck it, breaking **o** both its horns.
8: 8 height of its power, its large horn was broken **o**.
8:25 defeating many by catching them **o** guard.
11:30 warships from western coastlands will scare him **o**,
Hos 2: 2 Tell her to take **o** her garish makeup
2: 7 because I was better **o** with him than I am now.'
4:18 and **o** they go to find some prostitutes.
5:14 I will carry them **o**, and there will be no one left to
9: 3 You will be carried **o** to Egypt and Assyria,
10: 7 Samaria will be cut **o**, and its king will disappear
Joel 3: 5 and you have carried them **o** to your pagan
Am 3:14 The horns of the altar will be cut **o** and fall to the
5: 5 For the people of Gilgal will be dragged **o** into
Ob 1:11 help when foreign invaders carried **o** their wealth
Jnh 3: 6 down from his throne and took **o** his royal robes.
Mic 2: 8 You steal the shirts right **o** the backs of those who
3: 2 my people alive and tear the flesh **o** their bones.
3: 6 will close around you, cutting **o** all your visions.
7: 3 The people with money and influence pay them **o**,
Zec 3: 4 others standing there, "Take **o** his filthy clothes."
5: 7 When the heavy lead cover was lifted **o** the basket,
6: 7 The powerful horses were eager to be **o**, to patrol
11:16 meat of the fattest sheep and tear **o** their hooves.
13: 8 Two-thirds of the people in the land will be cut **o**
Mal 2:12 May the LORD cut **o** from the nation of Israel
Mt 4: 6 and said, "If you are the Son of God, jump **o**!
5:30 causes you to sin, cut it **o** and throw it away.
10:14 shake **o** the dust of that place from your feet as you
10:15 and Gomorrah will be better **o** on the judgment day
11: 1 he went **o** teaching and preaching in towns
11:22 and Sidon will be better **o** on the judgment day
11:24 Sodom will be better **o** on the judgment day than
12: 1 so they began breaking **o** heads of wheat
12:45 And so that person is worse **o** than before.
14:13 he went **o** by himself in a boat to a remote area to
18: 8 foot causes you to sin, cut it **o** and throw it away.
26:51 and slashed **o** an ear of the high priest's servant.
27:31 they took **o** the robe and put his own clothes on
27:64 we'll be worse **o** than we were at first."
Mk 2:23 his disciples began breaking **o** heads of wheat.
3: 9 and to have it ready in case he was crowded **o** the
5:20 So the man started **o** to visit the Ten Towns of that
6:11 shake **o** its dust from your feet as you leave.
6:27 So he sent an executioner to the prison to cut **o**
9:43 If your hand causes you to sin, cut it **o**. It is better
9:45 If your foot causes you to sin, cut it **o**. It is better to
11:13 He noticed a fig tree a little way **o** that was in full
14:47 and slashed **o** an ear of the high priest's servant.
14:52 they tore **o** his clothes, but he escaped and ran
15:20 they took **o** the purple robe and put his own clothes
Lk 4: 9 and said, "If you are the Son of God, jump **o**!
5:19 So they went up to the roof, took **o** some tiles,
6: 1 his disciples broke **o** heads of wheat, rubbed **o** the
husks in their hands, and ate the
7:38 fell on his feet, and she wiped them **o** with her hair.
9: 5 shake **o** its dust from your feet as you leave.
10:12 even wicked Sodom will be better **o** than such a
10:14 and Sidon will be better **o** on the judgment day
11:22 him of his weapons, and carries **o** his belongings.
11:26 And so that person is worse **o** than before."
18: 7 him day and night? Will he keep putting them **o**?
22:13 They went **o** to the city and found everything just
22:50 at the high priest's servant and cut **o** his right ear.
Jn 1:45 Philip went **o** to look for Nathanael and told him,
6:22 and that the disciples had gone **o** in their boat,
9:11 'Go to the pool of Siloam and wash **o** the mud.'
13: 4 So he got up from the table, took **o** his robe,
15: 2 He cuts **o** every branch that doesn't produce fruit,
18:10 a sword and slashed **o** the right ear of Malchus,
18:26 a relative of the man whose ear Peter had cut **o**,
Ac 3:23 to that Prophet will be cut **o** from God's people
7:33 "And the Lord said to him, 'Take **o** your sandals,
7:58 The official witnesses took **o** their coats and laid
9: 8 As Saul picked himself up **o** the ground, he found
10: 8 them what had happened and sent them **o** to Joppa.
12: 7 "Quick! Get up!" And the chains fell **o** his wrists.
13:51 But they shook **o** the dust of their feet against them
15:40 Paul chose Silas, and the believers sent them **o**,
16:26 flew open, and the chains of every prisoner fell **o**!
22:23 They yelled, threw **o** their coats, and tossed
27:17 across to the sandbars of Syrtis **o** the African coast,
27:32 So the soldiers cut the ropes and let the boat fall **o**.
27:35 God before them all, and broke **o** a piece and ate it.
27:40 So they cut **o** the anchors and left them in the sea.
28: 5 But Paul shook **o** the snake into the fire and was
Ro 2:25 you are no better **o** than an uncircumcised Gentile.
2:27 much better **o** than you Jews who are circumcised
9: 3 cut **o** from Christ!—if that would save them.
11:17 some of the Jews, have been broken **o**.
11:18 in to replace the branches that were broken **o**.
11:19 "those branches were broken **o** to make room for
11:20 were broken **o** because they didn't believe God,
11:22 But if you stop trusting, you also will be cut **o**.
15:24 go to Spain, and when I do, I will stop **o** in Rome.
1Co 11: 6 wear a head covering, she should cut **o** all her hair.
Gal 4: 1 those children are not much better **o** than slaves
4:17 They are trying to shut you **o** from me so that you
5: 4 keeping the law, you have been cut **o** from Christ!
Eph 4:22 throw **o** your old evil nature and your former way
Col 3: 9 for you have stripped **o** your old evil nature and all
Heb 12: 1 let us strip **o** every weight that slows us down,
2Pe 2: 6 of ashes and swept them **o** the face of the earth.
2:15 They have wandered **o** the right road and followed
2:20 its slave again, they are worse **o** than before.

OFFEND (2) [OFFENDED, OFFENDER, OFFENDERS, OFFENDS, OFFENSE, OFFENSES]

Mt 17:27 However, we don't want to **o** them, so go down to
Jn 6:61 so he said to them, "Does this **o** you?

OFFENDED (13) [OFFEND]

Ge 40: 1 Pharaoh's chief cup-bearer and chief baker **o** him.
1Sa 20: 1 How have I **o** your father that he is so determined
25:28 Please forgive me if I have **o** in any way.
Pr 18:19 It's harder to make amends with an **o** friend than to
Isa 3: 8 They have **o** his glorious presence among them.
Jnh 1: 7 Then the crew cast lots to see which of them had **o**
Mt 11: 6 'God blesses those who are not **o** by me.' "
13:57 And they were deeply **o** and refused to believe in
15:12 "Do you realize you **o** the Pharisees by what you
Mk 6: 3 They were deeply **o** and refused to believe in him.
Lk 7:23 'God blesses those who are not **o** by me.' "
Jn 7:21 on the Sabbath by healing a man, and you were **o**.
1Co 1:23 the Jews are **o**, and the Gentiles say it's all

OFFENDER (2) [OFFEND]

Ex 21:23 then the **o** must be punished according to the
21:23 If the result is death, the **o** must be executed.

OFFENDERS (1) [OFFEND]

Ezr 9: 2 the officials and leaders are some of the worst **o**."

OFFENDS (2) [OFFEND]

Ps 139:24 Point out anything in me that **o** you, / and lead me
Col 3:13 other's faults and forgive the person who **o** you.

OFFENSE (11) [OFFEND]

Lev 5:19 for they have been guilty of an **o** against the
17: 4 that person will be guilty of a capital **o**.
20: 9 must be put to death. They are guilty of a capital **o**.
20:11 woman must die, for they are guilty of a capital **o**.
20:12 contrary to nature and are guilty of a capital **o**.
20:13 a detestable act and are guilty of a capital **o**.
20:16 Both must die, for they are guilty of a capital **o**.
20:19 close relative. Both parties are guilty of a capital **o**.
20:20 and woman involved are guilty of a capital **o**
20:27 death by stoning. They are guilty of a capital **o**."
1Co 10:32 Don't give **o** to Jews or Gentiles or the church of

OFFENSES (4) [OFFEND]

Nu 18: 1 held responsible for any **o** related to the sanctuary.
18:23 and they will be held responsible for any **o** against
Pr 10:12 Hatred stirs up quarrels, but love covers all **o**.
Isa 44:22 I have scattered your **o** like the clouds. Oh,

OFFER (165) [OFFERED, OFFERING, OFFERINGS, OFFERS, PEACE-OFFERING]

Ex 3:18 wilderness to **o** sacrifices to the LORD our God.'
5: 3 so we can **o** sacrifices to the LORD our God.
5: 8 into the wilderness to **o** sacrifices to their God.
5:17 'Let us go, so we can **o** sacrifices to the LORD.'
8: 8 people go, so they can **o** sacrifices to the LORD."
8:25 Go ahead and **o** sacrifices to your God," he said.
8:26 The Egyptians would detest the sacrifices that we **o**
8:26 If we **o** them here where they can see us, they will
8:27 wilderness to **o** sacrifices to the LORD our God,
8:28 "I will let you go to **o** sacrifices to the LORD
13:15 That is why we now **o** all the firstborn males to the
20:24 **O** on such altars your sacrifices to me—your burnt
23: 5 do not walk by. Instead, stop and **o** to help.
29:28 whenever the people of Israel **o** up peace offerings
29:38 "This is what you are to **o** on the altar. **O** two
one-year-old lambs each day,
29:40 **o** two quarts of fine flour mixed with one quart of
29:40 also, **o** one quart of wine as a drink offering.
29:41 **O** the other lamb in the evening, along with the
29:42 **O** it in the LORD's presence at the Tabernacle
30: 9 Do not **o** any unholy incense on this altar, or any
34:25 "You must not **o** bread made with yeast as a
Lev 3: 1 The animal you **o** to the LORD must have no
5: 8 who will **o** one of the birds as the sin offering.
5:10 The priest will **o** the second bird as a whole burnt
7: 3 The priest will then **o** all its fat on the altar,
14:12 and **o** them as a guilt offering by lifting them up
14:19 "Then the priest must **o** the sin offering and again
14:20 and **o** it on the altar along with the grain offering.
14:30 "Then the priest will **o** the two turtledoves
15:30 The priest will **o** one for a sin offering
17: 8 If you **o** a whole burnt offering or a sacrifice
17: 9 entrance of the Tabernacle to **o** it to the LORD,
19: 5 **o** it properly so it will be accepted on your behalf.
19: 6 You must eat it on the same day you **o** it or on the
21: 8 them as holy because they **o** up food to your God.
21:17 defects will not qualify to **o** food to their God.
21:21 he has a blemish, he may not **o** food to his God.
22:18 If you **o** a whole burnt offering to the LORD,
22:21 you must **o** an animal that has no physical defects
23:13 you must also **o** one quart of wine as a drink
23:19 Then you must **o** one male goat as a sin offering
Nu 1:53 **o** the people of Israel protection from the
6:11 The priest will **o** one of the birds for a sin offering
6:14 and **o** these sacrifices to the LORD:
9: 6 so they could not **o** their Passover lambs that day.
9:11 They must **o** the Passover sacrifice one month
28: 3 you must **o** two one-year-old male lambs with no
28: 5 With each lamb you must **o** a grain offering of two
28: 8 **O** the second lamb in the evening with the same
28:15 on the first day of each month you must **o** one male
28:22 You must also **o** a male goat as a sin offering,
28:30 **o** one male goat to make atonement for yourselves.
Dt 12:14 There you must **o** your burnt offerings and do
12:27 You must **o** the meat and blood of your burnt
20:10 town to attack it, first **o** its people terms for peace.
26:12 "Every third year you must **o** a special tithe of
27: 6 On the altar you must **o** burnt offerings to the
28:68 There you will **o** to sell yourselves to your enemies
33:10 and **o** whole burnt offerings on the altar.
33:19 to **o** proper sacrifices there. / They benefit from the
Jos 2:14 "We **o** our own lives as a guarantee for your
1Sa 1:21 and their children went on their annual trip to **o** a
2:28 to **o** sacrifices on my altar, to burn incense, and to
9: 7 "But we don't have anything to **o** him,"
9: 8 We can at least **o** it to him and see what happens!"
10: 4 They will greet you and **o** you two of the loaves,
13:12 So I felt obliged to **o** the burnt offering myself
18:22 Why don't you accept the king's **o** and become his
18:26 David was delighted to accept the **o**. So before the
2Sa 15: 7 "Let me go to Hebron to **o** a sacrifice to the
1Ki 8:38 and if your people **o** a prayer concerning their
12:27 When they go to Jerusalem to **o** sacrifices at the
13: 1 was approaching the altar to **o** a sacrifice.
22:49 with your men." But Jehoshaphat refused the **o**.
2Ki 5:17 From now on I will never again **o** any burnt
10:19 for I am going to **o** a great sacrifice to Baal.
10:24 So they were all inside the temple to **o** sacrifices
17:32 priests to **o** sacrifices at the pagan shrines.
17:35 before them or serve them or **o** sacrifices to them.
17:36 and bow before him; **o** sacrifices to him alone.
1Ch 21:24 I will not **o** a burnt offering that has cost me
23:13 to **o** sacrifices in the LORD's presence, to serve
29:17 and I have watched your people **o** their gifts
2Ch 6:29 and if your people **o** a prayer concerning their
11:16 where they could **o** sacrifices to the LORD,
31: 2 and Levites into divisions to **o** the burnt offerings
35:12 so they could **o** them to the LORD according to
Ezr 6: 3 It must be rebuilt on the site where Jews used to **o**
6:10 Then they will be able to **o** acceptable sacrifices to
Ne 4: 2 build the wall in a day if they **o** enough sacrifices?
Job 1: 5 and **o** a burnt offering for each of them.
40:20 The mountains **o** it their best food, where all the
42: 8 servant Job and **o** a burnt offering for yourselves.
Ps 4: 5 **O** proper sacrifices, / and trust in the LORD.
27: 6 At his Tabernacle I will **o** sacrifices with shouts of
37:30 The godly **o** good counsel; / they know what is
56:12 O God, / and **o** a sacrifice of thanks for your help.
69:21 for food; / they **o** me sour wine to satisfy my thirst.
107:22 Let them **o** sacrifices of thanksgiving / and sing
116:12 What can I **o** the LORD / for all he has done for
116:17 I will **o** you a sacrifice of thanksgiving / and call
130: 4 But you **o** forgiveness, / that we might learn to fear
SS 8: 7 he owned, his **o** would be utterly despised."
Isa 1:15 Even though you **o** many prayers, I will not listen.
19:15 or poor, important or unknown, can **o** any help.
29: 1 Year after year you **o** your many sacrifices.
34: 6 the LORD will **o** a great sacrifice in the rich city
Jer 6:14 They **o** superficial treatments for my people's
7:18 and make cakes to **o** to the Queen of Heaven.

8:11 They **o** superficial treatments for my people's
11:12 will pray to their idols and **o** incense before them.
16: 7 No one will **o** a meal to comfort those who mourn
33:18 And there will always be Levitical priests to **o**
35: 2 one of the inner rooms, and **o** them some wine."
48:35 "for they **o** sacrifices at the pagan shrines and burn
La 4:17 but we were looking to nations that could **o** no help
Eze 20:31 For when you **o** gifts to them and give your little
42:13 It is there that the priests who **o** sacrifices to the
43:23 **o** another young bull that has no defects and a
43:24 and **o** them as a burnt offering to the LORD.
44:15 and **o** the fat and blood of the sacrifices,
44:27 the sanctuary, he must **o** a sin offering for himself,
46: 5 He is to **o** one gallon of olive oil for each half
46: 7 With each half bushel of flour he must **o** one
46:12 and he will **o** his sacrifices just as he does on
Da 2:46 and he commanded his people to **o** sacrifices
Hos 4:13 They **o** sacrifices to idols on the tops of mountains.
4:19 will die in shame because they **o** sacrifices to idols.
5: 6 and herds to **o** sacrifices to the LORD.
9: 4 None of the sacrifices you **o** there will please him.
9: 4 but they may not **o** it to the LORD.
14: 2 so that we may **o** you the sacrifice of praise.
Joel 1: 9 no grain or wine to **o** at the Temple of the LORD.
1:13 is no grain or wine to **o** at the Temple of your God.
2:14 give you so much that you will be able to **o** grain
Am 4: 4 and **o** your sacrifices to the idols at Bethel
4: 4 **O** sacrifices each morning and bring your tithes
Jnh 2: 9 But I will **o** sacrifices to you with songs of praise,
Mic 6: 7 Should we **o** him thousands of rams and tens of
Hag 2:14 they do and everything they **o** is defiled.
Mal 1: 8 And isn't it wrong to **o** animals that are crippled
1:11 All around the world they **o** sweet incense and pure
3: 3 so that they may once again **o** acceptable sacrifices
Mt 5:24 Then come and **o** your sacrifice to God.
Mk 12:33 This is more important than to **o** all of the burnt
Lk 6:29 If someone demands your coat, **o** your shirt also.
7:44 you didn't **o** me water to wash the dust from my
Jn 4:12 How can you **o** better water than he and his sons
Ac 13:46 of eternal life—well, we will **o** it to Gentiles.
22: 1 Paul said, "listen to me as I **o** my defense."
24:17 money to aid my people and to **o** sacrifices to God.
Ro 11:12 because the Jews turned down God's **o** of
15:16 and **o** you up as a fragrant sacrifice to God so that
Heb 2:17 then could **o** a sacrifice that would take away the
5: 3 That is why he has to **o** sacrifices, both for their
7:27 He does not need to **o** sacrifices every day like the
8: 3 And since every high priest is required to **o** gifts
8: 4 since there already are priests who **o** the gifts
9: 9 and sacrifices that the priests **o** are not able to
9:25 Nor did he enter heaven to **o** himself again
9:25 Place year after year to **o** the blood of an animal.
10:18 there is no need to **o** any more sacrifices.
13:15 let us continually **o** our sacrifice of praise to God
1Pe 2: 5 who **o** the spiritual sacrifices that please him

OFFERED (100) [OFFER]

Ge 46: 1 he **o** sacrifices to the God of his father, Isaac.
Ex 23:18 "Sacrificial blood must never be **o** together with
23:19 It must be **o** to the LORD your God.
40:29 On it he **o** a burnt offering and a grain offering,
Lev 2: 8 has been prepared before being **o** to the LORD,
4:28 with no physical defects. It will be **o** for their sin.
6:20 half to be **o** in the morning and half to be **o** in the evening.
7:15 meat must be eaten on the same day it is **o**.
21:22 However, he may eat from the food **o** to God,
22:22 or a scab must never be **o** to the LORD by fire on
22:23 or stunted, it may still be **o** as a freewill offering,
22:23 but it may not be **o** to fulfill a vow.
22:24 or is castrated, it may never be **o** to the LORD.
22:25 or defective animals from foreigners to be **o** as a
Nu 15: 5 For each lamb **o** as a whole burnt offering,
15:24 and it must be **o** along with the prescribed grain
18:15 or animal, that is **o** to the LORD will be yours.
23:14 and **o** a young bull and a ram on each altar.
23:30 and **o** a young bull and a ram on each altar.
28: 2 and **o** according to my instructions.
28:24 These will be **o** in addition to the regular whole
28:27 A special whole burnt offering will be **o** that day,
Dt 16: 6 It must be **o** at the place the LORD your God will
26:14 and I have not **o** any of it to the dead.
32:17 They **o** sacrifices to demons, non-gods, / to gods
Jdg 2: 5 and they **o** sacrifices to the LORD.
13:19 and **o** it on a rock as a sacrifice to the LORD.
1Sa 2:13 Whenever anyone **o** a sacrifice, Eli's sons would
6:15 and sacrifices were **o** to the LORD that day by the
7: 9 and **o** it to the LORD as a whole burnt offering.
11:15 Then they **o** peace offerings to the LORD,
17:25 reward the king has **o** to anyone who kills him?
2Sa 15:24 Then they **o** sacrifices there until everyone had
24:25 and **o** burnt offerings and peace offerings.
1Ki 3: 3 **o** sacrifices and burned incense at the local altars.
8:62 and all Israel with him **o** sacrifices to the LORD.
8:64 He **o** burnt offerings, grain offerings, and the fat of
9:25 Three times each year Solomon **o** burnt offerings
12:32 There at Bethel he himself **o** sacrifices to the
12:33 Jeroboam **o** sacrifices on the altar at Bethel.
22:43 and the people still **o** sacrifices and burned incense
2Ki 3:20 about the time when the morning sacrifice was **o**,
12: 3 and the people still **o** sacrifices and burned incense
14: 4 where the people **o** sacrifices and burned incense.
15: 4 where the people **o** sacrifices and burned incense.
15:35 where the people **o** sacrifices and burned incense.
16: 4 He **o** sacrifices and burned incense at the pagan
23: 5 They had also **o** incense to Baal, and to the sun,
1Ch 21:28 he **o** sacrifices there at Araunah's threshing floor.
2Ch 7: 4 and all the people **o** sacrifices to the LORD.
7: 5 King Solomon **o** a sacrifice of 22,000 oxen
8:13 Extra sacrifices were **o** on the Sabbaths, on new
28: 3 He **o** sacrifices in the valley of the son of Hinnom,
28: 4 He **o** sacrifices and burned incense at the pagan
28:23 He **o** sacrifices to the gods of Damascus who had
29:30 So they **o** joyous praise and bowed down in
Ezr 3: 5 They also **o** the regular burnt offerings
7:17 all of which will be **o** on the altar of the Temple of
8:35 They also **o** twelve goats as a sin offering.
Ne 12:43 Many sacrifices were **o** on that joyous day, for God
Ps 106:28 at Peor; / they even ate sacrifices **o** to the dead!
141: 2 Accept my prayer as incense **o** to you, / and my
Pr 1:25 ignored my advice and rejected the correction I **o**.
7:14 "I've **o** my sacrifices and just finished my vows.
Isa 1:29 **o** sacrifices to idols in your groves of sacred oaks.
Jer 32: 7 By law you have the right to buy it before it is **o** to
32: 8 By law you have the right to buy it before it is **o** to
Eze 6:13 and great oak where they **o** incense to their gods,
20:28 they **o** sacrifices and incense on every high hill
20:28 They roused my fury as they **o** up sacrifices to
44: 7 you profaned my Temple even as you **o** me my
44:24 assistants to boil the sacrifices **o** by the people."
Da 8:11 armies by canceling the daily sacrifices **o** to him
Hos 13:13 The people have been **o** new birth, but they are like
Jnh 1:16 and they **o** him a sacrifice and vowed to serve him.
Mal 1:10 so that these worthless sacrifices could not be **o**!
Mk 15:23 They **o** him wine drugged with myrrh, but he
Lk 2:24 So they **o** a sacrifice according to what was
19:44 because you have rejected the opportunity God **o**
Jn 6:51 this bread is my flesh, **o** so the world may live."
Ac 8:18 people's heads, he **o** money to buy this power.
15:29 You must abstain from eating food **o** to idols,
21:25 They should not eat food **o** to idols, nor consume
21:26 and sacrifices would be **o** for each of them.
Ro 11:15 For since the Jews' rejection meant that God **o**
1Co 8: 7 so when they eat food that has been **o** to idols,
10:20 What I am saying is that these sacrifices are **o** to
10:25 Don't ask whether or not it was **o** to idols, and
10:27 Eat whatever is **o** to you and don't ask any
10:28 warns you that this meat has been **o** to an idol.
Heb 5: 7 he **o** prayers and pleadings, with a loud cry
9:14 Christ **o** himself to God as a perfect sacrifice for
10:12 But our High Priest **o** himself to God as one
11:17 It was by faith that Abraham **o** Isaac as a sacrifice
Jas 2:21 because of what he did when he **o** his son Isaac on
5:15 And their prayer **o** in faith will heal the sick,
Rev 2:14 He taught them to worship idols by eating food **o**
2:20 eat food **o** to idols, and commit sexual sin.
8: 3 to be **o** on the gold altar before the throne.

OFFERING (603) [OFFER]

BURNT OFFERING (139) Ge 22:2,3,6,13; Ex 18:12; 29:18,25,42; 30:28; 31:9; 35:16; 40:6,10,29,29; Lev 1:3,9,10, 13,14,17; 3:5; 5:7,10; 6:9,9,10,12,12; 7:8,37; 8:18,21,28; 9:2, 3,7,12,14,16,17,22,24; 10:19; 12:6,8; 14:19,22,31; 15:15,30; 16:3,5,24,24; 17:8; 22:18; 23:12; Nu 6:11,14,16; 7:15,21,27, 33,39,45,51,57,63,69,75,81; 8:12; 15:3,3,5,8,24; 23:15; 28:6, 10,10,11,13,14,15,19,27,31; 29:2,8,11,13,16,19,22,25,28,31, 34,36,38; Dt 13:16; 18:10; Jdg 6:26; 11:31; 13:16,23; 1Sa 6:14; 7:9,10; 13:9,9,10,12; 2Sa 24:22; 2Ki 3:27; 10:25; 16:13, 15,15; 1Ch 6:49; 21:24; 2Ch 29:18,24,27,27; Ezr 8:35; Job 1:5; 42:8; Ps 51:16; Eze 43:24; 45:23,25; 46:2,4,12,13

DRINK OFFERING (30) Ex 29:40; Lev 23:13; Nu 6:17; 15:5,7,10,24; 28:7,8,9,10,14,15; 29:16,18,19,21,22,24,25,27, 28,30,31,33,34,37,38; 2Ki 16:13; Php 2:17

FRAGRANT OFFERING (1) Ex 29:41

FREEWILL OFFERING (8) Lev 7:16; 22:18,21,23; Nu 15:3; Dt 16:10; Ezr 1:4; 8:28

GRAIN OFFERING (64) Ex 40:29; Lev 2:1,4,5,6,8,9,10, 14,15; 5:13; 6:14,18,20,21; 7:9,37; 9:4,17; 10:12; 14:20,21, 31; 23:13; Nu 4:16; 6:17; 8:8; 15:4,9,24; 28:5,8,9,31; 29:11, 14,16,18,19,21,22,24,25,27,28,30,31,33,34,37,38; Jdg 13:19, 23; 2Ki 16:13,15,15; 1Ch 21:23; Eze 45:24,25; 46:5,7,11, 14,15

GUILT OFFERING (28) Lev 5:15,16,18,19; 6:6,17; 7:1,2,5,7,37; 14:12,13,14,17,21,21,24,25,28; 19:21,22; Nu 6:12; 1Sa 6:3,4,17; Ezr 10:19,19

HOLY OFFERING (3) Lev 10:17; 14:13; Nu 18:10

LORD'S* OFFERING (2) Nu 9:7,13

OFFERING MADE BY FIRE (14) Ex 29:41; Lev 1:9,13, 17; 2:2,9; 3:3,5,9,14,16; Nu 15:10; 28:6,8

PEACE OFFERING (39) Lev 3:1,3,6,9; 4:10,26,31,35; 7:12,13,18,20,29,32,33,37; 9:4,18,22; 19:5; 22:21; 23:19; Nu 6:14,17; 7:17,23,29,35,41,47,53,59,65,71,77,83; 15:8; Eze 46:2,12

SIN OFFERING (99) Ex 29:14; Lev 4:14,20,21,21,24, 25,29,32,33; 5:6,7,8,9,11,11,12; 6:17,25,25,30; 7:7,37; 8:2, 14; 9:2,3,7,8,10,15,22; 10:16,17,19,19; 14:13,19,22,31; 15:15,30; 16:3,5,6,9,11,11,15,25; 23:19; Nu 6:11,14,16; 7:16, 22,28,34,40,46,52,58,64,70,76,82; 8:8,12; 15:24,25,27; 28:15, 22; 29:5,11,11,16,19,22,25,28,31,34,38; 2Ch 29:21,23, 24,24; Ezr 6:17; 8:35; Eze 43:19,21,22,25; 44:27; 45:19,22,23,25

Ge 4: 4 best of his flock. The LORD accepted Abel's **o**,
22: 2 Sacrifice him there as a burnt **o** on one of the
22: 3 Then he chopped wood to build a fire for a burnt **o**
22: 6 Abraham placed the wood for the burnt **o** on
22:13 and sacrificed it as a burnt **o** on the altar in place of
35:14 He then poured wine over it as an **o** to God
Ex 18:12 Then Jethro presented a burnt **o** and gave sacrifices
25: 2 that everyone who wants to may bring me an **o**.
29:14 the dung) outside the camp, and burn it as a sin **o**.
29:18 This is a burnt **o** to the LORD, which is very
29:25 and burn it on the altar as a burnt **o** that will be
29:36 Each day you must sacrifice a young bull as an **o**
29:36 Afterward make an **o** to cleanse the altar.
29:40 olive oil; also, offer one quart of wine as a drink **o**.
29:41 will be a fragrant **o** to the LORD, an **o** made by fire.
29:42 "This is to be a daily burnt **o** given from
30:10 blood from the **o** made for the atonement of sin.
30:14 twentieth birthday must give this **o** to the LORD.
30:15 When this **o** is given to the LORD to make
30:28 the altar of burnt **o** with all its utensils,
31: 9 the altar of burnt **o** with all its utensils;
35:16 the altar of burnt **o**; the bronze grating of the altar
35:24 and bronze objects as their **o** to the LORD.
40: 6 Place the altar of burnt **o** in front of the Tabernacle
40:10 Sprinkle the anointing oil on the altar of burnt **o**
40:29 and he placed the altar of burnt **o** near the
40:29 On it he offered a burnt **o** and a grain **o**,
Lev 1: 3 "If your sacrifice for a whole burnt **o** is from the
1: 9 It is a whole burnt **o** made by fire, very pleasing to
1:10 "If your sacrifice for a whole burnt **o** is from the
1:13 It is a whole burnt **o** made by fire, very pleasing to
1:14 "If you bring a bird as a burnt **o** to the LORD,
1:17 It is a whole burnt **o** made by fire, very pleasing to
2: 1 "When you bring a grain **o** to the LORD, the **o** must consist of choice flour.
2: 2 Bring this **o** to one of Aaron's sons, and he will
2: 2 It is an **o** made by fire, very pleasing to the
2: 4 you present some kind of baked bread as a grain **o**,
2: 5 If your grain **o** is cooked on a griddle, it must be
2: 6 into pieces and pour oil on it; it is a kind of grain **o**.
2: 7 If your **o** is prepared in a pan, it also must be made
2: 8 "No matter how a grain **o** has been prepared
2: 9 The priests will take a token portion of the grain **o**
2: 9 and burn it on the altar as an **o** made by fire,
2:10 The rest of the grain **o** will be given to Aaron
2:11 or honey may be burned as an **o** to the LORD by
2:12 but these must never be burned on the altar as an **o**
2:14 "If you present a grain **o** to the LORD from the
2:15 Since it is a grain **o**, put olive oil on it and sprinkle
2:16 and burn it as an **o** given to the LORD by fire.
3: 1 "If you want to present a peace **o** from the herd,
3: 3 Part of this peace **o** must be presented to the LORD as an **o** made by fire.
3: 5 on the altar on top of the burnt **o** on the wood fire.
3: 5 It is an **o** made by fire, very pleasing to the
3: 6 "If you present a peace **o** to the LORD from the
3: 9 Part of this peace **o** must be presented to the LORD as an **o** made by fire.
3:11 the altar as food, an **o** given to the LORD by fire.
3:12 "If you bring a goat as your **o** to the LORD,
3:14 Part of this **o** must be presented to the LORD as an **o** made by fire.
3:16 burn them on the altar as food, an **o** made by fire;
4:10 done with the bull or cow sacrificed as a peace **o**.
4:14 the community must bring a young bull for a sin **o**
4:20 following the same procedure as with the sin **o** for
4:21 just as is done with the sin **o** for the high priest.
4:21 This is a sin **o** for the entire community of Israel.
4:23 he must bring as his **o** a male goat with no physical
4:24 offerings are slaughtered. This will be his sin **o**.
4:25 priest will dip his finger into the blood of the sin **o**,
4:26 fat on the altar, just as is done with the peace **o**.
4:28 they must bring as their **o** a female goat with no
4:29 They are to lay a hand on the head of the sin **o**
4:31 all the goat's fat, just as is done with the peace **o**.
4:32 "If any of the people bring a sheep as their sin **o**,
4:33 They are to lay a hand on the head of the sin **o**
4:35 just as is done with a sheep presented as a peace **o**.
5: 6 This will be a sin **o** to remove their sin,
5: 7 One of the birds will be a sin **o**, and the other will be a burnt **o**.
5: 8 who will offer one of the birds as the sin **o**.
5: 9 the blood of the sin **o** against the sides of the altar,
5:10 priest will offer the second bird as a whole burnt **o**,
5:11 bring two quarts of choice flour for their sin **o**.
5:11 Since it is a sin **o**, they must not mix it with olive
5:12 just like any other **o** given to the LORD by fire. This will be their sin **o**.
5:13 will belong to the priest, just as with the grain **o**."
5:15 to the LORD a ram from the flock as their guilt **o**.
5:16 for them with the ram sacrificed as a guilt **o**,
5:18 bring to the priest a ram from the flock as a guilt **o**.
5:19 This is a guilt **o**, for they have been guilty of an
6: 6 They must then bring a guilt **o** to the priest,
6: 6 This **o** must be a ram with no physical defects
6: 9 following instructions regarding the whole burnt **o**.
6: 9 The burnt **o** must be left on the altar until the next
6:10 on duty must clean out the ashes of the burnt **o**
6:12 the fire and arrange the daily whole burnt **o** on it.
6:12 peace offerings on top of this daily whole burnt **o**.
6:14 "These are the instructions regarding the grain **o**.
6:14 Aaron's sons must present this **o** to the LORD in
6:17 Like the sin **o** and the guilt offering, it is most
6:18 generation to generation, may eat of the grain **o**,
6:20 they must bring to the LORD a grain **o** of two
6:21 You must present this grain **o**, and it will be very
6:22 they will be inducted into office by **o** this same
6:25 sons these further instructions regarding the sin **o**.
6:25 The animal given as a sin **o** is most holy and must
6:29 males from a priest's family may eat of this **o**,
6:30 the blood of a sin **o** has been taken into the
7: 1 "These are the instructions for the guilt **o**, which is
7: 2 The animal sacrificed as a guilt **o** must be
7: 5 The priests will burn these parts on the altar as an **o** to the LORD made by fire. It is a guilt **o**.

7: 7 "For both the sin **o** and the guilt **o**, the meat
7: 8 In the case of the whole burnt **o**, the hide of the
7: 9 Any grain **o** that has been baked in an oven,
7:12 If you present your peace **o** as a thanksgiving **o**,
7:13 This peace **o** of thanksgiving must also be
7:16 if you bring an **o** to fulfill a vow or as a freewill **o**,
7:18 If any of the meat from this peace **o** is eaten on the
7:18 you will receive no credit for bringing it as an **o**.
7:20 but eats meat from a peace **o** that was presented to
7:25 Anyone who eats fat from an **o** given to the
7:29 When you present a peace **o** to the LORD,
7:30 Present it to him with your own hands as an **o**
7:32 You are to give the right thigh of your peace **o** to
7:33 the blood and offers the fat of the peace **o**.
7:37 These are the instructions for the whole burnt **o**, the grain **o**, the sin **o**, the guilt **o**, the ordination **o**, and the peace **o**.
8: 2 anointing oil, the bull for the sin **o**, the two rams,
8:14 Then Moses brought in the bull for the sin **o**,
8:18 the ram to the LORD for the whole burnt **o**,
8:21 the entire ram on the altar as a whole burnt **o**.
8:21 It was an **o** given to the LORD by fire,
8:28 and burned them on the altar on top of the burnt **o** as an ordination **o**.
8:28 It was an **o** given to the LORD by fire,
9: 2 "Take a young bull for a sin **o** and a ram for a whole burnt **o**,
9: 3 to take a male goat for a sin **o** for themselves
9: 3 and a year-old lamb for a whole burnt **o**,
9: 4 tell them to take a bull and a ram for a peace **o**
9: 4 and flour mixed with olive oil for a grain **o**.
9: 7 "Approach the altar and present your sin **o**
9: 7 and your whole burnt **o** to make atonement for
9: 8 and slaughtered the calf as a sin **o** for himself.
9:10 and the lobe of the liver from the sin **o**,
9:12 slaughtered the animal for the whole burnt **o**.
9:14 also burned them on the altar as a whole burnt **o**.
9:15 the people's goat and presented it as their sin **o**,
9:16 Then he brought the whole burnt **o** and presented it
9:17 He also brought the grain **o**, burning a handful of
9:17 in addition to the regular morning burnt **o**.
9:18 the bull and the ram for the people's peace **o**.
9:21 the breasts and right thighs as an **o** to the LORD,
9:22 Then, after presenting the sin **o**, the whole burnt **o**, and the peace **o**,
9:24 and consumed the burnt **o** and the fat on the altar.
10:12 "Take what is left of the grain **o** after the handful
10:16 know what had happened to the goat of the sin **o**,
10:17 "Why didn't you eat the sin **o** in the sanctuary
10:17 he demanded. "It is a holy **o**! It was given to you
10:19 "Today my sons presented both their sin **o** and their burnt **o** to the LORD,"
10:19 have approved if I had eaten the sin **o** today?"
12: 6 must bring a year-old lamb for a whole burnt **o**
12: 6 a young pigeon or turtledove for a purification **o**.
12: 8 One will be for the whole burnt **o** and the other for the purification **o**.
14:12 and offer them as a guilt **o** by lifting them up
14:13 As with the sin **o**, the guilt **o** will be given to the priest. It is a most holy **o**.
14:14 then take some of the blood from the guilt **o**
14:17 right foot, in addition to the blood of the guilt **o**.
14:19 "Then the priest must offer the sin **o** and again
14:19 the priest will slaughter the whole burnt **o**
14:20 and offer it on the altar along with the grain **o**.
14:21 two lambs must bring one male lamb for a guilt **o**,
14:21 of choice flour mixed with olive oil as a grain **o**
14:21 The guilt **o** will be presented by lifting it up,
14:22 One of the pair must be used for a sin **o** and the other for a whole burnt **o**.
14:24 The priest will take the lamb for the guilt **o**,
14:24 and lift them up before the LORD as an **o** to him.
14:25 the priest will slaughter the lamb for the guilt **o**
14:28 right foot, in addition to the blood of the guilt **o**.
14:31 One of them is for a sin **o** and the other for a whole burnt **o**,
14:31 to be presented along with the grain **o**.
15:15 one for a sin **o** and the other for a whole burnt **o**.
15:30 The priest will offer one for a sin **o** and the other for a whole burnt **o**.
16: 3 He must first bring a young bull for a sin **o** and a ram for a whole burnt **o**.
16: 5 then bring him two male goats for a sin **o** and a ram for a whole burnt **o**.
16: 6 "Aaron will present the bull as a sin **o**, to make
16: 9 the LORD will be presented by Aaron as a sin **o**.
16:11 "Then Aaron will present the young bull as a sin **o**
16:11 After he has slaughtered this bull for the sin **o**,
16:15 "Then Aaron must slaughter the goat as a sin **o** for
16:24 and go out to sacrifice his own whole burnt **o**
16:24 and the whole burnt **o** for the people.
16:25 He must also burn all the fat of the sin **o** on the
17: 4 the Tabernacle to present it as an **o** to the LORD,
17: 7 by **o** sacrifices to evil spirits out in the fields.
17: 8 If you offer a whole burnt **o** or a sacrifice
19: 5 "When you sacrifice a peace **o** to the LORD,
19: 7 If any of the **o** is eaten on the third day, it will be
19:21 must bring a ram as a guilt **o** and present it to the
19:22 the LORD with the sacrificial ram of the guilt **o**,
20: 4 And if the people of the community ignore this **o**
22:18 If you offer a whole burnt **o** to the LORD,
22:18 whether to fulfill a vow or as a freewill **o**,
22:21 "If you bring a peace **o** to the LORD from the
22:21 or flock, whether to fulfill a vow or as a freewill **o**,
22:23 or stunted, it may still be offered as a freewill **o**,
22:27 it will be acceptable as an **o** given to the LORD
22:29 When you bring a thanksgiving **o** to the LORD,
23: 8 the people must present an **o** to the LORD by fire.
23:12 physical defects as a whole burnt **o** to the LORD.
23:13 A grain **o** must accompany it consisting of three
23:13 It will be an **o** given to the LORD by fire, and it
23:13 you must also offer one quart of wine as a drink **o**.
23:14 until after you have brought this **o** to your God.
23:15 the day the bundle of grain was lifted up as an **o**,
23:16 and bring an **o** of new grain to the LORD.
23:17 of bread to be lifted up before the LORD as an **o**.
23:17 They will be an **o** to the LORD from the first of
23:19 Then you must offer one male goat as a sin **o**
23:19 and two one-year-old male lambs as a peace **o**.
23:36 and present another **o** to the LORD by fire.
24: 7 It will serve as a token **o**, to be burned in place of the bread as an **o** given to
27: 9 one that is acceptable as an **o** to the LORD—
27:11 one that is not acceptable as an **o** to the LORD—
Nu 4:16 the fragrant incense, the daily grain **o**,
5:15 **o** of two quarts of barley flour to be presented on
5:15 olive oil or frankincense, for it is a jealousy **o**—
5:15 an **o** of inquiry to find out if she is guilty.
5:18 must unbind her hair and place the **o** of inquiry—the jealousy **o**—
5:25 " 'Then the priest will take the jealousy **o** from
6:11 The priest will offer one of the birds for a sin **o** and the other for a burnt **o**.
6:12 must bring a one-year-old male lamb for a guilt **o**.
6:14 male lamb without defect for a burnt **o**,
6:14 female lamb without defect for a sin **o**, a ram without defect for a peace **o**,
6:16 the LORD: first the sin **o** and the burnt **o**;
6:17 then the ram for a peace **o**, along with the basket of
6:17 The priest must also make the prescribed grain **o** and drink **o**.
6:20 the gifts up before the LORD in a gesture of **o**.
7:12 leader of the tribe of Judah, presented his **o**.
7:13 The **o** consisted of a silver platter weighing about
7:15 a ram, and a one-year-old male lamb as a burnt **o**;
7:16 a male goat for a sin **o**;
7:17 and five one-year-old male lambs for a peace **o**.
7:17 This was the **o** brought by Nahshon son of
7:18 leader of the tribe of Issachar, presented his **o**.
7:19 The **o** consisted of a silver platter weighing about
7:21 a ram, and a one-year-old male lamb as a burnt **o**;
7:22 a male goat for a sin **o**;
7:23 and five one-year-old male lambs for a peace **o**.
7:23 This was the **o** brought by Nethanel son of Zuar.
7:24 leader of the tribe of Zebulun, presented his **o**.
7:25 The **o** consisted of a silver platter weighing about
7:27 a ram, and a one-year-old male lamb as a burnt **o**;
7:28 a male goat for a sin **o**;
7:29 and five one-year-old male lambs for a peace **o**.
7:29 This was the **o** brought by Eliab son of Helon.
7:30 leader of the tribe of Reuben, presented his **o**.
7:31 The **o** consisted of a silver platter weighing about
7:33 a ram, and a one-year-old male lamb as a burnt **o**;
7:34 a male goat for a sin **o**;
7:35 and five one-year-old male lambs for a peace **o**.
7:35 This was the **o** brought by Elizur son of Shedeur.
7:36 leader of the tribe of Simeon, presented his **o**.
7:37 The **o** consisted of a silver platter weighing about
7:39 a ram, and a one-year-old male lamb as a burnt **o**;
7:40 a male goat for a sin **o**;
7:41 and five one-year-old male lambs for a peace **o**.
7:41 This was the **o** brought by Shelumiel son of
7:42 leader of the tribe of Gad, presented his **o**.
7:43 The **o** consisted of a silver platter weighing about
7:45 a ram, and a one-year-old male lamb as a burnt **o**;
7:46 a male goat for a sin **o**;
7:47 and five one-year-old male lambs for a peace **o**.
7:47 This was the **o** brought by Eliasaph son of Deuel.
7:48 leader of the tribe of Ephraim, presented his **o**.
7:49 The **o** consisted of a silver platter weighing about
7:51 a ram, and a one-year-old male lamb as a burnt **o**;
7:52 a male goat for a sin **o**;
7:53 and five one-year-old male lambs for a peace **o**.
7:53 This was the **o** brought by Elishama son of
7:54 leader of the tribe of Manasseh, presented his **o**.
7:55 The **o** consisted of a silver platter weighing about
7:57 a ram, and a one-year-old male lamb as a burnt **o**;
7:58 a male goat for a sin **o**;
7:59 and five one-year-old male lambs for a peace **o**.
7:59 This was the **o** brought by Gamaliel son of
7:60 leader of the tribe of Benjamin, presented his **o**.
7:61 The **o** consisted of a silver platter weighing about
7:63 a ram, and a one-year-old male lamb as a burnt **o**;
7:64 a male goat for a sin **o**;
7:65 and five one-year-old male lambs for a peace **o**.
7:65 This was the **o** brought by Abidan son of Gideoni.
7:66 leader of the tribe of Dan, presented his **o**.
7:67 The **o** consisted of a silver platter weighing about
7:69 a ram, and a one-year-old male lamb as a burnt **o**;
7:70 a male goat for a sin **o**;
7:71 and five one-year-old male lambs for a peace **o**.
7:71 This was the **o** brought by Ahiezer son of
7:72 leader of the tribe of Asher, presented his **o**.
7:73 The **o** consisted of a silver platter weighing about
7:75 a ram, and a one-year-old male lamb as a burnt **o**;
7:76 a male goat for a sin **o**;
7:77 and five one-year-old male lambs for a peace **o**.
7:77 This was the **o** brought by Pagiel son of Ocran.
7:78 leader of the tribe of Naphtali, presented his **o**.
7:79 The **o** consisted of a silver platter weighing about
7:81 a ram, and a one-year-old male lamb as a burnt **o**;
7:82 a male goat for a sin **o**;
7:83 and five one-year-old male lambs for a peace **o**.
7:83 This was the **o** brought by Ahira son of Enan.
7:84 So this was the dedication **o** for the altar,
7:88 This was the dedication **o** for the altar after it was
8: 8 and a grain **o** of choice flour mixed with olive oil,
8: 8 along with a second young bull for a sin **o**.
8:11 LORD as a special **o** from the people of Israel,
8:12 One will be for a sin **o** and the other for a burnt **o**,
8:13 and present them as a special **o** to the LORD.
8:15 purified them and presented them as a special **o**.
8:21 presented them to the LORD as a special **o**.
9: 7 **o** at the proper time with the rest of the Israelites?"
9:13 to present the LORD's **o** at the proper time.
15: 3 and you want to please the LORD with a burnt **o** or any other **o** given by fire,
15: 3 When it is an ordinary burnt **o**, a sacrifice to fulfill a vow, a freewill **o**,
15: 4 **o** of two quarts of choice flour mixed with one
15: 5 For each lamb offered as a whole burnt **o**,
15: 5 must also present one quart of wine for a drink **o**.
15: 7 and give two and a half pints of wine for a drink **o**.
15: 8 "When you present a young bull as a burnt **o**
15: 8 of a special vow or as a peace **o** to the LORD,
15: 9 then the grain **o** accompanying it must include five
15:10 plus two quarts of wine for the drink **o**. This will be an **o** made by fire, very pleasing to the
15:12 Each of you must do this with each **o** you present.
15:13 If you native Israelites want to present an **o** by fire
15:14 living among you want to present an **o** by fire,
15:21 you are to present this **o** to the LORD each year
15:24 must present a young bull for a burnt **o**.
15:24 it must be offered along with the prescribed grain **o**
15:24 and drink **o** and with one male goat for a sin **o**.
15:25 and they have corrected it with their **o** given to the LORD by fire and by their sin **o**.
15:27 must bring a one-year-old female goat for a sin **o**.
16:35 and burned up the 250 men who were **o** incense.
18:10 You must eat it as a most holy **o**. All the males
18:17 and burn their fat as an **o** given by fire,
18:27 LORD will consider this to be your harvest **o**,
19:17 put some of the ashes from the burnt purification **o**
23:15 "Stand here by your burnt **o** while I go to meet the
28: 5 With each lamb you must offer a grain **o** of two
28: 6 This is the regular burnt **o** ordained at Mount Sinai,
28: 6 an **o** made by fire, very pleasing to the LORD.
28: 7 Along with it you must present the proper drink **o**,
28: 7 poured out in the Holy Place as an **o** to the
28: 8 second lamb in the evening with the same grain **o** and drink **o**.
28: 8 It, too, is an **o** made by fire, very pleasing to the
28: 9 They must be accompanied by a grain **o** of three
28: 9 of choice flour mixed with olive oil, and a drink **o**.
28:10 This is the whole burnt **o** to be presented each
28:10 in addition to the regular daily burnt **o** and its accompanying drink **o**.
28:11 present an extra burnt **o** to the LORD of two
28:13 This burnt **o** must be presented by fire, and it will
28:14 You must also give a drink **o** with each sacrifice:
28:14 Present this monthly burnt **o** on the first day of
28:15 must offer one male goat for a sin **o** to the LORD.
28:15 This is in addition to the regular daily burnt **o** and its accompanying drink **o**.
28:19 You must present as a burnt **o** to the LORD two
28:22 You must also offer a male goat as a sin **o**, to make
28:27 A special whole burnt **o** will be offered that day,
28:31 are in addition to the regular daily burnt **o** and its accompanying grain **o**.
29: 2 On that day you must present a burnt **o**,
29: 5 you must sacrifice a male goat as a sin **o**,
29: 8 You must present a burnt **o**, very pleasing to the
29:11 You must also sacrifice one male goat for a sin **o**.
29:11 This is in addition to the sin **o** of atonement
29:11 the regular daily burnt **o** with its grain **o**,
29:13 That day you must present a special whole burnt **o**
29:14 by a grain **o** of choice flour mixed with olive oil—
29:16 You must also sacrifice a male goat as a sin **o**,
29:16 in addition to the regular daily burnt **o** with its accompanying grain **o** and drink **o**.
29:18 must be accompanied by the prescribed grain **o** and drink **o**.
29:19 You must also sacrifice a male goat as a sin **o**,
29:19 in addition to the regular daily burnt **o** with its accompanying grain **o** and drink **o**.
29:21 must be accompanied by the prescribed grain **o** and drink **o**.
29:22 You must also sacrifice a male goat as a sin **o**,
29:22 in addition to the regular daily burnt **o** with its accompanying grain **o** and drink **o**.
29:24 must be accompanied by the prescribed grain **o** and drink **o**.
29:25 You must also sacrifice a male goat as a sin **o**,
29:25 in addition to the regular daily burnt **o** with its accompanying grain **o** and drink **o**.
29:27 must be accompanied by the prescribed grain **o** and drink **o**.
29:28 You must also sacrifice a male goat as a sin **o**,
29:28 in addition to the regular daily burnt **o** with its accompanying grain **o** and drink **o**.
29:30 must be accompanied by the prescribed grain **o** and drink **o**.
29:31 You must also sacrifice a male goat as a sin **o**,
29:31 in addition to the regular daily burnt **o** with its accompanying grain **o** and drink **o**.
29:33 must be accompanied by the prescribed grain **o** and drink **o**.
29:34 You must also sacrifice one male goat as a sin **o**, in addition to the regular daily burnt **o** with its accompanying grain **o** and drink **o**.
29:36 You must present a burnt **o**, very pleasing to the

29:37 must be accompanied by the prescribed grain **o** and drink **o**.
29:38 You must also sacrifice one male goat as a sin **o**, in addition to the regular daily burnt **o** with its accompanying grain **o** and drink **o**.
31:29 half to Eleazar the priest as an **o** to the LORD.
31:50 an **o** to the LORD from our share of the plunder—
Dt 12:17 of your flocks and herds, nor an **o** to fulfill a vow,
13:16 Put the entire town to the torch as a burnt **o** to the
16:10 Bring him a freewill **o** in proportion to the
18:10 never sacrifice your son or daughter as a burnt **o**.
23:18 your God any **o** from the earnings of a prostitute,
Jos 6:17 be completely destroyed as an **o** to the LORD.
Jdg 6:18 away until I come back and bring my **o** to you."
6:26 Sacrifice the bull as a burnt **o** on the altar, using as
11:31 I return in triumph. I will sacrifice it as a burnt **o**."
13:16 you may prepare a burnt **o** as a sacrifice to the
13:19 Then Manoah took a young goat and a grain **o**
13:23 he wouldn't have accepted our burnt **o** and grain **o**.
16:23 **o** sacrifices and praising their god, Dagon.
1Sa 2:16 The man **o** the sacrifice might reply, "Take as
6:3 "Send a guilt **o** so the plague will stop. Then,
6:4 "What sort of guilt **o** should we send?"
6:14 and sacrificed them to the LORD as a burnt **o**.
6:17 **o** to the LORD were gifts from the rulers of
7:9 and offered it to the LORD as a whole burnt **o**.
7:10 Just as Samuel was sacrificing the burnt **o**,
13:9 "Bring me the burnt **o** and the peace offerings!"
13:9 And Saul sacrificed the burnt **o** himself.
13:10 Just as Saul was finishing with the burnt **o**,
13:12 So I felt obliged to offer the burnt **o** myself before
15:22 Listening to him is much better than **o** the fat of
26:19 you up against me, then let him accept my **o**.
2Sa 15:12 While he was **o** the sacrifices, he sent for
24:22 "Here are oxen for the burnt **o**, and you can use
1Ki 18:33 and pour the water over the **o** and the wood."
18:36 At the customary time for **o** the evening sacrifice,
2Ki 3:27 and sacrificed him as a burnt **o** on the wall.
10:25 soon as Jehu had finished sacrificing the burnt **o**,
12:4 "Collect all the money brought as a sacred **o** to the
16:13 The king presented a burnt **o** and a grain **o**, poured a drink **o** over it,
16:15 the new altar for the morning sacrifices of burnt **o**,
16:15 the evening grain **o**, the king's burnt **o** and grain **o**,
18:31 These are the terms the king of Assyria is **o**:
23:10 a son or daughter in the fire as an **o** to Molech.
1Ch 6:49 They presented the offerings on the altar of burnt **o**
16:29 Bring your **o** and come to worship him.
21:23 And take the wheat for the grain **o**. I will give it all
21:24 I will not offer a burnt **o** that has cost me
21:26 fire from heaven to burn up the **o** on the altar.
25:3 of the harp, **o** thanks and praise to the LORD.
2Ch 28:25 the towns of Judah for **o** sacrifices to other gods.
29:18 the altar of burnt **o** with all its utensils,
29:21 and seven male goats as a sin **o** for the kingdom,
29:23 The male goats for the sin **o** were then brought
29:24 The priests then killed the goats as a sin **o**
29:24 king had specifically commanded that this burnt **o**
29:24 and sin **o** should be made for all Israel.
29:27 Then Hezekiah ordered that the burnt **o** be placed
29:27 As the burnt **o** was presented, songs of praise to the
35:14 busy from morning till night **o** the burnt offerings
Ezr 1:4 as well as a freewill **o** for the Temple of God in
6:17 And twelve male goats were presented as a sin **o**
7:15 which we are freely presenting as an **o** to the God
8:28 This silver and gold is a freewill **o** to the LORD,
8:35 They also offered twelve goats as a sin **o**.
8:35 All this was given as a burnt **o** to the LORD.
10:19 and they each acknowledged their guilt by **o** a ram as a guilt **o**.
Job 1:5 the morning and offer a burnt **o** for each of them.
42:8 my servant Job and offer a burnt **o** for yourselves.
Ps 51:16 or I would bring them. / If I brought you a burnt **o**,
54:6 I will sacrifice a voluntary **o** to you; / I will praise
96:8 Bring your **o** and come to worship him.
141:2 to you, / and my upraised hands as an evening **o**.
Isa 36:16 These are the terms the king of Assyria is **o**:
40:16 animals would not make an **o** worthy of our God.
53:10 Yet when his life is made an **o** for sin, he will have
66:3 When they sacrifice a lamb or bring an **o** of grain,
66:20 holy mountain in Jerusalem as an **o** to the LORD.
Jer 6:20 There is no use now in **o** me sweet incense from
11:17 provoking my anger by **o** incense to Baal."
32:29 where the people caused my fury to rise by **o**
Eze 16:25 **o** your body to every passerby in an endless stream
20:41 you will be as pleasing to me as an **o** of perfumed
27:17 **o** wheat from Minnith, early figs, honey, oil,
43:19 before me, are to be given a young bull for a sin **o**,
43:21 Then take the young bull for the sin **o** and burn it
43:22 sacrifice as a sin **o** a young male goat that has no
43:24 on them and offer them as a burnt **o** to the LORD.
43:25 a ram from the flock will be sacrificed as a sin **o**.
44:27 the sanctuary, he must offer a sin **o** for himself,
45:19 The priest will take some of the blood of this sin **o**
45:22 will provide a young bull as a sin **o** for himself
45:23 the feast he will prepare a burnt **o** to the LORD.
45:23 This daily **o** will consist of seven young bulls
45:23 A male goat will also be given each day for a sin **o**.
45:24 will provide a half bushel of flour as a grain **o**
45:25 will provide these same sacrifices for the sin **o**, the burnt **o**, and the grain **o**, along with the
46:2 while the priest offers his burnt **o** and peace **o**.
46:4 will present to the LORD a burnt **o** of six lambs
46:5 He will present a grain **o** of a half bushel of flour
46:7 he must bring a half bushel of flour for a grain **o**.
46:11 the grain **o** will be a half bushel of flour with each
46:12 offers a voluntary burnt **o** or peace **o** to the LORD,
46:13 must be sacrificed as a burnt **o** to the LORD.
46:14 a grain **o** must also be given to the LORD—
46:15 The lamb, the grain **o**, and the olive oil must be
Hos 3:1 have turned to other gods, **o** them choice gifts."
9:1 **o** sacrifices to other gods on every threshing floor.
11:2 **o** sacrifices to the images of Baal and burning
Am 4:5 Present your bread made with yeast as an **o** of
Mal 1:7 "You have despised my name by **o** defiled
1:9 But when you bring that kind of **o**, why should he
2:12 and yet brings an **o** to the LORD Almighty.
Mt 5:23 before the altar in the Temple, **o** a sacrifice to God,
8:4 Take along the **o** required in the law of Moses for
Mk 1:44 Take along the **o** required in the law of Moses for
Lk 2:22 Then it was time for the purification **o**, as required
5:14 Take along the **o** required in the law of Moses for
23:36 mocked him, too, by **o** him a drink of sour wine.
Ro 15:26 the believers in Greece have eagerly taken up an **o**
1Co 16:2 to what you have earned and save it for this **o**.
2Co 5:21 who never sinned, to be the **o** for our sin,
8:19 to accompany us as we take the **o** to Jerusalem—
9:2 in Greece were ready to send an **o** a year ago.
Php 2:17 **o** to complete the sacrifice of your faithful service
2Ti 4:6 my life has already been poured out as an **o** to
Heb 8:3 our High Priest must make an **o**, too.
10:11 **o** sacrifices that can never take away sins.
10:14 For by that one **o** he perfected forever all those
11:4 brought a more acceptable **o** to God than Cain did.
11:4 God accepted Abel's **o** to show that he was a
Rev 14:4 the people on the earth as a special **o** to God

OFFERINGS (415) [OFFER]

BURNT OFFERINGS (121) Ex 10:25; 20:24; 24:5; 30:9; 32:6; Lev 4:7,10,18,24,25,29,30,33,34; 6:25; 7:2; 14:13; 20:2; 23:18,18,37; Nu 7:87; 10:10; 23:3,6,17; 28:3,24,31; 29:6,39; Dt 12:6,11,13,14,27; 27:6; 33:10; Jos 8:31; 22:23,27, 28,29; Jdg 20:26; 21:4; 1Sa 6:15; 10:8; 15:22; 2Sa 6:17; 24:24,25; 1Ki 3:4,15; 8:64; 9:25; 10:5; 2Ki 5:17; 10:24; 16:15; 1Ch 16:1,40; 21:23,26; 22:1; 23:31; 29:21; 2Ch 1:6; 2:4; 7:1,7,7; 8:12; 9:4; 13:11; 23:18; 24:14,14; 29:7,28,31, 32,34,35; 30:15; 31:2,3; 35:12,14,16; Ezr 3:2,3,4,5,6; 6:9; 8:35; Ne 10:33; Ps 20:3; 40:6; 50:8; 51:19; 66:13,15; Isa 1:11; 43:23; 56:7; Jer 6:20; 7:21,22; 14:12; 17:26; 33:18; Eze 40:39,42; 43:27; 44:11; 45:15,17; Hos 6:6; Am 5:22; Mk 12:33

DRINK OFFERINGS (23) Ex 25:29; 30:9; 37:16; Lev 23:18,37; Nu 6:15; 28:24,31; 29:6,11,39; 2Ki 16:15; 1Ch 29:21; 2Ch 29:35; Ezr 7:17; Isa 57:6; Jer 7:18; 19:13; 32:29; 44:19; 52:19; Eze 20:28; 45:17

FREEWILL OFFERINGS (8) Lev 23:38; Nu 29:39; Dt 12:6,17; 2Ch 31:14; Ezr 1:6; 3:5; 7:16

GRAIN OFFERINGS (54) Ex 30:9; Lev 2:11,13,13; 6:23; 7:10; 23:18,37; Nu 6:15; 7:13,19,25,31,37,43,49,55,61,67,73, 79,87; 18:9; 28:12,20,28; 29:3,6,9,39; Jos 22:23,29; 1Ki 8:64; 1Ch 23:29; 2Ch 7:7; Ezr 7:17; Ne 10:33,37; 13:5,9; Isa 43:23; 57:6; Jer 14:12; 17:26; 33:18; 41:5; Eze 42:13; 44:29; 45:15,17; 46:20; Am 5:22; Heb 10:5,8

LORD'S* OFFERINGS (1) 1Sa 2:17

PEACE OFFERINGS (34) Ex 20:24; 24:5; 29:28; 32:6; Lev 6:12; 7:11,34; 10:14; 17:5; Nu 7:88; 10:10; 29:39; Dt 27:7; 1Sa 10:8; 11:15; 13:9; 2Sa 6:17; 24:25; 1Ki 3:15; 8:63, 64; 9:25; 2Ki 16:13; 1Ch 16:1; 21:26; 2Ch 7:7; 29:35; 30:22; 31:2; 33:16; Eze 43:27; 45:15,17; Am 5:22

SIN OFFERINGS (13) Lev 14:13; 16:27; Nu 7:87; 18:9; 2Ki 12:16; Ne 10:33; Ps 40:6; Eze 40:39; 42:13; 44:29; 45:17; 46:20; Hos 4:8

Ex 10:25 for sacrifices and burnt **o** to the LORD our God.
20:24 your burnt **o** and peace **o**, your sheep
24:5 the young men to sacrifice young bulls as burnt **o** and peace **o** to the LORD.
25:29 and bowls to be used in pouring out drink **o**.
28:38 regarding the sacred **o** of the people of Israel.
29:28 whenever the people of Israel offer up peace **o** or thanksgiving **o** to the LORD,
29:41 along with the same **o** of flour and wine as in the
30:9 or any burnt **o**, grain **o**, or drink **o**.
30:20 and before they approach the altar to burn **o** to the
32:6 got up early the next morning to sacrifice burnt **o** and peace **o**.
35:5 Everyone is invited to bring these **o** to the LORD:
35:21 they brought to the LORD their **o** of materials for
35:22 Some brought to the LORD their **o** of gold—
35:29 through Moses—brought their **o** to the LORD.
36:6 So the people stopped bringing their **o**.
37:16 utensils were to be used in pouring out drink **o**.
Lev 1:2 Whenever you present **o** to the LORD, you must
2:3 It will be considered a most holy part of the **o**
2:10 It will be considered a most holy part of the **o**
2:11 "Do not use yeast in any of the grain **o** you present
2:12 and honey to the **o** presented at harvesttime,
2:13 Season all your grain **o** with salt, to remind you of
2:13 Never forget to add salt to your grain **o**.
4:7 altar of burnt **o** at the entrance of the Tabernacle.
4:10 Then he must burn them on the altar of burnt **o**,
4:18 altar of burnt **o** at the entrance of the Tabernacle.
4:24 LORD at the place where burnt **o** are slaughtered.
4:25 put it on the horns of the altar of burnt **o**, and pour
4:29 and slaughter it at the place where burnt **o** are
4:30 put the blood on the horns of the altar of burnt **o**,
4:33 and slaughter it at the place where the burnt **o** are
4:34 the blood, put it on the horns of the altar of burnt **o**,
4:35 altar on top of the **o** given to the LORD by fire.
6:12 then burn the fat of the peace **o** on top of this daily
6:17 I have given it to the priests as their share of the **o**
6:18 because it is their regular share of the **o** given to
6:23 All such grain **o** of the priests must be entirely
6:25 at the place where the burnt **o** are slaughtered.
7:2 be slaughtered where the burnt **o** are slaughtered,
7:10 All other grain **o**, whether flour mixed with olive
7:11 of peace **o** that may be presented to the LORD.
7:34 It is their regular share of the peace **o** brought by
7:35 and his descendants from the **o** given to the
7:38 their **o** to the LORD in the wilderness of Sinai.
8:28 Moses then took all the **o** back and burned them on
8:31 with the bread that is in the basket of ordination **o**,
9:4 Tell them to present all these **o** to the LORD
9:7 Then present the **o** to make atonement for the
10:13 and your descendants as your regular share of the **o**
10:14 and daughters as your regular share of the peace **o**
10:15 LORD along with the fat of the **o** given by fire.
12:6 She must take her **o** to the priest at the entrance of
14:11 along with the **o**, before the LORD at the entrance
14:13 there in the sacred area at the place where sin **o** and burnt **o** are slaughtered.
14:23 the person being cleansed must bring the **o** to the
15:14 of the Tabernacle and give his **o** to the priest.
15:15 The priest will present the **o** there, one for a sin
16:27 "The bull and goat given as sin **o**, whose blood
17:5 so he can present them to the LORD as peace **o**.
20:2 If any among them devote their children as burnt **o**
21:6 they are the ones who present the **o** to the LORD
21:21 him from presenting **o** to the LORD by fire.
21:22 including the holy **o** and the most holy **o**.
22:4 they may not eat the sacred **o** until they have been
22:6 They must not eat any of the sacred **o** until they
22:7 they will be clean again and may eat the sacred **o**.
22:10 outside a priest's family may ever eat the sacred **o**,
22:12 priestly family, she may no longer eat the sacred **o**.
22:13 priests' families are allowed to eat the sacred **o**.
22:14 "Anyone who eats the sacred **o** without realizing it
22:15 No one may defile the sacred **o** brought to the
23:18 one bull, and two rams as burnt **o** to the LORD.
23:18 These whole burnt **o**, together with the accompanying grain **o** and drink **o**,
23:20 "The priest will lift up these **o** before the LORD,
23:20 These **o** are holy to the LORD and will belong to
23:25 you are to present **o** to the LORD by fire."
23:27 and present **o** to the LORD by fire.
23:36 you must present **o** to the LORD by fire.
23:37 to present all the various **o** to the LORD by fire—
23:37 whole burnt **o** and grain **o**, sacrificial meals and drink **o**—
23:38 And these **o** must be given in addition to your
23:38 the **o** you make to accompany your vows, and any freewill **o** that you present to the LORD.
24:9 for they represent a most holy portion of the **o**
26:31 and I will take no pleasure in your **o** of incense.
Nu 6:15 along with their prescribed grain **o** and drink **o**.
6:16 The priest will present these **o** before the LORD:
7:2 organized the census—came and brought their **o**.
7:13 These were both filled with grain **o** of choice flour
7:19 These were both filled with grain **o** of choice flour
7:25 These were both filled with grain **o** of choice flour
7:31 These were both filled with grain **o** of choice flour
7:37 These were both filled with grain **o** of choice flour
7:43 These were both filled with grain **o** of choice flour
7:49 These were both filled with grain **o** of choice flour
7:55 These were both filled with grain **o** of choice flour
7:61 These were both filled with grain **o** of choice flour
7:67 These were both filled with grain **o** of choice flour
7:73 These were both filled with grain **o** of choice flour
7:79 These were both filled with grain **o** of choice flour
7:87 male lambs were donated for the burnt **o**, along with their prescribed grain **o**.
7:87 Twelve male goats were brought for the sin **o**.
7:88 male lambs were donated for the peace **o**.
10:10 to rejoice over your burnt **o** and peace **o**.
16:15 and said to the LORD, "Do not accept their **o**!
18:8 I have given these **o** to you and your sons as your
18:9 You are allotted the portion of the most holy **o** that
18:9 From all the most holy **o**—including the grain **o**, sin **o**, and guilt **o**—
18:11 "All the other **o** presented to me by the Israelites
18:11 male and female alike, may eat of these **o**.
18:12 gifts brought by the people as **o** to the LORD—
18:19 I am giving you all these holy **o** that the people of
18:24 which have been set apart as **o** to the LORD.
23:3 said to Balak, "Stand here by your burnt **o**,
23:6 the king was standing beside his burnt **o** with all
23:17 of Moab were standing beside Balak's burnt **o**.
28:2 The **o** you present to me by fire on the altar are my
28:3 When you present your daily whole burnt **o** to the
28:12 These will be accompanied by grain **o** of choice
28:20 These will be accompanied by grain **o** of choice
28:23 You will present these **o** in addition to your regular
28:24 this is how you will prepare the food **o** to be
28:24 be offered in addition to the regular whole burnt **o** and drink **o**.
28:28 These will be accompanied by grain **o** of choice
28:31 These special burnt **o**, along with their drink **o**,
29:3 These must be accompanied by grain **o** of choice
29:6 addition to your regular monthly and daily burnt **o**,
29:6 given with their prescribed grain **o** and drink **o**.
29:6 These **o** are given to the LORD by fire and are
29:9 These **o** must be accompanied by the prescribed
29:9 grain **o** of choice flour mixed with olive oil—
29:11 its grain offering, and their accompanying drink **o**.
29:14 Each of these **o** must be accompanied by a grain
29:18 Each of these **o** of bulls, rams, and lambs must be
29:21 Each of these **o** of bulls, rams, and lambs must be
29:24 Each of these **o** of bulls, rams, and lambs must be
29:27 Each of these **o** of bulls, rams, and lambs must be
29:30 Each of these **o** of bulls, rams, and lambs must be

29:33 Each of these o of bulls, rams, and lambs must be
29:37 Each of these o must be accompanied by the
29:39 "You must present these o to the LORD at your
29:39 and o you present in connection with vows,
29:39 as freewill o, burnt o, grain o, drink o, or peace o."
Dt 12: 6 There you will bring to the LORD your burnt o, your special gifts, your o to fulfill a vow, your freewill o,
12: 6 and your o of the firstborn animals of your flocks
12:11 your burnt o, your sacrifices, your tithes,
12:11 your special gifts, and your o to fulfill a vow—
12:13 Be careful not to sacrifice your burnt o just
12:14 There you must offer your burnt o and do
12:17 "But your o must not be eaten at home—
12:17 a vow, nor your freewill o, nor your special gifts.
12:26 and your o given to fulfill a vow to the place the
12:27 and blood of your burnt o on the altar of the
18: 1 and Levites will eat from the o given to the
18: 3 from the oxen and sheep that the people bring as o:
18: 8 He may eat his share of the sacrifices and o,
27: 6 On the altar you must offer burnt o to the LORD
27: 7 Sacrifice peace o on it also, and feast there with
32:38 and drank the wine of their o? / Let those gods
33:10 before you / and offer whole burnt o on the altar.
Jos 8:31 Then on the altar they presented burnt o and peace o to the LORD.
13:14 their inheritance came from the o burned on the
22:23 Nor will we use it for our burnt o or grain o or peace o.
22:27 the LORD at his sanctuary with our burnt o, sacrifices, and peace o.
22:28 It is not for burnt o or sacrifices; it is a reminder of
22:29 from him by building our own altar for burnt o, grain o, or sacrifices.
Jdg 20:26 also brought burnt o and peace o to the LORD.
21: 4 and presented their burnt o and peace o on it.
1Sa 2:17 for they treated the LORD's o with contempt.
2:28 And I assigned the sacrificial o to you priests.
2:29 So why do you scorn my sacrifices and o? Why do
2:29 and they have become fat from the best o of my
3:14 his sons will never be forgiven by sacrifices or o."
6:15 Many burnt o and sacrifices were offered to the
10: 8 will join you there to sacrifice burnt o and peace o.
11:15 Then they offered peace o to the LORD, and Saul
13: 9 "Bring me the burnt offering and the peace o!"
15:22 your burnt o and sacrifices or your obedience to his
2Sa 6:17 David sacrificed burnt o and peace o to the LORD.
24:24 for I cannot present burnt o to the LORD my God
24:25 and offered burnt o and peace o.
1Ki 3: 2 At that time the people of Israel sacrificed their o
3: 4 went there and sacrificed one thousand burnt o.
3:15 where he sacrificed burnt o and peace o.
8:63 Solomon sacrificed peace o to the LORD
8:64 He offered burnt o, grain o, and the fat of peace o
8:64 presence was too small to handle so many o.
9:25 Three times each year Solomon offered burnt o and peace o to the LORD on the altar he had
10: 5 and the burnt o Solomon made at the Temple of
2Ki 5:17 From now on I will never again offer any burnt o
10:24 all inside the temple to offer sacrifices and burnt o.
12:16 the money that was contributed for guilt o and sin o was not brought into the LORD's
16:12 he inspected the altar and made o on it.
16:13 over it, and sprinkled the blood of peace o on it.
16:15 and grain offering, and the o of the people, including their drink o.
16:15 The blood from the burnt o and sacrifices should
1Ch 6:49 They presented the o on the altar of burnt offering
9:31 was entrusted with baking the bread used in the o.
16: 1 and they sacrificed burnt o and peace o before God.
16:40 They sacrificed the regular burnt o to the LORD
21:23 "Here are oxen for the burnt o, and you can use
21:26 and sacrificed burnt o and peace o.
22: 1 and the place of the altar for Israel's burnt o!"
23:29 the choice flour for the grain o, the wafers made
23:31 They assisted with the burnt o that were presented
29: 5 Who is willing to give o to the LORD today?"
29: 9 The people rejoiced over the o, for they had given
29:21 and a thousand male lambs as burnt o to the
29:21 They also brought drink o and many other
2Ch 1: 6 and sacrificed a thousand burnt o on it.
2: 4 and to sacrifice burnt o each morning and evening,
4: 6 He also made ten basins for water to wash the o,
7: 1 and burned up the burnt o and sacrifices,
7: 7 present burnt o and the fat from peace o there.
7: 7 altar he had built could not handle all the burnt o, grain o, and sacrificial fat.
8:12 Then Solomon sacrificed burnt o to the LORD on
9: 4 and the burnt o Solomon made at the Temple of
13:11 They present burnt o and fragrant incense to the
23:18 He also commanded them to present burnt o to the
24: 5 towns of Judah and collect the required annual o,
24:14 utensils for worship services and for burnt o,
24:14 And the burnt o were sacrificed continually in the
29: 7 and presenting burnt o at the sanctuary of the God
29:11 to lead the people in worship and make o to him."
29:28 trumpets blew, until all the burnt o were finished.
29:31 and thanksgiving o to the Temple of the LORD."
29:31 people brought their sacrifices and thanksgiving o,
29:31 those whose hearts were willing brought burnt o,
29:32 hundred rams, and two hundred lambs for burnt o.
29:34 were too few priests to prepare all the burnt o,
29:35 abundance of burnt o, along with the usual drink o,
29:35 and a great deal of fat from the many peace o.
30:15 and brought burnt o to the Temple of the LORD.
30:22 Peace o were sacrificed, and the people confessed
30:24 one thousand bulls and seven thousand sheep for o,
31: 2 into divisions to offer the burnt o and peace o,
31: 3 animals for the daily morning and evening burnt o,
31:14 was put in charge of distributing the freewill o of
33:16 and sacrificed peace o and thanksgiving o on it.
35: 5 assigned to you as they bring their o to the Temple.
35: 7 and young goats for the people's Passover o,
35: 8 young goats and three hundred bulls as Passover o.
35: 9 hundred bulls to the Levites for their Passover o.
35:12 They divided the burnt o among the people by their
35:13 and they boiled the holy o in pots, kettles,
35:14 busy from morning till night offering the burnt o
35:16 All the burnt o were sacrificed on the altar of the
Ezr 1: 6 many choice gifts in addition to all the freewill o.
3: 2 God of Israel so they could sacrifice burnt o on it,
3: 3 Then they immediately began to sacrifice burnt o
3: 4 sacrificing the burnt o specified for each day of the
3: 5 They also offered the regular burnt o
3: 5 and the o required for the new moon celebrations
3: 5 Freewill o were also sacrificed to the LORD by
3: 6 the priests had begun to sacrifice burnt o to the
6: 9 and lambs for the burnt o presented to the God of
7:16 as well as the freewill o of the people
7:17 and the appropriate grain o and drink o,
8:35 captivity sacrificed burnt o to the God of Israel.
Ne 10:33 for the regular grain o and burnt o;
10:33 for the o on the Sabbaths, the new moon
10:33 and the annual festivals; for the holy o;
10:33 and for the sin o to make atonement for Israel.
10:37 will bring the best of our flour and other grain o,
10:39 and the Levites must bring these o of grain,
13: 5 had previously been used for storing the grain o,
13: 5 Moses had decreed that these o belonged to the
13: 9 God's Temple, the grain o, and the frankincense.
Ps 20: 3 and look favorably on your burnt o. / *Interlude*
40: 6 You take no delight in sacrifices or o. / Now that
40: 6 you don't require burnt o or sin o.
50: 8 or the burnt o you constantly bring to my altar.
51:19 and with our whole burnt o; / and bulls will again
66:13 Now I come to your Temple with burnt o / to fulfill
66:15 That is why I am sacrificing burnt o to you—
Ecc 5: 1 Don't be a fool who doesn't realize that mindless o
Isa 1:11 the LORD. "Don't bring me any more burnt o!
1:11 I don't want to see the blood from your o of bulls
19:21 and will give their sacrifices and o to him.
43:23 You have not brought me lambs for burnt o.
43:23 and wearied you with my requests for grain o
56: 7 I will accept their burnt o and sacrifices,
57: 6 You worship them with drink o and grain o.
66: 3 their sins, are cursed. Their o will not be accepted.
Jer 6:20 expensive perfumes! I cannot accept your burnt o.
7:18 And they give drink o to their other idol gods!
7:21 says: "Away with your burnt o and sacrifices!
7:22 it was not burnt o and sacrifices I wanted from
14:12 When they present their burnt o and grain o to me,
17:26 the people will come with their burnt o
17:26 They will bring their grain o, incense,
17:26 and thanksgiving o to the LORD's Temple.
19:13 and where drink o were poured out to your
31:14 I will supply the priests with an abundance of o.
32:29 and by pouring out drink o to other gods.
33:11 of people bringing thanksgiving o to the LORD.
33:18 to offer burnt o and grain o and sacrifices to me."
41: 5 and had brought along grain o and incense.
44:19 pouring out drink o to her, and making cakes
52:19 pots, lampstands, dishes, bowls used for drink o,
Eze 20:26 to give their firstborn children as o to their gods—
20:28 and incense and poured out their drink o to them!
20:40 There I will require that you bring me all your o
40:39 slaughtered for the burnt o, sin o, and guilt o.
40:42 tables of hewn stone for preparation of the burnt o,
42:13 sacrifices to the LORD will eat the most holy o.
42:13 And they will use these rooms to store the grain o, sin o, and guilt o because these rooms are holy.
43:18 These will be the regulations for the burning of o
43:27 the priests will sacrifice on the altar the burnt o and peace o of the people.
44:11 may still slaughter the animals brought for burnt o
44:13 may not touch any of my holy things or the holy o,
44:29 the grain o, the sin o, and the guilt o.
45:15 These will be the grain o, burnt o, and peace o that will make atonement for the
45:16 of Israel must join the prince in bringing their o.
45:17 The prince will be required to provide o that are
45:17 He will provide the sin o, burnt o, grain o, drink o, and peace o to make reconciliation for the people
46:20 the priests will cook the meat from the guilt o and sin o and bake the flour from the grain o into bread.
Da 9:27 this time, he will put an end to the sacrifices and o.
Hos 4: 8 when the people sin and bring their sin o to them.
6: 6 to know God; that's more important than burnt o.
Joel 1: 9 The priests are mourning because there are no o.
Am 2: 8 they present o of wine purchased with stolen
4: 5 Then give your extra voluntary o so you can brag
5:22 I will not accept your burnt o and grain o.
5:22 I won't even notice all your choice peace o.
5:25 and o during the forty years in the wilderness,
Mic 4:13 will give all the wealth they acquired as o to me,
6: 6 Should we bow before God with o of yearling
Zep 3:10 the rivers of Ethiopia will come to present their o.
Mal 1:10 LORD Almighty, "and I will not accept your o.
1:11 sweet incense and pure o in honor of my name.
1:13 and mutilated, crippled and sick—presented as o!
1:13 Should I accept from you such o as these?"
2:13 because he pays no attention to your o,
3: 4 Then once more the LORD will accept the o
3: 8 have cheated me of the tithes and o due to me.
Mk 12:33 is more important than to offer all of the burnt o
1Co 9:13 meals from the food brought to the Temple as o?
9:13 serve at the altar get a share of the sacrificial o.
Heb 10: 5 "You did not want animal sacrifices and grain o.
10: 6 burned on the altar / or with other o for sin.
10: 8 or grain o or animals burned on the altar or other o for sin,

OFFERS (14) [OFFER]

Lev 6:26 The priest who o the sacrifice may eat his portion
7:33 the blood and o the fat of the peace offering.
Pr 3:16 She o you life in her right hand, and riches
3:32 to the LORD, but he o his friendship to the godly.
14:27 it o escape from the snares of death.
Isa 40:29 are tired and worn out; he o strength to the weak.
Eze 46: 2 by the gatepost while the priest o his burnt offering
46:12 Whenever the prince o a voluntary burnt offering
Jn 6:32 And now he o you the true bread from heaven.
Ro 2: 7 the glory and honor and immortality that God o.
Heb 5: 1 their gifts to God and o their sacrifices for sins.
9: 7 which he o to God to cover his own sins
1Jn 2:15 Stop loving this evil world and all that it o you,
2:16 For the world o only the lust for physical pleasure,

OFFICE (4) [OFFICER, OFFICER'S, OFFICERS, OFFICES, OFFICIAL, OFFICIAL'S, OFFICIALLY, OFFICIALS, OFFICIATE, OFFICIATING]

Lev 6:22 they will be inducted into o by offering this same
Jos 20: 6 priest who was in o at the time of the accident.
1Ch 9:26 all Levites, were in an o of great trust,
Isa 22:19 "Yes, I will drive you out of o," says the LORD.

OFFICER (45) [OFFICE]

Ge 37:36 to Potiphar, an o of Pharaoh, the king of Egypt.
2Sa 20:12 and Joab's o saw that a crowd was gathering
2Ki 7: 2 The o assisting the king said to the man of God,
7:17 The king appointed his o to control the traffic at
7:19 The king's o had replied, "That couldn't happen
9:25 Jehu said to Bidkar, his o, "Throw him into the
23:11 of Nathan-melech the eunuch, an o of the court.
25:19 he took an o of the Judean army, five of the king's
1Ch 9:11 Azariah was the chief o of the house of God.
26:24 son of Moses. He was the chief o of the treasuries.
27: 4 troops in his division, and Mikloth was his chief o.
27: 6 as the Thirty. His son Ammizabad was his chief o.
2Ch 24:11 and an o of the high priest counted the money
Ne 11: 9 Their chief o was Joel son of Zicri, who was
11:14 Their chief o was Zabdiel son of Haggedolim.
11:22 The chief o of the Levites in Jerusalem was Uzzi
Jer 39: 3 and Nebo-sarsekim, a chief o, and Nergal-sharezer,
39:13 and Nebushazban, a chief o, and Nergal-sharezer,
51:59 Jeremiah gave this message to Zedekiah's staff o,
52:25 he took an o of the Judean army, seven of the
Mt 5:25 into court, handed over to an o, and thrown in jail.
8: 5 a Roman o came and pleaded with him,
8: 8 Then the o said, "Lord, I am not worthy to have
8:13 Then Jesus said to the Roman o, "Go on home.
27:54 The Roman o and the other soldiers at the
Mk 15:39 When the Roman o who stood facing him saw how
15:44 so he called for the Roman military o in charge
15:45 The o confirmed the fact, and Pilate told Joseph he
Lk 7: 2 Now the highly valued slave of a Roman o was
7: 3 When the o heard about Jesus, he sent some
7: 6 at the house, the o sent some friends to say, "Lord,
12:58 and handed over to an o and thrown in jail.
Jn 4:53 And the o and his entire household believed in
18:12 So the soldiers, their commanding o,
Ac 10: 1 In Caesarea there lived a Roman army o named
10:22 "We were sent by Cornelius, a Roman o.
22:25 down to lash him, Paul said to the o standing there,
22:26 The o went to the commander and asked,
23:18 So the o did, explaining, "Paul, the prisoner,
24:23 He ordered an o to keep Paul in custody but to give
27: 1 placed in the custody of an army o named Julius,
27: 6 There the o found an Egyptian ship from
27:11 But the o in charge of the prisoners listened more
27:31 But Paul said to the commanding o
27:43 But the commanding o wanted to spare Paul,

OFFICER'S (1) [OFFICE]

Lk 7:10 And when the o friends returned to his house,

OFFICERS (87) [OFFICE]

Ge 50: 7 and advisers—all the senior o of Egypt.
Ex 15: 4 thrown into the sea. / The very best of Pharaoh's o
Dt 20: 5 "Then the o of the army will address the troops
20: 8 Then the o will also say, 'Is anyone terrified?
20: 9 When the o have finished saying this to their
29:10 your tribal leaders, your judges, your o, all the men
Jos 8:33 along with the leaders, o, and judges, were divided
23: 2 all the elders, leaders, judges, and o of Israel.
24: 1 along with their elders, leaders, judges, and o.
1Sa 8:15 and distribute it among his o and attendants.
18: 5 was applauded by the fighting men and o alike.
18:30 against them than all the rest of Saul's o.
21:11 But Achish's o weren't happy about his being
22: 6 holding his spear and surrounded by his o.
2Sa 8: 7 David brought the gold shields of Hadadezer's o to
11:11 and Joab and his o are camping in the open fields.
16: 6 He threw stones at the king and the king's o
16:11 Then David said to Abishai and the other o,
20:11 One of Joab's young o shouted to Amasa's troops,
24: 4 and his o went out to count the people of Israel.

1Ki 1:33 "Take Solomon and my **o** down to Gihon Spring.
9:22 government officials, **o** in his army,
14:27 he entrusted them to the care of the palace guard **o**.
20:12 "Prepare to attack!" Ben-hadad commanded his **o**.
20:23 After their defeat, Ben-hadad's **o** said to him,
20:31 Ben-hadad's **o** said to him, "Sir, we have heard
2Ki 3:11 One of King Joram's **o** replied, "Elisha son of
5:13 But his **o** tried to reason with him and said, "Sir,
6: 8 he would confer with his **o** and say, "We will
6:11 He called in his **o** and demanded, "Which of you
6:12 "It's not us, my lord," one of the **o** replied.
7:12 out of bed in the middle of the night and told his **o**,
7:13 One of his **o** replied, "We had better send out
9: 5 Jehu sitting in a meeting with the other army **o**.
9:11 Jehu went back to his fellow **o**, and one of them
10:25 he commanded his guards and **o**, "Go in and kill
10:25 and the guards and **o** dragged their bodies outside.
11:14 The **o** and trumpeters were surrounding him,
12:20 But his **o** plotted against him and assassinated him
23:30 Josiah's **o** took his body back in a chariot from
24:10 the **o** of King Nebuchadnezzar of Babylon came up
1Ch 12:18 join him, and he made them **o** over his troops.
12:28 twenty-two members of his family who were all **o**.
12:34 there were 1,000 **o** and 37,000 warriors armed with
18: 7 David brought the gold shields of Hadadezer's **o** to
26:26 the generals and captains and other **o** of the army.
27: 1 list of Israelite generals and captains, and their **o**,
27: 3 and was in charge of all the army **o** for the first
29: 6 and the king's administrative **o** all gave willingly.
2Ch 8: 9 **o** in his army, commanders of his chariots,
8:18 Hiram sent him ships commanded by his own **o**
23:13 The **o** and trumpeters were surrounding him,
32: 6 He appointed military **o** over the people and asked
32:21 the Assyrian army with all its commanders and **o**.
33:14 And he stationed his military **o** in all of the
Ne 2: 9 had sent along army **o** and horsemen to protect me.
4: 2 in front of his friends and the Samarian army **o**,
4:16 The **o** stationed themselves behind the people of
Est 1: 3 He invited all the military **o** of Media and Persia,
Isa 3: 3 army **o**, honorable citizens, advisers,
10:33 vast army of Assyria—**o** and high officials alike.
33:18 Assyrian **o** outside your walls counted your towers
Jer 26:21 When King Jehoiakim and the army **o** and officials
38:22 and given to the **o** of the Babylonian army.
39: 3 All the **o** of the Babylonian army came in and sat
39:13 king's adviser, and the other **o** of Babylon's king
41:16 and his **o** led away all the people they had
42: 1 Then all the army **o**, including Johanan son of
42: 8 called for Johanan son of Kareah and the army **o**,
43: 4 So Johanan and all the army **o** and all the people
43: 5 and his **o** took with them all the people who had
Eze 23:14 pictures of Babylonian military **o**, outfitted in
23:15 They were dressed like chariot **o** from the land of
23:23 handsome young captains, commanders, chariot **o**,
and other high-ranking **o**,
Da 4:36 My advisers and **o** sought me out, and I was
Na 2: 5 The king shouts to his **o**; they stumble in their
3:10 to see who would get the Egyptian **o** as servants.
Mt 8: 9 because I am under the authority of my superior **o**
Mk 6:21 army **o**, and the leading citizens of Galilee.
Lk 7: 8 because I am under the authority of my superior **o**,
Ac 21:32 his soldiers and **o** and ran down among the crowd.
23:17 Paul called one of the **o** and said, "Take this young
23:23 Then the commander called two of his **o**
25:23 accompanied by military **o** and prominent men of
27: 9 in the fall, and Paul spoke to the ship's **o** about it.
Tit 3: 1 your people to submit to the government and its **o**.

OFFICES (1) [OFFICE]

Ex 29:35 how you will ordain Aaron and his sons to their **o**.

OFFICIAL (29) [OFFICE]

2Ki 25: 8 captain of the guard, an **o** of the Babylonian king,
1Ch 27:24 was never recorded in King David's **o** records.
2Ch 31:13 and Azariah, the chief **o** in the Temple of God.
31:16 to the LORD's Temple to perform their **o** duties,
Ne 2:10 and Tobiah the Ammonite **o** heard of my arrival,
5:14 neither I nor my officials drew on our **o** food
Est 1:16 but also every **o** and citizen throughout your
2:19 and Mordecai had become a palace **o**,
3: 1 making him the most powerful **o** in the empire next
Ecc 5: 8 For every **o** is under orders from higher up,
Jer 36:12 and all the others with **o** responsibilities.
38: 7 Ebed-melech the Ethiopian, an important palace **o**,
52:12 captain of the guard, an **o** of the Babylonian king,
Da 1: 7 The chief **o** renamed them with these Babylonian
1: 8 He asked the chief **o** for permission to eat other
1: 9 Now God had given the chief **o** great respect for
1:11 been appointed by the chief **o** to look after Daniel,
1:18 the chief **o** brought all the young men to King
Mt 19: 7 say a man could merely write an **o** letter of divorce
23: 2 and the Pharisees are the **o** interpreters of the
Mk 10: 4 "He said a man merely has to write his wife an **o**
Jn 4:46 There was a government **o** in the city of
4:49 The **o** pleaded, "Lord, please come now before my
Ac 7:58 The **o** witnesses took off their coats and laid them
8: 1 Saul was one of the **o** witnesses at the killing of
15:25 to send you these **o** representatives, along with our
19:35 "Everyone knows that Ephesus is the **o** guardian
25:10 This is the **o** Roman court, so I ought to be tried
28: 7 belonging to Publius, the chief **o** of the island.

OFFICIAL'S (2) [OFFICE]

Mt 9:19 and the disciples were going to the **o** home,
9:23 When Jesus arrived at the **o** home, he noticed the

OFFICIALLY (1) [OFFICE]

Ezr 8:34 and weight, and the total weight was **o** recorded.

OFFICIALS (182) [OFFICE]

Ge 12:15 When the palace **o** saw her, they sang her praises
40: 2 Pharaoh became very angry with these **o**,
40:20 and he gave a banquet for all his **o** and household
41:34 Let Pharaoh appoint **o** over the land, and let them
45:16 was very happy to hear this and so were his **o**.
Ex 5:21 into this terrible situation with Pharaoh and his **o**.
7:20 As Pharaoh and all of his **o** watched, Moses raised
8: 9 want me to pray for you, your **o**, and your people.
9: 7 Pharaoh sent **o** to see whether it was true that none
9:14 to you and your **o** and all the Egyptian people.
9:20 Some of Pharaoh's **o** believed what the LORD
9:30 But as for you and your **o**, I know that you still do
9:34 and his **o** sinned yet again by stubbornly refusing
10: 1 I have made him and his **o** stubborn so I can
10: 6 and the homes of your **o** and all the houses of
10: 7 The court **o** now came to Pharaoh and appealed to
11: 3 He was respected by Pharaoh's **o** and the Egyptian
11: 8 All the **o** of Egypt will come running to me,
12:30 Pharaoh and his **o** and all the people of Egypt
14: 5 three days, Pharaoh and his **o** changed their minds.
Nu 22: 7 **o** of both Moab and Midian, set out and took
22: 8 So the **o** from Moab stayed there with Balaam.
22:13 next morning Balaam got up and told Balak's **o**,
22:14 So the Moabite **o** returned to King Balak
22:15 **o** than those he had sent the first time.
22:21 his donkey and started off with the Moabite **o**.
22:35 you to say." So Balaam went on with Balak's **o**.
22:40 the meat to Balaam and the **o** who were with him.
23: 6 beside his burnt offerings with all the **o** of Moab.
23:17 and the **o** of Moab were standing beside Balak's
Dt 1:15 appointed them to serve as judges and **o** over you.
16:18 and **o** for each of your tribes in all the towns the
31:28 and **o** of your tribes so that I can speak to them
Jos 22:14 In this delegation were ten high **o** of Israel,
22:21 the half-tribe of Manasseh answered these high **o**:
22:30 and the high **o** heard this from the tribes of
22:32 and the ten high **o** left the tribes of Reuben
2Sa 13:36 and the king and his **o** wept bitterly with them.
1Ki 1: 9 sons of King David—and all the royal **o** of Judah.
1:47 All the royal **o** went to King David
3:15 Then he invited all his **o** to a great banquet.
4: 2 and these were his high **o**: / Azariah son of Zadok
9:22 government **o**, officers in his army, commanders of
10: 5 the organization of his **o** and their splendid
10: 8 What a privilege for your **o** to stand here day after
11:17 and a few of his father's royal **o** had fled.
11:26 Jeroboam son of Nebat, one of Solomon's own **o**.
15:18 He sent it with some of his **o** to Ben-hadad son of
20: 6 But about this time tomorrow I will send my **o** to
21:14 The city **o** then sent word to Jezebel, "Naboth has
22: 3 During the visit, Ahab said to his **o**, "Do you
22: 9 So the king of Israel called one of his **o** and said,
2Ki 8: 6 So he directed one of his **o** to see to it that
9:28 His **o** took him by chariot to Jerusalem, where they
10: 1 and sent copies to Samaria, to the **o** of the city,
10:11 relatives living in Jezreel and all his important **o**,
18:18 but the king sent these **o** to meet with them:
19: 5 After King Hezekiah's **o** delivered the king's
22: 9 "Your **o** have given the money collected at the
24:12 his advisers, nobles, and **o**, and the queen mother,
24:15 along with his wives and **o**, the queen mother,
25:24 Gedaliah vowed to them that the Babylonian **o**
1Ch 13: 1 David consulted with all his **o**,
23: 4 Six thousand are to serve as **o** and judges.
24: 5 for there were many qualified **o** serving God in the
27:31 All these **o** were overseers of King David's
28: 1 David summoned all his **o** to Jerusalem—
28: 1 of the royal property and livestock, the palace **o**,
29:24 All the royal **o**, the army commanders,
2Ch 9: 4 the organization of his **o** and their splendid
9: 7 What a privilege for your **o** to stand here day after
17: 7 Jehoshaphat sent out his **o** to teach in all the towns
17: 7 These **o** included Ben-hail, Obadiah, Zechariah,
18: 2 who prepared a great banquet for him and his **o**.
18: 8 So the king of Israel called one of his **o** and said,
22: 8 he happened to meet some of Judah's **o**
24:11 became full, the Levites carried it to the king's **o**.
24:25 But his own **o** decided to kill him for murdering
26:11 the direction of Hananiah, one of the king's **o**.
28:21 and from the homes of his **o** and gave them to the
29:20 next morning King Hezekiah gathered the city **o**
29:30 and the **o** ordered the Levites to praise the LORD
30: 2 The king, his **o**, and all the community of
30:12 to unite in obeying the orders of the king and his **o**,
30:24 and the **o** donated one thousand bulls and ten
31: 8 When Hezekiah and his **o** came and saw these
32: 3 he consulted with his **o** and military advisers,
32: 9 sent **o** to Jerusalem with this message for Hezekiah
32:16 And Sennacherib's **o** further mocked the LORD
32:18 The Assyrian **o** who brought the letters shouted
32:19 These **o** talked about the God of Jerusalem as
33:24 At last Amon's own **o** plotted against him
34:13 others assisted as secretaries, **o**, and gatekeepers.
34:16 "Your **o** are doing everything they were assigned
35: 8 The king's **o** also made willing contributions to the
Ezr 5: 6 and the other **o** of the province west of the
6: 6 your colleagues and other **o** west of the Euphrates:
9: 2 the **o** and leaders are some of the worst offenders."
Ne 2:16 The city **o** did not know I had been out there
2:16 spoken to the religious and political leaders, the **o**,
4:19 I explained to the nobles and **o** and all the people,
5: 7 I spoke out against these nobles and **o**.
5:12 and **o** formally vow to do what they had promised.
5:14 neither I nor my **o** drew on our official food
5:16 And I required all my **o** to spend time working on
5:17 even though I regularly fed 150 Jewish **o** at my
6:17 and forth between Tobiah and the **o** of Judah.
11: 3 Here is a list of the names of the provincial **o** who
Est 1: 3 he gave a banquet for all his princes and **o**.
1: 3 as well as the noblemen and provincial **o**.
1: 5 special banquet for all the palace servants and **o**—
1:14 and Memucan—seven high **o** of Persia and Media.
1:18 of every one of us, your **o** throughout the empire,
3: 2 All the king's **o** would bow down before Haman to
3: 3 Then the palace **o** at the king's gate asked
3:12 and the local **o** of each province in their own
5:11 and how he had been promoted over all the other **o**
8: 9 and local **o** of all the 127 provinces stretching from
9: 3 and the royal **o** helped the Jews for fear of
Job 29:10 The highest **o** of the city stood quietly,
Isa 10:33 vast army of Assyria—officers and high **o** alike.
36: 3 These are the **o** who went out to meet with them:
37: 5 After King Hezekiah's **o** delivered the king's
Jer 1:18 None of the kings, **o**, priests, or people of Judah
2:26 Kings, **o**, priests, and prophets—all are alike in
4: 9 "the king and the **o** will tremble in fear.
8: 1 break open the graves of the kings and **o** of Judah,
17:25 and their **o** will always ride among the people of
21: 7 says the LORD, even after King Zedekiah, his **o**,
22: 2 Let your **o** and your people listen, too.
22: 4 and on horses, with his parade of **o** and subjects.
24: 8 his **o**, all the people left in Jerusalem, and those
25:18 of Judah, and their kings and **o** drank from the cup.
25:19 to Pharaoh, his **o**, his princes, and his people.
26:10 When the **o** of Judah heard what was happening,
26:11 and prophets presented their accusations to the **o**
26:16 Then the **o** and the people said to the priests
26:21 the army officers and **o** heard what he was saying,
29: 2 the queen mother, the court **o**, the leaders of Judah,
32:32 the kings, the **o**, the priests, and the prophets—
34:10 The **o** and all the people had obeyed the king's
34:19 whether you are **o** of Judah or Jerusalem, court **o**,
priests,
34:21 and his **o** to the army of the king of Babylon.
35: 4 was located next to the one used by the palace **o**,
36:12 palace where the administrative **o** were meeting.
36:14 the **o** sent Jehudi son of Nethaniah, grandson of
36:15 "Sit down and read the scroll to us," the **o** said,
36:19 and Jeremiah should both hide," the **o** told Baruch.
36:20 Then the **o** left the scroll for safekeeping in the
36:21 and read it to the king as all his **o** stood by.
36:24 Neither the king nor his **o** showed any signs of fear
36:31 I will punish him and his family and his **o**
37: 2 But neither King Zedekiah nor his **o** nor the people
37:14 wouldn't listen, and he took Jeremiah before the **o**.
37:18 What have I done against you, your **o**,
38: 4 So these **o** went to the king and said, "Sir,
38: 6 So the **o** took Jeremiah from his cell and lowered
38:25 My **o** may hear that I spoke to you. Then they may
38:27 it wasn't long before the king's **o** came to Jeremiah
41: 3 they went out and slaughtered all the Judean **o**
41:16 warriors, women, children, and palace **o**.
44:21 that you and your ancestors, your kings and **o**,
51:57 "I will make drunk her **o**, wise men, rulers,
Da 1: 3 who was in charge of the palace **o**,
3: 2 and all the provincial **o** to come to the dedication
3: 3 When all these **o** had arrived and were standing
6: 7 and other **o** have unanimously agreed that Your
6:11 The **o** went together to Daniel's house and found
11: 5 But one of this king's own **o** will become more
Mic 7: 3 **O** and judges alike demand bribes. The people
Na 3:17 Your princes and **o** are also like locusts,
Mt 20:25 and **o** lord it over the people beneath them.
Mk 10:42 and **o** lord it over the people beneath them.
Ac 5:21 When the high priest and his **o** arrived,
16:22 and the city **o** ordered them stripped and beaten
16:35 The next morning the city **o** sent the police to tell
16:38 the city **o** were alarmed to learn that Paul and Silas
17: 8 The people of the city, as well as the city **o**,
17: 9 But the **o** released Jason and the other believers
19:31 Some of the **o** of the province, friends of Paul,
1Pe 2:14 and the **o** he has appointed. For the king has sent

OFFICIATE (2) [OFFICE]

Nu 8:26 the Tabernacle, but they may not **o** in the service.
18: 4 but no one who is not a Levite may **o** with you.

OFFICIATING (2) [OFFICE]

Ex 35:19 for Aaron and his sons to wear while **o** as priests."
Lev 14:11 Then the **o** priest will present that person for

OFFSCOURING [KJV] See REFUSE

OFFSPRING (16) [OFF]

Ge 3:15 and your **o** and her **o** will be enemies.
12: 7 and said, "I am going to give this land to your **o**."
13:15 land to you and your **o** as a permanent possession.
17: 7 It will continue between me and your **o** forever.
17: 8 this land of Canaan to you and to your **o** forever.
24: 7 solemnly promised to give this land to my **o**.
30:39 all of their **o** were streaked, speckled, and spotted.
31:38 your sheep and goats so they produced healthy **o**.
Lev 22:28 a mother animal and her **o** on the same day,
Nu 24: 7 in buckets; / their **o** are supplied with all they need.
Job 11:12 any more than a wild donkey can bear human **o**!
39: 3 to give birth to their young and deliver their **o**.
Ps 109:13 May all his **o** die. / May his family name be blotted

Isa 57: 3 you **o** of adulterers and prostitutes!
Ac 17:28 As one of your own poets says, 'We are his **o**.'

OFTEN (44)

Ge 37: 2 he **o** tended his father's flocks with his half
42:34 and you may come as **o** as you like to buy
Ex 2:17 But other shepherds would **o** come and chase the
Nu 24: 1 so he did not resort to divination as he **o** did.
Dt 2:11 and the Anakites are **o** referred to as the Rephaites,
Ne 5: 8 How **o** must we redeem them?" And they had
Job 33:29 "Yes, God **o** does these things for people.
Ps 78:40 how **o** they rebelled against him in the desert
Pr 1:24 "I called you so **o**, but you didn't come. I reached
7:12 She is **o** seen in the streets and markets,
25:17 Don't visit your neighbors too **o**, or you will wear
Ecc 7:22 For you know how **o** you yourself have laughed at
8:14 good people are **o** treated as though they were
8:14 and wicked people are **o** treated as though they
9:11 The wise are **o** poor, and the skillful are not
9:12 in a snare, people are **o** caught by sudden tragedy.
Isa 57: 1 pass away; the godly **o** die before their time.
Mt 11:18 John the Baptist didn't drink wine and he **o** fasted,
17:15 He **o** falls into the fire or into the water.
18:21 how **o** should I forgive someone who sins against
23:37 How **o** I have wanted to gather your children
Mk 5: 4 was put into chains and shackles—as he **o** was—
9:10 but they **o** asked each other what he meant by
9:22 The evil spirit **o** makes him fall into the fire or into
Lk 2:19 these things in her heart and thought about them **o**.
5:16 But Jesus **o** withdrew to the wilderness for prayer.
7:33 John the Baptist didn't drink wine and he **o** fasted,
8:29 This spirit had **o** taken control of the man.
13:34 How **o** I have wanted to gather your children
15: 1 and other notorious sinners **o** came to listen to
Jn 12: 6 and he **o** took some for his own use.
Ac 3:10 beggar they had seen so **o** at the Beautiful Gate,
8:10 to the greatest, **o** spoke of him as "the Great One—
24:26 so he sent for him quite **o** and talked with him.
Ro 1: 9 God knows how **o** I pray for you. Day and night I
1Co 11:25 Do this in remembrance of me as **o** as you drink
2Co 11:23 I have worked harder, been put in jail more **o**,
11:27 **O** I have been hungry and thirsty and have gone
11:27 **O** I have shivered with cold, without enough
Php 3:18 For I have told you **o** before, and I say it again with
1Ti 5:23 sake of your stomach because you are sick so **o**.
2Ti 1:16 and all his family because he **o** visited
Phm 1: 7 so **o** refreshed the hearts of God's people.
Rev 11: 6 kind of plague upon the earth as **o** as they wish.

OG (23) [OG'S]

Nu 21:33 but King **O** of Bashan and all his people attacked
21:34 for I have given you victory over **O** and his entire
21:35 And Israel was victorious and killed King **O**,
32:33 the Amorites and the land of King **O** of Bashan—
Dt 1: 4 who had ruled in Heshbon, and King **O** of Bashan,
3: 1 where King **O** and his army attacked us at Edrei.
3: 2 for I have given you victory over **O** and his army,
3: 3 So the LORD our God handed King **O** and all his
3:11 King **O** of Bashan was the last of the giant
4:47 conquered his land and that of King **O** of Bashan—
29: 7 and King **O** of Bashan came out to fight against us,
31: 4 just as he destroyed Sihon and **O**, the kings of the
Jos 2:10 And we know what you did to Sihon and **O**,
9:10 and King **O** of Bashan (who lived in Ashtaroth).
12: 4 King **O** of Bashan, the last of the Rephaites,
12: 6 destroyed the people of King Sihon and King **O**.
13:12 and all the territory of King **O** of Bashan, who had
13:12 King **O** was the last of the Rephaites, for Moses
13:30 all of Bashan, all the former kingdom of King **O**,
1Ki 4:19 Sihon of the Amorites and King **O** of Bashan.
Ne 9:22 of Heshbon and the land of King **O** of Bashan.
Ps 135:11 Sihon king of the Amorites, / **O** king of Bashan,
136:20 and **O** king of Bashan. / His faithful love endures

OG'S (3) [OG]

Dt 3:10 which were part of **O** kingdom in Bashan.
3:13 of Gilead and all of Bashan—**O** former kingdom—
Jos 13:31 and King **O** royal cities of Ashtaroth and Edrei.

OH (98) [O] See Index of Articles, Etc.

OHAD (2)

Ge 46:10 were Jemuel, Jamin, **O**, Jakin, Zohar, and Shaul.
Ex 6:15 Jamin, **O**, Jakin, Zohar, and Shaul (whose mother

OHEL (1)

1Ch 3:20 **O**, Berekiah, Hasadiah, and Jushab-hesed.

OHOLAH (6) [SAMARIA]

Eze 23: 4 The older girl was named **O**, and her sister was
23: 4 for **O** is Samaria and Oholibah is Jerusalem.
23: 5 "Then **O** lusted after other lovers instead of me,
23:11 though Oholibah saw what had happened to **O**,
23:36 you must accuse **O** and Oholibah of all their awful
23:44 They slept with **O** and Oholibah, these shameless

OHOLIAB (5)

Ex 31: 6 "And I have appointed **O** son of Ahisamach,
35:34 has given both him and **O** son of Ahisamach,
36: 1 "Bezalel, **O**, and the other craftsmen whom the
36: 2 So Moses told Bezalel and **O** to begin the work,
38:23 He was assisted by **O** son of Ahisamach,

OHOLIBAH (8) [JUDAH]

Eze 23: 4 older girl was named Oholah, and her sister was **O**.
23: 4 for Oholah is Samaria and **O** is Jerusalem.
23:11 "Yet even though **O** saw what had happened to
23:18 "So I became disgusted with **O**, just as I was with
23:21 And so, **O**, you celebrated your former days as a
23:22 "Therefore, **O**, this is what the Sovereign LORD
23:36 must accuse Oholah and **O** of all their awful deeds.
23:44 They slept with Oholah and **O**, these shameless

OHOLIBAMAH (8)

Ge 36: 2 and **O**, the daughter of Anah and granddaughter of
36: 5 Esau and **O** had sons named Jeush, Jalam,
36:14 Esau also had sons through **O**, the daughter of
36:18 and his wife **O** became the leaders of the clans of
36:18 These are the clans descended from Esau's wife **O**,
36:25 son of Anah was Dishon, and **O** was his daughter.
36:41 **O**, Elah, Pinon,
1Ch 1:52 **O**, Elah, Pinon,

OIL (194) [OILS]

Ge 28:18 a memorial pillar. Then he poured olive **o** over it.
35:14 to God and anointed the pillar with olive **o**.
Ex 25: 6 olive **o** for the lamps; spices for the anointing **o**
and the fragrant incense;
27:20 "Tell the people of Israel to bring you pure olive **o**
29: 2 loaves of bread, thin cakes mixed with olive **o**, and
wafers with **o** poured over them.
29: 7 Then take the anointing **o** and pour it over his
29:21 the altar and mix it with some of the anointing **o**.
29:23 one loaf of bread, one cake mixed with olive **o**,
29:36 for it; make it holy by anointing it with **o**.
29:40 of fine flour mixed with one quart of olive **o**;
30:24 12-1/2 pounds of cassia, and one gallon of olive **o**.
30:25 Blend these ingredients into a holy anointing **o**.
30:26 Use this scented **o** to anoint the Tabernacle,
30:30 Use this **o** also to anoint Aaron and his sons,
30:31 of Israel, 'This will always be my holy anointing **o**.
30:33 Anyone who blends scented **o** like it or puts any of
31:11 the anointing **o**; and the special incense for the
35: 8 olive **o** for the lamps; spices for the anointing **o**
and the fragrant incense;
35:14 the lamp cups and the **o** for lighting;
35:15 the anointing **o** and fragrant incense;
35:28 They also brought spices and olive **o** for the light,
the anointing **o**, and the fragrant incense.
37:29 Then he made the sacred **o** for anointing the priests
39:37 the lamp cups and the **o** for lighting;
39:38 the gold altar; the anointing **o**; the fragrant incense;
40: 9 "Take the anointing **o** and sprinkle it on the
40:10 Sprinkle the anointing **o** on the altar of burnt
Lev 2: 1 You are to pour olive **o** on it and sprinkle it with
2: 2 will take a handful of the flour mixed with olive **o**,
2: 4 it must be made of choice flour mixed with olive **o**
2: 4 presented in the form of cakes mixed with olive **o**
or wafers spread with olive **o**.
2: 5 it must be made of choice flour and olive **o**, and it
2: 6 Break it into pieces and pour **o** on it; it is a kind of
2: 7 it also must be made of choice flour and olive **o**.
2:15 put olive **o** on it and sprinkle it with incense.
2:16 portion of the roasted grain mixed with olive **o**,
5:11 they must not mix it with olive **o** or put any
6:15 the choice flour that has been mixed with olive **o**
6:21 It must be cooked on a griddle with olive **o**, and it
7:10 whether flour mixed with olive **o** or dry flour,
7:12 all made without yeast and soaked with olive **o**.
8: 2 the anointing **o**, the bull for the sin offering,
8:10 Then Moses took the anointing **o** and anointed the
8:12 Then he poured some of the anointing **o** on
8:26 a cake of unleavened bread soaked with olive **o**,
and a thin wafer spread with olive **o**.
8:30 Next Moses took some of the anointing **o** and some
9: 4 and flour mixed with olive **o** for a grain offering.
10: 7 for the anointing **o** of the LORD is upon you."
14:10 with five quarts of choice flour mixed with olive **o**
and three-fifths of a pint of olive **o**.
14:12 priest will take one of the lambs and the olive **o**
14:15 "Then the priest will pour some of the olive **o** into
14:16 He will dip his right finger into the **o** and sprinkle
14:17 then put some of the **o** remaining in his left hand
14:18 The **o** remaining in the priest's hand will then be
14:21 choice flour mixed with olive **o** as a grain offering
and three-fifths of a pint of olive **o**.
14:24 lamb for the guilt offering, along with the olive **o**,
14:26 "The priest will also pour some of the olive **o** into
14:27 He will dip his right finger into the **o** and sprinkle
14:28 then put some of the olive **o** from his hand on the
14:29 The **o** that is still in the priest's hand will then be
21:10 who has had the anointing **o** poured on his head
21:12 because he has been made holy by the anointing **o**
23:13 of three quarts of choice flour mixed with olive **o**.
24: 2 to provide you with pure olive **o** for the lampstand,
Nu 4: 9 lamp snuffers, trays, and special jars of olive **o**.
4:16 will be responsible for the **o** of the lampstand,
4:16 the daily grain offering, and the anointing **o**.
5:15 Do not mix it with olive **o** or frankincense, for it is
6:15 cakes of choice flour mixed with olive **o** and
wafers spread with olive **o**—
7:13 grain offerings of choice flour mixed with olive **o**.
7:19 grain offerings of choice flour mixed with olive **o**.
7:25 grain offerings of choice flour mixed with olive **o**.
7:31 grain offerings of choice flour mixed with olive **o**.
7:37 grain offerings of choice flour mixed with olive **o**.
7:43 grain offerings of choice flour mixed with olive **o**.
7:49 grain offerings of choice flour mixed with olive **o**.
7:55 grain offerings of choice flour mixed with olive **o**.
7:61 grain offerings of choice flour mixed with olive **o**.
7:67 grain offerings of choice flour mixed with olive **o**.
7:73 grain offerings of choice flour mixed with olive **o**.
7:79 grain offerings of choice flour mixed with olive **o**.
8: 8 a grain offering of choice flour mixed with olive **o**,
11: 8 cakes tasted like they had been cooked in olive **o**.
15: 4 of choice flour mixed with one quart of olive **o**.
15: 6 flour mixed with two and a half pints of olive **o**,
15: 9 of choice flour mixed with two quarts of olive **o**,
18:12 the best of the olive **o**, wine, and grain.
28: 5 of choice flour mixed with one quart of olive **o**.
28: 9 of three quarts of choice flour mixed with olive **o**,
28:12 grain offerings of choice flour mixed with olive **o**
28:20 grain offerings of choice flour mixed with olive **o**
28:28 grain offerings of choice flour mixed with olive **o**
29: 3 grain offerings of choice flour mixed with olive **o**
29: 9 grain offerings of choice flour mixed with olive **o**
29:14 grain offering of choice flour mixed with olive **o**—
Dt 11:14 crops of grain, grapes for wine, and olives for **o**.
12:17 the tithe of your grain and new wine and olive **o**,
14:23 applies to your tithes of grain, new wine, olive **o**,
18: 4 the new wine, the olive **o**, and the wool at shearing
28:40 but you will never use the olive **o**, for the trees will
28:51 you no grain, new wine, olive **o**, calves, or lambs,
32:13 from the cliffs, / with olive **o** from the hard rock.
33:24 by his brothers; / may he bathe his feet in olive **o**.
Jdg 9: 9 'Should I quit producing the olive **o** that blesses
1Sa 10: 1 Then Samuel took a flask of olive **o** and poured it
16: 1 Now fill your horn with olive **o** and go to
16:13 Samuel took the olive **o** he had brought and poured
2Sa 1:21 shield of Saul will no longer be anointed with **o**.
1Ki 1:39 There Zadok the priest took a flask of olive **o** from
5:11 for his household and 110,000 gallons of olive **o**.
17:12 and a little cooking **o** in the bottom of the jug.
17:14 and **o** left in your containers until the time when
17:15 eat from her supply of flour and **o** for many days.
2Ki 4: 2 at all, except a flask of olive **o**," she replied.
4: 4 Pour olive **o** from your flask into the jars,
4: 6 he told her. And then the olive **o** stopped flowing.
4: 7 to her, "Now sell the olive **o** and pay your debts,
9: 1 he told him. "Take this vial of olive **o** with you,
9: 3 and pour the **o** over his head. Say to him, 'This is
9: 6 Then the young prophet poured the **o** over Jehu's
1Ch 9:29 as choice flour, wine, olive **o**, incense, and spices.
12:40 of flour, fig cakes, raisins, wine, olive **o**, cattle,
23:29 the cakes cooked in olive **o**, and the other mixed
27:28 Joash was responsible for the supplies of olive **o**.
2Ch 2:10 gallons of wine, and 110,000 gallons of olive **o**."
2:15 "Send along the wheat, barley, olive **o**, and wine
11:11 he stored supplies of food, olive **o**, and wine.
28:15 and drink, and dressed their wounds with olive **o**.
31: 5 of their crops and grain, new wine, olive **o**, honey,
32:28 storehouses for his grain, new wine, and olive **o**;
Ezr 3: 7 paying them with food, wine, and olive **o**.
6: 9 salt, wine, and olive **o** that they need each day.
7:22 550 gallons of wine, 550 gallons of olive **o**,
Ne 5:11 charged on their money, grain, wine, and olive **o**."
10:37 our fruit, and the best of our new wine and olive **o**.
10:39 and olive **o** to the Temple and place them in the
13: 5 and tithes of grain, new wine, olive **o**,
13:12 new wine, and olive **o** to the Temple storerooms.
Est 2:12 six months with **o** of myrrh, followed by six
Job 20:17 will never again enjoy abundant streams of olive **o**
24:11 They press out olive **o** without being allowed to
29: 6 and my olive groves poured out streams of olive **o**.
Ps 23: 5 me as a guest, / anointing my head with **o**.
45: 7 pouring out the **o** of joy on you more than on
89:20 I have anointed him with my holy **o**.
104:15 to make them glad, / olive **o** as lotion for their skin,
133: 2 harmony is as precious as the fragrant anointing **o**
Pr 5: 3 sweet as honey, and her mouth is smoother than **o**.
Isa 57: 9 You have given olive **o** and perfume to Molech as
Jer 31:12 wine, and **o**, and the healthy flocks and herds.
41: 8 barley, **o**, and honey that they had hidden away.
Eze 16:13 the finest foods—fine flour, honey, and olive **o**—
16:18 Then you used my **o** and incense to worship them.
16:19 the fine flour and **o** and honey I had given you,
23:41 and my **o** on a table that was spread before you.
27:17 from Minnith, early figs, honey, **o**, and balm.
32:14 and they will flow as smoothly as olive **o**,
45:14 one percent of your olive **o**,
45:24 and a gallon of olive **o** with each young bull
45:25 the grain offering, along with the required olive **o**.
46: 5 He is to offer one gallon of olive **o** for each half
46: 7 bushel of flour he must offer one gallon of olive **o**.
46:11 One gallon of **o** is to be given with each half
46:14 a third of a gallon of olive **o** to moisten the flour.
46:15 and the olive **o** must be given as a daily sacrifice
Hos 2: 5 for clothing of wool and linen, and for olive **o**.'
2: 8 she has—the grain, the wine, the olive **o**.
Joel 1:10 The grain, the wine, and the olive **o** are gone.
2:19 I am sending you grain and wine and olive **o**,
2:24 the presses will overflow with wine and olive **o**.
Mic 6: 7 of rams and tens of thousands of rivers of olive **o**?
6:15 but not get enough **o** to anoint yourselves.
Hag 2:12 to brush against some bread or stew, wine or **o**,
Zec 4: 2 "I see a solid gold lampstand with a bowl of **o** on
4:12 that pour out golden **o** through two gold tubes?"
Mt 25: 3 The five who were foolish took no **o** for their
25: 4 other five were wise enough to take along extra **o**.
25: 8 'Please give us some of your **o** because our lamps
25:10 "But while they were gone to buy **o**,
Mk 6:13 many sick people, anointing them with olive **o**.
Lk 7:46 You neglected the courtesy of olive **o** to anoint my
16: 6 'I owe him eight hundred gallons of olive **o**.'
Heb 1: 9 pouring out the **o** of joy on you more than on

Jas 5:14 anointing them with **o** in the name of the Lord.
Rev 6:6 day's pay. And don't waste the olive **o** and wine."
18:13 wine, olive **o**, fine flour, wheat, cattle, sheep,

OILS (4) [OIL]

2Ki 20:13 the silver, the gold, the spices, and the aromatic **o**.
Isa 39:2 the silver, the gold, the spices, and the aromatic **o**.
Eze 16:9 your blood, and I rubbed fragrant **o** into your skin.
Da 10:3 had drunk no wine, and had used no fragrant **o**.

OINTMENT (5) [OINTMENTS]

2Ki 20:7 "Make an **o** from figs and spread it over the boil."
Isa 38:21 "Make an **o** from figs and spread it over the boil,
Jer 46:11 Go up to Gilead to get **o**, O virgin daughter of
Jn 19:39 pounds of embalming **o** made from myrrh
Rev 3:18 And buy **o** for your eyes so you will be able to see.

OINTMENTS (4) [OINTMENT]

2Ch 16:14 laid on a bed perfumed with sweet spices and **o**,
Est 2:12 by six months with special perfumes and **o**.
Isa 1:6 and infected wounds—without any **o** or bandages.
Lk 23:56 and prepared spices and **o** to embalm him.

OLD (359) [OLDER, OLDEST, ONE-YEAR-OLD]

DAYS OF OLD (4) Ps 143:5; Isa 51:9; 63:11; Heb 11:2

OLD AGE (19) Ge 15:15; 21:2,7; 25:8; 35:29; 37:3; 44:20; Ru 4:15; 1Sa 2:31; 26:10; 1Ki 11:4; 15:23; 1Ch 29:28; 2Ch 24:15; Job 5:26; 21:7; Ps 71:9; 92:14; Lk 1:36

OLD MAN (23) Ge 24:1; 27:2; 43:27; 44:20; Jos 13:1; 23:2; Jdg 19:16,20,22,23; 1Sa 17:12; 28:14; 1Ki 13:13,18; 14:4; 2Ki 4:14; 1Ch 23:1; 2Ch 15:13; Job 42:17; Hos 7:9; Lk 1:18; Jn 3:4; Phm 1:9

OLD MEN (9) 2Ch 36:17; Ps 148:12; Jer 18:21; 26:17; La 5:12,14; Joel 2:28; Zec 8:4; Ac 2:17

Ge 5:3 When Adam was 130 years **o**, his son Seth was
5:6 When Seth was 105 years **o**, his son Enosh was
5:9 When Enosh was 90 years **o**, his son Kenan was
5:12 When Kenan was 70 years **o**, his son Mahalalel
5:15 When Mahalalel was 65 years **o**, his son Jared was
5:18 When Jared was 162 years **o**, his son Enoch was
5:21 When Enoch was 65 years **o**, his son Methuselah
5:25 When Methuselah was 187 years **o**, his son
5:28 When Lamech was 182 years **o**, his son Noah was
5:32 By the time Noah was 500 years **o**, he had three
6:4 who became the heroes mentioned in legends of **o**.
7:6 He was 600 years **o** when the flood came,
7:11 When Noah was 600 years **o**, on the seventeenth
8:13 when Noah was 601 years **o**, ten and a half months
9:29 He was 950 years **o** when he died.
11:10 When Shem was 100 years **o**, his son Arphaxad
11:12 When Arphaxad was 35 years **o**, his son Shelah
11:14 When Shelah was 30 years **o**, his son Eber was
11:16 When Eber was 34 years **o**, his son Peleg was
11:18 When Peleg was 30 years **o**, his son Reu was born.
11:20 When Reu was 32 years **o**, his son Serug was born.
11:22 When Serug was 30 years **o**, his son Nahor was
11:24 When Nahor was 29 years **o**, his son Terah was
11:26 When Terah was 70 years **o**, he became the father
12:4 Abram was seventy-five years **o** when he left
15:15 (But you will die in peace, at a ripe **o** age.)
16:16 Abram was eighty-six years **o** at that time.
17:1 When Abram was ninety-nine years **o**, the LORD
17:24 Abraham was ninety-nine years **o** at that time,
18:11 And since Abraham and Sarah were both very **o**,
18:12 when my master—my husband—is also so **o**?"
18:13 she say, 'Can an **o** woman like me have a baby?'
19:4 all the men of Sodom, young and **o**, came from all
19:31 And our father will soon be too **o** to have children.
21:2 and she gave a son to Abraham in his **o** age.
21:5 Abraham was one hundred years **o** at the time.
21:7 Yet I have given Abraham a son in his **o** age!"
23:1 When Sarah was 127 years **o**,
24:1 Abraham was now a very **o** man, and the LORD
24:36 When Sarah, my master's wife, was very **o**,
25:8 and he died at a ripe **o** age, joining his ancestors in
25:20 When Isaac was forty years **o**, he married
25:26 Isaac was sixty years **o** when the twins were born.
27:1 When Isaac was **o** and almost blind, he called for
27:2 "I am an **o** man now," Isaac said, "and I expect
35:8 Soon after this, Rebekah's **o** nurse, Deborah, died.
35:29 and he died at a ripe **o** age, joining his ancestors in
37:2 When Joseph was seventeen years **o**, he often
37:3 because Joseph had been born to him in his **o** age.
38:11 youngest son, Shelah, was **o** enough to marry her.
41:46 He was thirty years **o** when he entered the service
43:27 "How is your father—the **o** man you spoke about?
44:20 We said, 'Yes, we have a father, an **o** man, and a child of his **o** age,
47:8 "How **o** are you?" Pharaoh asked him.
47:9 but I am still not nearly as **o** as many of my
47:28 in Egypt, so he was 147 years **o** when he died.
50:22 in Egypt. Joseph was 110 years **o** when he died.
Ex 6:16 (Levi, their father, lived to be 137 years **o**.)
6:18 and Uzziel. (Kohath lived to be 133 years **o**.)
6:20 and Moses. (Amram lived to be 137 years **o**.)
7:7 Moses was eighty years **o**, and Aaron was
10:9 "Young and **o**, all of us will go," Moses replied.
38:26 This included all the men who were twenty years **o**
Lev 25:22 you will eat from the **o** crop until the new harvest
Nu 1:3 twenty years **o** or older who are able to go to war.
1:18 The men of Israel twenty years **o** or older were
1:20[-21] This is the number of men twenty years **o**
1:45 all the men of Israel who were twenty years **o**
3:15 Count every male who is one month **o** or older."
3:22 There were 7,500 males one month **o** or older
3:28 There were 8,600 males one month **o** or older
3:34 There were 6,200 males one month **o** or older
3:39 there were 22,000 males one month **o** or older.
3:40 all the firstborn sons in Israel who are one month **o**
3:43 number of firstborn sons who were one month **o**
14:29 none of you who are twenty years **o** or older
18:16 Redeem them when they are one month **o**.
26:2 of all the men of Israel who are twenty years **o**
26:4 "Count all the men of Israel twenty years **o**
26:62 men from the Levite clans who were one month **o**
32:11 no one who is twenty years **o** or older will ever see
33:39 Aaron was 123 years **o** when he died there on
Dt 2:14 **o** enough to fight in battle had died in the
28:50 and heartless nation that shows no respect for the **o**
31:2 "I am now 120 years **o** and am no longer able to
34:7 Moses was 120 years **o** when he died, yet his
Jos 5:4 because all the men who were **o** enough to bear
5:6 **o** enough to bear arms when they left Egypt had
6:21 and women, young and **o**, cattle, sheep, donkeys—
9:4 weathered saddlebags and **o** patched wineskins.
9:13 we filled them, but now they are **o** and cracked.
13:1 When Joshua was an **o** man, the LORD said to him, "You are growing **o**,
14:7 I was forty years **o** when Moses, the servant of the
14:10 in the wilderness. Today I am eighty-five years **o**.
23:1 all their enemies. Joshua, who was now very **o**,
23:2 of Israel. He said to them, "I am an **o** man now.
Jdg 6:25 your father's herd, the one that is seven years **o**.
8:32 Gideon died when he was very **o**, and he was
19:16 That evening an **o** man came home from his work
19:20 are welcome to stay with me," the **o** man said.
19:22 beating at the door and shouting to the **o** man,
19:23 The **o** man stepped outside to talk to them. "No,
Ru 1:12 parents' homes, for I am too **o** to marry again.
4:15 restore your youth and care for you in your **o** age.
1Sa 2:22 Now Eli was very **o**, but he was aware of what his
2:31 die before their time. None will live to a ripe **o** age.
4:15 who was ninety-eight years **o** and blind.
4:18 broke his neck and died, for he was **o** and very fat.
5:9 young and **o**, with a plague of tumors, and there
8:1 As Samuel grew **o**, he appointed his sons to be
8:5 "Look," they told him, "you are now **o**, and your
12:2 own sons, and I stand here, an **o**, gray-haired man.
13:1 Saul was thirty years **o** when he became king,
17:12 Jesse was an **o** man at that time, and he had eight
24:13 As that **o** proverb says, 'From evil people come
26:10 down someday, or he will die in battle or of **o** age.
28:14 "He is an **o** man wrapped in a robe," she replied.
2Sa 2:10 Ishbosheth was forty years **o** when he became
4:4 He was five years **o** when Saul and Jonathan were
5:4 David was thirty years **o** when he began to reign,
19:32 He was very **o**, about eighty, and very wealthy.
19:34 "No," he replied, "I am far too **o** for that.
19:35 I am eighty years **o** today, and I can no longer
1Ki 1:1 Now King David was very **o**, and no matter how
1:15 He was very **o** now, and Abishag was taking care
11:4 In Solomon's **o** age, they turned his heart to
13:11 there was an **o** prophet living in Bethel,
13:12 The **o** prophet asked them, "Which way did he
13:13 "Quick, saddle the donkey," the **o** man said.
13:14 The **o** prophet asked him, "Are you the man of
13:18 But the **o** prophet answered, "I am a prophet,
13:18 and water to drink.' " But the **o** man was lying to
13:20 a message from the LORD came to the **o** prophet.
13:25 reported it in Bethel, where the **o** prophet lived.
13:26 When the **o** prophet heard the report, he said,
14:4 He was an **o** man now and could no longer see.
14:21 He was forty-one years **o** when he became king,
15:23 *of Judah.* In his **o** age his feet became diseased.
22:42 He was thirty-five years **o** when he became king,
2Ki 3:21 every man who could fight, young and **o**,
4:14 doesn't have a son, and her husband is an **o** man."
8:17 Jehoram was thirty-two years **o** when he became
8:26 Ahaziah was twenty-two years **o** when he became
11:21 Joash was seven years **o** when he became king.
14:2 Amaziah was twenty-five years **o** when he became
15:2 He was sixteen years **o** when he became king,
15:33 He was twenty-five years **o** when he became king,
16:2 Ahaz was twenty years **o** when he became king,
16:14 Then King Ahaz removed the **o** bronze altar from
16:15 The **o** bronze altar will be only for my personal
17:40 not listen and continued to follow their **o** ways.
18:2 He was twenty-five years **o** when he became king,
21:1 Manasseh was twelve years **o** when he became
21:19 Amon was twenty-two years **o** when he became
22:1 Josiah was eight years **o** when he became king,
23:18 his bones or those of the **o** prophet from Samaria.
23:31 Jehoahaz was twenty-three years **o** when he
23:36 Jehoiakim was twenty-five years **o** when he
24:8 Jehoiachin was eighteen years **o** when he became
24:18 Zedekiah was twenty-one years **o** when he became
1Ch 2:21 When Hezron was sixty years **o**, he married
23:1 When David was an **o** man, he appointed his son
23:3 All the Levites who were thirty years **o** or older
23:24 Each had to be twenty years **o** or older to qualify
23:27 final instructions that all the Levites twenty years **o**
25:8 without regard to whether they were young or **o**,
29:28 He died at a ripe **o** age, having enjoyed long life,
2Ch 12:13 He was forty-one years **o** when he became king,
15:13 put to death—whether young or **o**, man or woman.
20:31 He was thirty-five years **o** when he became king,
21:5 Jehoram was thirty-two years **o** when he became
21:20 Jehoram was thirty-two years **o** when he became
22:2 Ahaziah was twenty-two years **o** when he became
24:1 Joash was seven years **o** when he became king,
24:15 Jehoiada lived to a very **o** age, finally dying at 130.
25:1 Amaziah was twenty-five years **o** when he became
25:5 that he had an army of 300,000 men twenty years **o**
27:1 Jotham was twenty-five years **o** when he became
27:8 He was twenty-five years **o** when he became king,
28:1 Ahaz was twenty years **o** when he became king,
29:1 Hezekiah was twenty-five years **o** when he became
31:15 dividing the gifts fairly among young and **o** alike.
31:16 also distributed the gifts to all males three years **o**
31:17 and to the Levites twenty years **o** or older who
33:1 Manasseh was twelve years **o** when he became
33:21 Amon was twenty-two years **o** when he became
34:1 Josiah was eight years **o** when he became king,
36:2 Jehoahaz was twenty-three years **o** when he
36:5 Jehoiakim was twenty-five years **o** when he
36:9 Jehoiachin was eighteen years **o** when he became
36:11 Zedekiah was twenty-one years **o** when he became
36:17 killing both young and **o**, men and women, healthy
Ezr 3:3 local residents, they rebuilt the altar at its **o** site.
3:8 The Levites who were twenty years **o** or older were
Ne 3:6 The **O** City Gate was repaired by Joiada son of
8:2 and all the children **o** enough to understand.
10:28 serve God, and who were **o** enough to understand
12:39 then past the Ephraim Gate to the **O** City Gate,
Est 3:13 young and **o**, including women and children—
Job 5:26 You will live to a good **o** age. You will not be
14:8 Though its roots have grown **o** in the earth and its
21:7 "The truth is that the wicked live to a good **o** age. They grow **o** and wealthy.
22:15 "Will you continue on the **o** paths where evil
32:6 "I am young and you are **o**, so I held back and did
42:17 he died, an **o** man who had lived a long, good life.
Ps 28:5 So he will tear them down like **o** buildings,
37:25 Once I was young, and now I am **o**. / Yet I have
58:9 God will sweep them away, both young and **o**,
71:9 And now, in my **o** age, don't set me aside.
71:18 Now that I am **o** and gray, / do not abandon me,
77:5 I think of the good **o** days, long since ended,
89:1 Young and **o** will hear of your faithfulness.
89:45 You have made him **o** before his time
92:14 Even in **o** age they will still produce fruit;
102:26 remain forever; / they will wear out like **o** clothing.
143:5 I remember the days of **o**. / I ponder all your great
148:12 young men and maidens, / **o** men and children.
Pr 20:29 the gray hair of experience is the splendor of the **o**.
23:22 despise your mother's experience when she is **o**.
Ecc 4:13 is better to be a poor but wise youth than to be an **o**
6:3 have a hundred children and live to be very **o**.
7:10 Don't long for "the good **o** days," for you don't
10:8 When you demolish an **o** wall, you could be bitten
11:8 When people live to be very **o**, let them rejoice in
12:1 Honor him in your youth before you grow **o**
12:2 the sun and moon and stars is dim to your **o** eyes,
SS 7:13 the new as well as **o**, for I have stored them up for
Isa 4:1 your name so we won't be mocked as **o** maids."
7:15 By the time this child is **o** enough to eat curds
8:4 before this child is **o** enough to say 'Papa'
11:1 yes, a new Branch bearing fruit from the **o** root.
20:4 them walk naked and barefoot, both young and **o**,
22:11 you build a reservoir for water from the **o** pool.
28:9 Are we little children, barely **o** enough to talk?
50:9 All my enemies will be destroyed like **o** clothes
51:9 Rouse yourself as in the days of **o** when you slew
63:11 Then they remembered those days of **o** when
65:17 no one will even think about the **o** ones anymore.
65:20 longer will babies die when only a few days **o**.
65:20 No longer will people be considered **o** at one
Jer 3:16 "you will no longer wish for 'the good **o** days'
6:16 Look for the **o**, godly way, and walk in it.
17:11 at the end of their lives, will become poor **o** fools.
18:21 Let their **o** men die in a plague, and let their young
20:10 Even my **o** friends are watching me, waiting for a
20:16 Let him be destroyed like the cities of **o** that the
26:17 Then some of the wise **o** men stood and spoke to
31:13 will dance for joy, and the men—**o** and young—
38:11 where he found some **o** rags and discarded
48:38 For I have smashed Moab like an **o**,
51:3 Young and **o** alike will be completely destroyed.
51:22 **o** people and children, young men and maidens.
52:1 Zedekiah was twenty-one years **o** when he became
La 2:21 young and **o**, boys and girls, killed by the swords
3:4 He has made my skin and flesh grow **o**. He has
5:12 and the **o** men are treated with contempt.
5:14 The **o** men no longer sit in the city gates; the young
Eze 9:6 **o** and young, girls and women and little children.
12:23 Now give them this new proverb to replace the **o**
13:18 the souls of my people, both young and **o** alike.
16:8 saw you again, you were **o** enough to be married.
21:26 The **o** order changes—now the lowly are exalted,
23:43 with worn-out, **o** prostitutes like these, let them!'
27:9 Wise **o** craftsmen from Gebal did all the caulking.
37:2 He led me around among the **o**, dry bones that
37:11 They are saying, 'We have become **o**, dry bones—
Hos 7:9 Israel is like an **o** man with graying hair,
7:9 unaware of how weak and **o** he has become.
8:8 they lie among the nations like an **o** pot that no one
Joel 2:28 will prophesy. Your **o** men will dream dreams.
Na 2:11 where the **o** and feeble and the young and tender
Zec 8:4 Once again **o** men and women will walk
14:10 the Benjamin Gate over to the site of the **o** gate,
Mt 2:16 and around Bethlehem who were two years **o**
9:16 And who would patch an **o** garment with unshrunk
9:16 the patch shrinks and pulls away from the **o** cloth,
9:17 And no one puts new wine into **o** wineskins.
9:17 The **o** skins would burst from the pressure,
13:52 the storehouse the new teachings as well as the **o**."

Mk 2:21 And who would patch an **o** garment with unshrunk
2:21 new patch shrinks and pulls away from the **o** cloth,
2:22 And no one puts new wine into **o** wineskins.
5:42 And the girl, who was twelve years **o**,
Lk 1:7 was barren, and now they were both very **o**.
1:17 the spirit and power of Elijah, the prophet of **o**.
1:18 I'm an **o** man now, and my wife is also well along
1:36 Elizabeth has become pregnant in her **o** age!
1:59 When the baby was eight days **o**, all the relatives
2:36 of Phanuel, of the tribe of Asher, and was very **o**.
2:37 She was now eighty-four years **o**. She never left
2:42 When Jesus was twelve years **o**, they attended the
3:23 Jesus was about thirty years **o** when he began his
5:36 a new garment and uses it to patch an **o** garment.
5:36 and the patch wouldn't even match the **o** garment.
5:37 And no one puts new wine into **o** wineskins.
5:37 The new wine would burst the **o** skins,
5:39 But no one who drinks the **o** wine seems to want
5:39 the fresh and the new. 'The **o** is better,' they say."
8:42 only child was dying, a little girl twelve years **o**.
Jn 3:4 "How can an **o** man go back into his mother's
8:57 The people said, "You aren't even fifty years **o**.
9:21 He is **o** enough to speak for himself. Ask him."
9:23 they said, "He is **o** enough to speak for himself.
21:18 But when you are **o**, you will stretch out your
Ac 2:17 see visions, / and your **o** men will dream dreams.
7:8 was circumcised when he was eight days **o**.
7:23 "One day when he was forty years **o**, he decided to
Ro 4:19 even though he knew that he was too **o** to be a
6:6 Our **o** sinful selves were crucified with Christ
6:18 Now you are free from sin, your **o** master, and you
7:5 When we were controlled by our **o** nature,
7:6 not in the **o** way by obeying the letter of the law,
7:18 so far as my **o** sinful nature is concerned.
1Co 5:8 not by eating the **o** bread of wickedness and evil,
2Co 3:6 The **o** way ends in death; in the new way, the Holy
3:7 That **o** system of law etched in stone led to death,
3:9 If the **o** covenant, which brings condemnation,
3:11 So if the **o** covenant, which has been set aside,
3:14 and even to this day whenever the **o** covenant is
5:14 we also believe that we have all died to the **o** life
5:17 are not the same anymore, for the **o** life is gone.
Gal 1:14 and I tried as hard as possible to follow all the **o**
2:18 I make myself guilty if I rebuild the **o** system I
5:17 The **o** sinful nature loves to do evil, which is just
Eph 4:22 throw off your **o** evil nature and your former way
Php 3:5 For I was circumcised when I was eight days **o**,
Col 3:9 for you have stripped off your **o** evil nature and all
1Ti 4:7 time arguing over godless ideas and **o** wives' tales.
5:9 must be a woman who is at least sixty years **o**
Phm 1:9 an **o** man, now in prison for the sake of Christ
Heb 1:11 They will wear out like **o** clothing.
1:12 You will roll them up like an **o** coat. / They will fade away like **o** clothing. / But you are always the same; / you will never grow **o**."
7:16 not by meeting the **o** requirement of belonging to
7:18 the **o** requirement about the priesthood was set
7:23 is that there were many priests under the **o** system.
8:6 the ministry of those who serve under the **o** laws,
8:8 But God himself found fault with the **o** one when
9:10 For that **o** system deals only with food and drink
9:13 Under the **o** system, the blood of goats and bulls
10:1 The **o** system in the law of Moses was only a
10:1 The sacrifices under the **o** system were repeated
10:11 Under the **o** covenant, the priest stands before the
11:2 God gave his approval to people in days of **o**
11:11 even though they were too **o** and Sarah was barren.
11:12 Abraham, who was too **o** to have any children—
11:21 was by faith that Jacob, when he was **o** and dying,
1Pe 1:14 Don't slip back into your **o** ways of doing evil;
3:5 That is the way the holy women of **o** made
2Pe 1:9 that God has cleansed them from their **o** life of sin.
1Jn 2:7 for it is an **o** one you have always had, right from
Rev 20:2 the dragon—that **o** serpent, the Devil, Satan—
21:1 for the **o** heaven and the **o** earth had disappeared.
21:4 For the **o** world and its evils are gone forever."

OLDER (71) [OLD]

Ge 10:21 were also born to Shem, the **o** brother of Japheth.
19:31 One day the **o** daughter said to her sister,
19:33 and the **o** daughter went in and slept with her
19:34 The next morning the **o** daughter said to her
19:37 When the **o** daughter gave birth to a son,
25:23 the descendants of your **o** son will serve the
27:1 he called for Esau, his **o** son, and said, "My son?"
27:19 Jacob replied, "It's Esau, your **o** son. I've done as
27:32 of course!" he replied. "It's Esau, your **o** son."
41:51 Joseph named his **o** son Manasseh, for he said,
42:3 So Joseph's ten **o** brothers went down to Egypt to
48:14 his left hand was on the head of Manasseh, the **o**.
48:18 "No, Father," he said, "this one over here is **o**.
Ex 2:10 Later, when he was **o**, the child's mother brought
38:26 all the men who were twenty years old or **o**,
Lev 27:7 A man **o** than sixty is valued at fifteen pieces of
27:7 a woman **o** than sixty is valued at ten pieces of
Nu 1:3 twenty years old or **o** who are able to go to war.
1:18 of Israel twenty years old or **o** were registered,
1:20[-21] years old or **o** who were able to go to war,
1:45 were twenty years old or **o** and able to go to war.
3:15 Count every male who is one month old or **o**."
3:22 one month old or **o** among these Gershonite clans.
3:28 one month old or **o** among these Kohathite clans.
3:34 one month old or **o** among these Merarite clans.
3:39 there were 22,000 males one month old or **o**.
3:40 firstborn sons in Israel who are one month old or **o**,
3:43 sons who were one month old or **o** was 22,273.
14:29 years old or **o** and were counted in the census
26:2 all the men of Israel who are twenty years old or **o**,
26:4 all the men of Israel twenty years old and **o**,
26:62 who were one month old or **o** numbered 23,000.
32:11 or **o** will ever see the land I solemnly promised to
Jos 17:1 of Manasseh, the descendants of Joseph's **o** son.
1Sa 14:49 had two daughters: Merab, who was **o**, and Michal.
18:17 "I am ready to give you my **o** daughter, Merab,
1Ki 2:22 You know that he is my **o** brother, and that he has
12:6 with the **o** men who had counseled his father,
12:7 The **o** counselors replied, "If you are willing to
12:13 for he rejected the advice of the **o** counselors
2Ki 4:18 One day when her child was **o**, he went out to visit
1Ch 6:28 The sons of Samuel were Joel (the **o**) and Abijah
23:3 who were thirty years old or **o** were counted,
23:24 or **o** to qualify for service in the house of the
23:27 twenty years old or **o** were registered for service.
2Ch 10:6 with the **o** men who had counseled his father,
10:7 The **o** counselors replied, "If you are good to the
10:13 for he rejected the advice of the **o** counselors
22:1 The marauding bands of Arabs had killed all the **o**
25:5 an army of 300,000 men twenty years old and **o**,
31:16 the gifts to all males three years old or **o**,
31:17 or **o** who were listed according to their jobs
Ezr 3:8 or **o** were put in charge of rebuilding the LORD's
3:12 Many of the **o** priests, Levites, and other leaders
Job 15:10 gray-haired men much **o** than your father!
32:4 the others to speak because they were **o** than he.
32:7 I thought, 'Those who are **o** should speak,
Pr 22:6 and when they are **o**, they will remain upon it.
Eze 16:46 "Your **o** sister was Samaria, who lived with her
23:4 The **o** girl was named Oholah, and her sister was
23:13 she was going, defiling herself just like her **o** sister.
Mt 21:28 A man with two sons told the **o** boy, 'Son, go out
Lk 15:25 "Meanwhile, the **o** son was in the fields working.
15:28 "The **o** brother was angry and wouldn't go in.
Jn 7:22 this tradition of circumcision is **o** than the law of
Ro 9:12 "The descendants of your **o** son will serve the
1Ti 5:1 Never speak harshly to an **o** man, but appeal to him
5:2 Treat the **o** women as you would your mother,
Tit 2:2 Teach the **o** men to exercise self-control, to be
2:3 teach the **o** women to live in a way that is
2:4 These **o** women must train the younger women to

OLDEST (60) [OLD]

Ge 10:15 Canaan's **o** son was Sidon, the ancestor of the
22:21 The **o** was named Uz, the next **o** was Buz,
24:2 in charge of his household, who was his **o** servant,
25:13 The **o** was Nebaioth, followed by Kedar, Abdeel,
29:16 Leah, who was the **o**, and her younger sister,
35:23 The sons of Leah were Reuben (Jacob's **o** son),
36:15 The sons of Esau's **o** son, Eliphaz,
38:6 When his **o** son, Er, grew up, Judah arranged his
43:33 them in the order of their ages, from **o** to youngest.
44:12 Joseph's servant began searching the **o** brother's
46:8 with him to Egypt: Reuben was Jacob's **o** son.
49:3 "Reuben, you are my **o** son, / the child of my
Ex 6:14 Israel's **o** son, included Hanoch, Pallu, Hezron,
11:5 from the **o** son of Pharaoh, who sits on the throne, to the **o** son of his lowliest slave.
Nu 26:5 the clans descended from Reuben, Jacob's **o** son:
Dt 21:17 He must give the customary double portion to his **o**
Jos 17:1 (Makir was Manasseh's **o** son and was the father of
Jdg 8:20 Turning to Jether, his **o** son, he said, "Kill them!"
1Sa 8:2 Joel and Abijah, his **o** sons, held court in
17:13 Jesse's three **o** sons—Eliab, Abinadab,
17:14 Since David's three **o** brothers were in the army,
17:28 But when David's **o** brother, Eliab, heard David
2Sa 3:2 The **o** was Amnon, whose mother was Ahinoam of
1Ki 16:34 he laid the foundations, his **o** son, Abiram, died.
2Ki 3:27 So he took his **o** son, who would have been the
1Ch 1:13 Canaan's **o** son was Sidon, the ancestor of the
1:29 The sons of Ishmael were Nebaioth (the **o**), Kedar,
2:3 But the **o** son, Er, was a wicked man,
2:25 the **o** son of Hezron, were Ram (the **o**), Bunah,
2:27 the **o** son of Jerahmeel, were Maaz, Jamin,
2:42 The **o** son of Caleb, the brother of Jerahmeel,
2:50 sons of Hur, the **o** son of Caleb's wife Ephrathah,
3:1 The **o** was Amnon, whose mother was Ahinoam of
3:15 The sons of Josiah were Johanan (the **o**),
5:1 The **o** son of Israel was Reuben. But since he
5:3 the **o** son of Israel, were Hanoch, Pallu, Hezron,
8:1 of age, included Bela (the **o**), Ashbel, Aharah,
8:30 and his **o** son was named Abdon. Jeiel's other sons
8:39 Ulam (the **o**), Jeush (the second), and Eliphelet
9:5 from the Shilonite clan, including Asaiah (the **o**)
9:31 a Levite and the **o** son of Shallum the Korahite,
9:36 and his **o** son was named Abdon. Jeiel's other sons
26:2 The sons of Meshelemiah were Zechariah (the **o**),
26:4 also gatekeepers, were Shemaiah (the **o**),
26:10 leader among his sons, though he was not the **o**.
2Ch 21:3 Jehoram became king because he was the **o**.
Ne 10:36 We agree to give to God our **o** sons
Job 1:13 and daughters were dining at the **o** brother's house,
1:18 and daughters were feasting in their **o** brother's
Ps 78:51 He killed the **o** son in each Egyptian family,
105:36 Then he killed the **o** child in each Egyptian home,
Jer 31:9 For I am Israel's father, and Ephraim is my **o** child.
Mt 22:25 The **o** married and then died without children,
Mk 12:20 The **o** of them married and then died without
Lk 20:29 The **o** married and then died without children.
Jn 8:9 slipped away one by one, beginning with the **o**,
Heb 12:16 He traded his birthright as the **o** son for a single

OLDNESS [KJV] See OLD (WAY)

OLIVE (172) [OLIVES]

Ge 8:11 the bird returned to him with a fresh **o** leaf in its
28:18 as a memorial pillar. Then he poured **o** oil over it.
35:14 offering to God and anointed the pillar with **o** oil.
Ex 23:11 The same applies to your vineyards and **o** groves.
25:6 **o** oil for the lamps; spices for the anointing oil
27:20 "Tell the people of Israel to bring you pure **o** oil
29:2 make loaves of bread, thin cakes mixed with **o** oil,
29:23 take one loaf of bread, one cake mixed with **o** oil,
29:40 quarts of fine flour mixed with one quart of **o** oil;
30:24 12-1/2 pounds of cassia, and one gallon of **o** oil.
35:8 **o** oil for the lamps; spices for the anointing oil
35:28 They also brought spices and **o** oil for the light,
Lev 2:1 You are to pour **o** oil on it and sprinkle it with
2:2 he will take a handful of the flour mixed with **o** oil,
2:4 it must be made of choice flour mixed with **o** oil
2:4 be presented in the form of cakes mixed with **o** oil or wafers spread with **o** oil.
2:5 it must be made of choice flour and **o** oil, and it
2:7 it also must be made of choice flour and **o** oil.
2:15 put **o** oil on it and sprinkle it with incense.
2:16 token portion of the roasted grain mixed with **o** oil,
5:11 they must not mix it with **o** oil or put any incense
6:15 of the choice flour that has been mixed with **o** oil
6:21 It must be cooked on a griddle with **o** oil, and it
7:10 whether flour mixed with **o** oil or dry flour,
7:12 all made without yeast and soaked with **o** oil.
8:26 a cake of unleavened bread soaked with **o** oil, and a thin wafer spread with **o** oil.
9:4 and flour mixed with **o** oil for a grain offering.
14:10 along with five quarts of choice flour mixed with **o** oil and three-fifths of a pint of **o** oil.
14:12 The priest will take one of the lambs and the **o** oil
14:15 "Then the priest will pour some of the **o** oil into
14:21 along with two quarts of choice flour mixed with **o**
14:21 a grain offering and three-fifths of a pint of **o** oil.
14:24 the lamb for the guilt offering, along with the **o** oil,
14:26 "The priest will also pour some of the **o** oil into
14:28 then put some of the **o** oil from his hand on the
23:13 of three quarts of choice flour mixed with **o** oil.
24:2 to provide you with pure **o** oil for the lampstand,
Nu 4:9 lamp snuffers, trays, and special jars of **o** oil.
5:15 Do not mix it with **o** oil or frankincense, for it is a
6:15 cakes of choice flour mixed with **o** oil and wafers spread with **o** oil—
7:13 grain offerings of choice flour mixed with **o** oil.
7:19 grain offerings of choice flour mixed with **o** oil.
7:25 grain offerings of choice flour mixed with **o** oil.
7:31 grain offerings of choice flour mixed with **o** oil.
7:37 grain offerings of choice flour mixed with **o** oil.
7:43 grain offerings of choice flour mixed with **o** oil.
7:49 grain offerings of choice flour mixed with **o** oil.
7:55 grain offerings of choice flour mixed with **o** oil.
7:61 grain offerings of choice flour mixed with **o** oil.
7:67 grain offerings of choice flour mixed with **o** oil.
7:73 grain offerings of choice flour mixed with **o** oil.
7:79 grain offerings of choice flour mixed with **o** oil.
8:8 and a grain offering of choice flour mixed with **o**
11:8 These cakes tasted like they had been cooked in **o**
15:4 of choice flour mixed with one quart of **o** oil.
15:6 flour mixed with two and a half pints of **o** oil,
15:9 of choice flour mixed with two quarts of **o** oil,
18:12 the LORD—the best of the **o** oil, wine, and grain.
28:5 of choice flour mixed with one quart of **o** oil.
28:9 of three quarts of choice flour mixed with **o** oil,
28:12 grain offerings of choice flour mixed with **o** oil—
28:20 grain offerings of choice flour mixed with **o** oil—
28:28 grain offerings of choice flour mixed with **o** oil—
29:3 grain offerings of choice flour mixed with **o** oil—
29:9 grain offerings of choice flour mixed with **o** oil—
29:14 a grain offering of choice flour mixed with **o** oil—
Dt 6:11 eat from vineyards and **o** trees you did not plant.
12:17 the tithe of your grain and new wine and **o** oil,
14:23 applies to your tithes of grain, new wine, **o** oil,
18:4 the new wine, the **o** oil, and the wool at shearing
24:20 When you beat the olives from your **o** trees,
28:40 You will grow **o** trees throughout your land,
28:40 but you will never use the **o** oil, for the trees will
28:51 you no grain, new wine, **o** oil, calves, or lambs,
32:13 from the cliffs, / with **o** oil from the hard rock.
33:24 by his brothers; / may he bathe his feet in **o** oil.
Jos 24:13 I gave you vineyards and **o** groves for food,
Jdg 9:8 a king. First they said to the **o** tree, 'Be our king!'
9:9 'Should I quit producing the **o** oil that blesses both
15:5 He also destroyed their grapevines and **o** trees.
1Sa 8:14 and vineyards and **o** groves and give them to his
10:1 Then Samuel took a flask of **o** oil and poured it
16:1 Now fill your horn with **o** oil and go to Bethlehem.
16:13 Samuel took the **o** oil he had brought and poured it
1Ki 1:39 There Zadok the priest took a flask of **o** oil from
5:11 for his household and 110,000 gallons of **o** oil.
6:23 Solomon placed two cherubim made of **o** wood,
6:31 Solomon made double doors of **o** wood with
6:33 Then he made four-sided doorposts of **o** wood for
2Ki 4:2 at all, except a flask of **o** oil," she replied.
4:4 Pour **o** oil from your flask into the jars,
4:6 he told her. And then the **o** oil stopped flowing.
4:7 said to her, "Now sell the **o** oil and pay your debts,
5:26 and clothing and **o** groves and vineyards and sheep
9:1 he told him. "Take this vial of **o** oil with you,
18:32 wine, bread and vineyards, **o** trees and honey—
1Ch 9:29 as choice flour, wine, **o** oil, incense, and spices.
12:40 of flour, fig cakes, raisins, wine, **o** oil, cattle,
23:29 the cakes cooked in **o** oil, and the other mixed
27:28 from Geder was in charge of the king's **o** groves
27:28 Joash was responsible for the supplies of **o** oil.

2Ch 2:10 gallons of wine, and 110,000 gallons of **o** oil."
2:15 "Send along the wheat, barley, **o** oil, and wine that
11:11 he stored supplies of food, **o** oil, and wine.
28:15 and drink, and dressed their wounds with **o** oil.
31: 5 of their crops and grain, new wine, **o** oil, honey,
32:28 storehouses for his grain, new wine, and **o** oil;
Ezr 3: 7 and Sidon, paying them with food, wine, and **o** oil.
6: 9 salt, wine, and **o** oil that they need each day.
7:22 of wheat, 550 gallons of wine, 550 gallons of **o** oil,
Ne 5:11 You must restore their fields, vineyards, **o** groves,
5:11 charged on their money, grain, wine, and **o** oil."
8:15 to get branches from **o**, wild **o**, myrtle, palm, and
9:25 cisterns already dug and vineyards and **o** groves
10:37 of our fruit, and the best of our new wine and **o** oil.
10:39 and **o** oil to the Temple and place them in the
13: 5 and tithes of grain, new wine, **o** oil,
13:12 new wine, and **o** oil to the Temple storerooms.
Job 15:33 like an **o** tree that sheds its blossoms so the fruit
20:17 He will never again enjoy abundant streams of **o**
24:11 They press out **o** oil without being allowed to taste
29: 6 and my **o** groves poured out streams of **o** oil.
Ps 52: 8 But I am like an **o** tree, / thriving in the house of
104:15 to make them glad, / **o** oil as lotion for their skin,
128: 3 as vigorous and healthy as young **o** trees.
Isa 41:19 cedar, acacia, myrtle, **o**, cypress, fir, and pine—
57: 9 You have given **o** oil and perfume to Molech as
Jer 11:16 the LORD, once called them a thriving **o** tree,
11:17 the LORD Almighty, who planted this **o** tree,
Eze 16:13 ate the finest foods—fine flour, honey, and **o** oil—
32:14 and they will flow as smoothly as **o** oil,
45:14 one percent of your **o** oil,
45:24 and a gallon of **o** oil with each young bull and ram.
45:25 the grain offering, along with the required **o** oil.
46: 5 He is to offer one gallon of **o** oil for each half
46: 7 bushel of flour he must offer one gallon of **o** oil.
46:14 a third of a gallon of **o** oil to moisten the flour.
46:15 and the **o** oil must be given as a daily sacrifice
Hos 2: 5 for clothing of wool and linen, and for **o** oil.'
2: 8 everything she has—the grain, the wine, the **o** oil.
2:22 the grain, the grapes, and the **o** trees for moisture.
14: 6 will spread out like those of beautiful **o** trees,
Joel 1:10 The grain, the wine, and the **o** oil are gone.
2:19 I am sending you grain and wine and **o** oil,
2:24 and the presses will overflow with wine and **o** oil.
Am 4: 9 Locusts devoured all your fig and **o** trees.
Mic 6: 7 of rams and tens of thousands of rivers of **o** oil?
Hab 3:17 even though the **o** crop fails, and the fields lie
Hag 2:19 and the **o** tree have produced their crops.
Zec 4: 3 And I see two **o** trees, one on each side of the
4:11 "What are these two **o** trees on each side of the
4:12 and what are the two **o** branches that pour out
Mt 26:36 Then Jesus brought them to an **o** grove called
Mk 6:13 many sick people, anointing them with **o** oil.
14:32 And they came to an **o** grove called Gethsemane,
Lk 7:46 You neglected the courtesy of **o** oil to anoint my
16: 6 'I owe him eight hundred gallons of **o** oil.'
Jn 18: 1 with his disciples and entered a grove of **o** trees.
18: 3 lanterns, and weapons, they arrived at the **o** grove.
18:26 "Didn't I see you out there in the **o** grove with
Ro 11:17 who were branches from a wild **o** tree,
11:17 sharing in God's rich nourishment of his special **o**
11:24 branches from a wild **o** tree and graft you into his
Rev 6: 6 a day's pay. And don't waste the **o** oil and wine."
11: 4 These two prophets are the two **o** trees and the two
18:13 wine, **o** oil, fine flour, wheat, cattle, sheep, horses,

OLIVES (28) [OLIVE]

Dt 7:13 grapes, and **o**, and great herds of cattle, sheep,
8: 8 fig trees, pomegranates, **o**, and honey.
11:14 crops of grain, grapes for wine, and **o** for oil.
24:20 When you beat the **o** from your olive trees,
24:20 Leave some of the **o** for the foreigners, orphans,
2Sa 15:30 walked up the road that led to the Mount of **O**,
15:32 of the Mount of **O** where people worshiped God,
1Ki 11: 7 On the Mount of **O**, east of Jerusalem, he even
Isa 17: 6 like the stray **o** left on the tree after the harvest.
24:13 like the stray **o** left on the tree or the few grapes
Jer 40:10 Harvest the grapes and summer fruits and **o**,
Mic 6:15 You will press your **o** but not get enough oil to
Hag 1:11 the grain and grapes and **o** and all your other crops,
Zec 14: 4 On that day his feet will stand on the Mount of **O**,
14: 4 And the Mount of **O** will split apart, making a
Mt 21: 1 came to the town of Bethphage on the Mount of **O**.
24: 3 Later, Jesus sat on the slopes of the Mount of **O**.
26:30 they sang a hymn and went out to the Mount of **O**.
Mk 11: 1 of Bethphage and Bethany, on the Mount of **O**.
13: 3 Jesus sat on the slopes of the Mount of **O** across
14:26 they sang a hymn and went out to the Mount of **O**.
Lk 19:29 of Bethphage and Bethany, on the Mount of **O**,
19:37 where the road started down from the Mount of **O**,
21:37 he returned to spend the night on the Mount of **O**.
22:39 upstairs room and went as usual to the Mount of **O**.
Jn 8: 1 Jesus returned to the Mount of **O**,
Ac 1:12 The apostles were at the Mount of **O** when this
Jas 3:12 Can you pick **o** from a fig tree or figs from a

OLIVET [KJV] See (MOUNT OF) OLIVES

OLIVEYARD [KJV] See OLIVE (GROVES)

OLYMPAS (1)

Ro 16:15 and to **O** and all the other believers who are with

OMAR (3)

Ge 36:11 were Teman, **O**, Zepho, Gatam, and Kenaz.
36:15 leaders of the clans of Teman, **O**, Zepho, Kenaz,
1Ch 1:36 **O**, Zepho, Gatam, Kenaz, and Amalek, who was

OMEGA (3)

Rev 1: 8 "I am the Alpha and the **O**—the beginning
21: 6 I am the Alpha and the **O**—the Beginning
22:13 I am the Alpha and the **O**, the First and the Last,

OMENS (1)

Dt 18:10 or sorcery, or allow them to interpret **o**,

OMER (1)

Ex 16:36 container used to measure the manna was an **o**,

OMINOUSLY (1)

Jer 48:16 "Calamity is coming fast to Moab; it threatens **o**.

OMNIPOTENT [KJV] See ALMIGHTY

OMRI (15) [OMRI'S]

1Ki 16:16 they chose **O**, commander of the army, as their
16:17 So **O** led the army of Israel away from Gibbethon
16:21 their king, while the other half supported **O**.
16:22 So Tibni was killed, and **O** became the next king.
16:23 **O** began to rule over Israel in the thirty-first year
16:24 Then **O** bought the hill now known as Samaria
16:25 But **O** did what was evil in the LORD's sight,
16:28 When **O** died, he was buried in Samaria. Then his
16:29 Ahab son of **O** began to rule over Israel in the
2Ki 8:26 was Athaliah, a granddaughter of King **O** of Israel.
1Ch 7: 8 Joash, Eliezer, Elioenai, **O**, Jeremoth, Abijah,
9: 4 son of **O**, son of Imri, son of Bani, a descendant of
27:18 (a brother of David) / Issachar | **O** son of Michael
2Ch 22: 2 was Athaliah, a granddaughter of King **O** of Israel.
Mic 6:16 "The only laws you keep are those of evil King **O**;

OMRI'S (2) [OMRI]

1Ki 16:22 But **O** supporters defeated the supporters of Tibni
16:27 The rest of the events in **O** reign, the extent of his

ON (1 of 3855) [ONTO, ONWARD] See also Index of Articles, Etc.

Nu 16: 1 and Abiram, the sons of Eliab, and **O** son of Peleth,

ONAM (4)

Ge 36:23 were Alvan, Manahath, Ebal, Shepho, and **O**.
1Ch 1:40 were Alvan, Manahath, Ebal, Shepho, and **O**.
2:26 wife named Atarah. She was the mother of **O**.
2:28 The sons of **O** were Shammai and Jada. The sons

ONAN (8) [ONAN'S]

Ge 38: 4 wife had another son, and she named him **O**.
38: 8 Then Judah said to Er's brother **O**, "You must
38: 9 But **O** was not willing to have a child who would
38:10 But the LORD considered it a wicked thing for **O**
46:12 of Judah were Er, **O**, Shelah, Perez, and Zerah.
46:12 (But Er and **O** had died in the land of Canaan.)
Nu 26:19 Judah had two sons, Er and **O**, who had died in the
1Ch 2: 3 Their names were Er, **O**, and Shelah.

ONAN'S (1) [ONAN]

Ge 38:10 his dead brother. So the LORD took **O** life, too.

ONCE (236) [ONE]

Ge 18:32 please do not get angry; I will speak but **o** more!
28: 2 Instead, go at **o** to Paddan-aram, to the house of
29:35 **O** again she became pregnant and had a son.
35: 9 God appeared to Jacob **o** again when he arrived at
37:33 Their father recognized it at **o**. "Yes," he said,
41:14 Pharaoh sent for Joseph at **o**, and he was brought
Ex 8: 1 "Go to Pharaoh **o** again and tell him, 'This is what
9:28 terrifying thunder and hail. I will let you go at **o**."
9:33 all at **o** the thunder and hail stopped,
10:17 "Forgive my sin only this **o**, and plead with the
10:20 But the LORD made Pharaoh stubborn **o** again,
10:27 So the LORD hardened Pharaoh's heart **o** more,
14: 4 And **o** again I will harden Pharaoh's heart, and he
17: 2 So **o** more the people grumbled and complained to
22:21 you yourselves were **o** foreigners in the land of
30:10 "**O** a year Aaron must purify the altar by placing
Lev 16:34 to make atonement for the Israelites **o** each year."
19:34 Remember that you were **o** foreigners in the land
Nu 13:30 "Let's go at **o** to take the land," he said. "We can
22:11 Come at **o** to curse them. Perhaps then I will be
Dt 2:10 and powerful race of giants called the Emites had **o**
2:20 too, was **o** considered the land of the Rephaites,
5:15 Remember that you were **o** slaves in Egypt
7:22 You will not clear them away all at **o**, for if you
10:10 And **o** again the LORD yielded to my pleas
10:19 for you yourselves were **o** foreigners in the land of
23:23 But **o** you have voluntarily made a vow, be careful
Jos 6: 3 Your entire army is to march around the city **o** a
6:11 the LORD was carried around the city **o** that day,
6:14 On the second day they marched around the city **o**
7:17 The Israelites set out at **o** to investigate
Jdg 1: 7 "I **o** had seventy kings with thumbs and big toes
3:12 **O** again the Israelites did what was evil in the
5:14 a land that **o** belonged to the Amalekites,
9: 8 **O** upon a time the trees decided to elect a king.
11:18 But they never **o** crossed the Arnon River into
13: 9 and the angel of God appeared **o** again to his wife
1Sa 1: 9 **O** when they were at Shiloh, Hannah went over to
1:19 and went to worship the LORD **o** more.
3: 8 and **o** more Samuel jumped up and ran to Eli.
16:11 "Send for him at **o**," Samuel said. "We will not
20: 9 was planning to kill you, I would tell you at **o**."
20:12 and let you know at **o** how he feels about you.
2Sa 4:10 **O** before, someone told me, 'Saul is dead,'
5:23 And **o** again David asked the LORD what to do.
7: 7 And I have never **o** complained to Israel's leaders,
9: 7 I will give you all the land that **o** belonged to your
14:26 He cut his hair only **o** a year, and then only
15:14 "Then we must flee at **o**, or it will be too late!"
15:16 So the king and his household set out at **o**. He left
17:16 He must go across at **o** into the wilderness beyond.
19:22 for celebration! I am **o** again the king of Israel!"
20:23 Joab **o** again became the commander of David's
21:15 **O** again the Philistines were at war with Israel.
23: 8 He **o** used his spear to kill eight hundred enemy
23: 9 **O** Eleazar and David stood together against the
23:13 **O** during harvesttime, when David was at the cave
23:18 He **o** used his spear to kill three hundred enemy
24: 1 **O** again the anger of the LORD burned against
1Ki 1:13 Go at **o** to King David and say to him, 'My lord,
10:22 **O** every three years the ships returned,
18: 4 **O** when Jezebel had tried to kill all the LORD's
18: 7 Obadiah recognized him at **o** and fell to the ground
2Ki 1:13 **O** more the king sent a captain with fifty men.
11:10 and shields that had **o** belonged to King David
13:21 **O** when some Israelites were burying a man,
1Ch 11:11 He **o** used his spear to kill three hundred enemy
11:15 **O** when David was at the rock near the cave of
11:20 He **o** used his spear to kill three hundred enemy
14:14 And **o** again David asked God what to do. "Do not
17: 6 And I never **o** complained to Israel's leaders,
2Ch 9:21 **O** every three years the ships returned,
14: 9 **O** an Ethiopian named Zerah attacked Judah with
23: 9 and shields that had **o** belonged to King David
24: 5 "Go at **o** to all the towns of Judah and collect the
Ezr 6:13 and their colleagues complied at **o** with the
9:10 For **o** again we have ignored your commands!
Ne 2:18 They replied at **o**, "Good! Let's rebuild the wall!"
9:28 and **o** more you let their enemies conquer them.
9:28 again for help, you listened **o** more from heaven.
9:30 So **o** again you allowed the pagan inhabitants of
13:12 And **o** more all the people of Judah began bringing
13:20 a variety of wares camped outside Jerusalem **o**
Est 8: 3 Now **o** more Esther came before the king,
Job 9: 3 would it be possible to answer him even **o** in a
34:32 evil I have done; tell me, and I will stop at **o**'?
Ps 37:25 **O** I was young, and now I am old. / Yet I have
52: 5 But God will strike you down **o** and for all.
71:21 me to even greater honor / and comfort me **o** again.
80:18 Revive us so we can call on your name **o** more.
89:19 You **o** spoke in a vision to your prophet and said,
119:106 I've promised it **o**, and I'll promise again: / I will
Pr 4: 3 For I, too, was **o** my father's son, tenderly loved by
7:22 He followed her at **o**, like an ox going to the
19:19 If you rescue them **o**, you will have to do it again.
SS 6:13 come back, that we may see you **o** again."
Isa 1:21 See how Jerusalem, **o** so faithful, has become a
1:21 **O** the home of justice and righteousness, she is
1:22 **O** like pure silver, you have become like worthless
1:22 **O** so pure, you are now like watered-down wine.
7:25 go to the fertile hillsides where the gardens **o** grew,
14: 1 of Jacob. Israel will be his special people **o** again.
14: 1 He will bring them back to settle **o** again in their
16: 8 Moab was **o** like a spreading grapevine.
16: 8 Her shoots **o** reached as far as the Dead Sea.
21: 4 The sleep I **o** enjoyed at night is now a faint
23: 7 How can this silent ruin be all that is left of your **o**
23:12 **O** you were a lovely city, but you will never again
29:17 the wilderness of Lebanon will be a fertile field **o**
35: 7 and rushes will flourish where desert jackals **o**
35: 8 And a main road will go through that **o** deserted
44:26 and the towns of Judah will be lived in **o** again,
47:12 you strike terror into the hearts of people **o** again.
55:13 Where **o** there were thorns, cypress trees will
60:15 "Though you were **o** despised and hated
Jer 3:16 "And when your land is **o** more filled with
7:12 " 'Go to the place at Shiloh where I **o** put the
11:16 the LORD, **o** called them a thriving olive tree,
23:14 as the people of Sodom and Gomorrah **o** were."
32:44 Yes, fields will **o** again be bought and sold—
33:10 Judah's other towns, there will be heard **o** more
33:12 will **o** more see shepherds leading sheep
33:13 **O** again their flocks will prosper in the towns of
34:16 women you had freed, making them slaves **o** again.
48:32 Your spreading vines **o** reached as far as the Dead
50:19 and to be satisfied **o** more on the hill country of
La 1: 1 **o** bustling with people, are now silent.
1: 1 **O** the queen of nations, she is now a slave.
1: 8 All who **o** honored her now despise her, for they
2:20 those they **o** bounced on their knees?
4: 5 The people who **o** ate only the richest foods now
4: 5 Those who **o** lived in palaces now search the
4: 7 Our princes were **o** glowing with health; they were
5:21 back to you again! Give us back the joys we **o** had!
Eze 11:17 and I will give you the land of Israel **o** again.
16:22 you have not **o** thought of the days long ago when
23: 2 **o** there were two sisters who were daughters of the
26:17 'O famous island city, / **o** ruler of the sea,
26:17 their naval power, / **o** spread fear around the world.
31: 3 Assyria, too, was **o** like a cedar of Lebanon,
32:23 These mighty men who **o** struck terror in the hearts
32:26 They **o** struck terror into the hearts of all people.
32:30 the sword. **O** a terror, they now lie there in shame.
33: 1 **O** again a message came to me from the LORD:

36:11 of Israel, I will bring people to live on you o again.
36:12 I will cause my people to walk on you o again,
36:38 The ruined cities will be crowded with people o
Da 2:16 Daniel went at o to see the king and requested
11:4 nor will the kingdom hold the authority it o had.
11:29 "Then at the appointed time he will o again invade
Hos 2:14 "But then I will win her back o again. I will lead
Joel 2:22 fig trees and grapevines will flourish o more.
2:23 O more the autumn rains will come, as well as the
2:26 O again you will have all the food you want,
Jnh 1:15 him into the raging sea, and the storm stopped at o!
2:7 I turned my thoughts o more to the LORD.
Mic 7:19 O again you will have compassion on us. You will
Na 1:12 O my people, I have already punished you o,
2:12 O Nineveh, you were o a mighty lion! You crushed
Zep 2:14 The city that o was so proud will become a pasture
2:15 This is the fate of that boisterous city, o so secure.
Zec 2:12 and he will o again choose Jerusalem to be his own
6:7 patrol the earth!" So they left at o on their patrol.
8:4 O again old men and women will walk Jerusalem's
8:12 O more I will make the remnant in Judah
9:7 will join my people, just as the Jebusites o did.
Mal 3:3 so that they may o again offer acceptable sacrifices
3:4 Then o more the LORD will accept the offerings
Mt 2:9 O again the star appeared to them, guiding them to
4:20 And they left their nets at o and went with him.
14:27 But Jesus spoke to them at o. "It's all right,"
27:63 we remember what that deceiver o said while he
Mk 1:18 And they left their nets at o and went with him.
3:6 At o the Pharisees went away and met with the
4:1 O again Jesus began teaching by the lakeshore.
4:15 but then Satan comes at o and takes it away from
5:30 Jesus realized at o that healing power had gone out
6:50 But Jesus spoke to them at o. "It's all right,"
6:54 The people standing there recognized him at o,
10:32 Jesus o more began to describe everything that was
Lk 4:33 O when he was in the synagogue, a man possessed
4:39 She got up at o and prepared a meal for them.
8:19 O when Jesus' mother and brothers came to see
11:1 O when Jesus had been out praying, one of his
14:5 into a pit, don't you proceed at o to get him out?"
15:29 and never o refused to do a single thing you told
18:18 O a religious leader asked Jesus this question:
23:2 They began at o to state their case: "This man has
Jn 9:17 Then the Pharisees o again questioned the man
9:27 man exclaimed. "I told you o. Didn't you listen?
10:31 O again the Jewish leaders picked up stones to kill
10:39 O again they tried to arrest him, but he got away
13:30 So Judas left at o, going out into the night.
18:7 O more he asked them, "Whom are you searching
21:17 O more he asked him, "Simon son of John,
Ac 10:33 So I sent for you at o, and it was good of you to
15:30 The four messengers went at o to Antioch,
16:10 So we decided to leave for Macedonia at o, for we
16:40 and encouraged them o more before leaving town.
17:14 The believers acted at o, sending Paul on to the
19:38 are in session and the judges can take the case at o.
28:1 O we were safe on shore, we learned that we were
Ro 6:10 He died o to defeat sin, and now he lives for the
6:17 O you were slaves of sin, but now you have
9:26 And, / "O they were told, / 'You are not my
11:30 O, you Gentiles were rebels against God, but when
1Co 16:2 until I get there and then try to collect it all at o.
2Co 5:16 O I mistakenly thought of Christ that way,
11:16 O again, don't think that I have lost my wits to talk
11:25 O I was stoned. Three times I was shipwrecked.
11:25 O I spent a whole night and a day adrift at sea.
Gal 4:9 back again and become slaves o more to the weak
Eph 2:1 O you were dead, doomed forever because of your
2:13 Though you o were far away from God, now you
5:8 For though your hearts were o full of darkness,
Php 3:7 I o thought all these things were so very important,
4:16 I was in Thessalonica you sent help more than o.
Col 1:21 This includes you who were o so far away from
1Th 2:5 Never o did we try to win you with flattery, as you
Tit 3:3 O we, too, were foolish and disobedient. We were
Heb 6:4 to repentance those who were o enlightened—
7:25 Therefore he is able, o and forever, to save
7:27 But Jesus did this o for all when he sacrificed
9:7 and only o a year, and always with blood, which he
9:12 O for all time he took blood into that Most Holy
9:26 He came o for all time, at the end of the age,
9:27 just as it is destined that each person dies only o
9:28 so also Christ died only o as a sacrifice to take
10:2 for the worshipers would have been purified o for
10:10 sacrifice of the body of Jesus Christ o for all time.
12:26 "O again I will shake not only the earth
1Pe 2:10 "O you were not a people; / now you are the
2:10 of God. / O you received none of God's mercy;
2:25 O you were wandering like lost sheep. But now
3:18 Christ also suffered when he died for our sins o for
Jude 1:3 God gave this unchanging truth o for all time to his

ONCE-DESOLATE (1) [DESOLATE, ONE]

Eze 38:12 I will go to those o cities that are again filled with

ONE (2167) [ONCE, ONCE-DESOLATE, ONE'S, ONE-FIFTH, ONE-FOURTH, ONE-ROOM, ONE-TENTH, ONE-THIRD, ONE-YEAR-OLD, ONES, ONESELF]

EVERY ONE (19) Ge 34:22; Jos 21:42; 1Sa 11:2; 2Sa 8:2; 1Ki 19:10,14; 2Ki 10:19; 2Ch 14:5; 20:23; Est 1:18; Ps 34:19; 104:27; 119:33; Isa 31:7; Jer 42:17; 44:11; Da 12:1; Lk 4:40; Jude 1:5

HOLY ONE (56) Nu 16:7; 2Ki 19:22; Job 6:10; Ps 71:22; 78:41; 89:18; Pr 9:10; 30:3; Isa 1:4; 5:19,24; 8:13; 10:17,20; 12:6; 17:7; 29:19,23; 30:11,12,15; 31:1; 37:23; 40:25; 41:14,16,20; 43:3,14,15; 45:11; 47:4; 48:17; 49:7,7; 54:5; 55:5; 57:15; 60:9,14; Jer 50:29; 51:5; Eze 39:7; Da 4:13,23; Hos 11:9,12; Hab 1:12; 3:3; Mk 1:24; Lk 4:34; Jn 6:69; 10:36; Ac 2:27; 13:35; Rev 16:5

LOVE ONE ANOTHER (7) 1Th 4:9; 1Jn 2:7; 3:11,23; 4:7; 2Jn 1:5,6

MIGHTY ONE (9) Ge 49:24; Ps 132:2,5; Isa 1:24; 10:34; 33:21; 49:26; 60:16; Lk 1:49

ONE ANOTHER (37) Ge 25:18; 42:1; Lev 19:11; Isa 13:8; 34:14; 41:6; Jer 9:4,20; 22:8; Eze 4:17; 24:23; Zep 3:13; Zec 7:9; Mt 21:38; Mk 12:7; Lk 8:25; Jn 10:41; 13:35; 1Co 3:3; Gal 5:13,15,15,26,26; Eph 4:32; 5:21; Php 2:2; 1Th 4:9; Heb 10:24; 13:4; 1Pe 3:8; 1Jn 2:7; 3:11,23; 4:7; 2Jn 1:5,6

ONE BODY (9) Ro 12:5,5; 1Co 6:16; 10:17; 12:12,20; Eph 2:16; 4:4; Col 3:15

ONE DAY (119) Ge 1:5; 4:23; 9:21; 18:1; 19:31; 24:2; 25:29; 26:26; 27:45; 30:14; 34:1; 37:3; 39:11; 48:1; Ex 3:1; Lev 24:10; Nu 1:1; 10:11,29; 15:32; 16:1; 27:1,12; Jos 10:35; Jdg 4:6; 9:1; 14:1; 16:1; 17:2,7; 19:1; Ru 2:2; 3:1; 1Sa 2:27; 9:3; 14:1; 15:1; 17:17; 18:17; 19:9; 22:5; 23:1,15; 27:5; 2Sa 2:12; 3:7; 4:5; 9:1; 12:4,23; 13:4; 1Ki 2:13; 11:29; 16:9; 20:29; 21:2; 2Ki 1:2; 4:1,8,11,18,38,42; 5:3; 6:1,26,28; 12:4; 14:8; 19:37; Est 2:21; Job 1:6,13; 2:1; Ps 73:17; Pr 7:6; Isa 37:38; Jer 28:1; 38:14; Eze 4:5,6; Mt 4:18; 5:1; 9:14; 12:38; 16:1; 17:22; Mk 1:9,16; 2:18; 7:1; 10:13; Lk 1:8; 3:21; 5:1,17; 6:12; 8:4,22; 9:1,18; 10:25; 11:14; 17:1,5,20; 18:1,15; 20:1; Ac 6:9; 7:23; 11:5; 13:2; 16:16; 21:7; 22:17; 26:12; Ro 14:5; 1Co 10:8

RIGHTEOUS ONE (5) Pr 21:12; Isa 24:16; Ac 3:14; 7:52; 22:14

THE EVIL ONE (8) Mt 6:13; 13:19,38; Jn 17:15; 2Th 3:3; 1Jn 3:12; 5:18,19

Ge 1:5 darkness "night." Together these made up o day.
1:9 "Let the waters beneath the sky be gathered into o
1:16 The greater o, the sun, presides during the day;
1:16 the lesser o, the moon, presides through the night.
2:5 any rain. And no o was there to cultivate the soil.
2:11 O of these branches is the Pishon, which flows
2:19 call them, and Adam chose a name for each o.
2:21 He took o of Adam's ribs and closed up the place
2:24 is joined to his wife, and the two are united into o.
4:23 O day Lamech said to Adah and Zillah, "Listen to
4:25 another son in place of Abel, the o Cain killed."
7:2 for sacrifice, and take o pair of each of the others.
7:4 O week from today I will begin forty days
7:10 O week later, the flood came and covered the
9:21 O day he became drunk on some wine he had
10:8 O of Cush's descendants was Nimrod,
11:1 At o time the whole world spoke a single language
14:5 O year later, Kedorlaomer and his allies arrived.
14:13 O of the men who escaped came and told Abram
14:23 you might say, 'I am the o who made Abram rich!'
15:3 so o of my servants will have to be my heir."
15:10 He cut each o down the middle and laid the halves
16:12 This son of yours will be a wild o—free
16:13 for she said, "I have seen the O who sees me!"
17:4 I will make you the father of not just o nation,
17:17 "How could I become a father at the age of o
18:1 O day about noon, as Abraham was sitting at the
18:10 Then o of them said, "About this time next year I
19:31 O day the older daughter said to her sister,
20:3 But o night God came to Abimelech in a dream
21:5 Abraham was o hundred years old at the time.
22:2 Sacrifice him there as a burnt offering on o of the
24:2 O day Abraham said to the man in charge of his
24:3 that you will not let my son marry o of these local
24:14 I will ask o of them for a drink. If she says, 'Yes,
24:14 let her be the o you have appointed as Isaac's wife.
24:21 or not she was the o the LORD intended him to
24:37 let Isaac marry o of the local Canaanite women.
24:44 let her be the o you have selected to be the wife of
24:63 O evening as he was taking a walk out in the
25:18 from Ishmael camped close to o another.
25:23 O nation will be stronger than the other;
25:25 so much hair that o would think he was wearing a
25:29 O day when Jacob was cooking some stew,
26:22 Abandoning that o, he dug another well,
26:26 O day Isaac had visitors from Gerar.
27:36 haven't you saved even o blessing for me?"
27:38 Esau pleaded, "Not o blessing left for me? O my
27:45 for you. Why should I lose both of you in o day?"
27:46 I'd rather die than see Jacob marry o of them."
28:2 and marry o of your uncle Laban's daughters.
28:9 and married o of Ishmael's daughters,
30:2 "He is the only o able to give you children!"
30:14 O day during the wheat harvest, Reuben found
30:31 Just do o thing, and I'll go back to work for you.
31:53 to punish either o of us who harms the other."
32:8 He thought, "If Esau attacks o group,
34:1 O day Dinah, Leah's daughter, went to visit some
34:16 live here and unite with you to become o people.
34:22 But they will consider staying here only on o
34:22 Every o of us men must be circumcised, just as
35:5 all the towns of that area, and no o attacked them.
36:20 o of the families native to the land of Seir:
36:35 He was the o who destroyed the Midianite army in
37:3 So o day he gave Joseph a special gift—a beautiful
37:5 O night Joseph had a dream and promptly reported
38:28 were being born, o of them reached out his hand,
38:28 appeared first, saying, "This o came out first."
39:9 No o here has more authority than I do! He has
39:11 O day, however, no o else was around when he was doing his work
40:5 O night the cup-bearer and the baker each had a
40:8 but there is no o here to tell us what they mean."
41:5 This time he saw seven heads of grain on o stalk,
41:8 but not o of them could suggest what they meant.
41:11 O night the chief baker and I each had a dream,
41:22 This time there were seven heads of grain on o
41:24 but not o of them could tell me what they mean."
41:44 but no o will move a hand or a foot in the entire
42:1 "Why are you standing around looking at o
42:13 and o of our brothers is no longer with us."
42:16 O of you go and get your brother! I'll keep the rest
42:19 really are. Only o of you will remain in the prison.
42:27 and o of them opened his sack to get some grain to
42:32 We are twelve brothers, sons of o father;
42:32 o brother has disappeared, and the youngest is with
42:33 Leave o of your brothers here with me, and take
42:35 there at the top of each o was the bag of money
43:29 your youngest brother, the o you told me about?
44:9 If you find his cup with any o of us, let that o die.
44:10 "except that only the o who stole it will be a slave.
44:18 "My lord, let me say just this o word to you.
44:28 and that o of them went away and never returned—
48:1 O day not long after this, word came to Joseph that
48:18 "No, Father," he said, "this o over here is older.
49:4 first no longer. / For you slept with o of my wives;
49:10 until the coming of the o to whom it belongs, / the o whom all nations will obey.
49:24 by the Mighty O of Jacob, / the Shepherd,
Ex 2:5 o of Pharaoh's daughters came down to bathe in
2:5 she told o of her servant girls to get it for her.
2:6 "He must be o of the Hebrew children," she said.
2:7 and find o of the Hebrew women to nurse the baby
2:11 he saw an Egyptian beating o of the Hebrew
2:12 After looking around to make sure no o was
2:13 like that?" Moses said to the o in the wrong.
2:21 In time, Reuel gave Moses o of his daughters,
3:1 O day Moses was tending the flock of his
3:14 God replied, "I AM THE O WHO ALWAYS IS.
6:25 Eleazar son of Aaron married o of the daughters of
8:2 across your entire land from o border to the other.
8:10 Then you will know that no o is as powerful as the
9:4 Not a single o of Israel's livestock will die!' "
10:6 of Egypt has there been a plague like this o!"
10:14 and there has never again been o like it.
10:15 Not o green thing remained, neither tree nor plant,
11:1 "I will send just o more disaster on Pharaoh
12:22 no o is allowed to leave the house until morning.
12:46 All who eat the lamb must eat it together in o
14:28 the Israelites into the sea, not a single o survived.
17:5 the o you used when you struck the water of the
18:16 an argument arises, I am the o who settles the case.
18:21 Appoint them as judges over groups of o thousand, o hundred, fifty, and ten.
18:25 They were put in charge of groups of o thousand, o hundred, fifty, and ten.
19:13 until they hear o long blast from the ram's horn.
20:10 On that day no o in your household may do any
21:8 since he is the o who broke the contract with her.
21:18 and o hits the other with a stone or fist,
22:1 For oxen the fine is five oxen for each o stolen.
22:1 For sheep the fine is four sheep for each o stolen.
22:3 the o who killed the thief is guilty of murder.
22:6 then the o who started the fire must pay for the lost
23:29 But I will not do this all in o year because the land
24:4 the altar, o for each of the twelve tribes of Israel.
25:19 end of the atonement cover, making it all o piece.
25:31 and its decorations will be o piece—
25:35 O blossom will be set beneath each pair of
25:36 and branches must all be o piece with the stem,
26:3 Join five of these sheets together into o set;
26:5 The fifty loops along the edge of o set are to match
26:9 Join five of these together into o set, and join the
26:28 will run all the way from o end of the Tabernacle
27:2 of the altar so the horns and altar are all o piece.
28:21 Each stone will represent o of the tribes of Israel,
29:15 and his sons must lay their hands on the head of o
29:23 take o loaf of bread, o cake mixed with olive oil,
29:23 and o wafer from the basket of yeastless bread that
29:39 o in the morning and the other in the evening.
29:40 With o of them, offer two quarts of fine flour mixed with o quart of
29:40 also, offer o quart of wine as a drink offering.
29:46 I am the o who brought them out of Egypt so that I
30:24 12-1/2 pounds of cassia, and o gallon of olive oil.
32:27 and forth from o end of the camp to the other,
33:18 Then Moses had o more request. "Please let me
33:20 directly at my face, for no o may see me and live."
34:3 No o else may come with you. In fact, no o is allowed anywhere on the mountain.
34:20 No o is allowed to appear before me without a gift.
34:24 No o will attack and conquer your land when you
36:8 O of the craftsmen then embroidered blue, purple,
36:10 Five of these sheets were joined together to make o
36:13 Thus the Tabernacle was joined together in o
36:16 joined five of these sheets together to make o set,
36:18 the roof covering was joined together in o piece.
36:29 They made two of these, o for each rear corner.
36:33 along each side, running from o end to the other.
37:8 a part of the atonement cover—it was all o piece.
37:17 lamp cups, blossoms, and buds were all of o piece.
37:21 O blossom was set beneath each pair of branches,
37:22 and branches were all o piece with the stem,
38:2 were four horns, o at each of the four corners, all of o piece with the rest.
39:14 each with the name of o of the twelve tribes of

Lev 2: 2 Bring this offering to **o** of Aaron's sons, and he
4:22 "If **o** of Israel's leaders does something forbidden
5: 7 **O** of the birds will be a sin offering, and the other
5: 8 who will offer **o** of the birds as the sin offering.
7:14 **O** of each kind of bread must be presented as a gift
11:45 am the **o** who brought you up from the land of
12: 8 **O** will be for the whole burnt offering
13: 2 be brought to Aaron the priest or to **o** of his sons.
14: 5 The priest will order **o** of the birds to be
14:10 and **o** female year-old lamb with no physical
14:12 The priest will take **o** of the lambs and the olive oil
14:21 lambs must bring **o** male lamb for a guilt offering,
14:22 **O** of the pair must be used for a sin offering
14:31 **O** of them is for a sin offering and the other for a
14:50 He will slaughter **o** of the birds over a clay pot that
15:15 **o** for a sin offering and the other for a whole burnt
15:30 The priest will offer **o** for a sin offering
16: 8 to the LORD and which **o** will be the scapegoat.
16:17 No **o** else is allowed inside the Tabernacle while
16:17 No **o** may enter until he comes out again after
19:11 not steal. "Do not cheat **o** another. "Do not lie.
21:18 No **o** who has a defect may come near to me,
22:10 "No **o** outside a priest's family may ever eat the
22:10 in a priest's home or is **o** of his hired servants.
22:15 No **o** may defile the sacred offerings brought to
23:13 you must also offer **o** quart of wine as a drink
23:18 **o** bull, and two rams as burnt offerings to the
23:19 Then you must offer **o** male goat as a sin offering
24:10 **O** day a man who had an Israelite mother and an
Egyptian father got into a fight with **o** of the
25:26 If there is no **o** to redeem the land but the person
25:27 has the right to redeem it from the **o** who bought it.
26:17 and you will run even when no **o** is chasing you!
26:26 so the bread from **o** oven will have to be stretched
26:36 and you will fall even when no **o** is pursuing you.
26:37 Yes, though no **o** is chasing you, you will stumble
27: 6 A boy between the ages of **o** month and five years
27: 9 **o** that is acceptable as an offering to the LORD—
27:10 neither a good animal for a bad **o** nor a bad animal
for a good **o**.
27:11 **o** that is not acceptable as an offering to the
27:33 and the substituted **o** will be considered holy
Nu 1: 1 **O** day in midspring, during the second year after
1: 4 assisted by **o** family leader from each tribe."
1:18 twenty years old or older were registered, **o** by **o**,
3:15 Count every male who is **o** month old or older."
3:22 There were 7,500 males **o** month old or older
3:28 There were 8,600 males **o** month old or older
3:34 There were 6,200 males **o** month old or older
3:39 there were 22,000 males **o** month old or older.
3:40 all the firstborn sons in Israel who are **o** month old
3:43 The total number of firstborn sons who were **o**
6:11 The priest will offer **o** of the birds for a sin offering
6:19 **o** cake made without yeast, and **o** wafer made
without yeast,
8:12 **O** will be for a sin offering and the other for a
9:11 They must offer the Passover sacrifice **o** month
10: 4 But if only **o** is blown, then only the leaders of the
10:11 **O** day in midspring, during the second year after
10:29 **O** day Moses said to his brother-in-law, Hobab son
11:32 too. No **o** gathered less than fifty bushels!
13: 2 Send **o** leader from each of the twelve ancestral
14:22 not **o** of these people will ever enter that land.
15: 4 of choice flour mixed with **o** quart of olive oil.
15: 5 you must also present **o** quart of wine for a drink
15:24 and with **o** male goat for a sin offering.
15:32 **O** day while the people of Israel were in the
16: 1 **O** day Korah son of Izhar, a descendant of Kohath
16: 7 will see whom the LORD chooses as his holy **o**."
16:11 The **o** you are really revolting against is the
16:15 and I have never hurt a single **o** of them."
16:22 angry with all the people when only **o** man sins?"
16:40 no **o** who was not a descendant of Aaron—
17: 2 **o** from each of Israel's ancestral tribes,
17: 3 for there must be **o** staff for the leader of each
18: 4 but no **o** who is not a Levite may officiate with
18:16 Redeem them when they are **o** month old.
22:19 But stay here **o** more night to see if the LORD has
25: 6 then **o** of the Israelite men brought a Midianite
26:62 The men from the Levite clans who were **o** month
26:64 Not **o** person that Moses and Aaron counted in this
27: 1 **O** day a petition was presented by the daughters of
27:12 **O** day the LORD said to Moses, "Climb to the
28: 4 **O** lamb will be sacrificed in the morning
28: 5 of choice flour mixed with **o** quart of olive oil.
28: 7 consisting of **o** quart of fermented drink with each
28:11 **o** ram, and seven one-year-old male lambs, all with
28:14 a half pints for the ram, and **o** quart for each lamb.
28:15 on the first day of each month you must offer **o**
28:19 **o** ram, and seven one-year-old male lambs, all with
28:27 It will consist of two young bulls, **o** ram, and seven
28:30 offer **o** male goat to make atonement for
29: 2 It will consist of **o** young bull, **o** ram, and seven
29: 8 It will consist of **o** young bull, **o** ram, and seven
29:11 You must also sacrifice **o** male goat for a sin
29:34 You must also sacrifice **o** male goat as a sin
29:36 It will consist of **o** young bull, **o** ram, and seven
29:38 You must also sacrifice **o** male goat as a sin
31: 4 tribe of Israel, send **o** thousand men into battle."
31: 5 So they chose **o** thousand men from each tribe of
31:28 Set apart **o** out of every five hundred as the
31:30 Also take **o** of every fifty of the captives, cattle,
31:47 Moses took **o** of every fifty prisoners and animals
31:49 battle under our command; not **o** of us is missing!
32:11 no **o** who is twenty years old or older will ever see
34:18 Also enlist **o** leader from each tribe to help them
35:30 but only if there is more than **o** witness.
35:30 No **o** may be put to death on the testimony of only
o witness.
36: 9 No inheritance may pass from **o** tribe to another;
Dt 1: 1 between Paran on **o** side and Tophel, Laban,
1:14 "You agreed that my plan was a good **o**.
1:23 I chose twelve scouts, **o** from each of your tribes.
1:35 'Not **o** of you from this entire wicked generation
4:32 Then search from **o** end of the heavens to the other.
4:34 Has any other god taken **o** nation for himself by
5:14 On that day no **o** in your household may do any
7:24 No **o** will be able to stand against you, and you
10:21 is your God, the **o** who is worthy of your praise,
10:21 the **o** who has done mighty miracles that you
11:25 No **o** will be able to stand against you,
12:14 will choose within **o** of your tribal territories.
13: 9 You must be the **o** to initiate the execution; then all
13:12 "Suppose you hear in **o** of the towns the LORD
17: 2 in **o** of your towns that the LORD your God is
17: 6 person to death on the testimony of only **o** witness.
19: 3 three districts, with **o** of these cities in each district.
19: 5 And suppose **o** of them swings an ax and the ax
19: 5 the slayer could flee to **o** of the cities of refuge
19:11 and then escapes to **o** of the cities of refuge.
19:15 of a crime on the testimony of just **o** witness.
21:15 but he loves **o** and not the other, and both have
22:19 They will fine him **o** hundred pieces of silver,
22:27 that she screamed, but there was no **o** to rescue her.
24: 5 He must be free to be at home for **o** year,
25: 1 and the judges declare that **o** is right and the other
25: 5 same property and **o** of them dies without a son,
25:11 and the wife of **o** tries to rescue her husband by
28: 7 They will attack you from **o** direction, but they will
28:25 You will attack your enemies from **o** direction,
28:26 and no **o** will be there to chase them away.
28:29 and no **o** will come to save you.
28:31 to your enemies, and no **o** will be there to help you.
28:55 is devouring—the flesh of **o** of his own children—
28:64 all the nations from **o** end of the earth to the other.
28:68 enemies as slaves, but no **o** will want to buy you."
31: 7 You are the **o** who will deliver it to them as their
31: 8 for the LORD is the **o** who goes before you.
32:30 How could **o** person chase a thousand of them,
32:36 strength is gone / and no **o** is left, slave or free.
32:39 I am the **o** who kills and gives life; / I am the **o**
who wounds and heals; / no **o** delivers from my
power!
33:16 and the favor of the **o** who appeared in the burning
33:20 "Blessed is the **o** who enlarges Gad's territory!
33:26 "There is no **o** like the God of Israel. / He rides
34: 6 but to this day no **o** knows the exact place.
Jos 1: 5 No **o** will be able to stand their ground against you
2:11 No **o** has the courage to fight after hearing such
2:19 But we swear that no **o** inside this house will be
3:12 Now choose twelve men, **o** from each tribe.
3:13 and the river will pile up there in **o** heap."
4: 2 "Now choose twelve men, **o** from each tribe.
4: 5 Each of you must pick up **o** stone and carry it out
4: 5 twelve stones in all, **o** for each of the twelve tribes.
4: 8 **o** for each tribe, just as the LORD had
5:14 "Neither **o**," he replied. "I am commander of the
6: 1 of the Israelites. No **o** was allowed to go in or out.
6: 5 When you hear the priests give **o** long blast on the
7:14 member of the guilty family must come **o** by **o**.
7:15 The **o** who has stolen what was set apart for
8:33 **O** group stood at the foot of Mount Gerizim,
10: 8 Not a single **o** of them will be able to stand up to
10:14 or since has there been a day like that **o**,
10:21 no **o** dared to speak a word against Israel.
10:28 the king. Not **o** person in the city was left alive.
10:35 They captured it in **o** day, and as at Lachish,
10:37 the entire population. Not **o** person was left alive.
11: 8 until not **o** enemy warrior was left alive.
11:10 (Hazor had at **o** time been the capital of the
11:19 No **o** in this region made peace with the Israelites
11:22 Not **o** was left in all the land of Israel, though some
15:16 daughter Acsah in marriage to the **o** who attacks
15:17 was the **o** who conquered it, so Acsah became
17:14 "Why have you given us only **o** portion of land
17:17 and strong, you will be given more than **o** portion.
18:14 **o** of the towns belonging to the tribe of Judah.
20: 3 person unintentionally can run to **o** of these cities
20: 3 and be protected from the relatives of the **o** who
20: 4 "Upon reaching **o** of these cities, the **o** who caused
the accidental death will appear
20: 6 Then the **o** declared innocent because the death
20: 6 the **o** found innocent is free to return home."
20: 9 person could take refuge in **o** of these cities.
21:42 Every **o** of these towns had pasturelands
22:14 officials of Israel, **o** from each of the ten tribes,
22:19 There is only **o** true altar of the LORD our God.
22:20 He was not the only **o** who died because of that
23: 9 for you, and no **o** has yet been able to defeat you.
23:10 Each **o** of you will put to flight a thousand of the
23:14 your God has come true. Not a single **o** has failed!
24:17 For the LORD our God is the **o** who rescued us
24:32 the sons of Hamor for **o** hundred pieces of silver.
Jdg 1:12 daughter Acsah in marriage to the **o** who attacks
1:13 was the **o** who conquered it, so Acsah became
3:29 and bravest warriors. Not **o** of them escaped.
4: 6 **O** day she sent for Barak son of Abinoam,
4:16 of Sisera's warriors. Not a single **o** was left alive.
6:16 Midianites as if you were fighting against **o** man."
6:25 your father's herd, the **o** that is seven years old.
6:31 and destroy the **o** who knocked down his altar!"
6:39 be angry with me, but let me make **o** more request.
7: 5 In **o** group put all those who cup water in their
7:14 friend said, "Your dream can mean only **o** thing—
7:19 and the **o** hundred men with him reached the outer
8:24 However, I have **o** request. Each of you can give
8:25 and each **o** threw in a gold earring he had gathered.
9: 1 **O** day Gideon's son Abimelech went to Shechem
9: 2 ruled by all seventy of Gideon's sons or by **o** man.
9: 5 and there, on **o** stone, they killed all seventy of his
9:18 killing his seventy sons on **o** stone.
12: 7 he died, he was buried in **o** of the towns of Gilead.
13: 6 He was like **o** of God's angels, terrifying to look
14: 1 **O** day when Samson was in Timnah, he noticed a
14: 3 "Isn't there **o** woman in our tribe or among all the
14: 3 his father, "Get her for me. She is the **o** I want."
14:14 "From the **o** who eats came something to eat;
15:19 Then he named that place "The Spring of the **O**
16: 1 **O** day Samson went to the Philistine city of Gaza
16: 9 She had hidden some men in **o** of the rooms of her
16:18 "Come back **o** more time," she said, "for he has
16:24 The **o** who killed so many of us is now in our
16:28 please strengthen me **o** more time so that I may
17: 2 **O** day he said to his mother, "I heard you curse
17: 2 Well, here they are. I was the **o** who took them."
17: 5 Then he installed **o** of his sons as the priest.
17: 7 **O** day a young Levite from Bethlehem in Judah
17:11 agreed to this and became like **o** of Micah's sons.
18:19 of Israel than just for the household of **o** man?"
18:28 There was no **o** to rescue the residents of the town,
19: 1 **O** day he brought home a woman from Bethlehem
19:15 town square, but no **o** took them in for the night.
19:18 the LORD. But no **o** has taken us in for the night,
19:29 Then he sent **o** piece to each tribe of Israel.
20: 1 came together in **o** large assembly and stood in the
20: 8 and replied, "Not **o** of us will return home.
20:10 **O** tenth of the men from each tribe will be chosen
21: 3 this happened? Now **o** of our tribes is missing!"
21: 6 "Today we have lost **o** of the tribes from our
21: 8 And they discovered that no **o** from Jabesh-gilead
21: 9 the people, no **o** from Jabesh-gilead was present.
21:21 and each of you can take **o** of them home to be
Ru 1: 4 **O** married a woman named Orpah, and the other a
2: 2 **O** day Ruth said to Naomi, "Let me go out into the
2:19 May the LORD bless the **o** who helped you!"
2:20 That man is **o** of our closest relatives, **o** of our
family redeemers."
3: 1 **O** day Naomi said to Ruth, "My daughter,
3:12 But there is **o** problem. While it is true that I am **o**
of your family
3:14 "No **o** must know that a woman was here at the
1Sa 2: 2 No **o** is holy like the LORD! / There is no **o** besides
you; / there is no Rock like
2: 7 The LORD makes **o** poor and another rich;
2: 7 he brings **o** down and lifts another up.
2: 9 in darkness. / No **o** will succeed by strength alone.
2:10 he increases the might of his anointed **o**."
2:20 take the place of this **o** she gave to the LORD."
2:27 **O** day a prophet came to Eli and gave him this
3: 2 **O** night Eli, who was almost blind by now,
3:20 All the people of Israel from **o** end of the land to
9: 3 **O** day Kish's donkeys strayed away, and he told
9: 4 So Saul took **o** of his servants and traveled all
9: 8 the servant said, "I have **o** small silver piece.
10: 3 **O** will be bringing three young goats, another will
10:12 But **o** of the neighbors responded, "It doesn't
10:24 No **o** in all Israel is his equal!" And all the people
11: 2 Nahash said, "but only on **o** condition.
11: 2 I will gouge out the right eye of every **o** of you as a
11: 7 and all of them came out together as **o**.
11:13 But Saul replied, "No **o** will be executed today,
12: 3 before the LORD and before his anointed **o**—
12: 5 and his anointed **o** are my witnesses,"
13:17 **O** went north toward Ophrah in the land of Shual,
14: 1 **O** day Jonathan said to the young man who carried
14: 3 No **o** realized that Jonathan had left the Israelite
14: 5 and the **o** on the south was in front of Geba.
14:24 on my enemies." So no **o** ate a thing all day,
14:28 But **o** of the men saw him and said, "Your father
14:35 an altar to the LORD, the first **o** he had ever built.
14:36 all night and destroy every last **o** of them."
14:39 But no **o** would tell him what the trouble was.
14:42 And Jonathan was shown to be the guilty **o**.
14:45 not **o** hair on his head will be touched,
15: 1 **O** day Samuel said to Saul, "I anointed you king
15:28 given it to someone else—**o** who is better than you.
16: 1 for I have selected **o** of his sons to be my new
16: 6 Samuel took **o** look at Eliab and thought,
16: 8 "This is not the **o** the LORD has chosen."
16: 9 "Neither is this the **o** the LORD has chosen."
16:12 And the LORD said, "This is the **o**; anoint him."
16:18 **O** of the servants said to Saul, "The son of Jesse is
16:21 and David became **o** of Saul's armor bearers.
17:17 **O** day Jesse said to David, "Take this half-bushel
17:25 The king will give him **o** of his daughters for a
18:17 **O** day Saul said to David, "I am ready to give you
18:25 "Tell David that all I want for the bride price is **o**
19: 9 But **o** day as Saul was sitting at home,
21: 1 you alone?" he asked. "Why is no **o** with you?"
21: 5 even on ordinary trips, how much more on this **o**!"
21:11 "Isn't he the **o** the people honor with dances,
22: 5 **O** day the prophet Gad told David,
22: 8 For not **o** of you has ever told me that my own son
22:20 **o** of the sons of Ahimelech, escaped and fled to
23: 1 **O** day news came to David that the Philistines
23:15 **O** day near Horesh, David received the news that
24: 6 a serious thing to attack the LORD's anointed **o**,
24:10 never harm him—he is the LORD's anointed **o**.'
24:14 Should he spend his time chasing **o** who is as
24:15 judge which of us is right and punish the guilty **o**.
25:14 **o** of Nabal's servants went to Abigail and told her,

25:17 so ill-tempered that no **o** can even talk to him!"
25:18 **o** hundred raisin cakes, and two hundred fig cakes.
25:22 May God deal with me severely if even **o** man of
25:34 not **o** of Nabal's men would be alive tomorrow
26: 5 David slipped over to Saul's camp **o** night to look
26: 9 innocent after attacking the LORD's anointed **o**?
26:11 But the LORD forbid that I should kill the **o** he
26:22 "Let **o** of your young men come over and get it.
26:23 in my power, for you are the LORD's anointed **o**.
27: 5 **O** day David said to Achish, "If it is all right with
27: 5 we would rather live in **o** of the country towns
27: 9 David didn't leave **o** person alive in the villages he
27:11 No **o** was left alive to come to Gath and tell where
29: 2 their troops in groups of **o** hundred and **o** thousand,
2Sa 1:10 Then I took his crown and **o** of his bracelets
1:14 you not afraid to kill the LORD's anointed **o**?"
1:15 Then David said to **o** of his men, "Kill him!"
1:16 that you killed the LORD's anointed **o**."
2:12 **O** day Abner led some of Ishbosheth's troops from
2:16 Each **o** grabbed his opponent by the hair and thrust
2:21 "Take on **o** of the younger men and strip him of
3: 7 **O** day Ishbosheth, Saul's son, accused Abner of
sleeping with **o** of his father's
3:14 for I bought her with the lives of **o** hundred
4: 5 **O** day Recab and Baanah, the sons of Rimmon
4: 9 the **o** who saves me from my enemies, I will tell
5: 2 was our king, you were the **o** who really led Israel.
7: 5 Are you the **o** to build me a temple to live in?
7: 6 been a tent, moving from **o** place to another.
7:12 you die, I will raise up **o** of your descendants,
7:13 He is the **o** who will build a house—a temple—
7:22 There is no **o** like you—there is no other God.
8: 2 to be executed for every **o** group to be spared.
8: 4 he crippled all but **o** hundred of the chariot horses.
9: 1 **O** day David began wondering if anyone in Saul's
9: 2 named Ziba, who had been **o** of Saul's servants.
9: 3 "Yes, **o** of Jonathan's sons is still alive,
9:11 with David, as though he were **o** of his own sons.
10: 6 and Zobah, **o** thousand from the king of Maacah,
11: 2 Late **o** afternoon David got out of bed after taking
11:25 David said. "The sword kills **o** as well as another!
11:27 her to the palace, and she became **o** of his wives.
12: 1 in a certain town. **O** was rich, and **o** was poor.
12: 4 **O** day a guest arrived at the home of the rich man.
12: 6 He must repay four lambs to the poor man for the **o**
12:23 I will go to him **o** day, but he cannot return to
13: 4 **O** day Jonadab said to Amnon,
13:13 And you would be called **o** of the greatest fools in
13:28 I'm the **o** who has given the command.
13:30 has killed all your sons; not **o** is left alive!"
14: 6 since no **o** was there to stop it, **o** of them was killed.
14: 7 But if I do that, I will have no **o** left, and my
14: 8 and I'll see to it that no **o** touches him."
14:12 "Please let me ask **o** more thing of you!" she said.
14:18 "I want to know **o** thing," the king replied. "Yes,
14:25 Now no **o** in Israel was as handsome as Absalom.
14:27 He had three sons and **o** daughter. His daughter's
15:12 **o** of David's counselors who lived in Giloh.
15:16 He left no **o** behind except ten of his concubines to
16: 1 **o** hundred clusters of raisins, **o** hundred bunches of
17:12 to the ground, so that not **o** of his men is left alive.
17:19 dry in the sun; so no **o** suspected they were there.
18:10 **O** of David's men saw what had happened and told
18:26 He shouted down, "Here comes another **o**!"
19: 7 not a single **o** of them will remain here tonight.
19:32 He was the **o** who provided food for the king
19:42 of Judah replied. "The king is **o** of our own tribe.
20:11 **O** of Joab's young officers shouted to Amasa's
20:19 I am **o** who is peace loving and faithful in Israel.
22: 3 my savior, the **o** who saves me from violence.
22:42 They called for help, but no **o** came to rescue them.
23: 7 **O** must be armed to chop them down; / they will
23:11 **O** time the Philistines gathered at Lehi
23:15 from the well in Bethlehem, the **o** by the gate."
23:19 though he was not **o** of the Three.
23:23 of the Thirty, though he was not **o** of the Three.
24:12 Choose **o** of these punishments, and I will do
24:17 "I am the **o** who has sinned and done wrong!
1Ki 2: 4 **o** of them will always sit on the throne of Israel.'
2:13 **O** day Adonijah, whose mother was Haggith,
2:16 So now I have just **o** favor to ask of you.
2:20 "I have **o** small request to make of you," she said.
2:45 and may **o** of David's descendants always sit on
3: 1 the king of Egypt, and married **o** of his daughters.
3: 4 and sacrificed **o** thousand burnt offerings.
3:12 and understanding mind such as no **o** else has ever
3:17 "Please, my lord," **o** of them began, "this woman
3:22 "No," the first woman said, "the dead **o** is yours,
and the living **o** is mine."
4: 7 Each of them arranged provisions for **o** month of
4:11 married to Taphath, **o** of Solomon's daughters.)
4:19 And there was **o** governor over the land of Judah.
4:23 **o** hundred sheep or goats, as well as deer, gazelles,
5: 6 there is no **o** among us who can cut timber like you
5:14 so that each man would be **o** month in Lebanon
6:36 so that there was **o** layer of cedar beams after every
7: 2 **O** of Solomon's buildings was called the Palace of
7: 8 quarters for Pharaoh's daughter, **o** of his wives.
7:12 so that there was **o** layer of cedar beams after every
7:21 **o** toward the south and **o** toward the north.
7:21 He named the **o** on the south Jakin, and the **o** on
the north Boaz.
7:32 to axles that had been cast as **o** unit with the cart.
7:34 and these, too, were cast as **o** unit with the cart.
7:35 and side panels were cast as **o** unit with the cart.
7:38 also made ten bronze basins, **o** for each cart.
8: 5 and oxen before the Ark in such numbers that no **o**

8:19 but you will not be the **o** to do it. **O** of your sons
will build it instead.'
8:32 the guilty party and acquit the **o** who is innocent.
8:56 Not **o** word has failed of all the wonderful
10:20 **o** standing on each end of each of the six steps.
11:11 away from you and give it to **o** of your servants.
11:13 And even so, I will let him be king of **o** tribe,
11:26 son of Nebat, **o** of Solomon's own officials.
11:29 **O** day as Jeroboam was leaving Jerusalem,
11:32 But I will leave him **o** tribe for the sake of my
11:34 the **o** whom I chose and who obeyed my
11:36 His son will have **o** tribe so that the descendants of
14: 2 so that no **o** will recognize you as the queen.
14:10 I will burn up your royal dynasty as **o** burns up
15:29 so that not **o** of the royal family was left,
16: 9 **O** day in Tirzah, Elah was getting drunk at the
18: 4 Obadiah had hidden **o** hundred of them in two
18: 6 Ahab went **o** way by himself, and Obadiah went
18:13 Has no **o** told you, my lord, about the time when
18:23 The prophets of Baal may choose whichever **o** they
18:25 Choose **o** of the bulls and prepare it and call on the
18:26 So they prepared **o** of the bulls and placed it on the
18:31 **o** to represent each of the tribes of Israel,
18:40 Don't let a single **o** escape!" So the people seized
19:10 your altars, and killed every **o** of your prophets.
19:14 your altars, and killed every **o** of your prophets.
20:25 Recruit another army like the **o** you lost. Give us
20:29 killed 100,000 Aramean foot soldiers in **o** day.
20:35 the LORD instructed **o** of the group of prophets to
20:41 and the king of Israel recognized him as **o** of the
21: 2 **O** day Ahab said to Naboth, "Since your vineyard
21:21 He will not let a single **o** of your male descendants,
21:25 No **o** else so completely sold himself to what was
22: 8 "There is still **o** prophet of the LORD, but I hate
22: 9 So the king of Israel called **o** of his officials
22:11 **O** of them, Zedekiah son of Kenaanah, made some
22:30 I will disguise myself so no **o** will recognize me,
2Ki 1: 2 **O** day Israel's new king, Ahaziah, fell through the
3:11 **O** of King Joram's officers replied, "Elisha son of
4: 1 **O** day the widow of **o** of Elisha's fellow
4: 5 many jars to her, and she filled **o** after another.
4: 6 "Bring me another jar," she said to **o** of her sons.
4: 8 **O** day Elisha went to the town of Shunem.
4:11 **O** day Elisha returned to Shunem, and he went up
4:18 **O** day when her child was older, he went out to
4:19 His father said to **o** of the servants, "Carry him
4:22 "Send **o** of the servants and a donkey so that I can
4:38 **O** day as the group of prophets was seated before
4:39 **O** of the young men went out into the field to
4:42 **O** day a man from Baal-shalishah brought the man
4:43 "Feed **o** hundred people with only this?"
5: 3 **O** day the girl said to her mistress, "I wish my
5:18 may the LORD pardon me in this **o** thing.
6: 1 **O** day the group of prophets came to Elisha
6: 5 But as **o** of them was chopping, his ax head fell
6:12 "It's not us, my lord," **o** of the officers replied.
6:14 So **o** night the king of Aram sent a great army with
6:26 **O** day as the king of Israel was walking along the
6:28 "This woman proposed that we eat my son **o** day
7: 5 to the camp of the Arameans, but no **o** was there!
7: 8 they went into **o** tent after another, eating,
7:10 gone out to the Aramean camp and no **o** was there!
7:13 **O** of his officers replied, "We had better send out
8: 5 her son—the very **o** Elisha brought back to life!"
8: 6 So he directed **o** of his officials to see to it that
8:18 for he had married **o** of Ahab's daughters.
8:26 became king, and he reigned in Jerusalem **o** year.
9: 5 Commander," he said. "For which **o** of us?"
9:10 the plot of land in Jezreel, and no **o** will bury her."
9:11 and **o** of them asked him, "What did that crazy
9:37 so that no **o** will be able to recognize her.' "
10: 9 "I am the **o** who conspired against my master
10:19 See to it that every **o** of them comes, for I am
10:21 and filled the temple of Baal from **o** end to the
10:22 "Be sure that every worshiper of Baal wears **o** of
10:25 and kill all of them. Don't let a single **o** escape!"
12: 4 **O** day King Joash said to the priests, "Collect all
14: 8 **O** day Amaziah sent this challenge to Israel's king
14:26 and how they had absolutely no **o** to help them.
15:13 Shallum reigned in Samaria only **o** month.
15:35 He was the **o** who rebuilt the upper gate of the
17:27 "Send **o** of the exiled priests from Samaria back to
17:28 So **o** of the priests who had been exiled from
17:39 He is the **o** who will rescue you from all your
18:14 than eleven tons of silver and about **o** ton of gold.
18:22 But isn't he the **o** who was insulted by King
18:32 arrange to take you to another land like this **o**—
18:35 Name just **o**! So what makes you think that the
19:22 It was the Holy **O** of Israel!
19:37 **O** day while he was worshiping in the temple of
21:13 I will wipe away the people of Jerusalem as **o**
21:16 filled from **o** end to the other with innocent blood.
23: 8 to the left of the city gate as **o** enters the city.
23:10 so no **o** could ever again use it to sacrifice a son
24:16 best troops and **o** thousand craftsmen and smiths,
1Ch 1:46 He was the **o** who destroyed the Midianite army in
2: 7 Achan son of Carmi, **o** of Zerah's descendants,
2:35 Sheshan gave **o** of his daughters to be the wife of
4:10 He was the **o** who prayed to the God of Israel,
4:19 **O** of her sons was the father of Keilah the Garmite,
4:21 Shelah was **o** of Judah's sons. The descendants of
5: 1 by sleeping with **o** of his father's concubines,
7:15 **O** of his descendants was Zelophehad, who had
9: 4 **O** family that returned was that of Uthai son of
11: 2 was our king, you were the **o** who really led Israel.
11:17 from the well in Bethlehem, the **o** by the gate."
11:21 though he was not **o** of the Three.

11:25 of the Thirty, though he was not **o** of the Three.
12:18 help you, / for your God is the **o** who helps you."
13: 5 of Israel, from **o** end of the country to the other,
15: 2 God this time, no **o** except the Levites may carry it.
16:13 O descendants of Jacob, God's chosen **o**.
16:20 between nations, / from **o** kingdom to another.
17: 4 You are not the **o** to build me a temple to live in.
17: 5 been a tent, moving from **o** place to another.
17:11 For when you die, I will raise up **o** of your sons,
17:12 He is the **o** who will build a house—a temple—
17:20 "O LORD, there is no **o** like you—there is no
18: 4 David captured **o** thousand chariots,
18: 4 he crippled all but **o** hundred of the chariot horses.
21:10 Choose **o** of these punishments, and I will do
21:17 said to God, "I am the **o** who called for the census!
21:17 I am the **o** who has sinned and done wrong!
22: 8 you will not be the **o** to build a Temple to honor
22:10 He is the **o** who will build a Temple to honor my
23:17 Eliezer had only **o** son, Rehabiah, the family
27: 1 Each division served for **o** month and had
29:11 We adore you as the **o** who is over all things.
2Ch 3:11 **O** wing of the first figure was 7-1/2 feet long,
3:11 touched **o** of the wings of the second figure.
3:12 the second figure had **o** wing 7-1/2 feet long that
3:16 He also made **o** hundred decorative pomegranates
3:17 **o** to the south of the entrance and the other to the
3:17 He named the **o** on the south Jakin, and the **o** on
the north Boaz.
4: 8 north wall. Then he molded **o** hundred gold basins.
5: 6 and oxen before the Ark in such numbers that no **o**
6: 9 but you will not be the **o** to do it. **O** of your sons
will build it instead.'
6:23 the guilty party, and acquit the **o** who is innocent.
6:42 O LORD God, do not reject your anointed **o**.
7:12 Then **o** night the LORD appeared to Solomon
9:19 **o** standing on each end of each of the six steps.
11:18 (Eliab was **o** of David's brothers, a son of Jesse.)
14: 5 as well as the incense altars from every **o** of
14: 6 No **o** tried to make war against him at this time,
14:11 no **o** but you can help the powerless against the
17:14 there were 300,000 troops organized in units of **o**
18: 7 "There is still **o** prophet of the LORD, but I hate
18: 8 So the king of Israel called **o** of his officials
18:10 **O** of them, Zedekiah son of Kenaanah, made some
18:29 I will disguise myself so no **o** will recognize me,
20: 6 and mighty; no **o** can stand against you!
20:14 the Spirit of the LORD came upon **o** of the men
20:23 allies from Mount Seir and killed every **o** of them.
20:24 Not a single **o** of the enemy had escaped.
21: 6 for he had married **o** of Ahab's daughters.
21:20 No **o** was sorry when he died. He was buried in the
22: 2 became king, and he reigned in Jerusalem **o** year.
26:11 the direction of Hananiah, **o** of the king's officials.
28:24 so that no **o** could worship there and
29:32 **o** hundred rams, and two hundred lambs for burnt
30: 3 Passover was normally celebrated **o** month earlier,
30:24 King Hezekiah gave the people **o** thousand bulls
30:24 and the officials donated **o** thousand bulls and ten
30:26 for Jerusalem had not seen a celebration like this **o**
32:12 and Jerusalem to worship at only the **o** altar at the
32:14 Name just **o** time when any god, anywhere,
32:19 Jerusalem as though he were **o** of the pagan gods,
Ezr 2:61 (This Barzillai had married **o** of the daughters of
3: 1 all the people assembled together as **o** person in
6:17 **o** hundred young bulls, two hundred rams, and four
8:15 I found that not **o** Levite had volunteered to come
9: 7 Our whole history has been **o** of great sin. That is
9:11 From **o** end to the other, the land is filled with
Ne 1: 2 Hanani, **o** of my brothers, came to visit me with
3:28 each **o** doing the section immediately opposite his
3:31 Malkijah, **o** of the goldsmiths, repaired the wall as
4:17 The common laborers carried on their work with **o**
4:17 supporting their load and **o** hand holding a weapon.
5:18 required at my expense for each day were **o** ox,
6: 2 meet them at **o** of the villages in the plain of Ono.
7:63 (This Barzillai had married **o** of the daughters of
8: 1 all the people assembled together as **o** person at the
12:24 **o** section responding to the other,
12:31 **O** of the choirs proceeded southward along the top
13:13 Zadok the scribe, and Pedaiah, **o** of the Levites,
13:15 **O** Sabbath day I saw some men of Judah treading
13:28 **O** of the sons of Joiada son of Eliashib the high
Est 1: 8 The only restriction on the drinking was that no **o**
1:18 Before this day is out, the wife of every **o** of us,
2:21 **O** day as Mordecai was on duty at the palace,
4: 2 for no **o** was allowed to enter while wearing
4: 5 **o** of the king's eunuchs who had been appointed as
6: 8 he should bring out **o** of the king's own royal
6: 9 Instruct **o** of the king's most noble princes to dress
7: 9 Then Harbona, **o** of the king's eunuchs, said,
9: 2 But no **o** could make a stand against them,
Job 1: 6 **O** day the angels came to present themselves
1:13 **O** day when Job's sons and daughters were dining
1:15 I am the only **o** who escaped to tell you."
1:16 I am the only **o** who escaped to tell you."
1:17 I am the only **o** who escaped to tell you."
1:19 are dead. I am the only **o** who escaped to tell you."
2: 1 **O** day the angels came again to present themselves
2:13 And no **o** said a word, for they saw that his
5: 1 "You may cry for help, but no **o** listens. You may
5: 4 far from help, with no **o** to defend them.
6:10 I have not denied the words of the Holy **O**.
6:14 "**O** should be kind to a fainting friend, but you
10: 7 not guilty, no **o** can rescue me from your power.
14: 4 Who can create purity in **o** born impure? No **o**!
17: 3 O God, since no **o** else will stand up for me.
18:17 perish from the earth. No **o** will remember them.

18:21 the place of **o** who rejected God.' "
19: 7 "I cry out for help, but no **o** hears me. I protest,
21:23 **O** person dies in prosperity and security,
21:31 No **o** rebukes them openly. No **o** repays them for what they have done.
23: 2 "My complaint today is still a bitter **o**, and I try
24:15 the twilight, for he says, 'No **o** will see me then.'
24:15 He masks his face so no **o** will know him.
24:18 own is cursed, so that no **o** enters their vineyard.
24:20 find him sweet to eat. No **o** will remember him.
27:15 with no **o** to mourn them, not even their wives.
28:13 No **o** knows where to find it, for it is not found
29:12 and the orphans who had no **o** to help them.
29:25 and as **o** who comforts those who mourn.
30:13 knowing full well that I have no **o** to help me.
30:24 "Surely no **o** would turn against the needy when
32:12 but not **o** of you has refuted Job or answered his
35:10 my Creator, the **o** who gives songs in the night?
35:11 Where is the **o** who makes us wiser than the
36:23 No **o** can tell him what to do. No **o** can say to him,
38:26 fall on barren land, in a desert where no **o** lives?
39:26 "Are you the **o** who makes the hawk soar
40:24 No **o** can catch it off guard or put a ring in its nose
41:10 And since no **o** dares to disturb the crocodile,
41:32 its wake. **O** would think the sea had turned white.
42: 2 that you can do anything, and no **o** can stop you.
42:12 six thousand camels, **o** thousand teams of oxen, and **o** thousand female donkeys.
Ps 2: 2 against the LORD / and against his anointed **o**.
2: 4 But the **o** who rules in heaven laughs. / The Lord
3: 3 my glory, and the **o** who lifts my head high.
5: 9 My enemies cannot speak **o** truthful word.
7: 2 tearing me to pieces with no **o** to rescue me.
10:15 Go after them until the last **o** is destroyed!
14: 1 and their actions are evil; / no **o** does good!
14: 2 he looks to see if there is even **o** with real understanding, / **o** who seeks for God.
14: 3 become corrupt. / No **o** does good, / not even **o**!
16:10 the dead / or allow your godly **o** to rot in the grave.
18:41 They called for help, but no **o** came to rescue them.
19: 6 The sun rises at **o** end of the heavens / and follows
19: 9 The laws of the LORD are true; / each **o** is fair.
22: 8 "Is this the **o** who relies on the LORD? / Then let
22:11 for trouble is near, / and no **o** else can help me.
25: 3 No **o** who trusts in you will ever be disgraced,
27: 4 The **o** thing I ask of the LORD— / the thing I seek
34:19 the LORD rescues them from each and every **o**.
34:20 from harm— / not **o** of their bones will be broken!
38:13 I am silent before them as **o** who cannot speak.
41: 9 Even my best friend, the **o** I trusted completely, / the **o** who shared my food,
49: 8 not come so easily, / for no **o** can ever pay enough
50:22 or I will tear you apart, / and no **o** will help you.
53: 1 and their actions are evil; / no **o** does good!
53: 2 he looks to see if there is even **o** with real understanding, / **o** who seeks for God.
53: 3 become corrupt. / No **o** does good, / not even **o**!
54: 4 my helper. / The Lord is the **o** who keeps me alive!
56: 8 You have recorded each **o** in your book.
62: 3 So many enemies against **o** man— / all of them
68:33 Sing to the **o** who rides across the ancient heavens,
69:20 If only **o** person would show some pity; / if only **o** would turn and comfort me.
71:11 and get him, / for there is no **o** to help him now."
71:22 I will sing for you with a lyre, / O Holy **O** of Israel.
72:12 help the oppressed, who have no **o** to defend them.
73:17 Then **o** day I went into your sanctuary, O God,
74: 9 are gone; / no **o** can tell us when it will end.
75: 3 I am the **o** who keeps its foundations firm.
75: 6 For no **o** on earth—from east or west, / or even
76:11 Let everyone bring tribute to the Awesome **O**.
77:19 mighty waters— / a pathway no **o** knew was there!
78:41 and frustrated the Holy **O** of Israel.
78:44 into blood, / so no **o** could drink from the streams.
79: 3 all around Jerusalem; / no **o** is left to bury the dead.
84: 9 Have mercy on the **o** you have anointed.
86: 9 All the nations—and you made each **o**—
87: 6 "This **o** has become a citizen of Jerusalem."
88: 4 I have been dismissed as **o** who is dead, / like a
89: 9 You are the **o** who rules the oceans. / When their
89:10 You are the **o** who crushed the great sea monster.
89:18 and he, the Holy **O** of Israel, has given us our king.
89:38 are you so angry with the **o** you chose as king?
89:48 No **o** can live forever; all will die. / No **o** can escape the power of the grave.
89:51 O LORD; / they mock the **o** you anointed as king.
94: 9 Is the **o** who made your ears deaf? / Is the **o** who formed your eyes blind?
102: T A prayer of **o** overwhelmed with trouble,
104:27 Every **o** of these depends on you / to give them
105: 6 O descendants of Jacob, God's chosen **o**.
105:13 between nations, / from **o** kingdom to another.
106:11 covered their enemies; / not **o** of them survived.
106:23 But Moses, his chosen **o**, stepped between the
107:12 they fell, and no **o** helped them rise again.
109:12 Let no **o** be kind to him; / let no **o** pity his fatherless children.
118:26 Bless the **o** who comes in the name of the LORD.
119:33 O LORD, / to follow every **o** of your principles.
119:162 in your word / like **o** who finds a great treasure.
121: 3 the **o** who watches over you will not sleep.
132: 2 the LORD. / He vowed to the Mighty **O** of Israel,
132: 5 a sanctuary for the Mighty **O** of Israel."
132:17 my anointed **o** will be a light for my people.
137: 3 "Sing us **o** of those songs of Jerusalem!"
137: 8 be destroyed. / Happy is the **o** who pays you back
137: 9 Happy is the **o** who takes your babies
142: 4 help me, / but no **o** gives me a passing thought!
142: 4 No **o** will help me; / no **o** cares a bit what happens
143: 2 servant to trial! / Compared to you, no **o** is perfect.
144:10 You are the **o** who rescued your servant David.
146: 6 He is the **o** who made heaven and earth, / the sea,
146: 6 He is the **o** who keeps every promise forever,
Pr 7: 6 I was looking out the window of my house **o** day
9:10 Knowledge of the Holy **O** results in understanding.
9:12 If you become wise, you will be the **o** to benefit.
9:12 If you scorn wisdom, you will be the **o** to suffer.
11:26 but they bless the **o** who sells to them in their time
14:10 and no **o** else can fully share its joy.
20: 6 but who can find **o** who is really faithful?
21:12 The Righteous **O** knows what is going on in the
23:30 It is the **o** who spends long hours in the taverns,
24:16 But **o** calamity is enough to lay the wicked low.
24:30 of a lazy person, the vineyard of **o** lacking sense.
25: 3 No **o** can discover the height of heaven, the depth
25:12 Valid criticism is as treasured by the **o** who heeds
28: 1 The wicked run away when no **o** is chasing them,
29: 4 to his nation, but **o** who demands bribes destroys it.
30: 3 human wisdom, nor do I know the Holy **O**.
Ecc 1:11 no **o** will remember what we are doing now.
3:22 No **o** will bring them back from death to enjoy life
4: 1 tears of the oppressed, with no **o** to comfort them.
4: 9 can accomplish more than twice as much as **o**;
4:10 If **o** person falls, the other can reach out and help.
4:11 from each other. But how can **o** be warm alone?
5:18 Even so, I have noticed **o** thing, at least, that is
7:28 Just **o** out of every thousand men I interviewed can be said to be upright, but not **o** woman!
8: 4 by great power. No **o** can resist or question it.
8:17 This reminded me that no **o** can discover
9: 1 no **o** knows whether or not God will show them
9: 3 It seems so tragic that **o** fate comes to all. That is
9:15 But afterward no **o** thought any more about him.
9:18 of war, but **o** sinner can destroy much that is good.
SS 1: 9 What a lovely filly you are, my beloved **o**!
2:10 'Rise up, my beloved, my fair **o**, and come away.
2:13 Arise, my beloved, my fair **o**, and come away.' "
3: 1 "**O** night as I lay in bed, I yearned deeply for my
3: 3 you seen him anywhere, this **o** I love so much?'
3: 8 Each **o** wears a sword on his thigh, ready to defend
4: 2 They are perfectly matched; not **o** is missing.
4: 9 I am overcome by **o** glance of your eyes, by a
4:12 You are like a spring that no **o** else can drink from,
5: 2 "**O** night as I was sleeping, my heart awakened in
5: 8 If you find my beloved **o**, tell him that I am sick
5: 9 what is it about your loved **o** that brings you to tell
6: 6 washed ewes, perfectly matched and not **o** missing.
6: 9 But I would still choose my dove, my perfect **o**,
6:12 myself in my princely bed with my beloved **o**."
7:10 "I am my lover's, the **o** he desires.
8: 1 who was watching, and no **o** would criticize me.
8:11 Each of them pays **o** thousand pieces of silver for
Isa 1: 4 They have despised the Holy **O** of Israel,
1:24 LORD Almighty, the Mighty **O** of Israel, says,
1:31 the straw on fire, and no **o** will be able to put it out.
3: 9 They are not **o** bit ashamed. How terrible it will be
5: 1 Now I will sing a song for the **o** I love about his
5:10 Ten measures of seed will yield only **o** measure of
5:19 They even mock the Holy **O** of Israel and say,
5:24 They have despised the word of the Holy **O** of
5:29 and no **o** will be there to rescue them.
6: 6 Then **o** of the seraphim flew over to the altar,
6:11 their cities are destroyed, with no **o** left in them.
7:24 The entire land will be **o** vast brier patch, a hunting
7:25 No **o** will go to the fertile hillsides where the
8: 8 It will submerge Immanuel's land from **o** end to
8:13 He alone is the Holy **O**. If you fear him, you need
9:19 are fuel for the fire, and no **o** spares anyone else.
10:14 No **o** can even flap a wing against me or utter a
10:17 The LORD, the Light of Israel and the Holy **O**,
10:20 Judah will trust the LORD, the Holy **O** of Israel.
10:34 The Mighty **O** will cut down the enemy as an ax
12: 6 For great is the Holy **O** of Israel who lives among
13: 8 They look helplessly at **o** another as the flames of
14: 8 is broken! No **o** will come to cut us down now!'
14:10 With **o** voice they all cry out, 'Now you are as
14:16 'Can this be the **o** who shook the earth
14:17 Is this the **o** who destroyed the world and made it
15: 1 In **o** night your cities of Ar and Kir will be
15: 8 is a land of weeping from **o** end to the other—
16: 5 **o** who always does what is just and right.
16:12 in their temples, but no **o** will come to save them.
17: 2 There will be no **o** to chase them away.
17: 7 and have respect for the Holy **O** of Israel.
19:18 **O** of these will be Heliopolis, the City of the Sun.
22:11 for help. He is the **o** who planned this long ago.
22:22 will open doors, and no **o** will be able to shut them;
22:22 close doors, and no **o** will be able to open them.
24:16 Hear them singing praises to the Righteous **O**!
26:18 no **o** has been born to populate the earth.
27:11 the **o** who made them will show them no pity
27:12 them together **o** by **o** like handpicked grain.
29:16 Should the thing that was created say to the **o** who
29:19 Those who are poor will rejoice in the Holy **O** of
29:23 they will recognize the holiness of the Holy **O** of
30: 5 your shame. He will not help you even **o** little bit."
30:11 more than enough about your 'Holy **O** of Israel.'
30:12 This is the reply of the Holy **O** of Israel:
30:15 The Sovereign LORD, the Holy **O** of Israel, says,
30:17 **O** of them will chase a thousand of you. Five of
31: 1 of looking to the LORD, the Holy **O** of Israel.
31: 4 "When a lion, even a young **o**, kills a sheep,
31: 7 I know the glorious day will come when every **o** of
33: 8 roads are deserted; no **o** travels them anymore.
33:14 "Which **o** of us," they cry, "can live here in the
33:21 The LORD will be our Mighty **O**. He will be like
34:10 to generation. No **o** will live there anymore.
34:14 Wild goats will bleat at **o** another among the ruins,
34:15 And the vultures will come, each **o** with its mate.
34:16 Not **o** of these birds and animals will be missing,
36: 7 But isn't he the **o** who was insulted by King
36:17 arrange to take you to another land like this **o**—
36:20 Name just **o**! So what makes you think that the
37:23 It was the Holy **O** of Israel!
37:38 **O** day while he was worshiping in the temple of
40:22 He is the **o** who spreads out the heavens like a
40:25 compare me? Who is my equal?" asks the Holy **O**.
40:26 He brings them out **o** after another, calling each by
40:28 No **o** can measure the depths of his understanding.
41: 6 They encourage **o** another with the words,
41: 8 as for you, Israel my servant, Jacob my chosen **o**,
41:14 your Redeemer. I am the Holy **O** of Israel.'
41:16 You will glory in the Holy **O** of Israel.
41:20 it is the LORD, the Holy **O** of Israel, who did it.
41:26 you admit that he was right? No **o** else said a word!
41:28 Not **o** of your idols told you this. Not **o** gave any
42: 1 He is my chosen **o**, and I am pleased with him.
42:22 are fair game for all and have no **o** to protect them.
42:23 Will not even **o** of you apply these lessons from
43: 3 your God, the Holy **O** of Israel, your Savior.
43:13 No **o** can oppose what I do. No **o** can reverse my
43:14 your Redeemer, the Holy **O** of Israel, says:
43:15 your Holy **O**, Israel's Creator and King.
43:25 am the **o** who blots out your sins for my own sake
43:26 and you can present your case if you have **o**.
44: 1 listen to me, Jacob my servant, Israel my chosen **o**.
44: 2 not be afraid. O Israel, my chosen **o**, do not fear.
44: 8 other God? No! There is no other Rock—not **o**!"
44:10 his own god—an idol that cannot help him **o** bit!
44:25 I am the **o** who exposes the false prophets as liars
45: 1 his anointed **o**, whose right hand he will empower.
45: 3 the God of Israel, the **o** who calls you by name.
45: 4 the sake of Jacob my servant, Israel my chosen **o**.
45: 7 I am the **o** who creates the light and makes the
45: 7 I am the **o** who sends good times and bad times.
45: 7 the LORD, am the **o** who does these things.
45: 9 Does the clay dispute with the **o** who shapes it,
45:11 the Creator and Holy **O** of Israel, says:
45:12 I am the **o** who made the earth and created people
45:19 dark corner so no **o** can understand what I mean.
45:21 but me—a just God and a Savior—no, not **o**!
46: 9 I alone! I am God, and there is no **o** else like me.
47: 1 "Come, Babylon, unconquered **o**, sit in the dust.
47: 4 is the LORD Almighty, is the Holy **O** of Israel.
47:10 'No **o** sees me,' you said. Your 'wisdom'
48:12 to me, O family of Jacob, Israel my chosen **o**!
48:17 your Redeemer, the Holy **O** of Israel, says:
49: 7 The LORD, the Redeemer and Holy **O** of Israel,
49: 7 says to the **o** who is despised and rejected by a nation, to the **o** who is the servant of rulers:
49: 7 the Holy **O** of Israel, chooses you."
49:26 and Redeemer, the Mighty **O** of Israel."
50: 3 I am the **o** who sends darkness out across the skies,
51:10 you not the same today, the **o** who dried up the sea,
51:12 "I, even I, am the **o** who comforts you. So why are
51:13 the **o** who put the stars in the sky and established
51:16 I am the **o** who says to Israel, 'You are mine!' "
51:18 Not **o** of your children is left alive to help you
52:14 so disfigured **o** would scarcely know he was a
53:12 I will give him the honors of **o** who is mighty
54: 5 He is your Redeemer, the Holy **O** of Israel,
55: 5 the LORD your God, the Holy **O** of Israel,
56: 5 For the name I give them is an everlasting **o**.
57: 1 their time. And no **o** seems to care or wonder why.
57: 1 No **o** seems to understand that God is protecting
57:15 The high and lofty **o** who inhabits eternity, the Holy **O**, says this:
59: 4 No **o** cares about being fair and honest.
59:16 He was amazed to see that no **o** intervened to help
60: 9 the Holy **O** of Israel, for he will fill you with
60:14 of the LORD, and Zion of the Holy **O** of Israel.
60:16 your Savior and Redeemer, the Mighty **O** of Israel.
63: 3 the winepress alone; no **o** was there to help me.
63: 5 I looked, but no **o** came to help my people. I was
63:11 "Where is the **o** who brought Israel through the
63:11 Where is the **o** who sent his Holy Spirit to be
63:12 Where is the **o** whose power divided the sea before
63:13 Where is the **o** who led them through the bottom of
64: 7 Yet no **o** calls on your name or pleads with you for
65:17 so wonderful that no **o** will even think about the
65:20 No longer will people be considered old at **o**
65:25 no **o** will be hurt or destroyed on my holy
Jer 1: 1 **o** of the priests from Anathoth, a town in the land
2: 6 and death, where no **o** lives or even travels?'
2:15 are now in ruins. No **o** lives in them anymore.
2:36 you flit from **o** ally to another asking for help.
3:14 **o** from here and two from there, from wherever
5: 1 If you can find even **o** person who is just
5:22 am the **o** who defines the ocean's sandy shoreline,
7:19 Am I the **o** they are hurting?" asks the LORD.
7:33 and no **o** will be left to scare them away.
9: 4 They all take advantage of **o** another and spread
9: 5 all fool and defraud each other; no **o** tells the truth.
9:11 will be ghost towns, with no **o** living in them."
9:12 so completely that no **o** even dares to travel
9:20 daughters to wail; teach **o** another how to lament.
9:22 after the harvest. No **o** will be left to bury them."
10: 6 LORD, there is no **o** like you! For you are great,
10: 7 the kingdoms of the world, there is no **o** like you.
10:20 home is gone, and no **o** is left to help me rebuild it.
10:23 is not his own. No **o** is able to plan his own course.

11:23 Not **o** of these plotters from Anathoth will survive,
12:11 The whole land is desolate, and no **o** even cares.
12:12 The sword of the LORD kills people from **o** end of the nation to the other. No **o** will escape!
13:14 I will smash them **o** against the other, even parents
13:19 their gates, and no **o** will be able to open them.
14:16 and war. There will be no **o** left to bury them.
16:4 No **o** will mourn for them or bury them, and they
16:6 this land. No **o** will bury them or mourn for them.
16:7 No **o** will offer a meal to comfort those who mourn
16:7 No **o** will send a cup of wine to console them.
17:6 on the salty flats where no **o** lives.
17:27 and no **o** will be able to put out the roaring
21:13 safe on our mountain! No **o** can touch us here."
22:6 you deserted, with no **o** living within your walls.
22:8 pass by the ruins of this city and say to **o** another,
22:20 they are all destroyed. Not **o** is left to help you.
23:4 Not a single **o** of them will be lost or missing,"
23:18 "But can you name even **o** of these prophets who
23:18 Has even **o** of them cared enough to listen?
23:23 Am I a God who is only in **o** place?"
23:33 "Suppose **o** of the people or **o** of the prophets or
24:2 **O** basket was filled with fresh, ripe figs,
25:26 northern countries, far and near, **o** after the other—
25:33 will fill the earth from **o** end to the other.
25:33 No **o** will mourn for them or gather up their bodies
28:1 **O** day in late summer of that same year—
29:28 predicting that our captivity will be a long **o**.
30:10 in their own land, and no **o** will make them afraid.
30:13 There is no **o** to help you or bind up your injury.
31:32 This covenant will not be like the **o** I made with
32:23 They have hardly done **o** thing you told them to!
32:39 And I will give them **o** heart and mind to worship
34:9 No **o** was to keep a fellow Judean in bondage.
35:2 Take them into **o** of the inner rooms, and offer
35:4 This room was located next to the **o** used by the
38:14 **O** day King Zedekiah sent for Jeremiah to meet
38:27 No **o** had overheard the conversation between
41:9 **o** made by King Asa when he fortified Mizpah to
42:17 That is the fate awaiting every **o** of you who insists
44:2 They now lie in ruins, and no **o** lives in them.
44:7 For not **o** of you will survive—not a man, woman,
44:10 No **o** has chosen to follow my law and the decrees
44:11 I have made up my mind to destroy every **o** of you!
46:18 "**o** is coming against Egypt who is as tall as Mount
48:2 No **o** will ever brag about Moab again, for there is
48:9 cities will be left empty, with no **o** living in them.
48:33 No **o** treads the grapes with shouts of joy. There is
49:4 your wealth and thought no **o** could ever harm you.
49:5 and no **o** will help your exiles as they flee.
49:7 of Teman? Is there no **o** left to give wise counsel?
49:18 says the LORD. "No **o** will live there anymore.
49:33 be desolate forever. No **o** will live there anymore."
50:3 and bring such destruction that no **o** will live in her
50:29 she has defied the LORD, the Holy **O** of Israel.
50:32 will stumble and fall, and no **o** will raise you up.
50:34 But the **o** who redeems them is strong. His name is
50:40 says the LORD. "No **o** will live there anymore.
51:3 No **o** will be spared! Young and old alike will be
51:5 was filled with sin against the Holy **O** of Israel."
51:43 she is a dry wilderness where no **o** lives or even
52:23 and a total of **o** hundred on the network around the
La 1:2 Among all her lovers, there is no **o** left to help her.
1:7 fell to her enemy, and there was no **o** to help her.
1:9 Now she lies in the gutter with no **o** to lift her out.
1:16 No **o** is here to comfort me; any who might
1:17 Jerusalem pleads for help, but no **o** comforts her.
1:21 heard my groans, but no **o** turned to comfort me.
2:22 the LORD's anger, no **o** has escaped or survived.
3:1 I am the **o** who has seen the afflictions that come
3:38 Is it not the Most High who helps **o** and harms
4:4 cry for bread, but no **o** has any to give them.
4:6 where utter disaster struck in a moment with no **o**
4:8 No **o** even recognizes them. Their skin sticks to
4:12 Not a king in all the earth—no **o** in all the world—
4:14 so defiled by blood that no **o** dared to touch them.
5:8 become our masters; there is no **o** left to rescue us.
Eze 1:11 **o** pair stretched out to touch the wings of the living
1:15 ground beneath them, **o** wheel belonging to each.
4:5 sins for 390 days—**o** day for each year of their sin.
4:6 for 40 days—**o** day for each year of Judah's sin.
4:17 so scarce that the people will look at **o** another in
7:5 With **o** blow after another I will bring total
7:13 Not **o** person whose life is twisted by sin will
7:14 but no **o** listens, for my fury is against them all.
9:2 **O** of them was dressed in linen and carried a
10:6 the man went in and stood beside **o** of the wheels.
10:7 Then **o** of the cherubim reached out his hand
12:23 give them this new proverb to replace the old **o**:
14:14 their righteousness would save no **o**
15:7 And I will see to it that if they escape from **o** fire,
16:4 When you were born, no **o** cared about you.
16:5 No **o** had the slightest interest in you; no **o** pitied
16:34 No **o** pays you; instead, you pay them!
16:57 to all the world, and you are the **o** who is scorned
17:5 "Then he planted **o** of its seedlings in fertile
18:4 The person who sins will be the **o** who dies.
18:20 The **o** who sins is the **o** who dies. The child will
18:25 of Israel. Am I the **o** who is unjust, or is it you?
19:3 She raised **o** of her cubs / to become a strong
20:31 even though you have come to me requesting **o**.
21:20 **o** road going to Ammon and its capital, Rabbah,
21:27 And it will not be restored until the **o** appears who
22:30 have to destroy the land, but I found no **o**.
30:22 his arms—the good arm along with the broken **o**—
33:24 'Abraham was only **o** man, and yet he gained
33:28 so ruined that no **o** will even travel through them.
34:6 of the earth, yet no **o** has gone to search for them.
34:17 I will judge between **o** sheep and another,
34:22 And I will judge between **o** sheep and another.
34:23 And I will set **o** shepherd over them, even my
34:28 will live in safety, and no **o** will make them afraid.
37:17 Now hold them together in your hand as **o** stick.
37:19 to Judah. I will make them **o** stick in my hand.'
37:22 I will unify them into **o** nation in the land.
37:22 **O** king will rule them all; no longer will they be
37:24 be their king, and they will have only **o** shepherd.
38:17 You are the **o** I was talking about long ago, when I
39:7 know that I am the LORD, the Holy **O** of Israel.
39:26 And then no **o** will bother them or make them
40:15 passage was 87-1/2 feet from **o** end to the other.
40:20 There was a gateway on the north just like the **o** on
40:44 **o** beside the north gateway, facing south,
41:6 **o** above the other, with thirty rooms on each level.
41:7 Each level was wider than the **o** below it,
41:11 feet wide. **O** door faced north and the other south.
41:19 **O** face—that of a man—looked toward the palm tree on **o** side.
42:3 **O** block of rooms overlooked the 35-foot width of
42:5 levels of rooms was narrower than the **o** beneath it
42:11 was the same length and width as the other **o**,
45:7 **O** section will share a border with the east side of
45:12 **O** shekel consists of twenty gerahs, and sixty shekels are equal to **o** mina.
45:13 **o** bushel of wheat or barley for every sixty you
45:14 **o** percent of your olive oil,
45:15 and **o** sheep for every two hundred in your flocks
46:4 LORD a burnt offering of six lambs and **o** ram,
46:5 He is to offer **o** gallon of olive oil for each half
46:6 he will bring **o** young bull, six lambs, and **o** ram, all with no physical defects.
46:7 With each half bushel of flour he must offer **o**
46:11 **O** gallon of oil is to be given with each half bushel
46:16 If the prince gives a gift of land to **o** of his sons,
46:17 But if he gives a gift of land to **o** of his servants,
48:31 be three gates, each **o** named after a tribe of Israel.
Da 2:1 **O** night during the second year of his reign,
2:11 No **o** except the gods can tell you your dream,
2:25 "I have found **o** of the captives from Judah who
2:44 will never be destroyed; no **o** will ever conquer it.
3:15 I will give you **o** more chance. If you bow down
4:5 But **o** night I had a dream that greatly frightened
4:13 I saw a messenger, a holy **o**, coming down from
4:18 tell me what it means, for no **o** else can help me.
4:23 a holy **o**, coming down from heaven and saying,
4:34 Most High and honored the **o** who lives forever.
4:35 No **o** can stop him or challenge him, / saying,
6:13 "That man Daniel, **o** of the captives from Judah,
6:17 so that no **o** could rescue Daniel from the lions.
7:5 It was rearing up on **o** side, and it had three ribs in
7:9 put in place and the Ancient **O** sat down to judge.
7:13 He approached the Ancient **O** and was led into his
7:16 So I approached **o** of those standing beside the
7:19 the **o** so different from the others and so terrifying.
7:22 until the Ancient **O** came and judged in favor of
8:1 following the **o** that had already appeared to me.
8:3 **O** of the horns was longer than the other,
8:3 it had begun to grow later than the shorter **o**.
8:4 and no **o** could stand against it or help its victims.
8:5 which had **o** very large horn between its eyes,
8:7 There was no **o** who could rescue the ram from the
8:9 From **o** of the prominent horns came a small horn
8:13 **O** of them said, "How long will the events of this
8:22 The four prominent horns that replaced the **o** large
9:12 a disaster like the **o** that happened in Jerusalem.
9:25 to rebuild Jerusalem until the Anointed **O** comes.
9:26 the Anointed **O** will be killed, appearing to have
9:27 with the people for a period of **o** set of seven,
10:7 I, Daniel, am the only **o** who saw this vision.
10:13 Then Michael, **o** of the archangels, came to help
10:16 Then the **o** who looked like a man touched my lips,
10:16 I said to the **o** standing in front of me, "I am
10:18 Then the **o** who looked like a man touched me
10:21 (There is no **o** to help me against these spirit
11:5 but **o** of this king's own officials will become more
11:7 But when **o** of her relatives becomes king of the
11:13 a fully equipped army far greater than the **o** he lost.
11:45 run out, and there will be no **o** to help him.
12:1 But at that time every **o** of your people whose
12:6 **O** of them asked the man dressed in linen,
12:7 and took this solemn oath by the **o** who lives
Hos 1:11 of Judah and Israel will unite under **o** leader,
2:10 No **o** will be able to rescue her from my hands.
4:2 violence everywhere, with **o** murder after another.
5:9 **O** thing is certain, Israel: When your day of
5:14 them off, and there will be no **o** left to rescue them.
7:7 They kill their kings **o** after another, and no **o** cries out to me for help.
8:8 they lie among the nations like an old pot that no **o**
11:9 I am the Holy **O** living among you, and I will not
11:12 still walks with God and is faithful to the Holy **O**.
12:8 No **o** can say I got it by cheating! My record is
14:8 I am the **o** who looks after you and cares for you.
Joel 2:3 them is nothing but desolation; not **o** thing escapes.
Am 4:2 Every last **o** of you will be dragged away like a
4:7 I sent rain on **o** town but withheld it from another.
4:7 Rain fell on **o** field, while another field withered
4:8 People staggered from **o** town to another for a
4:13 For the LORD is the **o** who shaped the
5:3 "When **o** of your cities sends a thousand men to
6:9 If there are ten men left in **o** house, they will all
6:10 **o** who is responsible for burning the dead—
7:14 "I'm not **o** of your professional prophets.
7:14 I certainly never trained to be **o**. I'm just a
8:6 Then you enslave poor people for a debt of **o** piece
9:1 will be slaughtered in battle. No **o** will escape!
9:9 sifted in a sieve, yet not **o** true kernel will be lost.
Ob 1:11 You acted as though you were **o** of Israel's
Jnh 3:7 "No **o**, not even the animals, may eat or drink
Mic 5:2 **o** whose origins are from the distant past.
5:7 rain falling on the grass, which no **o** can hold back.
5:8 be like helpless sheep, with no **o** to rescue them.
7:2 not **o** fair-minded person is left on the earth.
Na 1:9 He will destroy you with **o** blow; he won't need to
3:7 Yet no **o** anywhere will regret your destruction."
Hab 1:7 They do as they like, and no **o** can stop them.
1:12 O LORD my God, my Holy **O**, you who are
3:3 I see God, the Holy **O**, moving across the deserts
Zep 2:5 The LORD will destroy you until not **o** of you is
3:2 No **o** can tell it anything; it refuses all correction.
3:5 his justice is more evident, but no **o** takes notice—
3:13 never telling lies or deceiving **o** another.
3:13 in safety; there will be no **o** to make them afraid."
Hag 2:12 If **o** of you is carrying a holy sacrifice in his robes
Zec 4:2 each **o** having seven spouts with wicks.
4:3 I see two olive trees, **o** on each side of the bowl."
4:9 "Zerubbabel is the **o** who laid the foundation of
5:3 **O** side says that those who steal will be banished
7:9 and show mercy and kindness to **o** another.
7:14 so desolate that no **o** even traveled through it.
8:21 The people of **o** city will say to the people in
8:23 the world will clutch at the hem of **o** Jew's robe.
11:7 and named **o** Favor and the other Union.
13:4 "No **o** will be boasting then of a prophetic gift!
13:4 No **o** will wear prophet's clothes to try to fool the
14:9 On that day there will be **o** LORD—his name
14:10 south of Jerusalem, will become **o** vast plain.
Mal 1:14 but then sacrifices a defective **o** to the Lord.
2:15 Didn't the LORD make you **o** with your wife?
Mt 3:14 "I am the **o** who needs to be baptized by you,"
4:18 **O** day as Jesus was walking along the shore beside
5:1 **O** day as the crowds were gathering, Jesus went up
5:29 It is better for you to lose **o** part of your body than
5:30 It is better for you to lose **o** part of your body than
5:36 my head!' for you can't turn **o** hair white or black.
6:13 yield to temptation, / but deliver us from the evil **o**.
6:18 Then no **o** will suspect you are fasting, except your
6:24 "No **o** can serve two masters. For you will hate **o** and love the other, or be devoted to **o** and despise
7:29 for he taught as **o** who had real authority—
8:19 Then **o** of the teachers of religious law said to him,
8:28 so dangerous that no **o** could go through that area.
9:14 **O** day the disciples of John the Baptist came to
9:17 And no **o** puts new wine into old wineskins.
10:23 When you are persecuted in **o** town, flee to the
10:41 If you welcome a prophet as **o** who speaks for
10:42 And if you give even a cup of cold water to **o** of
11:14 he is Elijah, the **o** the prophets said would come.
11:27 No **o** really knows the Son except the Father, and no **o** really knows the Father except the Son
12:6 there is **o** here who is even greater than the
12:11 And he answered, "If you had **o** sheep, and it fell
12:13 and it became normal, just like the other **o**.
12:38 **O** day some teachers of religious law
13:3 He told many stories such as this **o**: "A farmer
13:19 Then the evil **o** comes and snatches the seed away
13:38 The weeds are the people who belong to the evil **o**.
15:14 and if **o** blind person guides another, they will both
16:1 **O** day the Pharisees and Sadducees came to test
16:14 others say Jeremiah or **o** of the other prophets."
17:4 **o** for you, **o** for Moses, **o** for Elijah."
17:22 **O** day after they had returned to Galilee, Jesus told
18:6 But if anyone causes **o** of these little ones who
18:10 "Beware that you don't despise a single **o** of these
18:12 "If a shepherd has **o** hundred sheep, and **o** wanders away and is lost, what will he do?
18:12 and go out into the hills to search for the lost **o**?
18:14 it is not my heavenly Father's will that even **o** of
18:16 take **o** or two others with you and go back again,
18:24 **o** of his debtors was brought in who owed him
19:5 is joined to his wife, and the two are united into **o**.'
19:6 Since they are no longer two but **o**, let no **o** separate them,
20:1 early **o** morning to hire workers for his vineyard.
20:7 "They replied, 'Because no **o** hired us.'
20:12 'Those people worked only **o** hour, and yet you've
20:13 "He answered **o** of them, 'Friend, I haven't been
20:21 to you, **o** at your right and the other at your left?"
21:9 Bless the **o** who comes in the name of the Lord!
21:24 to do these things if you answer **o** question,"
21:35 his servants, beat **o**, killed **o**, and stoned another.
21:38 they said to **o** another, 'Here comes the heir to this
22:5 their business, **o** to his farm, another to his store.
22:35 **O** of them, an expert in religious law, tried to trap
22:46 No **o** could answer him. And after that, no **o** dared to ask him any more questions.
23:8 call you 'Rabbi,' for you have only **o** teacher,
23:10 for there is only **o** master, the Messiah.
23:15 For you cross land and sea to make **o** convert,
23:39 'Bless the **o** who comes in the name of the
24:2 so completely demolished that not **o** stone will be
24:36 no **o** knows the day or the hour when these things
24:40 together in the field; **o** will be taken, the other left.
24:41 flour at the mill; **o** will be taken, the other left.
25:15 He gave five bags of gold to **o**, two bags of gold to another, and **o** bag of gold to the last—
25:18 But the servant who received the **o** bag of gold dug
25:24 "Then the servant with the **o** bag of gold came
25:28 and give it to the **o** with the ten bags of gold.
25:40 when you did it to **o** of the least of these my
26:14 Then Judas Iscariot, **o** of the twelve disciples,

26:21 he said, "The truth is, **o** of you will betray me."
26:22 **o** by **o** they began to ask him, "I'm not the **o**, am I,
26:23 "**O** of you who is eating with me now will betray
26:25 Judas, the **o** who would betray him, also asked,
"Teacher, I'm not the **o**, am I?"
26:40 you stay awake and watch with me even **o** hour?
26:47 as he said this, Judas, **o** of the twelve disciples,
26:48 "You will know which **o** to arrest when I go over
26:51 **O** of the men with Jesus pulled out a sword
26:69 "You were **o** of those with Jesus the Galilean."
26:73 over to him and said, "You must be **o** of them;
27:15 Now it was the governor's custom to release **o**
27:17 "Which **o** do you want me to release to you—
27:48 **O** of them ran and filled a sponge with sour wine,
27:57 a rich man from Arimathea who was **o** of Jesus'
Mk 1: 9 **O** day Jesus came from Nazareth in Galilee,
1:16 **O** day as Jesus was walking along the shores of the
1:22 for he taught as **o** who had real authority—
1:24 I know who you are—the Holy **O** sent from God!"
2: 2 visitors that there wasn't room for **o** more person,
2:18 **O** day some people came to Jesus and asked,
2:22 And no **o** puts new wine into old wineskins.
2:23 **O** Sabbath day as Jesus was walking through some
4: 2 the people by telling many stories such as this **o**:
4:14 The farmer I talked about is the **o** who brings
4:31 Though this is **o** of the smallest of seeds,
4:32 it grows to become **o** of the largest of plants,
5: 4 No **o** was strong enough to control him.
6:10 each village, be a guest in only **o** home," he said.
7: 1 **O** day some Pharisees and teachers of religious
7: 4 but **o** of many traditions they have clung to—
7:13 And this is only **o** example. There are many,
8:14 so there was only **o** loaf of bread with them in the
8:28 and others say you are **o** of the other prophets."
9: 2 No **o** else was there. As the men watched,
9: 5 **o** for you, **o** for Moses, and **o** for Elijah."
9:17 **O** of the men in the crowd spoke up and said,
9:38 told him to stop because he isn't **o** of our group."
9:39 "No **o** who performs miracles in my name will
9:42 "But if anyone causes **o** of these little ones who
9:43 It is better to enter heaven with only **o** hand than to
9:45 It is better to enter heaven with only **o** foot than to
10: 8 and the two are united into **o**.' Since they are no
longer two but **o**,
10: 9 let no **o** separate them, for God has joined them
10:13 **O** day some parents brought their children to Jesus
10:21 "You lack only **o** thing," he told him. "Go
10:37 "**o** at your right and the other at your left."
11: 9 Bless the **o** who comes in the name of the Lord!
11:14 to the tree, "May no **o** ever eat your fruit again!"
11:29 to do these things if you answer **o** question,"
12: 2 At grape-picking time he sent **o** of his servants to
12: 6 until there was only **o** left—his son whom he loved
12: 7 "But the farmers said to **o** another, 'Here comes
12:28 **O** of the teachers of religious law was standing
12:29 O Israel! The Lord our God is the **o** and only Lord.
12:32 spoken the truth by saying that there is only **o** God
12:34 no **o** dared to ask him any more questions.
13: 1 **o** of his disciples said, "Teacher, look at these
13: 2 so completely demolished that not **o** stone will be
13:32 no **o** knows the day or hour when these things will
14:10 Then Judas Iscariot, **o** of the twelve disciples,
14:18 Jesus said, "The truth is, **o** of you will betray me, **o**
of you who is here eating with me."
14:19 **o** by **o** they began to ask him, "I'm not the **o**, am I?
14:20 He replied, "It is **o** of you twelve, **o** who is eating
14:37 you stay awake and watch with me even **o** hour?
14:43 as he said this, Judas, **o** of the twelve disciples,
14:44 "You will know which **o** to arrest when I go over
14:66 **O** of the servant girls who worked for the high
14:67 then said, "You were **o** of those with Jesus,
14:69 the others, "That man is definitely **o** of them!"
14:70 "You must be **o** of them because you are from
15: 6 Now it was the governor's custom to release **o**
15: 7 **O** of the prisoners at that time was Barabbas,
15:36 **O** of them ran and filled a sponge with sour wine,
16: 4 looked up and saw that the stone—a very large **o**—
16:13 back to tell the others, but no **o** believed them.
Lk 1: 8 **O** day Zechariah was serving God in the Temple,
1:49 For he, the Mighty **O**, is holy, / and he has done
1:61 "There is no **o** in all your family by that name."
3:11 "If you have two coats, give **o** to the poor.
3:21 **O** day when the crowds were being baptized,
4:34 I know who you are—the Holy **O** sent from God."
4:40 the touch of his hand healed every **o**.
5: 1 **O** day as Jesus was preaching on the shore of the
5: 3 Stepping into **o** of the boats, Jesus asked Simon,
5:12 In **o** of the villages, Jesus met a man with an
5:17 **O** day while Jesus was teaching, some Pharisees
5:36 "No **o** tears a piece of cloth from a new garment
5:37 And no **o** puts new wine into old wineskins.
5:39 But no **o** who drinks the old wine seems to want
6: 1 **O** Sabbath day as Jesus was walking through some
6:10 He looked around at them **o** by **o** and then said
6:12 **O** day soon afterward Jesus went to a mountain to
6:29 If someone slaps you on **o** cheek, turn the other
6:39 "What good is it for **o** blind person to lead
6:39 The first **o** will fall into a ditch and pull the other
7:36 **O** of the Pharisees asked Jesus to come to his
7:41 five hundred pieces of silver to **o** and fifty pieces
7:43 "I suppose the **o** for whom he canceled the larger
8: 4 **O** day Jesus told this story to a large crowd that
8: 8 and produced a crop **o** hundred times as much as
8:16 "No **o** would light a lamp and then cover it up
8:22 **O** day Jesus said to his disciples, "Let's cross over
8:25 They said to **o** another, "Who is this man,
9: 1 **O** day Jesus called together his twelve apostles
9: 4 you enter each village, be a guest in only **o** home.
9:18 **O** day as Jesus was alone, praying, he came over to
9:19 and others say you are **o** of the other ancient
9:33 **o** for you, **o** for Moses, and **o** for Elijah."
9:35 the cloud said, "This is my Son, my Chosen **O**.
10: 7 Stay in **o** place, eating and drinking what they
10:22 No **o** really knows the Son except the Father, and
no **o** really knows the Father except the Son
10:25 **O** day an expert in religious law stood up to test
10:37 man replied, "The **o** who showed him mercy."
10:42 There is really only **o** thing worth being concerned
11: 1 **o** of his disciples came to him as he finished
11:14 **O** day Jesus cast a demon out of a man who
11:33 "No **o** lights a lamp and then hides it or puts it
11:37 **o** of the Pharisees invited him home for a meal.
12: 6 Yet God does not forget a single **o** of them.
13: 8 "The gardener answered, 'Give it **o** more chance.
13:10 **O** Sabbath day as Jesus was teaching in a
13:35 'Bless the **o** who comes in the name of the
14: 1 **O** Sabbath day Jesus was in the home of a leader
14:18 **O** said he had just bought a field and wanted to
14:33 So no **o** can become my disciple without giving up
15: 4 "If you had **o** hundred sheep, and **o** of them
strayed away and was lost in the
15: 4 to go and search for the lost **o** until you found it?
15: 7 heaven will be happier over **o** lost sinner who
15: 8 a woman has ten valuable silver coins and loses **o**.
15:10 of God's angels when even **o** sinner repents."
15:16 looked good to him. But no **o** gave him anything.
15:26 and he asked **o** of the servants what was going on.
15:29 And in all that time you never gave me even **o**
16: 5 He asked the first **o**, 'How much do you owe him?'
16: 6 and write another **o** for four hundred gallons.'
16: 7 and replace it with **o** for only eight hundred
16:13 "No **o** can serve two masters. For you will hate **o**
and love the other, or be devoted to **o** and despise
16:26 at its edge, and no **o** there can cross over to us.'
17: 1 **O** day Jesus said to his disciples, "There will
17: 2 in store for harming **o** of these little ones.
17: 5 **O** day the apostles said to the Lord, "We need
17:15 **O** of them, when he saw that he was healed,
17:20 **O** day the Pharisees asked Jesus, "When will the
17:34 That night two people will be asleep in **o** bed; **o**
will be taken away, and the other will be left.
17:35 together at the mill; **o** will be taken, the other left."
18: 1 **O** day Jesus told his disciples a story to illustrate
18:10 **O** was a Pharisee, and the other was a dishonest
18:15 **O** day some parents brought their little children to
18:22 "There is still **o** thing you lack," Jesus said.
19: 2 He was **o** of the most influential Jews in the
19:24 and give it to the **o** who earned the most.'
20: 1 **O** day as Jesus was teaching and preaching the
20:10 he sent **o** of his servants to collect his share of the
20:31 And so it went, **o** after the other, until each of the
20:40 ended their questions; no **o** dared to ask any more.
21: 6 so completely demolished that not **o** stone will be
22: 3 Judas Iscariot, who was **o** of the twelve disciples,
22:36 don't have a sword, sell your clothes and buy **o**!
22:47 led by Judas, **o** of his twelve disciples.
22:50 And **o** of them slashed at the high priest's servant
22:56 she said, "This man was **o** of Jesus' followers!"
22:58 looked at him and said, "You must be **o** of them!"
22:59 "This must be **o** of Jesus' disciples because he is a
23:18 and with **o** voice they shouted, "Kill him,
23:35 him save himself if he is really God's Chosen **O**,
23:39 **O** of the criminals hanging beside him scoffed,
24:18 Then **o** of them, Cleopas, replied, "You must be
Jn 1: 9 The **o** who is the true light, who gives light to
1:15 "This is the **o** I was talking about when I said,
1:16 brought to us—**o** gracious blessing after another!
1:18 No **o** has ever seen God. But his only Son, who is
1:30 He is the **o** I was talking about when I said,
1:31 I didn't know he was the **o**, but I have been
1:33 I didn't know he was the **o**, but when God sent me
1:33 upon someone, he is the **o** you are looking for.
1:33 He is the **o** who baptizes with the Holy Spirit.'
1:40 was **o** of these men who had heard what John said
2:25 No **o** needed to tell him about human nature.
3: 1 After dark **o** evening, a Jewish religious leader
3: 5 no **o** can enter the Kingdom of God without being
3:26 the **o** you said was the Messiah, is also baptizing
4:22 Samaritans know so little about the **o** you worship,
4:25 the Messiah will come—the **o** who is called Christ.
4:37 '**O** person plants and someone else harvests.'
4:52 "Yesterday afternoon at **o** o'clock his fever
5: 1 Afterward Jesus returned to Jerusalem for **o** of the
5: 5 **O** of the men lying there had been sick for
5: 7 "for I have no **o** to help me into the pool when the
5:38 you do not believe me—the **o** he sent to you.
6:29 wants you to do: Believe in the **o** he has sent."
6:33 The true bread of God is the **o** who comes down
6:35 No **o** who comes to me will ever be hungry again.
6:39 that I should not lose even **o** of all those he has
6:69 and we know you are the Holy **O** of God."
6:70 "I chose the twelve of you, but **o** is a devil."
6:71 son of Simon Iscariot, **o** of the Twelve, who would
7:13 But no **o** had the courage to speak favorably about
7:18 but those who seek to honor the **o** who sent them
7:27 no **o** will know where he comes from."
7:28 But I represent **o** you don't know, and he is true.
7:30 but no **o** laid a hand on him, because his time had
7:33 Then I will return to the **o** who sent me.
7:44 some wanted him arrested, but no **o** touched him.
7:48 "Is there a single **o** of us rulers or Pharisees who
8: 9 they slipped away **o** by **o**, beginning with the
8:10 Didn't even **o** of them condemn you?"
8:18 I am **o** witness, and my Father who sent me is the
8:25 "I am the **o** I have always claimed to be.
8:26 For I say only what I have heard from the **o** who
8:29 And the **o** who sent me is with me—he has not
9: 4 out the tasks assigned us by the **o** who sent me,
10:16 and there will be **o** flock with **o** shepherd.
10:18 No **o** can take my life from me. I lay down my life
10:28 never perish. No **o** will snatch them away from me,
10:29 than anyone else. So no **o** can take them from me.
10:30 The Father and I are **o**."
10:32 For which **o** of these good deeds are you killing
10:36 why do you call it blasphemy when the Holy **O**
10:41 didn't do miracles," they remarked to **o** another,
11: 3 telling him, "Lord, the **o** you love is very sick."
11:27 the **o** who has come into the world from God."
11:49 And **o** of them, Caiaphas, who was high priest that
11:50 be destroyed? Let this **o** man die for the people."
12: 4 But Judas Iscariot, **o** of his disciples—the **o** who
would betray him—said,
12:13 Bless the **o** who comes in the name of the Lord!
12:45 you see me, you are seeing the **o** who sent me.
13:16 Nor are messengers more important than the **o** who
13:18 to all of you; I know so well each **o** of you I chose.
13:18 'The **o** who shares my food has turned against me,'
13:21 "The truth is, **o** of you will betray me!"
13:23 **O** of Jesus' disciples, the **o** Jesus loved,
13:26 "It is the **o** to whom I give the bread dipped in the
13:35 Your love for **o** another will prove to the world
14: 6 No **o** can come to the Father except through me.
14:21 And I will reveal myself to each **o** of them."
15:24 signs among them that no **o** else could do,
16: 5 "But now I am going away to the **o** who sent me,
16:22 you will rejoice, and no **o** can rob you of that joy.
16:32 each **o** going his own way, leaving me alone.
17: 2 He gives eternal life to each **o** you have given him.
17: 3 true God, and Jesus Christ, the **o** you sent to earth.
17:12 I guarded them so that not **o** was lost, except the **o**
headed for destruction,
17:15 of the world, but to keep them safe from the evil **o**.
17:21 My prayer for all of them is that they will be **o**, just
as you and I are **o**, Father—
17:22 you gave me, so that they may be **o**, as we are—
17:23 I in them and you in me, all being perfected into **o**.
18: 8 "And since I am the **o** you want, let these others
18: 9 "I have not lost a single **o** of those you gave me."
18:14 Caiaphas was the **o** who had told the other Jewish
leaders, "Better that **o** should die for all."
18:17 asked Peter, "Aren't you **o** of Jesus' disciples?"
18:22 **O** of the Temple guards standing there struck Jesus
18:25 asked him again, "Aren't you **o** of his disciples?"
18:26 But **o** of the household servants of the high priest,
19:11 So the **o** who brought me to you has the greater
19:18 **o** on either side, with Jesus between them.
19:23 but it was seamless, woven in **o** piece from the top.
19:34 **O** of the soldiers, however, pierced his side with a
19:36 that say, "Not **o** of his bones will be broken,"
20: 2 and the other disciple, the **o** whom Jesus loved.
20:24 **O** of the disciples, Thomas (nicknamed the Twin),
21:12 And no **o** dared ask him if he really was the Lord
21:20 the **o** who had leaned over to Jesus during supper
Ac 1: 4 In **o** of these meetings as he was eating a meal with
1:17 Judas was **o** of us, chosen to share in the ministry
1:20 his home become desolate, with no **o** living in it.'
2: 1 the believers were meeting together in **o** place.
2:27 the dead / or allow your Holy **O** to rot in the grave.
2:30 and he knew God had promised with an oath that **o**
3: 1 and John went to the Temple **o** afternoon to take
3: 2 the Temple gate, the **o** called the Beautiful Gate,
3:14 You rejected this holy, righteous **o**, and instead
4:11 For Jesus is the **o** referred to in the Scriptures,
4:12 There is salvation in no **o** else! There is no other
4:32 All the believers were of **o** heart and mind,
4:36 the **o** the apostles nicknamed Barnabas (which
5:13 No **o** else dared to join them, though everyone had
5:23 but when we opened the gates, no **o** was there!"
5:34 But **o** member had a different perspective. He was
6: 9 But **o** day some men from the Synagogue of Freed
7: 5 no inheritance here, not even **o** square foot of land.
7:23 "**O** day when he was forty years old, he decided to
7:52 Name **o** prophet your ancestors didn't persecute!
7:52 who predicted the coming of the Righteous **O**—
8: 1 Saul was **o** of the official witnesses at the killing of
8:10 the greatest, often spoke of him as "the Great **O**—
8:31 "How can I, when there is no **o** to instruct me?"
9: 5 "I am Jesus, the **o** you are persecuting!
9: 7 the sound of someone's voice, but they saw no **o**!
10: 3 **O** afternoon about three o'clock, he had a vision in
10: 7 and a devout soldier, **o** of his personal attendants.
10:43 He is the **o** all the prophets testified about,
11: 5 "**O** day in Joppa," he said, "while I was praying,
11:28 **O** of them named Agabus stood up in **o** of the
13: 2 **O** day as these men were worshiping the Lord
13:23 "And it is **o** of King David's descendants, Jesus,
13:27 or realize that he is the **o** the prophets had written
13:35 'You will not allow your Holy **O** to rot in the
16:14 **O** of them was Lydia from Thyatira, a merchant of
16:16 **O** day as we were going down to the place of
17:23 And **o** of them had this inscription on it—'To an
17:26 From **o** man he created all the nations throughout
17:27 find him—though he is not far from any **o** of us.
17:28 As **o** of your own poets says, 'We are his
18: 9 **O** night the Lord spoke to Paul in a vision and told
18:10 and no **o** will harm you because many people here
19: 4 in Jesus, the **o** John said would come later."
19:32 were all shouting, some **o** thing and some another.
20:21 I have had **o** message for Jews and Gentiles alike—
21: 7 we greeted the believers but stayed only **o** day.
21: 8 **o** of the seven men who had been chosen to

21:16 originally from Cyprus and **o** of the early disciples.
21:34 Some shouted **o** thing and some another.
22: 8 'I am Jesus of Nazareth, the **o** you are persecuting.'
22:14 and to see the Righteous **O** and hear him speak.
22:17 "**O** day after I returned to Jerusalem, I was
22:22 then with **o** voice they shouted, "Away with such
23: 5 'Do not speak evil of any **o** who rules over
23:17 Paul called **o** of the officers and said, "Take this
24:21 except for **o** thing I said when I shouted out,
26: 2 that you are the **o** hearing my defense against all
26:12 "**O** day I was on such a mission to Damascus,
26:15 'I am Jesus, the **o** you are persecuting.
27:21 No **o** had eaten for a long time. Finally, Paul called
28:31 the Lord Jesus Christ. And no **o** tried to stop him.
Ro 1: 8 How I thank God through Jesus Christ for each **o**
1:10 **O** of the things I always pray for is the
2:29 a true Jew is **o** whose heart is right with God.
3:10 the Scriptures say, / "No **o** is good— / not even **o**.
3:11 No **o** has real understanding; / no **o** is seeking God.
3:12 gone wrong. / No **o** does good, / not even **o**."
3:20 For no **o** can ever be made right in God's sight by
3:30 There is only **o** God, and there is only **o** way of being accepted by him.
4:19 was too old to be a father at the age of **o** hundred
5: 7 Now, no **o** is likely to die for a good person,
5:15 For this **o** man, Adam, brought death to many
5:16 is very different from the result of that **o** man's sin.
5:17 The sin of this **o** man, Adam, caused death to rule
5:17 in triumph over sin and death through this **o** man,
5:18 Adam's **o** sin brought condemnation upon
5:18 but Christ's **o** act of righteousness makes all
5:19 Because **o** person disobeyed God, many people
5:19 But because **o** other person obeyed God,
6: 3 and were baptized to become **o** with Christ Jesus,
7: 4 And now you are united with the **o** who was raised
7:20 I don't want to do, I am not really the **o** doing it;
8:33 He is the **o** who has given us right standing with
8:34 for he is the **o** who died for us and was raised to
9:20 Should the thing that was created say to the **o** who
9:21 the same lump of clay to make **o** jar for decoration
11: 4 God's reply? He said, "You are not the only **o** left.
12: 5 We are all parts of his **o** body, and each of us has
12: 5 And since we are all **o** body in Christ, we belong to
12:13 children are in need, be the **o** to help them out.
13: 1 the government, for God is the **o** who put it there.
13: 9 are all summed up in this **o** commandment:
14: 2 **o** person believes it is all right to eat anything.
14: 5 some think **o** day is more holy than another day,
15: 6 Then all of you can join together with **o** voice,
16: 2 her in the Lord, as **o** who is worthy of high honor.
16: 4 I am not the only **o** who is thankful to them;
16: 8 whom I love as **o** of the Lord's own children,
16:17 And now I make **o** more appeal, my dear brothers
16:22 Tertius, the **o** who is writing this letter for Paul,
1Co 1: 9 and he is the **o** who invited you into this wonderful
1:10 I plead with you to be of **o** mind, united in thought
1:15 for now no **o** can say they were baptized in my
1:29 so that no **o** can ever boast in the presence of God.
1:30 He is the **o** who made us acceptable to God.
2:11 No **o** can know what anyone else is really thinking
2:11 and no **o** can know God's thoughts except God's
3: 3 You are jealous of **o** another and quarrel with each
3: 4 When **o** of you says, "I am a follower of Paul,"
3: 7 because he is the **o** who makes the seed grow.
3: 8 The **o** who plants and the **o** who waters work as a team with the same
3:11 For no **o** can lay any other foundation than the **o**
4: 6 you won't brag about **o** of your leaders at the
4:15 you about Christ, you have only **o** spiritual father.
5: 3 Concerning the **o** who has done this, I have
5: 6 Don't you realize that if even **o** person is allowed
6: 6 But instead, **o** Christian sues another—right in
6:16 to a prostitute, he becomes **o** body with her?
6:16 the Scriptures say, "The two are united into **o**."
6:17 is joined to the Lord becomes **o** spirit with him.
6:18 other sin so clearly affects the body as this **o** does.
8: 3 But the person who loves God is the **o** God knows
8: 4 a god and that there is only **o** God and no other.
8: 6 But we know that there is only **o** God, the Father,
8: 6 And there is only **o** Lord, Jesus Christ,
9:20 I become **o** of them so that I can bring them to
9:24 everyone runs, but only **o** person gets the prize.
10: 8 them did, causing 23,000 of them to die in **o** day.
10:17 we all eat from **o** loaf, showing that we are **o** body.
10:28 out of consideration for the conscience of the **o**
11: 3 But there is **o** thing I want you to know: A man is
12: 3 No **o** speaking by the Spirit of God can curse
12: 3 and no **o** is able to say, "Jesus is Lord," except by
12: 8 To **o** person the Spirit gives the ability to give wise
12:10 He gives **o** person the power to perform miracles,
12:11 It is the **o** and only Holy Spirit who distributes
12:12 but the many parts make up only **o** body.
12:13 all been baptized into Christ's body by **o** Spirit,
12:14 the body has many different parts, not just **o** part.
12:17 Or if your whole body were just **o** big ear,
12:19 strange thing a body would be if it had only **o** part!
12:20 Yes, there are many parts, but only **o** body.
12:26 If **o** part suffers, all the parts suffer with it, and if **o** part is honored, all the parts are glad.
12:27 and each **o** of you is a separate and necessary part
14: 3 But **o** who prophesies is helping others grow in the
14: 4 but **o** who speaks a word of prophecy strengthens
14: 7 For no **o** will recognize the melody unless the
14:26 When you meet, **o** will sing, another will teach,
14:26 **o** will speak in an unknown language,
14:27 They must speak **o** at a time, and someone must be
14:28 But if no **o** is present who can interpret, they must
14:30 from the Lord, the **o** who is speaking must stop.
14:31 **o** after the other, so that everyone will learn and be
15: 6 more than five hundred of his followers at **o** time,
15:41 The sun has **o** kind of glory, while the moon
2Co 1:19 He is the **o** whom Timothy, Silas, and I preached
3: 6 He is the **o** who has enabled us to represent his
6: 3 We try to live in such a way that no **o** will be
6: 3 and so no **o** can find fault with our ministry.
8: 8 to do it. This is **o** way to prove your love is real.
8:20 for we are anxious that no **o** should find fault with
9: 5 it to be a willing gift, not **o** given under pressure.
9: 6 But the **o** who plants generously will get a
9:10 For God is the **o** who gives seed to the farmer
10:16 are far beyond you, where no **o** else is working.
11: 2 For I promised you as a pure bride to **o** husband,
11: 4 about a different Jesus than the **o** we preach,
11: 4 or a different Spirit than the **o** you received,
11: 4 or a different kind of gospel than the **o** you
Gal 1: 8 who preaches any other message than the **o** we told
1: 9 If anyone preaches any other gospel than the **o** you
1:12 from Jesus Christ himself. No **o** else taught me.
1:14 I was **o** of the most religious Jews of my own age,
1:23 "The **o** who used to persecute us now preaches the
2:16 For no **o** will ever be saved by obeying the law."
2:21 I am not **o** of those who treats the grace of God as
3: 2 Let me ask you this **o** question: Did you receive
3:11 it is clear that no **o** can ever be right with God by
3:15 Just as no **o** can set aside or amend an irrevocable
3:28 you are all Christians—you are **o** in Christ Jesus.
4:22 **o** from his slave-wife and **o** from his freeborn wife.
5: 8 for he is the **o** who called you to freedom.
5: 9 But it takes only **o** wrong person among you to
5:13 but freedom to serve **o** another in love.
5:14 For the whole law can be summed up in this **o**
5:15 you are always biting and devouring **o** another,
5:15 watch out! Beware of destroying **o** another.
5:26 or irritate **o** another, or be jealous of **o** another.
6:12 you to be circumcised are doing it for just **o** reason.
Eph 1:14 This is just **o** more reason for us to praise our
2: 6 all because we are **o** with Christ Jesus.
2:14 and you Gentiles by making us all **o** people.
2:15 and Gentiles by creating in himself **o** new person
2:16 Together as **o** body, Christ reconciled both groups
4: 4 We are all **o** body, we have the same Spirit, and we
4: 5 There is only **o** Lord, **o** faith, **o** baptism,
4: 6 and there is only **o** God and Father, who is over us
4: 7 he has given each **o** of us a special gift according
4:10 The same **o** who came down is the **o** who
4:11 He is the **o** who gave these gifts to the church:
4:30 he is the **o** who has identified you as his own,
4:32 to each other, tenderhearted, forgiving **o** another,
5:21 you will submit to **o** another out of reverence for
5:29 No **o** hates his own body but lovingly cares for it,
5:31 joined to his wife, and the two are united into **o**."
5:32 illustration of the way Christ and the church are **o**.
6: 8 Remember that the Lord will reward each **o** of us
Php 2: 2 loving **o** another, and working together with **o** heart and purpose.
2:15 so that no **o** can speak a word of blame against
2:20 I have no **o** else like Timothy, who genuinely cares
3: 5 So I am a real Jew if there ever was **o**!
3: 9 and become **o** with him. I no longer count on my
3:13 but I am focusing all my energies on this **o** thing:
4: 8 let me say **o** more thing as I close this letter.
Col 1: 7 was the **o** who brought you the Good News.
1: 8 He is the **o** who told us about the great love for
1:13 For he has rescued us from the **o** who rules in the
1:16 Christ is the **o** through whom God created
2: 4 so that no **o** will be able to deceive you with
3:15 For as members of **o** body you are all called to live
4: 9 and much loved brother, **o** of your own people.
4:11 Jesus (the **o** we call Justus) also sends his
1Th 1:10 He is the **o** who has rescued us from the terrors of
2: 4 He is the **o** who examines the motives of our
4: 9 For God himself has taught you to love **o** another.
5:15 See that no **o** pays back evil for evil, but always try
2Th 2: 3 is revealed—the **o** who brings destruction.
2: 7 and it will remain secret until the **o** who is holding
3: 3 make you strong and guard you from the evil **o**.
1Ti 1:17 is the eternal King, the unseen **o** who never dies;
2: 5 For there is only **o** God and **o** Mediator who can
3: 3 peace loving, and not **o** who loves money.
4: 6 **o** who is fed by the message of faith and the true
5: 3 for any widow who has no **o** else to care for her.
5: 5 **o** who is truly alone in this world, has placed her
6:14 Then no **o** can find fault with you from now until
6:16 No **o** has ever seen him, nor ever will. To him be
2Ti 1:12 not ashamed of it, for I know the **o** in whom I trust,
2: 4 then you cannot satisfy the **o** who has enlisted you
2:15 **o** who does not need to be ashamed and who
4:16 I was brought before the judge, no **o** was with me.
Tit 1:12 **O** of their own men, a prophet from Crete, has said
3:12 As soon as **o** of them arrives, do your best to meet
Heb 2:10 **o** fit to bring them into their salvation.
3: 4 a builder, but God is the **o** who made everything.
5: 4 And no **o** can become a high priest simply
5: 7 to the **o** who could deliver him out of death.
6:13 Since there was no **o** greater to swear by, God took
7: 6 the **o** who had already received the promises of
7:13 For the **o** we are talking about belongs to a
7:23 When **o** priest died, another had to take his place.
8: 5 is only a copy, a shadow of the real **o** in heaven.
8: 6 for he is the **o** who guarantees for us a better
8: 8 But God himself found fault with the old **o** when
8: 9 This covenant will not be like the **o** / I made with
8:13 it means he has made the first **o** obsolete.
9:15 That is why he is the **o** who mediates the new
9:16 no **o** gets anything until it is proved that the person
9:17 no **o** can use the will to get any of the things
10:12 But our High Priest offered himself to God as **o**
10:14 For by that **o** offering he perfected forever all those
10:24 Think of ways to encourage **o** another to outbursts
10:30 For we know the **o** who said, / "I will take
10:37 the Coming **O** will come and not delay.
11:12 And so a whole nation came from this **o** man,
11:27 because he kept his eyes on the **o** who is invisible.
12:16 Make sure that no **o** is immoral or godless like
12:24 the **o** who mediates the new covenant between God
12:25 it that you obey God, the **o** who is speaking to you.
12:25 how terrible our danger if we reject the **O** who
13: 4 and remain faithful to **o** another in marriage.
Jas 1:13 no **o** who wants to do wrong should ever say,
2: 3 but you say to the poor **o**, "You can stand over
2:10 And the person who keeps all of the laws except **o**
2:19 it's enough just to believe that there is **o** God?
3: 8 but no **o** can tame the tongue. It is an
5:20 you can be sure that the **o** who brings that person
1Pe 3: 8 Finally, all of you should be of **o** mind, full of
3: 8 loving **o** another with tender hearts and humble
1Jn 1: 1 The **o** who existed from the beginning is the **o**
1: 2 This **o** who is life from God was shown to us,
1: 2 and announce to you that he is the **o** who is eternal
2: 1 is Jesus Christ, the **o** who pleases God completely.
2: 7 for it is an old **o** you have always had, right from
2: 7 This commandment—to love **o** another—
2:13 you know Christ, the **o** who is from the beginning.
2:14 you know Christ, the **o** who is from the beginning.
2:22 The **o** who says that Jesus is not the Christ.
3:11 from the beginning: We should love **o** another.
3:12 who belonged to the evil **o** and killed his brother.
3:17 But if **o** of you has money enough to live well
3:23 Jesus Christ, and love **o** another, just as he
4: 7 Dear friends, let us continue to love **o** another,
4:12 No **o** has ever seen God. But if we love each other,
5:18 and the evil **o** cannot get his hands on them.
5:19 us is under the power and control of the evil **o**.
2Jn 1: 5 urge you, dear lady, that we should love **o** another.
1: 5 but **o** we had from the beginning.
1: 6 and he has commanded us to love **o** another,
Jude 1: 5 he later destroyed every **o** of those who did not
1: 9 But even Michael, **o** of the mightiest of the angels,
Rev 1: 3 God blesses the **o** who reads this prophecy to the
1: 4 Grace and peace from the **o** who is, who always
1: 8 "I am the **o** who is, who always was, and who is still to come, the Almighty **O**."
1:18 I am the living **o** who died. Look, I am alive
2: 1 This is the message from the **o** who holds the
2: 1 the **o** who walks among the seven gold lampstands:
2: 8 This is the message from the **o** who is the First
2:12 This is the message from the **o** who has a sharp
2:17 And I will give to each **o** a white stone, and on the
2:17 that no **o** knows except the **o** who receives it.
2:23 And all the churches will know that I am the **o** who
3: 1 This is the message from the **o** who has the
3: 7 This is the message from the **o** who is holy
3: 7 and true. He is the **o** who has the key of David.
3: 7 He opens doors, and no **o** can shut them; he shuts doors, and no **o** can open them.
3: 8 and I have opened a door for you that no **o** can
3:11 you have, so that no **o** will take away your crown.
3:14 This is the message from the **o** who is the Amen—
3:15 hot nor cold. I wish you were **o** or the other!
3:19 I am the **o** who corrects and disciplines everyone I
4: 3 The **o** sitting on the throne was as brilliant as
4: 8 the **o** who always was, who is, and who is still to
4: 9 and honor and thanks to the **o** sitting on the throne, the **o** who lives forever and ever,
4:10 and worship the **o** who lives forever and ever.
5: 1 And I saw a scroll in the right hand of the **o** who
5: 3 But no **o** in heaven or on earth or under the earth
5: 4 because no **o** could be found who was worthy to
5: 5 But **o** of the twenty-four elders said to me,
5: 7 and took the scroll from the right hand of the **o**
5: 8 Each **o** had a harp, and they held gold bowls filled
5:13 and power / belong to the **o** sitting on the throne
6: 1 Then **o** of the four living beings called out with a
6: 4 And another horse appeared, a red **o**. Its rider was
6:16 and hide us from the face of the **o** who sits on the
7:13 Then **o** of the twenty-four elders asked me,
7:14 I said to him, "Sir, you are the **o** who knows."
10: 6 And he swore an oath in the name of the **o** who
11: 9 at their bodies. No **o** will be allowed to bury them.
11:17 God Almighty, / the **o** who is and who always was,
12: 9 or Satan, the **o** deceiving the whole world—
12:10 the **o** who accused our brothers and sisters before
13: 3 I saw that **o** of the heads of the beast seemed
13:17 And no **o** could buy or sell anything without that
13:18 Let the **o** who has understanding solve the number
14: 3 And no **o** could learn this song except those
14:15 and called out in a loud voice to the **o** sitting on the
14:16 So the **o** sitting on the cloud swung his sickle over
15: 7 And **o** of the four living beings handed each of the
15: 8 No **o** could enter the Temple until the seven angels
16: 5 O Holy **O**, who is and who always was.
17: 1 **O** of the seven angels who had poured out the
17:12 they will be appointed to their kingdoms for **o** brief
18:10 In **o** single moment God's judgment came on her."
18:11 for her, for there is no **o** left to buy their goods.
18:17 And in **o** single moment all the wealth of the city is
18:24 She was the **o** who slaughtered God's people all
19:11 And the **o** sitting on the horse was named Faithful
19:19 and their armies in order to fight against the **o**
19:21 out of the mouth of the **o** riding the white horse.
20:11 white throne, and I saw the **o** who was sitting on it.

21: 5 And the o sitting on the throne said, "Look,
21: 9 Then o of the seven angels who held the seven
21:27 no o who practices shameful idolatry
22: 8 am the o who saw and heard all these things.
22:11 Let the o who is doing wrong continue to do wrong; the o who is vile, continue to be vile; the o who is good, continue to do good; and the o who is holy, continue in holiness.
22:17 Let each o who hears them say, "Come."

ONE'S (9) [ONE]

Pr 10:27 Fear of the LORD lengthens o life, but the years
11: 9 Evil words destroy o friends; wise discernment
14:21 It is sin to despise o neighbors; blessed are those
18: 8 rumors are—but they sink deep into o heart.
26: 6 convey a message is as foolish as cutting off o feet
26:22 rumors are—but they sink deep into o heart.
Ecc 5:14 there is nothing left to pass on to o children.
Mic 2: 2 No o family or inheritance is safe with you around!
Ac 20:26 No o damnation can be blamed on me,

ONE-FIFTH (4) [FIFTH, ONE]

Ge 41:34 and let them collect o of all the crops during the
47:26 that Pharaoh should receive o of all the crops
Ex 30:13 His payment to the LORD will be o of an ounce
38:26 It came from the tax of o of an ounce of silver

ONE-FOURTH (1) [FOURTH, ONE]

Rev 6: 8 They were given authority over o of the earth,

ONE-ROOM (1) [ONE, ROOM]

Eze 40:44 Inside the inner courtyard there were two o

ONE-TENTH (3) [ONE, TEN]

Nu 18:28 You must present o of the tithe received from the
Dt 14:22 o of all the crops you harvest each year.
Eze 45:11 and the bath will each measure o of a homer.

ONE-THIRD (18) [ONE, THREE]

2Sa 18: 2 O were placed under Joab, o under Joab's brother Abishai son of Zeruiah, and o under Ittai the Gittite.
Rev 8: 7 upon the earth, and o of the earth was set on fire.
8: 7 O of the trees were burned, and all the grass was
8: 8 And o of the water in the sea became blood.
8: 9 And o of all things living in the sea died.
8: 9 And o of all the ships on the sea were destroyed.
8:10 It fell upon o of the rivers and on the springs of
8:11 It made o of the water bitter, and many people died
8:12 and o of the sun was struck, and o of the moon, and o of the stars, and they became dark.
8:12 And o of the day was dark and o of the night also.
9:15 and year were turned loose to kill o of all the
9:18 O of all the people on earth were killed by these
12: 4 His tail dragged down o of the stars, which he

ONE-YEAR-OLD (49) [OLD, ONE, YEAR]

Ex 12: 5 This animal must be a o male, either a sheep
29:38 to offer on the altar. Offer two o lambs each day,
Lev 23:18 present seven o lambs with no physical defects,
23:19 and two o male lambs as a peace offering.
Nu 6:12 and each must bring a o male lamb for a guilt
6:14 a o male lamb without defect for a burnt offering,
6:14 a o female lamb without defect for a sin offering,
7:15 a ram, and a o male lamb as a burnt offering;
7:17 and five o male lambs for a peace offering.
7:21 a ram, and a o male lamb as a burnt offering;
7:23 and five o male lambs for a peace offering.
7:27 a ram, and a o male lamb as a burnt offering;
7:29 and five o male lambs for a peace offering.
7:33 a ram, and a o male lamb as a burnt offering;
7:35 and five o male lambs for a peace offering.
7:39 a ram, and a o male lamb as a burnt offering;
7:41 and five o male lambs for a peace offering.
7:45 a ram, and a o male lamb as a burnt offering;
7:47 and five o male lambs for a peace offering.
7:51 a ram, and a o male lamb as a burnt offering;
7:53 and five o male lambs for a peace offering.
7:57 a ram, and a o male lamb as a burnt offering;
7:59 and five o male lambs for a peace offering.
7:63 a ram, and a o male lamb as a burnt offering;
7:65 and five o male lambs for a peace offering.
7:69 a ram, and a o male lamb as a burnt offering;
7:71 and five o male lambs for a peace offering.
7:75 a ram, and a o male lamb as a burnt offering;
7:77 and five o male lambs for a peace offering.
7:81 a ram, and a o male lamb as a burnt offering;
7:83 and five o male lambs for a peace offering.
7:87 and twelve o male lambs were donated for the
7:88 and sixty o male lambs were donated for the peace
15:27 the guilty person must bring a o female goat for a
28: 3 you must offer two o male lambs with no physical
28: 9 sacrifice two o male lambs with no physical
28:11 one ram, and seven o male lambs, all with no
28:19 one ram, and seven o male lambs, all with no
28:27 two young bulls, one ram, and seven o male lambs.
29: 2 one ram, and seven o male lambs, all with no
29: 8 one ram, and seven o male lambs, all with no
29:13 two rams, and fourteen o male lambs, all with no
29:17 two rams, and fourteen o male lambs, all with no
29:20 two rams, and fourteen o male lambs, all with no
29:23 young bulls, two rams, and fourteen o male lambs,
29:26 young bulls, two rams, and fourteen o male lambs,
29:29 young bulls, two rams, and fourteen o male lambs,
29:32 young bulls, two rams, and fourteen o male lambs,
29:36 one ram, and seven o male lambs, all with no

ONES (147) [ONE]

HOLY ONES (5) Dt 33:3; Da 4:17; 8:13; Zec 14:5; Jude 1:14

Ge 30:42 But he didn't do this with the weaker o,
30:42 to Laban, and the stronger o were Jacob's.
31: 8 his mind and said I could have the streaked o,
41: 4 Then the thin, ugly cows ate the fat o! At this point
41:20 ugly cows ate up the seven fat o that had come out
41:24 the withered heads swallowed up the plump o!
43: 8 and not only we, but you and our little o.
45:19 and little o and to bring your father here.
46: 5 They carried their little o and wives in the wagons
47:24 your households, and your little o."
Ex 6:27 They are the o who went to Pharaoh to ask
10:10 to be with you if you try to take your little o along!
34: 1 "Prepare two stone tablets like the first o.
34: 4 So Moses cut two tablets of stone like the first o.
Lev 14:42 Other stones will be brought in to replace the o that
21: 6 they are the o who present the offerings to the
Nu 14: 3 Our wives and little o will be carried off as slaves!
16: 7 You Levites are the o who have gone too far!"
16:27 tents with their wives and children and little o.
31:16 "These are the very o who followed Balaam's
31:16 They are the o who caused the plague to strike the
Dt 1:39 be captured, but they will be the o who occupy it.
10: 1 to me, 'Prepare two stone tablets like the first o,
10: 2 the same words that were on the o you smashed.
13:10 Stone the guilty o to death because they have tried
22: 6 on the ground or in a tree and there are young o
29:11 With you are your little o, your wives,
29:14 But you are not the only o with whom the LORD
33: 3 love the people; / all your holy o are in your hands.
Jdg 11: 7 "Aren't you the o who hated me and drove me
1Sa 2: 9 He will protect his godly o, / but the wicked will
14:41 and Saul were chosen as the guilty o,
2Sa 3:29 Joab and his family are the guilty o. May his
19:11 "Why are you the last o to reinstate the king?"
19:12 Why are you the last o to welcome me back?"
2Ki 3:19 conquer the best of their cities, even the fortified o.
2Ch 2: 3 "Send me cedar logs like the o that were supplied
20:13 Judah stood before the LORD with their little o,
Job 21:19 But I say that God should punish the o who sin,
Ps 30: 4 Sing to the LORD, all you godly o! / Praise his
31:23 Love the LORD, all you faithful o!
38:11 My loved o and friends stay away, fearing my
69:33 For the LORD hears the cries of his needy o;
74:21 these poor and needy o give praise to your name.
79: 2 for the birds of heaven. / The flesh of your godly o
83: 3 your people, / laying plans against your precious o.
85: 8 for he speaks peace to his people, his faithful o.
88:18 You have taken away my companions and loved o;
105:43 of Egypt with joy, / his chosen o with rejoicing.
106: 5 Let me share in the prosperity of your chosen o.
116:15 The LORD's loved o are precious to him;
119:21 You rebuke those cursed proud o / who wander
127: 2 for food to eat; / for God gives rest to his loved o.
148:14 made his people strong, / honoring his godly o—
149: 9 This is the glory of his faithful o.
Pr 8: 5 O foolish o, let me give you understanding.
Ecc 8:10 How strange that they were the very o who
Isa 1:26 and wise counselors like the o you used to have.
5: 4 give me wild grapes / when I expected sweet o?
32:10 a year—you careless o will suddenly begin to care.
33:15 The o who can live here are those who are honest
33:16 These are the o who will dwell on high. The rocks
46: 2 the idols and the o carrying them are bowed down.
46: 8 "Do not forget this, you guilty o.
50: 4 so that I know what to say to all these weary o.
51:21 But now listen to this, you afflicted o, who sit in a
65: 8 as good grapes are found among a cluster of bad o
65:17 no one will even think about the old o anymore.
Jer 2:29 You are the o who have rebelled, says the LORD.
12: 7 I have surrendered my dearest o to their enemies.
23: 1 and scattered the very o they were expected to care
28: 6 the treasures of this Temple and all our loved o.
31:30 those who eat the sour grapes will be the o whose
48: 4 Moab is being destroyed. Her little o will cry out.
La 4: 4 The parched tongues of their little o stick with
Eze 31:16 the o whose roots went deep into the water,
34:16 I will search for my lost o who strayed away,
41:21 and the o at the entrance of the Most Holy Place
44:16 They are the o who will enter my sanctuary
44:16 They are the o who will fulfill all my requirements.
Da 4:17 by the messengers; it is commanded by the holy o.
8:13 Then I heard two of the holy o talking to each
11:14 Lawless o among your own people will join them
Hos 2: 1 will call your sisters Ruhamah—'The o I love.'
13:16 their little o dashed to death against the ground,
Mic 1:16 for your little o will be exiled to distant lands.
3: 2 but you are the very o who hate good and love evil.
Hab 3:13 your chosen people, to save your anointed o.
Zep 1:13 They are the very o whose property will be
3:19 I will save the weak and helpless o; I will bring
Zec 1:10 "They are the o the LORD has sent out to patrol
4:14 "They represent the two anointed o who assist the
14: 5 my God will come, and all his holy o with him.
Mt 13:48 good fish into crates, and throw the bad o away.
18: 6 But if anyone causes one of these little o who
18:10 that you don't despise a single one of these little o.
18:14 will that even one of these little o should perish.
19:18 "Which o?" the man asked. And Jesus replied:
20:23 My Father has prepared those places for the o he
24:22 it will be shortened for the sake of God's chosen o.
24:24 so as to deceive, if possible, even God's chosen o.
24:31 and they will gather together his chosen o from the
25: 8 Then the five foolish o asked the others,
25:37 "Then these righteous o will reply, 'Lord,
25:41 on the left and say, 'Away with you, you cursed o,
Mk 3:13 and called the o he wanted to go with him.
9:42 "But if anyone causes one of these little o who
10:40 God has prepared those places for the o he has
13:20 But for the sake of his chosen o he has shortened
13:22 so as to deceive, if possible, even God's chosen o.
13:27 together his chosen o from all over the world—
Lk 1:51 How he scatters the proud and haughty o!
12:18 I'll tear down my barns and build bigger o.
16:10 in small matters, you won't be faithful in large o.
17: 2 in store for harming one of these little o.
Jn 14:21 Those who obey my commandments are the o who
20:30 signs besides the o recorded in this book.
Ac 7:52 They even killed the o who predicted the coming
Ro 11: 7 A few have—the o God has chosen—but the rest
1Co 3: 7 The o who do the planting or watering aren't
6: 8 you yourselves are the o who do wrong and cheat
2Co 2: 3 I will not be made sad by the very o who ought to
10:11 The o who say this must realize that we will be just
Gal 2: 4 false o, really—who came to spy on us and see our
Eph 2:11 You were called "the uncircumcised o" by the
Php 3: 3 the Spirit are the only o who are truly circumcised.
4:15 you Philippians were the only o who gave me
2Ti 2:20 and the cheap o are for everyday use.
Heb 2:11 and the o he makes holy have the same Father.
3:16 Weren't they the o Moses led out of Egypt?
7: 9 that Levi's descendants, the o who collect the tithe,
11:13 All these faithful o died without receiving what
11:35 Women received their loved o back again from
Jas 2: 5 Aren't they the o who will inherit the kingdom
2: 7 Aren't they the o who slander Jesus Christ,
2Pe 2:10 daring even to scoff at the glorious o without
2:11 speak out disrespectfully against the glorious o.
1Jn 5: 5 And the o who win this battle against the world are the o who believe that Jesus is the Son of God.
Jude 1: 8 and scoff at the power of the glorious o.
1:14 the Lord is coming / with thousands of his holy o.
1:19 and they are the o who are creating divisions
Rev 3: 9 They will acknowledge that you are the o I love.
7:14 "These are the o coming out of the great
13: 8 They are the o whose names were not written in
17:14 people are the called and chosen and faithful o."
22:17 Let the thirsty o come—anyone who wants to.

ONESELF (2) [ONE, SELF]

Pr 19: 8 To acquire wisdom is to love o; people who
28:26 Trusting o is foolish, but those who walk in

ONESIMUS (4)

Col 4: 9 I am also sending O, a faithful and much loved
Phm 1:10 My plea is that you show kindness to O. I think of
1:11 O hasn't been of much use to you in the past,
1:15 O ran away for a little while so you could have

ONESIPHORUS (2)

2Ti 1:16 May the Lord show special kindness to O and all
4:19 and Aquila and those living at the household of O.

ONIONS (1)

Nu 11: 5 melons, leeks, o, and garlic that we wanted.

ONLOOKERS (2) [LOOK]

Mk 2:12 the mat, and pushed his way through the stunned o.
9:25 When Jesus saw that the crowd of o was growing,

ONLY (732)

ONLY CHILD (3) Jdg 11:34; Pr 4:3; Lk 8:42

ONLY SON (12) Ge 22:2; Jer 6:26; Am 8:10; Zec 12:10; Lk 7:12; 9:38; Jn 1:14,18; 3:16,18; Heb 11:17; 1Jn 4:9

Ge 3: 3 "It's o the fruit from the tree at the center of the
6: 3 for such a long time, for they are o mortal flesh.
6: 9 the o blameless man living on earth at the time.
7:23 They were all destroyed, and o Noah was left alive,
17:12 This applies not o to members of your family,
18:28 Suppose there are o forty-five? Will you destroy
18:29 "Suppose there are o forty?" And the LORD
18:30 "Let me speak—suppose o thirty are found?"
18:31 let me continue—suppose there are o twenty?"
18:32 but once more! Suppose o ten are found there?"
19:14 But the young men thought he was o joking.
22: 2 "Take your son, your o son—yes, Isaac,
26:13 a rich man, and his wealth o continued to grow.
30: 2 "He is the o one able to give you children!"
31:12 'Look, and you will see that o the streaked,
34:12 I will pay it—o give me the girl as my wife."
34:22 But they will consider staying here o on one
39:18 "I was saved o by my screams. He ran out,
41:40 O I will have a rank higher than yours."
42:19 really are. O one of you will remain in the prison.
43: 8 and not o we, but you and our little ones.
44:10 "except that o the one who stole it will be a slave.
44:17 "O the man who stole the cup will be my slave.
47:22 The o land he didn't buy was that belonging to the
Ex 1:16 as they are born. Allow o the baby girls to live."
8: 9 Then o the frogs in the Nile River will remain
9:26 The o spot in all Egypt without hail that day was
10:11 O the men may go and serve the LORD, for that
10:17 "Forgive my sin o this once, and plead with the

11: 8 **O** then will I go!" Then, burning with anger,
12:15 you may eat **o** bread made without yeast.
12:18 **O** bread without yeast may be eaten from the
12:20 you live, eat **o** bread that has no yeast in it."
13: 6 For seven days you will eat **o** bread without yeast.
13: 7 Eat **o** bread without yeast during those seven days.
16:18 and those who gathered **o** a little had enough.
20:25 If you build altars from stone, use **o** uncut stones.
21: 2 buy a Hebrew slave, he is to serve for **o** six years.
21: 3 **o** he will go free in the seventh year.
23:25 "You must serve **o** the LORD your God. If you
31:15 Work six days **o**, but the seventh day must be a day
34:14 must worship no other gods, but **o** the LORD,
35: 2 Each week, work for six days **o**. The seventh day is
Lev 6:29 **O** males from a priest's family may eat of this
7:19 it may **o** be eaten by people who are ceremonially
13: 6 It was **o** a temporary rash. So after washing the
13:31 reveals that the infection is **o** skin-deep
13:39 If the patch is **o** a pale white, this is a harmless skin
22:13 **o** members of the priests' families are allowed to
22:19 it will be accepted **o** if it is a male animal with no
25:15 The seller will charge you **o** for the crop years left
25:23 You are **o** foreigners and tenants living with me.
25:33 the cities reserved for the Levites are the **o**
25:40 and they will serve you **o** until the Year of Jubilee.
25:52 If **o** a few years remain until the Year of Jubilee,
Nu 3: 4 this left **o** Eleazar and Ithamar to serve as priests
9:20 would stay over the Tabernacle for **o** a few days,
9:20 so the people would stay for **o** a few days.
9:21 Sometimes the cloud stayed **o** overnight
10: 4 But if **o** one is blown, then **o** the leaders of the
10: 8 **O** the priests, Aaron's descendants, are allowed to
11:18 and complaints: "If **o** we had meat to eat!
11:25 upon them, but that was the **o** time this happened.
12: 2 "Has the LORD spoken **o** through Moses?
14: 3 "Why is the LORD taking us to this country **o** to
14: 9 They are **o** helpless prey to us! They have no
14:30 The **o** exceptions will be Caleb son of Jephunneh
14:38 the land, **o** Joshua and Caleb remained alive.
14:42 You will **o** be crushed by your enemies
16:10 He has given this special ministry **o** to you
16:22 "Must you be angry with all the people when **o**
20:19 We **o** want to pass through your country
21:24 They went **o** as far as the Ammonite border
22:20 But be sure to do **o** what I tell you to do."
22:35 but you may say **o** what I tell you to say."
22:38 I will speak **o** the messages that God gives me."
23:13 There you will see **o** a portion of the nation of
24:13 I told you that I could say **o** what the LORD says!
26:65 The **o** exceptions were Caleb son of Jephunneh
31:18 **O** the young girls who are virgins may live;
32:12 The **o** exceptions are Caleb son of Jephunneh the
35:30 but **o** if there is more than one witness.
35:30 No one may be put to death on the testimony of **o**
Dt 1: 2 Normally it takes **o** eleven days to travel from
1:16 perfectly fair at all times, not **o** to fellow Israelites,
3:24 You have **o** begun to show me your greatness
4:12 but didn't see his form; there was **o** a voice.
4:26 You will live there **o** a short time; then you will be
4:27 the nations, where **o** a few of you will survive.
6:13 When you take an oath, you must use **o** his name.
9: 5 God will drive these nations out ahead of you **o**
10:22 down into Egypt, there were **o** seventy of them.
12:14 so **o** at the place the LORD will choose within
12:16 The **o** restriction is that you are not to eat the
12:23 The **o** restriction is never to eat the blood,
13: 4 Serve **o** the LORD your God and fear him alone.
13:18 "The LORD your God will be merciful **o** if you
15: 3 however, applies **o** to your fellow Israelites—
16: 3 For seven days eat **o** bread made without yeast,
17: 6 person to death on the testimony of **o** one witness.
17: 8 someone is guilty of murder or **o** of manslaughter,
20:15 But these instructions apply **o** to distant towns,
22:25 and he rapes her, then **o** the man should die.
24:12 is poor and has **o** a cloak to give as security,
28:67 In the morning you will say, 'If **o** it were night!'
28:67 in the evening you will say, 'If **o** it were morning!'
29:14 But you are not the **o** ones with whom the LORD
32:17 had not known before, / to gods **o** recently arrived,
Jos 1: 8 all that is written in it. **O** then will you succeed.
1:15 **O** then may you settle here on the east side of the
2:18 **o** if you leave this scarlet rope hanging from the
6:17 **O** Rahab the prostitute and the others in her house
6:24 **O** the things made from silver, gold, bronze,
7: 7 If **o** we had been content to stay on the other side!
7:11 And they have not **o** stolen them; they have also
8:23 **O** the king of Ai was taken alive and brought to
8:27 **O** the cattle and the treasures of the city were not
14: 4 **o** towns to live in and the surrounding pasturelands
17:14 "Why have you given us **o** one portion of land
22:19 There is **o** one true altar of the LORD our God.
22:20 He was not the **o** one who died because of that
22:29 **O** the altar of the LORD our God that stands in
Jdg 4: 8 told her, "I will go, but **o** if you go with me!"
7: 3 leaving **o** ten thousand who were willing to fight.
7: 6 **O** three hundred of the men drank from their
7:14 friend said, "Your dream can mean **o** one thing—
8:20 draw his sword, for he was **o** a boy and was afraid.
10: 6 Not **o** this, but they abandoned the LORD and no
10:15 you see fit, **o** rescue us today from our enemies."
11:34 home to Mizpah, his daughter—his **o** child—
15:11 "I **o** paid them back for what they did to me."
16: 3 But Samson stayed in bed **o** until midnight.
20:47 leaving **o** six hundred men who escaped to the rock
Ru 2:10 so kind to me?" she asked. "I am **o** a foreigner."
1Sa 2:18 Now Samuel, though **o** a boy, was the LORD's
2:30 But I will honor **o** those who honor me, and I will
5: 4 **O** the trunk of his body was left intact.
7: 3 Determine to obey **o** the LORD; then he will
7: 4 and Ashtoreth and worshiped **o** the LORD.
9:21 Saul replied, "But I'm **o** from Benjamin,
11: 2 "All right," Nahash said, "but **o** on one condition.
13:15 were still with him, he found **o** six hundred left!
14: 6 a battle whether he has many warriors or **o** a few!"
14:29 "A command like that **o** hurts us.
14:43 "It was **o** a little bit on the end of a stick.
15: 9 They destroyed **o** what was worthless or of poor
16:18 Not **o** that; he is brave and strong and has good
17:29 David replied. "I was **o** asking a question!"
17:33 You are **o** a boy, and he has been in the army since
17:40 Then, armed **o** with his shepherd's staff and sling,
17:50 triumphed over the Philistine giant with **o** a stone
18: 8 with ten thousands and me with **o** thousands.
18:13 and appointed him commander over **o** a thousand
19:16 they discovered that it was **o** an idol in the bed
20: 3 But I swear to you that I am **o** a step away from
20:39 what Jonathan meant; **o** Jonathan and David knew.
21: 9 "I **o** have the sword of Goliath the Philistine,
22:20 **O** Abiathar, one of the sons of Ahimelech, escaped
2Sa 2:26 Don't you realize the **o** thing we will gain is
2:27 "God **o** knows what would have happened if you
2:30 he discovered that **o** nineteen men were missing,
13:32 all your sons have been killed! It was **o** Amnon!
13:33 your sons aren't all dead! It was **o** Amnon."
14:26 He cut his hair **o** once a year, and then **o** because it
15:20 You arrived **o** yesterday, and now should I force
15:33 "If you go with me, you will **o** be a burden.
17: 2 everyone will run away. Then I will kill **o** the king,
17: 3 After all, it is **o** this man's life that you seek.
18: 3 Absalom's troops; they will be looking **o** for you.
18:33 If **o** I could have died instead of you! O Absalom,
19:11 that all Israel is ready, and **o** you are holding out.
19:28 my relatives and I could expect **o** death from you,
19:35 I would **o** be a burden to my lord the king.
23:21 Another time, armed **o** with a club, he killed a
1Ki 3:18 were alone; there were **o** two of us in the house.
11: 4 gods instead of trusting **o** in the LORD his God,
12:20 So **o** the tribe of Judah remained loyal to the
14:13 He is the **o** member of your family who will have a
14:13 for this child is the **o** good thing that the LORD,
16:15 Asa's reign in Judah, but he reigned **o** seven days.
17:12 And I have **o** a handful of flour left in the jar
18:22 "I am the **o** prophet of the LORD who is left,
20:24 **O** this time replace the kings with field
22:14 I will say **o** what the LORD tells me to say."
22:16 "How many times must I demand that you speak **o**
22:31 "Attack **o** the king of Israel!"
22:47 was no king in Edom at that time, **o** a deputy.
2Ki 3:18 But this is **o** a simple thing for the LORD, for he
3:25 Finally, **o** Kir-hareseth was left, but even that came
4:43 "Feed one hundred people with **o** this?"
5: 7 He is **o** trying to find an excuse to invade us
7: 1 five quarts of fine flour will cost **o** half an ounce of
7: 1 and ten quarts of barley grain will cost **o** half an
9:35 they found **o** her skull, her feet, and her hands.
10:23 "Make sure that **o** those who worship Baal are
13:19 Now you will be victorious **o** three times."
15:13 in Judah. Shallum reigned in Samaria **o** one month.
16:15 The old bronze altar will be **o** for my personal
17:18 **O** the tribe of Judah remained in the land.
17:36 Worship **o** the LORD, who brought you out of
17:39 You must worship **o** the LORD your God. He is
18:14 tribute money you demand if you will **o** go away."
18:22 and make everyone in Judah worship **o** at the altar
19:18 **o** idols of wood and stone shaped by human hands.
19:29 This year you will eat **o** what grows up by itself,
24:14 So **o** the poorest people were left in the land.
1Ch 6:49 **O** Aaron and his descendants served as priests.
7:15 was Zelophehad, who had **o** daughters.
11:23 Another time, armed with **o** a club, he killed an
23:17 Eliezer had **o** one son, Rehabiah, the family leader.
23:22 Eleazar died with no sons, **o** daughters.
24: 2 So **o** Eleazar and Ithamar were left to carry on as
29:14 and we give you **o** what you have already given us!
29:15 We are here for **o** a moment, visitors and strangers
2Ch 11:12 So **o** Judah and Benjamin remained under his
13:10 **O** the descendants of Aaron serve the LORD as
16:12 but sought help **o** from his physicians.
18:13 I will say **o** what my God tells me to say."
18:15 "How many times must I demand that you speak **o**
18:30 to his charioteers: "Attack **o** the king of Israel!"
21:17 **O** his youngest son, Ahaziah, was spared.
23: 6 **o** the priests and Levites on duty may enter the
24:24 Although the Arameans attacked with **o** a small
26: 7 God helped him not **o** with his wars against the
32:12 and Jerusalem to worship at **o** the one altar at the
33:17 the pagan shrines, but **o** to the LORD their God.
35:21 I **o** want to fight the nation with which I am at war.
36: 2 he became king, but he reigned **o** three months.
36: 9 but he reigned in Jerusalem **o** three months and ten
Ezr 10:15 **O** Jonathan son of Asahel and Jahzeiah son of
Ne 2:12 out during the night, taking **o** a few others with me.
4:16 **o** half my men worked while the other half stood
7: 4 And **o** a few houses were scattered throughout the
9:29 by which people will find life if **o** they obey.
9:33 and you gave us **o** what we deserved.
Est 1: 8 The **o** restriction on the drinking was that no one
1:16 "Queen Vashti has wronged not **o** the king
5:12 Queen Esther invited **o** me and the king himself to
7: 4 If we had **o** been sold as slaves, I could remain
Job 1:15 I am the **o** one who escaped to tell you."
1:16 I am the **o** one who escaped to tell you."
1:17 I am the **o** one who escaped to tell you."
1:19 are dead. I am the **o** one who escaped to tell you."
2: 4 for skin—he blesses you **o** because you bless him.
2:10 Should we accept **o** good things from the hand of
3:26 I have no rest; instead, **o** trouble comes."
9:15 would have no defense. I could **o** plead for mercy.
9:33 If **o** there were a mediator who could bring us
10: 4 Are your eyes **o** those of a human? Do you see
10:20 I have **o** a little time left, so leave me alone—
11: 5 If **o** God would speak; if **o** he would tell you what
11: 6 If **o** he would tell you the secrets of wisdom,
11:13 "If **o** you would prepare your heart and lift up
15:31 They are **o** fooling themselves, for emptiness will be their **o** reward.
15:35 and evil, and their hearts give birth **o** to deceit."
20: 5 and the joy of the godless has been **o** temporary?
23: 3 If **o** I knew where to find God, I would go to his
31:35 "If **o** I had someone who would listen to me
32:13 'He is too wise for us. **O** God can convince him.'
35: 8 No, your sins affect **o** people like yourself,
35: 8 and your good deeds affect **o** other people.
35:14 He will bring about justice if you will **o** wait.
36:25 has seen these things, but **o** from a distance.
40:19 amazing handiwork. **O** its Creator can threaten it.
Ps 2: 8 **O** ask, and I will give you the nations as your
8: 5 For you made us **o** a little lower than God,
14: 1 **O** fools say in their hearts, / "There is no God."
17:14 from those whose **o** concern is earthly gain.
24: 4 **O** those whose hands and hearts are pure, / who do
33:20 **O** he can help us, protecting us like a shield.
34: 2 I will boast **o** in the LORD; / let all who are
37: 8 Do not envy others— / it **o** leads to harm.
39: 7 where do I put my hope? / My **o** hope is in you.
40:11 My **o** hope is in your unfailing love
42: 3 Day and night, I have **o** tears for food, / while my
43: 2 For you are God, my **o** safe haven. / Why have you
44: 5 **O** by your power can we push back our enemies;
44: 5 **o** in your name can we trample our foes.
53: 1 **O** fools say in their hearts, / "There is no God."
68: 6 But for rebels, there is **o** famine and distress.
69:20 If **o** one person would show some pity; / if **o** one would turn and comfort me.
73: 8 They scoff and speak **o** evil; / in their pride they
73:20 Their present life is **o** a dream / that is gone when
76:10 Human opposition **o** enhances your glory, / for you
78:36 But they followed him **o** with their words;
80: 3 shine down upon us. / **O** then will we be saved.
80: 7 shine down upon us. / **O** then will we be saved.
80:19 shine down upon us. / **O** then will we be saved.
81: 8 stern warnings. / O Israel, if you would **o** listen!
88:18 and loved ones; / **o** darkness remains.
92: 6 **O** an ignorant person would not know this! / **O** a fool would not understand it.
92: 7 there is **o** eternal destruction ahead of them.
101: 6 **O** those who are above reproach / will be allowed
103:14 how weak we are; / he knows we are **o** dust.
116: 3 grave overtook me. / I saw **o** trouble and sorrow.
119: 3 with evil, / and they walk **o** in his paths.
119:43 of truth from me, / for my **o** hope is in your laws.
119:49 your promise to me, / for it is my **o** hope.
119:68 You are good and do **o** good; / teach me your
119:114 and my shield; / your word is my **o** source of hope.
119:118 your principles. / They are **o** fooling themselves.
119:161 but my heart trembles **o** at your word.
129: 6 on a rooftop, / turning yellow when **o** half grown,
139:19 O God, if **o** you would destroy the wicked!
Pr 1: 7 **O** fools despise wisdom and discipline.
2:21 For **o** the upright will live in the land, and those
4: 3 tenderly loved by my mother as an **o** child.
5:12 If **o** I had not demanded my own way!
5:15 your own well—share your love **o** with your wife.
9: 8 bother rebuking mockers; they will **o** hate you.
10:32 are helpful, but the wicked speak **o** what is corrupt.
11:23 to happiness, while the wicked can expect **o** wrath.
11:29 Those who bring trouble on their families inherit **o**
12: 3 never brings stability; **o** the godly have deep roots.
12:11 means prosperity; **o** fools idle away their time.
14:15 **O** simpletons believe everything they are told!
14:24 for the wise; the effort of fools yields **o** folly.
15: 2 makes learning a joy; fools spout **o** foolishness.
15: 5 **O** a fool despises a parent's discipline;
15: 7 **O** the wise can give good advice; fools cannot do
15:32 If you reject criticism, you **o** harm yourself;
18: 2 they **o** want to air their own opinions.
19:14 but **o** the LORD can give an understanding wife.
20: 3 is a mark of honor; **o** fools insist on quarreling.
21:11 A simpleton can learn **o** by seeing mockers
26:19 lies to a friend and then says, "I was **o** joking."
28:16 **O** a stupid prince will oppress his people, but a
28:20 But the person who wants to get rich quick will **o**
28:22 tries to get rich quick, but it **o** leads to poverty.
29:24 If you assist a thief, you are **o** hurting yourself.
Ecc 1:18 To increase knowledge **o** increases sorrow.
2: 2 "What good does it do to seek **o** pleasure?"
2: 3 I hoped to experience the **o** happiness most people
2:21 to earn it. This is not **o** foolish but highly unfair.
5: 2 for he is in heaven, and you are **o** here on earth.
5: 8 and matters of justice **o** get lost in red tape
5:15 People who live **o** for wealth come to the end of
7: 4 while the fool thinks **o** about having a good time
7:12 but it's important to know that **o** wisdom can save
9: 4 There is hope **o** for the living. For as they say,
9:14 There was a small town with **o** a few people living
10:17 and whose leaders feast **o** to gain strength for their
SS 6: 9 perfect one, the **o** beloved daughter of her mother!
8: 1 "Oh, if **o** you were my brother, who nursed at my
Isa 1:19 If you will **o** obey me and let me help you,
3:24 beauty will be gone. **O** shame will be left to them.
4: 1 **O** let us be called by your name so we won't be

5:10 Ten measures of seed will yield **o** one measure of
6:13 Even if **o** a tenth—a remnant—survive, it will be
8:17 from the people of Israel. My **o** hope is in him.
9:18 It burns not **o** briers and thorns but the forests,
10:19 **O** a few from all that mighty army will survive—
10:22 **o** a few of them will return at that time.
15:7 The desperate refugees take **o** the possessions they
17:6 **O** a few of its people will be left, like the stray
17:6 **O** two or three remain in the highest branches,
17:11 Your **o** harvest will be a load of grief and incurable
21:17 **O** a few of its courageous archers will survive.
24:13 left on the vine after harvest, **o** a remnant is left.
26:9 for God. / For **o** when you come to judge the earth
27:5 These enemies will be spared **o** if they surrender
27:8 but he has punished Israel **o** a little. He has exiled
28:12 rest in their own land if they would **o** obey him,
29:16 greater than you. You are **o** the jars he makes!
30:15 "**O** in returning to me and waiting for me will you
30:16 But the **o** swiftness you are going to see is the
35:8 It will be **o** for those who walk in God's ways;
35:9 be no other dangers. **O** the redeemed will follow it.
36:7 and make everyone in Judah worship **o** at the altar
37:19 **o** idols of wood and stone shaped by human hands.
37:30 This year you will eat **o** what grows up by itself,
38:19 **O** the living can praise you as I do today.
43:12 You are witnesses that I am the **o** God,"
45:14 and say, 'God is with you, and he is the **o** God.' "
45:19 I, the LORD, speak **o** what is true and right.
46:10 **O** I can tell you what is going to happen even
59:7 They think **o** about sinning. Wherever they go,
65:20 "No longer will babies die when **o** a few days old.
65:20 old at one hundred! **O** sinners will die that young!
Jer 2:5 foolish idols, **o** to become foolish themselves.
2:26 a thief, Israel feels shame **o** when she gets caught.
3:10 She has **o** pretended to be sorry,"
3:13 **O** acknowledge your guilt. Admit that you rebelled
3:23 **O** in the LORD our God will Israel ever find
6:26 and weep bitterly, as for the loss of an **o** son.
7:5 I will be merciful **o** if you stop your wicked
7:10 **o** to go right back to all those evils again?
7:23 be my people. **O** do as I say, and all will be well!'
8:15 We hoped for a time of healing, but found **o** terror.
9:3 And they **o** go from bad to worse! They care
10:10 But the LORD is the **o** true God, the living God.
13:16 you look for light, you will find **o** terrible darkness.
14:8 passing through the land, stopping **o** for the night?
14:12 In return, I will give them **o** war, famine,
14:19 We hoped for a time of healing but found **o** terror.
14:22 the LORD our God! **O** you can do such things.
23:23 Am I a God who is **o** in one place?"
25:5 **O** then will I let you live in this land that the
28:9 **O** when his predictions come true can it be known
30:5 the people crying; there is **o** fear and trembling.
33:21 **o** then will my covenant with David, my servant,
33:21 **O** then will he no longer have a descendant to
34:7 the **o** cities of Judah with their walls still standing.
36:32 in the fire. **O** this time, he added much more!
37:10 leaving **o** a handful of wounded survivors,
42:2 we are **o** a tiny remnant compared to what we were
44:8 You will **o** destroy yourselves and make
44:14 returning home to Judah, **o** a handful will escape."
44:28 "**O** a small number will escape death and return to
La 1:20 the sword kills, and at home there is **o** death.
4:5 The people who once ate **o** the richest foods now
Eze 12:12 in the wall, taking **o** what he can carry with him.
15:4 No, it can **o** be used for fuel, and even as fuel,
17:14 **O** by keeping her treaty with Babylon could Israel
18:23 I **o** want them to turn from their wicked ways
20:49 they are saying of me, 'He **o** talks in riddles!' "
24:5 Use **o** the best sheep from the flock and heap fuel
24:17 You may sigh but **o** quietly. Let there be no
28:2 But you are **o** a man and not a god, though you
33:11 I **o** want them to turn from their wicked ways
33:24 'Abraham was **o** one man, and yet he gained
33:31 their mouths, but their hearts seek **o** after money.
36:11 Not **o** the people, but your flocks and herds will
37:24 be their king, and they will have **o** one shepherd.
42:8 which extended for **o** 87-1/2 feet, while the inner
43:8 They put their idol altars right next to mine with **o**
44:3 **O** the prince himself may sit inside this gateway to
44:3 may come and go **o** through the gateway's foyer."
44:17 inner courtyard, they must wear **o** linen clothing.
44:22 They may choose their wives **o** from among the
44:26 But such a priest can **o** return to his Temple duties
45:10 You must use **o** honest weights and scales,
45:21 **O** bread without yeast may be eaten during that
46:17 the servant may keep it **o** until the Year of Jubilee,
46:17 **O** the gifts given to the prince's sons will be
Da 1:4 "Select **o** strong, healthy, and good-looking young
1:16 the attendant fed them **o** vegetables instead of the
6:5 "Our **o** chance of finding grounds for accusing
10:7 I, Daniel, am the **o** one who saw this vision.
11:24 of strongholds, but this will last for **o** a short while.
12:10 **O** those who are wise will know what it means.
Hos 2:12 where **o** wild animals will eat the fruit.
7:13 but they have **o** spoken lies about me.
9:7 and shows **o** hatred for those who love God.
10:9 night in Gibeah, there has been **o** sin and more sin!
Am 3:12 sheep from a lion's mouth will recover **o** two legs
3:12 in Samaria are rescued with **o** a broken chair
5:3 a thousand men to battle, **o** a hundred will return.
5:3 sends a hundred, **o** ten will come back alive."
5:18 who say, "If **o** the day of the LORD were here!
5:19 like a man who runs from a lion—**o** to meet a bear.
5:23 They are **o** noise to my ears. I will not listen to
6:3 but your actions **o** bring the day of judgment
7:2 will not survive, for we are **o** a small nation."
7:5 will not survive, for we are **o** a small nation."
8:10 heads as signs of sorrow, as if your **o** son had died.
Jnh 4:10 to put it there. And a plant is **o**, at best, short lived.
Mic 1:12 but **o** bitterness awaits them as the LORD's
3:11 can get; you priests teach God's laws **o** for a price;
5:2 are **o** a small village in Judah.
6:16 "The **o** laws you keep are those of evil King Omri;
6:16 the **o** example you follow is that of wicked King
Hag 2:16 for a twenty-bushel crop, you harvested **o** ten.
2:16 gallons from the winepress, you found **o** twenty.
Zec 1:15 I was **o** a little angry with my people,
7:6 don't think about me, but **o** of pleasing yourselves.
10:2 give false advice, fortune-tellers predict **o** lies,
11:12 whatever I am worth; but **o** if you want to."
12:10 have pierced and mourn for him as for an **o** son.
14:7 **O** the LORD knows how this could happen!
Mt 4:9 "if you will **o** kneel down and worship me."
4:10 worship the Lord your God; / serve **o** him.' "
5:46 If you love **o** those who love you, what good is
5:47 If you are kind **o** to your friends, how are you
6:7 They think their prayers are answered **o** by
6:16 I assure you, that is the **o** reward they will ever get.
7:13 "You can enter God's Kingdom **o** through the
7:14 and the road is narrow, and **o** a few ever find it.
8:9 I **o** need to say, 'Go,' and they go, or 'Come,'
9:24 "Go away, for the girl isn't dead; she's **o** asleep."
10:6 but **o** to the people of Israel—God's lost sheep.
10:28 They can **o** kill your body; they cannot touch your
10:28 Fear **o** God, who can destroy both soul and body in
10:29 Not even a sparrow, worth **o** half a penny, can fall
12:29 first tying him up. **O** then can his house be robbed!
12:39 But Jesus replied, "**O** an evil, faithless generation
12:39 but the **o** sign I will give them is the sign of the
13:58 And so he did **o** a few miracles there because of
14:17 "We have **o** five loaves of bread and two fish!"
15:24 "I was sent **o** to help the people of Israel—
16:4 **O** an evil, faithless generation would ask for a
16:4 but the **o** sign I will give them is the sign of the
17:8 when they looked, they saw **o** Jesus with them.
19:11 Jesus said. "**O** those whom God helps.
19:17 Jesus replied. "**O** God is good. But to answer your
20:12 'Those people worked **o** one hour, and yet you've
20:31 but they **o** shouted louder, "Lord, Son of David,
21:19 if there were any figs on it, but there were **o** leaves.
23:8 call you 'Rabbi,' for you have **o** one teacher,
23:9 for **o** God in heaven is your spiritual Father.
23:10 for there is **o** one master, the Messiah.
24:8 But all this will be **o** the beginning of the horrors to
24:36 in heaven or the Son himself. **O** the Father knows.
27:23 But the crowd **o** roared the louder, "Crucify him!"
Mk 3:27 first tying him up. **O** then can his house be robbed!
4:34 in his public teaching he taught **o** with parables,
5:39 he asked. "The child isn't dead; she is **o** asleep."
6:10 each village, be a guest in **o** one home," he said.
7:13 And this is **o** one example. There are many,
7:19 but **o** passes through the stomach and then comes
8:14 so there was **o** one loaf of bread with them in the
9:8 and Elijah were gone, and **o** Jesus was with them.
9:29 "This kind can be cast out **o** by prayer."
9:43 It is better to enter heaven with **o** one hand than to
9:45 It is better to enter heaven with **o** one foot than to
10:5 "He wrote those instructions **o** as a concession to
10:18 me good?" Jesus asked. "**O** God is truly good.
10:21 "You lack **o** one thing," he told him. "Go and sell
10:48 But he **o** shouted louder, "Son of David,
11:13 But there were **o** leaves because it was too early in
12:6 until there was **o** one left—his son whom he loved
12:29 O Israel! The Lord our God is the one and **o** Lord.
12:32 You have spoken the truth by saying that there is **o**
13:8 But all this will be **o** the beginning of the horrors to
13:32 in heaven or the Son himself. **O** the Father knows.
14:51 along behind, clothed **o** in a linen nightshirt.
15:14 But the crowd **o** roared the louder, "Crucify him!"
Lk 2:36 died when they had been married **o** seven years.
4:8 worship the Lord your God; / serve **o** him.' "
6:24 who are rich, / for you have your **o** happiness now.
6:33 And if you do good **o** to those who do good to you,
6:34 And if you lend money **o** to those who can repay
7:8 I **o** need to say, 'Go,' and they go, or 'Come,'
7:12 The boy who had died was the **o** son of a widow,
7:47 But a person who is forgiven little shows **o** little
8:42 His **o** child was dying, a little girl twelve years old.
8:52 the weeping! She isn't dead; she is **o** asleep."
9:4 you enter each village, be a guest in **o** one home.
9:13 "We have **o** five loaves of bread and two fish.
9:38 "Teacher, look at my boy, who is my **o** son.
10:42 There is really **o** one thing worth being concerned
11:29 But the **o** sign I will give them is the sign of the
12:4 They can **o** kill the body; they cannot do any more
12:48 they are doing wrong will be punished **o** lightly.
13:23 asked him, "Lord, will **o** a few be saved?"
14:29 you might complete **o** the foundation before
16:7 and replace it with one for **o** eight hundred
17:18 Does **o** this foreigner return to give glory to God?"
18:19 Jesus asked him. "**O** God is truly good.
18:39 but he **o** shouted louder, "Son of David,
19:20 "But the third servant brought back **o** the original
22:45 **o** to find them asleep, exhausted from grief.
24:18 "You must be the **o** person in Jerusalem who
Jn 1:8 was not the light; he was **o** a witness to the light.
1:14 seen his glory, the glory of the **o** Son of the Father.
1:18 But his **o** Son, who is himself God, is near to the
3:6 Humans can reproduce **o** human life, but the Holy
3:13 For **o** I, the Son of Man, have come to earth
3:16 so loved the world that he gave his **o** Son,
3:18 been judged for not believing in the **o** Son of God.
4:10 "If you **o** knew the gift God has for you and who I
4:20 insist that Jerusalem is the **o** place of worship,
5:19 He does **o** what he sees the Father doing.
5:43 readily accept others who represent **o** themselves.
6:13 There were **o** five barley loaves to start with,
6:46 **o** I, who was sent from God, have seen him.)
8:9 until **o** Jesus was left in the middle of the crowd
8:26 For I say **o** what I have heard from the one who
11:8 "**o** a few days ago the Jewish leaders in Judea
11:10 **O** at night is there danger of stumbling
11:18 Bethany was **o** a few miles down the road from
11:52 that Jesus' death would be not for Israel **o**,
14:22 why are you going to reveal yourself **o** to us
17:3 to know you, the **o** true God, and Jesus Christ,
17:20 "I am praying not **o** for these disciples but also for
18:31 "**O** the Romans are permitted to execute
21:8 for they were **o** out about three hundred feet.
21:23 He **o** said, "If I want him to remain alive until I
Ac 8:16 for they had **o** been baptized in the name of the
9:26 They thought he was **o** pretending to be a believer!
11:19 They preached the Good News, but **o** to Jews.
16:10 for we could **o** conclude that God was calling us to
18:25 However, he knew **o** about John's baptism.
19:26 And this is happening not **o** here in Ephesus
21:7 we greeted the believers but stayed **o** one day.
21:13 For I am ready not **o** to be jailed at Jerusalem
24:4 kindly give me your attention for **o** a moment as I
27:12 Phoenix was a good harbor with **o** a southwest
27:28 and found the water was **o** 120 feet deep.
27:28 little later they sounded again and found **o** 90 feet.
28:22 for the **o** thing we know about these Christians is
Ro 2:25 is worth something **o** if you obey God's law.
3:29 After all, God is not the God of the Jews **o**, is he?
3:30 There is **o** one God, and there is **o** one way of
being accepted by him.
3:30 He makes people right with himself **o** by faith,
3:31 **o** when we have faith do we truly fulfill the law.
4:9 Now then, is this blessing **o** for the Jews, or is it
4:10 Was he declared righteous **o** after he had been
4:12 but **o** if they have the same kind of faith Abraham
4:15 (The **o** way to avoid breaking the law is to have no
7:1 don't you know that the law applies **o** to a person
9:22 of his judgment and are fit **o** for destruction.
9:27 on the seashore, / **o** a small number will be saved.
11:4 God's reply? He said, "You are not the **o** one left.
11:25 but this will last **o** until the complete number of
14:2 has a sensitive conscience will eat **o** vegetables.
16:4 I am not the **o** one who is thankful to them; so are
1Co 1:12 or "I follow Peter," or "I follow **o** Christ."
1:22 because they believe **o** what agrees with their own
1:31 should boast **o** of what the Lord has done."
2:2 For I decided to concentrate **o** on Jesus Christ
2:14 because **o** those who have the Spirit can
3:5 Why, we're **o** servants. Through us God caused
4:15 you about Christ, you have **o** one spiritual father.
7:5 The **o** exception to this rule would be the
7:6 This is **o** my suggestion. It's not meant to be an
8:4 a god and that there is **o** one God and no other.
8:6 But we know that there is **o** one God, the Father,
8:6 And there is **o** one Lord, Jesus Christ,
9:6 Or is it **o** Barnabas and I who have to work to
9:9 Do you suppose God was thinking **o** about oxen
9:24 race everyone runs, but **o** one person gets the prize.
10:24 Don't think **o** of your own good. Think of other
12:11 and **o** Holy Spirit who distributes these gifts.
12:12 but the many parts make up **o** one body.
12:16 of the body because I am **o** an ear and not an eye,"
12:19 What a strange thing a body would be if it had **o**
12:20 Yes, there are many parts, but **o** one body.
13:1 I would **o** be making meaningless noise like a loud
13:9 Now we know **o** a little, and even the gift of
14:16 For if you praise God **o** in the spirit, how can those
15:19 And if we have hope in Christ **o** for this life,
15:37 but **o** a dry little seed of wheat or whatever it is
2Co 3:2 But the **o** letter of recommendation we need is you
3:5 Our **o** power and success come from God.
3:14 And this veil can be removed **o** by believing in
8:3 For I can testify that they gave not **o** what they
8:13 I **o** mean that there should be some equality.
8:15 and those who gathered **o** a little had enough."
9:4 **o** to find that you still weren't ready after all I had
9:6 a farmer who plants **o** a few seeds will get a small
10:12 But they are **o** comparing themselves with each
10:17 should boast **o** of what the Lord has done."
12:3 or just my spirit, I don't know; **o** God knows.
12:5 I am going to boast **o** about my weaknesses.
12:13 The **o** thing I didn't do, which I do in the other
Gal 1:19 And the **o** other apostle I met at that time was
2:10 The **o** thing they suggested was that we remember
3:2 for the Holy Spirit came upon you **o** after you
3:18 For if the inheritance could be received **o** by
3:19 But this system of law was to last **o** until the
3:22 so the **o** way to receive God's promise is to believe
5:9 But it takes **o** one wrong person among you to
5:12 I **o** wish that those troublemakers who want to
6:3 help someone in need, you are **o** fooling yourself.
6:8 Those who live **o** to satisfy their own sinful desires
6:13 They **o** want you to be circumcised so they can
Eph 2:5 (It is **o** by God's special favor that you have been
2:11 even though it affected **o** their bodies and not their
4:5 There is **o** one Lord, one faith, one baptism,
4:6 and there is **o** one God and Father, who is over us
5:9 For this light within you produces **o** what is good
Php 1:27 I come and see you again or **o** hear about you,
1:29 For you have been given not **o** the privilege of
2:4 Don't think **o** about your own affairs, but be
2:21 All the others care **o** for themselves and not for
3:3 For we who worship God in the Spirit are the **o**

4:15 you Philippians were the **o** ones who gave me
Col 2:17 For these rules were **o** shadows of the real thing,
2:19 and we grow **o** as we get our nourishment
3:2 Do not think **o** about things down here on earth.
4:11 These are the **o** Jewish Christians among my
1Th 1:5 it was not **o** with words but also with power,
2:8 so much that we gave you not **o** God's Good News
2Th 2:6 for he can be revealed **o** when his time comes.
1Ti 1:4 For these things **o** cause arguments; they don't
2:5 For there is **o** one God and one Mediator who can
5:6 But the widow who lives **o** for pleasure is
5:23 Don't drink **o** water. You ought to drink a little
6:15 from heaven by the blessed and **o** almighty God,
2Ti 2:23 in foolish, ignorant arguments that **o** start fights.
3:2 For people will love **o** themselves and their money.
4:11 **O** Luke is with me. Bring Mark with you when
Tit 1:11 from the truth. Such teachers **o** want your money.
Heb 1:14 But angels are **o** servants. They are spirits sent
2:10 And it was **o** right that God—who made everything
2:14 For **o** as a human being could he die, and **o** by
dying could he break the power of the
2:15 **O** in this way could he deliver those who have
3:5 faithful in God's house, but **o** as a servant.
4:3 For **o** we who believe can enter his place of rest.
5:12 You are like babies who drink **o** milk and cannot
7:21 **O** to Jesus did he say, / "The Lord has taken an
8:5 They serve in a place of worship that is **o** a copy,
9:7 But **o** the high priest goes into the Most Holy
9:7 and **o** once a year, and always with blood,
9:10 For that old system deals **o** with food and drink
9:10 external regulations that are in effect **o** until their
9:17 The will goes into effect **o** after the death of the
9:27 And just as it is destined that each person dies **o**
9:28 so also Christ died **o** once as a sacrifice to take
10:1 The old system in the law of Moses was **o** a
11:17 was ready to sacrifice his **o** son, Isaac,
12:26 "Once again I will shake not **o** the earth
12:27 will be shaken, so that **o** eternal things will be left.
Jas 1:22 If you don't obey, you are **o** fooling yourself.
3:13 so that **o** good deeds will pour forth.
4:3 is wrong—you want **o** what will give you pleasure.
1Pe 1:7 These trials are **o** to test your faith, to show that it
2:18 not **o** if they are kind and reasonable, but even if
3:20 **O** eight people were saved from drowning in that
1Jn 1:8 we are **o** fooling ourselves and refusing to accept
2:2 He takes away not **o** our sins but the sins of all the
2:16 For the world offers **o** the lust for physical
4:9 he loved us by sending his **o** Son into the world
4:21 has commanded that we must love not **o** him
5:6 the cross—not by water **o**, but by water and blood.
5:20 He is the **o** true God, and he is eternal life.
3Jn 1:10 He not **o** refuses to welcome the traveling teachers,
1:11 bad example influence you. Follow **o** what is good.
Jude 1:4 for they have turned against our **o** Master
1:12 They are shameless in the way they care **o** about
1:12 They are not **o** dead but doubly dead, for they have
Rev 19:12 was written on him, and **o** he knew what it meant.
21:27 but **o** those whose names are written in the Lamb's

ONO (5)

1Ch 8:12 Shemed (who built **O** and Lod and their villages),
Ezr 2:33 The citizens of Lod, Hadid, and **O** | 725
Ne 6:2 meet them at one of the villages in the plain of **O**.
7:37 The citizens of Lod, Hadid, and **O** | 721
11:35 Lod, **O**, and the Valley of Craftsmen.

ONSLAUGHT (1)

Da 11:15 south will not be able to stand in the face of the **o**.

ONTO (13) [ON]

Ex 8:3 even into your bedrooms and **o** your beds!
Nu 22:23 but Balaam beat it and turned it back **o** the road.
Jos 8:32 Joshua copied the law of Moses **o** the stones of the
2Sa 20:10 with it so that his insides gushed out **o** the ground.
Ps 133:2 ran down his beard / and **o** the border of his robe.
Eze 40:17 built against the walls, opening **o** the pavement.
42:3 Another block of rooms looked out **o** the pavement
Mt 13:48 the net is full, they drag it up **o** the shore, sit down,
27:5 Then Judas threw the money **o** the floor of the
Mk 7:33 Then, spitting **o** his own fingers, he touched the
Ac 28:3 driven out by the heat, fastened itself **o** his hand.
Gal 6:1 and humbly help that person back **o** the right path.
Rev 16:21 pounds fell from the sky **o** the people below.

ONWARD (4) [ON]

Job 17:9 The righteous will move **o** and forward, and those
Da 11:16 "The king of the north will march **o** unopposed;
Hab 3:10 and trembled. **O** swept the raging waters.
Hag 2:19 their crops. From this day **o** I will bless you."

ONYX (12)

Ge 2:12 aromatic resin and **o** stone are also found there.
Ex 25:7 **o** stones, and other stones to be set in the ephod
28:9 Take two **o** stones and engrave on them the names
28:20 fourth row will contain a beryl, an **o**, and a jasper.
35:9 **o** stones, and other stones to be set in the ephod
35:27 The leaders brought **o** stones and the other
39:6 The two **o** stones, attached to the shoulder-pieces
39:13 In the fourth row were a beryl, an **o**, and a jasper.
1Ch 29:2 iron, and wood, as well as great quantities of **o**,
Job 28:16 greater than precious **o** stone or sapphires.
Eze 28:13 beryl, **o**, jasper, sapphire, turquoise, and emerald—
Rev 21:20 the fifth **o**, the sixth carnelian, the seventh

OOZING (1)

Lev 21:20 a defective eye, or has **o** sores or scabs on his skin,

OPEN (159) [OPEN-MINDED, OPENED, OPENING, OPENLY, OPENS, REOPENED]

Ge 25:27 became a skillful hunter, a man of the **o** fields,
27:3 and a quiver full of arrows out into the **o** country,
27:27 "The smell of my son is the good smell of the **o**
29:2 flocks of sheep lying in an **o** field beside a well,
34:10 And you may live among us; the land is **o** to you!
Ex 9:21 for the word of the LORD left them out in the **o**.
14:16 and a path will **o** up before you through the sea.
Lev 13:10 and an **o** sore appears in the affected area,
13:14 But if any **o** sores appear, the infected person will
13:15 this pronouncement as soon as he sees an **o** sore
13:15 because **o** sores indicate the presence of a
13:16 if the **o** sores heal and turn white like the rest of the
13:29 or woman, has an **o** sore on the head or chin,
14:7 living bird free so it can fly away into the **o** fields.
14:53 he will release the living bird in the **o** fields outside
17:5 Israelites from sacrificing animals in the **o** fields.
22:22 injured, mutilated, or that has a growth, an **o** sore,
25:31 will be treated like property in the **o** fields.
Nu 16:31 when the ground suddenly split **o** beneath them.
24:4 the Almighty, / who falls down with eyes wide **o**:
24:16 the Almighty, / who falls down with eyes wide **o**:
Dt 20:11 If they accept your terms and **o** the gates to you,
Jos 8:17 after the Israelites, and the city was left wide **o**.
Jdg 20:31 About thirty Israelites died in the **o** fields
2Sa 3:29 generation be cursed with a man who has **o** sores
10:8 and Maacah positioned themselves to fight in the **o**
11:11 and his officers are camping in the **o** fields.
1Ki 6:18 decorated with carvings of gourds and **o** flowers.
6:29 carvings of cherubim, palm trees, and **o** flowers.
6:32 palm trees, and **o** flowers, and the doors were
6:35 palm trees, and **o** flowers, and the doors were
8:52 "May your eyes be **o** to my requests and to the
2Ki 6:17 "O LORD, **o** his eyes and let him see!"
6:20 "O LORD, now **o** their eyes and let them see."
8:12 to the ground, and rip **o** their pregnant women!"
9:3 Then **o** the door and run for your life!"
13:17 "**O** that eastern window," and he opened it.
15:16 and ripped **o** the pregnant women.
18:31 Make peace with me—**o** the gates and come out.
19:16 and hear! **O** your eyes, O LORD, and see!
1Ch 9:27 It was also their job to **o** the gates every morning.
19:9 kings positioned themselves to fight in the **o** fields.
2Ch 31:19 who were living in the **o** villages around the towns,
Ne 6:5 Sanballat's servant came with an **o** letter in his
7:3 "Do not leave the gates **o** during the hottest part of
8:5 When they saw him **o** the book, they all rose to
Job 7:5 and scabs. My flesh breaks **o**, full of pus.
24:1 "Why doesn't the Almighty **o** the court and bring
39:4 Their young grow up in the **o** fields, then leave
41:14 Who could pry **o** its jaws? For its teeth are terrible!
Ps 5:9 Their talk is foul, like the stench from an **o** grave.
22:13 their prey, / they come at me with **o** mouths.
24:7 **O** up, ancient gates! / **O** up, ancient doors,
24:9 **O** up, ancient gates! / **O** up, ancient doors,
34:15 who do right; / his ears are **o** to their cries for help.
58:9 and old, / faster than a pot heats on an **o** flame.
60:2 You have shaken our land and split it **o**.
78:1 to my teaching. / **O** your ears to what I am saying,
78:15 He split **o** the rocks in the wilderness / to give them
78:23 But he commanded the skies to **o**— / he opened the
81:10 **O** your mouth wide, and I will fill it with good
104:28 You **o** your hand to feed them, and they are
118:19 **O** for me the gates where the righteous enter,
119:18 **O** my eyes to see / the wonderful truths in your
119:131 I **o** my mouth, panting expectantly, / longing for
145:16 When you **o** your hand, / you satisfy the hunger
Pr 18:15 Intelligent people are always **o** to new ideas.
20:13 Keep your eyes **o**, and there will be plenty to eat!
27:5 An **o** rebuke is better than hidden love!
Ecc 5:1 of God, keep your ears **o** and your mouth shut!
SS 5:2 '**O** to me, my darling, my treasure, my lovely
5:5 I jumped up to **o** it. My hands dripped with
Isa 22:22 He will **o** doors, and no one will be able to shut
22:22 will close doors, and no one will be able to **o** them.
26:2 **O** the gates to all who are righteous;
35:5 he will **o** the eyes of the blind and unstop the ears
36:16 Make peace with me—**o** the gates and come out.
37:17 and hear! **O** your eyes, O LORD, and see!
41:18 I will **o** up rivers for them on high plateaus. I will
42:7 You will **o** the eyes of the blind and free the
45:8 **O** up, O heavens, and pour out your righteousness.
45:8 Let the earth **o** wide so salvation and righteousness
53:7 silent before the shearers, he did not **o** his mouth.
55:3 "Come to me with your ears wide **o**. Listen,
60:11 Your gates will stay **o** around the clock to receive
Jer 8:1 "the enemy will break **o** the graves of the kings
9:20 of the LORD; **o** your ears to what he has to say.
12:5 If you stumble and fall on **o** ground, what will you
13:19 close their gates, and no one will be able to **o** them.
26:18 Mount Zion will be plowed like an **o** field;
29:31 "Send an **o** letter to all the exiles in Babylon.
50:26 Break **o** her granaries. Crush her walls and houses
Eze 2:8 a rebel. **O** your mouth, and eat what I give you."
24:8 So I will splash her blood on a rock as an **o**
25:9 I will **o** up their eastern flank and wipe out their
29:5 You will lie unburied on the **o** ground, for I have
33:27 Those living in the **o** fields will be eaten by wild
37:12 I will **o** your graves of exile and cause you to rise
39:5 You will fall in the **o** fields, for I have spoken,
41:9 This left an **o** area between these side rooms
41:10 This **o** area measured 35 feet in width, and it went
42:14 the parts of the building complex **o** to the public."
46:1 but it will be **o** on Sabbath days and the days of
48:17 **O** lands will surround the city for 150 yards in
Da 6:10 with its windows **o** toward Jerusalem.
9:18 my request. **O** your eyes and see our wretchedness.
11:20 he will die, though neither in battle nor **o** conflict.
Hos 4:16 and unprotected, like a helpless lamb in an **o** field.
13:16 their pregnant women ripped **o** by swords."
Am 1:13 ripping **o** pregnant women with their swords.
Mic 3:12 of you, Mount Zion will be plowed like an **o** field;
4:10 for you must leave this city to live in the **o** fields.
Na 2:6 But too late! The river gates are **o**! The enemy has
Hab 3:9 of power! You split **o** the earth with flowing rivers!
Zep 2:14 and the cedar paneling will lie **o** to the wind
Zec 11:1 **O** your doors, Lebanon, so that fire may sweep
Mal 3:10 "I will **o** the windows of heaven for you.
Mt 13:12 To those who are **o** to my teaching,
16:19 and whatever you **o** on earth will be opened in
17:27 **O** the mouth of the first fish you catch, and you
25:11 they stood outside, calling, 'Sir, **o** the door for us!'
26:43 for they just couldn't keep their eyes **o**.
Mk 1:10 he saw the heavens split **o** and the Holy Spirit
4:25 To those who are **o** to my teaching,
14:40 for they just couldn't keep their eyes **o**.
Lk 8:16 No, lamps are mounted in the **o**, where they can be
8:18 To those who are **o** to my teaching,
8:40 of the lake the crowds received Jesus with **o** arms
12:36 Then you will be ready to **o** the door and let him in
13:25 and pleading, 'Lord, **o** the door for us!'
16:21 the dogs would come and lick his **o** sores.
Jn 1:51 you will all see heaven **o** and the angels of God
9:32 been able to **o** the eyes of someone born blind.
10:21 a demon! Can a demon **o** the eyes of the blind?"
Ac 1:18 and falling there, he burst **o**, spilling out his
8:32 silent before the shearers, / he did not **o** his mouth.
10:11 He saw the sky **o**, and something like a large sheet
12:13 and a servant girl named Rhoda came to **o** it.
16:26 All the doors flew **o**, and the chains of every
16:27 The jailer woke up to see the prison doors wide **o**.
26:18 to **o** their eyes so they may turn from darkness to
Ro 3:13 "Their talk is foul, like the stench from an **o** grave.
2Co 6:11 spoken honestly with you. Our hearts are **o** to you.
6:13 I would to my own children. **O** your hearts to us!
7:2 Please **o** your hearts to us. We have not done
Heb 9:8 was not **o** to the people as long as the first room
11:36 and their backs were cut **o** with whips.
1Pe 3:12 who do right, / and his ears are **o** to their prayers.
2Pe 1:11 And God will **o** wide the gates of heaven for you to
Rev 3:7 shut them; he shuts doors, and no one can **o** them.
3:20 If you hear me calling and **o** the door, I will come
4:1 as I looked, I saw a door standing **o** in heaven,
5:3 on earth or under the earth was able to **o** the scroll
5:4 one could be found who was worthy to **o** the scroll
5:5 He is worthy to **o** the scroll and break its seven
5:9 and break its seals and **o** it. / For you were killed,
15:5 in heaven, God's Tabernacle, was thrown wide **o**!

OPEN-MINDED (1) [MIND, OPEN]

Ac 17:11 And the people of Berea were more **o** than those in

OPENED (80) [OPEN]

Ge 3:5 "God knows that your eyes will be **o** when you eat
3:7 At that moment, their eyes were **o**, and they
8:6 Noah **o** the window he had made in the boat
21:19 Then God **o** Hagar's eyes, and she saw a well.
41:56 Joseph **o** up the storehouses and sold grain to the
42:27 and one of them **o** his sack to get some grain to
43:21 we stopped for the night and **o** our sacks.
44:11 sacks from the backs of their donkeys and **o** them.
Ex 2:6 As the princess **o** it, she found the baby boy.
14:21 and the LORD **o** up a path through the water with
Nu 16:32 The earth **o** up and swallowed the men, along with
22:31 Then the LORD **o** Balaam's eyes, and he saw the
26:10 But the earth **o** up and swallowed them with
Dt 11:6 when the earth **o** up and swallowed them,
Jdg 3:25 And when they **o** the door, they found their master
19:27 When her husband **o** the door to leave, he found
1Sa 3:15 got up and **o** the doors of the Tabernacle as usual.
2Sa 22:10 He **o** the heavens and came down; / dark storm
1Ki 17:20 tragedy on this widow who has **o** her home to me,
2Ki 4:35 time the boy sneezed seven times and **o** his eyes!
6:17 The LORD **o** his servant's eyes, and when he
7:2 "That couldn't happen even if the LORD **o** the
7:19 "That couldn't happen even if the LORD **o** the
9:10 Then the young prophet **o** the door and ran.
13:17 "Open that eastern window," and he **o** it.
Ne 11:17 who **o** the thanksgiving services with prayer;
13:19 not to be **o** until the Sabbath ended.
Job 31:32 away a stranger but have **o** my doors to everyone.
Ps 18:9 He **o** the heavens and came down; / dark storm
78:23 the skies to open— / he **o** the doors of heaven—
105:20 him free; / the ruler of the nation **o** his prison door.
105:41 He **o** up a rock, and water gushed out / to form a
106:17 Because of this, the earth **o** up; / it swallowed
SS 5:6 I **o** to my lover, but he was gone. I yearned for
7:12 vines have budded, whether the blossoms have **o**,
Isa 43:16 I am the LORD, who **o** a way through the waters,
45:1 Their fortress gates will be **o**, never again to shut
65:2 "I **o** my arms to my own people all day long,
Jer 50:25 "The LORD has **o** his armory and brought out
Eze 1:1 the heavens were **o** to me, and I saw visions of
3:2 So I **o** my mouth, and he fed me the scroll.
33:22 the LORD had taken hold of me and **o** my mouth,
40:25 and there was a foyer where the gateway passage **o**
41:11 Two doors **o** from the side rooms into the terrace

42: 2 whose entrance **o** toward the north, was 175 feet
44: 2 gate must remain closed; it will never again be **o**.
46:12 the east gateway to the inner courtyard will be **o**
Da 7:10 the court began its session, and the books were **o**.
10:16 my lips, and I **o** my mouth and began to speak.
Na 3:13 The gates of your land will be **o** wide to the enemy
Hab 2: 5 and wide, with their mouths **o** as wide as death,
Zec 13: 1 "On that day a fountain will be **o** for the dynasty
Mt 2:11 Then they **o** their treasure chests and gave him
3:16 the heavens were **o** and he saw the Spirit of God
7: 7 Keep on knocking, and the door will be **o**.
7: 8 finds. And the door is **o** to everyone who knocks.
16:19 and whatever you open on earth will be **o** in
27:52 and tombs **o**. The bodies of many godly men
Mk 7:34 up to heaven, he sighed and commanded, "Be **o**!"
Lk 3:21 was baptized. As he was praying, the heavens **o**,
11: 9 Keep on knocking, and the door will be **o**.
11:10 finds. And the door is **o** to everyone who knocks.
24:31 Suddenly, their eyes were **o**, and they recognized
24:45 Then he **o** their minds to understand these many
Jn 9:17 and demanded, "This man who **o** your eyes—
Ac 5:19 **o** the gates of the jail, and brought them out.
5:23 but when we **o** the gates, no one was there!"
7:56 I see the heavens **o** and the Son of Man standing in
9:40 he said, "Get up, Tabitha." And she **o** her eyes!
12:10 gate to the street, and this **o** to them all by itself.
12:16 When they finally went out and **o** the door,
14:27 and how he had **o** the door of faith to the Gentiles,
16:14 As she listened to us, the Lord **o** her heart, and she
Ro 10:21 God said, / "All day long I **o** my arms to them,
Heb 10:20 life-giving way that Christ has **o** up for us through
Rev 3: 8 and I have **o** a door for you that no one can shut.
9: 2 When he **o** it, smoke poured out as though from a
11:19 the Temple of God was **o** and the Ark of his
19:11 Then I saw heaven **o**, and a white horse was
20:12 And the books were **o**, including the Book of Life.

OPENING (16) [OPEN]

Ge 6:16 Construct an **o** all the way around the boat,
Ex 28:32 with an **o** for Aaron's head in the middle of it.
28:32 The **o** will be reinforced by a woven collar so it
39:23 with an **o** for Aaron's head in the middle of it.
39:23 The edge of this **o** was reinforced with a woven
Jos 10:18 "Cover the **o** of the cave with large rocks
10:22 "Remove the rocks covering the **o** of the cave
10:27 Then they covered the **o** of the cave with a large
1Ki 7:31 a round pedestal, and its **o** was 2-1/4 feet across;
Pr 17:14 Beginning a quarrel is like **o** a floodgate, so drop
Eze 8: 7 where I could see an **o** in the wall.
40:11 which was 17-1/2 feet wide at the **o** and 22-3/4 feet
40:17 were built against the walls, **o** onto the pavement.
Ac 9:25 in a large basket through an **o** in the city wall.
12:14 she was so overjoyed that, instead of **o** the door,
Rev 12:16 But the earth helped her by **o** its mouth

OPENLY (8) [OPEN]

2Sa 12:12 but I will do this to you **o** in the sight of all
Job 21:31 No one rebukes them **o**. No one repays them for
34:26 He **o** strikes them down for their wickedness.
Isa 3: 9 their guilt. They sin **o** like the people of Sodom.
Hos 1: 2 **o** committing adultery against the LORD by
Mt 10:32 I will **o** acknowledge that person before my Father
Mk 8:32 As he talked about this **o** with his disciples,
Lk 12: 8 will **o** acknowledge that person in the presence of

OPENS (7) [OPEN]

Nu 16:30 and the ground **o** up and swallows them and all
2Ch 20:16 of the valley that **o** into the wilderness of Jeruel.
Ps 146: 8 The LORD **o** the eyes of the blind. / The LORD
Pr 31:20 hand to the poor and **o** her arms to the needy.
Isa 50: 4 he wakens me and **o** my understanding to his will.
Jn 10: 3 The gatekeeper **o** the gate for him, and the sheep
Rev 3: 7 He **o** doors, and no one can shut them; he shuts

OPERATION (1)

Ex 39:40 all the articles used in the **o** of the Tabernacle;

OPERATION [KJV] See also DOING, MADE, POWER

OPHEL (5)

2Ch 27: 3 extensive rebuilding on the wall at the hill of **O**.
33:14 and continuing around the hill of **O**, where it was
Ne 3:26 and the Temple servants living on the hill of **O**,
3:27 great projecting tower and over to the wall of **O**.
11:21 were Ziha and Gishpa, all lived on the hill of **O**.

OPHIR (11)

Ge 10:29 **O**, Havilah, and Jobab.
1Ki 9:28 They sailed to **O** and brought back to Solomon
10:11 (When Hiram's ships brought gold from **O**,
22:48 built a fleet of trading ships to sail to **O** for gold.
1Ch 1:23 **O**, Havilah, and Jobab. All these were descendants
29: 4 I am donating more than 112 tons of gold from **O**
2Ch 8:18 These ships sailed to the land of **O** with Solomon's
9:10 of Hiram and Solomon brought gold from **O**,
Job 28:16 Its value is greater than all the gold of **O**,
Ps 45: 9 the queen, / wearing jewelry of finest gold from **O**!
Isa 13:12 be as scarce as gold—more rare than the gold of **O**.

OPHNI (1)

Jos 18:24 Kephar-ammoni, **O**, and Geba—twelve towns with

OPHRAH (8)

Jos 18:23 Avvim, Parah, **O**,
Jdg 6:11 LORD came and sat beneath the oak tree at **O**,
6:24 The altar remains in **O** in the land of the clan of
8:27 made a sacred ephod from the gold and put it in **O**,
8:32 Joash, at **O** in the land of the clan of Abiezer.
9: 5 He took the soldiers to his father's home at **O**,
1Sa 13:17 One went north toward **O** in the land of Shual,
1Ch 4:14 Meonothai was the father of **O**. Seraiah was the

OPINION (11) [OPINIONS]

Ex 23: 2 do not be swayed in your testimony by the **o** of the
2Sa 17: 6 Then he asked, "What is your **o**? Should we
1Ki 12: 8 and instead asked the **o** of the young men who had
2Ch 10: 8 and instead asked the **o** of the young men who had
Job 32:10 So listen to me and let me express my **o**.
Jn 7:43 So the crowd was divided in their **o** about him.
9:16 So there was a deep division of **o** among them.
Ac 14: 4 But the people of the city were divided in their **o**
25:25 But in my **o** he has done nothing worthy of death.
1Co 7:40 But in my **o** it will be better for her if she doesn't
9: 8 And this isn't merely human **o**. Doesn't God's law

OPINIONS (4) [OPINION]

1Ki 18:21 long are you going to waver between two **o**?
Pr 18: 2 in understanding; they only want to air their own **o**.
Ecc 12:12 There is no end of **o** ready to be expressed.
Jn 10:19 the people were again divided in their **o** about him.

OPPONENT (2) [OPPOSE]

2Sa 2:16 Each one grabbed his **o** by the hair and thrust his
1Ki 20:20 Each Israelite soldier killed his Aramean **o**,

OPPONENTS (5) [OPPOSE]

2Sa 22:49 reach of my enemies; / you save me from violent **o**.
Ps 18:48 reach of my enemies; / you save me from violent **o**.
92:11 own ears I have heard the defeat of my wicked **o**.
Pr 18:18 and settle disputes between powerful **o**.
Lk 21:15 and such wisdom that none of your **o** will be able

OPPORTUNITIES (3) [OPPORTUNITY]

2Co 2:12 News of Christ, the Lord gave me tremendous **o**.
9:10 the same way, he will give you many **o** to do good,
Col 4: 3 that God will give us many **o** to preach about his

OPPORTUNITY (26) [OPPORTUNITIES]

Ex 11: 9 But this will give me the **o** to do even more mighty
Jdg 14: 4 creating an **o** to disrupt the Philistines, who ruled
1Sa 24: 4 "Now's your **o**!" David's men whispered to him.
2Sa 12:14 given the enemies of the LORD great **o** to despise
Pr 10: 5 a youth who sleeps away the hour of **o** brings
Jer 46:17 king of Egypt, is a loudmouth who missed his **o**!'
Zep 2: 2 and your **o** is blown away like chaff.
Mt 10:18 This will be your **o** to tell them about me—yes,
Mk 13: 9 This will be your **o** to tell them about me.
14: 1 were still looking for an **o** to capture Jesus secretly
Lk 4:13 tempting Jesus, he left him until the next **o** came.
19:44 because you have rejected the **o** God offered you."
20:20 Watching for their **o**, the leaders sent secret agents
21:13 This will be your **o** to tell them about me.
22: 6 So he began looking for an **o** to betray Jesus
23: 8 Herod was delighted at the **o** to see Jesus,
Jn 11:15 because this will give you another **o** to believe in
Ac 3:12 Peter saw his **o** and addressed the crowd.
5:31 He did this to give the people of Israel an **o** to turn
25:16 They are given an **o** to defend themselves face to
Ro 1:10 One of the things I always pray for is the **o**,
Gal 6:10 Whenever we have the **o**, we should do good to
Eph 5:16 Make the most of every **o** for doing good in these
Col 4: 5 are not Christians, and make the most of every **o**.
Jas 1: 2 trouble comes your way, let it be an **o** for joy.
Rev 13:10 for here is your **o** to have endurance and faith.

OPPOSE (23) [OPPONENT, OPPONENTS, OPPOSED, OPPOSES, OPPOSING, OPPOSITE, OPPOSITION]

Ex 23:22 your enemies, and I will **o** those who **o** you.
Nu 24: 8 He devours all the nations that **o** him,
Est 6:13 against him. It will be fatal to continue to **o** him."
Job 30:12 These outcasts **o** me to my face. They send me
Ps 35: 1 O LORD, **o** those who **o** me. / Declare war
38:20 for good / and **o** me because I stand for the right.
55:18 waged against me, / even though many still **o** me.
Isa 43:13 No one can **o** what I do. No one can reverse my
50: 8 Who will dare to **o** me now? Where are my
59:14 Our courts **o** people who are righteous, and justice
Jer 49:19 can challenge me? What ruler can **o** my will?"
50:44 can challenge me? What ruler can **o** my will?"
Na 1: 2 He takes revenge on all who **o** him and furiously
Ac 26: 9 I could to **o** the followers of Jesus of Nazareth.
1Co 16: 9 are responding. But there are many who **o** me.
2Co 13: 8 Our responsibility is never to **o** the truth, but to
Gal 2:11 Peter came to Antioch, I had to **o** him publicly,
1Th 2:15 driven us out. They displease God and **o** everyone
1Ti 6:20 foolish discussions with those who **o** you with their
2Ti 2:25 They should gently teach those who **o** the truth.
Tit 1: 9 and show those who **o** it where they are wrong.

OPPOSED (5) [OPPOSE]

Ezr 10:15 and Jahzeiah son of Tikvah **o** this course of action,
Ac 18: 6 But when the Jews **o** him and insulted him,
26:11 so violently **o** to them that I even hounded them in
1Th 2: 2 even though we were surrounded by many who **o**
1Jn 3: 4 Those who sin are **o** to the law of God, for all sin

OPPOSES (5) [OPPOSE]

Job 31:23 For if the majesty of God **o** me, what hope is
Isa 41:11 and ashamed. Anyone who **o** you will die.
Mt 12:30 Anyone who isn't helping me **o** me, and anyone
Lk 11:23 "Anyone who isn't helping me **o** me, and anyone
1Jn 3: 4 to the law of God, for all sin **o** the law of God.

OPPOSING (2) [OPPOSE]

1Sa 15: 2 Amalek for **o** Israel when they came from Egypt.
Rev 2: 9 but you are rich! I know the slander of those **o** you.

OPPOSITE (38) [OPPOSE]

Ex 14: 2 Camp there along the shore, **o** Baal-zephon.
30: 4 Beneath the molding, on **o** sides of the altar,
30: 6 just outside the inner curtain, **o** the Ark's cover—
37:27 Two gold rings were placed on **o** sides,
40: 5 the inner curtain, **o** the Ark of the Covenant.
Nu 20:17 and never leave it until we have crossed the **o**
33: 7 **o** Baal-zephon, and camped near Migdol.
33:50 the Jordan River on the plains of Moab **o** Jericho,
1Sa 17: 3 and Israelites faced each other on **o** hills,
20:25 with Jonathan sitting **o** him and Abner beside him.
23:26 and David were now on **o** sides of a mountain.
26:13 David climbed the hill **o** the camp until he was at a
2Sa 2:13 facing each other from **o** sides of the pool.
20: 8 Amasa met them, coming from the **o** direction.
1Ki 20:29 The two armies camped **o** each other for seven
1Ch 6:78 of Reuben, east of the Jordan River **o** Jericho,
2Ch 3:12 one wing 7-1/2 feet long that touched the **o** wall.
Ne 3:16 He rebuilt the wall to a place **o** the royal cemetery
3:19 repaired another section of wall **o** the armory by
3:21 **o** the door of Eliashib's house to the side of the
3:25 carried on the work from a point **o** the buttress
3:27 who repaired another section **o** the great projecting
3:28 each one doing the section immediately **o** his own
3:31 and merchants, **o** the Inspection Gate.
12: 9 and Unni, stood **o** them during the service.
12:24 who stood **o** them during the ceremonies of praise
Est 9: 1 hoped to destroy them, but quite the **o** happened.
Eze 16:34 So you are the **o** of other prostitutes. No one pays
40:23 inner courtyard directly **o** this outer gateway.
40:27 And here again, directly **o** the outer gateway,
46: 9 they came in; they must always use the **o** gateway.
47:20 where the northern border begins, **o** Lebo-hamath.
48:21 extending in **o** directions to the eastern and western
Da 12: 5 and saw two others standing on **o** banks of the
Jnh 1: 3 and went in the **o** direction in order to get away
Gal 5:17 which is just **o** from what the Holy Spirit wants.
5:17 And the Spirit gives us desires that are **o** from what
Heb 10: 3 But just the **o** happened. Those yearly sacrifices

OPPOSITION (4) [OPPOSE]

Ge 26:21 there was a fight over it. So Isaac named it "**O**."
34:25 took their swords, entered the town without **o**,
Ps 76:10 Human **o** only enhances your glory, / for you use it
Pr 25:15 a prince, and soft speech can crush strong **o**.

OPPRESS (31) [OPPRESSED, OPPRESSES, OPPRESSING, OPPRESSION, OPPRESSIVE, OPPRESSOR, OPPRESSORS]

Ex 9: 2 If you continue to **o** them and refuse to let them go,
22:21 "Do not **o** foreigners in any way. Remember,
23: 9 "Do not **o** the foreigners living among you.
Nu 24:24 of Cyprus; / they will **o** both Assyria and Eber,
Dt 23:16 in whatever town they choose, and do not **o** them.
28:48 They will **o** you harshly until you are destroyed.
Jdg 10: 8 who began to **o** them that year. For eighteen years
2Sa 7:10 nations won't **o** them as they did in the past,
1Ch 16:21 Yet he did not let anyone **o** them. / He warned
17: 9 nations won't **o** them as they did in the past,
2Ch 16:10 that time, Asa also began to **o** some of his people.
Job 37:23 yet he is so just and merciful that he does not **o** us.
Ps 10: 2 Proud and wicked people viciously **o** the poor.
94: 5 They **o** your people, LORD, / hurting those you
105:14 Yet he did not let anyone **o** them. / He warned
119:122 for me. / Don't let those who are arrogant **o** me!
Pr 14:31 Those who **o** the poor insult their Maker, but those
28:16 Only a stupid prince will **o** his people, but a king
Isa 3:12 Children **o** my people, and women rule over them.
10:24 do not be afraid of the Assyrians when they **o** you
19:20 to the LORD for help against those who **o** them,
32: 7 including all the lies they use to **o** the poor in the
Jer 22:17 the innocent, the poor, and reign ruthlessly."
Eze 22:29 Even common people **o** the poor, rob the needy,
45: 8 "My princes will no longer **o** and rob my people;
Am 4: 1 you women who **o** the poor and crush the needy
5:12 You **o** good people by taking bribes and deprive
6:14 "It will **o** you bitterly throughout your land—
Zec 7:10 Do not **o** widows, orphans, foreigners, and poor
Mal 3: 5 who **o** widows and orphans, or who deprive the
Jas 2: 6 Isn't it the rich who **o** you and drag you into court?

OPPRESSED (43) [OPPRESS]

Ge 15:13 and they will be **o** as slaves for four hundred years.
Ex 1:12 But the more the Egyptians **o** them, the more
3: 9 and I have seen how the Egyptians have **o** them
Dt 28:29 You will be **o** and robbed continually, and no one
Jdg 4: 3 ruthlessly **o** the Israelites for twenty years.
6: 9 you from the Egyptians and from all who **o** you.
10: 8 For eighteen years they **o** all the Israelites east of

10:12 When they **o** you, you cried out to me, and I
1Sa 12: 3 Have I ever **o** you? Have I ever taken a bribe?
12: 4 "you have never cheated or **o** us in any way,
2Ki 13:22 King Hazael of Aram had **o** Israel during the entire
2Ch 28:20 he **o** King Ahaz instead of helping him.
Job 20:19 For he **o** the poor and left them destitute.
35: 9 "The **o** cry out beneath the wrongs that are done to
Ps 9: 9 The LORD is a shelter for the **o**, / a refuge in
10:18 You will bring justice to the orphans and the **o**,
12: 7 LORD, we know you will protect the **o**,
14: 6 The wicked frustrate the plans of the **o**,
37:14 and string their bows / to kill the poor and the **o**,
42: 9 must I wander in darkness, / **o** by my enemies?"
43: 2 I wander around in darkness, / **o** by my enemies?
69:33 he does not despise his people who are **o**.
72:12 he will help the **o**, who have no one to defend
76: 9 do evil, O God, / and to rescue the **o** of the earth.
82: 3 uphold the rights of the **o** and the destitute.
146: 7 who gives justice to the **o** / and food to the hungry.
Pr 31: 5 and be unable to give justice to those who are **o**.
Ecc 4: 1 I saw the tears of the **o**, with no one to comfort
5: 8 If you see a poor person being **o** by the powerful
Isa 1:17 Learn to do good. Seek justice. Help the **o**.
26: 6 The poor and **o** trample it underfoot.
52: 4 Now they have been **o** without cause by Assyria.
53: 7 He was **o** and treated harshly, yet he never said a
59:16 amazed to see that no one intervened to help the **o**.
Eze 22: 7 Orphans and widows are wronged and **o**.
Am 2: 7 in the dust and deny justice to those who are **o**.
5: 7 making it a bitter pill for the poor and **o**.
Zep 3:19 And I will deal severely with all who have **o** you.
Zec 2: 8 Almighty sent me against the nations who **o** you.
11: 7 flock intended for slaughter—the flock that was **o**.
Ac 10:38 and healing all who were **o** by the Devil,
1Co 9:22 When I am with those who are **o**, I share their
Heb 11:37 of sheep and goats, hungry and **o** and mistreated.

OPPRESSES (2) [OPPRESS]

Pr 28: 3 A poor person who **o** the poor is like a pounding
Eze 18:12 **o** the poor and helpless, steals from debtors by

OPPRESSING (10) [OPPRESS]

1Sa 10:18 and from all of the nations that were **o** you.
2Ki 13: 4 see how terribly the king of Aram was **o** Israel.
Ne 5: 7 "You are **o** your own relatives by charging them
Job 10: 3 What do you gain by **o** me? Why do you reject me,
Pr 22:16 A person who gets ahead by **o** the poor or by
Isa 58: 3 you are fasting. You keep right on **o** your workers.
58: 6 and to stop **o** those who work for you.
58: 9 "Stop **o** the helpless and stop making false
Mt 24:49 and begins **o** the other servants, partying,
Lk 12:45 and begins **o** the other servants, partying,

OPPRESSION (21) [OPPRESS]

Ex 3:17 I promise to rescue you from the **o** of the
Dt 26: 7 He heard us and saw our hardship, toil, and **o**.
28:33 You will suffer under constant **o** and harsh
Jdg 2:18 his people, who were burdened by **o** and suffering.
Ps 44:24 Why do you ignore our suffering and **o**?
72:14 He will save them from **o** and from violence,
107:39 through **o**, trouble, and sorrow,
119:134 Rescue me from the **o** of evil people; / then I can
Ecc 4: 1 Again I observed all the **o** that takes place in our
Isa 5: 7 find righteousness, / but instead he heard cries of **o**.
16: 4 When **o** and destruction have ceased and enemy
30:12 what I tell you and trust instead in **o** and lies,
43: 2 When you walk through the fire of **o**, you will not
51:13 Will you remain in constant dread of human **o**?
Jer 22:13 its walls and **o** into its doorframes and ceilings.
28:11 **o** from all the nations now subject to King
Eze 45: 9 your violence and **o** and do what is just and right.
Na 1:13 your chains and release you from Assyrian **o**."
Hab 2: 6 Now you will get what you deserve for your **o**
1Co 9:22 I share their **o** so that I might bring them to Christ.
Heb 11:25 He chose to share the **o** of God's people instead of

OPPRESSIVE (2) [OPPRESS]

Isa 25: 4 For the **o** acts of ruthless people are like a storm
59:13 We know how unfair and **o** we have been,

OPPRESSOR (2) [OPPRESS]

Pr 29:13 The poor and the **o** have this in common—
Zec 9: 8 No foreign **o** will ever again overrun my people's

OPPRESSORS (12) [OPPRESS]

Job 29:17 I broke the jaws of godless **o** and made them
Ps 71: 4 power of the wicked, / from the clutches of cruel **o**.
72: 4 the children of the needy, / and to crush their **o**.
82: 5 But these **o** know nothing; / they are so ignorant!
Ecc 4: 1 The **o** have great power, and the victims are
Isa 28:11 God will speak to them through foreign **o** who
63: 4 to avenge my people, to ransom them from their **o**.
Jer 20:13 I was poor and needy, he delivered me from my **o**.
21:12 who have been robbed; rescue them from their **o**.
22: 3 who have been robbed; rescue them from their **o**.
La 1: 5 Her **o** have become her masters, and her enemies
Lk 4:18 that the downtrodden will be freed from their **o**,

OPULENT (1)

Est 1: 4 a tremendous display of the **o** wealth and glory of

OR (1707) See Index of Articles, Etc.

ORACLE (2)

Pr 30: 1 An **o**. I am weary, O God; I am weary and worn
31: 1 of King Lemuel, an **o** that his mother taught him.

ORATOR (2)

Ex 6:12 How can I expect Pharaoh to listen? I'm no **o**!"
6:30 with the LORD, saying, "I can't do it! I'm no **o**.

ORBITS (1)

Jdg 5:20 The stars in their **o** fought against Sisera.

ORCHARD (2) [ORCHARDS]

SS 2: 3 my lover is like the finest apple tree in the **o**.
4:13 You are like a lovely **o** bearing precious fruit,

ORCHARDS (3) [ORCHARD]

Ne 9:25 and olive groves and **o** in abundance.
Eze 34:27 The **o** and fields of my people will yield bumper
Hos 2:12 I will destroy her vineyards and **o**, things she

ORDAIN (3) [ORDAINED, ORDINATION]

Ex 28:41 with these garments, and then anoint and **o** them.
29: 9 In this way, you will **o** Aaron and his sons.
29:35 "This is how you will **o** Aaron and his sons to

ORDAINED (10) [ORDAIN]

Ex 29:29 so they can be anointed and **o** in them.
32:29 "Today you have been **o** for the service of the
Lev 21:10 and has been **o** to wear the special priestly
Nu 28: 6 This is the regular burnt offering **o** at Mount Sinai,
Jdg 17:12 So Micah **o** the Levite as his personal priest,
1Sa 7: 1 it to the hillside home of Abinadab and **o** Eleazar,
1Ki 12:31 and **o** priests from the rank and file of the people—
Eze 28:14 I **o** and anointed you as the mighty angelic
48:11 This area is set aside for the **o** priests,
Ac 10:42 and to testify that Jesus is **o** of God to be the judge

ORDER (86) [ORDERED, ORDERING, ORDERS]

Ge 43:33 he seated them in the **o** of their ages,
Ex 1:15 gave this **o** to the Hebrew midwives, Shiphrah
1:22 Then Pharaoh gave this **o** to all his people:
5: 6 That same day Pharaoh sent this **o** to the slave
9:19 **O** your livestock and servants to come in from the
28:10 naming all the tribes in the **o** of their ancestors'
Lev 8:34 by the LORD in **o** to make atonement for you.
13:54 the priest will **o** the contaminated object to be
14: 5 The priest will **o** one of the birds to be slaughtered
14:40 the priest must **o** that the stones from those areas
18:23 to a male animal in **o** to have intercourse with it;
25:21 'I will **o** my blessing for you in the sixth year,
Nu 2:17 All the tribes are to travel in the same **o** that they
10:13 the LORD gave the **o** through Moses.
10:28 This was the **o** in which the tribes marched,
31:23 must be passed through fire in **o** to be made
Jos 22: 2 and you have obeyed every **o** I have given you.
Jdg 20:36 **o** to give those hiding in ambush more room to
1Sa 2: 8 is the LORD's, / and he has set the world in **o**.
2Sa 6:21 So I am willing to act like a fool in **o** to show my
14:24 But the king gave this **o**: "Absalom may go to his
15:16 ten of his concubines to keep the palace in **o**.
17:23 set his affairs in **o**, and hanged himself.
18: 5 And all the troops heard the king give this **o** to his
1Ki 12:18 to restore **o**, but all Israel stoned him to death.
15:17 and fortified Ramah in **o** to prevent anyone from
15:22 Then King Asa sent an **o** throughout Judah,
22:27 Give them this **o** from the king: 'Put this man in
2Ki 7:10 donkeys were tethered and the tents were all in **o**,
20: 1 Set your affairs in **o**, for you are going to die.
23:21 King Josiah then issued this **o** to all the people:
23:35 In **o** to get the silver and gold demanded as tribute
1Ch 8: 1 The sons of Benjamin, in **o** of age, included Bela
15:14 and the Levites purified themselves in **o** to bring
2Ch 10:18 who was in charge of the labor force, to restore **o**,
16: 1 and fortified Ramah in **o** to prevent anyone from
16: 9 **o** to strengthen those whose hearts are fully
18:26 Give them this **o** from the king: 'Put this man in
24: 6 levied this tax on the community of Israel in **o** to
24:21 to kill Zechariah, and by **o** of King Joash himself,
32:31 God withdrew from Hezekiah in **o** to test him
35: 3 He issued this **o** to the Levites, who had been set
Ne 5: 9 Should you not walk in the fear of our God in **o** to
10:28 the pagan people of the land in **o** to serve God,
13:22 and to guard the gates in **o** to preserve the holiness
Est 1:12 But when they conveyed the king's **o** to Queen
1:19 It should **o** that Queen Vashti be forever banished
3: 4 after day, but still he refused to comply with the **o**.
Job 11:10 or if he calls the court to **o**, who is going to stop
Ps 11: 3 The foundations of law and **o** have collapsed.
59: T soldiers to watch David's house in **o** to kill him.
71: 3 Give the **o** to save me, / for you are my rock
Isa 38: 1 Set your affairs in **o**, for you are going to die.
60:21 for I will plant them there with my own hands in **o**
La 4:10 and eaten them in **o** to survive the siege.
Eze 20:14 But again I held back in **o** to protect the honor of
21:26 The old **o** changes—now the lowly are exalted,
24: 6 So take the meat out chunk by chunk in whatever **o**
Da 4: 6 So I issued an **o** calling in all the wise men of
11:14 own people will join them in **o** to fulfill the vision,
11:17 He will give him a daughter in marriage in **o** to
Jnh 1: 3 and went in the opposite direction in **o** to get away
Mt 17:11 is indeed coming first to set everything in **o**.
27:58 And Pilate issued an **o** to release it to him.
Mk 7: 9 "You reject God's laws in **o** to hold on to your
7:13 you break the law of God in **o** to protect your own
9:12 is indeed coming first to set everything in **o**.
9:31 in **o** to spend more time with his disciples
Lk 1: 5 Zechariah was a member of the priestly **o** of
1: 8 in the Temple, for his **o** was on duty that week.
9:54 should we **o** down fire from heaven to burn them
16: 2 Get your report in **o**, because you are going to be
22:25 the kings and great men **o** their people around,
Jn 1:31 but I have been baptizing with water in **o** to point
Ac 18: 2 Claudius Caesar's **o** to deport all Jews from Rome.
20:30 Even some of you will distort the truth in **o** to draw
1Co 1:27 in **o** to shame those who think they are wise.
14:13 in **o** to tell people plainly what has been said.
14:40 be sure that everything is done properly and in **o**.
15:23 But there is an **o** to this resurrection: Christ was
Gal 1: 4 in **o** to rescue us from this evil world in which we
1Ti 4:10 and suffer much in **o** that people will believe the
Heb 6:11 in **o** to make certain that what you hope for will
10: 9 He cancels the first covenant in **o** to establish the
13:12 and died outside the city gates in **o** to make his
Rev 19:19 and their armies in **o** to fight against the one sitting

ORDERED (81) [ORDER]

Ge 42:25 then **o** his servants to fill the men's sacks with
43:31 himself under control. "Bring on the food!" he **o**.
Ex 5:10 "Pharaoh has **o** us not to provide straw for you.
6:13 But the LORD **o** Moses and Aaron to return to
Lev 10:18 eaten the meat in the sanctuary area as I **o** you."
Nu 23:30 So Balak did as Balaam **o** and offered a young bull
25: 5 So Moses **o** Israel's judges to execute everyone
Dt 3:26 'That's enough!' he **o**. 'Speak of it no more.
Ru 2:15 went back to work again, Boaz **o** his young men,
1Sa 14:17 "Find out who isn't here," Saul **o**. And when they
19:15 Saul **o**, "so I can kill him as he lies there!"
22:17 And he **o** his bodyguards, "Kill these priests of the
2Sa 4:12 So David **o** his young men to kill them, and they
1Ki 1:32 Then King David **o**, "Call Zadok the priest,
2:19 he **o** that a throne be brought for his mother,
2:25 So King Solomon **o** Benaiah son of Jehoiada to
22:26 King Ahab of Israel then **o**, "Arrest Micaiah
2Ki 10: 8 So Jehu **o**, "Pile them in two heaps at the entrance
10:20 Then Jehu **o**, "Prepare a solemn assembly to
11: 9 did everything just as Jehoiada the priest **o**.
11:15 Then Jehoiada the priest **o** the commanders who
14:13 Then Jehoash **o** his army to demolish six hundred
23:16 He **o** that the bones be brought out, and he burned
1Ch 15:16 David also **o** the Levite leaders to appoint a choir
22:17 Then David **o** all the leaders of Israel to assist
2Ch 18:25 King Ahab of Israel then **o**, "Arrest Micaiah
23: 8 people did everything just as Jehoiada the priest **o**.
23:14 Then Jehoiada the priest **o** the commanders who
25:23 Then Jehoash **o** his army to demolish six hundred
29:27 Then Hezekiah **o** that the burnt offering be placed
29:30 and the officials **o** the Levites to praise the LORD
35:16 on the altar of the LORD, as King Josiah had **o**.
Ezr 4:19 I have **o** a search to be made of the records
Est 2: 9 He quickly **o** a special menu for her and provided
4: 5 She **o** him to go to Mordecai and find out what was
5:14 Haman immensely, and he **o** the gallows set up.
6: 1 so he **o** an attendant to bring the historical records
6: 5 is out there." "Bring him in," the king **o**.
7: 9 "Then hang Haman on it!" the king **o**.
Ps 65: 9 a bountiful harvest of grain, / for you have **o** it so.
Jer 11:17 who planted this olive tree, have **o** it destroyed.
34: 9 He had **o** all the people to free their Hebrew
Da 1: 3 Then the king **o** Ashpenaz, who was in charge of
1:10 "My lord the king has **o** that you eat this food
1:18 When the three-year training period **o** by the king
2:24 who had been **o** to execute the wise men of
3:13 Nebuchadnezzar flew into a rage and **o** Shadrach,
3:20 Then he **o** some of the strongest men of his army to
6:23 and **o** that Daniel be lifted from the den.
Jnh 2:10 Then the LORD **o** the fish to spit up Jonah on the
Mt 5:40 If you are **o** to court and your shirt is taken from
18:25 so the king **o** that he, his wife, his children,
27:26 He **o** Jesus flogged with a lead-tipped whip,
Mk 1:34 and he **o** many demons to come out of their
15:15 He **o** Jesus flogged with a lead-tipped whip,
Lk 18:40 he stopped and **o** that the man be brought to him.
19:24 the king **o**, 'Take the money from this servant,
Jn 6:10 "Tell everyone to sit down," Jesus **o**. So all of
Ac 5:34 and **o** that the apostles be sent outside the council
5:40 Then they **o** them never again to speak in the name
8:38 He **o** the carriage to stop, and they went down into
10:42 And he **o** us to preach everywhere and to testify
12: 8 put on your coat and follow me," the angel **o**.
12:19 Herod Agrippa **o** a thorough search for him.
16:22 and the city officials **o** them stripped and beaten
16:23 The jailer was **o** to make sure they didn't escape.
21:33 arrested him and **o** him bound with two chains.
21:34 so he **o** Paul to be taken to the fortress.
22:24 and **o** him lashed with whips to make him confess
22:29 because he had **o** him bound and whipped.
22:30 and **o** the leading priests into session with the
23:10 **o** his soldiers to take him away from them
23:23 the commander called two of his officers and **o**,
23:31 So that night, as **o**, the soldiers took Paul as far as
23:35 Then the governor **o** him kept in the prison at
24:23 He **o** an officer to keep Paul in custody but to give
25:17 the case the very next day and **o** Paul brought in.
25:21 So I **o** him back to jail until I could arrange to send
25:23 men of the city. Festus **o** that Paul be brought in.

27:43 Then he **o** all who could swim to jump overboard
Rev 13:14 He **o** the people of the world to make a great statue

ORDERING (2) [ORDER]

Jn 19:31 so they asked Pilate to hasten their deaths by **o** that
Ac 23: 3 break the law yourself by **o** me struck like that?"

ORDERS (49) [ORDER]

Ex 2:15 he gave **o** to have Moses arrested and killed.
Nu 14:41 "Why are you now disobeying the LORD's **o** to
32:28 So Moses gave **o** to Eleazar, Joshua, and the tribal
Dt 2: 4 Give these **o** to the people: "You will be passing
Jos 2: 3 So the king of Jericho sent **o** to Rahab: "Bring out
6: 7 Then he gave **o** to the people: "March around the
8: 4 with these **o**: "Hide in ambush close behind the
8: 8 the LORD has commanded. You have your **o**."
Jdg 21:10 to Jabesh-gilead with **o** to kill everyone there,
1Ki 2:30 and said to Joab, "The king **o** you to come out!"
22:31 Now the king of Aram had issued these **o** to his
2Ki 22:12 Then he gave these **o** to Hilkiah the priest,
1Ch 14:12 their idols there, so David gave **o** to burn them up.
21: 2 David gave these **o** to Joab and his commanders:
22: 2 So David gave **o** to call together the foreigners
25: 2 who proclaimed God's messages by the king's **o**.
2Ch 18:30 Now the king of Aram had issued these **o** to his
20: 3 He also gave **o** that everyone throughout Judah
30:12 a strong desire to unite in obeying the **o** of the king
32: 1 giving **o** for his army to break through their walls.
34:20 Then he gave these **o** to Hilkiah, Ahikam son of
35:10 by their divisions, according to the king's **o**.
35:15 following the **o** given by David, Asaph, Heman,
Ezr 4:21 issue **o** to have these people stop their work.
6: 1 So King Darius issued **o** that a search be made in
8:21 I gave **o** for all of us to fast and humble ourselves
Ne 11:23 They were under royal **o**, which determined their
Est 1:15 for a queen who refuses to obey the king's **o**,
2:20 She was still following Mordecai's **o**, just as she
8: 5 send out a decree reversing Haman's **o** to destroy
Ps 91:11 For he **o** his angels / to protect you wherever you
147:15 He sends his **o** to the world— / how swiftly his
148: 6 and forever. / His **o** will never be revoked.
Ecc 5: 8 For every official is under **o** from higher up,
Isa 45:11 Do you give me **o** about the work of my hands?
Eze 9: 8 While they were carrying out their **o**, I was all
Da 2:12 and he sent out **o** to execute all the wise men of
5: 2 he gave **o** to bring in the gold and silver cups that
6: 7 Give **o** that for the next thirty days anyone who
6:16 So at last the king gave **o** for Daniel to be arrested
6:24 Then the king gave **o** to arrest the men who had
Joel 2:11 This is his mighty army, and they follow his **o**.
Am 7:12 Then Amaziah sent **o** to Amos: "Get out of here,
Mt 4: 6 Scriptures say, / 'He **o** his angels to protect you.
14: 9 in front of his guests, he issued the necessary **o**.
Mk 1:27 has such authority! Even evil spirits obey his **o**!"
Lk 4:10 'He **o** his angels to protect and guard you.
Ac 10:48 So he gave **o** for them to be baptized in the name
1Co 9:14 the Lord gave **o** that those who preach the Good

ORDINARY (14)

Ex 18:22 men can serve the people, resolving all the **o** cases.
29:33 The **o** people may not eat them, for these things are
30:32 It must never be poured on the body of an **o**
Lev 10:10 to distinguish between what is holy and what is **o**,
22:32 Do not treat my holy name as common and **o**.
Nu 15: 3 When it is an **o** burnt offering, a sacrifice to fulfill
1Sa 21: 5 And since they stay clean even on **o** trips,
28: 8 So Saul disguised himself by wearing **o** clothing
Ne 7: 5 the city, along with the **o** citizens, for registration.
Pr 22:29 They will serve kings rather than **o** people.
Jn 9:16 "But how could an **o** sinner do such miraculous
Ac 4:13 for they could see that they were **o** men who had
Ro 12:16 act important, but enjoy the company of **o** people.
1Co 6: 3 So you should surely be able to resolve **o**

ORDINATION (15) [ORDAIN]

Ex 29:22 "Since this is the ram for the **o** of Aaron and his
29:26 Then take the breast of Aaron's **o** ram, and lift it
29:27 "Set aside as holy the parts of the **o** ram that
29:27 lifted up before the LORD in the **o** ceremony.
29:31 "Take the ram used in the **o** ceremony, and boil its
29:33 and bread used for their atonement in the **o**
29:34 If any of the **o** meat or bread remains until the
29:35 The **o** ceremony will go on for seven days.
Lev 7:37 the sin offering, the guilt offering, the **o** offering,
8:22 presented the second ram, which was the ram of **o**.
8:28 altar on top of the burnt offering as an **o** offering.
8:29 This was Moses' share of the ram of **o**, just as the
8:31 with the bread that is in the basket of **o** offerings,
8:33 for that is the time it will take to complete the **o**
9: 1 After the **o** ceremony, on the eighth day,

ORE (1)

Job 28: 3 darkest regions of the earth as they search for **o**.

OREB (7)

Jdg 7:25 They captured **O** and Zeeb, the two Midianite generals, killing **O** at the rock of **O**,
7:25 Afterward the Israelites brought the heads of **O**
8: 3 God gave you victory over **O** and Zeeb,
Ps 83:11 Let their mighty nobles die as **O** and Zeeb did.
Isa 10:26 triumphed over the Midianites at the rock of **O**,

OREN (1)

1Ch 2:25 Ram (the oldest), Bunah, **O**, Ozem, and Ahijah.

ORGAN [KJV] See FLUTE

ORGANIZATION (2) [ORGANIZE]

1Ki 10: 5 the **o** of his officials and their splendid clothing,
2Ch 9: 4 the **o** of his officials and their splendid clothing,

ORGANIZE (2) [ORGANIZATION, ORGANIZED]

Ge 41:40 will manage my household and **o** all my people.
2Ch 25: 5 Another thing Amaziah did was to **o** the army,

ORGANIZED (7) [ORGANIZE]

Nu 7: 2 the tribal leaders who had **o** the census—came
2Ch 17:14 there were 300,000 troops **o** in units of one
26:11 of fighting men had been mustered and **o** by Jeiel,
31: 2 Hezekiah then **o** the priests and Levites into
32: 4 They **o** a huge work crew to stop the flow of the
35:10 **o** by their divisions, according to the king's orders.
Ne 12:31 of the wall and **o** two large choirs to give thanks.

ORGANS (18)

Ex 12: 9 roast it all, including the head, legs, and internal **o**.
29:13 Take all the fat that covers the internal **o**,
29:17 up the ram and wash off the internal **o** and the legs.
29:22 the fat tail and the fat that covers the internal **o**.
Lev 1: 9 But the internal **o** and legs must first be washed
1:13 The internal **o** and legs must first be washed with
3: 3 by fire. This includes the fat around the internal **o**,
3: 9 off near the backbone, the fat around the internal **o**,
3:14 This part includes the fat around the internal **o**,
4: 8 must remove all the fat around the bull's internal **o**,
4:11 its hide, meat, head, legs, internal **o**, and dung—
7: 3 the fat from the tail, the fat around the internal **o**,
8:16 He took all the fat around the internal **o**, the lobe of
8:21 After washing the internal **o** and the legs with
8:25 the fat around the internal **o**, the lobe of the liver,
9:14 Then he washed the internal **o** and the legs
9:19 fat from the tail and from around the internal **o**—
16:27 the animals' hides, the internal **o**, and the dung.

ORGIES (1)

Jer 3:23 worship of idols and our religious **o** on the hills

ORIGIN (3) [ORIGINAL, ORIGINALLY, ORIGINS]

1Sa 10:12 So that is the **o** of the saying "Is Saul a prophet?"
2Sa 5: 8 That is the **o** of the saying, "The blind
Job 38:24 Where is the path to the **o** of light? Where is the

ORIGINAL (18) [ORIGIN]

Lev 25:27 it back, the **o** owner may then return to the land.
25:28 But if the **o** owner cannot afford to redeem it,
25:28 the land will be returned to the **o** owner.
25:30 It will not be returned to the **o** owner in the Year of
25:31 and must be returned to the **o** owner in the Year of
27:10 then both the **o** animal and the substitute will be
27:24 to the **o** owner from whom you purchased it.
27:33 then both the **o** animal and the substituted one will
2Sa 4: 3 because the **o** people of Beeroth fled to Gittaim,
1Ch 11: 4 the Jebusites, **o** inhabitants of the land, lived.
2Ch 24:13 They restored the Temple of God according to its **o**
Ezr 2:68 the rebuilding of God's Temple on its **o** site,
6: 3 to offer their sacrifices, retaining the **o** foundations.
Ne 4: 6 At last the wall was completed to half its **o** height
Zec 14:10 But Jerusalem will be raised up in its **o** place
Lk 19:16 ten times as much as the **o** amount!
19:18 reported a good gain—five times the **o** amount.
19:20 "But the third servant brought back only the **o**

ORIGINALLY (4) [ORIGIN]

Jos 21: 4 were given thirteen towns that were **o** assigned to
Jdg 18:29 Israel's son, but it had **o** been called Laish.
Mt 19: 8 but it was not what God had **o** intended.
Ac 21:16 a man **o** from Cyprus and one of the early

ORIGINS (1) [ORIGIN]

Mic 5: 2 from you, one whose **o** are from the distant past.

ORION (3)

Job 9: 9 the Bear, **O**, the Pleiades, and the constellations of
38:31 Are you able to restrain the Pleiades or **O**?
Am 5: 8 LORD who created the stars, the Pleiades and **O**.

ORNAMENT (1) [ORNAMENTS]

Isa 3:17 The Lord will send a plague of scabs to **o** their

ORNAMENTS (9) [ORNAMENT]

Ex 33: 4 and refused to wear their jewelry and **o**.
33: 5 and **o** until I decide what to do with you."
Jdg 8:21 and took the royal **o** from the necks of their
2Sa 1:24 for he dressed you in fine clothing and gold **o**.
Isa 3:16 noses in the air, with tinkling **o** on their ankles.
3:18 their **o**, headbands, and crescent necklaces;
3:23 their mirrors, linen garments, head **o**, and shawls.
49:18 will be like jewels or bridal **o** for you to display.
Eze 16:17 and gold and silver **o** I had given you and made

ORPAH (2)

Ru 1: 4 One married a woman named **O**, and the other a
1:14 and **O** kissed her mother-in-law good-bye.

ORPHAN (4) [ORPHANED, ORPHANS]

Job 6:27 You would even send an **o** into slavery or sell a
31:21 If my arm has abused an **o** because I thought I
Ps 82: 3 "Give fair judgment to the poor and the **o**;
Isa 1:17 Seek justice. Help the oppressed. Defend the **o**.

ORPHANED (1) [ORPHAN]

La 5: 3 We are **o** and fatherless. Our mothers are widowed.

ORPHANS (34) [ORPHAN]

Ex 22:22 "Do not exploit widows or **o**.
Dt 10:18 He gives justice to **o** and widows. He shows love
14:29 the **o**, and the widows in your towns, so they can
16:11 the Levites from your towns, and the foreigners, **o**,
16:14 your servants, and with the Levites, foreigners, **o**,
24:17 be given to foreigners living among you and to **o**,
24:19 to get it. Leave it for the foreigners, **o**, and widows.
24:20 of the olives for the foreigners, **o**, and widows.
24:21 grapes for the foreigners, **o**, and widows.
26:12 foreigners, **o**, and widows so that they will have
26:13 foreigners, **o**, and widows, just as you commanded
27:19 who is unjust to foreigners, **o**, and widows.'
Job 22: 9 helping them and crushed the strength of **o**.
29:12 their need and the **o** who had no one to help them.
31:17 my food and refused to share it with hungry **o**?
31:18 No, from childhood I have cared for **o**, and all my
Ps 10:14 put their trust in you. / You are the defender of **o**.
10:18 You will bring justice to the **o** and the oppressed,
94: 6 They kill widows and foreigners / and murder **o**.
146: 9 He cares for the **o** and widows, / but he frustrates
Pr 23:10 Don't steal the land of defenseless **o** by moving the
Isa 1:23 and refuse to defend the **o** and the widows.
9:17 and no mercy on even the widows and **o**.
10: 2 deprive the poor, the widows, and the **o** of justice.
Jer 5:28 They refuse justice to **o** and deny the rights of the
7: 6 if you stop exploiting foreigners, **o**, and widows;
22: 3 Do not mistreat foreigners, **o**, and widows.
49:11 But I will preserve the **o** who remain among you.
Eze 22: 7 **O** and widows are wronged and oppressed.
Hos 14: 3 'our gods.' No, in you alone do the **o** find mercy."
Zec 7:10 oppress widows, **o**, foreigners, and poor people.
Mal 3: 5 who oppress widows and **o**, or who deprive the
Jn 14:18 No, I will not abandon you as **o**—I will come to
Jas 1:27 of God our Father means that we must care for **o**

OSEE [KJV] See HOSEA

OSHEA [KJV] See JOSHUA

OSPREY (2)

Lev 11:13 are detestable for you: the eagle, the vulture, the **o**,
Dt 14:12 birds you may not eat: the eagle, the vulture, the **o**,

OSSIFRAGE [KJV] See VULTURE

OSTRICH (4) [OSTRICHES]

Lev 11:16 the **o**, the nighthawk, the seagull, hawks of all
Dt 14:15 the **o**, the nighthawk, the seagull, hawks of all
Job 39:13 "The **o** flaps her wings grandly, but they are no
Mic 1: 8 I will howl like a jackal and wail like an **o**.

OSTRICHES (6) [OSTRICH]

Job 30:29 a brother to jackals and a companion to **o**.
Isa 13:21 **O** will live among the ruins, and wild goats will
34:13 will become a haunt for jackals and a home for **o**.
43:20 the jackals and **o**, too, for giving them water in the
Jer 50:39 "Soon this city of Babylon will be inhabited by **o**
La 4: 3 their children's cries, like the **o** of the desert.

OTHER (1038) [OTHER'S, OTHERS, OTHERS', OTHERWISE] See Index of Articles, Etc.

ANY OTHER (51) Ge 19:12; 49:16; Ex 20:3,5; 22:10; 23:13; Lev 5:12; 6:3; 7:24; 10:9; Nu 12:3; 15:3; 18:7; Dt 4:34; 5:7,9; 22:9; 24:5; 26:19; Jdg 13:4,7,14; Ru 2:8; 1Ki 6:7; 10:23; 2Ki 5:17; 12:12; 17:35,37; 18:33; 2Ch 2:5; 9:22; Ne 10:31; Est 3:8; Job 31:7; Ps 87:2; 135:5; 147:20; SS 1:1; Isa 36:18; 44:8; Da 11:37; Hag 2:12; Lk 21:29; Ro 13:9; 1Co 3:11; Gal 1:8,8,9; Eph 5:27; Heb 7:20

EACH OTHER (165) Ge 11:7; 25:22; 42:28; 48:20; Ex 18:13; 25:20; 26:35; 36:18; 37:9; Lev 25:14,17; 26:37; Jdg 6:29; 7:22; 10:18; Ru 3:14; 1Sa 14:20; 17:3,21; 20:23,41,42; 2Sa 2:13,15,17,26; 1Ki 7:4,5; 20:29; 2Ki 3:23; 7:3,9; 10:15; 1Ch 8:32; 9:38; 2Ch 12:15; 20:23; Ne 4:19; Est 9:19,22; Ps 12:2; 64:5; Pr 18:24; Ecc 4:11; 8:9; Isa 3:5; 11:13; 19:2; 65:5; Jer 9:5; 23:30,35; 46:12,16; 51:46; Eze 3:13; 38:21; 42:3; Da 2:43; 8:13; 11:27,27; Joel 2:8; Zep 3:13; Hag 2:22; Zec 7:10; 8:10,16,17; 11:9; 14:13; Mal 2:10,14; 3:16; Mt 24:7,10; Mk 9:10,50; 13:8; 14:56; Lk 2:15; 5:21; 12:1; 20:14; 21:10; 22:23; 24:32; Jn 4:33; 5:44; 6:52; 9:8; 11:47,56; 12:19; 13:22,34,34; 15:12,17; 16:17; Ac 2:12; 4:16; 7:26; 28:4; Ro 1:26,27; 12:5,10,10,16; 14:13,19; 15:5,7,32; 16:16; 1Co 3:3; 7:5; 11:33; 12:25; 15:41; 16:20; 2Co 10:12; 13:11,12; Gal 5:17; Eph 2:16; 4:2,25,32; Php 1:9; 2:2; Col 3:9,16; 1Th 3:12; 4:18; 5:11,11,13,15,26; 2Th 1:3; Heb 3:13; 10:25; 12:15; 13:1; Jas 4:11,11,11; 5:9,16,16; 1Pe 1:22,22; 3:8; 4:8; 5:5,14; 1Jn 1:7; 3:18; 4:11,12,19; Rev 2:4; 11:10

NO OTHER (37) Ex 9:14; 34:14; Nu 5:19; Dt 4:35,39; 1Sa 21:6; 2Sa 7:22; 1Ki 3:13; 8:60; 10:20; 1Ch 17:20; 2Ch 1:12; 9:19; Job 42:15; Ps 86:8; Isa 35:9; 43:10,11; 44:6,8; 45:5,6,6,18,21,22; Eze 31:14; Da 3:29; Hos 13:4; Mk 12:31,32; Ac 4:12; 1Co 6:18; 8:4; 11:16; Php 4:15; Heb 10:26

OTHER GODS (59) Ex 18:11; 20:3; 23:13; 34:14,16,16; Dt 5:7; 7:4; 8:19; 11:16; 13:6; 17:3; 28:14; 29:26; 30:17; 31:18,20; Jos 23:16; 24:2,16,20; Jdg 2:12,17,19; 10:13; 1Sa 8:8; 1Ki 9:6,9; 11:10; 14:9; 2Ki 17:7,35,37,38; 2Ch 7:19,22; 28:25; Ps 10:16; 16:4; 78:58; Jer 1:16; 2:25; 3:6; 10:11; 16:11; 22:9; 32:29; 35:15; 44:3; 46:25; Eze 6:9; 43:7; 44:12; Hos 1:2; 3:1; 4:10,12; 6:10; 9:1

OTHER NATIONS (42) Ex 23:24; Nu 23:9; Dt 7:7; 8:20; 9:4; 17:14; 18:12; 29:18; 32:21; Jos 24:18; 1Sa 8:5; 2Sa 7:14; 8:11; 2Ki 18:33; 19:12; 1Ch 16:26; 18:11; 2Ch 32:17; Ps 96:5; 111:6; 126:2; Isa 36:18; 37:12; 54:3; Jer 10:2,2; 25:9; 36:2; Eze 23:30; 25:8; 31:18; 32:19; 34:28; 36:13; Am 9:7,9; Mic 5:8; Zec 1:15; 14:18,19; Mal 1:11; Ro 10:19

OTHER PEOPLE (17) Ex 24:2; 33:16; Lev 20:24,26; Jos 7:9; 23:7; Ezr 10:25; Ne 13:24; Job 35:8; Ps 73:5; Jer 5:26; 41:10; Lk 13:2; Jn 11:33; Ro 14:18; 1Co 14:17; 1Ti 1:9

OTHER SIDE (31) Ge 32:23; Ex 14:26; Nu 32:19; Dt 3:25; Jos 2:1; 4:11; 7:7; Jdg 11:18; 1Sa 31:7; 2Sa 10:16; 2Ki 2:9; 1Ch 19:16; 2Ch 7:6; Eze 41:19; Zec 5:3; Mt 8:18,28; 14:22; 16:5; Mk 4:35; 5:1,21; 6:53; 8:13; Lk 8:22,37,40; 10:31,32; Jn 1:28; 3:26

OTHER'S (14) [OTHER] See Index of Articles, Etc.

OTHERS (372) [OTHER] See Index of Articles, Etc.

OTHERS' (1) [OTHER] See Index of Articles, Etc.

OTHERWISE (25) [OTHER]

Ge 14:23 **O** you might say, 'I am the one who made Abram
34:17 **O** we will take her and be on our way."
41:36 **O** disaster will surely strike the land, and all the
43:8 **O** we will all die of starvation—and not only we,
45:11 **O** you and your household will come to utter
Lev 20:22 **o** the land to which I am bringing you will vomit
22:9 **o** they will be subject to punishment and die for
Nu 4:20 **O** they must not approach the sanctuary and look
22:33 **o**, I would certainly have killed you by now
Dt 24:15 **O** they might cry out to the LORD against you,
2Sa 17:16 **O** he will die and his entire army with him."
Job 24:25 "Can anyone claim **o**? Who can prove me
Eze 47:14 **O** each tribe will receive an equal share. I swore
Mal 4:6 **O** I will come and strike the land with a curse."
Mt 26:41 and pray. **O** temptation will overpower you.
Mk 14:38 and pray. **O**, temptation will overpower you.
Lk 14:26 than your own life. **O**, you cannot be my disciple.
14:29 **O**, you might complete only the foundation before
22:46 and pray. **O**, temptation will overpower you."
Jn 8:55 If I said **o**, I would be as great a liar as you!
1Co 7:14 **O**, your children would not have a godly influence,
9:27 **O**, I fear that after preaching to others I myself
2Co 2:7 **O** he may become so discouraged that he won't be
Jas 4:16 **O** you will be boasting about your own plans,
1Jn 2:19 with us; **o** they would have stayed with us.

OTHNI (1)

1Ch 26:7 Their names were **O**, Rephael, Obed, and Elzabad.

OTHNIEL (9) [OTHNIEL'S]

Jos 15:17 **O**, the son of Caleb's brother Kenaz, was the one
15:18 When Acsah married **O**, she urged him to ask her
Jdg 1:13 **O**, the son of Caleb's younger brother Kenaz,
1:14 When Acsah married **O**, she urged him to ask her
3:9 His name was **O**, the son of Caleb's younger
3:10 of Aram, and the LORD gave **O** victory over him.
3:11 the land for forty years. Then **O** son of Kenaz died.
1Ch 4:13 The sons of Kenaz were **O** and Seraiah.
27:15 Heled, a descendant of **O** from Netophah,

OTHNIEL'S (3) [OTHNIEL]

Jos 15:17 one who conquered it, so Acsah became **O** wife.
Jdg 1:13 one who conquered it, so Acsah became **O** wife.
1Ch 4:13 and Seraiah. **O** sons were Hathath and Meonothai.

OUCHES [KJV] See FILIGREE, SETTINGS

OUGHT (20)

Dt 17:14 'We **o** to have a king like the other nations around
Jdg 18:14 and a cast idol. It's obvious what we **o** to do."
Jn 13:14 washed your feet, you **o** to wash each other's feet.
19:7 "By our laws he **o** to die because he called himself
Ac 24:19 and they **o** to be here to bring charges if they have
25:10 official Roman court, so I **o** to be tried right here.
26:9 "I used to believe that I **o** to do everything I could
1Co 7:36 But if a man thinks he **o** to marry his fiancée
2Co 1:8 I think you **o** to know, dear friends,
2:3 I will not be made sad by the very ones who **o** to
12:11 You **o** to be writing commendations for me,
Eph 5:28 husbands **o** to love their wives as they love their
2Th 3:7 For you know that you **o** to follow our example.
1Ti 5:23 You **o** to drink a little wine for the sake of your
Heb 4:1 so we **o** to tremble with fear that some of you
5:12 a long time now, and you **o** to be teaching others.
Jas 4:15 What you **o** to say is, "If the Lord wants us to,
4:17 it is sin to know what you **o** to do and then not do
1Jn 3:16 so we also **o** to give up our lives for our Christian
4:11 loved us that much, we surely **o** to love each other.

OUNCE (13) [OUNCES, TWELVE-OUNCE]

Ex 30:13 to the LORD will be one-fifth of an **o** of silver.
38:26 It came from the tax of one-fifth of an **o** of silver
1Sa 13:21 a quarter of an **o** of silver for sharpening a
13:21 and an eighth of an **o** for sharpening an ax,
2Ki 7:1 five quarts of fine flour will cost only half an **o** of
7:1 of barley grain will cost only half an **o** of silver."
7:16 fine flour were sold that day for half an **o** of silver,
7:16 of barley grain were sold for half an **o** of silver,
7:18 five quarts of fine flour will cost half an **o** of silver,
7:18 and ten quarts of barley grain will cost half an **o** of
Ezr 8:29 without an **o** lost, to the leading priests,
Ne 10:32 annual Temple tax of an eighth of an **o** of silver,
Ecc 10:1 an **o** of foolishness can outweigh a pound of

OUNCES (17) [OUNCE]

Nu 7:14 brought a gold container weighing about four **o**,
7:20 brought a gold container weighing about four **o**,
7:26 brought a gold container weighing about four **o**,
7:32 brought a gold container weighing about four **o**,
7:38 brought a gold container weighing about four **o**,
7:44 brought a gold container weighing about four **o**,
7:50 brought a gold container weighing about four **o**,
7:56 brought a gold container weighing about four **o**,
7:62 brought a gold container weighing about four **o**,
7:68 brought a gold container weighing about four **o**,
7:74 brought a gold container weighing about four **o**,
7:80 brought a gold container weighing about four **o**,
7:86 about four **o** for each of the gold containers that
2Ki 6:25 and a cup of dove's dung cost about two **o** of
15:20 demanding that each of them pay twenty **o** of silver
2Ch 3:9 They used gold nails that weighed about twenty **o**
Eze 4:10 eight **o** of food for each day, and eat it at set times.

OUR (1316) [WE] See Index of Articles, Etc.

OURS (23) [WE] See Index of Articles, Etc.

OURSELVES (42) [SELF, WE] See Index of Articles, Etc.

OUT (1977) [OUTER] See Index of Articles, Etc.

OUTBREAK (2)

2Sa 6:8 He named that place Perez-uzzah (which means "**o**
1Ch 13:11 He named that place Perez-uzzah (which means "**o**

OUTBURST (2) [OUTBURSTS]

Lev 19:24 will be devoted to the LORD as an **o** of praise.
Jer 20:8 I speak, the words come out in a violent **o**.

OUTBURSTS (3) [OUTBURST]

2Co 12:20 jealousy, **o** of anger, selfishness, backstabbing,
Gal 5:20 hostility, quarreling, jealousy, **o** of anger,
Heb 10:24 Think of ways to encourage one another to **o** of

OUTCAST (2) [OUTCASTS]

Jer 30:17 "Now you are called an **o**—'Jerusalem for whom
Eze 28:10 You will die like an **o** at the hands of foreigners.

OUTCASTS (15) [OUTCAST]

Job 30:8 They are nameless fools, **o** of civilization.
30:12 These **o** oppose me to my face. They send me
Isa 16:4 Let our **o** stay among you. Hide them from our
56:8 who brings back the **o** of Israel, says:
Eze 31:18 You will lie there among the **o** who have died by
32:19 So go down to the pit and lie there among the **o**.'
32:21 they lie among the **o**, all victims of the sword.'
32:24 its hordes who descended as **o** to the world below.
32:25 in the pit, all of them **o**, slaughtered by the sword.
32:26 But now they are **o**, all victims of the sword.
32:27 not buried in honor like the fallen heroes of the **o**,
32:28 Egypt, will lie crushed and broken among the **o**,
32:29 with the **o** who have gone down to the pit.
32:30 They lie there as **o** with all the other dead who
32:32 and his hordes will lie there among the **o** who have

OUTCROP (1)

SS 2:14 hiding behind some rocks, behind an **o** on the cliff.

OUTCRY (1)

1Sa 4:13 an **o** resounded throughout the town.

OUTDOORS (1)

Nu 19:16 And if someone **o** touches the corpse of someone

OUTER (39) [OUT]

Nu 4:25 the **o** covering of fine goatskin leather,
Jdg 7:19 and the one hundred men with him reached the **o**
1Ki 6:5 A complex of rooms was built against the **o** walls
2Ki 16:18 as well as the king's **o** entrance to the Temple of
2Ch 4:9 courtyard for the priests and the large **o** courtyard.
6:13 and had placed it at the center of the Temple's **o**
33:14 It was after this that Manasseh rebuilt the **o** wall of
Est 6:4 "Who is that in the **o** court?" the king inquired.
6:4 Haman had just arrived in the **o** court of the palace
8:15 and he wore an **o** cloak of fine linen and purple.
Eze 10:5 and could be heard clearly in the **o** courtyard.
40:17 the gateway into the **o** courtyard of the Temple.
40:19 Then the man measured across the Temple's **o** courtyard between the **o**
40:23 inner courtyard directly opposite this **o** gateway.
40:25 the gateway passage opened into the **o** courtyard.
40:27 And here again, directly opposite the **o** gateway,
40:31 The foyer of the south gateway faced into the **o**
40:34 Its foyer faced into the **o** courtyard. It had palm
40:37 Its foyer faced into the **o** courtyard, and it had palm
41:9 The **o** wall of the Temple's side rooms was 8-3/4
41:10 and the row of rooms along the **o** wall of the inner
41:20 the walls, including the **o** wall of the Holy Place.
42:1 We entered the **o** courtyard and came to a group of
42:3 looked out onto the pavement of the **o** courtyard.
42:7 There was an **o** wall that separated the rooms from the **o** courtyard;
42:8 This wall added length to the **o** block of rooms,
42:9 There was an entrance from the **o** courtyard to
42:10 courtyard between the Temple and the **o** courtyard.
42:14 they must not go directly to the **o** courtyard.
44:1 brought me back to the east gateway in the **o** wall,
44:19 When they return to the **o** courtyard where the
46:20 carrying the sacrifices through the **o** courtyard
46:21 Then he brought me back to the **o** courtyard
Mt 8:12 will be cast into **o** darkness, where there will be
22:13 and foot and throw him out into the **o** darkness,
25:30 Now throw this useless servant into **o** darkness,
Rev 11:2 But do not measure the **o** courtyard, for it has been

OUTFITTED (1)

Eze 23:14 military officers, **o** in striking red uniforms.

OUTGOINGS [KJV] See BORDERS, BOUNDARY, ENDED, ENDS, GATEWAYS

OUTLANDISH [KJV] See FOREIGN

OUTLAW (1) [OUTLAWED, OUTLAWS]

Pr 24:15 Do not lie in wait like an **o** at the home of the

OUTLAWED (1) [OUTLAW]

Isa 59:14 falls dead in the streets, and fairness has been **o**.

OUTLAWS (1) [OUTLAW]

1Sa 25:11 and give it to a band of **o** who come from who

OUTLINE (1)

Ac 24:4 a moment as I briefly **o** our case against this man.

OUTLIVED (2) [LIVE]

Jos 24:31 lifetime of Joshua and of the leaders who **o** him—
Jdg 2:7 the lifetime of Joshua and the leaders who **o** him—

OUTLYING (2)

1Ch 6:56 and **o** areas were given to Caleb son of Jephunneh.
2Ch 19:10 comes to you from fellow citizens in an **o** town,

OUTNUMBER (2) [NUMBER]

Ps 139:18 can't even count them; / they **o** the grains of sand!
Hab 1:4 The wicked far **o** the righteous, and justice is

OUTPOST (4) [OUTPOSTS]

1Sa 14:1 let's go over to where the Philistines have their **o**."
14:4 To reach the Philistine **o**, Jonathan had to go down
2Ki 17:9 from the smallest **o** to the largest walled city.
18:8 from their smallest **o** to their largest walled city.

OUTPOSTS (2) [OUTPOST]

Jdg 7:11 and went down to the **o** of the enemy camp.
1Sa 14:15 the field, including even the **o** and raiding parties.

OUTRAN (1) [RUN]

Jn 20:4 The other disciple **o** Peter and got there first.

OUTRUN (1) [RUN]

Am 2:15 Even warriors on horses won't be able to **o** the

OUTSIDE (147) [OUTSIDERS]

Ge 9:22 father was naked and went **o** and told his brothers.
15:5 Then the LORD brought Abram **o** beneath the
19:6 Lot stepped **o** to talk to them, shutting the door
19:16 two daughters and rushed them to safety **o** the city,
24:11 camels kneel down beside a well just **o** the village.
24:31 Why do you stand here **o** the village when we have
29:19 "I'd rather give her to you than to someone **o** the
33:18 in Canaan, and they set up camp just **o** the town.
34:28 hands on, both inside the town and **o** in the fields.
Ex 5:20 and Aaron, who were waiting **o** for them.
9:19 or animal left **o** will die beneath the hail.' "
12:46 You must not carry any of its meat **o**, and you may
25:11 Overlay it inside and **o** with pure gold, and put a
26:35 and lampstand across the room from each other **o**
27:21 The lampstand will be placed **o** the inner curtain of
29:14 the dung) **o** the camp, and burn it as a sin offering.
30:6 Place the incense altar just **o** the inner curtain,
33:7 tent known as the Tent of Meeting far **o** the camp.

40: 5 "Place the incense altar just **o** the inner curtain,
40: 8 Then set up the courtyard around the **o** of the tent,
40:22 side of the Holy Place, just **o** the inner curtain.
Lev 4:12 away to a ceremonially clean place **o** the camp,
4:21 then take what is left of the bull **o** the camp
6:11 and carry the ashes **o** the camp to a place that is
8:17 its hide, meat, and dung, was burned **o** the camp,
9:11 and the hide, however, he burned **o** the camp.
10: 4 away from the sanctuary to a place **o** the camp."
13:46 and must live in isolation **o** the camp.
13:55 whether it is contaminated on the inside or **o**.
14: 3 who will examine them at a place **o** the camp.
14: 8 they must still remain **o** their tents for seven days.
14:40 then be thrown into an area **o** the town designated
14:41 and the scrapings dumped in the unclean place **o**
14:53 he will release the living bird in the open fields **o**
16:27 for Israel, will be carried **o** the camp to be burned.
17: 3 or a lamb or a goat anywhere inside or **o** the camp
22:10 "No one **o** a priest's family may ever eat the
22:12 If a priest's daughter marries someone **o** the
24: 3 Aaron will set it up **o** the inner curtain of the Most
24:14 "Take the blasphemer **o** the camp, and tell all
24:23 they led the blasphemer **o** the camp and stoned him
Nu 15:35 The whole community must stone him **o** the
15:36 So the whole community took the man **o** the camp
19: 3 and it will be taken **o** the camp and slaughtered in
19: 9 and place them in a purified place **o** the camp.
31:13 of the people went to meet them **o** the camp.
31:19 or touched a dead body must stay **o** the camp for
35: 5 Measure off 3,000 feet **o** the town walls in every
35:27 and the victim's nearest relative finds him **o** the
Dt 23:12 "Mark off an area **o** the camp for a latrine.
24:11 Stand **o** and the owner will bring it out to you.
25: 5 a son, his widow must not marry **o** the family.
32:25 **O**, the sword will bring death, / and inside,
Jos 8:24 army finished killing all the men **o** the city,
Jdg 9:38 The men you mocked are right **o** the city! Go out
12: 9 He married his daughters to men **o** his clan
12: 9 and brought in thirty young women from **o** his clan
18:16 warriors from the tribe of Dan stood just **o** the gate,
19:23 The old man stepped **o** to talk to them. "No,
1Ki 2:36 But don't step **o** the city to go anywhere else.
2:46 Benaiah son of Jehoiada took Shimei **o** and killed
6:17 **o** the Most Holy Place, was 60 feet long.
7:31 it was decorated on the **o** with carvings of wreaths.
8: 8 main room—the Holy Place—but not from **o** it.
21:13 So he was dragged **o** the city and stoned to death.
21:19 dogs will lick your blood **o** the city just as they
2Ki 6:15 of God got up early the next morning and went **o**,
10:25 and the guards and officers dragged their bodies **o**.
19:32 They will not march **o** its gates with their shields
23: 4 The king had all these things burned **o** Jerusalem
23: 6 and took it **o** Jerusalem to the Kidron Valley,
1Ch 28:12 the **o** rooms, the treasuries of God's Temple,
2Ch 5: 9 main room—the Holy Place—but not from **o** it.
23: 6 must obey the LORD's instructions and stay **o**.
24: 8 and set **o** the gate leading to the Temple of the
32: 3 and they decided to stop the flow of the springs **o**
32: 5 and constructing a second wall **o** the first.
33:15 were in Jerusalem, and he dumped them **o** the city.
Ne 4:22 I also told everyone living **o** the walls to move into
11:16 who were in charge of the work **o** the Temple of
13:20 and tradesmen with a variety of wares camped **o**
Est 4: 2 He stood **o** the gate of the palace, for no one was
Job 31:34 to acknowledge my sin and would not go **o**?
Pr 8:34 me daily at my gates, waiting for me **o** my home!
22:13 saying, "If I go **o**, I might meet a lion in the street
26:13 "I can't go **o** because there might be a lion on the
Isa 33:18 Assyrian officers **o** your walls counted your towers
37:33 They will not march **o** its gates with their shields
Jer 22:19 dragged out of Jerusalem and dumped **o** the gate!
32:29 The Babylonians **o** the walls will come in and set
Eze 5:12 A third of them will be slaughtered by the enemy **o**
12: 4 Bring your baggage **o** during the day so they can
12: 7 In broad daylight I brought my pack **o**, filled with
16:49 while the poor and needy suffered **o** her door.
40:40 **O** the foyer, on each side of the stairs going up to
40:41 four inside and four **o**, where the sacrifices were
41: 5 There was a row of rooms along the **o** wall;
43:21 and burn it at the appointed place **o** the Temple
46: 2 will enter the foyer of the gateway from the **o**.
47: 2 The man brought me **o** the wall through the north
48:18 **O** the city there will be a farming area that
Mic 1:11 The people of Zaanan dare not come **o** their walls.
Zec 2: 4 Many will live **o** the city walls, with all their
Mt 9:25 When the crowd was finally **o**, Jesus went in
12:46 his mother and brothers were **o**, wanting to talk
12:47 told Jesus, "Your mother and your brothers are **o**,
13:36 Then, leaving the crowds **o**, Jesus went into the
23:25 You are so careful to clean the **o** of the cup
23:26 of the cup, and then the **o** will become clean, too.
23:27 beautiful on the **o** but filled on the inside with dead
24:17 A person **o** the house must not go inside to pack.
25:11 they stood **o**, calling, 'Sir, open the door for us!'
26:69 Meanwhile, as Peter was sitting **o** in the courtyard,
Mk 1:33 all over Capernaum gathered **o** the door to watch.
2: 2 room for one more person, not even **o** the door.
3:31 They stood **o** and sent word for him to come out
3:32 "Your mother and your brothers and sisters are **o**,
5:40 crowd laughed at him, but he told them all to go **o**.
11: 4 found the colt standing in the street, tied **o** a house.
13:15 A person **o** the house must not go back into the
Lk 1:10 was being burned, a great crowd stood **o**, praying.
2: 8 That night some shepherds were in the fields **o** the
8:20 told Jesus, "Your mother and your brothers are **o**,
11:39 so careful to clean the **o** of the cup and the dish,
11:40 Didn't God make the inside as well as the **o**?
13:25 Then you will stand **o** knocking and pleading,
17:31 On that day a person **o** the house must not go into
21:21 and those **o** the city should not enter it for shelter.
Jn 11:30 Now Jesus had stayed **o** the village, at the place
18:16 Peter stood **o** the gate. Then the other disciple
19: 4 Pilate went **o** again and said to the people, "I am
20:11 Mary was standing **o** the tomb crying, and as she
Ac 5: 9 Just **o** that door are the young men who buried
5:23 "The jail was locked, with the guards standing **o**,
5:34 and ordered that the apostles be sent **o** the council
10:17 Cornelius found the house and stood **o** at the gate.
16:13 On the Sabbath we went a little way **o** the city to a
1Co 5:13 God will judge those on the **o**; but as the Scriptures
6: 4 why do you go to **o** judges who are not respected
2Co 7: 5 **O** there was conflict from every direction,
1Ti 3: 7 people **o** the church must speak well of him so that
Heb 13:11 but the bodies of the animals were burned **o** the
13:12 and died **o** the city gates in order to make his
13:13 So let us go out to him **o** the camp and bear the
Rev 5: 1 was writing on the inside and the **o** of the scroll,
14:20 And the grapes were trodden in the winepress **o** the
22:15 **O** the city are the dogs—the sorcerers, the sexually

OUTSIDERS (4) [OUTSIDE]
Mk 4:11 these stories to conceal everything about it from **o**,
Lk 8:10 these stories to conceal everything about it from **o**,
1Co 5:12 It isn't my responsibility to judge **o**, but it certainly
Eph 2:11 Don't forget that you Gentiles used to be **o** by

OUTSKIRTS (5)
Nu 11: 1 among them and destroyed the **o** of the camp.
Jos 18:15 The southern boundary began at the **o** of
1Sa 14: 2 and his six hundred men were camped on the **o** of
17:20 He arrived at the **o** of the camp just as the Israelite
Ac 14:13 The temple of Zeus was located on the **o** of the

OUTSMART (1)
2Co 2:11 so that Satan will not **o** us. For we are very familiar

OUTSPREAD (1) [SPREAD]
1Ki 6:27 Their **o** wings reached from wall to wall,

OUTSTANDING (3)
Ne 11: 6 of Perez who lived in Jerusalem—all **o** men.
11:14 and 128 of his **o** associates. Their chief officer was
Isa 32: 5 Wealthy cheaters will not be respected as **o**

OUTSTRETCHED (1) [STRETCH]
Eze 1:11 Each had two pairs of **o** wings—one pair stretched

OUTWARD (5) [OUTWARDLY]
1Sa 16: 7 People judge by **o** appearance, but the LORD
1Ki 6: 3 It projected **o** 15 feet from the front of the Temple.
7:25 on a base of twelve bronze oxen, all facing **o**.
2Ch 4: 4 on a base of twelve bronze oxen, all facing **o**.
1Pe 3: 3 Don't be concerned about the **o** beauty that

OUTWARDLY (1) [OUTWARD]
Mt 23:28 You try to look like upright people **o**, but inside

OUTWEIGH (1) [WEIGH]
Ecc 10: 1 an ounce of foolishness can **o** a pound of wisdom

OUTWITTED (1)
Mt 2:16 when he learned that the wise men had **o** him.

OVATION (1)
Ac 12:22 The people gave him a great **o**, shouting, "It is the

OVEN (5) [OVENS]
Lev 7: 9 Any grain offering that has been baked in an **o**,
11:35 If it is a clay **o** or cooking pot, it must be smashed
26:26 so the bread from one **o** will have to be stretched to
La 5:10 skin has been blackened as though baked in an **o**.
Hos 7: 4 They are like an **o** that is kept hot even while the

OVENS (4) [OVEN]
Ex 8: 3 They will fill even your **o** and your kneading
Jos 9:12 "This bread was hot from the **o** when we left.
Ne 3:11 of Pahath-moab, who repaired the Tower of the **O**,
12:38 along the top of the wall past the Tower of the **O** to

OVER (1008) See Index of Articles, Etc.

OVERBEARING (1)
Pr 30:22 who becomes a king, / an **o** fool who prospers,

OVERBOARD (4)
Jnh 1: 5 for help and threw the cargo **o** to lighten the ship.
Ac 27:18 the ship, the crew began throwing the cargo **o**.
27:38 the ship further by throwing the cargo of wheat **o**.
27:43 Then he ordered all who could swim to jump **o**

OVERCHARGE [KJV] See OVERSTATING

OVERCHARGED (1)
Lk 19: 8 Lord, and if I have **o** people on their taxes,

OVERCOME (23) [OVERCOMES]
Ge 24:60 May your descendants **o** / all their enemies."
43:30 because he was **o** with emotion for his brother
Ex 15:16 terror and dread will **o** them. / Because of your
Nu 5:30 or if a man is **o** with jealousy and suspicion that his
2Sa 18:33 The king was **o** with emotion. He went up to his
Job 19: 5 You are trying to **o** me, using my humiliation as
Ps 31: 7 I am **o** with joy because of your unfailing love,
112: 6 Such people will not be **o** by evil circumstances.
119:133 steps by your word, / so I will not be **o** by any evil.
Ecc 9:18 A wise person can **o** weapons of war, but one
10: 4 don't quit! A quiet spirit can **o** even great mistakes.
SS 4: 9 I am **o** by one glance of your eyes, by a single bead
6: 5 Look away, for your eyes **o** me! Your hair, as it
Isa 35:10 and they will be **o** with joy and gladness.
51:11 and they will be **o** with joy and gladness.
Jer 23: 9 I stagger like a drunkard, like someone **o** by wine,
Eze 7:25 Terror and trembling will **o** my people. They will
Da 4:19 was **o** for a time, aghast at the meaning of the
8:27 Then I, Daniel, was **o** and lay sick for several days.
Lk 22:40 "Pray that you will not be **o** by temptation."
Jn 16:33 But take heart, because I have **o** the world."
Gal 6: 1 Dear friends, if a Christian is **o** by some sin,
Rev 13: 7 wage war against God's holy people and to **o** them.

OVERCOMES (1) [OVERCOME]
Pr 1:27 when calamity **o** you like a storm, when you are

OVERDO (1) [DO]
Ecc 6:11 words you speak, the less they mean. So why **o** it?

OVERDRIVE [KJV] See DRIVEN (TOO HARD)

OVERFLOW (15) [OVERFLOWED, OVERFLOWING, OVERFLOWS]
Job 40:11 Give vent to your anger. Let it **o** against the proud.
Ps 65:11 even the hard pathways **o** with abundance.
Pr 3:10 and your vats will **o** with the finest wine.
Isa 8: 8 This flood will **o** all its channels and sweep into
66:12 and prosperity will **o** Jerusalem like a river,"
Jer 13:17 My eyes will **o** with tears because the LORD's
14:17 this to them: 'Night and day my eyes **o** with tears.
47: 2 "A flood is coming from the north to **o** the land.
Joel 2:24 and the presses will **o** with wine and olive oil.
Zec 1:17 The towns of Israel will again **o** with prosperity,
Jn 15:11 will be filled with my joy. Yes, your joy will **o**!
Ro 15:13 May you **o** with hope through the power of the
Php 1: 9 I pray that your love for each other will **o** more
Col 2: 7 Let your lives **o** with thanksgiving for all he has
1Th 3:12 love grow and **o** to each other and to everyone else,

OVERFLOWED (3) [OVERFLOW]
1Ki 18:35 water ran around the altar and even **o** the trench.
Lk 7:13 the Lord saw her, his heart **o** with compassion.
2Co 8: 2 and deep poverty have **o** in rich generosity.

OVERFLOWING (8) [OVERFLOW]
Ge 41:49 After seven years, the granaries were filled to **o**.
Dt 28: 5 You will be blessed with baskets **o** with fruit,
Jos 3:15 the harvest season, and the Jordan was **o** its banks.
Ps 130: 7 is unfailing love / and an **o** supply of salvation.
Isa 41:16 And the joy of the LORD will fill you to **o**.
Jer 46: 7 like the Nile River at floodtime, **o** all the land?
Joel 3:13 The storage vats are **o** with the wickedness of these
Lk 12:17 In fact, his barns were full to **o**.

OVERFLOWS (5) [OVERFLOW]
Job 6:15 as a seasonal brook that **o** its banks in the spring
Ps 23: 5 my head with oil. / My cup **o** with blessings.
45: 1 My heart **o** with a beautiful thought! / I will recite
Hos 11: 8 My heart is torn within me, and my compassion **o**.
1Th 3:12 and to everyone else, just as our love **o** toward you.

OVERGROWN (4) [GROW]
Pr 24:31 I saw that it was **o** with thorns. It was covered with
Isa 5: 6 I will let it be **o** with briers and thorns.
17: 9 Their largest cities will be as deserted as **o** thickets.
32:13 For your land will be **o** with thorns and briers.

OVERHANGING (1) [HANG]
Isa 57: 5 sacrifices down in the valleys, under **o** rocks.

OVERHEARD (3) [HEAR]
Ge 27: 5 But Rebekah **o** the conversation. So when Esau left
27: 6 said to her son Jacob, "I **o** your father asking Esau
Jer 38:27 No one had **o** the conversation between Jeremiah

OVERJOYED (3) [JOY]
1Sa 6:13 and when they saw the Ark, they were **o**!
Da 6:23 The king was **o** and ordered that Daniel be lifted
Ac 12:14 she was so **o** that, instead of opening the door,

OVERLAID (37) [OVERLAY]
Ex 26:32 four posts made from acacia wood and **o** with gold.
26:37 five posts made from acacia wood and **o** with gold.
30: 5 are to be made of acacia wood and **o** with gold.
36:34 The frames and crossbars were all **o** with gold.
36:36 The posts were **o** with gold and set into four silver
36:38 their decorated tops and bands were **o** with gold.

37: 2 It was **o** with pure gold inside and out, and it had a
37: 4 poles from acacia wood and **o** them with gold.
37:11 It was **o** with pure gold, with a gold molding all
37:15 poles of acacia wood and **o** them with gold.
37:26 He **o** the top, sides, and horns of the altar with pure
37:28 were made of acacia wood and were **o** with gold.
38: 2 piece with the rest. This altar was **o** with bronze.
38: 6 were made of acacia wood and were **o** with bronze.
38:17 The tops of the posts were **o** with silver,
38:19 The tops of the posts were **o** with silver,
1Ki 6:20 Solomon **o** its walls and ceiling with pure gold. He also **o** the altar made of cedar.
6:21 Then he **o** the rest of the Temple's interior with
6:28 He **o** the two cherubim with gold.
6:30 The floor in both rooms was **o** with gold.
6:32 and open flowers, and the doors were **o** with gold.
6:35 and open flowers, and the doors were **o** with gold.
7:50 room of the Temple, with their fronts **o** with gold.
10:18 made a huge ivory throne and **o** it with pure gold.
2Ki 18:16 and from the doorposts he had **o** with gold,
2Ch 3: 4 of the foyer and the ceiling were **o** with pure gold.
3: 5 **o** with pure gold, and decorated with carvings of
3: 7 and thresholds throughout the Temple were **o** with
3: 8 Its interior was **o** with about twenty-three tons of
3: 9 The walls of the upper rooms were also **o** with
3:10 figures shaped like cherubim and **o** them with gold.
4: 9 the courtyard entrances and **o** them with bronze.
4:22 and the main room of the Temple, **o** with gold.
9:17 made a huge ivory throne and **o** it with pure gold.
Isa 40:19 **o** with gold, and decorated with silver chains?
Hab 2:19 They may be **o** with gold and silver, but they are

OVERLAPPING (1)
Job 41:15 The **o** scales on its back make a shield.

OVERLAY (10) [OVERLAID, OVERLAYING]
Ex 25:11 **O** it inside and outside with pure gold, and put a
25:13 poles from acacia wood, and **o** them with gold.
25:24 **O** it with pure gold and run a molding of gold
25:28 poles from acacia wood and **o** them with gold.
26:29 **O** the frames with gold and make gold rings to
26:29 the crossbars. **O** the crossbars with gold as well.
27: 2 all one piece. **O** the altar and its horns with bronze.
27: 6 poles from acacia wood, and **o** them with bronze.
30: 3 **O** the top, sides, and horns of the altar with pure
38:28 the rods and hooks and to **o** the tops of the posts.

OVERLAYING (2) [OVERLAY]
1Ki 6:22 So he finished **o** the entire Temple with gold,
1Ch 29: 4 and over 262 tons of refined silver to be used for **o**

OVERLIVED [KJV] See OUTLIVED

OVERLOOK (3) [OVERLOOKED, OVERLOOKING, OVERLOOKS]
Dt 9:27 **O** the stubbornness and sin of these people,
Ps 74:23 Don't **o** these things your enemies have said.
Eze 42:13 "These rooms that **o** the Temple from the north

OVERLOOKED (2) [OVERLOOK]
Eze 42: 3 One block of rooms **o** the 35-foot width of the
Ac 17:30 God **o** people's former ignorance about these

OVERLOOKING (7) [OVERLOOK]
Nu 23:28 Balaam to the top of Mount Peor, **o** the wasteland.
Jos 8:14 and attacked the Israelites at a place **o** the Jordan
18:18 the north side of the slope **o** the Jordan Valley.
Pr 9: 3 to come. She calls out from the heights **o** the city.
9:14 She sits in her doorway on the heights **o** the city.
19:11 restrain their anger; they earn esteem by **o** wrongs.
SS 7: 4 Your nose is as fine as the tower of Lebanon **o**

OVERLOOKS (2) [OVERLOOK]
Nu 21:20 valley in Moab where Pisgah Peak **o** the wasteland.
1Sa 26: 1 hiding on the hill of Hakilah, which **o** Jeshimon."

OVERNIGHT (10) [NIGHT]
Ge 24:54 the servant and the men with him stayed there **o**.
Ex 16:19 Then Moses told them, "Do not keep any of it **o**."
Nu 9:21 Sometimes the cloud stayed only **o** and moved on
22: 8 "Stay here **o**," Balaam said. "In the morning I
Dt 21:23 the body must never remain on the tree **o**.
24:12 a cloak to give as security, do not keep the cloak **o**.
Ps 4: 4 Think about it **o** and remain silent. / *Interlude*
Isa 10:29 are crossing the pass and are staying **o** at Geba.
13:20 and shepherds will not allow their sheep to stay **o**.
Mt 21:17 Then he returned to Bethany, where he stayed **o**.

OVERPAST [KJV] See PASSED, PAST

OVERPLUS [KJV] See BASED

OVERPOWER (6) [POWER]
Job 14:20 You always **o** them, and then they pass from the
Ps 89:22 not get the best of him, / nor will the wicked **o** him.
Mt 26:41 and pray. Otherwise temptation will **o** you.
Mk 14:38 and pray. Otherwise, temptation will **o** you.
Lk 22:46 and pray. Otherwise, temptation will **o** you."
1Ti 5:11 because their physical desires will **o** their devotion

OVERPOWERED (2) [POWER]
Jdg 16: 5 so strong and how he can be **o** and tied up
Jer 20: 7 You are stronger than I am, and you **o** me.

OVERPOWERS (2) [POWER]
Ps 55: 4 My heart is in anguish. / The terror of death **o** me.
Lk 11:22 until someone who is stronger attacks and **o** him,

OVERRAN (1) [RUN]
Ps 105:30 Then frogs **o** the land; / they were found even in

OVERRUN (5) [RUN]
Ex 10: 6 They will **o** your palaces and the homes of your
Isa 7:24 vast brier patch, a hunting ground **o** by wildlife.
34:13 Thorns will **o** its palaces; nettles will grow in its
Eze 25: 4 I will allow nomads from the eastern deserts to **o**
Zec 9: 8 No foreign oppressor will ever again **o** my

OVERSEE (1) [OVERSEERS, OVERSIGHT]
Nu 34:29 These are the men the LORD has appointed to **o**

OVERSEERS (2) [OVERSEE]
1Ch 27:31 All these officials were **o** of King David's
28: 1 the **o** of the royal property and livestock,

OVERSHADOW (2)
Job 3: 5 Let a black cloud **o** it, and let the darkness terrify
Lk 1:35 and the power of the Most High will **o** you.

OVERSIGHT (1) [OVERSEE]
Nu 3:32 with special responsibility for the **o** of the

OVERSPREAD [KJV] See SCATTERED

OVERSTATING (1)
2Co 2: 5 I am not **o** it when I say that the man who caused

OVERTAKE (6) [OVERTAKES, OVERTAKING, OVERTOOK]
Dt 28:45 will pursue and **o** you until you are destroyed.
32:35 disaster will arrive, / and their destiny will **o** them.'
Ps 34:21 Calamity will surely **o** the wicked, / and those who
35: 8 So let sudden ruin **o** them! / Let them be caught in
Isa 47:11 So disaster will **o** you suddenly, and you won't be
Rev 18: 8 and famine will **o** her in a single day.

OVERTAKES (2) [OVERTAKE]
Ps 112: 4 When darkness **o** the godly, light will come
Pr 1:26 in trouble! I will mock you when disaster **o** you—

OVERTAKING (1) [OVERTAKE]
Jdg 20:43 chasing them down, finally **o** them east of Gibeah.

OVERTHREW (4) [OVERTHROW]
Ex 15: 7 your majesty, / you **o** those who rose against you.
Jer 20:16 the cities of old that the LORD **o** without mercy.
31:28 I **o** it, destroyed it, and brought disaster upon it.
Heb 11:33 By faith these people **o** kingdoms, ruled with

OVERTHROW (6) [OVERTHREW, OVERTHROWN, OVERTHROWS]
2Ch 25: 8 God will **o** you, for he has the power to help
Jer 1:10 and tear them down, to destroy and **o** them.
Da 11:17 in marriage in order to **o** the kingdom from within,
11:24 He will plot the **o** of strongholds, but this will last
Hag 2:22 I will **o** royal thrones, destroying the power of
Zec 10: 5 they will **o** even the horsemen of the enemy.

OVERTHROWN (3) [OVERTHROW]
Ps 9: 3 in retreat; / they are **o** and destroyed before you.
Da 8:12 against the Temple ceremonies, and truth was **o**.
Ac 5:38 these things merely on their own, it will soon be **o**.

OVERTHROWS (1) [OVERTHROW]
Job 12:19 priests away stripped of status; he **o** the mighty.

OVERTOOK (1) [OVERTAKE]
Ps 116: 3 around my throat; / the terrors of the grave **o** me.

OVERTURN (3) [OVERTURNED, OVERTURNING, OVERTURNS]
Job 28: 9 tear apart flinty rocks and **o** the roots of mountains.
Isa 28:18 and I will **o** your deal to dodge the grave.
Hag 2:22 I will **o** their chariots and charioteers. The horses

OVERTURNED (1) [OVERTURN]
Ps 89:44 You have ended his splendor / and **o** his throne.

OVERTURNING (1) [OVERTURN]
Job 9: 5 he moves the mountains, **o** them in his anger.

OVERTURNS (1) [OVERTURN]
Job 34:25 and in the night he **o** them, destroying them.

OVERWHELM (8) [OVERWHELMED, OVERWHELMING, OVERWHELMS]
Dt 28:15 you today, all these curses will come and **o** you:
28:59 then the LORD will **o** both you and your children
Ps 55: 5 Fear and trembling **o** me. / I can't stop shaking.
64: 1 Do not let my enemies' threats **o** me.
69: 2 I am in deep water, / and the floods **o** me.
69:15 Don't let the floods **o** me, / or the deep waters
Pr 1:27 by trouble, and when anguish and distress **o** you.
Isa 8: 7 the Lord will **o** them with a mighty flood from the

OVERWHELMED (27) [OVERWHELM]
Ex 8: 4 You and your people will be **o** by frogs!' "
1Sa 18:10 in fact, a tormenting spirit from God **o** Saul,
2Ki 4:37 She fell at his feet, **o** with gratitude. Then she
Job 19:27 see him with my own eyes. I am **o** at the thought!
Ps 10:10 The helpless are **o** and collapse; / they fall beneath
55: 2 and answer me, / for I am **o** by my troubles.
61: 2 I will cry to you for help, / for my heart is **o**.
71:15 for I am **o** by how much you have done for me.
77: 3 of God, and I moan, / **o** with longing for his help.
88:16 Your fierce anger has **o** me. / Your terrors have cut
90: 7 wither beneath your anger; / we are **o** by your fury.
102: T A prayer of one **o** with trouble, pouring out
105:32 and flashes of lightning **o** the land.
119:20 I am **o** continually / with a desire for your laws.
119:139 I am **o** with rage, / for my enemies have
124: 4 have engulfed us; / a torrent would have **o** us.
124: 5 waters of their fury / would have **o** our very lives.
142: 3 For I am **o**, / and you alone know the way I should
Isa 61:10 I am **o** with joy in the LORD my God! For he has
Jer 45: 3 You have said, 'I am **o** with trouble! Haven't I had
50:12 But your homeland will be **o** with shame
Eze 3:15 I sat there among them for seven days, **o**.
Mk 5:42 and walked around! Her parents were absolutely **o**.
10:32 and the people following behind were **o** with fear.
Lk 1:12 Zechariah was **o** with fear.
8:56 Her parents were **o**, but Jesus insisted that they not
2Co 1: 8 We were crushed and completely **o**, and we

OVERWHELMING (5) [OVERWHELM]
Dt 26: 8 **o** terror, and miraculous signs and wonders.
Jer 32:21 and wonders, with great power and **o** terror.
Na 1: 8 But he sweeps away his enemies in an **o** flood.
Ro 8:37 **o** victory is ours through Christ, who loved us.
2Co 3:10 all compared with the **o** glory of the new covenant.

OVERWHELMS (2) [OVERWHELM]
Job 27:20 Terror **o** them, and they are blown away in the
Ps 38: 4 My guilt **o** me— / it is a burden too heavy to bear.

OWE (8) [OWED]
Ge 30:28 How much do I **o** you? Whatever it is, I'll pay it."
Ex 21: 2 and he will **o** you nothing for his freedom.
Lk 16: 5 He asked the first one, 'How much do you **o** him?'
16: 6 'I **o** him eight hundred gallons of olive oil.'
16: 7 " 'And how much do you **o** my employer?'
Ro 13: 7 Give to everyone what you **o** them: Pay your taxes
15:27 because they feel they **o** a real debt to them.
Phm 1:19 And I won't mention that you **o** me your very soul!

OWED (4) [OWE]
Ne 10:31 and to cancel the debts **o** to us by other Jews.
Mt 18:24 one of his debtors was brought in who **o** him
18:28 he went to a fellow servant who **o** him a few
Lk 16: 5 "So he invited each person who **o** money to his

OWL (11) [OWLS]
Lev 11:17 the little **o**, the cormorant, the great **o**,
11:18 the white **o**, the pelican, the carrion vulture,
Dt 14:16 the little **o**, the great **o**, the white **o**,
Ps 102: 6 I am like an **o** in the desert, / like a lonely **o** in a far-off wilderness.
Isa 34:11 It will be haunted by the horned **o**, the hawk, the screech **o**, and the raven.
34:15 There the **o** will make her nest and lay her eggs.

OWLS (1) [OWL]
Zep 2:14 **O** of many kinds will live among the ruins of its

OWN (802) [HOMEOWNER, OWNED, OWNER, OWNER'S, OWNERS, OWNERSHIP, OWNS, SHIPOWNERS]
Ge 1:25 each able to reproduce more of its **o** kind.
1:27 So God created people in his **o** image;
2:23 "She is part of my **o** flesh and bone!
10: 5 in various lands, each tribe with its **o** language.
15: 4 for you will have a son of your **o** to inherit
22:16 even your beloved son, I swear by my **o** self that
28: 4 May you **o** this land where we now are foreigners,
29:14 "Just think, my very **o** flesh and blood!"
30:30 When should I provide for my **o** family?"
30:40 Jacob added them to his **o** flock, thus separating
31:37 You have searched through everything I **o**.
31:43 But what can I do now to my **o** daughters
32: 5 and now I **o** oxen, donkeys, sheep, goats, and many
33:14 We will follow at our **o** pace and meet you at
38: 9 to have a child who would not be his **o** heir.
38:16 not realizing that she was his **o** daughter-in-law.
40: 5 had a dream, and each dream had its **o** meaning.
41:42 Then Pharaoh placed his **o** signet ring on Joseph's

43:32 The Egyptians sat at their **o** table
43:34 Their food was served to them from Joseph's **o**
46:30 for I have seen you with my **o** eyes and know you
46:32 them their flocks and herds and everything they **o**.'
48: 5 Now I am adopting as my **o** sons these two boys of
48: 6 children born to you in the future will be your **o**.
49: 4 of my wives; / you dishonored me in my **o** bed.
50:23 son Makir, who were treated as if they were his **o**.
Ex 1:21 feared God, he gave them families of their **o**.
3: 8 and lead them out of Egypt into their **o** good
5:22 "Why have you mistreated your **o** people like this,
6: 7 I will make you my **o** special people, and I will be
6: 8 Isaac, and Jacob. It will be your very **o** property.
6:12 "My **o** people won't listen to me anymore.
15:17 bring them in and plant them on your **o** mountain—
18:27 to his father-in-law, who returned to his **o** land.
19: 5 you will be my **o** special treasure from among all
21:35 Each will also **o** half of the dead bull.
22:31 "You are my **o** holy people. Therefore, do not eat
23: 9 Remember your **o** experience in the land of Egypt.
30:38 Those who make it for their **o** enjoyment will be
32:11 so angry with your **o** people whom you brought
32:13 You swore by your **o** self, 'I will make your
32:29 him even though it meant killing your **o** sons
33:13 don't forget that this nation is your very **o** people."
34: 5 down in a pillar of cloud and called out his **o** name,
34: 9 our sins. Accept us as your **o** special possession."
38:10 were twenty posts, each with its **o** bronze base,
Lev 6: 4 or a lost object that they claimed as their **o**,
7:30 Present it to him with your **o** hands as an offering
14:15 of the olive oil into the palm of his **o** left hand.
14:26 of the olive oil into the palm of his **o** left hand.
16:24 and go out to sacrifice his **o** whole burnt offering
20:26 set you apart from all other people to be my very **o**.
21:14 She must be a virgin from his **o** clan,
22:11 if the priest buys slaves with his **o** money,
22:33 you from Egypt, that I might be your very **o** God.
25:33 Levites are the only property they **o** in all Israel.
26:29 You will eat the flesh of your **o** sons
26:33 the nations and attack you with my **o** weapons.
Nu 1:16 These tribal leaders, heads of their **o** families,
1:20[-21] each listed according to his **o** clan and family:
1:52 designated camping area with its **o** family banner.
2: 2 "Each tribe will be assigned its **o** area in the camp,
6: 7 even if their **o** father, mother, brother, or sister has
10: 9 "When you arrive in your **o** land and go to war
10:30 not go. I must return to my **o** land and family."
15:39 following your **o** desires and going your **o** ways,
16:28 I have done—for I have not done them on my **o**.
17: 9 them to the people. Each man claimed his **o** staff.
18:27 as though it were the first grain from your **o**
18:27 threshing floor or wine from your **o** winepress.
18:30 it will be considered as though it came from your **o**
24:14 Now I am returning to my **o** people. But first let
27: 3 against the LORD. He died because of his **o** sin.
35:28 high priest, the slayer may return to his **o** property.
36: 6 as long as it is within their **o** ancestral tribe.
Dt 4:20 burning furnace of Egypt to become his **o** people
6:24 and to fear him for our **o** prosperity
7: 6 the LORD your God has chosen you to be his **o**
7:19 You saw it all with your **o** eyes! And remember the
8:16 this to humble you and test you for your **o** good.
8:17 so you would never think that it was your **o**
9:26 Sovereign LORD, do not destroy your **o** people.
10:13 and laws that I am giving you today for your **o**
11: 7 all the LORD's mighty deeds with your **o** eyes!
12:12 for they will have no inheritance of land as their **o**.
14: 2 and he has chosen you to be his **o** special treasure
18: 2 They will have no inheritance of their **o** among the
18:22 That prophet has spoken on his **o** and need not be
20: 1 and chariots and an army greater than your **o**,
24:16 Those worthy of death must be executed for their **o**
26:18 his **o** special treasure, just as he promised, and that
28:53 so severe that you will eat the flesh of your **o** sons
28:54 you will have no compassion for his **o** brother,
28:55 is devouring—the flesh of one of his **o** children—
28:56 the husband she loves and to her **o** son or daughter.
29: 2 "You have seen with your **o** eyes everything the
29:19 even though I am walking in my **o** stubborn way.'
29:22 both your **o** descendants and the foreigners who
32:19 He was provoked to anger by his **o** sons
32:49 giving to the people of Israel as their **o** possession.
Jos 2:14 "We offer our **o** lives as a guarantee for your
22: 9 They started the journey back to their **o** land of
22:29 or turn away from him by building our **o** altar for
24: 7 With your very **o** eyes you saw what I did.
24:28 sent the people away, each to his **o** inheritance.
Jdg 7: 2 me that they saved themselves by their **o** strength.
9: 2 And remember, I am your **o** flesh and blood!"
17: 6 so the people did whatever seemed right in their **o**
21:18 But we cannot give them our **o** daughters in
21:23 and carried them off to the land of their **o**
21:24 and families, and they returned to their **o** homes.
21:25 so the people did whatever seemed right in their **o**
Ru 2:11 and your **o** land to live here among complete
4: 6 "because this might endanger my **o** estate.
4:16 of the baby and cared for him as if he were her **o**.
1Sa 5:11 the Ark of the God of Israel back to its **o** country,
6: 2 the LORD? Tell us how to return it to its **o** land."
8:14 and olive groves and give them to his **o** servants.
8:16 the finest of your cattle and donkeys for his **o** use.
12: 2 I have selected him ahead of my **o** sons, and I
13:14 for the LORD has sought out a man after his **o**
14:39 will surely die, even if it is my **o** son Jonathan!"
17:38 Then Saul gave David his **o** armor—a bronze
17:54 but he stored the Philistine's armor in his **o** tent.)
20: 3 I swear it by the LORD and by your **o** soul!"
22: 8 For not one of you has ever told me that my **o** son
22: 8 My **o** son—encouraging David to try and kill me!"
22:23 here with me, and I will protect you with my **o** life,
24:10 This very day you can see with your **o** eyes it isn't
25: 6 to you, your family, and everything you **o**!
25: 8 Ask your **o** servants, and they will tell you this is
25:13 was David's reply as he strapped on his **o**.
25:26 and taking vengeance into your **o** hands,
25:33 and carrying out vengeance with my **o** hands.
26:23 The LORD gives his **o** reward for doing good
31: 4 not do it. So Saul took his **o** sword and fell on it.
31: 5 he fell on his **o** sword and died beside the king.
2Sa 4:11 who have killed an innocent man in his **o** house
and on his **o** bed?
5: 8 he told his **o** troops, "Go up through the water
7:10 It will be their **o** land where wicked nations won't
7:23 have you redeemed from slavery to be your **o**
9:11 with David, as though he were one of his **o** sons.
12: 3 It ate from the man's **o** plate and drank from his
12: 4 But instead of killing a lamb from his **o** flocks for
12:10 despised me by taking Uriah's wife to be your **o**.
12:11 will cause your **o** household to rebel against you.
12:30 king's head, and it was placed on David's **o** head.
14:13 because you have refused to bring home your **o**
14:24 "Absalom may go to his **o** house, but he must
15:21 and by your **o** life that I will go wherever you go,
16: 8 At last you will taste some of your **o** medicine,
16:11 the other officers, "My **o** son is trying to kill me.
19:12 my relatives, my **o** tribe, my **o** flesh and blood!
19:28 honored me among those who eat at your **o** table!
19:37 Then let me return again to die in my **o** town,
19:39 embraced him, Barzillai returned to his **o** home.
19:42 of Judah replied. "The king is one of our **o** tribe.
20: 7 from Joab's army and the king's **o** bodyguard.
20:14 Sheba had traveled across Israel to mobilize his **o**
1Ki 1:12 If you want to save your **o** life and the life of your
1:44 They had him ride on the king's **o** mule,
1:47 make Solomon's fame even greater than your **o**,
2:37 surely die; your blood will be on your **o** head."
3: 8 And here I am among your **o** chosen people,
4:25 each family had its **o** home and garden.
8:24 You made that promise with your **o** mouth,
8:24 and today you have fulfilled it with your **o** hands.
8:43 and fear you, just as your **o** people Israel do.
8:53 of the earth to be your **o** special possession."
10: 7 it until I arrived here and saw it with my **o** eyes.
10:13 all her attendants left and returned to their **o** land.
11:20 up in Pharaoh's palace among Pharaoh's **o** sons.
11:21 said to Pharaoh, "Let me return to my **o** country."
11:26 son of Nebat, one of Solomon's **o** officials.
12:16 Israel! Look out for your **o** house, O David!"
13: 8 "Even if you gave me half of everything you **o**,
13:23 the prophet saddled his **o** donkey for him,
13:30 He laid the body in his **o** grave, crying out in grief,
20:40 "Well, it's your **o** fault," the king replied.
20:40 "You have determined your **o** judgment."
2Ki 3:27 so they withdrew and returned to their **o** land.
8:20 revolted against Judah and crowned their **o** king.
10:24 you will pay for it with your **o** life."
12: 7 Don't use any more gifts for your **o** needs.
12:16 It was given to the priests for their **o** use.
13:16 and Elisha laid his **o** hands on the king's hands.
14: 6 Those worthy of death must be executed for their **o**
16: 3 of Israel, even sacrificing his **o** son in the fire.
17:17 They even sacrificed their **o** sons and daughters in
17:29 foreigners also continued to worship their **o** gods.
17:31 their **o** children as sacrifices to Adrammelech
18:27 so hungry and thirsty that they will eat their **o** dung
and drink their **o** urine."
18:31 each of you to continue eating from your **o** garden
and drinking from your **o** well.
19:30 will take root again in your **o** soil, and you will
19:33 The king will return to his **o** country by the road on
19:34 For my **o** honor and for the sake of my servant
19:36 of Assyria broke camp and returned to his **o** land.
20:15 "I showed them everything I **o**—all my treasures."
20:18 Some of your **o** descendants will be taken away
21: 6 Manasseh even sacrificed his **o** son in the fire.
21:23 Then Amon's **o** servants plotted against him
23:20 the priests of the pagan shrines on their **o** altars,
23:30 to Jerusalem and buried him in his **o** tomb.
1Ch 10: 4 not do it. So Saul took his **o** sword and fell on it.
10: 5 that Saul was dead, he fell on his **o** sword and died.
12:30 were 20,800 warriors, each famous in his **o** clan.
17: 9 It will be their **o** land where wicked nations won't
17:21 have you redeemed from slavery to be your **o**
19: 7 troops that Hanun had recruited from his **o** towns.
20: 2 king's head, and it was placed on David's **o** head.
29: 3 I am giving all of my **o** private treasures of gold
2Ch 4: 6 Sea itself, and not the basins, for their **o** washing.
6:15 You made that promise with your **o** mouth,
6:15 and today you have fulfilled it with your **o** hands.
6:33 and fear you, just as your **o** people Israel do.
8: 1 and his **o** royal palace were completed.
8:18 Hiram sent him ships commanded by his **o** officers
9: 6 it until I arrived here and saw it with my **o** eyes.
9:12 all her attendants left and returned to their **o** land.
10:16 Israel! Look out for your **o** house, O David!"
11:15 Jeroboam appointed his **o** priests to serve at the
13: 9 and the Levites and have appointed your **o** priests,
21: 8 revolted against Judah and crowned their **o** king.
21:13 And you have even killed your **o** brothers,
24:25 But his **o** officials decided to kill him for
25: 4 Those worthy of death must be executed for their **o**
25:14 He set them up as his **o** gods, bowed down in front
25:15 could not even save their **o** people from you?"
28: 3 of Hinnom, even sacrificing his **o** sons in the fire.
28:10 What about your **o** sins against the LORD your
28:11 you have taken, for they are your **o** relatives.
28:15 and took all the prisoners back to their **o** land—
31: 1 the Israelites returned to their **o** towns and homes.
32:21 So Sennacherib returned home in disgrace to his **o**
32:21 some of his **o** sons killed him there with a sword.
33: 6 Manasseh even sacrificed his **o** sons in the fire in
33:24 At last Amon's **o** officials plotted against him
34: 5 the bones of the pagan priests on their **o** altars,
Ezr 1: 7 and had placed in the temple of his **o** gods.
Ne 1: 6 Yes, even my **o** family and I have sinned!
3:10 of Harumaph repaired the wall beside his **o** house,
3:17 the building of the wall on behalf of his **o** district.
3:23 repaired the sections next to their **o** houses.
3:28 the section immediately opposite his **o** house.
3:29 of Immer also rebuilt the wall next to his **o** house,
3:30 of Berekiah rebuilt the wall next to his **o** house.
4: 4 May their scoffing fall back on their **o** heads,
5: 7 "You are oppressing your **o** relatives by charging
7: 3 regular posts and some in front of their **o** homes."
7:73 that is to say, all Israel—settled in their **o** towns."
9: 2 from all foreigners as they confessed their **o** sins
9:35 Even while they had their **o** kingdom, they did not
11: 3 live in their **o** homes in the various towns of Judah,
12:29 for the singers had built their **o** villages around
13:19 I also sent some of my **o** servants to guard the
Est 1:22 to each province in its **o** script and language,
2: 7 her into his family and raised her as his **o** daughter.
3:12 and the local officials of each province in their **o**
6: 8 he should bring out one of the king's **o** royal robes,
6: 8 as well as the king's **o** horse with a royal emblem
6: 9 him through the city square on the king's **o** horse.
6:11 it on Mordecai, placed him on the king's **o** horse,
7: 9 that stands seventy-five feet tall in his **o** courtyard.
Job 3: 5 let the darkness and utter gloom claim it for its **o**.
4:18 "If God cannot trust his **o** angels and has charged
5:13 He catches those who think they are wise in their **o**
9:20 my **o** mouth would pronounce me guilty.
9:31 I would be so filthy my **o** clothing would hate me.
9:35 without fear, but I cannot do that in my **o** strength.
10: 3 the work of your **o** hands, while sending joy
14:22 They are absorbed in their **o** pain and grief."
15: 6 why should I condemn you? Your **o** mouth does!
15:17 I will answer you from my **o** experience.
17: 5 They denounce their companions for their **o**
18: 7 Their **o** schemes will be their downfall.
19:17 to my wife. I am loathsome to my **o** family.
19:27 him for myself. Yes, I will see him with my **o** eyes.
19:28 go on persecuting me, saying, 'It's his **o** fault'?
20: 7 will perish forever, thrown away like his **o** dung.
21:16 But their prosperity is not of their **o** doing, so I will
21:19 not their children! Let them feel their **o** penalty.
21:20 Let their **o** eyes see their destruction. Let them
24: 6 They harvest a field they do not **o**, and they glean
24:18 Everything they **o** is cursed, so that no one enters
24:20 Even the sinner's **o** mother will forget him.
31:12 destroys to hell. It would wipe out everything I **o**.
31:25 happiness depend on my wealth and all that I **o**?
37:19 We are too ignorant to make our **o** arguments.
39:16 harsh toward her young, as if they were not her **o**.
40:14 praise you, for your **o** strength would save you.
42: 5 but now I have seen you with my **o** eyes.
Ps 5:10 Let them be caught in their **o** traps. / Drive them
7:16 violence for others, / but it falls on their **o** heads.
9:15 for others. / They have been caught in their **o** trap.
9:16 The wicked have trapped themselves in their **o**
12: 4 Our lips are our **o**—who can stop us?"
33:12 whose people he has chosen for his **o**.
35:14 or family, / as if I were grieving for my **o** mother.
35:20 who are minding their **o** business.
35:21 "Aha! / With our **o** eyes we saw him do it!"
36: 8 You feed them from the abundance of your **o**
37:15 be stabbed through the heart with their **o** swords,
38:11 Even my **o** family stands at a distance.
44: 1 O God, we have heard it with our **o** ears—
44: 3 it was not their **o** strength that gave them victory.
50:10 are mine, / and I **o** the cattle on a thousand hills.
50:20 and slander a brother— / your **o** mother's son.
58: 3 from birth they have lied and gone their **o** way.
64: 8 Their **o** words will be turned against them,
69: 8 Even my **o** brothers pretend they don't know me;
74: 1 so intense against the sheep of your **o** pasture?
74: 2 the tribe you redeemed as your **o** special
78:52 But he led his **o** people like a flock of sheep,
78:62 because he was so angry with his **o** people—
78:71 of Jacob's descendants— / God's **o** people, Israel.
81:12 stubborn way, / living according to their **o** desires.
83:12 for they said, "Let us seize for our **o** use
92:11 With my **o** eyes I have seen the downfall of my
92:11 with my **o** ears I have heard the defeat of my
92:13 For they are transplanted into the LORD's **o**
94:14 he will not abandon his **o** special possession.
101: 2 I will lead a life of integrity / in my **o** home.
106:40 and he abhorred his **o** special possession.
109:21 for the sake of your **o** reputation!
113: 8 among princes, / even the princes of his **o** people!
135: 4 Jacob for himself, / Israel for his **o** special treasure.
141:10 Let the wicked fall into their **o** snares, / but let me
Pr 1:18 for themselves; they booby-trap their **o** lives!
1:31 they must eat the bitter fruit of living their **o** way.
1:32 and their **o** complacency will destroy them.
3: 5 your heart; do not depend on your **o** understanding.
3: 7 Don't be impressed with your **o** wisdom. Instead,
5:12 If only I had not demanded my **o** way!
5:15 Drink water from your **o** well—share your love
5:22 An evil man is held captive by his **o** sins; they are
6:32 adultery is an utter fool, for he destroys his **o** soul.

9:15 to men going by who are minding their **o** business.
11:7 all perish, for they rely on their **o** feeble strength.
11:17 Your **o** soul is nourished when you are kind,
12:12 each other's loot, while the godly bear their **o** fruit.
12:13 The wicked are trapped by their **o** words,
14:1 a foolish woman tears hers down with her **o** hands.
14:10 Each heart knows its **o** bitterness, and no one else
16:2 People may be pure in their **o** eyes, but the LORD
16:4 The LORD has made everything for his **o**
18:2 they only want to air their **o** opinions.
19:3 People ruin their lives by their **o** foolishness
19:19 Short-tempered people must pay their **o** penalty.
21:13 of the poor will be ignored in their **o** time of need.
26:5 or they will become wise in their **o** estimation.
28:10 lead the upright into sin will fall into their **o** trap,
31:22 She quilts her **o** bedspreads. She dresses like
Ecc 3:11 God has made everything beautiful for its **o** time.
5:9 Even the king milks the land for his **o** profit!
7:29 but they have each turned to follow their **o**
9:3 Instead, they choose their **o** mad course, for they
SS 4:12 that no one else can drink from, a fountain of my **o**.
8:12 But as for my **o** vineyard, O Solomon, you can
Isa 3:9 They have brought about their **o** destruction.
4:1 We will provide our **o** food and clothing.
5:9 With my **o** ears I heard him say, "Many beautiful
9:20 They fight against their **o** neighbors to steal food,
9:20 In the end they will even eat their **o** children.
10:13 "By my **o** power and wisdom I have won these
10:13 By my **o** strength I have captured many lands,
13:14 rushing back to their **o** lands like hunted deer,
14:1 bring them back to settle once again in their **o** land.
17:8 for help or worship what their **o** hands have made.
28:12 God's people could have rest in their **o** land if they
28:21 unusual thing: He will destroy his **o** people!
28:25 barley, and spelt, each in its **o** section of his land?
30:20 You will see your teacher with your **o** eyes,
33:11 Your **o** breath will turn to fire and kill you.
36:12 so hungry and thirsty that they will eat their **o** dung and drink their **o** urine."
36:16 each of you to continue eating from your **o** garden and drinking from your **o** well.
37:31 will take root again in your **o** soil, and you will
37:34 The king will return to his **o** country by the road on
37:35 For my **o** honor and for the sake of my servant
37:37 of Assyria broke camp and returned to his **o** land.
39:4 "I showed them everything I **o**—all my treasures."
39:7 Some of your **o** descendants will be taken away
42:19 Who in all the world is as blind as my **o** people,
43:25 am the one who blots out your sins for my **o** sake
44:5 and will take the honored name of Israel as their **o**.
44:10 Who but a fool would make his **o** god—an idol that
45:23 I have sworn by my **o** name, and I will never go
48:9 Yet for my **o** sake and for the honor of my name,
48:11 I will rescue you for my sake—yes, for my **o** sake!
49:8 land of Israel and reassign it to its **o** people again.
49:26 I will feed your enemies with their **o** flesh.
49:26 They will be drunk with rivers of their **o** blood.
50:11 you who live in your **o** light and warm yourselves by your **o** fires.
53:4 were a punishment from God for his **o** sins!
53:6 We have left God's paths to follow our **o**.
56:11 are stupid shepherds, all following their **o** path,
58:13 Don't pursue your **o** interests on that day,
58:13 and don't follow your **o** desires or talk idly.
60:21 for I will plant them there with my **o** hands in order
61:3 them like strong and graceful oaks for his **o** glory.
62:4 delights in you and will claim you as his **o**.
62:8 The LORD has sworn to Jerusalem by his **o**
63:8 He said, "They are my very **o** people. Surely they
65:2 "I opened my arms to my **o** people all day long,
65:2 They follow their **o** evil paths and thoughts.
65:7 both for their **o** sins and for those of their
65:21 they build and eat the fruit of their **o** vineyards.
66:3 But those who choose their **o** ways, delighting in
Jer 2:19 Your **o** wickedness will punish you. You will see
3:15 And I will give you leaders after my **o** heart,
3:17 They will no longer stubbornly follow their **o** evil
3:19 'I would love to treat you as my **o** children!'
4:18 "Your **o** actions have brought this upon you.
4:18 This punishment is a bitter dose of your **o**
5:19 and gave yourselves to foreign gods in your **o** land.
5:19 will serve foreigners in a land that is not your **o**.'
6:19 It is the fruit of their **o** sin because they refuse to
7:3 your evil ways, I will let you stay in your **o** land.
7:6 worshiping idols as you now do to your **o** harm.
7:19 of all, they hurt themselves, to their **o** shame."
7:30 set up their abominable idols right in my **o** Temple,
9:14 they have stubbornly followed their **o** desires
10:16 including Israel, his **o** special possession.
10:23 I know, LORD, that a person's life is not his **o**. No one is able to plan his **o** course.
11:8 they stubbornly followed their **o** evil desires.
12:6 Even your **o** brothers, members of your **o** family,
12:15 I will bring them home to their **o** lands again, each nation to its **o** inheritance.
13:10 They stubbornly follow their **o** desires and worship
14:7 So please, help us for the sake of your **o** reputation.
14:14 They speak foolishness made up in their **o** lying
14:16 For I will pour out their **o** wickedness on them.
14:21 For the sake of your **o** name, LORD, do not
15:7 I will destroy my **o** people, because they refuse to
16:9 In your **o** lifetime, before your very eyes, I will put
16:12 You stubbornly follow your **o** evil desires
16:15 who brought the people of Israel back to their **o**
16:20 Can people make their **o** god? The gods they make
17:16 It is your message I have given them, not my **o**.
18:12 live as we want to, following our **o** evil desires."
18:18 We have our **o** priests and wise men and prophets.
19:9 Then those trapped inside will have to eat their **o**
22:5 I swear by my **o** name, says the LORD, that this
22:12 a distant land and never again see his **o** country."
23:3 I will bring them back into their **o** fold, and they
23:8 who brought the people of Israel back to their **o**
23:8 exiled them.' Then they will live in their **o** land."
23:11 I have seen their despicable acts right here in my **o**
23:17 And to those who stubbornly follow their **o** evil
23:36 For people are using it to give authority to their **o**
24:6 I have sent them into captivity for their **o** good.
25:29 the city where my **o** name is honored.
25:30 'The LORD will roar loudly against his **o** land
26:11 "You have heard with your **o** ears what a traitor he
26:12 Then Jeremiah spoke in his **o** defense.
27:11 to stay in their **o** country to farm the land as usual.
29:14 and bring you home again to your **o** land."
29:25 You wrote a letter on your **o** authority to
30:10 and will have peace and quiet in their **o** land,
30:21 They will have their **o** ruler again, and he will not
31:5 of Samaria and eat from your **o** gardens there.
31:17 "Your children will come again to their **o** land.
31:30 All people will die for their **o** sins—those who eat
32:15 Someday people will again **o** property here in this
32:34 set up their abominable idols right in my **o** Temple,
32:39 for their **o** good and for the good of all their
39:14 So Jeremiah stayed in Judah among his **o** people.
45:3 I am weary of my **o** sighing and can find no rest.'
48:26 Moab will wallow in her **o** vomit, ridiculed by all.
49:13 For I have sworn by my **o** name,"
50:16 sword of the enemy and rush back to their **o** lands.
50:19 And I will bring Israel home again to her **o** land,
51:9 Return now to your **o** land, for her judgment will
51:14 taken this vow and has sworn to it by his **o** name:
51:19 including his people, his **o** special possession.
51:34 our riches. He has thrown us out of our **o** country.
La 2:7 The Lord has rejected his **o** altar; he despises his **o** sanctuary.
2:20 "You are doing this to your **o** people!
3:14 My **o** people laugh at me. All day long they sing
4:10 Tenderhearted women have cooked their **o**
4:20 we could hold our **o** against any nation on earth!
Eze 3:10 let all my words sink deep into your **o** heart first.
3:21 will live, and you will have saved your **o** life, too."
5:10 Parents will eat their **o** children, and children will
12:25 I will fulfill my threat of destruction in your **o**
13:2 of Israel who are inventing their **o** prophecies.
13:3 prophets who are following their **o** imaginations
13:9 and they will never again see their **o** land.
13:17 women who prophesy from their **o** imaginations.
14:22 You will see with your **o** eyes how wicked they
16:6 helplessly kicking about in your **o** blood.
16:22 lay naked in a field, kicking about in your **o** blood.
16:32 who takes in strangers instead of her **o** husband.
18:20 Righteous people will be rewarded for their **o**
18:20 and wicked people will be punished for their **o**
21:30 No, I will destroy you in your **o** country, the land
21:32 and your blood will be spilled in your **o** land.
22:11 their daughters-in-law or who rape their **o** sisters.
23:29 deal with you in hatred and rob you of all you **o**,
28:25 The people of Israel will again live in their **o** land,
31:14 Let no other nation proudly exult in its **o**
32:2 heaving around in your **o** rivers, stirring up mud
33:4 to take action—well, it is their **o** fault if they die.
34:13 I will bring them back home to their **o** land of
35:6 for blood, I will give you a bloodbath of your **o**.
36:13 saying, 'Israel is a land that devours her **o** people!'
36:17 when the people of Israel were living in their **o**
36:20 and he couldn't keep them safe in his **o** land!'
37:14 and you will live and return home to your **o** land.
37:21 I will bring them home to their **o** land from the
39:26 home to live in peace and safety in their **o** land.
46:18 property to his sons, it must be from his **o** land,
Da 1:5 of the best food and wine from his **o** kitchens.
3:28 than serve or worship any god except their **o** God.
4:30 I, by my **o** mighty power, have built this beautiful
6:17 The king sealed the stone with his **o** royal seal
8:24 will become very strong, but not by his **o** power.
9:17 For your **o** sake, Lord, smile again on your
9:19 For your **o** sake, O my God, do not delay, for your
11:5 but one of this king's **o** officials will become more
11:9 king of the south but will soon return to his **o** land.
11:14 Lawless ones among your **o** people will join them
11:19 He will take refuge in his **o** fortresses but will
11:26 Those of his **o** household will bring his downfall.
Hos 2:4 And I will not love her children as I would my **o**
8:4 they have brought about their **o** destruction.
8:6 This calf you worship was crafted by your **o** hands!
11:6 destroy them, trapping them in their **o** evil plans.
Am 6:8 The Sovereign LORD has sworn by his **o** name,
6:13 "Didn't we take Karnaim by our **o** strength
8:7 Now the LORD has sworn this oath by his **o**
Ob 1:15 All your evil deeds will fall back on your **o** heads.
Jnh 1:14 you have sent this storm upon him for your **o** good
Mic 2:13 of your cities of captivity, back to your **o** land.
4:4 Everyone will live quietly in their **o** homes in
5:3 countrymen will return from exile to their **o** land.
5:13 so you will never again worship the work of your **o**
7:2 even setting traps for their **o** brothers.
7:6 Your enemies will be right in your **o** household.
7:10 With my **o** eyes I will see them trampled down like
Hab 1:5 For I am doing something in your **o** day,
1:11 are deeply guilty, for their **o** strength is their god."
2:18 How foolish to trust in something made by your **o**
3:14 With their **o** weapons, you destroyed those who
Zep 2:11 will worship the LORD, each in their **o** land.
3:4 Its prophets are arrogant liars seeking their **o** gain.
Hag 1:9 while you are all busy building your **o** fine houses.
Zec 1:8 brown, and white horses, each with its **o** rider.
1:17 comfort Zion and choose Jerusalem as his **o**.' "
2:9 crush them, and their **o** slaves will plunder them.'
2:12 will once again choose Jerusalem to be his **o** city.
13:3 his **o** father and mother will tell him, 'You must
13:3 Then his **o** father and mother will stab him.
Mal 3:17 day when I act, they will be my **o** special treasure.
Mt 6:34 for tomorrow will bring its **o** worries.
7:3 your friend's eye when you have a log in your **o**?
7:4 when you can't see past the log in your **o** eye?
7:5 First get rid of the log from your **o** eye,
8:20 but I, the Son of Man, have no home of my **o**,
8:22 Let those who are spiritually dead care for their **o**
9:1 and went back across the lake to his **o** town.
10:21 to death, fathers will betray their **o** children,
10:36 Your enemies will be right in your **o** household!
12:26 against himself. His **o** kingdom will not survive.
12:27 prince of demons, what about your **o** followers?
13:57 "A prophet is honored everywhere except in his **o** hometown and among his **o** family."
15:6 And so, by your **o** tradition, you nullify the direct
15:9 for they replace God's commands with their **o**
16:26 whole world but lose your **o** soul in the process?
17:25 Do kings tax their **o** people or the foreigners they
22:34 they thought up a fresh question of their **o** to ask
27:31 off the robe and put his **o** clothes on him again.
27:60 He placed it in his **o** new tomb, which had been
Mk 4:28 because the earth produces crops on its **o**. First a
6:4 "A prophet is honored everywhere except in his **o**
6:4 and among his relatives and his **o** family."
7:7 for they replace God's commands with their **o**
7:8 specific laws and substitute your **o** traditions."
7:9 God's laws in order to hold on to your **o** traditions.
7:13 you break the law of God in order to protect your **o**
7:27 "First I should help my **o** family, the Jews.
7:33 Then, spitting onto his **o** fingers, he touched the
8:36 whole world but lose your **o** soul in the process?
13:12 to death, fathers will betray their **o** children,
15:20 the purple robe and put his **o** clothes on him again.
Lk 1:56 three months and then went back to her **o** home.
2:3 All returned to their **o** towns to register for this
4:24 truth is, no prophet is accepted in his **o** hometown.
6:34 Even sinners will lend to their **o** kind for a full
6:41 your friend's eye when you have a log in your **o**?
6:42 when you can't see past the log in your **o** eye?
6:42 First get rid of the log from your **o** eye;
8:3 contributing from their **o** resources to support Jesus
9:25 but lose or forfeit your **o** soul in the process?
9:58 but I, the Son of Man, have no home of my **o**,
9:60 "Let those who are spiritually dead care for their **o**
10:34 Then he put the man on his **o** donkey and took him
11:19 prince of demons, what about your **o** followers?
12:15 Real life is not measured by how much we **o**."
14:26 follower you must love me more than your **o** father
14:26 brothers and sisters—yes, more than your **o** life.
14:27 be my disciple if you do not carry your **o** cross
16:12 why should you be trusted with money of your **o**?
17:8 and serve him his supper before eating his **o**.
Jn 1:11 Even in his **o** land and among his **o** people,
4:44 "A prophet is honored everywhere except in his **o**
5:30 the will of God who sent me; it is not merely my **o**.
5:31 "If I were to testify on my **o** behalf, my testimony
7:16 So Jesus told them, "I'm not teaching my **o** ideas,
7:17 my teaching is from God or is merely my **o**.
7:18 Those who present their **o** ideas are looking for
8:17 Your **o** law says that if two people agree about
8:28 realize that I am he and that I do nothing on my **o**,
8:42 from God. I am not here on my **o**, but he sent me.
9:2 Was it a result of his **o** sins or those of his
10:3 He calls his **o** sheep by name and leads them out.
10:4 After he has gathered his **o** flock, he walks ahead
10:14 I know my **o** sheep, and they know me,
10:34 "It is written in your **o** law that God said to certain
12:6 and he often took some for his **o** use.
12:49 I don't speak on my **o** authority. The Father who sent me gave me his **o** instructions
14:10 The words I say are not my **o**, but my Father who
14:24 And remember, my words are not my **o**.
16:13 He will not be presenting his **o** ideas; he will be
16:32 each one going his **o** way, leaving me alone.
18:9 He did this to fulfill his **o** statement: "I have not
18:31 take him away and judge him by your **o** laws,"
18:34 Jesus replied, "Is this your **o** question, or did
18:35 "Your **o** people and their leading priests brought
Ac 2:6 and they were bewildered to hear their **o** languages
2:11 And we all hear these people speaking in our **o**
2:30 **o** descendants would sit on David's throne as the
3:12 though we had made this man walk by our **o** power
3:22 up a Prophet like me from among your **o** people.
4:32 and they felt that what they owned was not their **o**;
5:38 and doing these things merely on their **o**,
7:21 daughter found him and raised him as her **o** son.
7:27 Moses aside and told him to mind his **o** business.
7:37 up a Prophet like me from among your **o** people.'
13:22 'David son of Jesse is a man after my **o** heart,
13:32 to our ancestors has come true in our **o** time,
13:41 and die! / For I am doing something in your **o** day,
14:16 he permitted all the nations to go their **o** ways,
17:28 As one of your **o** poets says, 'We are his
18:6 and said, "Your blood be upon your **o** heads—
20:34 these hands of mine have worked to pay my **o** way,
21:11 Paul's belt and bound his **o** feet and hands with it.
21:40 and he addressed them in their **o** language,
22:2 When they heard him speaking in their **o** language,
26:4 from my earliest childhood among my **o** people
26:17 And I will protect you from both your **o** people

27:34 "Please eat something now for your **o** good.
28:16 Paul was permitted to have his **o** private lodging,
28:19 had no desire to press charges against my **o** people.
28:30 next two years, Paul lived in his **o** rented house.
Ro 1: 7 and he has called you to be his very **o** people.
2:15 for their **o** consciences either accuse them or tell
2:26 all the rights and honors of being his **o** people?
7:13 It uses God's good commandment for its **o** evil
8: 3 He sent his **o** Son in a human body like ours,
8:15 You should behave instead like God's very **o**
8:27 for us believers in harmony with God's **o** will.
8:32 Since God did not spare even his **o** Son but gave
8:33 dares accuse us whom God has chosen for his **o**?
9:11 proves that God chooses according to his **o** plan,
10: 3 they are clinging to their **o** way of getting right
11: 2 No, God has not rejected his **o** people, whom he
11:24 wild olive tree and graft you into his **o** good tree—
11:32 For God has imprisoned all people in their **o**
14: 7 For we are not our **o** masters when we live or when
16: 8 whom I love as one of the Lord's **o** children,
16:13 whom the Lord picked out to be his very **o**;
16:18 they are serving their **o** personal interests.
1Co 1: 2 you who have been called by God to be his **o** holy
1:22 because they believe only what agrees with their **o**
2:11 can know God's thoughts except God's **o** Spirit.
3: 3 for you are still controlled by your **o** sinful desires.
3: 3 Doesn't that prove you are controlled by your **o**
3: 8 according to their **o** hard work.
3:19 who think they are wise / in their **o** cleverness."
4: 3 I don't even trust my **o** judgment on this point.
4: 7 you have accomplished something on your **o**?
4:11 many beatings, and we have no homes of our **o**.
4:12 We have worked wearily with our **o** hands to earn
6: 8 and cheat even your **o** Christian brothers
6:18 For sexual immorality is a sin against your **o** body.
7: 2 each man should have his **o** wife,
7: 2 and each woman should have her **o** husband.
9: 1 Haven't I seen Jesus our Lord with my **o** eyes?
9: 7 What soldier has to pay his **o** expenses? And have
9:17 If I were doing this of my **o** free will, then I would
10:24 Don't think only of your **o** good. Think of other
11: 7 for man is God's glory, made in God's **o** image,
11:21 For I am told that some of you hurry to eat your **o**
11:22 Don't you have your **o** homes for eating
13: 5 or rude. Love does not demand its **o** way. Love is
14:21 in the Scriptures, / "I will speak to my **o** people
16:21 is my greeting, which I write with my **o** hand—
2Co 1:12 on God's grace, not on our **o** earthly wisdom.
1:22 and he has identified us as his **o** by placing the
4: 7 our glorious power is from God and is not our **o**.
6:10 We **o** nothing, and yet we have everything.
6:13 I am talking now as I would to my **o** children.
7:13 In addition to our **o** encouragement, we were
8: 3 but far more. And they did it of their **o** free will.
9: 7 You must each make up your **o** mind as to how
11:26 I have faced danger from my **o** people, the Jews,
Gal 1:14 I was one of the most religious Jews of my **o** age,
3: 3 trying to become perfect by your **o** human effort?
3:20 but God acted on his **o** when he made his promise
4: 1 even though they actually **o** everything their father
4: 5 so that he could adopt us as his very **o** children.
4: 7 Now you are no longer a slave but God's **o** child.
4:15 I know you would gladly have taken out your **o**
4:23 was born as God's **o** fulfillment of his promise.
5:20 is wrong except those in your **o** little group,
6: 5 For we are each responsible for our **o** conduct.
6: 8 Those who live only to satisfy their **o** sinful desires
6:11 as I write these closing words in my **o** handwriting.
Eph 1: 5 **o** family by bringing us to himself through Jesus
1:13 he identified you as his **o** by giving you the Holy
1:14 and that he has purchased us to be his **o** people.
4:16 As each part does its **o** special work, it helps the
4:30 he is the one who has identified you as his **o**,
5:28 to love their wives as they love their **o** bodies.
5:29 No one hates his **o** body but lovingly cares for it,
Php 2: 4 Don't think only about your **o** affairs, but be
3: 1 of telling you this. I am doing this for your **o** good.
3: 4 If others have reason for confidence in their **o**
3: 9 I no longer count on my **o** goodness or my ability
3:21 and change them into glorious bodies like his **o**,
Col 1:22 his death on the cross in his **o** human body.
1:26 but now it has been revealed to his **o** holy people.
4: 9 and much loved brother, one of your **o** people.
4:18 Here is my greeting in my **o** handwriting—PAUL.
1Th 1: 4 and that he chose you to be his **o** people.
2: 7 as a mother feeding and caring for her **o** children.
2: 8 you not only God's Good News but our **o** lives,
2:11 treated each of you as a father treats his **o** children.
2:13 think of the words we spoke as being just our **o**.
2:14 you suffered persecution from your **o** countrymen.
2:14 suffered from their **o** people, the Jews.
2:15 For some of the Jews had killed their **o** prophets,
3: 7 in all of our **o** crushing troubles and suffering,
4:11 minding your **o** business and working with your
2Th 3:12 Settle down and get to work. Earn your **o** living.
3:17 is my greeting, which I write with my **o** hand—
1Ti 3: 4 He must manage his **o** family well, with children
3: 5 For if a man cannot manage his **o** household,
5: 1 him respectfully as though he were your **o** father.
5: 1 Talk to the younger men as you would to your **o**
5: 2 younger women with all purity as your **o** sisters.
5: 8 But those who won't care for their **o** relatives,
5:14 have children, and take care of their **o** homes.
2Ti 4: 3 They will follow their **o** desires and will look for
Tit 1:12 One of their **o** men, a prophet from Crete, has said
2:14 to cleanse us, and to make us his very **o** people,
Phm 1:10 I think of him as my **o** son because he became a
1:12 him back to you, and with him comes my **o** heart.
1:19 I, Paul, write this in my **o** handwriting: "I will
Heb 1: 3 The Son reflects God's **o** glory, and everything
3:12 Make sure that your **o** hearts are not evil
5: 3 both for their sins and for his **o** sins.
6:13 swear by, God took an oath in his **o** name, saying:
7: 5 the people, even though they are their **o** relatives.
7:27 They did this for their **o** sins first and then for the
9: 7 which he offers to God to cover his **o** sins
9:12 He took his **o** blood, and with it he secured our
10:30 also said, / "The Lord will judge his **o** people."
11:14 looking forward to a country they can call their **o**.
11:26 of the Messiah than to **o** the treasures of Egypt,
12: 7 remember that God is treating you as his **o**
13: 3 as though you feel their pain in your **o** bodies.
13:12 to make his people holy by shedding his **o** blood.
Jas 1:14 Temptation comes from the lure of our **o** evil
1:18 In his goodness he chose to make us his **o** children
4:16 Otherwise you will be boasting about your **o** plans,
1Pe 2: 9 God's holy nation, his very **o** possession.
2:24 He personally carried away our sins in his **o** body
4:17 and it must begin first among God's **o** children.
2Pe 1: 3 He has called us to receive his **o** glory
1:16 We have seen his majestic splendor with our **o**
2:10 He is especially hard on those who follow their **o**
3:17 I don't want you to lose your **o** secure footing.
1Jn 1: 1 We saw him with our **o** eyes and touched him with
our **o** hands.
4:14 we have seen with our **o** eyes and now testify that
Jude 1:10 tell them, and they bring about their **o** destruction.
Rev 13: 2 And the dragon gave him his **o** power and throne

OWNED (26) [OWN]

Ge 13: 1 Abram with his wife and Lot and all that they **o**,
13:18 Then Abram moved his camp to the oak grove **o**
14:12 who lived in Sodom—and took everything he **o**.
24:10 with him the best of everything his master **o**.
25: 5 Abraham left everything he **o** to his son Isaac.
32:10 I left home, I **o** nothing except a walking stick,
39: 6 administrative responsibility over everything he **o**.
Nu 16:32 were standing with them, and everything they **o**.
32: 1 of Reuben and Gad **o** vast numbers of livestock.
Jdg 10: 4 and they **o** thirty towns in the land of Gilead,
1Sa 25: 2 There was a wealthy man from Maon who **o**
25:21 the wilderness, and nothing he **o** was lost or stolen.
2Sa 12: 2 The rich man **o** many sheep and cattle.
12: 3 The poor man **o** nothing but a little lamb he had
1Ki 21: 1 and near the palace was a vineyard **o** by a man
2Ch 31: 5 of their fields. They brought a tithe of all they **o**.
Job 1: 3 He **o** seven thousand sheep, three thousand camels,
Ecc 2: 7 I also **o** great herds and flocks, more than any of
SS 8: 7 If a man tried to buy love with everything he **o**,
Jer 35: 9 or **o** vineyards or farms or planted crops.
Mt 13:44 and sold everything he **o** to get enough money to
13:46 great value, he sold everything he **o** and bought it!
Ac 4:32 and they felt that what they **o** was not their own;
4:34 because people who **o** land or houses sold them
4:37 He sold a field he **o** and brought the money to the
Heb 10:34 When all you **o** was taken from you, you accepted

OWNER (53) [OWN]

Ge 31:37 for all to see. Let them decide who is the real **o**!
Ex 21: 9 And if the slave girl's **o** arranges for her to marry
21:20 slave is beaten and dies, the **o** must be punished.
21:21 however, then the **o** should not be punished,
21:26 "If an **o** hits a male or female slave in the eye
21:27 And if an **o** knocks out the tooth of a male
21:28 such a case, however, the **o** will not be held liable.
21:29 that the **o** knew the bull had gored people in the
21:29 it must be stoned, and the **o** must also be killed.
21:30 the **o** of the bull to compensate for the loss of life.
21:30 The **o** will have to pay whatever is demanded.
21:32 the slave's **o** is to be given thirty silver coins in
21:34 The **o** of the well must pay in full for the dead
21:36 yet its **o** failed to keep it under control, the money
21:36 The **o** of the living bull must pay in full for the
22: 5 and the **o** lets it stray into someone else's field to
22: 5 then the animal's **o** must pay damages in the form
22:11 The **o** must accept the neighbor's word, and no
22:12 was stolen, payment must be made to the **o**.
22:14 or killed, and if the **o** was not there at the time,
22:15 But if the **o** is there, no payment is required.
23: 4 donkey that has strayed away, take it back to its **o**.
Lev 14:35 The **o** of such a house must then go to the priest
25:27 it back, the original **o** may then return to the land.
25:28 But if the original **o** cannot afford to redeem it,
25:28 then it will belong to the new **o** until the next Year
25:28 the land will be returned to the original **o**.
25:30 It will not be returned to the original **o** in the Year
25:31 and must be returned to the original **o** in the Year
27:24 to the original **o** from whom you purchased it.
Dt 22: 1 don't pretend not to see it. Take it back to its **o**.
22: 2 to someone nearby or you don't know who the **o**
is, keep it until the **o** comes looking for it;
24: 6 as a pledge, for the **o** uses it to make a living.
24:11 Stand outside and the **o** will bring it out to you.
24:13 Return the cloak to its **o** by sunset so your
1Ki 16:24 bought the hill now known as Samaria from its **o**,
Isa 1: 3 know their **o** and appreciate his care, but not my
Mt 20: 1 "For the Kingdom of Heaven is like the **o** of an
20: 7 "The **o** of the estate told them, 'Then go on out
21:37 "Finally, the **o** sent his son, thinking, 'Surely they
21:40 "When the **o** of the vineyard returns,"
Mk 12: 4 "The **o** then sent another servant, but they beat
12: 6 The **o** finally sent him, thinking, 'Surely they will
12: 9 "What do you suppose the **o** of the vineyard will
14:14 house he enters, say to the **o**, 'The Teacher asks,
Lk 5: 3 Jesus asked Simon, its **o**, to push it out into the
20:11 So the **o** sent another servant, but the same thing
20:13 " 'What will I do?' the **o** asked himself. 'I know!
20:15 "What do you suppose the **o** of the vineyard will
22:11 say to the **o**, 'The Teacher asks, Where is the guest
Ac 21:11 'So shall the **o** of this belt be bound by the Jewish
27:11 more to the ship's captain and the **o** than to Paul.

OWNER'S (1) [OWN]

Ex 21:21 not be punished, since the slave is the **o** property.

OWNERS (5) [OWN]

Ex 21:35 then the two **o** must sell the live bull and divide the
Job 31:39 or if I have stolen its crops or murdered its **o**,
Isa 5: 9 homes will stand deserted, the **o** dead or gone.
Lk 19:33 as they were untying it, the **o** asked them,
Col 4: 1 You slave **o** must be just and fair to your slaves.

OWNERSHIP (1) [OWN]

2Ch 21: 3 and also the **o** of some of Judah's fortified cities.

OWNS (12) [OWN]

Ge 24:36 and my master has given him everything he **o**.
38:25 "The man who **o** this identification seal
Ex 20:17 or donkey, or anything else your neighbor **o**."
22: 9 between two people as to who **o** a particular ox,
Lev 27:32 The LORD also **o** every tenth animal counted off
Dt 5:21 or donkey, or anything else your neighbor **o**.'
21:17 and who **o** the rights of the firstborn son,
2Sa 16: 4 "I give you everything Mephibosheth **o**."
Ps 95: 4 He **o** the depths of the earth, / and even the
La 1:10 taking everything precious that she **o**.
Mt 24:47 master will put that servant in charge of all he **o**.
Lk 12:44 master will put that servant in charge of all he **o**.

OX (46) [OXEN]

Ex 20:17 male or female servant, **o** or donkey,
21:33 to cover it, and then an **o** or a donkey falls into it.
22: 1 "A fine must be paid by anyone who steals an **o**
22: 4 If someone steals an **o** or a donkey or a sheep
22: 9 between two people as to who owns a particular **o**,
22:10 **o**, sheep, or any other animal, but it dies or is
23: 4 "If you come upon your enemy's **o** or donkey that
23:12 This will give your **o** and your donkey a chance to
Nu 7: 3 cart for every two leaders and an **o** for each leader.
22: 4 everything in sight, like an **o** devours grass!"
23:22 them out of Egypt; / he is like a strong **o** for them.
24: 8 up from Egypt, / drawing them along like a wild **o**.
Dt 5:21 or land, male or female servant, **o** or donkey,
14: 4 the animals you may eat: the **o**, the sheep, the goat,
14:26 you want—an **o**, a sheep, some wine, or beer.
17: 1 "Never sacrifice a sick or defective **o** or sheep to
22: 1 "If you see your neighbor's **o** or sheep wandering
22: 4 "If you see your neighbor's **o** or donkey lying on
22:10 "Do not plow with an **o** and a donkey harnessed
25: 4 "Do not keep an **o** from eating as it treads out the
28:31 Your **o** will be butchered before your eyes, but you
33:17 his power is like the horns of a wild **o**.
Jdg 3:31 He killed six hundred Philistines with an **o** goad.
1Sa 12: 3 anointed one—whose **o** or donkey have I stolen?
13:21 ounce for sharpening an ax, a sickle, or an **o** goad.)
2Sa 6:13 and waited so David could sacrifice an **o**
24:22 and **o** yokes for wood to build a fire on the altar.
Ne 5:18 required at my expense for each day were one **o**,
Job 24: 3 A poor widow must surrender her valuable **o** as
39: 9 "Will the wild **o** consent to being tamed? Will it
39:10 Can you hitch a wild **o** to a plow? Will it plow a
39:11 Can you go away and trust the **o** to do your work?
40:15 I made it, just as I made you. It eats grass like an **o**.
Ps 69:31 will please the LORD more than sacrificing an **o**
106:20 their glorious God / for a statue of a grass-eating **o**!
Pr 7:22 like an **o** going to the slaughter or like a trapped
Isa 1: 3 the donkey and the **o**—know their owner
46: 1 and Nebo, are being hauled away on **o** carts.
65:25 feed together. The lion will eat straw like the **o**.
66: 3 When such people sacrifice an **o**, it is no more
Eze 1:10 on the right side, the face of an **o** on the left side,
10:14 the first was the face of an **o**, the second was a
Lk 13:15 Don't you untie your **o** or your donkey from their
1Co 9: 9 "Do not keep an **o** from eating as it treads out the
1Ti 5:18 "Do not keep an **o** from eating as it treads out the
Rev 4: 7 the second looked like an **o**; the third had a human

OXEN (74) [OX]

Ge 20:14 Then Abimelech took sheep and **o** and servants—
21:27 Then Abraham gave sheep and **o** to Abimelech,
32: 5 and now I own **o**, donkeys, sheep, goats, and many
49: 6 murdered men, / and they crippled **o** just for sport.
Ex 22: 1 For **o** the fine is five **o** for each one stolen.
Lev 7:23 never eat fat, whether from **o** or sheep or goats.
Nu 7: 3 Together they brought six carts and twelve **o**.
7: 5 "Receive their gifts and use these **o** and carts for
7: 6 So Moses presented the carts and **o** to the Levites.
7: 7 and four **o** to the Gershonite division for their
7: 8 and eight **o** to the Merarite division for their work.
7: 9 none of the carts or **o** to the Kohathite division,
7:17 and two **o**, five rams, five male goats, and five
7:23 and two **o**, five rams, five male goats, and five
7:29 and two **o**, five rams, five male goats, and five
7:35 and two **o**, five rams, five male goats, and five
7:41 and two **o**, five rams, five male goats, and five
7:47 and two **o**, five rams, five male goats, and five
7:53 and two **o**, five rams, five male goats, and five

7:59 and two **o**, five rams, five male goats, and five
7:65 and two **o**, five rams, five male goats, and five
7:71 and two **o**, five rams, five male goats, and five
7:77 and two **o**, five rams, five male goats, and five
7:83 and two **o**, five rams, five male goats, and five
Dt 5:14 your **o** and donkeys and other livestock,
18:3 the priests may claim as their share from the **o**
Jdg 6:4 nothing to eat, taking all the sheep, **o**, and donkeys.
1Sa 11:7 He took two **o** and cut them into pieces and sent
11:7 "This is what will happen to the **o** of anyone who
2Sa 6:6 the **o** stumbled, and Uzzah put out his hand to
24:22 "Here are **o** for the burnt offering, and you can use
24:24 pieces of silver for the threshing floor and the **o**.
1Ki 1:9 where he sacrificed sheep, **o**, and fattened calves.
1:19 He has sacrificed many **o**, fattened calves,
1:25 Today he has sacrificed many **o**, fattened calves,
4:23 ten **o** from the fattening pens, twenty pasture-fed
7:25 The Sea rested on a base of twelve bronze **o**,
7:29 were decorated with carved lions, **o**, and cherubim.
7:29 and below the lions and **o** were wreath decorations.
7:44 the Sea and the twelve **o** under it,
8:5 and **o** before the Ark in such numbers that no one
8:63 peace offerings to the LORD numbering 22,000 **o**
19:19 son of Shaphat plowing a field with a team of **o**.
19:19 There were eleven teams of **o** ahead of him,
19:20 Elisha left the **o** standing there, ran after Elijah,
19:21 Elisha then returned to his **o**, killed them, and used
2Ki 5:26 and vineyards and sheep and **o** and servants?
16:17 removed the Sea from the backs of the bronze **o**
1Ch 12:40 brought food on donkeys, camels, mules, and **o**.
13:9 the **o** stumbled, and Uzzah put out his hand to
21:23 "Here are **o** for the burnt offerings, and you can
2Ch 4:3 its rim by two rows of figures that resembled **o**.
4:3 There were about six **o** per foot all the way around,
4:4 The Sea rested on a base of twelve bronze **o**,
4:15 the Sea and the twelve **o** under it,
5:6 and **o** before the Ark in such numbers that no one
7:5 King Solomon offered a sacrifice of 22,000 **o**
15:11 seven hundred **o** and seven thousand sheep
18:2 great numbers of sheep and **o** for the feast.
Ezr 8:35 They presented twelve **o** for the people of Israel,
Job 1:3 three thousand camels, five hundred teams of **o**,
1:14 "Your **o** were plowing, with the donkeys feeding
6:5 no green grass, and **o** low when they have no food.
42:12 six thousand camels, one thousand teams of **o**,
Ps 22:21 lions' jaws, / and from the horns of these wild **o**.
144:14 and may our **o** be loaded down with produce.
Isa 30:24 The **o** and donkeys that till the ground will eat
Jer 51:23 and flocks, farmers and **o**, captains and rulers.
Am 6:12 Can **o** be used to plow rocks? Stupid even to ask—
Lk 14:19 Another said he had just bought five pair of **o**
Jn 2:15 He drove out the sheep and **o**, scattered the money
Ac 14:13 and the crowd brought **o** and wreaths of flowers,
1Co 9:9 Do you suppose God was thinking only about **o**

OZEM (2)
1Ch 2:15 his sixth was **O**, and his seventh was David.
2:25 Ram (the oldest), Bunah, Oren, **O**, and Ahijah.

OZIAS [KJV] See UZZIAH

OZNI (1) [OZNITE]
Nu 26:16 The Oznite clan, named after its ancestor **O**.

OZNITE (1) [OZNI]
Nu 26:16 The **O** clan, named after its ancestor Ozni.

P

PAARAI (2)
2Sa 23:35 Hezro from Carmel; / **P** from Arba;
1Ch 11:37 Hezro from Carmel; / **P** son of Ezbai;

PACE (2)
Ge 33:14 We will follow at our own **p** and meet you at
2Sa 16:13 and Shimei kept **p** with them on a nearby hillside,

PACIFIED (1) [PEACE]
Est 7:10 set up for Mordecai, and the king's anger was **p**.

PACIFIES (1) [PEACE]
Pr 21:14 A secret gift calms anger; a secret bribe **p** fury.

PACK (14) [PACKED]
Ge 45:17 "Tell your brothers to load their **p** animals
2Ki 3:9 there was no water for the men or their **p** animals.
Ne 2:12 We took no **p** animals with us, except the donkey
Ps 22:16 My enemies surround me like a **p** of dogs; / an evil
Jer 10:17 "**P** your bag and prepare to leave; the siege is
46:19 **P** up! Get ready to leave for exile, you citizens of
Eze 12:3 **P** whatever you can carry on your back and leave
12:6 lift your **p** to your shoulders and walk away into
12:7 In broad daylight I brought my **p** outside,
12:7 and went out into the darkness with my **p** on my
Na 3:14 into the pits to trample clay, and **p** it into molds!
Mt 24:17 A person outside the house must not go inside to **p**.
Mk 13:15 the house must not go back into the house to **p**.
Lk 17:31 outside the house must not go into the house to **p**.

PACKED (5) [PACK]
1Sa 15:6 up from Egypt." So the Kenites **p** up and left.
25:18 She **p** them on donkeys and said to her servants,
Mk 2:2 so **p** with visitors that there wasn't room for one
Lk 15:13 "A few days later this younger son **p** all his
Ac 21:15 Shortly afterward we **p** our things and left for

PACT (5)
1Sa 18:4 and he sealed the **p** by giving him his robe, tunic,
20:42 for we have made a **p** in the LORD's name.
2Ki 11:4 He made a **p** with them and made them swear an
2Ch 23:1 and made a **p** with five army commanders:
Isa 33:8 The Assyrians have broken their peace **p** and care

PADDAN (1) [PADDAN-ARAM]
Ge 48:7 As I was returning from **P**, Rachel died in the land

PADDAN-ARAM (9) [PADDAN]
Ge 25:20 the daughter of Bethuel the Aramean from **P**
28:2 Instead, go at once to **P**, to the house of your
28:5 and he went to **P** to stay with his uncle Laban,
28:6 had blessed Jacob and sent him to **P** to find a wife,
28:7 that Jacob had obeyed his parents and gone to **P**.
31:18 of him—all the livestock he had acquired at **P**—
35:9 when he arrived at Bethel after traveling from **P**.
35:26 and Asher. These were the sons born to Jacob at **P**.
46:15 are the sons of Jacob who were born to Leah in **P**,

PADON (2)
Ezr 2:44 Keros, Siaha, **P**,
Ne 7:47 Keros, Siaha, **P**,

PAGAN (121) [PAGANS]
Ex 32:6 and indulged themselves in **p** revelry.
34:13 Instead, you must break down their **p** altars,
Lev 26:30 I will destroy your **p** shrines and cut down your
Nu 33:52 molten images and demolish all their **p** shrines.
Dt 7:5 you must break down their **p** altars and shatter
12:4 God in the way these **p** peoples worship their gods.
Jdg 14:3 Why must you go to the **p** Philistines to find a
15:18 of thirst and fall into the hands of these **p** people?"
1Sa 17:26 "Who is this **p** Philistine anyway, that he is
17:36 and bears, and I'll do it to this **p** Philistine, too,
31:4 and kill me before these **p** Philistines run me
31:9 the news of Saul's death in their **p** temple
1Ki 12:31 Jeroboam built shrines at the **p** high places
12:32 he appointed priests for the **p** shrines he had made.
13:2 On you he will sacrifice the priests from the **p**
13:32 and against the **p** shrines in the towns of Samaria
13:33 wanted to could become a priest for the **p** shrines.
14:23 They built **p** shrines and set up sacred pillars
14:24 **p** nations the LORD had driven from the land
15:14 Although the **p** shrines were not completely
22:43 however, he failed to remove all the **p** shrines,
2Ki 3:13 "Go to the **p** prophets of your father and mother!"
12:3 Yet even so, he did not destroy the **p** shrines,
14:4 Amaziah did not destroy the **p** shrines,
15:4 But he did not destroy the **p** shrines,
15:35 But he did not destroy the **p** shrines,
16:3 He imitated the detestable practices of the **p**
16:4 and burned incense at the **p** shrines and on the hills
17:8 They had imitated the practices of the **p** nations the
17:9 They built **p** shrines for themselves in all their
17:29 they placed their idols at the **p** shrines that the
17:32 priests to offer sacrifices at the **p** shrines.
18:4 He removed the **p** shrines, smashed the sacred
21:2 imitating the detestable practices of the **p** nations
21:3 He rebuilt the **p** shrines his father, Hezekiah,
21:4 He even built **p** altars in the Temple of the
21:9 **p** nations whom the LORD had destroyed when
22:17 people have abandoned me and worshiped **p** gods,
23:5 He did away with the **p** priests, who had been
23:5 for they had burned incense at the **p** shrines
23:8 He also defiled all the **p** shrines, where they had
23:9 The priests who had served at the **p** shrines were
23:13 The king also desecrated the **p** shrines east of
23:15 the **p** shrine that Jeroboam son of Nebat had made
23:19 Then Josiah demolished all the buildings at the **p**
23:20 He executed the priests of the **p** shrines on their
1Ch 10:4 and run me through before these **p** Philistines
2Ch 11:15 appointed his own priests to serve at the **p** shrines,
13:9 appointed your own priests, just like the **p** nations.
14:3 He removed the **p** altars and the shrines.
14:5 Asa also removed the **p** shrines, as well as the
15:17 Although the **p** shrines were not completely
17:6 He knocked down the **p** shrines and destroyed the
20:33 however, he failed to remove all the **p** shrines,
21:11 He had built **p** shrines in the hill country of Judah
21:11 and Judah to give themselves to **p** gods.
28:3 He imitated the detestable practices of the **p**
28:4 and burned incense at the **p** shrines and on the hills
28:24 then set up altars to **p** gods in every corner of
28:25 He made **p** shrines in all the towns of Judah for
30:14 to work and removed the **p** altars from Jerusalem.
31:1 and removed the **p** shrines and altars.
32:19 of Jerusalem as though he were one of the **p** gods,
33:2 imitating the detestable practices of the **p** nations
33:3 He rebuilt the **p** shrines his father Hezekiah had
33:4 He even built **p** altars in the Temple of the
33:9 and Jerusalem to do even more evil than the **p**
33:17 the people still sacrificed at the **p** shrines,
33:19 a list of the locations where he built **p** shrines
34:3 and Jerusalem, destroying all the **p** shrines,
34:5 Then he burned the bones of the **p** priests on their
34:7 He destroyed the **p** altars and the Asherah poles,
34:25 Judah have abandoned me and worshiped **p** gods,
36:14 They followed the **p** practices of the surrounding
Ezr 9:7 and our priests have been at the mercy of the **p**
10:2 for we have married these **p** women of the land.
10:3 a covenant with our God to divorce our **p** wives
10:10 "You have sinned, for you have married **p** women.
10:11 the people of the land and from these **p** women."
10:14 Everyone who has a **p** wife will come at the
10:17 dealing with all the men who had married **p** wives.
10:18 These are the priests who had married **p** wives:
10:44 Each of these men had a **p** wife, and some even
Ne 5:8 who have had to sell themselves to **p** foreigners,
9:30 So once again you allowed the **p** inhabitants of the
10:28 and all who had separated themselves from the **p**
10:30 "We promise not to let our daughters marry the **p**
13:25 children intermarry with the **p** people of the land.
Ps 44:2 You drove out the **p** nations / and gave all the land
79:1 O God, **p** nations have conquered your land,
79:10 Why should **p** nations be allowed to scoff, / asking,
80:8 you drove away the **p** nations and transplanted us
86:8 Nowhere among the **p** gods is there a god like you,
105:44 He gave his people the lands of **p** nations,
106:41 He handed them over to **p** nations, / and those who
Isa 27:9 has finished, all the **p** altars will be crushed to dust.
48:11 the **p** nations will not be able to claim that their
Jer 7:31 They have built the **p** shrines of Topheth in the
9:26 Like all these **p** nations, the people of Israel also
17:3 and treasures—together with your **p** shrines—
18:13 heard of such a thing, even among the **p** nations?
19:5 They have built **p** shrines to Baal, and there they
32:35 They have built **p** shrines to Baal in the valley of
48:35 "for they offer sacrifices at the **p** shrines and burn
Eze 6:3 war upon you, and I will destroy your **p** shrines.
6:6 I will destroy your **p** shrines, your altars,
16:24 you built a **p** shrine and put altars to idols in every
16:31 You build your **p** shrines on every street corner
16:39 They will knock down your **p** shrines and the altars
Hos 10:8 And the **p** shrines of Aven, the place of Israel's
Joel 3:5 and you have carried them off to your **p** temples.
Am 3:14 for its sins, I will destroy the **p** altars at Bethel.
5:26 No, your real interest was in your **p** gods—
7:9 The **p** shrines of your ancestors and the temples of
Mic 5:14 I will abolish your **p** shrines with their Asherah
Zep 1:8 princes of Judah and all those following **p** customs.
1:9 I will punish those who participate in **p** worship
Mt 18:17 treat that person as a **p** or a corrupt tax collector.
Ac 7:43 No, your real interest was in your **p** gods—
Ro 2:22 but do you steal from **p** temples?
1Co 10:7 and they indulged themselves in **p** revelry."

PAGANS (9) [PAGAN]
1Sa 14:6 "Let's go across to see those **p**," Jonathan said to
2Sa 1:20 of Ashkelon, / or the **p** will laugh in triumph.
Ps 106:35 Instead, they mingled among the **p** / and adopted
Mt 5:47 you different from anyone else? Even **p** do that.
6:32 Why be like the **p** who are so deeply concerned
1Co 5:1 something so evil that even the **p** don't do it.
10:19 Am I saying that the idols to whom the **p** bring
12:2 You know that when you were still **p** you were led
1Th 4:5 not in lustful passion as the **p** do, in their ignorance

PAGIEL (5)
Nu 1:13 Asher | **P** son of Ocran
2:27[-28] Asher | **P** son of Ocran | 41,500
7:72 On the eleventh day **P** son of Ocran, leader of the
7:77 This was the offering brought by **P** son of Ocran.
10:26 The tribe of Asher was led by **P** son of Ocran.

PAHATH-MOAB (6)
Ezr 2:6 The family of **P** (descendants of Jeshua and Joab)
8:4 From the family of **P**: Eliehoenai son of Zerahiah
10:30 From the family of **P**: Adna, Kelal, Benaiah,
Ne 3:11 Malkijah son of Harim and Hasshub son of **P**,
7:11 The family of **P** (descendants of Jeshua and Joab)
10:14 who signed were Parosh, **P**, Elam, Zattu, Bani,

PAID (57) [PAY]
Ge 23:16 So Abraham **p** Ephron the amount he had
30:16 "I have **p** for you with some mandrake roots my
30:26 You know I have fully **p** for them with my service
42:35 of each one was the bag of money **p** for the grain.
Ex 22:1 "A fine must be **p** by anyone who steals an ox
Lev 19:20 someone else's wife, compensation must be **p**.
24:20 does to hurt another person must be **p** back in kind.
Jdg 1:7 Now God has **p** me back for what I did to them."
11:28 But the king of Ammon **p** no attention to
15:11 "I only **p** them back for what they did to me."
1Sa 25:39 who has **p** back Nabal and kept me from doing it
2Sa 24:24 So David **p** him fifty pieces of silver for the
1Ki 12:15 So the king **p** no attention to the people's demands.
2Ki 12:12 and they **p** any other expenses related to the
12:14 It was **p** out to the workmen, who used it for the
15:19 But Menahem **p** him thirty-seven tons of silver to
24:1 and **p** him tribute for three years but then rebelled.
2Ch 10:15 So the king **p** no attention to the people's demands.
25:6 He also **p** about 7,500 pounds of silver to hire
25:9 "But what should I do about the silver I **p** to hire
26:8 The Meunites **p** annual tribute to him, and his fame

34:10 Then they **p** the workers who did the repairs
Ezr 6:4 All expenses will be **p** by the royal treasury.
Ne 8:3 All the people **p** close attention to the Book of the
Job 7:2 for the day to end, like a servant waiting to be **p**.
Ps 66:19 But God did listen! / He **p** attention to my prayer.
111:9 He has **p** a full ransom for his people. / He has
Pr 1:24 I reached out to you, but you **p** no attention.
1:30 and **p** no attention when I corrected them.
Isa 34:8 the year when Edom will be **p** back for all it did to
44:22 to me, for I have **p** the price to set you free."
Jer 3:8 she **p** no attention. She saw that I had divorced
5:3 You struck your people, but they **p** no attention.
32:10 weighed out the silver, and **p** him.
51:35 "May the people of Babylonia be **p** in full for all
Mic 3:11 you prophets won't prophesy unless you are **p**.
Mt 5:26 won't be free again until you have **p** the last penny.
18:30 and jailed until the debt could be **p** in full.
18:34 sent the man to prison until he had **p** every penny.
20:9 When those hired at five o'clock were **p**,
20:10 receive more. But they, too, were **p** a day's wage.
20:12 and yet you've **p** them just as much as you **p** us
27:6 "since it's against the law to accept money **p** for
Lk 12:59 you won't be free again until you have **p** the last
Jn 4:36 The harvesters are **p** good wages, and the fruit they
12:21 **p** a visit to Philip, who was from Bethsaida in
Ac 18:17 there in the courtroom. But Gallio **p** no attention.
Ro 13:6 For government workers need to be **p** so they can
1Co 9:10 Christian workers should be **p** by those they serve.
Col 3:25 you will be **p** back for the wrong you have done.
1Ti 5:17 Elders who do their work well should be **p** well,
Heb 7:8 of Jewish priests, tithes are **p** to men who will die.
7:9 **p** a tithe to Melchizedek through their ancestor
1Pe 1:18 For you know that God **p** a ransom to save you
1:18 And the ransom he **p** was not mere gold or silver.
1:19 He **p** for you with the precious lifeblood of Christ,

PAIN (49) [PAINED, PAINFUL, PAINLESS, PAINS]

Ge 3:16 "You will bear children with intense **p**
Jos 23:13 to you, a **p** in your side and a thorn in your eyes,
2Sa 1:9 my misery, for I am in terrible **p** and want to die.'
1Ch 4:10 all that I do, and keep me from all trouble and **p**!"
Job 6:10 Despite the **p**, I have not denied the words of the
9:28 I would dread all the **p** he would send. For I know
14:22 They are absorbed in their own **p** and grief."
15:20 "Wicked people are in **p** throughout their lives.
30:17 My weary nights are filled with **p** as though
33:19 Or God disciplines people with sickness and **p**,
Ps 25:18 Feel my **p** and see my trouble. / Forgive all my
38:6 I am bent over and racked with **p**. / My days are
38:17 I am on the verge of collapse, / facing constant **p**.
41:3 they are sick / and eases their **p** and discomfort.
48:6 like a woman writhing in the **p** of childbirth
69:26 they scoff at the **p** of those you have hurt.
69:29 I am suffering and in **p**. / Rescue me, O God,
73:14 trouble all day long; / every morning brings me **p**.
90:10 But even the best of these years are filled with **p**
109:22 I am poor and needy, / and my heart is full of **p**.
Pr 10:26 Lazy people are a **p** to their employer. They are
Ecc 2:23 Their days of labor are filled with **p** and grief;
11:10 So banish grief and **p**, but remember that youth,
SS 8:5 gave you birth, where in great **p** she delivered you.
Isa 17:11 only harvest will be a load of grief and incurable **p**.
21:3 My stomach aches and burns with **p**. Sharp pangs
26:17 about to give birth, / writhing and crying out in **p**.
Jer 4:19 My heart, my heart—I writhe in **p**! My heart
6:24 Fear and **p** have gripped us, like that of a woman
13:21 You will writhe in **p** like a woman giving birth!
45:3 with trouble! Haven't I had enough **p** already?
49:24 and **p** have gripped her as they do a woman giving
50:43 Fear and **p** have gripped him, like that of a woman
51:29 Babylon trembles and writhes in **p**, for everything
Eze 30:16 Pelusium will be racked with **p**; Thebes will be
30:24 he will lie there mortally wounded, groaning in **p**.
Mic 4:9 **P** has gripped you like it does a woman in labor.
4:10 Writhe and groan in terrible **p**, you people of
Mt 4:24 And whatever their illness and **p**, or if they were
8:6 servant lies in bed, paralyzed and racked with **p**."
Ro 8:23 also groan to be released from **p** and suffering.
2Co 2:2 For if I cause you **p** and make you sad, who is
7:9 but because the **p** caused you to have remorse
11:27 lived with weariness and **p** and sleepless nights.
Heb 13:3 as though you feel their **p** in your own bodies.
1Pe 4:1 So then, since Christ suffered physical **p**, you must
Rev 9:5 months with agony like the **p** of scorpion stings.
12:2 and she cried out in the **p** of labor as she awaited
21:4 will be no more death or sorrow or crying or **p**.

PAINED (1) [PAIN]

Ps 73:21 I had become, / how **p** I had been by all I had seen.

PAINFUL (9) [PAIN]

Ge 5:29 "He will bring us relief from the **p** labor of
1Ch 4:9 named him Jabez because his birth had been so **p**.
Job 6:25 Honest words are **p**, but what do your criticisms
Pr 17:21 It is **p** to be the parent of a fool; there is no joy for
2Co 2:1 I won't make them unhappy with another **p** visit."
2:4 How **p** it was to write that letter! Heartbroken,
7:8 for I know that it was **p** to you for a little while.
Php 1:17 intending to make my chains more **p** to me.
Heb 12:11 is enjoyable while it is happening—it is **p**!

PAINLESS (1) [PAIN]

Ps 73:4 They seem to live such a **p** life; / their bodies are

PAINS (10) [PAIN]

Ge 35:16 But Rachel's **p** of childbirth began while they were
1Sa 4:19 were dead, her labor **p** suddenly began.
Ps 120:5 It **p** me to live with these people from Kedar!
Isa 66:7 "Before the birth **p** even begin, Jerusalem gives
66:8 But by the time Jerusalem's birth **p** begin, the baby
Jn 16:21 It will be like a woman experiencing the **p** of labor.
Ro 8:22 in the **p** of childbirth right up to the present time.
Gal 4:19 I feel as if I am going through labor **p** for you
1Th 5:3 birth **p** begin when her child is about to be born.
Rev 16:11 and they cursed the God of heaven for their **p**

PAINTED (5) [PAINTINGS]

2Ki 9:30 she **p** her eyelids and fixed her hair and sat at a
Jer 22:14 throughout with fragrant cedar and **p** a lovely red.'
La 2:14 Instead, they **p** false pictures, filling you with false
Eze 23:14 She fell in love with pictures that were **p** on a
23:40 you bathed yourselves, **p** your eyelids,

PAINTINGS (1) [PAINTED]

Eze 23:16 When she saw these **p**, she longed to give herself

PAIR (20) [PAIRS]

Ge 6:19 Bring a **p** of every kind of animal—a male and a
7:2 for sacrifice, and take one **p** of each of the others.
7:3 and a female in each **p** to ensure that every kind of
8:19 kinds of animals and birds came out, **p** by **p**.
27:16 She made him a **p** of gloves from the hairy skin of
Ex 25:35 One blossom will be set beneath each **p** of
37:21 One blossom was set beneath each **p** of branches,
Lev 14:22 One of the **p** must be used for a sin offering
Dt 24:6 "It is wrong to take a **p** of millstones, or even just
Jdg 15:4 in pairs, and he fastened a torch to each **p** of tails.
Isa 6:6 and he picked up a burning coal with a **p** of tongs.
Eze 1:11 one **p** stretched out to touch the wings of the living
1:11 either side of it, and the other **p** covered its body.
Am 2:6 for silver and poor people for a **p** of sandals.
8:6 for a debt of one piece of silver or a **p** of sandals.
Lk 2:24 "either a **p** of turtledoves or two young pigeons."
10:4 or a traveler's bag, or even an extra **p** of sandals.
14:19 Another said he had just bought five **p** of oxen
Rev 6:5 and its rider was holding a **p** of scales in his hand.

PAIRS (9) [PAIR]

Ge 6:20 **P** of each kind of bird and each kind of animal,
7:2 Take along seven **p** of each animal that I have
7:3 Then select seven **p** of every kind of bird.
7:9 They came into the boat in **p**, male and female,
7:14 With them in the boat were **p** of every kind of
Jdg 15:4 He tied their tails together in **p**, and he fastened a
Eze 1:6 except that each had four faces and two **p** of wings.
1:11 Each had two **p** of outstretched wings—one pair
Lk 10:1 and sent them on ahead in **p** to all the towns

PALACE (193) [PALACES]

Ge 12:15 When the **p** officials saw her, they sang her praises
20:2 sent for her and had her brought to him at his **p**.
37:36 king of Egypt. Potiphar was captain of the **p** guard.
39:1 of Egypt. Potiphar was the captain of the **p** guard.
40:3 in the **p** of Potiphar, the captain of the guard.
41:10 and you imprisoned us in the **p** of the captain of
43:17 did as he was told and took them to Joseph's **p**.
43:19 As the brothers arrived at the entrance to the **p**,
43:24 The brothers were then led into the **p** and given
45:2 His sobs could be heard throughout the **p**,
45:2 and the news was quickly carried to Pharaoh's **p**.
Ex 7:23 Pharaoh returned to his **p** and put the whole thing
8:24 There were terrible swarms of flies in Pharaoh's **p**
10:11 And Pharaoh threw them out of the **p**.
Nu 22:18 "Even if Balak were to give me a **p** filled with
24:13 'Even if Balak were to give me a **p** filled with
1Sa 18:2 that day on Saul kept David with him at the **p**
2Sa 5:11 with carpenters and stonemasons to build him a **p**.
7:1 When the king was settled in his **p** and the LORD
7:2 "Here I am living in this beautiful cedar **p**,
9:7 and you may live here with me at the **p**!"
9:10 But Mephibosheth will live here at the **p** with
9:13 in both feet, moved to Jerusalem to live at the **p**.
11:2 a nap and went for a stroll on the roof of the **p**.
11:4 and when she came to the **p**, he slept with her.
11:8 even sent a gift to Uriah after he had left the **p**.
11:9 He stayed that night at the **p** entrance with some of
11:13 home to his wife. Again he slept at the **p** entrance.
11:27 David sent for her and brought her to the **p**,
12:20 After that, he returned to the **p** and ate.
15:16 except ten of his concubines to keep the **p** in order.
16:22 So they set up a tent on the **p** roof where everyone
20:3 When the king arrived at his **p** in Jerusalem,
1Ki 3:1 City of David until he could finish building his **p**
4:6 Ahishar was manager of **p** affairs. / Adoniram son
4:22 The daily food requirements for Solomon's **p** were
7:1 Solomon also built a **p** for himself, and it took him
7:2 One of Solomon's buildings was called the **P** of
9:1 the Temple of the LORD, as well as the royal **p**.
9:10 built the Temple of the LORD and the royal **p**,
9:15 the royal **p**, the Millo, the wall of Jerusalem,
9:24 from the City of David to the new **p** he had built
10:4 and when she saw the **p** he had built,
10:12 for the Temple of the LORD and the royal **p**,
10:17 The king placed these shields in the **P** of the Forest
10:21 as were all the utensils in the **P** of the Forest of
11:20 who was brought up in Pharaoh's **p** among
13:7 "Come to the **p** with me and have something to
14:26 the LORD and the royal **p** and stole everything,
14:27 and he entrusted them to the care of the **p** guard
15:18 treasuries of the LORD's Temple and the royal **p**.
16:9 drunk at the home of Arza, the supervisor of the **p**.
18:3 summoned Obadiah, who was in charge of the **p**.
20:6 tomorrow I will send my officials to search your **p**
21:1 King Ahab had a **p** in Jezreel, and near the **p** was a vineyard owned by a man
21:2 "Since your vineyard is so convenient to the **p**,
22:39 events in Ahab's reign and the story of the ivory **p**
2Ki 1:2 latticework of an upper room at his **p** in Samaria,
7:9 let's go back and tell the people at the **p**."
7:11 shouted the news to the people in the **p**.
9:31 When Jehu entered the gate of the **p**, she shouted at
9:34 Then Jehu went into the **p** and ate and drank.
10:5 So the **p** and city administrators, together with the
11:5 duty on the Sabbath are to guard the royal **p** itself.
11:6 And the final third must stand guard behind the **p**
11:6 These three groups will all guard the **p**.
11:16 and led her out to the gate where horses enter the **p**
11:19 went through the gate of the guards and into the **p**,
11:20 because Athaliah had been killed at the king's **p**.
12:18 treasuries of the LORD's Temple and the royal **p**.
14:14 of the LORD, as well as from the **p** treasury.
15:5 king's son Jotham was put in charge of the royal **p**,
15:25 and Arieh, in the citadel of the **p** at Samaria.
16:8 and the **p** treasury and sent it as a gift to the
16:18 inside the **p** for use on the Sabbath day,
18:15 in the Temple of the LORD and in the **p** treasury.
18:18 Eliakim son of Hilkiah, the **p** administrator,
18:37 the **p** administrator, Shebna the court secretary,
19:2 And he sent Eliakim the **p** administrator,
20:13 There was nothing in his **p** or kingdom that
20:15 "What did they see in your **p**?" Isaiah asked.
20:18 They will become eunuchs who will serve in the **p**
21:18 he was buried in the **p** garden, the garden of Uzza.
21:23 plotted against him and assassinated him in his **p**.
23:12 built on the **p** roof above the upper room of Ahaz.
24:13 from the LORD's Temple and the royal **p**.
25:9 the royal **p**, and all the houses of Jerusalem.
1Ch 14:1 with stonemasons and carpenters to build him a **p**.
17:1 Now when David was settled in his **p**, he said to
17:1 "Here I am living in this beautiful cedar **p**,
27:25 Azmaveth son of Adiel was in charge of the **p**
28:1 of the royal property and livestock, the **p** officials,
2Ch 2:1 a Temple for the LORD and a royal **p** for himself.
2:3 to my father, David, when he was building his **p**.
2:12 a Temple for the LORD and a royal **p** for himself.
7:11 the Temple of the LORD, as well as the royal **p**.
8:1 and his own royal **p** were completed.
8:11 from the City of David to the new **p** he had built
8:11 "My wife must not live in King David's **p**,
9:3 and when she saw the **p** he had built,
9:11 for the Temple of the LORD and the royal **p**,
9:16 The king placed these shields in the **P** of the Forest
9:20 as were all the utensils in the **P** of the Forest of
12:9 of the Temple of the LORD and of the royal **p**,
16:2 of the LORD's Temple and from the royal **p**.
21:17 carried away everything of value in the royal **p**,
23:5 Another third will go over to the royal **p**,
23:15 and led her out to the gate where horses enter the **p**
23:20 They went through the Upper Gate and into the **p**,
25:24 He also seized the treasures of the royal **p**,
26:21 His son Jotham was put in charge of the royal **p**,
28:7 Azrikam, the king's **p** commander; and Elkanah,
28:21 the royal **p**, and from the homes of his officials
33:20 When Manasseh died, he was buried at his **p**.
33:24 plotted against him and assassinated him in his **p**.
36:7 and he placed them in his **p** in Babylon.
36:18 from both the LORD's Temple and the royal **p**.
Est 1:5 the king gave a special banquet for all the **p**
1:5 and was held at Susa in the courtyard of the **p**
1:9 a banquet for the women of the **p** at the same time.
2:9 seven maids specially chosen from the king's **p**,
2:16 **p** in early winter of the seventh year of his reign,
2:19 and Mordecai had become a **p** official,
2:21 One day as Mordecai was on duty at the **p**, two of
3:3 Then the **p** officials at the king's gate asked
4:2 He stood outside the gate of the **p**, for no one was
4:6 out to Mordecai in the square in front of the **p** gate.
4:13 there in the **p** when all other Jews are killed.
4:14 but that you have been elevated to the **p** for just
5:1 her royal robes and entered the inner court of the **p**,
5:13 Mordecai the Jew just sitting there at the **p** gate."
6:4 Haman had just arrived in the outer court of the **p**
6:10 for Mordecai the Jew, who sits at the gate of the **p**.
6:12 Afterward Mordecai returned to the **p** gate,
7:7 to his feet in a rage and went out into the **p** garden.
7:8 just as the king returned from the **p** garden.
7:8 "Will he even assault the queen right here in the **p**,
9:4 For Mordecai had been promoted in the king's **p**,
Ps 45:15 enthusiastic procession / as they enter the king's **p**!
144:12 be like graceful pillars, / carved to beautify a **p**.
Isa 14:11 All the pleasant music in your **p** has ceased.
22:15 told me to confront Shebna, the **p** administrator,
32:14 The **p** and the city will be deserted, and busy towns
36:3 Eliakim son of Hilkiah, the **p** administrator,
36:22 the **p** administrator, Shebna the court secretary,
37:2 And he sent Eliakim the **p** administrator,
39:2 There was nothing in his **p** or kingdom that
39:4 "What did they see in your **p**?" asked Isaiah.
39:7 They will become eunuchs who will serve in the **p**
Jer 19:13 including the **p** of Judah's kings, will become like
22:4 The king will ride through the **p** gates in chariots
22:5 that this **p** will become a pile of rubble.' "
22:6 is what the LORD says concerning the royal **p**:
22:13 for Jehoiakim, who builds his **p** with forced labor.
22:14 'I will build a magnificent **p** with huge rooms

22:15 "But a beautiful **p** does not make a great king!
22:23 It may be nice to live in a beautiful **p** lined with
26:10 they rushed over from the **p** and sat down at the
27:18 and in the king's **p** and in the palaces of Jerusalem.
27:21 kept in the Temple and in the **p** of Judah's king:
30:18 The **p** will be reconstructed as it was before.
32: 2 in the courtyard of the guard in the royal **p**.
33: 4 and even the king's **p** to get materials to strengthen
35: 4 was located next to the one used by the **p** officials,
36:12 he went down to the secretary's room in the **p**
36:22 and the king was in a winterized part of the **p**,
37:17 secretly requested that Jeremiah come to the **p**,
37:21 in the courtyard of the guard in the royal **p**.
37:21 in the city. So Jeremiah was put in the **p** prison.
38: 7 the Ethiopian, an important **p** official,
38: 8 so Ebed-melech rushed from the **p** to speak with
38:11 and went to a room in the **p** beneath the treasury,
38:13 of the guard—the **p** prison—where he remained.
38:22 All the women left in your **p** will be brought out
39: 8 the Babylonians burned Jerusalem, including the **p**,
41:16 warriors, women, children, and **p** officials.
43: 9 at the entrance of Pharaoh's **p** here in Tahpanhes.
52:13 the royal **p**, and all the houses of Jerusalem.
Da 1: 3 who was in charge of the **p** officials,
1: 3 to bring to the **p** some of the young men of Judah's
1: 4 and have the poise needed to serve in the royal **p**.
4: 4 was living in my **p** in comfort and prosperity.
4:29 he was taking a walk on the flat roof of the royal **p**
5: 5 hand writing on the plaster wall of the king's **p**,
6:18 Then the king returned to his **p** and spent the night
Am 1: 4 So I will send down fire on King Hazael's **p**,
Na 2: 6 The enemy has entered! The **p** is about to collapse!
Mk 6:21 and he gave a party for his **p** aides, army officers,
Lk 11:21 who is completely armed, guards his **p**, it is safe—
Ac 7:10 and put him in charge of all the affairs of the **p**.
Php 1:13 including all the soldiers in the **p** guard,
4:22 too, especially those who work in Caesar's **p**.

PALACES (24) [PALACE]

Ex 10: 6 They will overrun your **p** and the homes of your
2Ch 36:19 down the walls of Jerusalem, burned all the **p**,
Job 3:15 I would rest with wealthy princes whose **p** were
Ps 45: 8 aloes, and cassia. / In **p** decorated with ivory,
122: 7 peace within your walls / and prosperity in your **p**.
Pr 30:28 to catch, / but they are found even in kings' **p**.
Isa 13: 2 march against Babylon to destroy the **p** of the high
13:22 and jackals will make their dens in its **p**.
23:13 torn down its **p**, and turned it into a heap of rubble.
25: 2 Beautiful **p** in distant lands disappear and will
34:13 Thorns will overrun its **p**; nettles will grow in its
Jer 6: 5 So let us attack by night and destroy her **p**!' "
17:27 The fire will spread to the **p**, and no one will be
27:18 and in the king's palace and in the **p** of Jerusalem.
49:27 Damascus that will burn up the **p** of Ben-hadad."
La 2: 5 He has destroyed her forts and **p**. He has brought
2: 7 He has given Jerusalem's **p** to her enemies.
4: 5 Those who once lived in **p** now search the garbage
Hos 8:14 "Israel has built great **p**, and Judah has fortified its
8:14 I will send down fire on their **p** and burn their
Am 3:15 summer houses, too—all their **p** filled with ivory.
Zep 2:14 of many kinds will live among the ruins of its **p**,
Mt 11: 8 Those who dress like that live in **p**, not out in the
Lk 7:25 beautiful clothes and live in luxury are found in **p**,

PALAL (1)

Ne 3:25 **P** son of Uzai carried on the work from a point

PALE (13)

Lev 13:39 If the patch is only a **p** white, this is a harmless
Nu 11: 7 like small coriander seeds, **p** yellow in color.
Est 7: 6 Haman grew **p** with fright before the king
Isa 29:22 "My people will no longer **p** with fear or be
Da 1:10 "If you become **p** and thin compared to the other
5: 6 and his face turned **p** with fear. Such terror gripped
5:10 live the king! Don't be so **p** and afraid about this.
7:28 by my thoughts and my face was **p** with fear,
10: 8 My strength left me, my face grew deathly **p**,
Joel 2: 6 grips all the people; every face grows **p** with fright.
Na 2:10 people stand aghast, their faces **p** and trembling.
Mt 6:16 who try to look **p** and disheveled so people will
Rev 6: 8 and saw a horse whose color was **p** green like a

PALESTINA, PALESTINE [KJV] See PHILISTIA

PALLU (5) [PALLUITE]

Ge 46: 9 of Reuben were Hanoch, **P**, Hezron, and Carmi.
Ex 6:14 included Hanoch, **P**, Hezron, and Carmi.
Nu 26: 5 The Palluite clan, named after its ancestor **P**.
26: 8 **P** was the ancestor of Eliab,
1Ch 5: 3 son of Israel, were Hanoch, **P**, Hezron, and Carmi.

PALLUITE (1) [PALLU]

Nu 26: 5 The **P** clan, named after its ancestor Pallu.

PALM (31) [PALMS]

Ex 15:27 there were twelve springs and seventy **p** trees.
Lev 14:15 of the olive oil into the **p** of his own left hand.
14:26 of the olive oil into the **p** of his own left hand.
23:40 and collect **p** fronds and other leafy branches
Nu 33: 9 are twelve springs of water and seventy **p** trees.
Jdg 4: 5 She would hold court under the **P** of Deborah,
1Ki 6:29 carvings of cherubim, **p** trees, and open flowers.
6:32 **p** trees, and open flowers, and the doors were
6:35 **p** trees, and open flowers, and the doors were
7:36 and **p** trees decorated the panels and supports
2Ch 3: 5 and decorated with carvings of **p** trees and chains.
Ne 8:15 from olive, wild olive, myrtle, **p**, and fig trees.
Ps 92:12 But the godly will flourish like **p** trees / and grow
SS 7: 7 You are tall and slim like a **p** tree, and your breasts
7: 8 'I will climb up into the **p** tree and take hold of its
Isa 9:14 the head and the tail, the **p** branch and the reed.
48:13 The **p** of my right hand spread out the heavens
Eze 40:16 dividing walls were decorated with carved **p** trees.
40:22 and the **p** tree decorations were identical to those
40:26 and there were **p** tree decorations along the
40:31 It had **p** tree decorations on its columns, and there
40:34 It had **p** tree decorations on its columns, and there
40:37 and it had **p** tree decorations on the columns.
41:18 and there was a **p** tree carving between each of the
41:19 of a man—looked toward the **p** tree on one side.
41:19 looked toward the **p** tree on the other side.
41:25 carved cherubim and **p** trees just as on the walls.
41:26 recessed windows decorated with carved **p** trees.
Joel 1:12 The pomegranate trees, **p** trees, and apple trees—
Jn 12:13 took **p** branches and went down the road to meet
Rev 7: 9 in white and held **p** branches in their hands.

PALMERWORM [KJV] See LOCUST

PALMS (3) [PALM]

Nu 24: 6 They spread before me like groves of **p**,
Dt 34: 3 Valley with Jericho—the city of **p**—as far as Zoar.
2Ch 28:15 back to their own land—to Jericho, the city of **p**.

PALSY [KJV] See PARALYZED

PALTI (5)

Nu 13: 9 Benjamin | **P** son of Raphu
1Sa 25:44 to a man from Gallim named **P** son of Laish.
2Sa 3:15 Michal away from her husband **P** son of Laish.
3:16 **P** followed along behind her as far as Bahurim,
3:16 Abner told him, "Go back home!" So **P** returned.

PALTIEL (1)

Nu 34:26 Issachar | **P** son of Azzan

PAMPERED (1)

Pr 29:21 A servant who is **p** from childhood will later

PAMPHYLIA (5)

Ac 2:10 Phrygia, **P**, Egypt, and the areas of Libya toward
13:13 and those with him left Paphos by ship for **P**,
14:24 Then they traveled back through Pisidia to **P**.
15:38 since John Mark had deserted them in **P** and had
27: 5 along the coast of the provinces of Cilicia and **P**,

PAN (2) [PANS]

Lev 2: 7 If your offering is prepared in a **p**, it also must be
7: 9 that has been baked in an oven, prepared in a **p**,

PANELED (9) [PANELING, PANELS]

1Ki 6:15 from floor to ceiling, was **p** with wood.
6:15 He **p** the walls and ceilings with cedar, and he used
6:16 and was **p** with cedar from floor to ceiling.
7: 7 It was **p** with cedar from floor to ceiling.
2Ch 3: 5 The main room of the Temple was **p** with cypress
Jer 22:14 **p** throughout with fragrant cedar and painted a
Eze 41:15 and the foyer of the Temple were all **p** with wood,
41:16 The inner walls of the Temple were **p** with wood
41:17 door leading into the Most Holy Place was also **p**.

PANELING (4) [PANELED]

1Ki 6:18 Cedar **p** completely covered the stone walls
6:18 and the **p** was decorated with carvings of gourds
Ps 74: 6 With axes and picks, / they smashed the carved **p**.
Zep 2:14 and the cedar **p** will lie open to the wind

PANELS (7) [PANELED]

1Ki 7:28 They were constructed with side **p** braced with
7:29 Both the **p** and the crossbars were decorated with
7:31 The **p** of the carts were square, not round.
7:32 Under the **p** were four wheels that were connected
7:35 and side **p** were cast as one unit with the cart.
7:36 and palm trees decorated the **p** and supports
2Ki 16:17 Then the king removed the side **p** and basins from

PANGS (4)

Isa 13: 8 Fear grips them with terrible **p**, like those of a
21: 3 Sharp **p** of horror are upon me, like the **p** of a
woman giving birth.
Mic 6:14 Your hunger **p** and emptiness will still remain.

PANIC (26) [PANICKED]

Ex 14:10 The people began to **p**, and they cried out to the
23:27 lands you invade, and they will **p** before you.
Dt 20: 3 as you go out to fight today! Do not lose heart or **p**.
28:28 will strike you with madness, blindness, and **p**.
Jos 10:10 The LORD threw them into a **p**, and the Israelites
Jdg 4:15 and all his charioteers and warriors into a **p**.
7:21 watched as all the Midianites rushed around in a **p**,
1Sa 5: 9 with a plague of tumors, and there was a great **p**.
14:15 Suddenly, **p** broke out in the Philistine army,
2Sa 17: 2 He and his troops will **p**, and everyone will run
17: 9 your men fall, there will be **p** among your troops,
1Ki 1:49 Then all of Adonijah's guests jumped up in **p** from
2Ki 25:26 well as the army commanders, fled in **p** to Egypt,
Ps 104:29 But if you turn away from them, they **p**.
Isa 7: 6 'We will invade Judah and throw its people into **p**.
31: 8 of God will strike them, and they will **p** and flee.
Jer 49:29 taken away. Everywhere shouts of **p** will be heard:
50:36 it strikes her mightiest warriors, **p** will seize them!
51:32 The fortifications are burning, and the army is in **p**.
51:46 But do not **p** when you hear the first rumor of
Eze 30: 9 Great **p** will come upon them on that day of
Zec 12: 4 I will cause every horse to **p** and every rider to lose
14:13 be terrified, stricken by the LORD with great **p**.
Mt 24: 6 And wars will break out near and far, but don't **p**.
Mk 13: 7 And wars will break out near and far, but don't **p**.
Lk 21: 9 when you hear of wars and insurrections, don't **p**.

PANICKED (3) [PANIC]

1Sa 4: 7 they **p**. "The gods have come into their camp!"
1Ki 20:20 and suddenly the entire Aramean army **p** and fled.
2Ki 7: 7 So they **p** and fled into the night, abandoning their

PANNAG [KJV] See (EARLY) FIGS

PANS (2) [PAN]

2Ch 35:13 kettles, and **p**, and brought them out quickly
Eze 15: 3 for making things, like pegs to hang up pots and **p**?

PANT (1) [PANTED, PANTING, PANTS]

Isa 42:14 I will gasp and **p** like a woman giving birth.

PANTED (1) [PANT]

Ge 32:26 But Jacob **p**, "I will not let you go unless you

PANTED, PANTETH [KJV] See BEATS, PANTING, PANTS, REELS

PANTHERS (1)

SS 4: 8 where lions have their dens and **p** prowl.

PANTING (2) [PANT]

Ps 119:131 I open my mouth, **p** expectantly, / longing for your
Jer 14: 6 The wild donkeys stand on the bare hills **p** like

PANTS (1) [PANT]

Ps 42: 1 As the deer **p** for streams of water, / so I long for

PAPA (1)

Isa 8: 4 before this child is old enough to say '**P**'

PAPERS (2)

Jer 32:16 Then after I had given the **p** to Baruch, I prayed to
2Ti 4:13 Also bring my books, and especially my **p**.

PAPHOS (2)

Ac 13: 6 across the entire island until finally they reached **P**,
13:13 and those with him left **P** by ship for Pamphylia,

PAPYRUS (2)

Ex 2: 3 she got a little basket made of **p** reeds
Job 8:11 "Can **p** reeds grow where there is no marsh?

PARABLE (1) [PARABLES]

Ps 78: 2 for I will speak to you in a **p**. / I will teach you

PARABLES (7) [PARABLE]

Pr 1: 6 in these proverbs, **p**, wise sayings, and riddles.
Hos 12:10 prophets to warn you with many visions and **p**."
Mt 13:34 he never spoke to them without using such **p**.
13:35 the prophecy that said, / "I will speak to you in **p**.
Mk 4:34 in his public teaching he taught only with **p**,
Jn 16:25 "I have spoken of these matters in **p**, but the time
16:29 "At last you are speaking plainly and not in **p**.

PARADE (4) [PARADING]

Jer 22: 4 and on horses, with his **p** of officials and subjects.
Mk 12:38 For they love to **p** in flowing robes and to have
Lk 20:46 For they love to **p** in flowing robes and to have
1Co 4: 9 like prisoners of war at the end of a victor's **p**,

PARADING (1) [PARADE]

Isa 1:12 Why do you keep **p** through my courts with your

PARADISE (3)

Lk 23:43 "I assure you, today you will be with me in **p**."
2Co 12: 4 But I do know that I was caught up into **p**
Rev 2: 7 will eat from the tree of life in the **p** of God.

PARAH (1)

Jos 18:23 Avvim, **P**, Ophrah,

PARALYZED (27)

Jos 5: 1 could cross, they lost heart and were **p** with fear.
7: 5 The Israelites were **p** with fear at this turn of
1Sa 25:37 As a result he had a stroke, and he lay on his bed **p**.
28:20 **p** with fright because of Samuel's words.
2Sa 4: 1 lost all courage, and his people were **p** with fear.
17:10 they have the heart of a lion, will be **p** with fear.

1Ki 13: 4 But instantly the king's hand became **p** in that
2Ki 10: 4 But they were **p** with fear and said, "Two kings
Ps 143: 4 I am losing all hope; / I am **p** with fear.
Pr 26: 7 of a fool, a proverb becomes as limp as a **p** leg.
Isa 13: 7 Every arm is **p** with fear. Even the strongest hearts
45: 1 Before him, mighty kings will be **p** with fear.
Hab 1: 4 The law has become **p** and useless, and there is no
Mt 4:24 by demons, or were epileptics, or were **p**—
8: 6 young servant lies in bed, **p** and racked with pain."
9: 2 Some people brought to him a **p** man on a mat.
9: 2 Jesus said to the **p** man, "Take heart, son!
9: 6 Then Jesus turned to the **p** man and said,
Mk 2: 3 Four men arrived carrying a **p** man on a mat.
2: 5 their faith, Jesus said to the **p** man, "My son,
2: 9 Is it easier to say to the **p** man, 'Your sins are
2:10 Then Jesus turned to the **p** man and said,
Lk 5:18 Some men came carrying a **p** man on a sleeping
5:24 Then Jesus turned to the **p** man and said,
Jn 5: 3 people—blind, lame, or **p**—lay on the porches.
Ac 8: 7 And many who had been **p** or lame were healed.
9:33 who had been **p** and bedridden for eight years.

PARAN (9) [EL-PARAN]

Ge 21:20 with the boy as he grew up in the wilderness of **P**.
Nu 10:12 until the cloud stopped in the wilderness of **P**.
12:16 left Hazeroth and camped in the wilderness of **P**.
13: 3 of Israel, from their camp in the wilderness of **P**.
13:26 people of Israel at Kadesh in the wilderness of **P**.
Dt 1: 1 between **P** on one side and Tophel, Laban,
33: 2 from Mount Seir; / he shone forth from Mount **P**
1Ki 11:18 They escaped from Midian and went to **P**,
Hab 3: 3 across the deserts from Edom and Mount **P**.

PARCEL (2) [PARCELS]

Jos 24:32 in the **p** of ground Jacob had bought from the sons
Jn 4: 5 near the **p** of ground that Jacob gave to his son

PARCELS (1) [PARCEL]

Jos 17: 5 Manasseh's inheritance came to ten **p** of land,

PARCHED (14)

Job 38:27 Who sends the rain that satisfies the **p** ground
Ps 63: 1 in this **p** and weary land / where there is no water.
69: 3 from crying for help; / my throat is **p** and dry.
143: 6 I thirst for you as **p** land thirsts for rain.
Isa 19: 5 flood the fields. The riverbed will be **p** and dry.
35: 7 The **p** ground will become a pool, and springs of
41:17 and their tongues are **p** from thirst, then I,
41:18 fed by springs will flow across the dry, **p** ground.
44: 3 to quench your thirst and to moisten your **p** fields.
Jer 14: 4 The ground is **p** and cracked for lack of rain.
La 4: 4 The **p** tongues of their little ones stick with thirst to
Joel 1:17 The seeds die in the **p** ground, and the grain crops
2:20 I will drive them back into the **p** wastelands,
Zep 2:13 Nineveh, a desolate wasteland, **p** like a desert.

PARDON (11) [PARDONED, PARDONS]

Ex 34: 9 but please **p** our iniquity and our sins.
Nu 14:19 Please **p** the sins of this people because of your
14:20 "I will **p** them as you have requested.
Dt 29:20 The LORD will not **p** such people. His anger
2Ki 5:18 However, may the LORD **p** me in this one thing.
5:18 my arm, may the LORD **p** me when I bow, too."
2Ch 30:18 "May the LORD, who is good, **p** those
Job 7:21 Why not just **p** my sin and take away my guilt?
Isa 55: 7 Yes, turn to our God, for he will abundantly **p**.
Jer 5: 7 "How can I **p** you? For even your children have
Joel 3:21 I will **p** my people's crimes, which I have not yet

PARDONED (3) [PARDON]

Ps 34:22 Everyone who trusts in him will be freely **p**.
Isa 40: 2 that her sad days are gone and that her sins are **p**.
Joel 3:21 my people's crimes, which I have not yet **p**;

PARDONS (1) [PARDON]

Mic 7:18 who **p** the sins of the survivors among his people?

PARENT (3) [GRANDPARENTS, PARENT'S, PARENTS, PARENTS']

Dt 8: 5 So you should realize that just as a **p** disciplines a
Pr 17:21 It is painful to be the **p** of a fool; there is no joy for
Eze 18:20 and the **p** will not be punished for the child's sins.

PARENT'S (4) [PARENT]

Pr 13: 1 A wise child accepts a **p** discipline; a young
15: 5 Only a fool despises a **p** discipline; whoever learns
Eze 18:19 you ask. 'Doesn't the child pay for the **p** sins?' No!
18:20 The child will not be punished for the **p** sins,

PARENTS (63) [PARENT]

Ge 28: 7 He also knew that Jacob had obeyed his **p**
38:11 his two brothers.) So Tamar went home to her **p**.
Ex 20: 5 but I punish the children for the sins of their **p** to
34: 7 but I punish the children for the sins of their **p** to
Lev 20: 4 to Molech and refuse to execute the guilty **p**,
Nu 14:18 but he punishes the children for the sins of their **p**
26:59 Amram and Jochebed became the **p** of Aaron,
Dt 5: 9 but I punish the children for the sins of their **p** to
24:16 "**P** must not be put to death for the sins of their
24:16 nor the children for the sins of their **p**.
33: 9 to you / than to their **p**, relatives, and children.
Jdg 14: 5 As Samson and his **p** were going down to Timnah,
1Sa 22: 4 and David's **p** stayed in Moab while David was
2Ki 14: 6 "**P** must not be put to death for the sins of their
14: 6 nor the children for the sins of their **p**.
2Ch 25: 4 "**P** must not be put to death for the sins of their
25: 4 nor the children for the sins of their **p**.
Job 39: 4 the open fields, then leave their **p** and never return.
Ps 78:57 and were as faithless as their **p** had been.
Pr 17: 6 glory of the aged; **p** are the pride of their children.
19:14 **P** can provide their sons with an inheritance of
23:25 So give your **p** joy! May she who gave you birth
28: 7 out worthless companions bring shame to their **p**.
28:24 Robbing your **p** and then saying, "What's wrong
Jer 13:14 even **p** against children, says the LORD.
31:29 'The **p** eat sour grapes, but their children's mouths
Eze 5:10 **P** will eat their own children, and children will eat
their **p**.
18: 2 'The **p** have eaten sour grapes, but their children's
18: 4 are mine to judge—both **p** and children alike.
Mal 4: 6 His preaching will turn the hearts of **p** to their
children, and the hearts of children to their **p**.
Mt 7: 9 You **p**—if your children ask for a loaf of bread,
10:21 and children will rise against their **p** and cause
15: 5 'You don't need to honor your **p** by caring for their
Mk 5:42 Her **p** were absolutely overwhelmed.
7:11 you say it is all right for people to say to their **p**,
7:12 You let them disregard their needy **p**.
10:13 One day some **p** brought their children to Jesus
13:12 and children will rise against their **p** and cause
Lk 2:22 so his **p** took him to Jerusalem to present him to
2:39 When Jesus' **p** had fulfilled all the requirements of
2:41 Every year Jesus' **p** went to Jerusalem for the
2:43 behind in Jerusalem. His **p** didn't miss him at first,
2:48 His **p** didn't know what to think. "Son!"
8:56 Her **p** were overwhelmed, but Jesus insisted that
18:15 One day some **p** brought their little children to
18:29 given up house or wife or brothers or **p** or children,
21:16 your **p**, brothers, relatives, and friends—will betray
Jn 9: 2 Was it a result of his own sins or those of his **p**?"
9:18 believe he had been blind, so they called in his **p**.
9:20 His **p** replied, "We know this is our son and that
Ac 7:19 and forced **p** to abandon their newborn babies
7:20 His **p** cared for him at home for three months.
Ro 1:30 new ways of sinning and are disobedient to their **p**.
2:28 true Jew just because you were born of Jewish **p** or
2Co 12:14 other way around; **p** supply food for their children.
Eph 6: 1 obey your **p** because you belong to the Lord,
Col 3:20 You children must always obey your **p**, for this is
1Ti 5: 4 at home and repay their **p** by taking care of them.
2Ti 3: 2 at God, disobedient to their **p**, and ungrateful.
Heb 11:23 It was by faith that Moses' **p** hid him for three
1Pe 1:23 Your new life did not come from your earthly **p**

PARENTS' (8) [PARENT]

Ge 38:11 again at that time but to return to her **p** home.
Lev 21:12 of his God by leaving it to attend his **p** funeral,
Dt 22:21 by being promiscuous while living in her **p** home.
Ru 1:12 No, my daughters, return to your **p** homes, for I am
Jer 32:18 though children suffer for their **p** sins.
Eze 20:18 and told them not to follow in their **p** footsteps,
Jn 9: 3 "It was not because of his sins or his **p** sins,"
2Co 12:14 little children don't pay for their **p** food.

PARKS (1)

Ecc 2: 5 I made gardens and **p**, filling them with all kinds of

PARMASHTA (1)

Est 9: 9 **P**, Arisai, Aridai, and Vaizatha—

PARMENAS (1)

Ac 6: 5 Holy Spirit), Philip, Procorus, Nicanor, Timon, **P**,

PARNACH (1)

Nu 34:25 Zebulun | Elizaphan son of **P**

PAROSH (6)

Ezr 2: 3 The family of **P** | 2,172
8: 3 From the family of **P**: Zechariah and 150 other
10:25 From the family of **P**: Ramiah, Izziah, Malkijah,
Ne 3:25 of the guard. Next to him were Pedaiah son of **P**
7: 8 The family of **P** | 2,172
10:14 The leaders who signed were **P**, Pahath-moab,

PARSHANDATHA (1)

Est 9: 7 They also killed **P**, Dalphon, Aspatha,

PARSIN (2)

Da 5:25 that was written: MENE, MENE, TEKEL, **P**.
5:28 ***P*** means 'divided'—your kingdom has been

PART (107) [APART, PARTED, PARTIAL, PARTITIONED, PARTS]

Ge 2:23 "She is **p** of my own flesh and bone!
17: 9 "Your **p** of the agreement," God told Abraham,
18:16 Abraham went with them **p** of the way.
Ex 37: 8 so they were actually a **p** of the atonement cover—
Lev 2: 3 It will be considered a most holy **p** of the offerings
2:10 It will be considered a most holy **p** of the offerings
3: 3 **P** of this peace offering must be presented to the
3: 9 **P** of this peace offering must be presented to the
3:14 **P** of this offering must be presented to the LORD
3:14 This **p** includes the fat around the internal organs,
7:29 bring **p** of it as a special gift to the LORD.
9:13 the head, and he burned each **p** on the altar.
24: 8 of the Israelites as a continual **p** of the covenant.
27:22 but which is not **p** of your ancestral property,
Nu 18:30 'When you present the best **p**, it will be considered
Dt 3:10 which were **p** of Og's kingdom in Bashan.
23:13 Each of you must have a spade as **p** of your
Jos 14: 8 For my **p**, I followed the LORD my God
19: 9 Their inheritance came from **p** of what had been
Jdg 2: 2 For your **p**, you were not to make any covenants
20:40 and saw the smoke rising into the sky from every **p**
21:23 They kidnapped the women who took **p** in the
Ru 2: 9 See which **p** of the field they are harvesting,
1Sa 9:12 He has just arrived to take **p** in a public sacrifice
20:29 He wanted to take **p** in a family sacrifice.
23:19 of Hakilah, which is in the southern **p** of Jeshimon.
30:12 They also gave him **p** of a fig cake and two
30:26 David sent **p** of the plunder to the leaders of Judah,
2Sa 4: 2 The town of Beeroth is now **p** of Benjamin
15:10 he sent secret messengers to every **p** of Israel to
20: 1 We want no **p** of this son of Jesse. Come on,
21: 2 They were not **p** of Israel but were all that was left
1Ki 7:24 and they had been cast as **p** of the tank.
2Ki 3:13 "I want no **p** of you," Elisha said to the king of
1Ch 4:39 in the east **p** of the valley, seeking pastureland for
28:19 "Every **p** of this plan," David told Solomon,
2Ch 4: 3 and they had been cast as **p** of the tank.
12:15 and in *The Record of Iddo the Seer,* which are **p**
13:13 Jeroboam had secretly sent **p** of his army around
Ezr 4: 3 "You may have no **p** in this work, for we have
Ne 6: 8 are lying. There is no truth in any **p** of your story."
7: 3 "Do not leave the gates open during the hottest **p**
10:35 "We promise always to bring the first **p** of every
12:27 They were to take **p** in the joyous occasion with
12:44 the gifts, the first **p** of the harvest, and the tithes.
13:31 and that the first **p** of the harvest was collected for
Job 21:14 We want no **p** of you and your ways.
Ps 16: 4 I will not take **p** in their sacrifices / or even speak
109:18 Cursing is as much a **p** of him as his clothing,
Pr 3: 9 and with the best **p** of everything your land
Ecc 9: 6 They no longer have a **p** in anything here on earth.
SS 4: 7 so beautiful, my beloved, so perfect in every **p**.
Isa 10: 7 my people as **p** of his plan to conquer the world.
14: 1 them there and become a **p** of the people of Israel.
21: 2 you Elamites and Medes, take **p** in the siege.
44:15 he uses **p** of the wood to make a fire to warm
44:16 He burns **p** of the tree to roast his meat and to keep
Jer 36:22 and the king was in a winterized **p** of the palace,
Eze 16:61 even though they are not **p** of our covenant.
18:12 worships idols and takes **p** in loathsome practices,
22: 9 and people who take **p** in lewd activities.
Da 11:41 Edom, and the best **p** of Ammon will escape.
Zec 11:15 "Go again and play the **p** of a worthless shepherd.
Mt 5:29 It is better for you to lose one **p** of your body than
5:30 It is better for you to lose one **p** of your body than
13:33 the yeast permeated every **p** of the dough."
13:53 telling these stories, he left that **p** of the country.
23:23 For you are careful to tithe even the tiniest **p** of
Mk 6: 1 Jesus left that **p** of the country and returned with
12:44 For they gave a tiny **p** of their surplus, but she,
Lk 11:42 For you are careful to tithe even the tiniest **p** of
13:21 the yeast permeated every **p** of the dough."
21: 4 For they have given a tiny **p** of their surplus,
22:22 Son of Man, must die since it is **p** of God's plan.
23:19 and for taking **p** in an insurrection in Jerusalem
Jn 8:35 of the family, but a son is **p** of the family forever.
10:26 believe me because you are not **p** of my flock.
17:16 They are not **p** of this world any more than I am.
Ac 3: 1 to take **p** in the three o'clock prayer service.
5: 2 He brought **p** of the money to the apostles, but he
8:21 You can have no **p** in this, for your heart is not
Ro 6:13 Do not let any **p** of your body become a tool of
12: 4 have many parts and each **p** has a special function,
12:18 Do your **p** to live in peace with everyone, as much
1Co 12:14 the body has many different parts, not just one **p**.
12:15 "I am not a **p** of the body because I am not a
12:15 that does not make it any less a **p** of the body.
12:16 "I am not **p** of the body because I am only an ear
12:16 would that make it any less a **p** of the body?
12:18 and he has put each **p** just where he wants it.
12:19 strange thing a body would be if it had only one **p**!
12:26 If one **p** suffers, all the parts suffer with it, and if
one **p** is honored, all the parts are glad.
12:27 each one of you is a separate and necessary **p** of it.
2Co 6:12 it is not because of a lack of love on our **p**, but
Gal 5:25 let us follow the Holy Spirit's leading in every **p** of
Eph 2:22 as **p** of this dwelling where God lives by his Spirit.
3: 6 and both are **p** of the same body and enjoy together
4:16 As each **p** does its own special work, it helps the
5:11 Take no **p** in the worthless deeds of evil
Col 3: 7 You used to do them when your life was still **p** of
Heb 9:11 by human hands and not **p** of this created world.
1Pe 2:21 This suffering is all **p** of what God has called you
1Jn 5:18 We know that those who have become **p** of God's
Rev 5: 6 of God that are sent out into every **p** of the earth.
18: 4 Do not take **p** in her sins, or you will be punished
18: 9 And the rulers of the world who took **p** in her

PARTAKE (1)

Jn 6:57 those who **p** of me will live because of me.

PARTED (5) [PART]

Ge 13:11 and servants and **p** company with his uncle Abram.
24:60 They blessed her with this blessing as she **p**:
Ps 136:13 Give thanks to him who **p** the Red Sea.
Hab 3: 8 LORD, that you struck the rivers and **p** the sea?
2Ti 1: 4 see you again, for I remember your tears as we **p**.

PARTHIANS (1)
Ac 2: 9 **P**, Medes, Elamites, people from Mesopotamia,

PARTIAL (1) [PART]
1Co 13:12 All that I know now is **p** and incomplete, but

PARTIALITY (8)
Ge 37: 4 brothers hated Joseph because of their father's **p**.
Dt 10:17 who shows no **p** and takes no bribes.
16:19 You must never twist justice or show **p**.
2Ch 19: 7 perverted justice, **p**, or the taking of bribes."
Pr 28:21 Showing **p** is never good, yet some will do wrong
Mal 2: 9 but have shown **p** in your interpretation of the
Ac 10:34 "I see very clearly that God doesn't show **p**.
Jas 3:17 good deeds. It shows no **p** and is always sincere.

PARTICIPATE (5) [PARTICIPATED, PARTICIPATION]
Ps 141: 4 evil things; / don't let me **p** in acts of wickedness.
Zep 1: 9 I will punish those who **p** in pagan worship
Ro 13:13 Don't **p** in wild parties and getting drunk, or in
Eph 5: 7 Don't **p** in the things these people do.
1Ti 5:22 Do not **p** in the sins of others. Keep yourself pure.

PARTICIPATED (2) [PARTICIPATE]
Jdg 3: 1 Israelites who had not **p** in the wars of Canaan.
Ne 12:43 The women and children also **p** in the celebration,

PARTICIPATION (1) [PARTICIPATE]
Gal 5:20 idolatry, **p** in demonic activities, hostility,

PARTICULAR (4) [PARTICULARLY]
Ge 25:28 Isaac loved Esau in **p** because of the wild game he
Ex 22: 9 dispute between two people as to who owns a **p** ox,
1Ch 25: 8 The musicians were appointed to their **p** term of
1Co 3:21 So don't take pride in following a **p** leader.

PARTICULARLY (1) [PARTICULAR]
1Ti 4:10 Savior of all people, and **p** of those who believe.

PARTIES (13) [PARTY]
Ex 22: 9 Both **p** must come before God for a decision,
Lev 20:13 penalty for homosexual acts is death to both **p**.
20:19 Both **p** are guilty of a capital offense.
1Sa 13:17 Three raiding **p** soon left the camp of the
14:15 including even the outposts and raiding **p**.
2Sa 4: 2 who were captains of Ishbosheth's raiding **p**.
Isa 5:12 furnish lovely music and wine at your grand **p**;
Jer 16: 8 "And do not go to their feasts and **p**. Do not eat
Mt 24:38 the people were enjoying banquets and **p**
Lk 17:27 the people enjoyed banquets and **p** and weddings
Ro 13:13 Don't participate in wild **p** and getting drunk,
Gal 5:21 envy, drunkenness, wild **p**, and other kinds of sin.
1Pe 4: 3 their feasting and drunkenness and wild **p**,

PARTITIONED (1) [PART]
1Ki 6:16 He **p** off an inner sanctuary—the Most Holy

PARTNER (7) [PARTNERS]
Zec 13: 7 against my shepherd, the man who is my **p**,
2Co 6:14 How can goodness be a **p** with wickedness?
6:15 How can a believer be a **p** with an unbeliever?
8:23 say that he is my **p** who works with me to help
Phm 1:17 So if you consider me your **p**, give him the same
1Pe 3: 7 but she is your equal **p** in God's gift of new life.
2Jn 1:11 Anyone who encourages him becomes a **p** in his

PARTNERS (9) [PARTNER]
Lk 5: 7 A shout for help brought their **p** in the other boat,
5:10 His **p**, James and John, the sons of Zebedee,
1Co 3: 9 We work together as **p** who belong to God.
10:20 And I don't want any of you to be **p** with demons.
2Co 6: 1 As God's **p**, we beg you not to reject this
Php 1: 5 because you have been my **p** in spreading the
1Pe 4:13 because these trials will make you **p** with Christ in
3Jn 1: 8 so that we may become **p** with them for the truth.
Rev 1: 9 In Jesus we are **p** in suffering and in the Kingdom

PARTRIDGE (1)
1Sa 26:20 Why does he hunt me down like a **p** on the

PARTS (38) [PART]
Ex 29:27 "Set aside as holy the **p** of the ordination ram that
29:28 these **p** will be the regular share of Aaron and his
Lev 7: 5 The priests will burn these **p** on the altar as an
9:20 He placed these fat **p** on top of the breasts of these
10:14 These **p** have been given to you and to your sons
Nu 31:27 Then divide the plunder into two **p**, and give half
Dt 18: 3 "These are the **p** the priests may claim as their
2Ch 26: 6 in the Ashdod area and in other **p** of Philistia.
Ne 4:13 So I placed armed guards behind the lowest **p** of
Est 1:22 He sent letters to all **p** of the empire, to each
Ps 139:13 You made all the delicate, inner **p** of my body
Isa 41: 7 Carefully they join the **p** together, then fasten the
49:19 "Even the most desolate **p** of your abandoned land
Eze 5: 1 Use a scale to weigh the hair into three equal **p**.
40:24 to the south gateway and measured its various **p**,
42:14 the **p** of the building complex open to the public."
Da 2:42 Some **p** of it will be as strong as iron, and others as
11: 4 will be broken apart and divided into four **p**.
Mt 24: 7 and earthquakes in many **p** of the world.
Mk 13: 8 and there will be earthquakes in many **p** of the
Jn 15: 6 Anyone who **p** from me is thrown away like a
Ro 12: 4 Just as our bodies have many **p** and each part has a
12: 5 We are all **p** of his one body, and each of us has
1Co 6:15 Don't you realize that your bodies are actually **p** of
12:12 The human body has many **p**, but the many **p** make up only one body.
12:14 Yes, the body has many different **p**, not just one
12:18 But God made our bodies with many **p**, and he has
12:20 Yes, there are many **p**, but only one body.
12:22 some of the **p** that seem weakest and least
12:23 And the **p** we regard as less honorable are those we
12:23 the eyes of others those **p** that should not be seen,
12:24 while other **p** do not require this special care.
12:24 and care are given to those **p** that have less dignity.
12:26 If one part suffers, all the **p** suffer with it, and if one part is honored, all the **p** are glad.
Eph 4:16 it helps the other **p** grow, so that the whole body is
2Pe 3:16 he meant, just as they do the other **p** of Scripture—

PARTY (19) [PARTIES, PARTYING]
Ge 21: 8 Abraham gave a big **p** to celebrate the happy
31:27 I would have given you a farewell **p**, with joyful
49: 6 May I never be a **p** to their wicked plans.
Jdg 14:10 Samson threw a **p** at Timnah, as was the custom of
14:15 Did you invite us to this **p** just to make us poor?"
Ru 4: 7 to remove his sandal and hand it to the other **p**.
1Sa 2:25 another person, God can mediate for the guilty **p**.
25:36 she found that Nabal had thrown a big **p** and was
2Sa 16: 5 As David and his **p** passed Bahurim, a man came
1Ki 2:32 For my father was no **p** to the deaths of Abner son
8:32 Punish the guilty **p** and acquit the one who is
2Ki 5:15 and his entire **p** went back to find the man of God.
2Ch 6:23 Punish the guilty **p**, and acquit the one who is
Ecc 10:19 A **p** gives laughter, and wine gives happiness,
Isa 3:22 **p** clothes, gowns, capes, and purses;
56:12 they say. "We will get some wine and have a **p**.
Mt 14: 6 But at a birthday **p** for Herod, Herodias' daughter
Mk 6:21 and he gave a **p** for his palace aides, army officers,
Lk 15:24 He was lost, but now he is found.' So the **p** began.

PARTYING (2) [PARTY]
Mt 24:49 the other servants, **p**, and getting drunk—
Lk 12:45 the other servants, **p**, and getting drunk—

PARUAH (1)
1Ki 4:17 Jehoshaphat son of **P**, in Issachar.

PARVAIM (1)
2Ch 3: 6 and with pure gold from the land of **P**.

PAS-DAMMIM (1) [EPHES-DAMMIM]
1Ch 11:13 with David in the battle against the Philistines at **P**.

PASACH (1)
1Ch 7:33 The sons of Japhlet were **P**, Bimhal, and Ashvath.

PASEAH (4)
1Ch 4:12 was the father of Beth-rapha, **P**, and Tehinnah.
Ezr 2:49 Uzza, **P**, Besai,
Ne 3: 6 The Old City Gate was repaired by Joiada son of **P**
7:51 Gazzam, Uzza, **P**,

PASHHUR (13)
1Ch 9:12 son of **P**, son of Malkijah, and Maasai son of
Ezr 2:38 The family of **P** | 1,247
10:22 From the family of **P**: Elioenai, Maaseiah, Ishmael,
Ne 7:41 The family of **P** | 1,247
10: 3 **P**, Amariah, Malkijah,
11:12 son of Zechariah, son of **P**, son of Malkijah;
Jer 20: 1 Now **P** son of Immer, the priest in charge of the
20: 3 The next day, when **P** finally released him, Jeremiah said, "**P**,
20: 6 **P**, you and all your household will go as captives
21: 1 when King Zedekiah sent **P** son of Malkijah
38: 1 Gedaliah son of **P**, Jehucal son of Shelemiah,
38: 1 and **P** son of Malkijah heard what Jeremiah had

PASS (84) [PASSED, PASSERBY, PASSES, PASSING]
Ge 15:17 and a flaming torch **p** between the halves of the
28: 4 May God **p** on to you and your descendants the
35:12 And I will **p** on to you the land I gave to Abraham
Ex 11: 4 About midnight I will **p** through Egypt.
12:12 On that night I will **p** through the land of Egypt
12:13 as a sign. When I see the blood, I will **p** over you.
12:23 For the LORD will **p** through the land and strike
12:23 the doorframe, the LORD will **p** over your home.
15:16 like a stone, / until your people **p** by, O LORD,
15:16 until the people whom you purchased **p** by.
19:12 Set boundary lines that the people may not **p**.
23: 1 "Do not **p** along false reports. Do not cooperate
33:19 "I will make all my goodness **p** before you,
Nu 20:17 Please let us **p** through your country. We will be
20:19 We only want to **p** through your country
20:20 "Stay out! You may not **p** through our land."
20:21 Because Edom refused to allow Israel to **p** through
27:11 **p** on his inheritance to the nearest relative in his
34: 4 then run south past Scorpion **P** in the direction of
36: 7 None of the inherited land may **p** from tribe to
36: 9 No inheritance may **p** from one tribe to another;
Dt 2:27 'Let us **p** through your land. We will stay on the
2:28 All we want is permission to **p** through your land.
2:29 Let us **p** through until we cross the Jordan into the
2:30 But King Sihon refused to allow you to **p** through,
4: 5 to me and commanded me to **p** them on to you.
4: 9 And be sure to **p** them on to your children
32:46 **P** them on as a command to your children so they
Jos 15: 3 ran south of Scorpion **P** into the wilderness of Zin
Jdg 1:36 The boundary of the Amorites ran from Scorpion **P**
8:13 After this, Gideon returned by way of Heres **P**.
11:17 Edom asking for permission to **p** through his land.
11:17 but he wouldn't let them **p** through either.
11:20 But King Sihon didn't trust Israel to **p** through his
1Sa 13:23 The **p** at Micmash had meanwhile been secured by
1Ki 9: 8 it will become an appalling sight for all who **p** by.
2Ch 7:21 it will become an appalling sight to all who **p** by.
Est 9:27 and to **p** it on to their descendants and to all who
Job 14:20 overpower them, and then they **p** from the scene.
34:20 At midnight they all **p** away; the mighty are
Ps 10: 8 in dark alleys, / murdering the innocent who **p** by.
80:12 our walls / so that all who **p** may steal our fruit?
129: 8 And may those who **p** by refuse to give them this
Ecc 5:14 there is nothing left to **p** on to one's children.
Isa 8:16 who will **p** it down to future generations.
10:29 They are crossing the **p** and are staying overnight
31: 5 and save the city; he will **p** over it and rescue it."
46:10 Everything I plan will come to **p**, for I do whatever
49: 7 "Kings will stand at attention when you **p** by.
57: 1 The righteous **p** away; the godly often die before
57:16 If I did, all people would **p** away—all the souls I
60:22 the LORD, will bring it all to **p** at the right time."
66:24 All who **p** by will view them with utter horror."
Jer 5:22 and roar, but they can never **p** the bounds I set.
18:16 All who **p** by will be astonished and shake their
19: 8 All who **p** by will be appalled and will gasp at the
22: 8 People from many nations will **p** by the ruins of
49:17 All who **p** by will be appalled and will gasp at the
50:13 All who **p** by will be horrified and will gasp at the
La 1:12 "Is it nothing to you, all you who **p** by?
2:15 All who **p** by jeer at you. They scoff and insult
Eze 3:17 from me, **p** it on to the people immediately.
26:18 The islands are dismayed as you **p** away.'
29:11 For forty years not a soul will **p** that way,
44: 2 No man will ever **p** through it, for the LORD,
Da 4:25 Seven periods of time will **p** while you live this
4:32 Seven periods of time will **p** while you live this
7:26 "But then the court will **p** judgment, and all his
9:25 **p** from the time the command is given to rebuild
Hos 4: 4 your finger at someone else and try to **p** the blame!
Joel 1: 3 **P** the awful story down from generation to
Am 5:17 for I will **p** through and destroy them all.
Zec 10:11 They will **p** safely through the sea of distress,
Mt 24:34 this generation will not **p** from the scene before all
Mk 8: 7 blessed these and told the disciples to **p** them out.
13:30 this generation will not **p** from the scene until all
14:35 the awful hour awaiting him might **p** him by.
Lk 21:32 this generation will not **p** from the scene until all
Ac 7:38 life-giving words on Mount Sinai to **p** on to us.
1Co 7:31 for this world and all it contains will **p** away.
11:23 and I **p** it on to you just as I received it.
Col 4:16 **p** it on to the church at Laodicea so they can read
2Ti 2: 2 people who are able to **p** them on to others.
2Pe 3:10 Then the heavens will **p** away with a terrible noise,

PASSAGE (18) [PASSAGES]
Ne 8: 8 being read, helping the people understand each **p**.
Eze 40: 7 alcoves on each side built into the gateway **p**.
40: 7 between them of 8-3/4 feet along the **p** wall.
40: 7 led to the foyer at the inner end of the gateway **p**,
40:10 three guard alcoves on each side of the gateway **p**.
40:11 the opening and 22-3/4 feet wide in the gateway **p**.
40:15 The full length of the gateway **p** was 87-1/2 feet
40:21 The gateway **p** was 87-1/2 feet long and 43-3/4
40:22 the foyer was at the inner end of the gateway **p**.
40:25 and there was a foyer where the gateway **p** opened
40:25 the gateway **p** was 87-1/2 feet long and 43-3/4 feet
40:29 the gateway **p** was 87-1/2 feet long and 43-3/4 feet
40:33 The gateway **p** measured 87-1/2 feet long
40:36 The gateway **p** measured 87-1/2 feet long
46: 2 He will worship inside the gateway **p** and then go
Ac 8:32 The **p** of Scripture he had been reading was this:
Heb 4: 5 But in the other **p** God said, "They will never
5: 6 And in another **p** God said to him, / "You are a

PASSAGES (1) [PASSAGE]
Lk 24:27 Then Jesus quoted **p** from the writings of Moses

PASSED (68) [PASS]
Ex 2:23 Years **p**, and the king of Egypt died.
7:25 An entire week **p** from the time the LORD turned
12:27 for he **p** over the homes of the Israelites in Egypt.
33:22 and cover you with my hand until I have **p**.
34: 6 He **p** in front of Moses and said, "I am the
Nu 13:22 they **p** first through the Negev and arrived at
31:23 must be **p** through fire in order to be made
Dt 2:14 So thirty-eight years **p** from the time we first
5: 5 He spoke to me, and I **p** his words on to you.
Jos 3:17 the middle of the riverbed as the people **p** by them.
15: 4 From there it **p** to Azmon, until it finally reached
15: 8 then **p** through the valley of the son of Hinnom,
15:10 **p** along to the town of Kesalon on the northern
15:11 It **p** Jabneel and ended at the Mediterranean Sea.
18:18 From there it **p** along the north side of the slope
19:14 The northern boundary of Zebulun **p** Hannathon
23: 1 The years **p**, and the LORD had given the people

Jdg 9:25 the hilltops and robbed everyone who **p** that way.
1Sa 4:20 but before she **p** away the midwives tried to
8:10 So Samuel **p** on the LORD's warning to the
9:14 entered the town, and as they **p** through the gates,
2Sa 3:1 As time **p** David became stronger and stronger,
15:23 the land as the king and his followers **p** by.
15:24 offered sacrifices there until everyone had **p** by.
16:5 As David and his party **p** Bahurim, a man came out
18:4 gate of the city as all the divisions of troops **p** by.
1Ki 18:1 After many months **p**, in the third year of the
19:11 And as Elijah stood there, the LORD **p** by,
19:21 He **p** around the meat to the other plowmen,
20:39 As the king **p** by, the prophet called out to him,
21:3 the inheritance that was **p** down by my ancestors."
2Ki 4:8 From then on, whenever he **p** that way, he would
25:6 at Riblah, where sentence was **p** against him.
Ne 12:37 They **p** the house of David and then proceeded to
Est 2:22 the plot and **p** the information on to Queen Esther.
3:2 Haman to show him respect whenever he **p** by,
Job 14:13 and forget me there until your anger has **p**.
Ps 139:16 moment was laid out / before a single day had **p**.
Isa 26:20 the LORD's anger against your enemies has **p**.
63:5 vengeance alone; unaided, I **p** down judgment.
Jer 25:3 I have faithfully **p** them on to you, but you have
52:9 of Hamath, where sentence was **p** against him.
Eze 16:8 And when I **p** by and saw you again, you were old
27:34 and your crew / have **p** away with you.
31:17 Its allies, too, were all destroyed and had **p** away.
36:34 lie empty and desolate—a shock to all who **p** by—
47:1 then **p** to the right of the altar on its south side.
Da 4:34 "After this time had **p**, I, Nebuchadnezzar,
Mal 2:6 They **p** on to the people all the truth they received
Mk 11:20 The next morning as they **p** by the fig tree he had
Lk 10:31 crossed to the other side of the road and **p** him by.
10:32 him lying there, but he also **p** by on the other side.
Jn 5:24 but they have already **p** from death into life.
6:11 gave thanks to God, and **p** them out to the people.
17:8 for I have **p** on to them the words you gave me;
Ac 12:10 They **p** the first and second guard posts and came
12:10 So they **p** through and started walking down the
20:2 he encouraged the believers in all the towns he **p**
20:15 The next day we **p** the island of Kios.
21:3 We sighted the island of Cyprus, **p** it on our left,
27:5 We **p** along the coast of the provinces of Cilicia
1Co 5:3 one who has done this, I have already **p** judgment
11:2 and you are following the Christian teaching I **p** on
15:3 I **p** on to you what was most important and what
15:3 and what had also been **p** on to me—
2Co 13:6 I hope you recognize that we have **p** the test
Heb 2:3 It was **p** on to us by those who heard him speak,
1Jn 3:14 it proves that we have **p** from death to eternal life.

PASSERBY (1) [PASS]

Eze 16:25 offering your body to every **p** in an endless stream

PASSES (11) [PASS]

Ex 33:22 As my glorious presence **p** by, I will put you in the
1Sa 24:3 At the place where the road **p** some sheepfolds,
Job 9:25 "My life **p** more swiftly than a runner. It flees
39:18 up to run, she **p** the swiftest horse with its rider.
Ps 7:8 The LORD **p** judgment on the nations.
102:11 My life **p** as swiftly as the evening shadows.
Pr 13:22 but the sinner's wealth **p** to the godly.
Jer 51:43 a dry wilderness where no one lives or even **p** by.
Eze 12:22 in Israel: 'Time **p**, making a liar of every prophet'?
Mt 15:17 "Anything you eat **p** through the stomach and
Mk 7:19 but only **p** through the stomach and then comes out

PASSING (15) [PASS]

Lev 25:46 **p** them on to your children as a permanent
Dt 2:4 "You will be **p** through the country belonging to
Jdg 3:26 Ehud escaped, **p** the idols on his way to Seirah.
Job 14:2 Like the shadow of a **p** cloud, we quickly
Ps 39:12 For I am your guest— / a traveler **p** through,
142:4 and help me, / but no one gives me a **p** thought!
144:4 like a breath of air; / our days are like a **p** shadow.
Pr 24:23 It is wrong to show favoritism when **p** judgment.
Jer 14:8 Why are you like someone **p** through the land,
Zep 2:15 Everyone **p** that way will laugh in derision
Mt 20:3 "At nine o'clock in the morning he was **p** through
27:39 And the people **p** by shouted abuse, shaking their
Mk 15:29 And the people **p** by shouted abuse, shaking their
1Co 7:36 has trouble controlling his passions and time is **p**,
3Jn 1:5 care of the traveling teachers who are **p** through,

PASSION (11) [PASSIONATE, PASSIONS]

2Ki 19:31 The **p** of the LORD Almighty will make this
Ps 69:9 **P** for your house burns within me, / so those who
Ecc 7:26 Her **p** is a trap, and her soft hands will bind you.
Isa 37:32 The **p** of the LORD Almighty will make this
57:5 You worship your idols with great **p** beneath every
63:15 Where is the **p** and the might you used to show on
Zec 8:2 and strong; I am consumed with **p** for Jerusalem!
Jn 1:13 This is not a physical birth resulting from human **p**
2:17 "**P** for God's house burns within me."
1Co 7:37 and there is no urgency and he can control his **p**,
1Th 4:5 not in lustful **p** as the pagans do, in their ignorance

PASSIONATE (7) [PASSION]

Ex 34:14 for he is a God who is **p** about his relationship with
Nu 25:11 by displaying **p** zeal among them on my behalf.
Isa 9:7 The **p** commitment of the LORD Almighty will
Zec 1:14 love for Jerusalem and Mount Zion is **p** and strong.
8:2 My love for Mount Zion is **p** and strong; I am

Rev 14:8 and made them drink the wine of her **p**
18:3 For all the nations have drunk the wine of her **p**

PASSIONS (3) [PASSION]

1Co 7:36 because he has trouble controlling his **p** and time is
Gal 5:24 Those who belong to Christ Jesus have nailed the **p**
Eph 2:3 following the **p** and desires of our evil nature.

PASSOVER (102)

Ex 12:11 Eat the food quickly, for this is the LORD's **P**.
12:21 to slaughter the lamb they have set apart for the **P**.
12:27 will reply, 'It is the celebration of the LORD's **P**,
12:43 "These are the regulations for the festival of **P**.
12:43 No foreigners are allowed to eat the **P** lamb.
12:48 among you who want to celebrate the LORD's **P**,
12:48 Then they may come and celebrate the **P** with you.
12:48 But an uncircumcised male may never eat of the **P**
34:25 And none of the meat of the **P** lamb may be kept
Lev 23:5 "First comes the LORD's **P**, which begins at
23:6 Then the day after the **P** celebration, the Festival of
Nu 9:2 "Tell the Israelites to celebrate the **P** at the proper
9:4 So Moses told the people to celebrate the **P**
9:6 so they could not offer their **P** lambs that day.
9:10 generations are ceremonially unclean at **P** time
9:10 they may still celebrate the LORD's **P**.
9:11 They must offer the **P** sacrifice one month later,
9:12 follow all the normal regulations concerning the **P**.
9:13 yet still refuse to celebrate the **P** at the regular
9:14 among you want to celebrate the **P** to the LORD,
28:16 early spring, you must celebrate the LORD's **P**.
33:3 after the first **P** celebration in early spring.
Dt 16:1 always celebrate the **P** at the proper time in early
16:2 Your **P** sacrifice may be from either the flock
16:4 And do not let any of the meat of the **P** lamb
16:5 "The **P** must not be eaten in the towns that the
Jos 5:10 they celebrated **P** on the evening of the fourteenth
2Ki 23:21 "You must celebrate the **P** to the LORD your
23:22 There had not been a **P** celebration like that since
23:23 This **P** was celebrated to the LORD in Jerusalem
2Ch 8:13 the **P** celebration, the Festival of Harvest,
30:1 at Jerusalem to celebrate the **P** of the LORD,
30:2 of Jerusalem decided to celebrate **P** in midspring.
30:3 **P** was normally celebrated one month earlier,
30:4 This plan for keeping the **P** seemed right to the
30:5 to Jerusalem to celebrate the **P** of the LORD,
30:13 assembled at Jerusalem in midspring to celebrate **P**
30:15 in midspring, the people slaughtered their **P** lambs.
30:17 the Levites had to slaughter their **P** lambs for them,
30:18 and they were allowed to eat the **P** meal anyway,
35:1 Then Josiah announced that the **P** of the LORD
35:1 The **P** lambs were slaughtered at twilight of that
35:6 Slaughter the **P** lambs, purify yourselves,
35:7 and young goats for the people's **P** offerings,
35:8 young goats and three hundred bulls as **P** offerings.
35:9 and five hundred bulls to the Levites for their **P**
35:10 When everything was ready for the **P** celebration,
35:11 The Levites then slaughtered the **P** lambs
35:13 Then they roasted the **P** lambs as prescribed;
35:16 The entire ceremony for the LORD's **P** was
35:17 All the Israelites present in Jerusalem celebrated **P**
35:18 of the prophet Samuel had there been such a **P**.
35:18 None of the kings of Israel had ever kept a **P** as
35:19 This **P** celebration took place in the eighteenth
Ezr 6:19 On April 21 the returned exiles celebrated **P**.
6:20 So they slaughtered the **P** lamb for all the returned
6:21 The **P** meal was eaten by the people of Israel who
6:22 They ate the **P** meal and celebrated the Festival of
Eze 45:21 day of the new year, you must celebrate the **P**.
45:22 On the day of **P** the prince will provide a young
Mt 26:2 the **P** celebration begins in two days, and I,
26:5 "But not during the **P**," they agreed, "or there
26:17 "Where do you want us to prepare the **P** supper?"
26:18 and I will eat the **P** meal with my disciples at your
26:19 as Jesus told them and prepared the **P** supper there.
27:15 to the crowd each year during the **P** celebration—
27:62 next day—on the first day of the **P** ceremonies—
Mk 14:1 It was now two days before the **P** celebration
14:2 "But not during the **P**," they agreed, "or there
14:12 Bread (the day the **P** lambs were sacrificed),
14:12 "Where do you want us to go to prepare the **P**
14:14 Where is the guest room where I can eat the **P**
14:16 had said, and they prepared the **P** supper there.
15:6 to release one prisoner each year at **P** time—
Lk 2:41 Jesus' parents went to Jerusalem for the **P** festival.
22:1 which begins with the **P** celebration, was drawing
22:7 Bread arrived, when the **P** lambs were sacrificed.
22:8 John ahead and said, "Go and prepare the **P** meal,
22:11 Where is the guest room where I can eat the **P**
22:13 had said, and they prepared the **P** supper there.
22:15 anxious to eat this **P** meal with you before my
Jn 2:13 It was time for the annual **P** celebration, and Jesus
2:23 signs he did in Jerusalem at the **P** celebration,
4:45 for they had been in Jerusalem at the **P** celebration
6:4 (It was nearly time for the annual **P** celebration.)
11:55 It was now almost time for the celebration of **P**,
11:55 the cleansing ceremony before the **P** began.
11:56 "What do you think? Will he come for the **P**?"
12:1 Six days before the **P** ceremonies began,
12:12 swept through the city. A huge crowd of **P** visitors
12:20 Greeks who had come to Jerusalem to attend the **P**
13:1 Before the **P** celebration, Jesus knew that his hour
18:28 and they wouldn't be allowed to celebrate the **P**
18:39 me to release someone from prison each year at **P**.
19:14 now about noon of the day of preparation for the **P**.
19:31 very special Sabbath at that, because it was the **P**),
19:42 because it was the day of preparation before the **P**

Ac 12:3 he arrested Peter during the **P** celebration
12:4 was to bring Peter out for public trial after the **P**.
20:6 As soon as the **P** season ended, we boarded a ship
1Co 5:7 Christ, our **P** Lamb, has been sacrificed for us.
Heb 11:28 commanded the people of Israel to keep the **P**

PAST (78)

Ge 18:11 and Sarah was long **p** the age of having children,
Ex 21:29 the owner knew the bull had gored people in the **p**,
21:36 But if the bull was known from **p** experience to
40:32 Whenever they walked **p** the altar to enter the
Nu 34:4 then run south **p** Scorpion Pass in the direction of
Dt 2:8 So we went **p** our relatives, the descendants of
32:7 days of long ago; / think about the generations **p**.
Jos 16:6 at the Mediterranean, ran east **p** Micmethath,
16:6 then curved eastward **p** Taanath-shiloh to the east
18:19 ran **p** the north slope of Beth-hoglah, and ended at
19:11 went west, going **p** Maralah, touching Dabbesheth,
19:34 The western boundary ran **p** Aznoth-tabor, then to
Jdg 9:37 And another group is coming down the road **p** the
2Sa 4:6 So Recab and Baanah slipped **p** the doorkeeper,
7:10 nations won't oppress them as they did in the **p**,
15:18 to let David's troops move **p** to lead the way.
15:34 just as I was your father's adviser in the **p**.'
16:1 David was just **p** the top of the hill when Ziba,
1Ch 17:9 nations won't oppress them as they did in the **p**,
Ezr 4:15 what a rebellious city this has been in the **p**.
4:19 **p** been a hotbed of insurrection against many
Ne 2:13 out through the Valley Gate, **p** the Jackal's Well,
12:38 along the top of the wall **p** the Tower of the Ovens
12:39 then **p** the Ephraim Gate to the Old City Gate,
12:39 **p** the Fish Gate and the Tower of Hananel,
Job 4:3 "In the **p** you have encouraged many a troubled
4:15 A spirit swept **p** my face. Its wind sent shivers up
Ps 25:6 which you have shown from long ages **p**.
41:13 of Israel, / who lives forever from eternal ages **p**.
57:1 of your wings / until this violent storm is **p**.
68:28 Display your power, O God, as you have in the **p**.
74:12 You, O God, are my king from ages **p**,
78:2 I will teach you hidden lessons from our **p**—
93:2 You yourself are from the everlasting **p**.
102:25 In ages **p** you laid the foundation of the earth,
Pr 8:23 I was appointed in ages **p**, at the very first,
Ecc 3:15 will exist in the future has already existed in the **p**.
5:20 who do this rarely look with sorrow on the **p**,
SS 2:11 For the winter is **p**, and the rain is over and gone.
Isa 16:4 Hide them from our enemies until the terror is **p**."
16:13 LORD has already said this about Moab in the **p**.
42:23 not even one of you apply these lessons from the **p**
44:8 Have I not proclaimed from ages **p** what my
48:7 They are brand new, not things from the **p**. So you
63:16 be our Father. You are our Redeemer from ages **p**.
65:22 It will not be like the **p**, when invaders took the
Jer 14:19 Why have you wounded us **p** all hope of healing?
21:2 and do a mighty miracle as he has done in the **p**.
25:3 "For the **p** twenty-three years—from the thirteenth
31:28 In the **p** I uprooted and tore down this nation.
33:11 the prosperity of this land to what it was in the **p**,
42:21 your God any better now than you have in the **p**.
Eze 18:22 All their **p** sins will be forgotten, and they will live
33:13 expecting their **p** righteousness to save them,
33:16 None of their **p** sins will be brought up again,
36:31 Then you will remember your **p** sins and hate
39:26 They will accept responsibility for their **p** shame
47:18 **p** the Dead Sea and as far south as Tamar.
Da 4:27 Break from your wicked **p** by being merciful to the
Hos 13:1 In the **p** when the tribe of Ephraim spoke,
Mic 5:2 from you, one whose origins are from the distant **p**.
Hab 1:11 They sweep **p** like the wind and are gone. But they
Hag 2:9 of this Temple will be greater than its **p** glory,
Zec 14:3 against those nations, as he has fought in times **p**.
Mt 7:4 when you can't see **p** the log in your own eye?
Mk 6:15 a prophet like the other great prophets of the **p**.
6:48 walking on the water. He started to go **p** them,
Lk 6:42 when you can't see **p** the log in your own eye?
18:36 When he heard the noise of a crowd going **p**,
Ac 27:7 the leeward side of Crete, **p** the cape of Salmone.
Php 1:20 always be bold for Christ, as I have been in the **p**,
1:30 You have seen me suffer for him in the **p**, and you
3:13 Forgetting the **p** and looking forward to what lies
Col 1:26 was kept secret for centuries and generations **p**,
Phm 1:11 Onesimus hasn't been of much use to you in the **p**,
1Pe 4:3 You have had enough in the **p** of the evil things
Rev 9:12 The first terror is **p**, but look, two more terrors are
11:14 The second terror is **p**, but look, now the third

PASTOR [KJV] See SHEPHERD

PASTORS (1)

Eph 4:11 the evangelists, and the **p** and teachers.

PASTRIES (1)

Ge 40:16 "there were three baskets of **p** on my head.

PASTURE (25) [PASTURE-FED, PASTURELAND, PASTURELANDS, PASTURES]

Ge 37:12 Joseph's brothers went to **p** their father's flocks at
47:4 in Egypt, for there is no **p** for our flocks in Canaan.
Nu 35:3 and the surrounding lands will provide **p** for their
2Sa 7:8 a shepherd boy, tending your sheep out in the **p**.
1Ch 17:7 a shepherd boy, tending your sheep out in the **p**.
Ps 65:12 The wilderness becomes a lush **p**,
74:1 so intense against the sheep of your own **p**?

79:13 Then we your people, the sheep of your **p**,
100: 3 we are his. / We are his people, the sheep of his **p**.
Isa 5:17 feed among the ruins; lambs and kids will **p** there.
14:30 I will feed the poor in my **p**; the needy will lie
65:10 and the valley of Achor will be a place to **p** herds.
Jer 49:19 of the Jordan, leaping on the sheep in the **p**.
50:44 of the Jordan, leaping on the sheep in the **p**.
La 1: 6 Her princes are like starving deer searching for **p**,
Eze 25: 5 And I will turn the city of Rabbah into a **p** for
34:31 You are my flock, the sheep of my **p**. You are my
Hos 4:16 as a heifer, so the LORD will put her out to **p**.
Joel 1:18 about confused because there is no **p** for them.
Mic 2:12 again like sheep in a fold, like a flock in its **p**.
Zep 2: 6 The coastal area will become a **p**, a place of
2: 7 The few survivors of the tribe of Judah will **p**
2:14 so proud will become a **p** for sheep and cattle.
Zec 10: 1 of rain so that every field becomes a lush **p**.
Mal 4: 2 go free, leaping with joy like calves let out to **p**.

PASTURE-FED (1) [PASTURE, FEED]

1Ki 4:23 twenty **p** cattle, one hundred sheep or goats,

PASTURELAND (11) [LAND, PASTURE]

Ge 13: 6 There were too many animals for the available **p**.
Lev 25:34 The strip of **p** around each of the Levitical cities
Nu 35: 4 The **p** assigned to the Levites around these towns
35: 5 This area will serve as the larger **p** for the towns.
35: 7 forty-eight towns with the surrounding **p** will be
Dt 11:15 He will give you lush **p** for your cattle to graze in,
1Ch 4:39 east part of the valley, seeking **p** for their flocks.
4:41 because they wanted its good **p** for their flocks.
Job 39: 8 The mountains are its **p**, where it searches for
Isa 30:23 wonderful harvests and plenty of **p** for your cattle.
Eze 34:14 I will give them good **p** on the high hills of Israel.

PASTURELANDS (39) [LAND, PASTURE]

Nu 35: 2 towns to live in, along with the surrounding **p**.
Jos 14: 4 and the surrounding **p** for their flocks and herds.
21: 2 to give us towns to live in and **p** for our cattle."
21: 3 their inheritance the following towns with their **p**.
21: 8 and **p** to the Levites by casting sacred lots.
21:11 hill country of Judah, along with its surrounding **p**.
21:13 The following towns with their **p** were given to the
21:17 the following towns with their surrounding **p**:
21:20 these towns and **p** from the tribe of Ephraim:
21:23 and **p** were allotted to the priests from the tribe of
21:25 the following towns with their **p** to the priests:
21:26 So ten towns with their **p** were given to the rest of
21:27 received two towns with their **p** from the half-tribe
21:29 Jarmuth, and En-gannim—four towns with their **p**.
21:31 Helkath, and Rehob—four towns and their **p**.
21:32 and Kartan—three towns with their **p**.
21:33 and their **p** were allotted to the clan of Gershon.
21:35 Dimnah, and Nahalal—four towns with their **p**.
21:37 and Mephaath—four towns with their **p**.
21:39 Heshbon, and Jazer—four towns with their **p**.
21:41 and **p** within Israelite territory given to the Levites
21:42 Every one of these towns had **p** surrounding it.
1Ch 6:55 included Hebron and its surrounding **p** in Judah,
6:57 the following towns, each with its surrounding **p**:
6:60 Geba, Alemeth, and Anathoth, each with its **p**.
6:64 Israel assigned all these towns and **p** to the Levites.
6:66 Ephraim these towns, each with its surrounding **p**:
6:70 of Manasseh: Aner and Bileam, each with its **p**.
6:71 Manasseh the town of Golan in Bashan with its **p** and Ashtaroth with its **p**.
6:73 Ramoth, and Anem, with their **p**.
6:75 Hukok, and Rehob, each with its **p**.
6:76 Hammon, and Kiriathaim, each with its **p**.
6:77 Kartah, Rimmono, and Tabor, each with its **p**.
6:79 Kedemoth, and Mephaath, each with its **p**.
6:81 Heshbon, and Jazer, each with its **p**.
13: 2 the priests and Levites in their towns and **p**.
Ps 83:12 "Let us seize for our own use / these **p** of God!"
Eze 48:15 homes, **p**, and common lands, with a city at the

PASTURES (21) [PASTURE]

1Ch 4:40 They found lush **p** there, and the land was quiet
Job 5:24 When you visit your **p**, nothing will be missing.
Ps 104:18 High in the mountains are **p** for the wild goats,
147: 8 and makes the green grass grow in mountain **p**.
Isa 32:20 Their flocks and herds will graze in green **p**.
35: 2 as lovely as Mount Carmel's **p** and the plain of
49: 9 grazing in green **p** and on hills that were
Jer 6: 3 around the city and divide your **p** for their flocks.
9:10 weep for the mountains and wail for the desert **p**.
23:10 The land itself is in mourning—its **p** are dried up.
25:36 in despair, for the LORD is spoiling their **p**.
Eze 34:14 in pleasant places and feed in lush mountain **p**.
34:18 Is it not enough for you to keep the best of the **p**
Joel 1:19 The fire has consumed the **p** and burned up all the
1:20 have dried up, and fire has consumed the **p**.
2:22 you animals of the field! The **p** will soon be green.
Am 1: 2 Suddenly, the lush **p** of the shepherds dry up.
Mic 7:14 and rule your people; lead your flock in green **p**.
7:14 Let them enjoy the fertile **p** of Bashan and Gilead
Na 1: 4 dry up, the lush **p** of Bashan and Carmel fade,
Jn 10: 9 be saved. Wherever they go, they will find green **p**.

PAT (1)

2Co 5:12 Are we trying to **p** ourselves on the back again?

PATARA (1)

Ac 21: 1 next day we reached Rhodes and then went to **P**.

PATCH (10) [PATCHED, PATCHES]

Lev 13: 2 or a shiny **p** on their skin that develops into a
13:39 If the **p** is only a pale white, this is a harmless skin
14:56 area of skin, in a skin rash, or in a shiny **p** of skin.
Isa 7:24 The entire land will be one vast brier **p**, a hunting
Mt 9:16 And who would **p** an old garment with unshrunk
9:16 For the **p** shrinks and pulls away from the old
Mk 2:21 And who would **p** an old garment with unshrunk
2:21 For the new **p** shrinks and pulls away from the old
Lk 5:36 a new garment and uses it to **p** an old garment.
5:36 and the **p** wouldn't even match the old garment.

PATCHED (2) [PATCH]

Jos 9: 4 with weathered saddlebags and old **p** wineskins.
9: 5 put on ragged clothes and worn-out, **p** sandals.

PATCHES (3) [PATCH]

Ge 30:35 that were speckled and spotted with any white **p**,
Lev 13:38 a man or woman, has shiny white **p** on the skin,
Isa 7:23 pieces of silver, will become **p** of briers and thorns.

PATH (99) [FOOTPATH, PATHS, PATHWAY, PATHWAYS]

Ge 24:48 because he had led me along the right **p** to find a
27:20 "Because the LORD your God put it in my **p**!"
49:17 beside the road, / a poisonous viper along the **p**,
Ex 14:16 and a **p** will open up before you through the sea.
14:21 and the LORD opened up a **p** through the water
Dt 5:33 Stay on the **p** that the LORD your God has
8:20 the LORD has destroyed other nations in your **p**,
9:16 How quickly you had turned from the **p** the
31:29 and will turn from the **p** I have commanded you to
Jos 2:10 For we have heard how the LORD made a dry **p**
Jdg 2:17 How quickly they turned away from the **p** of their
14: 8 he turned off the **p** to look at the carcass of the
2Sa 22:37 You have made a wide **p** for my feet / to keep
Job 12:24 leaves them wandering in a wasteland without a **p**.
18: 8 a net. They fall into a pit that's been dug in the **p**.
18:10 hidden in the ground. A rope lies coiled on their **p**.
19: 8 blocked my way and plunged my **p** into darkness.
28:26 laws of the rain and prepared a **p** for the lightning.
30:12 They send me sprawling; they lay traps in my **p**.
38:24 Where is the **p** to the origin of light? Where is the
38:25 of rain? Who laid out the **p** for the lightning?
Ps 1: 6 For the LORD watches over the **p** of the godly,
1: 6 but the **p** of the wicked leads to destruction.
5: 8 Lead me in the right **p**, O LORD, / or my enemies
17: 5 My steps have stayed on your **p**; / I have not
18:36 You have made a wide **p** for my feet / to keep
25: 4 Show me the **p** where I should walk, O LORD;
25: 8 he shows the proper **p** to those who go astray.
25:12 He will show them the **p** they should choose.
27:11 O LORD. / Lead me along the **p** of honesty,
35: 6 Make their **p** dark and slippery, / with the angel of
37:31 God's law, / so they will never slip from his **p**.
37:34 Travel steadily along his **p**. / He will honor you,
44:18 deserted you. / We have not strayed from your **p**.
50:23 If you keep to my **p**, / I will reveal to you the
57: 6 from distress. / They have dug a deep pit in my **p**,
66: 6 He made a dry **p** through the Red Sea, / and his
73:18 Truly, you put them on a slippery **p** / and send
106: 9 the Red Sea to divide, and a dry **p** appeared.
119:35 Make me walk along the **p** of your commands,
119:101 I have refused to walk on any **p** of evil, / that I may
119:105 word is a lamp for my feet / and a light for my **p**.
119:110 wicked have set their traps for me along your **p**,
139: 3 You chart the **p** ahead of me / and tell me where to
139:24 and lead me along the **p** of everlasting life.
Pr 1:31 They must experience the full terror of the **p** they
4:14 do as the wicked do or follow the **p** of evildoers.
4:26 Mark out a straight **p** for your feet; then stick to the **p** and stay safe.
5: 6 For she does not care about the **p** to life.
5:21 what a man does, examining every **p** he takes.
7: 8 He was strolling down the **p** by her house
7:25 toward her. Don't wander down her wayward **p**.
12:28 godly leads to life; their **p** does not lead to death.
14: 2 Those who follow the right **p** fear the LORD;
14: 2 those who take the wrong **p** despise him.
14:12 There is a **p** before each person that seems right,
15:10 Whoever abandons the right **p** will be severely
15:19 trouble all through life; the **p** of the upright is easy!
15:21 no sense; a sensible person stays on the right **p**.
15:24 The **p** of the wise leads to life above; they leave
16:17 The **p** of the upright leads away from evil; whoever follows that **p** is safe.
16:25 There is a **p** before each person that seems right,
16:29 their companions, leading them down a harmful **p**.
21: 8 The guilty walk a crooked **p**; the innocent travel a
22: 6 Teach your children to choose the right **p**,
Ecc 7:29 each turned to follow their own downward **p**."
Isa 3:12 They are leading you down a pretty garden **p** to
9:16 people have led them down the **p** of destruction.
11:15 The LORD will make a dry **p** through the Red
26: 7 who are righteous, / the **p** is not steep and rough.
42:16 I will lead blind Israel down a new **p**,
43:16 the waters, making a dry **p** through the sea.
51:10 making a **p** of escape when you saved your
56:11 are stupid shepherds, all following their own **p**,
63:17 why have you allowed us to turn from your **p**?
Jer 6:16 Travel its **p**, and you will find rest for your souls.
6:21 "I will put obstacles in my people's **p**. Fathers
8: 5 people keep going along their self-destructive **p**,
8: 6 All are running down the **p** of sin as swiftly as a
18:22 pit for me, and they have hidden traps along my **p**.
31:21 Mark well the **p** by which you came. Come back
La 1:13 He has placed a trap in my **p** and turned me back.
3: 9 He has blocked my **p** with a high stone wall.
3:11 He dragged me off the **p** and tore me with his
Eze 39:11 The **p** of those who travel there will be blocked by
Da 7:23 the whole world, trampling everything in its **p**.
Zep 1:17 you as helpless as a blind man searching for a **p**.
Mt 13:19 The seed that fell on the hard **p** represents those
Mk 4:15 The seed that fell on the hard **p** represents those
Lk 1:79 of death, / and to guide us to the **p** of peace."
8:12 The seed that fell on the hard **p** represents those
Jn 13:17 now do them! That is the **p** of blessing.
Ro 9:32 They stumbled over the great rock in their **p**.
14:13 will not put an obstacle in another Christian's **p**.
Gal 6: 1 and humbly help that person back onto the right **p**.
2Ti 2:18 They have left the **p** of truth, preaching the lie that
Heb 12:13 Mark out a straight **p** for your feet. Then those who

PATHROS (3)

Jer 44:15 a great crowd of all the Judeans living in **P**,
Eze 29:14 and bring its people back to the land of **P** in
30:14 I will destroy **P**, Zoan, and Thebes, and they will

PATHRUSITES (2)

Ge 10:14 **P**, Casluhites, and the Caphtorites, from whom the
1Ch 1:12 **P**, Casluhites, and the Caphtorites, from whom the

PATHS (28) [PATH]

Jdg 5: 6 and travelers stayed on crooked side **p**.
2Ki 17:19 They walked down the same evil **p** that Israel had
Job 13:27 You put my feet in stocks. You watch all my **p**.
22:15 "Will you continue on the old **p** where evil people
23:11 "For I have stayed in God's **p**; I have followed his
24:13 acknowledge its ways. They will not stay in its **p**.
Ps 23: 3 renews my strength. / He guides me along right **p**,
81:13 that Israel would follow me, walking in my **p**!
119: 3 with evil, / and they walk only in his **p**.
Pr 1:15 with them, my child! Stay far away from their **p**.
2: 8 He guards the **p** of justice and protects those who
2:13 turn from right ways to walk down dark and evil **p**.
2:19 her is doomed. He will never reach the **p** of life.
2:20 men instead, and stay on the **p** of the righteous.
3: 6 his will in all you do, and he will direct your **p**.
3:17 She will guide you down delightful **p**; all her ways
4:11 you wisdom's ways and lead you in straight **p**.
8:20 I walk in righteousness, in **p** of justice.
10: 9 but those who follow crooked **p** will slip and fall.
Isa 48:17 and leads you along the **p** you should follow.
49:11 And I will make my mountains into level **p** for
53: 6 We have left God's **p** to follow our own.
65: 2 They follow their own evil **p** and thoughts.
Jer 14:10 to wander far from me and do not follow in my **p**.
18:15 of good, and they walk the muddy **p** of sin.
23:12 "Therefore, their **p** will be dark and slippery.
Hos 14: 9 The **p** of the LORD are true and right,
Mal 2: 8 But not you! You have left God's **p**.

PATHWAY (11) [PATH, WAY]

Job 31: 7 If I have strayed from his **p**, or if my heart has
31:26 in the skies, or the moon walking down its silver **p**,
Ps 32: 8 "I will guide you along the best **p** for your life.
77:19 your **p** through the mighty waters— / a **p** no one knew was there!
Pr 10:17 People who accept correction are on the **p** to life,
Isa 43:19 I will make a **p** through the wilderness for my
Mt 3: 3 'Prepare a **p** for the Lord's coming! / Make a
Mk 1: 3 'Prepare a **p** for the Lord's coming! / Make a
Lk 3: 4 'Prepare a **p** for the Lord's coming! / Make a
Jn 1:23 'Prepare a straight **p** for the Lord's coming!' "

PATHWAYS (2) [PATH, WAY]

Ps 65:11 even the hard **p** overflow with abundance.
Ecc 11: 5 God's ways are as hard to discern as the **p** of the

PATIENCE (21) [PATIENT]

Ps 78:41 Again and again they tested God's **p**
78:56 did all this for them, / they continued to test his **p**.
95: 9 For there your ancestors tried my **p**; / they courted
106:14 desires ran wild, / testing God's **p** in that dry land.
Pr 25:15 **P** can persuade a prince, and soft speech can crush
Ecc 7: 8 is better than starting. **P** is better than pride.
Isa 7:13 You aren't satisfied to exhaust my **p**. You exhaust the **p** of God as well!
Mic 2: 7 Will the LORD have **p** with such behavior?
6: 3 Tell me why your **p** is exhausted! Answer me!
Ro 15: 5 May God, who gives this **p** and encouragement,
2Co 6: 6 our **p**, our kindness, our sincere love,
Gal 5:22 love, joy, peace, **p**, kindness, goodness,
Col 1:11 so that you will have all the **p** and endurance you
3:12 kindness, humility, gentleness, and **p**.
1Ti 1:16 example of his great **p** with even the worst sinners.
Tit 2: 2 have strong faith and be filled with love and **p**.
Heb 3: 8 when they tested God's **p** in the wilderness.
3: 9 There your ancestors tried my **p**, / even though
6:12 inherit God's promises because of their faith and **p**.
Jas 5:10 For examples of **p** in suffering, look at the

PATIENT (30) [PATIENCE, PATIENTLY]

Ge 44:18 Be **p** with me for a moment, for I know you could
Ru 3:18 Then Naomi said to her, "Just be **p**, my daughter,
Ne 9:30 your love, you were **p** with them for many years.
Job 4: 2 "Will you be **p** and let me say a word? For who

Pr 16:32 It is better to be **p** than powerful; it is better to
Mic 7: 9 I will be **p** as the LORD punishes me, for I have
Zep 3: 8 "Be **p**; the time is coming soon when I will stand
Mt 18:26 the king and begged him, 'Oh, sir, be **p** with me,
18:29 more time. 'Be **p** and I will pay it,' he pleaded.
Ro 2: 4 realize how kind, tolerant, and **p** God is with you?
9:22 but he also has the right to be very **p** with those
12:12 for you. Be **p** in trouble, and always be prayerful.
1Co 4:12 who curse us. We are **p** with those who abuse us.
13: 4 Love is **p** and kind. Love is not jealous or boastful
2Co 11: 1 I hope you will be **p** with me as I keep on talking
Eph 4: 2 Be **p** with each other, making allowance for each
1Th 5:14 care of those who are weak. Be **p** with everyone.
2Ti 2:24 to teach effectively and be **p** with difficult people.
3:10 You know my love and my **p** endurance.
Heb 10:36 **P** endurance is what you need now, so you will
Jas 5: 7 you must be **p** as you wait for the Lord's return.
5: 8 You, too, must be **p**. And take courage,
1Pe 2:20 you get no credit for being **p** if you are beaten for
2:20 suffer for doing right and are **p** beneath the blows,
2Pe 1: 6 Self-control leads to **p** endurance, and **p** endurance
leads to godliness.
3: 9 some people think. No, he is being **p** for your sake.
Rev 1: 9 and in the Kingdom and in **p** endurance.
2: 2 I have seen your hard work and your **p** endurance.
2:19 your faith, your service, and your **p** endurance.

PATIENTLY (21) [PATIENT]

Ps 27:14 Wait **p** for the LORD. / Be brave and courageous. / Yes, wait **p** for the LORD.
37: 7 of the LORD, / and wait **p** for him to act.
40: 1 I waited **p** for the LORD to help me, / and he
Isa 38:13 I waited **p** all night, / but I was torn apart as though
Hab 2: 3 If it seems slow, wait **p**, for it will surely take
Ac 26: 3 and controversies. Now please listen to me **p**!
Ro 8:25 we don't have yet, we must wait **p** and confidently.
15: 4 and encouragement as we wait **p** for God's
2Co 1: 6 Then you can **p** endure the same things we suffer.
6: 4 We **p** endure troubles and hardships and calamities
12:12 For I **p** did many signs and wonders and miracles
2Ti 4: 2 **P** correct, rebuke, and encourage your people with
Heb 6:15 Then Abraham waited **p**, and he received what
Jas 1:12 God blesses the people who **p** endure testing.
5: 7 They **p** wait for the precious harvest to ripen.
5:11 Job is an example of a man who endured **p**.
1Pe 2:19 of your conscience, you **p** endure unfair treatment.
3:20 God waited **p** while Noah was building his boat.
Rev 2: 3 You have **p** suffered for me without quitting.
14:12 God's holy people to endure persecution **p**

PATMOS (1)

Rev 1: 9 I was exiled to the island of **P** for preaching the

PATRIARCH (1) [PATRIARCHS]

Heb 7: 4 Even Abraham, the great **p** of Israel,

PATRIARCHS (2) [PATRIARCH]

Ac 7: 8 and Jacob was the father of the twelve **p** of the
Ro 11:16 And since Abraham and the other **p** were holy,

PATROBAS (1)

Ro 16:14 Phlegon, Hermes, **P**, Hermas, and the other

PATROL (4) [PATROLLED]

Zec 1:10 "They are the ones the LORD has sent out to **p**
6: 7 to be off, to **p** back and forth across the earth.
6: 7 And the LORD said, "Go and **p** the earth!" So they left at once on their **p**.

PATROLLED (2) [PATROL]

Ps 55:10 Its walls are **p** day and night against invaders,
Zec 1:11 "We have **p** the earth, and the whole earth is at

PATTERN (5) [PATTERNED]

Ex 25:40 to the **p** I have shown you here on the mountain.
Nu 9:16 This was the regular **p**—at night the cloud changed
Jos 6:14 to the camp. They followed this **p** for six days.
Php 3:17 Dear friends, **p** your lives after mine, and learn
2Ti 1:13 Hold on to the **p** of right teaching you learned from

PATTERNED (2) [PATTERN]

Ge 1:27 in his own image; / God **p** them after himself;
Ex 28:39 "Weave Aaron's **p** tunic from fine linen cloth.

PAU (2)

Ge 36:39 Hadad became king and ruled from the city of **P**.
1Ch 1:50 Hadad became king and ruled from the city of **P**.

PAUL (209) [PAUL'S, SAUL]

Ac 13: 9 Then Saul, also known as **P**, filled with the Holy
13:13 Now **P** and those with him left Paphos by ship for
13:14 and **P** traveled inland to Antioch of Pisidia.
13:16 So **P** stood, lifted his hand to quiet them,
13:42 As **P** and Barnabas left the synagogue that day,
13:43 who worshiped at the synagogue followed **P**
13:45 so they slandered **P** and argued against whatever
13:46 Then **P** and Barnabas spoke out boldly
13:50 and they incited a mob against **P** and Barnabas
14: 1 **P** and Barnabas went together to the synagogue
14: 2 stirred up distrust among the Gentiles against **P**
14: 8 **P** and Barnabas came upon a man with crippled
14: 9 He was listening as **P** preached, and **P** noticed him and realized he had faith to be
14:10 So **P** called to him in a loud voice, "Stand up!"
14:11 When the listening crowd saw what **P** had done,
14:12 that Barnabas was the Greek god Zeus and that **P**,
14:14 when Barnabas and **P** heard what was happening,
14:18 **P** and Barnabas could scarcely restrain the people
14:19 They stoned **P** and dragged him out of the city,
14:21 **P** and Barnabas returned again to Lystra, Iconium,
14:23 **P** and Barnabas also appointed elders in every
15: 1 While **P** and Barnabas were at Antioch of Syria,
15: 2 **P** and Barnabas, disagreeing with them,
15: 2 Finally, **P** and Barnabas were sent to Jerusalem,
15: 4 **P** and Barnabas were welcomed by the whole
15:12 as Barnabas and **P** told about the miraculous signs
15:22 and they sent them to Antioch of Syria with **P**
15:25 along with our beloved Barnabas and **P**,
15:35 **P** and Barnabas stayed in Antioch to assist many
15:36 After some time **P** said to Barnabas, "Let's return
15:38 But **P** disagreed strongly, since John Mark had
15:40 **P** chose Silas, and the believers sent them off,
16: 1 **P** and Silas went first to Derbe and then on to
16: 3 so **P** wanted him to join them on their journey.
16: 6 Next **P** and Silas traveled through the area of
16: 9 That night **P** had a vision. He saw a man from
16:14 her heart, and she accepted what **P** was saying.
16:18 This went on day after day until **P** got
16:19 so they grabbed **P** and Silas and dragged them
16:22 A mob quickly formed against **P** and Silas,
16:25 **P** and Silas were praying and singing hymns to
16:28 But **P** shouted to him, "Don't do it! We are all
16:29 to the dungeon and fell down before **P** and Silas.
16:36 So the jailer told **P**, "You and Silas are free to
16:37 But **P** replied, "They have publicly beaten us
16:38 the city officials were alarmed to learn that **P**
16:40 **P** and Silas then returned to the home of Lydia,
17: 1 Now **P** and Silas traveled through the towns of
17: 5 searching for **P** and Silas so they could drag them
17: 6 "**P** and Silas have turned the rest of the world
17:10 That very night the believers sent **P** and Silas to
17:11 the Scriptures day after day to check up on **P**
17:13 But when some Jews in Thessalonica learned that **P**
17:14 sending **P** on to the coast, while Silas and Timothy
17:15 Those escorting **P** went with him to Athens,
17:16 While **P** was waiting for them in Athens, he was
17:22 So **P**, standing before the Council, addressed them
17:32 When they heard **P** speak of the resurrection of a
18: 1 Then **P** left Athens and went to Corinth.
18: 3 **P** lived and worked with them, for they were
18: 4 Each Sabbath found **P** at the synagogue, trying to
18: 5 **P** spent his full time preaching and testifying to the
18: 6 **P** shook the dust from his robe and said,
18: 9 One night the Lord spoke to **P** in a vision and told
18:11 So **P** stayed there for the next year and a half,
18:12 some Jews rose in concerted action against **P**
18:13 They accused **P** of "persuading people to worship
18:14 But just as **P** started to make his defense,
18:18 **P** stayed in Corinth for some time after that and
18:18 **P** had shaved his head according to Jewish custom,
18:19 at the port of Ephesus, **P** left the others behind.
18:23 **P** went back to Galatia and Phrygia, visiting all the
19: 1 **P** traveled through the interior provinces.
19: 4 **P** said, "John's baptism was to demonstrate a
19: 6 Then when **P** laid his hands on them, the Holy
19: 8 Then **P** went to the synagogue and preached boldly
19: 9 so **P** left the synagogue and took the believers with
19:11 God gave **P** the power to do unusual miracles,
19:13 you by Jesus, whom **P** preaches, to come out!"
19:15 the spirit replied, "I know Jesus, and I know **P**.
19:21 Afterward **P** felt impelled by the Holy Spirit to go
19:26 this man **P** has persuaded many people that
19:30 **P** wanted to go in, but the believers wouldn't let
19:31 friends of **P**, also sent a message to him,
20: 1 **P** sent for the believers and encouraged them.
20: 7 **P** was preaching; and since he was leaving the next
20: 9 As **P** spoke on and on, a young man named
20:10 **P** went down, bent over him, and took him into his
20:11 And **P** continued talking to them until dawn;
20:13 **P** went by land to Assos, where he had arranged
20:16 **P** had decided against stopping at Ephesus this
21: 4 Holy Spirit that **P** should not go on to Jerusalem.
21:12 begged **P** not to go on to Jerusalem.
21:18 The next day **P** went in with us to meet with
21:19 **P** gave a detailed account of the things God had
21:26 So **P** agreed to their request, and the next day he
21:27 from the province of Asia saw **P** in the Temple
21:29 and they assumed **P** had taken him into the
21:30 **P** was dragged out of the Temple, and immediately
21:32 and the troops coming, they stopped beating **P**.
21:34 so he ordered **P** to be taken to the fortress.
21:35 so violent the soldiers had to lift **P** to their
21:37 As **P** was about to be taken inside, he said to the
21:39 "No," **P** replied, "I am a Jew from Tarsus in
21:40 so **P** stood on the stairs and motioned to the people
22: 1 "Brothers and esteemed fathers," **P** said,
22:22 The crowd listened until **P** came to that word,
22:24 The commander brought **P** inside and ordered him
22:25 As they tied **P** down to lash him, **P** said to the officer standing there,
22:27 So the commander went over and asked **P**,
22:27 Roman citizen?" "Yes, I certainly am," **P** replied.
22:29 The soldiers who were about to interrogate **P**
22:30 The next day the commander freed **P** from his
22:30 He had **P** brought in before them to try to find out
23: 1 Gazing intently at the high council, **P** began:
23: 2 those close to **P** to slap him on the mouth.
23: 3 But **P** said to him, "God will slap you,
23: 4 Those standing near **P** said to him, "Is that the
23: 5 the high priest," **P** replied, "for the Scriptures say,
23: 6 **P** realized that some members of the high council
23: 9 Pharisees jumped up to argue that **P** was all right.
23:10 and the men were tugging at **P** from both sides,
23:11 That night the Lord appeared to **P** and said, "Be encouraged, **P**.
23:12 oath to neither eat nor drink until they had killed **P**.
23:14 oath to neither eat nor drink until we have killed **P**.
23:15 commander to bring **P** back to the council again,"
23:16 of their plan and went to the fortress and told **P**.
23:17 **P** called one of the officers and said, "Take this
23:18 explaining, "**P**, the prisoner, called me over
23:20 "Some Jews are going to ask you to bring **P** before
23:24 Provide horses for **P** to ride, and get him safely to
23:31 as ordered, the soldiers took **P** as far as Antipatris.
23:33 they presented **P** and the letter to Governor Felix.
23:34 and then asked **P** what province he was from. "Cilicia," **P** answered.
24: 1 the lawyer Tertullus, to press charges against **P**.
24: 2 When **P** was called in, Tertullus laid charges against **P** in the following
24:10 **P** said, "I know, sir, that you have been a judge of
24:23 He ordered an officer to keep **P** in custody but to
24:24 Sending for **P**, they listened as he told them about
24:26 He also hoped that **P** would bribe him, so he sent
24:27 favor with the Jewish leaders, he left **P** in prison.
25: 2 met with him and made their accusations against **P**.
25: 3 They asked Festus as a favor to transfer **P** to
25: 4 But Festus replied that **P** was at Caesarea and he
25: 5 If **P** has done anything wrong, you can make your
25: 8 **P** denied the charges. "I am not guilty," he said.
25:10 But **P** replied, "No! This is the official Roman
25:17 case the very next day and ordered **P** brought in.
25:19 called Jesus who died, but whom **P** insists is alive.
25:21 But **P** appealed to the emperor. So I ordered him
25:23 of the city. Festus ordered that **P** be brought in.
26: 1 Then Agrippa said to **P**, "You may speak in your
26: 1 So **P**, with a gesture of his hand, started his
26:24 Suddenly, Festus shouted, "**P**, you are insane.
26:25 But **P** replied, "I am not insane, Most Excellent
26:29 **P** replied, "Whether quickly or not, I pray to God
27: 1 **P** and several other prisoners were placed in the
27: 3 Julius was very kind to **P** and let him go ashore to
27: 9 the fall, and **P** spoke to the ship's officers about it.
27:11 more to the ship's captain and the owner than to **P**.
27:21 Finally, **P** called the crew together and said, "Men,
27:24 and he said, 'Don't be afraid, **P**, for you will surely
27:31 But **P** said to the commanding officer
27:33 the early morning light, **P** begged everyone to eat.
27:43 But the commanding officer wanted to spare **P**,
28: 3 As **P** gathered an armful of sticks and was laying
28: 5 But **P** shook off the snake into the fire and was
28: 8 **P** went in and prayed for him, and laying his hands
28:15 When **P** saw them, he thanked God and took
28:16 **P** was permitted to have his own private lodging,
28:25 they left with this final word from **P**:
28:30 next two years, **P** lived in his own rented house.
Ro 1: 1 This letter is from **P**, Jesus Christ's slave,
16:22 Tertius, the one who is writing this letter for **P**,
1Co 1: 1 This letter is from **P**, chosen by the will of God to
1:12 Some of you are saying, "I am a follower of **P**."
1:13 be divided into pieces? Was I, **P**, crucified for you?
1:13 Were any of you baptized in the name of **P**?
3: 4 "I am a follower of **P**," and another says,
3: 5 Who is Apollos, and who is **P**, that we should be
3:22 **P** and Apollos and Peter; the whole world and life
16:21 my greeting, which I write with my own hand—**P**.
2Co 1: 1 This letter is from **P**, appointed by God to be an
10: 1 Now I, **P**, plead with you. I plead with the
10:10 For some say, "Don't worry about **P**. His letters
Gal 1: 1 This letter is from **P**, an apostle. I was not
5: 2 Listen! I, **P**, tell you this: If you are counting on
Eph 1: 1 This letter is from **P**, chosen by God to be an
3: 1 I, **P**, am a prisoner of Christ Jesus because of my
Php 1: 1 This letter is from **P** and Timothy, slaves of Christ
Col 1: 1 This letter is from **P**, chosen by God to be an
1:23 and I, **P**, have been appointed by God to proclaim
4:18 Here is my greeting in my own handwriting—**P**.
1Th 1: 1 This letter is from **P**, Silas, and Timothy. It is
2:18 and I, **P**, tried again and again, but Satan prevented
2Th 1: 1 This letter is from **P**, Silas, and Timothy. It is
3:17 my greeting, which I write with my own hand—**P**.
1Ti 1: 1 This letter is from **P**, an apostle of Christ Jesus,
2Ti 1: 1 This letter is from **P**, an apostle of Christ Jesus by
Tit 1: 1 This letter is from **P**, a slave of God and an apostle
Phm 1: 1 This letter is from **P**, in prison for preaching the
1: 9 So take this as a request from your friend **P**,
1:19 I, **P**, write this in my own handwriting: "I will
2Pe 3:15 This is just as our beloved brother **P** wrote to you

PAUL'S (14) [PAUL]

Ac 17: 2 As was **P** custom, he went to the synagogue
17:11 and they listened eagerly to **P** message.
17:33 That ended **P** discussion with them,
18:14 Gallio turned to **P** accusers and said, "Listen,
19:29 who were **P** traveling companions from
21:11 he took **P** belt and bound his own feet and hands
23:16 But **P** nephew heard of their plan and went to the
23:20 **P** nephew told him, "Some Jews are going to ask
24:10 Now it was **P** turn. The governor motioned for him
25: 6 and on the following day **P** trial began.
25: 7 On **P** arrival in court, the Jewish leaders from
25:14 Festus discussed **P** case with the king.
28:17 Three days after **P** arrival, he called together the
28:23 that day a large number of people came to **P** house.

PAULUS (1) [SERGIUS]
Ac 13: 7 Sergius **P**, a man of considerable insight

PAUSE (1) [PAUSED]
Da 11: 16 He will **p** in the glorious land of Israel, intent on

PAUSED (1) [PAUSE]
2Sa 15: 17 set out on foot, and they **p** at the edge of the city

PAVEMENT (10)
Ex 24: 10 Under his feet there seemed to be a **p** of brilliant
2Ki 16: 17 of the bronze oxen and placed it on the stone **p**.
Est 1: 6 and silver couches stood on a mosaic **p** of
Jer 43: 9 bury large rocks between the **p** stones at the
Eze 40: 17 A stone **p** ran along the walls of the courtyard,
40: 17 were built against the walls, opening onto the **p**.
40: 18 This **p** flanked the gates and extended out from the
40: 18 as the gateway entrance. This was the lower **p**.
42: 3 Another block of rooms looked out onto the **p** of
Jn 19: 13 the platform that is called the Stone **P** (in Hebrew,

PAW (1) [PAWS]
Job 28: 8 upon those treasures; no lion has set his **p** there.

PAWS (3) [PAW]
Lev 11: 27 on all fours, those that have **p** are unclean for you.
Job 39: 21 It **p** the earth and rejoices in its strength. When it
39: 24 Fiercely it **p** the ground and rushes forward into

PAY (185) [PAID, PAYING, PAYMENT, PAYMENTS, PAYS, REPAID, REPAY, REPAYING, REPAYMENT, REPAYS]
Ge 16: 5 The LORD will make you **p** for doing this to
23: 9 I want to **p** the full price, of course, whatever is
23: 13 Let me **p** the full price for the field so I can bury
29: 15 "You shouldn't work for me without **p** just
29: 20 So Jacob spent the next seven years working to **p**
30: 28 How much do I owe you? Whatever it is, I'll **p** it."
31: 39 You made me **p** for every animal stolen from the
34: 12 matter what dowry or gift you demand, I will **p** it—
38: 16 "How much will you **p** me?" Tamar asked.
43: 21 The money we had used to **p** for the grain was
50: 15 "Now Joseph will **p** us back for all the evil we did
Ex 2: 9 the princess told her. "I will **p** you for your help."
7: 1 LORD said to Moses, "**P** close attention to this.
21: 19 the assailant must **p** for time lost because of the
21: 19 of the injury and must **p** for the medical expenses.
21: 22 then the person responsible must **p** damages in the
21: 30 The owner will have to **p** whatever is demanded.
21: 34 The owner of the well must **p** in full for the dead
21: 36 The owner of the living bull must **p** in full for the
22: 3 "A thief who is caught must **p** in full for
22: 3 the thief must be sold as a slave to **p** the debt.
22: 4 then the thief must **p** double the value.
22: 5 then the animal's owner must **p** damages in the
22: 6 then the one who started the fire must **p** for the lost
22: 9 and the person whom God declares guilty must **p**
22: 14 the time, the person who borrowed it must **p** for it.
22: 16 he must **p** the customary dowry and accept her as
22: 17 the man must still **p** the money for her dowry.
23: 21 **P** attention to him, and obey all of his instructions.
30: 12 each man who is counted must **p** a ransom for
Lev 19: 13 "Always **p** your hired workers promptly.
22: 14 realizing it must **p** the priest for the amount eaten,
22: 16 the people and require them to **p** compensation.
24: 18 another person's animal must **p** it back in full—
26: 41 will be humbled, and they will **p** for their sins.
27: 8 but cannot afford to **p** the prescribed amount,
27: 8 to the priest and he will evaluate your ability to **p**.
27: 8 You will then **p** the amount decided by the priest.
27: 13 you must **p** the value set by the priest, plus 20
27: 15 you must **p** the value set by the priest, plus 20
27: 19 you must **p** the land's value as assessed by the
27: 31 tenth of the fruit or grain, you must **p** its value,
Nu 14: 33 In this way, they will **p** for your faithlessness,
18: 21 I will **p** them for their service in the Tabernacle
20: 19 of our livestock drinks your water, we will **p** for it.
22: 7 and took money with them to **p** Balaam to curse
22: 17 I will **p** you well and do anything you ask of me.
Dt 2: 6 **P** them for whatever food or water you use.
2: 28 We will **p** for every bite of food we eat and all the
22: 29 he must **p** fifty pieces of silver to her father.
24: 15 **P** them their wages each day before sunset
Jdg 5: 3 you kings! / **P** attention, you mighty rulers!
15: 10 We have come to **p** him back for what he did to
16: 28 so that I may **p** back the Philistines for the loss of
1Sa 25: 25 please don't **p** any attention to him.
1Ki 5: 6 and I will **p** your men whatever wages you ask.
5: 9 You can **p** me with food for my household."
20: 39 or **p** a fine of seventy-five pounds of silver!'
21: 2 in exchange, or if you prefer, I will **p** you for it."
2Ki 3: 4 They used to **p** the king of Israel an annual tribute
4: 7 to her, "Now sell the olive oil and **p** your debts,
10: 24 you will **p** for it with your own life."
12: 5 Let the priests take some of that money to **p** for
12: 11 who used it to **p** the people working on the
15: 20 demanding that each of them **p** twenty ounces of
17: 3 so Israel was forced to **p** heavy annual tribute to
17: 4 and by refusing to **p** the annual tribute to Assyria.
18: 7 the king of Assyria and refused to **p** him tribute.
18: 14 I will **p** whatever tribute money you demand if you
22: 5 Then they can use it to **p** workers to repair the
23: 33 He also demanded that Judah **p** 7,500 pounds of
23: 35 requiring them to **p** in proportion to their wealth.
2Ch 2: 10 I will **p** your men 100,000 bushels of crushed
Ezr 4: 13 for the Jews will then refuse to **p** their tribute,
6: 8 You must **p** the full construction costs without
7: 24 of God will be required to **p** taxes of any kind.'
Ne 5: 4 the limit on our fields and vineyards to **p** our taxes.
10: 32 we promise to obey the command to **p** the annual
Est 4: 7 **p** into the royal treasury for the destruction of the
Job 8: 8 **P** attention to the experience of our ancestors.
13: 6 Listen to my charge; **p** attention to my arguments.
21: 33 Many **p** their respects as the body is laid to rest
34: 2 wise men. **P** attention, you who have knowledge.
34: 19 and he doesn't **p** any more attention to the rich
Ps 5: 1 hear me as I pray; / **p** attention to my groaning.
17: 1 to my cry for help. / **P** attention to my prayer,
28: 4 **P** them back for all their evil deeds!
41: 10 Make me well again, so I can **p** them back!
49: 1 you people! / **P** attention, everyone in the world!
49: 8 not come so easily, / for no one can ever **p** enough
54: 2 listen to my prayer. / **P** attention to my plea.
119: 71 for it taught me to **p** attention to your principles.
130: 2 Hear my cry, O Lord. / **P** attention to my prayer.
Pr 4: 1 father's instruction. **P** attention and grow wise,
4: 20 **P** attention, my child, to what I say.
5: 1 My son, **p** attention to my wisdom; listen carefully
5: 13 Why didn't I **p** attention to those who gave me
6: 31 means selling everything in his house to **p** it back.
7: 24 to me, my sons, and **p** attention to my words.
13: 8 The rich can **p** a ransom, but the poor won't even
17: 4 wicked talk; liars **p** attention to destructive words.
17: 16 It is senseless to **p** tuition to educate a fool who has
19: 19 Short-tempered people must **p** their own penalty.
22: 27 If you can't **p** it, even your bed will be snatched
23: 1 with a ruler, **p** attention to what is put before you.
24: 29 "Now I can **p** them back for all their meanness to
30: 10 the person will curse you, and you will **p** for it.
Isa 30: 6 and camels loaded with treasure to **p** for Egypt's
30: 9 to **p** any attention to the LORD's instructions.
44: 21 "**P** attention, O Israel, for you are my servant.
55: 2 Why **p** for food that does you no good? Listen,
65: 7 insulted me on the hills. I will **p** them back in full!
Jer 6: 17 But you replied, 'No! We won't **p** attention!'
11: 8 But your ancestors did not **p** any attention;
14: 12 they fast in my presence, I will **p** no attention.
15: 10 to foreclose nor a borrower who refuses to **p**—
17: 23 They stubbornly refused to **p** attention and would
22: 5 But if you refuse to **p** attention to this warning,
La 3: 64 **P** them back, LORD, for all the evil they have
5: 4 We have to **p** for water to drink, and even firewood
Eze 16: 34 No one pays you; instead, you **p** them!
18: 19 'Doesn't the child **p** for the parent's sins?' No!
20: 19 'Follow my laws, **p** attention to my instructions,
22: 7 Resident foreigners are forced to **p** for protection.
29: 19 plundering everything they have to **p** his army.
35: 11 I will **p** back your angry deeds with mine.
40: 4 **P** close attention to everything I show you.
Joel 3: 4 and **p** you back for everything you have done.
3: 7 and I will **p** you back for all you have done.
Mic 1: 7 and they will now be carried away to **p** prostitutes
3: 5 but you declare war on anyone who refuses to **p**
6: 7 Should we sacrifice our firstborn children to **p** for
7: 3 The people with money and influence **p** them off,
Mt 17: 24 "Doesn't your teacher **p** the Temple tax?"
17: 27 a coin. Take the coin and **p** the tax for both of us."
18: 25 He couldn't **p**, so the king ordered that he,
18: 25 and everything he had be sold to **p** the debt.
18: 26 'Oh, sir, be patient with me, and I will **p** it all.'
18: 29 more time. 'Be patient and I will **p** it,' he pleaded.
20: 2 He agreed to **p** the normal daily wage and sent
20: 4 telling them he would **p** them whatever was right
20: 8 told the foreman to call the workers in and **p** them,
20: 10 When those hired earlier came to get their **p**,
20: 11 When they received their **p**, they protested,
20: 14 I wanted to **p** this last worker the same as you.
22: 17 Is it right to **p** taxes to the Roman government
24: 15 standing in the holy place"—reader, **p** attention!
24: 23 or 'There he is,' don't **p** any attention.
26: 15 "How much will you **p** me to betray Jesus to
Mk 4: 24 And be sure to **p** attention to what you hear.
5: 26 and had spent everything she had to **p** them,
12: 14 is it right to **p** taxes to the Roman government
12: 15 Should we **p** them, or should we not?" Jesus saw
13: 14 where it should not be"—reader, **p** attention!
13: 21 or, 'There he is,' don't **p** any attention.
Lk 3: 14 know they didn't do. And be content with your **p**."
8: 18 So be sure to **p** attention to what you hear.
10: 7 because those who work deserve their **p**.
10: 35 'I'll **p** the difference the next time I am here.'
14: 28 then checking to see if there is enough money to **p**
20: 22 is it right to **p** taxes to the Roman government
23: 2 them not to **p** their taxes to the Roman government
Jn 11: 19 and many of the people had come to **p** their
13: 29 and **p** for the food or to give some money to the
Ac 13: 8 and urged the governor to **p** no attention to what
20: 34 hands of mine have worked to **p** my own way,
21: 24 and **p** for them to have their heads shaved.
25: 13 his sister, Bernice, to **p** their respects to Festus.
Ro 11: 35 give him so much that he would have to **p** it back?
12: 17 Never **p** back evil for evil to anyone. Do things in
13: 6 **P** your taxes, too, for these same reasons.
13: 7 **P** your taxes and import duties, and give respect
13: 8 **P** all your debts, except the debt of love for others.
1Co 4: 6 If you **p** attention to the Scriptures, you won't brag
9: 7 What soldier has to **p** his own expenses? And have
9: 18 What then is my **p**? It is the satisfaction I get from
9: 19 not bound to obey people just because they **p** me,
2Co 12: 14 little children don't **p** for their parents' food.
Gal 4: 17 from me so that you will **p** more attention to them.
1Ti 5: 18 another place, "Those who work deserve their **p**!"
Jas 2: 9 But if you **p** special attention to the rich, you are
5: 4 field workers whom you have cheated of their **p**.
1Pe 3: 9 Instead, **p** them back with a blessing. That is what
2Pe 1: 19 **P** close attention to what they wrote, for their
Rev 6: 6 wheat bread or three loaves of barley for a day's **p**.

PAYING (16) [PAY]
Lev 5: 16 holy things they have defiled by **p** for the loss,
27: 2 to the LORD by **p** the value of that person,
27: 27 you may redeem it by **p** the priest's assessment of
1Sa 17: 25 and his whole family will be exempted from **p**
2Sa 16: 8 "The LORD is **p** you back for murdering Saul
1Ch 21: 24 to Araunah, "No, I insist on **p** what it is worth.
Ezr 3: 7 people of Tyre and Sidon, **p** them with food, wine,
Ps 49: 7 themselves from death / by **p** a ransom to God.
Isa 52: 3 Now I can redeem you without **p** for you."
Jer 22: 13 By not **p** wages, he builds injustice into its walls
32: 9 **p** Hanamel seventeen pieces of silver for it.
32: 25 **p** good money for it before these witnesses—
Da 6: 13 from Judah, is **p** no attention to you or your law.
Ro 13: 8 You can never finish **p** that! If you love your
Gal 6: 6 word of God should help their teachers by **p** them.
2Th 3: 8 We never accepted food from anyone without **p** for

PAYMENT (33) [PAY]
Ge 42: 25 to return each brother's **p** at the top of his sack.
47: 26 the priests' land, they were exempt from this **p**.
Ex 21: 11 may leave as a free woman without making any **p**.
21: 24 Similarly, the **p** must be hand for hand, foot for
21: 27 the slave should be released in **p** for the tooth.
21: 30 the dead person's relatives may accept **p** from the
21: 32 slave's owner is to be given thirty silver coins in **p**,
22: 3 If **p** is not made, the thief must be sold as a slave to
22: 11 the neighbor's word, and no **p** will be required.
22: 12 property was stolen, **p** must be made to the owner.
22: 13 be shown as evidence, and no **p** will be required.
22: 15 no **p** is required. And no **p** is required if the animal
22: 29 "You must make the necessary **p** for redemption
30: 13 His **p** to the LORD will be one-fifth of an ounce
Lev 23: 28 your God, and **p** will be made for your sins.
Nu 35: 31 you must never accept a ransom **p** for the life of
35: 32 And never accept a ransom **p** from someone who
Dt 15: 2 They must not demand **p** from their neighbors
22: 19 The **p** will be made to the woman's father.
27: 25 'Cursed is anyone who accepts **p** to kill an
Jdg 3: 18 After delivering the **p**, Ehud sent home those who
1Ki 5: 11 In return Solomon sent him an annual **p** of 100,000
9: 11 to King Hiram of Tyre as **p** for all the cedar
2Ki 12: 4 a **p** of vows, or a voluntary gift.
1Ch 21: 25 hundred pieces of gold in **p** for the threshing floor.
Isa 52: 3 "When I sold you into exile, I received no **p**.
Eze 16: 31 that you have not even demanded **p** for your love!
27: 15 they brought **p** in ivory tusks and ebony wood.
Hos 9: 7 punishment has come; the day of **p** is almost here.
12: 14 so their Lord will now sentence them to death in **p**
Mt 18: 28 grabbed him by the throat and demanded instant **p**.
1Co 9: 17 this of my own free will, then I would deserve **p**.

PAYMENTS (2) [PAY]
Lev 5: 16 When they give their **p** to the priest, he will make
Eze 16: 41 and end your **p** to your many lovers.

PAYS (9) [PAY]
2Sa 22: 48 He is the God who **p** back those who harm me;
Ps 18: 47 He is the God who **p** back those who harm me;
137: 8 be destroyed. / Happy is the one who **p** you back
SS 8: 11 Each of them **p** one thousand pieces of silver for
Isa 31: 4 it **p** no attention to the shepherd's shouts and noise.
45: 21 and state your proofs that idol worship **p**.
Eze 16: 34 No one **p** you; instead, you pay them!
Mal 2: 13 because he **p** no attention to your offerings,
1Th 5: 15 See that no one **p** back evil for evil, but always try

PEACE (350) [PACIFIED, PACIFIES, PACIFY, PEACE-OFFERING, PEACEABLY, PEACEFUL, PEACEFULLY, PEACEMAKER, PEACEMAKERS]
Ge 15: 15 (But you will die in **p**, at a ripe old age.)
26: 29 you well, and we sent you away from us in **p**.
26: 31 Then Isaac sent them home again in **p**.
31: 44 Come now, and we will make a **p** treaty, you and I,
Ex 18: 23 and all these people will go home in **p**."
20: 24 your burnt offerings and **p** offerings, your sheep
24: 5 as burnt offerings and **p** offerings to the LORD.
29: 28 whenever the people of Israel offer up **p** offerings
32: 6 to sacrifice burnt offerings and **p** offerings.
34: 15 If you make **p** with them, they will invite you to go
Lev 3: 1 "If you want to present a **p** offering from the herd,
3: 3 Part of this **p** offering must be presented to the
3: 6 "If you present a **p** offering to the LORD from
3: 9 Part of this **p** offering must be presented to the
4: 10 with the bull or cow sacrificed as a **p** offering.
4: 26 fat on the altar, just as is done with the **p** offering.
4: 31 the goat's fat, just as is done with the **p** offering.
4: 35 just as is done with a sheep presented as a **p**
6: 12 then burn the fat of the **p** offerings on top of this
7: 11 **p** offerings that may be presented to the LORD.
7: 12 If you present your **p** offering as a thanksgiving
7: 13 This **p** offering of thanksgiving must also be
7: 18 If any of the meat from this **p** offering is eaten on

7:20 but eats meat from a **p** offering that was presented
7:29 When you present a **p** offering to the LORD,
7:32 You are to give the right thigh of your **p** offering to
7:33 the blood and offers the fat of the **p** offering.
7:34 It is their regular share of the **p** offerings brought
7:37 the ordination offering, and the **p** offering.
9: 4 tell them to take a bull and a ram for a **p** offering
9:18 the bull and the ram for the people's **p** offering.
9:22 the whole burnt offering, and the **p** offering,
10:14 and daughters as your regular share of the **p**
17: 5 so he can present them to the LORD as **p**
19: 5 "When you sacrifice a **p** offering to the LORD,
22:21 "If you bring a **p** offering to the LORD from the
23:19 and two one-year-old male lambs as a **p** offering.
26: 6 "I will give you **p** in the land, and you will be able
Nu 6:14 sin offering, a ram without defect for a **p** offering,
6:17 then the ram for a **p** offering, along with the basket
6:26 LORD show you his favor / and give you his **p**.'
7:17 and five one-year-old male lambs for a **p** offering.
7:23 and five one-year-old male lambs for a **p** offering.
7:29 and five one-year-old male lambs for a **p** offering.
7:35 and five one-year-old male lambs for a **p** offering.
7:41 and five one-year-old male lambs for a **p** offering.
7:47 and five one-year-old male lambs for a **p** offering.
7:53 and five one-year-old male lambs for a **p** offering.
7:59 and five one-year-old male lambs for a **p** offering.
7:65 and five one-year-old male lambs for a **p** offering.
7:71 and five one-year-old male lambs for a **p** offering.
7:77 and five one-year-old male lambs for a **p** offering.
7:83 and five one-year-old male lambs for a **p** offering.
7:88 male lambs were donated for the **p** offerings.
10:10 rejoice over your burnt offerings and **p** offerings.
15: 8 of a special vow or as a **p** offering to the LORD,
25:12 I am making my special covenant of **p** with him.
29:39 grain offerings, drink offerings, or **p** offerings."
Dt 2:26 to King Sihon of Heshbon with this proposal of **p**:
20:10 a town to attack it, first offer its people terms for **p**.
20:12 But if they refuse to make **p** and prepare to fight,
27: 7 Sacrifice **p** offerings on it also, and feast there with
Jos 8:31 burnt offerings and **p** offerings to the LORD.
9: 6 distant land to ask you to make a **p** treaty with us."
9:11 our people to be their servants, and ask for **p**.'
9:15 went ahead and signed a **p** treaty with them,
10: 1 He also learned that the Gibeonites had made **p**
10: 4 "for they have made **p** with Joshua and the people
11:19 No one in this region made **p** with the Israelites
11:20 them to fight the Israelites instead of asking for **p**.
22:23 burnt offerings or grain offerings or **p** offerings.
22:27 our burnt offerings, sacrifices, and **p** offerings.
Jdg 3:11 So there was **p** in the land for forty years.
3:30 that day, and the land was at **p** for eighty years.
5:31 Then there was **p** in the land for forty years.
6:24 LORD there and named it "The LORD Is **P**."
8:28 about forty years—the land was at **p**.
18: 6 "Go in **p**," the priest replied. "For the LORD
20:26 burnt offerings and **p** offerings to the LORD.
21: 4 their burnt offerings and **p** offerings on it.
21:13 The Israelite assembly sent a **p** delegation to the
1Sa 7:14 And there was also **p** between Israel
10: 8 there to sacrifice burnt offerings and **p** offerings.
11: 1 But the citizens of Jabesh asked for **p**. "Make a
11:15 Then they offered **p** offerings to the LORD,
13: 9 "Bring me the burnt offering and the **p** offerings!"
16: 4 they asked. "Do you come in **p**?"
20:42 At last Jonathan said to David, "Go in **p**, for we
25: 6 "**P** and prosperity to you, your family,
25:35 accepted her gifts and told her, "Return home in **p**.
2Sa 6:17 burnt offerings and **p** offerings to the LORD.
7: 1 and the LORD had brought **p** to the land,
14:17 Yes, the king will give us **p** of mind again.' I know
20:19 I am one who is **p** loving and faithful in Israel.
20:21 hand him over to me, we will leave the city in **p**."
24:25 and offered burnt offerings and **p** offerings.
1Ki 2: 5 but it was done in a time of **p**, staining his belt
2: 6 him what you think best, but don't let him die in **p**.
2:13 she asked him. "No," he said, "I come in **p**.
2:33 and may the LORD grant **p** to David and his
3:15 he sacrificed burnt offerings and **p** offerings.
4:24 And there was **p** throughout the entire land.
4:25 all of Judah and Israel lived in **p** and safety.
5: 4 But now the LORD my God has given me **p** on
5:12 and Solomon made a formal alliance of **p**.
8:63 Solomon sacrificed **p** offerings to the LORD
8:64 grain offerings, and the fat of **p** offerings there,
9:25 and **p** offerings to the LORD on the altar he had
20:18 "whether they have come for **p** or for war."
22:17 master has been killed. Send them home in **p**.' "
22:44 Jehoshaphat also made **p** with the king of Israel.
2Ki 5:19 "Go in **p**," Elisha said. So Naaman started home
9:17 out a rider to find out if they are coming in **p**."
9:18 king wants to know whether you are coming in **p**."
9:18 Jehu replied, "What do you know about **p**?
9:19 king wants to know whether you come in **p**."
9:19 Jehu answered, "What do you know about **p**?
9:22 Joram demanded, "Do you come in **p**, Jehu?"
9:22 "How can there be **p** as long as the idolatry
9:31 at him, "Have you come in **p**, you murderer?
16:13 over it, and sprinkled the blood of **p** offerings on it.
18:31 Make **p** with me—open the gates and come out.
20:19 "At least there will be **p** and security during my
22:20 city until after you have died and been buried in **p**.
1Ch 12:17 and said, "If you have come in **p** to help me,
12:18 son of Jesse. / **P** and prosperity be with you,
16: 1 burnt offerings and **p** offerings before God.
21:26 and sacrificed burnt offerings and **p** offerings.
22: 9 But you will have a son who will experience **p**
22: 9 I will give him **p** with his enemies in all the
22: 9 and I will give **p** and quiet to Israel during his
22:18 "He has given you **p** with the surrounding nations.
23:25 "The LORD, the God of Israel, has given us **p**,
2Ch 7: 7 burnt offerings and the fat from **p** offerings there.
14: 1 next king. There was **p** in the land for ten years,
14: 5 So Asa's kingdom enjoyed a period of **p**.
18:16 master has been killed. Send them home in **p**.' "
20:30 So Jehoshaphat's kingdom was at **p**, for his God
29:35 and a great deal of fat from the many **p** offerings.
30:22 **P** offerings were sacrificed, and the people
31: 2 to offer the burnt offerings and **p** offerings,
32:22 So there was **p** at last throughout the land.
33:16 and sacrificed **p** offerings and thanksgiving
34:28 until after you have died and been buried in **p**.
Est 9:30 letters wishing **p** and security were sent to the Jews
Job 3:13 at birth, I would be at **p** now, asleep and at rest.
3:26 I have no **p**, no quietness. I have no rest; instead,
5:23 You will be at **p** with the stones of the field,
5:23 and its wild animals will be at **p** with you.
12: 6 But even robbers are left in **p**, and those who
21:13 in prosperity; then they go down to the grave in **p**.
22:21 If you agree with him, you will have **p** at last,
25: 2 and dreadful. He enforces **p** in the heavens.
Ps 4: 8 I will lie down in **p** and sleep, / for you alone,
29:11 The LORD blesses them with **p**.
34:14 do good. / Work hard at living in **p** with others.
35:20 They don't talk of **p**; / they plot against innocent
37:37 a wonderful future lies before those who love **p**.
85: 8 for he speaks **p** to his people, his faithful ones.
85:10 met together. / Righteousness and **p** have kissed!
119:165 Those who love your law have great **p** / and do not
120: 6 am tired of living here / among people who hate **p**.
120: 7 As for me, I am for **p**; / but when I speak, they are
122: 6 Pray for the **p** of Jerusalem. / May all who love
122: 7 O Jerusalem, may there be **p** within your walls
122: 8 and friends, I will say, / "**P** be with you."
125: 5 who do evil. / And let Israel have quietness and **p**.
128: 6 And may Israel have quietness and **p**.
147:14 He sends **p** across your nation / and satisfies you
Pr 1:33 But all who listen to me will live in **p** and safety,
10:10 cause trouble, but a bold reproof promotes **p**.
12:20 plotting evil; joy fills hearts that are planning **p**!
16: 7 he makes even their enemies live at **p** with them.
17: 1 A dry crust eaten in **p** is better than a great feast
29:17 and they will give you happiness and **p** of mind.
Ecc 3: 8 a time to hate. / A time for war and a time for **p**.
6: 5 Yet he would have had more **p** than he has in
Isa 9: 5 In that day of **p**, battle gear will no longer be
9: 6 Mighty God, Everlasting Father, Prince of **P**.
11: 6 live together; the leopard and the goat will be at **p**.
14:30 poor in my pasture; the needy will lie down in **p**.
26: 3 You will keep in perfect **p** all who trust in you,
26:12 LORD, you will grant us **p**, / for all we have
27: 5 if they surrender and beg for **p** and protection."
32:17 And this righteousness will bring **p**. Quietness
33: 7 for Assyria has refused their petition for **p**.
33: 8 The Assyrians have broken their **p** pact and care
36:16 Make **p** with me—open the gates and come out.
39: 8 "At least there will be **p** and security during my
48:18 Then you would have had **p** flowing like a gentle
48:22 "But there is no **p** for the wicked,"
52: 7 are the feet of those who bring good news of **p**
53: 5 He was beaten that we might have **p**. He was
54:14 enemies will stay far away; you will live in **p**.
55:12 You will live in joy and **p**. The mountains and hills
57: 2 For the godly who die will rest in **p**.
57:19 May they have **p**, both near and far, for I will heal
57:21 There is no **p** for the wicked," says my God.
59: 8 They do not know what true **p** is or what it means
59: 8 who follow them cannot experience a moment's **p**.
60:17 for iron. **P** and righteousness will be your leaders!
66:12 **P** and prosperity will overflow Jerusalem like a
Jer 4:10 what you said, for you promised **p** for Jerusalem.
6:14 They give assurances of **p** when all is war.
8:11 They give assurances of **p** when all is war.
8:15 We hoped for **p**, but no **p** came. We hoped for
9: 8 They promise **p** to their neighbors while planning
14:13 The LORD will surely send you **p**.' "
14:19 We hoped for **p**, but no **p** came. We hoped for
16: 5 I have removed my protection and **p** from them.
17:18 and terror on all who persecute me, but give me **p**.
23:17 'Don't worry! The LORD says you will have **p**!'
28: 9 So a prophet who predicts **p** must carry the burden
29: 7 And work for the **p** and prosperity of Babylon.
29: 7 held captive, for if Babylon has **p**, so will you."
30:10 Israel will return and will have **p** and quiet in their
31:24 and shepherds alike will live together in **p**
32:37 to this very city and let them live in **p** and safety.
33: 6 Jerusalem's damage and give her prosperity and **p**.
35:15 so that you might live in **p** here in the land I gave
46:27 Israel will return and will have **p** and quiet,
48:11 "From her earliest history, Moab has lived in **p**.
La 3:17 **P** has been stripped away, and I have forgotten
Eze 7:25 my people. They will look for **p** but will not find it.
12:24 and misleading predictions about **p** in Israel.
13:10 'All is peaceful!' when there is no **p** at all!
13:16 They were lying prophets who claimed **p** would
13:16 would come to Jerusalem when there was no **p**.
34:15 tend my sheep and cause them to lie down in **p**,
34:25 "I will make a covenant of **p** with them and drive
37:26 And I will make a covenant of **p** with them,
38: 8 which will be lying in **p** after her recovery from
38:14 When my people are living in **p** in their land,
39:26 against me after they come home to live in **p**
43:27 the burnt offerings and **p** offerings of the people.
45:15 and **p** offerings that will make atonement for the
45:17 and **p** offerings to make reconciliation for the
46: 2 the priest offers his burnt offering and **p** offering.
46:12 burnt offering or **p** offering to the LORD,
Da 4: 1 throughout the world: / "**P** and prosperity to you!
6:25 throughout the world: / "**P** and prosperity to you!
10:19 Be at **p**; take heart and be strong!" As he spoke
Hos 2:18 and bows, so you can live unafraid in **p** and safety.
Am 5:22 I won't even notice all your choice **p** offerings.
Ob 1: 7 They will promise you **p**, while plotting your
Mic 3: 5 You promise **p** for those who give you food,
4: 4 Everyone will live quietly in their own homes in **p**
5: 5 And he will be the source of our **p**.
7:14 Help them to live in **p** and prosperity.
Na 1:15 He is bringing a message of **p**. Celebrate your
Hag 2: 9 And in this place I will bring **p**. I, the LORD
Zec 1:11 patrolled the earth, and the whole earth is at **p**."
1:15 I am very angry with the other nations that enjoy **p**
3:10 your neighbor into your home to share your **p**
8:12 For I am planting seeds of **p** and prosperity among
8:16 in your courts that are just and that lead to **p**.
8:19 for the people of Judah. So love truth and **p**.
9:10 Your king will bring **p** to the nations. His realm
Mal 2: 5 covenant with the Levites was to bring life and **p**,
Mt 5: 9 God blesses those who work for **p**, / for they will
10:34 "Don't imagine that I came to bring **p** to the earth!
Mk 5:34 made you well. Go in **p**. You have been healed."
9:50 among yourselves and live in **p** with each other."
Lk 1:79 of death, / and to guide us to the path of **p**."
2:14 and **p** on earth to all whom God favors."
2:29 "Lord, now I can die in **p**! / As you promised me,
7:50 the woman, "Your faith has saved you; go in **p**."
8:48 to her, "your faith has made you well. Go in **p**."
12:51 Do you think I have come to bring **p** to the earth?
14:32 he will send a delegation to discuss terms of **p**.
19:38 **P** in heaven / and glory in highest heaven!"
19:42 wish that even today you would find the way of **p**.
19:42 But now it is too late, and **p** is hidden from you.
24:36 there among them. He said, "**P** be with you."
Jn 14:27 am leaving you with a gift—**p** of mind and heart.
14:27 And the **p** I give isn't like the **p** the world
16:33 told you all this so that you may have **p** in me.
20:19 there among them! "**P** be with you," he said.
20:21 He spoke to them again and said, "**P** be with you.
20:26 standing among them. He said, "**P** be with you."
Ac 9:31 The church then had **p** throughout Judea, Galilee,
10:36 that there is **p** with God through Jesus Christ,
12:20 So they sent a delegation to make **p** with him
16:36 "You and Silas are free to leave. Go in **p**."
24: 2 you have given **p** to us Jews and have enacted
Ro 1: 7 May grace and **p** be yours from God our Father
2:10 and honor and **p** from God for all who do good—
3:17 They do not know what true **p** is."
5: 1 we have **p** with God because of what Jesus Christ
8: 6 Holy Spirit controls your mind, there is life and **p**.
12:18 Do your part to live in **p** with everyone, as much as
14:17 a life of goodness and **p** and joy in the Holy Spirit.
15:13 you happy and full of **p** as you believe in him.
15:33 now may God, who gives us his **p**, be with you all.
16:20 The God of **p** will soon crush Satan under your
1Co 1: 3 and the Lord Jesus Christ give you his grace and **p**.
7:15 with them, for God wants his children to live in **p**.)
14:33 For God is not a God of disorder but of **p**, as in all
2Co 1: 2 and the Lord Jesus Christ give you his grace and **p**.
13:11 Live in harmony and **p**. Then the God of love and **p** will be with you.
Gal 1: 3 May grace and **p** be yours from God our Father
5:22 love, joy, **p**, patience, kindness, goodness,
6:16 and **p** be upon all those who live by this principle.
Eph 1: 2 May grace and **p** be yours, sent to you from God
2:14 For Christ himself has made **p** between us Jews
2:15 His purpose was to make **p** between Jews
2:17 He has brought this Good News of **p** to you
4: 3 Holy Spirit, and bind yourselves together with **p**.
6:15 put on the **p** that comes from the Good News,
6:23 May God give you **p**, dear friends, and love with
Php 1: 2 and the Lord Jesus Christ give you grace and **p**.
4: 7 If you do this, you will experience God's **p**,
4: 7 His **p** will guard your hearts and minds as you live
4: 9 saw me doing, and the God of **p** will be with you.
Col 1: 2 May God our Father give you grace and **p**.
1:20 He made **p** with everything in heaven and on earth
3:15 And let the **p** that comes from Christ rule in your
3:15 of one body you are all called to live in **p**.
1Th 1: 1 Lord Jesus Christ. May his grace and **p** be yours.
5:23 Now may the God of **p** make you holy in every
2Th 1: 2 and the Lord Jesus Christ give you grace and **p**.
3:16 May the Lord of **p** himself always give you his **p** no matter what happens.
1Ti 1: 2 Jesus our Lord give you grace, mercy, and **p**.
2: 2 so that we can live in **p** and quietness, in godliness
3: 3 He must be gentle, **p** loving, and not one who
2Ti 1: 2 Jesus our Lord give you grace, mercy, and **p**.
2:22 Pursue faith and love and **p**, and enjoy the
Tit 1: 4 and Christ Jesus our Savior give you grace and **p**.
Phm 1: 3 and the Lord Jesus Christ give you grace and **p**.
Heb 7: 2 He is also "king of **p**" because *Salem* means **p**."
12:14 Try to live in **p** with everyone, and seek to live a
13:20[-21] And now, may the God of **p**, who brought
Jas 3:17 It is also **p** loving, gentle at all times, and willing
3:18 those who are peacemakers will plant seeds of **p**
1Pe 1: 2 and more of God's special favor and wonderful **p**.
3:11 do good. / Work hard at living in **p** with others.
5:14 Christian love. **P** be to all of you who are in Christ.
2Pe 1: 2 and wonderful **p** as you come to know Jesus,
3:14 a pure and blameless life. And be at **p** with God.
2Jn 1: 3 May grace, mercy, and **p**, which come from God
3Jn 1:15 May God's **p** be with you. Your friends here send
Jude 1: 2 and more of God's mercy, **p**, and love.

Rev 1: 4 Grace and **p** from the one who is, who always was,
6: 4 and the authority to remove **p** from the earth.

PEACE-OFFERING (1) [OFFER, PEACE]
Nu 6: 18 and put it on the fire beneath the **p** sacrifice.

PEACEABLY (2) [PEACE]
Jdg 11: 13 to the Jordan. Now then, give back the land **p**."
1Th 5: 13 And remember to live **p** with each other.

PEACEFUL (15) [PEACE]
Ex 11: 7 it will be so **p** that not even a dog will bark.
Jdg 18: 7 like the Sidonians; they were **p** and secure.
18: 27 town of Laish, whose people were **p** and secure.
2Sa 17: 3 Then all the people will remain unharmed and **p**."
2Ki 11: 20 and the city was **p** because Athaliah had been
1Ch 4: 40 lush pastures there, and the land was quiet and **p**.
2Ch 14: 6 During those **p** years, he was able to build up the
23: 21 and the city was **p** because Athaliah had been
Ps 23: 2 in green meadows; / he leads me beside **p** streams.
Isa 9: 7 His ever expanding, **p** government will never end.
63: 14 As with cattle going down into a **p** valley,
Jer 25: 37 **P** meadows will be turned into a wasteland by the
Eze 13: 10 prophets deceive my people by saying, 'All is **p**!'
Zep 3: 13 They will live **p** lives, lying down to sleep in
1Th 5: 3 everything is **p** and secure," then disaster will fall

PEACEFULLY (1) [PEACE]
Jer 34: 5 but will die **p** among your people. They will burn

PEACEMAKER (1) [PEACE]
Ac 7: 26 He tried to be a **p**. 'Men,' he said, 'you are

PEACEMAKERS (1) [PEACE]
Jas 3: 18 And those who are **p** will plant seeds of peace

PEACOCKS (2)
1Ki 10: 22 loaded down with gold, silver, ivory, apes, and **p**.
2Ch 9: 21 loaded down with gold, silver, ivory, apes, and **p**.

PEACOCKS [KJV] See also OSTRICH

PEAK (5) [PEAKS]
Nu 21: 20 in Moab where Pisgah **P** overlooks the wasteland.
23: 14 took Balaam to the plateau of Zophim on Pisgah **P**.
Dt 3: 27 You can go to Pisgah **P** and view the land in every
34: 1 from the plains of Moab and climbed Pisgah **P**,
Mt 4: 8 Next the Devil took him to the **p** of a very high

PEAKS (5) [PEAK]
Ge 7: 20 more than twenty-two feet above the highest **p**.
8: 5 to go down, other mountain **p** began to appear.
2Ki 19: 23 yes, the remotest **p** of Lebanon.
Isa 37: 24 yes, the remotest **p** of Lebanon.
Jer 49: 16 Though you live among the **p** with the eagles,

PEARL (3) [MOTHER-OF-PEARL, PEARLS]
Mt 13: 45 the Kingdom of Heaven is like a **p** merchant on the
13: 46 When he discovered a **p** of great value, he sold
Rev 21: 21 were made of pearls—each gate from a single **p**!

PEARLS (9) [PEARL]
Job 28: 18 trying to get it. The price of wisdom is far above **p**.
Mt 7: 6 Don't give **p** to swine! They will trample the **p**, then turn and attack you.
13: 45 like a pearl merchant on the lookout for choice **p**.
1Ti 2: 9 or by wearing gold or **p** or expensive clothes.
Rev 17: 4 jewelry made of gold and precious gems and **p**.
18: 12 silver, jewels, **p**, fine linen, purple dye, silk,
18: 16 decked out with gold and precious stones and **p**!
21: 21 The twelve gates were made of **p**—each gate from

PECK (1)
Ge 40: 19 Then birds will come and **p** away at your flesh."

PEDAHEL (1)
Nu 34: 28 Naphtali | **P** son of Ammihud

PEDAHZUR (5)
Nu 1: 10 Manasseh son of Joseph | Gamaliel son of **P**
2: 20[-21] Manasseh | Gamaliel son of **P** | 32,200
7: 54 On the eighth day Gamaliel son of **P**, leader of the
7: 59 was the offering brought by Gamaliel son of **P**.
10: 23 tribe of Manasseh was led by Gamaliel son of **P**.

PEDAIAH (8)
2Ki 23: 36 was Zebidah, the daughter of **P** from Rumah.
1Ch 3: 18 Malkiram, **P**, Shenazzar, Jekamiah, Hoshama,
3: 19 The sons of **P** were Zerubbabel and Shimei.
27: 20 son of Azaziah / Manasseh (west) | Joel son of **P**
Ne 3: 25 of the guard. Next to him were **P** son of Parosh
8: 4 To his left stood **P**, Mishael, Malkijah, Hashum,
11: 7 son of Joed, son of **P**, son of Kolaiah, son of
13: 13 Zadok the scribe, and **P**, one of the Levites,

PEDESTAL (10)
Ex 30: 18 "Make a large bronze washbasin with a bronze **p**.
30: 28 all its utensils, and the large washbasin with its **p**.
31: 9 with all its utensils; the washbasin and its **p**;
35: 16 and utensils; the large washbasin with its **p**;
38: 8 and its bronze **p** were cast from bronze mirrors
39: 39 and utensils; the large washbasin and its **p**;
40: 11 the large washbasin and its **p** to make them holy.
Lev 8: 11 and all its utensils and the washbasin and its **p**,
1Ki 7: 31 1-1/2 feet above the cart's top like a round **p**,
Zec 5: 11 is ready, they will set the basket there on its **p**."

PEDIGREES (2)
1Ti 1: 4 in endless speculation over myths and spiritual **p**.
Tit 3: 9 involved in foolish discussions about spiritual **p**

PEELED (3)
Ge 30: 37 and **p** off strips of the bark to make white streaks
30: 38 Then he set up these **p** branches beside the
30: 41 Jacob set up the **p** branches in front of them.

PEEP (1)
Isa 10: 14 flap a wing against me or utter a **p** of protest."

PEERED (1)
Lk 24: 12 he **p** in and saw the empty linen wrappings;

PEG (6) [PEGS]
Jdg 4: 21 quietly crept up to him with a hammer and tent **p**.
4: 21 Then she drove the tent **p** through his temple
4: 22 there dead, with the tent **p** through his temple.
5: 26 Then with her left hand she reached for a tent **p**,
5: 26 She pounded the tent **p** through his head,
Zec 10: 4 the tent **p**, the battle bow, and all the rulers.

PEGS (10) [PEG]
Ex 26: 17 There will be two **p** on each frame so they can be
27: 19 including all the tent **p** used to support the
35: 18 the tent **p** of the Tabernacle and courtyard and their
36: 22 There were two **p** on each frame so they could be
38: 20 All the tent **p** used in the Tabernacle and courtyard
38: 31 and all the tent **p** used to hold the curtains of the
39: 40 at the courtyard entrance; the cords and tent **p**;
Nu 3: 37 of the courtyard and all their bases, **p**, and cords.
4: 32 **p**, cords, accessories, and everything else related to
Eze 15: 3 for making things, like **p** to hang up pots and pans?

PEKAH (13) [PEKAH'S]
2Ki 15: 25 Then **P** son of Remaliah, the commander of
15: 25 **P** assassinated the king, along with Argob
15: 25 at Samaria. **P** then became the next king of Israel.
15: 27 **P** son of Remaliah began to rule over Israel in the
15: 28 But **P** did what was evil in the LORD's sight.
15: 30 Then Hoshea son of Elah conspired against **P**
15: 37 of Aram and King **P** of Israel to attack Judah.
16: 5 and King **P** of Israel declared war on Ahaz.
2Ch 28: 6 In a single day **P** son of Remaliah, Israel's king,
Isa 7: 1 by King Rezin of Aram and King **P** of Israel,
7: 4 King Rezin of Aram and **P** son of Remaliah.
7: 9 is no stronger than its king, **P** son of Remaliah.
8: 6 over what will happen to King Rezin and King **P**.

PEKAH'S (3) [PEKAH]
2Ki 15: 31 The rest of the events in **P** reign and all his deeds
15: 32 Judah in the second year of King **P** reign in Israel.
16: 1 in the seventeenth year of King **P** reign in Israel.

PEKAHIAH (3) [PEKAHIAH'S]
2Ki 15: 22 Menahem died, his son **P** became the next king.
15: 23 **P** son of Menahem began to rule over Israel in the
15: 24 But **P** did what was evil in the LORD's sight.

PEKAHIAH'S (2) [PEKAHIAH]
2Ki 15: 25 the commander of **P** army, conspired against him.
15: 26 The rest of the events in **P** reign and all his deeds

PEKOD (2)
Jer 50: 21 the land of Merathaim and against the people of **P**.
Eze 23: 23 will come with all the Chaldeans from **P**

PELAIAH (3)
1Ch 3: 24 Eliashib, **P**, Akkub, Johanan, Delaiah, and Anani—
Ne 8: 7 Kelita, Azariah, Jozabad, Hanan, and **P**—
10: 10 Shebaniah, Hodiah, Kelita, **P**, Hanan,

PELALIAH (1)
Ne 11: 12 son of **P**, son of Amzi, son of Zechariah, son of

PELATIAH (5)
1Ch 3: 21 The sons of Hananiah were **P** and Jeshaiah.
4: 42 led by **P**, Neariah, Rephaiah, and Uzziel—
Ne 10: 22 **P**, Hanan, Anaiah,
Eze 11: 1 were Jaazaniah son of Azzur and **P** son of Benaiah,
11: 13 was still speaking, **P** son of Benaiah suddenly died.

PELEG (9)
Ge 10: 25 The first was named **P**—"division"—for during
11: 16 When Eber was 34 years old, his son **P** was born.
11: 17 After the birth of **P**, Eber lived another 430 years
11: 18 When **P** was 30 years old, his son Reu was born.
11: 19 **P** lived another 209 years and had other sons
1Ch 1: 19 The first was named **P**—"division"—for during
1: 25 Eber, **P**, Reu,
Lk 3: 35 Reu was the son of **P**. / **P** was the son of Eber.

PELET (2) [BETH-PELET]
1Ch 2: 47 Jotham, Geshan, **P**, Ephah, and Shaaph.
12: 3 Jeziel and **P**, sons of Azmaveth; / Beracah

PELETH (2)
Nu 16: 1 and Abiram, the sons of Eliab, and On son of **P**,
1Ch 2: 33 but Jonathan had two sons named **P** and Zaza.

PELICAN (2)
Lev 11: 18 the white owl, the **p**, the carrion vulture,
Dt 14: 17 the **p**, the carrion vulture, the cormorant,

PELICAN [KJV] See also OWL

PELON (4)
2Sa 23: 26 Helez from **P**; / Ira son of Ikkesh from Tekoa;
1Ch 11: 27 Shammah from Harod; / Helez from **P**;
11: 36 Hepher from Mekerah; / Ahijah from **P**;
27: 10 Helez, a descendant of Ephraim from **P**,

PELUSIUM (2)
Eze 30: 15 I will pour out my fury on **P**, the strongest fortress
30: 16 **P** will be racked with pain; Thebes will be torn

PEN (5) [PENS]
1Sa 6: 7 but shut their calves away from them in a **p**.
6: 10 to the cart, and their calves were shut up in a **p**.
Ps 45: 1 for my tongue is like the **p** of a skillful poet.
Lk 15: 23 And kill the calf we have been fattening in the **p**.
2Co 3: 3 It is written not with **p** and ink, but with the Spirit

PENALTIES (2) [PENALTY]
Ps 94: 2 Sentence the proud to the **p** they deserve.
Jer 25: 13 all the **p** announced by Jeremiah against the

PENALTY (22) [PENALTIES]
Lev 5: 6 and bring to the LORD as their **p** a female from
5: 7 or two young pigeons as the **p** for their sin.
5: 16 paying for the loss, plus an added **p** of 20 percent.
6: 5 they must restore the principal amount plus a **p** of
10: 7 under **p** of death, for the anointing oil of the
16: 2 whenever he chooses; the **p** for intrusion is death.
20: 13 "The **p** for homosexual acts is death to both
22: 14 the amount eaten, plus an added **p** of 20 percent.
Nu 5: 7 adding a **p** of 20 percent and returning it to the
Est 1: 15 "What **p** does the law provide for a queen who
Job 21: 19 not their children! Let them feel their own **p**.
34: 36 you deserve the maximum **p** for the wicked way
Pr 19: 19 Short-tempered people must pay their own **p**.
Eze 3: 18 the wicked, saying, 'You are under the **p** of death,'
22: 31 I will heap on them the full **p** for all their sins,
23: 49 worship of idols. Yes, you will suffer the full **p**!
Lk 23: 15 Nothing this man has done calls for the death **p**.
Ro 1: 27 suffered within themselves the **p** they so richly
1: 32 They are fully aware of God's death **p** for those
7: 10 me the way of life, instead gave me the death **p**.
Heb 9: 15 For Christ died to set them free from the **p** of the
Rev 18: 6 Give her a double **p** for all her evil deeds.

PENANCE (2) [REPENT]
Isa 58: 3 We have done much **p**, and you don't even notice
58: 5 yourselves by going through the motions of **p**,

PENCE [KJV] See DOLLARS, FORTUNE, PIECES

PENDANTS (1)
Jdg 8: 26 not including the crescents and **p**, the royal

PENETRATE (3) [PENETRATES]
Job 41: 13 its hide, and who can **p** its double layer of armor?
41: 17 They lock together so nothing can **p** them.
Pr 4: 21 of my words. Let them **p** deep within your heart,

PENETRATES (1) [PENETRATE]
Pr 20: 27 The LORD's searchlight **p** the human spirit,

PENIEL (6) [PENUEL]
Ge 32: 30 Jacob named the place **P**—"face of God"—
32: 31 The sun rose as he left **P**, and he was limping
Jdg 8: 8 From there Gideon went up to **P** and asked for
8: 9 So he said to the people of **P**, "After I return in
8: 17 He also knocked down the tower of **P** and killed all
1Ki 12: 25 Later he went and built up the town of **P**.

PENINNAH (6)
1Sa 1: 2 Elkanah had two wives, Hannah and **P**.
1: 2 **P** had children, while Hannah did not.
1: 4 he would give portions of the sacrifice to **P**
1: 6 But **P** made fun of Hannah because the LORD
1: 7 **P** would taunt Hannah as they went to the
1: 21 The next year Elkanah, **P**, and their children went

PENIS (1)
Dt 23: 1 "If a man's testicles are crushed or his **p** is cut off,

PENNIES (3) [PENNY]
Mk 12: 42 Then a poor widow came and dropped in two **p**.

Lk 12:6 is the price of five sparrows? A couple of **p**?
21:2 Then a poor widow came by and dropped in two **p**.

PENNY (5) [PENNIES]

Ge 31:42 you would have sent me off without a **p** to my
Mt 5:26 won't be free again until you have paid the last **p**.
10:29 Not even a sparrow, worth only half a **p**, can fall to
18:34 sent the man to prison until he had paid every **p**.
Lk 12:59 won't be free again until you have paid the last **p**."

PENNYWORTH [KJV] See FORTUNE

PENS (3) [PEN]

1Ki 4:23 ten oxen from the fattening **p**, twenty pasture-fed
Ps 50:9 your barns; / I want no more goats from your **p**.
78:70 his servant David, / calling him from the sheep **p**.

PENT (1)

Job 32:18 For I am **p** up and full of words, and the spirit

PENTECOST (3)

Ac 2:1 On the day of **P**, seven weeks after Jesus'
20:16 get to Jerusalem, if possible, for the Festival of **P**.
1Co 16:8 be staying here at Ephesus until the Festival of **P**,

PENUEL (2) [PENIEL]

1Ch 4:4 **P** (the father of Gedor), and Ezer (the father of
8:25 Iphdeiah, and **P** were the sons of Shashak.

PEOPLE (3697) [LAYPEOPLE, PEOPLE'S, PEOPLES]

ALL PEOPLE (37) Ge 3:20; Dt 2:25; Ps 62:12; 65:2; 148:11; Pr 8:4; 24:12; Ecc 6:7; Isa 2:17; 40:5; 57:16; Jer 4:2; 9:1; 10:14; 17:10; 31:30; 32:19; 51:17; Eze 18:4; 32:26; Joel 2:28; Zep 3:9; Mt 7:21; 16:27; Lk 2:31; 3:6; Ac 2:17; Ro 2:6; 3:9; 5:18,20,21; 11:32; 1Ti 2:1; 4:10; Tit 2:11; Heb 12:23

HOLY PEOPLE (30) Ex 22:31; Dt 7:6; 28:9; Isa 4:3; 52:11; 62:12; 63:18; Da 7:18,21,22,22,25,27; 8:24; 12:7; 1Co 1:2; Eph 1:1; 2:19; Col 1:2,12,26; 3:12; 2Th 1:10; Jude 1:3; Rev 11:18; 13:7; 14:12; 16:6; 17:6; 18:20

OTHER PEOPLE (17) Ex 24:2; 33:16; Lev 20:24,26; Jos 7:9; 23:7; Ezr 10:25; Ne 13:24; Job 35:8; Ps 73:5; Jer 5:26; 41:10; Lk 13:2; Jn 11:33; Ro 14:18; 1Co 14:17; 1Ti 1:9

PEOPLE ISRAEL (46) Dt 21:8,8; 26:15; 1Sa 10:1; 2Sa 5:2,12; 7:7,8,10; 1Ki 8:16,30,33,36,43,52,56,59,66; 14:7; 16:2; 1Ch 11:2; 14:2; 17:7,9; 2Ch 6:5,21,24,27,33; 7:10; 31:8; 35:3; Ne 1:6; Ps 79:7; 135:12; Isa 1:3; 56:8; 58:1; Jer 10:25; 12:14; 30:7; 31:36; La 4:3; Mic 6:2; Mt 2:6; Lk 2:32

PEOPLE OF ISRAEL (410) Ge 32:32; 47:27; 48:20; Ex 3:9,13,18; 5:6; 6:5,11,13,26; 7:2; 9:26; 10:23; 11:3; 12:28,33,35,37,40,50,51; 14:8,9,10,16,19,22,29,31; 15:1,19,22; 16:6,17,35; 17:1,7,8; 19:3; 20:22; 25:2,8,22; 27:20,21; 28:12,38; 29:28,43,45; 30:12,31; 31:13,16; 34:30; 35:29; 39:7,42; 40:36,38; Lev 10:14; 15:31; 16:5; 17:14; 22:32; 24:2,15; 25:42,46,55; Nu 1:53; 2:34; 3:12,38,42,45,45; 5:2,6,12; 6:1,23; 8:6,10,11,14,16,17; 9:17,17,22; 11:4; 13:26; 14:5; 15:1,18,32,38; 16:9,34,38; 17:6,12; 18:5,8,19,20,32; 19:2,9,10; 20:1,12,13,14,24; 21:2,4,31; 22:1,41; 24:2; 25:4,13; 26:62,63; 27:8,12,14; 28:1; 29:40; 31:16,30,42,54; 32:4,7,9,18,22; 33:3,40; 35:2,8,10,34; 36:2,13; Dt 1:1,5; 4:45; 5:1; 10:6; 27:14; 31:1,11,19,23,26; 32:9,49,51,52; 33:1; 34:8,9; Jos 4:7; 5:1; 8:33; 9:11,18,26,27; 10:4,12; 11:23; 22:20; 23:1; 24:1; Jdg 11:16,17; 1Sa 2:22,27,32; 3:20; 4:1; 7:3,16; 10:17; 13:22; 15:6; 27:12; 2Sa 3:19,21; 6:5; 15:6; 24:1,4; 1Ki 3:2; 6:1,13; 8:9; 9:7; 12:16,20; 14:15,18; 16:21; 18:19; 19:10,14; 2Ki 3:3; 8:12; 13:23; 17:6,9,11,22,24; 18:4; 1Ch 6:64; 13:5; 16:17; 2Ch 5:10; 6:11; 7:3,20; 13:12; 30:6,21; Ezr 6:16,21; 7:6,7,10,13; 8:25,35; 9:1; 10:5,25; Ne 13:18; Ps 68:26; 103:7; 105:10,24; 115:12; 122:4; 148:14; Isa 1:10; 2:5,6; 8:17; 9:9; 10:22; 14:1; 29:22; 33:24; 45:17,19; 48:20; 49:5,6; 60:9; 62:11; 65:9; Jer 3:20; 5:11; 7:15; 9:26; 11:17; 16:14,15; 23:7,8,13; 30:3; 31:2,31,33; 32:22; 50:4,33; 51:49; Eze 3:1,4,7; 4:3; 6:11; 7:7; 8:6,10; 9:9; 11:5; 12:6,9,10,27; 13:4; 14:4,6,11; 17:2; 18:25,29,29,30,31; 20:13,27,30,31,39,40,44; 22:18,24; 24:21; 25:14; 28:25; 33:7,10,11,20; 34:30; 35:5; 36:17,22,32; 37:11,21; 39:7,12, 22; 40:4; 43:7,10; 44:6,6,9; 45:16,17,22; 48:11; Hos 1:6; 4:1; 5:11; 7:8,11; 8:3,8,9,13; 9:1,16,17; 12:1,14; Joel 2:27; 3:16; Am 2:6,11; 3:1; 4:12; 5:1; 6:14; 7:11,17; 8:2; 9:14; Ob 1:17; Mic 5:3,9; Zep 3:13; Zec 9:1; 10:7; Mt 10:6; 15:24; 21:5; 27:9; Jn 12:15; Ac 2:22; 3:12,26; 4:10,27; 5:31; 7:23,37,38; 9:15; 10:36; 13:16,31; Ro 9:4,27; 10:19; 11:2; 2Co 3:7,13; Heb 4:11; 8:8,10; 11:22,28,29,30; 12.25, Rev 2.14

PEOPLE OF JUDAH (87) Jos 15:63; Jdg 1:19; 2Sa 1:18; 2:7; 19:15; 1Ki 4:20; 12:23; 14:22; 2Ki 14:10,21; 16:6; 17:19; 21:11,16; 23:2,35; 25:21,26; 1Ch 6:15; 9:1; 2Ch 14:4,7; 15:2,9; 17:5; 20:5,15,17,18,20; 24:24; 25:19; 26:1; 31:6; 33:9,16; 34:25,30; Ezr 4:4,6; 10:9; Ne 4:10,16; 11:25,30; 12:44; 13:12,16; Isa 8:6; 11:12; Jer 1:18; 3:18; 4:3; 7:30; 9:26; 11:2,9,12,13; 13:19; 17:20,25; 19:11; 20:4; 25:1; 26:18; 27:20; 31:23; 36:3,31; 43:9,10; 52:27; Eze 8:17; 25:12; Da 9:7; Hos 1:7,11; Joel 3:6,8; Am 2:4; Mic 1:16; Na 1:15; Zec 8:15,19; 12:4; Mal 3:4

PEOPLE OF THE LORD* (10) Nu 16:3; 27:17; Dt 14:1; 27:9; Jdg 5:11,13; 2Sa 6:21; Eze 36:20; Hos 8:1; Zep 2:10

Ge 1:26 Then God said, "Let us make **p** in our image,
1:27 So God created **p** in his own image;
3:20 because she would be the mother of all **p**
3:22 "The **p** have become as we are,
4:26 It was during his lifetime that **p** first began to
5:1 When God created **p**, he made them in the likeness
7:1 for among all the **p** of the earth, I consider you
7:21 all kinds of small animals, and all the **p**.
7:23 **p**, animals both large and small, and birds.
9:5 Animals that kill **p** must die, and any person who
9:19 From these three sons of Noah came all the **p** now
10:9 and **p** would speak of someone as being "like
10:25 for during his lifetime the **p** of the world were
10:32 The earth was populated with the **p** of these
11:2 As the **p** migrated eastward, they found a plain in
11:5 to see the city and the tower the **p** were building.
11:9 confused the **p** by giving them many languages,
12:5 and all the **p** who had joined his household at
13:13 The **p** of this area were unusually wicked
14:21 told him, "Give back my **p** who were captured.
18:20 "I have heard that the **p** of Sodom and Gomorrah
18:24 Suppose you find fifty innocent **p** there within the
18:26 "If I find fifty innocent **p** in Sodom,
19:25 eliminating all life—**p**, plants, and animals alike.
19:30 Lot left Zoar because he was afraid of the **p** there,
20:2 Abraham told **p** there that his wife, Sarah, was his
23:11 Here in the presence of my **p**, I give it to you.
23:12 Abraham bowed again to the **p** of the land,
26:22 another well, and the local **p** finally left him alone.
32:32 That is why even today the **p** of Israel don't eat
33:5 and asked, "Who are these **p** with you?"
34:16 and live here and unite with you to become one **p**.
34:30 "You have made me stink among all the **p** of this
35:5 terror from God came over the **p** in all the towns of
41:36 will surely strike the land, and all the **p** will die."
41:40 will manage my household and organize all my **p**.
41:49 that the **p** could not keep track of the amount.
41:55 Throughout the land of Egypt the **p** began to
41:57 And **p** from surrounding lands also came to Egypt
44:7 "What kind of **p** do you think we are, that you
47:15 When the **p** of Egypt and Canaan ran out of
47:21 all the **p** of Egypt became servants to Pharaoh.
47:23 Then Joseph said to the **p**, "See, I have bought you
47:27 So the **p** of Israel settled in the land of Goshen in
48:19 "Manasseh, too, will become a great **p**, but his
48:20 "The **p** of Israel will use your names to bless each
49:16 "Dan will govern his **p** / like any other tribe in
50:9 of chariots, cavalry, and **p** accompanied Joseph.
50:20 I have today so I could save the lives of many **p**.
Ex 1:9 He told his **p**, "These Israelites are becoming a
1:22 Then Pharaoh gave this order to all his **p**:
2:11 grown up, he went out to visit his **p**, the Israelites,
2:13 next day, as Moses was out visiting his **p** again,
3:7 "You can be sure I have seen the misery of my **p**
3:9 The cries of the **p** of Israel have reached me,
3:10 You will lead my **p**, the Israelites, out of Egypt."
3:13 "If I go to the **p** of Israel and tell them,
3:18 "The leaders of the **p** of Israel will accept your
4:11 "Who makes **p** so they can speak or not speak,
4:16 Aaron will be your spokesman to the **p**, and you
4:21 will make him stubborn so he will not let the **p** go.
5:1 'Let my **p** go, for they must go out into the
5:4 "distracting the **p** from their tasks?
5:5 Look, there are many **p** here in Egypt, and you are
5:6 and foremen he had set over the **p** of Israel:
5:7 "Do not supply the **p** with any more straw for
5:10 So the slave drivers and foremen informed the **p**:
5:12 So the **p** scattered throughout the land in search of
5:22 "Why have you mistreated your own **p** like this,
5:23 he has been even more brutal to your **p**.
6:1 my powerful hand upon him, he will let the **p** go.
6:5 sure that I have heard the groans of the **p** of Israel,
6:7 I will make you my own special **p**, and I will be
6:9 So Moses told the **p** what the LORD had said,
6:11 and tell him to let the **p** of Israel leave Egypt."
6:12 "My own **p** won't listen to me anymore.
6:13 and to demand that he let the **p** of Israel leave
6:26 "Lead all the **p** of Israel out of the land of Egypt,
6:27 permission to lead the **p** from the land of Egypt.
7:2 He will demand that the **p** of Israel be allowed to
7:14 and he continues to refuse to let the **p** go.
7:16 of the Hebrews, has sent me to say, "Let my **p** go,
8:1 Let my **p** go, so they can worship me.
8:4 and your **p** will be overwhelmed by frogs!' "
8:8 LORD to take the frogs away from me and my **p**.
8:8 I will let the **p** go, so they can offer sacrifices to
8:9 want me to pray for you, your officials, and your **p**.
8:18 And the gnats covered all the **p** and animals.
8:20 Let my **p** go, so they can worship me.
8:23 make a clear distinction between your **p** and my **p**.
8:29 of flies to disappear from you and all your **p**.
8:29 and refuse to let the **p** go to sacrifice to the
8:32 his heart again and refused to let the **p** go.
9:1 says: Let my **p** go, so they can worship me.
9:7 remained stubborn. He still refused to let the **p** go.
9:9 causing boils to break out on **p** and animals alike."
9:10 and terrible boils broke out on the **p** and animals
9:13 says: Let my **p** go, so they can worship me.
9:14 to you and your officials and all the Egyptian **p**.
9:17 But you are still lording it over my **p**, and you
9:22 on the **p**, the animals, and the crops."
9:25 fields was destroyed—**p**, animals, and crops alike.
9:26 the land of Goshen, where the **p** of Israel lived.
9:27 "The LORD is right, and my **p** and I are wrong.
9:35 Pharaoh refused to let the **p** leave, just as the
10:3 to me? Let my **p** go, so they can worship me.
10:20 stubborn once again, and he did not let the **p** go.
10:23 During all that time the **p** scarcely moved, for they
10:23 But there was light as usual where the **p** of Israel
11:3 the Egyptians to look favorably on the **p** of Israel,
11:3 by Pharaoh's officials and the Egyptian **p** alike.)
12:16 all the **p** must gather for a time of special worship.
12:27 and did not destroy us.' " Then all the **p** bowed
12:28 So the **p** of Israel did just as the LORD had
12:30 and all the **p** of Egypt woke up during the night,
12:33 All the Egyptians urged the **p** of Israel to get out of
12:35 And the **p** of Israel did as Moses had instructed
12:37 That night the **p** of Israel left Rameses and started
12:38 Many **p** who were not Israelites went with them,
12:39 because the **p** were rushed out of Egypt
12:40 The **p** of Israel had lived in Egypt for 430 years.
12:42 LORD to bring his **p** out from the land of Egypt,
12:50 So the **p** of Israel followed all the LORD's
12:51 And that very day the LORD began to lead the **p**
13:3 So Moses said to the **p**, "This is a day to
13:15 throughout the land of Egypt, both **p** and animals.
13:17 When Pharaoh finally let the **p** go, God did not
13:17 God said, "If the **p** are faced with a battle,
14:2 "Tell the **p** to march toward Pi-hahiroth between
14:8 and he chased after the **p** of Israel who had
14:9 The Egyptians caught up with the **p** of Israel as
14:10 the **p** of Israel could see them in the distance,
14:10 The **p** began to panic, and they cried out to the
14:13 But Moses told the **p**, "Don't be afraid. Just stand
14:15 are you crying out to me? Tell the **p** to get moving!
14:16 Then all the **p** of Israel will walk through on dry
14:19 angel of God, who had been leading the **p** of Israel,
14:22 So the **p** of Israel walked through the sea on dry
14:29 The **p** of Israel had walked through the middle of
14:31 When the **p** of Israel saw the mighty power that the
15:1 and the **p** of Israel sang this song to the LORD:
15:13 you will lead / this **p** whom you have ransomed.
15:14 and tremble; / anguish will grip the **p** of Philistia.
15:15 All the **p** of Canaan will melt with fear;
15:16 like a stone, / until your **p** pass by, O LORD,
15:16 until the **p** whom you purchased pass by.
15:19 But the **p** of Israel had walked through on dry
15:22 Then Moses led the **p** of Israel away from the Red
15:23 But the **p** couldn't drink it because it was bitter.
15:24 Then the **p** turned against Moses. "What are we
16:4 The **p** can go out each day and pick up as much
16:6 and Aaron called a meeting of all the **p** of Israel
16:10 And as Aaron spoke to the **p**, they looked out
16:17 So the **p** of Israel went out and gathered this food
16:21 The **p** gathered the food morning by morning,
16:22 The leaders of the **p** came and asked Moses why
16:27 Some of the **p** went out anyway to gather food,
16:28 "How long will these **p** refuse to obey my
16:30 So the **p** rested on the seventh day.
16:35 So the **p** of Israel ate manna for forty years until
17:1 the **p** of Israel left the Sin Desert and moved from
17:2 So once more the **p** grumbled and complained to
17:4 with the LORD, "What should I do with these **p**?
17:5 of the leaders of Israel and walk on ahead of the **p**.
17:6 Then the **p** will be able to drink." Moses did just
17:7 because the **p** of Israel argued with Moses
17:8 While the **p** of Israel were still at Rephidim,
18:1 things God had done for Moses and his **p**,
18:5 and the **p** were camped near the mountain of God.
18:8 and how the LORD had delivered his **p** from all
18:11 because his **p** have escaped from the proud
18:14 saw all that Moses was doing for the **p**,
18:14 The **p** have been standing here all day to get your
18:15 "Well, the **p** come to me to seek God's guidance.
18:16 I inform the **p** of God's decisions and teach them
18:18 going to wear yourself out—and the **p**, too.
18:22 These men can serve the **p**, resolving all the
18:23 and all these **p** will go home in peace."
18:25 all over Israel and made them judges over the **p**.
19:3 to the descendants of Jacob, the **p** of Israel:
19:7 and called together the leaders of the **p**
19:9 so the **p** themselves can hear me as I speak to you.
19:9 Moses told the LORD what the **p** had said.
19:10 "Go down and prepare the **p** for my visit.
19:11 for I will come down upon Mount Sinai as all the **p**
19:12 Set boundary lines that the **p** may not pass.
19:13 Any **p** or animals that cross the boundary must be
19:13 The **p** must stay away from the mountain until they
19:14 So Moses went down to the **p**. He purified them
19:16 blast from a ram's horn, and all the **p** trembled.
19:21 and warn the **p** not to cross the boundaries.
19:21 and warn the **p** not to cross the boundaries.
19:23 the **p** cannot come up on the mountain!"
19:24 or the **p** cross the boundaries to come up here.
19:25 So Moses went down to the **p** and told them what
20:1 Then God instructed the **p** as follows:
20:18 When the **p** heard the thunder and the loud blast of
20:21 As the **p** stood in the distance, Moses entered into
20:22 LORD said to Moses, "Say this to the **p** of Israel:
21:18 "Now suppose two **p** quarrel, and one hits the
21:22 "Now suppose two **p** are fighting, and in the
21:29 that the owner knew the bull had gored **p** in the
22:9 "Suppose there is a dispute between two **p** as to
22:31 "You are my own holy **p**. Therefore, do not eat
23:1 Do not cooperate with evil **p** by telling lies on the
23:6 "Do not twist justice against **p** simply
23:12 It will also allow the **p** of your household,
23:26 will be no miscarriages or infertility among your **p**,
23:27 "I will send my terror upon all the **p** whose lands
23:31 I will help you defeat the **p** now living in the land,
24:2 none of the other **p** are allowed to climb on the
24:3 When Moses had announced to the **p** all the
24:7 took the Book of the Covenant and read it to the **p**.
24:8 sprinkled the blood from the basins over the **p**
24:12 Then you will teach the **p** from them."
25:2 "Tell the **p** of Israel that everyone who wants to
25:8 "I want the **p** of Israel to build me a sacred
25:22 From there I will give you my commands for the **p**
27:20 "Tell the **p** of Israel to bring you pure olive oil for
27:21 This is a permanent law for the **p** of Israel, and it
28:1 and Ithamar, will be set apart from the common **p**.

28:12 of the ephod as memorial stones for the **p** of Israel.
28:29 the LORD will be reminded of his **p** continually.
28:30 for his **p** whenever he goes in before the LORD.
28:38 regarding the sacred offerings of the **p** of Israel.
28:38 always wear it so the LORD will accept the **p**.
29:28 whenever the **p** of Israel offer up peace offerings
29:33 The ordinary **p** may not eat them, for these things
29:43 I will meet the **p** of Israel there, and the Tabernacle
29:45 I will live among the **p** of Israel and be their God,
30:12 "Whenever you take a census of the **p** of Israel,
30:12 Then there will be no plagues among the **p** as you
30:31 And say to the **p** of Israel, 'This will always be my
31:13 "Tell the **p** of Israel to keep my Sabbath day,
31:16 The **p** of Israel must keep the Sabbath day forever.
32: 1 the mountain right away, the **p** went to Aaron.
32: 3 All the **p** obeyed Aaron and brought him their gold
32: 4 The **p** exclaimed, "O Israel, these are the gods
32: 5 When Aaron saw how excited the **p** were about it,
32: 6 So the **p** got up early the next morning to sacrifice
32: 7 The **p** you brought from Egypt have defiled
32: 9 have seen how stubborn and rebellious these **p** are.
32:11 so angry with your own **p** whom you brought from
32:12 terrible disaster you are planning against your **p**!
32:14 and didn't bring against his **p** the disaster he had
32:17 When Joshua heard the noise of the **p** shouting
32:20 mixed it with water. Then he made the **p** drink it.
32:21 "What did the **p** do to you?" he demanded.
32:22 "You yourself know these **p** and what a wicked
32:25 When Moses saw that Aaron had let the **p** get
32:28 and about three thousand **p** died that day.
32:30 The next day Moses said to the **p**, "You have
32:31 "Alas, these **p** have committed a terrible sin.
32:34 Now go, lead the **p** to the place I told you about.
32:34 But when I call the **p** to account, I will certainly
32:35 And the LORD sent a great plague upon the **p**
33: 1 "Now that you have brought these **p** out of Egypt,
33: 3 along with you, for you are a stubborn, unruly **p**.
33: 4 When the **p** heard these stern words, they went into
33: 5 to tell them, "You are an unruly, stubborn **p**.
33: 8 all the **p** would get up and stand in their tent
33:10 Then all the **p** would stand and bow low at their
33:12 'Take these **p** up to the Promised Land.'
33:13 don't forget that this nation is your very own **p**."
33:16 how will anyone ever know that your **p** and I have
33:16 and distinct from all other **p** on the earth?"
34: 9 Yes, this is an unruly and stubborn **p**, but please
34:10 And all the **p** around you will see the power of the
34:12 "Be very careful never to make treaties with the **p**
34:15 "Do not make treaties of any kind with the **p**
34:30 and the **p** of Israel saw the radiance of Moses'
34:32 Then all the **p** came, and Moses gave them the
34:34 Then he would give the **p** whatever instructions the
34:35 and the **p** would see his face aglow. Afterward he
35: 1 Now Moses called a meeting of all the **p** and told
35: 4 Then Moses said to all the **p**, "This is what the
35:20 So all the **p** left Moses and went to their tents to
35:29 So the **p** of Israel—every man and woman who
36: 3 Moses gave them the materials donated by the **p**
36: 6 So the **p** stopped bringing their offerings.
38:24 The **p** brought gifts of gold totaling about 2,200
38:29 The **p** also brought 5,310 pounds of bronze,
39: 7 to the LORD concerning the **p** of Israel.
39:42 So the **p** of Israel followed all of the LORD's
40:36 the **p** of Israel would set out on their journey,
40:38 fire in the cloud so all the **p** of Israel could see it.
Lev 4:13 the community's notice, all the **p** will be guilty.
4:20 this way, the priest will make atonement for the **p**,
4:32 "If any of the **p** bring a sheep as their sin offering,
5: 1 "If any of the **p** are called to testify about
5: 5 "When any of the **p** become aware of their guilt in
5:11 "If any of the **p** cannot afford to bring young
5:15 "If any of the **p** sin by unintentionally defiling the
6: 2 "Suppose some of the **p** sin against the LORD by
7:19 it may only be eaten by **p** who are ceremonially
8: 4 and all the **p** assembled at the Tabernacle entrance.
9: 5 So the **p** brought all of these things to the entrance
9: 7 present the offerings to make atonement for the **p**,
9:15 Next Aaron presented the sacrifices for the **p**.
9:22 Aaron raised his hands toward the **p** and blessed
9:23 when they came back out, they blessed the **p** again,
9:24 When the **p** saw all this, they shouted with joy
10: 3 before all the **p**.' " And Aaron was silent.
10:14 of the peace offerings presented by the **p** of Israel.
10:17 and for making atonement for the **p** before the
13: 2 "If some of the **p** notice a swelling or a rash
14: 8 "The **p** being purified must complete the cleansing
15:31 you will keep the **p** of Israel separate from things
16: 5 The **p** of Israel must then bring him two male goats
16:10 the wilderness, it will make atonement for the **p**.
16:15 must slaughter the goat as a sin offering for the **p**
16:24 and the whole burnt offering for the **p**.
16:24 he will make atonement for himself and for the **p**.
17: 7 The **p** must no longer be unfaithful to the LORD
17:14 That is why I have told the **p** of Israel never to eat
18: 2 "Say this to your **p**, the Israelites: I, the LORD,
18: 3 So do not act like the **p** in Egypt, where you used
18: 3 or like the **p** of Canaan, where I am taking you.
18:24 because this is how the **p** I am expelling from the
18:25 That is why I am punishing the **p** who live there,
18:27 by the **p** of the land where I am taking you,
18:28 as it will vomit out the **p** who live there now.
19:16 "Do not spread slanderous gossip among your **p**.
19:32 of God by standing up in the presence of elderly **p**
20: 2 they must be stoned to death by **p** of the
20: 4 And if the **p** of the community ignore this offering
20: 6 "If any among the **p** are unfaithful by consulting
20:23 Do not live by the customs of the **p** whom I will
20:24 your God, who has set you apart from all other **p**.
20:26 I have set you apart from all other **p** to be my very
22:16 by allowing unauthorized **p** to eat them.
22:16 The negligent priest would bring guilt upon the **p**
22:32 I must be treated as holy by the **p** of Israel. It is I,
23: 7 all the **p** must stop their regular work and gather
23: 8 the **p** must present an offering to the LORD by
23: 8 the **p** must again stop all their regular work to hold
23:24 You will call the **p** to a sacred assembly—
24: 2 "Command the **p** of Israel to provide you with
24:15 Say to the **p** of Israel: Those who blaspheme God
25:42 The **p** of Israel are my servants, whom I brought
25:46 but the **p** of Israel, your relatives, must never be
25:55 For the **p** of Israel are my servants, whom I
26: 9 will look favorably upon you and multiply your **p**
26:12 I will be your God, and you will be my **p**.
26:40 "But at last my **p** will confess their sins
26:43 At last the **p** will receive the due punishment for
Nu 1:16 own families, were chosen from among all the **p**.
1:18 All the **p** were registered according to their
1:19 So Moses counted the **p** there in the wilderness of
1:53 **p** of Israel protection from the LORD's fierce
2:34 So the **p** of Israel did everything just as the
3:12 for all the firstborn sons of the **p** of Israel.
3:38 for the sanctuary on behalf of the **p** of Israel.
3:42 So Moses counted the firstborn sons of the **p** of
3:45 in place of the firstborn sons of the **p** of Israel.
3:45 for the firstborn livestock of the **p** of Israel.
5: 2 "Command the **p** of Israel to remove anyone from
5: 4 and removed such **p** from the camp.
5: 6 instructions to the **p** of Israel: If any of the **p**—men
5:12 "Say to the **p** of Israel: 'Suppose a man's wife
5:21 "then may the **p** see that the LORD's curse is
5:27 her name will become a curse word among her **p**.
6: 1 "Speak to the **p** of Israel and give them these
6: 2 If some of the **p**, either men or women,
6:23 and his sons to bless the **p** of Israel with this
6:27 and his sons will designate the Israelites as my **p**,
8: 6 "Now set the Levites apart from the rest of the **p**
8:10 the **p** of Israel must lay their hands on them.
8:11 LORD as a special offering from the **p** of Israel,
8:14 you will set the Levites apart from the rest of the **p**
8:16 "Of all the **p** of Israel, the Levites are reserved for
8:17 For all the firstborn males among the **p** of Israel
are mine, both **p** and animals.
9: 4 So Moses told the **p** to celebrate the Passover
9:10 'If any of the **p** now or in future generations are
9:17 over the sacred tent, the **p** of Israel followed it.
9:17 wherever the cloud settled, the **p** of Israel camped.
9:20 few days, so the **p** would stay for only a few days.
9:21 the cloud lifted, the **p** broke camp and followed.
9:22 the **p** of Israel stayed in camp and did not move on.
10: 2 silver to be used for summoning the **p** to assemble
10: 3 the **p** will know that they are to gather before you
10: 7 But when you call the **p** to an assembly,
11: 1 The **p** soon began to complain to the LORD about
11: 2 The **p** screamed to Moses for help; and when he
11: 4 and the **p** of Israel also began to complain.
11: 8 The **p** gathered it from the ground and made flour
11:11 What did I do to deserve the burden of a **p** like
11:13 Where am I supposed to get meat for all these **p**?
11:14 I can't carry all these **p** by myself! The load is far
11:17 They will bear the burden of the **p** along with you,
11:18 "And tell the **p** to purify themselves, for tomorrow
11:24 and reported the LORD's words to the **p**.
11:29 I wish that all the LORD's **p** were prophets,
11:32 So the **p** went out and caught quail all that day
11:33 the anger of the LORD blazed against the **p**,
11:34 because they buried the **p** there who had craved
12:15 and the **p** waited until she was brought back before
13:18 and find out whether the **p** living there are strong
13:26 and the **p** of Israel at Kadesh in the wilderness of
13:28 But the **p** living there are powerful, and their cities
13:30 But Caleb tried to encourage the **p** as they stood
13:32 who go to live there. All the **p** we saw were huge.
14: 1 Then all the **p** began weeping aloud, and they cried
14: 5 fell face down on the ground before the **p** of Israel.
14: 9 and don't be afraid of the **p** of the land.
14:11 said to Moses, "How long will these **p** reject me?
14:13 you displayed in rescuing these **p** from Egypt.
14:14 who are well aware that you are with this **p**.
14:14 that you have appeared in full view of your **p** in the
14:15 Now if you slaughter all these **p**, the nations that
14:19 Please pardon the sins of this **p** because of your
14:22 not one of these **p** will ever enter that land.
14:39 the Israelites, there was much sorrow among the **p**.
14:44 But the **p** pushed ahead toward the hill country of
15: 1 Moses to give these instructions to the **p** of Israel:
15:18 "Give the **p** of Israel the following instructions:
15:32 One day while the **p** of Israel were in the
15:38 "Say to the **p** of Israel:
16: 3 anyone else among all these **p** of the LORD?"
16: 9 **p** of Israel to be near him as you serve in the
16: 9 and to stand before the **p** to minister to them?
16:21 "Get away from these **p** so that I may instantly
16:22 "Must you be angry with all the **p** when only one
16:24 "Then tell all the **p** to get away from the tents of
16:26 "Quick!" he told the **p**. "Get away from the tents
16:27 So all the **p** stood back from the tents of Korah,
16:34 All of the **p** of Israel fled as they heard their
16:38 then serve as a warning to the **p** of Israel."
16:41 saying, "You two have killed the LORD's **p**!"
16:42 As the **p** gathered to protest to Moses and Aaron,
16:45 "Get away from these **p** so that I can instantly
16:46 and carry it quickly among the **p** to make
16:47 did as Moses told him and ran out among the **p**.
16:49 But 14,700 **p** died in that plague, in addition to
17: 6 So Moses gave the instructions to the **p** of Israel,
17: 9 the LORD's presence, he showed them to the **p**.
17:12 Then the **p** of Israel said to Moses, "We are as
18: 5 anger will never again blaze against the **p** of Israel.
18: 8 holy gifts that are brought to me by the **p** of Israel.
18:12 "I also give you the harvest gifts brought by the **p**
18:13 All the firstfruits of the land that the **p** present to
18:19 I am giving you all these holy offerings that the **p**
18:20 of land or share of property among the **p** of Israel.
18:32 But be careful not to treat the holy gifts of the **p** of
19: 2 Tell the **p** of Israel to bring you a red heifer that
19: 9 They will be kept there for the **p** of Israel to use in
19:10 This is a permanent law for the **p** of Israel and any
19:19 Then on the seventh day the **p** being cleansed must
20: 1 In early spring the **p** of Israel arrived in the
20: 2 There was no water for the **p** to drink at that place,
20: 3 The **p** blamed Moses and said, "We wish we had
20: 4 Did you bring the LORD's **p** into this wilderness
20: 6 Moses and Aaron turned away from the **p** and went
20: 8 As the **p** watch, command the rock over there to
20: 8 get enough water from the rock to satisfy all the **p**
20:10 Then he and Aaron summoned the **p** to come
20:11 So all the **p** and their livestock drank their fill.
20:12 to demonstrate my holiness to the **p** of Israel,
20:13 because it was where the **p** of Israel argued with
20:14 message is from your relatives, the **p** of Israel:
20:24 He will not enter the land I am giving the **p** of
20:29 When the **p** realized that Aaron had died, all Israel
21: 2 Then the **p** of Israel made this vow to the LORD:
21: 2 "If you will help us conquer these **p**, we will
21: 4 Then the **p** of Israel set out from Mount Hor,
21: 4 of Edom. But the **p** grew impatient along the way,
21: 7 Then the **p** came to Moses and cried out,
21: 7 take away the snakes." So Moses prayed for the **p**.
21:16 "Assemble the **p**, and I will give them water."
21:29 Your destruction is certain, O **p** of Moab!
21:31 So the **p** of Israel occupied the territory of the
21:33 Og of Bashan and all his **p** attacked them at Edrei.
22: 1 Then the **p** of Israel traveled to the plains of Moab
22: 3 Israelites there were, he and his **p** were terrified.
22: 5 "A vast horde of **p** has arrived from Egypt.
22: 6 I know that blessings fall on the **p** you bless.
22: 6 I also know that the **p** you curse are doomed."
22:11 'A vast horde of **p** has come from Egypt and has
22:12 "You are not to curse these **p**, for I have blessed
22:17 ask of me. Just come and curse these **p** for me!"
22:41 From there he could see the **p** of Israel spread out
23: 9 from the hills. / I see a **p** who live by themselves,
23:10 Who can count even a fourth of Israel's **p**?
23:24 These **p** rise up like a lioness; / like a majestic lion
24: 2 where he saw the **p** of Israel camped, tribe by tribe.
24:14 Now I am returning to my own **p**. But first let me
24:14 what the Israelites will do to your **p** in the future."
24:17 It will crush the foreheads of Moab's **p**,
24:17 cracking the skulls of the **p** of Sheth.
24:20 Then Balaam looked over at the **p** of Amalek
25: 3 causing the LORD's anger to blaze against his **p**.
25: 4 so his fierce anger will turn away from the **p** of
25: 6 right before the eyes of Moses and all the **p**,
25: 9 but not before 24,000 **p** had died.
25:13 his God and made atonement for the **p** of Israel."
26:62 included in the total census figure of the **p** of Israel
26:63 So these are the census figures of the **p** of Israel as
27: 8 Moreover announce this to the **p** of Israel: 'If a
27:12 and look out over the land I have given the **p** of
27:14 When the **p** of Israel rebelled, you failed to
27:17 so the **p** of the LORD will not be like sheep
27:19 him with the responsibility of leading the **p**.
28: 1 "Give these instructions to the **p** of Israel:
28:18 festival you must call a sacred assembly of the **p**.
28:25 you must call another holy assembly of the **p**.
28:26 you must call a holy assembly of the **p**.
29: 1 You must call a solemn assembly of all the **p** on
29: 7 you must call another holy assembly of all the **p**.
29: 7 the Day of Atonement, the **p** must go without food,
29:12 must call yet another holy assembly of all the **p**,
29:35 the festival, call all the **p** to another holy assembly.
29:40 So Moses gave all of these instructions to the **p** of
31: 3 So Moses said to the **p**, "Choose some men to
31:11 the plunder and captives, both **p** and animals,
31:13 and all the leaders of the **p** went to meet them
31:16 and caused the **p** of Israel to rebel against the
31:16 who caused the plague to strike the LORD's **p**.
31:26 taken in the battle, including the **p** and animals.
31:27 who fought the battle and half to the rest of the **p**.
31:30 and goats in the half that belongs to the **p** of Israel.
31:42 The half of the plunder belonging to the **p** of Israel,
31:47 From the half-share given to the **p**, Moses took one
31:54 to the LORD that the **p** of Israel belong to him.
32: 2 Eleazar the priest, and the other leaders of the **p**.
32: 4 has conquered this whole area for the **p** of Israel.
32: 7 "Are you trying to discourage the rest of the **p** of
32: 9 they discouraged the **p** of Israel from entering the
32:17 they will be safe from any attacks by the local **p**.
32:18 We will not return to our homes until all the **p** of
32:22 to the LORD and to the rest of the **p** of Israel.
32:25 Then the **p** of Gad and Reuben replied, "We are
32:34 The **p** of Gad built the towns of Dibon, Ataroth,
32:37 The **p** of Reuben built the towns of Heshbon,
32:41 The **p** of Jair, another clan of the tribe of
33: 3 The **p** of Israel left defiantly, in full view of all the
33:14 where there was no water for the **p** to drink.
33:40 heard that the **p** of Israel were approaching his
33:52 you must drive out all the **p** living there. You must
33:55 But if you fail to drive out the **p** who live in the
34:17 the men who are to divide the land among the **p**:
35: 2 "Instruct the **p** of Israel to give to the Levites from

35: 8 These towns will come from the property of the **p**
35:10 “Say this to the **p** of Israel: ‘When you cross the
35:11 designate cities of refuge for **p** to flee to if they
35:34 the LORD, who lives among the **p** of Israel.’ ”
36: 2 divide the land by sacred lot among the **p** of Israel.
36:13 and regulations that the LORD gave to the **p** of
Dt 1: 1 **p** of Israel while they were in the wilderness east
1: 5 So Moses addressed the **p** of Israel while they were
1:15 Some were responsible for a thousand **p**, some for
1:28 They say that the **p** of the land are taller and more
1:38 Joshua son of Nun, will lead the **p** into the land.
2: 4 Give these orders to the **p**: “You will be passing
2:25 Beginning today I will make all **p** throughout the
2:33 to us, and we crushed him, his sons, and all his **p**.
3: 3 our God handed King Og and all his **p** over to us,
3: 6 We destroyed all the **p** in every town we
3:28 for he will lead the **p** across the Jordan.
4:10 where he told me, ‘Summon the **p** before me,
4:20 the burning furnace of Egypt to become his own **p**
4:32 from the time God created **p** on the earth until
4:45 and regulations that Moses gave to the **p** of Israel
4:46 He and his **p** had been destroyed by Moses
5: 1 Moses called all the **p** of Israel together and said,
5:28 to me, ‘I have heard what the **p** have said to you,
5:31 You will teach them to the **p** so they can obey
5:32 So Moses told the **p**, “You must obey all the
6:22 blows against Egypt and Pharaoh and all his **p**.
7: 4 They will lead your young **p** away from me to
7: 6 For you are a holy **p**, who belong to the LORD
7: 6 Of all the **p** on earth, the LORD your God has
7:19 will use this same power against the **p** you fear.
8: 3 He did it to teach you that **p** need more than bread
9: 5 upright **p** that you are about to occupy their land.
9: 6 for you are not—you are a stubborn **p**.
9:12 because the **p** you led out of Egypt have become
9:13 LORD said to me, ‘I have been watching this **p**,
9:26 ‘O Sovereign LORD, do not destroy your own **p**.
9:27 Overlook the stubbornness and sin of these **p**,
9:28 If you destroy these **p**, the Egyptians will say,
9:29 But they are your **p** and your special possession,
10: 6 “The **p** of Israel set out from the wells of the **p** of
10:11 and lead the **p** into the land I swore to give their
13: 9 to initiate the execution; then all the **p** must join in.
14: 1 “Since you are the **p** of the LORD your God,
15: 7 “But if there are any poor **p** in your towns when
16: 8 On the seventh day the **p** must assemble before the
16:18 They will judge the **p** fairly throughout the land.
17: 7 the first stones, and then all the **p** will join in.
17:16 and he must never send his **p** to Egypt to buy
18: 3 the oxen and sheep that the **p** bring as offerings:
18:10 And do not let your **p** practice fortune-telling
18:14 The **p** you are about to displace consult with
18:18 and he will tell the **p** everything I command him.
19:10 That way you will prevent the death of innocent **p**
20:10 a town to attack it, first offer its **p** terms for peace.
20:11 then all the **p** inside will serve you in forced labor.
20:18 This will keep the **p** of the land from teaching you
21: 8 forgive your **p** Israel whom you have redeemed.
21: 8 Do not charge your **p** Israel with the guilt of
22: 5 The LORD your God detests **p** who do this.
25: 1 “Suppose two **p** take a dispute to court,
26:15 and bless your **p** Israel and the land you have given
26:18 The LORD has declared today that you are his **p**,
27: 1 and the leaders of Israel charged the **p** as follows:
27: 9 Today you have become the **p** of the LORD your
27:11 That same day Moses gave this charge to the **p**:
27:12 Mount Gerizim to proclaim a blessing over the **p**.
27:14 Then the Levites must shout to all the **p** of Israel:
27:15 to the LORD.’ / And all the **p** will reply, ‘Amen.’
27:16 or mother.’ / And all the **p** will reply, ‘Amen.’
27:17 And all the **p** will reply, ‘Amen.’
27:18 on the road.’ / And all the **p** will reply, ‘Amen.’
27:19 and widows.’ / And all the **p** will reply, ‘Amen.’
27:20 his father.’ / And all the **p** will reply, ‘Amen.’
27:21 with an animal.’ / And all the **p** will reply, ‘Amen.’
27:22 or his mother.’ / And all the **p** will reply, ‘Amen.’
27:23 And all the **p** will reply, ‘Amen.’
27:24 in secret.’ / And all the **p** will reply, ‘Amen.’
27:25 And all the **p** will reply, ‘Amen.’
27:26 obeying them.’ / And all the **p** will reply, ‘Amen.’
28: 9 the LORD will establish you as his holy **p** as he
28:10 will see that you are a **p** claimed by the LORD,
29:13 He wants to confirm you today as his **p** and to
29:20 The LORD will not pardon such **p**. His anger
29:25 because the **p** of the land broke the covenant they
29:28 and fury the LORD uprooted his **p** from their land
31: 1 finished saying these things to all the **p** of Israel,
31: 5 The LORD will hand over to you the **p** who live
31: 7 For you will lead these **p** into the land that the
31:11 you must read this law to all the **p** of Israel when
31:16 these **p** will begin worshiping foreign gods,
31:19 words of this song, and teach it to the **p** of Israel.
31:21 I know what these **p** are like, even before they
31:23 You must bring the **p** of Israel into the land I swore
31:26 so it may serve as a witness against the **p** of Israel.
32: 6 repay the LORD, / you foolish and senseless **p**?
32: 9 For the **p** of Israel belong to the LORD; / Jacob is
32:15 the **p** grew heavy, plump, and stuffed!
32:28 the **p** are foolish, without understanding.
32:30 of them, / and two **p** put ten thousand to flight,
32:36 “Indeed, the LORD will judge his **p**, / and he will
32:43 on his enemies / and cleanse his land and his **p**.”
32:44 and recited all the words of this song to the **p**.
32:49 the land I am giving to the **p** of Israel as their own
32:51 You failed to demonstrate my holiness to the **p** of
32:52 but you may not enter the land I am giving to the **p**
33: 1 of God, gave to the **p** of Israel before his death:
33: 3 Indeed, you love the **p**; / all your holy ones are in
33: 5 in Israel— / when the leaders of the **p** assembled,
33: 7 the cry of Judah / and bring them again to their **p**.
33:12 “The **p** of Benjamin are loved by the LORD
33:18 “May the **p** of Zebulun prosper in their
33:18 May the **p** of Issachar prosper at home in their
33:19 They summon the **p** to the mountain / to offer
33:21 The **p** of Gad took the best land for themselves;
33:21 When the leaders of the **p** were assembled,
33:29 Who else is like you, a **p** saved by the LORD?
34: 8 The **p** of Israel mourned thirty days for Moses on
34: 9 So the **p** of Israel obeyed him and did everything
Jos 1: 2 you must lead my **p** across the Jordan River into
1: 6 for you will lead my **p** to possess all the land I
1:11 and tell the **p** to get their provisions ready.
2:10 Jordan River, whose **p** you completely destroyed.
2:24 “for all the **p** in the land are terrified of us.”
3: 3 giving these instructions to the **p**: “When you see
3: 5 Then Joshua told the **p**, “Purify yourselves,
3: 6 of the Covenant and lead the **p** across the river.”
3:14 When the **p** set out to cross the Jordan, the priests
3:16 Then all the **p** crossed over near the city of Jericho.
3:17 the middle of the riverbed as the **p** passed by them.
4: 1 When all the **p** were safely across the river,
4: 7 as a permanent memorial among the **p** of Israel.”
4:10 Meanwhile, the **p** hurried across the riverbed.
4:19 The **p** crossed the Jordan on the tenth day of the
5: 1 up the Jordan River so the **p** of Israel could cross,
5: 2 flint to make the Israelites a circumcised **p** again.”
6: 1 because the **p** were afraid of the Israelites.
6: 5 on the horns, have all the **p** give a mighty shout.
6: 5 and the **p** can charge straight into the city.”
6: 7 Then he gave orders to the **p**: “March around the
6: 8 After Joshua spoke to the **p**, the seven priests with
6:16 on their horns, Joshua commanded the **p**, “Shout!
6:20 When the **p** heard the sound of the horns,
7: 9 and all the other **p** living in the land hear about it,
7:13 Command the **p** to purify themselves in
8: 1 to you the king of Ai, his **p**, his city, and his land.
8: 9 But Joshua remained among the **p** in the camp that
8:33 the LORD, had given for blessing the **p** of Israel.
9: 3 But when the **p** of Gibeon heard what had
9:11 So our leaders and our **p** instructed us, ‘Prepare for
9:11 Go meet with the **p** of Israel and declare our **p** to
be their servants,
9:16 facts came out—these **p** of Gibeon lived nearby!
9:18 The **p** of Israel grumbled against their leaders
9:24 this entire land and destroy all the **p** living in it.
9:26 Joshua did not allow the **p** of Israel to kill them.
9:27 and water carriers for the **p** of Israel and for the
10: 2 and his **p** became very afraid when they heard all
10: 4 have made peace with Joshua and the **p** of Israel.”
10:12 Joshua prayed to the LORD in front of all the **p** of
10:40 the kings and **p** of the hill country, the Negev,
10:42 the God of Israel, was fighting for his **p**.
11:12 Joshua slaughtered all the other kings and their **p**,
11:14 cities for themselves, but they killed all the **p**.
11:23 He gave it to the **p** of Israel as their special
12: 6 and the Israelites had destroyed the **p** of King
12: 8 The **p** who lived in this region were the Hittites,
13: 2 The **p** still need to occupy the land of the
13: 6 “I will drive these **p** out of the land for the
13:13 But the Israelites failed to drive out the **p** of
14: 8 my brothers who went with me frightened the **p**
15:15 Then he fought against the **p** living in the town of
15:63 so the Jebusites live there among the **p** of Judah to
16:10 so the **p** of Gezer live as slaves among the **p**
17: 7 to the **p** living near the spring of Tappuah.
17:14 land when the LORD has given us so many **p**?”
19:47 captured it, slaughtered its **p**, and settled there.
22:20 Didn’t God punish all the **p** of Israel when Achan,
22:21 Then the **p** of Reuben, Gad, and the half-tribe of
22:25 Jordan River as a barrier between our **p** and your **p**.
22:34 The **p** of Reuben and Gad named the altar
23: 1 and the LORD had given the **p** of Israel rest from
23: 5 for the LORD your God will drive out all the **p**
23: 7 Make sure you do not associate with the other **p**
24: 1 Then Joshua summoned all the **p** of Israel to
24: 2 Joshua said to the **p**, “This is what the LORD,
24: 5 and afterward I brought you out as a free **p**.
24:16 The **p** replied, “We would never forsake the
24:19 Then Joshua said to the **p**, “You are not able to
24:21 But the **p** answered Joshua, saying, “No, we are
24:24 The **p** said to Joshua, “We will serve the LORD
24:25 So Joshua made a covenant with the **p** that day at
24:27 Joshua said to all the **p**, “This stone has heard
24:28 Then Joshua sent the **p** away, each to his own
Jdg 1: 8 killing all its **p** and setting the city on fire.
1:11 From there they marched against the **p** living in the
1:16 They settled among the **p** there, near the town of
1:19 The LORD was with the **p** of Judah, and they
1:19 But they failed to drive out the **p** living in the
plains because the **p** there had iron chariots.
1:20 And Caleb drove out the **p** living there, who were
1:21 live in Jerusalem among the **p** of Benjamin.
1:27 The tribe of Manasseh failed to drive out the **p**
1:32 the Canaanites dominated the land where the **p** of
1:33 the **p** of Beth-shemesh and Beth-anath were
1:33 forced to work as slaves for the **p** of Naphtali.
2: 2 you were not to make any covenants with the **p**
2: 3 I will no longer drive out the **p** living in your land.
2: 6 After Joshua sent the **p** away, each of the tribes left
2:12 worshiping the gods of the **p** around them.
2:15 as he promised. And the **p** were very distressed.
2:18 and rescued the **p** from their enemies throughout
2:18 For the LORD took pity on his **p**, who were
2:19 the judge died, the **p** returned to their corrupt ways,
2:20 “Because these **p** have violated the covenant I
3: 4 These **p** were left to test the Israelites—to see
5: 2 leaders take charge, / and the **p** gladly follow—
5: 6 and in the days of Jael, / **p** avoided the main roads,
5: 7 There were few **p** left in the villages of Israel—
5:11 Then the **p** of the LORD / marched down to the
5:13 The **p** of the LORD marched down against
5:23 ‘Let the **p** of Meroz be cursed,’ said the angel of
6: 3 Amalek, and the **p** of the east would attack Israel,
6:27 of his father’s household and the **p** of the town.
6:28 next morning, as the **p** of the town began to stir,
6:29 The **p** said to each other, “Who did this?”
6:33 and the **p** of the east formed an alliance against
7: 3 Therefore, tell the **p**, ‘Whoever is timid or afraid
7:12 and the **p** of the east had settled in the valley like a
8: 1 Then the **p** of Ephraim asked Gideon, “Why have
8: 9 So he said to the **p** of Peniel, “After I return in
9: 2 “Ask the **p** of Shechem whether they want to be
9: 3 So Abimelech’s uncles spoke to all the **p** of
9: 6 Then the **p** of Shechem and Beth-millo called a
9: 7 and shouted, “Listen to me, **p** of Shechem!
9: 9 the olive oil that blesses both God and **p**,
9:13 producing the wine that cheers both God and **p**,
9:20 and devour the **p** of Shechem and Beth-millo;
9:20 and may fire come out from the **p** of Shechem
9:23 trouble between Abimelech and the **p** of Shechem,
9:25 The **p** of Shechem set an ambush for Abimelech on
9:26 and gained the confidence of the **p** of Shechem.
9:36 there are **p** coming down from the hilltops!”
9:37 Gaal said, “No, **p** are coming down from the hills.
9:42 The next day the **p** of Shechem went out into the
9:43 When Abimelech saw the **p** coming out of the city,
9:45 He killed the **p**, leveled the city, and scattered salt
9:46 When the **p** who lived in the tower of Shechem
9:47 Someone reported to Abimelech that the **p** were
9:49 So all the **p** who had lived in the tower of Shechem
10:18 first will become ruler over all the **p** of Gilead.”
11: 8 we will make you ruler over all the **p** of Gilead.”
11: 9 will you really make me ruler over all the **p**?”
11:16 When the **p** of Israel arrived at Kadesh on their
11:17 through either. So the **p** of Israel stayed in Kadesh.
11:21 God of Israel, gave his **p** victory over King Sihon.
12: 6 because **p** from Ephraim cannot pronounce the
14:16 You have given my **p** a riddle, but you haven’t told
15:18 of thirst and fall into the hands of these pagan **p**?”
16:24 When the **p** saw him, they praised their god,
16:25 Half drunk by now, the **p** demanded, “Bring out
16:27 The temple was completely filled with **p**.
16:30 down on the Philistine leaders and all the **p**.
16:30 So he killed more **p** when he died than he had
17: 6 so the **p** did whatever seemed right in their own
18: 1 for they had not yet driven out the **p** who lived in
18: 7 where they noticed the **p** living carefree lives,
18: 7 The **p** were also wealthy because their land was
18:10 get there, you will find the **p** living carefree lives.
18:22 When the **p** from the tribe of Dan were quite a
18:27 town of Laish, whose **p** were peaceful and secure.
18:27 They attacked and killed all the **p** and burned the
18:28 Then the **p** of the tribe of Dan rebuilt the town
20: 2 The leaders of all the **p** and all the tribes of Israel
20: 2 took their positions in the assembly of the **p** of
20: 8 And all the **p** stood up together and replied,
20:13 this evil.” But the **p** of Benjamin would not listen.
20:18 “Which tribe should lead the attack against the **p**
20:48 in all the towns—the **p**, the cattle—everything.
21: 2 And the **p** went to Bethel and sat in the presence of
21: 4 Early the next morning the **p** built an altar
21: 9 For after they counted all the **p**, no one from
21:15 The **p** felt sorry for Benjamin because the LORD
21:25 so the **p** did whatever seemed right in their own
Ru 1: 6 his **p** in Judah by giving them good crops again.
1:10 they said. “We want to go with you to your **p**.”
1:15 “your sister-in-law has gone back to her **p** and to
1:16 Your **p** will be my **p**, and your God will be
3:14 but she got up before it was light enough for **p** to
4:11 the leaders and all the **p** standing there replied,
1Sa 2:22 of what his sons were doing to the **p** of Israel.
2:23 “I have been hearing reports from the **p** about the
2:24 The reports I hear among the LORD’s **p** are not
2:26 to gain favor with the LORD and with the **p**.
2:27 when the **p** of Israel were slaves in Egypt?
2:29 have become fat from the best offerings of my **p**!
2:32 envy as I pour out prosperity on the **p** of Israel.
3:20 All the **p** of Israel from one end of the land to the
4: 1 And Samuel’s words went out to all the **p** of Israel.
5: 6 Then the LORD began to afflict the **p** of Ashdod
5: 7 When the **p** realized what was happening,
5: 9 the LORD began afflicting its **p**, young and old,
5:10 but when the **p** of Ekron saw it coming they cried
5:11 So the **p** summoned the rulers again and begged
6:13 The **p** of Beth-shemesh were harvesting wheat in
6:14 So the **p** broke up the wood of the cart for a fire
6:15 to the LORD that day by the **p** of Beth-shemesh.
6:19 And the **p** mourned greatly because of what the
6:21 So they sent messengers to the **p** at Kiriath-jearim
7: 3 Then Samuel said to all the **p** of Israel, “If you are
7:16 He judged the **p** of Israel at each of these places.
8:10 Samuel passed on the LORD’s warning to the **p**.
8:19 But the **p** refused to listen to Samuel’s warning.
8:21 So Samuel told the LORD what the **p** had said,
8:22 a king.” Then Samuel agreed and sent the **p** home.
9: 6 He is held in high honor by all the **p**
9: 9 (In those days if **p** wanted a message from God,
9:16 Anoint him to be the leader of my **p**, Israel. He will
9:16 for I have looked down on my **p** in mercy and have
9:17 the man I told you about! He will rule my **p**.”
10: 1 has appointed you to be the leader of his **p** Israel.

10:17 Later Samuel called all the **p** of Israel to meet
10:24 Then Samuel said to all the **p**, "This is the man the
10:24 And all the **p** shouted, "Long live the king!"
10:25 Then Samuel told the **p** what the rights and duties
10:25 the LORD. Then Samuel sent the **p** home again.
11: 4 Saul's hometown, and told the **p** about their plight,
11: 7 And the LORD made the **p** afraid of Saul's anger,
11:12 Then the **p** exclaimed to Samuel, "Now where are
11:14 Then Samuel said to the **p**, "Come, let us all go to
12: 1 Then Samuel addressed the **p** again: "I have done
12: 9 But the **p** soon forgot about the LORD their God,
12:18 And all the **p** were terrified of the LORD and of
12:22 The LORD will not abandon his chosen **p**,
13: 4 and he warned the **p** that the Philistines now hated
13:14 has already chosen him to be king over his **p**,
13:22 So none of the **p** of Israel had a sword or spear,
14:40 and all of you stand over there." And the **p** agreed.
14:41 the guilty ones, and the **p** were declared innocent.
14:45 But the **p** broke in and said to Saul,
14:45 So the **p** rescued Jonathan, and he was not put to
15: 6 For you were kind to the **p** of Israel when they
15:24 for I was afraid of the **p** and did what they
15:30 and before my **p** by going with me to worship the
16: 7 **P** judge by outward appearance, but the LORD
17:47 the LORD does not need weapons to rescue his **p**.
19:24 The **p** who were watching exclaimed, "What?
21:11 "Isn't he the one the **p** honor with dances, singing,
23: 5 took all their livestock and rescued the **p** of Keilah.
24: 9 "Why do you listen to the **p** who say I am trying
24:13 old proverb says, 'From evil **p** come evil deeds.'
26:19 so I can no longer live among the LORD's **p**
27: 8 **p** who had lived near Shur, along the road to
27:12 "By now the **p** of Israel must hate him bitterly.
31: 9 and to the **p** throughout the land of Philistia.
31:11 But when the **p** of Jabesh-gilead heard what the
2Sa 1:18 Later he commanded that it be taught to all the **p** of
2: 7 be my strong and loyal subjects like the **p** of Judah,
3:18 'I have chosen David to save my **p** from the
3:19 Then he went to Hebron to tell David that all the **p**
3:21 "Let me go and call all the **p** of Israel to your side.
3:28 and my **p** are innocent of this crime against Abner.
3:32 and the king and all the **p** wept at his graveside.
3:34 a wicked plot." / All the **p** wept again for Abner.
3:36 This pleased the **p** very much. In fact,
3:38 Then King David said to the **p**, "Do you not
4: 1 all courage, and his **p** were paralyzed with fear.
4: 3 because the original **p** of Beeroth fled to Gittaim,
5: 2 told you, 'You will be the shepherd of my **p** Israel.
5:12 made his kingdom great for the sake of his **p** Israel.
6: 5 and all the **p** of Israel were celebrating before the
6:18 David blessed the **p** in the name of the LORD
6:21 me as the leader of Israel, the **p** of the LORD.
7: 7 to Israel's leaders, the shepherds of my **p** Israel.
7: 8 I chose you to lead my **p** Israel when you were just
7:10 provided a permanent homeland for my **p** Israel,
7:11 from the time I appointed judges to rule my **p**.
7:23 you redeemed from slavery to be your own **p**?
7:23 for yourself when you rescued your **p** from Egypt.
7:24 You made Israel your **p** forever, and you,
8: 2 He made the **p** lie down on the ground in a row,
10: 6 Now the **p** of Ammon realized how seriously they
10:12 Let us fight bravely to save our **p** and the cities of
12:31 He also made slaves of the **p** of Rabbah and forced
12:31 That is how he dealt with the **p** of all the
13:34 "I see a crowd of **p** coming from the Horonaim
14:13 "Why don't you do as much for all the **p** of God
14:16 us from those who would cut us off from God's **p**.
15: 2 When **p** brought a case to the king for judgment,
15: 4 Then **p** could bring their problems to me, and I
15: 5 And when **p** tried to bow before him,
15: 6 Absalom stole the hearts of all the **p** of Israel.
15:17 The king and his **p** set out on foot, and they
15:30 And the **p** who were with him covered their heads
15:32 of the Mount of Olives where **p** worshiped God,
16: 2 "The donkeys are for your **p** to ride on,
17: 3 and I will bring all the **p** back to you as a bride
17: 3 Then all the **p** will remain unharmed
17:22 and all the **p** with him went across the Jordan
19: 9 The **p** were saying, "The king saved us from our
19:15 the **p** of Judah came to Gilgal to meet him
19:39 So all the **p** crossed the Jordan with the king.
20:22 Then the woman went to the **p** with her wise
21: 3 Tell me so that the LORD will bless his **p** again."
21:12 he went to the **p** of Jabesh-gilead and asked for the
21:12 it was the **p** of Jabesh-gilead who had retrieved
22:44 over nations; / **p** I don't even know now serve me.
24: 1 "Go and count the **p** of Israel and Judah,"
24: 2 his army, "Take a census of all the **p** in the land—
24: 2 so that I may know how many **p** there are."
24: 3 times as many **p** in your kingdom as there are now!
24: 4 and his officers went out to count the **p** of Israel.
24: 9 Joab reported the number of **p** to the king.
24:15 Seventy thousand **p** died throughout the nation.
24:17 But these **p** are innocent—what have they done?
1Ki 1:39 and all the **p** shouted, "Long live King Solomon!"
1:40 And all the **p** returned with Solomon to Jerusalem,
3: 2 At that time the **p** of Israel sacrificed their
3: 8 And here I am among your own chosen **p**, a nation
3: 9 so that I can govern your **p** well
3:11 you have asked for wisdom in governing my **p**
3:28 and the **p** were awed as they realized the great
4: 7 food from the **p** for the king's household.
4:20 The **p** of Judah and Israel were as numerous as the
6: 1 This was 480 years after the **p** of Israel were
6:13 live among the **p** of Israel and never forsake my **p**."
8: 9 where the LORD made a covenant with the **p** of
8:16 'From the day I brought my **p** Israel out of Egypt,
8:16 I have chosen David to be king over my **p**.' "
8:30 and your **p** Israel when we pray toward this place.
8:33 "If your **p** Israel are defeated by their enemies
8:35 is no rain because your **p** have sinned against you,
8:36 and forgive the sins of your servants, your **p** Israel.
8:36 have given to your **p** as their special possession.
8:38 and if your **p** offer a prayer concerning their
8:39 Give your **p** whatever they deserve, for you alone
8:43 Then all the **p** of the earth will come to know and
fear you, just as your own **p** Israel do.
8:44 "If your **p** go out at your command to fight their
8:50 and forgive your **p** who have sinned against you.
8:51 for they are your **p**—your special possession—
8:52 to my requests and to the requests of your **p** Israel.
8:56 "Praise the LORD who has given rest to his **p**
8:59 may uphold my cause and the cause of his **p** Israel,
8:60 May **p** all over the earth know that the LORD is
8:61 And may you, his **p**, always be faithful to the
8:66 the festival was over, Solomon sent the **p** home.
8:66 been good to his servant David and to his **p** Israel.
9: 7 then I will uproot the **p** of Israel from this land I
9: 9 'Because his **p** forgot the LORD their God,
9:20 There were still some **p** living in the land who
10: 8 How happy these **p** must be! What a privilege for
10:24 **P** from every nation came to visit him and to hear
11: 2 The LORD had clearly instructed his **p** not to
12: 5 come back for my answer." So the **p** went away.
12: 6 he asked. "How should I answer these **p**?"
12: 7 "If you are willing to serve the **p** today and give
12: 9 "How should I answer these **p** who want me to
12:12 and all the **p** returned to hear Rehoboam's
12:14 He told the **p**, "My father was harsh on you,
12:16 O David!" So the **p** of Israel returned home.
12:20 When the **p** of Israel learned of Jeroboam's return
12:23 of Judah, and to all the **p** of Judah and Benjamin,
12:28 He said to the **p**, "It is too much trouble for you to
12:30 This became a great sin, for the **p** worshiped them,
12:31 ordained priests from the rank and file of the **p**—
13:25 **P** came by and saw the body lying in the road
13:33 to choose priests from the rank and file of the **p**.
14: 7 'I promoted you from the ranks of the common **p**
14: 7 and made you ruler over my **p** Israel.
14:15 He will uproot the **p** of Israel from this good land
14:18 When the **p** of Israel buried him, they mourned for
14:22 the **p** of Judah did what was evil in the LORD's
14:24 The **p** imitated the detestable practices of the
16: 2 out of the dust to make you ruler of my **p** Israel,
16: 2 You have aroused my anger by causing my **p** to
16:21 But now the **p** of Israel were divided into two
16:21 Half the **p** tried to make Tibni son of Ginath their
18:19 Now bring all the **p** of Israel to Mount Carmel,
18:20 So Ahab summoned all the **p** and the prophets to
18:21 follow him!" But the **p** were completely silent.
18:24 to the wood is the true God!" And all the **p** agreed.
18:30 Then Elijah called to the **p**, "Come over here!"
18:37 Answer me so these **p** will know that you,
18:39 And when the **p** saw it, they fell on their faces
18:40 So the **p** seized them all, and Elijah took them
19:10 But the **p** of Israel have broken their covenant with
19:14 But the **p** of Israel have broken their covenant with
20: 6 to search your palace and the homes of your **p**.
20: 8 to any more demands," the leaders and **p** advised.
20:42 and your **p** will die instead of his **p**."
21:12 and put Naboth at a prominent place before the **p**.
21:13 Then two scoundrels accused him before all the **p**
21:26 the **p** whom the LORD had driven from the land
22:43 and the **p** still offered sacrifices and burned
2Ki 3: 3 son of Nebat had led the **p** of Israel to commit.
3: 4 Mesha of Moab and his **p** were sheep breeders.
3:21 when the **p** of Moab heard about the three armies
4:43 "Feed one hundred **p** with only this?" But Elisha
6:10 of God, warning the **p** there to be on their guard.
6:30 the **p** could see that he was wearing sackcloth
7: 9 let's go back and tell the **p** at the palace."
7:11 Then the gatekeepers shouted the news to the **p** in
7:16 Then the **p** of Samaria rushed out and plundered
7:17 and trampled to death as the **p** rushed out.
7:20 it was, for the **p** trampled him to death at the gate!
8:12 "I know the terrible things you will do to the **p** of
9: 6 I anoint you king over the LORD's **p**, Israel.
10: 1 to the officials of the city, to the leaders of the **p**,
10:18 Then Jehu called a meeting of all the **p** of the city
11:12 and all the **p** clapped their hands and shouted,
11:13 heard all the noise made by the guards and the **p**,
11:14 and **p** from all over the land were rejoicing
11:17 and the **p** that they would be the LORD's **p**.
11:17 also made a covenant between the king and the **p**.
11:18 And all the **p** of the land went over to the temple of
11:19 and all the **p** of the land escorted the king from the
11:20 So all the **p** of the land rejoiced, and the city was
12: 3 and the **p** still offered sacrifices and burned
12: 8 agreed not to collect any more money from the **p**,
12:11 who used it to pay the **p** working on the LORD's
13:23 But the LORD was gracious to the **p** of Israel,
14: 4 where the **p** offered sacrifices and burned incense.
14:10 will bring disaster on you and the **p** of Judah?"
14:21 The **p** of Judah then crowned Amaziah's
15: 4 where the **p** offered sacrifices and burned incense.
15: 5 the royal palace, and he governed the **p** of the land.
15:29 and he took the **p** to Assyria as captives.
15:35 where the **p** offered sacrifices and burned incense.
16: 6 He drove out the **p** of Judah and sent Edomites to
16:15 and grain offering, and the offerings of the **p**,
17: 6 and the **p** of Israel were exiled to Assyria.
17: 7 of Israel because the **p** worshiped other gods,
17: 9 The **p** of Israel had also secretly done many things
17:11 So the **p** of Israel had done many evil things,
17:19 But even the **p** of Judah refused to obey the
17:22 And the **p** of Israel persisted in all the evil ways of
17:24 And the king of Assyria transported groups of **p**
17:24 in the towns of Samaria, replacing the **p** of Israel.
17:26 "The **p** whom you have resettled in the towns of
17:29 at the pagan shrines that the **p** of Israel had built.
17:31 And the **p** from Sepharvaim even burned their own
17:40 But the **p** would not listen and continued to follow
18: 4 because the **p** of Israel had begun to worship it by
18:26 speak in Hebrew, for the **p** on the wall will hear."
18:27 The **p** will become so hungry and thirsty that they
18:28 and shouted in Hebrew to the **p** on the wall,
18:33 ever saved their **p** from the king of Assyria?
18:35 has ever been able to save its **p** from my power?
18:36 But the **p** were silent and did not answer
19:12 Rezeph, and the **p** of Eden who were in Tel-assar?
19:26 That is why their **p** have so little power / and are
19:31 For a remnant of my **p** will spread out from
20: 5 "Go back to Hezekiah, the leader of my **p**.
21: 9 But the **p** refused to listen, and Manasseh led them
21:11 He has led the **p** of Judah into idolatry.
21:13 I will wipe away the **p** of Jerusalem as one wipes a
21:14 Then I will reject even those few of my **p** who are
21:16 Manasseh also murdered many innocent **p** until
21:16 This was in addition to the sin that he caused the **p**
21:24 But the **p** of the land killed all those who had
22: 4 have collected from the **p** at the LORD's Temple.
22: 7 of the money they receive, for they are honest **p**."
22:13 the LORD for me and for the **p** and for all Judah.
22:16 I will destroy this city and its **p**, just as I stated in
22:17 For my **p** have abandoned me and worshiped
22:19 you heard what I said against this city and its **p**,
23: 2 the Temple of the LORD with all the **p** of Judah
23: 2 all the **p** from the least to the greatest.
23: 3 and all the **p** pledged themselves to the covenant.
23:17 And the **p** of the town told him, "It is the tomb of
23:21 King Josiah then issued this order to all the **p**:
23:27 I will banish the **p** from my presence and reject my
23:30 Then the **p** anointed his son Jehoahaz and made
23:35 Jehoiakim collected a tax from the **p** of Judah,
24:14 So only the poorest **p** were left in the land.
24:20 finally banished the **p** of Jerusalem and Judah from
25:11 along with the rest of the **p** and the troops who had
25:12 **p** to stay behind in Judah to care for the vineyards
25:19 And of the **p** still hiding in the city, he took an
25:21 So the **p** of Judah were sent into exile from their
25:22 and grandson of Shaphan as governor over the **p**
25:26 Then all the **p** of Judah, from the least to the
1Ch 1:19 for during his lifetime the **p** of the world were
2:53 from whom came the **p** of Zorah and Eshtaol.
4:22 Jokim, the **p** of Cozeba, Joash, and Saraph,
5:26 to invade the land and lead away the **p** of Reuben,
6:15 who went into exile when the LORD sent the **p** of
6:64 So the **p** of Israel assigned all these towns
9: 1 The **p** of Judah were exiled to Babylon
9: 2 property in their former towns were common **p**.
9: 3 **P** from the tribes of Judah, Benjamin, Ephraim,
10: 9 and to the **p** throughout the land of Philistia.
10:11 But when the **p** of Jabesh-gilead heard what the
11: 2 told you, 'You will be the shepherd of my **p** Israel.
11: 5 The **p** of Jebus said to David, "You will never get
12:15 and drove out all the **p** living in the lowlands on
12:40 And **p** from as far away as Issachar, Zebulun,
13: 4 for the **p** could see it was the right thing to do.
13: 5 So David summoned all the **p** of Israel, from one
14: 2 his kingdom very great for the sake of his **p** Israel.
16: 2 David blessed the **p** in the name of the LORD.
16: 4 **p** in worship before the Ark of the LORD by
16:17 to the **p** of Israel as a never-ending treaty:
16:22 "Do not touch these **p** I have chosen, / and do not
16:36 And all the **p** shouted "Amen!" and praised the
16:43 Then all the **p** returned to their homes, and David
17: 6 to Israel's leaders, the shepherds of my **p**.
17: 7 I chose you to lead my **p** Israel when you were just
17: 9 provided a permanent homeland for my **p** Israel,
17:10 from the time I appointed judges to rule my **p**.
17:21 you redeemed from slavery to be your own **p**?
17:21 for yourself when you rescued your **p** from Egypt.
17:22 You chose Israel to be your **p** forever, and you,
19: 6 Now the **p** of Ammon realized how seriously they
19:13 Let us fight bravely to save our **p** and the cities of
20: 3 He also made slaves of the **p** of Rabbah and forced
20: 3 That is how he dealt with the **p** of all the
21: 2 "Take a census of all the **p** in the land—
21: 3 "May the LORD increase the number of his **p** a
21: 4 so Joab traveled throughout Israel to count the **p**.
21: 5 and reported the number of **p** to David. There were
21:14 and seventy thousand **p** died as a result.
21:17 But these **p** are innocent—what have they done?
21:17 and my family, but do not destroy your **p**."
22:18 and they are now subject to the LORD and his **p**.
28: 2 them as follows: "My brothers and my **p**!
29: 9 The **p** rejoiced over the offerings, for they had
29:12 and it is at your discretion that **p** are made great
29:14 But who am I, and who are my **p**, that we could
29:17 and I have watched your **p** offer their gifts
29:18 and Israel, make your **p** always want to obey you.
2Ch 1: 5 and the **p** gathered in front of it to consult the
1: 9 for you have made me king over a **p** as numerous
1:11 "Because your greatest desire is to help your **p**,
1:11 and knowledge to properly govern my **p**,
2:11 because the LORD loves his **p** that he has made
5:10 when the LORD made a covenant with the **p** of
6: 5 'From the day I brought my **p** out of Egypt, I have
6: 5 Nor have I chosen a king to lead my **p** Israel.
6:11 that the LORD made with the **p** of Israel."
6:18 "But will God really live on earth among **p**?

6:21 and your **p** Israel when we pray toward this place.
6:24 "If your **p** Israel are defeated by their enemies
6:26 is no rain because your **p** have sinned against you,
6:27 and forgive the sins of your servants, your **p** Israel.
6:27 have given to your **p** as their special possession.
6:29 and if your **p** offer a prayer concerning their
6:30 Give your **p** whatever they deserve, for you alone
6:33 Then all the **p** of the earth will come to know and
fear you, just as your own **p** Israel do.
6:34 "If your **p** go out at your command to fight their
6:39 and forgive your **p** who have sinned against you.
7: 3 When all the **p** of Israel saw the fire coming down
7: 4 and all the **p** offered sacrifices to the LORD.
7: 5 and all the **p** dedicated the Temple of God.
7:10 end of the celebration, Solomon sent the **p** home.
7:10 so good to David and Solomon and to his **p** Israel.
7:14 Then if my **p** who are called by my name will
7:20 then I will uproot the **p** of Israel from this land of
7:22 will be, 'Because his **p** abandoned the LORD,
8: 7 There were still some **p** living in the land who
8:14 He also assigned the Levites to lead the **p** in praise
9: 7 How happy these **p** must be! What a privilege for
10: 5 in three days for my answer." So the **p** went away.
10: 6 he asked. "How should I answer these **p**?"
10: 7 "If you are good to the **p** and show them kindness
10: 9 "How should I answer these **p** who want me to
10:12 and all the **p** returned to hear Rehoboam's
10:14 He told the **p**, "My father was harsh on you,
12: 7 "Since the **p** have humbled themselves, I will not
13:12 O **p** of Israel, do not fight against the LORD,
14: 4 He commanded the **p** of Judah to seek the LORD,
14: 7 Asa told the **p** of Judah, "Let us build towns
14:14 and terror from the LORD came upon the **p** there.
15: 2 "Listen, all you **p** of Judah and Benjamin!
15: 9 Then Asa called together all the **p** of Judah
15: 9 along with the **p** of Ephraim, Manasseh,
15:10 The **p** gathered at Jerusalem in late spring,
16:10 that time, Asa also began to oppress some of his **p**.
16:14 and at his funeral the **p** built a huge fire in his
17: 5 All the **p** of Judah brought gifts to Jehoshaphat,
17: 9 through all the towns of Judah, teaching the **p**.
19: 4 lived in Jerusalem, but he went out among the **p**,
19: 4 encouraging the **p** to return to the LORD, the God
19: 6 Remember that you do not judge to please **p**
20: 4 So **p** from all the towns of Judah came to
20: 5 Jehoshaphat stood before the **p** of Judah
20: 7 those who lived in this land when your **p** arrived?
20: 8 Your **p** settled here and built this Temple for you.
20:15 Listen, all you **p** of Judah and Jerusalem!
20:17 He is with you, O **p** of Judah and Jerusalem.
20:18 And all the **p** of Judah and Jerusalem did the same,
20:20 "Listen to me, all you **p** of Judah and Jerusalem!
20:21 After consulting the leaders of the **p**, the king
20:26 which got its name that day because the **p** praised
20:33 and the **p** never fully committed themselves to
21:11 and had led the **p** of Jerusalem and Judah to give
21:13 You have led the **p** of Jerusalem and Judah to
21:14 your **p**, your children, your wives, and all that is
21:19 His **p** did not build a great fire to honor him at his
22: 1 Then the **p** of Jerusalem made Ahaziah,
22: 9 was given a decent burial because the **p** said,
23: 6 The rest of the **p** must obey the LORD's
23: 8 and the **p** did everything just as Jehoiada the priest
23:12 When Athaliah heard the noise of the **p** running
23:13 and **p** from all over the land were rejoicing
23:13 were leading the **p** in a great celebration.
23:16 and the **p** that they would be the LORD's **p**.
23:17 And all the **p** went over to the temple of Baal
23:20 and all the **p** escorted the king from the Temple of
23:21 So all the **p** of the land rejoiced, and the city was
24: 9 telling the **p** to bring to the LORD the tax that
24:10 This pleased all the leaders and the **p**, and they
24:19 bring them back to him, but the **p** would not listen.
24:20 He stood before the **p** and said, "This is what God
24:24 The **p** of Judah had abandoned the LORD,
25: 7 with Israel. He will not help those **p** of Ephraim!
25:13 killing three thousand **p** and carrying off great
25:14 he brought with him idols taken from the **p** of Seir.
25:15 who could not even save their own **p** from you?"
25:19 will bring disaster on you and the **p** of Judah?"
26: 1 The **p** of Judah then crowned Amaziah's
26:21 the royal palace, and he governed the **p** of the land.
27: 2 the **p** continued in their corrupt ways.
28: 5 and to exile large numbers of his **p** to Damascus.
28:10 are planning to make slaves of these **p** from Judah
28:14 the plunder in the sight of all the leaders and **p**.
28:19 for he had encouraged his **p** to sin and had been
29:11 and to lead the **p** in worship and make offerings to
29:23 brought before the king and the assembly of **p**,
29:31 So the **p** brought their sacrifices and thanksgiving
29:32 The **p** brought to the LORD seventy bulls,
29:36 And Hezekiah and all the **p** rejoiced greatly
29:36 because of what God had done for the **p**,
30: 3 and the **p** had not yet assembled at Jerusalem.
30: 4 the Passover seemed right to the king and all the **p**.
30: 5 The **p** had not been celebrating it in great numbers
30: 6 "O **p** of Israel, return to the LORD, the God of
30:10 But most of the **p** just laughed at the messengers
30:12 God's hand was on the **p** in the land of Judah,
30:15 the **p** slaughtered their Passover lambs.
30:17 Since many of the **p** there had not purified
30:20 listened to Hezekiah's prayer and healed the **p**.
30:21 So the **p** of Israel who were present in Jerusalem
30:22 and the **p** confessed their sins to the LORD,
30:24 King Hezekiah gave the **p** one thousand bulls
30:27 Then the Levitical priests stood and blessed the **p**,
31: 4 he required the **p** in Jerusalem to bring the
31: 5 The **p** responded immediately and generously with
31: 6 The **p** who had moved to Judah from Israel,
31: 6 and the **p** of Judah themselves, brought in the
31: 8 they thanked the LORD and his **p** Israel!
31:10 "Since the **p** began bringing their gifts to the
31:10 plenty to spare, for the LORD has blessed his **p**."
32: 6 He appointed military officers over the **p**
32: 8 for us!" These words greatly encouraged the **p**.
32: 9 this message for Hezekiah and all the **p** in the city:
32:13 before me have done to all the **p** of the earth!
32:13 nations able to rescue their **p** from my power?
32:14 anywhere, was able to rescue his **p** from me!
32:15 has ever yet been able to rescue his **p** from me
32:17 nations failed to rescue their **p** from my power,
32:18 language to the **p** gathered on the walls of the city,
32:22 and the **p** of Jerusalem from King Sennacherib of
32:26 and the **p** of Jerusalem humbled themselves.
33: 9 But Manasseh led the **p** of Judah and Jerusalem to
33:10 The LORD spoke to Manasseh and his **p**, but they
33:16 He also encouraged the **p** of Judah to worship the
33:17 However, the **p** still sacrificed at the pagan shrines,
33:25 But the **p** of the land killed all those who had
34: 9 The gifts were brought by **p** from Manasseh,
34: 9 from all Judah, Benjamin, and the **p** of Jerusalem.
34:24 I will certainly destroy this city and its **p**.
34:25 For the **p** of Judah have abandoned me
34:27 you heard what I said against this city and its **p**.
34:28 and its **p** until after you have died and been buried
34:30 the Temple of the LORD with all the **p** of Judah
34:30 the Levites—all the **p** from the greatest to the least.
34:32 and the **p** of Benjamin to make a similar pledge.
34:32 As the **p** of Jerusalem did this, they renewed their
35: 3 serving the LORD your God and his **p** Israel.
35: 8 officials also made willing contributions to the **p**,
35:12 They divided the burnt offerings among the **p** by
35:13 brought them out quickly so the **p** could eat them.
35:18 all the priests and Levites, all the **p** of Jerusalem,
and **p** from all over Judah and Israel.
36: 1 Then the **p** of the land took Josiah's son Jehoahaz
36:14 and the **p** became more and more unfaithful.
36:15 for he had compassion on his **p** and his Temple.
36:16 But the **p** mocked these messengers of God
36:17 They had no pity on the **p**, killing both young
36:23 All of you who are the LORD's **p** may return to
Ezr 1: 3 All of you who are his **p** may return to Jerusalem
2:21 The **p** of Bethlehem | 123
2:22 The **p** of Netophah | 56
2:23 The **p** of Anathoth | 128
2:24 The **p** of Beth-azmaveth | 42
2:27 The **p** of Micmash | 122
2:60 of Delaiah, Tobiah, and Nekoda—a total of 652 **p**.
2:64 So a total of 42,360 **p** returned to Judah,
2:70 and some of the common **p** settled in villages near
2:70 The rest of the **p** returned to the other towns of
3: 1 all the **p** assembled together as one person in
3: 3 Even though the **p** were afraid of the local
3: 5 were also sacrificed to the LORD by the **p**.
3: 7 and bought cedar logs from the **p** of Tyre
3:11 Then all the **p** gave a great shout,
4: 4 and frighten the **p** of Judah to keep them from their
4: 6 him a letter of accusation against the **p** of Judah
4: 9 the **p** of Tarpel, the Persians, the Babylonians,
4: 9 and the **p** of Erech and Susa (that is, Elam).
4:10 They also sent greetings from the rest of the **p**
4:21 issue orders to have these **p** stop their work.
5: 4 They also asked for a list of the names of all the **p**
5:12 this Temple and exiled the **p** to Babylonia.
5:16 The **p** have been working on it ever since,
6:16 then dedicated with great joy by the **p** of Israel,
6:16 and the rest of the **p** who had returned from exile.
6:21 The Passover meal was eaten by the **p** of Israel
7: 6 the God of Israel, had given to the **p** of Israel.
7: 7 Some of the **p** of Israel, as well as some of the
7:10 teach those laws and regulations to the **p** of Israel.
7:13 "I decree that any of the **p** of Israel in my
7:16 as well as the freewill offerings of the **p**
7:25 the **p** in the province west of the Euphrates River.
7:25 If the **p** are not familiar with those laws, you must
8:15 for three days while I went over the lists of the **p**
8:16 and Meshullam, who were leaders of the **p**.
8:25 and the **p** of Israel had presented for the Temple of
8:35 They presented twelve oxen for the **p** of Israel,
8:36 who then cooperated by supporting the **p**
9: 1 came to me and said, "Many of the **p** of Israel,
9: 2 men of Israel have married women from these **p**
9: 4 sat with me because of this unfaithfulness of his **p**.
9:11 by the detestable practices of the **p** living there.
9:14 and intermarrying with **p** who do these detestable
10: 1 Temple of God, a large crowd of **p** from Israel—
10: 5 and all the **p** of Israel swear that they would do as
10: 9 all the **p** of Judah and Benjamin had gathered in
10: 9 and all the **p** were sitting in the square before the
10:11 Separate yourselves from the **p** of the land
10:25 These are the other **p** of Israel who were guilty:
Ne 1: 6 and see me praying night and day for your **p** Israel.
1:10 the **p** you rescued by your great power and might.
3: 2 **P** from the city of Jericho worked next to them,
3: 5 Next were the **p** from Tekoa, though their leaders
3: 7 from Meronoth, and **p** from Gibeon and Mizpah,
3:13 The **p** from Zanoah, led by Hanun,
3:27 Then came the **p** of Tekoa, who repaired another
4: 6 the entire city, for the **p** had worked very hard.
4:10 Then the **p** of Judah began to complain that the
4:13 I stationed the **p** to stand guard by families,
4:14 together the leaders and the **p** and said to them,
4:16 The officers stationed themselves behind the **p** of
4:19 I explained to the nobles and officials and all the **p**,
5:10 have been lending the **p** money and grain,
5:12 and demand nothing more from the **p**.
5:13 the LORD. And the **p** did as they had promised.
5:15 governors who had laid heavy burdens on the **p**,
5:15 Even their assistants took advantage of the **p**.
5:18 because the **p** were already having a difficult time.
5:19 O my God, all that I have done for these **p**,
7:27 The **p** of Anathoth | 128
7:28 The **p** of Beth-azmaveth | 42
7:31 The **p** of Micmash | 122
7:33 The **p** of Nebo | 52
7:62 of Delaiah, Tobiah, and Nekoda—a total of 642 **p**.
7:66 "So a total of 42,360 **p** returned to Judah,
7:72 The rest of the **p** gave 20,000 gold coins,
7:73 the Temple servants, along with some of the **p**—
8: 1 all the **p** assembled together as one person at the
8: 3 All the **p** paid close attention to the Book of the
8: 5 Ezra stood on the platform in full view of all the **p**.
8: 6 the great God, and all the **p** chanted, "Amen!
8: 7 instructed the **p** who were standing there.
8: 8 being read, helping the **p** understand each passage.
8: 9 and the Levites who were interpreting for the **p**
8: 9 All the **p** had been weeping as they listened to the
8:10 and share gifts of food with **p** who have nothing
8:11 too, quieted the **p**, telling them, "Hush!
8:12 So the **p** went away to eat and drink at a festive
8:15 telling the **p** to go to the hills to get branches from
8:16 So the **p** went out and cut branches and used them
9: 1 On October 31 the **p** returned for another
9: 5 Shebaniah, and Pethahiah—called out to the **p**:
9:10 against Pharaoh, his servants, and all his **p**,
9:11 You divided the sea for your **p** so they could walk
9:22 and you placed your **p** in every corner of the land.
9:24 Your **p** could deal with them as they pleased.
9:28 all was going well, your **p** turned to sin again,
9:28 Yet whenever your **p** cried to you again for help,
9:29 by which **p** will find life if only they obey.
10:28 The rest of the **p**—the priests, Levites, gatekeepers,
10:28 from the pagan **p** of the land in order to serve God,
10:30 to let our daughters marry the pagan **p** of the land,
10:31 We further promise that if the **p** of the land should
10:34 and the common **p** should bring wood to God's
10:39 The **p** and the Levites must bring these offerings of
11: 1 Now the leaders of the **p** were living in Jerusalem,
11: 1 A tenth of the **p** from the other towns of Judah
11: 2 And the **p** commended everyone who volunteered
11: 3 Most of the **p**, priests, Levites, Temple servants,
11: 4 but some of the **p** from Judah and Benjamin
11:25 Some of the **p** of Judah lived in Kiriath-arba with
11:30 So the **p** of Judah were living all the way from
11:31 Some of the **p** of Benjamin lived at Geba,
12:30 then the **p**, the gates, and the wall.
12:38 I followed them, with the other half of the **p**,
12:43 for God had given the **p** cause for great joy.
12:43 and the joy of the **p** of Jerusalem could be heard
12:44 for all the **p** of Judah valued the priests and Levites
12:47 the **p** brought a daily supply of food for the
13: 1 the **p** found a statement which said that no
13:12 And once more all the **p** of Judah began bringing
13:16 They were selling it on the Sabbath to the **p** of
13:18 Now you are bringing even more wrath upon the **p**
13:24 or some other **p** and could not speak the language
13:25 children intermarry with the pagan **p** of the land.
Est 3: 8 "There is a certain race of **p** scattered through all
3:11 "but go ahead and do as you like with these **p**."
3:14 in every province and made known to all the **p**,
4: 3 and wailed, and many **p** lay in sackcloth and ashes.
4: 8 go to the king to beg for mercy and plead for her **p**.
7: 3 is that my life and the lives of my **p** will be spared.
7: 4 For my **p** and I have been sold to those who would
8: 6 For how can I endure to see my **p** and my family
8:13 law in every province and proclaimed to all the **p**.
8:15 And the **p** of Susa celebrated the new decree.
8:17 And many of the **p** of the land became Jews
9: 6 They killed five hundred **p** in the fortress of Susa.
9:11 when the king was informed of the number of **p**
9:12 "The Jews have killed five hundred **p** in the
9:15 on March 8 and killed three hundred more **p**,
9:31 (The **p** decided to observe this festival, just as they
10: 3 because he worked for the good of his **p** and was a
Job 5: 7 **P** are born for trouble as predictably as sparks fly
6: 6 **P** complain when there is no salt in their food.
6:23 Have I asked you to save me from ruthless **p**?
10: 4 of a human? Do you see things as **p** see them?
12: 5 **P** who are at ease mock those in trouble. They give
a push to **p** who are stumbling.
13: 9 you think you can fool him as easily as you fool **p**?
14:10 "But when **p** die, they lose all strength.
14:12 **p** lie down and do not rise again. Until the heavens
15:20 "Wicked **p** are in pain throughout their lives.
15:27 "These wicked **p** are fat and rich,
16:10 **P** jeer and laugh at me. They slap my cheek in
17: 6 "God has made a mockery of me among the **p**;
18:20 **P** in the west are appalled at their fate; **p** in the east
20: 4 "Don't you realize that ever since **p** were first
21: 4 "My complaint is with God, not with **p**.
21:28 and wicked **p** who came to disaster because of
21:30 Evil **p** are spared in times of calamity and are
22:15 "Will you continue on the old paths where evil **p**
23: 7 Fair and honest **p** can reason with him, so I would
24: 2 Evil **p** steal land by moving the boundary markers.
24:13 "Wicked **p** rebel against the light. They refuse to
24:20 Wicked **p** are broken like a tree in the storm.
25: 6 How much less are mere **p**, who are but worms in
27:16 "Evil **p** may have all the money in the world,
28: 1 "**P** know how to mine silver and refine gold.
28: 6 "**P** know how to find sapphires and gold dust—

28:9 **P** know how to tear apart flinty rocks and overturn
28:12 "But do **p** know where to find wisdom?
28:20 "But do **p** know where to find wisdom?
30:5 and **p** shout after them as if they were thieves.
31:33 Have I tried to hide my sins as **p** normally do,
32:8 Surely it is God's Spirit within **p**, the breath of the
33:14 and again, though **p** do not recognize it.
33:15 in visions of the night when deep sleep falls on **p**
33:19 Or God disciplines **p** with sickness and pain,
33:29 "Yes, God often does these things for **p**.
34:8 He seeks the companionship of evil **p**. He spends
34:11 He repays **p** according to their deeds. He treats **p**
according to their ways.
34:21 "For God carefully watches the way **p** live;
34:30 from ruling so they cannot be a snare to the **p**.
34:31 "Why don't **p** say to God, 'I have sinned, but I
34:34 bright **p** will tell me, and wise **p** will hear me say,
35:8 No, your sins affect only **p** like yourself, and your
good deeds affect only other **p**.
36:20 cover of night, for that is when **p** will be destroyed.
36:31 By his mighty acts he governs the **p**, giving them
37:24 No wonder **p** everywhere fear him. **P** who are truly
wise show him reverence."
Ps 2:1 Why do the **p** waste their time with futile plans?
3:8 O LORD. / May your blessings rest on your **p**.
4:2 How long will you **p** ruin my reputation?
4:6 Many **p** say, "Who will show us better times?"
10:2 Proud and wicked **p** viciously oppress the poor.
10:4 These wicked **p** are too proud to seek God.
10:15 Break the arms of these wicked, evil **p**! / Go after
10:18 the oppressed, / so **p** can no longer terrify them.
14:4 do evil never learn? / They eat up my **p** like bread;
14:6 the oppressed, / but the LORD will protect his **p**.
14:7 For when the LORD restores his **p**, / Jacob will
15:5 the innocent. / Such **p** will stand firm forever.
16:3 The godly **p** in the land / are my true heroes!
17:4 kept me from going along with cruel and evil **p**.
17:9 Protect me from wicked **p** who attack me,
18:43 over nations; / **p** I don't even know now serve me.
22:22 and sisters. / I will praise you among all your **p**.
22:25 I will praise you among all the **p**; / I will fulfill my
22:27 **P** from every nation will bow down before him.
24:1 in it. / The world and all its **p** belong to him.
27:2 When evil **p** come to destroy me, / when my
28:8 The LORD protects his **p** / and gives victory to
28:9 Save your **p**! / Bless Israel, your special
29:11 The LORD gives his **p** strength. / The LORD
33:12 the LORD, / whose **p** he has chosen for his own.
34:9 Let the LORD's **p** show him reverence,
34:17 The LORD hears his **p** when they call to him for
35:15 I am attacked by **p** I don't even know; / they hurl
35:18 I will praise you before all the **p**.
35:20 don't talk of peace; / they plot against innocent **p**
36:6 You care for **p** and animals alike, O LORD.
37:7 him to act. / Don't worry about evil **p** who prosper
37:35 proud and evil **p** thriving like mighty trees.
39:11 When you discipline **p** for their sins, / their lives
40:9 I have told all your **p** about your justice. / I have
43:1 up my cause! / Defend me against these ungodly **p**.
44:4 and my God. / You command victories for your **p**.
44:12 You sold us—your precious **p**—for a pittance.
45:10 Forget your **p** and your homeland far away.
45:12 **P** of great wealth will entreat your favor.
48:11 Let the **p** on Mount Zion rejoice. / Let the towns of
49:1 Listen to this, all you **p**! / Pay attention,
49:20 **P** who boast of their wealth don't understand
50:4 and earth will be his witnesses / as he judges his **p**:
50:5 "Bring my faithful **p** to me— / those who made a
50:7 "O my **p**, listen as I speak. / Here are my charges
52:1 crime of yours, / you who have disgraced God's **p**?
52:9 wait for your mercies / in the presence of your **p**.
53:4 do evil never learn? / They eat up my **p** like bread;
53:6 For when God restores his **p**, / Jacob will shout
57:9 I will thank you, Lord, in front of all the **p**.
58:1 meaning of the word? / Do you judge the **p** fairly?
58:3 These wicked **p** are born sinners; / even from birth
59:11 Don't kill them, for my **p** soon forget such lessons;
60:5 right arm to save us, / and rescue your beloved **p**.
62:8 O my **p**, trust in him at all times. / Pour out your
62:12 O Lord, is yours. / Surely you judge all **p**
65:2 answer our prayers, / and to you all **p** will come.
66:5 what awesome miracles he does for his **p**!
66:6 the Red Sea, / and his **p** went across on foot.
67:2 your saving power among **p** everywhere.
67:7 bless us, / and **p** all over the world will fear him.
68:7 O God, when you led your **p** from Egypt,
68:10 There your **p** finally settled, / and with a bountiful
68:10 O God, / you provided for your needy **p**.
68:18 crowd of captives. / You received gifts from the **p**,
68:23 You, my **p**, will wash your feet in their blood,
68:26 Praise God, all you **p** of Israel;
68:35 God of Israel gives power and strength to his **p**.
69:33 he does not despise his **p** who are oppressed.
69:35 rebuild the towns of Judah. / His **p** will live there
72:2 Help him judge your **p** in the right way;
72:15 May the **p** always pray for him / and bless him all
73:5 They aren't troubled like other **p** / or plagued with
73:10 And so the **p** are dismayed and confused,
73:12 Look at these arrogant **p**— / enjoying a life of ease
73:15 this way, / I would have been a traitor to your **p**.
74:2 Remember that we are the **p** you chose in ancient
74:19 your doves. / Don't forget your afflicted **p** forever.
75:1 **P** everywhere tell of your mighty miracles.
75:3 When the earth quakes and its **p** live in turmoil,
77:15 You have redeemed your **p** by your strength,
77:20 You led your **p** along that road like a flock of
78:1 O my **p**, listen to my teaching. / Open your ears to
78:20 but he can't give his **p** bread and meat."
78:29 The **p** ate their fill. / He gave them what they
78:32 But in spite of this, the **p** kept on sinning.
78:52 But he led his own **p** like a flock of sheep,
78:60 the Tabernacle where he had lived among the **p**.
78:62 He gave his **p** over to be butchered by the sword,
78:62 because he was so angry with his own **p**—
78:71 of Jacob's descendants— / God's own **p**, Israel.
79:7 For they have devoured your **p** Israel,
79:13 Then we your **p**, the sheep of your pasture,
81:8 "Listen to me, O my **p**, while I give you stern
81:11 "But no, my **p** wouldn't listen. / Israel did not
81:13 But oh, that my **p** would listen to me! / Oh,
82:4 deliver them from the grasp of evil **p**.
83:3 They devise crafty schemes against your **p**,
83:7 and Amalekites, / and **p** from Philistia and Tyre.
85:2 You have forgiven the guilt of your **p**— / yes,
85:6 you revive us again, / so your **p** can rejoice in you?
85:8 for he speaks peace to his **p**, his faithful ones.
86:14 O God, insolent **p** rise up against me; / violent **p**
are trying to kill me.
87:7 At all the festivals, the **p** will sing, / "The source
89:19 I have selected him from the common **p** to be king.
89:50 I carry in my heart the insults of so many **p**.
90:3 You turn **p** back to dust, saying, / "Return to
90:5 You sweep **p** away like dreams that disappear
94:5 They oppress your **p**, LORD, / hurting those you
94:14 The LORD will not reject his **p**; / he will not
94:23 God will make the sins of evil **p** fall back upon
95:7 for he is our God. / We are the **p** he watches over,
95:10 'They are a **p** whose hearts turn away from me.
97:10 hate evil! / He protects the lives of his godly **p**
100:3 we are his. / We are his **p**, the sheep of his pasture.
101:5 I will not tolerate **p** who slander their neighbors.
102:14 For your **p** love every stone in her walls / and show
102:28 The children of your **p** / will live in security.
103:7 to Moses / and his deeds to the **p** of Israel.
104:14 the cattle. / You cause plants to grow for **p** to use.
104:23 Then **p** go off to their work; / they labor until the
105:10 to the **p** of Israel as a never-ending treaty:
105:15 "Do not touch these **p** I have chosen, / and do not
105:24 And the LORD multiplied the **p** of Israel
105:28 for they had defied his commands to let his **p** go.
105:37 But he brought his **p** safely out of Egypt,
105:37 there were no sick or feeble **p** among them.
105:43 So he brought his **p** out of Egypt with joy,
105:44 He gave his **p** the lands of pagan nations,
106:4 too, LORD, when you show favor to your **p**;
106:5 Let me rejoice in the joy of your **p**; / let me praise
106:12 Then at last his **p** believed his promises.
106:16 The **p** in the camp were jealous of Moses
106:19 The **p** made a calf at Mount Sinai; / they bowed
106:23 stepped between the LORD and the **p**.
106:24 The **p** refused to enter the pleasant land, / for they
106:40 is why the LORD's anger burned against his **p**,
106:48 Let all the **p** say, "Amen!" / Praise the LORD!
108:3 I will thank you, LORD, in front of all the **p**.
108:6 right arm to save me, / and rescue your beloved **p**.
109:25 I am an object of mockery to **p** everywhere;
110:3 that day of battle, / your **p** will serve you willingly.
111:1 with all my heart / as I meet with his godly **p**.
111:6 He has shown his great power to his **p** / by giving
111:9 He has paid a full ransom for his **p**. / He has
112:2 an entire generation of godly **p** will be blessed.
112:6 Such **p** will not be overcome by evil
113:8 among princes, / even the princes of his own **p**!
115:12 He will bless the **p** of Israel / and the family of
116:11 I cried out to you, / "These **p** are all liars!"
116:14 to the LORD / in the presence of all his **p**.
116:18 to the LORD / in the presence of all his **p**,
117:1 all you nations. / Praise him, all you **p** of the earth.
118:8 to trust the LORD / than to put confidence in **p**.
119:1 Happy are **p** of integrity, / who follow the law of
119:61 Evil **p** try to drag me into sin, / but I am firmly
119:69 Arrogant **p** have made up lies about me, / but in
119:78 Bring disgrace upon the arrogant **p** who lied about
119:85 These arrogant **p** who hate your law / have dug
119:115 Get out of my life, you evil-minded **p**, / for I intend
119:126 you to act, / for these evil **p** have broken your law.
119:134 Rescue me from the oppression of evil **p**; / then I
119:136 gush from my eyes / because **p** disobey your law.
119:150 Those lawless **p** are coming near to attack me;
119:161 Powerful **p** harass me without cause, / but my heart
120:2 O LORD, from liars / and from all deceitful **p**.
120:5 It pains me to live with these **p** from Kedar!
120:6 I am tired of living here / among **p** who hate peace.
122:4 All the **p** of Israel—the LORD's **p**—
124:2 not been on our side / when **p** rose up against us,
125:2 so the LORD surrounds and protects his **p**,
132:10 do not reject the king you chose for your **p**.
132:16 agents of salvation; / its godly **p** will sing for joy.
132:17 my anointed one will be a light for my **p**.
135:8 in each Egyptian home, / both **p** and animals
135:9 wonders in Egypt; / Pharaoh and all his **p** watched.
135:12 a special possession to his **p** Israel.
135:14 For the LORD will vindicate his **p** / and have
136:16 Give thanks to him who led his **p** through the
140:1 O LORD, rescue me from evil **p**. / Preserve me
146:3 Don't put your confidence in powerful **p**; / there is
148:11 kings of the earth and all **p**, / rulers and judges of
148:14 He has made his **p** strong, / honoring his godly
ones— / the **p** of Israel who are close to him.
149:2 O **p** of Jerusalem, exult in your King.
149:4 For the LORD delights in his **p**; / he crowns the
Pr 1:2 The purpose of these proverbs is to teach **p**
1:3 **p** will receive instruction in discipline,
1:4 They will give knowledge and purpose to young **p**.
1:18 But not these **p**! They set an ambush for
2:12 Wisdom will save you from evil **p**, from those
2:13 These **p** turn from right ways to walk down dark
3:4 Then you will find favor with both God and **p**,
3:31 Do not envy violent **p**; don't copy their ways.
3:32 Such wicked **p** are an abomination to the LORD,
4:16 for evil **p** cannot sleep until they have done their
5:9 and hand over to merciless **p** everything you have
6:12 Here is a description of worthless and wicked **p**:
8:4 to all of you! I am raising my voice to all **p**.
10:4 Lazy **p** are soon poor; hard workers get rich.
10:6 evil **p** cover up their harmful intentions.
10:9 **P** with integrity have firm footing, but those who
10:10 **P** who wink at wrong cause trouble, but a bold
10:11 to life; evil **p** cover up their harmful intentions.
10:13 Wise words come from the lips of **p** with
10:14 Wise **p** treasure knowledge, but the babbling of a
10:16 their lives, but evil **p** squander their money on sin.
10:17 **P** who accept correction are on the pathway to life,
10:26 Lazy **p** are a pain to their employer. They are like
11:3 Good **p** are guided by their honesty;
11:3 treacherous **p** are destroyed by their dishonesty.
11:6 The godliness of good **p** rescues them;
11:6 the ambition of treacherous **p** traps them.
11:18 Evil **p** get rich for the moment, but the reward of
11:19 Godly **p** find life; evil **p** find death.
11:20 The LORD hates **p** with twisted hearts, but he
11:21 You can be sure that evil **p** will be punished,
11:26 **P** curse those who hold their grain for higher
12:14 **P** can get many good things by the words they say;
12:18 Some **p** make cutting remarks, but the words of the
12:23 Wise **p** don't make a show of their knowledge,
12:27 Lazy **p** don't even cook the game they catch,
13:2 Good **p** enjoy the positive results of their words,
13:4 Lazy **p** want much but get little, but those who
13:6 Godliness helps **p** all through life, while the evil
13:13 **P** who despise advice will find themselves in
13:16 Wise **p** think before they act; fools don't and even
13:22 Good **p** leave an inheritance to their grandchildren,
14:14 get what they deserve; good **p** receive their reward.
14:19 Evil **p** will bow before good **p**; the wicked
14:34 exalts a nation, but sin is a disgrace to any **p**.
16:2 **P** may be pure in their own eyes, but the LORD
16:7 When the ways of **p** please the LORD, he makes
16:29 Violent **p** deceive their companions, leading them
17:11 Evil **p** seek rebellion, but they will be severely
17:24 Sensible **p** keep their eyes glued on wisdom,
18:15 Intelligent **p** are always open to new ideas. In fact,
18:16 it may bring you before important **p**!
19:3 **P** ruin their lives by their own foolishness and
19:8 **p** who cherish understanding will prosper.
19:11 **P** with good sense restrain their anger; they earn
19:19 Short-tempered **p** must pay their own penalty.
19:24 Some **p** are so lazy that they won't even lift a
21:2 **P** may think they are doing what is right,
21:10 Evil **p** love to harm others; their neighbors get no
21:25 The desires of lazy **p** will be their ruin, for their
22:24 Keep away from angry, short-tempered **p**,
22:29 They will serve kings rather than ordinary **p**.
23:6 Don't eat with **p** who are stingy; don't desire their
24:1 Don't envy evil **p**; don't desire their company.
24:12 And he will judge all **p** according to what they
24:24 will be cursed by many **p** and denounced by the
25:27 it is not good for **p** to think about all the honors
26:12 There is more hope for fools than for **p** who think
26:15 Some **p** are so lazy that they won't lift a finger to
26:16 Lazy **p** consider themselves smarter than seven
26:24 **P** with hate in their hearts may sound pleasant
28:5 Evil **p** don't understand justice, but those who
28:7 Young **p** who obey the law are wise; those who
28:11 Rich **p** picture themselves as wise, but their real
28:12 When the wicked take charge, **p** go into hiding.
28:13 **P** who cover over their sins will not prosper.
28:16 Only a stupid prince will oppress his **p**, but a king
28:23 the end, **p** appreciate frankness more than flattery.
28:28 When the wicked take charge, **p** hide.
29:2 When the godly are in authority, the **p** rejoice.
29:5 To flatter **p** is to lay a trap for their feet.
29:6 Evil **p** are trapped by sin, but the righteous escape,
29:18 When **p** do not accept divine guidance, they run
29:25 Fearing **p** is a dangerous trap, but to trust the
30:11 Some **p** curse their father and do not thank their
Ecc 1:3 What do **p** get for all their hard work?
2:3 I hoped to experience the only happiness most **p**
2:14 I saw that wise and foolish **p** share the same fate.
2:21 I must leave everything I gain to **p** who haven't
2:22 So what do **p** get for all their hard work?
3:9 What do **p** really get for all their hard work?
3:10 the various kinds of work God has given **p** to do.
3:11 **p** cannot see the whole scope of God's work from
3:12 So I concluded that there is nothing better for **p**
3:13 And **p** should eat and drink and enjoy the fruits of
3:14 God's purpose in this is that **p** should fear him.
3:18 Then I realized that God allows **p** to continue in
3:19 So **p** have no real advantage over the animals.
3:22 So I saw that there is nothing better for **p** than to
4:4 Then I observed that most **p** are motivated to
4:5 Foolish **p** refuse to work and almost starve.
4:9 Two **p** can accomplish more than twice as much as
4:10 But **p** who are alone when they fall are in real
5:11 you have, the more **p** come to help you spend it.
5:12 **P** who work hard sleep well, whether they eat little
5:15 **P** who live only for wealth come to the end of their
5:16 As **p** come into this world, so they depart.
5:18 It is good for **p** to eat well, drink a good glass of
5:20 **P** who do this rarely look with sorrow on the past,
6:2 God gives great wealth and honor to some **p**

6: 7 All **p** spend their lives scratching for food, but they
6: 8 do wise **p** really have any advantage over fools?
6: 8 Do poor **p** gain anything by being wise
7: 7 Extortion turns wise **p** into fools, and bribes
7:15 including the fact that some good **p** die young and
some wicked **p** live on and on.
7:29 I discovered that God created **p** to be upright,
8: 7 how can **p** avoid what they don't know is going to
8: 9 where **p** have the power to hurt each other.
8:10 I have seen wicked **p** buried with honor.
8:11 crime is not punished, **p** feel it is safe to do wrong.
8:14 good **p** are often treated as though they were
8:14 and wicked **p** are often treated as though they were
8:15 because there is nothing better for **p** to do in this
8:17 Not even the wisest **p** know everything, even if
9: 1 the actions of godly and wise **p** are in God's hands,
9: 2 Good **p** receive the same treatment as sinners,
9: 2 and **p** who take oaths are treated like **p** who
9: 3 That is why **p** are not more careful to be good.
9:12 **P** can never predict when hard times might come.
9:12 in a snare, **p** are often caught by sudden tragedy.
9:14 There was a small town with only a few **p** living in
10: 6 if they give foolish **p** great authority, and if they
fail to give **p** of proven worth their
10:14 Foolish **p** claim to know all about the future
11: 8 When **p** live to be very old, let them rejoice in
12: 9 was wise, he taught the **p** everything he knew.
Isa 1: 3 and appreciate his care, but not my **p** Israel.
1:10 of Israel! Listen to the law of our God, **p** of Israel.
1:10 just like the rulers and **p** of Sodom and Gomorrah.
1:27 the repentant **p** of Jerusalem will be redeemed.
2: 2 **P** from all over the world will go there to worship.
2: 5 Come, **p** of Israel, let us walk in the light of the
2: 6 The LORD has rejected the **p** of Israel
2: 8 The **p** bow down and worship these things they
2:17 The arrogance of all **p** will be brought low.
3: 5 **P** will take advantage of each other—man against
3: 5 Young **p** will revolt against authority,
3: 5 and nobodies will sneer at honorable **p**.
3: 9 their guilt. They sin openly like the **p** of Sodom.
3:12 Children oppress my **p**, and women rule over
3:12 O my **p**, can't you see what fools your rulers are?
3:13 presenting his case against his **p**!
3:14 your barns with grain extorted from helpless **p**.
3:15 How dare you grind my **p** into the dust like that!"
4: 2 and the fruit of the land will be the pride of its **p**.
4: 3 the destruction of Jerusalem, will be a holy **p**.
5: 3 "Now, you **p** of Jerusalem and Judah, / you have
5: 7 This is the story of the LORD's **p**. / They are the
5:13 So I will send my **p** into exile far away
5:13 will starve, and the common **p** will die of thirst.
5:25 why the anger of the LORD burns against his **p**.
5:25 and the rotting bodies of his **p** are thrown as
5:29 They will seize my **p** and carry them off into
6: 8 "Whom should I send as a messenger to my **p**?
6: 9 And he said, "Yes, go. But tell my **p** this:
6:10 Harden the hearts of these **p**. Close their ears,
7: 2 the hearts of the king and his **p** trembled with fear,
7: 6 'We will invade Judah and throw its **p** into panic.
7:20 off everything: your land, your crops, and your **p**.
7:22 The few **p** still left in the land will live on curds
8: 6 "The **p** of Judah have rejected my gentle care
8:14 and Judah he will be a stone that causes **p** to
8:14 And for the **p** of Jerusalem he will be a trap that
8:17 though he has turned away from the **p** of Israel.
8:18 the plans the LORD Almighty has for his **p**.
8:21 My **p** will be led away as captives, weary
9: 2 The **p** who walk in darkness will see a great light
9: 3 and its **p** will rejoice as **p** rejoice at
9: 4 For God will break the chains that bind his **p**
9: 9 and the **p** of Israel and Samaria will soon discover
9:13 the **p** will still not repent and turn to the LORD
9:16 For the leaders of the **p** have led them down the
9:19 The **p** are fuel for the fire, and no one spares
10: 6 Assyria will enslave my **p**, who are a godless
10: 7 He will merely think he is attacking my **p** as part
10:18 and they will waste away like sick **p** in a plague.
10:22 But though the **p** of Israel are as numerous as the
10:22 The LORD has rightly decided to destroy his **p**.
10:24 "My **p** in Jerusalem, do not be afraid of the
10:27 that day the LORD will end the bondage of his **p**.
10:29 All the **p** of Gibeah—the city of Saul—are running
10:30 Well may you scream in terror, you **p** of Gallim!
10:31 There go the **p** of Madmenah, all fleeing.
11: 9 so the earth will be filled with **p** who know the
11:11 bring back a remnant of his **p** for the second time,
11:12 He will gather the scattered **p** of Judah from the
12: 6 Let all the **p** of Jerusalem shout his praise with joy!
13:12 **P** will be as scarce as gold—more rare than the
13:18 The attacking armies will shoot down the young **p**
14: 1 of Jacob. Israel will be his special **p** once again.
14: 1 And **p** from many different nations will come
14: 1 them there and become a part of the **p** of Israel.
14: 2 The nations of the world will help the LORD's **p**
14: 3 In that wonderful day when the LORD gives his **p**
14: 6 You persecuted the **p** with unceasing blows of rage
14:20 have destroyed your nation and slaughtered your **p**.
14:25 my mountains. My **p** will no longer be their slaves.
14:32 and that the poor of his **p** will find refuge in its
15: 2 Your **p** in Dibon will mourn at their temples
15: 5 Its **p** flee to Zoar and Eglath-shelishiyah. Weeping,
16: 7 Yes, you **p** of Moab, mourn for the delicacies of
16:12 On the hilltops the **p** of Moab will pray in anguish
16:14 will be ended, and few of its **p** will be left alive."
17: 6 Only a few of its **p** will be left, like the stray olives
17: 6 Yes, Israel will be stripped bare of **p**,"
17: 7 Then at last the **p** will think of their Creator
17:14 of those who plunder and destroy the **p** of God.
18: 2 to your tall, smooth-skinned **p**, who are feared far
18: 7 from this tall, smooth-skinned **p**, who are feared
19:20 When the **p** cry to the LORD for help against
19:25 Almighty will say, "Blessed be Egypt, my **p**.
21: 5 They are spreading rugs for **p** to sit on. Everyone is
21:10 O my **p**, threshed and winnowed, I have told you
21:14 O **p** of Tema, bring food and water to these weary
22: 3 The **p** try to slip away, but they are captured,
22: 4 Let me cry for my **p** as I watch them being
22:21 And he will be a father to the **p** of Jerusalem
23: 2 you **p** of the coast and you merchants of Sidon.
23: 6 now to Tarshish! Wail, you **p** who live by the sea!
23:13 the land of Babylonia—the **p** of that land are gone!
24: 1 See how he is scattering the **p** over the face of the
24: 5 The earth suffers for the sins of its **p**, for they have
24: 6 Therefore, a curse consumes the earth and its **p**.
24:17 and snares will be your lot, you **p** of the earth.
24:23 in Jerusalem, in the sight of all the leaders of his **p**.
25: 4 For the oppressive acts of ruthless **p** are like a
25: 5 So the boastful songs of ruthless **p** are stilled.
25: 8 all insults and mockery against his land and **p**.
25: 9 In that day the **p** will proclaim, "This is our God.
25:11 God will push down Moab's **p** as a swimmer
26: 9 will **p** turn from wickedness and do what is right.
26:11 Show them your eagerness to defend your **p**.
26:19 fall like dew / on his **p** in the place of the dead!
26:20 Go home, my **p**, and lock your doors! Hide until
26:21 heaven to punish the **p** of the earth for their sins.
27: 6 The time is coming when my **p** will take root.
27:11 The **p** are like the dead branches of a tree,
27:11 stupid nation, for its **p** have turned away from God.
28: 1 for that city—the pride of a **p** brought low by wine.
28: 5 will be the pride and joy of the remnant of his **p**.
28:12 God's **p** could have rest in their own land if they
28:19 This message will bring terror to your **p**.
28:21 unusual thing: He will destroy his own **p**!
29: 13 so the Lord says, "These **p** say they are mine.
29:14 and even the most brilliant **p** lack understanding."
29:18 In that day deaf **p** will hear words read from a
29:18 and blind **p** will see through the gloom
29:22 who redeemed Abraham, says to the **p** of Israel,
29:22 "My **p** will no longer pale with fear or be
30: 9 For these **p** are stubborn rebels who refuse to pay
30:19 O **p** of Zion, who live in Jerusalem, you will weep
30:26 So it will be when the LORD begins to heal his **p**
30:29 But the **p** of God will sing a song of joy,
30:32 his **p** will keep time with the music of tambourines
31: 6 Therefore, my **p**, though you are such wicked
32: 7 The smooth tricks of evil **p** will be exposed,
32: 8 But good **p** will be generous to others and will be
32:18 My **p** will live in safety, quietly at home. They will
32:20 God will greatly bless his **p**. Wherever they plant
33:12 Your **p** will be burned up completely, like thorns
33:14 The sinners among my **p** shake with fear.
33:19 These fierce, violent **p** with a strange,
33:23 Their treasure will be divided by the **p** of God.
33:24 The **p** of Israel will no longer say, "We are sick
35: 8 of Holiness. Evil-hearted **p** will never travel on it.
36:11 speak in Hebrew, for the **p** on the wall will hear."
36:12 The **p** will become so hungry and thirsty that they
36:13 and shouted in Hebrew to the **p** on the wall,
36:18 ever saved their **p** from the king of Assyria?
36:20 has ever been able to save its **p** from my power?
36:21 But the **p** were silent and did not answer
37:12 Rezeph, and the **p** of Eden who were in Tel-assar?
37:27 That is why their **p** have so little power / and are
37:32 For a remnant of my **p** will spread out from
40: 1 "Comfort, comfort my **p**," says your God.
40: 5 will be revealed, and all **p** will see it together.
40: 6 "Shout that **p** are like the grass that dies away.
40: 7 the breath of the LORD. And so it is with **p**.
40:22 The **p** below must seem to him like grasshoppers!
40:23 He judges the great **p** of the world and brings them
42: 6 for I have given you to my **p** as the personal
42:11 of Kedar rejoice! / Let the **p** of Sela sing for joy;
42:19 Who in all the world is as blind as my own **p**,
42:19 Who is as blind as my chosen **p**, the servant of the
42:22 But what a sight his **p** are, for they have been
42:24 for the **p** would not go where he sent them,
43: 8 Bring out the **p** who have eyes but are blind,
43:19 through the wilderness for my **p** to come home.
43:20 in the desert, so that my chosen **p** can be refreshed.
43:22 "But, my dear **p**, you refuse to ask for my help.
44:15 rest of it and makes himself a god for **p** to worship!
44:25 I cause wise **p** to give bad advice, thus proving
45:12 one who made the earth and created **p** to live on it.
45:13 He will restore my city and free my captive **p**
45:17 But the LORD will save the **p** of Israel with
45:19 And I did not tell the **p** of Israel to ask me for
45:24 The **p** will declare, "The LORD is the source of
46: 2 The gods cannot protect the **p**, and the **p** cannot
protect the gods.
46: 6 Some **p** pour out their silver and gold and hire a
46:12 Listen to me, you stubborn, evil **p**!
47: 6 For I was angry with my chosen **p** and began their
47: 7 You did not care at all about my **p** or think about
47:12 you strike terror into the hearts of **p** once again.
48:20 LORD has redeemed his servants, the **p** of Israel.
49: 5 who commissioned me to bring his **p** of Israel back
49: 6 "You will do more than restore the **p** of Israel to
49: 8 the land of Israel and reassign it to its own **p** again.
49:12 See, my **p** will return from far away, from lands to
49:13 For the LORD has comforted his **p** and will have
49:19 abandoned land will soon be crowded with your **p**.
51: 4 "Listen to me, my **p**. Hear me, Israel, for my law
51: 6 The **p** of the earth will die like flies, but my
51:10 making a path of escape when you saved your **p**?
52: 1 and godless **p** will no longer enter your gates.
52: 4 "Long ago my **p** went to live as resident foreigners
52: 5 asks the LORD. "Why are my **p** enslaved again?
52: 6 But I will reveal my name to my **p**, and they will
52: 8 see the LORD bringing his **p** home to Jerusalem.
52: 9 joyful song, for the LORD has comforted his **p**.
52:11 You are the LORD's holy **p**. Purify yourselves,
53: 8 But who among the **p** realized that he was dying
55: 7 Let the **p** turn from their wicked deeds. Let them
56: 8 I will bring others, too, besides my **p** Israel."
56: 9 wild animals of the forest! Come and devour my **p**!
56:10 For the leaders of my **p**—the LORD's watchmen,
57:14 and stones so my **p** can return from captivity.' "
57:16 If I did, all **p** would pass away—all the souls I
57:17 I was angry and punished these greedy **p**.
58: 1 of a trumpet blast. Tell my **p** Israel of their sins!
58:12 Then you will be known as the **p** who rebuild their
59:10 No wonder we grope like blind **p** and stumble
59:14 Our courts oppose **p** who are righteous, and justice
60: 9 of Tarshish, reserved to bring the **p** of Israel home.
60:21 All your **p** will be righteous. They will possess
61: 8 I will faithfully reward my **p** for their suffering
61: 9 Everyone will realize that they are a **p** the LORD
62:10 Go out! Prepare the highway for my **p** to return!
62:11 "Tell the **p** of Israel, 'Look, your Savior is
62:12 They will be called the Holy **P** and the **P**
Redeemed by the LORD.
63: 4 For the time has come for me to avenge my **p**,
63: 5 I looked, but no one came to help my **p**. I was
63: 8 He said, "They are my very own **p**. Surely they
63:11 days of old when Moses led his **p** out of Egypt.
63:11 one who sent his Holy Spirit to be among his **p**?
63:14 You led your **p**, LORD, and gained a magnificent
63:18 How briefly your holy **p** possessed the holy place,
63:19 act as though we had never been known as your **p**?
64: 5 anger is heavy on us. How can **p** like us be saved?
64: 9 Look at us, we pray, and see that we are all your **p**.
65: 1 "**P** who never before inquired about me are now
65: 1 I am being found by **p** who were not looking for
65: 2 "I opened my arms to my own **p** all day long,
65: 9 I will preserve a remnant of the **p** of Israel and of
65:10 For my **p** who have searched for me, the plain of
65:15 Your name will be a curse word among my **p**,
65:18 a place of happiness. Her **p** will be a source of joy.
65:19 I will rejoice in Jerusalem and delight in my **p**.
65:20 No longer will **p** be considered old at one hundred!
65:21 **p** will live in the houses they build and eat the fruit
65:22 For my **p** will live as long as trees and will have
65:23 For they are **p** blessed by the LORD, and their
66: 3 When such **p** sacrifice an ox, it is no more
66:14 will see the good hand of the LORD on his **p**—
66:20 They will bring the remnant of your **p** back from
66:22 and earth will remain, so will you always be my **p**,
Jer 1: 3 the **p** of Jerusalem were taken away as captives.
1: 8 And don't be afraid of the **p**, for I will be with you
1:14 "for terror from the north will boil out on the **p** of
1:16 I will pronounce judgment on my **p** for all their
1:18 or **p** of Judah will be able to stand against you.
2: 3 All who harmed my **p** were considered guilty,
2: 4 Listen to the word of the LORD, **p** of Jacob—
2:11 Yet my **p** have exchanged their glorious God for
2:13 For my **p** have done two evil things: They have
2:31 "O my **p**, listen to the words of the LORD!
2:31 Why then do my **p** say, 'At last we are free from
2:32 Yet for years on end my **p** have forgotten me.
3:12 O Israel, my faithless **p**, come home to me again,
3:16 "And when your land is once more filled with **p**,"
3:18 In those days the **p** of Judah and Israel will return
3:20 But you have betrayed me, you **p** of Israel!
3:21 the weeping and pleading of Israel's **p**.
3:22 "Yes, we will come," the **p** reply, "for you are
4: 2 and all **p** will come and praise my name."
4: 3 This is what the LORD says to the **p** of Judah
4: 7 your land! Your towns will lie in ruins, empty of **p**.
4:10 the **p** have been deceived by what you said,
4:11 when the LORD will say to the **p** of Jerusalem,
4:17 for my **p** have rebelled against me,' " says the
4:22 "My **p** are foolish and do not know me,"
4:25 I looked, and all the **p** were gone. All the birds of
4:28 in black, because of my decree against my **p**.
4:29 the **p** flee in terror from the cities.
4:31 It is the cry of Jerusalem's **p** gasping for breath,
5: 3 You struck your **p**, but they paid no attention.
5: 7 I fed my **p** until they were fully satisfied. But they
5:11 The **p** of Israel and Judah are full of treachery
5:14 "Because the **p** are talking like this, I will give you
5:15 a **p** whose language you do not know,
5:19 "And when your **p** ask, 'Why is the LORD our
5:21 Listen, you foolish and senseless **p**—who have
5:23 "But my **p** have stubborn and rebellious hearts.
5:26 "Among my **p** are wicked men who lie in wait for
5:26 They are continually setting traps for other **p**.
5:31 an iron hand. And worse yet, my **p** like it that way!
6: 1 "Run for your lives, you **p** of Benjamin! Flee from
6:12 For I will punish the **p** of this land,"
6:19 all the earth! I will bring disaster upon my **p**.
6:26 Now my **p**, dress yourselves in sackcloth, and sit
6:27 that you may determine the quality of my **p**.
7: 2 LORD's Temple, and give this message to the **p**:
7:12 I did there because of all the wickedness of my **p**,
7:15 just as I did your relatives, the **p** of Israel.'
7:16 "Pray no more for these **p**, Jeremiah. Do not weep
7:20 Its **p**, animals, trees, and crops will be consumed
7:23 and I will be your God, and you will be my **p**.
7:24 "But my **p** would not listen to me. They kept on
7:26 But my **p** have not listened to me or even tried to

7:28 'This is the nation whose **p** will not obey the
7:30 "The **p** of Judah have sinned before my very
7:33 The corpses of my **p** will be food for the vultures
8: 1 the graves of the priests, prophets, and common **p**.
8: 2 the gods my **p** have loved, served, and worshiped.
8: 3 And the **p** of this evil nation who survive will wish
8: 4 "Jeremiah, say to the **p**, 'This is what the LORD
8: 4 When **p** fall down, don't they get up again?
8: 5 Then why do these **p** keep going along their
8: 7 return at the proper time each year. But not my **p**!
8:14 "Then the **p** will say, 'Why should we wait here to
8:16 the land and everything in it—cities and **p** alike.'
8:19 Listen to the weeping of my **p**; it can be heard all
8:19 the **p** ask. "Is her King no longer there?" "Oh,
8:20 is gone," the **p** cry, "yet we are not saved!"
8:21 I weep for the hurt of my **p**. I am stunned
8:22 Why is there no healing for the wounds of my **p**?
9: 1 and night for all my **p** who have been slaughtered.
9: 3 "My **p** bend their tongues like bows to shoot lies.
9:13 because my **p** have abandoned the instructions I
9:19 Hear the **p** of Jerusalem crying in despair, 'We are
9:26 Moabites, the **p** who live in distant places, and yes,
even the **p** of Judah.
9:26 the **p** of Israel also have uncircumcised hearts."
10: 7 Among all the wise **p** of the earth and in all the
10: 8 The wisest of **p** who worship idols are stupid
10:14 Compared to him, all **p** are foolish / and have no
10:21 The shepherds of my **p** have lost their senses.
10:25 For they have utterly devoured your **p** Israel,
11: 2 "Remind the **p** of Judah and Jerusalem about the
11: 4 then you will be my **p**, and I will be your God."
11: 9 a conspiracy against me among the **p** of Judah
11:12 Then the **p** of Judah and Jerusalem will pray to
11:13 Look now, **p** of Judah, you have as many gods as
11:14 "Pray no more for these **p**, Jeremiah. Do not weep
11:15 What right do my beloved **p** have to come to my
11:17 For the **p** of Israel and Judah have done evil,
12: 1 so prosperous? Why are evil **p** so happy?
12: 3 Drag these **p** away like helpless sheep to be
12: 4 Yet the **p** say, "The LORD won't do anything!"
12: 7 "I have abandoned my **p**, my special possession.
12: 8 My chosen **p** have roared at me like a lion of the
12: 9 My chosen **p** have become as disgusting to me as a
12:12 The sword of the LORD kills **p** from one end of
12:13 My **p** have planted wheat but are harvesting thorns.
12:14 reaching out for the inheritance I gave my **p** Israel,
12:16 if these nations quickly learn the ways of my **p**,
12:16 as they taught my **p** to swear by the name of Baal),
12:16 then they will be given a place among my **p**.
13:10 These wicked **p** refuse to listen to me.
13:11 "They were to be my **p**, my pride, my glory—
13:13 and the prophets, right on down to the common **p**.
13:19 The **p** of Judah will be taken away as captives.
14: 2 All the **p** sit on the ground in mourning, and a
14: 7 The **p** say, "LORD, our wickedness has caught
14: 9 here among us, LORD. We are known as your **p**.
14:10 So the LORD replies to his **p**, "You love to
14:10 Now I will no longer accept you as my **p**.
14:11 said to me, "Do not pray for these **p** anymore.
14:16 As for the **p** to whom they prophesy—their bodies
14:17 for my virgin daughter—my precious **p**—
14:18 I see the bodies of **p** slaughtered by the enemy.
14:18 there I see **p** who have died of starvation.
15: 1 and Samuel stood before me pleading for these **p**,
15: 4 I will make my **p** an object of horror to all the
15: 7 I will destroy my own **p**, because they refuse to
15:17 I never joined the **p** in their merry feasts. I sat
16:10 "When you tell the **p** all these things, they will
16:14 "when **p** who are taking an oath will no longer
16:14 who rescued the **p** of Israel from the land of
16:15 who brought the **p** of Israel back to their own land
16:20 Can **p** make their own god? The gods they make
17: 1 "My **p** act as though their evil ways are laws to be
17:10 I give all **p** their due rewards, according to what
17:15 **P** scoff at me and say, "What is this 'message
17:16 not abandoned my job as a shepherd for your **p**.
17:20 Say to all the **p**, 'Listen to this message from the
17:20 you kings of Judah and all you **p** of Judah
17:25 and their officials will always ride among the **p** of
17:26 the **p** will come with their burnt offerings
18:15 These can be counted on, but not my **p**! For they
18:17 I will scatter my **p** before their enemies as the east
18:18 Then the **p** said, "Come on, let's find a way to
19: 1 Then ask some of the leaders of the **p** and of the
19: 4 The **p** burn incense to foreign gods—idols never
19:11 so I will shatter the **p** of Judah and Jerusalem
19:12 This is what I will do to this place and its **p**,
19:14 the Temple of the LORD. He said to the **p** there,
20: 4 I will hand the **p** of Judah over to the king of
21: 6 upon this city, and both **p** and animals will die.
21: 8 "Tell all the **p**, 'This is what the LORD says:
21:12 Give justice to the **p** you judge! Help those who
22: 2 Let your officials and your **p** listen, too.
22: 8 **P** from many nations will pass by the ruins of this
23: 1 "I will send disaster upon the leaders of my **p**—
23: 7 says the LORD, "when **p** are taking an oath,
23: 7 who rescued the **p** of Israel from the land of
23: 8 who brought the **p** of Israel back to their own land
23:13 prophesied by Baal and led my **p** of Israel into sin.
23:14 These prophets are as wicked as the **p** of Sodom
23:16 This is my warning to my **p**," says the LORD
23:22 my words and turned my **p** from their evil ways.
23:27 they are trying to get my **p** to forget me,
23:32 dreams are flagrant lies that lead my **p** into sin.
23:32 and they have no message at all for my **p**,"
23:33 "Suppose one of the **p** or one of the prophets
23:36 For **p** are using it to give authority to their own
24: 7 They will be my **p**, and I will be their God,
24: 8 his officials, all the **p** left in Jerusalem, and those
25: 1 This message for all the **p** of Judah came to
25: 2 Jeremiah the prophet said to the **p** in Judah
25: 9 I will bring them all against this land and its **p**
25:12 punish the king of Babylon and his **p** for their sins,
25:14 the Babylonians, just as they enslaved my **p**.
25:14 in proportion to the suffering they cause my **p**."
25:19 to Pharaoh, his officials, his princes, and his **p**.
25:23 and Buz, and to the **p** who live in distant places.
25:31 He will judge all the **p** of the earth,
26: 2 and make an announcement to the **p** who have
26: 7 and all the **p** listened to Jeremiah as he spoke in
26: 8 and all the **p** at the Temple mobbed him.
26: 9 And all the **p** threatened him as he stood in front of
26:11 their accusations to the officials and the **p**.
26:16 and the **p** said to the priests and prophets,
26:17 of the wise old men stood and spoke to the **p** there.
26:18 He told the **p** of Judah, 'This is what the LORD
26:19 King Hezekiah and the **p** kill him for saying this?
27: 5 have made the earth and all its **p** and every animal.
27:11 But the **p** of any nation that submits to the king of
27:12 submit to the king of Babylon and his **p**," I said.
27:13 "Why do you insist on dying—you and your **p**?
27:16 Then I spoke to the priests and the **p** and said,
27:20 along with all the other important **p** of Judah
28: 1 in the Temple while all the priests and **p** listened.
28: 5 stood in front of all the priests and **p** at the Temple.
28: 7 words I speak to you in the presence of all these **p**.
28:15 has not sent you, but the **p** believe your lies.
29: 1 and all the **p** who had been exiled to Babylon by
29:23 these men have done terrible things among my **p**.
29:25 sent copies to the other priests and **p** in Jerusalem.
29:32 will see the good things I will do for my **p**,
30: 3 when I will restore the fortunes of my **p** of Israel
30: 5 I have heard the **p** crying; there is only fear
30: 7 It will be a time of trouble for my **p** Israel. Yet in
30: 9 For my **p** will serve the LORD their God
30:19 and I will multiply my **p** and make of them a great
30:22 You will be my **p**, and I will be your God."
31: 1 of all the families of Israel, and they will be my **p**.
31: 2 I will again come to give rest to the **p** of Israel."
31: 3 "I have loved you, my **p**, with an everlasting love.
31: 7 'Save your **p**, O LORD, the remnant of Israel!'
31:10 The LORD, who scattered his **p**, will gather them
31:14 I will satisfy my **p** with my bounty. I, the LORD,
31:23 the **p** of Judah and its cities will again say,
31:29 "The **p** will no longer quote this proverb:
31:30 All **p** will die for their own sins—those who eat the
31:31 "when I will make a new covenant with the **p** of
31:33 I will make with the **p** of Israel on that day,"
31:33 I will be their God, and they will be my **p**.
31:36 "I am as likely to reject my **p** Israel as I am to do
32:15 Someday **p** will again own property here in this
32:19 You are very aware of the conduct of all **p**,
32:22 You gave the **p** of Israel this land that you had
32:29 where the **p** caused my fury to rise by offering
32:32 the sins of the **p** of Jerusalem, the kings,
32:33 My **p** have turned their backs on me and have
32:37 I will surely bring my **p** back again from all the
32:38 They will be my **p**, and I will be their God.
32:43 a land where **p** and animals have all disappeared.'
33: 9 The **p** of the world will see the good I do for my **p**
33:10 and the **p** and animals have all disappeared.'
33:11 along with the joyous songs of **p** bringing
33:12 though it is now desolate and the **p** and animals
33:24 "Have you heard what **p** are saying?—
33:25 I would no more reject my **p** than I would change
34: 5 but will die peacefully among your **p**. They will
34: 8 after King Zedekiah made a covenant with the **p**,
34: 9 He had ordered all the **p** to free their Hebrew
34:10 and all the **p** had obeyed the king's command,
34:11 They took back the **p** they had freed, making them
34:19 court officials, priests, or common **p**—
35:13 Go and say to the **p** in Judah and Jerusalem,
36: 3 Perhaps the **p** of Judah will repent if they see in
36: 6 On that day **p** will be there from all over Judah.
36: 8 and read these messages from the LORD to the **p**
36: 9 **P** from all over Judah came to attend the services
36:10 Baruch read Jeremiah's words to all the **p** from the
36:13 about the messages Baruch was reading to the **p**,
36:31 I will pour out on them and on all the **p** of Judah
37: 2 **p** who were left in the land listened to what the
37:18 or the **p** that I should be imprisoned like this?
38: 1 heard what Jeremiah had been telling the **p**.
38: 4 men we have left, as well as that of all the **p**, too.
39:10 But Nebuzaradan left a few of the poorest **p** in
39:14 So Jeremiah stayed in Judah among his own **p**.
40: 3 For these **p** have sinned against the LORD
40: 5 Stay there with the **p** he rules. But it's up to you;
40: 7 over the poor **p** who were left behind in Judah,
40:11 that the king of Babylon had left a few **p** in Judah
41:10 and the other **p** who had been left under Gedaliah's
41:13 The **p** Ishmael had captured shouted for joy when
41:16 and his officers led away all the **p** they had
42: 1 and all the **p**, from the least to the greatest,
42: 8 of Kareah and the army officers, and for all the **p**,
42:18 and fury were poured out on the **p** of Jerusalem,
43: 1 message from the LORD their God to all the **p**,
43: 4 and all the **p** refused to obey the LORD's
43: 5 and his officers took with them all the **p** who had
43: 7 The **p** refused to obey the LORD and went to
43: 9 "While the **p** of Judah are watching, bury large
43:10 Then say to the **p** of Judah, 'The LORD
43:12 all their idols and carrying away the **p** as captives.
44: 5 But my **p** would not listen or turn back from their
44:21 and all the **p** were burning incense to idols in the
45: 5 I will bring great disaster upon all these **p**, but I
46:23 They will cut down her **p** like trees,"
47: 2 the land and everything in it—cities and **p** alike.
47: 2 **P** will scream in terror, and everyone in the land
47: 7 and the **p** living along the sea must be destroyed."
48:18 from your glory and sit in the dust, you **p** of Dibon,
48:19 The **p** of Aroer stand anxiously beside the road to
48:28 "You **p** of Moab, flee from your cities and towns!
48:32 "You **p** of Sibmah, rich in vineyards, I will weep
48:45 "The **p** flee as far as Heshbon but are unable to go
48:45 to devour the entire land with all its rebellious **p**.
48:46 The **p** of the god Chemosh are destroyed!
49: 3 the town of Ai is destroyed. Weep, O **p** of Rabbah!
49: 8 and flee! Hide in deep caves, you **p** of Dedan!
49:20 the LORD's plans for Edom and the **p** of Teman.
49:24 has become feeble, and all her **p** turn to flee.
49:30 "Hide yourselves in deep caves, you **p** of Hazor,
49:32 I will scatter to the winds these **p** who live in
49:36 and I will scatter the **p** of Elam to the four winds.
49:37 will bring great disaster upon the **p** of Elam,"
50: 3 will be gone; both **p** and animals will flee.
50: 4 "Then the **p** of Israel and Judah will join
50: 6 "My **p** have been lost sheep. Their shepherds have
50: 8 land of the Babylonians. Lead my **p** home again.
50:11 and are glad, you plunderers of my chosen **p**.
50:21 the land of Merathaim and against the **p** of Pekod.
50:28 Listen to the **p** who have escaped from Babylon,
50:31 I am your enemy, O proud **p**," says the Lord,
50:33 "The **p** of Israel and Judah have been wronged.
50:34 But the **p** of Babylon—there will be no rest for
50:35 "It will strike the **p** of Babylon—her princes
50:38 with idols, and the **p** are madly in love with them.
50:39 Never again will **p** live there; it will lie desolate
51: 1 destroyer against Babylon and the **p** of Babylonia.
51:17 Compared to him, all **p** are foolish / and have no
51:19 including his **p**, his own special possession.
51:22 old **p** and children, young men and maidens.
51:24 and the **p** of Babylonia for all the wrong they have
done to my **p** in Jerusalem,"
51:35 the violence she did to us," say the **p** of Jerusalem.
51:35 "May the **p** of Babylonia be paid in full for all the
51:38 drunken feasts, the **p** of Babylon roar like lions.
51:45 "Listen, my **p**, flee from Babylon.
51:49 "Just as Babylon killed the **p** of Israel and others
51:49 throughout the world, so must her **p** be killed.
51:51 "We are ashamed," the **p** say. "We are insulted
51:52 The groans of her wounded **p** will be heard
51:62 so that neither **p** nor animals will remain here.
51:64 'In this same way Babylon and her **p** will sink,
52: 3 finally banished the **p** of Jerusalem and Judah from
52:15 then took as exiles some of the poorest of the **p**
52:16 But Nebuzaradan allowed some of the poorest **p** to
52:25 And of the **p** still hiding in the city, he took an
52:27 So the **p** of Judah were sent into exile from their
La 1: 1 once bustling with **p**, are now silent.
1:11 Her **p** groan as they search for bread. They have
1:17 Regarding his **p**, the LORD has said, "Let their
1:18 Listen, **p** everywhere; look upon my anguish
2: 4 He bends his bow against his **p** as though he were
2:11 poured out, as I see what has happened to my **p**.
2:20 "You are doing this to your own **p**!
3:14 My own **p** laugh at me. All day long they sing their
3:33 For he does not enjoy hurting **p** or causing them
3:34 But the leaders of his **p** trampled prisoners
3:35 They deprived **p** of their God-given rights in
3:48 from my eyes because of the destruction of my **p**!
4: 3 the jackals feed their young, but not my **p** Israel.
4: 5 The **p** who once ate only the richest foods now beg
4: 6 The guilt of my **p** is greater than that of Sodom,
4:15 "Get away!" the **p** shouted at them. "You are
4:21 Are you rejoicing in the land of Uz, O **p** of Edom?
Eze 2: 4 They are a hard-hearted and stubborn **p**. But I am
3: 1 Then go and give its message to the **p** of Israel."
3: 4 of man, go to the **p** of Israel with my messages.
3: 5 I am not sending you to some foreign **p** whose
3: 6 I am not sending you to **p** with strange
3: 7 I am sending you to the **p** of Israel, but they won't
3:11 Then go to your **p** in exile and say to them, 'This is
3:17 message from me, pass it on to the **p** immediately.
3:20 If good **p** turn bad and don't listen to my warning,
3:25 with ropes so you cannot go out among the **p**.
4: 3 This will be a warning to the **p** of Israel.
4:12 While all the **p** are watching, bake it over a fire
4:16 drop by drop, and the **p** will drink it with dismay.
4:17 so scarce that the **p** will look at one another in
5: 2 to the wind, for I will scatter my **p** with the sword.
5:12 A third of your **p** will die in the city from famine
6: 4 be smashed. I will kill your **p** in front of your idols.
6: 8 "But I will let a few of my **p** escape destruction,
6:11 because of all the evil that the **p** of Israel have
7: 7 O **p** of Israel, the day of your destruction is
7:11 None of these proud and wicked **p** will survive.
7:23 "Prepare chains for my **p**, for the land is bloodied
7:25 Terror and trembling will overcome my **p**.
8: 6 Do you see the great sins the **p** of Israel are doing
8:10 I also saw the various idols worshiped by the **p** of
8:17 "Is it nothing to the **p** of Judah that they commit
9: 9 "The sins of the **p** of Israel and Judah are very
11: 1 son of Benaiah, who were leaders among the **p**.
11: 3 They say to the **p**, 'Is it not a good time to build
11: 5 "This is what the LORD says to the **p** of Israel:
11:15 the **p** still left in Jerusalem are talking about their
11:18 "When the **p** return to their homeland, they will
11:20 Then they will truly be my **p**, and I will be their
12: 3 in broad daylight so the **p** can see you,
12: 6 All of these actions will be a sign for the **p** of
12: 7 Then in the evening while the **p** looked on, I dug

12: 9 "Son of man, these rebels, the **p** of Israel,
12:10 Zedekiah in Jerusalem and for all the **p** of Israel.'
12:19 Give the **p** this message from the Sovereign
12:23 Give the **p** this message from the Sovereign
12:27 "Son of man, the **p** of Israel are saying,
13: 4 "O **p** of Israel, these prophets of yours are like
13:10 "These evil prophets deceive my **p** by saying,
13:10 It's as if the **p** have built a flimsy wall, and these
13:12 And when the wall falls, the **p** will cry out,
13:18 you women who are ensnaring the souls of my **p**,
13:19 You turn my **p** away from me for a few handfuls of
13:19 By lying to my **p** who love to listen to lies, you kill
13:20 which you use to ensnare my **p** like birds.
13:20 setting my **p** free like birds set free from a cage.
13:21 off the magic veils and save my **p** from your grasp.
13:23 For I will rescue my **p** from your grasp.
14: 4 will punish the **p** of Israel who set up idols in their
14: 5 and hearts of all my **p** who have turned from me to
14: 6 give the **p** of Israel this message from the
14: 8 I will turn against such **p** and make a terrible
14:10 evil **p** who claim to want my advice—
14:11 the **p** of Israel will learn not to stray from me,
14:11 They will be my **p**, and I will be their God,
14:13 suppose the **p** of a country were to sin against me,
14:13 and sending a famine to destroy both **p**
14:15 wild animals to devastate the land and kill the **p**.
14:16 no good—it wouldn't save the **p** from destruction.
14:18 LORD swears that they could not save the **p**.
14:19 the land, and the plague killed **p** and animals alike.
14:20 LORD swears that they could not save the **p**.
14:21 and plague—destroying all her **p** and animals.
15: 6 The **p** of Jerusalem are like grapevines growing
15: 8 because my **p** have been unfaithful to me,
16:55 and Samaria, and all their **p** will be restored,
17: 2 "Son of man, tell this story to the **p** of Israel.
18: 4 For all **p** are mine to judge—both parents
18: 7 to the hungry and provides clothes for **p** in need.
18:18 doing what was clearly wrong among his **p**.
18:20 Righteous **p** will be rewarded for their own
18:20 and wicked **p** will be punished for their own
18:21 But if wicked **p** turn away from all their sins
18:23 Sovereign LORD, that I like to see wicked **p** die?
18:24 if righteous **p** turn to sinful ways and start acting
18:25 Lord isn't being just!' Listen to me, O **p** of Israel.
18:26 When righteous **p** turn from being good and start
18:27 And if wicked **p** turn away from their wickedness,
18:28 decided to turn from their sins. Such **p** will not die.
18:29 And yet the **p** of Israel keep saying, 'The Lord is
18:29 O **p** of Israel, it is you who are unjust, not I.
18:30 "Therefore, I will judge each of you, O **p** of Israel,
18:31 new spirit. For why should you die, O **p** of Israel?
20: 9 at Israel's God, who had promised to deliver his **p**.
20:10 So I brought my **p** out of Egypt and led them into
20:12 them apart to be holy, making them my special **p**.
20:13 "But the **p** of Israel rebelled against me, and they
20:14 That way the nations who saw me lead my **p** out of
20:27 give the **p** of Israel this message from the
20:30 give the **p** of Israel this message from the
20:31 Should I listen to you or help you, O **p** of Israel?
20:39 "As for you, O **p** of Israel, this is what the
20:40 the **p** of Israel will someday worship me, and I will
20:44 You will know that I am the LORD, O **p** of Israel,
21: 3 about to unsheath my sword to destroy your **p**—
21: 6 "Son of man, groan before the **p**! Groan before
21: 9 of man, give the **p** this message from the LORD:
21:12 for that sword will slaughter my **p** and their
21:23 The **p** of Jerusalem will think it is a mistake,
21:23 But the king of Babylon will remind the **p** of their
22: 5 you will be mocked by **p** both far and near.
22: 9 **P** accuse others falsely and send them to their
22: 9 and **p** who take part in lewd activities.
22:18 the **p** of Israel are the worthless slag that remains
22:24 "Son of man, give the **p** of Israel this message:
22:25 They devour innocent **p**, seizing treasures
22:26 And they do not teach my **p** the difference between
22:29 Even common **p** oppress the poor, rob the needy,
23:45 But righteous **p** will judge these sister cities for
24:18 So I proclaimed this to the **p** the next morning,
24:19 Then the **p** asked, "What does all this mean?
24:21 and I was told to give this message to the **p** of
24:27 talk to him, and you will be a symbol for these **p**.
25: 2 the land of Ammon and prophesy against its **p**.
25: 6 and cheered with glee at the destruction of my **p**,
25: 8 Because the **p** of Moab have said that Judah is just
25:12 The **p** of Edom have sinned greatly by avenging
themselves against the **p** of Judah.
25:13 I will wipe out their **p**, cattle, and flocks with the
25:14 By the hand of my **p** of Israel, I will accomplish
25:15 The **p** of Philistia have acted against Judah out of
25:16 and utterly destroy the **p** who live by the sea.
26:11 They will butcher your **p**, and your famous pillars
26:13 will the sound of harps be heard among your **p**.
26:17 been destroyed! / Your **p**, with their naval power,
28:22 Give the **p** of Sidon this message from the
28:23 and your **p** will lie slaughtered within your walls.
28:25 The **p** of Israel will again live in their own land,
28:25 the nations of the world my holiness among my **p**.
29: 2 against Pharaoh the king and all the **p** of Egypt.
29: 6 "All the **p** of Egypt will discover that I am the
29: 8 O Egypt, and destroy both **p** and animals.
29:11 a soul will pass that way, neither **p** nor animals.
29:14 and bring its **p** back to the land of Pathros in
30: 8 And the **p** of Egypt will know that I am the
30:15 of Egypt, and I will stamp out the **p** of Thebes.
31: 2 message to Pharaoh, king of Egypt, and all his **p**:
31:14 They will land in the pit along with all the proud **p**
32: 3 I will send many **p** to catch you in my net and haul
32:13 Never again will **p** or animals disturb those waters
32:15 everything you have and strike down all your **p**,
32:22 lies there surrounded by the graves of all its **p**,
32:23 **p** everywhere are now dead at the hands of their
32:25 surrounded by the graves of all their **p**.
32:26 They once struck terror into the hearts of all **p**.
33: 2 "Son of man, give your **p** this message: When I
33: 2 a country, the **p** of that land choose a watchman.
33: 3 enemy coming, he blows the alarm to warn the **p**.
33: 6 and doesn't sound the alarm to warn the **p**,
33: 7 I am making you a watchman for the **p** of Israel.
33: 8 If I announce that some wicked **p** are sure to die
33:10 "Son of man, give the **p** of Israel this message:
33:11 I take no pleasure in the death of wicked **p**.
33:11 Turn! Turn from your wickedness, O **p** of Israel!
33:12 "Son of man, give your **p** this message: The good
works of righteous **p** will not save them
33:12 nor will the sins of evil **p** destroy them if they
33:13 When I tell righteous **p** that they will live, but
33:14 And suppose I tell some wicked **p** that they will
33:17 "Your **p** are saying, 'The Lord is not just,' but it is
33:18 I say, when righteous **p** turn to evil, they will die.
33:19 But if wicked **p** turn from their wickedness and do
33:20 O **p** of Israel, you are saying, 'The Lord is not
33:25 Now give these **p** this message from the Sovereign
33:30 of man, your **p** are whispering behind your back.
34:13 and by the rivers in all the places where **p** live.
34:17 "And as for you, O my flock, my **p**, this is what the
34:24 my servant David will be a prince among my **p**.
34:25 Then my **p** will be able to camp safely in the
34:26 I will cause my **p** and their homes around my holy
34:27 and fields of my **p** will yield bumper crops,
34:29 so my **p** will never again go hungry or be shamed
34:30 the **p** of Israel, are my **p**, says the Sovereign
34:31 You are my **p**, and I am your God,
35: 2 toward Mount Seir, and prophesy against its **p**.
35: 5 Your continual hatred for the **p** of Israel led you to
35: 8 and your streams will be filled with **p** slaughtered
35:15 you **p** of Mount Seir and all who live in Edom!
36:10 the ruined cities will be rebuilt and filled with **p**.
36:11 Not only the **p**, but your flocks and herds will also
36:11 of Israel, I will bring **p** to live on you once again.
36:12 I will cause my **p** to walk on you once again,
36:13 saying, 'Israel is a land that devours her own **p**!'
36:14 But you will never again devour your **p** or bereave
36:17 when the **p** of Israel were living in their own land,
36:20 the nations said, 'These are the **p** of the LORD,
36:21 which had been dishonored by my **p** throughout
36:22 give the **p** of Israel this message from the
36:28 You will be my **p**, and I will be your God.
36:32 O my **p** of Israel, you should be utterly ashamed of
36:33 I will bring **p** to live in your cities, and the ruins
36:35 And when I bring you back, **p** will say,
36:35 now have strong walls, and they are filled with **p**!'
36:38 The ruined cities will be crowded with **p** once
37: 3 of man, can these bones become living **p** again?"
37:11 "Son of man, these bones represent the **p** of Israel.
37:12 O my **p**, I will open your graves of exile and cause
37:13 When this happens, O my **p**, you will know that I
37:18 When your **p** ask you what your actions mean,
37:20 sticks you have inscribed, so the **p** can see them.
37:21 I will gather the **p** of Israel from among the
37:23 Then they will truly be my **p**, and I will be their
37:27 I will be their God, and they will be my **p**.
38: 8 and after the return of her **p** from many lands.
38:11 and destroy these **p** who live in such confidence!
38:12 **p** who have returned from exile in many nations.
38:12 many slaves, for the **p** are rich with cattle now,
38:14 When my **p** are living in peace in their land,
38:17 that in future days I would bring you against my **p**.
38:20 living things—all the fish, birds, animals, and **p**—
39: 7 I will make known my holy name among my **p** of
39: 9 "Then the **p** in the towns of Israel will go out
39:12 It will take seven months for the **p** of Israel to
39:22 And from that time on the **p** of Israel will know
39:25 I will end the captivity of my **p**; I will have mercy
39:28 Then my **p** will know that I am the LORD their
39:28 them home. I will leave none of my **p** behind.
40: 4 Then you will return to the **p** of Israel and tell them
43: 7 remain here forever, living among the **p** of Israel.
43:10 describe to the **p** of Israel the Temple I have shown
43:27 the burnt offerings and peace offerings of the **p**.
44: 6 And give these rebels, the **p** of Israel, this message
44: 6 O **p** of Israel, enough of your disgusting sins!
44: 7 into my sanctuary—**p** who have no heart for God.
44: 9 including those who live among the **p** of Israel,
44:11 for burnt offerings and be present to help the **p**.
44:12 But they encouraged my **p** to worship other gods,
44:14 and helping the **p** in a general way.
44:19 they return to the outer courtyard where the **p** are,
44:19 so they do not harm the **p** by transmitting holiness
44:23 They will teach my **p** the difference between what
44:24 judges to resolve any disagreements among my **p**.
44:29 and sacrifices brought to the Temple by the **p**—
45: 8 "My princes will no longer oppress and rob my **p**;
45: 8 they will assign the rest of the land to the **p**,
45: 9 Quit robbing and cheating my **p** out of their land!
45:15 will make atonement for the **p** who bring them,
45:16 All the **p** of Israel must join the prince in bringing
45:17 offerings to make reconciliation for the **p** of Israel.
45:22 as a sin offering for himself and the **p** of Israel.
46: 3 The common **p** will worship the LORD in front
46: 9 But when the **p** come in through the north gateway
46:10 will enter and leave with the **p** on these occasions.
46:18 for I do not want any of my **p** unjustly evicted
46:20 and harming the **p** by transmitting holiness to
46:24 assistants to boil the sacrifices offered by the **p**."
48:11 and did not go astray when the **p** of Israel
48:18 This farmland will produce food for the **p** working
Da 2:11 you your dream, and they do not live among **p**."
2:46 and he commanded his **p** to offer sacrifices
3: 4 "**P** of all races and nations and languages,
3: 7 all the **p**, whatever their race or nation or language,
3:10 You issued a decree requiring all the **p** to bow
3:29 If any **p**, whatever their race or nation or language,
4: 1 King Nebuchadnezzar sent this message to the **p** of
4:35 All the **p** of the earth / are nothing compared to
5:19 made him so great that **p** of all races and nations
6:25 Then King Darius sent this message to the **p** of
6:27 He rescues and saves his **p**; / he performs
7: 5 a voice saying to it, "Get up! Devour many **p**!"
7:14 so that **p** of every race and nation and language
7:18 the holy **p** of the Most High will be given the
7:21 this horn was waging war against the holy **p**
7:22 and judged in favor of the holy **p** of the Most High.
7:22 Then the time arrived for the holy **p** to take over
7:25 and wear down the holy **p** of the Most High.
7:27 will be given to the holy **p** of the Most High.
8:24 destroy powerful leaders and devastate the holy **p**.
9: 6 and ancestors and to all the **p** of the land.
9: 7 including the **p** of Judah and Jerusalem and all
9:15 your **p** from Egypt in a great display of power.
9:16 and your **p** because of our sins and the sins of our
9:19 for your **p** and your city bear your name."
9:20 and confessing my sin and the sins of my **p**,
9:24 seventy sets of seven has been decreed for your **p**
9:27 He will make a treaty with the **p** for a period of
10: 6 voice was like the roaring of a vast multitude of **p**.
10:14 to explain what will happen to your **p** in the future,
11:14 Lawless ones among your own **p** will join them in
11:28 On the way he will set himself against the **p** of the
11:30 But he will vent his anger against the **p** of the holy
11:32 But the **p** who know their God will be strong
12: 1 But at that time every one of your **p** whose name is
12: 7 When the shattering of the holy **p** has finally come
Hos 1: 2 This will illustrate the way my **p** have been untrue
1: 6 for I will no longer show love to the **p** of Israel
1: 7 their God, will show love to the **p** of Judah.
1: 9 LORD said, "Name him Lo-ammi—'Not my **p**'—
1: 9 for Israel is not my **p**, and I am not their God.
1:10 In that day its **p** will be like the sands of the
1:10 they were told, 'You are not my **p**,' it will be said,
1:11 Then the **p** of Judah and Israel will unite under one
1:11 when God will again plant his **p** in his land.
2: 1 day you will call your brothers Ammi—'My **p**.'
2:23 And to those I called 'Not my **p**,' I will say, 'Now
you are my **p**.'
3: 1 For the LORD still loves Israel even though the **p**
3: 5 But afterward the **p** will return to the LORD their
4: 1 Hear the word of the LORD, O **p** of Israel!
4: 6 My **p** are being destroyed because they don't know
4: 8 "The priests get fed when the **p** sin and bring their
4: 8 to them. So the priests are glad when the **p** sin!
4: 9 'Like priests, like **p**'—since the priests are wicked,
the **p** are wicked, too.
4: 9 both priests and **p** for all their wicked deeds.
4:11 and prostitution have robbed my **p** of their brains.
4:14 with whores and shrine prostitutes. O foolish **p**!
5: 1 For you have led the **p** into a snare by worshiping
5:11 The **p** of Israel will be crushed and broken by my
6:10 My **p** have defiled themselves by chasing after
6:11 I wanted so much to restore the fortunes of my **p**!
7: 2 Its **p** don't realize I am watching them. Their sinful
7: 3 The **p** make the king glad with their wickedness.
7: 8 "My **p** of Israel mingle with godless foreigners,
7:11 "The **p** of Israel have become like silly,
7:13 "How terrible it will be for my **p** who have
7:16 toward me. Then the **p** of Egypt will laugh at them.
8: 1 The enemy descends like an eagle on the **p** of the
8: 3 The **p** of Israel have rejected what is good,
8: 4 The **p** have appointed kings and princes, but not
8: 8 The **p** of Israel have been swallowed up; they lie
8: 9 The **p** of Israel have sold themselves to many
8:13 The **p** of Israel love their rituals of sacrifice,
8:13 I will call my **p** to account for their sins, and I will
9: 1 O **p** of Israel, do not rejoice as others do. For you
9: 7 "The prophets are crazy!" the **p** shout.
9: 9 The things my **p** do are as depraved as what they
9:14 O LORD, what should I request for your **p**?
9:16 The **p** of Israel are stricken. Their roots are dried
9:17 My God will reject the **p** of Israel because they
10: 1 But the more wealth the **p** got, the more they
10: 2 The hearts of the **p** are fickle; they are guilty
10: 5 The **p** of Samaria tremble for their calf idol at
10: 5 The **p** mourn over it, and the priests wail for it,
10: 6 and shamed because its **p** have trusted in this idol.
10:14 Now the terrors of war will rise among your **p**.
11: 5 "But since my **p** refuse to return to me, they will
11: 7 For my **p** are determined to desert me. They call
11:10 "For someday the **p** will follow the LORD.
11:10 and my **p** will return trembling from the west.
12: 1 The **p** of Israel feed on the wind; they chase after
12: 7 the **p** are like crafty merchants selling from
12:14 But the **p** of Israel have bitterly provoked the
13: 1 the **p** shook with fear because the other Israelite
13: 1 But the **p** of Ephraim sinned by worshiping Baal
13:13 The **p** have been offered new birth, but they are
13:15 It will blow hard against the **p** of Ephraim,
13:16 The **p** of Samaria must bear the consequences of
14: 7 My **p** will return again to the safety of their land.
14: 9 and right, and righteous **p** live by walking in them.
Joel 1: 2 Hear this, you leaders of the **p**! Everyone listen!
1:14 of fasting; call the **p** together for a solemn meeting.
1:14 and all the **p** into the Temple of the LORD your

2:6 Fear grips all the **p**; every face grows pale with
2:15 of fasting; call the **p** together for a solemn meeting.
2:17 will stand between the **p** and the altar, weeping. Let them pray, "Spare your **p**, LORD!
2:18 Then the LORD will pity his **p** and be indignant
2:21 Don't be afraid, my **p**! Be glad now and rejoice
2:23 Rejoice, you **p** of Jerusalem! Rejoice in the
2:26 Never again will my **p** be disgraced like this.
2:27 Then you will know that I am here among my **p** of
2:27 My **p** will never again be disgraced like this.
2:28 rains again, I will pour out my Spirit upon all **p**.
2:32 There will be **p** on Mount Zion in Jerusalem who
3:2 There I will judge them for harming my **p**,
3:3 They cast lots to decide which of my **p** would be
3:6 You have sold the **p** of Judah and Jerusalem to the
3:8 will sell your sons and daughters to the **p** of Judah,
3:13 are overflowing with the wickedness of these **p**."
3:16 But to his **p** of Israel, the LORD will be a
3:19 they attacked Judah and killed her innocent **p**.
3:21 will make my home in Jerusalem with my **p**."
Am 1:3 "The **p** of Damascus have sinned again and again,
1:3 They beat down my **p** in Gilead as grain is
1:5 and slaughter its **p** all the way to the valley of
1:5 and the **p** of Aram will return to Kir as slaves.
1:6 "The **p** of Gaza have sinned again and again,
1:6 They sent my **p** into exile, selling them as slaves in
1:8 I will slaughter the **p** of Ashdod and destroy the
1:9 "The **p** of Tyre have sinned again and again,
1:11 "The **p** of Edom have sinned again and again,
1:13 "The **p** of Ammon have sinned again and again,
2:1 "The **p** of Moab have sinned again and again,
2:2 The **p** will fall in the noise of battle, as the warriors
2:4 "The **p** of Judah have sinned again and again,
2:6 "The **p** of Israel have sinned again and again,
2:6 They have perverted justice by selling honest **p** for silver and poor **p** for a pair of sandals.
2:7 They trample helpless **p** in the dust and deny
2:9 "Yet think of all I did for my **p**! I destroyed the Amorites before my **p** arrived in
2:11 Can you deny this, my **p** of Israel?"
3:1 has spoken against you, O **p** of Israel and Judah—
3:3 Can two **p** walk together without agreeing on the
3:6 war trumpet blares, shouldn't the **p** be alarmed?
3:10 "My **p** have forgotten what it means to do right,"
4:8 **P** staggered from one town to another for a drink
4:12 God as he comes in judgment, you **p** of Israel!"
5:1 Listen, you **p** of Israel! Listen to this funeral song I
5:5 For the **p** of Gilgal will be dragged off into exile,
5:5 and the **p** of Bethel will come to nothing."
5:7 You wicked **p**! You twist justice, making it a bitter
5:10 How you despise **p** who tell the truth!
5:12 You oppress good **p** by taking bribes and deprive
5:15 Almighty will have mercy on his **p** who remain.
6:1 popular in Israel, you to whom the **p** go for help.
6:14 "O **p** of Israel, I am about to bring an enemy
7:2 "O Sovereign LORD, please forgive your **p**!
7:4 I saw him preparing to punish his **p** with a great
7:8 "I will test my **p** with this plumb line.
7:11 and the **p** of Israel will be sent away into exile.' "
7:15 and told me, 'Go and prophesy to my **p** in Israel.'
7:16 against Israel. Stop preaching against my **p**.'
7:17 And the **p** of Israel will certainly become captives
8:2 "This fruit represents my **p** of Israel—
8:6 Then you enslave poor **p** for a debt of one piece of
8:12 **P** will stagger everywhere from sea to sea,
9:1 so the roof will crash down on the **p** below.
9:5 touches the land and it melts, and all its **p** mourn.
9:8 I will uproot it and scatter its **p** across the earth.
9:14 I will bring my exiled **p** of Israel back from distant
Ob 1:16 Just as you swallowed up my **p** on my holy
1:17 And the **p** of Israel will come back to reclaim their
1:19 "Then my **p** living in the Negev will occupy the
1:19 And the **p** of Benjamin will occupy the land of
Jnh 1:2 because I have seen how wicked its **p** are."
3:5 The **p** of Nineveh believed God's message,
4:2 you could cancel your plans for destroying these **p**.
4:11 But Nineveh has more than 120,000 **p** living in
Mic 1:2 Attention! Let all the **p** of the world listen!
1:10 You **p** in Beth-leaphrah, roll in the dust to show
1:11 You **p** of Shaphir, go as captives into exile—
1:11 The **p** of Zaanan dare not come outside their walls.
1:11 The **p** of Beth-ezel mourn because the very
1:12 The **p** of Maroth anxiously wait for relief, but only
1:13 your swiftest chariots and flee, you **p** of Lachish.
1:15 You **p** of Mareshah, I will bring a conqueror to
1:16 Weep, you **p** of Judah! Shave your heads in
2:5 and the LORD's **p** will have no say in how the
2:6 "Don't say such things," the **p** say.
2:8 Yet to this very hour my **p** rise against me!
3:2 You skin my **p** alive and tear the flesh off their
3:5 "You are leading my **p** astray! You promise peace
4:1 **P** from all over the world will go there to worship.
4:6 "I will gather together my **p** who are lame,
4:8 As for you, O Jerusalem, the citadel of God's **p**,
4:9 He is dead! Have you no wise **p** to counsel you?
4:10 and groan in terrible pain, you **p** of Jerusalem,
5:3 The **p** of Israel will be abandoned to their enemies
5:4 Then his **p** will live there undisturbed, for he will
5:9 The **p** of Israel will stand up to their foes, and all
6:2 He has a case against his **p** Israel!
6:3 O my **p**, what have I done to make you turn from
6:5 "Don't you remember, my **p**, how King Balak of
6:8 No, O **p**, the LORD has already told you what is
7:2 The godly **p** have all disappeared; not one
7:3 The **p** with money and influence pay them off,
7:12 **P** from many lands will come and honor you—
7:14 O LORD, come and rule your **p**; lead your flock
7:18 who pardons the sins of the survivors among his **p**?
7:18 You cannot stay angry with your **p** forever,
Na 1:5 the earth trembles, and its **p** are destroyed.
1:12 O my **p**, I have already punished you once, and I
1:15 Celebrate your festivals, O **p** of Judah, and fulfill
2:8 The **p** are slipping away. "Stop, stop!"
2:8 someone shouts, but the **p** just keep on running.
2:10 The **p** stand aghast, their faces pale and trembling.
3:3 **P** stumble over them, scramble to their feet,
3:4 worship her false gods, enchanting **p** everywhere.
3:10 Thebes fell, and her **p** were led away as captives.
3:18 Your **p** are scattered across the mountains.
Hab 1:3 I am surrounded by **p** who love to argue and fight.
1:8 They are a fierce **p**, more fierce than wolves at
1:13 Should you be silent while the wicked destroy **p**
3:13 You went out to rescue your chosen **p**, to save your
3:16 day when disaster will strike the **p** who invade us.
Zep 1:3 "I will sweep away both **p** and animals alike.
1:7 The LORD has prepared his **p** for a great
1:18 He will make a terrifying end of all the **p** on earth.
2:7 For the LORD their God will visit his **p** in
2:8 "I have heard the taunts of the **p** of Moab
2:8 mocking my **p** and invading their borders.
2:9 Those of my **p** who are left will plunder them
2:10 for they have scoffed at the **p** of the LORD
2:11 Then **p** from nations around the world will worship
3:9 "On that day I will purify the lips of all **p**, so that
3:10 My scattered **p** who live beyond the rivers of
3:11 all the proud and arrogant **p** from among you.
3:13 The **p** of Israel who survive will do no wrong to
Hag 1:2 The **p** are saying, 'The time has not yet come to
1:12 and the whole remnant of God's **p** obeyed the
1:12 and the **p** worshiped the LORD in earnest.
1:13 gave the **p** this message from the LORD:
1:14 the high priest, and the whole remnant of God's **p**.
2:2 and to the remnant of God's **p** there in the land:
2:4 Take courage, all you **p** still left in the land,
2:14 "That is how it is with this **p** and this nation,
Zec 1:3 Therefore, say to the **p**, 'This is what the LORD
1:15 I was only a little angry with my **p**, but the nations
2:4 so full of **p** that it won't have room enough for
2:11 LORD on that day, and they, too, will be my **p**.
4:7 stone of the Temple in place, and the **p** will shout:
7:2 The **p** of Bethel had sent Sharezer
7:5 "Say to all your **p** and your priests, 'During those
7:7 and the towns of Judah were bustling with **p**,
7:10 oppress widows, orphans, foreigners, and poor **p**.
8:6 a small and discouraged remnant of God's **p**.
8:7 You can be sure that I will rescue my **p** from the
8:8 They will be my **p**, and I will be faithful and just
8:10 were no jobs and no wages for either **p** or animals.
8:11 But now I will not treat the remnant of my **p** as I
8:15 my decision to bless Jerusalem and the **p** of Judah.
8:19 festivals of joy and celebration for the **p** of Judah.
8:20 **P** from nations and cities around the world will
8:21 The **p** of one city will say to the people in another,
8:21 The people of one city will say to the **p** in another,
8:22 **P** from many nations, even powerful nations,
8:23 In those days ten **p** from nations and languages
9:1 including the **p** of Israel, are on the LORD.
9:7 And the Philistines of Ekron will join my **p**,
9:9 Rejoice greatly, O **p** of Zion! Shout in triumph, O **p** of Jerusalem! Look,
9:14 The LORD will appear above his **p**; his arrows
9:15 The LORD Almighty will protect his **p**, and they
9:16 the LORD their God will rescue his **p**,
10:2 So my **p** are wandering like lost sheep, without a
10:7 The **p** of Israel will become like mighty warriors,
10:12 I will make my **p** strong in my power, and they
12:4 I will watch over the **p** of Judah, but I will blind
12:5 'The **p** of Jerusalem have found strength in the
12:6 while the **p** living in Jerusalem remain secure.
12:7 so that the **p** of Jerusalem and the royal line of
12:8 On that day the LORD will defend the **p** of
12:10 the family of David and on all the **p** of Jerusalem.
13:1 the dynasty of David and for the **p** of Jerusalem,
13:4 one will wear prophet's clothes to try to fool the **p**.
13:8 Two-thirds of the **p** in the land will be cut off
13:9 I will say, 'These are my **p**,' and they will say,
14:12 Their **p** will become like walking corpses,
14:18 And if the **p** of Egypt refuse to attend the festival,
Mal 1:4 and their **p** will be called 'The **P** with Whom
1:11 But my name is honored by **p** of other nations
2:6 They passed on to the **p** all the truth they received
2:7 and **p** should go to them for instruction,
2:9 and humiliated in the eyes of all the **p**.
3:4 the offerings brought to him by the **p** of Judah
3:5 for these **p** do not fear me," says the LORD
3:8 "Should **p** cheat God? Yet you have cheated me!
3:17 "They will be my **p**," says the LORD Almighty.
Mt 1:21 him Jesus, for he will save his **p** from their sins."
2:6 who will be the shepherd for my **p** Israel.' "
3:5 **P** from Jerusalem and from every section of Judea
4:4 '**P** need more than bread for their life;
4:16 the **p** who sat in darkness / have seen a great light.
4:19 and I will show you how to fish for **p**!"
4:23 And he healed **p** who had every kind of sickness
4:25 **p** from Galilee, the Ten Towns, Jerusalem, from all
6:7 don't babble on and on as **p** of other religions do.
6:16 so **p** will admire them for their fasting.
7:6 "Don't give what is holy to unholy **p**. Don't give
7:11 If you sinful **p** know how to give good gifts to your
7:21 "Not all **p** who sound religious are really godly.
8:16 That evening many demon-possessed **p** were
9:2 Some **p** brought to him a paralyzed man on a mat.
9:12 Jesus replied, "Healthy **p** don't need a doctor—
9:12 "Healthy people don't need a doctor—sick **p** do."
9:32 some **p** brought to him a man who couldn't speak
9:35 he healed **p** of every sort of disease and illness.
10:6 but only to the **p** of Israel—God's lost sheep.
10:41 And if you welcome good and godly **p** because of
11:12 been forcefully advancing, and violent **p** attack it.
11:16 These **p** are like a group of children playing a
11:21 their **p** would have sat in deep repentance long
11:23 And you **p** of Capernaum, will you be exalted to
12:15 He left that area, and many **p** followed him.
12:41 The **p** of Nineveh will rise up against this
13:2 he sat and taught as the **p** listened on the shore.
13:10 do you always tell stories when you talk to the **p**?"
13:13 because **p** see what I do, but they don't really see.
13:15 For the hearts of these **p** are hardened, / and their
13:17 many prophets and godly **p** have longed to see
13:38 and the good seed represents the **p** of the
13:38 The weeds are the **p** who belong to the evil one.
13:49 and separate the wicked **p** from the godly,
14:5 because all the **p** believed John was a prophet.
14:19 Then he told the **p** to sit down on the grass. And he
14:19 each disciple, and the disciples gave them to the **p**.
14:22 the other side of the lake while he sent the **p** home.
14:35 and soon **p** were bringing all their sick to be
15:8 'These **p** honor me with their words, / but their
15:15 "Explain what you meant when you said **p** aren't
15:24 "I was sent only to help the **p** of Israel—
15:32 disciples to him and said, "I feel sorry for these **p**.
15:35 So Jesus told all the **p** to sit down on the ground.
15:39 Then Jesus sent the **p** home, and he got into a boat
16:13 "Who do **p** say that the Son of Man is?"
16:27 and will judge all **p** according to their deeds.
17:17 Jesus replied, "You stubborn, faithless **p**!
17:25 Do kings tax their own **p** or the foreigners they
20:3 and saw some **p** standing around doing nothing.
20:6 town again and saw some more **p** standing around.
20:12 'Those **p** worked only one hour, and yet you've
20:25 and officials lord it over the **p** beneath them.
21:5 "Tell the **p** of Israel, / 'Look, your King is coming
21:26 be mobbed, because the **p** think he was a prophet."
23:28 You try to look like upright **p** outwardly, but inside
23:29 and decorate the graves of the godly **p** your
23:35 **p** from righteous Abel to Zechariah son of
24:11 prophets will appear and will lead many **p** astray.
24:38 the **p** were enjoying banquets and parties
24:39 **P** didn't realize what was going to happen until the
26:28 which seals the covenant between God and his **p**.
26:47 by the leading priests and other leaders of the **p**.
26:57 Then the **p** who had arrested Jesus led him to the
27:9 the price at which he was valued by the **p** of
27:25 And all the **p** yelled back, "We will take
27:39 And the **p** passing by shouted abuse, shaking their
27:53 holy city of Jerusalem, and appeared to many **p**.
Mk 1:4 and was preaching that **p** should be baptized to
1:5 **P** from Jerusalem and from all over Judea traveled
1:17 and I will show you how to fish for **p**!"
1:21 day he went into the synagogue and taught the **p**.
1:32 and demon-possessed **p** were brought to Jesus.
1:33 And a huge crowd of **p** from all over Capernaum
1:34 So Jesus healed great numbers of sick **p** who had
1:39 and expelling demons from many **p**.
1:45 and **p** from everywhere came to him there.
2:15 (There were many **p** of this kind among the crowds
2:16 were Pharisees saw him eating with **p** like that,
2:17 "Healthy **p** don't need a doctor—sick **p** do.
2:18 One day some **p** came to Jesus and asked,
2:27 said to them, "The Sabbath was made to benefit **p**, and not **p** to benefit the Sabbath.
3:8 and vast numbers of **p** came to see him for
3:10 a result, many sick **p** were crowding around him,
4:2 He began to teach the **p** by telling many stories
4:33 and illustrations to teach the **p** as much as they
5:39 He went inside and spoke to the **p**. "Why all this
6:5 them except to place his hands on a few sick **p**
6:13 cast out many demons and healed many sick **p**,
6:14 because **p** everywhere were talking about him.
6:31 There were so many **p** coming and going that Jesus
6:33 But many **p** saw them leaving, and **p** from many towns ran ahead along the shore
6:41 the bread and fish to the disciples to give to the **p**.
6:45 the lake to Bethsaida, while he sent the **p** home.
6:54 The **p** standing there recognized him at once,
6:55 and began carrying sick **p** to him on mats.
7:7 'These **p** honor me with their lips, / but their hearts
7:11 But you say it is all right for **p** to say to their
7:32 and the **p** begged Jesus to lay his hands on the man
8:1 had gathered, and the **p** ran out of food again.
8:2 "I feel sorry for these **p**. They have been here with
8:6 So Jesus told all the **p** to sit down on the ground.
8:9 There were about four thousand **p** in the crowd that
8:12 "Why do you **p** keep demanding a miraculous
8:22 some **p** brought a blind man to Jesus, and they
8:24 "Yes," he said, "I see **p**, but I can't see them very
8:27 he asked them, "Who do **p** say I am?"
9:19 Jesus said to them, "You faithless **p**! How long
10:23 "How hard it is for rich **p** to get into the Kingdom
10:32 and the **p** following behind were overwhelmed
10:42 and officials lord it over the **p** beneath them.
10:48 "Be quiet!" some of the **p** yelled at him. But he
11:18 But they were afraid of him because the **p** were
11:32 For they were afraid that the **p** would start a riot,
12:35 Later, as Jesus was teaching the **p** in the Temple,
12:40 and then, to cover up the kind of **p** they really are,
12:41 in their money. Many rich **p** put in large amounts.
14:24 sealing the covenant between God and his **p**.
15:6 year at Passover time—anyone the **p** requested.
15:29 And the **p** passing by shouted abuse, shaking their
Lk 1:1 Many **p** have written accounts about the events

1:17 coming of the Lord, preparing the **p** for his arrival.
1:21 the **p** were waiting for Zechariah to come out,
1:36 **P** used to say she was barren, but she's already in
1:68 because he has visited his **p** and redeemed them.
1:77 You will tell his **p** how to find salvation
2:31 you have given to all **p**.
2:32 the nations, / and he is the glory of your **p** Israel!"
3: 3 preaching that **p** should be baptized to show that
3: 6 And then all **p** will see / the salvation sent from
3:14 and don't accuse **p** of things you know they didn't
3:18 warnings as he announced the Good News to the **p**.
4: 4 '**P** need more than bread for their life.' "
4:28 heard this, the **p** in the synagogue were furious.
4:32 too, the **p** were amazed at the things he said,
4:36 Amazed, the **p** exclaimed, "What authority
4:40 **p** throughout the village brought sick family
5:10 be afraid! From now on you'll be fishing for **p**!"
5:31 "Healthy **p** don't need a doctor—sick **p** do.
6:17 There were **p** from all over Judea and from
7:21 he cured many **p** of their various diseases,
7:25 **p** who wear beautiful clothes and live in luxury are
7:29 When they heard this, all the **p**,
7:41 "A man loaned money to two **p**—five hundred
8:15 good-hearted **p** who hear God's message, cling to
8:37 And all the **p** in that region begged Jesus to go
8:52 The house was filled with **p** weeping and wailing,
9: 5 If the **p** of the village won't receive your message
9:15 So the **p** all sat down.
9:16 the bread and fish to the disciples to give to the **p**.
9:18 and asked them, "Who do **p** say I am?"
9:41 "You stubborn, faithless **p**," Jesus said,
9:43 Awe gripped the **p** as they saw this display of
9:53 The **p** of the village refused to have anything to do
10:13 their **p** would have sat in deep repentance long
10:15 And you **p** of Capernaum, will you be exalted to
11:13 If you sinful **p** know how to give good gifts to your
11:30 What happened to him was a sign to the **p** of
11:30 that God has sent me, the Son of Man, to these **p**.
11:32 The **p** of Nineveh, too, will rise up against this
11:44 **P** walk over them without knowing the corruption
11:46 For you crush **p** beneath impossible religious
11:52 For you hide the key to knowledge from the **p**.
12: 5 who has the power to kill **p** and then throw them
12:30 These things dominate the thoughts of most **p**,
12:48 "But **p** who are not aware that they are doing
13: 1 **p** from Galilee as they were sacrificing at the
13: 2 were worse sinners than other **p** from Galilee?"
13:17 And all the **p** rejoiced at the wonderful things he
13:29 Then **p** will come from all over the world to take
14: 1 of the Pharisees. The **p** were watching him closely,
14: 3 is it permitted in the law to heal **p** on the Sabbath
15: 2 that he was associating with such despicable **p**—
17:26 the world will be like the **p** were in Noah's day.
17:27 the **p** enjoyed banquets and parties and weddings
17:28 **P** went about their daily business—eating
17:34 That night two **p** will be asleep in one bed;
18: 7 justice to his chosen **p** who plead with him day
18:24 "How hard it is for rich **p** to get into the Kingdom
19: 8 Lord, and if I have overcharged **p** on their taxes,
19:14 But his **p** hated him and sent a delegation after him
19:47 and the other leaders of the **p** began planning how
19:48 because all the **p** hung on every word he said.
20: 6 if we say it was merely human, the **p** will stone us,
20: 9 Now Jesus turned to the **p** again and told them this
20:26 So they failed to trap him in the presence of the **p**.
20:34 Jesus replied, "Marriage is for **p** here on earth.
20:47 and then, to cover up the kind of **p** they really are,
21: 1 he watched the rich **p** putting their gifts into the
21:23 be great distress in the land and wrath upon this **p**.
21:26 The courage of many **p** will falter because of the
22:25 the kings and great men order their **p** around,
22:25 and yet they are called 'friends of the **p**.'
22:66 At daybreak all the leaders of the **p** assembled,
23: 2 "This man has been leading our **p** to ruin by
23:13 and other religious leaders, along with the **p**,
23:30 **P** will beg the mountains to fall on them
23:34 Jesus said, "Father, forgive these **p**, because they
24:19 highly regarded by both God and all the **p**.
24:25 Then Jesus said to them, "You are such foolish **p**!
Jn 1:11 Even in his own land and among his own **p**,
1:15 John pointed him out to the **p**. He shouted to the
2:16 Then, going over to the **p** who sold doves, he told
2:23 many **p** were convinced that he was indeed the
2:24 because he knew what **p** were really like.
3: 8 so you can't explain how **p** are born of the Spirit."
3:23 water there and **p** kept coming to him for baptism.
3:26 one you said was the Messiah, is also baptizing **p**.
4:13 "**P** soon become thirsty again after drinking this
4:30 So the **p** came streaming from the village to see
4:36 and the fruit they harvest is **p** brought to eternal
4:48 and wonders before you **p** will believe in me?"
5: 3 Crowds of sick **p**—blind, lame, or paralyzed—
6: 5 Jesus soon saw a great crowd of **p** climbing the
6: 5 where can we buy bread to feed all these **p**?"
6:11 gave thanks to God, and passed them out to the **p**.
6:13 filled with the pieces of bread the **p** did not eat!
6:14 When the **p** saw this miraculous sign,
6:23 the Lord had blessed the bread and the **p** had eaten.
6:41 Then the **p** began to murmur in disagreement
6:44 For **p** can't come to me unless the Father who sent
6:52 Then the **p** began arguing with each other about
6:65 "That is what I meant when I said that **p** can't
7:12 "He's nothing but a fraud, deceiving the **p**."
7:25 Some of the **p** who lived there in Jerusalem said
8:12 Jesus said to the **p**, "I am the light of the world.
8:17 Your own law says that if two **p** agree about
8:31 Jesus said to the **p** who believed in him, "You are
8:48 The **p** retorted, "You Samaritan devil! Didn't we
8:52 The **p** said, "Now we know you are possessed by a
8:57 The **p** said, "You aren't even fifty years old.
10:19 the **p** were again divided in their opinions about
10:32 direction I have done many things to help the **p**.
10:34 own law that God said to certain leaders of the **p**,
10:35 So if those **p**, who received God's message,
11: 9 As long as it is light, **p** can walk safely. They can
11:19 and many of the **p** had come to pay their respects
11:31 When the **p** who were at the house trying to
11:33 her weeping and saw the other **p** wailing with her,
11:36 The **p** who were standing nearby said, "See how
11:42 but I said it out loud for the sake of all these **p**
11:45 Many of the **p** who were with Mary believed in
11:50 be destroyed? Let this one man die for the **p**."
11:54 Jesus stopped his public ministry among the **p**
11:55 and many **p** from the country arrived in Jerusalem
12: 9 When all the **p** heard of Jesus' arrival,
12:11 because of him that many of the **p** had deserted
12:15 "Don't be afraid, **p** of Israel. / Look, your King is
12:37 he had done, most of the **p** did not believe in him.
12:39 But the **p** couldn't believe, for as Isaiah also said,
12:42 Many **p**, including some of the Jewish leaders,
15:13 the greatest love is shown when **p** lay down their
15:21 The **p** of the world will hate you because you
18:20 I have been heard by **p** everywhere, and I teach
18:35 "Your own **p** and their leading priests brought you
18:38 Then he went out again to the **p** and told them,
19: 4 Pilate went outside again and said to the **p**, "I am
19:14 And Pilate said to the **p**, "Here is your king!"
19:20 Latin, and Greek, so that many **p** could read it.
Ac 1: 8 and will tell **p** about me everywhere—
1:19 death spread rapidly among all the **p** of Jerusalem,
2: 7 they exclaimed. "These **p** are all from Galilee,
2: 9 Medes, Elamites, **p** from Mesopotamia, Judea,
2:11 And we all hear these **p** speaking in our own
2:15 Some of you are saying these **p** are drunk. It isn't
2:15 **P** don't get drunk by nine o'clock in the morning.
2:17 God said, / I will pour out my Spirit upon all **p**.
2:22 "**P** of Israel, listen! God publicly endorsed Jesus
2:47 and enjoying the goodwill of all the **p**.
3: 2 so he could beg from the **p** going into the Temple.
3: 9 All the **p** saw him walking and heard him praising
3:12 "**P** of Israel," he said, "what is so astounding
3:22 up a Prophet like me from among your own **p**.
3:23 listen to that Prophet will be cut off from God's **p**
3:26 up his servant, he sent him first to you **p** of Israel,
4: 1 While Peter and John were speaking to the **p**,
4: 4 But many of the **p** who heard their message
4:10 and to all the **p** of Israel that he was healed in the
4:12 There is no other name in all of heaven for **p** to
4:25 Why did the **p** waste their time with futile plans?
4:27 and the **p** of Israel were all united against Jesus,
4:34 because **p** who owned land or houses sold them
5:12 many miraculous signs and wonders among the **p**.
5:14 And more and more **p** believed and were brought
5:15 sick **p** were brought out into the streets on beds
5:20 to the Temple and give the **p** this message of life!"
5:25 had jailed were out in the Temple, teaching the **p**.
5:26 for they were afraid the **p** would kill them if they
5:31 He did this to give the **p** of Israel an opportunity to
5:34 on religious law and was very popular with the **p**.
5:37 He got some **p** to follow him, but he was killed,
6: 8 amazing miracles and signs among the **p**.
7:17 the number of our **p** in Egypt greatly increased.
7:19 This king plotted against our **p** and forced parents
7:23 he decided to visit his relatives, the **p** of Israel.
7:34 sure that I have seen the misery of my **p** in Egypt.
7:35 so God sent back the same man his **p** had
7:37 "Moses himself told the **p** of Israel, 'God will
7:37 up a Prophet like me from among your own **p**.'
7:38 Moses was with the assembly of God's **p** in the
7:38 He was the mediator between the **p** of Israel
7:51 "You stubborn **p**! You are heathen at heart
8: 2 (Some godly **p** came and buried Stephen with loud
8: 5 of Samaria and told the **p** there about the Messiah.
8:10 The Samaritan **p**, from the least to the greatest,
8:12 But now the **p** believed Philip's message of Good
8:14 that the **p** of Samaria had accepted God's message,
8:19 he exclaimed, "so that when I lay my hands on **p**,
9:15 and to kings, as well as to the **p** of Israel.
9:32 and in his travels he came to the Lord's **p** in the
10:36 heard about the Good News for the **p** of Israel—
11:24 And large numbers of **p** were brought to the Lord.
11:26 church for a full year, teaching great numbers of **p**.
12:20 Now Herod was very angry with the **p** of Tyre
12:22 The **p** gave him a great ovation, shouting, "It is
13:16 "**P** of Israel," he said, "and you devout Gentiles
13:21 Then the **p** begged for a king, and God gave them
13:27 The **p** in Jerusalem and their leaders fulfilled
13:31 these are his witnesses to the **p** of Israel.
13:42 the **p** asked them to return again and speak about
14: 4 But the **p** of the city were divided in their opinion
14:14 their clothing in dismay and ran out among the **p**,
14:18 and Barnabas could scarcely restrain the **p** from
15:14 the Gentiles to take from them a **p** for himself.
16:13 where we supposed that some **p** met for prayer,
16:21 "They are teaching the **p** to do things that are
17: 2 in a row he interpreted the Scriptures to the **p**.
17: 8 The **p** of the city, as well as the city officials,
17:11 And the **p** of Berea were more open-minded than
18:10 because many **p** here in this city belong to me."
18:13 They accused Paul of "persuading **p** to worship
19: 4 John himself told the **p** to believe in Jesus, the one
19:10 so that **p** throughout the province of Asia—
19:12 that had touched his skin were placed on sick **p**,
19:26 this man Paul has persuaded many **p** that
19:32 Inside, the **p** were all shouting, some one thing
21:21 They say that you teach **p** not to circumcise their
21:28 This is the man who teaches against our **p** and tells
21:39 is an important city. Please, let me talk to these **p**."
21:40 on the stairs and motioned to the **p** to be quiet.
22: 9 The **p** with me saw the light but didn't hear the
22:18 for the **p** here won't believe you when you give
23:11 Just as you have told the **p** about me here in
24:17 I returned to Jerusalem with money to aid my **p**
25:16 that Roman law does not convict **p** without a trial.
26: 4 from my earliest childhood among my own **p**
26:17 And I will protect you from both your own **p**
26:18 for their sins and be given a place among God's **p**,
28: 2 The **p** of the island were very kind to us. It was
28: 4 The **p** of the island saw it hanging there and said to
28: 6 The **p** waited for him to swell up or suddenly drop
28: 9 Then all the other sick **p** on the island came
28:10 **p** put on board all sorts of things we would need
28:17 even though I had done nothing against our **p**
28:19 I had no desire to press charges against my own **p**.
28:23 and on that day a large number of **p** came to Paul's
28:26 'Go and say to my **p**, / You will hear my words,
28:27 For the hearts of these **p** are hardened, / and their
Ro 1: 7 and he has called you to be his very own **p**.
1:14 For I have a great sense of obligation to **p** in our culture and to **p** in other cultures,
1:18 wicked **p** who push the truth away from
1:20 **p** have seen the earth and sky and all that God
1:23 they worshiped idols made to look like mere **p**,
2: 1 "What terrible **p** you have been talking about!"
2: 6 will judge all **p** according to what they have done.
2:19 and a beacon light for **p** who are lost in darkness
2:26 them all the rights and honors of being his own **p**?
2:29 kind of change seeks praise from God, not from **p**.
3: 5 for **p** will see God's goodness when he declares us
3: 5 punish us?" (That is actually the way some **p** talk.)
3: 9 not at all, for we have already shown that all **p**,
3:19 for its purpose is to keep **p** from having excuses
3:30 He makes **p** right with himself only by faith,
4: 4 When **p** work, their wages are not a gift.
4: 5 But **p** are declared righteous because of their faith,
5:13 Yes, **p** sinned even before the law was given.
5:18 but Christ's one act of righteousness makes all **p**
5:19 person disobeyed God, many **p** became sinners.
5:19 many **p** will be made right in God's sight.
5:20 so that all **p** could see how sinful they were.
5:20 But as **p** sinned more and more, God's wonderful
5:21 So just as sin ruled over all **p** and brought them to
8:29 For God knew his **p** in advance, and he chose them
9: 3 for my **p**, my Jewish brothers and sisters. I would
9: 4 They are the **p** of Israel, chosen to be God's special
9: 5 Their ancestors were great **p** of God, and Christ
9:18 and he chooses to make some **p** refuse to listen.
9:19 "Why does God blame **p** for not listening?
9:25 "Those who were not my **p**, / I will now call my **p**.
9:26 "Once they were told, / 'You are not my **p**.'
9:27 "Though the **p** of Israel are as numerous as the
9:33 "I am placing a stone in Jerusalem that causes **p** to
10: 1 and my prayer to God is that the Jewish **p** might be
10: 3 For they don't understand God's way of making **p**
10:19 But did the **p** of Israel really understand? Yes,
10:20 "I was found by **p** / who were not looking for me.
11: 1 I ask, then, has God rejected his **p**, the Jews?
11: 2 No, God has not rejected his own **p**, whom he
11: 2 Elijah the prophet complained to God about the **p**
11:11 Did God's **p** stumble and fall beyond recovery?
11:28 Yet the Jews are still his chosen **p** because of his
11:32 For God has imprisoned all **p** in their own
12:14 If **p** persecute you because you are a Christian,
12:16 but enjoy the company of ordinary **p**.
13: 3 For the authorities do not frighten **p** who are doing
14:18 please God. And other **p** will approve of you, too.
14:23 But if **p** have doubts about whether they should eat
15:10 O you Gentiles, / along with his **p**, the Jews."
15:11 you Gentiles; / praise him, all you **p** of the earth."
16:17 Watch out for **p** who cause divisions and upset
16:18 Such **p** are not serving Christ our Lord; they are
16:18 and glowing words they deceive innocent **p**.
1Co 1: 2 who have been called by God to be his own holy **p**.
2:14 But **p** who aren't Christians can't understand these
3: 3 You are acting like **p** who don't belong to the
4: 9 to the entire world—to **p** and angels alike.
4:19 then I'll find out whether these arrogant **p** are just
5: 9 I told you not to associate with **p** who indulge in
5:10 You would have to leave this world to avoid **p** like
5:11 or a swindler. Don't even eat with such **p**.
6:10 thieves, greedy **p**, drunkards, abusers,
8: 5 According to some **p**, there are many so-called
9:19 This means I am not bound to obey **p** just
10: 7 "The **p** celebrated with feasting and drinking,
10:15 You are reasonable **p**. Decide for yourselves if
11:11 But in relationships among the Lord's **p**,
14: 2 you will be talking to God but not to **p**, since they
14: 9 If you talk to **p** in a language they don't
14:11 I will not understand **p** who speak those languages,
14:13 in order to tell **p** plainly what has been said.
14:17 no doubt, but it doesn't help the other **p** present.
14:21 in the Scriptures, / "I will speak to my own **p**
14:23 or **p** who don't understand these things come into
14:24 or **p** who don't understand these things come into
14:32 Remember that **p** who prophesy are in control of
15:19 this life, we are the most miserable **p** in the world.
15:23 when Christ comes back, all his **p** will be raised.
15:29 then what point is there in **p** being baptized for
16: 9 for a great work here, and many **p** are responding.
2Co 1:17 Or am I like **p** of the world who say yes when they
3: 1 Some **p** need to bring letters of recommendation

3: 7 yet it began with such glory that the **p** of Israel
3:13 so the **p** of Israel would not see the glory fading
4:15 as God's grace brings more and more **p** to Christ,
5:18 And God has given us the task of reconciling **p** to
6: 8 We serve God whether **p** honor us or despise us,
6:16 I will be their God, / and they will be my **p**.
7: 9 It was the kind of sorrow God wants his **p** to have,
9: 9 "Godly **p** give generously to the poor.
10: 5 proud argument that keeps **p** from knowing God.
10:18 When **p** boast about themselves, it doesn't count
11:13 These **p** are false apostles. They have fooled you
11:26 I have faced danger from my own **p**, the Jews,
Gal 1:10 Obviously, I'm not trying to be a **p** pleaser! No,
1:10 If I were still trying to please **p**, I would not be
1:23 All they knew was that **p** were saying, "The one
3:19 It was given to show **p** how guilty they are.
3:19 who was the mediator between God and the **p**.
3:20 Now a mediator is needed if two **p** enter into an
4:24 represents Mount Sinai where **p** first became
6:15 really have been changed into new and different **p**.
6:16 live by this principle. They are the new **p** of God.
Eph 1: 1 It is written to God's holy **p** in Ephesus, who are
1:14 and that he has purchased us to be his own **p**.
1:18 and glorious inheritance he has given to his **p**.
2:12 You were excluded from God's **p**, Israel, and you
2:14 us Jews and you Gentiles by making us all one **p**.
2:19 You are citizens along with all of God's holy **p**.
3:18 as all God's **p** should, how wide, how long,
4: 8 led a crowd of captives / and gave gifts to his **p**."
4:12 Their responsibility is to equip God's **p** to do his
5: 3 Such sins have no place among God's **p**.
5: 7 Don't participate in the things these **p** do.
5:12 to talk about the things that ungodly **p** do in secret.
6: 7 you were working for the Lord rather than for **p**.
6:12 For we are not fighting against **p** made of flesh
Php 1: 1 It is written to all of God's **p** in Philippi,
2:15 in a dark world full of crooked and perverse **p**.
2:29 and with great joy, and be sure to honor **p** like him.
Col 1: 2 It is written to God's holy **p** in the city of Colosse,
1: 4 in Christ Jesus and that you love all of God's **p**.
1:12 share the inheritance that belongs to God's holy **p**,
1:26 but now it has been revealed to his own holy **p**.
1:27 For it has pleased God to tell his **p** that the riches
2:18 These **p** claim to be so humble, but their sinful
3:12 Since God chose you to be the holy **p** whom he
3:23 you were working for the Lord rather than for **p**.
4: 9 and much loved brother, one of your own **p**.
1Th 1: 4 and sisters, and that he chose you to be his own **p**.
1: 8 the Lord is ringing out from you to **p** everywhere,
1: 8 for wherever we go we find **p** telling us about your
2: 4 Our purpose is to please God, not **p**. He is the one
2:14 Christ Jesus, suffered from their own **p**, the Jews.
4: 9 love that should be shown among God's **p**.
4:12 **p** who are not Christians will respect the way you
4:13 so you will not be full of sorrow like **p** who have
5: 3 When **p** are saying, "All is well; everything is
5: 7 the time for sleep and the time when **p** get drunk.
2Th 1:10 comes to receive glory and praise from his holy **p**.
3: 2 that we will be saved from wicked and evil **p**,
3:12 of the Lord Jesus Christ we appeal to such **p**—
1Ti 1: 4 Don't let **p** waste time in endless speculation over
1: 4 they don't help **p** live a life of faith in God.
1: 9 But they were not made for **p** who do what is right.
1: 9 They are for **p** who are disobedient and rebellious,
1: 9 who murder their father or mother or other **p**.
1:10 These laws are for **p** who are sexually immoral,
1:13 I hunted down his **p**, harming them in every way I
1:19 For some **p** have deliberately violated their
2: 1 I urge you, first of all, to pray for all **p**. As you
2: 5 and one Mediator who can reconcile God and **p**.
3: 7 **p** outside the church must speak well of him
3: 8 deacons must be **p** who are respected and have
3:15 you will know how **p** must conduct themselves in
4: 3 to be eaten with thanksgiving by **p** who know
4:10 and suffer much in order that **p** will believe the
4:10 is in the living God, who is the Savior of all **p**,
5: 8 we believe. Such **p** are worse than unbelievers.
5:24 Remember that some **p** lead sinful lives,
5:25 everyone knows how much good some **p** do,
6: 5 These **p** always cause trouble. Their minds are
6: 9 But **p** who long to be rich fall into temptation
6:10 And some **p**, craving money, have wandered from
6:21 Some **p** have wandered from the faith by following
2Ti 2: 2 Teach these great truths to trustworthy **p** who are
2:24 to teach effectively and be patient with difficult **p**.
3: 2 For **p** will love only themselves and their money.
3: 5 them godly. You must stay away from **p** like that.
3:13 But evil **p** and impostors will flourish. They will
4: 2 rebuke, and encourage your **p** with good teaching.
4: 3 For a time is coming when **p** will no longer listen
Tit 1:10 they engage in useless talk and deceive **p**.
1:12 has said about them, "The **p** of Crete are all liars;
1:14 and the commands of **p** who have turned their
1:16 Such **p** claim they know God, but they deny him
2:11 God has been revealed, bringing salvation to all **p**.
2:14 to cleanse us, and to make us his very own **p**,
2:15 these things and encourage your **p** to do them,
3: 1 Remind your **p** to submit to the government
3:11 For **p** like that have turned away from the truth.
3:14 For our **p** should not have unproductive lives.
Phm 1: 5 in the Lord Jesus and your love for all of God's **p**.
1: 7 so often refreshed the hearts of God's **p**.
Heb 2: 2 and the **p** were punished for every violation of the
2:12 and sisters. / I will praise you among all your **p**."
2:17 a sacrifice that would take away the sins of the **p**.
3:16 And who were those **p** who rebelled against God,
3:17 Wasn't it the **p** who sinned, whose bodies fell in
4: 6 So God's rest is there for **p** to enter. But those who
4: 9 So there is a special rest still waiting for the **p** of
4:11 who disobeys God, as the **p** of Israel did, will fall.
5: 2 he is human, he is able to deal gently with the **p**,
6: 6 It is impossible to bring such **p** to repentance again
6:16 When **p** take an oath, they call on someone greater
7: 5 in the law of Moses to collect a tithe from all the **p**,
7:27 their own sins first and then for the sins of the **p**.
8: 8 a new covenant / with the **p** of Israel and Judah.
8:10 with the **p** of Israel on that day, says the Lord:
8:10 I will be their God, / and they will be my **p**.
9: 7 and the sins the **p** have committed in ignorance.
9: 8 was not open to the **p** as long as the first room
9: 9 cleanse the consciences of the **p** who bring them.
9:15 mediates the new covenant between God and **p**,
9:19 For after Moses had given the **p** all of God's laws,
9:19 both the book of God's laws and all the **p**,
9:28 once as a sacrifice to take away the sins of many **p**.
10:16 with my **p** on that day, says the Lord: / I will put
10:21 have a great High Priest who rules over God's **p**,
10:25 as some **p** do, but encourage and warn each other,
10:29 Such **p** have insulted and enraged the Holy Spirit
who brings God's mercy to his **p**.
10:30 He also said, / "The Lord will judge his own **p**."
11: 2 God gave his approval to **p** in days of old
11:12 a nation with so many **p** that, like the stars of the
11:14 And obviously **p** who talk like that are looking
11:22 confidently spoke of God's bringing the **p** of Israel
11:25 He chose to share the oppression of God's **p**
11:28 It was by faith that Moses commanded the **p** of
11:29 It was by faith that the **p** of Israel went right
11:30 It was by faith that the **p** of Israel marched around
11:33 By faith these **p** overthrew kingdoms, ruled with
11:39 All of these **p** we have mentioned received God's
12: 3 Think about all he endured when sinful **p** did such
12:23 come to God himself, who is the judge of all **p**.
12:24 mediates the new covenant between God and **p**,
12:25 For if the **p** of Israel did not escape when they
13: 4 God will surely judge **p** who are immoral
13:12 to make his **p** holy by shedding his own blood.
Jas 1: 7 **P** like that should not expect to receive anything
1:11 wealthy **p** will fade away with all of their
1:12 God blesses the **p** who patiently endure testing.
2: 1 Jesus Christ if you favor some **p** more than others?
2:18 Now someone may argue, "Some **p** have faith;
3: 7 **P** can tame all kinds of animals and birds
4:13 you **p** who say, "Today or tomorrow we are going
5: 1 you rich **p**, weep and groan with anguish
5: 6 and killed good **p** who had no power to defend
1Pe 1: 1 I am writing to God's chosen **p** who are living as
1:24 the prophet says, / "**P** are like grass that dies away;
2: 4 He was rejected by the **p**, but he is precious to God
2: 8 also say, / "He is the stone that makes **p** stumble,
2: 9 But you are not like that, for you are a chosen **p**.
2:10 Once you were not a **p**; / now you are the **p** of God.
3: 9 Don't retaliate when **p** say unkind things about
3:16 Then if **p** speak evil against you, they will be
3:20 Only eight **p** were saved from drowning in that
4: 3 in the past of the evil things that godless **p** enjoy—
5: 3 Don't lord it over the **p** assigned to your care,
2Pe 2: 5 Then God destroyed the whole world of ungodly **p**
2: 6 an example of what will happen to ungodly **p**.
2: 9 the Lord knows how to rescue godly **p** from their
2:10 These **p** are proud and arrogant, daring even to
2:14 They make a game of luring unstable **p** into sin.
2:17 These **p** are as useless as dried-up springs of water
2:20 And when **p** escape from the wicked ways of the
3: 7 the day of judgment, when ungodly **p** will perish.
3: 9 slow about his promise to return, as some **p** think.
3:15 the Lord is waiting so that **p** have time to be saved.
3:17 be carried away by the errors of these wicked **p**.
1Jn 2:19 These **p** left our churches because they never really
2:22 Such **p** are antichrists, for they have denied the
3: 1 But the **p** who belong to this world don't know
3: 7 When **p** do what is right, it is because they are
3: 8 But when **p** keep on sinning, it shows they belong
4: 5 These **p** belong to this world, so they speak from
4:20 for if we don't love **p** we can see, how can we love
Jude 1: 3 unchanging truth once for all time to his holy **p**.
1: 4 because some godless **p** have wormed their way in
1: 4 The fate of such **p** was determined long ago,
1:10 But these **p** mock and curse the things they do not
1:12 When these **p** join you in fellowship meals
1:14 generations after Adam, prophesied about these **p**.
1:15 He will bring the **p** of the world / to judgment.
1:16 These **p** are grumblers and complainers,
Rev 2: 2 patient endurance. I know you don't tolerate evil **p**.
2:14 who showed Balak how to trip up the **p** of Israel.
2:15 **p** who follow the same teaching and commit the
5: 8 bowls filled with incense—the prayers of God's **p**!
5: 9 and your blood has ransomed **p** for God
5: 9 from every tribe and language and **p** and nation.
6:10 how long will it be before you judge the **p** who
6:10 When will you avenge our blood against these **p**?"
6:15 of the earth, the rulers, the generals, the wealthy **p**,
6:15 the **p** with great power, and every slave and every
7: 9 from every nation and tribe and **p** and language,
8: 3 given to him to mix with the prayers of God's **p**,
8:11 and many **p** died because the water was so bitter.
9: 4 but to attack all the **p** who did not have the seal of
9: 6 In those days **p** will seek death but will not find it.
9:10 that sting like scorpions, with power to torture **p**.
9:15 turned loose to kill one-third of all the **p** on earth.
9:18 One-third of all the **p** on earth were killed by these
9:19 had heads like snakes, with the power to injure **p**.
9:20 But the **p** who did not die in these plagues still
11:10 All the **p** who belong to this world will give
11:13 Seven thousand **p** died in that earthquake.
11:18 You will reward your prophets and your holy **p**,
13: 7 was allowed to wage war against God's holy **p**
13: 7 over every tribe and **p** and language and nation.
13: 8 And all the **p** who belong to this world worshiped
13:10 The **p** who are destined for prison will be arrested
13:14 he deceived all the **p** who belong to this world.
13:14 He ordered the **p** of the world to make a great
14: 4 They have been purchased from among the **p** on
14: 6 News to preach to the **p** who belong to this world
14: 6 this world—to every nation, tribe, language, and **p**.
14:12 Let this encourage God's holy **p** to endure
15: 2 And on it stood all the **p** who had been victorious
16: 6 For your holy **p** and your prophets have been
16:21 pounds fell from the sky onto the **p** below.
17: 2 and the **p** who belong to this world have been
17: 6 drunk with the blood of God's holy **p** who were
17: 8 And the **p** who belong to this world, whose names
17:14 and his **p** are the called and chosen and faithful
17:15 is sitting represent masses of **p** of every nation
18: 4 calling from heaven, "Come away from her, my **p**.
18: 6 Do to her as she has done to your **p**. Give her a
18:20 O holy **p** of God and apostles and prophets!
18:24 She was the one who slaughtered God's **p** all over
19: 8 represents the good deeds done by the **p** of God.)
20: 4 and the **p** sitting on them had been given the
20: 9 and surrounded God's **p** and the beloved city.
21: 3 "Look, the home of God is now among his **p**!
21: 3 He will live with them, and they will be his **p**.

PEOPLE'S (53) [PEOPLE]

Ge 6: 5 Now the LORD observed the extent of the **p**
8:21 even though **p** thoughts and actions are bent
Ex 7:19 in wooden bowls and stone pots in the **p** homes."
16:12 "I have heard the **p** complaints. Now tell them,
18:13 Moses sat as usual to hear the **p** complaints against
18:19 You should continue to be the **p** representative
19: 8 So Moses brought the **p** answer back to the
Lev 6:30 to make atonement in the Holy Place for the **p** sins,
9:15 He slaughtered the **p** goat and presented it as their
9:18 the bull and the ram for the **p** peace offering.
16:21 he will lay the **p** sins on the head of the goat;
16:22 the goat will carry all the **p** sins upon itself into a
1Ki 8:37 or if your **p** enemies are in the land besieging their
12:15 So the king paid no attention to the **p** demands.
2Ki 12: 9 The priests guarding the entrance put all of the **p**
2Ch 6:28 or if your **p** enemies are in the land besieging their
10:15 So the king paid no attention to the **p** demands.
35: 7 and young goats for the **p** Passover offerings,
Job 14:19 floods wash away the soil, so you destroy **p** hope.
33:13 You say, 'He does not respond to **p** complaints.'
Ps 94:11 The LORD knows **p** thoughts, / that they are
Ecc 8: 6 even as **p** troubles lie heavily upon them.
Isa 51: 7 Do not be afraid of **p** scorn or their slanderous talk.
Jer 6:14 They offer superficial treatments for my **p** mortal
6:18 all you nations. Take note of my **p** condition.
6:21 "I will put obstacles in my **p** path. Fathers
8:11 They offer superficial treatments for my **p** mortal
15:13 Because of all my **p** sins against me, I will hand
Eze 7:10 The **p** wickedness and pride have reached a
7:27 in despair, and the **p** hands will tremble with fear.
22:27 They actually destroy **p** lives for profit!
36: 8 heavy crops of fruit to prepare for my **p** return—
Hos 7: 3 The princes laugh about the **p** many lies.
Joel 3:21 I will pardon my **p** crimes, which I have not yet
Mic 1: 9 For my **p** wound is far too deep to heal. It has
3: 3 You eat my **p** flesh, cut away their skin, and break
Zec 9: 8 No foreign oppressor will ever again overrun my **p**
Mt 23:27 but filled on the inside with dead **p** bones
Lk 16:12 And if you are not faithful with other **p** money,
Ac 8:18 when the apostles placed their hands upon **p** heads,
12:23 because he accepted the **p** worship instead of
15: 8 God, who knows **p** hearts, confirmed that he
17:30 God overlooked **p** former ignorance about these
Ro 16:17 and upset **p** faith by teaching things that are
2Co 1:11 so many **p** prayers for our safety have been
3:14 But the **p** minds were hardened, and even to this
5:19 to himself, no longer counting **p** sins against them.
2Th 3:11 and wasting time meddling in other **p** business.
1Ti 5:13 getting into other **p** business and saying things they
2Ti 2:25 Perhaps God will change those **p** hearts, and they
3: 6 They are the kind who work their way into **p**
Heb 9:13 and the ashes of a young cow could cleanse **p**
1Pe 4:15 making trouble, or prying into other **p** affairs.

PEOPLES (26) [PEOPLE]

ALL...PEOPLES (6) Dt 4:19; Est 8:9; Ps 96:10; Isa 66:18; Jer 32:27; Rev 11:9

Ge 10: 5 Their descendants became the seafaring **p** in
Dt 2:12 In a similar way the **p** in Canaan were driven from
4:19 these heavenly bodies for all the **p** of the earth.
12: 4 God in the way these pagan **p** worship their gods.
13: 7 They might suggest that you worship the gods of **p**
32: 8 he established the boundaries of the **p**
1Ki 4:21 The conquered **p** of those lands sent tribute money
Ezr 2:25 The **p** of Kiriath-jearim, Kephirah, and Beeroth
2:26 The **p** of Ramah and Geba | 621
2:28 The **p** of Bethel and Ai | 223
9: 1 have not kept themselves separate from the other **p**
Ne 7:26 The **p** of Bethlehem and Netophah | 188
7:29 The **p** of Kiriath-jearim, Kephirah, and Beeroth
7:30 The **p** of Ramah and Geba | 621
7:32 The **p** of Bethel and Ai | 123
Est 8: 9 the scripts and languages of all the **p** of the empire,
Ps 96:10 and cannot be shaken. / He will judge all **p** fairly.

149: 7 on the nations / and punishment on the p,
Isa 66: 18 So I will gather all nations and p together, and they
Jer 32: 27 am the LORD, the God of all the p of the world.
Eze 34: 13 home to their own land of Israel from among the p
Joel 3: 8 and they will sell them to the p of Arabia, a nation
Hab 2: 5 greed they have gathered up many nations and p.
3: 7 I see the p of Cushan and Midian trembling in
Rev 10: 11 "You must prophesy again about many p, nations,
11: 9 And for three and a half days all p, tribes,

PEOR (9) [BAAL-PEOR, BETH-PEOR]

Nu 23: 28 So Balak took Balaam to the top of Mount P,
25: 3 long Israel was joining in the worship of Baal of P,
25: 5 everyone who had joined in worshiping Baal of P.
25: 18 deceit by tricking you into worshiping Baal of P,
25: 18 who was killed on the day of the plague at P."
31: 16 of Israel to rebel against the LORD at Mount P.
Dt 4: 3 everyone who had worshiped the god Baal of P.
Jos 22: 17 Was our sin at P not enough? We are not yet fully
Ps 106: 28 our ancestors joined in the worship of Baal at P;

PER (2)

1Ki 7: 24 There were about six gourds p foot all the way
2Ch 4: 3 There were about six oxen p foot all the way

PERAZIM (1) [BAAL-PERAZIM]

Isa 28: 21 as he did against the Philistines at Mount P

PERCEIVE (5) [PERCEIVED]

Nu 24: 17 present time. / I p him, but far in the distant future.
Isa 6: 9 will see what I do, but you will not p its meaning.'
Mt 13: 14 will see what I do, but you will not p its meaning.
Mk 4: 12 'They see what I do, / but they don't p its meaning.
Ac 28: 26 will see what I do, / but you will not p its meaning.

PERCEIVED (1) [PERCEIVE]

2Co 2: 15 But this fragrance is p differently by those being

PERCENT (10)

Lev 5: 16 paying for the loss, plus an added penalty of 20 p.
6: 5 a penalty of 20 p to the person they have harmed.
22: 14 the amount eaten, plus an added penalty of 20 p.
27: 13 you must pay the value set by the priest, plus 20 p.
27: 15 you must pay the value set by the priest, plus 20 p.
27: 19 land's value as assessed by the priest, plus 20 p.
27: 27 the priest's assessment of its worth, plus 20 p.
27: 31 the fruit or grain, you must pay its value, plus 20 p.
Nu 5: 7 adding a penalty of 20 p and returning it to the
Eze 45: 14 one p of your olive oil,

PERESH (2)

1Ch 7: 16 Maacah, gave birth to a son whom she named P.
7: 16 The sons of P were Ulam and Rakem.

PEREZ (18) [PEREZ-UZZAH, PEREZITE, PEREZITES, RIMMON-PEREZ]

Ge 38: 29 break out first?" And ever after, he was called P.
46: 12 of Judah were Er, Onan, Shelah, P, and Zerah.
46: 12 The sons of P were Hezron and Hamul.
Nu 26: 20 The Perezite clan, named after its ancestor P.
Ru 4: 12 woman who will be like those of our ancestor P,
4: 18 their ancestor P: / P was the father of Hezron.
1Ch 2: 4 Their names were P and Zerah. So Judah had five
2: 5 The sons of P were Hezron and Hamul.
4: 1 Some of the descendants of Judah were P, Hezron,
9: 4 son of Bani, a descendant of P son of Judah.
27: 3 He was a descendant of P and was in charge of all
Ne 11: 4 son of Mahalalel, of the family of P;
11: 6 There were also 468 descendants of P who lived in
Mt 1: 3 Judah was the father of P and Zerah (their mother
1: 3 P was the father of Hezron. / Hezron was the father
Lk 3: 33 Hezron was the son of P. / P was the son of Judah.

PEREZ-UZZAH (2) [PEREZ, UZZAH]

2Sa 6: 8 He named that place P (which means "outbreak
1Ch 13: 11 He named that place P (which means "outbreak

PEREZITE (1) [PEREZ]

Nu 26: 20 The P clan, named after its ancestor Perez.

PEREZITES (1) [PEREZ]

Nu 26: 21 These were the subclans descended from the P.

PERFECT (40) [PERFECTED, PERFECTING, PERFECTION, PERFECTIONS, PERFECTLY]

Dt 32: 4 He is the Rock; his work is p. / Everything he does
1Sa 29: 9 as I'm concerned, you're as p as an angel of God.
2Sa 14: 25 head to foot, he was the p specimen of a man.
22: 31 "As for God, his way is p. / All the LORD's
Job 22: 3 Would it be any gain to him if you were p?
Ps 18: 30 As for God, his way is p. / All the LORD's
19: 7 The law of the LORD is p, / reviving the soul.
64: 6 they say, / "We have devised the p plan!"
119: 138 Your decrees are p; / they are entirely worthy of
143: 2 servant to trial! / Compared to you, no one is p.
Ecc 11: 4 If you wait for p conditions, you will never get
SS 4: 7 so beautiful, my beloved, so p in every part.
6: 9 But I would still choose my dove, my p one,
Isa 26: 3 You will keep in p peace all who trust in you,
Eze 27: 3 You claimed, O Tyre, to be p in beauty.
43: 23 bull that has no defects and a p ram from the flock.
Zec 6: 13 and there will be p harmony between the two.
Mt 5: 48 you are to be p, even as your Father in heaven is p.
19: 21 "If you want to be p, go and sell all you have
Ro 12: 2 how good and pleasing and p his will really is.
1Co 8: 1 You think that everyone should agree with your p
13: 12 but then we will see everything with p clarity.
Gal 3: 3 why are you now trying to become p by your own
Col 1: 28 them to God, p in their relationship to Christ.
3: 14 Love is what binds us all together in p harmony.
4: 12 for you, asking God to make you strong and p,
Heb 2: 10 the suffering of Jesus, God made him a p leader,
5: 9 In this way, God qualified him as a p High Priest,
7: 19 For the law made nothing p, and now a better hope
7: 28 with an oath, and his Son has been made p forever.
9: 11 He has entered that great, p sanctuary in heaven,
9: 14 Christ offered himself to God as a p sacrifice for
10: 1 but they were never able to provide p cleansing for
10: 2 If they could have provided p cleansing,
12: 23 redeemed in heaven who have now been made p.
Jas 1: 17 is good and p comes to us from God above,
1: 25 But if you keep looking steadily into God's p law
1Jn 4: 17 And as we live in God, our love grows more p.
4: 18 love has no fear because p love expels all fear.

PERFECTED (4) [PERFECT]

Eze 16: 14 because the splendor I bestowed on you p your
Jn 17: 23 I in them and you in me, all being p into one.
Heb 10: 14 For by that one offering he p forever all those
1Jn 4: 18 and this shows that his love has not been p in us.

PERFECTING (1) [PERFECT]

Eze 27: 11 Their shields hung on your walls, p your splendor.

PERFECTION (5) [PERFECT]

Job 37: 16 how he balances the clouds with wonderful p
Ps 50: 2 From Mount Zion, the p of beauty, / God shines in
119: 96 Even p has its limits, / but your commands have no
Eze 28: 12 You were the p of wisdom and beauty.
Php 3: 12 these things or that I have already reached p!

PERFECTIONS (1) [PERFECT]

Ps 27: 4 the days of my life, / delighting in the LORD's p

PERFECTLY (17) [PERFECT]

Dt 1: 16 the judges, 'You must be p fair at all times,
1Sa 20: 3 "Your father knows p well about our friendship,
2Sa 3: 25 You know p well that he came to spy on you
2Ki 19: 11 You know p well what the kings of Assyria have
Ps 7: 11 God is a judge who is p fair. / He is angry with the
119: 142 Your justice is eternal, / and your law is p true.
SS 4: 2 They are p matched; not one is missing.
6: 6 washed ewes, p matched and not one missing.
Isa 37: 11 You know p well what the kings of Assyria have
Hab 1: 13 You are p just in this. But will you, who cannot
Mt 11: 30 For my yoke fits p, and the burden I give you is
Mk 5: 15 for he was sitting there fully clothed and p sane.
7: 35 Instantly the man could hear p and speak plainly!
Ro 7: 16 I know p well that what I am doing is wrong,
14: 14 and am p sure on the authority of the Lord Jesus
Eph 4: 16 his direction, the whole body is fitted together p.
Heb 6: 17 so that those who received the promise could be p

PERFORM (28) [PERFORMED, PERFORMING, PERFORMS]

Ex 4: 5 "P this sign, and they will believe you,"
4: 17 so you can p the miraculous signs I have shown
4: 21 and p the miracles I have empowered you to do.
4: 28 told him about the miraculous signs they were to p.
28: 43 or approach the altar in the Holy Place to p their
34: 10 I will p wonders that have never been done before
Lev 14: 4 he will p a purification ceremony, using two wild
14: 19 and again p the atonement ceremony for the person
Nu 8: 22 then on the Levites went into the Tabernacle to p
18: 2 and your sons as you p the sacred duties in front of
18: 5 "You yourselves must p the sacred duties within
Dt 3: 24 or on earth who can p such great deeds as yours?
30: 11 is not too difficult for you to understand or p.
34: 11 The LORD sent Moses to p all the miraculous
Jdg 16: 25 "Bring out Samson so he can p for us!"
1Ch 23: 28 helped p the ceremonies of purification,
2Ch 31: 16 who came daily to the LORD's Temple to p their
Ps 45: 4 and justice. / Go forth to p awe-inspiring deeds!
86: 10 For you are great and p great miracles. / You alone
Isa 41: 23 Or p a mighty miracle that will fill us with
66: 19 I will p a sign among them. And I will send those
Eze 24: 17 Do not p the rituals of mourning or accept any
Mt 24: 24 and p great miraculous signs and wonders so as to
Mk 6: 2 all his wisdom and the power to p such miracles?
13: 22 and p miraculous signs and wonders so as to
Lk 23: 8 and had been hoping for a long time to see him p a
1Co 12: 10 He gives one person the power to p miracles,
Rev 13: 14 And with all the miracles he was allowed to p on

PERFORMED (28) [PERFORM]

Ex 4: 30 and Moses p the miraculous signs as they watched.
7: 10 and they p the miracle just as the LORD had told
Lev 14: 23 p in the LORD's presence at the Tabernacle
16: 32 the atonement ceremony will be p by the anointed
Nu 8: 21 then p the rite of atonement over them to purify
14: 22 and the miraculous signs I p both in Egypt and in
19: 9 This ceremony is p for the removal of sin.
Dt 11: 3 and wonders he p in Egypt against Pharaoh and all
Jos 24: 17 He p mighty miracles before our very eyes.
1Sa 16: 5 Then Samuel p the purification rite for Jesse
2Sa 7: 23 You p awesome miracles and drove out the nations
1Ch 6: 49 and they p all the other duties related to the Most
17: 21 You p awesome miracles and drove out the nations
2Ch 5: 13 and singers p together in unison to praise
Ne 12: 45 They p the service of their God and the service of
Ps 105: 27 They p miraculous signs among the Egyptians,
135: 9 He p miraculous signs and wonders in Egypt;
Jer 32: 20 You p miraculous signs and wonders in the land of
Da 4: 2 and wonders the Most High God has p for me.
8: 27 Afterward I got up and p my duties for the king,
Mt 7: 22 in your name and p many miracles in your name.'
14: 6 Herodias' daughter p a dance that greatly pleased
Mk 6: 22 and p a dance that greatly pleased them all.
Ac 2: 43 and the apostles p many miraculous signs
6: 8 p amazing miracles and signs among the people.
8: 11 He was very influential because of the magic he p.
8: 13 amazed by the great miracles and signs Philip p.
Heb 9: 6 and out of the first room regularly as they p their

PERFORMING (7) [PERFORM]

Ex 10: 1 so I can continue to display my power by p
15: 11 so awesome in splendor, / p such wonders?
Nu 3: 7 p their sacred duties in and around the Tabernacle.
8: 26 fellow Levites by p guard duty at the Tabernacle,
Mk 7: 5 For they eat without first p the hand-washing
Lk 11: 38 p the ceremonial washing required by Jewish
Ac 5: 12 the apostles were p many miraculous signs

PERFORMS (7) [PERFORM]

Nu 16: 30 But if the LORD p a miracle and the ground
Job 5: 9 to understand. He p miracles without number.
9: 10 to understand. He p miracles without number.
Ps 111: 4 Who can forget the wonders he p? / How gracious
Da 6: 27 his people; / he p miraculous signs and wonders
Mk 9: 39 "No one who p miracles in my name will soon be
Jn 11: 47 "This man certainly p many miraculous signs.

PERFUME (27) [PERFUMED, PERFUMES]

Ru 3: 3 take a bath and put on p and dress in your nicest
2Sa 14: 2 mourning clothes and don't bathe or wear any p.
Pr 27: 9 The heartfelt counsel of a friend is as sweet as p
Ecc 7: 1 is more valuable than the most expensive p.
10: 1 Dead flies will cause even a bottle of p to stink!
SS 1: 12 on his couch, enchanted by the fragrance of my p.
4: 10 Your p is more fragrant than the richest of spices.
4: 14 myrrh and aloes, p from every incense tree,
4: 16 on my garden and waft its lovely p to my lover.
5: 5 My hands dripped with p, my fingers with lovely
Isa 3: 24 Instead of smelling of sweet p, they will stink.
57: 9 have given olive oil and p to Molech as your gift.
Am 6: 6 and you p yourselves with exotic fragrances,
Mt 26: 7 woman came in with a beautiful jar of expensive p
26: 12 She has poured this p on me to prepare my body
Mk 14: 3 woman came in with a beautiful jar of expensive p.
14: 3 She broke the seal and poured the p over his head.
14: 4 "Why was this expensive p wasted?" they asked.
Lk 7: 37 and brought a beautiful jar filled with expensive p.
7: 38 she kept kissing his feet and putting p on them.
7: 46 my head, but she has anointed my feet with rare p.
Jn 11: 2 This is the Mary who poured the expensive p on
12: 3 Then Mary took a twelve-ounce jar of expensive p
12: 5 "That p was worth a small fortune. It should have
2Co 2: 14 and to spread the Good News like a sweet p.
2: 16 those who are being saved we are a life-giving p.
Eph 5: 2 because that sacrifice was like sweet p to him.

PERFUMED (6) [PERFUME]

2Ch 16: 14 He was laid on a bed p with sweet spices
Ps 45: 8 Your robes are p with myrrh, aloes, and cassia.
Pr 7: 17 I've p my bed with myrrh, aloes, and cinnamon.
SS 5: 13 His lips are like p lilies. His breath is like myrrh.
Eze 20: 41 you will be as pleasing to me as an offering of p
Rev 18: 12 scarlet cloth, every kind of p wood, ivory goods,

PERFUMES (7) [PERFUME]

1Sa 8: 13 force them to cook and bake and make p for him.
Ne 3: 8 Beyond him was Hananiah, a manufacturer of p.
Est 2: 12 followed by six months with special p
SS 4: 13 orchard bearing precious fruit, with the rarest of p:
Isa 3: 20 their scarves, ankle chains, sashes, p, and charms;
Jer 6: 20 Keep your expensive p! I cannot accept your burnt
Eze 20: 28 They brought their p and incense and poured out

PERGA (2)

Ac 13: 13 ship for Pamphylia, landing at the port town of P.
14: 25 They preached again in P, then went on to Attalia.

PERGAMUM (2)

Rev 1: 11 Ephesus, Smyrna, P, Thyatira, Sardis,
2: 12 "Write this letter to the angel of the church in P.

PERHAPS (49)

Ge 16: 2 P I can have children through her." And Abram
32: 8 Esau attacks one group, p the other can escape."
32: 20 "P," Jacob hoped, "he will be friendly to us."
Ex 32: 30 P I will be able to obtain forgiveness for you."
Nu 22: 6 Then p I will be able to conquer them and drive
22: 11 P then I will be able to conquer them and drive
23: 27 P it will please God to let you curse them from
Dt 7: 17 P you will think to yourselves, 'How can we ever
1Sa 6: 5 P then he will stop afflicting you, your gods,

9: 6 go find him. **P** he can tell us which way to go."
14: 6 "**P** the LORD will help us, for nothing can hinder
24:12 **P** the LORD will punish you for what you are
2Sa 12:22 '**P** the LORD will be gracious to me and let the
14:15 I said to myself, '**P** the king will listen to me
16:12 And **p** the LORD will see that I am being
1Ki 18:27 **P** he is deep in thought, or he is relieving himself.
20:31 our heads. Then **p** King Ahab will let you live."
2Ki 2:16 **P** the Spirit of the LORD has left him on some
18:22 "But **p** you will say, 'We are trusting in the
19: 4 But **p** the LORD your God has heard the Assyrian
Job 1: 5 "**P** my children have sinned and have cursed God
Ecc 5:11 except **p** to watch it run through your fingers!
11: 6 you never know which will grow—**p** they all will.
Isa 26:11 **P** then they will be ashamed. / Let your fire
36: 7 "But **p** you will say, 'We are trusting in the
37: 4 But **p** the LORD your God has heard the Assyrian
Jer 21: 2 **P** the LORD will be gracious and do a mighty
21: 2 **P** he will force Nebuchadnezzar to withdraw his
26: 3 **P** they will listen and turn from their evil ways.
36: 3 **P** the people of Judah will repent if they see in
36: 7 **P** even yet they will turn from their evil ways
51: 8 and give her medicine. **P** she can yet be healed.
Eze 12: 3 for **p** they will even yet consider what this means,
Da 4:27 to the poor. **P** then you will continue to prosper."
Joel 2:14 **P** even yet he will give you a reprieve, sending you
2:14 **P** he will give you so much that you will be able to
Am 5:15 **P** even yet the LORD God Almighty will have
Jnh 3: 9 **P** even yet God will have pity on us and hold back
Zep 2: 3 **P** even yet the LORD will protect you from his
Mt 7: 5 then **p** you will see well enough to deal with the
Lk 6:42 then **p** you will see well enough to deal with the
Ac 4:17 But **p** we can stop them from spreading their
8:22 to the Lord. **P** he will forgive your evil thoughts,
17:27 and **p** feel their way toward him and find him—
23: 9 "**P** a spirit or an angel spoke to him."
1Co 16: 6 **p** all winter, and then you can send me on my way
2Co 12:19 **P** you think we are saying all this just to defend
2Ti 2:25 **P** God will change those people's hearts, and they
Phm 1:15 **P** you could think of it this way: Onesimus ran

PERIL (1) [PERILOUS]

Ps 31: 3 For the honor of your name, lead me out of this **p**.

PERILOUS (1) [PERIL]

Da 9:25 and strong defenses, despite the **p** times.

PERIOD (29) [PERIODS]

Ge 31:35 Rachel explained. "I'm having my monthly **p**."
41:29 The next seven years will be a **p** of great prosperity
50: 3 and there was a **p** of national mourning for seventy
50: 4 When the **p** of mourning was over,
50:10 with a seven-day **p** of mourning for Joseph's
Lev 12: 2 just as she is defiled during her menstrual **p**.
12: 5 just as she is defiled during her menstrual **p**.
15:13 he must count off a **p** of seven days.
15:19 "Whenever a woman has her menstrual **p**, she will
15:25 continues for many days beyond the normal **p**,
15:26 just as it would be during her normal menstrual **p**.
15:28 she must count off a **p** of seven days.
15:33 with a woman during her monthly menstrual **p**;
15:33 has had intercourse with a woman during her **p**."
18:19 with her during her **p** of menstrual impurity.
Nu 6: 6 during the entire **p** of their vow to the LORD,
Dt 34: 8 until the customary **p** of mourning was over.
Jos 11:21 During this **p**, Joshua destroyed all the descendants
2Sa 11: 4 the purification rites after having her menstrual **p**.)
11:27 When the **p** of mourning was over, David sent for
2Ch 14: 5 So Asa's kingdom enjoyed a **p** of peace.
Eze 18: 6 intercourse with a woman during her menstrual **p**.
Da 1: 5 They were to be trained for a three-year **p**, and
1:18 When the three-year training **p** ordered by the king
9:24 "A **p** of seventy sets of seven has been decreed for
9:26 "After this **p** of sixty-two sets of seven,
9:27 He will make a treaty with the people for a **p** of
Zec 2: 8 "After a **p** of glory, the LORD Almighty sent me
Ac 13:31 And he appeared over a **p** of many days to those

PERIODS (5) [PERIOD]

1Ch 9:25 villages came to share their duties for seven-day **p**.
Da 4:16 For seven **p** of time, let him have the mind of an
4:23 with the animals of the field for seven **p** of time.'
4:25 Seven **p** of time will pass while you live this way,
4:32 Seven **p** of time will pass while you live this way,

PERISH (32) [PERISHABLE, PERISHED, PERISHING]

1Sa 2: 9 his godly ones, / but the wicked will **p** in darkness.
Job 4: 7 "Stop and think! Does the innocent person **p**?
4: 9 They **p** by a breath from God. They vanish in a
6:18 nothing there to drink, and so they **p** in the desert.
18:17 All memory of their existence will **p** from the
20: 7 yet he will **p** forever, thrown away like his own
36:12 they will **p** in battle and die from lack of
Ps 37:20 But the wicked will **p**. / The LORD's enemies are
37:28 but the children of the wicked will **p**.
68: 2 in fire. / Let the wicked **p** in the presence of God.
73:27 But those who desert him will **p**, / for you destroy
80:16 May they **p** at the sight of your frown.
92: 9 Your enemies, LORD, will surely **p**;
102:26 Even they will **p**, but you remain forever;
Pr 11: 7 When the wicked die, their hopes all **p**, for they
12: 7 The wicked **p** and are gone, but the children of the
14:11 The house of the wicked will **p**, but the tent of the
Hos 9:11 or **p** in the womb or never even be conceived.
Mt 18:14 will that even one of these little ones should **p**.
Lk 13: 3 And you will also **p** unless you turn from your evil
13: 5 you again that unless you repent, you will also **p**."
21:18 But not a hair of your head will **p**!
Jn 3:16 so that everyone who believes in him will not **p**
10:28 I give them eternal life, and they will never **p**.
11:26 eternal life for believing in me and will never **p**.
Ac 8:20 "May your money **p** with you for thinking God's
27:34 own good. For not a hair of your heads will **p**."
Ro 8:13 For if you keep on following it, you will **p**. But if
Heb 1:11 Even they will **p**, but you remain forever.
2Pe 3: 7 the day of judgment, when ungodly people will **p**.
3: 9 He does not want anyone to **p**, so he is giving more
Jude 1:11 like Korah, they will **p** because of their rebellion.

PERISHABLE (5) [PERISH]

Jn 6:27 shouldn't be so concerned about **p** things like food.
1Co 15:50 These **p** bodies of ours are not able to live forever.
15:53 For our **p** earthly bodies must be transformed into
15:54 when our **p** earthly bodies have been transformed
2Co 4: 7 is held in **p** containers, that is, in our weak bodies.

PERISHED (1) [PERISH]

1Co 15:18 all who have died believing in Christ have **p**!

PERISHING (4) [PERISH]

Pr 31: 8 for themselves; ensure justice for those who are **p**.
2Co 2:15 differently by those being saved and by those **p**.
2:16 To those who are **p** we are a fearful smell of death
4: 3 is veiled from anyone, it is a sign that they are **p**.

PERIZZITES (23)

Ge 13: 7 time Canaanites and **P** were also living in the land.
15:20 Hittites, **P**, Rephaites,
34:30 of this land—among all the Canaanites and **P**.
Ex 3: 8 Hittites, Amorites, **P**, Hivites, and Jebusites live.
3:17 Hittites, Amorites, **P**, Hivites, and Jebusites—
23:23 Hittites, **P**, Canaanites, Hivites, and Jebusites,
33: 2 Amorites, Hittites, **P**, Hivites, and Jebusites.
34:11 the Amorites, Canaanites, Hittites, **P**, Hivites,
Dt 7: 1 Girgashites, Amorites, Canaanites, **P**, Hivites,
20:17 Amorites, Canaanites, **P**, Hivites, and Jebusites,
Jos 3:10 Hittites, Hivites, **P**, Girgashites, Amorites,
9: 1 Amorites, Canaanites, **P**, Hivites, and Jebusites,
11: 3 the kings of the Hittites; the kings of the **P**;
12: 8 the Amorites, the Canaanites, the **P**, the Hivites,
17:15 out land for yourselves in the forest where the **P**
24:11 the **P**, the Canaanites, the Hittites, the Girgashites,
Jdg 1: 4 gave them victory over the Canaanites and **P**,
1: 5 and the Canaanites and **P** were defeated.
3: 5 Hittites, Amorites, **P**, Hivites, and Jebusites,
1Ki 9:20 Hittites, **P**, Hivites, and Jebusites.
2Ch 8: 7 Amorites, **P**, Hivites, and Jebusites.
Ezr 9: 1 Hittites, **P**, Jebusites, Ammonites, Moabites,
Ne 9: 8 Hittites, Amorites, **P**, Jebusites, and Girgashites.

PERMANENT (48) [PERMANENTLY]

Ge 9:13 It is the sign of my **p** promise to you and to all the
13:15 land to you and your offspring as a **p** possession.
23: 9 so I may have a **p** burial place for my family."
23:18 They became Abraham's **p** possession by the
23:20 sold to Abraham by the Hittites as a **p** burial place.
49:30 bought from Ephron the Hittite for a **p** burial place.
50:13 This is the cave that Abraham had bought for a **p**
Ex 12:17 This festival will be a **p** regulation for you, to be
12:24 these instructions are **p** and must be observed by
17:14 "Write this down as a **p** record, and announce it to
27:21 This is a **p** law for the people of Israel, and it must
28:43 This law is **p** for Aaron and his descendants.
30:21 This is a **p** law for Aaron and his descendants,
31:17 It is a **p** sign of my covenant with them. For in six
Lev 3:17 This is a **p** law for you and all your descendants,
10: 9 This is a **p** law for you, and it must be kept by all
16:29 This is a **p** law for you, and it applies to those who
16:31 spend the day in fasting. This is a **p** law for you.
16:34 This is a **p** law for you, to make atonement for the
17: 7 This is a **p** law for them, to be kept generation after
23:14 This is a **p** law for you, and it must be observed
23:21 This is a **p** law for you, and it must be observed
23:31 This is a **p** law for you, and it must be observed
23:41 This is a **p** law for you, and it must be kept by all
24: 3 This is a **p** law for you, and it must be kept by all
25:23 the land must never be sold on a **p** basis because it
25:30 city will become the **p** property of the buyer.
25:34 may never be sold. It is their **p** ancestral property.
25:46 passing them on to your children as a **p**
Nu 10: 8 This is a **p** law to be followed from generation to
15:15 subject to the same laws. This is a **p** law for you.
18:23 any offenses against it. This is a **p** law among you.
19:10 This is a **p** law for the people of Israel and any
19:21 This is a **p** law. Those who sprinkle the water of
35:29 These are **p** laws for you to observe from
Jos 4: 7 These stones will stand as a **p** memorial among the
8:28 So Ai became a **p** mound of ruins, desolate to this
24:25 committing them to a **p** and binding contract
Ru 3: 1 it's time that I found a **p** home for you,
2Sa 7:10 And I have provided a **p** homeland for my people
1Ki 2: 7 Make them **p** guests of the king, for they took care
1Ch 17: 9 And I have provided a **p** homeland for my people
28: 8 and leave it to your children as a **p** inheritance.
Eze 46:14 to moisten the flour. This will be a **p** law for you.
46:17 Only the gifts given to the prince's sons will be **p**.
Lk 16:17 It is stronger and more **p** than heaven and earth.
Jn 8:35 A slave is not a **p** member of the family, but a son
Ac 7:46 and asked for the privilege of building a **p** Temple

PERMANENTLY (5) [PERMANENT]

Ex 25:15 be taken from the rings; they are to be left there **p**.
Nu 17:10 "Place Aaron's staff **p** before the Ark of the
1Sa 1:22 and leave him there with the LORD **p**."
1Ch 28: 2 LORD's covenant, God's footstool, could rest **p**.
Ps 77: 8 love gone forever? / Have his promises **p** failed?

PERMEATED (2)

Mt 13:33 of flour, the yeast **p** every part of the dough."
Lk 13:21 of flour, the yeast **p** every part of the dough."

PERMISSION (19) [PERMIT]

Ge 47: 4 We request **p** to live in the land of Goshen."
Ex 4:18 "With your **p**," Moses said, "I would like to go
6:27 They are the ones who went to Pharaoh to ask **p** to
Dt 2:28 All we want is **p** to pass through your land.
Jdg 11:17 king of Edom asking for **p** to pass through his land.
11:17 Then they asked the king of Moab for similar **p**,
11:19 asking for **p** to cross through his land to get to their
1Sa 20: 6 tell him I asked **p** to go home to Bethlehem for an
Ezr 3: 7 Sea to Joppa, for King Cyrus had given **p** for this.
5: 3 "Who gave you **p** to rebuild this Temple
5: 9 'Who gave you **p** to rebuild this Temple
Ne 13: 6 of Babylon, though I later received his **p** to return.
Est 9:13 give the Jews in Susa **p** to do again tomorrow as
La 3:37 Can anything happen without the Lord's **p**?
Da 1: 8 He asked the chief official for **p** to eat other things
Mk 5:13 Jesus gave them **p**. So the evil spirits came out of
Lk 8:32 to let them enter into the pigs. Jesus gave them **p**.
Jn 19:38 asked Pilate for **p** to take Jesus' body down.
19:38 When Pilate gave him **p**, he came and took the

PERMIT (8) [PERMISSION, PERMITS, PERMITTED, PERMITTING]

Ex 12:23 He will not **p** the Destroyer to enter and strike
Ezr 4:22 for we must not **p** the situation to get out of
Ps 55:22 of you. / He will not **p** the godly to slip and fall.
94:20 their side— / leaders who **p** injustice by their laws?
Mt 24:43 stay alert and not **p** the house to be broken into.
Lk 12:39 coming would not **p** the house to be broken into.
Ac 28: 4 he escaped the sea, justice will not **p** him to live."
Heb 7:12 is changed, the law must also be changed to **p** it.

PERMITS (1) [PERMIT]

Isa 41: 2 and **p** him to trample their kings underfoot.

PERMITTED (17) [PERMIT]

Lev 11:39 "If an animal that is **p** for eating dies and you
14: 4 using two wild birds of a kind **p** for food,
Ne 13: 1 or Moabite should ever be **p** to enter the assembly
Eze 44:25 brother, or unmarried sister. In such cases it is **p**.
Mt 13:11 "You have been **p** to understand the secrets of the
15:27 "but even dogs are **p** to eat crumbs that fall
19: 8 "Moses **p** divorce as a concession to your
Mk 4:11 "You are **p** to understand the secret about the
10: 4 "Well, he **p** it," they replied. "He said a man
11: 6 had told them to say, and they were **p** to take it.
Lk 8:10 "You have been **p** to understand the secrets of the
14: 3 is it **p** in the law to heal people on the Sabbath day,
Jn 18:31 "Only the Romans are **p** to execute someone,"
Ac 14:16 In earlier days he **p** all the nations to go their own
28:16 Paul was **p** to have his own private lodging,
Rev 13:15 He was **p** to give life to this statue so that it could
19: 8 She is **p** to wear the finest white linen."

PERMITTING (2) [PERMIT]

Ne 13:18 by **p** the Sabbath to be desecrated in this way!"
Rev 2:20 You are **p** that woman—that Jezebel who calls

PERPETUAL (2)

Ps 9: 6 have met their doom; / their cities are **p** ruins.
Jn 4:14 It becomes a **p** spring within them, giving them

PERPLEXED (6)

Lk 21:25 in turmoil, **p** by the roaring seas and strange tides.
Ac 2:12 They stood there amazed and **p**. "What can this
5:24 and the leading priests heard this, they were **p**,
10:17 Peter was very **p**. What could the vision mean?
25:20 I was **p** as to how to conduct an investigation of
2Co 4: 8 We are **p**, but we don't give up and quit.

PERSECUTE (15) [PERSECUTED, PERSECUTING, PERSECUTION, PERSECUTIONS, PERSECUTORS]

Job 19:22 Why must you **p** me as God does? Why aren't you
30:21 cruel toward me. You **p** me with your great power.
Ps 119:84 I wait? / When will you punish those who **p** me?
119:157 Many **p** and trouble me, / yet I have not swerved
140:12 I know the LORD will surely help those they **p**;
Jer 17:18 Bring shame and terror on all who **p** me, but give
Mt 5:44 love your enemies! Pray for those who **p** you!
Lk 11:49 to them, and they will kill some and **p** the others.'
Jn 15:20 they persecuted me, naturally they will **p** you.
Ac 7:52 Name one prophet your ancestors didn't **p**!
12: 1 About that time King Herod Agrippa began to **p**
Ro 12:14 If people **p** you because you are a Christian,
Gal 1:23 "The one who used to **p** us now preaches the very
5:11 as some say I do—why would the Jews **p** me?

2Th 1: 6 and in his justice he will punish those who **p** you.

PERSECUTED (27) [PERSECUTE]

Ps 109:16 all kindness to others; / he **p** the poor and needy,
129: 1 From my earliest youth my enemies have **p** me—
129: 2 from my earliest youth my enemies have **p** me,
Isa 14: 6 You **p** the people with unceasing blows of rage
Am 9: 9 "For I have commanded that Israel be **p** by the
Mt 5:10 God blesses those who are **p** because they live for
5:11 and **p** and lied about because you are my
5:12 And remember, the ancient prophets were **p**, too.
10:23 When you are **p** in one town, flee to the next.
13:21 or are **p** because they believe the word.
24: 9 "Then you will be arrested, **p**, and killed. You will
Mk 4:17 or are **p** because they believe the word.
Jn 15:20 Since they **p** me, naturally they will persecute you.
Ac 9:21 "Isn't this the same man who **p** Jesus' followers
22: 4 And I **p** the followers of the Way, hounding some
Ro 8:35 loves us if we have trouble or calamity, or are **p**,
1Co 15: 9 an apostle after the way I **p** the church of God.
Gal 1:13 Jewish religion—how I violently **p** the Christians.
4:29 And we who are born of the Holy Spirit are **p** by
4:29 as Isaac, the child of promise, was **p** by Ishmael,
5:11 The fact that I am still being **p** proves that I am
6:12 They don't want to be **p** for teaching that the cross
Php 3: 6 And zealous? Yes, in fact I harshly **p** the church.
1Th 2:15 Now they have **p** us and driven us out.
2Th 1: 7 And God will provide rest for you who are being **p**
2Ti 3:11 You know all about how I was **p** in Antioch,
Rev 2:10 put you to the test. You will be **p** for 'ten days.'

PERSECUTING (7) [PERSECUTE]

Job 19:28 "How dare you go on **p** me, saying, 'It's his own
Ac 9: 4 saying to him, "Saul! Saul! Why are you **p** me?"
9: 5 the voice replied, "I am Jesus, the one you are **p**!
22: 7 saying to me, 'Saul, Saul, why are you **p** me?'
22: 8 'I am Jesus of Nazareth, the one you are **p**.'
26:14 to me in Aramaic, 'Saul, Saul, why are you **p** me?
26:15 the Lord replied, 'I am Jesus, the one you are **p**.

PERSECUTION (9) [PERSECUTE]

Da 11:35 And some who are wise will fall victim to **p**.
Lk 21:12 all this occurs, there will be a time of great **p**.
Ac 8: 1 A great wave of **p** began that day, sweeping over
11:19 **p** after Stephen's death traveled as far as
1Th 2:14 you suffered **p** from your own countrymen.
2Th 1: 5 But God will use this **p** to show his justice. For he
2Ti 3:11 You know how much **p** and suffering I have
3:12 to live a godly life in Christ Jesus will suffer **p**.
Rev 14:12 Let this encourage God's holy people to endure **p**

PERSECUTIONS (4) [PERSECUTE]

Da 11:34 While all these **p** are going on, a little help will
Mk 10:30 sisters, mothers, children, and property—with **p**.
2Co 12:10 and with insults, hardships, **p**, and calamities.
2Th 1: 4 and faithfulness in all the **p** and hardships you are

PERSECUTORS (4) [PERSECUTE]

Dt 30: 7 will inflict all these curses on your enemies and **p**.
Ps 7: 1 my God. / Save me from my **p**—rescue me!
142: 6 for I am very low. / Rescue me from my **p**,
Jer 15:15 Punish my **p**! Don't let them kill me! Be merciful

PERSEVERANCE (1) [PERSEVERE]

1Ti 6:11 godly life, along with faith, love, **p**, and gentleness.

PERSEVERE (1) [PERSEVERANCE]

Rev 3:10 "Because you have obeyed my command to **p**,

PERSIA (25) [PERSIAN, PERSIANS]

2Ch 36:20 and his sons until the kingdom of **P** came to power.
36:22 In the first year of King Cyrus of **P**, the LORD
36:23 "This is what King Cyrus of **P** says: The LORD,
Ezr 1: 1 In the first year of King Cyrus of **P**, the LORD
1: 2 "This is what King Cyrus of **P** says: The LORD,
1: 8 the treasurer of **P**, to count these items and present
4: 3 of Israel, just as King Cyrus of **P** commanded us."
4: 5 went on during the entire reign of King Cyrus of **P**
4: 5 and lasted until King Darius of **P** took the throne.
4: 7 later during the reign of King Artaxerxes of **P**,
4:24 the second year of the reign of King Darius of **P**.
6:14 by Cyrus, Darius, and Artaxerxes, the kings of **P**.
7: 1 during the reign of King Artaxerxes of **P**,
9: 9 he caused the kings of **P** to treat us favorably.
Ne 12:22 During the reign of Darius II of **P**, a list was
Est 1: 3 He invited all the military officers of Media and **P**,
1:14 seven high officials of **P** and Media.
10: 2 *Book of the History of the Kings of Media and P.*
Eze 27:10 Men from distant **P**, Lydia, and Libya served in
38: 5 **P**, Ethiopia, and Libya will join you, too, with all
Da 8:20 ram represents the kings of Media and **P**.
10: 1 In the third year of the reign of King Cyrus of **P**,
10:13 spirit prince of the kingdom of **P** blocked my way.
10:13 there with the spirit prince of the kingdom of **P**.
10:20 fight against the spirit prince of the kingdom of **P**,

PERSIAN (3) [PERSIA]

Est 1:13 who knew all the **P** laws and customs, for he
Da 6:28 the reign of Darius and the reign of Cyrus the **P**.
11: 2 Three more **P** kings will reign, to be succeeded by

PERSIANS (6) [PERSIA]

Ezr 4: 9 the people of Tarpel, the **P**, the Babylonians,
Est 1:19 a law of the **P** and Medes that cannot be revoked.
Da 5:28 has been divided and given to the Medes and **P**."
6: 8 so it cannot be changed, a law of the Medes and **P**,
6:12 it is a law of the Medes and **P**, which cannot be
6:15 that according to the law of the Medes and the **P**,

PERSIS (1)

Ro 16:12 and to dear **P**, who has worked so hard for the

PERSIST (1) [PERSISTED, PERSISTENT]

Ro 2: 7 He will give eternal life to those who **p** in doing

PERSISTED (3) [PERSIST]

Ex 5: 3 But Aaron and Moses **p**. "The God of the
1Sa 17:34 But David **p**. "I have been taking care of my
2Ki 17:22 And the people of Israel **p** in all the evil ways of

PERSISTENT (4) [PERSIST]

Jdg 14:17 he told her the answer because of her **p** nagging.
Ps 15: 4 Those who despise **p** sinners, / and honor the
Eph 6:18 and be **p** in your prayers for all Christians
2Ti 4: 2 Be **p**, whether the time is favorable or not.

PERSON (434) [PERSON'S, PERSONAL, PERSONALLY, PERSONS]

Ge 2: 7 the breath of life. And the man became a living **p**.
9: 5 must die, and any **p** who murders must be killed.
9: 6 you must execute anyone who murders another **p**,
9: 6 for to kill a **p** is to kill a living being made in
25:27 while Jacob was the kind of **p** who liked to stay at
31:32 household gods, let the **p** who has taken them die!
Ex 9:19 Every **p** or animal left outside will die beneath the
16:16 much as it needs. Pick up two quarts for each **p**."
16:18 By gathering two quarts for each **p**, everyone had
16:22 the ground—four quarts for each **p** instead of two.
21:12 "Anyone who hits a **p** hard enough to cause death
21:14 if someone deliberately attacks and kills another **p**,
21:19 If the injured **p** is later able to walk again,
21:22 then the **p** responsible must pay damages in the
21:24 an eye is injured, injure the eye of the **p** who did it.
21:24 knock out the tooth of the **p** who did it.
22: 2 the process, the **p** who killed the thief is not guilty.
22: 9 and the **p** whom God declares guilty must pay
22:14 at the time, the **p** who borrowed it must pay for it.
23: 3 And do not slant your testimony in favor of a **p** just because that **p** is poor.
23: 7 Never put an innocent or honest **p** to death. I will
23: 8 A bribe always hurts the cause of the **p** who is in
30:32 must never be poured on the body of an ordinary **p**,
Lev 6: 5 a penalty of 20 percent to the **p** they have harmed.
7:21 that **p** must be cut off from the community."
13: 3 and the priest must pronounce the **p** ceremonially
13: 4 the priest will put the infected **p** in quarantine for
13: 5 then the priest will put the **p** in quarantine for
13: 6 the priest will pronounce the **p** ceremonially clean.
13: 6 the **p** will be considered free of disease.
13: 7 the infected **p** must return to be examined again.
13: 8 then he must pronounce this **p** ceremonially
13:11 and the priest must pronounce that **p** ceremonially
13:11 the **p** need not be quarantined for further
13:13 the priest must examine the infected **p** to see if the
13:13 he will pronounce the **p** ceremonially clean
13:14 the infected **p** will be pronounced ceremonially
13:16 the rest of the skin, the **p** must return to the priest.
13:17 then the priest will pronounce the **p** ceremonially
13:19 that **p** must go to the priest to be examined.
13:20 then the priest must pronounce that **p** ceremonially
13:21 then the priest is to put the **p** in quarantine for
13:22 the priest must pronounce the **p** ceremonially
13:23 and the priest will pronounce that **p** ceremonially
13:25 then pronounce that **p** ceremonially unclean,
13:26 then the priest is to put the infected **p** in quarantine
13:27 the priest must pronounce that **p** ceremonially
13:28 then pronounce the **p** ceremonially clean.
13:30 the priest must pronounce the infected **p**
13:31 then he must put the **p** in quarantine for seven
13:33 the infected **p** must shave off all hair except the
13:33 Then the priest must put the **p** in quarantine for
13:34 the priest must pronounce that **p** ceremonially
13:34 After washing clothes, that **p** will be clean.
13:35 But if the infection begins to spread after the **p** is
13:36 he must pronounce the infected **p** ceremonially
13:37 then pronounce the infected **p** ceremonially clean.
13:39 skin rash, and the **p** is ceremonially clean.
14: 7 bird's blood seven times over the **p** being purified,
14: 7 and the priest will pronounce that **p** to be
14:10 each **p** cured of the skin disease must bring two
14:11 Then the officiating priest will present that **p** for
14:18 before the LORD for the **p** being cleansed.
14:19 ceremony for the **p** cured of the skin disease.
14:20 the priest will make atonement for the **p** being
14:20 and the healed **p** will be ceremonially clean.
14:21 thus making atonement for the **p** being cleansed.
14:22 The **p** being cleansed must also bring two
14:22 or two young pigeons, whichever the **p** can afford.
14:23 the **p** being cleansed must bring the offerings to the
14:29 the priest will make atonement for the **p** being
14:30 young pigeons, whichever the **p** was able to afford.
14:31 before the LORD for the **p** being cleansed.
17: 4 that **p** will be guilty of a capital offense.
17: 4 Such a **p** has shed blood and must be cut off from
17:10 I will cut off such a **p** from the community,
21:11 must never defile himself by going near a dead **p**,
22:10 even if the **p** lives in a priest's home or is one of
24:19 "Anyone who injures another **p** must be dealt with
24:20 Whatever anyone does to hurt another **p** must be
24:21 but whoever kills another **p** must be put to death.
25:16 the **p** selling the land is actually selling you a
25:26 but the **p** who sold it manages to get enough
25:27 then that **p** has the right to redeem it from the one
27: 2 to the LORD by paying the value of that **p**,
27:28 whether a **p**, an animal, or an inherited field—
27:29 A **p** specially set apart by the LORD for
27:29 be redeemed. Such a **p** must be put to death.
Nu 3:47 collect five pieces of silver for each **p**, each piece
4:19 and assign a specific duty or load to each **p**.
5: 2 or who has been defiled by touching a dead **p**.
5: 6 betray the LORD by doing wrong to another **p**,
5: 7 and returning it to the **p** who was wronged.
5: 8 But if the **p** who was wronged is dead, and there
9: 6 been ceremonially defiled by touching a dead **p**,
9: 7 ceremonially unclean by touching a dead **p**.
12: 3 Now Moses was more humble than any other **p** on
15:27 the guilty **p** must bring a one-year-old female goat
15:28 The priest will make atonement for the guilty **p**
15:28 before the LORD, and that **p** will be forgiven.
18: 7 Any other **p** who comes too near the sanctuary will
19:16 or a grave, that **p** will be unclean for seven days.
19:18 That **p** must sprinkle the water on the tent, on all
19:18 or has touched a **p** who was killed or who died
19:19 and seventh days the ceremonially clean **p** must
19:22 and anyone that a defiled **p** touches will be
26:64 Not one **p** that Moses and Aaron counted in this
35: 6 where a **p** who has accidentally killed someone can
35:16 and kills another **p** with a piece of iron,
35:17 and kills another **p** with a large stone,
35:18 and kills another **p** with a wooden weapon.
35:20 premeditated hostility someone pushes another **p**
35:20 or throws a dangerous object and the **p** dies,
35:21 angrily hits another **p** with a fist and the **p** dies,
35:22 " 'But suppose someone pushes another **p** without
35:22 something that unintentionally hits another **p**,
35:23 though they were not enemies, and the **p** dies.
Dt 2:34 women, and children. Not a single **p** was spared.
15: 9 the loan and the needy **p** cries out to the LORD,
17: 6 But never put a **p** to death on the testimony of only
19: 5 the ax head flies off the handle, killing the other **p**.
19: 6 to chase down and kill the **p** who caused the death.
21: 8 Israel with the guilt of murdering an innocent **p**.'
25: 2 If the **p** in the wrong is sentenced to be flogged,
27:18 'Cursed is anyone who leads a blind **p** astray on
27:24 'Cursed is anyone who kills another **p** in secret.'
27:25 who accepts payment to kill an innocent **p**.'
28:29 just like a blind **p** groping in the darkness,
32:30 How could one **p** chase a thousand of them,
Jos 7:18 Zimri's family was brought forward **p** by **p**,
8:22 of them died. Not a single **p** survived or escaped.
10:28 the king. Not one **p** in the city was left alive.
10:37 the entire population. Not one **p** was left alive.
11:11 Not a single **p** was spared. And then Joshua burned
20: 3 Anyone who kills another **p** unintentionally can
20: 6 But the **p** who caused the death must stay in that
20: 9 Anyone who accidentally killed another **p** could
1Sa 2:25 If someone sins against another **p**, God can
10: 6 with them. You will be changed into a different **p**.
22:23 my own life, for the same **p** wants to kill us both."
27: 9 David didn't leave one **p** alive in the villages he
2Sa 6:20 to the servant girls like any indecent **p** might do!"
19:20 the very first **p** in all Israel to greet you."
23: 3 'The **p** who rules righteously, / who rules in the
1Ki 8:31 "If someone wrongs another **p** and is required to
2Ki 7:10 all in order, but there was not a single **p** around.
11: 8 Any unauthorized **p** who approaches you must be
2Ch 6:22 "If someone wrongs another **p** and is required to
23: 7 Any unauthorized **p** who enters the Temple must
32:12 Surely you must realize that Hezekiah is the very **p**
Ezr 3: 1 all the people assembled together as one **p** in
Ne 8: 1 all the people assembled together as one **p** at the
Job 1: 3 He was, in fact, the richest **p** in that entire area.
4: 7 "Stop and think! Does the innocent **p** perish?
4: 7 When has the upright **p** been destroyed?
4:17 before God? Can a **p** be pure before the Creator?'
8:20 God will not reject a **p** of integrity, nor will he
9: 2 But how can a **p** be declared innocent in the eyes
11: 2 Is a **p** proved innocent just by talking a lot?
11:10 If God comes along and puts a **p** in prison, or if he
11:12 An empty-headed **p** won't become wise any more
15: 7 "Were you the first **p** ever born? Were you born
15:16 a corrupt and sinful **p** with a thirst for wickedness!
16:21 and me, as a **p** mediates between friends.
18:21 They will say, 'This was the home of a wicked **p**,
21:23 One **p** dies in prosperity and security,
21:25 Another **p** dies in bitter poverty, never having
22: 2 to God? Can even a wise **p** be helpful to him?
26: 2 How you have saved a **p** who has no strength!
33: 7 I am not some great **p** to make you nervous
33:12 you yourself have said, 'God is greater than any **p**.'
33:23 from heaven is there to intercede for a **p**,
34:19 He doesn't care how great a **p** may be, and he
Ps 7:12 If a **p** does not repent, / God will sharpen his
69:20 in despair. / If only one **p** would show some pity;
75: 6 from the wilderness— / can raise another **p** up.
92: 6 Only an ignorant **p** would not know this! / Only a
109: 6 Arrange for an evil **p** to turn on him. / Send an
119: 9 How can a young **p** stay pure? / By obeying your
Pr 3:13 Happy is the **p** who finds wisdom and gains
6:19 out lies, / a **p** who sows discord among brothers.
10: 7 of the godly, but the name of a wicked **p** rots away.

10:22 The blessing of the LORD makes a **p** rich, and he
10:31 The godly **p** gives wise advice, but the tongue that
11:12 a neighbor; a **p** with good sense remains silent.
12: 8 Everyone admires a **p** with good sense, but a
12:16 but a wise **p** stays calm when insulted.
12:25 Worry weighs a **p** down; an encouraging word
cheers a **p** up.
13:15 A **p** with good sense is respected; a treacherous **p**
walks a rocky road.
14:12 There is a path before each **p** that seems right,
14:18 but the wise **p** is crowned with knowledge.
15: 2 The wise **p** makes learning a joy; fools spout only
15:14 A wise **p** is hungry for truth, while the fool feeds
15:18 starts fights; a cool-tempered **p** tries to stop them.
15:19 A lazy **p** has trouble all through life; the path of the
15:21 have no sense; a sensible **p** stays on the right path.
15:33 Fear of the LORD teaches a **p** to be wise;
16:25 There is a path before each **p** that seems right,
17:10 A single rebuke does more for a **p** of
17:27 A truly wise **p** uses few words; a **p** with
understanding is even-tempered.
18: 9 A lazy **p** is as bad as someone who destroys things.
19: 2 a **p** who moves too quickly may go the wrong way.
19: 6 everyone is the friend of a **p** who gives gifts!
19:15 A lazy **p** sleeps soundly—and goes hungry.
19:22 Loyalty makes a **p** attractive. And it is better to be
21:11 a wise **p** learns from instruction.
21:16 The **p** who strays from common sense will end up
21:27 God loathes the sacrifice of an evil **p**,
22: 3 A prudent **p** foresees the danger ahead and takes
22:13 The lazy **p** is full of excuses, saying, "If I go
22:16 A **p** who gets ahead by oppressing the poor or by
23:21 to poverty. Too much sleep clothes a **p** with rags.
24: 8 A **p** who plans evil will get a reputation as a
24:30 I walked by the field of a lazy **p**, the vineyard of
25:14 A **p** who doesn't give a promised gift is like clouds
25:19 Putting confidence in an unreliable **p** is like
25:20 Singing cheerful songs to a **p** whose heart is heavy
25:28 A **p** without self-control is as defenseless as a city
26:13 The lazy **p** is full of excuses, saying, "I can't go
26:14 forth on its hinges, so the lazy **p** turns over in bed.
26:21 A quarrelsome **p** starts fights as easily as hot
27: 7 Honey seems tasteless to a **p** who is full, but even
27: 8 A **p** who strays from home is like a bird that strays
27:12 A prudent **p** foresees the danger ahead and takes
27:19 is reflected in water, so the heart reflects the **p**.
27:21 and gold, but a **p** is tested by being praised.
28: 3 A poor **p** who oppresses the poor is like a
28: 8 A **p** who makes money by charging interest will
28: 9 The prayers of a **p** who ignores the law are
28:20 But the **p** who wants to get rich quick will only get
28:22 A greedy **p** tries to get rich quick, but it only leads
29: 9 If a wise **p** takes a fool to court, there will be
29:11 vent to anger, but a wise **p** quietly holds it back.
29:22 A hot-tempered **p** starts fights and gets into all
30:10 Never slander a **p** to his employer. If you do, the **p**
will curse you, and you will pay
Ecc 2:14 For the wise **p** sees, while the fool is blind. Yet I
2:16 For the wise **p** and the fool both die, and in the
4:10 If one **p** falls, the other can reach out and help.
4:12 A **p** standing alone can be attacked and defeated,
5: 8 If you see a poor **p** being oppressed by the
6:10 It was known long ago what each **p** would be.
7: 4 A wise **p** thinks much about death, while the fool
7: 5 It is better to be criticized by a wise **p** than to be
7:19 A wise **p** is stronger than the ten leading citizens of
7:20 There is not a single **p** in all the earth who is
8:12 But even though a **p** sins a hundred times and still
9:17 the quiet words of a wise **p** are better than the
9:18 A wise **p** can overcome weapons of war, but one
12:13 obey his commands, for this is the duty of every **p**.
Isa 10:15 Can the ax boast greater power than the **p** who
10:15 Is the saw greater than the **p** who saws? Can a
29: 8 A hungry **p** dreams of eating but is still hungry.
29: 8 A thirsty **p** dreams of drinking but is still faint
44:19 The **p** who made the idol never stops to reflect,
52:14 so disfigured one would scarcely know he was a **p**.
Jer 4:29 the cities have been abandoned—not a **p** remains!
5: 1 If you can find even one **p** who is just and honest,
23:34 I will punish that **p** along with his entire family.
26:15 lie on you, on this city, and on every **p** living in it.
46:19 will be destroyed, without a single **p** living there.
51:37 and contempt, without a single **p** living there.
La 3: 6 has buried me in a dark place, like a **p** long dead.
Eze 7:13 Not one **p** whose life is twisted by sin will recover.
18: 4 my rule: The **p** who sins will be the one who dies.
18:13 Should such a sinful **p** live? No! He must die
18:17 Such a **p** will not die because of his father's sins;
44:25 in the presence of a dead **p** unless it is his father,
Da 2:30 because I am wiser than any living **p** that I know
Hos 9: 4 just as food touched by a **p** in mourning is unclean.
Am 6:10 And the **p** will answer, "No!" Then he will say,
Ob 1: 8 At that time not a single wise **p** will be left in the
Mic 7: 2 not one fair minded **p** is left on the earth.
Hag 2:13 ceremonially unclean by touching a dead **p**
Mt 5:24 Go and be reconciled to that **p**. Then come
5:38 an eye is injured, injure the eye of the **p** who did it.
5:38 knock out the tooth of the **p** who did it.'
5:39 But I say, don't resist an evil **p**! If you are slapped
7:20 or a **p** is by the kind of fruit that is produced.
7:24 is wise, like a **p** who builds a house on solid rock.
7:26 it is foolish, like a **p** who builds a house on sand.
10:32 I will openly acknowledge that **p** before my Father
10:33 I will deny that **p** before my Father in heaven.
11:11 Yet even the most insignificant **p** in the Kingdom
12:12 And how much more valuable is a **p** than a sheep!
12:35 A good **p** produces good words from a good heart,
12:35 and an evil **p** produces evil words from an evil
12:43 "When an evil spirit leaves a **p**, it goes into the
12:44 Then it says, 'I will return to the **p** I came from.'
12:45 and they all enter the **p** and live there. And so that
p is worse off than before.
13:52 **p** who brings out of the storehouse the new
15:14 and if one blind **p** guides another, they will both
15:18 from an evil heart and defile the **p** who says them.
18: 6 it would be better for that **p** to be thrown into the
18: 7 but how terrible it will be for the **p** who does the
18:15 If the other **p** listens and confesses it, you have
won that **p** back.
18:17 If that **p** still refuses to listen, take your case to the
18:17 but the other **p** won't accept it, treat that **p** as a
pagan or a corrupt tax collector.
19:23 it is very hard for a rich **p** to get into the Kingdom
19:24 than for a rich **p** to enter the Kingdom of God!"
24:17 A **p** outside the house must not go inside to pack.
24:18 A **p** in the field must not return even to get a coat.
Mk 2: 2 visitors that there wasn't room for one more **p**,
8:38 If a **p** is ashamed of me and my message in these
8:38 will be ashamed of that **p** when I return in the
9:23 "Anything is possible if a **p** believes."
9:41 the Messiah, I assure you, that **p** will be rewarded.
9:42 it would be better for that **p** to be thrown into the
10:25 than for a rich **p** to enter the Kingdom of God!"
13:15 A **p** outside the house must not go back into the
13:16 A **p** in the field must not return even to get a coat.
16: 9 and the first **p** who saw him was Mary Magdalene,
Lk 6:39 "What good is it for one blind **p** to lead another?
6:45 A good **p** produces good deeds from a good heart,
6:45 and an evil **p** produces evil deeds from an evil
6:48 It is like a **p** who builds a house on a strong
6:49 and doesn't obey is like a **p** who builds a house
7:28 Yet even the most insignificant **p** in the Kingdom
7:47 But a **p** who is forgiven little shows only little
9:26 If a **p** is ashamed of me and my message, I,
9:26 will be ashamed of that **p** when I return in my
9:59 He said to another **p**, "Come, be my disciple."
11:24 "When an evil spirit leaves a **p**, it goes into the
11:24 it says, 'I will return to the **p** I came from.'
11:26 than itself, and they all enter the **p** and live there.
And so that **p** is worse off than before."
12: 8 will openly acknowledge that **p** in the presence of
12: 9 on earth, I will deny that **p** before God's angels.
12:21 a **p** is a fool to store up earthly wealth but not have
14: 9 The host will say, 'Let this **p** sit here instead.'
14:30 'There's the **p** who started that building and ran
16: 5 "So he invited each **p** who owed money to his
17: 1 but how terrible it will be for the **p** who does the
17:31 On that day a **p** outside the house must not go into
17:31 to pack. A **p** in the field must not return to town.
18:25 than for a rich **p** to enter the Kingdom of God!"
24:18 "You must be the only **p** in Jerusalem who hasn't
Jn 1:45 "We have found the very **p** Moses
4:37 'One **p** plants and someone else harvests.'
13:10 "A **p** who has bathed all over does not need to
16:21 because she has brought a new **p** into the world.
Ac 17:32 of the resurrection of a **p** who had been dead,
Ro 1:17 "It is through faith that a righteous **p** has life."
5: 7 Now, no one is likely to die for a good **p**,
5: 7 though someone might be willing to die for a **p**
5:19 Because one **p** disobeyed God, many people
5:19 But because one other **p** obeyed God, many people
7: 1 don't you know that the law applies only to a **p**
7:24 Oh, what a miserable **p** I am! Who will free me
10: 5 For Moses wrote that the law's way of making a **p**
12: 2 but let God transform you into a new **p** by
14: 2 one **p** believes it is all right to eat anything.
14: 5 Each **p** should have a personal conviction about
14:14 believes it is wrong, then for that **p** it is wrong.
14:20 to eat anything if it makes another **p** stumble.
16: 5 He was the very first **p** to become a Christian in
1Co 1:31 the Scriptures say, / "The **p** who wishes to boast
2:11 anyone else is really thinking except that **p** alone,
4: 2 a **p** who is put in charge as a manager must be
5: 3 Even though I am not there with you in **p**, I am
5: 6 Don't you realize that if even one **p** is allowed to
5: 7 Remove this wicked **p** from among you so that you
5:13 "You must remove the evil **p** from among you."
6:17 But the **p** who is joined to the Lord becomes one
7:38 So the **p** who marries does well, and the **p** who
doesn't marry does even better.
8: 3 But the **p** who loves God is the one God knows
9:24 a race everyone runs, but only one **p** gets the prize.
10:29 of conscience for you, but it is for the other **p**.
11:27 that **p** is guilty of sinning against the body
12: 8 To one **p** the Spirit gives the ability to give wise
12:10 He gives one **p** the power to perform miracles,
12:10 Still another **p** is given the ability to speak in
12:11 He alone decides which gift each **p** should have.
14: 4 A **p** who speaks in tongues is strengthened
14:30 and another **p** receives a revelation from the Lord,
15:45 "The first man, Adam, became a living **p**."
16:22 If anyone does not love the Lord, that **p** is cursed.
2Co 1:18 As surely as God is true, I am not that sort of **p**.
9: 7 For God loves the **p** who gives cheerfully.
10: 1 of you say I am bold in my letters but timid in **p**.
10:10 are demanding and forceful, but in **p** he is weak,
10:11 and forceful in **p** as we are in our letters.
10:17 the Scriptures say, / "The **p** who wishes to boast
11:16 if you do, listen to me, as you would to a foolish **p**,
Gal 1: 9 you welcomed, let God's curse fall upon that **p**.
3:11 "It is through faith that a righteous **p** has life."
5: 9 But it takes only one wrong **p** among you to infect
5:10 God will judge that **p**, whoever it is, who has been
6: 1 and humbly help that **p** back onto the right path.
Eph 2:15 and Gentiles by creating in himself one new **p**
4:24 display a new nature because you are a new **p**,
5: 5 or greedy **p** will inherit the Kingdom of Christ
5: 5 For a greedy **p** is really an idolater who worships
Col 3:13 other's faults and forgive the **p** who offends you.
2Th 2:15 strong grip on everything we taught you both in **p**
1Ti 6: 4 Such a **p** has an unhealthy desire to quibble over
Tit 3:10 After that, have nothing more to do with that **p**.
Heb 3: 3 just as a **p** who builds a fine house deserves more
5:13 And a **p** who is living on milk isn't very far along
7: 7 the **p** who has the power to bless is always greater
than the **p** who is blessed.
9:16 no one gets anything until it is proved that the **p**
9:17 effect only after the death of the **p** who wrote it.
9:17 While the **p** is still alive, no one can use the will to
9:27 And just as it is destined that each **p** dies only once
10:38 And a righteous **p** will live by faith. / But I will
Jas 2: 3 give special attention and a good seat to the rich **p**,
2:10 And the **p** who keeps all of the laws except one is
2:10 guilty as the **p** who has broken all of God's laws.
2:16 but then you don't give that **p** any food or clothing.
5:16 The earnest prayer of a righteous **p** has great power
5:20 you can be sure that the one who brings that **p** back
1Jn 2: 4 that **p** is a liar and does not live in the truth.
3:14 But a **p** who doesn't love them is still dead.
3:17 refuses to help—how can God's love be in that **p**?
4: 2 a human being, that **p** has the Spirit of God.
4: 3 not acknowledge Jesus, that **p** is not from God.
Such a **p** has the spirit of the Antichrist.
4:20 but hates another Christian, that **p** is a liar;
5:16 you should pray, and God will give that **p** life.
2Jn 1: 7 real body. Such a **p** is a deceiver and an antichrist.
Rev 2:23 searches out the thoughts and intentions of every **p**.
6:15 great power, and every slave and every free **p**—
22:18 God will add to that **p** the plagues described in this

PERSON'S (32) [PERSON]

Ex 21:30 the dead **p** relatives may accept payment from the
22: 6 gets out of control and goes into another **p** field,
Lev 13: 3 then examine the affected area of a **p** skin.
14:14 and put it on the tip of the healed **p** right ear,
14:17 in his left hand on the tip of the healed **p** right ear,
14:18 hand will then be poured over the healed **p** head.
14:25 and put some of its blood on the tip of the **p** right
14:28 oil from his hand on the lobe of the **p** right ear,
14:29 priest's hand will then be poured over the **p** head.
24:17 "Anyone who takes another **p** life must be put to
24:18 "Anyone who kills another **p** animal must pay it
Nu 35:12 a dead **p** relatives who want to avenge the death.
Dt 19:12 and handed over to the dead **p** avenger to be killed.
21: 8 Then they will be absolved of the guilt of this **p**
1Sa 16: 7 but the LORD looks at a **p** thoughts
Job 7: 1 A **p** life is long and hard, like that of a hired hand,
22: 2 "Can a **p** actions be of benefit to God? Can even a
Pr 13:23 A poor **p** farm may produce much food,
17: 9 Disregarding another **p** faults preserves love;
17:22 but a broken spirit saps a **p** strength.
18: 4 A **p** words can be life-giving water; words of true
18:20 the right words on a **p** lips bring satisfaction.
20: 5 Though good advice lies deep within a **p** heart,
22:26 Do not co-sign another **p** note or put up a
Ecc 8: 1 Wisdom lights up a **p** face, softening its hardness.
Isa 40:20 Or is a poor **p** wooden idol better? Can God be
Jer 10:23 I know, LORD, that a **p** life is not his own.
13:11 As a belt clings to a **p** waist, so I created Judah
Mk 7:21 For from within, out of a **p** heart, come evil
Jn 3:27 "God in heaven appoints each **p** work.
Col 2:23 when it comes to conquering a **p** evil thoughts
Rev 22:19 God will remove that **p** share in the tree of life

PERSONAL (37) [PERSON]

Ge 39: 1 a member of the **p** staff of Pharaoh, the king of
44: 2 Then put my **p** silver cup at the top of the youngest
44: 5 What do you mean by stealing my master's **p**
Lev 23:38 offerings must be given in addition to your **p** gifts,
Nu 11:28 who had been Moses' **p** assistant since his youth,
Jdg 17:12 So Micah ordained the Levite as his **p** priest,
18: 4 with Micah and that he was Micah's **p** priest.
1Sa 28: 2 "I will make you my **p** bodyguard for life."
2Sa 10: 9 He placed them under his **p** command and led
20:26 Ira the Jairite was David's **p** priest.
1Ki 1: 8 Shimei, Rei, and David's **p** bodyguard.
1:33 to Gihon Spring. Solomon is to ride on my **p** mule.
1:38 and Solomon rode on King David's **p** mule.
2Ki 3:11 is here. He used to be Elijah's **p** assistant."
10:11 all his important officials, **p** friends, and priests.
16:15 The old bronze altar will be only for my **p** use."
18:17 and his **p** representative from Lachish with a huge
18:19 Then the Assyrian king's **p** representative sent this
22:12 court secretary, and Asaiah the king's **p** adviser:
25:19 of the Judean army, five of the king's **p** advisers,
1Ch 19:10 He placed them under his **p** command and led
2Ch 1:11 and you did not ask for **p** wealth and honor
31: 3 The king also made a **p** contribution of animals for
34:20 court secretary, and Asaiah the king's **p** adviser:
35: 7 Then Josiah contributed from his **p** property thirty
Isa 36: 2 Then the king of Assyria sent his **p** representative
36: 4 Then the Assyrian king's **p** representative sent this
42: 6 for I have given you to my people as the **p**
56:11 their own path, all of them intent on **p** gain.
Jer 52:25 of the Judean army, seven of the king's **p** advisers,
Ac 10: 7 and a devout soldier, one of his **p** attendants.
12:20 made friends with Blastus, Herod's **p** assistant,
Ro 14: 5 Each person should have a **p** conviction about this
14:12 each of us will have to give a **p** account to God.
16:18 our Lord; they are serving their own **p** interests.

Gal 6: 4 then you will enjoy the **p** satisfaction of having
3Jn 1:15 Please give my **p** greetings to each of our friends

PERSONALLY (18) [PERSON]

Ge 43: 9 I **p** guarantee his safety. If I don't bring him back
Ex 33:14 the LORD replied, "I will **p** go with you, Moses.
33:15 Then Moses said, "If you don't go with us **p**,
Lev 26:24 and I will **p** strike you seven times over for your
Nu 18: 7 must **p** handle all the sacred service associated
Dt 4:37 and **p** brought you out of Egypt with a great
18:19 I will **p** deal with anyone who will not listen to the
Jos 24:31 those who had **p** experienced all that the LORD
2Sa 17:11 And I think that you should **p** lead the troops.
2Ch 26:16 and **p** burning incense on the altar.
Ps 87: 5 And the Most High will **p** bless this city.
Isa 63: 9 suffering he also suffered, and he **p** rescued them.
Hos 1: 7 I will **p** free them from their enemies without any
Ro 14:10 each of us will stand **p** before the judgment seat of
1Co 14: 4 A person who speaks in tongues is strengthened **p**
Gal 1:22 in the churches in Judea didn't know me **p**.
Col 2: 1 many other friends who have never known me **p**.
1Pe 2:24 He **p** carried away our sins in his own body on the

PERSONS (2) [PERSON]

Ac 7:14 relatives to come to Egypt, seventy-five **p** in all.
2Co 5:17 that those who become Christians become new **p**.

PERSPECTIVE (2)

Lk 18:27 "What is impossible from a human **p** is possible
Ac 5:34 But one member had a different **p**. He was a

PERSPIRE (1)

Eze 44:18 not wear anything that would cause them to **p**.

PERSUADE (6) [PERSUADED, PERSUADING, PERSUASIVE, PERSUASIVELY]

Jdg 19: 3 and an extra donkey to Bethlehem to **p** her to come
Pr 25:15 Patience can **p** a prince, and soft speech can crush
Mt 27: 1 and other leaders met again to discuss how to **p** the
Lk 1:16 And he will **p** many Israelites to turn to the Lord
Ac 21:14 When it was clear that we couldn't **p** him, we gave
2Co 5:11 fear of the Lord that we work so hard to **p** others.

PERSUADED (10) [PERSUADE]

2Ch 24:17 King Joash and **p** the king to listen to their advice.
Job 2: 3 even though you **p** me to harm him without
Jer 20: 7 O LORD, you **p** me, and I allowed myself to be
20: 7 you persuaded me, and I allowed myself to be **p**.
26:24 and **p** the court not to turn him over to the mob to
Mt 27:20 and other leaders **p** the crowds to ask for Barabbas
Lk 15:15 He **p** a local farmer to hire him to feed his pigs.
Ac 6:11 So they **p** some men to lie about Stephen, saying,
17: 4 Some who listened were **p** and became converts,
19:26 this man Paul has **p** many people that handmade

PERSUADING (1) [PERSUADE]

Ac 18:13 They accused Paul of "**p** people to worship God in

PERSUASIVE (3) [PERSUADE]

Pr 16:23 comes wise speech; the words of the wise are **p**.
1Co 2: 4 I did not use wise and **p** speeches, but the Holy
Col 2: 4 so that no one will be able to deceive you with **p**

PERSUASIVELY (1) [PERSUADE]

Ac 19: 8 arguing **p** about the Kingdom of God.

PERTAINS (1)

Da 8:19 What you have seen **p** to the very end of time.

PERUDA (2)

Ezr 2:55 returned from exile: / Sotai, Sophereth, **P**,
Ne 7:57 returned from exile: / Sotai, Sophereth, **P**,

PERVERSE (3) [PERVERT]

Ps 101: 4 I will reject **p** ideas / and stay away from every
Pr 4:24 Avoid all **p** talk; stay far from corrupt speech.
Php 2:15 God in a dark world full of crooked and **p** people.

PERVERSION (2) [PERVERT]

Lev 18:23 order to have intercourse with it; this is a terrible **p**.
Jude 1: 7 with sexual immorality and every kind of sexual **p**.

PERVERT (4) [PERVERSE, PERVERSION, PERVERTED, PERVERTING]

Job 17:12 night is day and day is night; how they **p** the truth!
Pr 17:23 The wicked accept secret bribes to **p** justice.
Isa 5:23 They take bribes to **p** justice. They let the wicked
29:21 And those who use trickery to **p** justice and tell lies

PERVERTED (8) [PERVERT]

1Sa 8: 3 for money. They accepted bribes and **p** justice.
2Ch 19: 7 for the LORD our God does not tolerate **p** justice,
Pr 6:14 Their **p** hearts plot evil. They stir up trouble
8:13 I hate pride, arrogance, corruption, and **p** speech.
La 3:36 They **p** justice in the courts. Do they think the Lord
Hos 10: 4 So **p** justice springs up among them like poisonous
Am 2: 6 They have **p** justice by selling honest people for
Hab 1: 4 and justice is **p** with bribes and trickery.

PERVERTING (1) [PERVERT]

Ac 13:10 will you never stop **p** the true ways of the Lord?

PESTILENCE (1)

Hab 3: 5 **P** marches before him; plague follows close

PESTLE (1)

Pr 27:22 you grind them like grain with mortar and **p**.

PET (1)

Job 41: 5 Can you make it a **p** like a bird, or give it to your

PETALS (3)

Ex 25:33 an almond blossom, complete with buds and **p**.
25:34 four almond blossoms, complete with buds and **p**.
37:19 an almond blossom, complete with buds and **p**.

PETER (191) [CEPHAS, PETER'S, SIMON]

Mt 4:18 Simon, also called **P**, and Andrew—fishing with a
10: 2 first Simon (also called **P**), / then Andrew (Peter's
14:28 Then **P** called to him, "Lord, if it's really you,
14:29 So **P** went over the side of the boat and walked on
15:15 Then **P** asked Jesus, "Explain what you meant
16:16 Simon **P** answered, "You are the Messiah, the Son
16:18 Now I say to you that you are **P**, and upon this
16:22 But **P** took him aside and corrected him.
16:23 Jesus turned to **P** and said, "Get away from me,
17: 1 Six days later Jesus took **P** and the two brothers,
17: 4 **P** blurted out, "Lord, this is wonderful! If you
17:24 the tax collectors for the Temple tax came to **P**
17:25 "Of course he does," **P** replied. Then he went into
17:25 to speak, Jesus asked him, "What do you think, **P**?
17:26 "They tax the foreigners," **P** replied. "Well,
18:21 Then **P** came to him and asked, "Lord, how often
19:27 Then **P** said to him, "We've given up everything
26:33 **P** declared, "Even if everyone else deserts you,
26:34 "**P**," Jesus replied, "the truth is, this very night,
26:35 "No!" **P** insisted. "Not even if I have to die with
26:37 He took **P** and Zebedee's two sons, James
26:40 He said to **P**, "Couldn't you stay awake and watch
26:58 **P** was following far behind and eventually came to
26:69 as **P** was sitting outside in the courtyard,
26:70 But **P** denied it in front of everyone. "I don't know
26:72 Again **P** denied it, this time with an oath. "I don't
26:74 **P** said, "I swear by God, I don't know the man."
Mk 3:16 the twelve he chose: / Simon (he renamed him **P**),
5:37 and wouldn't let anyone go with him except **P**
8:29 you say I am?" **P** replied, "You are the Messiah."
8:32 **P** took him aside and told him he shouldn't say
8:33 at his disciples and then said to **P** very sternly,
9: 2 Six days later Jesus took **P**, James, and John to the
9: 5 "Teacher, this is wonderful!" **P** exclaimed.
10:28 Then **P** began to mention all that he and the other
11:21 **P** remembered what Jesus had said to the tree on
13: 3 **P**, James, John, and Andrew came to him privately
14:29 **P** said to him, "Even if everyone else deserts you,
14:30 "**P**," Jesus replied, "the truth is, this very night,
14:31 "No!" **P** insisted. "Not even if I have to die with
14:33 He took **P**, James, and John with him, and he
14:37 "Simon!" he said to **P**. "Are you asleep?
14:54 **P** followed far behind and then slipped inside the
14:66 Meanwhile, **P** was below in the courtyard. One of
14:67 noticed **P** warming himself at the fire. She looked
14:68 **P** denied it. "I don't know what you're talking
14:70 **P** denied it again. A little later some other
bystanders began saying to **P**,
14:71 **P** said, "I swear by God, I don't know this man
16: 7 and give this message to his disciples, including **P**:
16: S they reported all these instructions briefly to **P**
Lk 5: 8 When Simon **P** realized what had happened,
6:14 Simon (he also called him **P**), / Andrew (Peter's
8:45 Everyone denied it, and **P** said, "Master,
8:51 Jesus wouldn't let anyone go in with him except **P**,
9:20 **P** replied, "You are the Messiah sent from God!"
9:28 About eight days later Jesus took **P**, James,
9:32 **P** and the others were very drowsy and had fallen
9:33 As Moses and Elijah were starting to leave, **P**,
12:41 **P** asked, "Lord, is this illustration just for us
18:28 **P** said, "We have left our homes and followed
22: 8 Jesus sent **P** and John ahead and said, "Go
22:33 **P** said, "Lord, I am ready to go to prison with you,
22:34 But Jesus said, "**P**, let me tell you something.
22:54 priest's residence, and **P** was following far behind.
22:55 and sat around it, and **P** joined them there.
22:57 **P** denied it. "Woman," he said, "I don't even
22:58 be one of them!" "No, man, I'm not!" **P** replied.
22:60 But **P** said, "Man, I don't know what you are
22:61 At that moment the Lord turned and looked at **P**.
22:61 Then **P** remembered that the Lord had said,
22:62 And **P** left the courtyard, crying bitterly.
24:12 However, **P** ran to the tomb to look. Stooping,
24:34 "The Lord has really risen! He appeared to **P**!"
Jn 1:42 but you will be called Cephas" (which means **P**).
6:68 Simon **P** replied, "Lord, to whom would we go?
13: 6 When he came to Simon **P**, **P** said to him, "Lord,
13: 8 "No," **P** protested, "you will never wash my
13: 9 Simon **P** exclaimed, "Then wash my hands
13:24 Simon **P** motioned to him to ask who would do
13:36 Simon **P** said, "Lord, where are you going?"
18:10 Then Simon **P** drew a sword and slashed off the
18:11 But Jesus said to **P**, "Put your sword back into its
18:15 Simon **P** followed along behind, as did another of
18:16 **P** stood outside the gate. Then the other disciple
18:16 the woman watching at the gate, and she let **P** in.
18:17 The woman asked **P**, "Aren't you one of Jesus'
18:18 And **P** stood there with them, warming himself.
18:25 Meanwhile, as Simon **P** was standing by the fire,
18:26 a relative of the man whose ear **P** had cut off,
18:27 Again **P** denied it. And immediately a rooster
20: 2 She ran and found Simon **P** and the other disciple,
20: 3 **P** and the other disciple ran to the tomb to see.
20: 4 The other disciple outran **P** and got there first.
20: 6 Then Simon **P** arrived and went inside. He also
21: 2 Simon **P**, Thomas (nicknamed the Twin),
21: 3 Simon **P** said, "I'm going fishing." "We'll come,
21: 7 Then the disciple whom Jesus loved said to **P**,
21: 7 When Simon **P** heard that it was the Lord, he put
21:11 So Simon **P** went aboard and dragged the net to the
21:15 After breakfast Jesus said to Simon **P**, "Simon son
21:15 "Yes, Lord," **P** replied, "you know I love you."
21:16 "Yes, Lord," **P** said, "you know I love you."
21:17 **P** was grieved that Jesus asked the question a third
21:20 **P** turned around and saw the disciple Jesus loved
21:21 **P** asked Jesus, "What about him, Lord?"
Ac 1:13 **P**, / John, / James, / Andrew, / Philip, / Thomas,
1:15 **P** stood up and addressed them as follows:
1:20 **P** continued, "This was predicted in the book of
2:14 Then **P** stepped forward with the eleven other
2:38 **P** replied, "Each of you must turn from your sins
2:40 Then **P** continued preaching for a long time,
2:41 Those who believed what **P** said were baptized
3: 1 **P** and John went to the Temple one afternoon to
3: 3 When he saw **P** and John about to enter, he asked
3: 4 **P** and John looked at him intently and **P** said,
3: 6 But **P** said, "I don't have any money for you.
3: 7 Then **P** took the lame man by the right hand
3:11 where he was holding tightly to **P** and John.
3:12 **P** saw his opportunity and addressed the crowd.
4: 1 While **P** and John were speaking to the people,
4: 2 They were very disturbed that **P** and John were
4: 8 Then **P**, filled with the Holy Spirit, said to them,
4:13 were amazed when they saw the boldness of **P**
4:15 So they sent **P** and John out of the council chamber
4:19 But **P** and John replied, "Do you think God wants
4:23 **P** and John found the other believers and told them
5: 3 Then **P** said, "Ananias, why has Satan filled your
5: 8 **P** asked her, "Was this the price you and your
5: 9 And **P** said, "How could the two of you even think
5:29 But **P** and the apostles replied, "We must obey
8:14 God's message, they sent **P** and John there.
8:17 Then **P** and John laid their hands upon these
8:20 But **P** replied, "May your money perish with you
8:25 Lord in Samaria, **P** and John returned to Jerusalem.
9:32 **P** traveled from place to place to visit the
9:34 **P** said to him, "Aeneas, Jesus Christ heals you!
9:38 But they had heard that **P** was nearby at Lydda,
9:39 So **P** returned with them; and as soon as he arrived,
9:40 But **P** asked them all to leave the room; then he
9:40 she opened her eyes! When she saw **P**, she sat up!
9:43 And **P** stayed a long time in Joppa, living with
10: 5 men down to Joppa to find a man named Simon **P**.
10: 9 nearing the city, **P** went up to the flat roof to pray.
10:13 Then a voice said to him, "Get up, **P**; kill and eat
10:14 "Never, Lord," **P** declared. "I have never in all
10:17 **P** was very perplexed. What could the vision
10:18 They asked if this was the place where Simon **P**
10:19 Meanwhile, as **P** was puzzling over the vision,
10:21 So **P** went down and said, "I'm the man you are
10:23 So **P** invited the men to be his guests for the night.
10:24 together his relatives and close friends to meet **P**.
10:25 As **P** entered his home, Cornelius fell to the floor
10:26 But **P** pulled him up and said, "Stand up! I'm a
10:28 **P** told them, "You know it is against the Jewish
10:32 send some men to Joppa and summon Simon **P**.
10:34 Then **P** replied, "I see very clearly that God
10:44 Even as **P** was saying these things, the Holy Spirit
10:45 The Jewish believers who came with **P** were
10:46 in tongues and praising God. Then **P** asked,
11: 2 But when **P** arrived back in Jerusalem, some of the
11: 4 Then **P** told them exactly what had happened.
11: 7 And I heard a voice say, 'Get up, **P**; kill and eat
11:13 'Send messengers to Joppa to find Simon **P**.
12: 3 he arrested **P** during the Passover celebration
12: 4 Herod's intention was to bring **P** out for public
12: 5 But while **P** was in prison, the church prayed very
12: 6 The night before **P** was to be placed on trial,
12: 7 in the cell, and an angel of the Lord stood before **P**.
12: 9 So **P** left the cell, following the angel. But all the
12:11 **P** finally realized what had happened. "It's really
12:14 and told everyone, "**P** is standing at the door!"
12:16 Meanwhile, **P** continued knocking. When they
12:18 among the soldiers about what had happened to **P**.
15: 7 **P** stood and addressed them as follows:
15:14 **P** has told you about the time God first visited the
1Co 1:12 are saying, "I follow Apollos," or "I follow **P**,"
3:22 Paul and Apollos and **P**; the whole world and life
9: 5 other disciples and the Lord's brothers and **P** do?
15: 5 He was seen by **P** and then by the twelve apostles.
Gal 1:18 that I finally went to Jerusalem for a visit with **P**
2: 7 just as he had given **P** the responsibility of
2: 8 For the same God who worked through **P** for the
2: 9 In fact, James, **P**, and John, who were known as
2:11 But when **P** came to Antioch, I had to oppose him
2:12 **P** wouldn't eat with the Gentiles anymore
2:14 I said to **P** in front of all the others, "Since you,
1Pe 1: 1 This letter is from **P**, an apostle of Jesus Christ.
2Pe 1: 1 This letter is from Simon **P**, a slave and apostle of

PETER'S (13) [PETER]

Mt 8:14 When Jesus arrived at **P** house,

8:14 **P** mother-in-law was in bed with a high fever.
10: 2 (also called Peter), / then Andrew (**P** brother),
26:75 Suddenly, Jesus' words flashed through **P** mind:
Mk 14:72 Suddenly, Jesus' words flashed through **P** mind:
Lk 6:14 (he also called him Peter), / Andrew (**P** brother),
Jn 1:40 Andrew, Simon **P** brother, was one of these men
1:44 was from Bethsaida, Andrew and **P** hometown.
6: 8 Then Andrew, Simon **P** brother, spoke up.
Ac 2:37 **P** words convicted them deeply, and they said to
5:15 so that **P** shadow might fall across some of them as
12:14 When she recognized **P** voice, she was
Gal 2:13 Then the other Jewish Christians followed **P**

PETHAHIAH (4)

1Ch 24:16 The nineteenth lot fell to **P**. / The twentieth lot fell
Ezr 10:23 Kelaiah (also called Kelita), **P**, Judah, and Eliezer.
Ne 9: 5 Sherebiah, Hodiah, Shebaniah, and **P**—
11:24 **P** son of Meshezabel, a descendant of Zerah son of

PETHOR (2)

Nu 22: 5 who was living in his native land of **P** near the
Dt 23: 4 they tried to hire Balaam son of Beor from **P** in

PETHUEL (1)

Joel 1: 1 The LORD gave this message to Joel son of **P**.

PETITION (4) [PETITIONS]

Nu 27: 1 One day a **p** was presented by the daughters of
36: 1 to Moses and the family leaders of Israel with a **p**.
Est 7: 3 my **p** is that my life and the lives of my people will
Isa 33: 7 for Assyria has refused their **p** for peace.

PETITIONS (1) [PETITION]

Hos 14: 2 Bring your **p**, and return to the LORD. Say to

PEULLETHAI (1)

1Ch 26: 5 Issachar (the seventh), and **P** (the eighth).

PHALEC [KJV] See PELEG

PHALLU [KJV] See PALLU

PHALTI(EL) [KJV] See PALTI, PALTIEL

PHANUEL (1)

Lk 2:36 She was the daughter of **P**, of the tribe of Asher,

PHARAOH (201) [PHARAOH'S]

Ge 12:15 their king, the **p**, and she was taken into his harem.
12:16 Then **P** gave Abram many gifts because of her—
12:18 So **P** called for Abram and accused him sharply.
12:20 **P** then sent them out of the country under armed
37:36 to Potiphar, an officer of **P**, the king of Egypt.
39: 1 a member of the personal staff of **P**, the king of
40: 2 **P** became very angry with these officials,
40:13 Within three days **P** will take you out of prison
40:14 Mention me to **P**, and ask him to let me out of
40:17 top basket were all kinds of bakery goods for **P**,
40:19 Three days from now **P** will cut off your head
41: 1 **P** dreamed that he was standing on the bank of the
41: 4 the fat ones! At this point in the dream, **P** woke up.
41: 7 Then **P** woke up again and realized it was a dream.
41: 8 **P** became very concerned as to what the dreams
41:14 **P** sent for Joseph at once, and he was brought
41:15 "I had a dream last night," **P** told him, "and none
41:17 So **P** told him the dream. "I was standing on the
41:25 dreams mean the same thing," Joseph told **P**.
41:34 Let **P** appoint officials over the land, and let them
41:37 Joseph's suggestions were well received by **P**
41:38 **P** said, "Who could do it better than Joseph?
41:39 Turning to Joseph, **P** said, "Since God has
41:41 And **P** said to Joseph, "I hereby put you in charge
41:42 Then **P** placed his own signet ring on Joseph's
41:43 **P** also gave Joseph the chariot of his
41:44 And **P** said to Joseph, "I am the king, but no one
41:45 **P** renamed him Zaphenath-paneah and gave him a
41:46 thirty years old when he entered the service of **P**,
41:55 They pleaded with **P** for food, and he told them,
42:15 I swear by the life of **P** that you will not leave
44:18 killed in an instant, as though you were **P** himself.
45: 8 And he has made me a counselor to **P**—manager of
45:16 The news soon reached **P**: "Joseph's brothers have
45:16 **P** was very happy to hear this and so were his
45:17 **P** said to Joseph, "Tell your brothers to load their
45:18 '**P** will assign to you the very best territory in the
45:21 Joseph gave them wagons, as **P** had commanded,
46: 5 and wives in the wagons **P** had provided for them.
46:31 and tell **P** that you have all come from the land of
46:33 So when **P** calls for you and asks you about your
47: 1 So Joseph went to see **P** and said, "My father
47: 2 of his brothers with him and presented them to **P**.
47: 3 **P** asked them, "What is your occupation?"
47: 5 And **P** said to Joseph, "Now that your family has
47: 7 and presented him to **P**, and Jacob blessed **P**.
47: 8 "How old are you?" **P** asked him.
47:10 Then Jacob blessed **P** again before he left.
47:11 his father and brothers, just as **P** had commanded.
47:19 for food; we will then become servants to **P**.
47:20 So Joseph bought all the land of Egypt for **P**.
47:20 so severe, and their land then belonged to **P**.
47:21 all the people of Egypt became servants to **P**.
47:22 for they were assigned food from **P** and didn't
47:23 "See, I have bought you and your land for **P**.
47:24 you harvest it, a fifth of your crop will belong to **P**.
47:26 that **P** should receive one-fifth of all the crops
47:26 But since **P** had not taken over the priests' land,
50: 4 and asked them to speak to **P** on his behalf.
50: 5 "Tell **P** that my father made me swear an oath.
50: 6 **P** agreed to Joseph's request. "Go and bury your
Ex 1:15 Then **P**, the king of Egypt, gave this order to the
1:22 Then **P** gave this order to all his people:
2:15 And sure enough, when **P** heard about it, he gave
2:15 But Moses fled from **P** and escaped to the land of
3:10 Now go, for I am sending you to **P**. You will lead
3:11 "But who am I to appear before **P**?" Moses asked
4:21 go to **P** and perform the miracles I have
5: 1 to Israel's leaders, Moses and Aaron went to see **P**.
5: 2 "Is that so?" retorted **P**. "And who is the LORD
5: 4 "Who do you think you are," **P** shouted,
5: 6 That same day **P** sent this order to the slave drivers
5:10 "**P** has ordered us not to provide straw for you.
5:15 So the Israelite foremen went to **P** and pleaded
5:17 But **P** replied, "You're just lazy! You obviously
5:19 Since **P** would not let up on his demands,
5:21 you for getting us into this terrible situation with **P**
5:23 Since I gave **P** your message, he has been even
6: 1 "Now you will see what I will do to **P**,"
6:11 "Go back to **P**, and tell him to let the people of
6:12 How can I expect **P** to listen? I'm no orator!"
6:13 LORD ordered Moses and Aaron to return to **P**,
6:27 They are the ones who went to **P** to ask permission
6:29 Give **P** the message I have given you."
6:30 I'm no orator. Why should **P** listen to me?"
7: 1 I will make you seem like God to **P**. Your brother,
7: 2 I say to you and have him announce it to **P**.
7: 3 But I will cause **P** to be stubborn so I can multiply
7: 4 Even then **P** will refuse to listen to you. So I will
7: 7 at the time they made their demands to **P**.
7: 9 "**P** will demand that you show him a miracle to
7:10 So Moses and Aaron went to see **P**, and they
7:10 Aaron threw down his staff before **P** and his court,
7:11 Then **P** called in his wise men and magicians,
7:14 the LORD said to Moses, "**P** is very stubborn,
7:15 So go to **P** in the morning as he goes down to the
7:20 As **P** and all of his officials watched, Moses raised
7:23 **P** returned to his palace and put the whole thing
8: 1 "Go to **P** once again and tell him, 'This is what the
8: 8 Then **P** summoned Moses and Aaron and begged,
8:10 "Do it tomorrow," **P** said. "All right,"
8:12 So Moses and Aaron left **P**, and Moses pleaded
8:15 But when **P** saw that the frogs were gone,
8:19 the finger of God!" the magicians exclaimed to **P**.
8:20 and meet **P** as he goes down to the river.
8:25 **P** hastily called for Moses and Aaron. "All right!
8:28 "All right, go ahead," **P** replied. "I will let you go
8:30 So Moses left **P** and asked the LORD to remove
8:32 But **P** hardened his heart again and refused to let
9: 1 "Go back to **P**," the LORD commanded Moses.
9: 7 **P** sent officials to see whether it was true that none
9: 8 and have Moses toss it into the sky while **P**
9:10 gathered soot from a furnace and went to see **P**.
9:10 As **P** watched, Moses tossed the soot into the air,
9:12 But the LORD made **P** even more stubborn,
9:13 Go to **P** and tell him, 'The LORD, the God of the
9:27 Then **P** urgently sent for Moses and Aaron.
9:33 So Moses left **P** and went out of the city. As he
9:34 When **P** saw this, he and his officials sinned yet
9:35 **P** refused to let the people leave, just as the
10: 1 "Return to **P** and again make your demands.
10: 3 So Moses and Aaron went to **P** and said, "This is
10: 7 The court officials now came to **P** and appealed to
10: 8 So Moses and Aaron were brought back to **P**.
10:10 **P** retorted, "The LORD will certainly need to be
10:11 And **P** threw them out of the palace.
10:16 **P** quickly sent for Moses and Aaron. "I confess
10:18 So Moses left **P** and pleaded with the LORD.
10:20 But the LORD made **P** stubborn once again,
10:24 Then **P** called for Moses. "Go and worship the
10:28 "Get out of here!" **P** shouted at Moses.
11: 1 "I will send just one more disaster on **P**
11: 1 After that, **P** will let you go. In fact, he will be
11: 4 So Moses announced to **P**, "This is what the
11: 5 from the oldest son of **P**, who sits on the throne,
11: 9 LORD had told Moses, "**P** will not listen to you.
12:29 from the firstborn son of **P**, who sat on the throne,
12:30 **P** and his officials and all the people of Egypt
12:31 **P** sent for Moses and Aaron during the night.
13:15 **P** refused to let us go, so the LORD killed all the
13:17 When **P** finally let the people go, God did not lead
14: 3 Then **P** will think, 'Those Israelites are confused.
14: 4 so I will receive great glory at the expense of **P**
14: 5 three days, **P** and his officials changed their minds.
14: 6 So **P** called out his troops and led the chase in his
14:10 As **P** and his army approached, the people of Israel
14:17 Then I will receive great glory at the expense of **P**
14:18 When I am finished with **P** and his army, all Egypt
14:28 the chariots and charioteers—the entire army of **P**.
18: 4 my helper; he delivered me from the sword of **P**."
18: 8 the LORD had done to rescue Israel from **P**
18:10 he has saved you from the Egyptians and from **P**.
Dt 6:22 blows against Egypt and **P** and all his people.
7: 8 power from your slavery under **P** in Egypt.
7:18 Just remember what the LORD your God did to **P**
11: 3 and wonders he performed in Egypt against **P**
29: 2 own eyes everything the LORD did in Egypt to **P**
34:11 and wonders in the land of Egypt against **P**,
1Sa 6: 6 Don't be stubborn and rebellious as **P**
1Ki 3: 1 Solomon made an alliance with **P**, the king of
11:18 Then they traveled to Egypt and went to **P**,
11:19 **P** grew very fond of Hadad, and he gave him a
11:21 he said to **P**, "Let me return to my own country."
11:22 "Why?" **P** asked him. "What do you lack here?
2Ki 18:21 The **p** of Egypt is completely unreliable!
23:29 While Josiah was king, **P** Neco, king of Egypt,
23:33 **P** Neco put Jehoahaz in prison at Riblah in the land
23:34 **P** Neco then installed Eliakim, another of Josiah's
23:35 the silver and gold demanded as tribute by **P** Neco,
Ne 9:10 displayed miraculous signs and wonders against **P**,
Ps 105:20 Then **P** sent for him and set him free; / the ruler of
135: 9 wonders in Egypt; / **P** and all his people watched.
136:15 but he hurled **P** and his army into the sea.
Isa 19:11 Will they dare tell **P** about their long line of wise
19:12 What has happened to your wise counselors, **P**?
30: 2 You have put your trust in **P** for his protection.
30: 3 But in trusting **P**, you will be humiliated
36: 6 The **P** of Egypt is completely unreliable!
Jer 25:19 I went to Egypt and spoke to **P**, his officials,
37: 5 At this time the army of **P** Hophra of Egypt
44:30 I will turn **P** Hophra, king of Egypt, over to his
46: 2 occasion of the battle of Carchemish when **P** Neco,
46:17 There they will say, '**P**, the king of Egypt, is a
46:25 I will punish its rulers and **P**, too, and all who trust
Eze 17:17 **P** and all his mighty army will fail to help Israel
29: 2 turn toward Egypt and prophesy against **P** the king
29: 3 I am your enemy, O **P**, king of Egypt—you great
30:21 "Son of man, I have broken the arm of **P**, the king
30:22 I am the enemy of **P**, the king of Egypt! I will
30:24 But I will break the arms of **P**, king of Egypt,
30:25 while the arms of **P** fall useless to his sides.
31: 2 "Son of man, give this message to **P**, king of
31:18 This will be the fate of **P** and all his teeming
32: 2 "Son of man, mourn for **P**, king of Egypt, and give
32:31 "When **P** arrives, he will be relieved to find that
32:32 And **P** and his hordes will lie there among the
Ac 7:10 And God gave him favor before **P**, king of Egypt.
7:10 so that **P** appointed him governor over all of Egypt
7:13 to his brothers, and they were introduced to **P**.
Ro 9:17 For the Scriptures say that God told **P**, "I have

PHARAOH'S (45) [PHARAOH]

Ge 12:17 But the LORD sent a terrible plague upon **P**
40: 1 **P** chief cup-bearer and chief baker offended him.
40:11 I was holding **P** wine cup in my hand, so I took the
40:11 the juice into it. Then I placed the cup in **P** hand."
40:20 **P** birthday came three days later, and he gave a
40:23 **P** cup-bearer, however, promptly forgot all about
41:14 of clothes, he went in and stood in **P** presence.
41:46 And when Joseph left **P** presence, he made a tour
45: 2 and the news was quickly carried to **P** palace.
47:14 and he brought the money to **P** treasure-house.
47:17 and donkeys of Egypt were in **P** possession.
47:25 "May it please you, sir, to let us be **P** servants."
50: 4 Joseph approached **P** advisers and asked them to
50: 7 a great number of **P** counselors and advisers—
Ex 2: 5 one of **P** daughters came down to bathe in the
5:20 As they left **P** court, they met Moses and Aaron,
7:13 **P** heart, however, remained hard and stubborn.
7:22 into blood. So **P** heart remained hard and stubborn.
8:18 **P** magicians tried to do the same thing with their
8:19 But **P** heart remained hard and stubborn.
8:24 There were terrible swarms of flies in **P** palace
9:20 Some of **P** officials believed what the LORD
10:27 So the LORD hardened **P** heart once more,
11: 3 He was respected by **P** officials and the Egyptian
11: 8 Then, burning with anger, Moses left **P** presence.
11:10 and Aaron did these miracles in **P** presence,
14: 4 And once again I will harden **P** heart, and he will
14: 8 The LORD continued to strengthen **P** resolve,
14: 9 All the forces in **P** army—all his horses, chariots,
14:23 all of **P** horses, chariots, and charioteers—
15: 4 **P** chariots and armies, / he has thrown into the sea.
/ The very best of **P** officers
15:19 When **P** horses, chariots, and charioteers rushed
Dt 6:21 you must tell them, 'We were **P** slaves in Egypt,
1Ki 7: 8 He also built similar living quarters for **P** daughter,
9:24 After Solomon moved his wife, **P** daughter,
11: 1 Besides **P** daughter, he married women from
11:20 who was brought up in **P** palace among **P**
2Ch 8:11 Solomon moved his wife, **P** daughter,
Jer 37: 7 that **P** army is about to return to Egypt, though he
37:11 left Jerusalem because of **P** approaching army,
43: 9 at the entrance of **P** palace here in Tahpanhes.
Ac 7:21 **P** daughter found him and raised him as her own
Heb 11:24 refused to be treated as the son of **P** daughter.

PHARES, PHAREZ [KJV] See PEREZ

PHARISEE (8) [PHARISEES]

Lk 7:39 When the **P** who was the host saw what was
7:40 "Simon," he said to the **P**, "I have something to
18:10 One was a **P**, and the other was a dishonest tax
18:11 The proud **P** stood by himself and prayed this
18:14 I tell you, this sinner, not the **P**, returned home
Jn 3: 1 a Jewish religious leader named Nicodemus, a **P**,
Ac 5:34 He was a **P** named Gamaliel, who was an expert on
23: 6 so he shouted, "Brothers, I am a **P**, as were all my

PHARISEES (89) [PHARISEE]

Mt 3: 7 But when he saw many **P** and Sadducees coming
5:20 than the teachers of religious law and the **P** do,
9:11 The **P** were indignant. "Why does your teacher eat
9:14 and asked him, "Why do we and the **P** fast,
9:34 But the **P** said, "He can cast out demons
12: 2 Some **P** saw them do it and protested,
12:10 The **P** asked Jesus, "Is it legal to work by healing

12:14 Then the **P** called a meeting and discussed plans
12:24 But when the **P** heard about the miracle, they said,
12:38 of religious law and **P** came to Jesus and said,
15: 1 Some **P** and teachers of religious law now arrived
15:12 "Do you realize you offended the **P** by what you
16: 1 One day the **P** and Sadducees came to test Jesus'
16: 6 "Beware of the yeast of the **P** and Sadducees."
16:11 'Beware of the yeast of the **P** and Sadducees.' "
16:12 or bread but about the false teaching of the **P**
19: 3 Some **P** came and tried to trap him with this
21:45 When the leading priests and **P** heard Jesus,
22:15 Then the **P** met together to think of a way to trap
22:34 But when the **P** heard that he had silenced the
22:41 Then, surrounded by the **P**, Jesus asked them a
23: 2 and the **P** are the official interpreters of the
23:13 will be for you teachers of religious law and you **P**.
23:15 will be for you teachers of religious law and you **P**.
23:23 will be for you teachers of religious law and you **P**.
23:25 will be for you teachers of religious law and you **P**.
23:26 Blind **P**! First wash the inside of the cup, and
23:27 will be for you teachers of religious law and you **P**.
23:29 will be for you teachers of religious law and you **P**.
27:62 the leading priests and **P** went to see Pilate.
Mk 2:16 who were **P** saw him eating with people like that,
2:18 John's disciples and the **P** sometimes fasted.
2:18 "Why do John's disciples and the **P** fast,
2:24 But the **P** said to Jesus, "They shouldn't be doing
3: 6 At once the **P** went away and met with the
7: 1 One day some **P** and teachers of religious law
7: 3 (The Jews, especially the **P**, do not eat until they
7: 5 So the **P** and teachers of religious law asked him,
8:11 When the **P** heard that Jesus had arrived,
8:15 "Beware of the yeast of the **P** and of Herod."
10: 2 Some **P** came and tried to trap him with this
12:13 The leaders sent some **P** and supporters of Herod
Lk 5:17 some **P** and teachers of religious law were sitting
5:21 the **P** and teachers of religious law said to each
5:30 But the **P** and their teachers of religious law
5:33 they declared, "and so do the disciples of the **P**.
6: 2 But some **P** said, "You shouldn't be doing that!
6: 7 and the **P** watched closely to see whether Jesus
7:30 But the **P** and experts in religious law had rejected
7:36 One of the **P** asked Jesus to come to his home for a
11:37 one of the **P** invited him home for a meal.
11:39 "You **P** are so careful to clean the outside of the
11:42 "But how terrible it will be for you **P**! For you are
11:43 "How terrible it will be for you **P**! For how you
11:53 the **P** and teachers of religious law were furious.
12: 1 and warned them, "Beware of the yeast of the **P**—
13:31 A few minutes later some **P** said to him, "Get out
14: 1 day Jesus was in the home of a leader of the **P**.
14: 3 Jesus asked the **P** and experts in religious law,
15: 2 This made the **P** and teachers of religious law
16:14 The **P**, who dearly loved their money,
17:20 One day the **P** asked Jesus, "When will the
19:39 But some of the **P** among the crowd said,
Jn 1:24 Then those who were sent by the **P**
4: 1 Jesus learned that the **P** had heard, "Jesus is
7:32 When the **P** heard that the crowds were murmuring
7:45 to arrest him returned to the leading priests and **P**.
7:47 "Have you been led astray, too?" the **P** mocked.
7:48 a single one of us rulers or **P** who believes in him?
8: 3 and **P** brought a woman they had caught in the act
8:13 The **P** replied, "You are making false claims about
9:13 Then they took the man to the **P**.
9:15 The **P** asked the man all about it. So he told them,
9:16 Some of the **P** said, "This man Jesus is not from
9:17 Then the **P** once again questioned the man who
9:40 The **P** who were standing there heard him
11:46 But some went to the **P** and told them what Jesus
11:47 and **P** called the high council together to discuss
11:57 and **P** had publicly announced that anyone seeing
12:19 Then the **P** said to each other, "We've lost. Look,
12:42 because of their fear that the **P** would expel them
18: 3 and **P** had given Judas a battalion of Roman
Ac 15: 5 then some of the men who had been **P** before their
23: 6 the high council were Sadducees and some were **P**,
23: 7 divided the council—the **P** against the Sadducees—
23: 8 or angels or spirits, but the **P** believe in all of these.
23: 9 Some of the teachers of religious law who were **P**
26: 5 they know that I have been a member of the **P**,
Php 3: 5 What's more, I was a member of the **P**,

PHAROSH [KJV] See PAROSH

PHARPAR (1)

2Ki 5:12 and **P** River of Damascus better than all the rivers

PHARZITES [KJV] See PEREZITE(S)

PHASEAH [KJV] See PASEAH

PHEBE [KJV] See PHOEBE

PHENICE [KJV] See PHOENIX, PHOENICIA(N)

PHENICIA [KJV] See PHOENICIA(N)

PHICOL (3)

Ge 21:22 About this time, Abimelech came with **P**, his army
21:32 Abimelech left with **P**, the commander of his
26:26 Ahuzzath, and also **P**, his army commander.

PHILADELPHIA (2)

Rev 1:11 Ephesus, Smyrna, Pergamum, Thyatira, Sardis, **P**,
3: 7 "Write this letter to the angel of the church in **P**.

PHILEMON (2)

Phm 1: 1 It is written to **P**, our much loved co-worker,
1: 4 I always thank God when I pray for you, **P**,

PHILETUS (1)

2Ti 2:17 Hymenaeus and **P** are examples of this.

PHILIP (33) [PHILIP'S]

Mt 10: 3 **P**, / Bartholomew, / Thomas, / Matthew (the tax
14: 3 Herodias (the former wife of Herod's brother **P**).
Mk 3:18 Andrew, / **P**, / Bartholomew, / Matthew, / Thomas,
Lk 3: 1 his brother **P** was ruler over Iturea and Traconitis;
6:14 Andrew (Peter's brother), / James, / John, / **P**,
Jn 1:43 He found **P** and said to him, "Come, be my
1:44 **P** was from Bethsaida, Andrew and Peter's
1:45 **P** went off to look for Nathanael and told him,
1:46 "Just come and see for yourself," **P** said.
1:48 "I could see you under the fig tree before **P** found
6: 5 Turning to **P**, he asked, "**P**, where can we buy
6: 6 He was testing **P**, for he already knew what he was
6: 7 **P** replied, "It would take a small fortune to feed
12:21 paid a visit to **P**, who was from Bethsaida in
12:22 **P** told Andrew about it, and they went together to
14: 8 **P** said, "Lord, show us the Father and we will be
14: 9 Jesus replied, "**P**, don't you even yet know who I
Ac 1:13 Peter, / John, / James, / Andrew, / **P**, / Thomas,
6: 5 **P**, Procorus, Nicanor, Timon, Parmenas,
8: 5 **P**, for example, went to the city of Samaria
8:13 He began following **P** wherever he went, and he
8:13 by the great miracles and signs **P** performed.
8:26 As for **P**, an angel of the Lord said to him,
8:29 The Holy Spirit said to **P**, "Go over and walk
8:30 **P** ran over and heard the man reading from the
8:31 And he begged **P** to come up into the carriage
8:34 The eunuch asked **P**, "Was Isaiah talking about
8:35 So **P** began with this same Scripture and then used
8:38 went down into the water, and **P** baptized him.
8:39 of the water, the Spirit of the Lord caught **P** away.
8:40 **P** found himself farther north at the city of Azotus!
21: 8 and stayed at the home of **P** the Evangelist,

PHILIP'S (2) [PHILIP]

Mk 6:17 She had been his brother **P** wife, but Herod had
Ac 8:12 But now the people believed **P** message of Good

PHILIPPI (6) [PHILIPPIANS]

Mt 16:13 When Jesus came to the region of Caesarea **P**,
Mk 8:27 and went up to the villages of Caesarea **P**.
Ac 16:12 From there we reached **P**, a major city of the
20: 6 we boarded a ship at **P** in Macedonia and five days
Php 1: 1 It is written to all of God's people in **P**,
1Th 2: 2 You know how badly we had been treated at **P** just

PHILIPPIANS (1) [PHILIPPI]

Php 4:15 you **P** were the only ones who gave me financial

PHILISTIA (14) [PHILISTINE]

Ex 15:14 and tremble; / anguish will grip the people of **P**.
Jdg 10: 6 the gods of Aram, Sidon, Moab, Ammon, and **P**.
1Sa 31: 9 and to the people throughout the land of **P**.
2Sa 8:12 Edom, Moab, Ammon, **P**, and Amalek—and from
1Ch 10: 9 and to the people throughout the land of **P**.
18:11 Edom, Moab, Ammon, **P**, and Amalek.
2Ch 26: 6 towns in the Ashdod area and in other parts of **P**.
Ps 83: 7 and Amalekites, / and people from **P** and Tyre.
87: 4 also **P** and Tyre, and even distant Ethiopia.
Isa 11:14 They will join forces to swoop down on **P** to the
Eze 16:57 by Edom and all her neighbors and by **P**.
25:15 The people of **P** have acted against Judah out of
Joel 3: 4 against me, Tyre and Sidon and you cities of **P**?
Am 3: 9 Announce this to the leaders of **P** and Egypt:

PHILISTIM [KJV] See PHILISTINE(S)

PHILISTINE (73) [PHILISTIA, PHILISTINE'S, PHILISTINES]

Ge 21:34 And Abraham lived in **P** country for a long time.
Ex 13:17 lead them on the road that runs through **P** territory,
Jos 13: 4 and includes the five **P** cities of Gaza, Ashdod,
Jdg 3: 3 the Philistines (those living under the five **P**
14: 1 was in Timnah, he noticed a certain **P** woman.
14: 2 "I want to marry a young **P** woman I saw in
16: 1 One day Samson went to the **P** city of Gaza
16: 8 So the **P** leaders brought Delilah seven new
16:18 told her the truth, so she sent for the **P** leaders.
16:18 So the **P** leaders returned and brought the money
16:23 The **P** leaders held a great festival,
16:27 All the **P** leaders were there, and there were about
16:30 And the temple crashed down on the **P** leaders
1Sa 5: 8 So they called together the rulers of the five **P**
6: 1 The Ark of the LORD remained in **P** territory
6:12 The **P** rulers followed them as far as the border of
6:16 The five **P** rulers watched all this and then returned
6:18 The five gold rats represented the five **P** cities
7: 7 When the **P** rulers heard that all Israel had gathered
13: 4 He announced that the **P** garrison at Geba had been
13:20 or sickles, they had to take them to a **P** blacksmith.
13:23 been secured by a contingent of the **P** army.
14: 4 To reach the **P** outpost, Jonathan had to go down
14:15 Suddenly, panic broke out in the **P** army, both in
14:19 and confusion in the **P** camp grew louder
14:21 Even the Hebrews who had gone over to the **P**
17: 4 Then Goliath, a **P** champion from Gath, came out
of the **P** ranks to face the forces of Israel.
17:16 the **P** giant strutted in front of the Israelite army.
17:21 the Israelite and **P** forces stood facing each other,
17:23 champion from Gath, come out from the **P** ranks,
17:26 "What will a man get for killing this **P** and putting
17:26 "Who is this pagan **P** anyway, that he is allowed
17:32 a thing," David told Saul. "I'll go fight this **P**!"
17:33 "There is no way you can go against this **P**.
17:36 and bears, and I'll do it to this pagan **P**, too,
17:37 of the lion and the bear will save me from this **P**!"
17:49 it from his sling and hit the **P** in the forehead.
17:50 So David triumphed over the **P** giant with only a
17:53 army returned and plundered the deserted **P** camp.
18:25 for the bride price is one hundred **P** foreskins!
18:30 Whenever the **P** army attacked, David was more
19: 5 about the time he risked his life to kill the **P** giant
21: 9 "I only have the sword of Goliath the **P**,
22:10 gave David food and the sword of Goliath the **P**."
23: 3 want to go to Keilah to fight the whole **P** army!"
28: 5 When Saul saw the vast **P** army, he became frantic
29: 1 The entire **P** army now mobilized at Aphek,
29: 2 As the **P** rulers were leading out their troops in
29: 3 But the **P** commanders demanded, "What are
29: 4 But the **P** commanders were angry. "Send him
29: 6 go with us, but the other **P** rulers won't hear of it.
29:11 while the **P** army went on to Jezreel.
31: 3 and the **P** archers caught up with him and wounded
2Sa 21:12 from the public square of the **P** city of Beth-shan.)
21:17 son of Zeruiah came to his rescue and killed the **P**.
23:13 the **P** army was camped in the valley of Rephaim.
23:14 and a **P** detachment had occupied the town of
23:16 So the Three broke through the **P** lines, drew some
1Ki 15:27 and the Israelite army were laying siege to the **P**
16:15 then engaged in attacking the **P** town of
1Ch 10: 3 and the **P** archers caught up with him and wounded
11:15 the **P** army was camped in the valley of Rephaim.
11:16 and a **P** detachment had occupied the town of
11:18 So the Three broke through the **P** lines, drew some
12:19 the **P** leaders refused to let David and his men go
14:16 and he struck down the **P** army all the way from
Isa 14:31 Weep, you **P** cities, for you are doomed! Melt in
20: 1 Sargon of Assyria captured the **P** city of Ashdod,
Jer 25:20 of Uz and the kings of the **P** cities of Ashkelon,
Am 6: 2 city of Hamath and on down to the **P** city of Gath.
Ob 1:19 in the foothills of Judah will possess the **P** plains
Zep 2: 4 these **P** cities, too, will be rooted out and left in

PHILISTINE'S (2) [PHILISTINE]

1Sa 17:54 but he stored the **P** armor in his own tent.)
17:57 Abner brought him to Saul with the **P** head still in

PHILISTINES (189) [PHILISTINE]

Ge 10:14 and the Caphtorites, from whom the **P** came.
21:32 and they returned home to the land of the **P**.
26: 1 to Gerar, where Abimelech, king of the **P**, lived.
26: 8 But some time later, Abimelech, king of the **P**,
26:14 many servants. Soon the **P** became jealous of him,
26:18 which the **P** had filled in after Abraham's death.
Jos 13: 2 The people still need to occupy the land of the **P**
Jdg 3: 3 the **P** (those living under the five Philistine rulers),
3:31 He killed six hundred **P** with an ox goad.
10: 7 and he handed them over to the **P**
10:11 the Amorites, the Ammonites, the **P**,
13: 1 so the LORD handed them over to the **P**,
13: 5 from birth. He will rescue Israel from the **P**."
14: 3 Why must you go to the pagan **P** to find a wife?"
14: 4 creating an opportunity to disrupt the **P**, who ruled
15: 3 blamed for everything I am going to do to you **P**."
15: 5 and let the foxes run through the fields of the **P**.
15: 6 the **P** demanded. "Samson," was the reply,
15: 6 So the **P** went and got the woman and her father
15: 8 So he attacked the **P** with great fury and killed
15: 9 The **P** retaliated by setting up camp in Judah
15:10 The men of Judah asked the **P**, "Why have you
15:10 The **P** replied, "We've come to capture Samson.
15:11 to Samson, "Don't you realize the **P** rule over us?
15:12 come to tie you up and hand you over to the **P**."
15:13 "We will tie you up and hand you over to the **P**,"
15:14 arrived at Lehi, the **P** came shouting in triumph.
15:15 lying on the ground and killed a thousand **P** with it.
15:20 judge for twenty years, while the **P** ruled the land.
16: 5 The leaders of the **P** went to her and said,
16: 9 "Samson! The **P** have come to capture you!"
16:12 "Samson! The **P** have come to capture you!"
16:14 "Samson! The **P** have come to capture you!"
16:20 "Samson! The **P** have come to capture you!"
16:21 So the **P** captured him and gouged out his eyes.
16:28 so that I may pay back the **P** for the loss of my
16:30 "Let me die with the **P**," he prayed.
1Sa 4: 1 At that time Israel was at war with the **P**.
4: 1 camped near Ebenezer, and the **P** were at Aphek.
4: 2 The **P** attacked and defeated the army of Israel,
4: 3 did the LORD allow us to be defeated by the **P**?"
4: 6 "What's going on?" the **P** asked. "What's all the
4: 9 Fight as you never have before, **P**! If you don't,
4:10 So the **P** fought desperately, and Israel was
5: 1 After the **P** captured the Ark of God, they took it
6: 2 Then the **P** called in their priests and diviners
6:17 The five gold tumors that were sent by the **P** as a
6:21 "The **P** have returned the Ark of the LORD.
7: 3 the LORD; then he will rescue you from the **P**."

7: 7 when they learned that the **P** were approaching.
7: 8 with the LORD our God to save us from the **P**!"
7:10 the burnt offering, the **P** arrived for battle.
7:10 and the **P** were thrown into such confusion that the
7:13 So the **P** were subdued and didn't invade Israel
7:13 LORD's powerful hand was raised against the **P**.
7:14 and Gath that the **P** had captured were restored to
7:14 along with the rest of the territory that the **P** had
9:16 He will rescue them from the **P**, for I have looked
10: 5 of God, where the garrison of the **P** is located,
12: 9 Hazor's army, and by the **P** and the king of Moab.
13: 3 and defeated the garrison of **P** at Geba.
13: 3 The news spread quickly among the **P** that Israel
13: 4 and he warned the people that the **P** now hated the
13: 5 The **P** mustered a mighty army of three thousand
13:11 and the **P** are at Micmash ready for battle.
13:12 So I said, 'The **P** are ready to march against us,
13:16 of Benjamin. The **P** set up their camp at Micmash.
13:17 Three raiding parties soon left the camp of the **P**.
13:19 The **P** wouldn't allow them for fear they would
14: 1 let's go over to where the **P** have their outpost."
14:11 When the **P** saw them coming, they shouted,
14:13 and the **P** fell back as Jonathan and his armor
14:16 the vast army of **P** began to melt away in every
14:20 out to the battle and found the **P** killing each other.
14:22 the chase when they saw the **P** running away.
14:31 and killed the **P** all day from Micmash to Aijalon,
14:36 "Let's chase the **P** all night and destroy every last
14:37 So Saul asked God, "Should we go after the **P**?
14:46 Saul called back the army from chasing the **P**, and
the **P** returned home.
14:47 Ammon, Edom, the kings of Zobah, and the **P**.
14:52 The Israelites fought constantly with the **P**
17: 1 The **P** now mustered their army for battle
17: 3 So the **P** and Israelites faced each other on
17: 8 to fight for you, and I will represent the **P**.
17:13 had already joined Saul's army to fight the **P**.
17:19 army at the valley of Elah, fighting against the **P**.
17:51 When the **P** saw that their champion was dead,
17:52 a great shout of triumph and rushed after the **P**,
17:52 and wounded **P** were strewn all along the road
18:17 "I'll send him out against the **P** and let them kill
18:21 another chance to see him killed by the **P**!"
18:27 and his men went out and killed two hundred **P**
19: 8 after that, and David led his troops against the **P**.
23: 1 One day news came to David that the **P** were at
23: 4 to Keilah, for I will help you conquer the **P**."
23: 5 They slaughtered the **P** and took all their livestock
23:27 an urgent message reached Saul that the **P** were
23:28 So Saul quit the chase and returned to fight the **P**.
24: 1 After Saul returned from fighting the **P**, he was
27: 1 The best thing for me to do is escape to the **P**.
27: 7 and they lived there among the **P** for a year
27:11 and again while he was living among the **P**.
28: 1 About that time the **P** mustered their armies for
28: 4 The **P** set up their camp at Shunem, and Saul
28:15 "The **P** are at war with us, and God has left me
28:19 and the army of Israel over to the **P** tomorrow,
29:11 So David headed back into the land of the **P**,
30:16 vast amount of plunder they had taken from the **P**
31: 1 Now the **P** attacked Israel, forcing the Israelites to
31: 2 The **P** closed in on Saul and his sons, and they
31: 4 and kill me before these pagan **P** run me through
31: 7 So the **P** moved in and occupied their towns.
31: 8 next day, when the **P** went out to strip the dead,
31:11 Jabesh-gilead heard what the **P** had done to Saul,
2Sa 1:20 announce the news in Gath, / or the **P** will rejoice.
3:14 for I bought her with the lives of one hundred **P**."
3:18 'I have chosen David to save my people from the **P**
5:17 When the **P** heard that David had been anointed
5:18 The **P** arrived and spread out across the valley of
5:19 asked the LORD, "Should I go out to fight the **P**?
5:20 went to Baal-perazim and defeated the **P** there.
5:21 The **P** had abandoned their idols there, so David
5:22 But after a while the **P** returned and again spread
5:24 is moving ahead of you to strike down the **P**."
5:25 and he struck down the **P** all the way from Gibeon
8: 1 and humbled the **P** by conquering Gath,
19: 9 "The king saved us from our enemies, the **P**,
21:12 and Jonathan had died in a battle with the **P**,
21:15 Once again the **P** were at war with Israel.
21:18 there was another battle against the **P** at Gob.
21:20 In another battle with the **P** at Gath, a huge man
21:22 These four **P** were descended from the giants of
23: 9 and David stood together against the **P** when the
23:10 He killed **P** until his hand was too tired to lift his
23:11 One time the **P** gathered at Lehi and attacked the
23:12 in the middle of the field and beat back the **P**.
1Ki 4:21 from the Euphrates River to the land of the **P**,
2Ki 8: 2 and lived in the land of the **P** for seven years.
18: 8 He also conquered the **P** as far distant as Gaza
1Ch 1:12 and the Caphtorites, from whom the **P** came.
10: 1 Now the **P** attacked Israel, forcing the Israelites to
10: 2 The **P** closed in on Saul and his sons, and they
10: 4 and run me through before these pagan **P** come
10: 7 So the **P** moved in and occupied their towns.
10: 8 The next day when the **P** went out to strip the
10:11 Jabesh-gilead heard what the **P** had done to Saul,
11:13 He was with David in the battle against the **P** at
11:14 in the middle of the field and beat back the **P**.
12:19 and joined David when he went with the **P** to fight
14: 8 When the **P** heard that David had been anointed
14: 9 The **P** had arrived in the valley of Rephaim
14:10 David asked God, "Should I go out to fight the **P**?
14:11 went to Baal-perazim and defeated the **P** there.
14:12 The **P** had abandoned their idols there, so David
14:13 a while, the **P** returned and raided the valley again.
14:15 God is moving ahead of you to strike down the **P**."
18: 1 and humbled the **P** by conquering Gath
20: 4 After this, war broke out with the **P** at Gezer.
20: 4 of the giants, and so the **P** were subdued.
20: 5 During another battle with the **P**, Elhanan son of
20: 6 In another battle with the **P** at Gath, a huge man
20: 8 These **P** were descendants of the giants of Gath,
2Ch 9:26 kings from the Euphrates River to the land of the **P**
17:11 Some of the **P** brought him gifts and silver as
21:16 Then the LORD stirred up the **P** and the Arabs,
26: 6 He declared war on the **P** and broke down the
26: 7 helped him not only with his wars against the **P**,
28:18 And the **P** had raided towns located in the foothills
28:18 its villages, and the **P** had occupied these towns.
Ps 56: T regarding the time the **P** seized him in Gath.
60: 8 be my slave. / I will shout in triumph over the **P**."
108: 9 be my slave. / I will shout in triumph over the **P**."
Isa 2: 6 who practice magic and divination, just like the **P**.
9:12 with Arameans from the east and **P** from the west.
14:29 Do not rejoice, you **P**, that the king who attacked
20: 5 How dismayed will be the **P**, who counted on the
28:21 as he did against the **P** at Mount Perazim
Jer 47: 1 to the prophet Jeremiah concerning the **P** of Gaza,
47: 4 "The time has come for the **P** to be destroyed,
47: 4 Yes, the LORD is destroying the **P**,
Eze 16:27 I handed you over to your enemies, the **P**, and even
25:16 raise my fist of judgment against the land of the **P**.
Am 1: 8 attack Ekron, and the few **P** still left will be killed.
9: 7 I brought the **P** from Crete and led the Arameans
Zep 2: 5 And how terrible it will be for you **P** who live
Zec 9: 6 of Ashdod. Thus, I will destroy the pride of the **P**.
9: 7 All the surviving **P** will worship our God and be
9: 7 And the **P** of Ekron will join my people, just as the

PHILOLOGUS (1)
Ro 16:15 Give my greetings to **P**, Julia, Nereus and his

PHILOSOPHERS (3) [PHILOSOPHY]
Ac 17:18 a debate with some of the Epicurean and Stoic **p**.
17:19 Then they took him to the Council of **P**. "Come
1Co 1:20 So where does this leave the **p**, the scholars,

PHILOSOPHY (1) [PHILOSOPHERS]
Col 2: 8 Don't let anyone lead you astray with empty **p**

PHINEHAS (26)
Ex 6:25 one of the daughters of Putiel, and she bore him **P**.
Nu 25: 7 When **P** son of Eleazar and grandson of Aaron the
25: 8 **P** thrust the spear all the way through the man's
25:11 "**P** son of Eleazar and grandson of Aaron the
31: 6 and **P** son of Eleazar the priest led them into battle.
Jos 22:13 they sent a delegation led by **P** son of Eleazar,
22:30 When **P** the priest and the high officials heard this
22:31 **P** son of Eleazar, the priest, replied to them,
22:32 Then **P** son of Eleazar, the priest, and the ten high
24:33 of Gibeah, which had been given to his son **P**.
Jdg 20:28 and **P** son of Eleazar and grandson of Aaron was
1Sa 1: 3 that time were the two sons of Eli—Hophni and **P**.
2:34 two sons, Hophni and **P**, to die on the same day!
4: 4 Hophni and **P**, the sons of Eli, helped carry the Ark
4:11 and Hophni and **P**, the two sons of Eli, were killed.
4:17 Your two sons, Hophni and **P**, were killed, too.
4:19 the wife of **P**, was pregnant and near her time of
14: 3 Ahitub was the son of **P** and the grandson of Eli,
1Ch 6: 4 Eleazar was the father of **P**. / **P** was the father of
Abishua.
6:50 descendants of Aaron were Eleazar, **P**, Abishua,
9:20 **P** son of Eleazar had been in charge of the
Ezr 7: 5 son of Abishua, son of **P**, son of Eleazar, son of
8: 2 From the family of **P**: Gershom. / From the family
8:33 son of Uriah the priest and to Eleazar son of **P**,
Ps 106:30 But **P** had the courage to step in, / and the plague

PHLEGON (1)
Ro 16:14 **P**, Hermes, Patrobas, Hermas, and the other

PHOEBE (1)
Ro 16: 1 Our sister **P**, a deacon in the church in Cenchrea,

PHOENICIA (5) [PHOENICIAN]
Isa 23:11 He has spoken out against **P** and depleted its
Mk 7:26 Since she was a Gentile, born in Syrian **P**,
Ac 11:19 after Stephen's death traveled as far as **P**,
15: 3 and they stopped along the way in **P** and Samaria
21: 2 boarded a ship sailing for the Syrian province of **P**.

PHOENICIAN (1) [PHOENICIA]
Ob 1:20 and occupy the **P** coast as far north as Zarephath.

PHOENIX (2)
Ac 27:12 most of the crew wanted to go to **P**, farther up the
27:12 **P** was a good harbor with only a southwest

PHRASE (2)
Jer 23:36 But stop using this **p**, 'prophecy from the LORD.'
23:38 Because you have used this **p**, "prophecy from the

PHRYGIA (3)
Ac 2:10 **P**, Pamphylia, Egypt, and the areas of Libya
16: 6 Next Paul and Silas traveled through the area of **P**
18:23 Paul went back to Galatia and **P**, visiting all the

PHUT [KJV] See PUT

PHYGELUS (1)
2Ti 1:15 deserted me; even **P** and Hermogenes are gone.

PHYSICAL (59) [PHYSICALLY]
Ex 12: 5 either a sheep or a goat, with no **p** defects.
29: 1 Take a young bull and two rams with no **p** defects.
Lev 1: 3 bring a bull with no **p** defects to the entrance of the
1:10 bring a male sheep or goat with no **p** defects.
3: 1 you offer to the LORD must have no **p** defects.
3: 6 or female, and it must have no **p** defects.
4: 3 to the LORD a young bull with no **p** defects.
4:23 he must bring as his offering a male goat with no **p**
4:28 as their offering a female goat with no **p** defects.
4:32 sin offering, it must be a female with no **p** defects.
5:15 The animal must have no **p** defects, and it must be
5:18 The animal must have no **p** defects, and it must be
6: 6 This offering must be a ram with no **p** defects
9: 2 both with no **p** defects, and present them to the
9: 3 for a whole burnt offering, each with no **p** defects.
14:10 and one female year-old lamb with no **p** defects,
21:17 his descendants who have **p** defects will not
21:21 his **p** defects disqualify him from presenting
21:23 Yet because of his **p** defect, he must never go
22:19 only if it is a male animal with no **p** defects.
22:20 Do not bring an animal with **p** defects, because it
22:21 you must offer an animal that has no **p** defects of
23:12 **p** defects as a whole burnt offering to the LORD.
23:18 present seven one-year-old lambs with no **p**
Nu 19: 2 to bring you a red heifer that has no **p** defects
28: 3 two one-year-old male lambs with no **p** defects.
28: 9 sacrifice two one-year-old male lambs with no **p**
28:11 one-year-old male lambs, all with no **p** defects.
28:19 one-year-old male lambs, all with no **p** defects.
28:31 Be sure that all the animals you sacrifice have no **p**
29: 2 one-year-old male lambs, all with no **p** defects.
29: 8 one-year-old male lambs, all with no **p** defects.
29:13 one-year-old male lambs, all with no **p** defects.
29:17 one-year-old male lambs, all with no **p** defects.
29:20 one-year-old male lambs, all with no **p** defects.
29:23 one-year-old male lambs, all with no **p** defects.
29:26 one-year-old male lambs, all with no **p** defects.
29:29 one-year-old male lambs, all with no **p** defects.
29:32 one-year-old male lambs, all with no **p** defects.
29:36 one-year-old male lambs, all with no **p** defects.
Dt 4:16 So do not corrupt yourselves by making a **p** image
Pr 20:30 **P** punishment cleanses away evil; such discipline
23:14 **P** discipline may well save them from death.
Eze 43:22 offering a young male goat that has no **p** defects.
43:25 None of these animals may have **p** defects of any
45:18 sacrifice a young bull with no **p** defects to purify
46: 4 of six lambs and one ram, all with no **p** defects.
46: 6 six lambs, and one ram, all with no **p** defects.
46:13 "Each morning a year-old lamb with no **p** defects
Mt 15:30 crippled, mute, and many others with **p** difficulties,
Jn 1:13 This is not a **p** birth resulting from human passion
Ro 9: 8 This means that Abraham's **p** descendants are not
Col 2:11 were "circumcised," but not by a **p** procedure.
1Ti 4: 8 **P** exercise has some value, but spiritual exercise is
5:11 because their **p** desires will overpower their
Heb 12:18 You have not come to a **p** mountain, to a place of
1Pe 3:18 He suffered **p** death, but he was raised to life in the
4: 1 So then, since Christ suffered **p** pain, you must arm
1Jn 2:16 For the world offers only the lust for **p** pleasure,

PHYSICALLY (1) [PHYSICAL]
Job 1:12 everything he possesses, but don't harm him **p**."

PHYSICIAN (2) [PHYSICIANS]
Jer 8:22 Is there no medicine in Gilead? Is there no **p** there?
Lk 4:23 you will quote me that proverb, '**P**, heal yourself'

PHYSICIANS (1) [PHYSICIAN]
2Ch 16:12 the LORD's help but sought help only from his **p**.

PI-HAHIROTH (4)
Ex 14: 2 "Tell the people to march toward **P** between
14: 9 as they were camped beside the shore near **P**,
Nu 33: 7 They left Etham and turned back toward **P**,
33: 8 They left **P** and crossed the Red Sea into the

PICK (25) [GRAPE-PICKING, HANDPICKED, PICKED, PICKER, PICKING, PICKS]
Ge 38:20 to her and to **p** up the pledges he had given her,
Ex 16: 4 and **p** up as much food as they need for that day.
16: 5 Tell them to **p** up twice as much as usual on the
16:16 as it needs. **P** up two quarts for each person."
16:29 Do not **p** up food from the ground on that day."
Lev 11:28 If you **p** up and move its carcass, you must
19: 9 and do not **p** up what the harvesters drop.
19:10 and do not **p** up the grapes that fall to the ground.
23:22 and do not **p** up what the harvesters drop.
Jos 4: 5 Each of you must **p** up one stone and carry it out
Ru 2:16 Let her **p** them up, and don't give her a hard
1Sa 13:21 ounce of silver for sharpening a plowshare or a **p**,
2Ki 13:18 Now **p** up the other arrows and strike them against
Isa 17:11 but you will never **p** any grapes from them.
Jer 6: 9 a second time to **p** the grapes that were missed."
12: 9 Bring on the wild beasts to **p** their corpses clean!
43:12 He will **p** clean the land of Egypt as a shepherd
Eze 39: 9 will go out and **p** up your small and large shields,
Mt 7:16 You don't **p** grapes from thornbushes, or figs from

Mk 2: 9 'Your sins are forgiven' or 'Get up, **p** up your mat,
8: 19 How many baskets of leftovers did you **p** up
8: 20 how many large baskets of leftovers did you **p**
Jn 5: 8 "Stand up, **p** up your sleeping mat, and walk!"
5: 11 said to me, '**P** up your sleeping mat and walk.' "
Jas 3: 12 Can you **p** olives from a fig tree or figs from a

PICKED (27) [PICK]

Ex 16: 21 the food they had not **p** up melted and disappeared.
Dt 1: 25 They **p** some of its fruit and brought it back to us.
24: 21 Do not glean the vines after they are **p**, but leave
Jdg 15: 15 Then he **p** up a donkey's jawbone that was lying
1Sa 17: 40 He **p** up five smooth stones from a stream and put
1Ki 8: 3 leaders of Israel arrived, the priests **p** up the Ark.
2Ki 2: 13 Then Elisha **p** up Elijah's cloak and returned to the
4: 37 Then she **p** up her son and carried him downstairs.
13: 18 So the king **p** them up and struck the ground three
Ps 102: 10 For you have **p** me up and thrown me out.
Isa 6: 6 and he **p** up a burning coal with a pair of tongs.
28: 4 snatched up, as an early fig is hungrily **p** and eaten.
Jnh 1: 15 Then the sailors **p** Jonah up and threw him into the
Zec 5: 9 and they **p** up the basket and flew with it into the
Mt 14: 20 and they **p** up twelve baskets of leftovers.
15: 37 they were full, and when the scraps were **p** up,
27: 6 The leading priests **p** up the money. "We can't put
Mk 6: 43 and they **p** up twelve baskets of leftover bread
8: 8 they were full, and when the scraps were **p** up,
Lk 5: 25 the man jumped to his feet, **p** up his mat,
9: 17 and they **p** up twelve baskets of leftovers!
Jn 8: 59 At that point they **p** up stones to kill him. But Jesus
10: 31 Once again the Jewish leaders **p** up stones to kill
Ac 9: 8 As Saul **p** himself up off the ground, he found that
17: 18 "This babbler has **p** up some strange ideas."
Ro 16: 13 whom the Lord **p** out to be his very own;
Rev 18: 21 Then a mighty angel **p** up a boulder as large as a

PICKER (1) [PICK]

Mic 7: 1 I feel like the fruit **p** after the harvest who can find

PICKING (2) [PICK]

Job 33: 10 God is **p** a quarrel with me, and he considers me to
Hos 7: 8 with godless foreigners, **p** up their evil ways.

PICKS (6) [PICK]

1Sa 13: 20 **p**, axes, or sickles, they had to take them to a
2Sa 12: 31 **p**, and axes, and to work in the brick kilns.
1Ch 20: 3 and forced them to labor with saws, **p**, and axes.
Ps 74: 6 With axes and **p**, / they smashed the carved
Isa 40: 15 He **p** up the islands as though they had no weight
Jer 43: 12 land of Egypt as a shepherd **p** fleas from his cloak.

PICTURE (8) [PICTURES]

Job 21: 24 the very **p** of good health.
Pr 28: 11 Rich people **p** themselves as wise, but their real
Isa 49: 16 Ever before me is a **p** of Jerusalem's walls in ruins.
Mt 22: 20 he asked, "Whose **p** and title are stamped on it?"
Mk 12: 16 he asked, "Whose **p** and title are stamped on it?"
Lk 20: 24 Whose **p** and title are stamped on it?" "Caesar's,"
Gal 3: 1 a signboard with a **p** of Christ dying on the cross.
1Pe 3: 21 And this is a **p** of baptism, which now saves you

PICTURES (3) [PICTURE]

La 2: 14 Instead, they painted false **p**, filling you with false
Eze 23: 14 She fell in love with **p** that were painted on a
23: 14 **p** of Babylonian military officers, outfitted in

PIECE (50) [PIECES, SHOULDER-PIECES]

Ge 23: 4 Please let me have a **p** of land for a burial plot."
25: 25 one would think he was wearing a **p** of clothing.
Ex 25: 19 end of the atonement cover, making it all one **p**.
25: 31 entire lampstand and its decorations will be one **p**
25: 36 and branches must all be one **p** with the stem,
27: 2 of the altar so the horns and altar are all one **p**.
30: 2 with horns at the corners carved from the same **p**
36: 13 Thus the Tabernacle was joined together in one **p**.
36: 18 the roof covering was joined together in one **p**.
37: 8 a part of the atonement cover—it was all one **p**.
37: 17 lamp cups, blossoms, and buds were all of one **p**.
37: 22 and branches were all one **p** with the stem,
37: 25 with its corner horns made from the same **p** of
38: 2 each of the four corners, all of one **p** with the rest.
Lev 9: 13 They handed the animal to him **p** by **p**,
13: 52 burn the linen or wool clothing or the **p** of leather
15: 23 whether it is her bedding or any **p** of furniture.
27: 16 "If you dedicate to the LORD a **p** of your
Nu 3: 47 each **p** weighing the same as the standard
5: 23 Then the priest will write these curses on a **p** of
18: 16 each **p** weighing the same as the standard
35: 16 and kills another person with a **p** of iron,
Jos 19: 49 the Israelites gave a special **p** of land to Joshua as
Jdg 19: 29 Then he sent one **p** to each tribe of Israel.
1Sa 9: 8 the servant said, "I have one small silver **p**.
9: 23 the **p** that had been set aside for the guest of honor.
14: 27 and he dipped a stick into a **p** of honeycomb
24: 4 David crept forward and cut off a **p** of Saul's robe.
24: 11 It is a **p** of your robe! I cut it off, but I didn't kill
1Ki 17: 12 that I don't have a single **p** of bread in the house.
Job 2: 8 Then Job scraped his skin with a **p** of broken
32: 17 No, I will say my **p**. I will speak my mind. I surely
Pr 28: 21 do wrong for something as small as a **p** of bread.
Isa 30: 14 You will be smashed like a **p** of pottery—shattered
so completely that there won't be a **p** left that is
51: 6 and the earth will wear out like a **p** of clothing.
Jer 2: 27 To an image carved from a **p** of wood they say,
Eze 13: 19 me for a few handfuls of barley or a **p** of bread.
45: 1 This **p** of land will be 8-1/3 miles long and 6-2/3
Hos 4: 12 They are asking a **p** of wood to tell them what to
Am 3: 12 mouth will recover only two legs and a **p** of ear.
8: 6 Then you enslave poor people for a debt of one **p**
Mic 2: 2 When you want a certain **p** of land, you find a way
Lk 5: 36 "No one tears a **p** of cloth from a new garment
24: 42 They gave him a **p** of broiled fish,
Jn 19: 23 but it was seamless, woven in one **p** from the top.
Ac 27: 35 God before them all, and broke off a **p** and ate it.
Eph 6: 13 Use every **p** of God's armor to resist the enemy in
Col 3: 14 And the most important **p** of clothing you must

PIECES (99) [PIECE]

Ge 20: 16 "I am giving your 'brother' a thousand **p** of silver
23: 15 "the land is worth four hundred **p** of silver,
23: 16 four hundred **p** of silver, as was publicly agreed.
33: 19 Shechem's father, for a hundred **p** of silver.
37: 28 out of the pit and sold him for twenty **p** of silver,
37: 33 and eaten him. Surely Joseph has been torn in **p**!"
44: 28 doubtless torn to **p** by some wild animal.
45: 22 changes of clothes and three hundred **p** of silver!
Ex 15: 6 right hand, O LORD, / dashes the enemy to **p**.
28: 7 It will consist of two **p**, front and back, joined at
29: 17 alongside the head and the other **p** of the body,
Lev 1: 6 When the animal has been skinned and cut into **p**,
1: 8 Aaron's sons will then put the **p** of the animal,
1: 12 Then you must cut the animal in **p**, and the priests
will lay the **p** of the sacrifice,
2: 6 Break it into **p** and pour oil on it; it is a kind of
6: 21 and it must be well mixed and broken into **p**.
8: 20 Next he cut the ram into **p** and burned the head,
some of its **p**,
11: 35 clay oven or cooking pot, it must be smashed to **p**.
27: 3 of twenty and sixty is valued at fifty **p** of silver;
27: 4 a woman of that age is valued at thirty **p** of silver.
27: 5 and twenty is valued at twenty **p** of silver;
27: 5 a girl of that age is valued at ten **p** of silver.
27: 6 and five years is valued at five **p** of silver;
27: 6 a girl of that age is valued at three **p** of silver.
27: 7 A man older than sixty is valued at fifteen **p** of
27: 7 a woman older than sixty is valued at ten **p** of
27: 16 fifty **p** of silver for an area that produces five
Nu 3: 47 collect five **p** of silver for each person, each piece
6: 20 and thigh **p** that were lifted up before the LORD.
18: 16 The redemption price is five **p** of silver, each piece
24: 8 that oppose him, / breaking their bones in **p**,
Dt 22: 19 They will fine him one hundred **p** of silver, for he
22: 29 he must pay fifty **p** of silver to her father. Then he
Jos 24: 32 the sons of Hamor for one hundred **p** of silver.
Jdg 16: 5 Then each of us will give you eleven hundred **p** of
17: 2 who stole eleven hundred **p** of silver from you.
17: 10 I will give you ten **p** of silver a year, plus a change
19: 29 a knife and cut his concubine's body into twelve **p**.
20: 6 So I cut her body into twelve **p** and sent the **p**
throughout the land of Israel,
1Sa 11: 7 He took two oxen and cut them into **p** and sent the
15: 33 And Samuel cut Agag to **p** before the LORD at
2Sa 18: 11 I would have rewarded you with ten **p** of silver
18: 12 "I wouldn't do it for a thousand **p** of silver,"
24: 24 So David paid him fifty **p** of silver for the
1Ki 10: 29 Jerusalem could be purchased for 600 **p** of silver,
10: 29 and horses could be bought for 150 **p** of silver.
11: 30 cloak he was wearing and tore it into twelve **p**.
11: 31 Then he said to Jeroboam, "Take ten of these **p**,
18: 23 and cut it into **p** and lay it on the wood of their
18: 33 He piled wood on the altar, cut the bull into **p**, and
laid the **p** on the wood.
2Ki 11: 18 demolished the altars and smashed the idols to **p**,
23: 12 to bits and scattered the **p** in the Kidron Valley.
1Ch 21: 25 So David gave Araunah six hundred **p** of gold in
2Ch 1: 17 Jerusalem could be purchased for 600 **p** of silver,
1: 17 and horses could be bought for 150 **p** of silver.
25: 12 them off, dashing them to **p** on the rocks below.
28: 24 from the Temple of God and broke them into **p**.
Job 16: 12 He took me by the neck and dashed me to **p**.
Ps 7: 2 a lion, / tearing me to **p** with no one to rescue me.
SS 8: 11 Each of them pays one thousand **p** of silver for its
8: 12 O Solomon, you can take my thousand **p** of silver.
8: 12 And I will give two hundred **p** of silver to those
Isa 7: 23 now worth as much as a thousand **p** of silver,
Jer 23: 29 not like a mighty hammer that smashes rock to **p**?
32: 9 paying Hanamel seventeen **p** of silver for it.
Eze 17: 7 but the victims of your injustice are the **p** of meat.
23: 34 Then you will smash it to **p** and beat your breast in
Da 2: 35 The **p** were crushed as small as chaff on a
Hos 3: 2 So I bought her back for fifteen **p** of silver
6: 1 He has torn us in **p**; now he will heal us. He has
6: 5 I sent my prophets to cut you to **p**. I have
13: 8 I will rip you to **p** like a bear whose cubs have
Am 6: 11 homes both great and small will be smashed to **p**.
Mic 1: 7 All her carved images will be smashed to **p**.
4: 13 so you can trample many nations to **p**.
Zec 11: 12 So they counted out for my wages thirty **p** of
Mt 14: 19 Breaking the loaves into **p**, he gave some of the
15: 36 the fish, thanked God for them, broke them into **p**,
21: 44 who stumbles over that stone will be broken to **p**,
26: 15 to you?" And they gave him thirty **p** of silver.
26: 26 Then he broke it in **p** and gave it to the disciples,
27: 3 So he took the thirty **p** of silver back to the leading
27: 9 that says, / "They took the thirty **p** of silver—
Mk 6: 41 Breaking the loaves into **p**, he kept giving the
8: 6 thanked God for them, broke them into **p**, and gave
14: 22 Then he broke it in **p** and gave it to the disciples,
Lk 7: 41 five hundred **p** of silver to one and fifty **p** to the
9: 16 Breaking the loaves into **p**, he kept giving the
10: 35 The next day he handed the innkeeper two **p** of
20: 18 who stumble over that stone will be broken to **p**,
22: 19 he broke it in **p** and gave it to the disciples, saying,
Jn 6: 13 but twelve baskets were filled with the **p** of bread
1Co 1: 13 Can Christ be divided into **p**? Was I, Paul,
Rev 16: 19 The great city of Babylon split into three **p**,

PIERCE (9) [PIERCED, PIERCES, PIERCING]

Ex 21: 6 him to the door and publicly **p** his ear with an awl.
Job 20: 24 He will try to escape, but God's arrow will **p** him.
41: 2 a rope through the nose or **p** its jaw with a spike?
Ps 42: 10 Their taunts **p** me like a fatal wound. / They scoff,
57: 4 whose teeth **p** like spears and arrows,
64: 7 them down. / Suddenly, his arrows will **p** them.
Pr 7: 23 awaiting the arrow that would **p** its heart. He was
Zec 11: 17 The sword will cut his arm and **p** his right eye!
Lk 2: 35 be revealed. And a sword will **p** your very soul."

PIERCED (12) [PIERCE]

2Ki 9: 24 The arrow **p** his heart, and he sank down dead in
Job 16: 13 and his arrows **p** me without mercy.
26: 13 and his power **p** the gliding serpent.
Ps 22: 16 closes in on me. / They have **p** my hands and feet.
120: 4 You will be **p** with sharp arrows / and burned with
Jer 4: 18 of your own medicine. It has **p** you to the heart!"
Eze 28: 8 home in the heart of the sea, **p** with many wounds.
Zec 12: 10 They will look on me whom they have **p**
Jn 19: 34 however, **p** his side with a spear, and blood
19: 37 and "They will look on him whom they **p**."
1Ti 6: 10 the faith and **p** themselves with many sorrows.
Rev 1: 7 everyone will see him—even those who **p** him.

PIERCES (3) [PIERCE]

2Ki 18: 21 that breaks beneath your weight and **p** your hand.
Job 16: 9 He gnashes his teeth at me and **p** me with his eyes.
Isa 36: 6 that breaks beneath your weight and **p** your hand.

PIERCING (4) [PIERCE]

Jdg 5: 26 the tent peg through his head, **p** his temples.
Job 39: 29 there it hunts its prey, keeping watch with **p** eyes.
Ps 45: 5 Your arrows are sharp, / **p** your enemies' hearts.
59: 7 their mouths, / the **p** swords that fly from their lips.

PIG (4) [PIG'S, PIGS]

Lev 11: 7 And the **p** may not be eaten, for though it has split
Dt 14: 8 And the **p** may not be eaten, for though it has split
Isa 66: 3 as putting a dog or the blood of a **p** on the altar!
2Pe 2: 22 its vomit," and "A washed **p** returns to the mud."

PIG'S (1) [PIG]

Pr 11: 22 but lacks discretion is like a gold ring in a **p** snout.

PIGEON (3) [PIGEONS]

Ge 15: 9 a three-year-old ram, a turtledove, and a young **p**."
Lev 1: 14 choose either a turtledove or a young **p**.
12: 6 and a young **p** or turtledove for a purification

PIGEONS (9) [PIGEON]

Lev 5: 7 or two young **p** as the penalty for their sin.
5: 11 cannot afford to bring young turtledoves or **p**,
12: 8 she must bring two turtledoves or two young **p**.
14: 22 must also bring two turtledoves or two young **p**,
14: 30 will offer the two turtledoves or the two young **p**,
15: 14 day he must bring two turtledoves or two young **p**
15: 29 she must bring two turtledoves or two young **p**
Nu 6: 10 or two young **p** to the priest at the entrance of the
Lk 2: 24 "either a pair of turtledoves or two young **p**."

PIGS (13) [PIG]

Mt 8: 30 A large herd of **p** was feeding in the distance,
8: 31 "If you cast us out, send us into that herd of **p**."
8: 32 the demons came out of the men and entered the **p**,
Mk 5: 11 There happened to be a large herd of **p** feeding on
5: 12 "Send us into those **p**," the evil spirits begged.
5: 13 evil spirits came out of the man and entered the **p**,
5: 13 and the entire herd of two thousand **p** plunged
5: 16 to the man and to the **p** told everyone about it,
Lk 8: 32 A large herd of **p** was feeding on the hillside
8: 32 pleaded with him to let them enter into the **p**.
8: 33 the demons came out of the man and entered the **p**,
15: 15 persuaded a local farmer to hire him to feed his **p**.
15: 16 so hungry that even the pods he was feeding the **p**

PILATE (64) [PILATE'S]

Mt 27: 2 Then they bound him and took him to **P**,
27: 11 Now Jesus was standing before **P**, the Roman
27: 13 their many charges against you?" **P** demanded.
27: 19 Just then, as **P** was sitting on the judgment seat,
27: 22 "But if I release Barabbas," **P** asked them,
27: 23 "Why?" **P** demanded. "What crime has he
27: 24 **P** saw that he wasn't getting anywhere and that a
27: 26 So **P** released Barabbas to them. He ordered Jesus
27: 58 went to **P** and asked for Jesus' body. And **P** issued
an order to release it to him.
27: 62 the leading priests and Pharisees went to see **P**.
27: 65 **P** replied, "Take guards and secure it the best you
Mk 15: 1 They bound Jesus and took him to **P**, the Roman
15: 2 **P** asked Jesus, "Are you the King of the Jews?"
15: 4 And **P** asked him, "Aren't you going to say
15: 8 The mob began to crowd in toward **P**, asking him
15: 9 I give you the King of the Jews?" **P** asked.

15:12 "But if I release Barabbas," **P** asked them,
15:14 "Why?" **P** demanded. "What crime has he
15:15 So **P**, anxious to please the crowd,
15:43 his courage and went to **P** to ask for Jesus' body.
15:44 **P** couldn't believe that Jesus was already dead,
15:45 the fact, and **P** told Joseph he could have the body.
Lk 3:1 **P** was governor over Judea; Herod Antipas was
13:1 About this time Jesus was informed that **P** had
23:1 Then the entire council took Jesus over to **P**,
23:3 So **P** asked him, "Are you the King of the Jews?"
23:4 **P** turned to the leading priests and to the crowd
23:6 "Oh, is he a Galilean?" **P** asked.
23:7 that he was, **P** sent him to Herod Antipas,
23:11 put a royal robe on him and sent him back to **P**.
23:12 Herod and **P**, who had been enemies before,
23:13 Then **P** called together the leading priests
23:20 **P** argued with them, because he wanted to release
23:24 So **P** sentenced Jesus to die as they demanded.
23:52 He went to **P** and asked for Jesus' body.
Jn 18:29 So **P**, the governor, went out to them and asked,
18:31 and judge him by your own laws," **P** told them.
18:33 Then **P** went back inside and called for Jesus to be
18:35 "Am I a Jew?" **P** asked. "Your own people
18:37 **P** replied, "You are a king then?" "You say that I
18:38 "What is truth?" **P** asked. Then he went out again
19:1 Then **P** had Jesus flogged with a lead-tipped whip.
19:4 **P** went outside again and said to the people,
19:5 the purple robe. And **P** said, "Here is the man!"
19:6 "Crucify! Crucify!" "You crucify him," **P** said.
19:8 When **P** heard this, he was more frightened than
19:10 "You won't talk to me?" **P** demanded.
19:12 Then **P** tried to release him, but the Jewish leaders
19:13 they said this, **P** brought Jesus out to them again.
19:13 Then **P** sat down on the judgment seat on the
19:14 And **P** said to the people, "Here is your king!"
19:15 **P** asked. "We have no king but Caesar,"
19:16 Then **P** gave Jesus to them to be crucified.
19:19 And **P** posted a sign over him that read, "Jesus of
19:21 Then the leading priests said to **P**, "Change it from
19:22 **P** replied, "What I have written, I have written.
19:31 so they asked **P** to hasten their deaths by ordering
19:38 asked **P** for permission to take Jesus' body down.
19:38 When **P** gave him permission, he came and took
Ac 3:13 whom you handed over and rejected before **P**,
4:27 Pontius **P** the governor, the Gentiles,
13:28 but they asked **P** to have him killed anyway.
1Ti 6:13 who gave a good testimony before Pontius **P**,

PILATE'S (3) [PILATE]

Mt 27:17 As the crowds gathered before **P** house that
Mk 15:5 But Jesus said nothing, much to **P** surprise.
Ac 3:13 before Pilate, despite **P** decision to release him.

PILDASH (1)

Ge 22:22 Kesed, Hazo, **P**, Jidlaph, and Bethuel.

PILE (23) [PILED, PILES, PILING]

Ge 31:46 his men to gather stones and **p** them up in a heap.
31:46 then sat down beside the **p** of stones to share a
31:47 They named it "Witness **P**," which is
31:48 "This **p** of stones will stand as a witness to remind
Dt 13:16 Then you must **p** all the plunder in the middle of
Jos 3:13 and the river will **p** up there in one heap."
4:3 and **p** them up at the place where you camp
10:27 the opening of the cave with a large **p** of stones,
1Sa 2:8 the poor from the dust— / yes, from a **p** of ashes!
20:19 you hid before, and wait there by the stone **p**.
20:20 and shoot three arrows to the side of the stone **p** as
20:41 from where he had been hiding near the stone **p**.
2Ki 10:8 "**P** them in two heaps at the entrance of the city
Ezr 6:11 and their house will be reduced to a **p** of rubble.
Job 8:17 Its roots grow down through a **p** of rocks to hold it
Ps 40:12 too many to count! / They **p** up so high
69:27 **P** their sins up high, / and don't let them go free.
Jer 9:6 They **p** lie upon lie and utterly refuse to come to
22:5 that this palace will become a **p** of rubble.' "
Eze 24:9 I myself will **p** up the fuel beneath her.
Hab 1:10 They simply **p** ramps of earth against their walls
Jn 15:6 Such branches are gathered into a **p** to be burned.
1Th 2:16 By doing this, they continue to **p** up their sins.

PILED (17) [PILE]

Ex 8:14 They were **p** into great heaps, and a terrible stench
15:8 At the blast of your breath, the waters **p** up!
Lev 26:30 I will leave your corpses **p** up beside your lifeless
Jos 4:20 It was there at Gilgal that Joshua **p** up the twelve
7:26 They **p** a great heap of stones over Achan,
8:29 They **p** a great heap of stones over him that can
Jdg 9:49 They **p** the branches against the walls of the temple
2Sa 18:17 pit in the forest and **p** a great heap of stones over it.
1Ki 18:33 He **p** wood on the altar, cut the bull into pieces,
2Ch 31:6 their God, and they **p** them up in great heaps.
Ezr 9:6 For our sins are **p** higher than our heads, and our
Isa 30:33 the Assyrian king; it has been **p** high with wood.
59:12 For our sins are **p** up before God and testify
Joel 2:24 The threshing floors will again be **p** high with
Hab 3:15 with your horses, and the mighty waters **p** high.
Zec 9:3 built a strong fortress and has **p** up so much silver
Rev 18:5 For her sins are **p** as high as heaven, and God is

PILES (5) [PILE]

Ge 11:3 "let's make great **p** of burnt brick and collect
Jos 2:6 up to the roof and hidden them beneath **p** of flax.)
Jdg 15:5 including the grain still in **p** and all that had been
2Ch 31:8 and his officials came and saw these huge **p**,
Ne 9:37 The lush produce of this land **p** up in the hands of

PILGRIMAGE (3) [PILGRIMS]

Ps 84:5 who set their minds on a **p** to Jerusalem.
119:54 music of my life / throughout the years of my **p**.
122:4 the LORD's people— / make their **p** here.

PILGRIMS (1) [PILGRIMAGE]

Isa 30:29 as when a flutist leads a group of **p** to Jerusalem—

PILGRIMS [KJV] See also ALIENS, NOMADS

PILHA (1)

Ne 10:24 Hallohesh, **P**, Shobek,

PILING (2) [PILE]

Jos 3:16 the water began **p** up at a town upstream called
Isa 30:1 that are not from my Spirit, thus **p** up your sins.

PILL (1)

Am 5:7 making it a bitter **p** for the poor and oppressed.

PILLAR (43) [PILLARS]

PILLAR OF CLOUD (14) Ex 13:21,22; 14:19,20; 33:9; 34:5; Nu 12:5; 14:14,14; Dt 1:33; 31:15; Ne 9:12,19; Ps 99:7

PILLAR OF FIRE (10) Ex 13:21,22; 14:20,24; Nu 9:15; 14:14; Dt 1:33; Ne 9:12,19; Ps 78:14

Ge 19:26 along behind him, and she became a **p** of salt.
28:18 used as a pillow and set it upright as a memorial **p**.
28:22 This memorial **p** will become a place for
31:13 the place where you anointed the **p** of stone
31:51 This heap of stones and this **p**
35:14 Jacob set up a stone **p** to mark the place where God
35:14 offering to God and anointed the **p** with olive oil.
Ex 13:21 a **p** of cloud during the day and a **p** of fire at night.
13:22 And the LORD did not remove the **p** of cloud or **p** of fire from their sight.
14:19 and the **p** of cloud also moved around behind
14:20 the **p** of cloud turned into a **p** of fire,
14:24 down on the Egyptian army from the **p** of fire
33:9 the **p** of cloud would come down and hover at the
34:5 Then the LORD came down in a **p** of cloud
Nu 9:15 over the Tabernacle appeared to be a **p** of fire.
12:5 Then the LORD descended in the **p** of cloud
14:14 people in the **p** of cloud that hovers over them.
14:14 They know that you go before them in the **p** of cloud by day and the **p** of fire by night.
Dt 1:33 by a **p** of fire at night and a **p** of cloud by day.
31:15 And the LORD appeared to them in a **p** of cloud
Jdg 9:6 a meeting under the oak beside the **p** at Shechem
2Ki 3:2 He at least tore down the sacred **p** of Baal that his
10:26 They dragged out the sacred **p** used in the worship
10:27 They broke down the sacred **p** of Baal
11:14 king standing in his place of authority by the **p**,
23:3 The king took his place of authority beside the **p**
25:17 The bronze capital on top of each **p** was 7-1/2 feet
2Ch 23:13 place of authority by the **p** at the Temple entrance.
34:31 The king took his place of authority beside the **p**
Ne 9:12 You led our ancestors by a **p** of cloud during the
9:12 and a **p** of fire at night so that they could find their
9:19 The **p** of cloud still led them forward by day,
9:19 and the **p** of fire showed them the way through the
Ps 78:14 he led them by a cloud, / and at night by a **p** of fire.
99:7 He spoke to them from the **p** of cloud, / and they
Jer 1:18 cannot be captured, like an iron **p** or a bronze wall.
52:22 The bronze capital on top of each **p** was 7-1/2 feet
1Ti 3:15 living God, which is the **p** and support of the truth.

PILLARS (58) [PILLAR]

Ex 24:4 He also set up twelve **p** around the altar, one for
34:13 smash the sacred **p** they worship, and cut down
Lev 26:1 not make idols or set up carved images, sacred **p**,
Nu 3:36 the crossbars, the **p**, the bases, and all the
4:31 the crossbars, the **p** with their bases,
Dt 7:5 down their pagan altars and shatter their sacred **p**.
12:3 Break down their altars and smash their sacred **p**.
16:22 And never set up sacred **p** for worship,
Jdg 16:25 the temple, between the two **p** supporting the roof.
16:26 by the hand, "Place my hands against the two **p**.
16:29 Then Samson put his hands on the center **p** of the
1Ki 7:2 cedar ceiling beams rested on four rows of cedar **p**.
7:3 by forty-five rafters that rested on three rows of **p**,
7:6 He also built the Hall of **P**, which was 75 feet long
7:6 covered by a canopy that was supported by **p**.
7:15 Huram cast two bronze **p**, each 27 feet tall and 18
7:16 For the tops of the **p** he made capitals of molded
7:18 the latticework to decorate the capitals over the **p**.
7:20 Each capital on the two **p** had two hundred
7:21 Huram set the **p** at the entrance of the Temple,
7:22 The capitals on the **p** were shaped like lilies. And so the work on the **p** was finished.
7:41 two **p**, / two bowl-shaped capitals on top of the **p**,
7:42 that were hung around the capitals on top of the **p**),
14:23 They built pagan shrines and set up sacred **p**
2Ki 17:10 They set up sacred **p** and Asherah poles at the top
18:4 removed the pagan shrines, smashed the sacred **p**,
23:14 He smashed the sacred **p** and cut down the
25:13 The Babylonians broke up the bronze **p**, the bronze
25:16 The bronze from the two **p**, the water carts,
25:17 Each of the **p** was 27 feet tall. The bronze capital
1Ch 18:8 He molded it into the bronze Sea, the **p**,
2Ch 3:15 Solomon made two **p** that were 27 feet tall,
3:16 and used them to decorate the tops of the **p**.
3:17 Then he set up the two **p** at the entrance of the
4:12 two **p**, / two bowl-shaped capitals on top of the **p**,
4:13 that were hung around the capitals on top of the **p**),
14:3 He smashed the sacred **p** and cut down the
31:1 and Manasseh, and they smashed the sacred **p**,
Est 1:6 ribbons to silver rings embedded in marble **p**.
Ps 89:14 Your throne is founded on two strong **p**—
144:12 May our daughters be like graceful **p**,
Pr 9:1 Wisdom has built her spacious house with seven **p**.
SS 5:15 His legs are like **p** of marble set in sockets of the
Jer 27:19 says about the bronze **p** in front of the Temple,
43:13 He will break down the sacred **p** standing in the
52:17 The Babylonians broke up the bronze **p**, the bronze
52:20 The bronze from the two **p**, the water carts,
52:21 Each of the **p** was 27 feet tall and 18 feet in
Eze 26:11 your people, and your famous **p** will topple.
43:9 and the sacred **p** erected to honor their kings,
Joel 2:30 and on the earth—blood and fire and **p** of smoke.
Mic 5:13 I will destroy all your idols and sacred **p**, so you
Gal 2:9 and John, who were known as **p** of the church,
Rev 3:12 All who are victorious will become **p** in the
10:1 shone like the sun, and his feet were like **p** of fire.

PILLED [KJV] See PEELED

PILLOW (4)

Ge 28:11 Jacob found a stone for a **p** and lay down to sleep.
28:18 He took the stone he had used as a **p** and set it
Ps 6:6 tears drench my bed; / my **p** is wet from weeping.
Am 3:12 rescued with only a broken chair and a tattered **p**.

PILOT (1)

Jas 3:4 a huge ship turn wherever the **p** wants it to go,

PILTAI (1)

Ne 12:17 **P** was leader of the family of Moadiah.

PIN (2)

1Sa 18:11 hurled it at David, intending to **p** him to the wall.
26:8 I'll **p** him to the ground, and I won't need to strike

PINE (3)

Isa 41:19 cedar, acacia, myrtle, olive, cypress, fir, and **p**—
60:13 the forests of cypress, fir, and **p**—to beautify my
Eze 27:6 They made your deck of **p** wood, brought from the

PINIONS (1)

Dt 32:11 to take them in / and carried them aloft on his **p**.

PINON (2)

Ge 36:41 Oholibamah, Elah, **P**,
1Ch 1:52 Oholibamah, Elah, **P**,

PINS [KJV] See PEGS, PURSES

PINT (2) [PINTS]

Lev 14:10 with olive oil and three-fifths of a **p** of olive oil.
14:21 a grain offering and three-fifths of a **p** of olive oil.

PINTS (3) [PINT]

Nu 15:6 flour mixed with two and a half **p** of olive oil,
15:7 give two and a half **p** of wine for a drink offering.
28:14 two and a half **p** for the ram, and one quart for

PIOUS (2)

Isa 1:13 even your most **p** meetings—are all sinful
58:2 Yet they act so **p**! They come to the Temple every

PIPES (1)

Da 3:5 flute, zither, lyre, harp, **p**, and other instruments,

PIRAM (1)

Jos 10:3 of Hebron, **P** of Jarmuth, Japhia of Lachish,

PIRATHON (5)

Jdg 12:13 After Elon died, Abdon son of Hillel, from **P**,
12:15 Then he died and was buried at **P** in Ephraim,
2Sa 23:30 Benaiah from **P**; / Hurai from Nahale-gaash;
1Ch 11:31 (from the tribe of Benjamin); / Benaiah from **P**;
27:14 Benaiah from **P** in Ephraim was commander of the

PISGAH (8)

Nu 21:20 Then they went to the valley in Moab where **P**
23:14 took Balaam to the plateau of Zophim on **P** Peak.
Dt 3:17 to the Dead Sea, with the slopes of **P** on the east.
3:27 You can go to **P** Peak and view the land in every
4:49 far south as the Dead Sea, below the slopes of **P**.)
34:1 from the plains of Moab and climbed **P** Peak,
Jos 12:3 Dead Sea, from Beth-jeshimoth to the slopes of **P**.
13:20 Beth-peor, the slopes of **P**, and Beth-jeshimoth.

PISHON (1)

Ge 2:11 One of these branches is the **P**, which flows around

PISIDIA (3)

Ac 13:14 and Paul traveled inland to Antioch of **P**.
14:21 again to Lystra, Iconium, and Antioch of **P**,
14:24 Then they traveled back through **P** to Pamphylia.

PISON [KJV] See PISHON

PISPAH (1)

1Ch 7:38 The sons of Jether were Jephunneh, **P**, and Ara.

PISS [KJV] See URINE

PISSETH [KJV] See MALE, MAN, MEN

PISTACHIO (1)

Ge 43:11 balm, honey, spices, myrrh, **p** nuts, and almonds.

PIT (54) [PITS]

Ge 37:20 let's kill him and throw him into a deep **p**.
37:22 Let's just throw him alive into this **p** here.
37:24 and threw him into the **p**. This **p** was normally used to store water, but it was
37:28 his brothers pulled Joseph out of the **p** and sold
37:29 Reuben returned to get Joseph out of the **p**.
2Sa 17: 9 He has probably already hidden in some **p** or cave.
18:17 They threw Absalom's body into a deep **p** in the
23:20 Another time he chased a lion down into a **p**.
1Ch 11:22 Another time he chased a lion down into a **p**.
Job 18: 8 They fall into a **p** that's been dug in the path.
Ps 7:15 They dig a **p** to trap others / and then fall into it
9:15 The nations have fallen into the **p** they dug for
30: 3 You kept me from falling into the **p** of death.
35: 7 I did them no wrong, / they dug a **p** for me.
35: 8 Let them fall to destruction in the **p** they dug for
40: 2 He lifted me out of the **p** of despair, / out of the
55:23 down to the **p** of destruction. / Murderers and liars
57: 6 from distress. / They have dug a deep **p** in my path,
69:15 waters swallow me, / or the **p** of death devour me.
88: 6 You have thrust me down to the lowest **p**,
94:13 troubled times / until a **p** is dug for the wicked.
Pr 1:12 prime of life, they will go down into the **p** of death.
22:14 The mouth of an immoral woman is a deep **p**;
23:27 A prostitute is a deep **p**; an adulterous woman is
Isa 14:19 those killed in battle. You will descend to the **p**.
Jer 18:22 For they have dug a **p** for me, and they have
La 3:53 They threw me into a **p** and dropped stones on me.
Eze 19: 4 heard about him, / and he was trapped in their **p**.
19: 8 out their nets for him / and captured him in their **p**.
26:20 I will send you to the **p** to lie there with those who
26:20 like those in the **p** who have entered the world of
28: 8 They will bring you down to the **p**, and you will
31:14 They will land in the **p** along with all the proud
31:16 were relieved to find it there with them in the **p**.
31:18 will be brought down to the **p** with all these other
32:18 in company with those who descend to the **p**.
32:19 So go down to the **p** and lie there among the
32:23 Their graves are in the depths of the **p**, and they
32:24 but now they lie in the **p** and share the humiliation
32:25 but now they lie in shame in the **p**, all of them
32:29 with the outcasts who have gone down to the **p**.
32:30 all the other dead who have descended to the **p**.
Hos 5: 2 You have dug a deep **p** to trap them at Acacia.
Mt 21:33 around it, dug a **p** for pressing out the grape juice,
Mk 12: 1 around it, dug a **p** for pressing out the grape juice,
Lk 8:31 Jesus not to send them into the Bottomless **P**.
14: 5 If your son or your cow falls into a **p**, don't you
Rev 9: 1 was given the key to the shaft of the bottomless **p**.
9:11 Their king is the angel from the bottomless **p**;
11: 7 the beast that comes up out of the bottomless **p**
17: 8 yet he will soon come up out of the bottomless **p**
20: 1 down from heaven with the key to the bottomless **p**
20: 3 The angel threw him into the bottomless **p**,

PITCH (4) [PITCHED]

Ex 2: 3 papyrus reeds and waterproofed it with tar and **p**.
Isa 34: 9 The streams of Edom will be filled with burning **p**,
Eze 25: 4 camps among you and **p** their tents on your land.
Da 11:45 and the sea and will **p** his royal tents there,

PITCHED (1) [PITCH]

Jdg 4:11 his tribe and **p** his tent by the Oak of Zaanannim,

PITCHER (2) [PITCHERS]

Mk 14:13 "a man carrying a **p** of water will meet you.
Lk 22:10 a man carrying a **p** of water will meet you.

PITCHERS (5) [PITCHER]

Ex 25:29 as well as **p** and bowls to be used in pouring out
37:16 dishes, bowls, and **p** to be placed on the table.
1Ch 28:17 sacrificial meat and for the basins, **p**, and dishes,
Jer 14: 3 The servants return with empty **p**, confused
Mk 7: 4 as their ceremony of washing cups, **p**, and kettles.)

PITHOM (1)

Ex 1:11 They forced them to build the cities of **P**

PITHON (2)

1Ch 8:35 Micah was the father of **P**, Melech, Tahrea,
9:41 The sons of Micah were **P**, Melech, Tahrea,

PITIED (4) [PITY]

2Ki 13:23 He **p** them because of his covenant with Abraham,
Ps 106:44 Even so, he **p** them in their distress / and listened
Eze 16: 5 interest in you; no one **p** you or cared for you.
20:17 I **p** them and held back from destroying them in

PITS (8) [PIT]

Ge 14:10 As it happened, the valley was filled with tar **p**.
14:10 and Gomorrah fled, some slipped into the tar **p**,
Ps 119:85 hate your law / have dug deep **p** for me to fall into.
140:10 or into deep **p** from which they can't escape.
Jer 2: 6 a land of deserts and **p**, of drought and death,
La 4: 5 lived in palaces now search the garbage **p** for food.
Na 3:14 Go into the **p** to trample clay, and pack it into
Zep 2: 9 of stinging nettles, salt **p**, and eternal desolation.

PITTANCE (1)

Ps 44:12 You sold us—your precious people—for a **p**.

PITY (32) [PITIED]

Ge 40:14 And please have some **p** on me when you are back
Dt 13: 8 they do this, do not give in or listen, and have no **p**.
19:21 You must never show **p**! Your rule should be life
25:12 her hand must be cut off without **p**.
28:50 no respect for the old and no **p** for the young.
Jdg 2:18 For the LORD took **p** on his people, who were
2Sa 12: 6 man for the one he stole and for having no **p**."
2Ch 36:17 They had no **p** on the people, killing both young
Job 41: 3 Will it beg you for mercy or implore you for **p**?
Ps 17:10 They are without **p**. / Listen to their boasting.
69:20 If only one person would show some **p**;
72:13 He feels **p** for the weak and the needy, / and he
90:13 long will you delay? / Take **p** on your servants!
102:13 on Jerusalem— / and now is the time to **p** her,
109:12 kind to him; / let no one **p** his fatherless children.
Isa 27:11 the one who made them will show them no **p**
Jer 13:14 I will not let my **p** or mercy or compassion keep
21: 7 them all without mercy, **p**, or compassion.'
Eze 5:11 I will show you no **p** at all because you have
7: 4 I will turn my eyes away and show no **p**,
7: 9 I will neither spare nor **p** you. I will repay you for
8:18 with them in fury. I will neither **p** nor spare them.
9: 5 is not marked. Show no mercy; have no **p**!
9:10 So I will not spare them or have any **p** on them.
Joel 2:18 Then the LORD will **p** his people and be
Jnh 3: 9 Perhaps even yet God will have **p** on us and hold
Zec 11: 6 I will no longer have **p** on the inhabitants of the
Mt 9:36 He felt great **p** for the crowds that came,
18:27 Then the king was filled with **p** for him, and he
Mk 1:41 Moved with **p**, Jesus touched him. "I want to,"
Lk 10:33 and when he saw the man, he felt deep **p**.
16:24 rich man shouted, 'Father Abraham, have some **p**!

PLACE (665) [PLACED, PLACES, PLACING]

HIGH PLACE (2) Eze 20:29,29

HOLY PLACE (77) Ex 26:33,33,34; 27:21; 28:29,35,43; 29:30; 31:11; 35:12,19; 39:1,34,41; 40:3,22,24,26; Lev 4:6; 6:30; 10:18; 16:2,16,17,20,23,27,33; 24:3; Nu 28:7; 1Ki 6:16,17,21,22; 7:49,50; 8:6,8; 1Ch 6:49; 2Ch 3:8,10,14; 4:20,22; 5:7,9,11; Ezr 9:8; Ps 24:3; Isa 57:15; 63:18; Eze 41:1,2,3,4,15,15,17,20,21,21,23,23,25; 42:14; 45:3; Da 9:24; Ob 1:17; Mt 24:15; Heb 9:2,3,7,8,12,25; 10:19; 13:11

MOST HOLY PLACE (42) Ex 26:33,34; 27:21; 35:12; 39:34; 40:3; Lev 4:6; 16:2,16,17,20,23,27,33; 24:3; 1Ki 6:16,17,21,22; 7:49,50; 8:6; 1Ch 6:49; 2Ch 3:8,10,14; 4:20,22; 5:7; Eze 41:4,15,17,21,23; 45:3; Da 9:24; Heb 9:3,7,8,12,25; 10:19

Ge 1: 9 the waters beneath the sky be gathered into one **p**
2:21 and closed up the **p** from which he had taken it.
4:12 the earth, constantly wandering from **p** to **p**."
4:25 "God has granted me another son in **p** of Abel,
8: 9 But the dove found no **p** to land because the water
11:28 he died in Ur of the Chaldeans, the **p** of his birth.
12: 6 they came to a **p** near Shechem and set up camp
13: 3 to the **p** between Bethel and Ai where they had
13: 4 This was the **p** where Abram had built the altar,
13: 9 stay in this area, then I'll move on to another **p**."
13:12 Lot moved his tents to a **p** near Sodom,
19:12 "Get them out of this **p**—sons-in-law, sons,
19:13 The stench of the **p** has reached the LORD,
19:27 and hurried out to the **p** where he had stood in the
20: 1 between Kadesh and Shur at a **p** called Gerar.
20:11 Abraham said, "I figured this to be a godless **p**.
20:15 and choose a **p** where you would like to live,"
21:17 God has heard the boy's cries from the **p** where
21:31 ever since, that **p** has been known as Beersheba—
21:33 worshiped the LORD, the Eternal God, at that **p**.
22: 3 and set out for the **p** where God had told him to go.
22: 4 of the journey, Abraham saw the **p** in the distance.
22: 9 When they arrived at the **p** where God had told
22:13 and sacrificed it as a burnt offering on the altar in **p**
22:14 Abraham named the **p** "The LORD Will
23: 4 in a foreign land, with no **p** to bury my wife.
23: 9 so I may have a permanent burial **p** for my
23:20 to Abraham by the Hittites as a permanent burial **p**.
24:31 all ready for you and a **p** prepared for the camels!"
26:25 He set up his camp at that **p**, and his servants dug a
28:11 At sundown he arrived at a good **p** to set up camp
28:16 woke up and said, "Surely the LORD is in this **p**,
28:17 was afraid and said, "What an awesome **p** this is!
28:19 He named the **p** Bethel—"house of God"—
28:22 This memorial pillar will become a **p** for
31:13 the **p** where you anointed the pillar of stone
31:49 This **p** was also called Mizpah, for Laban said,
32: 2 is God's camp!" So he named the **p** Mahanaim.
32:30 Jacob named the **p** Peniel—"face of God"—
33:17 and herds. That is why the **p** was named Succoth.
35:13 Then God went up from the **p** where he had
35:14 Jacob set up a stone pillar to mark the **p** where God
35:15 Jacob called the **p** Bethel—"house of God"—
39:14 Soon all the men around the **p** came running.
42:24 left the room and found a **p** where he could weep.
47: 6 choose any **p** you like for them to live. Give them
48:17 So he lifted it to **p** it on Manasseh's head instead.
49:30 from Ephron the Hittite for a permanent burial **p**.
50:11 renamed the **p** Abel-mizraim, for they said,
50:11 "This is a **p** of very deep mourning for these
50:13 burial **p** in the field of Ephron the Hittite,
Ex 13: 3 the day you left Egypt, the **p** of your slavery.
13:13 from the LORD by presenting a lamb in its **p**.
14:27 The water roared back into its usual **p**,
15:13 your strength / to the **p** where your holiness dwells.
15:17 the **p** you have made as your home, O LORD,
15:23 (That is why the **p** was called Marah, which means
16:33 Then store it in a sacred **p** as a reminder for all
17: 1 left the Sin Desert and moved from **p** to **p**.
17: 7 Moses named the **p** Massah—"the **p** of testing"—and Meribah—"the **p** of arguing"—
21:13 I will appoint a **p** where the slayer can run for
25:16 **p** inside it the stone tablets inscribed with the terms
25:17 the **p** of atonement—out of pure gold.
25:18 and **p** them at the two ends of the atonement cover.
25:21 **P** inside the Ark the stone tablets inscribed with
26:14 On top of these coverings **p** a layer of tanned ram
26:33 When the inner curtain is in **p**, put the Ark of the
26:33 This curtain will separate the Holy **P** from the Most Holy **P**.
26:34 "Then put the Ark's cover—the **p** of atonement—
26:34 of the Ark of the Covenant inside the Most Holy **P**.
26:35 **P** the table and lampstand across the room from
27:21 inner curtain of the Most Holy **P** in the Tabernacle.
28:29 into the presence of the LORD in the Holy **P**.
28:35 he enters the Holy **P** to minister to the LORD,
28:43 or approach the altar in the Holy **P** to perform their
29: 3 **P** these various kinds of bread in a single basket,
29: 6 And **p** on his head the turban with the gold
29:20 and **p** some of it on the tip of the right earlobes of
29:30 to minister in the Tabernacle and the Holy **P**.
29:31 and boil its meat in a sacred **p**.
30: 6 **P** the incense altar just outside the inner curtain,
30: 6 opposite the Ark's cover—the **p** of atonement—
31: 7 the Ark's cover—the **p** of atonement;
31:11 and the special incense for the Holy **P**.
32:34 Now go, lead the people to the **p** I told you about.
33:15 us personally, don't let us move a step from this **p**.
34:20 from the LORD by presenting a lamb in its **p**.
35:12 and its poles; the Ark's cover—the **p** of atonement;
35:12 curtain to enclose the Ark in the Most Holy **P**;
35:19 the priests to wear while ministering in the Holy **P**;
37: 6 he made the Ark's cover—the **p** of atonement.
37:14 These were made to hold the carrying poles in **p**.
38:31 pegs used to hold the curtains of the courtyard in **p**.
39: 1 to be worn while ministering in the Holy **P**.
39:34 the inner curtain that enclosed the Most Holy **P**;
39:35 the Ark's cover—the **p** of atonement;
39:41 to be worn while ministering in the Holy **P**—
40: 3 **P** the Ark of the Covenant inside, and install the
40: 3 curtain to enclose the Ark within the Most Holy **P**.
40: 5 "**P** the incense altar just outside the inner curtain,
40: 6 **P** the altar of burnt offering in front of the
40:20 the Ark's cover—the **p** of atonement—on top of it.
40:22 along the north side of the Holy **P**, just outside the
40:24 from the table on the south side of the Holy **P**.
40:26 in the Holy **P** in front of the inner curtain.
Lev 4: 6 in front of the inner curtain of the Most Holy **P**.
4:12 must be carried away to a ceremonially clean **p**
4:12 the camp, the **p** where the ashes are thrown.
4:24 and slaughter it before the LORD at the **p** where
4:29 and slaughter it at the **p** where burnt offerings are
4:33 and slaughter it at the **p** where the burnt offerings
6:11 and carry the ashes outside the camp to a **p** that is
6:16 and eaten in a sacred **p** within the courtyard of the
6:25 at the **p** where the burnt offerings are slaughtered.
6:26 a sacred **p** within the courtyard of the Tabernacle.
6:27 it must be washed off in a sacred **p**.
6:30 atonement in the Holy **P** for the people's sins,
7: 6 and it must be eaten in a sacred **p**, for it is most
10: 4 away from the sanctuary to a **p** outside the camp."
10:13 It must be eaten in a sacred **p**, for it has been given
10:14 and thigh that were lifted up may be eaten in any **p**
10:18 the animal's blood was not taken into the Holy **P**,
13:19 or a reddish white spot remains in its **p**,
13:45 Then, as they go from **p** to **p**, they must cover
14: 3 who will examine them at a **p** outside the camp.
14:13 there in the sacred area at the **p** where sin offerings
14:41 and the scrapings dumped in the unclean **p** outside
14:45 and plaster must be carried out of town to the **p**
16: 2 **P** behind the inner curtain whenever he chooses;
16: 2 the **p** of atonement—is there, and I myself am
16:13 the **p** of atonement—that rests on the Ark of the
16:16 he will make atonement for the Most Holy **P**,
16:17 goes in to make atonement for the Most Holy **P**.
16:20 finished making atonement for the Most Holy **P**,
16:23 he wore when he entered the Most Holy **P**,
16:24 bathe his entire body with water in a sacred **p**,
16:27 whose blood Aaron brought into the Most Holy **P**
16:32 high priest who serves in **p** of his ancestor Aaron.
16:33 and make atonement for the Most Holy **P**,
24: 3 inner curtain of the Most Holy **P** in the Tabernacle
24: 6 **P** the bread in the LORD's presence on the pure
24: 7 to be burned in **p** of the bread as an offering given
24: 9 who must eat them in a sacred **p**,
Nu 3:45 "Take the Levites in **p** of the firstborn sons of the
4: 6 they must put the carrying poles of the Ark in **p**.
4: 7 and **p** the dishes, spoons, bowls, cups,
4:14 Finally, the carrying poles must be put in **p**.

5:18 unbind her hair and **p** the offering of inquiry—
7:89 the **p** of atonement—that rests on the Ark of the
8: 2 he is to **p** them so their light shines forward."
8:16 I have claimed them for myself in **p** of all the
8:18 I claim the Levites in **p** of all the firstborn sons of
11: 3 area was known as Taberah—"the **p** of burning"—
11:34 So that **p** was called Kibroth-hattaavah—
16:46 and **p** burning coals on it from the altar.
17:10 "**P** Aaron's staff permanently before the Ark of
19: 9 and **p** them in a purified **p** outside the camp.
20: 2 was no water for the people to drink at that **p**,
20: 5 us leave Egypt and bring us here to this terrible **p**?
20: 9 He took the staff from the **p** where it was kept
20:13 This **p** was known as the waters of Meribah,
21: 3 and the **p** has been called Hormah ever since.
22:24 Then the angel of the LORD stood at a **p** where
22:26 and stood in a **p** so narrow that the donkey could
23:13 King Balak told him, "Come with me to another **p**.
23:17 So Balaam returned to the **p** where the king
23:27 "Come, I will take you to yet another **p**.
28: 7 poured out in the Holy **P** as an offering to the
Dt 1:17 they will react, for you are judging in the **p** of God.
1:31 for his child. Now he has brought you to this **p**.'
2:22 the Horites so they could settle there in their **p**.
10: 2 Then **p** the tablets in the sacred chest—the Ark of
10: 6 His son Eleazar became the high priest in his **p**.
12: 5 you must seek the LORD your God at the **p** he
12: 9 when you arrive in the **p** of rest the LORD your
12:11 to the **p** the LORD your God will choose for his
12:14 so only at the **p** the LORD will choose within one
12:18 of the LORD your God at the **p** he will choose.
12:21 It might happen that the **p** the LORD your God
12:26 and your offerings given to fulfill a vow to the **p**
13: 2 and the predicted signs or miracles take **p**.
13:10 you from the land of Egypt, the **p** of slavery.
14:23 Bring this tithe to the **p** the LORD your God
14:24 Now the **p** the LORD your God chooses for his
14:25 and take the money to the **p** the LORD your God
15:20 LORD your God each year at the **p** he chooses.
16: 2 at the **p** he chooses for his name to be honored.
16: 6 It must be offered at the **p** the LORD your God
16: 7 and eat it in the **p** the LORD your God chooses.
16:11 at the **p** he chooses for his name to be honored.
16:15 to honor the LORD your God at the **p** he chooses,
16:16 at the **p** he chooses on each of these occasions,
17: 8 Take such cases to the **p** the LORD your God will
17:10 The decision they make at the **p** the LORD
18: 6 wherever he is living, to the **p** the LORD chooses.
26: 2 and bring it to the **p** the LORD your God chooses
26: 9 He brought us to this **p** and gave us this land
26:10 Then **p** the produce before the LORD your God
26:15 Look down from your holy dwelling **p** in heaven
28:65 There among those nations you will find no **p** of
31:11 before the LORD your God at the **p** he chooses.
31:26 and **p** it beside the Ark of the Covenant of the
34: 6 in Moab, but to this day no one knows the exact **p**.
Jos 4: 3 and pile them up at the **p** where you camp
4: 8 They carried them to the **p** where they camped for
4: 9 at the **p** where the priests who carried the Ark of
5: 9 So that **p** has been called Gilgal to this day.
6:23 They moved her whole family to a safe **p** near the
7:26 That is why the **p** has been called the Valley of
8:14 and attacked the Israelites at a **p** overlooking the
10: 5 They moved all their troops into **p** and attacked
10:18 and **p** guards at the entrance to keep the kings
22:10 altar near the Jordan River at a **p** called Geliloth.
Jdg 2: 5 So they called the **p** "Weeping," and they offered
6:20 "**P** the meat and the unleavened bread on this
6:28 In their **p** a new altar had been built, and it had the
15:17 the jawbone; and the **p** was named Jawbone Hill.
15:19 Then he named that **p** "The Spring of the One
16:26 by the hand, "**P** my hands against the two pillars.
17: 8 that area of Ephraim, looking for a good **p** to live.
17: 9 in Judah, and I am looking for a **p** to live."
18: 1 And the tribe of Dan was trying to find a **p** to
18:12 They camped at a **p** west of Kiriath-jearim in
19:13 We will find a **p** to spend the night in either
20:22 and assembled at the same **p** they had fought the
20:30 third day and assembled at the same **p** as before.
Ru 1: 7 she set out from the **p** where she had been living,
1Sa 1: 9 Eli the priest was sitting at his customary **p** beside
2:20 to take the **p** of this one she gave to the LORD."
6: 8 and beside it **p** a chest containing the gold rats
9:19 "Go on up the hill ahead of me to the **p** of
10: 7 After these signs take **p**, do whatever you think is
19: 2 "you must find a hiding **p** out in the fields.
20:18 You will be missed when your **p** at the table is
20:19 toward evening, go to the **p** where you hid before,
20:25 He sat at his usual **p** against the wall,
20:25 and Abner beside him. But David's **p** was empty.
20:27 But when David's **p** was empty again the next day,
20:30 know that you want David to be king in your **p**,
23:23 even if I have to search every hiding **p** in Judah!"
23:28 the **p** where David was camped has been called the
24: 3 At the **p** where the road passes some sheepfolds,
24:18 for when the LORD put me in a **p** where you
2Sa 2:16 The **p** has been known ever since as the Field of
5:20 So David named that **p** Baal-perazim (which
6: 8 He named that **p** Perez-uzzah (which means
7: 6 always been a tent, moving from one **p** to another.
7:10 a secure **p** where they will never be disturbed.
14:20 He did it to **p** the matter before you in a different
19:13 you as commander of my army in **p** of Joab."
21: 5 to keep us from having any **p** at all in Israel.
22:20 He led me to a **p** of safety; / he rescued me
1Ki 1: 5 decided to make himself king in **p** of his aged
2:35 Benaiah to command the army in **p** of Joab,
2:35 and he installed Zadok the priest to take the **p** of
5: 5 told him, 'Your son, whom I will **p** on your throne,
5: 9 We will float them along the coast to whatever **p**
6:16 the Most Holy **P**—at the far end of the Temple.
6:17 outside the Most Holy **P**, was 60 feet long.
6:21 chains to protect the entrance to the Most Holy **P**.
6:22 the altar that belonged to the Most Holy **P**.
7:49 in front of the Most Holy **P**, the flower decorations,
7:50 the doors for the entrances to the Most Holy **P**
8: 1 also known as Zion, to its new **p** in the Temple.
8: 6 the Most Holy **P**—and placed it beneath the wings
8: 8 main room—the Holy **P**—but not from outside it.
8:16 **p** where a temple should be built to honor my
8:20 for I have become king in my father's **p**.
8:21 And I have prepared a **p** there for the Ark,
8:29 this **p** where you have said you would put your
8:29 you always hear the prayers I make toward this **p**.
8:30 and your people Israel when we pray toward this **p**.
11:36 the city I have chosen to be the **p** for my name.
11:37 And I will **p** you on the throne of Israel, and you
13: 8 not eat any food or drink any water in this **p**.
13:16 to eat any food or drink any water here in this **p**.
13:22 You came back to this **p** and ate food and drank
14:21 all the tribes of Israel as the **p** to honor his name.
17: 3 and hide by Kerith Brook at a **p** east of where it
20:42 now you must die in his **p**, and your people will
21: 9 and prayer and give Naboth a **p** of honor.
21:12 and put Naboth at a prominent **p** before the people.
2Ki 1:17 This took **p** in the second year of the reign of
4:10 Then he will have a **p** to stay whenever he comes
5:17 me to load two of my mules with earth from this **p**,
6: 1 this **p** where we meet with you is too small.
6: 2 There we can build a new **p** for us to meet."
6: 6 When he showed him the **p**, Elisha cut a stick
6: 8 will mobilize our forces at such and such a **p**."
6: 9 warn the king of Israel, "Do not go near that **p**,
6:10 So the king of Israel would send word to the **p**
8: 1 "Take your family and move to some other **p**,
11:14 king standing in his **p** of authority by the pillar,
21: 4 the **p** where the LORD had said his name should
21: 7 the very **p** where the LORD had told David
22:17 My anger is burning against this **p**, and it will not
22:20 **p**.' " So they took her message back to the king.
23: 3 The king took his **p** of authority beside the pillar
23:34 another of Josiah's sons, to reign in **p** of his father,
1Ch 6:49 all the other duties related to the Most Holy **P**.
11:13 The battle took **p** in a field full of barley,
13:11 He named that **p** Perez-uzzah (which means
14:11 So that **p** was named Baal-perazim (which means
15: 1 He also prepared a **p** for the Ark of God and set up
15: 3 Ark of the LORD to the **p** he had prepared for it.
15:12 the God of Israel, to the **p** I have prepared for it.
17: 5 always been a tent, moving from one **p** to another.
17: 9 a secure **p** where they will never be disturbed.
22: 1 and the **p** of the altar for Israel's burnt offerings!"
23:26 the Tabernacle and its utensils from **p** to **p**."
28:11 Ark's cover—the **p** of atonement—would be kept.
29:23 So Solomon took the throne of the LORD in **p** of
29:28 and honor. Then his son Solomon ruled in his **p**.
2Ch 1: 8 David, and now you have made me king in his **p**.
2: 4 It will be a **p** set apart to burn incense and sweet
2: 6 for him, except as a **p** to burn sacrifices to him?
3: 8 The Most Holy **P** was thirty feet wide,
3:10 with gold. These were placed in the Most Holy **P**.
3:14 Across the entrance of the Most Holy **P**,
4:20 to burn in front of the Most Holy **P** as prescribed;
4:22 the doors for the entrances to the Most Holy **P**
5: 2 also known as Zion, to its new **p** in the Temple.
5: 7 the Most Holy **P**—and placed it beneath the wings
5: 9 main room—the Holy **P**—but not from outside it.
5:11 Then the priests left the Holy **P**. All the priests
6: 5 **p** where a temple should be built to honor my
6:10 for I have become king in my father's **p**.
6:20 this **p** where you have said you would put your
6:20 you always hear the prayers I make toward this **p**.
6:21 and your people Israel when we pray toward this **p**.
6:40 be attentive to all the prayers made to you in this **p**.
6:41 arise and enter this resting **p** of yours,
7:12 and have chosen this Temple as the **p** for making
7:15 I will listen to every prayer made in this **p**,
12:13 all the tribes of Israel as the **p** to honor his name.
13:11 They **p** the Bread of the Presence on the holy table,
23:13 **p** of authority by the pillar at the Temple entrance.
31:16 regardless of their **p** in the genealogical records,
32:31 the remarkable events that had taken **p** in the land,
33: 4 the **p** where the LORD had said his name should
33: 7 the very **p** where God had told David and his son
34:25 My anger will be poured out against this **p**,
34:28 **p**.' " So they took her message back to the king.
34:31 The king took his **p** of authority beside the pillar
35:19 This Passover celebration took **p** in the eighteenth
Ezr 1: 4 Those who live in any **p** where Jewish survivors
5:15 him to return the utensils to their **p** in Jerusalem
6:12 as the **p** to honor his name destroy any king
9: 8 He has given us security in this holy **p**. Our God
10: 9 This took **p** on December 19, and all the people
Ne 1: 9 I will bring you back to the **p** I have chosen for my
3: 3 hung the doors, and put the bolts and bars in **p**.
3:16 He rebuilt the wall to a **p** opposite the royal
10:39 and **p** them in the sacred containers near the
Est 2: 9 and her maids into the best **p** in the harem.
4:14 for the Jews will arise from some other **p**,
Job 7:12 Am I a sea monster that you **p** a guard on me?
9: 6 He shakes the earth from its **p**, and its foundations
16: 4 I could say the same things if you were in my **p**.
18:21 wicked person, the **p** of one who rejected God.' "
26: 5 "The dead tremble in their **p** beneath the waters.
26: 6 There is no cover for the **p** of destruction.
29: 7 and took my **p** among the honored leaders.
31:22 then let my shoulder be wrenched out of **p**! Let my
34:13 in his care? Who has set the whole world in **p**?
Ps 1: 5 Sinners will have no **p** among the godly.
8: 3 the moon and the stars you have set in **p**—
18:19 He led me to a **p** of safety; / he rescued me
24: 3 of the LORD? / Who may stand in his holy **p**?
26: 8 LORD, / the **p** where your glory shines.
27: 5 He will **p** me out of reach on a high rock.
31: 8 me over to my enemy / but have set me in a safe **p**.
32: 7 For you are my hiding **p**; / you protect me from
43: 3 to your holy mountain, / to the **p** where you live.
59: 9 to rescue me, / for you, O God, are my **p** of safety.
59:16 my refuge, / a **p** of safety in the day of distress.
66:12 But you brought us to a **p** of great abundance.
74: 7 They utterly defiled the **p** that bears your holy
84: 1 How lovely is your dwelling **p**, / O LORD
84: 3 and raises her young— / at a **p** near your altar,
84: 6 it will become a **p** of refreshing springs,
88:11 In the **p** of destruction, can they proclaim your
91: 2 He alone is my refuge, my **p** of safety; / he is my
95:11 a vow: / 'They will never enter my **p** of rest.' "
132: 5 until I find a **p** to build a house for the LORD,
132: 7 Let us go to the dwelling **p** of the LORD;
132:11 "I will **p** your descendants on your throne.
132:14 "I will live here, for this is the **p** I desired.
139: 5 You **p** your hand of blessing on my head.
139: 8 if I go down to the **p** of the dead, you are there.
142: 5 O LORD. / I say, "You are my **p** of refuge.
Pr 4: 9 She will **p** a lovely wreath on your head; she will
14:26 he will be a **p** of refuge for their children.
25: 6 with the king or push for a **p** among the great.
Ecc 3:20 Both go to the same **p**—the dust from which they
4: 1 Again I observed all the oppression that takes **p** in
9:11 by chance, by being at the right **p** at the right time.
10: 6 people of proven worth their rightful **p** of dignity.
SS 8: 6 **P** me like a seal over your heart, or like a seal on
Isa 2: 2 will become the most important **p** on earth.
3:13 The LORD takes his **p** in court. He is the great
4: 6 daytime heat and a hiding **p** from storms and rain.
5: 6 I will make it a wild **p**. / I will not prune the vines
5: 8 who buy up property so others have no **p** to live.
11:10 for the land where he lives will be a glorious **p**.
13:13 the heavens, and the earth will move from its **p**.
14: 9 "In the **p** of the dead there is excitement over your
14:15 you will be brought down to the **p** of the dead,
14:23 a **p** of porcupines, filled with swamps and marshes.
18: 4 "I will watch quietly from my dwelling **p**—
18: 7 in Jerusalem, the **p** where his name dwells.
22:23 for I will drive him firmly in **p** like a tent stake.
26:19 fall like dew / on his people in the **p** of the dead!
28:20 For you have no **p** of refuge—the bed you have
30:33 Topheth—the **p** of burning—has long been ready
32:10 crop will fail, and the harvest will never take **p**.
33:20 you will see Zion as a **p** of worship
38:10 of my life, / must I now enter the **p** of the dead?
41: 7 then fasten the thing in **p** so it won't fall over.
45:18 the heavens and earth and put everything in **p**.
45:18 world to be lived in, not to be a **p** of empty chaos.
47:14 at all. Their hearth is not a **p** to sit for warmth.
57:15 and holy **p** with those whose spirits are contrite
62:12 And Jerusalem will be known as the Desirable **P**
63:18 briefly your holy people possessed the holy **p**,
65:10 and the valley of Achor will be a **p** to pasture
65:18 I will create Jerusalem as a **p** of happiness.
66: 1 as that? Could you build a dwelling **p** for me?
Jer 7:12 " 'Go to the **p** at Shiloh where I once put the
7:14 this **p** that I gave to you and your ancestors.
7:20 "I will pour out my terrible fury on this **p**.
7:32 "when that **p** will no longer be called Topheth
9:11 the LORD. "It will be a **p** haunted by jackals.
12:16 then they will be given a **p** among my people.
16: 2 "Do not marry or have children in this **p**.
19: 3 I will bring such a terrible disaster on this **p** that
19: 4 and turned this valley into a **p** of wickedness.
19: 4 And they have filled this **p** with the blood of
19: 6 when this **p** will no longer be called Topheth
19:12 This is what I will do to this **p** and its people,
23: 5 "when I will **p** a righteous Branch on King
23:23 Am I a God who is only in one **p**?"
25:35 You will find no **p** to hide; there will be no way to
26: 6 the **p** where the Tabernacle was located.
49:10 land of Edom, and there will be no **p** left to hide.
50: 7 their **p** of rest, the hope of their ancestors.'
La 1: 3 lives among foreign nations and has no **p** of rest.
1:10 the **p** the LORD had forbidden them to enter.
3: 6 He has buried me in a dark **p**, like a person long
5:18 is empty and desolate, a **p** haunted by jackals.
Eze 3:12 (May the glory of the LORD be praised in his **p**!)
4: 3 an iron griddle and **p** it between you and the city.
4: 4 your left side and **p** the sins of Israel on yourself.
5: 2 **P** a third of it at the center of your map of
6: 7 Then when the **p** is littered with corpses, you will
20:15 with milk and honey, the most beautiful **p** on earth.
20:29 'What is this high **p** where you are going?'
20:29 has been called Bamah—'high **p**'—ever since.)
26: 5 It will be a **p** for fishermen to spread their nets,
26:14 a bare rock, a **p** for fishermen to spread their nets.
28:16 from your **p** among the stones of fire.
32:25 They have a resting **p** among the slaughtered,
39:11 and they will change the name of the **p** to the
41: 1 After that, the man brought me into the Holy **P**,
41: 2 The Holy **P** itself was 70 feet long and 35 feet
41: 3 went into the inner room at the end of the Holy **P**.
41: 4 "This," he told me, "is the Most Holy **P**."
41:15 The Holy **P**, the Most Holy **P**, and the foyer of

41:17 leading into the Most Holy **P** was also paneled.
41:20 the walls, including the outer wall of the Holy **P**.
41:21 were square columns at the entrance to the Holy **P**,
41:21 and the ones at the entrance of the Most Holy **P**
41:23 Holy **P** and the Most Holy **P** had double doorways,
41:25 The doors leading into the Holy **P** were decorated
42:14 When the priests leave the Holy **P**, they must not
43:7 this is the **p** of my throne and the **p** where I will rest my feet.
43:21 and burn it at the appointed **p** outside the Temple
45:3 Within it the sanctuary of the Most Holy **P** will be
45:5 It will be their possession and a **p** for their towns.
46:19 He showed me a **p** at the extreme west end of these
Da 2:39 inferior to yours, will rise to take your **p**.
6:3 the king made plans to **p** him over the entire
7:9 I watched as thrones were put in **p** and the Ancient
8:8 In the large horn's **p** grew four prominent horns
8:17 As Gabriel approached the **p** where I was standing,
9:13 All the troubles he predicted have taken **p**.
9:24 prophetic vision, and to anoint the Most Holy **P**.
11:36 For what has been determined will surely take **p**.
Hos 1:10 Then, at the **p** where they were told, 'You are not
5:15 Then I will return to my **p** until they admit their
10:8 shrines of Aven, the **p** of Israel's sin, will crumble.
Joel 2:8 each other; each moves in exactly the right **p**.
Am 9:2 "Even if they dig down to the **p** of the dead,
Ob 1:17 a refuge for those who escape; it will be a holy **p**.
Mic 4:1 will become the most important **p** on earth.
Hab 2:3 seems slow, wait patiently, for it will surely take **p**.
Zep 2:6 a **p** of shepherd camps and enclosures for sheep.
2:9 Their land will become a **p** of stinging nettles,
2:15 it has become an utter ruin, a **p** where animals live!
Hag 2:7 I will fill this **p** with glory, says the LORD
2:9 And in this **p** I will bring peace. I, the LORD
Zec 4:7 will set the final stone of the Temple in **p**,
9:12 Come back to the **p** of safety, all you prisoners,
14:10 But Jerusalem will be raised up in its original **p**
Mt 2:9 and stopped over the **p** where the child was.
8:20 no home of my own, not even a **p** to lay my head."
10:14 shake off the dust of that **p** from your feet as you
10:15 better off on the judgment day than that **p** will be.
11:23 you will be brought down to the **p** of the dead.
14:15 came to him and said, "This is a desolate **p**,
21:13 'My Temple will be called a **p** of prayer,'
24:3 and asked, "When will all this take **p**?
24:15 that causes desecration standing in the holy **p**"—
24:34 pass from the scene before all these things take **p**.
24:51 In that **p** there will be weeping and gnashing of
25:33 He will **p** the sheep at his right hand and the goats
26:16 looking for the right time and **p** to betray Jesus.
26:64 sitting at God's right hand in the **p** of power
27:33 Then they went out to a **p** called Golgotha (which
Mk 5:10 and again not to send them to some distant **p**.
5:23 "Please come and **p** your hands on her; heal her
6:5 them except to **p** his hands on a few sick people
6:35 came to him and said, "This is a desolate **p**,
7:33 Jesus led him to a private **p** away from the crowd.
9:35 "Anyone who wants to be the first must take last **p**
11:17 'My Temple will be called a **p** of prayer for all
13:4 "When will all this take **p**? And will there be any
13:30 from the scene until all these events have taken **p**.
14:11 looking for the right time and **p** to betray Jesus.
14:15 That is the **p**; go ahead and prepare our supper
14:62 sitting at God's right hand in the **p** of power
15:22 And they brought Jesus to a **p** called Golgotha
15:25 in the morning when the crucifixion took **p**.
16:18 They will be able to **p** their hands on the sick
16:19 and sat down in the **p** of honor at God's right hand.
Lk 1:1 accounts about the events that took **p** among us.
3:3 Then John went from **p** to **p** on both sides of
4:17 and he unrolled the scroll to the **p** where it says:
9:12 There is nothing to eat here in this deserted **p**."
9:58 no home of my own, not even a **p** to lay my head."
10:7 Stay in one **p**, eating and drinking what they
10:15 you will be brought down to the **p** of the dead."
11:37 a meal. So he went in and took his **p** at the table.
14:10 'Friend, we have a better **p** than this for you!'
16:23 and his soul went to the **p** of the dead. There,
16:28 and I want him to warn them about this **p** of
17:23 of Man has returned and that he is in this **p** or that.
19:37 As they reached the **p** where the road started down
19:44 Your enemies will not leave a single stone in **p**,
19:46 'My Temple will be a **p** of prayer,'
21:7 "Teacher," they asked, "when will all this take **p**?
21:31 when you see the events I've described taking **p**,
21:32 from the scene until all these events have taken **p**.
22:12 That is the **p**. Go ahead and prepare our supper
22:51 And he touched the **p** where the man's ear had
22:69 will be sitting at God's right hand in the **p** of
23:33 Finally, they came to a **p** called The Skull.
Jn 1:28 This incident took **p** at Bethany, a village east of
1:39 in the afternoon when they went with him to the **p**,
4:20 Jews insist that Jerusalem is the only **p** of worship,
6:23 Several boats from Tiberias landed near the **p**
8:37 because my message does not find a **p** in your
10:40 He went beyond the Jordan River to stay near the **p**
11:30 outside the village, at the **p** where Martha met him.
11:54 He went to a **p** near the wilderness, to the village
14:2 and I am going to prepare a **p** for you.
16:21 her anguish gives **p** to joy because she has brought
18:2 Judas, the betrayer, knew this **p**, because Jesus had
19:17 Jesus went to the **p** called Skull Hill (in Hebrew,
19:20 The **p** where Jesus was crucified was near the city;
19:41 The **p** of crucifixion was near a garden,
20:12 and foot of the **p** where the body of Jesus had been
20:25 and **p** my hand into the wound in his side."
Ac 1:19 and they gave the **p** the Aramaic name
1:21 we must choose someone else to take Judas's **p**.
2:1 the believers were meeting together in one **p**.
5:31 Then God put him in the **p** of honor at his right
7:7 end they will come out and worship me in this **p**.'
7:49 the Lord. / 'Could you build a dwelling **p** for me?
7:55 and he saw Jesus standing in the **p** of honor at
7:56 and the Son of Man standing in the **p** of honor at
9:32 Peter traveled from **p** to **p** to visit the believers,
10:18 They asked if this was the **p** where Simon Peter
12:17 he said. And then he went to another **p**.
16:16 One day as we were going down to the **p** of prayer,
26:18 their sins and be given a **p** among God's people,
27:12 a poor **p** to spend the winter—most of the crew
27:21 you should have listened to me in the first **p**
Ro 5:2 Christ has brought us into this **p** of highest
8:34 and is sitting at the **p** of highest honor next to God,
9:29 And Isaiah said in another **p**, / "If the Lord
10:7 "You don't need to go to the **p** of the dead" (to
11:21 not spare the branches he put there in the first **p**,
15:10 And in another **p** it is written, / "Rejoice, O you
15:12 the Gentiles. / They will **p** their hopes on him."
1Co 7:35 this for your benefit, not to **p** restrictions on you.
15:2 something that was never true in the first **p**.
2Co 8:6 who encouraged your giving in the first **p**, to return
Gal 5:6 For when we **p** our faith in Christ Jesus, it makes
Eph 1:20 and seated him in the **p** of honor at God's right
5:3 Such sins have no **p** among God's people.
Php 1:7 of you, for you have a very special **p** in my heart.
Col 1:7 faithful servant, and he is helping us in your **p**.
3:1 where Christ sits at God's right hand in the **p** of
3:10 In its **p** you have clothed yourselves with a
1Ti 5:18 And in another **p**, "Those who work deserve their
Heb 1:3 he sat down in the **p** of honor at the right hand of
3:11 a vow: / 'They will never enter my **p** of rest.' "
3:18 he vowed that they would never enter his **p** of rest?
4:1 God's promise of entering his **p** of rest still stands,
4:2 Good News—that God has prepared a **p** of rest—
4:3 For only we who believe can enter his **p** of rest.
4:3 'They will never enter my **p** of rest,' " even
4:3 **p** of rest has been ready since he made the world.
4:5 God said, "They will never enter my **p** of rest."
4:7 So God set another time for entering his **p** of rest,
4:8 This new **p** of rest was not the land of Canaan,
4:11 Let us do our best to enter that **p** of rest.
7:19 and now a better hope has taken its **p**.
7:23 When one priest died, another had to take his **p**.
7:26 and he has been given the highest **p** of honor in
8:1 Our High Priest sat down in the **p** of highest honor
8:2 the true **p** of worship that was built by the Lord
8:5 They serve in a **p** of worship that is only a copy,
9:2 bread on the table. This was called the Holy **P**.
9:3 was the second room called the Most Holy **P**.
9:5 out over the Ark's cover, the **p** of atonement.
9:6 When these things were all in **p**, the priests went in
9:7 But only the high priest goes into the Most Holy **P**,
9:8 **P** was not open to the people as long as the first
9:12 for all time he took blood into that Most Holy **P**,
9:24 He did not go into the earthly **p** of worship, for that
9:25 **P** year after year to offer the blood of an animal.
10:12 Then he sat down at the **p** of highest honor at
10:19 we can boldly enter heaven's Most Holy **P**
11:16 But they were looking for a better **p**, a heavenly
12:2 Now he is seated in the **p** of highest honor beside
12:18 to a **p** of flaming fire, darkness, gloom,
13:11 of animals into the Holy **P** as a sacrifice for sin,
1Pe 3:22 He is seated in the **p** of honor next to God, and all
4:9 home with those who need a meal or a **p** to stay.
5:10 and he will **p** you on a firm foundation.
2Pe 1:19 their words are like a light shining in a dark **p**—
1Jn 1:10 and showing that his word has no **p** in our hearts.
5:21 keep away from anything that might take God's **p**
Jude 1:6 God gave them but left the **p** where they belonged.
1:9 (This took **p** when Michael was arguing with Satan
Rev 2:5 and remove your lampstand from its **p** among the
12:6 where God had prepared a **p** to give her care for
12:14 This allowed her to fly to a **p** prepared for her in
16:16 and their armies to a **p** called *Armageddon* in
20:11 fled from his presence, but they found no **p** to hide.

PLACED (150) [PLACE]

Ge 2:8 in the east, and there he **p** the man he had created.
2:9 At the center of the garden he **p** the tree of life
2:15 The LORD God **p** the man in the Garden of Eden
3:17 told you not to eat, I have **p** a curse on the ground.
9:2 will be afraid of you. I have **p** them in your power.
9:13 I have **p** my rainbow in the clouds. It is the sign of
22:6 Abraham **p** the wood for the burnt offering on
22:9 to go, he built an altar and **p** the wood on it.
30:35 He **p** them in the care of his sons,
40:11 juice into it. Then I **p** the cup in Pharaoh's hand."
41:42 Then Pharaoh **p** his own signet ring on Joseph's
41:42 and **p** the royal gold chain about his neck.
50:26 and his body was **p** in a coffin in Egypt.
Ex 16:34 He eventually **p** it for safekeeping in the Ark of the
26:35 The lampstand must be **p** on the south side,
27:21 The lampstand will be **p** outside the inner curtain
29:23 of yeastless bread that was **p** before the LORD.
36:11 Fifty blue loops were **p** along the edge of the last
37:7 and **p** them at the two ends of the atonement cover.
37:16 dishes, bowls, and pitchers to be **p** on the table.
37:27 Two gold rings were **p** on opposite sides,
39:25 Bells of pure gold were **p** between the
40:20 He **p** inside the Ark the stone tablets inscribed with
40:22 Next he **p** the table in the Tabernacle,
40:26 He also **p** the incense altar in the Tabernacle,
40:29 and he **p** the altar of burnt offering near the
40:30 Next he **p** the large washbasin between the
Lev 8:8 Then Moses **p** the chestpiece on Aaron and put the
8:9 He **p** on Aaron's head the turban with the gold
8:26 On top of these he **p** a loaf of unleavened bread,
8:26 without yeast that was **p** in the LORD's presence.
9:20 He **p** these fat parts on top of the breasts of these
Nu 4:10 and the bundle must be **p** on a carrying frame.
4:12 fine goatskin leather, and **p** on the carrying frame.
4:14 are to be **p** on the cloth, and a covering of fine
7:10 They each **p** their gifts before the altar.
16:18 **p** burning coals and incense on them,
Dt 1:21 He has **p** it in front of you. Go and occupy it as the
10:5 and **p** the tablets in the Ark of the Covenant,
Jos 22:25 The LORD has **p** the Jordan River as a barrier
Jdg 2:18 Whenever the LORD **p** a judge over Israel,
17:4 and an idol. And these were **p** in Micah's house.
1Sa 5:2 temple of Dagon and **p** it beside the idol of Dagon.
6:11 the gold rats and gold tumors were **p** on the cart.
6:15 tumors from the cart and **p** them on the large rock.
7:12 and **p** it between the towns of Mizpah
9:22 the great hall and **p** them at the head of the table,
9:24 So the cook brought it in and **p** it before Saul.
10:25 them down on a scroll and **p** it before the LORD.
21:6 the Bread of the Presence that was **p** before the
24:10 For the LORD **p** you at my mercy back there in
26:23 and I refused to kill you even when the LORD **p**
31:10 They **p** his armor in the temple of the Ashtoreths,
2Sa 6:3 They **p** the Ark of God on a new cart and brought
6:17 The Ark of the LORD was **p** inside the special
8:6 Then he **p** several army garrisons in Damascus,
8:14 He **p** army garrisons throughout Edom, and all the
10:9 He **p** them under his personal command and led
12:30 the king's head, and it was **p** on David's own head.
18:2 One-third were **p** under Joab, one-third under
20:3 he had left to keep house should be **p** in seclusion.
1Ki 2:24 confirmed me and **p** me on the throne of my father,
6:19 the Ark of the LORD's covenant would be **p**.
6:23 Within the inner sanctuary Solomon **p** two
6:27 Solomon **p** them side by side in the inner sanctuary
7:39 The Sea was **p** at the southeast corner of the
8:6 and **p** it beneath the wings of the cherubim.
8:9 tablets that Moses had **p** there at Mount Sinai,
10:9 in you and has **p** you on the throne of Israel.
10:17 The king **p** these shields in the Palace of the Forest
12:29 He **p** these calf idols at the southern and northern
18:26 they prepared one of the bulls and **p** it on the altar.
20:38 having **p** a bandage over his eyes to disguise
2Ki 10:7 They **p** their heads in baskets and presented them
11:12 the king's son, and **p** the crown on his head.
16:14 and **p** it on the north side of the new altar.
16:17 of the bronze oxen and **p** it on the stone pavement.
17:29 they **p** their idols at the pagan shrines that the
24:13 that King Solomon of Israel had **p** in the Temple.
1Ch 10:10 They **p** his armor in the temple of their gods,
18:6 Then he **p** several army garrisons in Damascus,
18:13 He **p** army garrisons throughout Edom, and all the
19:10 He **p** them under his personal command and led
20:2 the king's head, and it was **p** on David's own head.
28:16 on which the Bread of the Presence would be **p**
2Ch 3:10 with gold. These were **p** in the Most Holy Place.
4:7 Five were **p** against the south wall, and five were **p** against the north wall.
4:8 He also built ten tables and **p** them in the Temple,
4:10 The Sea was **p** near the southeast corner of the
5:7 and **p** it beneath the wings of the cherubim.
5:10 tablets that Moses had **p** there at Mount Sinai,
6:11 There I have **p** the Ark, and in the Ark is the
6:13 and had **p** it at the center of the Temple's outer
6:41 of yours, where your magnificent Ark has been **p**.
9:8 in you and has **p** you on the throne to rule for him.
9:16 The king **p** these shields in the Palace of the Forest
23:11 the king's son, and **p** the crown on his head.
29:27 Then Hezekiah ordered that the burnt offering be **p**
35:24 out of his chariot and **p** him in another chariot.
36:7 and he **p** them in his palace in Babylon.
Ezr 1:7 and had **p** in the temple of his own gods.
5:14 in Jerusalem and had **p** in the temple of Babylon.
Ne 4:13 So I **p** armed guards behind the lowest parts of the
9:22 and you **p** your people in every corner of the land.
10:38 to the Temple of our God and **p** in the storerooms.
13:5 a large storage room and **p** it at Tobiah's disposal.
Est 2:8 harem at the fortress of Susa and **p** in Hegai's care.
6:11 put it on Mordecai, **p** him on the king's own horse,
Job 20:4 that ever since people were first **p** on the earth,
39:6 I have **p** it in the wilderness; its home is the
Ps 2:6 "I have **p** my chosen king on the throne
19:4 The sun lives in the heavens / where God **p** it.
21:3 You **p** a crown of finest gold on his head.
104:5 You **p** the world on its foundation / so it would
105:18 feet with fetters / and **p** his neck in an iron collar.
136:6 Give thanks to him who **p** the earth on the water.
140:5 out a net; / they have **p** traps all along the way.
Pr 6:3 You have **p** yourself at your friend's mercy.
Isa 40:20 Can God be compared to an idol that must be **p** on
44:13 idol that cannot even move from where it is **p**!
59:17 and **p** the helmet of salvation on his head.
Jer 24:1 I saw two baskets of figs **p** in front of the
La 1:13 He has **p** a trap in my path and turned me back.
Eze 5:5 to Jerusalem. I **p** her at the center of the nations,
40:42 On these tables were **p** the butchering knives
Da 1:2 and **p** them in the treasure-house of his god in the
6:17 stone was brought and **p** over the mouth of the den.
7:25 and they will be **p** under his control for a time,
Mt 27:29 and they **p** a stick in his right hand as a scepter.
27:60 He **p** it in his own new tomb, which had been
Mk 4:21 A lamp is **p** on a stand, where its light will shine.
8:25 Then Jesus **p** his hands over the man's eyes again.

10:16 and **p** his hands on their heads and blessed them.
Lk 2:40 his years, and God **p** his special favor upon him.
23:55 and saw the tomb where they **p** his body.
Ac 8:18 the apostles **p** their hands upon people's heads,
12: 6 The night before Peter was to be **p** on trial, he was
13:29 him down from the cross and **p** him in a tomb.
19:12 or cloths that had touched his skin were **p** on sick
27: 1 and several other prisoners were **p** in the custody
Ro 13: 1 All governments have been **p** in power by God.
1Co 12:28 the members that God has **p** in the body of Christ:
1Ti 5: 5 is truly alone in this world, has **p** her hope in God.
Heb 7: 6 And Melchizedek **p** a blessing upon Abraham,
11:35 They **p** their hope in the resurrection to a better
Jas 4: 5 whom God has **p** within us, jealously longs for us
1Pe 1:21 your faith and hope can be **p** confidently in God.
Rev 6: 2 carried a bow, and a crown was **p** on his head.
7: 3 or the trees until we have **p** the seal of God on the

PLACES (60) [PLACE]

HIGH PLACES (2) 1Ki 12:31; Mic 1:3

Ge 25:16 listed according to the **p** they settled and camped.
36:40 clans of Esau, who lived in the **p** named for them:
Ex 16:29 On the Sabbath day you must stay in your **p**.
20:24 Build altars in the **p** where I remind you who I am,
Lev 21:23 near the altar, for this would desecrate my holy **p**.
26:31 your cities desolate and destroy your **p** of worship,
Nu 10:31 "You know the **p** in the wilderness where we
33: 2 identified by the different **p** they stopped along the
35:12 These cities will be **p** of protection from a dead
Dt 1:33 who goes before you looking for the best **p** to
2:37 all the **p** the LORD our God had commanded us
12: 2 you must destroy all the **p** where they worship
12: 3 Erase the names of their gods from those **p**!
Jos 2: 7 to the shallow crossing **p** of the Jordan River.
5: 7 those who had grown up to take their fathers' **p**.
Jdg 6: 2 where they made hiding **p** for themselves in caves
7:22 Those who were not killed fled to **p** as far away as
9:43 he and his men jumped up from their hiding **p**
1Sa 7:16 He judged the people of Israel at each of these **p**.
23:23 Discover his hiding **p**, and come back with a more
30:31 Hebron, and all the other **p** they had visited.
1Ki 12:31 Jeroboam built shrines at the pagan high **p**
20:34 and you may establish **p** of trade in Damascus,
2Ki 23:14 Then he desecrated these **p** by scattering human
2Ch 30:16 They took their **p** at the Temple according to the
35: 5 Then stand in your appointed holy **p** and help the
35:10 the priests and the Levites took their **p**,
35:15 descendants of Asaph, were in their assigned **p**,
Ezr 3:10 their robes and took their **p** to blow their trumpets.
Ne 12:40 to the Temple of God, where they took their **p**.
Job 34:24 asking anyone, and he sets up others in their **p**.
Ps 68: 6 God **p** the lonely in families; / he sets the prisoners
74: 8 So they burned down all the **p** where God was
Isa 7:19 also in the desolate valleys, caves, and thorny **p**.
65: 4 the graves and secret **p** to worship evil spirits.
Jer 9:26 the people who live in distant **p**, and yes,
25:23 and Buz, and to the people who live in distant **p**.
40:12 they began to return to Judah from the **p** to which
49:32 to the winds these people who live in distant **p**.
Eze 31:15 I made the deep **p** mourn, and I restrained the
34:12 and rescue them from all the **p** to which they were
34:13 and by the rivers in all the **p** where people live.
34:14 There they will lie down in pleasant **p** and feed in
34:25 people will be able to camp safely in the wildest **p**
37:21 land from the **p** where they have been scattered.
42:20 around it to separate the holy **p** from the common.
Hos 8:11 but these very altars became **p** for sinning!
Joel 3: 7 But I will bring them back again from all these **p** to
Mic 1: 3 and comes to earth, walking on the high **p**.
Hab 1: 8 Their horsemen race forward from distant **p**.
Mt 20:21 will you let my two sons sit in **p** of honor next to
20:23 My Father has prepared those **p** for the ones he has
Mk 1:45 He had to stay out in the secluded **p**, and people
10:37 we want to sit in **p** of honor next to you,"
10:40 God has prepared those **p** for the ones he has
Lk 3: 5 the curves, / and smooth out the rough **p**!
4:43 the Good News of the Kingdom of God in other **p**,
13:29 the world to take their **p** in the Kingdom of God.
Ro 15:22 so long because I have been preaching in these **p**.
2Co 10:16 and preach the Good News in other **p** that are far

PLACING (10) [PLACE]

Ex 30:10 "Once a year Aaron must purify the altar by **p** on
Jdg 18:21 on their way again, **p** their children, livestock,
1Sa 2: 8 treats them like princes, / **p** them in seats of honor.
2Ki 4:34 **p** his mouth on the child's mouth, his eyes on the
Isa 28:16 "Look! I am **p** a foundation stone in Jerusalem.
Ac 12: 4 **p** him under the guard of four squads of four
Ro 9:33 "I am **p** a stone in Jerusalem that causes people to
2Co 1:22 and he has identified us as his own by **p** the Holy
Heb 6: 1 away from evil deeds and **p** our faith in God.
1Pe 2: 6 express it, / "I am **p** a stone in Jerusalem,

PLAGUE (65) [PLAGUED, PLAGUES]

Ge 12:17 But the LORD sent a terrible **p** upon Pharaoh's
Ex 9: 3 the LORD will send a deadly **p** to destroy your
9: 5 The LORD announced that he would send the **p**
9:14 I will send a **p** that will really speak to you
9:15 I could have attacked you with a **p** that would have
10: 6 Never in the history of Egypt has there been a **p**
10:14 It was the worst locust **p** in Egyptian history,
10:17 LORD your God to take away this terrible **p**."
12:13 This **p** of death will not touch you when I strike the
32:35 And the LORD sent a great **p** upon the people
Lev 26:25 to your cities, I will send a **p** to destroy you there,
Nu 8:19 so no **p** will strike them when they approach the
11:33 and he caused a severe **p** to break out among them.
14:12 I will disown them and destroy them with a **p**.
14:37 were struck dead with a **p** before the LORD.
16:46 is blazing among them—the **p** has already begun."
16:47 The **p** indeed had already begun, but Aaron burned
16:48 the living and the dead until the **p** was stopped.
16:49 But 14,700 people died in that **p**, in addition to
16:50 Then because the **p** had stopped, Aaron returned to
25: 8 So the **p** against the Israelites was stopped,
25:18 who was killed on the day of the **p** at Peor."
26: 1 After the **p** had ended, the LORD said to Moses
31:16 They are the ones who caused the **p** to strike the
Dt 28:61 bring against you every sickness and **p** there is,
Jos 22:17 even after the **p** that struck the entire assembly of
1Sa 5: 6 and the nearby villages with a **p** of tumors.
5: 9 young and old, with a **p** of tumors, and there was a
5:11 For the **p** from God had already begun, and great
6: 3 "Send a guilt offering so the **p** will stop. Then, if the **p** doesn't stop, you will know that God didn't send the **p** after
6: 4 "Since the **p** has struck both you and your five
6: 9 we will know that the **p** was simply a coincidence
2Sa 24:13 or three days of severe **p** throughout your land?
24:15 So the LORD sent a **p** upon Israel that morning,
24:21 LORD there, so that the LORD will stop the **p**."
24:25 answered his prayer, and the **p** was stopped.
1Ch 21:12 or three days of severe **p** as the angel of the
21:14 So the LORD sent a **p** upon Israel, and seventy
21:22 to the LORD there, so that he will stop the **p**."
Job 9:23 He laughs when a **p** suddenly kills the innocent.
27:15 survive will be brought down to the grave by a **p**,
Ps 78:50 Egyptians' lives / but handed them over to the **p**.
91: 3 from every trap / and protect you from the fatal **p**.
91: 6 nor dread the **p** that stalks in darkness,
91:10 conquer you; / no **p** will come near your dwelling.
106:15 what they asked for, / but he sent a **p** along with it.
106:29 all these things, / so a **p** broke out among them.
106:30 had the courage to step in, / and the **p** was stopped.
Isa 3:17 The Lord will send a **p** of scabs to ornament their
10:16 will send a **p** among your proud troops,
10:18 and they will waste away like sick people in a **p**.
Jer 18:21 Let their old men die in a **p**, and let their young
21: 6 I will send a terrible **p** upon this city, and both
Eze 14:19 the land, and the **p** killed people and animals alike.
14:21 war, famine, beasts, and **p**—destroying all her
28:23 I will send a **p** against you, and blood will be
Hab 3: 5 marches before him; **p** follows close behind.
Zec 14:12 And the LORD will send a **p** on all the nations
14:15 This same **p** will strike the horses, mules, camels,
14:16 the enemies of Jerusalem who survive the **p** will go
14:18 the LORD will punish them with the same **p** that
Rev 11: 6 and to send every kind of **p** upon the earth as often
16:21 of the hailstorm, which was a very terrible **p**.

PLAGUED (1) [PLAGUE]

Ps 73: 5 or **p** with problems like everyone else.

PLAGUES (20) [PLAGUE]

Ex 30:12 Then there will be no **p** among the people as you
Dt 28:59 both you and your children with indescribable **p**.
28:59 These **p** will be intense and without relief,
Jos 24: 5 and Aaron, and I brought terrible **p** on Egypt;
1Sa 4: 8 with **p** when Israel was in the wilderness.
6: 6 go until God had ravaged them with dreadful **p**.
1Ki 8:37 or **p**, or crop disease, or attacks of locusts
2Ch 6:28 or **p**, or crop disease, or attacks of locusts
7:13 devour your crops, or I might send **p** among you.
Hos 13:14 O grave, bring forth your **p**! For I will not relent!
Am 4:10 "I sent **p** against you like the **p** I sent against
Rev 9:18 the people on earth were killed by these three **p**—
9:20 But the people who did not die in these **p** still
15: 1 Seven angels were holding the seven last **p**,
15: 6 the bowls of the seven **p** came from the Temple,
15: 8 angels had completed pouring out the seven **p**.
16: 9 cursed the name of God, who sent all of these **p**.
21: 9 the seven bowls containing the seven last **p** came
22:18 God will add to that person the **p** described in this

PLAIN (34) [PLAINLY, PLAINS]

Ge 11: 2 they found a **p** in the land of Babylonia and settled
13:12 to a place near Sodom, among the cities of the **p**.
14: 5 Zuzites in Ham, the Emites in the **p** of Kiriathaim,
19:25 along with the other cities and villages of the **p**,
19:28 He looked out across the **p** to Sodom
19:29 from the disaster that engulfed the cities on the **p**.
Dt 1: 7 the western foothills, the Negev, and the coastal **p**.
Jos 13: 9 to the **p** beyond Medeba, as far as Dibon.
13:16 the middle of the gorge) to the **p** beyond Medeba.
13:17 It included Heshbon and the other towns on the **p**
13:21 land of Reuben also included all the towns of the **p**
20: 8 Bezer, in the wilderness **p** of the tribe of Reuben;
Jdg 14:12 I will give you thirty **p** linen robes and thirty fancy
2Sa 18:23 Then Ahimaaz took a shortcut across the **p** of the
1Ch 5:16 and its villages, and throughout the Sharon **P**.
27:29 Shitrai was in charge of the cattle on the Sharon **P**.
2Ch 35:22 he led his army into battle on the **p** of Megiddo.
Ne 6: 2 to meet them at one of the villages in the **p** of Ono.
Ps 78:12 did for their ancestors in Egypt, on the **p** of Zoan.
78:43 signs in Egypt, / his wonders on the **p** of Zoan.
Pr 8: 9 My words are **p** to anyone with understanding,
Ecc 12:10 Indeed, the Teacher taught the **p** truth, and he did
Isa 33: 9 The **p** of Sharon is now a wilderness. Bashan
35: 2 as Mount Carmel's pastures and the **p** of Sharon.
65:10 the **p** of Sharon will again be filled with flocks,
Jer 47: 5 You remnant of the Mediterranean **p**, how long
Da 3: 1 and set it up on the **p** of Dura in the province of
Zec 14:10 south of Jerusalem, will become one vast **p**.
Lk 8:17 eventually be brought to light and made **p** to all.
1Co 2: 4 And my message and my preaching were very **p**.
14: 7 are examples of the need for speaking in **p**
Php 3:15 on some point, I believe God will make it **p** to you.
2Ti 1:10 And now he has made all of this **p** to us by the
Rev 20: 9 And I saw them as they went up on the broad **p** of

PLAINLY (17) [PLAIN]

Ge 26:28 "We can **p** see that the LORD is with you.
Ex 21: 5 But the slave may **p** declare, 'I love my master,
2Ch 29: 8 of dread, horror, and ridicule, as you can so **p** see.
Ps 62:11 God has spoken **p**, / and I have heard it many
Isa 28:22 has **p** told me that he is determined to crush you.
32: 4 who stammer in uncertainty will speak out **p**.
48:16 I have always told you **p** what would happen
Mt 16:21 then on Jesus began to tell his disciples **p** that he
Mk 7:35 Instantly the man could hear perfectly and speak **p**!
Jn 3:28 You yourselves know how **p** I told you that I am
10:24 us in suspense? If you are the Messiah, tell us **p**."
11:14 Then he told them **p**, "Lazarus is dead.
14: 2 for you. If this were not so, I would tell you **p**.
16:25 and I will tell you **p** all about the Father.
16:29 "At last you are speaking **p** and not in parables.
Ac 20:26 Let me say **p** that I have been faithful. No one's
1Co 14:13 in order to tell people **p** what has been said.

PLAINS (25) [PLAIN]

Ge 13:10 Lot took a long look at the fertile **p** of the Jordan
Nu 22: 1 Then the people of Israel traveled to the **p** of Moab
26: 3 camped on the **p** of Moab beside the Jordan River,
26:63 and Eleazar the priest on the **p** of Moab beside the
31:12 which was camped on the **p** of Moab beside the
33:48 and camped on the **p** of Moab beside the Jordan
33:49 as far as Abel-shittim on the **p** of Moab.
33:50 Jordan River on the **p** of Moab opposite Jericho,
35: 1 was camped beside the Jordan on the **p** of Moab,
36:13 camped on the **p** of Moab beside the Jordan River,
Dt 34: 1 Then Moses went to Mount Nebo from the **p** of
34: 8 mourned thirty days for Moses on the **p** of Moab,
Jos 4:13 and they crossed over to the **p** of Jericho in the
5:10 While the Israelites were camped at Gilgal on the **p**
13:32 Moses had made while he was on the **p** of Moab,
Jdg 1:19 they failed to drive out the people living in the **p**
1:34 and would not let them come down into the **p**.
1Ki 20:23 they won. But we can beat them easily on the **p**.
20:25 and men, and we will fight against them in the **p**.
20:28 the LORD is a god of the hills and not of the **p**.
2Ki 25: 5 after them and caught the king on the **p** of Jericho,
2Ch 26:10 of livestock in the foothills of Judah and on the **p**.
Jer 39: 5 the king and caught him on the **p** of Jericho.
52: 8 and caught King Zedekiah on the **p** of Jericho,
Ob 1:19 the foothills of Judah will possess the Philistine **p**

PLAITING [KJV] See (FANCY) HAIRSTYLES

PLAN (87) [PLANNED, PLANNING, PLANS]

Ge 18:17 "Should I hide my **p** from Abraham?"
32:20 **p** was to appease Esau with the presents before
Ex 2:14 Do you **p** to kill me as you killed that Egyptian
Dt 1:14 "You agreed that my **p** was a good one.
1Sa 23: 9 But David learned of Saul's **p** and told Abiathar
2Sa 15:27 king told Zadok the priest, "Look, here is my **p**.
17: 4 This **p** seemed good to Absalom and to all the
17:14 which really was the better **p**, so that he could
18: 4 "If you think that's the best **p**, I'll do it," the king
2Ki 10:19 But Jehu's **p** was to destroy all the worshipers of
1Ch 28: 9 and understands and knows every **p** and thought.
28:19 "Every part of this **p**," David told Solomon,
2Ch 30: 4 This **p** for keeping the Passover seemed right to the
Ezr 10:16 So this was the **p** that they followed. Ezra selected
Ne 2:19 Tobiah, and Geshem the Arab heard of our **p**,
6: 6 According to his reports, you **p** to be their king.
Est 2: 4 to the king, so he put the **p** into effect immediately.
Ps 7:16 it backfires on them. / They **p** violence for others,
10: 2 Let them be caught in the evil they **p** for others.
62: 4 They **p** to topple me from my high position.
64: 5 and **p** how to set their traps. / "Who will ever
64: 6 they say, / "We have devised the perfect **p**!"
Pr 12: 2 but he condemns those who **p** wickedness.
14:22 but if you **p** good, you will be granted unfailing
16:30 plot evil; without a word, they **p** their mischief.
31:15 and **p** the day's work for her servant girls.
Isa 8:12 Do not be afraid that some **p** conceived behind
10: 7 my people as part of his **p** to conquer the world.
14:26 I have a **p** for the whole earth, for my mighty
45:19 Israel to ask me for something I did not **p** to give.
46:10 Everything I **p** will come to pass, for I do whatever
53:10 But it was the LORD's good **p** to crush him
53:10 and the LORD's **p** will prosper in his hands.
Jer 10:23 is not his own. No one is able to **p** his own course.
29: 5 "Build homes, and **p** to stay. Plant gardens,
29:28 should build homes and **p** to stay for many years.
33:26 or change the **p** that David's descendants will rule
Eze 20:30 Do you **p** to pollute yourselves just as your
43:10 Tell them its appearance and its **p** so they will be
Da 11:17 the kingdom from within, but his **p** will fail.
Am 7: 6 Then the LORD turned from this **p**, too. "I won't
Mic 4:12 know the LORD's thoughts or understand his **p**.
Hab 1:12 are eternal—is your **p** in all of this to wipe us out?
2: 3 But these things I **p** won't happen right away.
Zec 12: 9 For my **p** is to destroy all the nations that come
Mk 10: 6 But God's **p** was seen from the beginning of

Lk 7:29 tax collectors, agreed that God's **p** was right,
7:30 and experts in religious law had rejected God's **p**
9:31 was about to fulfill God's **p** by dying in Jerusalem.
22:22 Son of Man, must die since it is part of God's **p**.
Jn 1:13 physical birth resulting from human passion or **p**—
13: 2 Simon Iscariot, to carry out his **p** to betray Jesus.
Ac 2:23 But you followed God's prearranged **p**.
4:28 did occurred according to your eternal will and **p**.
7:44 It was constructed in exact accordance with the **p**
23:16 But Paul's nephew heard of their **p** and went to the
25: 3 to Jerusalem. (Their **p** was to waylay and kill him.)
27:43 spare Paul, so he didn't let them carry out their **p**.
Ro 8: 3 But God put into effect a different **p** to save us.
9:11 proves that God chooses according to his own **p**,
15:21 I have been following the **p** spoken of in the
16:25 about Jesus Christ and his **p** for you Gentiles,
16:25 a **p** kept secret from the beginning of time.
1Co 1:25 This "foolish" **p** of God is far wiser than the
10:33 That is the **p** I follow, too. I try to please everyone
2Co 1:17 You may be asking why I changed my **p**. Hadn't I
10:13 is to stay within the boundaries of God's **p** for us,
10:13 and this **p** includes our working there with you.
Eph 1: 5 His unchanging **p** has always been to adopt us into
1: 9 God's secret **p** has now been revealed to us;
1: 9 it is a **p** centered on Christ, designed long ago
1:10 And this is his **p**: At the right time he will bring
3: 3 this letter, God himself revealed his secret **p** to me.
3: 4 you will understand what I know about this **p**
3: 6 And this is the secret **p**: The Gentiles have an
3: 9 I was chosen to explain to everyone this **p** that
3:11 This was his **p** from all eternity, and it has now
3:14 When I think of the wisdom and scope of God's **p**,
6:19 secret **p** that the Good News is for the Gentiles,
Col 2: 2 have complete understanding of God's secret **p**,
4: 3 many opportunities to preach about his secret **p**—
2Ti 1: 9 because that was his **p** long before the world
Jas 5:11 From his experience we see how the Lord's **p**
2Pe 1:12 I **p** to keep on reminding you of these things—
Rev 10: 7 his trumpet, God's mysterious **p** will be fulfilled.
17:17 For God has put a **p** into their minds, a **p** that will carry out his purposes.

PLANE (2)

Ge 30:37 and **p** trees and peeled off strips of the bark to
Eze 31: 8 equal to it; no **p** tree had boughs to compare.

PLANKS (4)

Ex 27: 8 The altar must be hollow, made from **p**. Be careful
38: 7 The altar was hollow and was made from **p**.
1Ki 6: 9 put in a ceiling made of beams and **p** of cedar.
Ac 27:44 and he told the others to try for it on **p** and debris

PLANNED (27) [PLAN]

Ex 14: 4 I have **p** this so I will receive great glory at the
Nu 24:11 I had **p** to reward you richly, but the LORD has
33:56 And I will do to you what I had **p** to do to
2Sa 21: 5 they replied, "It was Saul who **p** to destroy us,
1Ki 9: 1 He completed everything he had **p** to do.
2Ki 19:25 Long ago I **p** what I am now causing to happen,
2Ch 7:11 He completed everything he had **p** to do.
Job 23:14 So he will do for me all he has **p**. He controls my
Ps 75: 2 God says, "At the time I have **p**, / I will bring
140: 9 be destroyed / by the very evil they have **p** for me.
Isa 5:19 you can do. We want to see what you have **p**."
14:24 has sworn this oath: "It will all happen as I have **p**.
22:11 God for help. He is the one who **p** this long ago.
25: 1 You **p** them long ago, and now you have
37:26 Long ago I **p** what I am now causing to happen,
42:21 Through it he had **p** to show the world that he is
Jer 18: 8 its evil ways, I will not destroy it as I had **p**.
36: 3 in writing all the terrible things I have **p** for them.
51:29 for everything the LORD has **p** against her stands
Eze 39:10 They will take plunder from those who **p** to
Am 3: 6 comes to a city, isn't it because the LORD **p** it?
Mk 3: 2 on the Sabbath? If he did, they **p** to condemn him.
Lk 10: 1 in pairs to all the towns and villages he **p** to visit.
Ro 1:13 dear friends, that I **p** many times to visit you,
Gal 1: 4 He died for our sins, just as God our Father **p**,
Eph 2:10 so that we can do the good things he **p** for us long
1Pe 2: 8 so they meet the fate that has been **p** for them.

PLANNING (40) [PLAN]

Ge 24:42 if you are **p** to make my mission a success,
27:42 But someone got wind of what Esau was **p**
37:22 Reuben was secretly **p** to help Joseph escape,
Ex 14: 5 were not **p** to return to Egypt after three days,
32:12 this terrible disaster you are **p** against your people!
Jdg 20: 5 **p** to kill me, and they raped my concubine until she
1Sa 2:25 for the LORD was already **p** to put them to death.
19: 2 told him what his father was **p**.
20: 2 "I'm sure he's not **p** any such thing, for he always
20: 7 his temper, then you will know he was **p** to kill me.
20: 9 the slightest notion my father was **p** to kill you,
23:10 I have heard that Saul is **p** to come and destroy
1Ki 5: 5 So I am **p** to build a Temple to honor the name of
2Ki 6: 9 for the Arameans are **p** to mobilize their troops
2Ch 28:10 And now you are **p** to make slaves of these people
Ne 6: 6 and the Jews are **p** to rebel and that is why you are
Ps 28: 3 to their neighbors / while **p** evil in their hearts.
Pr 2:11 Wise **p** will watch over you. Understanding will
3:21 My child, don't lose sight of good **p** and insight.
12:20 are plotting evil; joy fills hearts that are **p** peace!
21: 5 Good **p** and hard work lead to prosperity, but hasty
Ecc 9:10 will be no work or **p** or knowledge or wisdom.
Isa 21: 3 I grow faint when I hear what God is **p**; I am
59:13 we have been, carefully **p** our deceitful lies.
Jer 9: 8 They promise peace to their neighbors while **p** to
11:19 I had no idea that they were **p** to kill me!
18:11 I am **p** disaster against you instead of good. So turn
18:19 help me! Listen to what they are **p** to do to me!
Zec 8:21 the LORD Almighty. We are **p** to go ourselves.'
Mt 12:15 But Jesus knew what they were **p**. He left that area,
Mk 11:18 what Jesus had done, they began **p** how to kill him.
Lk 19:47 and the other leaders of the people began **p** how to
Jn 7:35 "Where is he **p** to go?" they asked. "Maybe he is
8:22 Jewish leaders asked, "Is he **p** to commit suicide?
Ac 5:35 take care what you are **p** to do to these men!
Ro 12:12 Be glad for all God is **p** for you. Be patient in
15:24 I am **p** to go to Spain, and when I do, I will stop
1Co 16: 5 for I am **p** to travel through Macedonia.
Tit 3:12 I am **p** to send either Artemas or Tychicus to you.
Jude 1: 3 I had been eagerly **p** to write to you about the

PLANS (80) [PLAN]

Ge 37:18 him in the distance and made **p** to kill him.
43:18 they said. "He **p** to pretend that we stole it.
49: 6 May I never be a party to their wicked **p**.
Ex 25: 9 and its furnishings exactly according to the **p** I will
2Sa 15:35 Tell them the **p** that are being made to capture me,
1Ki 16: 9 half of the royal chariots, made **p** to kill him.
2Ki 6:11 has been informing the king of Israel of my **p**?"
25: 4 and all the soldiers made **p** to escape from the city.
1Ch 28:11 Then David gave Solomon the **p** for the Temple
28:12 David also gave Solomon all the **p** he had in mind
Ne 2:12 I had not told anyone about the **p** God had put in
2:16 I had not yet said anything to anyone about my **p**.
4: 8 They all made **p** to come and fight against
4:15 When our enemies heard that we knew of their **p**
Est 6:13 you will never succeed in your **p** against him.
Job 5:12 He frustrates the **p** of the crafty, so their efforts
Ps 2: 1 Why do the people waste their time with futile **p**?
14: 6 The wicked frustrate the **p** of the oppressed,
20: 4 he grant your heart's desire / and fulfill all your **p**.
33:10 The LORD shatters the **p** of the nations
33:11 But the LORD's **p** stand firm forever;
38:12 enemies lay traps for me; / they make **p** to ruin me.
40: 5 for us. / Your **p** for us are too numerous to list.
54: 5 May my enemies' **p** for evil be turned against
83: 3 your people, / laying **p** against your precious ones.
103:20 you mighty creatures who carry out his **p**,
119:26 I told you my **p**, and you answered. / Now teach
119:91 remain true today, / for everything serves your **p**.
138: 8 The LORD will work out his **p** for my life—
146: 4 and in a moment all their **p** come to an end.
146: 9 and widows, / but he frustrates the **p** of the wicked.
Pr 12: 5 The **p** of the godly are just; the advice of the
15:22 **P** go wrong for lack of advice; many counselors
16: 3 work to the LORD, and then your **p** will succeed.
16: 9 We can make our **p**, but the LORD determines
19:21 You can make many **p**, but the LORD's purpose
20:18 **P** succeed through good counsel; don't go to war
21:30 Human **p**, no matter how wise or well advised,
22:12 but he ruins the **p** of the deceitful.
24: 8 A person who **p** evil will get a reputation as a
Isa 8:10 develop your strategies, prepare your **p** of attack—
8:18 the **p** the LORD Almighty has for his people.
14:27 Almighty has spoken—who can change his **p**?
18: 5 your attack, while your **p** are ripening like grapes,
19: 3 will lose heart, and I will confuse their **p**.
19:17 for the LORD Almighty has laid out his **p** against
22:11 But all your feverish **p** are to no avail because you
29:15 for those who try to hide their **p** from the LORD,
30: 1 "You make **p** that are contrary to my will.
30: 1 You weave a web of **p** that are not from my Spirit,
59: 5 and energy spinning evil **p** that end up in deadly
Jer 19: 7 For I will upset the battle **p** of Judah and Jerusalem
23:20 will not diminish until it has finished all his **p**.
29:11 For I know the **p** I have for you,"
29:11 "They are **p** for good and not for disaster, to give
30:24 will not diminish until it has finished all his **p**.
40:12 They stopped at Mizpah to discuss their **p** with
46:13 about King Nebuchadnezzar's **p** to attack Egypt.
48: 2 In Heshbon **p** have been completed to destroy her.
49:20 Listen to the LORD's **p** for Edom and the people
50:45 Listen to the LORD's **p** against Babylon
51:12 for the LORD will fulfill all his **p** against
52: 7 and all the soldiers made **p** to escape from the city.
La 2: 8 He made careful **p** for their destruction, then he
3:61 You know all about the **p** they have made—
Eze 20:13 and I made **p** to utterly consume them in the desert.
Da 6: 3 the king made **p** to place him over the entire
11:17 He will make **p** to come with the might of his
Hos 11: 6 destroy them, trapping them in their own evil **p**.
Jnh 4: 1 This change of **p** upset Jonah, and he became very
4: 2 I knew how easily you could cancel your **p** for
Mic 2: 1 for you who lie awake at night, thinking up evil **p**.
Zec 1:16 and **p** will be made for the reconstruction of
7:10 And do not make evil **p** to harm each other.
Mt 12:14 called a meeting and discussed **p** for killing Jesus.
Mk 3: 6 and met with the supporters of Herod to discuss **p**
Ac 4:25 Why did the people waste their time with futile **p**?
1Co 1:25 of God is far wiser than the wisest of human **p**,
2Co 10: 3 but we don't wage war with human **p** and methods.
Jas 4:16 Otherwise you will be boasting about your own **p**,

PLANT (79) [PLANTED, PLANTER, PLANTING, PLANTS, REPLANT, TRANSPLANTED]

Ge 1:11 forth with every sort of grass and seed-bearing **p**.
47:23 will provide you with seed, so you can **p** the fields.
47:24 and use it to **p** the next year's crop and to feed
Ex 10:15 neither tree nor **p**, throughout the land of Egypt.
15:17 bring them in and **p** them on your own mountain—
23:10 "**P** and harvest your crops for six years,
Lev 19:19 Do not **p** your field with two kinds of seed.
19:23 "When you enter the land and **p** fruit trees,
25: 3 For six years you may **p** your fields and prune your
25: 4 Do not **p** your crops or prune your vineyards
25:11 do not **p** any seeds or store away any of the crops
25:20 since we are not allowed to **p** or harvest crops that
25:22 As you **p** the seed in the eighth year, you will still
26: 5 harvest will extend until it is time to **p** grain again.
26:16 You will **p** your crops in vain because your
27:16 assessed by the amount of seed required to **p** it—
Dt 6:11 eat from vineyards and olive trees you did not **p**.
22: 9 "Do not **p** any other crop between the rows of
28:30 You will **p** a vineyard, but you will never enjoy its
28:38 "You will **p** much but harvest little, for locusts
28:39 You will **p** vineyards and care for them, but you
Jos 24:13 olive groves for food, though you did not **p** them.
2Ki 19:29 But in the third year you will **p** crops and harvest
Job 4: 8 My experience shows that those who **p** trouble
8:16 so strong, like a lush **p** growing in the sunshine,
Ps 107:37 They sow their fields, **p** their vineyards,
126: 5 Those who **p** in tears / will harvest with shouts of
126: 6 They weep as they go to **p** their seed, / but they
Pr 22: 8 Those who **p** seeds of injustice will harvest
Ecc 3: 2 a time to die. / A time to **p** and a time to harvest.
11: 6 Be sure to stay busy and **p** a variety of crops,
Isa 17:10 You may **p** the finest imported grapevines,
17:11 that they blossom on the very morning you **p** them,
28:25 Does he not finally **p** his seeds for dill, cummin,
32:20 Wherever they **p** seed, bountiful crops will spring
37:30 But in the third year you will **p** crops and harvest
41:19 I will **p** trees—cedar, acacia, myrtle, olive, cypress,
60:21 for I will **p** them there with my own hands in order
Jer 1:10 You are to build others up and **p** them."
18: 9 I will build up and **p** a certain nation or kingdom,
24: 6 tear them down. I will **p** them and not uproot them.
29: 5 to stay. **P** gardens, and eat the food you produce.
29:28 He said we should **p** fruit trees, because we will
31: 5 Again you will **p** your vineyards on the mountains
31:28 But in the future I will **p** it and build it up,"
35: 7 And do not build houses or **p** crops or vineyards,
42:10 not tear you down; I will **p** you and not uproot you.
50:16 Lead from Babylon all those who **p** crops; send all
Eze 16: 7 And I helped you to thrive like a **p** in the field.
17:22 and I will **p** it on the top of Israel's highest
28:26 and build their homes and **p** their vineyards.
Hos 1:11 when God will again **p** his people in his land.
2:23 "At that time I will **p** a crop of Israelites and raise
10:12 I said, '**P** the good seeds of righteousness, and you
Am 9:14 They will **p** vineyards and gardens; they will eat
9:15 I will firmly **p** them there in the land I have given
Jnh 4: 6 And the LORD God arranged for a leafy **p** to
4: 6 and Jonah was very grateful for the **p**.
4: 7 at dawn the worm ate through the stem of the **p**,
4: 9 it right for you to be angry because the **p** died?"
4:10 the LORD said, "You feel sorry about the **p**,
4:10 to put it there. And a **p** is only, at best, short lived.
Mic 6:15 You will **p** crops but not harvest them. You will
Mt 6:26 They don't need to **p** or harvest or put food in
13: 3 as this one: "A farmer went out to **p** some seed.
15:13 "Every **p** not planted by my heavenly Father will
25:24 harvesting crops you didn't **p** and gathering crops
25:26 harvesting crops I didn't **p** and gathering crops I
Mk 4: 3 "Listen! A farmer went out to **p** some seed.
4: 5 with underlying rock. The **p** sprang up quickly,
Lk 8: 5 "A farmer went out to **p** some seed. As he
12:24 They don't need to **p** or harvest or put food in
19:21 isn't yours and harvesting crops you didn't **p**.'
Jn 4:38 I sent you to harvest where you didn't **p**;
1Co 3: 6 My job was to **p** the seed in your hearts,
15:36 it doesn't grow into a **p** unless it dies first.
15:37 And what you put in the ground is not the **p** that
15:38 A different kind of **p** grows from each kind of
Jas 3:18 And those who are peacemakers will **p** seeds of

PLANTED (57) [PLANT]

Ge 2: 8 Then the LORD God **p** a garden in Eden,
2: 9 And the LORD God **p** all sorts of trees in the
9:20 the Flood, Noah became a farmer and **p** a vineyard.
21:33 Then Abraham **p** a tamarisk tree at Beersheba,
26:12 harvested a hundred times more grain than he **p**,
Lev 11:37 If the dead body falls on seed grain to be **p** in the
Nu 24: 6 They are like aloes **p** by the LORD, / like cedars
Dt 11:10 where you **p** your seed and dug out irrigation
20: 6 Has anyone just **p** a vineyard but not yet eaten any
21: 4 plowed nor **p** with a stream running through it.
29:23 and salt, with nothing **p** and nothing growing,
Jdg 6: 3 Whenever the Israelites **p** their crops,
Job 31: 8 then let someone else harvest the crops I have **p**, and let all that I have **p** be uprooted.
Ps 1: 3 They are like trees **p** along the riverbank,
80:15 that you yourself have **p**, / this son you have raised
104:16 well cared for— / the cedars of Lebanon that he **p**.
105:44 and they harvested crops that others had **p**.
Ecc 3:11 He has **p** eternity in the human heart, but even so,
Isa 5: 2 cleared its stones, / and **p** it with choice vines.
61: 3 For the LORD has **p** them like strong
Jer 2:21 When I **p** you, I chose a vine of the purest stock—
11:17 the LORD Almighty, who **p** this olive tree,
12: 2 You have **p** them, and they have taken root
12:13 My people have **p** wheat but are harvesting thorns.
17: 8 They are like trees **p** along a riverbank, with roots
35: 9 or owned vineyards or farms or **p** crops.

45: 4 this nation that I built. I will uproot what I **p**.
Eze 17: 4 away to a city filled with merchants, where he **p** it.
17: 5 "Then he **p** one of its seedlings in fertile ground
17: 8 The vine did this even though it was already **p** in
19: 10 **p** by the water's edge. / It had lush, green foliage
36: 9 Your ground will be tilled and your crops **p**.
36: 36 rebuilt the ruins and **p** lush crops in the wilderness.
Hos 8: 7 "They have **p** the wind and will harvest the
Zep 1: 13 never drink wine from the vineyards they have **p**.
Hag 1: 6 You have **p** much but harvested little. You have
Mt 13: 8 and even a hundred times as much as had been **p**.
13: 23 or even a hundred times as much as had been **p**."
13: 24 "The Kingdom of Heaven is like a farmer who **p**
13: 25 his enemy came and **p** weeds among the wheat.
13: 27 the field where you **p** that good seed is full of
13: 31 "The Kingdom of Heaven is like a mustard seed **p**
13: 39 The enemy who **p** the weeds among the wheat is
15: 13 "Every plant not **p** by my heavenly Father will be
21: 33 A certain landowner **p** a vineyard, built a wall
Mk 4: 8 and even a hundred times as much as had been **p**."
4: 20 or even a hundred times as much as had been **p**."
4: 26 of God is like: A farmer **p** seeds in a field,
12: 1 "A man **p** a vineyard, built a wall around it,
Lk 8: 8 a crop one hundred times as much as had been **p**."
13: 6 "A man **p** a fig tree in his garden and came again
13: 19 It is like a tiny mustard seed **p** in a garden; it grows
20: 9 "A man **p** a vineyard, leased it out to tenant
Jn 12: 24 truth is, a kernel of wheat must be **p** in the soil.
1Co 9: 11 We have **p** good spiritual seed among you. Is it too
Jas 1: 21 and humbly accept the message God has **p** in your

PLANTER (1) [PLANT]
Jn 4: 36 What joy awaits both the **p** and the harvester alike!

PLANTING (8) [PLANT]
Ecc 2: 4 homes for myself and by **p** beautiful vineyards.
Isa 28: 24 Is he forever cultivating the soil and never **p** it?
30: 23 Then the LORD will bless you with rain at **p**
Am 5: 11 drink wine from the lush vineyards you are **p**.
Mic 1: 6 Her streets will be plowed up for **p** vineyards.
Zec 8: 12 For I am **p** seeds of peace and prosperity among
1Co 3: 7 The ones who do the **p** or watering aren't
15: 37 dry little seed of wheat or whatever it is you are **p**.

PLANTS (34) [PLANT]
Ge 1: 11 The seeds will then produce the kinds of **p**
1: 12 The land was filled with seed-bearing **p** and trees,
1: 12 and their seeds produced **p** and trees of like kind.
1: 29 I have given you the seed-bearing **p** throughout the
1: 30 and other green **p** to the animals and birds for their
2: 5 there were no **p** or grain growing on the earth,
19: 25 eliminating all life—people, **p**, and animals alike.
Ex 10: 15 They ate all the **p** and all the fruit on the trees that
Dt 32: 2 on tender grass, / like gentle showers on young **p**.
1Ki 4: 33 He could speak with authority about all kinds of **p**,
Job 40: 21 It lies down under the lotus **p**, hidden by the reeds.
40: 22 The lotus **p** give it shade among the willows beside
Ps 104: 14 the cattle. / You cause **p** to grow for people to use.
144: 12 sons flourish in their youth / like well-nurtured **p**.
Pr 16: 28 A troublemaker **p** seeds of strife; gossip separates
31: 16 and buys it; with her earnings she **p** a vineyard.
Isa 15: 6 banks are scorched, and the tender **p** are gone.
44: 14 he **p** the cedar in the forest to be nourished by the
61: 11 filled with young **p** springing up everywhere.
Da 4: 15 and let him live like an animal among the **p** of the
Hos 2: 22 chorus will sing together, 'Jezreel'—'God **p**!'
Mt 13: 5 with underlying rock. The **p** sprang up quickly,
13: 21 But like young **p** in such soil, their roots don't go
13: 32 but it becomes the largest of garden **p** and grows
13: 37 Son of Man, am the farmer who **p** the good seed.
Mk 4: 17 But like young **p** in such soil, their roots don't go
4: 32 it grows to become one of the largest of **p**,
Lk 8: 13 But like young **p** in such soil, their roots don't go
Jn 4: 37 'One person **p** and someone else harvests.'
1Co 3: 8 The one who **p** and the one who waters work as a
15: 39 And just as there are different kinds of seeds and **p**,
2Co 9: 6 a farmer who **p** only a few seeds will get a small
9: 6 But the one who **p** generously will get a generous
Rev 9: 4 They were told not to hurt the grass or **p** or trees

PLASTER (5) [PLASTERING, REPLASTERED]
Lev 14: 45 and **p** must be carried out of town to the place
Dt 27: 2 set up some large stones and coat them with **p**.
27: 4 these stones at Mount Ebal and coat them with **p**,
27: 8 On the stones coated with **p**, you must clearly
Da 5: 5 hand writing on the **p** wall of the king's palace,

PLASTERING (1) [PLASTER]
Lev 14: 48 areas have not reappeared after the fresh **p**,

PLATE (1) [PLATES, PLATTER, PLATTERS]
2Sa 12: 3 It ate from the man's own **p** and drank from his

PLATEAU (4) [PLATEAUS]
Nu 23: 14 So Balak took Balaam to the **p** of Zophim on
Dt 3: 10 We had now conquered all the cities on the **p**,
4: 43 Bezer on the wilderness **p** for the tribe of Reuben;
Jer 48: 21 All the cities of the **p** lie in ruins, too.

PLATEAUS (2) [PLATEAU]
Isa 41: 18 I will open up rivers for them on high **p**. I will give
Jer 48: 8 both on the **p** and in the valleys, for the LORD

PLATES (3) [PLATE]
Ex 25: 29 And make gold **p** and dishes, as well as pitchers
37: 16 using pure gold, he made the **p**, dishes, bowls,
Mk 7: 28 are given some crumbs from the children's **p**."

PLATFORM (5)
2Ch 6: 13 He had made a bronze **p** 7-1/2 feet long, 7-1/2 feet
6: 13 He stood on the **p** before the entire assembly,
Ne 8: 4 Ezra the scribe stood on a high wooden **p** that had
8: 5 Ezra stood on the **p** in full view of all the people.
Jn 19: 13 Then Pilate sat down on the judgment seat on the **p**

PLATTED [KJV] See MADE

PLATTER (14) [PLATE]
Ge 27: 18 Jacob carried the **p** of food to his father and said,
Nu 7: 13 The offering consisted of a silver **p** weighing about
7: 19 The offering consisted of a silver **p** weighing about
7: 25 The offering consisted of a silver **p** weighing about
7: 31 The offering consisted of a silver **p** weighing about
7: 37 The offering consisted of a silver **p** weighing about
7: 43 The offering consisted of a silver **p** weighing about
7: 49 The offering consisted of a silver **p** weighing about
7: 55 The offering consisted of a silver **p** weighing about
7: 61 The offering consisted of a silver **p** weighing about
7: 67 The offering consisted of a silver **p** weighing about
7: 73 The offering consisted of a silver **p** weighing about
7: 79 The offering consisted of a silver **p** weighing about
7: 85 about 3-1/4 pounds for each **p** and 1-3/4 pounds

PLATTERS (1) [PLATE]
Nu 7: 84 twelve silver **p**, twelve silver basins, and twelve

PLAY (21) [PLAYED, PLAYER, PLAYING, PLAYS, TRUMPET-PLAYING]
1Sa 16: 16 "Let us find a good musician to **p** the harp for you
16: 23 from God troubled Saul, David would **p** the harp.
18: 10 David began to **p** the harp, as he did whenever this
2Sa 19: 35 and I cannot hear the musicians as they **p**.
2Ki 3: 15 Now bring me someone who can **p** the harp."
1Ch 15: 20 Maaseiah, and Benaiah were chosen to **p** the lyres.
15: 21 Jeiel, and Azaziah were chosen to **p** the harps.
Job 32: 21 I won't **p** favorites or try to flatter anyone.
40: 20 it their best food, where all the wild animals **p**.
41: 5 like a bird, or give it to your little girls to **p** with?
Ps 33: 3 to him; / **p** skillfully on the harp and sing with joy.
58: 5 snake charmers, / no matter how skillfully they **p**.
81: 2 the tambourine. / **P** the sweet lyre and the harp.
104: 26 and Leviathan, which you made to **p** in the sea.
Isa 22: 13 But instead, you dance and **p**; you slaughter
Jer 9: 21 Children no longer **p** in the streets, and young men
Am 5: 7 and fair **p** are meaningless fictions to you.
Zec 8: 5 of the city will be filled with boys and girls at **p**.
11: 15 "Go again and **p** the part of a worthless shepherd.
Mt 22: 16 You are impartial and don't **p** favorites.
Mk 12: 14 you are. You are impartial and don't **p** favorites.

PLAYED (12) [PLAY]
1Sa 19: 9 upon him again. As David **p** his harp for the king,
2Ki 3: 15 While the harp was being **p**, the power of the
1Ch 15: 20 Obed-edom, and Jeiel. They **p** the harps and lyres.
16: 6 **p** the trumpets regularly before the Ark of God's
Ne 12: 35 and some priests who **p** trumpets. Then came
12: 42 They **p** and sang loudly and clearly under the
Hos 4: 12 They have **p** the prostitute, serving other gods
Mt 11: 17 'We **p** wedding songs and you weren't happy,
11: 17 so we **p** funeral songs, but you weren't sad.'
Lk 7: 32 'We **p** wedding songs and you weren't happy,
7: 32 so we **p** funeral songs, but you weren't sad.'
1Co 14: 7 the melody unless the notes are **p** clearly.

PLAYER (1) [PLAY]
1Sa 16: 18 said to Saul, "The son of Jesse is a talented harp **p**.

PLAYING (16) [PLAY]
Jdg 11: 34 meet him, **p** on a tambourine and dancing for joy.
1Sa 10: 5 They will be **p** a harp, a tambourine, a flute,
2Sa 6: 5 and **p** all kinds of musical instruments—
1Ki 1: 40 to Jerusalem, **p** flutes and shouting for joy.
1Ch 13: 8 singing and **p** all kinds of musical instruments—
15: 28 of cymbals, and loud **p** on harps and lyres.
25: 6 Their responsibilities included the **p** of cymbals,
2Ch 5: 12 and stood at the east side of the altar **p** cymbals,
5: 12 They were joined by 120 priests who were **p**
Ps 68: 25 with them are young women **p** tambourines.
Pr 28: 19 have plenty of food; **p** around brings poverty.
Jer 6: 11 even on children **p** in the streets, on gatherings of
Hos 2: 2 suggestive clothing and to stop **p** the prostitute.
Mt 11: 16 These people are like a group of children **p** a game
Lk 7: 32 They are like a group of children **p** a game in the
Rev 14: 2 It was like the sound of many harpists **p** together.

PLAYS (3) [PLAY]
1Sa 16: 17 "Find me someone who **p** well and bring him
Job 30: 31 My harp **p** sad music, and my flute accompanies
Eze 33: 32 a beautiful voice or **p** fine music on an instrument.

PLAZAS (1)
Mk 6: 56 they laid the sick in the market **p** and streets.

PLEA (7) [PLEAD, PLEADED, PLEADING, PLEADINGS, PLEADS, PLEAS]
Ps 6: 9 The LORD has heard my **p**; / the LORD will
17: 1 O LORD, hear my **p** for justice. / Listen to my
54: 2 listen to my prayer. / Pay attention to my **p**.
102: 1 LORD, hear my prayer! / Listen to my **p**!
143: 1 Hear my prayer, O LORD; / listen to my **p**!
Jer 42: 6 LORD our God to whom we send you with our **p**.
Phm 1: 10 My **p** is that you show kindness to Onesimus.

PLEAD (31) [PLEA]
Ge 44: 16 my lord, what can we say to you? How can we **p**?
Ex 8: 8 "**P** with the LORD to take the frogs away from
10: 17 and **p** with the LORD your God to take away this
1Sa 7: 8 "**P** with the LORD our God to save us from the
2Sa 14: 15 "But I have come to **p** with you for my son
18: 22 But Ahimaaz continued to **p** with Joab,
Est 4: 8 to the king to beg for mercy and **p** for her people.
7: 7 But Haman stayed behind to **p** for his life with
Job 9: 15 I would have no defense. I could only **p** for mercy.
19: 16 but he doesn't come; I even **p** with him!
Ps 55: 17 noon, and night / I **p** aloud in my distress,
142: 1 out to the LORD; / I **p** for the LORD's mercy.
Pr 18: 23 The poor **p** for mercy; the rich answer with insults.
Isa 19: 3 They will **p** with their idols for wisdom. They will
28: 23 Listen to me; listen as I **p**!
Jer 15: 11 Your enemies will ask you to **p** on their behalf in
44: 4 I sent my servants, the prophets, to **p** with them,
51: 36 "I will be your lawyer to **p** your case, and I will
La 2: 19 **P** for your children as they faint with hunger in the
3: 58 Lord, you are my lawyer! **P** my case! For you have
Da 9: 17 Listen as I **p**. For your own sake, Lord, smile again
Lk 18: 7 justice to his chosen people who **p** with him day
Ro 12: 1 I **p** with you to give your bodies to God.
1Co 1: 10 I **p** with you to be of one mind, united in thought
2Co 10: 1 Now I, Paul, **p** with you. I **p** with the gentleness and kindness that Christ
Gal 4: 12 I **p** with you to live as I do in freedom from these
Php 4: 2 And now I want to **p** with those two women,
1Ti 2: 1 **p** for God's mercy upon them, and give thanks.
Heb 7: 25 He lives forever to **p** with God on their behalf.
1Jn 2: 1 there is someone to **p** for you before the Father.

PLEADED (37) [PLEA]
Ge 18: 30 "Please don't be angry, my Lord," Abraham **p**.
25: 21 Isaac **p** with the LORD to give Rebekah a child
27: 38 Esau **p**, "Not one blessing left for me? O my
41: 55 They **p** with Pharaoh for food, and he told them,
Ex 4: 10 But Moses **p** with the LORD, "O Lord, I'm just
4: 13 But Moses again **p**, "Lord, please! Send someone
5: 15 Israelite foremen went to Pharaoh and **p** with him.
8: 12 and Moses **p** with the LORD about the frogs he
10: 18 So Moses left Pharaoh and **p** with the LORD.
17: 4 Then Moses **p** with the LORD, "What should I
32: 11 But Moses **p** with the LORD his God not to do it.
Nu 10: 31 "Please don't leave us," Moses **p**. "You know the
14: 13 they hear about it?" Moses **p** with the LORD.
16: 22 "O God, the God and source of all life," they **p**.
Dt 3: 23 "At that time I **p** with the LORD and said,
Jos 10: 6 they **p**. "Come quickly and save us!
Jdg 10: 15 But the Israelites **p** with the LORD and said,
1Sa 7: 9 He **p** with the LORD to help Israel,
11: 1 with us, and we will be your servants," they **p**.
15: 30 Then Saul **p** again, "I know I have sinned.
19: 4 "Please don't sin against David," Jonathan **p**.
2Sa 12: 17 The leaders of the nation **p** with him to get up
19: 19 "My lord the king, please forgive me," he **p**.
2Ki 1: 13 He **p** with him, "O man of God, please spare my
Jer 18: 20 though I **p** for them and tried to protect them from
Da 9: 3 the Lord God and **p** with him in prayer and fasting.
Hos 12: 4 and won. He wept and **p** for a blessing from him.
Jnh 1: 14 "O LORD," they **p**, "don't make us die for this
Mt 8: 5 a Roman officer came and **p** with him,
15: 25 But she came and worshiped him and **p** again,
18: 29 little more time. 'Be patient and I will pay it,' he **p**.
18: 32 you that tremendous debt because you **p** with me.
Lk 8: 32 and the demons **p** with him to let them enter into
18: 41 to do for you?" "Lord," he **p**, "I want to see!"
22: 32 But I have **p** in prayer for you, Simon, that your
Jn 4: 49 The official **p**, "Lord, please come now before my
1Th 2: 12 We **p** with you, encouraged you, and urged you to

PLEADING (18) [PLEA]
1Ki 1: 51 had seized the horns of the altar and that he was **p**,
Ps 27: 7 Listen to my **p**, O LORD. / Be merciful
77: 2 long I pray, with hands lifted toward heaven, **p**.
88: 9 O LORD; / I lift my **p** hands to you for mercy.
88: 13 I cry out to you. / I will keep on **p** day by day.
Jer 3: 21 the weeping and **p** of Israel's people.
4: 31 **p** for help, prostrate before their murderers.
15: 1 and Samuel stood before me **p** for these people,
La 3: 56 You listened to my **p**; you heard my weeping!
Da 9: 20 **p** with the LORD my God for Jerusalem, his holy
Hos 2: 21 "I will answer the **p** of the sky for clouds,
Mt 15: 22 **p**, "Have mercy on me, O Lord, Son of David!
Mk 5: 17 and the crowd began **p** with Jesus to go away
5: 23 **p** with him to heal his little daughter. "She is
Lk 13: 25 Then you will stand outside knocking and **p**,
Ac 16: 9 **p** with him, "Come over here and help us."
Ro 8: 34 at the place of highest honor next to God, **p** for us.
2Co 5: 20 as though Christ himself were here **p** with you,

PLEADINGS (3) [PLEA]
Ge 42: 21 We saw his terror and anguish and heard his **p**,

Mk 14:39 Jesus left them again and prayed, repeating his **p**.
Heb 5:7 he offered prayers and **p**, with a loud cry and tears,

PLEADS (5) [PLEA]

Jdg 6:31 Whoever **p** his case will be put to death by
Isa 64:7 one calls on your name or **p** with you for mercy.
La 1:17 Jerusalem **p** for help, but no one comforts her.
Hos 8:2 Now Israel **p** with me, 'Help us, for you are our
Ro 8:27 for the Spirit **p** for us believers in harmony with

PLEAS (4) [PLEA]

Ex 2:23 and their **p** for deliverance rose up to God.
Dt 10:10 And once again the LORD yielded to my **p**
Ps 102:17 prayers of the destitute. / He will not reject their **p**.
Isa 19:22 and he will listen to their **p** and heal them.

PLEASANT (22) [PLEASE]

Ge 49:15 sees how good the countryside is, / how **p** the land,
1Sa 16:12 for him. He was ruddy and handsome, with **p** eyes.
Job 36:11 throughout their lives. All their years will be **p**.
36:16 You have prospered in a wide and **p** valley.
Ps 16:6 The land you have given me is a **p** land. / What a
106:24 The people refused to enter the **p** land, / for they
133:1 How wonderful it is, how **p**, / when brothers live
Pr 3:24 You can lie down without fear and enjoy **p** dreams.
13:19 It is **p** to see dreams come true, but fools will not
26:24 People with hate in their hearts may sound **p**
27:14 If you shout a **p** greeting to your neighbor too early
Ecc 10:12 It is **p** to listen to wise words, but the speech of
SS 1:16 "What a lovely, **p** sight you are, my love, as we lie
2:14 For your voice is **p**, and your face is lovely."
7:6 you are, my beloved; how **p** for utter delight!
Isa 5:7 Israel and Judah are his **p** garden. / He expected
14:11 All the **p** music in your palace has ceased.
27:2 "In that day we will sing of the **p** vineyard.
Eze 34:14 There they will lie down in **p** places and feed in
Hos 4:13 They go up into the hills to burn incense in the **p**
9:13 watched Israel become as beautiful and **p** as Tyre.
Zec 7:14 The land that had been so **p** became a desert."

PLEASANTLY (3) [PLEASE]

2Ki 25:28 He spoke **p** to Jehoiachin and gave him
Jer 12:6 Do not trust them, no matter how **p** they speak.
52:32 He spoke **p** to Jehoiachin and gave him

PLEASE (239) [PLEASANT, PLEASANTLY, PLEASED, PLEASER, PLEASES, PLEASING, PLEASURE, PLEASURE-CRAZY, PLEASURES]

Ge 18:5 **P** stay awhile before continuing on your journey."
18:30 "**P** don't be angry, my Lord," Abraham pleaded.
18:32 Finally, Abraham said, "Lord, **p** do not get angry;
19:7 "**P**, my brothers," he begged, "don't do such a
19:18 "Oh no, my lords, **p**," Lot begged.
19:20 **P** let me go there instead; don't you see how small
23:4 **P** let me have a piece of land for a burial plot."
23:11 "No, sir," he said to Abraham, "**p** listen to me.
24:17 to her, the servant asked, "**P** give me a drink."
24:42 my mission a success, **p** guide me in a special way.
24:43 to draw water, "**P** give me a drink of water!"
24:45 filled the jug. So I said to her, '**P** give me a drink.'
30:27 "**P** don't leave me," Laban replied, "for I have
32:11 O LORD, **p** rescue me from my brother, Esau.
33:10 "No, **p** accept them," Jacob said, "for what a
33:11 **P** take my gifts, for God has been very generous to
34:8 he longs for her to be his wife. **P** let him marry her.
34:11 "**P** be kind to me, and let me have her as my
40:14 And **p** have some pity on me when you are back in
44:33 **P**, my lord, let me stay here as a slave instead of
47:25 "May it **p** you, sir, to let us be Pharaoh's
Ex 4:13 But Moses again pleaded, "Lord, **p**!
5:15 "**P** don't treat us like this," they begged.
9:28 **P** beg the LORD to end this terrifying thunder
10:7 **P** let the Israelites go to serve the LORD their
11:8 will come running to me, bowing low. '**P** leave!'
21:8 If she does not **p** the man who bought her, he may
32:32 But now, **p** forgive their sin—and if not, then blot
33:13 **P**, if this is really so, show me your intentions
33:18 "**P** let me see your glorious presence," he said.
34:9 favor in your sight, O Lord, then **p** go with us.
34:9 but **p** pardon our iniquity and our sins.
Nu 10:31 "**P** don't leave us," Moses pleaded. "You know
11:15 than treat me like this. **P** spare me this misery!"
12:11 **P** don't punish us for this sin we have so foolishly
14:17 "**P**, Lord, prove that your power is as great as you
14:19 **P** pardon the sins of this people because of your
15:3 and you want to **p** the LORD with a burnt
20:17 **P** let us pass through your country. We will be
22:6 **P** come and curse them for me because they are
22:16 **P** don't let anything stop you from coming.
23:27 Perhaps it will **p** God to let you curse them from
27:16 **p** appoint a new leader for the community.
32:5 **p** let us have this land as our property instead of
Dt 3:25 **P** let me cross the Jordan to see the wonderful land
12:8 "Today you are doing whatever you **p**, but that is
Jos 15:19 me land in the Negev; **p** give me springs as well."
Jdg 1:15 me land in the Negev; **p** give me springs as well."
4:19 "**P** give me some water," he said. "I'm thirsty."
6:39 Gideon said to God, "**P** don't be angry with me,
8:5 "Will you **p** give my warriors some food?
13:8 **p** let the man of God come back to us again
13:15 "**P** stay here until we can prepare a young goat for
16:6 "**P** tell me what makes you so strong and what it
16:10 Now **p** tell me how you can be tied up securely."
16:13 Won't you **p** tell me how you can be tied up
16:28 **p** strengthen me one more time so that I may pay
19:6 father said, "**P** stay the night and enjoy yourself."
21:22 in protest, we will tell them, '**P** be understanding.
Ru 2:13 "I hope I continue to **p** you, sir," she replied.
1Sa 1:16 **P** don't think I am a wicked woman! For I have
2:36 '**P**,' they will say, 'give us jobs among the priests
5:11 "**P** send the Ark of the God of Israel back to its
6:21 the Ark of the LORD. **P** come here and get it!"
9:18 "Can you **p** tell me where the seer's house is?"
14:41 **p** show us who is guilty and who is innocent.
15:25 Oh, **p**, forgive my sin now and go with me to
15:30 But **p**, at least honor me before the leaders
16:22 "**P** let David join my staff, for I am very pleased
19:4 "**P** don't sin against David," Jonathan pleaded.
20:8 your father. But **p** don't betray me to him!"
22:15 **P** don't accuse me and my family in this matter,
23:11 O LORD, God of Israel, **p** tell me."
25:8 So would you **p** be kind to us, since we have come
25:8 **P** give us any provisions you might have on
25:24 this matter, my lord. **P** listen to what I have to say.
25:25 ill-tempered man; **p** don't pay any attention to him.
25:28 **P** forgive me if I have offended in any way.
25:31 done these great things for you, **p** remember me!"
29:7 **P** don't upset them, but go back quietly."
2Sa 7:29 may it **p** you to bless me and my family so that our
13:6 "**P** let Tamar come to take care of me and cook
13:13 **P**, just speak to the king about it, and he will let
13:24 and his servants **p** come to celebrate the occasion
14:11 "**P** swear to me by the LORD your God that you
14:12 "**P** let me ask one more thing of you!" she said.
18:12 'For my sake, **p** don't harm young Absalom.'
18:22 with Joab, "Whatever happens, **p** let me go, too."
19:19 "My lord the king, **p** forgive me," he pleaded.
24:10 **P** forgive me, LORD, for doing this foolish
1Ki 2:16 **P** don't turn me down." "What is it?" she asked.
3:17 "**P**, my lord," one of them began, "this woman
3:26 my lord! Give her the child—**p** do not kill him!"
5:6 Now **p** command that cedars from Lebanon be cut
13:6 "**P** ask the LORD your God to restore my hand
17:10 "Would you **p** bring me a cup of water?"
17:21 my God, **p** let this child's life return to him."
20:32 '**P** let me live!' " The king of Israel responded,
2Ki 1:13 man of God, **p** spare my life and the lives of these,
1:14 the first two groups. But now **p** spare my life!"
2:9 "**P** let me become your rightful successor."
4:16 "**P** don't lie to me like that, O man of God."
5:15 world except in Israel. Now **p** accept my gifts."
5:17 but **p** allow me to load two of my mules with earth
6:3 "**P** come with us," someone suggested. "I will,"
6:18 Elisha prayed, "O LORD, **p** make them blind."
6:26 called to him, "**P** help me, my lord the king!"
18:26 "**P** speak to us in Aramaic, for we understand it
1Ch 4:10 **P** be with me in all that I do, and keep me from all
21:8 **P** forgive me for doing this foolish thing."
2Ch 1:9 **p** keep your promise to David my father,
10:7 show them kindness and do your best to **p** them,
19:6 you do not judge to **p** people but to **p** the LORD.
Ezr 4:12 "**P** be informed that the Jews who came here to
Ne 1:8 "**P** remember what you told your servant Moses:
1:11 O Lord, **p** hear my prayer! Listen to the prayers of
1:11 **P** grant me success now as I go to ask the king for
2:5 "If it **p** Your Majesty and if you are pleased with
2:7 I also said to the king, "If it **p** Your Majesty,
2:8 And **p** send a letter to Asaph, the manager of the
Est 1:19 So if it **p** the king, we suggest that you issue a
3:9 If it **p** Your Majesty, issue a decree that they be
5:4 "If it **p** Your Majesty, let the king and Haman
5:8 **p** come with Haman tomorrow to the banquet I
9:13 And Esther said, "If it **p** Your Majesty,
Job 2:6 "All right, do with him as you **p**," the LORD
13:5 **P** be quiet! That's the smartest thing you could do.
34:9 has even said, 'Why waste time trying to **p** God?'
Ps 28:1 **P** help me; don't refuse to answer me. / For if you
39:10 **P**, don't punish me anymore! / I am exhausted by
40:13 **P**, LORD, rescue me! / Come quickly, LORD,
55:2 **P** listen and answer me, / for I am overwhelmed by
60:11 Oh, **p** help us against our enemies, / for all human
69:31 For this will **p** the LORD more than sacrificing an
70:1 **P**, God, rescue me! / Come quickly, LORD,
70:5 I am poor and needy; / **p** hurry to my aid, O God.
71:12 don't stay away. / My God, **p** hurry to help me.
80:1 **P** listen, O Shepherd of Israel, / you who lead
108:12 Oh, **p** help us against our enemies, / for all human
116:4 the name of the LORD: / "**P**, LORD, save me!"
118:25 **P**, LORD, **p** save us. / **P**, LORD, **p** give us success.
119:8 will obey your principles. / **P** don't give up on me!
119:24 Your decrees **p** me; / they give me wise advice.
119:122 **P** guarantee a blessing for me. / Don't let those
141:1 O LORD, I am calling to you. **P** hurry!
Pr 16:7 When the ways of people **p** the LORD, he makes
Ecc 2:26 knowledge, and joy to those who **p** him.
2:26 the wealth away and gives it to those who **p** him.
7:26 Those who **p** God will escape from her, but sinners
Isa 36:11 "**P** speak to us in Aramaic, for we understand it
58:5 Do you really think this will **p** the LORD?
64:9 LORD. **P** don't remember our sins forever.
Jer 2:2 I remember how eager you were to **p** me as a
10:24 So correct me, LORD, but **p** be gentle. Do not
14:7 So **p**, help us for the sake of your own reputation.
14:9 known as your people. **P** don't abandon us now!"
14:21 not break your covenant with us. **P** don't forget us!
21:2 "**P** ask the LORD to help us.
37:3 "**P** pray to the LORD our God for us."
42:2 They said, "**P** pray to the LORD your God for us.
Eze 23:24 over to them so they can do with you as they **p**.
Da 2:7 They said again, "**P**, Your Majesty. Tell us the
4:27 "O King Nebuchadnezzar, **p** listen to me.
9:16 **p** turn your furious anger away from your city of
Hos 9:4 None of the sacrifices you offer there will **p** him.
Am 7:2 "O Sovereign LORD, **p** forgive your people!
7:5 Then I said, "O Sovereign LORD, **p** don't do it.
Mic 6:7 of rivers of olive oil? Would that **p** the LORD?
Zec 3:5 Then I said, "**P**, could he also have a clean turban
8:23 And they will say, '**P** let us walk with you, for we
Mt 13:36 "**P** explain the story of the weeds in the field."
25:8 '**P** give us some of your oil because our lamps are
Mk 5:23 "**P** come and place your hands on her; heal her
14:36 **P** take this cup of suffering away from me. Yet I
15:15 So Pilate, anxious to **p** the crowd,
Lk 4:6 because they are mine to give to anyone I **p**.
4:38 with a high fever. "**P** heal her," everyone begged.
5:8 before Jesus and said, "Oh, Lord, **p** leave me—
8:28 Most High God? **P**, I beg you, don't torture me!"
12:13 **p** tell my brother to divide our father's estate with
15:19 called your son. **P** take me on as a hired man." '
16:27 "Then the rich man said, '**P**, Father Abraham,
22:42 **p** take this cup of suffering away from me.
Jn 4:7 and Jesus said to her, "**P** give me a drink."
4:15 "**P**, sir," the woman said, "give me some of that
4:49 "Lord, **p** come now before my little boy dies."
Ac 9:38 men to beg him, "**P** come as soon as possible!"
21:39 an important city. **P**, let me talk to these people."
25:9 Then Festus, wanting to **p** the Jews, asked him,
26:3 and controversies. Now **p** listen to me patiently!
27:34 "**P** eat something now for your own good. For not
Ro 8:5 the Holy Spirit think about things that **p** the Spirit.
8:8 the control of their sinful nature can never **p** God.
14:6 And those who won't eat everything also want to **p**
14:8 While we live, we live to **p** the Lord. And when we
14:18 you serve Christ with this attitude, you will **p** God.
15:1 cannot just go ahead and do them to **p** ourselves.
15:2 We should **p** others. If we do what helps them,
15:3 For even Christ didn't **p** himself. As the Scriptures
16:5 **P** give my greetings to the church that meets in
16:7 Christians before I did. **P** give them my greetings.
16:14 And **p** give my greetings to Asyncritus, Phlegon,
1Co 7:32 doing the Lord's work and thinking how to **p** him.
7:33 his earthly responsibilities and how to **p** his wife.
7:34 earthly responsibilities and how to **p** her husband.
10:33 I follow, too. I try to **p** everyone in everything I do.
2Co 5:9 So our aim is to **p** him always, whether we are here
5:15 his new life will no longer live to **p** themselves.
5:15 Instead, they will live to **p** Christ, who died
7:2 **P** open your hearts to us. We have not done wrong
11:1 me as I keep on talking like a fool. **P** bear with me.
12:13 a burden to you. **P** forgive me for this wrong!
Gal 1:10 No, I am trying to **p** God. If I were still trying to **p** people, I would not be
6:8 But those who live to **p** the Spirit will harvest
Eph 3:13 So **p** don't despair because of what they are doing
6:6 but not just to **p** your masters when they are
Php 4:1 So **p** stay true to the Lord, my dear friends.
4:2 **P**, because you belong to the Lord, settle your
Col 1:10 the way you live will always honor and **p** the Lord,
3:22 Try to **p** them all the time, not just when they are
4:15 **P** give my greetings to our Christian brothers
1Th 2:4 Our purpose is to **p** God, not people. He is the one
2Th 2:2 **P** don't be so easily shaken and troubled by those
2Ti 4:9 **P** come as soon as you can.
Tit 2:9 obey their masters and do their best to **p** them.
3:15 **P** give my greetings to all of the believers who
Phm 1:20 **p** do me this favor for the Lord's sake.
1:22 **P** keep a guest room ready for me, for I am hoping
Heb 11:6 you see, it is impossible to **p** God without faith.
12:28 and **p** God by worshiping him with holy fear
13:22 **p** listen carefully to what I have said in this brief
1Pe 2:5 who offer the spiritual sacrifices that **p** him
1Jn 3:22 because we obey him and do the things that **p** him.
3Jn 1:15 **P** give my personal greetings to each of our friends

PLEASED (57) [PLEASE]

Ge 8:21 And the LORD was **p** with the sacrifice and said
47:29 son Joseph and said to him, "If you are **p** with me,
Nu 14:8 And if the LORD is **p** with us, he will bring us
Jdg 14:7 he talked with the woman and was very **p** with her.
1Sa 16:22 let David join my staff, for I am very **p** with him."
2Sa 3:36 This **p** the people very much. In fact, everything the king did **p** them!
19:6 had lived and all of us had died, you would be **p**.
1Ki 3:10 The Lord was **p** with Solomon's reply and was
5:7 Solomon's message, he was very **p** and said,
9:12 had given him, but he was not at all **p** with them.
1Ch 17:27 it has **p** you to bless me and my family so that our
28:4 the LORD was **p** to make me king over all Israel.
2Ch 24:10 This **p** all the leaders and the people, and they
Ne 2:5 it please Your Majesty and if you are **p** with me,
9:24 Your people could deal with them as they **p**.
Est 1:8 those who wished could have as much as they **p**,
5:8 If Your Majesty is **p** with me and wants to grant
5:14 This **p** Haman immensely, and he ordered the
7:3 "If Your Majesty is **p** with me and wants to grant
8:5 "If Your Majesty is **p** with me and if he thinks it is
9:5 and did as they **p** with those who hated them.
Ps 41:11 I know that you are **p** with me, / for you have not
51:16 You would not be **p** with sacrifices, / or I would
51:19 Then you will be **p** with worthy sacrifices
104:34 May he be **p** by all these thoughts about him,
105:22 He could instruct the king's aides as he **p**
Pr 16:13 The king is **p** with righteous lips; he loves those
20:23 double standards; he is not **p** by dishonest scales.
21:3 The LORD is more **p** when we do what is just
Isa 42:1 He is my chosen one, and I am **p** with him.
43:24 or **p** me with the fat from sacrifices.

Jer 37: 4 been imprisoned, so he could come and go as he **p**.
Da 8: 4 its victims. It did as it **p** and became very great.
Mal 1: 8 like that to your governor, and see how **p** he is!"
1:10 I am not at all **p** with you," says the LORD
Mt 3:17 is my beloved Son, and I am fully **p** with him."
11:26 Yes, Father, it **p** you to do it this way!
12:18 He is my Beloved, / and I am very **p** with him.
14: 6 daughter performed a dance that greatly **p** him,
17: 5 is my beloved Son, and I am fully **p** with him.
Mk 1:11 are my beloved Son, and I am fully **p** with you."
6:22 and performed a dance that greatly **p** them all.
Lk 3:22 are my beloved Son, and I am fully **p** with you."
10:21 Yes, Father, it **p** you to do it this way.
Ac 6: 5 This idea **p** the whole group, and they chose the
12: 3 When Herod saw how much this **p** the Jewish
1Co 10: 5 after all this, God was not **p** with most of them,
Gal 1:15 For it **p** God in his kindness to choose me and call
Eph 5: 2 And God was **p**, because that sacrifice was like
Col 1:19 For God in all his fullness was **p** to live in Christ,
1:27 For it has **p** God to tell his people that the riches
Heb 10: 6 you were not **p** with animals burned on the altar
10: 8 nor were you **p** with them" (though they are
1Pe 2:19 For God is **p** with you when, for the sake of your
2:20 are patient beneath the blows, God is **p** with you.
2Pe 1:17 "This is my beloved Son; I am fully **p** with him."

PLEASER (1) [PLEASE]

Gal 1:10 Obviously, I'm not trying to be a people **p**! No,

PLEASES (19) [PLEASE]

Ge 18: 3 "My lord," he said, "if it **p** you, stop here for a
Dt 12:25 because you will be doing what **p** the LORD.
12:28 because you will be doing what **p** the LORD your
Ezr 5:17 "So now, if it **p** the king, we request that you
Est 2: 4 the young woman who **p** you most will be made
6: 6 "What should I do to honor a man who truly **p**
Ps 135: 6 The LORD does whatever **p** him / throughout all
Pr 21: 1 directed by the LORD; he turns it wherever he **p**.
Isa 56: 4 who choose to do what **p** me and commit their
Da 4:35 He has the power to do as he **p** / among the angels
11:36 "The king will do as he **p**, exalting himself
Php 2:13 to obey him and the power to do what **p** him.
4:18 sacrifice that is acceptable to God and **p** him.
Col 3:20 obey your parents, for this is what **p** the Lord.
1Th 4: 1 name of the Lord Jesus to live in a way that **p** God,
1Ti 2: 3 This is good and **p** God our Savior,
5: 4 of them. This is something that **p** God very much.
1Jn 2: 1 He is Jesus Christ, the one who **p** God completely.
3Jn 1: 6 to send them on their way in a manner that **p** God.

PLEASING (74) [PLEASE]

Ex 29:18 offering to the LORD, which is very **p** to him.
29:25 as a burnt offering that will be **p** to the LORD.
Lev 1: 9 burnt offering made by fire, very **p** to the LORD.
1:13 burnt offering made by fire, very **p** to the LORD.
1:17 burnt offering made by fire, very **p** to the LORD.
2: 2 is an offering made by fire, very **p** to the LORD.
2: 9 made by fire, and it will be very **p** to the LORD.
2:12 burned on the altar as an offering **p** to the LORD.
3: 5 is an offering made by fire, very **p** to the LORD.
3:16 made by fire; these will be very **p** to the LORD.
4:31 on the altar, and it will be very **p** to the LORD.
6:15 on the altar, and it will be very **p** to the LORD.
6:21 grain offering, and it will be very **p** to the LORD.
8:21 given to the LORD by fire, very **p** to the LORD.
8:28 given to the LORD by fire, very **p** to the LORD.
17: 6 and it will be very **p** to the LORD.
23:13 to the LORD by fire, and it will be very **p** to him.
23:18 given to the LORD by fire and will be **p** to him.
Nu 15: 7 This sacrifice will be very **p** to the LORD.
15:10 be an offering made by fire, very **p** to the LORD.
15:13 present an offering by fire that is **p** to the LORD,
15:14 **p** to the LORD, they must follow the same
15:24 It will be **p** to the LORD, and it must be offered
18:17 as an offering given by fire, very **p** to the LORD.
28: 2 on the altar are my food, and they are very **p** to me.
28: 6 an offering made by fire, very **p** to the LORD.
28: 8 is an offering made by fire, very **p** to the LORD.
28:13 by fire, and it will be very **p** to the LORD.
28:24 to be presented by fire, very **p** to the LORD.
28:27 will be offered that day, very **p** to the LORD.
29: 2 present a burnt offering, very **p** to the LORD.
29: 6 given to the LORD by fire and are very **p** to him.
29: 8 present a burnt offering, very **p** to the LORD.
29:13 whole burnt offering by fire, very **p** to the LORD.
29:36 present a burnt offering, very **p** to the LORD.
Dt 13:18 I am giving you today, doing what is **p** to him.
1Sa 15:22 Samuel replied, "What is more **p** to the LORD:
1Ki 11:33 followed my ways and done what is **p** in my sight.
15: 5 For David had done what was **p** in the LORD's
15:11 Asa did what was **p** in the LORD's sight, as his
22:43 Asa. He did what was **p** in the LORD's sight.
2Ki 12: 2 All his life Joash did what was **p** in the LORD's
14: 3 Amaziah did what was **p** in the LORD's sight,
15: 3 He did what was **p** in the LORD's sight, just as
15:34 Jotham did what was **p** in the LORD's sight,
16: 2 He did not do what was **p** in the sight of the
17: 9 things that were not **p** to the LORD their God.
18: 3 He did what was **p** in the LORD's sight, just as
20: 3 be faithful to you and do what is **p** in your sight."
22: 2 He did what was **p** in the LORD's sight
2Ch 14: 2 for Asa did what was **p** and good in the sight of the
20:32 Asa. He did what was **p** in the LORD's sight.
24: 2 Joash did what was **p** in the LORD's sight
25: 2 Amaziah did what was **p** in the LORD's sight,
26: 4 He did what was **p** in the LORD's sight, just as
27: 2 He did what was **p** in the LORD's sight, just as
28: 1 He did not do what was **p** in the sight of the
29: 2 He did what was **p** in the LORD's sight, just as
31:20 doing what was **p** and good in the sight of the
34: 2 He did what was **p** in the LORD's sight
Ps 19:14 be **p** to you, / O LORD, my rock and my
66:15 to you— / the best of my rams as a **p** aroma.
141: 6 they will listen to my words and find them **p**.
SS 1: 3 How fragrant your cologne, and how **p** your name!
Isa 38: 3 be faithful to you and do what is **p** in your sight."
Eze 20:41 you will be as **p** to me as an offering of perfumed
Zec 7: 6 you don't think about me, but only of **p** yourselves.
Jn 8:29 For I always do those things that are **p** to him."
Ro 12: 2 know how good and **p** and perfect his will really is.
15:16 you might be pure and **p** to him by the Holy Spirit.
Eph 5:10 Try to find out what is **p** to the Lord.
Heb 11: 5 he was taken up, he was approved as **p** to God.
13:16 in need, for such sacrifices are very **p** to God.
13:20[-21] the power of Jesus Christ, all that is **p** to him.

PLEASURE (32) [PLEASE]

Lev 26:31 and I will take no **p** in your offerings of incense.
Dt 28:63 "Just as the LORD has found great **p** in helping
28:63 the LORD will find **p** in destroying you,
Ne 9:37 We serve them at their **p**, and we are in great
Job 7: 7 but a breath, and I will never again experience **p**.
22: 3 Is it any **p** to the Almighty if you are righteous?
Ps 5: 4 O God, you take no **p** in wickedness; / you cannot
16: 3 in the land / are my true heroes! / I take **p** in them!
Pr 10:23 for a fool, while wise conduct is a **p** to the wise.
21:17 Those who love **p** become poor; wine and luxury
23:24 cause for joy. What a **p** it is to have wise children.
Ecc 2: 1 I said to myself, "Come now, let's give **p** a try.
2: 2 I said. "What good does it do to seek only **p**?"
2:10 I even found great **p** in hard work, an additional
2:24 Then I realized that this **p** is from the hand of God.
4: 8 Why am I giving up so much **p** now?" It is all
5: 4 in following through, for God takes no **p** in fools.
Eze 33:11 I take no **p** in the death of wicked people.
Hag 1: 8 Then I will take **p** in it and be honored,
Mal 2:13 your offerings, and he doesn't accept them with **p**.
Mk 7:22 deceit, eagerness for lustful **p**, envy, slander,
2Co 12:21 sexual immorality, and eagerness for lustful **p**.
Gal 5:19 impure thoughts, eagerness for lustful **p**,
Eph 1: 5 through Jesus Christ. And this gave him great **p**.
1: 9 designed long ago according to his good **p**.
1Ti 5: 6 But the widow who lives only for **p** is spiritually
2Ti 3: 4 puffed up with pride, and love **p** rather than God.
Heb 10:38 But I will have no **p** in anyone who turns away."
Jas 4: 3 is wrong—you want only what will give you **p**.
1Jn 2:16 For the world offers only the lust for physical **p**,
Rev 4:11 and it is for your **p** that they exist and were
18: 7 She has lived in luxury and **p**, so match it now

PLEASURE-CRAZY (1) [PLEASE]

Isa 47: 8 "You are a **p** kingdom, living at ease and feeling

PLEASURES (6) [PLEASE]

Ps 16:11 and the **p** of living with you forever.
Lk 8:14 out by the cares and riches and **p** of this life.
Tit 2:12 instructed to turn from godless living and sinful **p**.
3: 3 became slaves to many wicked desires and evil **p**.
Heb 11:25 people instead of enjoying the fleeting **p** of sin.
2Pe 2:13 They love to indulge in evil **p** in broad daylight.

PLEDGE (25) [PLEDGED, PLEDGES]

Ge 38:17 "What **p** will you give me so I can be sure you
44:32 I made a **p** to my father that I would take care of
Ex 22:26 If you take your neighbor's cloak as a **p** of
Nu 30: 2 or makes a **p** under oath must never break it.
30: 3 or a **p** under oath while she is still living at her
30: 4 her father hears of the vow or **p** but says nothing,
30: 5 let her fulfill the vow or **p** on the day he hears of it,
30: 6 a vow or makes an impulsive **p** and later marries.
30: 7 If her husband learns of her vow or **p** and raises no
30: 8 her vow or impulsive **p** on the day he hears of it,
30:10 her husband's home when she makes a vow or **p**.
30:11 does nothing to stop her, her vow or **p** will stand.
30:12 her vow or **p** will be nullified, and the LORD will
30:15 than a day and then tries to nullify a vow or **p**,
Dt 24: 6 or even just the upper millstone, as a **p**,
24:17 and you must never accept a widow's garment in **p**
2Ch 34:32 and the people of Benjamin to make a similar **p**.
Job 22: 6 and then kept the clothing he gave you as a **p**.
24: 9 her breast; they take the baby as a **p** for a loan.
Ps 89:49 You promised it to David with a faithful **p**.
Isa 49: 8 help you. I will give you as a token and **p** to Israel.
Eze 18: 7 not keeping the items given in **p** by poor debtors,
18:12 to let them redeem what they have given in **p**,
33:15 For instance, they might give back a borrower's **p**,
1Ti 5:12 they would be guilty of breaking their previous **p**.

PLEDGED (4) [PLEDGE]

2Ki 23: 3 He **p** to obey the LORD by keeping all his
23: 3 and all the people **p** themselves to the covenant.
1Ch 29:24 and the sons of King David **p** their loyalty to King
2Ch 34:31 He **p** to obey the LORD by keeping all his

PLEDGES (7) [PLEDGE]

Ge 38:20 back to her and to pick up the **p** he had given her,
38:23 "Then let her keep the **p**!" Judah exclaimed.
Nu 30: 4 says nothing, then all her vows and **p** will stand.
30: 5 then all her vows and **p** will become invalid.
30: 7 the day he hears of it, her vows and **p** will stand.
30: 9 she must fulfill all her vows and **p** no matter what.
30:13 or nullify any vows or **p** she makes to deny herself.

PLEIADES (3)

Job 9: 9 the Bear, Orion, the **P**, and the constellations of the
38:31 the stars? Are you able to restrain the **P** or Orion?
Am 5: 8 the LORD who created the stars, the **P** and Orion.

PLENTIFUL (10) [PLENTY]

Ge 49:11 his clothes in wine / because his harvest is so **p**.
Dt 8: 9 It is a land where food is **p** and nothing is lacking.
1Ki 10:27 The king made silver as **p** in Jerusalem as stones.
2Ch 1:15 silver and gold were as **p** in Jerusalem as stones.
9:27 The king made silver as **p** in Jerusalem as stones.
Job 5:25 be many; your descendants will be as **p** as grass!
Ps 69:16 and take care of me, / for your mercy is so **p**.
78:27 birds as **p** as the sands along the seashore!
Jer 5:24 each spring and fall, assuring us of **p** harvests.'
Jn 12:24 many new kernels—a **p** harvest of new lives.

PLENTY (39) [PLENTIFUL, PLENTIFULLY]

Ge 24:25 we have **p** of straw and food for the camels,
27:28 May God always give you **p** of dew for healthy
33: 9 "Brother, I have **p**," Esau answered. "Keep what
41:53 At last the seven years of **p** came to an end.
41:54 but in Egypt there was **p** of grain in the
Ex 16: 3 had killed us there! At least there we had **p** to eat.
Dt 8:11 Beware that in your **p** you do not forget the
11:11 It is a land of hills and valleys with **p** of rain—
11:15 to graze in, and you yourselves will have **p** to eat.
Jdg 19:19 and **p** of bread and wine for ourselves."
1Ki 4:20 They were very contented, with **p** to eat and drink.
17:14 There will always be **p** of flour and oil left in your
2Ki 3:17 You will have **p** for yourselves and for your cattle
4:43 can eat, for the LORD says there will be **p** for all.
4:44 sure enough, there was **p** for all and some left over,
6: 2 to the Jordan River, where there are **p** of logs.
18:32 and vineyards, olive trees and honey—a land of **p**.
2Ch 31:10 we have had enough to eat and **p** to spare,
32: 4 kings of Assyria come here and find **p** of water?"
Ne 9:36 "So now today we are slaves here in the land of **p**
Job 20:22 "In the midst of **p**, he will run into trouble,
Ps 78:15 to give them **p** of water, as from a gushing spring.
147:14 and satisfies you with **p** of the finest wheat.
Pr 20:13 Keep your eyes open, and there will be **p** to eat!
28:19 Hard workers have **p** of food; playing around
Isa 1:19 and let me help you, then you will have **p** to eat.
30:23 and **p** of pastureland for your cattle.
36:17 and wine, bread and vineyards—a land of **p**.
Jer 44:17 For in those days we had **p** to eat, and we were
Eze 17: 8 and had **p** of water so it could grow into a splendid
Lk 13: 8 and I'll give it special attention and **p** of fertilizer.
16: 4 then I'll have **p** of friends to take care of me when
Jn 3:23 because there was **p** of water there and people kept
21: 6 side of the boat, and you'll get **p** of fish!"
Ac 22:28 the commander muttered, "and it cost me **p**!"
2Co 8:14 Right now you have **p** and can help them. Then at
9: 8 you need and **p** left over to share with others.
12: 6 I have **p** to boast about and would be no fool in
Php 4:12 it is with a full stomach or empty, with **p** or little.

PLIGHT (4)

Ge 30:22 Then God remembered Rachel's **p** and answered
1Sa 11: 4 and told the people about their **p**,
Ps 59: 4 to kill me. / Rise up and help me! Look on my **p**!
80:14 Look down from heaven and see our **p**.

PLOT (40) [PLOTS, PLOTTED, PLOTTERS, PLOTTING]

Ge 23: 4 Please let me have a piece of land for a burial **p**."
23:17 He bought the **p** of land belonging to Ephron at
Jdg 9:25 But someone warned Abimelech about their **p**.
1Sa 22:15 for I knew nothing of any **p** against you."
2Sa 3:34 you were murdered— / the victim of a wicked **p**."
2Ki 9:10 Jezebel, at the **p** of land in Jezreel, and no one will
9:36 'At the **p** of land in Jezreel, dogs will eat Jezebel's
Est 2:22 But Mordecai heard about the **p** and passed the
6: 2 of how Mordecai had exposed the **p** of Bigthana
8: 3 and begging him with tears to stop Haman's evil **p**
9:25 he issued a decree causing Haman's evil **p** to
Job 21:27 I know the schemes you **p** against me.
Ps 2: 2 the earth prepare for battle; / the rulers **p** together
21:11 Although they **p** against you, / their evil schemes
35:20 talk of peace; / they **p** against innocent people
37:12 The wicked **p** against the godly; / they snarl at
52: 2 All day long you **p** destruction. / Your tongue cuts
64: 6 As they **p** their crimes, they say, / "We have
140: 2 those who **p** evil in their hearts / and stir up trouble
Pr 3:29 Do not **p** against your neighbors, for they trust you.
6:14 Their perverted hearts **p** evil. They stir up trouble
14:22 If you **p** evil, you will be lost; but if you plan good,
16:30 With narrowed eyes, they **p** evil; without a word,
Ecc 8: 3 and don't take a stand with those who **p** evil.
Isa 29:20 be gone, and all those who **p** evil will be killed.
33:15 who refuse to listen to those who **p** murder,
Jer 2:33 "How you **p** and scheme to win your lovers.
26:21 But Uriah heard about the **p** and escaped to Egypt.
48: 2 about Moab again, for there is a **p** against her life.
Eze 22:25 Your princes **p** conspiracies just as lions stalk their
Da 11:24 He will **p** the overthrow of strongholds, but this
11:27 these kings will **p** against each other at the
Hos 7: 6 Their **p** smolders through the night, and in the
7:15 made them strong, yet now they **p** evil against me.

Am 7:10 "Amos is hatching a **p** against you right here on
Na 1:11 Who is this king of yours who dares to **p** evil
Jn 11:53 So from that time on the Jewish leaders began to **p**
Ac 9:24 But Saul was told about their **p**, and that they were
20:3 he discovered a **p** by some Jews against his life,
23:30 But when I was informed of a **p** to kill him,

PLOTS (11) [PLOT]
Ps 36:4 They lie awake at night, hatching sinful **p**.
64:2 Protect me from the **p** of the wicked,
Pr 6:18 a heart that **p** evil, / feet that race to do wrong,
Jer 5:27 filled with birds, their homes are filled with evil **p**.
11:18 Then the LORD told me about the **p** my enemies
18:23 you know all about their murderous **p** against me.
La 3:60 You have seen the **p** my enemies have laid against
3:62 the **p** my enemies whisper and mutter against me
Da 11:25 but to no avail, for **p** against him will succeed.
Zec 8:17 Do not make evil **p** to harm each other. And stop
Ac 20:19 the trials that came to me from the **p** of the Jews.

PLOTTED (14) [PLOT]
Nu 14:4 Then they **p** among themselves, "Let's choose a
1Ki 15:27 **p** against Nadab and assassinated him while he
2Ki 12:20 But his officers **p** against him and assassinated him
21:23 Then Amon's own servants **p** against him
2Ch 24:21 Then the leaders **p** to kill Zechariah, and by order
33:24 At last Amon's own officials **p** against him
Est 2:21 angry at King Xerxes and **p** to assassinate him.
6:2 They had **p** to assassinate the king.
9:24 had **p** to crush and destroy them on the day
Ps 105:25 and they **p** against the LORD's servants.
Jer 12:6 They have **p**, raising a cry against you. Do not trust
49:30 for King Nebuchadnezzar of Babylon has **p** against
Ac 7:19 This king **p** against our people and forced parents
9:29 Greek-speaking Jews, but they **p** to murder him.

PLOTTERS (1) [PLOT]
Jer 11:23 Not one of these **p** from Anathoth will survive,

PLOTTING (15) [PLOT]
2Sa 13:32 Absalom has been **p** this ever since Amnon raped
Ne 6:2 of Ono. But I realized they were **p** to harm me,
Ps 31:13 enemies conspire against me, / **p** to take my life.
56:5 I say; / they spend their days **p** ways to harm me.
63:9 But those **p** to destroy me will come to ruin.
71:10 against me. / They are **p** together to kill me.
109:20 for my accusers / who are **p** against my life.
140:4 those who are violent, / for they are **p** against me.
Pr 12:20 Deceit fills hearts that are **p** evil; joy fills hearts
24:2 For they spend their days **p** violence, and their
30:32 If you have been a fool by being proud or **p** evil,
Isa 59:4 They spend their time **p** evil deeds and then doing
Ob 1:7 will promise you peace, while **p** your destruction.
Lk 22:2 and teachers of religious law were actively **p**
Jn 7:1 Judea where the Jewish leaders were **p** his death.

PLOUGH [KJV] See PLOW

PLOW (17) [PLOWED, PLOWING, PLOWMEN, PLOWSHARE, PLOWSHARES]
Nu 19:2 physical defects and has never been yoked to a **p**.
Dt 21:3 cow that has never been trained or yoked to a **p**.
22:10 "Do not **p** with an ox and a donkey harnessed
1Sa 8:12 Some will be forced to **p** in his fields and harvest
1Ki 19:21 and used the wood from the **p** to build a fire to
Job 39:10 Can you hitch a wild ox to a **p**? Will it **p** a field for
Pr 20:4 If you are too lazy to **p** in the right season, you will
Isa 28:24 Does a farmer always **p** and never sow? Is he
61:5 and **p** your fields and tend your vineyards.
Jer 4:3 "**P** up the hard ground of your hearts!
31:18 a calf that needed to be trained for the yoke and **p**.
Hos 10:11 I will drive her in front of the **p**. Israel and Judah
10:12 **P** up the hard ground of your hearts, for now is the
Am 6:12 Can oxen be used to **p** rocks? Stupid even to ask—
Lk 9:62 "Anyone who puts a hand to the **p** and then looks
1Co 9:10 Just as farm workers who **p** fields and thresh the

PLOWED (9) [PLOW]
Dt 21:4 They must lead it to a valley that is neither **p** nor
Jdg 14:18 Samson replied, "If you hadn't **p** with my heifer,
Ps 65:10 You drench the **p** ground with rain,
129:3 with cuts, / as if a farmer had **p** long furrows.
Isa 5:2 He **p** the land, cleared its stones, / and planted it
Jer 26:18 Mount Zion will be **p** like an open field;
Hos 12:11 like the heaps of stone along the edges of a **p** field.
Mic 1:6 Her streets will be **p** up for planting vineyards.
3:12 of you, Mount Zion will be **p** like an open field;

PLOWING (7) [PLOW]
Ge 45:6 during which there will be neither **p** nor harvest.
Ex 34:21 even during the seasons of **p** and harvest.
1Sa 11:5 Saul was **p** in the field, and when he returned to
1Ki 19:19 and found Elisha son of Shaphat **p** a field with a
19:19 ahead of him, and he was **p** with the twelfth team.
Job 1:14 "Your oxen were **p**, with the donkeys feeding
Lk 17:7 "When a servant comes in from **p** or taking care of

PLOWMEN (1) [PLOW]
1Ki 19:21 He passed around the meat to the other **p**, and they

PLOWSHARE (1) [PLOW]
1Sa 13:21 a quarter of an ounce of silver for sharpening a **p**

PLOWSHARES (4) [PLOW]
1Sa 13:20 whenever the Israelites needed to sharpen their **p**,
Isa 2:4 All the nations will beat their swords into **p**
Joel 3:10 Beat your **p** into swords and your pruning hooks
Mic 4:3 All the nations will beat their swords into **p**

PLUCK (1) [PLUCKED]
Dt 23:25 And you may **p** a few heads of your neighbor's

PLUCKED (2) [PLUCK]
Pr 30:17 and despises a mother will be **p** out by ravens of
Eze 17:4 and **p** off its topmost shoot. Then he carried it

PLUMAGE (1)
Eze 17:7 eagle with broad wings and full **p** came along.

PLUMB (6)
Isa 28:17 and the **p** line of righteousness to check the
Am 7:7 beside a wall that had been built using a **p** line.
7:7 He was checking it with a **p** line to see if it was
7:8 what do you see?" I answered, "A **p** line."
7:8 "I will test my people with this **p** line.
Zec 4:10 work begin, to see the **p** line in Zerubbabel's hand.

PLUMP (6)
Ge 41:5 on one stalk, with every kernel well formed and **p**.
41:7 And these thin heads swallowed up the seven **p**,
41:22 on one stalk, and all seven heads were **p** and full.
41:24 And the withered heads swallowed up the **p** ones!
41:26 and the seven **p** heads of grain both represent
Dt 32:15 the people grew heavy, **p**, and stuffed!

PLUNDER (82) [PLUNDERED, PLUNDERERS, PLUNDERING]
Ge 31:26 "Are my daughters prisoners, the **p** of war,
49:19 by marauding bands, / but he will turn and **p** them.
49:27 and in the evening he divides the **p**."
Ex 3:22 In this way, you will **p** the Egyptians!"
15:9 with them, and destroy them. / I will divide the **p**,
Nu 31:9 their cattle and flocks and all their wealth as **p**.
31:11 After they had gathered the **p** and captives,
31:26 are to make a list of all the **p** taken in the battle,
31:27 Then divide the **p** into two parts, and give half to
31:32 The **p** remaining from the spoils that the fighting
31:36 So the half of the **p** given to the fighting men
31:42 The half of the **p** belonging to the people of Israel,
31:50 an offering to the LORD from our share of the **p**—
31:53 All the fighting men had taken some of the **p** for
Dt 2:35 We took all the livestock as **p** for ourselves,
3:7 for ourselves and took **p** from all the towns.
13:16 Then you must pile all the **p** in the middle of the
13:17 Keep none of the **p** that has been set apart for
20:14 all the women, children, livestock, and other **p**.
1Sa 14:32 That evening they flew upon the battle **p**
15:19 Why did you rush for the **p** and do exactly what
15:21 and **p** to sacrifice to the LORD your God in
30:16 because of the vast amount of **p** they had taken
30:22 didn't go with us, so they can't have any of the **p**.
30:26 David sent part of the **p** to the leaders of Judah,
2Sa 3:22 returned from a raid, bringing much **p** with them.
12:30 David took a vast amount of **p** from the city.
23:10 did not return until it was time to collect the **p**!
2Ki 3:23 and killed each other! Let's go and collect the **p**!"
21:14 and I will hand them over as **p** for their enemies.
1Ch 2:7 brought disaster on Israel by taking **p** that had been
5:21 The **p** taken from the Hagrites included 50,000
20:2 David took a vast amount of **p** from the city.
26:27 These men had dedicated some of the **p** they had
2Ch 14:13 the army of Judah carried off vast quantities of **p**.
14:14 vast quantities of **p** were taken from these towns,
15:11 of the animals they had taken as **p** in the battle—
20:25 and his men went out to gather the **p**.
20:25 so much **p** that it took them three days just to
24:23 Then they sent all the **p** back to their king in
25:13 and carrying off great quantities of **p**.
28:8 from Judah and took tremendous amounts of **p**,
28:14 and handed over the **p** in the sight of all the leaders
28:15 and distributed clothes from the **p** to the prisoners
Est 9:10 the enemy of the Jews. But they did not take any **p**.
9:15 hundred more people, though again they took no **p**.
9:16 those who hated them. But they did not take any **p**.
Ps 44:10 from our enemies / and allow them to **p** our land.
68:12 while the women of Israel divide the **p**.
Pr 16:19 with the poor than to share **p** with the proud.
Isa 1:7 foreigners **p** your fields and destroy everything
9:3 will shout with joy like warriors dividing the **p**.
10:6 It will **p** them, trampling them like dirt beneath its
11:14 they will attack and **p** the nations to the east.
17:14 This is the just reward of those who **p** and destroy
33:18 and estimated how much **p** they would get from
49:24 Who can snatch the **p** of war from the hands of a
49:25 be released, and the **p** of tyrants will be retrieved.
Jer 2:14 of slaves? Why has she been carried away as **p**?
12:12 Destroying armies **p** the land. The sword of the
15:13 over their wealth and treasures as **p** to the enemy.
17:3 as **p** to your enemies, for sin runs rampant in your
20:5 And I will let your enemies **p** Jerusalem.
30:16 Those who **p** you will be plundered, and those who
50:10 plundered until the attackers are glutted with **p**,"
51:53 I will send enemies to **p** her," says the LORD.
Eze 7:21 I will give it as **p** to foreigners from the most
25:7 against you. I will give you as **p** to many nations.
26:12 "They will **p** all your riches and merchandise
29:18 and his army won no **p** to compensate them for all
36:5 by gleefully taking my land for themselves as **p**.
38:12 I will capture vast amounts of **p** and take many
39:10 They will take **p** from those who plundered to **p** them
Da 11:24 distribute among his followers the **p** and wealth of
Am 3:11 their defenses. Then he will **p** all their fortresses."
Na 2:9 Loot the silver! **P** the gold! There seems no end to
2:12 your city and your homes with captives and **p**.
2:13 Never again will you bring back **p** from conquered
Hab 2:8 have plundered many nations; now they will **p** you.
Zep 2:9 Those of my people who are left will **p** them
Zec 2:9 to crush them, and their own slaves will **p** them.'

PLUNDERED (24) [PLUNDER]
Ge 14:11 victorious invaders then **p** Sodom and Gomorrah
34:27 Then all of Jacob's sons **p** the town because their
49:19 "Gad will be **p** by marauding bands, / but he will
Ex 12:36 like a victorious army, they **p** the Egyptians!
1Sa 14:48 saving Israel from all those who had **p** them.
17:53 army returned and **p** the deserted Philistine camp.
2Ki 7:16 of Samaria rushed out and **p** the Aramean camp.
Ps 7:4 betrayed a friend / or **p** my enemy without cause,
76:5 The mightiest of our enemies have been **p**.
Isa 21:2 I see you **p** and destroyed. Go ahead, you Elamites
33:9 a wilderness. Bashan and Carmel have been **p**.
Jer 4:30 What are you doing, you who have been **p**?
30:16 Those who plunder you will be **p**, and those who
50:10 Babylonia will be **p** until the attackers are glutted
50:37 When it strikes her treasures, they all will be **p**.
La 1:10 The enemy has **p** her completely,
Eze 23:46 and hand them over to be terrorized and **p**.
Hos 13:15 Every precious thing they have will be **p**
Ob 1:13 You shouldn't have **p** the land of Israel when they
Na 3:1 and lies! She is crammed with wealth to be **p**.
Hab 2:8 You have **p** many nations; now they will plunder
Zep 1:13 They are the very ones whose property will be **p**
Zec 14:1 your possessions will be **p** right in front of you!
14:2 will be taken, the houses **p**, and the women raped.

PLUNDERERS (1) [PLUNDER]
Jer 50:11 and are glad, you **p** of my chosen people.

PLUNDERING (2) [PLUNDER]
Isa 7:21 When they finally stop **p**, a farmer will be
Eze 29:19 **p** everything they have to pay his army.

PLUNGE (3) [PLUNGED, PLUNGES]
Job 9:31 you would **p** me into a muddy ditch, and I would
Pr 14:16 avoid danger; fools **p** ahead with great confidence.
1Ti 6:9 and harmful desires that **p** them into ruin

PLUNGED (7) [PLUNGE]
Jdg 3:21 to his right thigh, and **p** it into the king's belly.
2Sa 18:14 and **p** them into Absalom's heart as he dangled
Job 19:8 has blocked my way and **p** my path into darkness.
Mt 8:32 and the whole herd **p** down the steep hillside into
Mk 5:13 and the entire herd of two thousand pigs **p** down
Lk 8:33 and the whole herd **p** down the steep hillside into
Rev 16:10 of the beast, and his kingdom was **p** into darkness.

PLUNGES (2) [PLUNGE]
Mt 6:23 evil eye shuts out the light and **p** you into darkness.
Lk 11:34 evil eye shuts out the light and **p** you into darkness.

PLUS (14)
Ex 12:37 about 600,000 men, **p** all the women and children.
36:28 **p** an extra frame at each corner.
Lev 5:16 for the loss, **p** an added penalty of 20 percent.
6:5 they must restore the principal amount **p** a penalty
22:14 amount eaten, **p** an added penalty of 20 percent.
27:13 must pay the value set by the priest, **p** 20 percent.
27:15 must pay the value set by the priest, **p** 20 percent.
27:19 land's value as assessed by the priest, **p** 20 percent.
27:27 the priest's assessment of its worth, **p** 20 percent.
27:31 or grain, you must pay its value, **p** 20 percent.
Nu 15:10 **p** two quarts of wine for the drink offering.
Dt 3:12 **p** half of the hill country of Gilead with its towns,
Jdg 17:10 a year, **p** a change of clothes and your food."
Da 9:25 Seven sets of seven **p** sixty-two sets of seven will

PLY (1) [PLYING]
Ge 34:21 invite them to live here among us and **p** their trade.

PLYING (1) [PLY]
Ps 107:23 went off in ships, / **p** the trade routes of the world.

POCHERETH [KJV] See POKERETH-HAZZEBAIM

POCKET (1) [POCKETFUL, POCKETS]
Ex 28:30 Insert into the **p** of the chestpiece the Urim

POCKETFUL (1) [POCKET]
2Ki 4:39 and came back with a **p** of wild gourds.

POCKETS (1) [POCKET]
Hag 1:6 you were putting them in **p** filled with holes!

PODS (1)
Lk 15:16 so hungry that even the **p** he was feeding the pigs

POEM (2)

Ps 45: 1 I will recite a lovely **p** to the king,
Isa 38: 9 well again, he wrote this **p** about his experience:

POET (1) [POETS]

Ps 45: 1 for my tongue is like the pen of a skillful **p**.

POETS (2) [POET]

Nu 21:27 For this reason the ancient **p** wrote this about him:
Ac 17:28 As one of your own **p** says, 'We are his offspring.'

POINT (56) [POINTED, POINTING, POINTS]

Ge 22: 2 one of the mountains, which I will **p** out to you."
41: 4 fat ones! At this **p** in the dream, Pharaoh woke up.
Ex 7:19 "Tell Aaron to **p** his staff toward the waters of
8: 5 "Tell Aaron to **p** his shepherd's staff toward all
Nu 5:21 at this **p** the priest must put the woman under this
34: 4 Its southernmost **p** will be Kadesh-barnea,
Jos 3:16 And the water below that **p** flowed on to the Dead
7:14 and the LORD will **p** out the tribe to which the
7:14 its clans, and the LORD will **p** out the guilty clan.
7:14 and the LORD will **p** out the guilty family.
8:18 "**P** your spear toward Ai, for I will give you the
15: 1 the wilderness of Zin being its southernmost **p**.
15: 7 From that **p** it went through the valley of Achor to
Jdg 20:41 At this **p** Benjamin's warriors realized disaster was
1Sa 7:12 he said, "Up to this **p** the LORD has helped us!"
2Ch 20:24 So when the army of Judah arrived at the lookout **p**
Ne 3:21 **p** opposite the door of Eliashib's house to the side
3:25 Palal son of Uzai carried on the work from a **p**
Ps 25: 4 O LORD; / **p** out the right road for me to follow.
39: 2 the turmoil within me grew to the bursting **p**.
60: 4 honor you— / a rallying **p** in the face of attack.
139:24 **P** out anything in me that offends you, / and lead
Ecc 1:10 What can you **p** to that is new? How do you know
Isa 66: 9 Would I ever bring this nation to the **p** of birth
Jer 17: 1 inscribed with a diamond **p** on their stony hearts,
Eze 47: 3 go across. At that **p** the water was up to my ankles.
47:18 "The eastern border starts at a **p** between Hauran
47:20 border to the **p** where the northern border begins,
Hos 4: 4 "Don't **p** your finger at someone else and try to
Mt 4: 5 him to Jerusalem, to the highest **p** of the Temple,
16:23 You are seeing things merely from a human **p** of
18:15 sins against you, go privately and **p** out the fault.
26:38 "My soul is crushed with grief to the **p** of death.
26:56 At that **p**, all the disciples deserted him and fled.
Mk 8:33 You are seeing things merely from a human **p** of
14:34 "My soul is crushed with grief to the **p** of death.
15:11 But at this **p** the leading priests stirred up the mob
Lk 4: 9 to the highest **p** of the Temple, and said, "If you
15:11 To illustrate the **p** further, Jesus told them this
16:17 the law has lost its force in even the smallest **p**.
23:14 I have examined him thoroughly on this **p** in your
Jn 1:31 but I have been baptizing with water in order to **p**
5:39 give you eternal life. But the Scriptures **p** to me!
6:66 At this **p** many of his disciples turned away
8:59 At that **p** they picked up stones to kill him.
Ac 6:15 At this **p** everyone in the council stared at Stephen
Ro 4: 2 But from God's **p** of view Abraham had no basis at
7: 4 So then, dear friends, the **p** is this: The law no
1Co 4: 3 I don't even trust my own judgment on this **p**.
15:29 then what **p** is there in people being baptized for
Eph 2: 7 so God can always **p** to us as examples of the
Php 2:30 and he was at the **p** of death while trying to do for
3:15 If you disagree on some **p**, I believe God will make
1Ti 1: 6 But some teachers have missed this whole **p**.
Heb 8: 1 Here is the main **p**: Our High Priest sat down in the
Rev 3: 2 for even what is left is at the **p** of death.

POINTED (7) [POINT]

1Ki 13: 4 So he **p** at the man and shouted, "Seize that man!"
Job 41:26 sword can stop it, nor spear nor dart nor **p** shaft.
Mt 12:49 Then he **p** to his disciples and said, "These are my
24: 1 his disciples **p** out to him the various Temple
Jn 1:15 John **p** him out to the people. He shouted to the
Ac 25:16 I quickly **p** out to them that Roman law does not
Heb 7:17 And the psalmist **p** this out when he said of Christ,

POINTING (7) [POINT]

La 2:14 They did not try to hold you back from exile by **p**
Da 8: 8 horns **p** in the four directions of the earth.
Mic 3: 8 fearlessly **p** out Israel's sin and rebellion.
Mt 21:45 heard Jesus, they realized he was **p** at them—
Mk 12:12 because they realized he was **p** at them—
Lk 20:19 because they realized he was **p** at them—
Heb 9: 9 This is an illustration **p** to the present time.

POINTS (1) [POINT]

Ro 15:15 been bold enough to emphasize some of these **p**,

POISE (1) [POISED]

Da 1: 4 and have the **p** needed to serve in the royal palace.

POISED (9) [POISE]

Dt 33:20 Gad is **p** there like a lion / to tear off an arm
Isa 5:25 will not be satisfied. His fist is still **p** to strike!
9:12 will not be satisfied. His fist is still **p** to strike.
9:17 will not be satisfied. His fist is still **p** to strike.
9:21 will not be satisfied. His fist is still **p** to strike.
10: 4 will not be satisfied. His fist is still **p** to strike.
Jer 4:10 Yet the sword is even now **p** to strike them dead!"
Mt 3:10 Even now the ax of God's judgment is **p**, ready to
Lk 3: 9 Even now the ax of God's judgment is **p**, ready to

POISON (16) [POISONED, POISONING, POISONOUS]

Dt 32:32 Their grapes are **p**, / and their clusters are bitter.
32:33 is the venom of snakes, / the deadly **p** of vipers.
2Ki 4:40 cried out, "Man of God, there's **p** in this stew!"
Job 20:16 He will suck the **p** of snakes. The viper will kill
Ps 58: 4 They spit **p** like deadly snakes; / they are like
69:21 But instead, they give me **p** for food; / they offer
140: 3 like a snake; / the **p** of a viper drips from their lips.
Pr 5: 4 But the result is as bitter as **p**, sharp as a
26: 6 is as foolish as cutting off one's feet or drinking **p**!
Jer 8:14 and has given us a cup of **p** to drink because we
9:15 feed them with bitterness and give them **p** to drink.
23:15 feed them with bitterness and give them **p** to drink.
Am 6:12 how stupid you are when you turn justice into **p**
Ro 3:13 "The **p** of a deadly snake drips from their lips."
Heb 12:15 it springs up, many are corrupted by its **p**.
Jas 3: 8 It is an uncontrollable evil, full of deadly **p**.

POISONED (2) [POISON]

Job 6: 4 He has sent his **p** arrows deep within my spirit.
Jer 9: 8 For their tongues aim lies like **p** arrows.

POISONING (1) [POISON]

Ps 105:29 the nation's water into blood, / **p** all the fish.

POISONOUS (18) [POISON]

Ge 49:17 a snake beside the road, / a **p** viper along the path,
Nu 21: 6 So the LORD sent **p** snakes among them,
21: 8 "Make a replica of a **p** snake and attach it to the
Dt 8:15 and terrifying wilderness with **p** snakes
29:18 no root among you would bear bitter and **p** fruit.
32:24 of wild beasts, / by **p** snakes that glide in the dust.
2Ki 4:39 them into the kettle without realizing they were **p**.
Job 20:14 turns sour within him, a **p** venom in his stomach.
Ps 91:13 You will trample down lions and **p** snakes;
Pr 23:32 For in the end it bites like a **p** serpent; it stings like
Isa 11: 8 Babies will crawl safely among **p** snakes. Yes,
14:29 From that snake a **p** snake will be born, a fiery
30: 6 wilderness they go, where lions and **p** snakes live.
65:25 **P** snakes will strike no more. In those days, no one
Jer 8:17 "I will send these enemy troops among you like **p**
Hos 10: 4 So perverted justice springs up among them like **p**
Mk 16:18 and if they drink anything **p**, it won't hurt them.
Ac 28: 3 a **p** snake, driven out by the heat, fastened itself

POKERETH-HAZZEBAIM (2)

Ezr 2:57 Shephatiah, Hattil, **P**, and Ami.
Ne 7:59 Shephatiah, Hattil, **P**, and Ami.

POLE (27) [FLAGPOLE, POLES]

Ge 40:19 cut off your head and impale your body on a **p**.
40:22 he sentenced the chief baker to be impaled on a **p**,
41:13 the chief baker was executed and impaled on a **p**."
Nu 13:23 so large that it took two of them to carry it on a **p**
21: 8 of a poisonous snake and attach it to the top of a **p**.
21: 9 out of bronze and attached it to the top of a **p**.
Dt 16:21 "You must never set up an Asherah **p** beside the
Jdg 6:25 and cut down the Asherah **p** standing beside it.
6:26 using as fuel the wood of the Asherah **p** you cut
6:28 and that the Asherah **p** beside it was gone.
6:30 altar of Baal and for cutting down the Asherah **p**."
1Ki 15:13 because she had made an obscene Asherah **p**.
15:13 He cut down the **p** and burned it in the Kidron
16:33 Then he set up an Asherah **p**. He did more to
2Ki 13: 6 They even set up an Asherah **p** in Samaria.
17:16 They set up an Asherah **p** and worshiped Baal
21: 3 altars for Baal and set up an Asherah **p**,
21: 7 Manasseh even took an Asherah **p** he had made
23: 6 The king removed the Asherah **p** from the
23: 6 Then he ground the **p** to dust and threw the dust in
23: 7 the women wove coverings for the Asherah **p**.
23:15 the stones to dust and burned the Asherah **p**.
2Ch 15:16 because she had made an obscene Asherah **p**.
15:16 He cut down the **p**, broke it up, and burned it in the
Isa 27: 9 There won't be an Asherah **p** or incense altar left
Jn 3:14 And as Moses lifted up the bronze snake on a **p** in
3:14 so I, the Son of Man, must be lifted up on a **p**,

POLES (55) [POLE]

Ex 25:13 Make **p** from acacia wood, and overlay them with
25:14 Fit the **p** into the rings at the sides of the Ark to
25:15 These carrying **p** must never be taken from the
25:27 These rings will support the **p** used to carry the
25:28 Make these **p** from acacia wood and overlay them
27: 6 For moving the altar, make **p** from acacia wood,
27: 7 put the **p** into the rings at two sides of the altar
30: 4 attach two gold rings to support the carrying **p**.
30: 5 The **p** are to be made of acacia wood and overlaid
35:12 the Ark and its **p**; the Ark's cover—the place of
35:13 the table, its carrying **p**, and all of its utensils;
35:15 the incense altar and its carrying **p**; the anointing
35:16 grating of the altar and its carrying **p** and utensils;
37: 4 Then he made **p** from acacia wood and overlaid
37: 5 He put the **p** into the rings at the sides of the Ark to
37:14 These were made to hold the carrying **p** in place.
37:15 He made the carrying **p** of acacia wood
37:27 beneath the molding, to hold the carrying **p**.
37:28 The carrying **p** were made of acacia wood
38: 5 each side of the grating to support the carrying **p**.
38: 6 The carrying **p** themselves were made of acacia
38: 7 These **p** were inserted into the rings at the side of
39:35 the Ark of the Covenant and its carrying **p**;
39:39 bronze altar; the bronze grating; its **p** and utensils;
40:20 and then he attached the Ark's carrying **p**.
Nu 4: 6 they must put the carrying **p** of the Ark in place.
4: 8 Then they must insert the carrying **p** into the table.
4:11 Then they are to attach the carrying **p** to the altar.
4:14 Finally, the carrying **p** must be put in place.
Dt 7: 5 Cut down their Asherah **p** and burn their idols.
12: 3 Burn their Asherah **p** and cut down their carved
Jdg 3: 7 worshiped the images of Baal and the Asherah **p**.
1Ki 8: 7 forming a canopy over the Ark and its carrying **p**.
8: 8 These **p** were so long that their ends could be seen
14:15 angered the LORD by worshiping Asherah **p**.
14:23 up sacred pillars and Asherah **p** on every high hill
2Ki 17:10 sacred pillars and Asherah **p** at the top of every hill
18: 4 sacred pillars, and knocked down the Asherah **p**.
23:14 the sacred pillars and cut down the Asherah **p**.
1Ch 15:15 Ark of God on their shoulders with its carrying **p**,
2Ch 5: 8 forming a canopy over the Ark and its carrying **p**.
5: 9 These **p** were so long that their ends could be seen
14: 3 the sacred pillars and cut down the Asherah **p**.
17: 6 the pagan shrines and destroyed the Asherah **p**.
19: 3 for you have removed the Asherah **p** throughout
24:18 and they worshiped Asherah **p** and idols instead!
31: 1 cut down the Asherah **p**, and removed the pagan
33: 3 altars for the images of Baal and set up Asherah **p**.
33:19 and set up Asherah **p** and idols before he repented.
34: 3 the Asherah **p**, and the carved idols and cast
34: 4 He also made sure that the Asherah **p**, the carved
34: 7 He destroyed the pagan altars and the Asherah **p**,
Isa 17: 8 will never again bow down to their Asherah **p**
Jer 17: 2 go to worship at their sacred altars and Asherah **p**,
Mic 5:14 abolish your pagan shrines with their Asherah **p**

POLICE (3)

Ac 1:16 who guided the Temple **p** to arrest Jesus.
16:35 The next morning the city officials sent the **p** to
16:38 When the **p** made their report, the city officials

POLISHED (6)

Ezr 8:27 2 fine articles of **p** bronze, as precious as gold.
Eze 21: 9 the LORD: A sword is being sharpened and **p**.
21:11 Yes, the sword is now being sharpened and **p**;
21:15 It flashes like lightning; it is **p** for slaughter!
Da 10: 6 His arms and feet shone like **p** bronze, and his
Rev 2:18 like flames of fire, whose feet are like **p** bronze:

POLITICAL (5)

Ge 11: 6 advantage of their common language and **p** unity,
1Ch 23: 2 David summoned all the **p** leaders of Israel,
2Ch 1: 2 the army, the judges, and all the **p** and clan leaders.
Ne 2:16 I had not yet spoken to the religious and **p** leaders,
Da 11: 2 Using his wealth for **p** advantage, he will stir up

POLLUTE (3) [POLLUTED, POLLUTES, POLLUTING]

Eze 20:26 I let them **p** themselves with the very gifts I had
20:30 Do you plan to **p** yourselves just as your ancestors
20:31 you continue to **p** yourselves to this day.

POLLUTED (6) [POLLUTE]

Nu 35:33 ensure that the land where you live will not be **p**,
Ezr 9: 2 So the holy race has become **p** by these mixed
Ps 106:38 the idols of Canaan, / they **p** the land with murder.
Jer 3: 2 You have **p** the land with your prostitution
Eze 36:18 They **p** the land with murder and by worshiping
Zep 3: 1 **p** Jerusalem, the city of violence and crime.

POLLUTES (1) [POLLUTE]

Nu 35:33 live will not be polluted, for murder **p** the land.

POLLUTING (4) [POLLUTE]

Pr 25:26 it is like **p** a fountain or muddying a spring.
Eze 14:11 learn not to stray from me, **p** themselves with sin.
37:23 They will stop **p** themselves with their detestable
Da 11:31 **p** the sanctuary, putting a stop to the daily

POMEGRANATE (6) [POMEGRANATES]

1Sa 14: 2 outskirts of Gibeah, around the **p** tree at Migron.
SS 4: 3 Your cheeks behind your veil are like **p** halves—
6: 7 Your cheeks behind your veil are like **p** halves—
8: 2 give you spiced wine to drink, my sweet **p** wine.
Joel 1:12 The **p** trees, palm trees, and apple trees—yes,
Hag 2:19 and before the grapevine, the fig tree, the **p**,

POMEGRANATES (20) [POMEGRANATE]

Ex 28:33 Make **p** out of blue, purple, and scarlet yarn,
28:34 and **p** are to alternate all the way around the hem.
39:24 **P** were attached to the bottom edge of the robe.
39:25 Bells of pure gold were placed between the **p** along
39:26 with bells and **p** alternating all around the hem.
Nu 13:23 They also took samples of the **p** and figs.
20: 5 This land has no grain, figs, grapes, or **p**.
Dt 8: 8 of grapevines, fig trees, **p**, olives, and honey.
1Ki 7:18 He also made two rows of **p** that encircled the
7:20 Each capital on the two pillars had two hundred **p**
7:42 four hundred **p** that hung from the chains on the
7:42 **p** for each of the chain networks that were hung
2Ki 25:17 and was decorated with a network of bronze **p** all
2Ch 3:16 He also made one hundred decorative **p**
4:13 four hundred **p** that hung from the chains on the

4:13 p for each of the chain networks that were hung
SS 6:11 budding yet, or whether the p were blossoming.
7:12 have opened, and whether the p are in flower.
Jer 52:22 and was decorated with a network of bronze p all
52:23 There were ninety-six p on the sides, and a total of

POMP (2)

Isa 47:1 For your days of glory, p, and honor have ended.
Ac 25:23 and Bernice arrived at the auditorium with great p,

PONDER (2) [PONDERED]

Ps 111:2 All who delight in him should p them.
143:5 the days of old. / I p all your great works.

PONDERED (1) [PONDER]

Ps 119:59 I p the direction of my life, / and I turned to follow

PONTIUS (2) [PILATE]

Ac 4:27 Herod Antipas, P Pilate the governor, the Gentiles,
1Ti 6:13 who gave a good testimony before P Pilate,

PONTUS (3)

Ac 2:9 Judea, Cappadocia, P, the province of Asia,
18:2 born in P, who had recently arrived from Italy with
1Pe 1:1 who are living as foreigners in the lands of P,

POOL (20) [POOLS]

2Sa 2:13 and they met Abner at the p of Gibeon.
2:13 facing each other from opposite sides of the p.
3:26 They found him at the p of Sirah and brought him
4:12 and hung their bodies beside the p in Hebron.
1Ki 22:38 Then his chariot was washed beside the p of
2Ki 18:17 the aqueduct that feeds water into the upper p,
20:20 the extent of his power and how he built a p
Ne 2:14 I went to the Fountain Gate and to the King's P,
3:15 Then he repaired the wall of the p of Siloam near
Isa 7:3 of the aqueduct that feeds water into the upper p,
22:9 to be repaired. You store up water in the lower p.
22:11 you build a reservoir for water from the old p.
35:7 The parched ground will become a p, and springs
36:2 the aqueduct that feeds water into the upper p,
Jer 41:12 They caught up with him at the p near Gibeon.
Jn 5:2 near the Sheep Gate, was the p of Bethesda,
5:7 "for I have no one to help me into the p when the
9:7 and wash in the p of Siloam" (Siloam means
9:11 'Go to the p of Siloam and wash off the mud.'
Jas 3:12 and you can't draw fresh water from a salty p.

POOLS (8) [POOL]

Dt 8:7 into a good land of flowing streams and p of water,
2Ki 3:16 This dry valley will be filled with p of water!
Ps 84:6 where p of blessing collect after the rains!
107:35 But he also turns deserts into p of water, / the dry
114:8 He turned the rock into p of water; / yes, springs of
SS 7:4 Your eyes are like the sparkling p in Heshbon by
Isa 41:18 In the deserts they will find p of water. Rivers fed
42:15 the rivers into dry land / and will dry up all the p.

POOR (203) [IMPOVERISHED, POOREST, POVERTY]

Ex 23:3 in favor of a person just because that person is p.
23:6 justice against people simply because they are p.
23:11 Then let the p among you harvest any volunteer
30:15 must not give more, and the p must not give less.
Lev 19:10 Leave them for the p and the foreigners who live
19:15 neither favoring the p nor showing deference to the
23:22 Leave it for the p and the foreigners living among
Nu 13:20 How is the soil? Is it fertile or p? Are there many
Dt 15:4 There should be no p among you, for the LORD
15:7 "But if there are any p people in your towns when
15:11 There will always be some among you who are p.
15:11 you to share your resources freely with the p
24:12 If your neighbor is p and has only a cloak to give
24:14 "Never take advantage of p laborers,
24:15 because they are p and are counting on it.
Jdg 14:15 Did you invite us to this party just to make us p?"
Ru 3:10 not running after a younger man, whether rich or p.
1Sa 2:7 The LORD makes one p and another rich;
2:8 He lifts the p from the dust— / yes, from a pile of
15:9 destroyed only what was worthless or of p quality.
18:23 "How can a p man from a humble family afford
2Sa 12:1 in a certain town. One was rich, and one was p.
12:3 The p man owned nothing but a little lamb he had
12:4 he took the p man's lamb and killed it and served it
12:6 He must repay four lambs to the p man for the one
Ne 4:2 army officers, "What does this bunch of p,
Est 9:22 and by giving gifts to each other and to the p.
Job 3:19 Rich and p are there alike, and the slave is free
5:11 He gives prosperity to the p and humble, and he
5:15 He rescues the p from the cutting words of the
5:16 And so at last the p have hope, and the fangs of the
20:10 His children will beg from the p, for he must give
20:19 For he oppressed the p and left them destitute.
24:3 and they even take donkeys from the p
24:3 A p widow must surrender her valuable ox as
24:4 The p are kicked aside; the needy must hide
24:5 the p must spend all their time just getting enough
24:10 The p must go about naked, without any clothing.
24:14 The murderer rises in the early dawn to kill the p
29:12 For I helped the p in their need and the orphans
29:16 I was a father to the p and made sure that even
31:16 "Have I refused to help the p or crushed the hopes
34:19 pay any more attention to the rich than to the p.
34:28 So they cause the p to cry out, catching God's
Ps 9:18 the hopes of the p will not always be crushed.
10:2 Proud and wicked people viciously oppress the p.
12:5 the helpless, / and I have heard the groans of the p.
22:26 The p will eat and be satisfied. / All who seek the
35:10 Who else protects the p and needy from those who
37:14 string their bows / to kill the p and the oppressed,
40:17 As for me, I am p and needy, / but the Lord is
41:1 Oh, the joys of those who are kind to the p.
49:2 High and low, / rich and p—listen!
70:5 But I am p and needy; / please hurry to my aid,
72:2 in the right way; / let the p always be treated fairly.
72:4 Help him to defend the p, / to rescue the children
72:12 He will rescue the p when they cry to him;
74:21 let these p and needy ones give praise to your
82:3 "Give fair judgment to the p and the orphan;
82:4 Rescue the p and helpless; / deliver them from the
107:41 But he rescues the p from their distress
109:16 to others; / he persecuted the p and needy,
109:22 For I am p and needy, / and my heart is full of
113:7 and he lifts the p from the dirt / and the needy from
132:15 this city prosperous / and satisfy its p with food.
140:12 he will maintain the rights of the p.
Pr 10:4 Lazy people are soon p; hard workers get rich.
10:15 their fortress; the poverty of the p is their calamity.
13:7 Some who are p pretend to be rich; others who are rich pretend to be p.
13:8 pay a ransom, but the p won't even get threatened.
13:23 A p person's farm may produce much food,
14:20 The p are despised even by their neighbors,
14:21 one's neighbors; blessed are those who help the p.
14:31 Those who oppress the p insult their Maker, but those who help the p honor him.
15:15 For the p, every day brings trouble; for the happy
16:8 It is better to be p and godly than rich
16:19 It is better to live humbly with the p than to share
17:5 Those who mock the p insult their Maker;
17:18 It is p judgment to co-sign a friend's note,
18:23 The p plead for mercy; the rich answer with
19:1 It is better to be p and honest than to be a fool
19:7 If the relatives of the p despise them, how much
19:7 The p call after them, but they are gone.
19:17 If you help the p, you are lending to the LORD—
19:22 And it is better to be p than dishonest.
21:13 Those who shut their ears to the cries of the p will
21:17 Those who love pleasure become p; wine
22:2 The rich and the p have this in common:
22:7 Just as the rich rule the p, so the borrower is
22:9 those who are generous, because they feed the p.
22:16 A person who gets ahead by oppressing the p
22:22 Do not rob the p because they are p or exploit
28:3 A p person who oppresses the p is like a
28:6 It is better to be p and honest than rich
28:8 up in the hands of someone who is kind to the p.
28:11 as wise, but their real poverty is evident to the p.
28:15 A wicked ruler is as dangerous to the p as a lion
28:27 Whoever gives to the p will lack nothing. But a
29:7 The godly know the rights of the p; the wicked
29:13 The p and the oppressor have this in common—
29:14 A king who is fair to the p will have a long reign.
30:9 And if I am too p, I may steal and thus insult
30:14 They devour the p with teeth as sharp as swords
31:9 Yes, speak up for the p and helpless, and see that
31:20 She extends a helping hand to the p and opens her
Ecc 4:13 It is better to be a p but wise youth than to be an
5:8 If you see a p person being oppressed by the
6:8 Do p people gain anything by being wise
9:11 The wise are often p, and the skillful are not
9:15 There was a p, wise man living there who knew
9:16 those who are wise will be despised if they are p.
Isa 3:14 You have taken advantage of the p, filling your
10:2 They deprive the p, the widows, and the orphans of
10:30 army comes. P Anathoth, what a fate is yours!
11:4 He will defend the p and the exploited. He will
14:30 I will feed the p in my pasture; the needy will lie
14:32 and that the p of his people will find refuge in its
19:15 in Egypt, whether rich or p, important or unknown,
25:4 But to the p, O LORD, you are a refuge from the
26:6 The p and oppressed trample it underfoot.
29:19 Those who are p will rejoice in the Holy One of
32:7 including all the lies they use to oppress the p in
40:20 Or is a p person's wooden idol better? Can God be
41:17 "When the p and needy search for water and there
44:20 The p, deluded fool feeds on ashes. He is trusting
58:7 and to welcome p wanderers into your homes.
61:1 has appointed me to bring good news to the p.
Jer 2:34 is stained with the blood of the innocent and the p.
5:4 "But what can we expect from the p and ignorant?
5:28 justice to orphans and deny the rights of the p.
17:11 at the end of their lives, will become p old fools.
20:13 For though I was p and needy, he delivered me
22:16 that justice and help were given to the p and needy,
22:17 the innocent, oppress the p, and reign ruthlessly."
40:7 over the p people who were left behind in Judah,
49:9 who harvest grapes always leave a few for the p.
Eze 16:49 while the p and needy suffered outside her door.
18:7 not keeping the items given in pledge by p debtors,
18:7 and does not rob the p but instead gives food to the
18:12 oppresses the p and helpless, steals from debtors
18:16 and does not exploit the p, but instead is fair to
18:17 helps the p, does not lend money at interest,
22:29 Even common people oppress the p, rob the needy,
38:13 and seize their goods and make them p?'
Da 4:27 from your wicked past by being merciful to the p.
Am 2:6 people for silver and p people for a pair of sandals.
4:1 you women who oppress the p and crush the needy
5:7 making it a bitter pill for the p and oppressed.
5:11 You trample the p and steal what little they have
5:12 and deprive the p of justice in the courts.
8:4 to this, you who rob the p and trample the needy!
8:6 Then you enslave p people for a debt of one piece
Ob 1:5 who harvest grapes always leave a few for the p.
Hag 1:9 You hoped for rich harvests, but they were p.
Zec 7:10 oppress widows, orphans, foreigners, and p people.
Mt 11:5 and the Good News is being preached to the p.
19:21 and sell all you have and give the money to the p,
26:9 sold it for a fortune and given the money to the p."
26:11 You will always have the p among you, but I will
Mk 10:21 and sell all you have and give the money to the p,
12:42 Then a p widow came and dropped in two pennies.
12:43 this p widow has given more than all the others
12:44 but she, p as she is, has given everything she has."
14:5 for a small fortune and given the money to the p!"
14:7 You will always have the p among you, and you
Lk 3:11 "If you have two coats, give one to the p.
4:18 has appointed me to preach Good News to the p.
6:20 and said, / "God blesses you who are p,
7:22 and the Good News is being preached to the p.
14:13 Instead, invite the p, the crippled, the lame,
14:21 the streets and alleys of the city and invite the p,
18:22 "Sell all you have and give the money to the p,
19:8 "I will give half my wealth to the p, Lord,
21:2 Then a p widow came by and dropped in two
21:3 "this p widow has given more than all the rest of
21:4 but she, p as she is, has given everything she has."
Jn 12:5 have been sold and the money given to the p."
12:6 Not that he cared for the p—he was a thief who
12:8 You will always have the p among you, but I will
13:29 pay for the food or to give some money to the p.
Ac 9:36 doing kind things for others and helping the p.
10:4 and gifts to the p have not gone unnoticed by God!
10:31 and your gifts to the p have been noticed by God!
20:35 of how you can help the p by working hard.
27:12 a p place to spend the winter—most of the crew
1Co 11:22 to disgrace the church of God and shame the p?
13:3 If I gave everything I have to the p and even
13:12 Now we see things imperfectly as in a p mirror,
2Co 6:10 We are p, but we give spiritual riches to others.
8:9 he was very rich, yet for your sakes he became p,
9:9 "Godly people give generously to the p.
Gal 2:10 suggested was that we remember to help the p,
Jas 1:9 Christians who are p should be glad, for God has
2:2 and another comes in who is p and dressed in
2:3 but you say to the p one, "You can stand over
2:5 Hasn't God chosen the p in this world to be rich in
2:6 And yet, you insult the p man! Isn't it the rich who
Rev 3:17 and miserable and p and blind and naked.
13:16 great and small, rich and p, slave and free—

POOREST (5) [POOR]

2Ki 24:14 So only the p people were left in the land.
25:12 But the captain of the guard allowed some of the p
Jer 39:10 But Nebuzaradan left a few of the p people in
52:15 then took as exiles some of the p of the people
52:16 But Nebuzaradan allowed some of the p people to

POPLAR (1) [POPLARS]

Ge 30:37 Now Jacob took fresh shoots from p, almond,

POPLARS (1) [POPLAR]

Hos 4:13 in the pleasant shade of oaks, p, and other trees.

POPULAR (3)

Ecc 4:16 might become the leader of millions and be very p.
Am 6:1 You are famous and p in Israel, you to whom the
Ac 5:34 on religious law and was very p with the people.

POPULATE (1) [POPULATED, POPULATION, POPULATIONS, REPOPULATE]

Isa 26:18 the world; / no one has been born to p the earth.

POPULATED (2) [POPULATE]

Ge 10:32 The earth was p with the people of these nations
Zec 7:7 and the foothills of Judah were p areas?' "

POPULATION (22) [POPULATE]

Ge 6:1 When the human p began to grow rapidly on the
47:27 began to prosper there, and their p grew rapidly.
Ex 23:30 I will drive them out a little at a time until your p
Nu 15:26 for the entire p was involved in the sin.
26:54 each group's inheritance reflecting the size of its p.
Jos 5:3 and circumcised the entire male p of Israel at
8:25 So the entire p of Ai was wiped out that day—
10:32 Here, too, the entire p was slaughtered, just as at
10:37 at Eglon, they completely destroyed the entire p.
Jdg 9:51 tower inside the city, and the entire p fled to it.
1Ki 9:16 killing the Canaanite p and burning it down.
2Ki 15:16 He killed the entire p and ripped open the pregnant
16:9 capital of Damascus and led its p away as captives,
Ne 7:4 city was large and spacious, but the p was small.
Pr 14:28 A growing p is a king's glory; a dwindling nation
Jer 31:27 "when I will greatly increase the p and multiply
39:9 sent to Babylon the remnant of the p as well as
Eze 36:10 I will greatly increase the p of Israel,
Zec 10:8 are left, their p will grow again to its former size.
14:2 Half the p will be taken away into captivity,
Ac 9:35 Then the whole p of Lydda and Sharon turned to
21:30 The whole p of the city was rocked by these

POPULATIONS (1) [POPULATE]
Nu 26:53 the land among the tribes in proportion to their **p**,

POPULOUS [KJV] See NUMEROUS

PORATHA (1)
Est 9: 8 **P**, Adalia, Aridatha,

PORCH (1) [PORCHES]
1Ki 7: 6 There was a **p** at its front, covered by a canopy that

PORCHES (2) [PORCH]
Jn 5: 2 was the pool of Bethesda, with five covered **p**.
5: 3 blind, lame, or paralyzed—lay on the **p**.

PORCIUS (1) [FESTUS]
Ac 24:27 in this way; then Felix was succeeded by **P** Festus.

PORCUPINES (1)
Isa 14:23 a place of **p**, filled with swamps and marshes.

PORK (2)
Isa 65: 4 They also eat **p** and other forbidden foods.
66:17 feasting on **p** and rats and other forbidden meats,

PORPHYRY (1)
Est 1: 6 silver couches stood on a mosaic pavement of **p**,

PORT (8) [PORT, SEAPORT]
1Ki 9:26 a **p** near Elath in the land of Edom, along the shore
2Ch 20:36 Together they built a fleet of trading ships at the **p**
Isa 23:14 O ships of Tarshish, for your home **p** is destroyed!
Jnh 1: 3 He went down to the seacoast, to the **p** of Joppa,
Ac 13:13 ship for Pamphylia, landing at the **p** town of Perga.
18:19 When they arrived at the **p** of Ephesus, Paul left
18:22 The next stop was at the **p** of Caesarea. From there
27: 2 We left on a boat whose home **p** was

PORTABLE (1)
2Ki 16:17 the side panels and basins from the **p** water carts.

PORTION (32) [PORTIONED, PORTIONS]
Ge 41:48 Joseph took a **p** of all the crops grown in Egypt
48:22 And I give you an extra **p** beyond what I have
48:22 the **p** that I took from the Amorites with my sword
Lev 2: 2 the incense, and burn this token **p** on the altar fire.
2: 9 The priests will take a token **p** of the grain offering
2:14 to the LORD from the first **p** of your harvest,
2:16 The priests will take a token **p** of the roasted grain
5:12 who will scoop out a handful as a token **p**.
6:15 He will burn this token **p** on the altar, and it will be
6:26 The priest who offers the sacrifice may eat his **p** in
23:10 bring the priest some grain from the first **p** of your
24: 9 for they represent a most holy **p** of the offerings
Nu 5:26 He will take a handful as a token **p** and burn it on
18: 9 You are allotted the **p** of the most holy offerings
18: 9 that **p** belongs to you and your sons.
18:28 From this you must present the LORD's **p** to
18:32 tithes if you give the best **p** to the priests.
23:13 There you will see only a **p** of the nation of Israel.
34: 3 The southern **p** of your country will extend from
Dt 14:25 you may sell the tithe **p** of your crops and herds
21:17 He must give the customary double **p** to his oldest
Jos 15:17 the other **p** of which was in the territory of King
17:14 "Why have you given us only one **p** of land when
17:17 and strong, you will be given more than one **p**.
1Sa 1: 5 But he gave Hannah a special **p** because he loved
2Ch 31: 4 bring the prescribed **p** of their income to the priests
Ne 12:47 gave a **p** of what they received to the priests,
13: 5 olive oil, and the special **p** set aside for the priests.
Isa 61: 7 you will inherit a double **p** of prosperity
Eze 45: 1 aside a section of it for the LORD as his holy **p**.
45: 3 measure out a **p** of land 8-1/3 miles long and 3-1/3
48:12 It will be their special **p** when the land is

PORTIONED (1) [PORTION]
Eze 4:16 The water will be **p** out drop by drop,

PORTIONS (10) [PORTION]
Lev 7:36 **p** to the priests as their regular share from the time
8:27 and he presented the **p** by lifting them up before
Nu 6:20 These are holy **p** for the priest, along with the
18:29 Be sure to set aside the best **p** of the gifts given to
22:40 He sent **p** of the meat to Balaam and the officials
1Sa 1: 4 he would give **p** of the sacrifice to Peninnah
2Ch 31:19 men were appointed to distribute **p** to every male
35:14 till night offering the burnt offerings and the fat **p**.
Eze 12:19 and sip their tiny **p** of water in utter despair,
48:13 Together these **p** of land will measure 8-1/3 miles

PORTS (2) [PORT]
2Ch 8:17 to Ezion-geber and Elath, **p** in the land of Edom,
Ac 27: 2 it was scheduled to make several stops at **p** along

POSED (3)
Mt 22:23 is no resurrection after death. They **p** this question:
Mk 12:18 is no resurrection after death. They **p** this question:
Lk 20:28 They **p** this question: "Teacher, Moses gave us a

POSITION (24) [POSITIONED, POSITIONS]
Ge 40:13 and return you to your **p** as his chief cup-bearer.
40:21 then restored the chief cup-bearer to his former **p**,
41:13 I was restored to my **p** as cup-bearer, and the chief
50:20 He brought me to the high **p** I have today so I
Ex 14:19 the people of Israel, moved to a **p** behind them,
Nu 2:17 each in **p** under the appropriate family banner.
Jdg 7:21 Each man stood at his **p** around the camp
1Ki 2:27 So Solomon deposed Abiathar from his **p** as priest
13: 4 the king's hand became paralyzed in that **p**,
15:13 grandmother Maacah from her **p** as queen mother
2Ch 15:16 grandmother Maacah from her **p** as queen mother
Ne 6:11 "Should someone in my **p** run away from danger?
6:11 Should someone in my **p** enter the Temple to save
Ps 62: 4 They plan to topple me from my high **p**.
109: 8 years be few; / let his **p** be given to someone else.
Isa 22:19 "I will pull you down from your high **p**.
22:22 house of David—the highest **p** in the royal court.
Eze 26:20 Never again will you be given a **p** of respect here
Da 2:48 Then the king appointed Daniel to a high **p**
Na 2: 3 Watch as their glittering chariots move into **p**,
Jn 11:51 nation came from Caiaphas in his **p** as high priest.
Ac 1:20 And again, 'Let his **p** be given to someone else.'
Php 2: 7 he took the humble **p** of a slave and appeared in
2Th 2: 4 He will **p** himself in the temple of God,

POSITIONED (5) [POSITION]
Ge 48:13 Then he **p** the boys so Ephraim was at Jacob's left
2Sa 10: 8 and Maacah **p** themselves to fight in the open
10:17 The Arameans **p** themselves there in battle
1Ch 19: 9 while the other kings **p** themselves to fight in the
19:17 Jordan River, and **p** his troops in battle formation.

POSITIONS (10) [POSITION]
Jdg 20: 2 took their **p** in the assembly of the people of God.
1Ch 26: 6 ability who earned **p** of great authority in the clan.
2Ch 7: 6 The priests took their assigned **p**, and so did the
20:17 Take your **p**; then stand still and watch the
29:26 then took their **p** around the Temple with the
29:26 and the priests took their **p** with the trumpets.
Est 1:14 and held the highest **p** in the empire.
Eze 23:24 They will take up **p** on every side, surrounding you
Da 3:30 and Abednego to even higher **p** in the province of
11:39 appointing them to **p** of authority and dividing the

POSITIVE (1)
Pr 13: 2 Good people enjoy the **p** results of their words,

POSSESS (23) [DEMON-POSSESSED, POSSESSED, POSSESSES, POSSESSION, POSSESSIONS]
Ex 32:13 to your descendants, and they will **p** it forever.' "
Dt 11:29 LORD your God brings you into the land to **p** it,
30: 5 to your ancestors, and you will **p** that land again.
33:23 may you **p** the west and the south."
Jos 1: 6 for you will lead my people to **p** all the land I
1:15 **p** the land the LORD your God is giving them.
1Ch 28: 8 so that you may **p** this good land and leave it to
Ezr 9:11 **p** was totally defiled by the detestable practices of
Ps 37: 9 but those who trust in the LORD will **p** the land.
37:11 Those who are gentle and lowly will **p** the land;
37:16 and have little / than to be evil and **p** much.
Pr 16:22 Discretion is a life-giving fountain to those who **p**
Isa 34:17 They will **p** it forever, from generation to
57:13 But whoever trusts in me will **p** the land
60:21 They will **p** their land forever, for I will plant them
65: 9 of the people of Israel and of Judah to **p** my land.
Jer 30: 3 and they will **p** it and live here again.
Am 2:10 so you could **p** the land of the Amorites.
9:12 And Israel will **p** what is left of Edom and all the
Ob 1:19 Those living in the foothills of Judah will **p** the
Lk 4:36 "What authority and power this man's words **p**!
11:41 So give to the needy what you greedily **p**, and you
Jas 4: 2 and you can't **p** it, so you fight and quarrel to take

POSSESSED (28) [POSSESS]
Dt 3: 8 "We now **p** all the land of the two Amorite kings
Isa 63:18 How briefly your holy people **p** the holy place,
Jer 3:16 when you **p** the Ark of the LORD's covenant.
Eze 36: 3 all directions, and now you are **p** by many nations.
Mt 4:24 their illness and pain, or if they were **p** by demons,
8:28 two men who were **p** by demons met him.
9:32 who couldn't speak because he was **p** by a demon.
11:18 and he often fasted, and you say, 'He's demon **p**.'
Mk 1:23 A man **p** by an evil spirit was in the synagogue,
3:11 And whenever those **p** by evil spirits caught sight
3:22 "He's **p** by Satan, the prince of demons.
5: 2 a man **p** by an evil spirit ran out from a cemetery
5:15 when they saw the man who had been demon **p**,
5:18 the man who had been demon **p** begged to go,
7:25 to him whose little girl was **p** by an evil spirit.
9:17 because he is **p** by an evil spirit that won't let him
Lk 4:33 a man **p** by a demon began shouting at Jesus,
4:41 Some were **p** by demons; and the demons came out
7:33 and he often fasted, and you say, 'He's demon **p**.'
8:27 a man who was **p** by demons came out to meet
8:35 And they saw the man who had been **p** by demons
8:38 The man who had been demon **p** begged to go,
Jn 7:20 The crowd replied, "You're demon **p**!
8:48 Didn't we say all along that you were **p** by a
8:52 "Now we know you are **p** by a demon.
10:21 "This doesn't sound like a man **p** by a demon!
Ac 5:16 bringing their sick and those **p** by evil spirits,
19:15 But when they tried it on a man **p** by an evil spirit,

POSSESSES (1) [POSSESS]
Job 1:12 "Do whatever you want with everything he **p**,

POSSESSION (75) [POSSESS]
Ge 13:15 land to you and your offspring as a permanent **p**.
23:18 They became Abraham's permanent **p** by the
47:17 herds, and donkeys of Egypt were in Pharaoh's **p**.
48: 4 to you and your descendants as an everlasting **p**.'
Ex 21:16 whether they are caught in **p** of their victims
34: 9 and our sins. Accept us as your own special **p**."
Nu 33:53 Take **p** of the land and settle in it, because I have
34: 2 which I am giving you as your special **p**, these will
Dt 3:12 "When we took **p** of this land, I gave the territory
4:20 of Egypt to become his own people and special **p**;
4:21 LORD your God is giving you as your special **p**.
4:38 bring you in and give you their land as a special **p**,
9:26 They are your special **p**, redeemed from Egypt by
9:29 But they are your people and your special **p**,
10:11 to give their ancestors, so they may take **p** of it.'
12:10 the LORD your God is giving you as a special **p**.
15: 4 you in the land he is giving you as a special **p**.
19:10 the LORD your God is giving you as a special **p**,
19:14 the LORD your God is giving you as a special **p**,
20:16 the LORD your God is giving you as a special **p**,
21:23 the LORD your God is giving you as a special **p**.
24: 4 the LORD your God is giving you as a special **p**.
25:19 enemies in the land he is giving you as a special **p**,
26: 1 the LORD your God is giving you as a special **p**
31: 3 living there, and you will take **p** of their land.
32: 9 belong to the LORD; / Jacob is his special **p**.
32:10 he guarded them as his most precious **p**.
32:49 I am giving to the people of Israel as their own **p**.
33: 4 the law, / the special **p** of the assembly of Israel.
Jos 1:11 and take **p** of the land the LORD your God has
8: 7 jump up from your ambush and take **p** of the city,
11:23 He gave it to the people of Israel as their special **p**,
13: 6 So be sure to give this land to Israel as a special **p**,
14: 9 which you were just walking will be your special **p**
18: 3 "How long are you going to wait before taking **p**
19:47 But the tribe of Dan had trouble taking **p** of their
24: 8 victory over them, and you took **p** of their land.
Jdg 1:19 of Judah, and they took **p** of the hill country.
2: 6 each of the tribes left to take **p** of the land allotted
3:13 Eglon attacked Israel and took **p** of Jericho.
6:34 Then the Spirit of the LORD took **p** of Gideon.
18: 9 You should not hesitate to go and take **p** of it.
1Ki 8:36 you have given to your people as their special **p**.
8:51 for they are your people—your special **p**—
8:53 the nations of the earth to be your own special **p**."
21:18 be at Naboth's vineyard in Jezreel, taking **p** of it.
1Ch 16:18 give you the land of Canaan / as your special **p**."
2Ch 6:27 you have given to your people as their special **p**.
Ne 9:15 and take **p** of the land you had sworn to give them.
9:24 They went in and took **p** of the land. You subdued
Ps 2: 8 your inheritance, / the ends of the earth as your **p**.
28: 9 Save your people! / Bless Israel, your special **p**!
47: 4 the proud **p** of Jacob's descendants, whom he
69:35 His people will live there / and take **p** of the land.
74: 2 the tribe you redeemed as your own special **p**!
78:62 so angry with his own people—his special **p**.
79: 1 nations have conquered your land, your special **p**.
94:14 his people; / he will not abandon his own special **p**.
105:11 give you the land of Canaan / as your special **p**."
106:40 his people, / and he abhorred his own special **p**.
135:12 as an inheritance, / a special **p** to his people Israel.
136:22 a special **p** to his servant Israel. / His faithful love
Pr 7: 2 Guard my teachings as your most precious **p**.
Isa 19:25 I have made. Blessed be Israel, my special **p**!"
63:17 for we are your servants and your special **p**.
Jer 10:16 that exists, / including Israel, his own special **p**.
12: 7 "I have abandoned my people, my special **p**.
51:19 including his people, his own special **p**.
Eze 33:24 one man, and yet he gained **p** of the entire land!
33:24 surely the land should be given to us as a **p**.'
35:10 and Judah will be ours. We will take **p** of them.
45: 5 It will be their **p** and a place for their towns.
Zec 2: 8 who harms you harms my most precious **p**.
Jas 1:18 And we, out of all creation, became his choice **p**.
1Pe 2: 9 of priests, God's holy nation, his very own **p**.

POSSESSIONS (19) [POSSESS]
Ge 13:17 and explore the new **p** I am giving you."
14:16 Abram's nephew Lot with his **p**, and all the
31:21 Jacob took all his **p** with him and crossed the
32:23 they were on the other side, he sent over all his **p**.
34:23 we do this, all their flocks and **p** will become ours.
46: 1 So Jacob set out for Egypt with all his **p**.
47: 1 They came with all their flocks and herds and **p**,
Jdg 2:14 handed them over to marauders who stole their **p**.
18:21 their children, livestock, and **p** in front of them.
Job 15:29 and their **p** will no longer spread across the
Ps 105:21 he became ruler over all the king's **p**.
Isa 15: 7 The desperate refugees take only the **p** they can
Eze 12: 5 they are watching and carry your **p** out through it.
Zec 9: 4 But now the Lord will strip away Tyre's **p** and hurl
14: 1 for the day of the LORD is coming when your **p**
Mt 19:22 he went sadly away because he had many **p**.
Mk 10:22 and he went sadly away because he had many **p**.
Ac 2:45 They sold their **p** and shared the proceeds with
1Jn 2:16 the lust for everything we see, and pride in our **p**.

POSSIBILITY (1) [POSSIBLE]
Lk 22: 2 him without starting a riot, a **p** they greatly feared.

POSSIBLE (28) [POSSIBILITY, POSSIBLY]
Ge 39:10 with her, and he kept out of her way as much as **p**.
Ex 12:33 of Israel to get out of the land as quickly as **p**,
Ru 1:12 And even if it were **p**, and I were to get married
Job 9: 3 would it be **p** to answer him even once in a
Pr 11:24 It is **p** to give freely and become more wealthy,
Ecc 7:27 after looking into the matter from every **p** angle.
Isa 49:15 But even if that were **p**, I would not forget you!
53:11 my righteous servant will make it **p** for many to be
Mt 19:26 it is impossible. But with God everything is **p**."
24:24 and wonders so as to deceive, if **p**,
26:39 If it is **p**, let this cup of suffering be taken away
Mk 9:23 Jesus asked. "Anything is **p** if a person believes."
10:27 But not with God. Everything is **p** with God."
13:22 and wonders so as to deceive, if **p**,
14:35 He prayed that, if it were **p**, the awful hour
14:36 "Abba, Father," he said, "everything is **p** for you.
Lk 18:27 from a human perspective is **p** with God."
21:36 And pray that, if **p**, you may escape these horrors
Ac 9:38 two men to beg him, "Please come as soon as **p**!"
20:16 get to Jerusalem, if **p**, for the Festival of Pentecost.
Ro 12:18 part to live in peace with everyone, as much as **p**.
1Co 1:30 God alone made it **p** for you to be in Christ Jesus.
7:35 serve the Lord best, with as few distractions as **p**.
Gal 1:14 and I tried as hard as **p** to follow all the old
4:15 own eyes and given them to me if it had been **p**.
1Th 3:11 and our Lord Jesus make it **p** for us to come to you
2Th 1:12 This is all made **p** because of the undeserved favor
Heb 10: 4 For it is not **p** for the blood of bulls and goats to

POSSIBLY (5) [POSSIBLE]
Ge 34:14 They said to them, "We couldn't **p** allow this,
1Ki 2:22 "How can you **p** ask me to give Abishag to
Job 35: 7 great gift to him? What could you **p** give him?
Pr 6: 3 quick, get out of it if you **p** can! You have placed
Jn 3:12 how can you **p** believe if I tell you what is going

POST (2) [POSTED, POSTS]
Ex 38:17 Each **p** had a bronze base, and all the hooks
Isa 21: 8 my lord. Night after night I have remained at my **p**.

POSTED (4) [POST]
Isa 62: 6 O Jerusalem, I have **p** watchmen on your walls;
Mt 27:66 So they sealed the tomb and **p** guards to protect it.
Jn 19:19 And Pilate **p** a sign over him that read, "Jesus of
Ac 17: 9 and the other believers after they had **p** bail.

POSTS (42) [POST]
Ex 26:32 gold hooks set into four **p** made from acacia wood
26:32 overlaid with gold. The **p** will fit into silver bases.
26:37 Hang this curtain on gold hooks set into five **p**
26:37 with gold. The **p** will fit into five bronze bases.
27:10 They will be held up by twenty bronze **p** that fit
27:10 to the silver rods that are attached to the **p**.
27:11 150 feet of curtains held up by twenty **p** fitted into
27:12 75 feet long, supported by ten **p** set into ten bases.
27:14 feet long, supported by three **p** set into three bases.
27:15 feet long, supported by three **p** set into three bases.
27:16 It will be attached to four **p** that fit into four bases.
27:17 All the **p** around the courtyard must be connected
27:17 The **p** are to be set in solid bronze bases.
35:11 the clasps, frames, crossbars, **p**, and bases;
35:17 the walls of the courtyard; the **p** and their bases;
36:36 then attached to four gold hooks set into four **p** of
36:36 The **p** were overlaid with gold and set into four
36:38 This curtain was connected by five hooks to five **p**.
36:38 The **p** with their decorated tops and bands were
38:10 There were twenty **p**, each with its own bronze
38:11 with twenty bronze **p** and bases and with silver
38:12 walls were made from curtains supported by ten **p**
38:14 and was supported by three **p** set into three bases.
38:15 and was supported by three **p** set into three bases.
38:17 The tops of the **p** were overlaid with silver,
38:19 It was supported by four **p** set into four bronze
38:19 The tops of the **p** were overlaid with silver,
38:27 and for the **p** supporting the inner curtain required
38:28 the rods and hooks and to overlay the tops of the **p**.
38:30 which was used for casting the bases for the **p** at
38:31 Bronze was also used to make the bases for the **p**
39:33 the clasps, frames, crossbars, **p**, and bases;
39:40 the courtyard and the **p** and bases holding them up;
40:18 and attaching the crossbars and raising the **p**.
Nu 3:37 They were also responsible for the **p** of the
4:32 the **p** for the courtyard walls with their bases,
Jdg 16: 3 got up, took hold of the city gates with its two **p**,
1Ki 7:30 At each corner of the carts were supporting **p** for
2Ch 35:15 the gates and did not need to leave their **p** of duty,
Ne 7: 3 Some will serve at their regular **p** and some in
SS 3:10 Its **p** are of silver, its canopy is gold, and its seat is
Ac 12:10 They passed the first and second guard **p** and came

POT (32) [FIREPOT, POTS, POTSHERD, POTTER, POTTER'S, POTTERS, POTTERY, WATERPOTS]
Lev 6:28 If a clay **p** is used to boil the sacrificial meat,
11:33 "If such an animal dies and falls into a clay **p**, everything in the **p** will be defiled, and the **p** must
11:35 If it is a clay oven or cooking **p**, it must be
14: 5 over a clay **p** that is filled with fresh springwater.
14:50 He will slaughter one of the birds over a clay **p** that
15:12 Any clay **p** touched by the man with the discharge
Nu 11: 8 Then they boiled it in a **p** and made it into flat
Jdg 6:19 carrying the meat in a basket and the broth in a **p**,
1Sa 2:14 the servant would stick the fork into the **p**
Job 13:12 as ashes. Your defense is as fragile as a clay **p**.
41:20 like steam from a boiling **p** on a fire of dry rushes.
Ps 31:12 ignored as if I were dead, / as if I were a broken **p**.
58: 9 and old, / faster than a **p** heats on an open flame.
Pr 26:23 just as a pretty glaze covers a common clay **p**.
Isa 45: 9 Does a clay **p** ever argue with its maker?
45: 9 Does the **p** exclaim, 'How clumsy can you be!'?
Jer 1:13 And I replied, "I see a **p** of boiling water,
Eze 11: 3 Our city is like an iron **p**. Inside it we will be like
11: 7 This city is an iron **p**, but the victims of your
11:11 No, this city will not be an iron **p** for you, and you
24: 3 Put a **p** of water on the fire to boil.
24: 5 the flock and heap fuel on the fire beneath the **p**.
24: 5 Bring the **p** to a boil, and cook the bones along
24: 6 city of murderers! She is a **p** filled with corruption.
24:10 on the wood! Let the fire roar to make the **p** boil.
24:10 many spices. Then empty the **p** and burn the bones.
24:11 Now set the empty **p** on the coals to scorch away
Hos 8: 8 they lie among the nations like an old **p** that no one
Mic 3: 3 You chop them up like meat for the cooking **p**.
Zec 14:21 every cooking **p** in Jerusalem and Judah will be set

POTENTATE [KJV] See ALMIGHTY

POTIPHAR (11) [POTIPHAR'S]
Ge 37:36 Meanwhile, in Egypt, the traders sold Joseph to **P**,
37:36 king of Egypt. **P** was captain of the palace guard.
39: 1 he was purchased by **P**, a member of the personal
39: 1 of Egypt. **P** was the captain of the palace guard.
39: 3 **P** noticed this and realized that the LORD was
39: 4 **P** soon put Joseph in charge of his entire household
39: 5 the LORD began to bless **P** for Joseph's sake.
39: 6 So **P** gave Joseph complete administrative
39:19 After hearing his wife's story, **P** was furious!
40: 3 in the palace of **P**, the captain of the guard.
40: 4 and **P** assigned Joseph to take care of them.

POTIPHAR'S (1) [POTIPHAR]
Ge 39: 7 **P** wife began to desire him and invited him to

POTIPHERA (3)
Ge 41:45 the daughter of **P**, priest of Heliopolis.
41:50 to Joseph and his wife, Asenath, the daughter of **P**,
46:20 was Asenath, daughter of **P**, priest of Heliopolis.

POTS (18) [POT]
Ex 7:19 wooden bowls and stone **p** in the people's homes."
2Sa 17:28 cooking **p**, serving bowls, wheat and barley flour,
1Ki 7:40 He also made the necessary **p**, shovels, and basins.
7:45 the **p**, the shovels, and the basins. All these utensils
2Ki 25:14 They also took all the **p**, shovels, lamp snuffers,
2Ch 4:11 Huram-abi also made the necessary **p**, shovels,
4:16 the **p**, the shovels, the meat hooks, and all the
35:13 and they boiled the holy offerings in **p**, kettles,
Ps 2: 9 with an iron rod / and smash them like clay **p**.' "
Isa 27:11 and used for kindling beneath the cooking **p**.
Jer 18: 2 "Go down to the shop where clay **p** and jars are
52:18 They also took all the **p**, shovels, lamp snuffers,
52:19 firepans, basins, **p**, lampstands, dishes,
La 4: 2 their weight in gold, are now treated like **p** of clay.
Eze 15: 3 making things, like pegs to hang up **p** and pans?
Zec 14:20 And the cooking **p** in the Temple of the LORD
14:21 be free to use any of these **p** to boil their sacrifices.
Rev 2:27 with an iron rod and smash them like clay **p**.

POTSHERD (1) [POT]
Jer 19: 2 the son of Hinnom by the entrance to the **P** Gate,

POTTAGE [KJV] See STEW

POTTER (8) [POT]
Isa 29:16 He is the **P**, and he is certainly greater than you.
29:16 a jar ever say, "The **p** who made me is stupid"?
41:25 He will trample them as a **p** treads on clay.
64: 8 are our Father. We are the clay, and you are the **p**.
Jer 18: 3 he told me and found the **p** working at his wheel.
18: 4 so the **p** squashed the jar into a lump of clay
18: 6 can I not do to you as this **p** has done to his clay?
Ro 9:21 When a **p** makes jars out of clay, doesn't he have a

POTTER'S (3) [POT]
Jer 18: 6 As the clay is in the **p** hand, so are you in my hand.
Mt 27: 7 discussion they finally decided to buy the **p** field,
27:10 and purchased the **p** field, / as the Lord directed."

POTTERS (3) [POT]
1Ch 4:23 They were the **p** who lived in Netaim and Gederah.
Zec 11:13 And the LORD said to me, "Throw it to the **p**"—
11:13 and threw them to the **p** in the Temple of the

POTTERY (4) [POT]
Job 2: 8 Then Job scraped his skin with a piece of broken **p**
Isa 30:14 You will be smashed like a piece of **p**—shattered
Jer 25:34 has arrived; you will fall and shatter like fragile **p**.
32:14 and put them into a **p** jar to preserve them for a

POUCH (4)
Ex 28:16 two folds of cloth, forming a **p** nine inches square.
39: 9 It was doubled over to form a **p**, nine inches
1Sa 25:29 of the LORD your God, secure in his treasure **p**!
Job 14:17 My sins would be sealed in a **p**, and you would

POUNCE (6)
Ps 10: 9 they crouch silently, / waiting to **p** on the helpless.
Pr 6:11 and poverty will **p** on you like a bandit;
24:34 and poverty will **p** on you like a bandit;
Isa 5:29 Roaring like lions, they will **p** on their prey.
Jer 5: 6 attack them; a wolf from the desert will **p** on them.
Hab 1: 8 Like eagles they swoop down to **p** on their prey.

POUND (8) [POUNDED, POUNDING, POUNDS]
Jos 7:21 and a bar of gold weighing more than a **p**.
Ne 5:15 daily ration of food and wine, besides a **p** of silver.
Ps 93: 3 the mighty oceans roar as they **p** the shore.
Ecc 10: 1 an ounce of foolishness can outweigh a **p** of
Jer 51:55 Waves of enemies **p** against her; the noise of battle
Eze 21:12 **p** your thighs in anguish, for that sword will
26: 9 He will **p** your walls with battering rams
Na 3: 2 Wheels rumble, horses' hooves **p**, and chariots

POUNDED (1) [POUND]
Jdg 5:26 She **p** the tent peg through his head, piercing his

POUNDING (5) [POUND]
Nu 11: 8 by grinding it with hand mills or **p** it in mortars.
Ps 65: 7 You quieted the raging oceans / with their **p** waves
Pr 28: 3 A poor person who oppresses the poor is like a **p**
Isa 28:28 grain is easily crushed, so he doesn't keep on **p** it.
44:12 a sharp tool, **p** and shaping it with all his might.

POUNDS (79) [POUND]
Ex 25:39 You will need seventy-five **p** of pure gold for the
30:23 12-1/2 **p** of pure myrrh, 6-1/4 **p** each of cinnamon and of sweet cane,
30:24 12-1/2 **p** of cassia, and one gallon of olive oil.
37:24 was made from seventy-five **p** of pure gold.
38:24 people brought gifts of gold totaling about 2,200 **p**,
38:25 amount of silver that was given was about 7,545 **p**.
38:27 the inner curtain required 7,500 **p** of silver, about 75 **p** for each base.
38:28 The rest of the silver, about 45 **p**, was used to
38:29 The people also brought 5,310 **p** of bronze,
Nu 3:50 of Israel came to about thirty-four **p** in weight.
7:13 consisted of a silver platter weighing about 3-1/4 **p** and a silver basin of about 1-3/4 **p**.
7:19 consisted of a silver platter weighing about 3-1/4 **p** and a silver basin of about 1-3/4 **p**.
7:25 consisted of a silver platter weighing about 3-1/4 **p** and a silver basin of about 1-3/4 **p**.
7:31 consisted of a silver platter weighing about 3-1/4 **p** and a silver basin of about 1-3/4 **p**.
7:37 consisted of a silver platter weighing about 3-1/4 **p** and a silver basin of about 1-3/4 **p**.
7:43 consisted of a silver platter weighing about 3-1/4 **p** and a silver basin of about 1-3/4 **p**.
7:49 consisted of a silver platter weighing about 3-1/4 **p** and a silver basin of about 1-3/4 **p**.
7:55 consisted of a silver platter weighing about 3-1/4 **p** and a silver basin of about 1-3/4 **p**.
7:61 consisted of a silver platter weighing about 3-1/4 **p** and a silver basin of about 1-3/4 **p**.
7:67 consisted of a silver platter weighing about 3-1/4 **p** and a silver basin of about 1-3/4 **p**.
7:73 consisted of a silver platter weighing about 3-1/4 **p** and a silver basin of about 1-3/4 **p**.
7:79 consisted of a silver platter weighing about 3-1/4 **p** and a silver basin of about 1-3/4 **p**.
7:85 In all, the silver objects weighed about 60 **p**,
7:85 3-1/4 **p** for each platter and 1-3/4 **p** for each basin.
7:86 weight of the donated gold came to about three **p**,
31:52 as a gift to the LORD weighed about 420 **p**.
Jdg 8:26 The weight of the gold earrings was forty-three **p**,
1Sa 17: 5 and a coat of mail that weighed 125 **p**.
17: 7 with an iron spearhead that weighed fifteen **p**.
2Sa 12:30 with gems, and it weighed about seventy-five **p**.
14:26 When he weighed it out, it came to five **p**!
21:16 his bronze spearhead weighed more than seven **p**,
1Ki 9:14 Hiram had sent Solomon nine thousand **p** of gold.
10:10 Then she gave the king a gift of nine thousand **p** of
10:16 each containing over fifteen **p** of gold.
10:17 each containing nearly four **p** of gold.
16:24 from its owner, Shemer, for 150 **p** of silver.
20:39 either die or pay a fine of seventy-five **p** of silver!'
2Ki 5: 5 taking as gifts 750 **p** of silver, 150 **p** of gold, and
5:22 He would like 75 **p** of silver and two sets of
5:23 "By all means, take 150 **p** of silver,"
6:25 After a while even a donkey's head sold for two **p**
23:33 pay 7,500 **p** of silver and 75 **p** of gold as tribute.
1Ch 20: 2 with gems, and it weighed about seventy-five **p**.
2Ch 9: 9 Then she gave the king a gift of nine thousand **p** of
9:15 hammered gold, each containing over 15 **p** of gold.
9:16 each containing about 7-1/2 **p** of gold.
25: 6 He also paid about 7,500 **p** of silver to hire
27: 5 he received from them an annual tribute of 7,500 **p**
36: 3 from Judah of 7,500 **p** of silver and 75 **p** of gold.
Ezr 2:69 6,250 **p** of silver, and 100 robes for the priests.
7:22 You are to give him up to 7,500 **p** of silver,
8:26 7,500 **p** of silver utensils, / 7,500 **p** of gold,
Ne 7:71 gold coins and some 2,750 **p** of silver for the work.
7:72 about 2,500 **p** of silver, and 67 robes for the
Job 37: 1 "My heart **p** as I think of this. It leaps within me.
Jer 4:19 in pain! My heart **p** within me! I cannot be still.
Lk 19:13 and gave them ten **p** of silver to invest for him
Jn 19:39 bringing about seventy-five **p** of embalming
Rev 16:21 and hailstones weighing seventy-five **p** fell from

POUR (82) [DOWNPOUR, POURED, POURING, POURS]

Ex 4: 9 from the Nile River and **p** it out on the dry ground.
29: 7 Then take the anointing oil and **p** it over his head.
29:12 and **p** out the rest at the base of the altar.
Lev 2: 1 You are to **p** olive oil on it and sprinkle it with
2: 6 Break it into pieces and **p** oil on it; it is a kind of
4:25 and **p** out the rest of the blood at the base of the
4:30 and **p** out the rest of the blood at the base of the
4:34 and **p** out the rest of the blood at the base of the
14:15 "Then the priest will **p** some of the olive oil into
14:26 "The priest will also **p** some of the olive oil into
Nu 19:17 offering in a jar and **p** fresh water over them.
20: 8 command the rock over there to **p** out its water.
Dt 12:16 You must **p** it out on the ground like water.
12:24 Instead, **p** out the blood on the ground like water.
15:23 You must **p** it out on the ground like water.
28:24 and it will **p** down from the sky until you are
29:21 to **p** out on them all the covenant curses recorded
Jdg 6:20 bread on this rock, and **p** the broth over it."
1Sa 2:32 You will watch with envy as I **p** out prosperity on
1Ki 18:33 and **p** the water over the offering and the wood."
2Ki 4: 4 **P** olive oil from your flask into the jars,
9: 3 and **p** the oil over his head. Say to him, 'This is
2Ch 12: 7 I will not use Shishak to **p** out my anger on
Job 3:24 cannot eat for sighing; my groans **p** out like water.
10:17 You **p** out an ever-increasing volume of anger
16:20 My friends scorn me, but I **p** out my tears to God.
37: 6 to fall on the earth and tells the rain to **p** down.
Ps 10: 5 awaiting them. / They **p** scorn on all their enemies.
36:10 **P** out your unfailing love on those who love you;
62: 8 **P** out your heart to him, / for God is our refuge.
69:24 **P** out your fury on them; / consume them with
78:16 He made streams **p** from the rock,
79: 6 **P** out your wrath on the nations that refuse to
104:10 You make the springs **p** water into ravines,
142: 2 I **p** out my complaints before him / and tell him all
Pr 1:23 I'll **p** out the spirit of wisdom upon you and make
Isa 1:24 says, "I will **p** out my fury on you, my enemies!
44: 3 And I will **p** out my Spirit and my blessings on
45: 8 Open up, O heavens, and **p** out your righteousness.
46: 6 Some people **p** out their silver and gold and hire a
54: 9 so now I swear that I will never again **p** out my
Jer 6:11 "I will **p** out my fury over Jerusalem, even on
7:20 "I will **p** out my terrible fury on this place.
10:18 you from this land and **p** great troubles upon you.
10:25 **P** out your wrath on the nations that refuse to
14:16 For I will **p** out their own wickedness on them.
18:21 children starve! Let the sword **p** out their blood!
23: 2 Now I will **p** out judgment on you for the evil you
26: 3 withhold the disaster I am ready to **p** out on them
36:31 I will **p** out on them and on all the people of Judah
48:12 "when I will send troublemakers to **p** her from her jar. They will **p** her out, then shatter the jar!
La 2:19 cry out. **P** out your hearts like water to the Lord.
Eze 7: 8 Soon I will **p** out my fury to complete your
14:19 "Or suppose I were to **p** out my fury by sending an
20: 8 Then I threatened to **p** out my fury on them to
20:13 So I threatened to **p** out my fury on them, and I
20:21 So again I threatened to **p** out my fury on them in
21:31 I will **p** out my fury on you and blow on you with
22:31 So now I will **p** my fury on them,
30:15 I will **p** out my fury on Pelusium, the strongest
39:29 for I will **p** out my Spirit upon them,
Hos 2:21 which will **p** down water on the earth in answer to
5:10 So I will **p** my anger down on them like a
9: 4 you will not be allowed to **p** out wine as a sacrifice
Joel 2:28 rains again, I will **p** out my Spirit upon all people.
2:29 I will **p** out my Spirit even on servants, men
Ob 1:16 will swallow the punishment I **p** out on you.
Mic 5: 6 when they **p** over the borders to invade our land.
5:15 I will **p** out my vengeance on all the nations that
Zep 3: 8 and **p** out my fiercest anger and fury on them.
Zec 4:12 and what are the two olive branches that **p** out
12:10 "Then I will **p** out a spirit of grace and prayer on
Mal 3:10 I will **p** out a blessing so great you won't have
Lk 22:20 an agreement sealed with the blood I will **p** out for
Ac 2:17 God said, / I will **p** out my Spirit upon all people.
2:18 In those days I will **p** out my Spirit / upon all my
2:33 gave him the Holy Spirit to **p** out upon us, just as
Ro 2: 8 But he will **p** out his anger and wrath on those who
9:23 He also has the right to **p** out the riches of his glory
1Th 5: 9 our Lord Jesus Christ, not to **p** out his anger on us.
Jas 3:13 so that only good deeds will **p** forth.

POURED (86) [POUR]

Ge 25:11 God **p** out rich blessings on Isaac,
28:18 as a memorial pillar. Then he **p** olive oil over it.
35:14 He then **p** wine over it as an offering to God
Ex 29: 2 with olive oil, and wafers with oil **p** over them.
30:32 It must never be **p** on the body of an ordinary
Lev 4: 7 The rest of the bull's blood must be **p** out at the
4:18 then be **p** out at the base of the altar of burnt
8:12 Then he **p** some of the anointing oil on Aaron's
8:15 He **p** out the rest of the blood at the base of the
9: 9 He **p** out the rest of the blood at the base of the
14:18 hand will then be **p** over the healed person's head.
14:29 priest's hand will then be **p** over the person's head.
21:10 who has had the anointing oil **p** on his head
Nu 28: 7 **p** out in the Holy Place as an offering to the
Dt 12:27 The blood of your other sacrifices must be **p** out
Jos 8:19 the men in ambush jumped up and **p** into the city.
Jdg 5: 4 earth trembled / and the cloudy skies **p** down rain.
1Sa 7: 6 water from a well and **p** it out before the LORD.
10: 1 took a flask of olive oil and **p** it over Saul's head.
16:13 olive oil he had brought and **p** it on David's head.
2Sa 22: 9 Smoke **p** from his nostrils; / fierce flames leaped
23:16 to drink it. Instead, he **p** it out before the LORD.
1Ki 1:39 from the sacred tent and **p** it on Solomon's head.
13: 3 and its ashes will be **p** out on the ground."
13: 5 crack appeared in the altar, and the ashes **p** out,
2Ki 9: 6 Then the young prophet **p** the oil over Jehu's head
16:13 and a grain offering, **p** a drink offering over it,
1Ch 11:18 to drink it. Instead, he **p** it out before the LORD.
2Ch 34:21 The LORD's anger has been **p** out against us
34:25 My anger will be **p** out against this place,
Job 29: 6 and my olive groves **p** out streams of olive oil.
Ps 18: 8 Smoke **p** from his nostrils; / fierce flames leaped
22:14 My life is **p** out like water, / and all my bones are
68: 8 the earth trembled, and the heavens **p** rain
77:17 The clouds **p** down their rain; / the thunder rolled
85: 1 you have **p** out amazing blessings on your land!
133: 2 that was **p** over Aaron's head, / that ran down his
Pr 3:20 the earth burst forth, and the clouds **p** down rain.
Isa 29:10 For the LORD has **p** out on you a spirit of deep
32:15 until at last the Spirit is **p** down upon us from
42:25 That is why he **p** out such fury on them
51:20 The LORD has **p** out his fury; God has rebuked
Jer 19:13 and where drink offerings were **p** out to your
42:18 and fury were **p** out on the people of Jerusalem,
42:18 so they will be **p** out on you when you enter Egypt.
48:11 She has not been **p** from flask to flask, and she is
48:21 Judgment has been **p** out on them all—on Holon
La 2: 4 His fury is **p** out like fire on beautiful Jerusalem.
2:11 My heart is broken, my spirit **p** out, as I see what
4:11 is satisfied. His fiercest anger has now been **p** out.
Eze 20:28 and **p** out their drink offerings to them!
22:22 that I, the LORD, have **p** out my fury on you."
36:18 by worshiping idols, so I **p** out my fury on them.
Da 9:11 have been **p** out against us because of our sin.
9:27 until the end that has been decreed is **p** out on this
Hos 10: 1 the more they **p** it on the altars of their foreign
Joel 2:28 "Then after I have **p** out my rains again, I will
Zep 1:15 It is a day when the LORD's anger will be **p** out.
1:17 Your blood will be **p** out into the dust, and your
Mt 26: 7 jar of expensive perfume and **p** it over his head.
26:12 She has **p** this perfume on me to prepare my body
26:28 his people. It is **p** out to forgive the sins of many.
Mk 7: 3 do not eat until they have **p** water over their
14: 3 broke the seal and **p** the perfume over his head.
14:24 said to them, "This is my blood, **p** out for many,
Jn 11: 2 This is the Mary who **p** the expensive perfume on
13: 5 and **p** water into a basin. Then he began to wash
Ac 10:45 the Holy Spirit had been **p** out upon the Gentiles,
1Co 15:10 because God **p** out his special favor on me—
Eph 1: 6 God for the wonderful kindness he has **p** out on us
Php 2:17 But even if my life is to be **p** out like a drink
2Ti 4: 6 my life has already been **p** out as an offering to
Tit 3: 6 He generously **p** out the Spirit upon us because of
Jas 5:18 Then he prayed for rain, and down it **p**. The grass
Rev 8: 4 God from the altar where the angel had **p** them out.
9: 2 smoke **p** out as though from a huge furnace,
14:10 It is **p** out undiluted into God's cup of wrath.
16: 2 left the Temple and **p** out his bowl over the earth,
16: 3 Then the second angel **p** out his bowl on the sea,
16: 4 Then the third angel **p** out his bowl on the rivers
16: 6 been killed, and their blood was **p** out on the earth.
16: 8 Then the fourth angel **p** out his bowl on the sun,
16:10 Then the fifth angel **p** out his bowl on the throne of
16:12 Then the sixth angel **p** out his bowl on the great
16:17 Then the seventh angel **p** out his bowl into the air.
17: 1 One of the seven angels who had **p** out the seven

POURING (12) [POUR]

Ex 17: 6 Strike the rock, and water will come **p** out.
25:29 and bowls to be used in **p** out drink offerings.
37:16 These utensils were to be used in **p** out drink
1Sa 1:15 very sad, and I was **p** out my heart to the LORD.
Ps 45: 7 **p** out the oil of joy on you more than on anyone
102: T with trouble, **p** out problems before the LORD.
Jer 32:29 and by **p** out drink offerings to other gods.
44:19 **p** out drink offerings to her, and making cakes
Mic 1: 4 valleys like wax in a fire, like water **p** down a hill.
Heb 1: 9 **p** out the oil of joy on you more than on anyone
Jas 3:10 and cursing come **p** out of the same mouth.
Rev 15: 8 angels had completed **p** out the seven plagues.

POURS (10) [POUR]

Job 12:21 He **p** disgrace upon princes and confiscates
36:28 The rain **p** down from the clouds, and everyone
Ps 42: 8 Through each day the LORD **p** his unfailing love
75: 8 He **p** the wine out in judgment, / and all the wicked
85:12 Yes, the LORD **p** down his blessings. / Our land
107:40 the LORD **p** contempt on their princes,
Pr 6:19 a false witness who **p** out lies, / a person who sows
Isa 30:28 His anger **p** out like a flood on his enemies,
Am 5: 8 from the oceans and **p** it down as rain on the land.
9: 6 from the oceans and **p** it down as rain on the land.

POURTRAY(ED) [KJV] See DRAW, ENGRAVED, PICTURES

POUTED (1)

Jdg 16:15 Then Delilah **p**, "How can you say you love me

POVERTY (26) [POOR]

Ge 45:11 and your household will come to utter **p**.' "
Lev 25:35 "If any of your Israelite relatives fall into **p**
Job 21:25 Another person dies in bitter **p**, never having tasted
Pr 6:11 and **p** will pounce on you like a bandit;
6:26 For a prostitute will bring you to **p**, and sleeping
10:15 is their fortress; the **p** of the poor is their calamity.
13:18 ignore criticism, you will end in **p** and disgrace;
14:23 Work brings profit, but mere talk leads to **p**!
19: 4 makes many "friends"; **p** drives them away.
20:13 If you love sleep, you will end in **p**. Keep your
21: 5 lead to prosperity, but hasty shortcuts lead to **p**.
22:16 or by showering gifts on the rich will end in **p**.
23:21 for they are on their way to **p**. Too much sleep
24:34 and **p** will pounce on you like a bandit;
28:11 as wise, but their real **p** is evident to the poor.
28:19 have plenty of food; playing around brings **p**.
28:22 person tries to get rich quick, but it only leads to **p**.
28:27 will come upon those who close their eyes to **p**.
30: 8 to tell a lie. Second, give me neither **p** nor riches!
31: 7 Let them drink to forget their **p** and remember their
Ecc 4:14 might even become king, though he was born in **p**.
Isa 17: 4 of Israel will be very dim, for **p** will stalk the land.
Ac 4:34 There was no **p** among them, because people who
2Co 8: 2 and deep **p** have overflowed in rich generosity.
8: 9 so that by his **p** he could make you rich.
Rev 2: 9 "I know about your suffering and your **p**—but you

POWDER (1)

Ex 32:20 he ground it into **p** and mixed it with water.

POWER (426) [OVERPOWER, OVERPOWERED, OVERPOWERS, POWERFUL, POWERFULLY, POWERLESS, POWERS]

GREAT POWER (24) Ex 13:9,16; 15:16; 32:11; Ne 1:10; Job 30:21; Ps 20:6; 54:1; 66:7; 79:11; 111:6; Ecc 4:1; 8:4; Jer 21:5; 27:5; 32:17,21; Jnh 1:16; Mal 1:5; Mk 9:1; 13:26; Jas 5:16; Rev 6:15; 11:17

POWER OF GOD (12) Mt 22:29; Mk 12:24; Lk 11:20; Jn 9:3; Ac 8:10; Ro 1:16; 1Co 1:18,24; 2:5; 2Co 13:4; Col 2:12; 1Pe 5:6

Ge 9: 2 will be afraid of you. I have placed them in your **p**.
41:16 "It is beyond my **p** to do this," Joseph replied.
Ex 6: 6 I will redeem you with mighty **p** and great acts of
7: 5 When I show the Egyptians my **p** and force them
8:22 and that I have **p** even in the heart of your land.
9:16 that you might see my **p** and that my fame might
10: 1 so I can continue to display my **p** by performing
13: 3 the LORD has brought you out by his mighty **p**.
13: 9 LORD who rescued you from Egypt with great **p**.
13:14 'With mighty **p** the LORD brought us out of
13:16 who brought you out of Egypt with great **p**."
14:31 When the people of Israel saw the mighty **p** that
15: 6 "Your right hand, O LORD, / is glorious in **p**.
15: 9 will unsheath my sword; / my **p** will destroy them.'
15:16 Because of your great **p**, / they will be silent like a
18:10 He has rescued Israel from the **p** of Egypt!
20:20 has come in this way to show you his awesome **p**.
32:11 brought from the land of Egypt with such great **p**
34:10 And all the people around you will see the **p** of the
34:10 the awesome **p** I will display through you.
Lev 25:43 never exercise your **p** over them in a ruthless way.
26:37 You will have no **p** to stand before your enemies.
Nu 11:23 said to Moses, "Is there any limit to my **p**?
14:13 "They know full well the **p** you displayed in
14:17 prove that your **p** is as great as you have claimed it
22:38 "I have come, but I have no **p** to say just anything.
23:23 touch Jacob; / no sorcery has any **p** against Israel.
Dt 3:24 have only begun to show me your greatness and **p**.
4:34 miraculous signs, wonders, war, awesome **p**,
4:37 brought you out of Egypt with a great display of **p**.
5:15 LORD your God brought you out with amazing **p**
6:21 LORD brought us out of Egypt with amazing **p**.
7: 8 **p** from your slavery under Pharaoh in Egypt.
7:19 and the amazing **p** he used when he brought you
7:19 The LORD your God will use this same **p** against
7:24 He will put their kings in your **p**, and you will
8:18 your God who gives you **p** to become rich,
9:26 redeemed from Egypt by your mighty **p**
9:29 whom you brought from Egypt by your mighty **p**
11: 2 your God or seen his greatness and awesome **p**.
26: 8 LORD brought us out of Egypt with amazing **p**,
32:27 and say, / "Our **p** has triumphed!
32:39 and heals; / no one delivers from my **p**!
33:17 a young bull; / his **p** is like the horns of a wild ox.
34:12 Moses that the LORD demonstrated his mighty **p**
Jos 4:24 of the earth might know the **p** of the LORD,
Jdg 16:24 one who killed so many of us is now in our **p**!"
1Sa 10: 6 Spirit of the LORD will come upon you with **p**,
24: 4 'I will certainly put Saul into your **p**, to do with as
24:15 my advocate, and he will rescue me from your **p**!"
24:19 let his enemy get away when he had him in his **p**?
26:23 you even when the LORD placed you in my **p**,
2Sa 12: 7 king of Israel and saved you from the **p** of Saul.
1Ki 8:42 of you and of your mighty miracles and your **p**—
15:23 of the events in Asa's reign, the extent of his **p**,
16: 5 and the extent of his **p** are recorded in *The Book*
16:27 of the events in Omri's reign, the extent of his **p**,
22:45 events in Jehoshaphat's reign, the extent of his **p**,
2Ki 3:15 the **p** of the LORD came upon Elisha,
13: 8 and all his deeds, including the extent of his **p**,
13:12 including the extent of his **p** and his war with King
14:15 including the extent of his **p** and his war with King
14:28 his deeds, including the extent of his **p**, his wars,
15:19 gain his support in tightening his grip on royal **p**.
17: 4 So of Egypt to help him shake free of Assyria's **p**
17:36 you out of Egypt with such mighty miracles and **p**.

18:29 He will never be able to rescue you from my **p**.
18:34 and Ivvah? Did they rescue Samaria from my **p**?
18:35 has ever been able to save its people from my **p**?
19:19 Now, O LORD our God, rescue us from his **p**;
19:26 That is why their people have so little **p** / and are
20:20 including the extent of his **p** and how he built a
1Ch 29:11 is the greatness, the **p**, the glory, the victory,
29:12 **P** and might are in your hand, and it is at your
2Ch 13:20 So Jeroboam of Israel never regained his **p** during
25:8 for he has the **p** to help or to frustrate."
32:7 for there is a **p** far greater on our side!
32:13 nations able to rescue their people from my **p**?
32:15 much less will your God rescue you from my **p**!"
32:17 nations failed to rescue their people from my **p**,
36:20 and his sons until the kingdom of Persia came to **p**.
Ne 1:10 the people you rescued by your great **p** and might.
9:37 of our sins. They have **p** over us and our cattle.
Job 5:20 of famine, from the **p** of the sword in time of war.
10:7 I am not guilty, no one can rescue me from your **p**.
10:16 like a lion and display your awesome **p** against me.
12:6 and God has them in his **p**—live in safety!
12:13 "But true wisdom and **p** are with God; counsel
12:16 with him; deceivers and deceived are both in his **p**.
24:22 "God, in his **p**, drags away the rich. They may rise
26:12 By his **p** the sea grew calm. By his skill he crushed
26:13 and his **p** pierced the gliding serpent.
26:14 minor things he does, merely a whisper of his **p**.
26:14 Who can understand the thunder of his **p**?"
27:11 "I will teach you about God's **p**. I will not conceal
27:22 without mercy. They struggle to flee from its **p**.
30:21 toward me. You persecute me with your great **p**.
35:9 to them. They groan beneath the **p** of the mighty.
36:5 He is mighty in both **p** and understanding.
37:5 We cannot comprehend the greatness of his **p**.
37:7 working at such a time so they can recognize his **p**.
37:23 We cannot imagine the **p** of the Almighty, yet he is
Ps 20:6 his holy heaven / and rescue him by his great **p**.
21:13 We praise you, LORD, for all your glorious **p**.
40:10 I have talked about your faithfulness and saving **p**.
44:3 It was by your mighty **p** that they succeeded;
44:5 Only by your **p** can we push back our enemies;
45:6 and ever. / Your royal **p** is expressed in justice.
49:15 He will snatch me from the **p** of death.
54:1 Come with great **p**, O God, and rescue me!
59:11 stagger them with your **p**, and bring them to their
59:16 But as for me, I will sing about your **p**. / I will
62:11 heard it many times: / **P**, O God, belongs to you;
63:2 your sanctuary / and gazed upon your **p** and glory.
65:6 You formed the mountains by your **p** / and armed
66:3 Your enemies cringe before your mighty **p**.
66:7 For by his great **p** he rules forever. / He watches
67:2 your saving **p** among people everywhere.
68:28 Display your **p**, O God, as you have in the past.
68:34 Tell everyone about God's **p**. / His majesty shines
68:35 The God of Israel gives **p** and strength to his
69:29 and in pain. / Rescue me, O God, by your saving **p**.
71:4 My God, rescue me from the **p** of the wicked,
71:15 All day long I will proclaim your saving **p**,
71:18 Let me proclaim your **p** to this new generation,
75:10 but I will increase the **p** of the godly."
77:14 You demonstrate your awesome **p** among the
78:4 We will tell of his **p** and the mighty miracles he
78:26 and guided the south wind by his mighty **p**.
78:42 They forgot about his **p** / and how he rescued them
79:11 Demonstrate your great **p** by saving those
80:2 and Manasseh. / Show us your mighty **p**.
89:17 glorious strength. / Our **p** is based on your favor.
89:24 be with him, / and he will rise to **p** because of me.
89:48 No one can escape the **p** of the grave. / *Interlude*
90:11 Who can comprehend the **p** of your anger?
92:10 as a wild bull. / How refreshed I am by your **p**!
97:10 and rescues them from the **p** of the wicked.
98:1 has won a mighty victory / by his **p** and holiness.
106:8 of his name / and to demonstrate his mighty **p**.
106:42 and brought them under their cruel **p**.
107:24 They, too, observed the LORD's **p** in action,
111:6 He has shown his great **p** to his people / by giving
132:8 along with the Ark, the symbol of your **p**.
132:17 Here I will increase the **p** of David; / my anointed
138:7 against my angry enemies! / Your **p** will save me.
144:7 me from deep waters, / from the **p** of my enemies.
144:11 Rescue me from the **p** of my enemies.
145:11 they will celebrate examples of your **p**.
147:5 How great is our Lord! His **p** is absolute!
Pr 3:27 who deserve it when it's in your **p** to help them.
29:2 But when the wicked are in **p**, they groan.
Ecc 4:1 The oppressors have great **p**, and the victims are
8:4 The king's command is backed by great **p**. No one
8:8 None of us has the **p** to prevent the day of our
8:9 where people have the **p** to hurt each other.
Isa 10:5 of my anger. Its military **p** is a club in my hand.
10:13 "By my own **p** and wisdom I have won these
10:15 Can the ax boast greater **p** than the person who
14:5 For the LORD has crushed your wicked **p**
14:8 sing out this joyous song: 'Your **p** is broken!
14:11 Your might and **p** are gone; they were buried with
14:26 for my mighty **p** reaches throughout the world.
17:3 also be destroyed, and the **p** of Damascus will end.
20:5 who counted on the **p** of Ethiopia and boasted of
30:4 For though his **p** extends to Zoan and Hanes,
33:10 "I will stand up and show my **p** and might.
36:19 Did they rescue Samaria from my **p**?
36:20 has ever been able to save its people from my **p**?
37:20 Now, O LORD our God, rescue us from his **p**;
37:27 That is why their people have so little **p** / and are
40:10 Sovereign LORD is coming in all his glorious **p**.
40:29 He gives **p** to those who are tired and worn out;
44:7 them tell you if they can and thus prove their **p**.
46:7 no answer. It has no **p** to get anyone out of trouble.
50:2 Is it because I have no **p** to rescue? No, that is not
51:5 They will wait for me and long for my **p**.
52:6 to my people, and they will come to know its **p**.
52:10 The LORD will demonstrate his holy **p** before the
53:1 To whom will the LORD reveal his saving **p**?
55:4 He displayed my **p** by being my witness and a
55:13 it will be an everlasting sign of his **p** and love.
59:16 himself stepped in to save them with his mighty **p**
63:12 Where is the one whose **p** divided the sea before
Jer 2:16 have utterly destroyed Israel's glory and **p**.
10:6 For you are great, and your name is full of **p**.
10:12 But God made the earth by his **p**, / and he
10:14 they are frauds. / They have no life or **p** in them.
16:21 "So now I will show them my **p** and might,"
21:5 I myself will fight against you with great **p**, for I
23:10 For the prophets do evil and abuse their **p**.
26:14 As for me, I am helpless and in your **p**—do with
27:5 By my great **p** I have made the earth and all its
32:17 have made the heavens and earth by your great **p**.
32:21 with great **p** and overwhelming terror.
42:11 and will save you and rescue you from his **p**.
51:15 He made the earth by his **p**, / and he preserves it by
51:17 they are frauds. / They have no life or **p** in them.
La 2:17 enemies to rejoice over her and boast of their **p**.
Eze 17:16 the land of the king who put him in **p** and whose
20:22 who had seen my **p** in bringing them out of Egypt.
20:33 an iron fist in great anger and with awesome **p**.
21:10 far stronger than you have fallen beneath its **p**!
26:17 been destroyed! / Your people, with their naval **p**,
30:6 allies will fall, and the pride of their **p** will end.
33:28 her pride. Her arrogant **p** will come to an end.
39:21 inflicted on them and the **p** I have demonstrated.
Da 2:20 and ever, / for he alone has all wisdom and **p**.
2:37 has given you sovereignty, **p**, strength, and honor.
3:15 What god will be able to rescue you from my **p**
3:17 He will rescue us from your **p**, Your Majesty.
4:30 I, by my own mighty **p**, have built this beautiful
4:35 He has the **p** to do as he pleases / among the angels
6:27 He has rescued Daniel / from the **p** of the lions."
7:14 and royal **p** over all the nations of the world,
7:23 "This fourth beast is the fourth world **p** that will
7:26 and all his **p** will be taken away and completely
7:27 Then the sovereignty, **p**, and greatness of all the
8:7 one who could rescue the ram from the goat's **p**.
8:8 But at the height of its **p**, its large horn was broken
8:9 horns came a small horn whose **p** grew very great.
8:10 His **p** reached to the heavens where it attacked the
8:23 a fierce king, a master of intrigue, will rise to **p**.
8:24 He will become very strong, but not by his own **p**.
8:25 but he will be broken, though not by human **p**.
9:15 your people from Egypt in a great display of **p**.
11:3 "Then a mighty king will rise to **p** who will rule a
11:4 But at the height of his **p**, his kingdom will be
11:5 "The king of the south will increase in **p**, but one
11:21 "The next to come to **p** will be a despicable man
Hos 1:5 by breaking its military **p** in the Jezreel Valley."
Am 5:9 With blinding speed and **p** he destroys the strong,
6:13 we take Karnaim by our own strength and **p**?"
Jnh 1:16 sailors were awestruck by the LORD's great **p**,
Mic 2:1 of the wicked schemes you have **p** to accomplish.
3:8 I am filled with **p** and the Spirit of the LORD.
4:8 royal might and **p** will come back to you again.
7:16 They will be embarrassed that their **p** is
Na 1:3 The LORD is slow to get angry, but his **p** is great,
1:3 He displays his **p** in the whirlwind and the storm.
2:2 but the LORD will restore its honor and **p** again.
Hab 1:6 I am raising up the Babylonians to be a new **p** on
3:2 Show us your **p** to save us. And in your anger,
3:4 from his hands. He rejoices in his awesome **p**.
3:6 But his **p** is not diminished in the least!
3:9 You were commanding your weapons of **p**!
Hag 2:22 destroying the **p** of foreign kingdoms.
Zec 10:12 I will make my people strong in my **p**, and they
Mal 1:5 the LORD's great **p** reaches far beyond our
Mt 12:24 He gets his **p** from Satan, the prince of demons."
22:29 the Scriptures, and you don't know the **p** of God.
24:30 Son of Man arrive on the clouds of heaven with **p**
26:64 sitting at God's right hand in the place of **p**
Mk 3:22 That's where he gets the **p** to cast out demons."
5:30 Jesus realized at once that healing **p** had gone out
6:2 all his wisdom and the **p** to perform such miracles?
9:1 you see the Kingdom of God arrive in great **p**!"
12:24 the Scriptures, and you don't know the **p** of God.
13:26 the Son of Man arrive on the clouds with great **p**
14:62 sitting at God's right hand in the place of **p**
Lk 1:17 He will be a man with the spirit and **p** of Elijah,
1:35 and the **p** of the Most High will overshadow you.
4:14 returned to Galilee, filled with the Holy Spirit's **p**.
4:36 "What authority and **p** this man's words possess!
5:15 the report of his **p** spread even faster,
5:17 And the Lord's healing **p** was strongly with Jesus.
6:19 because healing **p** went out from him, and they
8:29 the wilderness, completely under the demon's **p**.
8:46 touched me, for I felt healing **p** go out from me."
9:1 and gave them **p** and authority to cast out demons
9:43 the people as they saw this display of God's **p**.
10:19 And I have given you authority over all the **p** of
11:15 He gets his **p** from Satan, the prince of demons!"
11:20 But if I am casting out demons by the **p** of God,
12:5 who has the **p** to kill people and then throw them
21:27 will see the Son of Man arrive on the clouds with **p**
22:53 the time when the **p** of darkness reigns."
22:69 be sitting at God's right hand in the place of **p**."
24:49 Spirit comes and fills you with **p** from heaven."
Jn 6:57 I live by the **p** of the living Father who sent me;
9:3 born blind so the **p** of God could be seen in him.
10:18 when I want to and also the **p** to take it again.
12:38 To whom will the Lord reveal his saving **p**?"
14:30 of this world approaches. He has no **p** over me,
19:10 "Don't you realize that I have the **p** to release you
19:11 "You would have no **p** over me at all unless it
Ac 1:8 you will receive **p** and will tell people about me
3:12 though we had made this man walk by our own **p**
4:7 in the two disciples and demanded, "By what **p**,
4:10 in the name and **p** of Jesus Christ from Nazareth,
4:30 Send your healing **p**; may miraculous signs
6:8 Stephen, a man full of God's grace and **p**,
8:10 spoke of him as "the Great One—the **P** of God."
8:18 people's heads, he offered money to buy this **p**.
8:19 "Let me have this **p**, too," he exclaimed, "so that
10:38 Jesus of Nazareth with the Holy Spirit and with **p**.
11:21 The **p** of the Lord was upon them, and a large
14:1 and preached with such **p** that a great number of
14:3 was true by giving them **p** to do miraculous signs
19:11 God gave Paul the **p** to do unusual miracles,
26:18 darkness to light, and from the **p** of Satan to God.
Ro 1:16 It is the **p** of God at work, saving everyone who
1:20 invisible qualities—his eternal **p** and divine nature.
3:9 whether Jews or Gentiles, are under the **p** of sin.
6:4 from the dead by the glorious **p** of the Father,
6:6 with Christ so that sin might lose its **p** in our lives.
6:7 died with Christ we were set free from the **p** of sin.
6:9 die again. Death no longer has any **p** over him.
6:22 But now you are free from the **p** of sin and have
7:4 The law no longer holds you in its **p**, because you
died to its **p** when you died with
7:6 with Christ, and we are no longer captive to its **p**.
7:8 If there were no law, sin would not have that **p**.
8:2 For the **p** of the life-giving Spirit has freed you
8:2 Christ Jesus from the **p** of sin that leads to death.
8:13 But if through the **p** of the Holy Spirit you turn
9:17 for the very purpose of displaying my **p** in you,
9:22 has every right to exercise his judgment and his **p**,
11:23 them back into the tree again. He has the **p** to do it.
11:36 everything exists by his **p** and is intended for his
13:1 All governments have been placed in **p** by God.
14:4 The Lord's **p** will help them do as they should.
15:13 May you overflow with hope through the **p** of the
15:19 as signs from God—all by the **p** of God's Spirit.
1Co 1:17 for fear that the cross of Christ would lose its **p**.
1:18 saved recognize this message as the very **p** of God.
1:24 Christ is the mighty **p** of God and the wonderful
2:5 so that you might trust the **p** of God rather than
4:19 big talkers or whether they really have God's **p**.
4:20 God is not just fancy talk; it is living by God's **p**.
5:4 and the **p** of the Lord Jesus will be with you as you
6:14 raise our bodies from the dead by his marvelous **p**,
7:22 the Lord has now set you free from the awful **p** of
12:9 and to someone else he gives the **p** to heal the sick.
12:10 He gives one person the **p** to perform miracles,
12:29 Does everyone have the **p** to do miracles?
14:2 You will be speaking by the **p** of the Spirit, but it
15:43 but when they are raised, they will be full of **p**.
15:56 that results in death, and the law gives sin its **p**.
2Co 3:5 Our only **p** and success come from God.
4:7 this light and **p** that now shine within us—
4:7 So everyone can see that our glorious **p** is from
6:6 our sincere love, and the **p** of the Holy Spirit.
6:7 the truth. God's **p** has been working in us.
12:9 all you need. My **p** works best in your weakness."
12:9 so that the **p** of Christ may work through me.
13:3 his dealings with you; he is a mighty **p** among you.
13:4 in weakness, he now lives by the mighty **p** of God.
13:4 are weak, but we live in him and have God's
p—the **p** we use in dealing with you.
Eph 1:19 greatness of his **p** for us who believe him. This is
the same mighty **p**
1:21 or authority or **p** or leader or anything else in this
2:2 the mighty prince of the **p** of the air.
3:7 By God's special favor and mighty **p**, I have been
3:18 And may you have the **p** to understand, as all
3:19 the fullness of life and **p** that comes from God.
3:20 By his mighty **p** at work within us, he is able to
6:10 A final word: Be strong with the Lord's mighty **p**.
6:18 and on every occasion in the **p** of the Holy Spirit.
Php 2:13 to obey him and the **p** to do what pleases him.
3:10 and experience the mighty **p** that raised him from
3:21 using the same mighty **p** that he will use to
Col 1:11 that you will be strengthened with his glorious **p**
1:29 as I depend on Christ's mighty **p** that works within
2:12 new life because you trusted the mighty **p** of God,
3:1 at God's right hand in the place of honor and **p**.
1Th 1:5 it was not only with words but also with **p**,
2Th 1:9 separated from the Lord and from his glorious **p**
1:11 And we pray that God, by his **p**, will fulfill all your
2:9 come to do the work of Satan with counterfeit **p**
1Ti 6:16 ever will. To him be honor and **p** forever. Amen.
2Ti 1:7 given us a spirit of fear and timidity, but of **p**, love,
1:10 who broke the **p** of death and showed us the way to
3:5 but they will reject the **p** that could make them
Heb 1:3 He sustains the universe by the mighty **p** of his
1:8 Your royal **p** is expressed in righteousness.
2:14 and only by dying could he break the **p** of the
Devil, who had the **p** of death.
4:12 For the word of God is full of living **p**. It is sharper
6:5 of the word of God and the **p** of the age to come—
7:7 the person who has the **p** to bless is always greater
7:16 but by the **p** of a life that cannot be destroyed.
9:14 For by the **p** of the eternal Spirit, Christ offered
9:26 to remove the **p** of sin forever by his sacrificial
13:20[-21] produce in you, through the **p** of Jesus Christ,
Jas 4:12 among us. He alone has the **p** to save or to destroy.

5: 6 and killed good people who had no **p** to defend
5:16 earnest prayer of a righteous person has great **p**
1Pe 1: 5 And God, in his mighty **p**, will protect you until
1:12 to you in the **p** of the Holy Spirit sent from heaven.
3:21 which now saves you by the **p** of Jesus Christ's
4:11 All glory and **p** belong to him forever and ever.
5: 6 So humble yourselves under the mighty **p** of God,
5:11 All **p** is his forever and ever. Amen.
2Pe 1: 3 his divine **p** gives us everything we need for living
1: 4 And by that same mighty **p**, he has given us all of
1:16 we told you about the **p** of our Lord Jesus Christ
2:11 even though they are far greater in **p** and strength
1Jn 5:19 and that the world around us is under the **p**
Jude 1: 8 and scoff at the **p** of the glorious ones.
1:25 Yes, glory, majesty, **p**, and authority belong to
Rev 4:11 Lord our God, / to receive glory and honor and **p**.
5:12 He is worthy to receive **p** and riches / and wisdom
5:13 also sang: / "Blessing and honor and glory and **p**
6:15 the people with great **p**, and every slave and every
7: 2 four angels who had been given **p** to injure land
7:12 and thanksgiving and honor and **p** and strength
9: 3 and they were given **p** to sting like scorpions.
9:10 that sting like scorpions, with **p** to torture people.
9:10 This **p** was given to them for five months.
9:19 Their **p** was in their mouths, but also in their tails.
9:19 had heads like snakes, with the **p** to injure people.
11: 3 And I will give **p** to my two witnesses, and they
11: 6 They have **p** to shut the skies so that no rain will
11: 6 And they have the **p** to turn the rivers and oceans
11:17 for now you have assumed your great **p**
12:10 the salvation and **p** and kingdom of our God,
13: 2 And the dragon gave him his own **p** and throne
13: 4 worshiped the dragon for giving the beast such **p**,
14:18 who has **p** to destroy the world with fire,
15: 8 was filled with smoke from God's glory and **p**.
17:12 ten horns are ten kings who have not yet risen to **p**;
17:13 They will all agree to give their **p** and authority to
19: 1 is from our God. Glory and **p** belong to him alone.
20: 6 For them the second death holds no **p**, but they will

POWERFUL (75) [POWER]

Ge 26:16 "for you have become too rich and **p** for us."
Ex 1:20 continued to multiply, growing more and more **p**.
6: 1 "When he feels my **p** hand upon him, he will let
8:10 Then you will know that no one is as **p** as the
19:16 there was a **p** thunder and lightning storm,
Nu 13:28 But the people living there are **p**, and their cities
Dt 1:28 of the land are taller and more **p** than we are,
2:10 and **p** race of giants called the Emites had once
2:21 They were a numerous and **p** race, as tall as the
7: 1 These seven nations are all more **p** than you.
7:17 nations that are so much more **p** than we are?'
9: 1 to nations much greater and more **p** than you.
9:14 a nation larger and more **p** than they are.'
Jos 23: 9 LORD has driven out great and **p** nations for you,
1Sa 7:13 the LORD's **p** hand was raised against the
2Sa 3: 6 Abner became a **p** leader among those who were
5:10 And David became more and more **p**,
22:18 He delivered me from my **p** enemies, / from those
1Ch 5: 2 descendants of Judah that became the most **p** tribe
11: 9 And David became more and more **p**,
2Ch 1: 1 his God was with him and made him very **p**.
13:21 Abijah of Judah grew more and more **p**.
17:12 became more and more **p** and built fortresses
20: 6 You are **p** and mighty; no one can stand against
26: 8 spread even to Egypt, for he had become very **p**.
26:15 helped him wonderfully until he became very **p**.
26:16 But when he had become **p**, he also became proud,
27: 6 King Jotham became **p** because he was careful to
Ezr 4:20 **P** kings have ruled over Jerusalem and the entire
Est 3: 1 making him the most **p** official in the empire next
9: 4 all the provinces as he became more and more **p**.
Job 1:19 a **p** wind swept in from the desert and hit the house
5:15 He saves them from the clutches of the **p**.
22: 8 you think the land belongs to the **p** and that those
25: 2 "God is **p** and dreadful. He enforces peace in the
40:16 See its **p** loins and the muscles of its belly.
Ps 18:17 He delivered me from my **p** enemies, / from those
29: 4 The voice of the LORD is **p**; / the voice of the
48: 7 of Tarshish / being shattered by a **p** east wind.
74:11 Unleash your **p** fist and deliver a deathblow.
89:13 **P** is your arm! / Strong is your hand! / Your right
110: 2 The LORD will extend your **p** dominion from
119:161 **P** people harass me without cause, / but my heart
136:12 He acted with a strong hand and **p** arm.
136:18 He killed **p** kings— / His faithful love endures
146: 3 Don't put your confidence in **p** people; / there is no
Pr 16:32 It is better to be patient than **p**; it is better to have
18:18 and settle disputes between **p** opponents.
24: 5 and a man of knowledge is more **p** than a strong
30:26 Rock badgers—they aren't **p**, / but they make their
Ecc 5: 8 If you see a poor person being oppressed by the **p**
Isa 14:31 be destroyed. A **p** army is coming out of the north.
60:16 **P** kings and mighty nations will bring the best of
Jer 6: 1 Warn everyone that a **p** army is coming from the
32:18 You are the great and **p** God, the LORD
Eze 34:16 But I will destroy those who are fat and **p**. I will
Da 2:10 And no king, however great and **p**, has ever asked
2:31 saw in front of you a huge and **p** statue of a man,
4: 3 How great are his signs, / how **p** his wonders!
8: 8 The goat became very **p**. But at the height of its
8:24 He will destroy **p** leaders and devastate the holy
11: 5 king's own officials will become more **p** than he
Joel 2: 2 a mighty army appears! How great and **p** they are!
Jnh 1: 4 suddenly the LORD flung a **p** wind over the sea,
Zec 6: 7 The **p** horses were eager to be off, to patrol back

8:22 People from many nations, even **p** nations,
Jn 10:29 them to me, and he is more **p** than anyone else.
Ac 4:33 And the apostles gave **p** witness to the resurrection
9:22 Saul's preaching became more and more **p**,
18:28 He refuted all the Jews with **p** arguments in public
19:20 about the Lord spread widely and had a **p** effect.
1Co 1:26 or **p**, or wealthy when God called you.
1:27 those who are powerless to shame those who are **p**.
2: 4 but the Holy Spirit was **p** among you.
4:10 you are so wise! We are weak, but you are so **p**!

POWERFULLY (5) [POWER]

Jdg 14: 6 At that moment the Spirit of the LORD **p** took
14:19 Then the Spirit of the LORD **p** took control of
15:14 But the Spirit of the LORD **p** took control of
Ac 13:17 in Egypt. Then he **p** led them out of their slavery.
Ro 1: 4 **p** raised him from the dead by means of the Holy

POWERLESS (8) [POWER]

Nu 22:18 I would be **p** to do anything against the will of the
24:13 I am **p** to do anything against the will of the
2Ch 14:11 no one but you can help the **p** against the mighty!
20:12 We are **p** against this mighty army that is about to
Ne 9:24 the Canaanites, who inhabited the land, were **p**!
Job 26: 2 "How you have helped the **p**! How you have
Mk 6:19 but without Herod's approval she was **p**.
1Co 1:27 And he chose those who are **p** to shame those who

POWERS (13) [POWER]

Ps 89: 7 The highest angelic **p** stand in awe of God.
Zec 1:19 "These horns represent the world **p** that scattered
Mt 16:18 my church, and all the **p** of hell will not conquer it.
24:29 from the sky, / and the **p** of heaven will be shaken.
Mk 13:25 from the sky, / and the **p** of heaven will be shaken.
Ro 8:38 and even the **p** of hell can't keep God's love away.
Gal 4: 3 We were slaves to the spiritual **p** of this world.
4: 9 to the weak and useless spiritual **p** of this world?
Eph 6:12 against those mighty **p** of darkness who rule this
Col 2: 8 human thinking and from the evil **p** of this world,
2:20 and he has set you free from the evil **p** of this
1Pe 3:22 and authorities and **p** are bowing before him.
2Pe 2:12 They laugh at the terrifying **p** they know so little

PRACTICALLY (1)

Ex 11: 1 so anxious to get rid of you that he will **p** force you

PRACTICE (20) [PRACTICED, PRACTICES, PRACTICING]

Lev 18:22 "Do not **p** homosexuality; it is a detestable sin.
18:30 and do not **p** any of these detestable activities.
19:26 its blood. "Do not **p** fortune-telling or witchcraft.
Dt 18:10 And do not let your people **p** fortune-telling
Job 1: 5 God in their hearts." This was Job's regular **p**.
Ps 119:34 your law; / I will put it into **p** with all my heart.
Ecc 8: 8 wickedness will certainly not rescue those who **p**
Isa 2: 6 with foreigners from the East who **p** magic
Jer 5:23 turned against me and have chosen to **p** idolatry.
Eze 13:23 that you never saw, nor will you **p** your magic.
Hos 6: 9 along the road to Shechem and **p** every kind of sin.
Mt 23: 3 So **p** and obey whatever they say to you, but don't
23: 3 their example. For they don't **p** what they teach.
Lk 11:28 all who hear the word of God and put it into **p**."
Ro 2: 8 all who refuse to obey the truth and **p** evil deeds.
1Co 9:25 All athletes **p** strict self-control. They do it to win a
2Co 1:24 to tell you exactly how to put your faith into **p**.
Php 4: 9 Keep putting into **p** all you learned from me
1Jn 5:18 part of God's family do not make a **p** of sinning,
Rev 21: 8 and the immoral, and those who **p** witchcraft,

PRACTICED (4) [PRACTICE]

Lev 18:27 "All these detestable activities are **p** by the people
2Ki 21: 6 He **p** sorcery and divination, and he consulted with
2Ch 33: 6 He **p** sorcery, divination, and witchcraft, and he
Jer 9: 5 With **p** tongues they tell lies; they wear themselves

PRACTICES (23) [PRACTICE]

Jdg 2:19 And they refused to give up their evil **p**
1Ki 14:24 The people imitated the detestable **p** of the pagan
22:46 who still continued their **p** from the days of his
2Ki 16: 3 He imitated the detestable **p** of the pagan nations
17: 8 They had imitated the **p** of the pagan nations the
17: 8 as well as the **p** the kings of Israel had introduced.
17:34 They follow their former **p** instead of truly
21: 2 imitating the detestable **p** of the pagan nations
2Ch 17: 4 instead of following the **p** of the kingdom of Israel.
28: 3 He imitated the detestable **p** of the pagan nations
33: 2 imitating the detestable **p** of the pagan nations
36:14 They followed the pagan **p** of the surrounding
Ezr 9: 1 They have taken up the detestable **p** of the
9:11 by the detestable **p** of the people living there.
Est 9:32 So the command of Esther confirmed the **p** of
Eze 5:11 you have defiled my Temple with idols and vile **p**.
7: 9 I will repay you for all your detestable **p**. Then you
14: 6 from your idols, and stop all your loathsome **p**.
18:12 worships idols and takes part in loathsome **p**,
Zep 3: 7 they continue their evil **p** from dawn till dusk
Zec 1: 4 Turn from your evil ways and stop all your evil **p**.'
Ac 19:18 who became believers confessed their sinful **p**.
Rev 21:27 no one who **p** shameful idolatry and dishonesty—

PRACTICING (2) [PRACTICE]

Ac 19:19 A number of them who had been **p** magic brought
2Th 3: 4 And we are confident in the Lord that you are **p** the

PRAISE (305) [PRAISED, PRAISES, PRAISING]

PRAISE THE LORD (5) Ps 68:19; Lk 1:46,68; Ro 15:11; Php 4:10

PRAISE (TO) THE LORD* (82) Ge 29:35; Dt 8:10; Ru 4:14; 1Sa 25:32,39; 1Ki 5:7; 8:56; 1Ch 16:4; 23:5; 25:3; 29:20; 2Ch 20:19,22; 29:27,30; 31:2; Ezr 3:10; 7:27; Ne 9:5; Ps 22:23; 26:12; 28:6; 31:21; 33:2; 34:1; 68:26; 98:5; 102:18; 103:1,2,20,21,22,22; 104:1,35,35; 105:45; 106:1,48; 107:8, 15,21,31; 111:1; 112:1; 113:1,9; 115:18,18; 116:19; 117:1,2; 135:1,3,19,19,20,20,21; 145:21; 146:1,1,2,10; 147:1,12,20; 148:1,1,5,7,14; 149:1,9; 150:1,6; Isa 12:1; 63:7; Jer 20:13; Joel 2:26; Zec 11:5

SING PRAISE (3) Ps 7:17; 47:6,6

Ge 24:27 "**P** be to the LORD, the God of my master,
29:35 for she said, "Now I will **p** the LORD!"
49: 8 "Judah, your brothers will **p** you. / You will defeat
Ex 15: 2 He is my God, and I will **p** him; / he is my father's
18:10 "**P** be to the LORD," Jethro said, "for he has
Lev 19:24 will be devoted to the LORD as an outburst of **p**.
Dt 8:10 **p** the LORD your God for the good land he has
10:21 He is your God, the one who is worthy of your **p**,
26:19 Then you will receive **p**, honor, and renown.
Ru 4:14 "**P** the LORD who has given you a family
1Sa 25:32 to Abigail, "**P** the LORD, the God of Israel,
25:39 he said, "**P** the LORD, who has paid back Nabal
2Sa 22: 4 I will call on the LORD, who is worthy of **p**,
22:50 O LORD, I will **p** you among the nations;
1Ki 5: 7 "**P** the LORD for giving David a wise son to be
8:56 "**P** the LORD who has given rest to his people
1Ch 16: 4 and giving thanks and **p** to the LORD,
16:25 Great is the LORD! He is most worthy of **p**!
16:32 Let the sea and everything in it shout his **p**!
16:33 Let the trees of the forest rustle with **p** before the
16:35 thank your holy name / and rejoice and **p** you."
16:42 and other instruments to accompany the songs of **p**
23: 5 and another four thousand will **p** the LORD with
23:30 the LORD to sing songs of thanks and **p** to him.
25: 3 of the harp, offering thanks and **p** to the LORD.
29:13 our God, we thank you and **p** your glorious name!
29:20 "Give **p** to the LORD your God!"
2Ch 5:13 and singers performed together in unison to **p**
8:14 He also assigned the Levites to lead the people in **p**
20:19 clans of Kohath and Korah stood to **p** the LORD,
20:22 At the moment they began to sing and give **p**,
23:12 the people running and the shouts of **p** to the king,
29:27 songs of **p** to the LORD were begun,
29:30 and the officials ordered the Levites to **p** the
29:30 So they offered joyous **p** and bowed down in
31: 2 and **p** to the LORD at the gates of the Temple.
Ezr 3:10 of Asaph, clashed their cymbals to **p** the LORD,
3:11 With **p** and thanks, they sang this song to the
7:27 **P** the LORD, the God of our ancestors, who made
7:28 And **p** him for demonstrating such unfailing love
Ne 9: 5 "Stand up and **p** the LORD your God, for he
9: 5 Then they continued, "**P** his glorious name!
12:24 stood opposite them during the ceremonies of **p**
12:46 choir directors to lead the choirs in hymns of **p**
Job 1:21 has taken it away. / **P** the name of the LORD!"
31:20 did they not **p** me for providing wool clothing to
36:24 glorify his mighty works, singing songs of **p**.
40:14 Then even I would **p** you, for your own strength
Ps 6: 5 remembers you? / Who can **p** you from the grave?
7:17 I will sing **p** to the name of the LORD Most
8: 2 taught children and nursing infants / to give you **p**.
9:14 so I can **p** you publicly at Jerusalem's gates,
10: 3 they **p** the greedy and curse the LORD.
18: 3 I will call on the LORD, who is worthy of **p**,
18:49 O LORD, I will **p** you among the nations;
21:13 We **p** you, LORD, for all your glorious power.
22:22 and sisters. / I will **p** you among all your people.
22:23 **P** the LORD, all you who fear him! / Honor him,
22:25 I will **p** you among all the people; / I will fulfill my
22:26 be satisfied. / All who seek the LORD will **p** him.
26:12 taken a stand, / and I will publicly **p** the LORD.
28: 6 **P** the LORD! / For he has heard my cry for
30: 1 I will **p** you, LORD, for you have rescued me.
30: 4 the LORD, all you godly ones! / **P** his holy name.
30: 9 the grave? / Can my dust **p** you from the grave?
31:21 **P** the LORD, / for he has shown me his unfailing
33: 1 with joy to the LORD, / for it is fitting to **p** him.
33: 2 **P** the LORD with melodies on the lyre;
33: 3 Sing new songs of **p** to him; / play skillfully on the
34: 1 I will **p** the LORD at all times. / I will constantly
35:10 I will **p** him from the bottom of my heart:
35:18 I will **p** you before all the people.
35:28 and goodness, / and I will **p** you all day long.
40: 3 me a new song to sing, / a hymn of **p** to our God.
42: 5 in God! / I will **p** him again— / my Savior and
42:11 I will **p** him again— / my Savior and my God!
43: 4 I will **p** you with my harp, / O God, my God!
43: 5 I will **p** him again— / my Savior and my God!
44: 8 and constantly **p** your name. / *Interlude*
45:17 Therefore, the nations will **p** you forever and ever.
47: 1 your hands for joy! / Shout to God with joyful **p**!
47: 6 Sing **p** to God, sing praises; / sing **p** to our King,
47: 7 is the King over all the earth. / **P** him with a psalm!
48: 1 is the LORD, / and how much we should **p** him
51:15 Unseal my lips, O Lord, / that I may **p** you.
52: 9 I will **p** you forever, O God, / for what you have
54: 6 offering to you; / I will **p** your name, O LORD,
56: 4 O God, I **p** your word. / I trust in God, so why
56:10 O God, I **p** your word. / Yes, LORD, I **p** your word.
63: 3 love is better to me than life itself; / how I **p** you!
63: 5 richest of foods. / I will **p** you with songs of joy.
63:11 All who trust in him will **p** him, / while liars will

64:10 And those who do what is right / will **p** him.
65: 1 What mighty **p**, O God, / belongs to you in Zion.
66:20 **P** God, who did not ignore my prayer / and did not
67: 3 May the nations **p** you, O God. / Yes, may all the nations **p** you.
67: 5 May the nations **p** you, O God. / Yes, may all the nations **p** you.
68:19 **P** the Lord; **p** God our savior! / For each day
68:26 **P** God, all you people of Israel; / **p** the LORD, the source of Israel's life.
68:35 and strength to his people. / **P** be to God!
69:30 Then I will **p** God's name with singing, / and I will
69:34 **P** him, O heaven and earth, / the seas and all that
71:14 for you to help me; / I will **p** you more and more.
71:16 I will **p** your mighty deeds, O Sovereign LORD.
71:22 Then I will **p** you with music on the harp,
72:17 nations be blessed through him / and bring him **p**.
74:21 let these poor and needy ones give **p** to your name.
86: 9 Lord; / they will **p** your great and holy name.
86:12 With all my heart I will **p** you, O Lord my God.
88:10 Do the dead get up and **p** you? / *Interlude*
89: 5 All heaven will **p** your miracles, LORD;
89: 5 myriads of angels will **p** you for your faithfulness.
89:12 Mount Tabor and Mount Hermon **p** your name.
95: 2 with thanksgiving. / Let us sing him psalms of **p**.
96: 4 Great is the LORD! He is most worthy of **p**!
96:11 Let the sea and everything in it shout his **p**!
96:12 with joy! / Let the trees of the forest rustle with **p**
97:12 be happy in the LORD / and **p** his holy name!
98: 4 all the earth; / break out in **p** and sing for joy!
98: 5 Sing your **p** to the LORD with the harp,
98: 7 Let the sea and everything in it shout his **p**!
99: 3 Let them **p** your great and awesome name.
100: 4 gates with thanksgiving; / go into his courts with **p**.
101: 1 and justice. / I will **p** you, LORD, with songs.
102:18 so that a nation yet to be created will **p** the
103: 1 **P** the LORD, I tell myself; / with my whole heart, I will **p** his holy name.
103: 2 **P** the LORD, I tell myself, / and never forget the
103:20 **P** the LORD, you angels of his, / you mighty
103:21 Yes, **p** the LORD, you armies of angels
103:22 **P** the LORD, everything he has created,
103:22 As for me—I, too, will **p** the LORD.
104: 1 **P** the LORD, I tell myself; / O LORD my God,
104:33 long as I live. / I will **p** my God to my last breath!
104:35 As for me—I will **p** the LORD! / **P** the LORD!
105:45 his principles / and obey his laws. / **P** the LORD!
106: 1 **P** the LORD! / Give thanks to the LORD,
106: 2 the LORD? / Who can ever **p** him half enough?
106: 5 let me **p** you with those who are your heritage.
106:12 his promises. / Then they finally sang his **p**.
106:47 can thank your holy name / and rejoice and **p** you.
106:48 Let all the people say, "Amen!" / **P** the LORD!
107: 8 Let them **p** the LORD for his great love / and for
107:15 Let them **p** the LORD for his great love / and for
107:21 Let them **p** the LORD for his great love / and for
107:31 Let them **p** the LORD for his great love / and for
109: 1 O God, whom I **p**, / don't stand silent and aloof
111: 1 **P** the LORD! / I will thank the LORD with all
111:10 come to all who obey him. / **P** his name forever!
112: 1 **P** the LORD! / Happy are those who fear the
113: 1 **P** the LORD! / Yes, give **p**, O servants of the LORD. / **P** the name of the LORD!
113: 3 from east to west— / **p** the name of the LORD.
113: 9 that she becomes a happy mother. / **P** the LORD!
115:18 But we can **p** the LORD / both now and forever! / **P** the LORD!
116:13 I will **p** the LORD's name for saving me.
116:19 in the heart of Jerusalem. / **P** the LORD!
117: 1 **P** the LORD, all you nations. / **P** him, all you people of the earth.
117: 2 of the LORD endures forever. / **P** the LORD!
118:28 You are my God, and I will **p** you! / You are my
119:164 I will **p** you seven times a day / because all your
119:171 Let my lips burst forth with **p**, / for you have
119:175 Let me live so I can **p** you, / and may your laws
135: 1 **P** the LORD! / **P** the name of the LORD! / **P** him, you who serve the LORD,
135: 3 **P** the LORD, for the LORD is good;
135:19 O Israel, **p** the LORD! / O priests of Aaron, **p** the LORD!
135:20 O Levites, **p** the LORD! / All you who fear the LORD, **p** the LORD!
135:21 for he lives here in Jerusalem. / **P** the LORD!
145: T A psalm of **p** of David.
145: 1 I will **p** you, my God and King, / and bless your
145: 2 will bless you every day, / and I will **p** you forever.
145: 3 Great is the LORD! He is most worthy of **p**!
145:21 I will **p** the LORD, / and everyone on earth will
146: 1 **P** the LORD! / **P** the LORD, I tell myself.
146: 2 I will **p** the LORD as long as I live. / I will sing
146:10 God is King in every generation! / **P** the LORD!
147: 1 **P** the LORD! / How good it is to sing praises to
147:12 **P** the LORD, O Jerusalem! / **P** your God, O Zion!
147:20 they do not know his laws. / **P** the LORD!
148: 1 **P** the LORD! / **P** the LORD from the heavens! / **P** him from the skies!
148: 2 **P** him, all his angels! / **P** him, all the armies of
148: 3 **P** him, sun and moon! / **P** him, all you twinkling
148: 4 **P** him, skies above! / **P** him, vapors high above the
148: 5 Let every created thing give **p** to the LORD,
148: 7 **P** the LORD from the earth, / you creatures of the
148:13 Let them all **p** the name of the LORD. / For his
148:14 of Israel who are close to him. / **P** the LORD!
149: 1 **P** the LORD! / Sing to the LORD a new song.
149: 3 **P** his name with dancing, / accompanied by
149: 9 is the glory of his faithful ones. / **P** the LORD!
150: 1 **P** the LORD! / **P** God in his heavenly dwelling; / **p** him in his mighty heaven!
150: 2 **P** him for his mighty works; / **p** his unequaled greatness!
150: 3 **P** him with a blast of the trumpet; / **p** him with the lyre and harp!
150: 4 **P** him with the tambourine and dancing;
150: 4 **p** him with stringed instruments and flutes!
150: 5 **P** him with a clash of cymbals; / **p** him with loud clanging cymbals.
150: 6 lives sing praises to the LORD! / **P** the LORD!
Pr 27: 2 Don't **p** yourself; let others do it!
28: 4 To reject the law is to **p** the wicked; to obey the
31:31 she has done. Let her deeds publicly declare her **p**.
SS 1: 4 are for him! We **p** his love even more than wine."
Isa 12: 1 "**P** the LORD! / He was angry with me,
12: 4 "Thank the LORD! / **P** his name! / Tell the world
12: 5 Make known his **p** around the world.
12: 6 Let all the people of Jerusalem shout his **p** with
24:14 Those in the west will **p** the LORD's majesty.
24:15 **p** the name of the LORD, the God of Israel.
25: 1 O LORD, I will honor and **p** your name, for you
26:15 We **p** you, LORD! / You have made our nation
38:18 For the dead cannot **p** you; / they cannot raise their voices in **p**.
38:19 Only the living can **p** you as I do today.
42: 8 I will not share my **p** with carved idols.
42:12 glorify the LORD; / let them sing his **p**.
57:19 Then words of **p** will be on their lips. May they
60:18 and **p** will be on the lips of all who enter there.
61: 3 joy instead of mourning, **p** instead of despair.
61:11 Everyone will **p** him! His righteousness will be
62: 7 Jerusalem the object of **p** throughout the earth.
63: 7 I will **p** the LORD for all he has done.
Jer 4: 2 and all people will come and **p** my name."
20:13 **P** the LORD! For though I was poor and needy,
31: 7 Shout out with **p** and joy: 'Save your people,
Da 2:20 saying, / "**P** the name of God forever and ever,
2:23 I thank and **p** you, God of my ancestors, / for you
3:28 "**P** to the God of Shadrach, Meshach,
4:37 **p** and glorify and honor the King of heaven.
Hos 14: 2 so that we may offer you the sacrifice of **p**.
Joel 2:26 and you will **p** the LORD your God, who does
Am 5:23 Away with your hymns of **p**! They are only noise
Jnh 2: 9 But I will offer sacrifices to you with songs of **p**,
Hab 3: 3 fills the heavens, and the earth is filled with his **p**!
Zep 3:20 They will **p** you as I restore your fortunes before
Zec 11: 5 sellers will say, '**P** the LORD, I am now rich!'
Mt 5:16 so that everyone will **p** your heavenly Father.
21: 9 him were shouting, / "**P** God for the Son of David!
21: 9 the name of the Lord! / **P** God in highest heaven!"
21:15 Temple shouting, "**P** God for the Son of David."
21:16 have taught children and infants to give you **p**.' "
25:21 The master was full of **p**. 'Well done, my good
Mk 11: 9 crowds all around him were shouting, / "**P** God!
11:10 our ancestor David! / **P** God in highest heaven!"
Lk 1:46 Mary responded, / "Oh, how I **p** the Lord.
1:68 "**P** the Lord, the God of Israel, / because he has
17:10 obey me you should say, 'We are not worthy of **p**.
17:15 back to Jesus, shouting, "**P** God, I'm healed!"
Jn 7:18 their own ideas are looking for **p** for themselves,
12:13 the road to meet him. They shouted, / "**P** God!
12:43 For they loved human **p** more than the **p** of
Ro 2:29 Whoever has that kind of change seeks **p** from
9: 5 rules over everything and is worthy of eternal **p**!
15: 6 giving **p** and glory to God, the Father of our Lord
15: 9 "I will **p** you among the Gentiles; / I will sing
15:11 And yet again, / "**P** the Lord, all you Gentiles; / **p** him, all you people of the earth."
1Co 4: 5 then God will give to everyone whatever **p** is due.
11:17 when I mention this next issue, I cannot **p** you.
11:22 Do you want me to **p** you? Well, I certainly do not!
14:16 For if you **p** God only in the spirit, how can those who don't understand you **p** God
2Co 1: 3 All **p** to the God and Father of our Lord Jesus
6: 8 or despise us, whether they slander us or **p** us.
Eph 1: 3 How we **p** God, the Father of our Lord Jesus
1: 6 So we **p** God for the wonderful kindness he has
1:12 first to trust in Christ should **p** our glorious God.
1:14 This is just one more reason for us to **p** our
Php 1:11 for this will bring much glory and **p** to God.
4: 8 about things that are excellent and worthy of **p**.
4:10 and how I **p** the Lord that you are concerned about
1Th 2: 6 As for **p**, we have never asked for it from you
2Th 1:10 comes to receive glory and **p** from his holy people.
Heb 2:12 and sisters. / I will **p** you among all your people."
3: 3 a fine house deserves more **p** than the house itself.
13:15 let us continually offer our sacrifice of **p** to God by
1Pe 1: 7 it will bring you much **p** and glory and honor on
4:16 **P** God for the privilege of being called by his
Rev 1: 5 All **p** to him who loves us and has freed us from
19: 5 "**P** our God, all his servants, from the least to the

PRAISED (41) [PRAISE]

Ge 24:48 I **p** the LORD, the God of my master, Abraham,
Jos 22:33 And all the Israelites were satisfied and **p** God
Jdg 16:24 the people saw him, they **p** their god, saying,
1Ch 16:36 the people shouted "Amen!" and **p** the LORD.
29:10 Then David **p** the LORD in the presence of the
29:10 our ancestor Israel, may you be **p** forever and ever!
29:20 And the entire assembly **p** the LORD, the God of
2Ch 5:13 their voices and **p** the LORD with these words:
7: 3 on the ground and worshiped and **p** the LORD,
20:26 which got its name that day because the people **p**
Ne 5:13 "Amen," and they **p** the LORD.
8: 6 Then Ezra **p** the LORD, the great God, and all the
Job 29:11 "All who heard of me **p** me. All who saw me
Ps 12: 8 strut about, / and evil is **p** throughout the land.
48:10 O God, / you will be **p** to the ends of the earth.
135:21 The LORD be **p** from Zion, / for he lives here in
Pr 27:21 and gold, but a person is tested by being **p**.
31:30 a woman who fears the LORD will be greatly **p**.
Ecc 7: 5 criticized by a wise person than to be **p** by a fool!
8:10 and are **p** in the very city where they committed
Isa 64:11 beautiful Temple where our ancestors **p** you has
Jer 51:41 is fallen—great Babylon, **p** throughout the earth!
Eze 3:12 (May the glory of the LORD be **p** in his place!)
Da 2:19 in a vision. Then Daniel **p** the God of heaven,
4:34 and I **p** and worshiped the Most High and honored
Mt 9: 8 They **p** God for sending a man with such great
15:31 could see again! And they **p** the God of Israel.
Mk 2:12 Then they all **p** God. "We've never seen anything
Lk 2:28 He took the child in his arms and **p** God, saying,
4:15 taught in their synagogues and was **p** by everyone.
5:26 And they **p** God, saying over and over again,
6:26 What sorrows await you who are **p** by the crowds,
6:26 for their ancestors also **p** false prophets.
7:16 fear swept the crowd, and they **p** God, saying,
13:13 could stand straight. How she **p** and thanked God!
18:43 praising God. And all who saw it **p** God, too.
23:47 he **p** God and said, "Surely this man was
Ac 21:20 After hearing this, they **p** God. But then they said,
Ro 1:25 but not the Creator himself, who is to be **p** forever.
2Co 8:18 He is highly **p** in all the churches as a preacher of
11:31 who is to be **p** forever, knows I tell the truth.

PRAISES (51) [PRAISE]

SING PRAISES (19) Ps 9:2,11; 30:12; 47:6,6; 59:17; 61:8; 68:4,32; 75:9; 81:1; 92:1; 115:17; 146:2; 147:1,7; 150:6; Ro 15:9; Jas 5:13

Ge 12:15 they sang her **p** to their king, the pharaoh, and she
1Ch 16: 9 Sing to him; yes, sing his **p**. / Tell everyone about
Ps 5:11 in you rejoice; / let them sing joyful **p** forever.
9: 2 of you. / I will sing **p** to your name, O Most High.
9:11 Sing **p** to the LORD who reigns in Jerusalem.
16: 9 is filled with joy, / and my mouth shouts his **p**!
22: 3 are holy. / The **p** of Israel surround your throne.
30:12 that I might sing **p** to you and not be silent.
34: 1 LORD at all times. / I will constantly speak his **p**.
47: 6 to God, sing **p**; / sing praise to our King, sing **p**!
57: 7 in you, O God; / no wonder I can sing your **p**!
57: 9 the people. / I will sing your **p** among the nations.
59:17 O my Strength, to you I sing **p**, / for you, O God,
61: 8 Then I will always sing **p** to your name / as I fulfill
66: 1 Shout joyful **p** to God, all the earth!
66: 4 on earth will worship you; / they will sing your **p**,
66: 8 whole world bless our God / and sing aloud his **p**.
68: 4 Sing **p** to God and to his name! / Sing loud **p** to him who rides the clouds.
68:32 of the earth. / Sing **p** to the Lord. / *Interlude*
71:23 I will shout for joy and sing your **p**, / for you have
75: 9 God has done; / I will sing **p** to the God of Israel.
81: 1 Sing **p** to God, our strength. / Sing to the God of
84: 4 can live in your house, / always singing your **p**.
92: 1 thanks to the LORD, / to sing **p** to the Most High.
102:21 will be celebrated in Zion, / his **p** in Jerusalem,
105: 2 Sing to him; yes, sing his **p**. / Tell everyone about
108: 1 in you, O God; / no wonder I can sing your **p**!
108: 3 the people. / I will sing your **p** among the nations.
115:17 The dead cannot sing **p** to the LORD, / for they
138: 1 all my heart; / I will sing your **p** before the gods.
144: 9 I will sing your **p** with a ten-stringed harp.
146: 2 I will sing **p** to my God even with my dying
147: 1 How good it is to sing **p** to our God!
147: 7 sing **p** to our God, accompanied by harps.
149: 1 Sing his **p** in the assembly of the faithful.
149: 6 Let the **p** of God be in their mouths, / and a sharp
150: 6 Let everything that lives sing **p** to the LORD!
Pr 31:28 children stand and bless her. Her husband **p** her:
SS 6: 9 see her; even queens and concubines sing her **p**!
Isa 24:16 Hear them singing **p** to the Righteous One! But my
38:20 I will sing his **p** with instruments / every day of my
42:10 Sing his **p** from the ends of the earth! / Sing,
42:11 Sela sing for joy; / shout **p** from the mountaintops!
44:15 He makes an idol and bows down and **p** it!
Jer 17:14 you alone can save. My **p** are for you alone!
Ac 2:26 is filled with joy, / and my mouth shouts his **p**!
Ro 15: 9 among the Gentiles; / I will sing **p** to your name."
Jas 3: 9 Sometimes it **p** our Lord and Father,
5:13 be thankful should continually sing **p** to the Lord.

PRAISING (29) [PRAISE]

Jdg 16:23 offering sacrifices and **p** their god, Dagon.
2Ch 7: 6 King David had made for **p** the LORD.
20:21 to the LORD and **p** him for his holy splendor.
Ezr 3:11 **p** the LORD because the foundation of the
Ps 27: 6 of joy, / singing and **p** the LORD with music.
47: 9 They join us in **p** the God of Abraham. / For all the
66:17 For I cried out to him for help, / **p** him as I spoke.
71: 6 cared for me. / No wonder I am always **p** you!
71: 8 That is why I can never stop **p** you; / I declare your
79:13 **p** your greatness from generation to generation.
109:30 thanks to the LORD, / **p** him to everyone.
140:13 Surely the godly are **p** your name, / for they will
Isa 62: 9 You raised it, and you will keep it, **p** the LORD.
Da 5:23 drinking wine from them while **p** gods of silver,
Lk 1:64 Zechariah could speak again, and he began **p** God.
2:13 vast host of others—the armies of heaven—**p** God:
2:20 and **p** God for what the angels had told them,
2:38 with Mary and Joseph, and she began **p** God.
5:25 his feet, picked up his mat, and went home **p** God.

18:43 the man could see, and he followed Jesus, **p** God.
19:37 **p** God for all the wonderful miracles they had
24:53 they spent all of their time in the Temple, **p** God.
Ac 2:47 all the while **p** God and enjoying the goodwill of
3: 8 Then, walking, leaping, and **p** God, he went into
3: 9 the people saw him walking and heard him **p** God.
4:21 without starting a riot. For everyone was **p** God
10:46 they heard them speaking in tongues and **p** God.
11:18 objections were answered and they began **p** God.
2Th 1:10 And you will be among those **p** him on that day,

PRAY (161) [PRAYED, PRAYER, PRAYERFUL, PRAYERS, PRAYING, PRAYS]

Ge 20: 7 and he will **p** for you, for he is a prophet.
Ex 8: 9 "Tell me when you want me to **p** for you,
8: 9 I will **p** that you and your houses will be rid of the
8:28 don't go too far away. Now hurry, and **p** for me."
9:29 the city, I will lift my hands and **p** to the LORD.
23:13 never **p** to or swear by any other gods.
Nu 21: 7 **P** that the LORD will take away the snakes."
1Sa 1: 9 to the Tabernacle after supper to **p** to the LORD.
7: 5 all of you. I will **p** to the LORD for you."
12:19 "**P** to the LORD your God for us, or we will
2Sa 7:27 I have been bold enough to **p** this prayer
1Ki 8:30 and your people Israel when we **p** toward this
8:33 on your name and **p** to you here in this Temple,
8:35 and then they **p** toward this Temple and confess
8:42 your power—and when they **p** toward this Temple,
8:44 and if they **p** to the LORD toward this city that
8:47 they may turn to you again in repentance and **p**,
8:48 and **p** toward the land you gave to their ancestors,
2Ki 19: 1 and went into the Temple of the LORD to **p**.
19: 4 for his words. Oh, **p** for those of us who are left!"
1Ch 17:25 I have been bold enough to **p** this prayer
2Ch 6:21 and your people Israel when we **p** toward this
6:24 on your name and **p** to you here in this Temple,
6:26 and then they **p** toward this Temple and confess
6:32 your great name and to **p** toward this Temple,
6:34 and if they **p** to you toward this city that you have
6:37 they may turn to you again in repentance and **p**,
6:38 and **p** toward the land you gave to their ancestors,
7:14 and **p** and seek my face and turn from their wicked
Ezr 6:10 to the God of heaven and **p** for me and my sons.
Job 8: 5 But if you **p** to God and seek the favor of the
21:15 we obey him? What good will it do us if we **p**?'
22:27 You will **p** to him, and he will hear you, and you
42: 8 My servant Job will **p** for you, and I will accept his
Ps 5: 1 O LORD, hear me as I **p**; / pay attention to my
5: 2 and my God, / for I will never **p** to anyone but you.
17: 6 will answer, O God. / Bend down and listen as I **p**.
72:15 May the people always **p** for him / and bless him
77: 2 All night long I **p**, with hands lifted toward heaven,
77: 4 don't let me sleep. / I am too distressed even to **p**!
116: 2 and listens, / I will **p** as long as I have breath!
119:145 I **p** with all my heart; answer me, LORD!
122: 6 **P** for the peace of Jerusalem. / May all who love
138: 3 When I **p**, you answer me; / you encourage me by
142: 5 Then I **p** to you, O LORD. / I say, "You are my
Isa 16:12 On the hilltops the people of Moab will **p** in
37: 1 and went into the Temple of the LORD to **p**.
37: 4 for his words. Oh, **p** for those of us who are left!"
45:20 their wooden idols and **p** to gods that cannot save!
62: 6 they will **p** to the LORD day and night for the
62: 6 of his promises. Take no rest, all you who **p**.
64: 9 Look at us, we **p**, and see that we are all your
Jer 7:16 "**P** no more for these people, Jeremiah. Do not weep or **p** for them, and don't beg me to
11:12 people of Judah and Jerusalem will **p** to their idols
11:14 "**P** no more for these people, Jeremiah. Do not weep or **p** for them, for I will not listen to
14:11 said to me, "Do not **p** for these people anymore.
27:18 let them **p** to the LORD Almighty about the gold
27:18 Let them **p** that these remaining articles will not be
29: 7 **P** to the LORD for that city where you are held
29:12 In those days when you **p**, I will listen.
37: 3 "Please **p** to the LORD our God for us."
42: 2 "Please **p** to the LORD your God for us.
42: 4 "I will **p** to the LORD your God, and I will tell
42:20 For you were deceitful when you sent me to **p** to
Eze 3:26 of your mouth so you won't be able to **p** for them,
Da 10:12 Since the first day you began to **p** for
Joel 2:17 Let them **p**, "Spare your people, LORD!
Jnh 1: 6 he shouted. "Get up and **p** to your god! Maybe he
3: 8 required to wear sackcloth and **p** earnestly to God.
Zep 2: 1 Gather together and **p**, you shameless nation.
Mt 5:44 love your enemies! **P** for those who persecute you!
6: 5 When you **p**, don't be like the hypocrites who love to **p** publicly
6: 6 But when you **p**, go away by yourself,
6: 6 the door behind you, and **p** to your Father secretly.
6: 7 "When you **p**, don't babble on and on as people of
6: 9 **P** like this: / Our Father in heaven, / may your
9:38 So **p** to the Lord who is in charge of the harvest;
14:23 Afterward he went up into the hills by himself to **p**.
19:13 so he could lay his hands on them and **p** for them.
24:20 And **p** that your flight will not be in winter or on
26:36 and he said, "Sit here while I go on ahead to **p**."
26:41 Keep alert and **p**. Otherwise temptation will
26:44 So he went back to **p** a third time, saying the same
Mk 1:35 and went out alone into the wilderness to **p**.
6:46 Afterward he went up into the hills by himself to **p**.
11:24 You can **p** for anything, and if you believe,
13:18 And **p** that your flight will not be in winter.
14:32 and Jesus said, "Sit here while I go and **p**."
14:38 Keep alert and **p**. Otherwise, temptation will
Lk 5:33 "John the Baptist's disciples always fast and **p**,"
6:12 day soon afterward Jesus went to a mountain to **p**,
6:28 **P** for the happiness of those who curse you. **P** for those who hurt you.
9:28 took Peter, James, and John to a mountain to **p**.
10: 2 **P** to the Lord who is in charge of the harvest,
11: 1 him as he finished and said, "Lord, teach us to **p**,
11: 2 He said, "This is how you should **p**: / "Father,
18:10 "Two men went to the Temple to **p**. One was a
21:36 And **p** that, if possible, you may escape these
22:40 "**P** that you will not be overcome by temptation."
22:46 he asked. "Get up and **p**. Otherwise,
Jn 12:27 Should I **p**, 'Father, save me from what lies
Ac 8:22 Turn from your wickedness and **p** to the Lord.
8:24 "**P** to the Lord for me," Simon exclaimed,
10: 9 nearing the city, Peter went up to the flat roof to **p**.
26:29 I **p** to God that both you and everyone here in this
Ro 1: 9 God knows how often I **p** for you. Day and night I
1:10 One of the things I always **p** for is the opportunity,
8:26 For we don't even know what we should **p** for, nor how we should **p**.
12:14 don't curse them; **p** that God will bless them.
15:13 So I **p** that God, who gives you hope, will keep
15:31 **P** that I will be rescued from those in Judea who
15:31 **P** also that the Christians there will be willing to
1Co 11:13 Is it right for a woman to **p** to God in public
14:13 **p** also for the gift of interpretation in order to tell
14:14 For if I **p** in tongues, my spirit is praying, but I
14:15 I will **p** in the spirit, and I will **p** in words I understand.
2Co 9:14 And they will **p** for you with deep affection
13: 7 We **p** to God that you will not do anything wrong.
13: 7 We **p** this, not to show that our ministry to you has
13: 9 What we **p** for is your restoration to maturity.
Eph 1:16 thanking God for you. I **p** for you constantly,
1:18 I **p** that your hearts will be flooded with light
1:19 I **p** that you will begin to understand the incredible
3:14 God's plan, I fall to my knees and **p** to the Father,
3:16 I **p** that from his glorious, unlimited resources he
3:17 And I **p** that Christ will be more and more at home
6:18 **P** at all times and on every occasion in the power
6:19 And **p** for me, too. Ask God to give me the right
6:20 But **p** that I will keep on speaking boldly for him,
Php 1: 4 I always **p** for you, and I make my requests with a
1: 9 I **p** that your love for each other will overflow
1:19 For I know that as you **p** for me and as the Spirit of
4: 6 worry about anything; instead, **p** about everything.
Col 1: 3 We always **p** for you, and we give thanks to God
1:11 We also **p** that you will be strengthened with his
4: 3 Don't forget to **p** for us, too, that God will give us
4: 4 **P** that I will proclaim this message as clearly as I
1Th 1: 2 thank God for all of you and **p** for you constantly.
3:10 Night and day we **p** earnestly for you, asking God
5:25 Dear brothers and sisters, **p** for us.
2Th 1:11 And we **p** that God, by his power, will fulfill all
3: 1 dear brothers and sisters, I ask you to **p** for us.
3: 1 **P** first that the Lord's message will spread rapidly
3: 2 **P**, too, that we will be saved from wicked and evil
1Ti 2: 1 I urge you, first of all, to **p** for all people. As you
2: 2 **P** this way for kings and all others who are in
2: 8 I want men to **p** with holy hands lifted up to God,
Phm 1: 4 I always thank God when I **p** for you, Philemon,
Heb 13:18 **P** for us, for our conscience is clear and we want to
Jas 5:14 elders of the church and have them **p** over them,
5:16 and **p** for each other so that you may be healed.
1Pe 1:17 to whom you **p** has no favorites when he judges.
1Jn 5:16 you should **p**, and God will give that person life.
5:16 and I am not saying you should **p** for those who
Jude 1:20 And continue to **p** as you are directed by the Holy

PRAYED (87) [PRAY]

Ge 20:17 Then Abraham **p** to God, and God healed
24:12 "O LORD, God of my master," he **p**. "Give me
24:42 "So this afternoon when I came to the spring I **p**
32: 9 Then Jacob **p**, "O God of my grandfather
Nu 11: 2 and when he **p** to the LORD, the fire stopped.
21: 7 take away the snakes." So Moses **p** for the people.
Dt 9:20 But I **p** for Aaron, and the LORD spared him.
9:26 I **p** to the LORD and said, 'O Sovereign LORD,
Jos 10:12 Joshua **p** to the LORD in front of all the people of
Jdg 13: 8 Then Manoah **p** to the LORD. He said, "Lord,
16:28 Then Samson **p** to the LORD,
16:30 "Let me die with the Philistines," he **p**.
1Sa 1:10 crying bitterly as she **p** to the LORD.
2: 1 Then Hannah **p**: / "My heart rejoices in the
14:41 Then Saul **p**, "O LORD, God of Israel,
23:10 And David **p**, "O LORD, God of Israel, I have
2Sa 7:18 David went in and sat before the LORD and **p**,
15:31 David **p**, "O LORD, let Ahithophel give
1Ki 8:12 Then Solomon **p**, "O LORD, you have said that
8:23 He **p**, "O LORD, God of Israel, there is no God
8:59 And may these words that I have **p** in the presence
13: 6 So the man of God **p** to the LORD, and the king's
18:36 Elijah the prophet walked up to the altar and **p**,
18:42 top of Mount Carmel and fell to the ground and **p**.
19: 4 under a solitary broom tree and **p** that he might die.
2Ki 4:33 and shut the door behind him and **p** to the LORD.
6:17 Then Elisha **p**, "O LORD, open his eyes and let
6:18 Elisha **p**, "O LORD, please make them blind."
6:20 Elisha **p**, "O LORD, now open their eyes and let
13: 4 Then Jehoahaz **p** for the LORD's help,
19:15 And Hezekiah **p** this prayer before the LORD:
20: 2 he turned his face to the wall and **p** to the LORD,
1Ch 4:10 He was the one who **p** to the God of Israel, "Oh,
17:16 David went in and sat before the LORD and **p**,
21:26 And when David **p**, the LORD answered him by
2Ch 6: 1 Then Solomon **p**, "O LORD, you have said that
6:14 He **p**, "O LORD, God of Israel, there is no God
20: 6 He **p**, "O LORD, God of our ancestors,
30:18 But King Hezekiah **p** for them, and they were
32:24 He **p** to the LORD, who healed him and gave him
33:13 And when he **p**, the LORD listened to him
Ezr 8:21 We **p** that he would give us a safe journey
8:23 and earnestly **p** that our God would take care of us,
9: 6 I **p**, "O my God, I am utterly ashamed; I blush to
10: 1 While Ezra **p** and made this confession, weeping
Ne 1: 4 I mourned, fasted, and **p** to the God of heaven.
4: 4 Then I **p**, "Hear us, O our God, for we are being
4: 9 But we **p** to our God and guarded the city day
6: 9 the work. So I **p** for strength to continue the work.
Job 42:10 When Job **p** for his friends, the LORD restored
Ps 18: 6 out to the LORD; / yes, I **p** to my God for help.
34: 4 I **p** to the LORD, and he answered me,
35:13 I grieved for them. / I even fasted and **p** for them,
38:16 I **p**, "Don't let my enemies gloat over me
41: 4 "O LORD," I **p**, "have mercy on me. / Heal me,
116:10 I believed in you, so I **p**, / "I am deeply troubled,
118: 5 In my distress I **p** to the LORD, / and the LORD
Isa 37:15 And Hezekiah **p** this prayer before the LORD:
38: 2 he turned his face to the wall and **p** to the LORD,
Jer 32:16 had given the papers to Baruch, I **p** to the LORD:
Da 6:10 He **p** three times a day, just as he had always done,
9: 4 I **p** to the LORD my God and confessed:
Jnh 2: 1 Then Jonah **p** to the LORD his God from inside
Zec 1:12 hearing this, the angel of the LORD **p** this prayer:
Mt 11:25 Then Jesus **p** this prayer: "O Father, Lord of
26:42 Again he left them and **p**, "My Father! If this cup
Mk 14:35 He **p** that, if it were possible, the awful hour
14:39 Then Jesus left them again and **p**, repeating his
Lk 6:12 to a mountain to pray, and he **p** to God all night.
18:11 proud Pharisee stood by himself and **p** this prayer:
18:13 and dared not even lift his eyes to heaven as he **p**.
22:41 about a stone's throw, and knelt down and **p**,
22:44 He **p** more fervently, and he was in such agony of
Ac 1:24 Then they all **p** for the right man to be chosen.
6: 6 who **p** for them as they laid their hands on them.
7:59 Stephen **p**, "Lord Jesus, receive my spirit."
8:15 they **p** for these new Christians to receive the Holy
9:40 them all to leave the room; then he knelt and **p**.
10: 2 to charity and was a man who regularly **p** to God.
12: 5 was in prison, the church **p** very earnestly for him.
14:23 elders in every church and **p** for them with fasting,
20:36 had finished speaking, he knelt and **p** with them.
21: 5 came down to the shore with us. There we knelt, **p**,
27:29 out four anchors from the stern and **p** for daylight.
28: 8 Paul went in and **p** for him, and laying his hands
Jas 5:17 and yet when he **p** earnestly that no rain would fall,
5:18 Then he **p** for rain, and down it poured. The grass

PRAYER (118) [PRAY]

Ge 24:42 when I came to the spring I prayed this **p**:
25:21 So the LORD answered Isaac's **p**, and his wife
Jdg 13: 9 God answered his **p**, and the angel of God
1Sa 1:11 my sorrow and answer my **p** and give me a son,
2Sa 7:27 I have been bold enough to pray this **p** because you
24:25 And the LORD answered his **p**, and the plague
1Ki 8:28 Listen to my **p** and my request, O LORD my
8:28 and the **p** that your servant is making to you today.
8:38 and if your people offer a **p** concerning their
9: 3 to him, "I have heard your **p** and your request.
17:22 The LORD heard Elijah's **p**, and the life of the
21: 9 for fasting and **p** and give Naboth a place of honor.
2Ki 13: 4 the LORD's help, and the LORD heard his **p**.
19:15 And Hezekiah prayed this **p** before the LORD:
19:20 I have heard your **p** about King Sennacherib of
20: 5 says: I have heard your **p** and seen your tears.
1Ch 5:20 and he answered their **p** because they trusted in
17:25 I have been bold enough to pray this **p** because you
21:28 David saw that the LORD had answered his **p**,
2Ch 6:19 Listen to my **p** and my request, O LORD my
6:19 and the **p** that your servant is making to you.
6:29 and if your people offer a **p** concerning their
7:12 "I have heard your **p** and have chosen this Temple
7:15 I will listen to every **p** made in this place,
30:20 And the LORD listened to Hezekiah's **p**
32:20 and the prophet Isaiah son of Amoz cried out in **p**
33:18 of the events of Manasseh's reign, his **p** to God,
33:19 Manasseh's **p**, the account of the way God
Ezr 8:23 our God would take care of us, and he heard our **p**.
Ne 1: 6 listen to my **p**! Look down and see me praying
1:11 O Lord, please hear my **p**! Listen to the prayers of
2: 4 can I help you?" With a **p** to the God of heaven,
11:17 who opened the thanksgiving services with **p**;
Job 11:13 your heart and lift up your hands to him in **p**!
16:17 Yet I am innocent, and my **p** is pure.
42: 8 for you, and I will accept his **p** on your behalf.
42: 9 and the LORD accepted Job's **p**.
Ps 4: 1 my distress. / Have mercy on me and hear my **p**.
6: 9 has heard my plea; / the LORD will answer my **p**.
17: T A **p** of David.
17: 1 Listen to my cry for help. / Pay attention to my **p**,
28: 2 Listen to my **p** for mercy / as I cry out to you for
39:12 Hear my **p**, O LORD! / Listen to my cries for
44:20 our God / or spread our hands in **p** to foreign gods,
54: 2 O God, listen to my **p**. / Pay attention to my plea.
55: 1 Listen to my **p**, O God. / Do not ignore my cry for
61: 1 O God, listen to my cry! / Hear my **p**!
63: 4 as long as I live, / lifting up my hands to you in **p**.
66:19 But God did listen! / He paid attention to my **p**.
66:20 Praise God, who did not ignore my **p** / and did not
69:13 O God, / answer my **p** with your sure salvation.
84: 8 O LORD God Almighty, hear my **p**. / Listen,
86: T A **p** of David.

86: 1 Bend down, O LORD, and hear my **p**;
86: 6 Listen closely to my **p**, O LORD; / hear my
88: 2 Now hear my **p**; / listen to my cry.
90: T A **p** of Moses, the man of God.
102: T A **p** of one overwhelmed with trouble, pouring out
102: 1 LORD, hear my **p**! / Listen to my plea!
118:21 I thank you for answering my **p** / and saving me!
119:170 Listen to my **p**; / rescue me as you promised.
120: 1 I cried out to him, and he answered my **p**.
130: 2 Hear my cry, O Lord. / Pay attention to my **p**.
141: 2 Accept my **p** as incense offered to you, / and my
141: 5 But I am in constant **p** / against the wicked
142: T regarding his experience in the cave. A **p**.
143: 1 Hear my **p**, O LORD; / listen to my plea!
143: 8 me where to walk, / for I have come to you in **p**.
Isa 1:15 From now on, when you lift up your hands in **p**,
37:15 And Hezekiah prayed this **p** before the LORD:
37:21 This is my answer to your **p** concerning King
38: 5 says: I have heard your **p** and seen your tears.
56: 7 and will fill them with joy in my house of **p**.
56: 7 because my Temple will be called a house of **p** for
La 2:19 water to the Lord. Lift up your hands to him in **p**.
Da 9: 3 Lord God and pleaded with him in **p** and fasting.
9:17 "O our God, hear your servant's **p**! Listen as I
10:12 heard in heaven. I have come in answer to your **p**.
Jnh 2: 7 And my earnest **p** went out to you in your holy
Hab 3: 1 This **p** was sung by the prophet Habakkuk:
3:19 This **p** is to be accompanied by stringed
Zec 1:12 the angel of the LORD prayed this **p**:
12:10 and **p** on the family of David and on all the people
Mt 6: 5 "And now about **p**. When you pray, don't be like
11:25 Then Jesus prayed this **p**: "O Father, Lord of
21:13 'My Temple will be called a place of **p**,'
21:22 you will receive whatever you ask for in **p**."
23: 5 On their arms they wear extra wide **p** boxes with
Mk 9:29 "This kind can be cast out only by **p**."
11:17 'My Temple will be called a place of **p** for all
Lk 1:13 For God has heard your **p**, and your wife,
2:37 and night, worshiping God with fasting and **p**.
5:16 But Jesus often withdrew to the wilderness for **p**.
11: 5 Then, teaching them more about **p**, he used this
18: 1 a story to illustrate their need for constant **p**
18:11 proud Pharisee stood by himself and prayed this **p**:
19:46 'My Temple will be a place of **p**,'
22:32 But I have pleaded in **p** for you, Simon, that your
Jn 17: 9 "My **p** is not for the world, but for those you have
17:21 My **p** for all of them is that they will be one,
Ac 1:14 They all met together continually for **p**, along with
2:42 sharing in the Lord's Supper and in **p**.
3: 1 to take part in the three o'clock **p** service.
4:24 were united as they lifted their voices in **p**:
4:31 After this **p**, the building where they were meeting
6: 4 Then we can spend our time in **p** and preaching
12:12 of John Mark, where many were gathered for **p**.
13: 3 So after more fasting and **p**, the men laid their
16:13 where we supposed that some people met for **p**,
16:16 One day as we were going down to the place of **p**,
Ro 1: 9 and night I bring you and your needs in **p** to God,
10: 1 and my **p** to God is that the Jewish people might be
1Co 7: 5 so they can give themselves more completely to **p**.
Col 4: 2 Devote yourselves to **p** with an alert mind and a
1Ti 4: 5 know it is made holy by the word of God and **p**.
5: 5 she asks God for help and spends much time in **p**.
Jas 5:15 And their **p** offered in faith will heal the sick,
5:16 The earnest **p** of a righteous person has great

PRAYERFUL (1) [PRAY]

Ro 12:12 for you. Be patient in trouble, and always be **p**.

PRAYERS (49) [PRAY]

Ge 30:17 And God answered her **p**. She became pregnant
30:22 and answered her **p** by giving her a child.
35: 3 God who answered my **p** when I was in distress.
1Sa 12:23 sin against the LORD by ending my **p** for you.
1Ki 8:29 May you always hear the **p** I make toward this
8:45 then hear their **p** from heaven and uphold their
8:49 then hear their **p** from heaven where you live.
8:54 When Solomon finished making these **p**
2Ch 6:20 May you always hear the **p** I make toward this
6:35 then hear their **p** from heaven and uphold their
6:39 then hear their **p** from heaven where you live.
6:40 be attentive to all the **p** made to you in this place.
Ne 1:11 Listen to the **p** of those of us who delight in
Ps 20: 5 our God. / May the LORD answer all your **p**.
35:13 prayed for them, / but my **p** returned unanswered.
65: 2 for you answer our **p**, / and to you all people will
65: 5 You faithfully answer our **p** with awesome deeds,
69:16 Answer my **p**, O LORD, / for your unfailing love
72:20 (This ends the **p** of David son of Jesse.)
80: 4 how long will you be angry and reject our **p**?
102:17 He will listen to the **p** of the destitute. / He will not
109: 7 let him be pronounced guilty. / Count his **p** as sins.
116: 1 the LORD because he hears / and answers my **p**.
Pr 15: 8 the wicked, but he delights in the **p** of the upright.
15:29 the wicked, but he hears the **p** of the righteous.
28: 9 The **p** of a person who ignores the law are
Isa 1:15 Even though you offer many **p**, I will not listen.
65:24 their needs, I will go ahead and answer their **p**!
La 3: 8 And though I cry and shout, he shuts out my **p**.
3:44 yourself in a cloud so our **p** cannot reach you.
Eze 36:37 I am ready to hear Israel's **p** for these blessings,
Mt 6: 7 They think their **p** are answered only by repeating
Mk 12:40 people they really are, they make long **p** in public.
Lk 20:47 people they really are, they make long **p** in public.
Ac 10: 4 "Your **p** and gifts to the poor have not gone
10:31 He told me, 'Cornelius, your **p** have been heard,
2Co 1:11 so many people's **p** for our safety have been
Eph 6:18 and be persistent in your **p** for all Christians
2Ti 1: 3 and day I constantly remember you in my **p**.
Phm 1:22 for I am hoping that God will answer your **p**
Heb 5: 7 he offered **p** and pleadings, with a loud cry
5: 7 And God heard his **p** because of his reverence for
13:19 I especially need your **p** right now so that I can
1Pe 3: 7 treat her as you should, your **p** will not be heard.
3:12 who do right, / and his ears are open to their **p**.
4: 7 Therefore, be earnest and disciplined in your **p**.
Rev 5: 8 bowls filled with incense—the **p** of God's people!
8: 3 given to him to mix with the **p** of God's people,
8: 4 of the incense, mixed with the **p** of the saints,

PRAYING (42) [PRAY]

Ge 24:15 As he was still **p**, a young woman named Rebekah
24:45 "Before I had finished **p** these words, I saw
1Sa 1:12 As she was **p** to the LORD, Eli watched her.
1:16 For I have been **p** out of great anguish
1:26 who stood here several years ago **p** to the LORD.
2Ch 7: 1 When Solomon finished **p**, fire flashed down from
Ne 1: 6 Look down and see me **p** night and day for your
Ps 14: 4 they wouldn't think of **p** to the LORD.
17: 6 I am **p** to you because I know you will answer,
42: 8 I sing his songs, / **p** to God who gives me life.
53: 4 like bread; / they wouldn't think of **p** to God.
69:13 But I keep right on **p** to you, LORD, / hoping this
109: 4 they try to destroy me— / even as I am **p** for them!
Isa 44:17 He falls down in front of it, worshiping and **p** to it.
62: 1 I will not stop **p** for her until her righteousness
Da 6:11 and found him **p** and asking for God's help.
9:20 I went on **p** and confessing my sin and the sins of
9:21 As I was **p**, Gabriel, whom I had seen in the earlier
9:23 The moment you began **p**, a command was given.
Mt 26:39 and fell face down on the ground, **p**, "My Father!
Mk 11:25 But when you are **p**, first forgive anyone you are
Lk 1:10 was being burned, a great crowd stood outside, **p**.
3:21 was baptized. As he was **p**, the heavens opened,
9:18 One day as Jesus was alone, **p**, he came over to his
9:29 And as he was **p**, the appearance of his face
11: 1 Once when Jesus had been out **p**, one of his
Jn 17:20 "I am **p** not only for these disciples but also for all
Ac 9:11 ask for Saul of Tarsus. He is **p** to me right now.
10:30 "Four days ago I was **p** in my house at three
11: 5 he said, "while I was **p**, I went into a trance
16:25 Paul and Silas were **p** and singing hymns to God,
22:17 I was **p** in the Temple, and I fell into a trance.
Ro 15:30 to join me in my struggle by **p** to God for me.
1Co 11: 4 man dishonors Christ if he covers his head while **p**
14:14 For if I pray in tongues, my spirit is **p**, but I don't
2Co 1:11 will rescue us because you are helping by **p** for us.
Col 1: 9 So we have continued **p** for you ever since we first
1Th 5:17 Keep on **p**.
2Th 1:11 And so we keep on **p** for you, that our God will
Phm 1: 6 And I am **p** that you will really put your generosity
Jas 5:13 you suffering? They should keep on **p** about it.
3Jn 1: 2 I am **p** that all is well with you and that your body

PRAYS (8) [PRAY]

Job 33:26 When he **p** to God, he will be accepted. And God
Isa 46: 7 And when someone **p** to it, there is no answer.
Da 6: 7 for the next thirty days anyone who **p** to anyone,
6:12 for the next thirty days anyone who **p** to anyone,
6:13 your law. He still **p** to his God three times a day."
Ro 8:26 But the Holy Spirit **p** for us with groanings that
1Co 11: 5 But a woman dishonors her husband if she **p**
Col 4:12 He always **p** earnestly for you, asking God to make

PREACH (53) [PREACHED, PREACHER, PREACHES, PREACHING]

Mic 2:11 to you, "I'll **p** to you the joys of wine and drink!"
Mt 3: 5 Valley went out to the wilderness to hear him **p**.
4:17 From then on, Jesus began to **p**, "Turn from your
Mk 1:14 Jesus went to Galilee to **p** God's Good News.
1:38 and I will **p** to them, too, because that is why I
3:14 calling them apostles. He sent them out to **p**,
16:15 all the world and **p** the Good News to everyone,
Lk 4:18 for he has appointed me to **p** Good News to the
4:43 "I must **p** the Good News of the Kingdom of God
5:15 and vast crowds came to hear him **p** and to be
9:60 and **p** the coming of the Kingdom of God."
16:16 "Until John the Baptist began to **p**, the laws of
22:35 "When I sent you out to **p** the Good News and you
Ac 5:42 they continued to teach and **p** this message:
8:25 along the way to **p** the Good News to them,
10:42 And he ordered us to **p** everywhere and to testify
13:44 turned out to hear them **p** the word of the Lord.
15: 7 among you some time ago to **p** to the Gentiles
16:10 that God was calling us to **p** the Good News there.
23:11 you must **p** the Good News in Rome."
Ro 1: 1 to be an apostle and sent out to **p** his Good News.
1:15 come to you in Rome, too, to **p** God's Good News.
3: 8 yet some slander me by saying this is what I **p**!
10: 8 which is the message we **p**—is already within easy
15:20 My ambition has always been to **p** the Good News
1Co 1:17 send me to baptize, but to **p** the Good News—
1:23 So when we **p** that Christ was crucified, the Jews
9:12 If you support others who **p** to you, shouldn't we
9:14 the Lord gave orders that those who **p** the Good
15:11 makes no difference whether I **p** or they **p**.
15:12 since we **p** that Christ rose from the dead, why are
2Co 2:12 when I came to the city of Troas to **p** the Good
2:17 are many of them—who **p** just to make money.
2:17 We **p** God's message with sincerity and with
4: 3 If the Good News we **p** is veiled from anyone,
4: 4 They don't understand the message we **p** about the
4: 5 about ourselves; we **p** Christ Jesus, the Lord.
4:13 But we continue to **p** because we have the same
10:16 and **p** the Good News in other places that are far
11: 4 even if they **p** about a different Jesus than the one
we **p**,
Gal 1:11 which I **p** is not based on mere human reasoning
Php 1:15 But others **p** about Christ with pure motives.
1:16 They **p** because they love me, for they know the
1:17 Those others do not have pure motives as they **p**
1:17 They **p** with selfish ambition, not sincerely,
Col 4: 3 that God will give us many opportunities to **p**
2Ti 2: 8 raised from the dead. This is the Good News I **p**.
2: 9 And because I **p** this Good News, I am suffering
4: 2 **P** the word of God. Be persistent, whether the time
4:17 that I might **p** the Good News in all its fullness for
Rev 14: 6 carrying the everlasting Good News to **p** to the

PREACHED (42) [PREACH]

Mt 11: 5 to life, and the Good News is being **p** to the poor.
24:14 And the Good News about the Kingdom will be **p**
26:13 wherever the Good News is **p** throughout the
Mk 2: 2 even outside the door. And he **p** the word to them.
13:10 And the Good News must first be **p** to every
14: 9 wherever the Good News is **p** throughout the
16:20 And the disciples went everywhere and **p**,
Lk 7:22 to life, and the Good News is being **p** to the poor.
16:16 now the Good News of the Kingdom of God is **p**,
Jn 5:33 to listen to John the Baptist, and he **p** the truth.
18:20 because I have **p** regularly in the synagogues
Ac 4:31 And they **p** God's message with boldness.
6: 7 God's message was **p** in ever-widening circles.
8:40 He **p** the Good News there and in every city along
9:27 and how he boldly **p** in the name of Jesus in
11:19 of Syria. They **p** the Good News, but only to Jews.
13: 5 to the Jewish synagogues and **p** the word of God.
13: 6 Afterward they **p** from town to town across the
13:24 John the Baptist **p** the need for everyone in Israel
14: 1 and **p** with such power that a great number of both
14: 7 and they **p** the Good News there.
14: 9 He was listening as Paul **p**, and Paul noticed him
14:25 They **p** again in Perga, then went on to Attalia.
15:21 For these laws of Moses have been **p** in Jewish
15:36 "Let's return to each city where we previously **p**
19: 8 and **p** boldly for the next three months,
20:25 I have **p** the Kingdom will ever see me again.
26:20 I **p** first to those in Damascus, then in Jerusalem
1Co 4:15 For I became your father in Christ Jesus when I **p**
15: 1 and sisters, of the Good News I **p** to you before.
15:11 The important thing is that you believed what we **p**
2Co 1:19 Silas, and I **p** to you, and he is the divine Yes—
6: 7 We have faithfully **p** the truth. God's power has
Gal 4:12 You did not mistreat me when I first **p** to you.
Php 1:18 remains that the message about Christ is being **p**,
Col 1:23 The Good News has been **p** all over the world,
1Th 2: 9 there as we **p** God's Good News among you.
2:13 thanking God that when we **p** his message to you,
1Pe 1:12 **p** to you in the power of the Holy Spirit sent from
1:25 And that word is the Good News that was **p** to you.
3:19 So he went and **p** to the spirits in prison—
4: 6 That is why the Good News was **p** even to those

PREACHER (4) [PREACH]

1Co 9:18 to anyone, never demanding my rights as a **p**.
2Co 8:18 He is highly praised in all the churches as a **p** of
1Ti 2: 7 as a **p** and apostle to teach the Gentiles about faith
2Ti 1:11 And God chose me to be a **p**, an apostle, and a

PREACHES (5) [PREACH]

Ac 19:13 you by Jesus, whom Paul **p**, to come out!"
Gal 1: 8 who **p** any other message than the one we told you
1: 8 comes from heaven and **p** any other message,
1: 9 If anyone **p** any other gospel than the one you
1:23 "The one who used to persecute us now **p** the very

PREACHING (66) [PREACH]

Ezr 6:14 and they were greatly encouraged by the **p** of the
Am 7:12 on back to the land of Judah and do your **p** there!
7:16 prophesy against Israel. Stop **p** against my people.'
Mal 4: 6 His **p** will turn the hearts of parents to their
Mt 3: 1 In those days John the Baptist began **p** in the
4:23 **p** everywhere the Good News about the Kingdom.
11: 1 and **p** in towns throughout the country.
11:12 And from the time John the Baptist began **p**
12:41 because they repented at the **p** of Jonah.
Mk 1: 4 and was **p** that people should be baptized to show
1:39 **p** in the synagogues and expelling demons from
Lk 3: 3 **p** that people should be baptized to show that they
3: 7 Here is a sample of John's **p** to the crowds that
4:44 travel around, **p** in synagogues throughout Judea.
5: 1 One day as Jesus was **p** on the shore of the Sea of
9: 6 the villages, **p** the Good News and healing the sick.
11:32 because they repented at the **p** of Jonah.
20: 1 was teaching and **p** the Good News in the Temple,
Ac 2:40 Then Peter continued **p** for a long time,
4:29 and give your servants great boldness in their **p**.
6: 2 "We apostles should spend our time **p**
6: 4 our time in prayer and **p** and teaching the word."
8: 4 went everywhere **p** the Good News about Jesus.
8:25 and **p** the word of the Lord in Samaria,
9:20 And immediately he began **p** about Jesus in the
9:22 Saul's **p** became more and more powerful,
9:28 in Jerusalem, **p** boldly in the name of the Lord.
10:37 in Galilee after John the Baptist began **p**.
11:20 and Cyrene began **p** to Gentiles about the Lord

14: 3 a long time, **p** boldly about the grace of the Lord.
14:21 After **p** the Good News in Derbe and making many
15:35 were teaching and **p** the word of the Lord there.
17:13 learned that Paul was **p** the word of God in Berea,
18: 5 Paul spent his full time **p** and testifying to the
18:26 and Aquila heard him **p** boldly in the synagogue,
19: 9 Then he began **p** daily at the lecture hall of
20: 7 Paul was **p**; and since he was leaving the next day,
26:21 The Jews arrested me in the Temple for **p** this,
Ro 15:22 so long because I have been **p** in these places.
1Co 1:21 he has used our foolish **p** to save all who believe.
2: 4 And my message and my **p** were very plain.
9:15 I would rather die than lose my distinction of **p**
9:16 For **p** the Good News is not something I can boast
9:18 It is the satisfaction I get from **p** the Good News
9:27 I fear that after **p** to others I myself might be
15:14 if Christ was not raised, then all our **p** is useless,
2Co 4: 5 We don't go around **p** about ourselves; we preach
11: 7 and honored you by **p** God's Good News to you
Gal 2: 2 I wanted them to understand what I had been **p** to
2: 6 who were there had nothing to add to what I was **p**.
2: 7 responsibility of **p** the Good News to the Gentiles,
2: 7 just as he had given Peter the responsibility of **p** to
2: 9 They encouraged us to keep **p** to the Gentiles,
5:11 if I were still **p** that you must be circumcised—
5:11 still **p** salvation through the cross of Christ alone.
Eph 3: 1 of Christ Jesus because of my **p** to you Gentiles.
6:20 I am in chains now for **p** this message as God's
Php 1:15 Some are **p** out of jealousy and rivalry. But others
2:22 his father, he has helped me in **p** the Good News.
1Th 2: 3 So you can see that we were not **p** with any deceit
2:16 by trying to keep us from **p** the Good News to the
1Ti 5:17 especially those who work hard at both **p**
2Ti 2:18 **p** the lie that the resurrection of the dead has
Phm 1: 1 in prison for **p** the Good News about Christ Jesus,
1:13 while I am in these chains for **p** the Good News,
Rev 1: 9 I was exiled to the island of Patmos for **p** the word

PREARRANGED (3) [ARRANGE]
Mt 26:48 Judas had given them a **p** signal: "You will know
Mk 14:44 Judas had given them a **p** signal: "You will know
Ac 2:23 But you followed God's **p** plan. With the help of

PRECAUTIONS (2) [CAUTIOUS]
Pr 22: 3 person foresees the danger ahead and takes **p**;
27:12 person foresees the danger ahead and takes **p**.

PRECEDE (2) [PRECEDED, PRECEDES]
Ps 139: 5 You both **p** and follow me. / You place your hand
Lk 1:17 He will **p** the coming of the Lord,

PRECEDED (1) [PRECEDE]
Jer 28: 8 The ancient prophets who **p** you and me spoke

PRECEDES (2) [PRECEDE]
Pr 15:33 teaches a person to be wise; humility **p** honor.
18:12 goes before destruction; humility **p** honor.

PRECIOUS (57)
Dt 32:10 he guarded them as his most **p** possession.
2Sa 23:17 "This water is as **p** as the blood of these men who
1Ki 10: 2 with spices, huge quantities of gold, and **p** jewels.
10:10 of gold, and great quantities of spices and **p** jewels.
10:11 brought rich cargoes of almug wood and **p** jewels.
1Ch 11:19 "This water is as **p** as the blood of these men who
29: 2 other **p** stones, costly jewels, and all kinds of fine
29: 8 They also contributed numerous **p** stones,
2Ch 9: 1 with spices, huge quantities of gold, and **p** jewels.
9: 9 of gold, and great quantities of spices and **p** jewels.
9:10 brought rich cargoes of almug wood and **p** jewels.
32:27 gold, **p** stones, and spices, and for his shields
Ezr 8:27 2 fine articles of polished bronze, as **p** as gold.
Job 22:24 for money, and throw your **p** gold into the river.
22:25 will be your treasure. He will be your **p** silver!
28:10 They cut tunnels in the rocks and uncover **p** stones.
28:16 of Ophir, greater than **p** onyx stone or sapphires.
29:24 at them. My look of approval was **p** to them.
Ps 22:20 a violent death; / spare my **p** life from these dogs.
36: 7 How **p** is your unfailing love, O God!
44:12 You sold us—your **p** people—for a pittance.
68:31 Let Egypt come with gifts of **p** metals;
72:14 and from violence, / for their lives are **p** to him.
83: 3 your people, / laying plans against your **p** ones.
116:15 The LORD's loved ones are **p** to him; / it grieves
133: 2 For harmony is as **p** as the fragrant anointing oil
139:17 How **p** are your thoughts about me, O God!
Pr 3:15 Wisdom is more **p** than rubies; nothing you desire
7: 2 Guard my teachings as your most **p** possession.
24: 4 its rooms are filled with all sorts of **p** riches
31:10 and capable wife? She is worth more than **p** rubies.
SS 4:13 You are like a lovely orchard bearing **p** fruit,
Isa 28:16 a tested and **p** cornerstone that is safe to build on.
43: 4 their lives for yours because you are **p** to me.
54:11 and make the walls of your houses from **p** jewels.
Jer 14:17 for my virgin daughter—my **p** people—
20: 5 the **p** jewels and gold and silver of your kings—
27:21 says about the **p** things kept in the Temple and in
La 1:10 her completely, taking everything **p** that she owns.
4: 2 See how the **p** children of Jerusalem, worth their
Eze 28:13 Your clothing was adorned with every **p** stone—
Da 11:38 on him gold, silver, **p** stones, and costly gifts.
Hos 13:15 Every **p** thing they have will be plundered
Joel 3: 5 taken my silver and gold and all my **p** treasures,
Mic 4: 8 The kingship will be restored to my **p** Jerusalem.
Zec 2: 8 'Anyone who harms you harms my most **p**
2Co 4: 7 But this **p** treasure—this light and power that now
Jas 5: 7 They patiently wait for the **p** harvest to ripen.
1Pe 1: 7 and your faith is far more **p** to God than mere gold.
1:19 He paid for you with the **p** lifeblood of Christ,
2: 4 by the people, but he is **p** to God who chose him.
2: 7 Yes, he is very **p** to you who believe. But for those
3: 4 of a gentle and quiet spirit, which is so **p** to God.
2Pe 1: 1 I am writing to all of you who share the same **p**
Rev 17: 4 jewelry made of gold and **p** gems and pearls.
18:16 decked out with gold and **p** stones and pearls!
21:11 with the glory of God and sparkled like a **p** gem,

PREDECESSOR (4) [PREDECESSORS]
Da 5: 2 to bring in the gold and silver cups that his **p**,
5:11 Your **p**, King Nebuchadnezzar, made him chief
5:13 you Daniel, who was exiled from Judah by my **p**,
5:18 majesty, glory, and honor to your **p**,

PREDECESSORS (1) [PREDECESSOR]
Da 11:24 and do something that none of his **p** ever did—

PREDESTINATE(D) [KJV] See CHOSE(N), UNCHANGING PLAN

PREDICAMENT (1)
Da 6:14 day looking for a way to get Daniel out of this **p**.

PREDICT (6) [PREDICTABLY, PREDICTED, PREDICTING, PREDICTION, PREDICTIONS, PREDICTS]
Ge 44: 5 silver drinking cup, which he uses to **p** the future?
Ecc 9:12 People can never **p** when hard times might come.
Isa 43: 9 Can any of them **p** something even a single day in
Mic 3: 6 making it impossible for you to **p** the future.
Zec 10: 2 gods give false advice, fortune-tellers **p** only lies,
Ac 11:28 **p** by the Spirit that a great famine was coming

PREDICTABLY (1) [PREDICT]
Job 5: 7 People are born for trouble as **p** as sparks fly

PREDICTED (27) [PREDICT]
Ge 40:22 baker to be impaled on a pole, just as Joseph had **p**.
41:54 seven years of famine began, just as Joseph had **p**.
Ex 7:13 He still refused to listen, just as the LORD had **p**.
7:22 to Moses and Aaron, just as the LORD had **p**.
8:15 to Moses and Aaron, just as the LORD had **p**.
8:19 wouldn't listen to them, just as the LORD had **p**.
9:12 and he refused to listen, just as the LORD had **p**.
9:35 to let the people leave, just as the LORD had **p**.
Dt 13: 2 and the **p** signs or miracles take place.
1Ki 13: 5 just as the man of God had **p** in his message from
2Ki 7:17 of God had **p** when the king came to his house.
23:16 tomb of the man of God who had **p** these things.
23:17 and **p** the very things that you have just done to the
Isa 41:26 Who else **p** this, making you admit that he was
43:12 First I **p** your deliverance; I declared what I would
Jer 26:20 And he **p** the same terrible disaster against the city
Eze 6:10 and that I was serious when I **p** that all this would
Da 9:13 come true. All the troubles he **p** have taken place.
Jnh 4: 3 than alive because nothing I **p** is going to happen."
Mk 9:13 he was badly mistreated, just as the Scriptures **p**."
Lk 24:26 Wasn't it clearly **p** by the prophets that the
Jn 12:38 This is exactly what Isaiah the prophet had **p**:
Ac 1:16 This was **p** long ago by the Holy Spirit,
1:20 "This was **p** in the book of Psalms, where it says,
2:16 what you see this morning was **p** centuries ago by
7:52 They even killed the ones who **p** the coming of the
15:15 of Gentiles agrees with what the prophets **p**.

PREDICTING (2) [PREDICT]
Jer 29:28 to Babylon, **p** that our captivity will be a long one.
Ac 2:31 into the future and **p** the Messiah's resurrection.

PREDICTION (3) [PREDICT]
Jn 11:52 It was a **p** that Jesus' death would be not for Israel
12:41 Isaiah was referring to Jesus when he made this **p**,
18:32 This fulfilled Jesus' **p** about the way he would die.

PREDICTIONS (14) [PREDICT]
Isa 8:20 "Check their **p** against my testimony,"
8:20 "If their **p** are different from mine, it is
43: 9 Where are the witnesses of such **p**? Who can verify
44:25 events to happen that are contrary to their **p**.
44:26 But I carry out the **p** of my prophets! When they
48: 3 suddenly I took action, and all my **p** came true.
48: 6 You have heard my **p** and seen them fulfilled,
Jer 5:13 Their **p** of disaster will fall on themselves!' "
10: 2 Do not be afraid of their **p**, even though other
17:15 talking about? Why don't your **p** come true?"
28: 9 Only when his **p** come true can it be known that he
Eze 12:24 and misleading **p** about peace in Israel.
Lk 18:31 all the **p** of the ancient prophets concerning the
Jn 10:41 "but all his **p** about this man have come true."

PREDICTS (2) [PREDICT]
Dt 18:22 If the prophet **p** something in the LORD's name
Jer 28: 9 So a prophet who **p** peace must carry the burden of

PREFECTS (3)
Da 3: 2 **p**, governors, advisers, counselors, judges,
3:27 Then the princes, **p**, governors, and advisers
6: 7 We administrators, **p**, princes, advisers, and other

PREFER (4) [PREFERENCE, PREFERENTIAL, PREFERRING]
Jos 24:15 Would you **p** the gods your ancestors served
1Ki 21: 2 in exchange, or if you **p**, I will pay you for it."
1Co 3: 4 of Paul," and another says, "I **p** Apollos,"
Phm 1: 9 but because of our love, I **p** just to ask you. So take

PREFERENCE (1) [PREFER]
1Ch 24: 5 means of sacred lots so that no **p** would be shown,

PREFERENTIAL (2) [PREFER]
2Ki 25:28 and gave him **p** treatment over all the other exiled
Jer 52:32 and gave him **p** treatment over all the other exiled

PREFERRING (1) [PREFER]
Heb 11:35 **p** to die rather than turn from God and be free.

PREFINISHED (1) [FINISH]
1Ki 6: 7 construction of the Temple were **p** at the quarry,

PREGNANCY (1) [PREGNANT]
Lk 1:26 In the sixth month of Elizabeth's **p**, God sent the

PREGNANT (54) [PREGNANCY]
Ge 4: 1 Adam slept with his wife, Eve, and she became **p**.
4:17 Then Cain's wife became **p** and gave birth to a
16: 4 So Abram slept with Hagar, and she became **p**.
16: 4 When Hagar knew she was **p**, she began to treat
16: 5 Now this servant of mine is **p**, and she despises
16:11 "You are now **p** and will give birth to a son.
19:36 So both of Lot's daughters became **p** by their
21: 2 Sarah became **p**, and she gave a son to Abraham in
25:21 Isaac's prayer, and his wife became **p** with twins.
29:32 So Leah became **p** and had a son. She named him
29:33 She soon became **p** again and had another son.
29:34 Again she became **p** and had a son. She named him
29:35 Once again she became **p** and had a son.
30: 5 Bilhah became **p** and presented him with a son.
30: 7 Then Bilhah became **p** again and gave Jacob a
30: 9 Leah realized that she wasn't getting **p** anymore,
30:17 She became **p** again and gave birth to her fifth son.
30:19 Then she became **p** again and had a sixth son.
30:23 She became **p** and gave birth to a son. "God has
38: 3 She became **p** and had a son, and Judah named the
38:18 then let him sleep with her, and she became **p**.
38:24 was **p** as a result of prostitution.
Ex 2: 2 The woman became **p** and gave birth to a son.
21:22 they hurt a **p** woman so her child is born
Lev 12: 2 When a woman becomes **p** and gives birth to a
Jdg 13: 2 His wife was unable to become **p**, and they had no
13: 3 you will soon become **p** and give birth to a son.
13: 5 You will become **p** and give birth to a son, and his
13: 7 'You will become **p** and give birth to a son.
Ru 4:13 with her, the LORD enabled her to become **p**,
1Sa 4:19 of Phinehas, was **p** and near her time of delivery.
2Sa 11: 5 When Bathsheba discovered that she was **p**,
12:24 She became **p** and gave birth to a son, and they
2Ki 4:17 But sure enough, the woman soon became **p**.
8:12 to the ground, and rip open their **p** women!"
15:16 entire population and ripped open the **p** women.
1Ch 7:23 his wife, and she became **p** and gave birth to a son.
Ps 7:14 The wicked conceive evil; / they are **p** with trouble
Isa 8: 3 with my wife, and she became **p** and had a son.
Hos 1: 3 and she became **p** and gave Hosea a son.
1: 6 Soon Gomer became **p** again and gave birth to a
1: 8 she again became **p** and gave birth to a second son.
2: 5 and became **p** in a shameful way.
13:16 their **p** women ripped open by swords."
Am 1:13 ripping open **p** women with their swords.
Mt 1:18 was still a virgin, she became **p** by the Holy Spirit.
24:19 How terrible it will be for **p** women and for
Mk 13:17 How terrible it will be for **p** women and for
Lk 1:24 became **p** and went into seclusion for five months.
1:31 You will become **p** and have a son, and you are to
1:36 your relative Elizabeth has become **p** in her old
2: 5 his fiancée, who was obviously **p** by this time.
21:23 How terrible it will be for **p** women and for
Rev 12: 2 She was **p**, and she cried out in the pain of labor as

PREMATURELY (1)
Ex 21:22 they hurt a pregnant woman so her child is born **p**.

PREMEDITATED (2)
Nu 35:20 So if in **p** hostility someone pushes another person
35:22 someone pushes another person without **p** hostility,

PREMISES (1)
Ecc 10:13 Since fools base their thoughts on foolish **p**,

PREPARATION (9) [PREPARE]
Ge 26:30 they ate and drank in **p** for the treaty ceremony.
Ex 12:16 may be done on these days except in the **p** of food.
Jos 7:13 Command the people to purify themselves in **p** for
Eze 40:42 There were also four tables of hewn stone for **p** of
Mk 15:42 on Friday, the day of **p**, the day before the Sabbath.
Lk 23:54 on Friday afternoon, the day of **p** for the Sabbath.

Jn 12: 7 "Leave her alone. She did it in **p** for my burial.
19:14 It was now about noon of the day of **p** for the
19:42 because it was the day of **p** before the Passover

PREPARATIONS (7) [PREPARE]

1Ch 12:39 for **p** had been made by their relatives for their
22: 5 the world. So I will begin making **p** for it now."
28: 2 I made the necessary **p** for building it,
29:19 this Temple, for which I have made all these **p**."
2Ch 35:14 The Levites took responsibility for all these **p**.
Eze 12: 3 Make your **p** in broad daylight so the people can
Na 3:15 But in the middle of your **p**, the fire will devour

PREPARE (70) [PREPARATION, PREPARATIONS, PREPARED, PREPARES, PREPARING]

Ge 18: 5 Let me **p** some food to refresh you. Please stay
27: 4 **P** it just the way I like it so it's savory and good,
27: 7 to **p** him a delicious meal of wild game. He wants
27: 9 I'll **p** your father's favorite dish from them.
43:16 me this noon. Take them inside and **p** a big feast."
Ex 19:10 "Go down and **p** the people for my visit.
34: 1 told Moses, "**P** two stone tablets like the first ones.
35:20 left Moses and went to their tents to **p** their gifts.
Nu 23: 1 and **p** seven young bulls and seven rams for a
23:29 me seven altars and **p** me seven young bulls
28:24 this is how you will **p** the food offerings to be
Dt 10: 1 said to me, '**P** two stone tablets like the first ones,
20:12 But if they refuse to make peace and **p** to fight,
Jos 9:11 and our people instructed us, '**P** for a long journey.
Jdg 13:15 "Please stay here until we can **p** a young goat for
13:16 you may **p** a burnt offering as a sacrifice to the
2Sa 13: 5 him to let Tamar come and **p** some food for you.
13: 7 and sent Tamar to Amnon's house to **p** some food
1Ki 5:18 and Hiram's builders **p** the timber and stone for the
18:23 I will **p** the other bull and lay it on the wood on the
18:25 Choose one of the bulls and **p** it and call on the
20:12 "**P** to attack!" Ben-hadad commanded his
2Ki 10: 3 be your king, and **p** to fight for Ahab's dynasty."
10:20 "**P** a solemn assembly to worship Baal!"
2Ch 29:34 But there were too few priests to **p** all the burnt
35: 6 purify yourselves, and **p** to help those who come.
Est 5: 8 Haman tomorrow to the banquet I will **p** for you.
Job 11:13 "If only you would **p** your heart and lift up your
Ps 2: 2 The kings of the earth **p** for battle; / the rulers plot
7:13 He will **p** his deadly weapons / and ignite his
23: 5 You **p** a feast for me / in the presence of my
35: 2 up your shield. / **P** for battle, and come to my aid.
59: 4 Despite my innocence, they **p** to kill me. / Rise up
Pr 31:15 She gets up before dawn to **p** breakfast for her
Isa 8: 9 all you nations. **P** for battle—and die! Yes, die!
8:10 develop your strategies, **p** your plans of attack—
21: 5 Quick! Grab your shields and **p** for battle!
62:10 Go out! **P** the highway for my people to return!
Jer 6: 4 They shout, '**P** for battle and attack at noon!
10:17 "Pack your bag and **p** to leave; the siege is about
46: 4 Harness the horses, and **p** to mount them. Put on
46: 4 sharpen your spears, and **p** your armor.
49:14 a coalition against Edom, and **p** for battle!"
50:14 "Yes, **p** to attack Babylon, all you nations round
51:12 **P** an ambush, for the LORD will fulfill all his
51:39 I will **p** a different kind of feast for them.
Eze 4:12 Each day **p** your bread as you would barley cakes.
7:23 "**P** chains for my people, for the land is bloodied
36: 8 heavy crops of fruit to **p** for my people's return—
45:23 On each of the seven days of the feast he will **p** a
Am 4:12 **P** to meet your God as he comes in judgment,
Mal 3: 1 my messenger, and he will **p** the way before me.
Mt 3: 3 '**P** a pathway for the Lord's coming! / Make a
11:10 before you, / and he will **p** your way before you.'
26:12 She has poured this perfume on me to **p** my body
26:17 "Where do you want us to **p** the Passover
Mk 1: 2 messenger before you, / and he will **p** your way.
1: 3 '**P** a pathway for the Lord's coming! / Make a
14:12 "Where do you want us to go to **p** the Passover
14:15 is the place; go ahead and **p** our supper there."
Lk 1:76 because you will **p** the way for the Lord.
3: 4 '**P** a pathway for the Lord's coming! / Make a
7:27 before you, / and he will **p** your way before you.'
9:52 ahead to a Samaritan village to **p** for his arrival.
17: 8 He must first **p** his master's meal and serve him his
22: 8 and said, "Go and **p** the Passover meal,
22:12 is the place. Go ahead and **p** our supper there."
Jn 1:23 '**P** a straight pathway for the Lord's coming!' "
3:28 I am here to **p** the way for him—that is all.
14: 2 Father's home, and I am going to **p** a place for you.

PREPARED (107) [PREPARE]

Ge 14: 8 **p** for battle in the valley of the Dead Sea
21:14 up early the next morning, **p** food for the journey,
24:31 all ready for you and a place **p** for the camels!"
26:30 So Isaac **p** a great feast for them, and they ate
27:31 Esau **p** his father's favorite meat dish and brought
32:13 he was for the night and **p** a present for Esau:
43:25 so they **p** their gifts for Joseph's arrival at noon.
46:29 Joseph **p** his chariot and traveled to Goshen to
Ex 12:11 you eat this meal, as though **p** for a long journey.
23:20 you to lead you safely to the land I have **p** for you.
35:25 who were skilled in sewing and spinning **p** blue,
Lev 2: 7 If your offering is **p** in a pan, it also must be made
2: 8 "No matter how a grain offering has been **p** before
6:17 Remember, this flour may never be **p** with yeast.
7: 9 offering that has been baked in an oven, **p** in a pan,
Nu 23: 4 "I have **p** seven altars and have sacrificed a young
26:63 figures of the people of Israel as **p** by Moses
Jos 22:12 and **p** to go to war against their brother tribes.
Jdg 9:52 the tower. But as he **p** to set fire to the entrance,
20:33 reached Baal-tamar, they turned and **p** to attack.
1Sa 9:25 to the roof of the house and **p** a bed for him there.
2Sa 6:17 inside the special tent that David had **p** for it.
1Ki 6:19 Solomon **p** the inner sanctuary in the rear of the
8:21 And I have **p** a place there for the Ark,
18:26 So they **p** one of the bulls and placed it on the
18:42 So Ahab **p** a feast. But Elijah climbed to the top of
20:12 his officers. So they **p** to attack the city.
2Ki 7:14 So two chariots with horses were **p**, and the king
1Ch 9:30 But it was the priests who **p** the spices and incense.
12:33 They were fully armed and **p** for battle
12:35 of Dan, there were 28,600 warriors, all **p** for battle.
12:36 there were 40,000 trained warriors, all **p** for battle.
15: 1 He also **p** a place for the Ark of God and set up a
15: 3 the Ark of the LORD to the place he had **p** for it.
15:12 the God of Israel, to the place I have **p** for it.
16: 1 Ark of God into the special tent David had **p** for it,
2Ch 1: 4 to the special tent he had **p** for it in Jerusalem.
18: 2 who **p** a great banquet for him and his officials.
26:13 They were **p** to assist the king against any enemy.
31:11 Hezekiah decided to have storerooms **p** in the
35:11 blood on the altar while the Levites **p** the animals.
35:14 Afterward the Levites **p** a meal for themselves
Ezr 5: 8 It is being rebuilt with specially **p** stones,
6: 4 Every three layers of specially **p** stones will be
Ne 8:10 gifts of food with people who have nothing **p**.
Est 5: 4 and Haman come today to a banquet I have **p** for
5:12 and the king himself to the banquet she **p** for us.
6: 4 king to hang Mordecai from the gallows he had **p**.
6:14 arrived to take Haman to the banquet Esther had **p**.
Job 13:18 I have **p** my case; I will be proved innocent.
28:26 the laws of the rain and **p** a path for the lightning.
Pr 9: 2 She has **p** a great banquet, mixed the wines,
21:31 The horses are **p** for battle, but the victory belongs
Isa 45: 5 I have **p** you, even though you do not know me,
Jer 8:13 All the good things I **p** for them will soon be gone.
41:17 near Bethlehem, where they **p** to leave for Egypt.
Eze 21:10 It is being **p** for terrible slaughter; it will flash like
21:11 and polished; it is being **p** for the executioner!
23:24 wagons, and a great army fully **p** for attack.
38: 7 "Get ready; be **p**! Keep all the armies around you
39:19 This is the sacrificial feast I have **p** for you.
40:41 where the sacrifices were cut up and **p**.
Da 9:14 LORD has brought against us the disaster he **p**,
Jnh 4: 7 But God also **p** a worm! The next morning at dawn
Zep 1: 7 The LORD has **p** his people for a great slaughter
Mt 8:12 those for whom the Kingdom was **p**—
8:15 left her. Then she got up and **p** a meal for him.
20:23 My Father has **p** those places for the ones he has
22: 2 of a king who **p** a great wedding feast for his son.
22: 4 'The feast has been **p**, and choice meats have been
24:42 So be **p**, because you don't know what day your
25: 7 "All the bridesmaids got up and **p** their lamps.
25:13 "So stay awake and be **p**, because you do not
25:34 inherit the Kingdom **p** for you from the foundation
25:41 into the eternal fire **p** for the Devil and his
26:19 as Jesus told them and **p** the Passover supper there.
Mk 1:31 and she got up and **p** a meal for them.
10:40 God has **p** those places for the ones he has
14:16 had said, and they **p** the Passover supper there.
Lk 4:39 She got up at once and **p** a meal for them.
12:35 "Be dressed for service and well **p**,
14:16 "A man **p** a great feast and sent out many
14:24 the smallest taste of what I had **p** for them.' "
15:27 the calf we were fattening and has **p** a great feast.
22:13 had said, and they **p** the Passover supper there.
23:56 Then they went home and **p** spices and ointments
24: 1 came to the tomb, taking the spices they had **p**.
Jn 12: 2 A dinner was **p** in Jesus' honor. Martha served,
Ac 4:26 The kings of the earth **p** for battle; / the rulers
9:37 Her friends **p** her for burial and laid her in an
10:10 But while lunch was being **p**, he fell into a trance.
14:13 and they **p** to sacrifice to the apostles at the city
Ro 9:23 upon those he **p** to be the objects of his mercy—
1Co 2: 9 what God has **p** / for those who love him."
2Co 3: 3 Clearly, you are a letter from Christ **p** by us.
5: 5 God himself has **p** us for this, and as a guarantee
Eph 6:15 from the Good News, so that you will be fully **p**.
Heb 4: 2 this Good News—that God has **p** a place of rest—
11:16 their God, for he has **p** a heavenly city for them.
1Pe 1:10 They prophesied about this gracious salvation **p** for
Rev 8: 6 Then the seven angels with the seven trumpets **p** to
9:15 And the four angels who had been **p** for this hour
12: 6 where God had **p** a place to give her care for 1,260
12:14 This allowed her to fly to a place **p** for her in the
19: 7 feast of the Lamb, and his bride has **p** herself.
19:17 Gather together for the great banquet God has **p**.
21: 2 of heaven like a beautiful bride **p** for her husband.

PREPARES (3) [PREPARE]

Dt 1:38 into the land. Encourage him as he **p** to enter it.
2Sa 22:35 He **p** me for battle; / he strengthens me to draw a
Ps 18:34 He **p** me for battle; / he strengthens me to draw a

PREPARING (20) [PREPARE]

Ge 19: 4 as they were **p** to retire for the night, all the men of
Jdg 10:17 in Gilead, **p** to attack Israel's army at Mizpah.
19: 9 and his concubine and servant were **p** to leave,
2Sa 24:16 But as the death angel was **p** to destroy Jerusalem,
1Ch 9:32 **p** the bread to be set on the table each Sabbath day.
21:15 But just as the angel was **p** to destroy it,
22: 2 and he assigned them the task of **p** blocks of stone
Job 15:24 in distress and anguish, like a king **p** for an attack.
Ps 85:13 as a herald before him, / **p** the way for his steps.
Isa 10:31 all fleeing. And the citizens of Gebim are **p** to run.
21: 5 Look! They are **p** a great feast. They are spreading
Jer 49:30 has plotted against you and is **p** to destroy you.
Am 7: 1 I saw him **p** to send a vast swarm of locusts over
7: 4 I saw him **p** to punish his people with a great fire.
Na 1:14 I am **p** a grave for you because you are despicable
Lk 1:17 coming of the Lord, **p** the people for his arrival.
10:40 was worrying over the big dinner she was **p**.
Ac 20: 3 He was **p** to sail back to Syria when he discovered
21:23 have taken a vow and are **p** to shave their heads.
2Ti 3:17 It is God's way of **p** us in every way,

PRESBYTERY [KJV] See ELDERS

PRESCRIBED (27)

Lev 5:10 following all the procedures that have been **p**.
9:16 whole burnt offering and presented it in the **p** way.
27: 8 such a vow but cannot afford to pay the **p** amount,
Nu 6:15 along with their **p** grain offerings and drink
6:17 The priest must also make the **p** grain offering
7:87 burnt offerings, along with their **p** grain offerings.
15:24 and it must be offered along with the **p** grain
29: 6 and they must be given with their **p** grain offerings
29: 9 These offerings must be accompanied by the **p**
29:18 and lambs must be accompanied by the **p** grain
29:21 and lambs must be accompanied by the **p** grain
29:24 and lambs must be accompanied by the **p** grain
29:27 and lambs must be accompanied by the **p** grain
29:30 and lambs must be accompanied by the **p** grain
29:33 and lambs must be accompanied by the **p** grain
29:37 must be accompanied by the **p** grain offering
2Ch 4:20 gold to burn in front of the Most Holy Place as **p**;
23:18 as **p** by the law of Moses, and to sing and rejoice
30: 5 celebrating it in great numbers as **p** in the law.
31: 4 he required the people in Jerusalem to bring the **p**
35:13 Then they roasted the Passover lambs as **p**;
Ezr 3: 4 They celebrated the Festival of Shelters as **p** in the
3:10 to praise the LORD, just as King David had **p**.
Ne 8:15 live during the festival, as it was **p** in the law.
12:36 They used the musical instruments **p** by David,
Est 2:12 she was given the **p** twelve months of beauty
9:27 these two **p** days at the appointed time each year.

PRESENCE (243) [PRESENT]

Ge 4:14 have banished me from my land and from your **p**;
4:16 So Cain left the LORD's **p** and settled in the land
19:27 to the place where he had stood in the LORD's **p**.
23:11 Here in the **p** of my people, I give it to you. Go
23:18 made in the **p** of the Hittite elders at the city gate.
24:40 'for the LORD, in whose **p** I have walked,
27: 7 He wants to bless Esau in the LORD's **p** before
41:14 of clothes, he went in and stood in Pharaoh's **p**.
41:46 And when Joseph left Pharaoh's **p**, he made a tour
Ex 11: 8 burning with anger, Moses left Pharaoh's **p**.
11:10 and Aaron did these miracles in Pharaoh's **p**,
16: 7 In the morning you will see the glorious **p** of the
16: 9 'Come into the LORD's **p**, and hear his reply to
18:12 all joined him in a sacrificial meal in God's **p**.
22:11 then take an oath of innocence in the **p** of the
24:11 In fact, they shared a meal together in God's **p**!
24:16 And the glorious **p** of the LORD rested upon
25:30 You must always keep the special Bread of the **P**
27:21 will keep the lamps burning in the LORD's **p** day
28:29 he goes into the **p** of the LORD in the Holy Place.
28:30 Aaron's heart when he goes into the LORD's **p**.
28:35 will tinkle as he goes in and out of the LORD's **p**.
29:11 then slaughter it in the LORD's **p** at the entrance
29:26 and lift it up in the LORD's **p** as a special gift to
29:42 Offer it in the LORD's **p** at the Tabernacle
29:43 the Tabernacle will be sanctified by my glorious **p**.
30: 8 he must again burn incense in the LORD's **p**.
33:18 "Please let me see your glorious **p**," he said.
33:22 As my glorious **p** passes by, I will put you in the
34: 5 "the LORD," as Moses stood there in his **p**.
35:13 and all of its utensils; the Bread of the **P**;
39:36 the table and all its utensils; the Bread of the **P**;
40:23 And he arranged the Bread of the **P** on the table
40:25 Then he set up the lamps in the LORD's **p**,
40:34 and the glorious **p** of the LORD filled it.
Lev 1: 5 Then slaughter the animal in the LORD's **p**,
1:11 on the north side of the altar in the LORD's **p**.
4: 4 and slaughter it there in the LORD's **p**.
4: 7 that stands in the LORD's **p** in the Tabernacle.
4:18 that stands in the LORD's **p** in the Tabernacle.
6:25 and must be slaughtered in the LORD's **p** at the
8:26 without yeast that was placed in the LORD's **p**.
8:29 took the breast and lifted it up in the LORD's **p**.
9: 5 and stood there in the LORD's **p**.
9: 6 the glorious **p** of the LORD will appear to you."
9:23 and the glorious **p** of the LORD appeared to the
9:24 Fire blazed forth from the LORD's **p**
10: 2 So fire blazed forth from the LORD's **p**
13:15 because open sores indicate the **p** of a contagious
14:23 in the LORD's **p** at the Tabernacle entrance.
16:13 There in the LORD's **p**, he will put the incense on
16:30 be cleansed from all your sins in the LORD's **p**.
19:32 "Show your fear of God by standing up in the **p** of
22: 3 by the Israelites, they must be cut off from my **p**.
24: 4 must be tended continually in the LORD's **p**.
24: 6 Place the bread in the LORD's **p** on the pure gold
Nu 3: 4 and Abihu died in the LORD's **p** in the
4: 7 where the Bread of the **P** is displayed, and place
14:10 Then the glorious **p** of the LORD appeared to all
14:22 They have seen my glorious **p** and the miraculous
16: 5 allow those who are chosen to enter his holy **p**.
16:19 Then the glorious **p** of the LORD appeared to the

16:38 because they were used in the LORD's **p**.
16:40 should ever enter the LORD's **p** to burn incense.
16:42 and the glorious **p** of the LORD appeared.
17: 7 Moses put the staffs in the LORD's **p** in the
17: 9 brought all the staffs out from the LORD's **p**,
19: 3 be taken outside the camp and slaughtered in his **p**.
20: 3 "We wish we had died in the LORD's **p** with our
20: 6 Then the glorious **p** of the LORD appeared to
Dt 10:10 I stayed on the mountain in the LORD's **p** for
12: 7 and your families will feast in the **p** of the LORD
12:12 and all your servants in the **p** of the LORD your
12:18 You must eat these in the **p** of the LORD your
12:18 celebrating in the **p** of the LORD your God in all
14:23 his name to be honored, and eat it there in his **p**.
14:26 Then feast there in the **p** of the LORD your God
15:20 and your family must eat these animals in the **p** of
17:18 a scroll for himself in the **p** of the Levitical priests.
25: 2 and be beaten in his **p** with the number of lashes
25: 9 the widow must walk over to him in the **p** of the
26: 5 then say in the **p** of the LORD your God,
26:13 Then you must declare in the **p** of the LORD your
29:15 this covenant with you who stand in his **p** today
Jos 4:13 over to the plains of Jericho in the LORD's **p**.
6: 8 horns started marching in the **p** of the LORD,
7:23 Then they laid them on the ground in the **p** of the
9:19 "We have sworn an oath in the **p** of the LORD,
18: 6 Then I will cast sacred lots in the **p** of the LORD
18: 8 sacred lots in the **p** of the LORD here at Shiloh."
18:10 Joshua cast sacred lots in the **p** of the LORD to
19:51 **p** of the LORD at the entrance of the Tabernacle
Jdg 5: 5 Even Mount Sinai shook in the **p** of the LORD,
11:11 At Mizpah, in the **p** of the LORD,
20: 1 and stood in the **p** of the LORD at Mizpah.
20:23 and wept in the **p** of the LORD until evening.
20:26 and wept in the **p** of the LORD and fasted until
21: 2 to Bethel and sat in the **p** of God until evening,
21: 5 our council in the **p** of the LORD at Mizpah?"
21: 5 they had taken a solemn oath in the LORD's **p**,
Ru 4: 4 then buy it here in the **p** of these witnesses.
1Sa 2:21 Samuel grew up in the **p** of the LORD.
6:20 "Who is able to stand in the **p** of the LORD,
18:13 Saul banned him from his **p** and appointed him
19:24 and all night, prophesying in the **p** of Samuel.
21: 6 the Bread of the **P** that was placed before the
26:20 I die on foreign soil, far from the **p** of the LORD?
2Sa 7:26 of your servant David be established in your **p**.
14:24 own house, but he must never come into my **p**."
1Ki 1:32 of Jehoiada." When they came into the king's **p**,
7:48 gold altar, / the gold table for the Bread of the **P**,
8:11 because the glorious **p** of the LORD filled the
8:59 And may these words that I have prayed in the **p** of
8:64 because the bronze altar in the LORD's **p** was too
8:65 of Shelters in the **p** of the LORD their God.
18:15 by the LORD Almighty, in whose **p** I stand,
2Ki 13:23 destroyed them or banished them from his **p**.
17:18 the LORD was angry, he swept them from his **p**.
23: 3 and renewed the covenant in the LORD's **p**.
23:27 I will banish the people from my **p** and reject my
24: 3 He had decided to remove Judah from his **p**
24:20 and Judah from his **p** and sent them into exile.
1Ch 13:10 on the Ark. So Uzzah died there in the **p** of God.
17:24 of your servant David be established in your **p**.
23:13 to offer sacrifices in the LORD's **p**, to serve the
23:31 of Levites served in the LORD's **p** at all times,
24: 6 the names and assignments in the **p** of the king,
24:31 It was done in the **p** of King David, Zadok,
28:16 table on which the Bread of the **P** would be placed
29:10 Then David praised the LORD in the **p** of the
29:22 and drank in the LORD's **p** with great joy that
2Ch 1: 6 went up to the bronze altar in the LORD's **p**
4:19 the gold altar; / the tables for the Bread of the **P**;
5:14 because the glorious **p** of the LORD filled the
7: 1 and the glorious **p** of the LORD filled the
7: 2 because the glorious **p** of the LORD filled it.
7: 3 and the glorious **p** of the LORD filling the
13:11 They place the Bread of the **P** on the holy table,
14:12 So the LORD defeated the Ethiopians in the **p** of
20: 9 we can come to stand in your **p** before this Temple
29:11 The LORD has chosen you to stand in his **p**,
29:18 and the table of the Bread of the **P** with all its
34:31 and renewed the covenant in the LORD's **p**.
36:12 and he refused to humble himself in the **p** of the
Ezr 9:15 such a condition none of us can stand in your **p**."
Ne 2: 1 I had never appeared sad in his **p** before this time.
4: 5 for they have provoked you to anger here in the **p**
10:33 This will provide for the Bread of the **P**;
13:28 the Horonite, so I banished him from my **p**.
Est 1:19 that Queen Vashti be forever banished from your **p**
Job 1:12 him physically." So Satan left the LORD's **p**.
2: 7 So Satan left the LORD's **p**, and he struck Job
13:16 If I were, I would be thrown from his **p**.
13:21 and don't terrify me with your awesome **p**.
23:15 No wonder I am so terrified in his **p**. When I think
26: 6 The underworld is naked in God's **p**. There is no
36:33 The thunder announces his **p**; the storm announces
Ps 5: 5 the proud will not be allowed to stand in your **p**,
9:19 defy you! / Let the nations be judged in your **p**!
15: 1 Who may enter your **p** on your holy hill?
16:11 me the way of life, / granting me the joy of your **p**
18:12 The brilliance of his **p** broke through the clouds,
21: 6 You have given him the joy of being in your **p**.
22:25 I will fulfill my vows in the **p** of those who
22:29 all mortals—those born to die—bow down in his **p**.
23: 5 prepare a feast for me / in the **p** of my enemies.
24: 6 They alone may enter God's **p** / and worship the
31:20 You hide them in the shelter of your **p**, / safe from
31:20 You shelter them in your **p**, / far from accusing
37: 7 Be still in the **p** of the LORD, / and wait patiently
41:12 you have brought me into your **p** forever.
51:11 Do not banish me from your **p**, / and don't take
52: 9 will wait for your mercies / in the **p** of your people.
56:13 So now I can walk in your **p**, O God, / in your
68: 2 in fire. / Let the wicked perish in the **p** of God.
68: 3 let the godly rejoice. / Let them be glad in God's **p**.
68: 4 His name is the LORD— / rejoice in his **p**!
89:15 for they will walk in the light of your **p**, LORD.
101: 7 and liars will not be allowed to enter my **p**.
102:28 Their children's children / will thrive in your **p**."
114: 7 Tremble, O earth, at the **p** of the Lord, / at the **p** of
the God of Israel.
116: 9 And so I walk in the LORD's **p** / as I live here on
116:14 promises to the LORD / in the **p** of all his people.
116:18 promises to the LORD / in the **p** of all his people,
118:20 Those gates lead to the **p** of the LORD,
139: 7 your spirit! / I can never get away from your **p**!
140:13 praising your name, / for they will live in your **p**.
Pr 8:30 was his constant delight, rejoicing always in his **p**.
Isa 3: 8 They have offended his glorious **p** among them.
26:17 out in pain. / When we are in your **p**, LORD,
33:14 "can live here in the **p** of this all-consuming fire?"
52:15 many nations. Kings will stand speechless in his **p**.
53: 2 My servant grew up in the LORD's **p** like a
64: 1 How the mountains would quake in your **p**!
Jer 5:22 Why do you not tremble in my **p**? I, the LORD,
14:12 When they fast in my **p**, I will pay no attention.
23:39 I will expel you from my **p**, along with this city
28: 7 words I speak to you in the **p** of all these people.
32:12 I did all this in the **p** of my cousin Hanamel,
52: 3 and Judah from his **p** and sent them into exile.
Eze 38:20 animals, and people—will quake in terror at my **p**.
41:22 "is the table that stands in the LORD's **p**."
44: 3 sit inside this gateway to feast in the LORD's **p**.
44:15 They will stand in my **p** and offer the fat and blood
44:25 in the **p** of a dead person unless it is his father,
Da 7:10 and a river of fire flowed from his **p**. Millions of
7:13 the Ancient One and was led into his **p**.
Hos 6: 2 he will restore us so we can live in his **p**.
9: 5 will you do on days of feasting in the LORD's **p**?
Joel 2:17 The priests, who minister in the LORD's **p**,
Jnh 2: 4 'O LORD, you have driven me from your **p**.
Mic 7:17 will fear him greatly, trembling in terror at his **p**.
Na 1: 5 In his **p** the mountains quake, and the hills melt
1: 6 and the mountains crumble to dust in his **p**.
Zep 1: 7 Stand in silence in the **p** of the Sovereign LORD,
Zec 3: 7 and out of my **p** along with these others standing
Mal 3:16 In his **p**, a scroll of remembrance was written to
Mt 18:10 angels are always in the **p** of my heavenly Father.
25:32 All the nations will be gathered in his **p**, and he
Lk 1: 9 the sanctuary and burn incense in the Lord's **p**.
1:19 "I am Gabriel! I stand in the very **p** of God.
12: 8 will openly acknowledge that person in the **p** of
15:10 there is joy in the **p** of God's angels when even one
19:27 them in and execute them right here in my **p**.' "
20:26 So they failed to trap him in the **p** of the people.
23:14 examined him thoroughly on this point in your **p**
Ac 2:28 and you will give me wonderful joy in your **p**.'
3:20 of refreshment will come from the **p** of the Lord,
Ro 9: 1 In the **p** of Christ, I speak with utter truthfulness—
1Co 1:29 so that no one can ever boast in the **p** of God.
2Co 7: 7 His **p** was a joy, but so was the news he brought of
Eph 1:23 who fills everything everywhere with his **p**.
3:12 in him, we can now come fearlessly into God's **p**,
Col 1:22 a result, he has brought you into the very **p** of God,
1Th 3: 9 Because of you we have great joy in the **p** of God.
1Ti 5:21 I solemnly command you in the **p** of God
Heb 10:22 let us go right into the **p** of God, with true hearts
1Jn 1: 7 But if we are living in the light of God's **p**, just as
Jude 1:24 and who will bring you into his glorious **p** innocent
Rev 9:13 horns of the gold altar that stands in the **p** of God.
14:10 and burning sulfur in the **p** of the holy angels
20:11 The earth and sky fled from his **p**, but they found

PRESENT (159) [PRESENCE, PRESENTATION, PRESENTED, PRESENTING, PRESENTS]

Ge 32:13 he was for the night and prepared a **p** for Esau:
32:18 They are a **p** for his master Esau! He is coming
34:20 father before the town leaders to **p** this proposal.
Ex 21: 1 "Here are some other instructions you must **p** to
21: 6 If he does this, his master must **p** him before God.
29: 3 and **p** them at the entrance of the Tabernacle,
29: 4 "**P** Aaron and his sons at the entrance of the
29: 8 Next **p** his sons, and dress them in their tunics
34: 2 and **p** yourself to me there on the top of the
Lev 1: 2 Whenever you **p** offerings to the LORD,
1: 5 will **p** the blood by sprinkling it against the sides
2: 4 "When you **p** some kind of baked bread as a grain
2: 8 bring it to the priests who will **p** it at the altar.
2:11 in any of the grain offerings you **p** to the LORD,
2:14 "If you **p** a grain offering to the LORD from the
3: 1 "If you want to **p** a peace offering from the herd,
3: 6 "If you **p** a peace offering to the LORD from the
3: 7 you bring a sheep as your gift, **p** it to the LORD
4: 4 He must **p** the bull to the LORD at the entrance of
4:14 and **p** it at the entrance of the Tabernacle.
6: 6 to the priest, who will **p** it before the LORD.
6:14 Aaron's sons must **p** this offering to the LORD in
6:21 You must **p** this grain offering, and it will be very
7:12 If you **p** your peace offering as a thanksgiving
7:29 When you **p** a peace offering to the LORD,
7:30 **P** it to him with your own hands as an offering
7:30 and **p** it to the LORD by lifting it up before him.
9: 2 no physical defects, and **p** them to the LORD.
9: 4 Tell them to **p** all these offerings to the LORD
9: 7 "Approach the altar and **p** your sin offering
9: 7 Then **p** the offerings to make atonement for the
12: 7 The priest will then **p** them to the LORD
14:11 Then the officiating priest will **p** that person for
15:14 and **p** himself to the LORD at the entrance of the
15:15 The priest will **p** the offerings there, one for a sin
15:29 and **p** them to the priest at the entrance of the
16: 2 and I myself am **p** in the cloud over the atonement
16: 6 "Aaron will **p** the bull as a sin offering, to make
16: 7 and **p** them to the LORD at the entrance of the
16:11 "Then Aaron will **p** the young bull as a sin
17: 4 the Tabernacle to **p** it as an offering to the LORD,
17: 5 so he can **p** them to the LORD as peace offerings.
18:23 and a woman must never **p** herself to a male
19:21 and **p** it to the LORD at the entrance of the
21: 6 they are the ones who **p** the offerings to the
23: 8 the people must **p** an offering to the LORD by
23:18 **p** seven one-year-old lambs with no physical
23:25 you are to **p** offerings to the LORD by fire."
23:27 and **p** offerings to the LORD by fire.
23:36 you must **p** offerings to the LORD by fire.
23:36 and **p** another offering to the LORD by fire.
23:37 **p** all the various offerings to the LORD by fire—
23:38 and any freewill offerings that you **p** to the
Nu 3: 6 and **p** them to Aaron the priest as his assistants.
5:16 " 'The priest must then **p** her before the LORD.
5:30 the husband must **p** his wife before the LORD,
6:16 The priest will **p** these offerings before the
8: 9 and **p** the Levites at the entrance of the Tabernacle.
8:11 Aaron must **p** the Levites to the LORD as a
8:12 of the young bulls and **p** them to the LORD.
8:13 and **p** them as a special offering to the LORD.
9:10 are on a journey and cannot be **p** at the ceremony,
9:13 to **p** the LORD's offering at the proper time.
15: 5 you must also **p** one quart of wine for a drink
15: 8 "When you **p** a young bull as a burnt offering
15:12 Each of you must do this with each offering you **p**.
15:13 If you native Israelites want to **p** an offering by fire
15:14 And if any foreigners living among you want to **p**
15:20 **P** a cake from the first of the flour you grind
15:21 you are to **p** this offering to the LORD each year
15:24 the whole community must **p** a young bull for a
16:16 and **p** yourself before the LORD with all your
16:17 on it, so you can **p** them before the LORD.
18:13 All the firstfruits of the land that the people **p** to
18:28 You must **p** one-tenth of the tithe received from
18:28 From this you must **p** the LORD's portion to
18:30 'When you **p** the best part, it will be considered as
24:17 I see him, but not in the **p** time. / I perceive him,
27:19 **P** him to Eleazar the priest before the whole
28: 2 The offerings you **p** to me by fire on the altar are
28: 3 When you **p** your daily whole burnt offerings to
28: 7 Along with it you must **p** the proper drink offering,
28:11 **p** an extra burnt offering to the LORD of two
28:14 **P** this monthly burnt offering on the first day of
28:19 You must **p** as a burnt offering to the LORD two
28:23 You will **p** these offerings in addition to your
28:26 when you **p** the first of your new grain to the
29: 2 On that day you must **p** a burnt offering,
29: 8 You must **p** a burnt offering, very pleasing to the
29:13 That day you must **p** a special whole burnt offering
29:36 You must **p** a burnt offering, very pleasing to the
29:39 "You must **p** these offerings to the LORD at your
29:39 and offerings you **p** in connection with vows,
Dt 33:10 to Israel. / They will **p** incense before you
Jos 7:14 In the morning you must **p** yourselves by tribes,
12: 2 This territory included half of the **p** area of Gilead,
22: 3 of the LORD your God up to the **p** day.
Jdg 15: 1 Samson took a young goat as a **p** to his wife.
21: 9 all the people, no one from Jabesh-gilead was **p**.
1Sa 10:19 **p** yourselves before the LORD by tribes
25:27 And here is a **p** I have brought to you and your
30:26 "Here is a **p** for you, taken from the LORD's
2Sa 24:24 for I cannot **p** burnt offerings to the LORD my
1Ki 18: 1 said to Elijah, "Go and **p** yourself to King Ahab.
18:15 I stand, that I will **p** myself to Ahab today."
2Ki 5: 6 "With this letter I **p** my servant Naaman.
2Ch 5:11 All the priests who were **p** had purified
7: 7 so they could **p** burnt offerings and the fat from
13:11 They **p** burnt offerings and fragrant incense to the
23:18 He also commanded them to **p** burnt offerings to
30:21 So the people of Israel who were **p** in Jerusalem
35:17 All the Israelites **p** in Jerusalem celebrated
Ezr 1: 8 to count these items and **p** them to Sheshbazzar,
8:29 Guard these treasures well until you **p** them,
Ne 10:36 We will **p** them to the priests who minister in the
13:18 so that our God brought the **p** troubles upon us
Job 1: 6 One day the angels came to **p** themselves before
2: 1 One day the angels came again to **p** themselves
5: 8 to you is this: Go to God and **p** your case to him.
23: 4 I would lay out my case and **p** my arguments.
Ps 73:20 Their **p** life is only a dream / that is gone when
Pr 4: 9 your head; she will **p** you with a beautiful crown."
Isa 43:26 and you can **p** your case if you have one.
Jer 14:12 When they **p** their burnt offerings and grain
36: 2 message you have given, right up to the **p** time.
44:15 Then all the women **p** and all the men who knew
Eze 43:24 You are to **p** them to the LORD, and the priests
44:11 for burnt offerings and be **p** to help the people.
46: 4 "Each Sabbath day the prince will **p** to the
46: 5 He will **p** a grain offering of a half bushel of flour
Hos 9: 4 All who **p** such sacrifices will be defiled.
Am 2: 8 they **p** offerings of wine purchased with stolen
4: 5 **P** your bread made with yeast as an offering of
Zep 3:10 rivers of Ethiopia will come to **p** their offerings.
Mt 11:13 of the Scriptures looked forward to this **p** time.
Lk 2:22 so his parents took him to Jerusalem to **p** him to

2:27 and Joseph came to **p** the baby Jesus to the Lord as
12:56 and the sky, but you can't interpret these **p** times.
Jn 7:18 Those who **p** their own ideas are looking for praise
Ac 1:13 Here is the list of those who were **p**: / Peter,
1:15 on a day when about 120 believers were **p**,
2: 4 And everyone **p** was filled with the Holy Spirit
21:18 and all the elders of the Jerusalem church were **p**.
25:24 Then Festus said, "King Agrippa and all **p**, this is
Ro 3:26 and just in this **p** time when he declares sinners to
8:22 as in the pains of childbirth right up to the **p** time.
1Co 3:22 and life and death; the **p** and the future.
4:13 like everybody's trash—right up to the **p** moment.
7:26 Because of the **p** crisis, I think it is best to remain
14:17 no doubt, but it doesn't help the other people **p**.
14:28 But if no one is **p** who can interpret, they must be
15:28 the Son will **p** himself to God, so that God,
2Co 4:14 us with Jesus and **p** us to himself along with you.
4:17 For our **p** troubles are quite small and won't last
5: 2 We grow weary in our **p** bodies, and we long for
Eph 5:27 He did this to **p** her to himself as a glorious church
Php 4:14 you have done well to share with me in my **p**
Col 1:28 for we want to **p** them to God, perfect in their
Heb 9: 9 This is an illustration pointing to the **p** time.

PRESENTATION (1) [PRESENT]

Ex 5: 1 After this **p** to Israel's leaders, Moses and Aaron

PRESENTED (101) [PRESENT]

Ge 30: 5 Bilhah became pregnant and **p** him with a son.
30:10 Soon Zilpah **p** him with another son.
31:54 Then Jacob **p** a sacrifice to God and invited
43:15 to Egypt, where they **p** themselves to Joseph.
47: 2 of his brothers with him and **p** them to Pharaoh.
47: 7 Jacob, and **p** him to Pharaoh, and Jacob blessed
Ex 13:12 and firstborn male animals must be **p** to the
18:12 Then Jethro **p** a burnt offering and gave sacrifices
35:22 They **p** gold objects of every kind to the LORD.
Lev 2: 4 It may be **p** in the form of cakes mixed with olive
2:12 and honey to the offerings **p** at harvesttime,
3: 3 Part of this peace offering must be **p** to the LORD
3: 9 Part of this peace offering must be **p** to the LORD
3:14 Part of this offering must be **p** to the LORD as an
4:35 just as is done with a sheep **p** as a peace offering.
6:17 as their share of the offerings **p** to me by fire.
7:11 of peace offerings that may be **p** to the LORD.
7:14 One of each kind of bread must be **p** as a gift to the
7:20 but eats meat from a peace offering that was **p** to
8: 6 Then he **p** Aaron and his sons and washed them
8:13 Next Moses **p** Aaron's sons and clothed them in
8:18 Then Moses **p** the ram to the LORD for the whole
8:22 Next Moses **p** the second ram, which was the ram
8:24 Next he **p** Aaron's sons and put some of the blood
8:27 and he **p** the portions by lifting them up before the
9:15 Next Aaron **p** the sacrifices for the people.
9:15 the people's goat and **p** it as their sin offering,
9:16 burnt offering and **p** it in the prescribed way.
10:12 after the handful has been **p** to the LORD by fire.
10:14 of the peace offerings **p** by the people of Israel.
10:19 "Today my sons **p** both their sin offering and their
14:21 The guilt offering will be **p** by lifting it up,
14:31 to be **p** along with the grain offering.
16: 9 to the LORD will be **p** by Aaron as a sin offering.
16:10 The goat chosen to be the scapegoat will be **p** to
22: 3 they approach the sacred food **p** by the Israelites,
22:30 Eat the entire sacrificial animal on the day it is **p**.
Nu 5:15 of two quarts of barley flour to be **p** on her behalf.
5:18 When he has **p** her before the LORD, he must
7: 3 They **p** these to the LORD in front of the
7: 6 So Moses **p** the carts and oxen to the Levites.
7:10 The leaders also **p** dedication gifts for the altar at
7:12 leader of the tribe of Judah, **p** his offering.
7:18 leader of the tribe of Issachar, **p** his offering.
7:24 leader of the tribe of Zebulun, **p** his offering.
7:30 leader of the tribe of Reuben, **p** his offering.
7:36 leader of the tribe of Simeon, **p** his offering.
7:42 of Deuel, leader of the tribe of Gad, **p** his offering.
7:48 leader of the tribe of Ephraim, **p** his offering.
7:54 leader of the tribe of Manasseh, **p** his offering.
7:60 leader of the tribe of Benjamin, **p** his offering.
7:66 leader of the tribe of Dan, **p** his offering.
7:72 leader of the tribe of Asher, **p** his offering.
7:78 leader of the tribe of Naphtali, **p** his offering.
8:15 purified them and **p** them as a special offering.
8:21 and Aaron **p** them to the LORD as a special
18:11 "All the other offerings **p** to me by the Israelites
18:18 and right thigh that are **p** by lifting them up before
27: 1 One day a petition was **p** by the daughters of
27:22 and **p** Joshua to Eleazar the priest and the whole
28:10 This is the whole burnt offering to be **p** each
28:13 This burnt offering must be **p** by fire, and it will be
28:24 you will prepare the food offerings to be **p** by fire,
31:52 the gold that the commanders **p** as a gift to the
Dt 31:14 Joshua went and **p** themselves at the Tabernacle.
Jos 8:31 Then on the altar they **p** burnt offerings and peace
24: 1 So they came and **p** themselves to God.
Jdg 6:19 he brought them out and **p** them to the angel,
21: 4 and **p** their burnt offerings and peace offerings on
21: 8 "Was anyone absent when we **p** ourselves to the
1Sa 1: 4 On the day Elkanah **p** his sacrifice, he would give
16:10 In the same way all seven of Jesse's sons were **p** to
18:27 and **p** all their foreskins to the king.
2Sa 4: 8 at Hebron and **p** Ishbosheth's head to David.
8:10 Joram **p** David with many gifts of silver, gold,
2Ki 10: 7 heads in baskets and **p** them to Jehu at Jezreel.
11:12 He **p** Joash with a copy of God's covenant
16:13 The king **p** a burnt offering and a grain offering,
1Ch 6:49 They **p** the offerings on the altar of burnt offering
18:10 Joram **p** David with many gifts of gold, silver,
23:31 They assisted with the burnt offerings that were **p**
2Ch 23:11 They **p** Joash with a copy of God's laws
25:14 down in front of them, and **p** sacrifices to them!
29:27 As the burnt offering was **p**, songs of praise to the
35:11 the Passover lambs and **p** the blood to the priests,
Ezr 6: 9 and lambs for the burnt offerings **p** to the God of
6:17 And twelve male goats were **p** as a sin offering for
7:11 King Artaxerxes had **p** a copy of this letter to Ezra,
7:16 and the priests that are **p** for the Temple of their
8:25 and the people of Israel had **p** for the Temple of
8:35 They **p** twelve oxen for the people of Israel,
Pr 16:21 and instruction is appreciated if it's well **p**.
Jer 26:11 and prophets **p** their accusations to the officials
Mal 1:13 and mutilated, crippled and sick—**p** as offerings!
Lk 20:41 Then Jesus **p** them with a question. "Why is it,"
Jn 19:35 it is **p** so that you also can believe.
Ac 6: 6 These seven were **p** to the apostles, who prayed for
23:33 they **p** Paul and the letter to Governor Felix.
Ro 15:19 I have fully **p** the Good News of Christ all the way
2Co 2:15 Our lives are a fragrance **p** by Christ to God.
Heb 1: 6 when he **p** his honored Son to the world, God said,

PRESENTING (11) [PRESENT]

Ex 13:13 from the LORD by **p** a lamb in its place.
34:20 from the LORD by **p** a lamb in its place.
Lev 9:22 Then, after **p** the sin offering, the whole burnt
21:21 his physical defects disqualify him from **p**
Nu 9: 7 But why should we be excluded from **p** the
31:50 So we are **p** the items of gold we captured as an
2Ch 29: 7 and **p** burnt offerings at the sanctuary of the God
Ezr 7:15 which we are freely **p** as an offering to the God of
Ps 69:31 an ox / or **p** a bull with its horns and hooves.
Isa 3:13 prosecuting attorney, **p** his case against his people!
Jn 16:13 He will not be **p** his own ideas; he will be telling

PRESENTS (7) [PRESENT]

Ge 24:53 He also gave valuable **p** to her mother and brother.
32:20 Esau with the **p** before meeting him face to face.
32:21 So the **p** were sent on ahead, and Jacob spent that
Lev 7: 9 or cooked on a griddle belongs to the priest who **p**
2Ch 32:23 with valuable **p** for King Hezekiah, too.
Heb 5: 1 He **p** their gifts to God and offers their sacrifices
Rev 11:10 All the people who belong to this world will give **p**

PRESERVE (18) [PRESERVED, PRESERVES, PRESERVING]

Ge 19:32 That way we will **p** our family line through our
45: 5 He sent me here ahead of you to **p** your lives.
48:16 May they **p** my name and the names of my
Dt 25: 7 'My husband's brother refuses to **p** his brother's
1Ki 19:18 Yet I will **p** seven thousand others in Israel who
Ne 9: 6 You **p** and give life to everything, and all the
13:22 and to guard the gates in order to **p** the holiness of
Ps 21: 4 He asked you to **p** his life, / and you have granted
89:29 I will **p** an heir for him; / his throne will be as
138: 7 you will **p** me against the anger of my enemies.
140: 1 evil people. / **P** me from those who are violent,
140: 4 **P** me from those who are violent, / for they are
Isa 65: 9 I will **p** a remnant of the people of Israel and of
Jer 32:14 and put them into a pottery jar to **p** them for a long
39:18 trusted me, I will **p** your life and keep you safe.
49:11 But I will **p** the orphans who remain among you.
50:20 or in Judah, for I will forgive the remnant I **p**.
Gal 2: 5 We wanted to **p** the truth of the Good News for

PRESERVED (7) [PRESERVE]

Ge 19:34 with him. That way our family line will be **p**."
Ex 29:29 "Aaron's sacred garments must be **p** for his
Jos 24:17 the wilderness among our enemies, he **p** us.
2Sa 22:44 You **p** me as the ruler over nations; / people I don't
Job 10:12 your unfailing love. My life was **p** by your care.
Ps 41:12 You have **p** my life because I am innocent;
Mt 9:17 That way both the wine and the wineskins are **p**."

PRESERVES (6) [PRESERVE]

Dt 33:12 them continuously / and **p** them from every harm."
Ps 121: 7 LORD keeps you from all evil / and **p** your life.
Pr 17: 9 Disregarding another person's faults **p** love;
22:12 The LORD **p** knowledge, but he ruins the plans
Jer 10:12 the earth by his power, / and he **p** it by his wisdom.
51:15 the earth by his power, / and he **p** it by his wisdom.

PRESERVING (1) [PRESERVE]

Ps 12: 7 **p** them forever from this lying generation,

PRESIDE (1) [PRESIDED, PRESIDES]

Isa 14:13 I will **p** on the mountain of the gods far away in

PRESIDED (2) [PRESIDE]

1Ki 4: 5 Azariah son of Nathan **p** over the district
Job 29:25 what they should do and **p** over them as their chief.

PRESIDES (3) [PRESIDE]

Ge 1:16 The greater one, the sun, **p** during the day;
1:16 the lesser one, the moon, **p** through the night.
Ps 82: 1 God **p** over heaven's court; / he pronounces

PRESS (6) [PRESSED, PRESSES, PRESSING, PRESSURE, PRESSURES]

Job 24:11 They **p** out olive oil without being allowed to taste
Ps 56: 1 have mercy on me. / The enemy troops **p** in on me.
Hos 6: 3 might know the LORD! Let us **p** on to know him!
Mic 6:15 You will **p** your olives but not get enough oil to
Ac 24: 1 and the lawyer Tertullus, to **p** charges against Paul.
28:19 even though I had no desire to **p** charges against

PRESSED (11) [PRESS]

Ge 18:29 Then Abraham **p** his request further.
Dt 16:13 has been threshed and the grapes have been **p**.
2Sa 13:25 Absalom **p** him, but the king wouldn't come,
Ne 5: 9 Then I **p** further, "What you are doing is not right!
Isa 62: 9 yourselves will drink the wine that you have **p**."
Jer 30: 6 hands **p** against their sides like women about to
Lk 5: 1 great crowds **p** in on him to listen to the word of
6:38 **p** down, shaken together to make room for more,
11:29 As the crowd **p** in on Jesus, he said, "These are
Ac 25:15 and other Jewish leaders **p** charges against him
2Co 4: 8 We are **p** on every side by troubles, but we are not

PRESSES (2) [PRESS]

Jer 48:33 are gone from fruitful Moab. The **p** yield no wine.
Joel 2:24 and the **p** will overflow with wine and olive oil.

PRESSING (6) [PRESS]

2Sa 13:27 But Absalom kept on **p** the king until he finally
Mt 21:33 a wall around it, dug a pit for **p** out the grape juice,
Mk 5:31 said to him, "All this crowd is **p** around you.
12: 1 a wall around it, dug a pit for **p** out the grape juice,
Lk 8:45 "Master, this whole crowd is **p** up against you."
13:22 as he went, always **p** on toward Jerusalem.

PRESSURE (7) [PRESS]

Ge 39:10 She kept putting **p** on him day after day, but he
Ex 3:19 of Egypt will not let you go except under heavy **p**.
Ps 119:143 As **p** and stress bear down on me, / I find joy in
Pr 24:10 If you fail under **p**, your strength is not very great.
Mt 9:17 The old skins would burst from the **p**,
2Co 9: 5 I want it to be a willing gift, not one given under **p**.
9: 7 Don't give reluctantly or in response to **p**. For God

PRESSURES (1) [PRESS]

Ex 18:23 you to do so, then you will be able to endure the **p**,

PRESTIGE (1)

Ac 19:27 all around the world—will be robbed of her **p**!"

PRESUMED (2)

Nu 35:16 it must be **p** to be murder, and the murderer must
35:18 It must be **p** to be murder, and the murderer must

PRETEND (14) [PRETENDED, PRETENDING, PRETENDS, PRETENSE]

Ge 43:18 they said. "He plans to **p** that we stole it.
Dt 22: 1 or sheep wandering away, don't **p** not to see it.
22: 3 your neighbor loses. Don't **p** you did not see it.
2Sa 13: 5 you what to do. Go back to bed and **p** you are sick.
14: 2 He said to her, "**P** you are in mourning;
Ps 50:16 my laws no longer, / and don't **p** that you obey me.
69: 8 Even my own brothers **p** they don't know me;
Pr 13: 7 Some who are poor **p** to be rich; others who are rich **p** to be poor.
26:25 Though they **p** to be kind, their hearts are full of all
Ac 23:15 "**P** you want to examine his case more fully.
Ro 12: 9 Don't just **p** that you love others. Really love them.
1Ti 4: 2 They **p** to be religious, but their consciences are
1Pe 2: 1 and deceit. Don't just **p** to be good!

PRETENDED (7) [PRETEND]

Ge 42: 7 them instantly, but he **p** to be a stranger.
1Sa 21:13 So he **p** to be insane, scratching on doors
2Sa 13: 6 So Amnon **p** to be sick. And when the king came
1Ki 2: 5 He **p** that it was an act of war, but it was done in a
Ps 34: T regarding the time he **p** to be insane in front of
Jer 3:10 She has only **p** to be sorry," says the LORD.
Ac 5:36 that fellow Theudas, who **p** to be someone great.

PRETENDING (8) [PRETEND]

1Ki 14: 5 wife will come here, **p** to be someone else.
14: 6 Why are you **p** to be someone else?" Then he told
Eze 33:31 So they come **p** to be sincere and sit before you
Lk 20:20 the leaders sent secret agents **p** to be honest men.
Ac 9:26 They thought he was only **p** to be a believer!
23:20 **p** they want to get some more information.
2Co 11:15 So it is no wonder his servants can also do it by **p**
1Th 2: 5 And God is our witness that we were not just **p** to

PRETENDS (2) [PRETEND]

Jer 29:27 from Anathoth, who **p** to be a prophet among you?
Gal 1: 7 that **p** to be the Good News but is not the Good

PRETENSE (2) [PRETEND]

Hos 4:15 Their worship is mere **p** as they take oaths in the
Am 5:21 "I hate all your show and **p**—the hypocrisy of

PRETTY (5)

Ge 29:17 Leah had **p** eyes, but Rachel was beautiful in every

Pr 7:21 So she seduced him with her **p** speech. With her
26:23 just as a **p** glaze covers a common clay pot.
Isa 3:12 They are leading you down a **p** garden path to
32:11 Strip off your **p** clothes, and wear sackcloth in

PREVAIL (6) [PREVAILED, PREVAILS]

Dt 16:20 Let true justice **p**, so you may live and occupy the
2Ch 14:11 are our God; do not let mere men **p** against you!"
Pr 19:21 many plans, but the LORD's purpose will **p**.
Isa 3:4 children to rule over them, and anarchy will **p**.
42:4 and righteousness **p** throughout the earth.
Eze 30:13 left in Egypt; anarchy will **p** throughout the land!

PREVAILED (2) [PREVAIL]

Ge 7:17 For forty days the floods **p**, covering the ground
Lk 23:23 and louder for Jesus' death, and their voices **p**.

PREVAILS (1) [PREVAIL]

Isa 24:16 I am discouraged, for evil still **p**, and treachery is

PREVENT (11) [PREVENTED, PREVENTING, PREVENTS]

Nu 17:10 complaints against me and **p** any further deaths."
Dt 17:20 This regular reading will **p** him from becoming
17:20 It will also **p** him from turning away from these
19:10 That way you will **p** the death of innocent people
1Ki 15:17 and fortified Ramah in order to **p** anyone from
2Ki 23:33 of Hamath to **p** him from ruling from Jerusalem.
2Ch 16:1 and fortified Ramah in order to **p** anyone from
Job 36:21 for it was to **p** you from getting into a life of evil
Ecc 8:8 None of us has the power to **p** the day of our death.
Mt 27:64 This will **p** his disciples from coming and stealing
Lk 11:52 and you **p** others from entering."

PREVENTED (4) [PREVENT]

2Sa 21:10 She **p** vultures from tearing at their bodies during
Ezr 5:5 the leaders of the Jews were not **p** from building
Ro 1:13 many times to visit you, but I was **p** until now.
1Th 2:18 and I, Paul, tried again and again, but Satan **p** us.

PREVENTING (1) [PREVENT]

Jdg 3:28 River across from Moab, **p** anyone from crossing.

PREVENTS (2) [PREVENT]

Job 34:30 He **p** the godless from ruling so they cannot be a
Lk 8:12 and **p** them from believing and being saved.

PREVIOUS (17) [PREVIOUSLY]

Ge 31:24 But the **p** night God had appeared to Laban in a
Lev 25:22 you will still be eating the produce of the **p** year.
26:10 the **p** year to make room for each new harvest.
Nu 26:64 in the **p** census taken in the wilderness of Sinai.
Dt 4:42 without having any **p** hostility could flee for safety.
19:4 kills a neighbor without harboring any **p** hatred,
Jdg 20:22 at the same place they had fought the **p** day.
1Sa 9:15 Now the LORD had told Samuel the **p** day,
2Ki 12:18 Jehoram, and Ahaziah, the **p** kings of Judah,
23:5 who had been appointed by the **p** kings of Judah,
Eze 3:20 Their **p** good deeds won't help them, and I will
18:24 All their **p** goodness will be forgotten, and they
33:22 The **p** evening the LORD had taken hold of me
Da 2:40 That kingdom will smash and crush all **p** empires,
Mk 11:21 what Jesus had said to the tree on the **p** day
Eph 3:5 God did not reveal it to **p** generations, but now he
1Ti 5:12 Then they would be guilty of breaking their **p**

PREVIOUSLY (11) [PREVIOUS]

Lev 9:15 their sin offering, just as he had done **p** for himself.
Dt 8:3 a food **p** unknown to you and your ancestors.
Jos 13:8 of the LORD, had **p** assigned this land to them.
14:15 (**P** Hebron had been called Kiriath-arba. It had
18:11 It lay between the territory **p** assigned to the tribes
Ne 13:5 The room had **p** been used for storing the grain
Isa 49:9 in green pastures and on hills that were **p** bare.
52:15 For they will see what they had not **p** been told
Jn 4:44 He had **p** said, "A prophet is honored everywhere
Ac 7:35 so God sent back the same man his people had **p**
15:36 "Let's return to each city where we **p** preached the

PREY (27)

Ge 49:9 is a young lion / that has finished eating its **p**.
Nu 14:9 They are only helpless **p** to us! They have no
23:24 They refuse to rest / until they have feasted on **p**,
2Ki 19:26 so little power / and are such easy **p** for you.
Job 9:26 swift boat, like an eagle that swoops down on its **p**.
28:7 treasures that no bird of **p** can see, no falcon's eye
38:39 "Can you stalk **p** for a lioness and satisfy the
39:29 From there it hunts its **p**, keeping watch with
Ps 22:13 Like roaring lions attacking their **p**, / they come at
57:4 who greedily devour human **p**— / whose teeth
Isa 5:29 Roaring like lions, they will pounce on their **p**.
37:27 so little power / and are such easy **p** for you.
46:11 I will call a swift bird of **p** from the east—a leader
Jer 2:30 have killed your prophets as a lion kills its **p**.
25:38 He has left his den like a lion seeking its **p**,
Eze 19:3 He learned to catch and devour **p**, / and he became
19:6 He learned to catch and devour **p**, / and he,
22:25 princes plot conspiracies just as lions stalk their **p**.
26:5 Tyre will become the **p** of many nations,
34:5 a shepherd. They are easy **p** for any wild animal.
34:10 their mouths; the sheep will no longer be their **p**.
34:28 They will no longer be **p** for other nations,
Hos 5:14 tear at Israel and Judah as a lion rips apart its **p**.
Am 3:4 lion growl in its den without first catching its **p**?
Hab 1:8 Like eagles they swoop down to pounce on their **p**.
3:14 like a whirlwind, thinking Israel would be easy **p**.
Zep 3:3 who by dawn have left no trace of their **p**.

PRICE (25) [PRICELESS, PRICES]

Ge 23:9 I want to pay the full **p**, of course, whatever is
23:13 Let me pay the full **p** for the field so I can bury my
Lev 25:15 the **p** of the land should be based on the number of
25:16 The more the years, the higher the **p**; the fewer the years, the lower the **p**.
25:27 The **p** of the land will be based on the number of
25:50 The **p** of their freedom will be based on the
Nu 3:48 and his sons as the redemption **p** for the extra
18:16 The redemption **p** is five pieces of silver,
1Sa 18:23 afford the bride **p** for the daughter of a king?"
18:25 "Tell David that all I want for the bride **p** is one
1Ki 10:28 acquired them from Cilicia at the standard **p**.
1Ch 21:22 me buy this threshing floor from you at its full **p**.
2Ch 1:16 acquired them from Cilicia at the standard **p**.
Job 28:18 to get it. The **p** of wisdom is far above pearls.
Pr 20:14 The buyer haggles over the **p**, saying,
27:26 and your goats will be sold for the **p** of a field.
Isa 44:22 return to me, for I have paid the **p** to set you free."
Mic 3:11 can get; you priests teach God's laws only for a **p**;
Mt 27:9 the **p** at which he was valued by the people of
Lk 12:6 "What is the **p** of five sparrows? A couple of
Ac 5:8 "Was this the **p** you and your husband received for your land?" "Yes," she replied, "that was the **p**."
1Co 6:20 for God bought you with a high **p**. So you must
7:23 God purchased you at a high **p**. Don't be enslaved

PRICELESS (3) [PRICE]

Da 11:8 idols with him, along with **p** gold and silver dishes.
Php 3:8 with the **p** gain of knowing Christ Jesus my Lord.
1Pe 1:4 For God has reserved a **p** inheritance for his

PRICES (1) [PRICE]

Pr 11:26 curse those who hold their grain for higher **p**,

PRICK (1)

Eze 28:24 Israel's scornful neighbors **p** and tear at her

PRICKS [KJV] See SPLINTERS, FIGHT (AGAINST)

PRIDE (62) [PROUD]

1Sa 17:28 I know about your **p** and dishonesty. You just want
2Sa 1:19 Your **p** and joy, O Israel, lies dead on the hills!
2Ch 32:26 Then Hezekiah repented of his **p**, and the people of
Job 20:6 Though the godless man's **p** reaches to the heavens
33:17 them to change their minds; he keeps them from **p**.
35:12 and God does not answer, it is because of their **p**.
Ps 59:12 is on their lips, / let them be captured by their **p**,
73:6 They wear **p** like a jeweled necklace, / and their
73:8 only evil; / in their **p** they seek to crush others.
101:5 their neighbors. / I will not endure conceit and **p**.
105:36 Egyptian home, / the **p** and joy of each family.
Pr 6:3 Now swallow your **p**; go and beg to have your
8:13 That is why I hate **p**, arrogance, corruption,
11:2 **P** leads to disgrace, but with humility comes
13:10 **P** leads to arguments; those who take advice are
16:5 The LORD despises **p**; be assured that the proud
16:18 **P** goes before destruction, and haughtiness before
17:6 of the aged; parents are the **p** of their children.
29:23 **P** ends in humiliation, while humility brings honor.
Ecc 7:8 is better than starting. Patience is better than **p**.
Isa 2:11 The day is coming when your **p** will be brought
2:17 Their **p** will lie in the dust. The LORD alone will
4:2 and the fruit of the land will be the **p** of its people.
9:9 soon discover it. In their **p** and arrogance they say,
16:6 much about? Its **p** and insolence are all gone now!
23:9 LORD Almighty has done it to destroy your **p**
25:11 He will end their **p** and all their evil works.
28:1 the **p** and joy of the drunkards of Israel!
28:1 that city—the **p** of a people brought low by wine.
28:3 the **p** and joy of the drunkards of Israel—
28:5 He will be the **p** and joy of the remnant of his
Jer 13:9 This illustrates how I will rot away the **p** of Judah
13:11 "They were to be my people, my **p**, my glory—
13:17 to listen, I will weep alone because of your **p**.
48:29 We have heard of the **p** of Moab, for it is very
50:32 O land of **p**, you will stumble and fall, and no one
Eze 7:10 people's wickedness and **p** have reached a climax.
16:49 Sodom's sins were **p**, laziness, and gluttony,
24:21 my Temple, the source of your security and **p**.
28:2 In your great **p** you claim, 'I am a god! I sit on a
28:17 Your heart was filled with **p** because of all your
30:6 allies will fall, and the **p** of their power will end.
32:12 They will shatter the **p** of Egypt, and all its hordes
33:28 I will destroy the land and demolish her **p**.
Da 5:20 when his heart and mind were hardened with **p**,
11:12 the king of the south will be filled with **p** and will
Am 6:8 "I despise the **p** and false glory of Israel, and I
8:7 sworn this oath by his own name, the **P** of Israel:
Zep 2:10 They will receive the wages of their **p**, for they
3:11 There will be no **p** on my holy mountain.
Zec 9:6 Thus, I will destroy the **p** of the Philistines.
10:11 The **p** of Assyria will be crushed, and the rule of
Mk 7:22 lustful pleasure, envy, slander, **p**, and foolishness.
Ro 4:2 point of view Abraham had no basis at all for **p**.
1Co 3:21 So don't take **p** in following a particular leader.
11:15 And isn't it obvious that long hair is a woman's **p**
15:31 This is as certain as my **p** in what the Lord Jesus
2Co 7:4 confidence in you, and my **p** in you is great.
1Th 2:20 For you are our **p** and joy.
1Ti 3:6 and the Devil will use that **p** to make him fall.
2Ti 3:4 their friends, be reckless, be puffed up with **p**,
1Jn 2:16 for everything we see, and **p** in our possessions.

PRIEST (466) [PRIEST'S, PRIESTHOOD, PRIESTLY, PRIESTS, PRIESTS']

AARON THE PRIEST (17) Ex 31:10; 38:21; 39:41; Lev 1:7; 13:2; Nu 3:6; 4:16,28,33; 7:8; 16:37; 18:28; 25:7,11; 26:1; 33:38; Jos 21:13

CHIEF PRIEST (2) 2Ki 25:18; Jer 52:24

ELEAZAR THE PRIEST (29) Nu 3:32; 16:39; 19:3,6; 26:3,63; 27:2,19,21,22; 31:6,12,13,21,26,29,31,41,51,54; 32:2; 34:17; Jos 14:1; 17:4; 19:51; 21:1; 22:13,31,32

EZRA THE PRIEST (6) Ezr 7:11,12; 10:10; Ne 8:2,9; 12:26

HIGH PRIEST (90) Ex 29:30; Lev 4:3,21; 16:32; 21:10,13; Nu 35:25,28,28,32; Dt 10:6; Jos 20:6; 2Ki 12:10; 22:4,8; 23:4; 1Ch 6:10; 2Ch 19:11; 24:6,11; 26:17; 31:10; 34:9,14; Ezr 7:5; Ne 3:1,20; 12:10,12; 13:28; Hag 1:1,12,14; 2:2,4; Zec 3:1,8; 6:11; Mt 26:3,57,62,63,65; Mk 2:26; 14:60,61,63,66; Jn 11:49,51; 18:13,15,19,22,24,26; Ac 4:6,6; 5:17,21,28; 7:1; 9:1; 22:5; 23:2,4,5; 24:1; Heb 2:17; 3:1; 4:14,15; 5:1,4,5,9,10; 6:20; 7:26; 8:1,3,3,6; 9:7,11,25; 10:12,21; 13:11

JEHOIADA THE PRIEST (18) 2Ki 11:4,9,9,15,18; 12:2,9; 1Ch 27:5; 2Ch 22:11; 23:1,8,8,14; 24:2,14,20,25; Jer 29:26

ZADOK THE PRIEST (11) 2Sa 15:27; 1Ki 1:8,26,32,34,38,39,44; 2:35; 1Ch 16:39; 24:6

Ge 14:18 the king of Salem and a **p** of God Most High,
41:45 the daughter of Potiphera, **p** of Heliopolis.
41:50 the daughter of Potiphera, **p** of Heliopolis.
46:20 daughter of Potiphera, **p** of Heliopolis.
Ex 2:16 Now it happened that the **p** of Midian had seven
3:1 Jethro, the **p** of Midian, and he went deep into the
18:1 the **p** of Midian and Moses' father-in-law,
28:3 from everyone else, so he may serve me as a **p**.
29:30 Whoever is the next high **p** after Aaron will wear
30:33 or puts any of it on someone who is not a **p** will be
31:10 beautifully stitched, holy garments for Aaron the **p**,
38:21 and Ithamar son of Aaron the **p** served as recorder.
39:41 the holy garments for Aaron the **p** and for his sons
40:13 anoint him, setting him apart to serve me as a **p**.
Lev 1:7 the sons of Aaron the **p** will build a wood fire on
1:15 The **p** will take the bird to the altar, twist off its
1:16 The **p** must remove the crop and the feathers
1:17 the **p** will tear the bird apart, though not
3:11 The **p** will burn them on the altar as food,
3:16 The **p** will burn them on the altar as food,
4:3 "If the high **p** sins, bringing guilt upon the entire
4:5 The **p** on duty will then take some of the animal's
4:7 The **p** will put some of the blood on the horns of
4:8 The **p** must remove all the fat around the bull's
4:16 The **p** will bring some of its blood into the
4:19 The **p** must remove all the animal's fat and burn it
4:20 same procedure as with the sin offering for the **p**.
4:20 this way, the **p** will make atonement for the people,
4:21 The **p** must then take what is left of the bull
4:21 just as is done with the sin offering for the high **p**.
4:25 Then the **p** will dip his finger into the blood of the
4:26 the **p** will make atonement for the leader's sin,
4:30 The **p** will then dip his finger into the blood,
4:31 Then the **p** will burn the fat on the altar, and it will
4:31 In this way, the **p** will make atonement for them,
4:34 The **p** will then dip his finger into the blood,
4:35 Then the **p** will burn the fat on the altar on top of
4:35 In this way, the **p** will make atonement for them,
5:6 their sin, and the **p** will make atonement for them.
5:8 They must bring them to the **p**, who will offer one
5:8 The **p** will wring its neck but without severing its
5:10 The **p** will offer the second bird as a whole burnt
5:10 the **p** will make atonement for those who are
5:12 They must take the flour to the **p**, who will scoop
5:13 the **p** will make atonement for those who are
5:13 The rest of the flour will belong to the **p**, just as
5:16 When they give their payments to the **p**, he will
5:18 they must bring to the **p** a ram from the flock as a
5:18 the **p** will make atonement for those who are
6:6 They must then bring a guilt offering to the **p**,
6:7 The **p** will then make atonement for them before
6:10 the **p** on duty must clean out the ashes of the burnt
6:12 Each morning the **p** will add fresh wood to the fire
6:15 The **p** on duty will take a handful of the choice
6:26 The **p** who offers the sacrifice may eat his portion
7:3 The **p** will then offer all its fat on the altar,
7:7 the meat of the sacrificed animal belongs to the **p**
7:8 hide of the sacrificed animal also belongs to the **p**.
7:9 or cooked on a griddle belongs to the **p** who
7:14 then belong to the **p** who sprinkles the altar with
7:31 Then the **p** will burn the fat on the altar,
7:32 right thigh of your peace offering to the **p** as a gift.
7:33 The right thigh must always be given to the **p** who
12:6 She must take her offerings to the **p** at the entrance
12:7 The **p** will then present them to the LORD
12:8 The **p** will sacrifice them, thus making atonement
13:2 they must be brought to Aaron the **p** or to one of
13:3 The **p** will then examine the affected area of a
13:3 and the **p** must pronounce the person ceremonially
13:4 the **p** will put the infected person in quarantine for
13:5 On the seventh day the **p** will make another
13:5 then the **p** will put the person in quarantine for

13: 6 The **p** will examine the skin again on the seventh
13: 6 the **p** will pronounce the person ceremonially
13: 7 this examination and pronouncement by the **p**,
13: 8 If the **p** notices that the rash has spread, then he
13: 9 skin disease must go to the **p** for an examination.
13:10 If the **p** sees that some hair has turned white
13:11 and the **p** must pronounce that person ceremonially
13:12 "Now suppose the **p** discovers after his
13:13 the **p** must examine the infected person to see if
13:15 The **p** must make this pronouncement as soon as
13:16 the rest of the skin, the person must return to the **p**.
13:17 then the **p** will pronounce the person ceremonially
13:19 that person must go to the **p** to be examined.
13:20 If the **p** finds the disease to be more than
13:20 then the **p** must pronounce that person
13:21 But if the **p** sees that there is no white hair in the
13:21 then the **p** is to put the person in quarantine for
13:22 the **p** must pronounce the person ceremonially
13:23 and the **p** will pronounce that person ceremonially
13:25 then the **p** must examine it. If the hair in the
13:25 The **p** must then pronounce that person
13:26 But if the **p** discovers that there is no white hair in
13:26 then the **p** is to put the infected person in
13:27 the **p** must pronounce that person ceremonially
13:28 The **p** must then pronounce the person
13:30 the **p** must examine the infection. If it appears to
13:30 the **p** must pronounce the infected person
13:33 Then the **p** must put the person in quarantine for
13:34 the **p** must pronounce that person ceremonially
13:36 the **p** must do another examination. If the infection
13:37 The **p** will then pronounce the infected person
13:39 the **p** must examine the affected area. If the patch
13:43 The **p** must examine him, and if he finds swelling
13:44 The **p** must pronounce him ceremonially unclean
13:49 and must be taken to the **p** to be examined.
13:50 affected spot, the **p** will put it away for seven days.
13:51 On the seventh day the **p** must inspect it again.
13:52 The **p** must burn the linen or wool clothing
13:53 "But if the **p** examines it again and the affected
13:54 the **p** will order the contaminated object to be
13:55 Then the **p** must inspect the object again. If he sees
13:56 But if the **p** sees that the affected area has faded
13:59 This is how the **p** will determine whether these
14: 2 who have been healed must be brought to the **p**,
14: 3 If the **p** finds that someone has been healed of the
14: 5 The **p** will order one of the birds to be slaughtered
14: 7 The **p** will also sprinkle the dead bird's blood
14: 7 and the **p** will pronounce that person to be
14: 7 the **p** will set the living bird free so it can fly away
14:11 Then the officiating **p** will present that person for
14:12 The **p** will take one of the lambs and the olive oil
14:13 the guilt offering will be given to the **p**.
14:14 The **p** will then take some of the blood from the
14:15 "Then the **p** will pour some of the olive oil into
14:17 The **p** will then put some of the oil remaining in
14:18 the **p** will make atonement before the LORD for
14:19 "Then the **p** must offer the sin offering and again
14:19 the **p** will slaughter the whole burnt offering
14:20 the **p** will make atonement for the person being
14:23 **p** for the cleansing ceremony to be performed in
14:24 The **p** will take the lamb for the guilt offering,
14:25 Then the **p** will slaughter the lamb for the guilt
14:26 "The **p** will also pour some of the olive oil into the
14:28 The **p** will then put some of the olive oil from his
14:29 the **p** will make atonement for the person being
14:30 "Then the **p** will offer the two turtledoves
14:31 the **p** will make atonement before the LORD for
14:35 of such a house must then go to the **p** and say,
14:36 Before the **p** examines the house, he must have the
14:36 Then the **p** will go in and inspect the house.
14:39 On the seventh day the **p** must return for another
14:40 the **p** must order that the stones from those areas
14:44 the **p** must return and inspect the house again.
14:48 "But if the **p** returns for his inspection and finds
14:49 To purify the house the **p** will need two birds,
14:53 this way, the **p** will make atonement for the house,
15:14 of the Tabernacle and give his offerings to the **p**.
15:15 The **p** will present the offerings there, one for a sin
15:15 the **p** will make atonement for the man before the
15:29 and present them to the **p** at the entrance of the
15:30 The **p** will offer one for a sin offering and the other
15:30 the **p** will make atonement for her before the
16:32 high **p** who serves in place of his ancestor Aaron.
17: 5 It will cause them to bring their sacrifices to the **p**
17: 6 That way the **p** will be able to sprinkle the blood
19:22 The **p** will then make atonement for him before the
21:10 "The high **p**, who has had the anointing oil poured
21:13 "The high **p** must marry a virgin.
22:11 However, if the **p** buys slaves with his own money,
22:14 realizing it must pay the **p** for the amount eaten,
22:16 The negligent **p** would bring guilt upon the people
23:10 bring the **p** some grain from the first portion of
23:11 the **p** will lift it up before the LORD so it may be
23:20 "The **p** will lift up these offerings before the
27: 8 go to the **p** and he will evaluate your ability to pay.
27: 8 You will then pay the amount decided by the **p**.
27:11 then you must bring the animal to the **p**.
27:13 you must pay the value set by the **p**, plus 20
27:14 to the LORD, the **p** must come to assess its value.
27:15 you must pay the value set by the **p**, plus 20
27:18 the **p** must assess the land's value in proportion to
27:19 you must pay the land's value as assessed by the **p**,
27:23 the **p** must assess its value based on the years until
27:27 the **p** may sell it to someone else for its assessed
Nu 3: 6 and present them to Aaron the **p** as his assistants.
3:32 Eleazar the **p**, Aaron's son, was the chief
3:38 Anyone other than a **p** or Levite who came too
4:16 "Eleazar son of Aaron the **p** will be responsible
4:28 directly responsible to Ithamar son of Aaron the **p**.
4:33 responsible to Ithamar son of Aaron the **p**."
5: 8 belongs to the LORD and must be given to the **p**,
5: 9 All the sacred gifts that the Israelites bring to a **p**
5:10 Each **p** may keep the sacred donations that he
5:15 the husband must bring his wife to the **p** with an
5:16 " 'The **p** must then present her before the
5:18 The **p** will stand before her, holding the jar of
5:19 The **p** will put the woman under oath and say to
5:21 at this point the **p** must put the woman under this
5:23 Then the **p** will write these curses on a piece of
5:25 " 'Then the **p** will take the jealousy offering from
5:30 and the **p** will apply this entire ritual law to her.
6:10 or two young pigeons to the **p** at the entrance of
6:11 The **p** will offer one of the birds for a sin offering
6:16 The **p** will present these offerings before the
6:17 The **p** must also make the prescribed grain offering
6:19 the **p** will take for each of them the boiled shoulder
6:20 The **p** will then lift the gifts up before the LORD
6:20 These are holy portions for the **p**, along with the
7: 8 under the leadership of Ithamar son of Aaron the **p**.
15:25 With it the **p** will make atonement for the whole
15:28 The **p** will make atonement for the guilty person
16:37 "Tell Eleazar son of Aaron the **p** to pull all the
16:39 So Eleazar the **p** collected the 250 bronze incense
18:28 must present the LORD's portion to Aaron the **p**.
19: 3 Give it to Eleazar the **p**, and it will be taken
19: 6 Eleazar the **p** must then take cedarwood, a hyssop
19: 7 "Then the **p** must wash his clothes and bathe
25: 7 of Eleazar and grandson of Aaron the **p** saw this,
25:11 and grandson of Aaron the **p** has turned my anger
26: 1 said to Moses and to Eleazar son of Aaron, the **p**,
26: 3 and Eleazar the **p** issued these census instructions
26:63 and Eleazar the **p** on the plains of Moab beside the
27: 2 before Moses, Eleazar the **p**, the tribal leaders,
27:19 Present him to Eleazar the **p** before the whole
27:21 is needed, Joshua will stand before Eleazar the **p**,
27:22 and presented Joshua to Eleazar the **p**
31: 6 and Phinehas son of Eleazar the **p** led them into
31:12 they brought them all to Moses and Eleazar the **p**,
31:13 Moses, Eleazar the **p**, and all the leaders of the
31:21 Then Eleazar the **p** said to the men who were in the
31:26 "You and Eleazar the **p** and the family leaders of
31:29 Give this share of their half to Eleazar the **p** as an
31:31 and Eleazar the **p** did as the LORD commanded
31:41 gave all the LORD's share to Eleazar the **p**,
31:51 and Eleazar the **p** received the gold from all the
31:54 and Eleazar the **p** accepted the gifts from the
32: 2 they came to Moses, Eleazar the **p**, and the other
33:38 Aaron the **p** was directed by the LORD to go up
34:17 the people: Eleazar the **p** and Joshua son of Nun.
35:25 live in a city of refuge until the death of the high **p**.
35:28 the city of refuge until the death of the high **p**.
35:28 But after the death of the high **p**, the slayer may
35:32 to his property before the death of the high **p**.
Dt 10: 6 His son Eleazar became the high **p** in his place.
17:12 or of the **p** who represents the LORD your God
20: 2 the **p** will come forward to speak with the troops.
26: 3 Go to the **p** in charge at that time and say to him,
26: 4 The **p** will then take the basket from your hand
Jos 14: 1 land in Canaan as allotted by Eleazar the **p**,
17: 4 These women came to Eleazar the **p**, Joshua son of
19:51 These are the territories that Eleazar the **p**,
20: 6 **p** who was in office at the time of the accident.
21: 1 tribe of Levi came to consult with Eleazar the **p**,
21:13 were given to the descendants of Aaron the **p**:
22:13 a delegation led by Phinehas son of Eleazar, the **p**.
22:30 When Phinehas the **p** and the high officials heard
22:31 Phinehas son of Eleazar, the **p**, replied to them,
22:32 Then Phinehas son of Eleazar, the **p**, and the ten
Jdg 17: 5 Then he installed one of his sons as the **p**.
17:10 Micah said, "and you can be a father and **p** to me.
17:12 So Micah ordained the Levite as his personal **p**,
17:13 "because I have a Levite serving as my **p**."
18: 4 with Micah and that he was Micah's personal **p**.
18: 6 "Go in peace," the **p** replied. "For the LORD
18:18 When the **p** saw the men carrying all the sacred
18:19 with us," they said. "Be a father and **p** to all of us.
18:19 Isn't it better to be a **p** for an entire tribe of Israel
18:20 The young **p** was quite happy to go with them,
18:24 "You've taken away all my gods and my **p**,
18:27 Then, with Micah's idols and his **p**, the men of
18:30 son of Gershom, a descendant of Moses, as their **p**.
20:28 son of Eleazar and grandson of Aaron was the **p**.)
1Sa 1: 9 Eli the **p** was sitting at his customary place beside
2:11 the LORD's helper, for he assisted Eli the **p**.
2:18 He wore a linen tunic just like that of a **p**.
2:28 Aaron from among all his relatives to be my **p**,
2:35 "Then I will raise up a faithful **p** who will serve
14: 3 (Among Saul's men was Ahijah the **p**, who was
14: 3 the **p** of the LORD who had served at Shiloh.)
14:19 But while Saul was talking to the **p**, the shouting
14:36 is best." But the **p** said, "Let's ask God first."
21: 1 went to the town of Nob to see Ahimelech the **p**.
21: 4 "We don't have any regular bread," the **p** replied.
21: 6 food available, the **p** gave him the holy bread—
21: 9 you killed in the valley of Elah," the **p** replied.
22: 9 he said, "I saw David talking to Ahimelech the **p**.
23: 6 Abiathar the **p** went to Keilah with David,
23: 9 and told Abiathar the **p** to bring the ephod
30: 7 Then he said to Abiathar the **p**, "Bring me the
2Sa 15:27 Then the king told Zadok the **p**, "Look, here is my
20:26 Ira the Jairite was David's personal **p**.
1Ki 1: 7 of Zeruiah and Abiathar the **p** into his confidence,
1: 8 and refused to support Adonijah were Zadok the **p**,
1:19 invited all your sons and Abiathar the **p** and Joab,
1:25 the commander of the army, and Abiathar the **p**.
1:26 neither were Zadok the **p**, Benaiah son of Jehoiada,
1:32 "Call Zadok the **p**, Nathan the prophet,
1:34 There Zadok the **p** and Nathan the prophet are to
1:38 So Zadok the **p**, Nathan the prophet, Benaiah son
1:39 There Zadok the **p** took a flask of olive oil from
1:42 Jonathan son of Abiathar the **p** arrived.
1:44 sent him down to Gihon Spring with Zadok the **p**,
2:22 and that he has Abiathar the **p** and Joab son of
2:26 Then the king said to Abiathar the **p**, "Go back to
2:27 Abiathar from his position as **p** of the LORD,
2:35 and he installed Zadok the **p** to take the place of
4: 2 high officials: / Azariah son of Zadok was the **p**.
4: 5 Zabud son of Nathan, a **p**, was a trusted adviser to
13:33 Anyone who wanted to could become a **p** for the
2Ki 11: 4 Jehoiada the **p** summoned the commanders,
11: 9 did everything just as Jehoiada the **p** ordered.
11: 9 off duty. They brought them all to Jehoiada the **p**,
11:15 Then Jehoiada the **p** ordered the commanders who
11:18 and they killed Mattan the **p** of Baal in front of the
11:18 Jehoiada the **p** stationed guards at the Temple of
12: 2 because Jehoiada the **p** instructed him.
12: 9 Then Jehoiada the **p** bored a hole in the lid of a
12:10 and the high **p** counted the money that had been
16:10 So he sent a model of the altar to Uriah the **p**,
16:15 He said to Uriah the **p**, "Use the new altar for the
16:16 Uriah the **p** did just as King Ahaz instructed him.
22: 4 "Go up to Hilkiah the high **p** and have him count
22: 8 Hilkiah the high **p** said to Shaphan the court
22:10 to the king, "Hilkiah the **p** has given me a scroll."
22:12 Then he gave these orders to Hilkiah the **p**,
22:14 So Hilkiah the **p**, Ahikam, Acbor, Shaphan,
23: 4 Then the king instructed Hilkiah the high **p**
23:24 Hilkiah the **p** had found in the LORD's Temple.
25:18 took with him as prisoners Seraiah the chief **p**,
1Ch 6:10 the high **p** at the Temple built by Solomon in
16:39 David stationed Zadok the **p** and his fellow priests
24: 6 Zadok the **p**, Ahimelech son of Abiathar,
27: 5 Benaiah son of Jehoiada the **p** was commander of
29:22 as their leader, and they anointed Zadok as their **p**.
2Ch 13: 9 You let anyone become a **p** these days!
13: 9 and seven rams can become a **p** of these so-called
15: 3 without a **p** to teach them, and without God's law.
19:11 "Amariah the high **p** will have final say in all
22:11 In this way, Jehosheba, the wife of Jehoiada the **p**,
23: 1 of Athaliah's reign, Jehoiada the **p** decided to act.
23: 8 did everything just as Jehoiada the **p** ordered.
23: 8 Jehoiada the **p** did not let anyone go home after
23:14 Then Jehoiada the **p** ordered the commanders who
23:17 and they killed Mattan the **p** of Baal in front of the
24: 2 sight throughout the lifetime of Jehoiada the **p**.
24: 6 So the king called for Jehoiada the high **p**
24:11 and an officer of the high **p** counted the money
24:14 the LORD during the lifetime of Jehoiada the **p**.
24:20 God came upon Zechariah son of Jehoiada the **p**.
24:25 to kill him for murdering the son of Jehoiada the **p**.
26:17 Azariah the high **p** went in after him with eighty
31:10 And Azariah the high **p**, from the family of Zadok,
34: 9 They gave Hilkiah the high **p** the money that had
34:14 As Hilkiah the high **p** was recording the money
34:18 to the king, "Hilkiah the **p** has given me a scroll."
Ezr 2:63 **p** who could consult the LORD about the matter
7: 5 son of Eleazar, son of Aaron the high **p**.
7:11 the **p** and scribe who studied and taught the
7:12 from Artaxerxes, the king of kings, to Ezra the **p**,
7:21 for he is a **p** and teacher of the law of the God of
7:24 I also decree that no **p**, Levite, singer, gatekeeper,
8:33 and entrusted to Meremoth son of Uriah the **p**
10:10 Then Ezra the **p** stood and said to them:
Ne 3: 1 Then Eliashib the high **p** and the other priests
3:20 to the door of the home of Eliashib the high **p**.
7:65 **p** who could consult the LORD about the matter
8: 2 So on October 8 Ezra the **p** brought the scroll of
8: 9 Nehemiah the governor, Ezra the **p** and scribe,
10:38 A **p**—a descendant of Aaron—will be with the
12: 1 Zerubbabel son of Shealtiel and Jeshua the high **p**:
12:10 Jeshua the high **p** was the father of Joiakim.
12:12 Now when Joiakim was high **p**, the family leaders
12:26 the governor and of Ezra the **p** and scribe.
13: 4 Before this had happened, Eliashib the **p**, who had
13:13 I put Shelemiah the **p**, Zadok the scribe,
13:28 **p** had married a daughter of Sanballat the
Ps 106:16 and envious of Aaron, the LORD's holy **p**.
110: 4 "You are a **p** forever in the line of Melchizedek."
Isa 8: 2 I asked Uriah the **p** and Zechariah son of
Jer 20: 1 the **p** in charge of the Temple of the LORD,
21: 1 son of Maaseiah, the **p**, to speak with him.
23:34 If any prophet, **p**, or anyone else says, 'I have a
29:25 the **p**, and you sent copies to the other priests
29:26 as the **p** in charge of the house of the LORD.
29:29 But when Zephaniah the **p** received Shemaiah's
37: 3 Jehucal son of Shelemiah and Zephaniah the **p**,
52:24 took with him as prisoners Seraiah the chief **p**,
Eze 1: 3 gave a message to me, Ezekiel son of Buzi, a **p**,
44:25 A **p** must never defile himself by being in the
44:26 But such a **p** can only return to his Temple duties
45:19 The **p** will take some of the blood of this sin
46: 2 Then he will stand by the gatepost while the **p**
Am 7:10 But when Amaziah, the **p** of Bethel, heard what
Hag 1: 1 and to Jeshua son of Jehozadak, the high **p**.
1:12 of Shealtiel, Jeshua son of Jehozadak, the high **p**,
1:14 of Judah, Jeshua son of Jehozadak, the high **p**,
2: 2 and to Jeshua son of Jehozadak, the high **p**,
2: 4 Take courage, Jeshua son of Jehozadak, the high **p**.
Zec 3: 1 Then the angel showed me Jeshua the high **p**
3: 8 Listen to me, O Jeshua the high **p**, and all you
6:11 on the head of Jeshua son of Jehozadak, the high **p**.

6:13 He will also serve as **p** from his throne, and there
Mt 8:4 "Go right over to the **p** and let him examine you.
26:3 meeting at the residence of Caiaphas, the high **p**,
26:57 the high **p**, where the teachers of religious law
26:62 Then the high **p** stood up and said to Jesus, "Well,
26:63 Then the high **p** said to him, "I demand in the
26:65 Then the high **p** tore his clothing to show his
Mk 1:44 "Go right over to the **p** and let him examine you.
2:26 God (during the days when Abiathar was high **p**),
14:60 Then the high **p** stood up before the others
14:61 Then the high **p** asked him, "Are you the Messiah,
14:63 Then the high **p** tore his clothing to show his
14:66 One of the servant girls who worked for the high **p**
Lk 1:5 It all begins with a Jewish **p**, Zechariah, who lived
5:14 "Go right to the **p** and let him examine you.
10:31 "By chance a Jewish **p** came along; but when he
Jn 11:49 of them, Caiaphas, who was high **p** that year, said,
11:51 came from Caiaphas in his position as high **p**.
18:13 the father-in-law of Caiaphas, the high **p** that year.
18:15 That other disciple was acquainted with the high **p**,
18:19 the high **p** began asking Jesus about his followers
18:22 "Is that the way to answer the high **p**?"
18:24 bound Jesus and sent him to Caiaphas, the high **p**.
18:26 But one of the household servants of the high **p**,
Ac 4:6 Annas the high **p** was there, along with Caiaphas,
4:6 Alexander, and other relatives of the high **p**.
5:17 The high **p** and his friends, who were Sadducees,
5:21 When the high **p** and his officials arrived,
5:28 the high **p** demanded. "Instead, you have filled all
7:1 Then the high **p** asked Stephen, "Are these
9:1 the Lord's followers, so he went to the high **p**.
14:13 The **p** of the temple and the crowd brought oxen
19:14 Seven sons of Sceva, a leading **p**, were doing this.
22:5 The high **p** and the whole council of leaders can
23:2 Instantly Ananias the high **p** commanded those
23:4 to him, "Is that the way to talk to God's high **p**?"
23:5 I didn't realize he was the high **p**," Paul replied,
24:1 Five days later Ananias, the high **p**, arrived with
Heb 2:17 be our merciful and faithful High **P** before God.
3:1 we declare to be God's Messenger and High **P**.
4:14 That is why we have a great High **P** who has gone
4:15 This High **P** of ours understands our weaknesses,
5:1 Now a high **p** is a man chosen to represent other
5:4 And no one can become a high **p** simply
5:5 Christ did not exalt himself to become High **P**.
5:6 passage God said to him, / "You are a **p** forever
5:9 In this way, God qualified him as a perfect High **P**,
5:10 And God designated him to be a High **P** in the line
6:20 He has become our eternal High **P** in the line of
7:1 the city of Salem and also a **p** of God Most High.
7:3 He remains a **p** forever, resembling the Son of
7:11 why did God need to send a different **p** from the
7:15 even more evident from the fact that a different **p**,
7:16 He became a **p**, not by meeting the old requirement
7:17 out when he said of Christ, / "You are a **p** forever
7:20 God took an oath that Christ would always be a **p**,
but he never did this for any other **p**.
7:21 will not break his vow: / 'You are a **p** forever.' "
7:23 When one **p** died, another had to take his place.
7:24 But Jesus remains a **p** forever; his priesthood will
7:26 He is the kind of high **p** we need because he is
8:1 Our High **P** sat down in the place of highest honor
8:3 And since every high **p** is required to offer gifts
8:3 our High **P** must make an offering, too.
8:4 If he were here on earth, he would not even be a **p**,
8:6 But our High **P** has been given a ministry that is
9:7 But only the high **p** goes into the Most Holy Place,
9:11 So Christ has now become the High **P** over all the
9:25 like the earthly high **p** who enters the Most Holy
10:11 the **p** stands before the altar day after day,
10:12 But our High **P** offered himself to God as one
10:21 And since we have a great High **P** who rules over
13:11 the high **p** brought the blood of animals into the

PRIEST'S (19) [PRIEST]

Lev 6:29 Only males from a **p** family may eat of this
7:6 All males from a **p** family may eat the meat,
13:31 if the **p** examination reveals that the infection is
14:18 The oil remaining in the **p** hand will then be
14:29 The oil that is still in the **p** hand will then be
21:9 If a **p** daughter becomes a prostitute, defiling her
22:10 "No one outside a **p** family may ever eat the
22:10 even if the person lives in a **p** home or is one of his
22:12 If a **p** daughter marries someone outside the
27:14 to assess its value. The **p** assessment will be final.
27:27 you may redeem it by paying the **p** assessment of
Mt 26:51 and slashed off an ear of the high **p** servant.
26:58 and eventually came to the courtyard of the high **p**
Mk 14:47 and slashed off an ear of the high **p** servant.
14:53 Jesus was led to the high **p** home where the leading
14:54 then slipped inside the gates of the high **p**
Lk 22:50 And one of them slashed at the high **p** servant
22:54 arrested him and led him to the high **p** residence,
Jn 18:10 off the right ear of Malchus, the high **p** servant.

PRIESTHOOD (12) [PRIEST]

Ex 40:15 Aaron's descendants are set apart for the **p** forever,
Nu 3:10 and his sons to carry out the duties of the **p**.
16:10 but now you are demanding the **p** as well!
18:1 be held liable for violations connected with the **p**.
18:7 I am giving you the **p** as your special gift of
Ne 13:29 for they have defiled the **p** and the promises
Heb 7:11 if the **p** of Levi could have achieved God's
7:11 and it was that **p** on which the law was based—
7:12 And when the **p** is changed, the law must also be
7:14 never mentioned Judah in connection with the **p**.
7:18 the old requirement about the **p** was set aside
7:24 Jesus remains a priest forever; his **p** will never end.

PRIESTLY (13) [PRIEST]

Lev 21:10 and has been ordained to wear the special **p**
22:12 daughter marries someone outside the **p** family,
Nu 20:26 There you will remove Aaron's **p** garments and put
20:28 Moses removed the **p** garments from Aaron
1Sa 2:28 and to wear the **p** garments as he served me.
22:18 priests in all, all still wearing their **p** tunics.
2Sa 6:14 the LORD with all his might, wearing a **p** tunic.
8:18 David's sons served as **p** leaders.
1Ki 12:31 those who were not from the **p** tribe of Levi.
1Ch 15:27 the song leader. David was also wearing a **p** tunic.
Zec 3:5 So they put a clean **p** turban on his head
Lk 1:5 Zechariah was a member of the **p** order of Abijah.
1:5 Elizabeth, was also from the **p** line of Aaron.

PRIESTS (504) [PRIEST]

LEVITICAL PRIESTS (15) Dt 17:9,18; 18:1; 21:5; 24:8; 27:9; Jos 3:3; 8:33; 2Ch 5:5; 23:18; 30:27; Jer 33:18,21; Eze 43:19; 44:15

PRIESTS AND LEVITES (34) Nu 18:22; Dt 18:1; 1Ki 8:4; 1Ch 13:2; 15:4; 23:2; 24:6; 28:13,21; 2Ch 8:15; 11:13; 23:4,6; 24:5; 29:4; 30:15; 31:2,4,9; 35:8,18; Ezr 1:5; 6:18,20; 7:13; 9:1; Ne 8:13; 12:1,30,44,44; 13:29,30; Isa 66:21

PRIESTS AND THE LEVITES (7) 1Ch 15:14; 24:31; 2Ch 13:10; 34:30; 35:10; Ezr 8:30; 10:5

Ge 47:22 land he didn't buy was that belonging to the **p**,
Ex 19:6 And you will be to me a kingdom of **p**, my holy
19:22 Even the **p** who regularly come near to the LORD
19:24 do not let the **p** or the people cross the boundaries
28:1 They will be my **p** and will minister to me.
28:4 sons to wear when they serve as **p** before me.
28:41 Set them apart as holy so they can serve as my **p**.
29:1 for the dedication of Aaron and his sons as **p**:
29:9 They will then be **p** forever. In this way, you will
29:44 and his sons as holy, that they may be my **p**.
30:30 so they can minister before me as **p**.
31:10 garments for his sons to wear as they minister as **p**;
35:19 the beautifully stitched clothing for the **p** to wear
35:19 and his sons to wear while officiating as **p**."
37:29 Then he made the sacred oil for anointing the **p**
39:1 For the **p**, the craftsmen made beautiful garments
40:15 as you did their father, so they may serve me as **p**.
40:30 so the **p** could use it to wash themselves.
Lev 1:5 in the LORD's presence, and Aaron's sons, the **p**,
1:9 Then the **p** will burn the entire sacrifice on the
1:11 Aaron's sons, the **p**, will sprinkle its blood against
1:12 and the **p** will lay the pieces of the sacrifice,
1:13 Then the **p** will burn the entire sacrifice on the
2:8 bring it to the **p** who will present it at the altar.
2:9 The **p** will take a token portion of the grain
2:16 The **p** will take a token portion of the roasted grain
3:2 the **p**, will then sprinkle the animal's blood against
6:17 I have given it to the **p** as their share of the
6:22 As the sons of the **p** replace their fathers, they will
6:23 All such grain offerings of the **p** must be entirely
7:5 The **p** will burn these parts on the altar as an
7:10 are to be shared among all the **p** and their sons.
7:34 designated the breast and the right thigh for the **p**.
7:35 they were appointed to serve the LORD as **p**.
7:36 **p** as their regular share from the time of the
16:33 the Tabernacle, the altar, the **p**, and the entire
21:1 "Tell the **p** to avoid making themselves
21:5 "The **p** must never shave their heads,
21:7 "The **p** must not marry women defiled by
21:7 for the **p** must be set apart to God as holy.
22:4 "If any of the **p** have a contagious skin disease
22:4 If any of the **p** become unclean by touching a
22:8 The **p** may never eat an animal that has died a
22:9 Warn all the **p** to follow these instructions
23:20 are holy to the LORD and will belong to the **p**.
27:20 or if the field is sold to someone else by the **p**,
27:21 the LORD. It will become the property of the **p**.
Nu 3:3 They were anointed and set apart to minister as **p**.
3:4 and Ithamar to serve as **p** with their father,
10:8 Only the **p**, Aaron's descendants, are allowed to
18:7 But you and your sons, the **p**, must personally
18:8 "I have put the **p** in charge of all the holy gifts that
18:20 "You **p** will receive no inheritance of land or share
18:22 Israelites other than the **p** and Levites are to stay
18:32 tithes if you give the best portion to the **p**.
25:13 he and his descendants will be **p** for all time,
Dt 17:9 where the Levitical **p** and the judge on duty will
17:18 scroll for himself in the presence of the Levitical **p**.
18:1 "Remember that the Levitical **p** and the rest of the
18:1 the **p** and Levites will eat from the offerings given
18:3 "These are the parts the **p** may claim as their share
18:4 You must also give to the **p** the first share of the
19:17 the accuser and accused must appear before the **p**
21:5 The Levitical **p** must go there also, for the LORD
24:8 and follow the instructions of the Levitical **p**;
27:9 and the Levitical **p** addressed all Israel as follows:
31:9 So Moses wrote down this law and gave it to the **p**,
Jos 3:3 "When you see the Levitical **p** carrying the Ark of
3:6 In the morning Joshua said to the **p**, "Lift up the
3:8 Give these instructions to the **p** who are carrying
3:13 The **p** will be carrying the Ark of the LORD,
3:14 the **p** who were carrying the Ark of the Covenant
3:15 But as soon as the feet of the **p** who were carrying
3:17 the **p** who were carrying the Ark of the LORD's
4:3 the **p** are standing in the middle of the Jordan
4:9 at the place where the **p** who carried the Ark of the
4:10 The **p** who were carrying the Ark stood in the
4:11 the **p** crossed over with the Ark of the LORD.
4:16 "Command the **p** carrying the Ark of the
4:18 And as soon as the **p** carrying the Ark of the
6:4 Seven **p** will walk ahead of the Ark, each carrying
6:4 the city seven times, with the **p** blowing the horns.
6:5 When you hear the **p** give one long blast on the
6:6 So Joshua called together the **p** and said, "Take up
6:6 and assign seven **p** to walk in front of it,
6:8 the seven **p** with the rams' horns started marching
6:8 And the **p** carrying the Ark of the LORD's
6:9 Armed guards marched both in front of the **p**
6:9 the Ark, with the **p** continually blowing the horns.
6:12 and the **p** again carried the Ark of the LORD.
6:13 The seven **p** with the rams' horns marched in front
6:13 Armed guards marched both in front of the **p** with
6:13 All this time the **p** were sounding their horns.
6:16 as the **p** sounded the long blast on their horns,
8:33 and between them stood the Levitical **p** carrying
18:7 Their role as **p** of the LORD is their inheritance.
21:17 From the tribe of Benjamin the **p** were given the
21:19 So thirteen towns were given to the **p**,
21:23 and pasturelands were allotted to the **p** from the
21:25 following towns with their pasturelands to the **p**:
Jdg 18:30 This family continued as **p** for the tribe of Dan
1Sa 1:3 The **p** of the LORD at that time were the two sons
2:13 or for their duties as **p**. Whenever anyone offered a
2:28 And I assigned the sacrificial offerings to you **p**.
2:30 branch of the tribe of Levi would always be my **p**.
2:31 to your family, so it will no longer serve as my **p**.
2:35 and his family will be **p** to my anointed kings
2:36 'give us jobs among the **p** so we will have enough
5:5 That is why to this day neither the **p** of Dagon nor
6:2 Then the Philistines called in their **p** and diviners
22:11 and all his family, who served as **p** at Nob.
22:17 "Kill these **p** of the LORD, for they are allies
22:17 But Saul's men refused to kill the LORD's **p**.
22:18 on them and killed them, eighty-five **p** in all,
22:19 Then he went to Nob, the city of the **p**, and killed
22:21 When he told David that Saul had killed the **p** of
2Sa 8:17 and Ahimelech son of Abiathar were the **p**.
15:35 Zadok and Abiathar, the **p**, are there. Tell them the
17:15 Hushai reported to Zadok and Abiathar, the **p**,
19:11 Then King David sent Zadok and Abiathar, the **p**,
20:25 court secretary. Zadok and Abiathar were the **p**.
1Ki 4:4 of the army. / Zadok and Abiathar were the **p**.
8:3 leaders of Israel arrived, the **p** picked up the Ark.
8:4 Then the **p** and Levites took the Ark of the
8:6 Then the **p** carried the Ark of the LORD's
8:10 As the **p** came out of the inner sanctuary, a cloud
8:11 The **p** could not continue their work
12:31 and ordained **p** from the rank and file of the
12:32 And it was at Bethel that he appointed **p** for the
13:2 On you he will sacrifice the **p** from the pagan
13:33 He continued to choose **p** from the rank and file of
2Ki 10:11 all his important officials, personal friends, and **p**.
10:19 and worshipers of Baal, and call together all his **p**.
12:4 One day King Joash said to the **p**, "Collect all the
12:5 Let the **p** take some of that money to pay for
12:6 the **p** still had not repaired the Temple.
12:7 called for Jehoiada and the other **p** and asked them,
12:8 So the **p** agreed not to collect any more money
12:9 The **p** guarding the entrance put all of the people's
12:16 It was given to the **p** for their own use.
17:27 "Send one of the exiled **p** from Samaria back to
17:28 So one of the **p** who had been exiled from Samaria
17:32 but they appointed from among themselves **p** to
19:2 and the leading **p**, all dressed in sackcloth,
23:2 all the people of Judah and Jerusalem, and the **p**,
23:4 instructed Hilkiah the high priest and the leading **p**
23:5 He did away with the pagan **p**, who had been
23:8 Josiah brought back to Jerusalem all the **p** of the
23:9 The **p** who had served at the pagan shrines were
23:9 allowed to eat unleavened bread with the other **p**.
23:20 He executed the **p** of the pagan shrines on their
1Ch 6:49 Only Aaron and his descendants served as **p**.
9:2 With them came some of the **p**, Levites,
9:10 Among the **p** who returned were Jedaiah,
9:12 Other returning **p** were Adaiah son of Jeroham,
9:13 In all, 1,760 **p** returned. They were heads of clans
9:30 But it was the **p** who prepared the spices
13:2 including the **p** and Levites in their towns
15:4 These are the **p** and Levites who were called
15:11 Then David summoned the **p**, Zadok and Abiathar,
15:14 So the **p** and the Levites purified themselves in
15:24 Benaiah, and Eliezer—all of whom were **p**—
16:6 The **p**, Benaiah and Jahaziel, played the trumpets
16:39 and his fellow **p** at the Tabernacle of the LORD
18:16 and Ahimelech son of Abiathar were the **p**.
23:2 together with the **p** and Levites, for the coronation
23:28 The work of the Levites was to assist the **p**,
23:32 And so, under the supervision of the **p**, the Levites
24:1 This is how Aaron's descendants, the **p**,
24:2 only Eleazar and Ithamar were left to carry on as **p**.
24:6 and the family leaders of the **p** and Levites.
24:31 and the family leaders of the **p** and the Levites.
27:17 Hashabiah son of Kemuel / Aaron (the **p**) | Zadok
28:13 concerning the work of the various divisions of **p**
28:21 The various divisions of **p** and Levites will serve in
2Ch 4:6 The **p** used the Sea itself, and not the basins,
4:9 Solomon also built a courtyard for the **p**
5:5 The Levitical **p** carried them all up to the Temple.
5:7 Then the **p** carried the Ark of the LORD's
5:11 Then the **p** left the Holy Place. All the **p** who were
5:12 They were joined by 120 **p** who were playing
5:14 The **p** could not continue their work
6:41 May your **p**, O LORD God, be clothed with
7:2 The **p** could not even enter the Temple of the

7: 6 The **p** took their assigned positions, and so did the
7: 6 the **p** blew the trumpets, while all Israel stood.
8: 14 In assigning the **p** to their duties,
8: 14 in praise and to assist the **p** in their daily duties.
8: 15 any way from David's commands concerning the **p**
11: 13 But all the **p** and Levites living among the northern
11: 14 would not allow them to serve the LORD as **p**.
11: 15 Jeroboam appointed his own **p** to serve at the
13: 9 And you have chased away the **p** of the LORD
13: 9 and the Levites and have appointed your own **p**,
13: 10 the descendants of Aaron serve the LORD as **p**,
13: 12 His **p** blow their trumpets and lead us into battle
13: 14 the LORD for help. Then the **p** blew the trumpets,
17: 8 He also sent out the **p**, Elishama and Jehoram.
19: 8 Jehoshaphat appointed some of the Levites and **p**
23: 4 When the **p** and Levites come on duty on the
23: 6 only the **p** and Levites on duty may enter the
23: 18 Jehoiada now put the Levitical **p** in charge of the
24: 5 He summoned the **p** and Levites and gave them
26: 17 in after him with eighty other **p** of the LORD,
26: 18 That is the work of the **p** alone, the sons of Aaron
26: 19 But as he was standing there with the **p** before the
26: 20 When Azariah and the other **p** saw the leprosy,
29: 4 He summoned the **p** and Levites to meet him at the
29: 16 The **p** went into the sanctuary of the Temple of the
29: 21 The king commanded the **p**, who were descendants
29: 22 and the **p** took the blood and sprinkled it on the
29: 24 The **p** then killed the goats as a sin offering
29: 26 and the **p** took their positions with the trumpets.
29: 34 But there were too few **p** to prepare all the burnt
29: 34 was finished and until more **p** had been purified.
29: 34 about purifying themselves than the **p**.
30: 3 but not enough **p** could be purified by that time,
30: 15 Then the **p** and Levites became ashamed, so they
30: 16 The Levites brought the sacrificial blood to the **p**,
30: 21 Each day the Levites and **p** sang to the LORD,
30: 24 Meanwhile, many more **p** purified themselves.
30: 25 including the **p**, the Levites, all who came from the
30: 27 Then the Levitical **p** stood and blessed the people,
31: 2 Hezekiah then organized the **p** and Levites into
31: 4 the prescribed portion of their income to the **p**
31: 9 come from?" Hezekiah asked the **p** and Levites.
31: 15 They distributed the gifts among the families of **p**
31: 17 And they distributed gifts to the **p** who were listed
31: 19 As for the **p**, the descendants of Aaron, who were
31: 19 to distribute portions to every male among the **p**
34: 5 Then he burned the bones of the pagan **p** on their
34: 30 Judah and Jerusalem and the **p** and the Levites—
35: 2 Josiah also assigned the **p** to their duties
35: 8 willing contributions to the people, **p**, and Levites.
35: 8 gave the **p** twenty-six hundred lambs and young
35: 10 the **p** and the Levites took their places,
35: 11 Passover lambs and presented the blood to the **p**,
35: 14 prepared a meal for themselves and for the **p**,
35: 14 because the **p** had been busy from morning till
35: 18 involving all the **p** and Levites, all the people of
36: 14 All the leaders of the **p** and the people became
Ezr 1: 5 Then God stirred the hearts of the **p** and Levites
2: 36 These are the **p** who returned from exile:
2: 61 Three families of **p**—Hobaiah, Hakkoz,
2: 62 so they were not allowed to serve as **p**.
2: 69 6,250 pounds of silver, and 100 robes for the **p**.
2: 70 So the **p**, the Levites, the singers, the gatekeepers,
3: 2 Then Jeshua son of Jehozadak with his fellow **p**
3: 6 the **p** had begun to sacrifice burnt offerings to the
3: 8 Jeshua son of Jehozadak and his fellow **p**, and all
3: 10 the **p** put on their robes and took their places to
3: 12 Many of the older **p**, Levites, and other leaders
6: 9 Give the **p** in Jerusalem whatever is needed in the
6: 16 great joy by the people of Israel, the **p**, the Levites,
6: 18 Then the **p** and Levites were divided into their
6: 20 The **p** and Levites had purified themselves
6: 20 returned exiles, for the other **p**, and for themselves.
7: 7 as well as some of the **p**, Levites, singers,
7: 13 including the **p** and Levites, may volunteer to
7: 16 and the **p** that are presented for the Temple of their
8: 15 the lists of the people and the **p** who had arrived.
8: 24 I appointed twelve leaders of the **p**—Sherebiah,
Hashabiah, and ten other **p**—
8: 28 And I said to these **p**, "You and these treasures
8: 29 without an ounce lost, to the leading **p**, the Levites,
8: 30 So the **p** and the Levites accepted the task of
9: 1 of Israel, and even some of the **p** and Levites,
9: 7 and our **p** have been at the mercy of the pagan
10: 5 and demanded that the leaders of the **p**
10: 18 These are the **p** who had married pagan wives:
Ne 3: 1 and the other **p** started to rebuild at the Sheep Gate.
3: 22 Then came the **p** from the surrounding region.
3: 28 The **p** repaired the wall up the hill from the Horse
5: 12 Then I called the **p** and made the nobles
7: 39 "These are the **p** who returned from exile:
7: 63 "Three families of **p**—Hobaiah, Hakkoz,
7: 64 so they were not allowed to serve as **p**.
7: 70 gold coins, 50 gold basins, and 530 robes for the **p**.
7: 72 2,500 pounds of silver, and 67 robes for the **p**.
7: 73 "So the **p**, the Levites, the gatekeepers,
8: 13 On October 9 the family leaders and the **p**
9: 32 and upon our kings and princes and **p** and prophets
9: 34 Our kings, princes, **p**, and ancestors did not obey
9: 38 are the names of our princes and Levites and **p**."
10: 1 son of Hacaliah. The **p** who signed were Zedekiah,
10: 8 Maaziah, Bilgai, and Shemaiah. These were the **p**.
10: 28 the **p**, Levites, gatekeepers, singers,
10: 34 the families of the **p**, Levites, and the common
10: 36 We will present them to the **p** who minister in the
10: 39 in the sacred containers near the ministering **p**,
11: 3 Most of the people, **p**, Levites, Temple servants,
11: 10 From the **p**: Jedaiah son of Joiarib; Jakin;
11: 20 The other **p**, Levites, and the rest of the Israelites
12: 1 Here is the list of the **p** and Levites who had
12: 7 These were the leaders of the **p** and their associates
12: 12 the family leaders of the **p** were as follows:
12: 22 and the **p** in the days of the following high **p**:
12: 30 The **p** and Levites first dedicated themselves,
12: 35 and some **p** who played trumpets. Then came
12: 41 We went together with the trumpet-playing **p**—
12: 44 from the fields as required by the law for the **p**
12: 44 for all the people of Judah valued the **p** and Levites
12: 47 gave a portion of what they received to the **p**,
13: 5 olive oil, and the special portion set aside for the **p**.
13: 29 and the promises and vows of the **p** and Levites.
13: 30 and assigned tasks to the **p** and Levites,
13: 31 the first part of the harvest was collected for the **p**.
Job 12: 19 He leads **p** away stripped of status; he overthrows
Ps 78: 64 Their **p** were slaughtered, / and their widows could
99: 6 Moses and Aaron were among his **p**; / Samuel also
115: 10 O **p** of Aaron, trust the LORD! / He is your
115: 12 people of Israel / and the family of Aaron, the **p**.
118: 3 Let Aaron's descendants, the **p**, repeat:
132: 9 Your **p** will be agents of salvation; / may your
132: 16 I will make its **p** the agents of salvation; / its godly
135: 19 the LORD! / O **p** of Aaron, praise the LORD!
Isa 23: 18 good food and fine clothing for the LORD's **p**.
24: 2 **P** and laypeople, servants and masters, maids
28: 7 The **p** and prophets reel and stagger from beer
37: 2 and the leading **p**, all dressed in sackcloth,
43: 28 That is why I have disgraced your **p** and assigned
61: 6 You will be called **p** of the LORD, ministers of
66: 21 I will appoint some of those who return to be my **p**
Jer 1: 1 one of the **p** from Anathoth, a town in the land of
1: 18 None of the kings, officials, **p**, or people of Judah
2: 8 The **p** did not ask, 'Where is the LORD?'
2: 26 Kings, officials, **p**, and prophets—all are alike in
4: 9 The **p** and the prophets will be struck with
5: 31 false prophecies, and the **p** rule with an iron hand.
6: 13 to them. Yes, even my prophets and **p** are like that!
8: 1 and the graves of the **p**, prophets, and common
8: 10 to them. Yes, even my prophets and **p** are like that.
13: 13 on David's throne and from the **p** and the prophets,
14: 18 The prophets and **p** continue with their work,
18: 18 We have our own **p** and wise men and prophets.
19: 1 leaders of the people and of the **p** to follow you.
23: 11 "The **p** are like the prophets, all ungodly,
23: 33 of the people or one of the prophets or **p** asks you,
26: 7 The **p**, the prophets, and all the people listened to
26: 8 the **p** and prophets and all the people at the Temple
26: 11 The **p** and prophets presented their accusations to
26: 16 and the people said to the **p** and prophets,
27: 16 Then I spoke to the **p** and the people and said,
28: 1 me publicly in the Temple while all the **p**
28: 5 to Hananiah as they stood in front of all the **p**
29: 1 a letter from Jerusalem to the elders, **p**, prophets,
29: 25 and you sent copies to the other **p** and people in
31: 14 I will supply the **p** with an abundance of offerings.
32: 32 the kings, the officials, the **p**, and the prophets—
33: 18 And there will always be Levitical **p** to offer burnt
33: 21 with the Levitical **p** who minister before me.
34: 19 officials of Judah or Jerusalem, court officials, **p**,
48: 7 Your god Chemosh, with his **p** and princes, will be
49: 3 Molech will be exiled along with his princes and **p**.
La 1: 4 The city gates are silent, her **p** groan, her young
1: 19 My **p** and leaders starved to death in the city,
2: 6 Kings and **p** fall together before his anger.
2: 20 Should **p** and prophets die within the Lord's
4: 13 because of the sins of her prophets and **p**,
4: 16 The **p** and leaders are no longer honored
Eze 7: 26 They will receive no teaching from the **p** and no
22: 26 Your **p** have violated my laws and defiled my holy
40: 45 for the **p** who supervise the Temple maintenance.
40: 46 south inner gate is for the **p** in charge of the altar—
42: 13 It is there that the **p** who offer sacrifices to the
42: 14 When the **p** leave the Holy Place, they must not go
43: 19 that time, the Levitical **p** of the family of Zadok,
43: 24 and the **p** are to sprinkle salt on them and offer
43: 27 the **p** will sacrifice on the altar the burnt offerings
44: 13 They may not approach me to minister as **p**.
44: 15 the Levitical **p** of the family of Zadok continued to
44: 21 The **p** must never drink wine before entering the
44: 22 among the virgins of Israel or the widows of the **p**.
44: 24 And the **p** themselves must obey my instructions
44: 28 "As to property, the **p** will not have any, for I
44: 29 sets apart for the LORD will belong to the **p**.
44: 30 all the gifts brought to the LORD will go to the **p**.
44: 30 the first of your flour must also be given to the **p**
44: 31 The **p** may never eat meat from any bird or animal
45: 4 set aside for the **p** who minister to the LORD in
46: 19 and led me to the sacred rooms assigned to the **p**,
46: 20 "This is where the **p** will cook the meat from the
48: 10 For the **p** there will be a strip of land measuring
48: 11 This area is set aside for the ordained **p**,
48: 13 same size and shape as that belonging to the **p**—
Hos 3: 4 and without sacrifices, temple, **p**, or even idols!
4: 4 the blame! Look, you **p**, my complaint is with you!
4: 6 It is all your fault, you **p**, for you yourselves refuse
4: 6 know me. Now I refuse to recognize you as my **p**.
4: 7 The more **p** there are, the more they sin against
4: 8 "The **p** get fed when the people sin and bring their
4: 8 to them. So the **p** are glad when the people sin!
4: 9 'Like **p**, like people'—since the **p** are wicked,
4: 9 So now I will punish both **p** and people for all their
5: 1 "Hear this, you **p** and all of Israel's leaders!
6: 9 Gangs of **p** murder travelers along the road to
10: 5 The people mourn over it, and the **p** wail for it,
Joel 1: 9 The **p** are mourning because there are no offerings.
1: 13 Dress yourselves in sackcloth, you **p**! Wail,
2: 17 The **p**, who minister in the LORD's presence,
Mic 3: 11 can get; you **p** teach God's laws only for a price;
Zep 1: 4 I will put an end to all the idolatrous **p**, so that
3: 4 Its **p** defile the Temple by disobeying God's laws.
Hag 2: 11 Ask the **p** this question about the law:
2: 12 will it also become holy?" The **p** replied, "No."
2: 13 will it be defiled?" And the **p** answered, "Yes."
Zec 3: 8 O Jeshua the high priest, and all you other **p**.
7: 3 and of the **p** at the Temple of the LORD
7: 5 "Say to all your people and your **p**, 'During those
Mal 1: 6 The LORD Almighty says to the **p**: "A son
2: 1 "Listen, you **p**; this command is for you!
2: 7 for the **p** are the messengers of the LORD
Mt 2: 4 He called a meeting of the leading **p** and teachers
12: 4 and they ate the special bread reserved for the **p**
12: 5 **p** on duty in the Temple may work on the Sabbath?
16: 21 and the leading **p** and the teachers of religious law.
20: 18 "the Son of Man will be betrayed to the leading **p**
21: 15 The leading **p** and the teachers of religious law saw
21: 23 the leading **p** and other leaders came up to him.
21: 45 When the leading **p** and Pharisees heard Jesus,
26: 3 At that same time the leading **p** and other leaders
26: 14 one of the twelve disciples, went to the leading **p**
26: 47 They had been sent out by the leading **p** and other
26: 59 the leading **p** and the entire high council were
27: 1 the leading **p** and other leaders met again to
27: 3 the thirty pieces of silver back to the leading **p**
27: 6 The leading **p** picked up the money. "We can't put
27: 12 But when the leading **p** and other leaders made
27: 20 the leading **p** and other leaders persuaded the
27: 41 The leading **p**, the teachers of religious law,
27: 62 the leading **p** and Pharisees went to see Pilate.
28: 11 had been guarding the tomb went to the leading **p**
Mk 2: 26 ate the special bread reserved for the **p** alone,
8: 31 and be rejected by the leaders, the leading **p**,
10: 33 "the Son of Man will be betrayed to the leading **p**
11: 18 When the leading **p** and teachers of religious law
11: 27 the leading **p**, the teachers of religious law,
14: 1 The leading **p** and the teachers of religious law
14: 10 went to the leading **p** to arrange to betray Jesus to
14: 11 The leading **p** were delighted when they heard why
14: 43 They had been sent out by the leading **p**,
14: 53 led to the high priest's home where the leading **p**,
14: 55 the leading **p** and the entire high council were
15: 1 Very early in the morning the leading **p**,
15: 3 Then the leading **p** accused him of many crimes,
15: 10 (For he realized by now that the leading **p** had
15: 11 But at this point the leading **p** stirred up the mob to
15: 31 The leading **p** and teachers of religious law also
Lk 1: 9 As was the custom of the **p**, he was chosen by lot
3: 2 Annas and Caiaphas were the high **p**. At this time a
6: 4 ate the special bread reserved for the **p** alone,
9: 22 the leading **p**, and the teachers of religious law.
17: 14 at them and said, "Go show yourselves to the **p**."
19: 47 but the leading **p**, the teachers of religious law,
20: 1 the leading **p** and teachers of religious law
20: 19 of religious law and the leading **p** heard this story,
22: 2 The leading **p** and teachers of religious law were
22: 4 and he went over to the leading **p** and captains of
22: 52 Then Jesus spoke to the leading **p** and captains of
22: 66 including the leading **p** and the teachers of
23: 4 Pilate turned to the leading **p** and to the crowd
23: 10 the leading **p** and the teachers of religious law
23: 13 Then Pilate called together the leading **p** and other
24: 20 But our leading **p** and other religious leaders
Jn 1: 19 testimony of John when the Jewish leaders sent **p**
7: 32 and the leading **p** sent Temple guards to arrest
7: 45 been sent to arrest him returned to the leading **p**
11: 47 Then the leading **p** and Pharisees called the high
11: 57 the leading **p** and Pharisees had publicly
12: 10 Then the leading **p** decided to kill Lazarus, too,
18: 3 The leading **p** and Pharisees had given Judas a
18: 35 own people and their leading **p** brought you here.
19: 6 the leading **p** and Temple guards began shouting,
19: 15 no king but Caesar," the leading **p** shouted back.
19: 21 Then the leading **p** said to Pilate, "Change it from
Ac 4: 1 the leading **p**, the captain of the Temple guard,
4: 23 and told them what the leading **p** and elders had
5: 24 of the Temple guard and the leading **p** heard this,
6: 7 and many of the Jewish **p** were converted, too.
9: 14 And we hear that he is authorized by the leading **p**
9: 21 and take them in chains to the leading **p**."
22: 30 and ordered the leading **p** into session with the
23: 14 They went to the leading **p** and other leaders
25: 2 where the leading **p** and other Jewish leaders met
25: 15 the leading **p** and other Jewish leaders pressed
26: 10 Authorized by the leading **p**, I caused many of the
26: 12 the authority and commission of the leading **p**.
Heb 7: 5 Now the **p**, who are descendants of Levi,
7: 8 In the case of Jewish **p**, tithes are paid to men who
7: 23 Another difference is that there were many **p** under
7: 27 to offer sacrifices every day like the other high **p**.
7: 28 Those who were high **p** under the law of Moses
8: 4 since there already are **p** who offer the gifts
9: 6 the **p** went in and out of the first room regularly as
9: 9 and sacrifices that the **p** offer are not able to
13: 10 We have an altar from which the **p** in the Temple
1Pe 2: 5 What's more, you are God's holy **p**, who offer the
2: 9 You are a kingdom of **p**, God's holy nation,
Rev 1: 6 and his **p** who serve before God his Father.
5: 10 caused them to become God's kingdom and his **p**.
20: 6 but they will be **p** of God and of Christ and will

PRIESTS' (8) [PRIEST]

Ge 47: 26 But since Pharaoh had not taken over the **p** land,

Lev 7:36 regular share from the time of the **p** anointing.
22:13 only members of the **p** families are allowed to eat
1Sa 22:19 the city of the priests, and killed the **p** families—
Ezr 2:63 The governor would not even let them eat the **p**
Ne 7:65 The governor would not even let them eat the **p**
Eze 48:12 Next to the **p** territory will lie the land where the
Mal 2:7 The **p** lips should guard knowledge, and people

PRIMARY (3)

Eze 43:12 built is holy. Yes, this is the **p** law of the Temple.
Mt 6:33 and make the Kingdom of God your **p** concern.
Lk 12:31 if you make the Kingdom of God your **p** concern.

PRIME (9)

Est 3:1 son of Hammedatha the Agagite to **p** minister,
10:3 Mordecai the Jew became the **p** minister,
Job 3:14 would rest with the world's kings and **p** ministers,
15:32 They will be cut down in the **p** of life, and all they
22:16 They were snatched away in the **p** of life,
40:19 It is a **p** example of God's amazing handiwork.
Pr 1:12 Though they are in the **p** of life, they will go down
Isa 38:10 I said, "In the **p** of my life, / must I now enter the
1Ti 1:16 so that Christ Jesus could use me as a **p** example of

PRINCE (59) [PRINCE'S, PRINCELY, PRINCES, PRINCESS]

Ge 23:6 "Certainly, for you are an honored **p** among us.
34:2 But when the local **p**, Shechem son of Hamor the
49:26 head of Joseph, / who is a **p** among his brothers.
Ex 2:14 "Who appointed you to be our **p** and judge?
Dt 33:16 crowning the brow of the **p** among his brothers.
Est 6:9 Have the **p** shout as they go, 'This is what
Job 31:37 I have done. I would come before him like a **p**.
Ps 82:7 You will fall as any **p**, / for all must die.' "
Pr 6:7 Even though they have no **p**, governor, or ruler to
19:6 Many beg favors from a **p**; everyone is the friend
25:15 Patience can persuade a **p**, and soft speech can
28:16 Only a stupid **p** will oppress his people, but a king
Isa 9:6 Mighty God, Everlasting Father, **P** of Peace.
Eze 7:27 The king and the **p** will stand helpless, weeping in
21:25 "O you corrupt and wicked **p** of Israel, your final
28:2 give the **p** of Tyre this message from the Sovereign
34:24 and my servant David will be a **p** among my
37:25 And my servant David will be their **p** forever.
38:2 the **p** who rules over the nations of Meshech
44:3 Only the **p** himself may sit inside this gateway to
45:7 special sections of land will be set apart for the **p**.
45:13 "This is the tax you must give to the **p**: one bushel
45:16 All the people of Israel must join the **p** in bringing
45:17 The **p** will be required to provide offerings that are
45:22 On the day of Passover the **p** will provide a young
45:24 The **p** will provide a half bushel of flour as a grain
45:25 the **p** will provide these same sacrifices for the sin
46:2 The **p** will enter the foyer of the gateway from the
46:4 "Each Sabbath day the **p** will present to the
46:8 "The **p** must enter the gateway through the foyer,
46:10 The **p** will enter and leave with the people on these
46:11 and as much flour as the **p** chooses to give with
46:12 Whenever the **p** offers a voluntary burnt offering
46:16 If the **p** gives a gift of land to one of his sons,
46:17 will be set free, and the land will return to the **p**.
46:18 And the **p** may never take anyone's property by
48:21 the sacred lands and the city, will belong to the **p**.
Da 6:1 and he appointed a **p** to rule over each province.
8:25 He will even take on the **P** of princes in battle,
10:13 But for twenty-one days the spirit **p** of the
10:13 and I left him there with the spirit **p** of the
10:20 Soon I must return to fight against the spirit **p** of
10:20 then against the spirit **p** of the kingdom of Greece.
10:21 these spirit princes except Michael, your spirit **p**.
11:22 armies will be swept away, including a covenant **p**.
Hos 3:4 that Israel will be a long time without a king or **p**,
Mt 9:34 because he is empowered by the **p** of demons."
10:25 the household, have been called the **p** of demons,
12:24 He gets his power from Satan, the **p** of demons."
12:27 And if I am empowered by the **p** of demons,
Mk 3:22 "He's possessed by Satan, the **p** of demons.
Lk 11:15 He gets his power from Satan, the **p** of demons!"
11:18 You say I am empowered by the **p** of demons.
11:19 And if I am empowered by the **p** of demons,
Jn 12:31 when the **p** of this world will be cast out.
14:30 talk to you, because the **p** of this world approaches.
16:11 because the **p** of this world has already been
Ac 5:31 put him in the place of honor at his right hand as **P**
Eph 2:2 the mighty **p** of the power of the air.

PRINCE'S (5) [PRINCE]

Eze 45:7 and western borders of the **p** lands will line up
45:8 These sections of land will be the **p** allotment.
46:17 Only the gifts given to the **p** sons will be
48:22 So the **p** land will include everything between the
48:23 Benjamin's territory lies just south of the **p** lands,

PRINCELY (1) [PRINCE]

SS 6:12 I found myself in my **p** bed with my beloved one."

PRINCES (82) [PRINCE]

Ge 17:20 Twelve **p** will be among his descendants.
Nu 21:18 Sing of this well, / which **p** dug, / which great
Jos 13:21 **p** living in the region who were allied with Sihon.
Jdg 5:15 The **p** of Issachar were with Deborah and Barak.
1Sa 2:8 from a pile of ashes! / He treats them like **p**,
2Ki 24:14 including all the **p** and the best of the soldiers,
2Ch 11:22 made Maacah's son Abijah chief among the **p**,
36:18 royal palace. He also took with him all the royal **p**.
Ezr 7:28 before the king, his council, and all his mighty **p**!
Ne 9:32 and upon our kings and **p** and priests and prophets
9:34 Our kings, **p**, priests, and ancestors did not obey
9:38 On this sealed document are the names of our **p**
Est 1:3 he gave a banquet for all his **p** and officials.
1:16 Memucan answered the king and his **p**,
1:21 The king and his **p** thought this made good sense,
2:18 he gave a banquet in Esther's honor for all his **p**
3:12 the king's secretaries and dictated letters to the **p**,
6:9 Instruct one of the king's most noble **p** to dress the
8:9 they wrote a decree to the Jews and to the **p**,
9:3 commanders of the provinces, the **p**, the governors,
Job 3:15 I would rest with wealthy **p** whose palaces were
12:21 He pours disgrace upon **p** and confiscates weapons
29:9 The **p** stood in silence and put their hands over
Ps 45:12 The **p** of Tyre will shower you with gifts.
76:12 For he breaks the spirit of **p** / and is feared by the
83:11 Let all their **p** die like Zebah and Zalmunna,
107:40 the LORD pours contempt on their **p**,
113:8 sets them among **p**, / even the **p** of his own people!
118:9 to trust the LORD / than to put confidence in **p**.
119:23 Even **p** sit and speak against me, / but I will
Pr 19:10 a fool to live in luxury or for a slave to rule over **p**!
Ecc 10:7 I have even seen servants riding like **p**—and **p** walking like servants.
Isa 3:14 and the **p** will be the first to feel the LORD's
10:8 He will say, 'Each of my **p** will soon be a king,
32:1 king is coming! And honest **p** will rule under him.
34:12 Land of Nothing, and its **p** soon will all be gone.
41:25 and I will give him victory over kings and **p**.
49:7 **P** will bow low because the LORD has chosen
Jer 24:1 to Babylon along with the **p** of Judah and all the
25:19 to Pharaoh, his officials, his **p**, and his people.
44:17 and **p** have always done in the towns of Judah
48:7 Your god Chemosh, with his priests and **p**, will be
49:3 your god Molech will be exiled along with his **p**
49:38 the LORD, "and I will destroy its king and **p**.
50:35 the people of Babylon—her **p** and wise men, too.
La 1:6 Her **p** are like starving deer searching for pasture,
2:9 Her kings and **p** have been exiled to distant lands;
4:7 Our **p** were once glowing with health; they were as
5:12 Our **p** are being hanged by their thumbs,
Eze 17:12 took away her king and **p**, and brought them to
19:1 "Sing this funeral song for the **p** of Israel:
22:25 Your **p** plot conspiracies just as lions stalk their
27:21 and the **p** of Kedar brought lambs and rams
32:29 "Edom is there with its kings and **p**. Mighty as
32:30 All the **p** of the north and the Sidonians are there,
39:18 and drink the blood of **p** as though they were rams,
45:8 "My **p** will no longer oppress and rob my people;
45:9 Enough, you **p** of Israel! Stop all your violence
Da 3:2 Then he sent messages to the **p**, prefects,
3:27 Then the **p**, prefects, governors, and advisers
6:2 and two others as administrators to supervise the **p**
6:3 capable than all the other administrators and **p**.
6:4 and **p** began searching for some fault in the way
6:6 the administrators and **p** went to the king and said,
6:7 We administrators, prefects, **p**, advisers, and other
8:25 He will even take on the Prince of **p** in battle,
9:6 and **p** and ancestors and to all the people of the
9:8 O LORD, we and our kings, **p**, and ancestors are
10:21 (There is no one to help me against these spirit **p**
Hos 7:3 The **p** laugh about the people's many lies.
7:5 "On royal holidays, the **p** get drunk. The king
8:4 The people have appointed kings and **p**, but not
Am 1:15 And their king and his **p** will go into exile together.
2:3 I will destroy their king and slaughter all their **p**.
Mic 5:5 seven rulers to watch over us, eight **p** to lead us.
Na 3:17 Your **p** and officials are also like locusts,
3:18 O Assyrian king, your **p** lie dead in the dust.
Hab 1:10 They scoff at kings and **p** and scorn all their
Zep 1:8 I will punish the leaders and **p** of Judah and all
Lk 1:52 He has taken **p** from their thrones / and exalted the

PRINCESS (10) [PRINCE]

Ex 2:5 When the **p** saw the little basket among the reeds,
2:6 As the **p** opened it, she found the baby boy.
2:7 Then the baby's sister approached the **p**. "Should I
2:8 "Yes, do!" the **p** replied. So the girl rushed home
2:9 child home and nurse him for me," the **p** told her.
2:10 the child's mother brought him back to the **p**,
2:10 The **p** named him Moses, for she said, "I drew
1Ch 4:18 was named Bithiah, and she was an Egyptian **p**.
Ps 45:13 The bride, a **p**, waits within her chamber,
Isa 47:1 never again will you be the lovely **p**, tender

PRINCIPAL (1)

Lev 6:5 they must restore the **p** amount plus a penalty of 20

PRINCIPLE (4) [PRINCIPLES]

Ex 21:31 "The same **p** applies if the bull gores a boy or a
Job 9:2 "Yes, I know this is all true in **p**. But how can a
Pr 18:1 snarling at every sound **p** of conduct.
Gal 6:16 and peace be upon all those who live by this **p**.

PRINCIPLES (29) [PRINCIPLE]

2Sa 22:23 before me; / I have never abandoned his **p**.
1Ch 29:19 decrees, and **p**, and to build this Temple, for which
Ps 18:22 before me; / I have never abandoned his **p**.
99:7 and they followed the decrees and **p** he gave them.
105:45 All this happened so they would follow his **p**
119:5 that my actions would consistently / reflect your **p**!
119:8 I will obey your **p**. / Please don't give up on me!
119:12 Blessed are you, O LORD; / teach me your **p**.
119:16 I will delight in your **p** / and not forget your word.
119:23 speak against me, / but I will meditate on your **p**.
119:26 and you answered. / Now teach me your **p**.
119:33 O LORD, / to follow every one of your **p**.
119:48 and love your commands. / I meditate on your **p**.
119:54 Your **p** have been the music of my life
119:64 is full of your unfailing love; / teach me your **p**.
119:68 You are good and do only good; / teach me your **p**.
119:71 for me, / for it taught me to pay attention to your **p**.
119:80 May I be blameless in keeping your **p**; / then I will
119:83 But I cling to your **p** and obey them.
119:112 I am determined to keep your **p**, / even forever,
119:117 then I will meditate on your **p** continually.
119:118 But you have rejected all who stray from your **p**.
119:124 with me in unfailing love, / and teach me your **p**.
119:135 Look down on me with love; / teach me all your **p**.
119:145 answer me, LORD! / I will obey your **p**.
119:155 for they do not bother with your **p**.
119:171 forth with praise, / for you have taught me your **p**.
147:19 his words to Jacob, / his **p** and laws to Israel.
Hos 12:6 Act on the **p** of love and justice, and always live in

PRIOR (2)

Jos 20:9 they could escape being killed in revenge **p** to
1Ch 9:18 **P** to this time, they were responsible for the King's

PRISCILLA (6)

Ac 18:2 had recently arrived from Italy with his wife, **P**.
18:18 the coast of Syria, taking **P** and Aquila with him.
18:26 When **P** and Aquila heard him preaching boldly in
Ro 16:3 Greet **P** and Aquila. They have been co-workers in
1Co 16:19 along with Aquila and **P** and all the others who
2Ti 4:19 Give my greetings to **P** and Aquila and those living

PRISON (76) [IMPRISON, IMPRISONED, IMPRISONMENT, PRISONER, PRISONERS, PRISONS]

Ge 39:20 and threw him into the **p** where the king's
39:22 and over everything that happened in the **p**.
40:3 and he put them in the **p** where Joseph was,
40:4 They remained in **p** for quite some time,
40:13 Within three days Pharaoh will take you out of **p**
40:20 and they were brought to him from the **p**.
42:16 I'll keep the rest of you here, bound in **p**.
42:17 So he put them all in **p** for three days.
42:19 really are. Only one of you will remain in the **p**.
Jdg 16:21 bronze chains and made to grind grain in the **p**.
16:25 So he was brought from the **p** and made to stand at
1Ki 22:27 'Put this man in **p**, and feed him nothing but bread
2Ki 17:4 he arrested him and put him in **p** for his rebellion.
23:33 Pharaoh Neco put Jehoahaz in **p** at Riblah in the
25:27 and released him from **p** on April 2 of that year.
25:29 Jehoiachin with new clothes to replace his **p** garb
2Ch 16:10 Hanani for saying this that he threw him into **p**.
18:26 'Put this man in **p**, and feed him nothing but bread
Job 11:10 If God comes along and puts a person in **p**, or if he
Ps 105:18 There in **p**, they bruised his feet with fetters
105:20 the ruler of the nation opened his **p** door.
107:16 For he broke down their **p** gates of bronze;
142:7 Bring me out of **p** / so I can thank you. / The godly
Ecc 4:14 Such a youth could come from **p** and succeed.
Isa 24:22 and put in **p** until they are tried and condemned.
42:7 the eyes of the blind and free the captives from **p**.
53:8 From **p** and trial they led him away to his death.
Jer 32:8 he would, Hanamel came and visited me in the **p**.
37:15 Jonathan's house had been converted into a **p**.
37:21 in the city. So Jeremiah was put in the palace **p**.
38:6 him by ropes into an empty cistern in the **p** yard.
38:13 of the guard—the palace **p**—where he remained.
39:14 sent messengers to bring Jeremiah out of the **p**.
39:15 message to Jeremiah while he was still in **p**:
52:11 Zedekiah remained there in **p** for the rest of his
52:31 and released him from **p** on March 31 of that year.
52:33 Jehoiachin with new clothes to replace his **p** garb
Mt 11:2 John the Baptist, who was now in **p**, heard about
14:10 So John was beheaded in the **p**,
18:34 Then the angry king sent the man to **p** until he had
25:36 you cared for me. I was in **p**, and you visited me.'
25:39 When did we ever see you sick or in **p**, and visit
25:43 I was sick and in **p**, and you didn't visit me.'
25:44 or thirsty or a stranger or naked or sick or in **p**,
27:16 This year there was a notorious criminal in **p**,
Mk 6:27 So he sent an executioner to the **p** to cut off John's
6:27 bring it to him. The soldier beheaded John in the **p**,
Lk 3:20 So Herod put John in **p**, adding this sin to his many
22:33 Peter said, "Lord, I am ready to go to **p** with you,
23:19 (Barabbas was in **p** for murder and for taking part
23:25 the man in **p** for insurrection and murder.
Jn 3:24 This was before John was put into **p**.
18:39 to release someone from **p** each year at Passover.
Ac 12:5 But while Peter was in **p**, the church prayed very
12:6 with others standing guard at the **p** gate.
16:23 severely beaten, and then they were thrown into **p**.
16:26 and the **p** was shaken to its foundations.
16:27 The jailer woke up to see the **p** doors wide open.
22:4 binding and delivering both men and women to **p**.
23:35 Then the governor ordered him kept in the **p** at
24:27 favor with the Jewish leaders, he left Paul in **p**.
26:10 many of the believers in Jerusalem to be sent to **p**.
Ro 16:7 and Junia, my relatives, who were in **p** with me.
Php 1:7 both when I was in **p** and when I was out,
Col 4:10 Aristarchus, who is in **p** with me, sends you his
2Ti 1:8 of me, either, even though I'm in **p** for Christ.
1:12 And that is why I am suffering here in **p**. But I am
1:16 He was never ashamed of me because I was in **p**.

Phm 1: 1 in **p** for preaching the Good News about Christ
1: 9 an old man, now in **p** for the sake of Christ Jesus.
1:10 a believer as a result of my ministry here in **p**.
Heb 13: 3 Don't forget about those in **p**. Suffer with them as
1Pe 3:19 So he went and preached to the spirits in **p**—
Rev 2:10 The Devil will throw some of you into **p** and put
13:10 The people who are destined for **p** will be arrested
20: 7 thousand years end, Satan will be let out of his **p**.

PRISONER (20) [PRISON]

1Ki 20:39 I was in the battle, and a man brought me a **p**.
20:40 busy doing something else, the **p** disappeared!"
2Ki 23:34 Jehoahaz was taken to Egypt as a **p**, where he died.
24:12 of Nebuchadnezzar's reign, he took Jehoiachin **p**.
1Ch 3:17 who was taken **p** by the Babylonians,
2Ch 33:11 the Assyrian armies, and they took Manasseh **p**.
36: 4 Then Neco took Jehoahaz to Egypt as a **p**.
Jer 26:23 They took him **p** and brought him back to King
36: 5 "I am a **p** here and unable to go to the Temple.
38:28 And Jeremiah remained a **p** in the courtyard of the
Mt 27:15 Now it was the governor's custom to release one **p**
Mk 15: 6 Now it was the governor's custom to release one **p**
15: 8 in toward Pilate, asking him to release a **p** as usual.
Ac 16:26 doors flew open, and the chains of every **p** fell off!
23:18 explaining, "Paul, the **p**, called me over and asked
25:14 "There is a **p** here," he told him, "whose case
25:27 For it doesn't seem reasonable to send a **p** to the
Eph 3: 1 am a **p** of Christ Jesus because of my preaching to
4: 1 Therefore I, a **p** for serving the Lord, beg you to
Phm 1:23 Epaphras, my fellow **p** in Christ Jesus, sends you

PRISONERS (35) [PRISON]

Ge 31:26 "Are my daughters **p**, the plunder of war, that you
39:20 and threw him into the prison where the king's **p**
39:22 the jailer put Joseph in charge of all the other **p**
Nu 21: 1 attacked the Israelites and took some of them as **p**.
31:47 Moses took one of every fifty **p** and animals
2Ki 6:22 "Do we kill **p** of war? Give them food and drink
25:18 The captain of the guard took with him as **p**
2Ch 28:13 "You must not bring the **p** here!" they declared.
28:14 So the warriors released the **p** and handed over the
28:15 and distributed clothes from the plunder to the **p**
28:15 and took all the **p** back to their own land—
Job 3:18 Even **p** are at ease in death, with no guards to curse
Ps 68: 6 in families; / he sets the **p** free and gives them joy.
79:11 Listen to the moaning of the **p**. / Demonstrate your
102:20 to hear the groans of the **p**, / to release those
107:10 and deepest gloom, / miserable **p** in chains.
146: 7 and food to the hungry. / The LORD frees the **p**.
Isa 10: 4 You will stumble along as **p** or lie among the dead.
14:17 world's greatest cities and had no mercy on his **p**?'
20: 4 will take away the Egyptians and Ethiopians as **p**.
45:14 all be yours. They will follow you as **p** in chains.
49: 9 Through you I am saying to the **p** of darkness,
61: 1 that captives will be released and **p** will be freed.
Jer 52:24 The captain of the guard took with him as **p**
La 3:34 But the leaders of his people trampled **p** underfoot.
Zec 9:11 I will free your **p** from death in a waterless
9:12 the place of safety, all you **p**, for there is yet hope!
Mk 15: 7 One of the **p** at that time was Barabbas,
Ac 16:25 hymns to God, and the other **p** were listening.
16:27 He assumed the **p** had escaped, so he drew his
27: 1 and several other **p** were placed in the custody of
27:11 But the officer in charge of the **p** listened more to
27:42 The soldiers wanted to kill the **p** to make sure they
1Co 4: 9 like **p** of war at the end of a victor's parade,
Gal 3:22 But the Scriptures have declared that we are all **p**

PRISONS (2) [PRISON]

Lk 21:12 You will be dragged into synagogues and **p**,
Jude 1: 6 God has kept them chained in **p** of darkness,

PRIVACY (1) [PRIVATE]

2Ki 6:12 the words you speak in the **p** of your bedroom!"

PRIVATE (16) [PRIVACY, PRIVATELY]

Ge 43:30 to cry. Going into his **p** room, he wept there.
Dt 18: 8 and offerings, even if he has a **p** source of income.
1Sa 21: 2 "The king has sent me on a **p** matter," David said.
1Ch 29: 3 I am giving all of my own **p** treasures of gold
Est 2:14 That evening she was taken to the king's **p** rooms,
2:21 who were guards at the door of the king's **p**
6: 2 who guarded the door to the king's **p** quarters.
Ps 105:30 they were found even in the king's **p** rooms.
SS 4:12 "You are like a **p** garden, my treasure, my bride!
Jer 40:15 Later Johanan had a **p** conference with Gedaliah
Joel 2:16 from his quarters and the bride from her **p** room.
Mt 2: 7 Then Herod sent a **p** message to the wise men,
Mk 7:33 Jesus led him to a **p** place away from the crowd.
Jn 18:20 and I teach nothing in **p** that I have not said in
Ac 28:16 Paul was permitted to have his own **p** lodging,
1Co 4: 5 secrets to light and will reveal our **p** motives.

PRIVATELY (10) [PRIVATE]

2Sa 3:27 him aside at the gateway as if to speak with him **p**.
Pr 25: 9 So discuss the matter with them **p**. Don't tell
Eze 24:23 You will mourn **p** for all the evil you have done.
Mt 17:19 Afterward the disciples asked Jesus **p**,
18:15 sins against you, go **p** and point out the fault.
20:17 he took the twelve disciples aside **p** and told them
24: 3 His disciples came to him **p** and asked,
Mk 13: 3 John, and Andrew came to him **p** and asked him,
1Co 14:28 church meeting and speak in tongues to God **p**.
Gal 2: 2 While I was there I talked **p** with the leaders of the

PRIVILEGE (19) [PRIVILEGED]

Ge 16: 5 though I myself gave her the **p** of sleeping with
23: 6 It will be a **p** to have you choose the finest of our
1Ki 10: 8 What a **p** for your officials to stand here day after
2Ch 9: 7 What a **p** for your officials to stand here day after
Ps 119:29 to myself; / give me the **p** of knowing your law.
Pr 25: 2 It is God's **p** to conceal things and the king's **p** to discover them.
Lk 14:15 "What a **p** it would be to have a share in the
Ac 7:46 and asked for the **p** of building a permanent
11:18 "God has also given the Gentiles the **p** of turning
Ro 1: 5 God has given us the **p** and authority to tell
5: 2 Christ has brought us into this place of highest **p**
9: 4 They have the **p** of worshiping him and receiving
2Co 8: 4 and again for the gracious **p** of sharing in the gift
Eph 3: 7 I have been given the wonderful **p** of serving him
Php 1:29 For you have been given not only the **p** of trusting
1:29 in Christ but also the **p** of suffering for him.
1Pe 1: 3 that God has given us the **p** of being born again.
4:16 Praise God for the **p** of being called by his

PRIVILEGED (2) [PRIVILEGE]

Job 22: 8 and that those who are **p** have a right to it!
Lk 10:23 "How **p** you are to see what you have seen.

PRIZE (10) [PRIZED]

Pr 4: 8 If you **p** wisdom, she will exalt you. Embrace her
1Co 9:24 race everyone runs, but only one person gets the **p**.
9:25 They do it to win a **p** that will fade away, but we do it for an eternal **p**.
Php 3:14 end of the race and receive the **p** for which God,
2Ti 2: 5 follows the rules or is disqualified and wins no **p**.
4: 8 And now the **p** awaits me—the crown of
4: 8 And the **p** is not just for me but for all who eagerly
Heb 11:40 for they can't receive the **p** at the end of the race
2Jn 1: 8 so that you do not lose the **p** for which we have

PRIZED (1) [PRIZE]

Rev 18:14 "The luxuries and splendor that you **p** so much

PROBABLY (5)

Ge 43:12 in your sacks, as it was **p** someone's mistake.
Jos 2: 5 If you hurry, you can **p** catch up with them."
2Sa 17: 8 Right now they are **p** as enraged as a mother bear
17: 9 He has **p** already hidden in some pit or cave.
Lk 4:23 "**P** you will quote me that proverb, 'Physician,

PROBE (1)

Job 10: 6 that you are in a hurry to **p** for my guilt, to search

PROBLEM (14) [PROBLEMS]

Lev 13:25 and the **p** appears to be more than skin-deep,
13:26 and the **p** appears to be no more than skin-deep
Ru 3:12 But there is one **p**. While it is true that I am one of
2Ki 2:19 "We have a **p**, my lord," they told him.
2Ch 15: 6 for God was troubling you with every kind of **p**.
Ne 5: 7 Then I called a public meeting to deal with the **p**.
Ecc 5:13 There is another serious **p** I have seen in the world.
5:16 And this, too, is a very serious **p**. As people come
Isa 59: 2 But there is a **p**—your sins have cut you off from
Mt 22:29 "Your **p** is that you don't know the Scriptures,
27: 4 do we care?" they retorted. "That's your **p**."
Mk 12:24 "Your **p** is that you don't know the Scriptures,
Jn 2: 3 so Jesus' mother spoke to him about the **p**.
2Co 6:12 If there is a **p** between us, it is not because of a

PROBLEMS (16) [PROBLEM]

Ex 18: 8 He also told him about the **p** they had faced along
24:14 If there are any **p** while I am gone, consult with
Dt 1:12 how can I settle all your quarrels and **p** by myself?
2Sa 15: 4 Then people could bring their **p** to me, and I would
2Ch 15: 5 safe to travel. **P** troubled the nation on every hand.
Ps 25:17 My **p** go from bad to worse. / Oh, save me from
73: 5 other people / or plagued with **p** like everyone else.
102: T with trouble, pouring out **p** before the LORD.
Da 5:12 explain riddles, and solve difficult **p**.
5:16 you can give interpretations and solve difficult **p**.
Mt 9:36 because their **p** were so great and they didn't know
13:21 but they wilt as soon as they have **p** or are
Mk 4:17 but they wilt as soon as they have **p** or are
Ro 5: 3 We can rejoice, too, when we run into **p** and trials,
1Co 7:28 I am trying to spare you the extra **p** that come with
Gal 6: 2 Share each other's troubles and **p**, and in this way

PROCEDURE (4) [PROCEED]

Lev 4:20 following the same **p** as with the sin offering for
15: 8 if he spits on you, you must undergo the same **p**.
Col 2:11 you were "circumcised," but not by a physical **p**.
2:11 It was a spiritual **p**—the cutting away of your

PROCEDURES (5) [PROCEED]

Lev 5:10 following all the **p** that have been prescribed.
Nu 15:14 to the LORD, they must follow the same **p**.
1Ch 23:31 all times, following all the **p** they had been given.
24:19 **p** established by their ancestor Aaron in obedience
1Co 16: 1 You should follow the same **p** I gave to the

PROCEED (5) [PROCEDURE, PROCEDURES, PROCEEDED, PROCEEDING, PROCEEDS, PROCESSION]

Ezr 10: 4 for it is your duty to tell us how to **p** in setting
Pr 21:29 put up a bold front, but the upright **p** with care.
Jer 23:25 last night.' And then they **p** to tell lies in my name.
Lk 13:33 tomorrow, and the next day I must **p** on my way.
14: 5 into a pit, don't you **p** at once to get him out?"

PROCEEDED (10) [PROCEED]

Ex 40:16 Moses **p** to do everything as the LORD had
Nu 21:18 left the wilderness and **p** on through Mattanah,
Jos 15: 6 then **p** north of Beth-arabah to the stone of Bohan.
15:11 then **p** to the slope of the hill north of Ekron,
18:13 and **p** down to Ataroth-addar to the top of the hill
18:17 From En-rogel the boundary **p** northeast to
2Ch 20:28 and trumpets and **p** to the Temple of the LORD.
Ne 12:31 One of the choirs **p** southward along the top of the
12:37 of David and then **p** to the Water Gate on the east.
12:40 were giving thanks then **p** to the Temple of God,

PROCEEDING (1) [PROCEED]

Jos 19:11 and **p** to the brook east of Jokneam.

PROCEEDS (1) [PROCEED]

Ac 2:45 and shared the **p** with those in need.

PROCESS (12)

Ge 50: 3 The embalming **p** took forty days, and there was a
Ex 21:22 and in the **p**, they hurt a pregnant woman so her
22: 2 act of breaking into a house and is killed in the **p**,
Lev 25: 5 or **p** the grapes that grow on your unpruned vines.
25:11 and do not **p** the grapes that grow on your
2Sa 11: 1 In the **p** they laid siege to the city of Rabbah.
1Ch 20: 1 In the **p** they laid siege to the city of Rabbah
Mt 16:26 the whole world but lose your own soul in the **p**?
18:24 In the **p**, one of his debtors was brought in who
Mk 8:36 the whole world but lose your own soul in the **p**?
9: 3 far whiter than any earthly **p** could ever make it.
Lk 9:25 but lose or forfeit your own soul in the **p**?

PROCESSION (12) [PROCEED]

2Sa 3:31 And King David himself walked behind the **p** to
Ne 12:36 the man of God. Ezra the scribe led this **p**.
Job 21:33 A great funeral **p** goes to the cemetery. Many pay
Ps 42: 4 leading a great **p** to the house of God,
45:15 What a joyful, enthusiastic **p** / as they enter the
68:24 Your **p** has come into view, O God— / the **p** of my God and King
Isa 60:11 of the world will be led as captives in a victory **p**.
Mt 21: 9 He was in the center of the **p**, and the crowds all
Mk 11: 9 He was in the center of the **p**, and the crowds all
Lk 7:12 A funeral **p** was coming out as he approached the
2Co 2:14 and leads us along in Christ's triumphal **p**.

PROCLAIM (32) [PROCLAIMED, PROCLAIMING, PROCLAIMS, PROCLAMATION]

Lev 25:10 as holy, a time to **p** release for all who live there.
Dt 27:12 and Benjamin must stand on Mount Gerizim to **p** a
27:13 and Naphtali must stand on Mount Ebal to **p** a
32: 3 I will **p** the name of the LORD; / how glorious is
2Sa 1:20 will rejoice. / Don't **p** it in the streets of Ashkelon,
1Ki 13:32 For the message the LORD told him to **p** against
1Ch 16: 8 Give thanks to the LORD and **p** his greatness.
16:23 Each day **p** the good news that he saves.
25: 1 and Jeduthun to **p** God's messages to the
Ps 50: 6 Then let the heavens **p** his justice, / for God
71:15 All day long I will **p** your saving power,
71:18 Let me **p** your power to this new generation,
75: 9 But as for me, I will always **p** what God has done;
88:11 place of destruction, can they **p** your faithfulness?
92: 2 It is good to **p** your unfailing love in the morning,
96: 2 Each day **p** the good news that he saves.
105: 1 Give thanks to the LORD and **p** his greatness.
145: 6 will be on every tongue; / I will **p** your greatness.
Isa 25: 9 In that day the people will **p**, "This is our God.
45:19 I publicly **p** bold promises. I do not whisper
Jer 23:28 but let my true messengers faithfully **p** my every
31:10 you nations of the world; **p** it in distant coastlands:
Am 3: 8 has spoken—I dare not refuse to **p** his message!
Mt 12:18 upon him, / and he will **p** justice to the nations.
24: 7 and kingdoms will **p** war against each other,
Mk 13: 8 and kingdoms will **p** war against each other,
Lk 4:18 He has sent me to **p** / that captives will be released,
21:10 and kingdoms will **p** war against each other.
Gal 1:16 so that I could **p** the Good News about Jesus to the
Col 1:23 and I, Paul, have been appointed by God to **p** it.
4: 4 Pray that I will **p** this message as clearly as I
1Jn 4:15 All who **p** that Jesus is the Son of God have God

PROCLAIMED (20) [PROCLAIM]

Nu 23:21 their God is with them; / he has been **p** their king.
Dt 4:13 He **p** his covenant, which he commanded you to
1Sa 31: 9 Then they **p** the news of Saul's death in their
2Sa 2: 9 There he **p** Ishbosheth king over Gilead, Jezreel,
1Ki 22:11 son of Kenaanah, made some iron horns and **p**,
2Ki 11:12 with a copy of God's covenant and **p** him king.
13:17 Then Elisha **p**, "This is the LORD's arrow,
1Ch 10: 9 Then they **p** the news of Saul's death before their
25: 2 who **p** God's messages by the king's orders.
25: 3 who **p** God's messages to the accompaniment of
2Ch 18:10 son of Kenaanah, made some iron horns and **p**,
23:11 Joash with a copy of God's laws and **p** him king.
Est 3:15 and it was **p** in the fortress of Susa.
8:13 as law in every province and **p** to all the people.
Isa 44: 8 Have I not **p** from ages past what my purposes are

51: 4 Hear me, Israel, for my law will be **p**, and my
Eze 24:18 So I **p** this to the people the next morning, and in
Da 5:29 and he was **p** the third highest ruler in the
Zec 7: 7 Isn't this the same message the LORD **p** through
2Pe 1:19 we have even greater confidence in the message **p**

PROCLAIMING (8) [PROCLAIM]
Est 1:22 **p** that every man should be the ruler of his home.
Ps 64: 9 will stand in awe, / **p** the mighty acts of God,
Jer 34: 8 covenant with the people, **p** freedom for the slaves.
Ac 28:31 **p** the Kingdom of God with all boldness
Col 1:25 by **p** his message in all its fullness to you Gentiles.
1Th 3: 2 and our brother in **p** the Good News of Christ.
Heb 13:15 of praise to God by **p** the glory of his name.
Rev 20: 4 their testimony about Jesus, for **p** the word of God.

PROCLAIMS (2) [PROCLAIM]
Dt 18:19 listen to the messages the prophet **p** on my behalf.
Ps 2: 7 The king **p** the LORD's decree: / "The LORD

PROCLAMATION (8) [PROCLAIM]
Ge 26:11 Then Abimelech made a public **p**: "Anyone who
2Ch 24: 9 Then a **p** was sent throughout Judah
30: 5 So they sent a **p** throughout all Israel,
36:22 stirring the heart of Cyrus to put this **p** into writing
Ezr 1: 1 stirring the heart of Cyrus to put this **p** into writing
10: 7 Then a **p** was made throughout Judah
Ne 8:15 He had said that a **p** should be made throughout
2Ti 1: 8 be ready to suffer with me for the **p** of the Good

PROCORUS (1)
Ac 6: 5 Holy Spirit), Philip, **P**, Nicanor, Timon, Parmenas,

PRODUCE (68) [PRODUCED, PRODUCES, PRODUCING, PRODUCTION, PRODUCTIVE, PRODUCTS, REPRODUCE]
Ge 1:11 The seeds will then **p** the kinds of plants and trees
3:19 All your life you will sweat to **p** food, until your
4: 3 Cain brought to the LORD a gift of his farm **p**,
31: 8 the whole flock began to **p** speckled lambs.
49:20 "Asher will **p** rich foods, / food fit for kings.
Ex 5:11 But you must **p** just as many bricks as before!"
30:35 refine it to **p** a pure and holy incense.
Lev 23:39 after you have harvested all the **p** of the land,
25: 6 the **p** that grows naturally during the Sabbath year.
25:12 eat the **p** that grows naturally in the fields that
25:21 so the land will **p** a bumper crop, enough to
25:22 you will still be eating the **p** of the previous year.
26: 4 then yield its crops, and the trees will **p** their fruit.
27:30 "A tenth of the **p** of the land, whether grain
Dt 6:11 will be richly stocked with goods you did not **p**.
22: 9 grapes from the vineyard or the **p** of the other crop.
26: 2 put some of the first **p** from each harvest into a
26:10 Then place the **p** before the LORD your God
30: 9 and your fields will **p** abundant harvests,
2Sa 9:10 and servants are to farm the land for him to **p** food
2Ch 31: 5 olive oil, honey, and all the **p** of their fields.
Ezr 9:12 You promised that we would enjoy the good **p** of
Ne 9:37 The lush **p** of this land piles up in the hands of the
10:37 We will store the **p** in the storerooms of the
13:15 grapes, figs, and all sorts of **p** to Jerusalem to sell.
13:15 So I rebuked them for selling their **p** on the
Ps 60: 7 Ephraim will **p** my warriors, / and Judah will **p** my kings.
92:14 Even in old age they will still **p** fruit; / they will
104:14 You allow them to **p** food from the earth—
108: 8 Ephraim will **p** my warriors, / and Judah will **p** my kings.
144:14 and may our oxen be loaded down with **p**.
Pr 13:23 A poor person's farm may **p** much food,
Isa 5:10 Ten acres of vineyard will not **p** even six gallons
7:22 and wild honey because that is all the land will **p**.
Jer 29: 5 plan to stay. Plant gardens, and eat the food you **p**.
Eze 17: 8 a splendid vine and **p** rich leaves and luscious fruit.
36: 8 But the mountains of Israel will **p** heavy crops of
48:18 This farmland will **p** food for the people working
Hag 2:17 and hail to destroy all the **p** of your labor.
Zec 8:12 The earth will **p** its crops, and the sky will release
Mt 3:10 every tree that does not **p** good fruit will be
7:18 A good tree can't **p** bad fruit, and a bad tree can't **p** good fruit.
7:19 So every tree that does not **p** good fruit is chopped
13:23 truly accept God's message and **p** a huge harvest—
13:26 When the crop began to grow and **p** grain,
21:43 and given to a nation that will **p** the proper fruit.
Mk 4:20 and accept God's message and **p** a huge harvest—
Lk 3: 9 every tree that does not **p** good fruit will be
6:43 "A good tree can't **p** bad fruit, and a bad tree can't **p** good fruit.
8:15 cling to it, and steadily **p** a huge harvest.
Jn 12:24 But its death will **p** many new kernels—a plentiful
15: 2 He cuts off every branch that doesn't **p** fruit,
15: 2 that do bear fruit so they will **p** even more.
15: 4 For a branch cannot **p** fruit if it is severed from the
15: 5 remain in me, and I in them, will **p** much fruit.
15: 8 My true disciples **p** much fruit. This brings great
15:16 I appointed you to go and **p** fruit that will last,
Ro 7: 4 As a result, you can **p** good fruit, that is,
2Co 4:17 Yet they **p** for us an immeasurably great glory that
9:10 and he will **p** a great harvest of generosity in you.
Gal 5:19 sinful nature, your lives will **p** these evil results:
5:22 controls our lives, he will **p** this kind of fruit in us:
Heb 13:20[-21] May he **p** in you, through the power of Jesus
2Pe 1: 5 Then your faith will **p** a life of moral excellence.

PRODUCED (23) [PRODUCE]
Ge 1:12 and their seeds **p** plants and trees of like kind.
2: 9 in the garden—beautiful trees that **p** delicious fruit.
30:12 Then Zilpah **p** a second son,
31:38 your sheep and goats so they **p** healthy offspring.
Nu 17: 8 of Levi, had sprouted, blossomed, and **p** almonds!
Dt 33:14 grow in the sun, / and the bounty **p** each month;
1Ki 5:10 So Hiram **p** for Solomon as much cedar
2Ch 26:15 And he **p** machines mounted on the walls of
Job 29: 6 In those days my cows **p** milk in abundance,
Eze 17: 6 It soon **p** strong branches and luxuriant leaves.
Hag 2:19 and the olive tree have **p** their crops.
Mt 7:20 a tree or a person is by the kind of fruit that is **p**.
13: 8 fell on fertile soil and **p** a crop that was thirty,
13:22 of this life and the lure of wealth, so no crop is **p**.
Mk 4: 7 choked out the tender blades so that it **p** no grain.
4: 8 seed fell on fertile soil and **p** a crop that was thirty,
4:19 and the desire for nice things, so no crop is **p**.
Lk 8: 8 and **p** a crop one hundred times as much as had
12:16 "A rich man had a fertile farm that **p** fine crops.
Ro 2:29 the body but a change of heart **p** by God's Spirit.
7: 5 and the law aroused these evil desires that **p** sinful
2Co 7:11 Just see what this godly sorrow **p** in you!
Php 1:11 those good things that are **p** in your life by Jesus

PRODUCES (15) [PRODUCE]
Lev 27:16 fifty pieces of silver for an area that **p** five bushels
Ne 10:37 to the Levites a tenth of everything our land **p**,
Pr 3: 9 and with the best part of everything your land **p**.
20: 1 Wine **p** mockers; liquor leads to brawls.
29:15 To discipline and reprimand a child **p** wisdom,
Isa 55:11 with my word. I send it out, and it always **p** fruit.
Mt 7:17 tree **p** good fruit, and an unhealthy tree **p** bad fruit.
12:35 A good person **p** good words from a good heart,
12:35 and an evil person **p** evil words from an evil heart.
Mk 4:28 because the earth **p** crops on its own. First a leaf
Lk 6:44 A tree is identified by the kind of fruit it **p**.
6:45 A good person **p** good deeds from a good heart,
6:45 and an evil person **p** evil deeds from an evil heart.
Eph 5: 9 For this light within you **p** only what is good

PRODUCING (10) [PRODUCE]
Ge 49:21 is a deer let loose, / **p** magnificent fawns.
Jdg 9: 9 'Should I quit **p** the olive oil that blesses both God
9:11 'Should I quit **p** my sweet fruit just to wave back
9:13 'Should I quit **p** the wine that cheers both God
Isa 55:10 **p** seed for the farmer and bread for the hungry.
Jer 17: 8 stay green, and they go right on **p** delicious fruit.
Eze 17:23 noble cedar, sending forth its branches and **p** seed.
Hos 4: 3 That is why your land is not **p**. It is filled with
8: 7 The stalks of wheat wither, **p** no grain. And if there
Jude 1:12 giving rain, promising much but **p** nothing.

PRODUCTION (1) [PRODUCE]
Ex 5: 8 But don't reduce their **p** quotas by a single brick.

PRODUCTIVE (3) [PRODUCE]
Dt 28: 4 will be blessed with many children and **p** fields.
Isa 59: 6 Nothing they do is **p**; all their activity is filled with
2Pe 1: 8 the more you will become **p** and useful in your

PRODUCTS (2) [PRODUCE]
Ge 43:11 do this. Fill your bags with the best **p** of the land.
2Ki 8: 9 with the finest **p** of Damascus as a gift for Elisha.

PROFANE (3) [PROFANED, PROFANING, PROFANITY]
Lev 18:21 for you must not **p** the name of your God.
19:12 swear a falsehood and so **p** the name of your God.
22: 2 me with great care, so they do not **p** my holy name.

PROFANED (2) [PROFANE]
Lev 20: 3 and **p** my holy name by giving their children to
Eze 44: 7 you **p** my Temple even as you offered me my food,

PROFANING (2) [PROFANE]
Lev 19: 8 you will answer for the sin of **p** what is holy to the
Ne 13:17 "Why are you **p** the Sabbath in this evil way?

PROFANITY (1) [PROFANE]
Ps 35:16 They mock me with the worst kind of **p**, / and they

PROFESS (1)
Ac 17: 7 for they **p** allegiance to another king, Jesus."

PROFESSIONAL (2)
Am 5:16 and summon **p** mourners to wail and lament.
7:14 Amos replied, "I'm not one of your **p** prophets.

PROFIT (6) [PROFITS]
Pr 3:14 For the **p** of wisdom is better than silver, and her
14:23 Work brings **p**, but mere talk leads to poverty!
Ecc 5: 9 Even the king milks the land for his own **p**!
Isa 33:15 and fair, who reject making a **p** by fraud,
Eze 22:27 They actually destroy people's lives for **p**!
Jas 4:13 a year. We will do business there and make a **p**."

PROFITS (2) [PROFIT]
Isa 23:18 But in the end her businesses will give their **p** to
Lk 19:15 had done with the money and what their **p** were.

PROFOUND (1)
Zec 12:12 "All Israel will weep in **p** sorrow, each family by

PROGRAM (2)
Ge 41:33 in Egypt and put him in charge of a nationwide **p**.
Ac 6: 2 of God, not administering a food **p**," they said.

PROGRESS (5) [PROGRESSING]
Nu 33: 2 Moses kept a written record of their **p**.
2Ch 24:13 renovation worked hard, and they made steady **p**.
Hos 10: 9 and more sin! You have made no **p** whatsoever.
1Ti 4:15 into your tasks so that everyone will see your **p**.
Heb 12: 1 especially the sin that so easily hinders our **p**.

PROGRESSING (1) [PROGRESS]
2Sa 11: 7 army were getting along and how the war was **p**.

PROHIBIT (1) [PROHIBITED]
Mt 18:18 Whatever you **p** on earth is prohibited in heaven,

PROHIBITED (1) [PROHIBIT]
Mt 18:18 Whatever you prohibit on earth is **p** in heaven,

PROJECT (8) [PROJECTED, PROJECTING, PROJECTS]
Ge 41:40 I hereby appoint you to direct this **p**. You will
Ex 36: 7 were more than enough to complete the whole **p**.
38:22 of the tribe of Judah, was in charge of the whole **p**,
Nu 1: 3 to go to war. You and Aaron are to direct the **p**,
1Ki 15:21 he abandoned his **p** of fortifying Ramah
1Ch 22:17 all the leaders of Israel to assist Solomon in this **p**.
2Ch 16: 5 he abandoned his **p** of fortifying Ramah.
2Co 8:11 Now you should carry this **p** through to completion

PROJECTED (2) [PROJECT]
1Ki 6: 3 It **p** outward 15 feet from the front of the Temple.
7:31 It **p** 1-1/2 feet above the cart's top like a round

PROJECTING (2) [PROJECT]
Ne 3:26 as the Water Gate toward the east and the **p** tower.
3:27 who repaired another section opposite the great **p**

PROJECTS (7) [PROJECT]
Ge 11: 3 They began to talk about construction **p**. "Come,"
1Ki 9:23 appointed 550 of them to supervise the various **p**.
2Ch 8: 1 and the great building **p** of the LORD's Temple
8:10 appointed 250 of them to supervise the various **p**.
14: 7 So they went ahead with these **p** and brought them
Ne 3:25 and the corner to the upper tower that **p** from the
Job 3:14 famous for their great construction **p**.

PROLONG (1)
Ps 85: 5 Will you **p** your wrath to distant generations?

PROMINENT (12)
Nu 16: 2 involving 250 other **p** leaders, all members of the
1Ki 21:12 and put Naboth at a **p** place before the people.
1Ch 7:40 They were all skilled warriors and **p** leaders.
9:33 The musicians, all **p** Levites, lived at the Temple.
9:34 and were listed as **p** leaders in their tribal
Eze 11: 1 where I saw twenty-five **p** men of the city.
Da 8: 8 In the large horn's place grew four **p** horns
8: 9 From one of the **p** horns came a small horn whose
8:22 The four **p** horns that replaced the one large horn
Mt 23: 6 and in the most **p** seats in the synagogue!
Ac 17:12 as did some of the **p** Greek women and many men.
25:23 by military officers and **p** men of the city.

PROMISCUITY (2) [PROMISCUOUS]
Lev 19:29 or the land will be filled with **p** and detestable
Eze 16:26 the flames of my anger with your increasing **p**.

PROMISCUOUS (2) [PROMISCUITY]
Dt 22:21 by being **p** while living in her parents' home.
SS 8: 9 But if she is **p**, we will shut her off from men."

PROMISE (124) [PROMISED, PROMISES, PROMISING]
Ge 9:11 I solemnly **p** never to send another flood to kill all
9:13 It is the sign of my permanent **p** to you and to all
26:24 I will do this because of my **p** to Abraham,
29:27 if you **p** to work another seven years for me."
38:26 because I didn't keep my **p** to let her marry my son
Ex 2:24 and remembered his covenant **p** to Abraham,
3:17 I **p** to rescue you from the oppression of the
Nu 11:21 and yet you **p** them meat for a whole month!
Dt 13: 1 about the future, and they **p** you signs or miracles,
Jos 1: 3 I **p** you what I promised Moses: 'Everywhere you
2:14 we will keep our **p** when the LORD gives us the
6:22 Then Joshua said to the two spies, "Keep your **p**.
9:21 So the Israelites kept their **p** to the Gibeonites.
14:10 these forty-five years since Moses made this **p**—
23:14 Deep in your hearts you know that every **p** of the
Jdg 11:10 leaders replied. "We **p** to do whatever you say."
11:36 "Father, you have made a **p** to the LORD.
15:12 "But **p** that you won't kill me yourselves."
1Sa 1:23 and may the LORD help you keep your **p**."
20:12 told David, "I **p** by the LORD, the God of Israel,
2Sa 7:21 For the sake of your **p** and according to your will,

7:25 my family. Confirm it as a **p** that will last forever.
1Ki 1:13 didn't you **p** me that my son Solomon would be
2: 4 then the LORD will keep the **p** he made to me:
6:12 I will fulfill through you the **p** I made to your
8:15 who has kept the **p** he made to my father, David.
8:24 You have kept your **p** to your servant David,
8:24 You made that **p** with your own mouth, and today
8:25 carry out your further **p** to your servant David,
8:26 fulfill this **p** to your servant David, my father.
9: 5 For I made this **p** to your father, David: 'You will
22:13 Be sure that you agree with them and **p** success."
1Ch 17:23 and my family. May it be a **p** that will last forever.
2Ch 1: 9 please keep your **p** to David my father,
6: 4 who has kept the **p** he made to my father, David.
6:15 You have kept your **p** to your servant David,
6:15 You made that **p** with your own mouth, and today
6:16 carry out your further **p** to your servant David,
6:17 God of Israel, fulfill this **p** to your servant David.
7:18 This is the same **p** I gave your father, David,
18:12 Be sure that you agree with them and **p** success."
Ne 5:13 of my robe and said, "If you fail to keep your **p**,
9:38 we are making a solemn **p** and putting it in writing.
10:30 "We **p** not to let our daughters marry the pagan
10:31 We further **p** that if the people of the land should
10:31 And we **p** not to do any work every seventh year
10:32 we **p** to obey the command to pay the annual
10:35 "We **p** always to bring the first part of every
10:37 And we **p** to bring to the Levites a tenth of
10:39 "So we **p** together not to neglect the Temple of
Ps 89:33 never stop loving him, / nor let my **p** to him fail.
98: 3 He has remembered his **p** to love and be faithful to
105:42 For he remembered his sacred **p** / to Abraham his
106:24 for they wouldn't believe his **p** to care for them.
119:38 Reassure me of your **p**, / which is for those who
119:49 Remember your **p** to me, / for it is my only hope.
119:50 Your **p** revives me; / it comforts me in all my
119:57 LORD, you are mine! / I **p** to obey your words!
119:106 I've promised it once, and I'll **p** again: / I will obey
119:123 to see the truth of your **p** fulfilled.
119:148 awake through the night, / thinking about your **p**.
132:11 swore to David / a **p** he will never take back:
146: 6 in them. / He is the one who keeps every **p** forever,
Pr 20:25 It is dangerous to make a rash **p** to God before
Ecc 5: 4 So when you make a **p** to God, don't delay in
5: 5 It is better to say nothing than to **p** something that
5: 6 messenger that the **p** you made was a mistake.
SS 2: 7 "**P** me, O women of Jerusalem, by the swift
3: 5 "**P** me, O women of Jerusalem, by the swift
5: 8 "Make this **p** to me, O women of Jerusalem!
8: 4 "I want you to **p**, O women of Jerusalem, not to
Jer 7: 4 But do not be fooled by those who repeatedly **p**
9: 8 They **p** peace to their neighbors while planning to
11: 5 so I could keep my **p** to your ancestors to give you
34: 4 "But listen to this **p** from the LORD,
Eze 13:19 and you **p** life to those who should not live.
38:19 I **p** a mighty shaking in the land of Israel on that
Ob 1: 7 They will **p** you peace, while plotting your
Mic 3: 5 You **p** peace for those who give you food, but you
Hag 2:19 I am giving you a **p** now while the seed is still in
Zec 9:12 I **p** this very day that I will repay you two mercies
Mt 5:37 To strengthen your **p** with a vow shows that
Lk 1:54 He has not forgotten his **p** to be merciful.
Ac 2:39 This **p** is to you and to your children, and even to
7: 5 God did **p**, however, that eventually the whole
7:17 near when God would fulfill his **p** to Abraham,
13:32 God's **p** to our ancestors has come true in our own
26: 6 the fulfillment of God's **p** made to our ancestors.
Ro 4:13 that God's **p** to give the whole earth to Abraham
4:14 So if you claim that God's **p** is for those who obey
4:14 And in that case, the **p** is also meaningless.
4:16 is the key! God's **p** is given to us as a free gift.
4:18 even though such a **p** seemed utterly impossible!
4:20 Abraham never wavered in believing God's **p**.
9: 6 has God failed to fulfill his **p** to the Jews?
9: 8 It is the children of the **p** who are considered to be
9:16 So receiving God's **p** is not up to us. We can't get
Gal 3:16 God gave the **p** to Abraham and his child.
3:16 And notice that it doesn't say the **p** was to his
3:16 But the **p** was to his child—and that, of course,
3:17 the law to Moses. God would be breaking his **p**.
3:18 it would not be the result of accepting God's **p**.
3:18 But God gave it to Abraham as a **p**.
3:19 coming of the child to whom God's **p** was made.
3:20 but God acted on his own when he made his **p** to
3:22 so the only way to receive God's **p** is to believe in
4:23 attempt to bring about the fulfillment of God's **p**.
4:23 wife was born as God's own fulfillment of his **p**.
4:28 dear brothers and sisters, are children of the **p**,
4:29 just as Isaac, the child of **p**, was persecuted by
Eph 3: 6 and enjoy together the **p** of blessings through
6: 2 first of the Ten Commandments that ends with a **p**.
6: 3 And this is the **p**: If you honor your father
Heb 4: 1 God's **p** of entering his place of rest still stands,
6:13 For example, there was God's **p** to Abraham.
6:17 so that those who received the **p** could be perfectly
6:18 So God has given us both his **p** and his oath.
6:18 for we can hold on to his **p** with confidence.
10:23 say we have, for God can be trusted to keep his **p**.
11: 9 and Jacob, to whom God gave the same **p**.
11:11 Abraham believed that God would keep his **p**.
12:26 shook the earth, but now he makes another **p**:
2Pe 2:19 They **p** freedom, but they themselves are slaves to
3: 9 The Lord isn't really being slow about his **p** to

PROMISED (226) [PROMISE]

Ge 14:22 Abram replied, "I have solemnly **p** the LORD,
18:19 and just. Then I will do for him all that I have **p**."
21: 1 Then the LORD did exactly what he had **p**.
24: 7 solemnly **p** to give this land to my offspring.
26: 3 just as I solemnly **p** Abraham, your father.
28: 4 and your descendants the blessings he **p** to
28:15 I have finished giving you everything I have **p**."
32: 9 and to my relatives, and you **p** to treat me kindly.
32:12 But you **p** to treat me kindly and to multiply my
38:17 send you a young goat from my flock," Judah **p**.
47:30 beside my ancestors." So Joseph **p** that he would.
50: 6 "Go and bury your father, as you **p**," he said.
Ex 8:13 And the LORD did as Moses had **p**. The frogs in
9:34 again by stubbornly refusing to do as they had **p**.
12:25 When you arrive in the land the LORD has **p** to
13:17 was the shortest way from Egypt to the **P** Land.
32:13 I will give them all of this land that I have **p** to
33: 1 lead them to the land I solemnly **p** Abraham,
33:12 telling me, 'Take these people up to the **P** Land.'
Lev 18:24 from the **P** Land have defiled themselves.
20:24 But I have **p** that you will inherit their land, a land
Nu 6:21 fulfill their special vow exactly as they have **p**."
10:29 the Midianite, "We are on our way to the **P** Land.
14:40 are ready to enter the land the LORD has **p** us."
23:19 to act? / Has he ever **p** and not carried it through?
32:11 or older will ever see the land I solemnly **p** to
Dt 1:11 you a thousand times more and bless you as he **p**!
1:21 the LORD, the God of your ancestors, has **p** you.
1:37 He said to me, 'You will never enter the **P** Land!
6: 3 as the LORD, the God of your ancestors, **p** you.
6:18 that the LORD solemnly **p** to give your ancestors.
6:23 so he could give us this land he had solemnly **p** to
7:12 love with you, as he solemnly **p** your ancestors.
9: 3 and drive them out, just as the LORD has **p**.
11:25 will send fear and dread ahead of you, as he **p** you,
12:20 your God enlarges your territory as he has **p**,
13:17 great nation, just as he solemnly **p** your ancestors.
15: 6 The LORD your God will bless you as he has **p**.
18: 2 himself is their inheritance, just as he **p** them.
19: 8 as he solemnly **p** your ancestors, and gives you all
the land he **p** them,
23:21 your God, be prompt in doing whatever you **p** him.
26:15 and honey—just as you solemnly **p** our ancestors.'
26:17 You have **p** to obey his laws, commands,
26:18 his own special treasure, just as he **p**, and that you
26:19 that is holy to the LORD your God, just as he **p**."
27: 3 as the LORD, the God of your ancestors, **p** you.
28: 9 you as his holy people as he solemnly **p** to do.
28:68 a journey I **p** you would never again make.
29:13 to confirm that he is your God, just as he **p** you,
31: 3 and he will go with you, just as the LORD **p**.
34: 4 "This is the land I **p** on oath to Abraham, Isaac,
Jos 1: 3 I promise you what I **p** Moses: 'Everywhere you
5: 7 not been circumcised on the way to the **P** Land—
13:14 Instead, as the LORD had **p** them,
13:33 the God of Israel, had **p** to be their inheritance.
14: 8 and discouraged them from entering the **P** Land.
14: 9 So that day Moses **p** me, 'The land of Canaan on
14:10 and well as he **p** for all these forty-five years since
14:12 to give me the hill country that the LORD **p** me.
21:44 just as he had solemnly **p** their ancestors.
22: 4 God has given the other tribes rest, as he **p** them.
23: 5 of them, just as the LORD your God **p** you.
23:10 LORD your God fights for you, just as he has **p**.
23:15 your God has given you the good things he **p**,
Jdg 1:20 city of Hebron was given to Caleb as Moses had **p**.
2:15 against them, bringing them defeat, just as he **p**.
6:36 are truly going to use me to rescue Israel as you **p**,
6:37 you are going to help me rescue Israel as you **p**."
11:36 You must do to me what you have **p**,
1Sa 2:30 I had **p** that your branch of the tribe of Levi would
22: 7 the news. "Has David **p** you fields and vineyards?
22: 7 Has he **p** to make you commanders in his army?
24:22 So David **p**, and Saul went home. But David
25:30 When the LORD has done all he **p** and has made
28:10 took an oath in the name of the LORD and **p**,
2Sa 3: 9 help David get all that the LORD has **p** him!
7:25 do as you have **p** concerning me and my family.
7:28 and you have **p** these good things to me,
9: 1 for he had **p** Jonathan that he would show kindness
14:13 all the people of God as you have **p** to do for me?
15: 8 I **p** to sacrifice to him in Hebron if he would bring
1Ki 2:24 David; he has established my dynasty as he **p**.
5:12 gave great wisdom to Solomon just as he had **p**.
8:20 "And now the LORD has done what he **p**,
8:56 who has given rest to his people Israel, just as he **p**.
13: 3 and he said, "The LORD has **p** to give this sign:
14:18 as the LORD had **p** through the prophet Ahijah.
15:29 just as the LORD had **p** concerning Jeroboam by
16:12 as the LORD had **p** through the prophet Jehu.
17:16 just as the LORD had **p** through Elijah.
21:29 done this, I will not do what I **p** during his lifetime.
22:38 licked the king's blood, just as the LORD had **p**.
2Ki 1:17 just as the LORD had **p** through Elijah.
4:44 and some left over, just as the LORD had **p**.
7:16 half an ounce of silver, just as the LORD had **p**.
8:19 and **p** that his descendants would continue to rule
10:17 just as the LORD had **p** through Elijah.
14:25 God of Israel, had **p** through Jonah son of Amittai,
20: 9 LORD will give you to prove he will do as he **p**.
22:20 I will not send the **p** disaster against this city until
23:16 This happened just as the LORD had **p** through
24: 2 just as the LORD had **p** through his prophets.
25:24 of Babylon, and all will go well for you," he **p**.
1Ch 11: 3 just as the LORD had **p** through Samuel.
11:10 just as the LORD had **p** concerning Israel.
12:23 king instead of Saul, just as the LORD had **p**.
17:23 do as you have **p** concerning me and my family.
17:26 And you have **p** these good things to me,
27:23 because the LORD had **p** to make the Israelites as
2Ch 6:10 "And now the LORD has done what he **p**,
21: 7 and **p** that his descendants would continue to rule
23: 3 The LORD has **p** that a descendant of David will
34:28 I will not send the **p** disaster against this city
34:31 He **p** to obey all the terms of the covenant that
Ezr 9:12 You **p** that if we avoided these things, we would
9:12 You **p** that we would enjoy the good produce of
Ne 5:12 and officials formally vow to do what they had **p**.
5:13 the LORD. And the people did as they had **p**.
9: 8 And you have done what you **p**, for you are always
9:23 and brought them into the land you had **p** to their
10:29 They solemnly **p** to carefully follow all the
Est 4: 7 and told him how much money Haman had **p** to
Ps 25:13 and their children will inherit the **P** Land.
47: 4 He chose the **P** Land as our inheritance, / the proud
54: 5 Do as you **p** and put an end to them.
60: 6 God has **p** this by his holiness: / "I will divide up
68: 9 O God, / to refresh the weary **P** Land.
89:49 You **p** it to David with a faithful pledge.
102:13 the time to pity her, / now is the time you **p** to help.
108: 7 God has **p** this by his holiness: / "I will divide up
119:41 your unfailing love, / the salvation that you **p** me.
119:58 I want your blessings. / Be merciful just as you **p**.
119:65 many good things for me, LORD, / just as you **p**.
119:76 love comfort me, / just as you **p** me, your servant.
119:106 I've **p** it once, and I'll promise again: / I will obey
119:107 O LORD; / restore my life again, just as you **p**.
119:116 LORD, sustain me as you **p**, that I may live!
119:154 my case; take my side! / Protect my life as you **p**.
119:169 to my cry; / give me the discerning mind you **p**.
119:170 Listen to my prayer; / rescue me as you **p**.
Pr 25:14 A person who doesn't give a **p** gift is like clouds
Isa 7:11 to prove that I will crush your enemies as I have **p**.
34:16 none will lack a mate, for the LORD has **p** this.
38: 7 LORD will give you to prove he will do as he **p**:
55: 3 all the mercies and unfailing love that I **p** to David.
58:14 and give you your full share of the inheritance I **p**
Jer 2: 7 my land and corrupted the inheritance I had **p** you.
4:10 by what you said, for you **p** peace for Jerusalem.
11: 6 your ancestors made, and do everything they **p**.
19:15 upon this city and its surrounding towns just as I **p**,
20: 6 and all your friends to whom you **p** that everything
25:13 I will bring upon them all the terrors I have **p** in
28:11 "The LORD has **p** that within two years he will
29:10 and do for you all the good things I have **p**,
32:22 land that you had **p** their ancestors long before—
32:42 upon them, so I will do all the good I have **p** them.
33:14 do for Israel and Judah all the good I have **p** them.
36:31 of Judah and Jerusalem all the disasters I have **p**,
38:16 So King Zedekiah secretly **p** him, "As surely as
La 1:21 Oh, bring the day you **p**, when you will destroy
Eze 20: 6 I **p** that I would bring her and her descendants out
20: 9 at Israel's God, who had **p** to deliver his people.
20:28 for when I brought them into the land I had **p**
20:42 brought you home to the land I **p** your ancestors,
36:36 For I, the LORD, have **p** this, and I will do it.
37:14 will see that I have done everything just as I **p**.
Am 9: 8 Yet I have **p** that I will never completely destroy
Mic 1:14 the kings of Israel, for it **p** help it could not give.
4: 4 nothing to fear. The LORD Almighty has **p** this!
7:20 and unfailing love as you **p** with an oath to our
Hab 2:13 Has not the LORD Almighty **p** that the wealth of
Hag 2: 5 just as I **p** when you came out of Egypt.
Zec 8:14 your ancestors angered me and I **p** to punish them,
Mt 14: 7 so he **p** with an oath to give her anything she
Mk 6:23 Then he **p**, "I will give you whatever you ask,
14:11 heard why he had come, and they **p** him a reward.
Lk 1:55 For he **p** our ancestors—Abraham and his
1:70 just as he **p** / through his holy prophets long ago.
2:29 "Lord, now I can die in peace! / As you **p** me,
2:38 who had been waiting for the **p** King to come
22: 5 was ready to help them, and they **p** him a reward.
24:49 I will send the Holy Spirit, just as my Father **p**.
Ac 1: 4 Jerusalem until the Father sends you what he **p**.
2:30 and he knew God had **p** with an oath that one of
2:33 And the Father, as he had **p**, gave him the Holy
3:21 all things, as God **p** long ago through his prophets.
3:25 and you are included in the covenant God **p** to
13:23 Jesus, who is God's **p** Savior of Israel!
13:34 For God had **p** to raise him from the dead,
13:34 'I will give you the sacred blessings I **p** to David.'
Ro 1: 2 This Good News was **p** long ago by God through
3:21 but by the way **p** in the Scriptures long ago.
4:18 When God **p** Abraham that he would become the
4:21 convinced that God was able to do anything he **p**.
8:23 his children, including the new bodies he has **p** us.
8:30 standing with himself, and he **p** them his glory.
9: 9 For God had **p**, "Next year I will return, and Sarah
11:17 So now you also receive the blessing God has **p**
2Co 9: 5 ahead of me to make sure the gift you **p** is ready.
11: 2 For I **p** you as a pure bride to one husband, Christ.
Gal 3: 8 God **p** this good news to Abraham long ago when
3:14 Gentiles with the same blessing he **p** to Abraham,
3:14 and we Christians receive the **p** Holy Spirit
5: 5 **p** to us who are right with God through faith.
Eph 1:13 giving you the Holy Spirit, whom he **p** long ago.
1:14 guarantee that he will give us everything he **p**
1:18 the wonderful future he has **p** to those he called.
2Ti 1: 1 sent out to tell others about the life he has **p**
Tit 1: 2 which God **p** them before the world began—
Heb 1: 2 God **p** everything to the Son as an inheritance,
6:15 waited patiently, and he received what God had **p**.
9:15 can receive the eternal inheritance God has **p** them.
9:17 no one can use the will to get any of the things **p** to
10:36 God's will. Then you will receive all that he has **p**.

11: 9 And even when he reached the land God **p** him,
11:13 ones died without receiving what God had **p** them,
11:18 though God had **p** him, "Isaac is the son through
11:33 with justice, and received what God had **p** them.
11:39 yet none of them received all that God had **p**.
Jas 1:12 of life that God has **p** to those who love him.
2: 5 inherit the kingdom God **p** to those who love him?
2Pe 1: 4 He has **p** that you will escape the decadence all
3: 4 "Jesus **p** to come back, did he? Then where is he?
3:13 to the new heavens and new earth he has **p**,
1Jn 2:25 in this fellowship we enjoy the eternal life he **p** us.

PROMISES (62) [PROMISE]

Nu 10:29 for the LORD has given wonderful **p** to Israel!"
Jos 21:45 All of the good **p** that the LORD had given Israel
1Sa 20:23 And may the LORD make us keep our **p** to each
2Sa 22:31 his way is perfect. / All the LORD's **p** prove true.
1Ki 8:23 You keep your **p** and show unfailing love to all
8:56 Not one word has failed of all the wonderful **p** he
2Ki 19:10 Don't let this God you trust deceive you with **p**
2Ch 6:14 You keep your **p** and show unfailing love to all
Ne 13:29 and the **p** and vows of the priests and Levites.
Ps 12: 6 The LORD's **p** are pure, / like silver refined in a
15: 4 the LORD / and keep their **p** even when it hurts.
18:30 his way is perfect. / All the LORD's **p** prove true.
55:20 friend of mine, he betrayed me; / he broke his **p**.
71:22 because you are faithful to your **p**, O God.
74:20 Remember your covenant **p**, / for the land is full of
77: 8 gone forever? / Have his **p** permanently failed?
91: 4 His faithful **p** are your armor and protection.
106:12 Then at last his people believed his **p**. / Then they
116:14 I will keep my **p** to the LORD / in the presence of
116:18 I will keep my **p** to the LORD / in the presence of
119:82 My eyes are straining to see your **p** come true.
119:140 Your **p** have been thoroughly tested; / that is why I
138: 2 and faithfulness, / because your **p** are backed
Pr 31: 2 O my son, O son of my womb, O son of my **p**,
Ecc 5: 2 And don't make rash **p** to God, for he is in heaven,
5: 4 pleasure in fools. Keep all the **p** you make to him.
Isa 19:21 They will make **p** to the LORD and keep them.
30: 7 Egypt's **p** are worthless! I call her the Harmless
33: 1 You expect others to respect their **p** to you, while you betray your **p** to them.
33: 8 and care nothing for the **p** they made before
37:10 Don't let this God you trust deceive you with **p**
45:19 I publicly proclaim bold **p**. I do not whisper
48: 1 You don't follow through on any of your **p**,
62: 6 LORD day and night for the fulfillment of his **p**.
Jer 44:25 Then go ahead and carry out your **p** and vows to
La 2:17 He has fulfilled the **p** of disaster he made long ago.
Da 9: 4 You always fulfill your **p** of unfailing love to those
11:23 By making deceitful **p**, he will make various
Hos 10: 4 and make **p** they don't intend to keep.
Mal 1:14 "Cursed is the cheat who **p** to give a fine ram from
Lk 1: 2 of what God has done in fulfillment of his **p**.
Ro 1:31 break their **p**, and are heartless and unforgiving.
3: 3 but just because they broke their **p**, does that mean God will break his **p**?
9: 4 of worshiping him and receiving his wonderful **p**.
11:28 his chosen people because of his **p** to Abraham,
15: 4 encouragement as we wait patiently for God's **p**.
15: 8 that God is true to the **p** he made to their ancestors.
2Co 1:20 For all of God's **p** have been fulfilled in him.
7: 1 Because we have these **p**, dear friends, let us
Gal 3:21 is there a conflict between God's law and God's **p**?
3:29 and now all the **p** God gave to him belong to you.
Eph 2:12 and you did not know the **p** God had made to
1Ti 4: 8 for it **p** a reward in both this life and the next.
Heb 6:12 example of those who are going to inherit God's **p**
7: 6 the one who had already received the **p** of God.
8: 6 us a better covenant with God, based on better **p**.
11:13 it all from a distance and welcomed the **p** of God.
11:17 Abraham, who had received God's **p**, was ready to
2Pe 1: 4 he has given us all of his rich and wonderful **p**.
1: 5 effort to apply the benefits of these **p** to your life.

PROMISING (8) [PROMISE]

1Ki 22:13 "Look, all the prophets are **p** victory for the king.
2Ch 18:12 "Look, all the prophets are **p** victory for the king.
Jer 32:40 with them, **p** not to stop doing good for them.
41: 8 them go by **p** to bring him their stores of wheat,
48:15 Her most **p** youth are doomed to slaughter,"
Eze 13:22 And you have encouraged the wicked by **p** them
2Pe 2:17 away by the wind—**p** much and delivering nothing.
Jude 1:12 without giving rain, **p** much but producing nothing.

PROMOTE (1) [PROMOTED, PROMOTES]

Tit 2: 1 **p** the kind of living that reflects right teaching.

PROMOTED (6) [PROMOTE]

1Ki 14: 7 'I **p** you from the ranks of the common people
Est 3: 1 King Xerxes **p** Haman son of Hammedatha the
5:11 and how he had been **p** over all the other officials
9: 4 For Mordecai had been **p** in the king's palace,
10: 2 the greatness of Mordecai, whom the king had **p**,
Da 3:30 Then the king **p** Shadrach, Meshach,

PROMOTES (1) [PROMOTE]

Pr 10:10 at wrong cause trouble, but a bold reproof **p** peace.

PROMPT (2) [PROMPTLY, PROMPTS]

Dt 23:21 be **p** in doing whatever you promised him.
Pr 13:24 your children, you will be **p** to discipline them.

PROMPTLY (4) [PROMPT]

Ge 37: 5 a dream and **p** reported the details to his brothers,
40:23 however, **p** forgot all about Joseph,
Lev 19:13 or rob anyone. "Always pay your hired workers **p**.
Dt 23:21 For the LORD your God demands that you **p**

PROMPTS (1) [PROMPT]

Job 20: 3 your insults, but now my spirit **p** me to reply.

PRONE (1)

Nu 15:39 and going your own ways, as you are **p** to do.

PRONOUNCE (31) [PRONOUNCED, PRONOUNCEMENT, PRONOUNCEMENTS, PRONOUNCES, PRONOUNCING]

Ge 27: 4 Then I will **p** the blessing that belongs to you,
Lev 13: 3 and the priest must **p** the person ceremonially
13: 6 the priest will **p** the person ceremonially clean.
13: 8 then he must **p** this person ceremonially unclean,
13:11 and the priest must **p** that person ceremonially
13:13 he will **p** the person ceremonially clean
13:17 then the priest will **p** the person ceremonially
13:20 then the priest must **p** that person ceremonially
13:22 the priest must **p** the person ceremonially unclean,
13:23 and the priest will **p** that person ceremonially
13:25 then **p** that person ceremonially unclean,
13:27 the priest must **p** that person ceremonially unclean,
13:28 priest must then **p** the person ceremonially clean.
13:30 the priest must **p** the infected person ceremonially
13:34 the priest must **p** that person ceremonially clean.
13:36 he must **p** the infected person ceremonially
13:37 then **p** the infected person ceremonially clean.
13:44 The priest must **p** him ceremonially unclean
14: 7 and the priest will **p** that person to be ceremonially
14:48 then he will **p** the house clean
Dt 10: 8 before the LORD, and to **p** blessings in his name.
11:29 you must **p** a blessing from Mount Gerizim and a
21: 5 and to **p** blessings in the LORD's name.
Jdg 12: 6 because people from Ephraim cannot **p** the word
1Ch 23:13 and to **p** blessings in his name forever.
Job 9:20 I am innocent, my own mouth would **p** me guilty.
23:10 tested me like gold in a fire, he will **p** me innocent.
Jer 1:16 I will **p** judgment on my people for all their evil—
4:12 blast sent by me! Now I will **p** your destruction!"
Joel 3:12 the LORD, will sit to **p** judgment on them all.
Zec 10: 2 and interpreters of dreams **p** comfortless

PRONOUNCED (13) [PRONOUNCE]

Ge 27:23 just like Esau's. So Isaac **p** his blessing on Jacob.
Lev 13:14 the infected person will be **p** ceremonially unclean.
13:35 begins to spread after the person is **p** clean,
14: 9 in water. Then they will be **p** ceremonially clean.
14:36 so everything inside will not be **p** unclean.
22: 4 the sacred offerings until they have been **p** clean.
2Ki 9:25 Ahab? The LORD **p** this message against him:
Ps 109: 7 case is called for judgment, / let him be **p** guilty.
133: 3 And the LORD has **p** his blessing, / even life
Jer 26:19 back the terrible disaster he had **p** against them.
36: 7 For the LORD's terrible anger has been **p** against
39: 5 There the king of Babylon **p** judgment upon
Gal 3:13 But Christ has rescued us from the curse **p** by the

PRONOUNCEMENT (2) [PRONOUNCE]

Lev 13: 7 to spread after this examination and **p** by the priest,
13:15 The priest must make this **p** as soon as he sees an

PRONOUNCEMENTS (1) [PRONOUNCE]

Eze 2:10 other words of sorrow, and **p** of doom.

PRONOUNCES (1) [PRONOUNCE]

Ps 82: 1 over heaven's court; / he **p** judgment on the judges:

PRONOUNCING (1) [PRONOUNCE]

2Ch 19: 6 "Always think carefully before **p** judgment.

PROOF (21) [PROVE]

Ex 3:12 And this will serve as **p** that I have sent you:
Nu 13:27 with milk and honey. Here is some of its fruit as **p**.
Dt 22:15 and mother must bring the **p** of her virginity to the
22:17 But here is the **p** of my daughter's virginity.'
2Ki 19:29 "Here is the **p** that the LORD will protect this
Job 16: 8 me to skin and bones—as **p**, they say, of my sins.
Isa 37:30 "Here is the **p** that the LORD will protect this
Jer 28: 9 who predicts peace must carry the burden of **p**.
44:29 And this is the **p** I give you, says the LORD,
Mt 8: 4 so everyone will have **p** of your healing."
Mk 1:44 so everyone will have **p** of your healing."
Lk 5:14 so everyone will have **p** of your healing."
Jn 3: 2 Your miraculous signs are **p** enough that God is
10:25 The **p** is what I do in the name of my Father.
Ac 11:23 When he arrived and saw this **p** of God's favor,
1Co 9: 2 for you are living **p** that I am the Lord's apostle.
2Co 12:12 I certainly gave you every **p** that I am truly an
13: 3 I will give you all the **p** you want that Christ
1Th 1: 5 you was further **p** of the truth of our message.
Heb 9:18 required under the first covenant as a **p** of death.
1Jn 4:13 And God has given us his Spirit as **p** that we live

PROOFS (2) [PROVE]

Isa 45:21 your case, and state your **p** that idol worship pays.
Ac 9:22 and the Jews in Damascus couldn't refute his **p**

PROPAGANDA (1)

Ac 4:17 perhaps we can stop them from spreading their **p**.

PROPER (33) [PROPERLY]

Lev 5:15 and it must be of the **p** value in silver as measured
5:18 no physical defects, and it must be of the **p** value.
23: 4 the holy occasions to be observed at the **p** time
23:37 and drink offerings—each on its **p** day.
Nu 9: 2 Israelites to celebrate the Passover at the **p** time,
9: 7 at the **p** time with the rest of the Israelites?"
9:13 to present the LORD's offering at the **p** time.
19:13 and do not purify themselves in the **p** way defile
28: 7 Along with it you must present the **p** drink
Dt 11:14 then he will send the rains in their **p** seasons
16: 1 always celebrate the Passover at the **p** time in early
28:12 The LORD will send rain at the **p** time from his
33:19 to offer **p** sacrifices there. / They benefit from the
1Ki 14:13 member of your family who will have a **p** burial,
1Ch 15:13 We failed to ask God how to move it in the **p**
23:31 The **p** number of Levites served in the LORD's
Ne 13:11 back again and restored them to their **p** duties.
13:31 of wood for the altar was brought at the **p** times
Est 1:20 will receive **p** respect from their wives!"
Job 5:26 old age. You will not be harvested until the **p** time!
38:32 Can you ensure the **p** sequence of the seasons
Ps 4: 5 Offer **p** sacrifices, / and trust in the LORD.
25: 8 he shows the **p** path to those who go astray.
Isa 14:20 You will not be given a **p** burial, for you have
Jer 8: 7 the crane. They all return at the **p** time each year.
Mt 21:43 and given to a nation that will produce the **p** fruit.
22:11 he noticed a man who wasn't wearing the **p** clothes
Lk 1:20 For my words will certainly come true at the **p**
22:14 Then at the **p** time Jesus and the twelve apostles
1Co 14:34 It is not **p** for them to speak. They should be
16:18 You must give **p** honor to all who serve so well.
1Ti 2: 6 message that God gave to the world at the **p** time.
5:20 so that others will have a **p** fear of God.

PROPERLY (7) [PROPER]

Lev 19: 5 offer it **p** so it will be accepted on your behalf.
22:29 it must be sacrificed **p** so it will be accepted on
2Ch 1:10 Give me wisdom and knowledge to rule them **p**,
1:11 for wisdom and knowledge to **p** govern my people,
30:19 even though they are not **p** cleansed for the
Est 1:15 the king's orders, **p** sent through his eunuchs?"
1Co 14:40 But be sure that everything is done **p** and in order.

PROPERTY (71)

Ge 34:10 with us. You are free to acquire **p** among us."
Ex 6: 8 Isaac, and Jacob. It will be your very own **p**.
9: 4 make a distinction between the **p** of the Israelites
10:26 All our **p** must go with us; not a hoof can be left
21:21 not be punished, since the slave is the owner's **p**.
22: 8 or not it was the neighbor who stole the **p**.
22:12 But if the animal or **p** was stolen, payment must be
Lev 5:15 by unintentionally defiling the LORD's sacred **p**,
6: 4 whether a security deposit, or **p** entrusted to them,
25:14 an agreement with a neighbor to buy or sell **p**,
25:30 city will become the permanent **p** of the buyer.
25:31 will be treated like **p** in the open fields.
25:33 And any **p** that can be redeemed by the Levites—
25:33 the cities reserved for the Levites are the only **p**
25:34 never be sold. It is their permanent ancestral **p**.
25:41 and they will return to their clan and ancestral **p**.
25:45 born in your land. You may treat them as your **p**,
27:16 dedicate to the LORD a piece of your ancestral **p**,
27:21 for the LORD. It will become the **p** of the priests.
27:22 but which is not part of your ancestral **p**,
Nu 18:20 of land or share of **p** among the people of Israel.
27: 4 Give us **p** along with the rest of our relatives."
27: 7 Assign them the **p** that would have been given to
32: 5 please let us have this land as our **p** instead of
32:29 you must give them the land of Gilead as their **p**.
35: 2 to the Levites from their **p** certain towns to live in,
35: 8 These towns will come from the **p** of the people of
35:28 the high priest, the slayer may return to his own **p**.
35:32 allowing the slayer to return to his **p** before the
36: 8 in line to inherit **p** must marry within their tribe,
36: 8 so that all the Israelites will keep their ancestral **p**.
Dt 2: 5 all the hill country around Mount Seir as their **p**,
2: 9 I have given them Ar as their **p**, and I will not give
2:19 I have given the land of Ammon to them as their **p**,
3:18 your God has given you this land as your **p**,
19:14 markers your ancestors set up to mark their **p**.
25: 5 "If two brothers are living together on the same **p**
27:17 'Cursed is anyone who steals **p** from a neighbor by
Ru 4: 9 I have bought from Naomi all the **p** of Elimelech,
4:10 and to inherit the family **p** here in his hometown.
1Sa 25: 2 Maon who owned **p** near the village of Carmel.
2Sa 14: 7 He doesn't deserve to inherit his family's **p**.'
2Ki 9:26 swear that I will repay him here on Naboth's **p**,
1Ch 9: 2 The first to return to their **p** in their former towns
27:31 these officials were overseers of King David's **p**.
28: 1 the overseers of the royal **p** and livestock,
2Ch 11:14 and **p** and moved to Judah and Jerusalem,
35: 7 Then Josiah contributed from his personal **p** thirty
Ezr 10: 8 forfeit all their **p** and be expelled from the
Ne 5:13 shake you from your homes and from your **p**!"
Est 3:13 The **p** of the Jews would be given to those who
8: 2 appointed Mordecai to be in charge of Haman's **p**.

8:11 and wives, and to take the **p** of their enemies.
Job 1:10 protected him and his home and his **p** from harm.
Pr 15:25 of the proud, but he protects the **p** of widows.
22:28 Do not steal your neighbor's **p** by moving the
Isa 5: 8 Destruction is certain for you who buy up **p**
Jer 32:15 Someday people will again own **p** here in this land
37:12 the land of Benjamin, to see the **p** he had bought.
Eze 44:28 "As to **p**, the priests will not have any, for I alone
46:18 And the prince may never take anyone's **p** by
46:18 If he gives **p** to his sons, it must be from his own
46:18 any of my people unjustly evicted from their **p**."
Zep 1:13 They are the very ones whose **p** will be plundered
Mt 19:29 or sisters or father or mother or children or **p**,
Mk 10:29 or sisters or mother or father or children or **p**,
10:30 brothers, sisters, mothers, children, and **p**—
12:40 But they shamelessly cheat widows out of their **p**,
Lk 20:47 But they shamelessly cheat widows out of their **p**,
Ac 5: 1 with his wife, Sapphira, sold some **p**.
5: 4 The **p** was yours to sell or not sell, as you wished.

PROPHECIES (13) [PROPHESY]

Nu 24:23 Balaam concluded his **p** by saying: / "Alas,
2Ch 24:27 story about the sons of Joash, the **p** about him,
Jer 5:31 the prophets give false **p**, and the priests rule with
18:18 him to teach the law and give us advice and **p**.
28: 6 He said, "Amen! May your **p** come true! I hope
36: 4 Baruch wrote down all the **p** that the LORD had
Eze 13: 2 prophets of Israel who are inventing their own **p**.
13: 6 And yet they expect him to fulfill their **p**!
Am 7:13 Don't bother us here in Bethel with your **p**,
Ac 13:29 "When they had fulfilled all the **p** concerning his
17: 3 and proving the **p** about the sufferings of the
1Th 5:20 Do not scoff at **p**,
1Ti 4:14 **p** spoken to you when the elders of the church laid

PROPHECY (56) [PROPHESY]

Nu 23: 7 This was the **p** Balaam delivered:
23:18 This was the **p** Balaam delivered: / "Rise up,
24: 3 and this is the **p** he delivered: / "This is the **p** of Balaam son of Beor, / the **p** of the man whose eyes
24:15 This is the **p** Balaam delivered: / "This is the
24:15 of Beor, / the **p** of the man whose eyes see clearly,
24:20 over at the people of Amalek and delivered this **p**:
Dt 18:21 'How will we know whether the **p** is from the
2Ch 9:29 *the Prophet* and in *The P of Ahijah from Shiloh,*
10:15 for it fulfilled the **p** of the LORD spoken to
36:22 the LORD fulfilled Jeremiah's **p** by stirring the
Ezr 1: 1 the LORD fulfilled Jeremiah's **p** by stirring the
Ne 6:12 but that he had uttered this **p** against me
Jer 23:31 prophets who say, 'This **p** is from the LORD!'
23:33 'What **p** has the LORD burdened you with now?'
23:34 or anyone else says, 'I have a **p** from the LORD,'
23:36 But stop using this phrase, '**p** from the LORD.'
23:38 they respond, 'This is a **p** from the LORD!'
23:38 you have used this phrase, "**p** from the LORD,"
32: 3 put him there because he continued to give this **p**:
48:47 This is the end of Jeremiah's **p** concerning Moab.
Eze 12:23 'The time has come for every **p** to be fulfilled!'
Da 4:33 That very same hour the **p** was fulfilled,
12: 4 But you, Daniel, keep this **p** a secret; seal up the
Mt 2:17 Herod's brutal action fulfilled the **p** of Jeremiah:
4:14 This fulfilled Isaiah's **p**:
12:17 This fulfilled the **p** of Isaiah concerning him:
13:14 This fulfills the **p** of Isaiah, which says: / 'You will
13:35 This fulfilled the **p** that said, / "I will speak to you
21: 4 This was done to fulfill the **p**,
27: 9 This fulfilled the **p** of Jeremiah that says,
Lk 1:67 was filled with the Holy Spirit and gave this **p**:
22:37 For the time has come for this **p** about me to be
Jn 2:17 Then his disciples remembered this **p** from the
11:51 This **p** that Jesus should die for the entire nation
12:14 and sat on it, fulfilling the **p** that said:
12:16 realize at the time that this was a fulfillment of **p**.
Ac 2:32 "This **p** was speaking of Jesus, whom God raised
13:27 and their leaders fulfilled **p** by condemning Jesus
21: 9 four unmarried daughters who had the gift of **p**.
21:10 who also had the gift of **p**, arrived from Judea.
24:14 and everything written in the books of **p**.
Ro 9:25 the Gentiles, God says in the **p** of Hosea,
1Co 13: 2 If I had the gift of **p**, and if I knew all the mysteries
13: 8 but **p** and speaking in unknown languages
13: 9 only a little, and even the gift of **p** reveals little!
14: 1 abilities the Spirit gives, especially the gift of **p**.
14: 4 but one who speaks a word of **p** strengthens the
14: 5 For **p** is a greater and more useful gift than
14: 6 special knowledge or some **p** or some teaching—
14:22 **p**, however, is for the benefit of believers,
2Pe 1:20 you must understand that no **p** in Scripture ever
Rev 1: 3 God blesses the one who reads this **p** to the church,
19:10 For the essence of **p** is to give a clear witness for
22: 7 Blessed are those who obey the **p** written in this

PROPHESIED (18) [PROPHESY]

Nu 11:25 They **p** as the Spirit rested upon them, but that was
11:26 out to the Tabernacle, so they **p** there in the camp.
24:21 Then he looked over at the Kenites and **p**:
1Sa 19:21 he sent other troops, but they, too, **p**!
2Ch 20:37 Then Eliezer son of Dodavahu from Mareshah **p**
Ezr 5: 1 and Zechariah son of Iddo **p** in the name of the
Isa 42: 9 Everything I **p** has come true, and now I will
Jer 23:13 for they **p** by Baal and led my people of Israel into
26:11 what a traitor he is, for he has **p** against this city."
26:18 **p** during the reign of King Hezekiah of Judah.
29:31 Since he has **p** to you when I did not send him
Zec 13: 3 for you have **p** lies in the name of the LORD.'
Mt 7:22 we **p** in your name and cast out demons in your
Ac 19: 6 on them, and they spoke in other tongues and **p**.
21: 4 These disciples **p** through the Holy Spirit that Paul
Gal 4:27 That is what Isaiah meant when he **p**, / "Rejoice,
1Pe 1:10 They **p** about this gracious salvation prepared for
Jude 1:14 generations after Adam, **p** about these people.

PROPHESIES (7) [PROPHESY]

1Ki 22: 8 He never **p** anything but bad news for me!
22:18 He never **p** anything but bad news for me."
2Ch 18: 7 He never **p** anything but bad news for me!
18:17 He never **p** anything but bad news for me."
Isa 8: 4 This name **p** that within a couple of years,
1Co 11: 5 if she prays or **p** without a covering on her head,
14: 3 But one who **p** is helping others grow in the Lord,

PROPHESY (52) [PROPHECIES, PROPHECY, PROPHESIED, PROPHESIES, PROPHESYING, PROPHET, PROPHET'S, PROPHETIC, PROPHETS, PROPHETS']

1Sa 10: 6 upon you with power, and you will **p** with them.
10:10 of God came upon Saul, and he, too, began to **p**.
19:20 came upon Saul's men, and they also began to **p**.
19:23 of God came upon Saul, and he, too, began to **p**!
Ne 6: 7 appointed prophets to **p** about you in Jerusalem,
Isa 42: 9 I prophesied has come true, and now I will **p** again.
Jer 14:14 They **p** of visions and revelations they have never
14:16 As for the people to whom they **p**—their bodies
23:16 "Do not listen to these prophets when they **p** to
23:21 for me. I have given them no message, yet they **p**.
25:30 "Now **p** all these things, and say to them,
26: 9 "What right do you have to **p** in the LORD's
26:12 "The LORD sent me to **p** against this Temple
29: 9 because they **p** lies in my name. I have not sent
Eze 4: 7 there with your arm bared and **p** her destruction.
6: 2 toward the mountains of Israel and **p** against them.
11: 4 son of man, **p** against them loudly and clearly."
13:17 also speak out against the women who **p** from their
20:46 out against it; **p** against the fields of the Negev.
21: 2 and **p** against Israel and her sanctuaries.
21:14 of man, **p** to them and clap your hands vigorously.
21:28 **p** concerning the Ammonites and their mockery.
25: 2 the land of Ammon and **p** against its people.
28:21 look toward the city of Sidon and **p** against it.
29: 2 turn toward Egypt and **p** against Pharaoh the king
30: 2 **p** and give this message from the Sovereign
34: 2 "Son of man, **p** against the shepherds, the leaders
35: 2 turn toward Mount Seir, and **p** against its people.
36: 1 "Son of man, **p** to Israel's mountains. Give them
36: 6 **p** to the hills and mountains, the ravines
38: 2 "Son of man, **p** against Gog of the land of Magog,
38:14 "Therefore, son of man, **p** against Gog. Give him
39: 1 "Son of man, **p** against Gog. Give him this
Joel 2:28 Your sons and daughters will **p**. Your old men will
Am 7:15 and told me, 'Go and **p** to my people in Israel.'
7:16 You say, 'Don't **p** against Israel. Stop preaching
Mic 2: 6 such things," the people say. "Don't **p** like that.
3:11 a price; you prophets won't **p** unless you are paid.
Mt 26:68 saying, "**P** to us, you Messiah! Who hit you that
Ac 2:17 Your sons and daughters will **p**, / your young men
2:18 men and women alike, / and they will **p**.
Ro 12: 6 So if God has given you the ability to **p**, speak out
1Co 12:10 to perform miracles, and to another the ability to **p**.
14: 5 but even more I wish you were all able to **p**.
14:29 Let two or three **p**, and let the others evaluate what
14:31 In this way, all who **p** will have a turn to speak,
14:32 Remember that people who **p** are in control of their
14:39 So, dear brothers and sisters, be eager to **p**,
2Pe 1:21 or because they wanted to **p**. It was the Holy Spirit
Rev 10:11 "You must **p** again about many peoples, nations,
11: 3 in sackcloth and will **p** during those 1,260 days."
11: 6 so that no rain will fall for as long as they **p**.

PROPHESYING (14) [PROPHESY]

Nu 11:27 to Moses, "Eldad and Medad are **p** in the camp!"
1Sa 10: 5 a flute, and a lyre, and they will be **p**.
10:13 When Saul had finished **p**, he climbed the hill to
19:20 and saw Samuel and the other prophets **p**,
19:24 all day and all night, **p** in the presence of Samuel.
1Ki 22:10 All of Ahab's prophets were **p** there in front of
2Ch 18: 9 All of Ahab's prophets were **p** there in front of
Jer 26:20 from Kiriath-jearim was also **p** for the LORD.
Zec 13: 3 If anyone begins **p** again, his own father
Mt 15: 7 Isaiah was **p** about you when he said,
Mk 7: 6 Isaiah was **p** about you when he said,
1Co 11: 4 Christ if he covers his head while praying or **p**.
14:24 But if all of you are **p** and unbelievers or people
14:30 But if someone is **p** and another person receives a

PROPHET (243) [PROPHESY]

FALSE PROPHET (5) Ac 13:6; Rev 16:13; 19:20,20; 20:10

Ge 20: 7 her husband, and he will pray for you, for he is a **p**.
Ex 7: 1 Your brother, Aaron, will be your **p**; he will speak
15:20 Then Miriam the **p**, Aaron's sister, took a
Dt 18:15 "The LORD your God will raise up for you a **p**
18:15 fellow Israelites, and you must listen to that **p**.
18:18 I will raise up a **p** like you from among their fellow
18:18 I will tell that **p** what to say, and he will tell the
18:19 to the messages the **p** proclaims on my behalf.
18:20 But any **p** who claims to give a message from
18:22 If the **p** predicts something in the LORD's name
18:22 That **p** has spoken on his own and need not be
34:10 There has never been another **p** like Moses,
Jdg 4: 4 was a **p** who had become a judge in Israel.
6: 8 the LORD sent a **p** to the Israelites. He said,
1Sa 2:27 One day a **p** came to Eli and gave him this
3:20 that Samuel was confirmed as a **p** of the LORD.
10:11 about it, they exclaimed, "What? Is Saul a **p**? How did the son of Kish become a **p**?"
10:12 matter who his father is; anyone can become a **p**."
10:12 So that is the origin of the saying "Is Saul a **p**?"
10:14 So we went to the **p** Samuel to ask him where they
19:24 watching exclaimed, "What? Is Saul a **p**, too?"
22: 5 One day the **p** Gad told David,
2Sa 7: 2 David summoned Nathan the **p**. "Look!"
12: 1 So the LORD sent Nathan the **p** to tell David this
12:25 and sent word through Nathan the **p** that his name
24:11 the word of the LORD came to the **p** Gad,
1Ki 1: 8 son of Jehoiada, Nathan the **p**, Shimei, Rei,
1:10 But he did not invite Nathan the **p**, or Benaiah,
1:11 Then Nathan the **p** went to Bathsheba,
1:22 still speaking with the king, Nathan the **p** arrived.
1:23 told him, "Nathan the **p** is here to see you."
1:32 "Call Zadok the priest, Nathan the **p**,
1:34 and Nathan the **p** are to anoint him king over
1:38 So Zadok the priest, Nathan the **p**, Benaiah son of
1:44 Nathan the **p**, and Benaiah son of Jehoiada,
11:29 the **p** Ahijah from Shiloh met him on the road,
12:15 son of Nebat through the **p** Ahijah from Shiloh.
13:11 As it happened, there was an old **p** living in Bethel,
13:12 The old **p** asked them, "Which way did he go?"
13:14 The old **p** asked him, "Are you the man of God
13:18 But the old **p** answered, "I am a **p**, too,
13:20 a message from the LORD came to the old **p**.
13:23 the **p** saddled his own donkey for him,
13:25 and reported it in Bethel, where the old **p** lived.
13:26 When the old **p** heard the report, he said, "It is the
13:27 Then the **p** said to his sons, "Saddle a donkey for
13:29 So the **p** laid the body of the man of God on the
13:31 Afterward the **p** said to his sons, "When I die,
14: 2 Then go to the **p** Ahijah at Shiloh—the man who
14:18 as the LORD had promised through the **p** Ahijah.
15:29 concerning Jeroboam by the **p** Ahijah from Shiloh.
16: 1 to King Baasha by the **p** Jehu son of Hanani:
16: 7 and his family through the **p** Jehu son of Hanani.
16:12 as the LORD had promised through the **p** Jehu.
18:22 "I am the only **p** of the LORD who is left,
18:36 Elijah the **p** walked up to the altar and prayed,
19:16 from Abel-meholah to replace you as my **p**.
20:13 Then a **p** came to see King Ahab and told him,
20:14 And the **p** replied, "This is what the LORD says:
20:14 attack first?" Ahab asked. "Yes," the **p** answered.
20:22 Afterward the **p** said to King Ahab, "Get ready for
20:35 "Strike me!" But the man refused to strike the **p**.
20:36 Then the **p** told him, "Because you have not
20:37 Then the **p** turned to another man and said,
20:37 So he struck the **p** and wounded him.
20:38 The **p** waited for the king beside the road,
20:39 the **p** called out to him, "Sir, I was in the battle,
20:41 Then the **p** pulled the bandage from his eyes,
20:42 And the **p** told him, "This is what the LORD
22: 7 "Isn't there a **p** of the LORD around, too?"
22: 8 "There is still one **p** of the LORD, but I hate him.
2Ki 3:11 "Is there no **p** of the LORD with us?
5: 3 "I wish my master would go to see the **p** in
5: 5 "Go and visit the **p**," the king told him. "I will
5: 8 and he will learn that there is a true **p** here in
5:13 if the **p** had told you to do some great thing,
6:12 "Elisha, the **p** in Israel, tells the king of Israel even
9: 1 Elisha the **p** had summoned a member of the group
9: 4 So the young **p** did as he was told and went to
9: 6 Then the young **p** poured the oil over Jehu's head
9:10 Then the young **p** opened the door and ran.
14:25 Jonah son of Amittai, the **p** from Gath-hepher.
19: 2 dressed in sackcloth, to the **p** Isaiah son of Amoz.
19: 6 the **p** replied, "Say to your master, 'This is what
20: 1 and the **p** Isaiah son of Amoz went to visit him.
20:14 Then Isaiah the **p** went to King Hezekiah
22:14 section of Jerusalem to consult with the **p** Huldah.
23:18 burn his bones or those of the old **p** from Samaria.
1Ch 17: 1 was settled in his palace, he said to Nathan the **p**,
29:29 *The Record of Nathan the* **P**, and *The Record of*
2Ch 9:29 are recorded in *The Record of Nathan the P*
10:15 son of Nebat by the **p** Ahijah from Shiloh.
12: 5 The **p** Shemaiah then met with Rehoboam
12:15 are recorded in *The Record of Shemaiah the P*
13:22 are recorded in *The Commentary of Iddo the P*.
15: 8 When Asa heard this message from Azariah the **p**,
18: 6 "Isn't there a **p** of the LORD around, too?
18: 7 "There is still one **p** of the LORD, but I hate him.
21:12 Then Elijah the **p** wrote Jehoram this letter:
25:15 the LORD very angry, and he sent a **p** to ask,
25:16 I have you killed!" So the **p** left with this warning:
26:22 to end, are recorded by the **p** Isaiah son of Amoz.
28: 9 But a **p** of the LORD named Oded was there in
29:25 through Gad, the king's seer, and the **p** Nathan.
32:20 and the **p** Isaiah son of Amoz cried out in prayer to
32:32 *P Isaiah Son of Amoz,* which is included in *The*
34:22 section of Jerusalem to consult with the **p** Huldah.
35:18 Never since the time of the **p** Samuel had there
35:25 The **p** Jeremiah composed funeral songs for Josiah,
36:12 humble himself in the presence of the **p** Jeremiah,
36:21 desolate for seventy years, just as the **p** had said.
Ne 6:14 And remember Noadiah the **p** and all the prophets
Ps 51: T regarding the time Nathan the **p** came to him after
89:19 You once spoke in a vision to your **p** and said,
Isa 37: 2 dressed in sackcloth, to the **p** Isaiah son of Amoz.
37: 6 the **p** replied, "Say to your master, 'This is what
38: 1 and the **p** Isaiah son of Amoz went to visit him.
39: 3 Then Isaiah the **p** went to King Hezekiah

Jer 20: 2 So he arrested Jeremiah the **p** and had him
23:34 If any **p**, priest, or anyone else says, 'I have a
25: 2 Jeremiah the **p** said to the people in Judah
28: 1 Hananiah son of Azzur, a **p** from Gibeon,
28: 9 So a **p** who predicts peace must carry the burden of
28:10 Then Hananiah the **p** took the yoke off Jeremiah's
28:15 Then Jeremiah the **p** said to Hananiah, "Listen,
29:26 to put anyone who claims to be a **p** in the stocks
29:27 who pretends to be a **p** among you?
34: 6 So Jeremiah the **p** delivered the message to King
35:15 I have sent you **p** after **p** to tell you to turn
38: 9 evil thing in putting Jeremiah the **p** into the cistern.
42: 2 Jeremiah the **p**. They said, "Please pray to the
43: 6 Also included were the **p** Jeremiah and Baruch.
45: 1 The **p** Jeremiah gave a message to Baruch son of
46: 1 the **p** from the LORD concerning foreign nations.
46:13 Then the LORD gave the **p** Jeremiah this
47: 1 This is the LORD's message to the **p** Jeremiah
49:34 This message concerning Elam came to the **p**
50: 1 The LORD gave Jeremiah the **p** this message
51:59 The **p** Jeremiah gave this message to Zedekiah's
Eze 2: 5 at least they will know they have had a **p** among
12:22 in Israel: 'Time passes, making a liar of every **p**'?
14: 4 fall into sin and then come to a **p** asking for help.
14: 7 and who then come to a **p** asking for my advice.
14: 9 And if a **p** is deceived and gives a message
14: 9 because I, the LORD, have deceived that **p**.
33:30 Let's go hear the **p** tell us what the LORD is
33:33 then they will know a **p** has been among them."
Da 9: 2 of the LORD, as recorded by Jeremiah the **p**,
Hos 9: 8 The **p** is a watchman for my God over Israel,
12:13 out of Egypt by a **p**, who guided and protected
Mic 2:11 Suppose a **p** full of lies were to say to you,
2:11 That's just the kind of **p** you would like!
Hab 1: 1 This is the message that the **p** Habakkuk received
3: 1 This prayer was sung by the **p** Habakkuk:
Hag 1: 1 the LORD gave a message through the **p** Haggai
1: 3 So the LORD sent this message through the **p**
1:12 It had been delivered by the **p** Haggai,
2: 1 the LORD sent another message through the **p**
2:10 the LORD sent this message to the **p** Haggai:
Zec 1: 1 the LORD gave this message to the **p** Zechariah
1: 7 the LORD sent another message to the **p**
13: 5 'No,' he will say. 'I'm not a **p**; I'm a farmer.
Mal 1: 1 the LORD gave to Israel through the **p** Malachi.
4: 5 I am sending you the **p** Elijah before the great
Mt 1:22 to fulfill the Lord's message through his **p**:
2: 5 they said, "for this is what the **p** wrote:
2:15 fulfilled what the Lord had spoken through the **p**:
10:41 If you welcome a **p** as one who speaks for God,
you will receive the same reward a **p** gets.
11: 9 looking for a **p**? Yes, and he is more than a **p**.
12:39 sign I will give them is the sign of the **p** Jonah.
13:57 "A **p** is honored everywhere except in his own
14: 5 because all the people believed John was a **p**.
16: 4 sign I will give them is the sign of the **p** Jonah."
21:11 "It's Jesus, the **p** from Nazareth in Galilee."
21:26 be mobbed, because the people think he was a **p**."
21:46 because the crowds considered Jesus to be a **p**.
24:15 when you will see what Daniel the **p** spoke about:
27:47 and thought he was calling for the **p** Elijah.
Mk 1: 2 In the book of the **p** Isaiah, God said, / "Look,
6: 4 "A **p** is honored everywhere except in his own
6:15 Others thought Jesus was the ancient **p** Elijah.
6:15 Still others thought he was a **p** like the other great
11:32 a riot, since everyone thought that John was a **p**.
14:65 "Who hit you that time, you **p**?" they jeered.
15:35 and thought he was calling for the **p** Elijah.
Lk 1:17 with the spirit and power of Elijah, the **p** of old.
1:76 little son, / will be called the **p** of the Most High,
2:36 Anna, a **p**, was also there in the Temple. She was
4:17 The scroll containing the messages of Isaiah the **p**
4:24 the truth is, no **p** is accepted in his own hometown.
4:27 Or think of the **p** Elisha, who healed Naaman,
7:16 saying, "A mighty **p** has risen among us,"
7:26 looking for a **p**? Yes, and he is more than a **p**.
7:39 he said to himself, "This proves that Jesus is no **p**.
9: 8 or some other ancient **p** risen from the dead."
11:29 sign I will give them is the sign of the **p** Jonah.
13:33 For it wouldn't do for a **p** of God to be killed
20: 6 stone us, because they are convinced he was a **p**."
22:64 and asked, "Who hit you that time, you **p**?"
24:19 "He was a **p** who did wonderful miracles.
Jn 1:21 "No," he replied. "Are you the **P**?" "No."
1:25 "If you aren't the Messiah or Elijah or the **P**,
4:19 "Sir," the woman said, "you must be a **p**.
4:44 "A **p** is honored everywhere except in his own
6:14 "Surely, he is the **P** we have been expecting!"
7:40 of them declared, "This man surely is the **P**."
7:52 see for yourself—no **p** ever comes from Galilee!"
9:17 he is?" The man replied, "I think he must be a **p**."
12:38 This is exactly what Isaiah the **p** had predicted:
Ac 2:16 morning was predicted centuries ago by the **p** Joel:
2:30 But he was a **p**, and he knew God had promised
3:22 'The Lord your God will raise up a **P** like me from
3:23 'Anyone who will not listen to that **P** will be cut
3:24 every **p** spoke about what is happening today.
7:37 'God will raise up a **P** like me from among your
7:48 in temples made by human hands. As the **p** says,
7:52 Name one **p** your ancestors didn't persecute!
8:28 he was reading aloud from the book of the **p**
8:30 and heard the man reading from the **p** Isaiah;
13: 6 met a Jewish sorcerer, a false **p** named Bar-Jesus.
13:20 judges ruled until the time of Samuel the **p**.
28:25 when he said to our ancestors through Isaiah the **p**,
Ro 9:27 Concerning Israel, Isaiah the **p** cried out,
10:16 for Isaiah the **p** said, "Lord, who has believed our
11: 2 Elijah the **p** complained to God about the people of
15:12 And the **p** Isaiah said, / "The heir to David's
1Co 12:29 Of course not. Is everyone a **p**? No. Are all
14:37 If you claim to be a **p** or think you are very
Tit 1:12 own men, a **p** from Crete, has said about them,
1Pe 1:24 As the **p** says, / "People are like grass that dies
1Jn 4: 2 If a **p** acknowledges that Jesus Christ became a
4: 3 If a **p** does not acknowledge Jesus, that person is
Rev 2:20 that Jezebel who calls herself a **p**—to lead my
16:13 the mouth of the dragon, the beast, and the false **p**.
19:20 and with him the false **p** who did mighty miracles
19:20 and his false **p** were thrown alive into the lake of
20:10 burns with sulfur, joining the beast and the false **p**.

PROPHET'S (3) [PROPHESY]

1Ki 13:19 some food and drank some water at the **p** home.
2Ki 4:32 child was indeed dead, lying there on the **p** bed.
Zec 13: 4 No one will wear **p** clothes to try to fool the

PROPHETIC (7) [PROPHESY]

Da 9:24 to confirm the **p** vision, and to anoint the Most
Zec 13: 4 "No one will be boasting then of a **p** gift! No one
Lk 21:22 and the **p** words of the Scriptures will be fulfilled.
1Ti 1:18 based on the **p** words spoken about you earlier.
Rev 22:10 "Do not seal up the **p** words you have written,
22:18 to everyone who hears the **p** words of this book:
22:19 And if anyone removes any of the words of this **p**

PROPHETS (264) [PROPHESY]

FALSE PROPHETS (21) Dt 13:5; Isa 44:25; Jer 23:9,28; 27:9,14; Eze 13:2,3; 14:10; 21:29; Hos 4:5; Mic 3:5; Zec 13:2; Mt 7:15; 24:11,24; Mk 13:22; Lk 6:26; 2Pe 2:1; 1Jn 4:1,4

SERVANTS THE PROPHETS (10) 2Ki 17:13; 21:10; Ezr 9:11; Jer 26:5; 44:4; Da 9:6,10; Am 3:7; Zec 1:6; Rev 10:7

Nu 11:29 I wish that all the LORD's people were **p**,
12: 6 Even with **p**, I the LORD communicate by
Dt 13: 1 "Suppose there are **p** among you, or those who
13: 2 If the **p** then say, 'Come, let us worship the gods of
13: 5 The false **p** or dreamers who try to lead you astray
1Sa 9: 9 and ask the seer," for **p** used to be called seers.)
10: 5 you will meet a band of **p** coming down from the
10:10 at Gibeah, they saw the **p** coming toward them.
19:20 and saw Samuel and the other **p** prophesying,
28: 6 either by dreams or by sacred lots or by the **p**.
28:15 God has left me and won't reply by **p** or dreams.
1Ki 18: 4 when Jezebel had tried to kill all the LORD's **p**,
18: 4 He had put fifty **p** in each cave and had supplied
18:13 when Jezebel was trying to kill the LORD's **p**?
18:19 with all 450 **p** of Baal and the 400 **p** of Asherah,
18:20 all the people and the **p** to Mount Carmel.
18:22 of the LORD who is left, but Baal has 450 **p**.
18:23 The **p** of Baal may choose whichever one they
18:25 Then Elijah said to the **p** of Baal, "You go first,
18:40 Then Elijah commanded, "Seize all the **p** of Baal.
19: 1 had done and that he had slaughtered the **p** of Baal.
19:10 down your altars, and killed every one of your **p**.
19:14 down your altars, and killed every one of your **p**.
20:35 the LORD instructed one of the group of **p** to say
20:41 the king of Israel recognized him as one of the **p**.
22: 6 So King Ahab summoned his **p**, about four
22:10 All of Ahab's **p** were prophesying there in front of
22:12 All the other **p** agreed. "Yes," they said, "go up
22:13 "Look, all the **p** are promising victory for the king.
22:22 will go out and inspire all Ahab's **p** to speak lies.'
22:23 has put a lying spirit in the mouths of your **p**.
2Ki 2: 3 The group of **p** from Bethel came to Elisha
2: 5 Then the group of **p** from Jericho came to Elisha
2: 7 Fifty men from the group of **p** also went
2:15 When the group of **p** from Jericho saw what
3:13 "Go to the pagan **p** of your father and mother!"
4: 1 One day the widow of one of Elisha's fellow **p**
4:38 One day as the group of **p** was seated before him,
4:42 "Give it to the group of **p** so they can eat."
4:43 "Give it to the group of **p** so they can eat,
5:22 **p** from the hill country of Ephraim have just
6: 1 One day the group of **p** came to Elisha and told
9: 1 had summoned a member of the group of **p**.
9: 7 I will avenge the murder of my **p** and all the
10:19 Summon all the **p** and worshipers of Baal, and call
17:13 Again and again the LORD had sent his **p**
17:13 and which I gave you through my servants the **p**."
17:23 just as all his **p** had warned would happen.
21:10 Then the LORD said through his servants the **p**:
23: 2 Judah and Jerusalem, and the priests, and the **p**—
24: 2 just as the LORD had promised through his **p**.
1Ch 16:22 people I have chosen, / and do not hurt my **p**."
2Ch 18: 5 So King Ahab summoned his **p**, four hundred of
18: 9 All of Ahab's **p** were prophesying there in front of
18:11 All the other **p** agreed. "Yes," they said, "go up
18:12 "Look, all the **p** are promising victory for the king.
18:21 will go out and inspire all Ahab's **p** to speak lies.'
18:22 has put a lying spirit in the mouths of your **p**.
20:20 Believe in his **p**, and you will succeed."
24:19 The LORD sent **p** to bring them back to him,
36:15 their ancestors, repeatedly sent his **p** to warn them,
36:16 They scoffed at the **p** until the LORD's anger
Ezr 5: 1 At that time the **p** Haggai and Zechariah son of
5: 2 And the **p** of God were with them and helped
6:14 encouraged by the preaching of the **p** Haggai
9:11 Your servants the **p** warned us that the land we
Ne 6: 7 He also reports that you have appointed **p** to
6:14 and all the **p** like her who have tried to intimidate
9:26 they killed the **p** who encouraged them to return to
9:30 You sent your Spirit, who, through the **p**,
9:32 and upon our kings and princes and priests and **p**
Ps 74: 9 evidence that you will save us. / All the **p** are gone;
105:15 people I have chosen, / and do not hurt my **p**."
Isa 3: 2 the heroes, soldiers, judges, **p**, diviners, elders,
9:15 of Israel are the head, and the lying **p** are the tail.
28: 7 The priests and **p** reel and stagger from beer
29:10 He has closed the eyes of your **p** and visionaries.
30:10 They tell the **p**, "Shut up! We don't want any
44:25 I am the one who exposes the false **p** as liars by
44:26 But I carry out the predictions of my **p**! When they
Jer 2: 8 against me, and the **p** spoke in the name of Baal,
2:26 Kings, officials, priests, and **p**—all are alike in
2:30 You yourselves have killed your **p** as a lion kills its
4: 9 The priests and the **p** will be struck with horror."
5:13 God's **p** are windbags full of words with no divine
5:31 the **p** give false prophecies, and the priests rule
6:13 to them. Yes, even my **p** and priests are like that!
7:25 Egypt until now, I have continued to send my **p**—
8: 1 the graves of the priests, **p**, and common people.
8:10 to them. Yes, even my **p** and priests are like that.
13:13 on David's throne and from the priests and the **p**,
14:13 their **p** are telling them, 'All is well—
14:14 LORD said, "These **p** are telling lies in my name.
14:15 says the LORD, I will punish these lying **p**,
14:18 The **p** and priests continue with their work,
18:18 We have our own priests and wise men and **p**.
23: 9 My heart is broken because of the false **p**, and I
23:10 dried up. For the **p** do evil and abuse their power.
23:11 "The priests are like the **p**, all ungodly,
23:13 "I saw that the **p** of Samaria were terribly evil,
23:14 But now I see that the **p** of Jerusalem are even
23:14 These **p** are as wicked as the people of Sodom
23:15 what the LORD Almighty says concerning the **p**:
23:15 because of Jerusalem's **p** that wickedness fills this
23:16 "Do not listen to these **p** when they prophesy to
23:18 "But can you name even one of these **p** who
23:21 "I have not sent these **p**, yet they claim to speak
23:25 "I have heard these **p** say, 'Listen to the dream I
23:26 If they are **p**, they are **p** of deceit,
23:28 Let these false **p** tell their dreams, but let my true
23:30 "I stand against these **p** who get their messages
23:31 these smooth-tongued **p** who say, 'This prophecy
23:33 of the people or one of the **p** or priests asks you,
23:37 "This is what you should say to the **p**: 'What is the
25: 4 "Again and again, the LORD has sent you his **p**,
26: 5 and if you will not listen to my servants, the **p**—
26: 7 The priests, the **p**, and all the people listened to
26: 8 the priests and **p** and all the people at the Temple
26:11 and **p** presented their accusations to the officials
26:16 and the people said to the priests and **p**,
27: 9 " 'Do not listen to your false **p**, fortune-tellers,
27:14 Do not listen to the false **p** who keep telling you,
27:15 is what the LORD says: I have not sent these **p**!
27:15 You will all die—you and all these **p**, too."
27:16 Do not listen to your **p** who claim that soon the
27:18 If they really are the LORD's **p**, let them pray to
28: 8 The ancient **p** who preceded you and me spoke
29: 1 a letter from Jerusalem to the elders, priests, **p**,
29: 8 "Do not let the **p** and mediums who are there in
29:15 You may claim that the LORD has raised up **p** for
29:19 I have spoken to them repeatedly through my **p**.
29:21 the God of Israel, says about your **p**—
32:32 the kings, the officials, the priests, and the **p**—
37:19 Where are your **p** now who told you the king of
44: 4 again I sent my servants, the **p**, to plead with them,
La 2: 9 Her **p** receive no more visions from the LORD.
2:14 Your "**p**" have said so many foolish things,
2:20 and **p** die within the Lord's Temple?
4:13 because of the sins of her **p** and priests,
Eze 7:26 They will look in vain for a vision from the **p**.
13: 2 speak against the false **p** of Israel who are
13: 3 Destruction is certain for the false **p** who are
13: 4 these **p** of yours are like jackals digging around in
13: 9 I will raise my fist against all the lying **p**, and they
13:10 "These evil **p** deceive my people by saying,
13:10 and these **p** are trying to hold it together by
13:16 They were lying **p** who claimed peace would come
14: 9 I will stand against such **p** and cut them off from
14:10 False **p** and hypocrites—evil people who claim to
21:29 and false **p** have given false visions
22:28 And your **p** announce false visions and speak false
38:17 when I announced through Israel's **p** that in future
Da 9: 2 I, Daniel, was studying the writings of the **p**.
9: 6 We have refused to listen to your servants the **p**,
9:10 the laws he gave us through his servants the **p**.
Hos 4: 5 just as you might at night, and so will your false **p**.
6: 5 I sent my **p** to cut you to pieces. I have slaughtered
9: 7 "The **p** are crazy!" the people shout.
12:10 I sent my **p** to warn you with many visions
Am 2:11 I chose some of your sons to be **p** and others to be
2:12 drink your wine, and you said to my **p**, 'Shut up!'
3: 7 first of all, I warn you through my servants the **p**.
7:14 "I'm not one of your professional **p**.
Mic 3: 5 This is what the LORD says to you false **p**:
3: 6 The sun will set for you **p**, and your day will come
3:11 a price; you **p** won't prophesy unless you are paid.
Zep 3: 4 Its **p** are arrogant liars seeking their own gain.
Zec 1: 4 would not listen when the earlier **p** said to them,
1: 5 "Your ancestors and their **p** are now long dead.
1: 6 But all the things I said through my servants the **p**
7: 3 They were to ask this question of the **p** and of the
7: 7 through the **p** years ago when Jerusalem
7:12 had sent them by his Spirit through the earlier **p**.
8: 9 You have heard what the **p** have been saying about
13: 2 I will remove from the land all false **p**
Mt 2: 4 "Where did the **p** say the Messiah would be
2:23 This fulfilled what was spoken by the **p** concerning

5:12 And remember, the ancient **p** were persecuted, too.
5:17 abolish the law of Moses or the writings of the **p**.
7:12 a summary of all that is taught in the law and the **p**.
7:15 "Beware of false **p** who come disguised as
11:14 I say, he is Elijah, the one the **p** said would come.
13:17 many **p** and godly people have longed to see
16:14 and others say Jeremiah or one of the other **p**."
22:40 and all the demands of the **p** are based on these
23:29 For you build tombs for the **p** your ancestors killed
23:30 never would have joined them in killing the **p**.'
23:31 the descendants of those who murdered the **p**.
23:34 I will send you **p** and wise men and teachers of
23:37 the city that kills the **p** and stones God's
24:11 And many false **p** will appear and will lead many
24:24 For false messiahs and false **p** will rise up
26:56 the words of the **p** as recorded in the Scriptures."
Mk 6:15 he was a prophet like the other great **p** of the past.
8:28 and others say you are one of the other **p**."
13:22 For false messiahs and false **p** will rise up
Lk 1:70 just as he promised / through his holy **p** long ago.
6:23 the ancient **p** were also treated that way by your
6:26 for their ancestors also praised false **p**.
9:19 and others say you are one of the other ancient **p**
10:24 many **p** and kings have longed to see and hear
11:47 For you build tombs for the very **p** your ancestors
11:49 'I will send **p** and apostles to them, and they will
11:50 of all God's **p** from the creation of the world—
13:28 Jacob, and all the **p** within the Kingdom of God,
13:34 the city that kills the **p** and stones God's
16:16 and the messages of the **p** were your guides.
16:29 'Moses and the **p** have warned them.
16:31 'If they won't listen to Moses and the **p**,
18:31 all the predictions of the ancient **p** concerning the
22:37 everything written about me by the **p** will come
24:25 so hard to believe all that the **p** wrote in the
24:26 Wasn't it clearly predicted by the **p** that the
24:27 passages from the writings of Moses and all the **p**,
24:44 and the **p** and in the Psalms must all come true."
Jn 1:45 the very person Moses and the **p** wrote about!
8:52 Even Abraham and the **p** died, but you say that
8:53 who died? Are you greater than the **p**, who died?
Ac 3:18 But God was fulfilling what all the **p** had declared
3:21 all things, as God promised long ago through his **p**.
3:25 You are the children of those **p**, and you are
7:42 as their gods! In the book of the **p** it is written,
10:43 He is the one all the **p** testified about, saying that
11:27 some **p** traveled from Jerusalem to Antioch.
13:1 Among the **p** and teachers of the church at Antioch
13:15 readings from the books of Moses and from the **P**,
13:27 or realize that he is the one the **p** had written about,
15:15 of Gentiles agrees with what the **p** predicted.
15:32 Then Judas and Silas, both being **p**,
26:22 I teach nothing except what the **p** and Moses said
26:27 King Agrippa, do you believe the **p**? I know you
28:23 the five books of Moses and the books of the **p**.
Ro 1:2 ago by God through his **p** in the holy Scriptures.
11:3 they have killed your **p** and torn down your altars.
11:26 Do you remember what the **p** said about this?
16:26 But now as the **p** foretold and as the eternal God
1Co 12:28 first are apostles, / second are **p**, / third are
Eph 2:20 built on the foundation of the apostles and the **p**.
3:5 it by the Holy Spirit to his holy apostles and **p**.
4:11 the apostles, the **p**, the evangelists, and the pastors
1Th 2:15 For some of the Jews had killed their own **p**,
Heb 1:1 and in many ways to our ancestors through the **p**.
11:32 Samson, Jephthah, David, Samuel, and all the **p**.
Jas 5:10 look at the **p** who spoke in the name of the Lord.
1Pe 1:10 This salvation was something the **p** wanted to
2Pe 1:19 confidence in the message proclaimed by the **p**.
1:20 in Scripture ever came from the **p** themselves
1:21 It was the Holy Spirit who moved the **p** to speak
2:1 But there were also false **p** in Israel, just as there
3:2 and understand what the holy **p** said long ago
1Jn 4:1 from God. For there are many false **p** in the world.
4:4 have already won your fight with these false **p**,
Rev 10:7 just as he announced it to his servants the **p**."
11:4 These two **p** are the two olive trees and the two
11:5 fire flashes from the mouths of the **p** and consumes
11:10 the death of the two **p** who had tormented them.
11:18 You will reward your **p** and your holy people,
16:6 For your holy people and your **p** have been killed,
18:20 O holy people of God and apostles and **p**!
18:24 In her streets the blood of the **p** was spilled.
22:6 Lord God, who tells his **p** what the future holds,
22:9 of God, just like you and your brothers the **p**,

PROPHETS' (2) [PROPHESY]

Ac 13:27 though they hear the **p** words read every Sabbath.
13:40 Be careful! Don't let the **p** words apply to you.

PROPITIATION [KJV] See SATISFY (ANGER), SACRIFICE

PROPORTION (11)

Lev 27:18 the priest must assess the land's value in **p** to the
Nu 26:53 "Divide the land among the tribes in **p** to their
33:54 among the clans by sacred lot and in **p** to their size.
35:8 Each tribe will give in **p** to its inheritance."
Dt 16:10 Bring him a freewill offering in **p** to the blessings
2Ki 23:35 requiring them to pay in **p** to their wealth.
Ps 28:4 Measure it out in **p** to their wickedness.
90:15 Give us gladness in **p** to our former misery!
Jer 25:14 I will punish them in **p** to the suffering they cause
Eze 39:24 and punished them in **p** to the vileness of their sins.
Mt 25:15 dividing it in **p** to their abilities—and then left on

PROPOSAL (3) [PROPOSE]

Ge 34:20 his father before the town leaders to present this **p**.
Dt 2:26 to King Sihon of Heshbon with this **p** of peace:
Jdg 9:3 And after listening to their **p**, they decided in favor

PROPOSE (1) [PROPOSAL, PROPOSED]

2Co 8:10 a year ago, for you were the first to **p** this idea,

PROPOSED (3) [PROPOSE]

Jos 18:4 report of their **p** divisions of the inheritance.
1Ki 22:49 At that time Ahaziah son of Ahab **p** to
2Ki 6:28 "This woman **p** that we eat my son one day

PROPOSITIONED (1)

Ge 38:16 So he stopped and **p** her to sleep with him,

PROPPED (2)

1Ki 22:35 and Ahab was **p** up in his chariot facing the
2Ch 18:34 and Ahab **p** himself up in his chariot facing the

PROSECUTE (1) [PROSECUTING]

Mic 6:2 He will **p** them to the full extent of the law.

PROSECUTING (1) [PROSECUTE]

Isa 3:13 He is the great **p** attorney, presenting his case

PROSELYTE [KJV] See CONVERT

PROSPER (34) [PROSPERED, PROSPERITY, PROSPEROUS, PROSPERS]

Ge 47:27 And before long, they began to **p** there, and their
Dt 5:29 they and their descendants would **p** forever.
22:7 the mother go, so you may **p** and enjoy a long life.
28:63 has found great pleasure in helping you to **p**
29:9 so that you will **p** in everything you do.
33:18 "May the people of Zebulun **p** in their expeditions
33:18 May the people of Issachar **p** at home in their tents.
2Ch 24:20 the LORD's commands so that you cannot **p**?
Job 8:20 a person of integrity, nor will he make evildoers **p**.
Ps 1:3 leaves never wither, / and in all they do, they **p**.
37:3 Then you will live safely in the land and **p**.
37:7 him to act. / Don't worry about evil people who **p**
73:3 when I saw them **p** despite their wickedness.
73:16 So I tried to understand why the wicked **p**.
122:6 peace of Jerusalem. / May all who love this city **p**.
128:5 May you see Jerusalem **p** as long as you live.
140:11 Don't let liars **p** here in our land. / Cause disaster
Pr 11:11 Upright citizens bless a city and make it **p**,
11:25 The generous **p** and are satisfied; those who
13:4 but those who work hard will **p** and be satisfied.
16:20 Those who listen to instruction will **p**; those who
17:20 The crooked heart will not **p**; the twisted tongue
19:8 people who cherish understanding will **p**.
28:13 People who cover over their sins will not **p**. But if
Isa 52:13 See, my servant will **p**; he will be highly exalted.
53:10 and the LORD's plan will **p** in his hands.
55:11 all I want it to, and it will **p** everywhere I send it.
Jer 30:20 Their children will **p** as they did long ago. I will
33:13 Once again their flocks will **p** in the towns of the
La 1:5 have become her masters, and her enemies **p**,
Eze 17:9 Should I let this vine grow and **p**? No! I will pull it
Da 4:27 to the poor. Perhaps then you will continue to **p**."
Hos 1:10 Yet the time will come when Israel will **p**
Ac 13:17 chose our ancestors and made them **p** in Egypt.

PROSPERED (5) [PROSPER]

1Ch 29:23 David, and he **p** greatly, and all Israel obeyed him.
Job 36:16 You have **p** in a wide and pleasant valley.
Jer 12:2 have planted them, and they have taken root and **p**.
Eze 31:5 It **p** and grew long thick branches because of all
Da 6:28 So Daniel **p** during the reign of Darius

PROSPERITY (53) [PROSPER]

Ge 9:27 of Japheth, / and may he share the **p** of Shem;
41:26 heads of grain both represent seven years of **p**.
41:29 The next seven years will be a period of great **p**
41:30 so great that all the **p** will be forgotten and wiped
Dt 6:24 and to fear him for our own **p** and well-being,
30:15 Today I am giving you a choice between **p**
1Sa 2:32 You will watch with envy as I pour out **p** on the
25:6 "Peace and **p** to you, your family, and everything
1Ki 10:7 and **p** are far greater than what I was told.
1Ch 12:18 your side, son of Jesse. / Peace and **p** be with you,
Ezr 9:12 and leave this **p** to our children as an inheritance
Job 5:11 He gives **p** to the poor and humble, and he takes
10:3 own hands, while sending joy and **p** to the wicked?
20:21 gorging himself; therefore, his **p** will not endure.
21:13 They spend their days in **p**; then they go down to
21:16 But their **p** is not of their own doing, so I will have
21:23 One person dies in **p** and security,
30:15 and my **p** has vanished as a cloud before a strong
36:11 then they will be blessed with **p** throughout their
Ps 21:3 You welcomed him back with success and **p**.
25:13 They will live in **p**, / and their children will inherit
41:2 and keeps them alive. / He gives them **p**
72:3 May the mountains yield **p** for all, / and may the
72:7 May there be abundant **p** until the end of time.
106:5 Let me share in the **p** of your chosen ones.
122:7 be peace within your walls / and **p** in your palaces.
Pr 12:11 Hard work means **p**; only fools idle away their
21:5 Good planning and hard work lead to **p**, but hasty
28:25 causes fighting; trusting the LORD leads to **p**.
Ecc 7:14 Enjoy **p** while you can. But when hard times strike,
Isa 54:13 teach all your citizens, and their **p** will be great.
61:7 you will inherit a double portion of **p**
66:12 and **p** will overflow Jerusalem like a river,"
Jer 29:7 And work for the peace and **p** of Babylon. Pray to
32:44 For someday I will restore **p** to them. I,
33:6 heal Jerusalem's damage and give her **p** and peace.
33:11 For I will restore the **p** of this land to what it was
39:16 I will send disaster, not **p**. You will see its
La 3:17 been stripped away, and I have forgotten what **p** is.
Eze 29:14 I will restore the **p** of Egypt and bring its people
31:14 Let no other nation proudly exult in its own **p**,
Da 4:1 throughout the world: / "Peace and **p** to you!
4:4 was living in my palace in comfort and **p**.
6:25 throughout the world: / "Peace and **p** to you!
Hos 7:14 begging foreign gods for crops and **p**.
Joel 3:1 when I restore the **p** of Judah and Jerusalem,"
Am 5:18 That day will not bring light and **p**, but darkness
Mic 4:4 will live quietly in their own homes in peace and **p**,
7:14 in green pastures. Help them to live in peace and **p**.
Zep 2:7 his people in kindness and restore their **p** again.
Zec 1:17 The towns of Israel will again overflow with **p**,
3:10 into your home to share your peace and **p**."
8:12 For I am planting seeds of peace and **p** among you.

PROSPEROUS (19) [PROSPER]

Ge 29:6 "He's well and **p**. Look, here comes his daughter
48:20 'May God make you as **p** as Ephraim
Dt 5:33 and **p** lives in the land you are about to enter
6:10 filled with large, **p** cities that you did not build.
8:12 For when you have become full and **p** and have
30:5 He will make you even more **p** and numerous than
31:20 There they will become **p**; they will eat all the food
33:28 So Israel will live in safety, / **p** Jacob in security,
Ezr 9:12 avoided these things, we would become a **p** nation.
Job 1:10 You have made him **p** in everything he does.
Ps 30:6 When I was **p** I said, / "Nothing can stop me
37:11 will possess the land; / they will live in **p** security.
132:15 I will make this city **p** / and satisfy its poor with
Jer 12:1 Why are the wicked so **p**? Why are evil people
13:12 you don't need to tell us how **p** we will be!'
22:21 "When you were **p**, I warned you, but you replied,
Eze 36:11 I will make you even more **p** than you were before.
Hos 10:1 How **p** Israel is—a luxuriant vine loaded with fruit!
Lk 6:25 sorrows await you who are satisfied and **p** now,

PROSPERS (1) [PROSPER]

Pr 30:22 who becomes a king, / an overbearing fool who **p**,

PROSTITUTE (45) [PROSTITUTE'S, PROSTITUTED, PROSTITUTES, PROSTITUTING, PROSTITUTION]

Ge 34:31 "Should he treat our sister like a **p**?" they retorted
38:15 noticed her as he went by and thought she was a **p**,
38:21 "Where can I find the **p** who was sitting beside the
38:21 "We've never had a **p** here," they replied.
38:22 the village had claimed they didn't have a **p** there.
Lev 19:29 "Do not defile your daughter by making her a **p**,
21:9 If a priest's daughter becomes a **p**, defiling her
Dt 23:17 or woman may ever become a temple **p**.
23:18 your God any offering from the earnings of a **p**,
Jos 2:1 set out and came to the house of a **p** named Rahab
6:17 Only Rahab the **p** and the others in her house will
6:25 So Joshua spared Rahab the **p** and her relatives
Jdg 11:1 He was the son of Gilead, but his mother was a **p**.
11:2 they said, "for you are the son of a **p**."
16:1 Philistine city of Gaza and spent the night with a **p**.
Pr 6:26 For a **p** will bring you to poverty, and sleeping
23:27 A **p** is a deep pit; an adulterous woman is
SS 1:7 For why should I wander like a **p** among the flocks
Isa 1:21 how Jerusalem, once so faithful, has become a **p**.
23:15 come back to life and sing sweet songs like a **p**.
Jer 2:33 The most experienced **p** could learn from you!
3:2 You sit like a **p** beside the road waiting for a client.
3:3 For you are a **p** and are completely unashamed.
Eze 16:15 You gave yourself as a **p** to every man who came
16:20 Was it not enough that you should be a **p**?
16:30 do such things as these, acting like a shameless **p**.
16:31 You have been worse than a **p**, so eager for sin that
16:35 "Therefore, you **p**, listen to this message from the
23:19 remembering her youth when she was a **p** in
Hos 1:2 he said to him, "Go and marry a **p**, so some of her
2:2 and suggestive clothing and to stop playing the **p**.
2:5 For their mother is a shameless **p** and became
4:12 They have played the **p**, serving other gods
4:15 "Though Israel is a **p**, may Judah avoid such guilt.
5:3 You have left me as a **p** leaves her husband;
5:4 You are a **p** through and through, and you cannot
Am 7:17 your wife will become a **p** in this city, and your
1Co 6:15 which belongs to Christ, and join it to a **p**?
6:16 don't you know that if a man joins himself to a **p**,
Heb 11:31 It was by faith that Rahab the **p** did not die with all
Jas 2:25 Rahab the **p** is another example of this. She was
Rev 17:1 the judgment that is going to come on the great **p**,
17:15 "The waters where the **p** is sitting represent
17:16 ten kings who will reign with him—all hate the **p**.
19:2 He has punished the great **p** who corrupted the

PROSTITUTE'S (1) [PROSTITUTE]

Jos 6:22 Go to the **p** house and bring her out, along with all

PROSTITUTED (7) [PROSTITUTE]

Jdg 2:17 listen to the judges but **p** themselves to other gods,

8:27 But soon all the Israelites **p** themselves by
8:33 the Israelites **p** themselves by worshiping the
Jer 2:20 you have **p** yourselves by bowing down to idols.
3:1 But you have **p** yourself with many lovers,
Eze 16:28 You have **p** yourselves with the Assyrians, too.
23:7 so she **p** herself with the most desirable men of

PROSTITUTES (25) [PROSTITUTE]

Ex 34:15 They are spiritual **p**, committing adultery against
1Ki 3:16 two **p** came to the king to have an argument
14:24 There were even shrine **p** throughout the land.
15:12 He banished the shrine **p** from the land
22:38 where the **p** bathed, and dogs came and licked the
22:46 He banished from the land the rest of the shrine **p**,
2Ki 23:7 He also tore down the houses of the shrine **p** that
Pr 29:3 but if he hangs around with **p**, his wealth is wasted.
Isa 57:3 you offspring of adulterers and **p**!
Eze 16:33 **P** charge for their services—but not you! You give
16:34 So you are the opposite of other **p**. No one pays
23:3 They became **p** in Egypt. Even as young girls,
23:43 to sleep with worn-out, old **p** like these, let them!'
23:44 with Oholah and Oholibah, these shameless **p**,
Hos 4:10 Though they do a big business as **p**, they will have
4:14 the same thing, sinning with whores and shrine **p**.
4:18 their drinking bouts and off they go to find some **p**.
9:1 to your God, hiring yourselves out like **p**,
Joel 3:3 They traded young boys for **p** and little girls for
Mic 1:7 and they will now be carried away to pay **p**
Mt 21:31 and **p** will get into the Kingdom of God before you
21:32 didn't believe him, while tax collectors and **p** did.
Lk 15:30 comes back after squandering your money on **p**,
1Co 6:9 idol worshipers, adulterers, male **p**, homosexuals,
Rev 17:5 Mother of All **P** and Obscenities in the World."

PROSTITUTING (2) [PROSTITUTE]

Eze 20:30 Do you intend to keep **p** yourselves by worshiping
23:30 You brought all this on yourself by **p** yourself to

PROSTITUTION (23) [PROSTITUTE]

Ge 38:24 his daughter-in-law, was pregnant as a result of **p**.
Lev 20:5 along with all those who commit **p** by worshiping
21:7 "The priests must not marry women defiled by **p**
21:14 a divorced woman, or a woman defiled by **p**.
Jer 3:2 You have polluted the land with your **p**
3:8 now Judah, too, has left me and given herself to **p**.
Eze 16:16 for idols, where you carried out your acts of **p**.
16:25 body to every passerby in an endless stream of **p**.
16:28 And after your **p** there you still were not satisfied.
16:36 Because you have exposed yourself in **p** to all your
16:41 I will see to it that you stop your **p** and end your
23:8 left Egypt, she did not leave her spirit of **p** behind.
23:11 abandoning herself to her lust and **p**.
23:14 "Then she carried her **p** even further. She fell in
23:19 She turned to even greater **p**, remembering her
23:27 to the lewdness and **p** you brought from Egypt.
23:29 The shame of your **p** will be exposed to all the
23:35 the consequences of all your lewdness and **p**."
23:49 You will be fully repaid for all your **p**—
Hos 3:3 live in my house for many days and stop your **p**.
4:11 and **p** have robbed my people of their brains.
4:13 "That is why your daughters turn to **p**, and your
Mic 1:7 were bought with the money earned by her **p**,

PROSTRATE (3)

Dt 9:18 forty days and nights I lay **p** before the LORD,
2Sa 13:31 jumped up, tore his robe, and fell **p** on the ground.
Jer 4:31 pleading for help, **p** before their murderers.

PROTECT (82) [PROTECTED, PROTECTING, PROTECTION, PROTECTIVE, PROTECTOR, PROTECTS]

Ge 15:1 to him, "Do not be afraid, Abram, for I will **p** you,
28:15 be with you, and I will **p** you wherever you go.
28:20 and **p** me on this journey and give me food
33:15 let me leave some of my men to guide and **p** you."
Ex 37:9 stretched out above the atonement cover to **p** it.
Lev 26:6 from your land and **p** you from your enemies.
Nu 6:24 'May the LORD bless you / and **p** you.
35:25 They must **p** the slayer from the avenger, and they
Dt 3:18 armed and ready to **p** your Israelite relatives.
7:15 And the LORD will **p** you from all sickness.
13:8 or listen, and have no pity. Do not spare or **p** them.
23:14 your God moves around in your camp to **p** you
28:52 the walls you trusted to **p** you—are knocked down.
1Sa 2:9 He will **p** his godly ones, / but the wicked will
22:23 here with me, and I will **p** you with my own life,
26:16 because you failed to **p** your master, the LORD's
1Ki 6:21 and he made gold chains to **p** the entrance to the
2Ki 19:29 "Here is the proof that the LORD will **p** this city
Ezr 8:21 that he would give us a safe journey and **p** us,
8:22 and **p** us from enemies along the way.
Ne 2:9 sent along army officers and horsemen to **p** me.
4:9 and guarded the city day and night to **p** ourselves.
Ps 5:11 let them sing joyful praises forever. / **P** them,
12:7 LORD, we know you will **p** the oppressed,
14:6 the oppressed, / but the LORD will **p** his people.
17:9 **P** me from wicked people who attack me,
23:4 Your rod and your staff / **p** and comfort me.
25:20 **P** me! Rescue my life from them! / Do not let me
25:21 May integrity and honesty **p** me, / for I put my
32:7 you are my hiding place; / you **p** me from trouble.
35:17 their fierce attacks. / **P** my life from these lions!
46:5 be destroyed. / God will **p** it at the break of day.
59:1 **P** me from those who have come to destroy me.
64:2 **P** me from the plots of the wicked,
86:2 **P** me, for I am devoted to you. / Save me, for I
91:3 from every trap / and **p** you from the fatal plague.
91:11 he orders his angels / to **p** you wherever you go.
91:14 love me. / I will **p** those who trust in my name.
94:16 Who will **p** me from the wicked? / Who will stand
110:5 The Lord stands at your right hand to **p** you.
119:86 **P** me from those who hunt me down without
119:154 take my side! / **P** my life as you promised.
125:2 Just as the mountains surround and **p** Jerusalem,
Pr 4:6 turn your back on wisdom, for she will **p** you.
6:22 can lead you. When you sleep, they will **p** you.
20:28 Unfailing love and faithfulness **p** the king;
27:18 workers who **p** their employer's interests will be
28:17 will drive him into the grave. Don't **p** him!
Isa 7:9 If you want me to **p** you, learn to believe what I
7:20 these Assyrians you have hired to **p** you—and use
16:3 **P** us from their relentless attack. Do not betray us.
20:6 For we counted on Egypt to **p** us from the king of
37:30 "Here is the proof that the LORD will **p** this city
42:22 are fair game for all and have no one to **p** them.
46:2 The gods cannot **p** the people, and the people cannot **p** the gods.
52:12 and the God of Israel will **p** you from behind.
58:8 and the glory of the LORD will **p** you from
Jer 15:20 will not conquer you, for I will **p** and deliver you.
18:20 for them and tried to **p** them from your anger.
38:12 "Put these rags under your armpits to **p** you from
41:9 Mizpah to **p** himself against King Baasha of Israel.
45:5 all these people, but I will **p** you wherever you go.
Eze 20:9 didn't do it, for I acted to **p** the honor of my name.
20:14 But again I held back in order to **p** the honor of my
20:22 I withdrew my judgment against them to **p** the
36:22 I am doing it to **p** my holy name, which you
Zep 2:3 Perhaps even yet the LORD will **p** you from his
Zec 9:8 guard my Temple and **p** it from invading armies.
9:15 The LORD Almighty will **p** his people, and they
10:2 lost sheep, without a shepherd to **p** and guide them.
11:6 the land into a wilderness, and I will not **p** them."
Mt 4:6 the Scriptures say, / 'He orders his angels to **p** you.
26:53 ask my Father for thousands of angels to **p** us,
27:66 So they sealed the tomb and posted guards to **p** it.
Mk 7:13 you break the law of God in order to **p** your own
Lk 4:10 'He orders his angels to **p** and guard you.
Ac 21:35 soldiers had to lift Paul to their shoulders to **p** him.
26:17 And I will **p** you from both your own people
1Co 12:23 So we carefully **p** from the eyes of others those
1Pe 1:5 will **p** you until you receive this salvation,
Rev 3:10 I will **p** you from the great time of testing that will

PROTECTED (14) [PROTECT]

Jos 6:17 in her house will be spared, for she **p** our spies.
20:3 and be **p** from the relatives of the one who was
1Sa 25:21 We **p** his flocks in the wilderness, and nothing he
1Ki 1:44 son of Jehoiada, **p** by the king's bodyguard.
Ezr 8:31 And the gracious hand of our God **p** us and saved
Job 1:10 You have always **p** him and his home and his
11:18 have hope. You will be **p** and will rest in safety.
Ps 140:7 my strong savior, / you **p** me on the day of battle.
Hos 12:13 out of Egypt by a prophet, who guided and **p** them.
Na 3:8 surrounded by rivers, **p** by water on all sides?
Ac 26:22 But God **p** me so that I am still alive today to tell
1Th 5:8 **p** by the body armor of faith and love,
Rev 7:16 and they will be fully **p** from the scorching
12:14 be cared for and **p** from the dragon for a time,

PROTECTING (8) [PROTECT]

Dt 33:29 He is your **p** shield / and your triumphant sword!
Job 24:21 advantage of the childless who have no **p** sons.
Ps 33:20 to save us. / Only he can help us, **p** us like a shield.
63:7 I sing for joy in the shadow of your **p** wings.
71:3 Be to me a **p** rock of safety, / where I am always
89:40 You have broken down the walls **p** him / and laid
Pr 2:7 He is their shield, **p** those who walk with integrity.
Isa 57:1 No one seems to understand that God is **p** them

PROTECTION (33) [PROTECT]

Ge 19:8 leave these men alone, for they are under my **p**."
Nu 1:53 people of Israel **p** from the LORD's fierce anger.
14:9 They have no **p**, but the LORD is with us!
35:12 These cities will be places of **p** from a dead
35:15 These cities are for the **p** of Israelites,
1Sa 22:3 and mother live here under royal **p** until I know
25:16 day and night they were like a wall of **p** to us
27:2 and went to live at Gath under the **p** of King
2Sa 22:3 my God is my rock, in whom I find **p**. / He is my
22:31 He is a shield for all who look to him for **p**.
Ps 2:12 an instant. / But what joy for all who find **p** in him!
7:1 I come to you for **p**, O LORD my God. / Save me
11:1 I trust in the LORD for **p**. / So why do you say to
18:2 my savior; / my God is my rock, in whom I find **p**.
18:30 He is a shield for all who look to him for **p**.
31:1 O LORD, I have come to you for **p**; / don't let me
31:4 my enemies set for me, / for I find **p** in you alone.
31:19 so much for those who come to you for **p**,
57:1 on me, O God, have mercy! / I look to you for **p**.
61:7 May he reign under God's **p** forever.
71:7 because you have been my strength and **p**.
89:18 Yes, our **p** comes from the LORD, / and he,
91:4 His faithful promises are your armor and **p**.
Pr 19:23 the LORD gives life, security, and **p** from harm.
30:5 proves true. He defends all who come to him for **p**.
Isa 27:5 only if they surrender and beg for peace and **p**."
30:2 You have put your trust in Pharaoh for his **p**.
33:21 He will be like a wide river of **p** that no enemy can
Jer 16:5 "for I have removed my **p** and peace from them.
La 2:3 The Lord has withdrawn his **p** as the enemy
4:20 We had foolishly boasted that under his **p** we could
Eze 22:7 Resident foreigners are forced to pay for **p**.
Mk 6:20 a good and holy man, so he kept him under his **p**.

PROTECTIVE (4) [PROTECT]

Ezr 9:9 He has given us a **p** wall in Judah and Jerusalem.
Ps 101:6 I will keep a **p** eye on the godly, / so they may
121:5 The LORD stands beside you as your **p** shade.
Gal 3:23 We were kept in **p** custody, so to speak, until we

PROTECTOR (2) [PROTECT]

Ps 84:9 O God, look with favor upon the king, our **p**!
84:11 For the LORD God is our light and **p**. / He gives

PROTECTS (18) [PROTECT]

Ezr 8:22 the king, "Our God **p** all those who worship him,
Ps 27:1 The LORD **p** me from danger— / so why should I
28:8 The LORD **p** his people / and gives victory to his
31:23 For the LORD **p** those who are loyal to him,
34:20 For the LORD **p** them from harm— / not one of
35:10 Who else **p** the poor and needy from those who
41:2 The LORD **p** them / and keeps them alive.
97:10 hate evil! / He **p** the lives of his godly people
116:6 The LORD **p** those of childlike faith; / I was
125:2 so the LORD surrounds and **p** his people,
127:1 builders is useless. / Unless the LORD **p** a city,
145:20 The LORD **p** all those who love him, / but he
146:9 The LORD **p** the foreigners among us. / He cares
Pr 2:8 of justice and **p** those who are faithful to him.
10:29 The LORD **p** the upright but destroys the wicked.
15:25 of the proud, but he **p** the property of widows.
Mt 23:37 together as a hen **p** her chicks beneath her wings,
Lk 13:34 together as a hen **p** her chicks beneath her wings,

PROTEST (6) [PROTESTED]

Nu 16:42 As the people gathered to **p** to Moses and Aaron,
Jdg 21:22 when their fathers and brothers come to us in **p**,
Ne 5:1 and their wives raised a cry of **p** against their
Job 19:7 but no one hears me. I **p**, but there is no justice.
Isa 10:14 even flap a wing against me or utter a peep of **p**."
Jer 30:15 Why do you **p** your punishment—this wound that

PROTESTED (18) [PROTEST]

Ex 3:13 But Moses **p**, "If I go to the people of Israel
4:1 But Moses **p** again, "Look, they won't believe me!
5:22 So Moses went back to the LORD and **p**,
19:23 Moses **p**. "You already told them not to.
Nu 11:28 **p**, "Moses, my master, make them stop!"
1Sa 17:39 "I can't go in these," he **p**. "I'm not used to
20:2 "That's not true!" Jonathan **p**. "I'm sure he's not
1Ki 18:9 "Oh, sir," Obadiah **p**, "what harm have I done to
2Ki 4:16 "No, my lord!" she **p**. "Please don't lie to me like
Job 35:16 Job, you have **p** in vain. You have spoken like a
Jer 37:14 "That's not true!" Jeremiah **p**. "I had no intention
Mt 12:2 Some Pharisees saw them do it and **p**,
20:11 When they received their pay, they **p**,
Lk 9:13 "You feed them." "Impossible!" they **p**.
20:16 such a thing should ever happen," his listeners **p**.
23:40 But the other criminal **p**, "Don't you fear God
Jn 13:8 "No," Peter **p**, "you will never wash my feet!"
Ac 28:19 But when the Jewish leaders **p** the decision,

PROUD (103) [PRIDE, PROUDEST, PROUDLY]

Ex 18:11 because his people have escaped from the **p**
Dt 8:14 Do not become **p** at that time and forget the
17:20 regular reading will prevent him from becoming **p**
1Sa 2:3 "Stop acting so **p** and haughty! / Don't speak with
2Sa 22:28 but your eyes are on the **p** to humiliate them.
2Ki 14:10 indeed destroyed Edom and are very **p** about it.
19:22 At whom did you look in such **p** condescension?
2Ch 25:19 You may be very **p** of your conquest of Edom,
26:16 he also became **p**, which led to his downfall.
32:25 to the kindness shown him, and he became **p**.
Ne 9:16 But our ancestors were a **p** and stubborn lot,
9:29 but they became **p** and obstinate and disobeyed
Job 38:11 will you come. Here your **p** waves must stop!'
40:11 vent to your anger. Let it overflow against the **p**.
40:12 Humiliate the **p** with a glance; walk on the wicked
Ps 5:5 the **p** will not be allowed to stand in your presence,
10:2 **P** and wicked people viciously oppress the poor.
10:4 These wicked people are too **p** to seek God.
12:3 flattery to an end / and silence their **p** tongues.
18:27 those who are humble, / but you humiliate the **p**.
31:18 those **p** and arrogant lips that accuse the godly.
36:11 Don't let the **p** trample me; / don't let the wicked
37:35 **p** and evil people thriving like mighty trees.
40:4 the LORD, / who have no confidence in the **p**,
47:4 the **p** possession of Jacob's descendants, whom he
73:3 For I envied the **p** / when I saw them prosper
75:4 "I warned the **p**, 'Stop your boasting!' / I told the
94:2 Sentence the **p** to the penalties they deserve.
119:21 You rebuke those cursed **p** ones / who wander
119:51 The **p** hold me in utter contempt, / but I do not turn
123:4 We have had our fill of the scoffing of the **p**
131:1 LORD, my heart is not **p**; / my eyes are not
138:6 the humble, / but he keeps his distance from the **p**.
140:5 The **p** have set a trap to catch me; / they have
Pr 15:25 The LORD destroys the house of the **p**, but he
16:5 be assured that the **p** will be punished.
16:19 with the poor than to share plunder with the **p**.
21:4 Haughty eyes, a **p** heart, and evil actions are all

21:24 Mockers are **p** and haughty; they act with
30:13 They are **p** beyond description and disdainful.
30:32 If you have been a fool by being **p** or plotting evil,
Isa 2:12 In that day the LORD Almighty will punish the **p**,
5:15 brought down to the dust; the **p** will be humbled.
10:12 and punish him—for he is **p** and arrogant.
10:16 will send a plague among your **p** troops,
13:11 I will crush the arrogance of the **p**
16:6 the **p** land we have heard so much about?
24:21 and the **p** rulers of the nations on earth.
26:5 He humbles the **p** / and brings the arrogant city to
28:3 The **p** city of Samaria—the pride and joy of the
30:28 He will sift out the **p** nations. He will bridle them
37:23 At whom did you look in such **p** condescension?
43:14 be forced to flee in those ships they are so **p** of.
Jer 13:15 Listen! Do not be **p**, for the LORD has spoken.
43:2 of Kareah and all the other **p** men said to Jeremiah,
49:4 You are **p** of your fertile valleys, but they will soon
49:16 You are **p** that you inspire fear in others. And you
are **p** because you live in a rock fortress
50:31 I am your enemy, O **p** people," says the Lord,
Eze 7:11 None of these **p** and wicked people will survive.
7:20 They were **p** of their gold jewelry and used it to
7:24 I will break down their **p** fortresses and defile their
16:50 She was **p** and did loathsome things, so I wiped her
16:56 In your **p** days you held Sodom in contempt.
28:5 very rich, and your riches have made you very **p**.
30:18 When I come to break the **p** strength of Egypt,
31:10 Because it became **p** and arrogant, and because it
31:14 They will land in the pit along with all the **p** people
31:16 And all the other **p** trees of Eden, the most
Da 4:37 and he is able to humble those who are **p**."
Hos 13:6 were satisfied, then you became **p** and forgot me.
Ob 1:3 You are **p** because you live in a rock fortress
Na 2:13 Never again will the voices of your **p** messengers
Hab 2:4 "Look at the **p**! They trust in themselves, and their
Zep 2:14 so **p** will become a pasture for sheep and cattle.
3:11 I will remove all the **p** and arrogant people from
Zec 10:3 and glorious, like a **p** warhorse in battle.
Lk 1:51 How he scatters the **p** and haughty ones!
14:11 For the **p** will be humbled, but the humble will be
16:3 to go out and dig ditches, and I'm too **p** to beg.
18:11 The **p** Pharisee stood by himself and prayed this
18:14 For the **p** will be humbled, but the humble will be
Ro 1:30 haters of God, insolent, **p**, and boastful.
2:23 You are so **p** of knowing the law, but you dishonor
11:25 so that you will not feel **p** and start bragging.
1Co 5:2 And you are so **p** of yourselves! Why aren't you
13:4 and kind. Love is not jealous or boastful or **p**
2Co 1:14 you will be **p** of us in the same way we are **p**
5:12 No, we are giving you a reason to be **p** of us,
7:14 I had told him how **p** I was of you—and you didn't
10:5 With these weapons we break down every **p**
12:7 Satan to torment me and keep me from getting **p**.
Eph 2:11 who were **p** of their circumcision, even though it
Php 2:16 I will be **p** that I did not lose the race and that my
Col 2:18 but their sinful minds have made them **p**.
1Th 2:19 and joy, and what is our **p** reward and crown?
1Ti 3:6 because he might be **p** of being chosen so soon,
6:17 Tell those who are rich in this world not to be **p**
2Ti 3:2 They will be boastful and **p**, scoffing at God,
Jas 4:6 Scriptures say, / "God sets himself against the **p**,
1Pe 5:5 in humility, for / "God sets himself against the **p**,
2Pe 2:10 These people are **p** and arrogant, daring even to

PROUDEST (1) [PROUD]

Job 41:34 Of all the creatures, it is the **p**. It is the king of

PROUDLY (10) [PROUD]

Job 31:36 I would face the accusation **p**. I would treasure it
36:9 He shows them their sins, for they have behaved **p**.
Isa 44:5 Some will **p** claim, 'I belong to the LORD.'
64:6 When we **p** display our righteous deeds, we find
Eze 31:14 Let no other nation **p** exult in its own prosperity,
35:13 In saying that, you boasted **p** against me, and I
Mic 2:3 none of you will ever again walk **p** in the streets."
Zep 3:2 It **p** refuses to listen even to the voice of the
2Co 10:7 as those who **p** declare that they belong to Christ.
2Th 1:4 We **p** tell God's other churches about your

PROVE (58) [PROOF, PROOFS, PROVED, PROVEN, PROVES, PROVING]

Ge 42:34 If you **p** to be what you say, then I will give you
44:16 How can we plead? How can we **p** our innocence?
Ex 7:9 show him a miracle to **p** that God has sent you.
9:14 I will **p** to you that there is no other God like me in
9:29 This will **p** to you that the earth belongs to the
10:2 among the Egyptians to **p** that I am the LORD."
Nu 14:17 **p** that your power is as great as you have claimed it
Dt 8:2 humbling you and testing you to **p** your character,
13:14 and can **p** that such a detestable act has occurred
Jdg 6:17 show me a sign to **p** that it is really the LORD
6:37 **p** it to me in this way. I will put some wool on the
1Sa 2:34 And to **p** that what I have said will come true,
18:17 But first you must **p** yourself to be a real warrior
2Sa 22:31 way is perfect. / All the LORD's promises **p** true.
1Ki 13:3 That same day the man of God gave a sign to **p** his
18:36 **p** today that you are God in Israel and that I am
18:36 **P** that I have done all this at your command.
2Ki 20:8 "What sign will the LORD give to **p** that he will
20:9 will give you to **p** he will do as he promised.
Ezr 2:59 they could not **p** that they or their families were
Ne 7:61 they could not **p** that they or their families were
Job 9:20 Though I am blameless, it would **p** me wicked.
13:19 If you could **p** me wrong, I would remain silent
24:25 anyone claim otherwise? Who can **p** me wrong?"
Ps 18:30 way is perfect. / All the LORD's promises **p** true.
Ecc 3:21 For who can **p** that the human spirit goes upward
7:25 I was determined to **p** to myself that wickedness is
Isa 7:11 to **p** that I will crush your enemies as I have
38:7 will give you to **p** he will do as he promised:
38:22 "What sign will **p** that I will go to the Temple of
44:7 them tell you if they can and thus **p** their power.
49:8 This will **p** that I will reestablish the land of Israel
La 3:59 done to me, LORD. Be my judge, and **p** me right.
Mal 3:10 room to take it in! Try it! Let me **p** it to you!
Mt 3:8 **P** by the way you live that you have really turned
9:6 I will **p** that I, the Son of Man, have the authority
12:38 we want you to show us a miraculous sign to **p** that
Mk 2:10 I will **p** that I, the Son of Man, have the authority
8:11 "Give us a miraculous sign from heaven to **p**
Lk 3:8 **P** by the way you live that you have really turned
5:24 I will **p** that I, the Son of Man, have the authority
23:39 **P** it by saving yourself—and us, too, while you're
Jn 2:18 from God, show us a miraculous sign to **p** it."
7:4 can do such wonderful things, **p** it to the world!"
13:35 Your love for one another will **p** to the world that
Ac 24:13 These men certainly cannot **p** the things they
25:7 made many serious accusations they couldn't **p**.
26:20 and **p** they have changed by the good things they
1Co 1:22 because they want a sign from heaven to **p** it is
3:3 Doesn't that **p** you are controlled by your own
2Co 8:8 to do it. This is one way to **p** your love is real.
8:24 and **p** to all the churches that our boasting about
9:13 For your generosity to them will **p** that you are
2Th 3:17 I do this at the end of all my letters to **p** that they
Jas 2:14 you have faith if you don't **p** it by your actions?
2Pe 1:10 work hard to **p** that you really are among those
3Jn 1:11 Remember that those who do good **p** that they are
1:11 and those who do evil **p** that they do not know

PROVED (22) [PROVE]

Dt 22:20 are true, and her virginity could not be **p**.
Ne 9:8 When he had **p** himself faithful, you made a
Job 6:15 you have **p** as unreliable as a seasonal brook that
6:21 You, too, have **p** to be of no help. You have seen
11:2 Is a person **p** innocent just by talking a lot?
13:18 I have prepared my case; I will be **p** innocent.
Ps 51:4 You will be **p** right in what you say, / and your
Jer 44:25 of Heaven, and you have **p** it by your actions.
Da 6:3 Daniel soon **p** himself more capable than all the
Lk 20:37 even Moses **p** this when he wrote about the
Ac 1:3 and **p** to them in many ways that he was actually
14:3 The Lord **p** their message was true by giving them
17:31 and he **p** to everyone who this is by raising him
18:27 he **p** to be of great benefit to those who, by God's
Ro 3:4 Scriptures say, "He will be **p** right in what he says,
2Co 6:6 We have **p** ourselves by our purity,
7:14 and now my boasting to Titus has also **p** true!
11:6 this by now, for we have **p** it again and again.
Php 2:22 But you know how Timothy has **p** himself. Like a
Heb 2:2 God delivered through angels has always **p** true,
9:16 no one gets anything until it is **p** that the person
1Jn 2:19 they left us, it **p** that they do not belong with us.

PROVEN (1) [PROVE]

Ecc 10:6 and if they fail to give people of **p** worth their

PROVENDER [KJV] See FOOD, FED, FEED, FODDER

PROVERB (13) [PROVERBIAL, PROVERBS]

Ge 22:14 This name has now become a **p**: "On the mountain
Dt 28:37 a **p** and a mockery among all the nations to which
1Sa 24:13 As that old **p** says, 'From evil people come evil
Pr 26:7 of a fool, a **p** becomes as limp as a paralyzed leg.
26:9 A **p** in a fool's mouth is as dangerous as a
Jer 31:29 "The people will no longer quote this **p**:
Eze 12:22 "Son of man, what is that **p** they quote in Israel:
12:23 I will put an end to this **p**, and you will soon stop
12:23 Now give them this new **p** to replace the old one:
18:2 "Why do you quote this **p** in the land of Israel:
18:3 you will not say this **p** anymore in Israel.
Joel 2:17 Don't let their name become a **p** of unbelieving
Lk 4:23 "Probably you will quote me that **p**, 'Physician,

PROVERBIAL (2) [PROVERB]

Ge 10:9 His name became **p**, and people would speak of
Jer 29:22 Their terrible fate will become **p**, so that whenever

PROVERBS (13) [PROVERB]

1Ki 4:32 He composed some 3,000 **p** and wrote 1,005
Ps 49:4 I listen carefully to many **p** / and solve riddles with
Pr 1:1 These are the **p** of Solomon, David's son, king of
1:2 The purpose of these **p** is to teach people wisdom
1:3 Through these **p**, people will receive instruction in
1:4 These **p** will make the simpleminded clever.
1:5 Let those who are wise listen to these **p**
1:6 by exploring the depth of meaning in these **p**,
10:1 The **p** of Solomon: A wise child brings joy to a
25:1 These are more **p** of Solomon, collected by the
Ecc 12:9 he knew. He collected **p** and classified them.
Eze 16:44 Everyone who makes up **p** will say of you,
2Pe 2:22 They make these **p** come true: "A dog returns to

PROVES (11) [PROVE]

1Sa 24:11 This **p** that I am not trying to harm you and that I
1Ki 1:52 Solomon replied, "If he **p** himself to be loyal,
Pr 13:24 discipline your children, it **p** you don't love them;
30:5 Every word of God **p** true. He defends all who
Mt 3:9 the descendants of Abraham.' That **p** nothing.
Lk 3:8 the descendants of Abraham.' That **p** nothing.
7:39 said to himself, "This **p** that Jesus is no prophet.
Jn 8:47 Since you don't, it **p** you aren't God's children."
Ro 9:11 (This message **p** that God chooses according to his
Gal 5:11 The fact that I am still being persecuted **p** that I am
1Jn 3:14 it **p** that we have passed from death to eternal life.

PROVIDE (34) [PROVIDED, PROVIDES, PROVIDING, PROVISION, PROVISIONS]

Ge 22:8 "God will **p** a lamb, my son," Abraham answered.
22:14 Abraham named the place "The LORD Will **P**."
30:30 about me? When should I **p** for my own family?"
47:23 I will **p** you with seed, so you can plant the fields.
Ex 5:10 "Pharaoh has ordered us not to **p** straw for you.
Lev 24:2 "Command the people of Israel to **p** you with pure
Nu 35:3 and the surrounding lands will **p** pasture for their
Dt 32:38 and help you! / Let them **p** you with shelter!
1Ki 20:10 if there remains enough dust from Samaria to **p**
1Ch 22:14 "I have worked hard to **p** materials for building
Ezr 6:9 without fail, **p** them with the wheat, salt, wine,
7:23 Be careful to **p** whatever the God of heaven
Ne 10:33 This will **p** for the Bread of the Presence;
10:33 It will also **p** for the other items necessary for the
Est 1:15 "What penalty does the law **p** for a queen who
Ps 65:9 not run dry; / they **p** a bountiful harvest of grain,
104:11 They **p** water for all the animals, / and the wild
Pr 19:14 Parents can **p** their sons with an inheritance of
27:26 your sheep will **p** wool for clothing, and your goats
Isa 4:1 marry you! We will **p** our own food and clothing.
4:5 Then the LORD will **p** shade for Jerusalem
23:18 will not be hoarded but will be used to **p** good food
Eze 45:17 The prince will be required to **p** offerings that are
45:17 He will **p** the sin offerings, burnt offerings,
45:22 On the day of Passover the prince will **p** a young
45:24 The prince will **p** a half bushel of flour as a grain
45:25 the prince will **p** these same sacrifices for the sin
Lk 10:7 in one place, eating and drinking what they **p** you.
12:29 Don't worry whether God will **p** it for you.
Ac 23:24 **P** horses for Paul to ride, and get him safely to
27:3 to visit with friends so they could **p** for his needs.
2Co 9:8 And God will generously **p** all you need. Then you
2Th 1:7 And God will **p** rest for you who are being
Heb 10:1 but they were never able to **p** perfect cleansing for

PROVIDED (23) [PROVIDE]

Ge 22:14 "On the mountain of the LORD it will be **p**."
24:32 and **p** water for the camel drivers to wash their
46:5 and wives in the wagons Pharaoh had **p** for them.
Ex 16:32 **p** in the wilderness when he brought you out of
Dt 2:7 and **p** for your every need so that you lacked
Ru 3:1 permanent home for you, so that you will be **p** for.
2Sa 7:10 And I have **p** a permanent homeland for my people
19:32 He was the one who **p** food for the king during his
1Ki 1:5 So he **p** himself with chariots and horses
4:27 The district governors faithfully **p** food for King
1Ch 5:2 the most powerful tribe and **p** a ruler for the nation,
17:9 And I have **p** a permanent homeland for my people
22:3 David **p** large amounts of iron for the nails that
22:4 He also **p** innumerable cedar logs, for the men of
2Ch 11:23 He **p** them with generous provisions and arranged
26:14 Uzziah **p** the entire army with shields, spears,
28:15 They **p** clothing and sandals to wear, gave them
Ne 13:7 that he had **p** Tobiah with a room in the courtyards
Est 2:9 menu for her and **p** her with beauty treatments.
Ps 68:10 O God, / you **p** for your needy people.
Eze 41:8 a terrace, which **p** a foundation for the side rooms.
Hos 2:9 and ripened grain I generously **p** each harvest
Heb 10:2 If they could have **p** perfect cleansing,

PROVIDES (5) [PROVIDE]

Job 38:41 Who **p** food for the ravens when their young cry
Ps 147:8 the heavens with clouds, / **p** rain for the earth,
Jer 31:35 It is the LORD who **p** the sun to light the day
Eze 18:7 to the hungry and **p** clothes for people in need.
18:16 this son feeds the hungry, **p** clothes for the needy,

PROVIDING (4) [PROVIDE]

Lev 21:6 **p** God with his food, and they must remain holy.
1Ki 4:7 They were responsible for **p** food from the people
Job 31:20 did they not praise me for **p** wool clothing to keep
Isa 33:6 **p** a rich store of salvation, wisdom,

PROVINCE (60) [PROVINCES, PROVINCIAL]

Ezr 4:10 and throughout the neighboring lands of the **p** west
4:11 from your loyal subjects in the **p** west of the
4:16 the **p** west of the Euphrates River will be lost to
4:17 and throughout the **p** west of the Euphrates River.
4:20 and the entire **p** west of the Euphrates River
5:3 governor of the **p** west of the Euphrates,
5:6 and the other officials of the **p** west of the
5:8 of the Temple of the great God in the **p** of Judah.
6:2 But it was at the fortress at Ecbatana in the **p** of
6:6 governor of the **p** west of the Euphrates River,
6:8 without delay from my taxes collected in your **p**
6:13 governor of the **p** west of the Euphrates River,
7:16 and gold which you may obtain from the **p** of
7:21 hereby send this decree to all the treasurers in the **p**
7:25 all the people in the **p** west of the Euphrates River.
8:36 and the governors of the **p** west of the Euphrates
Ne 1:3 well for those who returned to the **p** of Judah.
2:7 give me letters to the governors of the **p** west of

2: 9 When I came to the governors of the **p** west of the
3: 7 the headquarters of the governor of the **p** west of the
Est 1:22 to each **p** in its own script and language,
2: 3 Let the king appoint agents in each **p** to bring these
3:12 and the local officials of each **p** in their own scripts
3:14 A copy of this decree was to be issued in every **p**
8:11 or **p** who might attack them or their children
8:13 this decree was to be recognized as law in every **p**
8:17 In every city and **p**, wherever the king's decree
Isa 19: 2 city against city, **p** against **p**.
Da 2:48 He made Daniel ruler over the whole **p** of
2:49 be in charge of all the affairs of the **p** of Babylon,
3: 1 and set it up on the plain of Dura in the **p** of
3:12 whom you have put in charge of the **p** of Babylon.
3:30 and Abednego to even higher positions in the **p** of
6: 1 and he appointed a prince to rule over each **p**.
8: 2 in the **p** of Elam, standing beside the Ulai River.
Ac 2: 9 Judea, Cappadocia, Pontus, the **p** of Asia,
6: 9 Alexandria, Cilicia, and the **p** of Asia.
16: 6 told them not to go into the **p** of Asia at that time.
16: 7 of Mysia, they headed for the **p** of Bithynia,
19:10 so that people throughout the **p** of Asia—
19:22 while he stayed awhile longer in the **p** of Asia.
19:26 only here in Ephesus but throughout the entire **p**!
19:27 goddess worshiped throughout the **p** of Asia
19:31 Some of the officials of the **p**, friends of Paul,
20: 4 and Trophimus, who were from the **p** of Asia.
20:16 didn't want to spend further time in the **p** of Asia.
20:18 "You know that from the day I set foot in the **p** of
21: 2 There we boarded a ship sailing for the Syrian **p** of
21:27 Jews from the **p** of Asia saw Paul in the Temple
23:34 read it and then asked Paul what **p** he was from.
24:19 But some Jews from the **p** of Asia were there—
27: 2 stops at ports along the coast of the **p** of Asia.
27: 5 and Pamphylia, landing at Myra, in the **p** of Lycia.
Ro 16: 5 first person to become a Christian in the **p** of Asia.
1Co 16:19 The churches here in the **p** of Asia greet you
2Co 1: 8 about the trouble we went through in the **p** of Asia.
2Ti 1:15 all the Christians who came here from the **p** of
1Pe 1: 1 Galatia, Cappadocia, the **p** of Asia, and Bithynia.
Rev 1: 4 is from John to the seven churches in the **p** of Asia.

PROVINCES (25) [PROVINCE]

Ezr 2: 1 Here is the list of the Jewish exiles of the **p** who
Ne 7: 6 "Here is the list of the Jewish exiles of the **p** who
Est 1: 1 who reigned over 127 **p** stretching from India to
2:18 and declaring a public festival for the **p**.
3: 8 people scattered through all the **p** of your empire.
3:12 to the princes, the governors of the respective **p**,
3:13 and sent by messengers into all the **p** of the empire.
4: 3 And as news of the king's decree reached all the **p**,
8: 5 destroy the Jews throughout all the **p** of the king.
8: 9 and local officials of all the 127 **p** stretching from
8:12 The day chosen for this event throughout all the **p**
9: 2 **p** to defend themselves against anyone who might
9: 3 And all the commanders of the **p**, the princes,
9: 4 and his fame spread throughout all the **p** as he
9:12 that here, what has happened in the rest of the **p**?
9:16 the other Jews throughout the king's **p** had
9:17 Throughout the **p** this was done on March 7.
9:20 the Jews near and far, throughout all the king's **p**,
9:28 and celebrated by every family throughout the **p**
9:30 throughout the 127 **p** of the empire of Xerxes.
Ecc 2: 8 and gold, the treasure of many kings and **p**.
Da 6: 1 Mede decided to divide the kingdom into 120 **p**,
Ac 19: 1 in Corinth, Paul traveled through the interior **p**.
27: 5 We passed along the coast of the **p** of Cilicia
Gal 1:21 I went north into the **p** of Syria and Cilicia.

PROVINCIAL (7) [PROVINCE]

1Ki 20:14 The troops of the **p** commanders will do it."
20:15 So Ahab mustered the troops of the 232 **p**
20:17 the troops of the **p** commanders marched out of the
20:19 But by now Ahab's **p** commanders had led the
Ne 11: 3 Here is a list of the names of the **p** officials who
Est 1: 3 and Persia, as well as the noblemen and **p** officials.
Da 3: 2 and all the **p** officials to come to the dedication of

PROVING (2) [PROVE]

Isa 44:25 people to give bad advice, thus **p** them to be fools.
Ac 17: 3 and **p** the prophecies about the sufferings of the

PROVISION (1) [PROVIDE]

Ex 16:32 forever as a treasured memorial of the LORD's **p**.

PROVISIONS (9) [PROVIDE]

Ge 42:25 of his sack. He also gave them **p** for their journey.
45:21 and he supplied them with **p** for the journey.
Jos 1:11 the camp and tell the people to get their **p** ready.
9: 5 And they took along dry, moldy bread for **p**.
Jdg 7: 8 So Gideon collected the **p** and rams' horns of the
1Sa 25: 8 Please give us any **p** you might have on hand."
1Ki 4: 7 Each of them arranged **p** for one month of the year.
2Ch 11:23 He provided them with generous **p** and arranged
Ne 5:18 The **p** required at my expense for each day were

PROVOKE (2) [PROVOKED, PROVOKING]

Dt 32:21 I will **p** their fury by blessing the foolish Gentiles.
Job 12: 6 robbers are left in peace, and those who **p** God—

PROVOKED (6) [PROVOKE]

Dt 32:16 foreign gods; / they **p** his fury with detestable acts.
32:19 He was **p** to anger by his own sons and daughters.
32:21 they have **p** my fury with useless idols.
Ne 4: 5 for they have **p** you to anger here in the presence
Jer 7:29 and forsaken this generation that has **p** his fury.'
Hos 12:14 But the people of Israel have bitterly **p** the

PROVOKING (1) [PROVOKE]

Jer 11:17 **p** my anger by offering incense to Baal."

PROW (1)

Ac 27:30 they were going to put out anchors from the **p**.

PROWL (4) [PROWLED, PROWLS]

Ps 59: 6 snarling like vicious dogs / as they **p** the streets.
59:14 snarling like vicious dogs / as they **p** the streets.
104:20 when all the forest animals **p** about.
SS 4: 8 where lions have their dens and panthers **p**.

PROWLED (1) [PROWL]

Eze 19: 6 He **p** among the other lions / and became a leader

PROWLS (2) [PROWL]

Ge 49:27 "Benjamin is a wolf that **p**. / He devours his
1Pe 5: 8 He **p** around like a roaring lion, looking for some

PRUDENT (4)

Dt 4: 6 'What other nation is as wise and **p** as this!'
Pr 14:15 they are told! The **p** carefully consider their steps.
22: 3 A **p** person foresees the danger ahead and takes
27:12 A **p** person foresees the danger ahead and takes

PRUNE (3) [PRUNED, PRUNES, PRUNING]

Lev 25: 3 and **p** your vineyards and harvest your crops,
25: 4 or **p** your vineyards during that entire year.
Isa 5: 6 I will not **p** the vines or hoe the ground.

PRUNED (1) [PRUNE]

Jn 15: 3 You have already been **p** for greater fruitfulness by

PRUNES (1) [PRUNE]

Jn 15: 2 and he **p** the branches that do bear fruit so they will

PRUNING (4) [PRUNE]

Isa 2: 4 into plowshares and their spears into **p** hooks.
18: 5 the LORD will cut you off as though with **p**
Joel 3:10 into swords and your **p** hooks into spears.
Mic 4: 3 into plowshares and their spears into **p** hooks.

PRUNINGHOOKS [KJV] See PRUNING (SHEARS)

PRY (1) [PRYING]

Job 41:14 Who could **p** open its jaws? For its teeth are

PRYING (1) [PRY]

1Pe 4:15 making trouble, or **p** into other people's affairs.

PSALM (104) [PSALMIST, PSALMS]

Ps 3: T A **p** of David, regarding the time David fled from
4: T A **p** of David, to be accompanied by stringed
5: T A **p** of David, to be accompanied by the flute.
6: T A **p** of David, to be accompanied by an
7: T A **p** of David, which he sang to the LORD
8: T A **p** of David, to be accompanied by a stringed
9: T A **p** of David, to be sung to the tune "Death of the
11: T For the choir director: A **p** of David.
12: T A **p** of David, to be accompanied by an
13: T For the choir director: A **p** of David.
14: T For the choir director: A **p** of David.
15: T A **p** of David.
16: T A **p** of David.
18: T A **p** of David, the servant of the LORD.
19: T For the choir director: A **p** of David.
20: T For the choir director: A **p** of David.
21: T For the choir director: A **p** of David.
22: T A **p** of David, to be sung to the tune "Doe of the
23: T A **p** of David.
24: T A **p** of David.
25: T A **p** of David.
26: T A **p** of David.
27: T A **p** of David.
28: T A **p** of David.
29: T A **p** of David.
30: T A **p** of David, sung at the dedication of the
31: T For the choir director: A **p** of David.
32: T A **p** of David.
34: T A **p** of David, regarding the time he pretended to
35: T A **p** of David.
36: T A **p** of David, the servant of the LORD.
37: T A **p** of David.
38: T A **p** of David, to bring us to the LORD's
39: T For Jeduthun, the choir director: A **p** of David.
40: T For the choir director: A **p** of David.
41: T For the choir director: A **p** of David.
42: T choir director: A **p** of the descendants of Korah.
44: T choir director: A **p** of the descendants of Korah.
45: T A **p** of the descendants of Korah, to be sung to the
46: T A **p** of the descendants of Korah, to be sung by
47: T choir director: A **p** of the descendants of Korah.
47: 7 is the King over all the earth. / Praise him with a **p**!
48: T A **p** of the descendants of Korah. A song.
49: T choir director: A **p** of the descendants of Korah.
50: T A **p** of Asaph.
51: T A **p** of David, regarding the time Nathan the
52: T A **p** of David, regarding the time Doeg the
55: T A **p** of David, to be accompanied by stringed
56: T A **p** of David, regarding the time the Philistines
57: T A **p** of David, regarding the time he fled from Saul
58: T A **p** of David, to be sung to the tune "Do Not
59: T A **p** of David, regarding the time Saul sent soldiers
60: T A **p** of David useful for teaching,
61: T A **p** of David, to be accompanied by stringed
62: T For Jeduthun, the choir director: A **p** of David.
63: T A **p** of David, regarding a time when David was in
64: T For the choir director: A **p** of David.
65: T For the choir director: A **p** of David. A song.
66: T For the choir director: A **p**. A song.
67: T A **p**, to be accompanied by stringed instruments.
68: T For the choir director: A **p** of David. A song.
69: T A **p** of David, to be sung to the tune "Lilies."
70: T A **p** of David, to bring us to the LORD's
72: T A **p** of Solomon.
73: T A **p** of Asaph.
74: T A **p** of Asaph.
75: T A **p** of Asaph, to be sung to the tune "Do Not
76: T A **p** of Asaph, to be accompanied by stringed
77: T For Jeduthun, the choir director: A **p** of Asaph.
78: T A **p** of Asaph.
79: T A **p** of Asaph.
80: T A **p** of Asaph, to be sung to the tune "Lilies of the
81: T A **p** of Asaph, to be accompanied by a stringed
82: T A **p** of Asaph.
83: T A **p** of Asaph. A song.
84: T A **p** of the descendants of Korah, to be
85: T choir director: A **p** of the descendants of Korah.
87: T A **p** of the descendants of Korah. A song.
88: T A **p** of the descendants of Korah, to be sung to the
88: T A **p** of Heman the Ezrahite. A song.
89: T A **p** of Ethan the Ezrahite.
92: T A **p** to be sung on the LORD's Day. A song.
98: T A **p**.
100: T A **p** of thanksgiving.
101: T A **p** of David.
103: T A **p** of David.
108: T A **p** of David. A song.
109: T For the choir director: A **p** of David.
110: T A **p** of David.
122: T A song for the ascent to Jerusalem. A **p** of David.
124: T A song for the ascent to Jerusalem. A **p** of David.
127: T song for the ascent to Jerusalem. A **p** of Solomon.
131: T A song for the ascent to Jerusalem. A **p** of David.
133: T A song for the ascent to Jerusalem. A **p** of David.
138: T A **p** of David.
139: T For the choir director: A **p** of David.
140: T For the choir director: A **p** of David.
141: T A **p** of David.
142: T A **p** of David, regarding his experience in the cave.
143: T A **p** of David.
144: T A **p** of David.
145: T A **p** of praise of David.
Ac 13:33 This is what the second **p** is talking about when it
13:35 Another **p** explains more fully, saying, 'You will

PSALMIST (4) [PSALM]

2Sa 23: 1 by the God of Jacob, / David, the sweet **p** of Israel.
Ro 15: 9 That is what the **p** meant when he wrote: / "I will
2Co 4:13 because we have the same kind of faith the **p** had
Heb 7:17 And the **p** pointed this out when he said of Christ,

PSALMS (7) [PSALM]

2Ch 29:30 Levites to praise the LORD with the **p** of David
Ps 95: 2 with thanksgiving. / Let us sing him **p** of praise.
Lk 20:42 For David himself wrote in the book of **P**:
24:44 and the prophets and in the **P** must all come true."
Ac 1:20 "This was predicted in the book of **P**, where it
Eph 5:19 Then you will sing **p** and hymns and spiritual
Col 3:16 Sing **p** and hymns and spiritual songs to God with

PSYCHICS (11)

Lev 19:31 "Do not rely on mediums and **p**, for you will be
20: 6 by consulting and following mediums or **p**,
20:27 as mediums or **p** must be put to death by stoning.
Dt 18:11 or cast spells, or function as mediums or **p**, or call
1Sa 28: 3 banned all mediums and **p** from the land of Israel.
28: 9 has expelled all the mediums and **p** from the land.
2Ki 21: 6 and he consulted with mediums and **p**.
23:24 Josiah also exterminated the mediums and **p**,
2Ch 33: 6 and he consulted with mediums and **p**.
Isa 8:19 find out the future by consulting mediums and **p**?
19: 3 mediums, and **p** to show them which way to turn.

PTOLEMAIS (1)

Ac 21: 7 The next stop after leaving Tyre was **P**, where we

PUAH (5) [PUITE]

Ge 46:13 of Issachar were Tola, **P**, Jashub, and Shimron.
Ex 1:15 order to the Hebrew midwives, Shiphrah and **P**:
Nu 26:23 The Puite clan, named after its ancestor **P**.
Jdg 10: 1 Tola, the son of **P** and descendant of Dodo,
1Ch 7: 1 of Issachar were Tola, **P**, Jashub, and Shimron.

PUBLIC (54) [PUBLICITY, PUBLICLY]

Ge 21:30 "They are my gift to you as a **p** confirmation that I
26:11 Then Abimelech made a **p** proclamation:
1Sa 9:12 He has just arrived to take part in a **p** sacrifice up

2Sa 12:11 and he will go to bed with them in **p** view.
21:12 the **p** square of the Philistine city of Beth-shan.)
2Ki 10:27 the temple of Baal, converting it into a **p** toilet.
15:10 assassinated him in **p**, and became the next king.
23: 6 pole to dust and threw the dust in the **p** cemetery.
1Ch 26:29 and his sons were appointed to serve as **p**
Ne 5: 7 Then I called a **p** meeting to deal with the problem.
11:24 was the king's agent in all matters of **p**
Est 2:18 and declaring a **p** festival for the provinces.
8:17 and declared a **p** festival and holiday.
Job 30:28 I stand in the **p** square and cry for help.
Pr 1:20 shouts in the streets. She cries out in the **p** square.
5:14 of utter ruin, and now I must face **p** disgrace."
5:16 Why spill the water of your springs in **p**,
19:26 or chase away their mother are a **p** disgrace and an
Isa 42: 2 be gentle—he will not shout or raise his voice in **p**.
47: 2 and strip off your robe. Expose yourself to **p** view.
Jer 29:21 "I will turn them over to Nebuchadnezzar for a **p**
Eze 22: 2 of murderers? Denounce her terrible deeds in **p**,
24:22 You will not mourn in **p** or console yourselves by
42:14 the parts of the building complex open to the **p**."
48:15 the sacred Temple area, will be allotted for **p** use—
Hos 2:10 I will strip her naked in **p**, while all her lovers look
Am 5:16 "There will be crying in all the **p** squares and in
Mt 10:26 will be revealed; all that is secret will be made **p**.
11:16 a group of children playing a game in the **p** square.
12:19 not fight or shout; / he will not raise his voice in **p**.
Mk 4:34 in his **p** teaching he taught only with parables,
12:40 people they really are, they make long prayers in **p**.
Lk 1:80 wilderness until he began his **p** ministry to Israel.
3:23 thirty years old when he began his **p** ministry.
7:32 a group of children playing a game in the **p** square.
10:11 from our feet as a **p** announcement of your doom.
12: 2 will be revealed; all that is secret will be made **p**.
16:15 Then he said to them, "You like to look good in **p**,
20:47 people they really are, they make long prayers in **p**.
Jn 7: 4 "You can't become a **p** figure if you hide like this!
7:10 also went, though secretly, staying out of **p** view.
7:13 had the courage to speak favorably about him in **p**,
7:26 But here he is, speaking in **p**, and they say nothing
11:54 Jesus stopped his **p** ministry among the people
18:20 I teach nothing in private that I have not said in **p**.
Ac 10:41 not to the general **p**, but to us whom God had
12: 4 Herod's intention was to bring Peter out for **p** trial
17:17 and he spoke daily in the **p** square to all who
18:28 all the Jews with powerful arguments in **p** debate.
19:19 incantation books and burned them at a **p** bonfire.
19:27 I'm not just talking about the loss of **p** respect for
1Co 11:13 Is it right for a woman to pray to God in **p** without
Heb 6: 6 again by rejecting him, holding him up to **p** shame.
10:33 Sometimes you were exposed to **p** ridicule

PUBLICAN [KJV] See TAX (COLLECTOR)

PUBLICITY (1) [PUBLIC]

Mk 9:30 traveled through Galilee. Jesus tried to avoid all **p**

PUBLICK [KJV] See PUBLICLY

PUBLICLY (33) [PUBLIC]

Ge 23: 9 full price, of course, whatever is **p** agreed upon,
23:10 speaking **p** before all the elders of the town.
23:16 four hundred pieces of silver, as was **p** agreed.
Ex 21: 6 him to the door and **p** pierce his ear with an awl.
Lev 20:17 Both of them must be **p** cut off from the
Nu 27:19 and **p** commission him with the responsibility of
Dt 25: 3 more than forty lashes would **p** humiliate your
Ru 4: 7 to the other party. This **p** validated the transaction.
2Sa 17:23 Ahithophel was **p** disgraced when Absalom
Ps 9:14 so I can praise you **p** at Jerusalem's gates,
26:12 taken a stand, / and I will **p** praise the LORD.
89:45 before his time / and **p** disgraced him. / *Interlude*
107:32 Let them exalt him **p** before the congregation
Pr 25: 7 than to be sent to the end of the line, **p** disgraced!
31:31 she has done. Let her deeds **p** declare her praise.
Isa 45:19 I **p** proclaim bold promises. I do not whisper
Jer 28: 1 addressed me **p** in the Temple while all the priests
Eze 5: 8 I will punish you **p** while all the nations watch.
Mt 1:19 the engagement quietly, so as not to disgrace her **p**.
6: 1 Don't do your good deeds **p**, to be admired,
6: 5 don't be like the hypocrites who love to pray **p** on
10:32 "If anyone acknowledges me **p** here on earth,
Mk 1:45 Jesus that he couldn't enter a town anywhere **p**.
Lk 3:19 John also **p** criticized Herod Antipas, ruler of
12: 8 If anyone acknowledges me **p** here on earth,
Jn 11:57 and Pharisees had **p** announced that anyone seeing
Ac 2:22 God **p** endorsed Jesus of Nazareth by doing
16:37 "They have **p** beaten us without trial and jailed
19: 9 rejected his message and **p** spoke against the Way,
20:20 telling you the truth, either **p** or in your homes.
21:26 Then he **p** announced the date when their vows
Gal 2:11 Peter came to Antioch, I had to oppose him **p**,
Col 2:15 He shamed them **p** by his victory over them on the

PUBLISH (3) [PUBLISHED]

1Ch 16:24 **P** his glorious deeds among the nations.
Ps 96: 3 **P** his glorious deeds among the nations.
Jer 46:14 **P** it in the cities of Migdol, Memphis,

PUBLISHED (1) [PUBLISH]

Est 1:20 When this decree is **p** throughout your vast empire,

PUBLIUS (1) [PUBLIUS'S]

Ac 28: 7 where we landed was an estate belonging to **P**,

PUBLIUS'S (1) [PUBLIUS]

Ac 28: 8 **P** father was ill with fever and dysentery.

PUCKER (3)

Jer 31:29 but their children's mouths **p** at the taste.'
31:30 sour grapes will be the ones whose mouths will **p**.
Eze 18: 2 but their children's mouths **p** at the taste'?

PUDENS (1)

2Ti 4:21 and so do **P**, Linus, Claudia, and all the brothers

PUFF (2) [PUFFED]

Ps 62: 9 them on the scales, / they are lighter than a **p** of air.
Jer 22:22 And now your allies have all disappeared with a **p**

PUFFED (2) [PUFF]

2Co 12: 7 But to keep me from getting **p** up, I was given a
2Ti 3: 4 their friends, be reckless, be **p** up with pride,

PUITE (1) [PUAH]

Nu 26:23 The **P** clan, named after its ancestor Puah.

PUL (1) [TIGLATH-PILESER]

1Ch 5:26 So the God of Israel caused King **P** of Assyria

PULL (24) [PULLED, PULLING, PULLS]

Nu 16:37 "Tell Eleazar son of Aaron the priest to **p** all the
Dt 25: 9 **p** his sandal from his foot, and spit in his face.
Jdg 6:25 **P** down your father's altar to Baal, and cut down
Ru 2:16 And **p** out some heads of barley from the bundles
2Sa 11:15 is fiercest. Then **p** back so that he will be killed."
1Ki 13: 4 in that position, and he couldn't **p** it back.
Ps 31: 4 **P** me from the trap my enemies set for me,
52: 5 and for all. / He will **p** you from your home
69:14 **P** me out of the mud; / don't let me sink any
69:14 who hate me, / and **p** me from these deep waters.
Isa 11: 8 in a nest of deadly snakes and **p** it out unharmed.
22:19 "I will **p** you down from your high position.
22:25 I will **p** out the stake that seemed so firm.
50: 6 and my cheeks to those who **p** out my beard.
62:10 Smooth out the road; **p** out the boulders; raise a
Jer 22:24 signet ring on my right hand, I would **p** you off.
38:10 and **p** Jeremiah out of the cistern before he dies."
51:44 and **p** from his mouth what he has taken.
Eze 17: 9 and prosper? No! I will **p** it out, roots and all!
17: 9 I will **p** it out easily enough—it won't take a strong
Am 9: 2 place of the dead, I will reach down and **p** them up.
Mt 12:11 wouldn't you get to work and **p** it out?
13:28 " 'Shall we **p** out the weeds?' they asked.
Lk 6:39 one will fall into a ditch and **p** the other down also.

PULLED (25) [PULL]

Ge 19:10 reached out and **p** Lot in and bolted the door.
37:23 when Joseph arrived, they **p** off his beautiful robe
37:28 his brothers **p** Joseph out of the pit and sold him
Dt 25:10 as 'the family of the man whose sandal was **p** off'!
Jdg 3:21 **p** out the dagger strapped to his right thigh,
16:14 But Samson woke up, **p** back the loom shuttle,
1Sa 17:51 he ran over and **p** Goliath's sword from its sheath.
2Sa 20:12 So he **p** him off the road into a field and threw a
1Ki 20:41 Then the prophet **p** the bandage from his eyes,
Ezr 6:11 in any way will have a beam **p** from their house.
9: 3 I tore my clothing, **p** hair from my head and beard,
Ne 13:25 on them. I beat some of them and **p** out their hair.
Job 20:25 The arrow is **p** from his body, and the arrowhead
SS 5: 5 my fingers with lovely myrrh, as I **p** back the bolt.
Jer 38:13 they **p** him out. So Jeremiah was returned to the
Da 7: 4 As I watched, its wings were **p** off, and it was left
Zec 6: 2 The first chariot was **p** by red horses, the second
Mt 26:51 One of the men with Jesus **p** out a sword
Mk 14:47 But someone **p** out a sword and slashed off an ear
Jn 21: 8 with the boat and **p** the loaded net to the shore,
Ac 10:16 Then the sheet was **p** up again to heaven.
10:26 But Peter **p** him up and said, "Stand up! I'm a
11:10 and all it contained was **p** back up to heaven.
27:13 So they **p** up anchor and sailed along close to
Jude 1:12 doubly dead, for they have been **p** out by the roots.

PULLEY (1)

Ecc 12: 6 at the spring and the **p** is broken at the well.

PULLING (3) [PULL]

Ne 4: 2 Look at those charred stones they are **p** out of the
Eze 26:10 through your broken gates, **p** chariots behind them.
Ac 23:10 at Paul from both sides, **p** him this way and that.

PULLS (2) [PULL]

Mt 9:16 the patch shrinks and **p** away from the old cloth,
Mk 2:21 new patch shrinks and **p** away from the old cloth,

PULSE [KJV] See VEGETABLES

PULVERIZE (1)

Isa 28:28 it under the wheels of a cart, but he doesn't **p** it.

PUNCHES (1)

1Co 9:26 every step. I am not like a boxer who misses his **p**.

PUNISH (140) [PUNISHED, PUNISHES, PUNISHING, PUNISHMENT, PUNISHMENTS]

Ge 15:14 But I will **p** the nation that enslaves them, and in
31:53 to **p** either one of us who harms the other."
50:19 be afraid of me. Am I God, to judge and **p** you?
Ex 19:24 to come up here. If they do, I will **p** them."
20: 5 but I **p** the children for the sins of their parents to
32:34 to account, I will certainly **p** them for their sins."
34: 7 but I **p** the children for the sins of their parents to
Lev 26:16 I will **p** you. You will suffer from sudden terrors,
26:18 I will **p** you for your sins seven times over.
26:28 I will **p** you seven times over for your sins.
Nu 12:11 Please don't **p** us for this sin we have so foolishly
Dt 5: 9 but I **p** the children for the sins of their parents to
7:10 But he does not hesitate to **p** and destroy those
22:18 The judges must then **p** the man.
Jos 22:20 Didn't God **p** all the people of Israel when Achan,
22:23 it for this purpose, may the LORD himself **p** us.
Jdg 10:15 **P** us as you see fit, only rescue us today from our
Ru 1:17 May the LORD **p** me severely if I allow anything
1Sa 3:17 And may God **p** you if you hide anything from
24:12 Perhaps the LORD will **p** you for what you are
24:15 judge which of us is right and **p** the guilty one.
2Sa 7:14 If he sins, I will use other nations to **p** him.
1Ki 2:44 King David. May the LORD **p** you for them.
8:32 **P** the guilty party and acquit the one who is
11:39 But I will **p** the descendants of David because of
17:18 Have you come here to **p** my sins by killing my
2Ki 19: 4 the living God and will **p** him for his words.
2Ch 6:23 **P** the guilty party, and acquit the one who is
22: 7 a fatal mistake, for God had decided to **p** Ahaziah.
Job 21: 9 are safe from every fear, and God does not **p** them.
21:19 you say, 'at least God will **p** their children!'
21:19 But I say that God should **p** the ones who sin,
Ps 10:12 Arise, O LORD! / **P** the wicked, O God! / Do not
10:14 grief they cause. / You take note of it and **p** them.
39:10 Please, don't **p** me anymore! / I am exhausted by
59: 5 the God of Israel, / rise up to **p** hostile nations.
89:32 then I will **p** their sin with the rod, / and their
94:10 He punishes the nations—won't he also **p** you?
110: 6 He will **p** the nations / and fill them with their
119:84 When will you **p** those who persecute me?
Pr 17:26 for being good or to **p** nobles for being honest!
19:25 If you **p** a mocker, the simpleminded will learn a
Ecc 8: 3 For the king will **p** those who disobey him.
Isa 2:12 In that day the LORD Almighty will **p** the proud,
10:12 he will turn against the king of Assyria and **p** him
13:11 will **p** the world for its evil and the wicked for their
24:21 In that day the LORD will **p** the fallen angels in
26:21 The LORD is coming from heaven to **p** the
27: 1 swift sword and **p** Leviathan, the swiftly moving
37: 4 the living God and will **p** him for his words.
54:15 it will not be because I sent them to **p** you.
59: 9 That is why God doesn't **p** those who injure us.
64:12 to help us? Will you continue to be silent and **p** us?
66:16 The LORD will **p** the world by fire and by his
Jer 2:19 Your own wickedness will **p** you. You will see
2:35 Now I will **p** you severely because you claim you
5: 9 Should I not **p** them for this?" asks the LORD.
5:29 Should I not **p** them for this?" asks the LORD.
6:12 For I will **p** the people of this land,"
9: 9 Should I not **p** them for this?" asks the LORD.
9:25 "when I will **p** all those who are circumcised in
11:22 "I will **p** them! Their young men will die in battle,
14:10 all your wickedness and will **p** you for your sins."
14:15 says the LORD, I will **p** these lying prophets,
15:15 **P** my persecutors! Don't let them kill me!
16:18 I will **p** them doubly for all their sins, because they
21:14 And I myself will **p** you for your sinfulness,
23:34 I will **p** that person along with his entire family.
25:12 I will **p** the king of Babylon and his people for
25:14 I will **p** them in proportion to the suffering they
25:29 I have begun to **p** Jerusalem, the city where my
27: 8 I will **p** any nation that refuses to be his slave,
29:32 I will **p** him and his family. None of his
30:15 I have had to **p** you because your sins are many
30:20 before me, and I will **p** anyone who hurts them.
31:20 "I had to **p** him, but I still love him. I long for him
36:31 I will **p** him and his family and his officials
44:13 I will **p** them in Egypt just as I punished them in
44:29 will happen to you and that I will **p** you here:
46:25 "I will **p** Amon, the god of Thebes, and all the
46:25 I will **p** its rulers and Pharaoh, too, and all who
49: 2 I will **p** you for this," says the LORD,
49: 8 when I bring disaster on Edom, I will **p** you, too!
50:18 "Now I will **p** the king of Babylon and his land,
51:44 And I will **p** Bel, the god of Babylon, and pull
51:47 For the time is surely coming when I will **p** this
La 1:22 **P** them, as you have punished me for all my sins.
Eze 5: 8 I will **p** you publicly while all the nations watch.
5: 9 I will **p** you more severely than I have punished
5:10 And I will **p** you by scattering the few who survive
9: 1 "Bring on the men appointed to **p** the city!
14: 4 will **p** the people of Israel who set up idols in their
14: 7 I, the LORD, will **p** all those, both Israelites
16:38 I will **p** you for your murder and adultery. I will
16:41 your homes and **p** you in front of many women.
17:19 I will **p** him for breaking my covenant
23:31 I will **p** you with the same terrors that destroyed
28:26 And when I **p** the neighboring nations that treated
30:19 And so I will greatly **p** Egypt, and they will know
35:11 I will **p** you for all your acts of anger, envy,
36:19 I scattered them to many lands to **p** them for the
38:22 I will **p** you and your hordes with disease

Hos 1: 4 for I am about to **p** King Jehu's dynasty to avenge
2:13 I will **p** her for all the times she deserted me,
4: 9 So now I will **p** both priests and people for all their
4:14 Why should I **p** them? For you men are doing the
7:12 from the sky. I will **p** them for all their evil ways.
8:13 people to account for their sins, and I will **p** them.
9: 9 will not forget. He will surely **p** them for their sins.
10:10 I will call out the armies of the nations to **p** you for
11: 9 I will not **p** you as much as my burning anger tells
12: 2 He is about to **p** Jacob for all his deceitful ways.
Joel 2:13 is filled with kindness and is eager not to **p** you.
Am 3: 2 That is why I must **p** you for all your sins."
3:14 "On the very day I **p** Israel for its sins, I will
7: 4 I saw him preparing to **p** his people with a great
Mic 7: 9 and **p** my enemies for all the evil they have done to
Hab 1:12 have decreed the rise of these Babylonians to **p**
Zep 1: 8 "I will **p** the leaders and princes of Judah and all
1: 9 I will **p** those who participate in pagan worship
1:12 to find and **p** those who sit contented in their sins,
3: 7 however much I **p** them, they continue their evil
Zec 8:14 ancestors angered me and I promised to **p** them,
10: 3 against your shepherds, and I will **p** these leaders.
14:18 the LORD will **p** them with the same plague that
Mal 2:17 LORD favors evildoers since he does not **p** them.
3:15 and those who dare God to **p** them go free of
Ac 4:21 because they didn't know how to **p** them without
7: 7 'But I will **p** the nation that enslaves them,'
Ro 2: 2 in his justice, will **p** anyone who does such things.
2:12 God will **p** the Gentiles when they sin,
2:12 And he will **p** the Jews when they sin, for they do
3: 5 Isn't it unfair, then, for God to **p** us?" (That is
3:25 and just when he did not **p** those who sinned in
13: 4 for that very purpose, to **p** those who do wrong.
2Co 7:11 such zeal, and such a readiness to **p** the wrongdoer.
10: 6 And we will **p** those who remained disobedient
2Th 1: 6 and in his justice he will **p** those who persecute
1Pe 2:14 For the king has sent them to **p** all who do wrong
Jude 1: 7 and are a warning of the eternal fire that will **p** all

PUNISHED (76) [PUNISH]

Ge 3:14 "Because you have done this, you will be **p**.
4:24 If anyone who kills Cain is to be **p** seven times,
4:24 anyone who takes revenge against me will be **p**
Ex 21:20 slave is beaten and dies, the owner must be **p**.
21:21 however, then the owner should not be **p**,
21:23 then the offender must be **p** according to the
Lev 24:15 will suffer the consequences of their guilt and be **p**.
Jdg 9:24 God **p** Abimelech and the men of Shechem for
9:56 God **p** Abimelech for the evil he had done against
9:57 God also **p** the men of Shechem for all their evil.
1Ki 8:35 and turn from their sins because you have **p** them,
2Ki 17:20 He **p** them by handing them over to their attackers
1Ch 21: 7 displeased with the census, and he **p** Israel for it.
2Ch 6:26 and turn from their sins because you have **p** them,
Ezr 7:26 and the law of the king will be **p** immediately by
9:13 "Now we are being **p** because of our wickedness
9:13 But we have actually been **p** far less than we
Ne 9:33 Every time you **p** us you were being just. We have
Job 27: 7 "May my enemy be **p** like the wicked,
31:11 For lust is a shameful sin, a crime that should be **p**.
31:28 If so, I should be **p** by the judges, for it would
Ps 34:21 and those who hate the righteous will be **p**.
69:26 To those you have **p**, they add insult to injury;
91: 8 your eyes; / you will see how the wicked are **p**.
99: 8 but you **p** them when they went wrong.
103:10 He has not **p** us for all our sins, / nor does he deal
118:18 The LORD has **p** me severely, / but he has not
Pr 10:13 with understanding, but fools will be **p** with a rod.
11:21 You can be sure that evil people will be **p**,
15:10 abandons the right path will be severely **p**;
16: 5 despises pride; be assured that the proud will be **p**.
17: 5 who rejoice at the misfortune of others will be **p**.
17:11 people seek rebellion, but they will be severely **p**.
19:29 Mockers will be **p**, and the backs of fools will be
21:11 A simpleton can learn only by seeing mockers **p**;
21:18 Sometimes the wicked are **p** to save the godly,
29:24 You will be **p** if you report the crime, but you will
Ecc 8: 5 Those who obey him will not be **p**. Those who are
8:11 When a crime is not **p**, people feel it is safe to do
Isa 27: 7 Has the LORD **p** Israel in the same way he has **p**
her enemies?
27: 8 but he has **p** Israel only a little. He has exiled her
40: 2 the LORD has **p** her in full for all her sins."
57:17 I was angry and **p** these greedy people. I withdrew
Jer 2:30 I have **p** your children, but it did them no good.
6: 6 This is the city to be **p**, for she is wicked through
8:12 They will be humbled when they are **p**,
44:13 I will punish them in Egypt just as I **p** them in
50:18 and his land, just as I **p** the king of Assyria.
La 1: 5 for the LORD has **p** Jerusalem for her many sins.
1:22 Punish them, as you have **p** me for all my sins.
3:39 complain when we are **p** for our sins?
Eze 5: 9 I will punish you more severely than I have **p**
14:10 to want my advice—will all be **p** for their sins.
18:20 The child will not be **p** for the parent's sins,
18:20 and the parent will not be **p** for the child's sins.
18:20 and wicked people will be **p** for their own
35: 5 when I had already **p** them for all their sins.
39:24 and **p** them in proportion to the vileness of their
Hos 10: 2 the people are fickle; they are guilty and must be **p**.
Na 1:12 O my people, I have already **p** you once, and I will
Zec 1:15 but the nations **p** them far beyond my intentions.
14:19 and the other nations will all be **p** if they don't go
Lk 12:47 The servant will be severely **p**, for though he knew
12:48 that they are doing wrong will be **p** only lightly.
Jn 3:20 fear their sins will be exposed and they will be **p**.
Ac 22: 5 from there to Jerusalem, in chains, to be **p**.
Ro 2: 1 When you say they are wicked and should be **p**,
13: 4 of course you should be afraid, for you will be **p**.
13: 5 to keep from being **p** and to keep a clear
2Co 2: 6 He was **p** enough when most of you were united in
2Th 1: 9 They will be **p** with everlasting destruction,
Heb 2: 2 and the people were **p** for every violation of the
1Pe 4: 6 so that although their bodies were **p** with death,
Rev 18: 4 not take part in her sins, or you will be **p** with her.
19: 2 He has **p** the great prostitute who corrupted the

PUNISHES (6) [PUNISH]

Nu 14:18 but he **p** the children for the sins of their parents to
Job 36:13 Even when he **p** them, they refuse to cry out to him
Ps 31:23 to him, / but he harshly **p** all who are arrogant.
94:10 He **p** the nations—won't he also punish you?
Mic 7: 9 I will be patient as the LORD **p** me, for I have
Heb 12: 6 and he **p** those he accepts as his children."

PUNISHING (9) [PUNISH]

Ge 44:16 God is **p** us for our sins. My lord, we have all
Lev 18:25 That is why I am **p** the people who live there,
Jdg 8:16 **p** them with thorns and briers from the wilderness.
Job 11: 6 God is doubtless **p** you far less than you deserve!
32: 2 that he had sinned and that God was right in **p** him.
Ps 11: 6 **p** them with burning sulfur and scorching winds.
Isa 5:23 They let the wicked go free while **p** the innocent.
Jer 6:15 They will be humbled beneath my **p** anger,"
2Pe 2: 9 even while **p** the wicked right up until the day of

PUNISHMENT (73) [PUNISH]

Ge 4:13 to the LORD, "My **p** is too great for me to bear!
4:15 for I will give seven times your **p** to anyone who
Lev 5: 1 they will be held responsible and be subject to **p**.
22: 9 otherwise they will be subject to **p** and die for
26:43 At last the people will receive the due **p** for their
Dt 19:19 the accuser will receive the **p** intended for the
1Sa 25:39 it myself. Nabal has received the **p** for his sin."
Job 8: 4 sinned against him, so their **p** was well deserved.
9:34 and I would no longer live in terror of his **p**.
19:29 you yourselves are in danger of **p** for your attitude.
37:13 either as a **p** or as a sign of his unfailing love.
Ps 10: 5 They do not see your **p** awaiting them. / They pour
17:14 May they have their **p** in full. / May their children
28: 4 Give them the **p** they so richly deserve!
39: 9 I won't say a word. / For my **p** is from you.
109:20 May those curses become the LORD's **p** for my
120: 3 will God do to you? / How will he increase your **p**?
149: 7 vengeance on the nations / and **p** on the peoples,
Pr 16: 4 for his own purposes, even the wicked for **p**.
20:30 Physical **p** cleanses away evil; such discipline
24:22 Who knows where the **p** from the LORD
Isa 1: 5 Why do you continue to invite **p**? Must you rebel
3:11 you deserve. Your well-earned **p** is on the way."
9:13 For after all this **p**, the people will still not repent
28:22 So scoff no more, or your **p** will be even greater.
47: 6 and began their **p** by letting them fall into your
53: 4 And we thought his troubles were a **p** from God
53: 8 dying for their sins—that he was suffering their **p**?
66:15 He will bring **p** with the fury of his anger
Jer 1:12 and I will surely carry out my threats of **p**."
4:18 This **p** is a bitter dose of your own medicine.
11:23 disaster upon them when their time of **p** comes."
22:18 this is the LORD's decree of **p** against King
23:12 disaster upon them when their time of **p** comes.
30:15 Why do you protest your **p**—this wound that has
42:10 For I am sorry for all the **p** I have had to bring
46:21 a day of great disaster for Egypt, a time of great **p**.
51: 6 Save yourselves! Don't get trapped in her **p**!
51:56 For the LORD is a God who gives just **p**, and he
La 1: 9 with no thought of the **p** that would follow.
4:22 O Jerusalem, your **p** will end; you will soon return
4:22 But Edom, your **p** is just beginning; soon your
5: 7 We have suffered the **p** they deserved!
Eze 4:17 in terror, and they will waste away under their **p**.
7: 8 Soon I will pour out my fury to complete your **p**
7:11 Their violence will fall back on them as **p** for their
7:27 and they will receive the **p** they so richly deserve.
16:58 This is your **p** for all your disgusting sins,
21:24 with sin. So now the time of your **p** has come!
23:45 They will sentence them to all the **p** they deserve.
39:21 Everyone will see the **p** I have inflicted on them
39:23 it was **p** for sin, for they acted in treachery against
Hos 5: 9 When your day of **p** comes, you will become a
6:11 "O Judah, a harvest of **p** is also waiting for you,
9: 7 The time of Israel's **p** has come; the day of
13:12 have been collected and stored away for **p**.
Am 8: 2 fruit represents my people of Israel—ripe for **p**! I
will not delay their **p** again.
Ob 1:16 and the surrounding nations will swallow the **p** I
Mic 7: 4 day is coming swiftly now. Your time of **p** is here.
Mt 25:46 And they will go away into eternal **p**,
Mk 12:40 Because of this, their **p** will be the greater."
Lk 17: 2 the **p** in store for harming one of these little ones.
20:47 Because of this, their **p** will be the greater."
Ac 13:11 And now the Lord has laid his hand of **p** upon you,
Ro 2: 5 So you are storing up terrible **p** for yourself
3:25 For God sent Jesus to take the **p** for our sins
4:15 But the law brings **p** on those who try to obey it.
5:10 we will certainly be delivered from eternal **p** by his
13: 2 land are refusing to obey God, and **p** will follow.
1Co 4:21 Should I come with **p** and scolding, or should I
2Co 11:15 In the end they will get every bit of **p** their wicked
Heb 10:29 Think how much more terrible the **p** will be for

PUNISHMENTS (5) [PUNISH]

Dt 21: 5 And they are to decide all lawsuits and **p**.
2Sa 24:12 Choose one of these **p**, and I will do it.' "
1Ch 21:10 Choose one of these **p**, and I will do it.' "
Eze 14:21 all four of these fearsome **p** fall upon Jerusalem—
Rev 16: 7 Lord God Almighty, your **p** are true and just."

PUNON (2)

Nu 33:42 Then they left Zalmonah and camped at **P**.
33:43 They left **P** and camped at Oboth.

PUNY (2)

Ps 147:10 how **p** in his sight is the strength of a man.
Isa 31: 3 Their horses are **p** flesh, not mighty spirits!

PURAH (2)

Jdg 7:10 go down to the camp with your servant **P**.
7:11 So Gideon took **P** and went down to the outposts

PURCHASE (10) [PURCHASED]

Ge 47:17 But at least they were able to **p** food for that year.
Lev 25:44 you may **p** male or female slaves from among the
25:45 You may also **p** the children of such resident
Ru 4: 5 your **p** of the land from Naomi also requires that
4: 7 transferring a right of **p** to remove his sandal
Ezr 7:17 are to be used specifically for the **p** of bulls,
Jer 32:10 I signed and sealed the deed of **p** before witnesses,
32:11 which contained the terms and conditions of the **p**,
1Co 1:30 and holy, and he gave himself to **p** our freedom.
1Ti 2: 6 He gave his life to **p** freedom for everyone. This is

PURCHASED (20) [PURCHASE]

Ge 17:12 and the foreign-born servants whom you have **p**.
25:10 This was the field Abraham had **p** from the
39: 1 he was **p** by Potiphar, a member of the personal
Ex 12:44 But any slave who has been **p** may eat it if he has
15:16 O LORD, / until the people whom you **p** pass by.
Lev 27:22 you dedicate to the LORD a field that you have **p**
27:24 released to the original owner from whom you **p** it.
1Ki 10:29 to Jerusalem could be **p** for 600 pieces of silver,
2Ch 1:17 to Jerusalem could be **p** for 600 pieces of silver,
34:11 and masons and **p** cut stone for the walls
Job 28:17 It cannot be **p** with jewels mounted in fine gold.
Am 2: 8 they present offerings of wine **p** with stolen
Mt 27:10 and **p** the potter's field, / as the Lord directed."
Mk 16: 1 went out and **p** burial spices to put on Jesus' body.
Ac 20:28 God's flock—his church, **p** with his blood—
1Co 7:23 God **p** you at a high price. Don't be enslaved by
Eph 1: 7 so rich in kindness that he **p** our freedom through
1:14 and that he has **p** us to be his own people.
Col 1:14 God has **p** our freedom with his blood and has
Rev 14: 4 They have been **p** from among the people on the

PURE (125) [PURE-BLOODED, PURELY, PUREST, PURIFICATION, PURIFIED, PURIFIES, PURIFY, PURIFYING, PURITY]

PURE GOLD (43) Ex 25:11,17,24,36,38,39; 28:14,22,36; 30:3; 36:34; 37:2,6,11,16,22,23,24,26; 39:15,25,30; Lev 24:4,6; 1Ki 6:20,21; 7:50; 10:18; 2Ki 25:15; 2Ch 3:4,5,6,8,9; 4:20,21,22; 9:17; Pr 8:10; Jer 52:19; Da 10:5; Rev 21:18,21

Ge 2:12 The gold of that land is exceptionally **p**;
Ex 25:11 Overlay it inside and outside with **p** gold, and put a
25:17 the place of atonement—out of **p** gold.
25:24 Overlay it with **p** gold and run a molding of gold
25:31 "Make a lampstand of **p**, hammered gold.
25:36 the stem, and they must be hammered from **p** gold.
25:38 and trays must also be made of **p** gold.
25:39 You will need seventy-five pounds of **p** gold for
27:20 "Tell the people of Israel to bring you **p** olive oil
28:14 and two cords made of **p** gold will be attached to
28:22 to the ephod, make braided cords of **p** gold.
28:36 "Next make a medallion of **p** gold.
30: 3 the top, sides, and horns of the altar with **p** gold,
30:23 12-1/2 pounds of **p** myrrh, 6-1/4 pounds each of
30:34 mollusk scent, galbanum, and **p** frankincense—
30:35 refine it to produce a **p** and holy incense.
36:34 used to hold the crossbars were made of **p** gold.
37: 2 It was overlaid with **p** gold inside and out, and it
37: 6 Then, from **p** gold, he made the Ark's cover—
37:11 It was overlaid with **p** gold, with a gold molding
37:16 Next, using **p** gold, he made the plates, dishes,
37:17 the lampstand, again using **p**, hammered gold.
37:22 the stem, and they were hammered from **p** gold.
37:23 the lamp snuffers, and the trays, all of **p** gold.
37:24 was made from seventy-five pounds of **p** gold.
37:26 and horns of the altar with **p** gold and ran a gold
39:15 to the ephod, they made braided cords of **p** gold.
39:25 Bells of **p** gold were placed between the
39:30 they made the sacred medallion of **p** gold to be
Lev 24: 2 to provide you with **p** olive oil for the lampstand,
24: 4 The lamps on the **p** gold lampstand must be tended
24: 6 Place the bread in the LORD's presence on the **p**
24: 7 Sprinkle some **p** frankincense near each row.
Nu 5:28 But if she has not defiled herself and is **p**, she will
31:23 through fire in order to be made ceremonially **p**.
2Sa 22:27 To the **p** you show yourself **p**, / but to the
1Ki 6:20 Solomon overlaid its walls and ceiling with **p** gold.
6:21 the rest of the Temple's interior with **p** gold,
7:50 basins, dishes, and firepans, all of **p** gold.
10:18 a huge ivory throne and overlaid it with **p** gold.
2Ki 25:15 and all the other utensils made of **p** gold or silver.
2Ch 3: 4 the foyer and the ceiling were overlaid with **p** gold.

3: 5 overlaid with **p** gold, and decorated with carvings
3: 6 and with **p** gold from the land of Parvaim.
3: 8 overlaid with about twenty-three tons of **p** gold.
3: 9 of the upper rooms were also overlaid with **p** gold.
4:20 and their lamps of **p** gold to burn in front of the
4:21 flower decorations, lamps, and tongs, all of **p** gold;
4:22 basins, dishes, and firepans, all of **p** gold;
9:17 a huge ivory throne and overlaid it with **p** gold.
Job 4:17 Can a person be **p** before the Creator?'
8: 6 if you are **p** and live with complete integrity,
11: 4 You claim, 'My teaching is **p**,' and 'I am clean in
15:14 Can a mortal be **p**? Can a human be just?
15:15 Even the heavens cannot be absolutely **p** in his
15:16 How much less **p** is a corrupt and sinful person
16:17 Yet I am innocent, and my prayer is **p**.
17: 9 and those with **p** hearts will become stronger
22:30 Then even sinners will be rescued by your **p**
25: 4 claim to be righteous? Who in all the earth is **p**?
33: 9 You said, 'I am **p**; I am innocent; I have not
Ps 12: 6 The LORD's promises are **p**, / like silver refined
18:26 To the **p** you show yourself **p**, / but to the
19: 9 Reverence for the LORD is **p**, / lasting forever.
24: 4 Only those whose hands and hearts are **p**, / who do
32:11 Shout for joy, all you whose hearts are **p**!
73: 1 God is good to Israel, / to those whose hearts are **p**.
73:13 Was it for nothing that I kept my heart **p** / and kept
119: 9 How can a young person stay **p**? / By obeying your
Pr 8:10 rather than silver, and knowledge over **p** gold.
15:26 thoughts of the wicked, but he delights in **p** words.
16: 2 People may be **p** in their own eyes, but the LORD
20: 9 cleansed my heart; I am **p** and free from sin"?
20:11 way they act, whether their conduct is **p** and right.
22:11 Anyone who loves a **p** heart and gracious speech is
30:12 They feel **p**, but they are filthy and unwashed.
Isa 1:22 Once like **p** silver, you have become like worthless
1:22 Once so **p**, you are now like watered-down wine.
Jer 13:27 Jerusalem! How long will it be before you are **p**?"
52:19 and all the other utensils made of **p** gold or silver.
Eze 47: 8 waters of the Dead Sea and make them fresh and **p**.
Da 10: 5 with a belt of **p** gold around his waist.
11:35 and cleansed and made **p** until the time of the end,
Zec 13: 9 bring that group through the fire and make them **p**,
Mal 1:11 and **p** offerings in honor of my name.
Mt 5: 8 God blesses those whose hearts are **p**, / for they
6:22 your body. A **p** eye lets sunshine into your soul.
Lk 11:34 A **p** eye lets sunshine into your soul. But an evil
Jn 17:17 Make them **p** and holy by teaching them your
Ro 15:16 so that you might be **p** and pleasing to him by the
1Co 1:30 He made us **p** and holy, and he gave himself to
5: 7 person from among you so that you can stay **p**.
2Co 11: 2 For I promised you as a **p** bride to one husband,
11: 3 that somehow you will be led away from your **p**
Php 1:10 so that you may live **p** and blameless lives until
1:15 But others preach about Christ with **p** motives.
1:17 Those others do not have **p** motives as they preach
1:18 But whether or not their motives are **p**, the fact
4: 8 Think about things that are **p** and lovely
1Th 2:10 that we were **p** and honest and faultless toward all
1Ti 1: 5 be filled with love that comes from a **p** heart,
5:22 participate in the sins of others. Keep yourself **p**.
2Ti 2:21 If you keep yourself **p**, you will be a utensil God
2:22 of those who call on the Lord with **p** hearts.
Tit 1:15 Everything is **p** to those whose hearts are **p**.
1:15 But nothing is **p** to those who are corrupt
2: 5 to live wisely and be **p**, to take care of their homes,
Heb 10:22 and our bodies have been washed with **p** water.
Jas 1:27 **P** and lasting religion in the sight of God our
3:17 wisdom that comes from heaven is first of all **p**.
1Pe 1: 4 **p** and undefiled, beyond the reach of change
1: 7 to test your faith, to show that it is strong and **p**.
2: 2 You must crave **p** spiritual milk so that you can
3: 2 by watching your **p**, godly behavior.
2Pe 3:14 make every effort to live a **p** and blameless life.
1Jn 3: 3 And all who believe this will keep themselves **p**,
just as Christ is **p**.
Rev 14: 4 For they are spiritually undefiled, **p** as virgins,
19:14 The armies of heaven, dressed in **p** white linen,
21:18 of jasper, and the city was **p** gold, as clear as glass.
21:21 And the main street was **p** gold, as clear as glass.
22: 1 And the angel showed me a **p** river with the water

PURE-BLOODED (1) [BLOOD, PURE]

Php 3: 5 having been born into a **p** Jewish family that is a

PURELY (1) [PURE]

2Co 10: 2 those who think we act from **p** human motives.

PUREST (3) [PURE]

Job 28:19 for it. Its value is greater than the **p** gold.
Pr 8:19 My gifts are better than the **p** gold, my wages
Jer 2:21 When I planted you, I chose a vine of the **p** stock

PURGE (6) [PURGED]

Dt 17: 7 In this way, you will **p** all evil from among you.
19:13 **P** the guilt of murder from Israel so all may go
Jdg 20:13 so we can execute them and **p** Israel of this evil."
Isa 27: 9 The LORD did this to **p** away Israel's sin.
Eze 20:38 I will **p** you of all those who rebel and sin against
22:15 among the nations and **p** you of your wickedness.

PURGED (2) [PURGE]

Dt 17:12 be put to death. Such evil must be **p** from Israel.
Ne 13:30 So I **p** out everything foreign and assigned tasks to

PURGETH [KJV] See PRUNES

PURIFICATION (26) [PURE]

Lev 12: 4 of her **p** from the blood of childbirth is completed.
12: 4 During this time of **p**, she must not touch anything
12: 4 not go to the sanctuary until her time of **p** is over.
12: 6 "When the time of **p** is completed for either a son
12: 6 and a young pigeon or turtledove for a **p** offering.
12: 8 burnt offering and the other for the **p** offering.
14: 2 by those seeking **p** from a contagious skin disease.
14: 4 he will perform a **p** ceremony, using two wild
Nu 8: 7 Do this by sprinkling them with the water of **p**.
19: 9 of Israel to use in the water for the **p** ceremony.
19:12 on the third and seventh days with the water of **p**;
19:13 Since the water of **p** was not sprinkled on them,
19:17 put some of the ashes from the burnt **p** offering in
19:20 Since the water of **p** has not been sprinkled on
19:21 Those who sprinkle the water of **p** must afterward
19:21 and anyone who touches the water of **p** will remain
31:23 then be further purified with the water of **p**.
1Sa 16: 5 Then Samuel performed the **p** rite for Jesse and his
21: 7 was there that day for ceremonial **p**.
2Sa 11: 4 (She had just completed the **p** rites after having her
1Ch 23:28 side rooms, helped perform the ceremonies of **p**,
Ne 12:45 the service of their God and the service of **p**,
Lk 2:22 Then it was time for the **p** offering, as required by
Ac 21:24 to the Temple and join them in the **p** ceremony,
21:26 and the next day he went through the **p** ritual with
24:18 me in the Temple as I was completing a **p** ritual.

PURIFIED (40) [PURE]

Ex 19:14 He **p** them for worship and had them wash their
Lev 12: 5 then wait another sixty-six days to be **p** from the
14: 7 bird's blood seven times over the person being **p**,
14: 8 "The people being **p** must complete the cleansing
14:52 After he has **p** the house in this way,
22: 6 offerings until they have **p** their bodies with water.
Nu 8:15 because you have **p** them and presented them as a
8:21 The Levites **p** themselves and washed their
19: 9 and place them in a **p** place outside the camp.
19:12 with the water of purification; then they will be **p**.
31:23 then be further **p** with the water of purification.
31:23 But everything that burns must be **p** by the water
31:24 seventh day you must wash your clothes and be **p**.
1Ch 15:14 and the Levites **p** themselves in order to bring the
2Ch 5:11 All the priests who were present had **p** themselves,
29:15 their fellow Levites, and they **p** themselves.
29:17 Then they **p** the Temple of the LORD itself,
29:18 "We have **p** the Temple of the LORD, the altar
29:19 of the altar of the LORD, **p** and ready for use."
29:34 was finished and until more priests had been **p**.
30: 3 but not enough priests could be **p** by that time,
30:15 so they **p** themselves and brought burnt offerings
30:17 Since many of the people there had not **p**
30:18 Issachar, and Zebulun had not **p** themselves.
30:24 Meanwhile, many more priests **p** themselves.
34: 5 their own altars, and so he **p** Judah and Jerusalem.
34: 8 his reign, after he had **p** the land and the Temple,
Ezr 6:20 The priests and Levites had **p** themselves and were
Ne 13: 9 Then I demanded that the rooms be **p**, and I
Ps 12: 6 silver refined in a furnace, / **p** seven times over.
66:10 you have **p** us like silver melted in a crucible.
Eze 47:11 But the marshes and swamps will not be **p**;
Da 12:10 Many will be **p**, cleansed, and refined by these
Zec 13: 9 just as gold and silver are refined and **p** by fire.
Mk 9:49 "For everyone will be **p** with fire.
Heb 9:22 nearly everything was **p** by sprinkling with blood.
9:23 in heaven—had to be **p** by the blood of animals.
9:23 But the real things in heaven had to be **p** with far
10: 2 for the worshipers would have been **p** once for all
Rev 3:18 to buy gold from me—gold that has been **p** by fire.

PURIFIES (2) [PURE]

Pr 20:30 cleanses away evil; such discipline **p** the heart.
1Pe 1: 7 It is being tested as fire tests and **p** gold—and your

PURIFY (34) [PURE]

Ex 19:10 **P** them today and tomorrow, and have them wash
19:22 come near to the LORD must **p** themselves,
29:36 **P** the altar by making atonement for it; make it
30:10 "Once a year Aaron must **p** the altar by placing on
Lev 8:15 finger he put it on the four horns of the altar to **p** it.
14:49 To **p** the house the priest will need two birds,
Nu 8:21 the rite of atonement over them to **p** them.
11:18 "And tell the people to **p** themselves,
19:12 They must **p** themselves on the third and seventh
19:13 and do not **p** themselves in the proper way defile
19:20 and do not **p** themselves will be cut off from the
31:19 You must **p** yourselves and your captives on the
31:20 **p** all your clothing and everything made of leather,
Jos 3: 5 Then Joshua told the people, "**P** yourselves,
7:13 Command the people to **p** themselves in
1Sa 16: 5 **P** yourselves and come with me to the sacrifice."
1Ch 15:12 You must **p** yourselves and all your fellow Levites,
2Ch 29: 5 **P** yourselves, and **p** the Temple of the LORD,
29:15 Then they began to **p** the Temple of the LORD,
34: 3 twelfth year, he began to **p** Judah and Jerusalem,
35: 6 Slaughter the Passover lambs, **p** yourselves,
Ne 13:22 Then I commanded the Levites to **p** themselves
Job 1: 5 they lasted several days—Job would **p** his children.
Ps 51: 2 Wash me clean from my guilt. / **P** me from my sin.
51: 7 **P** me from my sins, and I will be clean; / wash me,
Isa 52:11 **P** yourselves, you who carry home the vessels of
66:17 "Those who '**p**' themselves in a sacred garden,
Jer 6:29 But it will never **p** and cleanse them because there
Eze 45:18 sacrifice a young bull with no physical defects to **p**
Zep 3: 9 "On that day I will **p** the lips of all people, so that
Mal 3: 3 He will **p** the Levites, refining them like gold
Heb 9:14 will **p** our hearts from deeds that lead to death
Jas 4: 8 you sinners; **p** your hearts, you hypocrites.

PURIFYING (2) [PURE]

2Ch 29:34 conscientious about **p** themselves than the priests.
31:18 For they had all been faithful in **p** themselves.

PURIM (6)

Est 3: 7 lots were cast (the lots were called ***p***)
9:24 by casting lots (the lots were called ***p***).
9:26 (That is why this celebration is called **P**, because it
9:29 Mordecai's letter to establish the Festival of **P**.
9:31 These letters established the Festival of **P**—
9:32 command of Esther confirmed the practices of **P**,

PURITY (11) [PURE]

Job 14: 4 Who can create **p** in one born impure? No one!
Ps 86:11 Grant me **p** of heart, / that I may honor you.
Pr 17: 3 Fire tests the **p** of silver and gold, but the LORD
27:21 Fire tests the **p** of silver and gold, but a person is
Jer 6:29 because there is no **p** in them to refine.
1Co 5: 8 but by eating the new bread of **p** and truth.
2Co 6: 6 We have proved ourselves by our **p**,
7: 1 And let us work toward complete **p** because we
1Ti 4:12 way you live, in your love, your faith, and your **p**.
5: 2 and treat the younger women with all **p** as your
6:14 that you obey his commands with all **p**. Then no

PURLOINING [KJV] See STEAL

PURPLE (47)

Ex 25: 4 blue, **p**, and scarlet yarn; fine linen; goat hair for
26: 1 are to be decorated with blue, **p**, and scarlet yarn,
26:31 into the cloth using blue, **p**, and scarlet yarn.
26:36 designs into it, using blue, **p**, and scarlet yarn.
27:16 beautiful embroidery in blue, **p**, and scarlet yarn.
28: 5 and embroidered with gold thread and blue, **p**,
28: 6 embroidered with gold thread and blue, **p**,
28: 8 cloth embroidered with gold thread and blue, **p**,
28:15 cloth embroidered with gold thread and blue, **p**,
28:33 pomegranates out of blue, **p**, and scarlet yarn,
35: 6 blue, **p**, and scarlet yarn; fine linen; goat hair for
35:23 Others brought blue, **p**, and scarlet yarn, fine linen,
35:25 **p**, and scarlet yarn, and fine linen cloth, and they
35:35 designers, weavers, and embroiderers in blue, **p**,
36: 8 One of the craftsmen then embroidered blue, **p**,
36:35 embroidered into it with blue, **p**, and scarlet yarn.
36:37 and embroidered with blue, **p**, and scarlet yarn.
38:18 and embroidered with blue, **p**, and scarlet yarn.
38:23 at engraving, designing, and embroidering blue, **p**,
39: 1 beautiful garments of blue, **p**, and scarlet cloth—
39: 2 and embroidered with gold thread and blue, **p**,
39: 3 it into the linen with the blue, **p**, and scarlet yarn.
39: 5 fine linen cloth; blue, **p**, and scarlet yarn; and gold
39: 8 and embroidered with gold thread and blue, **p**,
39:24 were finely crafted of blue, **p**, and scarlet yarn.
39:29 and embroidered with blue, **p**, and scarlet yarn,
Nu 4:13 and the altar must then be covered with a **p** cloth.
2Ch 2: 7 someone who is expert at dyeing **p**, scarlet,
2:14 He is an expert in dyeing **p**, blue, and scarlet cloth
3:14 hung a curtain made of fine linen and blue, **p**,
Est 1: 6 fastened by **p** ribbons to silver rings embedded in
8:15 and he wore an outer cloak of fine linen and **p**.
SS 3:10 is gold, and its seat is upholstered in **p** cloth.
Jer 10: 9 Then they dress these gods in royal **p** robes made
Eze 27: 7 and **p** awnings made bright with dyes from the
27:16 **p** dyes, embroidery, fine linen, and jewelry of coral
Da 5: 7 and tell me what it means will be dressed in **p**
5:16 you will be clothed in **p** robes of royal honor,
5:29 Daniel was dressed in **p** robes,
Mk 15:17 They dressed him in a **p** robe and made a crown of
15:20 they took off the **p** robe and put his own clothes on
Jn 19: 2 it on his head, and they put a royal **p** robe on him.
19: 5 out wearing the crown of thorns and the **p** robe.
Ac 16:14 from Thyatira, a merchant of expensive **p** cloth.
Rev 17: 4 The woman wore **p** and scarlet clothing
18:12 silver, jewels, pearls, fine linen, **p** dye, silk,
18:16 like a woman clothed in finest **p** and scarlet linens,

PURPOSE (52) [PURPOSES]

Ge 8:20 and birds that had been approved for that **p**.
24:12 Help me to accomplish the **p** of my journey.
Lev 5: 4 vow of any kind, whether its **p** is for good or bad,
7:24 be eaten, though it may be used for any other **p**.
Dt 14:23 The **p** of tithing is to teach you always to fear the
Jos 22:23 If we have built it for this **p**, may the LORD
22:29 in front of the Tabernacle may be used for that **p**."
Ru 2:16 from the bundles and drop them on **p** for her.
1Ch 12:31 18,000 men were sent for the express **p** of helping
12:38 the single **p** of making David the king of Israel.
23:31 and evening on the altar set aside for that **p**,
Ps 57: 2 Most High, / to God who will fulfill his **p** for me.
Pr 1: 2 The **p** of these proverbs is to teach people wisdom
1: 4 They will give knowledge and **p** to young people.
19:21 make many plans, but the LORD's **p** will prevail.
Ecc 3:14 God's **p** in this is that people should fear him.
Isa 45:13 I will raise up Cyrus to fulfill my righteous **p**,
49: 4 spent my strength for nothing and to no **p** at all.
Eze 48: 8 of Judah is the land set aside for a special **p**.
Da 4:17 The **p** of this decree is that the whole world may

Mal 2: 5 “The **p** of my covenant with the Levites was to
Mt 5:18 of God’s law will remain until its **p** is achieved.
Lk 13:32 and the third day I will accomplish my **p**.
Jn 6:27 For God the Father has sent me for that very **p**.”
10:10 The thief’s **p** is to steal and kill and destroy. My **p** is to give life in all its fullness.
18:37 you are right,” Jesus said. “I was born for that **p**.
Ac 17:27 “His **p** in all of this was that the nations should
Ro 3: 5 “But,” some say, “our sins serve a good **p**,
3:19 for its **p** is to keep people from having excuses
8:28 and are called according to his **p** for them.
9:17 “I have appointed you for the very **p** of displaying
10: 4 For Christ has accomplished the whole **p** of the
11:11 His **p** was to make his salvation available to the
13: 4 authorities are established by God for that very **p**,
14: 9 Christ died and rose again for this very **p**, so that
1Co 1:10 you to be of one mind, united in thought and **p**.
3: 8 one who waters work as a team with the same **p**.
9:26 So I run straight to the goal with **p** in every step.
2Co 7:12 My **p** was not to write about who did the wrong
Eph 1:12 God’s **p** was that we who were the first to trust in
2:15 His **p** was to make peace between Jews
3:10 God’s **p** was to show his wisdom in all its rich
6:22 I am sending him to you for just this **p**. He will let
Php 2: 2 and working together with one heart and **p**.
1Th 2: 4 Our **p** is to please God, not people. He is the one
1Ti 1: 5 The **p** of my instruction is that all the Christians
2Ti 2:21 you will be a utensil God can use for his **p**.
3:10 Timothy, and how I live, and what my **p** in life is.
1Pe 1:20 God chose him for this **p** long before the world
5:12 My **p** in writing is to encourage you and assure
Jude 1:18 **p** in life is to enjoy themselves in every evil way

PURPOSES (10) [PURPOSE]

Job 23:13 and who can turn him from his **p**?
Pr 16: 4 The LORD has made everything for his own **p**,
Isa 10:12 king of Assyria to accomplish his **p** in Jerusalem,
14:24 It will come about according to my **p**.
44: 8 Have I not proclaimed from ages past what my **p**
Jn 2: 6 they were used for Jewish ceremonial **p** and held
Ro 7:13 uses God’s good commandment for its own evil **p**.
1Th 2: 3 preaching with any deceit or impure **p** or trickery.
Heb 7:11 priesthood of Levi could have achieved God’s **p**—
Rev 17:17 into their minds, a plan that will carry out his **p**.

PURSES (2)

Isa 3:22 party clothes, gowns, capes, and **p**;
Lk 12:33 And the **p** of heaven have no holes in them.

PURSUE (11) [PURSUED, PURSUERS, PURSUES, PURSUING, PURSUIT, PURSUITS]

Dt 28:22 These devastations will **p** you until you die.
28:45 all these curses will **p** and overtake you until you
Ps 4: 2 How long will you **p** lies? / *Interlude*
23: 6 Surely your goodness and unfailing love will **p** me
Pr 15: 9 of the wicked, but he loves those who **p** godliness.
Isa 58:13 Don’t **p** your own interests on that day, but enjoy
Jer 29:18 Yes, I will **p** them with war, famine, and disease,
50:21 **P**, kill, and completely destroy them, as I have
La 5: 5 Those who **p** us are at our heels; we are exhausted
1Ti 6:11 **P** a godly life, along with faith, love, perseverance,
2Ti 2:22 **P** faith and love and peace, and enjoy the

PURSUED (3) [PURSUE]

2Ch 13:19 Abijah and his army **p** Jeroboam’s troops
14:13 Asa and his army **p** them as far as Gerar, and
Rev 12:13 he **p** the woman who had given birth to the child.

PURSUERS (1) [PURSUE]

Jos 8:20 direction of the wilderness now turned on their **p**.

PURSUES (2) [PURSUE]

Pr 21:21 Whoever **p** godliness and unfailing love will find
Na 1: 8 He **p** his foes into the darkness of night.

PURSUING (3) [PURSUE]

Lev 26:36 and you will fall even when no one is **p** you.
Ps 35: 6 with the angel of the LORD **p** them.
La 1: 6 for pasture, too weak to run from the **p** enemy.

PURSUIT (3) [PURSUE]

Ge 31:23 a group of his relatives and set out in hot **p**.
1Sa 30:10 so David continued the **p** with his four hundred
2Sa 2:19 He was relentless and single-minded in his **p**.

PURSUITS (1) [PURSUE]

Ps 2:12 and you will be destroyed in the midst of your **p**—

PUS (1)

Job 7: 5 and scabs. My flesh breaks open, full of **p**.

PUSH (13) [PUSHED, PUSHES, PUSHING]

Dt 15:17 an awl and **p** it through his earlobe into the door.
2Ki 4:27 Gehazi began to **p** her away, but the man of God
Job 12: 5 They give a **p** to people who are stumbling.
Ps 36:11 trample me; / don’t let the wicked **p** me around.
44: 5 Only by your power can we **p** back our enemies;
Pr 25: 6 with the king or **p** for a place among the great.
Isa 25:11 God will **p** down Moab’s people as a swimmer
Eze 34:21 For you fat sheep **p** and butt and crowd my sick
Am 6: 3 You **p** away every thought of coming disaster,
Lk 4:29 was built. They intended to **p** him over the cliff,
5: 3 asked Simon, its owner, to **p** it out into the water.
5:18 They tried to **p** through the crowd to Jesus,
Ro 1:18 wicked people who **p** the truth away from

PUSHED (6) [PUSH]

Nu 14:44 But the people **p** ahead toward the hill country of
Jdg 16:29 the temple and **p** against them with all his might.
19:25 Levite took his concubine and **p** her out the door.
Zec 5: 8 and he **p** her back into the basket and closed the
Mk 2:12 and **p** his way through the stunned onlookers.
Ac 7:27 “But the man in the wrong **p** Moses aside and told

PUSHES (4) [PUSH]

Nu 35:20 So if in premeditated hostility someone **p** another
35:22 “ ‘But suppose someone **p** another person without
Isa 25:11 people as a swimmer **p** down water with his hands.
Mk 4:28 First a leaf blade **p** through, then the heads of

PUSHING (1) [PUSH]

Ac 17:18 Others said, “He’s **p** some foreign religion.”

PUT (558) [PUTS, PUTTING]

Ge 4:15 Then the LORD **p** a mark on Cain to warn
6: 3 “My Spirit will not **p** up with humans for such a
6:16 Then **p** three decks inside the boat—bottom, middle, and upper—and **p** a door in the side.
10: 6 of Ham were Cush, Mizraim, **P**, and Canaan.
24:23 “Would your father have any room to **p** us up for
27:20 “Because the LORD your God **p** it in my path!”
31:17 So Jacob **p** his wives and children on camels.
35: 2 wash yourselves, and **p** on clean clothing.
37:34 Then Jacob tore his clothes and **p** on sackcloth.
38:19 her veil, and **p** on her widow’s clothing as usual.
39: 4 Potiphar soon **p** Joseph in charge of his entire
39: 5 From the day Joseph was **p** in charge, the LORD
39:22 the jailer **p** Joseph in charge of all the other
40: 3 and he **p** them in the prison where Joseph was,
41:33 and **p** him in charge of a nationwide program.
41:41 “I hereby **p** you in charge of the entire land of
41:43 So Joseph was **p** in charge of all Egypt.
42:17 So he **p** them all in prison for three days.
43:23 the God of your ancestors, must have **p** it there.
44: 1 and **p** each man’s money back into his sack.
44: 2 Then **p** my personal silver cup at the top of the
47: 6 **p** them in charge of my livestock, too.”
48:18 over here is older. **P** your right hand on his head.”
48:20 In this way, Jacob **p** Ephraim ahead of Manasseh.
Ex 1:10 We must find a way to **p** an end to this. If we don’t
1:11 their slaves and **p** brutal slave drivers over them,
2: 3 She **p** the baby in the basket and laid it among the
4: 6 said to Moses, “**P** your hand inside your robe.”
4: 7 “Now **p** your hand back into your robe again,”
4:20 Moses took his wife and sons, **p** them on a donkey,
7:23 to his palace and **p** the whole thing out of his mind.
14:31 and **p** their faith in him and his servant Moses.
16:33 “Get a container and **p** two quarts of manna into it.
18:25 They were **p** in charge of groups of one thousand,
21:12 hard enough to cause death must be **p** to death.
21:14 be dragged even from my altar and **p** to death.
21:15 who strikes father or mother must be **p** to death.
21:17 who curses father or mother must be **p** to death.
23: 7 Never **p** an innocent or honest person to death.
25:11 pure gold, and **p** a molding of gold all around it.
25:21 Then **p** the atonement cover on top of the Ark.
25:25 **P** a rim about three inches wide around the top edge, and **p** a gold molding all around the rim.
25:26 and **p** the rings at the four corners by the four legs,
26: 4 **P** loops of blue yarn along the edge of the last
26:10 **P** fifty loops along the edge of the last sheet in
26:14 and over them **p** a layer of fine goatskin leather.
26:33 is in place, **p** the Ark of the Covenant behind it.
26:34 “Then **p** the Ark’s cover—the place of
27: 7 **p** the poles into the rings at two sides of the altar.
29: 5 Then **p** Aaron’s tunic on him, along with the
29:20 Also **p** it on their right thumbs and the big toes of
29:24 **P** all these in the hands of Aaron and his sons to be
30:18 **P** it between the Tabernacle and the altar, and fill it
30:36 and **p** some of it in front of the Ark of the
31:15 anyone who works on the Sabbath must be **p** to
33:22 I will **p** you in the cleft of the rock and cover you
34:33 speaking with them, he **p** a veil over his face.
34:35 Afterward he would **p** the veil on again until he
37: 5 He **p** the poles into the rings at the sides of the Ark
39:17 The two gold cords were **p** through the gold rings
40:18 Moses **p** it together by setting its frames into their
40:19 the Tabernacle framework and **p** on the roof layers,
Lev 1: 8 Aaron’s sons will then **p** the pieces of the animal,
2:15 **p** olive oil on it and sprinkle it with incense.
4: 7 The priest will **p** some of the blood on the horns of
4:18 then **p** some of the blood on the horns of the
4:25 **p** it on the horns of the altar of burnt offerings,
4:30 **p** the blood on the horns of the altar of burnt
4:34 **p** it on the horns of the altar of burnt offerings,
5:11 not mix it with olive oil or **p** any incense on it.
6:10 of the burnt offering and **p** them beside the altar.
8: 8 and **p** the Urim and the Thummim inside it.
8:15 and with his finger he **p** it on the four horns of the
8:23 its blood and **p** it on the lobe of Aaron’s right ear,
8:24 and **p** some of the blood on the lobe of their right
9: 9 his finger into it and **p** it on the horns of the altar.
10: 1 and Abihu **p** coals of fire in their incense burners
11:32 It must be **p** into water, and it will remain defiled
13: 4 the priest will **p** the infected person in quarantine
13: 5 then the priest will **p** the person in quarantine for
13:21 then the priest is to **p** the person in quarantine for
13:26 then the priest is to **p** the infected person in
13:31 then he must **p** the person in quarantine for seven
13:33 Then the priest must **p** the person in quarantine for
13:50 the priest will **p** it away for seven days.
14:14 and **p** it on the tip of the healed person’s right ear,
14:17 then **p** some of the oil remaining in his left hand on
14:25 and **p** some of its blood on the tip of the person’s
14:28 then **p** some of the olive oil from his hand on the
16: 4 must wash his entire body and **p** on his linen tunic
16: 4 his waist and **p** the linen turban on his head.
16:13 he will **p** the incense on the burning coals so that a
16:24 **p** on his garments, and go out to sacrifice his own
16:32 He will **p** on the holy linen garments
19: 4 Do not **p** your trust in idols or make gods of metal
19:20 freed at the time, the couple will not be **p** to death.
20: 9 curse their father or mother must be **p** to death.
20:10 both the man and the woman must be **p** to death.
20:12 with his daughter-in-law, both must be **p** to death.
20:15 he must be **p** to death, and the animal must be
20:16 with it, she and the animal must both be **p** to death.
20:27 or psychics must be **p** to death by stoning.
24:12 They **p** the man in custody until the LORD’s will
24:17 who takes another person’s life must be **p** to death.
24:21 but whoever kills another person must be **p** to
27:29 be redeemed. Such a person must be **p** to death.
Nu 1:50 You must **p** the Levites in charge of the Tabernacle
4: 6 they must **p** the carrying poles of the Ark in place.
4:14 Finally, the carrying poles must be **p** in place.
5:19 The priest will **p** the woman under oath and say to
5:21 at this point the priest must **p** the woman under this
6:18 and **p** it on the fire beneath the peace-offering
6:19 and **p** them all into the Nazirite’s hands.
11:17 is upon you, and I will **p** the Spirit upon them also.
11:25 was upon Moses and **p** it upon the seventy leaders.
11:29 and that the LORD would **p** his Spirit upon them
15:35 said to Moses, “The man must be **p** to death!
17: 4 **P** these staffs in the Tabernacle in front of the Ark
17: 5 Then I will finally **p** an end to this murmuring
17: 7 Moses **p** the staffs in the LORD’s presence in the
17:10 This should **p** an end to their complaints against
18: 7 comes too near the sanctuary will be **p** to death.”
18: 8 “I have **p** the priests in charge of all the holy gifts
19:17 **p** some of the ashes from the burnt purification
20:26 Aaron’s priestly garments and **p** them on Eleazar,
20:28 garments from Aaron and **p** them on Eleazar,
35:30 No one may be **p** to death on the testimony of only
35:31 to execution; murderers must always be **p** to death.
Dt 7:24 He will **p** their kings in your power, and you will
13: 5 or dreamers who try to lead you astray must be **p**
13: 9 You must **p** them to death! You must be the one to
13:16 **P** the entire town to the torch as a burnt offering to
17: 6 But never **p** a person to death on the testimony of
17:12 the LORD your God must be **p** to death.
22:12 “You must **p** tassels on the four corners of your
24:16 “Parents must not be **p** to death for the sins of
26: 2 **p** some of the first produce from each harvest into
32:30 of them, / and two people **p** ten thousand to flight,
33: 8 the Levites. / You **p** them to the test at Massah
Jos 1:18 and does not obey your every command will be **p**
9: 5 They **p** on ragged clothes and worn-out,
10:24 “Come and **p** your feet on the kings’ necks.”
23:10 Each one of you will **p** to flight a thousand of the
24: 7 I **p** darkness between you and the Egyptians.
24:14 **P** away forever the idols your ancestors worshiped
Jdg 6:31 Whoever pleads his case will be **p** to death by
6:37 I will **p** some wool on the threshing floor tonight.
7: 5 In one group **p** all those who cup water in their
7: 5 In the other group **p** all those who kneel down
8:27 a sacred ephod from the gold and **p** it in Ophrah,
9:48 from a tree, and he **p** them on his shoulder.
10:16 Then the Israelites **p** aside their foreign gods
16: 3 He **p** them on his shoulders and carried them all
16:29 Then Samson **p** his hands on the center pillars of
19:28 So he **p** her body on his donkey and took her
Ru 3: 3 take a bath and **p** on perfume and dress in your
3:15 into the cloak and helped her **p** it on her back.
1Sa 2:25 for the LORD was already planning to **p** them to
2:31 I will **p** an end to your family, so it will no longer
4:12 and **p** dust on his head to show his grief.
6: 8 **P** the Ark of the LORD on the cart, and beside it
14:45 rescued Jonathan, and he was not **p** to death.
17:39 David **p** it on, strapped the sword over it, and took
17:40 from a stream and **p** them in his shepherd’s bag.
19:13 Then she took an idol and **p** it in his bed, covered it
19:13 and **p** a cushion of goat’s hair at its head.
20:32 “Why should he be **p** to death?”
24: 4 ‘I will certainly **p** Saul into your power, to do with
24:18 for when the LORD **p** me in a place where you
26:12 because the LORD had **p** Saul’s men into a deep
2Sa 1: 2 and **p** dirt on his head to show that he was in
1: 9 ‘Come over here and **p** me out of my misery,
2:14 “Let’s have a few of our warriors **p** on an
3:31 with him, “Tear your clothes and **p** on sackcloth.
6: 6 and Uzzah **p** out his hand to steady the Ark of
12:20 washed himself, **p** on lotions, and changed his
13:18 So the servant **p** her out. She was wearing a long,
13:19 now Tamar tore her robe and **p** ashes on her head.
15:32 and **p** dirt on his head as a sign of mourning.
17:19 The man’s wife **p** a cloth over the top of the well
1Ki 2:25 to execute him, and Adonijah was **p** to death.
6: 9 Solomon **p** in a ceiling made of beams and planks
8:29 this place where you have said you would **p** your
11:28 he **p** him in charge of the labor force from the
18: 4 He had **p** fifty prophets in each cave and had
20:32 So they **p** on sackcloth and ropes and went to the

21:12 and **p** Naboth at a prominent place before the
22:23 the LORD has **p** a lying spirit in the mouths of
22:27 '**P** this man in prison, and feed him nothing
2Ki 4:13 Does she want me to **p** in a good word for her to
4:38 "**P** on a large kettle and make some stew for these
4:39 and **p** them into the kettle without realizing they
5:12 better than all the rivers of Israel **p** together?
10:15 So Jehonadab **p** out his hand, and Jehu helped him
10:19 worshipers who fail to come will be **p** to death."
11: 2 Jehosheba **p** Joash and his nurse in a bedroom to
12: 9 The priests guarding the entrance **p** all of the
12:10 brought to the LORD's Temple and **p** it into bags.
13:16 Then Elisha told the king of Israel to **p** his hand on
14: 6 "Parents must not be **p** to death for the sins of
15: 5 The king's son Jotham was **p** in charge of the royal
17: 4 arrested him and **p** him in prison for his rebellion.
18:11 to Assyria and **p** them in colonies in Halah,
18:27 do not surrender, this city will be **p** under siege.
19: 1 he tore his clothes and **p** on sackcloth and went
19:28 heard for myself, / I will **p** my hook in your nose
23:33 Pharaoh Neco **p** Jehoahaz in prison at Riblah in the
25:21 the king of Babylon had them all **p** to death.
1Ch 1: 8 of Ham were Cush, Mizraim, **P**, and Canaan.
6:31 the house of the LORD after he **p** the Ark there.
13: 9 and Uzzah **p** out his hand to steady the Ark.
21:16 and the leaders of Israel **p** on sackcloth to show
21:27 to the angel, who **p** the sword back into its sheath.
26:15 and his sons were **p** in charge of the storehouses.
26:30 were **p** in charge of the Israelite lands west of the
26:32 and **p** them in charge of the tribes of Reuben
2Ch 4: 7 that had been given and **p** them in the Temple.
6:20 this place where you have said you would **p** your
11:12 He also **p** shields and spears in these towns as a
15:13 the God of Israel, would be **p** to death—
16: 7 "Because you have **p** your trust in the king of
18:22 the LORD has **p** a lying spirit in the mouths of
18:26 '**P** this man in prison, and feed him nothing
20:37 the ships met with disaster and never **p** out to sea.
22:11 She **p** Joash and his nurse in a bedroom. In this
23:18 Jehoiada now **p** the Levitical priests in charge of
25: 4 "Parents must not be **p** to death for the sins of
26:21 His son Jotham was **p** in charge of the royal
28:15 They **p** those who were weak on donkeys and took
31:12 Conaniah the Levite was **p** in charge, assisted by
31:14 was **p** in charge of distributing the freewill
33: 5 He **p** these altars for the stars of heaven in both
33:11 They **p** a ring through his nose, bound him in
34:13 were **p** in charge of the laborers of the various
36:22 heart of Cyrus to **p** this proclamation into writing
Ezr 1: 1 heart of Cyrus to **p** this proclamation into writing
3: 8 or older were **p** in charge of rebuilding the
3:10 the priests **p** on their robes and took their places to
6: 5 and **p** into God's Temple as they were before."
Ne 1:11 **P** it into his heart to be kind to me." In those days
2:12 I had not told anyone about the plans God had **p** in
3: 3 hung the doors, and **p** the bolts and bars in place.
13:13 I **p** Shelemiah the priest, Zadok the scribe,
Est 2: 4 the king, so he **p** the plan into effect immediately.
3: 9 so they can **p** it into the royal treasury.
4: 1 he tore his clothes, **p** on sackcloth and ashes,
5: 1 Esther **p** on her royal robes and entered the inner
6:11 So Haman took the robe and **p** it on Mordecai,
8:15 Then Mordecai **p** on the royal robe of blue
9: 1 So on March 7 the two decrees of the king were **p**
Job 6: 2 be weighed and my troubles be **p** on the scales,
13:27 You **p** my feet in stocks. You watch all my paths.
21: 5 be stunned. **P** your hand over your mouth in shock.
28: 3 They know how to **p** light into darkness
29: 9 in silence and **p** their hands over their mouths.
31:24 "Have I **p** my trust in money or felt secure
34:13 Who **p** the world in his care? Who has set the
40: 4 I will **p** my hand over my mouth in silence.
40:10 **p** on your robes of state, your majesty
40:24 it off guard or **p** a ring in its nose and lead it away.
41: 1 crocodile with a hook or **p** a noose around its jaw?
42:15 And their father **p** them into his will along with
Ps 8: 6 You **p** us in charge of everything you made,
10:14 punish them. / The helpless **p** their trust in you.
22: 5 They **p** their trust in you and were never
25: 5 who saves me. / All day long I **p** my hope in you.
25:21 and honesty protect me, / for I **p** my hope in you.
26: 2 **P** me on trial, LORD, and cross-examine me.
31: 1 to you for protection; / don't let me be **p** to shame.
31:24 all you who **p** your hope in the LORD!
32: 1 rebellion is forgiven, / whose sin is **p** out of sight!
35: 2 **P** on your armor, and take up your shield.
39: 7 And so, Lord, where do I **p** my hope? / My only
40: 3 They will **p** their trust in the LORD.
40:14 try to destroy me / be humiliated and **p** to shame.
42: 5 Why so sad? / I will **p** my hope in God!
42:11 Why so sad? / I will **p** my hope in God!
43: 5 Why so sad? / I will **p** my hope in God!
45: 3 **P** on your sword, O mighty warrior! / You are
53: 5 You will **p** them to shame, for God has rejected
54: 5 Do as you promised and **p** an end to them.
56: 3 But when I am afraid, / I **p** my trust in you.
70: 2 try to destroy me / be humiliated and **p** to shame.
73:18 Truly, you **p** them on a slippery path / and send
85: 4 of our salvation. / **P** aside your anger against us.
86:17 Then those who hate me will be **p** to shame,
105:21 Joseph was **p** in charge of all the king's household;
118: 8 trust the LORD / than to **p** confidence in people.
118: 9 trust the LORD / than to **p** confidence in princes.
118:27 Bring forward the sacrifice and **p** it on the altar.
119:31 LORD, don't let me be **p** to shame!
119:34 I will **p** it into practice with all my heart.
119:74 cause for joy, / for I have **p** my hope in your word.
119:81 but I have **p** my hope in your word.
119:147 I cry out for help and **p** my hope in your words.
127: 5 He will not be **p** to shame when he confronts his
130: 5 counting on him. / I have **p** my hope in his word.
131: 3 O Israel, **p** your hope in the LORD— / now
137: 2 We **p** away our lyres, / hanging them on the
146: 3 Don't **p** your confidence in powerful people;
147:11 those who **p** their hope in his unfailing love.
Pr 3:35 The wise inherit honor, but fools are **p** to shame!
6: 4 Don't **p** it off. Do it now! Don't rest until you do.
21:29 The wicked **p** up a bold front, but the upright
22:26 or **p** up a guarantee for someone else's loan.
23: 1 with a ruler, pay attention to what is **p** before you.
23: 2 If you are a big eater, **p** a knife to your throat,
27:23 and **p** your heart into caring for your herds,
Ecc 5:14 or they are **p** into risky investments that turn sour,
Isa 1:31 straw on fire, and no one will be able to **p** it out.
11: 8 a little child will **p** its hand in a nest of deadly
21: 6 "**P** a watchman on the city wall to shout out what
23: 4 But now you are **p** to shame, city of Sidon,
24:22 and **p** in prison until they are tried and condemned.
30: 2 You have **p** your trust in Pharaoh for his
36:12 do not surrender, this city will be **p** under siege.
37: 1 he tore his clothes and **p** on sackcloth and went
37:29 heard for myself, / I will **p** my hook in your nose
42: 1 am pleased with him. I have **p** my Spirit upon him.
44: 9 No wonder those who worship them are **p** to
45:18 the heavens and earth and **p** everything in place.
48:14 He will use him to **p** an end to the empire of
49:23 Those who wait for me will never be **p** to shame."
51:13 the one who **p** the stars in the sky and established
51:16 And I have **p** my words in your mouth and hidden
51:23 But I will **p** that cup into the hands of those who
52: 1 **P** on your beautiful clothes, O holy city of
52:11 **P** Babylon behind you, with everything it
53: 9 like a criminal; he was **p** in a rich man's grave.
59:17 He **p** on righteousness as his body armor
65:16 For I will **p** aside my anger and forget the evil of
66: 5 'Be joyful in him!' But they will be **p** to shame.
Jer 1: 9 and said, "See, I have **p** my words in your mouth!
4: 8 So **p** on clothes of mourning and weep with broken
6:21 "I will **p** obstacles in my people's path. Fathers
7:12 " 'Go to the place at Shiloh where I once **p** the
7:34 I will **p** an end to the happy singing and laughter in
13: 1 and buy a linen belt and **p** it around your waist,
13: 2 the LORD directed me and **p** it around my waist.
13:25 have forgotten me and **p** your trust in false gods.
16: 9 I will **p** an end to the happy singing and laughter in
17: 5 "Cursed are those who **p** their trust in mere
17:27 and no one will be able to **p** out the roaring
20: 2 and **p** in stocks at the Benjamin Gate of the
27: 6 I have **p** everything, even the wild animals,
27: 8 and serve him; **p** your neck under Babylon's yoke!
28: 4 yoke that the king of Babylon has **p** on your necks.
28:14 I have **p** a yoke of iron on the necks of all these
28:14 I have **p** everything, even the wild animals,
29:26 You are responsible to **p** anyone who claims to be
31:21 "Set up road signs; **p** up guideposts. Mark well the
31:33 "I will **p** my laws in their minds, and I will write
32: 3 King Zedekiah had **p** him there because he
32:14 and **p** them into a pottery jar to preserve them for a
32:40 I will **p** a desire in their hearts to worship me,
37:16 Jeremiah was **p** into a dungeon cell, where he
37:21 in the city. So Jeremiah was **p** in the palace prison.
38:12 "**P** these rags under your armpits to protect you
39:14 They **p** him under the care of Gedaliah son of
46: 4 **P** on your helmets, sharpen your spears,
48:35 "I will **p** an end to Moab," says the LORD,
48:37 their hands and **p** on clothes made of sackcloth.
49: 3 **P** on your clothes of mourning. Weep and wail,
51: 3 Don't let the archers **p** on their armor or draw their
52:27 the king of Babylon had them all **p** to death.
Eze 8: 3 He **p** out what seemed to be a hand and took me by
9: 4 and **p** a mark on the foreheads of all those who
10: 7 He **p** the coals into the hands of the man in linen
11:19 singleness of heart and **p** a new spirit within them.
12: 3 So now **p** on a demonstration to show them what it
12:23 I will **p** an end to this proverb, and you will soon
15: 5 useless both before and after being **p** into the fire!
16:24 and **p** altars to idols in every town square.
17:16 the land of the king who **p** him in power
18:31 **P** all your rebellion behind you, and get for
20:48 have set this fire. It will not be **p** out."
21:13 It will **p** them all to the test! So now the Sovereign
21:19 **P** a signpost on the road that comes out of Babylon
21:22 They will **p** up siege towers and build ramps
23:27 I will **p** a stop to the lewdness and prostitution you
23:40 your eyelids, and **p** on your finest jewels for them.
23:41 and **p** my incense and my oil on a table that was
23:42 who **p** bracelets on your wrists and beautiful
23:48 I will **p** an end to lewdness and idolatry in the land,
24: 3 **P** a pot of water on the fire to boil.
29: 4 I will **p** hooks in your jaws and drag you out on the
29: 7 When she **p** her weight on you, you gave way,
30:21 His arm has not been **p** in a cast so that it may
30:24 of Babylon's king and **p** my sword in his hand.
30:25 And when I **p** my sword in the hand of Babylon's
36:26 and right desires, and I will **p** a new spirit in you.
36:27 And I will **p** my Spirit in you so you will obey my
37: 6 I will **p** flesh and muscles on you and cover you
37: 6 I will **p** breath into you, and you will come to life.
37:14 I will **p** my Spirit in you, and you will live
37:26 and I will **p** my Temple among them forever.
38: 4 and **p** hooks into your jaws to lead you out to your
42:14 They must **p** on other clothes before entering the
43: 8 They **p** their idol altars right next to mine with
43: 9 Now let them **p** away their idols and the sacred
44:19 them in the sacred rooms and **p** on other clothes
45:19 and **p** it on the doorposts of the Temple,
Da 2:38 and has **p** even the animals and birds under your
3:12 whom you have **p** in charge of the province of
7: 9 I watched as thrones were **p** in place
9:24 and your holy city to **p** down rebellion,
9:27 he will **p** an end to the sacrifices and offerings.
11:18 But a commander from another land will **p** an end
Hos 1: 5 I will **p** an end to Israel's independence by
2:11 I will **p** an end to her annual festivals, her new
2:13 **p** on her earrings and jewels, and went out looking
4:16 as a heifer, so the LORD will **p** her out to pasture.
10:11 Now I will **p** a heavy yoke on her tender neck.
Jnh 3:10 When God saw that they had **p** a stop to their evil
4:10 the plant, though you did nothing to **p** it there.
Mic 5:12 I will **p** an end to all witchcraft; there will be no
Na 3: 9 The nations of **P** and Libya also helped
Zep 1: 4 I will **p** an end to all the idolatrous priests, so that
Zec 3: 5 So they **p** a clean priestly turban on his head
6:11 Then **p** the crown on the head of Jeshua son of
7:11 and **p** their fingers in their ears to keep from
Mal 3: 5 At that time I will **p** you on trial. I will be a ready
Mt 5:15 Instead, **p** it on a stand and let it shine for all.
6:26 don't need to plant or harvest or **p** food in barns
12:18 pleased with him. / I will **p** my Spirit upon him,
13:30 and burn them and to **p** the wheat in the barn.' "
15: 4 speaks evil of father or mother must be **p** to death.'
16:24 you must **p** aside your selfish ambition,
17:17 How long must I **p** up with you? Bring the boy to
18: 2 child over to him and **p** the child among them.
19:15 And he **p** his hands on their heads and blessed
21:41 "He will **p** the wicked men to a horrible death
24:47 the master will **p** that servant in charge of all he
25:27 you should at least have **p** my money into the bank
26: 4 how to capture Jesus secretly and **p** him to death.
26:52 "**P** away your sword," Jesus told him.
26:59 lie about Jesus, so they could **p** him to death.
27: 6 "We can't **p** it in the Temple treasury," they said,
27:20 to be released and for Jesus to be **p** to death.
27:28 They stripped him and **p** a scarlet robe on him.
27:29 a crown of long, sharp thorns and **p** it on his head,
27:31 off the robe and **p** his own clothes on him again.
Mk 4:21 anyone light a lamp and then **p** it under a basket
5: 4 Whenever he was **p** into chains and shackles—
7:10 speaks evil of father or mother must be **p** to death.'
7:33 He **p** his fingers into the man's ears. Then,
8:34 "you must **p** aside your selfish ambition,
9:19 How long must I **p** up with you? Bring the boy to
9:36 Then he **p** a little child among them.
12:41 their money. Many rich people **p** in large amounts.
14: 1 to capture Jesus secretly and **p** him to death.
14:55 testify against Jesus, so they could **p** him to death.
15:17 a crown of long, sharp thorns and **p** it on his head.
15:20 purple robe and **p** his own clothes on him again.
16: 1 and purchased burial spices to **p** on Jesus' body.
Lk 3:20 So Herod **p** John in prison, adding this sin to his
5:38 New wine must be **p** into new wineskins.
8:16 a lamp and then cover it up or **p** it under a bed.
9:23 you must **p** aside your selfish ambition,
9:41 "how long must I be with you and **p** up with you?
10:34 Then he **p** the man on his own donkey and took
11:28 who hear the word of God and **p** it into practice."
11:33 it is **p** on a lampstand to give light to all who enter
12:24 don't need to plant or harvest or **p** food in barns
12:37 **p** on an apron, and serve them as they sit and eat!
12:44 the master will **p** that servant in charge of all he
14:12 "When you **p** on a luncheon or a dinner," he said,
15:22 Bring the finest robe in the house and **p** it on him.
23:11 Then they **p** a royal robe on him and sent him back
Jn 3:24 This was before John was **p** into prison.
8: 3 act of adultery. They **p** her in front of the crowd.
11:34 "Where have you **p** him?" he asked them.
12:46 so that all who **p** their trust in me will no longer
13:12 he **p** on his robe again and sat down and asked,
18:11 said to Peter, "**P** your sword back into its sheath.
19: 2 a crown of long, sharp thorns and **p** it on his head,
and they **p** a royal purple robe on him.
19:29 **p** it on a hyssop branch, and held it up to his lips.
20: 2 and I don't know where they have **p** him!"
20:13 "and I don't know where they have **p** him."
20:15 tell me where you have **p** him, and I will go
20:25 **p** my fingers into them, and place my hand into the
20:27 to Thomas, "**P** your finger here and see my hands.
P your hand into the wound in my side.
21: 7 he **p** on his tunic (for he had stripped for work),
Ac 3: 2 Each day he was **p** beside the Temple gate, the one
5:18 They arrested the apostles and **p** them in the jail.
5:31 Then God **p** him in the place of honor at his right
6: 3 We will **p** them in charge of this business.
7:10 and **p** him in charge of all the affairs of the palace.
7:57 Then they **p** their hands over their ears,
10:39 They **p** him to death by crucifying him,
12: 8 told him, "Get dressed and **p** on your sandals."
12: 8 "Now **p** on your coat and follow me," the angel
12:21 Herod **p** on his royal robes, sat on his throne,
13:18 He **p** up with them through forty years of
16:24 took no chances but **p** them into the inner dungeon
27: 6 that was bound for Italy, and he **p** us on board.
27:30 they were going to **p** out anchors from the prow.
28:10 people **p** on board all sorts of things we would
Ro 1:19 God has **p** this knowledge in their hearts.
4: 7 is forgiven, / whose sins are **p** out of sight.
8: 3 But God **p** into effect a different plan to save us.
11: 8 "God has **p** them into a deep sleep.
11:21 For if God did not spare the branches he **p** there in
13: 1 the government, for God is the one who **p** it there.
14:13 will not **p** an obstacle in another Christian's path.

1Co 3:13 Everyone's work will be **p** through the fire to see
4: 1 have been **p** in charge of explaining God's secrets.
4: 2 a person who is **p** in charge as a manager must be
4: 9 But sometimes I think God has **p** us apostles on
7:17 You must accept whatever situation the Lord has **p**
9:12 We would rather **p** up with anything than **p** an
10: 9 Nor should we **p** Christ to the test, as some of them
12:18 and he has **p** each part just where he wants it.
12:24 So God has **p** the body together in such a way that
13:11 But when I grew up, I **p** away childish things.
15:24 having **p** down all enemies of every kind.
15:36 When you **p** a seed into the ground, it doesn't grow
15:37 And what you **p** in the ground is not the plant that
16: 2 each of you should **p** aside some amount of money
2Co 1:24 tell you exactly how to **p** your faith into practice.
3:13 who **p** a veil over his face so the people of Israel
5: 2 and we long for the day when we will **p** on our
5: 3 but we will **p** on new heavenly bodies.
6: 5 have been beaten, been **p** in jail, faced angry mobs,
10: 8 And I will not be **p** to shame by having my work
11:20 You **p** up with it when they make you their slaves,
11:20 take advantage of you, **p** on airs, and slap you in
11:23 I have worked harder, been **p** in jail more often,
Gal 3: 7 then, are all those who **p** their faith in God.
3: 9 All who **p** their faith in Christ share the same
3:23 until we could **p** our faith in the coming Savior.
3:24 Let me **p** it another way. The law was our guardian
Eph 1:22 And God has **p** all things under the authority of
2:16 and our hostility toward each other was **p** to death.
4:25 So **p** away all falsehood and "tell your neighbor
6:11 **P** on all of God's armor so that you will be able to
6:15 **p** on the peace that comes from the Good News,
6:17 **P** on salvation as your helmet, and take the sword
Php 2:12 to **p** into action God's saving work in your lives,
3: 3 We **p** no confidence in human effort. Instead,
Col 3: 5 So **p** to death the sinful, earthly things lurking
1Ti 5: 9 A widow who is **p** on the list for support must be a
5:16 of them and not **p** the responsibility on the church.
Phm 1: 6 And I am praying that you will really **p** your
Heb 2:13 He also said, "I will **p** my trust in him." And in
8:10 says the Lord: / I will **p** my laws in their minds
8:13 It is now out of date and ready to be **p** aside.
10:16 says the Lord: / I will **p** my laws in their hearts
10:28 **p** to death without mercy on the testimony of two
11:34 strong in battle and **p** whole armies to flight.
1Jn 4:16 God loves us, and we have **p** our trust in him.
Rev 2:10 some of you into prison and **p** you to the test.
17:17 For God has **p** a plan into their minds, a plan that

PUTEOLI (1)
Ac 28:13 so the following day we sailed up the coast to **P**.

PUTHITES (1)
1Ch 2:53 the Ithrites, **P**, Shumathites, and Mishraites,

PUTIEL (1)
Ex 6:25 son of Aaron married one of the daughters of **P**,

PUTS (10) [PUT]
Ex 30:33 or **p** any of it on someone who is not a priest will
Job 11:10 If God comes along and **p** a person in prison,
33:11 He **p** my feet in the stocks and watches every
Isa 41: 2 He **p** entire armies to the sword. He scatters them
Mt 9:17 And no one **p** new wine into old wineskins.
Mk 2:22 And no one **p** new wine into old wineskins.
Lk 5:37 And no one **p** new wine into old wineskins.
9:62 "Anyone who **p** a hand to the plow and then looks
11:33 a lamp and then hides it or **p** it under a basket.
3Jn 1:10 when they do help, he **p** them out of the church.

PUTTING (21) [PUT]
Ge 39:10 She kept **p** pressure on him day after day, but he
Nu 35:19 The victim's nearest relative is responsible for **p**
1Sa 17:26 this Philistine and **p** an end to his abuse of Israel?"
1Ki 20:31 by wearing sackcloth and **p** ropes on our heads.
Ne 9:38 are making a solemn promise and **p** it in writing.
Est 9:29 wrote another letter **p** the queen's full authority
Ps 47: 3 nations before us, / **p** our enemies beneath our feet.
Pr 25:19 **P** confidence in an unreliable person is like
Isa 2:22 Stop **p** your trust in mere humans. They are as frail
66: 3 it is as bad as **p** a dog or the blood of a pig on the
Jer 38: 9 "these men have done a very evil thing in **p**
Da 11:31 the sanctuary, **p** a stop to the daily sacrifices,
Hab 2: 9 **p** your families beyond the reach of danger.
Hag 1: 6 Your wages disappear as though you were **p** them
Mal 2:16 "It is as cruel as **p** on a victim's bloodstained
Lk 7:38 she kept kissing his feet and **p** perfume on them.
18: 7 with him day and night? Will he keep **p** them off?
21: 1 he watched the rich people **p** their gifts into the
Ac 27: 4 **P** out to sea from there, we encountered headwinds
Eph 6:14 **p** on the sturdy belt of truth and the body armor of
Php 4: 9 Keep **p** into practice all you learned from me

PUZZLED (4) [PUZZLING]
Ex 16:15 The Israelites were **p** when they saw it. "What is
Lk 9: 7 he was worried and **p** because some were saying,
24: 4 They were **p**, trying to think what could have
Jn 7:35 The Jewish leaders were **p** by this statement.

PUZZLING (1) [PUZZLED]
Ac 10:19 Meanwhile, as Peter was **p** over the vision,

PYGARG [KJV] See IBEX

PYRRHUS (1)
Ac 20: 4 They were Sopater of Berea, the son of **P**;

Q

QUACKS (1)
Job 13: 4 me with lies. As doctors, you are worthless **q**.

QUAIL (6)
Ex 16:13 That evening vast numbers of **q** arrived
Nu 11:31 Now the LORD sent a wind that brought **q** from
11:31 were **q** flying about three feet above the ground.
11:32 So the people went out and caught **q** all that day
11:32 They spread the **q** out all over the camp.
Ps 105:40 They asked for meat, and he sent them **q**; / he gave

QUAKE (6) [EARTHQUAKE, EARTHQUAKES, QUAKED, QUAKES]
Ps 29: 8 The voice of the LORD makes the desert **q**;
99: 1 between the cherubim. / Let the whole earth **q**!
Isa 31: 9 Even their generals will **q** with terror and flee
64: 1 How the mountains would **q** in your presence!
Eze 38:20 and people—will **q** in terror at my presence.
Na 1: 5 In his presence the mountains **q**, and the hills melt

QUAKED (7) [QUAKE]
Jdg 5: 5 The mountains **q** at the coming of the LORD.
2Sa 22: 8 "Then the earth **q** and trembled; / the foundations of the heavens shook; / they **q** because of his anger.
Ps 18: 7 Then the earth **q** and trembled; / the foundations of the mountains shook; / they **q** because of his anger.
77:16 and trembled! / The sea **q** to its very depths.
Isa 64: 3 And oh, how the mountains **q**!

QUAKES (2) [QUAKE]
Ps 75: 3 When the earth **q** and its people live in turmoil,
Joel 2:10 The earth **q** as they advance, and the heavens

QUALIFIED (5) [QUALIFY]
2Ki 10: 3 select the best **q** of King Ahab's sons to be your
1Ch 24: 5 for there were many **q** officials serving God in the
26: 8 were very capable men, well **q** for their work.
Ro 3: 6 If God is not just, how is he **q** to judge the world?
Heb 5: 9 In this way, God **q** him as a perfect High Priest,

QUALIFY (3) [QUALIFIED]
Lev 21:17 defects will not **q** to offer food to their God.
Nu 4: 3 of thirty and fifty who **q** to work in the Tabernacle.
1Ch 23:24 or older to **q** for service in the house of the

QUALITIES (2) [QUALITY]
Mk 9:50 You must have the **q** of salt among yourselves
Ro 1:20 They can clearly see his invisible **q**—his eternal

QUALITY (2) [HIGH-QUALITY, QUALITIES]
1Sa 15: 9 destroyed only what was worthless or of poor **q**.
Jer 6:27 that you may determine the **q** of my people.

QUANTITIES (11) [QUANTITY]
1Ki 10: 2 with spices, huge **q** of gold, and precious jewels.
10:10 of gold, and great **q** of spices and precious jewels.
1Ch 29: 2 bronze, iron, and wood, as well as great **q** of onyx,
2Ch 4:18 Such great **q** of bronze were used that its weight
9: 1 with spices, huge **q** of gold, and precious jewels.
9: 9 of gold, and great **q** of spices and precious jewels.
14:13 and the army of Judah carried off vast **q** of
14:14 vast **q** of plunder were taken from these towns,
25:13 and carrying off great **q** of plunder.
Zec 14:14 great **q** of gold and silver and fine clothing.
Rev 18:12 She bought great **q** of gold, silver, jewels, pearls,

QUANTITY (1) [QUANTITIES]
Rev 8: 3 And a great **q** of incense was given to him to mix

QUARANTINE (6) [QUARANTINED]
Lev 13: 4 the priest will put the infected person in **q** for
13: 5 then the priest will put the person in **q** for seven
13:21 then the priest is to put the person in **q** for seven
13:26 then the priest is to put the infected person in **q** for
13:31 then he must put the person in **q** for seven days.
13:33 Then the priest must put the person in **q** for

QUARANTINED (1) [QUARANTINE]
Lev 13:11 the person need not be **q** for further observation

QUARREL (9) [QUARRELING, QUARRELS, QUARRELSOME]
Ge 45:24 he called after them, "Don't **q** along the way!"
Ex 21:18 "Now suppose two people **q**, and one hits the
2Ch 35:21 king of Judah? I have no **q** with you today!
Job 33:10 God is picking a **q** with me, and he considers me to
Pr 17:14 Beginning a **q** is like opening a floodgate, so drop
17:19 Anyone who loves to **q** loves sin; anyone who
1Co 3: 3 are jealous of one another and **q** with each other.
2Ti 2:24 The Lord's servants must not **q** but must be kind to
Jas 4: 2 so you fight and **q** to take it away from them.

QUARRELING (6) [QUARREL]
Job 22:21 "Stop **q** with God! If you agree with him, you will
Pr 20: 3 a fight is a mark of honor; only fools insist on **q**.
Isa 58: 4 good is fasting when you keep on fighting and **q**?
2Co 12:20 I am afraid that I will find **q**, jealousy, outbursts of
Gal 5:20 hostility, **q**, jealousy, outbursts of anger,
Tit 3: 2 not speak evil of anyone, and they must avoid **q**.

QUARRELS (9) [QUARREL]
Dt 1:12 But how can I settle all your **q** and problems by
Pr 10:12 Hatred stirs up **q**, but love covers all offenses.
18: 6 Fools get into constant **q**; they are asking for a
22:10 Throw out the mocker, and fighting, **q**, and insults
26:20 for lack of fuel, and **q** disappear when gossip stops.
30:33 to the nose causes bleeding, so anger causes **q**.
1Co 3: 5 who is Paul, that we should be the cause of such **q**?
Tit 3: 9 or in **q** and fights about obedience to Jewish laws.
Jas 4: 1 What is causing the **q** and fights among you?

QUARRELSOME (1) [QUARREL]
Pr 26:21 A **q** person starts fights as easily as hot embers

QUARRIED (1) [QUARRY]
1Ki 5:17 the stonecutters **q** and shaped costly blocks of

QUARRIES (1) [QUARRY]
Jos 7: 5 the Israelites from the city gate as far as the **q**,

QUARRY (3) [QUARRIED, QUARRIES]
1Ki 6: 7 of the Temple were prefinished at the **q**,
Ecc 10: 9 When you work in a **q**, stones might fall and crush
Isa 51: 1 Consider the **q** from which you were mined,

QUART (8) [QUARTS]
Ex 29:40 offer two quarts of fine flour mixed with one **q** of
29:40 also, offer one **q** of wine as a drink offering.
Lev 23:13 you must also offer one **q** of wine as a drink
Nu 15: 4 of choice flour mixed with one **q** of olive oil.
15: 5 you must also present one **q** of wine for a drink
28: 5 of choice flour mixed with one **q** of olive oil.
28: 7 consisting of one **q** of fermented drink with each
28:14 a half pints for the ram, and one **q** for each lamb.

QUARTER (1) [QUARTERS]
1Sa 13:21 a **q** of an ounce of silver for sharpening a

QUARTERS (6) [QUARTER]
1Ki 7: 8 Solomon's living **q** surrounded a courtyard behind
7: 8 He also built similar living **q** for Pharaoh's
2Ki 23:11 They were near the **q** of Nathan-melech the
Est 2:21 were guards at the door of the king's private **q**—
6: 2 who guarded the door to the king's private **q**.
Joel 2:16 Call the bridegroom from his **q** and the bride from

QUARTS (48) [QUART]
Ex 16:16 much as it needs. Pick up two **q** for each person."
16:18 By gathering two **q** for each person, everyone had
16:22 the ground—four **q** for each person instead of two.
16:32 "Take two **q** of manna and keep it forever as a
16:33 "Get a container and put two **q** of manna into it.
16:36 the manna was an omer, which held about two **q**.)
29:40 offer two **q** of fine flour mixed with one quart of
Lev 5:11 they must bring two **q** of choice flour for their sin
6:20 LORD a grain offering of two **q** of choice flour,
14:10 along with five **q** of choice flour mixed with olive
14:21 along with two **q** of choice flour mixed with olive
23:13 of three **q** of choice flour mixed with olive oil.
23:17 These loaves must be baked from three **q** of choice
24: 5 choice flour, using three **q** of flour for each loaf.
Nu 5:15 two **q** of barley flour to be presented on her behalf.
15: 4 **q** of choice flour mixed with one quart of olive oil.
15: 6 give three **q** of choice flour mixed with two and a
15: 9 **q** of choice flour mixed with two **q** of olive oil,
15:10 plus two **q** of wine for the drink offering. This will
28: 5 **q** of choice flour mixed with one quart of olive oil.
28: 9 of three **q** of choice flour mixed with olive oil,
28:12 five **q** with each bull, three **q** with the ram,
28:13 and two **q** with each lamb. This burnt offering
28:14 two **q** of wine with each bull, two and a half pints
28:20 five **q** with each bull, three **q** with the ram,
28:21 and two **q** with each of the seven lambs.
28:28 five **q** with each bull, three **q** with the ram,
28:29 and two **q** with each of the seven lambs.
29: 3 five **q** with the bull, three **q** with the ram,
29: 4 and two **q** with each of the seven lambs.
29: 9 five **q** of choice flour with the bull, three **q** of choice flour with the ram,
29:10 and two **q** of choice flour with each of the seven
29:14 five **q** for each of the thirteen bulls, three **q** for each of the two rams,
29:15 and two **q** for each of the fourteen lambs.
2Ki 7: 1 five **q** of fine flour will cost only half an ounce of
7: 1 and ten **q** of barley grain will cost only half an
7:16 So it was true that five **q** of fine flour were sold

7:16 and ten **q** of barley grain were sold for half an
7:18 five **q** of fine flour will cost half an ounce of silver,
7:18 and ten **q** of barley grain will cost half an ounce of
Eze 46:14 and a half **q** of flour with a third of a gallon of

QUARTUS (1)

Ro 16:23 his greetings, and so does **Q**, a Christian brother.

QUATERNIONS [KJV] See SQUADS (OF FOUR SOLDIERS)

QUAVERING (1)

Ecc 12: 4 yourself will be deaf and tuneless, with a **q** voice.

QUEEN (62) [QUEEN'S, QUEENLY, QUEENS]

1Ki 10: 1 When the **q** of Sheba heard of Solomon's
10: 4 When the **q** of Sheba realized how wise Solomon
10:10 so many spices brought in as those the **q** of Sheba
10:13 King Solomon gave the **q** of Sheba whatever she
11:19 and he gave him a wife—the sister of **Q** Tahpenes.
14: 2 so that no one will recognize you as the **q**.
15:13 Maacah from her position as **q** mother
2Ki 9:30 When Jezebel, the **q** mother, heard that Jehu had
10:13 to visit the sons of King Ahab and the **q** mother."
24:12 nobles, and officials, and the **q** mother,
24:15 along with his wives and officials, the **q** mother,
2Ch 9: 1 When the **q** of Sheba heard of Solomon's
9: 3 When the **q** of Sheba realized how wise Solomon
9: 9 as fine as those the **q** of Sheba gave to Solomon.
9:12 King Solomon gave the **q** of Sheba whatever she
15:16 Maacah from her position as **q** mother
Ne 2: 6 The king, with the **q** sitting beside him, asked,
Est 1: 9 **Q** Vashti gave a banquet for the women of the
1:11 to bring **Q** Vashti to him with the royal crown on
1:12 But when they conveyed the king's order to **Q**
1:15 "What must be done to **Q** Vashti?" the king
1:15 "What penalty does the law provide for a **q** who
1:16 "**Q** Vashti has wronged not only the king but also
1:17 **Q** Vashti has refused to appear before the king.
1:18 will hear what the **q** did and will start talking to
1:19 It should order that **Q** Vashti be forever banished
1:19 and that you choose another **q** more worthy than
2: 4 you most will be made **q** instead of Vashti."
2:17 on her head and declared her **q** instead of Vashti.
2:22 the plot and passed the information on to **Q** Esther.
4: 4 When **Q** Esther's maids and eunuchs came
5: 2 When he saw **Q** Esther standing there in the inner
5: 3 the king asked her, "What do you want, **Q** Esther?
5:12 **Q** Esther invited only me and the king himself to
7: 1 the king and Haman went to **Q** Esther's banquet.
7: 2 asked her, "Tell me what you want, **Q** Esther.
7: 3 And so **Q** Esther replied, "If Your Majesty is
7: 6 grew pale with fright before the king and **q**.
7: 7 stayed behind to plead for his life with **Q** Esther,
7: 8 In despair he fell on the couch where **Q** Esther was
7: 8 "Will he even assault the **q** right here in the
8: 1 of Haman, the enemy of the Jews, to **Q** Esther.
8: 7 Then King Xerxes said to **Q** Esther and Mordecai
9:12 he called for **Q** Esther and said, "The Jews have
9:29 Then **Q** Esther, the daughter of Abihail, along with
9:31 decreed by both Mordecai the Jew and **Q** Esther.
Ps 45: 9 At your right side stands the **q**, / wearing jewelry
Isa 47: 5 Never again will you be known as the **q** of
47: 7 'I will reign forever as **q** of the world!'
Jer 7:18 and make cakes to offer to the **Q** of Heaven.
29: 2 the **q** mother, the court officials, the leaders of
44:17 We will burn incense to the **Q** of Heaven
44:18 But ever since we quit burning incense to the **Q** of
44:19 "do you suppose that we were worshiping the **Q** of
44:25 your devotion and sacrifices to the **Q** of Heaven,
La 1: 1 Once the **q** of nations, she is now a slave.
Eze 16:13 than ever. You looked like a **q**, and so you were!
Da 5:10 But when the **q** mother heard what was happening,
Mt 12:42 The **q** of Sheba will also rise up against this
Lk 11:31 "The **q** of Sheba will rise up against this
Ac 8:27 a eunuch of great authority under the **q** of Ethiopia.
Rev 18: 7 and sorrows. She boasts, 'I am **q** on my throne.

QUEEN'S (1) [QUEEN]

Est 9:29 wrote another letter putting the **q** full authority

QUEENLY (2) [QUEEN]

SS 7: 1 beautiful are your sandaled feet, O **q** maiden.
7: 5 A king is held captive in your **q** tresses.

QUEENS (4) [QUEEN]

SS 6: 8 all **q**, and eighty concubines and unnumbered
6: 9 see her; even **q** and concubines sing her praises!
Isa 49:23 Kings and **q** will serve you. They will care for all
Jer 44: 9 the sins of the kings and **q** of Judah, and the sins

QUENCH (7) [QUENCHED]

Ps 104:11 the animals, / and the wild donkeys **q** their thirst.
SS 8: 7 Many waters cannot **q** love; neither can rivers
Isa 42: 3 crush those who are weak or **q** the smallest hope.
44: 3 For I will give you abundant water to **q** your thirst
Hos 9: 2 The grapes you gather will not **q** your thirst.
Am 5: 6 Your gods in Bethel certainly won't be able to **q**
Mt 12:20 crush those who are weak, / or **q** the smallest hope.

QUENCHED (4) [QUENCH]

2Ki 22:17 is burning against this place, and it will not be **q**.'
Job 18: 6 The lamp hanging above them will be **q**.
Eze 20:47 The terrible flames will not be **q**; they will scorch
Heb 11:34 **q** the flames of fire, and escaped death by the edge

QUESTION (54) [QUESTIONED, QUESTIONING, QUESTIONS]

Ge 31:32 relatives of ours, I will give it back without **q**."
1Sa 17:29 David replied. "I was only asking a **q**!"
17:31 Then David's **q** was reported to King Saul,
1Ki 22: 7 too? I would like to ask him the same **q**."
2Ch 18: 6 too? I would like to ask him the same **q**."
Ecc 8: 4 is backed by great power. No one can resist or **q** it.
Isa 45:11 Holy One of Israel, says: "Do you **q** what I do?
Jer 30: 6 Now let me ask you a **q**: Do men give birth to
Hag 2:11 Ask the priests this **q** about the law:
Zec 7: 3 They were to ask this **q** of the prophets and of the
Mt 2: 3 Herod was deeply disturbed by their **q**, as was all
19: 3 Pharisees came and tried to trap him with this **q**:
19:16 Someone came to Jesus with this **q**: "Teacher,
19:17 But to answer your **q**, you can receive eternal life
21:24 authority to do these things if you answer one **q**,"
21:27 "Then I won't answer your **q** either."
22:16 with the supporters of Herod, to ask him this **q**:
22:23 is no resurrection after death. They posed this **q**:
22:34 they thought up a fresh **q** of their own to ask him.
22:35 in religious law, tried to trap him with this **q**:
22:41 surrounded by the Pharisees, Jesus asked them a **q**:
Mk 10: 2 Pharisees came and tried to trap him with this **q**:
10:19 But as for your **q**, you know the commandments:
11:29 authority to do these things if you answer one **q**,"
11:33 "Then I won't answer your **q** either."
12:18 is no resurrection after death. They posed this **q**:
Lk 6: 9 Then Jesus said to his critics, "I have a **q** for you.
10:25 law stood up to test Jesus by asking him this **q**:
18:18 Once a religious leader asked Jesus this **q**:
18:20 But as for your **q**, you know the commandments:
20: 3 "Let me ask you a **q** first," he replied.
20: 8 "Then I won't answer your **q** either."
20:28 They posed this **q**: "Teacher, Moses gave us a law
20:41 Then Jesus presented them with a **q**. "Why is it,"
22:68 And if I ask you a **q**, you won't answer.
23: 9 He asked Jesus **q** after **q**, but Jesus refused
Jn 18:21 Why are you asking me this **q**? Ask those who
18:34 Jesus replied, "Is this your own **q**, or did others
21:16 Jesus repeated the **q**: "Simon son of John, do you
21:17 Peter was grieved that Jesus asked the **q** a third
Ac 15: 2 to talk to the apostles and elders about this **q**.
15: 6 and church elders got together to decide this **q**.
15:27 tell you what we have decided concerning your **q**.
18:15 But since it is merely a **q** of words and names
Ro 4: 1 What were his experiences concerning this **q** of
1Co 9: 3 This is my answer to those who **q** my authority as
15:36 What a foolish **q**! When you put a seed into the
2Co 10:16 Then there will be no **q** about being in someone
Gal 2: 4 Even that **q** wouldn't have come up except for
3: 2 Let me ask you this one **q**: Did you receive the
1Ti 3:16 Without **q**, this is the great mystery of our faith:
Heb 6:16 them to it. And without any **q** that oath is binding.
7: 7 And without **q**, the person who has the power to

QUESTIONED (4) [QUESTION]

Dt 19:18 They must be closely **q**, and if the accuser is found
Job 31:14 What could I say when he **q** me about it?
Jn 9:17 Then the Pharisees once again **q** the man who had
Ac 4: 9 are we being **q** because we've done a good deed

QUESTIONING (1) [QUESTION]

Ac 15:10 Why are you now **q** God's way by burdening the

QUESTIONS (22) [QUESTION]

Ex 18:19 before God, bringing him their **q** to be decided.
1Ki 10: 1 of the LORD, she came to test him with hard **q**.
10: 3 Solomon answered all her **q**; nothing was too hard
2Ch 9: 1 she came to Jerusalem to test him with hard **q**.
9: 2 Solomon answered all her **q**; nothing was too hard
Job 38: 2 "Who is this that **q** my wisdom with such ignorant
38: 3 Brace yourself, because I have some **q** for you,
40: 7 "Brace yourself, because I have some **q** for you,
42: 3 'Who is this that **q** my wisdom with such
42: 4 I have some **q** for you, and you must answer
Mt 22:18 "Whom are you trying to fool with your trick **q**?
22:46 after that, no one dared to ask him any more **q**.
Mk 12:15 "Who are you trying to fool with your trick **q**?
12:34 after that, no one dared to ask him any more **q**.
Lk 2:46 religious teachers, discussing deep **q** with them.
3:16 John answered their **q** by saying, "I baptize with
11:53 that time on they grilled him with many hostile **q**,
20:40 And that ended their **q**; no one dared to ask any
1Co 7: 1 Now about the **q** you asked in your letter. Yes,
10:27 is offered to you and don't ask any **q** about it.
14:35 If they have any **q** to ask, let them ask their
1Pe 1:10 even though they had many **q** as to what it all

QUIBBLE (1)

1Ti 6: 4 Such a person has an unhealthy desire to **q** over the

QUICK (30) [QUICK-TEMPERED, QUICKLY]

Ge 18: 6 ran back to the tent and said to Sarah, "**Q**!
19:14 tell his daughters' fiancés, "**Q**, get out of the city!
41:14 After a **q** shave and change of clothes, he went in
Ex 9:19 **Q**! Order your livestock and servants to come in
32: 7 Then the LORD told Moses, "**Q**! Go down the
Nu 16:26 "**Q**!" he told the people. "Get away from the
16:46 "**Q**, take an incense burner and place burning
Jdg 9:48 "**Q**, do as I have done!" he told his men.
2Sa 17:16 "**Q**!" he told them. "Find David and urge him not
17:21 "**Q**!" they told him, "cross the Jordan tonight!"
20: 6 **Q**, take my troops and chase after him before he
1Ki 13:13 "**Q**, saddle the donkey," the old man said.
20:33 The men were **q** to grasp at this straw of hope,
22: 9 of Israel called one of his officials and said, "**Q**!
2Ki 9:21 "**Q**! Get my chariot ready!" King Joram
2Ch 18: 8 of Israel called one of his officials and said, "**Q**!
Pr 6: 3 **q**, get out of it if you possibly can! You have
13: 3 will have a long life; a **q** retort can ruin everything.
28:20 But the person who wants to get rich **q** will only
28:22 A greedy person tries to get rich **q**, but it only
SS 2:15 "**Q**! Catch all the little foxes before they ruin the
Isa 5:19 and do something! **Q**, show us what you can do.
21: 5 Everyone is eating and drinking. **Q**! Grab your
Jer 9:18 **Q**! Begin your weeping! Let the tears flow from
Mic 1:13 **Q**! Use your swiftest chariots and flee, you people
Lk 15:22 "But his father said to the servants, '**Q**!
19: 5 by name. "Zacchaeus!" he said. "**Q**, come down!
Ac 12: 7 him on the side to awaken him and said, "**Q**!
Ro 3:15 "They are **q** to commit murder.
Jas 1:19 Dear friends, be **q** to listen, slow to speak,

QUICK [KJV] See also ACTIVELY, ALIVE, LIVING

QUICK-TEMPERED (3) [QUICK, TEMPER]

Pr 12:16 A fool is **q**, but a wise person stays calm when
Ecc 7: 9 Don't be **q**, for anger is the friend of fools.
Tit 1: 7 He must not be arrogant or **q**; he must not be a

QUICKEN [KJV] See (GIVE, SPARE) LIFE, REVIVE

QUICKLY (104) [QUICK]

Ge 24:18 and she **q** lowered the jug for him to drink.
24:20 So she **q** emptied the jug into the watering trough
24:46 She **q** lowered the jug from her shoulder so I could
24:64 looked up and saw Isaac, she **q** dismounted.
27:20 "How were you able to find it so **q**, my son?"
29:12 So Rachel **q** ran and told her father, Laban.
44:11 They **q** took their sacks from the backs of their
45: 2 and the news was **q** carried to Pharaoh's palace.
45:13 everything you have seen, and bring him to me **q**."
45:17 and return **q** to their homes in Canaan.
Ex 1: 7 they multiplied so **q** that they soon filled the land.
1:12 the more **q** the Israelites multiplied!
1:19 their babies so **q** that we cannot get there in time!
2:18 "How did you get the flocks watered so **q** today?"
10:16 Pharaoh **q** sent for Moses and Aaron. "I confess
12:11 Eat the food **q**, for this is the LORD's Passover.
12:33 of Israel to get out of the land as **q** as possible,
Nu 16:46 and carry it **q** among the people to make atonement
Dt 4:26 you will **q** disappear from the land you are
7:22 the wild animals would multiply too **q** for you.
9: 3 so that you will **q** conquer them and drive them
9:16 How **q** you had turned from the path the LORD
11:17 Then you will **q** die in that good land the LORD
Jos 8:19 into the city. They **q** captured it and set it on fire.
9: 2 These kings **q** combined their armies to fight
10: 6 The men of Gibeon **q** sent messengers to Joshua at
10: 6 they pleaded. "Come **q** and save us!
23:16 and you will **q** be wiped out from the good land he
Jdg 2:17 How **q** they turned away from the path of their
2:23 That is why the LORD did not **q** drive the nations
13:10 So she **q** ran and told her husband, "The man who
1Sa 13: 3 The news spread **q** among the Philistines that
17:48 closer to attack, David **q** ran out to meet him.
20:38 So the boy **q** gathered up the arrows and ran back
25:18 She **q** gathered two hundred loaves of bread,
25:23 she **q** got off her donkey and bowed low before
25:42 **Q** getting ready, she took along five of her servant
1Ki 1:49 the banquet table and **q** went their separate ways.
3:28 Word of the king's decision spread **q** throughout
12:18 he **q** jumped into his chariot and fled to Jerusalem.
18:45 a terrific rainstorm, and Ahab left **q** for Jezreel.
2Ki 4:29 Go **q** and lay the staff on the child's face."
9:13 They **q** spread out their cloaks on the bare steps
2Ch 10:18 he **q** jumped into his chariot and fled to Jerusalem.
29:36 for everything had been accomplished so **q**.
35:13 and brought them out **q** so the people could eat
Est 2: 9 He **q** ordered a special menu for her and provided
5: 5 and said, "Tell Haman to come **q** to a banquet,
Job 14: 2 the shadow of a passing cloud, we **q** disappear.
24:18 "But they disappear from the earth as **q** as foam is
Ps 22:19 You are my strength; come **q** to my aid!
31: 2 Bend down and listen to me; / rescue me **q**.
38:22 Come **q** to help me, O Lord my savior.
40:13 rescue me! / Come **q**, LORD, and help me.
55: 8 How **q** I would escape— / far away from this wild
69:17 answer me **q**, for I am in deep trouble!
70: 1 rescue me! / Come **q**, LORD, and help me.
79: 8 Let your tenderhearted mercies **q** meet our needs,
81:14 How **q** I would then subdue their enemies!
102: 2 your ear / and answer me **q** when I call to you,
106:13 Yet how **q** they forgot what he had done!
143: 7 Come **q**, LORD, and answer me, / for my
Pr 13:11 Wealth from get-rich-quick schemes **q** disappears;
19: 2 a person who moves too **q** may go the wrong way.
Ecc 7: 6 Indeed, a fool's laughter is **q** gone, like thorns
SS 8:14 "Come **q**, my love! Move like a swift gazelle
Isa 40: 6 Their beauty fades as **q** as the beauty of flowers in
58: 8 Yes, your healing will come **q**. Your godliness will
58: 9 will answer. 'Yes, I am here,' he will **q** reply.

Jer 12:16 And if these nations **q** learn the ways of my
Eze 15: 4 be used for fuel, and even as fuel, it burns too **q**.
17: 5 where it would grow as **q** as a willow tree.
Da 2:25 Then Arioch **q** took Daniel to the king and said,
Joel 3:11 Come **q**, all you nations everywhere!
Mt 5:25 Come to terms **q** with your enemy before it is too
13: 5 soil with underlying rock. The plants sprang up **q**,
13:22 but all too **q** the message is crowded out by the
14:35 The news of their arrival spread **q** throughout the
21:20 and asked, "How did the fig tree wither so **q**?"
28: 7 go **q** and tell his disciples he has been raised from
28: 8 The women ran **q** from the tomb. They were very
Mk 1:28 The news of what he had done spread **q** through
2: 1 and the news of his arrival spread **q** through the
4: 5 soil with underlying rock. The plant sprang up **q**,
4:19 but all too **q** the message is crowded out by the
Lk 1:58 The word spread **q** to her neighbors and relatives
8:14 but all too **q** the message is crowded out by the
14:21 'Go **q** into the streets and alleys of the city
18: 8 I tell you, he will grant justice to them **q**! But when
19: 6 Zacchaeus **q** climbed down and took Jesus to his
Jn 9: 4 All of us must **q** carry out the tasks assigned us by
Ac 16:22 A mob **q** formed against Paul and Silas,
19:17 The story of what happened spread **q** all through
22:29 The soldiers who were about to interrogate Paul **q**
24:11 You can **q** discover that it was no more than
25:16 I **q** pointed out to them that Roman law does not
26:28 you think you can make me a Christian so **q**?"
26:29 Paul replied, "Whether **q** or not, I pray to God that
Ro 9:28 his sentence upon the earth / **q** and with finality."
Gal 5: 9 a little yeast spreads **q** through the whole batch of
Tit 3:12 do your best to meet me at Nicopolis as **q** as you
1Pe 1:24 their beauty fades as **q** as the beauty of
Rev 3:11 Look, I am coming **q**. Hold on to what you have,
11:14 is past, but look, now the third terror is coming **q**.

QUIET (39) [QUIETED, QUIETER, QUIETLY, QUIETNESS]

Ex 17: 2 to drink!" they demanded. "**Q**!" Moses replied.
Dt 27: 9 all Israel as follows: "O Israel, be **q** and listen!
Jdg 16: 2 They kept **q** during the night, saying to themselves,
18:19 "Be **q** and come with us," they said. "Be a father
1Sa 16:16 The harp music will **q** you, and you will soon be
2Ki 2: 3 "**Q**!" Elisha answered. "Of course I know it."
2: 5 "**Q**!" he answered again. "Of course I know it."
1Ch 4:40 pastures there, and the land was **q** and peaceful.
22: 9 I will give peace and **q** to Israel during his reign.
2Ch 25:16 Be **q** now before I have you killed!"
Est 4:14 If you keep **q** at a time like this, deliverance for the
7: 4 we had only been sold as slaves, I could remain **q**,
Job 6:24 I want is a reasonable answer—then I will keep **q**.
13: 5 Please be **q**! That's the smartest thing you could
34:29 When he is **q**, who can make trouble? But when he
Ps 9:16 themselves in their own snares. / ***Q Interlude***
55: 7 far away / to the **q** of the wilderness. / *Interlude*
131: 2 just as a small child is **q** with its mother.
Ecc 3: 7 to mend. / A time to be **q** and a time to speak up.
9:17 the **q** words of a wise person are better than the
10: 4 A **q** spirit can overcome even great mistakes.
Isa 14: 7 But at last the land is at rest and is **q**. Finally it can
33:20 You will see Jerusalem, a city **q** and secure.
Jer 30:10 and will have peace and **q** in their own land,
31: 9 They will walk beside **q** streams and not stumble.
46:27 Israel will return and will have peace and **q**,
Am 5:13 So those who are wise will keep **q**, for it is an evil
Mt 20:31 The crowd told them to be **q**, but they only shouted
Mk 4:39 the wind and said to the water, "**Q** down!"
10:48 "Be **q**!" some of the people yelled at him. But he
Lk 19:40 He replied, "If they kept **q**, the stones along the
Ac 12:17 He motioned for them to **q** down and told them
13:16 So Paul stood, lifted his hand to **q** them,
19:35 At last the mayor was able to **q** them down enough
21:40 on the stairs and motioned to the people to be **q**.
1Co 4:21 or should I come with **q** love and gentleness?
1Th 4:11 to live a **q** life, minding your own business
Heb 12:11 But afterward there will be a **q** harvest of right
1Pe 3: 4 the unfading beauty of a gentle and **q** spirit,

QUIETED (3) [QUIET]

Ne 8:11 the Levites, too, **q** the people, telling them, "Hush!
Ps 65: 7 You **q** the raging oceans / with their pounding
131: 2 But I have stilled and **q** myself, / just as a small

QUIETER (1) [QUIET]

Mk 6:32 They left by boat for a **q** spot.

QUIETLY (26) [QUIET]

Jdg 4:21 Jael **q** crept up to him with a hammer and tent peg.
Ru 3: 7 Then Ruth came **q**, uncovered his feet, and lay
1Sa 12: 7 Now stand here **q** before the LORD as I remind
29: 7 Please don't upset them, but go back **q**."
2Sa 15:27 and Abiathar should return **q** to the city with your
Job 16:12 "I was living **q** until he broke me apart. He took
29:10 The highest officials of the city stood **q**,
Ps 62: 1 I wait **q** before God, / for my salvation comes from
62: 5 I wait **q** before God, / for my hope is in him.
119:95 kill me, / I will **q** keep my mind on your decrees.
Pr 29:11 vent to anger, but a wise person **q** holds it back.
Isa 18: 4 "I will watch **q** from my dwelling place—
18: 4 as **q** as the heat rises on a summer day, or as the
32:18 My people will live in safety, **q** at home. They will
La 3:26 So it is good to wait **q** for salvation from the
Eze 24:17 You may sigh but only **q**. Let there be no wailing
Mic 4: 4 Everyone will live **q** in their own homes in peace
Hab 3:16 I will wait **q** for the coming day when disaster will
Mt 1:19 a just man, decided to break the engagement **q**,
Mk 7:30 her little girl was lying **q** in bed, and the demon
Lk 2:19 but Mary **q** treasured these things in her heart
8:35 been possessed by demons sitting **q** at Jesus' feet,
9:10 Then he slipped **q** away with them toward the town
22: 6 so they could arrest him **q** when the crowds
1Ti 2:11 should listen and learn **q** and submissively.
2:12 or have authority over them. Let them listen **q**.

QUIETNESS (6) [QUIET]

Job 3:26 I have no peace, no **q**. I have no rest; instead,
Ps 125: 5 who do evil. / And let Israel have **q** and peace.
128: 6 And may Israel have **q** and peace.
Isa 30:15 In **q** and confidence is your strength. But you
32:17 **Q** and confidence will fill the land forever.
1Ti 2: 2 so that we can live in peace and **q**, in godliness

QUILTS (1)

Pr 31:22 She **q** her own bedspreads. She dresses like royalty

QUIRINIUS (1)

Lk 2: 2 (This was the first census taken when **Q** was

QUIT (11) [QUITTING]

Jdg 9: 9 'Should I **q** producing the olive oil that blesses
9:11 'Should I **q** producing my sweet fruit just to wave
9:13 'Should I **q** producing the wine that cheers both
1Sa 23:28 So Saul **q** the chase and returned to fight the
Ecc 10: 4 If your boss is angry with you, don't **q**! A quiet
Jer 7: 3 Even now, if you **q** your evil ways, I will let you
22: 3 **Q** your evil deeds! Do not mistreat foreigners,
44:18 But ever since we **q** burning incense to the Queen
Eze 45: 9 **Q** robbing and cheating my people out of their
2Co 4: 8 We are perplexed, but we don't give up and **q**.
Col 3:21 they will become discouraged and **q** trying.

QUITE (18)

Ge 22:19 where Abraham lived for **q** some time.
39: 4 So Joseph naturally became **q** a favorite with him.
40: 4 They remained in prison for **q** some time,
Jdg 18:20 The young priest was **q** happy to go with them,
18:22 When the people from the tribe of Dan were **q** a
1Sa 3: 1 were very rare, and visions were **q** uncommon.
Ne 5:15 This was **q** a contrast to the former governors who
Est 9: 1 to destroy them, but **q** the opposite happened.
Mt 7:29 **q** unlike the teachers of religious law.
20:26 But among you it should be **q** different.
Mk 1:22 **q** unlike the teachers of religious law.
10:43 But among you it should be **q** different.
Ac 24:22 Felix, who was **q** familiar with the Way,
24:26 so he sent for him **q** often and talked with him.
2Co 4:17 For our present troubles are **q** small and won't last
12:10 I am **q** content with my weaknesses and with
1Th 5: 2 for you know **q** well that the day of the Lord will
2Pe 3:16 mean something **q** different from what he meant,

QUITTING (1) [QUIT]

Rev 2: 3 You have patiently suffered for me without **q**.

QUIVER (4) [QUIVERED, QUIVERS]

Ge 27: 3 and a **q** full of arrows out into the open country,
Ps 127: 5 How happy is the man whose **q** is full of them!
Isa 49: 2 of his hand. I am like a sharp arrow in his **q**.
Eze 21:21 They will cast lots by shaking arrows from the **q**.

QUIVERED (1) [QUIVER]

Hab 3:16 inside when I heard all this; my lips **q** with fear.

QUIVERS (1) [QUIVER]

Job 39:25 It **q** at the noise of battle and the shout of the

QUOTA (2) [QUOTAS]

Ex 5:13 "Meet your daily **q** of bricks, just as you did
5:18 but you must still deliver the regular **q** of bricks."

QUOTAS (2) [QUOTA]

Ex 5: 8 But don't reduce their production **q** by a single
5:14 "Why haven't you met your **q** either yesterday

QUOTE (4) [QUOTED, QUOTING]

Jer 31:29 "The people will no longer **q** this proverb.
Eze 12:22 "Son of man, what is that proverb they **q** in Israel:
18: 2 "Why do you **q** this proverb in the land of Israel:
Lk 4:23 "Probably you will **q** me that proverb, 'Physician,

QUOTED (3) [QUOTE]

Lk 24:27 Then Jesus **q** passages from the writings of Moses
Ac 2:29 to himself when he spoke these words I have **q**,
Heb 4: 7 David a long time later in the words already **q**:

QUOTING (1) [QUOTE]

Eze 12:23 an end to this proverb, and you will soon stop **q** it.

R

RAAMAH (5)

Ge 10: 7 Cush were Seba, Havilah, Sabtah, **R**, and Sabteca.
10: 7 The descendants of **R** were Sheba and Dedan.
1Ch 1: 9 Cush were Seba, Havilah, Sabtah, **R**, and Sabteca.
1: 9 The descendants of **R** were Sheba and Dedan.
Eze 27:22 of Sheba and **R** came with all kinds of spices,

RAAMSES [KJV] See RAMESES

RABBAH (18)

Dt 3:11 It can still be seen in the Ammonite city of **R**.)
Jos 13:25 as far as the town of Aroer just west of **R**.
15:60 also Kiriath-baal (that is, Kiriath-jearim) and **R**—
2Sa 11: 1 In the process they laid siege to the city of **R**.
12:26 army were successfully ending their siege of **R**,
12:27 "I have fought against **R** and captured its water
12:29 So David led the rest of his army to **R** and captured
12:31 He also made slaves of the people of **R** and forced
17:27 was warmly greeted by Shobi son of Nahash of **R**,
1Ch 20: 1 In the process they laid siege to the city of **R**
20: 2 When David arrived at **R**, he removed the crown
20: 3 He also made slaves of the people of **R** and forced
Jer 49: 2 says the LORD, "by destroying your city of **R**.
49: 3 the town of Ai is destroyed. Weep, O people of **R**!
Eze 21:20 one road going to Ammon and its capital, **R**,
21:21 uncertain whether to attack Jerusalem or **R**.
25: 5 And I will turn the city of **R** into a pasture for
Am 1:14 So I will send down fire on the walls of **R**, and all

RABBI (3)

Mt 23: 7 get on the streets, and they enjoy being called '**R**.'
23: 8 Don't ever let anyone call you '**R**,' for you have
Jn 1:38 They replied, "**R**" (which means Teacher),

RABBITH (1)

Jos 19:20 **R**, Kishion, Ebez,

RABBLE (2)

Nu 11: 4 Then the foreign **r** who were traveling with the
Dt 13:13 that some worthless **r** among you have led their

RABMAG [KJV] See (CHIEF) OFFICER

RABSARIS [KJV] See (FIELD) COMMANDER

RACAL (1)

1Sa 30:29 **R**, the towns of the Jerahmeelites, the towns of the

RACE (35) [RACED, RACES, RACING]

Ge 6: 2 of God saw the beautiful women of the human **r**
6: 7 "I will completely wipe out this human **r** that I
Dt 2:10 and powerful **r** of giants called the Emites had
2:10 were as tall as the Anakites, another **r** of giants.
2:21 They were a numerous and powerful **r**, as tall as
32: 8 to the nations, / when he divided up the human **r**,
Ezr 9: 2 So the holy **r** has become polluted by these mixed
Est 3: 8 "There is a certain **r** of people scattered through
Ps 14: 2 looks down from heaven / on the entire human **r**;
19: 5 It rejoices like a great athlete / eager to run the **r**.
33:13 down from heaven / and sees the whole human **r**.
53: 2 looks down from heaven / on the entire human **r**;
Pr 6:18 a heart that plots evil, / feet that **r** to do wrong,
Ecc 1:13 God has dealt a tragic existence to the human **r**.
9:11 The fastest runner doesn't always win the **r**,
Isa 6: 5 for I am a sinful man and a member of a sinful **r**.
41: 4 directing the affairs of the human **r** as each new
Jer 12: 5 makes you tired, how will you **r** against horses?
Da 3: 7 the people, whatever their **r** or nation or language,
3:29 any people, whatever their **r** or nation or language,
4: 1 sent this message to the people of every **r**
6:25 Darius sent this message to the people of every **r**
7:14 so that people of every **r** and nation and language
Na 2: 4 The chariots **r** recklessly along the streets
Hab 1: 8 Their horsemen **r** forward from distant places.
Mt 24:22 is shortened, the entire human **r** will be destroyed.
Mk 13:20 of calamity, the entire human **r** will be destroyed.
Ro 5:12 Adam sinned, sin entered the entire human **r**.
1Co 9:24 Remember that in a **r** everyone runs, but only one
Php 2:16 I will be proud that I did not lose the **r** and that my
3:14 I strain to reach the end of the **r** and receive the
2Ti 4: 7 I have fought a good fight, I have finished the **r**,
Heb 11:40 for they can't receive the prize at the end of the **r**
until we finish the **r**.
12: 1 And let us run with endurance the **r** that God has

RACED (1) [RACE]

Ac 9:42 The news **r** through the whole town, and many

RACES (3) [RACE]

Isa 21: 4 My mind reels; my heart **r**. The sleep I once
Da 3: 4 "People of all **r** and nations and languages,
5:19 made him so great that people of all **r** and nations

RACHAB [KJV] See RAHAB

RACHEL (41) [RACHEL'S]

Ge 29: 6 here comes his daughter **R** with the sheep."
29: 9 **R** arrived with her father's sheep, for she was a
29: 11 Then Jacob kissed **R**, and tears came to his eyes.
29: 12 So **R** quickly ran and told her father, Laban.
29: 16 who was the oldest, and her younger sister, **R**.
29: 17 but **R** was beautiful in every way, with a lovely
29: 18 Since Jacob was in love with **R**, he told her father,
29: 18 "I'll work for you seven years if you'll give me **R**,
29: 20 spent the next seven years working to pay for **R**.
29: 25 raged at Laban. "I worked seven years for **R**.
29: 27 the bridal week is over, and you can have **R**, too—
29: 28 Jacob had married Leah, Laban gave him **R**, too.
29: 29 And Laban gave **R** a servant, Bilhah, to be her
29: 30 So Jacob slept with **R**, too, and he loved her more
29: 31 LORD let her have a child, while **R** was childless.
30: 1 When **R** saw that she wasn't having any children,
30: 3 Then **R** told him, "Sleep with my servant, Bilhah,
30: 4 So **R** gave him Bilhah to be his wife, and Jacob
30: 6 **R** named him Dan, for she said, "God has
30: 8 **R** named him Naphtali, for she said, "I have had
30: 14 **R** begged Leah to give some of them to her.
30: 15 **R** said, "I will let him sleep with you tonight in
30: 25 Soon after Joseph was born to **R**, Jacob said to
31: 4 Jacob called **R** and Leah out to the field where he
31: 14 **R** and Leah said, "That's fine with us!
31: 19 **R** stole her father's household gods and took them
31: 32 But Jacob didn't know that **R** had taken them.
31: 34 **R** had taken the household gods and had stuffed
31: 35 "Forgive my not getting up, Father," **R** explained.
33: 2 and her children next, and **R** and Joseph last.
33: 7 Finally, **R** and Joseph came and made their bows.
35: 18 **R** was about to die, but with her last breath she
35: 19 So **R** died and was buried on the way to Ephrath
35: 24 The sons of **R** were Joseph and Benjamin.
46: 19 The sons of Jacob's wife **R** were Joseph
46: 22 were the descendants of Jacob and his wife **R**.
46: 25 the servant given to **R** by her father, Laban.
48: 7 from Paddan, **R** died in the land of Canaan.
Ru 4: 11 woman who is now coming into your home like **R**
Jer 31: 15 **R** weeps for her children, refusing to be
Mt 2: 18 **R** weeps for her children, / refusing to be

RACHEL'S (5) [RACHEL]

Ge 30: 22 Then God remembered **R** plight and answered her
31: 33 didn't find the gods. Finally, he went into **R** tent.
35: 16 But **R** pains of childbirth began while they were
35: 25 sons of Bilhah, **R** servant, were Dan and Naphtali.
1Sa 10: 2 you will see two men beside **R** tomb at Zelzah,

RACING (3) [RACE]

Isa 5: 26 the earth, and they will come **r** toward Jerusalem.
63: 13 They were like fine stallions **r** through the desert,
Jer 12: 5 to me, "If **r** against mere men makes you tired,

RACKED (4)

Ps 38: 6 I am bent over and **r** with pain. / My days are filled
La 1: 13 has made me desolate, **r** with sickness all day long.
Eze 30: 16 Pelusium will be **r** with pain; Thebes will be torn
Mt 8: 6 servant lies in bed, paralyzed and **r** with pain."

RACKETEERS (1)

Eze 22: 12 There are hired murderers, loan **r**, and extortioners

RADDAI (1)

1Ch 2: 14 his fourth was Nethanel, his fifth was **R**,

RADIANCE (4) [RADIANT, RADIATES]

Ex 34: 30 and the people of Israel saw the **r** of Moses' face,
Ps 50: 2 the perfection of beauty, / God shines in glorious **r**.
Isa 60: 3 your light. Mighty kings will come to see your **r**.
Lk 2: 9 and the **r** of the Lord's glory surrounded them.

RADIANT (6) [RADIANCE]

Ps 19: 5 It bursts forth like a **r** bridegroom / after his
34: 5 Those who look to him for help will be **r** with joy;
80: 1 above the cherubim, / display your **r** glory
Pr 4: 22 and **r** health to anyone who discovers their
Jer 31: 12 They will be **r** because of the many gifts the
Lk 11: 36 no dark corners, then your whole life will be **r**,

RADIATES (1) [RADIANCE]

SS 7: 5 and the sheen of your hair **r** royalty.

RAFTERS (4) [RAFTS]

1Ki 7: 3 It had a cedar roof supported by forty-five **r** that
2Ch 34: 11 stone for the walls and timber for the **r** and beams.
Ps 104: 3 you lay out the **r** of your home in the rain clouds.
Ecc 10: 18 lets the roof leak, and soon the **r** begin to rot.

RAFTS (3) [RAFTERS]

1Ki 5: 9 to the Mediterranean Sea and build them into **r**.
5: 9 Then we will break the **r** apart and deliver the
2Ch 2: 16 and will float the logs in **r** down the coast of the

RAG (3) [RAGGED, RAGS]

La 1: 8 so she has been tossed away like a filthy **r**.
1: 17 Let them be thrown away like a filthy **r**!"
Eze 36: 17 To me their conduct was as filthy as a bloody **r**.

RAGAU [KJV] See REU

RAGE (26) [ENRAGED, RAGED, RAGES, RAGING]

Ge 30: 2 Jacob flew into a **r**. "Am I God?" he asked.
Nu 22: 27 In a fit of **r** Balaam beat it again with his staff.
24: 10 King Balak flew into a **r** against Balaam.
1Sa 14: 23 and the battle continued to **r** even out beyond
20: 30 Saul boiled with **r** at Jonathan. "You stupid son of
2Ki 5: 12 So Naaman turned and went away in a **r**.
2Ch 25: 10 with Judah, and they returned home in a great **r**.
Ne 4: 1 the wall. He flew into a **r** and mocked the Jews,
Est 3: 5 or show him respect, he was filled with **r**.
7: 7 Then the king jumped to his feet in a **r** and went
Ps 2: 1 Why do the nations **r**? / Why do the people waste
6: 1 me in your anger / or discipline me in your **r**.
37: 8 Stop your anger! / Turn from your **r**! / Do not envy
38: 1 me in your anger! / Don't discipline me in your **r**!
78: 49 his fierce anger— / all his fury, **r**, and hostility.
119: 139 I am overwhelmed with **r**, / for my enemies have
Isa 8: 21 they will **r** and shake their fists at heaven and curse
14: 6 persecuted the people with unceasing blows of **r**
Da 3: 13 Then Nebuchadnezzar flew into a **r** and ordered
3: 19 Abednego that his face became distorted with **r**.
Na 1: 6 His **r** blazes forth like fire, and the mountains
Lk 6: 11 the enemies of Jesus were wild with **r** and began to
Ac 4: 25 your servant, saying, / 'Why did the nations **r**?
7: 54 and they shook their fists in **r**.
Eph 4: 31 of all bitterness, **r**, anger, harsh words, and slander,
Col 3: 8 **r**, malicious behavior, slander, and dirty language.

RAGED (8) [RAGE]

Ge 29: 25 "What sort of trick is this?" Jacob **r** at Laban.
Nu 11: 1 Fire from the LORD **r** among them and destroyed
2Sa 18: 8 The battle **r** all across the countryside, and more
1Ki 22: 35 The battle **r** all that day, and Ahab was propped up
2Ki 19: 27 you do. / I know the way you have **r** against me.
2Ch 18: 34 The battle **r** all that day, and Ahab propped himself
Isa 37: 28 you do. / I know the way you have **r** against me.
Ac 27: 20 The terrible storm **r** unabated for many days,

RAGES (2) [RAGE]

Ezr 8: 22 but his fierce anger **r** against those who abandon
Ps 50: 3 in his way, / and a great storm **r** around him.

RAGGED (2) [RAG]

Jos 9: 5 They put on **r** clothes and worn-out,
Mic 2: 8 making them as **r** as men who have just come

RAGING (16) [RAGE]

2Sa 5: 20 "He burst through my enemies like a **r** flood!"
1Ch 14: 11 "He used me to burst through my enemies like a **r**
Job 40: 23 It is not disturbed by **r** rivers, not even when the
Ps 38: 7 A **r** fever burns within me, / and my health is
42: 7 I hear the tumult of the **r** seas / as your waves
65: 7 You quieted the **r** oceans / with their pounding
93: 4 But mightier than the violent **r** of the seas,
124: 5 Yes, the **r** waters of their fury / would have
Jer 49: 23 Their hearts are troubled like a wild sea in a **r**
La 2: 3 He consumes the whole land of Israel like a **r** fire.
Hos 7: 6 and in the morning it flames forth like a **r** fire.
Ob 1: 18 At that time Israel will be a **r** fire, and Edom,
Jnh 1: 15 picked Jonah up and threw him into the **r** sea,
Hab 3: 10 and trembled. Onward swept the **r** waters.
Lk 8: 24 So Jesus rebuked the wind and the **r** waves.
Heb 10: 27 and the **r** fire that will consume his enemies.

RAGS (6) [RAG]

Pr 23: 21 Too much sleep clothes a person with **r**.
Isa 30: 22 You will throw them out like filthy **r**. "Ugh!"
64: 6 our righteous deeds, we find they are but filthy **r**.
Jer 38: 11 where he found some old **r** and discarded clothing.
38: 12 "Put these **r** under your armpits to protect you
Jas 5: 2 and your fine clothes are moth-eaten **r**.

RAGUEL [KJV] See REUEL

RAHAB (10) [RAHAB'S]

Jos 2: 1 and came to the house of a prostitute named **R**
2: 3 So the king of Jericho sent orders to **R**: "Bring out
2: 4 **R**, who had hidden the two men, replied,
2: 8 that night, **R** went up on the roof to talk with them.
6: 17 Only **R** the prostitute and the others in her house
6: 23 The young men went in and brought out **R**,
6: 25 So Joshua spared **R** the prostitute and her relatives
Mt 1: 5 Salmon was the father of Boaz (his mother was **R**).
Heb 11: 31 It was by faith that **R** the prostitute did not die with
Jas 2: 25 **R** the prostitute is another example of this.

RAHAB'S (1) [RAHAB]

Jos 2: 15 Then, since **R** house was built into the city wall,

RAHAM (2)

1Ch 2: 44 Shema was the father of **R**. **R** was the father of Jorkeam.

RAHEL [KJV] See RACHEL

RAID (4) [RAIDED, RAIDERS, RAIDING]

1Sa 27: 10 "Where did you make your **r** today?"
30: 1 they found that the Amalekites had made a **r** into
2Sa 3: 22 and some of David's troops returned from a **r**,
Pr 24: 15 And don't **r** the house where the godly live.

RAIDED (5) [RAID]

1Ch 14: 9 had arrived in the valley of Rephaim and **r** it.
14: 13 the Philistines returned and **r** the valley again.
2Ch 25: 13 the hired troops that Amaziah had sent home **r**
28: 18 And the Philistines had **r** towns located in the
Job 1: 15 when the Sabeans **r** us. They stole all the animals

RAIDERS (8) [RAID]

2Ki 5: 2 Now groups of Aramean **r** had invaded the land of
6: 23 the Aramean **r** stayed away from the land of Israel.
13: 20 Groups of Moabite **r** used to invade the land each
13: 21 were burying a man, they spied a band of these **r**.
24: 2 and Ammonite **r** against Judah to destroy it,
1Ch 12: 21 They helped David chase down bands of **r**,
Job 1: 17 "Three bands of Chaldean **r** have stolen your
Isa 16: 4 have ceased and enemy **r** have disappeared,

RAIDING (7) [RAID]

Jdg 15: 9 setting up camp in Judah and **r** the town of Lehi.
1Sa 13: 17 Three **r** parties soon left the camp of the
14: 15 the field, including even the outposts and **r** parties.
23: 27 Saul that the Philistines were **r** Israel again.
27: 8 and his men spent their time **r** the Geshurites,
30: 14 We were on our way back from **r** the Kerethites in
2Sa 4: 2 who were captains of Ishbosheth's **r** parties.

RAILINGS (1)

1Ki 10: 12 The king used the almug wood to make **r** for the

RAIMENT [KJV] See CLOAK, CLOTH(ED, -ES, -ING), COATS, GARB, GARMENT(S), ROBE(S)

RAIN (98) [RAINBOW, RAINED, RAINFALL, RAINING, RAINS, RAINSTORM, RAINY]

Ge 2: 5 the earth, for the LORD God had not sent any **r**.
7: 4 today I will begin forty days and forty nights of **r**.
7: 11 and the **r** fell in mighty torrents from the sky.
7: 12 The **r** continued to fall for forty days and forty
Ex 16: 4 I'm going to **r** down food from heaven for you.
Dt 11: 11 It is a land of hills and valleys with plenty of **r**—
11: 17 He will shut up the sky and hold back the **r**,
28: 12 The LORD will send **r** at the proper time from his
28: 24 The LORD will turn your **r** into sand and dust,
32: 2 My teaching will fall on you like **r**; / my speech
32: 2 My words will fall like **r** on tender grass,
33: 13 with the choice gift of **r** from the heavens,
Jdg 5: 4 and the cloudy skies poured down **r**.
1Sa 12: 17 You know that it does not **r** at this time of the year
12: 17 I will ask the LORD to send thunder and **r** today.
12: 18 to the LORD, and the LORD sent thunder and **r**.
2Sa 1: 21 let there be no dew or **r** upon you or your slopes.
22: 12 veiling his approach with dense **r** clouds.
1Ki 8: 35 "If the skies are shut up and there is no **r**
8: 36 and send **r** on your land that you have given to
17: 1 or **r** during the next few years unless I give the
17: 14 containers until the time when the LORD sends **r**
18: 1 to King Ahab. Tell him that I will soon send **r**!"
18: 44 If you don't hurry, the **r** will stop you!' "
2Ki 3: 17 You will see neither wind nor **r**, says the LORD,
2Ch 6: 26 "If the skies are shut up and there is no **r**
6: 27 and send **r** on your land that you have given to
7: 13 times I might shut up the heavens so that no **r** falls,
Job 5: 10 He gives **r** for the earth. He sends water for the
12: 15 If he holds back the **r**, the earth becomes a desert.
20: 23 of trouble. May God **r** down his anger upon him.
26: 8 He wraps the **r** in his thick clouds, and the clouds
28: 25 and determined how much **r** should fall.
28: 26 He made the laws of the **r** and prepared a path for
29: 23 They longed for me to speak as they longed for **r**.
29: 23 for my words were as refreshing as the spring **r**.
36: 27 draws up the water vapor and then distills it into **r**.
36: 28 The **r** pours down from the clouds, and everyone
37: 6 to fall on the earth and tells the **r** to pour down.
38: 25 "Who created a channel for the torrents of **r**?
38: 26 Who makes the **r** fall on barren land, in a desert
38: 27 Who sends the **r** that satisfies the parched ground
38: 28 "Does the **r** have a father? Where does dew come
38: 34 "Can you shout to the clouds and make it **r**?
Ps 18: 11 veiling his approach with dense **r** clouds.
65: 10 You drench the plowed ground with **r**,
68: 8 the earth trembled, and the heavens poured **r**
68: 9 You sent abundant **r**, O God, / to refresh the weary
77: 17 The clouds poured down their **r**; / the thunder
104: 3 you lay out the rafters of your home in the **r**
104: 13 You send **r** on the mountains from your heavenly
105: 32 Instead of **r**, he sent murderous hail, / and flashes
135: 7 over the earth. / He sends the lightning with the **r**
143: 6 I thirst for you as parched land thirsts for **r**.
147: 8 the heavens with clouds, / provides **r** for the earth,
Pr 3: 20 earth burst forth, and the clouds poured down **r**.
16: 15 there is life; his favor refreshes like a gentle **r**.
25: 14 gift is like clouds and wind that don't bring **r**.
25: 23 As surely as a wind from the north brings **r**,
26: 1 more than snow with summer or **r** with harvest.
28: 3 poor is like a pounding **r** that destroys the crops.
SS 2: 11 For the winter is past, and the **r** is over and gone.
Isa 4: 6 daytime heat and a hiding place from storms and **r**.
5: 6 command the clouds / to drop no more **r** on it."
24: 4 dries up, the crops wither, the skies refuse to **r**.

25: 4 you are a shelter from the **r** and the heat.
28: 2 Like a mighty hailstorm and a torrential **r**,
30:23 Then the LORD will bless you with **r** at planting
44:14 the cedar in the forest to be nourished by the **r**.
55:10 "The **r** and snow come down from the heavens
Jer 5:24 for he gives us **r** each spring and fall, assuring us
10:13 over the earth. / He sends the lightning with the **r**
14: 1 explaining why he was holding back the **r**:
14: 4 The ground is parched and cracked for lack of **r**.
14:22 Can any of the foreign gods send us **r**? Does it fall
51:16 over the earth. / He sends the lightning with the **r**
Eze 22:24 like an uncleared wilderness or a desert without **r**.
38:22 I will send torrential **r**, hailstones, fire, and burning
39: 6 And I will **r** down fire on Magog and on all your
Hos 2:21 down water on the earth in answer to its cries for **r**.
Am 4: 7 "I kept the **r** from falling when you needed it the
4: 7 I sent **r** on one town but withheld it from another.
4: 7 **R** fell on one field, while another field withered
5: 8 from the oceans and pours it down as **r** on the land.
9: 6 from the oceans and pours it down as **r** on the land.
Mic 5: 7 sent by the LORD or like **r** falling on the grass,
Zec 10: 1 Ask the LORD for **r** in the spring, and he will
10: 1 who makes storm clouds that drop showers of **r**
14:17 the King, the LORD Almighty, will have no **r**.
Mt 5:45 and he sends **r** on the just and on the unjust,
7:25 Though the **r** comes in torrents and the floodwaters
Lk 4:25 when there was no **r** for three and a half years
Ac 14:17 such as sending you **r** and good crops and giving
Heb 6: 7 When the ground soaks up the **r** that falls on it
Jas 5:17 and yet when he prayed earnestly that no **r** would
5:18 Then he prayed for **r**, and down it poured.
Jude 1:12 like clouds blowing over dry land without giving **r**,
Rev 11: 6 so that no **r** will fall for as long as they prophesy.

RAINBOW (6) [RAIN]

Ge 9:13 I have placed my **r** in the clouds. It is the sign of
9:14 over the earth, the **r** will be seen in the clouds,
9:16 When I see the **r** in the clouds, I will remember the
Eze 1:28 a glowing halo, like a **r** shining through the clouds.
Rev 4: 3 the glow of an emerald circled his throne like a **r**.
10: 1 surrounded by a cloud, with a **r** over his head.

RAINED (4) [RAIN]

Ge 19:24 Then the LORD **r** down fire and burning sulfur
Ps 78:24 and **r** down manna for them to eat. / He gave them
78:27 He **r** down meat as thick as dust— / birds as
Lk 17:29 Then fire and burning sulfur **r** down from heaven

RAINFALL (1) [RAIN]

1Ki 17: 7 dried up, for there was no **r** anywhere in the land.

RAINING (2) [RAIN]

Ezr 10: 9 the seriousness of the matter and because it was **r**.
Ps 18:12 the clouds, / **r** down hail and burning coals.

RAINS (16) [RAIN]

Ge 8: 2 ceased their gushing, and the torrential **r** stopped.
Lev 26: 4 I will send the seasonal **r**. The land will then yield
Dt 11:14 then he will send the **r** in their proper seasons
2Sa 23: 4 like the refreshing **r** that bring tender grass from
Ps 11: 6 He **r** down blazing coals on the wicked,
72: 6 May his reign be as refreshing as the springtime **r**
84: 6 where pools of blessing collect after the **r**!
Ecc 11: 3 When the clouds are heavy, the **r** come down.
Jer 3: 3 That is why even the spring **r** have failed. For you
Hos 6: 3 of dawn or the coming of **r** in early spring."
Joel 2:23 For the **r** he sends are an expression of his grace.
2:23 Once more the autumn **r** will come, as well as the
r of spring.
2:28 "Then after I have poured out my **r** again, I will
Mt 7:27 When the **r** and floods come and the winds beat
Jas 5: 7 Consider the farmers who eagerly look for the **r** in

RAINSTORM (3) [RAIN, STORM]

1Ki 18:41 a good meal! For I hear a mighty **r** coming!"
18:45 A heavy wind brought a terrific **r**, and Ahab left
Eze 13:11 A heavy **r** will undermine it; great hailstones

RAINY (3) [RAIN]

Ezr 10:13 This is the **r** season, so we cannot stay out here
Pr 27:15 is as annoying as the constant dripping on a **r** day.
Ac 28: 2 It was cold and **r**, so they built a fire on the shore

RAISE (55) [RAISED, RAISES, RAISING]

Ex 10:12 "**R** your hand over the land of Egypt to bring on
14:26 said to Moses, "**R** your hand over the sea again.
17:16 "They have dared to **r** their fist against the
Dt 18:15 "The LORD your God will **r** up for you a
18:18 I will **r** up a prophet like you from among their
25: 9 'This is what happens to a man who refuses to **r** up
32:40 Now I **r** my hand to heaven / and declare,
1Sa 2:35 "Then I will **r** up a faithful priest who will serve
2Sa 7:12 when you die, I will **r** up one of your descendants,
1Ki 14:14 And the LORD will **r** up a king over Israel who
2Ki 4:28 a son. And didn't I tell you not to **r** my hopes?"
19:22 Against whom did you **r** your voice?
1Ch 17:11 For when you die, I will **r** up one of your sons,
Ps 75: 4 I told the wicked, 'Don't **r** your fists!
75: 6 from the wilderness— / can **r** another person up.
107:38 How he blesses them! / They **r** large families there,
Isa 11:12 He will **r** a flag among the nations for Israel to
18: 3 When I **r** my battle flag on the mountain, let all the
37:23 Against whom did you **r** your voice?
38:18 praise you; / they cannot **r** their voices in praise.
42: 2 he will not shout or **r** his voice in public.
45:13 I will **r** up Cyrus to fulfill my righteous purpose,
62:10 out the boulders; **r** a flag for all the nations to see.
Jer 15: 6 I will **r** my clenched fists to destroy you.
30: 9 and David their king, whom I will **r** up for them.
50: 2 **R** a signal flag so everyone will know that Babylon
50:32 will stumble and fall, and no one will **r** you up.
51:12 **R** the battle flag against Babylon!
51:25 "I will **r** my fist against you, to roll you down
Eze 13: 9 I will **r** my fist against all the lying prophets,
25:13 I will **r** my fist of judgment against Edom.
25:16 I will **r** my fist of judgment against the land of the
35: 3 and I will **r** my fist against you to destroy you
Da 11: 7 he will **r** an army and enter the fortress of the king
11:25 and **r** a great army against the king of the south.
Hos 2:23 plant a crop of Israelites and **r** them for myself!
5: 8 **R** the battle cry in Beth-aven! Lead on into battle,
Am 5: 2 forsaken on the ground, / with none to **r** her up."
Zec 2: 9 I will **r** my fist to crush them, and their own slaves
Mt 10: 8 Heal the sick, **r** the dead, cure those with leprosy,
12:19 or shout; / he will not **r** his voice in public.
Jn 2:19 this temple, and in three days I will **r** it up."
5:21 He will even **r** from the dead anyone he wants to,
6:39 but that I should **r** them to eternal life at the last
6:40 eternal life—that I should **r** them at the last day."
6:44 and at the last day I will **r** them from the dead.
6:54 have eternal life, and I will **r** them at the last day.
Ac 3:22 'The Lord your God will **r** up a Prophet like me
7:37 'God will **r** up a Prophet like me from among your
13:34 For God had promised to **r** him from the dead,
24:15 that he will **r** both the righteous and the ungodly.
26: 8 incredible to any of you that God can **r** the dead?
1Co 6:14 And God will **r** our bodies from the dead by his
2Co 1: 9 rely on ourselves, but on God who can **r** the dead.
4:14 who raised our Lord Jesus will also **r** us with Jesus

RAISED (117) [RAISE]

Ex 7:20 Moses **r** his staff and hit the water of the Nile.
10:13 So Moses **r** his staff, and the LORD caused an
14:21 Then Moses **r** his hand over the sea,
14:27 sun began to rise, Moses **r** his hand over the sea.
15:12 You **r** up your hand, / and the earth swallowed our
Lev 9:22 Aaron **r** his hands toward the people and blessed
Nu 20:11 Then Moses **r** his hand and struck the rock twice
Dt 9:17 So I **r** the stone tablets and dashed them to the
Jdg 2:16 Then the LORD **r** up judges to rescue the
3: 9 for help, the LORD **r** up a man to rescue them.
3:15 for help, the LORD **r** up a man to rescue them.
1Sa 7:13 the LORD's powerful hand was **r** against the
2Sa 12: 3 He **r** that little lamb, and it grew up with his
1Ki 8:54 where he had been kneeling with his hands **r**
11:14 Then the LORD **r** up Hadad the Edomite,
11:23 God also **r** up Rezon son of Eliada to be an enemy
2Ki 10: 6 where they had been **r** since childhood.
13: 5 So the LORD **r** up a deliverer to rescue the
2Ch 5:13 they **r** their voices and praised the LORD with
Ezr 10:12 Then the whole assembly **r** their voices
Ne 5: 1 and their wives **r** a cry of protest against their
Est 2: 7 her into his family and **r** her as his own daughter.
Job 38:15 and it stops the arm that is **r** in violence.
Ps 60: 4 But you have **r** a banner for those who honor you
80:15 have planted, / this son you have **r** for yourself.
118:16 The strong right arm of the LORD is **r** in triumph.
Isa 1: 2 "The children I **r** and cared for have turned against
5:25 That is why he has **r** his fist to crush them.
10:26 or when the LORD's staff was **r** to drown the
49:11 The highways will be **r** above the valleys.
49:21 Who bore these children? Who **r** them for me?' "
62: 9 You **r** it, and you will keep it, praising the LORD.
Jer 29:15 You may claim that the LORD has **r** up prophets
La 2:22 enemy has killed all the children I bore and **r**."
Eze 19: 3 She **r** one of her cubs / to become a strong young
36: 7 I have **r** my hand and sworn an oath that those
44:12 So I have **r** my hand and taken an oath that they
Da 12: 7 **r** both his hands toward heaven and took this
Hos 10:13 cultivated wickedness and **r** a thriving crop of sins.
Zec 14:10 But Jerusalem will be **r** up in its original place
Mt 11: 5 are cured, the deaf hear, the dead are **r** to life,
16:21 be killed, and he would be **r** on the third day.
17: 9 the Son of Man, have been **r** from the dead."
17:23 but three days later he will be **r** from the dead."
20:19 But on the third day he will be **r** from the dead."
26:32 But after I have been **r** from the dead, I will go
27:52 and women who had died were **r** from the dead
27:63 'After three days I will be **r** from the dead.'
28: 6 He has been **r** from the dead, just as he said would
28: 7 and tell his disciples he has been **r** from the dead,
Mk 12:26 But now, as to whether the dead will be **r**—
14:28 But after I am **r** from the dead, I will go ahead of
16: 6 He has been **r** from the dead! Look, this is where
Lk 7:22 are cured, the deaf hear, the dead are **r** to life,
9:22 but three days later I will be **r** from the dead."
20:35 For those worthy of being **r** from the dead won't
20:36 They are children of God **r** up to new life.
20:37 But now, as to whether the dead will be **r**—
Jn 2:22 After he was **r** from the dead, the disciples
12: 1 home of Lazarus—the man he had **r** from the dead.
12: 9 to see Lazarus, the man Jesus had **r** from the dead.
14:20 When I am **r** to life again, you will know that I am
21:14 to his disciples since he had been **r** from the dead.
Ac 2:24 the horrors of death and **r** him back to life again,
2:32 whom God **r** from the dead, and we all are
3:15 You killed the author of life, but God **r** him to life.
3:26 When God **r** up his servant, he sent him first to
4:10 man you crucified, but whom God **r** from the dead.
5:30 The God of our ancestors **r** Jesus from the dead
7:21 daughter found him and **r** him as her own son.
10:40 but God **r** him to life three days later. Then God
13:30 But God **r** him from the dead!
13:33 in that God **r** Jesus. This is what the second psalm
13:37 someone whom God **r** and whose body did not
27:40 **r** the foresail, and headed toward shore.
Ro 1: 4 **r** him from the dead by means of the Holy Spirit.
4:25 and he was **r** from the dead to make us right with
6: 4 And just as Christ was **r** from the dead by the
6: 5 with him in his death, we will also be **r** as he was.
7: 4 And now you are united with the one who was **r**
8:11 of God, who **r** Jesus from the dead, lives in you.
8:11 And just as he **r** Christ from the dead, he will give
8:34 is the one who died for us and was **r** to life for us
10: 9 and believe in your heart that God **r** him from the
1Co 6:14 just as he **r** our Lord from the dead.
15: 4 and he was **r** from the dead on the third day,
15:13 of the dead, then Christ has not been **r** either.
15:14 And if Christ was not **r**, then all our preaching is
15:15 for we have said that God **r** Christ from the grave,
15:16 resurrection of the dead, then Christ has not been **r**.
15:17 And if Christ has not been **r**, then your faith is
15:20 But the fact is that Christ has been **r** from the dead.
15:20 a great harvest of those who will be **r** to life again.
15:23 Christ was **r** first; then when Christ comes back,
all his people will be **r**.
15:29 If the dead will not be **r**, then what point is there in
15:35 But someone may ask, "How will the dead be **r**?
15:43 but when they are **r**, they will be full of glory.
15:43 They are weak now, but when they are **r**, they will
15:44 but when they are **r**, they will be spiritual bodies.
15:52 the Christians who have died will be **r** with
2Co 4:14 We know that the same God who **r** our Lord Jesus
5:15 live to please Christ, who died and was **r** for them.
Gal 1: 1 from God the Father, who **r** Jesus from the dead.
Eph 1:20 that **r** Christ from the dead and seated him in the
2: 5 he gave us life when he **r** Christ from the dead.
2: 6 For he **r** us from the dead along with Christ,
Php 2: 9 God **r** him up to the heights of heaven and gave
3:10 and experience the mighty power that **r** him from
Col 2:12 And with him you were **r** to a new life because you
2:12 mighty power of God, who **r** Christ from the dead.
3: 1 Since you have been **r** to new life with Christ,
1Th 1:10 from heaven—Jesus, whom God **r** from the dead.
4:14 we believe that Jesus died and was **r** to life again,
2Ti 2: 8 David's family and that he was **r** from the dead.
1Pe 1:21 And because God **r** Christ from the dead and gave
3:18 physical death, but he was **r** to life in the Spirit.

RAISES (5) [RAISE]

Nu 30: 7 and **r** no objections on the day he hears of it,
1Sa 2: 6 he brings some down to the grave but **r** others up.
Job 12:23 He **r** up nations, and he destroys them. He makes
Ps 84: 3 and **r** her young— / at a place near your altar,
Pr 8: 1 calls out! Hear as understanding **r** her voice!

RAISIN (1) [RAISINS]

1Sa 25:18 one hundred **r** cakes, and two hundred fig cakes.

RAISING (13) [RAISE]

Ex 40:18 and attaching the crossbars and **r** the posts.
Jdg 21: 2 until evening, **r** their voices and weeping bitterly.
1Ki 8:38 or sorrow, **r** their hands toward this Temple,
2Ch 6:29 or sorrow, **r** their hands toward this Temple,
Pr 8: 4 to you, to all of you! I am **r** my voice to all people.
Jer 4:16 **r** a battle cry against the towns of Judah.
12: 6 They have plotted, **r** a cry against you. Do not trust
50: 9 I am **r** up an army of great nations from the north.
Eze 26: 8 a ramp, and **r** a roof of shields against you.
43: 7 or by **r** monuments in honor of their dead kings.
47:22 joined you and are **r** their families among you.
Hab 1: 6 I am **r** up the Babylonians to be a new power on
Ac 17:31 and he proved to everyone who this is by **r** him

RAISINS (8) [RAISIN]

Nu 6: 3 grape juice, and they must not eat grapes or **r**.
Jdg 13:14 She must not eat grapes or **r**, drink wine or any
1Sa 30:12 gave him part of a fig cake and two clusters of **r**
2Sa 6:19 a loaf of bread, a cake of dates, and a cake of **r**.
16: 1 one hundred clusters of **r**, one hundred bunches of
1Ch 12:40 of flour, fig cakes, **r**, wine, olive oil, cattle,
16: 3 a loaf of bread, a cake of dates, and a cake of **r**.
SS 2: 5 me with your love—your '**r**' and your 'apples'—

RAKEM (1)

1Ch 7:16 The sons of Peresh were Ulam and **R**.

RAKKATH (1)

Jos 19:35 were Ziddim, Zer, Hammath, **R**, Kinnereth,

RAKKON (1)

Jos 19:46 also **R** along with the territory across from Joppa.

RALLY (4) [RALLYING]

2Ch 14:13 so many Ethiopians fell that they were unable to **r**.
Isa 11:10 The nations will **r** to him, for the land where he
11:12 a flag among the nations for Israel to **r** around.
Da 11:11 will **r** against the vast forces assembled by the king

RALLYING (1) [RALLY]

Ps 60: 4 who honor you— / a **r** point in the face of attack.

RAM (97) [RAM'S, RAMS, RAMS']

Ge 15: 9 a three-year-old **r**, a turtledove, and a young
22:13 and saw a **r** caught by its horns in a bush.
22:13 So he took the **r** and sacrificed it as a burnt
31:38 In all those years I never touched a single **r** of
Ex 25: 5 tanned **r** skins and fine goatskin leather;
26:14 On top of these coverings place a layer of tanned **r**
29:17 Cut up the **r** and wash off the internal organs
29:19 "Now take the other **r** and have Aaron and his
29:22 "Since this is the **r** for the ordination of Aaron
29:22 of Aaron and his sons, take the fat of the **r**,
29:26 Then take the breast of Aaron's ordination **r**,
29:27 "Set aside as holy the parts of the ordination **r** that
29:31 "Take the **r** used in the ordination ceremony,
35: 7 tanned **r** skins and fine goatskin leather;
35:23 Some gave tanned **r** skins or fine goatskin leather.
36:19 The first was made of tanned **r** skins,
39:34 the layers of tanned **r** skins and fine goatskin
Lev 5:15 they must bring to the LORD a **r** from the flock
5:16 he will make atonement for them with the **r**
5:18 they must bring to the priest a **r** from the flock as a
6: 6 This offering must be a **r** with no physical defects
8:18 Then Moses presented the **r** to the LORD for the
8:20 Next he cut the **r** into pieces and burned the head,
8:21 Moses burned the entire **r** on the altar as a whole
8:22 Next Moses presented the second **r**, which was the **r** of ordination.
8:29 This was Moses' share of the **r** of ordination,
9: 2 a sin offering and a **r** for a whole burnt offering,
9: 4 tell them to take a bull and a **r** for a peace offering
9:18 the bull and the **r** for the people's peace offering.
9:19 Then he took the fat of the bull and the **r**—the fat
16: 3 a sin offering and a **r** for a whole burnt offering.
16: 5 a sin offering and a **r** for a whole burnt offering.
19:21 must bring a **r** as a guilt offering and present it to
19:22 LORD with the sacrificial **r** of the guilt offering,
22:19 It may be either a bull, a **r**, or a male goat.
22:27 "When a bull or a **r** or a male goat is born, it must
Nu 5: 8 given to the priest, along with a **r** for atonement.
6:14 a **r** without defect for a peace offering,
6:17 then the **r** for a peace offering, along with the
6:19 take for each of them the boiled shoulder of the **r**,
7:15 He brought a young bull, a **r**, and a one-year-old
7:21 He brought a young bull, a **r**, and a one-year-old
7:27 He brought a young bull, a **r**, and a one-year-old
7:33 He brought a young bull, a **r**, and a one-year-old
7:39 He brought a young bull, a **r**, and a one-year-old
7:45 He brought a young bull, a **r**, and a one-year-old
7:51 He brought a young bull, a **r**, and a one-year-old
7:57 He brought a young bull, a **r**, and a one-year-old
7:63 He brought a young bull, a **r**, and a one-year-old
7:69 He brought a young bull, a **r**, and a one-year-old
7:75 He brought a young bull, a **r**, and a one-year-old
7:81 He brought a young bull, a **r**, and a one-year-old
15: 6 "If the sacrifice is a **r**, give three quarts of choice
15:11 each sacrificial bull, **r**, lamb, or young goat.
23: 2 them sacrificed a young bull and a **r** on each altar.
23: 4 sacrificed a young bull and a **r** on each altar."
23:14 and offered a young bull and a **r** on each altar.
23:30 and offered a young bull and a **r** on each altar.
28:11 one **r**, and seven one-year-old male lambs, all with
28:12 five quarts with each bull, three quarts with the **r**,
28:14 two and a half pints for the **r**, and one quart for
28:19 one **r**, and seven one-year-old male lambs, all with
28:20 five quarts with each bull, three quarts with the **r**,
28:27 It will consist of two young bulls, one **r**, and seven
28:28 five quarts with each bull, three quarts with the **r**,
29: 2 It will consist of one young bull, one **r**, and seven
29: 3 five quarts with the bull, three quarts with the **r**,
29: 8 It will consist of one young bull, one **r**, and seven
29: 9 the bull, three quarts of choice flour with the **r**,
29:36 It will consist of one young bull, one **r**, and seven
Ru 4:19 Hezron was the father of **R**. / **R** was the father of
1Ch 2: 9 The sons of Hezron were Jerahmeel, **R**, and Caleb.
2:10 **R** was the father of Amminadab.
2:25 were **R** (the oldest), Bunah, Oren, Ozem,
2:27 The sons of **R**, the oldest son of Jerahmeel,
Ezr 10:19 their guilt by offering a **r** as a guilt offering.
Job 32: 2 Barakel the Buzite, of the clan of **R**, became angry.
Eze 43:23 that has no defects and a perfect **r** from the flock.
43:25 and a **r** from the flock will be sacrificed as a sin
45:24 a gallon of olive oil with each young bull and **r**.
46: 4 LORD a burnt offering of six lambs and one **r**,
46: 5 offering of a half bushel of flour to go with the **r**
46: 6 six lambs, and one **r**, all with no physical defects.
46: 7 With the **r** he must bring another half bushel of
46:11 another half bushel of flour with each **r**, and as
Da 8: 3 I saw in front of me a **r** with two long horns
8: 4 The **r** butted everything out of its way to the west,
8: 6 headed toward the two-horned **r** that I had seen
8: 7 The goat charged furiously at the **r** and struck it,
8: 7 Now the **r** was helpless, and the goat knocked it
8: 7 There was no one who could rescue the **r** from the
8:20 The two-horned **r** represents the kings of Media
Mal 1:14 "Cursed is the cheat who promises to give a fine **r**
Mt 1: 3 the father of Hezron. / Hezron was the father of **R**.
1: 4 **R** was the father of Amminadab.

RAM'S (9) [RAM]

Ex 19:13 until they hear one long blast from the **r** horn.
19:16 There was a long, loud blast from a **r** horn, and all
Lev 8:19 Then Moses took the **r** blood and sprinkled it
Jos 6: 4 will walk ahead of the Ark, each carrying a **r** horn.
6: 6 to walk in front of it, each carrying a **r** horn."
Jdg 6:34 He blew a **r** horn as a call to arms, and the men of
7:16 and gave each man a **r** horn and a clay jar with a
Ps 98: 6 with trumpets and the sound of the **r** horn.
Hos 5: 8 "Blow the **r** horn in Gibeah! Sound the alarm in

RAMAH (36)

Jos 18:25 Also Gibeon, **R**, Beeroth,
19: 8 as Baalath-beer (also known as **R** of the Negev).
19:29 Then the boundary turned toward **R**
19:36 Adamah, **R**, Hazor,
Jdg 4: 5 which stood between **R** and Bethel in the hill
19:13 a place to spend the night in either Gibeah or **R**."
1Sa 1: 1 There was a man named Elkanah who lived in **R** in
1:19 Then they returned home to **R**. When Elkanah
2:11 and Hannah returned home to **R** without Samuel.
7:17 Then he would return to his home at **R**, and he
7:17 And Samuel built an altar to the LORD at **R**.
8: 4 the leaders of Israel met at **R** to discuss the matter
15:34 Then Samuel went home to **R**, and Saul returned to
16:13 him from that day on. Then Samuel returned to **R**.
19:18 So David got away and went to **R** to see Samuel,
19:19 report reached Saul that David was at Naioth in **R**,
19:22 Saul himself went to **R** and arrived at the great
19:22 "They are at Naioth in **R**," someone told him.
20: 1 David now fled from Naioth in **R** and found
25: 1 his funeral. They buried him near his home at **R**.
28: 3 He was buried in **R**, his hometown. And Saul had
1Ki 15:17 and fortified **R** in order to prevent anyone from
15:21 he abandoned his project of fortifying **R**
15:22 timbers that Baasha had been using to fortify **R**.
1Ch 27:27 Shimei from **R** was in charge of the king's
2Ch 16: 1 and fortified **R** in order to prevent anyone from
16: 5 he abandoned his project of fortifying **R**.
16: 6 timbers that Baasha had been using to fortify **R**.
Ezr 2:26 The peoples of **R** and Geba | 621
Ne 7:30 The peoples of **R** and Geba | 621
11:33 Hazor, **R**, Gittaim,
Isa 10:29 Fear strikes the city of **R**. All the people of
Jer 31:15 "A cry of anguish is heard in **R**—mourning
40: 1 captain of the guard, had released him at **R**.
Hos 5: 8 Sound the alarm in **R**! Raise the battle cry in
Mt 2:18 "A cry of anguish is heard in **R**— / weeping

RAMATH-MIZPEH (1)

Jos 13:26 It extended from Heshbon to **R** and Betonim,

RAMATHAIM-ZOPHIM [KJV] See RAMAH

RAMESES (5)

Ge 47:11 the land of **R**—to his father and brothers, just as
Ex 1:11 of Pithom and **R** as supply centers for the king.
12:37 That night the people of Israel left **R** and started
Nu 33: 3 They set out from the city of **R** on the morning
33: 5 After leaving **R**, the Israelites set up camp at

RAMIAH (1)

Ezr 10:25 **R**, Izziah, Malkijah, Mijamin, Eleazar, Hashabiah,

RAMOTH (5) [RAMOTH-GILEAD, RAMOTH-NEGEV, REMETH]

Dt 4:43 **R** in Gilead for the tribe of Gad; Golan in Bashan
Jos 20: 8 **R** in Gilead, in the territory of the tribe of Gad;
21:38 From the tribe of Gad they received **R** in Gilead (a
1Ch 6:73 **R**, and Anem, with their pasturelands.
6:80 of Gad, they received **R** in Gilead, Mahanaim,

RAMOTH-GILEAD (20) [GILEAD, RAMOTH]

1Ki 4:13 Ben-geber, in **R**, including the Towns of Jair
22: 3 the Arameans are still occupying our city of **R**?
22: 4 "Will you join me in fighting against **R**?"
22: 6 "Should I go to war against **R** or not?"
22:12 "Yes," they said, "go up to **R** and be victorious,
22:15 "Micaiah, should we go to war against **R** or not?"
22:20 'Who can entice Ahab to go into battle against **R**
22:29 Jehoshaphat of Judah led their armies against **R**.
2Ki 8:28 Israel in his war against King Hazael of Aram at **R**.
9: 1 "Get ready to go to **R**," he told him. "Take this
9: 4 young prophet did as he was told and went to **R**.
9:14 (Now Joram had been with the army at **R**,
2Ch 18: 2 Jehoshaphat to join forces with him to attack **R**.
18: 3 "Will you join me in fighting against **R**?"
18: 5 "Should we go to war against **R** or not?"
18:11 "Yes," they said, "go up to **R** and be victorious.
18:14 "Micaiah, should we go to war against **R** or not?"
18:19 King Ahab of Israel to go into battle against **R**
18:28 Jehoshaphat of Judah led their armies against **R**.
22: 5 They went out to fight King Hazael of Aram at **R**,

RAMOTH-NEGEV (1) [NEGEV, RAMOTH]

1Sa 30:27 and his men had been: Bethel, **R**, Jattir,

RAMP (2) [RAMPS]

2Sa 20:15 and built a **r** against the city wall and began
Eze 26: 8 constructing a **r**, and raising a roof of shields

RAMPANT (3)

Ps 55:11 threats and cheating are **r** in the streets.
Jer 17: 3 to your enemies, for sin runs **r** in your land.
Mt 24:12 Sin will be **r** everywhere, and the love of many

RAMPARTS (3)

La 2: 8 the **r** and walls have fallen down before him.
Na 2: 1 Sound the alarm! Man the **r**! Muster your defenses,
Lk 19:43 Before long your enemies will build **r** against your

RAMPS (8) [RAMP]

2Ki 25: 1 the city and built siege **r** against its walls.
Isa 23:13 They have built siege **r** against its walls, torn down
Jer 6: 6 Build **r** against the walls of Jerusalem. This is the
32:24 "See how the siege **r** have been built against the
52: 4 the city and built siege **r** against its walls.
Eze 4: 2 Build siege **r** against the city walls. Surround it
21:22 and build **r** against the walls to reach the top.
Hab 1:10 They simply pile **r** of earth against their walls

RAMS (67) [RAM]

Ge 30:40 the streaked and dark-colored **r** in Laban's flock.
32:14 twenty male goats, two hundred ewes, twenty **r**,
Ex 29: 1 a young bull and two **r** with no physical defects.
29: 3 along with the young bull and the two **r**.
29:15 must lay their hands on the head of one of the **r**
Lev 8: 2 the bull for the sin offering, the two **r**,
23:18 and two **r** as burnt offerings to the LORD.
Nu 7:17 and two oxen, five **r**, five male goats, and five
7:23 and two oxen, five **r**, five male goats, and five
7:29 and two oxen, five **r**, five male goats, and five
7:35 and two oxen, five **r**, five male goats, and five
7:41 and two oxen, five **r**, five male goats, and five
7:47 and two oxen, five **r**, five male goats, and five
7:53 and two oxen, five **r**, five male goats, and five
7:59 and two oxen, five **r**, five male goats, and five
7:65 and two oxen, five **r**, five male goats, and five
7:71 and two oxen, five **r**, five male goats, and five
7:77 and two oxen, five **r**, five male goats, and five
7:83 and two oxen, five **r**, five male goats, and five
7:87 Twelve bulls, twelve **r**, and twelve one-year-old
7:88 Twenty-four young bulls, sixty **r**, sixty male goats,
23: 1 seven young bulls and seven **r** for a sacrifice."
23:29 me seven young bulls and seven **r** for a sacrifice."
29:13 It will consist of thirteen young bulls, two **r**,
29:14 thirteen bulls, three quarts for each of the two **r**,
29:17 sacrifice twelve young bulls, two **r**, and fourteen
29:18 Each of these offerings of bulls, **r**, and lambs must
29:20 of the festival, sacrifice eleven young bulls, two **r**,
29:21 Each of these offerings of bulls, **r**, and lambs must
29:23 day of the festival, sacrifice ten young bulls, two **r**,
29:24 Each of these offerings of bulls, **r**, and lambs must
29:26 of the festival, sacrifice nine young bulls, two **r**,
29:27 Each of these offerings of bulls, **r**, and lambs must
29:29 of the festival, sacrifice eight young bulls, two **r**,
29:30 Each of these offerings of bulls, **r**, and lambs must
29:32 of the festival, sacrifice seven young bulls, two **r**,
29:33 Each of these offerings of bulls, **r**, and lambs must
Dt 32:14 He gave them choice **r** and goats from Bashan,
1Sa 15:22 to him is much better than offering the fat of **r**.
2Ki 3: 4 of 100,000 lambs and the wool of 100,000 **r**.
1Ch 29:21 day they brought a thousand bulls, a thousand **r**,
2Ch 13: 9 and seven **r** can become a priest of these so-called
17:11 and the Arabs brought seventy-seven hundred **r**
29:21 They brought seven bulls, seven **r**, seven lambs,
29:22 Next they killed the **r** and sprinkled their blood on
29:32 one hundred **r**, and two hundred lambs for burnt
Ezr 6: 9 **r**, and lambs for the burnt offerings presented to
6:17 one hundred young bulls, two hundred **r**, and four
7:17 **r**, lambs, and the appropriate grain offerings
8:35 as well as ninety-six **r** and seventy-seven lambs.
Job 42: 8 young bulls and seven **r** and go to my servant Job
Ps 66:15 to you— / the best of my **r** as a pleasing aroma.
114: 4 The mountains skipped like **r**, / the little hills like
114: 6 Why, mountains, did you skip like **r**? / Why,
Isa 1:11 I don't want the fat from your **r** or other animals.
1:11 blood from your offerings of bulls and **r** and goats.
34: 6 for killing lambs and goats and **r** for a sacrifice.
60: 7 and the **r** of Nebaioth will be brought for my altars.
Jer 6: 6 "Cut down the trees for battering **r**.
51:40 to the slaughter, like **r** and goats to be sacrificed.
Eze 4: 2 Surround it with enemy camps and battering **r**.
21:22 With battering **r** they will go against the gates,
26: 9 He will pound your walls with battering **r**
27:21 and **r** and goats in trade for your goods.
39:18 drink the blood of princes as though they were **r**,
45:23 seven young bulls and seven **r** without any defects.
Mic 6: 7 Should we offer him thousands of **r** and tens of

RAMS' (4) [RAM]

Jos 6: 8 the seven priests with the **r** horns started marching
6:13 The seven priests with the **r** horns marched in front
Jdg 7: 8 and **r** horns of the other warriors and sent them
7:18 As soon as my group blows the **r** horns, those of

RAN (103) [RUN]

Ge 16: 6 So Sarai treated her harshly, and Hagar **r** away.
18: 2 He got up and **r** to meet them, welcoming them by
18: 6 So Abraham **r** back to the tent and said to Sarah,
18: 7 Then Abraham **r** out to the herd and chose a fat
24:20 the watering trough and **r** down to the well again.
24:28 The young woman **r** home to tell her family about
29:12 So Rachel quickly **r** and told her father, Laban.
33: 4 Then Esau **r** to meet him and embraced him
39:12 She was left holding it as he **r** from the house.
39:15 loud cries, he **r** and left his shirt behind with me."
39:18 my screams. He **r** out, leaving his shirt behind!"
47:15 the people of Egypt and Canaan **r** out of money,
Ex 4: 3 Moses was terrified, so he turned and **r** away.
37:12 of the table, and a gold molding **r** around the rim.
37:26 pure gold and **r** a gold molding around the edge.
Nu 11:27 A young man **r** and reported to Moses, "Eldad
16:47 did as Moses told him and **r** out among the people.
Jos 7:22 They **r** to the tent and found the stolen goods
15: 3 **r** south of Scorpion Pass into the wilderness of Zin

16: 2 it **r** over to Ataroth in the territory of the Arkites.
16: 5 From there it **r** to Upper Beth-horon,
16: 6 at the Mediterranean, **r** east past Micmethath,
18:14 then **r** south along the western edge of the hill
18:15 From there it **r** westward to the spring at the waters
18:19 **r** past the north slope of Beth-hoglah, and ended at
19:27 and **r** as far as Zebulun in the valley of Iphtah-el,
19:33 Its boundary **r** from Heleph, from the oak at
19:34 The western boundary **r** past Aznoth-tabor, then to
Jdg 1:36 The boundary of the Amorites **r** from Scorpion
4:17 Meanwhile, Sisera **r** to the tent of Jael, the wife of
7:21 rushed around in a panic, shouting as they **r**.
9:40 but he was defeated and **r** away. Many of
11:34 **r** out to meet him, playing on a tambourine
13: 6 The woman **r** and told her husband, "A man of
13:10 So she quickly **r** and told her husband, "The man
13:11 Manoah **r** back with his wife and asked, "Are you
20:42 So they **r** toward the wilderness, but the Israelites
1Sa 3: 5 He jumped up and **r** to Eli. "Here I am. What do
3: 6 "Samuel!" Again Samuel jumped up and **r** to Eli.
3: 8 and once more Samuel jumped up and **r** to Eli.
4:12 A man from the tribe of Benjamin **r** from the
17:48 closer to attack, David quickly **r** out to meet him.
17:51 he **r** over and pulled Goliath's sword from its
17:51 that their champion was dead, they turned and **r**.
19: 8 He attacked them with such fury that they all **r**
20:36 So the boy **r**, and Jonathan shot an arrow beyond
20:38 gathered up the arrows and **r** back to his master.
29: 3 the man who **r** away from King Saul of Israel.
2Sa 10:14 they **r** from Abishai and retreated into the city.
13:34 He **r** to tell the king, "I see a crowd of people
18:21 what you have seen." The man bowed and **r** off.
1Ki 2:28 he **r** to the sacred tent of the LORD and caught
18:35 and the water **r** around the altar and even
18:46 and **r** ahead of Ahab's chariot all the way to the
19:20 **r** after Elijah, and said to him, "First let me go
22:35 The blood from his wound **r** down to the floor of
22:36 as the sun was setting, the cry **r** through his troops:
2Ki 3:24 and attacked the Moabites, who turned and **r**.
9:10 Then the young prophet opened the door and **r**.
1Ch 19:15 they **r** from Abishai and retreated into the city.
21:20 His four sons, who were with him, **r** away and hid.
2Ch 32: 4 cutting off the brook that **r** through the fields.
Ps 48: 5 were stunned; / they were terrified and **r** away.
106:14 In the wilderness, their desires **r** wild,
133: 2 poured over Aaron's head, / that **r** down his beard
Eze 40:17 A stone pavement **r** along the walls of the
42: 4 Between the two blocks of rooms **r** a walkway
Da 10: 7 they were suddenly terrified and **r** away to hide.
Jnh 4: 2 do this, LORD? That is why I **r** away to Tarshish!
Mt 27:48 One of them **r** and filled a sponge with sour wine,
28: 8 The women **r** quickly from the tomb. They were
28: 9 And they **r** to him, held his feet, and worshiped
Mk 5: 2 a man possessed by an evil spirit **r** out from a
5: 6 He **r** to meet Jesus and fell down before him.
5:14 spreading the news as they **r**.
6:33 and people from many towns **r** ahead along the
6:55 and they **r** throughout the whole area and began
8: 1 had gathered, and the people **r** out of food again.
9:15 he came toward them, and then they **r** to greet him.
9:26 A murmur **r** through the crowd, "He's dead."
14:50 all his disciples deserted him and **r** away.
14:52 off his clothes, but he escaped and **r** away naked.
15:36 One of them **r** and filled a sponge with sour wine,
Lk 2:16 They **r** to the village and found Mary and Joseph.
8:34 spreading the news as they **r**.
14:30 and **r** out of money before it was finished!'
15:14 About the time his money **r** out, a great famine
15:20 he **r** to his son, embraced him, and kissed him.
19: 4 So he **r** ahead and climbed a sycamore tree beside
24:12 However, Peter **r** to the tomb to look. Stooping,
24:24 Some of our men **r** out to see, and sure enough,
Jn 2: 3 The wine supply **r** out during the festivities,
20: 2 She **r** and found Simon Peter and the other
20: 3 Peter and the other disciple **r** to the tomb to see.
Ac 7:11 misery for our ancestors, as they **r** out of food.
8:30 Philip **r** over and heard the man reading from the
12:14 the door, she **r** back inside and told everyone,
13:50 against Paul and Barnabas and **r** them out of town.
14:14 clothing in dismay and **r** out among the people,
16:29 the jailer called for lights and **r** to the dungeon
21:32 and officers and **r** down among the crowd.
27:41 But the ship hit a shoal and **r** aground. The bow of
Phm 1:15 Onesimus **r** away for a little while so you could

RANDOMLY (2)
1Ki 22:34 however, **r** shot an arrow at the Israelite troops,
2Ch 18:33 however, **r** shot an arrow at the Israelite troops,

RANG (1) [RING]
Rev 19: 3 Again and again their voices **r**, "Hallelujah!

RANGE (1)
Hab 2: 5 They **r** far and wide, with their mouths opened as

RANGING [KJV] See ATTACKING

RANK (11) [HIGH-RANKING, RANKS]
Ge 41:40 Only I will have a **r** higher than yours."
49: 3 You are first on the list in **r** and honor.
2Sa 23: 9 Next in **r** among the Three was Eleazar son of
23:11 Next in **r** was Shammah son of Agee from Harar.
1Ki 12:31 and ordained priests from the **r** and file of the
13:33 He continued to choose priests from the **r** and file
1Ch 11:12 Next in **r** among the Three was Eleazar son of
24:31 by means of sacred lots, without regard to age or **r**.
Est 1:20 husbands everywhere, whatever their **r**,
Joel 2: 7 Straight forward they march, never breaking **r**.
Lk 22:26 those who are the greatest should take the lowest **r**,

RANKS (5) [RANK]
1Sa 17: 4 came out of the Philistine **r** to face the forces of
17:22 and hurried out to the **r** to greet his brothers.
17:23 from Gath, come out from the Philistine **r**,
1Ki 14: 7 'I promoted you from the **r** of the common people
Pr 30:27 have no king, / but they march like an army in **r**.

RANSACKED (3)
Dt 2:35 along with anything of value from the towns we **r**.
1Ki 14:26 He **r** the Temple of the LORD and the royal
Zep 1:13 plundered by the enemy, whose homes will be **r**.

RANSOM (15) [RANSOMED, RANSOMS]
Ex 30:12 each man who is counted must pay a **r** for himself
Nu 35:31 you must never accept a **r** payment for the life of
35:32 And never accept a **r** payment from someone who
Job 33:24 not make him die, for I have found a **r** for his life.'
Ps 25:22 O God, **r** Israel / from all its troubles.
49: 7 themselves from death / by paying a **r** to God.
111: 9 He has paid a full **r** for his people. / He has
Pr 13: 8 The rich can pay a **r**, but the poor won't even get
Isa 43: 3 Ethiopia, and Seba as a **r** for your freedom.
63: 4 avenge my people, to **r** them from their oppressors.
Hos 13:14 Should I **r** them from the grave? Should I redeem
Mt 20:28 serve others, and to give my life as a **r** for many."
Mk 10:45 serve others, and to give my life as a **r** for many."
1Pe 1:18 For you know that God paid a **r** to save you from
1:18 And the **r** he paid was not mere gold or silver.

RANSOMED (5) [RANSOM]
Ex 15:13 love you will lead / this people whom you have **r**.
Isa 35:10 Those who have been **r** by the LORD will return
43: 1 "Do not be afraid, for I have **r** you. I have called
51:11 Those who have been **r** by the LORD will return
Rev 5: 9 were killed, and your blood has **r** people for God

RANSOMS (1) [RANSOM]
Ps 103: 4 He **r** me from death / and surrounds me with love

RANTING (1)
Pr 29: 9 there will be **r** and ridicule but no satisfaction.

RAPE (3) [RAPED, RAPES, RAPING]
Ge 39:14 she sobbed. "He tried to **r** me, but I screamed.
La 5:11 Our enemies **r** the women and young girls in
Eze 22:11 their daughters-in-law or who **r** their own sisters.

RAPED (9) [RAPE]
Ge 34: 2 Hamor the Hivite, saw her, he took her and **r** her.
34: 7 and furious that their sister had been **r**.
Dt 22:27 Since the man **r** her out in the country, it must be
Jdg 20: 5 and they **r** my concubine until she was dead.
2Sa 13:14 and since he was stronger than she was, he **r** her.
13:32 plotting this ever since Amnon **r** his sister Tamar.
Isa 13:16 and their wives **r** by the attacking hordes.
Jer 13:22 That is why you have been **r** and destroyed by
Zec 14: 2 be taken, the houses plundered, and the women **r**.

RAPES (1) [RAPE]
Dt 22:25 and he **r** her, then only the man should die.

RAPHA (1) [BETH-RAPHA]
1Ch 8: 2 Nohah, and **R**.

RAPHU (1)
Nu 13: 9 Benjamin | Palti son of **R**

RAPIDLY (9) [RAPID]
Ge 6: 1 When the human population began to grow **r** on
30:43 As a result, Jacob's flocks increased **r**, and he
47:27 to prosper there, and their population grew **r**.
48: 1 word came to Joseph that his father was failing **r**.
1Sa 13: 8 Saul realized that his troops were **r** slipping away.
Ac 1:19 The news of his death spread **r** among all the
6: 1 But as the believers **r** multiplied, there were
12:24 But God's Good News was spreading **r**, and there
2Th 3: 1 Pray first that the Lord's message will spread **r**

RAPING (2) [RAPE]
Dt 22:28 "If a man is caught in the act of **r** a young woman
Jdg 19:25 her all night, taking turns **r** her until morning.

RARE (4) [RARELY, RARER, RAREST]
1Sa 3: 1 those days messages from the LORD were very **r**,
SS 5: 9 "O woman of **r** beauty, what is it about your loved
Isa 13:12 as scarce as gold—more **r** than the gold of Ophir.
Lk 7:46 but she has anointed my feet with **r** perfume.

RARELY (2) [RARE]
Job 21:17 They **r** have trouble, and God skips them when he
Ecc 5:20 People who do this **r** look with sorrow on the past,

RARER (1) [RARE]
Pr 20:15 Wise speech is **r** and more valuable than gold

RAREST (3) [RARE]
SS 4:13 bearing precious fruit, with the **r** of perfumes:
6: 1 "O **r** of beautiful women, where has your lover
7:13 and the **r** fruits are at our doors, the new as well as

RASCAL (1)
Lk 16: 8 "The rich man had to admire the dishonest **r** for

RASE [KJV] See LEVEL

RASH (11) [RASHLY]
Lev 5: 4 "Or if they make a **r** vow of any kind, whether its
13: 2 "If some of the people notice a swelling or a **r**
13: 6 It was only a temporary **r**. So after washing the
13: 7 But if the **r** continues to spread after this
13: 8 If the priest notices that the **r** has spread, then he
13:12 that a **r** has broken out all over someone's skin,
13:39 patch is only a pale white, this is a harmless skin **r**,
14:56 in a swollen area of skin, in a skin **r**, or in a shiny
Pr 20:25 It is dangerous to make a **r** promise to God before
Ecc 5: 2 And don't make **r** promises to God, for he is in
Ac 19:36 no matter what is said. Don't do anything **r**.

RASHLY (1) [RASH]
Job 6: 3 all the sands of the sea. That is why I spoke so **r**.

RATE (1)
Ac 27:29 At this **r** they were afraid we would soon be driven

RATHER (41)
Ge 27:46 I'd **r** die than see Jacob marry one of them."
29:19 "I'd **r** give her to you than to someone outside the
Ex 21: 5 my wife, and my children. I would **r** not go free.'
Nu 11:15 I'd **r** you killed me than treat me like this.
32:19 We would **r** live here on the east side where we
Dt 12: 5 **R**, you must seek the LORD your God at the
Jdg 11:27 **R**, you have wronged me by attacking me.
1Sa 18:17 and let them kill him **r** than doing it myself."
27: 5 we would **r** live in one of the country towns
2Ch 1:11 but **r** you asked for wisdom and knowledge to
Job 7:15 I would **r** die of strangulation than go on and on
Ps 84:10 I would **r** be a gatekeeper in the house of my God
147:11 **R**, the LORD's delight is in those who honor him,
Pr 8:10 "Choose my instruction **r** than silver,
22:29 They will serve kings **r** than ordinary people.
Ecc 6: 9 Enjoy what you have **r** than desiring what you
Isa 28:27 never used on dill; **r**, it is beaten with a light stick.
48:10 **R**, I have refined you in the furnace of suffering.
Jer 8: 3 will wish to die **r** than live where I will send them.
Da 3:28 and were willing to die **r** than serve
Jnh 4: 3 I'd **r** be dead than alive because nothing I
Lk 4:27 **r** than the many lepers in Israel who needed help."
Jn 10: 1 **r** than going through the gate, must surely be a
Ac 4:19 "Do you think God wants us to obey you **r** than
5:29 "We must obey God **r** than human authority.
17:20 "You are saying some **r** startling things, and we
Ro 15:20 **r** than where a church has already been started by
1Co 2: 5 so that you might trust the power of God **r** than
9:12 We would **r** put up with anything than put an
9:15 I would **r** die than lose my distinction of preaching
14:19 But in a church meeting I would much **r** speak five
2Co 4:18 **r**, we look forward to what we have not yet seen.
5: 8 and we would **r** be away from these bodies, for
5:12 ministry **r** than having a sincere heart before God.
11:30 I would **r** boast about the things that show how
Gal 2:18 **R**, I make myself guilty if I rebuild the old system
Eph 6: 4 **R**, bring them up with the discipline
6: 7 as though you were working for the Lord **r** than for
Col 3:23 as though you were working for the Lord **r** than for
2Ti 3: 4 puffed up with pride, and love pleasure **r** than God.
Heb 11:35 preferring to die **r** than turn from God and be free.

RATIFIED (2)
Jos 9:15 and the leaders of Israel **r** their agreement with a
Ne 10: 1 The document was **r** and sealed with the following

RATION (4)
Lev 26:26 They will **r** your food by weight, and even if you
Ne 5:15 demanding a daily **r** of food and wine, besides a
Eze 4:10 **R** this out to yourself, eight ounces of food for
Da 1: 5 The king assigned them a daily **r** of the best food

RATS (6)
1Sa 6: 4 five rulers, make five gold tumors and five gold **r**,
6: 8 and beside it place a chest containing the gold **r**
6:11 of the LORD and the chest containing the gold **r**
6:15 and the chest containing the gold **r** and gold
6:18 The five gold **r** represented the five Philistine
Isa 66:17 feasting on pork and **r** and other forbidden meats,

RATTLE (1) [RATTLING]
Job 39:23 The arrows **r** against it, and the spear and javelin

RATTLING (1) [RATTLE]
Eze 37: 7 as I spoke, there was a **r** noise all across the valley.

RAVAGED (7) [RAVAGES]
Jos 11:14 and cattle of the **r** cities for themselves,
1Sa 6: 4 five gold rats, just like those that have **r** your land.
6: 6 They wouldn't let Israel go until God had **r** them
Isa 3:26 The city will be like a **r** woman, huddled on the

Jer 12:10 “Many rulers have r my vineyard, trampling down
32:43 ‘It has been r by the Babylonians, a land where
33:10 You say, ‘This land has been r, and the people

RAVAGES (3) [RAVAGED]

2Ki 19:30 left in Judah, who have escaped the r of the siege,
Isa 37:31 left in Judah, who have escaped the r of the siege,
Jer 46:26 But afterward the land will recover from the r of

RAVE (1) [RAVED]

1Sa 18:10 and he began to r like a madman.

RAVED (1) [RAVE]

1Ki 18:29 They r all afternoon until the time of the evening

RAVEN (2) [RAVENS]

Ge 8: 7 and released a r that flew back and forth until the
Isa 34:11 horned owl, the hawk, the screech owl, and the r.

RAVENOUS (1)

Zep 3: 3 Its judges are like r wolves at evening time,

RAVENS (8) [RAVEN]

Lev 11:15 r of all kinds,
Dt 14:14 r of all kinds,
1Ki 17: 4 Drink from the brook and eat what the r bring you,
17: 6 The r brought him bread and meat each morning
Job 38:41 Who provides food for the r when their young cry
Ps 147: 9 and the young r cry to him for food.
Pr 30:17 and despises a mother will be plucked out by r of
Lk 12:24 Look at the r. They don't need to plant or harvest

RAVIN [KJV] See PLUNDER, PROWLS

RAVINE (6) [RAVINES]

Jos 16: 8 following the Kanah R to the Mediterranean Sea.
17: 9 side of the Kanah R to the Mediterranean Sea.
17:10 The land south of the r belonged to Ephraim,
17:10 and the land north of the r belonged to Manasseh,
1Sa 25:20 As she was riding her donkey into a mountain r,
Isa 15: 7 they can carry and flee across the R of Willows.

RAVINES (9) [RAVINE]

Nu 21:14 town of Waheb in the area of Suphah, and the r;
21:15 and its r, which extend as far as the settlement of
Job 30: 6 So now they live in frightening r and in caves
Ps 104:10 You make the springs pour water into r,
Eze 6: 3 to the mountains and hills and to the r and valleys:
31:12 across the mountains and valleys and r of the land.
32: 6 the way to the mountains, filling the r to the brim.
36: 4 speaks to the hills and mountains, r and valleys,
36: 6 the hills and mountains, the r and valleys of Israel.

RAVISH (1) [RAVISHED]

Dt 28:30 engaged to a woman, but another man will r her.

RAVISHED (2) [RAVISH]

SS 4: 9 You have r my heart, my treasure, my bride.
Eze 30: 4 The land of Ethiopia will be r.

RAW (3)

Ex 12: 9 The meat must never be eaten r or boiled; roast it
1Sa 2:15 He would demand r meat before it had been boiled
Eze 29:18 and their shoulders were r and blistered.

RAY (2) [RAYS]

Isa 50:10 without a r of light, trust in the LORD and rely
Am 5:20 and hopeless day, without a r of joy or hope.

RAYS (1) [RAY]

Hab 3: 4 R of brilliant light flash from his hands.

RAZOR (3)

Ps 52: 2 Your tongue cuts like a sharp r; / you're an expert
Isa 7:20 In that day the Lord will take this “r”—
Eze 5: 1 and use it as a r to shave your head and beard.

REACH (38) [REACHED, REACHES, REACHING]

Ge 49:22 beside a fountain. / His branches r over the wall.
Ex 3:20 So I will r out and strike at the heart of Egypt with
Dt 9: 1 They live in cities with walls that r to the sky!
Jos 3: 8 ‘When you r the banks of the Jordan River, take a
10:20 remnant that managed to r their fortified cities.
1Sa 14: 4 To r the Philistine outpost, Jonathan had to go
2Sa 20: 6 he gets into a fortified city where we can't r him.”
22:49 You hold me safe beyond the r of my enemies;
Job 6: 9 I wish he would r out his hand and kill me.
29:19 For I am like a tree whose roots r the water,
Ps 18:48 You hold me safe beyond the r of my enemies;
27: 5 He will place me out of r on a high rock.
31: 2 a fortress where my enemies cannot r me.
61: 3 a fortress where my enemies cannot r me.
62: 7 He is my refuge, a rock where no enemy can r me.
90:10 years are given to us! / Some may even r eighty.
143: 6 I r out for you. / I thirst for you as parched land
144: 7 R down from heaven and rescue me; / deliver me
Pr 2:19 her is doomed. He will never r the paths of life.
Ecc 4:10 If one person falls, the other can r out and help.
Isa 49:10 and scorching desert winds will not r them
Jer 17: 8 a riverbank, with roots that r deep into the water.
25:31 His cry of judgment will r the ends of the earth,
La 3:44 yourself in a cloud so our prayers cannot r you.
Eze 21:22 and build ramps against the walls to r the top.
Am 9: 2 place of the dead, I will r down and pull them up.
Ob 1: 3 ‘Who can ever r us way up here?’ you ask
Hab 2: 9 putting your families beyond the r of danger.
Zec 14: 5 flee through this valley, for it will r across to Azal.
Mt 12:13 Then he said to the man, “R out your hand.”
Mk 3: 5 Then he said to the man, “R out your hand.”
Lk 5:19 but they couldn't r him. So they went up to the
6:10 and then said to the man, “R out your hand.”
17:23 “Reports will r you that the Son of Man has
Ro 10: 8 the message we preach—is already within easy r.
Gal 4: 2 They have to obey their guardians until they r
Php 3:14 I strain to r the end of the race and receive the
1Pe 1: 4 and undefiled, beyond the r of change and decay.

REACHED (91) [REACH]

Ge 19:10 But the two angels r out and pulled Lot in
19:13 The stench of the place has r the LORD, and he
19:23 The sun was rising as Lot r the village.
28:12 he dreamed of a stairway that r from earth to
34: 5 Word soon r Jacob that his daughter had been
38:24 word r Judah that Tamar, his daughter-in-law,
38:28 they were being born, one of them r out his hand,
42: 5 to buy food, for the famine had r Canaan as well.
45:16 The news soon r Pharaoh: “Joseph's brothers have
48:14 But Jacob crossed his arms as he r out to lay his
Ex 3: 9 The cries of the people of Israel have r me, and I
4: 4 So Moses r out and grabbed it, and it became a
14: 5 When word r the king of Egypt that the Israelites
18: 1 Word soon r Jethro, the priest of Midian
30:14 All who have r their twentieth birthday must give
Dt 1:20 ‘You have now r the land that the LORD our God
17:11 After they have interpreted the law and r a verdict,
Jos 9:17 once to investigate and r their towns in three days.
10:11 hailstorm that continued until they r Azekah.
15: 1 tribe of Judah r southward to the border of Edom,
15: 4 to Azmon, until it finally r the brook of Egypt,
Jdg 3:19 But when Ehud r the stone carvings near Gilgal,
3:21 Ehud r with his left hand, pulled out the dagger
5:26 Then with her left hand she r for a tent peg,
5:26 and with her right hand she r for the workman's
7:19 and the one hundred men with him r the outer edge
8: 5 When they r Succoth, Gideon asked the leaders of
19:11 It was late in the day when they r Jebus,
20: 3 (Word soon r the land of Benjamin that the other
20:33 When the main group of Israelite warriors r
1Sa 9:27 When they r the edge of town, Samuel told Saul to
19:19 When the report r Saul that David was at Naioth in
20:37 When the boy had almost r the arrow,
22: 6 The news of his arrival in Judah soon r Saul.
23:13 Word soon r Saul that David had escaped, so he
23:27 an urgent message r Saul that the Philistines were
27: 4 Word soon r Saul that David had fled to Gath,
30:21 When they r Besor Brook and met the two hundred
2Sa 2:32 they traveled all night and r Hebron at daybreak.
4: 4 When news of the battle r the capital, the child's
5: 8 message from the defenders of the city r David,
13:30 on the way back to Jerusalem, this report r David:
15:32 As they r the spot at the top of the Mount of Olives
16:14 so they rested when they r the Jordan River.
19: 1 Word soon r Joab that the king was weeping
22: 7 heard me from his sanctuary; / my cry r his ears.
22:17 “He r down from heaven and rescued me;
1Ki 1:51 Word soon r Solomon that Adonijah had seized
2:29 When news of this r King Solomon, he sent
6:27 Their outspread wings r from wall to wall,
11:21 When the news r Hadad in Egypt that David
12:18 When this news r King Rehoboam, he quickly
20:12 This reply of Ahab's r Ben-hadad and the other
2Ki 6: 7 said to him. And the man r out and grabbed it.
19:23 choicest cypress trees. / I have r its farthest corners
2Ch 10:18 When this news r King Rehoboam, he quickly
29:17 and in eight days they had r the foyer of the
Ezr 9: 6 than our heads, and our guilt has r to the heavens.
Est 4: 3 And as news of the king's decree r all the
Ps 18: 6 heard me from his sanctuary; / my cry r his ears.
18:16 He r down from heaven and rescued me; / he drew
Pr 1:24 I r out to you, but you paid no attention.
Isa 16: 8 Her shoots once r as far as the Dead Sea.
24:11 crying out for wine. Joy has r its lowest ebb.
37:24 choicest cypress trees. / I have r its farthest corners
Jer 41: 6 When he r them, he said, “Oh, come and see what
48:32 Your spreading vines once r as far as the Dead
Eze 7:10 people's wickedness and pride have r a climax.
10: 7 Then one of the cherubim r out his hand and took
22: 4 has come! You have r the end of your years.
Da 8:10 His power r to the heavens where it attacked the
Mic 1: 9 It has r into Judah, even to the gates of Jerusalem.
Mt 10:23 will return before you have r all the towns of
12:13 The man r out his hand, and it became normal,
14:31 Instantly Jesus r out his hand and grabbed him.
Mk 3: 5 The man r out his hand, and it became normal
10:46 And so they r Jericho. Later, as Jesus and his
Lk 5:13 Jesus r out and touched the man. “I want to,”
6:10 The man r out his hand, and it became normal
9: 7 When reports of Jesus' miracles r Herod Antipas,
17:11 he r the border between Galilee and Samaria.
19:37 As they r the place where the road started down
Ac 11: 1 Soon the news r the apostles and other believers in
13: 6 across the entire island until finally they r Paphos,
16:12 From there we r Philippi, a major city of the
21: 1 The next day we r Rhodes and then went to Patara.
21:31 word r the commander of the Roman regiment that
21:35 As they r the stairs, the mob grew so violent the
Php 3:12 these things or that I have already r perfection!
Heb 11: 9 And even when he r the land God promised him,
Jas 5: 4 The cries of the reapers have r the ears of the Lord

REACHES (13) [REACH]

Ge 11: 4 Let's build a great city with a tower that r to the
Job 20: 6 Though the godless man's pride r to the heavens
Ps 36: 5 your faithfulness r beyond the clouds.
57:10 as the heavens. / Your faithfulness r to the clouds.
71:19 O God, r to the highest heavens.
108: 4 the heavens. / Your faithfulness r to the clouds.
Isa 14:26 for my mighty power r throughout the world.
Jer 51:53 Though Babylon r as high as the heavens,
Eze 5:10 the few who survive to the far r of the earth.
Da 4:22 your greatness r up to heaven, and your rule to the
Mic 1:12 judgment r even to the gates of Jerusalem.
Mal 1: 5 the LORD's great power r far beyond our
Lk 12:58 try to settle the matter before it r the judge, or you

REACHETH [KJV] See EXTENDS, REACHED, REACHES, SPREAD, TOUCHES, TOUCHING

REACHING (9) [REACH]

Ge 49:26 r to the utmost bounds of the everlasting hills.
Ex 28:42 be worn next to their bodies, r from waist to thigh.
Jos 20: 4 “Upon r one of these cities, the one who caused
1Sa 17:49 R into his shepherd's bag and taking out a stone,
Jer 12:14 “As for all the evil nations r out for the
Eze 2: 9 Then I looked and saw a hand r out to me, and it
31:10 set itself so high above the others, r to the clouds,
Da 4:11 r high into the heavens for all the world to see.
4:20 r high into the heavens for all the world to see.

REACT (1) [REACTED, REACTION]

Dt 1:17 Don't be afraid of how they will r, for you are

REACTED (1) [REACT]

Ac 5:17 who were Sadducees, r with violent jealousy.

REACTION (1) [REACT]

2Ki 5: 8 the man of God, heard about the king's r,

READ (76) [READER, READING, READINGS, READS]

Ex 24: 7 the Book of the Covenant and r it to the people.
Dt 17:19 the law with him and r it daily as long as he lives.
31:11 you must r this law to all the people of Israel when
Jos 8:34 Joshua then r to them all the blessings and curses
8:35 Every command Moses had ever given was r to the
2Sa 15:10 soon as you hear the trumpets,” his message r,
2Ki 5: 7 When the king of Israel r it, he tore his clothes in
19:14 After Hezekiah received the letter and r it, he went
22: 8 Hilkiah gave the scroll to Shaphan, and he r it.
22:10 given me a scroll.” So Shaphan r it to the king.
22:16 and its people, just as I stated in the scroll you r.
23: 2 There the king r to them the entire Book of the
2Ch 34:18 given me a scroll.” So Shaphan r it to the king.
34:24 All the curses written in the scroll you have r will
34:30 There the king r to them the entire Book of the
Ezr 4:18 The letter you sent has been translated and r to me.
4:23 When this letter from King Artaxerxes was r to
Ne 8: 3 and r aloud to everyone who could understand.
8: 8 They r from the Book of the Law of God
8: 8 clearly explained the meaning of what was being r,
8:18 Ezra r from the Book of the Law of God on each
9: 3 God was r aloud to them for about three hours.
13: 1 that same day, as the Book of Moses was being r,
13: 3 When this law was r, all those of mixed ancestry
Est 6: 1 records of his kingdom so they could be r to him.
Isa 29:11 When you give it to those who can r, they will say, “We can't r it because it is sealed.”
29:12 When you give it to those who cannot r, they will say, “Sorry, we don't know how to r.”
29:18 In that day deaf people will hear words r from a
37:14 After Hezekiah received the letter and r it, he went
Jer 10: 2 “Do not act like other nations who try to r their
29:29 he took it to Jeremiah and r it to him.
36: 6 and r the messages from the LORD that are on
36: 8 and r these messages from the LORD to the
36:10 Baruch r Jeremiah's words to all the people from
36:14 to ask Baruch to come and r the messages to them,
36:15 “Sit down and r the scroll to us,” the officials
36:21 and r it to the king as all his officials stood by.
51:61 get to Babylon, r aloud everything on this scroll.
Da 5: 7 “Whoever can r this writing and tell me what it
5: 8 none of them could r the writing or tell him what it
5:15 and enchanters have tried to r this writing on the
5:16 If you can r these words and tell me their meaning,
Hab 2: 2 so that a runner can r it and tell everyone else.
Mt 12: 3 “Haven't you ever r in the Scriptures what King
12: 5 And haven't you ever r in the law of Moses that
16: 3 but you can't r the obvious signs of the times!
19: 4 “Haven't you r the Scriptures?” Jesus replied.
21:16 “Haven't you ever r the Scriptures? For they say,
21:42 “Didn't you ever r this in the Scriptures?
22:31 haven't you ever r about this in the Scriptures?
27:37 It r: “This is Jesus, the King of the Jews.”
Mk 2:25 “Haven't you ever r in the Scriptures what King
12:10 Didn't you ever r this in the Scriptures?
12:26 haven't you ever r about this in the writings of

15:26 charge against him. It **r**: "The King of the Jews."
Lk 4:16 on the Sabbath and stood up to **r** the Scriptures.
6:3 "Haven't you ever **r** in the Scriptures what King
10:26 does the law of Moses say? How do you **r** it?"
16:29 Your brothers can **r** their writings anytime they
Jn 19:19 And Pilate posted a sign over him that **r**, "Jesus of
19:20 Latin, and Greek, so that many people could **r** it.
Ac 13:27 though they hear the prophets' words **r** every
15:31 that day as they **r** this encouraging message.
23:34 He **r** it and then asked Paul what province he was
2Co 3:2 and everyone can **r** it and recognize our good work
3:14 to this day whenever the old covenant is being **r**,
3:15 Yes, even today when they **r** Moses' writings,
Eph 3:4 As you **r** what I have written, you will understand
Col 4:16 After you have **r** this letter, pass it on to the church at Laodicea so they can **r** it,
4:16 And you should **r** the letter I wrote to them.
1Th 5:27 I command you in the name of the Lord to **r** this
Rev 5:3 under the earth was able to open the scroll and **r** it.
5:4 found who was worthy to open the scroll and **r** it.

READER (2) [READ]

Mt 24:15 standing in the holy place"—**r**, pay attention!
Mk 13:14 standing where it should not be"—**r**, pay attention!

READILY (1) [READY]

Jn 5:43 even though you **r** accept others who represent

READINESS (1) [READY]

2Co 7:11 such zeal, and such a **r** to punish the wrongdoer.

READING (11) [READ]

Dt 17:20 This regular **r** will prevent him from becoming
Jer 36:13 about the messages Baruch was **r** to the people,
36:16 By the time Baruch had finished **r**, they were badly
36:23 Whenever Jehudi finished **r** three or four columns,
51:63 Then, when you have finished **r** the scroll, tie it to
Mt 16:3 You are good at **r** the weather signs in the sky,
Ac 8:28 he was **r** aloud from the book of the prophet Isaiah.
8:30 and heard the man **r** from the prophet Isaiah;
8:30 he asked, "Do you understand what you are **r**?"
8:32 The passage of Scripture he had been **r** was this:
1Ti 4:13 I get there, focus on **r** the Scriptures to the church,

READINGS (1) [READ]

Ac 13:15 After the usual **r** from the books of Moses

READS (1) [READ]

Rev 1:3 God blesses the one who **r** this prophecy to the

READY (128) [ALREADY, READILY, READINESS]

Ge 18:8 When the food was **r**, he took some cheese curds
24:31 the village when we have a room all **r** for you
30:41 Whenever the stronger females were **r** to mate,
37:13 send you to them." "I'm **r** to go," Joseph replied.
44:1 When his brothers were **r** to leave, Joseph gave
Ex 19:11 Be sure they are **r** on the third day, for I will come
19:15 "Get **r** for an important event two days from now.
34:2 Be **r** in the morning to come up Mount Sinai
Nu 14:40 but now we are **r** to enter the land the LORD has
Dt 3:18 armed and **r** to protect your Israelite relatives.
9:8 at Mount Sinai, where he was **r** to destroy you.
9:19 for you, for the LORD was **r** to destroy you.
9:25 and nights when he was **r** to destroy you.
Jos 1:11 and tell the people to get their provisions **r**.
4:13 were **r** for battle, and they crossed over to the
8:4 in ambush close behind the city and be **r** for action.
Jdg 4:14 Then Deborah said to Barak, "Get **r**!
19:5 up early, **r** to leave, but the woman's father said,
19:8 **r** to leave, and again the woman's father said,
Ru 1:6 and her daughters-in-law got **r** to leave Moab to
1Sa 9:26 So Saul got **r**, and he and Samuel left the house
13:11 and the Philistines are at Micmash **r** for battle.
13:12 I said, 'The Philistines are **r** to march against us,
18:17 "I am **r** to give you my older daughter, Merab,
23:20 Come down whenever you're **r**, O king, and we
25:42 Quickly getting **r**, she took along five of her
2Sa 19:11 For I have heard that all Israel is **r**, and only you
1Ki 20:22 "Get **r** for another attack by the king of Aram next
2Ki 4:29 Then Elisha said to Gehazi, "Get **r** to travel;
9:1 "Get **r** to go to Ramoth-gilead," he told him.
9:21 "Quick! Get my chariot **r**!" King Joram
11:11 themselves around the king, with their weapons **r**.
16:11 and it was **r** for the king when he returned from
19:3 It is like when a child is **r** to be born,
2Ch 23:10 the guards around the king, with their weapons **r**.
26:11 **r** to march into battle, unit by unit.
29:19 of the altar of the LORD, purified and **r** for use."
35:10 When everything was **r** for the Passover
Est 3:14 so that they would be **r** to do their duty on the
8:13 That way the Jews would be **r** on that day to take
Job 3:8 those who are **r** to rouse the sea monster—
8:12 still flowering, not **r** to be cut, they begin to wither.
15:28 They will live in abandoned houses that are **r** to
17:1 and I am near death. The grave is **r** to receive me.
32:19 cask without a vent. My words are **r** to burst out!
Ps 46:1 and strength, / always **r** to help in times of trouble.
86:5 O Lord, you are so good, so **r** to forgive, / so full
109:31 **r** to save them from those who condemn them.
119:173 Stand **r** to help me, / for I have chosen to follow
Pr 22:18 deep within yourself, always **r** on your lips.
25:4 and the sterling will be **r** for the silversmith.
Ecc 12:12 There is no end of opinions **r** to be expressed.
SS 3:8 **r** to defend the king against an attack during the
Isa 5:28 arrows will be sharp and their bows **r** for battle.
14:31 of the north. Each soldier rushes forward **r** to fight.
30:33 of burning—has long been **r** for the Assyrian king;
37:3 It is like when a child is **r** to be born,
41:1 Come now and speak. The court is **r** for your case.
46:13 For I am **r** to set things right, not in the distant
46:13 I am **r** to save Jerusalem and give my glory to
55:3 I am **r** to make an everlasting covenant with you.
Jer 6:25 The enemy is everywhere, and they are **r** to kill.
26:3 Then I will be able to withhold the disaster I am **r**
38:12 you from the ropes." Then when Jeremiah was **r**,
46:19 Get **r** to leave for exile, you citizens of Egypt!
Eze 22:2 "Son of man, are you **r** to judge Jerusalem?
22:2 Are you **r** to judge this city of murderers?
36:37 I am **r** to hear Israel's prayers for these blessings,
36:37 and I am **r** to grant them their requests.
38:7 "Get **r**; be prepared! Keep all the armies around
Joel 3:9 Say to the nations far and wide: "Get **r** for war!
Ob 1:1 was sent to the nations to say, "Get **r**, everyone!
Na 3:14 Get **r** for the siege! Store up water!
Zec 5:11 And when the temple is **r**, they will set the basket
Mal 3:5 I will be a **r** witness against all sorcerers
Mt 3:10 of God's judgment is poised, **r** to sever your roots.
3:12 He is **r** to separate the chaff from the grain with his
22:3 guests were invited, and when the banquet was **r**,
22:4 meats have been cooked. Everything is **r**. Hurry!'
22:8 he said to his servants, 'The wedding feast is **r**,
24:44 You also must be **r** all the time. For the Son of
25:10 and those who were **r** went in with him to the
Mk 3:9 and to have it **r** in case he was crowded off the
4:29 And as soon as the grain is **r**, the farmer comes
Lk 3:9 of God's judgment is poised, **r** to sever your roots.
3:17 He is **r** to separate the chaff from the grain with his
12:36 Then you will be **r** to open the door and let him in
12:37 There will be special favor for those who are **r**
12:38 will be special favor for his servants who are **r**!
12:40 You must be **r** all the time, for the Son of Man will
14:17 When all was **r**, he sent his servant around to
22:5 They were delighted that he was **r** to help them,
22:33 Peter said, "Lord, I am **r** to go to prison with you,
Jn 4:35 all around us and are **r** now for the harvest.
6:15 Jesus saw that they were **r** to take him by force
7:8 I am not yet **r** to go to this festival, because my
9:31 but he is **r** to hear those who worship him and do
13:37 Lord?" he asked. "I am **r** to die for you."
14:3 When everything is **r**, I will come and get you,
Ac 21:13 For I am **r** not only to be jailed at Jerusalem
23:21 than forty men hiding along the way **r** to jump him
23:21 They are **r**, expecting you to agree to their
23:23 "Get two hundred soldiers **r** to leave for Caesarea
1Co 3:2 handle anything stronger. And you still aren't **r**,
14:27 and someone must be **r** to interpret what they are
2Co 6:2 Indeed, God is **r** to help you right now.
9:2 in Greece were **r** to send an offering a year ago.
9:3 these brothers just to be sure that you really are **r**,
9:4 only to find that you still weren't **r** after all I had
9:5 of me to make sure the gift you promised is **r**.
1Ti 5:10 are in trouble? Has she always been **r** to do good?
6:18 always being **r** to share with others whatever God
2Ti 1:8 be **r** to suffer with me for the proclamation of the
2:21 and you will be **r** for the Master to use you for
Tit 3:1 should be obedient, always **r** to do what is good.
Phm 1:22 Please keep a guest room **r** for me, for I am hoping
Heb 4:3 place of rest has been **r** since he made the world.
4:4 We know it is **r** because the Scriptures mention the
8:5 For when Moses was getting **r** to build the
8:13 It is now out of date and **r** to be put aside.
11:17 was **r** to sacrifice his only son, Isaac,
Jas 1:4 you will be strong in character and **r** for anything.
5:5 your hearts are nice and fat, **r** for the slaughter.
1Pe 3:15 your Christian hope, always be **r** to explain it.
4:1 the same attitude he had, and be **r** to suffer, too.
Rev 12:4 **r** to devour the baby as soon as it was born.
16:15 who keep their robes **r** so they will not need to
18:5 and God is **r** to judge her for her evil deeds.

REAFFIRM (3) [AFFIRM]

1Sa 11:14 let us all go to Gilgal to **r** Saul's kingship."
20:17 And Jonathan made David **r** his vow of friendship
Eze 16:62 And I will **r** my covenant with you, and you will

REAIAH (4)

1Ch 4:2 Shobal's son **R** was the father of Jahath.
5:5 Micah, **R**, Baal,
Ezr 2:47 Giddel, Gahar, **R**,
Ne 7:50 **R**, Rezin, Nekoda,

REAL (45) [REALITIES, REALITY, REALLY]

Ge 31:37 for all to see. Let them decide who is the **r** owner!
Dt 8:3 **r** life comes by feeding on every word of the
1Sa 18:17 But first you must prove yourself to be a **r** warrior
Job 10:13 " 'Yet your **r** motive—I know this was your
28:28 to forsake evil is **r** understanding.' "
Ps 14:2 he looks to see if there is even one with **r**
53:2 he looks to see if there is even one with **r**
55:10 but the **r** danger is wickedness within the city.
Pr 12:21 No **r** harm befalls the godly, but the wicked have
18:24 but a **r** friend sticks closer than a brother.
28:11 as wise, but their **r** poverty is evident to the poor.
Ecc 3:19 So people have no **r** advantage over the animals.
4:10 But people who are alone when they fall are in **r**
Jer 16:20 The gods they make are not **r** gods at all!"
Am 5:26 No, your **r** interest was in your pagan gods—
Mt 7:29 for he taught as one who had **r** authority—
Mk 1:22 for he taught as one who had **r** authority—
Lk 8:23 to swamp them, and they were in **r** danger.
12:15 **R** life is not measured by how much we own."
Jn 8:41 you are obeying your **r** father when you act that
10:13 is merely hired and has no **r** concern for the sheep.
Ac 7:43 No, your **r** interest was in your pagan gods—
25:26 the emperor? For there is no **r** charge against him.
Ro 3:11 No one has **r** understanding; / no one is seeking
15:27 because they feel they owe a **r** debt to them.
1Co 1:10 Let there be **r** harmony so there won't be divisions
6:7 To have such lawsuits at all is a **r** defeat for you.
8:7 are accustomed to thinking of idols as being **r**,
8:7 they think of it as the worship of **r** gods, and their
10:19 to whom the pagans bring sacrifices are **r** gods
14:12 ask God for those that will be of **r** help to the
16:16 and others like them who serve with such **r**
2Co 8:8 to do it. This is one way to prove your love is **r**.
Gal 3:7 The **r** children of Abraham, then, are all those who
Php 3:5 So I am a **r** Jew if there ever was one!
Col 2:17 For these rules were only shadows of the **r** thing,
3:3 and your **r** life is hidden with Christ in God.
3:4 And when Christ, who is your **r** life, is revealed to
1Ti 6:19 for the future so that they may take hold of **r** life.
Heb 8:5 is only a copy, a shadow of the **r** one in heaven.
9:23 But the **r** things in heaven had to be purified with
9:24 for that was merely a copy of the **r** Temple in
1Jn 3:16 We know what **r** love is because Christ gave up his
4:10 This is **r** love. It is not that we loved God, but that
2Jn 1:7 believe that Jesus Christ came to earth in a **r** body.

REALITIES (1) [REAL]

Col 3:1 life with Christ, set your sights on the **r** of heaven,

REALITY (1) [REAL]

Heb 10:1 not the **r** of the good things Christ has done for us.

REALIZATION (1) [REALIZE]

Mk 5:33 trembling at the **r** of what had happened to her,

REALIZE (72) [REALIZATION, REALIZED, REALIZING]

Ge 45:3 They were stunned to **r** that Joseph was standing
Ex 4:5 "Then they will **r** that the LORD, the God of
7:5 Israelites go, they will **r** that I am the LORD."
10:7 their God! Don't you **r** that Egypt lies in ruins?"
16:6 "In the evening you will **r** that it was the LORD
16:29 "Do they not **r** that I have given them the seventh
Lev 5:3 even if they don't **r** they have been defiled,
6:5 When they **r** their guilt, they must restore the
Nu 14:40 "We **r** that we have sinned, but now we are ready
22:34 I did not **r** you were standing in the road to block
Dt 4:35 so you would **r** that the LORD is God
8:5 So you should **r** that just as a parent disciplines a
Jos 8:14 But he didn't **r** there was an ambush behind the
Jdg 13:16 (Manoah didn't **r** it was the angel of the LORD.)
14:4 and mother didn't **r** the LORD was at work in
15:11 "Don't you **r** the Philistines rule over us?
16:20 But he didn't **r** the LORD had left him.
20:34 so heavy that Benjamin didn't **r** the impending
1Sa 12:17 Then you will **r** how wicked you have been in
24:20 And now I **r** that you are surely going to be king,
2Sa 2:26 Don't you **r** the only thing we will gain is
3:38 "Do you not **r** that a great leader and a great man
1Ki 1:11 "Did you **r** that Haggith's son, Adonijah,
22:3 "Do you **r** that the Arameans are still occupying
2Ki 5:26 "Don't you **r** that I was there in spirit when
2Ch 13:5 Don't you **r** that the LORD, the God of Israel,
32:12 Surely you must **r** that Hezekiah is the very person
32:13 "Surely you must **r** what I and the other kings of
Job 20:4 "Don't you **r** that ever since people were first
38:18 Do you **r** the extent of the earth? Tell me about it if
Ps 73:11 "Does God **r** what is going on?" they ask.
Pr 5:6 a crooked trail and doesn't even **r** where it leads.
9:18 But the men don't **r** that her former guests are now
Ecc 1:17 But now I **r** that even this was like chasing the
5:1 Don't be a fool who doesn't **r** that mindless
6:4 I **r** that his birth would have been meaningless
7:14 hard times strike, **r** that both come from God.
7:14 That way you will **r** that nothing is certain in this
Isa 61:9 Everyone will **r** that they are a people the LORD
Eze 20:4 Make them **r** how loathsome the actions of their
Hos 2:8 She doesn't **r** that it was I who gave her everything
7:2 Its people don't **r** I am watching them. Their sinful
Mic 7:17 They will come to **r** what lowly creatures they
Mt 5:3 "God blesses those who **r** their need for him,
15:12 "Do you **r** you offended the Pharisees by what you
24:39 People didn't **r** what was going to happen until the
26:53 Don't you **r** that I could ask my Father for
Jn 8:28 then you will **r** that I am he and that I do nothing
8:37 Yes, I **r** that you are descendants of Abraham.
10:38 Then you will **r** that the Father is in me, and I am
12:16 His disciples didn't **r** at the time that this was a
19:10 "Don't you **r** that I have the power to release you
Ac 3:17 I **r** that what you did to Jesus was done in
7:25 Moses assumed his brothers would **r** that God had
12:9 it was a vision. He didn't **r** it was really happening.
13:27 or **r** that he is the one the prophets had written
23:5 I didn't **r** he was the high priest," Paul replied,
28:28 So I want you to **r** that this salvation from God is
Ro 2:4 Don't you **r** how kind, tolerant, and patient God is
6:16 Don't you **r** that whatever you choose to obey
1Co 3:16 Don't you **r** that all of you together are the temple
5:6 Don't you **r** that if even one person is allowed to

6: 3 Don't you r that we Christians will judge angels?
6:15 Don't you r that your bodies are actually parts of
8: 7 However, not all Christians r this. Some are
2Co 10:11 The ones who say this must r that we will be just
11: 6 I think you r this by now, for we have proved it
Eph 1:18 I want you to r what a rich and glorious
1Ti 1:16 Then others will r that they, too, can believe in
2Ti 3:16 and to make us r what is wrong in our lives.
Jas 4: 4 Don't you r that friendship with this world makes
Rev 3:17 And you don't r that you are wretched

REALIZED (76) [REALIZE]

Ge 30: 9 Leah r that she wasn't getting pregnant anymore,
39: 3 and r that the LORD was with Joseph,
41: 7 Then Pharaoh woke up again and r it was a dream.
Ex 2:14 because he r that everyone knew what he had
4:31 And when they r that the LORD had seen their
Nu 20:29 When the people r that Aaron had died, all Israel
24: 1 By now Balaam r that the LORD intended to
Jdg 6:22 When Gideon r that it was the angel of the
13:21 Manoah finally r it was the angel of the LORD,
16:18 Delilah r he had finally told her the truth, so she
20:41 At this point Benjamin's warriors r disaster was
1Sa 3: 8 Then Eli r it was the LORD who was calling the
5: 7 When the people r what was happening, they cried
13: 8 Saul r that his troops were rapidly slipping away.
14: 3 No one r that Jonathan had left the Israelite camp.
18:28 When the king r how much the LORD was with
20:33 So at last Jonathan r that his father was really
28:14 Saul r that it was Samuel, and he fell to the ground
30: 3 and r what had happened to their families,
31: 5 When his armor bearer r that Saul was dead,
2Sa 5:12 And David r that the LORD had made him king
10: 6 Now the people of Ammon r how seriously they
10:15 The Arameans now r that they were no match for
10:19 and his Aramean allies r they had been defeated by
12:19 saw them whispering, he r what had happened.
14: 1 Joab r how much the king longed to see Absalom.
1Ki 3:15 Then Solomon woke up and r it had been a dream.
3:28 and the people were awed as they r the great
10: 4 When the queen of Sheba r how wise Solomon
12:16 When all Israel r that the king had rejected their
22:33 the charioteers r he was not the king of Israel,
1Ch 10: 5 When his armor bearer r that Saul was dead,
14: 2 And David r that the LORD had made him king
19: 6 Now the people of Ammon r how seriously they
19:16 The Arameans now r that they were no match for
19:19 When the servants of Hadadezer r they had been
2Ch 9: 3 When the queen of Sheba r how wise Solomon
10:16 When all Israel r that the king had rejected their
13:14 When Judah r that they were being attacked from
18:32 As soon as the charioteers r he was not the king of
32: 2 When Hezekiah r that Sennacherib also intended
33:13 Manasseh had finally r that the LORD alone is
Ne 6: 2 of Ono. But I r they were plotting to harm me,
6:12 I r that God had not spoken to him, but that he had
6:16 They r that this work had been done with the help
13:23 About the same time I r that some of the men of
Ps 73:21 Then I r how bitter I had become, / how pained I
Ecc 2:24 Then I r that this pleasure is from the hand of God.
3:18 Then I r that God allows people to continue in
9:16 Then I r that though wisdom is better than
SS 6:12 Before I r it, I found myself in my princely bed
Isa 53: 8 But who among the people r that he was dying for
Mt 17:13 Then the disciples r he had been speaking of John
21:45 heard Jesus, they r he was pointing at them—
27: 3 r that Jesus had been condemned to die,
Mk 5:30 Jesus r at once that healing power had gone out
12:12 because they r he was pointing at them—
12:28 He r that Jesus had answered well, so he asked,
15:10 (For he r by now that the leading priests had
16:13 When they r who he was, they rushed back to tell
Lk 1:22 Then they r from his gestures that he must have
5: 8 When Simon Peter r what had happened, he fell to
8:47 When the woman r that Jesus knew, she began to
20:19 because they r he was pointing at them—
Jn 4:53 Then the father r it was the same time that Jesus
16:19 Jesus r they wanted to ask him, so he said,
18: 4 Jesus fully r all that was going to happen to him.
20: 9 then they hadn't r that the Scriptures said he would
Ac 3:10 When they r he was the lame beggar they had seen
12:11 Peter finally r what had happened. "It's really
14: 9 Paul noticed him and r he had faith to be healed.
19:34 But when the crowd r he was a Jew, they started
23: 6 Paul r that some members of the high council were
Ro 7: 9 I r I had broken the law and was a sinner,
Gal 2:19 the law, I r I could never earn God's approval.
Rev 12:13 And when the dragon r that he had been thrown

REALIZING (6) [REALIZE]

Ge 38:16 not r that she was his own daughter-in-law.
Lev 22:14 "Anyone who eats the sacred offerings without r it
2Ki 4:39 and put them into the kettle without r they were
Ps 64: 9 acts of God, / r all the amazing things he does.
Mk 12:34 R this man's understanding, Jesus said to him,
Heb 13: 2 have done this have entertained angels without r it!

REALLY (171) [REAL]

Ge 3: 1 "R?" he asked the woman. "Did God r say you
must not eat any of the fruit in
27:21 I want to touch you to make sure you r are Esau."
27:24 "Are you r my son Esau?" he asked. "Yes,
38:11 (But Judah didn't r intend to do this because he
42:19 We'll see how honorable you r are. Only one of
45:12 so can my brother Benjamin, that I r am Joseph!
Ex 4: 5 and the God of Jacob—r has appeared to you."
9:14 I will send a plague that will r speak to you
33:13 Please, if this is r so, show me your intentions
Lev 25:23 on a permanent basis because it r belongs to me.
Nu 16:11 The one you are r revolting against is the LORD!
Dt 8: 2 or not you would r obey his commands.
32: 5 when they act like that, are they r his children?
Jdg 6:17 show me a sign to prove that it is r the LORD
11: 9 will you r make me ruler over all the people?"
15: 2 "I r thought you hated her," her father explained,
Ru 1:19 their arrival. "Is it r Naomi?" the women asked.
1Sa 7: 3 "If you are r serious about wanting to return to the
12:21 that cannot help or rescue you—they r are useless!
17:55 whose son is he?" "I r don't know," Abner said.
18:22 to David, "The king r likes you, and so do we.
18:25 Vengeance on my enemies is all I r want."
20:33 So at last Jonathan realized that his father was r
23:12 "Will these men of Keilah r betray me and my
24:16 Saul called back, "Is that r you, my son David?"
27:11 alive to come to Gath and tell where he had r been.
2Sa 5: 2 was our king, you were the one who r led Israel.
7:20 You know what I am r like, Sovereign LORD.
10: 3 "Do you r think these men are coming here to
15: 3 would say, "You've r got a strong case here!
17:14 which r was the better plan, so that he could bring
1Ki 1:27 Has my lord r done this without letting any of his
3:26 Then the woman who r was the mother of the
8:27 "But will God r live on earth? Why,
18: 7 "Is it r you, my lord Elijah?" he asked.
1Ch 11: 2 was our king, you were the one who r led Israel.
17:18 you have honored me? You know what I am r like.
19: 3 "Do you r think these men are coming here to
2Ch 2: 6 But who can r build him a worthy home? Not even
6:18 "But will God r live on earth among people?
13: 8 Do you r think you can stand against the kingdom
32:31 order to test him and to see what was r in his heart.
Est 5: 6 said to Esther, "Now tell me what you r want.
Job 12: 2 "You r know everything, don't you? And when
13:14 take my life in my hands and say what I r think.
36:29 Can anyone r understand the spreading of the
Ps 36: 2 they cannot see how wicked they r are.
73:15 If I had r spoken this way, / I would have been a
142: 5 my place of refuge. / You are all I r want in life.
Pr 20: 6 but who can find one who is r faithful?
Ecc 1: 4 Generations come and go, but nothing r changes.
2:11 There was nothing r worthwhile anywhere.
3: 9 What do people r get for all their hard work?
6: 8 do wise people r have any advantage over fools?
7:23 am determined to be wise." But it didn't r work.
10:14 But who can r know what is going to happen?
Isa 26:12 for all we have accomplished is r from you.
42:20 to act on it. You hear, but you don't r listen."
44: 9 These highly valued objects are r worthless.
58: 5 Do you r think this will please the LORD?
Jer 7: 9 Do you r think you can steal, murder,
14:19 rejected Judah? Do you r hate Jerusalem?
17: 9 desperately wicked. Who r knows how bad it is?
27:18 If they r are the LORD's prophets, let them pray
28: 9 can it be known that he is r from the LORD."
Eze 20: 4 loathsome the actions of their ancestors r were.
23:43 Then I said, 'If they r want to sleep with worn-out,
23:45 will judge these sister cities for what they r are—
32: 2 but you are r just a sea monster, heaving around in
33:25 Do you r think the land should be yours?
Mic 3: 4 Do you r expect him to listen? After all the evil
7:17 come to realize what lowly creatures they r are.
Na 3: 6 with filth and show the world how vile you r are.
Zec 7: 5 was it r for me that you were fasting?
Mal 1: 2 says the LORD. But you retort, "R?
Mt 3: 8 Prove by the way you live that you have r turned
6:23 If the light you think you have is r darkness,
7:15 but are r wolves that will tear you apart.
7:21 "Not all people who sound religious are r godly.
11: 3 "Are you r the Messiah we've been waiting for,
11:27 No one r knows the Son except the Father, and no
one r knows the Father except the Son
13:13 because people see what I do, but they don't r see.
13:13 They hear what I say, but they don't r hear,
14:28 Then Peter called to him, "Lord, if it's r you,
14:33 "You r are the Son of God!" they exclaimed.
Mk 9: 6 He didn't r know what to say, for they were all
11:23 All that's required is that you r believe and do not
12:40 and then, to cover up the kind of people they r are,
Lk 3: 8 Prove by the way you live that you have r turned
7:39 If God had r sent him, he would know what kind
8:10 'They see what I do, / but they don't r see;
10:22 No one r knows the Son except the Father, and no
one r knows the Father except the Son
10:42 There is r only one thing worth being concerned
11:35 Make sure that the light you think you have is not r
20:47 and then, to cover up the kind of people they r are,
23:35 "let him save himself if he is r God's Chosen One,
24:34 "The Lord has r risen! He appeared to Peter!"
24:39 You can see that it's r me. Touch me and make
Jn 2:24 because he knew what people were r like.
7:26 Can it be that our leaders know that he r is the
12:44 you trust me, you are r trusting God who sent me.
14:28 If you r love me, you will be very happy for me,
21:12 And no one dared ask him if he r was the Lord
Ac 12: 9 was a vision. He didn't realize it was r happening.
12:11 "It's r true!" he said to himself. "The Lord has
17:11 and Silas, to see if they were r teaching the truth.
Ro 7: 6 Now we can r serve God, not in the old way by
7:13 So we can see how terrible sin r is.
7:15 for I r want to do what is right, but I don't do it.
7:20 I don't want to do, I am not r the one doing it;
7:25 In my mind I r want to obey God's law, but
8:19 day when God will reveal who his children r are.
10:19 But did the people of Israel r understand? Yes,
11: 6 God's wonderful kindness would not be what it r
12: 2 how good and pleasing and perfect his will r is.
12: 9 R love them. Hate what is wrong. Stand on the
1Co 2:11 No one can know what anyone else is r thinking
4: 8 I wish you r were on your thrones already, for
4:19 big talkers or whether they r have God's power.
8: 1 it is love that r builds up the church.
8: 2 to know all the answers doesn't r know very much.
8: 4 we all know that an idol is not r a god and that
11:22 What? Is this r true? Don't you have your own
11:22 Or do you r want to disgrace the church of God
11:34 If you are r hungry, eat at home so you won't
12:10 the ability to know whether it is r the Spirit of God
12:22 and least important are r the most necessary.
14:25 declaring, "God is r here among you."
2Co 1:17 of the world who say yes when they r mean no?
7:12 you could show how much you r do care for us.
8:12 If you are r eager to give, it isn't important how
9: 1 I r don't need to write to you about this gift for the
9: 3 these brothers just to be sure that you r are ready,
10:10 in person he is weak, and his speeches are r bad!"
13: 5 Examine yourselves to see if your faith is r
13: 9 We are glad to be weak, if you are r strong.
Gal 2: 4 false ones, r—who came to spy on us and see our
4:21 under the law. Do you know what the law r says?
5: 1 So Christ has r set us free. Now make sure that
6: 3 you are only fooling yourself. You are r a nobody.
6:13 And even those who advocate circumcision don't r
6:15 What counts is whether we r have been changed
Eph 3:18 how long, how high, and how deep his love r is.
5: 5 For a greedy person is r an idolater who worships
Php 1:10 For I want you to understand what r matters,
1:22 service for Christ. I r don't know which is better.
3:10 I can r know Christ and experience the mighty
3:18 shows they are r enemies of the cross of Christ.
1Th 5: 1 I r don't need to write to you about how and when
2Th 3:17 of all my letters to prove that they r are from me.
Phm 1: 6 And I am praying that you will r put your
1:13 I r wanted to keep him here with me while I am in
Heb 4:12 and desires. It exposes us for what we r are.
6: 9 like this, we r don't believe that it applies to you.
12: 8 are illegitimate and are not r his children after all.
Jas 1: 6 ask him, be sure that you r expect him to answer,
1Pe 1:22 So see to it that you r do love each other intensely
2Pe 1:10 work hard to prove that you r are among those
3: 9 The Lord isn't r being slow about his promise to
1Jn 2: 5 But those who obey God's word r do love him.
2:19 because they never r belonged with us;
3: 1 allows us to be called his children, and we r are!
3: 2 we will be like him, for we will see him as he r is.
3:15 Anyone who hates another Christian is r a
3:18 we love each other; let us r show it by our actions.
5: 3 his commandments, and r, that isn't difficult.
Rev 2: 9 but they r aren't because theirs is a synagogue of
2:24 as they call them—depths of Satan, r).

REALM (7) [REALMS]

1Ki 9:19 and Lebanon and throughout the entire r.
2Ch 8: 6 and Lebanon and throughout the entire r.
Ezr 7:23 risk bringing God's anger against the r of the king
Est 1:18 end to the contempt and anger throughout your r.
9:27 the Jews throughout the r agreed to inaugurate this
Da 11: 9 "Later the king of the north will invade the r of
Zec 9:10 His r will stretch from sea to sea and from the

REALMS (5) [REALM]

Eph 1: 3 us with every spiritual blessing in the heavenly r
1:20 of honor at God's right hand in the heavenly r.
2: 6 and we are seated with him in the heavenly r—
3:10 to all the rulers and authorities in the heavenly r.
6:12 and against wicked spirits in the heavenly r.

REAP (3) [REAPERS]

Gal 6: 7 get away with it. You will always r what you sow!
6: 9 for we will r a harvest of blessing at the
Jas 3:18 plant seeds of peace and r a harvest of goodness.

REAPERS (1) [REAP]

Jas 5: 4 The cries of the r have reached the ears of the Lord

REAPPEARANCE (1) [APPEAR]

Rev 17: 8 will be amazed at the r of this beast who had died.

REAPPEARED (1) [APPEAR]

Lev 14:48 and finds that the affected areas have not r after

REAPPEARS (2) [APPEAR]

Lev 13:57 If the spot r at a later time, however, the mildew is
14:43 "But if the mildew r after all these things have

REAR (12) [REARED, REARING]

Ex 26:27 Also make five crossbars for the r of the
36:27 which was its r, was made from six frames,
36:29 They made two of these, one for each r corner.
Nu 2:31 They are to bring up the r whenever the Israelites
10:25 They served as the r guard for all the tribal camps.
Jos 8:22 came out and started killing the enemy from the r.
10:19 chasing the enemy and cut them down from the r.
1Sa 29: 2 and his men marched at the r with King Achish.
1Ki 6: 5 all the way around the sides and r of the building.
6:19 Solomon prepared the inner sanctuary in the r of

2Ch 13:14 they were being attacked from the front and the r,
Joel 2:20 Those in the r will go into the Dead Sea; those at

REARED (1) [REAR]
Eze 19: 2 lay down among the young lions / and r her cubs.

REARING (1) [REAR]
Da 7: 5 It was r up on one side, and it had three ribs in its

REASON (41) [REASONABLE, REASONED, REASONING, REASONS]
Ge 33:15 "There is no r for you to be so kind to me,"
Ex 9:16 But I have let you live for this r—that you might
Lev 18:28 Do not give the land a r to vomit you out for
22: 5 someone who is ceremonially unclean for any r,
Nu 21:14 For this r *The Book of the Wars of the LORD*
21:27 For this r the ancient poets wrote this about him:
Dt 25: 8 town will then summon him and try to r with him.
28:66 with no r to believe that you will see the morning
1Sa 19: 5 man like David? There is no r for it at all!"
2Sa 16:11 Shouldn't this relative of Saul have even more r to
1Ki 20:39 if for any r he gets away, you will either die
2Ki 5:13 But his officers tried to r with him and said,
1Ch 5: 1 For this r, Reuben is not listed in the genealogy as
Job 1: 9 "Yes, Job fears God, but not without good r!
9:14 I should try to answer God or even r with him?
9:17 For he attacks me without r, and he multiplies my
15:12 What has captured your r? What has weakened
23: 7 Fair and honest people can r with him, so I would
36: 9 he takes the trouble to show them the r. He shows
Ps 109: 3 hateful words, / and they fight against me for no r.
Ecc 7:25 to find wisdom and to understand the r for things.
Isa 50: 2 No, that is not the r! For I can speak to the sea
64: 2 Then your enemies would learn the r for your
Jer 44:23 The very r all these terrible things have happened
Eze 7:12 There is no r for buyers to rejoice over the
Mt 18:23 "For this r, the Kingdom of Heaven can be
19: 3 a man be allowed to divorce his wife for any r?"
Lk 23:22 I have found no r to sentence him to death. I will
Jn 12:18 That was the main r so many went out to meet
12:27 lies ahead'? But that is the very r why I came!
Ro 13:11 Another r for right living is that you know how
1Co 4:17 That is the very r I am sending Timothy—to help
2Co 1:23 The r I didn't return to Corinth was to spare you
5:12 No, we are giving you a r to be proud of us,
Gal 6:12 you to be circumcised are doing it for just one r.
Eph 1:14 This is just one more r for us to praise our glorious
Php 1:26 you will have even more r to boast about what
3: 4 If others have r for confidence in their own efforts,
Heb 13:17 Give them r to do this joyfully and not with
Jas 4: 2 And yet the r you don't have what you want is that
5:13 And those who have r to be thankful should

REASONABLE (4) [REASON]
Job 6:24 "All I want is a r answer—then I will keep quiet.
Ac 25:27 For it doesn't seem r to send a prisoner to the
1Co 10:15 You are r people. Decide for yourselves if what I
1Pe 2:18 not only if they are kind and r, but even if they are

REASONED (2) [REASON]
Ac 24:25 As he r with them about righteousness
1Co 13:11 a child, I spoke and thought and r as a child does.

REASONING (1) [REASON]
Gal 1:11 which I preach is not based on mere human r

REASONS (4) [REASON]
Ecc 5:20 on the past, for God has given them r for joy.
Jnh 1:14 sent this storm upon him for your own good r."
Ro 13: 5 So you must obey the government for two r:
13: 6 Pay your taxes, too, for these same r.

REASSIGN (1) [ASSIGN]
Isa 49: 8 the land of Israel and r it to its own people again.

REASSURE (2) [ASSURE]
Ps 119:38 R me of your promise, / which is for those who
Lk 1: 4 to r you of the truth of all you were taught.

REASSURED (3) [ASSURE]
1Sa 12:20 "Don't be afraid," Samuel r them. "You have
23:17 "Don't be afraid," Jonathan r him. "My father
Lk 2:10 but the angel r them. "Don't be afraid!" he said.

REASSURING (1) [ASSURE]
Ge 50:21 And he spoke very kindly to them, r them.

REBA (2)
Nu 31: 8 Evi, Rekem, Zur, Hur, and R—died in the battle.
Jos 13:21 Evi, Rekem, Zur, Hur, and R—princes living in the

REBEKAH (27) [REBEKAH'S]
Ge 22:23 Bethuel became the father of R.
24:15 a young woman named R arrived with a water jug
24:16 Now R was very beautiful, and she was a virgin;
24:29 Now R had a brother named Laban.
24:45 I saw R coming along with her water jug on her
24:51 Here is R; take her and go. Yes, let her be the wife
24:53 and gold jewelry and lovely clothing for R.
24:55 "But we want R to stay at least ten days,"
24:57 "we'll call R and ask her what she thinks."
24:58 So they called R. "Are you willing to go with this
24:59 So they said good-bye to R and sent her away with
24:61 Then R and her servants mounted the camels
24:64 When R looked up and saw Isaac, she quickly
24:65 my master." So R covered her face with her veil.
24:67 And Isaac brought R into his mother's tent,
25:20 When Isaac was forty years old, he married R,
25:21 Isaac pleaded with the LORD to give R a child
25:28 wild game he brought home, but R favored Jacob.
26: 7 And when the men there asked him about R,
26: 8 looked out a window and saw Isaac fondling R.
26:35 Esau's wives made life miserable for Isaac and R.
27: 5 But R overheard the conversation. So when Esau
27:13 "Let the curse fall on me, dear son," said R.
27:42 of what Esau was planning and reported it to R.
27:46 Then R said to Isaac, "I'm sick and tired of these
49:31 There Isaac and his wife, R, are buried. And there I
Ro 9:10 When he grew up, he married R, who gave birth to

REBEKAH'S (3) [REBEKAH]
Ge 24:59 The woman who had been R childhood nurse went
29:12 was her cousin on her father's side, her aunt R son.
35: 8 Soon after this, R old nurse, Deborah, died.

REBEL (26) [REBELLED, REBELLING, REBELLION, REBELLIONS, REBELLIOUS, REBELS]
Ex 23:21 Do not r against him, for he will not forgive your
Nu 14: 9 Do not r against the LORD, and don't be afraid
31:16 and caused the people of Israel to r against the
Jos 22:18 If you r against the LORD today, he will be angry
22:19 But do not r against the LORD or draw us into
22:29 Far be it from us to r against the LORD or turn
Jdg 9:31 and now they are inciting the city to r against you.
1Sa 12:14 and if you do not r against the LORD's
12:15 But if you r against the LORD's commands
2Sa 12:11 will cause your own household to r against you.
1Ki 11:26 Another r leader was Jeroboam son of Nebat,
Ne 6: 6 and the Jews are planning to r and that is why you
Job 24:13 "Wicked people r against the light. They refuse to
Ps 5:10 because of their many sins, / for they r against you.
39: 8 my rebellion, / for even fools mock me when I r.
66: 7 movement of the nations; / let no r rise in defiance.
106:43 but they continued to r against him,
Pr 17:21 parent of a fool; there is no joy for the father of a r.
29:21 is pampered from childhood will later become a r.
Isa 1: 5 Must you r forever? Your head is injured, and your
50: 5 to me, and I have listened. I do not r or turn away.
Jer 29:32 my people, for he has taught you to r against me.
Eze 2: 8 Do not join them in being a r. Open your mouth,
20:38 I will purge you of all those who r and sin against
Jn 19:12 Anyone who declares himself a king is a r against
Tit 1:10 For there are many who r against right teaching;

REBELLED (52) [REBEL]
Ge 14: 4 but now in the thirteenth year they r.
Nu 20: 2 at that place, so they r against Moses and Aaron.
20:24 because the two of you r against my instructions
27: 3 Korah's followers, who r against the LORD.
27:14 for you both r against my instructions in the
27:14 When the people of Israel r, you failed to
Dt 1:26 "But you r against the command of the LORD
1:43 you again r against the LORD's command
9: 7 until now, you have constantly r against him.
9:23 But you r against the command of the LORD
31:27 I am still with you, you have r against the LORD.
2Sa 18:31 rescued you from all those who r against you."
2Ki 3: 5 the king of Moab r against the king of Israel.
3: 7 "The king of Moab has r against me. Will you
24: 1 and paid him tribute for three years but then r.
24:20 Then Zedekiah r against the king of Babylon.
2Ch 36:13 He also r against King Nebuchadnezzar,
Ne 9:17 they r and appointed a leader to take them back to
9:26 all this, they were disobedient and r against you.
Ps 68:18 the people, / even from those who r against you.
78:40 Oh, how often they r against him in the desert
78:56 They r against the Most High / and refused to
106: 7 Instead, they r against him at the Red Sea.
107:11 They r against the words of God,
Isa 59:13 We know that we have r against the LORD.
63:10 But they r against him and grieved his Holy Spirit.
65: 2 to my own people all day long, but they have r.
66:24 they will see the dead bodies of those who have r
Jer 2:29 You are the ones who have r, says the LORD.
3:13 Admit that you r against the LORD your God
4:17 for my people have r against me,' " says the
28:16 because you have r against the LORD."
48:26 like a drunkard, for she has r against the LORD.
52: 3 Then Zedekiah r against the king of Babylon.
La 1:18 LORD is right," she groans, "for I r against him.
1:20 and my soul despairs, for I have r against you.
3:42 "We have sinned and r, and you have not forgiven
Eze 2: 3 Their ancestors have r against me from the
5: 6 but she has r against my regulations and has been
17:15 this man of Israel's royal family r against Babylon,
20: 8 "But they r against me and would not listen.
20:13 "But the people of Israel r against me, and they
20:21 "But their children, too, r against me.
Da 9: 5 We have r against you and scorned your
9: 9 and forgiving, even though we have r against him.
Hos 6: 7 you broke my covenant and r against me.
7:13 Let them die, for they have r against me. I wanted
11: 2 But the more I called to him, the more he r,
13:16 of their guilt because they r against their God.
Heb 3: 8 your hearts against him / as Israel did when they r,
3:15 hearts against him / as Israel did when they r."
3:16 And who were those people who r against God,

REBELLING (5) [REBEL]
Dt 9:24 you have been r against the LORD as long as I
Ne 2:19 are you doing, r against the king like this?"
Ps 78:17 their sin, / r against the Most High in the desert.
Jer 2:17 And you have brought this on yourselves by r
Eze 2: 3 to the nation of Israel, a nation that is r against me.

REBELLION (40) [REBEL]
Ex 34: 7 thousands by forgiving every kind of sin and r.
Lev 16:16 because of the defiling sin and r of the Israelites.
16:21 confess over it all the sins and r of the Israelites.
Nu 14:18 in unfailing love, forgiving every kind of sin and r.
14:36 Then the ten scouts who had incited the r against
16: 2 They incited a r against Moses, involving 250
Dt 13: 5 for they encourage r against the LORD your God,
Jos 22:16 the LORD and build an altar in r against him?
22:19 or draw us into your r by building another altar for
22:22 We have not built the altar in r against the
24:19 jealous God. He will not forgive your r and sins.
1Sa 15:23 R is as bad as the sin of witchcraft,
2Sa 15:10 every part of Israel to stir up a r against the king.
1Ki 11:27 This is the story behind his r. Solomon was
2Ki 17: 4 he arrested him and put him in prison for his r.
Ezr 4:19 In fact, r and sedition are normal there!
Job 13:23 have I done wrong? Show me my r and my sin.
34:37 For now you have added r and blasphemy against
Ps 32: 1 Oh, what joy for those / whose r is forgiven,
32: 5 to myself, "I will confess my r to the LORD."
32: 6 let all the godly confess their r to you while there
39: 8 Rescue me from my r, / for even fools mock me
74:23 have said. / Their uproar of r grows ever louder.
107:17 Some were fools in their r; / they suffered for their
Pr 17:11 Evil people seek r, but they will be severely
Jer 5: 6 For their r is great, and their sins are many.
33: 8 against me, and I will forgive all their sins of r.
Eze 18:31 Put all your r behind you, and get for yourselves a
21:23 king of Babylon will remind the people of their r.
Da 8:13 How long will the r that causes desecration stop
9:24 for your people and your holy city to put down r,
Hos 10:10 I will attack you, too, for your r and disobedience.
Am 7:10 is intolerable. It will lead to r all across the land.
Mic 1: 5 Because of the sins and r of Israel and Judah.
1: 5 Who is to blame for Israel's r? Samaria, its capital
3: 8 fearlessly pointing out Israel's sin and r.
Ac 21:38 "Aren't you the Egyptian who led a r some time
2Th 2: 3 For that day will not come until there is a great r
Jude 1:11 And like Korah, they will perish because of their r.
1:15 they have done in r / and of all the insults that

REBELLIONS (2) [REBEL]
Am 5:12 For I know the vast number of your sins and r.
Ac 24: 5 to riots and r against the Roman government.

REBELLIOUS (24) [REBEL]
Ex 32: 9 "I have seen how stubborn and r these people are.
Dt 21:18 r son who will not obey his father or mother,
21:20 son of ours is stubborn and r and refuses to obey.
31:27 For I know how r and stubborn you are. Even now,
31:27 How much more r will you be after my death!
1Sa 6: 6 Don't be stubborn and r as Pharaoh
Ezr 4:12 to Jerusalem from Babylon are rebuilding this r
4:15 where you will discover what a r city this has been
Ps 25: 7 Forgive the r sins of my youth; / look instead
75: 5 at the heavens / or speak with r arrogance.' "
78: 8 like their ancestors— / stubborn, r, and unfaithful,
103:12 He has removed our r acts / as far away from us as
Pr 7:11 She was the brash, r type who never stays at home.
Isa 30: 1 "Destruction is certain for my r children,"
Jer 5:23 "But my people have stubborn and r hearts.
48:45 to devour the entire land with all its r people.
49: 4 You r daughter, you trusted in your wealth
Eze 2: 7 But they won't listen, for they are completely r!
3:26 you won't be able to pray for them, for they are r.
12: 2 but they won't listen because they are r.
Zep 3: 1 How terrible it will be for r, polluted Jerusalem,
2Co 10: 5 With these weapons we conquer their r ideas,
1Ti 1: 9 They are for people who are disobedient and r,
Tit 1: 6 children must be believers who are not wild or r.

REBELS (32) [REBEL]
Nu 17:10 before the Ark of the Covenant as a warning to r.
20:10 gather at the rock. "Listen, you r!" he shouted.
Jos 1:18 Anyone who r against your word and does not
Jdg 11: 3 Soon he had a large band of r following him.
2Sa 18:28 who has handed over the r who dared to stand
1Ki 11:24 and had become the leader of a gang of r.
Ps 68: 6 But for r, there is only famine and distress.
106:17 and buried Abiram and the other r.
Pr 24:21 and the king, and don't associate with r.
Isa 1:23 Your leaders are r, the companions of thieves.
30: 9 For these people are stubborn r who refuse to pay
31: 6 though you are such wicked r, come and return to
48: 8 You have been r from your earliest childhood,
Jer 6:28 Are they not the worst of r, full of slander?
23:17 They keep saying to these r who despise my word,
50:21 the land of r, a land that I will judge!
Eze 2: 5 they listen or not—for remember, they are r—
2: 6 by their dark scowls. For remember, they are r!
3: 9 their angry looks, even though they are such r."
3:27 will listen, but some will ignore you, for they are r.

12: 2 you live among **r** who could see the truth if they
12: 3 what this means, even though they are such **r**.
12: 9 "Son of man, these **r**, the people of Israel,
12:25 There will be no more delays, you **r** of Israel!
17:12 "Say to these **r** of Israel: Don't you understand the
24: 3 Then show these **r** an illustration; give them a
44: 6 And give these **r**, the people of Israel, this message
Hos 9:15 love them no more because all their leaders are **r**.
Zep 3:11 for you will no longer be **r** against me.
Lk 22:37 'He was counted among those who were **r**.' Yes,
Ro 11:30 Once, you Gentiles were **r** against God, but when
11:31 And now, in the same way, the Jews are the **r**,

REBIRTH (1) [BEAR]

Jn 1:13 human passion or plan—this **r** comes from God.

REBORN (1) [BEAR]

Jn 1:13 They are **r**! This is not a physical birth resulting

REBUFFED (1)

Isa 60:15 you were once despised and hated and **r** by all,

REBUILD (45) [BUILD]

Jos 6:26 who tries to **r** the city of Jericho. / At the cost of
1Ki 18:32 and he used the stones to **r** the LORD's altar.
Ezr 1: 3 in Judah to **r** this Temple of the LORD,
1: 5 and Benjamin to return to Jerusalem to **r** the
3: 2 his family began to **r** the altar of the God of Israel
5: 3 "Who gave you permission to **r** this Temple
5: 9 'Who gave you permission to **r** this Temple
5:15 and to **r** the Temple of God there as it had been
5:17 issued a decree to **r** God's Temple in Jerusalem.
6: 8 leaders of the Jews as they **r** this Temple of God.
6:22 so that he helped them to **r** the Temple of God,
9: 9 so that we were able to **r** the Temple of our God
Ne 2: 5 send me to Judah to **r** the city where my ancestors
2:17 Let us **r** the wall of Jerusalem and rid ourselves of
2:18 They replied at once, "Good! Let's **r** the wall!"
3: 1 and the other priests started to **r** at the Sheep Gate.
Ps 51:18 on Zion and help her; / **r** the walls of Jerusalem.
69:35 and **r** the towns of Judah. / His people will live
102:16 For the LORD will **r** Jerusalem. / He will appear
Ecc 3: 3 time to heal. / A time to tear down and a time to **r**.
Isa 9:10 in ruins now, but we will **r** it better than before.
14:21 and conquer the land or **r** the cities of the world."
54:11 I will **r** you on a foundation of sapphires and make
57:14 I will say, '**R** the road! Clear away the rocks
58:12 Your children will **r** the deserted ruins of your
58:12 Then you will be known as the people who **r** their
60:10 "Foreigners will come to **r** your cities. Kings
61: 4 They will **r** the ancient ruins, repairing cities long
Jer 3:16 and there will be no need to **r** the Ark.
10:20 My home is gone, and no one is left to help me **r** it.
31: 4 I will **r** you, my virgin Israel. You will again be
33: 7 the fortunes of Judah and Israel and **r** their cities.
Eze 22:30 "I looked for someone who might **r** the wall of
Da 9:25 to **r** Jerusalem until the Anointed One comes.
Am 9:11 but I will **r** its walls and restore its former glory.
9:14 and they will **r** their ruined cities and live in them
Hag 1: 2 'The time has not yet come to **r** the LORD's
1: 8 into the hills, bring down timber, and **r** my house.
Zec 6:15 Many will come from distant lands to **r** the Temple
Mal 1: 4 "We have been shattered, but we will **r** the ruins."
1: 4 "They may try to **r**, but I will demolish them
Mt 26:61 the Temple of God and **r** it in three days.' "
Mk 15:29 can destroy the Temple and **r** it in three days,
Ac 15:16 From the ruins I will **r** it, / and I will restore it,
Gal 2:18 I make myself guilty if I **r** the old system I already

REBUILDING (16) [BUILD]

1Ki 11:27 Solomon was **r** the Millo and repairing the walls of
2Ch 8: 2 Solomon now turned his attention to **r** the towns
8: 5 **r** their walls and installing barred gates.
27: 3 and also did extensive **r** on the wall at the hill of
Ezr 2:68 toward the **r** of God's Temple on its original site,
3: 8 or older were put in charge of **r** the LORD's
4: 1 and Benjamin heard that the exiles were **r** a
4:12 to Jerusalem from Babylon are **r** this rebellious
5: 2 the task of **r** the Temple of God in Jerusalem.
5:11 and we are **r** the Temple that was built here many
Ne 2:20 We his servants will start **r** this wall. But you have
3:14 After **r** it, he hung the doors and installed the bolts
4: 1 angry when he learned that we were **r** the wall.
6: 1 enemies found out that I had finished **r** the wall
Ps 147: 2 The LORD is **r** Jerusalem / and bringing the
Zec 8:13 but instead get on with **r** the Temple!

REBUILT (48) [BUILD]

Nu 21:27 city of Sihon! / May it be restored and **r**.
32:38 names of some of the towns they conquered and **r**.
Dt 13:16 town must remain a ruin forever; it may never be **r**.
Jos 19:50 country of Ephraim. He **r** the town and lived there.
Jdg 18:28 Then the people of the tribe of Dan **r** the town
21:23 Then they **r** their towns and lived in them.
1Ki 9:17 So Solomon **r** the city of Gezer.) He also built up
16:34 his reign that Hiel, a man from Bethel, **r** Jericho.
2Ki 14:22 Uzziah **r** the town of Elath and restored it to Judah.
15:35 He was the one who **r** the upper gate of the Temple
21: 3 He **r** the pagan shrines his father, Hezekiah,
1Ch 11: 8 while Joab **r** the rest of Jerusalem.
2Ch 8: 4 He **r** Tadmor in the desert and built towns in the
8: 6 He also **r** Baalath and other supply centers at this
26: 2 Uzziah **r** the town of Elath and restored it to Judah.
27: 3 Jotham **r** the Upper Gate to the LORD's Temple
33: 3 He **r** the pagan shrines his father Hezekiah had
33:14 It was after this that Manasseh **r** the outer wall of
Ezr 3: 3 of the local residents, they **r** the altar at its old site.
4:13 But we wish you to know that if this city is **r**
4:16 We declare that if this city is **r** and its walls are
4:21 That city must not be **r** except at my express
5: 8 It is being **r** with specially prepared stones,
5:13 a decree that the Temple of God should be **r**.
6: 3 It must be **r** on the site where Jews used to offer
6: 7 Let it be **r** on its former site, and do not hinder the
Ne 3:13 led by Hanun, **r** the Valley Gate, hung its doors,
3:15 He **r** it, roofed it, hung its doors, and installed its
3:15 and he **r** the wall as far as the stairs that descend
3:16 He **r** the wall to a place opposite the royal
3:21 and grandson of Hakkoz **r** another section of the
3:24 who **r** another section of the wall from Azariah's
3:29 Next Zadok son of Immer also **r** the wall next to
3:30 while Meshullam son of Berekiah **r** the wall next
Job 12:14 What he destroys cannot be **r**. When he closes in
Ps 28: 5 down like old buildings, / and they will never be **r**!
Isa 25: 2 in distant lands disappear and will never be **r**.
44:28 He will command that Jerusalem be **r** and that the
Jer 30:18 your fortunes, Jerusalem will be **r** on her ruins.
31:38 the LORD, "when all Jerusalem will be **r** for me,
Eze 26:14 You will never be **r**, for I, the LORD,
35: 9 you desolate forever. Your cities will never be **r**.
36:10 and the ruined cities will be **r** and filled with
36:33 people to live in your cities, and the ruins will be **r**.
36:36 **r** the ruins and planted lush crops in the
Da 9:25 Jerusalem will be **r** with streets and strong
Mic 7:11 In that day, Israel, your cities will be **r**, and your
Zec 1:16 My Temple will be **r**, says the LORD Almighty,

REBUKE (22) [REBUKED, REBUKES, REBUKING]

Job 26:11 The foundations of heaven tremble at his **r**.
Ps 6: 1 O LORD, do not **r** me in your anger
38: 1 O LORD, don't **r** me in your anger!
50:21 you thought I didn't care. / But now I will **r** you,
68:30 **R** these enemy nations— / these wild animals
104: 7 At the sound of your **r**, the water fled;
119:21 You **r** those cursed proud ones / who wander from
Pr 15:12 Mockers don't love those who **r** them, so they stay
17:10 A single **r** does more for a person of understanding
27: 5 An open **r** is better than hidden love!
30: 6 Do not add to his words, or he may **r** you, and you
Isa 66:15 fury of his anger and the flaming fire of his hot **r**.
Eze 5:15 the LORD turns against a nation in furious **r**.
25:17 I will execute terrible vengeance against them to **r**
Mal 2: 3 I will **r** your descendants and splatter your faces
Lk 17: 3 If another believer sins, **r** him; then if he repents,
19:39 **r** your followers for saying things like that!"
2Co 1:23 return to Corinth was to spare you from a severe **r**.
Eph 5:11 of evil and darkness; instead, **r** and expose them.
2Ti 4: 2 Patiently correct, **r**, and encourage your people
Tit 1:13 So **r** them as sternly as necessary to make them
Jude 1: 9 of blasphemy, but simply said, "The Lord **r** you."

REBUKED (17) [REBUKE]

Ge 37:10 father as well as his brothers, and his father **r** him.
1Sa 24: 7 So David sharply **r** his men and did not let them
Ne 13:15 So I **r** them for selling their produce on the
Ps 9: 5 You have **r** the nations and destroyed the wicked;
76: 6 When you **r** them, O God of Jacob, / their horses
Pr 9: 8 But the wise, when **r**, will love you all the more.
Isa 51:20 LORD has poured out his fury; God has **r** them.
Mt 8:26 Then he stood up and **r** the wind and waves,
17:18 Then Jesus **r** the demon in the boy, and it left him.
Mk 4:39 he **r** the wind and said to the water,
9:25 of onlookers was growing, he **r** the evil spirit.
16:14 He **r** them for their unbelief—their stubborn
Lk 8:24 So Jesus **r** the wind and the raging waves.
9:42 But Jesus **r** the evil spirit and healed the boy.
9:55 But Jesus turned and **r** them.
1Ti 5:20 Anyone who sins should be **r** in front of the whole
2Pe 2:16 course when his donkey **r** him with a human voice.

REBUKES (5) [REBUKE]

Job 21:31 No one **r** them openly. No one repays them for
Ps 2: 5 Then in anger he **r** them, / terrifying them with his
Pr 9: 7 Anyone who **r** a mocker will get a smart retort.
9: 7 Anyone who **r** the wicked will get hurt.
Zec 3: 2 the LORD, who has chosen Jerusalem, **r** you.

REBUKING (2) [REBUKE]

Pr 9: 8 So don't bother **r** mockers; they will only hate you.
Lk 4:39 Standing at her bedside, he spoke to the fever, **r** it,

RECAB (11) [RECABITE, RECABITES]

2Sa 4: 2 Now there were two brothers, Baanah and **R**,
4: 5 One day **R** and Baanah, the sons of Rimmon from
4: 6 So **R** and Baanah slipped past the doorkeeper,
4: 9 But David said to **R** and Baanah, "As surely as the
2Ki 10:15 When Jehu left there, he met Jehonadab son of **R**,
10:23 into the temple of Baal with Jehonadab son of **R**.
1Ch 2:55 from Hammath, the father of the family of **R**.
Ne 3:14 The Dung Gate was repaired by Malkijah son of **R**,
Jer 35: 6 because Jehonadab son of **R**, our ancestor, gave us
35:16 The families of **R** have obeyed their ancestor
35:19 Jehonadab son of **R** will always have descendants

RECABITE (1) [RECAB]

Jer 35: 3 and sons—representing all the **R** families.

RECABITES (3) [RECAB]

Jer 35: 2 "Go to the settlement where the families of the **R**
35:14 The **R** do not drink wine because their ancestor
35:18 Then Jeremiah turned to the **R** and said, "This is

RECAH (1)

1Ch 4:12 of Ir-nahash. These were the descendants of **R**.

RECALL (1)

Ps 77:11 I **r** all you have done, O LORD; / I remember

RECAPTURED (1) [CAPTURE]

2Ki 13:25 Then Jehoash son of Jehoahaz **r** from Ben-hadad

RECEDE (1)

Ge 8: 3 So the flood gradually began to **r**. After 150 days,

RECEIPT (OF CUSTOM) [KJV] See TAX-COLLECTION

RECEIVE (120) [RECEIVED, RECEIVES, RECEIVING]

Ge 47:26 that Pharaoh should **r** one-fifth of all the crops
Ex 14: 4 so I will **r** great glory at the expense of Pharaoh
14:17 Then I will **r** great glory at the expense of Pharaoh
Lev 7:18 and you will **r** no credit for bringing it as an
26:43 At last the people will **r** the due punishment for
Nu 7: 5 "**R** their gifts and use these oxen and carts for the
14:24 His descendants will **r** their full share of that land.
18:20 "You priests will **r** no inheritance of land or share
18:23 But the Levites will **r** no inheritance of land among
18:24 That is why I said they would **r** no inheritance of
18:26 'When you **r** the tithes from the Israelites, give a tenth of the tithes you **r**—
Dt 11:28 You will **r** a curse if you reject the commands of
15: 5 You will **r** this blessing if you carefully obey the
19:19 the accuser will **r** the punishment intended for the
26:19 Then you will **r** praise, honor, and renown.
Jos 18: 7 However, the Levites will not **r** any land.
18: 7 and the half-tribe of Manasseh won't **r** any more
Jdg 4: 9 you have made this choice, you will **r** no honor.
2Sa 19:37 and **r** whatever good things you want to give
1Ki 2:45 But may I **r** the LORD's rich blessings, and may
2Ki 5:26 Is this the time to **r** money and clothing and olive
10: 2 and weapons. As soon as you **r** this letter,
19: 7 and the king will **r** a report from Assyria telling
22: 7 supervisors to keep account of the money they **r**,
Ne 10:38 will be with the Levites as they **r** these tithes.
Est 1:20 their rank, will **r** proper respect from their wives!"
Job 17: 1 and I am near death. The grave is ready to **r** me.
27:13 "This is what the wicked will **r** from God; this is
33:26 And God will **r** him with joy and restore him to
Ps 24: 5 They will **r** the LORD's blessing / and have right
37:18 and they will **r** a reward that lasts forever.
Pr 1: 3 people will **r** instruction in discipline,
1: 5 And let those who understand **r** guidance
14:14 get what they deserve; good people **r** their reward.
24:26 It is an honor to **r** an honest reply.
28:13 they confess and forsake them, they will **r** mercy.
Ecc 5:19 And it is a good thing to **r** wealth from God
9: 2 Good people **r** the same treatment as sinners,
Isa 3:10 Tell them, "You will **r** a wonderful reward!"
18: 7 will **r** gifts from this land divided by rivers,
37: 7 I myself will make sure that the king will **r** a report
50:11 own fires. This is the reward you will **r** from me:
60:11 Your gates will stay open around the clock to **r** the
Jer 46:10 will **r** a sacrifice today in the north country beside
La 2: 9 Her prophets **r** no more visions from the LORD.
Eze 3:17 Whenever you **r** a message from me, pass it on to
7:26 They will **r** no teaching from the priests and no
7:27 and they will **r** the punishment they so richly
47:14 Otherwise each tribe will **r** an equal share. I swore
47:22 and they will **r** an inheritance among the tribes.
48: 1 of the tribes of Israel and the territory each is to **r**.
Da 4:26 This means that you will **r** your kingdom back
12:13 you will rise again to **r** the inheritance set aside for
Hos 3: 5 and they will **r** his good gifts in the last days.
14: 2 to him, "Forgive all our sins and graciously **r** us,
Zep 2:10 They will **r** the wages of their pride, for they have
Zec 6:13 and he will **r** royal honor and will rule as king
Mal 2: 2 I will curse even the blessings you **r**. Indeed,
Mt 5: 6 and thirsty for justice, / for they will **r** it in full.
10:41 for God, you will **r** the same reward a prophet gets.
13:20 those who hear the message and **r** it with joy.
19:17 you can **r** eternal life if you keep the
19:29 will **r** a hundred times as much in return and will
20:10 to get their pay, they assumed they would **r** more.
21:22 you will **r** whatever you ask for in prayer."
Mk 4:16 those who hear the message and **r** it with joy.
10:30 will **r** now in return, a hundred times over, houses,
Lk 6:38 If you give, you will **r**. Your gift will return to you
9: 5 If the people of the village won't **r** your message
10:25 "Teacher, what must I do to **r** eternal life?"
Jn 11: 4 of God. I, the Son of God, will **r** glory from this."
13:31 and God will **r** glory because of all that happens to
14:17 The world at large cannot **r** him, because it isn't
16:24 Ask, using my name, and you will **r**, and you will
20:22 on them and said to them, "**R** the Holy Spirit.
Ac 1: 8 you will **r** power and will tell people about me
2:38 Then you will **r** the gift of the Holy Spirit.
7:59 Stephen prayed, "Lord Jesus, **r** my spirit."
8:15 they prayed for these new Christians to **r** the Holy
8:19 my hands on people, they will **r** the Holy Spirit!"

19: 2 "Did you **r** the Holy Spirit when you believed?"
20:35 'It is more blessed to give than to **r**.' "
22:13 beside me and said, 'Brother Saul, **r** your sight.'
26:18 Then they will **r** forgiveness for their sins and be
Ro 4: 4 wages are not a gift. Workers earn what they **r**.
4:16 And we are certain to **r** it, whether or not we
5:17 to rule over us, but all who **r** God's wonderful,
6:16 or you can choose to obey God and **r** his approval.
11:17 So now you also **r** the blessing God has promised
16: 2 **R** her in the Lord, as one who is worthy of high
1Co 3:14 work survives the fire, that builder will **r** a reward.
2Co 4:15 and God will **r** more and more glory.
5:10 We will each **r** whatever we deserve for the good
5:15 so that those who **r** his new life will no longer live
Gal 3: 2 Did you **r** the Holy Spirit by keeping the law?
3:14 and we Christians **r** the promised Holy Spirit
3:22 so the only way to **r** God's promise is to believe in
5: 5 But we who live by the Spirit eagerly wait to **r**
Php 3:14 the end of the race and **r** the prize for which God,
4:17 What I want is for you to **r** a well-earned reward
2Th 1:10 when he comes to **r** glory and praise from his holy
1Ti 1:16 that they, too, can believe in him and **r** eternal life.
4: 4 any of it. We may **r** it gladly, with thankful hearts.
2Ti 3:15 and they have given you the wisdom to **r** the
Heb 1:14 from God to care for those who will **r** salvation.
4:16 There we will **r** his mercy, and we will find grace
9:15 so that all who are invited can **r** the eternal
10:36 Then you will **r** all that he has promised.
11:19 a sense, Abraham did **r** his son back from the dead.
11:40 for they can't **r** the prize at the end of the race until
Jas 1: 7 People like that should not expect to **r** anything
1:12 Afterward they will **r** the crown of life that God
1Pe 1: 5 will protect you until you **r** this salvation,
2Pe 1: 3 He has called us to **r** his own glory and goodness!
1Jn 3:22 And we will **r** whatever we request because we
2Jn 1: 8 Be diligent so that you will **r** your full reward.
Jude 1: 2 May you **r** more and more of God's mercy, peace,
Rev 4:11 O Lord our God, / to **r** glory and honor and power.
5:12 He is worthy to **r** power and riches / and wisdom

RECEIVED (118) [RECEIVE]

Ge 31:15 He sold us, and what he **r** for us has disappeared.
41:37 Joseph's suggestions were well **r** by Pharaoh
49:28 Each **r** a blessing that was appropriate to him.
50:17 When Joseph **r** the message, he broke down
Lev 25:51 they will repay most of what they **r** when they sold
Nu 9: 8 "Wait here until I have **r** instructions for you from
18:28 You must present one-tenth of the tithe **r** from the
23:20 I **r** a command to bless; / he has blessed, and I
31:51 and Eleazar the priest **r** the gold from all the
32:18 people of Israel have **r** their inheritance of land.
32:19 on the east side where we have **r** our inheritance."
34:14 and half the tribe of Manasseh have already **r** their
Dt 3:17 They also **r** the Jordan Valley, including the Jordan
16:10 in proportion to the blessings you have **r** from him.
28:47 enthusiasm for the abundant benefits you have **r**,
Jos 13: 8 and Gad had already **r** their inheritance on the east
14: 2 and a half tribes **r** their inheritance by means of
15:48 Judah also **r** the following towns in the hill
16: 4 Manasseh and Ephraim, **r** their inheritance.
17: 6 because the female descendants of Manasseh **r** an
18: 7 for they have already **r** their inheritance,
19: 9 So the tribe of Simeon **r** an inheritance within the
21: 6 The clan of Gershon **r** thirteen towns from the
21: 7 The clan of Merari **r** twelve cities from the tribes
21:27 **r** two towns with their pasturelands from the
21:28 From the tribe of Issachar they **r** Kishion,
21:30 From the tribe of Asher they **r** Mishal, Abdon,
21:32 From the tribe of Naphtali they **r** Kedesh in Galilee
21:36 From the tribe of Reuben they **r** Bezer, Jahaz,
21:38 From the tribe of Gad they **r** Ramoth in Gilead (a
1Sa 9:27 for I have **r** a special message for you from God."
17:27 And David **r** the same reply as before: "What you
17:30 asked them the same thing and **r** the same answer.
23:15 David **r** the news that Saul was on the way to Ziph
25:39 it myself. Nabal has **r** the punishment for his sin."
1Ki 5: 7 When Hiram **r** Solomon's message, he was very
5: 8 "I have **r** your message, and I will do as you have
10:14 Each year Solomon **r** about twenty-five tons of
10:15 This did not include the additional revenue he **r**
2Ki 19: 9 Soon afterward King Sennacherib **r** word that King
19:14 After Hezekiah **r** the letter and read it, he went up
1Ch 6:61 The remaining descendants of Kohath **r** ten towns
6:62 The descendants of Gershon **r** by sacred lots
6:63 The descendants of Merari **r** by sacred lots twelve
6:66 The descendants of Kohath **r** from the territory of
6:71 The descendants of Gershon **r** from the territory of
6:74 From the territory of Asher, they **r** Mashal, Abdon,
6:77 The remaining descendants of Merari **r** from the
6:78 they **r** Bezer (a desert town), Jahaz,
6:80 of Gad, they **r** Ramoth in Gilead, Mahanaim,
2Ch 9:13 Each year Solomon **r** about 25 tons of gold.
9:14 This did not include the additional revenue he **r**
27: 5 he **r** from them an annual tribute of 7,500 pounds
Ezr 4:20 of the Euphrates River and have **r** vast tribute,
Ne 12:47 in turn, gave a portion of what they **r** to the priests,
13: 6 though I later **r** his permission to return.
Job 29:16 and made sure that even strangers **r** a fair trial.
Ps 68:18 a crowd of captives. / You **r** gifts from the people,
Isa 13: 1 Isaiah son of Amoz **r** this message concerning the
37: 9 Soon afterward King Sennacherib **r** word that King
37:14 After Hezekiah **r** the letter and read it, he went up
52: 3 "When I sold you into exile, I **r** no payment.
56: 5 than the honor they would have **r** by having sons
Jer 13: 8 Then I **r** this message from the LORD:
29:29 But when Zephaniah the priest **r** Shemaiah's letter,
44: 1 This is the message Jeremiah **r** concerning the
50:43 The king of Babylon has **r** reports about the
Eze 23:10 the land as a sinner who had **r** what she deserved.
Am 1: 1 He **r** this message in visions two years before the
Hab 1: 1 This is the message that the prophet Habakkuk **r**
Zec 1: 6 'We have **r** what we deserved from the LORD
6: 9 Then I **r** another message from the LORD:
Mal 2: 6 They passed on to the people all the truth they **r**
Mt 6: 2 they have **r** all the reward they will ever get.
10: 8 and cast out demons. Give as freely as you have **r**!
20: 9 at five o'clock were paid, each **r** a full day's wage.
20:11 When they **r** their pay, they protested,
25:16 The servant who **r** the five bags of gold began
25:18 But the servant who **r** the one bag of gold dug a
25:22 "Next came the servant who had **r** the two bags of
Lk 8:40 On the other side of the lake the crowds **r** Jesus
Jn 10:35 So if those people, who **r** God's message,
Ac 1:18 (Judas bought a field with the money he **r** for his
5: 8 the price you and your husband **r** for your land?"
7:53 though you **r** it from the hands of angels."
8:17 upon these believers, and they **r** the Holy Spirit.
8:33 He was humiliated and **r** no justice. / Who can
10:47 now that they have **r** the Holy Spirit just as we
11: 1 and other believers in Judea that the Gentiles had **r**
22: 5 For I **r** letters from them to our Jewish brothers in
Ro 9:11 anything good or bad, she **r** a message from God.
15:27 Since the Gentiles **r** the wonderful spiritual
1Co 11:23 himself said, and I pass it on to you just as I **r** it.
12:13 by one Spirit, and we have all **r** the same Spirit.
2Co 7: 7 he brought of the encouragement he **r** from you.
11: 4 or a different Spirit than the one you **r**, or a
12: 1 about the visions and revelations I **r** from the Lord.
12: 7 even though I have **r** wonderful revelations from
Gal 3: 9 faith in Christ share the same blessing Abraham **r**
3:18 For if the inheritance could be **r** only by keeping
Eph 1:11 of Christ, we have **r** an inheritance from God,
Col 1:23 Don't drift away from the assurance you **r** when
1Th 1: 6 So you **r** the message with joy from the Holy Spirit
1Ti 4:14 Do not neglect the spiritual gift you **r** through the
Heb 6:15 waited patiently, and he **r** what God had promised.
6:17 so that those who **r** the promise could be perfectly
7: 6 the one who had already **r** the promises of God.
10:26 if we deliberately continue sinning after we have **r**
11:17 Abraham, who had **r** God's promises, was ready to
11:33 with justice, and **r** what God had promised them.
11:35 Women **r** their loved ones back again from death.
11:39 All of these people we have mentioned **r** God's
11:39 yet none of them **r** all that God had promised.
1Pe 2:10 Once you **r** none of God's mercy; / now you have
r his mercy."
2Pe 1:17 And he **r** honor and glory from God the Father
1Jn 2:27 But you have **r** the Holy Spirit, and he lives within
Rev 2:28 They will have the same authority I **r** from my

RECEIVES (9) [RECEIVE]

Nu 5:10 priest may keep the sacred donations that he **r**."
Job 12: 4 I am a man who calls on God and **r** an answer.
Pr 18:22 wife finds a treasure and **r** favor from the LORD.
Mt 7: 8 For everyone who asks, **r**. Everyone who seeks,
Lk 11:10 For everyone who asks, **r**. Everyone who seeks,
Jn 16:14 glory by revealing to you whatever he **r** from me.
16:15 Spirit will reveal to you whatever he **r** from me.
1Co 14:30 and another person **r** a revelation from the Lord,
Rev 2:17 name that no one knows except the one who **r** it.

RECEIVING (7) [RECEIVE]

Dt 9: 9 That was when I was on the mountain **r** the tablets
Lk 18:30 as well as **r** eternal life in the world to come."
Ac 11:18 privilege of turning from sin and **r** eternal life."
Ro 9: 4 of worshiping him and **r** his wonderful promises.
9:16 So **r** God's promise is not up to us. We can't get it
Heb 11:13 All these faithful ones died without **r** what God
12:28 Since we are **r** a kingdom that cannot be destroyed,

RECENTLY (6)

Ge 32: 4 I have been living with Uncle Laban until **r**,
Dt 32:17 had not known before, / to gods only **r** arrived,
1Sa 21: 4 young men have not slept with any women **r**."
Jer 34:15 **R** you repented and did what was right,
Ac 18: 2 who had **r** arrived from Italy with his wife,
3Jn 1: 3 Some of the brothers **r** returned and made me very

RECESSED (4)

1Ki 6: 4 made narrow, **r** windows throughout the Temple.
Eze 40:16 There were **r** windows that narrowed inward
41:16 as were the frames of the **r** windows. The inner
41:26 On both sides of the foyer there were **r** windows

RECITE (3) [RECITED, RECITING]

Ps 40: 5 If I tried to **r** all your wonderful deeds, / I would
45: 1 I will **r** a lovely poem to the king,
50:16 God says to the wicked: / "**R** my laws no longer,

RECITED (3) [RECITE]

Dt 31:30 So Moses **r** this entire song to the assembly of
32:44 and **r** all the words of this song to the people.
Ps 119:13 I have **r** aloud / all the laws you have given us.

RECITING (1) [RECITE]

Dt 32:45 When Moses had finished **r** these words to Israel,

RECKLESS (1) [RECKLESSLY]

2Ti 3: 4 betray their friends, be **r**, be puffed up with pride,

RECKLESSLY (3) [RECKLESS]

2Ki 9:20 be Jehu son of Nimshi, for he is driving so **r**."
Pr 26:10 or a bystander is like an archer who shoots **r**.
Na 2: 4 The chariots race **r** along the streets and through

RECKONING (4)

Jer 50:31 the LORD Almighty. "Your day of **r** has arrived.
Eze 21:25 wicked prince of Israel, your final day of **r** is here!
21:29 the wicked for whom the day of final **r** has come.
22:14 and courageous will you be in my day of **r**?

RECLAIM (1) [CLAIM]

Ob 1:17 And the people of Israel will come back to **r** their

RECLINING (1)

Est 7: 8 he fell on the couch where Queen Esther was **r**,

RECLUSE (1)

Pr 18: 1 A **r** is self-indulgent, snarling at every sound

RECOGNITION (1) [RECOGNIZE]

Est 6: 3 or **r** did we ever give Mordecai for this?"

RECOGNIZE (45) [RECOGNITION, RECOGNIZED, RECOGNIZES, RECOGNIZING]

Ge 27:23 But he did not **r** Jacob because Jacob's hands felt
38:25 stick is the father of my child. Do you **r** them?"
42: 8 Joseph's brothers didn't **r** him, but Joseph
Dt 32:31 our enemies is not like our Rock, / as even they **r**.
Ru 3:14 it was light enough for people to **r** each other.
1Ki 14: 2 so that no one will **r** you as the queen.
22:30 I will disguise myself so no one will **r** me,
2Ki 9:37 of Jezreel, so that no one will be able to **r** her.' "
1Ch 16:28 O nations of the world, **r** the LORD,
16:28 **r** that the LORD is glorious and strong.
2Ch 18:29 I will disguise myself so no one will **r** me,
35:22 his royal robes so the enemy would not **r** him.
Job 33:14 speaks again and again, though people do not **r** it.
37: 7 working at such a time so they can **r** his power.
Ps 51: 3 For I **r** my shameful deeds— / they haunt me day
79: 6 Pour out your wrath on the nations that refuse to **r**
96: 7 O nations of the world, **r** the LORD;
96: 7 **r** that the LORD is glorious and strong.
Isa 29:23 they will **r** the holiness of the Holy One of Israel.
32: 6 Everyone will **r** ungodly fools for what they are.
52: 6 Then at last they will **r** that it is I who speaks to
Jer 10:25 Pour out your wrath on the nations that refuse to **r**
24: 7 I will give them hearts that will **r** me as the
Eze 6: 9 They will **r** how grieved I am by their unfaithful
Hos 4: 6 to know me. Now I refuse to **r** you as my priests.
Mk 16:12 but they didn't **r** him at first because he had
Lk 2:12 And this is how you will **r** him: You will find a
Jn 1:10 through him, the world didn't **r** him when he came.
10: 4 and they follow him because they **r** his voice.
10: 5 will run from him because they don't **r** his voice."
10:27 My sheep **r** my voice; I know them, and they
14:17 because it isn't looking for him and doesn't **r** him.
18:37 All who love the truth **r** that what I say is true."
20:14 behind her. It was Jesus, but she didn't **r** him.
Ac 13:27 They didn't **r** him or realize that he is the one the
27:39 When morning dawned, they didn't **r** the coastline,
1Co 1:18 But we who are being saved **r** this message as the
14: 7 For no one will **r** the melody unless the notes are
14:37 you should **r** that what I am saying is a command
14:38 But if you do not **r** this, you will not be
2Co 3: 2 can read it and **r** our good work among you.
10: 7 You must **r** that we belong to Christ just as much
13: 6 I hope you **r** that we have passed the test and are
2Ti 3: 9 Someday everyone will **r** what fools they are,
Heb 5:14 who have trained themselves to **r** the difference

RECOGNIZED (20) [RECOGNIZE]

Ge 37:18 they **r** him in the distance and made plans to kill
37:33 Their father **r** it at once. "Yes," he said, "it is my
42: 7 Joseph **r** them instantly, but he pretended to be a
42: 8 brothers didn't recognize him, but Joseph **r** them.
1Sa 18:15 When Saul **r** this, he became even more afraid of
26:17 Saul **r** David's voice and called out, "Is that you,
1Ki 18: 7 Obadiah **r** him at once and fell to the ground
20:41 and the king of Israel **r** him as one of the prophets.
Est 8:13 A copy of this decree was to be **r** as law in every
Job 2:12 they saw Job from a distance, they scarcely **r** him.
Mt 17:12 I tell you, he has already come, but he wasn't **r**,
Mk 6:54 The people standing there **r** him at once,
Lk 24:31 Suddenly, their eyes were opened, and they **r** him.
24:35 and how they had **r** him as he was breaking the
Ac 4:13 They also **r** them as men who had been with Jesus.
12:14 When she **r** Peter's voice, she was so overjoyed
1Co 11:19 so that those of you who are right will be **r**!
14:38 But if you do not recognize this, you will not be **r**.
Gal 2: 9 **r** the gift God had given me, and they accepted
Heb 7: 4 **r** how great Melchizedek was by giving him a

RECOGNIZES (1) [RECOGNIZE]

La 4: 8 No one even **r** them. Their skin sticks to their

RECOGNIZING (2) [RECOGNIZE]

Da 9:13 our God by turning from our sins and **r** his truth.
Lk 24:16 who he was, because God kept them from **r** him.

RECOMMEND (1) [RECOMMENDATION]
Ecc 8:15 So I **r** having fun, because there is nothing better

RECOMMENDATION (4) [RECOMMEND]
1Co 16: 3 When I come I will write letters of **r** for the
2Co 3: 1 Some people need to bring letters of **r** with them or ask you to write letters of **r** for them.
3: 2 But the only letter of **r** we need is you yourselves!

RECONCILE (2) [RECONCILED, RECONCILIATION, RECONCILING]
1Sa 29: 4 Is there any better way for him to **r** himself with
1Ti 2: 5 and one Mediator who can **r** God and people.

RECONCILED (6) [RECONCILE]
2Sa 13:39 And David, now **r** to Amnon's death, longed to be
Ps 119:79 Let me be **r** / with all who fear you and know your
Mt 5:24 Go and be **r** to that person. Then come and offer
2Co 5:20 were here pleading with you, "Be **r** to God!"
Eph 2:16 Christ **r** both groups to God by means of his death,
Col 1:20 and by him God **r** everything to himself. He made

RECONCILIATION (3) [RECONCILE]
2Sa 16:21 know that you have insulted him beyond hope of **r**,
Pr 14: 9 of guilt, but the godly acknowledge it and seek **r**.
Eze 45:17 and peace offerings to make **r** for the people of

RECONCILING (2) [RECONCILE]
2Co 5:18 And God has given us the task of **r** people to him.
5:19 For God was in Christ, **r** the world to himself,

RECONSTRUCTED (1) [RECONSTRUCTION]
Jer 30:18 on her ruins. The palace will be **r** as it was before.

RECONSTRUCTION (1) [RECONSTRUCTED]
Zec 1:16 and plans will be made for the **r** of Jerusalem.'

RECORD (35) [RECORDED, RECORDER, RECORDING, RECORDS]
Ex 17:14 "Write this down as a permanent **r**, and announce
32:32 if not, then blot me out of the **r** you are keeping."
Nu 26: 4 This is the census **r** of all the descendants of Israel
26:57 This is the census **r** for the Levites who were
33: 2 Moses kept a written **r** of their progress.
1Sa 25:31 don't let this be a blemish on your **r**. Then you
1Ch 6:54 This is a **r** of the towns and territory assigned by
9: 1 All Israel was listed in the genealogical **r** in *The*
11:11 Here is the **r** of David's mightiest men: The first
29:29 are written in *The **R** of Samuel the Seer, The **R** of Nathan the Prophet,* and *The **R** of Gad the Seer.*
2Ch 9:29 are recorded in *The **R** of Nathan the Prophet*
12:15 are recorded in *The **R** of Shemaiah the Prophet* and in *The **R** of Iddo the Seer,* which are part of the genealogical **r**.
20:34 are recorded in *The **R** of Jehu Son of Hanani,*
24:27 and the **r** of his restoration of the Temple of God
33:19 and unfaithfulness are recorded in *The **R** of the*
Ne 7: 5 I had found the genealogical **r** of those who had
Ps 32: 2 for those / whose **r** the LORD has cleared of sin,
87: 4 I will **r** Egypt and Babylon among those who know
109:14 may his mother's sins never be erased from the **r**.
130: 3 LORD, if you kept a **r** of our sins, / who, O Lord,
Pr 18:17 Any story sounds true until someone sets the **r**
Jer 22:30 Let the **r** show that this man Jehoiachin was
30: 2 Write down for the **r** everything I have said to you,
Eze 13: 9 I will blot their names from Israel's **r** books,
Hos 12: 8 one can say I got it by cheating! My **r** is spotless!"
Mal 3:16 a scroll of remembrance was written to **r** the names
Mt 1: 1 This is a **r** of the ancestors of Jesus the Messiah,
19: 4 "They **r** that from the beginning 'God made them
1Co 13: 5 and it keeps no **r** of when it has been wronged.
Col 2:14 He canceled the **r** that contained the charges
Heb 7: 3 There is no **r** of his father or mother or any of his

RECORDED (73) [RECORD]
Nu 3: 1 and Moses as it was **r** when the LORD spoke to
Dt 29:21 to pour out on them all the covenant curses **r** in
29:27 bringing down on it all the curses **r** in this book.
Jos 10:13 Is this event not **r** in *The Book of Jashar*?
24:26 Joshua **r** these things in the Book of the Law of
2Sa 1:18 of the Bow, and it is **r** in *The Book of Jashar.*
1Ki 11:41 are **r** in *The Book of the Acts of Solomon.*
14:19 are **r** in *The Book of the History of the Kings of*
14:29 and all his deeds are **r** in *The Book of the History*
15: 7 and all his deeds are **r** in *The Book of the History*
15:23 and the names of the cities he built are **r** in *The*
15:31 and all his deeds are **r** in *The Book of the History*
16: 5 and the extent of his power are **r** in *The Book of*
16:14 and all his deeds are **r** in *The Book of the History*
16:20 and his conspiracy are **r** in *The Book of the*
16:27 and all his deeds are **r** in *The Book of the History*
22:39 and the cities he built are **r** in *The Book of the*
22:45 and the wars he waged are **r** in *The Book of the*
2Ki 1:18 The rest of the events in Ahaziah's reign are **r** in
8:23 and all his deeds are **r** in *The Book of the History*
10:34 and achievements are **r** in *The Book of the*
12:19 and all his deeds are **r** in *The Book of the History*
13: 8 are **r** in *The Book of the History of the Kings of*
13:12 are **r** in *The Book of the History of the Kings of*
14:15 are **r** in *The Book of the History of the Kings of*
14:18 The rest of the events in Amaziah's reign are **r** in
14:28 are **r** in *The Book of the History of the Kings of*
15: 6 and all his deeds are **r** in *The Book of the History*
15:11 The rest of the events in Zechariah's reign are **r** in
15:15 are **r** in *The Book of the History of the Kings of*
15:21 and all his deeds are **r** in *The Book of the History*
15:26 and all his deeds are **r** in *The Book of the History*
15:31 and all his deeds are **r** in *The Book of the History*
15:36 and all his deeds are **r** in *The Book of the History*
16:19 and his deeds are **r** in *The Book of the History of*
20:20 are **r** in *The Book of the History of the Kings of*
21:17 are **r** in *The Book of the History of the Kings of*
21:25 and all his deeds are **r** in *The Book of the History*
23:28 and all his deeds are **r** in *The Book of the History*
24: 5 and all his deeds are **r** in *The Book of the History*
1Ch 4:33 and these names are **r** in their family genealogy.
27:24 The final total was never **r** in King David's official
2Ch 9:29 are **r** in *The Record of Nathan the Prophet*
12:15 are **r** in *The Record of Shemaiah the Prophet*
13:22 are **r** in *The Commentary of Iddo the Prophet.*
16:11 are **r** in *The Book of the Kings of Judah*
20:34 are **r** in *The Record of Jehu Son of Hanani,*
25:26 are **r** in *The Book of the Kings of Judah*
26:22 to end, are **r** by the prophet Isaiah son of Amoz.
27: 7 are **r** in *The Book of the Kings of Israel*
28:26 are **r** in *The Book of the Kings of Judah*
32:32 and his acts of devotion are **r** in *The Vision of the*
33:18 are **r** in *The Book of the Kings of Israel.*
33:19 and unfaithfulness are **r** in *The Record of the*
35:12 to the instructions **r** in the Book of Moses.
35:25 a tradition and are **r** in *The Book of Laments.*
35:27 are **r** in *The Book of the Kings of Israel*
36: 8 are **r** in *The Book of the Kings of Israel*
Ezr 6:18 following all the instructions **r** in the Book of
8:34 and weight, and the total weight was officially **r**.
Ne 12:23 The heads of the Levite families were **r** in *The*
Est 2:23 This was all duly **r** in *The Book of the History of*
9:20 Mordecai **r** these events and sent letters to the Jews
10: 2 are **r** in *The Book of the History of the Kings of*
Ps 56: 8 in your bottle. / You have **r** each one in your book.
102:18 Let this be **r** for future generations, / so that a
139:16 Every day of my life was **r** in your book.
Jer 51:60 Jeremiah had **r** on a scroll all the terrible disasters
Da 9: 2 word of the LORD, as **r** by Jeremiah the prophet,
Mt 26:56 the words of the prophets as **r** in the Scriptures."
Jn 20:30 miraculous signs besides the ones **r** in this book.
21:24 disciple who saw these events and **r** them here.
Rev 20:15 And anyone whose name was not found **r** in the

RECORDER (1) [RECORD]
Ex 38:21 and Ithamar son of Aaron the priest served as **r**.

RECORDING (1) [RECORD]
2Ch 34:14 As Hilkiah the high priest was **r** the money

RECORDS (17) [RECORD]
Dt 1: 1 This book **r** the words that Moses spoke to all the
1Ch 4:22 These names all come from ancient **r**.
5:17 All of these were listed in the genealogical **r**
26:31 of the Hebronites according to the genealogical **r**.
26:31 year of David's reign, a search was made in the **r**,
27:24 total was never recorded in King David's official **r**.
2Ch 31:16 regardless of their place in the genealogical **r**,
31:17 who were listed in the genealogical **r** by families,
31:18 to all the families listed in the genealogical **r**,
31:19 and to all the Levites listed in the genealogical **r**.
Ezr 2:62 But they had lost their genealogical **r**, so they were
4:15 We suggest that you search your ancestors' **r**,
4:19 I have ordered a search to be made of the **r**
Ne 7:64 But they had lost their genealogical **r**, so they were
Est 6: 1 so he ordered an attendant to bring the historical **r**
6: 2 In those **r** he discovered an account of how
9:32 of Purim, and it was all written down in the **r**.

RECOUNT (2)
Jdg 5:11 They **r** the righteous victories of the LORD,
Heb 11:32 It would take too long to **r** the stories of the faith

RECOVER (16) [RECOVERED, RECOVERS, RECOVERY]
Jdg 11:26 Why have you made no effort to **r** it before now?
1Sa 30: 8 You will surely **r** everything that was taken from
2Ki 1: 2 the god of Ekron, to ask whether he would **r**.
8: 9 king of Aram, has sent me to ask you if he will **r**."
8:10 And Elisha replied, "Go and tell him, 'You will **r**.'
8:14 "He told me that you will surely **r**."
8:29 he returned to Jezreel to **r** from his wounds.
9:15 and had returned to Jezreel to **r** from his wounds.)
20: 1 are going to die. You will not **r** from this illness."
2Ch 22: 6 Joram returned to Jezreel to **r** from his wounds,
Isa 38: 1 are going to die. You will not **r** from this illness."
38:21 and spread it over the boil, and Hezekiah will **r**."
Jer 46:26 But afterward the land will **r** from the ravages of
Eze 7:13 Not one person whose life is twisted by sin will **r**.
Am 3:12 a sheep from a lion's mouth will **r** only two legs
2Co 2: 7 so discouraged that he won't be able to **r**.

RECOVERED (15) [RECOVER]
Ge 14:16 Abram and his allies **r** everything—the goods that
14:20 gave Melchizedek a tenth of all the goods he had **r**.
14:21 may keep for yourself all the goods you have **r**."
Ex 22: 4 steals an ox or a donkey or a sheep and it is **r** alive,
Lev 14:32 those who have **r** from a contagious skin disease
Nu 21: 9 were bitten looked at the bronze snake, they **r**!
Jdg 8:28 of how Israel subdued Midian, which never **r**.
2Ki 13:25 on three occasions, and so **r** the Israelite towns.
14:25 Jeroboam II **r** the territories of Israel between
14:28 and how he **r** for Israel both Damascus
16: 6 At that time the king of Edom **r** the town of Elath
20: 7 it over the boil." They did this, and Hezekiah **r**!
2Ch 29:19 We have also **r** all the utensils taken by King Ahaz
Ecc 1:15 cannot be righted. What is missing cannot be **r**.
Isa 39: 1 that Hezekiah had been very sick and that he had **r**.

RECOVERS (1) [RECOVER]
Ex 21:21 If the slave **r** after a couple of days, however,

RECOVERY (3) [RECOVER]
Eze 38: 8 which will be lying in peace after her **r** from war
Ro 11:11 Did God's people stumble and fall beyond **r**?
Rev 13: 3 the heads of the beast seemed wounded beyond **r**

RECRUIT (1) [RECRUITED, RECRUITMENT]
1Ki 20:25 **R** another army like the one you lost. Give us the

RECRUITED (2) [RECRUIT]
1Ki 1: 5 and horses and **r** fifty men to run in front of him.
1Ch 19: 7 troops that Hanun had **r** from his own towns.

RECRUITMENT (2) [RECRUIT]
2Ki 25:19 who was in charge of **r**, and sixty other citizens.
Jer 52:25 who was in charge of **r**, and sixty other citizens.

RECTANGULAR (1)
1Ki 7: 5 All the doorways were **r** in frame; they were in

RED (60) [BLOODRED, RED-HOT, REDDISH]
RED SEA (32) Ex 10:19; 13:18; 15:4,22; 23:31; Nu 14:25; 21:4; 33:8,10,11; Dt 1:40; 2:1; 11:4; Jos 2:10; 4:23; 24:6; Jdg 11:16; 1Ki 9:26; 2Ch 8:17; Ne 9:9; Ps 66:6; 77:16; 106:7,9, 22; 114:3,5; 136:13; Isa 11:15; Jer 49:21; Ac 7:36; Heb 11:29

Ge 25:25 The first was very **r** at birth. He was covered with
25:30 Give me some of that **r** stew you've made."
25:30 was how Esau got his other name, Edom—"**R**.")
Ex 10:19 west wind that blew the locusts out into the **R** Sea.
13:18 a route through the wilderness toward the **R** Sea,
15: 4 have been drowned in the **R** Sea.
15:22 led the people of Israel away from the **R** Sea,
23:31 And I will fix your boundaries from the **R** Sea to
28:17 The first row will contain a **r** carnelian,
39:10 In the first row were a **r** carnelian, a chrysolite,
Nu 14:25 for the wilderness in the direction of the **R** Sea."
19: 2 Tell the people of Israel to bring you a **r** heifer that
21: 4 taking the road to the **R** Sea to go around the land
33: 8 and crossed the **R** Sea into the wilderness beyond.
33:10 They left Elim and camped beside the **R** Sea.
33:11 They left the **R** Sea and camped in the Sin Desert.
Dt 1:40 on back through the wilderness toward the **R** Sea.'
2: 1 and set out across the wilderness toward the **R** Sea,
11: 4 how he drowned them in the **R** Sea as they were
Jos 2:10 for you through the **R** Sea when you left Egypt.
4:23 just as he did at the **R** Sea when he dried it up until
24: 6 But when your ancestors arrived at the **R** Sea,
Jdg 11:16 their journey from Egypt after crossing the **R** Sea,
1Ki 9:26 in the land of Edom, along the shore of the **R** Sea.
2Ki 3:22 across the water, making it look as **r** as blood.
2Ch 8:17 in the land of Edom, along the shore of the **R** Sea.
Ne 9: 9 and you heard their cries from beside the **R** Sea.
Job 16:16 My eyes are **r** with weeping; darkness covers my
38:14 as the light approaches, and the dawn is robed in **r**.
41:18 it flashes light! Its eyes are like the **r** of dawn.
Ps 66: 6 He made a dry path through the **R** Sea, / and his
77:16 When the **R** Sea saw you, O God, / its waters
106: 7 Instead, they rebelled against him at the **R** Sea.
106: 9 He commanded the **R** Sea to divide, and a dry path
106:22 in that land, / such awesome deeds at the **R** Sea.
114: 3 The **R** Sea saw them coming and hurried out of
114: 5 What's wrong, **R** Sea, that made you hurry out of
136:13 Give thanks to him who parted the **R** Sea.
Ecc 5: 8 and matters of justice only get lost in **r** tape
Isa 1:18 Even if you are stained as **r** as crimson, I can make
11:15 The LORD will make a dry path through the **R**
15: 9 The stream near Dibon runs **r** with blood, but I am
63: 1 the city of Bozrah, with his clothing stained **r**?
63: 2 Why are your clothes so **r**, as if you have been
Jer 22:14 with fragrant cedar and painted a lovely **r**.'
49:21 of despair will be heard all the way to the **R** Sea.
Eze 23:14 military officers, outfitted in striking **r** uniforms.
28:13 **r** carnelian, chrysolite, white moonstone, beryl,
Na 2: 3 Shields flash **r** in the sunlight! The attack begins!
Zec 1: 8 I saw a man sitting on a **r** horse that was standing
1: 8 Behind him were **r**, brown, and white horses,
6: 2 The first chariot was pulled by **r** horses, the second
Mt 16: 2 '**R** sky at night means fair weather tomorrow,
16: 3 **r** sky in the morning means foul weather all day.'
Ac 7:36 through the **R** Sea, and back and forth through the
Heb 11:29 the **R** Sea as though they were on dry ground.
Rev 6: 4 And another horse appeared, a **r** one. Its rider was
6:12 as black cloth, and the moon became as **r** as blood.
9:17 The riders wore armor that was fiery **r** and sky
12: 3 I saw a large **r** dragon with seven heads and ten

RED-HOT (1) [RED]
Ps 102: 3 like smoke, / and my bones burn like **r** coals.

REDDISH (6) [RED]
Lev 13:19 or a r white spot remains in its place,
13:24 becoming either a shiny r white or white,
13:42 if a r white infection appears on the front
13:43 and if he finds swelling around the r white sore,
13:49 or the leather has turned bright green or a r color,
14:37 bright green or r streaks on the walls of the house

REDEDICATE (1) [DEDICATE]
Nu 6:12 They must r themselves to the LORD for the full

REDEEM (36) [REDEEMED, REDEEMER, REDEEMERS, REDEEMS, REDEMPTION]
Ex 6:6 I will r you with mighty power and great acts of
13:13 its neck. However, you must r every firstborn son.
34:20 its neck. However, you must r every firstborn son.
Lev 25:26 If there is no one to r the land but the person who
25:27 then that person has the right to r it from the one
25:28 But if the original owner cannot afford to r it,
25:29 city has the right to r it for a full year after its sale.
25:32 "The Levites always have the right to r any house
25:49 They may also r themselves if they can get the
27:13 If you want to r the animal, you must pay the value
27:15 If you wish to r the house, you must pay the value
27:19 If you decide to r the dedicated field, you must pay
27:20 But if you decide not to r the field, or if the field is
27:27 you may r it by paying the priest's assessment of
27:27 If you do not r it, the priest may sell it to someone
27:31 If you want to r the LORD's tenth of the fruit
Nu 3:46 To r the 273 firstborn sons of Israel who are in
18:15 But you must always r your firstborn sons
18:16 R them when they are one month old.
18:17 you may not r the firstborn of cattle, sheep,
Ru 3:13 If he is willing to r you, then let him marry you.
4:4 to you about it so that you can r it if you wish.
4:4 because I am next in line to r it after you." The man replied, "All right, I'll r it."
4:6 "Then I can't r it," the family redeemer replied,
4:6 my own estate. You r the land; I cannot do it."
Ne 5:8 "The rest of us are doing all we can to r our
5:8 How often must we r them?" And they had
Ps 34:22 But the LORD will r those who serve him.
49:7 Yet they cannot r themselves from death
49:15 But as for me, God will r my life. / He will snatch
Isa 52:3 Now I can r you without paying for you."
Eze 18:12 steals from debtors by refusing to let them r what
Hos 7:13 I wanted to r them, but they have only spoken lies
13:14 Should I r them from death? O death, bring forth
Mic 4:10 he will r you from the grip of your enemies.

REDEEMED (38) [REDEEM]
Ex 13:13 A firstborn male donkey may be r from the
13:15 except that the firstborn sons are always r.'
34:20 A firstborn male donkey may be r from the
Lev 25:24 be a stipulation that the land can be r at any time.
25:30 But if it is not r within a year, then the house
25:31 Such a house may be r at any time and must be
25:33 And any property that can be r by the Levites—
25:54 If any Israelites have not been r by the time the
27:20 to someone else by the priests, it can never be r.
27:28 or an inherited field—must never be sold or r.
27:29 apart by the LORD for destruction cannot be r.
27:33 one will be considered holy and cannot be r."
Dt 9:26 r from Egypt by your mighty power and glorious
15:15 the land of Egypt and the LORD your God r you!
21:8 forgive your people Israel whom you have r.
24:18 in Egypt and that the LORD your God r you.
2Sa 7:23 have you r from slavery to be your own people?
1Ch 17:21 have you r from slavery to be your own people?
Ps 71:23 for joy and sing your praises, / for you have r me.
74:2 the tribe you r as your own special possession!
77:15 You have r your people by your strength,
106:10 from their enemies / and r them from their foes.
107:2 Has the LORD r you? Then speak out!
Isa 1:27 the repentant people of Jerusalem will be r.
29:22 That is why the LORD, who r Abraham, says to
35:9 will be no other dangers. Only the r will follow it.
44:23 For the LORD has r Jacob and is glorified in
48:20 of the earth that the LORD has r his servants,
52:9 has comforted his people. He has r Jerusalem.
62:12 the Holy People and the People R by the LORD.
63:9 In his love and mercy he r them. He lifted them up
Jer 31:11 For the LORD has r Israel from those too strong
La 3:58 my lawyer! Plead my case! For you have r my life.
Mic 6:4 you out of Egypt and r you from your slavery.
Zec 10:8 to them, they will come running, for I have r them.
Lk 1:68 because he has visited his people and r them.
Heb 12:23 And you have come to the spirits of the r in heaven
Rev 14:3 those 144,000 who had been r from the earth.

REDEEMER (24) [REDEEM]
Lev 25:25 then a close relative, a kinsman r, may buy it back
Ru 3:9 your covering over me, for you are my family r."
4:1 When the family r he had mentioned came by,
4:3 And Boaz said to the family r, "You know Naomi,
4:6 "Then I can't redeem it," the family r replied,
4:8 So the other family r drew off his sandal as he said
4:14 "Praise the LORD who has given you a family r
Job 19:25 "But as for me, I know that my R lives, and that
Ps 19:14 be pleasing to you, / O LORD, my rock and my r.
78:35 was their rock, / that their r was the Most High.
Pr 23:11 for their R is strong. He himself will bring their
Isa 41:14 for I will help you. I am the LORD, your R.
43:14 The LORD your R, the Holy One of Israel,
44:6 Israel's King and R, the LORD Almighty, says:
44:24 The LORD, your R and Creator, says: "I am the
47:4 Our R, whose name is the LORD Almighty,
48:17 "The LORD, your R, the Holy One of Israel,
49:7 The LORD, the R and Holy One of Israel, says to
49:26 the LORD, am your Savior and R, the Mighty
54:5 He is your R, the Holy One of Israel, the God of
54:8 compassion on you," says the LORD, your R.
59:20 "The R will come to Jerusalem,"
60:16 the LORD, am your Savior and R, the Mighty
63:16 still be our Father. You are our R from ages past.

REDEEMERS (2) [REDEEM]
Ru 2:20 one of our closest relatives, one of our family r."
3:12 While it is true that I am one of your family r,

REDEEMS (1) [REDEEM]
Jer 50:34 But the one who r them is strong. His name is the

REDEMPTION (9) [REDEEM]
Ex 22:29 "You must make the necessary payment for r of
Lev 25:48 they still retain the right of r. They may be bought
25:52 will repay a relatively small amount for their r.
Nu 3:48 and his sons as the r price for the extra firstborn
3:49 So Moses collected r money for the firstborn sons
3:51 And Moses gave the r money to Aaron and his
18:16 The r price is five pieces of silver, each piece
Ps 49:8 R does not come so easily, / for no one can ever
Eph 4:30 that you will be saved on the day of r.

REDOUND [KJV] See MORE (AND MORE)

REDUCE (6) [REDUCED]
Ge 31:39 to you and ask you to r the count of your flock?
Ex 5:8 But don't r their production quotas by a single
21:10 he may not r her food or clothing or fail to sleep
2Ki 10:32 At about that time the LORD began to r the size
Jer 21:10 by the king of Babylon, and he will r it to ashes.'
Zep 1:3 I will r the wicked to heaps of rubble, along with

REDUCED (13) [REDUCE]
Ge 31:15 He has r our rights to those of foreign women.
31:41 get the flock. And you have r my wages ten times!
Nu 36:3 this way, the total area of our tribal land will be r.
Jdg 6:6 So Israel was r to starvation by the Midianites.
1Sa 1:7 Hannah would finally be r to tears and would not
2Ki 13:7 Jehoahaz's army was r to fifty mounted troops,
Ezr 6:11 and their house will be r to a pile of rubble.
Job 16:8 You have r me to skin and bones—as proof,
19:20 I have been r to skin and bones and have escaped
Ps 102:5 of my groaning, / I am r to skin and bones.
Jer 26:18 like an open field; Jerusalem will be r to rubble!
Eze 16:27 I struck you with my fist and r your boundaries.
Mic 3:12 like an open field; Jerusalem will be r to rubble!

REED (5) [REEDS]
1Ki 14:15 Then the LORD will shake Israel like a r
Isa 9:14 the head and the tail, the palm branch and the r.
Eze 29:6 for you collapsed like a r when Israel looked to
Mt 11:7 Did you find him weak as a r, moved by every
Lk 7:24 Did you find him weak as a r, moved by every

REEDS (8) [REED]
Ex 2:3 she got a little basket made of papyrus r
2:3 and laid it among the r along the edge of the Nile
2:5 the princess saw the little basket among the r,
Job 8:11 "Can papyrus r grow where there is no marsh?
40:21 It lies down under the lotus plants, hidden by the r.
Ps 68:30 these wild animals lurking in the r,
Isa 19:6 streams of Egypt will become foul with rotting r
35:7 Marsh grass and r and rushes will flourish where

REEFS (1)
Jude 1:12 they are like dangerous r that can shipwreck you.

REEL (2) [REELED, REELING, REELS]
Isa 28:7 The priests and prophets r and stagger from beer
Eze 23:33 You will r like a drunkard beneath the awful blows

REELAIAH (2)
Ezr 2:2 Seraiah, R, Mordecai, Bilshan, Mispar, Bigvai,
Ne 7:7 Seraiah, R, Nahamani, Mordecai, Bilshan, Mispar,

REELED (1) [REEL]
Ps 107:27 They r and staggered like drunkards / and were at

REELING (1) [REEL]
Ps 60:3 hard on us, / making us drink wine that sent us r.

REELS (1) [REEL]
Isa 21:4 My mind r; my heart races. The sleep I once

REESTABLISH (2) [ESTABLISH]
Isa 49:8 This will prove that I will r the land of Israel
Zec 10:6 and save Israel; I will r them because I love them.

REESTABLISHED (1) [ESTABLISH]
Da 4:36 sought me out, and I was r as head of my kingdom,

REFER (4) [REFERENCE, REFERRED, REFERRING]
Eze 10:13 I heard someone r to the wheels as "the whirling
Mt 7:21 They may r to me as 'Lord,' but they still won't
11:10 John is the man to whom the Scriptures r when
Lk 7:27 John is the man to whom the Scriptures r when

REFERENCE (2) [REFER]
Ac 13:36 Now this is not a r to David, for after David had
13:37 No, it was a r to someone else—someone whom

REFERRED (6) [REFER]
Ge 16:13 Thereafter, Hagar r to the LORD, who had
Dt 2:11 and the Anakites are often r to as the Rephaites,
2:20 though the Ammonites r to them as Zamzummites.
25:10 Ever afterward his family will be r to as 'the
Lk 20:37 he r to the Lord as 'the God of Abraham, the God
Ac 4:11 For Jesus is the one r to in the Scriptures, where it

REFERRING (3) [REFER]
Ex 4:26 she was r to the circumcision.)
Jn 12:41 Isaiah was r to Jesus when he made this prediction,
Ac 2:29 David wasn't r to himself when he spoke these

REFINE (3) [REFINED, REFINER, REFINES, REFINING]
Ex 30:35 r it to produce a pure and holy incense.
Job 28:1 "People know how to mine silver and r gold.
Jer 6:29 because there is no purity in them to r.

REFINED (10) [REFINE]
1Ch 28:18 he designated the amount of r gold for the altar of
29:4 and over 262 tons of r silver to be used for
Ps 12:6 promises are pure, / like silver r in a furnace,
Isa 48:10 I have r you but not in the way silver is r.
48:10 Rather, I have r you in the furnace of suffering.
Da 11:35 they will be r and cleansed and made pure until the
12:10 will be purified, cleansed, and r by these trials.
Zec 13:9 just as gold and silver are r and purified by fire.
Rev 1:15 His feet were as bright as bronze r in a furnace,

REFINER (1) [REFINE]
Mal 3:3 He will sit and judge like a r of silver,

REFINES (1) [REFINE]
Mal 3:2 For he will be like a blazing fire that r metal

REFINING (3) [REFINE]
Ecc 7:3 than laughter, for sadness has a r influence on us.
Jer 6:29 The r fire grows hotter. But it will never purify
Mal 3:3 will purify the Levites, r them like gold or silver,

REFLECT (11) [REFLECTED, REFLECTING, REFLECTS]
Ex 25:37 and set them so they r their light forward.
Job 37:18 he makes the skies r the heat like a giant mirror.
Ps 119:5 my actions would consistently / r your principles!
119:15 study your commandments / and r on your ways.
119:55 I r at night on who you are, O LORD, / and I
Isa 13:8 as the flames of the burning city r on their faces.
44:19 The person who made the idol never stops to r,
Mt 12:37 The words you say now r your fate then;
2Co 3:18 so that we can be mirrors that brightly r the glory
3:18 and more like him and r his glory even more.
Tit 2:7 Let everything you do r the integrity

REFLECTED (3) [REFLECT]
Nu 8:3 up the seven lamps so they r their light forward,
Pr 27:19 As a face is r in water, so the heart reflects the
Lk 1:66 Everyone who heard about it r on these events

REFLECTING (1) [REFLECT]
Nu 26:54 each group's inheritance r the size of its

REFLECTS (3) [REFLECT]
Pr 27:19 face is reflected in water, so the heart r the person.
Tit 2:1 promote the kind of living that r right teaching.
Heb 1:3 The Son r God's own glory, and everything about

REFORMS (1)
Ac 24:2 given peace to us Jews and have enacted r for us.

REFRAIN (2)
Dt 23:22 However, it is not a sin to r from making a vow.
1Co 7:5 and wife to r from sexual intimacy for a limited

REFRAINETH [KJV] See TURN (OFF)

REFRESH (6) [REFRESHED, REFRESHES, REFRESHING, REFRESHMENT]
Ge 18:5 Let me prepare some food to r you. Please stay
Ps 68:9 O God, / to r the weary Promised Land.
Pr 11:25 those who r others will themselves be refreshed.
Isa 32:2 He will r her as a river in the desert and as the cool
57:15 I r the humble and give new courage to those with
2Pe 3:1 your wholesome thinking and r your memory.

REFRESHED (11) [REFRESH]

Ex 23:12 including your slaves and visitors, to be **r**.
31:17 but he rested on the seventh day and was **r**."
2Ki 19:24 and **r** myself with their water. / I even stopped up
Job 6:18 The caravans turn aside to be **r**, but there is
29:19 the water, whose branches are **r** with the dew.
Ps 92:10 strong as a wild bull. / How **r** I am by your power!
110:7 But he himself will be **r** from brooks along the
Pr 11:25 those who refresh others will themselves be **r**.
Isa 37:25 and **r** myself with their water. / I even stopped up
43:20 in the desert, so that my chosen people can be **r**.
Phm 1:7 kindness has so often **r** the hearts of God's people.

REFRESHES (1) [REFRESH]

Pr 16:15 there is life; his favor **r** like a gentle rain.

REFRESHING (10) [REFRESH]

2Sa 23:4 like the **r** rains that bring tender grass from the
Job 29:23 for my words were as **r** as the spring rain.
Ps 72:6 May his reign be as **r** as the springtime rains—
84:6 of Weeping, / it will become a place of **r** springs,
133:3 Harmony is as **r** as the dew from Mount Hermon
Pr 9:17 "Stolen water is **r**; food eaten in secret tastes the
18:4 words of true wisdom are as **r** as a bubbling brook.
25:13 Faithful messengers are as **r** as snow in the heat of
SS 4:15 as **r** as the streams from the Lebanon mountains."
Hos 14:5 I will be to Israel like a **r** dew from heaven. It will

REFRESHMENT (1) [REFRESH]

Ac 3:20 Then wonderful times of **r** will come from the

REFUGE (63) [REFUGEE, REFUGEES]

CITIES OF REFUGE (12) Nu 35:6,11,13; Dt 4:41; 19:2,5,7,9,11; Jos 20:2,7,8

CITY OF REFUGE (13) Nu 35:25,26,28,32; Dt 19:6,12; Jos 21:13,21,27,32,38; 1Ch 6:57,67

Nu 35:6 "You must give the Levites six cities of **r**, where a
35:11 designate cities of **r** for people to flee to if they
35:13 Designate six cities of **r** for yourselves,
35:25 live in a city of **r** until the death of the high priest.
35:26 " 'But if the slayer leaves the city of **r**,
35:28 The slayer should have stayed inside the city of **r**
35:32 payment from someone who has fled to a city of **r**,
Dt 4:41 Then Moses set apart three cities of **r** east of the
19:2 Then you must set apart three cities of **r** in the land
19:5 the slayer could flee to one of the cities of **r**
19:6 If the distance to the nearest city of **r** was too far,
19:7 I am commanding you to set aside three cities of **r**.
19:9 you must designate three additional cities of **r**.
19:11 and then escapes to one of the cities of **r**.
19:12 have the murderer brought back from the city of **r**
23:15 escape from their masters and take **r** with you,
32:37 are their gods, / the rocks they fled to for **r**?
33:27 The eternal God is your **r**, / and his everlasting
Jos 20:2 "Now tell the Israelites to designate the cities of **r**,
20:7 The following cities were designated as cities of **r**:
20:8 the following cities were designated as cities of **r**:
20:9 another person could take **r** in one of these cities.
21:13 Hebron (a city of **r** for those who accidentally
21:21 Shechem (a city of **r** for those who accidentally
21:27 Golan in Bashan (a city of **r**) and Be-eshterah.
21:32 they received Kedesh in Galilee (a city of **r**),
21:38 Gad they received Ramoth in Gilead (a city of **r**),
Jdg 9:46 they took **r** within the walls of the temple of
Ru 2:12 under whose wings you have come to take **r**,
1Ch 6:57 Hebron (a city of **r**), Libnah, Jattir, Eshtemoa,
6:67 Shechem (a city of **r** in the hill country of
Ps 5:11 But let all who take **r** in you rejoice; / let them sing
9:9 a shelter for the oppressed, / a **r** in times of trouble.
16:1 me safe, O God, / for I have come to you for **r**.
17:7 those who seek **r** from their enemies.
46:1 God is our **r** and strength, / always ready to help in
52:T told Saul that Ahimelech had given **r** to David.
59:16 of your unfailing love. / For you have been my **r**,
59:17 to you I sing praises, / for you, O God, are my **r**,
61:3 for you are my safe **r**, / a fortress where my
62:7 He is my **r**, a rock where no enemy can reach me.
62:8 Pour out your heart to him, / for God is our **r**.
71:1 O LORD, you are my **r**; / never let me be
91:2 He alone is my **r**, my place of safety; / he is my
91:9 If you make the LORD your **r**, / if you make the
104:18 and the rocks form a **r** for rock badgers.
119:114 You are my **r** and my shield; / your word is my
141:8 You are my **r**; don't let them kill me.
142:5 O LORD. / I say, "You are my place of **r**.
144:2 stands before me as a shield, and I take **r** in him.
Pr 14:26 he will be a place of **r** for their children.
14:32 by their sins, but the godly have a **r** when they die.
Isa 14:32 and that the poor of his people will find **r** in its
25:4 to the poor, O LORD, you are a **r** from the storm.
28:15 for we have built a strong **r** made of lies
28:17 Your **r** looks strong, but since it is made of lies,
28:20 For you have no place of **r**—the bed you have
Jer 16:19 and fortress, my **r** in the day of trouble!
Da 11:19 He will take **r** in his own fortresses but will
Joel 3:16 the LORD will be a welcoming **r** and a strong
Ob 1:17 "But Jerusalem will become a **r** for those who
Na 1:7 is good. When trouble comes, he is a strong **r**.
Heb 6:18 we who have fled to him for **r** can take new

REFUGEE (1) [REFUGE]

Eze 24:26 And on that day a **r** from Jerusalem will come to

REFUGEES (5) [REFUGE]

Nu 21:29 of Chemosh! / Chemosh has left his sons as **r**,
Isa 15:7 The desperate **r** take only the possessions they can
16:1 Moab's **r** at Sela send lambs to Jerusalem as a
21:14 of Tema, bring food and water to these weary **r**.
Jer 48:5 Her **r** will climb the hills of Luhith,

REFUSAL (1) [REFUSE]

Mk 16:14 their stubborn **r** to believe those who had seen him

REFUSE (138) [REFUSAL, REFUSED, REFUSES, REFUSING]

Ge 4:7 But if you **r** to respond correctly, then watch out!
24:41 you go to my relatives and they **r** to let her come,
43:32 Egyptians despise Hebrews and **r** to eat with them.
Ex 7:4 Even then Pharaoh will **r** to listen to you. So I will
7:14 and he continues to **r** to let the people go.
8:2 If you **r**, then listen carefully to this: I will send
8:21 If you **r**, I will send swarms of flies throughout
8:29 and **r** to let the people go to sacrifice to the
9:2 you continue to oppress them and **r** to let them go,
9:17 lording it over my people, and you **r** to let them go.
10:3 says: How long will you **r** to submit to me?
10:4 If you **r**, watch out! For tomorrow I will cover the
16:28 "How long will these people **r** to obey my
Lev 5:1 but they **r** to testify, they will be held responsible
20:4 to Molech and **r** to execute the guilty parents,
26:21 then you remain hostile toward me and **r** to obey,
26:27 "If after this you still **r** to listen and still remain
Nu 9:13 yet still **r** to celebrate the Passover at the regular
16:12 the sons of Eliab, but they replied, "We **r** to come!
23:24 like a majestic lion they stand. / They **r** to rest
32:30 But if they **r** to cross over and march ahead of you,
Dt 15:9 Do not be mean-spirited and **r** someone a loan
15:9 If you **r** to make the loan and the needy person
20:12 But if they **r** to make peace and prepare to fight,
28:15 "But if you **r** to listen to the LORD your God
28:45 "If you **r** to listen to the LORD your God and to
28:55 He will **r** to give them a share of the flesh he is
28:58 "If you **r** to obey all the terms of this law that are
30:17 But if your heart turns away and you **r** to listen,
Ru 1:13 for them to grow up and **r** to marry someone else?
1Sa 12:15 the LORD's commands and **r** to listen to him,
1Ki 2:20 he asked. "You know I won't **r** you."
Ezr 4:13 for the Jews will then **r** to pay their tribute,
Ne 10:31 or on any other holy day, we will **r** to buy it.
Est 3:8 and they **r** to obey even the laws of the king.
Job 16:6 defend myself. And it does not help if I **r** to speak.
24:13 They **r** to acknowledge its ways. They will not stay
24:21 protecting sons. They **r** to help the needy widows.
36:12 But if they **r** to listen to him, they will perish in
36:13 he punishes them, they **r** to cry out to him for help.
Ps 15:3 Those who **r** to slander others / or harm their
15:5 and who **r** to accept bribes to testify against the
26:5 who do evil, / and I **r** to join in with the wicked.
28:1 Please help me; don't **r** to answer me. / For if you
36:3 They **r** to act wisely or do what is good.
50:17 For you **r** my discipline / and treat my laws like
55:19 For my enemies **r** to change their ways;
58:4 deadly snakes; / they are like cobras that **r** to listen,
79:6 Pour out your wrath on the nations that **r** to
95:10 away from me. / They **r** to do what I tell them.'
101:3 I will **r** to look at / anything vile and vulgar.
129:8 And may those who pass by **r** to give them this
141:5 it is soothing medicine. / Don't let me **r** it.
Pr 11:15 is dangerous; it is better to **r** than to suffer later.
13:24 If you **r** to discipline your children, it proves you
21:7 Because the wicked **r** to do what is just,
21:25 people will be their ruin, for their hands **r** to work.
Ecc 4:5 Foolish people **r** to work and almost starve.
Isa 1:15 you lift up your hands in prayer, I will **r** to look.
1:23 and **r** to defend the orphans and the widows.
1:28 for they **r** to come to the LORD.
3:8 speak out against the LORD and **r** to obey him.
13:20 Nomads will **r** to camp there, and shepherds will
24:4 earth dries up, the crops wither, the skies **r** to rain.
28:11 Since they **r** to listen, God will speak to them
30:9 For these people are stubborn rebels who **r** to pay
33:15 who **r** to listen to those who plot murder,
42:18 Why won't you listen? Why do you **r** to see?
42:20 and understand what is right but **r** to act on it.
43:22 "But, my dear people, you **r** to ask for my help.
48:6 and seen them fulfilled, but you **r** to admit it.
60:12 For the nations that **r** to be your allies will be
64:12 After all this, LORD, must you still **r** to help us?
Jer 2:25 Why do you **r** to turn from all this running after
2:30 but it did them no good. They still **r** to obey.
5:28 They **r** justice to orphans and deny the rights of the
6:19 fruit of their own sin because they **r** to listen to me.
7:28 obey the LORD their God and who **r** to be taught.
9:3 They **r** to stand up for the truth. And they only go
9:6 pile lie upon lie and utterly **r** to come to me,"
10:25 Pour out your wrath on the nations that **r** to
13:10 These wicked people **r** to listen to me.
13:17 And if you still **r** to listen, I will weep alone
15:7 because they **r** to turn back to me from all their
16:12 follow your own evil desires and **r** to listen to me.
17:27 do not listen to me and **r** to keep the Sabbath holy,
18:17 my back on them and **r** to notice their distress."
22:5 But if you **r** to pay attention to this warning,
25:28 And if they **r** to accept the cup, tell them,
29:19 For they **r** to listen to me, though I have spoken to
35:14 to you again and again, and you **r** to listen or obey.
35:17 Because you **r** to listen or answer when I call,
38:18 But if you **r** to surrender, you will not escape!
38:21 But if you **r** to surrender, this is what the LORD
42:5 us if we **r** to obey whatever he tells us to do!
42:13 "But if you **r** to obey the LORD your God
48:10 Cursed be those who **r** to do the work the LORD
50:33 Their captors hold them and **r** to let them go.
La 3:45 You have discarded us as **r** and garbage among the
Eze 3:19 and they keep on sinning and **r** to repent,
33:4 Then if those who hear the alarm **r** to take action—
Da 3:11 That decree also states that those who **r** to obey
3:14 that you **r** to serve my gods or to worship the gold
3:15 But if you **r**, you will be thrown immediately into
Hos 4:6 you priests, for you yourselves **r** to know me. Now I **r** to recognize you as my priests.
4:14 You will be destroyed, for you **r** to understand.
11:5 "But since my people **r** to return to me, they will
Am 3:8 has spoken—I dare not **r** to proclaim his message!
Mic 5:15 vengeance on all the nations that **r** to obey me."
Zec 14:18 And if the people of Egypt **r** to attend the festival,
14:18 that he sends on the other nations who **r** to go.
Mt 6:15 But if you **r** to forgive others, your Father will not
10:38 If you **r** to take up your cross and follow me,
12:41 greater than Jonah is here—and you **r** to repent.
12:42 than Solomon is here—and you **r** to listen to him.
18:35 will do to you if you **r** to forgive your brothers
Lk 11:31 than Solomon is here—and you **r** to listen to him.
11:32 greater than Jonah is here—and you **r** to repent.
Jn 4:9 for Jews **r** to have anything to do with Samaritans.
5:23 But if you **r** to honor the Son, then you are
5:40 Yet you **r** to come to me so that I can give you this
5:43 representing my Father, and you **r** to welcome me,
20:23 If you **r** to forgive them, they are unforgiven."
Ac 18:15 you take care of it. I **r** to judge such matters."
25:11 done something worthy of death, I don't **r** to die.
Ro 1:31 They **r** to understand, break their promises, and are
2:8 who **r** to obey the truth and practice evil deeds.
9:18 and he chooses to make some people **r** to listen.
13:2 So those who **r** to obey the laws of the land are
15:31 be rescued from those in Judea who **r** to obey God.
Eph 2:2 He is the spirit at work in the hearts of those who **r**
2Th 1:8 and on those who **r** to obey the Good News of our
2:10 because they **r** to believe the truth that would save
3:14 Take note of those who **r** to obey what we say in
Heb 3:10 away from me. / They **r** to do what I tell them.'
Jas 1:27 in their troubles, and **r** to let the world corrupt us.
1Pe 3:1 even those who **r** to accept the Good News.

REFUSED (166) [REFUSE]

Ge 39:8 But Joseph **r**. "Look," he told her, "my master
39:10 on him day after day, but he **r** to sleep with her,
48:19 But his father **r**. "I know what I'm doing,
Ex 1:17 they **r** to obey the king and allowed the boys to
4:23 worship me. But since you have **r**, be warned!
7:13 He still **r** to listen, just as the LORD had
7:16 Until now, you have **r** to listen to him.
7:22 He **r** to listen to Moses and Aaron, just as the
8:15 He **r** to listen to Moses and Aaron, just as the
8:32 hardened his heart again and **r** to let the people go.
9:7 remained stubborn. He still **r** to let the people go.
9:12 and he **r** to listen, just as the LORD had
9:35 Pharaoh **r** to let the people leave, just as the
13:15 Pharaoh **r** to let us go, so the LORD killed all the
33:4 and **r** to wear their jewelry and ornaments.
Nu 20:21 Because Edom **r** to allow Israel to pass through
21:23 But King Sihon **r** to let them cross his land.
22:14 and reported, "Balaam **r** to come with us."
Dt 1:26 command of the LORD your God and **r** to go in.
1:32 all he did, you **r** to trust the LORD your God,
1:45 and wept before the LORD, but he **r** to listen.
2:30 But King Sihon **r** to allow you to pass through,
9:23 LORD your God and **r** to trust him or obey him.
Jdg 2:19 And they **r** to give up their evil practices
9:9 But it **r**, saying, 'Should I quit producing the olive
9:11 But the fig tree also **r**, saying, 'Should I quit
12:2 the beginning of the dispute, but you **r** to come!"
21:5 vowing that anyone who **r** to come must die.
1Sa 8:19 But the people **r** to listen to Samuel's warning.
10:27 And they despised him and **r** to bring him gifts.
15:11 not been loyal to me and has again **r** to obey me."
20:34 the table in fierce anger and **r** to eat all that day,
22:17 But Saul's men **r** to kill the LORD's priests.
26:23 and I **r** to kill you even when the LORD placed
28:6 but the LORD **r** to answer him, either by dreams
28:23 But Saul **r**. The men who were with him also urged
2Sa 2:21 But Asahel **r** and kept right on chasing Abner.
3:35 David had **r** to eat anything the day of the funeral,
12:17 with him to get up and eat with them, but he **r**.
12:21 the baby was still living, you wept and **r** to eat.
13:9 she set the serving tray before him, he **r** to eat.
14:13 because you have **r** to bring home your own
14:29 to ask him to intercede for him, but Joab **r** to come.
14:29 for him a second time, but again Joab **r** to come.
17:23 publicly disgraced when Absalom **r** his advice.
19:27 Ziba has slandered me by saying that I **r** to come.
22:42 They cried to the LORD, but he **r** to answer them.
23:16 But he **r** to drink it. Instead, he poured it out before
1Ki 1:8 and **r** to support Adonijah were Zadok the priest,
11:6 he **r** to follow the LORD completely, as his
12:19 The northern tribes of Israel have **r** to be ruled by a
18:18 for you have **r** to obey the commands of the
20:35 "Strike me!" But the man **r** to strike the prophet.
21:4 went to bed with his face to the wall and **r** to eat!
21:6 to sell me his vineyard or to trade it, and he **r**!"
22:49 with your men." But Jehoshaphat **r** the offer.
2Ki 5:16 Naaman urged him to take the gifts, Elisha **r**.
10:31 He **r** to turn from the sins of idolatry that Jeroboam
13:11 He **r** to turn from the sins of idolatry that Jeroboam

14:11 But Amaziah **r** to listen, so King Jehoash of Israel
14:24 He **r** to turn from the sins of idolatry that Jeroboam
15: 9 He **r** to turn from the sins of idolatry that Jeroboam
15:16 because its citizens **r** to surrender the town.
15:18 he **r** to turn from the sins of idolatry that Jeroboam
15:24 He **r** to turn from the sins of idolatry that Jeroboam
15:28 He **r** to turn from the sins of idolatry that Jeroboam
17:14 and **r** to believe in the LORD their God.
17:19 But even the people of Judah **r** to obey the
18: 7 the king of Assyria and **r** to pay him tribute.
18:12 For they had **r** to listen to the LORD their God.
21: 9 But the people **r** to listen, and Manasseh led them
21:22 and he **r** to follow the LORD's ways.
1Ch 11:18 But David **r** to drink it. Instead, he poured it out
12:19 the Philistine leaders **r** to let David and his men go
2Ch 10:19 The northern tribes of Israel have **r** to be ruled by a
15:13 They agreed that anyone who **r** to seek the
26:19 and **r** to set down the incense burner he was
35:22 But Josiah **r** to listen to Neco, to whom God had
36:12 and he **r** to humble himself in the presence of the
Ne 3: 5 people from Tekoa, though their leaders **r** to help.
5:16 to working on the wall and **r** to acquire any land.
5:18 Yet I **r** to claim the governor's food allowance
9:16 stubborn lot, and they **r** to obey your commands.
9:17 "They **r** to listen and did not remember the
9:29 turned their backs on you and **r** to listen.
9:35 but they **r** to turn from their wickedness.
Est 1:12 the king's order to Queen Vashti, she **r** to come.
1:17 that Queen Vashti has **r** to appear before the king.
3: 2 But Mordecai **r** to bow down or show him respect.
3: 4 after day, but still he **r** to comply with the order.
4: 4 clothing to him to replace the sackcloth, but he **r** it.
Job 22: 7 You must have **r** water for the thirsty and food for
31:13 if I have **r** to hear their complaints,
31:16 "Have I **r** to help the poor or crushed the hopes of
31:17 my food and **r** to share it with hungry orphans?
31:34 so that I **r** to acknowledge my sin and would not
32: 1 Job's three friends **r** to reply further to him
32: 2 because Job **r** to admit that he had sinned
Ps 18:41 They cried to the LORD, but he **r** to answer them.
30: 1 You **r** to let my enemies triumph over me.
32: 3 When I **r** to confess my sin, / I was weak
78:10 God's covenant, / and they **r** to live by his law.
78:32 kept on sinning. / They **r** to believe in his miracles.
78:56 against the Most High / and **r** to follow his decrees.
89:43 his sword useless / and have **r** to help him in battle.
106:24 The people **r** to enter the pleasant land, / for they
106:25 grumbled in their tents / and **r** to obey the LORD.
109:16 For he **r** all kindness to others; / he persecuted the
119:87 me off, / but I **r** to abandon your commandments.
119:101 I have **r** to walk on any path of evil, / that I may
Isa 7:12 But the king **r**. "No," he said, "I wouldn't test the
33: 7 for Assyria has **r** their petition for peace.
42:25 on fire and burned, but they still **r** to understand.
Jer 3:13 Confess that you **r** to follow me. I, the LORD,
5: 3 You crushed them, but they **r** to turn from sin.
5: 3 with faces set like stone; they have **r** to repent.
7:13 not listen. I called out to you, but you **r** to answer.
9:13 I gave them; they have **r** to obey my law.
11: 8 And because they **r** to obey, I brought upon them
11:10 They have **r** to listen to me and are worshiping
17:23 They stubbornly **r** to pay attention and would not
19:15 because you have stubbornly **r** to listen to me."
32:23 in it, but they **r** to obey you or follow your law.
32:33 have turned their backs on me and have **r** to return.
34:18 Because you have **r** the terms of our covenant,
35: 6 but they **r**. "No," they said. "We don't drink
35:16 but you have **r** to listen to me.'
40:14 assassinate you?" But Gedaliah **r** to believe them.
43: 4 and all the people **r** to obey the LORD's
43: 7 The people **r** to obey the LORD and went to
Eze 5: 6 She has **r** to obey the laws I gave her to follow.
5: 7 Since you have **r** to obey my laws and regulations
11:12 For you have **r** to obey me; instead, you have
20:13 and they **r** to obey my laws there in the wilderness.
20:21 They **r** to keep my laws and follow my
24:13 And now, because I tried to cleanse you but you **r**,
Da 6:18 He **r** his usual entertainment and couldn't sleep at
9: 6 We have **r** to listen to your servants the prophets,
9:13 But we have **r** to seek mercy from the LORD our
Am 7:17 Because you have **r** to listen, your wife will
Hag 2:17 Yet, even so, you **r** to return to me,
Zec 7:13 "Since they **r** to listen when I called to them,
Mt 13:57 they were deeply offended and **r** to believe in him.
21:32 you **r** to turn from your sins and believe him.
22: 3 everyone that it was time to come. But they all **r**!
25:45 when you **r** to help the least of these my brothers
27:34 but when he had tasted it, he **r** to drink it.
Mk 1:34 who he was, he **r** to allow the demons to speak.
6: 3 were deeply offended and **r** to believe in him.
15:23 offered him wine drugged with myrrh, but he **r** it.
Lk 7:30 plan for them, for they had **r** John's baptism.
9:53 The people of the village **r** to have anything to do
12:47 for though he knew his duty, he **r** to do it.
14: 4 When they **r** to answer, Jesus touched the sick man
15:29 and never once **r** to do a single thing you told me
23: 9 question after question, but Jesus **r** to answer.
Ro 1:28 When they **r** to acknowledge God, he abandoned
11:30 but when the Jews **r** his mercy, God was merciful
Gal 2: 5 But we **r** to listen to them for a single moment.
Heb 10:28 Anyone who **r** to obey the law of Moses was put to
11:24 **r** to be treated as the son of Pharaoh's daughter.
11:31 with all the others in her city who **r** to obey God.
12:25 did not escape when they **r** to listen to Moses,
Rev 2:13 And you **r** to deny me even when Antipas,
9:20 in these plagues still **r** to turn from their evil deeds.
16:11 But they **r** to repent of all their evil deeds.

REFUSES (37) [REFUSE]

Ge 17:14 Anyone who **r** to be circumcised will be cut off
Ex 22:17 But if her father **r** to let her marry him, the man
Nu 30: 5 But if her father **r** to let her fulfill the vow
30: 8 But if her husband **r** to accept her vow
30:12 But if her husband **r** to accept it on the day he
Dt 21:20 of ours is stubborn and rebellious and **r** to obey.
25: 7 But if the dead man's brother **r** to marry the
25: 7 'My husband's brother **r** to preserve his brother's
name in Israel—he **r** to marry me.'
25: 9 'This is what happens to a man who **r** to raise up a
1Sa 11: 7 happen to the oxen of anyone who **r** to follow Saul
Ezr 7:26 Anyone who **r** to obey the law of your God
Est 1:15 for a queen who **r** to obey the king's orders,
Pr 10: 3 but he **r** to satisfy the craving of the wicked.
13: 1 a parent's discipline; a young mocker **r** to listen.
29: 1 Whoever stubbornly **r** to accept criticism will
Ecc 4:13 than to be an old and foolish king who **r** all advice.
Isa 40:27 How can you say God **r** to hear your case?
Jer 12:17 But any nation who **r** to obey me will be uprooted
15:10 to foreclose nor a borrower who **r** to pay—
18:10 then that nation turns to evil and **r** to obey me,
27: 8 I will punish any nation that **r** to be his slave,
27:13 every nation that **r** to submit to Babylon's king?
Eze 18:10 be a robber or murderer and **r** to do what is right.
18:15 Suppose this son **r** to worship idols on the
Da 3: 6 Anyone who **r** to obey will immediately be thrown
Mic 3: 5 but you declare war on anyone who **r** to pay you.
Zep 3: 2 It proudly **r** to listen even to the voice of the
3: 2 No one can tell it anything; it **r** all correction.
Zec 14:17 And any nation anywhere in the world that **r** to
Mt 18:17 If that person still **r** to listen, take your case to the
Mk 16:16 But anyone who **r** to believe will be condemned.
Lk 10:10 But if a town **r** to welcome you, go out into its
1Co 11: 6 Yes, if she **r** to wear a head covering, she should
1Th 4: 8 Anyone who **r** to live by these rules is not
1Jn 3:17 and sees a brother or sister in need and **r** to help—
3Jn 1:10 He not only **r** to welcome the traveling teachers,

REFUSING (22) [REFUSE]

Ex 9:34 and his officials sinned yet again by stubbornly **r**
Nu 14:22 but again and again they tested me by **r** to listen.
2Ki 17: 4 and by **r** to pay the annual tribute to Assyria.
2Ch 36:13 **r** to turn to the LORD, the God of Israel.
Ps 78: 8 and unfaithful, / **r** to give their hearts to God.
Isa 1:20 But if you keep turning away and **r** to listen,
56: 2 who honor my Sabbath days of rest by **r** to work.
Jer 8: 5 **r** to turn back, even though I have warned them?
31:15 Rachel weeps for her children, **r** to be comforted—
44:23 **r** to obey him and follow his instructions, laws,
Eze 18:12 steals from debtors by **r** to let them redeem what
Da 3:12 They have defied Your Majesty by **r** to serve your
9:11 your law and turned away, **r** to listen to your voice.
Am 2: 4 rejected the laws of the LORD, **r** to obey him.
Ob 1:11 **r** to lift a finger to help when foreign invaders
Mt 2:18 **r** to be comforted—for they are dead."
25:45 my brothers and sisters, you were **r** to help me.'
Ro 2: 5 because of your stubbornness in **r** to turn from
13: 2 to obey the laws of the land are **r** to obey God,
2Th 3:11 **r** to work and wasting time meddling in other
1Jn 1: 8 are only fooling ourselves and **r** to accept the truth.
Rev 13:15 Then the statue commanded that anyone **r** to

REFUTE (1) [REFUTED]

Ac 9:22 and the Jews in Damascus couldn't **r** his proofs

REFUTED (2) [REFUTE]

Job 32:12 but not one of you has **r** Job or answered his
Ac 18:28 He **r** all the Jews with powerful arguments in

REGAIN (2) [GAIN]

1Sa 28:22 so you can **r** your strength for the trip back."
Pr 25:10 Then you will never **r** your good reputation.

REGAINED (2) [GAIN]

2Ch 13:20 So Jeroboam of Israel never **r** his power during
Ac 9:18 like scales fell from Saul's eyes, and he **r** his sight.

REGARD (8) [REGARDED, REGARDING, REGARDLESS, REGARDS]

Lev 6: 2 Or suppose they have been dishonest with **r** to a
1Ch 24:31 by means of sacred lots, without **r** to age or rank.
25: 8 without **r** to whether they were young or old,
26:13 without **r** to age or training, for it was all decided
Eze 28: 3 You **r** yourself as wiser than Daniel and think no
Da 11:37 He will have no **r** for the gods of his ancestors,
Ac 5:13 to join them, though everyone had high **r** for them.
1Co 12:23 And the parts we **r** as less honorable are those we

REGARDED (2) [REGARD]

Ps 106:31 So he has been **r** as a righteous man / ever since
Lk 24:19 highly **r** by both God and all the people.

REGARDING (27) [REGARD]

Ge 17:15 Then God added, "**R** Sarai, your wife—her name
Ex 28:38 thus bearing the guilt connected with any errors **r**
Lev 6: 9 and his sons the following instructions **r** the whole
6:14 "These are the instructions **r** the grain offering.
6:25 and his sons these further instructions **r** the sin
7:11 "These are the instructions **r** the different kinds of
11:46 "These are the instructions **r** the land animals,
23: 2 "Give the Israelites instructions **r** the LORD's
23:44 So Moses gave these instructions **r** the annual
Nu 4:27 and his sons will direct the Gershonites **r** their
1Ch 28:14 David gave instructions **r** how much gold
Ps 3: T **r** the time David fled from his son Absalom.
34: T **r** the time he pretended to be insane in front of
51: T **r** the time Nathan the prophet came to him after
52: T **r** the time Doeg the Edomite told Saul that
54: T **r** the time the Ziphites came and said to Saul,
56: T **r** the time the Philistines seized him in Gath.
57: T **r** the time he fled from Saul and went into the
59: T **r** the time Saul sent soldiers to watch David's
60: T **r** the time David fought Aram-naharaim
63: T **r** a time when David was in the wilderness of
142: T A psalm of David, **r** his experience in the cave.
La 1:17 **R** his people, the LORD has said, "Let their
Ac 16: 4 explaining the decision **r** the commandments that
23:29 I soon discovered it was something **r** their
Ro 10:21 But **r** Israel, God said, / "All day long I opened
Eph 3: 4 you will understand what I know about this plan **r**

REGARDLESS (2) [REGARD]

2Ch 31:16 **r** of their place in the genealogical records,
Mt 22:16 You teach about the way of God **r** of the

REGARDS (1) [REGARD]

Ro 16:10 And give my best **r** to the members of the

REGEM (1)

1Ch 2:47 The sons of Jahdai were **R**, Jotham, Geshan,

REGEMMELECH (1)

Zec 7: 2 The people of Bethel had sent Sharezer and **R**,

REGENERATION [KJV] See WASHING (AWAY OF SINS)

REGIMENT (3) [REGIMENTS]

Ac 10: 1 who was a captain of the Italian **R**.
21:31 word reached the commander of the Roman **r** that
27: 1 officer named Julius, a captain of the Imperial **R**.

REGIMENTS (1) [REGIMENT]

2Ch 26:12 leaders commanded these **r** of seasoned warriors.

REGION (38) [REGIONAL, REGIONS]

Ge 14: 1 About this time war broke out in the **r**.
Nu 21:32 they captured all the towns in the **r** and drove out
32:41 and changed the name of that **r** to the Towns of
Dt 3: 4 the entire Argob **r** in his kingdom of Bashan.
3:13 (The Argob **r** of Bashan used to be known as the
3:14 acquired the whole Argob **r** in Bashan all the way
3:14 Jair renamed this **r** after himself, calling it the
Jos 10:40 So Joshua conquered the whole **r**—the kings
11:16 So Joshua conquered the entire **r**—the hill country,
11:19 No one in this **r** made peace with the Israelites
12: 8 The people who lived in this **r** were the Hittites,
13:21 princes living in the **r** who were allied with Sihon.
Jdg 1:27 the Canaanites were determined to stay in that **r**.
11:21 of all the land of the Amorites, who lived in that **r**,
1Sa 9: 5 Finally, they entered the **r** of Zuph, and Saul said
1Ki 4:13 in Gilead, and in the Argob **r** of Bashan,
1Ch 4:39 who traveled to the **r** of Gedor, in the east part of
4:40 descendants had been living in the **r** of Gedor.
2Ch 8: 4 and built towns in the **r** of Hamath as supply
Ne 3:22 Then came the priests from the surrounding **r**.
Jer 44:15 Judeans living in Pathros, the southern **r** of Egypt
Mt 4:13 Sea of Galilee, in the **r** of Zebulun and Naphtali.
9:31 But instead, they spread his fame all over the **r**.
15:21 and went north to the **r** of Tyre and Sidon.
15:39 into a boat and crossed over to the **r** of Magadan.
16:13 When Jesus came to the **r** of Caesarea Philippi,
19: 1 left Galilee and went southward to the **r** of Judea
Mk 1:39 So he traveled throughout the **r** of Galilee,
5:20 the man started off to visit the Ten Towns of that **r**
7:24 Jesus left Galilee and went north to the **r** of Tyre.
7:31 to the Sea of Galilee and the **r** of the Ten Towns.
8:10 and crossed over to the **r** of Dalmanutha.
9:30 Leaving that **r**, they traveled through Galilee.
10: 1 and went southward to the **r** of Judea
Lk 4:37 done spread like wildfire throughout the whole **r**.
8:37 And all the people in that **r** begged Jesus to go
Ac 13:49 So the Lord's message spread throughout that **r**.
14: 6 They went to the **r** of Lycaonia, to the cities of

REGIONAL (1) [REGION]

1Ch 27:25 Jonathan son of Uzziah was in charge of the **r**

REGIONS (6) [REGION]

Dt 1: 7 of the Amorites and to all the neighboring **r**—
2Ki 15:29 He also conquered the **r** of Gilead, Galilee,
Job 28: 3 darkest **r** of the earth as they search for ore.
Jer 22:20 Search for them in the **r** east of the river. See,
25:22 and Sidon, and the kings of the **r** across the sea.
Ro 15:23 But now I have finished my work in these **r**,

REGISTER (2) [REGISTERED, REGISTERS, REGISTRATION]

Nu 3:40 who are one month old or older, and **r** each name.
Lk 2: 3 All returned to their own towns to **r** for this census.

REGISTERED (6) [REGISTER]
Ex 38:26 silver collected from each of those r in the census.
Nu 1:18 All the people were r according to their ancestry
1:18 The men of Israel twenty years old or older were r,
1Ch 23:24 leaders of their family groups, r carefully by name.
23:27 twenty years old or older were r for service.
Lk 10:20 because your names are r as citizens of heaven."

REGISTERS (1) [REGISTER]
Ps 87:6 When the LORD r the nations, / he will say,

REGISTRATION (1) [REGISTER]
Ne 7:5 of the city, along with the ordinary citizens, for r.

REGRET (2)
Na 3:7 Yet no one anywhere will r your destruction."
2Co 7:10 We will never r that kind of sorrow.

REGROUPED (2) [GROUP]
2Sa 2:25 Abner's troops from the tribe of Benjamin r there
10:15 that they were no match for Israel. So when they r,

REGULAR (62) [REGULARLY]
Ex 5:18 but you must still deliver the r quota of bricks."
20:9 week are set apart for your daily duties and r work,
29:28 these parts will be the r share of Aaron and his
30:10 This will be a r, annual event from generation to
Lev 6:18 because it is their r share of the offerings given to
6:22 It is the LORD's r share, and it must be
7:34 It is their r share of the peace offerings brought by
7:36 r share from the time of the priests' anointing.
9:17 in addition to the r morning burnt offering.
10:13 and your descendants as your r share of the
10:14 and daughters as your r share of the peace
23:7 all the people must stop their r work and gather for
23:8 the people must again stop all their r work to hold
23:21 you must stop all your r work and gather for a
23:25 You must do no r work on that day. Instead,
23:35 on the first day, and all your r work must stop.
23:36 and no r work may be done that day.
23:38 in addition to the LORD's r Sabbath days.
Nu 9:13 yet still refuse to celebrate the Passover at the r
9:16 This was the r pattern—at night the cloud changed
18:8 offerings to you and your sons as your r share.
18:11 before the altar also belong to you as your r share.
18:19 and daughters, to be eaten as your r share.
28:6 This is the r burnt offering ordained at Mount
28:10 in addition to the r daily burnt offering and its
28:15 This is in addition to the r daily burnt offering
28:18 None of your r work may be done on that day.
28:23 offerings in addition to your r morning sacrifices.
28:24 These will be offered in addition to the r whole
28:25 None of your r work may be done on that day.
28:26 None of your r work may be done on that day.
28:31 are in addition to the r daily burnt offering and its
29:1 people on that day, and no r work may be done.
29:6 These special sacrifices are in addition to your r
29:7 must go without food, and no r work may be done.
29:11 and the r daily burnt offering with its grain
29:12 and on that day no r work may be done.
29:16 in addition to the r daily burnt offering with its
29:19 in addition to the r daily burnt offering with its
29:22 in addition to the r daily burnt offering with its
29:25 in addition to the r daily burnt offering with its
29:28 in addition to the r daily burnt offering with its
29:31 in addition to the r daily burnt offering with its
29:34 in addition to the r daily burnt offering with its
29:35 You must do no r work on that day.
29:38 in addition to the r daily burnt offering with its
Dt 5:13 week are set apart for your daily duties and r work,
17:20 This r reading will prevent him from becoming
1Sa 21:4 "We don't have any r bread," the priest replied.
2Ki 12:4 whether it is a r assessment, a payment of vows,
25:30 The Babylonian king also gave him a r allowance
1Ch 12:14 among them could take on a hundred r troops,
16:40 They sacrificed the r burnt offerings to the LORD
Ezr 3:5 They also offered the r burnt offerings
Ne 7:3 Jerusalem to act as guards, everyone on a r watch.
7:3 Some will serve at their r posts and some in front
10:33 for the r grain offerings and burnt offerings;
10:34 at r times each year—the families of the priests,
Job 1:5 God in their hearts." This was Job's r practice.
Jer 52:34 The Babylonian king also gave him a r allowance
Da 1:19 So they were appointed to his r staff of advisers.
Mk 3:14 Then he selected twelve of them to be his r

REGULARLY (11) [REGULAR]
Ex 2:16 daughters who came r to this well to draw water
19:22 Even the priests who r come near to the LORD
2Sa 9:11 from that time on, Mephibosheth ate r with David,
1Ch 16:6 played the trumpets r before the Ark of God's
16:37 and his fellow Levites to minister r before the Ark
Ne 5:17 even though I r fed 150 Jewish officials at my
Eze 44:20 it off completely. Instead, they must trim it r.
Jn 18:20 because I have preached r in the synagogues
Ac 5:12 And the believers were meeting r at the Temple in
10:2 to charity and was a man who r prayed to God.
Heb 9:6 and out of the first room r as they performed their

REGULATION (2) [REGULATIONS]
Ex 12:17 This festival will be a permanent r for you, to be
Lev 7:36 This r applies throughout the generations to

REGULATIONS (80) [REGULATION]
Ge 26:5 all my requirements, commands, r, and laws."
Ex 12:19 These same r apply to the foreigners living with
12:43 "These are the r for the festival of Passover.
24:3 all the teachings and r the LORD had given him,
Lev 18:4 You must obey all my r and be careful to keep my
18:5 If you obey my laws and r, you will find life
18:26 You must strictly obey all of my laws and r,
19:37 You must be careful to obey all of my laws and r,
20:22 "You must carefully obey all my laws and r;
24:22 "These same r apply to Israelites by birth
25:18 securely in the land, keep my laws and obey my r.
26:15 rejecting my laws and treating my r with contempt,
26:43 for they rejected my r and despised my laws.
26:46 These are the laws, r, and instructions that the
Nu 9:3 all my laws and r concerning this celebration."
9:12 They must follow all the normal r concerning the
9:14 they must follow these same laws and r.
15:16 The same instructions and r will apply both to you
30:16 These are the r the LORD gave Moses
35:24 the assembly must follow these r in making a
36:13 and r that the LORD gave to the people of Israel
Dt 4:1 to these laws and r that I am about to teach you.
4:5 and r when you arrive in the land you are about to
4:8 and r as fair as this body of laws that I am giving
4:14 and r you must obey in the land you are about to
4:45 and r that Moses gave to the people of Israel when
5:1 to all the laws and r I am giving you today.
5:31 so I can give you all my commands, laws, and r.
6:1 and r that the LORD your God told me to teach
6:20 and r that the LORD our God has given us?'
7:11 laws, and r I am giving you today.
7:12 "If you listen to these r and obey them faithfully,
8:11 your God and disobey his commands, r, and laws.
11:1 obey all his requirements, laws, r, and commands.
11:32 to obey all the laws and r I am giving you today.
12:1 and r you must obey as long as you live in the land
26:16 has commanded you to obey all these laws and r.
26:17 and r by walking in his ways and doing everything
30:16 his commands, laws, and r by walking in his ways.
33:10 Now let them teach your r to Jacob; / let them give
33:21 the LORD's justice / and obeyed his r for Israel."
1Ki 2:3 Keep each of the laws, commands, r,
6:12 if you keep all my laws and r and obey all my
8:58 laws, and r that he gave our ancestors.
9:4 my commands and keeping my laws and r,
11:33 He has not obeyed my laws and r as his father,
2Ki 17:34 the LORD and obeying the laws, r, instructions,
17:37 Be careful to obey all the laws, r, instructions,
23:3 r, and laws with all his heart and soul.
1Ch 6:32 following all the r handed down to them.
22:13 and r that the LORD gave to Israel through
28:7 to obey my commands and r as he does now,
2Ch 7:17 did and obey all my commands, laws, and r,
8:14 Solomon followed the r of his father, David.
19:10 of God's instructions, commands, laws, or r,
30:16 according to the r found in the law of Moses,
33:8 the instructions, laws, and r given through Moses
34:31 r, and laws with all his heart and soul.
Ezr 7:10 to teach those laws and r to the people of Israel.
Ne 1:7 and r that you gave us through your servant
9:13 You gave them r and instructions that were just,
9:29 They did not follow your r, by which people will
10:29 laws, and r of the LORD their Lord.
Eze 5:6 but she has rebelled against my r and has been
5:7 Since you have refused to obey my laws and r
11:20 so they will obey my laws and r. Then they will
18:9 and faithfully obeys my laws and r. Anyone who
18:17 money at interest, and obeys all my r and laws.
37:24 They will obey my r and keep my laws.
43:18 These will be the r for the burning of offerings
44:5 Listen to everything I tell you about the r
44:24 Their decisions must be based on my r.
Da 9:5 against you and scorned your commands and r.
Mal 4:4 and r that I gave him on Mount Sinai for all Israel.
Lk 1:6 to obey all of the Lord's commandments and r.
Gal 2:4 to force us, like slaves, to follow their Jewish r.
5:3 you must obey all of the r in the whole law of
Heb 9:1 there were r for worship and a sacred tent here on
9:8 By these r the Holy Spirit revealed that the Most
9:10 external r that are in effect only until their

REHABIAH (4)
1Ch 23:17 R, the family leader. R had numerous descendants.
24:21 From the descendants of R, the leader was Isshiah.
26:25 His relatives through Eliezer were R, Jeshaiah,

REHEARSE [KJV] See ANNOUNCE, RECOUNT

REHOB (10) [BETH-REHOB]
Nu 13:21 the land from the wilderness of Zin as far as R,
Jos 19:28 Abdon, R, Hammon, Kanah, and as far as Greater
19:30 Ummah, Aphek, and R—twenty-two towns with
21:31 Helkath, and R—four towns and their pasturelands.
Jdg 1:31 Sidon, Ahlab, Aczib, Helbah, Aphik, and R.
2Sa 8:3 also destroyed the forces of Hadadezer son of R,
8:12 and from Hadadezer son of R, king of Zobah.
10:8 from Zobah and R and the men from Tob
1Ch 6:75 Hukok, and R, each with its pasturelands.
Ne 10:11 Mica, R, Hashabiah,

REHOBOAM (49) [REHOBOAM'S]
1Ki 11:43 David. Then his son R became the next king.
12:1 R went to Shechem, where all Israel had gathered
12:3 the whole assembly of Israel went to speak with R.
12:5 R replied, "Give me three days to think this over.
12:6 Then King R went to discuss the matter with the
12:8 But R rejected the advice of the elders and instead
12:13 But R spoke harshly to them, for he rejected the
12:17 But R continued to rule over the Israelites who
12:18 King R sent Adoniram, who was in charge of the
12:18 When this news reached King R, he quickly
12:21 When R arrived at Jerusalem, he mobilized the
12:23 "Say to R son of Solomon, king of Judah, and to
12:27 they will again give their allegiance to King R of
14:21 Meanwhile, R son of Solomon was king in Judah.
14:27 Afterward R made bronze shields as substitutes,
14:30 There was constant war between R and Jeroboam.
14:31 When R died, he was buried among his ancestors
1Ch 3:10 The descendants of Solomon were R, Abijah,
2Ch 9:31 David. Then his son R became the next king.
10:1 R went to Shechem, where all Israel had gathered
10:3 and all Israel went together to speak with R.
10:5 R replied, "Come back in three days for my
10:6 Then King R went to discuss the matter with the
10:8 But R rejected the advice of the elders and instead
10:13 But R spoke harshly to them, for he rejected the
10:17 But R continued to rule over the Israelites who
10:18 King R sent Adoniram, who was in charge of the
10:18 When this news reached King R, he quickly
11:1 When R arrived at Jerusalem, he mobilized the
11:3 "Say to R son of Solomon, king of Judah, and to
11:5 R remained in Jerusalem and fortified various
11:11 R strengthened their defenses and stationed
11:13 among the northern tribes of Israel sided with R.
11:17 and for three years they supported R son of
11:18 R married his cousin Mahalath, the daughter of
11:20 Later R married another cousin, Maacah,
11:21 R loved Maacah more than any of his other wives
11:22 R made Maacah's son Abijah chief among the
11:23 R also wisely gave responsibilities to his other
12:1 But when R was firmly established and strong,
12:5 then met with R and Judah's leaders,
12:10 King R later replaced them with bronze shields
12:12 Because R humbled himself, the LORD's anger
12:13 King R firmly established himself in Jerusalem
12:15 R and Jeroboam were continually at war with each
12:16 When R died, he was buried in the City of David.
13:7 defying Solomon's son R when he was young
Mt 1:7 Solomon was the father of R. / R was the father of

REHOBOAM'S (9) [REHOBOAM]
1Ki 12:12 and all the people returned to hear R decision,
14:21 R mother was Naamah, an Ammonite woman.
14:22 During R reign, the people of Judah did what was
14:25 In the fifth year of King R reign, King Shishak of
14:29 The rest of the events in R reign and all his deeds
2Ch 10:12 and all the people returned to hear R decision,
12:2 Jerusalem in the fifth year of King R reign.
12:13 R mother was Naamah, a woman from Ammon.
12:15 The rest of the events of R reign, from beginning

REHOBOTH (2) [REHOBOTH-IR]
Ge 36:37 Shaul from the city of R on the Euphrates River
1Ch 1:48 Shaul from the city of R on the Euphrates River

REHOBOTH-IR (1) [REHOBOTH]
Ge 10:11 reign to Assyria, where he built Nineveh, R, Calah,

REHUM (7)
Ezr 2:2 Reelaiah, Mordecai, Bilshan, Mispar, Bigvai, R,
4:8 R the governor and Shimshai the court secretary
4:17 "To R the governor, Shimshai the court secretary,
4:23 this letter from King Artaxerxes was read to R,
Ne 3:17 working under the supervision of R son of Bani.
7:7 Nahamani, Mordecai, Bilshan, Mispar, Bigvai, R,
10:25 R, Hashabnah, Maaseiah,

REI (1)
1Ki 1:8 son of Jehoiada, Nathan the prophet, Shimei, R,

REIGN (243) [REIGNED, REIGNING, REIGNS]
Ge 10:11 From there he extended his r to Assyria, where he
Ex 15:18 The LORD will r forever and ever!"
Dt 17:20 and his descendants will r for many generations in
1Sa 12:12 and said that you wanted a king to r over you,
2Sa 5:4 David was thirty years old when he began to r,
21:1 There was a famine during David's r that lasted for
1Ki 1:37 and may he make Solomon's r even greater than
6:1 during the fourth year of Solomon's r,
6:37 in midspring of the fourth year of Solomon's r.
6:38 detail by midautumn of the eleventh year of his r.
8:25 as you have done, they will always r over Israel.'
11:25 Israel's bitter enemy for the rest of Solomon's r,
11:25 hated Israel intensely and continued to r in Aram.
11:34 I will let Solomon r for the rest of his life.
11:36 David my servant will continue to r in Jerusalem,
11:41 The rest of the events in Solomon's r,
14:19 The rest of the events of Jeroboam's r, all his wars
14:22 During Rehoboam's r, the people of Judah did
14:25 In the fifth year of King Rehoboam's r,
14:29 The rest of the events in Rehoboam's r and all his
15:1 in the eighteenth year of Jeroboam's r in Israel.
15:6 and Jeroboam throughout Abijam's r.
15:7 The rest of the events in Abijam's r and all his
15:9 in the twentieth year of Jeroboam's r in Israel.
15:23 The rest of the events in Asa's r, the extent of his

15:25 Israel in the second year of King Asa's **r** in Judah.
15:28 Nadab in the third year of King Asa's **r** in Judah,
15:31 The rest of the events in Nadab's **r** and all his
15:33 Israel in the third year of King Asa's **r** in Judah.
16:5 The rest of the events in Baasha's **r** and the extent
16:8 in the twenty-sixth year of King Asa's **r** in Judah.
16:10 the twenty-seventh year of King Asa's **r** in Judah.
16:14 The rest of the events in Elah's **r** and all his deeds
16:15 the twenty-seventh year of King Asa's **r** in Judah,
16:20 The rest of the events of Zimri's **r** and his
16:23 in the thirty-first year of King Asa's **r** in Judah.
16:27 The rest of the events in Omri's **r**, the extent of his
16:29 in the thirty-eighth year of King Asa's **r** in Judah.
16:34 It was during his **r** that Hiel, a man from Bethel,
22:39 The rest of the events in Ahab's **r** and the story of
22:41 Judah in the fourth year of King Ahab's **r** in Israel.
22:43 During his **r**, however, he failed to remove all the
22:45 The rest of the events in Jehoshaphat's **r**,
22:51 seventeenth year of King Jehoshaphat's **r** in Judah.
2Ki 1:17 This took place in the second year of the **r** of
1:18 The rest of the events in Ahaziah's **r** are recorded
3:1 eighteenth year of King Jehoshaphat's **r** in Judah.
8:16 Judah in the fifth year of King Joram's **r** in Israel.
8:20 During Jehoram's **r**, the Edomites revolted against
8:23 The rest of the events in Jehoram's **r** and all his
8:25 in the twelfth year of King Joram's **r** in Israel.
9:29 Ahaziah's **r** over Judah had begun in the eleventh year of King Joram's **r** in Israel.
10:34 The rest of the events in Jehu's **r** and all his deeds
11:4 In the seventh year of Athaliah's **r**,
12:1 in the seventh year of King Jehu's **r** in Israel.
12:6 But by the twenty-third year of Joash's **r**,
12:19 The rest of the events in Joash's **r** and all his
13:1 in the twenty-third year of King Joash's **r** in Judah.
13:8 The rest of the events in Jehoahaz's **r** and all his
13:10 the thirty-seventh year of King Joash's **r** in Judah.
13:12 The rest of the events in Jehoash's **r** and all his
13:22 Israel during the entire **r** of King Jehoahaz.
14:1 the second year of the **r** of King Jehoash of Israel.
14:15 The rest of the events in Jehoash's **r**,
14:18 The rest of the events in Amaziah's **r** are recorded
14:23 in the fifteenth year of King Amaziah's **r** in Judah.
14:28 The rest of the events in the **r** of Jeroboam II
15:1 year of the **r** of King Jeroboam II of Israel.
15:6 The rest of the events in Uzziah's **r** and all his
15:8 the thirty-eighth year of King Uzziah's **r** in Judah.
15:11 The rest of the events in Zechariah's **r** are
15:13 the thirty-ninth year of King Uzziah's **r** in Judah.
15:15 The rest of the events in Shallum's **r**, including his
15:17 the thirty-ninth year of King Uzziah's **r** in Judah.
15:18 During his entire **r**, he refused to turn from the sins
15:21 The rest of the events in Menahem's **r** and all his
15:23 in the fiftieth year of King Uzziah's **r** in Judah.
15:26 The rest of the events in Pekahiah's **r** and all his
15:27 the fifty-second year of King Uzziah's **r** in Judah.
15:29 During his **r**, King Tiglath-pileser of Assyria
15:31 The rest of the events in Pekah's **r** and all his
15:32 in the second year of King Pekah's **r** in Israel.
15:36 The rest of the events in Jotham's **r** and all his
16:1 in the seventeenth year of King Pekah's **r** in Israel.
16:19 The rest of the events in Ahaz's **r** and his deeds
17:1 in the twelfth year of King Ahaz's **r** in Judah.
17:6 Finally, in the ninth year of King Hoshea's **r**,
18:1 in the third year of King Hoshea's **r** in Israel.
18:9 During the fourth year of Hezekiah's **r**, which was the seventh year of King Hoshea's **r** in
18:10 during the sixth year of King Hezekiah's **r**
18:10 and the ninth year of King Hoshea's **r** in Israel,
18:13 In the fourteenth year of King Hezekiah's **r**,
20:20 The rest of the events in Hezekiah's **r**,
21:17 The rest of the events in Manasseh's **r** and all his
21:25 The rest of the events in Amon's **r** and all his
22:3 In the eighteenth year of his **r**, King Josiah sent
23:23 during the eighteenth year of King Josiah's **r**.
23:28 The rest of the events in Josiah's **r** and all his
23:34 another of Josiah's sons, to **r** in place of his father,
24:1 During Jehoiakim's **r**, King Nebuchadnezzar of
24:5 The rest of the events in Jehoiakim's **r** and all his
24:10 During Jehoiachin's **r**, the officers of King
24:12 In the eighth year of Nebuchadnezzar's **r**, he took
25:1 January 15, during the ninth year of Zedekiah's **r**,
25:2 siege until the eleventh year of King Zedekiah's **r**.
25:8 was the nineteenth year of Nebuchadnezzar's **r**,
1Ch 4:41 But during the **r** of King Hezekiah of Judah,
5:10 During the **r** of Saul, the Reubenites defeated the
13:3 our God, for we neglected it during the **r** of Saul."
22:9 I will give peace and quiet to Israel during his **r**.
26:31 (In the fortieth year of David's **r**, a search was
29:29 All the events of King David's **r**, from beginning
29:30 These accounts include the mighty deeds of his **r**
2Ch 1:15 During Solomon's **r**, silver and gold were as
3:2 during the fourth year of Solomon's **r**.
6:16 as you have done, they will always **r** over Israel.'
9:29 The rest of the events of Solomon's **r**,
12:2 Jerusalem in the fifth year of King Rehoboam's **r**.
12:15 The rest of the events of Rehoboam's **r**,
13:1 in the eighteenth year of Jeroboam's **r** in Israel.
13:22 The rest of the events of Abijah's **r**, including his
15:9 Many had moved to Judah during Asa's **r** when
15:10 in late spring, during the fifteenth year of Asa's **r**.
15:19 no more war until the thirty-fifth year of Asa's **r**.
16:1 In the thirty-sixth year of Asa's **r**, King Baasha of
16:11 The rest of the events of Asa's **r**, from beginning
16:12 In the thirty-ninth year of his **r**, Asa developed a
16:13 So he died in the forty-first year of his **r**.
17:7 In the third year of his **r**, Jehoshaphat sent out his
20:33 During his **r**, however, he failed to remove all the
20:34 The rest of the events of Jehoshaphat's **r**,
21:8 During Jehoram's **r**, the Edomites revolted against
23:1 In the seventh year of Athaliah's **r**,
23:3 "The time has come for the king's son to **r**!
25:26 The rest of the events of Amaziah's **r**,
26:22 The rest of the events of Uzziah's **r**,
27:7 The rest of the events of Jotham's **r**, including his
28:26 The rest of the events of Ahaz's **r** and all his
29:3 In the very first month of the first year of his **r**,
32:32 The rest of the events of Hezekiah's **r** and his acts
33:18 The rest of the events of Manasseh's **r**, his prayer
34:3 During the eighth year of his **r**, while he was still
34:8 In the eighteenth year of his **r**, after he had purified
35:19 took place in the eighteenth year of Josiah's **r**.
35:26 The rest of the events of Josiah's **r** and his acts of
36:8 The rest of the events of Jehoiakim's **r**,
Ezr 4:5 This went on during the entire **r** of King Cyrus of
4:6 Years later when Xerxes began his **r**, the enemies
4:7 And even later during the **r** of King Artaxerxes of
4:24 the second year of the **r** of King Darius of Persia.
5:13 Cyrus of Babylon, during the first year of his **r**,
6:3 "In the first year of King Cyrus's **r**, a decree was
6:15 during the sixth year of King Darius's **r**.
7:1 during the **r** of King Artaxerxes of Persia,
7:7 him in the seventh year of King Artaxerxes' **r**.
8:1 me from Babylon during the **r** of King Artaxerxes:
Ne 1:1 of the twentieth year of King Artaxerxes' **r**,
2:1 during the twentieth year of King Artaxerxes' **r**,
5:14 thirty-second year of the **r** of King Artaxerxes—
12:22 During the **r** of Darius II of Persia, a list was
13:6 year of the **r** of King Artaxerxes of Babylon,
Est 1:3 In the third year of his **r**, he gave a banquet for all
2:16 palace in early winter of the seventh year of his **r**,
2:23 in *The Book of the History of King Xerxes' **R**.*
3:7 during the twelfth year of King Xerxes' **r**,
Ps 61:7 May he **r** under God's protection forever.
72:6 May his **r** be as refreshing as the springtime rains
72:7 May all the godly flourish during his **r**. / May there
72:8 May he **r** from sea to sea, / and from the Euphrates
93:5 The nature of your **r**, O LORD, is holiness
145:12 and about the majesty and glory of your **r**.
146:10 The LORD will **r** forever. / O Jerusalem,
Pr 8:15 Because of me, kings **r**, and rulers make just laws.
22:8 will harvest disaster, and their **r** of terror will end.
25:5 and his **r** will be made secure by justice.
28:16 but a king will have a long **r** if he hates dishonesty
29:14 A king who is fair to the poor will have a long **r**.
Isa 7:1 During the **r** of Ahaz son of Jotham and grandson
16:5 From that throne a faithful king will **r**, one who
36:1 In the fourteenth year of King Hezekiah's **r**,
47:7 'I will **r** forever as queen of the world!'
Jer 1:2 the thirteenth year of King Josiah's **r** in Judah.
1:3 He continued to give messages throughout the **r** of
1:3 until the eleventh year of King Zedekiah's **r** in
3:6 During the **r** of King Josiah, the LORD said to
22:15 Why did your father, Josiah, **r** so long? Because he
22:17 the innocent, oppress the poor, and **r** ruthlessly."
25:1 during the fourth year of Jehoiakim's **r** over Judah.
25:1 King Nebuchadnezzar of Babylon began his **r**.
26:1 LORD early in the **r** of Jehoiakim son of Josiah,
26:18 during the **r** of King Hezekiah of Judah.
27:1 LORD early in the **r** of Zedekiah son of Josiah,
28:1 the fourth year of the **r** of Zedekiah, king of
32:1 the LORD in the tenth year of the **r** of Zedekiah,
32:1 This was also the eighteenth year of the **r** of King
33:21 then will he no longer have a descendant to **r** on
36:9 during the fifth year of the **r** of Jehoiakim son of
39:1 of King Zedekiah's **r** that King Nebuchadnezzar
45:1 the fourth year of the **r** of Jehoiakim son of Josiah,
46:2 the fourth year of the **r** of Jehoiakim son of Josiah,
49:34 the beginning of the **r** of King Zedekiah of Judah.
51:59 This was during the fourth year of Zedekiah's **r**.
52:4 January 15, during the ninth year of Zedekiah's **r**,
52:5 siege until the eleventh year of King Zedekiah's **r**.
52:12 was the nineteenth year of Nebuchadnezzar's **r**,
52:28 the seventh year of Nebuchadnezzar's **r** was 3,023.
Da 1:1 During the third year of King Jehoiakim's **r** in
1:21 there until the first year of King Cyrus's **r**.
2:1 One night during the second year of his **r**,
5:11 During Nebuchadnezzar's **r**, this man was found to
5:26 God has numbered the days of your **r** and has
6:28 So Daniel prospered during the **r** of Darius and the **r** of Cyrus the Persian.
7:1 during the first year of King Belshazzar's **r** in
8:1 During the third year of King Belshazzar's **r**,
9:1 It was the first year of the **r** of Darius the Mede,
9:2 During the first year of his **r**, I, Daniel,
10:1 In the third year of the **r** of King Cyrus of Persia,
11:1 and defense since the first year of the **r** of Darius
11:2 Three more Persian kings will **r**, to be succeeded
11:20 but after a very brief **r**, he will die, though neither
Hag 1:1 August 29 of the second year of King Darius's **r**,
1:15 21 of the second year of King Darius's **r**.
2:10 18 of the second year of King Darius's **r**,
Zec 1:1 midautumn of the second year of King Darius's **r**,
1:7 February 15 of the second year of King Darius's **r**,
7:1 December 7 of the fourth year of King Darius's **r**,
Mt 2:1 of Bethlehem in Judea, during the **r** of King Herod.
Lk 1:33 And he will **r** over Israel forever; his Kingdom will
3:1 It was now the fifteenth year of the **r** of Tiberius,
Ac 11:28 (This was fulfilled during the **r** of Claudius.)
1Co 15:25 For Christ must **r** until he humbles all his enemies
2Ti 2:12 If we endure hardship, / we will **r** with him.
Rev 5:10 and his priests. / And they will **r** on the earth."
11:15 and of his Christ, and he will **r** forever and ever."
11:17 assumed your great power / and have begun to **r**.
17:10 the seventh is yet to come, but his **r** will be brief.
17:12 kingdoms for one brief moment to **r** with the beast.
17:16 which represent ten kings who will **r** with him—
20:6 and of Christ and will **r** with him a thousand years.
22:5 shine on them. And they will **r** forever and ever.

REIGNED (77) [REIGN]

Jos 13:10 who **r** in Heshbon, and extended as far as the
13:12 Og of Bashan, who had **r** in Ashtaroth and Edrei.
13:21 Sihon was the Amorite king who had **r** in Heshbon
1Sa 13:1 when he became king, and he **r** for forty-two years.
2Sa 5:4 when he began to reign, and he **r** forty years in all.
5:5 He had **r** over Judah from Hebron for seven years
5:5 and from Jerusalem he **r** over all Israel and Judah
8:15 David **r** over all Israel and was fair to everyone.
1Ki 2:11 He had **r** over Israel for forty years, seven of them
14:20 Jeroboam **r** in Israel twenty-two years.
14:21 and he **r** seventeen years in Jerusalem,
15:2 He **r** in Jerusalem three years. His mother was
15:10 He **r** in Jerusalem forty-one years.
15:25 Asa's reign in Judah. He **r** in Israel two years.
15:33 in Judah. Baasha **r** in Tirzah twenty-four years.
16:8 Asa's reign in Judah. He **r** in Israel two years.
16:15 Asa's reign in Judah, but he **r** only seven days.
16:23 He **r** twelve years in all, six of them in Tirzah.
16:29 reign in Judah. He **r** in Samaria twenty-two years.
22:42 and he **r** in Jerusalem twenty-five years.
22:51 reign in Judah. He **r** in Samaria two years.
2Ki 3:1 reign in Judah. He **r** in Samaria twelve years.
8:17 he became king, and he **r** in Jerusalem eight years.
8:26 he became king, and he **r** in Jerusalem one year.
10:36 Jehu **r** over Israel from Samaria for twenty-eight
12:1 He **r** in Jerusalem forty years. His mother was
13:1 reign in Judah. He **r** in Samaria seventeen years.
13:10 reign in Judah. He **r** in Samaria sixteen years.
14:2 and he **r** in Jerusalem twenty-nine years.
14:23 in Judah. Jeroboam **r** in Samaria forty-one years.
15:2 and he **r** in Jerusalem fifty-two years.
15:8 reign in Judah. He **r** in Samaria six months.
15:13 in Judah. Shallum **r** in Samaria only one month.
15:17 Uzziah's reign in Judah. He **r** in Samaria ten years.
15:23 reign in Judah. He **r** in Samaria two years.
15:27 reign in Judah. He **r** in Samaria twenty years.
15:33 became king, and he **r** in Jerusalem sixteen years.
16:2 became king, and he **r** in Jerusalem sixteen years.
17:1 Ahaz's reign in Judah. He **r** in Samaria nine years.
18:2 and he **r** in Jerusalem twenty-nine years.
21:1 and he **r** in Jerusalem fifty-five years.
21:19 he became king, and he **r** in Jerusalem two years.
22:1 and he **r** in Jerusalem thirty-one years.
23:31 became king, and he **r** in Jerusalem three months.
23:36 became king, and he **r** in Jerusalem eleven years.
24:8 became king, and he **r** in Jerusalem three months.
24:18 became king, and he **r** in Jerusalem eleven years.
1Ch 3:4 in Hebron, where he **r** seven and a half years.
3:4 to Jerusalem, where he **r** another thirty-three years.
18:14 David **r** over all Israel and was fair to everyone.
29:26 So David son of Jesse **r** over all Israel.
2Ch 1:13 at the hill of Gibeon, and he **r** over Israel.
12:13 and he **r** seventeen years in Jerusalem,
13:2 He **r** in Jerusalem three years. His mother was
20:31 and he **r** in Jerusalem twenty-five years.
21:5 he became king, and he **r** in Jerusalem eight years.
21:20 he became king, and he **r** in Jerusalem eight years.
22:1 So Ahaziah son of Jehoram **r** as king of Judah.
22:2 he became king, and he **r** in Jerusalem one year.
24:1 he became king, and he **r** in Jerusalem forty years.
25:1 and he **r** in Jerusalem twenty-nine years.
26:3 and he **r** in Jerusalem fifty-two years.
27:1 became king, and he **r** in Jerusalem sixteen years.
27:8 became king, and he **r** in Jerusalem sixteen years.
28:1 became king, and he **r** in Jerusalem sixteen years.
29:1 of Judah, and he **r** in Jerusalem twenty-nine years.
33:1 and he **r** in Jerusalem fifty-five years.
33:21 he became king, and he **r** in Jerusalem two years.
34:1 and he **r** in Jerusalem thirty-one years.
36:2 when he became king, but he **r** only three months.
36:5 became king, and he **r** in Jerusalem eleven years.
36:9 but he **r** in Jerusalem only three months and ten
36:11 became king, and he **r** in Jerusalem eleven years.
Est 1:1 who **r** over 127 provinces stretching from India to
Jer 52:1 became king, and he **r** in Jerusalem eleven years.
Ac 13:21 of the tribe of Benjamin, who **r** for forty years.
Rev 20:4 and they **r** with Christ for a thousand years.

REIGNING (1) [REIGN]

1Co 4:8 thrones already, for then we would be **r** with you!

REIGNS (13) [REIGN]

2Ch 11:17 the LORD as they had done during the **r** of David
Job 10:22 a land of utter gloom where confusion **r**
Ps 9:7 But the LORD **r** forever, / executing judgment
9:11 Sing praises to the LORD who **r** in Jerusalem.
29:10 the floodwaters. / The LORD **r** as king forever.
47:8 God **r** above the nations, / sitting on his holy
59:13 will know / that God **r** in Israel. / *Interlude*
Isa 1:1 to Isaiah son of Amoz during the **r** of Uzziah,
52:7 and salvation, the news that the God of Israel **r**!
Da 2:44 "During the **r** of those kings, the God of heaven
Lk 22:53 the time when the power of darkness **r**."
Rev 17:10 Five kings have already fallen, the sixth now **r**,
19:6 For the Lord our God, the Almighty, **r**.

REINED (1)

2Ki 9:23 Then King Joram **r** the chariot horses around

REINFORCE (1) [REINFORCED]
Jer 51:12 **R** the guard and station the watchmen. Prepare an

REINFORCED (3) [REINFORCE]
Ex 28:32 The opening will be **r** by a woven collar so it will
39:23 The edge of this opening was **r** with a woven
2Ch 32: 5 He also **r** the Millo in the City of David

REINSTATE (1)
2Sa 19:11 "Why are you the last ones to **r** the king?

REJECT (46) [REJECTED, REJECTING, REJECTION, REJECTS]
Lev 26:44 I will not utterly **r** or despise them while they are
Nu 14:11 said to Moses, "How long will these people **r** me?
Dt 11:28 You will receive a curse if you **r** the commands of
17:12 Anyone arrogant enough to **r** the verdict of the
2Sa 13:16 "To **r** me now is a greater wrong than what you
1Ki 9: 7 I will **r** this Temple that I have set apart to honor
2Ki 21:14 Then I will **r** even those few of my people who are
23:27 my presence and **r** my chosen city of Jerusalem
1Ch 28: 9 But if you forsake him, he will **r** you forever.
2Ch 6:42 O LORD God, do not **r** your anointed one.
7:20 I will **r** this Temple that I have set apart to honor
Job 8:20 God will not **r** a person of integrity, nor will he
10: 3 Why do you **r** me, the work of your own hands,
Ps 27: 9 yourself from me. / Do not **r** your servant in anger.
44:23 Why do you sleep? / Get up! Do not **r** us forever.
80: 4 how long will you be angry and **r** our prayers?
88:14 O LORD, why do you **r** me? / Why do you turn
94:14 The LORD will not **r** his people; / he will not
101: 4 I will **r** perverse ideas / and stay away from every
102:17 prayers of the destitute. / He will not **r** their pleas.
119:53 furious with the wicked, / those who **r** your law.
132:10 do not **r** the king you chose for your people.
Pr 15:32 If you **r** criticism, you only harm yourself; but if
28: 4 To **r** the law is to praise the wicked; to obey the
Isa 7:15 to choose what is right and **r** what is wrong.
33:15 and fair, who **r** making a profit by fraud,
57:20 "But those who still **r** me are like the restless sea.
Jer 31:36 "I am as likely to **r** my people Israel as I am to do
33:25 I would no more **r** my people than I would change
Eze 14: 7 who **r** me and set up idols in their hearts so they
Hos 8: 5 "O Samaria, I **r** this calf—this idol you have
9:17 My God will **r** the people of Israel because they
Zec 3: 2 "I, the LORD, **r** your accusations, Satan.
Mk 7: 9 "You **r** God's laws in order to hold on to your
Jn 6:37 given me will come to me, and I will never **r** them.
12:48 But all who **r** me and my message will be judged
2Co 4: 2 We **r** all shameful and underhanded methods.
6: 1 we beg you not to **r** this marvelous message of
Gal 4:14 to you, you did not **r** me and turn me away.
1Ti 4: 4 God created is good, we should not **r** any of it.
2Ti 3: 5 but they will **r** the power that could make them
4: 4 They will **r** the truth and follow strange myths.
Heb 12:25 how terrible our danger if we **r** the One who
1Pe 2: 7 to you who believe. But for those who **r** him,
2Pe 2:21 then **r** the holy commandments that were given to
1Jn 2:11 Those who **r** other Christians are wandering in

REJECTED (74) [REJECT]
Lev 26:43 for they **r** my regulations and despised my laws.
Nu 11:20 For you have **r** the LORD, who is here among
1Sa 10:19 so much for you, you have **r** me and said,
15:23 because you have **r** the word of the LORD, he has **r** you from being king."
15:26 Since you have **r** the LORD's command, he has **r** you from being the king of Israel."
16: 1 I have **r** him as king of Israel. Now fill your horn
16: 7 by his appearance or height, for I have **r** him.
1Ki 12: 8 But Rehoboam **r** the advice of the elders
12:13 to them, for he **r** the advice of the older counselors
12:16 When all Israel realized that the king had **r** their
2Ki 17:15 They **r** his laws and the covenant he had made
17:20 So the LORD **r** all the descendants of Israel.
2Ch 10: 8 But Rehoboam **r** the advice of the elders
10:13 to them, for he **r** the advice of the older counselors
10:16 When all Israel realized that the king had **r** their
Job 18:21 a wicked person, the place of one who **r** God.' "
34:33 But you have **r** him! The choice is yours, not mine.
Ps 53: 5 You will put them to shame, for God has **r** them.
60: 1 You have **r** us, O God, and broken our defenses.
60:10 Have you **r** us, O God? / Will you no longer march
74: 1 O God, why have you **r** us forever? / Why is your
77: 7 Has the Lord **r** me forever? / Will he never again
78:59 he was very angry, / and he **r** Israel completely.
78:67 But he **r** Joseph's descendants; / he did not choose
89:38 But now you have **r** him. / Why are you so angry
108:11 Have you **r** us, O God? / Will you no longer march
118:22 The stone **r** by the builders / has now become the
119:118 But you have **r** all who stray from your principles.
Pr 1:25 ignored my advice and **r** the correction I offered.
1:30 They **r** my advice and paid no attention when I
Isa 2: 6 The LORD has **r** the people of Israel
5:24 for they have **r** the law of the LORD Almighty.
8: 6 "The people of Judah have **r** my gentle care
49: 7 says to the one who is despised and **r** by a nation,
53: 3 He was despised and **r**—a man of sorrows,
Jer 2:37 for the LORD has **r** the nations you trust.
5: 5 But the leaders, too, had utterly **r** their God.
5:19 'You **r** him and gave yourselves to foreign gods in
6:19 to listen to me. They have **r** all my instructions.
6:30 I will label them '**R** Silver' because I, the LORD,
7:29 For the LORD has **r** and forsaken this generation
8: 9 their sin, for they have **r** the word of the LORD.
14:19 LORD, have you completely **r** Judah? Do you
La 2: 7 The Lord has **r** his own altar; he despises his own
5:22 Or have you utterly **r** us? Are you angry with us
Eze 20:16 I told them this because they had **r** my laws,
Hos 8: 3 The people of Israel have **r** what is good, and now
Am 2: 4 They have **r** the laws of the LORD, refusing to
Zec 10: 6 It will be as though I had never **r** them, for I am
Mal 1: 3 and I **r** Esau and devastated his hill country.
Mt 21:42 'The stone **r** by the builders / has now become the
Mk 8:31 suffer many terrible things and be **r** by the leaders,
12:10 'The stone **r** by the builders / has now become the
Lk 2:34 to Mary, "This child will be **r** by many in Israel,
7:30 and experts in religious law had **r** God's plan for
9:22 "I will be **r** by the leaders, the leading priests,
17:25 must suffer terribly and be **r** by this generation.
19:44 because you have **r** the opportunity God offered
20:17 'The stone **r** by the builders / has now become the
Ac 3:13 Jesus whom you handed over and **r** before Pilate,
3:14 You **r** this holy, righteous one, and instead
4:11 where it says, / 'The stone that you builders **r**
7:35 man his people had previously **r** by demanding,
7:39 "But our ancestors **r** Moses and wanted to return
13:46 But since you have **r** it and judged yourselves
19: 9 But some **r** his message and publicly spoke against
Ro 9:13 of the Scriptures, "I loved Jacob, but I **r** Esau."
11: 1 I ask, then, has God **r** his people, the Jews?
11: 2 No, God has not **r** his own people, whom he chose
Heb 12:17 when he wanted his father's blessing, he was **r**.
1Pe 2: 4 He was **r** by the people, but he is precious to God
2: 7 reject him, / "The stone that was **r** by the builders

REJECTING (6) [REJECT]
Lev 26:15 and if you break my covenant by **r** my laws
1Sa 8: 7 LORD replied, "for it is me they are **r**, not you.
Lk 10:16 accepting me. And anyone who rejects you is **r** me.
10:16 And anyone who rejects me is **r** God who sent
1Th 4: 8 rules is not disobeying human rules but is **r** God,
Heb 6: 6 nailing the Son of God to the cross again by **r** him,

REJECTION (1) [REJECT]
Ro 11:15 For since the Jews' **r** meant that God offered

REJECTS (5) [REJECT]
Jdg 12: 4 "The men of Gilead are nothing more than **r** from
Ecc 4:16 then the next generation grows up and **r** him!
Lk 10:16 And anyone who **r** you is rejecting me.
10:16 And anyone who **r** me is rejecting God who sent
1Jn 2: 9 but **r** another Christian is still in darkness.

REJOICE (116) [JOY]
Lev 23:40 Then **r** before the LORD your God for seven
Nu 10:10 and at the beginning of each month to **r** over your
Dt 12: 7 and you will **r** in all you have accomplished
32:43 "**R** with him, O heavens, / and let all the angels of
2Sa 1:20 the news in Gath, / or the Philistines will **r**.
1Ch 16:10 in his holy name; / O worshipers of the LORD, **r**!
16:31 Let the heavens be glad, and let the earth **r**!
16:35 can thank your holy name / and **r** and praise you."
29:17 our hearts and **r** when you find integrity there.
2Ch 6:41 and may your saints **r** in your goodness.
23:18 and to sing and **r** as David had instructed.
Est 9:19 when they **r** and send gifts to each other.
Ps 2:11 LORD with reverent fear, / and **r** with trembling.
5:11 But let all who take refuge in you **r**; / let them sing
9:14 so I can **r** that you have rescued me.
13: 4 defeated him!" / Don't let them **r** at my downfall.
13: 5 I will **r** because you have rescued me.
14: 7 Jacob will shout with joy, and Israel will **r**.
22:26 Their hearts will **r** with everlasting joy.
25: 2 be disgraced, / or let my enemies **r** in my defeat.
32:11 So **r** in the LORD and be glad, all you who obey
33:21 In him our hearts **r**, / for we are trusting in his holy
35: 9 Then I will **r** in the LORD. / I will be glad
35:19 let my treacherous enemies / **r** over my defeat.
35:26 May those who **r** at my troubles / be humiliated
38:16 my enemies gloat over me / or **r** at my downfall."
48:11 Let the people on Mount Zion **r**. / Let the towns of
51: 8 joy again; / you have broken me— / now let me **r**.
53: 6 Jacob will shout with joy, and Israel will **r**.
58:10 The godly will **r** when they see injustice avenged.
63:11 But the king will **r** in God. / All who trust in him
64:10 The godly will **r** in the LORD / and find shelter in
66: 6 went across on foot. / Come, let us **r** in who he is.
68: 3 But let the godly **r**. / Let them be glad in God's
68: 4 His name is the LORD— / **r** in his presence!
85: 6 you revive us again, / so your people can **r** in you?
89:16 They **r** all day long in your wonderful reputation.
89:42 his enemies against him / and made them all **r**.
96:11 Let the heavens be glad, and let the earth **r**!
97: 1 The LORD is king! Let the earth **r**!
104:34 these thoughts about him, / for I **r** in the LORD.
105: 3 in his holy name; / O worshipers of the LORD, **r**!
106: 5 Let me **r** in the joy of your people; / let me praise
106:47 can thank your holy name / and **r** and praise you.
118:24 the LORD has made. / We will **r** and be glad in it.
119:162 I **r** in your word / like one who finds a great
149: 2 O Israel, **r** in your Maker. / O people of Jerusalem,
149: 5 Let the faithful **r** in this honor. / Let them sing for
Pr 2:14 They **r** in doing wrong, and they enjoy evil as it
5:18 of blessing for you. **R** in the wife of your youth.
17: 5 those who **r** at the misfortune of others will be
23:15 My child, how I will **r** if you become wise.
24:17 Do not **r** when your enemies fall into trouble.
29: 2 When the godly are in authority, the people **r**.
Ecc 11: 8 live to be very old, let them **r** in every day of life.
Isa 9: 3 and its people will **r** as people **r** at
13: 3 to these armies, and they will **r** when I am exalted.
14:29 Do not **r**, you Philistines, that the king who
23:12 He says, "Never again will you **r**, O daughter of
25: 9 we trusted. Let us **r** in the salvation he brings!"
29:19 Those who are poor will **r** in the Holy One of
35: 1 Even the wilderness will **r** in those days.
42:11 you desert towns; / let the villages of Kedar **r**!
49:13 Sing for joy, O heavens! **R**, O earth! Burst into
62: 5 Then God will **r** over you as a bridegroom rejoices
63: 7 I will **r** in his great goodness to Israel, which he
65:13 You will be sad and ashamed, but they will **r**.
65:18 Be glad; **r** forever in my creation! And look!
65:19 I will **r** in Jerusalem and delight in my people.
66:10 "**R** with Jerusalem! Be glad with her, all you who
66:14 When you see these things, your heart will **r**.
Jer 11:15 their destruction? They actually **r** in doing evil!
32:41 I will **r** in doing good to them and will faithfully
50:11 "You **r** and are glad, you plunderers of my chosen
51:48 The heavens and earth will **r**, for out of the north
La 2:17 and caused her enemies to **r** over her and boast of
Eze 7:12 There is no reason for buyers to **r** over the bargains
35:14 The whole world will **r** when I make you desolate.
35:15 Now I will **r** at yours! You will be wiped out,
Hos 9: 1 O people of Israel, do not **r** as others do. For you
Joel 2:21 Be glad now and **r** because the LORD has done
2:23 **R**, you people of Jerusalem! **R** in the LORD your God!
Hab 1:15 and dragged out in their nets while they **r**?
3:18 yet I will **r** in the LORD! I will be joyful in the
Zep 3:14 Be glad and **r** with all your heart, O daughter of
3:17 He will **r** over you with great gladness. With his
Zec 2:10 The LORD says, "Shout and **r**, O Jerusalem,
9: 9 **R** greatly, O people of Zion! Shout in triumph,
10: 7 and be glad; their hearts will **r** in the LORD.
Mt 18:13 he will surely **r** over it more than over the
Lk 1:14 and many will **r** with you at his birth,
1:47 How I **r** in God my Savior!
6:23 "When that happens, **r**! Yes, leap for joy! For a
10:20 But don't **r** just because evil spirits obey you;
10:20 **r** because your names are registered as citizens of
15: 6 and neighbors to **r** with you because your lost
15: 9 will call in her friends and neighbors to **r** with her
Jn 16:20 is going to happen to me, but the world will **r**.
16:22 then you will **r**, and no one can rob you of that joy.
Ro 5: 3 We can **r**, too, when we run into problems
5:11 So now we can **r** in our wonderful new
15:10 in another place it is written, / "**R**, O you Gentiles,
2Co 13:11 **R**. Change your ways. Encourage each other.
Gal 4:27 when he prophesied, / "**R**, O childless woman!
Php 1:18 the message about Christ is being preached, so I **r**. And I will continue to **r**.
2:17 if I am to die for you), I will **r**, and I want to share
2:18 And you should be happy about this and **r** with me.
4: 4 Always be full of joy in the Lord. I say it again—**r**!
Rev 12:12 **R**, O heavens! And you who live in the heavens, **r**!
18:20 But you, O heaven, **r** over her fate. And you also **r**, O holy people of God and apostles
19: 7 Let us be glad and **r** and honor him. For the time

REJOICED (18) [JOY]
2Ki 11:20 So all the people of the land **r**, and the city was
1Ch 29: 9 The people **r** over the offerings, for they had given
2Ch 23:21 So all the people of the land **r**, and the city was
29:36 And Hezekiah and all the people **r** greatly
30:25 The entire assembly of Judah **r**,
Est 8:17 the Jews **r** and had a great celebration and declared
Job 31:29 "Have I ever **r** when my enemies came to ruin
Ps 97: 8 Jerusalem has heard and **r**, / and all the cities of
119:14 I have **r** in your decrees / as much as in riches.
Eze 26: 2 Tyre has **r** over the fall of Jerusalem, saying,
35:15 You **r** at the desolation of Israel's inheritance.
Ob 1:12 You shouldn't have **r** because they were suffering
Lk 1:58 had been very kind to her, and everyone **r** with her.
13:17 And all the people **r** at the wonderful things he did.
Jn 5:35 brightly for a while, and you benefited and **r**.
8:56 Your ancestor Abraham **r** as he looked forward to
Ac 7:41 sacrificed to it and **r** in this thing they had made.
16:34 He and his entire household **r** because they all

REJOICES (12) [JOY]
1Sa 2: 1 "My heart **r** in the LORD! / Oh, how the LORD
Job 39:21 It paws the earth and **r** in its strength. When it
Ps 19: 5 after his wedding. / It **r** like a great athlete
21: 1 How the king **r** in your strength, O LORD!
48: 2 in elevation— / the whole earth **r** to see it!
104:31 last forever! / The LORD **r** in all he has made!
Pr 14:35 A king **r** in servants who know what they are
Isa 62: 5 Then God will rejoice over you as a bridegroom **r**
Hab 3: 4 flash from his hands. He **r** in his awesome power.
Zec 4:10 for the LORD **r** to see the work begin,
Jn 3:29 A bridegroom's friend **r** with him. I am the
1Co 13: 6 about injustice but **r** whenever the truth wins out.

REJOICING (12) [JOY]
Dt 16:14 This festival will be a happy time of **r** with your
1Ki 1:45 and the whole city is celebrating and **r**.
2Ki 11:14 and people from all over the land were **r**
2Ch 23:13 and people from all over the land were **r**
Ps 105:43 out of Egypt with joy, / his chosen ones with **r**.
109:28 But I, your servant, will go right on **r**!
Pr 8:30 I was his constant delight, **r** always in his presence.
Isa 8: 6 and are **r** over what will happen to King Rezin
Jer 31:13 will comfort them and exchange their sorrow for **r**.

La 4:21 Are you **r** in the land of Uz, O people of Edom?
Ac 5:41 The apostles left the high council **r** that God had
8:39 never saw him again but went on his way **r**.

REJOINS (1) [JOIN]

Lev 25:10 that belonged to your ancestors and **r** your clan.

REKEM (5)

Nu 31:8 Evi, **R**, Zur, Hur, and Reba—died in the battle.
Jos 13:21 Evi, **R**, Zur, Hur, and Reba—princes living in the
18:27 **R**, Irpeel, Taralah,
1Ch 2:43 of Hebron were Korah, Tappuah, **R**, and Shema.
2:44 father of Jorkeam. **R** was the father of Shammai.

RELATE (2) [RELATED, RELATION, RELATIONS, RELATIONSHIP, RELATIONSHIPS, RELATIVE, RELATIVELY, RELATIVES]

Nu 4:4 at the Tabernacle will **r** to the most sacred objects.
Da 8:17 have seen in your vision **r** to the time of the end."

RELATED (21) [RELATE]

Lev 25:49 a nephew, or anyone else who is closely **r**.
Nu 3:26 the cords, and all the equipment **r** to their use.
3:31 inner curtain, and all the equipment **r** to their use.
3:36 the bases, and all the equipment **r** to their use.
4:32 accessories, and everything else **r** to their use.
18:1 responsible for any offenses **r** to the sanctuary.
Ru 3:12 there is another man who is more closely **r** to you
2Ki 8:27 because he was **r** by marriage to the family of
12:12 and they paid any other expenses **r** to the Temple's
1Ch 6:49 and they performed all the other duties **r** to the
26:30 They were responsible for all matters **r** to the
26:32 They were responsible for all matters **r** to the
28:20 He will see to it that all the work **r** to the Temple
2Ch 4:16 the shovels, the meat hooks, and all the **r** utensils.
5:1 When Solomon had finished all the work **r** to
8:16 So Solomon made sure that all the work **r** to
Est 8:1 for Esther had told the king how they were **r**.
Ac 19:25 along with others employed in **r** trades,
1Co 15:22 Everyone dies because all of us are **r** to Adam,
15:22 But all who are **r** to Christ, the other man, will be
Heb 7:6 But Melchizedek, who was not even **r** to Levi,

RELATION (1) [RELATE]

1Co 16:2 amount of money in **r** to what you have earned

RELATIONS (4) [RELATE]

Ex 22:19 "Anyone who has sexual **r** with an animal must be
1Ki 1:4 care of him. But the king had no sexual **r** with her.
1Co 7:5 So do not deprive each other of sexual **r**. The only
Rev 17:2 The rulers of the world have had immoral **r** with

RELATIONSHIP (11) [RELATE]

Ge 5:24 He enjoyed a close **r** with God throughout his life.
6:9 God's will and enjoyed a close **r** with him.
Ex 34:14 for he is a God who is passionate about his **r** with
Jos 22:28 it is a reminder of the **r** both of us have with the
Eze 23:17 became disgusted with them and broke off their **r**.
Lk 12:21 up earthly wealth but not have a rich **r** with God."
Ro 2:17 you are relying on God's law for your special **r**
4:13 but on the new **r** with God that comes by faith.
5:11 So now we can rejoice in our wonderful new **r**
1Co 7:24 a believer, stay there in your new **r** with God.
Col 1:28 to present them to God, perfect in their **r** to Christ.

RELATIONSHIPS (3) [RELATE]

Nu 30:16 LORD gave Moses concerning **r** between a man
Ro 1:27 instead of having normal sexual **r** with women,
1Co 11:11 But in **r** among the Lord's people, women are not

RELATIVE (26) [RELATE]

Lev 18:6 must never have sexual intercourse with a close **r**,
18:12 father's sister, because she is your father's close **r**.
18:13 because she is your mother's close **r**.
20:19 or his father's sister, he has violated a close **r**.
21:1 ceremonially unclean by touching a dead **r**
21:2 unless it is a close **r**—mother or father, son
25:25 then a close **r**, a kinsman redeemer, may buy it
25:48 They may be bought back by a close **r**—
Nu 27:11 pass on his inheritance to the nearest **r** in his clan.
35:19 The victim's nearest **r** is responsible for putting the
35:21 the victim's nearest **r** must execute the murderer
35:24 the slayer and the avenger, the victim's nearest **r**.
35:27 and the victim's nearest **r** finds him outside the
Jdg 9:3 in favor of Abimelech because he was their **r**.
9:18 to be your king just because he is your **r**.
Ru 2:1 who was a **r** of Naomi's husband, Elimelech
2:3 to Boaz, the **r** of her father-in-law, Elimelech.
3:2 Boaz is a close **r** of ours, and he's been very kind
4:3 She is selling the land that belonged to our **r**
2Sa 16:11 Shouldn't this **r** of Saul have even more reason to
Ne 13:4 of our God and who was also a **r** of Tobiah,
Pr 27:10 It is better to go to a neighbor than to a **r** who lives
Am 6:10 And when a close **r**—one who is responsible for
Lk 1:36 your **r** Elizabeth has become pregnant in her old
Jn 18:26 a **r** of the man whose ear Peter had cut off, asked,
Ro 16:11 Greet Herodion, my **r**. Greet the Christians in the

RELATIVELY (1) [RELATE]

Lev 25:52 then they will repay a **r** small amount for their

RELATIVES (157) [RELATE]

Ge 12:1 "Leave your country, your **r**, and your father's
13:8 got to stop," he said. "After all, we are close **r**!
14:13 Mamre and his **r**, Eshcol and Aner, were Abram's
19:12 "Do you have any other **r** here in the city?"
24:4 Go instead to my homeland, to my **r**, and find a
24:5 then take Isaac there to live among your **r**?"
24:27 for he has led me straight to my master's **r**."
24:38 I was to come to his **r** here in this far-off land,
24:40 you must get a wife for my son from among my **r**,
24:41 But if you go to my **r** and they refuse to let her
24:48 to find a wife from the family of my master's **r**.
29:15 work for me without pay just because we are **r**.
31:3 of your father and grandfather and to your **r** there,
31:23 he gathered a group of his **r** and set out in hot
31:32 I swear before all these **r** of ours, I will give it back
31:37 it out here in front of us, before our **r**, for all to see.
32:9 you told me to return to my land and to my **r**,
49:8 your enemies. / All your **r** will bow before you.
Ex 21:30 the dead person's **r** may accept payment from the
Lev 10:4 and carry the bodies of your **r** away from the
10:6 your **r**, may mourn for Nadab and Abihu,
18:17 They are close **r**, and to do this would be a horrible
19:17 not nurse hatred in your heart for any of your **r**.
21:4 As a husband among his **r**, he must not defile
25:25 If any of your Israelite **r** go bankrupt and are
25:35 "If any of your Israelite **r** fall into poverty
25:36 fear of God by letting them live with you as your **r**.
25:37 do not charge your **r** interest on anything you lend
25:39 "If any of your Israelite **r** go bankrupt and sell
25:46 but the people of Israel, your **r**, must never be
25:47 and if some of your Israelite **r** go bankrupt and sell
25:53 foreigner to treat any of your Israelite **r** ruthlessly.
Nu 5:8 and there are no near **r** to whom restitution can be
18:1 and your **r** from the tribe of Levi will be held
18:2 "Bring your **r** of the tribe of Levi to assist you
18:21 As for the tribe of Levi, your **r**, I will pay them for
20:14 "This message is from your **r**, the people of Israel:
27:4 Give us property along with the rest of our **r**."
27:7 an inheritance of land along with their father's **r**.
35:12 a dead person's **r** who want to avenge the death.
Dt 2:4 the country belonging to your **r** the Edomites,
2:8 So we went past our **r**, the descendants of Esau,
3:18 armed and ready to protect your Israelite **r**.
15:2 not demand payment from their neighbors or **r**,
23:7 or the Egyptians, because the Edomites are your **r**,
33:9 loyal to you / than to their parents, **r**, and children.
Jos 2:18 your father, mother, brothers, and all your **r**—
6:23 brothers, and all the other **r** who were with her.
6:25 and her **r** who were with her in the house,
20:3 and be protected from the **r** of the one who was
20:3 for the **r** may seek to avenge the killing.
20:5 If the **r** of the victim come to avenge the killing,
22:8 "Share with your **r** back home the great wealth
Jdg 1:3 The leaders of Judah said to their **r** from the tribe
16:31 his brothers and other **r** went down to get his body.
18:8 returned to Zorah and Eshtaol, their **r** asked them,
20:23 "Should we fight against our **r** from Benjamin
20:28 "Should we fight against our **r** from Benjamin
Ru 2:20 That man is one of our closest **r**, one of our family
1Sa 2:28 I chose your ancestor Aaron from among all his **r**
11:3 "If none of our **r** will come to save us, we will
22:1 Soon his brothers and other **r** joined him there.
2Sa 19:12 Yet you are my **r**, my own tribe, my own flesh
19:28 All my **r** and I could expect only death from you,
1Ki 12:24 Do not fight against your **r**, the Israelites. Go back
16:11 He even destroyed distant **r** and friends.
2Ki 10:11 Then Jehu killed all of Ahab's **r** living in Jezreel
10:13 he met some **r** of King Ahaziah of Judah.
10:13 And they replied, "We are **r** of King Ahaziah.
1Ch 5:7 Beerah's **r** are listed in their genealogy by their
5:13 Their **r**, the leaders of seven other clans,
6:48 Their **r**, also Levites, were appointed to various
7:22 them a long time, and his **r** came to comfort him.
9:6 From the Zerahite clan, Jeuel returned with his **r**.
9:17 Akkub, Talmon, Ahiman, and their **r**.
9:19 He and his **r**, the Korahites, were responsible for
9:25 their **r** in the villages came to share their duties for
12:2 They were all **r** of Saul from the tribe of Benjamin.
12:29 of Benjamin, Saul's **r**, there were 3,000 warriors.
12:32 there were 200 leaders of the tribe with their **r**.
12:39 for preparations had been made by their **r** for their
25:9 of the Asaph clan and twelve of his sons and **r**.
25:9 lot fell to Gedaliah and twelve of his sons and **r**.
25:10 lot fell to Zaccur and twelve of his sons and **r**.
25:11 fourth lot fell to Zeri and twelve of his sons and **r**.
25:12 lot fell to Nethaniah and twelve of his sons and **r**.
25:13 lot fell to Bukkiah and twelve of his sons and **r**.
25:14 lot fell to Asarelah and twelve of his sons and **r**.
25:15 lot fell to Jeshaiah and twelve of his sons and **r**.
25:16 lot fell to Mattaniah and twelve of his sons and **r**.
25:17 lot fell to Shimei and twelve of his sons and **r**.
25:18 lot fell to Uzziel and twelve of his sons and **r**.
25:19 lot fell to Hashabiah and twelve of his sons and **r**.
25:20 lot fell to Shubael and twelve of his sons and **r**.
25:21 lot fell to Mattithiah and twelve of his sons and **r**.
25:22 lot fell to Jerimoth and twelve of his sons and **r**.
25:23 lot fell to Hananiah and twelve of his sons and **r**.
25:24 fell to Joshbekashah and twelve of his sons and **r**.
25:25 lot fell to Hanani and twelve of his sons and **r**.
25:26 lot fell to Mallothi and twelve of his sons and **r**.
25:27 lot fell to Eliathah and twelve of his sons and **r**.
25:28 lot fell to Hothir and twelve of his sons and **r**.
25:29 lot fell to Geddalti and twelve of his sons and **r**.
25:30 lot fell to Mahazioth and twelve of his sons and **r**.
25:31 fell to Romamti-ezer and twelve of his sons and **r**.
26:7 Their **r**, Elihu and Semakiah, were also very
26:9 eighteen sons and **r** were also very capable men.
26:11 Hosah's sons and **r**, who served as gatekeepers,
26:25 His **r** through Eliezer were Rehabiah, Jeshaiah,
26:26 and his **r** were in charge of the treasuries that held
26:28 and his **r** also cared for the items dedicated to the
26:30 He and his **r**—seventeen hundred capable men—
26:32 hundred capable men among the **r** of Jeriah.
2Ch 11:4 Do not fight against your **r**. Go back home,
22:8 and Ahaziah's **r** who were attending Ahaziah.
28:11 captives you have taken, for they are your own **r**.
29:34 so their **r** the Levites helped them until the work
30:7 your ancestors and **r** who abandoned the LORD,
30:9 your **r** and your children will be treated mercifully
Ezr 3:9 were supervised by Jeshua with his sons and **r**,
8:17 to ask him and his **r** and the Temple servants to
Ne 4:23 not I, nor my **r**, nor my servants, nor the guards
5:7 "You are oppressing your own **r** by charging them
5:8 **r** who have had to sell themselves to pagan
11:8 there were Gabbai and Sallai, and a total of 928 **r**.
Est 4:14 from some other place, but you and your **r** will die.
Job 19:13 "My **r** stay far away, and my friends have turned
Pr 19:7 If the **r** of the poor despise them, how much more
27:10 you won't have to ask your **r** for assistance.
Isa 58:7 and do not hide from **r** who need your help.
66:5 "Your close **r** hate you and throw you out for
Jer 7:15 into exile, just as I did your **r**, the people of Israel.'
29:16 your **r** who were not exiled to Babylon.
Eze 11:15 left in Jerusalem are talking about their **r** in exile,
18:18 for being cruel and robbing close **r**, doing what
Da 11:7 But when one of her **r** becomes king of the south,
Am 1:11 They chased down their **r**, the Israelites,
Ob 1:10 Because of the violence you did to your close **r** in
1:11 For you deserted your **r** in Israel during their time
1:12 gloated when they exiled your **r** to distant lands.
1:13 have gloated over the destruction of your **r**,
Mk 6:4 and among his **r** and his own family."
Lk 1:58 and **r** heard that the Lord had been very kind to her,
1:59 all the **r** and friends came for the circumcision
2:44 they started to look for him among their **r**
14:12 invite your friends, brothers, **r**, and rich neighbors.
21:16 your parents, brothers, **r**, and friends—will betray
Ac 4:6 John, Alexander, and other **r** of the high priest.
7:3 God told him, 'Leave your native land and your **r**,
7:14 Jacob, and all his **r** to come to Egypt,
7:23 he decided to visit his **r**, the people of Israel.
10:24 was waiting for him and had called together his **r**
Ro 16:7 Then there are Andronicus and Junia, my **r**,
16:21 and Lucius, Jason, and Sosipater, my **r**,
1Ti 5:8 But those who won't care for their own **r**,
5:16 If a Christian woman has **r** who are widows,
Heb 7:5 all the people, even though they are their own **r**.

RELAX (2) [RELAXED]

Ge 43:23 "**R**. Don't worry about it," the household manager
2Sa 11:8 Then he told Uriah, "Go on home and **r**."

RELAXED (1) [RELAX]

Pr 14:30 A **r** attitude lengthens life; jealousy rots it away.

RELAY (2)

1Ki 20:2 Ben-hadad sent messengers into the city to **r** this
Est 4:10 to go back and **r** this message to Mordecai,

RELEASE (43) [RELEASED, RELEASES]

Ge 8:17 **R** all the animals and birds so they can breed
43:14 that he might **r** Simeon and return Benjamin.
Lev 14:53 he will **r** the living bird in the open fields outside
25:10 as holy, a time to proclaim **r** for all who live there.
26:22 I will **r** wild animals that will kill your children
Dt 15:2 or relatives, for the LORD's time of **r** has arrived.
15:3 This **r** from debt, however, applies only to your
15:9 a loan because the year of **r** is close at hand.
15:13 "When you **r** a male servant, do not send him
15:18 "Do not consider it a hardship when you **r** your
31:10 the Year of **R**, during the Festival of Shelters,
Jos 20:5 the leaders must not **r** the accused to them,
Job 14:14 through my struggle I would eagerly wait for **r**.
29:17 godless oppressors and made them **r** their victims.
Ps 102:20 of the prisoners, / to **r** those condemned to die.
144:6 **R** your lightning bolts and scatter your enemies! / **R** your arrows and confuse them!
Isa 42:7 You will **r** those who sit in dark dungeons.
Na 1:13 your chains and **r** you from Assyrian oppression."
Zec 8:12 will produce its crops, and the sky will **r** the dew.
Mt 27:15 Now it was the governor's custom to **r** one
27:17 "Which one do you want me to **r** to you—
27:21 "Which of these two do you want me to **r** to
27:22 "But if I **r** Barabbas," Pilate asked them,
27:58 And Pilate issued an order to **r** it to him.
Mk 7:26 She begged him to **r** her child from the demon's
15:6 Now it was the governor's custom to **r** one
15:8 toward Pilate, asking him to **r** a prisoner as usual.
15:11 mob to demand the **r** of Barabbas instead of Jesus.
15:12 "But if I **r** Barabbas," Pilate asked them,
Lk 23:16 So I will have him flogged, but then I will **r** him."
23:18 they shouted, "Kill him, and **r** Barabbas to us!"
23:20 argued with them, because he wanted to **r** Jesus.
Jn 18:39 But you have a custom of asking me to **r** someone
18:39 So if you want me to, I'll **r** the King of the Jews."
19:10 "Don't you realize that I have the power to **r** you
19:12 Then Pilate tried to **r** him, but the Jewish leaders
19:12 "If you **r** this man, you are not a friend of Caesar.
Ac 3:13 before Pilate, despite Pilate's decision to **r** him.
3:14 and instead demanded the **r** of a murderer.

16:37 Certainly not! Let them come themselves to **r** us!"
28:18 The Romans tried me and wanted to **r** me, for they
Rev 9:14 "**R** the four angels who are bound at the great

RELEASED (27) [RELEASE]
Ge 8:7 and **r** a raven that flew back and forth until the
8:10 Seven days later, Noah **r** the dove again.
8:12 A week later, he **r** the dove again, and this time it
43:23 Then he **r** Simeon and brought him out to them.
Ex 21:27 the slave should be **r** in payment for the tooth.
Lev 27:21 When the field is **r** in the Year of Jubilee, it will be
27:24 In the Year of Jubilee the field will be **r** to the
2Ki 25:27 and **r** him from prison on April 2 of that year.
2Ch 28:14 So the warriors **r** the prisoners and handed over the
Ps 78:26 He **r** the east wind in the heavens / and guided the
Isa 49:25 LORD says, "The captives of warriors will be **r**,
51:14 Soon all you captives will be **r**! Imprisonment,
61:1 and to announce that captives will be **r**
Jer 20:3 The next day, when Pashhur finally **r** him,
40:1 captain of the guard, had **r** him at Ramah.
52:31 and **r** him from prison on March 31 of that year.
Mt 18:27 pity for him, and he **r** him and forgave his debt.
27:20 persuaded the crowds to ask for Barabbas to be **r**
27:26 So Pilate **r** Barabbas to them. He ordered Jesus
Mk 15:15 anxious to please the crowd, **r** Barabbas to them.
Lk 4:18 that captives will be **r**, / that the blind will see,
23:25 As they had requested, he **r** Barabbas, the man in
Ac 2:24 God **r** him from the horrors of death and raised
17:9 But the officials **r** Jason and the other believers
Ro 7:6 But now we have been **r** from the law, for we died
8:23 also groan to be **r** from pain and suffering.
Rev 20:3 Afterward he would be **r** again for a little while.

RELEASES (4) [RELEASE]
Job 12:15 a desert. If he **r** the waters, they flood the earth.
Ps 135:7 with the rain / and **r** the wind from his storehouses.
Jer 10:13 with the rain / and **r** the wind from his storehouses.
51:16 with the rain / and **r** the wind from his storehouses.

RELEGATED (1)
Eze 44:14 and are **r** to doing maintenance work and helping

RELENT (3) [RELENTED, RELENTLESS, RELENTLESSLY]
Hos 13:14 O grave, bring forth your plagues! For I will not **r**!
Am 7:2 Unless you **r**, Israel will not survive, for we are
7:5 Unless you **r**, Israel will not survive, for we are

RELENTED (4) [RELENT]
2Sa 24:16 the LORD **r** and said to the angel, "Stop!
1Ch 21:15 the LORD **r** and said to the death angel, "Stop!
Ps 106:45 with them / and **r** because of his unfailing love.
Am 7:3 So the LORD **r** and did not fulfill the vision.

RELENTLESS (4) [RELENT]
Jdg 20:43 and were **r** in chasing them down,
2Sa 2:19 He was **r** and single-minded in his pursuit.
Isa 16:3 Protect us from their **r** attack. Do not betray us.
25:5 or like the **r** heat of the desert. But you silence the

RELENTLESSLY (2) [RELENT]
Job 30:17 as though something were **r** gnawing at my bones.
Ps 31:15 Rescue me from those who hunt me down **r**.

RELIABLE (3) [RELY]
1Ch 9:22 appointed their ancestors because they were **r** men.
Pr 13:17 into trouble, but a **r** messenger brings healing.
2Ti 2:2 that have been confirmed by many **r** witnesses.

RELIED (1) [RELY]
2Ch 16:8 At that time you **r** on the LORD, and he handed

RELIEF (16) [RELIEVE]
Ge 5:29 "He will bring us **r** from the painful labor of
33:10 "for what a **r** it is to see your friendly smile.
43:1 But there was no **r** from the terrible famine
Dt 28:59 These plagues will be intense and without **r**,
1Sa 8:18 you will beg for **r** from this king you are
2Ch 12:7 destroy them and will soon give them some **r**.
Ezr 9:8 our eyes and granted us some **r** from our slavery.
Est 9:16 They gained **r** from all their enemies,
9:22 a time when the Jews gained **r** from their enemies,
Job 3:22 It is a blessed **r** when they finally die, when they
32:20 I must speak to find **r**, so let me give my answers.
Ps 22:2 Every night you hear my voice, but I find no **r**.
94:13 You give them **r** from troubled times / until a pit is
Mic 1:12 The people of Maroth anxiously wait for **r**,
Ac 11:29 So the believers in Antioch decided to send **r** to the
Rev 14:11 and ever, and they will have no **r** day or night,

RELIES (1) [RELY]
Ps 22:8 "Is this the one who **r** on the LORD? / Then let

RELIEVE (3) [RELIEF, RELIEVED, RELIEVING]
Dt 23:13 Whenever you **r** yourself, you must dig a hole with
1Sa 24:3 Saul went into a cave to **r** himself.
Ps 81:6 "Now I will **r** your shoulder of its burden;

RELIEVED (3) [RELIEVE]
Eze 31:16 were **r** to find it there with them in the pit.
32:31 he will be **r** to find that he is not alone in having
Ac 20:12 taken home unhurt, and everyone was greatly **r**.

RELIEVING (1) [RELIEVE]
1Ki 18:27 Perhaps he is deep in thought, or he is **r** himself.

RELIGION (12) [RELIGIONS, RELIGIOUS]
Da 6:5 be in connection with the requirements of his **r**."
Hos 5:7 Now their false **r** will devour them, along with
Ac 17:18 Others said, "He's pushing some foreign **r**."
17:19 "Come and tell us more about this new **r**,"
25:19 It was something about their **r** and about someone
26:5 member of the Pharisees, the strictest sect of our **r**.
Gal 1:13 what I was like when I followed the Jewish **r**—
1:14 as possible to follow all the old traditions of my **r**.
1Ti 6:5 tell the truth. To them **r** is just a way to get rich.
6:6 Yet true **r** with contentment is great wealth.
Jas 1:26 are just fooling yourself, and your **r** is worthless.
1:27 and lasting **r** in the sight of God our Father means

RELIGIONS (1) [RELIGION]
Mt 6:7 don't babble on and on as people of other **r** do.

RELIGIOUS (104) [RELIGION]
Ex 5:1 the wilderness to hold a **r** festival in my honor.' "
1Ki 12:32 Jeroboam also instituted a **r** festival in Bethel,
12:33 He instituted a **r** festival for Israel, and he went up
2Ki 17:27 Let him teach the new residents the **r** customs of
17:33 they continued to follow the **r** customs of the
Ne 2:16 I had not yet spoken to the **r** and political leaders,
Ecc 9:2 ceremonially clean or unclean, **r** or irreligious.
Jer 3:23 Our worship of idols and our **r** orgies on the hills
Eze 6:6 and all the other **r** objects you have made.
45:17 provide offerings that are given at the **r** festivals,
46:9 to worship the LORD during the **r** festivals,
Am 2:8 At their **r** festivals, they lounge around in clothing
5:21 the hypocrisy of your **r** festivals and solemn
8:5 and the **r** festivals to end so you can get back to
Mt 2:4 of the leading priests and teachers of **r** law.
5:20 unless you obey God better than the teachers of **r**
7:21 "Not all people who sound **r** are really godly.
7:29 real authority—quite unlike the teachers of **r** law.
8:19 Then one of the teachers of **r** law said to him,
9:3 some of the teachers of **r** law said among
12:38 One day some teachers of **r** law and Pharisees
13:52 "Every teacher of **r** law who has become a
15:1 and teachers of **r** law now arrived from Jerusalem
16:21 and the leading priests and the teachers of **r** law.
17:10 "Why do the teachers of **r** law insist that Elijah
20:18 to the leading priests and the teachers of **r** law.
21:15 and the teachers of **r** law saw these wonderful
21:41 The **r** leaders replied, "He will put the wicked
22:35 One of them, an expert in **r** law, tried to trap him
23:2 "The teachers of **r** law and the Pharisees are the
23:4 They crush you with impossible **r** demands
23:13 "How terrible it will be for you teachers of **r** law
23:15 how terrible it will be for you teachers of **r** law
23:23 "How terrible it will be for you teachers of **r** law
23:25 "How terrible it will be for you teachers of **r** law
23:27 "How terrible it will be for you teachers of **r** law
23:29 "How terrible it will be for you teachers of **r** law
23:34 you prophets and wise men and teachers of **r** law.
26:57 where the teachers of **r** law and other leaders had
27:41 The leading priests, the teachers of **r** law,
28:12 A meeting of all the **r** leaders was called, and they
Mk 1:22 real authority—quite unlike the teachers of **r** law.
2:6 But some of the teachers of **r** law who were sitting
2:16 But when some of the teachers of **r** law who were
3:22 But the teachers of **r** law who had arrived from
7:1 and teachers of **r** law arrived from Jerusalem to
7:5 So the Pharisees and teachers of **r** law asked him,
8:31 the leading priests, and the teachers of **r** law.
9:11 "Why do the teachers of **r** law insist that Elijah
9:14 as some teachers of **r** law were arguing with them.
10:33 to the leading priests and the teachers of **r** law.
11:18 and teachers of **r** law heard what Jesus had done,
11:27 the leading priests, the teachers of **r** law,
12:28 One of the teachers of **r** law was standing there
12:32 The teacher of **r** law replied, "Well said, Teacher.
12:35 "Why do the teachers of **r** law claim that the
12:38 "Beware of these teachers of **r** law! For they love
14:1 and the teachers of **r** law were still looking for an
14:43 the teachers of **r** law, and the other leaders.
14:53 other leaders, and teachers of **r** law had gathered.
15:1 other leaders, and teachers of **r** law—
15:31 and teachers of **r** law also mocked Jesus.
Lk 2:46 was in the Temple, sitting among the **r** teachers,
5:17 and teachers of **r** law were sitting nearby.
5:21 and teachers of **r** law said to each other.
5:30 and their teachers of **r** law complained bitterly to
5:33 The **r** leaders complained that Jesus' disciples
6:7 The teachers of **r** law and the Pharisees watched
7:30 and experts in **r** law had rejected God's plan for
9:22 the leading priests, and the teachers of **r** law.
10:25 One day an expert in **r** law stood up to test Jesus
11:45 "Teacher," said an expert in **r** law, "you have
11:46 "how terrible it will be for you experts in **r** law!
11:46 For you crush people beneath impossible **r**
11:52 "How terrible it will be for you experts in **r** law!
11:53 the Pharisees and teachers of **r** law were furious.
14:3 Jesus asked the Pharisees and experts in **r** law,
15:2 and teachers of **r** law complain that he was
18:18 Once a **r** leader asked Jesus this question:
19:47 but the leading priests, the teachers of **r** law,
20:1 the leading priests and teachers of **r** law and other
20:19 When the teachers of **r** law and the leading priests
20:39 remarked some of the teachers of **r** law who were
20:46 "Beware of these teachers of **r** law! For they love
22:2 and teachers of **r** law were actively plotting Jesus'
22:66 the leading priests and the teachers of **r** law.
23:10 and the teachers of **r** law stood there shouting their
23:13 together the leading priests and other **r** leaders,
23:51 with the decision and actions of the other **r** leaders.
24:20 our leading priests and other **r** leaders arrested him
Jn 3:1 a Jewish **r** leader named Nicodemus, a Pharisee,
8:3 the teachers of **r** law and Pharisees brought a
Ac 4:5 and elders and teachers of **r** law met in Jerusalem.
5:34 who was an expert on **r** law and was very popular
6:12 the crowds, the elders, and the teachers of **r** law.
13:50 leaders stirred up both the influential **r** women
17:22 "Men of Athens, I notice that you are very **r**,
23:9 Some of the teachers of **r** law who were Pharisees
23:29 discovered it was something regarding their **r** law
Gal 1:14 I was one of the most **r** Jews of my own age,
1Ti 4:2 They pretend to be **r**, but their consciences are
2Ti 3:5 They will act as if they are **r**, but they will reject
Heb 9:6 room regularly as they performed their **r** duties.
Jas 1:26 If you claim to be **r** but don't control your tongue,

RELISH (1)
Pr 1:22 How long will you mockers **r** your mocking?

RELOCATED (1) [LOCATED]
Ezr 4:10 noble Ashurbanipal had deported and **r** in Samaria

RELUCTANTLY (1)
2Co 9:7 Don't give **r** or in response to pressure. For God

RELY (6) [RELIABLE, RELIED, RELIES, RELYING]
Lev 19:31 "Do not **r** on mediums and psychics, for you will
Job 39:12 Can you **r** on it to return, bringing your grain to the
Ps 33:18 who fear him, / those who **r** on his unfailing love.
Pr 11:7 all perish, for they **r** on their own feeble strength.
Isa 50:10 of light, trust in the LORD and **r** on your God.
2Co 1:9 But as a result, we learned not to **r** on ourselves,

RELYING (1) [RELY]
Ro 2:17 you are **r** on God's law for your special

REMAIN (131) [REMAINED, REMAINING, REMAINS]
Ge 38:11 She was to **r** a widow until his youngest son,
42:19 you really are. Only one of you will **r** in the prison.
Ex 8:9 Then only the frogs in the Nile River will **r** alive."
Lev 11:25 your clothes, and you will **r** defiled until evening.
11:28 your clothes, and you will **r** defiled until evening.
11:32 put into water, and it will **r** defiled until evening.
11:35 It has become defiled, and it will **r** that way.
11:40 your clothes. Then you will **r** defiled until evening.
14:8 they must still **r** outside their tents for seven days.
15:5 and you will **r** ceremonially defiled until evening.
15:6 in water. You will then **r** defiled until evening.
15:10 in water, and you will **r** defiled until evening.
15:11 in water, and you will **r** defiled until evening.
15:16 and he will **r** ceremonially defiled until evening.
15:17 must be washed, and it will **r** defiled until evening.
15:18 must bathe, and they will **r** defiled until evening.
15:21 in water, and you will **r** defiled until evening.
15:24 He will **r** defiled for seven days, and any bed on
15:27 in water, and you will **r** defiled until evening.
17:15 Then you will **r** ceremonially unclean until
19:6 Any leftovers that **r** until the third day must be
20:21 his brother, and the guilty couple will **r** childless.
21:6 providing God with his food, and they must **r** holy.
22:6 they will **r** defiled until evening. They must not eat
25:51 If many years still **r**, they will repay most of what
25:52 If only a few years **r** until the Year of Jubilee,
26:21 "If even then you **r** hostile toward me and refuse
26:27 still refuse to listen and still **r** hostile toward me,
Nu 19:7 though he will **r** ceremonially unclean until
19:8 in water, and he, too, will **r** unclean until evening.
19:10 and he will **r** ceremonially unclean until evening.
19:20 has not been sprinkled on them, they **r** defiled.
19:21 water of purification will **r** defiled until evening.
33:55 those who **r** will be like splinters in your eyes
36:7 for the inheritance of every tribe must **r** fixed as it
Dt 13:16 That town must **r** a ruin forever; it may never be
16:4 of the Passover lamb **r** until the next morning.
21:13 Then she must **r** in your home for a full month,
21:23 the body must never **r** on the tree overnight.
22:19 The woman will then **r** the man's wife, and he may
Jos 1:14 and cattle may **r** here on the east side of the Jordan
7:12 I will not **r** with you any longer unless you destroy
Jdg 6:39 This time let the fleece **r** dry while the ground
21:7 How can we find wives for the few who **r**,
21:16 "How can we find wives for the few who **r**,
1Sa 26:9 For who can **r** innocent after attacking the
2Sa 17:3 Then all the people will **r** unharmed
19:7 not a single one of them will **r** here tonight.
2Ki 17:23 off to the land of Assyria, where they **r** to this day.
1Ch 5:26 and the Gozan River, where they **r** to this day.
Est 7:4 If we had only been sold as slaves, I could **r** quiet,
Job 3:9 Let its morning stars **r** dark. Let it hope for light,
11:3 Should I **r** silent while you babble on? When you
13:19 could prove me wrong, I would **r** silent until I die.
32:16 now that you are silent? Must I also **r** silent?
41:11 Who will confront me and **r** safe?

Ps 4: 4 Think about it overnight and r silent. / *Interlude*
22: 1 have you forsaken me? / Why do you r so distant?
27: 3 no fear. / Even if they attack me, / I r confident.
92:14 will still produce fruit; / they will r vital and green.
102:26 Even they will perish, but you r forever; / they will
103: 9 will not constantly accuse us, / nor r angry forever.
109:15 May these sins always r before the LORD,
119:91 Your laws r true today, / for everything serves
119:101 path of evil, / that I may r obedient to your word.
Pr 2:21 the land, and those who have integrity will r in it.
22: 6 and when they are older, they will r upon it.
Isa 6:13 Israel will r a stump, like a tree that is cut down,
14:30 you out with famine. I will destroy the few who r.
15: 9 both those who try to run and those who r behind.
17: 6 Only two or three r in the highest branches, four
22:18 and there your glorious chariots will r, broken
51:13 Will you r in constant dread of human oppression?
54:10 hills disappear, but even then I will r loyal to you.
62: 1 my heart yearns for Jerusalem, I cannot r silent.
66:22 "As surely as my new heavens and earth will r,
Jer 6: 9 Even the few who r in Israel will be gleaned again,
17:25 and on horses, and this city will r forever.
49:11 But I will preserve the orphans who r among you.
51:62 so that neither people nor animals will r here.
La 5:19 But LORD, you r the same forever! Your throne
Eze 24:13 you will r filthy until my fury against you has been
24:23 Your heads must r covered, and your sandals must
29:14 But Egypt will r an unimportant, minor kingdom.
37:28 And since my Temple will r among them forever,
43: 7 I will r here forever, living among the people of
44: 2 the LORD said to me, "This gate must r closed;
44: 2 of Israel, entered here. Thus, it must always r shut.
48:21 "The areas that r, to the east and to the west of the
Da 12:12 who wait and r until the end of the 1,335 days!
Joel 3:20 "But Judah will r forever, and Jerusalem will
Am 5:15 Almighty will have mercy on his people who r.
Mic 6:14 Your hunger pangs and emptiness will still r.
Zec 5: 4 And my curse will r in that house until it is
11: 9 And those who r will devour each other!"
12: 6 while the people living in Jerusalem r secure.
Mal 2:15 guard yourself; r loyal to the wife of your youth.
2:16 "So guard yourself; always r loyal to your wife."
Mt 5:18 even the smallest detail of God's law will r until
24:35 earth will disappear, but my words will r forever.
Mk 13:31 earth will disappear, but my words will r forever.
Lk 21:33 earth will disappear, but my words will r forever.
Jn 6:56 All who eat my flesh and drink my blood r in me,
9:41 "But you r guilty because you claim you can see.
12:46 so that all who put their trust in me will no longer r
15: 4 R in me, and I will r in you. For a branch
15: 5 Those who r in me, and I in them, will produce
15: 7 if you stay joined to me and my words r in you,
15: 9 you even as the Father has loved me. R in my love.
15:10 When you obey me, you r in my love, just as I
obey my Father and r in his love.
21:22 "If I want him to r alive until I return,
21:23 only said, "If I want him to r alive until I return,
Ac 3:21 For he must r in heaven until the time for the final
13:43 men urged them, "By God's grace, r faithful."
1Co 7:11 leave him, let her r single or else go back to him.
7:26 present crisis, I think it is best to r just as you are.
1Th 3: 8 us new life, knowing you r strong in the Lord.
4:17 and r on the earth will be caught up in the clouds
to meet the Lord in the air and r with him forever.
2Th 2: 7 and it will r secret until the one who is holding it
2Ti 3:14 But you must r faithful to the things you have been
Heb 1:11 Even they will perish, but you r forever.
3: 6 our courage and r confident in our hope in Christ.
8: 9 They did not r faithful to my covenant, / so I
13: 4 and r faithful to one another in marriage.
1Jn 2:24 So you must r faithful to what you have been
Jude 1: 5 he later destroyed every one of those who did not r
Rev 2:10 R faithful even when facing death, and I will give
14:12 endure persecution patiently and r firm to the end,

REMAINED (70) [REMAIN]

Ge 18:22 but the LORD r with Abraham for a while.
40: 4 They r in prison for quite some time, and Potiphar
49:24 But his bow r strong, / and his arms were
Ex 7:13 Pharaoh's heart, however, r hard and stubborn.
7:22 into blood. So Pharaoh's heart r hard and stubborn.
8:19 But Pharaoh's heart r hard and stubborn.
8:31 swarms to disappear. Not a single fly r in the land!
9: 7 after he found it to be true, his heart r stubborn.
10:15 Not one green thing r, neither tree nor plant,
10:19 Not a single locust r in all the land of Egypt.
Nu 9:18 Then they r where they were as long as the cloud
9:19 If the cloud r over the Tabernacle for a long time,
14:24 He has r loyal to me, and I will bring him into the
14:38 explored the land, only Joshua and Caleb r alive.
21:35 his sons, and his subjects; not a single survivor r.
36:12 their inheritance of land r within their ancestral
Jos 8: 9 But Joshua r among the people in the camp that
11:22 though some still r in Gaza, Gath, and Ashdod.
18: 2 But there r seven tribes who had not yet been
Jdg 5:17 Gilead r east of the Jordan. / And Dan, why did he
8:10 all that r of the allied armies of the east—
18:31 Dan as long as the Tabernacle of God r at Shiloh.
1Sa 6: 1 The Ark of the LORD r in Philistine territory
7: 2 The Ark r in Kiriath-jearim for a long time—
18:29 and he r David's enemy for the rest of his life.
23:25 and he r there in the wilderness of Maon.
25:13 and two hundred r behind to guard their
2Sa 2:10 Meanwhile, the tribe of Judah r loyal to David.
6:11 The Ark of the LORD r there with the family of
6:23 daughter of Saul, r childless throughout her life.
1Ki 1: 8 But among those who r loyal to David and refused
12:20 So only the tribe of Judah r loyal to the family of
15:14 Asa r faithful to the LORD throughout his life.
2Ki 2:22 The water has r wholesome ever since, just as
11: 3 and his nurse r hidden in the Temple of the
17:18 his presence. Only the tribe of Judah r in the land.
18: 6 He r faithful to the LORD in everything, and he
25:11 then took as exiles those who r in the city,
1Ch 12:29 Most of the Benjaminites had r loyal to Saul until
13:14 The Ark of God r there with the family of
2Ch 11: 5 Rehoboam r in Jerusalem and fortified various
11:12 So only Judah and Benjamin r under his control.
15:17 Asa r fully committed to the LORD throughout
22:12 Joash r hidden in the Temple of God for six years
Ezr 4:24 and it r at a standstill until the second year of the
Ne 6: 1 finished rebuilding the wall and that no gaps r—
Ps 50:21 While you did all this, I r silent, / and you thought
Ecc 2: 9 I r clear-eyed so that I could evaluate all these
Isa 21: 8 my lord. Night after night I have r at my post.
Jer 37:16 put into a dungeon cell, where he r for many days.
38:13 of the guard—the palace prison—where he r.
38:28 And Jeremiah r a prisoner in the courtyard of the
52:11 Zedekiah r there in prison for the rest of his life.
52:15 poorest of the people and those who r in the city,
Da 1:21 Daniel r there until the first year of King Cyrus's
2:49 of Babylon, while Daniel r in the king's court.
Mal 2:14 though she r your faithful companion, the wife of
Mt 1:25 but she r a virgin until her son was born.
26:63 But Jesus r silent. Then the high priest said to him,
27:12 made their accusations against him, Jesus r silent.
Lk 22:28 You have r true to me in my time of trial.
Jn 7: 9 So Jesus r in Galilee.
Ac 9: 9 He r there blind for three days. And all that time
17:14 on to the coast, while Silas and Timothy r behind.
2Co 10: 6 And we will punish those who r disobedient after
1Th 3: 7 because you have r strong in your faith.
2Ti 4: 7 I have finished the race, and I have r faithful.
Heb 10:32 Remember how you r faithful even though it
2Pe 3: 4 everything has r exactly the same since the world
Rev 2:13 of Satan is located, and yet you have r loyal to me.

REMAINING (26) [REMAIN]

Ex 36:16 and the six r sheets were joined to make a second
Lev 10:12 Then Moses said to Aaron and his r sons, Eleazar
10:16 angry with Eleazar and Ithamar, Aaron's r sons.
14:17 then put some of the oil r in his left hand on the tip
14:18 The oil r in the priest's hand will then be poured
Nu 4:12 All the r utensils of the sanctuary must be wrapped
31:32 The plunder r from the spoils that the fighting men
34:13 be divided up among the nine and a half r tribes.
Dt 24:21 but leave any r grapes for the foreigners, orphans,
Jos 14: 1 The r tribes of Israel inherited land in Canaan as
17: 2 to the r families within the tribe of Manasseh:
18: 3 before taking possession of the r land the LORD,
23: 7 associate with the other people still r in the land.
23:12 with the survivors of these nations r among you,
Jdg 5:17 sat unmoved at the seashore, / r in his harbors.
1Sa 30:10 the pursuit with his four hundred r troops.
2Ki 7:13 Let them take five of the r horses. If something
1Ch 6:61 The r descendants of Kohath received ten towns
6:70 The r descendants of Kohath were assigned these
6:77 The r descendants of Merari received from the
2Ch 24:14 they brought the r money to the king and Jehoiada.
Job 7:16 on living. Oh, leave me alone for these few r days.
Isa 6: 2 covered their feet, and with the r two they flew.
Jer 27:18 Let them pray that these r articles will not be
Eze 17:21 and those r in the city will be scattered to the four
19:14 and devoured its fruit. / None of the r limbs

REMAINS (42) [REMAIN]

Ge 8:22 As long as the earth r, there will be springtime
Ex 29:34 of the ordination meat or bread r until the morning,
Lev 13:19 or a reddish white spot r in its place,
Dt 11:21 so that as long as the sky r above the earth, you
Jos 4: 9 were standing. The memorial r there to this day.
7:26 heap of stones over Achan, which r to this day.
10:27 a large pile of stones, which r to this very day.
13: 1 are growing old, and much land r to be conquered.
13: 4 The land of the Avvites in the south also r to be
Jdg 6:24 The altar r in Ophrah in the land of the clan of
6:28 had been built, and it had the r of a sacrifice on it.
1Sa 31:13 Then they took their r and buried them beneath the
1Ki 20:10 if there r enough dust from Samaria to provide
1Ch 10:12 Then they buried their r beneath the oak tree at
Job 16: 6 as it is, my grief r no matter how I defend myself.
18: 5 "The truth r that the light of the wicked will be
20:20 Of all the things he dreamed about, nothing r.
23:13 his mind concerning me r unchanged,
Ps 73:26 grow weak, / but God r the strength of my heart;
88:18 my companions and loved ones; / only darkness r.
103:17 But the love of the LORD r forever / with those
Pr 11:12 a neighbor; a person with good sense r silent.
14:13 a heavy heart; when the laughter ends, the grief r.
Jer 4:29 the cities have been abandoned—not a person r!
25:20 of Ashkelon, Gaza, Ekron, and what r of Ashdod.
Eze 7: 3 No hope r, for I will unleash my anger against you.
22:18 the people of Israel are the worthless slag that r
24:12 But it's hopeless; the corruption r. So throw it into
32: 9 "And when I bring your shattered r to distant
Hag 2: 5 My Spirit r among you, just as I promised when
Jn 3:36 eternal life, but the wrath of God r upon them."
1Co 7:29 The time that r is very short, so husbands should
2Co 3:11 which r forever, has far greater glory.
Php 1:18 the fact r that the message about Christ is being
Col 1:24 for I am completing what r of Christ's sufferings
2Ti 2:13 If we are unfaithful, / he r faithful, / for he cannot
Heb 7: 3 He r a priest forever, resembling the Son of God.
7:24 But Jesus r a priest forever; his priesthood will
1Pe 1: 7 So if your faith r strong after being tried by fiery
Rev 3: 2 Strengthen what little r, for even what is left is at
17:16 her naked, eat her flesh, and burn her r with fire.
18: 9 as they see the smoke rising from her charred r.

REMALIAH (6)

2Ki 15:25 Then Pekah son of R, the commander of
15:27 Pekah son of R began to rule over Israel in the
2Ch 28: 6 In a single day Pekah son of R, Israel's king,
Isa 7: 1 of Aram and King Pekah of Israel, the son of R.
7: 4 King Rezin of Aram and Pekah son of R.
7: 9 is no stronger than its king, Pekah son of R.

REMARKABLE (2)

2Ch 32:31 about the r events that had taken place in the land,
Jer 33: 3 and I will tell you some r secrets about what is

REMARKED (5) [REMARKS]

2Sa 23:15 David r longingly to his men, "Oh, how I would
1Ch 11:17 David r longingly to his men, "Oh, how I would
Ne 4: 3 the Ammonite, who was standing beside him, r,
Lk 20:39 r some of the teachers of religious law who were
Jn 10:41 "John didn't do miracles," they r to one another,

REMARKS (1) [REMARKED]

Pr 12:18 Some people make cutting r, but the words of the

REMARRIES (2) [MARRY]

Mk 10:12 And if a woman divorces her husband and r,
Ro 7: 3 that law and does not commit adultery when she r.

REMARRY (1) [MARRY]

1Ti 5:11 their devotion to Christ and they will want to r.

REMEDY (2)

1Sa 16:15 Some of Saul's servants suggested a r. "It is clear
2Ch 36:16 could no longer be restrained and there was no r.

REMEMBER (225) [REMEMBERED, REMEMBERING, REMEMBERS, REMEMBRANCE]

Ge 6:21 And r, take enough food for your family and for all
9:15 and I will r my covenant with you and with
9:16 I will r the eternal covenant between God
43: 5 R that the man said, 'You won't be allowed to
Ex 12:14 "You must r this day forever. Each year you will
12:22 And r, no one is allowed to leave the house until
12:24 "R, these instructions are permanent and must be
12:42 to generation, to r the LORD's deliverance.
13: 3 said to the people, "This is a day to r forever—
13: 3 mighty power. (R, you are not to use any yeast.)
13:11 And r these instructions when the LORD brings
20: 8 "R to observe the Sabbath day by keeping it holy.
20:23 R, you must not make or worship idols of silver
22:21 R, you yourselves were once foreigners in the land
23: 9 R your own experience in the land of Egypt.
23:13 And r, never pray to or swear by any other gods.
24: 2 And r, none of the other people are allowed to
31:13 It helps you to r that I am the LORD, who makes
32:13 R your covenant with your servants—Abraham,
34:22 And you must r to celebrate the Festival of Harvest
Lev 3:16 the LORD. R, all the fat belongs to the LORD.
6:13 R, the fire must be kept burning on the altar at all
6:17 R, this flour may never be prepared with yeast.
8:35 R, you must stay at the entrance of the Tabernacle
19:34 R that you were once foreigners in the land of
23:27 "R that the Day of Atonement is to be celebrated
23:39 R that the first day and closing eighth day of the
25:23 And r, the land must never be sold on a permanent
25:37 R, do not charge your relatives interest on anything
26:42 Then I will r my covenant with Jacob, with Isaac,
26:42 and with Abraham, and I will r the land.
26:45 I will r my ancient covenant with their ancestors,
Nu 10: 9 so the LORD your God will r you and rescue you
11: 5 "We r all the fish we used to eat for free in Egypt.
15:40 The tassels will help you r that you must obey all
24:12 "Don't you r what I told your messengers?
Dt 4:20 R that the LORD rescued you from the burning
4:39 So r this and keep it firmly in mind: The LORD
5:15 R that you were once slaves in Egypt and that the
7:18 Just r what the LORD your God did to Pharaoh
7:19 R the great terrors the LORD your God sent
7:19 And r the miraculous signs and wonders,
8: 2 R how the LORD your God led you through the
8:18 Always r that it is the LORD your God who gives
9: 7 "R how angry you made the LORD your God out
9: 8 R how angry you made the LORD at Mount
9:27 but r instead your servants Abraham, Isaac,
12:12 And r the Levites who live in your towns, for they
15:15 R that you were slaves in the land of Egypt
15:18 R that for six years they have given you the
16: 3 so that you will r the day you departed from Egypt
16:12 R that you were slaves in Egypt, so be careful to
18: 1 "R that the Levitical priests and the rest of the
24: 9 R what the LORD your God did to Miriam as you
24:18 Always r that you were slaves in Egypt and that
24:22 R that you were slaves in the land of Egypt.
26:11 R to include the Levites and the foreigners living
29:16 "Surely you r how we lived in the land of Egypt
32: 7 R the days of long ago; / think about the

Jos 1:13 "**R** what Moses, the servant of the LORD,
14: 6 "**R** what the LORD said to Moses, the man of
14:12 You will **r** that as scouts we found the Anakites
Jdg 2:10 or **r** the mighty things he had done for Israel.
9: 2 one man. And **r**, I am your own flesh and blood!"
16:28 to the LORD, "Sovereign LORD, **r** me again.
1Sa 1:26 "Sir, do you **r** me?" Hannah asked. "I am the
25:31 has done these great things for you, please **r** me!"
2Sa 17: 8 And **r** that your father is an experienced soldier.
19:43 **R**, we were the first to speak of bringing him back
1Ki 2: 8 "And **r** Shimei son of Gera, the Benjaminite from
2:44 "You surely **r** all the wicked things you did to my
2Ki 9:25 Do you **r** when you and I were riding along behind
20: 3 "**R**, O LORD, how I have always tried to be
2Ch 6:42 **R** your unfailing love for your servant David."
16: 8 Don't you **r** what happened to the Ethiopians
19: 6 **R** that you do not judge to please people but to
23: 6 **R**, only the priests and Levites on duty may enter
Ne 1: 8 "Please **r** what you told your servant Moses:
4:14 **R** the Lord, who is great and glorious, and fight for
5:19 **R**, O my God, all that I have done for these people,
6:14 **R**, O my God, all the evil things that Tobiah
6:14 And **r** Noadiah the prophet and all the prophets
9:17 and did not **r** the miracles you had done for them.
13:14 **R** this good deed, O my God, and do not forget all
13:22 **R** this good deed also, O my God!
13:29 **R** them, O my God, for they have defiled the
13:31 for the priests. / **R** this in my favor, O my God.
Est 8: 8 But **r** that whatever is written in the king's name
Job 7: 7 O God, **r** that my life is but a breath, and I will
10: 9 **R** that I am made of dust—will you turn me back
18:17 will perish from the earth. No one will **r** them.
24:20 will find him sweet to eat. No one will **r** him.
Ps 20: 3 May he **r** all your gifts / and look favorably on
25: 6 **R**, O LORD, your unfailing love and compassion,
42: 4 My heart is breaking / as I **r** how it used to be:
42: 6 deeply discouraged, / but I will **r** your kindness—
74: 2 **R** that we are the people you chose in ancient
74: 2 And **r** Jerusalem, your home here on earth.
74:20 **R** your covenant promises, / for the land is full of
74:22 **R** how these fools insult you all day long.
77:11 O LORD; / I **r** your wonderful deeds of long ago.
89:47 **R** how short my life is, / how empty and futile this
106: 4 **R** me, too, LORD, when you show favor to your
119:49 **R** your promise to me, / for it is my only hope.
132: 1 LORD, **r** David / and all that he suffered.
137: 6 if I fail to **r** you, / if I don't make Jerusalem my
137: 7 O LORD, **r** what the Edomites did / on the day
143: 5 I **r** the days of old. / I ponder all your great works.
Pr 31: 7 to forget their poverty and **r** their troubles no more.
Ecc 1:11 We don't **r** what happened in those former times.
1:11 no one will **r** what we are doing now.
11: 8 But let them also **r** that the dark days will be many.
11: 9 But **r** that you must give an account to God for
11:10 So banish grief and pain, but **r** that youth, with a
12: 2 It will be too late then to **r** him, when the light of
12: 6 Yes, **r** your Creator now while you are young,
Isa 38: 3 "**R**, O LORD, how I have always tried to be
57:11 How is it that you don't even **r** me or think about
64: 9 with us, LORD. Please don't **r** our sins forever.
Jer 2: 2 I **r** how eager you were to please me as a young
11: 6 and say, '**R** the covenant your ancestors made,
14:10 I will **r** all your wickedness and will punish you
31:34 their wickedness and will never again **r** their sins."
50: 6 their way and cannot **r** how to get back to the fold.
51:50 **R** the LORD, even though you are in a far-off
La 3:21 Yet I still dare to hope when I **r** this:
5: 1 LORD, **r** everything that has happened to us.
Eze 2: 5 whether they listen or not—for **r**, they are rebels—
2: 6 by their dark scowls. For **r**, they are rebels!
6: 9 they are exiled among the nations, they will **r** me.
16:61 Then you will **r** with shame all the evil you have
16:63 You will **r** your sins and cover your mouth in
23:27 on those things or fondly **r** your time in Egypt.
36:31 Then you will **r** your past sins and hate yourselves
36:32 But **r**, says the Sovereign LORD, I am not doing
43:11 as they watch so they will be sure to **r** them.
Mic 6: 5 "Don't you **r**, my people, how King Balak of
6: 5 And **r** your journey from Acacia to Gilgal, when I,
Hab 3: 2 power to save us. And in your anger, **r** your mercy.
Hag 2: 3 Is there anyone who can **r** this house—
Zec 10: 9 the nations, still they will **r** me in distant lands.
Mal 4: 4 "**R** to obey the instructions of my servant Moses,
Mt 5:12 And **r**, the ancient prophets were persecuted,
5:23 and you suddenly **r** that someone has something
16: 9 Don't you **r** the five thousand I fed with five
16:10 Don't you **r** the four thousand I fed with seven
27:63 we **r** what that deceiver once said while he was
28: 7 You will see him there. **R**, I have told you."
Mk 8:18 can't you hear?' Don't you **r** anything at all?
Lk 6:23 And **r**, the ancient prophets were also treated that
9:44 "Listen to me and **r** what I say. The Son of Man is
10: 3 and **r** that I am sending you out as lambs among
16:25 **r** that during your lifetime you had everything you
17:32 **R** what happened to Lot's wife!
23:42 **r** me when you come into your Kingdom."
24: 6 Don't you **r** what he told you back in Galilee,
Jn 14:24 And **r**, my words are not my own. This message is
14:28 **R** what I told you: I am going away, but I will
15:18 world hates you, **r** it hated me before it hated you.
15:20 Do you **r** what I told you? 'A servant is not greater
16: 4 so that when they happen, you will **r** I warned you.
Ac 1: 4 he promised. **R**, I have told you about this before.
20:31 **R** the three years I was with you—my constant
20:35 You should **r** the words of the Lord Jesus: 'It is
Ro 8: 9 (And **r** that those who do not have the Spirit of
11: 1 **R** that I myself am a Jew, a descendant of
11: 2 Do you **r** what the Scriptures say about this?
11: 4 And do you **r** God's reply? He said, "You are not
11:18 broken off. **R**, you are just a branch, not the root.
11:20 Yes, but **r**—those branches, the Jews, were broken
11:26 Do you **r** what the prophets said about this?
14:10 **R**, each of us will stand personally before the
14:20 **R**, there is nothing wrong with these things in
15: 8 **R** that Christ came as a servant to the Jews to show
1Co 1:16 of Stephanas. I don't **r** baptizing anyone else.)
1:26 **R**, dear brothers and sisters, that few of you were
7:16 You wives must **r** that your husbands might be
7:16 And you husbands must **r** that your wives might be
7:22 And **r**, if you were a slave when the Lord called
9:24 **R** that in a race everyone runs, but only one person
10:13 But **r** that the temptations that come into your life
14:32 **R** that people who prophesy are in control of their
2Co 8:15 Do you **r** what the Scriptures say about this?
9: 6 **R** this—a farmer who plants only a few seeds will
Gal 2:10 The only thing they suggested was that we **r** to
4:13 Surely you **r** that I was sick when I first brought
6: 7 **R** that you can't ignore God and get away with it.
Eph 4:30 **R**, he is the one who has identified you as his own,
6: 8 **R** that the Lord will reward each one of us for the
6: 9 **r**, you both have the same Master in heaven,
Php 4: 5 in all you do. **R**, the Lord is coming soon.
Col 3:13 **R**, the Lord forgave you, so you must forgive
3:24 **R** that the Lord will give you an inheritance as
4: 1 **R** that you also have a Master—in heaven.
4:18 in my own handwriting—PAUL. **R** my chains.
1Th 2: 9 Don't you **r**, dear brothers and sisters, how hard
3: 6 He reports that you **r** our visit with joy and that
4: 2 For you **r** what we taught you in the name of the
5:13 And **r** to live peaceably with each other.
2Th 2: 5 Don't you **r** that I told you this when I was with
1Ti 5:24 **R** that some people lead sinful lives, and everyone
2Ti 1: 3 Night and day I constantly **r** you in my prayers.
1: 4 to see you again, for I **r** your tears as we parted.
1:13 And **r** to live in the faith and love that you have in
Heb 8:12 and I will never again **r** their sins."
10:17 Then he adds, / "I will never again **r** / their sins
10:32 **R** how you remained faithful even though it meant
10:35 what happens. **R** the great reward it brings you!
12: 7 **r** that God is treating you as his own children.
13: 7 **R** your leaders who first taught you the word of
Jas 1:13 And **r**, no one who wants to do wrong should ever
1:22 And **r**, it is a message to obey, not just to listen to.
2:12 **r** that you will be judged by the law of love,
2:21 Don't you **r** that our ancestor Abraham was
4:17 **R**, it is sin to know what you ought to do and
1Pe 1:17 And **r** that the heavenly Father to whom you pray
3:17 **R**, it is better to suffer for doing good, if that is
4: 5 But just **r** that they will have to face God, who will
5: 9 **R** that Christians all over the world are going
2Pe 1:15 to you. I want you to **r** them long after I am gone.
3: 2 I want you to **r** and understand what the holy
3: 4 Why, as far back as anyone can **r**, everything has
3:15 And **r**, the Lord is waiting so that people have time
3Jn 1:11 **R** that those who do good prove that they are
Jude 1:17 must **r** what the apostles of our Lord Jesus Christ

REMEMBERED (31) [REMEMBER]

Ge 8: 1 But God **r** Noah and all the animals in the boat.
30:22 Then God **r** Rachel's plight and answered her
42: 9 And he **r** the dreams he had had many years
Ex 2:24 their cries and **r** his covenant promise to Abraham,
6: 5 to the Egyptians. I have **r** my covenant with them.
1Sa 1:19 slept with Hannah, the LORD **r** her request,
Ezr 3:12 Levites, and other leaders **r** the first Temple,
Est 9:28 These days would be **r** and kept from generation to
Ps 49:13 of fools, / though they will be **r** as being so wise.
78:35 Then they **r** that God was their rock, / that their
78:39 For he **r** that they were merely mortal, / gone in a
98: 3 He has **r** his promise to love and be faithful to
105:42 For he **r** his sacred promise / to Abraham his
106:45 He **r** his covenant with them / and relented
112: 6 Those who are righteous will be long **r**.
136:23 He **r** our utter weakness. / His faithful love endures
Ecc 9: 5 They have no further reward, nor are they **r**.
Isa 23:16 and sing her songs, so that she will again be **r**.
54: 4 and the sorrows of widowhood will be **r** no more,
63:11 Then they **r** those days of old when Moses led his
Jer 32:20 in the land of Egypt—things still **r** to this day!
Eze 16:43 because you have not **r** your youth but have
33:13 save them, then none of their good deeds will be **r**.
Da 11:20 "His successor will be **r** as the king who sent a tax
Mk 11:21 Peter **r** what Jesus had said to the tree on the
Lk 22:61 Then Peter **r** that the Lord had said,
24: 8 Then they **r** that he had said this.
Jn 2:17 Then his disciples **r** this prophecy from the
2:22 from the dead, the disciples **r** that he had said this.
12:16 they **r** that these Scriptures had come true before
Rev 16:19 And so God **r** all of Babylon's sins, and he made

REMEMBERING (3) [REMEMBER]

Ps 78: 7 set its hope anew on God, / **r** his glorious miracles
Eze 23:19 **r** her youth when she was a prostitute in Egypt.
Lk 1:72 our ancestors / by **r** his sacred covenant with them,

REMEMBERS (5) [REMEMBER]

Ps 6: 5 For in death, who **r** you? / Who can praise you
111: 5 to those who trust him; / he always **r** his covenant.
115:12 The LORD **r** us, / and he will surely bless us.
La 1: 7 and wandering, Jerusalem **r** her ancient splendor.
2Co 7:15 Now he cares for you more than ever when he **r**

REMEMBRANCE (6) [REMEMBER]

Ps 38: T A psalm of David, to bring us to the LORD's **r**.
70: T A psalm of David, to bring us to the LORD's **r**.
Mal 3:16 a scroll of **r** was written to record the names of
Lk 22:19 is my body, given for you. Do this in **r** of me."
1Co 11:24 which is given for you. Do this in **r** of me."
11:25 Do this in **r** of me as often as you drink it."

REMETH (1) [JARMUTH, RAMOTH]

Jos 19:21 **R**, En-gannim, En-haddah, and Beth-pazzez.

REMIND (28) [REMINDED, REMINDER, REMINDERS, REMINDING]

Ge 31:48 "This pile of stones will stand as a witness to **r** us
Ex 12:17 for it will **r** you that I brought your forces out of
13: 9 Let it **r** you always to keep the LORD's
20:24 Build altars in the places where I **r** you who I am,
Lev 2:13 offerings with salt, to **r** you of God's covenant.
22: 3 **R** them that if any of their descendants are
23:43 This will **r** each new generation of Israelites that
Nu 10:10 The trumpets will **r** the LORD your God of his
15:39 The tassels will **r** you of the commands of the
Jos 4: 7 'They **r** us that the Jordan River stopped flowing
22:27 It will **r** our descendants and your descendants that
1Sa 12: 7 Now stand here quietly before the LORD as I **r**
Ps 39: 4 **r** me how brief my time on earth will be.
39: 4 **R** me that my days are numbered, / and that my
Jer 11: 2 "**R** the people of Judah and Jerusalem about the
Eze 20:12 It was to **r** them that I, the LORD, had set them
20:20 for they are a sign to **r** you that I am the LORD
21:23 But the king of Babylon will **r** the people of their
29:16 Egypt's shattered condition will **r** Israel of how
Jn 14:26 and will **r** you of everything I myself have told
1Co 4:17 He will **r** you of what I teach about Christ Jesus in
15: 1 Now let me **r** you, dear brothers and sisters,
2Ti 1: 6 This is why I **r** you to fan into flames the spiritual
2:14 **R** everyone of these things, and command them in
Tit 3: 1 **R** your people to submit to the government and its
2Pe 3: 3 I want to **r** you that in the last days there will be
Jude 1: 5 I must **r** you—and you know it well—that even
1: 6 And I **r** you of the angels who did not stay within

REMINDED (7) [REMIND]

Ge 41: 9 "Today I have been **r** of my failure," he said.
Ex 4:21 Then the LORD **r** him, "When you arrive back in
28:29 the LORD will be **r** of his people continually.
Ecc 8:17 This **r** me that no one can discover everything God
Da 6:12 went back to the king and **r** him about his law.
Jn 5:34 though I have **r** you about John's testimony so you
Heb 10: 3 Those yearly sacrifices **r** them of their sins year

REMINDER (12) [REMIND]

Ex 13: 9 This annual festival will be a visible **r** to you,
13:16 It is a visible **r** that it was the LORD who brought
16:33 Then store it in a sacred place as a **r** for all future
28:12 these names before the LORD as a constant **r**.
Nu 31:54 and brought the gold to the Tabernacle as a **r** to the
Dt 6: 8 Tie them to your hands as a **r**, and wear them on
11:18 Tie them to your hands as a **r**, and wear them on
Jos 22:28 it is a **r** of the relationship both of us have with the
24:26 As a **r** of their agreement, he took a huge stone
1Sa 6:18 still stands in the field of Joshua as a **r** of what
Pr 7: 3 Tie them on your fingers as a **r**. Write them deep
Ro 15:15 knowing that all you need is this **r** from me.

REMINDERS (2) [REMIND]

Ex 39: 7 These stones served as **r** to the LORD concerning
Ac 14:17 There were always his **r**, such as sending you rain

REMINDING (3) [REMIND]

Ac 14:22 **r** them that they must enter into the Kingdom of
2Pe 1:12 I plan to keep on **r** you of these things—
1:13 I believe I should keep on **r** you of these things as

REMISSION [KJV] See also FORGIVE(N), FORGIVENESS

REMMON, REMMON-METHOAR [KJV] See RIMMON

REMNANT (38) [REMNANTS]

Jos 10:20 and wiped out the five armies except for a tiny **r**
Jdg 5:13 "Down from Tabor marched the **r** against the
8:10 and Zalmunna were in Karkor with a **r** of 15,000
21:13 **r** of Benjamin who were living at the rock of
1Sa 11:11 The **r** of their army was so badly scattered that no
2Ki 19:31 For a **r** of my people will spread out from
2Ch 34: 9 Ephraim, and from all the **r** of Israel, as well as
34:21 for me and for all the **r** of Israel and Judah.
Ezr 9: 8 our God has allowed a few of us to survive as a **r**.
9:13 have allowed some of us to survive as a **r**.
9:14 us until even this little **r** no longer survives.
9:15 before you in our guilt as nothing but an escaped **r**,
Isa 6:13 a **r**—survive, it will be invaded again and burned.
10:21 A **r** of them will return to the Mighty God.
11:11 In that day the Lord will bring back a **r** of his
11:16 He will make a highway from Assyria for the **r**
24:13 grapes left on the vine after harvest, only a **r** is left.
28: 5 He will be the pride and joy of the **r** of his people.
37:32 For a **r** of my people will spread out from
65: 9 I will preserve a **r** of the people of Israel and of

66:20 They will bring the **r** of your people back from
Jer 23: 3 But I will gather together the **r** of my flock from
31: 7 'Save your people, O LORD, the **r** of Israel!'
39: 9 sent to Babylon the **r** of the population as well as
42: 2 we are only a tiny **r** compared to what we were
42:15 then this is what the LORD says to the **r** of Judah.
42:19 "Listen, you **r** of Judah. The LORD has told you:
44:12 I will take this **r** of Judah that insisted on coming
47: 5 You **r** of the Mediterranean plain, how long will
50:20 or in Judah, for I will forgive the **r** I preserve.
Eze 5: 4 A fire will then spread from this **r** and destroy all
Mic 5: 8 The **r** of Israel will go out among the nations
Hag 1:12 and the whole **r** of God's people obeyed the
1:14 the high priest, and the whole **r** of God's people.
2: 2 and to the **r** of God's people there in the land:
Zec 8: 6 a small and discouraged **r** of God's people.
8:11 But now I will not treat the **r** of my people as I
8:12 Once more I will make the **r** in Judah and Israel

REMNANTS (1) [REMNANT]
Eze 33:24 the scattered **r** of Judah living among the ruined

REMODEL (1)
Am 5:15 is good; **r** your courts into true halls of justice.

REMORSE (8)
Isa 22:12 and to wear clothes of sackcloth to show your **r**.
Jer 44:10 To this very hour you have shown no **r**
Eze 7:18 They will shave their heads in sorrow and **r**.
Zec 11: 5 The buyers will slaughter their sheep without **r**.
Mt 11:21 and throwing ashes on their heads to show their **r**.
27: 3 had been condemned to die, he was filled with **r**.
Lk 10:13 and throwing ashes on their heads to show their **r**.
2Co 7: 9 but because the pain caused you to have **r**

REMOTE (4) [REMOTEST]
Jdg 19: 1 living in a **r** area of the hill country of Ephraim.
19:18 "We are on our way home to a **r** area in the hill
Isa 41: 5 in fear. **R** lands tremble and mobilize for war.
Mt 14:13 he went off by himself in a boat to a **r** area to be

REMOTEST (2) [REMOTE]
2Ki 19:23 highest mountains— / yes, the **r** peaks of Lebanon.
Isa 37:24 highest mountains— / yes, the **r** peaks of Lebanon.

REMOVAL (2) [REMOVE]
Nu 19: 9 This ceremony is performed for the **r** of sin.
1Pe 3:21 Baptism is not a **r** of dirt from your body; it is an

REMOVE (54) [REMOVAL, REMOVED, REMOVES, REMOVING]
Ge 30:32 and **r** all the sheep and goats that are speckled
Ex 8:30 and asked the LORD to **r** all the flies.
12:15 On the very first day you must **r** every trace of
13:22 And the LORD did not **r** the pillar of cloud
33: 5 **R** your jewelry and ornaments until I decide what
33:23 Then I will **r** my hand, and you will see me from
Lev 1:16 The priest must **r** the crop and the feathers
4: 8 The priest must **r** all the fat around the bull's
4:19 The priest must **r** all the animal's fat and burn it on
4:31 Those who are guilty must **r** all the goat's fat,
4:35 Those who are guilty must **r** all the sheep's fat,
5: 6 This will be a sin offering to **r** their sin,
26: 6 I will **r** the wild animals from your land
Nu 5: 2 "Command the people of Israel to **r** anyone from
5: 3 **R** them so they will not defile the camp, where I
19:17 "To **r** the defilement, put some of the ashes from
20:26 There you will **r** Aaron's priestly garments and put
Dt 13: 5 you must execute them to **r** the evil from among
Jos 7:13 You will never defeat your enemies until you **r**
10:22 "**R** the rocks covering the opening of the cave
Ru 4: 7 transferring a right of purchase to **r** his sandal
1Ki 2:31 This will **r** the guilt of his senseless murders from
22:43 however, he failed to **r** all the pagan shrines,
2Ki 23: 4 and the Temple gatekeepers to **r** from the
24: 3 He had decided to **r** Judah from his presence
2Ch 20:33 however, he failed to **r** all the pagan shrines,
29: 5 **R** all the defiled things from the sanctuary.
Job 13:21 **R** your hand from me, and don't terrify me with
Ps 51: 9 keep looking at my sins. / **R** the stain of my guilt.
Pr 25: 4 **R** the dross from silver, and the sterling will be
25: 5 **R** the wicked from the king's court, and his reign
Isa 1:18 matter how deep the stain of your sins, I can **r** it.
1:25 and skim off your slag. I will **r** all your impurities.
25: 7 In that day he will **r** the cloud of gloom,
25: 8 He will **r** forever all insults and mockery against
47: 2 grind the corn. **R** your veil and strip off your robe.
52: 2 **R** the slave bands from your neck, O captive
Jer 28: 2 I will **r** the yoke of the king of Babylon from your
Eze 11:18 they will **r** every trace of their detestable idol
Hos 2:18 I will **r** all weapons of war from the land,
Joel 2:20 I will **r** these armies from the north and send them
Zep 3:11 I will **r** all the proud and arrogant people from
3:15 For the LORD will **r** his hand of judgment
Zec 3: 9 and I will **r** the sins of this land in a single day.
9:10 I will **r** the battle chariots from Israel
13: 2 I will **r** from the land all false prophets
Mt 13:41 and they will **r** from my Kingdom everything that
1Co 5: 7 **R** this wicked person from among you so that you
5:13 "You must **r** the evil person from among you."
Heb 9:26 to **r** the power of sin forever by his sacrificial
Rev 2: 5 and **r** your lampstand from its place among the
6: 4 and the authority to **r** peace from the earth.
21: 4 He will **r** all of their sorrows, and there will be no
22:19 God will **r** that person's share in the tree of life

REMOVED (46) [REMOVE]
Ge 30:23 birth to a son. "God has **r** my shame," she said.
30:35 and **r** all the male goats that were speckled
Ex 34:34 the LORD, he **r** the veil until he came out again.
Lev 3: 4 lobe of the liver, which is to be **r** with the kidneys.
3:10 lobe of the liver, which is to be **r** with the kidneys.
3:15 lobe of the liver, which is to be **r** with the kidneys.
7: 4 lobe of the liver, which is to be **r** with the kidneys.
14:40 must order that the stones from those areas be **r**.
14:42 will be brought in to replace the ones that were **r**,
Nu 4:13 "The ashes must be **r** from the altar, and the altar
5: 4 and **r** such people from the camp.
20:28 Moses **r** the priestly garments from Aaron and put
2Sa 7:15 him as I took it from Saul, whom I **r** before you.
12:30 David **r** the crown from the king's head, and it was
1Ki 15:12 the land and **r** all the idols his ancestors had made.
15:14 Although the pagan shrines were not completely **r**,
2Ki 16:14 Then King Ahaz **r** the old bronze altar from the
16:17 Then the king **r** the side panels and basins from the
16:17 He also **r** the Sea from the backs of the bronze
16:18 he also **r** the canopy that had been constructed
18: 4 He **r** the pagan shrines, smashed the sacred pillars,
23: 6 The king **r** the Asherah pole from the LORD's
23:11 He **r** from the entrance of the LORD's Temple
1Ch 20: 2 at Rabbah, he **r** the crown from the king's head,
2Ch 14: 3 He **r** the pagan altars and the shrines. He smashed
14: 5 Asa also **r** the pagan shrines, as well as the incense
15: 8 and **r** all the idols in the land of Judah
15:17 Although the pagan shrines were not completely **r**
19: 3 for you have **r** the Asherah poles throughout the
30:14 set to work and **r** the pagan altars from Jerusalem.
31: 1 Asherah poles, and **r** the pagan shrines and altars.
33:15 Manasseh also **r** the foreign gods from the hills
34:33 So Josiah **r** all detestable idols from the entire land
Job 19: 9 me of my honor and **r** the crown from my head.
34:20 pass away; the mighty are **r** without human hand.
Ps 103:12 He has **r** our rebellious acts / as far away from us
Pr 2:22 But the wicked will be **r** from the land,
10:30 but the wicked will be **r** from the land.
Isa 6: 7 Now your guilt is **r**, and your sins are forgiven."
Jer 16: 5 "for I have **r** my protection and peace from them.
Mt 8:17 "He took our sicknesses and **r** our diseases."
Ac 13:22 But God **r** him from the kingship and replaced him
23:27 that he was a Roman citizen, I **r** him to safety.
1Co 5: 2 And why haven't you **r** this man from your
2Co 3:14 And this veil can be **r** only by believing in Christ.
3:18 And all of us have had that veil **r** so that we can be

REMOVES (5) [REMOVE]
Lev 11:36 But anyone who **r** the dead body will be defiled.
Job 12:18 He **r** the royal robe of kings. With ropes around
12:20 trusted adviser, and he **r** the insight of the elders.
Da 2:21 he **r** kings and sets others on the throne.
Rev 22:19 And if anyone **r** any of the words of this prophetic

REMOVING (4) [REMOVE]
Ge 19:29 **r** him from the disaster that engulfed the cities on
29: 3 wait for all the flocks to arrive before **r** the stone.
Lev 10:17 It was given to you for **r** the guilt of the
Est 3:10 confirming his decision by **r** his signet ring from

REMPHAN [KJV] See REPHAN

RENAMED (11) [NAME]
Ge 26:18 Isaac **r** them, using the names Abraham had given
41:45 Pharaoh **r** him Zaphenath-paneah and gave him a
50:11 **r** the place Abel-mizraim, for they said,
Nu 13:24 At that time the Israelites **r** the valley Eshcol—
32:42 and he **r** that area Nobah after himself.
Dt 3:14 Jair **r** this region after himself, calling it the Towns
Jos 19:47 They **r** the city Dan after their ancestor.
Jdg 18:29 They **r** the town Dan after their ancestor,
Ne 9: 7 him from Ur of the Chaldeans and **r** him Abraham.
Da 1: 7 The chief official **r** them with these Babylonian
Mk 3:16 of the twelve he chose: / Simon (he **r** him Peter),

RENDER (3) [RENDERED]
1Ki 3:28 God had given him to **r** decisions with justice.
2Ch 19: 6 He will be with you when you **r** the verdict in each
Zec 8:16 **R** verdicts in your courts that are just and that lead

RENDERED (1) [RENDER]
Lk 18: 7 Even he **r** a just decision in the end, so don't you

RENEW (6) [RENEWAL, RENEWED, RENEWS]
Nu 6:11 Then they must **r** their vow that day and let their
1Ki 15:19 "Let us **r** the treaty that existed between your
2Ch 16: 3 "Let us **r** the treaty that existed between your
Ps 51:10 a clean heart, O God. / **R** a right spirit within me.
119:40 **R** my life with your goodness.
126: 4 our fortunes, LORD, / as streams **r** the desert.

RENEWAL (1) [RENEW]
Eph 4:23 there must be a spiritual **r** of your thoughts

RENEWED (11) [RENEW]
1Sa 23:18 So the two of them **r** their covenant of friendship
2Ki 23: 3 and **r** the covenant in the LORD's presence.
2Ch 34:31 and **r** the covenant in the LORD's presence.
34:32 they **r** their covenant with God, the God of their
Job 29:20 bestowed on me, and my strength is continually **r**.'
Ps 94:19 your comfort gave me **r** hope and cheer.
103: 5 with good things. / My youth is **r** like the eagle's!
110: 3 your vigor will be **r** each day like the morning
Pr 3: 8 Then you will gain **r** health and vitality.
2Co 4:16 bodies are dying, our spirits are being **r** every day.
Col 3:10 nature that is continually being **r** as you learn more

RENEWS (1) [RENEW]
Ps 23: 3 He **r** my strength. / He guides me along right

RENOUNCED (1) [RENOUNCES]
Ps 89:39 You have **r** your covenant with him, / for you have

RENOUNCES (1) [RENOUNCED]
Jer 18: 8 but then that nation **r** its evil ways, I will not

RENOVATION (2)
2Ch 24:13 So the men in charge of the **r** worked hard,
34:10 they paid the workers who did the repairs and **r**.

RENOWN (2)
Dt 26:19 Then you will receive praise, honor, and **r**.
Zep 3:19 I will give glory and **r** to my former exiles,

RENT (1) [RENTAL, RENTED, RENTS]
Am 5:11 what little they have through taxes and unfair **r**.

RENTAL (1) [RENT]
Ex 22:15 because this loss was covered by the **r** fee.

RENTED (2) [RENT]
Ex 22:15 And no payment is required if the animal was **r**
Ac 28:30 the next two years, Paul lived in his own **r** house.

RENTS (1) [RENT]
SS 8:11 at Baal-hamon, which he **r** to some farmers there.

REOPENED (2) [OPEN]
Ge 26:18 He **r** the wells his father had dug,
2Ch 29: 3 Hezekiah **r** the doors of the Temple of the LORD

REPAID (7) [PAY]
Ge 44: 4 'Why have you **r** an act of kindness with such
1Sa 24:17 man than I am, for you have **r** me good for evil.
25:21 was lost or stolen. But he has **r** me evil for good.
2Ch 24:22 That was how King Joash **r** Jehoiada for his love
Jer 51:35 May Babylon be **r** for all the violence she did to
Eze 23:49 You will be fully **r** for all your prostitution—
Lk 18:30 will be **r** many times over in this life, as well as

REPAIR (11) [REPAIRED, REPAIRING, REPAIRS]
Dt 19: 3 Keep the roads to these cities in good **r** so that
2Ki 22: 5 Then they can use it to pay workers to **r** the
22: 6 and the cut stone needed to **r** the Temple.
2Ch 24: 4 Joash decided to **r** and restore the Temple of the
24: 5 so that we can **r** the Temple of your God.
34: 8 to **r** the Temple of the LORD his God.
Ezr 9: 9 to rebuild the Temple of our God and **r** its ruins.
Pr 29: 1 accept criticism will suddenly be broken beyond **r**.
Jer 19:11 of Judah and Jerusalem beyond all hope of **r**.
Eze 22:28 to them. They **r** cracked walls with whitewash!
Na 3:14 the defenses! Make bricks to **r** the walls!

REPAIRED (25) [REPAIR]
1Ki 18:30 They all crowded around him as he **r** the altar of
2Ki 12: 6 Joash's reign, the priests still had not **r** the Temple.
12: 7 and asked them, "Why haven't you **r** the Temple?
2Ch 15: 8 And he **r** the altar of the LORD, which stood in
29: 3 the doors of the Temple of the LORD and **r** them.
Ne 3: 4 and grandson of Hakkoz **r** the next section of wall.
3: 6 The Old City Gate was **r** by Joiada son of Paseah
3:10 Next Jedaiah son of Harumaph **r** the wall beside
3:11 of Pahath-moab, who **r** the Tower of the Ovens,
3:12 of Hallohesh and his daughters **r** the next section.
3:13 They also **r** the fifteen hundred feet of wall to the
3:14 The Dung Gate was **r** by Malkijah son of Recab,
3:15 leader of the Mizpah district, **r** the Fountain Gate.
3:15 Then he **r** the wall of the pool of Siloam near the
3:19 **r** another section of wall opposite the armory by
3:20 who **r** an additional section from the buttress to the
3:23 and grandson of Ananiah **r** the sections next to
3:26 who **r** the wall as far as the Water Gate toward the
3:27 who **r** another section opposite the great projecting
3:28 The priests **r** the wall up the hill from the Horse
3:30 the sixth son of Zalaph, **r** another section,
3:31 **r** the wall as far as the housing for the Temple
3:32 and merchants **r** the wall from that corner to the
4: 7 and that the gaps in the wall were being **r**,
Isa 22: 9 the walls of Jerusalem to see what needs to be **r**.

REPAIRING (4) [REPAIR]
1Ki 11:27 the Millo and **r** the walls of the city of his father,
2Ki 12:12 and cut stone for **r** the LORD's Temple,
2Ch 32: 5 by **r** the wall wherever it was broken down
Isa 61: 4 the ancient ruins, **r** cities long ago destroyed.

REPAIRS (5) [REPAIR]

2Ki 12: 5 to pay for whatever r are needed at the Temple."
12: 8 and they also agreed not to undertake the r of the
12:14 out to the workmen, who used it for the Temple r.
2Ch 24:14 When all the r were finished, they brought the
34:10 Then they paid the workers who did the r

REPAY (37) [PAY]

Lev 25:51 they will r most of what they received when they
25:52 then they will r a relatively small amount for their
Dt 32: 6 Is this the way you r the LORD, / you foolish
32:35 I will take vengeance; I will r those who deserve it.
32:41 on my enemies / and r those who hate me.
2Sa 3:39 So may the LORD r these wicked men for their
12: 6 He must r four lambs to the poor man for the one
1Ki 2:32 Then the LORD will r him for the murders of two
2Ki 9:26 'I solemnly swear that I will r him here on
Ne 5:11 R the interest you charged on their money, grain,
Ps 35:12 They r me with evil for the good I do. / I am sick
37:21 The wicked borrow and never r, / but the godly are
38:20 They r me evil for good / and oppose me because I
Pr 17:13 If you r evil for good, evil will never leave your
19:17 you are lending to the LORD—and he will r you!
Isa 59:18 He will r his enemies for their evil deeds. His fury
65: 6 I will not stand silent; I will r them in full! Yes, I will r them—
Jer 18:20 Should they r evil for good? They have set a trap
51: 6 LORD's time for vengeance; he will fully r her.
51:24 I will r Babylon and the people of Babylonia for
Eze 7: 9 I will r you for all your detestable practices.
9:10 I will fully r them for all they have done."
11:21 I will r them fully for their sins, says the Sovereign
16:43 I will fully r you for all of your sins,
Zec 9:12 I promise this very day that I will r you two
Lk 6:34 And if you lend money only to those who can r
6:35 And don't be concerned that they might not r.
7:42 But neither of them could r him, so he kindly
14:12 For they will r you by inviting you back.
14:14 you for inviting those who could not r you."
Ro 12:19 take vengeance; / I will r those who deserve it,"
1Ti 5: 4 at home and r their parents by taking care of them.
Phm 1:19 write this in my own handwriting: "I will r it."
Heb 10:30 I will r those who deserve it." He also said,
1Pe 3: 9 Don't r evil for evil. Don't retaliate when people
Rev 22:12 reward is with me, to r all according to their deeds.

REPAYING (1) [PAY]

Eze 7: 4 and show no pity, r you in full for all your evil.

REPAYMENT (1) [PAY]

Ex 22:26 If you take your neighbor's cloak as a pledge of r,

REPAYS (2) [PAY]

Job 21:31 No one r them for what they have done.
34:11 He r people according to their deeds. He treats

REPEAT (9) [REPEATED, REPEATEDLY, REPEATING, REPEATS]

Ex 12:20 I r, during those days you must not eat anything
31:15 I r: Because the LORD considers it a holy day,
Lev 11:12 I r, any marine animal that does not have both fins
Dt 6: 7 R them again and again to your children.
27: 3 I r, you will soon cross the river to enter the land
Ps 118: 2 Let the congregation of Israel r: / "His faithful
118: 3 Let Aaron's descendants, the priests, r:
118: 4 Let all who fear the LORD r: / "His faithful love
Jer 19: 2 and r to them the words that I give you.

REPEATED (8) [REPEAT]

Jdg 11:11 Jephthah r what he had said to the leaders.
2Ki 4:43 But Elisha r, "Give it to the group of prophets
17:12 despite the LORD's specific and r warnings.
Ps 109:30 But I will give r thanks to the LORD,
Jer 27:12 Then I r this same message to King Zedekiah of
Jn 21:16 Jesus r the question: "Simon son of John, do you
Ac 10:16 The same vision was r three times. Then the sheet
Heb 10: 1 The sacrifices under the old system were r again

REPEATEDLY (9) [REPEAT]

2Ch 36:15 of their ancestors, r sent his prophets to warn them,
Ne 9:28 In your wonderful mercy, you rescued them r!
Ps 40:16 your salvation / r shout, "The LORD is great!"
70: 4 who love your salvation / r shout, "God is great!"
Jer 7: 4 But do not be fooled by those who r promise your
7:13 says the LORD, I spoke to you about it r, but you
29:19 though I have spoken to them r through my
Lk 18: 3 A widow of that city came to him r, appealing for
Ac 27:41 while the stern was r smashed by the force of the

REPEATING (4) [REPEAT]

Isa 28:13 r it over and over, a line at a time, in very simple
Jer 11: 7 out of Egypt, r over and over again to this day:
Mt 6: 7 They think their prayers are answered only by r
Mk 14:39 Jesus left them again and prayed, r his pleadings.

REPEATS (3) [REPEAT]

Jdg 5:29 her wise women, / and she r these words to herself:
Pr 26:11 As a dog returns to its vomit, so a fool r his folly.
Ecc 1: 9 History merely r itself. It has all been done before.

REPENT (20) [PENANCE, REPENTANCE, REPENTANT, REPENTED, REPENTS]

Ps 7:12 If a person does not r, / God will sharpen his
50:22 R, all of you who ignore me, / or I will tear you
Isa 9:13 the people will still not r and turn to the LORD
Jer 5: 3 with faces set like stone; they have refused to r.
36: 3 Perhaps the people of Judah will r if they see in
Eze 3:19 and they keep on sinning and refuse to r,
3:21 But if you warn them and they r, they will live,
14: 6 R and turn away from your idols, and stop all your
33: 9 But if you warn them to r and they don't r,
33:12 will the sins of evil people destroy them if they r
Mt 12:41 greater than Jonah is here—and you refuse to r.
Lk 11:32 greater than Jonah is here—and you refuse to r.
13: 5 No, and I tell you again that unless you r, you will
2Pe 3: 9 so he is giving more time for everyone to r.
Rev 2:16 R, or I will come to you suddenly and fight against
2:21 I gave her time to r, but she would not turn away
9:21 And they did not r of their murders or their
16: 9 these plagues. They did not r and give him glory.
16:11 But they refused to r of all their evil deeds.

REPENTANCE (14) [REPENT]

1Ki 8:47 they may turn to you again in r and pray, 'We have
2Ki 22:19 your clothing in despair and wept before me in r.
2Ch 6:37 they may turn to you again in r and pray, 'We have
34:27 your clothing in despair and wept before me in r.
Job 42: 6 I said, and I sit in dust and ashes to show my r."
Jer 36:24 showed any signs of fear or r at what they heard.
La 3:40 our ways. Let us turn again in r to the LORD.
Mt 11:21 their people would have sat in deep r long ago,
Lk 10:13 their people would have sat in deep r long ago,
24:47 take this message of r to all the nations,
2Co 7:10 But sorrow without r is the kind that results in
Heb 6: 4 For it is impossible to restore to r those who were
6: 6 It is impossible to bring such people to r again
12:17 It was too late for r, even though he wept bitter

REPENTANT (3) [REPENT]

Ps 51:17 A broken and r heart, O God, / you will not
Isa 1:27 the r people of Jerusalem will be redeemed.
57:15 and give new courage to those with r hearts.

REPENTED (9) [REPENT]

2Ch 32:26 Then Hezekiah r of his pride, and the people of
33:19 and set up Asherah poles and idols before he r.
Ps 78:34 rest finally sought him. / They r and turned to God.
Jer 34:15 Recently you r and did what was right,
Zec 1: 6 As a result, they r and said, 'We have received
Mt 12:41 because they r at the preaching of Jonah.
Lk 11:32 because they r at the preaching of Jonah.
22:32 So when you have r and turned to me again,
2Co 12:21 because many of you who sinned earlier have not r

REPENTS (2) [REPENT]

Lk 15:10 of God's angels when even one sinner r."
17: 3 believer sins, rebuke him; then if he r, forgive him.

REPHAEL (1)

1Ch 26: 7 Their names were Othni, R, Obed, and Elzabad.

REPHAH (1)

1Ch 7:25 Ephraim's line of descent was R, Resheph, Telah,

REPHAIAH (7) [REPHAIAH'S]

1Ch 3:21 were Pelatiah and Jeshaiah. Jeshaiah's son was R.
4:42 led by Pelatiah, Neariah, R, and Uzziel—
7: 2 were Uzzi, R, Jeriel, Jahmai, Ibsam, and Shemuel.
8:37 Binea was the father of R. / R was the father of Eleasah.
9:43 Binea's son was R. / Rephaiah's son was Eleasah.
Ne 3: 9 R son of Hur, the leader of half the district of

REPHAIAH'S (2) [REPHAIAH]

1Ch 3:21 R son was Arnan. Arnan's son was Obadiah.
9:43 R son was Eleasah. / Eleasah's son was Azel.

REPHAIM (8)

Jos 15: 8 and on up to the northern end of the valley of R.
18:16 of Hinnom, at the northern end of the valley of R.
2Sa 5:18 and spread out across the valley of R.
5:22 and again spread out across the valley of R.
23:13 the Philistine army was camped in the valley of R.
1Ch 11:15 the Philistine army was camped in the valley of R.
14: 9 The Philistines had arrived in the valley of R
Isa 17: 5 the grainfields in the valley of R after the harvest.

REPHAIMS [KJV] REPHAITES

REPHAITES (9)

Ge 14: 5 They conquered the R in Ashteroth-karnaim,
15:20 Hittites, Perizzites, R,
Dt 2:11 and the Anakites are often referred to as the R,
2:20 too, was once considered the land of the R,
3:11 King Og of Bashan was the last of the giant R.
3:13 of Bashan used to be known as the land of the R.
Jos 12: 4 the last of the R, lived at Ashtaroth and Edrei.
13:12 King Og was the last of the R, for Moses had
17:15 in the forest where the Perizzites and R live."

REPHAN (1)

Ac 7:43 the shrine of Molech, / the star god R,

REPHIDIM (5)

Ex 17: 1 Eventually they came to R, but there was no water
17: 8 While the people of Israel were still at R,
19: 2 After breaking camp at R, they came to the base of
Nu 33:14 They left Alush and camped at R, where there was
33:15 They left R and camped in the wilderness of Sinai.

REPLACE (19) [REPLACED, REPLACING]

Lev 6:22 As the sons of the priests r their fathers, they will
14:42 Other stones will be brought in to r the ones that
1Ki 19:16 from Abel-meholah to r you as my prophet.
20:24 Only this time r the kings with field commanders!
2Ki 25:29 He supplied Jehoiachin with new clothes to r his
Est 4: 4 She sent clothing to him to r the sackcloth, but he
Job 8:19 its life, and others spring up from the earth to r it.
Ps 90:15 to our former misery! / R the evil years with good.
Isa 9:10 We will r the broken bricks with cut stone,
22:20 call my servant Eliakim son of Hilkiah to r you.
Jer 29:26 'The LORD has appointed you to r Jehoiada as
52:33 He supplied Jehoiachin with new clothes to r his
Eze 12:23 Now give them this new proverb to r the old one:
Mt 15: 9 for they r God's commands with their own
Mk 7: 7 for they r God's commands with their own
Lk 16: 7 and r it with one for only eight hundred bushels.'
Ac 1:25 as an apostle to r Judas the traitor in this ministry,
Ro 11:18 grafted in to r the branches that were broken off.
Heb 8: 7 have been no need for a second covenant to r it.

REPLACED (5) [REPLACE]

1Sa 21: 6 It had just been r that day with fresh bread.
2Ch 12:10 King Rehoboam later r them with bronze shields
Jer 28:13 but you have r it with a yoke of iron.
Da 8:22 The four prominent horns that r the one large horn
Ac 13:22 him from the kingship and r him with David,

REPLACING (3) [REPLACE]

2Sa 17:25 r Joab, who had been commander under David.
1Ki 2:12 succeeded him as king, r his father, David,
2Ki 17:24 in the towns of Samaria, r the people of Israel.

REPLANT (1) [PLANT]

Jer 32:41 and wholeheartedly r them in this land.

REPLASTERED (1) [PLASTER]

Lev 14:42 ones that were removed, and the walls will be r.

REPLENISH (1)

Ps 104:30 new life is born / to r all the living of the earth.

REPLENISH [KJV] See also FILL

REPLICA (1)

Nu 21: 8 "Make a r of a poisonous snake and attach it to the

REPLIED (670) [REPLY]

Ge 3:10 He r, "I heard you, so I hid. I was afraid because I
3:13 "The serpent tricked me," she r. "That's why I
4:13 Cain r to the LORD, "My punishment is too
4:15 The LORD r, "They will not kill you, for I will
14:22 Abram r, "I have solemnly promised the LORD,
15: 2 But Abram r, "O Sovereign LORD, what good
15: 8 But Abram r, "O Sovereign LORD, how can I be
16: 6 Abram r, "Since she is your servant, you may deal
16: 8 "I am running away from my mistress," she r.
17:19 But God r, "Sarah, your wife, will bear you a son.
18: 9 they asked him. "In the tent," Abraham r.
18:26 And the LORD r, "If I find fifty innocent people
18:29 And the LORD r, "I will not destroy it if there
18:30 And the LORD r, "I will not destroy it if there
20: 6 "Yes, I know you are innocent," God r. "That is
21:24 Abraham r, "All right, I swear to it!"
21:30 Abraham r, "They are my gift to you as a public
22: 1 "Abraham!" God called. "Yes," he r. "Here I
22: 7 Isaac said, "Father?" "Yes, my son," Abraham r.
23: 5 The Hittites r to Abraham,
23:13 and he r to Ephron as everyone listened. "No,
24:24 "My father is Bethuel," she r. "My grandparents
24:50 Then Laban and Bethuel r, "The LORD has
24:58 they asked her. And she r, "Yes, I will go."
24:65 asked the servant. And he r, "It is my master."
25:31 Jacob r, "All right, but trade me your birthright for
26: 9 would kill me to get her from me," Isaac r.
26:28 They r, "We can plainly see that the LORD is
27: 1 and said, "My son?" "Yes, Father?" Esau r.
27:11 "But Mother!" Jacob r. "He won't be fooled that
27:19 Jacob r, "It's Esau, your older son. I've done as
27:20 the LORD your God put it in my path!" Jacob r.
27:24 son Esau?" he asked. "Yes, of course," Jacob r.
27:32 of course!" he r. "It's Esau, your older son."
29: 5 the grandson of Nahor?" "Yes, we do," they r.
29: 8 until all the flocks and shepherds are here," they r.
29:19 "Agreed!" Laban r. "I'd rather give her to you
29:26 younger daughter ahead of the firstborn," Laban r.
30:15 But Leah angrily r, "Wasn't it enough that you
30:27 "Please don't leave me," Laban r, "for I have
30:29 Jacob r, "You know how faithfully I've served
30:31 Jacob r, "Don't give me anything at all. Just do
30:34 "All right," Laban r. "It will be as you have
31:11 said to me, 'Jacob!' And I r, 'Yes, I'm listening!'

31:43 Then Laban **r** to Jacob, "These women are my
32:27 is your name?" the man asked. He **r**, "Jacob."
32:29 Jacob asked him. "Why do you ask?" the man **r**.
33: 5 God has graciously given to me," Jacob **r**.
33: 8 Jacob **r**, "They are gifts, my lord, to ensure your
33:13 But Jacob **r**, "You can see, my lord, that some of
37:13 send you to them." "I'm ready to go," Joseph **r**.
37:16 "For my brothers and their flocks," Joseph **r**.
38:18 She **r**, "I want your identification seal, your cord,
38:21 "We've never had a prostitute here," they **r**.
40: 8 And they **r**, "We both had dreams last night,
40: 8 dreams is God's business," Joseph **r**.
41:16 "It is beyond my power to do this," Joseph **r**.
42: 7 "From the land of Canaan," they **r**.
42:38 But Jacob **r**, "My son will not go down with you,
43: 7 specifically asked us about our family," they **r**.
43:28 "Yes," they **r**. "He is alive and well." Then they
44:10 "Fair enough," the man **r**, "except that only the
44:26 we **r**, 'We can't unless you let our youngest
46: 2 "Jacob! Jacob!" he called. "Here I am," Jacob **r**.
47: 3 And they **r**, "We are shepherds like our ancestors.
47: 9 Jacob **r**, "I have lived for 130 hard years, but I am
47:16 "Well, then," Joseph **r**, "since your money is
Ex 2: 8 "Yes, do!" the princess **r**. So the girl rushed home
2:14 "Who do you think you are?" the man **r**.
3: 4 "Moses! Moses!" "Here I am!" Moses **r**.
3:14 God **r**, "I AM THE ONE WHO ALWAYS IS.
4: 2 in your hand?" "A shepherd's staff," Moses **r**.
4:18 are still alive." "Go with my blessing," Jethro **r**.
5:17 But Pharaoh **r**, "You're just lazy! You obviously
8: 9 "You set the time!" Moses **r**. "Tell me when you
8:10 "All right," Moses **r**, "it will be as you have said.
8:26 But Moses **r**, "That won't do! The Egyptians
8:28 "All right, go ahead," Pharaoh **r**. "I will let you
9:29 "All right," Moses **r**. "As soon as I leave the city,
10: 9 "Young and old, all of us will go," Moses **r**.
10:29 "Very well," Moses **r**. "I will never see you
16:23 He **r**, "The LORD has appointed tomorrow as a
17: 2 to drink!" they demanded. "Quiet!" Moses **r**.
18:15 Moses **r**, "Well, the people come to me to seek
32:18 But Moses **r**, "No, it's neither a cry of victory nor
32:22 "Don't get upset, sir," Aaron **r**. "You yourself
32:33 The LORD **r** to Moses, "I will blot out whoever
33:14 And the LORD **r**, "I will personally go with you,
33:17 And the LORD **r** to Moses, "I will indeed do
33:19 The LORD **r**, "I will make all my goodness pass
34:10 The LORD **r**, "All right. This is the covenant I
Nu 10:30 But Hobab **r**, "No, I will not go. I must return to
11:29 But Moses **r**, "Are you jealous for my sake?
16:12 and Abiram, the sons of Eliab, but they **r**,
20:20 But the king of Edom **r**, "Stay out! You may not
22:38 Balaam **r**, "I have come, but I have no power to
23:12 But Balaam **r**, "Can I say anything except what
23:26 But Balaam **r**, "Didn't I tell you that I must do
27: 6 And the LORD **r** to Moses,
27:18 The LORD **r**, "Take Joshua son of Nun, who has
32:25 Then the people of Gad and Reuben **r**, "We are
Jos 2: 4 the two men, **r**, "The men were here earlier,
2:21 "I accept your terms," she **r**. And she sent them
5:14 "Neither one," he **r**. "I am commander of the
5:15 The commander of the LORD's army **r**,
7:20 Achan **r**, "I have sinned against the LORD,
9: 7 The Israelites **r** to these Hivites, "How do we
9: 8 They **r**, "We will be your servants." "But who
9:19 But the leaders **r**, "We have sworn an oath in the
9:24 They **r**, "We did it because we were told that the
17:15 Joshua **r**, "If the hill country of Ephraim is not
22:31 Phinehas son of Eleazar, the priest, **r** to them,
24:16 The people **r**, "We would never forsake the
24:22 "Yes," they **r**, "we are accountable."
Jdg 4: 9 "Very well," she **r**, "I will go with you. But since
6:13 "Sir," Gideon **r**, "if the LORD is with us,
6:15 "But Lord," Gideon **r**, "how can I rescue Israel?
6:17 Gideon **r**, "If you are truly going to help me,
6:23 "It is all right," the LORD **r**. "Do not be afraid.
8: 2 But Gideon **r**, "What have I done compared to
8: 6 But the leaders of Succoth **r**, "You haven't caught
8:18 what were they like?" "Like you," they **r**.
8:23 But Gideon **r**, "I will not rule over you, nor will
8:25 "Gladly!" they **r**. They spread out a cloak,
9:13 But the grapevine **r**, 'Should I quit producing the
9:15 And the thornbush **r**, 'If you truly want to make
9:36 Zebul **r**, "It's just the shadows of the hills that
10:11 The LORD **r**, "Did I not rescue you from the
11: 8 "Because we need you," they **r**. "If you will lead
11:10 "The LORD is our witness," the leaders **r**.
13:11 to my wife the other day?" "Yes," he **r**, "I am."
13:13 The angel of the LORD **r**, "Be sure your wife
13:16 "I will stay," the angel of the LORD **r**, "but I
13:18 do you ask my name?" the angel of the LORD **r**.
14:16 given the answer to my father or mother," he **r**.
14:18 Samson **r**, "If you hadn't plowed with my heifer,
15:10 The Philistines **r**, "We've come to capture
15:11 But Samson **r**, "I only paid them back for what
15:13 and hand you over to the Philistines," they **r**.
16: 7 Samson **r**, "If I am tied up with seven new
16:11 Samson **r**, "If I am tied up with brand-new ropes
16:13 Samson **r**, "If you weave the seven braids of my
17: 2 LORD bless you for admitting it," his mother **r**.
17: 9 And he **r**, "I am a Levite from Bethlehem in
18: 6 "Go in peace," the priest **r**. "For the LORD will
18: 9 The men **r**, "Let's attack! We have seen the land,
18:24 "What do you mean, What do I want?" Micah **r**.
19:18 have been in Bethlehem in Judah," the man **r**.
20: 8 And all the people stood up together and **r**,
Ru 1:11 But Naomi **r**, "Why should you go on with me?
1:16 But Ruth **r**, "Don't ask me to leave you and turn
2: 4 "The LORD bless you!" the harvesters **r**.
2: 6 And the foreman **r**, "She is the young woman
2:11 "Yes, I know," Boaz **r**. "But I also know about
2:13 "I hope I continue to please you, sir," she **r**.
3: 5 "I will do everything you say," Ruth **r**.
3: 9 he demanded. "I am your servant Ruth," she **r**.
4: 4 after you." The man **r**, "All right, I'll redeem it."
4: 6 "Then I can't redeem it," the family redeemer **r**,
4:11 the leaders and all the people standing there **r**,
1Sa 1:15 "Oh no, sir!" she **r**, "I'm not drunk! But I am
3: 4 called out, "Samuel! Samuel!" "Yes?" Samuel **r**.
3: 5 What do you need?" "I didn't call you," Eli **r**.
3:10 And Samuel **r**, "Yes, your servant is listening."
3:16 "Samuel, my son." "Here I am," Samuel **r**.
3:18 anything back. "It is the LORD's will," Eli **r**.
4:17 "Israel has been defeated," the messenger **r**.
5: 8 The rulers discussed it and **r**, "Move it to the city
8: 7 "Do as they say," the LORD **r**, "for it is me they
8:22 and the LORD **r**, "Do as they say, and give them
9: 7 we don't have anything to offer him," Saul **r**.
9:12 "Yes," they **r**. "Stay right on this road. He is at
9:19 "I am the seer!" Samuel **r**. "Go on up the hill
9:21 Saul **r**, "But I'm only from Benjamin, the smallest
10:14 the donkeys," Saul **r**, "but we couldn't find them.
10:16 "He said the donkeys had been found," Saul **r**.
10:22 And the LORD **r**, "He is hiding among the
11: 3 **r** the leaders of Jabesh. "If none of our relatives
11:13 But Saul **r**, "No one will be executed today,
12: 4 "No," they **r**, "you have never cheated
12: 5 me of robbing you." "Yes, it is true," they **r**.
13:11 Saul **r**, "I saw my men scattering from me,
14: 7 "Do what you think is best," the youth **r**.
14:36 His men **r**, "We'll do whatever you think is best."
15:22 But Samuel **r**, "What is more pleasing to the
15:26 But Samuel **r**, "I will not return with you!
16: 2 "Take a heifer with you," the LORD **r**, "and say
16: 5 "Yes," Samuel **r**. "I have come to sacrifice to the
16:11 you have?" "There is still the youngest," Jesse **r**.
17:29 "What have I done now?" David **r**. "I was only
17:33 "Don't be ridiculous!" Saul **r**. "There is no way
17:58 And David **r**, "His name is Jesse, and we live in
18:23 When Saul's men said these things to David, he **r**,
19:17 Saul demanded of Michal. "I had to," Michal **r**.
20: 5 David **r**, "Tomorrow we celebrate the new moon
20:11 "Come out to the field with me," Jonathan **r**.
20:28 Jonathan **r**, "David earnestly asked me if he could
21: 4 "We don't have any regular bread," the priest **r**.
21: 5 "Don't worry," David **r**. "I never allow my men
21: 9 you killed in the valley of Elah," the priest **r**.
21: 9 is nothing like it!" David **r**. "Give it to me!"
22:14 "But sir," Ahimelech **r**, "is there anyone among
23: 4 and again the LORD **r**, "Go down to Keilah,
23:12 And the LORD **r**, "Yes, they will betray you."
25:32 David **r** to Abigail, "Praise the LORD, the God
26: 6 Joab's brother. "I'll go with you," Abishai **r**.
26:17 And David **r**, "Yes, my lord the king.
26:22 "Here is your spear, O king," David **r**. "Let one
28: 7 His advisers **r**, "There is a medium at Endor."
28:11 want me to call up?" "Call up Samuel," Saul **r**.
28:14 "He is an old man wrapped in a robe," she **r**.
28:15 "Because I am in deep trouble," Saul **r**.
28:16 But Samuel **r**, "Why ask me if the LORD has left
30:13 am an Egyptian—the slave of an Amalekite," he **r**.
30:15 The young man **r**, "If you swear by God's name
2Sa 1: 3 "I escaped from the Israelite camp," the man **r**.
1: 4 The man **r**, "Our entire army fled. Many men are
1: 8 to me, 'Who are you?' I **r**, 'I am an Amalekite.'
1:13 And he **r**, "I am a foreigner, an Amalekite,
2: 1 And the LORD **r**, "Yes." Then David asked,
2: 1 should I go to?" And the LORD **r**, "Hebron."
2:20 "Is that you, Asahel?" "Yes, it is," he **r**.
3:13 "All right," David **r**, "but I will not negotiate
5:19 over to me?" The LORD **r**, "Yes, go ahead.
5:23 "Do not attack them straight on," the LORD **r**.
7: 3 Nathan **r**, "Go ahead and do what you have in
9: 2 the king asked. "Yes sir, I am," Ziba **r**.
9: 3 Ziba **r**, "Yes, one of Jonathan's sons is still alive,
9:10 who had fifteen sons and twenty servants, **r**,
11:11 Uriah **r**, "The Ark and the armies of Israel
12:13 Nathan **r**, "Yes, but the LORD has forgiven you,
12:19 "Is the baby dead?" he asked. "Yes," they **r**.
12:22 David **r**, "I fasted and wept while the child was
13:25 The king **r**, "No, my son. If we all came,
14: 5 the king asked. "I am a widow," she **r**.
14: 9 "Oh, thank you, my lord," she **r**. "And I'll take
14:11 "As surely as the LORD lives," he **r**, "not a hair
14:13 She **r**, "Why don't you do as much for all the
14:18 "I want to know one thing," the king **r**. "Yes,
14:19 And the woman **r**, "My lord the king, how can I
14:32 And Absalom **r**, "Because I wanted you to ask the
15:15 "We are with you," his advisers **r**. "Do what you
15:22 David **r**, "All right, come with us." So Ittai
16: 2 And Ziba **r**, "The donkeys are for your people to
16: 3 "He stayed in Jerusalem," Ziba **r**. "He said,
16: 4 Mephibosheth owns." "Thank you, sir," Ziba **r**.
16:18 is chosen by the LORD and by Israel," Hushai **r**.
17: 7 "Well," Hushai **r**, "this time I think Ahithophel
17:20 She **r**, "They were here, but they crossed the
18:12 do it for a thousand pieces of silver," the man **r**.
18:22 too." "Why should you go, my son?" Joab **r**.
18:25 and the king **r**, "If he is alone, he has news."
18:26 The king **r**, "He also will have news."
18:27 good man and comes with good news," the king **r**.
18:29 Ahimaaz **r**, "When Joab told me to come,
18:32 And the Cushite **r**, "May all of your enemies,
19:26 Mephibosheth **r**, "My lord the king, my servant
19:29 "All right," David **r**. "My decision is that you
19:34 "No," he **r**, "I am far too old for that.
19:42 "Why not?" the men of Judah **r**. "The king is one
19:43 "But there are ten tribes in Israel," the others **r**.
20:17 "I am," he **r**. So she said, "Listen carefully to
20:20 And Joab **r**, "Believe me, I don't want to destroy
20:21 "All right," the woman **r**, "we will throw his
21: 4 "Well, money won't do it," the Gibeonites **r**.
21: 5 Then they **r**, "It was Saul who planned to destroy
24: 3 But Joab **r** to the king, "May the LORD your
24:14 "This is a desperate situation!" David **r** to Gad.
24:21 And David **r**, "I have come to buy your threshing
24:24 But the king **r** to Araunah, "No, I insist on buying
1Ki 1:17 She **r**, "My lord, you vowed to me by the LORD
1:36 "Amen!" Benaiah son of Jehoiada **r**.
1:43 "Not at all!" Jonathan **r**. "Our lord King David
1:52 Solomon **r**, "If he proves himself to be loyal,
2:15 He **r**, "As you know, the kingdom was mine;
2:17 He **r**, "Speak to King Solomon on my behalf,
2:18 "All right," Bathsheba **r**. "I will speak to the king
2:21 marry Abishag, the girl from Shunem," she **r**.
2:31 "Do as he said," the king **r**. "Kill him there
2:38 Shimei **r**, "Your sentence is fair; I will do
2:42 And you **r**, 'The sentence is fair; I will do as you
3: 6 Solomon **r**, "You were wonderfully kind to my
3:11 So God **r**, "Because you have asked for wisdom in
11:22 "Nothing is wrong," he **r**. "But even so, I must
12: 5 Rehoboam **r**, "Give me three days to think this
12: 7 The older counselors **r**, "If you are willing to
12:10 The young men **r**, "This is what you should tell
13:14 who came from Judah?" "Yes," he **r**, "I am."
13:16 "No, I cannot," he **r**. "I am not allowed to eat any
17:19 But Elijah **r**, "Give me your son." And he took
18: 8 "Yes, it is," Elijah **r**. "Now go and tell your
18:18 "I have made no trouble for Israel," Elijah **r**.
19:10 Elijah **r**, "I have zealously served the LORD God
19:14 He **r** again, "I have zealously served the LORD
19:20 then I will go with you!" Elijah **r**, "Go on back!
20: 4 "All right, my lord," Ahab **r**. "All that I have is
20:14 And the prophet **r**, "This is what the LORD says:
20:33 and they **r**, "Yes, your brother Ben-hadad!"
20:40 "Well, it's your own fault," the king **r**.
21: 3 But Naboth **r**, "The LORD forbid that I should
22: 4 And Jehoshaphat **r** to King Ahab, "Why,
22: 6 or not?" They all **r**, "Go right ahead!
22: 8 King Ahab **r**, "There is still one prophet of the
22:14 But Micaiah **r**, "As surely as the LORD lives,
22:15 or not?" And Micaiah **r**, "Go right ahead!
22:16 But the king **r** sharply, "How many times must I
22:22 "And the spirit **r**, 'I will go out and inspire all
22:25 And Micaiah **r**, "You will find out soon enough
22:28 But Micaiah **r**, "If you return safely, the LORD
2Ki 1: 6 They **r**, "A man came up to us and told us to go
1: 8 They **r**, "He was a hairy man, and he wore a
1:10 But Elijah **r** to the captain, "If I am a man of God,
1:12 Elijah **r**, "If I am a man of God, let fire come
2: 2 But Elisha **r**, "As surely as the LORD lives
2: 4 But Elisha **r** again, "As surely as the LORD lives
2: 6 But again Elisha **r**, "As surely as the LORD lives
2: 9 And Elisha **r**, "Please let me become your rightful
2:10 "You have asked a difficult thing," Elijah **r**.
3: 7 And Jehoshaphat **r**, "Why, of course! You and I
3: 8 attack from the wilderness of Edom," Joram **r**.
3:11 One of King Joram's officers **r**, "Elisha son of
3:14 Elisha **r**, "As surely as the LORD Almighty
4: 2 "Nothing at all, except a flask of olive oil," she **r**.
4:13 "No," she **r**, "my family takes good care of me."
5:16 But Elisha **r**, "As surely as the LORD lives,
5:25 Gehazi?" "I haven't been anywhere," he **r**.
6:12 "It's not us, my lord," one of the officers **r**.
6:28 She **r**, "This woman proposed that we eat my son
7: 1 Elisha **r**, "Hear this message from the LORD!
7: 2 But Elisha **r**, "You will see it happen, but you
7:13 One of his officers **r**, "We had better send out
7:19 The king's officer had **r**, "That couldn't happen
8:10 And Elisha **r**, "Go and tell him, 'You will
8:12 Elisha **r**, "I know the terrible things you will do to
8:13 Then Hazael **r**, "How could a nobody like me ever
8:14 And Hazael **r**, "He told me that you will surely
9: 5 of us?" Jehu asked. "For you, Commander," he **r**.
9:11 know the way such a man babbles on," Jehu **r**.
9:18 Jehu **r**, "What do you know about peace?
9:22 Jehu **r**, "How can there be peace as long as the
10:13 And they **r**, "We are relatives of King Ahaziah.
10:15 "Yes, I am," Jehonadab **r**. "If you are,"
14: 9 But King Jehoash of Israel **r** to King Amaziah of
18:27 But Sennacherib's representative **r**, "My master
19: 6 the prophet **r**, "Say to your master, 'This is what
20: 9 Isaiah **r**, "This is the sign that the LORD will
20:10 shadow always moves forward," Hezekiah **r**.
20:14 Hezekiah **r**, "They came from the distant land of
20:15 Isaiah asked. "They saw everything," Hezekiah **r**.
23:18 Josiah **r**, "Leave it alone. Don't disturb his
1Ch 14:10 The LORD **r**, "Yes, go ahead. I will give you the
14:14 "Do not attack them straight on," God **r**.
17: 2 Nathan **r**, "Go ahead with what you have in mind,
21: 3 But Joab **r**, "May the LORD increase the number
21:13 "This is a desperate situation!" David **r** to Gad.
21:24 But the king **r** to Araunah, "No, I insist on paying
2Ch 1: 8 Solomon **r** to God, "You have been so faithful
10: 5 Rehoboam **r**, "Come back in three days for my
10: 7 The older counselors **r**, "If you are good to the
10:10 The young men **r**, "This is what you should tell
18: 3 And Jehoshaphat **r**, "Why, of course! You and I
18: 5 They all **r**, "Go ahead, for God will give you a
18: 7 King Ahab **r**, "There is still one prophet of the
18:13 But Micaiah **r**, "As surely as the LORD lives,
18:14 or not?" And Micaiah **r**, "Go right ahead!

18:15 But the king **r** sharply, "How many times must I
18:21 "And the spirit **r**, 'I will go out and inspire all
18:24 And Micaiah **r**, "You will find out soon enough,
18:27 But Micaiah **r**, "If you return safely, the LORD
25: 9 The man of God **r**, "The LORD is able to give
25:18 But King Jehoash of Israel **r** to King Amaziah of
31:10 the high priest, from the family of Zadok, **r**,
Ezr 4: 3 Jeshua, and the other leaders of Israel **r**,
Ne 2: 3 but I **r**, "Long live the king! Why shouldn't I be
2: 5 I **r**, "If it please Your Majesty and if you are
2:18 They **r** at once, "Good! Let's rebuild the wall!"
2:20 But I **r**, "The God of heaven will help us succeed.
5:12 Then they **r**, "We will give back everything
6: 3 so I **r** by sending this message to them: "I am
6:11 But I **r**, "Should someone in my position run away
Est 5: 4 And Esther **r**, "If it please Your Majesty,
5: 7 Esther **r**, "This is my request and deepest wish.
6: 3 His attendants **r**, "Nothing has been done."
6: 5 So the attendants **r** to the king, "Haman is out
6: 7 So he **r**, "If the king wishes to honor someone,
7: 3 And so Queen Esther **r**, "If Your Majesty is
7: 6 Esther **r**, "This wicked Haman is our enemy."
Job 1: 9 Satan **r** to the LORD, "Yes, Job fears God,
2: 4 Satan **r** to the LORD, "Skin for skin—he blesses
2:10 But Job **r**, "You talk like a godless woman.
4: 1 Then Eliphaz the Temanite **r** to Job:
8: 1 Then Bildad the Shuhite **r** to Job:
11: 1 Then Zophar the Naamathite **r** to Job:
15: 1 Then Eliphaz the Temanite **r**:
18: 1 Then Bildad the Shuhite **r**:
20: 1 Then Zophar the Naamathite **r**:
22: 1 Then Eliphaz the Temanite **r**:
25: 1 Then Bildad the Shuhite **r**:
40: 3 Then Job **r** to the LORD,
42: 1 Then Job **r** to the LORD:
Isa 6:11 And he **r**, "Until their cities are destroyed, with no
36:12 But Sennacherib's representative **r**, "My master
37: 6 the prophet **r**, "Say to your master, 'This is what
39: 3 Hezekiah **r**, "They came from the distant land of
39: 4 asked Isaiah. "They saw everything," Hezekiah **r**.
49: 4 I **r**, "But my work all seems so useless! I have
Jer 1: 7 "Don't say that," the LORD **r**, "for you must go
1:11 And I **r**, "I see a branch from an almond tree."
1:13 And I **r**, "I see a pot of boiling water, tipping from
6:17 But you **r**, 'No! We won't pay attention!'
11: 5 the land you live in today.' " Then I **r**, "So be it,
12: 5 Then the LORD **r** to me, "If racing against mere
15:11 The LORD **r**, "All will be well with you,
15:19 The LORD **r**, "If you return to me, I will restore
18:12 But they **r**, "Don't waste your breath. We will
21: 3 Jeremiah **r**, "Go back to King Zedekiah and tell
22:21 I warned you, but you **r**, 'Don't bother me.'
24: 3 I **r**, "Figs, some very good and some very bad."
38:20 Jeremiah **r**, "You won't be handed over to them if
42: 4 "All right," Jeremiah **r**. "I will pray to the
Eze 37: 3 "O Sovereign LORD," I **r**, "you alone know the
Da 2: 8 The king **r**, "I can see through your trick! You are
2:10 The astrologers **r** to the king, "There isn't a man
2:27 Daniel **r**, "There are no wise men, enchanters,
3:16 Shadrach, Meshach, and Abednego **r**,
4:19 Belteshazzar **r**, "Oh, how I wish the events
6:12 "Yes," the king **r**, "that decision stands; it is a
8:14 The other **r**, "It will take twenty-three hundred
10:20 He **r**, "Do you know why I have come? Soon I
Am 7: 8 And the Lord **r**, "I will test my people with this
7:14 But Amos **r**, "I'm not one of your professional
8: 2 he asked. I **r**, "A basket full of ripe fruit."
Jnh 4: 4 The LORD **r**, "Is it right for you to be angry
Hab 1: 5 The LORD **r**, "Look at the nations and be
Hag 2:12 will it also become holy?" The priests **r**, "No."
Zec 1: 9 those horses for?" "I will show you," the angel **r**.
1:19 He **r**, "These horns represent the world powers
1:21 The angel **r**, "The blacksmiths have come to
2: 2 He **r**, "I am going to measure Jerusalem, to see
4: 5 you know?" the angel asked. "No, my lord," I **r**.
4:13 "Don't you know?" he asked. "No, my lord," I **r**.
5: 2 the angel asked. "I see a flying scroll," I **r**.
5: 6 He **r**, "It is a basket for measuring grain, and it is
5:11 He **r**, "To the land of Babylonia where they will
6: 5 He **r**, "These are the four spirits of heaven who
Mt 9:12 When he heard this, Jesus **r**, "Healthy people
12:25 Jesus knew their thoughts and **r**, "Any kingdom at
12:39 But Jesus **r**, "Only an evil, faithless generation
13:29 "He **r**, 'No, you'll hurt the wheat if you do.
14:16 But Jesus **r**, "That isn't necessary—you feed
15: 3 Jesus **r**, "And why do you, by your traditions,
15:13 Jesus **r**, "Every plant not planted by my heavenly
15:27 "Yes, Lord," she **r**, "but even dogs are permitted
15:33 The disciples **r**, "And where would we get enough
15:34 They **r**, "Seven, and a few small fish."
16: 2 He **r**, "You know the saying, 'Red sky at night
16:14 "Well," they **r**, "some say John the Baptist,
16:17 Jesus **r**, "You are blessed, Simon son of John,
17:11 Jesus **r**, "Elijah is indeed coming first to set
17:17 Jesus **r**, "You stubborn, faithless people!
17:25 "Of course he does," Peter **r**. Then he went into
17:26 "They tax the foreigners," Peter **r**. "Well, then,"
18:22 "No!" Jesus **r**, "seventy times seven!
19: 4 "Haven't you read the Scriptures?" Jesus **r**.
19: 8 Jesus **r**, "Moses permitted divorce as a concession
19:17 Jesus **r**. "Only God is good. But to answer your
19:18 "Which ones?" the man asked. And Jesus **r**:
19:20 all these commandments," the young man **r**.
19:28 And Jesus **r**, "I assure you that when I, the Son of
20: 7 "They **r**, 'Because no one hired us.' "The owner
20:21 She **r**, "In your Kingdom, will you let my two
20:22 to drink?" "Oh yes," they **r**, "we are able!"
21:11 And the crowds **r**, "It's Jesus, the prophet from
21:16 "Yes," Jesus **r**. "Haven't you ever read the
21:24 these things if you answer one question," Jesus **r**.
21:27 So they finally **r**, "We don't know." And Jesus
21:31 They **r**, "The first, of course." Then Jesus
21:41 The religious leaders **r**, "He will put the wicked
22:21 "Caesar's," they **r**. "Well, then," he said,
22:29 Jesus **r**, "Your problem is that you don't know the
22:37 Jesus **r**, " 'You must love the Lord your God with
22:42 son is he?" They **r**, "He is the son of David."
25: 9 But the others **r**, 'We don't have enough for all of
25:26 "But the master **r**, 'You wicked and lazy servant!
26:10 But Jesus **r**, "Why berate her for doing such a
26:23 He **r**, "One of you who is eating with me now will
26:34 "Peter," Jesus **r**, "the truth is, this very night,
26:64 Jesus **r**, "Yes, it is as you say. And in the future
27:11 asked him. Jesus **r**, "Yes, it is as you say."
27:65 Pilate **r**, "Take guards and secure it the best you
Mk 1:38 But he **r**, "We must go on to other towns as well,
2:19 Jesus **r**, "Do wedding guests fast while celebrating
2:25 But Jesus **r**, "Haven't you ever read in the
3:33 Jesus **r**, "Who is my mother? Who are my
4:11 He **r**, "You are permitted to understand the secret
5: 9 And the spirit **r**, "Legion, because there are many
7: 6 Jesus **r**, "You hypocrites! Isaiah was prophesying
7:28 She **r**, "That's true, Lord, but even the dogs under
8: 5 bread do you have?" he asked. "Seven," they **r**.
8:28 "Well," they **r**, "some say John the Baptist,
8:29 you say I am?" Peter **r**, "You are the Messiah."
9:21 the boy's father. He **r**, "Since he was very small.
9:24 The father instantly **r**, "I do believe, but help me
9:29 Jesus **r**, "This kind can be cast out only by
10: 4 "Well, he permitted it," they **r**. "He said a man
10:20 "Teacher," the man **r**, "I've obeyed all these
10:29 And Jesus **r**, "I assure you that everyone who has
11:29 these things if you answer one question," Jesus **r**.
11:33 So they finally **r**, "We don't know." And Jesus
12:16 and title are stamped on it?" "Caesar's," they **r**.
12:24 Jesus **r**, "Your problem is that you don't know the
12:29 Jesus **r**, "The most important commandment is
12:32 The teacher of religious law **r**, "Well said,
13: 2 Jesus **r**, "These magnificent buildings will be
13: 5 Jesus **r**, "Don't let anyone mislead you,
14: 6 But Jesus **r**, "Leave her alone. Why berate her for
14:20 He **r**, "It is one of you twelve, one who is eating
14:30 "Peter," Jesus **r**, "the truth is, this very night,
15: 2 of the Jews?" Jesus **r**, "Yes, it is as you say."
Lk 1:35 The angel **r**, "The Holy Spirit will come upon you,
3:11 John **r**, "If you have two coats, give one to the
3:13 "Show your honesty," he **r**. "Make sure you
3:14 John **r**, "Don't extort money, and don't accuse
4: 8 Jesus **r**, "The Scriptures say, / 'You must worship
4:43 But he **r**, "I must preach the Good News of the
5: 5 "Master," Simon **r**, "we worked hard all last
5:10 also amazed. Jesus **r** to Simon, "Don't be afraid!
6: 3 Jesus **r**, "Haven't you ever read in the Scriptures
7:40 "All right, Teacher," Simon **r**, "go ahead."
8:10 He **r**, "You have been permitted to understand the
8:21 Jesus **r**, "My mother and my brothers are all those
8:30 "Legion," he **r**—for the man was filled with many
9:14 the ground in groups of about fifty each," Jesus **r**.
9:19 "Well," they **r**, "some say John the Baptist,
9:20 Peter **r**, "You are the Messiah sent from God!"
9:58 But Jesus **r**, "Foxes have dens to live in, and birds
9:60 Jesus **r**, "Let those who are spiritually dead care
10:26 Jesus **r**, "What does the law of Moses say?
10:30 Jesus **r** with an illustration: "A Jewish man was
10:37 The man **r**, "The one who showed him mercy."
11:28 He **r**, "But even more blessed are all who hear the
12:14 Jesus **r**, "Friend, who made me a judge over you
12:42 And the Lord **r**, "I'm talking to any faithful,
13:15 But the Lord **r**, "You hypocrite! You work on the
13:23 "Lord, will only a few be saved?" He **r**,
13:32 Jesus **r**, "Go tell that fox that I will keep on
14:16 Jesus **r** with this illustration: "A man prepared a
15:29 but he **r**, 'All these years I've worked hard for you
16: 6 The man **r**, 'I owe him eight hundred gallons of
16:30 "The rich man **r**, 'No, Father Abraham! But if
17:20 Jesus **r**, "The Kingdom of God isn't ushered in
17:37 Jesus **r**, "Just as the gathering of vultures shows
18:21 The man **r**, "I've obeyed all these commandments
18:27 He **r**, "What is impossible from a human
18:29 "Yes," Jesus **r**, "and I assure you, everyone who
19:26 " 'Yes,' the king **r**, 'but to those who use well
19:34 And the disciples simply **r**, "The Lord needs it."
19:40 He **r**, "If they kept quiet, the stones along the road
20: 3 "Let me ask you a question first," he **r**.
20: 7 Finally they **r**, "We don't know."
20:24 and title are stamped on it?" "Caesar's," they **r**.
20:34 Jesus **r**, "Marriage is for people here on earth.
21: 8 He **r**, "Don't let anyone mislead you. For many
22:10 He **r**, "As soon as you enter Jerusalem, a man
22:35 did you lack anything?" "No," they **r**.
22:38 "Lord," they **r**, "we have two swords among us."
22:58 be one of them!" "No, man, I'm not!" Peter **r**.
22:67 But he **r**, "If I tell you, you won't believe me.
22:70 And he **r**, "You are right in saying that I am."
23: 3 of the Jews?" Jesus **r**, "Yes, it is as you say."
23:43 And Jesus **r**, "I assure you, today you will be with
24:18 Then one of them, Cleopas, **r**, "You must be the
Jn 1:21 they asked. "Are you Elijah?" "No," he **r**.
1:23 John **r** in the words of Isaiah: / "I am a voice
1:38 They **r**, "Rabbi" (which means Teacher),
1:48 And Jesus **r**, "I could see you under the fig tree
1:49 Nathanael **r**, "Teacher, you are the Son of God—
2:19 "All right," Jesus **r**. "Destroy this temple, and in
3: 3 Jesus **r**, "I assure you, unless you are born again,
3: 5 Jesus **r**, "The truth is, no one can enter the
3:10 Jesus **r**, "You are a respected Jewish teacher,
3:27 John **r**, "God in heaven appoints each person's
4:10 Jesus **r**, "If you only knew the gift God has for
4:13 Jesus **r**, "People soon become thirsty again after
4:17 "I don't have a husband," the woman **r**.
4:21 Jesus **r**, "Believe me, the time is coming when it
4:52 when the boy had begun to feel better, and they **r**,
5:11 He **r**, "The man who healed me said to me,
5:17 But Jesus **r**, "My Father never stops working,
5:19 Jesus **r**, "I assure you, the Son can do nothing by
6: 7 Philip **r**, "It would take a small fortune to feed
6:26 Jesus **r**, "The truth is, you want to be with me
6:28 They **r**, "What does God want us to do?"
6:30 They **r**, "You must show us a miraculous sign if
6:35 Jesus **r**, "I am the bread of life. No one who comes
6:43 But Jesus **r**, "Don't complain about what I said.
6:68 Simon Peter **r**, "Lord, to whom would we go?
7: 6 Jesus **r**, "Now is not the right time for me to go.
7:20 The crowd **r**, "You're demon possessed!
7:21 Jesus **r**, "I worked on the Sabbath by healing a
7:52 They **r**, "Are you from Galilee, too?
8:13 The Pharisees **r**, "You are making false claims
8:25 Jesus **r**, "I am the one I have always claimed to be.
8:34 Jesus **r**, "I assure you that everyone who sins is a
8:39 "No," Jesus **r**, "for if you were children of
8:41 They **r**, "We were not born out of wedlock!
9:12 is he now?" they asked. "I don't know," he **r**.
9:17 The man **r**, "I think he must be a prophet."
9:20 His parents **r**, "We know this is our son and that
9:25 "I don't know whether he is a sinner," the man **r**.
9:30 "Why, that's very strange!" the man **r**.
9:41 you were blind, you wouldn't be guilty," Jesus **r**.
10:25 Jesus **r**, "I have already told you, and you don't
10:33 They **r**, "Not for any good work, but for
10:34 Jesus **r**, "It is written in your own law that God
11: 9 Jesus **r**, "There are twelve hours of daylight every
12: 7 Jesus **r**, "Leave her alone. She did it in preparation
12:23 Jesus **r**, "The time has come for the Son of Man to
12:35 Jesus **r**, "My light will shine out for you just a
13: 7 Jesus **r**, "You don't understand now why I am
13: 8 Jesus **r**, "But if I don't wash you, you won't
13:10 Jesus **r**, "A person who has bathed all over does
13:36 And Jesus **r**, "You can't go with me now, but you
14: 9 Jesus **r**, "Philip, don't you even yet know who I
14:23 Jesus **r**, "All those who love me will do what I
18: 5 "Jesus of Nazareth," they **r**. "I am he,"
18: 7 And again they **r**, "Jesus of Nazareth."
18:20 Jesus **r**, "What I teach is widely known, because I
18:23 Jesus **r**, "If I said anything wrong, you must give
18:31 to execute someone," the Jewish leaders **r**.
18:34 Jesus **r**, "Is this your own question, or did others
18:37 Pilate **r**, "You are a king then?" "You say that I
19: 7 The Jewish leaders **r**, "By our laws he ought to die
19:22 Pilate **r**, "What I have written, I have written.
20:13 "Because they have taken away my Lord," she **r**,
20:25 But he **r**, "I won't believe it unless I see the nail
21: 5 have you caught any fish?" "No," they **r**.
21:15 "Yes, Lord," Peter **r**, "you know I love you."
21:22 Jesus **r**, "If I want him to remain alive until I
Ac 1: 7 "The Father sets those dates," he **r**, "and they are
2:38 Peter **r**, "Each of you must turn from your sins
4:19 But Peter and John **r**, "Do you think God wants us
5: 8 your land?" "Yes," she **r**, "that was the price."
5:29 But Peter and the apostles **r**, "We must obey God
8:20 But Peter **r**, "May your money perish with you for
8:31 The man **r**, "How can I, when there is no one to
9: 5 And the voice **r**, "I am Jesus, the one you are
9:10 a vision, calling, "Ananias!" "Yes, Lord!" he **r**.
10: 4 And the angel **r**, "Your prayers and gifts to the
10:30 Cornelius **r**, "Four days ago I was praying in my
10:34 Then Peter **r**, "I see very clearly that God doesn't
11: 8 " 'Never, Lord,' I **r**. 'I have never eaten anything
16:31 They **r**, "Believe on the Lord Jesus and you will
16:37 But Paul **r**, "They have publicly beaten us without
19: 2 "No," they **r**, "we don't know what you mean.
19: 3 he asked. And they **r**, "The baptism of John."
19:15 the spirit **r**, "I know Jesus, and I know Paul.
21:39 "No," Paul **r**, "I am a Jew from Tarsus in Cilicia,
22: 8 And he **r**, 'I am Jesus of Nazareth, the one you are
22:27 a Roman citizen?" "Yes, I certainly am," Paul **r**.
23: 5 the high priest," Paul **r**, "for the Scriptures say,
24:25 Felix was terrified. "Go away for now," he **r**.
25: 4 But Festus **r** that Paul was at Caesarea and he
25:10 But Paul **r**, "No! This is the official Roman court,
25:12 Festus conferred with his advisers and then **r**,
25:22 And Festus **r**, "You shall—tomorrow!"
26:15 "And the Lord **r**, 'I am Jesus, the one you are
26:25 But Paul **r**, "I am not insane, Most Excellent
26:29 Paul **r**, "Whether quickly or not, I pray to God that
28:21 They **r**, "We have heard nothing against you.

REPLIES (6) [REPLY]

2Sa 19:43 and the men of Judah were very harsh in their **r**.
Ps 12: 5 The LORD **r**, "I have seen violence done to the
Isa 21:12 The watchman **r**, "Morning is coming, but night
Jer 9:13 The LORD **r**, "This has happened because my
14:10 So the LORD **r** to his people, "You love to
Mal 1: 2 And the LORD **r**, "I showed my love for you by

REPLY (86) [REPLIED, REPLIES]

Ge 24:44 and she will **r**, "Certainly! And I'll water your
24:52 At this **r**, Abraham's servant bowed to the ground
32:18 You should **r**, 'These belong to your servant Jacob.
Ex 12:27 And you will **r**, 'It is the celebration of the
16: 9 and hear his **r** to your complaints.' "

19:19 and God thundered his **r** for all to hear.
Nu 9:9 This was the LORD's **r**:
Dt 27:15 the LORD.' / And all the people will **r**, 'Amen.'
27:16 or mother.' / And all the people will **r**, 'Amen.'
27:17 And all the people will **r**, 'Amen.'
27:18 on the road.' / And all the people will **r**, 'Amen.'
27:19 and widows.' / And all the people will **r**, 'Amen.'
27:20 his father.' / And all the people will **r**, 'Amen.'
27:21 an animal.' / And all the people will **r**, 'Amen.'
27:22 or his mother.' / And all the people will **r**, 'Amen.'
27:23 And all the people will **r**, 'Amen.'
27:24 in secret.' / And all the people will **r**, 'Amen.'
27:25 And all the people will **r**, 'Amen.'
27:26 obeying them.' / And all the people will **r**, 'Amen.'
Jos 22:28 If they say this, our descendants can **r**, 'Look at
Jdg 5:29 A **r** comes from her wise women, / and she repeats
15:6 "Samson," was the **r**, "because his father-in-law
1Sa 2:16 The man offering the sacrifice might **r**, "Take as
14:37 us defeat them?" But God made no **r** that day.
17:27 And David received the same **r** as before:
17:45 David shouted in **r**, "You come to me with sword,
25:9 gave this message to Nabal and waited for his **r**.
25:13 was David's **r** as he strapped on his own.
27:10 And David would **r**, "Against the south of Judah,
28:15 has left me and won't **r** by prophets or dreams.
1Ki 3:10 The Lord was pleased with Solomon's **r** and was
5:8 Then he sent this **r** to Solomon: / "I have received
18:26 answer us!" But there was no **r** of any kind.
18:29 but still there was no **r**, no voice, no answer.
20:12 This **r** of Ahab's reached Ben-hadad and the other
2Ch 2:11 King Hiram sent this letter of **r** to Solomon:
Ezr 4:17 Then Artaxerxes made this **r**: / "To Rehum the
Ne 6:4 same message, and each time I gave the same **r**.
6:8 My **r** was, "You know you are lying. There is no
Est 4:13 Mordecai sent back this **r** to Esther: "Don't think
4:15 Then Esther sent this **r** to Mordecai:
Job 13:22 I will answer! Or let me speak to you, and you **r**.
20:2 "I must **r** because I am greatly disturbed.
20:3 your insults, but now my spirit prompts me to **r**.
22:13 But you **r**, 'That's why God can't see what I am
23:5 Then I would listen to his **r** and understand what
32:1 Job's three friends refused to **r** further to him
32:5 But when he saw that they had no further **r**,
Ps 38:14 I choose to hear nothing, / and I make no **r**.
Pr 15:23 Everyone enjoys a fitting **r**; it is wonderful to say
24:26 It is an honor to receive an honest **r**.
SS 5:6 him anywhere. I called to him, but there was no **r**.
Isa 3:7 "No!" he will **r**. "I can't help. I don't have any
9:11 The LORD will **r** to their bragging by bringing
30:12 This is the **r** of the Holy One of Israel:
58:9 will answer. 'Yes, I am here,' he will quickly **r**.
Jer 3:22 "Yes, we will come," the people **r**, "for you are
5:19 you must **r**, 'You rejected him and gave yourselves
6:16 But you **r**, 'No, that's not the road we want!'
13:12 And they will **r**, 'Of course, you don't need to tell
16:11 Tell them that this is the LORD's **r**: It is
23:33 You must **r**, 'You are the burden! The LORD
33:25 But this is the LORD's **r**: I would no more reject
42:7 Ten days later, the LORD gave his **r** to Jeremiah.
42:9 God of Israel, with your request, and this is his **r**:
48:20 "And the **r** comes back, 'Moab lies in ruins;
Eze 20:1 They sat down in front of me to wait for his **r**.
Hos 2:23 Then they will **r**, 'You are our God!' "
Joel 2:19 He will **r**, "Look! I am sending you grain
Mt 7:23 But I will **r**, 'I never knew you. Go away;
15:23 But Jesus gave her no **r**—not even a word.
22:12 without wedding clothes?' And the man had no **r**.
22:22 His **r** amazed them, and they went away.
22:34 that he had silenced the Sadducees with his **r**,
25:37 "Then these righteous ones will **r**, 'Lord, when did
25:44 "Then they will **r**, 'Lord, when did we ever see
27:21 the crowd shouted back their **r**: "Barabbas!"
Mk 12:17 be given to God." This **r** completely amazed them.
14:61 Jesus made no **r**. Then the high priest asked him,
Lk 13:25 door for us!' But he will **r**, 'I do not know you.'
13:27 And he will **r**, 'I tell you, I don't know you.
16:7 'A thousand bushels of wheat,' was the **r**. 'Here,'
21:15 that none of your opponents will be able to **r**!
Ac 7:2 This was Stephen's **r**: "Brothers and honorable
Ro 11:4 And do you remember God's **r**? He said, "You are
1Co 6:12 But I **r**, "Not everything is good for you."

REPOPULATE (1) [POPULATE]

Ge 9:7 Now you must have many children and **r** the earth.

REPORT (45) [REPORTED, REPORTING, REPORTS]

Ge 24:56 and I want to **r** back to my master."
Ex 22:10 and there is no eyewitness to **r** just what happened.
Nu 13:27 This was their **r** to Moses: "We arrived in the land
Dt 1:28 Our scouts have demoralized us with their **r**.
Jos 14:7 I returned and gave from my heart a good **r**,
18:4 They will return to me with a written **r** of their
18:8 Then return to me with your written **r**, and I will
1Sa 17:26 talked to some others standing there to verify the **r**.
19:19 When the **r** reached Saul that David was at Naioth
23:23 and come back with a more definite **r**.
2Sa 11:18 Then Joab sent a battle **r** to David.
11:19 "**R** all the news of the battle to the king.
11:22 went to Jerusalem and gave a complete **r** to David.
13:30 the way back to Jerusalem, this **r** reached David:
20:4 Judah within three days and to **r** back at that time.
1Ki 13:26 When the old prophet heard the **r**, he said, "It is
2Ki 6:13 And the **r** came back: "Elisha is at Dothan."
9:15 don't let anyone escape to Jezreel to **r** what we
19:1 When King Hezekiah heard their **r**, he tore his
19:7 and the king will receive a **r** from Assyria telling
2Ch 29:18 went to King Hezekiah and gave him this **r**:
35:4 **R** for duty according to the family divisions of
Ezr 5:5 from building until a **r** was sent to Darius
Ne 6:7 "You can be very sure that this **r** will get back to
Est 2:22 king about it and gave Mordecai credit for the **r**.
Pr 22:21 and bring an accurate **r** to those who sent you.
29:24 You will be punished if you **r** the crime, but you
Isa 37:1 When King Hezekiah heard their **r**, he tore his
37:7 **r** from Assyria telling him that he is needed at
Jer 20:10 And they say, "If you say anything, we will **r** it."
Am 1:2 This is his **r** of what he saw and heard:
Mt 9:26 The **r** of this miracle swept through the entire
25:22 with the **r**, 'Sir, you gave me two bags of gold to
Lk 5:15 the **r** of his power spread even faster,
7:17 The **r** of what Jesus had done that day spread all
16:2 Get your **r** in order, because you are going to be
24:22 and they came back with an amazing **r**.
24:33 When they arrived, they were greeted with the **r**,
Jn 11:57 that anyone seeing Jesus must **r** him immediately
19:35 This **r** is from an eyewitness giving an accurate
Ac 15:22 Syria with Paul and Barnabas to **r** on this decision.
16:38 When the police made their **r**, the city officials
1Co 5:1 I can hardly believe the **r** about the sexual
2Co 2:13 brother Titus hadn't yet arrived with a **r** from you.
3Jn 1:10 I will **r** some of the things he is doing

REPORTED (35) [REPORT]

Ge 27:42 of what Esau was planning and **r** it to Rebekah.
37:2 But Joseph **r** to his father some of the bad things
37:5 a dream and promptly **r** the details to his brothers,
Nu 11:24 went out and **r** the LORD's words to the people.
11:27 A young man ran and **r** to Moses, "Eldad
13:26 They **r** to the whole community what they had
14:39 When Moses **r** the LORD's words to the
22:14 the Moabite officials returned to King Balak and **r**,
Dt 1:25 And they **r** that the land the LORD our God had
Jos 2:23 and **r** to Joshua all that had happened to them.
Jdg 9:47 Someone **r** to Abimelech that the people were
1Sa 14:33 Someone **r** to Saul, "Look, the men are sinning
17:31 Then David's question was **r** to King Saul,
18:24 When Saul's men **r** this back to the king,
2Sa 17:15 Then Hushai **r** to Zadok and Abiathar, the priests,
24:9 Joab **r** the number of people to the king.
1Ki 13:25 and they went and **r** it in Bethel, where the old
20:17 As they approached, Ben-hadad's scouts **r** to him,
2Ki 22:9 Shaphan returned to the king and **r**,
1Ch 21:5 and **r** the number of people to David. There were
25:6 Asaph, Jeduthun, and Heman **r** directly to the king.
2Ch 34:16 Shaphan took the scroll to the king and **r**,
Eze 9:11 who carried the writer's case, **r** back and said,
Zec 1:11 Then the other riders **r** to the angel of the LORD,
Mk 6:38 They came back and **r**, "We have five loaves of
16:S Then they **r** all these instructions briefly to Peter
Lk 10:17 disciples returned, they joyfully **r** to him, "Lord,
14:22 had done this, he **r**, 'There is still room for more.'
19:16 The first servant **r** a tremendous gain—ten times as
19:18 "The next servant also **r** a good gain—five times
20:20 something that could be **r** to the Roman governor
Ac 5:22 were gone. So they returned to the council and **r**,
14:27 called the church together and **r** about their trip,
15:4 They **r** on what God had been doing through their
Rev 1:2 John faithfully **r** the word of God

REPORTING (2) [REPORT]

2Ki 11:9 The commanders took charge of the men **r** for duty
2Ch 23:8 The commanders took charge of the men **r** for duty

REPORTS (19) [REPORT]

Ge 18:21 going down to see whether or not these **r** are true.
Ex 23:1 "Do not pass along false **r**. Do not cooperate with
Nu 13:32 So they spread discouraging **r** about the land
14:36 by spreading discouraging **r** about the land
Dt 2:25 When they hear **r** about you, they will tremble
1Sa 2:23 "I have been hearing **r** from the people about the
2:24 The **r** I hear among the LORD's people are not
Ne 6:6 According to his **r**, you plan to be their king.
6:7 He also **r** that you have appointed prophets to
Isa 30:10 We don't want any more of your **r**." They say,
Jer 6:24 We have heard **r** about the enemy, and we are
50:43 The king of Babylon has received **r** about the
Lk 1:2 They used as their source material the **r** circulating
9:7 When **r** of Jesus' miracles reached Herod Antipas,
17:23 "**R** will reach you that the Son of Man has
17:23 Don't believe such **r** or go out to look for him.
Ac 17:8 city officials, were thrown into turmoil by these **r**.
28:21 from Judea or **r** from anyone who has arrived here.
1Th 3:6 He **r** that you remember our visit with joy and that

REPOSE (1)

Job 21:33 the body is laid to rest and the earth gives sweet **r**.

REPRESENT (25) [REPRESENTATIVE, REPRESENTATIVES, REPRESENTED, REPRESENTING, REPRESENTS]

Ge 17:6 I will give you millions of descendants who will **r**
41:26 and the seven plump heads of grain both **r** seven
41:27 and the seven withered heads of grain **r** seven
Ex 28:21 Each stone will **r** one of the tribes of Israel,
34:27 for they **r** the terms of my covenant with you
Lev 24:9 for they **r** a most holy portion of the offerings
1Sa 17:8 to fight for you, and I will **r** the Philistines.
1Ki 18:31 twelve stones, one to **r** each of the tribes of Israel,
Ezr 10:16 Ezra selected leaders to **r** their families,
Jer 24:5 The good figs **r** the exiles I sent from Judah to the
24:8 "**r** King Zedekiah of Judah, his officials,
40:10 I will stay at Mizpah to **r** you before the
Eze 37:11 "Son of man, these bones **r** the people of Israel.
Da 7:17 "These four huge beasts **r** four kingdoms that will
Zec 1:19 "These horns **r** the world powers that scattered
4:10 For these seven lamps **r** the eyes of the LORD
4:14 "They **r** the two anointed ones who assist the Lord
Jn 5:43 even though you readily accept others who **r** only
7:28 But I **r** one you don't know, and he is true.
2Co 3:6 He is the one who has enabled us to **r** his new
Heb 5:1 Now a high priest is a man chosen to **r** other
Rev 17:9 The seven heads of the beast **r** the seven hills of
17:9 where this woman rules. They also **r** seven kings.
17:15 "The waters where the prostitute is sitting **r**
17:16 which **r** ten kings who will reign with him—

REPRESENTATIVE (18) [REPRESENT]

Ex 18:19 You should continue to be the people's **r** before
23:21 forgive your sins. He is my **r**—he bears my name.
2Ki 18:17 and his personal **r** from Lachish with a huge army
18:19 Then the Assyrian king's personal **r** sent this
18:26 of Hilkiah, Shebna, and Joah said to the king's **r**,
18:27 But Sennacherib's **r** replied, "My master wants
18:37 the king and told him what the Assyrian **r** had said.
19:4 has heard the Assyrian **r** defying the living God
19:8 the Assyrian **r** left Jerusalem and went to consult
Isa 36:2 Then the king of Assyria sent his personal **r** with a
36:4 Then the Assyrian king's personal **r** sent this
36:11 Shebna, and Joah said to the king's **r**,
36:12 But Sennacherib's **r** replied, "My master wants
36:22 the king and told him what the Assyrian **r** had said.
37:4 has heard the Assyrian **r** defying the living God
37:8 the Assyrian **r** left Jerusalem and went to consult
Jn 14:26 But when the Father sends the Counselor as my **r**
Col 3:17 you do or say, let it be as a **r** of the Lord Jesus,

REPRESENTATIVES (3) [REPRESENT]

Ezr 10:16 their families, designating each of the **r** by name.
Ac 15:25 to send you these official **r**, along with our beloved
2Co 8:23 help you. And these brothers are **r** of the churches.

REPRESENTED (3) [REPRESENT]

Jdg 21:5 "Was any tribe of Israel not **r** when we held our
1Sa 6:18 The five gold rats **r** the five Philistine cities
Da 2:39 great kingdom, **r** by the bronze belly and thighs,

REPRESENTING (7) [REPRESENT]

Lev 17:11 It is the blood, **r** life, that brings you atonement.
23:20 together with the loaves **r** the first of your later
Nu 17:8 **r** the tribe of Levi, had sprouted, blossomed,
Jer 35:3 his brothers and sons—**r** all the Recabite families.
Jn 5:43 For I have come to you **r** my Father, and you
Rev 13:17 the name of the beast or the number **r** his name.
15:2 the beast and his statue and the number **r** his name.

REPRESENTS (28) [REPRESENT]

Dt 17:12 or of the priest who **r** the LORD your God must
21:17 who **r** the strength of his father's manhood
Isa 52:11 with everything it **r**, for it is unclean to you.
Eze 37:16 'This stick **r** Judah and its allied tribes.' Then take
37:16 on it: 'This stick **r** the northern tribes of Israel.'
Da 8:20 The two-horned ram **r** the kings of Media
8:21 The shaggy male goat **r** the king of Greece,
8:21 and the large horn between its eyes **r** the first king
Am 8:2 LORD said, "This fruit **r** my people of Israel—
Mt 13:19 The seed that fell on the hard path **r** those who
13:20 The rocky soil **r** those who hear the message
13:22 The thorny ground **r** those who hear and accept the
13:23 The good soil **r** the hearts of those who truly
13:38 and the good seed **r** the people of the Kingdom.
Mk 4:15 The seed that fell on the hard path **r** those who
4:16 The rocky soil **r** those who hear the message
4:18 The thorny ground **r** those who hear and accept the
4:20 But the good soil **r** those who hear and accept
Lk 8:12 The seed that fell on the hard path **r** those who
8:13 The rocky soil **r** those who hear the message with
8:14 The thorny ground **r** those who hear and accept the
8:15 But the good soil **r** honest, good-hearted people
Gal 4:24 **r** Mount Sinai where people first became enslaved
4:26 the free woman, **r** the heavenly Jerusalem.
Heb 1:3 and everything about him **r** God exactly.
9:8 and the entire system it **r** were still in use.
Rev 17:18 And this woman you saw in your vision **r** the great
19:8 (Fine linen **r** the good deeds done by the people of

REPRIEVE (1)

Joel 2:14 Perhaps even yet he will give you a **r**, sending you

REPRIMAND (1)

Pr 29:15 To discipline and **r** a child produces wisdom,

REPROACH (1)

Ps 101:6 Only those who are above **r** / will be allowed to

REPROBATE(S) [KJV] See COUNTERFEIT, EVIL, REJECTED, WORTHLESS

REPRODUCE (3) [PRODUCE]

Ge 1:25 small animals, each able to **r** more of its own kind.
8:17 so they can breed and **r** in great numbers."

Jn 3: 6 Humans can **r** only human life, but the Holy Spirit

REPROOF (1) [REPROVE]

Pr 10: 10 wrong cause trouble, but a bold **r** promotes peace.

REPROOF, REPROVE [KJV] See also ACCUSE, CONVICT, CONVINCE, CORRECT, DECIDE, EXPOSE, PROVE, REBUKE(D)

REPROVE (2) [REPROOF]

Ps 141: 5 a kindness! / If they **r** me, it is soothing medicine.
Pr 19: 25 if you **r** the wise, they will be all the wiser.

REPTILES (5)

1Ki 4: 33 could also speak about animals, birds, **r**, and fish.
Ps 148: 10 wild animals and all livestock, / **r** and birds,
Ac 10: 12 In the sheet were all sorts of animals, **r**, and birds.
11: 6 I saw all sorts of small animals, wild animals, **r**,
Jas 3: 7 tame all kinds of animals and birds and **r** and fish,

REPULSIVE (1)

Job 19: 17 My breath is **r** to my wife. I am loathsome to my

REPUTATION (23)

Dt 1: 13 understanding, and a good **r**, and I will appoint
2Sa 14: 2 So he sent for a woman from Tekoa who had a **r**
1Ki 10: 1 When the queen of Sheba heard of Solomon's **r**,
1Ch 5: 24 Each of these men had a great **r** as a warrior
2Ch 9: 1 When the queen of Sheba heard of Solomon's **r**,
Ne 9: 10 You have a glorious **r** that has never been
13: 13 These men had an excellent **r**, and it was their job
Ps 4: 2 How long will you people ruin my **r**? / How long
89: 16 They rejoice all day long in your wonderful **r**.
109: 21 O Sovereign LORD, / for the sake of your own **r**!
Pr 3: 4 both God and people, and you will gain a good **r**.
22: 1 Choose a good **r** over great riches, for being held
24: 8 A person who plans evil will get a **r** as a
25: 10 of gossip. Then you will never regain your good **r**.
Ecc 7: 1 A good **r** is more valuable than the most expensive
Isa 63: 12 lifted up his hand, establishing his **r** forever?
63: 14 LORD, and gained a magnificent **r**."
Jer 14: 7 So please, help us for the sake of your own **r**.
Eze 39: 25 mercy on Israel, for I am jealous for my holy **r**!
Lk 11: 8 you what you want so his **r** won't be damaged.
Gal 2: 6 their **r** as great leaders made no difference to me,
1Ti 3: 2 exhibit self-control, live wisely, and have a good **r**.
Rev 3: 1 you do, and that you have a **r** for being alive—

REQUEST (62) [REQUESTED, REQUESTING, REQUESTS]

Ge 18: 29 Then Abraham pressed his **r** further.
19: 21 "All right," the angel said, "I will grant your **r**.
19: 29 But God had listened to Abraham's **r** and kept Lot
24: 14 This is my **r**. I will ask one of them for a drink.
30: 6 He has heard my **r** and given me a son."
34: 19 and Shechem lost no time in acting on this **r**,
47: 4 We **r** permission to live in the land of Goshen."
47: 29 most solemnly that you will honor this, my last **r**:
50: 6 Pharaoh agreed to Joseph's **r**. "Go and bury your
Ex 33: 18 Then Moses had one more **r**. "Please let me see
Nu 21: 3 The LORD heard their **r** and gave them victory
22: 5 He sent this message to **r** that Balaam come to help
Dt 5: 28 "The LORD heard your **r** and said to me, 'I have
Jos 10: 14 when the LORD answered such a **r** from a human
Jdg 6: 39 be angry with me, but let me make one more **r**.
8: 24 However, I have one **r**. Each of you can give me
11: 17 But their **r** was denied. Then they asked the king of
1Sa 1: 17 May the God of Israel grant the **r** you have asked
1: 19 slept with Hannah, the LORD remembered her **r**,
1: 27 to give me this child, and he has given me my **r**.
8: 6 Samuel was very upset with their **r** and went to the
12: 13 asked for him, and the LORD has granted your **r**.
2Sa 14: 22 your approval, for you have granted me this **r**!"
1Ki 2: 17 my behalf, for I know he will do anything you **r**.
2: 20 "I have one small **r** to make of you," she said.
2: 23 dead if Adonijah has not sealed his fate with this **r**.
8: 28 Listen to my prayer and my **r**, O LORD my God.
9: 3 said to him, "I have heard your prayer and your **r**.
12: 16 all Israel realized that the king had rejected their **r**,
15: 20 Ben-hadad agreed to King Asa's **r** and sent his
2Ki 2: 10 I am taken from you, then you will get your **r**.
1Ch 4: 10 all trouble and pain!" And God granted him his **r**.
2Ch 6: 19 Listen to my prayer and my **r**, O LORD my God.
10: 16 all Israel realized that the king had rejected their **r**,
16: 4 Ben-hadad agreed to King Asa's **r** and sent his
33: 13 listened to him and was moved by his **r** for help.
Ezr 5: 17 we **r** that you search in the royal archives of
Est 5: 3 do you want, Queen Esther? What is your **r**?
5: 6 What is your **r**? I will give it to you, even if it is
5: 7 Esther replied, "This is my **r** and deepest wish.
5: 8 is pleased with me and wants to grant my **r**,
7: 2 me what you want, Queen Esther. What is your **r**?
7: 3 is pleased with me and wants to grant my **r**,
Job 6: 8 "Oh, that I might have my **r**, that God would grant
Ps 21: 4 to preserve his life, / and you have granted his **r**.
Jer 42: 9 the God of Israel, with your **r**, and this is his reply:
Eze 17: 15 sending ambassadors to Egypt to **r** a great army
20: 1 some of the leaders of Israel came to **r** a message
Da 2: 49 At Daniel's **r**, the king appointed Shadrach,
9: 18 "O my God, listen to me and hear my **r**.
10: 12 before your God, your **r** has been heard in heaven.
Hos 9: 14 O LORD, what should I **r** for your people?
Mt 15: 28 to her, "your faith is great. Your **r** is granted."
20: 21 "What is your **r**?" he asked. She replied, "In your
27: 64 So we **r** that you seal the tomb until the third day.
Jn 15: 7 you may ask any **r** you like, and it will be granted!
16: 23 and he will grant your **r** because you use my name.
Ac 21: 26 So Paul agreed to their **r**, and the next day he went
23: 21 They are ready, expecting you to agree to their **r**."
2Co 8: 17 He welcomed our **r** that he visit you again. In fact,
Phm 1: 9 So take this as a **r** from your friend Paul, an old
1Jn 3: 22 And we will receive whatever we **r** because we

REQUESTED (20) [REQUEST]

Ex 10: 11 and serve the LORD, for that is what you **r**."
12: 31 all of you! Go and serve the LORD as you have **r**.
Nu 14: 20 LORD said, "I will pardon them as you have **r**.
Dt 18: 16 For this is what you yourselves **r** of the LORD
18: 17 LORD said to me, 'Fine, I will do as they have **r**.
1Ki 12: 12 hear Rehoboam's decision, just as the king had **r**.
2Ch 1: 12 give you the wisdom and knowledge you **r**.
4: 16 of the LORD, just as King Solomon had **r**.
10: 12 hear Rehoboam's decision, just as the king had **r**.
Est 2: 14 he had especially enjoyed her and **r** her by name.
5: 5 to come quickly to a banquet, as Esther has **r**."
Ps 21: 2 you have held back nothing that he **r**.
137: 3 Our tormentors **r** a joyful hymn: / "Sing us one of
Jer 36: 15 to us," the officials said, and Baruch did as they **r**.
37: 17 Later King Zedekiah secretly **r** that Jeremiah come
Da 2: 16 went at once to see the king and **r** more time
Mk 15: 6 each year at Passover time—anyone the people **r**.
Lk 23: 25 As they had **r**, he released Barabbas, the man in
Ac 9: 2 He **r** letters addressed to the synagogues in
23: 15 to bring Paul back to the council again," they **r**.

REQUESTING (1) [REQUEST]

Eze 20: 31 message even though you have come to me **r** one.

REQUESTS (14) [REQUEST]

1Ki 8: 30 May you hear the humble and earnest **r** from me
8: 52 "May your eyes be open to my **r** and to the **r** of your people Israel.
8: 54 finished making these prayers and **r** to the LORD,
2Ch 6: 21 May you hear the humble and earnest **r** from me
Ezr 7: 21 'You are to give Ezra whatever he **r** of you, for he
Ne 2: 8 And the king granted these **r**, because the gracious
Ps 5: 3 Each morning I bring my **r** to you and wait
Isa 43: 23 and wearied you with my **r** for grain offerings
Eze 36: 37 and I am ready to grant them their **r**.
Lk 18: 5 she is wearing me out with her constant **r**!' "
Php 1: 4 for you, and I make my **r** with a heart full of joy
1Ti 2: 1 As you make your **r**, plead for God's mercy upon
1Jn 5: 15 if we know he is listening when we make our **r**,

REQUIRE (9) [REQUIRED, REQUIREMENT, REQUIREMENTS, REQUIRES, REQUIRING]

Ge 34: 11 my wife," he begged. "I will give whatever you **r**.
Ex 10: 26 And we won't know which sacrifices he will **r**
Lev 22: 16 upon the people and **r** them to pay compensation.
Nu 5: 26 Then he will **r** the woman to drink the water.
Dt 10: 12 Israel, what does the LORD your God **r** of you?
Ps 40: 6 you don't **r** burnt offerings or sin offerings.
Eze 20: 40 There I will **r** that you bring me all your offerings
1Co 12: 24 while other parts do not **r** this special care. So God
Col 2: 23 may seem wise because they **r** strong devotion,

REQUIRED (59) [REQUIRE]

Ex 22: 11 the neighbor's word, and no payment will be **r**.
22: 13 be shown as evidence, and no payment will be **r**.
22: 15 But if the owner is there, no payment is **r**. And no payment is **r** if the animal was rented
38: 27 and for the posts supporting the inner curtain **r**
Lev 14: 32 normally **r** for the ceremony of cleansing."
15: 5 you will be **r** to wash your clothes and bathe in
15: 6 you will be **r** to wash your clothes and bathe in
15: 10 you will be **r** to wash your clothes and bathe in
15: 11 then you will be **r** to wash your clothes and bathe
15: 27 You will be **r** to wash your clothes and bathe in
27: 16 its value will be assessed by the amount of seed **r**
Nu 4: 31 They will be **r** to carry the frames of the
5: 22 And the woman will be **r** to say, "Yes, let it be
6: 21 beyond what is **r** by their normal Nazirite vow,
7: 9 since they were **r** to carry the sacred objects of the
19: 2 "Here is another ritual law **r** by the LORD:
1Ki 8: 31 and is **r** to take an oath of innocence in front of the
2Ki 12: 15 No accounting was **r** from the construction
2Ch 6: 22 and is **r** to take an oath of innocence in front of the
24: 5 towns of Judah and collect the **r** annual offerings,
24: 9 of God, had **r** of the Israelites in the wilderness.
31: 3 and for the other annual festivals as **r** in the law of
31: 4 he **r** the people in Jerusalem to bring the prescribed
34: 32 And he **r** everyone in Jerusalem and the people of
34: 33 and **r** everyone to worship the LORD their God.
Ezr 3: 5 and the offerings **r** for the new moon celebrations
7: 24 or other worker in this Temple of God will be **r** to
Ne 5: 16 And I **r** all my officials to spend time working on
5: 18 The provisions **r** at my expense for each day were
8: 18 held a solemn assembly, as the law of Moses **r**.
10: 34 on the altar of the LORD our God, as **r** in the law.
12: 44 these from the fields as **r** by the law for the priests
12: 45 as **r** by the laws of David and his son Solomon,
Ps 81: 4 For this is **r** by the laws of Israel; / it is a law of the
Eze 45: 17 The prince will be **r** to provide offerings that are
45: 25 and the grain offering, along with the **r** olive oil.
Jnh 3: 8 Everyone is **r** to wear sackcloth and pray earnestly
Mt 8: 4 Take along the offering **r** in the law of Moses for
Mk 1: 44 Take along the offering **r** in the law of Moses for
7: 3 their cupped hands, as **r** by their ancient traditions.
11: 23 All that's **r** is that you really believe and do not
12: 33 of the burnt offerings and sacrifices **r** in the law."
Lk 2: 22 as **r** by the law of Moses after the birth of a child;
2: 24 So they offered a sacrifice according to what was **r**
2: 27 to present the baby Jesus to the Lord as the law **r**,
5: 14 Take along the offering **r** in the law of Moses for
11: 38 the ceremonial washing **r** by Jewish custom.
12: 48 Much is **r** from those to whom much is given, and much more is **r** from those to whom much
23: 56 so they rested all that day as **r** by the law.
Ac 15: 5 and be **r** to follow the law of Moses.
1Co 7: 15 or wife is not **r** to stay with them,
Heb 8: 3 And since every high priest is **r** to offer gifts
8: 4 since there already are priests who offer the gifts **r**
9: 18 That is why blood was **r** under the first covenant as
10: 8 them" (though they are **r** by the law of Moses).
Rev 13: 12 And he **r** all the earth and those who belong to this
13: 16 He **r** everyone—great and small, rich and poor,

REQUIREMENT (5) [REQUIRE]

Nu 27: 11 Israelites must observe this as a general legal **r**,
31: 21 "The LORD has given Moses this **r** of the law:
Ro 8: 4 so that the **r** of the law would be fully
Heb 7: 16 not by meeting the old **r** of belonging to the tribe
7: 18 the old **r** about the priesthood was set aside

REQUIREMENTS (11) [REQUIRE]

Ge 26: 5 Abraham listened to me and obeyed all my **r**,
Dt 11: 1 must love the LORD your God and obey all his **r**,
1Ki 2: 3 Observe the **r** of the LORD your God and follow
4: 22 The daily food **r** for Solomon's palace were 150
Eze 44: 16 They are the ones who will fulfill all my **r**.
Da 6: 5 will be in connection with the **r** of his religion."
Zec 3: 7 If you follow my ways and obey my **r**, then you
Lk 2: 39 When Jesus' parents had fulfilled all the **r** of the
Ac 15: 28 to us to lay no greater burden on you than these **r**:
Ro 8: 8 you will fulfill all the **r** of God's law.
13: 10 wrong to anyone, so love satisfies all of God's **r**.

REQUIRES (14) [REQUIRE]

Ge 38: 8 as our law **r** of the brother of a man who has died.
Lev 8: 35 for seven days, doing everything the LORD **r**.
Dt 10: 12 He **r** you to fear him, to live according to his will,
Ru 4: 5 your purchase of the land from Naomi also **r** that
Ne 10: 36 of all our herds and flocks, just as the law **r**.
Ps 122: 4 thanks to the name of the LORD / as the law **r**.
Ecc 10: 10 Since a dull ax **r** great strength, sharpen the blade.
Jer 5: 5 the LORD's ways and what God **r** of them."
8: 7 They do not know what the LORD **r** of them.
Da 2: 11 This is an impossible thing the king **r**. No one
Mic 6: 8 told you what is good, and this is what he **r**:
Lk 3: 13 more taxes than the Roman government **r** you to."
Jn 14: 31 but I will do what the Father **r** of me, so that the
Ro 10: 5 right with God **r** obedience to all of its commands.

REQUIRING (4) [REQUIRE]

1Ki 15: 22 **r** that everyone, without exception, help to carry
2Ki 23: 35 **r** them to pay in proportion to their wealth.
Da 1: 20 In all matters **r** wisdom and balanced judgment,
3: 10 You issued a decree **r** all the people to bow down

REQUISITION (1)

Ezr 7: 20 you may **r** funds from the royal treasury.

REQUITE(D), REQUITING [KJV] See also PAID (BACK), PAY (BACK), REPAY, REPAYING, REPAYMENT, RETURNED, REWARD

REREWARD [KJV] See REAR (GUARD)

RESCUE (174) [RESCUED, RESCUES, RESCUING]

Ge 32: 11 O LORD, please **r** me from my brother, Esau.
37: 21 But Reuben came to Joseph's **r**. "Let's not kill
Ex 3: 8 So I have come to **r** them from the Egyptians
3: 17 I promise to **r** you from the oppression of the
5: 23 your people. You have not even begun to **r** them!"
14: 13 stand where you are and watch the LORD **r** you.
18: 8 the LORD had done to **r** Israel from Pharaoh
Nu 10: 9 will remember you and **r** you from your enemies.
Dt 22: 27 that she screamed, but there was no one to **r** her.
25: 11 and the wife of one tries to **r** her husband by
Jos 10: 7 Israelite army left Gilgal and set out to **r** Gibeon.
Jdg 2: 16 Then the LORD raised up judges to **r** the
3: 9 for help, the LORD raised up a man to **r** them.
3: 15 for help, the LORD raised up a man to **r** them.
6: 14 strength you have and **r** Israel from the Midianites.
6: 15 "But Lord," Gideon replied, "how can I **r** Israel?
6: 36 "If you are truly going to use me to **r** Israel as you
6: 37 then I will know that you are going to help me **r**
7: 7 "With these three hundred men I will **r** you
10: 1 of Puah and descendant of Dodo, came to **r** Israel.
10: 11 "Did I not **r** you from the Egyptians, the Amorites,
10: 13 served other gods. So I will not **r** you anymore.
10: 14 Let them **r** you in your hour of distress!"
10: 15 as you see fit, only **r** us today from our enemies."
13: 5 from birth. He will **r** Israel from the Philistines."
18: 28 There was no one to **r** the residents of the town,

1Sa 7: 3 then he will **r** you from the Philistines.”
9: 16 He will **r** them from the Philistines, for I have
11: 9 to say, “We will **r** you by noontime tomorrow!”
12: 8 he sent Moses and Aaron to **r** them from Egypt
12: 10 and you alone if you will **r** us from our enemies.’
12: 21 worthless idols that cannot help or **r** you—
17: 47 the LORD does not need weapons to **r** his people.
24: 15 my advocate, and he will **r** me from your power!”
26: 24 yours today. May he **r** me from all my troubles.”
2Sa 14: 16 and **r** us from those who would cut us off from
21: 17 But Abishai son of Zeruiah came to his **r**
22: 28 You **r** those who are humble, / but your eyes are
22: 42 They called for help, but no one came to **r** them.
2Ki 11: 15 of the Temple, and kill anyone who tries to **r** her.
13: 5 So the LORD raised up a deliverer to **r** the
16: 7 and **r** me from the attacking armies of Aram
17: 39 He is the one who will **r** you from all your
18: 29 He will never be able to **r** you from my power.
18: 30 in the LORD by saying, ‘The LORD will **r** us!
18: 32 to mislead you by saying, ‘The LORD will **r** us!’
18: 34 and Ivvah? Did they **r** Samaria from my power?
18: 35 So what makes you think that the LORD can **r**
19: 19 Now, O LORD our God, **r** us from his power;
20: 6 and I will **r** you and this city from the king of
1Ch 16: 35 Gather and **r** us from among the nations,
2Ch 20: 9 to you to save us, and you will hear us and **r** us.’
23: 14 of the Temple, and kill anyone who tries to **r** her.
32: 11 ‘The LORD our God will **r** us from the king of
32: 13 Were any of the gods of those nations able to **r**
32: 14 anywhere, was able to **r** his people from me!
32: 15 no god of any nation has ever yet been able to **r** his
32: 15 How much less will your God **r** you from my
32: 17 “Just as the gods of all the other nations failed to **r**
Job 5: 19 He will **r** you again and again so that no evil can
6: 23 Have I ever asked you to **r** me from my enemies?
10: 7 I am not guilty, no one can **r** me from your power.
Ps 3: 2 So many are saying, / “God will never **r** him!”
3: 7 Arise, O LORD! / **R** me, my God! / Slap all my
6: 4 Return, O LORD, and **r** me. / Save me because of
7: 1 my God. / Save me from my persecutors—**r** me!
7: 2 a lion, / tearing me to pieces with no one to **r** me.
12: 5 Now I will rise up to **r** them, / as they have longed
14: 7 that salvation would come from Mount Zion to **r**
17: 13 **R** me from the wicked with your sword!
18: 27 You **r** those who are humble, / but you humiliate
18: 41 They called for help, but no one came to **r** them.
20: 6 his holy heaven / and **r** him by his great power.
22: 8 loves him so much, / let the LORD **r** him!”
22: 20 **R** me from a violent death; / spare my precious life
25: 15 for he alone can **r** me from the traps of my
25: 20 Protect me! **R** my life from them! / Do not let me
31: 1 to shame. / **R** me, for you always do what is right.
31: 2 Bend down and listen to me; / **r** me quickly.
31: 5 **R** me, LORD, for you are a faithful God.
31: 15 **R** me from those who hunt me down relentlessly.
35: 17 and do nothing? / **R** me from their fierce attacks.
39: 8 **R** me from my rebellion, / for even fools mock me
40: 13 Please, LORD, **r** me! / Come quickly, LORD,
43: 1 ungodly people. / **R** me from these unjust liars.
50: 15 me in your times of trouble, / and I will **r** you,
53: 6 that salvation would come from Mount Zion to **r**
54: 1 Come with great power, O God, and **r** me!
54: 7 For you will **r** me from my troubles / and help me
55: 16 But I will call on God, / and the LORD will **r** me.
59: 1 **R** me from my enemies, O God. / Protect me from
59: 2 **R** me from these criminals; / save me from these
59: 9 You are my strength; I wait for you to **r** me,
60: 5 right arm to save us, / and **r** your beloved people.
69: 14 sink any deeper! / **R** me from those who hate me,
69: 18 Come and **r** me; / free me from all my enemies.
69: 29 and in pain. / **R** me, O God, by your saving power.
70: 1 Please, God, **r** me! / Come quickly, LORD,
71: 2 **R** me! Save me from my enemies, for you are just.
71: 4 My God, **r** me from the power of the wicked,
72: 4 to defend the poor, / to **r** the children of the needy,
72: 12 He will **r** the poor when they cry to him; / he will
72: 13 for the weak and the needy, / and he will **r** them.
76: 9 O God, / and to **r** the oppressed of the earth.
80: 2 Show us your mighty power. / Come to **r** us!
82: 4 **R** the poor and helpless; / deliver them from the
91: 3 For he will **r** you from every trap / and protect you
91: 14 The LORD says, “I will **r** those who love me.
91: 15 them in trouble. / I will **r** them and honor them.
108: 6 right arm to save me, / and **r** your beloved people.
109: 21 **R** me because you are so faithful and good.
119: 134 **R** me from the oppression of evil people; / then I
119: 153 Look down upon my sorrows and **r** me, / for I have
119: 170 Listen to my prayer; / **r** me as you promised.
120: 2 **R** me, O LORD, from liars / and from all
140: 1 O LORD, **r** me from evil people. / Preserve me
142: 6 for I am very low. / **R** me from my persecutors,
144: 7 Reach down from heaven and **r** me; / deliver me
144: 11 **R** me from the power of my enemies.
Pr 19: 19 If you **r** them once, you will have to do it again.
24: 11 **R** those who are unjustly sentenced to death;
Ecc 8: 8 wickedness will certainly not **r** those who practice
Isa 5: 29 into captivity, and no one will be there to **r** them.
19: 20 he will send them a savior who will **r** them.
26: 18 We have done nothing to **r** the world;
31: 5 and save the city; he will pass over it and **r** it.”
36: 14 deceive you. He will never be able to **r** you.
36: 15 in the LORD by saying, ‘The LORD will **r** us!
36: 18 mislead you by saying, ‘The LORD will **r** us!’
36: 19 Did they **r** Samaria from my power?
36: 20 So what makes you think that the LORD can **r**
37: 20 Now, O LORD our God, **r** us from his power;
38: 6 and I will **r** you and this city from the king of
44: 17 worshiping and praying to it. “**R** me!” he says.
48: 11 I will **r** you for my sake—yes, for my own sake!
50: 2 Is it because I have no power to **r**? No, that is not
56: 1 is right and good, for I am coming soon to **r** you.
Jer 15: 21 wicked men. I will **r** you from their cruel hands.”
21: 12 have been robbed; **r** them from their oppressors.
22: 3 have been robbed; **r** them from their oppressors.
39: 17 but I will **r** you from those you fear so much.
42: 11 and will save you and **r** you from his power.
La 5: 8 become our masters; there is no one left to **r** us.
Eze 13: 23 For I will **r** my people from your grasp.
34: 10 I will **r** my flock from their mouths; the sheep will
34: 12 and **r** them from all the places to which they were
34: 22 So I will **r** my flock, and they will no longer be
Da 3: 15 What god will be able to **r** you from my power
3: 17 He will **r** us from your power, Your Majesty.
3: 28 He sent his angel to **r** his servants who trusted in
3: 29 There is no other god who can **r** like this!”
6: 16 your God, whom you worship continually, **r** you.”
6: 17 so that no one could **r** Daniel from the lions.
6: 20 worship continually, able to **r** you from the lions?”
8: 7 There was no one who could **r** the ram from the
Hos 2: 10 No one will be able to **r** her from my hands.
5: 14 them off, and there will be no one left to **r** them.
Am 3: 12 “A shepherd who tries to **r** a sheep from a lion’s
5: 18 then the LORD would **r** us from all our
Mic 4: 10 But the LORD will **r** you there; he will redeem
5: 6 They will **r** us from the Assyrians when they pour
5: 8 will be like helpless sheep, with no one to **r** them.
Hab 3: 13 You went out to **r** your chosen people, to save your
Zec 8: 7 You can be sure that I will **r** my people from the
8: 13 Now I will **r** you and make you both a symbol
9: 16 the LORD their God will **r** his people,
Lk 2: 25 eagerly expected the Messiah to come and **r** Israel.
24: 21 he was the Messiah who had come to **r** Israel.
Ac 7: 25 would realize that God had sent him to **r** them,
7: 34 So I have come to **r** them. Now go, for I will send
2Co 1: 11 He will **r** us because you are helping by praying
Gal 1: 4 in order to **r** us from this evil world in which we
2Pe 2: 9 the Lord knows how to **r** godly people from their
Jude 1: 23 **R** others by snatching them from the flames of

RESCUED (87) [RESCUE]

Ge 34: 26 They **r** Dinah from Shechem’s house and returned
Ex 2: 19 “An Egyptian **r** us from the shepherds,” they told
6: 7 God who has **r** you from your slavery in Egypt.
13: 9 it was the LORD who **r** you from Egypt with
14: 30 This was how the LORD **r** Israel from the
18: 10 He has **r** Israel from the power of Egypt!
20: 2 your God, who **r** you from slavery in Egypt.
Lev 22: 33 It was I who **r** you from Egypt, that I might be
23: 43 in shelters when I **r** them from the land of Egypt.
Nu 32: 11 ‘Of all those I **r** from Egypt, no one who is twenty
Dt 4: 20 Remember that the LORD **r** you from the burning
5: 6 your God, who **r** you from slavery in Egypt.
6: 12 who **r** you from slavery in the land of Egypt.
7: 8 That is why the LORD **r** you with such amazing
8: 14 who **r** you from slavery in the land of Egypt.
13: 10 who **r** you from the land of Egypt, the place of
Jos 22: 31 you have **r** Israel from being destroyed by the
24: 10 Balaam bless you, and so I **r** you from Balak.
24: 17 For the LORD our God is the one who **r** us
Jdg 2: 18 and **r** the people from their enemies throughout the
3: 31 After Ehud, Shamgar son of Anath **r** Israel.
6: 9 and **r** you from the Egyptians and from all who
8: 22 will be our rulers, for you have **r** us from Midian.”
8: 34 who had **r** them from all their enemies surrounding
9: 17 and risked his life when he **r** you from the
10: 12 oppressed you, you cried out to me, and I **r** you.
1Sa 10: 18 you from Egypt and **r** you from the Egyptians
11: 13 for today the LORD has **r** Israel!”
14: 39 I vow by the name of the LORD who **r** Israel that
14: 45 So the people **r** Jonathan, and he was not put to
23: 5 took all their livestock and **r** the people of Keilah.
30: 18 the Amalekites had taken, and he **r** his two wives.
2Sa 7: 23 You made a great name for yourself when you **r**
18: 31 Today the LORD has **r** you from all those who
22: 1 after the LORD had **r** him from all his enemies
22: 17 “He reached down from heaven and **r** me;
22: 20 of safety; / he **r** me because he delights in me.
1Ki 1: 29 LORD lives, who has **r** me from every danger,
2Ki 18: 33 Have the gods of other nations **r** them—
1Ch 17: 21 You made a great name for yourself when you **r**
2Ch 32: 22 That is how the LORD **r** Hezekiah and the people
Ne 1: 10 the people you **r** by your great power and might.
9: 27 you sent them deliverers who **r** them from their
9: 28 In your wonderful mercy, you **r** them repeatedly!
Job 22: 30 Then even sinners will be **r** by your pure hands.”
33: 28 God **r** me from the grave, and now my life is filled
Ps 9: 14 so I can rejoice that you have **r** me.
13: 5 I will rejoice because you have **r** me.
18: T on the day the LORD **r** him from all his enemies
18: 16 He reached down from heaven and **r** me; / he drew
18: 19 of safety; / he **r** me because he delights in me.
22: 4 Our ancestors trusted in you, / and you **r** them.
30: 1 I will praise you, LORD, for you have **r** me.
56: 13 For you have **r** me from death; / you have kept my
78: 42 his power / and how he **r** them from their enemies.
81: 10 your God, / who **r** you from the land of Egypt.
86: 13 You have **r** me from the depths of death!
106: 10 So he **r** them from their enemies / and redeemed
107: 6 in their trouble, / and he **r** them from their distress.
118: 5 and the LORD answered me and **r** me.
144: 10 You are the one who **r** your servant David.
Pr 28: 18 The honest will be **r** from harm, but those who are
Ecc 9: 15 who knew how to save the town, and so it was **r**.
Isa 37: 12 Have the gods of other nations **r** them—
38: 17 suffer this anguish, / for you have **r** me from death
59: 11 We look to be **r**, but it is far away from us.
63: 9 he also suffered, and he personally **r** them.
Jer 16: 14 who **r** the people of Israel from the land of Egypt.’
23: 7 who **r** the people of Israel from the land of Egypt.’
34: 13 ago when I **r** them from their slavery in Egypt.
41: 16 his officers led away all the people they had **r**—
Eze 34: 27 and **r** them from those who enslaved them,
Da 6: 27 in the heavens and on earth. / He has **r** Daniel
12: 1 people whose name is written in the book will be **r**.
Hos 12: 9 your God, who **r** you from your slavery in Egypt.
13: 4 your God, who **r** you from your slavery in Egypt.
Am 2: 10 It was I who **r** you from Egypt and led you through
3: 1 and Judah—the entire family I **r** from Egypt:
3: 12 So it will be when the Israelites in Samaria are **r**
Mic 7: 15 like those I did when I **r** you from slavery in
Lk 1: 74 We have been **r** from our enemies, / so we can
Ro 15: 31 Pray that I will be **r** from those in Judea who
Gal 3: 13 But Christ has **r** us from the curse pronounced by
Col 1: 13 For he has **r** us from the one who rules in the
1Th 1: 10 He is the one who has **r** us from the terrors of the
2Pe 2: 7 God **r** Lot out of Sodom because he was a good
Jude 1: 5 that even though the Lord **r** the whole nation of

RESCUES (24) [RESCUE]

2Sa 22: 49 and **r** me from my enemies. / You hold me safe
Job 5: 15 He **r** the poor from the cutting words of the strong.
33: 30 He **r** them from the grave so they may live in the
36: 15 by means of their suffering, he **r** those who suffer.
Ps 18: 48 and **r** me from my enemies. / You hold me safe
33: 19 He **r** them from death / and keeps them alive in
34: 7 LORD guards all who fear him, / and he **r** them.
34: 17 to him for help. / He **r** them from all their troubles.
34: 18 he **r** those who are crushed in spirit.
34: 19 but the LORD **r** them from each and every one.
35: 9 in the LORD. / I will be glad because he **r** me.
35: 10 Who else **r** the weak and helpless from the strong?
41: 1 the poor. / The LORD **r** them in times of trouble.
41: 2 them prosperity / and **r** them from their enemies.
55: 18 He **r** me and keeps me safe / from the battle waged
68: 20 The Sovereign LORD **r** us from death.
97: 10 and **r** them from the power of the wicked.
107: 41 But he **r** the poor from their distress / and increases
145: 19 fear him; / he hears their cries for help and **r** them.
Pr 11: 6 The godliness of good people **r** them; the ambition
11: 8 God **r** the godly from danger, but he lets the
11: 9 one’s friends; wise discernment **r** the godly.
Da 6: 27 He **r** and saves his people; / he performs
Zec 9: 16 rescue his people, just as a shepherd **r** his sheep.

RESCUING (6) [RESCUE]

Ex 2: 17 came to their aid, **r** the girls from the shepherds.
Nu 14: 13 “They know full well the power you displayed in **r**
Dt 4: 34 for himself by **r** it from another by means of trials,
Ps 37: 40 The LORD helps them, / **r** them from the wicked.
57: 3 save me, / **r** me from those who are out to get me.
Da 9: 15 you brought lasting honor to your name by **r** your

RESEMBLE (1) [RESEMBLED, RESEMBLING]

Isa 40: 18 What image might we find to **r** him?

RESEMBLED (3) [RESEMBLE]

1Ki 7: 26 its rim flared out like a cup and **r** a lily blossom.
2Ch 4: 3 below its rim by two rows of figures that **r** oxen.
4: 5 its rim flared out like a cup and **r** a lily blossom.

RESEMBLING (1) [RESEMBLE]

Heb 7: 3 He remains a priest forever, **r** the Son of God.

RESEN (1)

Ge 10: 12 and **R**—the main city of the empire,

RESENT (1) [RESENTMENT]

Jas 1: 5 he will gladly tell you. He will not **r** your asking.

RESENTMENT (3) [RESENT]

Job 5: 2 Surely **r** destroys the fool, and jealousy kills the
36: 13 For the godless are full of **r**. Even when he
Pr 27: 3 but the **r** caused by a fool is heavier than both.

RESERVATION (1) [RESERVE]

Dt 26: 16 You must commit yourself to them without **r**.

RESERVE (1) [RESERVATION, RESERVED]

Pr 5: 17 You should **r** it for yourselves. Don’t share it with

RESERVED (16) [RESERVE]

Ex 12: 42 This night had been **r** by the LORD to bring his
30: 37 It is **r** for the LORD, and you must treat it as
Lev 25: 33 the cities **r** for the Levites are the only property
Nu 3: 38 toward the sunrise was **r** for the tents of Moses
3: 41 The Levites will be **r** for me as substitutes for the
8: 16 all the people of Israel, the Levites are **r** for me.
Dt 10: 9 or inheritance **r** for them among the other Israelite
Job 38: 23 I have **r** it for the time of trouble, for the day of
Ps 25: 14 Friendship with the LORD is **r** for those who fear
61: 5 You have given me an inheritance **r** for those who
Isa 60: 9 of Tarshish, **r** to bring the people of Israel home.
Jer 17: 4 The wonderful inheritance I have **r** for you will
Mt 12: 4 and they ate the special bread **r** for the priests
Mk 2: 26 ate the special bread **r** for the priests alone, and

Lk 6: 4 ate the special bread **r** for the priests alone, and
1Pe 1: 4 For God has **r** a priceless inheritance for his

RESERVOIR (3) [RESERVOIRS]
Ne 3:16 opposite the royal cemetery as far as the water **r**
Isa 22:11 you build a **r** for water from the old pool.
Na 2: 8 Nineveh is like a leaking water **r**! The people are

RESERVOIRS (3) [RESERVOIR]
Ex 7:19 of Egypt—all its rivers, canals, marshes, and **r**.
Ps 33: 7 sea its boundaries / and locked the oceans in vast **r**.
Ecc 2: 6 I built **r** to collect the water to irrigate my many

RESETTLE (3) [RESETTLED, RESETTLING, SETTLE]
Ne 11: 2 everyone who volunteered to **r** in Jerusalem.
Ob 1:20 to their homeland and **r** the villages of the Negev.
Zec 10:10 and Assyria and **r** them in Gilead and Lebanon.

RESETTLED (3) [RESETTLE]
2Ki 17:24 and **r** them in the towns of Samaria,
17:26 "The people whom you have **r** in the towns of
Ne 11: 4 people from Judah and Benjamin **r** in Jerusalem.

RESETTLING (1) [RESETTLE]
2Ki 16: 9 led its population away as captives, **r** them in Kir.

RESHEPH (1)
1Ch 7:25 line of descent was Rephah, **R**, Telah, Tahan,

RESIDENCE (4) [RESIDENT, RESIDENTS]
Ex 25: 8 "I want the people of Israel to build me a sacred **r**
Da 4:30 have built this beautiful city as my royal **r** and as
Mt 26: 3 and other leaders were meeting at the **r** of
Lk 22:54 they arrested him and led him to the high priest's **r**,

RESIDENT (8) [RESIDENCE]
Lev 25:35 support them as you would a **r** foreigner and allow
25:40 hired servants or as **r** foreigners who live with you,
25:45 You may also purchase the children of such **r**
25:47 "If a **r** foreigner becomes rich, and if some of your
25:53 You must not allow a **r** foreigner to treat any of
Nu 35:15 of Israelites, **r** foreigners, and traveling merchants.
Isa 52: 4 "Long ago my people went to live as **r** foreigners
Eze 22: 7 **R** foreigners are forced to pay for protection.

RESIDENTS (13) [RESIDENCE]
Ge 50:11 The local **r**, the Canaanites, renamed the place
Jdg 1:31 The tribe of Asher also failed to drive out the **r** of
1:33 The tribe of Naphtali also failed to drive out the **r**
18:28 There was no one to rescue the **r** of the town,
21:12 Among the **r** of Jabesh-gilead they found four
2Ki 17:27 Let him teach the new **r** the religious customs of
17:28 and taught the new **r** how to worship the LORD.
17:32 These new **r** worshiped the LORD, but they
17:41 So while these new **r** worshiped the LORD,
Ezr 3: 3 Even though the people were afraid of the local **r**,
4: 4 Then the local **r** tried to discourage and frighten
Ne 7: 3 Appoint the **r** of Jerusalem to act as guards,
Ac 2:14 all of you, fellow Jews and **r** of Jerusalem!

RESIDUE [KJV] See LEFT, OTHER, REMAIN(S), REMAINDER, REMAINING, REMNANT, REST, SOME, SURVIVOR(S)

RESIN (2) [RESINOUS]
Ge 2:12 aromatic **r** and onyx stone are also found there.
Ex 30:34 **r** droplets, mollusk scent, galbanum, and pure

RESINOUS (1) [RESIN]
Ge 6:14 "Make a boat from **r** wood and seal it with tar,

RESIST (9) [RESISTANCE, RESISTING, RESISTS]
Jdg 2:14 all around, and they were no longer able to **r** them.
Ps 139:21 hate you? / Shouldn't I despise those who **r** you?
Ecc 8: 4 by great power. No one can **r** or question it.
Da 11:32 who know their God will be strong and will **r** him.
Mt 5:39 But I say, don't **r** an evil person! If you are slapped
Lk 22:51 But Jesus said, "Don't **r** anymore." And he
Ac 7:51 to the truth. Must you forever **r** the Holy Spirit?
Eph 6:13 Use every piece of God's armor to **r** the enemy in
Jas 4: 7 before God. **R** the Devil, and he will flee from you.

RESISTANCE (1) [RESIST]
Isa 22: 3 All your leaders flee. They surrender without **r**.

RESISTING (1) [RESIST]
Nu 22:32 block your way because you are stubbornly **r** me.

RESISTS (1) [RESIST]
Hos 13:13 but they are like a child who **r** being born.

RESOLD (2) [SELL]
1Ki 10:29 of these were then **r** to the kings of the Hittites
2Ch 1:17 of these were then **r** to the kings of the Hittites

RESOLUTELY (1)
Lk 9:51 his return to heaven, Jesus **r** set out for Jerusalem.

RESOLVE (4) [RESOLVED, RESOLVING]
Ex 14: 8 The LORD continued to strengthen Pharaoh's **r**,
Ne 6: 9 imagining that they could break our **r** and stop the
Eze 44:24 "They will serve as judges to **r** any disagreements
1Co 6: 3 So you should surely be able to **r** ordinary

RESOLVED (1) [RESOLVE]
Lk 9:53 do with Jesus because he had **r** to go to Jerusalem.

RESOLVING (1) [RESOLVE]
Ex 18:22 men can serve the people, **r** all the ordinary cases.

RESORT (1) [RESORTED]
Nu 24: 1 so he did not **r** to divination as he often did.

RESORTED (1) [RESORT]
Jos 9: 4 they **r** to deception to save themselves. They sent

RESOUNDED (1)
1Sa 4:13 had happened, an outcry **r** throughout the town.

RESOURCE (1) [RESOURCES]
1Ch 29: 2 Using every **r** at my command, I have gathered as

RESOURCES (4) [RESOURCE]
Dt 15:11 That is why I am commanding you to share your **r**
Lk 8: 3 contributing from their own **r** to support Jesus
16: 9 use your worldly **r** to benefit others and make
Eph 3:16 unlimited **r** he will give you mighty inner strength

RESPECT (51) [RESPECTED, RESPECTFUL, RESPECTFULLY, RESPECTS]
Ge 31:53 God of his father, Isaac, to **r** the boundary line.
Ex 9:21 But those who had no **r** for the word of the
28:40 sashes, and headdresses to give them dignity and **r**.
Lev 19: 3 Each of you must show **r** for your mother
19:14 your fear of God by treating the deaf with **r**
19:32 of elderly people and showing **r** for the aged.
Dt 28:50 and heartless nation that shows no **r** for the old
1Sa 2:12 Now the sons of Eli were scoundrels who had no **r**
2Sa 1: 2 He fell to the ground before David in deep **r**.
2Ki 3:14 I would not bother with you except for my **r** for
Ezr 10: 3 and by the others who **r** the commands of our God.
Est 1:20 their rank, will receive proper **r** from their wives!"
3: 2 Haman to show him **r** whenever he passed by,
3: 2 But Mordecai refused to bow down or show him **r**.
3: 5 that Mordecai would not bow down or show him **r**,
Job 29: 8 saw me, and even the aged rose in **r** at my coming.
29:10 of the city stood quietly, holding their tongues in **r**.
34:27 following him. They have no **r** for any of his ways.
Pr 3:22 they fill you with life and bring you honor and **r**.
13:13 themselves in trouble; those who **r** it will succeed.
Isa 17: 7 their Creator and have **r** for the Holy One of Israel.
33: 1 You expect others to **r** their promises to you,
33: 8 made before witnesses. They have no **r** for anyone.
59:19 Then at last they will **r** and glorify the name of the
Jer 5:22 Do you have no **r** for me? Why do you not tremble
35:18 have obeyed your ancestor Jehonadab in every **r**,
Eze 26:20 Never again will you be given a position of **r** here
Da 1: 9 Now God had given the chief official great **r** for
Mal 1: 6 but where are the honor and **r** I deserve?
1: 7 by saying the altar of the LORD deserves no **r**.
Mt 21:37 sent his son, thinking, 'Surely they will **r** my son.'
Mk 12: 6 sent him, thinking, 'Surely they will **r** my son.'
Lk 20:13 I'll send my cherished son. Surely they will **r** him.'
Jn 8:16 my judgment would be correct in every **r** because I
Ac 19:27 I'm not just talking about the loss of public **r** for
Ro 10:12 Jew and Gentile are the same in this **r**. They all
13: 7 and give **r** and honor to all to whom it is due.
1Co 16:10 When Timothy comes, treat him with **r**. He is
16:16 to **r** them fully and others like them who serve
2Co 7:15 and welcomed him with such **r** and deep concern.
Eph 5:33 he loves himself, and the wife must **r** her husband.
6: 5 obey your earthly masters with deep **r** and fear.
1Th 4:12 people who are not Christians will **r** the way you
1Ti 3: 4 family well, with children who **r** and obey him.
3:13 as deacons will be rewarded with **r** from others
6: 1 who are slaves should give their masters full **r**
Tit 2: 2 to be worthy of **r**, and to live wisely.
Heb 2:17 it was necessary for Jesus to be in every **r** like us,
12: 9 Since we **r** our earthly fathers who disciplined us,
1Pe 2:17 Show **r** for everyone. Love your Christian brothers and sisters. Fear God. Show **r** for the king.

RESPECTED (19) [RESPECT]
Ge 34:19 Shechem was a highly **r** member of his family,
Ex 11: 3 He was **r** by Pharaoh's officials and the Egyptian
Dt 1:15 and **r** men you had selected from your tribes
2Ch 32:23 then on King Hezekiah became highly **r** among the
Pr 13:15 A person with good sense is **r**; a treacherous
Isa 32: 5 Wealthy cheaters will not be **r** as outstanding
La 4:16 and leaders are no longer honored and **r**.
Eze 29:21 to revive, and then at last your words will be **r**.
Mk 6:20 And Herod **r** John, knowing that he was a good
Lk 7: 3 he sent some **r** Jewish leaders to ask him to come
14: 8 What if someone more **r** than you has also been
Jn 3:10 Jesus replied, "You are a **r** Jewish teacher, and yet
Ac 6: 3 and select seven men who are well **r** and are full of
10:22 the God of Israel and is well **r** by all the Jews.
Ro 16: 7 They are **r** among the apostles and became
1Co 6: 4 why do you go to outside judges who are not **r** by
1Ti 3: 8 deacons must be people who are **r** and have
3:11 their wives must be **r** and must not speak evil of
5:10 She must be well **r** by everyone because of the

RESPECTER [KJV] See PARTIALITY

RESPECTFUL (2) [RESPECT]
Lk 11:43 and the **r** greetings from everyone as you walk
1Pe 3:16 But you must do this in a gentle and **r** way.

RESPECTFULLY (3) [RESPECT]
Ex 18: 7 He bowed to him **r** and greeted him warmly.
Mt 20:20 to Jesus with her sons. She knelt **r** to ask a favor.
1Ti 5: 1 but appeal to him **r** as though he were your own

RESPECTIVE (2)
Jos 17:11 Taanach, and Megiddo, with their **r** villages.
Est 3:12 to the princes, the governors of the **r** provinces,

RESPECTS (5) [RESPECT]
Job 21:33 Many pay their **r** as the body is laid to rest
Mal 1: 6 son honors his father, and a servant **r** his master.
Lk 20:36 will never die again. In these **r** they are like angels.
Jn 11:19 and many of the people had come to pay their **r**
Ac 25:13 with his sister, Bernice, to pay their **r** to Festus.

RESPOND (17) [RESPONDED, RESPONDING, RESPONDS, RESPONSE]
Ge 4: 7 You will be accepted if you **r** in the right way.
4: 7 But if you refuse to **r** correctly, then watch out!
Nu 23: 3 and I will go to see if the LORD will **r** to me.
1Sa 4:20 But she did not answer or **r** in any way.
2Ch 32:25 But Hezekiah did not **r** appropriately to the
Job 19:12 cry for help, yet God does not **r** to their moaning.
33:13 You say, 'He does not **r** to people's complaints.'
35:15 cry out against him because he does not **r** in anger?
Ps 20: 1 In times of trouble, may the LORD **r** to your cry.
20: 9 to our king, O LORD! / **R** to our cry for help.
Isa 30:19 He will **r** instantly to the sound of your cries.
49: 8 "At just the right time, I will **r** to you. On the day
Jer 7:27 out your warnings, but do not expect them to **r**.
17:23 to pay attention and would not **r** to discipline.
23:38 But suppose they **r**, 'This is a prophecy from the
Hos 6: 3 Then he will **r** to us as surely as the arrival of
1Co 4:13 We **r** gently when evil things are said about us.

RESPONDED (36) [RESPOND]
Ge 44: 7 "What are you talking about?" the brothers **r**.
Ex 10:19 The LORD **r** by sending a strong west wind that
19: 8 They all **r** together, "We will certainly do
24: 7 They all **r** again, "We will do everything the
Nu 32:16 But they **r** to Moses, "We simply want to build
Dt 1:22 "But you **r**, 'First, let's send out scouts to explore
Jos 11: 4 All these kings **r** by mobilizing their warriors
Jdg 6:35 summoning their warriors, and all of them **r**.
12: 4 The leaders of Ephraim **r**, "The men of Gilead are
1Sa 10:12 But one of the neighbors **r**, "It doesn't matter who
16:20 Jesse **r** by sending David to Saul, along with a
25:41 She bowed low to the ground and **r**, "Yes, I am
2Sa 19:14 all the leaders of Judah, and they **r** unanimously.
1Ki 15:18 Asa **r** by taking all the silver and gold that was left
20:32 'Please let me live!' " The king of Israel **r**,
2Ki 10: 6 Jehu **r** with a second letter: "If you are on my side
2Ch 16: 2 Asa **r** by taking the silver and gold from the
31: 5 The people **r** immediately and generously with the
Ezr 5: 2 and Jeshua son of Jehozadak **r** by beginning the
Ne 5:13 The whole assembly **r**, "Amen," and they praised
Job 9:16 And even if I summoned him and he **r**, he would
Jer 28: 5 Jeremiah **r** to Hananiah as they stood in front of all
Mt 4: 7 Jesus **r**, "The Scriptures also say, 'Do not test the
9:15 Jesus **r**, "Should the wedding guests mourn while
21:27 And Jesus **r**, "Then I won't answer your question
22:43 Jesus **r**, "Then why does David, speaking under
Mk 9:12 Jesus **r**, "Elijah is indeed coming first to set
10: 5 But Jesus **r**, "He wrote those instructions only as a
11:33 And Jesus **r**, "Then I won't answer your question
Lk 1:38 Mary **r**, "I am the Lord's servant, and I am willing
1:46 Mary **r**, / "Oh, how I praise the Lord.
4:12 Jesus **r**, "The Scriptures also say, 'Do not test the
19: 9 Jesus **r**, "Salvation has come to this home today,
20: 8 And Jesus **r**, "Then I won't answer your question
Jn 7:46 never heard anyone talk like this!" the guards **r**.
11:40 Jesus **r**, "Didn't I tell you that you will see God's

RESPONDING (2) [RESPOND]
Ne 12:24 and thanksgiving, one section **r** to the other,
1Co 16: 9 door for a great work here, and many people are **r**.

RESPONDS (1) [RESPOND]
Ps 27: 8 And my heart **r**, "LORD, I am coming."

RESPONSE (4) [RESPOND]
1Ki 20: 9 the messengers returned to Ben-hadad with the **r**.
Job 32:15 You sit there baffled, with no further **r**.
2Co 9: 7 Don't give reluctantly or in **r** to pressure. For God
12:20 like what I find, and then you won't like my **r**.

RESPONSIBILITIES (15) [RESPONSIBLE]
Nu 18: 4 The Levites must join with you to fulfill their **r** for
27:23 his hands on him and commissioned him to his **r**,
Dt 24: 5 drafted into the army or given any other special **r**.
1Ch 9:33 They were exempt from other **r** there since they

25: 6 Their **r** included the playing of cymbals, lyres,
2Ch 11:23 Rehoboam also wisely gave **r** to his other sons
Isa 28: 7 make stupid mistakes as they carry out their **r**.
Jer 36:12 son of Hananiah, and all the others with official **r**.
Mt 25:21 so now I will give you many more **r**.
25:23 so now I will give you many more **r**.
Lk 16:10 even a little, you won't be honest with greater **r**.
Ac 25: 1 Festus arrived in Caesarea to take over his new **r**,
1Co 7:33 He has to think about his earthly **r** and how to
7:34 woman must be concerned about her earthly **r**
1Ti 3:10 they should be given other **r** in the church as a test

RESPONSIBILITY (30) [RESPONSIBLE]

Ge 17: 9 and all your descendants have this continual **r**.
39: 6 So Potiphar gave Joseph complete administrative **r**
Ex 34:11 Your **r** is to obey all the commands I am giving
Nu 3:32 with special **r** for the oversight of the sanctuary.
3:38 who had the final **r** for the sanctuary on behalf of
4:16 and everything in it will be Eleazar's **r**."
27:19 and publicly commission him with the **r** of leading
2Sa 14: 9 "And I'll take the **r** if you are criticized for
1Ch 26:14 The **r** for the east gate went to Meshelemiah
2Ch 35:14 The Levites took **r** for all these preparations.
Ne 7: 2 I gave the **r** of governing Jerusalem to my brother
Pr 24:12 Don't try to avoid **r** by saying you didn't know
Isa 22:24 He will be loaded down with **r**, and he will bring
Jer 26:15 The **r** for such a deed will lie on you, on this city,
Eze 33: 5 the warning but wouldn't listen, so the **r** is theirs.
39:26 They will accept **r** for their past shame
Mt 24:45 to whom the master can give the **r** of managing his
27:24 innocent of the blood of this man. The **r** is yours!"
27:25 people yelled back, "We will take **r** for his death—
Lk 12:42 sensible servant to whom the master gives the **r** of
Ro 12: 8 given you leadership ability, take the **r** seriously.
1Co 5:12 It isn't my **r** to judge outsiders, but it certainly is
2Co 13: 8 Our **r** is never to oppose the truth, but to stand for
Gal 2: 7 They saw that God had given me the **r** of
2: 7 just as he had given Peter the **r** of preaching to the
Eph 4:12 Their **r** is to equip God's people to do his work
Col 1:25 God has given me the **r** of serving his church by
1Ti 3: 1 wants to be an elder, he desires an honorable **r**.
5: 4 their first **r** is to show godliness at home and repay
5:16 take care of them and not put the **r** on the church.

RESPONSIBLE (62) [RESPONSIBILITIES, RESPONSIBILITY]

Ge 21:26 Abimelech said. "And I have no idea who is **r**.
37:27 Let's not be **r** for his death; after all, he is our
42:37 bring Benjamin back to you. I'll be **r** for him."
44:31 We will be **r** for bringing his gray head down to
Ex 21:22 then the person **r** must pay damages in the amount
Lev 5: 1 they will be held **r** and be subject to punishment.
5:17 if it is done unintentionally, they will be held **r**.
17:16 wash your clothes and bathe, you will be held **r**."
Nu 1:53 The Levites are **r** to stand guard around the
3:25 These two clans were **r** to care for the tent of the
3:28 They were **r** for the care of the sanctuary.
3:31 These four clans were **r** for the care of the Ark,
3:36 These two clans were **r** for the care of the frames
3:37 They were also **r** for the posts of the courtyard
4:16 "Eleazar son of Aaron the priest will be **r** for the
4:26 The Gershonites are **r** for transporting all these
4:28 They will be directly **r** to Ithamar son of Aaron the
4:33 They are directly **r** to Ithamar son of Aaron the
18: 1 be held **r** for any offenses related to the sanctuary.
18:23 and they will be held **r** for any offenses against it.
32:15 you will be **r** for destroying this entire nation!"
35:19 The victim's nearest relative is **r** for putting the
Dt 1:15 Some were **r** for a thousand people, some for a
19:10 and you will not be held **r** for murder.
2Sa 3:37 and Israel knew that David was not **r** for Abner's
1Ki 4: 7 They were **r** for providing food from the people for
1Ch 9:13 They were **r** for ministering at the house of God.
9:18 they were **r** for the King's Gate on the east side.
9:19 were **r** for guarding the entrance to the sanctuary,
9:21 been **r** for guarding the entrance to the Tabernacle.
9:23 were **r** for guarding the entrance to the house of
9:26 for they were **r** for the rooms and treasuries at the
9:29 Others were **r** for the furnishings, the items in the
23:29 They were also **r** to check all the weights
26:30 They were **r** for all matters related to the things of
26:32 They were **r** for all matters related to the things of
27:27 Zabdi from Shepham was **r** for the grapes
27:28 of Judah. Joash was **r** for the supplies of olive oil.
27:29 Shaphat son of Adlai was **r** for the cattle in the
27:32 Jehiel the Hacmonite was **r** to teach the king's
Ne 12:44 They were **r** to collect these from the fields as
Pr 17:18 a friend's note, to become **r** for a neighbor's debts.
Jer 23: 4 Then I will appoint **r** shepherds to care for them,
29:26 You are **r** to put anyone who claims to be a
Eze 3:18 And I will hold you **r**, demanding your blood for
3:20 and I will hold you **r**, demanding your blood for
11: 2 these are the men who are **r** for the wicked counsel
33: 6 alarm to warn the people, he is **r** for their deaths.
33: 8 in their sins, but I will hold you **r** for their deaths.
33: 9 will die in their sins, but you will not be held **r**.
34:10 and I will hold them **r** for what has happened to
39:28 **r** for sending them away to exile and **r** for bringing
Da 6: 4 He was faithful and honest and always **r**.
Am 6:10 relative—one who is **r** for burning the dead—
Jnh 1:14 And don't hold us **r** for his death, because it isn't
Lk 11:50 "And you of this generation will be held **r** for the
Ro 14: 4 They are **r** to the Lord, so let him tell them
1Co 11: 3 A man is **r** to Christ, a woman is **r** to her husband, and Christ is **r** to God.

Gal 6: 5 For we are each **r** for our own conduct.

REST (334) [RESTED, RESTING, RESTLESS, RESTS]

Ge 8: 4 the boat came to **r** on the mountains of Ararat.
14:10 the tar pits, while the **r** escaped into the mountains.
16:12 he will live at odds with the **r** of his brothers."
18: 4 **R** in the shade of this tree while my servants get
42:16 I'll keep the **r** of you here, bound in prison.
42:19 The **r** of you may go on home with grain for your
44: 9 And all the **r** of us will be your master's slaves
44:10 stole it will be a slave. The **r** of you may go free."
44:17 The **r** of you may go home to your father."
Ex 4: 7 out this time, it was as healthy as the **r** of his body.
14: 7 along with the **r** of the chariots of Egypt, each with
16:23 LORD has appointed tomorrow as a day of **r**,
16:23 On this day we will **r** from our normal daily tasks.
16:29 them the seventh day, the Sabbath, as a day of **r**?
20:10 but the seventh day is a day of **r** dedicated to the
23:11 but let the land **r** and lie fallow during the seventh
23:11 Leave the **r** for the animals to eat. The same
23:12 "Work for six days, and **r** on the seventh.
23:12 will give your ox and your donkey a chance to **r**.
29:12 and pour out the **r** at the base of the altar.
29:20 Sprinkle the **r** of the blood on the sides of the altar.
31:15 but the seventh day must be a day of total **r**.
33:14 I will give you **r**—everything will be fine for
34:21 aside for work, but on the Sabbath day you must **r**,
35: 2 The seventh day is a day of total **r**, a holy day that
38: 2 each of the four corners, all of one piece with the **r**.
38:28 The **r** of the silver, about 45 pounds, was used to
Lev 2: 3 The **r** of the flour will be given to Aaron and his
2:10 The **r** of the grain offering will be given to Aaron
4: 7 The **r** of the bull's blood must be poured out at the
4:11 But the **r** of the bull—its hide, meat, head, legs,
4:18 The **r** of the blood must then be poured out at the
4:25 and pour out the **r** of the blood at the base of the
4:30 and pour out the **r** of the blood at the base of the
4:34 and pour out the **r** of the blood at the base of the
5: 9 and the **r** will be drained out at the base of the
5:13 The **r** of the flour will belong to the priest, just as
6:16 the **r** of the flour will belong to Aaron and his sons
8:15 He poured out the **r** of the blood at the base of the
8:17 The **r** of the bull, including its hide, meat,
8:24 then sprinkled the **r** of the blood against the sides
8:31 "Boil the **r** of the meat at the Tabernacle entrance,
9: 9 He poured out the **r** of the blood at the base of the
10: 6 However, the **r** of the Israelites, your relatives,
13:16 sores heal and turn white like the **r** of the skin,
16:31 It will be a Sabbath day of total **r**, and you will
19: 3 you must always observe my Sabbath days of **r**,
19:30 "Keep my Sabbath days of **r** and show reverence
23: 3 It is the LORD's Sabbath day of complete **r**,
23:24 you are to celebrate a day of complete **r**.
23:32 This will be a Sabbath day of total **r** for you,
23:32 This time of **r** and fasting will begin the evening
23:39 eighth day of the festival will be days of total **r**.
25: 4 land will enjoy a Sabbath year of **r** to the LORD.
25: 5 The land is to have a year of total **r**.
26: 2 You must keep my Sabbath days of **r** and show
26:34 Then the land will finally **r** and enjoy its Sabbaths.
26:35 it will take the **r** you never allowed it to take every
26:43 And the land will enjoy its years of Sabbath **r** as it
Nu 1:49 do not include them when you count the **r** of the
8: 6 "Now set the Levites apart from the **r** of the
8:14 you will set the Levites apart from the **r** of the
9: 1 and the **r** of the Israelites were in the wilderness of
9: 7 at the proper time with the **r** of the Israelites?"
10:33 ahead of them to show them where to stop and **r**.
15:33 before Moses, Aaron, and the **r** of the community.
23:24 like a majestic lion they stand. / They refuse to **r**
27: 4 Give us property along with the **r** of our
27:21 and the **r** of the community of Israel will discover
31:27 fought the battle and half to the **r** of the people.
32: 7 "Are you trying to discourage the **r** of the people
32:22 to the LORD and to the **r** of the people of Israel.
32:30 then they must accept land with the **r** of you in the
Dt 3:13 Then I gave the **r** of Gilead and all of Bashan—
3:20 When the LORD has given security to the **r** of the
5:14 but the seventh day is a day of **r** dedicated to the
5:14 your male and female servants must **r** as you do.
12: 9 when you arrive in the place of **r** the LORD your
12:10 When he gives you **r** and security from all your
18: 1 and the **r** of the tribe of Levi will not be given an
25:19 when the LORD your God has given you **r** from
28:65 nations you will find no place of security and **r**.
33:16 May these blessings **r** on Joseph's head,
Jos 1:13 'The LORD your God is giving you **r** and has
1:15 the LORD gives **r** to them as he has given **r** to you,
4:14 and for the **r** of his life they revered him as much
7:21 my tent, with the silver buried deeper than the **r**."
7:22 had said, with the silver buried beneath the **r**.
10:19 The **r** of you continue chasing the enemy and cut
11:23 the tribes. So the land finally had **r** from war.
13:27 and the **r** of the kingdom of King Sihon of
14:15 of the Anakites.) And the land had **r** from war.
17: 6 (The land of Gilead was given to the **r** of the male
21:20 The **r** of the Kohathite clan from the tribe of Levi
21:26 were given to the **r** of the Kohathite clan.
21:34 The **r** of the Levites—the Merari clan—were given
21:44 And the LORD gave them **r** on every side,
22: 4 the LORD your God has given the other tribes **r**,
22: 9 and the half-tribe of Manasseh left the **r** of Israel at
22:11 When the **r** of Israel heard they had built the altar
23: 1 and the LORD had given the people of Israel **r**
Jdg 8:28 Throughout the **r** of Gideon's lifetime—

9: 1 said to them and to the **r** of his mother's family,
14:17 with him and kept it up for the **r** of the celebration.
16:26 against the two pillars. I want to **r** against them."
20:10 and the **r** of us will take revenge on Gibeah for this
Ru 2: 7 except for a few minutes' **r** over there in the
3:18 The man won't **r** until he has followed through on
1Sa 7:14 along with the **r** of the territory that the Philistines
7:15 Samuel continued as Israel's judge for the **r** of his
13: 2 the army of Israel and sent the **r** of the men home.
13:15 but the **r** of the troops went with Saul to meet the
14:21 in with Saul, Jonathan, and the **r** of the Israelites.
18:29 and he remained David's enemy for the **r** of his
18:30 against them than all the **r** of Saul's officers.
2Sa 2: 9 the land of the Ashurites, and all the **r** of Israel.
3:10 go ahead and give David the **r** of Saul's kingdom.
10:10 He left the **r** of the army under the command of his
12:28 Now bring the **r** of the army and finish the job,
12:29 So David led the **r** of his army to Rabbah
14: 7 Now the **r** of the family is demanding, 'Let us have
23:10 The **r** of the army did not return until it was time to
1Ki 3:13 will be compared to you for the **r** of your life!
6:21 Then he overlaid the **r** of the Temple's interior
8:56 "Praise the LORD who has given **r** to his people
11:25 Rezon was Israel's bitter enemy for the **r** of
11:34 I will let Solomon reign for the **r** of his life.
11:41 The **r** of the events in Solomon's reign,
14:19 The **r** of the events of Jeroboam's reign, all his
14:29 The **r** of the events in Rehoboam's reign and all
15: 7 The **r** of the events in Abijam's reign and all his
15:23 The **r** of the events in Asa's reign, the extent of his
15:31 The **r** of the events in Nadab's reign and all his
16: 5 The **r** of the events in Baasha's reign
16:14 The **r** of the events in Elah's reign and all his
16:20 The **r** of the events of Zimri's reign and his
16:27 The **r** of the events in Omri's reign, the extent of
20:15 Then he called out the **r** of his army of seven
20:30 The **r** fled behind the walls of Aphek, but the wall
22:39 The **r** of the events in Ahab's reign and the story of
22:45 The **r** of the events in Jehoshaphat's reign,
22:46 He banished from the land the **r** of the shrine
2Ki 1:18 The **r** of the events in Ahaziah's reign are
4:11 to Shunem, and he went up to his room to **r**.
7:13 than if they stay here and die with the **r** of us."
8:23 The **r** of the events in Jehoram's reign and all his
10:34 The **r** of the events in Jehu's reign and all his
11: 1 she set out to destroy the **r** of the royal family.
11: 2 and stole him away from among the **r** of the king's
12:19 The **r** of the events in Joash's reign and all his
13: 8 The **r** of the events in Jehoahaz's reign and all his
13:12 The **r** of the events in Jehoash's reign and all his
14:15 The **r** of the events in Jehoash's reign,
14:18 The **r** of the events in Amaziah's reign are
14:28 The **r** of the events in the reign of Jeroboam II
15: 6 The **r** of the events in Uzziah's reign and all his
15:11 The **r** of the events in Zechariah's reign are
15:15 The **r** of the events in Shallum's reign,
15:21 The **r** of the events in Menahem's reign and all his
15:26 The **r** of the events in Pekahiah's reign and all his
15:31 The **r** of the events in Pekah's reign and all his
15:36 The **r** of the events in Jotham's reign and all his
16:19 The **r** of the events in Ahaz's reign and his deeds
20:20 The **r** of the events in Hezekiah's reign,
21:17 The **r** of the events in Manasseh's reign and all his
21:25 The **r** of the events in Amon's reign and all his
23:28 The **r** of the events in Josiah's reign and all his
24: 5 The **r** of the events in Jehoiakim's reign and all
25:11 along with the **r** of the people and the troops who
25:29 him to dine at the king's table for the **r** of his life.
1Ch 11: 8 while Joab rebuilt the **r** of Jerusalem.
19:11 He left the **r** of the army under the command of his
22: 9 will have a son who will experience peace and **r**.
28: 2 God's footstool, could **r** permanently.
2Ch 9:29 The **r** of the events of Solomon's reign,
12:15 The **r** of the events of Rehoboam's reign,
13:22 The **r** of the events of Abijah's reign, including his
14: 6 for the LORD was giving him **r** from his
14: 7 our God, and he has given us **r** from our enemies."
15:15 And the LORD gave them **r** from their enemies
16:11 The **r** of the events of Asa's reign, from beginning
20:30 for his God had given him **r** on every side.
20:34 The **r** of the events of Jehoshaphat's reign,
22:10 she set out to destroy the **r** of Judah's royal family.
22:11 and stole him away from among the **r** of the king's
23: 6 The **r** of the people must obey the LORD's
25:26 The **r** of the events of Amaziah's reign,
26:22 The **r** of the events of Uzziah's reign,
27: 7 The **r** of the events of Jotham's reign, including his
28:26 The **r** of the events of Ahaz's reign and all his
32:32 The **r** of the events of Hezekiah's reign and his
33:18 The **r** of the events of Manasseh's reign, his prayer
34:33 And throughout the **r** of his lifetime, they did not
35:26 The **r** of the events of Josiah's reign and his acts of
36: 8 The **r** of the events of Jehoiakim's reign,
36:21 The land finally enjoyed its Sabbath **r**,
Ezr 2:70 The **r** of the people returned to the other towns of
4:10 They also sent greetings from the **r** of the people
6:16 and the **r** of the people who had returned from
Ne 5: 8 "The **r** of us are doing all we can to redeem our
6: 1 and the **r** of our enemies found out that I had
7:72 The **r** of the people gave 20,000 gold coins,
10:28 The **r** of the people—the priests, Levites,
11: 1 live there, too, while the **r** stayed where they were.
11:20 and the **r** of the Israelites lived wherever their
Est 2:14 She would live there for the **r** of her life,
9:12 what has happened in the **r** of the provinces?
Job 3:13 at birth, I would be at peace now, asleep and at **r**.
3:14 I would **r** with the world's kings and prime

3:15 I would **r** with wealthy princes whose palaces were
3:17 cease from troubling, and the weary are at **r**.
3:26 I have no **r**; instead, only trouble comes."
11:18 You will be protected and will **r** in safety.
14: 6 So give us a little **r**, won't you? Turn away your
17:16 me to the grave. We will **r** together in the dust!"
21:33 Many pay their respects as the body is laid to **r**
37:19 so much, so teach the **r** of us what to say to God.
Ps 3: 8 O LORD. / May your blessings **r** on your people.
23: 2 He lets me **r** in green meadows; / he leads me
55: 6 wings like a dove; / then I would fly away and **r**!
78:34 God killed some of them, the **r** finally sought him.
91: 1 will find **r** in the shadow of the Almighty.
95:11 a vow: / 'They will never enter my place of **r**.' "
104:22 At dawn they slink back / into their dens to **r**.
116: 7 Now I can **r** again, / for the LORD has been
127: 2 for food to eat; / for God gives **r** to his loved ones.
132: 3 "I will not go home; / I will not let myself **r**.
139: 3 path ahead of me / and tell me where to stop and **r**.
Pr 4:16 They cannot **r** unless they have caused someone to
6: 4 Don't put it off. Do it now! Don't **r** until you do.
6:10 more slumber, a little folding of the hands to **r**—
19:20 instruction you can, and be wise the **r** of your life.
24:33 more slumber, a little folding of the hands to **r**—
Ecc 2:23 with pain and grief; even at night they cannot **r**.
SS 1: 7 flock today? Where will you **r** your sheep at noon?
Isa 5:27 They will run without stopping for **r** or sleep.
9: 6 And the government will **r** on his shoulders.
10:32 But the enemy stops at Nob for the **r** of that day.
11: 2 And the Spirit of the LORD will **r** on him—
14: 3 when the LORD gives his people **r** from sorrow
14: 7 But at last the land is at **r** and is quiet. Finally it
23:12 Even if you flee to Cyprus, you will find no **r**."
25:10 For the LORD's good hand will **r** on Jerusalem.
28:12 God's people could have **r** in their own land if they
32:18 live in safety, quietly at home. They will be at **r**.
34:14 the ruins, and night creatures will come there to **r**.
44:15 he takes the **r** of it and makes himself a god for
44:19 and roast my meat. How can the **r** of it be a god?
49:21 were killed, and the **r** were carried away into exile.
56: 2 Blessed are those who honor my Sabbath days of **r**
56: 6 and do not desecrate the Sabbath day of **r**,
57: 2 For the godly who die will **r** in peace.
62: 6 of his promises. Take no **r**, all you who pray.
62: 7 Give the LORD no **r** until he makes Jerusalem
63:14 the Spirit of the LORD gave them **r**.
65:11 because the **r** of you have forsaken the LORD
Jer 6:16 Travel its path, and you will find **r** for your souls.
26:15 **r** assured that you will be killing an innocent man!
31: 2 I will again come to give **r** to the people of Israel."
31:25 For I have given **r** to the weary and joy to the
41:11 and the **r** of the guerrilla leaders heard what
45: 3 I am weary of my own sighing and can find no **r**.'
47: 6 sword of the LORD, when will you be at **r** again?
Go back into your sheath; **r** and be still!
50: 7 their place of **r**, the hope of their ancestors.'
50:34 will defend them and give them **r** again in Israel.
50:34 people of Babylon—there will be no **r** for them!
52:11 Zedekiah remained there in prison for the **r** of his
52:15 along with the **r** of the craftsmen and the troops
52:33 him to dine at the king's table for the **r** of his life.
La 1: 3 lives among foreign nations and has no place of **r**.
2:18 Give yourselves no **r** from weeping day or night.
5: 5 at our heels; we are exhausted but are given no **r**.
Eze 20:12 And I gave them my Sabbath days of **r** as a sign
22: 8 my holy things and violate my Sabbath days of **r**.
34:18 Must you also trample down the **r**? Is it not enough
34:18 Must you also muddy the **r** with your feet?
43: 7 of my throne and the place where I will **r** my feet.
45: 8 they will assign the **r** of the land to the people,
48:11 the people of Israel and the **r** of the Levites did.
48:23 "These are the territories allotted to the **r** of the
Da 6:14 He spent the **r** of the day looking for a way to get
12:13 You will **r**, and then at the end of the days,
Hab 2: 5 is treacherous, and the arrogant are never at **r**.
Zep 1: 3 along with the **r** of humanity," says the LORD.
2: 7 They will lie down to **r** in the abandoned houses in
Zec 12: 7 The LORD will give victory to the **r** of Judah
12: 7 will not have greater honor than the **r** of Judah.
Mt 11:28 and carry heavy burdens, and I will give you **r**.
11:29 and gentle, and you will find **r** for your souls.
12:43 it goes into the desert, seeking **r** but finding none.
27:49 But the **r** said, "Leave him alone. Let's see
Mk 6:31 get away from the crowds for a while and **r**."
Lk 11:24 a person, it goes into the desert, searching for **r**.
21: 3 "this poor widow has given more than all the **r** of
Jn 1:39 to the place, and they stayed there the **r** of the day.
11:13 Jesus meant Lazarus was having a good night's **r**,
Ac 15:17 so that the **r** of humanity might find the Lord,
17: 6 and Silas have turned the **r** of the world upside
Ro 11: 7 has chosen—but the **r** were made unresponsive.
11:15 that God offered salvation to the **r** of the world,
1Co 7:12 Now, I will speak to the **r** of you, though I do not
2Co 2:13 But I couldn't **r** because my dear brother Titus
7: 5 When we arrived in Macedonia there was no **r** for
10: 6 disobedient after the **r** of you became loyal
Eph 2: 2 You used to live just like the **r** of the world,
Php 4: 3 worked with Clement and the **r** of my co-workers,
2Th 1: 7 And God will provide **r** for you who are being
3:13 And I say to the **r** of you, dear brothers and sisters,
Heb 3:11 a vow: / 'They will never enter my place of **r**.' "
3:18 vowed that they would never enter his place of **r**?
3:19 So we see that they were not allowed to enter his **r**
4: 1 God's promise of entering his place of **r** still
4: 2 Good News—that God has prepared a place of **r**—
4: 3 For only we who believe can enter his place of **r**.
4: 3 'They will never enter my place of **r**,' " even
4: 3 place of **r** has been ready since he made the world.
4: 5 God said, "They will never enter my place of **r**."
4: 6 So God's **r** is there for people to enter. But those
4: 7 So God set another time for entering his place of **r**,
4: 8 This new place of **r** was not the land of Canaan,
4: 8 not have spoken later about another day of **r**.
4: 9 So there is a special **r** still waiting for the people of
4:10 For all who enter into God's **r** will find **r** from
4:11 Let us do our best to enter that place of **r**.
11: 7 By his faith he condemned the **r** of the world
1Pe 4: 2 And you won't spend the **r** of your life chasing
Rev 2:24 But I also have a message for the **r** of you in
6:11 And they were told to **r** a little longer until the full
12:17 and he declared war against the **r** of her children—
14:13 for they will **r** from all their toils and trials;
20: 5 (The **r** of the dead did not come back to life until

RESTED (25) [REST]

Ge 2: 2 having finished his task, God **r** from all his work.
2: 3 because it was the day when he **r** from his work of
Ex 16:30 So the people **r** on the seventh day.
20:11 everything in them; then he **r** on the seventh day.
24:16 And the glorious presence of the LORD **r** upon
31:17 but he **r** on the seventh day and was refreshed."
38: 4 Next he made a bronze grating that **r** on a ledge
40:38 The cloud of the LORD **r** on the Tabernacle
Nu 11:25 They prophesied as the Spirit **r** upon them, but that
11:26 were still in the camp when the Spirit **r** upon them.
Jos 5: 8 they **r** in the camp until they were healed.
Jdg 19:15 They **r** in the town square, but no one took them in
2Sa 16:14 so they **r** when they reached the Jordan River.
1Ki 7: 2 The great cedar ceiling beams **r** on four rows of
7: 3 by forty-five rafters that **r** on three rows of pillars,
7:25 The Sea **r** on a base of twelve bronze oxen,
2Ch 4: 4 The Sea **r** on a base of twelve bronze oxen,
Ezr 8:32 safely in Jerusalem, where we **r** for three days.
Est 9:17 Then on the following day they **r**, celebrating their
9:18 and then **r** on the third day, making that their day
Eze 9: 3 where it had **r**, and moved to the entrance of the
41: 6 The supports for these rooms **r** on ledges in the
Lk 23:56 so they **r** all that day as required by the law.
Heb 4: 4 "On the seventh day God **r** from all his work."
4:10 their labors, just as God **r** after creating the world.

RESTING (9) [REST]

Ge 49:14 a strong beast of burden, / **r** among the sheepfolds.
Ex 27: 5 down into the firebox, **r** it on the ledge built there.
1Ki 6: 6 by beams **r** on ledges built out from the wall.
2Ch 6:41 LORD God, arise and enter this **r** place of yours,
Eze 32:25 They have a **r** place among the slaughtered,
Mt 26:45 Still **r**? Look, the time has come. I, the Son of
Mk 14:41 third time he said, "Still sleeping? Still **r**? Enough!
Jn 1:32 like a dove from heaven and **r** upon him.
1:33 the Holy Spirit descending and **r** upon someone,

RESTITUTION (4)

Lev 5:16 then make **r** for whatever holy things they have
24:21 "Whoever kills an animal must make full **r**,
Nu 5: 7 their sin and make full **r** for what they have done,
5: 8 and there are no near relatives to whom **r** can be

RESTLESS (3) [REST]

Job 30:27 My heart is troubled and **r**. Days of affliction have
Isa 57:20 "But those who still reject me are like the **r** sea.
Jer 2:23 You are like a **r** female camel, desperate for a

RESTORATION (6) [RESTORE]

2Ki 12:12 paid any other expenses related to the Temple's **r**.
22: 5 to the men assigned to supervise the Temple's **r**.
2Ch 24:27 and the record of his **r** of the Temple of God are
34:10 to supervise the **r** of the LORD's Temple.
Ac 3:21 in heaven until the time for the final **r** of all things,
2Co 13: 9 What we pray for is your **r** to maturity.

RESTORE (55) [RESTORATION, RESTORED, RESTORES, RESTORING]

Lev 6: 5 they must **r** the principal amount plus a penalty of
Dt 30: 3 then the LORD your God will **r** your fortunes.
Ru 4:15 May this child **r** your youth and care for you in
1Ki 12:18 to **r** order, but all Israel stoned him to death.
12:21 the army of Israel and to **r** the kingdom to himself.
13: 6 "Please ask the LORD your God to **r** my hand
2Ch 10:18 who was in charge of the labor force, to **r** order,
11: 1 the army of Israel and to **r** the kingdom to himself.
24: 4 decided to repair and **r** the Temple of the LORD.
24:12 and carpenters to **r** the Temple of the LORD.
Ezr 5: 3 to rebuild this Temple and **r** this structure?"
5: 9 to rebuild this Temple and **r** this structure?'
Ne 5:11 You must **r** their fields, vineyards, olive groves,
Job 8: 6 he will rise up and **r** your happy home.
33:26 receive him with joy and **r** him to good standing.
Ps 6: 3 at heart. / How long, O LORD, until you **r** me?
13: 3 my God! / **R** the light to my eyes, or I will die.
51:12 **R** to me again the joy of your salvation, / and make
60: 1 have been angry with us; now **r** us to your favor.
71:20 much hardship, / but you will **r** me to life again
71:21 You will **r** me to even greater honor / and comfort
119:93 for you have used them to **r** my joy and health.
119:107 O LORD; / **r** my life again, just as you promised.
126: 4 **R** our fortunes, LORD, / as streams renew the
Isa 45:13 He will **r** my city and free my captive people—
49: 6 "You will do more than **r** the people of Israel to
Jer 15:19 I will **r** you so you can continue to serve me.
29:14 "I will end your captivity and **r** your fortunes.
30: 3 For the time is coming when I will **r** the fortunes
30:18 again from your captivity and **r** your fortunes,
31:18 Turn me again to you and **r** me, for you alone are
32:44 For someday I will **r** prosperity to them. I,
33: 7 I will **r** the fortunes of Judah and Israel and rebuild
33:11 For I will **r** the prosperity of this land to what it
33:26 I will **r** them to their land and have mercy on
48:47 But in the latter days I will **r** the fortunes of
49: 6 But afterward I will **r** the fortunes of the
49:39 But in the latter days I will **r** the fortunes of
La 5:21 **R** us, O LORD, and bring us back to you again!
Eze 16:53 "But someday I will **r** the fortunes of Sodom and
Samaria, and I will **r** you, too.
29:14 I will **r** the prosperity of Egypt and bring its people
Hos 6: 2 he will **r** us so we can live in his presence.
6:11 I wanted so much to **r** the fortunes of my people!
Joel 3: 1 when I **r** the prosperity of Judah and Jerusalem,"
Am 9:11 "In that day I will **r** the fallen kingdom of David.
9:11 but I will rebuild its walls and **r** its former glory.
Na 2: 2 but the LORD will **r** its honor and power again.
Zep 2: 7 his people in kindness and **r** their prosperity again.
3:20 They will praise you as I **r** your fortunes before
Ac 1: 6 you going to free Israel now and **r** our kingdom?"
15:16 and I will **r** the fallen kingdom of David.
15:16 From the ruins I will rebuild it, / and I will **r** it,
Heb 6: 4 For it is impossible to **r** to repentance those who
1Pe 5:10 little while, he will **r**, support, and strengthen you,

RESTORED (28) [RESTORE]

Ge 40:21 then **r** the chief cup-bearer to his former position,
41:13 I was **r** to my position as cup-bearer, and the chief
Nu 21:27 city of Sihon! / May it be **r** and rebuilt.
1Sa 7:14 and Gath that the Philistines had captured were **r** to
2Ki 5:10 Then your skin will be **r**, and you will be healed of
8: 6 see to it that everything she had lost was **r** to her,
14:22 Uzziah rebuilt the town of Elath and **r** it to Judah.
2Ch 24:13 They **r** the Temple of God according to its original
26: 2 Uzziah rebuilt the town of Elath and **r** it to Judah.
29:35 So the Temple of the LORD was **r** to service.
33:16 Then he **r** the altar of the LORD and sacrificed
34:11 They **r** what earlier kings of Judah had allowed to
Ne 13:11 back again and **r** them to their proper duties.
Job 22:23 the Almighty and clean up your life, you will be **r**.
42:10 prayed for his friends, the LORD **r** his fortunes.
Ps 30: 2 I cried out to you for help, / and you **r** my health.
85: 1 on your land! / You have **r** the fortunes of Israel.
126: 1 When the LORD **r** his exiles to Jerusalem,
Isa 38:16 it leads to life and health. / You have **r** my health
44:28 Jerusalem be rebuilt and that the Temple be **r**."
Eze 16:55 Sodom and Samaria, and all their people will be **r**,
and at that time you also will be **r**.
21:27 And it will not be **r** until the one appears who has
Da 8:14 and mornings; then the Temple will be **r**."
Mic 4: 8 The kingship will be **r** to my precious Jerusalem.
Mk 8:25 the man stared intently, his sight was completely **r**,
Lk 7:21 and he cast out evil spirits and **r** sight to the blind.
Ro 5:10 For since we were **r** to friendship with God by the

RESTORES (2) [RESTORE]

Ps 14: 7 For when the LORD **r** his people, / Jacob will
53: 6 For when God **r** his people, / Jacob will shout with

RESTORING (1) [RESTORE]

2Ch 35:20 After Josiah had finished **r** the Temple, King Neco

RESTRAIN (9) [RESTRAINED, RESTRAINT]

Job 9:13 And God does not **r** his anger. The mightiest
37: 4 He does not **r** the thunder when he speaks.
38:31 the stars? Are you able to **r** the Pleiades or Orion?
Ps 36: 1 their hearts. / They have no fear of God to **r** them.
Pr 19:11 People with good sense **r** their anger; they earn
Ecc 2:10 I wanted, I took. I did not **r** myself from any joy.
Jer 2:24 the wind at mating time. Who can **r** your lust?
Ac 14:18 and Barnabas could scarcely **r** the people from
Ro 3:18 "They have no fear of God to **r** them."

RESTRAINED (6) [RESTRAIN]

2Ch 36:16 until the LORD's anger could no longer be **r**
Est 5:10 However, he **r** himself and went on home. Then he
Isa 42:14 "I have long been silent; / yes, I have **r** myself.
Eze 31:15 the deep places mourn, and I **r** the mighty waters.
Da 8:12 But the army of heaven was **r** from destroying him
Mk 5: 3 man lived among the tombs and could not be **r**,

RESTRAINT (1) [RESTRAIN]

Job 30:11 He has humbled me, so they have thrown off all **r**.

RESTRICTION (3) [RESTRICTIONS]

Dt 12:16 The only **r** is that you are not to eat the blood.
12:23 The only **r** is never to eat the blood, for the blood
Est 1: 8 The only **r** on the drinking was that no one should

RESTRICTIONS (1) [RESTRICTION]

1Co 7:35 saying this for your benefit, not to place **r** on you.

RESTS (5) [REST]

Ex 30: 6 of atonement—that **r** on the Ark of the Covenant.
Lev 16:13 of atonement—that **r** on the Ark of the Covenant.
Nu 7:89 of atonement—that **r** on the Ark of the Covenant.
Ps 16: 9 mouth shouts his praises! / My body **r** in safety.
Ac 2:26 my mouth shouts his praises! / My body **r** in hope.

RESULT (60) [RESULTED, RESULTING, RESULTS]
Ge 30:43 As a r, Jacob's flocks increased rapidly, and he
38:24 was pregnant as a r of prostitution.
Ex 17:13 As a r, Joshua and his troops were able to crush
21:23 If the r is death, the offender must be executed.
Lev 10:16 As a r, he became very angry with Eleazar
15:31 so they will not die as a r of defiling my
18:25 As a r, the entire land has become defiled. That is
Jos 17:5 As a r, Manasseh's inheritance came to ten parcels
1Sa 19:5 the LORD brought a great victory to Israel as a r?
25:37 As a r he had a stroke, and he lay on his bed
2Sa 4:4 she was running, and he became crippled as a r.)
2Ki 3:27 As a r, the anger against Israel was great, so they
6:25 As a r there was a great famine in the city. After a
1Ch 21:14 and seventy thousand people died as a r.
2Ch 14:14 As a r, vast quantities of plunder were taken from
31:21 As a r, he was very successful.
Est 2:8 As a r of the king's decree, Esther, along with
Pr 5:4 But the r is as bitter as poison, sharp as a
10:28 The hopes of the godly r in happiness,
Ecc 7:27 "I came to this r after looking into the matter from
Jer 5:27 evil plots. And the r? Now they are great and rich.
Da 8:12 As a r, sacrilege was committed against the
11:29 the south, but this time the r will be different.
Zec 1:6 As a r, they repented and said, 'We have received
Mt 23:35 As a r, you will become guilty of murdering all the
Mk 1:45 As a r, such crowds soon surrounded Jesus that he
3:10 As a r, many sick people were crowding around
Jn 9:2 Was it a r of his own sins or those of his parents?"
11:54 As a r, Jesus stopped his public ministry among
Ac 5:15 As a r of the apostles' work, sick people were
8:12 As a r, many men and women were baptized.
17:12 As a r, many Jews believed, as did some of the
18:2 They had been expelled from Italy as a r of
28:10 As a r we were showered with honors, and when
Ro 1:21 The r was that their minds became dark
1:24 As a r, they did vile and degrading things with
1:27 as a r, suffered within themselves the penalty they
5:16 And the r of God's gracious gift is very different from the r of that one man's sin.
6:21 And what was the r? It was not good, since now
6:22 things that lead to holiness and r in eternal life.
7:4 As a r, you can produce good fruit, that is,
11:5 A few are being saved as a r of God's kindness in
1Co 11:21 As a r, some go hungry while others get drunk.
2Co 1:9 But as a r, we learned not to rely on ourselves,
1:11 As a r, many will give thanks to God because
Gal 3:18 then it would not be the r of accepting God's
Php 3:10 As a r, I can really know Christ and experience the
Col 1:22 As a r, he has brought you into the very presence
1Th 1:7 As a r, you yourselves became an example to all
3:13 As a r, Christ will make your hearts strong,
4:12 As a r, people who are not Christians will respect
1Ti 1:19 as a r, their faith has been shipwrecked.
2:14 who was deceived by Satan, and sin was the r.
Phm 1:10 because he became a believer as a r of my ministry
Jas 2:20 When will you ever learn that faith that does not r
1Pe 1:2 As a r, you have obeyed Jesus Christ and are
2Pe 3:16 parts of Scripture—and the r is disaster for them.
1Jn 4:19 We love each other as a r of his loving us first.
Rev 18:3 have grown rich as a r of her luxurious living."

RESULTED (2) [RESULT]
1Ki 13:34 and r in the destruction of Jeroboam's kingdom
2Co 4:12 the face of death, but it has r in eternal life for you.

RESULTING (3) [RESULT]
Jn 1:13 This is not a physical birth r from human passion
Ro 5:21 and r in eternal life through Jesus Christ our Lord.
7:5 evil desires that produced sinful deeds, r in death.

RESULTS (12) [RESULT]
Ex 21:22 If no further harm r, then the person responsible
21:23 But if any harm r, then the offender must be
Pr 9:10 Knowledge of the Holy One r in understanding.
13:2 Good people enjoy the positive r of their words,
Mt 11:19 But wisdom is shown to be right by what r from
21:36 to collect for him, but the r were the same.
Ro 1:13 I want to work among you and see good r, just as I
1Co 15:10 out his special favor on me—and not without r.
15:56 For sin is the sting that r in death, and the law
2Co 7:10 But sorrow without repentance is the kind that r in
Gal 5:19 sinful nature, your lives will produce these evil r:
Jas 5:16 righteous person has great power and wonderful r.

RESURRECTED (1) [RESURRECTION]
1Co 15:42 and decay, will be different when they are r,

RESURRECTION (37) [RESURRECTED]
Mt 22:23 a group of Jews who say there is no r after death.
22:28 So tell us, whose wife will she be in the r? For she
22:31 as to whether there will be a r of the dead—
27:53 after Jesus' r. They left the cemetery, went into
Mk 12:18 a group of Jews who say there is no r after death.
12:23 So tell us, whose wife will she be in the r? For all
Lk 14:14 Then at the r of the godly, God will reward you for
20:27 a group of Jews who say there is no r after death.
20:33 So tell us, whose wife will she be in the r? For all
Jn 11:24 "when everyone else rises, on r day."
11:25 Jesus told her, "I am the r and the life. Those who
Ac 1:22 is chosen will join us as a witness of Jesus' r."
2:1 the day of Pentecost, seven weeks after Jesus' r,
2:31 into the future and predicting the Messiah's r.
4:2 the authority of Jesus, that there is a r of the dead.
4:33 And the apostles gave powerful witness to the r of
17:18 When he told them about Jesus and his r,
17:32 When they heard Paul speak of the r of a person
23:6 on trial because my hope is in the r of the dead!"
23:8 for the Sadducees say there is no r or angels
24:21 because I believe in the r of the dead!' "
1Co 15:12 why are some of you saying there will be no r of
15:13 For if there is no r of the dead, then Christ has not
15:15 but that can't be true if there is no r of the dead.
15:16 If there is no r of the dead, then Christ has not
15:21 now the r from the dead has begun through another
15:23 But there is an order to this r: Christ was raised
15:32 of Ephesus—if there will be no r from the dead?
15:32 If there is no r, / "Let's feast and get drunk,
15:42 It is the same way for the r of the dead. Our earthly
Php 3:11 somehow, I can experience the r from the dead!
2Ti 2:18 preaching the lie that the r of the dead has already
Heb 6:2 of hands, the r of the dead, and eternal judgment.
11:35 They placed their hope in the r to a better life.
1Pe 3:21 now saves you by the power of Jesus Christ's r.
Rev 20:5 This is the first r. (The rest of the dead did not
20:6 Blessed and holy are those who share in the first r.

RETAIN (1) [RETAINING, RETAINS]
Lev 25:48 they still r the right of redemption. They may be

RETAINING (1) [RETAIN]
Ezr 6:3 to offer their sacrifices, r the original foundations.

RETAINS (1) [RETAIN]
Lev 25:29 that time, the seller r the right to buy it back.

RETALIATE (2) [RETALIATED]
1Pe 2:23 He did not r when he was insulted. When he
3:9 Don't r when people say unkind things about you.

RETALIATED (1) [RETALIATE]
Jdg 15:9 The Philistines r by setting up camp in Judah

RETIRE (2) [RETIREMENT]
Ge 19:4 as they were preparing to r for the night,
Nu 8:25 and they must r at the age of fifty.

RETIREMENT (1) [RETIRE]
Nu 8:26 After r they may assist their fellow Levites by

RETORT (3) [RETORTED]
Pr 9:7 Anyone who rebukes a mocker will get a smart r.
13:3 will have a long life; a quick r can ruin everything.
Mal 1:2 says the LORD. But you r, "Really?

RETORTED (10) [RETORT]
Ge 4:9 Where is Abel?" "I don't know!" Cain r.
34:31 he treat our sister like a prostitute?" they r angrily.
Ex 5:2 "Is that so?" r Pharaoh. "And who is the LORD
10:10 Pharaoh r, "The LORD will certainly need to be
2Sa 6:21 David r to Michal, "I was dancing before the
2Ki 6:27 LORD doesn't help you, what can I do?" he r.
Jnh 4:9 "Yes," Jonah r, "even angry enough to die!"
Mt 27:4 "What do we care?" they r. "That's your
Jn 8:48 The people r, "You Samaritan devil! Didn't we
18:30 him over to you if he weren't a criminal!" they r.

RETREAT (4) [RETREATED, RETREATING]
Ps 9:3 My enemies turn away in r; / they are overthrown
44:10 You make us r from our enemies / and allow them
56:9 very day I call to you for help, / my enemies will r.
Da 11:18 to his insolence and will cause him to r in shame.

RETREATED (6) [RETREAT]
Jos 10:11 As the Amorites r down the road from Beth-horon,
Jdg 20:36 The Israelites had r from Benjamin's warriors in
1Sa 4:3 the army of Israel r to their camp, and their leaders
2Sa 2:29 and his men r through the Jordan Valley.
10:14 they ran from Abishai and r into the city.
1Ch 19:15 they ran from Abishai and r into the city.

RETREATING (1) [RETREAT]
Jos 7:5 and they killed about thirty-six who were r down

RETRIEVED (2)
2Sa 21:12 it was the people of Jabesh-gilead who had r their
Isa 49:25 be released, and the plunder of tyrants will be r.

RETURN (324) [RETURNED, RETURNING, RETURNS]
Ge 3:19 Then you will r to the ground from which you
3:19 were made from dust, and to the dust you will r."
15:16 After four generations your descendants will r here
16:9 "R to your mistress and submit to her authority."
18:10 of them said, "About this time next year I will r,
18:14 About a year from now, just as I told you, I will r,
20:7 Now r her to her husband, and he will pray for
20:7 But if you don't r her to him, you can be sure that
24:56 But he said, "Don't hinder my r. The LORD has
31:3 "R to the land of your father and grandfather
31:13 this country and r to the land you came from.' "
32:9 you told me to r to my land and to my relatives,
38:11 again at that time but to r to her parents' home.
40:13 and r you to your position as his chief cup-bearer.
42:25 but he also gave secret instructions to r each
43:14 that he might release Simeon and r Benjamin.
44:33 of the boy, and let the boy r with his brothers.
44:34 For how can I r to my father if the boy is not with
45:9 "Hurry, r to my father and tell him, 'This is what
45:17 and r quickly to their homes in Canaan.
50:5 his burial is complete, I will r without delay."
Ex 3:12 you will r here to worship God at this very
4:19 said to him, "Do not be afraid to r to Egypt,
6:13 LORD ordered Moses and Aaron to r to Pharaoh,
10:1 "R to Pharaoh and again make your demands.
13:17 they might change their minds and r to Egypt."
14:5 were not planning to r to Egypt after three days,
22:26 a pledge of repayment, you must r it by nightfall.
22:27 If you do not r it and your neighbor cries out to me
32:30 but I will r to the LORD on the mountain.
33:11 Afterward Moses would r to the camp,
Lev 13:7 the infected person must r to be examined again.
13:16 the rest of the skin, the person must r to the priest.
14:8 and may r to live inside the camp.
14:39 On the seventh day the priest must r for another
14:44 the priest must r and inspect the house again.
16:19 Israel's defilement and r it to its former holiness.
16:26 and bathe in water. Then he may r to the camp.
25:13 In the Year of Jubilee each of you must r to the
25:27 it back, the original owner may then r to the land.
25:41 and they will r to their clan and ancestral property.
Nu 10:30 will not go. I must r to my own land and family."
10:36 Ark was set down, he would say, "R, O LORD,
12:14 camp for seven days, and after that she may r."
14:3 as slaves! Let's get out of here and r to Egypt!"
14:41 the LORD's orders to r to the wilderness?
19:7 Afterward he may r to the camp, though he will
31:24 and be purified. Then you may r to the camp."
32:18 We will not r to our homes until all the people of
32:22 then you may r when the land is finally subdued
35:28 high priest, the slayer may r to his own property.
35:32 allowing the slayer to r to his property before the
Dt 3:20 then you may r here to the land I have given you.'
4:30 you will finally r to the LORD your God
5:30 Go and tell them to r to their tents.
10:1 of wood to keep them in. R to me on the mountain,
17:16 LORD has told you, 'You must never r to Egypt.'
22:2 it until the owner comes looking for it; then r it.
23:11 bathe himself, and at sunset he may r to the camp.
23:15 and take refuge with you, do not force them to r.
24:13 R the cloak to its owner by sunset so your
30:2 If at that time you r to the LORD your God,
30:5 He will r you to the land that belonged to your
Jos 18:4 They will r to me with a written report of their
18:8 Then r to me with your written report, and I will
20:6 the one found innocent is free to r home."
Jdg 5:28 Through the window she watched for his r, saying,
6:18 LORD answered, "I will stay here until you r."
8:7 I will r and tear your flesh with the thorns
8:9 "After I r in victory, I will tear down this tower."
11:31 out of my house to greet me when I r in triumph.
20:8 and replied, "Not one of us will r home.
Ru 1:6 got ready to leave Moab to r to her homeland.
1:12 No, my daughters, r to your parents' homes,
1Sa 6:2 the LORD? Tell us how to r it to its own land."
7:3 "If you are really serious about wanting to r to the
7:17 Then he would r to his home at Ramah, and he
15:26 But Samuel replied, "I will not r with you!
18:2 him at the palace and wouldn't let him r home.
22:5 "Leave the stronghold and r to the land of Judah."
25:35 accepted her gifts and told her, "R home in peace.
2Sa 1:2 On the third day after David's r, a man arrived
1:22 they did not r from battle empty-handed.
2:6 May the LORD be loyal to you in r and reward
8:13 After his r he destroyed eighteen thousand
11:12 told him, "and tomorrow you may r to the army."
12:23 I will go to him one day, but he cannot r to me."
15:27 and Abiathar should r quietly to the city with your
15:34 R to Jerusalem and tell Absalom, 'I will now be
19:14 They sent word to the king, "R to us, and bring
19:37 Then let me r again to die in my own town,
23:10 The rest of the army did not r until it was time to
1Ki 5:11 In r Solomon sent him an annual payment of
8:34 and r them to this land you gave their ancestors.
11:21 said to Pharaoh, "Let me r to my own country."
11:22 he replied. "But even so, I must r home."
12:20 When the people of Israel learned of Jeroboam's r
12:26 the kingdom will r to the dynasty of David.
13:9 and do not r to Judah by the same way you
13:17 and do not r to Judah by the same way you
14:28 them along and then r them to the guardroom.
17:21 my God, please let this child's life r to him."
22:27 and water until I r safely from the battle!' "
22:28 But Micaiah replied, "If you r safely, the LORD
22:36 ran through his troops: "It's all over—r home!"
2Ki 19:7 Then I will make him want to r to his land,
19:28 and my bridle in your mouth. / I will make you r
19:33 The king will r to his own country by the road on
1Ch 9:2 The first to r to their property in their former
2Ch 6:25 and r them to this land you gave their ancestors.
12:11 them along and then r them to the guardroom.
18:26 and water until I r safely from the battle!' "
18:27 But Micaiah replied, "If you r safely, the LORD
19:4 encouraging the people to r to the LORD,
28:11 Listen to me and r these captives you have taken,
30:6 "O people of Israel, r to the LORD, the God of
30:6 so that he will r to the few of us who have
30:9 For if you r to the LORD, your relatives and your
30:9 their captors, and they will be able to r to this land.

30: 9 If you **r** to him, he will not continue to turn his
33:13 So the LORD let Manasseh **r** to Jerusalem and to
36:23 All of you who are the LORD's people may **r** to
Ezr 1: 3 All of you who are his people may **r** to Jerusalem
1: 5 and Benjamin to **r** to Jerusalem to rebuild the
5:15 The king instructed him to **r** the utensils to their
7:13 may volunteer to **r** to Jerusalem with you.
7:28 And I gathered some of the leaders of Israel to **r**
Ne 1: 9 But if you **r** to me and obey my commands,
2: 6 When will you **r**?" So the king agreed, and I set a
9:26 they killed the prophets who encouraged them to **r**
9:29 You warned them to **r** to your law, but they
13: 6 though I later received his permission to **r**.
Job 10:21 the land of darkness and utter gloom, never to **r**.
16:22 must go down that road from which I will never **r**.
22:23 If you **r** to the Almighty and clean up your life,
39: 4 open fields, then leave their parents and never **r**.
39:12 Can you rely on it to **r**, bringing your grain to the
Ps 6: 4 **R**, O LORD, and rescue me. / Save me because of
22:27 earth will acknowledge the LORD and **r** to him.
51:13 teach your ways to sinners, / and they will **r** to you.
78:39 gone in a moment like a breath of wind, never to **r**.
85: 8 But let them not **r** to their foolish ways.
90: 3 turn people back to dust, saying, / "**R** to dust!"
109: 5 They **r** evil for good, / and hatred for my love.
109:19 Now may his curses **r** and cling to him like
126: 6 but they sing as they **r** with the harvest.
146: 4 When their breathing stops, they **r** to the earth,
Pr 7:20 with him, and he won't **r** until later in the month."
Ecc 3:20 from which they came and to which they must **r**.
4: 9 as much as one; they get a better **r** for their labor.
11: 1 Give generously, for your gifts will **r** to you later.
12: 7 For then the dust will **r** to the earth, and the spirit
will **r** to God who gave it.
SS 6:13 "**R**, **r** to us, O maid of Shulam. Come back,
Isa 10:21 A remnant of them will **r** to the Mighty God.
10:22 the seashore, only a few of them will **r** at that time.
14: 2 of the world will help the LORD's people to **r**,
23:17 She will **r** again to all her evil ways around the
26:14 are dead and gone. / Never again will they **r**!
27:13 and Egypt will **r** to Jerusalem to worship the
30: 6 All this, and Egypt will give you nothing in **r**.
31: 6 are such wicked rebels, come and **r** to the LORD.
35:10 been ransomed by the LORD will **r** to Jerusalem,
37: 7 Then I will make him want to **r** to his land,
37:29 and my bridle in your mouth. / I will make you **r**
37:34 The king will **r** to his own country by the road on
44:22 Oh, **r** to me, for I have paid the price to set you
49:12 See, my people will **r** from far away, from lands to
49:20 The generations born in exile will **r** and say,
51:11 been ransomed by the LORD will **r** to Jerusalem,
57:14 and stones so my people can **r** from captivity.' "
62:10 Go out! Prepare the highway for my people to **r**!
63:17 **R** and help us, for we are your servants and your
66:21 "And I will appoint some of those who **r** to be my
Jer 3: 7 that after she had done all this she would **r** to me.
3:14 "**R** home, you wayward children,"
3:18 and Israel will **r** together from exile in the north.
3:18 They will **r** to the land I gave their ancestors as an
8: 7 the crane. They all **r** at the proper time each year.
12:15 But afterward I will **r** and have compassion on all
14: 3 The servants **r** with empty pitchers, confused
14:12 In **r**, I will give them only war, famine,
15:19 "If you **r** to me, I will restore you so you can
22:10 For he will never **r** to see his native land again.
22:11 and was taken away as a captive: "He will never **r**.
22:27 You will never again **r** to the land of your desire.
24: 7 be their God, for they will **r** to me wholeheartedly.
30:10 and your children will **r** from their exile.
30:10 Israel will **r** and will have peace and quiet in their
31: 8 about to give birth. A great company will **r**!
31:21 back again, my virgin Israel; **r** to your cities here.
32:33 turned their backs on me and have refused to **r**.
37: 7 that Pharaoh's army is about to **r** to Egypt,
40: 5 then **r** to Gedaliah son of Ahikam and grandson of
40:12 they began to **r** to Judah from the places to which
44:28 will escape death and **r** to Judah from Egypt.
46:27 and your children will **r** from their exile.
46:27 Israel will **r** and will have peace and quiet,
51: 9 **R** now to your own land, for her judgment will be
La 4:22 punishment will end; you will soon **r** from exile.
Eze 7:13 should survive, they will never **r** to their business.
11:18 "When the people **r** to their homeland, they will
21: 5 and it will not **r** to its sheath until its work is
21:30 Should I **r** my sword to its sheath before I deal
24:27 your voice will suddenly **r** so you can talk to him,
33:15 **r** what they have stolen, and obey my life-giving
35: 7 killing off all who try to escape and any who **r**.
36: 8 heavy crops of fruit to prepare for my people's **r**—
37:14 and you will live and **r** home to your own land.
38: 8 and after the **r** of her people from many lands.
40: 4 Then you will **r** to the people of Israel and tell
44:19 When they **r** to the outer courtyard where the
44:26 But such a priest can only **r** to his Temple duties
46:17 will be set free, and the land will **r** to the prince.
Da 10:20 Soon I must **r** to fight against the spirit prince of
11: 9 king of the south but will soon **r** to his own land.
11:13 the king of the north will **r** with a fully equipped
11:28 of the north will then **r** home with great riches.
11:30 scare him off, and he will withdraw and **r** home.
Hos 1:11 one leader, and they will **r** from exile together.
2: 7 'I might as well **r** to my husband because I was
2:15 I will **r** her vineyards to her and transform the
3: 5 But afterward the people will **r** to the LORD their
5: 4 Your deeds won't let you **r** to your God. You are a
5:15 Then I will **r** to my place until they admit their
6: 1 "Come, let us **r** to the LORD! He has torn us in
7:10 yet he doesn't **r** to the LORD his God or even try
11: 5 "But since my people refuse to **r** to me, they will
11:10 and my people will **r** trembling from the west.
11:11 Flying like doves, they will **r** from Assyria.
14: 1 **R**, O Israel, to the LORD your God, for your sins
14: 2 Bring your petitions, and **r** to the LORD. Say to
14: 7 My people will **r** again to the safety of their land.
Joel 2:13 **R** to the LORD your God, for he is gracious
Am 1: 5 and the people of Aram will **r** to Kir as slaves.
4: 6 But still you wouldn't **r** to me," says the LORD.
4: 8 But still you wouldn't **r** to me," says the LORD.
4: 9 But still you wouldn't **r** to me," says the LORD.
4:10 But still you wouldn't **r** to me," says the LORD.
4:11 But still you wouldn't **r** to me," says the LORD.
5: 3 a thousand men to battle, only a hundred will **r**.
Ob 1:20 The exiles of Israel will **r** to their land and occupy
1:20 exiled in the north will **r** to their homeland
Mic 5: 3 Then at last his fellow countrymen will **r** from
Hag 2:17 Yet, even so, you refused to **r** to me,
Zec 1: 3 **R** to me, and I will **r** to you, says the LORD
Mal 3: 7 Now **r** to me, and I will **r** to you,"
3: 7 'How can we **r** when we have never gone away?'
Mt 2:12 because God had warned them in a dream not to **r**
2:13 "Stay there until I tell you to **r**, because Herod is
8:21 "Lord, first let me **r** home and bury my father."
10:23 will **r** before you have reached all the towns of
12:44 Then it says, 'I will **r** to the person I came from.'
17:10 that Elijah must **r** before the Messiah comes?"
19:29 will receive a hundred times as much in **r** and will
24: 3 there be any sign ahead of time to signal your **r**
24:18 A person in the field must not **r** even to get a coat.
24:33 you can know his **r** is very near, right at the door.
24:50 the master will **r** unannounced and unexpected.
25:13 because you do not know the day or hour of my **r**.
Mk 8:38 will be ashamed of that person when I **r** in the
9:11 that Elijah must **r** before the Messiah comes?"
10:30 will receive now in **r**, a hundred times over,
11: 3 just say, 'The Lord needs it and will **r** it soon.' "
13:16 A person in the field must not **r** even to get a coat.
13:29 you can be sure that his **r** is very near, right at the
13:34 and he told the gatekeeper to watch for his **r**.
13:35 For you do not know when the homeowner will **r**
13:37 I say to you I say to everyone: Watch for his **r**!"
Lk 6:34 sinners will lend to their own kind for a full **r**.
6:38 Your gift will **r** to you in full measure,
9:26 will be ashamed of that person when I **r** in my
9:51 As the time drew near for his **r** to heaven,
9:59 "Lord, first let me **r** home and bury my father."
10: 6 if they are not, the blessing will **r** to you.
11:24 it says, 'I will **r** to the person I came from.'
12:36 as though you were waiting for your master to **r**
12:37 favor for those who are ready and waiting for his **r**.
12:46 the master will **r** unannounced and unexpected.
15:27 We are celebrating because of his safe **r**.'
17:18 Does only this foreigner **r** to give glory to God?"
17:31 to pack. A person in the field must not **r** to town.
18: 8 But when I, the Son of Man, **r**, how many will I
19:12 to a distant empire to be crowned king and then **r**.
Jn 3:13 have come to earth and will **r** to heaven again.
4: 3 So he left Judea to **r** to Galilee.
6:62 if you see me, the Son of Man, **r** to heaven again?
7:33 little longer. Then I will **r** to the one who sent me.
13: 1 had come to leave this world and **r** to his Father.
13: 3 that he had come from God and would **r** to God.
16:28 and I will leave the world and **r** to the Father."
21:22 "If I want him to remain alive until I **r**,
21:23 only said, "If I want him to remain alive until I **r**,
Ac 1:11 And someday, just as you saw him go, he will **r**!"
7:39 ancestors rejected Moses and wanted to **r** to Egypt.
13:42 the people asked them to **r** again and speak about
15:16 'Afterward I will **r**, / and I will restore the fallen
15:36 "Let's **r** to each city where we previously
20: 3 his life, so he decided to **r** through Macedonia.
25: 5 he said, "Those of you in authority can **r** with me.
Ro 9: 9 For God had promised, "Next year I will **r**,
15:27 they feel the least they can do in **r** is help them
1Co 1: 7 you eagerly wait for the **r** of our Lord Jesus Christ.
9:11 too much to ask, in **r**, for mere food and clothing?
2Co 1:16 on my way to Macedonia and again on my **r** trip.
1:23 The reason I didn't **r** to Corinth was to spare you
8: 6 to **r** to you and encourage you to complete your
11: 7 News to you without expecting anything in **r**?
Php 1:26 Then when I **r** to you, you will have even more
3:20 And we are eagerly waiting for him to **r** as our
1Th 1: 3 and your continual anticipation of the **r** of our Lord
5:10 whether we are dead or alive at the time of his **r**.
2Ti 1:12 what I have entrusted to him until the day of his **r**.
1:18 show him special kindness on the day of Christ's **r**.
4: 8 will give me on that great day of his **r**.
4: 8 for all who eagerly look forward to his glorious **r**.
Phm 1:22 will answer your prayers and let me **r** to you soon.
Jas 5: 7 you must be patient as you wait for the Lord's **r**.
1Pe 1:13 that will come to you at the **r** of Jesus Christ.
2Pe 3: 9 Lord isn't really being slow about his promise to **r**,
Jude 1:16 and they flatter others to get favors in **r**.

RETURNED (313) [RETURN]

Ge 8: 9 So it **r** to the boat, and Noah held out his hand
8:11 the bird **r** to him with a fresh olive leaf in its beak.
14:17 As Abram **r** from his victory over Kedorlaomer
18:33 with Abraham, and Abraham **r** to his tent.
20:14 them to Abraham, and he **r** his wife, Sarah, to him.
21:32 and they **r** home to the land of the Philistines.
22:19 Then they **r** to Abraham's young men and traveled
24:62 home was in the Negev, had **r** from Beer-lahairoi.
27:30 had left his father, Esau **r** from his hunting trip.
31:55 and blessed them. Then he **r** home.
32: 6 The messengers **r** with the news that Esau was on
34: 5 fields herding cattle so he did nothing until they **r**.
34:26 Dinah from Shechem's house and **r** to their camp.
37:29 time later, Reuben **r** to get Joseph out of the pit.
38:22 So Hirah **r** to Judah and told him that he couldn't
43:10 and **r** twice by this time if you had let him come
43:18 because of the money **r** to us in our sacks,"
44:13 loaded the donkeys again, and **r** to the city.
44:16 My lord, we have all **r** to be your slaves—we
44:24 So we **r** to our father and told him what you had
44:28 and that one of them went away and never **r**—
45:25 And they left Egypt and **r** to their father, Jacob,
50:14 Then Joseph **r** to Egypt with his brothers and all
Ex 2:18 When the girls **r** to Reuel, their father, he asked,
4:29 So Moses and Aaron **r** to Egypt and called the
7:23 Pharaoh **r** to his palace and put the whole thing out
18:27 to his father-in-law, who **r** to his own land.
19: 7 Moses **r** from the mountain and called together the
32:31 So Moses **r** to the LORD and said, "Alas,
34:35 Afterward he would put the veil on again until he **r**
Lev 25:28 the land will be **r** to the original owner.
25:30 It will not be **r** to the original owner in the Year of
25:31 and must be **r** to the original owner in the Year of
25:33 Levitical cities—must be **r** in the Year of Jubilee.
Nu 11:30 Then Moses **r** to the camp with the leaders of
13:25 After exploring the land for forty days, the men **r**
16:50 Aaron **r** to Moses at the entrance of the
22:14 So the Moabite officials **r** to King Balak
23: 6 When Balaam **r**, the king was standing beside his
23:17 So Balaam **r** to the place where the king
24:25 Then Balaam and Balak **r** to their homes.
31:14 military commanders who had **r** from the battle.
Dt 1:45 Then you **r** and wept before the LORD, but he
28:31 Your donkey will be driven away, never to be **r**.
Jos 2:16 until the men who are searching for you have **r**;
2:22 but they finally **r** to the city without success.
6:11 then everyone **r** to spend the night in the camp.
6:14 marched around the city once and **r** to the camp.
7: 3 When they **r**, they told Joshua, "It's a small town,
10:15 and the Israelite army **r** to their camp at Gilgal.
10:21 Then the Israelites **r** safely to their camp at
10:43 and the Israelite army **r** to their camp at Gilgal.
14: 7 I **r** and gave from my heart a good report,
18: 9 Then they **r** to Joshua in the camp at Shiloh.
22:32 and **r** to the land of Canaan to tell the Israelites
Jdg 2:19 the judge died, the people **r** to their corrupt ways,
3:24 the king's servants **r** and found the doors to the
7:15 Then he **r** to the Israelite camp and shouted,
8:13 After this, Gideon **r** by way of Heres Pass.
8:15 Gideon then **r** to Succoth and said to the leaders,
8:29 Then Gideon son of Joash **r** home.
9:55 he was dead, they disbanded and **r** to their homes.
11:34 When Jephthah **r** home to Mizpah, his daughter—
11:39 When she **r** home, her father kept his vow, and she
14: 2 When he **r** home, he told his father and mother,
14: 8 Later, when he **r** to Timnah for the wedding,
16:18 So the Philistine leaders **r** and brought the money
17: 3 He **r** the money to her, and she said, "I now
18: 8 When the men **r** to Zorah and Eshtaol,
19: 2 to him and **r** to her father's home in Bethlehem.
19:26 At daybreak the woman **r** to the house where her
20:48 Then the Israelites **r** and slaughtered every living
21:14 Then the men of Benjamin **r** to their homes,
21:24 and families, and they **r** to their own homes.
Ru 1:22 So Naomi **r** from Moab, accompanied by her
3:15 her put it on her back. Then Boaz **r** to the town.
1Sa 1:19 Then they **r** home to Ramah. When Elkanah slept
2:11 and Hannah **r** home to Ramah without Samuel.
2:20 Before they **r** home, Eli would bless Elkanah
6:16 watched all this and then **r** to Ekron that same day.
6:21 "The Philistines have **r** the Ark of the LORD.
9:25 After the feast, when they had **r** to the town,
10:26 When Saul **r** to his home at Gibeah, a band of men
11: 5 and when he **r** to town, he asked,
14:46 chasing the Philistines, and the Philistines **r** home.
15:34 home to Ramah, and Saul **r** to his house at Gibeah.
16:13 him from that day on. Then Samuel **r** to Ramah.
17:53 Then the Israelite army **r** and plundered the
20:42 Then David left, and Jonathan **r** to the city.
23:18 Then Jonathan **r** home, while David stayed at
23:24 So the men of Ziph **r** home ahead of Saul.
23:28 So Saul quit the chase and **r** to fight the Philistines.
24: 1 After Saul **r** from fighting the Philistines, he was
25:12 So David's messengers **r** and told him what Nabal
26:25 Then David went away, and Saul **r** home.
30:12 and nights. It wasn't long before his strength **r**.
2Sa 1: 1 David **r** from his victory over the Amalekites
2:30 Meanwhile, Joab and his men also **r** home.
3:16 Abner told him, "Go back home!" So Palti **r**.
3:22 Joab and some of David's troops **r** from a raid,
5:22 But after a while the Philistines **r** and again spread
6:20 When David **r** home to bless his family,
10:14 After the battle was over, Joab **r** to Jerusalem.
11: 4 having her menstrual period.) Then she **r** home.
12:15 After Nathan **r** to his home, the LORD made
12:20 the LORD. After that, he **r** to the palace and ate.
12:31 Then David and his army **r** to Jerusalem.
15:37 So David's friend Hushai **r** to Jerusalem,
17:20 for them without success and **r** to Jerusalem.
18:16 and his men **r** from chasing the army of Israel.
19:39 and embraced him, Barzillai **r** to his own home.
20:22 back from the attack, and they all **r** to their homes.
Joab **r** to the king at Jerusalem.
24: 8 and twenty days and then **r** to Jerusalem.
1Ki 1:40 And all the people **r** with Solomon to Jerusalem,
1:45 They have just **r**, and the whole city is celebrating

2:30 So Benaiah **r** to the king and told him what Joab
2:34 So Benaiah son of Jehoiada **r** to the sacred tent
2:41 had left Jerusalem and had gone to Gath and **r**.
3:15 He **r** to Jerusalem and stood before the Ark of the
10:13 and all her attendants left and **r** to their own land.
10:22 Once every three years the ships **r**, loaded down
12: 2 he **r** from Egypt, for he had fled to Egypt to escape
12:12 and all the people **r** to hear Rehoboam's decision,
12:16 O David!" So the people of Israel **r** home.
14:17 So Jeroboam's wife **r** to Tirzah, and the child died
17:22 and the life of the child **r**, and he came back to life!
18:43 and looked, but he **r** to Elijah and said,
19:21 Elisha then **r** to his oxen, killed them, and used the
20: 5 Soon Ben-hadad's messengers **r** again and said,
20: 9 the messengers **r** to Ben-hadad with the response.
2Ki 1: 5 When the messengers **r** to the king, he asked them, "Why have you **r** so soon?"
2:13 and **r** to the bank of the Jordan River.
2:18 Elisha was still at Jericho when they **r**. "Didn't I
2:25 went to Mount Carmel and finally **r** to Samaria.
3:27 so they withdrew and **r** to their own land.
4:11 One day Elisha **r** to Shunem, and he went up to his
4:15 When the woman **r**, Elisha said to her as she stood
4:30 unless you go with me." So Elisha **r** with her.
4:31 He **r** to meet Elisha and told him, "The child is
4:38 Elisha now **r** to Gilgal, but there was a famine in
7:15 to escape. The scouts **r** and told the king about it.
8: 3 After the famine ended she **r** to the land of Israel,
8:29 he **r** to Jezreel to recover from his wounds.
9:15 and had **r** to Jezreel to recover from his wounds.)
9:36 When they **r** and told Jehu, he stated, "This fulfills
14:14 He also took hostages and **r** to Samaria.
16:11 and it was ready for the king when he **r** from
16:12 When the king **r**, he inspected the altar and made
17:28 who had been exiled from Samaria **r** to Bethel
19:36 of Assyria broke camp and **r** to his own land.
22: 9 Shaphan **r** to the king and reported,
23:20 altars to desecrate them. Finally, he **r** to Jerusalem.
24: 7 The king of Egypt never **r** after that, for the king of
1Ch 9: 4 One family that **r** was that of Uthai son of
9: 5 Others **r** from the Shilonite clan, including Asaiah
9: 6 From the Zerahite clan, Jeuel **r** with his relatives.
9: 6 In all, 690 families from the tribe of Judah **r**.
9: 9 In all, 956 families from the tribe of Benjamin **r**.
9:10 Among the priests who **r** were Jedaiah, Jehoiarib,
9:13 In all, 1,760 priests **r**. They were heads of clans
9:14 The Levites who **r** were Shemaiah son of Hasshub,
9:17 The gatekeepers who **r** were Shallum, Akkub,
14:13 the Philistines **r** and raided the valley again.
16:43 Then all the people **r** to their homes, and David **r** home to bless his family.
19:15 retreated into the city. Then Joab **r** to Jerusalem.
20: 3 Then David and his army **r** to Jerusalem.
21: 4 Israel to count the people. Then he **r** to Jerusalem
2Ch 1:13 Then Solomon **r** to Jerusalem from the Tabernacle
9:12 and all her attendants left and **r** to their own land.
9:21 Once every three years the ships **r**, loaded down
10: 2 he **r** from Egypt, for he had fled to Egypt to escape
10:12 and all the people **r** to hear Rehoboam's decision,
10:16 your own house, O David!" So all Israel **r** home.
20:27 Then they **r** to Jerusalem, with Jehoshaphat
22: 6 Joram **r** to Jezreel to recover from his wounds,
25:10 angry with Judah, and they **r** home in a great rage.
25:14 When King Amaziah **r** from defeating the
25:24 along with hostages, and then **r** to Samaria.
28: 9 there in Samaria when the army of Israel **r** home.
28:15 the city of palms. Then they **r** to Samaria.
31: 1 the Israelites **r** to their own towns and homes.
32:21 So Sennacherib **r** home in disgrace to his own
34: 7 the land of Israel and then **r** to Jerusalem.
Ezr 1:11 to Jerusalem when the exiles **r** there from Babylon.
2: 1 provinces who **r** from their captivity to Jerusalem
2: 2 This is the number of the men of Israel who **r** from
2:36 These are the priests who **r** from exile:
2:40 These are the Levites who **r** from exile:
2:43 of the following Temple servants **r** from exile:
2:55 of these servants of King Solomon **r** from exile:
2:59 Another group **r** to Jerusalem at this time from the
2:61 Hakkoz, and Barzillai—also **r** to Jerusalem.
2:64 So a total of 42,360 people **r** to Judah,
2:70 The rest of the people **r** to the other towns of Judah
3: 8 was made up of everyone who had **r** from exile,
5: 5 a report was sent to Darius and he **r** his decision.
5:14 King Cyrus **r** the gold and silver utensils that
6:16 and the rest of the people who had **r** from exile.
6:19 On April 21 the **r** exiles celebrated Passover.
6:20 So they slaughtered the Passover lamb for all the **r**
6:21 eaten by the people of Israel who had **r** from exile
8:35 Then the exiles who had **r** from captivity sacrificed
10: 6 because of the unfaithfulness of the **r** exiles.
10: 7 and Jerusalem that all the **r** exiles should come to
Ne 1: 3 "Things are not going well for those who **r** to the
4:15 frustrated them, we all **r** to our work on the wall.
7: 5 record of those who had first **r** to Judah.
7: 6 provinces who **r** from their captivity to Jerusalem
7: 7 This is the number of men of Israel who **r** from
7:39 "These are the priests who **r** from exile:
7:43 "These are the Levites who **r** from exile:
7:46 of the following Temple servants **r** from exile:
7:57 of these servants of King Solomon **r** from exile:
7:61 "Another group **r** to Jerusalem at this time from
7:63 Hakkoz, and Barzillai—also **r** to Jerusalem.
7:66 "So a total of 42,360 people **r** to Judah,
8:17 So everyone who had **r** from captivity lived in
9: 1 On October 31 the people **r** for another
12: 1 and Levites who had **r** with Zerubbabel son of
12: 8 The Levites who had **r** with them were Jeshua,
13: 6 for I had **r** to the king in the thirty-second year of
13:10 the worship services had all **r** to work their fields.
Est 4: 9 So Hathach **r** to Esther with Mordecai's message.
6:12 Afterward Mordecai **r** to the palace gate,
7: 8 just as the king **r** from the palace garden.
Ps 35:13 prayed for them, / but my prayers **r** unanswered.
60: T and Joab **r** and killed twelve thousand Edomites in
106:11 Then the water **r** and covered their enemies;
Isa 11:16 just as he did for Israel long ago when they **r** from
37:37 of Assyria broke camp and **r** to his own land.
Jer 3:10 her faithless sister Judah has never sincerely **r** to
11:10 They have **r** to the sins of their forefathers.
19:14 Then Jeremiah **r** from Topheth where he had
27:16 taken from my Temple will be **r** from Babylon.
37:21 commanded that Jeremiah not be **r** to the dungeon.
38:13 So Jeremiah was **r** to the courtyard of the guard—
39: 1 and his army **r** to besiege Jerusalem.
40: 6 So Jeremiah **r** to Gedaliah son of Ahikam at
40:15 will happen then to the Judeans who have **r**?
43: 5 **r** from the nearby countries to which they had fled.
Eze 38:12 people who have **r** from exile in many nations.
Da 1: 2 When Nebuchadnezzar **r** to Babylon, he took with
4:34 My sanity **r**, and I praised and worshiped the Most
4:36 "When my sanity **r** to me, so did my honor
6:18 Then the king **r** to his palace and spent the night
Zec 1:16 I have **r** to show mercy to Jerusalem. My Temple
4: 1 Then the angel who had been talking with me **r**
Mt 2:21 So Joseph **r** immediately to Israel with Jesus
4:12 had been arrested, he left Judea and **r** to Galilee.
13:54 He **r** to Nazareth, his hometown. When he taught
15:29 Jesus **r** to the Sea of Galilee and climbed a hill
17:22 One day after they had **r** to Galilee, Jesus told
21:17 Then he **r** to Bethany, where he stayed overnight.
21:23 When Jesus **r** to the Temple and began teaching,
25:11 Later, when the other five bridesmaids **r**,
25:19 "After a long time their master **r** from his trip
26:40 Then he **r** to the disciples and found them asleep.
26:43 He **r** to them again and found them sleeping,
Mk 2: 1 Several days later Jesus **r** to Capernaum,
3:20 When Jesus **r** to the house where he was staying,
6: 1 of the country and **r** with his disciples to Nazareth,
6:30 The apostles **r** to Jesus from their ministry tour
14:37 Then he **r** and found the disciples asleep.
14:40 Again he **r** to them and found them sleeping,
14:41 When he **r** to them the third time he said,
Lk 1:23 his term of service was over, and then he **r** home.
2: 3 All **r** to their own towns to register for this census.
2:15 When the angels had **r** to heaven, the shepherds
2:39 of the Lord, they **r** home to Nazareth in Galilee.
2:51 Then he **r** to Nazareth with them and was obedient
4:14 Then Jesus **r** to Galilee, filled with the Holy
4:39 and immediately her temperature **r** to normal.
7:10 And when the officer's friends **r** to his house,
8:37 So Jesus **r** to the boat and left, crossing back to the
8:55 And at that moment her life **r**, and she immediately
9:10 When the apostles **r**, they told Jesus everything
10:17 When the seventy-two disciples **r**, they joyfully
11:14 who couldn't speak, and the man's voice **r** to him.
14:21 "The servant **r** and told his master what they had
15:20 "So he **r** home to his father. And while he was still
15:24 for this son of mine was dead and has now **r** to life.
15:25 When he **r** home, he heard music and dancing in
17:23 "Reports will reach you that the Son of Man has **r**
18:14 not the Pharisee, **r** home justified before God.
19:15 "When he **r**, the king called in the servants to
21:37 and each evening he **r** to spend the night on the
22:45 At last he stood up again and **r** to the disciples,
24:52 and then **r** to Jerusalem filled with great joy.
Jn 5: 1 Afterward Jesus **r** to Jerusalem for one of the
7:45 had been sent to arrest him **r** to the leading priests
8: 1 Jesus **r** to the Mount of Olives,
11:28 Then she left him and **r** to Mary. She called Mary
Ac 5:22 were gone. So they **r** to the council and reported,
8:25 the Lord in Samaria, Peter and John **r** to Jerusalem.
9:39 So Peter **r** with them; and as soon as he arrived,
12:25 they **r** to Antioch, taking John Mark with them.
13:13 There John Mark left them and **r** to Jerusalem.
14:21 Paul and Barnabas **r** again to Lystra, Iconium,
14:26 Finally, they **r** by ship to Antioch of Syria,
16:40 Paul and Silas then **r** to the home of Lydia,
17:15 then they **r** to Berea with a message for Silas
21: 5 When we **r** to the ship at the end of the week,
21: 6 Then we went aboard, and they **r** home.
22:17 "One day after I **r** to Jerusalem, I was praying in
23:32 They **r** to the fortress the next morning,
24:17 I **r** to Jerusalem with money to aid my people
25: 6 Eight or ten days later he **r** to Caesarea, and on the
Gal 1:17 into Arabia and later **r** to the city of Damascus.
1Th 3: 6 Now Timothy has just **r**, bringing the good news
3Jn 1: 3 Some of the brothers recently **r** and made me very

RETURNING (27) [RETURN]

Ge 42:24 **R**, he talked some more with them. He then chose
43:21 as we were **r** home, we stopped for the night
48: 7 As I was **r** from Paddan, Rachel died in the land of
Lev 16:28 and bathe himself in water before **r** to the camp.
Nu 5: 7 20 percent and **r** it to the person who was wronged.
24:14 Now I am **r** to my own people. But first let me tell
1Sa 18: 6 army was **r** home after David had killed Goliath.
27: 9 and clothing before **r** home to see King Achish.
2Ki 9:18 "The rider has met them, but he is not **r**."
9:20 "The rider has met them, but he isn't **r** either!
1Ch 9:12 Other **r** priests were Adaiah son of Jeroham,
12:20 who defected to David as he was **r** to Ziklag:
2Ch 14:15 and camels before finally **r** to Jerusalem.
15: 2 and he went out to meet King Asa as he was **r**
28:12 with this and confronted the men **r** from battle.
Ezr 1: 8 to Sheshbazzar, the leader of the exiles **r** to Judah.
Isa 11:11 **r** them to the land of Israel from Assyria,
23: 1 O ships of Tarshish, **r** home from distant lands!
30:15 "Only in **r** to me and waiting for me will you be
Jer 44:14 Of those who fled to Egypt with dreams of **r** home
Da 10:18 a man touched me again, and I felt my strength **r**.
Zec 8: 3 I am **r** to Mount Zion, and I will live in Jerusalem.
Mt 21:18 as Jesus was **r** to Jerusalem, he was hungry,
Ac 8:28 and he was now **r**. Seated in his carriage, he was
19:21 to Macedonia and Achaia before **r** to Jerusalem.
25: 4 at Caesarea and he himself would be **r** there soon.
Heb 7: 1 When Abraham was **r** home after winning a great

RETURNS (31) [RETURN]

Lev 14:48 "But if the priest **r** for his inspection and finds that
22:13 support her, and she **r** to live in her father's home,
25:10 when each of you **r** to the lands that belonged to
2Sa 17: 3 the people back to you as a bride **r** to her husband.
Pr 26:11 As a dog **r** to its vomit, so a fool repeats his folly.
Ecc 1: 7 Then the water **r** again to the rivers and flows
Eze 44:27 The first day he **r** to work and enters the inner
Da 11: 8 When he **r** again to Egypt, he will carry back their
Mt 12:44 So it **r** and finds its former home empty, swept,
21:40 "When the owner of the vineyard **r**," Jesus asked,
24:37 "When the Son of Man **r**, it will be like it was in
24:46 If the master **r** and finds that the servant has done a
Lk 11:25 So it **r** and finds that its former home is all swept
12:43 If the master **r** and finds that the servant has done a
15: 7 heaven will be happier over one lost sinner who **r**
17:24 For when the Son of Man **r**, you will know it
17:26 "When the Son of Man **r**, the world will be like
17:30 usual' right up to the hour when the Son of Man **r**.
1Co 1: 8 on the great day when our Lord Jesus Christ **r**.
4: 5 to conclusions before the Lord **r** as to whether
5: 5 and he himself will be saved when the Lord **r**.
16:11 on his way with your blessings when he **r** to me.
Php 1:10 may live pure and blameless lives until Christ **r**.
2:16 tightly to the word of life, so that when Christ **r**,
1Th 4:15 We who are still living when the Lord **r** will not
1Ti 6:14 with you from now until our Lord Jesus Christ **r**.
1Pe 5: 1 will share his glory and his honor when he **r**.
2Pe 2:22 "A dog **r** to its vomit," and "A washed pig **r** to the mud."
1Jn 2:28 to live in fellowship with Christ so that when he **r**,
3: 2 even imagine what we will be like when Christ **r**.

REU (7)

Ge 11:18 When Peleg was 30 years old, his son **R** was born.
11:19 After the birth of **R**, Peleg lived another 209 years
11:20 When **R** was 32 years old, his son Serug was born.
11:21 **R** lived another 207 years and had other sons
1Ch 1:25 Eber, Peleg, **R**,
Lk 3:35 Serug was the son of **R**. / **R** was the son of Peleg.

REUBEN (79) [REUBEN'S, REUBENITE, REUBENITES]

Ge 29:32 She named him **R**, for she said, "The LORD has
30:14 **R** found some mandrakes growing in a field
35:22 While he was there, **R** slept with Bilhah,
35:23 The sons of Leah were **R** (Jacob's oldest son),
37:21 But **R** came to Joseph's rescue. "Let's not kill
37:22 **R** was secretly planning to help Joseph escape,
37:29 time later, **R** returned to get Joseph out of the pit.
42:22 **R** asked. "But you wouldn't listen. And now we
42:37 Then **R** said to his father, "You may kill my two
46: 8 went with him to Egypt: **R** was Jacob's oldest son.
46: 9 The sons of **R** were Hanoch, Pallu, Hezron,
48: 5 They will inherit from me just as **R** and Simeon
49: 3 "**R**, you are my oldest son, / the child of my
Ex 1: 2 **R**, Simeon, Levi, Judah,
6:14 The descendants of **R**, Israel's oldest son,
6:14 Their descendants became the clans of **R**.
Nu 1: 5 chosen for the task: / **R** | Elizur son of Shedeur
2:10[-11] "The divisions of **R**, Simeon, and Gad are to
2:10[-11] **R** | Elizur son of Shedeur | 46,500
7:30 leader of the tribe of **R**, presented his offering.
10:18 Then the tribes that camped with **R** set out with
13: 4 of the leaders: / **R** | Shammua son of Zaccur
16: 1 of Eliab, and On son of Peleth, from the tribe of **R**.
26: 5 These were the clans descended from **R**,
26: 7 The men from all the clans of **R** numbered 43,730.
32: 1 Now the tribes of **R** and Gad owned vast numbers
32:25 Then the people of Gad and **R** replied, "We are
32:29 and **R** who are able to fight the LORD's battles
32:31 The tribes of Gad and **R** said again, "Sir, we will
32:33 So Moses assigned to the tribes of Gad, **R**, and half
32:37 The people of **R** built the towns of Heshbon,
34:14 The families of the tribes of **R**, Gad, and half the
Dt 3:12 Gilead with its towns, to the tribes of **R** and Gad.
3:16 And to the tribes of **R** and Gad I gave the area
4:43 Bezer on the wilderness plateau for the tribe of **R**;
11: 6 and Abiram (the sons of Eliab, a descendant of **R**)
27:13 And the tribes of **R**, Gad, Asher, Zebulun, Dan,
29: 8 their land and gave it to the tribes of **R** and Gad
33: 6 Moses said this about the tribe of **R**:
33: 6 "Let the tribe of **R** live and not die out,
Jos 1:12 Then Joshua called together the tribes of **R**, Gad,
4:12 The armed warriors from the tribes of **R**, Gad,
12: 6 And Moses gave their land to the tribes of **R**,
13: 8 Half the tribe of Manasseh and the tribes of **R**
13:15 the following area to the families of the tribe of **R**.
13:21 The land of **R** also included all the towns of the
13:23 marked the western boundary for the tribe of **R**.
13:23 as an inheritance to the families of the tribe of **R**.

18: 7 And the tribes of Gad, **R**, and the half-tribe of
20: 8 Bezer, in the wilderness plain of the tribe of **R**;
21: 7 Merari received twelve cities from the tribes of **R**,
21:36 From the tribe of **R** they received Bezer, Jahaz,
22: 1 Then Joshua called together the tribes of **R**, Gad,
22: 9 So the men of **R**, Gad, and the half-tribe of
22:10 before they crossed the Jordan River, **R**, Gad,
22:13 They crossed the river to talk with the tribes of **R**,
22:15 they said to the tribes of **R**, Gad, and the half-tribe
22:21 Then the people of **R**, Gad, and the half-tribe of
22:30 the high officials heard this from the tribes of **R**,
22:32 and the ten high officials left the tribes of **R**
22:33 and spoke no more of war against **R** and Gad.
22:34 The people of **R** and Gad named the altar
Jdg 5:15 rushing into the valley. / But in the tribe of **R**
5:16 In the tribe of **R** / there was great indecision.
2Ki 10:33 including all of Gilead, Gad, **R**, and Manasseh.
1Ch 2: 1 The sons of Israel were **R**, Simeon, Levi, Judah,
5: 1 The oldest son of Israel was **R**. But since he
5: 1 **R** is not listed in the genealogy as the firstborn son.
5: 3 The sons of **R**, the oldest son of Israel,
5:18 were 44,760 skilled warriors in the armies of **R**,
5:26 to invade the land and lead away the people of **R**,
6:63 sacred lots twelve towns from the territories of **R**,
6:78 From the territory of **R**, east of the Jordan River
12:37 where the tribes of **R** and Gad and the half-tribe of
26:32 and put them in charge of the tribes of **R** and Gad
27:16 and their leaders: / **R** | Eliezer son of Zicri
Eze 48: 6 and then **R**,
48:31 The first will be named for **R**, the second for
Rev 7: 5 12,000 / from **R** | 12,000 / from Gad | 12,000

REUBEN'S (3) [REUBEN]

Nu 2:16 So the total of all the troops on **R** side of the camp
Jos 15: 6 to the stone of Bohan. (Bohan was **R** son.)
18:17 down to the stone of Bohan. (Bohan was **R** son.)

REUBENITE (1) [REUBEN]

1Ch 11:42 the **R** leader who had thirty men with him;

REUBENITES (5) [REUBEN]

Nu 32: 6 all the fighting?" Moses asked the **R** and Gadites.
1Ch 5: 6 Beerah was the leader of the **R** when they were
5: 8 These **R** lived in the area that stretches from Aroer
5:10 reign of Saul, the **R** defeated the Hagrites in battle.
5:11 Across from the **R** in the land of Bashan lived the

REUEL (11) [JETHRO]

Ge 36: 4 Esau and Basemath had a son named **R**.
36:10 and **R**, the son of Esau's wife Basemath.
36:13 The sons of **R** were Nahath, Zerah, Shammah,
36:17 The sons of Esau's son **R** became the leaders of
36:17 clans in the land of Edom were descended from **R**,
Ex 2:18 When the girls returned to **R**, their father,
2:21 In time, **R** gave Moses one of his daughters,
Nu 10:29 his brother-in-law, Hobab son of **R** the Midianite,
1Ch 1:35 of Esau were Eliphaz, **R**, Jeush, Jalam, and Korah.
1:37 The sons of **R** were Nahath, Zerah, Shammah,
9: 8 son of Shephatiah, son of **R**, son of Ibnijah.

REUMAH (1)

Ge 22:24 had four other children from his concubine **R**.

REUNITED (1) [UNITE]

2Sa 13:39 longed to be **r** with his son Absalom.

REVEAL (25) [REVEALED, REVEALER, REVEALING, REVEALS, REVELATION, REVELATIONS]

Ex 6: 3 though I did not **r** my name, the LORD, to them.
1Sa 2:27 "Didn't I **r** myself to your ancestors when the
Job 20:27 The heavens will **r** his guilt, and the earth will give
Ps 50:23 to my path, / I will **r** to you the salvation of God."
Isa 8:18 **r** the plans the LORD Almighty has for his
42: 1 Spirit upon him. He will **r** justice to the nations.
52: 6 But I will **r** my name to my people, and they will
53: 1 To whom will the LORD **r** his saving power?
Eze 28:22 and I will **r** my glory by what happens to you.
28:22 against you and **r** my holiness among you,
28:25 I will **r** to the nations of the world my holiness
36:23 And when I **r** my holiness through you before their
Da 2:47 for you have been able to **r** this secret."
11: 2 "Now then, I will **r** the truth to you. Three more
Mt 11:27 and those to whom the Son chooses to **r** him."
Lk 2:32 He is a light to **r** God to the nations, / and he is the
10:22 and those to whom the Son chooses to **r** him."
Jn 12:38 To whom will the Lord **r** his saving power?"
14:21 And I will **r** myself to each one of them."
14:22 why are you going to **r** yourself only to us and not
16:15 this is what I mean when I say that the Spirit will **r**
Ro 8:19 day when God will **r** who his children really are.
1Co 4: 5 secrets to light and will **r** our private motives.
Eph 3: 5 God did not **r** it to previous generations, but now
Heb 3: 5 was an illustration of the truths God would **r** later.

REVEALED (48) [REVEAL]

Ge 41:39 "Since God has **r** the meaning of the dreams to
Dt 29:29 but the **r** things belong to us and our descendants
2Sa 7:27 because you have **r** that you will build a house for
1Ch 17:25 because you have **r** that you will build a house for
Ps 98: 2 and has **r** his righteousness to every nation!
103: 7 He **r** his character to Moses / and his deeds to the
147:19 He has **r** his words to Jacob, / his principles
Isa 22:14 The LORD Almighty has **r** to me that this sin will
40: 5 Then the glory of the LORD will be **r**, and all
Jer 38:21 to surrender, this is what the LORD has **r** to me:
La 4:22 is just beginning; soon your many sins will be **r**.
Eze 20: 5 When I chose Israel and **r** myself to her in Egypt,
Da 2:19 That night the secret was **r** to Daniel in a vision.
2:23 of you / and **r** to us what the king demanded."
Ob 1: 1 This is the vision that the Sovereign LORD **r** to
Mt 10:26 For the time is coming when everything will be **r**;
16:17 because my Father in heaven has **r** this to you.
Lk 2:26 The Holy Spirit had **r** to him that he would not die
2:35 the deepest thoughts of many hearts will be **r**.
4: 5 and **r** to him all the kingdoms of the world in a
12: 2 The time is coming when everything will be **r**;
Jn 17:26 And I have **r** you to them and will keep on
Ac 7:13 they went, Joseph **r** his identity to his brothers,
Ro 8:39 the love of God that is **r** in Christ Jesus our Lord.
9: 4 God **r** his glory to them. He made covenants with
1Co 2:10 because God has **r** them to us by his Spirit,
15:51 But let me tell you a wonderful secret God has **r** to
Gal 1:16 Then he **r** his Son to me so that I could proclaim
2: 2 I went there because God **r** to me that I should go.
Eph 1: 9 God's secret plan has now been **r** to us; it is a plan
3: 3 in this letter, God himself **r** his secret plan to me.
3: 5 but now he has **r** it by the Holy Spirit to his holy
Col 1:26 but now it has been **r** to his own holy people.
3: 4 who is your real life, is **r** to the whole world,
2Th 2: 3 against God and the man of lawlessness is **r**—
2: 6 for he can be **r** only when his time comes.
2: 8 Then the man of lawlessness will be **r**,
1Ti 3: 9 They must be committed to the **r** truths of the
5:24 But there are others whose sin will not be **r** until
6:15 For at the right time Christ will be **r** from heaven
Tit 1: 3 And now at the right time he has **r** this Good
2:11 For the grace of God has been **r**, bringing salvation
2:13 our great God and Savior, Jesus Christ, will be **r**.
Heb 9: 8 By these regulations the Holy Spirit **r** that the Most
1Pe 1: 5 It will be **r** on the last day for all to see.
1: 7 and honor on the day when Jesus Christ is **r** to the
1Jn 5: 6 And Jesus Christ was **r** as God's Son by his
Rev 15: 4 for your righteous deeds have been **r**."

REVEALER (2) [REVEAL]

Da 2:29 The **r** of mysteries has shown you what is going to
2:47 God of gods, the Lord over kings, a **r** of mysteries,

REVEALING (5) [REVEAL]

Pr 11:13 A gossip goes around **r** secrets, but those who are
Mt 11:25 so wise and clever, and for **r** it to the childlike.
Lk 10:21 so wise and clever, and for **r** it to the childlike.
Jn 16:14 He will bring me glory by **r** to you whatever he
17:26 have revealed you to them and will keep on **r** you.

REVEALS (8) [REVEAL]

Lev 13:31 if the priest's examination **r** that the infection is
Nu 23: 3 Then I will tell you whatever he **r** to me."
Ps 48: 3 Jerusalem's towers. / He **r** himself as her defender.
111: 3 Everything he does **r** his glory and majesty.
Da 2:22 He **r** deep and mysterious things / and knows what
2:28 But there is a God in heaven who **r** secrets, and he
Am 4:13 stirs up the winds, and **r** his every thought.
1Co 13: 9 only a little, and even the gift of prophecy **r** little!

REVEL (1) [REVELING, REVELRY]

2Pe 2:13 They **r** in deceitfulness while they feast with you.

REVELATION (8) [REVEAL]

Ro 3: 2 the Jews were entrusted with the whole **r** of God.
1Co 14: 6 But if I bring you some **r** or some special
14:26 another will tell some special **r** God has given,
14:30 and another person receives a **r** from the Lord,
Gal 1:12 For my message came by a direct **r** from Jesus
2Th 2: 2 a **r**, or a letter supposedly from us, don't believe
Rev 1: 1 This is a **r** from Jesus Christ, which God gave him
1: 1 so that John could share the **r** with God's other

REVELATIONS (3) [REVEAL]

Jer 14:14 of visions and **r** they have never seen or heard.
2Co 12: 1 about the visions and **r** I received from the Lord.
12: 7 even though I have received wonderful **r** from

REVELING (1) [REVEL]

Isa 22: 2 What do I see in this **r** city? Bodies are lying

REVELRY (3) [REVEL]

Ex 32: 6 and drinking, and indulged themselves in pagan **r**.
Am 6: 7 led away as captives. Suddenly, all your **r** will end.
1Co 10: 7 and they indulged themselves in pagan **r**."

REVENGE (18) [VENGEANCE]

Ge 4:24 anyone who takes **r** against me will be punished
Lev 19:18 "Never seek **r** or bear a grudge against anyone,
Jos 20: 9 they could escape being killed in **r** prior to
Jdg 15: 7 Samson vowed, "I will take my **r** on you,
20:10 and the rest of us will take **r** on Gibeah for this
1Sa 14:24 before I have full **r** on my enemies."
2Sa 3:27 and killed Abner in **r** for killing his brother Asahel.
4: 8 Today the LORD has given you **r** on Saul and his
21: 4 we don't want to see the Israelites executed in **r**."
Est 8:13 be ready on that day to take **r** on their enemies.
Job 31:30 No, I have never cursed anyone or asked for **r**.
Ps 8: 2 They silence your enemies / who were seeking **r**.
Jer 20:10 they say, "and then we will get our **r** on him."
Eze 25:15 of Philistia have acted against Judah out of **r**
25:17 And when I have inflicted my **r**, then they will
Joel 3: 4 Are you trying to take **r** on me? If you are,
Na 1: 2 He takes **r** on all who oppose him and furiously
Mk 6:19 Herodias was enraged and wanted John killed in **r**,

REVENUE (2)

1Ki 10:15 This did not include the additional **r** he received
2Ch 9:14 This did not include the additional **r** he received

REVERE (1) [REVERED, REVERENCE, REVERENT]

Isa 25: 3 will declare your glory; ruthless nations will **r** you.

REVERED (5) [REVERE]

Jos 4:14 and for the rest of his life they **r** him as much as they had **r** Moses.
1Ch 16:25 worthy of praise! / He is to be **r** above all gods.
Ps 96: 4 worthy of praise! / He is to be **r** above all the gods.
Mal 2: 5 and they greatly **r** me and stood in awe of my

REVERENCE (17) [REVERE]

Lev 19:30 days of rest and show **r** toward my sanctuary,
26: 2 Sabbath days of rest and show **r** for my sanctuary.
Jos 5:14 At this, Joshua fell with his face to the ground in **r**.
Job 4: 6 Does your **r** for God give you no confidence?
15: 4 Have you no fear of God, no **r** for him?
22: 4 Is it because of your **r** for him that he accuses
37:24 fear him. People who are truly wise show him **r**."
Ps 19: 9 **R** for the LORD is pure, / lasting forever.
22:23 Show him **r**, all you descendants of Israel!
34: 9 Let the LORD's people show him **r**, / for those
111:10 **R** for the LORD is the foundation of true
Jer 44:10 To this very hour you have shown no remorse or **r**.
Zep 3: 7 I thought, 'Surely they will have **r** for me now!
Mal 2: 5 This called for **r** from them, and they greatly
Eph 5:21 you will submit to one another out of **r** for Christ.
Php 2:12 in your lives, obeying God with deep **r** and fear.
Heb 5: 7 God heard his prayers because of his **r** for God.

REVERENT (3) [REVERE]

Ps 2:11 Serve the LORD with **r** fear, / and rejoice with
Col 3:22 them willingly because of your **r** fear of the Lord.
1Pe 1:17 So you must live in **r** fear of him during your time

REVERSE (3) [REVERSING]

Nu 23:20 to bless; / he has blessed, and I cannot **r** it!
Isa 43:13 can oppose what I do. No one can **r** my actions."
1Co 7:18 before he became a believer should not try to **r** it.

REVERSING (1) [REVERSE]

Est 8: 5 send out a decree **r** Haman's orders to destroy the

REVIEW (1)

Isa 43:26 Let us **r** the situation together, and you can present

REVIVE (7) [REVIVED, REVIVES, REVIVING]

Ps 80:18 **R** us so we can call on your name once more.
85: 6 Won't you **r** us again, / so your people can rejoice
119:25 completely discouraged; / **r** me by your word.
Pr 25:13 of summer. They **r** the spirit of their employer.
Isa 23:17 Yes, after seventy years the LORD will **r** Tyre.
61: 4 They will **r** them, though they have been empty for
Eze 29:21 when I will cause the ancient glory of Israel to **r**,

REVIVED (4) [REVIVE]

Ge 45:27 loaded with the food sent by Joseph, his spirit **r**.
Jdg 15:19 the ground at Lehi, and Samson was **r** as he drank.
2Ki 13:21 the dead man **r** and jumped to his feet!
Ezr 9: 9 He **r** us so that we were able to rebuild the Temple

REVIVES (1) [REVIVE]

Ps 119:50 Your promise **r** me; / it comforts me in all my

REVIVING (1) [REVIVE]

Ps 19: 7 The law of the LORD is perfect, / **r** the soul.

REVOKED (6)

Est 1:19 a law of the Persians and Medes that cannot be **r**.
8: 8 and sealed with his ring can never be **r**."
Ps 148: 6 and forever. / His orders will never be **r**.
Da 6: 8 of the Medes and Persians, which cannot be **r**."
6:12 of the Medes and Persians, which cannot be **r**."
Zec 11:10 showing that I had **r** the covenant I had made with

REVOLT (7) [REVOLTED, REVOLTING]

1Sa 13: 3 quickly among the Philistines that Israel was in **r**,
22:13 Why did you encourage him to **r** against me
1Ki 2:28 Joab had also joined Adonijah's **r**.
Isa 3: 5 Young people will **r** against authority,
Eze 2: 3 and they are still in **r** to this very day.
17:14 so Israel would not become strong again and **r**.
Lk 23:14 this man to me, accusing him of leading a **r**.

REVOLTED (10) [REVOLT]

Jdg 9:18 But now you have **r** against my father and his
9:23 and the people of Shechem, and they **r**.
1Sa 14:21 who had gone over to the Philistine army **r**

2Sa 20:21 of Ephraim, who has **r** against King David.
2Ki 8:20 the Edomites **r** against Judah and crowned their
8:22 The town of Libnah **r** about that same time.
18: 7 He **r** against the king of Assyria and refused to pay
2Ch 21: 8 the Edomites **r** against Judah and crowned their
21:10 The town of Libnah **r** about that same time,
Hos 8: 1 have broken my covenant and **r** against my law.

REVOLTING (2) [REVOLT]

Nu 16:11 The one you are really **r** against is the LORD!
Gal 4:14 But even though my sickness was **r** to you, you did

REVOLVES (1)

Eze 38:12 and they think the whole world **r** around them!'

REWARD (89) [REWARDED, REWARDS]

Ge 15: 1 for I will protect you, and your **r** will be great."
Nu 22:37 "Didn't you believe me when I said I would **r** you
24:11 I had planned to **r** you richly, but the LORD has kept you from your **r**."
Ru 1: 8 And may the LORD **r** you for your kindness to
2:12 wings you have come to take refuge, **r** you fully."
1Sa 17:25 And have you heard about the huge **r** the king has
17:27 hearing is true. That is the **r** for killing the giant."
24:19 May the LORD **r** you well for the kindness you
25:28 The LORD will surely **r** you with a lasting
26:23 The LORD gives his own **r** for doing good
30:20 "These all belong to David as his **r**!" they said.
2Sa 2: 6 to you in return and **r** you with his unfailing love!
2: 6 And I, too, will **r** you for what you have done.
3: 8 by not betraying you to David, is this my **r**—
4:10 at Ziklag. That's the **r** I gave him for his news!
4:11 Now what **r** should I give the wicked men who
18:22 Joab replied. "There will be no **r** for you."
2Ch 20:11 Now see how they **r** us! For they have come to
Est 6: 3 "What **r** or recognition did we ever give Mordecai
Job 15:31 for emptiness will be their only **r**.
Ps 19:11 there is great **r** for those who obey them.
37:18 and they will receive a **r** that lasts forever.
58:11 "There truly is a **r** for those who live for God;
94:15 and those who are upright will have a **r**.
127: 3 are a gift from the LORD; / they are a **r** from him.
128: 4 That is the LORD's **r** / for those who fear him.
Pr 11:18 for the moment, but the **r** of the godly will last.
14:14 get what they deserve; good people receive their **r**.
25:22 coals on their heads, and the LORD will **r** you.
28:20 The trustworthy will get a rich **r**. But the person
31:31 **R** her for all she has done. Let her deeds publicly
Ecc 2:10 in hard work, an additional **r** for all my labors.
9: 5 They have no further **r**, nor are they remembered.
9: 9 The wife God gives you is your **r** for all your
Isa 3:10 Tell them, "You will receive a wonderful **r**!"
17:14 This is the just **r** of those who plunder and destroy
32: 9 Listen to me, and I will tell you of your **r**.
40:10 See, he brings his **r** with him as he comes.
45:13 and free my captive people—and not for a **r**!
49: 4 in the LORD's hand; I will trust God for my **r**."
50:11 own fires. This is the **r** you will receive from me:
61: 8 I will faithfully **r** my people for their suffering
62:11 See, he brings his **r** with him as he comes.' "
Jer 31:16 "Do not weep any longer, for I will **r** you.
32:19 and you **r** them according to their deeds.
Eze 29:20 I have given him the land of Egypt as a **r** for his
Da 11:30 and **r** those who forsake the covenant.
11:39 and dividing the land among them as their **r**.
Mic 2: 3 "I will **r** your evil with evil; you won't be able to
Mt 5:12 Be very glad! For a great **r** awaits you in heaven.
6: 1 then you will lose the **r** from your Father in
6: 2 they have received all the **r** they will ever get.
6: 4 and your Father, who knows all secrets, will **r** you.
6: 5 I assure you, that is all the **r** they will ever get.
6: 6 your Father, who knows all secrets, will **r** you.
6:16 I assure you, that is the only **r** they will ever get.
6:18 your Father, who knows all secrets, will **r** you.
10:41 you will receive the same **r** a prophet gets.
10:41 of their godliness, you will be given a **r** like theirs.
24:46 the servant has done a good job, there will be a **r**.
Mk 14:11 why he had come, and they promised him a **r**.
Lk 6:23 leap for joy! For a great **r** awaits you in heaven.
6:35 Then your **r** from heaven will be very great,
12:43 the servant has done a good job, there will be a **r**.
14:14 God will **r** you for inviting those who could not
16: 9 your generosity stores up a **r** for you in heaven.
19:17 so you will be governor of ten cities as your **r**.'
22: 5 ready to help them, and they promised him a **r**.
1Co 3:14 work survives the fire, that builder will receive a **r**.
Eph 2: 9 Salvation is not a **r** for the good things we have
6: 8 Remember that the Lord will **r** each one of us for
Php 4: 1 see you, for you are my joy and the **r** for my work.
4:17 What I want is for you to receive a well-earned **r**
Col 3:24 the Lord will give you an inheritance as your **r**,
1Th 2:19 and joy, and what is our proud **r** and crown?
1Ti 4: 8 for it promises a **r** in both this life and the next.
Heb 10:35 what happens. Remember the great **r** it brings you!
11:26 for he was looking ahead to the great **r** that God
1Pe 1: 9 Your **r** for trusting him will be the salvation of
1:17 He will judge or **r** you according to what you do.
3:14 suffer for doing what is right, God will **r** you for it.
5: 4 your **r** will be a never-ending share in his glory
2Pe 2:13 Their destruction is their **r** for the harm they have
2Jn 1: 8 Be diligent so that you will receive your full **r**.
Rev 11:18 It is time to judge the dead and **r** your servants.
11:18 You will **r** your prophets and your holy people,
16: 6 their murderers blood to drink. It is their just **r**."
22:12 "See, I am coming soon, and my **r** is with me,

REWARDED (15) [REWARD]

Ge 30:18 "God has **r** me for giving my servant to my
2Sa 18:11 I would have **r** you with ten pieces of silver and a
22:21 The LORD **r** me for doing right;
22:25 The LORD **r** me for doing right, / because of my
2Ch 15: 7 and courageous, for your work will be **r**."
Job 20:18 His labors will not be **r**. His wealth will bring him
Ps 18:20 The LORD **r** me for doing right;
18:24 The LORD **r** me for doing right, / because of the
Pr 11:31 If the righteous are **r** here on earth, how much
27:18 who protect their employer's interests will be **r**.
Eze 18:20 Righteous people will be **r** for their own goodness,
Mt 10:42 of the least of my followers, you will surely be **r**."
Mk 9:41 to the Messiah, I assure you, that person will be **r**.
1Co 3: 8 Yet they will be **r** individually, according to their
1Ti 3:13 Those who do well as deacons will be **r** with

REWARDS (3) [REWARD]

Ps 111:10 The **r** of wisdom come to all who obey him.
Jer 17:10 I give all people their due **r**, according to what
Heb 11: 6 a God and that he **r** those who sincerely seek him.

REZEPH (2)

2Ki 19:12 such nations as Gozan, Haran, **R**, and the people of
Isa 37:12 such nations as Gozan, Haran, **R**, and the people of

REZIA [KJV] See RIZIA

REZIN (9) [REZIN'S]

2Ki 15:37 In those days the LORD began to send King **R** of
16: 5 Then King **R** of Aram and King Pekah of Israel
16: 9 resettling them in Kir. They also killed King **R**.
Ezr 2:48 **R**, Nekoda, Gazzam,
Ne 7:50 Reaiah, **R**, Nekoda,
Isa 7: 1 Jerusalem was attacked by King **R** of Aram
7: 4 King **R** of Aram and Pekah son of Remaliah.
7: 8 And Damascus is no stronger than its king, **R**.
8: 6 and are rejoicing over what will happen to King **R**

REZIN'S (1) [REZIN]

Isa 9:11 will reply to their bragging by bringing **R** enemies,

REZON (5)

1Ki 11:23 God also raised up **R** son of Eliada to be an enemy
11:23 **R** had fled from his master, King Hadadezer of
11:24 **R** and his men fled to Damascus, where he became
11:25 **R** was Israel's bitter enemy for the rest of
11:25 **R** hated Israel intensely and continued to reign in

RHEGIUM (1)

Ac 28:13 From there we sailed across to **R**. A day later a

RHESA (2)

Lk 3:27 Joanan was the son of **R**. / **R** was the son of Zerubbabel.

RHODA (1)

Ac 12:13 and a servant girl named **R** came to open it.

RHODES (1)

Ac 21: 1 The next day we reached **R** and then went to

RHYTHM (1)

Ex 15:20 a tambourine and led all the women in **r** and dance.

RIB (1) [RIBS]

Ge 2:22 Then the LORD God made a woman from the **r**

RIBAI (2)

2Sa 23:29 Ithai son of **R** from Gibeah (from the tribe of
1Ch 11:31 Ithai son of **R** from Gibeah (from the tribe of

RIBBAND [KJV] See CORD

RIBBON (1) [RIBBONS]

SS 4: 3 Your lips are like a **r** of scarlet. Oh, how beautiful

RIBBONS (1) [RIBBON]

Est 1: 6 fastened by purple **r** to silver rings embedded in

RIBLAH (11)

Nu 34:11 then down to **R** on the east side of Ain. From there
2Ki 23:33 Pharaoh Neco put Jehoahaz in prison at **R** in the
25: 6 They brought him to the king of Babylon at **R**,
25:20 took them all to the king of Babylon at **R**.
25:21 And there at **R**, in the land of Hamath, the king of
Jer 39: 5 of Babylon, who was at **R** in the land of Hamath.
52: 9 They brought him to the king of Babylon at **R**,
52:10 There at **R**, the king of Babylon made Zedekiah
52:26 took them all to the king of Babylon at **R**.
52:27 And there at **R** in the land of Hamath, the king of
Eze 6:14 from the wilderness in the south to **R** in the north.

RIBS (2) [RIB]

Ge 2:21 He took one of Adam's **r** and closed up the place
Da 7: 5 and it had three **r** in its mouth between its teeth.

RICH (149) [ENRICH, ENRICHED, GET-RICH-QUICK, RICHER, RICHES, RICHEST, RICHLY, RICHNESS]

Ge 13: 2 for Abram was very **r** in livestock, silver, and gold.
14:23 you might say, 'I am the one who made Abram **r**!'
25:11 God poured out **r** blessings on Isaac,
26:13 He became a **r** man, and his wealth only continued
26:16 "for you have become too **r** and powerful for us."
27:17 with its **r** aroma, and some freshly baked bread.
49:20 "Asher will produce **r** foods, / food fit for kings.
Ex 30:15 the **r** must not give more, and the poor must not
34: 6 to anger and **r** in unfailing love and faithfulness.
Lev 19:15 favoring the poor nor showing deference to the **r**.
25:47 "If a resident foreigner becomes **r**, and if some of
Nu 14: 8 It is a **r** land flowing with milk and honey, and he
14:18 LORD is slow to anger and **r** in unfailing love,
Dt 1:17 you make decisions, never favor those who are **r**;
8:18 your God who gives you power to become **r**,
28:12 **r** treasury in the heavens to bless all the work you
33:23 "O Naphtali, you are **r** in favor / and full of the
Ru 3:10 running after a younger man, whether **r** or poor.
1Sa 2: 7 The LORD makes one poor and another **r**;
9: 1 Kish was a **r**, influential man from the tribe of
2Sa 12: 1 in a certain town. One was **r**, and one was poor.
12: 2 The **r** man owned many sheep and cattle.
12: 4 One day a guest arrived at the home of the **r** man.
1Ki 2:45 But may I receive the LORD's **r** blessings,
10:11 they also brought **r** cargoes of almug wood
2Ki 15:20 Menahem extorted the money from the **r** of Israel,
2Ch 9:10 they also brought **r** cargoes of almug wood
Job 1:10 in everything he does. Look how **r** he is!
3:19 **R** and poor are there alike, and the slave is free
15:27 "These wicked people are fat and **r**,
15:29 They will not continue to be **r**. Their wealth will
21:28 You will tell me of **r** and wicked people who came
24:22 "God, in his power, drags away the **r**. They may
27:19 "The wicked go to bed **r** but wake up to find that
34:19 and he doesn't pay any more attention to the **r** than
Ps 22:29 Let the **r** of the earth feast and worship. / Let all
49: 2 High and low, / **r** and poor—listen!
49:16 So don't be dismayed when the wicked grow **r**,
62:10 Don't try to get **r** / by extortion or robbery.
65: 9 of the earth and water it, / making it **r** and fertile.
109:18 or as the water he drinks, / or the **r** food he eats.
128: 2 How happy you will be! How **r** your life!
Pr 10: 4 Lazy people are soon poor; hard workers get **r**.
10:15 The wealth of the **r** is their fortress; the poverty of
10:22 The blessing of the LORD makes a person **r**,
11:16 women obtain wealth, and violent men get **r**.
11:18 Evil people get **r** for the moment, but the reward of
13: 7 Some who are poor pretend to be **r**; others who are **r** pretend to be poor.
13: 8 The **r** can pay a ransom, but the poor won't even
14:20 their neighbors, while the **r** have many "friends."
16: 8 is better to be poor and godly than **r** and dishonest.
18:11 The **r** think of their wealth as an impregnable
18:23 poor plead for mercy; the **r** answer with insults.
22: 2 The **r** and the poor have this in common:
22: 7 Just as the **r** rule the poor, so the borrower is
22:16 or by showering gifts on the **r** will end in poverty.
23: 4 Don't weary yourself trying to get **r**. Why waste
28: 6 is better to be poor and honest than **r** and crooked.
28:11 **R** people picture themselves as wise, but their real
28:20 The trustworthy will get a **r** reward. But the person who wants to get **r** quick will only
28:22 A greedy person tries to get **r** quick, but it only
30: 9 For if I grow **r**, I may deny you and say, "Who is
Ecc 5:12 But the **r** are always worrying and seldom get a
7:11 Being wise is as good as being **r**; in fact, it is
10:20 And don't make fun of a **r** man, either.
Isa 3:24 They will wear rough sackcloth instead of **r** robes.
5: 1 My beloved has a vineyard / on a **r** and fertile hill.
5: 4 more could I have done / to cultivate a **r** harvest?
19:15 whether **r** or poor, important or unknown,
28: 1 It sits in a **r** valley, but its glorious beauty will
33: 6 providing a **r** store of salvation, wisdom,
34: 6 the LORD will offer a great sacrifice in the **r** city
53: 9 like a criminal; he was put in a **r** man's grave.
Jer 5:27 And the result? Now they are great and **r**.
8:13 I will take away their **r** harvests of figs and grapes.
9:23 man in his might, or the **r** man in his riches.
48:32 "You people of Sibmah, **r** in vineyards, I will
51:13 You are a city **r** with water, a great center of
Eze 17: 8 and produce **r** leaves and luscious fruit.
26: 2 She who controlled the **r** trade routes to the east
27:18 Damascus traded for your **r** variety of goods,
28: 5 Yes, your wisdom has made you very **r**, and your
38:12 many slaves, for the people are **r** with cattle now,
Da 1:13 other young men who are eating the king's **r** food.
1:16 fed them only vegetables instead of the **r** foods
10: 3 All that time I had eaten no **r** food or meat,
11:24 his followers the plunder and wealth of the **r**.
Hos 12: 8 Israel boasts, "I am **r**, and I've gotten it all by
Ob 1:13 and making yourselves **r** at their expense.
Mic 6:10 Will there be no end of your getting **r** by cheating?
6:12 The **r** among you have become wealthy through
Hab 1:16 "These nets are the gods who have made us **r**!"
2: 9 "How terrible it will be for you who get **r** by
Hag 1: 9 You hoped for **r** harvests, but they were poor.
Zec 11: 5 sellers will say, 'Praise the LORD, I am now **r**!'
Mal 3:15 For those who do evil get **r**, and those who dare
Mt 19:23 it is very hard for a **r** person to get into the
19:24 than for a **r** person to enter the Kingdom of God!"
27:57 a **r** man from Arimathea who was one of Jesus'
Mk 10:23 "How hard it is for **r** people to get into the

10:25 than for a **r** person to enter the Kingdom of God!"
12:41 their money. Many **r** people put in large amounts.
Lk 1:53 and sent the **r** away with empty hands.
6:24 "What sorrows await you who are **r**, / for you
12:16 "A **r** man had a fertile farm that produced fine
12:21 but not have a **r** relationship with God."
14:12 your friends, brothers, relatives, and **r** neighbors.
16: 1 "A **r** man hired a manager to handle his affairs,
16: 8 "The **r** man had to admire the dishonest rascal for
16:19 "There was a certain **r** man who was splendidly
16:21 As Lazarus lay there longing for scraps from the **r**
16:22 The **r** man also died and was buried,
16:24 "The **r** man shouted, 'Father Abraham, have some
16:27 "Then the **r** man said, 'Please, Father Abraham,
16:30 "The **r** man replied, 'No, Father Abraham! But if
18:23 heard this, he became sad because he was very **r**.
18:24 "How hard it is for **r** people to get into the
18:25 than for a **r** person to enter the Kingdom of God!"
19: 2 tax-collecting business, and he had become very **r**.
21: 1 he watched the **r** people putting their gifts into the
Jn 1:16 We have all benefited from the **r** blessings he
Ro 11:17 sharing in God's **r** nourishment of his special olive
1Co 4: 8 You are already **r**! Without us you have become
2Co 8: 2 and deep poverty have overflowed in **r** generosity.
8: 9 Though he was very **r**, yet for your sakes he
8: 9 so that by his poverty he could make you **r**.
Eph 1: 7 so **r** in kindness that he purchased our freedom
1:18 I want you to realize what a **r** and glorious
2: 4 But God is so **r** in mercy, and he loved us so very
3:10 God's purpose was to show his wisdom in all its **r**
1Ti 6: 5 the truth. To them religion is just a way to get **r**.
6: 9 But people who long to be **r** fall into temptation
6:17 Tell those who are **r** in this world not to be proud
6:18 They should be **r** in good works and should give
Jas 1:10 And those who are **r** should be glad, for God has
2: 3 special attention and a good seat to the **r** person,
2: 5 Hasn't God chosen the poor in this world to be **r** in
2: 6 Isn't it the **r** who oppress you and drag you into
2: 9 But if you pay special attention to the **r**, you are
5: 1 you **r** people, weep and groan with anguish
2Pe 1: 4 he has given us all of his **r** and wonderful
Rev 2: 9 your suffering and your poverty—but you are **r**!
3:17 You say, 'I am **r**. I have everything I want. I don't
3:18 Then you will be **r**. And also buy white garments
13:16 great and small, **r** and poor, slave and free—
18: 3 and merchants throughout the world have grown **r**
18:19 great city! She made us all **r** from her great wealth.

RICHER (4) [RICH]

1Ki 10:23 So King Solomon became **r** and wiser than any
2Ch 9:22 So King Solomon became **r** and wiser than any
Da 11: 2 to be succeeded by a fourth, far **r** than the others.
Hos 10: 1 The **r** the harvests they brought in, the more

RICHES (45) [RICH]

Ge 31:16 The **r** God has given you from our father are
Dt 33:14 with the **r** that grow in the sun, / and the bounty
33:19 sacrifices there. / They benefit from the **r** of the sea
1Ki 3:11 or **r** for yourself or the death of your enemies—
3:13 give you what you did not ask for—**r** and honor!
1Ch 29:12 **R** and honor come from you alone, for you rule
2Ch 1:12 And I will also give you **r**, wealth, and honor such
18: 1 Now Jehoshaphat enjoyed great **r** and high esteem,
Job 15:31 Let them no longer trust in empty **r**. They are only
Ps 49: 6 They trust in their wealth / and boast of great **r**.
49:12 They will not last long despite their **r**— / they will
73:12 enjoying a life of ease while their **r** multiply.
119:14 I have rejoiced in your decrees / as much as in **r**.
Pr 3:16 life in her right hand, and **r** and honor in her left.
8:18 Unending **r**, honor, wealth, and justice are mine to
11: 4 **R** won't help on the day of judgment, but right
21:17 become poor; wine and luxury are not the way to **r**.
22: 1 Choose a good reputation over great **r**, for being
22: 4 True humility and fear of the LORD lead to **r**,
23: 5 For **r** can disappear as though they had the wings
24: 4 its rooms are filled with all sorts of precious **r**
27:24 for **r** don't last forever, and the crown might not be
30: 8 to tell a lie. Second, give me neither poverty nor **r**!
Ecc 5:13 **R** are sometimes hoarded to the harm of the saver,
Isa 8: 4 and Samaria and carry away their **r**."
10:14 By my greatness I have robbed their nests of **r**
45: 3 you treasures hidden in the darkness—secret **r**.
61: 6 treasures of the nations and will boast in their **r**.
Jer 9:23 mighty man in his might, or the rich man in his **r**.
17:11 Sooner or later they will lose their **r** and, at the end
51:34 like a great monster and filled his belly with our **r**.
Eze 26:12 "They will plunder all your **r** and merchandise
27:27 your **r** and wares, your sailors and helmsmen,
28: 5 very rich, and your **r** have made you very proud.
Da 11:28 of the north will then return home with great **r**.
Lk 8:14 out by the cares and **r** and pleasures of this life.
16:11 who will trust you with the true **r** of heaven?
Ro 9:23 He also has the right to pour out the **r** of his glory
10:12 who generously gives his **r** to all who ask for them.
11:33 How great are his **r** and wisdom and knowledge!
2Co 6:10 We are poor, but we give spiritual **r** to others.
Eph 3: 6 the Jews in all the **r** inherited by God's children.
Php 4:19 me will supply all your needs from his glorious **r**,
Col 1:27 For it has pleased God to tell his people that the **r**
Rev 5:12 He is worthy to receive power and **r** / and wisdom

RICHEST (5) [RICH]

Job 1: 3 He was, in fact, the **r** person in that entire area.
Ps 63: 5 You satisfy me more than the **r** of foods. / I will
SS 4:10 Your perfume is more fragrant than the **r** of spices.
La 4: 5 The people who once ate only the **r** foods now beg
Da 11:24 Without warning he will enter the **r** areas of the

RICHLY (14) [RICH]

Ge 17:16 Yes, I will bless her **r**, and she will become the
22:17 I will bless you **r**. I will multiply your descendants
24:35 "And the LORD has blessed my master **r**;
Nu 22:37 believe me when I said I would reward you **r**?"
24:11 I had planned to reward you **r**, but the LORD has
Dt 6:11 The houses will be **r** stocked with goods you did
1Ch 26: 5 (the eighth). God had **r** blessed Obed-edom.
Ps 28: 4 Give them the punishment they so **r** deserve!
67: 6 its harvests, / and God, our God, will **r** bless us.
115:14 May the LORD **r** bless / both you and your
Eze 7:27 they will receive the punishment they so **r** deserve.
Ro 1:27 within themselves the penalty they so **r** deserved.
1Ti 6:17 who **r** gives us all we need for our enjoyment.
Heb 6:14 "I will certainly bless you **r**, / and I will multiply

RICHNESS (1) [RICH]

Col 3:16 in all their **r**, live in your hearts and make you

RID (25)

Ge 21:10 and demanded, "Get **r** of that servant and her son.
Ex 6: 1 so anxious to get **r** of them that he will force them
8: 9 that you and your houses will be **r** of the frogs.
11: 1 so anxious to get **r** of you that he will practically
Lev 26:10 **r** of the leftovers from the previous year to make
Jdg 9:29 If I were in charge, I would get **r** of Abimelech.
1Sa 7: 3 get **r** of your foreign gods and your images of
Ne 2:17 of Jerusalem and **r** ourselves of this disgrace!"
Job 11:14 Get **r** of your sins and leave all iniquity behind
Jer 32:31 but anger me, so I am determined to get **r** of it.
Eze 20: 7 I said to them, 'Each of you, get **r** of your idols.
20: 8 They did not get **r** of their idols or forsake the gods
Zec 11: 8 I got **r** of their three evil shepherds in a single
13: 2 I will get **r** of every trace of idol worship
Mt 7: 4 let me help you get **r** of that speck in your eye,'
7: 5 First get **r** of the log from your own eye,
Lk 6:42 let me help you get **r** of that speck in your eye,'
6:42 First get **r** of the log from your own eye;
Ro 13:12 So don't live in darkness. Get **r** of your evil deeds.
Gal 1:13 the Christians. I did my best to get **r** of them.
4:30 "Get **r** of the slave and her son, for the son of the
Eph 4:31 Get **r** of all bitterness, rage, anger, harsh words,
Col 3: 8 But now is the time to get **r** of anger, rage,
Jas 1:21 So get **r** of all the filth and evil in your lives,
1Pe 2: 1 So get **r** of all malicious behavior and deceit.

RIDDEN (2) [RIDE]

Mk 11: 2 you will see a colt tied there that has never been **r**.
Lk 19:30 you will see a colt tied there that has never been **r**.

RIDDLE (8) [RIDDLES]

Jdg 14:12 Samson said to them, "Let me tell you a **r**. If you solve my **r** during these seven days of the
14:13 "All right," they agreed, "let's hear your **r**."
14:15 "Get the answer to the **r** from your husband,
14:16 You have given my people a **r**, but you haven't
14:18 you wouldn't have found the answer to my **r**!"
14:19 their clothing to the men who had answered his **r**.
Eze 17:12 Don't you understand the meaning of this **r** of the

RIDDLES (5) [RIDDLE]

Nu 12: 8 I speak to him face to face, directly and not in **r**!
Ps 49: 4 and solve **r** with inspiration from a harp.
Pr 1: 6 in these proverbs, parables, wise sayings, and **r**.
Eze 20:49 they are saying of me, 'He only talks in **r**!' "
Da 5:12 He can interpret dreams, explain **r**, and solve

RIDE (19) [RIDDEN, RIDER, RIDERS, RIDES, RIDING, RODE]

Nu 22:30 "But I am the same donkey you always **r** on,"
Dt 32:13 He made them **r** over the highlands; / he let them
Jdg 5:10 "You who **r** on fine donkeys / and sit on fancy
2Sa 16: 2 "The donkeys are for your people to **r** on,
1Ki 1:33 Solomon is to **r** on my personal mule.
1:44 They had him **r** on the king's own mule,
2Ki 18:23 he will give you two thousand horses for them to **r**
Ps 45: 4 In your majesty, **r** out to victory, / defending truth,
66:12 You sent troops to **r** across our broken bodies.
104: 3 your chariots; / you **r** upon the wings of the wind.
139: 9 If I **r** the wings of the morning, / if I dwell by the
Isa 36: 8 he will give you two thousand horses for them to **r**
66:20 They will **r** on horses, in chariots and wagons,
Jer 6:23 As they **r** forward, the noise of their army is like a
17:25 and their officials will always **r** among the people
22: 4 The king will **r** through the palace gates in chariots
50:42 As they **r** forward, the noise of their army is like a
Lk 19:35 and threw their garments over it for him to **r** on.
Ac 23:24 Provide horses for Paul to **r**, and get him safely to

RIDER (16) [RIDE]

Ge 49:17 that bites the horse's heels / so the **r** is thrown off.
Ex 15: 1 he has thrown both horse and **r** into the sea.
15:21 he has thrown both horse and **r** into the sea."
2Ki 9:17 "Send out a **r** to find out if they are coming in
9:18 So a **r** went out to meet Jehu and said, "The king
9:18 "The **r** has met them, but he is not returning."
9:19 So the king sent out a second **r**. He rode up to them
9:20 The watchman exclaimed, "The **r** has met them,
Job 39:18 up to run, she passes the swiftest horse with its **r**.
Jer 51:21 destroying the horse and **r**, the chariot
Zec 1: 8 brown, and white horses, each with its own **r**.
12: 4 every horse to panic and every **r** to lose his nerve.
Rev 6: 2 Its **r** carried a bow, and a crown was placed on his
6: 4 Its **r** was given a mighty sword and the authority to
6: 5 and its **r** was holding a pair of scales in his hand.
6: 8 And Death was the name of its **r**, who was

RIDERS (6) [RIDE]

Eze 39:20 feast on horses, **r**, and valiant warriors,
Hag 2:22 The horses will fall, and their **r** will kill each other.
Zec 1:11 Then the other **r** reported to the angel of the
Rev 9:17 I saw the horses and the **r** sitting on them.
9:17 The **r** wore armor that was fiery red and sky blue
19:18 captains, and strong warriors; of horses and their **r**;

RIDES (4) [RIDE]

Lev 15: 9 Any blanket on which the man **r** will be defiled.
Dt 33:26 He **r** across the heavens to help you,
Ps 68: 4 Sing loud praises to him who **r** the clouds.
68:33 Sing to the one who **r** across the ancient heavens,

RIDGES (1)

Ps 65:10 with rain, / melting the clods and leveling the **r**.

RIDICULE (7) [RIDICULED, RIDICULING, RIDICULOUS]

1Ki 9: 7 an object of mockery and **r** among the nations.
2Ch 29: 8 of dread, horror, and **r**, as you can so plainly see.
Pr 29: 9 there will be ranting and **r** but no satisfaction.
Jer 23:40 And I will make you an object of **r**, and your
48:27 Did you not make Israel the object of your **r**?
48:39 She has become an object of **r**, an example of ruin
Heb 10:33 Sometimes you were exposed to public **r** and were

RIDICULED (2) [RIDICULE]

Jer 48:26 Moab will wallow in her own vomit, **r** by all.
Mk 15:32 who were being crucified with Jesus **r** him.

RIDICULING (3) [RIDICULE]

2Ki 19:22 do you think you have been insulting and **r**?
Isa 37:23 do you think you have been insulting and **r**?
Lk 23:11 and his soldiers began mocking and **r** Jesus.

RIDICULOUS (1) [RIDICULE]

1Sa 17:33 "Don't be **r**!" Saul replied. "There is no way you

RIDING (12) [RIDE]

Nu 22:22 his way. As Balaam and two servants were **r** along,
1Sa 25:20 As she was **r** her donkey into a mountain ravine,
2Ki 9:25 when you and I were **r** along behind his father,
Ne 2:12 with us, except the donkey that I myself was **r**.
Ecc 10: 7 I have even seen servants **r** like princes—
Isa 19: 1 is advancing against Egypt, **r** on a swift cloud.
30:16 They will give us swift horses for **r** into battle.'
Eze 23:23 and other high-ranking officers, **r** their horses.
27:14 From Togarmah came **r** horses, chariot horses,
Zec 9: 9 and victorious, yet he is humble, **r** on a donkey—
Mt 21: 5 is coming to you. / He is humble, **r** on a donkey—
Rev 19:21 came out of the mouth of the one **r** the white horse.

RIE [KJV] See SPELT

RIFLED [KJV] See PLUNDERED

RIGHT (690) [RIGHT-HAND, RIGHTED, RIGHTFUL, RIGHTFULLY, RIGHTLY, RIGHTS]

DO WHAT IS...RIGHT (44) Ge 18:19,25; Ex 15:26; Dt 6:18; 1Ki 8:36; 2Ch 6:27; 19:11; Ps 11:7; 15:2; 26:11; 31:1; 64:10; 84:11; 106:3; Pr 21:3; Ecc 8:5; Isa 26:9; 56:1; Jer 18:11; 21:12; 22:3; 23:5; 33:15; Eze 18:10,21,27; 33:14,19; 45:9; Da 4:27; Mic 2:7; 6:8; Zep 2:3; Jn 3:21; Ac 10:35; Ro 6:13; 7:15,21; 1Ti 1:9; 2Ti 3:16; Heb 5:14; 1Pe 3:6; 1Jn 2:29; 3:7

IN THE RIGHT (8) Ge 4:7; 38:26; Ex 23:8; Ps 5:8; 72:2; Pr 20:4; Da 9:7; Rev 5:1

NOT RIGHT (8) 1Ki 15:3; 2Ki 7:9; Ne 5:9; Job 33:12; Hos 10:9; Ac 8:21; Ro 14:23; Jas 3:10

RIGHT HAND (65) Ge 48:13,14,17,18; Ex 15:6,6; Lev 8:23; 14:14,17,25,28; Dt 33:2; Jdg 5:26; 2Sa 20:9; 1Ki 2:19; Ps 18:35; 21:8; 48:10; 63:8; 73:23; 74:11; 89:13; 110:1,5; 137:5; Pr 3:16; SS 2:6; 8:3; Isa 41:10,13; 45:1; 48:13; Jer 22:24; Zec 3:1; Mt 6:3; 22:44; 25:33; 26:64; 27:29; Mk 12:36; 14:62; 16:19; Lk 6:6; 20:42; 22:69; Ac 2:33,34; 3:7; 5:31; 7:55,56; Eph 1:20; Col 3:1; Heb 1:3,13; 8:1; 10:12; Rev 1:16,17,20; 2:1; 5:1,7; 10:5; 13:16

Ge 4: 7 You will be accepted if you respond in the **r** way.
18: 5 "All **r**," they said. "Do as you have said."
18:19 the way of the LORD and do what is **r** and just.
18:25 not the Judge of all the earth do what is **r**?"
19:15 Get out of here **r** now, or you will be caught in the
19:21 "All **r**," the angel said, "I will grant your request.
21:24 Abraham replied, "All **r**, I swear to it!"
22: 5 will worship there, and then we will come **r** back."
24:33 "All **r**," Laban said, "tell us your mission."
24:48 because he had led me along the **r** path to find a
25:31 Jacob replied, "All **r**, but trade me your birthright
25:33 "Well then, swear to me **r** now that it is mine."
30:34 "All **r**," Laban replied. "It will be as you have
32:18 for his master Esau! He is coming **r** behind us.' "

32:20 'Your servant Jacob is **r** behind us.' " Jacob's
38:26 were his and said, "She is more in the **r** than I am,
42:24 and had him tied up **r** before their eyes.
43:23 have put it there. We collected your money all **r**."
45:9 all the land of Egypt. Come down to me **r** away!
48:13 Jacob's left hand and Manasseh was at his **r** hand.
48:14 So his **r** hand was on the head of Ephraim,
48:17 his father had laid his **r** hand on Ephraim's head.
48:18 over here is older. Put your **r** hand on his head."
Ex 4:14 "All **r**," he said. "What about your brother,
8:10 "All **r**," Moses replied, "it will be as you have
8:25 "All **r**! Go ahead and offer sacrifices to your
8:28 "All **r**, go ahead," Pharaoh replied. "I will let you
9:27 "The LORD is **r**, and my people and I are wrong.
9:29 "All **r**," Moses replied. "As soon as I leave the
10:8 "All **r**, go and serve the LORD your God,"
15:6 "Your **r** hand, O LORD, / is glorious in power. / Your **r** hand, O LORD,
15:26 the LORD your God and do what is **r** in his sight,
23:8 hurts the cause of the person who is in the **r**.
27:14 The curtain on the **r** side will be 22-1/2 feet long,
29:20 and place some of it on the tip of the **r** earlobes of
29:20 Also put it on their **r** thumbs and the big toes of their **r** feet.
29:22 the two kidneys with their fat, and the **r** thigh.
32:1 failed to come back down the mountain **r** away,
34:10 The LORD replied, "All **r**. This is the covenant I
38:14 The curtain on the **r** side was 22-1/2 feet long
Lev 7:32 You are to give the **r** thigh of your peace offering
7:33 The **r** thigh must always be given to the priest who
7:34 designated the breast and the **r** thigh for the priests.
8:23 of its blood and put it on the lobe of Aaron's **r** ear,
8:23 thumb of his **r** hand, and the big toe of his **r** foot.
8:24 and put some of the blood on the lobe of their **r**
8:24 of their **r** hands, and the big toe of their **r** feet.
8:25 two kidneys with their fat, along with the **r** thigh.
9:21 and **r** thighs as an offering to the LORD,
14:14 and put it on the tip of the healed person's **r** ear,
14:14 of the **r** hand, and on the big toe of the **r** foot.
14:16 He will dip his **r** finger into the oil and sprinkle it
14:17 his left hand on the tip of the healed person's **r** ear,
14:17 of the **r** hand, and on the big toe of the **r** foot,
14:25 some of its blood on the tip of the person's **r** ear,
14:25 of the **r** hand, and on the big toe of the **r** foot.
14:27 He will dip his **r** finger into the oil and sprinkle
14:28 oil from his hand on the lobe of the person's **r** ear,
14:28 of the **r** hand, and on the big toe of the **r** foot,
15:31 defiling my Tabernacle that is **r** there among them.
18:18 if your wife dies, then it is all **r** to marry her sister.
25:27 then that person has the **r** to redeem it from the one
25:29 has the **r** to redeem it for a full year after its sale.
25:29 that time, the seller retains the **r** to buy it back.
25:32 "The Levites always have the **r** to redeem any
25:48 they still retain the **r** of redemption. They may be
Nu 16:3 What **r** do you have to act as though you are
18:18 and **r** thigh that are presented by lifting them up
22:37 Why didn't you come **r** away?" Balak asked
25:6 **r** before the eyes of Moses and all the people,
27:7 "The daughters of Zelophehad are **r**. You must
36:5 the LORD: "The men of the tribe of Joseph are **r**.
Dt 4:34 God did for you in Egypt, **r** before your very eyes.
5:28 what the people have said to you, and they are **r**.
6:18 Do what is **r** and good in the LORD's sight,
21:9 and doing what is **r** in the LORD's sight,
25:1 and the judges declare that one is **r** and the other is
33:2 with flaming fire at his **r** hand.
Jos 4:23 For the LORD your God dried up the river **r**
9:22 in a distant land when you live **r** here among us?
9:25 are at your mercy—do whatever you think is **r**."
22:24 'What **r** do you have to worship the LORD,
22:27 have the **r** to worship the LORD at his sanctuary
24:23 "All **r** then," Joshua said, "destroy the idols
Jdg 3:16 and he strapped it to his **r** thigh, keeping it hidden
3:21 pulled out the dagger strapped to his **r** thigh,
5:26 and with her **r** hand she reached for the workman's
6:23 "It is all **r**," the LORD replied. "Do not be
7:20 and the horns in their **r** hands and shouted,
9:16 and that you have done **r** by Gideon and all of his
9:38 The men you mocked are **r** outside the city!
11:27 who is judge, decide today which of us is **r**—
14:13 "All **r**," they agreed, "let's hear your riddle."
15:12 over to the Philistines." "All **r**," Samson said.
16:3 and lifted them, bar and all, **r** out of the ground.
17:6 so the people did whatever seemed **r** in their own
21:25 so the people did whatever seemed **r** in their own
Ru 2:2 And Naomi said, "All **r**, my daughter, go ahead."
2:8 Stay **r** here with us when you gather grain;
2:8 Stay **r** behind the women working in my field.
2:15 "Let her gather grain **r** among the sheaves without
2:22 Stay with his workers **r** through the whole harvest.
4:4 But if you don't want it, let me know **r** away,
4:4 The man replied, "All **r**, I'll redeem it."
4:7 transferring a **r** of purchase to remove his sandal
1Sa 9:10 "All **r**," Saul agreed, "let's try it!" So they
9:12 "Yes," they replied. "Stay **r** on this road. He is at
11:2 "All **r**," Nahash said, "but only on one condition.
11:2 I will gouge out the **r** eye of every one of you as a
12:3 and I will make **r** whatever I have done wrong."
12:13 All **r**, here is the king you have chosen. Look him
12:23 I will continue to teach you what is good and **r**.
14:8 "All **r** then," Jonathan told him. "We will cross
14:12 "Come on, climb **r** behind me," Jonathan said to
14:13 and his armor bearer killed them **r** and left.
16:17 "All **r**," Saul said. "Find me someone who plays
17:37 Saul finally consented. "All **r**, go ahead," he said.
24:15 May the LORD judge which of us is **r** and punish
26:7 So David and Abishai went **r** into Saul's camp
27:5 day David said to Achish, "If it is all **r** with you,
2Sa 2:14 of hand-to-hand combat." "All **r**," Joab agreed.
2:21 But Asahel refused and kept **r** on chasing Abner.
3:13 "All **r**," David replied, "but I will not negotiate
14:21 "All **r**, go and bring back the young man
15:9 "All **r**," the king told him. "Go and fulfill your
15:22 David replied, "All **r**, come with us." So Ittai
17:8 **R** now they are probably as enraged as a mother
18:23 he begged. Joab finally said, "All **r**, go ahead."
18:29 "Is he all **r**?" Ahimaaz replied, "When Joab told
18:32 the king demanded. "Is he all **r**?" And the Cushite
19:29 "All **r**," David replied. "My decision is that you
19:43 "So we have ten times as much **r** to the king as
20:9 and took him by the beard with his **r** hand as
20:21 "All **r**," the woman replied, "we will throw his
21:6 "All **r**," the king said, "I will do it."
22:21 The LORD rewarded me for doing **r**;
22:25 The LORD rewarded me for doing **r**, / because of
1Ki 2:18 "All **r**," Bathsheba replied. "I will speak to the
2:19 brought for his mother, and she sat at his **r** hand.
2:26 and you suffered **r** along with him through all his
3:9 and know the difference between **r** and wrong.
3:24 All **r**, bring me a sword." So a sword was brought
3:26 But the other woman said, "All **r**, he will be
8:18 'It is **r** for you to want to build the Temple to
8:36 Teach them to do what is **r**, and send rain on your
11:38 my ways and do whatever I consider to be **r**,
15:3 and his heart was not **r** with the LORD his God,
20:4 "All **r**, my lord," Ahab replied. "All that I have is
22:6 or not?" They all replied, "Go **r** ahead!
22:15 or not?" And Micaiah replied, "Go **r** ahead!
22:19 of heaven around him, on his **r** and on his left.
2Ki 1:11 the king says that you must come down **r** away."
2:17 and he finally said, "All **r**, send them."
4:22 I can hurry to the man of God and come **r** back."
4:23 festival nor a Sabbath." But she said, "It's all **r**."
4:26 meet her and ask her, 'Is everything all **r** with you,
4:41 he threw it into the kettle and said, "Now it's all **r**;
5:17 Then Naaman said, "All **r**, but please allow me to
5:21 meet him. "Is everything all **r**?" Naaman asked.
6:2 us to meet." "All **r**," he told them, "go ahead."
6:19 This isn't the **r** city! Follow me, and I will take
7:9 Finally, they said to each other, "This is not **r**.
9:11 did that crazy fellow want? Is everything all **r**?"
11:8 must be killed. Stay **r** beside the king at all times."
22:2 He did not turn aside from doing what was **r**.
1Ch 12:2 sling stones with their left hand as well as their **r**.
13:4 for the people could see it was the **r** thing to do.
2Ch 6:8 'It is **r** for you to want to build the Temple to
6:27 Teach them to do what is **r**, and send rain on your
12:6 and said, "The LORD is **r** in doing this to us!"
18:14 or not?" And Micaiah replied, "Go **r** ahead!
18:18 on his throne with all the armies of heaven on his **r**
19:11 may the LORD be with those who do what is **r**."
23:7 must be killed. Stay **r** beside the king at all times."
24:5 Do not delay!" But the Levites did not act **r** away.
29:12 Then these Levites got **r** to work: / From the clan
30:4 This plan for keeping the Passover seemed **r** to the
34:2 He did not turn aside from doing what was **r**.
Ezr 10:12 raised their voices and answered, "Yes, you are **r**;
Ne 5:9 I pressed further, "What you are doing is not **r**!
8:4 To his **r** stood Mattithiah, Shema, Anaiah, Uriah,
Est 7:8 "Will he even assault the queen **r** here in the
8:5 Majesty is pleased with me and if he thinks it is **r**,
Job 1:12 "All **r**, you may test him," the LORD said to
2:6 "All **r**, do with him as you please," the LORD
6:5 Don't I have a **r** to complain? Wild donkeys bray
6:30 Don't I know the difference between **r** and wrong?
8:3 twist justice? Does the Almighty twist what is **r**?
15:3 It isn't **r** to speak so foolishly. What good do such
22:8 and that those who are privileged have a **r** to it!
27:5 I will never concede that you are **r**; until I die,
32:2 had sinned and that God was **r** in punishing him.
33:12 "In this you are not **r**, and I will show you why.
34:4 So let us discern for ourselves what is **r**; let us
35:2 "Do you think it is **r** for you to claim, 'I am
40:8 and condemn me so you can say you are **r**?
40:10 All **r** then, put on your robes of state, your majesty
42:7 for you have not been **r** in what you said about me,
42:8 for you have not been **r** in what you said about me,
Ps 5:8 Lead me in the **r** path, O LORD, / or my enemies
7:10 saving those whose hearts are true and **r**.
11:2 They shoot from the shadows at those who do **r**.
11:7 Those who do what is **r** will see his face.
15:2 Those who lead blameless lives / and do what is **r**,
16:8 I will not be shaken, for he is **r** beside me.
17:2 me innocent, / for you know those who do **r**.
17:15 But because I have done what is **r**, I will see you.
18:20 The LORD rewarded me for doing **r**;
18:24 The LORD rewarded me for doing **r**, / because of
18:35 Your **r** hand supports me; / your gentleness has
19:8 The commandments of the LORD are **r**,
21:8 Your strong **r** hand will seize all those who hate
23:3 renews my strength. / He guides me along **r** paths,
24:5 and have **r** standing with God their savior.
25:4 O LORD; / point out the **r** road for me to follow.
25:8 The LORD is good and does what is **r**; / he shows
25:9 He leads the humble in what is **r**, / teaching them
26:11 But I am not like that; I do what is **r**. / So in your
31:1 Rescue me, for you always do what is **r**.
34:15 eyes of the LORD watch over those who do **r**;
37:14 and the oppressed, / to slaughter those who do **r**.
37:30 good counsel; / they know what is **r** from wrong.
38:20 for good / and oppose me because I stand for the **r**.
40:17 but the Lord is thinking about me **r** now.
45:7 You love what is **r** and hate what is wrong.
45:9 At your **r** side stands the queen, / wearing jewelry
48:10 Your strong **r** hand is filled with victory.
51:4 You will be proved **r** in what you say, / and your
51:10 a clean heart, O God. / Renew a **r** spirit within me.
60:5 Use your strong **r** arm to save us, / and rescue your
63:8 your strong **r** hand holds me securely.
64:10 And those who do what is **r** / will praise him.
69:13 But I keep **r** on praying to you, LORD,
72:2 Help him judge your people in the **r** way;
72:3 hills be fruitful, / because the king does what is **r**.
73:23 I still belong to you; / you are holding my **r** hand.
74:11 Why do you hold back your strong **r** hand?
84:11 LORD withhold / from those who do what is **r**.
89:13 Your **r** hand is lifted high in glorious strength.
97:11 shines on the godly, / and joy on those who do **r**.
106:3 deal justly with others / and always do what is **r**.
108:6 Use your strong **r** arm to save me, / and rescue
109:28 But I, your servant, will go **r** on rejoicing!
110:1 said to my Lord, / "Sit in honor at my **r** hand
110:5 The Lord stands at your **r** hand to protect you.
118:15 The strong **r** arm of the LORD has done glorious
118:16 The strong **r** arm of the LORD is raised in
118:16 The strong **r** arm of the LORD has done glorious
119:121 of my enemies, / for I have done what is just and **r**.
119:128 Truly, each of your commandments is **r**. / That is
119:172 about your word, / for all your commands are **r**.
137:5 let my **r** hand forget its skill upon the harp.
147:1 praises to our God! / How delightful and how **r**!
Pr 1:3 good conduct, and doing what is **r**, just, and fair.
2:9 Then you will understand what is **r**, just, and fair,
2:9 and you will know how to find the **r** course of
2:13 These people turn from **r** ways to walk down dark
3:16 She offers you life in her **r** hand, and riches
8:6 excellent things to tell you. Everything I say is **r**,
10:2 has no lasting value, but **r** living can save your life.
11:4 but **r** living is a safeguard against death.
14:2 Those who follow the **r** path fear the LORD;
14:12 There is a path before each person that seems **r**,
15:10 Whoever abandons the **r** path will be severely
15:21 no sense; a sensible person stays on the **r** path.
15:23 it is wonderful to say the **r** thing at the **r** time!
16:1 our thoughts, but the LORD gives the **r** answer.
16:25 There is a path before each person that seems **r**,
18:20 the **r** words on a person's lips bring satisfaction.
19:10 It isn't **r** for a fool to live in luxury or for a slave to
20:4 If you are too lazy to plow in the **r** season, you will
20:11 way they act, whether their conduct is pure and **r**.
21:2 People may think they are doing what is **r**,
21:3 is just and **r** than when we give him sacrifices.
22:6 Teach your children to choose the **r** path,
23:16 my heart will thrill when you speak what is **r**
23:19 and be wise. Keep your heart on the **r** course.
Ecc 8:5 are wise will find a time and a way to do what is **r**.
9:11 by chance, by being at the **r** place at the **r** time.
10:2 The hearts of the wise lead them to do **r**,
SS 2:6 is under my head, and his **r** hand embraces me.
2:7 of the wild, not to awaken love until the time is **r**.
3:5 of the wild, not to awaken love until the time is **r**."
8:3 my head and your **r** hand would embrace me.
8:4 not to awaken love until the time is **r**."
Isa 7:14 All **r** then, the Lord himself will choose the sign.
7:15 he will know enough to choose what is **r** and reject
7:16 But before he knows **r** from wrong, the two kings
13:16 Their little children will be dashed to death **r**
16:5 will reign, one who always does what is just and **r**.
26:9 will people turn from wickedness and do what is **r**.
31:4 and noise. It just goes **r** on eating.
41:10 I will uphold you with my victorious **r** hand.
41:13 I am holding you by your **r** hand—I, the LORD
41:26 predicted this, making you admit that he was **r**?
42:20 You see and understand what is **r** but refuse to act
45:1 his anointed one, whose **r** hand he will empower.
45:19 I, the LORD, speak only what is true and **r**.
46:13 to set things **r**, not in the distant future, but **r** now!
48:13 The palm of my **r** hand spread out the heavens
49:8 "At just the **r** time, I will respond to you.
51:7 you who know **r** from wrong and cherish my law
56:1 "Do what is **r** and good, for I am coming soon to
57:8 You have climbed **r** into bed with these detestable
57:17 myself from them, but they went **r** on sinning.
58:3 You keep **r** on oppressing your workers.
60:22 the LORD, will bring it all to pass at the **r** time."
Jer 1:12 And the LORD said, "That's **r**, and it means that
3:5 you talk, and keep **r** on doing all the evil you can."
4:22 but they have no talent at all for doing **r**!"
6:16 So now the LORD says, "Stop **r** where you are!
7:10 only to go **r** back to all those evils again?
7:30 "They have set up their abominable idols **r** in my
11:15 What **r** do my beloved people have to come to my
13:13 the prophets, **r** on down to the common people.
14:9 to save us? You are **r** here among us, LORD.
17:8 and they go **r** on producing delicious fruit.
18:11 your evil ways, each of you, and do what is **r**.' "
20:6 you promised that everything would be all **r**."
21:4 I will bring your enemies **r** into the heart of this
21:12 Do what is **r**, or my anger will burn like an
22:3 Be fair-minded and just. Do what is **r**!
22:15 Because he was just and **r** in all his dealings.
22:24 Even if you were the signet ring on my **r** hand,
23:5 He will do what is just and **r** throughout the land.
23:11 I have seen their despicable acts **r** here in my own
26:9 "What **r** do you have to prophesy in the LORD's
32:7 By law you have the **r** to buy it before it is offered
32:8 By law you have the **r** to buy it before it is offered
32:33 year after year, I taught them **r** from wrong,
32:34 They have set up their abominable idols **r** in my
33:15 he will do what is just and **r** throughout the land.
34:15 Recently you repented and did what was **r**,

36: 2 message you have given, **r** up to the present time.
38: 5 "All **r**," he said. "Do as you like.
42: 4 "All **r**," Jeremiah replied. "I will pray to the
44: 5 They kept **r** on burning incense to these gods.
La 1:18 "And the LORD is **r**," she groans, "for I
3:59 to me, LORD. Be my judge, and prove me **r**.
Eze 1:10 the face of a lion on the **r** side, the face of an ox on
4: 6 turn over and lie on your **r** side for 40 days—
4:15 "All **r**," the LORD said. "You may bake your
9: 6 the mark. Begin your task **r** here at the Temple."
13:14 I will break down your wall **r** to the foundation,
18: 5 a certain man is just and does what is lawful and **r**,
18:10 a robber or murderer and refuses to do what is **r**.
18:19 For if the child does what is **r** and keeps my laws,
18:21 begin to obey my laws and do what is just and **r**,
18:27 obey the law, and do what is just and **r**, they will
20:39 go **r** ahead and worship your idols, but then don't
21:16 O sword, slash to the **r**, and slash to the left,
21:27 until the one appears who has the **r** to judge it.
23:11 her sister, she followed **r** in her footsteps.
33:14 they turn from their sins and do what is just and **r**.
33:16 for they have done what is just and **r**, and they will
33:19 from their wickedness and do what is just and **r**,
34:10 I will take away their **r** to feed the flock, along
with their **r** to feed themselves.
36:26 I will give you a new heart with new and **r** desires,
43: 8 They put their idol altars **r** next to mine with only a
45: 9 and oppression and do what is just and **r**.
47: 1 then passed to the **r** of the altar on its south side.
Da 4:27 please listen to me. Stop sinning and do what is **r**.
9: 7 "Lord, you are in the **r**; but our faces are covered
Hos 10: 9 Was it not **r** that the wicked men of Gibeah were
14: 9 The paths of the LORD are true and **r**,
Joel 2: 8 each other; each moves in exactly the **r** place.
Am 3:10 people have forgotten what it means to do **r**,"
7:10 "Amos is hatching a plot against you **r** here on
Jnh 4: 4 "Is it **r** for you to be angry about this?"
4: 9 "Is it **r** for you to be angry because the plant
Mic 2: 7 If you would do what is **r**, you would find my
2: 8 You steal the shirts **r** off the backs of those who
3: 1 of Israel! You are supposed to know **r** from wrong,
3: 9 of Israel! You hate justice and twist all that is **r**.
6: 8 to do what is **r**, to love mercy, and to walk humbly
7: 6 Your enemies will be **r** in your own household.
Hab 2: 3 But these things I plan won't happen **r** away.
Zep 2: 3 who uphold justice. Walk humbly and do what is **r**.
Zec 3: 1 Satan was there at the angel's **r** hand,
11:17 The sword will cut his arm and pierce his **r** eye!
11:17 become useless, and his **r** eye completely blind!"
12: 6 They will burn up all the neighboring nations **r**
14: 1 possessions will be plundered **r** in front of you!
Mal 1:12 you are saying it's all **r** to defile the Lord's table.
Mt 3:15 be done, because we must do everything that is **r**."
5:39 If you are slapped on the **r** cheek, turn the other,
6: 3 don't tell your left hand what your **r** hand is doing.
8: 4 "Go **r** over to the priest and let him examine you.
8:29 You have no **r** to torture us before God's appointed
8:32 "All **r**, go!" Jesus commanded them.
9: 8 crowd as they saw this happen **r** before their eyes.
9:28 They went **r** into the house where he was staying,
10:19 because you will be given the **r** words at the **r**
10:36 Your enemies will be **r** in your own household!
11:19 But wisdom is shown to be **r** by what results from
12:12 a sheep! Yes, it is **r** to do good on the Sabbath."
12:34 could evil men like you speak what is good and **r**?
13:37 "All **r**," he said. "I, the Son of Man,
13:56 All his sisters live **r** here among us. What makes
14:27 "It's all **r**," he said. "I am here! Don't be afraid."
14:29 "All **r**, come," Jesus said. So Peter went over the
15:26 "It isn't **r** to take food from the children and throw
16:28 And I assure you that some of you standing here **r**
18:17 If the church decides you are **r**, but the other
20: 4 telling them he would pay them whatever was **r** at
20:21 to you, one at your **r** and the other at your left?"
20:23 "But I have no **r** to say who will sit on the thrones
22:17 Is it **r** to pay taxes to the Roman government
22:44 said to my Lord, / Sit in honor at my **r** hand
24:33 you can know his return is very near, **r** at the door.
24:38 and weddings **r** up to the time Noah entered his
25:17 The servant with two bags of gold also went **r** to
25:33 He will place the sheep at his **r** hand and the goats
25:34 Then the King will say to those on the **r**, 'Come,
26:16 Judas began looking for the **r** time and place to
26:64 sitting at God's **r** hand in the place of power
27:29 and they placed a stick in his **r** hand as a scepter.
28:14 stand up for you and everything will be all **r**."
Mk 1:30 a high fever. They told Jesus about her **r** away.
1:44 "Go **r** over to the priest and let him examine you.
2: 4 the sick man on his mat, **r** down in front of Jesus.
6: 3 and Simon. And his sisters live **r** here among us."
6:25 the head of John the Baptist, **r** now, on a tray!"
6:50 "It's all **r**," he said. "I am here! Don't be afraid."
7:11 But you say it is all **r** for people to say to their
7:25 **R** away a woman came to him whose little girl was
7:27 It isn't **r** to take food from the children and throw
9: 1 "I assure you that some of you standing here **r**
10:37 "one at your **r** and the other at your left."
10:40 but I have no **r** to say who will sit on the thrones
12:14 is it **r** to pay taxes to the Roman government
12:36 said to my Lord, / Sit in honor at my **r** hand
13:29 be sure that his return is very near, **r** at the door.
14:11 So he began looking for the **r** time and place to
14:62 sitting at God's **r** hand in the place of power
16: 5 and there on the **r** sat a young man clothed in a
16:19 and sat down in the place of honor at God's **r**
Lk 1:11 standing to the **r** of the incense altar.
5:14 "Go **r** to the priest and let him examine you.
5:19 into the crowd, still on his mat, **r** in front of Jesus.
6: 6 a man with a deformed **r** hand was in the
7:29 unjust tax collectors, agreed that God's plan was **r**,
7:35 But wisdom is shown to be **r** by the lives of those
7:40 "All **r**, Teacher," Simon replied, "go ahead."
7:43 canceled the larger debt." "That's **r**," Jesus said.
8:50 be afraid. Just trust me, and she will be all **r**."
9:27 And I assure you that some of you standing here **r**
10:28 "**R**!" Jesus told him. "Do this and you will live!"
11:48 agree with your ancestors that what they did was **r**.
12:54 you say, 'Here comes a shower.' And you are **r**.
12:57 "Why can't you decide for yourselves what is **r**?
17:27 and weddings **r** up to the time Noah entered his
17:30 it will be 'business as usual' **r** up to the hour when
18:42 And Jesus said, "All **r**, you can see! Your faith has
19:11 that the Kingdom of God would begin **r** away.
19:27 and execute them **r** here in my presence.' "
20:21 we know that you speak and teach what is **r**
20:22 is it **r** to pay taxes to the Roman government
20:42 said to my Lord, / Sit in honor at my **r** hand
21:15 for I will give you the **r** words and such wisdom
22:29 has granted me a Kingdom, I now grant you the **r**
22:50 at the high priest's servant and cut off his **r** ear.
22:69 will be sitting at God's **r** hand in the place of
22:70 And he replied, "You are **r** in saying that I am."
Jn 1:12 he gave the **r** to become children of God.
1:25 or the Prophet, what **r** do you have to baptize?"
1:26 but **r** here in the crowd is someone you do not
2:18 "What **r** do you have to do these things?"
2:19 "All **r**," Jesus replied. "Destroy this temple,
3:21 But those who do what is **r** come to the light
4:17 the woman replied. Jesus said, "You're **r**!
7: 6 Jesus replied, "Now is not the **r** time for me to go.
7:24 Think this through and you will see that I am **r**."
8: 7 so he stood up again and said, "All **r**, stone her.
10:18 For I have the **r** to lay it down when I want to
13:13 You call me 'Teacher' and 'Lord,' and you are **r**,
18:10 drew a sword and slashed off the **r** ear of Malchus,
18:37 say that I am a king, and you are **r**," Jesus said.
Ac 1:24 Then they all prayed for the **r** man to be chosen.
2:25 I will not be shaken, for he is **r** beside me.
2:33 throne of highest honor in heaven, at God's **r** hand.
2:34 said to my Lord, / Sit in honor at my **r** hand
3: 7 Then Peter took the lame man by the **r** hand
4:14 had been healed was standing **r** there among them,
5:31 Then God put him in the place of honor at his **r**
7:55 standing in the place of honor at God's **r** hand.
7:56 standing in the place of honor at God's **r** hand!"
8:21 no part in this, for your heart is not **r** before God.
9:11 ask for Saul of Tarsus. He is praying to me **r** now.
10:35 he accepts those who fear him and do what is **r**.
11: 5 corners from the sky. And it came **r** down to me.
13:39 is freed from all guilt and declared **r** with God—
18:17 and had beaten him **r** there in the courtroom.
23: 9 Pharisees jumped up to argue that Paul was all **r**.
25:10 official Roman court, so I ought to be tried **r** here.
25:11 neither you nor anyone else has a **r** to turn me over
28:25 "The Holy Spirit was **r** when he said to our
Ro 1:17 This Good News tells us how God makes us **r** in
1:32 yet they go **r** ahead and do them anyway.
2:13 Those who obey the law will be declared **r** in
2:14 they show that in their hearts they know **r** from
2:15 accuse them or tell them they are doing what is **r**.
2:18 you know **r** from wrong because you have been
2:29 a true Jew is one whose heart is **r** with God.
3: 4 "He will be proved **r** in what he says,
3:20 For no one can ever be made **r** in God's sight by
3:21 shown us a different way of being **r** in his sight—
3:22 We are made **r** in God's sight when we trust in
3:25 We are made **r** with God when we believe that
3:26 time when he declares sinners to be **r** in his sight
3:28 So we are made **r** with God through faith and not
3:30 He makes people **r** with himself only by faith,
4:11 They are made **r** with God by faith.
4:25 and he was raised from the dead to make us **r** with
5: 1 since we have been made **r** in God's sight by faith,
5: 6 Christ came at just the **r** time and died for us
5: 9 And since we have been made **r** in God's sight by
5:18 of righteousness makes all people **r** in God's sight
5:19 many people will be made **r** in God's sight.
5:21 giving us **r** standing with God and resulting in
6:13 And use your whole body as a tool to do what is **r**
6:20 you weren't concerned with doing what was **r**.
7:12 But still, the law itself is holy and **r** and good.
7:15 for I really want to do what is **r**, but I don't do it.
7:18 matter which way I turn, I can't make myself do **r**.
7:21 to be a fact of life that when I want to do what is **r**,
8:10 is alive because you have been made **r** with God.
8:22 in the pains of childbirth **r** up to the present time.
8:30 And he gave them **r** standing with himself, and he
8:33 He is the one who has given us **r** standing with
9:21 doesn't he have a **r** to use the same lump of clay to
9:22 God has every **r** to exercise his judgment and his
9:22 but he also has the **r** to be very patient with those
9:23 He also has the **r** to pour out the riches of his glory
9:30 The Gentiles have been made **r** with God by faith,
9:31 so hard to get **r** with God by keeping the law,
9:32 Because they were trying to get **r** with God by
10: 3 God's way of making people **r** with himself.
10: 3 they are clinging to their own way of getting **r** with
10: 4 All who believe in him are made **r** with God.
10: 5 **r** with God requires obedience to all of its
10: 6 But the way of getting **r** with God through faith
10:10 in your heart that you are made **r** with God,
13: 3 authorities do not frighten people who are doing **r**,
13:11 Another reason for **r** living is that you know how
13:12 Clothe yourselves with the armor of **r** living,
14: 1 don't argue with them about what they think is **r**
14: 2 one person believes it is all **r** to eat anything.
14: 3 Those who think it is all **r** to eat anything must not
14: 4 so let him tell them whether they are **r** or wrong.
14:16 condemned for doing something you know is all **r**.
14:22 themselves by doing something they know is all **r**.
14:23 If you do anything you believe is not **r**, you are
15:17 So it is **r** for me to be enthusiastic about all Christ
16:19 I want you to see clearly what is **r** and to stay
1Co 1: 8 He will keep you strong **r** up to the end, and he
4:13 everybody's trash—**r** up to the present moment.
6: 1 of taking it to other Christians to decide who is **r**?
6: 6 Christian sues another—**r** in front of unbelievers!
6:11 You have been made **r** with God because of what
7: 3 which is her **r** as a married woman, nor should the
7:36 his passions and time is passing, it is all **r**;
9: 4 Don't we have the **r** to live in your homes
9: 5 Don't we have the **r** to bring a Christian wife along
9: 7 his crop and doesn't have the **r** to eat some of it?
9:12 shouldn't we have an even greater **r** to be
supported? Yet we have never used this **r**.
11:13 Is it **r** for a woman to pray to God in public
11:19 so that those of you who are **r** will be recognized!
16: 7 want to make just a short visit and then go **r** on.
16:12 but he was not willing to come **r** now.
16:12 He will be seeing you later, when the time is **r**.
2Co 3: 9 is the new covenant, which makes us **r** with God!
4:18 So we don't look at the troubles we can see **r** now;
5:13 And if we are in our **r** minds, it is for your benefit.
5:21 so that we could be made **r** with God through
6: 2 For God says, / "At just the **r** time, I heard you.
6: 2 Indeed, God is ready to help you **r** now.
7:11 have done everything you could to make things **r**.
8:14 **R** now you have plenty and can help them. Then at
13: 7 because we want you to do **r** even if we ourselves
Gal 2:16 Christians know that we become **r** with God,
2:17 But what if we seek to be made **r** with God
3:10 But those who depend on the law to make them **r**
3:11 it is clear that no one can ever be **r** with God by
3:21 we could have been made **r** with God by obeying
3:23 shown to us as the way of becoming **r** with God,
3:24 through faith in Christ, we are made **r** with God.
4: 4 But when the **r** time came, God sent his Son,
4:20 How I wish I were there with you **r** now, so that I
5: 2 If you are counting on circumcision to make you **r**
5: 4 For if you are trying to make yourselves **r** with
5: 5 promised to us who are **r** with God through faith.
6: 1 and humbly help that person back onto the **r** path.
Eph 1:10 At the **r** time he will bring everything together
1:20 and seated him in the place of honor at God's **r**
4:19 They don't care anymore about **r** and wrong,
5: 9 you produces only what is good and **r** and true.
6: 1 you belong to the Lord, for this is the **r** thing to do.
6: 9 same way, you masters must treat your slaves **r**.
6:19 Ask God to give me the **r** words as I boldly explain
Php 1: 7 It is **r** that I should feel as I do about all of you,
3: 9 For God's way of making us **r** with himself
4: 8 your thoughts on what is true and honorable and **r**.
Col 3: 1 where Christ sits at God's **r** hand in the place of
4: 6 so that you will have the **r** answer for everyone.
1Th 2: 7 As apostles of Christ we certainly had a **r** to make
2Th 1: 3 and sisters, we always thank God for you, as is **r**,
3: 9 It wasn't that we didn't have the **r** to ask you to
1Ti 1: 9 they were not made for people who do what is **r**.
1:10 do anything else that contradicts the **r** teaching
4:16 Stay true to what is **r**, and God will save you
6:11 all these evil things, and follow what is **r** and good.
6:15 For at the **r** time Christ will be revealed from
2Ti 1:13 Hold on to the pattern of **r** teaching you learned
2:22 Follow anything that makes you want to do **r**.
3:16 It straightens us out and teaches us to do what is **r**.
4: 3 when people will no longer listen to **r** teaching.
Tit 1: 3 And now at the **r** time he has revealed this Good
1: 9 then he will be able to encourage others with **r**
1:10 For there are many who rebel against **r** teaching;
2: 1 promote the kind of living that reflects **r** teaching.
2:12 with self-control, **r** conduct, and devotion to God,
2:14 own people, totally committed to doing what is **r**.
Phm 1: 8 of Christ because it is the **r** thing for you to do,
Heb 1: 3 he sat down in the place of honor at the **r** hand of
1: 9 You love what is **r** and hate what is wrong.
1:13 as he did to his Son, / "Sit in honor at my **r** hand
2:10 And it was only **r** that God—who made everything
5:13 and doesn't know much about doing what is **r**.
5:14 themselves to recognize the difference between **r**
and wrong, and then do what is **r**.
6:11 Our great desire is that you will keep **r** on loving
8: 1 place of highest honor in heaven, at God's **r** hand.
10:12 at the place of highest honor at God's **r** hand.
10:22 let us go **r** into the presence of God, with true
11: 7 rest of the world and was made **r** in God's sight.
11:27 Moses kept **r** on going because he kept his eyes on
11:29 It was by faith that the people of Israel went **r**
12:10 But God's discipline is always **r** and good for us
12:11 But afterward there will be a quiet harvest of **r**
13:10 the priests in the Temple on earth have no **r** to eat.
13:19 I especially need your prayers **r** now so that I can
Jas 1:20 Your anger can never make things **r** in God's
2:21 our ancestor Abraham was declared **r** with God
2:24 you see, we are made **r** with God by what we do,
2:25 She was made **r** with God by her actions—
3:10 Surely, my brothers and sisters, this is not **r**!
4:11 not a judge who can decide whether the law is **r**
4:12 So what **r** do you have to condemn your neighbor?
1Pe 2:14 all who do wrong and to honor those who do **r**.
2:20 But if you suffer for doing **r** and are patient
2:24 so we can be dead to sin and live for what is **r**.

3: 6 You are her daughters when you do what is **r**
3: 12 The eyes of the Lord watch over those who do **r**,
3: 14 But even if you suffer for doing what is **r**, God will
4: 19 keep on doing what is **r**, and trust yourself to the
2Pe 1: 1 our God and Savior, who makes us **r** with God.
2: 9 even while punishing the wicked **r** up until the day
2: 15 They have wandered off the **r** road and followed
2: 21 It would be better if they had never known the **r**
3: 13 a world where everyone is **r** with God.
1Jn 2: 7 one you have always had, **r** from the beginning.
2: 29 Since we know that God is always **r**, we also know that all who do what is **r** are his
3: 7 When people do what is **r**, it is because they are
3: 12 and his brother had been doing what was **r**.
Rev 1: 16 He held seven stars in his **r** hand, and a sharp
1: 17 But he laid his **r** hand on me and said, "Don't be
1: 20 meaning of the seven stars you saw in my **r** hand
2: 1 the one who holds the seven stars in his **r** hand,
3: 2 Your deeds are far from **r** in the sight of God.
5: 1 And I saw a scroll in the **r** hand of the one who
5: 7 and took the scroll from the **r** hand of the one
10: 2 He stood with his **r** foot on the sea and his left foot
10: 5 the sea and on the land lifted his **r** hand to heaven.
13: 16 to be given a mark on the **r** hand or on the

RIGHT-HAND (2) [HAND, RIGHT]

2Ki 12: 9 and set it on the **r** side of the altar at the entrance
Jn 21: 6 "Throw out your net on the **r** side of the boat,

RIGHTED (1) [RIGHT]

Ecc 1: 15 What is wrong cannot be **r**. What is missing cannot

RIGHTEOUS (130) [RIGHTEOUSLY, RIGHTEOUSNESS]

RIGHTEOUS DEEDS (3) Ps 71:24; Isa 64:6; Rev 15:4

RIGHTEOUS MAN (6) Ge 6:9; Ps 106:31; Lk 2:25; 23:50; Heb 11:4; 2Pe 2:8

RIGHTEOUS ONE (5) Pr 21:12; Isa 24:16; Ac 3:14; 7:52; 22:14

Ge 6: 9 Noah was a **r** man, the only blameless man living
7: 1 people of the earth, I consider you alone to be **r**.
15: 6 and the LORD declared him **r** because of his
Nu 23: 10 Let me die like the **r**; / let my life end like theirs."
Dt 6: 25 For we are **r** when we obey all the commands the
9: 4 has given us this land because we are so **r**!'
9: 5 It is not at all because you are such **r**,
9: 6 is not giving you this good land because you are **r**,
24: 13 And the LORD your God will count it as a **r** act.
Jdg 5: 11 They recount the **r** victories of the LORD,
1Ki 2: 32 him for the murders of two men who were more **r**
Job 6: 29 Stop assuming my guilt, for I am **r**. Don't be
17: 9 The **r** will move onward and forward, and those
22: 3 Is it any pleasure to the Almighty if you are **r**?
22: 19 "Now the **r** will be happy to see the wicked
25: 4 a mere mortal stand before God and claim to be **r**?
27: 17 But the **r** will wear that clothing, and the innocent
35: 2 it is right for you to claim, 'I am **r** before God'?
35: 3 Yet you also ask, 'What's the use of living a **r** life?
Ps 7: 8 Declare me **r**, O LORD, / for I am innocent,
7: 9 look deep within the mind and heart, / O **r** God.
11: 3 and order have collapsed. / What can the **r** do?"
11: 5 The LORD examines both the **r** and the wicked.
11: 7 For the LORD is **r**, and he loves justice.
22: 31 His **r** acts will be told to those yet unborn.
34: 19 The **r** face many troubles, / but the LORD rescues
34: 21 and those who hate the **r** will be punished.
52: 6 The **r** will see it and be amazed. / They will laugh
69: 28 of Life; / don't let them be counted among the **r**.
71: 24 I will tell about your **r** deeds / all day long,
94: 15 Judgment will come again for the **r**, / and those
94: 21 They attack the **r** / and condemn the innocent to
106: 31 So he has been regarded as a **r** man / ever since
112: 4 They are generous, compassionate, and **r**.
112: 6 Those who are **r** will be long remembered.
118: 19 Open for me the gates where the **r** enter, / and I
119: 7 When I learn your **r** laws, / I will thank you by
119: 137 O LORD, you are **r**, / and your decisions are fair.
143: 1 Answer me because you are faithful and **r**.
145: 17 The LORD is **r** in everything he does; / he is
146: 8 bent beneath their loads. / The LORD loves the **r**.
Pr 2: 20 of good men instead, and stay on the paths of the **r**.
4: 18 The way of the **r** is like the first gleam of dawn,
8: 16 lead with my help, and nobles make **r** judgments.
9: 9 be wiser. Teach the **r**, and they will learn more.
11: 31 If the **r** are rewarded here on earth, how much
13: 21 chases sinners, while blessings chase the **r**!
15: 29 from the wicked, but he hears the prayers of the **r**.
16: 13 The king is pleased with **r** lips; he loves those who
21: 12 The **R** One knows what is going on in the homes
29: 6 trapped by sin, but the **r** escape, shouting for joy.
Ecc 9: 2 whether they are **r** or wicked, good or bad,
Isa 1: 27 Because the LORD is just and **r**, the repentant
24: 16 Hear them singing praises to the **R** One! But my
26: 2 Open the gates to all who are **r**; / allow the faithful
26: 7 But for those who are **r**, / the path is not steep
32: 1 Look, a **r** king is coming! And honest princes will
42: 21 it he had planned to show the world that he is **r**.
45: 13 I will raise up Cyrus to fulfill my **r** purpose,
51: 6 salvation lasts forever. My **r** rule will never end!
53: 11 my **r** servant will make it possible for many to be counted **r**,
57: 1 The **r** pass away; the godly often die before their
57: 12 your so-called good deeds that you consider so **r**.
58: 2 You would almost think this was a **r** nation that
59: 14 Our courts oppose people who are **r**, and justice is
60: 21 All your people will be **r**. They will possess their
64: 6 When we proudly display our **r** deeds, we find
Jer 9: 24 understand that I am the LORD who is just and **r**,
20: 12 You know those who are **r**, and you examine the
23: 5 "when I will place a **r** Branch on King David's
31: 23 LORD bless you—O **r** home, O holy mountain!'
33: 15 At that time I will bring to the throne of David a **r**
Eze 13: 22 You have discouraged the **r** with your lies, when I
16: 51 sisters ever did. They seem **r** compared to you!
18: 20 **R** people will be rewarded for their own goodness,
18: 22 will live because of the **r** things they have done.
18: 24 if **r** people turn to sinful ways and start acting like
18: 26 When **r** people turn from being good and start
21: 3 to destroy your people—the **r** and the wicked alike.
21: 4 Yes, I will not spare even the **r**! I will make a clean
23: 45 But **r** people will judge these sister cities for what
33: 12 The good works of **r** people will not save them if
33: 13 When I tell **r** people that they will live, but
33: 18 I say, when **r** people turn to evil, they will die.
Hos 14: 9 and right, and **r** people live by walking in them.
Am 5: 24 of justice, a river of **r** living that will never run dry.
Hab 1: 4 The wicked far outnumber the **r**, and justice is
1: 13 wicked destroy people who are more **r** than they?
2: 4 lives are crooked; but the **r** will live by their faith.
Zec 9: 9 He is **r** and victorious, yet he is humble, riding on
Mal 2: 6 they walked with me, living good and **r** lives,
3: 18 you will again see the difference between the **r**
Mt 23: 35 people from **r** Abel to Zechariah son of Barachiah,
25: 37 "Then these **r** ones will reply, 'Lord, when did we
25: 46 but the **r** will go into eternal life."
Lk 1: 6 Zechariah and Elizabeth were **r** in God's eyes,
2: 25 He was a **r** man and very devout. He was filled
15: 7 to God than over ninety-nine others who are **r**
23: 50 Now there was a good and **r** man named Joseph.
Jn 17: 25 "O **r** Father, the world doesn't know you, but I do;
Ac 3: 14 You rejected this holy, **r** one, and instead
7: 52 the ones who predicted the coming of the **R** One—
22: 14 his will and to see the **R** One and hear him speak.
24: 15 that he will raise both the **r** and the ungodly.
Ro 1: 17 "It is through faith that a **r** person has life."
4: 3 believed God, so God declared him to be **r**."
4: 5 But people are declared **r** because of their faith,
4: 6 of an undeserving sinner who is declared to be **r**:
4: 9 We have been saying he was declared **r** by God
4: 10 Was he declared **r** only after he had been
4: 11 already accepted him and declared him to be **r**—
4: 22 of Abraham's faith, God declared him to be **r**.
4: 23 wonderful truth—that God declared him to be **r**—
4: 24 assuring us that God will also declare us to be **r** if
Gal 3: 6 so God declared him **r** because of his faith."
3: 11 "It is through faith that a **r** person has life."
Eph 4: 24 created in God's likeness—**r**, holy, and true.
1Ti 3: 16 and was shown to be **r** by the Spirit. / He was seen
2Ti 4: 8 crown of righteousness that the Lord, the **r** Judge,
Heb 10: 38 And a **r** person will live by faith. / But I will have
11: 4 Abel's offering to show that he was a **r** man.
Jas 2: 23 believed God, so God declared him to be **r**."
5: 16 The earnest prayer of a **r** person has great power
1Pe 4: 18 And / "If the **r** are barely saved, / what chance will
2Pe 2: 5 Noah warned the world of God's **r** judgment.
2: 8 he was a **r** man who was distressed by the
1Jn 3: 7 it is because they are **r**, even as Christ is **r**.
Rev 15: 4 for your **r** deeds have been revealed."

RIGHTEOUSLY (1) [RIGHTEOUS]

2Sa 23: 3 'The person who rules **r**, / who rules in the fear of

RIGHTEOUSNESS (71) [RIGHTEOUS]

1Ki 10: 9 made you king so you can rule with justice and **r**."
2Ch 9: 8 made you king so you can rule with justice and **r**."
Job 29: 14 **R** covered me like a robe, and I wore justice like a
36: 3 I will give you many illustrations of the **r** of my
Ps 36: 6 Your **r** is like the mighty mountains, / your justice
71: 15 I will tell everyone about your **r**. / All day long I
71: 19 Your **r**, O God, reaches to the highest heavens.
72: 1 to the king, O God, / and **r** to the king's son.
85: 10 truth have met together. / **R** and peace have kissed!
85: 11 from the earth, / and **r** smiles down from heaven.
85: 13 **R** goes as a herald before him, / preparing the way
88: 12 in the land of forgetfulness talk about your **r**?
89: 14 is founded on two strong pillars—**r** and justice.
89: 16 your wonderful reputation. / They exult in your **r**.
96: 13 to judge the earth. / He will judge the world with **r**
97: 2 **R** and justice are the foundation of his throne.
97: 6 The heavens declare his **r**; / every nation sees his
98: 2 his victory / and has revealed his **r** to every nation!
99: 4 have acted with justice / and **r** throughout Israel.
103: 6 The LORD gives **r** / and justice to all who are
111: 3 reveals his glory and majesty. / His **r** never fails.
143: 11 save me. / In your **r**, bring me out of this distress.
145: 7 they will sing with joy of your **r**.
Pr 8: 20 I walk in **r**, in paths of justice.
Isa 1: 21 Once the home of justice and **r**, she is now filled
5: 7 he found bloodshed. / He expected to find **r**,
5: 16 The holiness of God is displayed by his **r**.
28: 17 and the plumb line of **r** to check the foundation
32: 16 will rule in the wilderness and **r** in the fertile field.
32: 17 And this **r** will bring peace. Quietness
33: 5 he will make Jerusalem his home of justice and **r**.
42: 4 stop until truth and **r** prevail throughout the earth.
42: 6 the LORD, have called you to demonstrate my **r**.
45: 8 Open up, O heavens, and pour out your **r**.
45: 8 so salvation and **r** can sprout up together.
45: 24 "The LORD is the source of all my **r**
48: 18 flowing like a gentle river and **r** rolling like waves.
51: 8 at them as it eats wool. But my **r** will last forever.
59: 17 He put on **r** as his body armor and placed the
60: 17 stones for iron. Peace and **r** will be your leaders!
61: 10 clothing of salvation and draped me in a robe of **r**.
61: 11 His **r** will be like a garden in early spring,
62: 1 I will not stop praying for her until her **r** shines
62: 2 The nations will see your **r**. Kings will be blinded
Jer 23: 6 And this is his name: 'The LORD Is Our **R**.'
33: 16 And their motto will be 'The LORD is our **r**!'
Eze 14: 14 their **r** would save no one but themselves,
14: 20 the people. They alone would be saved by their **r**.
22: 30 might rebuild the wall of **r** that guards the land.
33: 13 then they sin, expecting their past **r** to save them,
Da 9: 24 to sin, to atone for guilt, to bring in everlasting **r**,
12: 3 and those who turn many to **r** will shine like stars
Hos 2: 19 showing you **r** and justice, unfailing love
10: 12 I said, 'Plant the good seeds of **r**, and you will
10: 12 that he may come and shower **r** upon you.'
Am 5: 7 **R** and fair play are meaningless fictions to you.
6: 12 into poison and make bitter the sweet fruit of **r**.
Mic 7: 9 of my darkness into the light, and I will see his **r**.
Mal 4: 2 the Sun of **R** will rise with healing in his wings.
Lk 1: 75 in holiness and **r** forever.
Jn 16: 8 and of God's **r**, and of the coming judgment.
16: 10 **R** is available because I go to the Father, and you
Ac 24: 25 As he reasoned with them about **r** and self-control
Ro 5: 17 gracious gift of **r** will live in triumph over sin
5: 18 but Christ's one act of **r** makes all people right in
6: 18 and you have become slaves to your new master, **r**.
6: 19 Now you must choose to be slaves of **r** so that you
2Co 6: 7 We have **r** as our weapon, both to attack and to
Eph 6: 14 sturdy belt of truth and the body armor of God's **r**.
2Ti 4: 8 the crown of **r** that the Lord, the righteous Judge,
Heb 1: 8 and ever. / Your royal power is expressed in **r**.

RIGHTFUL (2) [RIGHT]

2Ki 2: 9 "Please let me become your **r** successor."
Ecc 10: 6 people of proven worth their **r** place of dignity.

RIGHTLY (2) [RIGHT]

Isa 10: 22 The LORD has **r** decided to destroy his people.
Jas 4: 12 who made the law, can **r** judge among us.

RIGHTS (18) [RIGHT]

Ge 25: 33 thereby selling all his **r** as the firstborn to his
31: 15 He has reduced our **r** to those of foreign women.
Dt 21: 17 and who owns the **r** of the firstborn son,
1Sa 10: 25 Then Samuel told the people what the **r** and duties
Job 27: 2 vow by the living God, who has taken away my **r**,
34: 5 'I am innocent, but God has taken away my **r**.
Ps 82: 3 uphold the **r** of the oppressed and the destitute.
140: 12 they persecute; / he will maintain the **r** of the poor.
Pr 29: 7 The godly know the **r** of the poor; the wicked
Isa 1: 17 Defend the orphan. Fight for the **r** of widows.
Jer 5: 28 justice to orphans and deny the **r** of the poor.
La 3: 35 They deprived people of their God-given **r** in
Mic 2: 9 and stripped their children of all their God-given **r**.
Ro 2: 26 won't God give them all the **r** and honors of being
8: 23 when God will give us our full **r** as his children,
1Co 9: 15 Yet I have never used any of these **r**. And I am not
9: 18 to anyone, never demanding my **r** as a preacher.
Php 2: 6 he did not demand and cling to his **r** as God.

RIGID (1)

Mk 9: 18 at the mouth and grind his teeth and become **r**.

RIGOUR [KJV] See (MORE) BITTER, RUTHLESSLY

RIM (15) [RIMS]

Ex 25: 25 Put a **r** about three inches wide around the top edge, and put a gold molding all around the **r**.
25: 27 close to the **r** around the top. These rings will
37: 12 A **r** about 3 inches wide was attached along the
37: 12 of the table, and a gold molding ran around the **r**.
37: 14 next to the **r**. These were made to hold the carrying
1Ki 7: 23 a large round tank, 15 feet across from **r** to **r**;
7: 24 The Sea was encircled just below its **r** by two rows
7: 26 and its **r** flared out like a cup and resembled a lily
7: 35 Around the top of each cart there was a **r** 9 inches
2Ch 4: 2 a large round tank, 15 feet across from **r** to **r**;
4: 3 The Sea was encircled just below its **r** by two rows
4: 5 and its **r** flared out like a cup and resembled a lily

RIMMON (11) [DIMNAH, EN-RIMMON, GATH-RIMMON, HADAD-RIMMON, RIMMON-PEREZ]

Jos 15: 32 Lebaoth, Shilhim, Ain, and **R**. In all, there were
19: 7 It also included Ain, **R**, Ether, and Ashan—
19: 13 Eth-kazin, and **R** and turned toward Neah.
Jdg 20: 45 fled into the wilderness toward the rock of **R**,
20: 47 six hundred men who escaped to the rock of **R**,
21: 13 of Benjamin who were living at the rock of **R**.
2Sa 4: 2 They were sons of **R**, who was a Benjaminite from
4: 5 and Baanah, the sons of **R** from Beeroth,
2Ki 5: 18 goes into the temple of the god **R** to worship there
1Ch 4: 32 also lived in Etam, Ain, **R**, Token, and Ashan—
Zec 14: 10 north of Judah, to **R**, south of Jerusalem,

RIMMON-PEREZ (2) [PEREZ, RIMMON]

Nu 33: 19 They left Rithmah and camped at **R**.
33: 20 They left **R** and camped at Libnah.

RIMMONO (1) [DIMNAH]
1Ch 6:77 Kartah, **R**, and Tabor, each with its pasturelands.

RIMS (2) [RIM]
1Ki 7:33 The axles, spokes, **r**, and hubs were all cast from
Eze 1:18 The **r** of the four wheels were awesomely tall,

RING (23) [EARRING, NOSE-RING, RANG, RINGING, RINGS]
Ge 24:22 he gave her a gold **r** for her nose and two large
24:47 Milcah.' So I gave her the **r** and the bracelets.
41:42 Then Pharaoh placed his own signet **r** on Joseph's
Ex 26:24 and firmly attached at the top with a single **r**,
27: 4 a bronze grating, with a metal **r** at each corner.
36:29 and firmly attached at the top with a single **r**,
1Sa 26: 5 were sleeping inside a **r** formed by the slumbering
2Ch 33:11 They put a **r** through his nose, bound him in
Est 3:10 confirming his decision by removing his signet **r**
3:12 in the name of King Xerxes, sealed with his **r**,
8: 2 The king took off his signet **r**—which he had taken
8: 8 you want, and seal it with the king's signet **r**.
8: 8 and sealed with his **r** can never be revoked."
8:10 and sealed the message with the king's signet **r**.
Job 40:24 it off guard or put a **r** in its nose and lead it away.
42:11 of them brought him a gift of money and a gold **r**.
Pr 11:22 but lacks discretion is like a gold **r** in a pig's snout.
Jer 19: 3 that the ears of those who hear about it will **r**!
22:24 Even if you were the signet **r** on my right hand,
Eze 7: 7 It will **r** with shouts of anguish, not shouts of joy.
16:12 a **r** for your nose and earrings for your ears, and a
Hag 2:23 I will treat you like a signet **r** on my finger,
Lk 15:22 Get a **r** for his finger, and sandals for his feet.

RINGING (1) [RING]
1Th 1: 8 And now the word of the Lord is **r** out from you to

RINGLEADER (1) [LEAD]
Ac 24: 5 He is a **r** of the sect known as the Nazarenes.

RINGLEADERS (1) [LEAD]
Nu 25: 4 "Seize all the **r** and execute them before the

RINGS (35) [RING]
Ex 25:12 Cast four **r** of gold for it, and attach them to its four feet, two **r** on each side.
25:14 Fit the poles into the **r** at the sides of the Ark to
25:15 carrying poles must never be taken from the **r**;
25:26 Make four gold **r**, and put the **r** at the four corners by the four legs,
25:27 These **r** will support the poles used to carry the
26:29 and make gold **r** to support the crossbars.
27: 7 put the poles into the **r** at two sides of the altar.
28:23 Then make two gold **r** and attach them to the top
28:24 The two gold cords will go through the **r** on the
28:26 Then make two more gold **r**, and attach them to the
28:27 And make two more gold **r** and attach them to the
28:28 Then attach the bottom **r** of the chestpiece to the **r** on the ephod with blue cords.
30: 4 attach two gold **r** to support the carrying poles.
35:22 medallions, earrings, **r** from their fingers,
36:34 The **r** used to hold the crossbars were made of pure
37: 3 Four gold **r** were fastened to its four feet, two **r** at each side.
37: 5 He put the poles into the **r** at the sides of the Ark to
37:13 Then he cast four **r** of gold and attached them to
37:27 Two gold **r** were placed on opposite sides,
38: 5 Four **r** were cast for each side of the grating to
38: 7 These poles were inserted into the **r** at the side of
39:16 They also made two gold **r** and attached them to
39:17 The two gold cords were put through the gold **r** on
39:19 Two more gold **r** were attached to the lower inside
39:20 Then two gold **r** were attached to the ephod near
39:21 Blue cords were used to attach the bottom **r** of the chestpiece to the **r** on the ephod.
Nu 31:50 armbands, bracelets, **r**, earrings, and necklaces.
Est 1: 6 fastened by purple ribbons to silver **r** embedded in
Isa 3:21 their **r**, jewels,
Jer 51:55 against her; the noise of battle **r** through the city.

RINGSTRAKED [KJV] See SPECKLED

RINNAH (1)
1Ch 4:20 of Shimon were Amnon, **R**, Ben-hanan, and Tilon.

RINSED (2) [RINSING]
Lev 6:28 it must be scoured and **r** thoroughly with water.
15:12 and every wooden utensil he touches must be **r**

RINSING (1) [RINSED]
Lev 15:11 If the man touches you without first **r** his hands,

RIOT (11) [RIOTING, RIOTOUS, RIOTS]
Mt 14: 5 have executed John, but he was afraid of a **r**,
26: 5 the Passover," they agreed, "or there will be a **r**."
27:24 getting anywhere and that a **r** was developing.
Mk 11:32 they were afraid that the people would start a **r**,
14: 2 the Passover," they agreed, "or there will be a **r**."
Lk 20:19 But they were afraid there would be a **r** if they
22: 2 But they wanted to kill him without starting a **r**,
Ac 4:21 know how to punish them without starting a **r**.
17: 5 from the streets to form a mob and start a **r**.
21:30 by these accusations, and a great **r** followed.
24:12 nor did I incite a **r** in any synagogue or on the

RIOTING (2) [RIOT]
Ac 19:40 of being charged with **r** by the Roman government,
24:18 There was no crowd around me and no **r**.

RIOTOUS (1) [RIOT]
Am 8: 3 In that day the **r** sounds of singing in the Temple

RIOTS (2) [RIOT]
Lk 23: 5 "But he is causing **r** everywhere he goes, all over
Ac 24: 5 inciting the Jews throughout the world to **r**

RIP (2) [RIPPED, RIPPING, RIPS]
2Ki 8:12 to the ground, and **r** open their pregnant women!"
Hos 13: 8 I will **r** you to pieces like a bear whose cubs have

RIPE (21) [RIPEN, RIPENED, RIPENING, RIPENS]
Ge 15:15 (But you will die in peace, at a **r** old age.)
25: 8 and he died at a **r** old age, joining his ancestors in
35:29 and he died at a **r** old age, joining his ancestors in
40:10 and soon there were clusters of **r** grapes.
Ex 9:31 barley were destroyed because the barley was **r**
Nu 13:20 to be the season for harvesting the first **r** grapes.)
Dt 28:40 for the trees will drop the fruit before it is **r**.
1Sa 2:31 die before their time. None will live to a **r** old age.
1Ch 29:28 He died at a **r** old age, having enjoyed long life,
Job 15:33 vine whose grapes are harvested before they are **r**,
Jer 24: 2 One basket was filled with fresh, **r** figs,
Eze 44:30 The first of the **r** fruits and all the gifts brought to
Hos 9:10 it was like seeing the first **r** figs of the season!
Joel 3:13 Now let the sickle do its work, for the harvest is **r**.
Am 8: 1 In it I saw a basket filled with **r** fruit.
8: 2 he asked. I replied, "A basket full of **r** fruit."
8: 2 represents my people of Israel—**r** for punishment!
Na 3:12 They will be devoured like the **r** figs that fall into
Mal 3:11 Your grapes will not shrivel before they are **r**,"
Rev 14:15 for you to harvest; the crop is **r** on the earth."
14:18 of the earth, for they are fully **r** for judgment."

RIPEN (1) [RIPE]
Jas 5: 7 They patiently wait for the precious harvest to **r**.

RIPENED (1) [RIPE]
Hos 2: 9 and **r** grain I generously provided each harvest

RIPENING (2) [RIPE]
Isa 18: 5 your attack, while your plans are **r** like grapes,
Jn 4:35 Vast fields are **r** all around us and are ready now

RIPENS (1) [RIPE]
Mk 4:28 heads of wheat are formed, and finally the grain **r**.

RIPHATH (2)
Ge 10: 3 of Gomer were Ashkenaz, **R**, and Togarmah.
1Ch 1: 6 of Gomer were Ashkenaz, **R**, and Togarmah.

RIPPED (4) [RIP]
Jdg 14: 6 and he **r** the lion's jaws apart with his bare hands.
1Ki 14: 8 I **r** the kingdom away from the family of David
2Ki 15:16 entire population and **r** open the pregnant women.
Hos 13:16 their pregnant women **r** open by swords."

RIPPING (1) [RIP]
Am 1:13 **r** open pregnant women with their swords.

RIPS (1) [RIP]
Hos 5:14 tear at Israel and Judah as a lion **r** apart its prey.

RISE (109) [ARISE, ARISES, ARISING, AROSE, RISEN, RISES, RISING, ROSE, UPRAISED, UPRISING]
Ex 12:39 out of Egypt and had no time to wait for bread to **r**.
14:27 So as the sun began to **r**, Moses raised his hand
Lev 16:13 so that a cloud of incense will **r** over the Ark's
Nu 23:18 "**R** up, Balak, and listen! / Hear me, son of Zippor.
23:24 These people **r** up like a lioness; / like a majestic
24:17 far in the distant future. / A star will **r** from Jacob;
24:19 A ruler will **r** in Jacob / who will destroy the
Dt 1:28 and that the walls of their towns **r** high into the
33:11 strike down their foes so they never **r** again."
Jdg 5:31 But may those who love you **r** like the sun at full
Job 8: 6 he will **r** up and restore your happy home.
9: 7 the sun won't **r** and the stars won't shine.
14:12 people lie down and do not **r** again.
24:12 The groans of the dying **r** from the city,
24:22 They may **r** high, but they have no assurance in
38:12 to appear and caused the dawn to **r** in the east?
Ps 12: 5 Now I will **r** up to rescue them, / as they have
20: 8 and collapse, / but we will **r** up and stand firm.
35:23 Wake up! **R** to my defense! / Take up my case,
36:12 They have been thrown down, never to **r** again.
44:26 **R** up! Come and help us! / Save us because of your
59: 4 to kill me. / **R** up and help me! Look on my plight!
59: 5 the God of Israel, / **r** up to punish hostile nations.
66: 7 of the nations; / let no rebel **r** in defiance.
75: 7 he decides who will **r** and who will fall.
82: 8 **R** up, O God, and judge the earth, / for all the
86:14 O God, insolent people **r** up against me;
89: 9 When their waves **r** in fearful storms, you subdue
89:24 with him, / and he will **r** to power because of me.
107:12 they fell, and no one helped them **r** again.
119:62 At midnight I **r** to thank you / for your just laws.
119:147 I **r** early, before the sun is up; / I cry out for help
135: 7 He causes the clouds to **r** over the earth. / He sends
Pr 24:16 trip seven times, but each time they will **r** again.
Ecc 1: 5 sun rises and sets and hurries around to **r** again.
SS 2:10 '**R** up, my beloved, my fair one, and come away.
Isa 8:15 of them will stumble and fall, never to **r** again.
10:25 and then my anger will **r** up to destroy them."
13:20 Babylon will never **r** again. Generation after
14:21 Do not let them **r** and conquer the land or rebuild
19: 5 The waters of the Nile will fail to **r** and flood the
24:20 It falls and will not **r** again, for its sins are very
26:19 belong to God will live; / their bodies will **r** again!
26:19 who sleep in the earth / will **r** up and sing for joy!
31: 2 He will **r** against those who are wicked, and he
34:10 never end; the smoke of its burning will **r** forever.
52: 2 **R** from the dust, O Jerusalem. Remove the slave
Jer 10:13 He causes the clouds to **r** over the earth.
25:27 and vomit, and you will fall to **r** no more,
32:29 where the people caused my fury to **r** by offering
48: 5 while cries of terror **r** from Horonaim below.
51: 2 They will come from every side to **r** against her in
51:16 He causes the clouds to **r** over the earth.
51:64 and her people will sink, never again to **r**,
La 2:19 **R** during the night and cry out. Pour out your
Eze 29:15 never again great enough to **r** above its neighbors.
37:12 open your graves of exile and cause you to **r** again.
38:18 says the Sovereign LORD, my fury will **r**!
Da 2:39 inferior to yours, will **r** to take your place.
2:39 bronze belly and thighs, will **r** to rule the world.
8:23 a fierce king, a master of intrigue, will **r** to power.
11: 3 "Then a mighty king will **r** to power who will rule
12: 2 those whose bodies lie dead and buried will **r** up,
12:13 you will **r** again to receive the inheritance set aside
Hos 10:14 Now the terrors of war will **r** among your people.
Joel 2:20 The stench of their rotting bodies will **r** over the
Am 5: 2 "The virgin Israel has fallen, / never to **r** again!
8: 8 The land will **r** up like the Nile River at floodtime,
8:14 and Beersheba will fall down, never to **r** again."
Mic 2: 1 You **r** at dawn and hurry to carry out any of the
2: 8 Yet to this very hour my people **r** against me!
4:13 "**R** up and destroy the nations, O Jerusalem!"
7: 8 my enemies! For though I fall, I will **r** again.
Hab 1:12 you have decreed the **r** of these Babylonians to
2: 7 Suddenly, your debtors will **r** up in anger.
Mal 4: 2 the Sun of Righteousness will **r** with healing in his
Mt 7:25 the rain comes in torrents and the floodwaters **r**
10:21 and children will **r** against their parents and cause
12:41 The people of Nineveh will **r** up against this
12:42 The queen of Sheba will also **r** up against this
22:30 For when the dead **r**, they won't be married.
24:24 For false messiahs and false prophets will **r** up
Mk 8:31 be killed, and three days later he would **r** again.
9:31 but three days later he will **r** from the dead."
10:34 and kill him, but after three days he will **r** again."
12:25 For when the dead **r**, they won't be married.
13:12 and children will **r** against their parents and cause
13:22 For false messiahs and false prophets will **r** up
Lk 6:48 When the floodwaters **r** and break against the
8:23 and while he was sleeping the wind began to **r**.
11:31 "The queen of Sheba will **r** up against this
11:32 will **r** up against this generation on judgment day
18:33 and kill him, but on the third day he will **r** again."
24: 7 and that he would **r** again the third day?"
24:46 and die and **r** again from the dead on the third day.
Jn 5:29 and they will **r** again. Those who have done good **r** to eternal life, and those who have continued in evil will **r** to judgment.
11:23 Jesus told her, "Your brother will **r** again."
20: 9 that the Scriptures said he would **r** from the dead.
Ac 17:26 He decided beforehand which should **r** and fall,
24:10 The governor motioned for him to **r** and speak.
26:23 and be the first to **r** from the dead as a light to Jews
1Co 15:29 Why do it unless the dead will someday **r** again?
Eph 5:14 "Awake, O sleeper, / **r** up from the dead,
Col 1:18 He is the first of all who will **r** from the dead,
1Th 4:15 **r** to meet him ahead of those who are in their
4:16 all the Christians who have died will **r** from their
Rev 1: 5 witness to these things, the first to **r** from the dead,

RISEN (11) [RISE]
Isa 14:22 "I, myself, have **r** against him! I will destroy his
Jer 51:42 The sea has **r** over Babylon; she is covered by its
Mt 14:24 for a strong wind had **r**, and they were fighting
Mk 9: 9 seen until he, the Son of Man, had **r** from the dead.
16:14 to believe those who had seen him after he had **r**.
Lk 7:16 saying, "A mighty prophet has **r** among us,"
9: 8 or some other ancient prophet **r** from the dead."
9:19 one of the other ancient prophets **r** from the dead."
24: 6 He isn't here! He has **r** from the dead! Don't you
24:34 "The Lord has really **r**! He appeared to Peter!"
Rev 17:12 His ten horns are ten kings who have not yet **r** to

RISES (19) [RISE]
Job 24:14 The murderer **r** in the early dawn to kill the poor
39:27 Is it at your command that the eagle **r** to the
41:25 When it **r**, the mighty are afraid, gripped by terror.
Ps 19: 6 The sun **r** at one end of the heavens / and follows
65: 8 From where the sun **r** to where it sets, / you inspire
Ecc 1: 5 The sun **r** and sets and hurries around to rise again.
Isa 2:19 When the LORD **r** to shake the earth, his enemies

2:21 and the glory of his majesty as he **r** to shake the
18: 4 as quietly as the heat **r** on a summer day, or as the
Jer 14: 2 in mourning, and a great cry **r** from Jerusalem.
Eze 43:14 From the gutter the altar **r** 3-1/2 feet to a ledge that
43:14 From the lower ledge the altar **r** 7 feet to the upper
43:15 The top of the altar, the hearth, **r** still 7 feet higher,
Am 9: 5 The ground **r** like the Nile River at floodtime,
Lk 16:31 they won't listen even if someone **r** from the
Jn 11:24 "Yes," Martha said, "when everyone else **r**,
Heb 12:15 Watch out that no bitter root of unbelief **r** up
Jas 1:11 The hot sun **r** and dries up the grass; the flower
Rev 14:11 The smoke of their torment **r** forever and ever,

RISING (15) [RISE]

Ge 19:23 The sun was **r** as Lot reached the village.
19:28 as from a furnace, **r** from the cities there.
Jos 8:21 had succeeded and that smoke was **r** from the city,
Jdg 20:40 and saw the smoke **r** into the sky from every part
1Ki 18:44 "I saw a little cloud about the size of a hand **r**
Isa 30:27 with anger, surrounded by a thick, **r** smoke.
Jer 6:22 A great nation is **r** against you from far-off lands.
25:32 A great whirlwind of fury is **r** from the most
46: 7 "Who is this, **r** like the Nile River at floodtime,
50:41 and many kings are **r** against you from far-off
Eze 43:15 with a horn **r** up from each of the four corners.
Mk 9:10 each other what he meant by "**r** from the dead."
Ac 17: 3 sufferings of the Messiah and his **r** from the dead.
Rev 13: 1 And now in my vision I saw a beast **r** up out of the
18: 9 as they see the smoke **r** from her charred remains.

RISK (6) [RISKED, RISKING, RISKS, RISKY]

1Sa 28:21 "Sir, I obeyed your command at the **r** of my life.
2Sa 21:17 Why should we **r** snuffing out the light of Israel?"
Ezr 7:23 for why should we **r** bringing God's anger against
Pr 20: 2 a lion's roar; to rouse his anger is to **r** your life.
La 5: 9 We must hunt for food in the wilderness at the **r** of
Ac 19:31 begging him not to **r** his life by entering the

RISKED (9) [RISK]

Jdg 5:18 But Zebulun **r** his life, / as did Naphtali,
9:17 and **r** his life when he rescued you from the
12: 3 So I **r** my life and went to battle without you,
1Sa 19: 5 Have you forgotten about the time he **r** his life to
2Sa 23:17 of these men who **r** their lives to bring it to me."
1Ch 11:19 of these men who **r** their lives to bring it to me."
Ac 15:26 who have **r** their lives for the sake of our Lord
Ro 16: 4 In fact, they **r** their lives for me. I am not the only
Php 2:30 For he **r** his life for the work of Christ, and he was

RISKING (1) [RISK]

1Co 15:30 And why should we ourselves be continually **r** our

RISKS (2) [RISK]

Ecc 10: 9 with each stroke of your ax! Such are the **r** of life.
11: 2 for you do not know what **r** might lie ahead.

RISKY (1) [RISK]

Ecc 5:14 or they are put into **r** investments that turn sour,

RISSAH (2)

Nu 33:21 They left Libnah and camped at **R**.
33:22 They left **R** and camped at Kehelathah.

RITE (2) [RITES]

Nu 8:21 then performed the **r** of atonement over them to
1Sa 16: 5 Then Samuel performed the purification **r** for Jesse

RITES (1) [RITE]

2Sa 11: 4 (She had just completed the purification **r** after

RITHMAH (2)

Nu 33:18 They left Hazeroth and camped at **R**.
33:19 They left **R** and camped at Rimmon-perez.

RITUAL (11) [RITUALLY, RITUALS]

Nu 5:29 " 'This is the **r** law for dealing with jealousy.
5:30 and the priest will apply this entire **r** law to her.
6:13 "This is the **r** law of the Nazirites.
6:21 "This is the **r** law of the Nazirites. If any Nazirites
19: 2 "Here is another **r** law required by the LORD:
19:14 "This is the **r** law that applies when someone dies
Mk 7: 2 the usual Jewish **r** of hand washing before eating.
Ac 21:26 and the next day he went through the purification **r**
24:18 in the Temple as I was completing a purification **r**.
Heb 9:10 deals only with food and drink and **r** washing—
9:13 could cleanse people's bodies from **r** defilement.

RITUALLY (2) [RITUAL]

Nu 18:15 and the firstborn males of **r** unclean animals.
Eze 44:26 return to his Temple duties after being **r** cleansed

RITUALS (3) [RITUAL]

Eze 24:17 Do not perform the **r** of mourning or accept any
44: 8 kept the laws I gave you concerning these sacred **r**,
Hos 8:13 The people of Israel love their **r** of sacrifice,

RIVAL (3) [RIVALRY, RIVALS]

Ge 25:23 "The sons in your womb will become two **r**
1Sa 28:17 taken the kingdom from you and given it to your **r**,
SS 5:15 strong as the cedars of Lebanon. None can **r** him.

RIVALRY (1) [RIVAL]

Php 1:15 Some are preaching out of jealousy and **r**.

RIVALS (1) [RIVAL]

Lev 18:18 a woman and her sister because they will be **r**.

RIVER (297) [RIVER'S, RIVERBANK, RIVERBED, RIVERS, RIVERSIDE]

Ge 2:10 A **r** flowed from the land of Eden,
15:18 the border of Egypt to the great Euphrates **R**—
31:21 possessions with him and crossed the Euphrates **R**,
32:22 and eleven sons across the Jabbok **R**.
36:37 city of Rehoboth on the Euphrates **R** became king.
41: 1 that he was standing on the bank of the Nile **R**.
41: 2 cows suddenly came up out of the **r**
41: 3 Then seven other cows came up from the **r**,
41:17 "I was standing on the bank of the Nile **R**,"
41:18 healthy-looking cows came up out of the **r**
41:19 But then seven other cows came up from the **r**.
41:20 the seven fat ones that had come out of the **r** first,
50:10 near the Jordan **R**, they held a very great
Ex 1:22 all the newborn Israelite boys into the Nile **R**.
2: 3 it among the reeds along the edge of the Nile **R**.
2: 5 Pharaoh's daughters came down to bathe in the **r**,
4: 9 then take some water from the Nile **R** and pour it
7:15 Pharaoh in the morning as he goes down to the **r**.
7:17 the Nile with this staff, and the **r** will turn to blood.
7:18 The fish in it will die, and the **r** will stink.
7:20 of the Nile. Suddenly, the whole **r** turned to blood!
7:21 The fish in the **r** died, and the water became
7:24 drinking water, for they couldn't drink from the **r**.
8: 3 The Nile **R** will swarm with them. They will come up out of the **r** and into your
8: 9 Then only the frogs in the Nile **R** will remain
8:11 the frogs will be destroyed, except those in the **r**."
8:20 and meet Pharaoh as he goes down to the **r**.
23:31 and from the southern deserts to the Euphrates **R**.
Nu 21:13 Then they moved to the far side of the Arnon **R**,
21:14 area of Suphah, and the ravines; and the Arnon **R**
21:24 their land from the Arnon **R** to the Jabbok **R**.
21:26 and seized all his land as far as the Arnon **R**.
22: 1 plains of Moab and camped east of the Jordan **R**,
22: 5 in his native land of Pethor near the Euphrates **R**.
22:36 town on the Arnon **R** at the border of his land.
26: 3 camped on the plains of Moab beside the Jordan **R**,
26:63 priest on the plains of Moab beside the Jordan **R**,
27:12 "Climb to the top of the mountains east of the **r**,
31:12 camped on the plains of Moab beside the Jordan **R**,
32: 5 instead of giving us land across the Jordan **R**."
33:47 and camped in the mountains east of the **r**,
33:48 They left the mountains east of the **r** and camped on the plains of Moab beside the Jordan **R**,
33:49 Along the Jordan **R** they camped from
33:50 While they were camped near the Jordan **R** on the
33:51 'When you cross the Jordan **R** into the land of
34:12 and then along the Jordan **R** to the Dead Sea.
34:15 on the east side of the Jordan **R**, across from
35:14 three on the east side of the Jordan **R** and three on
36:13 camped on the plains of Moab beside the Jordan **R**,
Dt 1: 1 they were in the wilderness east of the Jordan **R**.
1: 5 they were in the land of Moab east of the Jordan **R**.
1: 7 and all the way to the great Euphrates **R**.
2:37 away from the Ammonites along the Jabbok **R**
3: 8 of the two Amorite kings east of the Jordan **R**—
3:16 all the way to the Jabbok **R** on the Ammonite
3:17 including the Jordan **R** and its eastern banks,
3:20 your God is giving them across the Jordan **R**,
3:27 but you may not cross the Jordan **R**.
4:21 He vowed that I would never cross the Jordan **R**
4:22 the land, I will die here on this side of the **r**.
4:41 set apart three cities of refuge east of the Jordan **R**,
4:46 in the valley near Beth-peor east of the Jordan **R**.
9: 1 Today you are about to cross the Jordan **R** to
11:24 and from the Euphrates **R** in the east to the
11:30 (These two mountains are west of the Jordan **R** in
12:10 You will soon cross the Jordan **R** and live in the
27: 2 When you cross the Jordan **R** and enter the land
27: 3 you will soon cross the **r** to enter the land the
27:12 "When you cross the Jordan **R**, the tribes of
31: 2 has told me that I will not cross the Jordan **R**.
32:47 the land you are crossing the Jordan **R** to occupy."
32:49 "Go to Moab, to the mountains east of the **r**,
Jos 1: 2 you must lead my people across the Jordan **R** into
1: 4 from the Euphrates **R** on the east to the
1:11 In three days you will cross the Jordan **R** and take
1:14 may remain here on the east side of the Jordan **R**,
1:15 east side of the Jordan **R** in the land that Moses,
2: 1 out the land on the other side of the Jordan **R**,
2: 7 to the shallow crossing places of the Jordan **R**.
2:10 the two Amorite kings east of the Jordan **R**,
2:23 down from the hill country, crossed the Jordan **R**,
3: 1 and arrived at the banks of the Jordan **R**,
3: 6 of the Covenant and lead the people across the **r**."
3: 8 'When you reach the banks of the Jordan **R**,
3: 8 take a few steps into the **r** and stop.' "
3:11 the whole earth, will lead you across the Jordan **R**!
3:13 and the **r** will pile up there in one heap."
4: 1 When all the people were safely across the **r**,
4: 7 'They remind us that the Jordan **R** stopped flowing
4: 8 twelve stones from the middle of the Jordan **R**,
4:10 of the **r** until all of the LORD's instructions,
4:18 the Jordan **R** flooded its banks as before.
4:20 up the twelve stones taken from the Jordan **R**.
4:23 For the LORD your God dried up the **r** right
5: 1 heard how the LORD had dried up the Jordan **R**
7: 7 why did you bring us across the Jordan **R** if you
9:10 to the two Amorite kings east of the Jordan **R**—
12: 1 These are the kings east of the Jordan **R** who had
12: 2 the middle of the Arnon Gorge to the Jabbok **R**,
12: 2 area of Gilead, which lies north of the Jabbok **R**.
13:23 The Jordan **R** marked the western boundary for the
13:27 The Jordan **R** was the western border, extending as
13:32 of Moab, across the Jordan **R**, east of Jericho.
14: 3 and a half tribes on the east side of the Jordan **R**.
15: 5 along the Dead Sea to the mouth of the Jordan **R**.
15: 5 bay where the Jordan **R** empties into the Dead Sea,
16: 1 of Joseph extended from the Jordan **R** near Jericho,
16: 7 touched Jericho, and ended at the Jordan **R**.
17: 5 the land of Gilead and Bashan across the Jordan **R**,
18: 7 gave them on the east side of the Jordan **R**."
18:12 The northern boundary began at the Jordan **R**,
18:19 which is the southern end of the Jordan **R**.
18:20 The eastern boundary was the Jordan **R**. This was
19:22 and Beth-shemesh, ending at the Jordan **R**—
19:33 and as far as Lakkum, ending at the Jordan **R**.
19:34 of Asher on the west, and the Jordan **R** on the east.
20: 8 On the east side of the Jordan **R**, across from
22: 4 gave you on the east side of the Jordan **R**.
22:10 before they crossed the Jordan **R**, Reuben, Gad,
22:10 altar near the Jordan **R** at a place called Geliloth.
22:11 had built the altar at Geliloth west of the Jordan **R**,
22:13 They crossed the **r** to talk with the tribes of
22:19 land is defiled, then join us on our side of the **r**,
22:25 The LORD has placed the Jordan **R** as a barrier
23: 4 from the Jordan **R** to the Mediterranean Sea in the
24: 2 and Nahor, lived beyond the Euphrates **R**,
24:11 "When you crossed the Jordan **R** and came to
24:14 when they lived beyond the Euphrates **R**
Jdg 3:28 of the shallows of the Jordan **R** across from Moab,
4: 7 with his chariots and warriors, to the Kishon **R**.
4:13 from Harosheth-haggoyim to the Kishon **R**.
5:21 The Kishon **R** swept them away— / that ancient **r**,
7:24 Cut them off at the shallows of the Jordan **R** at
8: 4 then crossed the Jordan **R** with his three hundred
10: 8 of the Jordan **R** in the land of the Amorites (that is,
11:13 stole my land from the Arnon **R** to the Jabbok **R**
11:18 and camped on the other side of the Arnon **R**.
11:18 But they never once crossed the Arnon **R** into
11:22 from the Arnon **R** to the Jabbok **R**, and from
11:26 to Aroer and in all the towns along the Arnon **R**.
12: 6 and kill him at the shallows of the Jordan **R**.
1Sa 13: 7 Some of them crossed the Jordan **R** and escaped
2Sa 2:29 They crossed the Jordan **R**, traveling all through
8: 3 to strengthen his control along the Euphrates **R**.
10:16 Hadadezer from the other side of the Euphrates **R**.
10:17 he mobilized all Israel, crossed the Jordan **R**,
15:28 I will stop at the shallows of the Jordan **R** and wait
16:14 so they rested when they reached the Jordan **R**.
17:16 not to stay at the shallows of the Jordan **R** tonight.
17:22 him went across the Jordan **R** during the night,
17:24 and was leading his troops across the Jordan **R**.
19:15 And when he arrived at the Jordan **R**, the people of
19:15 to Gilgal to meet him and escort him across the **r**.
19:18 hard ferrying the king's household across the **r**,
19:18 As the king was about to cross the **r**, Shimei fell
19:36 Just to go across the **r** with you is all the honor I
19:40 half the army of Israel escorted him across the **r**.
20: 2 and escorted him from the Jordan **R** to Jerusalem.
1Ki 2: 8 When he came down to meet me at the Jordan **R**,
4:21 from the Euphrates **R** to the land of the Philistines,
4:24 over all the kingdoms west of the Euphrates **R**,
14:15 and will scatter them beyond the Euphrates **R**,
17: 3 at a place east of where it enters the Jordan **R**.
2Ki 2: 6 for the LORD has told me to go to the Jordan **R**."
2: 7 as Elijah and Elisha stopped beside the Jordan **R**.
2: 8 The **r** divided, and the two of them went across on
2:13 and returned to the bank of the Jordan **R**.
2:14 Then the **r** divided, and Elisha went across.
5:10 and wash yourself seven times in the Jordan **R**.
5:12 Aren't the Abana **R** and Pharpar **R** of Damascus
5:14 So Naaman went down to the Jordan **R** and dipped
6: 2 Let's go down to the Jordan **R**, where there are
6: 5 of them was chopping, his ax head fell into the **r**.
7:15 They went all the way to the Jordan **R**, following a
10:33 east of the Jordan **R**, including all of Gilead,
17: 6 along the banks of the Habor **R** in Gozan,
18:11 along the banks of the Habor **R** in Gozan,
23:29 went to the Euphrates **R** to help the king of
24: 7 from the brook of Egypt to the Euphrates **R**.
1Ch 1:48 city of Rehoboth on the Euphrates **R** became king.
5: 9 edge of the desert that stretches to the Euphrates **R**.
5:26 Habor, Hara, and the Gozan **R**, where they remain
6:78 of Reuben, east of the Jordan **R** opposite Jericho,
12:15 They crossed the Jordan **R** during its seasonal
12:37 From the east side of the Jordan **R**—
18: 3 to strengthen his control along the Euphrates **R**.
19:16 troops from the other side of the Euphrates **R**.
19:17 he mobilized all Israel, crossed the Jordan **R**,
26:30 charge of the Israelite lands west of the Jordan **R**.
26:32 David sent them to the east side of the Jordan **R**
2Ch 9:26 He ruled over all the kings from the Euphrates **R** to
35:20 to do battle at Carchemish on the Euphrates **R**,
Ezr 4:10 lands of the province west of the Euphrates **R**.
4:11 subjects in the province west of the Euphrates **R**.
4:16 the province west of the Euphrates **R** will be lost to
4:17 throughout the province west of the Euphrates **R**.
4:20 and the entire province west of the Euphrates **R**
5: 6 west of the Euphrates **R** sent to King Darius:
6: 6 governor of the province west of the Euphrates **R**,
6:13 governor of the province west of the Euphrates **R**,
7:21 treasurers in the province west of the Euphrates **R**:
7:25 the people in the province west of the Euphrates **R**.

8:36 governors of the province west of the Euphrates **R**,
Ne 2:7 governors of the province west of the Euphrates **R**,
2:9 governors of the province west of the Euphrates **R**,
3:7 governor of the province west of the Euphrates **R**.
Job 14:11 from a lake and as a **r** disappears in drought,
22:24 and throw your precious gold into the **r**.
24:18 the earth as quickly as foam is swept down a **r**.
33:18 from the grave, from crossing over the **r** of death.
Ps 46:4 A **r** brings joy to the city of our God, / the sacred
72:8 and from the Euphrates **R** to the ends of the earth.
78:16 the rock, / making the waters flow down like a **r**!
80:11 our limbs east to the Euphrates **R**.
83:9 or as you did to Sisera and Jabin at the Kishon **R**.
105:41 to form a **r** through the dry and barren land.
114:3 The water of the Jordan **R** turned away.
114:5 What happened, Jordan **R**, that you turned away?
Isa 8:7 them with a mighty flood from the Euphrates **R**—
11:15 He will wave his hand over the Euphrates **R**,
16:2 birds at the shallow crossings of the Arnon **R**.
18:1 of the Nile. Its winged sailboats glide along the **r**,
27:12 from the Euphrates **R** in the east to the brook of
32:2 He will refresh her as a **r** in the desert and as the
33:21 He will be like a wide **r** of protection that no
48:18 you would have had peace flowing like a gentle **r**
66:12 and prosperity will overflow Jerusalem like a **r**,"
Jer 13:4 belt you are wearing, and go to the Euphrates **R**.
22:20 Search for them in the regions east of the **r**. See,
46:2 and his army were defeated beside the Euphrates **R**
46:6 By the Euphrates **R** to the north they stumble
46:7 "Who is this, rising like the Nile **R** at floodtime,
46:10 today in the north country beside the Euphrates **R**.
48:20 and wail! Tell it by the banks of the Arnon **R**:
51:36 avenge you. I will dry up her **r**, her water supply,
51:63 tie it to a stone, and throw it into the Euphrates **R**.
La 2:18 O walls of Jerusalem! Let your tears flow like a **r**.
Eze 1:1 the Judean exiles beside the Kebar **R** in Babylon,
1:3 there beside the Kebar **R** in the land of the
3:15 of Judean exiles in Tel-abib, beside the Kebar **R**.
3:23 as I had seen it in my first vision by the Kebar **R**.
10:15 same living beings I had seen beside the Kebar **R**.
10:20 the God of Israel when I was by the Kebar **R**.
17:5 of its seedlings in fertile ground beside a broad **r**,
29:3 For you have said, 'The Nile **R** is mine; I made it
29:9 "Because you said, 'The Nile **R** is mine; I made
29:10 I am now the enemy of both you and your **r**.
30:12 I will dry up the Nile **R** and hand the land over to
43:3 first by the Kebar **R** and then when he came to
47:5 and the **r** was too deep to cross without swimming.
47:7 trees were now growing on both sides of the **r**!
47:8 "This **r** flows east through the desert into the
47:9 Everything that touches the water of this **r** will
47:12 of fruit trees will grow along both sides of the **r**.
47:12 For they are watered by the **r** flowing from the
47:18 and runs southward along the Jordan **R** between
Da 7:10 and a **r** of fire flowed from his presence.
8:2 the province of Elam, standing beside the Ulai **R**.
8:3 a ram with two long horns standing beside the **r**.
8:6 ram that I had seen standing beside the **r**.
8:16 I heard a human voice calling out from the Ulai **R**,
10:4 as I was standing beside the great Tigris **R**,
12:5 two others standing on opposite banks of the **r**.
12:6 in linen, who was now standing above the **r**,
12:7 dressed in linen, who was standing above the **r**,
Am 5:24 a **r** of righteous living that will never run dry.
8:8 The land will rise up like the Nile **R** at floodtime,
9:5 The ground rises like the Nile **R** at floodtime,
Mic 7:12 and from Egypt all the way to the Euphrates **R**,
Na 2:6 But too late! The **r** gates are open! The enemy has
Zec 9:10 and from the Euphrates **R** to the ends of the earth.
Mt 3:6 their sins, he baptized them in the Jordan **R**.
3:13 Then Jesus went from Galilee to the Jordan **R** to be
4:15 Naphtali, / beside the sea, beyond the Jordan **R**—
4:25 from all over Judea, and from east of the Jordan **R**.
19:1 of Judea and into the area east of the Jordan **R**.
Mk 1:5 their sins, he baptized them in the Jordan **R**.
1:9 and he was baptized by John in the Jordan **R**.
3:8 Jerusalem, Idumea, from east of the Jordan **R**,
10:1 of Judea and into the area east of the Jordan **R**.
Lk 3:3 from place to place on both sides of the Jordan **R**,
4:1 full of the Holy Spirit, left the Jordan **R**.
Jn 1:28 a village east of the Jordan **R**, where John was
3:26 the man you met on the other side of the Jordan **R**,
10:40 He went beyond the Jordan **R** to stay near the
Rev 9:14 angels who are bound at the great Euphrates **R**."
12:16 and swallowing the **r** that gushed out from the
16:12 poured out his bowl on the great Euphrates **R**,
22:1 And the angel showed me a pure **r** with the water
22:2 On each side of the **r** grew a tree of life,

RIVER'S (1) [RIVER]

Jos 3:15 carrying the Ark touched the water at the **r** edge,

RIVERBANK (9) [RIVER]

Ex 2:5 the river, and her servant girls walked along the **r**.
7:15 to the river. Stand on the **r** and meet him there.
7:24 Then the Egyptians dug wells along the **r** to get
Ps 1:3 They are like trees planted along the **r**,
Isa 19:7 All the greenery along the **r** will wither and blow
44:4 will thrive like watered grass, like willows on a **r**.
Jer 17:8 They are like trees planted along a **r**, with roots
Eze 47:6 what I had seen, then he led me back along the **r**.
Ac 16:13 Sabbath we went a little way outside the city to a **r**,

RIVERBED (6) [RIVER]

Jos 3:16 flowed on to the Dead Sea until the **r** was dry.
3:17 the middle of the **r** as the people passed by them.
4:10 Meanwhile, the people hurried across the **r**.
4:16 the Ark of the Covenant to come up out of the **r**."
4:18 of the LORD's covenant came up out of the **r**,
Isa 19:5 and flood the fields. The **r** will be parched and dry.

RIVERS (42) [RIVER]

Ex 7:19 of Egypt—all its **r**, canals, marshes, and reservoirs.
8:5 Aaron to point his shepherd's staff toward all the **r**,
2Ki 5:12 better than all the **r** of Israel put together?
19:24 I even stopped up the **r** of Egypt / so that my
Job 20:17 streams of olive oil or **r** of milk and honey.
40:23 It is not disturbed by raging **r**, not even when the
Ps 36:8 letting them drink from your **r** of delight.
65:9 and fertile. / The **r** of God will not run dry;
74:15 gush forth, / and you dried up **r** that never run dry.
78:44 For he turned their **r** into blood, / so no one could
89:25 the west / to the Tigris and Euphrates **r** in the east.
98:8 Let the **r** clap their hands in glee! / Let the hills
107:33 He changes **r** into deserts, / and springs of water
119:136 **R** of tears gush from my eyes / because people
137:1 Beside the **r** of Babylon, we sat and wept / as we
Ecc 1:7 The **r** run into the sea, but the sea is never full.
1:7 Then the water returns again to the **r** and flows
SS 8:7 waters cannot quench love; neither can **r** drown it.
Isa 18:2 Take a message to your land divided by **r**, to your
18:7 will receive gifts from this land divided by **r**,
37:25 I even stopped up the **r** of Egypt / so that my
41:18 I will open up **r** for them on high plateaus. I will
41:18 **R** fed by springs will flow across the dry,
42:15 I will turn the **r** into dry land / and will dry up all
43:2 When you go through **r** of difficulty, you will not
43:19 come home. I will create **r** for them in the desert!
44:27 When I speak to the **r** and say, 'Be dry!' they will
49:26 They will be drunk with **r** of their own blood.
50:2 I can turn **r** into deserts covered with dying fish.
Eze 32:2 heaving around in your own **r**, stirring up mud
34:13 and by the **r** in all the places where people live.
Mic 6:7 of rams and tens of thousands of **r** of olive oil?
Na 1:4 At his command the oceans and **r** dry up, the lush
3:8 surrounded by **r**, protected by water on all sides?
Hab 3:8 LORD, that you struck the **r** and parted the sea?
3:9 of power! You split open the earth with flowing **r**!
Zep 3:10 My scattered people who live beyond the **r** of
Jn 7:38 For the Scriptures declare that **r** of living water
2Co 11:26 I have faced danger from flooded **r** and from
Rev 8:10 It fell upon one-third of the **r** and on the springs of
11:6 And they have the power to turn the **r** and oceans
16:4 Then the third angel poured out his bowl on the **r**

RIVERSIDE (1) [RIVER]

Nu 24:6 groves of palms, / like fruitful gardens by the **r**.

RIZIA (1)

1Ch 7:39 The sons of Ulla were Arah, Hanniel, and **R**.

RIZPAH (4)

2Sa 3:7 one of his father's concubines, a woman named **R**.
21:8 whose mother was **R** daughter of Aiah.
21:10 Then **R**, the mother of two of the men,
21:11 When David learned what **R**, Saul's concubine,

ROAD (130) [CROSSROADS, ROADS, ROADWAY]

Ge 16:7 Hagar beside a desert spring along the **r** to Shur.
38:14 Then she sat beside the **r** at the entrance to the
38:21 sitting beside the **r** at the entrance to the village?"
48:7 So with great sorrow I buried her there beside the **r**
49:17 He will be a snake beside the **r**, / a poisonous viper
Ex 13:17 God did not lead them on the **r** that runs through
Nu 20:17 We will stay on the king's **r** and never leave it
20:19 Israelites answered, "We will stay on the main **r**.
21:1 heard that the Israelites were approaching on the **r**
21:4 taking the **r** to the Red Sea to go around the land of
21:22 We will stay on the king's **r** until we have crossed
22:22 so he sent the angel of the LORD to stand in the **r**
22:23 standing in the **r** with a drawn sword in his hand.
22:23 The donkey bolted off the **r** into a field,
22:23 but Balaam beat it and turned it back onto the **r**.
22:24 where the **r** narrowed between two vineyard walls.
22:26 the angel of the LORD moved farther down the **r**
22:34 I did not realize you were standing in the **r** to block
Dt 2:8 and avoided the **r** through the Arabah Valley that
2:27 We will stay on the main **r** and won't turn off into
22:4 see your neighbor's ox or donkey lying on the **r**,
27:18 anyone who leads a blind person astray on the **r**.'
Jos 2:7 **r** leading to the shallow crossing places of the
2:22 chasing them had searched everywhere along the **r**,
10:10 Then the Israelites chased the enemy along the **r** to
10:11 As the Amorites retreated down the **r** from
Jdg 5:10 And you who must walk along the **r**, listen!
9:37 And another group is coming down the **r** past the
20:45 but Israel killed five thousand of them along the **r**.
21:19 along the east side of the **r** that goes from Bethel to
Ru 1:7 and they took the **r** that would lead them back to
1Sa 4:13 Eli was waiting beside the **r** to hear the news of the
6:12 the cows went straight along the **r** toward
9:12 "Yes," they replied. "Stay right on this **r**. He is at
17:52 were strewn all along the **r** from Shaaraim,
24:3 At the place where the **r** passes some sheepfolds,
26:3 Saul camped along the **r** beside the hill of Hakilah,
27:8 along the **r** to Egypt, since ancient times.
2Sa 2:24 near Giah, along the **r** to the wilderness of Gibeon.
13:34 from the Horonaim **r** along the side of the hill."
15:24 the Covenant of God and set it down beside the **r**.
15:30 David walked up the **r** that led to the Mount of
20:12 But Amasa lay in his blood in the middle of the **r**,
20:12 So he pulled him off the **r** into a field and threw a
1Ki 11:29 the prophet Ahijah from Shiloh met him on the **r**,
13:12 So they told their father which **r** the man of God
13:24 His body lay there on the **r**, with the donkey
13:25 People came by and saw the body lying in the **r**
13:28 and he went out and found the body lying in the **r**.
20:38 The prophet waited for the king beside the **r**,
2Ki 2:23 As he was walking along the **r**, a group of boys
9:27 was happening, he fled along the **r** to Beth-haggan.
12:20 and assassinated him at Beth-millo on the **r** to
18:17 near the **r** leading to the field where cloth is
19:28 make you return / by the **r** on which you came.' "
19:33 The king will return to his own country by the **r** on
Job 16:22 For soon I must go down that **r** from which I will
22:28 and light will shine on the **r** ahead of you.
30:13 They block my **r** and do everything they can to
Ps 25:4 O LORD; / point out the right **r** for me to follow.
77:19 Your **r** led through the sea, / your pathway through
77:20 You led your people along that **r** like a flock of
Pr 2:18 Entering her house leads to death; it is the **r** to hell.
7:27 Her house is the **r** to the grave. Her bedroom is the
13:15 is respected; a treacherous person walks a rocky **r**.
20:24 How can we understand the **r** we travel? It is the
21:8 a crooked path; the innocent travel a straight **r**.
22:5 The deceitful walk a thorny, treacherous **r**;
26:13 go outside because there might be a lion on the **r**!
Isa 7:3 near the **r** leading to the field where cloth is
9:1 which lies along the **r** that runs between the Jordan
15:5 Weeping, they climb the **r** to Luhith.
15:5 Their crying can be heard all along the **r** to
26:7 and you smooth out the **r** ahead of them.
35:8 And a main **r** will go through that once deserted
36:2 near the **r** leading to the field where cloth is
37:29 make you return / by the **r** on which you came.' "
37:34 The king will return to his own country by the **r** on
40:3 a straight, smooth **r** through the desert for our God.
42:16 and smooth out the **r** ahead of them. / Yes, I will
57:14 I will say, 'Rebuild the **r**! Clear away the rocks
62:10 Smooth out the **r**; pull out the boulders; raise a flag
Jer 3:2 You sit like a prostitute beside the **r** waiting for a
6:16 But you reply, 'No, that's not the **r** we want!'
8:4 When they start down the wrong **r** and discover
25:5 'Turn from the evil **r** you are traveling and from
31:21 "Set up **r** signs; put up guideposts. Mark well the
48:19 The people of Aroer stand anxiously beside the **r**
La 3:9 He has twisted the **r** before me with many detours.
Eze 21:19 Put a signpost on the **r** that comes out of Babylon
where the **r** forks into two—
21:20 one **r** going to Ammon and its capital, Rabbah,
48:1 Its boundary line follows the Hethlon **r** to
Hos 2:6 I will block the **r** to make her lose her way.
6:9 Gangs of priests murder travelers along the **r** to
13:7 like a lion, or like a leopard that lurks along the **r**.
Mt 3:3 Lord's coming! / Make a straight **r** for him!' "
7:14 and the **r** is narrow, and only a few ever find it.
9:9 As Jesus was going down the **r**, he saw Matthew
15:32 them away hungry, or they will faint along the **r**."
20:30 Two blind men were sitting beside the **r**.
20:32 Jesus stopped in the **r** and called, "What do you
21:8 Most of the crowd spread their coats on the **r**
21:8 branches from the trees and spread them on the **r**.
21:19 and he noticed a fig tree beside the **r**. He went over
Mk 1:3 Lord's coming! / Make a straight **r** for him!' "
8:3 without feeding them, they will faint along the **r**.
9:33 "What were you discussing out on the **r**?"
10:46 was sitting beside the **r** as Jesus was going by.
10:52 could see! Then he followed Jesus down the **r**.
11:8 Many in the crowd spread their coats on the **r**
Lk 3:4 for the Lord's coming! / Make a straight **r** for him!
10:4 And don't stop to greet anyone on the **r**.
10:30 beat him up, and left him half dead beside the **r**.
10:31 he crossed to the other side of the **r** and passed him
18:35 a blind beggar was sitting beside the **r**.
19:4 and climbed a sycamore tree beside the **r**,
19:36 Then the crowds spread out their coats on the **r**
19:37 As they reached the place where the **r** started down
19:40 the stones along the **r** would burst into cheers!"
24:32 feel strangely warm as he talked with us on the **r**
24:35 appeared to them as they were walking along the **r**
Jn 11:18 Bethany was only a few miles down the **r** from
12:13 palm branches and went down the **r** to meet him.
Ac 8:26 "Go south down the desert **r** that runs from
9:17 who appeared to you on the **r**, has sent me so that
22:6 "As I was on the **r**, nearing Damascus, about noon
1Co 1:18 sounds to those who are on the **r** to destruction.
Jas 2:25 and sent them safely away by a different **r**.
2Pe 2:15 They have wandered off the right **r** and followed

ROADS (9) [ROAD]

Lev 26:22 numbers will dwindle and your **r** will be deserted.
Dt 19:3 Keep the **r** to these cities in good repair so that
Jdg 5:6 in the days of Jael, / people avoided the main **r**,
20:31 and along the **r** leading to Bethel and Gibeah.
20:32 the men of Benjamin would chase them along the **r**
Job 19:12 His troops advance. They build up **r** to attack me.
Isa 33:8 Your **r** are deserted; no one travels them anymore.
Jer 6:25 Don't go out to the fields! Don't travel the **r**!
La 1:4 The **r** to Jerusalem are in mourning, no longer

ROADWAY (1) [ROAD, WAY]

Nu 22:31 standing in the **r** with a drawn sword in his hand.

ROAM (2) [ROAMING]

Jdg 11:37 But first let me go up and **r** in the hills and weep
SS 3: 2 I said to myself, 'I will get up now and **r** the city,

ROAMING (1) [ROAM]

1Sa 23:13 left Keilah and began **r** the countryside.

ROAR (28) [ROARED, ROARING, ROARS]

Ps 46: 3 Let the oceans **r** and foam. / Let the mountains
93: 3 O LORD. / The mighty oceans **r** like thunder;
93: 3 the mighty oceans **r** as they pound the shore.
104:21 Then the young lions **r** for their food, / but they are
Pr 19:12 The king's anger is like a lion's **r**, but his favor is
20: 2 The king's fury is like a lion's **r**; to rouse his anger
Isa 17:13 But though they **r** like breakers on a beach,
25: 5 the desert. But you silence the **r** of foreign nations.
51:15 who stirs up the sea, causing its waves to **r**.
66:15 and his swift chariots of destruction **r** like a
Jer 4:19 of enemy trumpets and the **r** of their battle cries.
5:22 The waves may toss and **r**, but they can never pass
10:22 Hear the terrifying **r** of great armies as they roll
25:30 'The LORD will **r** loudly against his own land
48: 3 then the **r** of battle will surge against Horonaim,
51:38 drunken feasts, the people of Babylon **r** like lions.
Eze 19: 7 the land trembled in fear / when they heard him **r**.
24:10 on the wood! Let the fire **r** to make the pot boil.
43: 2 The sound of his coming was like the **r** of rushing
Hos 11:10 I will **r** like a lion, and my people will return
Joel 2: 5 like the **r** of a fire sweeping across a field,
3:16 The LORD's voice will **r** from Zion and thunder
Am 3: 4 Does a lion ever **r** in a thicket without first finding
5: 6 If you don't, he will **r** through Israel like a fire,
Ob 1:18 The fire will **r** across the field,
Lk 23:18 Then a mighty **r** rose from the crowd, and with one
Rev 10: 3 And he gave a great shout, like the **r** of a lion.
19: 6 or the **r** of mighty ocean waves, or the crash of

ROARED (14) [ROAR]

Ex 14:27 The water **r** back into its usual place,
1Sa 17:43 "Am I a dog," he **r** at David, "that you come at
Est 7: 8 in the palace, before my very eyes?" the king **r**.
Ps 77:18 Your thunder **r** from the whirlwind; / the lightning
93: 3 The mighty oceans have **r**, O LORD.
Jer 2:15 Lions have **r** against her. The land has been
12: 8 My chosen people have **r** at me like a lion of the
Eze 1:24 As they flew their wings **r** like waves crashing
Am 3: 8 The lion has **r**—tremble in fear! The Sovereign
Mt 27:23 But the crowd only **r** the louder, "Crucify him!"
Mk 15:14 But the crowd only **r** the louder, "Crucify him!"
Lk 19:22 the king **r**. 'Hard, am I? If you knew so much
Rev 9: 9 and their wings **r** like an army of chariots rushing
11:19 Lightning flashed, thunder crashed and **r**;

ROARING (20) [ROAR]

Job 37: 4 Then comes the **r** of the thunder—the tremendous
Ps 22:13 Like **r** lions attacking their prey, / they come at me
118:12 like bees; / they blazed against me like a **r** flame.
Isa 5:29 **R** like lions, they will pounce on their prey.
5:30 will growl over their victims like the **r** of the sea.
21: 1 Disaster is **r** down on you from the desert, like a
Jer 4:12 It is a **r** blast sent by me! Now I will pronounce
6:23 ride forward, the noise of their army is like a **r** sea.
17: 4 For you have kindled my anger into a **r** fire that
17:27 and no one will be able to put out the **r** flames.' "
31:35 the night. It is he who stirs the sea into **r** waves.
50:42 ride forward, the noise of their army is like a **r** sea.
Da 3:23 securely tied, fell down into the **r** flames.
10: 6 and his voice was like the **r** of a vast multitude of
Zep 3: 3 Its leaders are like **r** lions hunting for their
Zec 11: 3 Hear the young lions **r**, for their thickets in the
Lk 21:25 perplexed by the **r** seas and strange tides.
Ac 2: 2 there was a sound from heaven like the **r** of a
1Pe 5: 8 He prowls around like a **r** lion, looking for some
Rev 14: 2 And I heard a sound from heaven like the **r** of a

ROARS (2) [ROAR]

Ps 83:14 As a fire **r** through a forest / and as a flame sets
Am 1: 2 "The LORD's voice **r** from his Temple on

ROAST (6) [ROASTED, ROASTING]

Ex 12: 8 That evening everyone must eat **r** lamb with bitter
12: 9 **r** it all, including the head, legs, and internal
Dt 16: 7 **R** the lamb and eat it in the place the LORD your
1Ki 19:21 wood from the plow to build a fire to **r** their flesh.
Isa 44:16 He burns part of the tree to **r** his meat and to keep
44:19 and used it to bake my bread and **r** my meat.

ROASTED (9) [ROAST]

Ge 18: 8 took some cheese curds and milk and the **r** meat,
Lev 2:14 bring kernels of new grain that have been **r** on a
2:16 The priests will take a token portion of the **r** grain
23:14 Do not eat any bread or **r** grain or fresh kernels on
Jos 5:11 and **r** grain harvested from the land.
1Sa 17:17 "Take this half-bushel of **r** grain and these ten
25:18 five dressed sheep, nearly a bushel of **r** grain,
2Sa 17:28 wheat and barley flour, **r** grain, beans, lentils,
2Ch 35:13 Then they **r** the Passover lambs as prescribed;

ROASTING (1) [ROAST]

1Sa 2:15 it had been boiled so that it could be used for **r**.

ROB (15) [ROBBED, ROBBER, ROBBERS, ROBBERY, ROBBING]

Lev 19:13 "Do not cheat or **r** anyone. "Always pay your
1Ki 21:19 Must you **r** him, too? Because you have done this,
Ps 35:10 and needy from those who want to **r** them?"
Pr 22:22 Do not **r** the poor because they are poor or exploit
Isa 10: 2 Yes, they **r** widows and fatherless children!
Eze 18: 7 and does not **r** the poor but instead gives food to
18:16 but instead is fair to debtors and does not **r** them.
22:29 **r** the needy, and deprive foreigners of justice.
23:29 deal with you in hatred and **r** you of all you own,
38:13 'Who are you to **r** them of silver and gold?
45: 8 princes will no longer oppress and **r** my people;
Am 8: 4 to this, you who **r** the poor and trample the needy!
Mt 12:29 man's house and **r** him without first tying him up.
Mk 3:27 man's house and **r** him without first tying him up.
Jn 16:22 you will rejoice, and no one can **r** you of that joy.

ROBBED (22) [ROB]

Ge 31: 1 "Jacob has **r** our father!" they said. "All his
Dt 28:29 You will be oppressed and **r** continually, and no
Jdg 9:25 the hilltops and **r** everyone who passed that way.
2Sa 17: 8 as a mother bear who has been **r** of her cubs.
Ezr 9: 7 captured, **r**, and disgraced, just as we are today.
Ps 89:41 Everyone who comes along has **r** him / while his
Pr 17:12 It is safer to meet a bear **r** of her cubs than to
Isa 10:14 By my greatness I have **r** their nests of riches
38:10 of the dead? / Am I to be **r** of my normal years?"
42:22 for they have been **r**, enslaved, imprisoned,
42:24 Who allowed Israel to be **r** and hurt? Was it not the
Jer 5:25 Your sin has **r** you of all these good things.
21:12 Help those who have been **r**; rescue them from
22: 3 Help those who have been **r**; rescue them from
Eze 23: 8 their lusts with her and **r** her of her virginity.
Da 11:33 die by fire and sword, or they will be jailed and **r**.
Hos 4:11 and prostitution have **r** my people of their brains.
Ob 1: 5 "If thieves came at night and **r** you, they would
Mt 12:29 first tying him up. Only then can his house be **r**!
Mk 3:27 first tying him up. Only then can his house be **r**!
Ac 19:27 all around the world—will be **r** of her prestige!"
2Co 11: 8 I "**r**" other churches by accepting their

ROBBER (5) [ROB]

Pr 6:11 a bandit; scarcity will attack you like an armed **r**.
23:28 She hides and waits like a **r**, looking for another
24:34 a bandit; scarcity will attack you like an armed **r**.
Eze 18:10 suppose that man has a son who grows up to be a **r**
Jn 10: 1 through the gate, must surely be a thief and a **r**!

ROBBERS (5) [ROB]

Job 12: 6 But even **r** are left in peace, and those who
Eze 7:22 I will hide my eyes as these **r** invade my treasured
Hos 6: 9 Its citizens are bands of **r**, lying in ambush for their
Jn 10: 8 others who came before me were thieves and **r**.
2Co 11:26 have faced danger from flooded rivers and from **r**.

ROBBERY (3) [ROB]

Ps 55:11 Murder and **r** are everywhere there; / threats
62:10 Don't try to get rich / by extortion or **r**. / And if
Isa 61: 8 the LORD, love justice. I hate **r** and wrongdoing.

ROBBING (6) [ROB]

1Sa 12: 5 "that you can never accuse me of **r** you."
Pr 1:19 who are greedy for gain. It ends up **r** them of life.
28:24 **R** your parents and then saying, "What's wrong
Eze 5:17 animals will attack you, **r** you of your children.
18:18 for being cruel and **r** close relatives, doing what
45: 9 Quit **r** and cheating my people out of their land!

ROBE (73) [ROBED, ROBES, WHITE-ROBED]

Ge 9:23 Shem and Japheth took a **r**, held it over their
37: 3 day he gave Joseph a special gift—a beautiful **r**.
37:23 Joseph arrived, they pulled off his beautiful **r**
37:31 brothers killed a goat and dipped the **r** in its blood.
37:32 They took the beautiful **r** to their father and asked
37:32 they told him. "It's Joseph's **r**, isn't it?"
37:33 "Yes," he said, "it is my son's **r**. A wild animal
Ex 4: 6 said to Moses, "Put your hand inside your **r**."
4: 7 "Now put your hand back into your **r** again,"
28: 4 an ephod, a **r**, an embroidered tunic, a turban,
28:31 "Make the **r** of the ephod entirely of blue cloth,
28:33 scarlet yarn, and attach them to the hem of the **r**,
28:35 Aaron will wear this **r** whenever he enters the Holy
29: 5 along with the embroidered **r** of the ephod,
39:22 The **r** of the ephod was woven entirely of blue
39:24 were attached to the bottom edge of the **r**.
39:25 between the pomegranates along the hem of the **r**,
39:26 This **r** was to be worn when Aaron ministered to
Lev 8: 7 He dressed him in the **r** of the ephod, along with
Jos 7:21 For I saw a beautiful **r** imported from Babylon,
7:24 the silver, the **r**, the bar of gold, his sons,
1Sa 15:27 at him to try to hold him back and tore his **r**.
18: 4 and he sealed the pact by giving him his **r**, tunic,
24: 4 David crept forward and cut off a piece of Saul's **r**.
24: 5 began bothering him because he had cut Saul's **r**.
24:11 It is a piece of your **r**! I cut it off, but I didn't kill
28:14 "He is an old man wrapped in a **r**," she replied.
2Sa 13:18 She was wearing a long, beautiful **r**, as was the
13:19 But now Tamar tore her **r** and put ashes on her
13:31 The king jumped up, tore his **r**, and fell prostrate
2Ki 2:12 disappeared from sight, Elisha tore his **r** in two.
1Ch 15:27 David was dressed in a **r** of fine linen, as were the
Ne 5:13 I shook out the fold of my **r** and said, "If you fail
Est 6: 9 most noble princes to dress the man in the king's **r**
6:10 "Hurry and get the **r** and my horse, and do just as
6:11 So Haman took the **r** and put it on Mordecai,
8:15 Then Mordecai put on the royal **r** of blue
Job 1:20 Job stood up and tore his **r** in grief. Then he
12:18 He removes the royal **r** of kings. With ropes
29:14 Righteousness covered me like a **r**, and I wore
Ps 104: 2 you are dressed in a **r** of light. / You stretch out the
133: 2 ran down his beard / and onto the border of his **r**.
SS 5: 3 "But I said, 'I have taken off my **r**. Should I get
Isa 6: 1 and the train of his **r** filled the Temple.
47: 2 the corn. Remove your veil and strip off your **r**.
51: 9 Wake up, LORD! **R** yourself with strength!
61:10 of salvation and draped me in a **r** of righteousness.
Eze 5: 3 Keep just a bit of the hair and tie it up in your **r**.
Zec 8:23 the world will clutch at the hem of one Jew's **r**.
Mt 9:20 up behind him. She touched the fringe of his **r**,
9:21 for she thought, "If I can just touch his **r**, I will be
14:36 him to let them touch even the fringe of his **r**,
27:28 They stripped him and put a scarlet **r** on him.
27:31 they took off the **r** and put his own clothes on him
Mk 5:27 through the crowd and touched the fringe of his **r**.
6:56 him to let them at least touch the fringe of his **r**,
15:17 They dressed him in a purple **r** and made a crown
15:20 they took off the purple **r** and put his own clothes
16: 5 on the right sat a young man clothed in a white **r**.
Lk 8:44 up behind Jesus and touched the fringe of his **r**.
15:22 Bring the finest **r** in the house and put it on him.
23:11 Then they put a royal **r** on him and sent him back
Jn 13: 4 So he got up from the table, took off his **r**,
13:12 he put on his **r** again and sat down and asked,
19: 2 on his head, and they put a royal purple **r** on him.
19: 5 out wearing the crown of thorns and the purple **r**.
19:23 They also took his **r**, but it was seamless, woven in
19:24 among themselves and threw dice for my **r**."
Ac 18: 6 Paul shook the dust from his **r** and said,
Rev 1:13 He was wearing a long **r** with a gold sash across
6:11 Then a white **r** was given to each of them.
19:13 He was clothed with a **r** dipped in blood, and his
19:16 On his **r** and thigh was written this title: King of

ROBED (4) [ROBE]

Job 38:14 as the light approaches, and the dawn is **r** in red.
Ps 93: 1 He is **r** in majesty. / Indeed, the LORD is **r** in majesty and armed with
104: 1 you are! / You are **r** with honor and with majesty;

ROBES (50) [ROBE]

Jdg 5:30 There are gorgeous **r** for Sisera, / and colorful, beautifully embroidered **r** for me.'
14:12 I will give you thirty plain linen **r** and thirty fancy **r**.
14:13 then you must give me thirty linen **r** and thirty fancy **r**."
1Sa 28: 8 by wearing ordinary clothing instead of his royal **r**.
2Sa 10: 4 cut off their **r** at the buttocks, and sent them back
1Ki 10: 5 their splendid clothing, the cup-bearers and their **r**,
22:10 Jehoshaphat of Judah, dressed in their royal **r**,
22:30 one will recognize me, but you wear your royal **r**."
22:32 charioteers saw Jehoshaphat in his royal **r**,
2Ki 10:22 every worshiper of Baal wears one of these **r**." So **r** were given to them.
1Ch 19: 4 shaved their beards, cut off their **r** at the buttocks,
2Ch 5:12 were dressed in fine linen **r** and stood at the east
9: 4 their splendid clothing, the cup-bearers and their **r**,
18: 9 Jehoshaphat of Judah, dressed in their royal **r**,
18:29 one will recognize me, but you wear your royal **r**."
18:31 charioteers saw Jehoshaphat in his royal **r**,
35:22 He laid aside his royal **r** so the enemy would not
Ezr 2:69 6,250 pounds of silver, and 100 **r** for the priests.
3:10 the priests put on their **r** and took their places to
Ne 7:70 50 gold basins, and 530 **r** for the priests.
7:72 2,500 pounds of silver, and 67 **r** for the priests.
Est 5: 1 Esther put on her royal **r** and entered the inner
6: 8 he should bring out one of the king's own royal **r**,
Job 2:12 they tore their **r** and threw dust into the air over
40:10 put on your **r** of state, your majesty and splendor.
Ps 45: 8 Your **r** are perfumed with myrrh, aloes, and cassia.
45:14 In her beautiful **r**, she is led to the king,
Isa 3:24 They will wear rough sackcloth instead of rich **r**.
22:21 He will have your royal **r**, your title, and your
59:17 He clothed himself with the **r** of vengeance
63: 1 Who is this in royal **r**, marching in the greatness of
Jer 10: 9 Then they dress these gods in royal purple **r** made
Eze 26:16 and take off their royal **r** and beautiful clothing.
Da 5: 7 it means will be dressed in purple **r** of royal honor
5:16 you will be clothed in purple **r** of royal honor,
5:29 Daniel was dressed in purple **r**,
Jnh 3: 6 down from his throne and took off his royal **r**.
Hag 2:12 If one of you is carrying a holy sacrifice in his **r**
Mt 23: 5 and they wear extra long tassels on their **r**.
Mk 12:38 For they love to parade in flowing **r** and to have
Lk 20:46 For they love to parade in flowing **r** and to have
24: 4 two men appeared to them, clothed in dazzling **r**.
Ac 12:21 Herod put on his royal **r**, sat on his throne,
Rev 7:14 They washed their **r** in the blood of the Lamb
16:15 who keep their **r** ready so they will not need to
22:14 Blessed are those who wash their **r** so they can

ROBOAM [KJV] See REHOBOAM

ROCK (117) [ROCKED, ROCKS, ROCKY]

Ge 49:24 One of Jacob, / the Shepherd, the **R** of Israel.
Ex 17: 6 I will meet you by the **r** at Mount Sinai.
17: 6 Strike the **r**, and water will come pouring out.

33:21 "Stand here on this **r** beside me.
33:22 I will put you in the cleft of the **r** and cover you
Lev 11: 5 The same is true of the **r** badger
Nu 20: 8 command the **r** over there to pour out its water.
20: 8 You will get enough water from the **r** to satisfy all
20:10 summoned the people to come and gather at the **r**.
20:10 "Must we bring you water from this **r**?"
20:11 his hand and struck the **r** twice with the staff,
Dt 8:15 so hot and dry. He gave you water from the **r**!
14: 7 may not eat the camel, the hare, or the **r** badger.
32: 4 He is the **R**; his work is perfect. / Everything he
32:13 from the cliffs, / with olive oil from the hard **r**.
32:15 they made light of the **R** of their salvation.
32:18 You neglected the **R** who had fathered you;
32:30 thousand to flight, / unless their **R** had sold them,
32:31 But the **r** of our enemies is not like our **R**,
Jdg 6:20 the meat and the unleavened bread on this **r**,
6:21 and fire flamed up from the **r** and consumed all he
7:25 Midianite generals, killing Oreb at the **r** of Oreb,
13:19 and offered it on a **r** as a sacrifice to the LORD.
15: 8 Then he went to live in a cave in the **r** of Etam.
15:11 down to get Samson at the cave in the **r** of Etam.
15:13 with two new ropes and led him away from the **r**.
20:16 each of whom could sling a **r** and hit a target
20:45 The survivors fled into the wilderness toward the **r**
20:47 leaving only six hundred men who escaped to the **r**
21:13 of Benjamin who were living at the **r** of Rimmon.
1Sa 2: 2 is no one besides you; / there is no **R** like our God.
6:14 a man named Joshua and stopped beside a large **r**.
6:15 from the cart and placed them on the large **r**.
6:18 The large **r** at Beth-shemesh, where they set the
23:25 went even farther into the wilderness to the great **r**,
23:28 was camped has been called the **R** of Escape.
2Sa 21:10 spread sackcloth on a **r** and stayed there the entire
22: 2 "The LORD is my **r**, my fortress, and my savior;
22: 3 my God is my **r**, in whom I find protection.
22:32 the LORD? / Who but our God is a solid **r**?
22:47 Blessed be my **r**! / May God, the **r** of my
salvation, be exalted!
23: 3 God of Israel spoke. / The **R** of Israel said to me:
1Ch 11:15 Once when David was at the **r** near the cave of
Ne 9:15 and water from the **r** when they were thirsty.
Job 19:24 and filled with lead, engraved forever in the **r**.
28:18 and valuable **r** crystal are worthless in trying to get
38:30 For the water turns to ice as hard as **r**,
41:24 Its heart is as hard as **r**, as hard as a millstone.
Ps 18: 2 The LORD is my **r**, my fortress, and my savior;
18: 2 my God is my **r**, in whom I find protection.
18:31 the LORD? / Who but our God is a solid **r**?
18:46 The LORD lives! Blessed be my **r**!
19:14 to you, / O LORD, my **r** and my redeemer.
27: 5 He will place me out of reach on a high **r**.
28: 1 O LORD, you are my **r** of safety. / Please help
31: 2 rescue me quickly. / Be for me a great **r** of safety,
31: 3 You are my **r** and my fortress. / For the honor of
42: 9 "O God my **r**," I cry, / "Why have you forsaken
61: 2 Lead me to the towering **r** of safety,
62: 2 He alone is my **r** and my salvation, / my fortress
62: 6 He alone is my **r** and my salvation, / my fortress
62: 7 is my refuge, a **r** where no enemy can reach me.
71: 3 Be to me a protecting **r** of safety, / where I am
71: 3 to save me, / for you are my **r** and my fortress.
78:16 He made streams pour from the **r**,
78:20 Yes, he can strike a **r** so water gushes out, / but he
78:35 Then they remembered that God was their **r**,
81:16 I would satisfy you with wild honey from the **r**."
89:26 my Father, / my God, and the **R** of my salvation.'
92:15 He is my **r**! / There is nothing but goodness in
94:22 my God is a mighty **r** where I can hide.
95: 1 Let us give a joyous shout to the **r** of our salvation!
104:18 and the rocks form a refuge for **r** badgers.
105:41 He opened up a **r**, and water gushed out / to form a
114: 8 He turned the **r** into pools of water; / yes, springs
of water came from solid **r**.
144: 1 Bless the LORD, who is my **r**. / He gives me
Pr 30:19 through the sky, / how a snake slithers on a **r**,
30:26 **R** badgers—they aren't powerful, / but they make
Isa 8:14 people to stumble and a **r** that makes them fall.
10:26 triumphed over the Midianites at the **r** of Oreb,
17:10 God who can save you—the **R** who can hide you.
22:16 building a beautiful tomb for yourself in the **r**?
26: 4 for the LORD GOD is the eternal **R**.
30:29 the mountain of the LORD—to the **R** of Israel.
32: 2 and as the cool shadow of a large **r** in a hot
44: 8 other God? No! There is no other **R**—not one!"
48:21 He divided the **r**, and water gushed out for them to
51: 1 you were mined, the **r** from which you were cut!
Jer 23:29 "Is it not like a mighty hammer that smashes **r** to
49:16 And you are proud because you live in a **r** fortress
Eze 3: 9 I have made you as hard as **r**! So don't be afraid of
24: 8 So I will splash her blood on a **r** as an open
26: 4 I will scrape away its soil and make it a bare **r**!
26:14 I will make your island a bare **r**, a place for
Da 2:34 a **r** was cut from a mountain by supernatural
2:35 But the **r** that knocked the statue down became a
2:45 That is the meaning of the **r** cut from the mountain
Ob 1: 3 You are proud because you live in a **r** fortress
Hab 1:12 O LORD our **R**, you have decreed the rise of
Mt 7:24 like a person who builds a house on solid **r**.
7:25 it won't collapse, because it is built on **r**.
13: 5 Other seeds fell on shallow soil with underlying **r**.
16:18 are Peter, and upon this **r** I will build my church,
27:60 new tomb, which had been carved out of the **r**.
Mk 4: 5 Other seed fell on shallow soil with underlying **r**.
15:46 laid it in a tomb that had been carved out of the **r**.
Lk 6:48 on a strong foundation laid upon the underlying **r**.
8: 6 Other seed fell on shallow soil with underlying **r**.
23:53 laid it in a new tomb that had been carved out of **r**.
Ro 9:32 They stumbled over the great **r** in their path.
9:33 people to stumble, / and a **r** that makes them fall.
1Co 10: 4 For they all drank from the miraculous **r** that
traveled with them, and that **r** was Christ.
1Pe 2: 8 people stumble, / the **r** that will make them fall."

ROCKED (1) [ROCK]

Ac 21:30 The whole population of the city was **r** by these

ROCKS (39) [ROCK]

Nu 24:21 are strongly situated; / your nest is set in the **r**.
Dt 32:37 are their gods, / the **r** they fled to for refuge?
Jos 10:18 "Cover the opening of the cave with large **r**
10:22 "Remove the **r** covering the opening of the cave
1Sa 13: 6 tried to hide in caves, holes, **r**, tombs, and cisterns.
24: 2 for David and his men near the **r** of the wild goats.
1Ki 19:11 It was such a terrible blast that the **r** were torn
2Ch 25:12 them off, dashing them to pieces on the **r** below.
Job 8:17 Its roots grow down through a pile of **r** to hold it
14:18 and crumble and as **r** fall from a cliff,
18: 4 to be abandoned? Will it make **r** fall from a cliff?
24: 8 and they huddle against the **r** for want of a home.
28: 9 People know how to tear apart flinty **r**
28:10 They cut tunnels in the **r** and uncover precious
30: 6 frightening ravines and in caves and among the **r**.
37: 8 The wild animals hide in the **r** or in their dens.
Ps 78:15 He split open the **r** in the wilderness / to give them
104:18 and the **r** form a refuge for rock badgers.
137: 9 takes your babies / and smashes them against the **r**!
141: 7 as a farmer breaks up the soil and brings up **r**,
SS 2:14 "My dove is hiding behind some **r**, behind an
Isa 2:10 Crawl into caves in the **r**. Hide from the terror of
2:19 They will hide in caves in the **r** from the terror of
2:21 and hide among the jagged **r** at the tops of cliffs.
5: 2 and carved a winepress in the nearby **r**.
33:16 The **r** of the mountains will be their fortress of
57: 5 down in the valleys, under overhanging **r**.
57:14 Clear away the **r** and stones so my people can
Jer 13: 4 Euphrates River. Hide it there in a hole in the **r**."
43: 9 bury large **r** between the pavement stones at the
48:28 the caves like doves that nest in the clefts of the **r**.
Eze 24: 7 leaving blood on the **r** for all to see.
Am 6:12 Can horses gallop over **r**? Can oxen be used to
plow **r**? Stupid even to ask—
Mt 27:51 from top to bottom. The earth shook, **r** split apart,
Ac 27:29 would soon be driven against the **r** along the shore,
27:39 and wondered if they could get between the **r**
Rev 6:15 in the caves and among the **r** of the mountains.
6:16 And they cried to the mountains and the **r**,

ROCKY (7) [ROCK]

1Sa 14: 4 Jonathan had to go down between two **r** cliffs that
Job 39:28 on the cliffs, making its home on a distant, **r** crag.
Pr 13:15 is respected; a treacherous person walks a **r** road.
30:26 but they make their homes among the **r** cliffs.
Mt 13:20 The **r** soil represents those who hear the message
Mk 4:16 The **r** soil represents those who hear the message
Lk 8:13 The **r** soil represents those who hear the message

ROD (15) [RODS]

Jdg 5:14 from Zebulun came those who carry the **r** of
Ps 2: 9 You will break them with an iron **r** / and smash
23: 4 Your **r** and your staff / protect and comfort me.
89:32 then I will punish their sin with the **r**, / and their
Pr 10:13 but fools will be punished with a **r**.
14: 3 The talk of fools is a **r** for their backs,
26: 3 with a bridle, and a fool with a **r** to his back!
Isa 30:31 be shattered. He will strike them down with his **r**.
La 3: 1 that come from the **r** of the LORD's anger.
Eze 40: 3 in his hand a measuring tape and a measuring **r**.
40: 5 The man took a measuring **r** that was 10-1/2 feet
Mic 5: 1 With a **r** they will strike the leader of Israel in the
Rev 2:27 They will rule the nations with an iron **r** and smash
12: 5 to a boy who was to rule all nations with an iron **r**.
19:15 He ruled them with an iron **r**, and he trod the

RODANIM (2)

Ge 10: 4 of Javan were Elishah, Tarshish, Kittim, and **R**.
1Ch 1: 7 of Javan were Elishah, Tarshish, Kittim, and **R**.

RODE (14) [RIDE]

Jdg 10: 4 His thirty sons **r** around on thirty donkeys,
12:14 and thirty grandsons, who **r** on seventy donkeys.
2Sa 18: 9 but as he **r** beneath the thick branches of a great
1Ki 1:38 and Solomon **r** on King David's personal mule.
13:14 he **r** after the man of God and found him sitting
2Ki 9:16 into a chariot and **r** to Jezreel to find King Joram,
9:19 He **r** up to them and demanded, "The king wants
9:21 and King Ahaziah of Judah **r** out in their chariots
9:27 Jehu **r** after him, shouting, "Shoot him, too!"
10:16 to the LORD." So Jehonadab **r** along with him.
Est 8:10 who **r** horses especially bred for the king's service.
8:14 the messengers **r** out swiftly on horses bred for the
Ac 8:36 As they **r** along, they came to some water,
Rev 6: 2 He **r** out to win many battles and gain the victory.

RODS (12) [ROD]

Ex 27:10 to the silver **r** that are attached to the posts.
27:11 fitted into bronze bases, with silver hooks and **r**.
27:17 the courtyard must be connected by silver **r**,
38:10 were silver hooks and **r** to hold up the curtains.
38:11 and bases and with silver hooks and **r**.
38:12 by ten posts and bases and with silver hooks and **r**.
38:17 a bronze base, and all the hooks and **r** were silver.
38:17 and the **r** to hold up the curtains were solid silver.
38:19 and the hooks and **r** were also made of silver.
38:28 was used to make the **r** and hooks and to overlay
Ac 16:22 ordered them stripped and beaten with wooden **r**.
2Co 11:25 Three times I was beaten with **r**. Once I was

ROEBUCK (1) [ROEBUCKS]

Dt 14: 5 the deer, the gazelle, the **r**, the wild goat, the ibex,

ROEBUCKS (1) [ROEBUCK]

1Ki 4:23 hundred sheep or goats, as well as deer, gazelles, **r**,

ROES [KJV] See DEER, GAZELLE

ROGELIM (2)

2Sa 17:27 of Lo-debar, and by Barzillai the Gileadite from **R**.
19:31 Barzillai the Gileadite now arrived from **R** to

ROHGAH (1)

1Ch 7:34 sons of Shomer were Ahi, **R**, Hubbah, and Aram.

ROLE (1)

Jos 18: 7 Their **r** as priests of the LORD is their

ROLL (15) [ROLLED, ROLLED-UP, ROLLING, ROLLS]

Ge 29: 8 "We don't **r** away the stone and begin the
1Sa 14:33 Saul said. "Find a large stone and **r** it over here.
Pr 26:27 If you **r** a boulder down on others, it will **r** back
and crush you.
Jer 4:20 Waves of destruction **r** over the land, until it lies in
10:22 Hear the terrifying roar of great armies as they **r**
25:34 **R** in the dust, you leaders of the flock!
51:25 fist against you, to **r** you down from the heights.
Eze 27:30 as they throw dust on their heads and **r** in ashes.
38: 9 will **r** down on them like a storm and cover the
Mic 1: 6 I will **r** the stones of her walls down into the valley
1:10 **r** in the dust to show your anguish and despair.
Mk 16: 3 On the way they were discussing who would **r** the
Jn 11:39 "**R** the stone aside," Jesus told them. But Martha,
Heb 1:12 You will **r** them up like an old coat. / They will

ROLLED (20) [ROLL]

Ge 29: 3 the stone would be **r** back over the mouth of the
29:10 Jacob went over to the well and **r** away the stone
Jos 5: 9 "Today I have **r** away the shame of your slavery
24:26 and **r** it beneath the oak tree beside the Tabernacle
1Ki 3:19 But her baby died during the night when she **r** over
Ps 77:17 their rain; / the thunder **r** and crackled in the sky.
Isa 28:27 A threshing wheel is never **r** on cummin; instead,
La 3:16 grind my teeth on gravel. He has **r** me in the dust.
Mt 27:60 Then he **r** a great stone across the entrance as he
28: 2 from heaven and **r** aside the stone and sat on it.
Mk 15:46 the rock. Then he **r** a stone in front of the entrance.
16: 4 a very large one—had already been **r** aside.
Lk 4:20 He **r** up the scroll, handed it back to the attendant,
24: 2 the stone covering the entrance had been **r** aside.
Jn 5: 9 was healed! He **r** up the mat and began walking!
11:38 It was a cave with a stone **r** across its entrance.
11:41 So they **r** the stone aside. Then Jesus looked up to
20: 1 and found that the stone had been **r** away from the
Rev 6:14 And the sky was **r** up like a scroll and taken away.
16:18 Then the thunder crashed and **r**, and lightning

ROLLED-UP (1) [ROLL]

Isa 34: 4 above will melt away and disappear like a **r** scroll.

ROLLING (2) [ROLL]

Isa 48:18 like a gentle river and righteousness **r** like waves.
Rev 14: 2 of a great waterfall or the **r** of mighty thunder.

ROLLS (3) [ROLL]

Job 36:29 and the thunder that **r** forth from heaven?
37: 2 the thunder of God's voice as it **r** from his mouth.
37: 3 It **r** across the heavens, and his lightning flashes

ROMAMTI-EZER (2)

1Ch 25: 4 Jerimoth, Hananiah, Hanani, Eliathah, Geddalti, **R**,
25:31 The twenty-fourth lot fell to **R** and twelve of his

ROMAN (49) [ROME]

Mt 8: 5 a **R** officer came and pleaded with him,
8:13 Then Jesus said to the **R** officer, "Go on home.
22:17 Is it right to pay taxes to the **R** government
22:19 Here, show me the **R** coin used for the tax."
27: 1 the **R** government to sentence Jesus to death.
27: 2 bound him and took him to Pilate, the **R** governor.
27:11 Jesus was standing before Pilate, the **R** governor.
27:26 then turned him over to the **R** soldiers to crucify
27:54 The **R** officer and the other soldiers at the
Mk 12:14 is it right to pay taxes to the **R** government or not?
12:15 Show me a **R** coin, and I'll tell you."
15: 1 and took him to Pilate, the **R** governor.
15:15 then turned him over to the **R** soldiers to crucify
15:39 When the **R** officer who stood facing him saw how
15:44 so he called for the **R** military officer in charge
Lk 2: 1 At that time the **R** emperor, Augustus, decreed that
a census should be taken throughout the **R** Empire.
3: 1 year of the reign of Tiberius, the **R** emperor.

3:13 "Make sure you collect no more taxes than the **R**
7:2 Now the highly valued slave of a **R** officer was
19:2 He was one of the most influential Jews in the **R**
20:20 something that could be reported to the **R** governor
20:22 is it right to pay taxes to the **R** government
20:24 "Show me a **R** coin. Whose picture and title are
23:1 council took Jesus over to Pilate, the **R** governor.
23:2 them not to pay their taxes to the **R** government
23:37 When the captain of the **R** soldiers handling the
23:47 When the captain of the **R** soldiers handling the
Jn 11:48 and then the **R** army will come and destroy both
18:3 and Pharisees had given Judas a battalion of **R**
18:28 Then he was taken to the headquarters of the **R**
Ac 10:1 In Caesarea there lived a **R** army officer named
10:22 "We were sent by Cornelius, a **R** officer.
11:28 great famine was coming upon the entire **R** world.
16:12 city of the district of Macedonia and a **R** colony;
16:21 people to do things that are against **R** customs."
16:37 without trial and jailed us—and we are **R** citizens.
16:38 to learn that Paul and Silas were **R** citizens.
19:40 being charged with rioting by the **R** government,
21:31 word reached the commander of the **R** regiment
22:25 "Is it legal for you to whip a **R** citizen who hasn't
22:26 "What are you doing? This man is a **R** citizen!"
22:27 and asked Paul, "Tell me, are you a **R** citizen?"
22:29 withdrew when they heard he was a **R** citizen,
23:27 When I learned that he was a **R** citizen, I removed
24:5 to riots and rebellions against the **R** government.
25:8 Jewish laws or the Temple or the **R** government."
25:10 This is the official **R** court, so I ought to be tried
25:16 I quickly pointed out to them that **R** law does not
28:17 and handed over to the **R** government,

ROMANS (6) [ROME]

Mt 20:19 Then they will hand him over to the **R** to be
Mk 10:33 sentence him to die and hand him over to the **R**.
Lk 18:32 He will be handed over to the **R** to be mocked,
Jn 18:31 "Only the **R** are permitted to execute someone,"
Ac 21:11 leaders in Jerusalem and turned over to the **R**.'"
28:18 The **R** tried me and wanted to release me, for they

ROME (13) [ROMAN, ROMANS]

Ac 2:10 visitors from **R** (both Jews and converts to
18:2 Claudius Caesar's order to deport all Jews from **R**.
19:21 "And after that," he said, "I must go on to **R**!"
19:40 And if **R** demands an explanation, we won't know
23:11 you must preach the Good News in **R**."
28:14 stay with them seven days. And so we came to **R**.
28:15 The believers in **R** had heard we were coming,
28:16 When we arrived in **R**, Paul was permitted to have
Ro 1:7 dear friends in **R**. God loves you dearly, and he has
1:15 So I am eager to come to you in **R**, too, to preach
15:24 to go to Spain, and when I do, I will stop off in **R**.
2Ti 1:17 When he came to **R**, he searched everywhere until
1Pe 5:13 Your sister church here in **R** sends you greetings,

ROOF (33) [ROOFED, ROOFING, ROOFS, ROOFTOP, ROOFTOPS]

Ge 6:16 all the way around the boat, 18 inches below the **r**.
Ex 26:12 An extra half sheet of this **r** covering will be left to
26:14 goatskin leather. This will complete the **r** covering.
36:14 a **r** covering was made from eleven sheets of cloth
36:18 the **r** covering was joined together in one piece.
36:19 Then they made two more layers for the **r**
40:19 the Tabernacle framework and put on the **r** layers,
Dt 22:8 on your household if someone falls from the **r**.
Jos 2:6 (But she had taken them up to the **r** and hidden
2:8 Rahab went up on the **r** to talk with them.
Jdg 9:51 themselves in and climbed up to the **r** of the tower.
9:53 a woman on the **r** threw down a millstone that
16:25 between the two pillars supporting the **r**.
16:27 and there were about three thousand on the **r** who
1Sa 9:25 Samuel took Saul up to the **r** of the house
2Sa 11:2 a nap and went for a stroll on the **r** of the palace.
16:22 So they set up a tent on the palace **r** where
18:24 the watchman climbed to the **r** of the gateway by
1Ki 7:3 It had a cedar **r** supported by forty-five rafters that
2Ki 4:10 Let's make a little room for him on the **r**
23:12 on the palace **r** above the upper room of Ahaz.
2Ch 3:4 pure gold. The **r** of the foyer was thirty feet high.
Ps 22:15 My tongue sticks to the **r** of my mouth. / You have
102:7 I lie awake, / lonely as a solitary bird on the **r**.
137:6 May my tongue stick to the **r** of my mouth
Ecc 10:18 Laziness lets the **r** leak, and soon the rafters begin
Eze 3:26 And I will make your tongue stick to the **r** of your
26:8 a ramp, and raising a **r** of shields against you.
Da 4:29 he was taking a walk on the flat **r** of the royal
Am 9:1 so the **r** will crash down on the people below.
Mk 2:4 so they dug through the clay **r** above his head.
Lk 5:19 So they went up to the **r**, took off some tiles,
Ac 10:9 nearing the city, Peter went up to the flat **r** to pray.

ROOFED (1) [ROOF]

Ne 3:15 He rebuilt it, **r** it, hung its doors, and installed its

ROOFS (3) [ROOF]

Ne 8:16 and used them to build shelters on the **r** of their
La 4:4 little ones stick with thirst to the **r** of their mouths.
Zep 1:5 For they go up to their **r** and bow to the sun,

ROOFTOP (2) [ROOF]

Dt 22:8 must have a barrier around the edge of its flat **r**.
Ps 129:6 May they be as useless as grass on a **r**,

ROOFTOPS (4) [ROOF]

Isa 22:1 is happening? Why is everyone running to the **r**?
65:3 They burn incense on the **r** of their homes.
Jer 19:13 all the houses where you burned incense on the **r**
32:29 my fury to rise by offering incense to Baal on the **r**

ROOM (99) [ONE-ROOM, ROOMS, STOREROOMS]

Ge 24:23 "Would your father have any **r** to put us up for the
24:25 food for the camels, and we have a **r** for guests."
24:31 the village when we have a **r** all ready for you
26:22 So Isaac called it "**R** Enough," for he said, "At last the LORD has made **r** for us,
42:24 Now he left the **r** and found a place where he could
43:30 to cry. Going into his private **r**, he wept there.
Ex 26:35 and lampstand across the **r** from each other outside
Lev 26:10 the previous year to make **r** for each new harvest.
Jdg 3:19 servants to be silent and sent them all out of the **r**.
3:20 to Eglon as he was sitting alone in a cool upstairs **r**
3:24 and found the doors to the upstairs **r** locked.
16:12 The men were hiding in the **r** as before, and again
20:36 give those hiding in ambush more **r** to maneuver.
2Sa 13:8 she went to the **r** where he was lying down so he
18:33 He went up to his **r** over the gateway and burst into
19:5 Then Joab went to the king's **r** and said to him,
1Ki 6:17 The main **r** of the Temple, outside the Most Holy
6:27 their inner wings touched at the center of the **r**.
6:29 and the main **r** were decorated with carvings of
7:36 the panels and supports wherever there was **r**,
7:50 the Most Holy Place and the main **r** of the Temple,
8:8 from the front entrance of the Temple's main **r**—
17:19 carried him up to the upper **r**, where he lived,
17:23 Then Elijah brought him down from the upper **r**
20:30 Ben-hadad fled into the city and hid in a secret **r**.
22:25 when you find yourself hiding in some secret **r**!"
2Ki 1:2 fell through the latticework of an upper **r** at his
4:10 Let's make a little **r** for him on the roof and furnish
4:11 returned to Shunem, and he went up to his **r** to rest.
4:35 and walked back and forth in the **r** a few times.
5:27 When Gehazi left the **r**, he was leprous; his skin
9:2 Call him into a back **r** away from his friends,
23:12 built on the palace roof above the upper **r** of Ahaz.
2Ch 3:5 The main **r** of the Temple was paneled with
3:13 and faced out toward the main **r** of the Temple.
4:22 the Most Holy Place and the main **r** of the Temple,
5:9 from the front entrance of the Temple's main **r**—
18:24 when you find yourself hiding in some secret **r**!"
Ezr 10:6 and went to the **r** of Jehohanan son of Eliashib.
Ne 3:31 Then he continued as far as the upper **r** at the
13:5 had converted a large storage **r** and placed it at
13:5 The **r** had previously been used for storing the
13:7 that he had provided Tobiah with a **r** in the
13:8 and threw all of Tobiah's belongings from the **r**.
SS 2:9 looking in through the window, gazing into the **r**.
Isa 49:20 born in exile will return and say, 'We need more **r**!
Jer 7:32 so many bodies in Topheth that there won't be **r**
19:11 bury the bodies in Topheth until there is no more **r**.
35:4 and we went into the **r** assigned to the sons of
35:4 This **r** was located next to the one used by the
35:4 directly above the **r** of Maaseiah son of Shallum,
36:10 from the Temple **r** of Gemariah son of Shaphan.
36:10 This **r** was just off the upper courtyard of the
36:12 he went down to the secretary's **r** in the palace
36:20 for safekeeping in the **r** of Elishama the secretary
36:21 Jehudi brought it from Elishama's **r** and read it to
38:11 and went to a **r** in the palace beneath the treasury,
Eze 8:8 into the wall and uncovered a door to a hidden **r**.
23:42 From your **r** came the sound of many men
40:38 **r** where the meat for sacrifices was washed before
41:1 the Holy Place, the large main **r** of the Temple,
41:3 Then he went into the inner **r** at the end of the
41:3 extended 12-1/4 feet to the corners of the inner **r**.
41:4 The inner **r** was 35 feet square. "This," he told
41:5 along the outside wall; each **r** was 7 feet wide.
Da 6:10 and knelt down as usual in his upstairs **r**,
7:8 were wrenched out, roots and all, to make **r** for it.
Joel 2:16 from his quarters and the bride from her private **r**.
Zec 2:4 so full of people that it won't have **r** enough for
10:10 There won't be enough **r** for them all!
Mal 3:10 so great you won't have enough **r** to take it in!
Mk 2:2 packed with visitors that there wasn't **r** for one
5:40 and his three disciples into the **r** where the girl was
14:14 Where is the guest **r** where I can eat the Passover
14:15 He will take you upstairs to a large **r** that is already
Lk 2:7 because there was no **r** for them in the village inn.
6:38 pressed down, shaken together to make **r** for more,
11:33 on a lampstand to give light to all who enter the **r**.
12:18 Then I'll have **r** enough to store everything.
14:22 done this, he reported, 'There is still **r** for more.'
22:11 Where is the guest **r** where I can eat the Passover
22:12 He will take you upstairs to a large **r** that is already
22:39 Jesus left the upstairs **r** and went as usual to the
Jn 13:31 As soon as Judas left the **r**, Jesus said, "The time
Ac 1:13 Then they went to the upstairs **r** of the house
9:37 prepared her for burial and laid her in an upstairs **r**.
9:39 soon as he arrived, they took him to the upstairs **r**.
9:39 The **r** was filled with widows who were weeping
9:40 But Peter asked them all to leave the **r**; then he
20:8 The upstairs **r** where we met was lighted with
Ro 11:19 "those branches were broken off to make **r** for
1Co 14:9 You might as well be talking to an empty **r**.
Phm 1:22 Please keep a guest **r** ready for me. I am hoping
Heb 9:2 In the first **r** were a lampstand, a table, and loaves
9:3 and behind the curtain was the second **r** called the
9:4 In that **r** were a gold incense altar and a wooden
9:6 and out of the first **r** regularly as they performed
9:8 was not open to the people as long as the first **r**

ROOMS (52) [ROOM]

Jdg 16:9 She had hidden some men in one of the **r** of her
1Ki 6:5 A complex of **r** was built against the outer walls of
6:6 The **r** were connected to the walls of the Temple
6:10 there was a complex of **r** on three sides of the
6:30 The floor in both **r** was overlaid with gold.
1Ch 9:26 for they were responsible for the **r** and treasuries at
23:28 They also took care of the courtyards and side **r**,
28:11 the treasuries, the upstairs **r**, the inner **r**,
28:12 the outside **r**, the treasuries of God's Temple, and the **r** for the dedicated gifts.
2Ch 3:9 The walls of the upper **r** were also overlaid with
Ne 13:9 Then I demanded that the **r** be purified, and I
Est 2:14 That evening she was taken to the king's private **r**,
Ps 105:30 they were found even in the king's private **r**.
Pr 24:4 Through knowledge its **r** are filled with all sorts of
Jer 22:14 'I will build a magnificent palace with huge **r**
35:2 Take them into one of the inner **r**, and offer them
Eze 8:12 of Israel are doing with their idols in dark **r**?
40:17 and thirty **r** were built against the walls,
41:5 There was a row of **r** along the outside wall;
41:6 These **r** were built in three levels, one above the other, with thirty **r** on each level.
41:6 The supports for these **r** rested on ledges in the
41:8 which provided a foundation for the side **r**.
41:9 The outer wall of the Temple's side **r** was 8-3/4
41:9 This left an open area between these side **r**
41:10 and the row of **r** along the outer wall of the inner
41:11 Two doors opened from the side **r** into the terrace
42:1 and came to a group of **r** against the north wall of
42:3 One block of **r** overlooked the 35-foot width of the
42:3 Another block of **r** looked out onto the pavement
42:4 Between the two blocks of **r** ran a walkway 17-1/2
42:5 Each of the two upper levels of **r** was narrower
42:7 There was an outer wall that separated the **r** from
42:8 This wall added length to the outer block of **r**,
42:8 the **r** toward the Temple—extended for 175 feet.
42:9 from the outer courtyard to these **r** from the east.
42:10 **r** just south of the inner courtyard between the
42:10 These **r** were arranged just like the **r** on the
42:11 There was a walkway between the two blocks of **r**
42:11 This complex of **r** was the same length and width
42:12 in the wall facing the doors of the inner block of **r**,
42:13 "These **r** that overlook the Temple from the north
42:13 And they will use these **r** to store the grain
42:13 and guilt offerings because these **r** are holy.
44:19 They must leave them in the sacred **r** and put on
46:19 and led me to the sacred **r** assigned to the priests,
46:19 me a place at the extreme west end of these **r**.
Jn 14:2 There are many **r** in my Father's home, and I am
Heb 9:2 There were two **r** in this tent. In the first room

ROOSTED (1)

Eze 31:13 The birds **r** on its fallen trunk, and the wild

ROOSTER (13)

Pr 30:31 the strutting **r**, / the male goat, / a king as he leads
Mt 26:34 "the truth is, this very night, before the **r** crows,
26:74 know the man." And immediately the **r** crowed.
26:75 "Before the **r** crows, you will deny me three
Mk 14:30 truth is, this very night, before the **r** crows twice,
14:68 went out into the entryway. Just then, a **r** crowed.
14:72 And immediately the **r** crowed the second time.
14:72 "Before the **r** crows twice, you will deny me three
Lk 22:34 The **r** will not crow tomorrow morning until you
22:60 And as soon as he said these words, the **r** crowed.
22:61 "Before the **r** crows tomorrow morning, you will
Jn 13:38 No, before the **r** crows tomorrow morning,
18:27 Peter denied it. And immediately a **r** crowed.

ROOT (13) [ROOTED, ROOTS]

Dt 29:18 and so that no **r** among you would bear bitter
2Ki 19:30 will take **r** again in your own soil, and you will
Ps 80:9 ground for us, / and we took **r** and filled the land.
Isa 11:1 yes, a new Branch bearing fruit from the old **r**.
27:6 The time is coming when my people will take **r**.
37:31 will take **r** again in your own soil, and you will
40:24 They hardly get started, barely taking **r**, when he
53:2 sprouting from a **r** in dry and sterile ground.
Jer 12:2 planted them, and they have taken **r** and prospered.
Eze 17:6 It took **r** there and grew into a low, spreading vine.
Ro 11:18 Remember, you are just a branch, not the **r**.
1Ti 6:10 For the love of money is at the **r** of all kinds of
Heb 12:15 Watch out that no bitter **r** of unbelief rises up

ROOTED (2) [ROOT]

Zep 2:4 too, will be **r** out and left in desolation.
Mt 15:13 not planted by my heavenly Father will be **r** up,

ROOTS (40) [ROOT]

Ge 30:14 growing in a field and brought the **r** to his mother,
30:15 Now will you steal my son's mandrake **r**, too?"
30:15 with you tonight in exchange for the mandrake **r**."
30:16 "I have paid for you with some mandrake **r** my
Job 8:17 Its **r** grow down through a pile of rocks to hold it
14:8 Though its **r** have grown old in the earth and its
18:16 Their **r** will dry up, and their branches will wither.
28:9 apart flinty rocks and overturn the **r** of mountains.
29:19 For I am like a tree whose **r** reach the water,
30:4 and they burn the **r** of shrubs for heat.
Pr 12:3 never brings stability; only the godly have deep **r**.

Isa 5:24 Their **r** will rot and their flowers wither, for they
Jer 17:8 a riverbank, with **r** that reach deep into the water.
Eze 17:6 toward the eagle, and its **r** grew down beneath it.
17:7 So the vine sent its **r** and branches out toward him
17:9 and prosper? No! I will pull it out, **r** and all!
31:5 thick branches because of all the water at its **r**.
31:7 for its **r** went deep into abundant water.
31:16 the ones whose **r** went deep into the water,
Da 4:15 But leave the stump and the **r** in the ground,
4:23 But leave the stump and the **r** in the ground,
4:26 But the stump and the **r** were left in the ground.
7:8 were wrenched out, **r** and all, to make room for it.
Hos 9:16 Their **r** are dried up; they will bear no more fruit.
14:5 it will send **r** deep into the soil like the cedars in
Am 2:9 but I destroyed their fruit and dug out their **r**.
Jnh 2:6 I sank down to the very **r** of the mountains. I was
Mal 4:1 They will be consumed like a tree—**r** and all.
Mt 3:10 of God's judgment is poised, ready to sever your **r**.
13:6 because the **r** had no nourishment in the shallow
13:21 plants in such soil, their **r** don't go very deep.
Mk 4:6 because the **r** had no nourishment in the shallow
4:17 plants in such soil, their **r** don't go very deep.
11:20 the disciples noticed it was withered from the **r**.
Lk 3:9 of God's judgment is poised, ready to sever your **r**.
8:13 plants in such soil, their **r** don't go very deep.
Ro 11:16 For if the **r** of the tree are holy, the branches will
Eph 3:17 May your **r** go down deep into the soil of God's
Col 2:7 Let your **r** grow down into him and draw up
Jude 1:12 for they have been pulled out by the **r**.

ROPE (8) [ROPES]

Jos 2:15 she let them down by a **r** through the window.
2:18 only if you leave this scarlet **r** hanging from the
2:21 leaving the scarlet **r** hanging from the window.
2Sa 8:2 he measured them off in groups with a length of **r**.
Job 18:10 hidden in the ground. A **r** lies coiled on their path.
41:2 Can you tie it with a **r** through the nose or pierce
Jer 38:11 to the cistern and lowered them to Jeremiah on a **r**.
Jn 4:11 "But sir, you don't have a **r** or a bucket," she said,

ROPES (24) [ROPE]

Jdg 15:13 So they tied him up with two new **r** and led him
15:14 and he snapped the **r** on his arms as if they were
16:11 "If I am tied up with brand-new **r** that have never
16:12 So Delilah took new **r** and tied him up with them.
16:12 But Samson snapped the **r** from his arms as if they
2Sa 17:13 Then we can take **r** and drag the walls of the city
22:6 The grave wrapped its **r** around me; / death itself
1Ki 20:31 by wearing sackcloth and putting **r** on our heads.
20:32 So they put on sackcloth and **r** and went to the
Job 12:18 With **r** around their waist, they are led away.
28:4 They descend on **r**, swinging back and forth.
Ps 18:4 The **r** of death surrounded me; / the floods of
18:5 The grave wrapped its **r** around me; / death itself
Pr 5:22 by his own sins; they are **r** that catch and hold him.
Isa 3:24 They will wear **r** for sashes, and their well-set hair
Jer 38:6 and lowered him by **r** into an empty cistern in the
38:12 under your armpits to protect you from the **r**."
La 1:14 "He wove my sins into **r** to hitch me to a yoke of
Eze 3:25 There you will be bound with **r** so you cannot go
4:8 I will tie you up with **r** so you won't be able to turn
Hos 11:4 I led Israel along with my **r** of kindness and love.
Jn 2:15 Jesus made a whip from some **r** and chased them
Ac 27:17 Then we banded the ship with **r** to strengthen the
27:32 So the soldiers cut the **r** and let the boat fall off.

ROSE (37) [RISE]

Ge 7:18 As the waters **r** higher and higher above the
32:31 The sun **r** as he left Peniel, and he was limping
Ex 2:23 and their pleas for deliverance **r** up to God.
15:7 you overthrew those who **r** against you.
Nu 14:2 Their voices **r** in a great chorus of complaint
Jdg 3:20 you from God!" As King Eglon **r** from his seat,
1Ki 2:19 The king **r** from his throne to meet her, and he
2Ki 6:6 Then the ax head **r** to the surface and floated.
1Ch 21:1 Satan **r** up against Israel and caused David to take
28:2 David **r** and stood before them and addressed them
Ne 8:5 they saw him open the book, they all **r** to their feet.
Est 8:4 scepter to Esther. So she **r** and stood before him
Job 29:8 and even the aged **r** in respect at my coming.
Ps 78:21 against Jacob. / Yes, his anger **r** against Israel,
78:31 the anger of God **r** against them, / and he killed
78:65 Then the Lord **r** up as though waking from sleep,
104:8 Mountains **r** and valleys sank / to the levels you
107:25 He spoke, and the winds **r**, / stirring up the waves.
124:2 not been on our side / when people **r** up against us,
SS 2:1 "I am the **r** of Sharon, the lily of the valley."
Jer 44:3 all their wickedness, my anger **r** high against them.
Eze 1:21 the living beings flew into the air, the wheels **r** up.
9:3 Then the glory of the God of Israel **r** up from
10:4 Then the glory of the LORD **r** up from above the
10:15 Then the cherubim **r** upward. These were the same
10:16 When they **r** into the air, the wheels stayed beside
11:22 and **r** into the air with their wheels beside them,
41:7 to the narrowing of the Temple wall as it **r** higher.
Mk 16:9 It was early on Sunday morning when Jesus **r** from
Lk 23:18 Then a mighty roar **r** from the crowd, and with one
Ac 10:41 and drank with him after he **r** from the dead.
18:12 some Jews **r** in concerted action against Paul
Ro 6:9 We are sure of this because Christ **r** from the dead,
14:9 Christ died and **r** again for this very purpose,
1Co 15:12 since we preach that Christ **r** from the dead,
1Pe 1:3 because Jesus Christ **r** again from the dead.
Rev 11:12 And they **r** to heaven in a cloud as their enemies

ROSH (1)

Ge 46:21 Beker, Ashbel, Gera, Naaman, Ehi, **R**, Muppim,

ROT (12) [ROTS, ROTTEN, ROTTING]

Lev 26:39 Those still left alive will **r** away in enemy lands
Ps 16:10 or allow your godly one to **r** in the grave.
49:14 Their bodies will **r** in the grave, / far from their
Pr 28:2 When there is moral **r** within a nation,
Ecc 10:18 lets the roof leak, and soon the rafters begin to **r**.
Isa 5:24 Their roots will **r** and their flowers wither, for they
25:10 will be crushed like trampled straw and left to **r**.
Jer 13:9 This illustrates how I will **r** away the pride of
Hos 5:12 I will sap Judah's strength as dry **r** weakens wood.
Ac 2:27 or allow your Holy One to **r** in the grave.
2:31 and that his body would not **r** in the grave.
13:35 'You will not allow your Holy One to **r** in the

ROTE (1)

Isa 29:13 to nothing more than human laws learned by **r**.

ROTS (2) [ROT]

Pr 10:7 the godly, but the name of a wicked person **r** away.
14:30 relaxed attitude lengthens life; jealousy **r** it away.

ROTTEN (6) [ROT]

Job 41:27 iron is nothing but straw, and bronze is **r** wood.
Isa 48:8 your earliest childhood, **r** through and through.
Jer 24:8 "But the **r** figs," the LORD said,
24:8 I will treat them like spoiled figs, too **r** to eat.
Ro 7:18 I know I am **r** through and through so far as my
Eph 4:22 which is **r** through and through, full of lust

ROTTING (9) [ROT]

Job 13:28 I waste away like **r** wood, like a moth-eaten coat.
Isa 5:25 and the **r** bodies of his people are thrown as
19:6 and the streams of Egypt will become foul with **r**
34:3 and the stench of **r** bodies will fill the land.
Jer 29:17 and disease upon them and make them like **r** figs—
Joel 2:20 The stench of their **r** bodies will rise over the
Zep 1:17 and your bodies will lie there **r** on the ground."
Zec 14:12 become like walking corpses, their flesh **r** away.
Jas 5:2 Your wealth is **r** away, and your fine clothes are

ROUGH (7) [ROUGHER, ROUGHS]

Isa 3:24 They will wear **r** sackcloth instead of rich robes.
26:7 who are righteous, / the path is not steep and **r**.
40:4 out the curves and smooth off the **r** spots.
Da 9:3 I wore **r** sackcloth and sprinkled myself with
Lk 3:5 the curves, / and smooth out the **r** places!
Jn 6:18 upon them as they rowed, and the sea grew very **r**.
Ac 27:7 We had several days of **r** sailing, and after great

ROUGHLY (3)

Ge 42:7 "Where are you from?" he demanded **r**.
42:30 "The man who is ruler over the land spoke very **r**
Ac 5:26 would kill them if they treated the apostles **r**.

ROUND (6) [ROUNDED, ROUNDS, WELL-ROUNDED]

1Ki 7:23 Then Huram cast a large **r** tank, 15 feet across
7:31 It projected 1-1/2 feet above the cart's top like a **r**
7:31 The panels of the carts were square, not **r**.
2Ch 4:2 Then he cast a large **r** tank, 15 feet across from rim
SS 5:14 His arms are like **r** bars of gold, set with
Jer 50:14 prepare to attack Babylon, all you nations **r** about.

ROUNDABOUT (1) [AROUND]

2Ki 3:9 and all three armies traveled along a **r** route

ROUNDED (5) [ROUND]

1Sa 30:20 His troops **r** up all the flocks and herds and drove
1Ki 7:20 beside the **r** surface next to the latticework.
10:19 The throne had six steps and a **r** back. On both
SS 7:1 Your **r** thighs are like jewels, the work of a skilled
Isa 24:22 They will be **r** up and put in prison until they are

ROUNDS (2) [ROUND]

SS 3:3 The watchmen stopped me as they made their **r**,
5:7 watchmen found me as they were making their **r**;

ROUSE (8) [AROUSE, AROUSED, AROUSING, ROUSED, ROUSES, ROUSING]

Ge 49:9 lies down; / like a lioness—who will dare to **r** him?
Dt 32:21 Now I will **r** their jealousy by blessing other
Job 3:8 those who are ready to **r** the sea monster—
Pr 20:2 like a lion's roar; to **r** his anger is to risk your life.
Isa 51:9 **R** yourself as in the days of old when you slew
Eze 38:14 in peace in their land, then you will **r** yourself.
Ro 10:19 "I will **r** your jealousy by blessing other nations.
1Co 10:22 Do you dare to **r** the Lord's jealousy as Israel did?

ROUSED (8) [ROUSE]

Dt 32:21 They have **r** my jealousy by worshiping non-gods;
Jos 8:10 Early the next morning Joshua **r** his men
Job 14:12 they will not wake up nor be **r** from their sleep.
Eze 20:28 They **r** my fury as they offered up sacrifices to
Da 8:18 But Gabriel **r** me with a touch and helped me to
Mt 25:6 At midnight they were **r** by the shout, 'Look,
Ac 6:12 Naturally, this **r** the crowds, the elders,
21:27 saw Paul in the Temple and **r** a mob against him.

ROUSES (1) [ROUSE]

Dt 32:11 Like an eagle that **r** her chicks / and hovers over

ROUSING (1) [ROUSE]

Eze 8:17 their noses at me, and **r** my fury against them?

ROUTE (6) [ROUTES]

Ex 13:18 So God led them along a **r** through the wilderness
Dt 1:22 They will advise us on the best **r** to take and decide
2:8 "Then as we traveled northward along the desert **r**
Jdg 8:11 Gideon circled around by the caravan **r** east of
2Ki 3:8 Then Jehoshaphat asked, "What **r** will we take?"
3:9 and all three armies traveled along a roundabout **r**

ROUTED (6)

1Sa 31:7 beyond the Jordan saw that their army had been **r**
2Ki 14:12 Judah was **r** by the army of Israel, and its army
1Ch 10:7 the Jezreel Valley saw that their army had been **r**
2Ch 13:15 and the Israelite army and **r** them before Abijah
25:22 Judah was **r** by the army of Israel, and its army
Ps 78:66 He **r** his enemies / and sent them to eternal shame.

ROUTES (4) [ROUTE]

Ps 107:23 went off in ships, / plying the trade **r** of the world.
Jer 51:32 All the escape **r** are blocked. The fortifications are
Eze 21:19 and trace two **r** on it for the sword of Babylon's
26:2 She who controlled the rich trade **r** to the east has

ROVE (1)

Isa 3:16 Their eyes **r** among the crowds, flirting with the

ROW (16) [ROWED, ROWING, ROWS]

Ex 28:17 The first **r** will contain a red carnelian,
28:18 The second **r** will contain a turquoise, a sapphire,
28:19 The third **r** will contain a jacinth, an agate, and an
28:20 The fourth **r** will contain a beryl, an onyx, and a
39:10 In the first **r** were a red carnelian, a chrysolite,
39:11 In the second **r** were a turquoise, a sapphire,
39:12 In the third **r** were a jacinth, an agate, and an
39:13 In the fourth **r** were a beryl, an onyx, and a jasper.
Lev 24:6 arrange the loaves in two rows, with six in each **r**.
24:7 Sprinkle some pure frankincense near each **r**.
2Sa 8:2 He made the people lie down on the ground in a **r**,
1Ki 7:3 rested on three rows of pillars, fifteen in each **r**.
Eze 41:5 There was a **r** of rooms along the outside wall;
41:10 and the **r** of rooms along the outer wall of the inner
Jnh 1:13 the sailors tried even harder to **r** the boat ashore.
Ac 17:2 and for three Sabbaths in a **r** he interpreted the

ROWED (1) [ROW]

Jn 6:18 Soon a gale swept down upon them as they **r**,

ROWING (2) [ROW]

Eze 27:26 Your oarsmen are **r** your ship of state into a
Mk 6:48 **r** hard and struggling against the wind and waves.

ROWS (14) [ROW]

Ex 28:17 Four **r** of gemstones will be attached to it. The first
39:10 Four **r** of gemstones were set across it. In the first
Lev 24:6 and arrange the loaves in two **r**, with six in each
Dt 22:9 "Do not plant any other crop between the **r** of
1Ki 7:2 The great cedar ceiling beams rested on four **r** of
7:3 by forty-five rafters that rested on three **r** of pillars,
7:4 On each of the side walls there were three **r** of
7:18 He also made two **r** of pomegranates that encircled
7:20 two hundred pomegranates in two **r** around them,
7:24 The Sea was encircled just below its rim by two **r**
7:42 **r** of pomegranates for each of the chain networks
2Ch 4:3 The Sea was encircled just below its rim by two **r**
4:13 **r** of pomegranates for each of the chain networks
Jer 5:10 "Go down the **r** of the vineyards and destroy

ROYAL (150) [ROYALTY]

Ge 41:35 and grain of these good years into the **r**
41:42 and placed the **r** gold chain about his neck.
Jos 10:2 as large as the **r** cities and larger than Ai.
13:31 and King Og's **r** cities of Ashtaroth and Edrei.
Jdg 8:21 and took the **r** ornaments from the necks of their
8:26 and pendants, the **r** clothing of the kings,
1Sa 22:3 and mother live here under **r** protection until I
27:5 of the country towns instead of here in the **r** city."
28:8 by wearing ordinary clothing instead of his **r** robes.
2Sa 8:16 Jehoshaphat son of Ahilud was the **r** historian.
20:24 Jehoshaphat son of Ahilud was the **r** historian.
1Ki 1:9 of King David—and all the **r** officials of Judah.
1:46 Solomon is now sitting on the **r** throne as king.
1:47 All the **r** officials went to King David
4:3 Jehoshaphat son of Ahilud was the **r** historian.
4:28 and straw for the **r** horses in the stables.
9:1 the Temple of the LORD, as well as the **r** palace.
9:10 built the Temple of the LORD and the **r** palace,
9:15 the **r** palace, the Millo, the wall of Jerusalem,
10:12 for the Temple of the LORD and the **r** palace,
11:14 a member of Edom's **r** family, to be an enemy
11:17 and a few of his father's **r** officials had fled.
14:10 I will burn up your **r** dynasty as one burns up trash
14:26 the LORD and the **r** palace and stole everything,
15:18 of the LORD's Temple and the **r** palace.
15:29 so that not one of the **r** family was left,

16: 9 who commanded half of the **r** chariots,
16:11 Zimri immediately killed the entire **r** family of
22:10 Jehoshaphat of Judah, dressed in their **r** robes,
22:30 will recognize me, but you wear your **r** robes."
22:32 charioteers saw Jehoshaphat in his **r** robes,
2Ki 11: 1 she set out to destroy the rest of the **r** family.
11: 5 duty on the Sabbath are to guard the **r** palace itself.
11:19 and the king took his seat on the **r** throne.
12:18 of the LORD's Temple and the **r** palace.
15: 5 The king's son Jotham was put in charge of the **r**
15:19 gain his support in tightening his grip on **r** power.
18:18 and Joah son of Asaph, the **r** historian.
18:37 and Joah son of Asaph, the **r** historian, went back
24:13 from the LORD's Temple and the **r** palace.
25: 9 the **r** palace, and all the houses of Jerusalem.
25:25 grandson of Elishama, who was of the **r** family,
1Ch 18:15 Jehoshaphat son of Ahilud was the **r** historian.
27:33 Ahithophel was the **r** adviser. Hushai the Arkite
28: 1 the overseers of the **r** property and livestock,
29:24 All the **r** officials, the army commanders,
2Ch 2: 1 Temple for the LORD and a **r** palace for himself.
2:12 Temple for the LORD and a **r** palace for himself.
7:11 the Temple of the LORD, as well as the **r** palace.
8: 1 and his own **r** palace were completed.
9:11 for the Temple of the LORD and the **r** palace,
12: 9 of the Temple of the LORD and of the **r** palace,
16: 2 of the LORD's Temple and from the **r** palace.
18: 9 Jehoshaphat of Judah, dressed in their **r** robes,
18:29 will recognize me, but you wear your **r** robes."
18:31 charioteers saw Jehoshaphat in his **r** robes,
21:17 and carried away everything of value in the **r**
21:20 in the City of David, but not in the **r** cemetery.
22:10 she set out to destroy the rest of Judah's **r** family.
23: 5 Another third will go over to the **r** palace,
23:20 and they seated the king on the **r** throne.
24:25 in the City of David, but not in the **r** cemetery.
25:24 He also seized the treasures of the **r** palace,
26:21 His son Jotham was put in charge of the **r** palace,
28:21 the **r** palace, and from the homes of his officials
28:27 was buried in Jerusalem but not in the **r** cemetery.
32:33 he was buried in the upper area of the **r** cemetery,
34: 8 and Joah son of Joahaz, the **r** historian,
35:22 He laid aside his **r** robes so the enemy would not
35:24 He was buried there in the **r** cemetery. And all
36:18 from both the LORD's Temple and the **r** palace.
36:18 He also took with him all the **r** princes.
Ezr 5:17 we request that you search in the **r** archives of
6: 4 All expenses will be paid by the **r** treasury.
7:20 you may requisition funds from the **r** treasury.
Ne 3:16 He rebuilt the wall to a place opposite the **r**
11:23 They were under **r** orders, which determined their
Est 1: 7 and there was an abundance of **r** wine, just as the
1:11 to bring Queen Vashti to him with the **r** crown on
2: 3 beautiful young women into the **r** harem at Susa.
2:16 When Esther was taken to King Xerxes at the **r**
2:17 so delighted with her that he set the **r** crown on her
3: 9 so they can put it into the **r** treasury.
4: 7 into the **r** treasury for the destruction of the Jews.
5: 1 Esther put on her **r** robes and entered the inner
5: 1 The king was sitting on his **r** throne,
6: 8 he should bring out one of the king's own **r** robes,
6: 8 as well as the king's own horse with a **r** emblem
8:15 Then Mordecai put on the **r** robe of blue and white
9: 3 and the **r** officials helped the Jews for fear of
10: 3 and was a friend at the **r** court for all of them.
Job 12:18 He removes the **r** robe of kings. With ropes around
Ps 2:12 Submit to God's **r** son, or he will become angry,
45: 6 and ever. / Your **r** power is expressed in justice.
45:10 Listen to me, O **r** daughter; take to heart what I
45:11 For your **r** husband delights in your beauty;
93: 5 Your **r** decrees cannot be changed. / The nature of
132:12 I teach them, / then your **r** line will never end."
Isa 7: 2 The news had come to the **r** court: "Aram is allied
7:13 Isaiah said, "Listen well, you **r** family of David!
9: 6 These will be his **r** titles: Wonderful Counselor,
22:21 He will have your **r** robes, your title, and your
22:22 of David—the highest position in the **r** court.
36: 3 and Joah son of Asaph, the **r** historian.
36:22 and Joah son of Asaph, the **r** historian, went back
63: 1 Who is this in **r** robes, marching in the greatness of
Jer 10: 9 Then they dress these gods in **r** purple robes made
21:11 "Say to the **r** family of Judah, 'Listen to this
22: 6 Now this is what the LORD says concerning the **r**
32: 2 in the courtyard of the guard in the **r** palace.
37:21 in the courtyard of the guard in the **r** palace.
38: 6 It belonged to Malkijah, a member of the **r** family.
39: 4 and his **r** guard saw the Babylonians in the city
41: 1 of Elishama, who was a member of the **r** family,
43:10 He will spread his **r** canopy over them.
52:13 the **r** palace, and all the houses of Jerusalem.
Eze 17:13 He made a treaty with a member of the **r** family
17:15 this man of Israel's **r** family rebelled against
26:16 and take off their **r** robes and beautiful clothing.
Da 1: 3 palace some of the young men of Judah's **r** family
1: 4 and have the poise needed to serve in the **r** palace.
1: 5 of them would be made his advisers in the **r** court.
4:29 he was taking a walk on the flat roof of the **r**
4:30 have built this beautiful city as my **r** residence
4:30 and as an expression of my **r** splendor."
5: 7 it means will be dressed in purple robes of **r** honor
5:16 you will be clothed in purple robes of **r** honor,
5:20 he was brought down from his **r** throne
6:17 The king sealed the stone with his own **r** seal
7:14 and **r** power over all the nations of the world,
11:20 who sent a tax collector to maintain the **r** splendor,
11:21 man who is not directly in line for **r** succession.
11:45 and the sea and will pitch his **r** tents there,
Hos 5: 1 Listen, all you men of the **r** family!
7: 5 "On **r** holidays, the princes get drunk. The king
Am 7:13 especially not here where the **r** sanctuary is!"
Jnh 3: 6 down from his throne and took off his **r** robes.
Mic 4: 8 your **r** might and power will come back to you
Hag 2:22 I will overthrow **r** thrones, destroying the power of
Zec 6:13 and he will receive **r** honor and will rule as king
12: 7 and the **r** line of David will not have greater honor
12: 8 And the **r** descendants will be like God,
Lk 1:69 from the **r** line of his servant David,
23:11 Then they put a **r** robe on him and sent him back to
Jn 7:42 the Messiah will be born of the **r** line of David,
19: 2 it on his head, and they put a **r** purple robe on him.
Ac 12:21 Herod put on his **r** robes, sat on his throne,
Ro 1: 3 as a man, born into King David's **r** family line.
Heb 1: 8 Your **r** power is expressed in righteousness.
Jas 2: 8 it is good when you truly obey our Lord's **r**

ROYALTY (2) [ROYAL]
Pr 31:22 She dresses like **r** in gowns of finest cloth.
SS 7: 5 and the sheen of your hair radiates **r**.

RUBBED (4) [RUBBING]
Eze 16: 4 and you were never washed, **r** with salt,
16: 9 off your blood, and I **r** fragrant oils into your skin.
29:18 against Tyre that the warriors' heads were **r** bare
Lk 6: 1 **r** off the husks in their hands, and ate the grains.

RUBBING (1) [RUBBED]
Pr 25:20 jacket in cold weather or **r** salt in a wound.

RUBBISH (1) [RUBBLE]
Ne 4: 2 at those charred stones they are pulling out of the **r**

RUBBLE (21) [RUBBISH]
2Ki 19:25 you should crush fortified cities into heaps of **r**.
Ezr 6:11 and their house will be reduced to a pile of **r**.
Ne 2:14 but my donkey couldn't get through the **r**.
4:10 so much **r** to be moved that we could never get it
Isa 23:13 down its palaces, and turned it into a heap of **r**.
25: 2 of ruins. Cities with strong walls are turned to **r**.
37:26 you should crush fortified cities into heaps of **r**.
Jer 22: 5 that this palace will become a pile of **r**.' "
26:18 like an open field; Jerusalem will be reduced to **r**!
49:13 will become an object of horror and a heap of **r**;
50:26 Crush her walls and houses into heaps of **r**.
51:25 I am finished, you will be nothing but a heap of **r**.
51:37 and Babylon will become a heap of **r**, haunted by
Da 2: 5 your houses will be demolished into heaps of **r**!
3:29 and their houses will be crushed into heaps of **r**.
Hos 5: 9 of punishment comes, you will become a heap of **r**.
Mic 1: 6 will make the city of Samaria a heap of **r**.
3:12 like an open field; Jerusalem will be reduced to **r**!
Zep 1: 3 I will reduce the wicked to heaps of **r**, along with
2:14 **R** will block all the doorways, and the cedar
Rev 16:19 and cities around the world fell into heaps of **r**.

RUBIES (6)
Pr 3:15 Wisdom is more precious than **r**; nothing you
8:11 For wisdom is far more valuable than **r**.
20:15 speech is rarer and more valuable than gold and **r**.
31:10 capable wife? She is worth more than precious **r**.
Isa 54:12 I will make your towers of sparkling **r** and your
Eze 27:16 embroidery, fine linen, and jewelry of coral and **r**.

RUDDER (1) [RUDDERS]
Jas 3: 4 And a tiny **r** makes a huge ship turn wherever the

RUDDERS (1) [RUDDER]
Ac 27:40 Then they lowered the **r**, raised the foresail,

RUDDY (1) [RUDDY-FACED]
1Sa 16:12 He was **r** and handsome, with pleasant eyes.

RUDDY-FACED (1) [FACE, RUDDY]
1Sa 17:42 sneering in contempt at this **r** boy.

RUDE (1)
1Co 13: 5 or **r**. Love does not demand its own way. Love is

RUDIMENTS [KJV] See EVIL POWERS

RUFUS (2)
Mk 15:21 (Simon is the father of Alexander and **R**.)
Ro 16:13 Greet **R**, whom the Lord picked out to be his very

RUGGED (2)
Ps 68:16 Why do you look with envy, O **r** mountains,
SS 2:17 like a gazelle or a young stag on the **r** mountains."

RUGS (1)
Isa 21: 5 They are spreading **r** for people to sit on.

RUHAMAH (1)
Hos 2: 1 And you will call your sisters **R**—'The ones I

RUIN (52) [RUINED, RUINING, RUINS]
Dt 13:16 That town must remain a **r** forever; it may never be
29:19 my own stubborn way.' This would lead to utter **r**!
2Ki 3:19 and **r** all their good land with stones."
2Ch 22: 4 family became his advisers, and they led him to **r**.
28:23 they led to his **r** and the **r** of all Israel.
34:11 earlier kings of Judah had allowed to fall into **r**.
Job 15:23 saying, 'Where is it?' They know their **r** is certain.
31:29 "Have I ever rejoiced when my enemies came to **r**
34:24 He brings the mighty to **r** without asking anyone,
Ps 4: 2 How long will you people **r** my reputation?
35: 8 So let sudden **r** overtake them! / Let them be
38:12 lay traps for me; / they make plans to **r** me.
63: 9 But those plotting to destroy me will come to **r**.
78:45 to consume them / and hordes of frogs to **r** them.
Pr 5:14 I have come to the brink of utter **r**, and now I must
7:26 For she has been the **r** of many; numerous men
13: 3 have a long life; a quick retort can **r** everything.
18: 7 The mouths of fools are their **r**; their lips get them
19: 3 People **r** their lives by their own foolishness
19:18 there is hope. If you don't, you will **r** their lives.
21:25 The desires of lazy people will be their **r**, for their
26:28 tongue hates its victims, and flattery causes **r**.
31: 3 your strength on women, on those who **r** kings.
Ecc 5: 7 And there is **r** in a flood of empty words. Fear God
10:12 but the speech of fools brings them to **r**.
SS 2:15 Catch all the little foxes before they **r** the vineyard
Isa 23: 7 How can this silent **r** be all that is left of your once
42:23 lessons from the past and see the **r** that awaits you?
Jer 25: 9 an object of horror and contempt and a **r** forever.
25:18 they have been a desolate **r**, an object of horror,
44: 6 streets of Jerusalem, and now they are a desolate **r**.
44:22 a desolate **r** without a single inhabitant—as it is
48:39 of ridicule, an example of **r** to all her neighbors.
Eze 5:14 "So I will turn you into a **r**, a mockery in the eyes
26:19 LORD says: I will make Tyre an uninhabited **r**.
27:27 On that day of vast **r**, everyone on board sinks into
Am 6: 6 caring nothing at all that your nation is going to **r**.
Mic 6:13 wound you! I will bring you to **r** for all your sins.
6:16 an example of you, bringing you to complete **r**.
Na 3: 7 back in horror and say, 'Nineveh lies in utter **r**.'
Zep 1:15 and anguish, a day of **r** and desolation,
2:15 But now, look how it has become an utter **r**,
3: 6 cities are now deserted; their streets are in silent **r**.
Hag 1:11 your cattle and to **r** everything you have worked
Lk 23: 2 "This man has been leading our people to **r** by
Ro 14:15 Don't let your eating **r** someone for whom Christ
1Co 3:17 God will bring **r** upon anyone who ruins this
Eph 5:18 be drunk with wine, because that will **r** your life.
1Ti 6: 9 and harmful desires that plunge them into **r**
2Ti 2:14 are useless, and they can **r** those who hear them.
Jas 3: 6 It is full of wickedness that can **r** your whole life.

RUINED (27) [RUIN]
Nu 17:12 said to Moses, "We are as good as dead! We are **r**!
Job 15:28 but their cities will be **r**. They will live in
Ps 105:33 He **r** their grapevines and fig trees / and shattered
109:10 may they be evicted from their **r** homes.
Isa 3:14 "You have **r** Israel, which is my vineyard.
13:21 Wild animals of the desert will move into the **r**
19:13 The leaders of Egypt have **r** the land with their
Jer 4:27 "The whole land will be **r**, but I will not destroy it
9:12 Why has the land been **r** so completely that no one
9:19 people of Jerusalem crying in despair, 'We are **r**!
49: 4 of your fertile valleys, but they will soon be **r**."
La 3:47 with fear, for we are trapped, desolate, and **r**."
Eze 30: 7 cities will be in ruins, surrounded by other **r** cities.
33:24 the scattered remnants of Judah living among the **r**
33:28 so **r** that no one will even travel through them.
33:29 When I have **r** the land because of their disgusting
36: 4 and to **r** wastes and long-deserted cities that have
36:10 and the **r** cities will be rebuilt and filled with
36:35 The **r** cities now have strong walls, and they are
36:38 The **r** cities will be crowded with people once
Joel 1: 5 All the grapes are **r**, and all your new wine is
1:10 The fields are **r** and empty of crops. The grain,
1:11 and barley—yes, all the field crops—are **r**.
Am 9:14 and they will rebuild their **r** cities and live in them
Mic 2: 4 "We are finished, / completely **r**! / God has
2:10 for you have filled it with sin and **r** it completely.
Zec 11: 2 Weep, you cypress trees, for all the **r** cedars;

RUINING (4) [RUIN]
Am 4: 7 when you needed it the most, **r** all your crops.
Mt 9:17 from the pressure, spilling the wine and **r** the skins.
Mk 2:22 the wineskins, spilling the wine and **r** the skins.
Lk 5:37 the old skins, spilling the wine and **r** the skins.

RUINS (58) [RUIN]
Ex 9:25 It left all of Egypt in **r**. Everything left in the fields
10: 7 their God! Don't you realize that Egypt lies in **r**?"
Lev 26:33 will become desolate, and your cities will lie in **r**.
26:35 As the land lies in **r**, it will take the rest you never
Jos 8:28 So Ai became a permanent mound of **r**, desolate to
1Sa 30: 3 When David and his men saw the **r** and realized
Ezr 9: 9 to rebuild the Temple of our God and repair its **r**.
Ne 2: 3 For the city where my ancestors are buried is in **r**,
2:17 It lies in **r**, and its gates are burned. Let us rebuild
Ps 9: 6 have met their doom; / their cities are perpetual **r**.
74: 3 Walk through the awful **r** of the city; / see how the
79: 1 holy Temple / and made Jerusalem a heap of **r**.
89:40 and laid in **r** every fort defending him.
Pr 22:12 but he **r** the plans of the deceitful.
Isa 1: 7 Your country lies in **r**, and your cities are burned.
3: 6 you be our leader! Take charge of this heap of **r**!"
3: 8 Judah and Jerusalem will lie in **r** because they
5:17 In those days flocks will feed among the **r**; lambs
9:10 "Our land lies in **r** now, but we will rebuild it

13:21 Ostriches will live among the **r**, and wild goats
17: 1 will disappear! It will become a heap of **r**.
24:12 The city is left in **r**, with its gates battered down.
25: 2 You turn mighty cities into heaps of **r**. Cities with
34:13 The **r** will become a haunt for jackals and a home
34:14 Wild goats will bleat at one another among the **r**,
49:16 before me is a picture of Jerusalem's walls in **r**.
52: 9 Let the **r** of Jerusalem break into joyful song,
58:12 Your children will rebuild the deserted **r** of your
61: 4 They will rebuild the ancient **r**, repairing cities
Jer 2:15 has been destroyed, and the cities are now in **r**.
4: 7 Your towns will lie in **r**, empty of people.
4:26 The cities lay in **r**, crushed by the LORD's fierce
9:11 "I will make Jerusalem into a heap of **r**,"
22: 8 People from many nations will pass by the **r** of this
30:18 your fortunes, Jerusalem will be rebuilt on her **r**.
44: 2 They now lie in **r**, and no one lives in them.
47: 5 of Gaza will be demolished; Ashkelon will lie in **r**.
48: 1 is certain for the city of Nebo; it will soon lie in **r**.
48:20 "And the reply comes back, 'Moab lies in **r**;
48:21 All the cities of the plateau lie in **r**, too.
51:43 Her cities now lie in **r**; she is a dry wilderness
Eze 13: 4 of yours are like jackals digging around in the **r**.
26:20 Your city will lie in **r**, buried beneath the earth,
30: 7 by desolate nations, and its cities will be in **r**,
30:14 Zoan, and Thebes, and they will lie in **r**,
33:27 as I live, those living in the **r** will die by the sword.
36:33 to live in your cities, and the **r** will be rebuilt.
36:36 rebuilt the **r** and planted lush crops in the
Da 9:18 See how your city lies in **r**—for everyone knows
Am 9:11 It is now like a house in **r**, but I will rebuild its
Zep 2:14 Owls of many kinds will live among the **r** of its
Hag 1: 4 in luxurious houses while my house lies in **r**?
1: 9 Because my house lies in **r**, says the LORD
Zec 14: 2 and half will be left among the **r** of the city.
Mal 1: 4 have been shattered, but we will rebuild the **r**."
Lk 6:49 that house, it will crumble into a heap of **r**."
Ac 15:16 From the **r** I will rebuild it, / and I will restore it,
1Co 3:17 God will bring ruin upon anyone who **r** this

RULE (130) [RULED, RULER, RULER'S, RULERS, RULES, RULING]

Lev 17: 5 This **r** will stop the Israelites from sacrificing
26:17 They will **r** over you, and you will run even when
Nu 8:24 "This is the **r** the Levites must follow: They must
Dt 15: 6 You will **r** many nations, but they will not **r** over you!
19:21 Your **r** should be life for life, eye for eye, tooth for
Jdg 8:23 "I will not **r** over you, nor will my son. The LORD will **r** over you!
15:11 "Don't you realize the Philistines **r** over us?
1Sa 9:17 the man I told you about! He will **r** my people."
11:12 are those men who said Saul shouldn't **r** over us?
24:20 to be king, and Israel will flourish under your **r**.
2Sa 3:21 Then you will be able to **r** over everything your
7:11 from the time I appointed judges to **r** my people.
19:10 whom we anointed to **r** over us, is dead.
1Ki 10: 9 so you can **r** with justice and righteousness."
11:37 and you will **r** over all that your heart desires.
12:17 But Rehoboam continued to **r** over the Israelites
15: 1 Abijam began to **r** over Judah in the eighteenth
15: 4 and he gave Abijam a son to **r** after him in
15: 9 Asa began to **r** over Judah in the twentieth year of
15:25 Nadab son of Jeroboam began to **r** over Israel in
15:33 Baasha began to **r** over Israel in the third year of
16: 8 Elah son of Baasha began to **r** over Israel from
16:15 Zimri began to **r** over Israel from Tirzah in the
16:23 Omri began to **r** over Israel in the thirty-first year
16:29 Ahab son of Omri began to **r** over Israel in the
22:41 Jehoshaphat son of Asa began to **r** over Judah in
22:51 Ahaziah son of Ahab began to **r** over Israel in the
2Ki 3: 1 Ahab's son Joram began to **r** over Israel in the
8:16 **r** over Judah in the fifth year of King Joram's reign
8:19 that his descendants would continue to **r** forever.
8:25 Ahaziah son of Jehoram began to **r** over Judah in
12: 1 Joash began to **r** over Judah in the seventh year of
13: 1 Jehoahaz son of Jehu began to **r** over Israel in the
13:10 Jehoash son of Jehoahaz began to **r** over Israel in
14: 1 Amaziah son of Joash began to **r** over Judah in the
14:23 began to **r** over Israel in the fifteenth year of King
15: 1 Uzziah son of Amaziah began to **r** over Judah in
15: 8 Zechariah son of Jeroboam II began to **r** over
15:13 Shallum son of Jabesh began to **r** over Israel in the
15:17 Menahem son of Gadi began to **r** over Israel in the
15:23 Pekahiah son of Menahem began to **r** over Israel in
15:27 Pekah son of Remaliah began to **r** over Israel in
15:30 He began to **r** over Israel in the twentieth year of
15:32 Jotham son of Uzziah began to **r** over Judah in the
16: 1 Ahaz son of Jotham began to **r** over Judah in the
17: 1 Hoshea son of Elah began to **r** over Israel in the
18: 1 Hezekiah son of Ahaz began to **r** over Judah in the
1Ch 16:14 our God. / His **r** is seen throughout the land.
17:10 from the time I appointed judges to **r** my people.
22:12 law of the LORD your God as you **r** over Israel.
28: 4 For he has chosen the tribe of Judah to **r**, and from
29:12 come from you alone, for you **r** over everything.
2Ch 1:10 me wisdom and knowledge to **r** them properly,
9: 8 and has placed you on the throne to **r** for him.
9: 8 so you can **r** with justice and righteousness."
10:17 But Rehoboam continued to **r** over the Israelites
12:13 himself in Jerusalem and continued to **r**.
13: 1 Abijah began to **r** over Judah in the eighteenth year
21: 7 that his descendants would continue to **r** forever.
Ps 9: 8 world with justice / and **r** the nations with fairness.
49:14 In the morning the godly will **r** over them.
89:25 I will extend his **r** from the Mediterranean Sea in
102:12 But you, O LORD, will **r** forever. / Your fame
105: 7 our God. / His **r** is seen throughout the land.
110: 2 from Jerusalem; / you will **r** over your enemies.
125: 3 The wicked will not **r** the godly, / for
136: 8 the sun to **r** the day, / His faithful love endures
136: 9 and the moon and stars to **r** the night. / His faithful
145:13 You **r** generation after generation. / The LORD is
Pr 16:12 for his **r** depends on his justice.
17: 2 A wise slave will **r** over the master's shameful
19:10 to live in luxury or for a slave to **r** over princes!
22: 7 Just as the rich **r** the poor, so the borrower is
31:26 and kindness is the **r** when she gives instructions.
Isa 3: 4 Then he will appoint children to **r** over them,
3:12 oppress my people, and women **r** over them.
9: 7 He will **r** forever with fairness and justice from the
11: 4 He will **r** against the wicked and destroy them with
14: 2 will be captured, and Israel will **r** over its enemies.
14: 5 crushed your wicked power and broken your evil **r**.
24:23 He will **r** gloriously in Jerusalem, in the sight of all
32: 1 is coming! And honest princes will **r** under him.
32:16 Justice will **r** in the wilderness and righteousness
40:10 He will **r** with awesome strength. See, he brings
51: 5 I will **r** the nations. They will wait for me and long
51: 6 lasts forever. My righteous **r** will never end!
52: 5 Those who **r** them shout in exultation.
Jer 5:31 and the priests **r** with an iron hand.
22:30 will ever sit on the throne of David to **r** in Judah.
27: 7 and great kings will conquer and **r** over Babylon.
33:26 or change the plan that David's descendants will **r**
51:28 and the armies of all the countries they **r**.
Eze 18: 4 both parents and children alike. And this is my **r**:
20:33 I will **r** you with an iron fist in great anger
37:22 One king will **r** them all; no longer will they be
Da 2:39 bronze belly and thighs, will rise to **r** the world.
4: 3 will last forever, / his **r** through all generations.
4:22 up to heaven, and your **r** to the ends of the earth.
4:34 His **r** is everlasting, / and his kingdom is eternal.
5:21 and appoints anyone he desires to **r** over them.
6: 1 and he appointed a prince to **r** over each province.
6:26 will never be destroyed, / and his **r** will never end.
7:14 obey him. His **r** is eternal—it will never end.
7:18 the kingdom, and they will **r** forever and ever."
7:23 is the fourth world power that will **r** the earth.
7:24 Its ten horns are ten kings that will **r** that empire.
7:27 They will **r** forever, and all rulers will serve
8:23 "At the end of their **r**, when their sin is at its
11: 3 "Then a mighty king will rise to power who will **r**
11: 5 than he and will **r** his kingdom with great strength.
Ob 1:21 in Jerusalem to **r** over the mountains of Edom.
Mic 4: 7 will **r** from Jerusalem as their king forever."
5: 6 They will **r** Assyria with drawn swords and enter
7:14 O LORD, come and **r** your people; lead your
Zec 6:13 royal honor and will **r** as king from his throne.
10:11 will be crushed, and the **r** of Egypt will end.
Ro 5:17 of this one man, Adam, caused death to **r** over us,
15:12 throne will come, / and he will **r** over the Gentiles.
1Co 7: 5 The only exception to this **r** would be the
7: 6 my suggestion. It's not meant to be an absolute **r**.
7:17 first called you. This is my **r** for all the churches.
Eph 4:10 so that his **r** might fill the entire universe.
6:12 against those mighty powers of darkness who **r**
Col 3:15 And let the peace that comes from Christ **r** in your
2Th 3:10 Even while we were with you, we gave you this **r**:
Rev 2:27 They will **r** the nations with an iron rod and smash
12: 5 She gave birth to a boy who was to **r** all nations
13: 7 And he was given authority to **r** over every tribe

RULED (52) [RULE]

Ge 36:31 These are the kings who **r** in Edom before there
36:32 Bela son of Beor, who **r** from his city of Dinhabah.
36:35 Bedad became king and **r** from the city of Avith.
36:39 Hadad became king and **r** from the city of Pau.
Nu 21:34 King Sihon of the Amorites, who **r** in Heshbon."
Dt 1: 4 who had **r** in Heshbon, and King Og of Bashan, who had **r** in Ashtaroth and Edrei.
3: 2 King Sihon of the Amorites, who **r** in Heshbon.'
Jos 12: 5 He **r** a territory stretching from Mount Hermon to
Jdg 9: 2 they want to be **r** by all seventy of Gideon's sons
9:22 After Abimelech had **r** over Israel for three years,
11:19 King Sihon of the Amorites, who **r** from Heshbon,
14: 4 the Philistines, who **r** over Israel at that time.
15:20 for twenty years, while the Philistines **r** the land.
Ru 1: 1 In the days when the judges **r** in Israel, a man from
2Sa 2:10 and he **r** from Mahanaim for two years.
2:11 and he **r** as king of Judah for seven and a half
1Ki 4:21 King Solomon **r** all the kingdoms from the
11:42 Solomon **r** in Jerusalem over all Israel for forty
12:19 The northern tribes of Israel have refused to be **r**
14:19 of Jeroboam's reign, all his wars and how he **r**,
2Ki 11: 3 for six years while Athaliah **r** over the land.
17: 2 but not as much as the kings of Israel who **r** before
23:22 like that since the time when the judges **r** in Israel,
1Ch 1:43 These are the kings who **r** in Edom before there
1:43 Bela son of Beor, who **r** from his city of Dinhabah.
1:46 Bedad became king and **r** from the city of Avith.
1:50 Hadad became king and **r** from the city of Pau.
2:22 who **r** twenty-three towns in the land of Gilead.
4:22 and Saraph, who **r** over Moab and Jashubi-lehem.
17:13 from him as I took it from Saul, who **r** before you.
29:27 He **r** Israel for forty years in all, seven years from
29:28 and honor. Then his son Solomon **r** in his place.
2Ch 9:26 He **r** over all the kings from the Euphrates River to
9:30 Solomon **r** in Jerusalem over all Israel for forty
10:19 The northern tribes of Israel have refused to be **r**
20:31 So Jehoshaphat **r** over the land of Judah. He was
22:12 of God for six years while Athaliah **r** over the land.
Ezr 4:20 Powerful kings have **r** over Jerusalem
Est 1: 2 At that time he **r** his empire from his throne at the
Ps 106:41 and those who hated them **r** over them.
Ecc 1: 1 King David's son, who **r** in Jerusalem.
1:16 I am wiser than any of the kings who **r** in
2: 9 So I became greater than any of the kings who **r** in
Isa 26:13 O LORD our God, others have **r** us, / but we
Jer 34: 1 came with all the armies from the kingdoms he **r**,
Eze 34: 4 Instead, you have **r** them with force and cruelty.
Da 11: 4 It will not be **r** by the king's descendants, nor will
Ac 13:20 judges **r** until the time of Samuel the prophet.
Ro 5:21 So just as sin **r** over all people and brought them to
Heb 11:33 these people overthrew kingdoms, **r** with justice,
Rev 19:15 He **r** them with an iron rod, and he trod the

RULER (51) [RULE]

Ge 42:30 "The man who is **r** over the land spoke very
42:33 Then the man, the **r** of the land, told us, 'This is
45: 8 of his entire household and **r** over all Egypt.
45:26 told him. "And he is **r** over all the land of Egypt!"
Nu 24:19 A **r** will rise in Jacob / who will destroy the
Jdg 8:22 Then the Israelites said to Gideon, "Be our **r**!
10:18 first will become **r** over all the people of Gilead."
11: 8 we will make you **r** over all the people of Gilead."
11: 9 will you really make me **r** over all the people?"
11:11 and he became their **r** and commander of the army.
2Sa 22:44 You preserved me as the **r** over nations; / people I
1Ki 1:35 for I have appointed him to be **r** over Israel
14: 7 and made you **r** over my people Israel.
16: 2 "I lifted you out of the dust to make you **r** of my
1Ch 5: 2 powerful tribe and provided a **r** for the nation,
2Ch 20: 6 You are **r** of all the kingdoms of the earth. You are
Est 1:22 proclaiming that every man should be the **r** of his
Ps 18:43 You appointed me as the **r** over nations;
105:20 the **r** of the nation opened his prison door.
105:21 he became **r** over all the king's possessions.
Pr 6: 7 have no prince, governor, or **r** to make them work,
17: 7 fitting for a fool; even less are lies fitting for a **r**.
23: 1 When dining with a **r**, pay attention to what is put
28:15 A wicked **r** is as dangerous to the poor as a lion
29:12 If a **r** honors liars, all his advisers will be wicked.
Jer 30:21 They will have their own **r** again, and he will not
49:19 can challenge me? What **r** can oppose my will?"
50:44 can challenge me? What **r** can oppose my will?"
Eze 26:17 'O famous island city, / once **r** of the sea,
39: 1 O Gog, **r** of the nations of Meshech and Tubal.
Da 2:38 He has made you the **r** over all the inhabited world
2:48 He made Daniel **r** over the whole province of
4:31 is for you! You are no longer **r** of this kingdom.
5: 7 He will become the third highest **r** in the
5:16 You will become the third highest **r** in the
5:29 and he was proclaimed the third highest **r** in the
9:26 and a **r** will arise whose armies will destroy the
Am 1: 5 I will destroy the **r** in Beth-eden, and the people of
Mic 5: 2 Yet a **r** of Israel will come from you, one whose
Mt 2: 6 village in Judah, / for a **r** will come from you
2:22 But when he learned that the new **r** was Herod's
Lk 3: 1 over Judea; Herod Antipas was **r** over Galilee; his brother Philip was **r** over Iturea and Traconitis; Lysanias was **r** over Abilene.
3:19 **r** of Galilee, for marrying Herodias, his brother's
Ac 7:27 'Who made you a **r** and judge over us?' he asked.
7:35 'Who made you a **r** and judge over us?'
7:35 Moses was sent to be their **r** and savior.
Eph 1:21 Now he is far above any **r** or authority or power
Col 2:10 He is the Lord over every **r** and authority in the
Rev 3:14 and true witness, the **r** of God's creation:

RULER'S (4) [RULE]

Ge 49:10 from Judah, / nor the **r** staff from his descendants,
Pr 29:26 Many seek the **r** favor, but justice comes from the
Eze 19:11 very strong, / strong enough to be a **r** scepter.
19:14 is strong enough to be a **r** scepter.' This is a

RULERS (69) [RULE]

Nu 21:28 in Moab; / it destroyed the **r** of the Arnon heights.
Jdg 3: 3 Philistines (those living under the five Philistine **r**),
5: 3 "Listen, you kings! / Pay attention, you mighty **r**!
8:14 he write down the names of all the seventy-seven **r**
8:22 and your son and your grandson will be our **r**,
1Sa 5: 8 So they called together the **r** of the five Philistine
5: 8 The **r** discussed it and replied, "Move it to the city
5:11 So the people summoned the **r** again and begged
6: 4 the plague has struck both you and your five **r**,
6:12 The Philistine **r** followed them as far as the border
6:16 The five Philistine **r** watched all this and
6:17 to the LORD were gifts from the **r** of Ashdod,
6:18 which were controlled by the five **r**.
7: 7 When the Philistine **r** heard that all Israel had
29: 2 As the Philistine **r** were leading out their troops in
29: 6 with us, but the other Philistine **r** won't hear of it.
2Ch 12: 8 better it is to serve me than to serve earthly **r**."
23:20 Then the commanders, nobles, **r**, and all the people
Ps 2: 2 of the earth prepare for battle; / the **r** plot together
2:10 act wisely! / Be warned, you **r** of the earth!
45:16 You will make them **r** over many lands.
47: 9 The **r** of the world have gathered together.
58: 1 Justice—do you **r** know the meaning of the word?
68:27 Then comes a great throng of **r** from Judah / and all the **r** of Zebulun and Naphtali.
148:11 the earth and all people, / **r** and judges of the earth,
Pr 8:15 Because of me, kings reign, and **r** make just laws.
8:16 **R** lead with my help, and nobles make righteous
31: 4 to guzzle wine. **R** should not crave liquor.
Ecc 10: 5 world go by. Kings and **r** make a grave mistake

Isa 1:10 You act just like the **r** and people of Sodom
3:12 O my people, can't you see what fools your **r** are?
16:8 The wine from those vineyards used to make the **r**
24:21 the heavens and the proud **r** of the nations on earth.
28:14 from the LORD, you scoffing **r** in Jerusalem.
49:7 by a nation, to the one who is the servant of **r**:
60:10 rebuild your cities. Kings and **r** will send you aid.
Jer 2:8 The judges ignored me, the **r** turned against me,
12:10 "Many **r** have ravaged my vineyard,
13:21 the LORD sets your foreign allies over you as **r**?
46:25 I will punish its **r** and Pharaoh, too, and all who
51:23 and flocks, farmers and oxen, captains and **r**.
51:57 wise men, **r**, captains, and warriors,"
La 2:2 He has brought to dust the kingdom and all its **r**.
Eze 26:16 All the seaport **r** will step down from their thrones
30:13 There will be no **r** left in Egypt; anarchy will
Da 7:27 rule forever, and all **r** will serve and obey them."
9:12 you warned you would do against us and our **r**.
Mic 3:11 You **r** govern for the bribes you can get;
5:5 we will appoint seven **r** to watch over us,
Zec 10:4 the tent peg, the battle bow, and all the **r**.
Lk 12:11 in the synagogues and before **r** and authorities,
Jn 7:48 "Is there a single one of us **r** or Pharisees who
Ac 4:5 The next day the council of all the **r** and elders
4:26 earth prepared for battle; / the **r** gathered together
1Co 2:6 and not the kind that appeals to the **r** of this world,
2:8 But the **r** of this world have not understood it;
Eph 3:10 show his wisdom in all its rich variety to all the **r**
6:12 but against the evil **r** and authorities of the unseen
Col 1:16 we can't see—kings, kingdoms, **r**, and authorities.
2:15 this way, God disarmed the evil **r** and authorities.
Rev 1:5 and the commander of all the **r** of the world.
6:15 of the earth, the **r**, the generals, the wealthy people,
16:14 These miracle-working demons caused all the **r** of
16:16 And they gathered all the **r** and their armies to a
17:2 The **r** of the world have had immoral relations with
18:3 The **r** of the world have committed adultery with
18:9 And the **r** of the world who took part in her
21:24 and the **r** of the world will come and bring their

RULES (42) [RULE]

Ex 22:28 blaspheme God or curse anyone who **r** over you.
Jdg 13:12 what kind of **r** should govern the boy's life
2Sa 23:3 'The person who **r** righteously, / who **r** in the fear of God,
1Ki 21:18 "Go down to meet King Ahab, who **r** in Samaria.
2Ch 7:18 'You will never fail to have a successor who **r** over
Job 38:33 the laws of the universe and how God **r** the earth?
Ps 2:4 But the one who **r** in heaven laughs. / The Lord
11:4 his holy Temple; / the LORD still **r** from heaven.
22:28 For the LORD is king! / He **r** all the nations.
29:10 The LORD **r** over the floodwaters. / The LORD
66:7 For by his great power he **r** forever. / He watches
89:9 You are the one who **r** the oceans. / When their
103:19 his throne; / from there he **r** over everything.
119:9 By obeying your word and following its **r**.
Jer 23:5 He will be a King who **r** with wisdom. He will do
40:5 Stay there with the people he **r**. But it's up to you;
Eze 38:2 the prince who **r** over the nations of Meshech
Da 4:17 the Most High **r** over the kingdoms of the world
4:25 until you learn that the Most High **r** over the
4:26 back again when you have learned that heaven **r**.
4:32 until you learn that the Most High **r** over the
5:21 until he learned that the Most High God **r** the
Jn 5:16 began harassing Jesus for breaking the Sabbath **r**.
5:18 In addition to disobeying the Sabbath **r**, he had
Ac 23:5 'Do not speak evil of any one who **r** over you.' "
Ro 5:21 to death, now God's wonderful kindness **r** instead,
9:5 who **r** over everything and is worthy of eternal
Col 1:13 For he has rescued us from the one who **r** in the
2:17 For these **r** were only shadows of the real thing,
2:20 So why do you keep on following **r** of the world,
2:22 Such **r** are mere human teaching about things that
2:23 These **r** may seem wise because they require
1Th 4:8 Anyone who refuses to live by these **r** is not disobeying human **r**
2Ti 2:5 Follow the Lord's **r** for doing his work, just as an athlete either follows the **r** or is
Heb 10:21 And since we have a great High Priest who **r** over
13:9 not from ceremonial **r** about food, which don't
Rev 1:6 everlasting glory! He **r** forever and ever! Amen!
17:9 the seven hills of the city where this woman **r**.
17:18 the great city that **r** over the kings of the earth."

RULING (6) [RULE]

1Ki 15:18 the king of Aram, who was **r** in Damascus,
2Ki 23:33 of Hamath to prevent him from **r** from Jerusalem.
2Ch 16:2 who was **r** in Damascus, along with this message:
22:9 of Ahaziah's family was capable of **r** the kingdom.
Job 34:30 He prevents the godless from **r** so they cannot be a
Isa 10:8 my princes will soon be a king, **r** a conquered land.

RUMAH (1)

2Ki 23:36 was Zebidah, the daughter of Pedaiah from **R**.

RUMBLE (3) [RUMBLING, RUMBLINGS]

Jer 47:3 and the **r** of wheels as the chariots rush by.
Na 3:2 Wheels **r**, horses' hooves pound, and chariots
Rev 4:5 came flashes of lightning and the **r** of thunder.

RUMBLING (3) [RUMBLE]

Eze 3:12 lifted me up, and I heard a loud **r** sound behind me.
3:13 each other and the **r** of their wheels beneath them.
Joel 2:5 like the **r** of chariots, like the roar of a fire

RUMBLINGS (1) [RUMBLE]

Ac 6:1 rapidly multiplied, there were **r** of discontent.

RUMOR (6) [RUMORS]

Job 28:22 'We have heard a **r** of where wisdom can be
Jer 51:46 But do not panic when you hear the first **r** of
Eze 7:26 will follow calamity; **r** will follow **r**.
Lk 16:1 but soon a **r** went around that the manager was
Jn 21:23 So the **r** spread among the community of believers

RUMORS (9) [RUMOR]

Ps 31:13 I have heard the many **r** about me, / and I am
Pr 18:8 What dainty morsels **r** are—but they sink deep into
26:22 What dainty morsels **r** are—but they sink deep into
Isa 23:1 it is gone! The **r** you heard in Cyprus are all true.
58:9 making false accusations and spreading vicious **r**!
Jer 18:18 Let's spread **r** about him and ignore what he
20:10 I have heard the many **r** about me. They call me
51:46 For **r** will keep coming year by year.
Ac 21:24 Then everyone will know that the **r** are all false

RUMP (1)

Eze 24:4 the **r** and the shoulder and all the most tender cuts.

RUMP [KJV] See also TAIL

RUN (102) [OUTRAN, OUTRUN, OVERRAN, OVERRUN, RAN, RUNNER, RUNNERS, RUNNING, RUNS]

Ge 15:16 when the sin of the Amorites has **r** its course."
19:17 "**R** for your lives!" the angels warned. "Do not
39:5 All his household affairs began to **r** smoothly,
39:23 making everything **r** smoothly and successfully.
Ex 21:13 I will appoint a place where the slayer can **r** for
25:24 it with pure gold and **r** a molding of gold around it.
26:26 "Make crossbars of acacia wood to **r** across the
26:28 will **r** all the way from one end of the Tabernacle
30:3 and **r** a gold molding around the entire altar.
Lev 26:17 and you will **r** even when no one is chasing you!
26:36 You will **r** as though chased by a warrior with a
Nu 34:4 then **r** south past Scorpion Pass in the direction of
34:7 Mediterranean Sea and **r** eastward to Mount Hor,
34:10 will start at Hazar-enan and **r** south to Shepham,
34:11 From there the boundary will **r** down along the
Jos 8:5 as they did before, and we will **r** away from them.
20:3 person unintentionally can **r** to one of these cities
Jdg 15:5 and let the foxes **r** through the fields of the
20:32 But the Israelites had agreed in advance to **r** away
1Sa 8:11 into his army and make them **r** before his chariots.
17:24 army saw him, they began to **r** away in fright.
25:10 There are lots of servants these days who **r** away
31:4 and kill me before these pagan Philistines **r** me
2Sa 2:18 David's forces that day. Asahel could **r** like a deer,
10:13 his troops attacked, the Arameans began to **r** away.
15:1 and he hired fifty footmen to **r** ahead of him.
17:2 his troops will panic, and everyone will **r** away.
18:3 "If we have to turn and **r**—and even if half of us
18:19 "Let me **r** to the king with the good news that the
22:41 You made them turn and **r**; / I have destroyed all
1Ki 1:5 and recruited fifty men to **r** in front of him.
2Ki 4:26 **R** out to meet her and ask her, 'Is everything all
9:3 Then open the door and **r** for your life!"
1Ch 10:4 and **r** me through before these pagan Philistines
19:14 his troops attacked, the Arameans began to **r** away.
Ezr 7:20 If you **r** short of money for anything necessary for
Ne 6:11 "Should someone in my position **r** away from
Job 20:22 "In the midst of plenty, he will **r** into trouble,
30:1 by young men whose fathers are not worthy to **r**
39:18 But whenever she jumps up to **r**, she passes the
39:22 it is unafraid. It does not **r** from the sword.
Ps 18:40 You made them turn and **r**; / I have destroyed all
19:5 It rejoices like a great athlete / eager to **r** the race.
21:12 For they will turn and **r** / when they see your
65:9 and fertile. / The rivers of God will not **r** dry;
68:1 Let those who hate God **r** for their lives.
74:15 and you dried up rivers that never **r** dry.
102:9 of my food. / My tears **r** down into my drink
119:32 will help me, / I will **r** to follow your commands.
143:9 from my enemies, LORD; / I **r** to you to hide me.
Pr 4:12 by wisdom, you won't limp or stumble as you **r**.
5:8 **R** from her! Don't go near the door of her house!
18:10 is a strong fortress; the godly **r** to him and are safe.
28:1 The wicked **r** away when no one is chasing them,
29:18 people do not accept divine guidance, they **r** wild.
Ecc 1:7 The rivers **r** into the sea, but the sea is never full.
4:6 especially when in the long **r** everything is
5:11 except perhaps to watch it **r** through your fingers!
SS 1:4 Take me with you. Come, let's **r**! Bring me into
2:17 **R** like a gazelle or a young stag on the rugged
Isa 5:27 They will **r** without stopping for rest or sleep.
10:31 And the citizens of Gebim are preparing to **r**.
13:14 Everyone will **r** until exhausted, rushing back to
13:15 Anyone who is captured will be **r** through with a
15:9 both those who try to **r** and those who remain
22:8 You **r** to the armory for your weapons.
28:16 Whoever believes need never **r** away again.
40:31 They will **r** and not grow weary. They will walk
59:7 Their feet **r** to do evil, and they rush to commit
Jer 4:5 '**R** for your lives! Flee to the fortified cities!'
4:29 They hide in the bushes and **r** for the mountains.
5:1 "**R** up and down every street in Jerusalem,"
6:1 "**R** for your lives, you people of Benjamin!
14:17 has been **r** through with a sword and lies mortally
18:14 from the crags of Mount Hermon ever **r** dry?
20:4 to Babylon or **r** them through with the sword.
46:5 The bravest of its fighting men **r** without a
46:21 They turn and **r**, for it is a day of great disaster for
47:3 Terrified fathers **r** madly, without a backward
51:45 **R** from the LORD's fierce anger.
La 1:6 too weak to **r** from the pursuing enemy.
Eze 16:40 a mob to stone you and **r** you through with swords.
47:15 "The northern border will **r** from the
47:16 then it will **r** to Berothah and Sibraim, which are
47:17 So the northern border will **r** from the
Da 11:45 but while he is there, his time will suddenly **r** out,
Hos 2:5 'I'll **r** after other lovers and sell myself to them for
Joel 2:4 They look like tiny horses, and they **r** as fast.
2:9 They swarm over the city and **r** along its walls.
Am 2:16 men will drop their weapons and **r** for their lives.
5:14 Do what is good and **r** from evil—that you may
5:24 a river of righteous living that will never **r** dry.
Jn 10:5 they will **r** from him because they don't recognize
10:12 A hired hand will **r** when he sees a wolf coming.
Ac 27:15 so they gave up and let it **r** before the gale.
Ro 5:3 too, when we **r** into problems and trials,
1Co 6:18 **R** away from sexual sin! No other sin so clearly
9:24 You also must **r** in such a way that you will win.
9:26 So I **r** straight to the goal with purpose in every
1Ti 6:11 so **r** from all these evil things, and follow what is
2Ti 2:22 **R** from anything that stimulates youthful lust.
Heb 12:1 And let us **r** with endurance the race that God has

RUNNER (3) [RUN]

Job 9:25 "My life passes more swiftly than a **r**. It flees
Ecc 9:11 The fastest **r** doesn't always win the race,
Hab 2:2 so that a **r** can read it and tell everyone else.

RUNNERS (1) [RUN]

Am 2:14 Your fastest **r** will not get away. The strongest

RUNNING (40) [RUN]

Ge 16:8 "I am **r** away from my mistress," she replied.
24:17 **R** over to her, the servant asked, "Please give me a
39:14 Soon all the men around the place came **r**.
Ex 11:8 All the officials of Egypt will come **r** to me,
36:33 along each side, **r** from one end to the other.
Dt 21:4 plowed nor planted with a stream **r** through it.
Jos 7:12 That is why the Israelites are **r** from their enemies
8:6 'The Israelites are **r** away from us as they did
19:27 of Iphtah-el, **r** north to Beth-emek and Neiel.
Ru 3:10 now than ever by not **r** after a younger man,
1Sa 14:22 the chase when they saw the Philistines **r** away.
20:36 "Start **r**," he told the boy, "so you can find the
22:17 They knew he was **r** away from me, but they didn't
2Sa 4:4 But she fell and dropped him as she was **r**, and he
10:14 And when the Ammonites saw the Arameans **r**,
18:24 As he looked, he saw a lone man **r** toward them.
18:26 the watchman saw another man **r** toward them.
1Ki 6:3 feet wide, **r** across the entire width of the Temple.
2Ki 5:21 When Naaman saw him **r** after him, he climbed
1Ch 19:15 And when the Ammonites saw the Arameans **r**,
2Ch 3:4 feet wide, **r** across the entire width of the Temple.
23:12 When Athaliah heard the noise of the people **r**
Isa 10:29 of Gibeah—the city of Saul—are **r** for their lives.
22:1 is happening? Why is everyone **r** to the rooftops?
52:12 You will not leave in a hurry, **r** for your lives.
55:5 and they will come **r** to obey, because I,
Jer 2:24 not even need to search, for you come **r** to them!
2:25 Why do you refuse to turn from all this **r** after
8:6 All are **r** down the path of sin as swiftly as a horse
51:31 Messengers from every side come **r** to the king to
Am 8:12 **r** here and going there, but they will not find it.
Jnh 1:10 Then he told them that he was **r** away from the
Na 2:8 someone shouts, but the people just keep on **r**.
Zec 10:8 When I whistle to them, they will come **r**, for I
14:4 making a wide valley **r** from east to west,
Mk 10:17 a man came **r** up to Jesus, knelt down, and asked,
Lk 6:38 together to make room for more, and **r** over.
14:29 you might complete only the foundation before **r**
Ac 2:6 they came **r** to see what it was all about,
Ro 13:11 living is that you know how late it is; time is **r** out.

RUNS (17) [RUN]

Ex 13:17 God did not lead them on the road that **r** through
2Sa 18:27 "The first man **r** like Ahimaaz son of Zadok,"
Pr 20:26 like wheat, then **r** the crushing wheel over them.
Isa 9:1 which lies along the road that **r** between the Jordan
15:9 The stream near Dibon **r** red with blood, but I am
33:3 The enemy **r** at the sound of your voice. When you
Jer 17:3 to your enemies, for sin **r** rampant in your land.
Eze 43:20 upper ledge, and the curb that **r** around that ledge.
47:18 and **r** southward along the Jordan River between
48:1 then **r** on to Hazar-enan on the border of
48:28 The southern border of Gad **r** from Tamar to the
Hos 2:7 When she **r** after her lovers, she won't be able to
Am 5:19 In that day you will be like a man who **r** from a
Lk 10:35 'If his bill **r** higher than that,' he said, 'I'll pay the
Jn 10:13 The hired hand **r** away because he is merely hired
Ac 8:26 "Go south down the desert road that **r** from
1Co 9:24 Remember that in a race everyone **r**, but only one

RURAL (2)

Ne 10:37 Levites who collect the tithes in all our **r** towns.
Est 9:19 **r** Jews living in unwalled villages celebrate an

RUSH (15) [RUSHED, RUSHES, RUSHING]

Ex 14:26 Then the waters will **r** back over the Egyptian

Jdg 21:21 out for their dances, **r** out from the vineyards,
1Sa 15:19 Why did you **r** for the plunder and do exactly what
2Ki 7:15 had thrown away in their mad **r** to escape.
Ne 4:20 blast of the trumpet, **r** to wherever it is sounding.
Job 30:14 all directions. They **r** upon me when I am down.
Pr 1:16 They **r** to commit crimes. They hurry to commit
Isa 17:12 The armies **r** forward like waves thundering
41: 7 The craftsmen **r** to make new idols. The carver
59: 7 feet run to do evil, and they **r** to commit murder.
Jer 47: 3 and the rumble of wheels as the chariots **r** by.
50:16 sword of the enemy and **r** back to their own lands.
Da 12: 4 Many will **r** here and there, and knowledge will
Na 3: 2 Hear the crack of the whips as the chariots **r**
Gal 1:16 to me, I did not **r** out to consult with anyone else;

RUSHED (35) [RUSH]

Ge 19:14 So Lot **r** out to tell his daughters' fiancés, "Quick,
19:16 two daughters and **r** them to safety outside the city,
24:30 and when he heard her story, he **r** out to the spring,
29:13 he **r** out to meet him and greeted him warmly.
31:31 "I **r** away because I was afraid," Jacob answered.
Ex 2: 8 So the girl **r** home and called the baby's mother.
12:39 because the people were **r** out of Egypt
15:19 chariots, and charioteers **r** into the sea,
Nu 16:25 and **r** over to the tents of Dathan and Abiram,
25: 8 and **r** after the man into his tent. Phinehas thrust
Jdg 7:21 and watched as all the Midianites **r** around in a
20:37 Then those who were in hiding **r** in from all sides
1Sa 4:14 Eli asked. The messenger **r** over to Eli,
14:20 and his six hundred men **r** out to the battle
17:52 a great shout of triumph and **r** after the Philistines,
30:17 David and his men **r** in among them
2Sa 3:24 he **r** to see the king. "What have you done?"
19:17 They **r** down to the Jordan to arrive ahead of the
1Ki 1:50 so he **r** to the sacred tent and caught hold of the
2Ki 3:24 the army of Israel **r** out and attacked the Moabites,
7:16 Then the people of Samaria **r** out and plundered
7:17 and trampled to death as the people **r** out.
2Ch 26:20 the other priests saw the leprosy, they **r** him out.
Jer 26:10 they **r** over from the palace and sat down at the
38: 8 so Ebed-melech **r** from the palace to speak with
Am 7:10 was saying, he **r** a message to King Jeroboam:
Hab 3:14 you destroyed those who **r** out like a whirlwind,
Mt 28: 8 and they **r** to find the disciples to give them the
Mk 5:14 as they ran. Everyone **r** out to see for themselves.
16:13 they **r** back to tell the others, but no one believed
Lk 8:29 simply broke them and **r** out into the wilderness,
24: 9 So they **r** back to tell his eleven disciples—
Ac 3:11 They all **r** out to Solomon's Colonnade, where he
7:57 out his voice with their shouts, they **r** at him.
19:29 Everyone **r** to the amphitheater, dragging along

RUSHES (7) [RUSH]

Job 39:24 and **r** forward into battle when the trumpet blows.
40:23 not even when the swelling Jordan **r** down upon it.
41:20 like steam from a boiling pot on a fire of dry **r**.
Isa 14:31 of the north. Each soldier **r** forward ready to fight.
19: 6 of Egypt will become foul with rotting reeds and **r**.
35: 7 and **r** will flourish where desert jackals once lived.
Jer 4:13 Our enemy **r** down on us like a storm wind!

RUSHING (7) [RUSH]

Jdg 5:15 They followed Barak, **r** into the valley.
Ps 39: 6 and all our busy **r** ends in nothing.
Isa 13:14 **r** back to their own lands like hunted deer,
Jer 8: 6 the path of sin as swiftly as a horse **r** into battle!
Eze 43: 2 The sound of his coming was like the roar of **r**
Na 2: 5 their haste, **r** to the walls to set up their defenses.
Rev 9: 9 and their wings roared like an army of chariots **r**

RUSTLE (2) [RUSTLED]

1Ch 16:33 Let the trees of the forest **r** with praise before the
Ps 96:12 with joy! / Let the trees of the forest **r** with praise

RUSTLED (1) [RUSTLE]

Rev 7: 1 Not a leaf **r** in the trees, and the sea became as

RUSTY (2)

Mt 6:19 where they can be eaten by moths and get **r**,
6:20 or **r** and where they will be safe from thieves.

RUTH (26)

Ru 1: 4 named Orpah, and the other a woman named **R**.
1:14 But **R** insisted on staying with Naomi.
1:16 But **R** replied, "Don't ask me to leave you
1:18 So when Naomi saw that **R** had made up her mind
1:22 accompanied by her daughter-in-law **R**, the young
2: 2 One day **R** said to Naomi, "Let me go out into the
2: 3 So **R** went out to gather grain behind the
2: 8 Boaz went over and said to **R**, "Listen,
2:10 **R** fell at his feet and thanked him warmly.
2:15 When **R** went back to work again, Boaz ordered
2:17 So **R** gathered barley there all day, and when she
2:18 **R** also gave her the food that was left over from
2:19 So **R** told her mother-in-law about the man in
2:21 Then **R** said, "What's more, Boaz even told me to
2:23 So **R** worked alongside the women in Boaz's fields
3: 1 One day Naomi said to **R**, "My daughter, it's time
3: 5 "I will do everything you say," **R** replied.
3: 7 Then **R** came quietly, uncovered his feet, and lay
3: 9 he demanded. "I am your servant **R**," she replied.
3:14 So **R** lay at Boaz's feet until the morning, but she
3:16 When **R** went back to her mother-in-law,
3:16 **R** told Naomi everything Boaz had done for her,
4: 5 land from Naomi also requires that you marry **R**,
4:10 And with the land I have acquired **R**, the Moabite
4:13 So Boaz married **R** and took her home to live with
Mt 1: 5 Boaz was the father of Obed (his mother was **R**).

RUTHLESS (9) [RUTHLESSLY]

Ex 1:14 They were **r** with the Israelites, forcing them to
Lev 25:43 never exercise your power over them in a **r** way.
Job 6:23 Have I asked you to save me from **r** people?
Isa 25: 3 will declare your glory; **r** nations will revere you.
25: 4 For the oppressive acts of **r** people are like a storm
25: 5 So the boastful songs of **r** people are stilled.
29: 5 your **r** enemies will be driven away like chaff
Eze 7:24 I will bring the most **r** of nations to occupy their
30:11 He and his armies—**r** among the nations—

RUTHLESSLY (3) [RUTHLESS]

Lev 25:53 foreigner to treat any of your Israelite relatives **r**.
Jdg 4: 3 **r** oppressed the Israelites for twenty years.
Jer 22:17 the innocent, oppress the poor, and reign **r**."

S

SABACHTHANI (2)

Mt 27:46 *"Eli, Eli, lema s?"* which means, "My God,
Mk 15:34 *"Eloi, Eloi, lema s?"* which means, "My God,

SABAOTH [KJV] See ALMIGHTY

SABBATH (144) [SABBATHS]

Ex 16:23 tomorrow as a day of rest, a holy **S** to the LORD.
16:25 your food for today, for today is a **S** to the LORD.
16:26 the food for six days, but the seventh day is a **S**.
16:27 to gather food, even though it was the **S** day.
16:29 given them the seventh day, the **S**, as a day of rest?
16:29 On the **S** day you must stay in your places.
20: 8 "Remember to observe the **S** day by keeping it
20:11 That is why the LORD blessed the **S** day and set
31:13 "Tell the people of Israel to keep my **S** day,
31:13 for the **S** is a sign of the covenant between me
31:14 Yes, keep the **S** day, for it is holy. Anyone who
31:15 anyone who works on the **S** must be put to death.
31:16 The people of Israel must keep the **S** day forever.
34:21 set aside for work, but on the **S** day you must rest,
Lev 16:31 It will be a **S** day of total rest, and you will spend
19: 3 and you must always observe my **S** days of rest,
19:30 "Keep my **S** days of rest and show reverence
23: 3 It is the LORD's **S** day of complete rest, a holy
23: 4 In addition to the **S**, the LORD has established
23:11 On the day after the **S**, the priest will lift it up
23:15 "From the day after the **S**, the day the bundle of
23:16 Keep counting until the day after the seventh **S**,
23:32 This will be a **S** day of total rest for you, and on
23:38 in addition to the LORD's regular **S** days.
24: 8 Every **S** day this bread must be laid out before the
25: 2 the land itself must observe a **S** to the LORD
25: 4 but during the seventh year the land will enjoy a **S**
25: 6 the produce that grows naturally during the **S** year.
25: 8 "In addition, you must count off seven **S** years,
26: 2 You must keep my **S** days of rest and show
26:34 Then at last the land will make up for its missed **S**
26:43 And the land will enjoy its years of **S** rest as it lies
Nu 15:32 they caught a man gathering wood on the **S** day.
28: 9 "On the **S** day, sacrifice two one-year-old male
28:10 whole burnt offering to be presented each **S** day,
Dt 5:12 " 'Observe the **S** day by keeping it holy,
5:15 God has commanded you to observe the **S** day.
2Ki 4:23 "It is neither a new moon festival nor a **S**."
11: 5 A third of you who are on duty on the **S** are to
11: 7 The other two units who are off duty on the **S** must
11: 9 took charge of the men reporting for duty that **S**,
16:18 constructed inside the palace for use on the **S** day,
1Ch 9:32 the bread to be set on the table each **S** day.
23:31 that were presented to the LORD on **S** days,
2Ch 23: 4 the priests and Levites come on duty on the **S**,
23: 8 took charge of the men reporting for duty that **S**,
31: 3 as well as for the weekly **S** festivals and monthly
36:21 The land finally enjoyed its **S** rest, lying desolate
Ne 9:14 them concerning the laws of your holy **S**.
10:31 or grain to be sold on the **S** or on any other holy
13:15 One **S** day I saw some men of Judah treading their
13:15 I rebuked them for selling their produce on the **S**.
13:16 They were selling it on the **S** to the people of
13:17 "Why are you profaning the **S** in this evil way?
13:18 by permitting the **S** to be desecrated in this way!"
13:19 Friday evening, not to be opened until the **S** ended.
13:19 no merchandise could be brought in on the **S** day.
13:21 And that was the last time they came on the **S**.
13:22 the gates in order to preserve the holiness of the **S**.
Isa 1:13 Your celebrations of the new moon and the **S** day,
56: 2 Blessed are those who honor my **S** days of rest by
56: 4 For I say this to the eunuchs who keep my **S** days
56: 6 worship him and do not desecrate the **S** day of rest,
58:13 "Keep the **S** day holy. Don't pursue your own
58:13 but enjoy the **S** and speak of it with delight as the
Jer 17:21 on your trade at Jerusalem's gates on the **S** day.
17:22 Do not do your work on the **S**, but make it a holy
17:24 do not carry on your trade or work on the **S** day,
17:27 do not listen to me and refuse to keep the **S** holy,
17:27 and if on the **S** day you bring loads of merchandise
La 2: 6 out all memory of the holy festivals and **S** days.
Eze 20:12 And I gave them my **S** days of rest as a sign
20:13 And they also violated my **S** days. So I threatened
20:16 ignored my will for them, and violated my **S** days.
20:20 and keep my **S** days holy, for they are a sign to
20:21 given them life. And they also violated my **S** days.
20:24 They scorned my instructions by violating my **S**
22: 8 my holy things and violate my **S** days of rest.
22:26 They disregard my **S** days so that my holy name is
23:38 they defiled my Temple and violated my **S** day!
44:24 and they will see to it that the **S** is set apart as a
45:17 the new moon celebrations, the **S** days, and all
46: 1 but it will be open on **S** days and the days of new
46: 3 the LORD in front of this gateway on **S** days
46: 4 "Each **S** day the prince will present to the LORD
46:12 and he will offer his sacrifices just as he does on **S**
Hos 2:11 her new moon celebrations, and her **S** days—
Am 8: 5 You can't wait for the **S** day to be over
Mt 12: 1 was walking through some grainfields on the **S**.
12: 2 the law to work by harvesting grain on the **S**."
12: 5 priests on duty in the Temple may work on the **S**?
12: 8 For I, the Son of Man, am master even of the **S**."
12:10 "Is it legal to work by healing on the **S** day?"
12:11 you had one sheep, and it fell into a well on the **S**,
12:12 than a sheep! Yes, it is right to do good on the **S**."
24:20 that your flight will not be in winter or on the **S**.
Mk 1:21 and every **S** day he went into the synagogue
2:23 One **S** day as Jesus was walking through some
2:24 the law to work by harvesting grain on the **S**."
2:27 said to them, "The **S** was made to benefit people,
and not people to benefit the **S**.
2:28 And I, the Son of Man, am master even of the **S**!"
3: 2 Since it was the **S**, Jesus' enemies watched him
3: 2 Would he heal the man's hand on the **S**? If he did,
3: 4 and asked, "Is it legal to do good deeds on the **S**,
6: 2 The next **S** he began teaching in the synagogue,
15:42 the day of preparation, the day before the **S**.
16: 1 when the **S** ended, Mary Magdalene and Salome
Lk 4:16 he went as usual to the synagogue on the **S**
4:31 and taught there in the synagogue every **S** day.
6: 1 One **S** day as Jesus was walking through some
6: 2 the law to work by harvesting grain on the **S**."
6: 5 "I, the Son of Man, am master even of the **S**."
6: 6 On another **S** day, a man with a deformed right
6: 7 to see whether Jesus would heal the man on the **S**,
6: 9 Is it legal to do good deeds on the **S**, or is it a day
13:10 One **S** day as Jesus was teaching in a synagogue,
13:14 indignant that Jesus had healed her on the **S** day.
13:14 "Come on those days to be healed, not on the **S**."
13:15 "You hypocrite! You work on the **S** day!
13:15 your ox or your donkey from their stalls on the **S**
13:16 Wasn't it necessary for me, even on the **S** day,
14: 1 One **S** day Jesus was in the home of a leader of the
14: 3 is it permitted in the law to heal people on the **S**
14: 5 and asked, "Which of you doesn't work on the **S**?
23:54 Friday afternoon, the day of preparation for the **S**.
23:56 But by the time they were finished it was the **S**,
Jn 5: 9 But this miracle happened on the **S** day.
5:10 man who was cured, "You can't work on the **S**!
5:16 began harassing Jesus for breaking the **S** rules.
5:18 In addition to disobeying the **S** rules, he had
7:21 "I worked on the **S** by healing a man,
7:22 But you work on the **S**, too, when you obey
7:23 time for circumcising your son falls on the **S**,
7:23 for making a man completely well on the **S**?
9:14 as it happened, Jesus had healed the man on a **S**.
9:16 Jesus is not from God, for he is working on the **S**."
19:31 which was the **S** (and a very special **S** at that,
Ac 13:14 On the **S** they went to the synagogue for the
13:27 though they hear the prophets' words read every **S**.
15:21 in every city on every **S** for many generations."
16:13 On the **S** we went a little way outside the city to a
18: 4 Each **S** found Paul at the synagogue, trying to

SABBATHS (6) [SABBATH]

Lev 26:34 Then the land will finally rest and enjoy its **S**.
2Ch 2: 4 offerings each morning and evening, on the **S**,
8:13 Extra sacrifices were offered on the **S**, on new
Ne 10:33 for the offerings on the **S**, the new moon
Ac 17: 2 and for three **S** in a row he interpreted the
Col 2:16 certain holy days or new-moon ceremonies or **S**.

SABEANS (2)

Job 1:15 when the **S** raided us. They stole all the animals
Isa 45:14 Ethiopians, and **S** will be subject to you.

SABTAH (2)

Ge 10: 7 Cush were Seba, Havilah, **S**, Raamah, and Sabteca.
1Ch 1: 9 Cush were Seba, Havilah, **S**, Raamah, and Sabteca.

SABTECA (2)

Ge 10: 7 Cush were Seba, Havilah, Sabtah, Raamah, and **S**.
1Ch 1: 9 Cush were Seba, Havilah, Sabtah, Raamah, and **S**.

SACAR (1)

1Ch 26: 4 Joah (the third), **S** (the fourth), Nethanel (the fifth),

SACHET (1)

SS 1:13 My lover is like a s of myrrh lying between my

SACK (10) [SACKCLOTH, SACKED, SACKS]

Ge 42:25 to return each brother's payment at the top of his s.
42:27 and one of them opened his s to get some grain to
42:27 to feed the donkeys, he found his money in the s.
42:28 "My money is here in my s!" They were filled
44: 1 and put each man's money back into his s.
44: 2 silver cup at the top of the youngest brother's s,
44:12 servant began searching the oldest brother's s,
44:12 the youngest. The cup was found in Benjamin's s!
44:16 and our brother who had your cup in his s."
2Ki 4:42 brought the man of God a s of fresh grain

SACKBUT [KJV] See LYRE

SACKCLOTH (39) [CLOTH, SACK]

Ge 37:34 Then Jacob tore his clothes and put on s.
Lev 11:32 the object is made of wood, cloth, leather, or s.
2Sa 3:31 were with him, "Tear your clothes and put on s.
21:10 spread s on a rock and stayed there the entire
1Ki 20:31 So let's humble ourselves by wearing s and putting
20:32 So they put on s and ropes and went to the king of
21:27 he tore his clothing, dressed in s, and fasted.
21:27 He even slept in s and went about in deep
2Ki 6:30 the people could see that he was wearing s
19: 1 he tore his clothes and put on s and went into the
19: 2 and the leading priests, all dressed in s,
1Ch 21:16 and the leaders of Israel put on s to show their
Ne 9: 1 This time they fasted and dressed in s
Est 4: 1 he tore his clothes, put on s and ashes, and went
4: 3 and wailed, and many people lay in s and ashes.
4: 4 She sent clothing to him to replace the s, but he
Job 16:15 Here I sit in s. I have surrendered, and I sit in the
Ps 69:11 When I dress in s to show sorrow, / they make fun
Isa 3:24 They will wear rough s instead of rich robes.
15: 3 They will wear s as they wander the streets.
22:12 and to wear clothes of s to show your remorse.
32:11 off your pretty clothes, and wear s in your grief.
37: 1 he tore his clothes and put on s and went into the
37: 2 and the leading priests, all dressed in s,
58: 5 You dress in s and cover yourselves with ashes.
Jer 6:26 Now my people, dress yourselves in s, and sit
48:37 slash their hands and put on clothes made of s.
La 2:10 Jerusalem sit on the ground in silence, clothed in s.
Eze 7:18 They will dress themselves in s; horror and shame
27:31 in grief because of you and dress themselves in s.
Da 9: 3 I wore rough s and sprinkled myself with ashes.
Joel 1:13 Dress yourselves in s, you priests! Wail, you who
1:13 Come, spend the night in s, you ministers of my
Jnh 3: 5 go without food and wear s to show their sorrow.
3: 6 He dressed himself in s and sat on a heap of ashes.
3: 8 Everyone is required to wear s and pray earnestly
Mt 11:21 clothed in s and throwing ashes on their heads to
Lk 10:13 clothed in s and throwing ashes on their heads to
Rev 11: 3 and they will be clothed in s and will prophesy

SACKED (1) [SACK]

Isa 13:16 Their homes will be s and their wives raped by the

SACKS (10) [SACK]

Ge 42:25 then ordered his servants to fill the men's s with
42:35 As they emptied out the s, there at the top of each
43:12 Take double the money that you found in your s,
43:18 because of the money returned to us in our s,"
43:21 we stopped for the night and opened our s,
43:21 we had used to pay for the grain was there in our s.
43:22 We have no idea how the money got into our s."
44: 1 "Fill each of their s with as much grain as they can
44: 8 we bring back the money we found in our s?
44:11 They quickly took their s from the backs of their

SACRED (179)

Ex 16:33 Then store it in a s place as a reminder for all
25: 8 "I want the people of Israel to build me a s
25:10 a s chest 3-3/4 feet long, 2-1/4 feet wide, and 2-1/4
26: 9 is to be doubled over at the entrance of the s tent.
26:36 from fine linen for the entrance of the s tent,
28:38 regarding the s offerings of the people of Israel.
29:29 "Aaron's s garments must be preserved for his
29:31 ordination ceremony, and boil its meat in a s place.
34:13 smash the s pillars they worship, and cut down
35:11 including the s tent and its coverings, the clasps,
35:19 the s garments for Aaron and his sons to wear
36:37 made another curtain for the entrance to the s tent.
37:29 Then he made the s oil for anointing the priests
39: 1 This same cloth was used for Aaron's s garments,
39:30 they made the s medallion of pure gold to be worn
39:33 the s tent with all its furnishings, the clasps,
39:38 the curtain for the entrance of the s tent;
Lev 5:15 unintentionally defiling the LORD's s property,
6:16 and eaten in a s place within the courtyard of the
6:26 in a s place within the courtyard of the Tabernacle.
6:27 it must be washed off in a s place.
7: 6 and it must be eaten in a s place, for it is most holy.
10:13 It must be eaten in a s place, for it has been given
14:13 then slaughter the lamb there in the s area at the
16: 4 linen turban on his head. These are his s garments.
16: 8 He is to cast s lots to determine which goat will be
16:24 must bathe his entire body with water in a s place,
22: 2 and his sons to treat the s gifts that the Israelites set
22: 3 approach the s food presented by the Israelites,
22: 4 they may not eat the s offerings until they have
22: 6 They must not eat any of the s offerings until they
22: 7 will be clean again and may eat the s offerings.
22:10 a priest's family may ever eat the s offerings,
22:12 she may no longer eat the s offerings.
22:13 priests' families are allowed to eat the s offerings.
22:14 "Anyone who eats the s offerings without
22:15 No one may defile the s offerings brought to the
23: 7 stop their regular work and gather for a s assembly.
23: 8 stop all their regular work to hold a s assembly."
23:21 all your regular work and gather for a s assembly.
23:24 You will call the people to a s assembly—
23:27 must humble yourselves, gather for a s assembly,
23:35 It will begin with a s assembly on the first day,
23:36 you must gather again for a s assembly and present
23:37 Celebrate them by gathering in s assemblies to
24: 9 male descendants, who must eat them in a s place,
26: 1 not make idols or set up carved images, s pillars,
27:23 then give the assessed value of the land as a s
Nu 3: 7 performing their s duties in and around the
3: 8 They will also maintain all the furnishings of the s
4: 4 at the Tabernacle will relate to the most s objects.
4:15 covering the sanctuary and all the s utensils,
4:15 But they must not touch the s objects, or they will
4:19 and not die when they approach the most s objects.
4:20 and look at the s objects for even a moment,
5: 9 All the s gifts that the Israelites bring to a priest
5:10 Each priest may keep the s donations that he
7: 9 since they were required to carry the s objects of
9:17 When the cloud lifted from over the s tent,
10:21 carrying the s objects from the Tabernacle.
18: 2 and your sons as you perform the s duties in front
18: 3 they must be careful not to touch any of the s
18: 5 "You yourselves must perform the s duties within
18: 7 must personally handle all the s service associated
27:21 determine the LORD's will by means of s lots.
28:18 On the first day of the festival you must call a s
33:54 You must distribute the land among the clans by s
33:54 The decision of the s lot is final. In this way,
34:13 you are to divide among yourselves by s lot.
36: 2 the LORD instructed you to divide the land by s
Dt 7: 5 down their pagan altars and shatter their s pillars.
10: 1 and make a s chest of wood to keep them in.
10: 2 Then place the tablets in the s chest—the Ark of
12: 3 Break down their altars and smash their s pillars.
12:26 Take your s gifts and your offerings given to fulfill
16:22 And never set up s pillars for worship,
26:13 'I have taken the s gift from my house and have
31:15 in a pillar of cloud at the entrance to the s tent.
33: 8 "O LORD, you have given the s lots / to your
Jos 6:19 or iron is s to the LORD and must be brought into
14: 2 tribes received their inheritance by means of s lots,
18: 6 Then I will cast s lots in the presence of the
18: 8 and I will assign the land to the tribes by casting s
18:10 Joshua cast s lots in the presence of the LORD to
19:51 s lots in the presence of the LORD at the entrance
21: 8 and pasturelands to the Levites by casting s lots.
21:10 the tribe of Levi, since the s lot fell to them first:
Jdg 8:27 Gideon made a s ephod from the gold and put it in
17: 5 and he made a s ephod and some household idols.
18:14 "There is a shrine here with a s ephod,
18:17 the s ephod, the household idols, and the cast idol.
18:18 When the priest saw the men carrying all the s
18:20 so he took along the s ephod, the household idols,
1Sa 28: 6 either by dreams or by s lots or by the prophets.
1Ki 1:39 the priest took a flask of olive oil from the s tent
1:50 so he rushed to the s tent and caught hold of the
2:28 he ran to the s tent of the LORD and caught hold
2:30 Benaiah went into the s tent of the LORD and
2:34 So Benaiah son of Jehoiada returned to the s tent
8: 4 along with the Tabernacle and all its s utensils,
14:23 They built pagan shrines and set up s pillars
2Ki 3: 2 He at least tore down the s pillar of Baal that his
10:26 They dragged out the s pillar used in the worship
10:27 They broke down the s pillar of Baal and wrecked
12: 4 "Collect all the money brought as a s offering to
12:18 King Joash collected all the s objects that
17:10 They set up s pillars and Asherah poles at the top
18: 4 removed the pagan shrines, smashed the s pillars,
23:14 He smashed the s pillars and cut down the Asherah
1Ch 6:54 and territory assigned by means of s lots to the
6:61 of the half-tribe of Manasseh by means of s lots.
6:62 The descendants of Gershon received by s lots
6:63 The descendants of Merari received by s lots
6:65 were also assigned by means of s lots.
23:29 They were in charge of the s bread that was set out
24: 5 assigned to the various groups by means of s lots
24:31 they were assigned to their duties by means of s
25: 8 their particular term of service by means of s lots,
26:13 for it was all decided by means of s lots.
2Ch 5: 5 along with the special tent and all its s utensils.
14: 3 He smashed the s pillars and cut down the Asherah
31: 1 and Manasseh, and they smashed the s pillars,
Ezr 2:63 the LORD about the matter by means of s lots.
Ne 7:65 the LORD about the matter by means of s lots.
8: 9 For today is a s day before the LORD your God."
8:10 This is a s day before our Lord. Don't be dejected
8:11 "Hush! Don't weep! For this is a s day."
10:34 "We have cast s lots to determine when—
10:39 and place them in the s containers near the
11: 1 and Benjamin were chosen by s lots to live there,
Ps 46: 4 the city of our God, / the s home of the Most High.
66:14 yes, the s vows you heard me make / when I was in
81: 3 Sound the trumpet for a s feast / when the moon is
105:42 For he remembered his s promise / to Abraham his
Isa 1:29 offered sacrifices to idols in your groves of s oaks.
1:29 of all the sins you committed in your s gardens.
65: 3 to my face by worshiping idols in their s gardens.
66:17 "Those who 'purify' themselves in a s garden,
Jer 17: 2 Even their children go to worship at their s altars
36: 9 This happened on the day of s fasting held in late
43:13 He will break down the s pillars standing in the
La 1:10 She has seen foreigners violate her s Temple,
4: 1 The s gemstones lie scattered in the streets!
Eze 36:38 I will multiply them like the s flocks that fill
43: 9 and the s pillars erected to honor their kings,
44: 8 kept the laws I gave you concerning these s rituals,
44:19 They must leave them in the s rooms and put on
44:24 obey my instructions and laws at all the s festivals,
45: 3 Within the larger s area, measure out a portion of
45: 5 The strip of s land next to it, also 8-1/3 miles long
45: 6 "Adjacent to the larger s area will be a section of
45: 7 will share a border with the east side of the s lands
46:11 "So at the special feasts and s festivals, the grain
46:19 and led me to the s rooms assigned to the priests,
48:12 when the land is distributed, the most s land of all.
48:15 south of the s Temple area, will be allotted for
48:18 miles to the west along the border of the s area.
48:20 entire area—including the s lands and the city—
48:21 to the east and to the west of the s lands
48:22 except for the areas set aside for the s lands
Da 1: 2 he took with him some of the s objects from the
7:25 He will try to change their s festivals and laws,
Mic 1: 7 to pieces. All her s treasures will be burned up.
5:13 I will destroy all your idols and s pillars, so you
Zec 14:20 will be as s as the basins used beside the altar.
Mt 5:34 it is a s vow because heaven is God's throne.
5:35 it is a s vow because the earth is his footstool.
23:17 the gold, or the Temple that makes the gold s?
23:19 gift on the altar, or the altar that makes the gift s?
Mk 16: S himself sent them out from east to west with the s
Lk 1:72 by remembering his s covenant with them,
Ac 13:34 'I will give you the s blessings I promised to
1Co 9:17 But God has chosen me and given me this s trust,
1Ti 1: 9 who consider nothing s and defile what is holy,
2Ti 3: 2 and ungrateful. They will consider nothing s.
Heb 8: 2 There he ministers in the s tent, the true place of
9: 1 regulations for worship and a s tent here on earth.
9:21 he sprinkled blood on the s tent and on everything
10:20 Christ has opened up for us through the s curtain,

SACRIFICE (172) [SACRIFICED, SACRIFICES, SACRIFICIAL, SACRIFICING]

Ge 7: 2 animal that I have approved for eating and for s,
7: 8 approved for eating and s and those that were not—
8:21 And the LORD was pleased with the s and said to
22: 2 S him there as a burnt offering on one of the
22: 7 said the boy, "but where is the lamb for the s?"
22:10 and lifted it up to kill his son as a s to the LORD.
31:54 Then Jacob presented a s to God and invited
Ex 8:29 and refuse to let the people go to s to the
12: 3 family must choose a lamb or a young goat for a s.
23:15 Everyone must bring me a s at that time.
24: 5 Then he sent some of the young men to s young
29:36 Each day you must s a young bull as an offering
32: 6 So the people got up early the next morning to s
34:25 "You must not offer bread made with yeast as a s
Lev 1: 3 "If your s for a whole burnt offering is from the
1: 9 Then the priests will burn the entire s on the altar.
1:10 "If your s for a whole burnt offering is from the
1:12 and the priests will lay the pieces of the s,
1:13 Then the priests will burn the entire s on the altar.
6:22 offering this same s on the day they are anointed.
6:26 The priest who offers the s may eat his portion in a
7:12 the usual animal s must be accompanied by various
7:18 It will have no value as a s, and you will receive no
12: 8 The priest will s them, thus making atonement for
16:24 and go out to s his own whole burnt offering
17: 8 If you offer a whole burnt offering or a s
18:21 "Do not give any of your children as a s to
19: 5 "When you s a peace offering to the LORD,
22:25 from foreigners to be offered as a s to your God.
23:12 That same day you must s a year-old male lamb
23:13 Along with this s, you must also offer one quart of
Nu 6:18 and put it on the fire beneath the peace-offering s.
9:11 They must offer the Passover s one month later,
15: 3 the s must be an animal from your flocks of sheep
15: 3 a s to fulfill a vow, a freewill offering,
15: 3 or a special s at any of the annual festivals,
15: 6 "If the s is a ram, give three quarts of choice flour
15: 7 This s will be very pleasing to the LORD.
15: 8 or a s in fulfillment of a special vow or as a peace
23: 1 prepare seven young bulls and seven rams for a s."
23:29 me seven young bulls and seven rams for a s."
28: 9 s two one-year-old male lambs with no physical
28:14 You must also give a drink offering with each s:
28:31 Be sure that all the animals you s have no physical
29: 5 you must s a male goat as a sin offering,
29:11 You must also s one male goat for a sin offering.
29:16 You must also s a male goat as a sin offering,
29:17 s twelve young bulls, two rams, and fourteen
29:19 You must also s a male goat as a sin offering,
29:20 day of the festival, s eleven young bulls, two rams,
29:22 You must also s a male goat as a sin offering,
29:23 day of the festival, s ten young bulls, two rams,
29:25 You must also s a male goat as a sin offering,
29:26 day of the festival, s nine young bulls, two rams,
29:28 You must also s a male goat as a sin offering,
29:29 day of the festival, s eight young bulls, two rams,
29:31 You must also s a male goat as a sin offering,
29:32 day of the festival, s seven young bulls, two rams,
29:34 You must also s one male goat as a sin offering,
29:38 You must also s one male goat as a sin offering,
Dt 12:13 Be careful not to s your burnt offerings just

15:21 with it, you must not s it to the LORD your God.
16: 2 Your Passover s may be from either the flock
16: 6 S it there as the sun goes down on the anniversary
17: 1 "Never s a sick or defective ox or sheep to the
18:10 never s your son or daughter as a burnt offering.
27: 7 S peace offerings on it also, and feast there with
Jdg 6:26 S the bull as a burnt offering on the altar, using as
6:28 had been built, and it had the remains of a s on it.
11:31 I return in triumph. I will s it as a burnt offering."
13:16 you may prepare a burnt offering as a s to the
13:19 and offered it on a rock as a s to the LORD.
1Sa 1: 3 and s to the LORD Almighty at the Tabernacle.
1: 4 On the day Elkanah presented his s, he would give portions of the s to Peninnah
1:21 on their annual trip to offer a s to the LORD.
1:24 They brought along a three-year-old bull for the s
2:13 Whenever anyone offered a s, Eli's sons would
2:16 The man offering the s might reply, "Take as
2:19 to him when she came with her husband for the s.
9:12 He has just arrived to take part in a public s up on
9:19 "Go on up the hill ahead of me to the place of s,
10: 8 I will join you there to s burnt offerings and peace
15:15 "But they are going to s them to the LORD your
15:21 and plunder to s to the LORD your God in
15:22 to his voice? Obedience is far better than s.
16: 2 "and say that you have come to make a s to the
16: 3 Invite Jesse to the s, and I will show you which of
16: 5 Samuel replied. "I have come to s to the LORD.
16: 5 Purify yourselves and come with me to the s."
20: 6 to go home to Bethlehem for an annual family s.
20:29 He wanted to take part in a family s. His brother
2Sa 6:13 they stopped and waited so David could s an ox
15: 7 "Let me go to Hebron to offer a s to the LORD in
15: 8 I promised to s to him in Hebron if he would bring
24:23 and may the LORD your God accept your s."
1Ki 13: 1 as Jeroboam was approaching the altar to offer a s.
13: 2 On you he will s the priests from the pagan shrines
18:29 raved all afternoon until the time of the evening s,
18:36 At the customary time for offering the evening s,
2Ki 3:20 the next day at about the time when the morning s
10:19 for I am going to offer a great s to Baal.
23:10 so no one could ever again use it to s a son
1Ch 28:13 Temple which were to be used for worship and s.
2Ch 2: 4 and to s burnt offerings each morning and evening,
7: 5 King Solomon offered a s of 22,000 oxen
28:23 of Aram, so they will help me, too, if I s to them."
29:21 to s the animals on the altar of the LORD.
Ezr 3: 2 God of Israel so they could s burnt offerings on it,
3: 3 Then they immediately began to s burnt offerings
3: 6 the priests had begun to s burnt offerings to the
9: 4 utterly appalled until the time of the evening s.
9: 5 At the time of the s, I stood up from where I had
Ps 50:13 I don't need the bulls you s; / I don't need the
50:23 But giving thanks is a s that truly honors me.
51:17 The s you want is a broken spirit. / A broken
54: 6 I will s a voluntary offering to you; / I will praise
56:12 O God, / and offer a s of thanks for your help.
66:15 And I will s bulls and goats. / *Interlude*
116:17 I will offer you a s of thanksgiving / and call on the
118:27 Bring forward the s and put it on the altar.
Pr 15: 8 The LORD hates the s of the wicked, but he
21:27 God loathes the s of an evil person,
Isa 34: 6 used for killing lambs and goats and rams for a s.
34: 6 the LORD will offer a great s in the rich city of
40:16 fuel to consume a s large enough to honor him.
66: 3 When such people s an ox, it is no more acceptable than a human s.
66: 3 When they s a lamb or bring an offering of grain,
Jer 7:31 where they s their little sons and daughters in the
32:35 and there they s their sons and daughters to
44:17 of Heaven and s to her just as much as we like—
46:10 will receive a s today in the north country beside
Eze 16:19 You set before them as a lovely s the fine flour
43:22 s as a sin offering a young male goat that has no
43:27 the priests will s on the altar the burnt offerings
45:18 s a young bull with no physical defects to purify
46:15 and the olive oil must be given as a daily s every
Da 9:21 came swiftly to me at the time of the evening s.
12:11 "From the time the daily s is taken away
Hos 8:13 The people of Israel love their rituals of s, but to
9: 4 you will not be allowed to pour out wine as a s to
12:11 And in Gilgal, too, they s bulls; their altars are
13: 2 "S to these," they cry, "and kiss the calf idols!"
14: 2 receive us, so that we may offer you the s of praise.
Jnh 1:16 and they offered him a s and vowed to serve him.
Mic 6: 7 Should we s our firstborn children to pay for the
Hag 2:12 If one of you is carrying a holy s in his robes
Mt 5:23 before the altar in the Temple, offering a s to God,
5:24 leave your s there beside the altar. Go and be
5:24 to that person. Then come and offer your s to God.
Lk 2:24 So they offered a s according to what was required
Ac 14:13 and they prepared to s to the apostles at the city
Ro 8: 3 over us by giving his Son as a s for our sins.
12: 1 Let them be a living and holy s—the kind he will
15:16 and offer you up as a fragrant s to God so that you
Eph 5: 2 and gave himself as a s to take away your sins.
5: 2 because that s was like sweet perfume to him.
Php 2:17 to complete the s of your faithful service (that is,
4:18 They are a sweet-smelling s that is acceptable to
Heb 2:17 then could offer a s that would take away the sins
9:14 Christ offered himself to God as a perfect s for our
9:28 so also Christ died only once as a s to take away
10:10 the s of the body of Jesus Christ once for all time.
10:12 Priest offered himself to God as one s for sins,
10:26 there is no other s that will cover these sins.
11:17 It was by faith that Abraham offered Isaac as a s
11:17 God's promises, was ready to s his only son, Isaac,
13:11 blood of animals into the Holy Place as a s for sin,
13:15 let us continually offer our s of praise to God by
1Jn 2: 2 He is the s for our sins. He takes away not only our
4:10 and sent his Son as a s to take away our sins.

SACRIFICED (67) [SACRIFICE]

Ge 8:20 built an altar to the LORD and s on it the animals
22:13 and s it as a burnt offering on the altar in place of
Ex 32: 8 like a calf, and they have worshiped and s to it.
Lev 4:10 is done with the bull or cow s as a peace offering.
5:16 he will make atonement for them with the ram s as
7: 2 The animal s as a guilt offering must be
7: 7 the meat of the s animal belongs to the priest in
7: 8 the hide of the s animal also belongs to the priest.
7:14 sprinkles the altar with blood from the s animal.
16: 8 to determine which goat will be s to the LORD
16: 9 The goat chosen to be s to the LORD will be
22:29 it must be s properly so it will be accepted on your
Nu 22:40 where the king s cattle and sheep. He sent portions
23: 2 and the two of them s a young bull and a ram on
23: 4 and have s a young bull and a ram on each altar."
28: 4 One lamb will be s in the morning and the other in
Dt 16: 2 and it must be s to the LORD your God at the
1Sa 2:13 While the meat of the s animal was still boiling,
6:14 and s them to the LORD as a burnt offering.
13: 9 And Saul s the burnt offering himself.
2Sa 6:17 And David s burnt offerings and peace offerings to
1Ki 1: 9 where he s sheep, oxen, and fattened calves.
1:19 He has s many oxen, fattened calves, and sheep,
1:25 Today he has s many oxen, fattened calves,
3: 2 At that time the people of Israel s their offerings at
3: 4 king went there and s one thousand burnt offerings.
3:15 where he s burnt offerings and peace offerings.
8: 5 and the entire community of Israel s sheep
8:63 Solomon s peace offerings to the LORD
2Ki 3:27 and s him as a burnt offering on the wall.
17:17 They even s their own sons and daughters in the
21: 6 Manasseh even s his own son in the fire.
1Ch 15:26 they s seven bulls and seven lambs.
16: 1 and they s burnt offerings and peace offerings
16:40 They s the regular burnt offerings to the LORD
21:26 and s burnt offerings and peace offerings.
2Ch 1: 6 and s a thousand burnt offerings on it.
5: 6 and the entire community of Israel s sheep
8:12 Then Solomon s burnt offerings to the LORD on
15:11 On that day they s to the LORD some of the
24:14 And the burnt offerings were s continually in the
30:22 Peace offerings were s, and the people confessed
33: 6 Manasseh even s his own sons in the fire in the
33:16 and s peace offerings and thanksgiving offerings
33:17 However, the people still s at the pagan shrines,
33:22 and s to all the idols his father had made.
34: 4 and scattered over the graves of those who had s to
35:16 All the burnt offerings were s on the altar of the
Ezr 3: 5 Freewill offerings were also s to the LORD by the
4: 2 We have s to him ever since King Esarhaddon of
6:17 two hundred rams, and four hundred lambs were s.
8:35 Then the exiles who had returned from captivity s
Ps 51:19 and bulls will again be s on your altar.
106:37 They even s their sons / and their daughters to the
Jer 51:40 lambs to the slaughter, like rams and goats to be s.
Eze 16:20 you had borne to me—and s them to your gods.
43:25 and a ram from the flock will be s as a sin offering.
46:13 must be s as a burnt offering to the LORD.
Mk 14:12 Bread (the day the Passover lambs were s),
Lk 22: 7 Bread arrived, when the Passover lambs were s.
Ac 7:41 and they s to it and rejoiced in this thing they had
15:20 and tell them to abstain from eating meat s to idols,
1Co 5: 7 Christ, our Passover Lamb, has been s for us.
8: 1 Now let's talk about food that has been s to idols.
8: 4 Should we eat meat that has been s to idols?
13: 3 everything I have to the poor and even s my body,
Heb 7:27 But Jesus did this once for all when he s himself on

SACRIFICES (197) [SACRIFICE]

Ge 46: 1 he offered s to the God of his father, Isaac.
Ex 3:18 the wilderness to offer s to the LORD our God.'
5: 3 so we can offer s to the LORD our God.
5: 8 going into the wilderness to offer s to their God.
5:17 'Let us go, so we can offer s to the LORD.'
8: 8 the people go, so they can offer s to the LORD."
8:25 Go ahead and offer s to your God," he said.
8:26 The Egyptians would detest the s that we offer to
8:27 the wilderness to offer s to the LORD our God,
8:28 "I will let you go to offer s to the LORD your
10:25 "we must take our flocks and herds for s and burnt
10:26 We will have to choose our s for the LORD our
10:26 And we won't know which s he will require until
18:12 presented a burnt offering and gave s to God.
20:24 Offer on such altars your s to me—your burnt
22:20 "Anyone who s to any god other than the LORD
38: 1 The altar for burning animal s also was constructed
Lev 7:21 and then eats meat from the LORD's s,
9:15 Next Aaron presented the s for the people.
14:32 but who cannot afford to bring the s normally
17: 3 If any Israelite s a bull or a lamb or a goat
17: 5 It will cause them to bring their s to the priest at
17: 7 by offering s to evil spirits out in the fields.
Nu 6:14 and offer these s to the LORD: a one-year-old
25: 2 These women invited them to attend s to their
28:23 offerings in addition to your regular morning s.
29: 6 These special s are in addition to your regular
29:39 These are in addition to the s and offerings you
Dt 12: 6 your s, your tithes, your special gifts,
12:11 your s, your tithes, your special gifts,
12:27 The blood of your other s must be poured out
12:31 burned their sons and daughters as s to their gods.
18: 8 He may eat his share of the s and offerings, even if
32:17 They offered s to demons, non-gods, / to gods they
32:38 now are those gods, / who ate the fat of their s
33:19 to offer proper s there. / They benefit from the
Jos 22:26 So we decided to build the altar, not for burnt s,
22:27 with our burnt offerings, s, and peace offerings.
22:28 It is not for burnt offerings or s; it is a reminder of
22:29 own altar for burnt offerings, grain offerings, or s.
Jdg 2: 5 and they offered s to the LORD.
16:23 offering s and praising their god, Dagon.
1Sa 2:28 to offer s on my altar, to burn incense, and to wear
2:29 So why do you scorn my s and offerings? Why do
3:14 and his sons will never be forgiven by s
6:15 and s were offered to the LORD that day by the
15:22 your burnt offerings and s or your obedience to his
2Sa 15:12 While he was offering the s, he sent for
15:24 Then they offered s there until everyone had
1Ki 3: 3 offered s and burned incense at the local altars.
8:62 and all Israel with him offered s to the LORD.
12:27 When they go to Jerusalem to offer s at the Temple
12:32 There at Bethel he himself offered s to the calves
12:33 Jeroboam offered s on the altar at Bethel.
22:43 and the people still offered s and burned incense
2Ki 5:17 or s to any other god except the LORD.
10:24 So they were all inside the temple to offer s
12: 3 and the people still offered s and burned incense
14: 4 where the people offered s and burned incense.
15: 4 where the people offered s and burned incense.
15:35 where the people offered s and burned incense.
16: 4 He offered s and burned incense at the pagan
16:15 "Use the new altar for the morning s of burnt
16:15 and s should be sprinkled over the new altar.
17:31 burned their own children as s to Adrammelech
17:32 themselves priests to offer s at the pagan shrines.
17:35 bow before them or serve them or offer s to them.
17:36 and bow before him; offer s to him alone.
25:14 and all the other bronze utensils used for making s
1Ch 21:28 he offered s there at Araunah's threshing floor.
23:13 to offer s in the LORD's presence, to serve the
29:21 and many other s on behalf of Israel.
2Ch 2: 6 Temple for him, except as a place to burn s to him?
7: 1 and burned up the burnt offerings and s,
7: 4 the king and all the people offered s to the LORD.
7:12 have chosen this Temple as the place for making s.
8:13 The number of s varied from day to day according
8:13 Extra s were offered on the Sabbaths, on new
11:16 where they could offer s to the LORD, the God of
25:14 down in front of them, and presented s to them!
28: 3 He offered s in the valley of the son of Hinnom,
28: 4 He offered s and burned incense at the pagan
28:23 He offered s to the gods of Damascus who had
28:25 all the towns of Judah for offering s to other gods.
29:31 Now bring your s and thanksgiving offerings to the
29:31 So the people brought their s and thanksgiving
29:33 six hundred bulls and three thousand sheep as s.
32:12 one altar at the Temple and to make s on it alone.
Ezr 2:63 s until there was a priest who could consult the
6: 3 rebuilt on the site where Jews used to offer their s,
6:10 Then they will be able to offer acceptable s to the
Ne 4: 2 can build the wall in a day if they offer enough s?
7:65 s until there was a priest who could consult the
12:43 Many s were offered on that joyous day, for God
Ps 4: 5 Offer proper s, / and trust in the LORD.
16: 4 I will not take part in their s / or even speak the
27: 6 At his Tabernacle I will offer s with shouts of joy,
40: 6 You take no delight in s or offerings. / Now that
50: 5 those who made a covenant with me by giving s."
50: 8 I have no complaint about your s / or the burnt
51:16 You would not be pleased with s, / or I would
51:19 Then you will be pleased with worthy s / and with
106:28 Baal at Peor; / they even ate s offered to the dead!
107:22 Let them offer s of thanksgiving / and sing joyfully
Pr 7:14 "I've offered my s and just finished my vows.
21: 3 do what is just and right than when we give him s.
Isa 1:11 "I am sick of your s," says the LORD.
1:12 parading through my courts with your worthless s?
1:14 I hate all your festivals and s. I cannot stand the
1:29 offered s to idols in your groves of sacred oaks.
19:21 and will give their s and offerings to him.
29: 1 of David. Year after year you offer your many s.
43:23 You have not honored me with s, though I have not
43:24 fragrant incense or pleased me with the fat from s.
56: 7 I will accept their burnt offerings and s,
57: 5 You slaughter your children as human s down in
Jer 6:20 Your s have no sweet fragrance for me."
7:21 says: "Away with your burnt offerings and s!
7:22 was not burnt offerings and s I wanted from them.
11:15 immoral things? Can their s avert their destruction?
17:26 people will come with their burnt offerings and s.
19: 5 to Baal, and there they burn their sons as s to Baal.
33:18 burnt offerings and grain offerings and s to me."
44:25 up your devotion and s to the Queen of Heaven,
48:35 "for they offer s at the pagan shrines and burn
52:18 and all the other bronze utensils used for making s
Eze 16:36 because you have slaughtered your children as s to
20:28 they offered s and incense on every high hill
20:28 They roused my fury as they offered up s to their
20:31 and give your little children to be burned as s,
20:40 bring me all your offerings and choice gifts and s.
21:21 They will inspect the livers of their animal s.
23:37 and murder by burning their children as s on their
40:38 for s was washed before being taken to the altar.
40:41 four outside, where the s were cut up and prepared.
42:13 It is there that the priests who offer s to the
44: 7 as you offered me my food, the fat and blood of s.
44:15 in my presence and offer the fat and blood of the s,

44:29 and **s** brought to the Temple by the people—
45:25 the prince will provide these same **s** for the sin
46:12 and he will offer his **s** just as he does on Sabbath
46:20 They will do it here to avoid carrying the **s** through
46:24 assistants to boil the **s** offered by the people."
Da 2:46 and he commanded his people to offer **s** and burn
8:11 armies by canceling the daily **s** offered to him
8:13 rebellion that causes desecration stop the daily **s**?
9:27 this time, he will put an end to the **s** and offerings.
11:31 the sanctuary, putting a stop to the daily **s**,
Hos 3:4 a king or prince, and without **s**, temple, priests,
4:13 They offer **s** to idols on the tops of mountains.
4:19 will die in shame because they offer **s** to idols.
5:6 their flocks and herds to offer **s** to the LORD.
6:6 I want you to be merciful; I don't want your **s**.
8:13 of sacrifice, but to me their **s** are all meaningless!
9:1 offering **s** to other gods on every threshing floor.
9:4 None of the **s** you offer there will please him.
9:4 Such **s** will be unclean, just as food touched by a
9:4 All who present such **s** will be defiled. They may
11:2 offering **s** to the images of Baal and burning
Am 4:4 and offer your **s** to the idols at Bethel and Gilgal.
4:4 Offer **s** each morning and bring your tithes every
5:25 "Was it to me you were bringing **s** and offerings
Jnh 2:9 But I will offer **s** to you with songs of praise,
Zec 14:21 will be free to use any of these pots to boil their **s**.
Mal 1:7 "You have despised my name by offering defiled **s**
1:7 "Then you ask, 'How have we defiled the **s**?'
1:8 When you give blind animals as **s**, isn't that
1:10 so that these worthless **s** could not be offered!
1:14 his flock but then **s** a defective one to the Lord.
2:3 splatter your faces with the dung of your festival **s**,
3:3 so that they may once again offer acceptable **s** to
Mt 9:13 'I want you to be merciful; I don't want your **s**.'
12:7 'I want you to be merciful; I don't want your **s**.'
Mk 12:33 of the burnt offerings and **s** required in the law."
Jn 2:14 merchants selling cattle, sheep, and doves for **s**;
Ac 7:42 it is written, / 'Was it to me you were bringing **s**
21:26 and **s** would be offered for each of them.
24:17 with money to aid my people and to offer **s** to God.
1Co 10:18 of Israel; all who eat the **s** are united by that act.
10:19 the idols to whom the pagans bring **s** are real gods
and that these **s** are of some value?
10:20 What I am saying is that these **s** are offered to
Heb 5:1 their gifts to God and offers their **s** for sins.
5:3 That is why he has to offer **s**, both for their sins
7:27 He does not need to offer **s** every day like the other
8:3 every high priest is required to offer gifts and **s**,
9:9 and **s** that the priests offer are not able to cleanse
9:23 purified with far better **s** than the blood of animals.
10:1 The **s** under the old system were repeated again
10:2 perfect cleansing, the **s** would have stopped,
10:3 Those yearly **s** reminded them of their sins year
10:5 "You did not want animal **s** and grain offerings.
10:8 "You did not want animal **s** or grain offerings
10:11 after day, offering **s** that can never take away sins.
10:18 been forgiven, there is no need to offer any more **s**.
13:16 those in need, for such **s** are very pleasing to God.
1Pe 2:5 who offer the spiritual **s** that please him because of

SACRIFICIAL (25) [SACRIFICE]

Ex 18:12 They all joined him in a **s** meal in God's presence.
23:18 "**S** blood must never be offered together with
23:18 And no **s** fat may be left unoffered until the next
Lev 6:27 or anyone who touches the **s** meat will become
6:27 and if the **s** blood splatters anyone's clothing,
6:28 If a clay pot is used to boil the **s** meat, it must be
19:22 the LORD with the **s** ram of the guilt offering,
22:30 Eat the entire **s** animal on the day it is presented.
23:37 and grain offerings, **s** meals and drink offerings—
Nu 15:11 instructions for what is to accompany each **s** bull,
1Sa 2:28 And I assigned the **s** offerings to you priests.
1Ch 28:17 solid gold meat hooks used to handle the **s** meat
2Ch 2:4 spices before him, to display the special **s** bread,
7:7 all the burnt offerings, grain offerings, and **s** fat.
30:16 The Levites brought the **s** blood to the priests,
Isa 22:13 you slaughter **s** animals, feast on meat, and drink
40:16 All Lebanon's **s** animals would not make an
Jer 7:18 children gather wood and the fathers build **s** fires.
Eze 39:17 Say to them: Gather together for my great **s** feast.
39:19 This is the **s** feast I have prepared for you.
40:39 where the **s** animals were slaughtered for the burnt
40:42 and other implements and the **s** animals.
40:43 and set on the tables where the **s** meat was to be
1Co 9:13 who serve at the altar get a share of the **s** offerings.
Heb 9:26 to remove the power of sin forever by his **s** death

SACRIFICING (16) [SACRIFICE]

Ex 34:15 committing adultery against me by **s** to their gods.
Lev 17:5 This rule will stop the Israelites from **s** animals in
1Sa 1:25 After **s** the bull, they took the child to Eli.
7:10 Just as Samuel was **s** the burnt offering,
1Ki 11:8 to use for burning incense and **s** to their gods.
2Ki 10:25 As soon as Jehu had finished **s** the burnt offering,
16:3 the kings of Israel, even **s** his own son in the fire.
2Ch 28:3 the son of Hinnom, even **s** his own sons in the fire.
Ezr 3:4 **s** the burnt offerings specified for each day of the
Ps 66:15 That is why I am **s** burnt offerings to you—
69:31 For this will please the LORD more than **s** an ox
106:38 and daughters. / By **s** them to the idols of Canaan,
Eze 16:21 Must you also slaughter my children by **s** them to
Lk 13:1 Galilee as they were **s** at the Temple in Jerusalem.
Ac 14:18 could scarcely restrain the people from **s** to them.
Ro 3:25 believe that Jesus shed his blood, **s** his life for us.

SACRILEGE (1) [SACRILEGIOUS]

Da 8:12 **s** was committed against the Temple ceremonies,

SACRILEGE [KJV] See also STEAL (FROM PAGAN TEMPLES)

SACRILEGIOUS (5) [SACRILEGE]

Da 9:27 he will set up a **s** object that causes desecration,
11:31 and setting up the **s** object that causes desecration.
12:11 and the **s** object that causes desecration is set up to
Mt 24:15 the **s** object that causes desecration standing in the
Mk 13:14 "The time will come when you will see the **s**

SAD (24) [SADLY, SADNESS]

1Sa 1:8 Why be so **s** just because you have no children?
1:15 But I am very **s**, and I was pouring out my heart to
1:18 and began to eat again, and she was no longer **s**.
2Ch 35:25 and to this day choirs still sing these **s** songs about
Ne 2:1 I had never appeared **s** in his presence before this
2:2 So the king asked me, "Why are you so **s**?
2:3 "Long live the king! Why shouldn't I be **s**?
8:10 Don't be dejected and **s**, for the joy of the LORD
Job 30:31 My harp plays **s** music, and my flute accompanies
Ps 35:14 I was **s**, as though they were my friends or family,
42:5 Why am I discouraged? / Why so **s**? / I will put my
42:11 Why am I discouraged? / Why so **s**? / I will put my
43:5 Why am I discouraged? / Why so **s**? / I will put my
Isa 40:2 Tell her that her **s** days are gone and that her sins
65:13 You will be **s** and ashamed, but they will rejoice.
Eze 27:32 they wail and mourn, they sing this **s** funeral song:
Mt 11:17 so we played funeral songs, but you weren't **s**.'
Lk 7:32 so we played funeral songs, but you weren't **s**.'
18:23 heard this, he became **s** because he was very rich.
Jn 16:6 Instead, you are very **s**.
Ac 20:38 **s** most of all because he had said that they would
Ro 12:15 happy with them. If they are **s**, share their sorrow.
2Co 2:2 For if I cause you pain and make you **s**, who is
2:3 I will not be made **s** by the very ones who ought to

SADDLE (6) [SADDLEBAGS, SADDLED]

Ge 31:34 and had stuffed them into her camel **s**,
Jdg 5:10 fine donkeys / and sit on fancy **s** blankets, listen!
2Sa 19:26 '**S** my donkey so that I can go with the king.'
1Ki 13:13 "Quick, **s** the donkey," the old man said.
13:27 the prophet said to his sons, "**S** a donkey for me."
Eze 27:20 Dedan traded their expensive **s** blankets with you.

SADDLEBAGS (1) [SADDLE]

Jos 9:4 loading their donkeys with weathered **s** and old

SADDLED (9) [SADDLE]

Ge 22:3 He **s** his donkey and took two of his servants with
Nu 22:21 So the next morning Balaam **s** his donkey
Jdg 19:10 So he took his two **s** donkeys and his concubine
2Sa 17:23 So he **s** his donkey, went to his hometown, set his
1Ki 2:40 he **s** his donkey and went to Gath to search for
13:13 And when they had **s** the donkey for him,
13:23 the prophet **s** his own donkey for him,
13:27 "Saddle a donkey for me." So they **s** a donkey,
2Ki 4:24 So she **s** the donkey and said to the servant,

SADDUCEES (14)

Mt 3:7 saw many Pharisees and **S** coming to be baptized,
16:1 and **S** came to test Jesus' claims by asking him to
16:6 "Beware of the yeast of the Pharisees and **S**."
16:11 'Beware of the yeast of the Pharisees and **S**.' "
16:12 but about the false teaching of the Pharisees and **S**.
22:23 That same day some **S** stepped forward—a group
22:34 heard that he had silenced the **S** with his reply,
Mk 12:18 Then the **S** stepped forward—a group of Jews who
Lk 20:27 Then some **S** stepped forward—a group of Jews
Ac 4:1 and some of the **S** came over to them.
5:17 The high priest and his friends, who were **S**,
23:6 that some members of the high council were **S**
23:7 divided the council—the Pharisees against the **S**—
23:8 for the **S** say there is no resurrection or angels

SADLY (2) [SAD]

Mt 19:22 he went **s** away because he had many possessions.
Mk 10:22 and he went **s** away because he had many

SADNESS (15) [SAD]

Jdg 21:6 The Israelites felt deep **s** for Benjamin and said,
1Sa 2:33 Those who are left alive will live in **s** and grief,
2Sa 15:23 There was deep **s** throughout the land as the king
19:2 the joy of that day's victory was turned into deep **s**.
Job 6:2 "If my **s** could be weighed and my troubles be put
9:27 if I decided to end my **s** and be cheerful,
Ps 31:10 I am dying from grief; / my years are shortened by **s**.
Ecc 7:3 than laughter, for **s** has a refining influence on us.
Jer 15:10 Then I said, "What **s** is mine, my mother. Oh,
16:6 will not cut themselves or shave their heads in **s**.
La 1:7 And now in the midst of her **s** and wandering,
Hos 4:3 It is filled with **s**, and all living things are
Lk 24:17 They stopped short, **s** written across their faces.
1Co 7:30 Happiness or **s** or wealth should not keep anyone
Jas 4:9 Let there be **s** instead of laughter, and gloom

SADOC [KJV] See ZADOK

SAFE (73) [SAVE]

Ge 6:18 But I solemnly swear to keep you **s** in the boat,
19:29 had listened to Abraham's request and kept Lot **s**,
Nu 32:17 so they will be **s** from any attacks by the local
Dt 19:4 the slayer may flee to any of these cities and be **s**.
19:5 could flee to one of the cities of refuge and be **s**.
29:19 thinking, 'I am **s**, even though I am walking in my
Jos 6:23 They moved her whole family to a **s** place near the
Ru 2:22 You will be **s** there, unlike in other fields."
1Sa 25:29 you are **s** in the care of the LORD your God,
26:13 hill opposite the camp until he was at a **s** distance.
27:1 will stop hunting for me, and I will finally be **s**."
30:23 He has kept us **s** and helped us defeat the enemy.
2Sa 5:6 you out!" For the Jebusites thought they were **s**.
7:11 And I will keep you **s** from all your enemies.
22:33 God is my strong fortress; / he has made my way **s**.
22:49 You hold me **s** beyond the reach of my enemies;
2Ch 15:5 During those dark times, it was not **s** to travel.
Ezr 8:21 We prayed that he would give us a **s** journey
Job 5:21 You will be **s** from slander and will have no fear of
5:24 You will know that your home is kept **s**. When you
21:9 Their homes are **s** from every fear, and God does
41:11 Who will confront me and remain **s**?
Ps 4:8 for you alone, O LORD, will keep me **s**.
16:1 Keep me **s**, O God, / for I have come to you for
18:32 arms me with strength; / he has made my way **s**.
18:48 You hold me **s** beyond the reach of my enemies;
20:1 May the God of Israel keep you **s** from all harm.
31:8 over to my enemy / but have set me in a **s** place.
31:20 **s** from those who conspire against them.
31:21 He kept me **s** when my city was under attack.
37:28 abandon the godly. / He will keep them **s** forever,
43:2 For you are God, my only **s** haven. / Why have you
48:8 It is the city of our God; / he will make it **s** forever.
55:18 He rescues me and keeps me **s** / from the battle
61:3 for you are my **s** refuge, / a fortress where my
61:4 **s** beneath the shelter of your wings!
78:53 He kept them **s** so they were not afraid;
Pr 2:11 watch over you. Understanding will keep you **s**.
3:23 They keep you **s** on your way and keep your feet
4:26 path for your feet; then stick to the path and stay **s**.
16:17 away from evil; whoever follows that path is **s**.
18:10 is a strong fortress; the godly run to him and are **s**.
28:26 is foolish, but those who walk in wisdom are **s**.
Ecc 8:11 is not punished, people feel it is **s** to do wrong.
Isa 8:14 He will keep you **s**. But to Israel and Judah he will
10:3 you turn for help? Where will your treasures be **s**?
11:6 Calves and yearlings will be **s** among lions, and a
28:16 and precious cornerstone that is **s** to build on.
Jer 5:17 your fortified cities, which you think are so **s**.
7:10 before me in my Temple and chant, "We are **s**!"—
15:21 I will certainly keep you **s** from these wicked men.
21:13 Jerusalem that boasts, "We are **s** on our mountain!
39:18 I will preserve your life and keep you **s**.
40:9 Gedaliah assured them that it would be **s** for them
Eze 11:3 Inside it we will be like meat—**s** from all harm.'
11:7 And you are not **s**, for I will soon drag you from
11:11 pot for you, and you will not be the meat, **s** inside.
36:20 and he couldn't keep them **s** in his own land!'
Hos 10:13 that great armies could make your nation **s**!
Mic 2:2 one's family or inheritance is **s** with you around!
Zec 2:4 with all their livestock—and yet they will be **s**.
8:10 No traveler was **s** from the enemy, for there were
14:11 **s** at last, never again to be cursed and destroyed.
Mt 3:9 Don't just say, 'We're **s**—we're the descendants of
6:20 or rusty and where they will be **s** from thieves.
Lk 3:8 Don't just say, 'We're **s**—we're the descendants of
11:21 is completely armed, guards his palace, it is **s**—
12:33 Your treasure will be **s**—no thief can steal it
15:27 We are celebrating because of his **s** return.'
19:20 amount of money and said, 'I hid it and kept it **s**.
Jn 17:12 During my time here, I have kept them **s**. I guarded
17:15 of the world, but to keep them **s** from the evil one.
Ac 28:1 Once we were **s** on shore, we learned that we were

SAFEGUARD (1) [GUARD, SAVE]

Pr 11:4 of judgment, but right living is a **s** against death.

SAFEKEEPING (5) [KEEP, SAVE]

Ex 16:34 He eventually placed it for **s** in the Ark of the
Lev 6:2 that an item entrusted to their **s** has been lost
Ezr 5:14 and delivered into the **s** of a man named
Jer 36:20 Then the officials left the scroll for **s** in the room of
Mt 25:18 in the ground and hid the master's money for **s**.

SAFELY (49) [SAVE]

Ge 7:18 above the ground, the boat floated **s** on the surface.
28:15 I will someday bring you **s** back to this land.
28:21 and if he will bring me back **s** to my father, then I
33:18 Then they arrived **s** at Shechem, in Canaan,
Ex 18:1 how the LORD had brought them **s** out of Egypt.
23:20 I am sending my angel before you to lead you **s** to
Nu 14:8 he will bring us **s** into that land and give it to us.
14:31 Well, I will bring them **s** into the land, and they
32:17 until we have brought them **s** to their inheritance.
Dt 20:1 who brought you **s** out of Egypt, is with you!
Jos 4:1 When all the people were **s** across the river,
10:21 Then the Israelites returned **s** to their camp at
2Sa 3:21 heart desires." So David sent Abner **s** on his way.
22:34 a deer, / leading me **s** along the mountain heights.
1Ki 22:27 and water until I return **s** from the battle!' "
22:28 But Micaiah replied, "If you return **s**, the LORD
2Ki 17:7 who had brought them **s** out of their slavery in
2Ch 18:26 and water until I return **s** from the battle!' "
18:27 But Micaiah replied, "If you return **s**, the LORD

19: 1 When King Jehoshaphat of Judah arrived s home
Ezr 8:32 So at last we arrived s in Jerusalem, where we
Ne 2: 7 instructing them to let me travel s through their
Job 29: 3 before me and I walked s through the darkness.
Ps 18:33 a deer, / leading me s along the mountain heights.
22: 9 Yet you brought me s from my mother's womb
37: 3 Then you will live s in the land and prosper.
78:52 of sheep, / guiding them s through the wilderness.
105:37 But he brought his people s out of Egypt,
107:30 that stillness / as he brought them s into harbor!
136:14 He led Israel s through, / His faithful love endures
Isa 11: 8 Babies will crawl s among poisonous snakes.
41: 3 He chases them away and goes on s, though he is
51:16 in your mouth and hidden you s within my hand.
Jer 2: 6 'Where is the LORD who brought us s out of
Eze 28:26 They will live s in Israel and build their homes
34:16 strayed away, and I will bring them s home again.
34:25 Then my people will be able to camp s in the
39: 6 and on all your allies who live s on the coasts.
Hab 3:19 as a deer and bring me s over the mountains.
Zec 8: 8 I will bring them home again to live s in Jerusalem.
10:11 They will pass s through the sea of distress,
Jn 11: 9 As long as it is light, people can walk s. They can
Ac 23:24 for Paul to ride, and get him s to Governor Felix."
27:39 get between the rocks and get the ship s to shore.
27:44 the broken ship. So everyone escaped s ashore!
1Co 10: 1 and he brought them all s through the waters of the
2Ti 4:18 and will bring me s to his heavenly Kingdom.
Jas 2:25 and sent them s away by a different road.
1Pe 3:18 but he died for sinners that he might bring us s

SAFER (1) [SAVE]
Pr 17:12 It is s to meet a bear robbed of her cubs than to

SAFETY (60) [SAVE]
Ge 19:16 and rushed them to s outside the city,
43: 9 I personally guarantee his s. If I don't bring him
Ex 21:13 will appoint a place where the slayer can run for s.
Nu 35: 6 who has accidentally killed someone can flee for s.
35:15 accidentally kills someone may flee there for s.
Dt 4:42 having any previous hostility could flee for s.
19: 3 who has killed someone can flee there for s.
33:12 and live in s beside him. / He surrounds them
33:28 So Israel will live in s, / prosperous Jacob in
Jos 2:14 offer our own lives as a guarantee for your s,"
2:17 the men told her, "We can guarantee your s
1Sa 4:13 for his heart trembled for the s of the Ark of God.
12:11 and Samuel to save you, and you lived in s.
2Sa 3:23 there visiting the king and had been sent away in s,
22:20 He led me to a place of s; / he rescued me
23: 5 He will constantly look after my s and success.
1Ki 4:25 all of Judah and Israel lived in peace and s.
2Ki 13: 5 Then Israel lived in s again as they had in former
2Ch 11:12 and spears in these towns as a further s measure.
Job 5:11 to the poor and humble, and he takes sufferers to s.
11:18 have hope. You will be protected and will rest in s.
12: 6 and God has them in his power—live in s!
24: 4 kicked aside; the needy must hide together for s.
Ps 3: 5 I lay down and slept. / I woke up in s,
11: 1 do you say to me, / "Fly to the mountains for s!
16: 9 my mouth shouts his praises! / My body rests in s.
18:19 He led me to a place of s; / he rescued me
28: 1 O LORD, you are my rock of s. / Please help me;
31: 2 rescue me quickly. / Be for me a great rock of s,
59: 9 to rescue me, / for you, O God, are my place of s.
59:16 been my refuge, / a place of s in the day of distress.
61: 2 Lead me to the towering rock of s,
69:36 and those who love him will live there in s.
71: 3 Be to me a protecting rock of s, / where I am
91: 2 He alone is my refuge, my place of s; / he is my
101: 6 eye on the godly, / so they may dwell with me in s.
107: 7 He led them straight to s, / to a city where they
144: 2 and my fortress, / my tower of s, my deliverer.
Pr 1:33 But all who listen to me will live in peace and s,
11:14 a nation falls; with many counselors, there is s.
18:11 they imagine it is a high wall of s.
29:25 a dangerous trap, but to trust the LORD means s.
Isa 32:18 My people will live in s, quietly at home.
33:16 rocks of the mountains will be their fortress of s.
Jer 7: 4 be fooled by those who repeatedly promise your s
23: 2 "Instead of leading my flock to s, you have
23: 6 day Judah will be saved, and Israel will live in s.
32:37 to this very city and let them live in peace and s.
33:16 Judah will be saved, and Jerusalem will live in s.
Eze 34:27 yield bumper crops, and everyone will live in s.
34:28 They will live in s, and no one will make them
39:26 home to live in peace and s in their own land.
Hos 2:18 and bows, so you can live unafraid in peace and s.
14: 7 My people will return again to the s of their land.
Zep 3:13 will live peaceful lives, lying down to sleep in s;
Zec 9:12 Come back to the place of s, all you prisoners,
Mk 16:18 They will be able to handle snakes with s, and if
Ac 23:27 that he was a Roman citizen, I removed him to s.
27:24 God in his goodness has granted s to everyone
2Co 1:11 so many people's prayers for our s have been

SAFFRON (1)
SS 4:14 nard and s, calamus and cinnamon, myrrh

SAID (2363) [SAY] See Index of Articles, Etc.
GOD SAID (47) Ge 1:3,6,9,11,14,20,24,26,29; 2:18; 3:14, 22; 6:13; 8:15; 9:12,17; 17:3; 31:11; 35:1,11; Ex 13:17; Dt 1:6; Jdg 6:20; 1Ki 3:5; 12:22; 13:8; 2Ki 4:27; 1Ch 17:3; 28:3; 2Ch 1:11; Jnh 4:9; Mt 22:31; Mk 1:2; 12:26; Lk 12:20; Jn 10:34; Ac 2:17; 3:25; 13:22; Ro 9:15; 10:21; 2Co 6:16; Heb 1:5,6; 4:3,5; 5:6

JESUS SAID (102) Mt 3:15; 8:4,7,13,20; 9:2,9; 11:28; 12:3; 14:29,31; 15:28; 16:24; 17:26; 19:11,14,23; 21:6; 23:1; 26:50,55; 27:14; 28:10; Mk 2:5,14; 3:3; 4:35; 5:19; 6:31,37; 9:19,39; 10:24,39,52; 11:14,22; 12:17,34; 14:18,32,62; 15:5; Lk 5:20,27; 6:9; 7:43,48,50; 8:22,38; 9:13,41,43,50; 10:37; 12:22; 13:18; 16:19; 17:1,19; 18:22,42; 19:11; 21:5; 22:15,34,48,51; 23:34; 24:25; Jn 1:42,47; 4:7,17; 6:32,53,70; 8:11,12,21,28,31,49; 9:37; 10:32; 13:26,31; 18:5,8,11,37; 19:11; 20:16,17; 21:10,12,15,16,17,19,23

LORD SAID (9) Isa 21:6; Lk 10:41; 11:39; 18:6; Ac 7:33; 8:26; 9:11,15; 22:21

LORD* SAID (253) Ge 4:10; 6:3,7; 7:1; 13:14; 15:4; 16:9; 18:13,28,31,32; 31:3; Ex 4:6,7,8,19; 6:10,26; 7:1,8,14,19; 8:1,5,16; 9:8,13,20,22; 10:1,12,21; 11:1; 12:43; 13:1; 14:15,26; 16:4,11; 17:5; 19:9,24; 20:22; 24:12; 25:1; 30:11,17,22; 32:9; 33:1; 34:27; Lev 4:1; 5:14; 6:1,8,19,24; 7:22,28; 8:1; 10:8; 11:1; 12:1; 13:1; 14:1,33; 15:1; 16:2; 17:1; 18:1; 20:1; 21:1,16; 22:1,17,26; 23:1,26,33; 24:1,13; 25:1; 27:1; Nu 3:5,11,40,44; 4:1,17,21; 5:5,11; 6:1,22; 7:4,11; 8:1,5; 10:1; 11:16,23; 12:6,14; 14:11,20,26; 15:35,37; 16:20,23,36,44; 17:1,10; 18:20; 19:1; 20:7,12,23; 21:16,34; 25:10,16; 26:1,52; 27:12; 28:1; 31:1,25; 33:50; 34:1,16; 35:1,9; Dt 1:42; 2:2,17,24,31; 6:19; 9:12,13; 10:1,11; 18:17; 31:14,16; 32:48; 34:4; Jos 4:1; 5:9; 6:2; 7:10; 8:1,18; 10:8; 11:6; 13:1; 14:6,12; 20:1; 24:27; Jdg 6:16,25; 7:2,9; 20:23,28; 1Sa 3:11; 9:17; 15:10,19; 16:1,7,12; 23:11; 2Sa 7:4; 21:1; 1Ki 9:3; 11:11; 17:2,8; 18:1; 19:9; 21:17; 22:17,20; 2Ki 1:15; 9:26; 10:30; 21:10; 1Ch 22:8; 2Ch 11:2; 18:16,19; Job 1:12; 2:6; 40:1; Ps 2:7; 89:3; 110:1; Isa 7:3; 8:1,3; 20:3; Jer 1:11,12,14; 3:6,11; 11:6; 13:1,6; 14:11,14; 15:1; 17:19; 18:13; 19:1; 22:1; 24:3,8; 25:27; 26:2; 27:2; 31:3; 37:2; Eze 4:15; 8:5,12; 10:6; 21:8; 23:36; 24:25; 43:7; 44:2,5; Hos 1:4,6,9; 3:1; Am 7:8; 8:2; Jnh 4:10; Hab 2:2; Zec 3:2; 6:7; 11:13,15; Mt 22:44; Mk 12:36; Lk 20:42; Ac 2:34

SAIL (11) [FORESAIL, SAILBOATS, SAILED, SAILING, SAILOR, SAILORS, SAILS]
1Ki 9:27 Hiram sent experienced crews of sailors to s the
22:48 Jehoshaphat also built a fleet of trading ships to s
22:48 But the ships never set s, for they were wrecked at
22:49 "Let my men s an expedition with your men."
Ps 65: 5 on earth, / even those who s on distant seas.
Isa 42:10 Sing, all you who s the seas, / all you who live in
Ac 18:21 God willing." Then he set s from Ephesus.
20: 3 He was preparing to s back to Syria when he
27: 1 When the time came, we set s for Italy. Paul
28:10 with honors, and when the time came to s,
28:11 s on another ship that had wintered at the island—

SAILBOATS (1) [SAIL]
Isa 18: 1 of the Nile. Its winged s glide along the river,

SAILED (15) [SAIL]
1Ki 9:28 They s to Ophir and brought back to Solomon
10:22 The king had a fleet of trading ships that s with
2Ch 8:18 These ships s to the land of Ophir with Solomon's
Ac 13: 4 of Seleucia and then s for the island of Cyprus.
15:39 took John Mark with him and s for Cyprus.
16:11 and s straight across to the island of Samothrace,
18:18 to the Christians and s for the coast of Syria,
20:14 He joined us there and we s together to Mitylene.
21: 1 Ephesian elders, we s straight to the island of Cos.
27: 4 so we s north of Cyprus between the island
27: 7 so we s down to the leeward side of Crete,
27:13 they pulled up anchor and s along close to shore.
27:16 We s behind a small island named Cauda,
28:13 From there we s across to Rhegium. A day later a
28:13 so the following day we s up the coast to Puteoli.

SAILING (6) [SAIL]
Ps 104:26 See the ships s along, / and Leviathan, which you
Isa 23: 3 s over deep waters. They brought you grain from
Jnh 1: 4 But as the ship was s along, suddenly the LORD
Ac 21: 2 There we boarded a ship s for the Syrian province
27: 7 We had several days of rough s, and after great
27:24 has granted safety to everyone s with you.'

SAILOR (1) [SAIL]
Pr 23:34 You will stagger like a s tossed at sea, clinging to a

SAILORS (16) [SAIL]
1Ki 9:27 Hiram sent experienced crews of s to sail the ships
2Ch 8:18 and manned by experienced crews of s.
9:21 of trading ships manned by the s sent by Hiram.
Ps 107:26 sank again to the depths; / the s cringed in terror.
Eze 27:27 your riches and wares, your s and helmsmen,
27:29 the s and helmsmen come to stand on the shore.
Jnh 1: 5 the desperate s shouted to their gods for help
1:10 The s were terrified when they heard this. "Oh,
1:13 the s tried even harder to row the boat ashore.
1:15 Then the s picked Jonah up and threw him into the
1:16 The s were awestruck by the LORD's great
Ac 27:13 from the south, the s thought they could make it.
27:17 The s were afraid of being driven across to the
27:27 across the Sea of Adria, the s sensed land was near.
27:30 Then the s tried to abandon the ship; they lowered
27:31 "You will all die unless the s stay aboard."

SAILS (2) [SAIL]
Isa 33:23 The enemies' s hang loose on broken masts with
Eze 27: 7 Your s were made of Egypt's finest linen, and they

SAINTS (2)
2Ch 6:41 and may your s rejoice in your goodness.
Rev 8: 4 of the incense, mixed with the prayers of the s,

SAKE (61) [SAKES]
Ge 18:26 in Sodom, I will spare the entire city for their s."
18:31 "Then I will not destroy it for the s of the
18:32 "Then, for the s of the ten, I will not destroy it."
39: 5 the LORD began to bless Potiphar for Joseph's s.
Nu 11:29 But Moses replied, "Are you jealous for my s?
Dt 14: 1 or shave the hair above your foreheads for the s of
2Sa 5:12 and had made his kingdom great for the s of his
7:21 For the s of your promise and according to your
18: 5 "For my s, deal gently with young Absalom."
18:12 king say to you and Abishai and Ittai, 'For my s,
1Ki 11:12 But for the s of your father, David, I will not do
11:13 for the s of my servant David and for the s of Jerusalem,
11:32 But I will leave him one tribe for the s of my servant David and for the s of Jerusalem,
11:34 For the s of my servant David, the one whom I
15: 4 But for David's s, the LORD his God allowed his
2Ki 19:34 my own honor and for the s of my servant David,
20: 6 my honor and for the s of my servant David.' "
1Ch 14: 2 and had made his kingdom very great for the s of
17:19 For my s, O LORD, and according to your will,
Ps 44:22 For your s we are killed every day; / we are being
69: 7 For I am mocked and shamed for your s;
79: 9 and forgive our sins / for the s of your name.
109:21 for the s of your own reputation!
122: 8 For the s of my family and friends, I will say,
122: 9 For the s of the house of the LORD our God,
132:10 For the s of your servant David, / do not reject the
Isa 37:35 my own honor and for the s of my servant David,
43:25 am the one who blots out your sins for my own s
45: 4 It is for the s of Jacob my servant, Israel my
48: 9 Yet for my own s and for the honor of my name,
48:11 I will rescue you for my s—yes, for my own s!
Jer 14: 7 So please, help us for the s of your own reputation.
14:21 For the s of your own name, LORD, do not
15:15 "LORD, you know I am suffering for your s.
Eze 28:17 You corrupted your wisdom for the s of your
Da 9:17 For your own s, Lord, smile again on your desolate
9:19 For your own s, O my God, do not delay, for your
Mt 19:12 and some choose not to marry for the s of the
19:29 or mother or children or property, for my s,
24:22 But it will be shortened for the s of God's chosen
Mk 5: 7 Most High God? For God's s, don't torture me!"
8:35 But if you give up your life for my s and for the s of the Good News,
10:29 or property, for my s and for the Good News,
13:20 But for the s of his chosen ones he has shortened
Lk 18:29 or children, for the s of the Kingdom of God,
Jn 11:15 And for your s, I am glad I wasn't there,
11:42 but I said it out loud for the s of all these people
Ac 15:26 who have risked their lives for the s of our Lord
21:13 but also to die for the s of the Lord Jesus."
Ro 8:36 "For your s we are killed every day;
1Ti 5:23 You ought to drink a little wine for the s of your
Phm 1: 9 an old man, now in prison for the s of Christ Jesus.
1:20 please do me this favor for the Lord's s.
Heb 11:26 He thought it was better to suffer for the s of the
1Pe 2:13 For the Lord's s, accept all authority—the king as
2:19 with you when, for the s of your conscience,
2Pe 3: 9 people think. No, he is being patient for your s.

SAKES (3) [SAKE]
Ge 18:24 will you still destroy it, and not spare it for their s?
Isa 43:14 "For your s I will send an invading army against
2Co 8: 9 he was very rich, yet for your s he became poor,

SAKIA (1)
1Ch 8:10 Jeuz, S, and Mirmah. These sons all became the

SAKKUTH (1)
Am 5:26 S your king god and Kaiwan your star god—

SALAH [KJV] See SHELAH

SALAMIS (1)
Ac 13: 5 There, in the town of S, they went to the Jewish

SALATHIEL [KJV] See SHEALTIEL

SALE (3) [SELL]
Ge 42: 6 of all Egypt and in charge of the s of the grain,
Lev 25:24 "With every s of land there must be a stipulation
25:29 has the right to redeem it for a full year after its s.

SALECAH (4)
Dt 3:10 and Bashan as far as the towns of S and Edrei,
Jos 12: 5 stretching from Mount Hermon to S in the north
13:11 all of Mount Hermon, all of Bashan as far as S,
1Ch 5:11 of Gad, who were spread as far east as S.

SALEM (3) [JERUSALEM]
Ge 14:18 the king of S and a priest of God Most High,
Heb 7: 1 This Melchizedek was king of the city of S
7: 2 also "king of peace" because *S* means "peace."

SALIM (1)
Jn 3:23 near S, because there was plenty of water there

SALIVA (1)
Jn 9: 6 Then he spit on the ground, made mud with the s,

SALLAI (1)
Ne 11: 8 and after him there were Gabbai and S, and a total

SALLU (4)
1Ch 9: 7 From the tribe of Benjamin came S son of
Ne 11: 7 S son of Meshullam, son of Joed, son of Pedaiah,
12: 7 S, Amok, Hilkiah, and Jedaiah. These were the
12:20 Kallai was leader of the family of S. / Eber was

SALMA (2)
1Ch 2:51 S (the father of Bethlehem), and Hareph (the father
2:54 The descendants of S were Bethlehem,

SALMON (8)
Ru 4:20 father of Nahshon. / Nahshon was the father of S.
4:21 S was the father of Boaz. / Boaz was the father of
1Ch 2:11 Nahshon was the father of S. / S was the father of Boaz.
Mt 1: 4 father of Nahshon. / Nahshon was the father of S.
1: 5 S was the father of Boaz (his mother was Rahab).
Lk 3:32 Boaz was the son of S. / S was the son of Nahshon.

SALMONE (1)
Ac 27: 7 to the leeward side of Crete, past the cape of S.

SALOME (2)
Mk 15:40 of James the younger and of Joseph), and S.
16: 1 Mary Magdalene and S and Mary the mother of

SALT (28) [SALTY]
Ge 19:26 along behind him, and she became a pillar of s.
Lev 2:13 Season all your grain offerings with s, to remind
2:13 Never forget to add s to your grain offerings.
11: 9 whether taken from fresh water or s water.
Dt 29:23 They will find its soil turned into sulfur and s,
Jos 15:62 Nibshan, the City of S, and En-gedi—six towns
Jdg 9:45 leveled the city, and scattered s all over the ground.
2Sa 8:13 eighteen thousand Edomites in the Valley of S.
2Ki 2:20 Elisha said, "Bring me a new bowl with s in it."
2:21 the town with water and threw the s into it.
14: 7 killed ten thousand Edomites in the Valley of S.
1Ch 18:12 eighteen thousand Edomites in the Valley of S.
2Ch 25:11 his courage and led his army to the Valley of S,
Ezr 6: 9 without fail, provide them with the wheat, s, wine,
7:22 gallons of olive oil, and an unlimited supply of s.
Job 6: 6 People complain when there is no s in their food.
Ps 60: T twelve thousand Edomites in the Valley of S.
Pr 25:20 jacket in cold weather or rubbing s in a wound.
Eze 16: 4 and you were never washed, rubbed with s,
43:24 and the priests are to sprinkle s on them and offer
47:11 will not be purified; they will be sources of s.
Zep 2: 9 of stinging nettles, s pits, and eternal desolation.
Mt 5:13 "You are the s of the earth. But what good is s if it has lost its flavor?
Mk 9:50 S is good for seasoning. But if it loses its flavor,
9:50 You must have the qualities of s among yourselves
Lk 14:34 "S is good for seasoning. But if it loses its flavor,
14:35 Flavorless s is good neither for the soil nor for

SALTY (6) [SALT]
Ps 107:34 He turns the fruitful land into s wastelands,
Jer 17: 6 on the s flats where no one lives.
Eze 47: 8 The waters of this stream will heal the s waters of
Mk 9:50 if it loses its flavor, how do you make it s again?
Lk 14:34 if it loses its flavor, how do you make it s again?
Jas 3:12 and you can't draw fresh water from a s pool.

SALU (1)
Nu 25:14 the Midianite woman was named Zimri son of S,

SALUTATION(S) [KJV] See GREET, GREETED, GREETING

SALUTE(TH) [KJV] See GREET, GREETED, GREETING, VISIT, WELCOME

SALUTED (1)
Mk 15:18 Then they s, yelling, "Hail! King of the Jews!"

SALVATION (126) [SAVE]
Ge 49:18 I trust in you for s, O LORD!
Dt 32:15 they made light of the Rock of their s.
2Sa 22: 3 He is my shield, the strength of my s, and my
22:36 You have given me the shield of your s; / your help
22:47 my rock! / May God, the rock of my s, be exalted!
1Ch 16:35 Cry out, "Save us, O God of our s! / Gather
2Ch 6:41 your priests, O LORD God, be clothed with s,
Ps 14: 7 that s would come from Mount Zion to rescue
18: 2 He is my shield, the strength of my s, and my
18:35 You have given me the shield of your s.
18:46 be my rock! / May the God of my s be exalted!
27: 1 The LORD is my light and my s— / so why
27: 9 me now; don't abandon me, / O God of my s!
35: 3 Let me hear you say, / "I am your s!"
40:16 and gladness. / May those who love your s
50:23 to my path, / I will reveal to you the s of God."
51:12 Restore to me again the joy of your s, / and make
53: 6 that s would come from Mount Zion to rescue
62: 1 quietly before God, / for my s comes from him.
62: 2 He alone is my rock and my s, / my fortress where
62: 6 He alone is my rock and my s, / my fortress where
62: 7 My s and my honor come from God alone.
69:13 O God, / answer my prayer with your sure s.
70: 4 and gladness. / May those who love your s
74:12 my king from ages past, / bringing s to the earth.
79: 9 Help us, O God of our s! / Help us for the honor of
85: 4 Now turn to us again, O God of our s. / Put aside
85: 7 unfailing love, O LORD, / and grant us your s.
85: 9 Surely his s is near to those who honor him;
88: 1 O LORD, God of my s, / I have cried out to you
89:26 are my Father, / my God, and the Rock of my s.'
91:16 them with a long life / and give them my s."
95: 1 Let us give a joyous shout to the rock of our s!
98: 3 The whole earth has seen the s of our God.
103:17 fear him. / His s extends to the children's children
106: 4 favor to your people; / come to me with your s.
116:13 I will lift up a cup symbolizing his s; / I will praise
119:41 your unfailing love, / the s that you promised me.
119:81 I faint with longing for your s; / but I have put my
119:155 The wicked are far from s, / for they do not bother
119:166 I long for your s, LORD, / so I have obeyed your
119:174 O LORD, I have longed for your s, / and your law
130: 7 is unfailing love / and an overflowing supply of s.
132: 9 Your priests will be agents of s; / may your loyal
132:16 I will make its priests the agents of s; / its godly
149: 4 in his people; / he crowns the humble with s.
Isa 11:10 throne will be a banner of s to all the world.
12: 2 my strength and my song; / he has become my s."
12: 3 joy you will drink deeply from the fountain of s!
25: 9 we trusted. Let us rejoice in the s he brings!"
26: 1 We are surrounded by the walls of God's s.
33: 2 our strength each day and our s in times of trouble.
33: 6 providing a rich store of s, wisdom,
45: 8 Let the earth open wide so s and righteousness can
45:17 will save the people of Israel with eternal s.
45:22 Let all the world look to me for s! For I am God;
49: 6 and you will bring my s to the ends of the earth."
49: 8 respond to you. On the day of s, I will help you.
51: 5 Your s is on the way. I will rule the nations.
51: 6 the earth will die like flies, but my s lasts forever.
51: 8 My s will continue from generation to
52: 7 feet of those who bring good news of peace and s,
52:10 The ends of the earth will see the s of our God.
58: 8 do these things, your s will come like the dawn.
59:17 body armor and placed the helmet of s on his head.
60:18 S will surround you like city walls, and praise will
61:10 For he has dressed me with the clothing of s
62: 1 the dawn, and her s blazes like a burning torch.
63: 1 "It is I, the LORD, announcing your s! It is I,
Jer 3:23 Only in the LORD our God will Israel ever find s.
La 3:26 So it is good to wait quietly for s from the LORD.
Jnh 2: 9 For my s comes from the LORD alone."
Hab 3: 8 No, you were sending your chariots of s!
3:18 in the LORD! I will be joyful in the God of my s.
Mk 16: S and unfailing message of s that gives eternal life.
Lk 1:77 You will tell his people how to find s
3: 6 then all people will see / the s sent from God.' "
19: 9 Jesus responded, "S has come to this home today,
21:28 stand straight and look up, for your s is near!"
Jn 4:22 know all about him, for s comes through the Jews.
Ac 4:12 There is s in no one else! There is no other name in
13:26 who fear the God of Israel—this s is for us!
13:47 to bring s to the farthest corners of the earth.' "
28:28 So I want you to realize that this s from God is also
Ro 5: 4 strengthens our confident expectation of s.
10: 8 S that comes from trusting Christ—which is the
11:11 His purpose was to make his s available to the
11:12 because the Jews turned down God's offer of s,
11:15 meant that God offered s to the rest of the world,
13:11 for the coming of our s is nearer now than when
13:12 is almost gone; the day of s will soon be here.
1Co 1:24 But to those called by God to s, both Jews
2Co 1: 6 down with troubles, it is for your benefit and s!
6: 2 On the day of s, I helped you." Indeed, God is
6: 2 ready to help you right now. Today is the day of s.
7:10 our lives to help us turn away from sin and seek s.
Gal 1:11 I solemnly assure you that the Good News of s
5:11 still preaching s through the cross of Christ alone.
Eph 2: 9 S is not a reward for the good things we have done,
6:17 Put on s as your helmet, and take the sword of the
Php 1:11 May you always be filled with the fruit of your s—
1Th 5: 8 and wearing as our helmet the confidence of our s.
2Th 2:13 chose you to be among the first to experience s,
2:13 a s that came through the Spirit who makes you
2:14 He called you to s when we told you the Good
2Ti 2:10 I am willing to endure anything if it will bring s
3:15 receive the s that comes by trusting in Christ Jesus.
Tit 1:10 true of those who insist on circumcision for s.
2:11 of God has been revealed, bringing s to all people.
Heb 1:14 sent from God to care for those who will receive s.
2: 3 s that was announced by the Lord Jesus himself?
2:10 a perfect leader, one fit to bring them into their s.
5: 9 and he became the source of eternal s for all those
6: 9 are meant for better things, things that come with s.
9:12 his own blood, and with it he secured our s forever.
9:28 This time he will bring s to all those who are
10:39 and seal their fate. We have faith that assures our s.
1Pe 1: 5 will protect you until you receive this s,
1: 9 Your reward for trusting him will be the s of your
1:10 This s was something the prophets wanted to know
1:10 They prophesied about this gracious s prepared for
2: 2 so that you can grow into the fullness of your s.
Jude 1: 3 planning to write to you about the s we all share.
Rev 7:10 "S comes from our God on the throne and from
12:10 the s and power and kingdom of our God,
19: 1 S is from our God. Glory and power belong to him

SAMARIA (119) [OHOLAH, SAMARIAN, SAMARITAN, SAMARITANS]
1Ki 13:32 and against the pagan shrines in the towns of S will
16:24 Then Omri bought the hill now known as S from
16:24 city on it and called the city S in honor of Shemer.
16:28 When Omri died, he was buried in S. Then his son
16:29 reign in Judah. He reigned in S twenty-two years.
16:32 First he built a temple and an altar for Baal in S.
18: 2 the famine had become very severe in S.
20: 1 They went to besiege S, the Israelite capital,
20:10 if there remains enough dust from S to provide
20:17 to him, "Some troops are coming from S."
20:34 of trade in Damascus, as my father did in S."
20:43 So the king of Israel went home to S angry
21:18 "Go down to meet King Ahab, who rules in S.
22:10 on thrones at the threshing floor near the gate of S.
22:37 and his body was taken to S and buried there.
22:38 Then his chariot was washed beside the pool of S,
22:51 reign in Judah. He reigned in S two years.
2Ki 1: 2 the latticework of an upper room at his palace in S,
1: 3 "Go and meet the messengers of the king of S
2:25 went to Mount Carmel and finally returned to S.
3: 1 reign in Judah. He reigned in S twelve years.
3: 6 mustered the army of Israel and marched from S.
5: 3 wish my master would go to see the prophet in S.
6:19 man you are looking for." And he led them to S.
6:20 As soon as they had entered S, Elisha prayed,
6:20 and they discovered that they were in S.
6:24 of Aram mobilized his entire army and besieged S.
7: 1 By this time tomorrow in the markets of S,
7:16 Then the people of S rushed out and plundered the
7:18 "By this time tomorrow in the markets of S,
10: 1 Now Ahab had seventy sons living in the city of S.
10: 1 So Jehu wrote a letter and sent copies to S,
10: 6 the king were being cared for by the leaders of S,
10:12 Then Jehu set out for S. Along the way, while he
10:17 When Jehu arrived in S, he killed everyone who
10:35 Jehu died, he was buried with his ancestors in S.
10:36 Jehu reigned over Israel from S for twenty-eight
13: 1 reign in Judah. He reigned in S seventeen years.
13: 6 They even set up an Asherah pole in S.
13: 9 he was buried in S with his ancestors.
13:10 reign in Judah. He reigned in S sixteen years.
13:13 he was buried with his ancestors in S.
14:14 He also took hostages and returned to S.
14:16 he was buried with his ancestors in S.
14:23 in Judah. Jeroboam reigned in S forty-one years.
15: 8 reign in Judah. He reigned in S six months.
15:13 in Judah. Shallum reigned in S only one month.
15:14 Then Menahem son of Gadi went to S from Tirzah
15:17 Uzziah's reign in Judah. He reigned in S ten years.
15:23 Uzziah's reign in Judah. He reigned in S two years.
15:25 and Arieh, in the citadel of the palace at S.
15:27 reign in Judah. He reigned in S twenty years.
17: 1 Ahaz's reign in Judah. He reigned in S nine years.
17: 5 the entire land, and for three years he besieged S.
17: 6 in the ninth year of King Hoshea's reign, S fell,
17:24 and resettled them in the towns of S,
17:24 So the Assyrians took over S and the other towns
17:27 "Send one of the exiled priests from S back to
17:28 So one of the priests who had been exiled from S
18: 9 attacked Israel and began a siege on the city of S.
18:10 ninth year of King Hoshea's reign in Israel, S fell.
18:34 and Ivvah? Did they rescue S from my power?
21:13 judge Jerusalem by the same standard I used for S
23:18 burn his bones or those of the old prophet from S.
23:19 buildings at the pagan shrines in the towns of S,
2Ch 18: 2 A few years later, he went to S to visit Ahab,
18: 9 on thrones at the threshing floor near the gate of S.
22: 9 and they found him hiding in the city of S.
25:13 raided several of the towns of Judah between S
25:24 along with hostages, and then returned to S.
28: 8 amounts of plunder, which they took back to S.
28: 9 there in S when the army of Israel returned home.
28:15 the city of palms. Then they returned to S.
Ezr 4:10 Ashurbanipal had deported and relocated in S
4:17 and their colleagues living in S and throughout the
Isa 7: 9 Israel is no stronger than its capital, S.
7: 9 And S is no stronger than its king, Pekah son of
8: 4 and S and carry away their riches."
9: 9 and the people of Israel and S will soon discover it.
10: 9 And we will destroy S just as we did Damascus.
10:10 were far greater than those in Jerusalem and S.
10:11 So when we have defeated S and her gods, we will
28: 1 Destruction is certain for the city of S—the pride
28: 3 The proud city of S—the pride and joy of the
36:19 of Sepharvaim? Did they rescue S from my power?
Jer 23:13 "I saw that the prophets of S were terribly evil,
31: 5 will plant your vineyards on the mountains of S
41: 5 eighty men arrived from Shechem, Shiloh, and S.
Eze 16:46 "Your older sister was S, who lived with her
16:51 "Even S did not commit half your sins. You have
16:53 I will restore the fortunes of Sodom and S,
16:55 Yes, your sisters, Sodom and S, and all their
16:61 your sisters, S and Sodom, to be your daughters,
23: 4 I am speaking of S and Jerusalem, for Oholah is S and Oholibah is Jerusalem.
23:33 of sorrow and distress, just as your sister S did.
Hos 7: 1 S is filled with liars, thieves, and bandits!

8: 5 "O S, I reject this calf—this idol you have made.
10: 5 The people of S tremble for their calf idol at
10: 7 S will be cut off, and its king will disappear like a
13:16 The people of S must bear the consequences of
Am 3: 9 "Take your seats now on the hills around S,
3:12 So it will be when the Israelites in S are rescued
4: 1 Listen to me, you "fat cows" of S, you women
6: 1 and think you are secure in Jerusalem and S!
8:14 those who worship and swear by the idols of S,
Ob 1:19 and take over the fields of Ephraim and S.
Mic 1: 1 The messages concerned both S and Jerusalem,
1: 5 is to blame for Israel's rebellion? S, its capital city!
1: 6 will make the city of S a heap of rubble.
Lk 17:11 he reached the border between Galilee and S.
Jn 4: 4 He had to go through S on the way.
Ac 1: 8 in Jerusalem, throughout Judea, in S, and to the
8: 1 believers except the apostles fled into Judea and S.
8: 5 went to the city of S and told the people there
8:14 that the people of S had accepted God's message,
8:25 and preaching the word of the Lord in S,
9:31 Galilee, and S, and it grew in strength
15: 3 the way in Phoenicia and S to visit the believers.

SAMARIAN (1) [SAMARIA]

Ne 4: 2 in front of his friends and the S army officers,

SAMARITAN (10) [SAMARIA]

Lk 9:52 He sent messengers ahead to a S village to prepare
10:33 "Then a despised S came along, and when he saw
10:34 the S soothed his wounds with medicine
17:16 him for what he had done. This man was a S.
Jn 4: 5 Eventually he came to the S village of Sychar,
4: 7 Soon a S woman came to draw water, and Jesus
4: 9 to Jesus, "You are a Jew, and I am a S woman.
8:48 The people retorted, "You S devil! Didn't we say
Ac 8:10 The S people, from the least to the greatest,
8:25 And they stopped in many S villages along the way

SAMARITANS (5) [SAMARIA]

Mt 10: 5 "Don't go to the Gentiles or the S,
Jn 4: 9 for Jews refuse to have anything to do with S.
4:20 while we S claim it is here at Mount Gerizim,
4:22 You S know so little about the one you worship,
4:39 Many S from the village believed in Jesus

SAME (354)

Ge 11: 1 spoke a single language and used the s words.
17:26 Both were circumcised the s day,
18:25 treating the innocent and the guilty exactly the s!
20:12 we both have the s father, though different
32:19 Jacob gave the s instructions to each of the
32:19 "You are all to say the s thing to Esau when you
33:16 So Esau started back to Seir that s day.
41:23 Then out of the s stalk came seven withered heads,
41:25 "Both dreams mean the s thing," Joseph told
Ex 5: 6 That s day Pharaoh sent this order to the slave
6:26 and Moses named in this list are the s Aaron
6:30 This is the s Moses who had argued with the
7:11 and they did the s thing with their secret arts.
8: 7 But the magicians were able to do the s thing with
8:18 Pharaoh's magicians tried to do the s thing with
12:19 These s regulations apply to the foreigners living
12:42 land of Egypt, so this s night now belongs to him.
12:47 of Israel must celebrate this festival at the s time.
21:31 "The s principle applies if the bull gores a boy
23:11 The s applies to your vineyards and olive groves.
26: 2 feet wide. All ten sheets must be exactly the s size.
26: 8 All eleven of these sheets must be exactly the s
26:24 Both of these corner frames will be made the s
27:11 It will be the s on the north side of the courtyard—
28: 8 And the sash will be made of the s materials:
28:11 Engrave these names in the s way a gemcutter
28:15 Use the s materials as you did for the ephod:
29:41 along with the s offerings of flour and wine as in
30: 2 with horns at the corners carved from the s piece of
30:34 weighing out the s amounts of each.
34: 1 I will write on them the s words that were on the
36: 9 Each sheet was exactly the s size—forty-two feet
36:15 Each sheet was exactly the s size—forty-five feet
37:25 with its corner horns made from the s piece of
39: 1 This s cloth was used for Aaron's sacred garments,
39: 5 They also made an elaborate woven sash of the s
39: 8 The chestpiece was made in the s style as the
Lev 4:20 following the s procedure as with the sin offering
6:22 they will be inducted into office by offering this s
7:15 The animal's meat must be eaten on the s day it is
7:16 the meat may be eaten on that s day,
11: 5 The s is true of the rock badger
15: 7 The s instructions apply if you touch the man who
15: 8 he spits on you, you must undergo the s procedure.
15:22 The s applies if you touch an object on which she
16:16 and he will do the s for the entire Tabernacle,
18: 9 whether she was brought up in the s family
19: 6 You must eat it on the s day you offer it or on the
19:10 It is the s with your grape crop—do not strip every
22:28 a mother animal and her offspring on the s day,
23:12 That s day you must sacrifice a year-old male lamb
23:21 That s day, you must stop all your regular work
24:22 "These s regulations apply to Israelites by birth
Nu 2:17 All the tribes are to travel in the s order that they
3:47 each piece weighing the s as the standard sanctuary
9:14 they must follow these s laws and regulations.
9:14 The s laws apply both to you and to the foreigners
15:14 to the LORD, they must follow the s procedures.
15:15 and foreigners are the s before the LORD and are
subject to the s laws.
15:16 The s instructions and regulations will apply both
15:29 This s law applies both to native Israelites
16:40 the s thing would happen to him as happened to
18:16 each piece weighing the s as the standard sanctuary
21:34 You will do the s to him as you did to King Sihon
22:30 "But I am the s donkey you always ride on,"
26: 9 and Abiram are the s community leaders who
28: 8 Offer the second lamb in the evening with the s
32:14 a brood of sinners, doing exactly the s thing!
35:18 The s is true if someone strikes and kills another
Dt 3: 5 We also took many unwalled villages at the s time.
3:21 He will do the s to all the kingdoms on the west
7:19 The LORD your God will use this s power
10: 2 and I will write on the tablets the s words that were
10: 4 They were the s words the LORD had spoken to
15:17 "You must do the s for your female servants.
21:23 You must bury the body that s day, for anyone
22: 3 Do the s if you find your neighbor's donkey,
25: 5 "If two brothers are living together on the s
27:11 That s day Moses gave this charge to the people:
32:48 That s day the LORD said to Moses,
Jos 10:28 That s day Joshua completely destroyed the city of
Jdg 8: 8 and asked for food, but he got the s answer.
20:22 and assembled at the s place they had fought the
20:30 third day and assembled at the s place as before.
Ru 1:15 her people and to her gods. You should do the s."
1Sa 1: 7 Year after year it was the s—Peninnah would taunt
2:34 Hophni and Phinehas, to die on the s day!
4: 8 They are the s gods who destroyed the Egyptians
4:12 and arrived at Shiloh later that s day.
5: 4 But the next morning the s thing happened—
6:16 all this and then returned to Ekron that s day.
8: 8 And now they are giving you the s treatment.
16:10 In the s way all seven of Jesse's sons were
17:27 And David received the s reply as before:
17:30 asked them the s thing and received the s answer.
19:21 prophesied! The s thing happened a third time!
22:23 own life, for the s person wants to kill us both."
29: 5 Isn't this the s David about whom the women of
31: 6 and his troops all died together that s day.
2Sa 2:13 About the s time, Joab son of Zeruiah led David's
7: 4 But that s night the LORD said to Nathan,
1Ki 3:17 them began, "this woman and I live in the s house.
7: 8 behind this hall; they were built the s way.
7:37 All ten water carts were the s size and were made
alike, for each was cast from the s mold.
8:64 That s day the king dedicated the central area of
13: 3 That s day the man of God gave a sign to prove his
13: 5 At the s time a wide crack appeared in the altar,
13: 9 and do not return to Judah by the s way you
13:17 and do not return to Judah by the s way you
15: 3 He committed the s sins as his father before him,
18:34 he said, "Do the s thing again!" And when they
20:25 Give us the s number of horses, chariots, and men,
22: 7 too? I would like to ask him the s question."
2Ki 8:22 The town of Libnah revolted about that s time.
17:19 They walked down the s evil paths that Israel had
17:41 And to this day their descendants do the s.
21:13 I will judge Jerusalem by the s standard I used for
21:13 and by the s measure I used for the family of Ahab.
21:21 worshiping the s idols that his father had
1Ch 17: 3 But that s night God said to Nathan,
2Ch 3:12 In the s way, the second figure had one wing 7-1/2
7:18 This is the s promise I gave your father, David,
18: 6 too? I would like to ask him the s question."
20:18 all the people of Judah and Jerusalem did the s,
21:10 The town of Libnah revolted about that s time,
29:22 the altar. And finally, they did the s with the lambs.
30:12 At the s time, God's hand was on the people in the
34: 6 He did the s thing in the towns of Manasseh,
35:12 the Book of Moses. They did the s with the bulls.
Ne 5: 5 We belong to the s family, and our children are just
6: 4 Four times they sent the s message, and each time
I gave the s reply.
13: 1 On that s day, as the Book of Moses was being
13:23 About the s time I realized that some of the men of
Est 1: 9 banquet for the women of the palace at the s time.
1:18 and will start talking to their husbands the s way.
4:16 night or day. My maids and I will do the s.
8: 1 On that s day King Xerxes gave the estate of
8:14 The s decree was also issued at the fortress of
Job 4: 8 plant trouble and cultivate evil will harvest the s.
9:22 Innocent or wicked, it is all the s to him. That is
15:18 men who have heard the s thing from their fathers,
16: 4 I could say the s things if you were in my place.
21:26 are buried in the s dust, both eaten by the s worms.
33: 6 "Look, you and I are the s before God. I, too,
Ps 17:14 in full. / May their children inherit more of the s,
102:27 But you are always the s; / your years never end.
Pr 24:14 In the s way, wisdom is sweet to your soul. If you
27:18 In the s way, workers who protect their employer's
Ecc 2:12 and anyone else would come to the s conclusions I
2:14 I saw that wise and foolish people share the s fate.
3:19 For humans and animals both breathe the s air,
3:20 Both go to the s place—the dust from which they
4:11 two under the s blanket can gain warmth from each
7: 1 In the s way, the day you die is better than the day
9: 2 The s destiny ultimately awaits everyone,
9: 2 Good people receive the s treatment as sinners,
Isa 19:23 their lands, and they will worship the s God.
24:13 Throughout the earth the story is the s—
27: 7 Has the LORD punished Israel in the s way he
28:27 He doesn't thresh all his crops the s way. A heavy
29: 8 In the s way, your enemies will dream of a
31: 4 In the s way, the LORD Almighty will come
51:10 Are you not the s today, the one who dried up the
55:11 It is the s with my word. I send it out, and it always
Jer 26:20 And he predicted the s terrible disaster against the
27:12 Then I repeated this s message to King Zedekiah of
28: 1 One day in late summer of that s year—the fourth
33:21 The s is true for my covenant with the Levitical
51:64 'In this s way Babylon and her people will sink,
La 5:19 But LORD, you remain the s forever!
Eze 1:16 All four wheels looked the s; each wheel had a
10:10 All four wheels looked the s; each wheel had a
10:15 These were the s living beings I had seen beside
10:20 These were the s living beings I had seen beneath
17:10 It will die in the s good soil where it had grown
23: 2 two sisters who were daughters of the s mother.
23:31 I will punish you with the s terrors that destroyed
23:32 You will drink from the s cup of terror as your
25:11 And in the s way, I will bring my judgment down
40:10 Each had the s measurements, and the dividing
40:18 courtyard the s distance as the gateway entrance.
40:24 and he found they were exactly the s as in the
40:28 and found that it had the s measurements as the
40:29 and foyer were the s size as those in the others.
40:32 and found that it had the s measurements as the
40:33 and foyer were the s size as those of the others,
40:35 and found that it had the s measurements as the
40:36 and foyer of this gateway had the s measurements
40:36 as in the others and the s window arrangements.
42:11 This complex of rooms was the s length and width
42:11 the other one, and it had the s entrances and doors.
42:17 the north side and got the s measurement.
42:18 The south side was the s length,
45:25 the prince will provide these s sacrifices for the sin
46: 8 the foyer, and he must leave the s way he came.
46: 9 They must never leave by the s gateway they came
48:13 The land allotted to the Levites will be the s size
48:25 Next is the territory of Issachar with the s eastern
48:27 just south of Zebulun with the s borders to the east
Da 4:33 That very s hour the prophecy was fulfilled,
Hos 4:14 For you men are doing the s thing, sinning with
Am 2: 4 They have been led astray by the s lies that
2: 7 Both father and son sleep with the s woman,
Mic 5:10 "At that s time," says the LORD, "I will destroy
Hag 2: 1 Then on October 17 of that s year, the LORD sent
Zec 7: 7 Isn't this the s message the LORD proclaimed
14:15 This s plague will strike the horses, mules, camels,
14:18 the LORD will punish them with the s plague that
Mal 2:10 Are we not all children of the s Father? Are we not
2:10 Are we not all created by the s God? Then why are
Mt 5:16 In the s way, let your good deeds shine out for all
5:19 and teach others to do the s,
8:13 And the young servant was healed that s hour.
10:41 you will receive the s reward a prophet gets.
13: 1 Later that s day, Jesus left the house and went
18:14 In the s way, it is not my heavenly Father's will
20: 5 and again around three o'clock he did the s thing.
20:14 I wanted to pay this last worker the s as you.
21:36 to collect for him, but the results were the s.
22:23 That s day some Sadducees stepped forward—
22:45 him Lord, how can he be his son at the s time?"
23: 8 and all of you are on the s level as brothers
26: 3 At that s time the leading priests and other leaders
26:35 And all the other disciples vowed the s.
26:44 back to pray a third time, saying the s things again.
27:44 with him also shouted the s insults at him.
Mk 12:37 him Lord, how can he be his son at the s time?"
14:31 never deny you!" And all the others vowed the s.
Lk 10:37 Then Jesus said, "Yes, now go and do the s."
11:48 was right. You would have done the s yourselves.
15: 7 In the s way, heaven will be happier over one lost
15:10 In the s way, there is joy in the presence of God's
17:10 In the s way, when you obey me you should say,
20:11 sent another servant, but the s thing happened;
20:12 A third man was sent and the s thing happened.
20:44 him Lord, how can he be his son at the s time?"
23:15 Herod came to the s conclusion and sent him back
24:13 That s day two of Jesus' followers were walking to
Jn 4:53 Then the father realized it was the s time that Jesus
6:11 to the people. Afterward he did the s with the fish.
6:57 in the s way, those who partake of me will live
9: 8 blind beggar asked each other, "Is this the s man—
9: 9 And the beggar kept saying, "I am the s man!"
14:12 anyone who believes in me will do the s works I
15:12 I command you to love each other in the s way that
Ac 3:13 This is the s Jesus whom you handed over
3:17 in ignorance; and the s can be said of your leaders.
7:35 so God sent back the s man his people had
8:35 So Philip began with this s Scripture and then used
9:21 "Isn't this the s man who persecuted Jesus'
10:16 The s vision was repeated three times.
11:17 And since God gave these Gentiles the s gift he
15:11 We believe that we are all saved the s way,
16:33 That s hour the jailer washed their wounds, and he
26: 7 and day, and they share the s hope I have.
26:29 here in this audience might become the s as I am,
Ro 2: 1 for you do these very s things.
3:22 And we all can be saved in this s way, no matter
4:12 but only if they have the s kind of faith Abraham
8:11 he will give life to your mortal body by this s Spirit
9:21 doesn't he have a right to use the s lump of clay to
10:12 Jew and Gentile are the s in this respect. They all
have the s Lord, who generously gives his
11: 5 It is the s today, for not all the Jews have turned
11: 9 David spoke of this s thing when he said,
11:31 And now, in the s way, the Jews are the rebels,
13: 6 Pay your taxes, too, for these s reasons.
14: 5 In the s way, some think one day is more holy than
1Co 3: 8 and the one who waters work as a team with the s

7: 7 just as I do. But we are not all the s.
7:34 In the s way, a woman who is no longer married
9: 8 human opinion. Doesn't God's law say the s thing?
9:14 In the s way, the Lord gave orders that those who
9:20 I do the s, even though I am not subject to the law,
10: 3 And all of them ate the s miraculous food,
10: 4 and all of them drank the s miraculous water.
10:12 be careful, for you too may fall into the s sin.
11: 5 on her head, for this is the s as shaving her head.
11:16 and all the churches of God feel the s way about it.
11:25 In the s way, he took the cup of wine after supper,
12: 4 but it is the s Holy Spirit who is the source of them
12: 5 in the church, but it is the s Lord we are serving.
12: 6 but it is the s God who does the work through all
12:13 by one Spirit, and we have all received the s Spirit.
14: 9 And it's the s for you. If you talk to people in a
15:42 It is the s way for the resurrection of the dead.
16: 1 You should follow the s procedures I gave to the
2Co 1: 4 we will be able to give them the s comfort God has
1: 6 Then you can patiently endure the s things we
1:14 you will be proud of us in the s way we are proud
4:13 because we have the s kind of faith the psalmist
4:14 We know that the s God who raised our Lord Jesus
5:17 They are not the s anymore, for the old life is gone.
8:16 I am thankful to God that he has given Titus the s
9:10 In the s way, he will give you many opportunities
12:18 For we both have the s Spirit and walk in each
other's steps, doing things the s way.
Gal 2: 8 For the s God who worked through Peter for the
3: 6 In the s way, "Abraham believed God, so God
3: 9 All who put their faith in Christ share the s
3:14 God has blessed the Gentiles with the s blessing he
6: 1 And be careful not to fall into the s temptation
Eph 1:19 us who believe him. This is the s mighty power
2:18 may come to the Father through the s Holy Spirit
3: 6 and both are part of the s body and enjoy together
4: 4 We are all one body, we have the s Spirit, and we
have all been called to the s glorious future.
4:10 The s one who came down is the one who
5:25 And you husbands must love your wives with the s
5:28 In the s way, husbands ought to love their wives as
6: 9 And in the s way, you masters must treat your
6: 9 remember, you both have the s Master in heaven,
Php 2: 5 Your attitude should be the s that Christ Jesus had.
3:21 using the s mighty power that he will use to
4:19 And this s God who takes care of me will supply
Col 1: 6 This s Good News that came to you is going out all
1Ti 3: 8 In the s way, deacons must be people who are
3:11 In the s way, their wives must be respected
5: 8 especially those living in the s household,
5:25 In the s way, everyone knows how much good
Tit 2: 6 In the s way, encourage the young men to live
Phm 1:17 give him the s welcome you would give me if I
Heb 1:12 But you are always the s; / you will never grow
2:11 and the ones he makes holy have the s Father.
2:13 And in the s context he said, "Here I am—
4:15 for he faced all of the s temptations we do, yet he
5: 2 For he is subject to the s weaknesses they have.
9:21 And in the s way, he sprinkled blood on the sacred
10:33 you helped others who were suffering the s things.
11: 9 and Jacob, to whom God gave the s promise.
13: 8 Jesus Christ is the s yesterday, today, and forever.
Jas 2:11 For the s God who said, "Do not commit
3:10 and cursing come pouring out of the s mouth.
1Pe 3: 1 In the s way, you wives must accept the authority
3: 7 In the s way, you husbands must give honor to
4: 1 you must arm yourselves with the s attitude he had,
5: 9 are going through the s kind of suffering you are.
2Pe 1: 1 I am writing to all of you who share the s precious
1: 4 And by that s mighty power, he has given us all of
2: 7 But at the s time, God rescued Lot out of Sodom
3: 4 everything has remained exactly the s since the
1Jn 2: 7 one another—is the s message you heard before.
3Jn 1:12 We ourselves can say the s for him, and you know
Rev 2:15 In the s way, you have some Nicolaitans among
you—people who follow the s teaching and
commit the s sins.
2:28 They will have the s authority I received from my
4: 1 and the s voice I had heard before spoke to me
11:13 And in the s hour there was a terrible earthquake

SAMGAR (1)

Jer 39: 3 Nergal-sharezer of S, and Nebo-sarsekim, a chief

SAMLAH (4)

Ge 36:36 S from the city of Masrekah became king.
36:37 When S died, Shaul from the city of Rehoboth on
1Ch 1:47 S from the city of Masrekah became king.
1:48 When S died, Shaul from the city of Rehoboth on

SAMOS (1)

Ac 20:15 The following day, we crossed to the island of S.

SAMOTHRACE (1)

Ac 16:11 and sailed straight across to the island of S,

SAMPLE (2) [SAMPLES]

Ex 23:19 bring me a choice s of the first day's harvest.
Lk 3: 7 Here is a s of John's preaching to the crowds that

SAMPLES (3) [SAMPLE]

Nu 13:20 and bring back s of the crops you see."
13:23 They also took s of the pomegranates and figs.
Eze 44:30 The first s of each grain harvest and the first of

SAMSON (53) [SAMSON'S]

Jdg 13:24 When her son was born, they named him S.
14: 1 One day when S was in Timnah, he noticed a
14: 3 But S told his father, "Get her for me. She is the
14: 5 As S and his parents were going down to Timnah,
14: 5 a young lion attacked S near the vineyards of
14: 7 When S arrived in Timnah, he talked with the
14:10 S threw a party at Timnah, as was the custom of
14:12 S said to them, "Let me tell you a riddle. If you
14:18 the men of the town came to S with their answer:
14:18 S replied, "If you hadn't plowed with my heifer,
14:19 But S was furious about what had happened,
15: 1 S took a young goat as a present to his wife.
15: 3 S said, "This time I cannot be blamed for
15: 6 "S," was the reply, "because his father-in-law
15: 7 "Because you did this," S vowed, "I will take my
15:10 The Philistines replied, "We've come to capture S.
15:11 went down to get S at the cave in the rock of Etam.
15:11 They said to S, "Don't you realize the Philistines
15:11 But S replied, "I only paid them back for what
15:12 you over to the Philistines." "All right," S said.
15:14 As S arrived at Lehi, the Philistines came shouting
15:14 Spirit of the LORD powerfully took control of S,
15:16 And S said, / "With the jawbone of a donkey,
15:18 Now S was very thirsty, and he cried out to the
15:19 the ground at Lehi, and S was revived as he drank.
15:20 S was Israel's judge for twenty years,
16: 1 One day S went to the Philistine city of Gaza
16: 2 Word soon spread that S was there, so the men of
16: 3 But S stayed in bed only until midnight. Then he
16: 4 Later S fell in love with a woman named Delilah,
16: 5 "Find out from S what makes him so strong
16: 6 So Delilah said to S, "Please tell me what makes
16: 7 S replied, "If I am tied up with seven new
16: 8 new bowstrings, and she tied S up with them.
16: 9 of the rooms of her house, and she cried out, "S!
16: 9 But S snapped the bowstrings as if they were string
16:11 S replied, "If I am tied up with brand-new ropes
16:12 room as before, and again Delilah cried out, "S!
16:12 But S snapped the ropes from his arms as if they
16:13 S replied, "If you weave the seven braids of my
16:14 it with the loom shuttle. Again she cried out, "S!
16:14 But S woke up, pulled back the loom shuttle,
16:17 Finally, S told her his secret. "My hair has never
16:19 Delilah lulled S to sleep with his head in her lap,
16:20 Then she cried out, "S! The Philistines have come
16:23 "Our god has given us victory over our enemy S!"
16:25 "Bring out S so he can perform for us!"
16:26 S said to the servant who was leading him by the
16:27 three thousand on the roof who were watching S
16:28 Then S prayed to the LORD,
16:29 Then S put his hands on the center pillars of the
16:31 S had been Israel's judge for twenty years.
Heb 11:32 Barak, S, Jephthah, David, Samuel, and all the

SAMSON'S (4) [SAMSON]

Jdg 14:15 On the fourth day they said to S wife,
14:16 So S wife came to him in tears and said,
14:20 the man who had been S best man at the wedding.
15: 6 "because his father-in-law from Timnah gave S

SAMUEL (143) [SAMUEL'S]

1Sa 1:20 She named him S, for she said, "I asked the
2:11 and Hannah returned home to Ramah without S.
2:18 Now S, though only a boy, was the LORD's
2:21 S grew up in the presence of the LORD.
2:26 Meanwhile, as young S grew taller, he also
3: 1 the boy S was serving the LORD by assisting Eli.
3: 3 and S was sleeping in the Tabernacle near the Ark
3: 4 Suddenly, the LORD called out, "S! S!" "Yes?"
"Yes?" S replied.
3: 6 Then the LORD called out again, "S!" Again S
jumped up and ran to Eli.
3: 7 S did not yet know the LORD because he had
3: 8 and once more S jumped up and ran to Eli.
3: 9 So he said to S, "Go and lie down again, and if
3: 9 your servant is listening.' " So S went back to
3:10 And the LORD came and called as before, "S! S!"
3:10 And S replied, "Yes, your servant is listening."
3:11 Then the LORD said to S, "I am about to do a
3:15 S stayed in bed until morning, then got up
3:16 But Eli called out to him, "S, my son." "Here I
am," S replied.
3:18 So S told Eli everything; he didn't hold anything
3:19 As S grew up, the LORD was with him,
3:19 and everything S said was wise and helpful.
3:20 that S was confirmed as a prophet of the LORD.
3:21 and gave messages to S there at the Tabernacle.
7: 3 Then S said to all the people of Israel, "If you are
7: 5 Then S told them, "Come to Mizpah, all of you.
7: 6 So it was at Mizpah that S became Israel's judge.
7: 8 to save us from the Philistines!" they begged S.
7: 9 So S took a young lamb and offered it to the
7:10 Just as S was sacrificing the burnt offering,
7:12 S then took a large stone and placed it between the
7:15 S continued as Israel's judge for the rest of his life.
7:17 And S built an altar to the LORD at Ramah.
8: 1 As S grew old, he appointed his sons to be judges
8: 4 Israel met at Ramah to discuss the matter with S.
8: 6 S was very upset with their request and went to the
8:10 So S passed on the LORD's warning to the
8:11 "This is how a king will treat you," S said.
8:21 So S told the LORD what the people had said,
8:22 a king." Then S agreed and sent the people home.
9:14 S was coming out toward them to climb the hill.
9:15 Now the LORD had told S the previous day,
9:17 When S noticed Saul, the LORD said,
9:18 Just then Saul approached S at the gateway
9:19 "I am the seer!" S replied. "Go on up the hill
9:22 Then S brought Saul and his servant into the great
9:23 S then instructed the cook to bring Saul the finest
9:24 it before Saul. "Go ahead and eat it," S said.
9:24 before I invited these others!" So Saul ate with S.
9:25 S took Saul up to the roof of the house
9:26 the next morning, S called up to Saul, "Get up!
9:26 got ready, and he and S left the house together.
9:27 of town, S told Saul to send his servant on ahead.
9:27 After the servant was gone, S said, "Stay here,
10: 1 Then S took a flask of olive oil and poured it over
10:14 So we went to the prophet S to ask him where they
10:16 But Saul didn't tell his uncle that S had anointed
10:17 Later S called all the people of Israel to meet
10:20 So S called the tribal leaders together before the
10:24 Then S said to all the people, "This is the man the
10:25 Then S told the people what the rights and duties
10:25 the LORD. Then S sent the people home again.
11: 7 who refuses to follow Saul and S into battle!"
11:12 Then the people exclaimed to S, "Now where are
11:14 Then S said to the people, "Come, let us all go to
12: 1 Then S addressed the people again: "I have done
12: 5 his anointed one are my witnesses," S declared,
12: 6 who appointed Moses and Aaron," S continued.
12:11 Barak, Jephthah, and S to save you, and you lived
12:18 So S called to the LORD, and the LORD sent
12:18 the people were terrified of the LORD and of S.
12:19 God for us, or we will die!" they cried out to S.
12:20 "Don't be afraid," S reassured them. "You have
13: 8 for S, as S had instructed him earlier, but S still
13:10 was finishing with the burnt offering, S arrived.
13:11 but S said, "What is this you have done?"
13:13 "How foolish!" S exclaimed. "You have
13:15 S then left Gilgal and went on his way, but the rest
15: 1 One day S said to Saul, "I anointed you king of
15:10 Then the LORD said to S,
15:11 S was so deeply moved when he heard this that he
15:12 Early the next morning S went to find Saul.
15:13 When S finally found him, Saul greeted him
15:14 and lowing of cattle I hear?" S demanded.
15:16 Then S said to Saul, "Stop! Listen to what the
15:17 And S told him, "Although you may think little of
15:22 But S replied, "What is more pleasing to the
15:26 But S replied, "I will not return with you!
15:27 As S turned to go, Saul grabbed at him to try to
15:28 And S said to him, "See? The LORD has torn the
15:31 So S finally agreed and went with him, and Saul
15:32 Then S said, "Bring King Agag to me."
15:33 But S said, "As your sword has killed the sons of
15:33 And S cut Agag to pieces before the LORD at
15:34 Then S went home to Ramah, and Saul returned to
15:35 S never went to meet with Saul again, but he
16: 1 Finally, the LORD said to S, "You have mourned
16: 2 But S asked, "How can I do that? If Saul hears
16: 4 So S did as the LORD instructed him. When he
16: 5 "Yes," S replied. "I have come to sacrifice to the
16: 5 Then S performed the purification rite for Jesse
16: 6 they arrived, S took one look at Eliab and thought,
16: 7 But the LORD said to S, "Don't judge by his
16: 8 Abinadab to step forward and walk in front of S.
16: 8 But S said, "This is not the one the LORD has
16: 9 Next Jesse summoned Shammah, but S said,
16:10 way all seven of Jesse's sons were presented to S.
16:10 But S said to Jesse, "The LORD has not chosen
16:11 Then S asked, "Are these all the sons you have?"
16:11 "Send for him at once," S said. "We will not sit
16:13 S took the olive oil he had brought and poured it
16:13 him from that day on. Then S returned to Ramah.
19:18 So David got away and went to Ramah to see S,
19:18 Then S took David with him to live at Naioth.
19:20 But when they arrived and saw S and the other
19:22 "Where are S and David?" he demanded.
19:24 and all night, prophesying in the presence of S.
25: 1 Now S died, and all Israel gathered for his funeral.
28: 3 Meanwhile, S had died, and all Israel had mourned
28:11 want me to call up?" "Call up S," Saul replied.
28:12 When the woman saw S, she screamed,
28:14 Saul realized that it was S, and he fell to the
28:15 S asked. "Because I am in deep trouble,"
28:16 But S replied, "Why ask me if the LORD has left
1Ch 6:27 Eliab, Jeroham, Elkanah, and S.
6:28 The sons of S were Joel (the older) and Abijah (the
6:33 His genealogy was traced back through Joel, S,
9:22 and S the seer had appointed their ancestors
11: 3 just as the LORD had promised through S.
26:28 the items dedicated to the LORD by S the seer,
29:29 to end, are written in *The Record of S the Seer,*
2Ch 35:18 Never since the time of the prophet S had there
Ps 99: 6 among his priests; / S also called on his name.
Jer 15: 1 and S stood before me pleading for these people,
Ac 3:24 "Starting with S, every prophet spoke about what
13:20 judges ruled until the time of S the prophet.
Heb 11:32 Barak, Samson, Jephthah, David, S, and all the

SAMUEL'S (5) [SAMUEL]

1Sa 4: 1 And S words went out to all the people of Israel.
7:13 And throughout S lifetime, the LORD's powerful
8:19 But the people refused to listen to S warning.
10: 9 his heart, and all S signs were fulfilled that day.
28:20 paralyzed with fright because of S words.

SANBALLAT (9) [SANBALLAT'S]

Ne 2:10 But when S the Horonite and Tobiah the

2:19 But when S, Tobiah, and Geshem the Arab heard
4: 1 S was very angry when he learned that we were
4: 7 But when S and Tobiah and the Arabs,
6: 1 When S, Tobiah, Geshem the Arab, and the rest of
6: 2 S and Geshem sent me a message asking me to
6:12 against me because Tobiah and S had hired him.
6:14 all the evil things that Tobiah and S have done.
13:28 priest had married a daughter of S the Horonite,

SANBALLAT'S (1) [SANBALLAT]
Ne 6: 5 S servant came with an open letter in his hand,

SANCTIFIED (1) [SANCTIFY]
Ex 29:43 and the Tabernacle will be s by my glorious

SANCTIFY (1) [SANCTIFIED, SANCTIFYING]
Ex 30:29 S them to make them entirely holy. After this,

SANCTIFYING (2) [SANCTIFY]
Ex 30:30 s them so they can minister before me as priests.
40:10 the altar of burnt offering and its utensils, s them.

SANCTUARIES (3) [SANCTUARY]
Eze 7:24 down their proud fortresses and defile their s.
21: 2 and prophesy against Israel and her s.
28:18 You defiled your s with your many sins and your

SANCTUARY (96) [SANCTUARIES]
Ex 15:17 the s, O Lord, that your hands have made.
36: 3 donated by the people for the completion of the s.
38:27 The 100 bases for the frames of the s walls and for
Lev 5:15 in silver as measured by the standard s shekel.
10: 4 away from the s to a place outside the camp."
10:17 "Why didn't you eat the sin offering in the s
10:18 you should have eaten the meat in the s area as I
12: 4 And she must not go to the s until her time of
16: 3 "When Aaron enters the s area, he must follow
19:30 days of rest and show reverence toward my s,
20: 3 because they have defiled my s and profaned my
21:12 He must not desecrate the s of his God by leaving
26: 2 Sabbath days of rest and show reverence for my s.
27:25 be measured in terms of the standard s shekel.
Nu 3:10 Anyone else who comes too near the s must be
3:28 They were responsible for the care of the s.
3:31 the altars, the various utensils used in the s,
3:32 special responsibility for the oversight of the s.
3:38 who had the final responsibility for the s on behalf
3:38 or Levite who came too near the s was to be
3:47 each piece weighing the same as the standard s
4:12 All the remaining utensils of the s must be
4:15 and his sons have finished covering the s
4:20 Otherwise they must not approach the s and look at
8:19 plague will strike them when they approach the s."
18: 1 held responsible for any offenses related to the s.
18: 5 must perform the sacred duties within the s
18: 7 Any other person who comes too near the s will be
18:16 each piece weighing the same as the standard s
19:20 for they have defiled the s of the LORD.
31: 6 They carried along the holy objects of the s
Jos 22:27 have the right to worship the LORD at his s with
2Sa 22: 7 He heard me from his s; / my cry reached his ears.
1Ki 6:16 He partitioned off an inner s—the Most Holy
6:19 Solomon prepared the inner s in the rear of the
6:20 This inner s was 30 feet long, 30 feet wide, and 30
6:23 Within the inner s Solomon placed two cherubim
6:27 Solomon placed them side by side in the inner s of
6:29 All the walls of the inner s and the main room were
6:31 For the entrance to the inner s, Solomon made
8: 6 LORD's covenant into the inner s of the Temple—
8:10 As the priests came out of the inner s, a cloud
1Ch 9:19 were responsible for guarding the entrance to the s,
9:29 the items in the s, and the supplies such as choice
22:19 Build the s of the LORD God so that you can
24: 5 the s from among the descendants of both Eleazar
28:10 LORD has chosen you to build a Temple as his s.
28:11 and the inner s where the Ark's cover—
2Ch 5: 7 LORD's covenant into the inner s of the Temple—
26:16 his God by entering the s of the LORD's Temple
26:18 Get out of the s, for you have sinned. The LORD
29: 5 Remove all the defiled things from the s.
29: 7 and presenting burnt offerings at the s of the God
29:16 The priests went into the s of the Temple of the
Ps 15: 1 Who may worship in your s, LORD? / Who may
18: 6 He heard me from his s; / my cry reached his ears.
20: 2 May he send you help from his s / and strengthen
26: 8 I love your s, LORD, / the place where your glory
27: 5 when troubles come; / he will hide me in his s.
28: 2 for help, / as I lift my hands toward your holy s.
61: 4 Let me live forever in your s, / safe beneath the
63: 2 I have seen you in your s / and gazed upon your
68:17 the Lord came from Mount Sinai into his s.
68:24 of my God and King / as he goes into the s.
68:35 God is awesome in his s. / The God of Israel gives
73:17 Then one day I went into your s, O God, / and I
74: 3 the city; / see how the enemy has destroyed your s.
74: 7 They set the s on fire, burning it to the ground.
78:69 There he built his towering s, / as solid
96: 6 surround him; / strength and beauty are in his s.
102:19 from his heavenly s. / He looked to the earth from
114: 2 the land of Judah became God's s, / and Israel
132: 5 the LORD, / a s for the Mighty One of Israel."
132: 8 Arise, O LORD, and enter your s, / along with the
Isa 6: 4 and the entire s was filled with smoke.
60:13 forests of cypress, fir, and pine—to beautify my s.
La 2: 7 has rejected his own altar; he despises his own s.
Eze 11:16 I will be a s to you during your time in exile.
44: 7 have brought uncircumcised foreigners into my s—
44: 8 you have hired foreigners to take charge of my s.
44: 9 will enter my s if they have not been circumcised
44:16 They are the ones who will enter my s
44:27 to work and enters the inner courtyard and the s,
45: 3 Within it the s of the Most Holy Place will be
45: 4 for the priests who minister to the LORD in the s.
Da 9:17 own sake, Lord, smile again on your desolate s.
11:31 polluting the s, putting a stop to the daily
Am 7:13 especially not here where the royal s is!"
Mal 2:11 beloved s by marrying women who worship idols.
Mt 23:35 in the Temple between the altar and the s.
Lk 1: 9 he was chosen by lot to enter the s and burn
1:11 Zechariah was in the s when an angel of the Lord
1:22 that he must have seen a vision in the Temple s.
11:51 who was killed between the altar and the s.
Heb 6:19 through the curtain of heaven into God's inner s.
9:11 He has entered that great, perfect s in heaven,

SAND (21) [SANDBARS, SANDS, SANDY]
Ge 22:17 like the stars of the sky and the s on the seashore.
41:49 There was so much grain, like s on the seashore,
Ex 2:12 Moses killed the Egyptian and buried him in the s.
Lev 11:30 common lizard, the s lizard, and the chameleon.
Dt 28:24 The LORD will turn your rain into s and dust,
33:19 of the sea / and the hidden treasures of the s."
Jos 11: 4 covered the landscape like the s on the seashore.
Jdg 7:12 Their camels were like grains of s on the
1Sa 13: 5 and as many warriors as the grains of s along the
2Sa 17:11 have an army as numerous as the s on the seashore.
1Ki 4:20 and Israel were as numerous as the s on the
Ps 139:18 even count them; / they outnumber the grains of s!
Pr 27: 3 A stone is heavy and s is weighty,
Isa 10:22 of Israel are as numerous as the s on the seashore,
Jer 15: 8 "There will be more widows than the grains of s
33:22 and the s on the seashores cannot be measured,
Hab 1: 9 the desert, sweeping captives ahead of them like s.
Mt 7:26 it is foolish, like a person who builds a house on s.
Ro 9:27 of Israel are as numerous as the s on the seashore,
Heb 11:12 like the stars of the sky and the s on the seashore,
Rev 20: 8 a mighty host, as numberless as s along the shore.

SANDAL (6) [SANDALED, SANDALS]
Ge 14:23 so much as a single thread or s thong from you.
Dt 25: 9 pull his s from his foot, and spit in his face.
25:10 as 'the family of the man whose s was pulled off'!
Ru 4: 7 transferring a right of purchase to remove his s
4: 8 So the other family redeemer drew off his s as he
Isa 5:27 Not a belt will be loose, not a s thong broken.

SANDALED (1) [SANDAL]
SS 7: 1 "How beautiful are your s feet, O queenly maiden.

SANDALS (20) [SANDAL]
Ex 3: 5 "Take off your s, for you are standing on holy
12:11 Wear your s, and carry your walking sticks in your
Dt 29: 5 yet your clothes and s did not wear out.
Jos 5:15 "Take off your s, for this is holy ground."
9: 5 put on ragged clothes and worn-out, patched s.
9:13 And our clothing and s are worn out from our long,
1Ki 2: 5 staining his belt and s with the blood of war.
2Ch 28:15 They provided clothing and s to wear, gave them
Isa 20: 2 "Take off all your clothes, including your s."
Eze 16:10 and s made of fine leather.
24:17 Do not uncover your head or take off your s.
24:23 remain covered, and your s must not be taken off.
Am 2: 6 people for silver and poor people for a pair of s.
8: 6 for a debt of one piece of silver or a pair of s.
Mt 10:10 with an extra coat and s or even a walking stick.
Mk 6: 9 He told them to wear s but not to take even an
Lk 10: 4 or a traveler's bag, or even an extra pair of s.
15:22 on him. Get a ring for his finger, and s for his feet.
Ac 7:33 "And the Lord said to him, 'Take off your s,
12: 8 angel told him, "Get dressed and put on your s."

SANDBARS (1) [SAND]
Ac 27:17 across to the s of Syrtis off the African coast,

SANDS (5) [SAND]
Ge 32:12 become as numerous as the s along the seashore—
Job 6: 3 they would be heavier than all the s of the sea.
Ps 78:27 birds as plentiful as the s along the seashore!
Isa 48:19 Then you would have become as numerous as the s
Hos 1:10 In that day its people will be like the s of the

SANDY (1) [SAND]
Jer 5:22 am the one who defines the ocean's s shoreline,

SANE (2) [SANITY]
Mk 5:15 he was sitting there fully clothed and perfectly s.
Lk 8:35 demons sitting quietly at Jesus' feet, clothed and s.

SANG (26) [SING]
Ge 12:15 they s her praises to their king, the pharaoh,
Ex 15: 1 and the people of Israel s this song to the LORD:
15:21 And Miriam s this song: / "I will sing to the
Nu 21:17 There the Israelites s this song: / "Spring up,
Jdg 5: 1 and Barak son of Abinoam s this song:
1Sa 18: 6 and they s and danced for joy with tambourines
2Sa 3:33 Then the king s this funeral song for Abner:
22: 1 David s this song to the LORD after the LORD
22: 2 These are the words he s: / "The LORD is my
2Ch 20:21 This is what they s: / "Give thanks to the LORD;
29:28 assembly worshiped the LORD as the singers s
30:21 Each day the Levites and priests s to the LORD,
Ezr 3:11 and thanks, they s this song to the LORD:
Ne 12:42 They played and s loudly and clearly under the
Job 38: 7 as the morning stars s together and all the angels
Ps 7: T which he s to the LORD concerning Cush of the
18: T He s this song to the LORD on the day the
106:12 his promises. / Then they finally s his praise.
126: 2 We were filled with laughter, / and we s for joy.
Isa 6: 3 In a great chorus they s, "Holy, holy, holy is the
Mt 26:30 Then they s a hymn and went out to the Mount of
Mk 14:26 Then they s a hymn and went out to the Mount of
Rev 5: 9 And they s a new song with these words:
5:12 And they s in a mighty chorus: / "The Lamb is
5:13 They also s: / "Blessing and honor and glory
14: 3 This great choir s a wonderful new song in front of

SANITY (2) [SANE]
Da 4:34 My s returned, and I praised and worshiped the
4:36 "When my s returned to me, so did my honor

SANK (14) [SINK]
Ex 15: 5 covered them; / they s to the bottom like a stone.
15:10 They s like lead / in the mighty waters.
Jdg 5:27 He s, he fell, / he lay dead at her feet.
1Sa 17:49 The stone s in, and Goliath stumbled and fell face
2Ki 9:24 his heart, and he s down dead in his chariot.
Ne 9:11 They s like stones beneath the mighty waters.
Ps 104: 8 Mountains rose and valleys s / to the levels you
107:26 and s again to the depths; / the sailors cringed in
Jer 38: 6 of mud at the bottom, and Jeremiah s down into it.
38:22 When your feet s in the mud, they left you to your
Jnh 2: 3 ocean depths, and I s down to the heart of the sea.
2: 5 "I s beneath the waves, and death was very near.
2: 6 I s down to the very roots of the mountains. I was
Ac 20: 9 he s into a deep sleep and fell three stories to his

SANSANNAH (1)
Jos 15:31 Ziklag, Madmannah, S,

SAP (1) [SAPPED, SAPS]
Hos 5:12 I will s Judah's strength as dry rot weakens wood.

SAPH (2)
2Sa 21:18 As they fought, Sibbecai from Hushah killed S,
1Ch 20: 4 As they fought, Sibbecai from Hushah killed S,

SAPHIR [KJV] See SHAPHIR

SAPPED (2) [SAP]
La 1:14 The Lord s my strength and gave me to my
Hos 7: 9 Worshiping foreign gods has s their strength,

SAPPHIRA (1)
Ac 5: 1 Ananias who, with his wife, S, sold some property.

SAPPHIRE (7) [SAPPHIRES]
Ex 24:10 feet there seemed to be a pavement of brilliant s,
28:18 contain a turquoise, a s, and a white moonstone.
39:11 row were a turquoise, a s, and a white moonstone.
Eze 1:26 was what looked like a throne made of blue s.
10: 1 I saw what appeared to be a throne of blue s above
28:13 beryl, onyx, jasper, s, turquoise, and emerald—
Rev 21:19 the second s, the third agate, the fourth emerald,

SAPPHIRES (4) [SAPPHIRE]
Job 28: 6 "People know how to find s and gold dust—
28:16 of Ophir, greater than precious onyx stone or s.
SS 5:14 His body is like bright ivory, aglow with s.
Isa 54:11 I will rebuild you on a foundation of s and make

SAPS (2) [SAP]
Pr 12: 4 and crown; a shameful wife s his strength.
17:22 but a broken spirit s a person's strength.

SARAH (32) [SARAH'S, SARAI, SARAI'S]
Ge 17:15 longer be Sarai; from now on you will call her S.
17:17 "Besides, S is ninety; how could she have a
17:19 But God replied, "S, your wife, will bear you a
17:21 be born to you and S about this time next year."
18: 6 So Abraham ran back to the tent and said to S,
18: 9 "Where is S, your wife?" they asked him.
18:10 I will return, and your wife S will have a son."
18:10 Now S was listening to this conversation from the
18:11 And since Abraham and S were both very old,
18:11 and S was long past the age of having children,
18:13 the LORD said to Abraham, "Why did S laugh?
18:14 as I told you, I will return, and S will have a son."
18:15 S was afraid, so she denied that she had laughed.
20: 2 told people there that his wife, S, was his sister.
20:14 to Abraham, and he returned his wife, S, to him.
20:16 Then he turned to S. "Look," he said, "I am
21: 2 S became pregnant, and she gave a son to
21: 6 And S declared, "God has brought me laughter!
21: 9 But S saw Ishmael—the son of Abraham and her
21:12 Do just as S says, for Isaac is the son through
23: 1 When S was 127 years old,
23:19 So Abraham buried S there in Canaan, in the cave
24:36 When S, my master's wife, was very old, she gave

25:10 from the Hittites, where he had buried his wife **S**.
49:31 There Abraham and his wife **S** are buried.
Isa 51: 2 Yes, think about your ancestors Abraham and **S**,
Ro 4:19 to be a father at the age of one hundred and that **S**,
9: 9 "Next year I will return, and **S** will have a son."
Gal 4:26 But **S**, the free woman, represents the heavenly
Heb 11:11 It was by faith that **S** together with Abraham was
11:11 even though they were too old and **S** was barren.
1Pe 3: 6 For instance, **S** obeyed her husband, Abraham,

SARAH'S (1) [SARAH]

Ge 25:12 of Abraham through Hagar, **S** Egyptian servant.

SARAI (15) [SARAH]

Ge 11:29 Meanwhile, Abram married **S**, and his brother
11:30 Now **S** was not able to have any children.
11:31 Terah took his son Abram, his daughter-in-law **S**,
12: 5 He took his wife, **S**, his nephew Lot, and all his
12:11 Abram said to **S**, "You are a very beautiful
12:17 plague upon Pharaoh's household because of **S**,
16: 1 But **S**, Abram's wife, had no children. So **S** took
her servant, an Egyptian woman named
16: 2 me from having any children," **S** said to Abram.
16: 3 So **S**, Abram's wife, took Hagar the Egyptian
16: 4 she began to treat her mistress **S** with contempt.
16: 5 Then **S** said to Abram, "It's all your fault!
16: 6 So **S** treated her harshly, and Hagar ran away.
17:15 Then God added, "Regarding **S**, your wife—her
name will no longer be **S**;

SARAI'S (1) [SARAH]

Ge 16: 8 The angel said to her, "Hagar, **S** servant,

SARAPH (1)

1Ch 4:22 Joash, and **S**, who ruled over Moab

SARDINE [KJV] See CARNELIAN

SARDIS (3)

Rev 1:11 Ephesus, Smyrna, Pergamum, Thyatira, **S**,
3: 1 "Write this letter to the angel of the church in **S**.
3: 4 "Yet even in **S** there are some who have not soiled

SARDITES [KJV] See SEREDITE

SARDIUS [KJV] See CARNELIAN

SAREPTA [KJV] See ZAREPHATH

SARGON (1)

Isa 20: 1 In the year when King **S** of Assyria captured the

SARID (2)

Jos 19:10 boundary of Zebulun's inheritance started at **S**.
19:12 the boundary line went east from **S** to the border of

SARON [KJV] See SHARON

SARUCH [KJV] See SERUG

SASH (13) [SASHES]

Ex 28: 4 a robe, an embroidered tunic, a turban, and a **s**.
28: 8 And the **s** will be made of the same materials:
28:27 gold rings and attach them to the ephod near the **s**.
28:28 securely to the ephod above the beautiful **s**.
28:39 linen as well. Also make him an embroidered **s**.
29: 5 the ephod itself, the chestpiece, and the **s**.
39: 5 They also made an elaborate woven **s** of the same
39:20 gold rings were attached to the ephod near the **s**.
39:21 held securely to the ephod above the beautiful **s**.
Lev 8: 7 embroidered tunic and tied the **s** around his waist.
8: 7 and attached the ephod with its decorative **s**.
16: 4 He must tie the linen **s** around his waist and put the
Rev 1:13 He was wearing a long robe with a gold **s** across

SASHES (7) [SASH]

Ex 28:40 "Then for Aaron's sons, make tunics, **s**,
29: 9 with their woven **s** and their headdresses. They will
39:29 The **s** were made of fine linen cloth
Lev 8:13 their **s**, and their turbans, just as the LORD had
Pr 31:24 linen garments and **s** to sell to the merchants.
Isa 3:20 ankle chains, **s**, perfumes, and charms;
3:24 They will wear ropes for **s**, and their well-set hair

SAT (95) [SIT]

Ge 21:16 and **s** down by herself about a hundred yards away.
31:46 then **s** down beside the pile of stones to share a
38:14 Then she **s** beside the road at the entrance to the
43:32 The Egyptians **s** at their own table
48: 2 gathered his strength and **s** up in bed to greet him.
Ex 2:15 Moses arrived in Midian, he **s** down beside a well.
12:29 the firstborn son of Pharaoh, who **s** on the throne,
18:13 Moses **s** as usual to hear the people's complaints
Lev 15: 6 If you sit where the man with the discharge has **s**,
Jdg 5:17 he stay home? / Asher **s** unmoved at the seashore,
6:11 and **s** beneath the oak tree at Ophrah,
19: 6 So the two of them **s** down together and had
21: 2 and **s** in the presence of God until evening,
Ru 2:14 So she **s** with his harvesters, and Boaz gave her
4: 1 I want to talk to you." So they **s** down together.
1Sa 20:24 new moon festival began, the king **s** down to eat.
20:25 He **s** at his usual place against the wall,
28:23 and got up from the ground and **s** on the couch.
2Sa 2:13 The two groups **s** down there, facing each other
7:18 went in and **s** before the LORD and prayed,
19: 8 So the king went out and **s** at the city gate, and as
1Ki 2:19 When he **s** down on his throne again, he ordered
2:19 brought for his mother, and she **s** at his right hand.
7: 7 where Solomon **s** to hear legal matters.
19: 4 He **s** down under a solitary broom tree and prayed
2Ki 9:30 her eyelids and fixed her hair and **s** at a window.
1Ch 17:16 went in and **s** before the LORD and prayed,
Ezr 9: 3 my head and beard, and **s** down utterly shocked.
9: 4 and **s** with me because of this unfaithfulness of his
9: 4 And I **s** there utterly appalled until the time of the
9: 5 I stood up from where I had **s** in mourning with my
10:16 the leaders **s** down to investigate the matter.
Ne 1: 4 When I heard this, I **s** down and wept. In fact,
Est 3:15 Then the king and Haman **s** down to drink,
Job 2: 8 a piece of broken pottery as he **s** among the ashes.
2:13 Then they **s** on the ground with him for seven days
Ps 107:10 Some **s** in darkness and deepest gloom,
137: 1 Beside the rivers of Babylon, we **s** and wept
Jer 15:17 I **s** alone because your hand was on me. I burst
26:10 and **s** down at the New Gate of the Temple to hold
39: 3 army came in and **s** in triumph at the Middle Gate:
Eze 3:15 I **s** there among them for seven days,
20: 1 They **s** down in front of me to wait for his reply.
23:41 You **s** with them on a beautifully embroidered
Da 7: 9 put in place and the Ancient One **s** down to judge.
7: 9 He **s** on a fiery throne with wheels of blazing fire,
Jnh 3: 6 himself in sackcloth and **s** on a heap of ashes.
Mt 4:16 the people who **s** in darkness / have seen a great
5: 1 with his disciples and **s** down to teach them.
8:27 The disciples just **s** there in awe. "Who is this?"
11:21 their people would have **s** in deep repentance long
13: 2 where he **s** and taught as the people listened on the
15:29 the Sea of Galilee and climbed a hill and **s** down.
21: 7 threw their garments over the colt, and he **s** on it.
24: 3 Jesus **s** on the slopes of the Mount of Olives.
26:20 Jesus **s** down at the table with the twelve disciples.
26:58 He went in, **s** with the guards, and waited to see
27:36 Then they **s** around and kept guard as he hung
28: 2 from heaven and rolled aside the stone and **s** on it.
Mk 4: 1 got into a boat and **s** down and spoke from there.
6:40 So they **s** in groups of fifty or a hundred.
9:35 He **s** down and called the twelve disciples over to
11: 7 and threw their garments over it, and he **s** on it.
12:41 and **s** and watched as the crowds dropped in their
13: 3 Jesus **s** on the slopes of the Mount of Olives across
14:54 For a while he **s** with the guards, warming himself
16: 5 and there on the right **s** a young man clothed in a
16:19 and **s** down in the place of honor at God's right
Lk 4:20 handed it back to the attendant, and **s** down.
5: 3 So he **s** in the boat and taught the crowds from
7:15 Then the dead boy **s** up and began to talk to those
7:36 so Jesus accepted the invitation and **s** down to eat.
9:15 So the people all **s** down.
10:13 their people would have **s** in deep repentance long
10:39 Her sister, Mary, **s** at the Lord's feet, listening to
11:38 His host was amazed to see that he **s** down to eat
22:14 and the twelve apostles **s** down together at the
22:55 guards lit a fire in the courtyard and **s** around it,
24:30 As they **s** down to eat, he took a small loaf of
Jn 4: 6 **s** wearily beside the well about noontime.
6: 3 the hills and **s** down with his disciples around him.
6:10 five thousand—**s** down on the grassy slopes.
8: 2 soon gathered, and he **s** down and taught them.
12: 2 Martha served, and Lazarus **s** at the table with him.
12:14 Jesus found a young donkey and **s** on it,
13:12 he put on his robe again and **s** down and asked,
19:13 Then Pilate **s** down on the judgment seat on the
Ac 9:40 opened her eyes! When she saw Peter, she **s** up!
12:21 **s** on his throne, and made a speech to them.
16:13 and we **s** down to speak with some women who
Heb 1: 3 he **s** down in the place of honor at the right hand of
8: 1 Our High Priest **s** down in the place of highest
10:12 Then he **s** down at the place of highest honor at
Rev 3:21 was victorious and **s** with my Father on his throne.
4: 4 surrounded him, and twenty-four elders **s** on them.

SATAN (65) [SATAN'S]

1Ch 21: 1 **S** rose up against Israel and caused David to take a
Job 1: 6 the LORD, and **S** the Accuser came with them.
1: 7 have you come from?" the LORD asked **S**.
1: 7 And **S** answered the LORD, "I have been going
1: 8 Then the LORD asked **S**, "Have you noticed my
1: 9 **S** replied to the LORD, "Yes, Job fears God,
1:12 you may test him," the LORD said to **S**.
1:12 him physically." So **S** left the LORD's presence.
2: 1 the LORD, and **S** the Accuser came with them.
2: 2 have you come from?" the LORD asked **S**.
2: 2 And **S** answered the LORD, "I have been going
2: 3 Then the LORD asked **S**, "Have you noticed my
2: 4 **S** replied to the LORD, "Skin for skin—
2: 6 do with him as you please," the LORD said to **S**.
2: 7 So **S** left the LORD's presence, and he struck Job
Zec 3: 1 **S** was there at the angel's right hand,
3: 2 And the LORD said to **S**, "I, the LORD, reject your
accusations, **S**.
Mt 4:10 "Get out of here, **S**," Jesus told him.
12:24 He gets his power from **S**, the prince of demons."
12:26 And if **S** is casting out **S**, he is fighting against
16:23 turned to Peter and said, "Get away from me, **S**!
Mk 1:13 He was there for forty days, being tempted by **S**.
3:22 "He's possessed by **S**, the prince of demons.
3:23 by way of illustration, "How can **S** cast out **S**?
3:26 And if **S** is fighting against himself, how can he
4:15 but then **S** comes at once and takes it away from
8:33 said to Peter very sternly, "Get away from me, **S**!
Lk 10:18 "I saw **S** falling from heaven as a flash of
11:15 He gets his power from **S**, the prince of demons!"
11:18 But if **S** is fighting against himself by empowering
11:21 For when **S**, who is completely armed, guards his
13:16 in which **S** has held her for eighteen years?"
22: 3 Then **S** entered into Judas Iscariot, who was one of
22:31 "Simon, Simon, **S** has asked to have all of you,
Jn 13:27 as Judas had eaten the bread, **S** entered into him.
Ac 5: 3 Peter said, "Ananias, why has **S** filled your heart?
26:18 darkness to light, and from the power of **S** to God.
Ro 16:20 The God of peace will soon crush **S** under your
1Co 7: 5 so that **S** won't be able to tempt them because of
2Co 2:11 so that **S** will not outsmart us. For we are very
4: 4 **S**, the god of this evil world, has blinded the minds
11:14 Even **S** can disguise himself as an angel of light.
12: 7 a messenger from **S** to torment me and keep me
Eph 2: 2 full of sin, obeying **S**, the mighty prince of the
6:16 shield to stop the fiery arrows aimed at you by **S**.
1Th 2:18 Paul, tried again and again, but **S** prevented us.
2Th 2: 9 This evil man will come to do the work of **S** with
1Ti 1:20 I turned them over to **S** so they would learn not to
2:14 not Adam, who was deceived by **S**, and sin was the
5:15 them have already gone astray and now follow **S**.
1Jn 2:13 because you have won your battle with **S**.
2:14 your hearts, and you have won your battle with **S**.
Jude 1: 9 did not dare accuse **S** of blasphemy, but simply
1: 9 (This took place when Michael was arguing with **S**
Rev 2: 9 really aren't because theirs is a synagogue of **S**.
2:13 in the city where that great throne of **S** is located,
2:24 as they call them—depths of **S**, really).
3: 9 I will force those who belong to **S**—those liars who
12: 9 the ancient serpent called the Devil, or **S**, the one
20: 2 seized the dragon—that old serpent, the Devil, **S**—
20: 3 so **S** could not deceive the nations anymore until
20: 7 thousand years end, **S** will be let out of his prison.

SATAN'S (2) [SATAN]

1Co 5: 5 cast this man out of the church and into **S** hands,
Rev 2:13 was martyred among you by **S** followers.

SATIATE(D) [KJV] See REST, SATISFIED, SATISFY

SATISFACTION (7) [SATISFY]

Pr 18:20 the right words on a person's lips bring **s**.
29: 9 to court, there will be ranting and ridicule but no **s**.
Ecc 2:20 It was not the answer to my search for **s** in this life.
2:24 than to enjoy food and drink and to find **s** in work.
6: 3 But if he finds no **s** in life and in the end does not
1Co 9:18 It is the **s** I get from preaching the Good News
Gal 6: 4 then you will enjoy the personal **s** of having done

SATISFIED (44) [SATISFY]

Lev 26:26 and even if you have food to eat, you will not be **s**.
Dt 14:29 the widows in your towns, so they can eat and be **s**.
Jos 22:30 and the half-tribe of Manasseh, they were **s**.
22:33 And all the Israelites were **s** and praised God
Jdg 15: 7 my revenge on you, and I won't stop until I'm **s**!"
Job 19:22 as God does? Why aren't you **s** with my anguish?
20:20 He was always greedy but never **s**. Of all the things
29:22 they had nothing to add, for my counsel **s** them.
Ps 17:15 I will see you. / When I awake, I will be fully **s**,
22:26 The poor will eat and be **s**. / All who seek the
104:28 You open your hand to feed them, and they are **s**.
Pr 11:25 The generous prosper and are **s**; those who refresh
13: 4 but those who work hard will prosper and be **s**.
27:20 Just as Death and Destruction are never **s**, so
human desire is never **s**.
30:15 are three other things—no, four!—that are never **s**:
Ecc 1: 8 No matter how much we see, we are never **s**.
Isa 5:25 But even then the LORD's anger will not be **s**.
7:13 of David! You aren't **s** to exhaust my patience.
9:12 But even then the LORD's anger will not be **s**.
9:17 But even then the LORD's anger will not be **s**.
9:21 But even then the LORD's anger will not be **s**.
10: 4 But even then the LORD's anger will not be **s**.
53:11 that is accomplished by his anguish, he will be **s**.
56:11 And they are as greedy as dogs, never **s**. They are
Jer 5: 7 I fed my people until they were fully **s**. But they
46:10 The sword will devour until it is **s**, yes, drunk with
50:19 and to be **s** once more on the hill country of
La 4:11 But now the anger of the LORD is **s**. His fiercest
Eze 5:13 Then at last my anger will be spent, and I will be **s**.
13:15 and those who covered it with whitewash will be **s**.
16:28 after your prostitution there you still were not **s**.
16:29 land of Babylonia—but you still weren't **s**!
23: 8 when the Egyptians **s** their lusts with her
24:13 remain filthy until my fury against you has been **s**.
27:33 you traded / **s** the needs of many nations.
Hos 13: 6 But when you had eaten and were **s**, then you
Hab 2: 5 opened as wide as death, but they are never **s**.
Lk 1:53 He has **s** the hungry with good things / and sent the
6:21 you who are hungry now, / for you will be **s**.
6:25 What sorrows await you who are **s** and prosperous
Jn 14: 8 "Lord, show us the Father and we will be **s**."
Heb 13: 5 from the love of money; be **s** with what you have.
2Pe 2:14 adultery with their eyes, and their lust is never **s**.

SATISFIES (7) [SATISFY]

Job 5: 5 and their wealth **s** the thirst of many others,
38:27 Who sends the rain that **s** the parched ground

Ps 107: 9 For he **s** the thirsty / and fills the hungry with good
147:14 and **s** you with plenty of the finest wheat.
Pr 18:20 Words satisfy the soul as food **s** the stomach;
Ac 17:25 breath to everything, and he **s** every need there is.
Ro 13:10 to anyone, so love **s** all of God's requirements.

SATISFY (31) [SATISFACTION, SATISFIED, SATISFIES, SATISFYING]

Nu 11:22 all our flocks and herds, would that **s** them?
20: 8 You will get enough water from the rock to **s** all
Job 38:39 prey for a lioness and **s** the young lions' appetites
Ps 63: 5 You **s** me more than the richest of foods. / I will
69:21 for food; / they offer me sour wine to **s** my thirst.
81:16 I would **s** you with wild honey from the rock."
90:14 **S** us in the morning with your unfailing love,
91:16 I will **s** them with a long life / and give them my
132:15 this city prosperous / and **s** its poor with food.
145:16 you **s** the hunger and thirst of every living thing.
Pr 5:19 a graceful deer. Let her breasts **s** you always.
6:35 There is no compensation or bribe that will **s** him.
10: 3 but he refuses to **s** the craving of the wicked.
18:20 Words **s** the soul as food satisfies the stomach;
30: 8 nor riches! Give me just enough to **s** my needs.
30:20 an adulterous woman can **s** her sexual appetite,
Isa 13: 3 I am exalted. I have called them to **s** my anger."
35: 7 a pool, and springs of water will **s** the thirsty land.
60:16 bring the best of their goods to **s** your every need.
Jer 31:14 I will **s** my people with my bounty. I, the LORD,
Eze 7:19 It will neither **s** nor feed them, for their love of
20: 8 Then I threatened to pour out my fury on them to **s**
21:17 too, will clap my hands, and I will **s** my fury.
23:18 before them and gave herself to **s** their lusts.
Joel 2:19 and wine and olive oil, enough to **s** your needs.
Mic 7: 1 or a single fig can be found to **s** my hunger.
Hag 1: 6 have wine to drink, but not enough to **s** your thirst.
Ro 3:25 for our sins and to **s** God's anger against us.
Gal 5:13 not freedom to **s** your sinful nature, but freedom to
6: 8 Those who live only to **s** their own sinful desires
2Ti 2: 4 then you cannot **s** the one who has enlisted you in

SATISFYING (3) [SATISFY]

Pr 3: 2 for they will give you a long and **s** life.
3:17 you down delightful paths; all her ways are **s**.
Jas 5: 5 your years on earth in luxury, **s** your every whim.

SATYRS [KJV] See (WILD) GOATS

SAUCE (1)

Jn 13:26 the one to whom I give the bread dipped in the **s**."

SAUL (341) [SAUL'S]

1Sa 9: 2 His son **S** was the most handsome man in Israel—
9: 3 and he told **S**, "Take a servant with you, and go
9: 4 So **S** took one of his servants and traveled all
9: 5 of Zuph, and **S** said to his servant, "Let's go home.
9: 7 we don't have anything to offer him," **S** replied.
9:10 "All right," **S** agreed, "let's try it!" So they
9:11 So **S** and his servant asked, "Is the seer here
9:17 When Samuel noticed **S**, the LORD said,
9:18 Just then **S** approached Samuel at the gateway
9:21 **S** replied, "But I'm only from Benjamin,
9:22 Then Samuel brought **S** and his servant into the
9:23 then instructed the cook to bring **S** the finest cut of
9:24 So the cook brought it in and placed it before **S**.
9:24 I invited these others!" So **S** ate with Samuel.
9:25 Samuel took **S** up to the roof of the house
9:26 the next morning, Samuel called up to **S**, "Get up!
9:26 So **S** got ready, and he and Samuel left the house
9:27 Samuel told **S** to send his servant on ahead.
10: 1 He kissed **S** on the cheek and said, "I am doing
10: 9 As **S** turned and started to leave, God changed his
10:10 When **S** and his servant arrived at Gibeah,
10:10 Then the Spirit of God came upon **S**, and he,
10:11 about it, they exclaimed, "What? Is **S** a prophet?
10:12 So that is the origin of the saying "Is **S** a
10:13 When **S** had finished prophesying, he climbed the
10:14 **S** replied, "but we couldn't find them.
10:16 "He said the donkeys had been found," **S** replied.
10:16 But **S** didn't tell his uncle that Samuel had
10:21 And finally **S** son of Kish was chosen from among
10:26 When **S** returned to his home at Gibeah, a band of
10:27 and refused to bring him gifts. But **S** ignored them.
11: 5 **S** was plowing in the field, and when he returned
11: 6 Then the Spirit of God came mightily upon **S**,
11: 7 to the oxen of anyone who refuses to follow **S**
11: 8 When **S** mobilized them at Bezek, he found that
11: 9 So **S** sent the messengers back to Jabesh-gilead to
11:11 But before dawn the next morning, **S** arrived,
11:12 "Now where are those men who said **S** shouldn't
11:13 But **S** replied, "No one will be executed today,
11:15 and **S** and all the Israelites were very happy.
13: 1 **S** was thirty years old when he became king,
13: 2 **S** selected three thousand special troops from the
13: 3 so **S** sounded the call to arms throughout Israel.
13: 4 Israelite army mobilized again and met **S** at Gilgal.
13: 7 Meanwhile, **S** stayed at Gilgal, and his men were
13: 8 **S** waited there seven days for Samuel, as Samuel
13: 8 **S** realized that his troops were rapidly slipping
13: 9 And **S** sacrificed the burnt offering himself.
13:10 Just as **S** was finishing with the burnt offering,
13:10 **S** went out to meet and welcome him,
13:11 **S** replied, "I saw my men scattering from me,
13:15 but the rest of the troops went with **S** to meet the
13:15 When **S** counted the men who were still with him,
13:16 **S** and Jonathan and the troops with them were
13:22 had a sword or spear, except for **S** and Jonathan.
14: 2 **S** and his six hundred men were camped on the
14:17 "Find out who isn't here," **S** ordered. And when
14:18 Then **S** shouted to Ahijah, "Bring the ephod
14:19 But while **S** was talking to the priest, the shouting
14:19 So **S** said to Ahijah, "Never mind; let's get
14:20 Then **S** and his six hundred men rushed out to the
14:21 the Philistine army revolted and joined in with **S**,
14:24 because **S** had made them take an oath, saying,
14:33 Someone reported to **S**, "Look, the men are
14:33 "That is very wrong," **S** said. "Find a large stone
14:35 And **S** built an altar to the LORD, the first one he
14:36 Then **S** said, "Let's chase the Philistines all night
14:37 So **S** asked God, "Should we go after the
14:38 Then **S** said to the leaders, "Something's wrong!
14:40 Then **S** said, "Jonathan and I will stand over here,
14:41 Then **S** prayed, "O LORD, God of Israel,
14:41 and **S** were chosen as the guilty ones,
14:42 Then **S** said, "Now choose between me
14:43 what you have done," **S** demanded of Jonathan.
14:44 "Yes, Jonathan," **S** said, "you must die! May God
14:45 But the people broke in and said to **S**,
14:46 Then **S** called back the army from chasing the
14:47 Now when **S** had secured his grasp on Israel's
14:52 So whenever **S** saw a young man who was brave
15: 1 One day Samuel said to **S**, "I anointed you king of
15: 4 So **S** mobilized his army at Telaim. There were
15: 5 Then **S** went to the city of Amalek and lay in wait
15: 6 **S** sent this message to the Kenites: "Move away
15: 7 Then **S** slaughtered the Amalekites from Havilah
15: 9 **S** and his men spared Agag's life and kept the best
15:11 "I am sorry that I ever made **S** king, for he has not
15:12 Early the next morning Samuel went to find **S**.
15:12 "**S** went to Carmel to set up a monument to
15:13 finally found him, **S** greeted him cheerfully.
15:15 the best of the sheep and cattle," **S** admitted.
15:16 Then Samuel said to **S**, "Stop! Listen to what the
15:16 told me last night!" "What was it?" **S** asked.
15:20 "But I did obey the LORD," **S** insisted.
15:24 Then **S** finally admitted, "Yes, I have sinned.
15:27 **S** grabbed at him to try to hold him back and tore
15:30 Then **S** pleaded again, "I know I have sinned.
15:31 and went with him, and **S** worshiped the LORD.
15:34 to Ramah, and **S** returned to his house at Gibeah.
15:35 Samuel never went to meet with **S** again, but he
15:35 And the LORD was sorry he had ever made **S**
16: 1 to Samuel, "You have mourned long enough for **S**.
16: 2 can I do that? If **S** hears about it, he will kill me."
16:14 Now the Spirit of the LORD had left **S**,
16:17 "All right," **S** said. "Find me someone who plays
16:18 One of the servants said to **S**, "The son of Jesse is
16:19 So **S** sent messengers to Jesse to say, "Send me
16:20 Jesse responded by sending David to **S**, along with
16:21 So David went to **S** and served him. **S** liked David
16:22 Then **S** sent word to Jesse asking, "Please let
16:23 the tormenting spirit from God troubled **S**,
16:23 Then **S** would feel better, and the tormenting spirit
17: 2 **S** countered by gathering his troops near the valley
17:11 When **S** and the Israelites heard this, they were
17:15 David went back and forth between working for **S**
17:19 David's brothers were with **S** and the Israelite
17:31 Then David's question was reported to King **S**,
17:32 "Don't worry about a thing," David told **S**.
17:33 "Don't be ridiculous!" **S** replied. "There is no
17:37 **S** finally consented. "All right, go ahead," he said.
17:38 Then **S** gave David his own armor—a bronze
17:55 As **S** watched David go out to fight Goliath,
17:57 Abner brought him to **S** with the Philistine's head
17:58 "Tell me about your father, my boy," **S** said.
18: 1 After David had finished talking with **S**, he met
18: 2 From that day on **S** kept David with him at the
18: 5 Whatever **S** asked David to do, David did it
18: 5 So **S** made him a commander in his army,
18: 6 along the way to celebrate and to cheer for King **S**,
18: 7 This was their song: / "**S** has killed his thousands,
18: 8 This made **S** very angry. "What's this?" he said.
18: 9 So from that time on **S** kept a jealous eye on
18:10 a tormenting spirit from God overwhelmed **S**,
18:10 this happened. But **S**, who had a spear in his hand,
18:12 for **S** was afraid of him, and he was jealous
18:13 **S** banned him from his presence and appointed him
18:15 When **S** recognized this, he became even more
18:17 One day **S** said to David, "I am ready to give you
18:17 For **S** thought to himself, "I'll send him out
18:19 **S** gave Merab in marriage to Adriel, a man from
18:20 and **S** was delighted when he heard about it.
18:21 **S** said to himself. But to David he said, "I have a
18:22 Then **S** told his men to say confidentially to David,
18:25 But what **S** had in mind was that David would be
18:27 the king. So **S** gave Michal to David to be his wife.
19: 1 **S** now urged his servants and his son Jonathan to
19: 6 So **S** listened to Jonathan and vowed, "As surely
19: 7 Then he took David to see **S**, and everything was
19: 9 But one day as **S** was sitting at home,
19:10 **S** hurled his spear at David in an attempt to kill
19:11 Then **S** sent troops to watch David's house.
19:15 **S** ordered, "so I can kill him as he lies there!"
19:17 **S** demanded of Michal. "I had to," Michal replied.
19:18 and he told him all that **S** had done to him.
19:19 When the report reached **S** that David was at
19:21 When **S** heard what had happened, he sent other
19:22 **S** himself went to Ramah and arrived at the great
19:23 the way to Naioth the Spirit of God came upon **S**,
19:24 watching exclaimed, "What? Is **S** a prophet, too?"
20:26 **S** didn't say anything about it that day, for he said
20:27 was empty again the next day, **S** asked Jonathan,
20:30 **S** boiled with rage at Jonathan. "You stupid son of
20:33 Then **S** hurled his spear at Jonathan, intending to
21:10 So David escaped from **S** and went to King Achish
21:11 singing, '**S** has killed his thousands, and David his
22: 6 The news of his arrival in Judah soon reached **S**.
22: 7 of Benjamin!" **S** shouted when he heard the news.
22:11 King **S** immediately sent for Ahimelech and all his
22:12 they arrived, **S** shouted at him, "Listen to me,
22:13 **S** demanded. "Why did you give him food and a
22:21 When he told David that **S** had killed the priests of
22:22 I saw Doeg there that day, I knew he would tell **S**.
23: 7 **S** soon learned that David was at Keilah. "Good!"
23: 8 So **S** mobilized his entire army to march to Keilah
23:10 I have heard that **S** is planning to come and destroy
23:11 And will **S** actually come as I have heard?
23:12 of Keilah really betray me and my men to **S**?"
23:13 Word soon reached **S** that David had escaped,
23:14 **S** hunted him day after day, but God didn't let him
23:15 David received the news that **S** was on the way to
23:19 But now the men of Ziph went to **S** in Gibeah
23:21 "The LORD bless you," **S** said. "At last
23:24 So the men of Ziph returned home ahead of **S**.
23:25 When David heard that **S** and his men were
23:25 in the wilderness of Maon. But **S** kept after him.
23:26 Just as **S** and his men began to close in on David
23:27 an urgent message reached **S** that the Philistines
23:28 So **S** quit the chase and returned to fight the
24: 1 After **S** returned from fighting the Philistines,
24: 2 So **S** chose three thousand special troops from
24: 3 **S** went into a cave to relieve himself.
24: 4 'I will certainly put **S** into your power, to do with
24: 7 rebuked his men and did not let them kill **S**.
24: 7 After **S** had left the cave and gone on his way,
24: 8 And when **S** looked around, David bowed low
24: 9 Then he shouted to **S**, "Why do you listen to the
24:16 **S** called back, "Is that really you, my son David?"
24:22 So David promised, and **S** went home. But David
25:44 **S**, meanwhile, had given his daughter Michal,
26: 1 Now some messengers from Ziph came back to **S**
26: 2 So **S** took three thousand of his best troops
26: 3 **S** camped along the road beside the hill of Hakilah,
26: 5 **S** and his general, Abner son of Ner, were sleeping
26:10 Surely the LORD will strike **S** down someday,
26:14 Then he shouted down to Abner and **S**, "Wake up,
26:17 **S** recognized David's voice and called out, "Is that
26:21 Then **S** confessed, "I have sinned. Come back
26:25 And **S** said to David, "Blessings on you, my son
26:25 Then David went away, and **S** returned home.
27: 1 to himself, "Someday **S** is going to get me.
27: 1 Then **S** will stop hunting for me, and I will finally
27: 4 Word soon reached **S** that David had fled to Gath,
28: 3 And **S** had banned all mediums and psychics from
28: 4 and **S** and the armies of Israel camped at Gilboa.
28: 5 When **S** saw the vast Philistine army, he became
28: 7 **S** then said to his advisers, "Find a woman who is
28: 8 So **S** disguised himself by wearing ordinary
28: 9 "You know that **S** has expelled all the mediums
28:10 But **S** took an oath in the name of the LORD
28:11 want me to call up?" "Call up Samuel," **S** replied.
28:12 she screamed, "You've deceived me! You are **S**!"
28:14 "What does he look like?" **S** asked. "He is an old
28:14 **S** realized that it was Samuel, and he fell to the
28:15 "Because I am in deep trouble," **S** replied.
28:20 **S** fell full length on the ground, paralyzed with
28:23 But **S** refused. The men who were with him also
28:25 She brought the meal to **S** and his men, and they
29: 3 the man who ran away from King **S** of Israel.
29: 5 '**S** has killed his thousands, and David his ten
31: 2 The Philistines closed in on **S** and his sons,
31: 3 The fighting grew very fierce around **S**,
31: 4 **S** groaned to his armor bearer, "Take your sword
31: 4 not do it. So **S** took his own sword and fell on it.
31: 5 When his armor bearer realized that **S** was dead,
31: 6 So **S**, three of his sons, his armor bearer, and his
31: 7 had been routed and that **S** and his sons were dead,
31: 8 they found the bodies of **S** and his three sons on
31:11 heard what the Philistines had done to **S**,
31:12 and took the bodies of **S** and his sons down from
2Sa 1: 1 After the death of **S**, David returned from his
1: 4 and **S** and his son Jonathan have been killed."
1: 5 "How do you know that **S** and Jonathan are
1: 6 I saw **S** there leaning on his spear with the enemy
1:12 They mourned and wept and fasted all day for **S**
1:17 Then David composed a funeral song for **S**
1:21 the shield of **S** will no longer be anointed with oil.
1:22 Both **S** and Jonathan killed their strongest foes;
1:23 How beloved and gracious were **S** and Jonathan!
1:24 O women of Israel, weep for **S**, / for he dressed
2: 4 heard that the men of Jabesh-gilead had buried **S**,
2: 7 And now that **S** is dead, I ask you to be my strong
3: 1 a long war between those who had been loyal to **S**
4: 4 He was five years old when **S** and Jonathan were
4: 8 the son of your enemy **S** who tried to kill you.
4: 8 Today the LORD has given you revenge on **S**
4:10 Once before, someone told me, '**S** is dead,'
5: 2 For a long time, even while **S** was our king,
6:16 Michal, the daughter of **S**, looked down from her
6:23 So Michal, the daughter of **S**, remained childless
7:15 love will not be taken from him as I took it from **S**,
9: 7 the land that once belonged to your grandfather **S**,
9: 9 master's grandson everything that belonged to **S**
12: 7 king of Israel and saved you from the power of **S**.
16: 3 get back the kingdom of my grandfather **S**.' "
16: 8 "The LORD is paying you back for murdering **S**
16:11 Shouldn't this relative of **S** have even more reason
19:17 including Ziba, the servant of **S**, and Ziba's fifteen
21: 1 "The famine has come because **S** and his family

21: 2 but **S**, in his zeal, had tried to wipe them out.
21: 5 they replied, "It was **S** who planned to destroy us,
21:12 and asked for the bones of **S** and his son Jonathan.
21:12 (When **S** and Jonathan had died in a battle with the
21:13 So David brought the bones of **S** and Jonathan,
22: 1 had rescued him from all his enemies and from **S**.
1Ch 5:10 During the reign of **S**, the Reubenites defeated the
8:33 was the father of **S**. **S** was the father of Jonathan,
9:39 was the father of **S**. **S** was the father of Jonathan,
10: 2 The Philistines closed in on **S** and his sons,
10: 3 The fighting grew very fierce around **S**,
10: 4 **S** groaned to his armor bearer, "Take your sword
10: 4 not do it. So **S** took his own sword and fell on it.
10: 5 When his armor bearer realized that **S** was dead,
10: 6 So **S** and his three sons died there together,
10: 7 had been routed and that **S** and his sons were dead,
10: 8 they found the bodies of **S** and his sons on Mount
10:11 heard what the Philistines had done to **S**,
10:12 their warriors went out and brought the bodies of **S**
10:13 So **S** died because he was unfaithful to the
11: 2 For a long time, even while **S** was our king,
12: 1 at Ziklag while he was hiding from **S** son of Kish.
12: 2 They were all relatives of **S** from the tribe of
12:19 he went with the Philistines to fight against **S**.
12:19 cost us our lives if David switches loyalties to **S**
12:23 all eager to see David become king instead of **S**,
12:29 Most of the Benjaminites had remained loyal to **S**
13: 3 for we neglected it during the reign of **S**."
15:29 Michal, the daughter of **S**, looked down from her
17:13 my unfailing love from him as I took it from **S**,
26:28 **S** son of Kish, Abner son of Ner, and Joab son of
Ps 18: T rescued him from all his enemies and from **S**.
52: T regarding the time Doeg the Edomite told **S** that
54: T regarding the time the Ziphites came and said to **S**,
57: T regarding the time he fled from **S** and went into the
59: T regarding the time **S** sent soldiers to watch David's
Isa 10:29 the city of **S**—are running for their lives.
Ac 7:58 and laid them at the feet of a young man named **S**.
8: 1 **S** was one of the official witnesses at the killing of
8: 3 **S** was going everywhere to devastate the church.
9: 1 **S** was uttering threats with every breath.
9: 4 and heard a voice saying to him, "**S**! **S**!
9: 5 "Who are you, sir?" **S** asked. And the voice
9: 7 The men with **S** stood speechless with surprise,
9: 8 As **S** picked himself up off the ground, he found
9:11 of Judas. When you arrive, ask for **S** of Tarsus.
9:15 For **S** is my chosen instrument to take my message
9:17 So Ananias went and found **S**. He laid his hands
on him and said, "Brother **S**,
9:19 **S** stayed with the believers in Damascus for a few
9:24 But **S** was told about their plot, and that they were
9:26 When **S** arrived in Jerusalem, he tried to meet with
9:27 and told them how **S** had seen the Lord on the way
9:27 also told them what the Lord had said to **S**
9:28 Then the apostles accepted **S**, and after that he was
11:25 Then Barnabas went on to Tarsus to find **S**.
11:30 and **S** to take to the elders of the church in
12:25 and **S** had finished their mission in Jerusalem,
13: 1 companion of King Herod Antipas), and **S**.
13: 2 and **S** for the special work I have for them."
13: 4 **S** and Barnabas went down to the seaport of
13: 7 The governor invited Barnabas and **S** to visit him,
13: 8 urged the governor to pay no attention to what **S**
13: 9 Then **S**, also known as Paul, filled with the Holy
13:21 and God gave them **S** son of Kish, a man of the
22: 7 to me, '**S**, **S**, why are you persecuting me?'
22:13 to me and stood beside me and said, 'Brother **S**,
26:14 in Aramaic, '**S**, **S**, why are you persecuting me?

SAUL'S (62) [SAUL]

1Sa 10: 1 took a flask of olive oil and poured it over **S** head.
10:14 **S** uncle asked him. "We went to look for the
11: 4 **S** hometown, and told the people about their plight,
11: 7 And the LORD made the people afraid of **S**
11:14 let us all go to Gilgal to reaffirm **S** kingship."
13: 2 The other thousand went with **S** son Jonathan to
14: 3 (Among **S** men was Ahijah the priest, who was
14:16 **S** lookouts in Gibeah saw a strange sight—the vast
14:49 **S** sons included Jonathan, Ishbosheth,
14:50 **S** wife was Ahinoam, the daughter of Ahimaaz.
14:50 The commander of **S** army was his cousin Abner,
14:51 Ner, and **S** father, Kish, were brothers;
14:52 with the Philistines throughout **S** lifetime.
16:15 Some of **S** servants suggested a remedy. "It is
16:21 and David became one of **S** armor bearers.
17:13 had already joined **S** army to fight the Philistines.
17:14 in the army, they stayed with **S** forces all the time.
18:20 **S** daughter Michal had fallen in love with David,
18:23 When **S** men said these things to David, he replied,
18:24 When **S** men reported this back to the king,
18:30 against them than all the rest of **S** officers.
19:20 the Spirit of God came upon **S** men, and they also
21: 7 Now Doeg the Edomite, **S** chief herdsman,
22: 9 who was standing there with **S** men, spoke up.
22:17 But **S** men refused to kill the LORD's priests.
23: 9 But David learned of **S** plan and told Abiathar the
24: 4 David crept forward and cut off a piece of **S** robe.
24: 5 began bothering him because he had cut **S** robe.
26: 3 David was hiding. But David knew of **S** arrival,
26: 5 David slipped over to **S** camp one night to look
26: 7 So David and Abishai went right into **S** camp
26:12 the spear and jug of water that were near **S** head.
26:12 because the LORD had put **S** men into a deep
31: 9 So they cut off **S** head and stripped off his armor.
31: 9 Then they proclaimed the news of **S** death in their
2Sa 2: 8 But Abner son of Ner, the commander of **S** army,
2: 8 had already gone to Mahanaim with **S** son
3: 1 while **S** dynasty became weaker and weaker.
3: 6 leader among those who were loyal to **S** dynasty.
3: 7 One day Ishbosheth, **S** son, accused Abner of
3:10 go ahead and give David the rest of **S** kingdom.
3:13 my wife Michal, **S** daughter, when you come."
3:14 then sent this message to Ishbosheth, **S** son:
4: 4 (**S** son Jonathan had a son named Mephibosheth,
9: 1 One day David began wondering if anyone in **S**
9: 2 man named Ziba, who had been one of **S** servants.
9: 3 asked him, "Is anyone still alive from **S** family?
9: 6 he was Jonathan's son and **S** grandson.
9: 9 Then the king summoned **S** servant Ziba and said,
16: 5 It was Shimei son of Gera, a member of **S** family.
19:24 Now Mephibosheth, **S** grandson, arrived from
21: 6 So let seven of **S** sons or grandsons be handed over
21: 7 who was **S** grandson, because of the oath David
21: 8 But he gave them **S** two sons Armoni
21: 8 He also gave them the five sons of **S** daughter
21:11 learned what Rizpah, **S** concubine, had done,
21:14 He buried them all in the tomb of Kish, **S** father,
1Ch 10: 9 So they stripped off **S** armor and cut off his head.
10: 9 Then they proclaimed the news of **S** death before
12:29 **S** relatives, there were 3,000 warriors.
Ac 9:18 Instantly something like scales fell from **S** eyes,
9:22 **S** preaching became more and more powerful,

SAVE (181) [SAFE, SAFEGUARD, SAFEKEEPING, SAFELY, SAFER, SAFETY, SALVATION, SAVED, SAVER, SAVES, SAVING, SAVIOR]

Ge 50:20 I have today so I could **s** the lives of many people.
Dt 28:29 robbed continually, and no one will come to **s** you.
Jos 9: 4 they resorted to deception to **s** themselves.
10: 6 they pleaded. "Come quickly and **s** us!
1Sa 4: 3 into battle with us, it will **s** us from our enemies."
4: 8 Who can **s** us from these mighty gods of Israel?
7: 8 "Plead with the LORD our God to **s** us from the
10:27 men who complained, "How can this man **s** us?"
11: 3 "If none of our relatives will come to **s** us, we will
12:11 Barak, Jephthah, and Samuel to **s** you, and you
17:37 and the bear will **s** me from this Philistine!"
23: 2 "Yes, go and **s** Keilah," the LORD told him.
2Sa 3:18 'I have chosen David to **s** my people from the
10:12 Let us fight bravely to **s** our people and the cities
22:49 of my enemies; / you **s** me from violent opponents.
1Ki 1:12 If you want to **s** your own life and the life of your
18: 5 and valley to see if we can find enough grass to **s**
2Ki 14:27 he used Jeroboam II, the son of Jehoash, to **s** them.
18:35 What god of any nation has ever been able to **s** its
1Ch 16:35 Cry out, "**S** us, O God of our salvation! / Gather
19:13 Let us fight bravely to **s** our people and the cities
2Ch 18:31 But Jehoshaphat cried out to the LORD to **s** him,
20: 9 We can cry out to you to **s** us, and you will hear us
25:15 who could not even **s** their own people from you?"
Ne 6:11 in my position enter the Temple to **s** his life?
Job 2: 4 A man will give up everything he has to **s** his life.
5:20 He will **s** you from death in time of famine,
6:23 Have I asked you to **s** me from ruthless people?
13:16 But this is what will **s** me: that I am not godless.
22:29 you say, 'Help him up,' God will **s** the downcast.
40:14 praise you, for your own strength would **s** you.
Ps 6: 4 rescue me. / **S** me because of your unfailing love.
7: 1 my God. / **S** me from my persecutors—rescue me!
9:14 **S** me, so I can praise you publicly at Jerusalem's
17: 7 You **s** with your strength / those who seek refuge
17:14 **S** me by your mighty hand, O LORD,
18:48 of my enemies; / you **s** me from violent opponents.
22: 8 Then let the LORD **s** him! / If the LORD loves
25:17 go from bad to worse. / Oh, **s** me from them all!
26:11 I do what is right. / So in your mercy, **s** me.
28: 9 **S** your people! / Bless Israel, your special
31:16 on your servant. / In your unfailing love, **s** me.
33:16 The best-equipped army cannot **s** a king, / nor is
great strength enough to **s** a warrior.
33:17 you victory— / for all its strength, it cannot **s** you.
33:20 We depend on the LORD alone to **s** us. / Only he
44: 6 my bow; / I do not count on my sword to **s** me.
44:26 and help us! / **S** us because of your unfailing love.
55:23 liars will die young, / but I am trusting you to **s** me.
57: 3 He will send help from heaven to **s** me,
59: 2 from these criminals; / **s** me from these murderers.
60: 5 Use your strong right arm to **s** us, / and rescue your
69: 1 **S** me, O God, / for the floodwaters are up to my
69:35 For God will **s** Jerusalem / and rebuild the towns of
71: 2 **S** me from my enemies, for you are just.
71: 3 Give the order to **s** me, / for you are my rock
72:14 He will **s** them from oppression and from violence,
74: 9 as evidence that you will **s** us. / All the prophets
79: 9 Oh, **s** us and forgive our sins / for the sake of your
86: 2 **S** me, for I serve you and trust you. / You are my
86:16 to your servant; / yes, **s** me, for I am your servant.
106:47 O LORD our God, **s** us! / Gather us back from
108: 6 Use your strong right arm to **s** me, / and rescue
109:26 my God! / **S** me because of your unfailing love.
109:31 ready to **s** them from those who condemn them.
116: 4 name of the LORD: / "Please, LORD, **s** me!"
118:25 Please, LORD, please **s** us. / Please, LORD,
119:94 I am yours; **s** me! / For I have applied myself to
119:146 I cry out to you; **s** me, / that I may obey your
119:149 O LORD, hear my cry; / in your justice, **s** my life.
138: 7 against my angry enemies! / Your power will **s** me.
143: 9 **S** me from my enemies, LORD; / I run to you to
143:11 For the glory of your name, O LORD, **s** me.
144:11 **S** me from the fatal sword! / Rescue me from the
Pr 2:12 Wisdom will **s** you from evil people, from those
2:16 Wisdom will **s** you from the immoral woman,
6: 5 **S** yourself like a deer escaping from a hunter,
10: 2 no lasting value, but right living can **s** your life.
11:30 life-giving fruit, and those who **s** lives are wise.
12: 6 but the words of the godly **s** lives.
21:18 Sometimes the wicked are punished to **s** the godly,
23:14 Physical discipline may well **s** them from death.
Ecc 7:12 but it's important to know that only wisdom can **s**
9:15 wise man living there who knew how to **s** the
Isa 12: 2 See, God has come to **s** me. / I will trust in him
16:12 in their temples, but no one will come to **s** them.
17:10 Because you have turned from the God who can **s**
31: 5 He will defend and **s** the city; he will pass over it
33:22 and our king. He will care for us and **s** us.
35: 4 to destroy your enemies. He is coming to **s** you."
36:20 What god of any nation has ever been able to **s** its
45:17 But the LORD will **s** the people of Israel with
45:20 their wooden idols and pray to gods that cannot **s**!
46: 4 will care for you. I will carry you along and **s** you.
46:13 I am ready to **s** Jerusalem and give my glory to
47:13 stand up and **s** you from what the future holds.
47:14 They cannot even **s** themselves! You will get no
49:25 those who fight you, and I will **s** your children.
50: 2 Was I too weak to **s** you? Is that why the house is
57:12 so righteous. None of them will benefit or **s** you.
59: 1 The LORD is not too weak to **s** you, and he is not
59:16 So he himself stepped in to **s** them with his mighty
63: 1 It is I, the LORD, who is mighty to **s**!"
Jer 2:27 but in times of trouble they cry out for me to **s**
2:28 When danger comes, let them **s** you if they can!
11:12 But the idols will not **s** them when disaster strikes!
14: 9 Are you also confused? Are you helpless to **s** us?
17:14 you alone can heal me; you alone can **s**.
30:11 For I am with you and will **s** you, says the LORD.
31: 7 '**S** your people, O LORD, the remnant of Israel!'
42:11 For I am with you and will **s** you and rescue you
51: 6 Flee from Babylon! **S** yourselves! Don't get
51: 9 helped her if we could, but nothing can **s** her now.
51:45 my people, flee from Babylon. **S** yourselves!
La 1:19 even as they searched for food to **s** their lives.
4:17 We looked in vain for our allies to come and **s** us,
Eze 13:21 the magic veils and **s** my people from your grasp.
14:14 their righteousness would **s** no one but themselves,
14:16 it wouldn't **s** the people from destruction.
14:18 the Sovereign LORD swears that they could not **s**
14:20 the Sovereign LORD swears that they could not **s**
18:27 and do what is just and right, they will **s** their lives.
33:12 The good works of righteous people will not **s**
33:13 expecting their past righteousness to **s** them,
37:23 for I will **s** them from their sinful backsliding.
Da 3:17 the God whom we serve is able to **s** us.
6:14 the law, and he tried to find a way to **s** Daniel.
Hos 13:10 the land? You asked for them, now let them **s** you!
14: 3 Assyria cannot **s** us, nor can our strength in battle.
Am 2:14 Even the mightiest warriors will be unable to **s**
Mic 6:14 And though you try to **s** your money, it will come
6:14 You will **s** a little, but I will give it to those who
7: 7 I wait confidently for God to **s** me, and my God
Hab 1: 2 "Violence!" I cry, but you do not come to **s**.
2:19 be for you who beg lifeless wooden idols to **s** you.
3: 2 Show us your power to **s** us. And in your anger,
3:13 your chosen people, to **s** your anointed ones.
Zep 2: 3 Beg the LORD to **s** you—all you who are humble,
3:19 I will **s** the weak and helpless ones; I will bring
Zec 10: 6 "I will strengthen Judah and **s** Israel; I will
Mt 1:21 him Jesus, for he will **s** his people from their sins."
8:25 to him and woke him up, shouting, "Lord, **s** us!
14:30 and began to sink. "**S** me, Lord!" he shouted.
27:40 **s** yourself and come down from the cross!"
27:42 they scoffed, "but he can't **s** himself!
27:49 Let's see whether Elijah will come and **s** him."
Mk 3: 4 doing harm? Is this a day to **s** life or to destroy it?"
15:30 **s** yourself and come down from the cross!"
15:31 they scoffed, "but he can't **s** himself!
Lk 6: 9 doing harm? Is this a day to **s** life or to destroy it?"
17:33 life will lose it, and whoever loses this life will **s** it.
19:10 come to seek and **s** those like him who are lost."
22:20 wine is the token of God's new covenant to **s** you
23:35 "let him **s** himself if he is really God's Chosen
23:37 "If you are the King of the Jews, **s** yourself!"
Jn 3:17 his Son into the world to condemn it, but to **s** it.
12:27 Should I pray, 'Father, **s** me from what lies ahead'?
12:47 for I have come to **s** the world and not to judge it.
Ac 2:40 "**S** yourselves from this generation that has gone
4:12 in all of heaven for people to call on to **s** them."
Ro 5: 9 he will certainly **s** us from God's judgment.
8: 3 The law of Moses could not **s** us, because of our
8: 3 But God put into effect a different plan to **s** us.
9: 3 cut off from Christ!—if that would **s** them.
10:14 But how can they call on him to **s** them unless they
11:14 and in that way I might **s** some of them.
1Co 1:21 he has used our foolish preaching to **s** all who
16: 2 to what you have earned and **s** it for this offering.
Gal 6:12 for teaching that the cross of Christ alone can **s**.
Php 3: 9 to obey God's law, but I trust Christ to **s** me.
1Th 5: 9 For God decided to **s** us through our Lord Jesus
2Th 2:10 they refuse to believe the truth that would **s** them.
1Ti 1:15 Christ Jesus came into the world to **s** sinners—
4:16 and God will **s** you and those who hear you.
Heb 7:25 to **s** everyone who comes to God through him.
11: 7 It was by faith that Noah built an ark to **s** his
Jas 1:21 your hearts, for it is strong enough to **s** your souls.
2:14 by your actions? That kind of faith can't **s** anyone.
4:12 He alone has the power to **s** or to destroy.
5:20 that person back will **s** that sinner from death
1Pe 1:18 For you know that God paid a ransom to **s** you

SAVED (115) [SAVE]

Ge 19:19 "You have been so kind to me and s my life,
19:20 you see how small it is? Then my life will be s."
27:36 Oh, haven't you s even one blessing for me?"
39:18 "I was s only by my screams. He ran out,
47:19 Just give us grain so that our lives may be s and
47:25 "You have s our lives!" they exclaimed. "May it
Ex 18:10 "for he has s you from the Egyptians and from
Lev 7:15 None of it may be s for the next morning.
Dt 33:29 Who else is like you, a people s by the LORD?
Jdg 7:2 the Israelites will boast to me that they s
1Sa 14:23 So the LORD s Israel that day, and the battle
14:45 to Saul, "Should Jonathan, who s Israel today, die?
17:37 The LORD who s me from the claws of the lion
2Sa 12:7 king of Israel and s you from the power of Saul.
18:19 the LORD has s him from his enemy Absalom."
19:5 "We s your life today and the lives of your sons,
19:9 "The king s us from our enemies, the Philistines,
2Ki 18:33 Have the gods of any other nations ever s their
1Ch 11:14 So the LORD s them by giving them a great
Ezr 8:31 and s us from enemies and bandits along the way.
Est 7:9 the man who s the king from assassination."
Job 26:2 How you have s a person who has no strength!
Ps 22:5 You heard their cries for help and s them.
80:3 face shine down upon us. / Only then will we be s.
80:7 face shine down upon us. / Only then will we be s.
80:19 face shine down upon us. / Only then will we be s.
81:7 You cried to me in trouble, and I s you;
106:8 Even so, he s them— / to defend the honor of his
107:2 Tell others he has s you from your enemies.
107:13 in their trouble, / and he s them from their distress.
107:19 in their trouble, / and he s them from their distress.
107:28 in their trouble, / and he s them from their distress.
116:6 I was facing death, and then he s me.
116:8 He has s me from death, / my eyes from tears,
119:117 Sustain me, and I will be s; / then I will meditate
136:24 He s us from our enemies. / His faithful love
Isa 25:9 "This is our God. We trusted in him, and he s us.
30:15 returning to me and waiting for me will you be s.
36:18 Have the gods of any other nations ever s their
43:12 what I would do, and then I did it—I s you.
44:26 When they say Jerusalem will be s and the towns
51:10 making a path of escape when you s your people?
64:5 anger is heavy on us. How can people like us be s?
Jer 4:14 cleanse your hearts that you may be s.
8:20 is gone," the people cry, "yet we are not s!"
23:6 In that day Judah will be s, and Israel will live in
30:7 for my people Israel. Yet in the end, they will be s!
33:16 In that day Judah will be s, and Jerusalem will live
Eze 3:19 But you will have s your life because you did what
3:21 will live, and you will have s your own life, too."
14:16 Those three alone would be s, but the land would
14:18 could not save the people. They alone would be s.
14:20 They alone would be s by their righteousness.
33:5 to the warning, they could have s their lives.
Joel 2:32 who calls on the name of the LORD will be s.
Mt 10:22 to me. But those who endure to the end will be s.
19:25 "Then who in the world can be s?" they asked.
24:13 But those who endure to the end will be s.
27:42 "He s others," they scoffed, "but he can't save
Mk 10:26 "Then who in the world can be s?" they asked.
13:13 to me. But those who endure to the end will be s.
15:31 "He s others," they scoffed, "but he can't save
16:16 Anyone who believes and is baptized will be s.
Lk 1:71 Now we will be s from our enemies / and from all
7:50 Jesus said to the woman, "Your faith has s you;
8:12 and prevents them from believing and being s.
13:23 asked him, "Lord, will only a few be s?"
18:26 this said, "Then who in the world can be s?"
23:35 "He s others," they said, "let him save himself if
Jn 5:34 you about John's testimony so you might be s.
10:9 the gate. Those who come in through me will be s.
Ac 2:21 who calls on the name of the Lord / will be s.'
2:47 Lord added to their group those who were being s.
11:14 tell you how you and all your household will be s!'
12:11 "The Lord has sent his angel and s me from Herod
15:1 circumcision taught by Moses, you cannot be s."
15:11 We believe that we are all s the same way,
16:17 and they have come to tell you how to be s."
16:30 and asked, "Sirs, what must I do to be s?"
16:31 "Believe on the Lord Jesus and you will be s,
Ro 3:22 And we all can be s in this same way, no matter
4:1 concerning this question of being s by faith?
8:24 Now that we are s, we eagerly look forward to this
9:27 on the seashore, / only a small number will be s.
10:1 prayer to God is that the Jewish people might be s.
10:9 that God raised him from the dead, you will be s.
10:10 it is by confessing with your mouth that you are s.
10:13 who calls on the name of the Lord will be s."
11:5 A few are being s as a result of God's kindness in
11:6 And if they are s by God's kindness, then it is not
11:26 And so all Israel will be s. Do you remember what
1Co 1:18 But we who are being s recognize this message as
3:15 The builders themselves will be s, but like
5:5 and he himself will be s when the Lord returns.
10:33 for me, but what is best for them so they may be s.
2Co 2:15 fragrance is perceived differently by those being s
2:16 But to those who are being s we are a life-giving
Gal 2:16 For no one will ever be s by obeying the law."
2:21 For if we could be s by keeping the law, then there
Eph 2:5 only by God's special favor that you have been s!)
2:8 God s you by his special favor when you believed.
4:30 guaranteeing that you will be s on the day of
Php 1:28 but that you are going to be s, even by God
3:2 who say you must be circumcised to be s.
3:12 when I will finally be all that Christ Jesus s me for
1Th 2:16 News to the Gentiles, for fear some might be s.
2Th 3:2 that we will be s from wicked and evil people,
1Ti 2:4 for he wants everyone to be s and to understand the
2:15 But women will be s through childbearing and by
2Ti 1:9 It is God who s us and chose us to live a holy life.
4:17 Gentiles to hear. And he s me from certain death.
Tit 3:5 He s us, not because of the good things we did,
1Pe 3:20 Only eight people were s from drowning in that
4:18 And / "If the righteous are barely s, / what chance
2Pe 3:15 Lord is waiting so that people have time to be s.

SAVER (1) [SAVE]

Ecc 5:13 Riches are sometimes hoarded to the harm of the s,

SAVES (18) [SAVE]

2Sa 4:9 the one who s me from my enemies, I will tell you
22:3 my savior, the one who s me from violence.
22:4 is worthy of praise, / for he s me from my enemies.
1Ch 16:23 Each day proclaim the good news that he s.
Job 5:15 He s them from the clutches of the powerful.
Ps 18:3 is worthy of praise, / for he s me from my enemies.
20:6 Now I know that the LORD s his anointed king.
25:5 and teach me, / for you are the God who s me.
37:39 The LORD s the godly; / he is their fortress in
37:40 He s them, / and they find shelter in him.
51:14 Forgive me for shedding blood, O God who s;
68:20 Our God is a God who s! / The Sovereign LORD
96:2 Each day proclaim the good news that he s.
Pr 14:25 A truthful witness s lives, but a false witness is a
Da 6:27 He rescues and s his people; / he performs
1Co 15:2 And it is this Good News that s you if you firmly
Eph 1:13 heard the truth, the Good News that God s you.
1Pe 3:21 which now s you by the power of Jesus Christ's

SAVING (16) [SAVE]

1Sa 9:24 "I was s it for you even before I invited these
14:48 s Israel from all those who had plundered them.
Ps 7:10 my shield, / s those whose hearts are true and right.
40:10 I have talked about your faithfulness and s power.
67:2 your s power among people everywhere.
69:29 and in pain. / Rescue me, O God, by your s power.
71:15 All day long I will proclaim your s power,
79:11 Demonstrate your great power by s those
116:13 I will praise the LORD's name for s me.
118:21 I thank you for answering my prayer / and s me!
Isa 53:1 To whom will the LORD reveal his s power?
Mic 1:14 gift to Moresheth-gath; there is no hope of s it.
Lk 23:39 Prove it by s yourself—and us, too, while you're at
Jn 12:38 To whom will the Lord reveal his s power?"
Ro 1:16 power of God at work, s everyone who believes—
Php 2:12 to put into action God's s work in your lives,

SAVIOR (54) [SAVE]

2Sa 22:2 "The LORD is my rock, my fortress, and my s;
22:3 my high tower, my s, the one who saves me from
Ps 18:2 The LORD is my rock, my fortress, and my s;
24:5 and have right standing with God their s.
38:22 Come quickly to help me, O Lord my s.
40:17 You are my helper and my s. / Do not delay,
42:5 hope in God! / I will praise him again— / my S and
42:11 I will praise him again— / my S and my God!
43:5 I will praise him again— / my S and my God!
65:5 our prayers with awesome deeds, / O God our s.
68:19 Praise the Lord; praise God our s! / For each day
70:5 to my aid, O God. / You are my helper and my s;
106:21 They forgot God, their s, / who had done such
140:7 O Sovereign LORD, my strong s, / you protected
Isa 19:20 he will send them a s who will rescue them.
43:3 your God, the Holy One of Israel, your S.
43:11 I am the LORD, and there is no other S.
45:15 Truly, O God of Israel, our S, you work in strange
45:21 but me—a just God and a S—no, not one!
49:26 the LORD, am your S and Redeemer, the Mighty
60:16 the LORD, am your S and Redeemer, the Mighty
62:11 the people of Israel, 'Look, your S is coming.
63:8 will not be false again." And he became their S.
Jer 14:8 O Hope of Israel, our S in times of trouble!
Hos 13:4 You have no God but me, for there is no other s.
Zep 3:17 He is a mighty s. He will rejoice over you with
Lk 1:47 How I rejoice in God my S!
1:69 He has sent us a mighty S / from the royal line of
2:11 The S—yes, the Messiah, the Lord—has been born
2:30 I have seen the S
Jn 4:42 what you told us. He is indeed the S of the world."
Ac 5:31 place of honor at his right hand as Prince and S.
7:35 Moses was sent to be their ruler and s.
13:23 Jesus, who is God's promised S of Israel!
Gal 3:23 until we could put our faith in the coming S.
Eph 5:23 his body, the church; he gave his life to be her S.
Php 3:20 we are eagerly waiting for him to return as our S.
1Ti 1:1 appointed by the command of God our S and by
2:3 This is good and pleases God our S,
4:10 is in the living God, who is the S of all people,
2Ti 1:10 our S, who broke the power of death and showed
Tit 1:3 It is by the command of God our S that I have been
1:4 and Christ Jesus our S give you grace and peace.
2:10 Then they will make the teaching about God our S
2:13 event when the glory of our great God and S,
3:4 But then God our S showed us his kindness
3:6 upon us because of what Jesus Christ our S did.
2Pe 1:1 our God and S, who makes us right with God.
1:11 eternal Kingdom of our Lord and S Jesus Christ.
2:20 and S Jesus Christ and then get tangled up with sin
3:2 our Lord and S commanded through your apostles.
3:18 and knowledge of our Lord and S Jesus Christ.
1Jn 4:14 the Father sent his Son to be the S of the world.
Jude 1:25 All glory to him, who alone is God our S,

SAVORED (1) [SAVORY]

Job 20:13 He s it, holding it long in his mouth.

SAVORY (1) [SAVORED]

Ge 27:4 Prepare it just the way I like it so it's s and good,

SAVOUR [KJV] See AROMA, FRAGRANCE, FRAGRANT, ODOR, SMELL, TASTE

SAW (510) [SAWED, SAWS, SEE]

Ge 1:4 And God s that it was good. Then he separated the
1:10 and the water "seas." And God s that it was good.
1:12 and trees of like kind. And God s that it was good.
1:18 from the darkness. And God s that it was good.
1:21 and every kind of bird. And God s that it was good.
1:25 more of its own kind. And God s that it was good.
1:31 and he s that it was excellent in every way.
6:2 the sons of God s the beautiful women of the
6:5 and he s that all their thoughts were consistently
6:12 and he s violence and depravity everywhere.
9:22 s that his father was naked and went outside
12:15 When the palace officials s her, they sang her
15:12 He s a terrifying vision of darkness and horror.
15:17 Abram s a smoking firepot and a flaming torch
19:1 When he s them, he stood up to meet them.
19:28 and Gomorrah and s columns of smoke and fumes,
21:9 But Sarah s Ishmael—the son of Abraham and her
21:19 Then God opened Hagar's eyes, and she s a well.
22:4 of the journey, Abraham s the place in the distance.
22:13 and s a ram caught by its horns in a bush.
24:30 When he s the nose-ring and the bracelets on his
24:45 I s Rebekah coming along with her water jug on
24:63 meditating, he looked up and s the camels coming.
24:64 When Rebekah looked up and s Isaac, she quickly
26:8 out a window and s Isaac fondling Rebekah.
28:12 And he s the angels of God going up and down on
29:2 He s in the distance three flocks of sheep lying in
30:1 When Rachel s that she wasn't having any
31:10 and s that the male goats mating with the flock
32:2 When Jacob s them, he exclaimed, "This is God's
32:25 When the man s that he couldn't win the match,
33:1 Jacob s Esau coming with his four hundred men.
34:2 Hamor the Hivite, s her, he took her and raped her.
37:18 When Joseph's brothers s him coming,
39:13 When she s that she had his shirt and that he had
40:8 Joseph replied. "Tell me what you s."
40:9 "In my dream," he said, "I s a vine in front of me.
40:16 When the chief baker s that the first dream had
41:5 This time he s seven heads of grain on one stalk,
42:21 We s his terror and anguish and heard his
43:16 When Joseph s that Benjamin was with them,
43:18 They were badly frightened when they s where
45:27 and when he s the wagons loaded with the food
48:17 But Joseph was upset when he s that his father had
Ex 2:2 She s what a beautiful baby he was and kept him
2:5 When the princess s the little basket among the
2:11 and he s how hard they were forced to work.
2:11 he s an Egyptian beating one of the Hebrew slaves.
2:13 his people again, he s two Hebrew men fighting.
3:4 When the LORD s that he had caught Moses'
8:15 But when Pharaoh s that the frogs were gone,
9:34 When Pharaoh s this, he and his officials sinned
14:31 When the people of Israel s the mighty power that
16:15 The Israelites were puzzled when they s it.
18:14 When Moses' father-in-law s all that Moses was
20:18 and when they s the lightning and the smoke
24:10 There they s the God of Israel. Under his feet there
24:11 And though Israel's leaders s God, he did not
24:17 The Israelites at the foot of the mountain s an
32:5 When Aaron s how excited the people were about
32:19 near the camp, Moses s the calf and the dancing.
32:25 When Moses s that Aaron had let the people get
34:30 and the people of Israel s the radiance of Moses'
Lev 9:24 When the people s all this, they shouted with joy
Nu 12:10 with leprosy. When Aaron s what had happened,
13:28 We also s the descendants of Anak who are living
13:32 go to live there. All the people we s were huge.
13:33 We even s giants there, the descendants of Anak.
16:42 the Tabernacle and s that the cloud had covered it,
22:3 And when they s how many Israelites there were,
22:23 Balaam's donkey suddenly s the angel of the
22:25 When the donkey s the angel of the LORD
22:27 This time when the donkey s the angel, it lay down
22:31 and he s the angel of the LORD standing in the
22:33 Three times the donkey s me and shied away;
24:2 where he s the people of Israel camped, tribe by
25:7 of Eleazar and grandson of Aaron the priest s this,
32:1 So when they s that the lands of Jazer and Gilead
Dt 1:19 and terrifying wilderness, which you yourselves s,
1:30 will fight for you, just as you s him do in Egypt.
1:31 And you s how the LORD your God cared for
4:3 You s what the LORD did to you at Baal-peor,
7:19 You s it all with your own eyes! And remember
26:7 He heard us and s our hardship, toil,
32:19 "The LORD s this and was filled with loathing.
Jos 5:13 and s a man facing him with sword in hand.
7:21 For I s a beautiful robe imported from Babylon,
8:14 When the king of Ai s the Israelites across the
8:21 and the other Israelites s that the ambush had
24:7 With your very own eyes you s what I did.
Jdg 4:23 So on that day Israel s God subdue Jabin,
9:36 When Gaal s them, he said to Zebul, "Look,

9:43 When Abimelech s the people coming out of the
9:55 When Abimelech's men s that he was dead,
11:35 When he s her, he tore his clothes in anguish.
13:20 When Manoah and his wife s this, they fell with
14: 2 "I want to marry a young Philistine woman I s in
16:24 When the people s him, they praised their god,
18:18 When the priest s the men carrying all the sacred
18:26 When Micah s that there were too many of them
19:17 When he s the travelers sitting in the town square,
19:30 Everyone who s it said, "Such a horrible crime has
20:36 Then the Benjaminites s that they were beaten.
20:40 and s the smoke rising into the sky from every part
Ru 1:18 So when Naomi s that Ruth had made up her mind
1Sa 4: 5 When the Israelites s the Ark of the Covenant of
5:10 but when the people of Ekron s it coming they
6:13 and when they s the Ark, they were overjoyed!
10:10 they s the prophets coming toward them.
13: 6 When the men of Israel s the vast number of
13:11 Saul replied, "I s my men scattering from me,
14:11 When the Philistines s them coming, they shouted,
14:16 Saul's lookouts in Gibeah s a strange sight—
14:22 the chase when they s the Philistines running away.
14:28 But one of the men s him and said, "Your father
14:52 So whenever Saul s a young man who was brave
17:23 with them, he s Goliath, the champion from Gath,
17:24 As soon as the Israelite army s him, they began to
17:51 When the Philistines s that their champion was
19:20 But when they arrived and s Samuel and the other
21: 1 Ahimelech trembled when he s him. "Why are you
22: 9 he said, "I s David talking to Ahimelech the priest.
22:22 When I s Doeg there that day, I knew he would tell
25:20 she s David and his men coming toward her.
25:23 When Abigail s David, she quickly got off her
25:25 But I never even s the messengers you sent.
28: 5 When Saul s the vast Philistine army, he became
28:12 When the woman s Samuel, she screamed,
28:21 When the woman s how distraught he was,
30: 3 When David and his men s the ruins and realized
31: 7 and beyond the Jordan s that their army had been
2Sa 1: 6 I s Saul there leaning on his spear with the enemy
1: 7 When he turned and s me, he cried out for me to
2:20 When Abner looked back and s him coming,
2:23 and stood still when they s Asahel lying there.
6:16 When she s King David leaping and dancing
10: 9 When Joab s that he would have to fight on two
10:14 And when the Ammonites s the Arameans running,
12:19 But when David s them whispering, he realized
13:20 Her brother Absalom s her and asked, "Is it true
13:34 Then the watchman on the Jerusalem wall s a great
17:18 But a boy s them leaving En-rogel to go to David,
18:10 One of David's men s what had happened and told
Joab, "I s Absalom dangling in a tree."
18:11 "You s him there and didn't kill him?
18:24 he looked, he s a lone man running toward them.
18:26 the watchman s another man running toward them.
20:12 and Joab's officer s that a crowd was gathering
24:17 When David s the angel, he said to the LORD,
24:20 When Araunah s the king and his men coming
1Ki 3:21 the morning light, I s that it wasn't my son at all."
10: 4 and when she s the palace he had built,
10: 7 it until I arrived here and s it with my own eyes.
11:28 and when Solomon s how industrious he was,
13:25 People came by and s the body lying in the road
16:18 When Zimri s that the city had been taken, he went
17:10 he s a widow gathering sticks, and he asked her,
18: 7 was walking along, he s Elijah coming toward him.
18:17 Ahab asked when he s him.
18:39 And when the people s it, they fell on their faces
18:44 "I s a little cloud about the size of a hand rising
19: 6 and s some bread baked on hot stones
22:17 "In a vision I s all Israel scattered on the
22:19 I s the LORD sitting on his throne with all the
22:32 So when the Aramean charioteers s Jehoshaphat in
2Ki 2:12 Elisha s it and cried out, "My father! My father!
2:15 When the group of prophets from Jericho s what
3:26 When the king of Moab s that he was losing the
4:25 God at Mount Carmel, Elisha s her in the distance.
5:21 When Naaman s him running after him, he climbed
6:17 he s that the hillside around Elisha was filled with
6:21 When the king of Israel s them, he shouted to
9:17 The watchman on the tower of Jezreel s Jehu
9:26 murder of Naboth and his sons that I s yesterday.'
9:27 When King Ahaziah of Judah s what was
9:32 looked up and s her at the window and shouted,
11:14 And she s the newly crowned king standing in his
11:14 When Athaliah s all this, she tore her clothes in
14:26 For the LORD s the bitter suffering of everyone
20:15 "They s everything," Hezekiah replied.
1Ch 10: 7 When the Israelites in the Jezreel Valley s that
15:29 When she s King David dancing and leaping for
19:10 When Joab s that he would have to fight on two
19:15 And when the Ammonites s the Arameans running,
21:16 and s the angel of the LORD standing between
21:20 wheat at the time, turned and s the angel there.
21:21 When Araunah s the king approaching, he left his
21:28 When David s that the LORD had answered his
2Ch 7: 3 When all the people of Israel s the fire coming
9: 3 and when she s the palace he had built,
9: 6 it until I arrived here and s it with my own eyes.
12: 7 When the LORD s their change of heart, he gave
15: 9 they s that the LORD his God was with him.
18:16 "In a vision I s all Israel scattered on the
18:18 I s the LORD sitting on his throne with all the
18:31 So when the Aramean charioteers s Jehoshaphat in
23:13 And she s the newly crowned king standing in his
23:13 When Athaliah s all this, she tore her clothes in
26:20 When Azariah and the other priests s the leprosy,
31: 8 and his officials came and s these huge piles,
34: 4 He s to it that the altars for the images of Baal
Ezr 3:12 and they wept aloud when they s the new Temple's
Ne 8: 5 When they s him open the book, they all rose to
9: 9 "You s the sufferings and sorrows of our ancestors
13:15 One Sabbath day I s some men of Judah treading
Est 2:15 and she was admired by everyone who s her.
3: 5 When Haman s that Mordecai would not bow
5: 2 When he s Queen Esther standing there in the inner
5: 9 But when he s Mordecai sitting at the gate,
Job 2:12 When they s Job from a distance, they scarcely
2:13 for they s that his suffering was too great for
28:27 he had done all this, he s wisdom and measured it.
29: 8 The young stepped aside when they s me, and even
29:11 of me praised me. All who s me spoke well of me.
31:19 Whenever I s someone who was homeless
32: 5 But when he s that they had no further reply,
Ps 35:21 "Aha! / With our own eyes we s him do it!"
48: 5 But when they s it, they were stunned; / they were
73: 3 when I s them prosper despite their wickedness.
77:16 When the Red Sea s you, O God, / its waters
114: 3 The Red Sea s them coming and hurried out of
116: 3 grave overtook me. / I s only trouble and sorrow.
139:16 You s me before I was born. / Every day of my life
Pr 7: 7 and s a simpleminded young man who lacked
24:31 I s that it was overgrown with thorns. It was
Ecc 2:14 Yet I s that wise and foolish people share the same
3:22 So I s that there is nothing better for people than to
4: 1 I s the tears of the oppressed, with no one to
Isa 2: 1 This is another vision that Isaiah son of Amoz s
6: 1 In the year King Uzziah died, I s the Lord. He was
10:15 Is the s greater than the person who saws? Can a
39: 4 "They s everything," Hezekiah replied.
52:14 Many were amazed when they s him—beaten
63: 5 I was amazed and appalled at what I s. So I
Jer 3: 7 And though her faithless sister Judah s this,
3: 8 She s that I had divorced faithless Israel and sent
23:13 "I s that the prophets of Samaria were terribly evil,
24: 1 I s two baskets of figs placed in front of the
39: 4 and his royal guard s the Babylonians in the city
41:13 had captured shouted for joy when they s Johanan
44: 2 You s what I did to Jerusalem and to all the towns
Eze 1: 1 were opened to me, and I s visions of God.
1: 4 I s a great storm coming toward me from the north,
1:15 I s four wheels on the ground beneath them,
1:28 When I s it, I fell face down in the dust, and I
2: 9 Then I looked and I s a hand reaching out to me,
2:10 and I s that both sides were covered with funeral
3:23 and went, and there I s the glory of the LORD,
8: 2 I s a figure that appeared to be a man.
8:10 and s the walls engraved with all kinds of snakes,
8:10 I also s the various idols worshiped by the people
10: 1 I s what appeared to be a throne of blue sapphire
11: 1 where I s twenty-five prominent men of the city.
13:23 no longer talk of seeing visions that you never s,
16: 6 "But I came by and s you there, helplessly kicking
16: 8 And when I passed by and s you again, you were
19: 5 'When the mother lion s / that all her hopes for him
20:14 That way the nations who s me lead my people out
20:28 every high hill and under every green tree they s!
23:11 "Yet even though Oholibah s what had happened
23:13 I s the way she was going, defiling herself just like
23:16 When she s these paintings, she longed to give
40: 3 I s a man whose face shone like bronze standing
44: 4 and s that the glory of the LORD filled the
46:21 of its four corners. In each corner I s an enclosure.
47: 1 There I s a stream flowing eastward from beneath
Da 2:28 and the visions you s as you lay on your bed.
2:31 in your vision you s in front of you a huge
2:41 and toes you s that were a combination of iron
3:27 and s that the fire had not touched them.
4: 5 I s visions that terrified me as I lay in my bed.
4:10 I s a large tree in the middle of the earth.
4:13 I s a messenger, a holy one, coming down from
4:20 You s a tree growing very tall and strong,
4:23 "Then you s a messenger, a holy one,
5: 5 At that very moment they s the fingers of a human
5: 5 The king himself s the hand as it wrote,
7: 1 had a dream and s visions as he lay in his bed.
7: 1 He wrote the dream down, and this is what he s.
7: 2 s a great storm churning the surface of a great sea,
7: 5 Then I s a second beast, and it looked like a bear.
7: 7 I s a fourth beast, terrifying, dreadful, and very
7:13 I s someone who looked like a man coming with
8: 1 Belshazzar's reign, I, Daniel, s another vision,
8: 3 I s in front of me a ram with two long horns
10: 5 I looked up and s a man dressed in linen clothing,
10: 7 I, Daniel, am the only one who s this vision.
10: 7 The men with me s nothing, but they were
12: 5 and s two others standing on opposite banks of the
Hos 5:13 "When Israel and Judah s how sick they were,
9:10 When I s your ancestors, it was like seeing the first
Am 1: 2 This is his report of what he s and heard:
7: 1 I s him preparing to send a vast swarm of locusts
7: 4 I s him preparing to punish his people with a great
7: 7 I s the Lord standing beside a wall that had been
8: 1 In it I s a basket filled with ripe fruit.
9: 1 Then I s a vision of the Lord standing beside the
Jnh 3:10 When God s that they had put a stop to their evil
Zec 1: 8 I s a man sitting on a red horse that was standing
1:18 Then I looked up and s four animal horns.
2: 1 I s a man with a measuring line in his hand.
5: 1 up again and s a scroll flying through the air.
5: 9 I looked up and s two women flying toward us,
6: 1 and s four chariots coming from between two
Mt 2: 7 he learned the exact time when they first s the star.
2:10 When they s the star, they were filled with joy!
3: 7 But when he s many Pharisees and Sadducees
3:16 and he s the Spirit of God descending like a dove
4:18 beside the Sea of Galilee, he s two brothers—
4:21 A little farther up the shore he s two other brothers,
9: 8 Fear swept through the crowd as they s this happen
9: 9 he s Matthew sitting at his tax-collection booth.
12: 2 Some Pharisees s them do it and protested,
14:26 When the disciples s him, they screamed in terror,
17: 8 when they looked, they s only Jesus with them.
18:31 "When some of the other servants s this, they were
20: 3 and s some people standing around doing nothing.
20: 6 and s some more people standing around.
21:15 and the teachers of religious law s these wonderful
21:20 The disciples were amazed when they s this
21:32 And even when you s this happening, you refused
21:38 "But when the farmers s his son coming, they said
26: 8 The disciples were indignant when they s this.
27:24 Pilate s that he wasn't getting anywhere and that a
28: 4 The guards shook with fear when they s him,
28:17 When they s him, they worshiped him—but some
Mk 1:10 he s the heavens split open and the Holy Spirit
1:16 he s Simon and his brother, Andrew, fishing with a
1:19 A little farther up the shore Jesus s Zebedee's sons,
2:14 he s Levi son of Alphaeus sitting at his
2:16 were Pharisees s him eating with people like that,
5: 6 Jesus was still some distance away, the man s him.
5:15 but they were frightened when they s the man who
5:38 Jesus s the commotion and the weeping
6:33 But many people s them leaving, and people from
6:48 He s that they were in serious trouble, rowing hard
6:49 but when they s him walking on the water,
6:50 They were all terrified when they s him. But Jesus
6:51 They were astonished at what they s.
9:20 But when the evil spirit s Jesus, it threw the child
9:25 When Jesus s that the crowd of onlookers was
9:38 we s a man using your name to cast out demons,
10:14 But when Jesus s what was happening, he was very
12:15 Jesus s through their hypocrisy and said, "Who are
14:69 The servant girl s him standing there and began
15:39 When the Roman officer who stood facing him s
15:47 and Mary the mother of Joseph s where Jesus'
16: 4 they arrived, they looked up and s that the stone—
16: 9 and the first person who s him was Mary
Lk 5:12 When the man s Jesus, he fell to the ground,
5:27 he s a tax collector named Levi sitting at his
7:13 When the Lord s her, his heart overflowed with
7:39 When the Pharisee who was the host s what was
8:28 As soon as he s Jesus, he shrieked and fell to the
8:34 When the herdsmen s it, they fled to the nearby
8:35 And they s the man who had been possessed by
9:32 Now they woke up and s Jesus' glory and the two
9:43 Awe gripped the people as they s this display of
9:49 we s someone using your name to cast out demons.
10:18 "I s Satan falling from heaven as a flash of
10:31 but when he s the man lying there, he crossed to
10:33 and when he s the man, he felt deep pity.
13:11 he s a woman who had been crippled by an evil
13:12 When Jesus s her, he called her over and said,
15:20 still a long distance away, his father s him coming.
16:23 he s Lazarus in the far distance with Abraham.
17:15 One of them, when he s that he was healed,
18:43 praising God. And all who s it praised God, too.
19:41 closer to Jerusalem and Jesus s the city ahead,
20:14 "But when the farmers s his son, they said to each
20:23 He s through their trickery and said,
22:49 When the other disciples s what was about to
23:47 handling the executions s what had happened,
23:48 came to see the crucifixion s all that had happened,
23:55 and s the tomb where they placed his body.
24:12 he peered in and s the empty linen wrappings;
Jn 1:29 The next day John s Jesus coming toward him
1:32 "I s the Holy Spirit descending like a dove from
1:34 I s this happen to Jesus, so I testify that he is the
1:38 Jesus looked around and s them following.
2:14 In the Temple area he s merchants selling cattle,
2:14 and he s money changers behind their counters.
5: 6 When Jesus s him and knew how long he had been
6: 2 because they s his miracles as he healed the sick.
6: 5 Jesus soon s a great crowd of people climbing the
6:14 When the people s this miraculous sign,
6:15 Jesus s that they were ready to take him by force
6:19 or four miles out when suddenly they s Jesus
6:24 When the crowd s that Jesus wasn't there, nor his
6:26 I fed you, not because you s the miraculous sign.
8:38 I am telling you what I s when I was with my
8:56 forward to my coming. He s it and was glad."
9: 1 he s a man who had been blind from birth.
11:31 at the house trying to console Mary s her leave
11:32 When Mary arrived and s Jesus, she fell down at
11:33 When Jesus s her weeping and s the other people
wailing with her,
11:45 Mary believed in Jesus when they s this happen.
15:24 they s all that I did and yet hated both of us—
19: 6 When they s him, the leading priests and Temple
19:26 When Jesus s his mother standing there beside the
19:33 they s that he was dead already, so they didn't
20: 5 and looked in and s the linen cloth lying there,
20: 8 other disciple also went in, and he s and believed—
20:12 She s two white-robed angels sitting at the head
20:14 her shoulder and s someone standing behind her.
20:20 They were filled with joy when they s their Lord!
20:30 Jesus' disciples s him do many other miraculous
21: 4 At dawn the disciples s Jesus standing on the
21: 9 they s that a charcoal fire was burning and fish
21:20 and s the disciple Jesus loved following them—
21:24 This is that disciple who s these events
Ac 1:11 And someday, just as you s him go, he will

3: 3 When he s Peter and John about to enter, he asked
3: 9 All the people s him walking and heard him
3:12 Peter s his opportunity and addressed the crowd.
4:13 were amazed when they s the boldness of Peter
5:10 the young men came in and s that she was dead,
7:24 he s an Egyptian mistreating a man of Israel.
7:26 them again and s two men of Israel fighting.
7:31 Moses s it and wondered what it was. As he went
7:55 upward into heaven and s the glory of God,
7:55 and he s Jesus standing in the place of honor at
8:18 When Simon s that the Holy Spirit was given when
8:39 The eunuch never s him again but went on his way
9: 7 the sound of someone's voice, but they s no one!
9:35 and Sharon turned to the Lord when they s Aeneas
9:40 she opened her eyes! When she s Peter, she sat up!
10: 3 he had a vision in which he s an angel of God
10:11 He s the sky open, and something like a large sheet
11: 5 I was praying, I went into a trance and s a vision.
11: 6 I s all sorts of small animals, wild animals, reptiles,
11:23 When he arrived and s this proof of God's favor,
12: 3 When Herod s how much this pleased the Jewish
13:12 When the governor s what had happened,
13:45 But when the Jewish leaders s the crowds,
14:11 When the listening crowd s what Paul had done,
16: 9 He s a man from Macedonia in northern Greece,
17:16 he was deeply troubled by all the idols he s
17:23 for as I was walking along I s your many altars.
21:27 from the province of Asia s Paul in the Temple
21:32 When the mob s the commander and the troops
22: 9 The people with me s the light but didn't hear the
22:18 I s a vision of Jesus saying to me, 'Hurry!
24:18 My accusers s me in the Temple as I was
27:39 but they s a bay with a beach and wondered if they
28: 4 The people of the island s it hanging there and said
28: 6 had waited a long time and s no harm come to him,
28:15 When Paul s them, he thanked God and took
1Co 1:21 Since God in his wisdom s to it that the world
15: 8 Last of all, I s him, too, long after the others,
Gal 2: 7 They s that God had given me the responsibility of
2:14 When I s that they were not following the truth of
Php 4: 9 from me and heard from me and s me doing,
Heb 3: 9 even though they s my miracles for forty years.
11:13 but they s it all from a distance and welcomed the
11:23 They s that God had given them an unusual child,
2Pe 2: 8 man who was distressed by the wickedness he s
1Jn 1: 1 We s him with our own eyes and touched him with
Rev 1: 2 and the testimony of Jesus Christ—everything he s.
1:12 was speaking to me, I s seven gold lampstands.
1:17 When I s him, I fell at his feet as dead. But he laid
1:20 This is the meaning of the seven stars you s in my
4: 1 as I looked, I s a door standing open in heaven,
4: 2 and I s a throne in heaven and someone sitting on
5: 1 And I s a scroll in the right hand of the one who
5: 2 And I s a strong angel, who shouted with a loud
5: 6 I looked and I s a Lamb that had been killed
6: 2 I looked up and s a white horse. Its rider carried a
6: 5 And I looked up and s a black horse, and its rider
6: 8 and s a horse whose color was pale green like a
6: 9 I s under the altar the souls of all who had been
7: 1 Then I s four angels standing at the four corners of
7: 2 And I s another angel coming from the east,
7: 9 After this I s a vast crowd, too great to count,
8: 2 And I s the seven angels who stand before God,
9: 1 and I s a star that had fallen to earth from the sky,
9:17 I s the horses and the riders sitting on them.
10: 1 Then I s another mighty angel coming down from
12: 1 I s a woman clothed with the sun, with the moon
12: 3 I s a large red dragon with seven heads and ten
13: 1 And now in my vision I s a beast rising up out of
13: 3 I s that one of the heads of the beast seemed
13:11 Then I s another beast come up out of the earth.
14: 1 Then I s the Lamb standing on Mount Zion,
14: 6 And I s another angel flying through the heavens,
14:14 Then I s the Son of Man sitting on a white cloud.
15: 1 Then I s in heaven another significant event,
15: 2 I s before me what seemed to be a crystal sea
15: 5 Then I looked and s that the Temple in heaven,
16:13 And I s three evil spirits that looked like frogs leap
17: 3 There I s a woman sitting on a scarlet beast that
17: 8 The beast you s was alive but isn't now. And yet
17:18 And this woman you s in your vision represents the
18: 1 After all this I s another angel come down from
19:11 Then I s heaven opened, and a white horse was
19:17 Then I s an angel standing in the sun, shouting to
19:19 Then I s the beast gathering the kings of the earth
20: 1 Then I s an angel come down from heaven with the
20: 4 Then I s thrones, and the people sitting on them
20: 4 And I s the souls of those who had been beheaded
20: 4 And I s the souls of those who had not worshiped
20: 9 And I s them as they went up on the broad plain of
20:11 And I s a great white throne, and I s the one who was sitting on it.
20:12 I s the dead, both great and small, standing before
21: 1 Then I s a new heaven and a new earth, for the old
21: 2 And I s the holy city, the new Jerusalem,
22: 8 am the one who s and heard all these things.
22: 8 And when I s and heard these things, I fell down to

SAWED (1) [SAW]

Heb 11:37 Some died by stoning, and some were s in half;

SAWS (3) [SAW]

2Sa 12:31 people of Rabbah and forced them to labor with s,
1Ch 20: 3 people of Rabbah and forced them to labor with s,
Isa 10:15 Is the saw greater than the person who s? Can a

SAY (823) [SAID, SAYING, SAYINGS, SAYS] See Index of Articles, Etc.

SAYING (9 of 263) [SAY] See also Index of Articles, Etc.

Dt 9: 2 You've heard the s, 'Who can stand up to the
1Sa 10:12 So that is the origin of the s "Is Saul a prophet?"
2Sa 5: 8 That is the origin of the s, "The blind and the lame
20:18 Then she continued, "There used to be a s, 'If you
Mt 16: 2 He replied, "You know the s, 'Red sky at night
Jn 4:37 You know the s, 'One person plants and someone
1Ti 1:15 This is a true s, and everyone should believe it:
3: 1 It is a true s that if someone wants to be an elder,
2Ti 2:11 This is a true s: / If we die with him, / we will also

SAYINGS (8) [SAY]

Job 26: 4 Where have you gotten all these wise s?
Pr 1: 2 and discipline, and to help them understand wise s.
1: 6 in these proverbs, parables, wise s, and riddles.
22:18 For it is good to keep these s deep within yourself,
22:20 I have written thirty s for you, filled with advice
24:23 Here are some further s of the wise: It is wrong to
31: 1 These are the s of King Lemuel, an oracle that his
Ecc 12:11 The collected s of the wise are like guidance from

SAYS (842) [SAY] See Index of Articles, Etc.

GOD SAYS (15) Ge 3:3; Ex 20:19; Dt 5:27; Jos 3:9; 2Ch 24:20; Ps 50:16; 75:2,10; Jer 42:20; Zec 11:4; Mt 15:4; Ac 10:15; 11:9; Ro 9:25; 2Co 6:2

LORD SAYS (4) Ps 68:22; Isa 29:13; Lk 2:23; Ac 15:17

LORD* SAYS (234) Ge 22:16; Ex 4:22; 7:17; 8:1,20; 11:4; 16:16; Nu 24:13; 2Sa 7:5; 24:12; 1Ki 12:24; 13:2,21; 20:13,14,28,42; 21:19; 22:5,11,19; 2Ki 1:4,16; 2:21; 3:16; 4:43; 7:1; 9:3; 19:6,32; 20:1; 22:16; 1Ch 17:4; 21:10; 2Ch 11:4; 12:5; 18:4,10,18; 20:15; 34:24; Ps 32:8; 91:14; 95:8; Isa 1:2; 7:7; 16:14; 28:16; 33:10; 37:6,33; 38:1; 45:1,2,14; 49:8,22,25; 52:3,4; 65:1,13; 66:1; Jer 2:2,5; 3:12; 4:3,27; 6:16,21,22; 7:20; 8:4; 9:22,23; 10:2; 12:14; 13:9; 15:2; 16:3; 17:1,5,21; 18:11; 20:4; 21:8,12; 22:3,6,11,13,30; 23:17,33, 38; 26:4; 27:15,16; 28:13,16; 29:16,31; 30:5,12,18; 31:7,15, 16; 32:3; 33:10,17; 34:4,17; 36:29,30; 37:9; 38:2; 42:15; 45:4; 47:2; 49:1,12,15,23,28; 50:2; 51:1,36; Eze 2:4; 3:11,27; 4:13; 5:5,7; 6:3,11; 7:2,5; 11:5,7; 12:10; 13:3,8,13,18,20; 14:21; 15:6; 16:36,59; 17:19,22; 20:39; 21:7,24; 23:22,28,32, 46; 24:6,9,21; 25:6,8,12,15; 26:3,7,15,19; 28:6,25; 29:8,19; 30:6,10,13,22; 31:10,15; 32:3,11; 34:10,11,17,20; 35:14; 36:2,5,13,33,37; 37:5,9,19; 38:10,17; 39:25; 43:18; 44:9; 45:9,18; 46:1,16; 47:13; Hos 9:10,15; 10:9; 14:4; Joel 2:12,25; Am 1:3,6,9,11,13; 2:1,4,6; 3:12; 5:3,4; 7:17; Ob 1:2; Mic 2:3; 3:5; Na 1:12,14; Zep 3:8; Zec 1:16; 2:6,10; 4:6; 8:3

SAYS THE LORD (15) Isa 19:4; 21:16; Jer 49:5; 50:31; Am 3:13; Ro 12:19; 14:11; 1Co 14:21; 2Co 6:17,18; Heb 8:8,9,10; 10:16; Rev 1:8

SAYS THE LORD* (239) 2Ki 3:17; 9:26; 19:33; 20:17; 22:19; 2Ch 34:27; Isa 1:11,18; 8:20; 17:3,6; 22:19; 30:1; 31:9; 37:34; 39:6; 41:21; 43:10,12; 48:22; 49:18; 54:1,8,10; 55:8; 56:1; 57:19; 59:20,21; 65:7,8; 66:12,17,20,22; Jer 2:12,29; 3:1,10,14,16,20,22; 4:1,9,17,22; 5:1,11,15,18; 6:12,15; 7:11,13,30,32; 8:1,12,17; 9:3,6,11,25; 10:18; 11:11; 13:11,14,25; 14:15; 15:3,6,9; 16:5,14,16,21; 17:24; 19:6,12; 21:7,10,14; 22:5,24; 23:1,4,5,7,11,16,30,32; 25:7,12; 27:8,22; 29:9,11,14,19,23; 30:8,10,11,17,21; 31:1,17,27,28,31,32, 33,34,38; 32:30; 33:11,14; 34:5; 42:11; 44:26,29; 46:5,23,28; 48:12,25,30,35,40,43,44,47; 49:2,2,6,13,16,18,26,30,31,32, 37,38,39; 50:4,10,20,21,30,35,40; 51:20,24,25,26,39,48,52, 53; Eze 16:58; Hos 2:13,16,21; 11:11; Joel 3:1; Am 3:10; 4:6,8,9,10,11; 5:27; 6:14; 9:8,13,15; Ob 1:8; Mic 4:6,13; 5:10; 7:15; Na 2:13; Zep 1:2,3,8,10; 2:9,12; Hag 1:8,9,13; 2:4,4,4,7,8,9,14,17,23,23; Zec 1:3,16; 2:5; 3:9,10; 4:6; 7:13; 8:11,14,17; 11:6; 12:4; 13:2,7,8; Mal 1:2,8,10,11,13,14; 2:2,4,8,16,16; 3:1,5,7,10,11,12,13,17; 4:3

SAYS THE SOVEREIGN LORD* (71) Eze 5:11; 11:8,21; 12:25; 13:8; 14:11,23; 15:8; 16:8,14,19,23,30,43,48,63; 17:12,16; 18:3,9,30,32; 20:31,33,36,40,44; 21:26; 22:12,31; 23:35; 24:14; 25:13,16; 26:5; 29:20; 30:6; 32:14,31; 33:11; 34:8,15,30,31; 35:6,11; 36:7,14,15,23,32; 38:18,21; 39:5,8,10,13,17,20,29; 43:19,27; 44:12,15,27; 45:15; 48:29; Am 3:11; 4:5; 8:9,11

SCAB (1) [SCABS]

Lev 22:22 or a s must never be offered to the LORD by fire

SCAB [KJV] See also RASH, SCURVY

SCABS (3) [SCAB]

Lev 21:20 defective eye, or has oozing sores or s on his skin,
Job 7: 5 My skin is filled with worms and s. My flesh
Isa 3:17 The Lord will send a plague of s to ornament their

SCAFFOLD [KJV] See PLATFORM

SCALE (5) [SCALES]

Lev 27: 3 here is the s of values to be used. A man between
2Sa 22:30 can crush an army; / with my God I can s any wall.
Ps 18:29 can crush an army; / with my God I can s any wall.
Eze 5: 1 Use a s to weigh the hair into three equal parts.
Joel 2: 7 like warriors and s city walls like trained soldiers.

SCALES (21) [SCALE]

Lev 11: 9 you may eat whatever has both fins and s,
11:10 eat marine animals that do not have both fins and s.
11:12 have both fins and s is strictly forbidden to you.
19:36 Your s and weights must be accurate.
Dt 14: 9 you may eat whatever has both fins and s.
14:10 eat marine animals that do not have both fins and s.
25:13 "You must use accurate s when you weigh out
Job 6: 2 could be weighed and my troubles be put on the s,
31: 6 Let God judge me on the s of justice, for he knows
41:15 The overlapping s on its back make a shield.
41:30 Its belly is covered with s as sharp as glass.
Ps 62: 9 nothing in his sight. / If you weigh them on the s,
Pr 20:23 double standards; he is not pleased by dishonest s.
Isa 40:15 They are but a drop in the bucket, dust on the s.
Eze 29: 4 you out on the land with fish sticking to your s.
45:10 You must use only honest weights and s,
Hos 12: 7 are like crafty merchants selling from dishonest s—
Am 8: 5 in false measures and weigh it out on dishonest s.
Mic 6:11 I tolerate all your merchants who use dishonest s
Ac 9:18 Instantly something like s fell from Saul's eyes,
Rev 6: 5 and its rider was holding a pair of s in his hand.

SCALL [KJV] See INFECTION

SCANDAL (1) [SCANDALOUS]

Pr 16:27 Scoundrels hunt for s; their words are a destructive

SCANDALOUS (1) [SCANDAL]

Am 3: 9 and witness the s spectacle of all Israel's crimes."

SCAPEGOAT (3) [GOAT]

Lev 16: 8 to the LORD and which one will be the s.
16:10 The goat chosen to be the s will be presented to the
16:26 out into the wilderness as a s must wash his clothes

SCAR (2)

Lev 13:23 does not spread, it is merely the s from the boil,
13:28 and has faded, it is simply a s from the burn.

SCARCE (3) [SCARCELY, SCARCITY]

Isa 13:12 People will be as s as gold—more rare than the
Eze 4:16 of man, I will cause food to be very s in Jerusalem.
4:17 so s that the people will look at one another in

SCARCELY (6) [SCARCE]

Ex 10:23 During all that time the people s moved, for they
Job 2:12 saw Job from a distance, they s recognized him.
25: 5 even the moon and stars s shine compared to him.
Isa 52:14 so disfigured one would s know he was a person.
Jer 51:41 The world can s believe its eyes at her fall!
Ac 14:18 and Barnabas could s restrain the people from

SCARCITY (2) [SCARCE]

Pr 6:11 a bandit; s will attack you like an armed robber.
24:34 a bandit; s will attack you like an armed robber.

SCARE (2)

Jer 7:33 and no one will be left to s them away.
Da 11:30 For warships from western coastlands will s him

SCARECROW (1)

Jer 10: 5 There stands their god like a helpless s in a garden!

SCARLET (51)

Ge 38:28 and the midwife tied a s thread around the wrist of
38:30 Then the baby with the s thread on his wrist was
Ex 25: 4 blue, purple, and s yarn; fine linen; goat hair for
26: 1 are to be decorated with blue, purple, and s yarn,
26:31 into the cloth using blue, purple, and s yarn.
26:36 designs into it, using blue, purple, and s yarn.
27:16 beautiful embroidery in blue, purple, and s yarn.
28: 5 with gold thread and blue, purple, and s yarn.
28: 6 with gold thread and blue, purple, and s yarn.
28: 8 with gold thread and blue, purple, and s yarn.
28:15 with gold thread and blue, purple, and s yarn.
28:33 Make pomegranates out of blue, purple, and s yarn,
35: 6 blue, purple, and s yarn; fine linen; goat hair for
35:23 Others brought blue, purple, and s yarn, fine linen,
35:25 purple, and s yarn, and fine linen cloth, and they
35:35 in blue, purple, and s yarn on fine linen cloth.
36: 8 purple, and s cherubim into them.
36:35 embroidered into it with blue, purple, and s yarn.
36:37 and embroidered with blue, purple, and s yarn.
38:18 and embroidered with blue, purple, and s yarn.
38:23 purple, and s yarn on fine linen cloth.
39: 1 beautiful garments of blue, purple, and s cloth—
39: 2 with gold thread and blue, purple, and s yarn.
39: 3 it into the linen with the blue, purple, and s yarn.
39: 5 fine linen cloth; blue, purple, and s yarn; and gold
39: 8 with gold thread and blue, purple, and s yarn.
39:24 were finely crafted of blue, purple, and s yarn.
39:29 and embroidered with blue, purple, and s yarn,
Lev 14: 4 some cedarwood, a s cloth, and a hyssop branch.
14: 6 the cedarwood, the s cloth, and the hyssop branch,
14:49 some cedarwood, a s cloth, and a hyssop branch.
14:51 dip the cedarwood, the hyssop branch, the s cloth,
Nu 4: 8 They must spread a s cloth over that, and finally a
4: 8 of fine goatskin leather on top of the s cloth.
19: 6 and s thread and throw them into the fire where the
Jos 2:18 only if you leave this s rope hanging from the
2:21 leaving the s rope hanging from the window.
2Ch 2: 7 who is expert at dyeing purple, s, and blue cloth;
2:14 blue, and s cloth and in working with linen.

3:14 made of fine linen and blue, purple, and s yarn,
SS 4:3 Your lips are like a ribbon of s. Oh, how beautiful
Na 2:3 The attack begins! See their s uniforms!
Mt 27:28 They stripped him and put a s robe on him.
Heb 9:19 using branches of hyssop bushes and s wool.
Rev 17:3 There I saw a woman sitting on a s beast that had
17:4 The woman wore purple and s clothing
17:11 The s beast that was alive and then died is the
17:16 The s beast and his ten horns—which represent ten
17:17 agree to give their authority to the s beast,
18:12 jewels, pearls, fine linen, purple dye, silk, s cloth,
18:16 like a woman clothed in finest purple and s linens,

SCARS (2)
Zec 13:6 'Then what are those s on your chest?'
Gal 6:17 For I bear on my body the s that show I belong to

SCARVES (1)
Isa 3:20 Gone will be their s, ankle chains, sashes,

SCATTER (39) [SCATTERED, SCATTERING, SCATTERS]
Ge 49:7 for it is cruel. / Therefore, I will s their descendants
Lev 26:33 I will s you among the nations and attack you with
Nu 16:37 are holy. Also tell him to s the burning incense
Dt 4:27 For the LORD will s you among the nations,
28:7 one direction, but they will s from you in seven!
28:25 one direction, but you will s from them in seven!
28:64 For the LORD will s you among all the nations
32:26 I decided to s them, / so even the memory of them
1Ki 14:15 and will s them beyond the Euphrates River,
Ne 1:8 'If you sin, I will s you among the nations.
Ps 53:5 God will s the bones of your enemies. / You will
68:1 Arise, O God, and s your enemies. / Let those who
68:30 tribute from us. / S the nations that delight in war.
106:27 that he would s their descendants among the
144:6 Release your lightning bolts and s your enemies!
Ecc 3:5 A time to s stones and a time to gather stones.
Isa 41:16 will blow them all away; a whirlwind will s them.
Jer 9:16 I will s them around the world, and they will be
13:24 "I will s you, just as chaff is scattered by the
18:17 I will s my people before their enemies as the east
29:18 and disease, and I will s them around the world.
32:37 all the countries where I will s them in my fury.
49:32 I will s to the winds these people who live in
49:36 and I will s the people of Elam to the four winds.
Eze 5:2 S another third across your map and slash at it with
5:2 S the last third to the wind, for I will s my people with the sword.
5:12 And I will s a third to the winds and chase them
6:5 of your idols and s your bones around your altars.
10:2 of glowing coals and s them over the city."
12:14 I will s his servants and guards to the four winds
12:15 And when I s them among the nations, they will
20:23 I vowed I would s them among all the nations
22:15 I will s you among the nations and purge you of
29:12 I will s the Egyptians to distant lands.
30:23 I will s the Egyptians to many lands throughout the
30:26 I will s the Egyptians among the nations.
Da 4:14 its branches! Shake off its leaves, and s its fruit!
Am 9:8 I will uproot it and s its people across the earth.

SCATTERED (84) [SCATTER]
Ge 9:19 of Noah came all the people now s across the earth.
11:8 In that way, the LORD s them all over the earth;
25:18 Ishmael's descendants were s across the country
Ex 5:12 So the people s throughout the land in search of
Nu 10:35 "Arise, O LORD, and let your enemies be s!
Dt 30:3 you back from all the nations where he has s you.
Jdg 9:45 leveled the city, and s salt all over the ground.
1Sa 11:11 so badly s that no two of them were left together.
14:14 and their bodies were s over about half an acre.
2Sa 22:15 He shot his arrows and s his enemies;
1Ki 22:17 "In a vision I saw all Israel s on the mountains,
2Ki 9:37 Her body will be s like dung on the field of Jezreel,
14:12 army of Israel, and its army s and fled for home.
23:12 them to bits and s the pieces in the Kidron Valley.
2Ch 18:16 "In a vision I saw all Israel s on the mountains,
25:22 army of Israel, and its army s and fled for home.
34:4 and s over the graves of those who had sacrificed
Ne 7:4 And only a few houses were s throughout the city.
Est 3:8 "There is a certain race of people s through all the
Job 4:11 will starve, and the cubs of the lioness will be s.
Ps 1:4 They are like worthless chaff, s by the wind.
18:14 He shot his arrows and s his enemies;
44:11 be slaughtered; / you have s us among the nations.
68:14 The Almighty s the enemy kings / like a blowing
89:10 You s your enemies with your mighty arm.
92:9 LORD, will surely perish; / all evildoers will be s.
141:7 so the bones of the wicked will be s without a
Isa 11:12 He will gather the s people of Judah from the ends
17:13 They will flee like chaff s by the wind or like dust
44:22 I have s your offenses like the clouds. Oh, return to
Jer 3:14 and two from there, from wherever you are s.
5:10 and destroy them, but leave a s few alive.
8:2 or buried but will be s on the ground like dung.
9:22 "Bodies will be s across the fields like dung,
10:21 they fail completely, and their flocks are s.
13:24 just as chaff is s by the winds blowing in from the
16:4 and they will lie s on the ground like dung.
23:1 and s the very ones they were expected to care
25:33 bury them. They will be s like dung on the ground.
30:11 completely destroy the nations where I have s you,
31:10 The LORD, who s his people, will gather them
40:15 Why should the few of us who are still left be s
50:17 "The Israelites are like sheep that have been s by
La 4:1 The sacred gemstones lie s in the streets!
4:16 The LORD himself has s them, and he no longer
Eze 6:8 and they will be s among the nations of the world.
6:13 When their dead lie s among their idols and altars,
11:16 Although I have s you in the countries of the
11:17 gather you back from the nations where you are s,
17:21 and those remaining in the city will be s to the four
20:34 will bring you out from the lands where you are s.
28:25 them from the distant lands where I have s them.
29:13 again from the nations to which they have been s.
31:12 Its branches were s across the mountains
33:24 the s remnants of Judah living among the ruined
34:5 So my sheep have been s without a shepherd.
34:12 I will be like a shepherd looking for his s flock.
34:12 all the places to which they were s on that dark
34:21 and hungry flock until they are s to distant lands.
36:19 I s them to many lands to punish them for the evil
36:20 But when they were s among the nations,
36:22 which you dishonored while you were s among the
37:2 They were s everywhere across the ground.
37:21 own land from the places where they have been s.
Da 9:7 and Jerusalem and all Israel, s near and far,
Am 8:3 Dead bodies will be s everywhere. They will be
Na 3:18 the dust. Your people are s across the mountains.
Zep 3:10 My s people who live beyond the rivers of Ethiopia
Zec 1:19 "These horns represent the world powers that s
1:21 have come to terrify the four horns that s
2:6 from the north, for I have s you to the four winds.
7:14 I s them as with a whirlwind among the distant
10:9 Though I have s them like seeds among the
13:7 Strike down the shepherd, and the sheep will be s,
Mt 13:4 As he s it across his field, some seeds fell on a
26:31 and the sheep of the flock will be s.'
Mk 4:4 As he s it across his field, some seed fell on a
14:27 will strike the Shepherd, / and the sheep will be s.'
Lk 8:5 As he s it across his field, some seed fell on a
Jn 2:15 s the money changers' coins over the floor,
11:52 of all the children of God s around the world.
16:32 when you will be s, each one going his own way,
Ac 5:37 but he was killed, too, and all his followers were s.
Jas 1:1 It is written to Jewish Christians s among the

SCATTERING (7) [SCATTER]
Ge 11:4 us together and keep us from s all over the world."
11:9 them many languages, thus s them across the earth.
1Sa 13:11 Saul replied, "I saw my men s from me, and you
2Ki 23:14 Then he desecrated these places by s human bones
Isa 24:1 See how he is s the people over the face of the
Eze 5:10 And I will punish you by s the few who survive to
Joel 3:2 for s my inheritance among the nations, and for

SCATTERS (5) [SCATTER]
Ps 147:16 white wool; / he s frost upon the ground like ashes.
Isa 41:2 to the sword. He s them in the wind with his bow.
Jer 18:17 people before their enemies as the east wind s dust.
Lk 1:51 How he s the proud and haughty ones!
Jn 10:12 And so the wolf attacks them and s the flock.

SCAVENGE (1)
Ps 59:15 They s for food / but go to sleep unsatisfied.

SCENE (5)
Job 14:20 overpower them, and then they pass from the s.
Hab 1:6 the Babylonians to be a new power on the world s.
Mt 24:34 this generation will not pass from the s before all
Mk 13:30 this generation will not pass from the s until all
Lk 21:32 this generation will not pass from the s until all

SCENT (4) [SCENTED]
Ex 30:34 resin droplets, mollusk s, galbanum, and pure
Job 14:9 at the s of water it may bud and sprout again like a
SS 4:11 The s of your clothing is like that of the mountains
7:8 grape clusters, and the s of your breath like apples.

SCENTED (3) [SCENT]
Ex 30:26 Use this s oil to anoint the Tabernacle, the Ark of
30:33 Anyone who blends s oil like it or puts any of it on
SS 5:13 His cheeks are like sweetly s beds of spices.

SCEPTER (9) [SCEPTERS]
Ge 49:10 The s will not depart from Judah, / nor the ruler's
Nu 24:17 will rise from Jacob; / a s will emerge from Israel.
Est 4:11 doomed to die unless the king holds out his gold s.
5:2 he welcomed her, holding out the gold s to her.
8:4 Again the king held out the gold s to Esther.
Jer 48:17 See how the strong s is broken, how the beautiful
Eze 19:11 very strong, / strong enough to be a ruler's s.
19:14 is strong enough to be a ruler's s.' This is a funeral
Mt 27:29 and they placed a stick in his right hand as a s.

SCEPTERS (1) [SCEPTER]
Nu 21:18 leaders hollowed out / with their s and staffs."

SCEVA (1)
Ac 19:14 Seven sons of S, a leading priest, were doing this.

SCHEDULE (2) [SCHEDULED]
1Sa 13:21 (The s of charges was as follows: a quarter of an
Jer 33:20 the night so that they do not come on their usual s,

SCHEDULED (3) [SCHEDULE]
Ezr 10:14 Everyone who has a pagan wife will come at the s
Est 3:13 This was s to happen nearly a year later on March
Ac 27:2 it was s to make several stops at ports along the

SCHEME (5) [SCHEMERS, SCHEMES, SCHEMING]
1Sa 26:19 But if this is simply a human s, then may those
Jer 2:33 "How you plot and s to win your lovers. The most
Eze 38:10 to your mind, and you will devise a wicked s.
Mic 7:3 pay them off, and together they s to twist justice.
Jas 4:2 what you don't have, so you s and kill to get it.

SCHEMERS (1) [SCHEME]
Pr 14:17 short-tempered do foolish things, and s are hated.

SCHEMES (13) [SCHEME]
Job 5:13 so that their cunning s are thwarted.
18:7 be shortened. Their own s will be their downfall.
21:27 your thoughts. I know the s you plot against me.
Ps 21:11 plot against you, / their evil s will never succeed.
26:10 Their hands are dirty with wicked s, / and they
33:10 the plans of the nations / and thwarts all their s.
37:7 people who prosper / or fret about their wicked s.
83:3 They devise crafty s against your people,
140:8 Do not let their evil s succeed, O God.
Pr 13:11 Wealth from get-rich-quick s quickly disappears;
24:9 The s of a fool are sinful; everyone despises a
Mic 2:1 and hurry to carry out any of the wicked s you
2Co 2:11 For we are very familiar with his evil s.

SCHEMING (2) [SCHEME]
Ps 64:2 of the wicked, / from the s of those who do evil.
Na 1:9 Why are you s against the LORD? He will

SCHISM [KJV] See HARMONY

SCHOLARS (2)
Da 2:21 gives wisdom to the wise / and knowledge to the s.
1Co 1:20 the s, and the world's brilliant debaters?

SCHOOL [KJV] See (LECTURE) HALL

SCHOOLMASTER [KJV] See GUARDIAN, TEACHER

SCIENCE (1)
Da 1:17 for learning the literature and s of the time.

SCIENCE [KJV] See also KNOWLEDGE

SCOFF (19) [SCOFFED, SCOFFERS, SCOFFING, SCOFFS]
1Ki 9:8 They will s and ask, 'Why did the LORD do such
Ps 42:10 They s, "Where is this God of yours?"
59:8 you laugh at them. / You s at all the hostile nations.
69:10 I weep and fast before the LORD, / they s at me.
69:26 they s at the pain of those you have hurt.
73:8 They s and speak only evil; / in their pride they
74:18 See how these enemies s at you, LORD.
79:10 Why should pagan nations be allowed to s,
Isa 28:22 So s no more, or your punishment will be even
66:5 LORD be honored!' they s. 'Be joyful in him!'
Jer 17:15 People s at me and say, "What is this 'message
La 2:15 They s and insult Jerusalem, saying, "Is this the
2:16 They s and grind their teeth and say, "We have
Eze 36:30 nations be able to s at your land for its famines.
Hab 1:10 They s at kings and princes and scorn all their
1Th 5:20 Do not s at prophecies,
1Ti 1:13 even though I used to s at the name of Christ.
2Pe 2:10 daring even to s at the glorious ones without
Jude 1:8 and s at the power of the glorious ones.

SCOFFED (11) [SCOFF]
1Ki 18:27 to shout louder," he s, "for surely he is a god!
2Ch 36:16 They s at the prophets until the LORD's anger
Ne 2:19 the Arab heard of our plan, they s contemptuously.
Eze 25:3 Because you s when my Temple was desecrated,
Zep 2:10 for they have s at the people of the LORD
Mt 27:42 "He saved others," they s, "but he can't save
Mk 15:31 "He saved others," they s, "but he can't save
Lk 16:14 dearly loved their money, naturally s at all this.
23:35 The crowd watched, and the leaders laughed and s.
23:39 One of the criminals hanging beside him s,
Jn 7:3 your followers can see your miracles!" they s.

SCOFFERS (3) [SCOFF]
Ps 1:1 or stand around with sinners, / or join in with s.
2Pe 3:3 last days there will be s who will laugh at the truth
Jude 1:18 that in the last times there would be s whose

SCOFFING (4) [SCOFF]
Ne 4:4 May their s fall back on their own heads, and may
Ps 123:4 We have had our fill of the s of the proud
Isa 28:14 from the LORD, you s rulers in Jerusalem.
2Ti 3:2 They will be boastful and proud, s at God,

SCOFFS (3) [SCOFF]
2Ki 19:21 of Jerusalem / s and shakes her head as you flee.

Ps 2: 4 who rules in heaven laughs. / The Lord s at them.
Isa 37:22 of Jerusalem / s and shakes her head as you flee.

SCOLDED (1) [SCOLDING]
Mk 14: 5 the money to the poor!" And they s her harshly.

SCOLDING (1) [SCOLDED]
1Co 4:21 Should I come with punishment and s, or should I

SCOOP (2) [SCOOPED, SCOOPS]
Lev 5:12 who will s out a handful as a token portion.
Pr 6:27 Can a man s fire into his lap and not be burned?

SCOOPED (1) [SCOOP]
Jdg 14: 9 He s some of the honey into his hands and ate it

SCOOPS (2) [SCOOP]
Ru 3:15 He measured out six s of barley into the cloak
3:17 "He gave me these six s of barley and said,

SCOPE (2)
Ecc 3:11 people cannot see the whole s of God's work from
Eph 3:14 When I think of the wisdom and s of God's plan,

SCORCH (3) [SCORCHED, SCORCHER, SCORCHING]
Eze 20:47 they will s everything from south to north.
24:11 Now set the empty pot on the coals to s away the
Rev 16: 8 on the sun, causing it to s everyone with its fire.

SCORCHED (4) [SCORCH]
2Ki 19:26 grass sprouting on a housetop, / easily s by the sun.
Isa 15: 6 The grassy banks are s, and the tender plants are
37:27 grass sprouting on a housetop, / easily s by the sun.
Da 3:27 heads was singed, and their clothing was not s.

SCORCHER (1) [SCORCH]
Lk 12:55 the south wind blows, you say, 'Today will be a s.'

SCORCHING (7) [SCORCH]
Ge 31:40 I worked for you through the s heat of the day
Dt 28:22 with s heat and drought, and with blight
Ps 11: 6 punishing them with burning sulfur and s winds.
Isa 49:10 and s desert winds will not reach them anymore.
Jnh 4: 8 grew hot, God sent a s east wind to blow on Jonah.
Mt 20:12 as you paid us who worked all day in the s heat.'
Rev 7:16 and they will be fully protected from the s

SCORN (16) [SCORNED, SCORNFUL, SCORNING]
1Sa 2:29 So why do you s my sacrifices and offerings?
Job 16:20 My friends s me, but I pour out my tears to God.
22:19 and the innocent will laugh them to s.
Ps 10: 5 awaiting them. / They pour s on all their enemies.
44:13 We are an object of s and derision to the nations
64: 8 who see it happening will shake their heads in s.
79: 4 an object of s and derision to those around us.
79:12 our neighbors / for the s they have hurled at you.
80: 6 You have made us the s of neighboring nations.
119:22 Don't let them s and insult me, / for I have obeyed
Pr 9:12 If you s wisdom, you will be the one to suffer.
Isa 51: 7 Do not be afraid of people's s or their slanderous
Jer 6:10 they cannot hear. They s the word of the LORD.
Eze 23:32 the world will mock and s you in your desolation.
34:29 or be shamed by the s of foreign nations.
Hab 1:10 scoff at kings and princes and s all their defenses.

SCORNED (8) [SCORN]
Ps 22: 6 and not a man. / I am s and despised by all!
31:11 I am s by all my enemies / and despised by my
44:14 butt of their jokes; / we are s by the whole world.
Eze 16:57 to all the world, and you are the one who is s—
20:24 They s my instructions by violating my Sabbath
Da 9: 5 against you and s your commands and regulations.
Mal 3: 7 you have s my laws and failed to obey them.
Lk 18: 9 who had great self-confidence and s everyone else:

SCORNFUL (1) [SCORN]
Eze 28:24 No longer will Israel's s neighbors prick and tear at

SCORNING (2) [SCORN]
2Ch 32:17 The king also sent letters s the LORD, the God of
Ps 107:11 the words of God, / s the counsel of the Most High.

SCORPION (5) [SCORPIONS]
Nu 34: 4 then run south past S Pass in the direction of Zin.
Jos 15: 3 ran south of S Pass into the wilderness of Zin
Jdg 1:36 The boundary of the Amorites ran from S Pass to
Lk 11:12 Or if they ask for an egg, do you give them a s?
Rev 9: 5 five months with agony like the pain of s stings.

SCORPIONS (9) [SCORPION]
Dt 8:15 terrifying wilderness with poisonous snakes and s,
1Ki 12:11 My father used whips on you, but I'll use s!' "
12:14 My father used whips on you, but I'll use s!"
2Ch 10:11 My father used whips on you, but I'll use s!' "
10:14 My father used whips on you, but I'll use s!"
Eze 2: 6 and barbed like briers, and they sting like s.
Lk 10:19 you can walk among snakes and s and crush them.
Rev 9: 3 and they were given power to sting like s.
9:10 They had tails that sting like s, with power to

SCOUNDREL (1) [SCOUNDRELS]
2Sa 16: 7 "Get out of here, you murderer, you s!"

SCOUNDRELS (6) [SCOUNDREL]
1Sa 2:12 Now the sons of Eli were s who had no respect for
1Ki 21:10 Find two s who will accuse him of cursing God
21:13 Then two s accused him before all the people of
2Ch 13: 7 Then a whole gang of s joined him,
Ps 120: 5 How I suffer among these s of Meshech! / It pains
Pr 16:27 S hunt for scandal; their words are a destructive

SCOURED (1)
Lev 6:28 it must be s and rinsed thoroughly with water.

SCOURGES (1)
Isa 9: 4 that bind his people and the whip that s them,

SCOURGES, SCOURGETH, SCOURGING(S) [KJV] See BEAT, FLOG(GED), HIT, STRIKE

SCOUT (1) [SCOUTED, SCOUTING, SCOUTS]
Jdg 18: 2 and Eshtaol, to s out a land for them to settle in.

SCOUTED (2) [SCOUT]
Nu 32: 9 they went up to the valley of Eshcol and s the land,
Jdg 18:14 The five men who had s out the land around Laish

SCOUTING (1) [SCOUT]
Dt 1:36 of the land he walked over during his s mission.'

SCOUTS (10) [SCOUT]
Nu 14:36 Then the ten s who had incited the rebellion
Dt 1:22 'First, let's send out s to explore the land for us.
1:23 so I chose twelve s, one from each of your tribes.
1:28 Our s have demoralized us with their report.
Jos 14:12 You will remember that as s we found the Anakites
18: 5 The s will map the land into seven sections,
1Ki 20:17 they approached, Ben-hadad's s reported to him,
2Ki 7:13 "We had better send out s to check into this.
7:14 and the king sent s to see what had happened to the
7:15 to escape. The s returned and told the king about it.

SCOWLS (1)
Eze 2: 6 Do not be dismayed by their dark s. For remember,

SCRAMBLE (1)
Na 3: 3 stumble over them, s to their feet, and fall again.

SCRAPE (1) [SCRAPED, SCRAPINGS]
Eze 26: 4 I will s away its soil and make it a bare rock!

SCRAPED (2) [SCRAPE]
Lev 14:41 Next the inside walls of the entire house must be s
Job 2: 8 Then Job s his skin with a piece of broken pottery

SCRAPINGS (1) [SCRAPE]
Lev 14:41 and the s dumped in the unclean place outside the

SCRAPS (4)
Jdg 1: 7 and big toes cut off, eating s from under my table.
Mt 15:37 they were full, and when the s were picked up,
Mk 8: 8 they were full, and when the s were picked up,
Lk 16:21 As Lazarus lay there longing for s from the rich

SCRATCH (2) [SCRATCHING]
Ge 3:17 All your life you will struggle to s a living from it.
Da 6:23 Not a s was found on him because he had trusted in

SCRATCHING (2) [SCRATCH]
1Sa 21:13 be insane, s on doors and drooling down his beard.
Ecc 6: 7 All people spend their lives s for food, but they

SCRAWNY (1)
Eze 34:20 surely judge between the fat sheep and the s sheep.

SCREAM (7) [SCREAMED, SCREAMING, SCREAMS]
Dt 22:24 The woman is guilty because she did not s for help.
Isa 10:30 Well may you s in terror, you people of Gallim!
13: 6 S in terror, for the LORD's time has arrived—
Jer 47: 2 People will s in terror, and everyone in the land
Eze 8:18 And though they s for mercy, I will not listen."
Mk 5: 7 He gave a terrible s, shrieking, "Why are you
Lk 9:39 An evil spirit keeps seizing him, making him s.

SCREAMED (8) [SCREAM]
Ge 39:14 she sobbed. "He tried to rape me, but I s.
Nu 11: 2 The people s to Moses for help; and when he
Dt 22:27 it must be assumed that she s, but there was no one
1Sa 28:12 woman saw Samuel, she s, "You've deceived me!
Mt 14:26 saw him, they s in terror, thinking he was a ghost.
Mk 1:26 the evil spirit s and threw the man into a
6:49 the water, they s in terror, thinking he was a ghost.
9:26 Then the spirit s and threw the boy into another

SCREAMING (7) [SCREAM]
Ge 39:14 she began s. Soon all the men around the place
Jer 18:22 Let s be heard from their homes as warriors come
Mic 4: 9 But why are you now s in terror? Have you no king
Mt 8:29 They began s at him, "Why are you bothering us,
Mk 5: 5 and in the hills, s and hitting himself with stones.
Lk 8:28 s, "Why are you bothering me, Jesus, Son of the
Ac 8: 7 spirits were cast out, s as they left their victims.

SCREAMS (3) [SCREAM]
Ge 39:18 "I was saved only by my s. He ran out, leaving his
Nu 16:34 of the people of Israel fled as they heard their s,
Eze 26:15 as the s of the wounded echo in the continuing

SCREECH (1)
Isa 34:11 the horned owl, the hawk, the s owl, and the raven.

SCRIBE (9) [SCRIBE'S, SCRIBES]
1Ch 27:32 to the king, a man of great insight, and a s.
Ezr 7: 6 This Ezra was a s, well versed in the law of Moses,
7:11 the priest and s who studied and taught the
Ne 8: 1 They asked Ezra the s to bring out the Book of the
8: 4 Ezra the s stood on a high wooden platform that
8: 9 Nehemiah the governor, Ezra the priest and s,
12:26 the governor and of Ezra the priest and s.
12:36 the man of God. Ezra the s led this procession.
13:13 Zadok the s, and Pedaiah, one of the Levites,

SCRIBES (1) [SCRIBE]
1Ch 2:55 and the families of s living at Jabez—

SCRIP [KJV] See BAG

SCRIPT (1) [SCRIPTS]
Est 1:22 to each province in its own s and language,

SCRIPTS (2) [SCRIPT]
Est 3:12 the local officials of each province in their own s
8: 9 The decree was written in the s and languages of

SCRIPTURE (13) [SCRIPTURES]
Mt 9:13 "Now go and learn the meaning of this S:
12: 7 aren't guilty if you knew the meaning of this S:
23: 5 wear extra wide prayer boxes with S verses inside,
Lk 4:21 "This S has come true today before your very
Jn 12:34 "We understood from S that the Messiah would
19:24 This fulfilled the S that says, "They divided my
Ac 8:32 The passage of S he had been reading was this:
8:35 So Philip began with this same S and then used
13:34 This is stated in the S that says, 'I will give you the
1Ti 5:18 For the S says, "Do not keep an ox from eating as
2Ti 3:16 All S is inspired by God and is useful to teach us
2Pe 1:20 you must understand that no prophecy in S ever
3:16 he meant, just as they do the other parts of S—

SCRIPTURES (131) [SCRIPTURE]
Mt 4: 4 But Jesus told him, "No! The S say, / 'People need
4: 6 you are the Son of God, jump off! For the S say,
4: 7 Jesus responded, "The S also say, 'Do not test the
4:10 of here, Satan," Jesus told him. "For the S say,
11:10 John is the man to whom the S refer when they
11:13 all the teachings of the S looked forward to this
12: 3 "Haven't you ever read in the S what King David
19: 4 "Haven't you read the S?" Jesus replied.
21:13 He said, "The S declare, 'My Temple will be
21:16 "Haven't you ever read the S? For they say,
21:42 asked them, "Didn't you ever read this in the S?
22:29 "Your problem is that you don't know the S,
22:31 haven't you ever read about this in the S?
23: 2 the Pharisees are the official interpreters of the S.
26:24 Son of Man, must die, as the S declared long ago.
26:31 will desert me," Jesus told them. "For the S say,
26:54 how would the S be fulfilled that describe what
26:56 the words of the prophets as recorded in the S."
Mk 2:25 "Haven't you ever read in the S what King David
4:12 so that the S might be fulfilled: / 'They see what I
9:12 then is it written in the S that the Son of Man must
9:13 he was badly mistreated, just as the S predicted."
11:17 He taught them, "The S declare, 'My Temple will
12:10 Didn't you ever read this in the S? / 'The stone
12:24 "Your problem is that you don't know the S,
14:21 Son of Man, must die, as the S declared long ago.
14:27 will desert me," Jesus told them. "For the S say,
14:49 But these things are happening to fulfill what the S
Lk 4: 4 The S say, 'People need more than bread for their
4: 8 Jesus replied, "The S say, / 'You must worship the
4:10 For the S say, / 'He orders his angels to protect
4:12 Jesus responded, "The S also say, 'Do not test the
4:16 on the Sabbath and stood up to read the S.
6: 3 "Haven't you ever read in the S what King David
7:27 John is the man to whom the S refer when they
8:10 it from outsiders, so that the S might be fulfilled:
19:46 He told them, "The S declare, 'My Temple will be
20:17 at them and said, "Then what do the S mean?
21:22 and the prophetic words of the S will be fulfilled.
24:25 hard to believe all that the prophets wrote in the S.
24:27 explaining what all the S said about himself.
24:32 with us on the road and explained the S to us?"

24:45 he opened their minds to understand these many S.
Jn 2:17 his disciples remembered this prophecy from the S:
2:22 said this. And they believed both Jesus and the S.
5:39 "You search the S because you believe they give you eternal life. But the S point to me!
6:31 As the S say, 'Moses gave them bread from
6:45 As it is written in the S, 'They will all be taught by
7:38 For the S declare that rivers of living water will
7:42 For the S clearly state that the Messiah will be
7:52 Search the S and see for yourself—no prophet ever
10:35 And you know that the S cannot be altered. So if
12:16 they remembered that these S had come true before
13:18 The S declare, 'The one who shares my food has
15:25 This has fulfilled what the S said: 'They hated me
17:12 the one headed for destruction, as the S foretold.
19:28 and to fulfill the S he said, "I am thirsty."
19:36 These things happened in fulfillment of the S that
20: 9 then they hadn't realized that the S said he would
Ac 1:16 it was necessary for the S to be fulfilled concerning
4:11 For Jesus is the one referred to in the S, where it
17: 2 and for three Sabbaths in a row he interpreted the S
17:11 They searched the S day after day to check up on
18:24 an eloquent speaker who knew the S well,
18:28 Using the S, he explained to them, "The Messiah
23: 5 was the high priest," Paul replied, "for the S say,
28:23 of God and taught them about Jesus from the S—
Ro 1: 2 ago by God through his prophets in the holy S.
1:17 As the S say, "It is through faith that a righteous
2:24 No wonder the S say, "The world blasphemes the
3: 4 As the S say, "He will be proved right in what he
3:10 As the S say, / "No one is good— / not even one.
3:21 the law but by the way promised in the S long ago.
4: 3 For the S tell us, "Abraham believed God, so God
4:17 That is what the S mean when God told him,
8:36 (Even the S say, "For your sake we are killed
9: 7 For the S say, "Isaac is the son through whom
9:13 In the words of the S, "I loved Jacob, but I
9:17 For the S say that God told Pharaoh, "I have
9:33 God warned them of this in the S when he said,
10: 8 In fact, the S say, "The message is close at hand;
10:11 As the S tell us, "Anyone who believes in him will
10:15 That is what the S mean when they say,
11: 2 Do you remember what the S say about this?
11: 8 As the S say, / "God has put them into a deep
12:20 Instead, do what the S say: / "If your enemies are
14:11 For the S say, / " 'As surely as I live,'
15: 3 As the S say, "Those who insult you are also
15: 4 Such things were written in the S long ago to teach
15:21 I have been following the plan spoken of in the S,
1Co 1:19 As the S say, / "I will destroy human wisdom
1:31 As the S say, / "The person who wishes to boast
2: 9 That is what the S mean when they say, / "No eye
3:19 As the S say, / "God catches those who think they
4: 6 If you pay attention to the S, you won't brag about
5:13 but as the S say, "You must remove the evil
6:16 For the S say, "The two are united into one."
10: 7 For the S say, "The people celebrated with
14:21 It is written in the S, / "I will speak to my own
15: 3 that Christ died for our sins, just as the S said.
15: 4 raised from the dead on the third day, as the S said.
15:27 For the S say, "God has given him authority over
15:45 The S tell us, "The first man, Adam, became a
15:54 will never die—then at last the S will come true:
2Co 8:15 Do you remember what the S say about this?
9: 9 As the S say, / "Godly people give generously to
10:17 As the S say, / "The person who wishes to boast
13: 1 As the S say, "The facts of every case must be
Gal 3: 8 the S looked forward to this time when God would
3:10 for the S say, "Cursed is everyone who does not
3:11 For the S say, "It is through faith that a righteous
3:13 For it is written in the S, "Cursed is everyone who
3:22 But the S have declared that we are all prisoners of
4:22 The S say that Abraham had two sons, one from
4:30 But what do the S say about that? "Get rid of the
Eph 4: 8 That is why the S say, / "When he ascended to the
5:31 As the S say, "A man leaves his father and mother
1Ti 4:13 I get there, focus on reading the S to the church,
2Ti 3:15 You have been taught the holy S from childhood,
Heb 2: 6 For somewhere in the S it says, / "What is man
4: 4 it is ready because the S mention the seventh day,
5:12 the basic things a beginner must learn about the S.
10: 7 just as it is written about me in the S.' "
Jas 2: 8 obey our Lord's royal command found in the S:
2:23 And so it happened just as the S say:
4: 5 What do you think the S mean when they say that
4: 6 As the S say, / "God sets himself against the
1Pe 2: 6 As the S express it, / "I am placing a stone in
2: 8 And the S also say, / "He is the stone that makes
3:10 For the S say, / "If you want a happy life and good

SCROLL (67)

Dt 17:18 he must copy these laws on a s for himself in the
1Sa 10:25 He wrote them down on a s and placed it before
2Ki 22: 8 Then Hilkiah gave the s to Shaphan, and he read it.
22:10 to the king, "Hilkiah the priest has given me a s."
22:13 Ask him about the words written in this s that has
22:13 our ancestors have not obeyed the words in this s.
22:13 We have not been doing what this s says we must
22:16 and its people, just as I stated in the s you read.
23: 3 the terms of the covenant that were written in the s,
23:24 s that Hilkiah the priest had found in the LORD's
2Ch 34:15 Then Hilkiah gave the s to Shaphan.
34:16 Shaphan took the s to the king and reported,
34:18 to the king, "Hilkiah the priest has given me a s."
34:21 Ask him about the words written in this s that has
34:21 We have not been doing what this s says we must
34:24 All the curses written in the s you have read will
34:31 the terms of the covenant that were written in the s.
Ezr 6: 2 in the province of Media that a s was found.
Ne 8: 2 So on October 8 Ezra the priest brought the s of the
Ps 40: 7 And this has been written about me in your s:
Isa 34: 4 will melt away and disappear like a rolled-up s.
Jer 36: 2 "Get a s, and write down all my messages against
36: 6 the messages from the LORD that are on this s.
36:14 too. So Baruch took the s and went to them.
36:15 "Sit down and read the s to us," the officials said,
36:18 and I wrote down his words with ink on this s."
36:20 Then the officials left the s for safekeeping in the
36:21 The king sent Jehudi to get the s. Jehudi brought it
36:23 king took his knife and cut off that section of the s.
36:23 by section, until the whole s was burned up.
36:25 and Gemariah begged the king not to burn the s,
36:27 After the king had burned Jeremiah's s,
36:28 "Get another s, and write everything again just as you did on the s
36:29 You burned the s because it said the king of
36:32 Then Jeremiah took another s and dictated again to
36:32 He wrote everything that had been on the s King
51:60 Jeremiah had recorded on a s all the terrible
51:61 get to Babylon, read aloud everything on this s.
51:63 Then, when you have finished reading the s,
Eze 2: 9 and saw a hand reaching out to me, and it held a s.
3: 1 "Son of man, eat what I am giving you—eat this s!
3: 2 So I opened my mouth, and he fed me the s.
Zec 5: 1 looked up again and saw a s flying through the air.
5: 2 the angel asked. "I see a flying s," I replied.
5: 3 "This s contains the curse that is going out over
Mal 3:16 a s of remembrance was written to record the
Lk 4:17 The s containing the messages of Isaiah the
4:17 and he unrolled the s to the place where it says:
4:20 He rolled up the s, handed it back to the attendant,
Rev 5: 1 And I saw a s in the right hand of the one who was
5: 1 was writing on the inside and the outside of the s,
5: 2 "Who is worthy to break the seals on this s
5: 3 on earth or under the earth was able to open the s
5: 4 one could be found who was worthy to open the s
5: 5 He is worthy to open the s and break its seven
5: 7 and took the s from the right hand of the one sitting
5: 8 And as he took the s, the four living beings
5: 9 "You are worthy to take the s / and break its seals
6: 1 the Lamb broke the first of the seven seals on the s.
6:14 And the sky was rolled up like a s and taken away.
10: 2 And in his hand was a small s, which he had
10: 8 and take the unrolled s from the angel who is
10: 9 and asked him to give me the little s.
10:10 So I took the little s from the hands of the angel,
22: 7 are those who obey the prophecy written in this s."
22: 9 as well as all who obey what is written in this s.

SCRUTINIZED (1)

Ps 17: 3 You have s me and found nothing amiss,

SCUM (4)

Ps 119:119 All the wicked of the earth are the s you skim off;
Mt 9:11 "Why does your teacher eat with such s?"
Mk 2:16 to his disciples, "Why does he eat with such s?"
Lk 5:30 "Why do you eat and drink with such s?"

SCURRIES (2) [SCURRY]

Lev 5: 2 or an animal that s along the ground—
11:41 "Consider detestable any animal that s along the

SCURRY (3) [SCURRIES]

Lev 11:29 "Of the small animals that s or creep on the
11:44 any of these animals that s along the ground.
Hos 2:18 the birds and the animals that s along the ground

SCURVY (1)

Dt 28:27 the boils of Egypt and with tumors, s, and the itch,

SCURVY [KJV] See also (OPEN) SORE

SEA (300) [SEABED, SEACOAST, SEACOASTS, SEAFARING, SEAPORT, SEAS, SEASHORE, SEASHORES, SEAWEED]

DEAD SEA (25) Ge 14:3,8; Nu 34:3,12; Dt 3:17; 4:49; Jos 3:16; 12:3; 15:2,5,5; 18:19; 2Ki 14:25; 2Ch 20:2; Isa 16:8; Jer 48:32; Eze 39:11; 47:8,8,9,10,10,18; Joel 2:20; Zec 14:8

GREAT SEA (5) Ge 1:21; Job 26:12; Ps 89:10; Da 7:2; Am 9:3

RED SEA (32) Ex 10:19; 13:18; 15:4,22; 23:31; Nu 14:25; 21:4; 33:8,10,11; Dt 1:40; 2:1; 11:4; Jos 2:10; 4:23; 24:6; Jdg 11:16; 1Ki 9:26; 2Ch 8:17; Ne 9:9; Ps 66:6; 77:16; 106:7,9, 22; 114:3,5; 136:13; Isa 11:15; Jer 49:21; Ac 7:36; Heb 11:29

Ge 1:21 So God created great s creatures and every sort of
1:26 the fish in the s, the birds in the sky, and all the
14: 3 in Siddim Valley (that is, the valley of the Dead S).
14: 8 prepared for battle in the valley of the Dead S
49: 4 But you are as unruly as the waves of the s,
49:13 "Zebulun will settle on the shores of the s
Ex 10:19 west wind that blew the locusts out into the Red S.
13:18 a route through the wilderness toward the Red S,
14: 2 toward Pi-hahiroth between Migdol and the s
14: 3 are trapped between the wilderness and the s!'
14:16 and a path will open up before you through the s.
14:17 and they will follow the Israelites into the s.
14:21 Then Moses raised his hand over the s,
14:22 So the people of Israel walked through the s on dry
14:23 followed them across the bottom of the s.
14:26 said to Moses, "Raise your hand over the s again.
14:27 sun began to rise, Moses raised his hand over the s.
14:28 Egyptians who had chased the Israelites into the s,
14:29 walked through the middle of the s on dry land,
15: 1 he has thrown both horse and rider into the s.
15: 4 and armies, / he has thrown into the s.
15: 4 have been drowned in the Red S.
15: 8 in the middle of the s the waters became hard.
15:10 with a blast of your breath, / the s covered them.
15:19 chariots, and charioteers rushed into the s,
15:21 he has thrown both horse and rider into the s."
15:22 led the people of Israel away from the Red S,
20:11 the earth, the s, and everything in them;
23:31 boundaries from the Red S to the Mediterranean S,
Nu 11:22 Even if we caught all the fish in the s, would that
11:31 LORD sent a wind that brought quail from the s
13:29 live along the coast of the Mediterranean S
14:25 for the wilderness in the direction of the Red S."
21: 4 taking the road to the Red S to go around the land
33: 8 and crossed the Red S into the wilderness beyond.
33:10 They left Elim and camped beside the Red S.
33:11 They left the Red S and camped in the Sin Desert.
34: 3 boundary will begin on the east at the Dead S.
34: 5 the brook of Egypt and end at the Mediterranean S.
34: 6 will be the coastline of the Mediterranean S.
34: 7 boundary will begin at the Mediterranean S
34:11 down along the eastern edge of the S of Galilee,
34:12 and then along the Jordan River to the Dead S.
Dt 1:40 on back through the wilderness toward the Red S.'
2: 1 and set out across the wilderness toward the Red S,
3:17 the way from the S of Galilee down to the Dead S,
4:49 of the Jordan Valley as far south as the Dead S,
11: 4 how he drowned them in the Red S as they were
11:24 in the east to the Mediterranean S in the west.
30:13 It is not beyond the s, so far away that you must
30:13 'Who will cross the s to bring it to us so we can
33:19 They benefit from the riches of the s
34: 2 land of Judah, extending to the Mediterranean S;
Jos 1: 4 on the east to the Mediterranean S on the west,
2:10 for you through the Red S when you left Egypt.
3:16 flowed on to the Dead S until the riverbed was dry.
4:23 just as he did at the Red S when he dried it up until
9: 1 and along the coast of the Mediterranean S as far
12: 3 far north as the western shores of the S of Galilee and as far south as the Dead S,
13:27 extending as far north as the S of Galilee.
15: 2 boundary began at the south bay of the Dead S,
15: 4 which it followed to the Mediterranean S.
15: 5 The eastern boundary extended along the Dead S
15: 5 where the Jordan River empties into the Dead S,
15:11 passed Jabneel and ended at the Mediterranean S.
15:12 was the shoreline of the Mediterranean S.
15:47 and along the coast of the Mediterranean S.
16: 3 then to Gezer and on over to the Mediterranean S.
16: 6 then on to the Mediterranean S. The northern
16: 8 the Kanah Ravine to the Mediterranean S.
17: 9 side of the Kanah Ravine to the Mediterranean S.
17:10 with the Mediterranean S forming Manasseh's
18:19 and ended at the north bay of the Dead S,
19:29 of Tyre and came to the Mediterranean S at Hosah.
23: 4 from the Jordan River to the Mediterranean S in
24: 6 But when your ancestors arrived at the Red S,
24: 7 I brought the s crashing down on the Egyptians,
Jdg 11:16 their journey from Egypt after crossing the Red S,
2Sa 22:16 of his breath, / the bottom of the s could be seen,
1Ki 5: 9 the Lebanon mountains to the Mediterranean S
7:23 15 feet across from rim to rim; it was called the S.
7:24 The S was encircled just below its rim by two rows
7:25 The S rested on a base of twelve bronze oxen,
7:26 The walls of the S were about three inches thick,
7:39 The S was placed at the southeast corner of the
7:44 the S and the twelve oxen under it,
9:26 in the land of Edom, along the shore of the Red S.
18:43 to his servant, "Go and look out toward the s."
18:44 cloud about the size of a hand rising from the s."
2Ki 14:25 of Israel between Lebo-hamath and the Dead S,
16:17 He also removed the S from the backs of the
25:13 and the bronze S that were at the LORD's
25:16 water carts, and the S was too great to be weighed.
1Ch 16:32 Let the s and everything in it shout his praise!
18: 8 He molded it into the bronze S, the pillars,
2Ch 2:16 down the coast of the Mediterranean S to Joppa.
4: 2 15 feet across from rim to rim; it was called the S.
4: 3 The S was encircled just below its rim by two rows
4: 4 The S rested on a base of twelve bronze oxen,
4: 5 The walls of the S were about three inches thick,
4: 6 five to the south of the S and five to the north.
4: 6 The priests used the S itself, and not the basins,
4:10 The S was placed near the southeast corner of the
4:15 the S and the twelve oxen under it,
8:17 in the land of Edom, along the shore of the Red S.
20: 2 is marching against you from beyond the Dead S.
20:37 the ships met with disaster and never put out to s.
Ezr 3: 7 and floated along the coast of the Mediterranean S
Ne 9: 9 and you heard their cries from beside the Red S.
9:11 You divided the s for your people so they could
9:11 you hurled their enemies into the depths of the s.
Job 3: 8 those who are ready to rouse the s monster—
6: 3 they would be heavier than all the sands of the s.
7:12 Am I a s monster that you place a guard on me?
9: 8 out the heavens and marches on the waves of the s.
11: 9 It is broader than the earth and wider than the s.
12: 8 will instruct you. Let the fish of the s speak to you.
26:12 By his power the s grew calm. By his skill he crushed the great s monster.
28:14 says the ocean. 'Nor is it here,' says the s.

36:30 around him and how it lights up the depths of the s.
38: 8 "Who defined the boundaries of the s as it burst
41:32 its wake. One would think the s had turned white.
Ps 8: 8 the birds in the sky, the fish in the s,
18:15 of your breath, / the bottom of the s could be seen,
29: 3 The voice of the LORD echoes above the s.
29: 3 The LORD thunders over the mighty s.
33: 7 He gave the s its boundaries / and locked the
46: 2 and the mountains crumble into the s.
66: 6 He made a dry path through the Red S, / and his
68:22 I will bring them up from the depths of the s.
72: 8 May he reign from s to s, / and from the
74:13 You split the s by your strength / and smashed the
s monster's heads.
77:16 When the Red S saw you, O God, / its waters
77:16 and trembled! / The s quaked to its very depths.
77:19 Your road led through the s, / your pathway
78:13 For he divided the s before them and led them
78:53 not afraid; / but the s closed in upon their enemies.
80:11 spread our branches west to the Mediterranean S,
89:10 You are the one who crushed the great s monster.
89:25 I will extend his rule from the Mediterranean S in
95: 5 The s belongs to him, for he made it. / His hands
96:11 Let the s and everything in it shout his praise!
98: 7 Let the s and everything in it shout his praise!
104:26 and Leviathan, which you made to play in the s.
106: 7 Instead, they rebelled against him at the Red S.
106: 9 He commanded the Red S to divide, and a dry path
106: 9 He led Israel across the s bottom that was as dry as
106:22 in that land, / such awesome deeds at the Red S.
114: 3 The Red S saw them coming and hurried out of
114: 5 What's wrong, Red S, that made you hurry out of
136:13 Give thanks to him who parted the Red S.
136:15 but he hurled Pharaoh and his army into the s.
146: 6 and earth, / the s, and everything in them.
Pr 23:34 You will stagger like a sailor tossed at s,
Ecc 1: 7 The rivers run into the s, but the s is never full.
1: 7 returns again to the rivers and flows again to the s.
Isa 5:30 growl over their victims like the roaring of the s.
9: 1 the road that runs between the Jordan and the s,
10:26 was raised to drown the Egyptian army in the s.
11: 9 And as the waters fill the s, so the earth will be
11:15 LORD will make a dry path through the Red S.
16: 8 Her shoots once reached as far as the Dead S.
23: 2 merchants of Sidon. Your traders crossed the s,
23: 4 are put to shame, city of Sidon, fortress on the s.
23: 4 For the s says, "Now I am childless; I have no
23: 6 to Tarshish! Wail, you people who live by the s!
24:15 In the coastlands of the s, praise the name of the
27: 1 the coiling, writhing serpent, the dragon of the s.
41: 1 in silence before me, you lands beyond the s.
41: 5 The lands beyond the s watch in fear.
42: 4 Even distant lands beyond the s will wait for his
43:16 the waters, making a dry path through the s.
50: 2 For I can speak to the s and make it dry!
51:10 you not the same today, the one who dried up the s,
51:15 who stirs up the s, causing its waves to roar.
57:20 those who still reject me are like the restless s.
63:11 is the one who brought Israel through the s,
63:12 Where is the one whose power divided the s before
63:13 the one who led them through the bottom of the s?
66:19 and to all the lands beyond the s that have not
Jer 6:23 the noise of their army is like a roaring s.
25:22 and the kings of the regions across the s.
27:19 the bronze S in the Temple courtyard, the bronze
31:35 It is he who stirs the s into roaring waves.
46:18 as tall as Mount Tabor or Mount Carmel by the s!
47: 7 and the people living along the s must be
48:32 spreading vines once reached as far as the Dead S,
49:21 of despair will be heard all the way to the Red S.
49:23 Their hearts are troubled like a wild s in a raging
50:42 the noise of their army is like a roaring s.
51:42 The s has risen over Babylon; she is covered by its
52:17 and the bronze S that were at the LORD's
52:20 and the S with the twelve bulls beneath it was too
La 2:13 For your wound is as deep as the s. Who can heal
Eze 25:16 and utterly destroy the people who live by the s.
26: 3 like the waves of the s crashing against your
26:12 and timbers and even your dust into the s.
26:17 'O famous island city, / once ruler of the s,
27: 3 that mighty gateway to the s, the trading center of
27: 4 You extended your boundaries into the s.
27:26 You are shipwrecked in the heart of the s!
27:27 everyone on board sinks into the depths of the s.
27:28 "Your cities by the s tremble as your helmsmen
27:32 a city as Tyre, / now silent at the bottom of the s?
27:34 are a wrecked ship, / broken at the bottom of the s.
28: 2 I sit on a divine throne in the heart of the s.'
28: 8 die there on your island home in the heart of the s,
32: 2 but you are really just a s monster, heaving around
39:11 in the Valley of the Travelers, east of the Dead S.
47: 8 into the Jordan Valley, where it enters the Dead S.
47: 8 this stream will heal the salty waters of the Dead S
47: 9 Fish will abound in the Dead S, for its waters will
47:10 will stand along the shores of the Dead S,
47:10 Fish of every kind will fill the Dead S, just as they
47:18 past the Dead S and as far south as Tamar.
Da 7: 2 saw a great storm churning the surface of a great s,
11:45 and the s and will pitch his royal tents there,
Joel 2:20 Those in the rear will go into the Dead S; those at
Am 7: 4 The fire had burned up the depths of the s and was
8:12 People will stagger everywhere from s to s,
9: 3 I will send the great s serpent after them to bite
Jnh 1: 4 the LORD flung a powerful wind over the s,
1: 9 the God of heaven, who made the s and the land."
1:12 "Throw me into the s," Jonah said, "and it will
1:13 But the stormy s was too violent for them, and they
1:15 picked Jonah up and threw him into the raging s,
2: 3 ocean depths, and I sank down to the heart of the s.
Hab 2:14 as the waters fill the s, with an awareness of the
3: 8 that you struck the rivers and parted the s?
3:15 You trampled the s with your horses,
Zep 1: 3 the birds of the air and the fish in the s will die.
Zec 9: 4 and hurl its fortifications into the Mediterranean S.
9:10 His realm will stretch from s to s and from the
10:11 They will pass safely through the s of distress, for
the waves of the s will be held back.
14: 8 half toward the Dead S and half toward the
Mt 4:13 he went to Capernaum, beside the S of Galilee,
4:15 beside the s, beyond the Jordan River—
4:18 walking along the shore beside the S of Galilee,
15:29 Jesus returned to the S of Galilee and climbed a
18: 6 the s with a large millstone tied around the neck.
21:21 'May God lift you up and throw you into the s,'
23:15 For you cross land and s to make one convert,
Mk 1:16 was walking along the shores of the S of Galilee,
7:31 then back to the S of Galilee and the region of the
9:42 the s with a large millstone tied around the neck.
11:23 'May God lift you up and throw you into the s,'
Lk 5: 1 was preaching on the shore of the S of Galilee,
17: 2 It would be better to be thrown into the s with a
17: 6 'May God uproot you and throw you into the s,'
Jn 6: 1 the S of Galilee, also known as the S of Tiberias.
6:18 them as they rowed, and the s grew very rough.
21: 1 again to the disciples beside the S of Galilee.
Ac 4:24 Sovereign Lord, Creator of heaven and earth, the s,
7:36 through the Red S, and back and forth through the
14:15 who made heaven and earth, the s, and everything
27: 4 Putting out to s from there, we encountered
27:14 they called it) caught the ship and blew it out to s.
27:17 so they lowered the s anchor and were thus driven
27:27 as we were being driven across the S of Adria,
27:40 So they cut off the anchors and left them in the s.
28: 4 Though he escaped the s, justice will not permit
1Co 10: 1 safely through the waters of the s on dry ground.
10: 2 they were all baptized in the cloud and the s.
2Co 11:25 Once I spent a whole night and a day adrift at s.
Heb 11:29 the Red S as though they were on dry ground.
Jas 1: 6 is as unsettled as a wave of the s that is driven
Jude 1:13 They are like wild waves of the s, churning up the
Rev 4: 6 In front of the throne was a shiny s of glass,
5:13 and on earth and under the earth and in the s.
7: 1 in the trees, and the s became as smooth as glass.
7: 2 who had been given power to injure land and s,
7: 3 Don't hurt the land or the s or the trees until we
8: 8 and a great mountain of fire was thrown into the s.
8: 8 And one-third of the water in the s became blood.
8: 9 And one-third of all things living in the s died.
8: 9 And one-third of all the ships on the s were
10: 2 He stood with his right foot on the s and his left
10: 5 Then the mighty angel standing on the s and on the
10: 6 and everything in it, and the s and everything in it.
10: 8 scroll from the angel who is standing on the s
12:12 rejoice! But terror will come on the earth and the s.
12:18 Then he stood waiting on the shore of the s.
13: 1 in my vision I saw a beast rising up out of the s.
14: 7 Worship him who made heaven and earth, the s,
15: 2 I saw before me what seemed to be a crystal s
16: 3 the second angel poured out his bowl on the s,
16: 3 the blood of a corpse. And everything in the s died.
20:13 The s gave up the dead in it, and death
21: 1 earth had disappeared. And the s was also gone.

SEABED (1) [SEA]
Ex 14:21 blew all that night, turning the s into dry land.

SEACOAST (1) [COAST, SEA]
Jnh 1: 3 He went down to the s, to the port of Joppa,

SEACOASTS (1) [COAST, SEA]
Lk 6:17 and from as far north as the s of Tyre and Sidon.

SEAFARING (1) [SEA]
Ge 10: 5 Their descendants became the s peoples in various

SEAGULL (2)
Lev 11:16 the ostrich, the nighthawk, the s, hawks of all
Dt 14:15 the ostrich, the nighthawk, the s, hawks of all

SEAL (28) [SEALED, SEALING, SEALS]
Ge 6:14 "Make a boat from resinous wood and s it with tar,
38:18 "I want your identification s, your cord,
38:25 "The man who owns this identification s
Ex 28:11 names in the same way a gemcutter engraves a s.
28:21 tribe will be engraved on it as though it were a s.
39: 6 tribes of Israel, just as initials are engraved on a s.
39:14 The stones were engraved like a s, each with the
1Ki 21: 8 sealed them with his s, and sent them to the elders
Est 8: 8 you want, and s it with the king's signet ring.
Ps 60: 2 S the cracks before it completely collapses.
SS 8: 6 Place me like a s over your heart, or like a s on
your arm.
Da 6:17 The king sealed the stone with his own royal s
12: 4 a secret; s up the book until the time of the end.
Mt 27:64 So we request that you s the tomb until the third
Mk 14: 3 She broke the s and poured the perfume over his
Heb 10:39 those who turn their backs on God and s their fate.
Rev 6: 3 When the Lamb broke the second s, I heard the
6: 5 When the Lamb broke the third s, I heard the third
6: 7 And when the Lamb broke the fourth s, I heard the
6: 9 And when the Lamb broke the fifth s, I saw under
6:12 I watched as the Lamb broke the sixth s, and there
7: 2 from the east, carrying the s of the living God.
7: 3 or the trees until we have placed the s of God on
7: 4 And I heard how many were marked with the s of
8: 1 When the Lamb broke the seventh s, there was
9: 4 but to attack all the people who did not have the s
22:10 "Do not s up the prophetic words you have

SEALED (28) [SEAL]
Dt 29:12 with you today, and he has s it with an oath.
1Sa 18: 4 and he s the pact by giving him his robe, tunic,
2Sa 23: 5 His agreement is eternal, final, s. / He will
1Ki 2:23 "May God strike me dead if Adonijah has not s his
21: 8 s them with his seal, and sent them to the elders
Ne 9:38 On this s document are the names of our princes
10: 1 was ratified and s with the following names:
Est 3:12 signed in the name of King Xerxes, s with his ring,
8: 8 and s with his ring can never be revoked."
8:10 and s the message with the king's signet ring.
Job 14:17 My sins would be s in a pouch, and you would
Ps 141: 3 of what I say, O LORD, / and keep my lips s.
Isa 5: 9 But the LORD Almighty has s your awful fate.
6: 5 Then I said, "My destruction is s, for I am a sinful
29:11 All these future events are a s book to them.
29:11 they will say, "We can't read it because it is s."
Jer 32:10 and s the deed of purchase before witnesses,
32:11 Then I took the s deed and an unsealed copy of the
32:14 Take both this s deed and the unsealed copy,
32:44 and sold—deeds signed and s and witnessed—
Da 6:17 The king s the stone with his own royal seal
Hos 13: 1 by worshiping Baal and thus s their destruction.
Zec 9:11 of the covenant I made with you, s with blood,
Mt 27:66 So they s the tomb and posted guards to protect it.
Lk 22:20 an agreement s with the blood I will pour out for
1Co 11:25 and you, s by the shedding of my blood.
Rev 5: 1 outside of the scroll, and it was s with seven seals.
7: 4 There were 144,000 who were s from all the tribes

SEALING (2) [SEAL]
Dt 32:34 up these things, / s them away within my treasury.
Mk 14:24 s the covenant between God and his people.

SEALS (7) [SEAL]
Da 6:17 with his own royal seal and the s of his nobles,
Mt 26:28 which s the covenant between God and his people.
Rev 5: 1 of the scroll, and it was sealed with seven s.
5: 2 "Who is worthy to break the s on this scroll
5: 5 is worthy to open the scroll and break its seven s."
5: 9 and break its s and open it. / For you were killed,
6: 1 the Lamb broke the first of the seven s on the

SEAMLESS (1) [SEAMS]
Jn 19:23 They also took his robe, but it was s, woven in one

SEAMS (1) [SEAMLESS]
Isa 54: 3 For you will soon be bursting at the s.

SEAPORT (2) [PORT, SEA]
Eze 26:16 All the s rulers will step down from their thrones
Ac 13: 4 and Barnabas went down to the s of Seleucia

SEARCH (80) [SEARCHED, SEARCHES, SEARCHING, SEARCHLIGHT]
Ge 31:33 Laban went first into Jacob's tent to s there,
31:35 So despite his thorough s, Laban didn't find them.
Ex 5:12 So the people scattered throughout the land in s of
Dt 4:29 From there you will s again for the LORD your
4:29 And if you s for him with all your heart and soul,
4:32 "S all of history, from the time God created people
4:32 Then s from one end of the heavens to the other.
Jos 7:22 So Joshua sent some men to make a s. They ran to
Jdg 6:29 And after asking around and making a careful s,
1Sa 23:15 news that Saul was on the way to Ziph to s for him
23:23 even if I have to s every hiding place in Judah!"
24: 2 and went to s for David and his men near the rocks
26:20 Why has the king of Israel come out to s for a
1Ki 2:40 saddled his donkey and went to Gath to s for them.
20: 6 tomorrow I will send my officials to s your palace
2Ki 2:16 and fifty of our strongest men will s the wilderness
1Ch 16:11 S for the LORD and for his strength, / and keep
26:31 year of David's reign, a s was made in the records,
2Ch 16: 9 The eyes of the LORD s the whole earth in order
Ezr 4:15 We suggest that you s your ancestors' records,
4:19 I have ordered a s to be made of the records
5:17 we request that you s in the royal archives of
6: 1 So King Darius issued orders that a s be made in
Est 2: 2 "Let us s the empire to find beautiful young
Job 3:21 They s for death more eagerly than for hidden
10: 6 in a hurry to probe for my guilt, to s for my sin?
24: 5 They go into the desert to s for food for their
28: 3 darkest regions of the earth as they s for ore.
Ps 40:16 But may all who s for you / be filled with joy
63: 1 O God, you are my God; / I earnestly s for you.
70: 4 But may all who s for you / be filled with joy
77: 6 I s my soul and think about the difference now.
105: 4 S for the LORD and for his strength, / and keep
119: 2 his decrees / and s for him with all their hearts.
139:23 S me, O God, and know my heart; / test me
Pr 1:28 Even though they anxiously s for me, they will not
2: 4 S for them as you would for lost money or hidden
8:17 love me. Those who s for me will surely find me.
11:27 If you s for good, you will find favor; but if you s
for evil, it will find you!

Ecc 1:13 I devoted myself to s for understanding and to
2:20 It was not the answer to my s for satisfaction in
3: 6 A time to s and a time to lose. / A time to keep
8:16 In my s for wisdom, I tried to observe everything
SS 3: 2 in all its streets and squares.' But my s was in vain.
Isa 26: 9 All night long I s for you; / earnestly I seek for
34:16 S the book of the LORD, and see what he will do.
41:17 "When the poor and needy s for water and there is
57:10 You grew weary in your s, but you never gave up.
Jer 2:24 Those who desire you do not even need to s,
5: 1 "Look high and low; s throughout the city!
16:16 "I am sending for hunters who will s for them in
17:10 s all hearts and examine secret motives.
22:20 S for them in Lebanon. Shout for them at Bashan.
22:20 S for them in the regions east of the river. See,
La 1:11 Her people groan as they s for bread. They have
4: 5 Those who once lived in palaces now s the garbage
Eze 34: 6 face of the earth, yet no one has gone to s for them.
34: 8 you didn't s for my sheep when they were lost.
34:11 LORD says: I myself will s and find my sheep.
34:16 I will s for my lost ones who strayed away, and I
39:14 special crews will be appointed to s the land for
Hos 2: 7 She will s for them but not find them. Then she
5:15 For as soon as trouble comes, they will s for me."
Am 9: 3 Mount Carmel, I will s them out and capture them.
Zep 1:12 "I will s with lanterns in Jerusalem's darkest
Zec 4:10 eyes of the LORD that s all around the world."
Mt 2: 8 "Go to Bethlehem and s carefully for the child.
10:11 s for a worthy man and stay in his home until you
18:12 and go out into the hills to s for the lost one?
Lk 2:45 they went back to Jerusalem to s for him there.
2:49 "But why did you need to s?" he asked.
15: 4 to go and s for the lost one until you found it?
Jn 5:39 "You s the Scriptures because you believe they
7:34 You will s for me but not find me. And you won't
7:36 when he says, 'You will s for me but not find me,'
7:52 S the Scriptures and see for yourself—no prophet
8:21 going away. You will s for me and die in your sin.
13:33 Then, though you s for me, you cannot come to
Ac 12:19 Herod Agrippa ordered a thorough s for him.

SEARCHED (20) [SEARCH]

Ge 31:33 and then he s the tents of the two concubines,
31:34 So although Laban s all the tents, he couldn't find
31:37 You have s through everything I own. Now show
Jos 2:22 The men who were chasing them had s everywhere
1Ki 1: 3 So they s throughout the country for a beautiful
18:10 LORD your God that the king has s every nation
2Ki 2:17 So fifty men s for three days but did not find
2Ch 22: 9 Then Jehu's men s for Ahaziah, and they found
Ps 37:36 Though I s for them, I could not find them!
77: 2 When I was in deep trouble, / I s for the Lord.
Ecc 7:25 I s everywhere, determined to find wisdom and to
SS 5: 6 I s for him, but I couldn't find him anywhere.
Isa 26:16 LORD, in distress we s for you. / We were bowed
65:10 For my people who have s for me, the plain of
La 1:19 the city, even as they s for food to save their lives.
Eze 22:30 I s for someone to stand in the gap in the wall
Ob 1: 6 and cranny of Edom will be s and looted.
Lk 4:42 The crowds s everywhere for him, and when they
Ac 17:11 They s the Scriptures day after day to check up on
2Ti 1:17 came to Rome, he s everywhere until he found me.

SEARCHES (4) [SEARCH]

Job 39: 8 its pastureland, where it s for every blade of grass.
Ps 9:10 have never abandoned anyone who s for you.
1Co 2:10 and his Spirit s out everything and shows us even
Rev 2:23 will know that I am the one who s out the thoughts

SEARCHING (16) [SEARCH]

Ge 44:12 Joseph's servant began s the oldest brother's sack,
Jos 2:16 "Hide there for three days until the men who are s
1Sa 23:25 David heard that Saul and his men were s for him,
1Ch 16:11 the LORD and for his strength, / and keep on s.
Ps 10: 8 They are always s / for some helpless victim.
105: 4 the LORD and for his strength, / and keep on s.
SS 3: 2 the city, s for him in all its streets and squares.'
Jer 5: 3 LORD, you are s for honesty. You struck your
La 1: 6 Her princes are like starving deer s for pasture,
Da 6: 4 and princes began s for some fault in the way
Am 8:12 s for the word of the LORD, running here
Zep 1:17 I will make you as helpless as a blind man s for a
Lk 2:48 and I have been frantic, s for you everywhere."
11:24 leaves a person, it goes into the desert, s for rest.
Jn 18: 7 more he asked them, "Whom are you s for?"
Ac 17: 5 s for Paul and Silas so they could drag them out to

SEARCHLIGHT (1) [LIGHT, SEARCH]

Pr 20:27 The LORD's s penetrates the human spirit,

SEARING (1)

Isa 49:10 The s sun and scorching desert winds will not

SEAS (18) [SEA]

Ge 1:10 named the dry ground "land" and the water "s."
Ne 9: 6 You made the earth and the s and everything in
Job 38:16 "Have you explored the springs from which the s
Ps 24: 2 For he laid the earth's foundation on the s
42: 7 I hear the tumult of the raging s / as your waves
65: 5 on earth, / even those who sail on distant s.
69:34 and earth, / the s and all that move in them.
93: 4 But mightier than the violent raging of the s,
104: 9 Then you set a firm boundary for the s, / so they
107:24 in action, / his impressive works on the deepest s.
135: 6 and earth, / and on the s and in their depths.
Pr 8:29 I was there when he set the limits of the s, so they
Isa 23:11 The LORD holds out his hand over the s.
42:10 Sing, all you who sail the s, / all you who live in
Eze 26:19 waves of enemy attack. Great s will swallow you.
Mic 7:12 and from many distant s and mountains.
Lk 21:25 perplexed by the roaring s and strange tides.
2Co 11:26 in the cities, in the deserts, and on the stormy s.

SEASHORE (16) [SEA, SHORE]

Ge 22:17 like the stars of the sky and the sand on the s.
32:12 become as numerous as the sands along the s—
41:49 There was so much grain, like sand on the s,
Jos 11: 4 covered the landscape like the sand on the s.
Jdg 5:17 did he stay home? / Asher sat unmoved at the s,
7:12 Their camels were like grains of sand on the s—
1Sa 13: 5 as many warriors as the grains of sand along the s!
2Sa 17:11 have an army as numerous as the sand on the s.
1Ki 4:20 and Israel were as numerous as the sand on the s.
Ps 78:27 birds as plentiful as the sands along the s!
Isa 10:22 of Israel are as numerous as the sand on the s,
48:19 become as numerous as the sands along the s—
Jer 15: 8 more widows than the grains of sand along the s.
Hos 1:10 that day its people will be like the sands of the s—
Ro 9:27 of Israel are as numerous as the sand on the s,
Heb 11:12 like the stars of the sky and the sand on the s,

SEASHORES (1) [SEA, SHORE]

Jer 33:22 and the sand on the s cannot be measured,

SEASON (19) [SEASONAL, SEASONED, SEASONING, SEASONS]

Ge 31:10 During the mating s, I had a dream and saw that
38:27 In due s the time of Tamar's delivery arrived,
Ex 23:16 of the Final Harvest at the end of the harvest s.
34:22 of the Final Harvest at the end of the harvest s.
Lev 2:13 S all your grain offerings with salt, to remind you
26: 5 Your threshing s will extend until the grape
Nu 13:20 (It happened to be the s for harvesting the first ripe
Dt 16:13 observed for seven days at the end of the harvest s,
Jos 3:15 Now it was the harvest s, and the Jordan was
2Sa 21:10 on a rock and stayed there the entire harvest s.
Ezr 10:13 This is the rainy s, so we cannot stay out here
Ps 1: 3 the riverbank, / bearing fruit each s without fail.
Pr 20: 4 If you are too lazy to plow in the right s, you will
Ecc 3: 1 a s for every activity under heaven.
3:17 "In due s God will judge everyone, both good
Hos 2: 9 ripened grain I generously provided each harvest s.
9:10 it was like seeing the first ripe figs of the s!
Mk 11:13 because it was too early in the s for fruit.
Ac 20: 6 As soon as the Passover s ended, we boarded a

SEASONAL (4) [SEASON]

Lev 26: 4 I will send the s rains. The land will then yield its
1Ch 12:15 They crossed the Jordan River during its s flooding
Job 6:15 you have proved as unreliable as a s brook that
Jer 15:18 Your help seems as uncertain as a s brook.

SEASONED (3) [SEASON]

2Ch 13: 3 led by King Abijah, fielded 400,000 s warriors,
17:13 and stationed an army of s troops at Jerusalem.
26:12 leaders commanded these regiments of s warriors.

SEASONING (2) [SEASON]

Mk 9:50 Salt is good for s. But if it loses its flavor, how do
Lk 14:34 "Salt is good for s. But if it loses its flavor,

SEASONS (6) [SEASON]

Ge 1:14 They will be signs to mark off the s, the days,
Ex 34:21 even during the s of plowing and harvest.
Dt 11:14 then he will send the rains in their proper s so you
Job 38:32 Can you ensure the proper sequence of the s
Ps 104:19 You made the moon to mark the s / and the sun
Gal 4:10 or don't do on certain days or months or s or years.

SEAT (14) [SEATED, SEATS]

Jdg 3:20 you from God!" As King Eglon rose from his s,
Ru 4: 1 So Boaz went to the town gate and took a s there.
1Sa 4:18 Eli fell backward from his s beside the gate.
1Ki 10:19 On both sides of the s were armrests,
2Ki 11:19 and the king took his s on the royal throne.
2Ch 9:18 On both sides of the s were armrests,
SS 3:10 is gold, and its s is upholstered in purple cloth.
Mt 27:19 Just then, as Pilate was sitting on the judgment s,
Lk 12:37 I tell you, he himself will s them, put on an apron,
14: 8 a wedding feast, don't always head for the best s.
14: 9 and will have to take whatever s is left at the foot
Jn 19:13 Then Pilate sat down on the judgment s on the
Ro 14:10 will stand personally before the judgment s of God.
Jas 2: 3 special attention and a good s to the rich person,

SEATED (9) [SEAT]

Ge 43:33 he s them in the order of their ages,
2Ki 4:38 One day as the group of prophets was s before him,
2Ch 23:20 the palace, and they s the king on the royal throne.
SS 2: 3 I am s in his delightful shade, and his fruit is
Ac 8:28 S in his carriage, he was reading aloud from the
Eph 1:20 and s him in the place of honor at God's right hand
2: 6 and we are s with him in the heavenly realms—
Heb 12: 2 Now he is s in the place of highest honor beside
1Pe 3:22 He is s in the place of honor next to God, and all

SEATS (6) [SEAT]

1Sa 2: 8 them like princes, / placing them in s of honor.
Am 3: 9 "Take your s now on the hills around Samaria,
Mt 23: 6 and in the most prominent s in the synagogue!
Mk 12:39 And how they love the s of honor in the
Lk 11:43 For how you love the s of honor in the synagogues
20:46 And how they love the s of honor in the

SEAWEED (1) [SEA, WEED]

Jnh 2: 5 around me, and s wrapped itself around my head.

SEBA (4)

Ge 10: 7 The descendants of Cush were S, Havilah, Sabtah,
1Ch 1: 9 The descendants of Cush were S, Havilah, Sabtah,
Ps 72:10 The eastern kings of Sheba and S / will bring him
Isa 43: 3 Ethiopia, and S as a ransom for your freedom.

SEBAM (1)

Nu 32: 3 Dibon, Jazer, Nimrah, Heshbon, Elealeh, S, Nebo,

SEBAT [KJV] See FEBRUARY

SECACAH (1)

Jos 15:61 there were the towns of Beth-arabah, Middin, S,

SECLUDED (1) [SECLUSION]

Mk 1:45 He had to stay out in the s places, and people from

SECLUSION (3) [SECLUDED]

2Sa 20: 3 he had left to keep house should be placed in s.
Ps 139:15 You watched me as I was being formed in utter s,
Lk 1:24 became pregnant and went into s for five months.

SECOND (130) [TWO]

Ge 1: 8 the space "sky." This happened on the s day.
2:13 The s branch is the Gihon, which flows around the
4: 2 Later she gave birth to a s son and named him
7:11 years old, on the seventeenth day of the s month,
30: 7 became pregnant again and gave Jacob a s son.
30:12 Then Zilpah produced a s son,
41: 5 Soon he fell asleep again and had a s dream.
41:52 Joseph named his s son Ephraim, for he said,
Ex 4: 8 they will believe the s," the LORD said.
18: 4 The name of his s son was Eliezer, for Moses had
26: 3 one set; then join the other five sheets into a s set.
26: 9 into one set, and join the other six into a s set.
26: 9 The sixth sheet of the s set is to be doubled over at
28:18 The s row will contain a turquoise, a sapphire,
36:10 one set, and a s set was made of the other five.
36:12 matched the loops along the edge of the s set.
36:16 six remaining sheets were joined to make a s set.
36:19 and the s was made of fine goatskin leather.
39:11 In the s row were a turquoise, a sapphire, and a
Lev 5:10 The priest will offer the s bird as a whole burnt
7:16 and whatever is left over may be eaten on the s
8:22 Next Moses presented the s ram, which was the
22:30 Don't leave any of it until the s day. I am the
Nu 1: 1 during the s year after Israel's departure from
2:16 These three tribes will be s in line whenever the
7:18 On the s day Nethanel son of Zuar, leader of the
8: 8 along with a s young bull for a sin offering.
9: 1 during the s year after Israel's departure from
10: 6 When you sound the signal a s time, the tribes on
10:11 during the s year after Israel's departure from
28: 8 Offer the s lamb in the evening with the same grain
29:17 "On the s day of this seven-day festival,
Dt 24: 3 and the s husband also divorces her or dies,
Jos 6:14 On the s day they marched around the city once
10:32 And the LORD gave it to them on the s day.
19: 1 The s allotment of land went to the families of the
Jdg 6:25 "Take the s best bull from your father's herd,
2Sa 3: 3 The s was Kileab, whose mother was Abigail,
14:29 Absalom sent for him a s time, but again Joab
1Ki 6: 6 the s floor 9 feet wide, and the top floor 10-1/2 feet
6: 8 There were winding stairs going up to the s floor,
6: 8 and another flight of stairs between the s and third
9: 2 Then the LORD appeared to Solomon a s time,
15:25 Israel in the s year of King Asa's reign in Judah.
2Ki 1:17 This took place in the s year of the reign of
9:19 So the king sent out a s rider. He rode up to them
10: 6 Jehu responded with a s letter: "If you are on my
14: 1 in the s year of the reign of King Jehoash of Israel.
15:32 Judah in the s year of King Pekah's reign in Israel.
1Ch 2:13 his s was Abinadab, his third was Shimea,
2:26 Jerahmeel had a s wife named Atarah. She was the
2:42 Caleb's s son was Mareshah, the father of Hebron.
3: 1 The s was Kileab, whose mother was Abigail from
3:15 Jehoiakim (the s), Zedekiah (the third),
6:28 of Samuel were Joel (the older) and Abijah (the s).
6:44 Heman's s assistant was Ethan from the clan of
8:39 Ulam (the oldest), Jeush (the s), and Eliphelet (the
12: 9 was their leader. / Obadiah was s. / Eliab was third.
16: 5 His assistants were Zechariah (the s), then Jeiel,
23:19 Amariah (the s), Jahaziel (the third),
23:20 Micah (the family leader) and Isshiah (the s).
24: 7 first lot fell to Jehoiarib. / The s lot fell to Jedaiah.
25: 9 The s lot fell to Gedaliah and twelve of his sons
26: 2 Jediael (the s), Zebadiah (the third), Jathniel (the
26: 4 Jehozabad (the s), Joah (the third), Sacar (the
26:11 His other sons included Hilkiah (the s),
27: 4 of Ahoah, was commander of the s division,
27: 4 which was on duty during the s month.
2Ch 3:11 feet long, touched one of the wings of the s figure.

3:12 the s figure had one wing 7-1/2 feet long that
32:5 and constructing a s wall outside the first.
Ezr 3:8 during the s year after they arrived in Jerusalem.
4:24 and it remained at a standstill until the s year of the
Ne 12:38 The s choir went northward around the other way
Est 2:14 and the next morning she was brought to the s
2:19 young women had been transferred to the s harem
9:18 continued killing their enemies on the s day also,
Job 42:12 So the LORD blessed Job in the s half of his life
42:14 the s Keziah, and the third Keren-happuch.
Pr 30:8 to tell a lie. S, give me neither poverty nor riches!
Isa 11:11 bring back a remnant of his people for the s time,
Jer 6:9 as when a harvester checks each vine a s time to
33:1 of the guard, the LORD gave him this s message:
Eze 1:16 each wheel had a s wheel turning crosswise within
10:10 each wheel had a s wheel turning crosswise within
10:14 first was the face of an ox, the s was a human face,
43:22 "On the s day, sacrifice as a sin offering a young
45:7 and the s section will share a border on the west
48:31 for Reuben, the s for Judah, and the third for Levi.
Da 2:1 One night during the s year of his reign,
7:5 Then I saw a s beast, and it looked like a bear.
Hos 1:8 again became pregnant and gave birth to a s son.
Jnh 3:1 Then the LORD spoke to Jonah a s time:
Hag 1:1 On August 29 of the s year of King Darius's reign,
1:15 This was on September 21 of the s year of King
2:10 On December 18 of the s year of King Darius's
2:20 The LORD sent this s message to Haggai on
Zec 1:1 In midautumn of the s year of King Darius's reign,
1:7 Then on February 15 of the s year of King
2:3 Then the angel who was with me went to meet a s
6:2 was pulled by red horses, the s by black horses,
Mt 22:25 so the s brother married the widow.
22:39 A s is equally important: 'Love your neighbor as
Mk 12:21 So the s brother married the widow, but soon he
12:31 The s is equally important: 'Love your neighbor as
14:72 And immediately the rooster crowed the s time.
Jn 4:54 This was Jesus' s miraculous sign in Galilee after
9:24 So for the s time they called in the man who had
Ac 7:13 The s time they went, Joseph revealed his identity
12:10 They passed the first and s guard posts and came to
13:33 This is what the s psalm is talking about when it
1Co 12:28 first are apostles, / s are prophets, / third are
15:47 while Christ, the s man, came from heaven.
2Co 13:2 had been sinning when I was there on my s visit.
Tit 3:10 divisions among you, give a first and s warning.
Heb 8:7 there would have been no need for a s covenant to
9:3 and behind the curtain was the s room called the
10:9 the first covenant in order to establish the s.
2Pe 3:1 This is my s letter to you, dear friends, and in both
Rev 2:11 Whoever is victorious will not be hurt by the s
4:7 the s looked like an ox; the third had a human face;
6:3 When the Lamb broke the s seal, I heard the s living being say, "Come!"
8:8 Then the s angel blew his trumpet, and a great
11:14 The s terror is past, but look, now the third terror is
16:3 Then the s angel poured out his bowl on the sea,
20:6 For them the s death holds no power, but they will
20:14 lake of fire. This is the s death—the lake of fire.
21:8 that burns with fire and sulfur. This is the s death."
21:19 the s sapphire, the third agate, the fourth emerald,

SECOND-CLASS (1) [TWO]

Isa 56:3 Do not let them think that I consider them s

SECOND-IN-COMMAND (6) [COMMAND, TWO]

Ge 41:43 Pharaoh also gave Joseph the chariot of his s,
1Ch 5:12 and Shapham was s, along with Janai and Shaphat.
12:3 of Shemaah from Gibeah; his brother Joash was s.
24:23 was the leader, Amariah was s, Jahaziel was third,
2Ch 28:7 palace commander; and Elkanah, the king's s.
Ne 11:9 by Judah son of Hassenuah, s over the city.

SECRET (60) [SECRETLY, SECRETS]

Ge 42:25 but he also gave s instructions to return each
Ex 7:11 and they did the same thing with their s arts.
7:22 But again the magicians of Egypt used their s arts,
8:7 were able to do the same thing with their s arts.
8:18 tried to do the same thing with their s arts,
Dt 27:24 'Cursed is anyone who kills another person in s.'
29:29 "There are s things that belong to the LORD our
Jdg 3:19 to Eglon and said, "I have a s message for you."
16:9 a fire. So the s of his strength was not discovered.
16:17 Finally, Samson told her his s. "My hair has never
2Sa 15:10 he sent s messengers to every part of Israel to stir
1Ki 20:30 Ben-hadad fled into the city and hid in a s room.
22:25 when you find yourself hiding in some s room!"
2Ch 18:24 when you find yourself hiding in some s room!"
Est 2:20 to keep her nationality and family background a s.
Job 4:12 "This truth was given me in s, as though
15:8 Were you listening at God's s council? Do you
Ps 90:8 before you— / our s sins—and you see them all.
Pr 9:17 is refreshing; food eaten in s tastes the best!"
17:23 The wicked accept s bribes to pervert justice.
21:14 A s gift calms anger; a s bribe pacifies fury.
Ecc 12:14 including every s thing, whether good or bad.
Isa 45:3 you treasures hidden in the darkness—s riches.
65:4 the graves and s places to worship evil spirits.
Jer 17:10 search all hearts and examine s motives.
Eze 28:3 than Daniel and think no s is hidden from you.
Da 2:18 to show them his mercy by telling them the s,
2:19 That night the s was revealed to Daniel in a vision.
2:30 any living person that I know the s of your dream,
2:47 for you have been able to reveal this s."
12:4 But you, Daniel, keep this prophecy a s; seal up the
Mt 6:4 Give your gifts in s, and your Father, who knows
6:18 except your Father, who knows what you do in s.
10:26 will be revealed; all that is s will be made public.
Mk 4:11 "You are permitted to understand the s about the
4:22 now hidden or s will eventually be brought to light.
7:24 He tried to keep it s that he was there, but he
Lk 8:17 or s will eventually be brought to light and made
12:2 will be revealed; all that is s will be made public.
20:20 the leaders sent s agents pretending to be honest
Jn 19:38 who had been a s disciple of Jesus (because he
Ro 2:16 by Jesus Christ, will judge everyone's s life.
16:25 a plan kept s from the beginning of time.
1Co 2:7 the wisdom we speak of is the s wisdom of God,
14:25 As they listen, their s thoughts will be laid bare,
15:51 But let me tell you a wonderful s God has revealed
Eph 1:9 God's s plan has now been revealed to us; it is a
3:3 this letter, God himself revealed his s plan to me.
3:6 And this is the s plan: The Gentiles have an equal
3:9 of all things, had kept s from the beginning.
5:12 to talk about the things that ungodly people do in s.
6:19 s plan that the Good News is for the Gentiles,
Php 4:12 I have learned the s of living in every situation,
Col 1:26 This message was kept s for centuries
1:27 of Christ are for you Gentiles, too. For this is the s:
2:2 they have complete understanding of God's s plan,
4:3 us many opportunities to preach about his s plan—
2Th 2:7 and it will remain s until the one who is holding it
Rev 10:4 "Keep s what the seven thunders said. Do not

SECRETARIES (4) [SECRETARY]

1Ki 4:3 and Ahijah, the sons of Shisha, were court s.
2Ch 34:13 Still others assisted as s, officials, and gatekeepers.
Est 3:12 On April 17 Haman called in the king's s
8:9 So on June 25 the king's s were summoned.

SECRETARY (27) [SECRETARIES, SECRETARY'S]

2Sa 8:17 Abiathar were the priests. Seraiah was the court s.
20:25 Sheva was the court s. Zadok and Abiathar were
2Ki 12:10 the court s and the high priest counted the money
18:18 Shebna the court s, and Joah son of Asaph,
18:37 Shebna the court s, and Joah son of Asaph,
19:2 Shebna the court s, and the leading priests,
22:3 of Azaliah and grandson of Meshullam, the court s,
22:8 Hilkiah the high priest said to Shaphan the court s,
22:12 Acbor son of Micaiah, Shaphan the court s,
25:19 the army commander's chief s, who was in charge
1Ch 18:16 Abiathar were the priests. Seraiah was the court s.
24:6 acted as s and wrote down the names
2Ch 24:11 Then the court s and an officer of the high priest
26:11 the s of the army, and his assistant, Maaseiah.
34:15 Hilkiah said to Shaphan the court s, "I have found
34:20 Acbor son of Micaiah, Shaphan the court s,
Ezr 4:8 and Shimshai the court s wrote the letter,
4:17 "To Rehum the governor, Shimshai the court s,
Isa 36:3 Shebna the court s, and Joah son of Asaph,
36:22 Shebna the court s, and Joah son of Asaph,
37:2 Shebna the court s, and the leading priests,
Jer 36:12 Elishama the s was there, along with Delaiah son
36:20 for safekeeping in the room of Elishama the s
36:32 another scroll and dictated again to his s Baruch.
37:15 and imprisoned in the house of Jonathan the s.
37:20 back to the dungeon in the house of Jonathan the s,
52:25 the army commander's chief s, who was in charge

SECRETARY'S (1) [SECRETARY]

Jer 36:12 he went down to the s room in the palace where the

SECRETLY (22) [SECRET]

Ge 31:20 They set out s and never told Laban they were
31:27 Why did you slip away s? I would have given you
37:22 Reuben was s planning to help Joseph escape,
Dt 13:6 or closest friend comes to you s and says,
27:15 who carves or casts idols and s sets them up.
28:57 she has borne, so that she herself can s eat them.
Jos 2:1 Then Joshua s sent out two spies from the Israelite
2Sa 12:12 You did it s, but I will do this to you openly in the
20:8 he s slipped the dagger from its sheath.
2Ki 17:9 The people of Israel had also s done many things
2Ch 13:13 Jeroboam had s sent part of his army around
23:2 These men traveled s throughout Judah
Job 31:27 and been s enticed in my heart to worship them?
Jer 37:17 Later King Zedekiah s requested that Jeremiah
38:16 So King Zedekiah s promised him, "As surely as
40:15 with Gedaliah and volunteered to kill Ishmael s.
Mt 6:6 the door behind you, and pray to your Father s.
26:4 to discuss how to capture Jesus s and put him to
Mk 14:1 still looking for an opportunity to capture Jesus s
Jn 7:10 Jesus also went, though s, staying out of public
Ac 16:37 So now they want us to leave s? Certainly not!
2Th 2:7 For this lawlessness is already at work s, and it will

SECRETS (16) [SECRET]

Job 11:6 If only he would tell you the s of wisdom, for true
Ps 25:14 With them he shares the s of his covenant.
44:21 have known it, / for he knows the s of every heart.
Pr 11:13 A gossip goes around revealing s, but those who
20:19 A gossip tells s, so don't hang around with
Isa 48:6 not mentioned before, s you have not yet heard.
Jer 33:3 and I will tell you some remarkable s about what is
Da 2:28 But there is a God in heaven who reveals s, and he
Mt 6:4 and your Father, who knows all s, will reward you.
6:6 your Father, who knows all s, will reward you.
6:18 your Father, who knows all s, will reward you.
13:11 "You have been permitted to understand the s of
Lk 8:10 "You have been permitted to understand the s of
1Co 2:10 out everything and shows us even God's deep s.
4:1 have been put in charge of explaining God's s.
4:5 he will bring our deepest s to light and will reveal

SECT (3)

Ac 24:5 He is a ringleader of the s known as the Nazarenes.
24:14 I admit that I follow the Way, which they call a s.
26:5 of the Pharisees, the strictest s of our religion.

SECTION (33) [SECTIONS]

Ge 13:9 Take your choice of any s of the land you want,
Jos 18:6 to decide which s will be assigned to each tribe.
18:9 into seven sections, listing the towns in each s.
18:10 to determine which tribe should have each s.
2Ki 22:14 and Asaiah went to the newer Mishneh s of
25:4 Then a s of the city wall was broken down, and all
2Ch 34:22 and the other men went to the newer Mishneh s of
Ne 3:4 and grandson of Hakkoz repaired the next s of
3:8 They left out a s of Jerusalem as far as the Broad
3:11 of the Ovens, in addition to another s of the wall.
3:12 of Hallohesh and his daughters repaired the next s.
3:19 repaired another s of wall opposite the armory by
3:20 who repaired an additional s from the buttress to
3:21 and grandson of Hakkoz rebuilt another s of the
3:24 who rebuilt another s of the wall from Azariah's
3:27 who repaired another s opposite the great
3:28 each one doing the s immediately opposite his own
3:30 the sixth son of Zalaph, repaired another s,
12:24 and thanksgiving, one s responding to the other,
Isa 28:25 barley, and spelt, each in its own s of his land?
Jer 36:23 king took his knife and cut off that s of the scroll.
36:23 He then threw it into the fire, s by s,
52:7 Then a s of the city wall was broken down, and all
Eze 45:1 you must set aside a s of it for the LORD as his
45:2 A s of this land, measuring 875 feet by 875 feet,
45:6 "Adjacent to the larger sacred area will be a s of
45:7 One s will share a border with the east side of the
45:7 and the second s will share a border on the west
Zep 1:10 and echo throughout the newer Mishneh s of the
Mt 3:5 People from Jerusalem and from every s of Judea
Jn 8:20 in the s of the Temple known as the Treasury.
10:23 walking through the s known as Solomon's

SECTIONS (7) [SECTION]

Jos 18:5 The scouts will map the land into seven s,
18:9 and mapped the entire territory into seven s,
2Ki 10:32 King Hazael conquered several s of the country
Ne 3:23 and grandson of Ananiah repaired the s next to
Eze 45:7 "Two special s of land will be set apart for the
45:8 These s of land will be the prince's allotment.
Da 8:22 Empire will break into four s with four kings,

SECU (1)

1Sa 19:22 went to Ramah and arrived at the great well in S.

SECULAR (1)

1Co 6:1 file a lawsuit and ask a s court to decide the matter,

SECUNDUS (1)

Ac 20:4 Aristarchus and S, from Thessalonica; Gaius,

SECURE (27) [SECURED, SECURELY, SECURITY]

Jdg 18:7 like the Sidonians; they were peaceful and s.
18:27 town of Laish, whose people were peaceful and s.
1Sa 25:29 of the LORD your God, s in his treasure pouch!
2Sa 7:10 a s place where they will never be disturbed.
7:16 before me, and your throne will be s forever.' "
1Ch 17:9 a s place where they will never be disturbed.
17:14 for all time, and his throne will be s forever.' "
Job 31:24 my trust in money or felt s because of my gold?
Ps 30:7 O LORD, made me as s as a mountain.
89:36 will go on forever; / his throne is as s as the sun,
125:1 Those who trust in the LORD are as s as Mount
Pr 14:26 Those who fear the LORD are s; he will be a
20:28 protect the king; his throne is made s through love.
25:5 and his reign will be made s by justice.
27:24 and the crown might not be s for the next
Isa 33:20 You will see Jerusalem, a city quiet and s.
47:8 living at ease and feeling s,
47:10 "You felt s in all your wickedness. 'No one sees
Jer 15:20 but I will make you as s as a fortified wall.
Eze 27:24 carpets bound with cords and made s.
Da 11:6 marriage to the king of the north to s the alliance,
Am 6:1 and think you are s in Jerusalem and Samaria!
Zep 2:15 This is the fate of that boisterous city, once so s.
Zec 12:6 while the people living in Jerusalem remain s.
Mt 27:65 "Take guards and s it the best you can."
1Th 5:3 everything is peaceful and s," then disaster will
2Pe 3:17 I don't want you to lose your own s footing.

SECURED (4) [SECURE]

1Sa 13:23 The pass at Micmash had meanwhile been s by a
14:47 Now when Saul had s his grasp on Israel's throne,
1Ch 19:7 and s the support of the king of Maacah and his
Heb 9:12 own blood, and with it he s our salvation forever.

SECURELY (13) [SECURE]

Ex 28:28 This will hold the chestpiece s to the ephod above

39:21 the chestpiece was held **s** to the ephod above the
Lev 25:18 "If you want to live **s** in the land, keep my laws
25:19 and you will eat your fill and live **s** in it.
26:5 You will eat your fill and live **s** in your land.
Jdg 16:5 and how he can be overpowered and tied up **s**.
16:6 so strong and what it would take to tie you up **s**."
16:10 Now please tell me how you can be tied up **s**."
16:13 you please tell me how you can be tied up **s**?"
Ps 63:8 behind you; / your strong right hand holds me **s**.
Jer 10:4 and then fasten it **s** with hammer and nails
Da 3:23 So Shadrach, Meshach, and Abednego, **s** tied,
1Jn 5:18 for God's Son holds them **s**, and the evil one

SECURITY (25) [SECURE]

Lev 6:2 have been dishonest with regard to a **s** deposit,
6:4 taken by theft or extortion, whether a **s** deposit,
Dt 3:20 When the LORD has given **s** to the rest of the
12:10 he gives you rest and **s** from all your enemies,
24:10 do not enter your neighbor's house to claim the **s**.
24:12 neighbor is poor and has only a cloak to give as **s**,
28:65 among those nations you will find no place of **s**
33:28 Israel will live in safety, / prosperous Jacob in **s**,
Ru 1:9 May the LORD bless you with the **s** of another
2Ki 20:19 there will be peace and **s** during my lifetime."
Ezr 9:8 He has given us **s** in this holy place. Our God has
Est 9:30 and **s** were sent to the Jews throughout the 127
Job 8:15 They cling to their home for **s**, but it won't last.
18:14 They are torn from the **s** of their tent, and they are
21:23 One person dies in prosperity and **s**,
24:23 They may be allowed to live in **s**, but God is
Ps 37:11 possess the land; / they will live in prosperous **s**.
69:22 become a snare, / and let their **s** become a trap.
102:28 will live in **s**. / Their children's children
Pr 3:26 for the LORD is your **s**. He will keep your foot
19:23 the LORD gives life, **s**, and protection from harm.
Isa 39:8 there will be peace and **s** during my lifetime."
Eze 24:21 my Temple, the source of your **s** and pride.
Hab 2:9 You believe your wealth will buy **s**, putting your
Zec 1:15 angry with the other nations that enjoy peace and **s**.

SEDITION (2)

Ezr 4:15 because of its long history of **s** against the kings
4:19 In fact, rebellion and **s** are normal there!

SEDITIONS [KJV] See DIVISIONS

SEDUCE (1) [SEDUCED, SEDUCES, SEDUCING, SEDUCTIVE, SEDUCTIVELY]

Pr 6:25 lust for her beauty. Don't let her coyness **s** you.

SEDUCED (5) [SEDUCE]

Dt 4:19 of heaven—don't be **s** by them and worship them.
Job 31:9 "If my heart has been **s** by a woman, or if I have
36:18 But watch out, or you may be **s** with wealth.
Pr 7:21 So she **s** him with her pretty speech. With her
Rev 14:8 because she **s** the nations of the world and made

SEDUCES (1) [SEDUCE]

Ex 22:16 "If a man **s** a virgin who is not engaged to anyone

SEDUCING (1) [SEDUCE]

1Sa 2:22 that his sons were **s** the young women who assisted

SEDUCTIVE (1) [SEDUCE]

Ecc 7:26 I discovered that a **s** woman is more bitter than

SEDUCTIVELY (1) [SEDUCE]

Pr 7:10 woman approached him, dressed **s** and sly of heart.

SEE (875) [FORESEES, SAW, SEEING, SEEN, SEES, SHORTSIGHTED, SIGHT, SIGHTED, SIGHTS]

Ge 2:19 He brought them to Adam to **s** what he would call
4:14 All who **s** me will try to kill me!"
8:8 Then he sent out a dove to **s** if it could find dry
9:16 When I **s** the rainbow in the clouds, I will
9:23 the other way so they wouldn't **s** him naked.
11:5 But the LORD came down to **s** the city
12:12 When the Egyptians **s** you, they will say, 'This is
13:14 "Look as far as you can **s** in every direction.
16:6 your servant, you may deal with her as you **s** fit."
18:21 I am going down to **s** whether or not these reports
19:20 **S**, there is a small village nearby. Please let me go
there instead; don't you **s** how small it is?"
24:7 and he will **s** to it that you find a young woman
24:13 **S**, here I am, standing beside this spring,
26:28 "We can plainly **s** that the LORD is with you.
27:12 He'll **s** that I'm trying to trick him, and then he'll
27:46 I'd rather die than **s** Jacob marry one of them."
30:33 This will make it easy for you to **s** whether or not I
30:38 so Laban's flocks would **s** them as they came to
31:12 'Look, and you will **s** that only the streaked,
31:37 here in front of us, before our relatives, for all to **s**.
31:50 or if you take other wives, but God will **s** it.
32:19 all to say the same thing to Esau when you **s** him.
33:10 "for what a relief it is to **s** your friendly smile.
33:13 But Jacob replied, "You can **s**, my lord, that some
37:14 "Go and **s** how your brothers and the flocks are
37:20 Then we'll **s** what becomes of all his dreams!"
42:9 You have come to **s** how vulnerable our land has
42:19 We'll **s** how honorable you really are. Only one of
43:3 couldn't **s** him again unless Benjamin came along.
43:5 and **s** me unless your brother is with you.' "
44:21 you said to us, 'Bring him here so I can **s** him.'
44:23 'You may not **s** me again unless your youngest
44:26 We won't be allowed to **s** the man in charge of the
44:34 I cannot bear to **s** what this would do to him."
45:12 "You can **s** for yourselves, and so can my brother
45:28 Joseph is alive! I will go and **s** him before I die."
46:3 for I will **s** to it that you become a great nation
47:1 So Joseph went to **s** Pharaoh and said, "My father
47:23 "**S**, I have bought you and your land for Pharaoh.
48:10 half blind because of his age and could hardly **s**.
48:11 to Joseph, "I never thought I would **s** you again,
48:11 but now God has let me **s** your children, too."
50:23 He lived to **s** three generations of descendants of
Ex 2:4 watching to **s** what would happen to him.
3:3 that bush burning up? I must go over to **s** this."
3:21 And I will **s** to it that the Egyptians treat you well.
4:11 or not speak, hear or not hear, **s** or not **s**?
5:1 Moses and Aaron went to **s** Pharaoh.
5:19 the Israelite foremen could **s** that they were in
6:1 "Now you will **s** what I will do to Pharaoh,"
7:10 So Moses and Aaron went to **s** Pharaoh, and they
8:26 If we offer them here where they can **s** us,
9:7 Pharaoh sent officials to **s** whether it was true that
9:10 soot from a furnace and went to **s** Pharaoh.
9:16 that you might **s** my power and that my fame might
10:5 so many that you won't be able to **s** the ground.
10:10 ones along! I can **s** through your wicked intentions.
10:23 the people scarcely moved, for they could not **s**.
10:28 "Don't ever let me **s** you again! The day you do,
10:29 Moses replied. "I will never **s** you again."
12:13 as a sign. When I **s** the blood, I will pass over you.
14:10 the people of Israel could **s** them in the distance,
14:13 The Egyptians that you **s** today will never be seen
14:30 And the Israelites could **s** the bodies of the
16:4 I will test them in this to **s** whether they will follow
16:7 In the morning you will **s** the glorious presence of
16:10 they could **s** the awesome glory of the LORD.
16:32 later generations will be able to **s** the bread that the
19:21 They must not come up here to **s** the LORD,
20:26 the skirts of your clothing and **s** your nakedness.
23:5 If you **s** the donkey of someone who hates you
23:8 makes you ignore something that you clearly **s**.
23:20 "**S**, I am sending my angel before you to lead you
33:18 "Please let me **s** your glorious presence," he said.
33:20 directly at my face, for no one may **s** me and live."
33:23 remove my hand, and you will **s** me from behind.
34:10 And all the people around you will **s** the power of
34:35 and the people would **s** his face aglow.
40:38 in the cloud so all the people of Israel could **s** it.
Lev 13:13 the priest must examine the infected person to **s** if
26:32 it will be utterly shocked at the destruction they **s**.
Nu 5:21 "then may the people **s** that the LORD's curse is
11:23 Now you will **s** whether or not my word comes
13:18 **S** what the land is like and find out whether the
13:20 and bring back samples of the crops you **s**."
13:27 "We arrived in the land you sent us to **s**, and it is
14:23 They will never even **s** the land I swore to give
16:7 Then we will **s** whom the LORD chooses as his
22:19 But stay here one more night to **s** if the LORD
22:41 From there he could **s** the people of Israel spread
23:3 and I will go to **s** if the LORD will respond to me.
23:9 I **s** them from the cliff tops; / I watch them from
23:9 the hills. / I **s** a people who live by themselves,
23:13 There you will **s** only a portion of the nation of
24:3 the prophecy of the man whose eyes **s** clearly,
24:15 the prophecy of the man whose eyes **s** clearly,
24:17 I **s** him, but not in the present time. / I perceive
28:2 **S** to it that they are brought at the appointed times
32:11 or older will ever **s** the land I solemnly promised to
Dt 1:35 to **s** the good land I swore to give your ancestors,
1:36 He will **s** this land because he has followed the
3:25 Please let me cross the Jordan to **s** the wonderful
3:28 He will give them the land you now **s** before you.'
4:12 You heard his words but didn't **s** his form;
4:15 You did not **s** the LORD's form on the day he
4:19 And when you look up into the sky and **s** the sun,
4:28 gods that neither **s** nor hear nor eat nor smell.
4:32 **S** if anything as great as this has ever happened
4:36 He let you **s** his great fire here on earth so he could
9:16 There below me I could **s** the gold calf you had
11:3 They weren't there to **s** the miraculous signs
11:4 They didn't **s** what the LORD did to the armies of
11:5 They didn't **s** how the LORD cared for you in the
11:6 They weren't there to **s** what he did to Dathan
13:3 The LORD your God is testing you to **s** if you
18:16 or **s** this blazing fire for fear you would die.
21:7 did not shed this blood, nor did we **s** it happen.
21:11 And suppose you **s** among the captives a beautiful
22:1 "If you **s** your neighbor's ox or sheep wandering
away, don't pretend not to **s** it.
22:3 your neighbor loses. Don't pretend you did not **s** it.
22:4 "If you **s** your neighbor's ox or donkey lying on
23:14 He must not **s** any shameful thing among you,
28:10 Then all the nations of the world will **s** that you are
28:66 with no reason to believe that you will **s** the
28:67 terror at the awesome horrors you **s** around you.
29:4 that understand, nor eyes that **s**, nor ears that hear!
29:22 will **s** the devastation of the land and the diseases
32:20 'I will abandon them; / I will **s** to their end!
32:52 So you will **s** the land from a distance, but you
34:4 I have now allowed you to **s** it, but you will not
Jos 3:3 "When you **s** the Levitical priests carrying the Ark
9:12 we left. But now, as you can **s**, it is dry and moldy.
14:10 "Now, as you can **s**, the LORD has kept me alive
Jdg 2:22 to **s** whether or not they would obey the LORD as
3:4 to **s** whether they would obey the commands the
10:15 Punish us as you **s** fit, only rescue us today from
11:23 "So you **s**, it was the LORD, the God of Israel,
Ru 1:15 "**S**," Naomi said to her, "your sister-in-law has
2:9 **S** which part of the field they are harvesting,
3:3 but don't let Boaz **s** you until he has finished his
1Sa 5:3 But when the citizens of Ashdod went to **s** it the
9:8 can at least offer it to him and **s** what happens!"
10:2 you will **s** two men beside Rachel's tomb at
10:3 you will **s** three men coming toward you who are
12:16 and **s** the great thing the LORD is about to do.
14:6 "Let's go across to **s** those pagans," Jonathan said
14:8 told him. "We will cross over and let them **s** us.
14:29 **S** how much better I feel now that I have eaten this
15:28 And Samuel said to him, "**S**? The LORD has torn
17:18 **S** how your brothers are getting along, and bring
17:28 and dishonesty. You just want to **s** the battle!"
17:39 over it, and took a step or two to **s** what it was like,
18:21 "Here's another chance to **s** him killed by the
19:7 Then he took David to **s** Saul, and everything was
19:18 David got away and went to Ramah to **s** Samuel,
21:1 David went to the city of Nob to **s** Ahimelech the
24:10 This very day you can **s** with your own eyes it isn't
27:9 and clothing before returning home to **s** King
28:2 "Now you will **s** for yourself what we can do."
28:13 be afraid!" the king told her. "What do you **s**?"
28:13 "I **s** a god coming up out of the earth," she said.
2Sa 3:24 he rushed to **s** the king. "What have you done?"
13:5 When your father comes to **s** you, ask him to let
13:6 And when the king came to **s** him, Amnon asked
13:34 "I **s** a crowd of people coming from the Horonaim
14:1 Joab realized how much the king longed to **s**
14:8 and I'll **s** to it that no one touches him."
14:24 into my presence." So Absalom did not **s** the king.
14:28 for two years without getting to **s** the king.
14:32 me back from Geshur if he didn't intend to **s** me.
14:32 Let me **s** the king; if he finds me guilty of
15:25 "he will bring me back to **s** the Ark
16:12 And perhaps the LORD will **s** that I am being
16:16 Arkite arrived, he went immediately to **s** Absalom.
16:22 a tent on the palace roof where everyone could **s** it,
17:5 the Arkite. Let's **s** what he thinks about this."
21:4 "And we don't want to **s** the Israelites executed in
1Ki 1:23 told him, "Nathan the prophet is here to **s** you."
1:48 to sit on my throne while I am still alive to **s** it.' "
2:13 came to **s** Bathsheba, Solomon's mother.
9:12 Hiram came from Tyre to **s** the towns Solomon had
12:10 was hard on you, just wait and **s** what I'll be like!
14:4 He was an old man now and could no longer **s**.
15:19 **S**, I am sending you a gift of silver and gold.
18:5 and valley to **s** if we can find enough grass to save
18:43 returned to Elijah and said, "I didn't **s** anything."
20:13 Then a prophet came to **s** King Ahab and told him,
20:13 the LORD says: Do you **s** all these enemy forces?
21:29 "Do you **s** how Ahab has humbled himself before
22:23 "So you **s**, the LORD has put a lying spirit in the
2Ki 1:14 **S** how the fire from heaven has destroyed the first
2:10 "If you **s** me when I am taken from you, then you
2:19 in beautiful natural surroundings, as you can **s**.
3:17 You will **s** neither wind nor rain, says the LORD,
5:3 "I wish my master would go to **s** the prophet in
6:1 came to Elisha and told him, "As you can **s**,
6:17 "O LORD, open his eyes and let him **s**!"
6:20 "O LORD, now open their eyes and let them **s**."
6:30 the people could **s** that he was wearing sackcloth
7:2 But Elisha replied, "You will **s** it happen, but you
7:14 and the king sent scouts to **s** what had happened to
7:19 the man of God had said, "You will **s** it happen,
8:3 and she went to **s** the king about getting back her
8:6 So he directed one of his officials to **s** to it that
9:17 to Joram, "I **s** a company of troops coming!"
10:16 with me, and **s** how devoted I am to the LORD."
10:19 **S** to it that every one of them comes, for I am
11:13 she hurried to the LORD's Temple to **s** what was
13:4 The LORD could **s** how terribly the king of Aram
18:37 and they went in to **s** the king and told him what
19:16 and hear! Open your eyes, O LORD, and **s**!
20:13 He also took them to **s** his armory and showed
20:15 "What did they **s** in your palace?" Isaiah asked.
22:20 You will not **s** the disaster I am going to bring on
1Ch 12:17 then may the God of our ancestors **s** and judge
12:23 They were all eager to **s** David become king
13:4 for the people could **s** it was the right thing to do.
28:20 He will **s** to it that all the work related to the
29:18 **S** to it that their love for you never changes.
2Ch 10:10 was hard on you, just wait and **s** what I'll be like!
13:12 So you **s**, God is with us. He is our leader.
16:3 **S**, I am sending you a gift of silver and gold.
18:22 "So you **s**, the LORD has put a lying spirit in the
20:10 "And now **s** what the armies of Ammon, Moab,
20:11 Now **s** how they reward us! For they have come to
20:24 lying on the ground for as far as they could **s**.
23:12 she hurried to the LORD's Temple to **s** what was
24:22 "May the LORD **s** what they are doing and hold
29:8 horror, and ridicule, as you can so plainly **s**.
30:7 an object of derision, as you yourselves can **s**.
32:31 to test him and to **s** what was really in his heart.
34:28 You will not **s** the disaster I am going to bring on
Ezr 4:14 and we do not want to **s** you dishonored in this
Ne 1:6 Look down and **s** me praying night and day for
Est 2:3 will **s** that they are all given beauty treatments.
3:4 So they spoke to Haman about this to **s** if he would
4:16 it is against the law, I will go in to **s** the king.
5:13 "But all this is meaningless as long as I **s**
8:6 For how can I endure to **s** my people and my
Job 3:9 but in vain; may it never **s** the morning light.
3:16 like a baby who never lives to **s** the light?

4:16 It stopped, but I couldn't **s** its shape. There was a
5:14 they **s** no better in the daytime than at night.
7:8 You **s** me now, but not for long. Your eyes will be
9:11 Yet when he comes near, I cannot **s** him. When he moves on, I do not **s** him go.
10:4 of a human? Do you **s** things as people **s** them?
17:8 The upright are astonished when they **s** me.
19:26 my body has decayed, yet in my body I will **s** God!
19:27 I will **s** him for myself. Yes, I will **s** him with my
20:9 Neither his friends nor his family will ever **s** him
21:8 They live to **s** their children grow to maturity,
21:20 Let their own eyes **s** their destruction. Let them
22:11 That is why you cannot **s** in the darkness,
22:13 'That's why God can't **s** what I am doing!
22:14 thick clouds swirl about him, and he cannot **s** us.
22:19 "Now the righteous will be happy to **s** the wicked
23:9 I do not **s** him in the north, for he is hidden. I turn
24:15 the twilight, for he says, 'No one will **s** me then.'
28:7 treasures that no bird of prey can **s**, no falcon's eye
31:35 who would listen to me and try to **s** my side!
33:32 want to hear it, for I am anxious to **s** you justified.
35:5 up into the sky and **s** the clouds high above you.
35:14 And it is even more false to say he doesn't **s** what
36:30 **S** how he spreads the lightning around him
40:16 **S** its powerful loins and the muscles of its belly.
42:16 living to **s** four generations of his children
Ps 8:3 at the night sky and **s** the work of your fingers—
9:13 **S** how I suffer at the hands of those who hate me.
10:5 They do not **s** your punishment awaiting them.
10:14 But you do **s** the trouble and grief they cause.
11:7 Those who do what is right will **s** his face.
14:2 he looks to **s** if there is even one with real
17:15 because I have done what is right, I will **s** you.
17:15 will be fully satisfied, / for I will **s** you face to face.
21:12 and run / when they **s** your arrows aimed at them.
25:18 Feel my pain and **s** my trouble. / Forgive all my
25:19 **S** how many enemies I have, / and how viciously
27:13 Yet I am confident that I will **s** the LORD's
31:11 When they **s** me on the street, / they turn the other
34:8 Taste and **s** that the LORD is good. / Oh, the joys
36:2 they cannot **s** how wicked they really are.
36:9 are the fountain of life, / the light by which we **s**.
37:34 you the land. / You will **s** the wicked destroyed.
40:3 Many will **s** what he has done and be astounded.
40:12 They pile up so high / I can't **s** my way out.
44:16 our mockers. / All we **s** are our vengeful enemies.
46:8 Come, **s** the glorious works of the LORD:
46:8 **S** how he brings destruction upon the world
48:2 in elevation— / the whole earth rejoices to **s** it!
49:9 to live forever / and never **s** the grave.
49:19 before them / and never again **s** the light of day.
50:18 When you **s** a thief, you help him, / and you spend
52:6 The righteous will **s** it and be amazed. / They will
53:2 he looks to **s** if there is even one with real
55:9 their speech, / for I **s** violence and strife in the city.
58:8 like a stillborn child who will never **s** the sun.
58:10 The godly will rejoice when they **s** injustice
64:8 All who **s** it happening will shake their heads in
66:5 Come and **s** what our God has done,
69:23 Let their eyes go blind so they cannot **s**, / and let
69:32 The humble will **s** their God at work and be glad.
74:3 **s** how the enemy has destroyed your sanctuary.
74:9 We **s** no miraculous signs / as evidence that you
74:18 **S** how these enemies scoff at you, LORD.
80:14 Look down from heaven and **s** our plight.
83:2 Don't you **s** what your arrogant enemies are doing?
90:8 before you— / our secret sins—and you **s** them all.
90:16 Let us **s** your miracles again; / let our children **s** your glory at work.
91:8 But you will **s** it with your eyes; / you will **s** how the wicked are punished.
104:26 **S** the ships sailing along, / and Leviathan,
107:42 The godly will **s** these things and be glad,
107:43 they will **s** in our history the faithful love of the
109:25 when they **s** me, they shake their heads.
109:27 Let them **s** that this is your doing, / that you
112:10 The wicked will be infuriated when they **s** this.
115:5 they have mouths, / or **s**, though they have eyes!
118:23 is the LORD's doing, / and it is marvelous to **s**.
119:18 Open my eyes to **s** / the wonderful truths in your
119:82 My eyes are straining to **s** your promises come
119:123 My eyes strain to **s** your deliverance, / to **s** the truth of your promise fulfilled.
119:159 **S** how I love your commandments, LORD.
128:5 May you **s** Jerusalem prosper as long as you live.
135:16 they have mouths, / or **s**, though they have eyes!
Pr 13:19 It is pleasant to **s** dreams come true, but fools will
14:8 The wise look ahead to **s** what is coming, but fools
20:12 Ears to hear and eyes to **s**—both are gifts from the
22:29 Do you **s** any truly competent workers? They will
23:33 You will **s** hallucinations, and you will say crazy
25:7 publicly disgraced! Just because you **s** something,
26:26 by trickery, it will finally come to light for all to **s**.
29:16 But the godly will live to **s** the tyrant's downfall.
31:9 the poor and helpless, and **s** that they get justice.
Ecc 1:8 No matter how much we **s**, we are never satisfied.
3:11 people cannot **s** the whole scope of God's work
3:18 they can **s** for themselves that they are no better
5:8 If you **s** a poor person being oppressed by the
11:7 Light is sweet; it's wonderful to **s** the sun!
SS 1:6 in the hot sun. Now **s** what it has done to me!
2:4 so everyone can **s** how much he loves me.
2:14 Let me **s** you; let me hear your voice. For your
3:11 **S** the crown with which his mother crowned him
6:9 The young women are delighted when they **s** her;
6:11 and out to the valley to **s** the new growth brought
6:11 I wanted to **s** whether the grapevines were budding
6:13 come back, that we may **s** you once again."
7:12 Let us **s** whether the vines have budded,
Isa 1:7 plunder your fields and destroy everything they **s**.
1:11 I don't want to **s** the blood from your offerings of
1:16 and be clean! Let me no longer **s** your evil deeds.
1:21 **S** how Jerusalem, once so faithful, has become a
3:12 my people, can't you **s** what fools your rulers are?
3:17 the LORD will make them bald for all to **s**!
5:19 you can do. We want to **s** what you have planned."
6:7 He touched my lips with it and said, "**S**, this coal
6:9 You will **s** what I do, but you will not perceive its
6:10 That way, they will not **s** with their eyes, hear with
9:2 The people who walk in darkness will **s** a great
12:2 **S**, God has come to save me. / I will trust in him
13:2 "**S** the flags waving as the enemy attacks.
13:9 For **s**, the day of the LORD is coming—
14:9 and mighty kings long dead are there to **s** you.
21:2 I **s** an awesome vision: I **s** you plundered and
22:2 What do I **s** in this reveling city? Bodies are lying
22:9 You inspect the walls of Jerusalem to **s** what needs
24:1 **S** how he is scattering the people over the face of
26:11 you threaten. / They do not **s** your upraised fist.
26:21 They will be brought out for all to **s**.
29:15 "The LORD can't **s** us," you say to yourselves.
29:18 and blind people will **s** through the gloom
29:23 For when they **s** their many children and material
30:16 But the only swiftness you are going to **s** is the
30:20 You will **s** your teacher with your own eyes,
31:9 with terror and flee when they **s** the battle flags,"
32:3 Then everyone who can **s** will be looking for God,
33:17 Your eyes will **s** the king in all his splendor,
33:17 and you will **s** a land that stretches into the
33:20 you will **s** Zion as a place of worship
33:20 You will **s** Jerusalem, a city quiet and secure.
34:16 the book of the LORD, and **s** what he will do.
36:22 and they went in to **s** the king and told him what
37:17 and hear! Open your eyes, O LORD, and **s**! "
38:11 I said, "Never again will I **s** the LORD GOD
38:11 land of the living. / Never again will I **s** my friends
39:2 He also took them to **s** his armory and showed
39:4 "What did they **s** in your palace?" asked Isaiah.
40:5 will be revealed, and all people will **s** it together.
40:10 **S**, he brings his reward with him as he comes.
40:26 And he counts them to **s** that none are lost or have
40:27 how can you say the LORD does not **s** your
41:11 "**S**, all your angry enemies lie there, confused
41:20 Everyone will **s** this miracle and understand that it
41:29 **S**, they are all foolish, worthless things. Your idols
42:18 Why won't you listen? Why do you refuse to **s**?
42:20 You **s** and understand what is right but refuse to
42:23 from the past and **s** the ruin that awaits you?
43:19 **S**, I have already begun! Do you not **s** it?
44:9 that this is so, for their idols neither **s** nor know.
44:18 Their eyes are closed, and they cannot **s**.
49:12 **S**, my people will return from far away, from lands
49:16 **S**, I have written your name on my hand.
49:18 Look and **s**, for all your children will come back to
49:22 "**S**, I will give a signal to the godless nations.
50:9 **S**, the Sovereign LORD is on my side! Who will
51:22 "**S**, I am taking the terrible cup from your hands.
52:8 for before their very eyes they **s** the LORD
52:10 The ends of the earth will **s** the salvation of our
52:13 **S**, my servant will prosper; he will be highly
52:15 For they will **s** what they had not previously been
57:13 Let's **s** if your idols can do anything for you when
59:16 He was amazed to **s** that no one intervened to help
60:1 Let your light shine for all the nations to **s**!
60:3 Mighty kings will come to **s** your radiance.
60:4 "Look and **s**, for everyone is coming home!
60:8 "And what do I **s** flying like clouds to Israel,
62:2 The nations will **s** your righteousness. Kings will
62:3 LORD will hold you in his hands for all to **s**—
62:10 out the boulders; raise a flag for all the nations to **s**.
62:11 **S**, he brings his reward with him as he comes.' "
63:15 look down from heaven and **s** us from your holy,
64:9 at us, we pray, and **s** that we are all your people.
66:14 When you **s** these things, your heart will rejoice.
66:14 Everyone will **s** the good hand of the LORD on
66:15 **S**, the LORD is coming with fire, and his swift
66:18 "I can **s** what they are doing, and I know what
66:18 and peoples together, and they will **s** my glory.
66:24 they will **s** the dead bodies of those who have
Jer 1:9 Then the LORD touched my mouth and said, "**S**,
1:11 said to me, "Look, Jeremiah! What do you **s**?"
1:11 And I replied, "I **s** a branch from an almond tree."
1:13 to me again and asked, "What do you **s** now?"
1:13 And I replied, "I **s** a pot of boiling water,
1:18 For **s**, today I have made you immune to their
2:10 to the land of Kedar. Think about what you **s** there.
2:10 **S** if anyone has ever heard of anything as strange
2:19 You will **s** what an evil, bitter thing it is to forsake
5:21 who have eyes but do not **s**, who have ears but do
6:22 "**S** a great army marching from the north!
7:11 I **s** all the evil going on there, says the LORD.
7:12 **S** what I did there because of all the wickedness of
7:17 Do you not **s** what they are doing throughout the
7:18 **S** how the women knead dough and make cakes to
9:7 Therefore, the LORD Almighty says, "**S**, I will
10:20 been taken away, and I will never **s** them again.
11:16 olive tree, beautiful to **s** and full of good fruit.
11:20 Let me **s** your vengeance against them, for I have
12:3 know my heart. You **s** me and test my thoughts.
13:20 **S** the armies marching down from the north!
14:18 I **s** the bodies of people slaughtered by the enemy.
14:18 there I **s** people who have died of starvation.
16:17 I am watching them closely, and I **s** every sin.
19:8 and will gasp at the destruction they **s** there.
19:9 I will **s** to it that your enemies lay siege to the city
20:12 Let me **s** your vengeance against them, for I have
22:10 For he will never return to **s** his native land again.
22:12 a distant land and never again **s** his own country."
22:20 **S**, they are all destroyed. Not one is left to help
22:22 Surely at last you will **s** your wickedness and be
23:14 But now I **s** that the prophets of Jerusalem are even
23:23 "Do they think I cannot **s** what they are doing?
24:3 LORD said to me, "What do you **s**, Jeremiah?"
24:6 I will **s** that they are well treated, and I will bring
29:32 None of his descendants will **s** the good things I
32:24 "**S** how the siege ramps have been built against the
33:9 The people of the world will **s** the good I do for my
33:12 will once more **s** shepherds leading sheep
34:22 I will **s** to it that all the towns of Judah are
35:3 So I went to **s** Jaazaniah son of Jeremiah
36:3 Perhaps the people of Judah will repent if they **s** in
37:12 land of Benjamin, to **s** the property he had bought.
39:12 "**S** that he isn't hurt," he had said. "Look after
39:16 not prosperity. You will **s** its destruction,
40:4 are welcome. I will **s** that you are well cared for.
40:8 So they came to **s** Gedaliah at Mizpah. These are
41:6 come and **s** what has happened to Gedaliah!"
42:18 And you will never **s** your homeland again.'
48:17 **S** how the strong scepter is broken,
48:39 is broken! Hear the wailing! **S** the shame of Moab!
48:44 I will **s** to it that you do not get away, for the time
49:17 and will gasp at the destruction they **s** there.
50:13 and will gasp at the destruction they **s** there.
50:31 "**S**, I am your enemy, O proud people,"
La 1:9 "LORD, **s** my deep misery," she cries.
1:11 look," she mourns, "and **s** how I am despised.
1:12 and **s** if there is any suffering like mine,
1:20 "LORD, **s** my anguish! My heart is broken
1:21 they were happy to **s** what you had done.
2:11 poured out, as I **s** what has happened to my people.
2:21 "**S** them lying in the streets—young and old,
3:36 in the courts. Do they think the Lord didn't **s** it?
4:2 **S** how the precious children of Jerusalem,
5:1 that has happened to us. **S** all the sorrows we bear!
Eze 1:8 Beneath each of their wings I could **s** human
5:15 They will **s** what happens when the LORD turns
8:6 of man," he said, "do you **s** what they are doing?
8:6 Do you **s** the great sins the people of Israel are
8:6 and you will **s** even greater sins than these!"
8:7 where I could **s** an opening in the wall.
8:9 "and **s** the unspeakable wickedness going on in
8:12 They are saying, 'The LORD doesn't **s** us;
9:4 and sigh because of the sins they **s** around them."
9:9 They are saying, 'The LORD doesn't **s** it!
12:2 you live among rebels who could **s** the truth if they
12:3 in broad daylight so the people can **s** you,
12:12 and his eyes will never **s** his homeland again.
12:13 though he will never **s** it, and he will die there.
12:24 "Then you will **s** what becomes of all the false
13:9 and they will never again **s** their own land.
14:22 You will **s** with your own eyes how wicked they
14:23 When you meet them and **s** their behavior, you will
15:7 And I will **s** to it that if they escape from one fire,
16:41 I will **s** to it that you stop your prostitution and end
18:23 that I like to **s** wicked people die?
20:48 And all the world will **s** that I, the LORD,
24:7 leaving blood on the rocks for all to **s**.
36:9 **S**, I am concerned for you, and I will come to help
37:14 You will **s** that I have done everything just as I
37:20 you have inscribed, so the people can **s** them.
39:15 set up beside them so the burial crews will **s** them
39:21 Everyone will **s** the punishment I have inflicted on
40:2 From there I could **s** what appeared to be a city
40:5 I could **s** a wall completely surrounding the
44:24 and they will **s** to it that the Sabbath is set apart as
47:2 There I could **s** the stream flowing out through the
Da 1:13 **s** how we look compared to the other young men
2:8 The king replied, "I can **s** through your trick!
2:16 Daniel went at once to **s** the king and requested
2:24 Then Daniel went in to **s** Arioch, who had been
3:25 "I **s** four men, unbound, walking around in the
4:11 high into the heavens for all the world to **s**.
4:20 high into the heavens for all the world to **s**.
5:23 gods that neither **s** nor hear nor know anything at
9:7 faces are covered with shame, just as you **s** us now.
9:18 Open your eyes and **s** our wretchedness.
9:18 **S** how your city lies in ruins—for everyone knows
Hos 7:2 Their sinful deeds are all around them; I **s** them all!
Joel 2:28 will dream dreams. Your young men will **s** visions.
Am 5:24 Instead, I want to **s** a mighty flood of justice,
6:2 Go over to Calneh and **s** what happened there.
7:7 He was checking it with a plumb line to **s** if it was
7:8 the LORD said to me, "Amos, what do you **s**?"
8:2 "What do you **s**, Amos?" he asked. I replied,
Jnh 1:7 Then the crew cast lots to **s** which of them had
2:4 How will I ever again **s** your holy Temple?'
3:3 a city so large that it took three days to **s** it all.
4:5 and made a shelter to sit under as he waited to **s** if
Mic 1:16 be snatched away, and you will never **s** them again.
6:16 treated with contempt, mocked by all who **s** you."
7:9 into the light, and I will **s** his righteousness.
7:10 Then my enemies will **s** that the LORD is on my
7:10 With my own eyes I will **s** them trampled down
Na 2:3 The attack begins! **S** their scarlet uniforms!
3:3 **S** the flashing swords and glittering spears in the
3:5 so all the earth will **s** your nakedness and shame.
3:7 All who **s** you will shrink back in horror and say,
3:10 Soldiers cast lots to **s** who would get the Egyptian
3:15 you like locusts, devouring everything they **s**.
Hab 1:3 Must I forever **s** this sin and misery all around me?
1:3 Wherever I look, I **s** destruction and violence.

2: 1 and wait to s what the LORD will say to me
3: 3 I s God, the Holy One, moving across the deserts
3: 7 I s the peoples of Cushan and Midian trembling in
Zec 2: 2 to s how wide and how long it is."
3: 4 to Jeshua he said, "S, I have taken away your sins,
4: 2 "What do you s now?" he asked. I answered,
4: 2 "I s a solid gold lampstand with a bowl of oil on
4: 3 And I s two olive trees, one on each side of the
4:10 for the LORD rejoices to s the work begin,
4:10 to s the plumb line in Zerubbabel's hand.
5: 2 "What do you s?" the angel asked. "I s a flying scroll," I replied.
9: 5 The city of Ashkelon will s Tyre fall and will be
10: 7 Their children, too, will s it all and be glad;
Mal 1: 5 When you s the destruction for yourselves,
1: 8 that to your governor, and s how pleased he is!"
3:18 Then you will again s the difference between the
Mt 2: 7 to the wise men, asking them to come s him.
5: 8 those whose hearts are pure, / for they will s God.
5:14 on a mountain, glowing in the night for all to s.
5:16 let your good deeds shine out for all to s,
6: 5 and in the synagogues where everyone can s them.
7: 4 when you can't s past the log in your own eye?
7: 5 then perhaps you will s well enough to deal with
9:28 asked them, "Do you believe I can make you s?"
9:30 And suddenly they could s! Jesus sternly warned
11: 5 the blind s, the lame walk, the lepers are cured,
11: 7 this man in the wilderness that you went out to s?
11: 8 Or were you expecting to s a man dressed in
12:22 healed the man so that he could both speak and s.
13:13 because people s what I do, but they don't really s.
13:14 but you will not understand; / you will s what I do,
13:15 have closed their eyes— / so their eyes cannot s,
13:16 "But blessed are your eyes, because they s;
13:17 many prophets and godly people have longed to s
15:31 and those who had been blind could s again!
16:28 here right now will not die before you s me,
20:33 "Lord," they said, "we want to s!"
20:34 and touched their eyes. Instantly they could s!
21: 2 he said, "and you will s a donkey tied there,
21:19 He went over to s if there were any figs on it,
21:42 This is the Lord's doing, / and it is marvelous to s.'
22: 9 out to the street corners and invite everyone you s.'
23:39 you this, you will never s me again until you say,
24: 2 But he told them, "Do you s all these buildings?
24:15 "The time will come when you will s what Daniel
24:21 the world has ever seen or will ever s again.
24:25 S, I have warned you.
24:30 And they will s the Son of Man arrive on the
24:33 when you s the events I've described beginning to
25:37 when did we ever s you hungry and feed you?
25:39 When did we ever s you sick or in prison, and visit
25:44 when did we ever s you hungry or thirsty or a
26:18 the city," he told them, "you will s a certain man.
26:46 Up, let's be going. S, my betrayer is here!"
26:58 and waited to s what was going to happen to Jesus.
26:64 And in the future you will s me, the Son of Man,
27:49 Let's s whether Elijah will come and save him."
27:62 the leading priests and Pharisees went to s Pilate.
28: 1 and the other Mary went out to s the tomb.
28: 6 would happen. Come, s where his body was lying.
28: 7 You will s him there. Remember, I have told you."
28:10 to leave for Galilee, and they will s me there."
Mk 1: 5 all over Judea traveled out into the wilderness to s
3: 8 and vast numbers of people came to s him for
4:12 'They s what I do, / but they don't perceive its
5:14 they ran. Everyone rushed out to s for themselves.
5:32 But he kept on looking around to s who had done
7:18 "Can't you s that what you eat won't defile you?
8:11 Testing him to s if he was from God,
8:18 'You have eyes—can't you s? You have ears—
8:23 on him and asked, "Can you s anything now?"
8:24 he said, "I s people, but I can't s them very clearly.
8:25 and he could s everything clearly.
9: 1 you s the Kingdom of God arrive in great power!"
10:51 "Teacher," the blind man said, "I want to s!"
10:52 healed you." And instantly the blind man could s!
11: 2 you will s a colt tied there that has never been
11:13 so he went over to s if he could find any figs on it.
12:11 is the Lord's doing, / and it is marvelous to s.' "
13:14 "The time will come when you will s the
13:26 Then everyone will s the Son of Man arrive on the
13:29 when you s the events I've described beginning to
14:42 Up, let's be going. S, my betrayer is here!"
14:62 Jesus said, "I am, and you will s me, the Son of
15:32 from the cross so we can s it and believe him!"
15:36 Let's s whether Elijah will come and take him
16: 7 You will s him there, just as he told you before he
Lk 2:15 Let's s this wonderful thing that has happened,
3: 6 And then all people will s / the salvation sent from
4:18 that captives will be released, / that the blind will s,
6: 7 and the Pharisees watched closely to s whether
6: 8 "Come and stand here where everyone can s."
6:42 when you can't s past the log in your own eye?
6:42 then perhaps you will s well enough to deal with
7:22 the blind s, the lame walk, the lepers are cured,
7:24 this man in the wilderness that you went out to s?
7:25 Or were you expecting to s a man dressed in
8:10 'They s what I do, / but they don't really s;
8:19 when Jesus' mother and brothers came to s him,
8:20 your brothers are outside, and they want to s you."
8:35 for they wanted to s for themselves what had
9: 9 I hear such strange stories?" And he tried to s him.
9:27 will not die before you s the Kingdom of God."
9:31 They were glorious to s. And they were speaking
10:23 "How privileged you are to s what you have seen.
10:24 many prophets and kings have longed to s and hear
11:16 sign from heaven to s if he was from God.
11:38 His host was amazed to s that he sat down to eat
12:54 "When you s clouds beginning to form in the
13: 6 and again to s if there was any fruit on it,
13:28 of teeth, for you will s Abraham, Isaac, Jacob,
13:35 And you will never s me again until you say,
14:28 then checking to s if there is enough money to pay
18: 5 I'm going to s that she gets justice, because she is
18:41 do for you?" "Lord," he pleaded, "I want to s!"
18:42 And Jesus said, "All right, you can s! Your faith
18:43 Instantly the man could s, and he followed Jesus,
19: 3 at Jesus, but he was too short to s over the crowds.
19:30 you will s a colt tied there that has never been
21:20 "And when you s Jerusalem surrounded by
21:26 because of the fearful fate they s coming upon the
21:27 Then everyone will s the Son of Man arrive on the
21:31 when you s the events I've described taking place,
23: 8 Herod was delighted at the opportunity to s Jesus,
23: 8 and had been hoping for a long time to s him
23:48 And when the crowd that came to s the crucifixion
24:24 Some of our men ran out to s, and sure enough,
24:39 You can s that it's really me. Touch me and make
24:39 ghosts don't have bodies, as you s that I do!"
24:40 As he spoke, he held out his hands for them to s,
Jn 1:33 'When you s the Holy Spirit descending
1:39 "Come and s," he said. It was about four o'clock
1:46 "Just come and s for yourself," Philip said.
1:48 "I could s you under the fig tree before Philip
1:50 the fig tree? You will s greater things than this."
1:51 you will all s heaven open and the angels of God
3: 3 born again, you can never s the Kingdom of God."
3:21 so everyone can s that they are doing what God
4:30 So the people came streaming from the village to s
4:40 When they came out to s him, they begged him to
6:22 began gathering on the shore, waiting to s Jesus.
6:40 For it is my Father's will that all who s his Son
6:62 Then what will you think if you s me, the Son of
7: 3 "Go where your followers can s your miracles!"
7:24 Think this through and you will s that I am right."
7:52 Search the Scriptures and s for yourself—
9:11 the mud.' I went and washed, and now I can s!"
9:15 and when it was washed away, I could s!"
9:19 Was he born blind? If so, how can he s?"
9:21 but we don't know how he can s or who healed
9:25 "But I know this: I was blind, and now I can s!"
9:39 and to show those who think they s that they are
9:41 you remain guilty because you claim you can s.
11: 9 They can s because they have the light of this
11:15 to believe in me. Come, let's go s him."
11:28 "The Teacher is here and wants to s you."
11:34 asked them. They told him, "Lord, come and s."
11:36 nearby said, "S how much he loved him."
11:40 "Didn't I tell you that you will s God's glory if
11:56 They wanted to s Jesus, and as they talked in the
12: 9 they flocked to s him and also to s Lazarus,
12:35 in the darkness, you cannot s where you are going.
12:40 hardened their hearts— / so their eyes cannot s,
12:45 For when you s me, you are seeing the one who
14: 9 seen the Father! So why are you asking to s him?
14:19 In just a little while the world will not s me again,
16:10 I go to the Father, and you will s me no more.
16:16 while I will be gone, and you won't s me anymore.
16:16 just a little while after that, you will s me again."
16:17 'You won't s me, and then you will s me'?
16:19 while I will be gone, and you won't s me anymore.
16:19 just a little while after that, you will s me again.
16:20 turn to wonderful joy when you s me again.
16:22 You have sorrow now, but I will s you again;
17:24 given me to be with me, so they can s my glory.
18:26 "Didn't I s you out there in the olive grove with
19:24 "Let's not tear it but throw dice to s who gets it."
20: 3 Peter and the other disciple ran to the tomb to s.
20:20 As he spoke, he held out his hands for them to s,
20:25 "I won't believe it unless I s the nail wounds in his
20:27 to Thomas, "Put your finger here and s my hands.
21: 4 on the beach, but they couldn't s who he was.
Ac 1:10 As they were straining their eyes to s him,
2: 6 they came running to s what it was all about,
2:16 what you s this morning was predicted centuries
2:17 will prophesy, / your young men will s visions,
2:33 to pour out upon us, just as you s and hear today.
4:13 for they could s that they were ordinary men who
7:31 As he went to s, the voice of the Lord called out to
7:56 I s the heavens opened and the Son of Man
8:23 for I can s that you are full of bitterness and held
9:12 laying his hands on him so that he can s again."
10:34 "I s very clearly that God doesn't show partiality.
15:36 to s how the new believers are getting along."
16:27 The jailer woke up to s the prison doors wide open.
17:11 to s if they were really teaching the truth.
20:25 I have preached the Kingdom will ever s me again.
20:38 because he had said that they would never s him
22:13 your sight.' And that very hour I could s him!
22:14 and to s the Righteous One and hear him speak.
23: 9 "We s nothing wrong with him," they shouted.
28:26 but you will not understand; / you will s what I do,
28:27 have closed their eyes— / so their eyes cannot s,
Ro 1:10 God willing, to come at last to s you.
1:13 I want to work among you and s good results,
1:20 They can clearly s his invisible qualities—
2: 4 Can't you s how kind he has been in giving you
3: 5 for people will s God's goodness when he declares
5:20 so that all people could s how sinful they were.
7:13 So we can s how terrible sin really is.
7:25 is in Jesus Christ our Lord. So you s how it is:
9:18 So you s, God shows mercy to some just
11: 8 very day he has shut their eyes so they do not s,
11:10 Let their eyes go blind so they cannot s, / and let
12:17 Do things in such a way that everyone can s you
15:21 who have never been told about him will s,
15:26 For you s, the believers in Greece have eagerly
15:28 of theirs, I will come to s you on my way to Spain.
16: 1 church in Cenchrea, will be coming to s you soon.
16:19 I want you to s clearly what is right and to stay
1Co 3:13 day to s what kind of work each builder has done.
3:13 Everyone's work will be put through the fire to s
8:10 You s, this is what can happen: Weak Christians
8:10 this food will s you eating in the temple of an idol.
13:12 Now we s things imperfectly as in a poor mirror,
13:12 then we will s everything with perfect clarity.
14:22 So you s that speaking in tongues is a sign, not for
15:21 So you s, just as death came into the world through
2Co 1:16 wanted to stop and s you on my way to Macedonia
2:17 You s, we are not like those hucksters—and there
3:13 so the people of Israel would not s the glory fading
4: 4 so they are unable to s the glorious light of the
4: 7 So everyone can s that our glorious power is from
4:18 So we don't look at the troubles we can s right
4:18 For the troubles we s will soon be over,
7:11 Just s what this godly sorrow produced in you!
7:11 such alarm, such longing to s me, such zeal,
7:13 we were especially delighted to s how happy Titus
8:17 In fact, he himself was eager to go and s you.
12: 6 of me than what they can actually s in my life
13: 5 Examine yourselves to s if your faith is really
Gal 2: 4 to spy on us and s our freedom in Christ Jesus.
3: 1 For you used to s the meaning of Jesus Christ's
Eph 3:10 They will s this when Jews and Gentiles are joined
Php 1:27 whether I come and s you again or only hear about
2:24 the Lord that I myself will come to s you soon.
2:26 him home again, for he has been longing to s you,
2:28 for I know you will be glad to s him, and that will
4: 1 and sisters, I love you and long to s you,
4: 5 Let everyone s that you are considerate in all you
Col 1:16 He made the things we can s and the things we can see and the things we can't s—
1Th 2: 3 So you can s that we were not preaching with any
2:17 because of our intense longing to s you again.
3: 6 you want to s us just as much as we want to s you.
3:10 asking God to let us s you again to fill up anything
5:15 S that no one pays back evil for evil, but always try
1Ti 4:15 your tasks so that everyone will s your progress.
2Ti 1: 4 I long to s you again, for I remember your tears as
Tit 3:13 S that they are given everything they need.
Heb 2: 9 What we do s is Jesus, who "for a little while was
3:19 So we s that they were not allowed to enter his rest
11: 1 It is the evidence of things we cannot yet s.
11: 3 that what we now s did not come from anything
11: 6 So, you s, it is impossible to please God without
12:14 for those who are not holy will not s the Lord.
12:25 S to it that you obey God, the one who is speaking
13:23 here soon, I will bring him with me to s you.
Jas 1:24 You s yourself, walk away, and forget what you
2:15 Suppose you s a brother or sister who needs food
2:17 So you s, it isn't enough just to have faith.
2:18 "I can't s your faith if you don't have good deeds,
2:22 You s, he was trusting God so much that he was
2:24 So you s, we are made right with God by what we
5:11 From his experience we s how the Lord's plan
1Pe 1: 5 It will be revealed on the last day for all to s.
1: 8 Though you do not s him, you trust him; and even
1:20 final days, he was sent to the earth for all to s.
1:22 So s to it that you really do love each other
2:12 they will s your honorable behavior, and they will
3:16 they will be ashamed when they s what a good life
2Pe 2: 9 So you s, the Lord knows how to rescue godly
1Jn 2:16 the lust for everything we s, and pride in our
3: 1 S how very much our heavenly Father loves us,
3: 2 will be like him, for we will s him as he really is.
4: 1 You must test them to s if the spirit they have
4:20 for if we don't love people we can s, how can we
5:16 If you s any Christian sinning in a way that does
3Jn 1:14 For I hope to s you soon, and then we will talk face
Rev 1: 7 And everyone will s him—even those who pierced
1:11 It said, "Write down what you s, and send it to the
1:12 When I turned to s who was speaking to me,
2:19 And I can s your constant improvement in all these
3:18 buy ointment for your eyes so you will be able to s.
9:20 and wood—idols that neither s nor hear nor walk!
17: 6 I could s that she was drunk—drunk with the blood
18: 9 they s the smoke rising from her charred remains.
22: 4 And they will s his face, and his name will be
22:12 "S, I am coming soon, and my reward is with me,

SEED (55) [SEED-BEARING, SEEDLING, SEEDLINGS, SEEDS]

Ge 47:23 I will provide you with s, so you can plant the
Ex 16:31 It was white like coriander s, and it tasted like
Lev 11:37 If the dead body falls on s grain to be planted in
11:37 in the field, the s will still be considered clean.
11:38 But if the s is wet when the dead body falls on it, the s will be defiled.
19:19 Do not plant your field with two kinds of s.
25:22 As you plant the s in the eighth year, you will still
27:16 its value will be assessed by the amount of s
27:16 for an area that produces five bushels of barley s.
Dt 11:10 where you planted your s and dug out irrigation
Ps 126: 6 They weep as they go to plant their s, / but they
Isa 5:10 Ten measures of s will yield only one measure of
6:13 but the stump will be a holy s that will grow
32:20 Wherever they plant s, bountiful crops will spring
55:10 producing s for the farmer and bread for the
Jer 4: 3 Do not waste your good s among thorns.

Eze 17:23 sending forth its branches and producing s.
Hag 2:19 I am giving you a promise now while the s is still
Mt 13: 3 as this one: "A farmer went out to plant some s.
13:19 The s that fell on the hard path represents those
13:19 and snatches the s away from their hearts.
13:24 is like a farmer who planted good s in his field.
13:27 the field where you planted that good s is full of
13:31 "The Kingdom of Heaven is like a mustard s
13:37 Son of Man, am the farmer who plants the good s.
13:38 and the good s represents the people of the
17:20 even if you had faith as small as a mustard s you
Mk 4: 3 "Listen! A farmer went out to plant some s.
4: 4 some s fell on a footpath, and the birds came
4: 5 Other s fell on shallow soil with underlying rock.
4: 7 Other s fell among thorns that shot up and choked
4: 8 Still other s fell on fertile soil and produced a crop
4:15 The s that fell on the hard path represents those
4:31 It is like a tiny mustard s. Though this is one of the
Lk 8: 5 "A farmer went out to plant some s. As he
8: 5 some s fell on a footpath, where it was stepped on,
8: 6 Other s fell on shallow soil with underlying rock.
8: 6 This s began to grow, but soon it withered and died
8: 7 Other s fell among thorns that shot up and choked
8: 8 Still other s fell on fertile soil. This s grew and produced a crop one hundred
8:11 the meaning of the story: The s is God's message.
8:12 The s that fell on the hard path represents those
13:19 It is like a tiny mustard s planted in a garden;
17: 6 "Even if you had faith as small as a mustard s,"
Jn 12:24 the soil. Unless it dies it will be alone—a single s.
1Co 3: 6 My job was to plant the s in your hearts,
3: 7 because he is the one who makes the s grow.
9:11 We have planted good spiritual s among you.
15:36 When you put a s into the ground, it doesn't grow
15:37 but only a dry little s of wheat or whatever it is you
15:38 different kind of plant grows from each kind of s.
2Co 9:10 For God is the one who gives s to the farmer
Heb 7:10 the s from which he came was in Abraham's loins

SEED-BEARING (4) [BEAR, SEED]

Ge 1:11 burst forth with every sort of grass and s plant.
1:11 And let there be trees that grow s fruit. The seeds
1:12 The land was filled with s plants and trees,
1:29 I have given you the s plants throughout the earth

SEEDLING (1) [SEED]

Job 14: 9 of water it may bud and sprout again like a new s.

SEEDLINGS (1) [SEED]

Eze 17: 5 "Then he planted one of its s in fertile ground

SEEDS (23) [SEED]

Ge 1:11 The s will then produce the kinds of plants
1:12 and their s produced plants and trees of like kind.
Lev 25:11 do not plant any s or store away any of the crops
Nu 6: 4 from a grapevine, not even the grape s or skins.
11: 7 The manna looked like small coriander s,
Pr 16:28 A troublemaker plants s of strife; gossip separates
22: 8 Those who plant s of injustice will harvest disaster,
Isa 28:25 Does he not finally plant his s for dill, cumin,
Hos 10:12 I said, 'Plant the good s of righteousness, and you
Joel 1:17 The s die in the parched ground, and the grain
Zec 8:12 For I am planting s of peace and prosperity among
10: 9 Though I have scattered them like s among the
Mt 13: 4 some s fell on a footpath, and the birds came
13: 5 Other s fell on shallow soil with underlying rock.
13: 7 Other s fell among thorns that shot up and choked
13: 8 But some s fell on fertile soil and produced a crop
13:32 It is the smallest of all s, but it becomes the largest
Mk 4:26 of God is like: A farmer planted s in a field,
4:27 the s sprouted and grew without the farmer's help,
4:31 Though this is one of the smallest of s,
1Co 15:39 And just as there are different kinds of s
2Co 9: 6 a farmer who plants only a few s will get a small
Jas 3:18 And those who are peacemakers will plant s of

SEEING (18) [SEE]

Ge 33:10 your friendly smile. It is like s the smile of God!
1Sa 1:13 S her lips moving but hearing no sound, he thought
26:12 and Abishai got away without anyone s them
Pr 21:11 A simpleton can learn only by s mockers punished;
Eze 13:23 But you will no longer talk of s visions that you
Hos 9:10 it was like s the first ripe figs of the season!
Mt 9: 2 S their faith, Jesus said to the paralyzed man,
16:23 You are s things merely from a human point of
Mk 2: 5 S their faith, Jesus said to the paralyzed man,
8:33 You are s things merely from a human point of
Lk 5:20 S their faith, Jesus said to the man, "Son, your sins
24:37 terribly frightened, thinking they were s a ghost!
Jn 9: 7 So the man went and washed, and came back s!
11:57 that anyone s Jesus must report him immediately
12:45 when you see me, you are s the one who sent me.
1Co 16:11 I am looking forward to s him soon, along with the
16:12 He will be s you later, when the time is right.
2Co 5: 7 That is why we live by believing and not by s.

SEEK (57) [SEEKING, SEEKS, SOUGHT]

Ex 18:15 the people come to me to s God's guidance.
Lev 19:18 "Never s revenge or bear a grudge against anyone,
Dt 12: 5 you must s the LORD your God at the place he
Jos 20: 3 for the relatives may s to avenge the killing.
1Sa 25:29 "Even when you are chased by those who s your
2Sa 17: 3 After all, it is only this man's life that you s.
2Ki 22:18 "But go to the king of Judah who sent you to s the
1Ch 22:19 Now s the LORD your God with all your heart.
28: 9 and thought. If you s him, you will find him.
2Ch 7:14 and pray and s my face and turn from their wicked
12:14 for he did not s the LORD with all his heart.
14: 4 He commanded the people of Judah to s the
15: 2 Whenever you s him, you will find him. But if you
15:12 Then they entered into a covenant to s the LORD,
15:13 They agreed that anyone who refused to s the
16:12 he did not s the LORD's help but sought help
20: 4 towns of Judah came to Jerusalem to s the LORD.
34: 3 Josiah began to s the God of his ancestor David.
34:26 "But go to the king of Judah who sent you to s the
Job 8: 5 if you pray to God and s the favor of the Almighty,
Ps 10: 4 These wicked people are too proud to s God.
17: 7 those who s refuge from their enemies.
22:26 All who s the LORD will praise him.
27: 4 thing I ask of the LORD— / the thing I s most—
69: 4 These enemies who s to destroy me / are doing
69:32 and be glad. / Let all who s God's help live in joy.
73: 8 only evil; / in their pride they s to crush others.
122: 9 I will s what is best for you, O Jerusalem.
Pr 3: 6 S his will in all you do, and he will direct your
14: 9 but the godly acknowledge it and s reconciliation.
17:11 Evil people s rebellion, but they will be severely
28: 7 those who s out worthless companions bring shame
29:10 hate the honest, but the upright s out the honest.
29:26 Many s the ruler's favor, but justice comes from
Ecc 2: 2 "What good does it do to s only pleasure?"
Isa 1:17 Learn to do good. S justice. Help the oppressed.
26: 9 night long I search for you; / earnestly I s for God.
51: 1 who hope for deliverance—all who s the LORD!
55: 6 S the LORD while you can find him. Call on him
Jer 22:25 I will hand you over to those who s to kill you,
29:13 for me in earnest, you will find me when you s me.
La 3:25 good to those who wait for him and s him.
Eze 33:31 their mouths, but their hearts s only after money.
Da 9:13 But we have refused to s mercy from the LORD
Hos 10:12 for now is the time to s the LORD, that he may
Zep 1: 6 ask for the LORD's guidance or s my blessings."
Zec 7: 2 along with their men, to s the LORD's favor.
8:21 LORD to bless us and to s the LORD Almighty.
8:22 will come to Jerusalem to s the LORD Almighty
Lk 19:10 have come to s and save those like him who are
Jn 7:18 but those who s to honor the one who sent them are
Ac 17:27 in all of this was that the nations should s after God
2Co 7:10 lives to help us turn away from sin and s salvation.
Gal 2:17 But what if we s to be made right with God
Heb 11: 6 and that he rewards those who sincerely s him.
12:14 with everyone, and s to live a clean and holy life,
Rev 9: 6 In those days people will s death but will not find

SEEKING (17) [SEEK]

Lev 14: 2 those s purification from a contagious skin disease.
Jdg 20:27 And the Israelites went up s direction from the
1Ch 4:39 part of the valley, s pastureland for their flocks.
2Ch 19: 3 and you have committed yourself to s God."
Ps 8: 2 They silence your enemies / who were s revenge.
Ecc 2: 3 While still s wisdom, I clutched at foolishness.
Jer 25:38 He has left his den like a lion s its prey, and their
45: 5 Are you s great things for yourself? Don't do it!
50: 4 "weeping and s the LORD their God.
Da 11:27 S nothing but each other's harm, these kings will
Zep 3: 4 Its prophets are arrogant liars s their own gain.
Mal 3: 1 Then the Lord you are s will suddenly come to his
Mt 12:43 it goes into the desert, s rest but finding none.
Jn 6:27 Spend your energy s the eternal life that I, the Son
Ro 2: 7 s after the glory and honor and immortality that
3:11 No one has real understanding; / no one is s God.
9:30 God by faith, even though they were not s him.

SEEKS (7) [SEEK]

Job 34: 8 He s the companionship of evil people. He spends
Ps 14: 2 one with real understanding, / one who s for God.
53: 2 one with real understanding, / one who s for God.
Pr 14: 6 A mocker s wisdom and never finds it,
Mt 7: 8 who asks, receives. Everyone who s, finds.
Lk 11:10 who asks, receives. Everyone who s, finds.
Ro 2:29 Whoever has that kind of change s praise from

SEEM (29) [SEEMED, SEEMS]

Ex 7: 1 I will make you s like God to Pharaoh.
Nu 16: 9 Does it s a small thing to you that the God of Israel
2Sa 19: 6 You s to love those who hate you and hate those
Job 8:16 The godless s so strong, like a lush plant growing
Ps 10: 4 to seek God. / They s to think that God is dead.
73: 4 They s to live such a painless life; / their bodies are
Pr 17:28 they keep their mouths shut, they s intelligent.
Ecc 6: 7 for food, but they never s to have enough.
Isa 24:23 brightness of the sun and moon will s to fade away.
40:22 The people below must s to him like grasshoppers!
58: 2 Temple every day and s delighted to hear my laws.
Jer 13:13 in this land so confused that they will s drunk—
Eze 16:51 sisters ever did. They s righteous compared to you!
16:52 In comparison, you make your sisters s innocent!
Hag 2: 3 it look to you now? It must s like nothing at all!
Zec 8: 6 All this may s impossible to you now, a small
Mt 19:30 But many who s to be important now will be the
Mk 10:31 But many who s to be important now will be the
Lk 10:40 doesn't it s unfair to you that my sister just sits
24:17 "You s to be in a deep discussion about
Ac 25:27 For it doesn't s reasonable to send a prisoner to the
26: 8 Why does it s incredible to any of you that God
1Co 12:22 some of the parts that s weakest and least
2Co 10: 8 I may s to be boasting too much about the
11: 4 You s to believe whatever anyone tells you,
13: 7 to do right even if we ourselves s to have failed.
Col 2:23 These rules may s wise because they require strong
1Ti 1: 7 are talking about, even though they s so confident.
Heb 5:11 But you don't s to listen, so it's hard to make you

SEEMED (22) [SEEM]

Ge 29:20 her was so strong that it s to him but a few days.
Ex 24:10 Under his feet there s to be a pavement of brilliant
Dt 1:23 This s like a good idea to me, so I chose twelve
Jdg 17: 6 so the people did whatever s right in their own
21:25 so the people did whatever s right in their own
1Sa 7: 2 because it s that the LORD had abandoned them.
2Sa 13: 2 and it s impossible that he could ever fulfill his
16:23 For every word Ahithophel spoke s as wise as
17: 4 This plan s good to Absalom and to all the other
2Ch 30: 4 This plan for keeping the Passover s right to the
Ps 73:22 I must have s like a senseless animal to you.
Isa 22:25 time comes, I will pull out the stake that s so firm.
Eze 8: 3 He put out what s to be a hand and took me by the
Da 7:20 This was the horn that s greater than the others
Na 3: 9 the source of her strength, which s without limit.
Lk 5:17 (It s that these men showed up from every village
Ac 15:25 So it s good to us, having unanimously agreed on
15:28 "For it s good to the Holy Spirit and to us to lay no
17:21 s to spend all their time discussing the latest ideas.)
Ro 4:18 even though such a promise s utterly impossible!
Rev 13: 3 I saw that one of the heads of the beast s wounded
15: 2 I saw before me what s to be a crystal sea mixed

SEEMLY [KJV] See RIGHT

SEEMS (19) [SEEM]

2Sa 15:26 with me, then let him do what s best to him."
Pr 14:12 There is a path before each person that s right,
16:25 There is a path before each person that s right,
17: 8 A bribe s to work like magic for those who give it;
27: 7 Honey s tasteless to a person who is full, but even
Ecc 9: 3 It s so tragic that one fate comes to all. That is why
Isa 49: 4 I replied, "But my work all s so useless! I have
57: 1 their time. And no one s to care or wonder why.
57: 1 No one s to understand that God is protecting them
Jer 15:18 Your help s as uncertain as a seasonal brook.
Eze 16:28 too. It s you can never find enough new lovers!
Na 2: 9 There s no end to Nineveh's many treasures—
Hab 2: 3 If it s slow, wait patiently, for it will surely take
Lk 5:39 But no one who drinks the old wine s to want the
Ro 7:21 It s to be a fact of life that when I want to do what
1Co 1:22 God's way s foolish to the Jews because they want
16: 4 And if it s appropriate for me also to go along,
2Co 5:13 If it s that we are crazy, it is to bring glory to God.
12:15 even though it s that the more I love you, the less

SEEN (214) [SEE]

Ge 9:14 over the earth, the rainbow will be s in the clouds,
16:13 for she said, "I have s the One who sees me!"
31:12 For I have s all that Laban has done to you.
31:42 But God has s your cruelty and my hard work.
32:30 for he said, "I have s God face to face, yet my life
35:20 over her grave, and it can be s there to this day.
37:16 their flocks," Joseph replied. "Have you s them?"
41:19 I've never s such ugly animals in all the land of
44:28 by some wild animal. I have never s him since.
45:13 Tell him about everything you have s, and bring
46:30 for I have s you with my own eyes and know you
Ex 3: 7 "You can be sure I have s the misery of my people
3: 9 and I have s how the Egyptians have oppressed
3:16 and have s what is happening to you in Egypt.
4:31 And when they realized that the LORD had s
14:13 The Egyptians that you see today will never be s
19: 4 'You have s what I did to the Egyptians. You know
32: 9 "I have s how stubborn and rebellious these
33:23 see me from behind. But my face will not be s."
Nu 13:26 reported to the whole community what they had s
14:22 They have s my glorious presence
27:13 After you have s it, you will die as Aaron your
Dt 1:28 They have even s giants there—the descendants of
3:11 It can still be s in the Ammonite city of Rabbah.)
3:21 'You have s all that the LORD your God has
4: 9 Be very careful never to forget what you have s the
5:24 Today we have s God speaking to humans, and yet
10:21 done mighty miracles that you yourselves have s.
11: 2 your God or s his greatness and awesome power.
11: 7 But you have s all the LORD's mighty deeds with
29: 2 "You have s with your own eyes everything the
29:17 You have s their detestable idols made of wood,
Jos 5:12 manna appeared that day, and it was never s again.
8:29 heap of stones over him that can still be s today.
23: 3 You have s everything the LORD your God has
Jdg 2: 7 those who had s all the great things the LORD
5: 8 the city gates. / Yet not a shield or spear could be s
6:22 I have s the angel of the LORD face to face!"
13:22 to his wife, "We will die, for we have s God!"
18: 9 We have s the land, and it is very good.
1Sa 10: 2 about you and is asking, 'Have you s my son?'
17:25 "Have you s the giant?" the men were asking.
23:22 of where he is staying and who has s him there,
2Sa 17:17 so as not to be s entering and leaving the city.
17:20 asked her, "Have you s Ahimaaz and Jonathan?"
18:21 from Cush, "Go tell the king what you have s."
22:16 of his breath, / the bottom of the sea could be s,
1Ki 8: 8 so long that their ends could be s from the front
2Ki 20: 5 says: I have heard your prayer and s your tears.
1Ch 16:14 our God. / His rule is s throughout the land.
2Ch 5: 9 so long that their ends could be s from the front
30:26 for Jerusalem had not s a celebration like this one

Job 6:21 You have s my calamity, and you are afraid.
7:10 gone forever from their home—never to be s again.
13:1 I have s many instances such as you describe.
27:12 I don't need to, for you yourselves have s all this;
31:7 or if my heart has lusted for what my eyes have s,
36:25 Everyone has s these things, but only from a
38:17 are located? Have you s the gates of utter gloom?
38:22 Have you s where the hail is made and stored?
42:5 but now I have s you with my own eyes.
Ps 12:5 "I have s violence done to the helpless,
18:15 of your breath, / the bottom of the sea could be s,
31:7 your unfailing love, / for you have s my troubles,
35:21 They shout that they have s me doing wrong.
37:25 I am old. / Yet I have never s the godly forsaken,
37:25 nor s their children begging for bread.
37:35 I myself have s it happen— / proud and evil people
48:8 the city's glory, / but now we have s it ourselves—
63:2 I have s you in your sanctuary / and gazed upon
69:19 and disgrace. / You have s all my enemies
73:21 had become, / how pained I had been by all I had s.
92:11 With my own eyes I have s the downfall of my
94:1 O God of vengeance, let your glorious justice be s!
95:9 they courted my wrath though they had s my many
98:3 The whole earth has s the salvation of our God.
105:7 our God. / His rule is s throughout the land.
Pr 7:12 She is often s in the streets and markets,
Ecc 4:3 For they have never s all the evil that is done in our
5:13 There is another serious problem I have s in the
6:1 There is another serious tragedy I have s in our
6:5 and he would never have s the sun or known of its
7:15 In this meaningless life, I have s everything,
8:10 I have s wicked people buried with honor.
10:5 There is another evil I have s as I have watched the
10:7 I have even s servants riding like princes—
SS 3:3 'Have you s him anywhere, this one I love
Isa 6:5 Yet I have s the King, the LORD Almighty!"
38:5 says: I have heard your prayer and s your tears.
48:6 have heard my predictions and s them fulfilled,
57:18 I have s what they do, but I will heal them anyway!
64:4 no ear has heard and no eye has s a God like you,
66:8 Who has ever s or heard of anything as strange as
66:19 sea that have not heard of my fame or s my glory.
Jer 3:6 said to me, "Have you s what fickle Israel does?
14:14 and revelations they have never s or heard.
23:11 I have s their despicable acts right here in my own
La 1:8 for they have s her stripped naked and humiliated.
1:10 She has s foreigners violate her sacred Temple,
3:1 I am the one who has s the afflictions that come
3:59 You have s the wrong they have done to me,
3:60 You have s the plots my enemies have laid against
Eze 3:23 just as I had s it in my first vision by the Kebar
8:4 was there, just as I had s it before in the valley.
8:12 have you s what the leaders of Israel are doing
8:15 "Have you s this?" he asked. "But I will show
8:17 "Have you s this, son of man?" he asked. "Is it
10:15 These were the same living beings I had s beside
10:20 These were the same living beings I had s beneath
10:22 were just like the faces of the beings I had s at the
13:3 their own imaginations and have s nothing at all!
16:50 so I wiped her out, as you have s.
20:22 had s my power in bringing them out of Egypt.
26:16 ground trembling with horror at what they have s.
32:9 remains to distant nations that you have never s,
40:4 of Israel and tell them everything you have s."
43:3 This vision was just like the others I had s, first by
47:6 He told me to keep in mind what I had s, then he
Da 7:15 I, Daniel, was troubled by all I had s, and my
8:6 headed toward the two-horned ram that I had s
8:17 "you must understand that the events you have s in
8:19 What you have s pertains to the very end of time.
9:21 Gabriel, whom I had s in the earlier vision,
10:16 "I am terrified by the vision I have s, my lord,
11:19 but will stumble and fall, and he will be s no more.
Hos 6:10 Yes, I have s a horrible thing in Israel: My people
Joel 2:2 The likes of them have not been s before and never will be s again.
Jnh 1:2 because I have s how wicked its people are."
Mt 2:2 We have s his star as it arose, and we have come to
4:16 people who sat in darkness / have s a great light.
8:10 I haven't s faith like this in all the land of Israel!
11:4 and tell him about what you have heard and s—
13:17 longed to see and hear what you have s and heard,
17:9 "Don't tell anyone what you have s until I, the Son
24:21 of greater horror than anything the world has ever s
Mk 2:12 "We've never s anything like this before!"
5:16 Those who had s what happened to the man
9:9 he told them not to tell anyone what they had s
10:6 But God's plan was s from the beginning of
16:11 told them that Jesus was alive and that she had s him,
16:14 their stubborn refusal to believe those who had s
Lk 1:22 he must have s a vision in the Temple sanctuary.
2:20 and because they had s the child, just as the angel
2:26 he would not die until he had s the Lord's Messiah.
2:30 I have s the Savior
5:26 over again, "We have s amazing things today."
7:9 I haven't s faith like this in all the land of Israel!"
7:16 and "We have s the hand of God at work today."
7:22 to John and tell him what you have s and heard—
8:16 where they can be s by those entering the house.
8:36 Then those who had s what happened told the
9:36 They didn't tell anyone what they had s until long
10:23 "How privileged you are to see what you have s.
10:24 longed to see and hear what you have s and heard,
19:37 God for all the wonderful miracles they had s.
24:23 and they had s angels who told them Jesus is alive!
Jn 1:14 And we have s his glory, the glory of the only Son
1:18 No one has ever s God. But his only Son, who is
1:50 because I told you I had s you under the fig tree?
3:11 I am telling you what we know and have s,
3:32 He tells what he has s and heard, but how few
4:45 and had s all his miraculous signs.
5:37 have never heard his voice or s him face to face,
6:36 haven't believed in me even though you have s me.
6:46 (Not that anyone has ever s the Father; only I, who was sent from God, have s him.)
7:11 at the festival and kept asking if anyone had s him.
8:57 How can you say you have s Abraham?"
9:3 born blind so the power of God could be s in him.
9:37 "You have s him," Jesus said, "and he is
12:17 Those in the crowd who had s Jesus call Lazarus
14:7 From now on you know him and have s him!"
14:9 Anyone who has s me has s the Father! So why
14:11 at least believe because of what you have s me do.
20:18 the disciples and told them, "I have s the Lord!"
20:25 They told him, "We have s the Lord!" But he
20:29 told him, "You believe because you have s me.
20:29 Blessed are those who haven't s me and believe
Ac 3:10 they realized he was the lame beggar they had s
4:20 stop telling about the wonderful things we have s
7:34 You can be sure that I have s the misery of my
9:27 and told them how Saul had s the Lord on the way
19:26 As you have s and heard, this man Paul has
21:29 (For earlier that day they had s him in the city with
22:15 telling the whole world what you have s and heard.
Ro 1:20 people have s the earth and sky and all that God
1Co 2:9 when they say, / "No eye has s, no ear has heard,
9:1 Haven't I s Jesus our Lord with my own eyes?
12:23 the eyes of others those parts that should not be s,
15:5 He was s by Peter and then by the twelve apostles.
15:6 he was s by more than five hundred of his
15:7 Then he was s by James and later by all the
2Co 4:6 glory of God that is s in the face of Jesus Christ.
4:10 so that the life of Jesus may also be s in our bodies.
4:18 rather, we look forward to what we have not yet s.
Php 1:30 You have s me suffer for him in the past, and you
1Ti 3:16 He was s by angels / and was announced to the
6:16 No one has ever s him, nor ever will. To him be
Heb 2:8 is left out. But we have not yet s all of this happen.
11:3 now see did not come from anything that can be s.
1Pe 1:8 You love him even though you have never s him.
2Pe 1:16 We have s his majestic splendor with our own
1Jn 1:1 from the beginning is the one we have heard and s.
1:2 life from God was shown to us, and we have s him.
1:3 you about what we ourselves have actually s
4:12 No one has ever s God. But if we love each other,
4:14 we have s with our own eyes and now testify that
4:20 how can we love God, whom we have not s?
Rev 1:19 Write down what you have s—both the things that
2:2 I have s your hard work and your patient
11:19 and the Ark of his Covenant could be s inside the
21:22 No temple could be s in the city, for the Lord God

SEER (18) [SEER'S, SEERS]

1Sa 9:9 they would say, "Let's go and ask the s,"
9:11 and his servant asked, "Is the s here today?"
9:19 "I am the s!" Samuel replied. "Go on up the hill
2Sa 24:11 came to the prophet Gad, who was David's s.
1Ch 9:22 and Samuel the s had appointed their ancestors
21:9 Then the LORD spoke to Gad, David's s.
25:5 All these were the sons of Heman, the king's s,
26:28 the items dedicated to the LORD by Samuel the s,
29:29 to end, are written in *The Record of Samuel the S,*
29:29 *the Prophet,* and *The Record of Gad the S.*
2Ch 9:29 and also in *The Visions of Iddo the S,* concerning
12:15 and in *The Record of Iddo the S,* which are part
16:7 At that time Hanani the s came to King Asa
19:2 Jehu son of Hanani the s went out to meet him.
29:25 through Gad, the king's s, and the prophet Nathan.
29:30 LORD with the psalms of David and Asaph the s.
35:15 Asaph, Heman, and Jeduthun, the king's s.
Am 7:12 "Get out of here, you s! Go on back to the land of

SEER'S (1) [SEER]

1Sa 9:18 "Can you please tell me where the s house is?"

SEERS (5) [SEER]

1Sa 9:9 and ask the seer," for prophets used to be called s.)
2Ki 17:13 his prophets and s to warn both Israel and Judah:
2Ch 33:18 and the words the s spoke to him in the name of
33:19 *S.* It includes a list of the locations where he built
Mic 3:7 Then you s will cover your faces in shame,

SEES (42) [SEE]

Ge 16:13 to her, as "the God who s me," for she said, "I have seen the One who s me!"
44:31 When he s that the boy is not with us, our father
49:15 When he s how good the countryside is,
Ex 4:14 you now. And when he s you, he will be very glad.
12:23 But when he s the blood on the top and sides of the
Lev 13:10 If the priest s that some hair has turned white
13:15 this pronouncement as soon as he s an open sore
13:21 But if the priest s that there is no white hair in the
13:55 If he s that the affected area has not changed
13:56 But if the priest s that the affected area has faded
14:44 If he s that the affected areas have spread, the walls
Nu 12:8 and not in riddles! He s the LORD as he is.
24:4 words of God, / who s a vision from the Almighty,
24:16 the Most High, / who s a vision from the Almighty,
Dt 32:36 his servants, / when he s their strength is gone
2Sa 15:25 "If the LORD s fit," David said, "he will bring
1Ki 14:13 God of Israel, s in the entire family of Jeroboam.
1Ch 28:9 For the LORD s every heart and understands
Job 31:4 He s everything I do and every step I take.
34:21 the way people live; he s everything they do.
Ps 22:7 Everyone who s me mocks me. / They sneer
33:13 down from heaven / and s the whole human race.
37:13 for he s their day of judgment coming.
97:4 out across the world. / The earth s and trembles.
97:6 his righteousness; / every nation s his glory.
Pr 1:17 When a bird s a trap being set, it stays away.
5:21 For the LORD s clearly what a man does,
24:12 For God knows all hearts, and he s you. He keeps
Ecc 2:14 For the wise person s, while the fool is blind.
Isa 21:6 a watchman on the city wall to shout out what he s.
21:7 Tell him to sound the alert when he s chariots
47:10 'No one s me,' you said. Your 'wisdom'
53:11 When he s all that is accomplished by his anguish,
La 3:50 until the LORD looks down from heaven and s.
Eze 18:14 has a son who s his father's wickedness
33:3 When the watchman s the enemy coming, he blows
33:6 But if the watchman s the enemy coming
Lk 14:10 Then when your host s you, he will come and say,
Jn 5:19 He does only what he s the Father doing.
10:12 A hired hand will run when he s a wolf coming.
1Jn 3:17 and s a brother or sister in need and refuses to

SEGUB (3)

1Ki 16:34 it by setting up the gates, his youngest son, S, died.
1Ch 2:21 the daughter of Makir. They had a son named S.
2:22 S was the father of Jair, who ruled twenty-three

SEIR (38)

Ge 14:6 and the Horites in Mount S, as far as El-paran at
32:3 to his brother, Esau, in Edom, the land of S.
33:14 will follow at our own pace and meet you at S."
33:16 So Esau started back to S that same day.
36:8 known as Edom) settled in the hill country of S.
36:9 the Edomites, who live in the hill country of S.
36:20 of the tribes that descended from S the Horite,
36:20 one of the families native to the land of S:
36:21 These were the Horite clans, the descendants of S,
36:30 after their clan leaders, who lived in the land of S.
Nu 24:18 taken over, / and S, its enemy, will be conquered,
Dt 1:2 Sinai to Kadesh-barnea, going by way of Mount S.
1:44 and battered you all the way from S to Hormah.
2:1 and we wandered around Mount S for a long time.
2:4 the descendants of Esau, who live in S.
2:5 the hill country around Mount S as their property,
2:8 the descendants of Esau, who live in S,
2:12 In earlier times the Horites had lived at Mount S,
2:22 helped the descendants of Esau at Mount S,
2:29 The descendants of Esau at Mount S allowed us to
33:2 and dawned upon us from Mount S; / he shone
Jos 11:17 which leads up to S, to Baal-gad at the foot of
12:7 of Lebanon to Mount Halak, which leads up to S.
15:10 The border circled west of Baalah to Mount S,
24:4 To Esau I gave the hill country of S, while Jacob
Jdg 5:4 "LORD, when you set out from S / and marched
1Ch 1:38 The sons of S were Lotan, Shobal, Zibeon, Anah,
4:42 from the tribe of Simeon went to Mount S,
2Ch 20:10 armies of Ammon, Moab, and Mount S are doing.
20:22 and Mount S to start fighting among themselves.
20:23 Ammon turned against their allies from Mount S
20:23 After they had finished off the army of S,
25:11 they killed ten thousand Edomite troops from S.
25:14 brought with him idols taken from the people of S.
Eze 35:2 "Son of man, turn toward Mount S, and prophesy
35:3 I am your enemy, O Mount S, and I will raise my
35:7 I will make Mount S utterly desolate, killing off all
35:15 you people of Mount S and all who live in Edom!

SEIRAH (1)

Jdg 3:26 Ehud escaped, passing the idols on his way to S.

SEIZE (15) [SEIZED, SEIZES, SEIZING, SEIZURES]

Ge 43:18 Then he will s us as slaves and take our donkeys."
Nu 25:4 "S all the ringleaders and execute them before the
1Ki 13:4 he pointed at the man and shouted, "S that man!"
18:40 Elijah commanded, "S all the prophets of Baal.
2Ki 6:13 where Elisha is, and we will send troops to s him."
Job 13:11 into your heart? Does not your fear of him s you?
Ps 21:8 Your strong right hand will s all those who hate
55:15 Let death s my enemies by surprise; / let the grave
83:12 for they said, "Let us s for our own use
109:11 May creditors s his entire estate, / and strangers
Isa 5:29 They will s my people and carry them off into
22:17 For the LORD is about to s you and hurl you
Jer 50:36 it strikes her mightiest warriors, panic will s them!
Eze 38:13 their cattle and s their goods and make them poor?'
Mic 2:2 want a certain piece of land, you find a way to s it.

SEIZED (18) [SEIZE]

Ge 19:16 the angels s his hand and the hands of his wife
34:28 They s all the flocks and herds and donkeys—
Nu 21:26 and s all his land as far as the Arnon River.
31:9 and children and s their cattle and flocks and all
2Sa 4:10 good news. But I s him and killed him at Ziklag.
10:4 So Hanun s David's ambassadors and shaved off
1Ki 1:51 Word soon reached Solomon that Adonijah had s
18:40 So the people s them all, and Elijah took them
2Ki 11:16 So they s her and led her out to the gate where
1Ch 19:4 So Hanun s David's ambassadors and shaved their
2Ch 23:15 So they s her and led her out to the gate where
25:24 He also s the treasures of the royal palace,
Ps 56:T regarding the time the Philistines s him in Gath.

Jer 38:23 You will be s by the king of Babylon, and this city
48:41 "Her cities will fall; her strongholds will be s.
Mt 22: 6 Others s his messengers and treated them
Ac 23:27 This man was s by the Jews, and they were about
Rev 20: 2 He s the dragon—that old serpent, the Devil,

SEIZES (1) [SEIZE]
Mk 9:18 And whenever this evil spirit s him, it throws him

SEIZING (2) [SEIZE]
Eze 22:25 innocent people, s treasures and extorting wealth.
Lk 9:39 An evil spirit keeps s him, making him scream.

SEIZURES (1) [SEIZE]
Mt 17:15 on my son, because he has s and suffers terribly.

SELA (4) [JOKTHEEL]
Jdg 1:36 of the Amorites ran from Scorpion Pass to S
2Ki 14: 7 He also conquered S and changed its name to
Isa 16: 1 Moab's refugees at S send lambs to Jerusalem as a
42:11 of Kedar rejoice! / Let the people of S sing for joy;

SELA-HAMMAHLEKOTH [KJV] See ROCK (OF ESCAPE)

SELAH [KJV] See INTERLUDE

SELDOM (1)
Ecc 5:12 are always worrying and s get a good night's sleep.

SELECT (9) [SELECTED, SELECTS]
Ge 7: 3 Then s seven pairs of every kind of bird.
Dt 17:15 be sure that you s as king the man the LORD your
21: 3 Then the leaders of that town must s a young cow
Jos 18: 4 S three men from each tribe, and I will send them
1Ki 12:21 armies of Judah and Benjamin—180,000 s troops
2Ki 10: 3 s the best qualified of King Ahab's sons to be your
2Ch 11: 1 armies of Judah and Benjamin—180,000 s troops
Da 1: 4 "S only strong, healthy, and good-looking young
Ac 6: 3 and s seven men who are well respected and are

SELECTED (13) [SELECT]
Ge 24:44 let her be the one you have s to be the wife of my
Lev 27:33 The tenth animal must not be s on the basis of
Dt 1:15 and respected men you had s from your tribes
1Sa 12: 2 I have s him ahead of my own sons, and I stand
13: 2 Saul s three thousand special troops from the army
16: 1 for I have s one of his sons to be my new king."
2Ch 2: 7 of Judah and Jerusalem who were s by my father,
3: 1 of Araunah the Jebusite, the site that David had s.
Ezr 10:16 Ezra s leaders to represent their families,
Est 3: 7 And the day s was March 7, nearly a year later.
Ps 89:19 I have s him from the common people to be king.
Mk 3:14 Then he s twelve of them to be his regular
Ro 9:24 even upon us, whom he s, both from the Jews

SELECTS (1) [SELECT]
Isa 44:14 He cuts down cedars; he s the cypress and the oak;

SELED (2)
1Ch 2:30 sons of Nadab were S and Appaim. S died without

SELEUCIA (1)
Ac 13: 4 and Barnabas went down to the seaport of S

SELF (3) [HERSELF, HIMSELF, ITSELF, MYSELF, ONESELF, OURSELVES, SELFISH, SELFISHNESS, SELVES, THEMSELVES, YOURSELF, YOURSELVES]
Ge 22:16 even your beloved son, I swear by my own s that
Ex 32:13 You swore by your own s, 'I will make your
Job 17: 7 and I am but a shadow of my former s.

SELF-CONDEMNED (1) [CONDEMN]
2Sa 1:16 "You die s," David said, "for you yourself

SELF-CONFIDENCE (1) [CONFIDENCE]
Lk 18: 9 Then Jesus told this story to some who had great s

SELF-CONTROL (15) [CONTROL]
Pr 5:23 He will die for lack of s; he will be lost because of
16:32 it is better to have s than to conquer a city.
25:28 A person without s is as defenseless as a city with
Ac 24:25 and s and the judgment to come,
1Co 7: 5 be able to tempt them because of their lack of s.
9:25 All athletes practice strict s. They do it to win a
Gal 5:23 gentleness, and s. Here there is no conflict with the
1Ti 3: 2 He must exhibit s, live wisely, and have a good
3:11 They must exercise s and be faithful in everything
2Ti 3: 3 they will slander others and have no s;
Tit 2: 2 Teach the older men to exercise s, to be worthy of
2:12 We should live in this evil world with s,
1Pe 1:13 So think clearly and exercise s. Look forward to
2Pe 1: 6 Knowing God leads to s. S leads to patient endurance, and patient endurance

SELF-DENIAL (1) [DENY]
Col 2:18 Don't let anyone condemn you by insisting on s.

SELF-DESTRUCTIVE (1) [DESTROY]
Jer 8: 5 Then why do these people keep going along their s

SELF-DISCIPLINE (1) [DISCIPLINE]
2Ti 1: 7 of fear and timidity, but of power, love, and s.

SELF-IMPORTANT (1) [IMPORTANT]
Pr 12: 9 is better to be a nobody with a servant than to be s

SELF-INDULGENCE (1) [INDULGE]
Mt 23:25 but inside you are filthy—full of greed and s!

SELF-INDULGENT (1) [INDULGE]
Pr 18: 1 A recluse is s, snarling at every sound principle of

SELF-SUFFICIENT (3) [SUFFICIENT]
Isa 47: 8 You say, 'I'm s and not accountable to anyone!
47:10 and claim, 'I am s and not accountable to anyone!'
Jer 49:31 "Go up and attack those s nomadic tribes,"

SELFISH (10) [SELF]
1Sa 30:23 Don't be s with what the LORD has given us.
Jer 22:17 "But you! You are full of s greed and dishonesty!
Mt 16:24 you must put aside your s ambition, shoulder your
Mk 8:34 he told them, "you must put aside your s ambition,
Lk 9:23 you must put aside your s ambition, shoulder your
Gal 5:20 jealousy, outbursts of anger, s ambition, divisions,
Php 1:17 They preach with s ambition, not sincerely,
2: 3 Don't be s; don't live to make a good impression
Jas 3:14 and there is s ambition in your hearts,
3:16 For wherever there is jealousy and s ambition,

SELFISHNESS (2) [SELF]
2Co 12:20 outbursts of anger, s, backstabbing, gossip, conceit,
Jas 3:15 For jealousy and s are not God's kind of wisdom.

SELFSAME [KJV] See SAME, THAT, VERY

SELL (38) [RESOLD, SALE, SELLER, SELLERS, SELLING, SELLS, SOLD]
Ge 37:27 Let's s Joseph to those Ishmaelite traders. Let's not
47:22 food from Pharaoh and didn't need to s their land.
Ex 21: 8 But he is not allowed to s her to foreigners,
21:35 then the two owners must s the live bull and divide
Lev 25:14 an agreement with a neighbor to buy or s property,
25:25 and are forced to s some inherited land,
25:39 relatives go bankrupt and s themselves to you,
25:47 go bankrupt and s themselves to such a foreigner,
27:27 the priest may s it to someone else for its assessed
Dt 14:21 living among you, or you may s it to a foreigner.
14:25 you may s the tithe portion of your crops and herds
21:14 You may not s her or treat her as a slave, for you
28:68 There you will offer to s yourselves to your
1Ki 21: 6 "I asked Naboth to s me his vineyard or to trade it,
21:15 "You know the vineyard Naboth wouldn't s you?
2Ki 4: 7 to her, "Now s the olive oil and pay your debts,
Ne 5: 5 Yet we must s our children into slavery just to get
5: 8 who have had to s themselves to pagan foreigners,
13:15 figs, and all sorts of produce to Jerusalem to s.
Job 6:27 even send an orphan into slavery or s a friend.
41: 6 try to buy it? Will they s it in their shops?
Pr 23:23 Get the truth and don't ever s it; also get wisdom,
31:24 linen garments and sashes to s to the merchants.
Isa 50: 1 "Did I s you as slaves to my creditors?
Jer 32:15 and will buy and s houses and vineyards
Hos 2: 5 and s myself to them for food and drink,
Joel 3: 8 I will s your sons and daughters to the people of
3: 8 and they will s them to the peoples of Arabia,
Am 8: 6 And you mix the wheat you s with chaff swept
Zep 1:11 market area, for all who buy and s there will die.
Mt 19:21 go and s all you have and give the money to the
Mk 10:21 "Go and s all you have and give the money to the
Lk 12:33 "S what you have and give to those in need.
18:22 "S all you have and give the money to the poor,
22:36 don't have a sword, s your clothes and buy one!
Ac 5: 4 The property was yours to s or not s, as you
Rev 13:17 no one could buy or s anything without that mark,

SELLER (2) [SELL]
Lev 25:15 The s will charge you only for the crop years left
25:29 that time, the s retains the right to buy it back.

SELLERS (3) [SELL]
Isa 24: 2 buyers and s, lenders and borrowers, bankers
Eze 7:12 they find or for s to grieve over their losses,
Zec 11: 5 The s will say, 'Praise the LORD, I am now rich!'

SELLING (18) [SELL]
Ge 25:33 thereby s all his rights as the firstborn to his
Lev 25:16 the person s the land is actually s you a
Ru 4: 3 She is s the land that belonged to our relative
Ne 5: 8 but you are s them back into slavery again.
13:15 So I rebuked them for s their produce on the
13:16 They were s it on the Sabbath to the people of
Pr 6:31 even if it means s everything in his house to pay it
Hos 12: 7 the people are like crafty merchants s from
Am 1: 6 my people into exile, s them as slaves in Edom.
1: 9 with Israel, s whole villages as slaves to Edom.
2: 6 They have perverted justice by s honest people for
Mt 21:12 the money changers and the stalls of those s doves.
Mk 11:15 the money changers and the stalls of those s doves,
Lk 17:28 and drinking, buying and s, farming and building—
Jn 2:14 In the Temple area he saw merchants s cattle,
Ac 5: 4 And after s it, the money was yours to give away.
Rev 18:15 The merchants who became wealthy by s her these

SELLS (5) [SELL]
Ex 21: 7 "When a man s his daughter as a slave, she will
22: 1 who steals an ox or sheep and then kills or s it.
Lev 25:29 "Anyone who s a house inside a walled city has
Dt 24: 7 a fellow Israelite and treats him as a slave or s him,
Pr 11:26 but they bless the one who s to them in their time

SELVEDGE [KJV] See EDGE

SELVES (1) [SELF]
Ro 6: 6 Our old sinful s were crucified with Christ so that

SEM [KJV] See SHEM

SEMAKIAH (1)
1Ch 26: 7 Their relatives, Elihu and S, were also very

SEMEIN (2)
Lk 3:26 Mattathias was the son of S. / S was the son of

SEMEN (5)
Ge 38: 9 he spilled the s on the ground to keep her from
Lev 15:16 "Whenever a man has an emission of s, he must
15:17 or leather that comes in contact with the s must be
15:32 defiled by a genital discharge or an emission of s;
22: 4 a corpse, or are defiled by an emission of s,

SENAAH (2)
Ezr 2:35 The citizens of S | 3,630
Ne 7:38 The citizens of S | 3,930

SENATE [KJV] See HIGH COUNCIL

SEND (291) [SENDING, SENDS, SENT]
Ge 9:11 I solemnly promise never to s another flood to kill
9:14 When I s clouds over the earth, the rainbow will be
24: 7 He will s his angel ahead of you, and he will see to
24:40 will s his angel with you and will make your
24:54 next morning, he said, "S me back to my master."
27:45 he forgets what you have done, I will s for you.
37:13 I'm going to s you to them." "I'm ready to go,"
38:17 "I'll s you a young goat from my flock,"
38:17 will you give me so I can be sure you will s it?"
38:23 "We tried our best to s her the goat.
43: 8 Judah said to his father, "S the boy with me,
Ex 4:13 again pleaded, "Lord, please! S someone else."
5:22 own people like this, Lord? Why did you s me?
8: 2 I will s vast hordes of frogs across your entire land
8:21 I will s swarms of flies throughout Egypt.
9: 3 the LORD will s a deadly plague to destroy your
9: 5 The LORD announced that he would s the plague
9:14 I will s a plague that will really speak to you
9:18 So tomorrow at this time I will s a hailstorm worse
11: 1 "I will s just one more disaster on Pharaoh
23:27 "I will s my terror upon all the people whose lands
23:28 I will s hornets ahead of you to drive out the
33: 2 And I will s an angel before you to drive out the
33:12 But you haven't told me whom you will s with me.
Lev 16:21 then he will s it out into the wilderness, led by a
16:26 "The man chosen to s the goat out into the
26: 4 I will s the seasonal rains. The land will then yield
26:25 I will s armies against you to carry out these
26:25 to your cities, I will s a plague to destroy you there,
26:36 of a leaf driven by the wind will s you fleeing.
Nu 13: 2 "S men to explore the land of Canaan, the land I
13: 2 S one leader from each of the twelve ancestral
22:37 "Did I not s you an urgent invitation? Why didn't
31: 4 tribe of Israel, s one thousand men into battle."
35:25 and they must s the slayer back to live in a city of
Dt 1:22 'First, let's s out scouts to explore the land for us.
7:20 then the LORD your God will s hornets to drive
11:14 then he will s the rains in their proper seasons
11:25 for the LORD your God will s fear and dread
15:13 a male servant, do not s him away empty-handed.
17:16 and he must never s his people to Egypt to buy
28:12 The LORD will s rain at the proper time from his
28:20 "The LORD himself will s against you curses,
28:21 The LORD will s diseases among you until none
28:48 your enemies whom the LORD will s against you.
28:68 Then the LORD will s you back to Egypt in ships,
29:22 and the diseases the LORD will s against it.
32:24 I will s against them wasting famine,
Jos 1:16 command us, and we will go wherever you s us.
18: 4 and I will s them out to survey the unconquered
Jdg 7: 7 over the Midianites. S all the others home."
8: 1 Why didn't you s for us when you first went out to
1Sa 2:13 Eli's sons would s over a servant with a
5:11 "Please s the Ark of the God of Israel back to its
6: 3 "S the Ark of the God of Israel back, along with a
6: 3 "S a guilt offering so the plague will stop. Then,
6: 3 you will know that God didn't s the plague after
6: 4 "What sort of guilt offering should we s?"
6:20 cried out. "Where can we s the Ark from here?"
9:16 "About this time tomorrow I will s you a man
9:19 what you want to know and s you on your way.
9:27 Samuel told Saul to s his servant on ahead.
11: 3 "Give us seven days to s messengers throughout

12:17 I will ask the LORD to s thunder and rain today.
16:11 "S for him at once," Samuel said. "We will not
16:19 to say, "S me your son David, the shepherd."
17:10 of Israel! S me a man who will fight with me!"
18:17 "I'll s him out against the Philistines and let them
20:21 Then I will s a boy to bring the arrows back.
29: 4 "S him back!" they demanded. "He can't go into
2Sa 11: 6 sent word to Joab: "S me Uriah the Hittite."
14:19 "Did Joab s you here?" And the woman replied,
15:36 and they will s their sons Ahimaaz and Jonathan to
18: 3 stay here in the city and s us help if we need it."
1Ki 8:36 and s rain on your land that you have given to your
18: 1 to King Ahab. Tell him that I will soon s rain!"
20: 6 But about this time tomorrow I will s my officials
22:17 master has been killed. S them home in peace.' "
2Ki 1:16 Why did you s messengers to Baal-zebub, the god
2:16 some valley." "No," Elisha said, "don't s them."
2:17 and he finally said, "All right, s them."
4:22 "S one of the servants and a donkey so that I can
5: 5 "I will s a letter of introduction for you to carry to
5: 8 S Naaman to me, and he will learn that there is a
6:10 So the king of Israel would s word to the place
6:13 Elisha is, and we will s troops to seize him."
6:22 and drink and s them home again to their master."
7:13 "We had better s out scouts to check into this.
9:17 "S out a rider to find out if they are coming in
15:37 In those days the LORD began to s King Rezin of
17:27 "S one of the exiled priests from Samaria back to
21: 8 I will not s them into exile from this land that I
22:20 I will not s the promised disaster against this city
1Ch 13: 2 let us s messages to all the Israelites throughout the
2Ch 2: 3 "S me cedar logs like the ones that were supplied
2: 7 "So s me a master craftsman who can work with
2: 8 Also s me cedar, cypress, and almug logs from
2: 8 at cutting timber. I will s my men to help them.
2:15 "S along the wheat, barley, olive oil, and wine that
6:27 and s rain on your land that you have given to your
7:13 your crops, or I might s plagues among you.
18:16 master has been killed. S them home in peace.' "
33: 8 I will not s them into exile from this land that I
34:28 I will not s the promised disaster against this city
36:22 into writing and to s it throughout his kingdom:
Ezr 1: 1 into writing and to s it throughout his kingdom:
5:17 then let the king s us his decision in this matter."
7:21 hereby s this decree to all the treasurers in the
8:17 and the Temple servants to s us ministers for the
10: 3 and to s them away with their children.
Ne 2: 5 s me to Judah to rebuild the city where my
2: 8 And please s a letter to Asaph, the manager of the
Est 8: 5 s out a decree reversing Haman's orders to destroy
8: 8 and s a message to the Jews in the king's name,
9:19 when they rejoice and s gifts to each other.
Job 6:27 You would even s an orphan into slavery or sell a
9:28 I would dread all the pain he would s. For I know
14:20 You disfigure them in death and s them away.
30:12 They s me sprawling; they lay traps in my path.
Ps 20: 2 May he s you help from his sanctuary
43: 3 S out your light and your truth; / let them guide
55:23 But you, O God, will s the wicked / down to the pit
57: 3 He will s help from heaven to save me,
57: 3 My God will s forth his unfailing love
73:18 and s them sliding over the cliff to destruction.
86:17 S me a sign of your favor. / Then those who hate
104:13 You s rain on the mountains from your heavenly
104:20 You s the darkness, and it becomes night,
104:30 When you s your Spirit, new life is born
109: 6 to turn on him. / S an accuser to bring him to trial.
Isa 3:17 The Lord will s a plague of scabs to ornament their
5:13 So I will s my people into exile far away
5:26 He will s a signal to the nations far away. He will
6: 8 "Whom should I s as a messenger to my people?
6: 8 will go for us?" And I said, "Lord, I'll go! S me."
10: 3 What will you do when I s desolation upon you
10:16 will s a plague among your proud troops,
16: 1 Moab's refugees at Sela s lambs to Jerusalem as a
19:20 he will s them a savior who will rescue them.
22:17 He is going to s you into captivity, you strong
28: 2 For the Lord will s the mighty Assyrian army
31: 2 In his wisdom, the LORD will s great disaster;
43:14 "For your sakes I will s an invading army against
48:15 I will s him on this errand and will help him
55:11 my word. I s it out, and it always produces fruit.
55:11 I want it to, and it will prosper everywhere I s it.
60:10 rebuild your cities. Kings and rulers will s you aid.
66: 4 I will s great troubles against them—all the things
66:19 And I will s those who survive to be messengers to
Jer 1: 7 "for you must go wherever I s you and say
4: 6 S a signal toward Jerusalem: 'Flee now! Do not
6: 1 alarm in Tekoa! S up a signal at Beth-hakkerem!
7:15 And I will s you into exile, just as I did your
7:25 until now, I have continued to s my prophets—
8: 3 wish to die rather than live where I will s them.
8:17 "I will s these enemy troops among you like
14: 3 The nobles s servants to get water, but all the wells
14:13 The LORD will surely s you peace.' "
14:14 I did not s them or tell them to speak. I did not give
14:22 Can any of the foreign gods s us rain? Does it fall
15: 3 "I will s four kinds of destroyers against them,"
15: 3 "I will s the sword to kill, the dogs to drag away,
16: 7 No one will s a cup of wine to console them.
16:13 this land and s you away into a foreign land where you
17: 4 and I will s you away as captives to a foreign land.
17:16 I have not urged you to s disaster. It is your
20: 4 I will s terror upon you and all your friends,
21: 6 I will s a terrible plague upon this city, and both
23: 1 "I will s disaster upon the leaders of my people—
23:32 I did not s or appoint them, and they have no
24: 9 taunted and cursed, wherever I s them.
24:10 I will s war, famine, and disease until they have
25:15 and make all the nations to whom I s you drink
25:16 crazed by the warfare I will s against them."
27: 3 Then s messages to the kings of Edom, Moab,
27: 8 I will s war, famine, and disease upon that nation
27:10 you from your land and s you far away to die.
27:22 to Babylon and will stay there until I s for them,
29:17 "I will s war, famine, and disease upon them
29:18 In every nation where I s them, I will make them
29:31 "S an open letter to all the exiles in Babylon.
29:31 Since he has prophesied to you when I did not s
35:17 I will s upon Judah and Jerusalem all the disasters I
37:20 Don't s me back to the dungeon in the house of
38:26 just tell them you begged me not to s you back to
39:16 I will s disaster, not prosperity. You will see its
42: 6 we will obey the LORD our God to whom we s
48:12 "when I will s troublemakers to pour her from her
50:16 all those who plant crops; s all the harvesters away.
50:29 "S out a call for archers to come to Babylon.
51:53 I will s enemies to plunder her," says the LORD.
Eze 12:14 to the four winds and s the sword after them.
14:15 "Or suppose I were to s an invasion of dangerous
22: 9 accuse others falsely and s them to their death.
23:22 I will s your lovers against you—those very
26:20 I will s you to the pit to lie there with those who
28:23 I will s a plague against you, and blood will be
30: 9 At that time I will s swift messengers in ships to
32: 3 I will s many people to catch you in my net
32:18 For I will s them down to the world below in
34:26 And I will s showers, showers of blessings,
38:22 I will s torrential rain, hailstones, fire, and burning
Hos 8:14 I will s down fire on their palaces and burn their
14: 5 it will s roots deep into the soil like the cedars in
Joel 2:20 these armies from the north and s them far away.
Am 1: 4 So I will s down fire on King Hazael's palace,
1: 7 So I will s down fire on the walls of Gaza, and all
1:10 So I will s down fire on the walls of Tyre, and all
1:12 So I will s down fire on Teman, and the fortresses
1:14 So I will s down fire on the walls of Rabbah,
2: 2 So I will s down fire on the land of Moab, and all
2: 5 So I will s down fire on Judah, and all the
5:27 So I will s you into exile, to a land east of
7: 1 I saw him preparing to s a vast swarm of locusts
8:11 "when I will s a famine on the land—
9: 3 I will s the great sea serpent after them to bite
Jnh 1: 4 causing a violent storm that threatened to s them to
Mic 1:14 S a farewell gift to Moresheth-gath; there is no
Zec 12: 2 nations that s their armies to besiege Jerusalem.
14:12 And the LORD will s a plague on all the nations
Mt 8:31 "If you cast us out, s us into that herd of pigs."
9:38 ask him to s out more workers for his fields."
13:41 I, the Son of Man, will s my angels, and they will
14:15 S the crowds away so they can go to the villages
15:23 Then his disciples urged him to s her away.
15:32 I don't want to s them away hungry, or they will
19: 7 write an official letter of divorce and s her away?"
21: 3 needs them,' and he will immediately s them."
22:16 They decided to s some of their disciples,
23:34 I will s you prophets and wise men and teachers of
24:31 And he will s forth his angels with the sound of a
26:53 to protect us, and he would s them instantly?
Mk 5:10 and again not to s them to some distant place.
5:12 "S us into those pigs," the evil spirits begged.
6:36 S the crowds away so they can go to the nearby
8: 3 And if I s them home without feeding them,
10: 4 wife an official letter of divorce and s her away."
13:27 And he will s forth his angels to gather together his
Lk 8:31 The demons kept begging Jesus not to s them into
9:12 "S the crowds away to the nearby villages
10: 2 and ask him to s out more workers for his fields.
11:49 'I will s prophets and apostles to them, and they
14:32 he will s a delegation to discuss terms of peace.
16:24 S Lazarus over here to dip the tip of his finger in
16:27 Father Abraham, s him to my father's home.
20:13 asked himself. 'I know! I'll s my cherished son.
24:49 "And now I will s the Holy Spirit, just as my
Jn 3:17 God did not s his Son into the world to condemn it,
15:26 "But I will s you the Counselor—the Spirit of
16: 7 go away, he will come because I will s him to you.
20:21 with you. As the Father has sent me, so I s you."
Ac 3:20 and he will s Jesus your Messiah to you again.
4:30 S your healing power; may miraculous signs
7:34 to rescue them. Now go, for I will s you to Egypt.'
7:43 So I will s you into captivity / far away in
10: 5 Now s some men down to Joppa to find a man
10:22 A holy angel instructed him to s for you so you can
10:32 Now s some men to Joppa and summon Simon
11:13 'S messengers to Joppa to find Simon Peter.
11:29 So the believers in Antioch decided to s relief to
15:25 to s you these official representatives, along with
22:21 for I will s you far away to the Gentiles!' "
25:21 to jail until I could arrange to s him to Caesar."
25:25 his case to the emperor, and I decided to s him.
25:27 For it doesn't seem reasonable to s a prisoner to
26:17 Yes, I am going to s you to the Gentiles,
Ro 15:24 for a little while, you can s me on my way again.
16:16 All the churches of Christ s you their greetings.
16:21 my relatives, s you their good wishes.
16:22 s my greetings, too, as a Christian brother.
1Co 1:17 For Christ didn't s me to baptize, but to preach the
16: 6 then you can s me on my way to the next
16:11 S him on his way with your blessings when he
2Co 1:16 Then you could s me on my way to Judea.
9: 2 in Greece were ready to s an offering a year ago.
9: 5 So I thought I should s these brothers ahead of me
13:12 All the Christians here s you their greetings.
Php 2:19 Jesus is willing, I hope to s Timothy to you soon.
2:23 I hope to s him to you just as soon as I find out
2:25 I thought I should s Epaphroditus back to you.
2:28 So I am all the more anxious to s him back to you,
4:21 The brothers who are with me here s you their
4:22 And all the other Christians s their greetings,
2Th 2:11 So God will s great deception upon them, and they
Tit 3:12 I am planning to s either Artemas or Tychicus to
Heb 7:11 why did God need to s a different priest from the
13:24 The Christians from Italy s you their greetings.
3Jn 1: 6 You do well to s them on their way in a manner
1:15 with you. Your friends here s you their greetings.
Rev 1:11 down what you see, and s it to the seven churches:
11: 6 and to s every kind of plague upon the earth as

SENDING (61) [SEND]

Ex 3:10 Now go, for I am s you to Pharaoh. You will lead
10:19 The LORD responded by s a strong west wind
23:20 I am s my angel before you to lead you safely to
Jdg 6:14 rescue Israel from the Midianites. I am s you!"
1Sa 16:20 Jesse responded by s David to Saul, along with a
20:22 leave immediately, for the LORD is s you away.
25:39 Then David wasted no time in s messengers to
2Sa 13:26 how about s my brother Amnon instead?"
1Ki 15:19 my father. See, I am s you a gift of silver and gold.
18: 9 "what harm have I done to you that you are s me
1Ch 21:26 the LORD answered him by s fire from heaven to
2Ch 2:13 "I am s you a master craftsman named Huram-abi.
16: 3 my father. See, I am s you a gift of silver and gold.
Ne 6: 3 so I replied by s this message to them: "I am doing
Job 10: 3 while s joy and prosperity to the wicked?
30:23 And I know that you are s me to my death—
Isa 11:15 s a mighty wind to divide it into seven streams that
Jer 16:16 "But now I am s for many fishermen who will
16:16 "I am s for hunters who will search for them in the
25:27 rise no more, for I am s terrible wars against you.'
Eze 2: 3 he said, "I am s you to the nation of Israel,
2: 4 But I am s you to say to them, 'This is what the
3: 5 I am not s you to some foreign people whose
3: 6 I am not s you to people with strange and difficult
3: 7 I am s you to the people of Israel, but they won't
14:13 and s a famine to destroy both people and animals
14:19 "Or suppose I were to pour out my fury by s an
17:15 s ambassadors to Egypt to request a great army
17:23 s forth its branches and producing seed.
39:28 responsible for s them away to exile
Joel 2:14 s you a blessing instead of this terrible curse.
2:19 I am s you grain and wine and olive oil, enough to
Mic 6: 9 of destruction are coming; the LORD is s them.
Hab 3: 8 No, you were s your chariots of salvation!
Zec 5: 4 I am s this curse into the house of every thief
Mal 3: 1 I am s my messenger, and he will prepare the way
4: 5 I am s you the prophet Elijah before the great
Mt 9: 8 They praised God for s a man with such great
10:16 "Look, I am s you out as sheep among wolves.
11:10 they say, / 'Look, I am s my messenger before you,
Mk 1: 2 "Look, I am s my messenger before you,
Lk 7:27 they say, / 'Look, I am s my messenger before you,
10: 3 and remember that I am s you out as lambs among
Jn 17:18 sent me into the world, I am s them into the world.
Ac 14:17 such as s you rain and good crops and giving you
15:27 So we are s Judas and Silas to tell you what we
17:14 s Paul on to the coast, while Silas and Timothy
24:24 S for Paul, they listened as he told them about faith
Ro 5: 8 But God showed his great love for us by s Christ to
1Co 4:17 That is the very reason I am s Timothy—to help
10: 1 God guided all of them by s a cloud that moved
2Co 8:18 We are also s another brother with Titus. He is
8:22 And we are also s with them another brother who
9: 3 But I am s these brothers just to be sure that you
Gal 1: 2 All the Christians here join me in s greetings to the
Eph 6:22 I am s him to you for just this purpose. He will let
Php 2:26 Now I am s him home again, for he has been
Col 4: 9 I am also s Onesimus, a faithful and much loved
Phm 1:12 I am s him back to you, and with him comes my
1Jn 4: 9 God showed how much he loved us by s his only
Rev 16: 5 "You are just in s this judgment, O Holy One,

SENDS (36) [SEND]

Dt 24: 1 a letter of divorce, gives it to her, and s her away.
28:37 among all the nations to which the LORD s you.
1Ki 17:14 containers until the time when the LORD s rain
2Ki 5: 7 and said, "This man s me a leper to heal!
Job 5:10 gives rain for the earth. He s water for the fields.
9:12 If he s death to snatch someone away, who can
37:10 God's breath s the ice, freezing wide expanses of
38:27 Who s the rain that satisfies the parched ground
Ps 135: 7 over the earth. / He s the lightning with the rain
147:14 He s peace across your nation / and satisfies you
147:15 He s his orders to the world— / how swiftly his
147:16 He s the snow like white wool; / he scatters frost
147:18 it all melts. / He s his winds, and the ice thaws.
Isa 9:18 too. Its burning s up vast clouds of smoke.
45: 7 I am the one who s good times and bad times.
50: 3 I am the one who s darkness out across the skies,
Jer 10:13 over the earth. / He s the lightning with the rain
29: 4 s this message to all the captives he has exiled to
51:16 over the earth. / He s the lightning with the rain
Joel 2:23 For the rains he s are an expression of his grace.
Am 5: 3 "When one of your cities s a thousand men to
5: 3 When a town s a hundred, only ten will come back
Zec 14:18 that he s on the other nations who refuse to go.
Mt 5:45 and he s rain on the just and on the unjust, too.
Jn 13:16 more important than the one who s them.
14:26 But when the Father s the Counselor as my
Ac 1: 4 "Do not leave Jerusalem until the Father s you

Ro 16:23 s you his greetings, and so does Quartus,
Col 4:10 s you his greetings, and so does Mark,
4:11 Jesus (the one we call Justus) also s his greetings.
4:12 a servant of Christ Jesus, s you his greetings.
4:14 Dear Doctor Luke s his greetings, and so does
2Ti 4:21 Eubulus s you greetings, and so do Pudens, Linus,
Tit 3:15 Everybody here s greetings. Please give my
Phm 1:23 fellow prisoner in Christ Jesus, s you his greetings.
1Pe 5:13 Your sister church here in Rome s you greetings,

SENEH (1)

1Sa 14:4 two rocky cliffs that were called Bozez and S.

SENIOR (1)

Ge 50:7 and advisers—all the s officers of Egypt.

SENIR (4) [BAAL-HERMON, HERMON]

Dt 3:9 Sirion by the Sidonians; the Amorites call it S.)
1Ch 5:23 Bashan to Baal-hermon, S, and Mount Hermon.
SS 4:8 from Mount S and Mount Hermon, where lions
Eze 27:5 like a great ship built of the finest cypress from S.

SENNACHERIB (14) [SENNACHERIB'S]

2Ki 18:13 King S of Assyria came to attack the fortified cities
19:9 Soon afterward King S received word that King
19:20 I have heard your prayer about King S of Assyria.
19:36 Then King S of Assyria broke camp and returned
2Ch 32:1 out this work, King S of Assyria invaded Judah.
32:2 When Hezekiah realized that S also intended to
32:9 Then King S of Assyria, while still besieging the
32:10 "This is what King S of Assyria says: What are
32:21 So S returned home in disgrace to his own land.
32:22 and the people of Jerusalem from King S of
Isa 36:1 King S of Assyria came to attack the fortified cities
37:9 Soon afterward King S received word that King
37:21 to your prayer concerning King S of Assyria.
37:37 Then King S of Assyria broke camp and returned

SENNACHERIB'S (5) [SENNACHERIB]

2Ki 18:27 But S representative replied, "My master wants
19:16 Listen to S words of defiance against the living
2Ch 32:16 And S officials further mocked the LORD God
Isa 36:12 But S representative replied, "My master wants
37:17 Listen to S words of defiance against the living

SENSE (23) [SENSED, SENSELESS, SENSES, SENSIBLE, SENSITIVE]

Dt 32:28 "Israel is a nation that lacks s; / the people are
1Sa 25:33 Thank God for your good s! Bless you for keeping
Est 1:21 The king and his princes thought this made good s,
Job 18:2 stop talking? Speak s if you want us to answer!
Ps 119:73 Now give me the s to follow your commands.
Pr 2:7 He grants a treasure of good s to the godly. He is
7:7 a simpleminded young man who lacked common s.
8:5 Let me give you common s. O foolish ones,
10:21 but fools are destroyed by their lack of common s.
11:12 a neighbor; a person with good s remains silent.
12:8 Everyone admires a person with good s, but a
13:15 A person with good s is respected; a treacherous
15:21 Foolishness brings joy to those who have no s;
19:11 People with good s restrain their anger; they earn
21:16 The person who strays from common s will end up
24:3 by wisdom and becomes strong through good s.
24:30 of a lazy person, the vineyard of one lacking s.
30:2 too ignorant to be human, and I lack common s.
Isa 32:4 Even the hotheads among them will be full of s
Da 1:4 are gifted with knowledge and good s, and have
Ac 2:43 A deep s of awe came over them all,
Ro 1:14 For I have a great s of obligation to people in our
Heb 11:19 And in a s, Abraham did receive his son back from

SENSED (1) [SENSE]

Ac 27:27 across the Sea of Adria, the sailors s land was near.

SENSELESS (8) [SENSE]

Dt 32:6 you repay the LORD, / you foolish and s people?
1Ki 2:31 This will remove the guilt of his s murders from
Ps 32:9 Do not be like a s horse or mule / that needs a bit
49:10 wise must finally die, / just like the foolish and s,
73:22 I must have seemed like a s animal to you.
Pr 17:16 It is s to pay tuition to educate a fool who has no
Jer 4:22 "They are s children who have no understanding.
5:21 Listen, you foolish and s people—who have eyes

SENSES (6) [SENSE]

Job 39:25 It s the battle even at a distance. It quivers at the
Jer 10:21 The shepherds of my people have lost their s.
Lk 15:17 "When he finally came to his s, he said to himself,
1Co 15:34 Come to your s and stop sinning. For to your
Gal 3:3 Have you lost your s? After starting your Christian
2Ti 2:26 Then they will come to their s and escape from the

SENSIBLE (7) [SENSE]

1Sa 25:3 his wife, Abigail, was a s and beautiful woman.
Pr 10:19 for it fosters sin. Be s and turn off the flow!
15:20 S children bring joy to their father; foolish children
15:21 have no sense; a s person stays on the right path.
17:24 S people keep their eyes glued on wisdom, but a
Mt 24:45 "Who is a faithful, s servant, to whom the master
Lk 12:42 s servant to whom the master gives the

SENSITIVE (1) [SENSE]

Ro 14:2 But another believer who has a s conscience will

SENT (718) [SEND]

Ge 2:5 the earth, for the LORD God had not s any rain.
3:23 and he s Adam out to cultivate the ground from
8:1 He s a wind to blow across the waters,
8:8 Then he s out a dove to see if it could find dry
12:17 But the LORD s a terrible plague upon Pharaoh's
12:20 then s them out of the country under armed escort
19:13 reached the LORD, and he has s us to destroy it."
20:2 So King Abimelech s for her and had her brought
20:13 When God s me to travel far from my father's
21:14 He s her away with their son, and she walked out
24:59 and s her away with Abraham's servant and his
25:6 sons of his concubines and s them off to the east,
26:27 since you s me from your land in a most unfriendly
26:29 you well, and we s you away from us in peace.
26:31 Then Isaac s them home again in peace.
27:42 She s for Jacob and told him, "Esau is threatening
28:5 So Isaac s Jacob away, and he went to
28:6 and s him to Paddan-aram to find a wife,
31:42 you would have s me off without a penny to my
32:3 Jacob now s messengers to his brother, Esau,
32:5 I have s these messengers to inform you of my
32:21 So the presents were s on ahead, and Jacob spent
32:22 during the night Jacob got up and s his two wives,
32:23 on the other side, he s over all his possessions.
37:14 So Jacob s him on his way, and Joseph traveled to
38:25 to kill her, she s this message to her father-in-law:
40:20 He s for his chief cup-bearer and chief baker,
41:14 Pharaoh s for Joseph at once, and he was brought
45:5 He s me here ahead of you to preserve your lives.
45:7 God has s me here to keep you and your families
45:8 Yes, it was God who s me here, not you! And he
45:23 He s his father ten donkeys loaded with the good
45:24 So he s his brothers off, and as they left, he called
45:27 saw the wagons loaded with the food s by Joseph,
46:28 Jacob s Judah on ahead to meet Joseph and get
50:16 So they s this message to Joseph: "Before your
Ex 3:12 And this will serve as proof that I have s you:
3:13 'The God of your ancestors has s me to you,'
3:14 Just tell them, 'I AM has s me to you.' "
3:15 of Isaac, and the God of Jacob—has s me to you.'
4:31 were soon convinced that the LORD had s Moses
5:6 That same day Pharaoh s this order to the slave
7:9 show him a miracle to prove that God has s you.
7:16 the Hebrews, has s me to say, "Let my people go,
8:12 pleaded with the LORD about the frogs he had s.
9:7 Pharaoh s officials to see whether it was true that
9:23 and the LORD s thunder and hail, and lightning
9:23 The LORD s a tremendous hailstorm against all
9:27 Then Pharaoh urgently s for Moses and Aaron.
10:16 Pharaoh quickly s for Moses and Aaron.
12:31 Pharaoh s for Moses and Aaron during the night.
15:26 then I will not make you suffer the diseases I s on
18:2 time before this, Moses had s his wife, Zipporah,
24:5 Then he s some of the young men to sacrifice
32:35 And the LORD s a great plague upon the people
36:6 and this message was s throughout the camp:
Lev 16:10 When it is s away into the wilderness, it will make
Nu 11:31 Now the LORD s a wind that brought quail from
13:3 He s out twelve men, all tribal leaders of Israel,
13:16 These are the names of the men Moses s to explore
13:17 Moses gave the men these instructions as he s them
13:27 "We arrived in the land you s us to see, and it is
16:28 "By this you will know that the LORD has s me
16:29 die a natural death, then the LORD has not s me.
20:14 he s ambassadors to the king of Edom with this
20:16 and s an angel who brought us out of Egypt.
21:6 So the LORD s poisonous snakes among them,
21:21 The Israelites now s ambassadors to King Sihon of
21:32 After Moses s men to explore the Jazer area,
22:5 s messengers to Balaam son of Beor, who was
22:5 He s this message to request that Balaam come to
22:10 of Zippor, king of Moab, has s me this message:
22:15 This time he s a larger number of even more
22:15 officials than those he had s the first time.
22:22 so he s the angel of the LORD to stand in the road
22:40 He s portions of the meat to Balaam
31:6 Then Moses s them out, a thousand men from each
32:8 This is what your ancestors did when I s them from
Dt 2:26 "Then from the wilderness of Kedemoth I s
7:19 great terrors the LORD your God s against them.
9:23 And at Kadesh-barnea the LORD s you out with
34:11 The LORD s Moses to perform all the miraculous
Jos 2:1 Then Joshua secretly s out two spies from the
2:3 So the king of Jericho s orders to Rahab:
2:3 They are spies s here to discover the best way to
2:21 And she s them on their way, leaving the scarlet
6:25 because she had hidden the spies Joshua s to
7:2 Joshua s some of his men from Jericho to spy out
7:4 So approximately three thousand warriors were s,
7:22 So Joshua s some men to make a search. They ran
8:3 thousand fighting men and s them out at night
8:12 That night Joshua s five thousand men to lie in
9:4 They s ambassadors to Joshua, loading their
10:3 So King Adoni-zedek of Jerusalem s messengers to
10:6 The men of Gibeon quickly s messengers to Joshua
11:1 he s urgent messages to the following kings:
14:7 s me from Kadesh-barnea to explore the land of
14:11 I am as strong now as I was when Moses s me on
22:6 So Joshua blessed them and s them home.
22:7 As Joshua s them away, he blessed them
22:13 they s a delegation led by Phinehas son of Eleazar,
24:5 "Then I s Moses and Aaron, and I brought terrible
24:12 And I s hornets ahead of you to drive out the two
24:28 Then Joshua s the people away, each to his own
Jdg 1:23 They s spies to Bethel (formerly known as Luz),
2:6 After Joshua s the people away, each of the tribes
3:15 The Israelites s Ehud to deliver their tax money to
3:18 Ehud s home those who had carried the tax money.
3:19 servants to be silent and s them all out of the room.
4:6 One day she s for Barak son of Abinoam,
6:8 the LORD s a prophet to the Israelites. He said,
6:35 He also s messengers throughout Manasseh,
7:8 horns of the other warriors and s them home.
7:23 Then Gideon s for the warriors of Naphtali, Asher,
7:24 Gideon also s messengers throughout the hill
9:31 He s messengers to Abimelech in Arumah,
11:5 the leaders of Gilead s for Jephthah in the land of
11:12 Then Jephthah s messengers to the king of
11:14 Jephthah s this message back to the Ammonite
11:17 they s messengers to the king of Edom asking for
11:19 "Then Israel s messengers to King Sihon of the
12:1 over to Zaphon. They s this message to Jephthah:
16:18 told her the truth, so she s for the Philistine leaders.
19:29 Then he s one piece to each tribe of Israel.
20:6 and s the pieces throughout the land of Israel,
20:12 The Israelites s messengers to the tribe of
20:38 They s up a large cloud of smoke from the town,
21:10 So they s twelve thousand warriors to
21:13 The Israelite assembly s a peace delegation to the
Ru 1:21 to suffer and the Almighty has s such tragedy?"
1Sa 4:4 So they s men to Shiloh to bring back the Ark of
5:10 So they s the Ark of God to the city of Ekron,
6:9 a coincidence and was not s by the LORD at all."
6:17 The five gold tumors that were s by the Philistines
6:21 So they s messengers to the people at
8:22 Then Samuel agreed and s the people home.
10:25 Then Samuel s the people home again.
11:7 and s the messengers to carry them throughout
11:9 So Saul s the messengers back to Jabesh-gilead to
12:8 he s Moses and Aaron to rescue them from Egypt
12:11 Then the LORD s Gideon, Barak, Jephthah,
12:18 to the LORD, and the LORD s thunder and rain.
13:2 the army of Israel and s the rest of the men home.
15:6 Saul s this message to the Kenites: "Move away
15:18 And the LORD s you on a mission and told you,
16:12 So Jesse s for him. He was ruddy and handsome,
16:14 and the LORD s a tormenting spirit that filled him
16:19 So Saul s messengers to Jesse to say, "Send me
16:22 Then Saul s word to Jesse asking, "Please let
17:31 was reported to King Saul, and the king s for him.
19:11 Then Saul s troops to watch David's house.
19:15 lies there!" And he s them back to David's house.
19:20 he s troops to capture him. But when they arrived
19:21 he s other troops, but they, too, prophesied!
21:2 "The king has s me on a private matter,"
22:11 King Saul immediately s for Ahimelech and all his
25:5 he s ten of his young men to Carmel. He told them
25:14 "David s men from the wilderness to talk to our
25:25 But I never even saw the messengers you s.
25:32 the God of Israel, who has s you to meet me today!
25:40 "David has s us to ask if you will marry him."
26:4 so he s out spies to watch his movements.
30:26 David s part of the plunder to the leaders of Judah,
30:27 The gifts were s to the leaders of the following
2Sa 2:5 he s them this message: "May the LORD bless
3:12 Then Abner s messengers to David, saying,
3:14 David then s this message to Ishbosheth,
3:21 So David s Abner safely on his way.
3:23 visiting the king and had been s away in safety,
3:26 and s messengers to catch up with Abner.
5:11 Then King Hiram of Tyre s messengers to David,
5:11 a palace. Hiram also s many cedar logs for lumber.
8:10 he s his son Joram to congratulate David on his
9:5 So David s for him and brought him from Makir's
10:2 So David s ambassadors to express sympathy to
10:3 David has s them to spy out the city so that they
10:4 the buttocks, and s them back to David in shame.
10:5 he s messengers to tell the men to stay at Jericho
10:7 he s Joab and the entire Israelite army to fight
11:1 David s Joab and the Israelite army to destroy the
11:3 He s someone to find out who she was, and he was
11:4 Then David s for her; and when she came to the
11:5 was pregnant, she s a message to inform David.
11:6 So David s word to Joab: "Send me Uriah the
11:8 David even s a gift to Uriah after he had left the
11:18 Then Joab s a battle report to David.
11:27 David s for her and brought her to the palace,
12:1 So the LORD s Nathan the prophet to tell David
12:25 and s word through Nathan the prophet that his
12:27 Joab s messengers to tell David, "I have fought
13:7 and s Tamar to Amnon's house to prepare some
13:25 the king wouldn't come, though he s his thanks.
14:2 So he s for a woman from Tekoa who had a
14:19 from you. Yes, Joab s me and told me what to say.
14:21 So the king s for Joab and told him, "All right,
14:29 Then Absalom s for Joab to ask him to intercede
14:29 Absalom s for him a second time, but again Joab
15:10 he s secret messengers to every part of Israel to stir
15:12 he was offering the sacrifices, he s for Ahithophel,
19:11 Then King David s Zadok and Abiathar,
19:14 They s word to the king, "Return to us, and bring
24:15 So the LORD s a plague upon Israel that
1Ki 1:44 The king s him down to Gihon Spring with Zadok
2:29 he s Benaiah son of Jehoiada to execute him.
2:36 The king then s for Shimei and told him, "Build a
2:42 So he s for Shimei and demanded, "Didn't I make
4:21 The conquered peoples of those lands s tribute
4:34 And kings from every nation s their ambassadors
5:1 Hiram s ambassadors to congratulate him.

5: 2 Then Solomon s this message back to Hiram:
5: 8 Then he s this reply to Solomon: / "I have
5:11 In return Solomon s him an annual payment of
5:14 He s them to Lebanon in shifts, ten thousand every
8:66 the festival was over, Solomon s the people home.
9:14 Hiram had s Solomon nine thousand pounds of
9:27 Hiram s experienced crews of sailors to sail the
12: 3 The leaders of Israel s for Jeroboam, and the whole
12:18 King Rehoboam s Adoniram, who was in charge of
15:18 He s it with some of his officials to Ben-hadad son
15:20 Asa's request and s his armies to attack Israel.
15:22 Then King Asa s an order throughout Judah,
19: 2 So Jezebel s this message to Elijah: "May the gods
20: 2 Ben-hadad s messengers into the city to relay this
20: 7 I already agreed when he s the message demanding
20:10 Then Ben-hadad s this message to Ahab:
20:11 The king of Israel s back this answer: "A warrior
21: 8 and s them to the elders and other leaders of the
21:14 The city officials then s word to Jezebel,
2Ki 1: 2 So he s messengers to the temple of Baal-zebub,
1: 9 Then he s an army captain with fifty soldiers to
1:11 So the king s another captain with fifty men.
1:13 Once more the king s a captain with fifty men.
3: 7 he s this message to King Jehoshaphat of Judah:
4:22 She s a message to her husband: "Send one of the
5: 8 about the king's reaction, he s this message to him:
5:10 But Elisha s a messenger out to him with this
5:22 "but my master has s me to tell you that two
5:23 and s two of his servants to carry the gifts for
5:24 the gifts from the servants and s the men back.
6:14 So one night the king of Aram s a great army with
6:23 feast for them and then s them home to their king.
6:32 when the king s a messenger to summon him.
6:32 to the leaders, "A murderer has s a man to kill me.
7:14 and the king s scouts to see what had happened to
8: 9 of Aram, has s me to ask you if he will recover."
9:19 So the king s out a second rider. He rode up to
10: 1 So Jehu wrote a letter and s copies to Samaria,
10: 5 of the king's sons, s this message to Jehu:
10:21 He s messengers throughout all Israel summoning
12:18 He s them all to Hazael, along with all the gold in
14: 8 One day Amaziah s this challenge to Israel's king
14: 9 "Out in the Lebanon mountains a thistle s a
14:19 But his enemies s assassins after him, and they
16: 6 the people of Judah and s Edomites to live there,
16: 7 King Ahaz s messengers to King Tiglath-pileser of
16: 8 and s it as a gift to the Assyrian king.
16:10 So he s a model of the altar to Uriah the priest,
17:13 Again and again the LORD had s his prophets
17:25 the LORD s lions among them to kill some of
17:26 So a message was s to the king of Assyria:
17:26 He has s lions among them to destroy them
18:14 King Hezekiah s this message to the king of
18:17 Nevertheless the king of Assyria s his commander
18:18 but the king s these officials to meet with them:
18:19 Then the Assyrian king's personal representative s
19: 2 And he s Eliakim the palace administrator,
19: 9 he s this message back to Hezekiah in Jerusalem:
19:20 Then Isaiah son of Amoz s this message to
20:12 of Babylon, s Hezekiah his best wishes and a gift,
22: 3 King Josiah s Shaphan son of Azaliah
22:15 has spoken! Go and tell the man who s you,
22:18 "But go to the king of Judah who s you to seek the
24: 2 Then the LORD s bands of Babylonian, Aramean,
24:20 and Judah from his presence and s them into exile.
25:21 So the people of Judah were s into exile from their
1Ch 6:15 who went into exile when the LORD s the people
12:19 much discussion, they s them back, for they said,
12:31 18,000 men were s for the express purpose of
14: 1 Now King Hiram of Tyre s messengers to David,
14: 1 a palace. Hiram also s many cedar logs for lumber.
18:10 he s his son Joram to congratulate David on his
19: 2 So David s ambassadors to express sympathy to
19: 3 David has s them to spy out the land so that they
19: 4 the buttocks, and s them back to David in shame.
19: 5 he s messengers to tell the men to stay at Jericho
19: 6 and the Ammonites s thirty-eight tons of silver to
19: 8 he s Joab and all his warriors to fight them.
21:14 So the LORD s a plague upon Israel, and seventy
21:15 And God s an angel to destroy Jerusalem. But just
22: 6 Then David s for his son Solomon and instructed
26:32 King David s them to the east side of the Jordan
2Ch 2: 3 Solomon also s this message to King Hiram at
2:11 King Hiram s this letter of reply to Solomon:
7:10 end of the celebration, Solomon s the people home.
8:18 Hiram s him ships commanded by his own officers
9:21 of trading ships manned by the sailors s by Hiram.
10: 3 The leaders of Israel s for Jeroboam, and he
10:18 King Rehoboam s Adoniram, who was in charge of
13:13 Jeroboam had secretly s part of his army around
16: 2 He s it to King Ben-hadad of Aram, who was
16: 4 Asa's request and s his armies to attack Israel.
17: 7 Jehoshaphat s out his officials to teach in all the
17: 8 He s Levites along with them, including Shemaiah,
17: 8 He also s out the priests, Elishama and Jehoram.
24: 9 Then a proclamation was s throughout Judah
24:19 The LORD s prophets to bring them back to him,
24:23 Then they s all the plunder back to their king in
25:10 the hired troops and s them back to Ephraim.
25:13 the hired troops that Amaziah had s home raided
25:15 the LORD very angry, and he s a prophet to ask,
25:17 King Amaziah of Judah s this challenge to Israel's
25:18 a thistle s a message to a mighty cedar tree:
25:27 But his enemies s assassins after him, and they
30: 1 King Hezekiah now s word to all Israel and Judah,
30: 5 So they s a proclamation throughout all Israel,
30: 6 messengers were s throughout Israel and Judah.
32: 9 s officials to Jerusalem with this message for
32:17 The king also s letters scorning the LORD,
32:21 And the LORD s an angel who destroyed the
33:11 So the LORD s the Assyrian armies, and they
34:23 has spoken! Go and tell the man who s you,
34:26 "But go to the king of Judah who s you to seek the
35:21 But King Neco s ambassadors to Josiah with this
36:15 repeatedly s his prophets to warn them,
Ezr 4: 7 s a letter to Artaxerxes in the Aramaic language,
4:10 They also s greetings from the rest of the people
4:11 This is a copy of the letter they s him:
4:14 in this way, we have s you this information.
4:18 The letter you s has been translated and read to me.
5: 5 from building until a report was s to Darius
5: 6 west of the Euphrates River s to King Darius:
6: 3 a decree was s out concerning the Temple of God
6: 6 So King Darius s this message: / "To Tattenai,
8:16 So I s for Eliezer, Ariel, Shemaiah, Elnathan,
8:16 I also s for Joiarib and Elnathan, who were very
8:17 I s them to Iddo, the leader of the Levites at
8:18 they s us a man named Sherebiah, along with
8:19 They also s Hashabiah, together with Jeshaiah
Ne 2: 9 had s along army officers and horsemen to protect
6: 2 and Geshem s me a message asking me to meet
6: 4 Four times they s the same message, and each time
6:19 And Tobiah s many threatening letters to
9:20 You s your good Spirit to instruct them, and you
9:27 you s them deliverers who rescued them from their
9:30 You s your Spirit, who, through the prophets,
11:36 Some of the Levites who lived in Judah were s to
13:19 I also s some of my own servants to guard the
Est 1:15 king's orders, properly s through his eunuchs?"
1:22 He s letters to all parts of the empire, to each
3:13 and s by messengers into all the provinces of the
4: 4 She s clothing to him to replace the sackcloth,
4: 5 Then Esther s for Hathach, one of the king's
4:13 Mordecai s back this reply to Esther: "Don't think
4:15 Then Esther s this reply to Mordecai:
8:10 He s the letters by swift messengers, who rode
9:20 these events and s letters to the Jews near and far,
9:30 and security were s to the Jews throughout the 127
Job 4:15 swept past my face. Its wind s shivers up my spine.
6: 4 He has s his poisoned arrows deep within my
22: 9 You must have s widows away without helping
31:23 That would be better than facing the judgment s by
36:21 getting into a life of evil that God s this suffering.
Ps 34: T be insane in front of Abimelech, who s him away.
35: 5 the wind— / a wind s by the angel of the LORD.
59: T regarding the time Saul s soldiers to watch David's
60: 3 on us, / making us drink wine that s us reeling.
66:12 You s troops to ride across our broken bodies.
68: 9 You s abundant rain, O God, / to refresh the weary
78:45 He s vast swarms of flies to consume them
78:66 routed his enemies / and s them to eternal shame.
88: 8 friends to loathe me; / you have s them all away.
105:17 Then he s someone to Egypt ahead of them—
105:20 Then Pharaoh s for him and set him free; / the ruler
105:26 But the LORD s Moses his servant, / along with
105:32 Instead of rain, he s murderous hail, / and flashes
105:40 They asked for meat, and he s them quail;
106:15 they asked for, / but he s a plague along with it.
119:71 The suffering you s was good for me, / for it taught
Pr 9: 3 She has s her servants to invite everyone to come.
22:21 and bring an accurate report to those who s you.
25: 7 It is better to wait for an invitation than to be s to
SS 1: 6 and s me out to tend the vineyards in the hot sun.
Isa 6:12 Do not stop until the LORD has s everyone away
7:10 the LORD s this message to King Ahaz:
10: 7 of Assyria will not know that it is I who s him.
18: 2 and ambassadors are s in fast boats down the Nile.
19:14 The LORD has s a spirit of foolishness on them,
23: 7 Think of all the colonists you s to distant lands.
36: 2 Then the king of Assyria s his personal
36: 4 Then the Assyrian king's personal representative s
37: 2 And he s Eliakim the palace administrator,
37: 9 he s this message back to Hezekiah in Jerusalem:
37:21 Then Isaiah son of Amoz s this message to
38:15 could I say? / For he himself had s this sickness.
39: 1 of Babylon, s Hezekiah his best wishes and a gift.
42:24 for the people would not go where he s them,
48:16 and his Spirit have s me with this message:
50: 1 because I divorced her and s her away?
54:15 it will not be because I s them to punish you.
61: 1 He has s me to comfort the brokenhearted and to
61: 2 He has s me to tell those who mourn that the time
62:11 The LORD has s this message to every land:
63:11 Where is the one who s his Holy Spirit to be
Jer 3: 8 that I had divorced faithless Israel and s her away.
4:12 It is a roaring blast s by me! Now I will pronounce
11:16 But now I have s the fury of their enemies to burn
14:15 spoken in my name even though I never s them.
21: 1 when King Zedekiah s Pashhur son of Malkijah
23:21 "I have not s these prophets, yet they claim to
24: 5 The good figs represent the exiles I s from Judah to
24: 6 I have s them into captivity for their own good.
25: 4 and again, the LORD has s you his prophets,
25:17 drink from it—every nation the LORD s me to.
26: 5 for I s them again and again to warn you, but you
26:12 "The LORD s me to prophesy against this
26:15 For it is absolutely true that the LORD s me to
26:21 he was saying, the king s someone to kill him.
26:22 Then King Jehoiakim s Elnathan son of Acbor to
27:15 what the LORD says: I have not s these prophets!
28:15 The LORD has not s you, but the people believe
29: 3 He s the letter with Elasah son of Shaphan
29: 9 in my name. I have not s them," says the LORD.
29:14 I will gather you out of the nations where I s you
29:24 The LORD s this message to Shemaiah the
29:25 and you s copies to the other priests and people in
29:28 Jeremiah s a letter here to Babylon, predicting that
30:16 and all your enemies will be s into exile.
32: 6 At that time the LORD s me a message. He said,
32:23 That is why you have s this terrible disaster upon
32:42 Just as I have s all these calamities upon them,
35:15 I have s you prophet after prophet to tell you to
36: 4 So Jeremiah s for Baruch son of Neriah, and as
36:14 the officials s Jehudi son of Nethaniah, grandson of
36:21 The king s Jehudi to get the scroll. Jehudi brought
37: 3 King Zedekiah s Jehucal son of Shelemiah
37: 7 who s you to ask me what is going to happen,
38:14 One day King Zedekiah s for Jeremiah to meet him
39: 7 him in chains, and s him away to exile in Babylon.
39: 9 s to Babylon the remnant of the population as well
39:14 s messengers to bring Jeremiah out of the prison.
40: 1 and Judah who were being s to exile in Babylon.
40:14 has s Ishmael son of Nethaniah to assassinate
42: 9 He said to them, "You s me to the LORD,
42:20 For you were deceitful when you s me to pray to
44: 4 "Again and again I s my servants, the prophets,
47: 7 But how can it be still when the LORD has s it on
49:14 that an ambassador was s to the nations to say,
52: 3 and Judah from his presence and s them into exile.
52:27 So the people of Judah were s into exile from their
52:30 In his twenty-third year he s Nebuzaradan,
La 1:13 "He has s fire from heaven that burns in my bones.
Eze 12:11 be driven from their homes and s away into exile.
13: 6 even though the LORD never s them.
17: 7 So the vine s its roots and branches out toward him
23:16 so she s messengers to Babylonia to invite them to
23:40 "You sisters s messengers to distant lands to get
27:16 "Aram s merchants to buy your wares.
30:11 the nations—have been s to demolish the land.
31:16 for I s it down to the grave with all the others like
39:23 then know why Israel was s away to exile—
Da 2:12 and he s out orders to execute all the wise men of
2:13 men were s to find and kill Daniel and his friends.
3: 2 Then he s messages to the princes, prefects,
3:28 He s his angel to rescue his servants who trusted in
4: 1 King Nebuchadnezzar s this message to the people
5:24 So God has s this hand to write a message.
6:22 My God s his angel to shut the lions' mouths
6:25 Then King Darius s this message to the people of
10:11 Stand up, for I have been s to you." When he said
11:20 s a tax collector to maintain the royal splendor,
Hos 6: 5 I s my prophets to cut you to pieces. I have
12:10 I s my prophets to warn you with many visions
Joel 2:25 It was I who s this great destroying army against
Am 1: 6 They s my people into exile, selling them as slaves
4: 7 I s rain on one town but withheld it from another.
4:10 "I s plagues against you like the plagues I s
7:11 and the people of Israel will be s away into
7:12 Then Amaziah s orders to Amos: "Get out of here,
Ob 1: 1 that an ambassador was s to the nations to say,
Jnh 1:14 you have s this storm upon him for your own good
3: 7 and his nobles s this decree throughout the city:
4: 8 God s a scorching east wind to blow on Jonah.
Mic 4:10 You will soon be s into exile in distant Babylon.
5: 7 They will be like dew s by the LORD or like rain
6: 4 I s Moses, Aaron, and Miriam to help you.
Hag 1: 3 So the LORD s this message through the prophet
1:12 whom the LORD their God had s,
2: 1 the LORD s another message through the prophet
2:10 the LORD s this message to the prophet Haggai:
2:17 I s blight and mildew and hail to destroy all the
2:20 The LORD s this second message to Haggai on
Zec 1: 7 the LORD s another message to the prophet
1:10 "They are the ones the LORD has s out to patrol
2: 8 the LORD Almighty s me against the nations who
2: 9 will know that the LORD Almighty has s me."
2:11 and you will know that the LORD Almighty s me
4: 9 you will know that the LORD Almighty has s me.
7: 2 The people of Bethel had s Sharezer
7: 4 The LORD Almighty s me this message:
7:12 or the messages that the LORD Almighty had s
Mal 2: 4 Then at last you will know it was I who s you this
Mt 2: 7 Then Herod s a private message to the wise men,
2:16 He s soldiers to kill all the boys in and around
10: 5 Jesus s the twelve disciples out with these
10:40 welcomes me is welcoming the Father who s me.
11: 2 was doing. So he s his disciples to ask Jesus,
14:22 and cross to the other side of the lake while he s
15:24 "I was s only to help the people of Israel—
15:39 Then Jesus s the people home, and he got into a
18:34 Then the angry king s the man to prison until he
20: 2 pay the normal daily wage and s them out to work.
21: 1 the Mount of Olives. Jesus s two of them on ahead.
21:34 At the time of the grape harvest he s his servants to
21:36 So the landowner s a larger group of his servants to
21:37 "Finally, the owner s his son, thinking,
22: 3 he s his servants to notify everyone that it was time
22: 4 So he s other servants to tell them, 'The feast has
22: 7 He s out his army to destroy the murderers
26:47 They had been s out by the leading priests
27:19 on the judgment seat, his wife s him this message:
27:24 So he s for a bowl of water and washed his hands
Mk 1:24 I know who you are—the Holy One s from God!"
1:43 Then Jesus s him on his way and told him sternly,
3:14 calling them apostles. He s them out to preach,
3:31 They stood outside and s word for him to come out
6: 7 disciples together and s them out two by two,
6:17 For Herod had s soldiers to arrest and imprison
6:27 So he s an executioner to the prison to cut off
6:45 the lake to Bethsaida, while he s the people home.
8: 9 that day, and he s them home after they had eaten.

8:26 Jesus s him home, saying, "Don't go back into the
9:37 welcomes me welcomes my Father who s me."
11: 1 the Mount of Olives. Jesus s two of them on ahead.
12: 2 At grape-picking time he s one of his servants to
12: 3 beat him up, and s him back empty-handed.
12: 4 "The owner then s another servant, but they beat
12: 5 The next servant he s was killed. Others who were
s were either beaten or killed,
12: 6 The owner finally s him, thinking, 'Surely they
12:13 The leaders s some Pharisees and supporters of
14:13 So Jesus s two of them into Jerusalem to make the
14:43 They had been s out by the leading priests,
16: S Afterward Jesus himself s them out from east to
Lk 1:19 It was he who s me to bring you this good news!
1:26 God s the angel Gabriel to Nazareth, a village in
1:53 and s the rich away with empty hands.
1:69 He has s us a mighty Savior / from the royal line of
3: 6 all people will see / the salvation s from God.' "
4:18 He has s me to proclaim / that captives will be
4:26 Yet Elijah was not s to any of them. He was s
instead to a widow of Zarephath—
4:34 I know who you are—the Holy One s from God."
4:43 in other places, too, because that is why I was s."
7: 3 he s some respected Jewish leaders to ask him to
7: 6 the house, the officer s some friends to say, "Lord,
7:19 and he s them to the Lord to ask him, "Are you the
7:20 and said to him, "John the Baptist s us to ask,
7:39 If God had really s him, he would know what kind
9: 2 Then he s them out to tell everyone about the
9:20 Peter replied, "You are the Messiah s from God!"
9:48 who welcomes me welcomes my Father who s me.
9:52 He s messengers ahead to a Samaritan village to
10: 1 and s them on ahead in pairs to all the towns
10:16 And anyone who rejects me is rejecting God who s
11:30 sign to the people of Nineveh that God had s him.
11:30 What happens to me will be a sign that God has s
14: 4 the sick man and healed him and s him away.
14:16 prepared a great feast and s out many invitations.
14:17 he s his servant around to notify the guests that it
16:30 But if someone is s to them from the dead,
19:14 and s a delegation after him to say they did not
19:29 on the Mount of Olives, he s two disciples ahead.
20:10 he s one of his servants to collect his share of the
20:10 beat him up, and s him back empty-handed.
20:11 So the owner s another servant, but the same thing
20:12 A third man was s and the same thing happened.
20:20 the leaders s secret agents pretending to be honest
21:24 or s away as captives to all the nations of the
22: 8 Jesus s Peter and John ahead and said, "Go
22:35 "When I s you out to preach the Good News
23: 7 that he was, Pilate s him to Herod Antipas,
23:11 put a royal robe on him and s him back to Pilate.
23:15 came to the same conclusion and s him back to us.
Jn 1: 6 God s John the Baptist
1:19 of John when the Jewish leaders s priests
1:22 so we can give an answer to those who s us.
1:24 Then those who were s by the Pharisees
1:33 but when God s me to baptize with water, he told
3: 2 "we all know that God has s you to teach us.
3:34 For he is s by God. He speaks God's words,
4:34 of God, who s me, and from finishing his work.
4:38 I s you to harvest where you didn't plant;
5:23 are certainly not honoring the Father who s him.
5:24 and believe in God who s me have eternal life.
5:30 because it is according to the will of God who s
5:33 you s messengers to listen to John the Baptist,
5:36 and they testify that the Father has s me.
5:38 you do not believe me—the one he s to you.
6:27 For God the Father has s me for that very
6:29 God wants you to do: Believe in the one he has s."
6:38 down from heaven to do the will of God who s me,
6:44 me unless the Father who s me draws them to me,
6:46 only I, who was s from God, have seen him.)
6:57 I live by the power of the living Father who s me;
7:16 my own ideas, but those of God who s me.
7:18 but those who seek to honor the one who s them
7:29 I have come from him, and he s me to you."
7:32 and the leading priests s Temple guards to arrest
7:33 Then I will return to the one who s me.
7:45 The Temple guards who had been s to arrest him
8:16 not alone—I have with me the Father who s me.
8:18 and my Father who s me is the other."
8:26 say only what I have heard from the one who s me,
8:29 And the one who s me is with me—he has not
8:42 from God. I am not here on my own, but he s me.
9: 4 out the tasks assigned us by the one who s me,
9: 7 wash in the pool of Siloam" (Siloam means S).
10:36 One who was s into the world by the Father says,
11: 3 So the two sisters s a message to Jesus telling him,
11:42 standing here, so they will believe you s me."
12:44 trust me, you are really trusting God who s me.
12:45 you see me, you are seeing the one who s me.
12:49 The Father who s me gave me his own instructions
13:20 welcomes me is welcoming the Father who s me."
14:24 This message is from the Father who s me.
15:21 belong to me, for they don't know God who s me.
16: 5 "But now I am going away to the one who s me,
17: 3 true God, and Jesus Christ, the one you s to earth.
17: 8 that I came from you, and they believe you s me.
17:18 As you s me into the world, I am sending them into
17:21 will be in us, and the world will believe you s me.
17:23 Then the world will know that you s me and will
17:25 but I do; and these disciples know you s me.
18:24 Then Annas bound Jesus and s him to Caiaphas,
20:21 with you. As the Father has s me, so I send you."
Ac 3:26 his servant, he s him first to you people of Israel,
4:15 So they s Peter and John out of the council
5:21 Then they s for the apostles to be brought for trial.
5:34 and ordered that the apostles be s outside the
7:12 still grain in Egypt, so he s his sons to buy some.
7:14 Then Joseph s for his father, Jacob, and all his
7:25 would realize that God had s him to rescue them,
7:35 so God s back the same man his people had
7:35 Moses was s to be their ruler and savior.
8:14 God's message, they s Peter and John there.
9:17 has s me so that you may get your sight back
9:30 and s him on to his hometown of Tarsus.
9:38 so they s two men to beg him, "Please come as
10: 8 them what had happened and s them off to Joppa.
10:17 then the men s by Cornelius found the house
10:20 without hesitation. All is well, for I have s them."
10:22 They said, "We were s by Cornelius, a Roman
10:29 So I came as soon as I was s for. Now tell me why
you s for me."
10:33 So I s for you at once, and it was good of you to
11:11 then three men who had been s from Caesarea
11:12 arrived at the home of the man who had s for us.
11:22 what had happened, they s Barnabas to Antioch.
12:11 "The Lord has s his angel and saved me from
12:20 So they s a delegation to make peace with him
13: 3 laid their hands on them and s them on their way.
13: 4 S out by the Holy Spirit, Saul and Barnabas went
13:15 those in charge of the service s them this message:
15: 2 Finally, Paul and Barnabas were s to Jerusalem,
15: 3 The church s the delegates to Jerusalem, and they
15:22 and they s them to Antioch of Syria with Paul
15:33 then Judas and Silas were s back to Jerusalem,
15:33 of the Christians, to those who had s them.
15:40 Paul chose Silas, and the believers s them off,
16:35 The next morning the city officials s the police to
17:10 That very night the believers s Paul and Silas to
19:22 He s his two assistants, Timothy and Erastus,
19:31 friends of Paul, also s a message to him,
20: 1 Paul s for the believers and encouraged them.
20:17 he s a message to the elders of the church at
23:22 the commander warned the young man as he s him
23:30 of a plot to kill him, I immediately s him on to you.
24:26 so he s for him quite often and talked with him.
26:10 I caused many of the believers in Jerusalem to be s
Ro 1: 1 be an apostle and s out to preach his Good News.
3:25 For God s Jesus to take the punishment for our sins
8: 3 He s his own Son in a human body like ours,
10:15 how will anyone go and tell them without being s?
13: 4 The authorities are s by God to help you. But if
1Co 10:10 for that is why God s his angel of death to destroy
2Co 2:17 And we know that the God who s us is watching
7: 8 I am no longer sorry that I s that letter to you,
7: 9 Now I am glad I s it, not because it hurt you,
12:12 that I am truly an apostle, s to you by God himself.
12:17 Did any of the men I s to you take advantage of
12:18 Titus to visit you and s our other brother with him,
Gal 4: 4 God s his Son, born of a woman, subject to the
4: 5 God s him to buy freedom for us who were slaves
4: 6 God has s the Spirit of his Son into your hearts,
Eph 1: 2 s to you from God our Father and Jesus Christ our
Php 4:16 Even when I was in Thessalonica you s help more
4:18 I am generously supplied with the gifts you s me
Col 4: 8 I have s him on this special trip to let you know
1Th 3: 2 and we s Timothy to visit you. He is our co-worker
3: 2 We s him to strengthen you, to encourage you in
3: 5 I s Timothy to find out whether your faith was still
2Ti 1: 1 s out to tell others about the life he has promised
4:12 I s Tychicus to Ephesus.
Tit 1: 1 I have been s to bring faith to those God has
Heb 1:14 They are spirits s from God to care for those who
Jas 2:25 and s them safely away by a different road.
1Pe 1:12 you in the power of the Holy Spirit s from heaven.
1:20 these final days, he was s to the earth for all to see.
2:14 For the king has s them to punish all who do wrong
1Jn 4:10 and s his Son as a sacrifice to take away our sins.
4:14 and now testify that the Father s his Son to be the
3Jn 1: 9 I s a brief letter to the church about this,
Rev 1: 1 An angel was s to God's servant John so that John
5: 6 which are the seven spirits of God that are s out
16: 9 the name of God, who s all of these plagues.
22: 6 has s his angel to tell you what will happen
22:16 have s my angel to give you this message for the

SENTENCE (18) [SENTENCED, SENTENCING]

Dt 17:11 a verdict, the s they impose must be fully executed;
19: 6 even though there was no death s and the first
1Ki 2:38 Shimei replied, "Your s is fair; I will do whatever
2:42 And you replied, 'The s is fair; I will do as you
2Ki 25: 6 at Riblah, where s was passed against him.
Ps 94: 2 S the proud to the penalties they deserve.
Jer 26:16 "This man does not deserve the death s,
52: 9 land of Hamath, where s was passed against him.
Eze 23:45 They will s them to all the punishment they
Hos 4: 5 As a s for your crimes, you will stumble in broad
12:14 so their Lord will now s them to death in payment
Mt 20:18 teachers of religious law. They will s him to die.
27: 1 the Roman government to s Jesus to death.
Mk 10:33 They will s him to die and hand him over to the
Lk 23:22 I have found no reason to s him to death. I will
Ac 25:15 charges against him and asked me to s him.
28:18 release me, for they found no cause for the death s.
Ro 9:28 For the Lord will carry out his s upon the earth

SENTENCED (9) [SENTENCE]

Ge 40:22 but he s the chief baker to be impaled on a pole,
Dt 25: 2 If the person in the wrong is s to be flogged,
Ps 76: 8 From heaven you s your enemies; / the earth
Pr 24:11 Rescue those who are unjustly s to death;
Jer 32: 4 taken to the king of Babylon to be judged and s.
34: 3 before the king of Babylon to be judged and s.
Lk 12:58 or you may be s and handed over to an officer
23:24 So Pilate s Jesus to die as they demanded.
Ac 12:19 Herod interrogated the guards and s them to death.

SENTENCING (1) [SENTENCE]

2Ch 32:11 s you to death by famine and thirst!

SENTINELS (1)

Eze 27:11 and from Helech stood on your walls as s.

SENTRIES (3) [SENTRY]

Ps 127: 1 protects a city, / guarding it with s will do no good.
130: 6 more than s long for the dawn, / yes, more than s
long for the dawn.

SENTRY (2) [SENTRIES]

Jer 37:13 a s arrested him and said, "You are defecting to
37:13 The s making the arrest was Irijah son of

SENUAH [KJV] See HASSENUAH

SEORIM (1)

1Ch 24: 8 third lot fell to Harim. / The fourth lot fell to S.

SEPARATE (30) [SEPARATED, SEPARATELY, SEPARATES, SEPARATING, SEPARATION]

Ge 1: 6 space between the waters, to s water from water."
1: 7 God made this space to s the waters above from
1:14 "Let bright lights appear in the sky to s the day
1:18 and the night, and to s the light from the darkness.
13: 9 of any section of the land you want, and we will s.
43:32 and his brothers were served at a s table.
Ex 26:33 This curtain will s the Holy Place from the Most
Lev 15:31 you will keep the people of Israel from things
Dt 29:21 The LORD will s them from all the tribes of
Jos 14: 4 The tribe of Joseph had become two s tribes—
Ru 1:17 me severely if I allow anything but death to s us!"
1Ki 1:49 the banquet table and quickly went their s ways.
Ezr 9: 1 have not kept themselves s from the other peoples
10:11 S yourselves from the people of the land and from
Pr 18:19 Arguments s friends like a gate locked with iron
27:22 You cannot s fools from their foolishness,
Eze 42:20 all around it to s the holy places from the common.
Zec 12:12 by itself, with the husbands and wives in s groups.
Mt 3:12 He is ready to s the chaff from the grain with his
13:49 will come and s the wicked people from the godly,
19: 6 they are no longer two but one, let no one s them,
25:32 and he will s them as a shepherd separates the
Mk 10: 9 let no one s them, for God has joined them
Lk 3:17 He is ready to s the chaff from the grain with his
Ro 8:35 Can anything ever s us from Christ's love? Does it
8:38 And I am convinced that nothing can ever s us
8:39 nothing in all creation will ever be able to s us
1Co 12:27 and each one of you is a s and necessary part of it.
2Co 6:17 and s yourselves from them, says the Lord.
Eph 2:14 broken down the wall of hostility that used to s us.

SEPARATED (15) [SEPARATE]

Ge 1: 4 it was good. Then he s the light from the darkness.
32:16 of animals by itself, s by a distance in between.
Nu 31:42 which Moses had s from the half belonging to the
2Sa 14:14 to bring us back when we have been s from him.
1Ki 8:53 you told your servant Moses that you had s Israel
Ne 4:19 and we are widely s from each other along the
9: 2 Those of Israelite descent s themselves from all
10:28 and all who had s themselves from the pagan
Job 26:10 He created the horizon when he s the waters;
Eze 42: 7 There was an outer wall that s the rooms from the
Mt 13:40 "Just as the weeds are s out and burned, so it will
Ac 15:39 disagreement over this was so sharp that they s.
Col 1:21 s from him by your evil thoughts and actions,
1Th 2:17 after we were s from you for a little while (though
2Th 1: 9 forever s from the Lord and from his glorious

SEPARATELY (1) [SEPARATE]

Zec 12:14 of the surviving families from Judah will mourn s,

SEPARATES (3) [SEPARATE]

Pr 16:28 plants seeds of strife; gossip s the best of friends.
17: 9 preserves love; telling about them s close friends.
Mt 25:32 and he will separate them as a shepherd s the sheep

SEPARATING (5) [SEPARATE]

Ge 30:40 his own flock, thus s the lambs from Laban's flock.
2Ki 2:11 It drove between them, s them, and Elijah was
Eze 34:17 one sheep and another, s the sheep from the goats.
40:10 and the dividing walls s them were also identical.
Lk 16:26 And besides, there is a great chasm s us.

SEPARATION (3) [SEPARATE]

Ex 28: 2 Make special clothing for Aaron to show his s to
Nu 6: 7 because it is the symbol of their s to God.
6:13 At the conclusion of their time of s as Nazirites,

SEPHAR (1)

Ge 10:30 from Mesha toward the eastern hills of S.

SEPHARVAIM (6)
2Ki 17:24 and S and resettled them in the towns of Samaria,
17:31 And the people from S even burned their own
18:34 And what about the gods of S, Hena, and Ivvah?
19:13 What happened to the kings of S, Hena,
Isa 36:19 and Arpad? And what about the gods of S?
37:13 What happened to the kings of S, Hena,

SEPTEMBER (2)
Eze 8: 1 Then on S 17, during the sixth year of King
Hag 1:15 This was on S 21 of the second year of King

SEPULCHRE(S) [KJV] See also BURIAL PLACE, GRAVE(S), TOMB(S)

SEQUENCE (1)
Job 38:32 Can you ensure the proper s of the seasons

SERAH (3)
Ge 46:17 Ishvi, and Beriah. Their sister was named S.
Nu 26:46 Asher also had a daughter named S.
1Ch 7:30 Ishvi, and Beriah. They had a sister named S.

SERAIAH (21)
2Sa 8:17 were the priests. S was the court secretary.
2Ki 25:18 guard took with him as prisoners S the chief priest,
25:23 of Kareah, S son of Tanhumeth the Netophathite,
1Ch 4:13 The sons of Kenaz were Othniel and S.
4:14 S was the father of Joab, the founder of the Valley
4:35 Jehu son of Joshibiah, son of S, son of Asiel,
6:14 Azariah was the father of S. / S was the father of
18:16 were the priests. S was the court secretary.
Ezr 2: 2 S, Reelaiah, Mordecai, Bilshan, Mispar, Bigvai,
7: 1 He was the son of S, son of Azariah, son of
Ne 7: 7 S, Reelaiah, Nahamani, Mordecai, Bilshan,
10: 2 S, Azariah, Jeremiah,
11:11 and S son of Hilkiah, son of Meshullam, son of
12: 1 and Jeshua the high priest: / S, Jeremiah, Ezra,
12:12 Meraiah was leader of the family of S.
Jer 36:26 commanded his son Jerahmeel, S son of Azriel,
40: 8 and Jonathan, sons of Kareah, S son of Tanhumeth,
51:59 S son of Neriah and grandson of Mahseiah,
51:61 He said to S, "When you get to Babylon,
52:24 guard took with him as prisoners S the chief priest,

SERAPHIM (2)
Isa 6: 2 Hovering around him were mighty s, each with six
6: 6 Then one of the s flew over to the altar, and he

SERED (2) [SEREDITE]
Ge 46:14 The sons of Zebulun were S, Elon, and Jahleel.
Nu 26:26 The Seredite clan, named after its ancestor S.

SEREDITE (1) [SERED]
Nu 26:26 The S clan, named after its ancestor Sered.

SERGIUS (1) [PAULUS]
Ac 13: 7 S Paulus, a man of considerable insight

SERIES (1)
Ex 7: 4 So I will crush Egypt with a s of disasters,

SERIOUS (22) [SERIOUSLY, SERIOUSNESS]
Ex 5:19 the Israelite foremen could see that they were in s
1Sa 2:17 So the sin of these young men was very s in the
7: 3 "If you are really s about wanting to return to the
24: 6 "It is a s thing to attack the LORD's anointed
30: 6 David was now in s trouble because his men were
2Sa 13:12 You know what a s crime it is to do such a thing in
2Ch 16:12 year of his reign, Asa developed a s foot disease.
Job 13:10 you will be in s trouble with him if even in your
Ps 106:32 angered the LORD, / causing Moses s trouble.
Pr 28:14 but the stubborn are headed for s trouble.
28:24 wrong with that?" is as s as committing murder.
Ecc 5:13 There is another s problem I have seen in the
5:16 And this, too, is a very s problem. As people come
6: 1 There is another s tragedy I have seen in our world.
Eze 6:10 and that I was s when I predicted that all this
Da 2: 5 the king said to the astrologers, "I am s about this.
2: 8 because you know I am s about what I said.
Mk 6:48 He saw that they were in s trouble, rowing hard
12:27 the living, not the dead. You have made a s error."
Ac 18:14 a case involving some wrongdoing or a s crime,
19:23 s trouble developed in Ephesus concerning the
25: 7 and made many s accusations they couldn't prove.

SERIOUSLY (7) [SERIOUS]
2Sa 10: 6 Now the people of Ammon realized how s they
2Ki 1: 2 at his palace in Samaria, and he was s injured.
1Ch 19: 6 Now the people of Ammon realized how s they
28:10 So take this s. The LORD has chosen you to build
Mal 2: 2 because you have not taken my warning s.
Ac 21:20 and they all take the law of Moses very s.
Ro 12: 8 you leadership ability, take the responsibility s.

SERIOUSNESS (2) [SERIOUS]
Ezr 10: 9 because of the s of the matter and because it was
Tit 2: 7 you do reflect the integrity and s of your teaching.

SERJEANTS [KJV] See POLICE

SERPENT (16) [SERPENTS]
Ge 3: 1 Now the s was the shrewdest of all the creatures
3: 4 "You won't die!" the s hissed.
3:13 "The s tricked me," she replied. "That's why I ate
3:14 So the LORD God said to the s, "Because you
2Ki 18: 4 He broke up the bronze s that Moses had made,
18: 4 incense to it. The bronze s was called Nehushtan.
Job 26:13 and his power pierced the gliding s.
Pr 23:32 For in the end it bites like a poisonous s; it stings
Isa 14:29 snake will be born, a fiery s to destroy you!
27: 1 the swiftly moving s, the coiling, writhing s, the dragon of the sea.
Jer 46:22 Silent as a s gliding away, Egypt flees.
Am 9: 3 I will send the great sea s after them to bite
2Co 11: 3 to Christ, just as Eve was deceived by the s.
Rev 12: 9 the ancient s called the Devil, or Satan, the one
20: 2 He seized the dragon—that old s, the Devil, Satan

SERPENTS (1) [SERPENT]
Ps 91:13 you will crush fierce lions and s under your feet!

SERUG (7)
Ge 11:20 When Reu was 32 years old, his son S was born.
11:21 After the birth of S, Reu lived another 207 years
11:22 When S was 30 years old, his son Nahor was born.
11:23 S lived another 200 years and had other sons
1Ch 1:26 S, Nahor, Terah,
Lk 3:35 Nahor was the son of S. / S was the son of Reu.

SERVANT (358) [SERVANT'S, SERVANTS]

MOSES, THE SERVANT (16) Dt 34:5; Jos 1:13,15; 8:33; 11:12; 12:6; 13:8; 14:7; 18:7; 22:2,4; 1Ch 6:49; 2Ch 24:6,9; Da 9:11; Rev 15:3

SERVANT DAVID (31) 2Sa 7:5,8,26; 1Ki 8:24,25,26,66; 11:13,32,34,38; 14:8; 2Ki 19:34; 20:6; 1Ch 17:4,7,24; 2Ch 6:15,16,17,42; Ps 78:70; 89:20; 132:10; 144:10; Isa 37:35; Eze 34:23,24; 37:24,25; Lk 1:69

SERVANT JACOB (5) Ge 32:4,18,20; Eze 28:25; 37:25

SERVANT MOSES (13) Ex 14:31; Nu 12:7; Jos 1:2; 9:24; 11:15; 1Ki 8:53,56; 2Ki 18:12; 21:8; Ne 1:7,8; 10:29; Mal 4:4

SERVANT OF GOD (6) 1Ch 6:49; 2Ch 24:9; Da 9:11; Rev 15:3; 19:10; 22:9

SERVANT OF THE LORD* (18) Dt 34:5; Jos 1:13,15; 8:33; 11:12; 12:6; 13:8; 14:7; 18:7; 22:2,4; 24:29; Jdg 2:8; 1Ki 18:12; 2Ch 24:6; Ps 18:T; 36:T; Isa 42:19

Ge 9:26 the LORD my God; / and may Canaan be his s.
9:27 the prosperity of Shem; / and let Canaan be his s."
15: 2 a son, Eliezer of Damascus, a s in my household,
15: 4 said to him, "No, your s will not be your heir,
16: 1 So Sarai took her s, an Egyptian woman named
16: 2 Sarai said to Abram. "Go and sleep with my s.
16: 3 took Hagar the Egyptian s and gave her to Abram
16: 5 Now this s of mine is pregnant, and she despises
16: 6 Abram replied, "Since she is your s, you may deal
16: 8 The angel said to her, "Hagar, Sarai's s,
18: 7 chose a fat calf and told a s to hurry and butcher it.
21: 9 the son of Abraham and her Egyptian s Hagar—
21:10 and demanded, "Get rid of that s and her son.
21:12 "Do not be upset over the boy and your s wife.
24: 2 in charge of his household, who was his oldest s,
24: 5 The s asked, "But suppose I can't find a young
24: 9 So the s took a solemn oath that he would follow
24:11 There the s made the camels kneel down beside a
24:17 Running over to her, the s asked, "Please give me
24:21 The s watched her in silence, wondering whether
24:33 But Abraham's s said, "I don't want to eat until I
24:34 "I am Abraham's s," he explained.
24:52 Abraham's s bowed to the ground and worshiped
24:54 and the s and the men with him stayed there
24:59 and sent her away with Abraham's s and his men.
24:61 mounted the camels and left with Abraham's s.
24:65 she asked the s. And he replied, "It is my master."
24:66 Then the s told Isaac the whole story.
25:12 of Abraham through Hagar, Sarah's Egyptian s.
26:24 because of my promise to Abraham, my s."
29:24 And Laban gave Leah a s, Zilpah, to be her maid.
29:29 And Laban gave Rachel a s, Bilhah, to be her
30: 3 Then Rachel told him, "Sleep with my s, Bilhah,
30: 9 so she gave her s, Zilpah, to Jacob to be his wife.
30:18 "God has rewarded me for giving my s to my
32: 4 'Humble greetings from your s Jacob!
32:10 and unfailing love you have shown to me, your s.
32:18 You should reply, 'These belong to your s Jacob.
32:20 'Your s Jacob is right behind us.' " Jacob's plan
35:25 sons of Bilhah, Rachel's s, were Dan and Naphtali.
35:26 The sons of Zilpah, Leah's s, were Gad and Asher.
41:12 man who was a s of the captain of the guard.
44:12 Joseph's s began searching the oldest brother's
46:18 the s given to Leah by her father, Laban.
46:25 the s given to Rachel by her father, Laban.
Ex 2: 5 and her s girls walked along the riverbank.
2: 5 she told one of her s girls to get it for her.
14:31 and put their faith in him and his s Moses.
20:17 neighbor's wife, male or female s, ox or donkey,
Lev 25:50 whatever it would cost to hire a s for that number
Nu 11:11 "Why are you treating me, your s, so miserably?
12: 7 But that is not how I communicate with my s
14:24 But my s Caleb is different from the others. He has
Dt 3:24 'O Sovereign LORD, I am your s. You have only
5:21 or land, male or female s, ox or donkey,
15:12 Israelite man or woman voluntarily becomes your s
15:12 in the seventh year you must set that s free.
15:13 "When you release a male s, do not send him
15:16 But suppose your s says, 'I will not leave you,'
15:17 into the door. After that, he will be your s for life.
34: 5 So Moses, the s of the LORD, died there in the
Jos 1: 1 After the death of Moses the LORD's s,
1: 2 "Now that my s Moses is dead, you must lead my
1:13 the s of the LORD, commanded you:
1:15 land that Moses, the s of the LORD, gave you."
5:14 Joshua said. "What do you want your s to do?"
8:31 LORD's s had written in the Book of the Law:
8:33 the s of the LORD, had given for blessing the
9:24 instructed his s Moses to conquer this entire land
11:12 just as Moses, the s of the LORD,
11:15 As the LORD had commanded his s Moses,
12: 6 Moses, the s of the LORD, and the Israelites had
13: 8 for Moses, the s of the LORD, had previously
14: 7 forty years old when Moses, the s of the LORD,
18: 7 which Moses, the s of the LORD,
22: 2 as Moses, the s of the LORD, commanded you,
22: 4 home now to the land Moses, the s of the LORD,
24:29 after this, Joshua son of Nun, the s of the LORD,
Jdg 2: 8 of Nun, the s of the LORD, died at the age of 110.
7:10 to attack, go down to the camp with your s Purah.
15:18 this great victory by the strength of your s.
16:26 Samson said to the s who was leading him by the
19: 3 her husband took a s and an extra donkey to
19: 9 and his concubine and s were preparing to leave,
19:11 and the man's s said to him, "It's getting too late
Ru 3: 9 he demanded. "I am your s Ruth," she replied.
1Sa 2:13 Eli's sons would send over a s with a
2:14 the s would stick the fork into the pot and demand
2:15 Sometimes the s would come even before the
2:16 Then the s would demand, "No, give it to me now,
3: 9 your s is listening.' " So Samuel went back to
3:10 And Samuel replied, "Yes, your s is listening."
9: 3 and he told Saul, "Take a s with you, and go look
9: 5 of Zuph, and Saul said to his s, "Let's go home.
9: 6 But the s said, "I've just thought of something!
9: 8 "Well," the s said, "I have one small silver piece.
9:11 So Saul and his s asked, "Is the seer here today?"
9:22 Samuel brought Saul and his s into the great hall
9:27 of town, Samuel told Saul to send his s on ahead.
9:27 After the s was gone, Samuel said, "Stay here,
10:10 When Saul and his s arrived at Gibeah, they saw
25:42 she took along five of her s girls as attendants,
26:19 But now let my lord the king listen to his s.
2Sa 6:20 He exposed himself to the s girls like any indecent
7: 5 "Go and tell my s David, 'This is what the
7: 8 "Now go and say to my s David, 'This is what the
7:26 And may the dynasty of your s David be
7:28 you have promised these good things to me, your s.
7:29 For when you grant a blessing to your s,
9: 6 bowed low in great fear and said, "I am your s."
9: 9 Then the king summoned Saul's s Ziba and said,
13:17 He shouted for his s and demanded, "Throw this
13:18 So the s put her out. She was wearing a long,
16: 1 the s of Mephibosheth, caught up with him.
17:17 Arrangements had been made for a s girl to bring
19:17 including Ziba, the s of Saul, and Ziba's fifteen
19:26 "My lord the king, my s Ziba deceived me.
20:17 So she said, "Listen carefully to your s."
1Ki 1:19 of the army. But he did not invite your s Solomon.
1:26 But I myself, your s, was not invited; neither were
8:24 You have kept your promise to your s David,
8:25 carry out your further promise to your s David,
8:26 fulfill this promise to your s David, my father.
8:28 and the prayer that your s is making to you today.
8:53 you told your s Moses that you had separated Israel
8:56 wonderful promises he gave through his s Moses.
8:66 because the LORD had been good to his s David
11:13 for the sake of my s David and for the sake of
11:32 But I will leave him one tribe for the sake of my s
11:34 For the sake of my s David, the one whom I chose
11:36 so that the descendants of David my s will
11:38 obey my laws and commands, as my s David did,
14: 8 But you have not been like my s David,
18:12 Yet I have been a true s of the LORD all my life.
18:36 that you are God in Israel and that I am your s.
18:43 Then he said to his s, "Go and look out toward the
18:43 The s went and looked, but he returned to Elijah
18:44 Finally the seventh time, his s told him, "I saw a
19: 3 a town in Judah, and he left his s there.
20:32 of Israel and begged, "Your s Ben-hadad says,
2Ki 4:12 He said to his s Gehazi, "Tell the woman I want to
4:20 So the s took him home, and his mother held him
4:24 So she saddled the donkey and said to the s,
4:38 he said to his s, "Put on a large kettle and make
4:43 "What?" his s exclaimed. "Feed one hundred
5: 6 "With this letter I present my s Naaman.
5:20 But Gehazi, Elisha's s, said to himself,
6:15 When the s of the man of God got up early the next
8: 4 was talking with Gehazi, the s of the man of God.
8: 9 He went in to him and said, "Your s Ben-hadad,
9:36 which he spoke through his s Elijah from Tishbe:
10:10 The LORD declared through his s Elijah that this
16: 7 "I am your s and your vassal. Come up and rescue
18:12 all the laws the LORD had given through his s
19:34 For my own honor and for the sake of my s David,
20: 6 my honor and for the sake of my s David.' "
21: 8 the whole law that was given through my s
1Ch 2:34 He also had an Egyptian s named Jarha.
6:49 that Moses, the s of God, had given them.
16:13 O children of Israel, God's s, / O descendants of
17: 4 "Go and tell my s David, 'This is what the
17: 7 "Now go and say to my s David, 'This is what the
17:24 And may the dynasty of your s David be
17:26 you have promised these good things to me, your s.

2Ch 1: 3 the LORD's s, had constructed in the wilderness.
6: 15 You have kept your promise to your s David,
6: 16 carry out your further promise to your s David,
6: 17 God of Israel, fulfill this promise to your s David.
6: 19 the cry and the prayer that your s is making to you.
6: 42 Remember your unfailing love for your s David."
13: 6 who was a mere s of David's son Solomon,
24: 6 Moses, the s of the LORD, levied this tax on the
24: 9 the s of God, had required of the Israelites in the
32: 16 mocked the LORD God and his s Hezekiah,
Ezr 7: 24 that no priest, Levite, singer, gatekeeper, Temple s,
Ne 1: 7 and regulations that you gave us through your s
1: 8 "Please remember what you told your s Moses:
2: 5 and if you are pleased with me, your s,
6: 5 Sanballat's s came with an open letter in his hand,
9: 14 And you commanded them, through Moses your s,
10: 29 to obey the law of God as issued by his s Moses.
Job 1: 8 asked Satan, "Have you noticed my s Job?
2: 3 asked Satan, "Have you noticed my s Job?
7: 2 longs for the day to end, like a s waiting to be paid.
19: 15 The s girls consider me a stranger. I am like a
19: 16 I call my s, but he doesn't come; I even plead with
42: 7 right in what you said about me, as my s Job was.
42: 8 young bulls and seven rams and go to my s Job
42: 8 My s Job will pray for you, and I will accept his
42: 8 right in what you said about me, as my s Job was."
Ps 18: T A psalm of David, the s of the LORD.
27: 9 yourself from me. / Do not reject your s in anger.
31: 16 Let your favor shine on your s. / In your unfailing
35: 27 "Great is the LORD, / who enjoys helping his s."
36: T A psalm of David, the s of the LORD.
60: 8 Moab will become my lowly s, / and Edom will be
69: 17 Don't hide from your s; / answer me quickly,
78: 70 He chose his s David, / calling him from the sheep
86: 16 Give strength to your s; / yes, save me, for I am
your s.
89: 3 a solemn agreement with David, my chosen s.
89: 20 I have found my s David. / I have anointed him
105: 6 O children of Abraham, God's s, / O descendants
105: 26 But the LORD sent Moses his s, / along with
105: 42 remembered his sacred promise / to Abraham his s.
108: 9 Moab will become my lowly s, / and Edom will be
109: 28 But I, your s, will go right on rejoicing!
116: 16 O LORD, I am your s; / yes, I am your s, the son of
119: 17 Be good to your s, / that I may live and obey your
119: 76 love comfort me, / just as you promised me, your s.
119: 124 I am your s; / deal with me in unfailing love,
119: 125 Give discernment to me, your s; / then I will
132: 10 For the sake of your s David, / do not reject the
136: 22 a special possession to his s Israel. / His faithful
143: 2 Don't bring your s to trial! / Compared to you,
143: 12 and destroy all my foes, / for I am your s.
144: 10 You are the one who rescued your s David.
Pr 11: 29 only the wind. The fool will be a s to the wise.
12: 9 It is better to be a nobody with a s than to be
22: 7 rule the poor, so the borrower is s to the lender.
29: 19 For a s, mere words are not enough—discipline is
29: 21 A s who is pampered from childhood will later
30: 23 a husband, / a s girl who supplants her mistress.
31: 15 and plan the day's work for her s girls.
Ecc 7: 21 on others—you may hear your s laughing at you.
Isa 20: 3 "My s Isaiah has been walking around naked
22: 20 then I will call my s Eliakim son of Hilkiah to
37: 35 For my own honor and for the sake of my s David,
41: 8 "But as for you, Israel my s, Jacob my chosen one,
42: 1 "Look at my s, whom I strengthen. He is my
42: 19 all the world is as blind as my own people, my s?
42: 19 as blind as my chosen people, the s of the LORD?
43: 10 O Israel!" says the LORD. "And you are my s.
44: 1 "But now, listen to me, Jacob my s, Israel my
44: 2 O Jacob, my s, do not be afraid. O Israel,
44: 21 "Pay attention, O Israel, for you are my s. I,
45: 4 It is for the sake of Jacob my s, Israel my chosen
49: 3 He said to me, "You are my s, Israel, and you will
49: 5 who formed me in my mother's womb to be his s,
49: 7 by a nation, to the one who is the s of rulers:
50: 10 Who among you fears the LORD and obeys his s?
52: 13 See, my s will prosper; he will be highly exalted.
53: 2 My s grew up in the LORD's presence like a
53: 11 my righteous s will make it possible for many to be
Jer 27: 6 to King Nebuchadnezzar of Babylon, who is my s.
30: 10 "So do not be afraid, Jacob, my s; do not be
33: 21 will my covenant with David, my s, be broken.
33: 22 my s, and the Levites who minister before me."
33: 26 abandon the descendants of Jacob or David, my s,
43: 10 I will surely bring my s Nebuchadnezzar, king of
46: 27 "But do not be afraid, Jacob, my s; do not be
46: 28 Fear not, Jacob, my s," says the LORD, "for I
Eze 28: 25 live in their own land, the land I gave my s Jacob.
34: 23 will set one shepherd over them, even my s David.
34: 24 and my s David will be a prince among my people.
37: 24 "My s David will be their king, and they will have
37: 25 their ancestors lived, the land I gave my s Jacob.
37: 25 And my s David will be their prince forever.
46: 17 the s may keep it only until the Year of Jubilee,
46: 17 At that time the s will be set free, and the land will
Da 6: 20 called out in anguish, "Daniel, s of the living God!
9: 11 the s of God, have been poured out against us
10: 17 can someone like me, your s, talk to you, my lord?
Na 2: 7 been decreed, and all the s girls mourn its capture.
Hag 2: 23 will honor you, Zerubbabel son of Shealtiel, my s.
Zec 3: 8 Soon I am going to bring my s, the Branch.
Mal 1: 6 son honors his father, and a s respects his master.
4: 4 "Remember to obey the instructions of my s
Mt 8: 6 "Lord, my young s lies in bed, paralyzed
8: 8 word from where you are, and my s will be healed!
8: 13 And the young s was healed that same hour.
10: 24 than the teacher. A s is not greater than the master.
10: 25 The s shares the master's fate. And since I,
12: 18 "Look at my S, / whom I have chosen. / He is my
18: 28 he went to a fellow s who owed him a few
18: 29 His fellow s fell down before him and begged for a
18: 32 in the man he had forgiven and said, 'You evil s!
18: 33 Shouldn't you have mercy on your fellow s,
20: 26 wants to be a leader among you must be your s,
23: 11 The greatest among you must be a s.
24: 45 "Who is a faithful, sensible s, to whom the master
24: 46 and finds that the s has done a good job,
24: 47 the master will put that s in charge of all he owns.
24: 48 But if the s is evil and thinks, 'My master won't be
24: 51 He will tear the s apart and banish him with the
25: 16 The s who received the five bags of gold began
25: 17 The s with two bags of gold also went right to
25: 18 But the s who received the one bag of gold dug a
25: 20 The s to whom he had entrusted the five bags of
25: 21 full of praise. 'Well done, my good and faithful s.
25: 22 "Next came the s who had received the two bags
25: 23 master said, 'Well done, my good and faithful s.
25: 24 "Then the s with the one bag of gold came
25: 26 "But the master replied, 'You wicked and lazy s!
25: 28 Take the money from this s and give it to the one
25: 30 Now throw this useless s into outer darkness,
26: 51 and slashed off an ear of the high priest's s.
26: 69 in the courtyard, a s girl came over and said to him,
26: 71 another s girl noticed him and said to those
Mk 9: 35 must take last place and be the s of everyone else."
10: 43 wants to be a leader among you must be your s,
12: 3 But the farmers grabbed the s, beat him up,
12: 4 "The owner then sent another s, but they beat him
12: 5 The next s he sent was killed. Others who were
14: 47 and slashed off an ear of the high priest's s.
14: 66 One of the s girls who worked for the high priest
14: 69 The s girl saw him standing there and began telling
Lk 1: 38 Mary responded, "I am the Lord's s, and I am
1: 48 For he took notice of his lowly s girl, / and now
1: 54 And how he has helped his s Israel! / He has not
1: 69 mighty Savior / from the royal line of his s David,
7: 7 word from where you are, and my s will be healed.
12: 42 sensible s to whom the master gives the
12: 43 and finds that the s has done a good job,
12: 44 the master will put that s in charge of all he owns.
12: 45 But if the s thinks, 'My master won't be back for a
12: 46 He will tear the s apart and banish him with the
12: 47 The s will be severely punished, for though he
14: 17 he sent his s around to notify the guests that it was
14: 21 "The s returned and told his master what they had
14: 22 After the s had done this, he reported, 'There is
17: 7 "When a s comes in from plowing or taking care
17: 9 And the s is not even thanked, because he is
19: 16 The first s reported a tremendous gain—ten times
19: 17 the king exclaimed. 'You are a trustworthy s.
19: 18 "The next s also reported a good gain—five times
19: 20 "But the third s brought back only the original
19: 22 " 'You wicked s!' the king roared. 'Hard, am I?
19: 24 the king ordered, 'Take the money from this s,
19: 25 master,' they said, 'that s has enough already!'
20: 10 But the farmers attacked the s, beat him up,
20: 11 So the owner sent another s, but the same thing
22: 26 the lowest rank, and the leader should be like a s.
22: 27 by his servants. But not here! For I am your s.
22: 50 And one of them slashed at the high priest's s
22: 56 A s girl noticed him in the firelight and began
Jn 13: 16 How true it is that a s is not greater than the
15: 20 'A s is not greater than the master.' Since they
18: 10 off the right ear of Malchus, the high priest's s.
Ac 3: 13 who has brought glory to his s Jesus by doing this.
3: 26 When God raised up his s, he sent him first to you
4: 25 through our ancestor King David, your s, saying,
4: 27 against Jesus, your holy s, whom you anointed.
4: 30 be done through the name of your holy s Jesus."
12: 13 the gate, and a s girl named Rhoda came to open it.
26: 16 For I have appeared to you to appoint you as my s
Ro 15: 8 Remember that Christ came as a s to the Jews to
1Co 9: 19 yet I have become a s of everyone so that I can
Gal 1: 10 trying to please people, I would not be Christ's s.
Col 1: 7 He is Christ's faithful s, and he is helping us in
4: 12 Epaphras, from your city, a s of Christ Jesus,
1Ti 4: 6 you will be doing your duty as a worthy s of Christ
Heb 3: 5 certainly faithful in God's house, but only as a s.
Rev 1: 1 An angel was sent to God's s John so that John
15: 3 of Moses, the s of God, and the song of the Lamb:
19: 10 For I am a s of God, just like you and other
22: 9 I am a s of God, just like you and your brothers the

SERVANT'S (2) [SERVANT]

2Ki 6: 17 The LORD opened his s eyes, and when he
Da 9: 17 "O our God, hear your s prayer! Listen as I plead.

SERVANTS (243) [SERVANT]

SERVANTS, THE PROPHETS (10) 2Ki 17:13; 21:10; Ezr 9:11; Jer 26:5; 44:4; Da 9:6,10; Am 3:7; Zec 1:6; Rev 10:7

TEMPLE SERVANTS (15) Ezr 2:43,58,70; 7:7; 8:17,20,20; Ne 3:26,31; 7:46,60,73; 10:28; 11:3,21

Ge 9: 25 May they be the lowest of s / to the descendants of
12: 16 sheep, cattle, donkeys, male and female s,
13: 11 He went there with his flocks and s and parted
15: 3 so one of my s will have to be my heir."
17: 12 but also to the s born in your household
17: 12 and the foreign-born s whom you have purchased.
17: 27 whether they were born there or bought as s.
18: 4 Rest in the shade of this tree while my s get some
20: 8 and hastily called a meeting of all his s.
20: 14 Then Abimelech took sheep and oxen and s—
21: 25 s had taken violently from Abraham's s.
22: 3 saddled his donkey and took two of his s with him,
24: 35 and gold, and many s and camels and donkeys.
24: 61 Then Rebekah and her s mounted the camels
26: 14 and goats, great herds of cattle, and many s.
26: 15 These were the wells that had been dug by the s of
26: 25 set up his camp at that place, and his s dug a well.
26: 32 That very day Isaac's s came and told him about a
27: 29 May many nations become your s. May you be the
27: 37 and have declared that all his brothers will be his s.
30: 43 very wealthy, with many s, camels, and donkeys.
32: 5 donkeys, sheep, goats, and many s, both men
32: 16 He told his s to lead them on ahead, each group of
32: 17 will ask, 'Where are you going? Whose s are you?
36: 6 children, household s, cattle, and flocks—
42: 25 then ordered his s to fill the men's sacks with
47: 19 for food; we will then become s to Pharaoh.
47: 21 all the people of Egypt became s to Pharaoh.
47: 25 "May it please you, sir, to let us be Pharaoh's s."
50: 17 So we, the s of the God of your father, beg you to
Ex 9: 19 your livestock and s to come in from the fields.
9: 20 brought their livestock and s in from the fields.
12: 45 Hired s and visiting foreigners may not eat it.
20: 10 your sons and daughters, your male and female s,
32: 13 Remember your covenant with your s—Abraham,
Lev 22: 10 lives in a priest's home or is one of his hired s.
25: 6 your male and female slaves, your hired s,
25: 40 Treat them instead as hired s or as resident
25: 42 The people of Israel are my s, whom I brought out
25: 53 The foreigner must treat them as s hired on a
25: 55 For the people of Israel are my s, whom I brought
Nu 22: 22 his way. As Balaam and two s were riding along,
32: 25 "We are your s and will follow your instructions
Dt 5: 14 your male and female s, your oxen and donkeys
5: 14 All your male and female s must rest as you do.
9: 27 but remember instead your s Abraham, Isaac,
12: 12 and all your s in the presence of the LORD your
12: 18 Eat them there with your children, your s,
15: 17 for life. "You must do the same for your female s.
15: 18 not consider it a hardship when you release your s.
16: 11 all your s, the Levites from your towns,
16: 14 your s, and with the Levites, foreigners, orphans,
29: 2 to Pharaoh and all his s and his whole country—
32: 36 and he will change his mind about his s,
32: 43 for he will avenge the blood of his s,
33: 8 given the sacred lots / to your faithful s the Levites.
34: 11 against Pharaoh, all his s, and his entire land.
Jos 9: 8 They replied, "We will be your s." "But who are
9: 11 of Israel and declare our people to be their s,
10: 6 to Joshua at Gilgal, "Don't abandon your s now!"
Jdg 3: 19 So the king commanded his s to be silent and sent
3: 24 the king's s returned and found the doors to the
3: 26 While the s were waiting, Ehud escaped,
6: 27 So Gideon took ten of his s and did as the LORD
9: 28 Why should we be Abimelech's s? He's merely the
9: 38 'Who is Abimelech, and why should we be his s?'
1Sa 8: 14 and olive groves and give them to his own s.
9: 4 So Saul took one of his s and traveled all through
11: 1 with us, and we will be your s," they pleaded.
16: 15 Some of Saul's s suggested a remedy. "It is clear
16: 18 One of the s said to Saul, "The son of Jesse is a
19: 1 Saul now urged his s and his son Jonathan to
22: 14 "is there anyone among all your s who is as
25: 8 Ask your own s, and they will tell you this is true.
25: 10 There are lots of s these days who run away from
25: 14 one of Nabal's s went to Abigail and told her,
25: 18 She packed them on donkeys and said to her s,
25: 41 I am even willing to become a slave to David's s!"
2Sa 8: 2 The Moabites who were spared became David's s
9: 2 a man named Ziba, who had been one of Saul's s.
9: 10 and s are to farm the land for him to produce food
9: 10 Ziba, who had fifteen sons and twenty s, replied,
9: 12 of Ziba's household were Mephibosheth's s.
11: 9 the palace entrance with some of the king's other s.
13: 9 "Everyone get out of here," Amnon told his s.
13: 24 and his s please come to celebrate the occasion
14: 30 So Absalom said to his s, "Go and set fire to
14: 31 "Why did your s set my field on fire?"
19: 17 of Saul, and Ziba's fifteen sons and twenty s.
1Ki 1: 27 any of his s know who should be the next king?"
5: 9 My s will bring the logs from the Lebanon
8: 32 then hear from heaven and judge between your s—
8: 36 hear from heaven and forgive the sins of your s,
11: 11 away from you and give it to one of your s.
2Ki 1: 13 spare my life and the lives of these, your fifty s.
4: 19 His father said to one of the s, "Carry him home to
4: 22 "Send one of the s and a donkey so that I can
5: 23 and sent two of his s to carry the gifts for Gehazi.
5: 24 Gehazi took the gifts from the s and sent the men
5: 26 and vineyards and sheep and oxen and s?
9: 7 and all the LORD's s who were killed by Jezebel.
10: 5 "We are your s and will do anything you tell us.
17: 13 and which I gave you through my s the prophets."
20: 7 Then Isaiah said to Hezekiah's s, "Make an
21: 10 Then the LORD said through his s the prophets:
21: 23 Then Amon's own s plotted against him
1Ch 19: 19 When the s of Hadadezer realized they had been
21: 3 do you want to do this? Are they not all your s?
2Ch 6: 23 then hear from heaven and judge between your s—
6: 27 hear from heaven and forgive the sins of your s,
36: 20 and they became s to the king and his sons until the
Ezr 2: 43 The descendants of the following Temple s
2: 55 The descendants of these s of King Solomon
2: 58 the Temple s and the descendants of Solomon's s
numbered 392.
2: 65 in addition to 7,337 s and 200 singers, both men

2:70 the singers, the gatekeepers, the Temple s,
5:11 'We are the s of the God of heaven and earth,
7: 7 Levites, singers, gatekeepers, and Temple s,
8:17 and the Temple s to send us ministers for the
8:20 and 220 Temple s. The Temple s were assistants to
9:11 Your s the prophets warned us that the land we
Ne 1:10 "We are your s, the people you rescued by your
2:20 We his s will start rebuilding this wall. But you
3:26 and the Temple s living on the hill of Ophel,
3:31 the wall as far as the housing for the Temple s
4:22 and their s could go on guard duty at night as well
4:23 not I, nor my relatives, nor my s, nor the guards
7:46 "The descendants of the following Temple s
7:57 "The descendants of these s of King Solomon
7:60 the Temple s and the descendants of Solomon's s numbered 392.
7:67 in addition to 7,337 s and 245 singers, both men
7:73 the gatekeepers, the singers, the Temple s,
9:10 wonders against Pharaoh, his s, and all his people,
10:28 the priests, Levites, gatekeepers, singers, Temple s,
11: 3 Most of the people, priests, Levites, Temple s,
11: 3 and descendants of Solomon's s continued to live
11:21 However, the Temple s, whose leaders were Ziha
13:19 I also sent some of my own s to guard the gates
Est 1: 5 the king gave a special banquet for all the palace s
2:18 banquet in Esther's honor for all his princes and s,
Job 1: 3 hundred female donkeys, and he employed many s.
1:17 raiders have stolen your camels and killed your s.
31:13 "If I have been unfair to my male or female s,
31:15 For God created both me and my s. He created us
31:31 My s have never let others go hungry.
Ps 79: 2 They have left the bodies of your s / as food for the
79:10 for they have spilled the blood of your s.
89:50 Consider, Lord, how your s are disgraced! / I carry
90:13 How long will you delay? / Take pity on your s!
104: 4 are your messengers; / flames of fire are your s.
105:25 and they plotted against the LORD's s.
113: 1 the LORD! / Yes, give praise, O s of the LORD.
123: 2 just as s keep their eyes on their master,
132: 9 agents of salvation; / may your loyal s sing for joy.
134: 1 bless the LORD, all you s of the LORD,
135:14 his people / and have compassion on his s.
Pr 9: 3 She has sent her s to invite everyone to come.
14:35 A king rejoices in s who know what they are
27:27 goats' milk for you, your family, and your s.
Ecc 10: 7 I have even seen s riding like princes—and princes walking like s.
Isa 24: 2 s and masters, maids and mistresses, buyers
38:21 Isaiah had said to Hezekiah's s, "Make an
48:20 of the earth that the LORD has redeemed his s,
54:17 These benefits are enjoyed by the s of the LORD;
61: 5 Foreigners will be your s. They will feed your
63:17 for we are your s and your special possession.
65: 8 not destroy all Israel. For I still have true s there.
65:13 "You will starve, but my s will eat. You will be
65:14 cry in sorrow and despair, while my s sing for joy.
65:15 destroy you and call his true s by another name.
Jer 14: 3 The nobles send s to get water, but all the wells are
14: 3 The s return with empty pitchers, confused
26: 5 and if you will not listen to my s, the prophets—
44: 4 "Again and again I sent my s, the prophets,
Eze 12:14 I will scatter his s and guards to the four winds
46:17 But if he gives a gift of land to one of his s,
Da 3:26 and Abednego, s of the Most High God, come out!
3:28 He sent his angel to rescue his s who trusted in
9: 6 We have refused to listen to your s the prophets,
9:10 the laws he gave us through his s the prophets.
11:43 and the Libyans and Ethiopians will be his s.
Joel 2:29 I will pour out my Spirit even on s, men
Am 3: 7 first of all, I warn you through my s the prophets.
Na 3:10 to see who would get the Egyptian officers as s.
Zec 1: 6 But all the things I said through my s the prophets
Mt 13:27 The farmer's s came and told him, 'Sir, the field
18:23 to date with s who had borrowed money from him.
18:31 "When some of the other s saw this, they were
21:34 At the time of the grape harvest he sent his s to
21:35 But the farmers grabbed his s, beat one, killed one,
21:36 So the landowner sent a larger group of his s to
22: 3 he sent his s to notify everyone that it was time to
22: 4 So he sent other s to tell them, 'The feast has been
22: 8 And he said to his s, 'The wedding feast is ready,
22:10 "So the s brought in everyone they could find,
24:49 and begins oppressing the other s, partying,
25:14 He called together his s and gave them money to
Mk 12: 2 At grape-picking time he sent one of his s to
Lk 12:38 there will be special favor for his s who are ready!
12:45 and begins oppressing the other s, partying,
15:22 "But his father said to the s, 'Quick!
15:26 and he asked one of the s what was going on.
17:10 We are s who have simply done our duty.' "
19:13 he called together ten s and gave them ten pounds
19:15 the king called in the s to whom he had given the
20:10 he sent one of his s to collect his share of the crop.
22:27 the master sits at the table and is served by his s.
Jn 2: 5 But his mother told the s, "Do whatever he tells
2: 7 Jesus told the s, "Fill the jars with water."
2: 9 of course, the s knew), he called the bridegroom
4:51 some of his s met him with the news that his son
12:26 and follow me, because my s must be where I am.
15:15 I no longer call you s, because a master doesn't confide in his s.
18:18 and the household s were standing around a
18:26 But one of the household s of the high priest,
Ac 2:18 upon all my s, men and women alike, / and they
4:29 and give your s great boldness in their preaching.
10: 7 Cornelius called two of his household s and a
16:17 "These men are s of the Most High God,
Ro 14: 4 Who are you to condemn God's s? They are
1Co 3: 5 Why, we're only s. Through us God caused you to
4: 1 and me as mere s of Christ who have been put in
2Co 4: 5 All we say about ourselves is that we are your s
11:15 So it is no wonder his s can also do it by
12:19 We tell you this as Christ's s, and we know that
2Ti 2:24 The Lord's s must not quarrel but must be kind to
Heb 1: 7 swift as the wind, / and s made of flaming fire."
1:14 But angels are only s. They are spirits sent from
Rev 1: 1 John could share the revelation with God's other s.
2:20 who calls herself a prophet—to lead my s astray.
6:11 full number of the s of Jesus had been martyred.
7: 3 placed the seal of God on the foreheads of his s."
10: 7 It will happen just as he announced it to his s the
11:18 It is time to judge the dead and reward your s.
19: 2 and he has avenged the murder of his s."
19: 5 "Praise our God, all his s, from the least to the
22: 3 the Lamb will be there, and his s will worship him.

SERVE (188) [SERVED, SERVES, SERVICE, SERVICES, SERVING]

Ge 17: 1 s me faithfully and live a blameless life.
25:23 the descendants of your older son will s the
27:40 You will s your brother for a time, but then you
31:13 the pillar of stone and made a vow to s me.
Ex 3:12 And this will s as proof that I have sent you:
10: 7 Please let the Israelites go to s the LORD their
10: 8 go and s the LORD your God," he said.
10:11 Only the men may go and s the LORD, for that is
12:13 have smeared on your doorposts will s as a sign.
12:31 Go and s the LORD as you have requested.
18:22 These men can s the people, resolving all the
21: 2 buy a Hebrew slave, he is to s for only six years.
23:24 gods of these other nations or s them in any way,
23:25 "You must s only the LORD your God. If you
28: 3 from everyone else, so he may s me as a priest.
28: 4 sons to wear when they s as priests before me.
28:41 Set them apart as holy so they can s as my priests.
40:13 anoint him, setting him apart to s me as a priest.
40:15 as you did their father, so they may s me as priests.
Lev 7:35 they were appointed to s the LORD as priests.
24: 7 It will s as a token offering, to be burned in place
25:40 and they will s you only until the Year of Jubilee.
Nu 3: 4 and Ithamar to s as priests with their father,
3: 7 They will s Aaron and the whole community,
4:23 and fifty who are eligible to s in the Tabernacle.
4:30 and fifty who are eligible to s in the Tabernacle.
4:37 clans who were eligible to s at the Tabernacle.
4:41 clans who were eligible to s at the Tabernacle.
8:19 They will s in the Tabernacle on behalf of the
16: 9 be near him as you s in the LORD's Tabernacle
16:38 then s as a warning to the people of Israel."
18:23 The Levites must s at the Tabernacle, and they will
35: 5 This area will s as the larger pastureland for the
Dt 1:15 and appointed them to s as judges and officials
6:13 You must fear the LORD your God and s him.
13: 4 S only the LORD your God and fear him alone.
20:11 then all the people inside will s you in forced labor.
28:46 These horrors will s as a sign and warning among
28:48 you will s your enemies whom the LORD will
29:26 They turned to s and worship other gods that were
30:17 and if you are drawn away to s and worship other
31:19 to sing it, so it may s as a witness against them.
31:26 so it may s as a witness against the people of
Jos 22: 5 and s him with all your heart and all your soul."
24:14 "So honor the LORD and s him wholeheartedly.
24:14 Euphrates River and in Egypt. S the LORD alone.
24:15 But if you are unwilling to s the LORD, then choose today whom you will s.
24:15 as for me and my family, we will s the LORD."
24:18 So we, too, will s the LORD, for he alone is our
24:19 "You are not able to s the LORD, for he is a holy
24:20 If you forsake the LORD and s other gods,
24:21 saying, "No, we are determined to s the LORD!"
24:22 "You have chosen to s the LORD." "Yes,"
24:24 said to Joshua, "We will s the LORD our God.
Jdg 2:13 They abandoned the LORD to s Baal
9:28 S the men of Hamor, who are Shechem's true descendants. Why should we s Abimelech?
1Sa 2:31 to your family, so it will no longer s as my priests.
2:35 "Then I will raise up a faithful priest who will s
27:12 Now he will have to stay here and s me forever!"
2Sa 16:19 "And anyway, why shouldn't I s you? I helped
22:44 over nations; / people I don't even know now s me.
1Ki 4:21 and continued to s him throughout his lifetime.
9:21 and they s in the labor force to this day.
9:22 Instead, he assigned them to s as fighting men,
12: 7 "If you are willing to s the people today and give
17: 1 of Israel, lives—the God whom I worship and s—
2Ki 3:14 surely as the LORD Almighty lives, whom I s,
5:16 whom I s, I will not accept any gifts."
17:35 or bow before them or s them or offer sacrifices to
20:18 They will become eunuchs who will s in the palace
23: 9 not allowed to s at the LORD's altar in Jerusalem,
25:24 "Live in the land and s the king of Babylon,
1Ch 23: 4 Six thousand are to s as officials and judges.
23:13 in the LORD's presence, to s the LORD,
26:29 and his sons were appointed to s as public
28: 9 Worship and s him with your whole heart and with
28:21 of priests and Levites will s in the Temple of God.
2Ch 8: 8 and they s in the labor force to this day.
8: 9 Instead, he assigned them to s as fighting men,
11:14 and his sons would not allow them to s the LORD
11:15 Jeroboam appointed his own priests to s at the
12: 8 so that they can learn how much better it is to s me than to s earthly rulers."
13:10 Only the descendants of Aaron s the LORD as
17:19 These were the troops stationed in Jerusalem to s
19: 8 and clan leaders in Israel to s as judges in
23: 4 the Sabbath, a third of them will s as gatekeepers.
35: 3 who had been set apart to s the LORD and were
Ezr 2:62 so they were not allowed to s as priests.
6:18 divisions to s at the Temple of God in Jerusalem,
Ne 7: 3 Some will s at their regular posts and some in front
7:64 so they were not allowed to s as priests.
9:35 they did not s you even though you showered your
9:37 We s them at their pleasure, and we are in great
10:28 the pagan people of the land in order to s God,
Ps 2:11 S the LORD with reverent fear, / and rejoice with
18:43 over nations; / people I don't even know now s me.
22:30 Future generations will also s him. / Our children
34:22 But the LORD will redeem those who s him.
72:11 will bow before him, / and all nations will s him.
86: 2 Save me, for I s you and trust you. / You are my
101: 6 who are above reproach / will be allowed to s me.
101: 7 I will not allow deceivers to s me, / and liars will
103:21 you armies of angels / who s him and do his will!
110: 3 day of battle, / your people will s you willingly.
134: 1 you who s as night watchmen in the house of the
135: 1 the LORD! / Praise him, you who s the LORD,
135: 2 you who s in the house of the LORD,
Pr 22:29 They will s kings rather than ordinary people.
23: 8 You will vomit up the delicious food they s,
Isa 14: 2 and those who come to live in their land will s
39: 7 They will become eunuchs who will s in the palace
41: 9 back from the ends of the earth so you can s me.
49:23 Kings and queens will s you. They will care for all
56: 6 to the LORD and s him and love his name,
65: 9 Those I choose will inherit it and s me there.
Jer 5:19 Now you will s foreigners in a land that is not your
15:19 I will restore you so you can continue to s me.
25:11 and her neighboring lands will s the king of
27: 7 All the nations will s him and his son and his
27: 8 So you must submit to Babylon's king and s him;
30: 9 For my people will s the LORD their God
35:19 of Recab will always have descendants who s me.
40: 9 "Stay here, and s the king of Babylon," he said,
Eze 20:32 all around us, who s idols of wood and stone.'
44:14 They are to s as the Temple caretakers and are
44:15 These men will s as my ministers. They will stand
44:16 enter my sanctuary and approach my table to s me.
44:24 "They will s as judges to resolve any
Da 1: 4 and have the poise needed to s in the royal palace.
3:12 They have defied Your Majesty by refusing to s
3:14 that you refuse to s my gods or to worship the gold
3:17 the God whom we s is able to save us.
3:18 Your Majesty can be sure that we will never s your
3:28 and were willing to die rather than s
7:27 rule forever, and all rulers will s and obey them."
Hos 11: 5 go back to Egypt and will be forced to s Assyria.
Joel 1:13 Wail, you who s before the altar! Come,
Jnh 1:16 they offered him a sacrifice and vowed to s him.
Zec 6:13 He will also s as priest from his throne, and there
Mal 1:13 You say, 'It's too hard to s the LORD,' and you
3:18 between those who s God and those who do not."
Mt 4:10 must worship the Lord your God; / s only him.' "
6:24 "No one can s two masters. For you will hate one
6:24 the other. You cannot s both God and money.
20:28 of Man, came here not to be served but to s others,
Mk 10:45 of Man, came here not to be served but to s others,
Lk 1:74 from our enemies, / so we can s God without fear,
4: 8 must worship the Lord your God; / s only him.' "
12:37 put on an apron, and s them as they sit and eat!
16:13 "No one can s two masters. For you will hate one
16:13 the other. You cannot s both God and money."
17: 8 and s him his supper before eating his own.
Ac 7:42 away from them and gave them up to s the sun,
17:25 and human hands can't s his needs—for he has no
27:23 to whom I belong and whom I s stood beside me,
Ro 1: 9 whom I s with all my heart by telling others the
3: 5 "But," some say, "our sins s a good purpose,
7: 6 Now we can really s God, not in the old way by
9:12 "The descendants of your older son will s the
12: 7 If your gift is that of serving others, s them well.
12:11 lazy in your work, but s the Lord enthusiastically.
14:18 If you s Christ with this attitude, you will please
1Co 7:35 I want you to do whatever will help you s the Lord
9:10 Christian workers should be paid by those they s.
9:13 And those who s at the altar get a share of the
16:16 and others like them who s with such real
16:18 You must give proper honor to all who s so well.
2Co 4:11 under constant danger of death because we s Jesus,
6: 8 We s God whether people honor us or despise us,
11: 8 their contributions so I could s you at no cost.
11:23 They say they s Christ? I know I sound like a
Gal 4:24 Now these two women s as an illustration of God's
5:13 sinful nature, but freedom to s one another in love.
Eph 6: 5 S them sincerely as you would s Christ.
1Th 1: 9 and how you turned away from idols to s the true
1Ti 1:12 me trustworthy and appointing me to s him,
3:10 If they do well, then they may s as deacons.
2Ti 1: 3 He is the God I s with a clear conscience, just as
Heb 7:13 whose members do not s at the altar.
8: 5 They s in a place of worship that is only a copy,
8: 6 to the ministry of those who s under the old laws,
1Pe 5: 2 get out of it, but because you are eager to s God.
5: 5 And all of you, s each other in humility, for
Rev 1: 6 and his priests who s before God his Father.

SERVED (65) [SERVE]

Ge 18: 8 and the roasted meat, and he s it to the men.
24:33 Then supper was s. But Abraham's servant said,

27:25 ate it. He also drank the wine that Jacob s him.
27:33 "Then who was it that just s me wild game?
30:29 "You know how faithfully I've s you through
39: 2 and blessed him greatly as he s in the home of his
43:32 and his brothers were s at a separate table.
43:34 Their food was s to them from Joseph's own table.
Ex 38: 8 women who s at the entrance of the Tabernacle.
38:21 and Ithamar son of Aaron the priest s as recorder.
39: 7 These stones s as reminders to the LORD
Nu 10:25 They s as the rear guard for all the tribal camps.
26:10 This s as a warning to the entire nation of Israel.
Dt 28:47 Because you have not s the LORD your God with
Jos 24:15 Would you prefer the gods your ancestors s
24:31 Israel s the LORD throughout the lifetime of
Jdg 2: 7 And the Israelites s the LORD throughout the
10: 6 abandoned the LORD and no longer s him at all.
10:10 you as our God and have s the images of Baal."
10:13 Yet you have abandoned me and s other gods.
10:16 put aside their foreign gods and s the LORD.
1Sa 2:28 and to wear the priestly garments as he s me.
12: 2 I have s as your leader since I was a boy.
14: 3 the priest of the LORD who had s at Shiloh.)
16:21 So David went to Saul and s him. Saul liked David
22:11 and all his family, who s as priests at Nob.
2Sa 8:18 David's sons s as priestly leaders.
12: 4 man's lamb and killed it and s it to his guest."
1Ki 19:10 "I have zealously s the LORD God Almighty.
19:14 "I have zealously s the LORD God Almighty.
22:53 He s Baal and worshiped him, arousing the anger
2Ki 4: 1 cried out to him, "My husband who s you is dead,
23: 9 The priests who had s at the pagan shrines were
1Ch 6:33 These are the men who s, along with their sons:
6:49 Only Aaron and his descendants s as priests.
9:18 These men s as gatekeepers for the camps of the
18:17 David's sons s as the king's chief assistants.
23:28 of Aaron, as they s at the house of the LORD.
23:28 and s in many other ways in the house of God.
23:31 The proper number of Levites s in the LORD's
26:11 Hosah's sons and relatives, who s as gatekeepers,
26:12 other Levites, they s at the house of the LORD.
27: 1 who s the king by supervising the army divisions
27: 1 Each division s for one month and had twenty-four
2Ch 19:11 will assist you in making sure that justice is s.
30:22 for the skill they displayed as they s the LORD.
34: 9 who s as gatekeepers at the Temple of God.
34:12 The workers s faithfully under the leadership of
Ne 11:22 whose family s as singers at God's Temple.
12:26 These all s in the days of Joiakim son of Jeshua,
Est 1: 7 Drinks were s in gold goblets of many designs,
Job 29:15 I s as eyes for the blind and feet for the lame.
Isa 26:14 Those we s before are dead and gone.
Jer 8: 2 the gods my people have loved, s, and worshiped.
16:11 They worshiped other gods and s them.
Eze 27:10 Lydia, and Libya s in your great army.
Mt 20:28 of Man, came here not to be s but to serve others,
Mk 10:45 of Man, came here not to be s but to serve others,
Lk 22:27 the master sits at the table and is s by his servants.
Jn 12: 2 Martha s, and Lazarus sat at the table with him.
21:13 Then Jesus s them the bread and the fish.
Ac 13:36 for after David had s his generation according to
2Co 11:23 I sound like a madman, but I have s him far more!
1Ti 5:10 to strangers? Has she s other Christians humbly?
Heb 3: 2 just as Moses s faithfully and was entrusted with

SERVES (6) [SERVE]

Lev 16:32 high priest who s in place of his ancestor Aaron.
Dt 15:12 becomes your servant and s you for six years,
Jos 12: 2 which s as a boundary for the Ammonites.
Ps 119:91 remain true today, / for everything s your plans.
Jn 2:10 "Usually a host s the best wine first," he said.
Col 4: 7 He is a faithful helper who s the Lord with me.

SERVICE (53) [SERVE]

Ge 30:26 You know I have fully paid for them with my s to
41:46 He was thirty years old when he entered the s of
Ex 32:29 "Today you have been ordained for the s of the
Nu 4:24 of the Gershonites will be in the areas of general s
4:35 and fifty years of age who were eligible for s in the
4:39 and fifty years of age who were eligible for s in the
4:43 and fifty years of age who were eligible for s in the
4:45 from the Merarite clans who were eligible for s.
4:47 and fifty years of age who were eligible for s in the
8:11 of Israel, thus dedicating them to the LORD's s.
8:26 the Tabernacle, but they may not officiate in the s.
18: 6 They are dedicated to the LORD for s in the
18: 7 must personally handle all the sacred s associated
18: 7 giving you the priesthood as your special gift of s.
18:21 I will pay them for their s in the Tabernacle with
1Ki 22: 4 yours to command. Even my horses are at your s."
2Ki 3: 7 yours to command. Even my horses are at your s."
1Ch 7: 2 the total number of men available for military s
7: 4 The total number of men available for military s
7: 5 The total number of men available for military s
7: 7 The total number of men available for military s
7: 9 there were 20,200 men available for military s
7:11 included 17,200 men available for military s.
7:40 There were 26,000 men available for military s
23:24 or older to qualify for s in the house of the
23:27 twenty years old or older were registered for s.
23:32 and faithfully carried out their duties of s at the
24: 1 the priests, were divided into groups for s.
25: 8 their particular term of s by means of sacred lots,
26:30 of the LORD and the s of the king in that area.
26:32 related to the things of God and the s of the king.
2Ch 17:16 son of Zicri, who volunteered for the LORD's s,
29:35 So the Temple of the LORD was restored to s.
31:21 In all that he did in the s of the Temple of God
Ezr 7:19 to you for the s of the Temple of your God,
Ne 12: 9 and Unni, stood opposite them during the s.
12:45 They performed the s of their God and the s of purification,
Est 8:10 who rode horses especially bred for the king's s.
8:14 rode out swiftly on horses bred for the king's s.
Lk 1:23 He stayed at the Temple until his term of s was
12:35 "Be dressed for s and well prepared,
Jn 16: 2 who kill you will think they are doing God a s.
Ac 3: 1 afternoon to take part in the three o'clock prayer s.
13:15 those in charge of the s sent them this message:
17: 2 As was Paul's custom, he went to the synagogue s,
Ro 15:17 Christ Jesus has done through me in my s to God.
1Co 12: 5 There are different kinds of s in the church, but it
16:15 and they are spending their lives in s to other
2Co 8:19 a s that glorifies the Lord and shows our eagerness
Php 1:22 Yet if I live, that means fruitful s for Christ.
2:17 to complete the sacrifice of your faithful s (that is,
Rev 2:19 your love, your faith, your s, and your patient

SERVICES (7) [SERVE]

Dt 15:18 you the s worth double the wages of hired workers,
2Ch 24:14 utensils for worship s and for burnt offerings,
Ne 11:17 who opened the thanksgiving s with prayer;
13:10 and the singers who were to conduct the worship s
Jer 36: 9 People from all over Judah came to attend the s at
Eze 16:33 Prostitutes charge for their s—but not you!
Ac 13:14 the Sabbath they went to the synagogue for the s.

SERVILE [KJV] See OCCUPATION, WORK

SERVING (28) [SERVE]

Ge 43:34 He gave the largest s to Benjamin—five times as
Nu 3: 8 s in the Tabernacle on behalf of all the Israelites.
8:24 They must begin s in the Tabernacle at the age of
18:31 for it is your compensation for s in the Tabernacle.
Dt 17: 3 by s other gods or by worshiping the sun,
18: 7 just like his fellow Levites who are s the LORD
Jos 23:16 LORD your God by worshiping and s other gods,
Jdg 17:13 "because I have a Levite s as my priest."
1Sa 3: 1 the boy Samuel was s the LORD by assisting Eli.
2Sa 13: 9 But when she set the s tray before him, he refused
17:28 cooking pots, s bowls, wheat and barley flour,
1Ch 24: 5 for there were many qualified officials s God in the
2Ch 35: 3 spend your time s the LORD your God and his
Ne 2: 1 King Artaxerxes' reign, I was s the king his wine.
Jer 34:14 every Hebrew slave must be freed after s six years.
Hos 4:12 the prostitute, s other gods and deserting their God.
Mal 3:14 "You have said, 'What's the use of s God?
Lk 1: 8 One day Zechariah was s God in the Temple,
Ro 12: 7 If your gift is that of s others, serve them well.
16:18 Such people are not s Christ our Lord; they are s their own personal interests.
1Co 12: 5 in the church, but it is the same Lord we are s.
Eph 3: 7 I have been given the wonderful privilege of s him
4: 1 Therefore I, a prisoner for s the Lord, beg you to
Col 1:25 God has given me the responsibility of s his church
3:24 as your reward, and the Master you are s is Christ.
Tit 2: 3 a way that is appropriate for someone s the Lord.
Rev 7:15 throne of God, s him day and night in his Temple.

SERVITOR [KJV] See SERVANT

SESSION (3)

Da 7:10 Then the court began its s, and the books were
Ac 19:38 the courts are in s and the judges can take the case
22:30 and ordered the leading priests into s with the

SET (476) [SETS, SETTING, SETTINGS, WELL-SET]

Ge 1:17 God s these lights in the heavens to light the earth,
12: 6 and s up camp beside the oak at Moreh.
12: 8 and s up camp in the hill country between Bethel
19: 3 He s a great feast before them, complete with fresh
21:28 ewe lambs and s them off by themselves,
22: 3 and s out for the place where God had told him to
24:10 ten of Abraham's camels with gifts and s out,
26:25 He s up his camp at that place, and his servants
28:11 At sundown he arrived at a good place to s up
28:18 as a pillow and s it upright as a memorial pillar.
30:38 Then he s up these peeled branches beside the
30:41 Jacob s up the peeled branches in front of them.
31:18 and s out on his journey to the land of Canaan,
31:20 They s out secretly and never told Laban they were
31:23 a group of his relatives and s out in hot pursuit.
31:25 of Gilead, he s up his camp not far from Jacob's.
31:37 S it out here in front of us, before our relatives,
31:45 So Jacob took a stone and s it up as a monument.
33:18 and they s up camp just outside the town.
35: 5 When they s out again, terror from God came over
35:14 Jacob s up a stone pillar to mark the place where
35:20 Jacob s up a stone monument over her grave,
41:16 will tell you what it means and will s you at ease."
44: 3 and s out on their journey with their loaded
46: 1 So Jacob s out for Egypt with all his possessions.
Ex 5: 6 and foremen he had s over the people of Israel:
8: 9 "You s the time!" Moses replied. "Tell me when
12:21 the lamb they have s apart for the Passover.
16:23 want today, and s aside what is left for tomorrow."
19: 2 to the base of Mount Sinai and s up camp there.
19:12 S boundary lines that the people may not pass.
19:23 You told me to s boundaries around the mountain
20: 9 Six days a week are s apart for your daily duties
20:11 blessed the Sabbath day and s it apart as holy.
21: 2 S him free in the seventh year, and he will owe you
24: 4 He also s up twelve pillars around the altar, one for
25: 7 and other stones to be s in the ephod
25:35 One blossom will be s beneath each pair of
25:37 and s them so they reflect their light forward.
26: 3 Join five of these sheets together into one s;
26: 3 then join the other five sheets into a second s.
26: 4 blue yarn along the edge of the last sheet in each s.
26: 5 The fifty loops along the edge of one s are to
26: 9 Join five of these together into one s, and join the other six into a second s.
26: 9 The sixth sheet of the second s is to be doubled
26:10 loops along the edge of the last sheet in each s,
26:30 "S up this Tabernacle according to the design you
26:32 Hang this inner curtain on gold hooks s into four
26:35 and the table must be s toward the north.
26:37 Hang this curtain on gold hooks s into five posts
27:12 feet long, supported by ten posts s into ten bases.
27:14 supported by three posts s into three bases.
27:15 supported by three posts s into three bases.
27:17 The posts are to be s in solid bronze bases.
28: 1 will be s apart from the common people.
28: 3 that will s Aaron apart from everyone else,
28:20 and a jasper. All these stones will be s in gold.
28:36 S APART AS HOLY TO THE LORD.
28:41 S them apart as holy so they can serve as my
29:17 S them alongside the head and the other pieces of
29:21 and their clothing will be s apart as holy to the
29:27 "S aside as holy the parts of the ordination ram
29:33 not eat them, for these things are s apart and holy.
29:44 and I will s apart Aaron and his sons as holy,
33: 7 It was Moses' custom to s up the tent known as the
34:21 "Six days are s aside for work, but on the Sabbath
35: 9 and other stones to be s in the ephod
36:10 of these sheets were joined together to make one s, and a second s was made of the other five.
36:11 placed along the edge of the last sheet in each s.
36:12 The fifty loops along the edge of the first s of
36:12 matched the loops along the edge of the second s.
36:13 made to connect the loops on the edge of each s.
36:16 joined five of these sheets together to make one s,
36:16 remaining sheets were joined to make a second s.
36:17 loops along the edge of the last sheet in each s.
36:36 then attached to four gold hooks s into four posts
36:36 overlaid with gold and s into four silver bases.
37:21 One blossom was s beneath each pair of branches,
38:14 and was supported by three posts s into three
38:15 and was supported by three posts s into three
38:19 It was supported by four posts s into four bronze
39: 6 of the ephod, were s in gold filigree.
39:10 Four rows of gemstones were s across it.
39:13 a jasper. Each of these gemstones was s in gold.
39:30 S APART AS HOLY TO THE LORD.
40: 2 "S up the Tabernacle on the first day of the new
40: 4 And bring in the lampstand, and s up the lamps.
40: 5 S up the curtain made for the entrance of the
40: 7 S the large washbasin between the Tabernacle
40: 8 Then s up the courtyard around the outside of the
40:15 Aaron's descendants are s apart for the priesthood
40:17 So the Tabernacle was s up on the first day of the
40:20 He also s the Ark's cover—the place of
40:21 and s up the inner curtain to shield it from view,
40:24 He s the lampstand in the Tabernacle across from
40:25 Then he s up the lamps in the LORD's presence,
40:33 And he s up the curtain at the entrance of the
40:36 the people of Israel would s out on their journey,
Lev 7:35 It has been s apart for Aaron and his descendants
8:15 he s the altar apart as holy and made atonement for
14: 7 the priest will s the living bird free so it can fly
20: 7 So s yourselves apart to be holy, for I, the LORD,
20:24 who has s you apart from all other people.
20:26 I have s you apart from all other people to be my
21: 6 They must be s apart to God as holy and must
21: 7 for the priests must be s apart to God as holy.
22: 2 that the Israelites s apart for me with great care,
22: 7 After all, this food has been s aside for them.
24: 3 Aaron will s it up outside the inner curtain of the
25:10 This year will be s apart as holy, a time to proclaim
25:54 and their children must be s free at that time.
26: 1 "Do not make idols or s up carved images,
27:13 you must pay the value s by the priest, plus 20
27:15 you must pay the value s by the priest, plus 20
27:21 be holy, a field specially s apart for the LORD.
27:28 anything specially s apart by the LORD—
27:28 Anything devoted in this way has been s apart for
27:29 A person specially s apart by the LORD for
27:30 to the LORD and must be s apart to him as holy.
27:32 and flocks. They are s apart to him as holy.
Nu 1:51 the Levites will take it down and s it up again.
2:17 "Then the Levites will s out from the middle of
2:34 Each clan and family s up camp and marched
3: 3 were anointed and s apart to minister as priests.
3:13 I s apart for myself all the firstborn in Israel of
6: 5 for they are holy and s apart to the LORD.
6: 8 This applies as long as they are s apart to the
7: 1 On the day Moses s up the Tabernacle, he anointed it and s it apart as holy, along with all
8: 3 He s up the seven lamps so they reflected their
8: 6 "Now s the Levites apart from the rest of the
8:14 you will s the Levites apart from the rest of the
8:17 I s them apart for myself on the night I killed all
9:15 The Tabernacle was s up, and on that day the cloud
10:12 So the Israelites s out from the wilderness of Sinai
10:18 Then the tribes that camped with Reuben s out
10:21 the Tabernacle would already be s up at its new
10:22 Then the tribes that camped with Ephraim s out

10:25 the tribes that camped with Dan **s** out under their
10:35 And whenever the Ark **s** out, Moses would cry,
10:36 And when the Ark was **s** down, he would say,
14:25 Tomorrow you must **s** out for the wilderness in the
14:40 and **s** out for the hill country of Canaan.
15:19 But you must **s** some aside as a gift to the LORD.
15:20 first of the flour you grind and **s** it aside as a gift,
16:3 Everyone in Israel has been **s** apart by the LORD,
18:14 "Whatever is specially **s** apart for the LORD also
18:17 are holy and have been **s** apart for the LORD.
18:24 which have been **s** apart as offerings to the
18:29 Be sure to **s** aside the best portions of the gifts
21:4 Then the people of Israel **s** out from Mount Hor,
21:12 to the valley of Zered Brook and **s** up camp.
22:7 **s** out and took money with them to pay Balaam to
23:9 live by themselves, / **s** apart from other nations.
24:21 are strongly situated; / your nest is **s** in the rocks.
31:28 **S** apart one out of every five hundred as the
33:3 They **s** out from the city of Rameses on the
33:5 the Israelites **s** up camp at Succoth.
Dt 2:1 and **s** out across the wilderness toward the Red
4:41 Then Moses **s** apart three cities of refuge east of
5:13 Six days a week are **s** apart for your daily duties
7:26 then you will be **s** apart for destruction just like
7:26 such things, for they are **s** apart for destruction.
10:6 "The people of Israel **s** out from the wells of the
10:8 At that time the LORD **s** apart the tribe of Levi to
11:24 Wherever you **s** your feet, the land will be yours.
13:17 Keep none of the plunder that has been **s** apart for
14:2 You have been **s** apart as holy to the LORD your
14:21 for you are **s** apart as holy to the LORD your
14:22 "You must **s** aside a tithe of your crops—
15:12 in the seventh year you must **s** that servant free.
15:19 "You must **s** aside for the LORD your God all
16:21 "You must never **s** up an Asherah pole beside the
16:22 And never **s** up sacred pillars for worship,
19:2 Then you must **s** apart three cities of refuge in the
19:7 That is why I am commanding you to **s** aside three
19:14 markers your ancestors **s** up to mark their property.
26:4 and **s** it before the altar of the LORD your God.
27:2 **s** up some large stones and coat them with plaster.
27:4 **s** up these stones at Mount Ebal and coat them with
Jos 2:1 So the two men **s** out and came to the house of a
3:14 When the people **s** out to cross the Jordan,
6:18 Do not take any of the things **s** apart for
6:26 cost of his youngest son, / he will **s** up its gates."
7:1 But Israel was unfaithful concerning the things **s**
7:11 the things that I commanded to be **s** apart for me.
7:12 For now Israel has been **s** apart for destruction.
7:12 things among you that were **s** apart for destruction.
7:13 O Israel, are things **s** apart for the LORD.
7:15 The one who has stolen what was **s** apart for
8:2 for yourselves. **S** an ambush behind the city."
8:3 So Joshua and the army of Israel **s** out to attack Ai.
8:8 **S** the city on fire, as the LORD has commanded.
8:19 the city. They quickly captured it and **s** it on fire.
9:17 The Israelites **s** out at once to investigate
10:7 army left Gilgal and **s** out to rescue Gibeon.
10:13 of the sky, and it did not **s** as on a normal day.
18:1 gathered at Shiloh and **s** up the Tabernacle.
20:9 These cities were **s** apart for Israelites as well as
22:20 sinned by stealing the things **s** apart for the
Jdg 5:4 "LORD, when you **s** out from Seir / and marched
9:25 The people of Shechem **s** an ambush for
9:43 into three groups and **s** an ambush in the fields.
9:49 against the walls of the temple and **s** them on fire.
9:52 But as he prepared to **s** fire to the entrance,
17:5 Micah **s** up a shrine, and he made a sacred ephod
18:11 So six hundred warriors from the tribe of Dan **s** out
18:30 Then they **s** up the carved image, and they
20:29 So the Israelites **s** an ambush all around Gibeah.
Ru 1:7 With her two daughters-in-law she **s** out from the
1Sa 2:8 is the LORD's, / and he has **s** the world in order.
5:3 the Ark of the LORD! So they **s** the idol up again.
6:18 where they **s** the Ark of the LORD,
9:23 the piece that had been **s** aside for the guest of
13:16 The Philistines **s** up their camp at Micmash.
15:12 "Saul went to Carmel to **s** up a monument to
17:20 and **s** out early the next morning with the gifts.
28:4 The Philistines **s** up their camp at Shunem,
30:9 So David and his six hundred men **s** out, and they
2Sa 2:24 out what had happened, they **s** out after Abner.
3:10 I should **s** him up as king over Israel as well as
8:11 and gold he had **s** apart from the other nations he
12:30 The crown was made of gold and **s** with gems,
13:9 But when she **s** the serving tray before him,
14:30 "Go and **s** fire to Joab's barley field, the field next
14:30 So they **s** his field on fire, as Absalom had
14:31 "Why did your servants **s** my field on fire?"
15:16 So the king and his household **s** out at once.
15:17 The king and his people **s** out on foot, and they
15:24 the Covenant of God and **s** it down beside the road.
16:22 So they **s** up a tent on the palace roof where
17:23 **s** his affairs in order, and hanged himself.
17:26 and the Israelite army **s** up camp in the land of
20:7 and Joab **s** out after Sheba with an elite guard from
1Ki 7:21 Huram **s** the pillars at the entrance of the Temple,
9:3 I have **s** apart this Temple you have built so that
9:7 I will reject this Temple that I have **s** apart to honor
14:23 They built pagan shrines and **s** up sacred pillars
16:33 Then he **s** up an Asherah pole. He did more to
18:23 lay it on the wood on the altar, but not **s** fire to it.
18:25 name of your god. But do not **s** fire to the wood."
20:27 Israel then mustered its army, **s** up supply lines,
20:34 So they made a treaty, and Ben-hadad was **s** free.
22:48 But the ships never **s** sail, for they were wrecked at
2Ki 3:2 the sacred pillar of Baal that his father had **s** up.
5:21 So Gehazi **s** off after him. When Naaman saw him
10:12 Then Jehu **s** out for Samaria. Along the way,
11:1 she **s** out to destroy the rest of the royal family.
12:9 and **s** it on the right-hand side of the altar at the
13:6 They even **s** up an Asherah pole in Samaria.
17:10 They **s** up sacred pillars and Asherah poles at the
17:16 They **s** up an Asherah pole and worshiped Baal
20:1 **S** your affairs in order, for you are going to die.
21:3 altars for Baal and **s** up an Asherah pole,
21:7 pole he had made and **s** it up in the Temple,
1Ch 2:7 plunder that had been **s** apart for the LORD.
9:32 the bread to be **s** on the table each Sabbath day.
15:1 of God and **s** up a special tent there to shelter it.
16:40 and evening on the altar **s** aside for that purpose,
20:2 The crown was made of gold and **s** with gems,
23:13 and his descendants were **s** apart to dedicate the
23:29 They were in charge of the sacred bread that was **s**
2Ch 2:4 It will be a place **s** apart to burn incense and sweet
3:17 Then he **s** up the two pillars at the entrance of the
7:16 this Temple and **s** it apart to be my home forever.
7:20 I will reject this Temple that I have **s** apart to honor
22:10 she **s** out to destroy the rest of Judah's royal
23:6 Temple of the LORD, for they are **s** apart as holy.
24:8 and **s** outside the gate leading to the Temple of the
25:14 He **s** them up as his own gods, bowed down in
26:18 the sons of Aaron who are **s** apart for this work.
26:19 and refused to **s** down the incense burner he was
28:24 then **s** up altars to pagan gods in every corner of
30:8 Come to his Temple which he has **s** apart as holy
30:14 They **s** to work and removed the pagan altars from
30:17 lambs for them, to **s** them apart for the LORD.
33:3 for the images of Baal and **s** up Asherah poles.
33:7 idol he had made and **s** it up in God's Temple,
33:19 and **s** up Asherah poles and idols before he
35:3 who had been **s** apart to serve the LORD
36:19 Then his army **s** fire to the Temple of God,
Ezr 8:28 and these treasures have been **s** apart as holy to the
Ne 2:6 So the king agreed, and I **s** a date for my departure.
3:1 They dedicated it and **s** up its doors,
3:6 They laid the beams, **s** up the doors, and installed
9:37 in the hands of the kings whom you have **s** over us
13:5 and the special portion **s** aside for the priests.
Est 2:17 so delighted with her that he **s** the royal crown on
5:14 "**S** up a gallows that stands seventy-five feet tall,
5:14 and he ordered the gallows **s** up.
7:9 "Haman has **s** up a gallows that stands
7:10 So they hanged Haman on the gallows he had **s** up
Job 16:12 dashed me to pieces. Then he **s** me up as his target.
26:10 the waters; he **s** the boundaries for day and night.
28:8 upon those treasures; no lion has **s** his paw there.
33:24 God will be gracious and say, '**S** him free. Do not
34:13 in his care? Who has **s** the whole world in place?
Ps 4:3 The LORD has **s** apart the godly for himself.
8:3 the moon and the stars you have **s** in place—
31:4 Pull me from the trap my enemies **s** for me,
31:8 over to my enemy / but have **s** me in a safe place.
34:6 and he heard me. / He **s** me free from all my fears.
35:8 Let them be caught in the snare they **s** for me!
40:2 and the mire. / He **s** my feet on solid ground
57:6 My enemies have **s** a trap for me. / I am weary
59:3 They have **s** an ambush for me. / Fierce enemies
64:5 and plan how to **s** their traps. / "Who will ever
69:22 Let the bountiful table **s** before them become a
71:2 you are just. / Turn your ear to listen and **s** me free.
71:9 And now, in my old age, don't **s** me aside.
74:4 battle cries; / there they **s** up their battle standards.
74:7 They **s** the sanctuary on fire, burning it to the
74:17 You **s** the boundaries of the earth, / and you make
78:7 So each generation can **s** its hope anew on God,
81:5 for Israel / when he attacked Egypt to **s** us free.
84:5 who **s** their minds on a pilgrimage to Jerusalem.
104:9 Then you **s** a firm boundary for the seas, / so they
104:19 the seasons / and the sun that knows when to **s**.
105:20 Then Pharaoh sent for him and **s** him free;
119:110 The wicked have **s** their traps for me along your
140:5 The proud have **s** a trap to catch me; / they have
141:9 Keep me out of the traps they have **s** for me,
142:3 Wherever I go, / my enemies have **s** traps for me.
Pr 1:17 When a bird sees a trap being **s**, it stays away.
1:18 They **s** an ambush for themselves; they booby-trap
7:9 as the day was fading, as the dark of night **s** in.
8:28 I was there when he **s** the clouds above, when he
8:29 I was there when he **s** the limits of the seas, so they
9:2 a great banquet, mixed the wines, and **s** the table.
22:28 ancient boundary markers **s** up by your ancestors.
26:27 If you **s** a trap for others, you will get caught in it
SS 5:12 beside brooks of water; they are **s** like jewels.
5:14 arms are like round bars of gold, **s** with chrysolite.
5:15 His legs are like pillars of marble **s** in sockets of
7:2 is lovely, like a heap of wheat **s** about with lilies.
Isa 1:31 Your evil deeds are the spark that will **s** the straw
14:13 to heaven and **s** my throne above God's stars.
30:33 like fire from a volcano, will **s** it ablaze.
38:1 **S** your affairs in order, for you are going to die.
42:25 They were **s** on fire and burned, but they still
44:22 to me, for I have paid the price to **s** you free."
46:7 and when they **s** it down, it stays there.
46:13 For I am ready to **s** things right, not in the distant
50:7 Therefore, I have **s** my face like a stone,
51:16 I **s** all the stars in space and established the earth.
57:8 you have **s** up your idols and worship them instead
60:20 The sun will never **s**; the moon will not go down.
Jer 1:5 Before you were born I **s** you apart and appointed
1:15 They will **s** their thrones at the gates of the city.
5:3 They are determined, with faces **s** like stone;
5:22 and roar, but they can never pass the bounds I **s**.
6:3 They will **s** up camp around the city and divide
6:17 I **s** watchmen over you who said, 'Listen for the
7:30 "They have **s** up their abominable idols right in
12:3 to be butchered! **S** them aside to be slaughtered!
17:27 as on other days, then I will **s** fire to these gates.
18:20 They have **s** a trap to kill me, though I pleaded for
31:21 "**S** up road signs; put up guideposts. Mark well the
32:29 outside the walls will come in and **s** fire to the city.
32:34 They have **s** up their abominable idols right in my
34:17 I will **s** you free to be destroyed by war, famine,
35:5 I **s** cups and jugs of wine before them and invited
41:12 they took all their men and **s** out to stop him.
43:10 I will **s** his throne on these stones that I have
43:12 He will **s** fire to the temples of Egypt's gods,
49:38 I will **s** my throne in Elam," says the LORD,
50:24 Listen, Babylon, for I have **s** a trap for you.
Eze 2:2 came into me as he spoke and **s** me on my feet.
3:24 Then the Spirit came into me and **s** me on my feet.
4:1 take a large brick and **s** it down in front of you.
4:10 ounces of food for each day, and eat it at **s** times.
4:11 a jar of water for each day, and drink it at **s** times.
13:20 setting my people free like birds **s** free from a cage.
14:3 these leaders have **s** up idols in their hearts.
14:4 will punish the people of Israel who **s** up idols in
14:7 who reject me and **s** up idols in their hearts so they
15:6 they are useless, I have **s** them aside to be burned!
16:19 You **s** before them as a lovely sacrifice the fine
20:12 that I, the LORD, had **s** them apart to be holy,
20:47 I will **s** you on fire, O forest, and every tree will be
20:48 world will see that I, the LORD, have **s** this fire.
24:11 Now **s** the empty pot on the coals to scorch away
25:4 They will **s** up their camps among you and pitch
28:13 beautifully crafted for you and **s** in the finest gold.
30:8 that I am the LORD when I have **s** Egypt on fire
30:16 Yes, I will **s** fire to all Egypt! Pelusium will be
31:10 and because it **s** itself so high above the others,
34:23 And I will **s** one shepherd over them, even my
37:28 have **s** Israel apart for myself to be holy."
39:15 a marker will be **s** up beside them so the burial
40:2 of Israel and **s** me down on a very high mountain.
40:43 and **s** on the tables where the sacrificial meat was
42:6 each of the upper levels was **s** back from the level
44:24 and they will see to it that the Sabbath is **s** apart as
45:1 you must **s** aside a section of it for the LORD as
45:2 feet by 875 feet, will be **s** aside for the Temple.
45:4 **s** aside for the priests who minister to the LORD
45:6 This will be **s** aside to be a city where anyone in
45:7 "Two special sections of land will be **s** apart for
46:17 At that time the servant will be **s** free, and the land
48:8 "South of Judah is the land **s** aside for a special
48:9 "The area **s** aside for the LORD's Temple will be
48:11 This area is **s** aside for the ordained priests,
48:14 for it belongs to the LORD; it is **s** apart as holy.
48:22 except for the areas **s** aside for the sacred lands
48:29 These are the allotments that will be **s** aside for
Da 2:44 the God of heaven will **s** up a kingdom that will
3:1 and **s** it up on the plain of Dura in the province of
3:2 to come to the dedication of the statue he had **s** up.
3:3 before the image King Nebuchadnezzar had **s** up,
3:7 the statue that King Nebuchadnezzar had **s** up.
3:12 or to worship the gold statue you have **s** up."
3:14 my gods or to worship the gold statue I have **s** up?
3:18 or worship the gold statue you have **s** up."
9:27 with the people for a period of one **s** of seven,
9:27 he will **s** up a sacrilegious object that causes
11:28 On the way he will **s** himself against the people of
11:44 and he will **s** out in great anger to destroy many as
12:11 that causes desecration is **s** up to be worshiped,
12:13 you will rise again to receive the inheritance **s**
Ob 1:7 Your trusted friends will **s** traps for you, and you
Mic 2:5 Others will **s** your boundaries then,
3:6 The sun will **s** for you prophets, and your day will
Na 2:5 rushing to the walls to **s** up their defenses.
3:13 wide to the enemy and **s** on fire and burned.
Zec 3:9 Now look at the jewel I have **s** before Jeshua,
4:7 Then Zerubbabel will **s** the final stone of the
5:11 they will **s** the basket there on its pedestal."
9:4 Tyre will be **s** on fire and burned to the ground.
14:20 S APART AS HOLY TO THE LORD.
14:21 and Judah will be **s** apart as holy to the LORD
Mt 10:35 I have come to **s** a man against his father, and a
17:11 "Elijah is indeed coming first to **s** everything in
Mk 9:12 "Elijah is indeed coming first to **s** everything in
14:15 you upstairs to a large room that is already **s** up.
Lk 9:51 to heaven, Jesus resolutely **s** out for Jerusalem.
10:8 town welcomes you, eat whatever is **s** before you
22:12 you upstairs to a large room that is already **s** up.
Jn 5:45 Yes, Moses, on whom you **s** your hopes.
8:32 will know the truth, and the truth will **s** you free."
8:33 to anyone on earth. What do you mean, '**s** free'?"
Ac 16:34 them into his house and **s** a meal before them.
17:31 For he has **s** a day for judging the world with
18:21 God willing." Then he **s** sail from Ephesus.
20:18 "You know that from the day I **s** foot in the
20:32 and give you an inheritance with all those he has **s**
26:18 God's people, who are **s** apart by faith in me.'
26:32 "He could be **s** free if he hadn't appealed to
27:1 When the time came, we **s** sail for Italy. Paul
28:11 It was three months after the shipwreck that we **s**
28:23 So a time was **s**, and on that day a large number of
Ro 6:7 For when we died with Christ we were **s** free from
6:15 So since God's grace has **s** us free from the law,
1Co 6:11 washed away, and you have been **s** apart for God.
7:14 a godly influence, but now they are **s** apart for him.
7:22 the Lord has now **s** you free from the awful power
2Co 3:11 which has been **s** aside, was full of glory,
7:13 the way you welcomed him and **s** his mind at ease.
Gal 3:15 Just as no one can **s** aside or amend an irrevocable

4: 2 until they reach whatever age their father s.
5: 1 So Christ has really s us free. Now make sure that
Col 2:20 and he has s you free from the evil powers of this
3: 1 with Christ, s your sights on the realities of heaven,
2Ti 4: 1 and the dead when he appears to s up his
Heb 4: 7 So God s another time for entering his place of
7:18 the old requirement about the priesthood was s
7:26 He has now been s apart from sinners, and he has
9:15 For Christ died to s them free from the penalty of
12: 1 with endurance the race that God has s before us.
Jas 2:12 judged by the law of love, the law that s you free.
3: 5 it can do. A tiny spark can s a great forest on fire.
3: 6 flame of destruction, for it is s on fire by hell itself.
2Pe 3:12 the day when God will s the heavens on fire
Rev 8: 7 the earth, and one-third of the earth was s on fire.

SETH (10)

Ge 4:25 She named him **S**, for she said, "God has granted
4:26 When **S** grew up, he had a son and named him
5: 3 Adam was 130 years old, his son **S** was born, and
S was the very image of his father.
5: 4 After the birth of **S**, Adam lived another 800 years,
5: 6 When **S** was 105 years old, his son Enosh was
5: 7 **S** lived another 807 years, and he had other sons
1Ch 1: 1 The descendants of Adam were **S**, Enosh,
Lk 3:38 Enosh was the son of **S**. / **S** was the son of Adam.

SETHUR (1)

Nu 13:13 Asher | **S** son of Michael

SETS (34) [SET]

Ex 26: 6 to fasten the loops of the two s of sheets together,
26:11 In this way, the two s will become a single unit.
36:18 so the two s of sheets were firmly attached to each
Lev 16:22 After the man s it free in the wilderness, the goat
Nu 8: 2 "Tell Aaron that when he s up the seven lamps in
Dt 27:15 who carves or casts idols and secretly s them up.
1Ki 7: 5 in frame; they were in s of three, facing each other.
7:17 Each capital was decorated with seven s of
2Ki 5: 5 of silver, 150 pounds of gold, and ten s of clothing.
5:22 of silver and two s of clothing to give to them."
5:23 He gave him two s of clothing, tied up the money
Job 34:24 asking anyone, and he s up others in their places.
Ps 65: 8 From where the sun rises to where it s,
68: 6 he s the prisoners free and gives them joy.
83:14 a forest / and as a flame s mountains ablaze,
113: 8 He s them among princes, / even the princes of his
Pr 10:26 in the eyes or vinegar that s the teeth on edge.
16:11 fairness in every business deal; he s the standard.
18:17 Any story sounds true until someone s the record
Ecc 1: 5 The sun rises and s and hurries around to rise
Jer 13:21 How will you feel when the LORD s up your foreign
Eze 44:29 Whatever anyone s apart for the LORD will
Da 2:21 he removes kings and s others on the throne.
9:24 "A period of seventy s of seven has been decreed
9:25 Seven s of seven plus sixty-two s of seven will
9:26 "After this period of sixty-two s of seven,
11: 3 and accomplish everything he s out to do.
Zec 12: 6 of Judah like a brazier that s a woodpile ablaze
Jn 8:36 So if the Son s you free, you will indeed be free.
Ac 1: 7 "The Father s those dates," he replied, "and they
Jas 1:25 the law that s you free—and if you do what it says
4: 6 Scriptures say, / "God s himself against the proud,
1Pe 5: 5 in humility, for / "God s himself against the proud,

SETTER [KJV] See PUSHING

SETTING (26) [SET]

Ex 31: 5 in cutting and s gemstones and in carving wood.
35:33 in cutting and s gemstones and in carving wood.
40:13 and anoint him, s him apart to serve me as a priest.
40:18 Moses put it together by s its frames into their
Nu 6: 2 s themselves apart to the LORD in a special way,
Jdg 1: 8 killing all its people and s the city on fire.
15: 9 The Philistines retaliated by s up camp in Judah
19:14 The sun was s as they came to Gibeah, a town in
1Sa 7:16 s up his court first at Bethel, then at Gilgal, and
28: 9 from the land. Why are you s a trap for me?"
1Ki 16:34 And when he finally completed it by s up the gates,
18:23 it on the wood of their altar, but without s fire to it.
18:24 The god who answers by s fire to the wood is the
22:36 Just as the sun was s, the cry ran through his
2Ki 4: 4 into the jars, s the jars aside as they are filled."
2Ch 18:34 until evening. Then just as the sun was s he died.
Ezr 10: 4 for it is your duty to tell us how to proceed in s
Ps 11: 2 their bows / and s their arrows in the bowstrings.
44: 2 you crushed their enemies, / s our ancestors free.
SS 1:10 are your cheeks, with your earrings s them afire!
Jer 5:26 They are continually s traps for other people.
34:17 Since you have not obeyed me by s your
Eze 13:20 s my people free like birds set free from a cage.
43:26 atonement for the altar, thus s it apart for holy use.
Da 11:31 and s up the sacrilegious object that causes
Mic 7: 2 all murderers, even s traps for their own brothers.

SETTINGS (5) [SET]

Ex 28:11 engraves a seal. Mount the stones in gold s.
28:13 The s are to be made of gold filigree,
28:14 be attached to the s on the shoulders of the ephod.
28:25 and the ends of the cords will be tied to the gold s
39:18 and the ends of the cords were tied to the gold s on

SETTLE (35) [RESETTLE, SETTLED, SETTLEMENT, SETTLEMENTS, SETTLERS, SETTLES, SETTLING]

Ge 19: 9 We let you s among us, and now you are trying to
20:16 This will s any claim against me in this matter."
34:10 the land is open to you! **S** here and trade with us.
34:23 let's agree to this so they will s here among us."
35: 1 to Jacob, "Now move on to Bethel and s there.
49:13 "Zebulun will s on the shores of the sea / and will
Nu 15: 2 "When you finally s in the land I am going to give
33:53 Take possession of the land and s in it, because I
Dt 1:12 But how can I s all your quarrels and problems by
2:22 the Horites so they could s there in their place.
17:14 is giving you, and you will conquer it and s there.
19: 1 will displace them and s in their towns and homes.
32: 2 fall on you like rain; / my speech will s like dew.
Jos 1:15 then may you s here on the east side of the Jordan
Jdg 4: 5 and the Israelites came to her to s their disputes.
18: 1 And the tribe of Dan was trying to find a place to s,
18: 2 and Eshtaol, to scout out a land for them to s in.
Ru 3:18 has followed through on this. He will s it today."
1Sa 15: 2 'I have decided to s accounts with the nation of
17: 8 "Do you need a whole army to s this?
17: 8 We will s this dispute in single combat!
2Sa 20:18 used to be a saying, 'If you want to s an argument,
Ps 107:36 He brings the hungry to s there / and build their
Pr 18:18 and s disputes between powerful opponents.
Isa 2: 4 The LORD will s international disputes.
7:19 They will s in the fertile areas and also in the
14: 1 He will bring them back to s once again in their
Jer 40:10 **S** in any town you wish, and live off the land.
48:11 She is like wine that has been allowed to s.
Hos 5: 2 I will s with all of you for what you have done.
Mic 4: 3 The LORD will s international disputes.
Zep 2:14 and cattle. All sorts of wild animals will s there.
Lk 12:58 try to s the matter before it reaches the judge,
Php 4: 2 you belong to the Lord, s your disagreement.
2Th 3:12 we command them: **S** down and get to work.

SETTLED (39) [SETTLE]

Ge 4:16 the LORD's presence and s in the land of Nod,
11: 2 found a plain in the land of Babylonia and s there.
11:31 stopped instead at the village of Haran and s there.
20: 1 and s for a while between Kadesh and Shur at a
24:10 the village where Abraham's brother Nahor had s.
25:11 on Isaac, who s near Beer-lahairoi in the Negev.
25:16 listed according to the places they s and camped.
36: 8 (also known as Edom) s in the hill country of Seir.
37: 1 So Jacob s again in the land of Canaan, where his
47:27 So the people of Israel s in the land of Goshen in
Ex 2:21 the invitation, and he s down to live with them.
12:49 or a foreigner who has s among you."
14:20 The cloud s between the Israelite and Egyptian
40:35 because the cloud had s down over it,
Nu 9:17 And wherever the cloud s, the people of Israel
21:25 all the towns of the Amorites and s in them,
Dt 26: 1 and you have conquered it and s there,
Jos 19:47 captured it, slaughtered its people, and s there.
21:43 their ancestors, and they conquered it and s there.
Jdg 1:16 They s among the people there, near the town of
7:12 and the people of the east had s in the valley like a
2Sa 2: 3 to Judah, and they s near the town of Hebron.
7: 1 When the king was s in his palace and the LORD
1Ki 3:16 prostitutes came to the king to have an argument s.
2Ki 17: 6 They were s in colonies in Halah, along the banks
1Ch 9: 3 Ephraim, and Manasseh came and s in Jerusalem.
17: 1 Now when David was s in his palace, he said to
2Ch 8: 2 Hiram had given him, and he s Israelites in them.
15: 9 Manasseh, and Simeon who had s among them.
20: 8 Your people s here and built this Temple for you.
Ezr 2:70 and some of the common people s in villages near
3: 1 when the Israelites had s in their towns,
Ne 7:73 that is to say, all Israel—s in their own towns."
7:73 when the Israelites had s in their towns,
Ps 68:10 There your people finally s, / and with a bountiful
78:55 by lot. / He s the tribes of Israel into their homes.
Mk 9:33 and his disciples s in the house where they would
Ac 2: 3 or tongues of fire appeared and s on each of them.
19:39 other matters, they can be s in a legal assembly.

SETTLEMENT (4) [SETTLE]

Lev 25:31 a house in a village—a s without fortified walls—
Nu 21:15 which extend as far as the s of Ar on the border of
2Ki 18:14 then demanded a s of more than eleven tons of
Jer 35: 2 "Go to the s where the families of the Recabites

SETTLEMENTS (1) [SETTLE]

1Ch 5:10 Then they moved into the Hagrite s all along the

SETTLERS (1) [SETTLE]

2Ki 17:25 But since these foreign s did not worship the

SETTLES (1) [SETTLE]

Ex 18:16 an argument arises, I am the one who s the case.

SETTLING (1) [SETTLE]

Mt 3:16 Spirit of God descending like a dove and s on him.

SEVEN (364) [SEVEN-DAY, SEVENFOLD, SEVENS, SEVENTH, 7]

SEVEN DAYS (81) Ge 8:10; 31:23; Ex 12:15,15,19; 13:6,7; 22:30; 23:15; 29:30,35,37; 34:18; Lev 8:33,35; 12:2; 13:4,21, 26,31,33,50; 14:8,38; 15:13,19,24,28; 22:27; 23:6,8,34,40; Nu 6:9; 12:14,14,15; 19:11,14,16; 28:24; 31:19; Dt 16:3,4,13, 15; Jdg 14:12; 1Sa 10:8; 11:3; 13:8; 31:13; 1Ki 8:65,65; 16:15; 20:29; 2Ki 3:9; 1Ch 10:12; 2Ch 7:8,9,9; 30:21,22,23; 35:17; Ezr 6:22; Ne 8:17,18; Est 1:5; Job 2:13; Isa 30:26; Eze 3:15,16; 43:25,26; 44:26; 45:21,23,25; Ac 21:27; 28:14; Heb 11:30

SEVEN TIMES (31) Ge 4:15,24; 33:3; Lev 4:6,17; 8:11; 14:7,16,27,51; 16:14,19; 26:18,24,28; Nu 19:4; Jos 6:4,15; 1Ki 18:43,43; 2Ki 4:35; 5:10,14; Ps 12:6; 119:164; Pr 6:31; 24:16; Isa 30:26; Da 3:19; Mt 18:21; Lk 17:4

SEVEN YEARS (28) Ge 29:18,20,25,27,30; 41:26,27,29,30, 36,47,49,53,54; Lev 25:8; Nu 13:22; Jdg 6:1,25; 12:9; 2Sa 5:5; 1Ki 6:38; 2Ki 8:1,2; 11:21; 1Ch 29:27; 2Ch 24:1; Eze 39:9; Lk 2:36

Ge 4:15 for I will give s times your punishment to anyone
4:24 If anyone who kills Cain is to be punished s times,
7: 2 Take along s pairs of each animal that I have
7: 3 Then select s pairs of every kind of bird.
8:10 **S** days later, Noah released the dove again.
21:28 But when Abraham took s additional ewe lambs
29:18 "I'll work for you s years if you'll give me Rachel,
29:20 So Jacob spent the next s years working to pay for
29:25 raged at Laban. "I worked s years for Rachel.
29:27 if you promise to work another s years for me."
29:28 So Jacob agreed to work s more years. A week
29:30 then stayed and worked the additional s years.
31:23 He caught up with them s days later in the hill
33: 3 his brother, he bowed low s times before him.
41: 2 In his dream, s fat, healthy-looking cows suddenly
41: 3 Then s other cows came up from the river,
41: 5 This time he saw s heads of grain on one stalk,
41: 6 s more heads appeared on the stalk,
41: 7 And these thin heads swallowed up the s plump,
41:18 "Suddenly, s fat, healthy-looking cows came up
41:19 But then s other cows came up from the river.
41:20 ugly cows ate up the s fat ones that had come out
41:22 This time there were s heads of grain on one stalk,
and all s heads were plump and full.
41:23 Then out of the same stalk came s withered heads,
41:26 The s fat cows and the s plump heads of grain both
represent s years of prosperity.
41:27 The s thin, ugly cows and the s withered heads of
grain represent s years of famine.
41:29 The next s years will be a period of great
41:30 But afterward there will be s years of famine
41:34 one-fifth of all the crops during the s good years.
41:36 That way there will be enough to eat when the s
41:47 for the next s years there were bumper crops
41:49 After s years, the granaries were filled to
41:53 At last the s years of plenty came to an end.
41:54 Then the s years of famine began, just as Joseph
45: 6 These two years of famine will grow to s,
46:25 These s were the descendants of Jacob through
Ex 2:16 Now it happened that the priest of Midian had s
12:15 For s days, you may eat only bread made without
12:15 s days of the festival will be cut off from the
12:19 During those s days, there must be no trace of
13: 6 For s days you will eat only bread without yeast.
13: 7 Eat only bread without yeast during those s days.
22:30 Leave the newborn animal with its mother for s
23:15 For s days you are to eat bread made without yeast,
25:37 Then make the s lamps for the lampstand, and set
29:30 s days before beginning to minister in the
29:35 The ordination ceremony will go on for s days.
29:37 Make atonement for the altar every day for s days.
34:18 the Festival of Unleavened Bread for s days,
37:23 He also made the s lamps, the lamp snuffers,
Lev 4: 6 and sprinkle it s times before the LORD in front
4:17 and sprinkle it s times before the LORD in front
8:11 He sprinkled the altar s times, anointing it and all
8:33 Do not leave the Tabernacle entrance for s days,
8:35 of the Tabernacle day and night for s days,
12: 2 she will be ceremonially unclean for s days,
13: 4 put the infected person in quarantine for s days.
13: 5 will put the person in quarantine for s more days.
13:21 priest is to put the person in quarantine for s days.
13:26 to put the infected person in quarantine for s days.
13:31 then he must put the person in quarantine for s
13:33 put the person in quarantine for another s days,
13:50 affected spot, the priest will put it away for s days.
13:54 to be washed and then isolated for s more days.
14: 7 The priest will also sprinkle the dead bird's blood s
14: 8 they must still remain outside their tents for s days.
14:16 the oil and sprinkle it s times before the LORD.
14:27 and sprinkle some of it s times before the LORD.
14:38 he will leave the house and lock it up for s days.
14:51 and he will sprinkle the house s times.
15:13 he must count off a period of s days.
15:19 she will be ceremonially unclean for s days.
15:24 He will remain defiled for s days, and any bed on
15:28 she must count off a period of s days.
16:14 and then s times against the front of the Ark.
16:19 into the blood and sprinkle it s times over the altar.
22:27 is born, it must be left with its mother for s days.
23: 6 This festival to the LORD continues for s days,
23: 8 On each of the next s days, the people must present
23:15 was lifted up as an offering, count off s weeks.
23:18 present s one-year-old lambs with no physical
23:34 This festival to the LORD will last for s days.
23:36 On each of the s festival days, you must present
23:40 Then rejoice before the LORD your God for s
23:42 During the s festival days, all of you who are
25: 8 "In addition, you must count off s Sabbath years,
25: 8 s years times s, adding up to forty-nine years
26:18 I will punish you for your sins s times over.

26:21 I will inflict you with s more disasters for your
26:24 and I will personally strike you s times over for
26:28 I will punish you s times over for your sins.
Nu 6:9 they must wait for s days and then shave their
8:2 "Tell Aaron that when he sets up the s lamps in
8:3 He set up the s lamps so they reflected their light
12:14 wouldn't she have been defiled for s days?
12:14 Banish her from the camp for s days, and after that
12:15 So Miriam was excluded from the camp for s days,
13:22 (The ancient town of Hebron was founded s years
19:4 and sprinkle it s times toward the front of the
19:11 body will be ceremonially unclean for s days.
19:14 will be ceremonially unclean for s days.
19:16 or a grave, that person will be unclean for s days.
23:1 said to King Balak, "Build me s altars here, and prepare s young bulls and s rams for a sacrifice."
23:4 "I have prepared s altars and have sacrificed a
23:14 He built s altars there and offered a young bull
23:29 "Build me s altars and prepare me s young bulls and s rams for a sacrifice."
28:11 one ram, and s one-year-old male lambs, all with
28:19 one ram, and s one-year-old male lambs, all with
28:21 and two quarts with each of the s lambs.
28:24 On each of the s days of the festival, this is how
28:27 one ram, and s one-year-old male lambs.
28:29 and two quarts with each of the s lambs.
29:2 one ram, and s one-year-old male lambs, all with
29:4 and two quarts with each of the s lambs.
29:8 one ram, and s one-year-old male lambs, all with
29:10 and two quarts of choice flour with each of the s
29:32 of the festival, sacrifice s young bulls, two rams,
29:36 one ram, and s one-year-old male lambs, all with
31:19 a dead body must stay outside the camp for s days.
Dt 7:1 These s nations are all more powerful than you.
16:3 For s days eat only bread made without yeast,
16:4 in any house throughout your land for s days.
16:9 "Count off s weeks from the beginning of your
16:13 must be observed for s days at the end of the
16:15 For s days celebrate this festival to honor the
28:7 one direction, but they will scatter from you in s!
28:25 one direction, but you will scatter from them in s!
Jos 6:4 S priests will walk ahead of the Ark, each carrying
6:4 day you are to march around the city s times,
6:6 and assign s priests to walk in front of it,
6:8 the s priests with the rams' horns started marching
6:13 The s priests with the rams' horns marched in
6:15 But this time they went around the city s times.
18:2 But there remained s tribes who had not yet been
18:5 The scouts will map the land into s sections,
18:9 and mapped the entire territory into s sections,
Jdg 6:1 handed them over to the Midianites for s years.
6:25 from your father's herd, the one that is s years old.
12:9 to marry his sons. Ibzan judged Israel for s years.
14:12 If you solve my riddle during these s days of the
16:7 "If I am tied up with s new bowstrings that have
16:8 So the Philistine leaders brought Delilah s new
16:13 "If you weave the s braids of my hair into the
16:13 Delilah wove the s braids of his hair into the fabric
20:15 to join the s hundred warriors who lived there.
20:16 S hundred of Benjamin's warriors were
Ru 4:15 and who has been better to you than s sons!"
1Sa 2:5 now full. / The barren woman now has s children;
6:1 remained in Philistine territory s months in all.
10:8 to Gilgal ahead of me and wait for me there s days.
11:3 "Give us s days to send messengers throughout
13:8 Saul waited there s days for Samuel, as Samuel
16:10 In the same way all s of Jesse's sons were
31:13 tamarisk tree at Jabesh, and they fasted for s days.
2Sa 2:11 and he ruled as king of Judah for s and a half years.
5:5 He had reigned over Judah from Hebron for s years
10:18 This time David's forces killed s hundred
21:6 So let s of Saul's sons or grandsons be handed over
21:9 So all s of them died together at the beginning of
21:16 his bronze spearhead weighed more than s pounds,
1Ki 2:11 s of them in Hebron and thirty-three in Jerusalem.
6:38 of his reign. So it took s years to build the Temple.
7:17 Each capital was decorated with s sets of
8:65 s days for the dedication of the altar and s days for the Festival of Shelters.
11:3 He had s hundred wives and three hundred
16:15 Asa's reign in Judah, but he reigned only s days.
18:43 S times Elijah told him to go and look, and s times
19:18 Yet I will preserve s thousand others in Israel who
20:15 Then he called out the rest of his army of s
20:29 The two armies camped opposite each other for s
2Ki 3:9 route through the wilderness for s days.
3:26 he led s hundred of his warriors in a desperate
4:35 This time the boy sneezed s times and opened his
5:10 and wash yourself s times in the Jordan River.
5:14 to the Jordan River and dipped himself s times,
8:1 for a famine on Israel that will last for s years."
8:2 and lived in the land of the Philistines for s years.
11:21 Joash was s years old when he became king.
24:16 He also took s thousand of the best troops and one
1Ch 3:4 in Hebron, where he reigned s and a half years.
3:24 Akkub, Johanan, Delaiah, and Anani—s in all.
5:13 the leaders of s other clans, were Michael,
10:12 the oak tree at Jabesh, and they fasted for s days.
11:23 he killed an Egyptian warrior who was s and a half
15:26 they sacrificed s bulls and s lambs.
18:4 s thousand charioteers, and twenty thousand foot
19:18 This time David's forces killed s thousand
29:27 s years from Hebron and thirty-three years from
2Ch 7:8 For the next s days they celebrated the Festival of
7:9 had celebrated the dedication of the altar for s days and the Festival of Shelters for s days.
13:9 and s rams can become a priest of these so-called
15:11 s hundred oxen and s thousand sheep and goats.
24:1 Joash was s years old when he became king,
29:21 brought s bulls, s rams, s lambs, and s male goats
30:21 of Unleavened Bread for s days with great joy.
30:22 So for s days the celebration continued.
30:23 then decided to continue the festival another s
30:24 thousand bulls and s thousand sheep for offerings,
35:17 and the Festival of Unleavened Bread for s days.
Ezr 6:22 the Festival of Unleavened Bread for s days.
7:14 and my Council of S hereby instruct you to
Ne 8:17 lived in these shelters for the s days of the festival,
8:18 Law of God on each of the s days of the festival.
Est 1:5 It lasted for s days and was held at Susa in the
1:10 and Carcas, the s eunuchs who attended him,
1:14 s high officials of Persia and Media.
2:9 He also assigned her s maids specially chosen from
Job 1:2 He had s sons and three daughters.
1:3 He owned s thousand sheep, three thousand
2:13 Then they sat on the ground with him for s days
42:8 Now take s young bulls and s rams and go to my
42:13 He also gave Job s more sons and three more
Ps 12:6 silver refined in a furnace, / purified s times over.
119:164 I will praise you s times a day / because all your
Pr 6:16 things the LORD hates—no, s things he detests:
6:31 he will be fined s times as much as he stole,
9:1 Wisdom has built her spacious house with s pillars.
24:16 They may trip s times, but each time they will rise
26:16 Lazy people consider themselves smarter than s
Isa 4:1 S women will fight over each of them and say,
11:15 sending a mighty wind to divide it into s streams
30:26 will be s times brighter—like the light of s days!
Jer 15:9 The mother of s grows faint and gasps for breath;
52:25 the Judean army, s of the king's personal advisers,
Eze 3:15 I sat there among them for s days, overwhelmed.
3:16 At the end of the s days, the LORD gave me a
39:9 for fuel. There will be enough to last them s years!
39:12 It will take s months for the people of Israel to
39:14 At the end of the s months, special crews will be
40:22 There were s steps leading up to the gateway
40:26 This gateway also had a stairway of s steps leading
43:25 "Every day for s days a male goat, a young bull,
43:26 Do this each day for s days to cleanse and make
44:26 being ritually cleansed and then waiting for s days.
45:21 the Passover. This festival will last for s days.
45:23 On each of the s days of the feast he will prepare a
45:23 This daily offering will consist of s young bulls and s rams without any defects.
45:25 "During the s days of the Festival of Shelters,
Da 3:19 He commanded that the furnace be heated s times
4:16 For s periods of time, let him have the mind of an
4:23 Let him eat grass with the animals of the field for s
4:25 S periods of time will pass while you live this way,
4:32 S periods of time will pass while you live this way,
9:24 "A period of seventy sets of s has been decreed for
9:25 S sets of seven plus sixty-two sets of s plus sixty-two sets of s will
9:26 "After this period of sixty-two sets of s,
9:27 a treaty with the people for a period of one set of s,
Mic 5:5 we will appoint s rulers to watch over us,
Zec 3:9 have set before Jeshua, a single stone with s facets.
4:2 are s lamps, each one having s spouts with wicks.
4:10 For these s lamps represent the eyes of the LORD
Mt 12:45 Then the spirit finds s other spirits more evil than
15:34 They replied, "S, and a few small fish."
15:36 Then he took the s loaves and the fish,
15:37 there were s large baskets of food left over!
16:10 Don't you remember the four thousand I fed with s
18:21 I forgive someone who sins against me? S times?"
18:22 "No!" Jesus replied, "seventy times s!
22:25 Well, there were s brothers. The oldest married
22:28 For she was the wife of all s of them!"
Mk 8:5 bread do you have?" he asked. "S," they replied.
8:6 Then he took the s loaves, thanked God for them,
8:8 there were s large baskets of food left over!
8:20 "And when I fed the four thousand with s loaves,
8:20 of leftovers did you pick up?" "S," they said.
12:20 Well, there were s brothers. The oldest of them
12:23 in the resurrection? For all s were married to her."
16:9 the woman from whom he had cast out s demons.
Lk 2:36 had died when they had been married only s years.
8:2 from whom he had cast out s demons;
11:26 Then the spirit finds s other spirits more evil than
17:4 Even if he wrongs you s times a day and each time
20:29 Well, there were s brothers. The oldest married
20:31 until each of the s had married her and died,
20:33 in the resurrection? For all s were married to her!"
24:13 to the village of Emmaus, s miles out of Jerusalem.
Ac 2:1 day of Pentecost, s weeks after Jesus' resurrection,
6:3 and select s men who are well respected and are
6:6 These s were presented to the apostles, who prayed
13:19 Then he destroyed s nations in Canaan and gave
19:14 S sons of Sceva, a leading priest, were doing this.
21:8 one of the s men who had been chosen to distribute
21:27 The s days were almost ended when some Jews
28:14 who invited us to stay with them s days.
Ro 11:4 I have s thousand others who have never bowed
Heb 11:30 the people of Israel marched around Jericho s days,
2Pe 2:5 except for Noah and his family of s.
Jude 1:14 Now Enoch, who lived s generations after Adam,
Rev 1:4 This letter is from John to the s churches in the
1:11 down what you see, and send it to the s churches:
1:12 who was speaking to me, I saw s gold lampstands.
1:16 He held s stars in his right hand, and a sharp
1:20 This is the meaning of the s stars you saw in my right hand and the s gold lampstands: The s stars are the angels of the s churches, and the s lampstands are the s churches.
2:1 This is the message from the one who holds the s
2:1 the one who walks among the s gold lampstands:
3:1 has the sevenfold Spirit of God and the s stars:
4:5 And in front of the throne were s lampstands with burning flames. They are the s spirits of God.
5:1 outside of the scroll, and it was sealed with s seals.
5:5 is worthy to open the scroll and break its s seals."
5:6 He had s horns and s eyes, which are the s spirits
6:1 the Lamb broke the first of the s seals on the scroll.
8:2 And I saw the s angels who stand before God, and they were given s trumpets.
8:6 Then the s angels with the s trumpets prepared
10:3 And when he shouted, the s thunders answered.
10:4 When the s thunders spoke, I was about to write.
10:4 "Keep secret what the s thunders said. Do not
11:13 S thousand people died in that earthquake.
12:3 I saw a large red dragon with s heads and ten horns, with s crowns on his heads.
13:1 It had s heads and ten horns, with ten crowns on its
15:1 S angels were holding the s last plagues,
15:6 The s angels who were holding the bowls of the s plagues came from the Temple,
15:7 s angels a gold bowl filled with the terrible wrath
15:8 No one could enter the Temple until the s angels had completed pouring out the s plagues.
16:1 voice shouting from the Temple to the s angels,
16:1 and empty out the s bowls of God's wrath on the
17:1 One of the s angels who had poured out the s
17:3 a woman sitting on a scarlet beast that had s heads
17:7 and of the beast with s heads and ten horns.
17:9 The s heads of the beast represent the s hills of
17:9 this woman rules. They also represent s kings.
17:11 He is like the other s, and he, too, will go to his
21:9 Then one of the s angels who held the s bowls containing the s last plagues came

SEVEN-DAY (7) [DAY, SEVEN]

Ge 50:10 with a s period of mourning for Joseph's father.
Lev 23:39 you will begin to celebrate this s festival to the
23:41 You must observe this s festival to the LORD
Nu 28:17 the following day a joyous, s festival will begin,
29:12 the Festival of Shelters, a s festival to the LORD.
29:17 "On the second day of this s festival,
1Ch 9:25 the villages came to share their duties for s periods.

SEVENFOLD (3) [SEVEN]

Ps 79:12 O Lord, take s vengeance on our neighbors
Rev 1:4 is still to come; from the s Spirit before his throne;
3:1 This is the message from the one who has the s

SEVENTEEN (9) [SEVENTEENTH, 17]

Ge 37:2 When Joseph was s years old, he often tended his
47:28 Jacob lived for s years after his arrival in Egypt,
2Sa 8:4 David captured s hundred charioteers and twenty
1Ki 14:21 became king, and he reigned s years in Jerusalem,
2Ki 13:1 reign in Judah. He reigned in Samaria s years.
1Ch 26:30 He and his relatives—s hundred capable men—
2Ch 8:18 and brought back to Solomon almost s tons of
12:13 became king, and he reigned s years in Jerusalem,
Jer 32:9 paying Hanamel s pieces of silver for it.

SEVENTEENTH (5) [SEVENTEEN]

Ge 7:11 600 years old, on the s day of the second month,
1Ki 22:51 in the s year of King Jehoshaphat's reign in Judah.
2Ki 16:1 Judah in the s year of King Pekah's reign in Israel.
1Ch 24:15 The s lot fell to Hezir. / The eighteenth lot fell to
25:24 The s lot fell to Joshbekashah and twelve of his

SEVENTH (82) [SEVEN]

SEVENTH DAY (39) Ge 2:2,3; Ex 12:16; 13:6; 16:26,29, 30; 20:10,11; 24:16; 31:15,17; 35:2; Lev 13:5,6,34,51; 14:9, 39; 23:3,8; Nu 7:48; 19:12,19; 28:25; 29:32; 31:24; Dt 5:14; 16:8; Jos 6:4,15; Jdg 14:17,18; 2Sa 12:18; 1Ki 20:29; Est 1:10; Eze 45:20; Heb 4:4,4

SEVENTH YEAR (20) Ex 21:2,3,4; 23:11; Lev 25:2,4,20; 26:35; Dt 15:1,12; 31:10; 2Ki 11:4; 12:1; 18:9; 2Ch 23:1; Ezr 7:7; Ne 10:31; Est 2:16; Jer 52:28; Eze 20:1

Ge 2:2 On the s day, having finished his task, God rested
2:3 And God blessed the s day and declared it holy,
Ex 12:16 the first day of the festival, and again on the s day,
13:6 Then on the s day, you will celebrate a great feast
16:26 the food for six days, but the s day is a Sabbath.
16:29 "Do they not realize that I have given them the s
16:30 So the people rested on the s day.
20:10 but the s day is a day of rest dedicated to the
20:11 everything in them; then he rested on the s day.
21:2 Set him free in the s year, and he will owe you
21:3 only he will go free in the s year.
21:4 then the man will be free in the s year, but his wife
23:11 let the land rest and lie fallow during the s year.
23:12 "Work for six days, and rest on the s. This will
24:16 On the s day the LORD called to Moses from the
31:15 days only, but the s day must be a day of total rest.
31:17 but he rested on the s day and was refreshed."
35:2 The s day is a day of total rest, a holy day that
Lev 13:5 On the s day the priest will make another
13:6 The priest will examine the skin again on the s day.
13:34 and he will examine the infection again on the s
13:51 On the s day the priest must inspect it again.
14:9 On the s day, they must again shave off all their
14:39 On the s day the priest must return for another
23:3 but on the s day all work must come to a complete
23:8 On the s day, the people must again stop all their
23:16 Keep counting until the day after the s Sabbath,

25: 2 observe a Sabbath to the LORD every s year.
25: 4 but during the s year the land will enjoy a Sabbath
25: 20 you might ask, 'What will we eat during the s year,
26: 35 allowed it to take every s year while you lived in it.
Nu 7: 48 On the s day Elishama son of Ammihud, leader of
19: 12 the third and s days with the water of purification;
19: 12 But if they do not do this on the third and s days,
19: 12 they will continue to be unclean even after the s
19: 19 and s days the ceremonially clean person must
19: 19 Then on the s day the people being cleansed must
28: 25 On the s day of the festival you must call another
29: 32 "On the s day of the festival, sacrifice seven
31: 19 and your captives on the third and s days.
31: 24 On the s day you must wash your clothes and be
Dt 5: 14 but the s day is a day of rest dedicated to the
15: 1 "At the end of every s year you must cancel your
15: 12 in the s year you must set that servant free.
16: 8 On the s day the people must assemble before the
31: 10 "At the end of every s year, the Year of Release,
Jos 6: 4 On the s day you are to march around the city
6: 15 On the s day the Israelites got up at dawn
6: 16 The s time around, as the priests sounded the long
19: 40 The s and last allotment of land went to the
Jdg 14: 17 At last, on the s day, he told her the answer
14: 18 So before sunset of the s day, the men of the town
2Sa 12: 18 Then on the s day the baby died. David's advisers
1Ki 18: 44 Finally the s time, his servant told him, "I saw a
20: 29 for seven days, and on the s day the battle began.
2Ki 11: 4 In the s year of Athaliah's reign,
12: 1 Joash began to rule over Judah in the s year of
18: 9 which was the s year of King Hoshea's reign in
1Ch 2: 15 his sixth was Ozem, and his s was David.
12: 11 Attai was sixth. / Eliel was s.
24: 10 The s lot fell to Hakkoz. / The eighth lot fell to
25: 14 The s lot fell to Asarelah and twelve of his sons
26: 3 Jehohanan (the sixth), and Eliehoenai (the s).
26: 5 Ammiel (the sixth), Issachar (the s), and Peullethai
27: 10 from Pelon, was commander of the s division,
27: 10 which was on duty during the s month.
2Ch 23: 1 In the s year of Athaliah's reign,
Ezr 7: 7 traveled up to Jerusalem with him in the s year of
Ne 10: 31 And we promise not to do any work every s year
Est 1: 10 On the s day of the feast, when King Xerxes was
2: 16 palace in early winter of the s year of his reign,
Jer 52: 28 The number of captives taken to Babylon in the s
Eze 20: 1 during the s year of King Jehoiachin's captivity,
45: 20 Do this also on the s day of the new year for
Heb 4: 4 is ready because the Scriptures mention the s day,
4: 4 "On the s day God rested from all his work."
Rev 8: 1 When the Lamb broke the s seal, there was silence
10: 7 But when the s angel blows his trumpet,
11: 15 Then the s angel blew his trumpet, and there were
16: 17 Then the s angel poured out his bowl into the air.
17: 10 the sixth now reigns, and the s is yet to come,
21: 20 the s chrysolite, the eighth beryl, the ninth topaz,

SEVENTY (44) [70]

Ge 46: 27 there were s members of Jacob's family in the land
50: 3 and there was a period of national mourning for s
Ex 1: 5 in Egypt. In all, Jacob had s direct descendants.
15: 27 where there were twelve springs and s palm trees.
24: 1 Nadab, Abihu, and s of Israel's leaders.
24: 9 and s of the leaders of Israel went up the mountain.
Nu 11: 16 "Summon before me s of the leaders of Israel.
11: 24 Then he gathered the s leaders and stationed them
11: 25 that was upon Moses and put it upon the s leaders.
33: 9 there are twelve springs of water and s palm trees.
Dt 10: 22 went down into Egypt, there were only s of them.
Jdg 1: 7 "I once had s kings with thumbs and big toes cut
8: 30 He had s sons, for he had many wives.
9: 2 they want to be ruled by all s of Gideon's sons
9: 4 They gave him s silver coins from the temple of
9: 5 on one stone, they killed all s of his half brothers.
9: 18 his descendants, killing his s sons on one stone.
9: 24 and the men of Shechem for murdering Gideon's s
9: 56 done against his father by murdering his s brothers.
12: 14 and thirty grandsons, who rode on s donkeys.
1Sa 6: 19 But the LORD killed s men from Beth-shemesh
2Sa 24: 15 S thousand people died throughout the nation.
1Ki 5: 15 Solomon also enlisted s thousand common
2Ki 10: 1 Now Ahab had s sons living in the city of Samaria.
10: 6 Now the s sons of the king were being cared for by
10: 7 the leaders killed all s of the king's sons.
1Ch 21: 14 upon Israel, and s thousand people died as a result.
2Ch 2: 2 He enlisted a force of s thousand common laborers,
29: 32 The people brought to the LORD s bulls,
36: 21 lying desolate for s years, just as the prophet had
Ps 90: 10 S years are given to us! / Some may even reach
Isa 23: 15 For s years, the length of a king's life, Tyre will be
23: 17 Yes, after s years the LORD will revive Tyre.
Jer 25: 11 lands will serve the king of Babylon for s years.
25: 12 "Then, after the s years of captivity are over,
29: 10 "The truth is that you will be in Babylon for s
Eze 8: 11 S leaders of Israel were standing there with
9: 6 So they began by killing the s leaders.
Da 9: 2 that Jerusalem must lie desolate for s years.
9: 24 "A period of s sets of seven has been decreed for
Zec 1: 12 for s years now you have been angry with
7: 5 'During those s years of exile, when you fasted
Mt 18: 22 "No!" Jesus replied, "s times seven!
Ac 23: 23 Also take two hundred spearmen and s horsemen.

SEVENTY-FIVE (12) [75]

Ge 12: 4 Abram was s years old when he left Haran.
Ex 25: 39 You will need s pounds of pure gold for the
37: 24 was made from s pounds of pure gold.
2Sa 12: 30 and set with gems, and it weighed about s pounds.
1Ki 20: 39 will either die or pay a fine of s pounds of silver!'
1Ch 20: 2 and set with gems, and it weighed about s pounds.
Est 5: 14 "Set up a gallows that stands s feet tall,
7: 9 "Haman has set up a gallows that stands s feet tall
9: 16 killing s thousand of those who hated them.
Jn 19: 39 bringing about s pounds of embalming ointment
Ac 7: 14 all his relatives to come to Egypt, s persons in all.
Rev 16: 21 and hailstones weighing s pounds fell from the sky

SEVENTY-SEVEN (5)

Ge 4: 24 revenge against me will be punished s times!"
Jdg 8: 14 that he write down the names of all the s rulers
2Ch 17: 11 and the Arabs brought s hundred rams and s hundred male goats.
Ezr 8: 35 of Israel, as well as ninety-six rams and s lambs.

SEVENTY-TWO (2) [72]

Lk 10: 1 The Lord now chose s other disciples and sent
10: 17 When the s disciples returned, they joyfully

SEVER (2) [SEVERED, SEVERING]

Mt 3: 10 of God's judgment is poised, ready to s your roots.
Lk 3: 9 of God's judgment is poised, ready to s your roots.

SEVERAL (38)

Ge 4: 4 while Abel brought s choice lambs from the best of
14: 15 and attacked during the night from s directions.
Jos 10: 3 of Jerusalem sent messengers to s other kings:
17: 9 (S towns in Manasseh's territory belonged to the
Jdg 11: 2 Gilead's wife also had s sons, and when these half
1Sa 1: 26 "I am the woman who stood here s years ago
6: 15 S men of the tribe of Levi lifted the Ark of the
2Sa 8: 6 Then he placed s army garrisons in Damascus,
11: 17 And Uriah was killed along with s other Israelite
2Ki 6: 10 there to be on their guard. This happened s times.
10: 32 King Hazael conquered s sections of the country
23: 16 he noticed s tombs in the side of the hill.
1Ch 15: 1 David now built s buildings for himself in the City
18: 6 Then he placed s army garrisons in Damascus,
2Ch 11: 23 and arranged for each of them to have s wives.
25: 13 raided s of the towns of Judah between Samaria
Job 1: 5 and sometimes they lasted s days—Job would
Jer 26: 22 to Egypt along with s other men to capture Uriah.
Da 8: 27 Daniel, was overcome and lay sick for s days.
Mt 22: 1 Jesus told them s other stories to illustrate the
Mk 2: 1 S days later Jesus returned to Capernaum,
Lk 20: 9 and moved to another country to live for s years.
24: 10 Joanna, Mary the mother of James, and s others.
Jn 6: 23 S boats from Tiberias landed near the place where
11: 55 from the country arrived in Jerusalem s days early
21: 2 S of the disciples were there—Simon Peter,
Ac 1: 14 of Jesus, s other women, and the brothers of Jesus.
10: 48 Cornelius asked him to stay with them for s days.
16: 12 and a Roman colony; we stayed there s days.
19: 1 he came to Ephesus, where he found s believers.
19: 19 The value of the books was s million dollars.
20: 4 S men were traveling with him. They were Sopater
21: 10 During our stay of s days, a man named Agabus,
24: 17 "After s years away, I returned to Jerusalem with
25: 14 During their stay of s days, Festus discussed Paul's
27: 1 and s other prisoners were placed in the custody of
27: 2 it was scheduled to make s stops at ports along the
27: 7 We had s days of rough sailing, and after great

SEVERE (23) [SEVERELY]

Ge 12: 10 At that time there was a s famine in the land,
26: 1 Now a s famine struck the land, as had happened
41: 56 So with s famine everywhere in the land,
41: 57 because the famine was s throughout the world.
47: 4 our flocks in Canaan. The famine is very s there.
47: 20 sold him their fields because the famine was so s,
Ex 9: 24 like that, with such s hail and continuous lightning.
Nu 11: 33 and he caused a s plague to break out among them.
Dt 28: 53 so s that you will eat the flesh of your own sons
Ru 1: 1 in Judah left the country because of a s famine.
2Sa 24: 13 or three days of s plague throughout your land?
1Ki 18: 2 the famine had become very s in Samaria.
2Ki 25: 3 the famine in the city had become very s,
1Ch 21: 12 or three days of s plague as the angel of the
2Ch 21: 15 You yourself will be stricken with a s intestinal
21: 18 struck Jehoram with the s intestinal disease.
Jer 52: 6 the famine in the city had become very s,
Eze 5: 16 and more s until every crumb of food is gone.
Ro 11: 22 Notice how God is both kind and s. He is s to those who disobeyed, but kind to you as
2Co 1: 23 return to Corinth was to spare you from a s rebuke.
Col 2: 23 strong devotion, humility, and s bodily discipline.
1Th 1: 6 Spirit in spite of the s suffering it brought you.

SEVERED (1) [SEVER]

Jn 15: 4 For a branch cannot produce fruit if it is s from the

SEVERELY (15) [SEVERE]

Ru 1: 17 May the LORD punish me s if I allow anything
1Sa 25: 22 May God deal with me s if even one man of his
31: 3 archers caught up with him and wounded him s.
1Ch 10: 3 archers caught up with him and wounded him s.
2Ch 24: 25 Arameans withdrew, leaving Joash s wounded.
Ps 118: 18 The LORD has punished me s, / but he has not
Pr 15: 10 Whoever abandons the right path will be s
17: 11 people seek rebellion, but they will be s punished.
Jer 2: 35 Now I will punish you s because you claim you
31: 18 'You disciplined me s, but I deserved it.
Eze 5: 9 I will punish you more s than I have punished
Zep 3: 19 And I will deal s with all who have oppressed you.
Mt 15: 22 has a demon in her, and it is s tormenting her."
Lk 12: 47 The servant will be s punished, for though he knew
Ac 16: 23 They were s beaten, and then they were thrown

SEVERING (1) [SEVER]

Lev 5: 8 its neck but without s its head from the body.

SEWAGE (1)

Jdg 3: 23 down the latrine and escaped through the s access.

SEWING (1)

Ex 35: 25 All the women who were skilled in s and spinning

SEX (5) [SEXUAL, SEXUALLY]

Ge 19: 5 Bring them out so we can have s with them."
Jdg 19: 22 is staying with you so we can have s with him."
Pr 5: 16 your springs in public, having s with just anyone?
Ro 1: 26 the women turned against the natural way to have s and instead indulged in s with each other.

SEXUAL (58) [SEX]

Ex 19: 15 And until then, abstain from having s intercourse."
22: 19 "Anyone who has s relations with an animal must
Lev 15: 18 After having s intercourse, both the man
15: 24 If a man has s intercourse with her during this
18: 6 "You must never have s intercourse with a close
18: 7 Do not violate your father by having s intercourse
18: 8 Do not have s intercourse with any of your father's
18: 9 "Do not have s intercourse with your sister or half
18: 10 "Do not have s intercourse with your
18: 11 Do not have s intercourse with the daughter of any
18: 13 Do not have s intercourse with your aunt,
18: 14 by having s intercourse with his wife;
18: 15 Do not have s intercourse with your
18: 17 "Do not have s intercourse with both a woman
18: 19 "Do not violate a woman by having s intercourse
18: 20 "Do not defile yourself by having s intercourse
18: 23 "A man must never defile himself by having s
19: 20 "If a man has s intercourse with a slave girl who is
20: 15 "If a man has s intercourse with an animal,
20: 17 "If a man has s intercourse with his sister,
20: 19 "If a man has s intercourse with his aunt,
Dt 22: 23 to be married, and he has s intercourse with her.
27: 20 'Cursed is anyone who has s intercourse with his
27: 21 'Cursed is anyone who has s intercourse with an
27: 22 'Cursed is anyone who has s intercourse with his
27: 23 'Cursed is anyone who has s intercourse with his
1Ki 1: 4 of him. But the king had no s relations with her.
Pr 30: 20 an adulterous woman can satisfy her s appetite,
Ecc 12: 5 and withered, dragging along without any s desire.
Hos 3: 3 you will not have s intercourse with anyone,
Mt 15: 19 adultery, all other s immorality, theft, lying,
Mk 7: 21 come evil thoughts, s immorality, theft, murder,
Ac 15: 20 from s immorality, and from consuming blood
15: 29 meat of strangled animals, and from s immorality.
21: 25 and they should stay away from all s immorality."
Ro 1: 27 instead of having normal s relationships with
1Co 5: 1 I can hardly believe the report about the s
5: 9 not to associate with people who indulge in s sin.
5: 10 talking about unbelievers who indulge in s sin,
5: 11 who claims to be a Christian yet indulges in s sin,
6: 9 Those who indulge in s sin, who are idol
6: 13 But our bodies were not made for s immorality.
6: 18 Run away from s sin! No other sin so clearly
6: 18 For s immorality is a sin against your own body.
7: 2 But because there is so much s immorality,
7: 3 The husband should not deprive his wife of s
7: 5 So do not deprive each other of s relations.
7: 5 and wife to refrain from s intimacy for a limited
10: 8 And we must not engage in s immorality as some
2Co 12: 21 s immorality, and eagerness for lustful pleasure.
Gal 5: 19 s immorality, impure thoughts, eagerness for
Eph 5: 3 Let there be no s immorality, impurity, or greed
Col 3: 5 Have nothing to do with s sin, impurity, lust,
1Th 4: 3 to be holy, so you should keep clear of all s sin.
Jude 1: 7 which were filled with s immorality and every kind of s perversion.
Rev 2: 14 food offered to idols and by committing s sin.
2: 20 eat food offered to idols, and commit s sin.

SEXUALLY (2) [SEX]

1Ti 1: 10 These laws are for people who are s immoral,
Rev 22: 15 the sorcerers, the s immoral, the murderers,

SHAALABBIN (1) [SHAALBIM]

Jos 19: 42 S, Aijalon, Ithlah,

SHAALBIM (2) [SHAALABBIN]

Jdg 1: 35 Aijalon, and S, but when the descendants of Joseph
1Ki 4: 9 Ben-deker, in Makaz, S, Beth-shemesh,

SHAALBON (2)

2Sa 23: 32 Eliahba from S; / the sons of Jashen;
1Ch 11: 33 Azmaveth from Bahurim; / Eliahba from S;

SHAALIM (1)

1Sa 9: 4 the land of Shalishah, the S area, and the entire

SHAAPH (2)
1Ch 2:47 were Regem, Jotham, Geshan, Pelet, Ephah, and S.
2:49 She also gave birth to S (the father of Madmannah)

SHAARAIM (3) [SHARUHEN]
Jos 15:36 S, Adithaim, Gederah, and Gederothaim. In all,
1Sa 17:52 Philistines were strewn all along the road from S,
1Ch 4:31 Beth-marcaboth, Hazar-susim, Beth-biri, and S.

SHAASHGAZ (1)
Est 2:14 There she would be under the care of S, another of

SHABBETHAI (3)
Ezr 10:15 and Meshullam and S the Levite supported them.
Ne 8:7 Jamin, Akkub, S, Hodiah, Maaseiah, Kelita,
11:16 S and Jozabad, who were in charge of the work

SHABBY (1)
Jas 2:2 comes in who is poor and dressed in s clothes.

SHACK (1)
Jer 9:2 and forget them and live in a s in the desert,

SHACKLED (1) [SHACKLES]
Lk 8:29 Even when he was s with chains, he simply broke

SHACKLES (3) [SHACKLED]
Ps 149:8 to bind their kings with s / and their leaders with
Mk 5:4 Whenever he was put into chains and s—as he
5:4 the chains from his wrists and smashed the s.

SHADE (16) [SHADED, SHADING]
Ge 18:4 Rest in the s of this tree while my servants get
21:15 water was gone, she left the boy in the s of a bush.
Jdg 9:15 make me your king, come and take shelter in my s.
Job 40:22 The lotus plants give it s among the willows beside
Ps 80:10 The mountains were covered with our s;
121:5 LORD stands beside you as your protective s.
SS 2:3 I am seated in his delightful s, and his fruit is
Isa 4:5 Then the LORD will provide s for Jerusalem
25:5 You cool the land with the s of a cloud.
Eze 31:3 full of thick branches that cast deep forest s with
31:6 and in its s all the wild animals gave birth to their
31:17 the grave—all those nations that had lived in its s.
Da 4:12 Wild animals lived in its s, and birds nested in its
4:14 Chase the animals from its s and the birds from its
4:21 Wild animals lived in its s, and birds nested in its
Hos 4:13 the hills to burn incense in the pleasant s of oaks,

SHADED (1) [SHADE]
SS 1:17 s by cedar trees and spreading firs."

SHADING (1) [SHADE]
Jnh 4:6 leaves over Jonah's head, s him from the sun.

SHADOW (30) [SHADOWS]
1Ki 20:25 There's not a s of a doubt that we will beat them."
2Ki 20:9 Would you like the s on the sundial to go forward
20:10 "The s always moves forward," Hezekiah replied.
20:11 and he caused the s to move ten steps backward on
1Ch 29:15 Our days on earth are like a s, gone so soon
Job 8:9 so little. Our days on earth are as transient as a s.
14:2 Like the s of a passing cloud, we quickly
17:7 with weeping, and I am but a s of my former self.
Ps 17:8 of your eye. / Hide me in the s of your wings.
34:5 with joy; / no s of shame will darken their faces.
36:7 All humanity finds shelter / in the s of your wings.
57:1 I will hide beneath the s of your wings
63:7 I sing for joy in the s of your protecting wings.
91:1 Most High / will find rest in the s of the Almighty.
109:23 I am fading like a s at dusk; / I am falling like a
144:4 like a breath of air; / our days are like a passing s.
Isa 9:2 on all who live in the land where death casts its s.
25:7 of gloom, the s of death that hangs over the earth.
32:2 and as the cool s of a large rock in a hot and weary
38:8 I will cause the sun's s to move ten steps backward
38:8 So the s on the sundial moved backward ten steps.
49:2 He has hidden me in the s of his hand. I am like a
La 2:1 The Lord in his anger has cast a dark s over
Eze 31:6 All the great nations of the world lived in its s.
31:12 All those who lived beneath its s went away
Mt 4:16 those who lived in the land where death casts its s,
Lk 1:79 to those who sit in darkness and in the s of death,
Ac 5:15 so that Peter's s might fall across some of them as
Heb 8:5 that is only a copy, a s of the real one in heaven.
10:1 The old system in the law of Moses was only a s of

SHADOWS (11) [SHADOW]
Jdg 9:36 "It's just the s of the hills that look like men."
Ps 11:2 They shoot from the s at those who do right.
39:6 We are merely moving s, / and all our busy rushing
102:11 My life passes as swiftly as the evening s. / I am
104:23 they labor until the evening s fall again.
Ecc 8:13 Their days will never grow long like the evening s.
SS 2:17 Before the dawn comes and the s flee away,
4:6 Before the dawn comes and the s flee away,
Jer 6:4 the day is fading, and the evening s are falling.
Col 2:17 For these rules were only s of the real thing,
Jas 1:17 Unlike them, he never changes or casts shifting s.

SHADRACH (14) [HANANIAH]
Da 1:7 Hananiah was called S. / Mishael was called
2:49 Daniel's request, the king appointed S, Meshach,
3:12 there are some Jews—S, Meshach, and Abednego
3:13 Nebuchadnezzar flew into a rage and ordered S,
3:14 to them, "Is it true, S, Meshach, and Abednego,
3:16 S, Meshach, and Abednego replied,
3:19 Nebuchadnezzar was so furious with S, Meshach,
3:20 some of the strongest men of his army to bind S,
3:23 So S, Meshach, and Abednego, securely tied,
3:26 "S, Meshach, and Abednego, servants of the Most
3:26 So S, Meshach, and Abednego stepped out of the
3:28 "Praise to the God of S, Meshach, and Abednego!
3:29 speak a word against the God of S, Meshach,
3:30 Then the king promoted S, Meshach,

SHAFT (4)
1Sa 17:7 The s of his spear was as heavy and thick as a
Job 28:4 They sink a mine s into the earth far from where
41:26 sword can stop it, nor spear nor dart nor pointed s.
Rev 9:1 and he was given the key to the s of the bottomless

SHAGEE (2)
2Sa 23:33 Jonathan son of S from Harar; / Ahiam son of
1Ch 11:34 from Gizon; / Jonathan son of S from Harar;

SHAGGY (1)
Da 8:21 The s male goat represents the king of Greece,

SHAHARAIM (1) [SHAHARAIM'S]
1Ch 8:8 After S divorced his wives Hushim and Baara,

SHAHARAIM'S (1) [SHAHARAIM]
1Ch 8:11 S wife Hushim had already given birth to Abitub

SHAHAZUMAH (1)
Jos 19:22 S, and Beth-shemesh, ending at the Jordan River—

SHAKE (37) [SHAKEN, SHAKES, SHAKING, SHAKY, SHOOK]
Ge 27:40 but then you will s loose from him and be free."
Jdg 16:20 "I will do as before and s myself free."
1Sa 4:5 shout of joy was so loud that it made the ground s!
1Ki 14:15 Then the LORD will s Israel like a reed whipped
2Ki 17:4 So of Egypt to help him s free of Assyria's power
Ne 5:13 may God s you from your homes and from your
Job 16:4 my criticisms against you and s my head at you.
Ps 22:7 mocks me. / They sneer and s their heads, saying,
64:8 All who see it happening will s their heads in
109:25 when they see me, they s their heads.
Isa 2:19 When the LORD rises to s the earth, his enemies
2:21 and the glory of his majesty as he rises to s the
7:2 trembled with fear, just as trees s in a storm.
8:21 they will rage and s their fists at heaven and curse
13:13 For I will s the heavens, and the earth will move
33:14 The sinners among my people s with fear.
Jer 18:16 and s their heads in amazement at its utter
49:21 The earth will s with the noise of Edom's fall,
50:46 The earth will s with the noise of Babylon's fall,
Eze 26:10 and your walls will s as the horses gallop through
27:36 of the nations / s their heads at the sight of you,
31:16 I made the nations s with fear at the sound of its
Da 4:14 its branches! S off its leaves, and scatter its fruit!
Joel 3:16 and the earth and heavens will begin to s.
Am 9:1 Temple columns so hard that the foundation will s.
Na 2:10 of its wealth. Hearts melt in horror, and knees s.
3:12 that fall into the mouths of those who s the trees.
Zep 2:15 that way will laugh in derision or s a defiant fist.
Hag 2:6 In just a little while I will again s the heavens
2:6 the earth. I will s the oceans and the dry land, too.
2:7 I will s all the nations, and the treasures of all the
2:21 that I am about to s the heavens and the earth.
Zec 9:5 Gaza will s with terror, and so will Ekron, for their
Mt 10:14 s off the dust of that place from your feet as you
Mk 6:11 to you, s off its dust from your feet as you leave.
Lk 9:5 enter it, s off its dust from your feet as you leave.
Heb 12:26 "Once again I will s not only the earth

SHAKEN (21) [SHAKE]
1Sa 17:11 heard this, they were terrified and deeply s.
1Ch 16:30 The world is firmly established and cannot be s.
Ps 16:8 with me. / I will not be s, for he is right beside me.
33:11 stand firm forever; / his intentions can never be s.
60:2 You have s our land and split it open.
62:2 my salvation, / my fortress where I will never be s.
62:6 my salvation, / my fortress where I will not be s.
82:5 are in darkness, / the whole world is s to the core.
93:1 The world is firmly established; / it cannot be s.
96:10 The world is firmly established and cannot be s.
Isa 24:18 you from the heavens. The world is s beneath you.
Da 5:9 face turned ashen white. His nobles, too, were s.
Mt 24:29 from the sky, / and the powers of heaven will be s.
Mk 13:25 from the sky, / and the powers of heaven will be s.
Lk 6:38 pressed down, s together to make room for more,
Ac 2:25 with me. / I will not be s, for he is right beside me.
16:26 and the prison was s to its foundations.
2Th 2:2 Please don't be so easily s and troubled by those
Heb 12:27 This means that the things on earth will be s,
Rev 6:13 green figs falling from trees s by mighty winds.
11:19 and the world was s by a mighty earthquake.

SHAKES (7) [SHAKE]
2Ki 19:21 of Jerusalem / scoffs and s her head as you flee.
Job 9:6 He s the earth from its place, and its foundations
Ps 29:8 desert quake; / the LORD s the desert of Kadesh.
Isa 10:32 that day. He s his fist at Mount Zion in Jerusalem.
23:11 He s the kingdoms of the earth. He has spoken out
37:22 of Jerusalem / scoffs and s her head as you flee.
Hab 3:6 When he stops, the earth s. When he looks,

SHAKING (5) [SHAKE]
Ps 55:5 and trembling overwhelm me. / I can't stop s.
Eze 21:21 They will cast lots by s arrows from the quiver.
38:19 I promise a mighty s in the land of Israel on that
Mt 27:39 by shouted abuse, s their heads in mockery.
Mk 15:29 by shouted abuse, s their heads in mockery.

SHAKY (1) [SHAKE]
Heb 12:12 your tired hands and stand firm on your s legs.

SHALISHAH (1) [BAAL-SHALISHAH]
1Sa 9:4 the land of S, the Shaalim area, and the entire land

SHALL (11)
Mt 11:16 "How s I describe this generation? These people
13:28 " 'S we pull out the weeds?' they asked.
Lk 7:31 "How s I describe this generation?" Jesus asked.
Jn 18:11 S I not drink from the cup the Father has given
Ac 21:11 'So s the owner of this belt be bound by the Jewish
22:10 "I said, 'What s I do, Lord?' And the Lord told
25:12 have appealed to Caesar, and to Caesar you s go!"
25:22 And Festus replied, "You s—tomorrow!"
25:26 But what s I write the emperor? For there is no real
Ro 9:30 Well then, what s we say about these things?
1Co 14:15 Well then, what s I do? I will do both. I will pray

SHALLOW (7) [SHALLOWS]
Jos 2:7 to the s crossing places of the Jordan River.
Isa 16:2 birds at the s crossings of the Arnon River.
Mt 13:5 Other seeds fell on s soil with underlying rock.
13:6 because the roots had no nourishment in the s soil.
Mk 4:5 Other seed fell on s soil with underlying rock.
4:6 because the roots had no nourishment in the s soil.
Lk 8:6 Other seed fell on s soil with underlying rock.

SHALLOWS (6) [SHALLOW]
Jdg 3:28 And the Israelites took control of the s of the
7:24 Cut them off at the s of the Jordan River at
12:5 Jephthah captured the s of the Jordan,
12:6 take him and kill him at the s of the Jordan River.
2Sa 15:28 I will stop at the s of the Jordan River and wait
17:16 and urge him not to stay at the s of the Jordan

SHALLUM (24) [SHALLUM'S]
2Ki 15:10 Then S son of Jabesh conspired against Zechariah,
15:13 S son of Jabesh began to rule over Israel in the
15:13 in Judah. S reigned in Samaria only one month.
22:14 She was the wife of S son of Tikvah and grandson
1Ch 2:40 the father of Sismai. / Sismai was the father of S.
2:41 S was the father of Jekamiah. / Jekamiah was the
4:25 The descendants of Shaul were S, Mibsam,
6:12 the father of Zadok. / Zadok was the father of S.
6:13 S was the father of Hilkiah. / Hilkiah was the
9:17 The gatekeepers who returned were S, Akkub,
9:17 and their relatives. S was the chief gatekeeper.
9:19 S was the son of Kore, a descendant of Abiasaph,
9:31 a Levite and the oldest son of S the Korahite,
2Ch 28:12 Jehizkiah son of S, and Amasa son of Hadlai—
34:22 She was the wife of S son of Tikvah and grandson
Ezr 2:42 The gatekeepers of the families of S, Ater, Talmon,
7:2 son of S, son of Zadok, son of Ahitub,
10:24 gatekeepers who were guilty: S, Telem, and Uri.
10:42 S, Amariah, and Joseph.
Ne 3:12 S son of Hallohesh and his daughters repaired the
3:15 S son of Col-hozeh, the leader of the Mizpah
7:45 The gatekeepers of the families of S, Ater, Talmon,
Jer 32:7 "Your cousin Hanamel son of S will come and say
35:4 directly above the room of Maaseiah son of S,

SHALLUM'S (1) [SHALLUM]
2Ki 15:15 The rest of the events in S reign, including his

SHALMAI (2)
Ezr 2:46 Hagab, S, Hanan,
Ne 7:48 Lebanah, Hagabah, S,

SHALMAN (1)
Hos 10:14 just as they did when S destroyed Beth-arbel.

SHALMANESER (2) [SHALMANESER'S]
2Ki 17:3 King S of Assyria attacked and defeated King
18:9 King S of Assyria attacked Israel and began a siege

SHAMA (1)
1Ch 11:44 S and Jeiel, the sons of Hotham, from Aroer;

SHAMBLES (1)
Na 2:10 Soon the city is an empty s, stripped of its wealth.

SHAMBLES [KJV] See also MARKETPLACE

SHAME (98) [ASHAMED, SHAMED, SHAMEFUL, SHAMEFULLY, SHAMELESS, SHAMELESSLY, SHAMING]

Ge 2:25 wife were both naked, neither of them felt any **s**.
3:7 and they suddenly felt **s** at their nakedness.
30:23 birth to a son. "God has removed my **s**," she said.
Jos 5:9 "Today I have rolled away the **s** of your slavery in
2Sa 10:4 at the buttocks, and sent them back to David in **s**.
13:13 Where could I go in my **s**? And you would be
1Ch 19:4 at the buttocks, and sent them back to David in **s**.
Job 8:22 Those who hate you will be clothed with **s**,
10:15 I am filled with **s** and misery so that I can't hold
Ps 6:10 and terrified. / May they suddenly turn back in **s**.
31:1 to you for protection; / don't let me be put to **s**.
34:5 with joy; / no shadow of **s** will darken their faces.
35:26 triumph over me / be covered with **s** and dishonor.
40:14 who try to destroy me / be humiliated and put to **s**.
40:15 Let them be horrified by their **s**, / for they said,
44:15 constant humiliation; / **s** is written across our faces.
53:5 You will put them to **s**, for God has rejected them.
70:2 who try to destroy me / be humiliated and put to **s**.
70:3 Let them be horrified by their **s**, / for they said,
71:13 May humiliation and **s** cover / those who want to
78:66 He routed his enemies / and sent them to eternal **s**.
86:17 Then those who hate me will be put to **s**, / for you,
119:31 to your decrees. / LORD, don't let me be put to **s**!
127:5 He will not be put to **s** when he confronts his
132:18 I will clothe his enemies with **s**, / but he will be a
Pr 3:35 The wise inherit honor, but fools are put to **s**!
6:33 disgrace are his lot. His **s** will never be erased.
10:5 who sleeps away the hour of opportunity brings **s**.
13:5 godly hate lies; the wicked come to **s** and disgrace.
18:3 When the wicked arrive, contempt, **s**, and disgrace
18:13 What a **s**, what folly, to give advice before
28:7 those who seek out worthless companions bring **s**
30:32 about it—cover your mouth with your hand in **s**.
Isa 1:29 **S** will cover you when you think of the times you
3:24 beauty will be gone. Only **s** will be left to them.
20:4 their buttocks uncovered, to the **s** of Egypt.
23:4 But now you are put to **s**, city of Sidon, fortress on
30:5 it will all turn out to your **s**. He will not help you
42:17 them their gods— / they will be turned away in **s**.
43:28 Israel a future of complete destruction and **s**.
44:9 No wonder those who worship them are put to **s**.
44:11 worship idols will stand before the LORD in **s**,
44:11 a god. Together they will stand in terror and **s**.
47:3 You will be naked and burdened with **s**. I will take
49:23 Those who wait for me will never be put to **s**."
50:6 I do not hide from **s**, for they mock me and spit in
54:4 "Fear not; you will no longer live in **s**. The **s** of
your youth and the sorrows of widowhood
61:7 Instead of **s** and dishonor, you will inherit a double
66:5 'Be joyful in him!' But they will be put to **s**.
Jer 2:26 a thief, Israel feels **s** only when she gets caught.
3:25 Let us now lie down in **s** and dishonor, for we
7:19 of all, they hurt themselves, to their own **s**."
11:13 Your altars of **s**—altars for burning incense to your
12:13 They will harvest a crop of **s**, for the fierce anger
13:26 I myself will expose you to **s**.
17:18 Bring **s** and terror on all who persecute me,
20:18 life has been filled with trouble, sorrow, and **s**.
46:12 The nations have heard of your **s**. The earth is
48:39 it is broken! Hear the wailing! See the **s** of Moab!
50:12 But your homeland will be overwhelmed with **s**
La 2:10 young women of Jerusalem hang their heads in **s**.
Eze 7:18 in sackcloth; horror and **s** will cover them.
16:61 Then you will remember with **s** all the evil you
16:63 and **s** when I forgive you of all that you have done,
23:29 The **s** of your prostitution will be exposed to all the
32:25 but now they lie in **s** in the pit, all of them outcasts,
32:30 of the sword. Once a terror, they now lie there in **s**.
36:6 because you have suffered **s** before the surrounding
36:7 nations will soon have their turn at suffering **s**.
39:26 They will accept responsibility for their past **s**
44:13 for they must bear the **s** of all the sins they have
Da 9:7 but our faces are covered with **s**, just as you see us
9:8 and ancestors are covered with **s** because we have
11:18 to his insolence and will cause him to retreat in **s**.
12:2 some to everlasting life and some to **s**
Hos 4:18 Their love for **s** is greater than their love for honor.
4:19 They will die in **s** because they offer sacrifices to
Ob 1:10 be destroyed completely and filled with **s** forever.
Mic 1:8 walk around naked and barefoot in sorrow and **s**.
3:7 Then you seers will cover your faces in **s**, and you
Na 3:5 so all the earth will see your nakedness and **s**.
Hab 2:15 so that you can gloat over their nakedness and **s**.
2:16 and all your glory will be turned to **s**.
Zep 3:5 but no one takes notice—the wicked know no **s**.
1Co 1:27 foolish in order to **s** those who think they are wise.
1:27 And he chose those who are powerless to **s** those
4:14 I am not writing these things to **s** you, but to warn
5:2 Why aren't you mourning in sorrow and **s**?
6:5 I am saying this to **s** you. Isn't there anyone in all
11:22 want to disgrace the church of God and **s** the poor?
15:34 For to your **s** I say that some of you don't even
2Co 10:8 And I will not be put to **s** by having my work
Php 1:20 hope that I will never do anything that causes me **s**,
Tit 2:5 Then they will not bring **s** on the word of God.
Heb 6:6 again by rejecting him, holding him up to public **s**.
1Pe 4:16 But it is no **s** to suffer for being a Christian.
1Jn 2:28 full of courage and not shrink back from him in **s**.

SHAMED (14) [SHAME]

Ps 69:7 For I am mocked and **s** for your sake;
71:24 who tried to hurt me / has been **s** and humiliated.
Jer 8:9 These wise teachers will be **s** by exile for their sin,
17:13 who turn away from you will be disgraced and **s**.
20:11 They will be **s** and thoroughly humiliated.
Eze 34:29 go hungry or be **s** by the scorn of foreign nations.
36:15 and you will no longer be **s** by them or cause your
Hos 10:6 Israel will be laughed at and **s** because its people
Hab 2:10 you have **s** your name and forfeited your lives.
Zep 3:19 to my former exiles, who have been mocked and **s**.
Lk 13:17 This **s** his enemies. And all the people rejoiced at
Col 2:15 He **s** them publicly by his victory over them on the
1Ti 6:1 the name of God and his teaching will not be **s**.
Rev 3:18 so you will not be **s** by your nakedness.

SHAMEFACEDNESS [KJV] See (NOT DRAW) ATTENTION

SHAMEFUL (30) [SHAME]

Ex 23:24 utterly conquer them and break down their **s** idols.
Dt 22:17 He has accused her of **s** things, claiming that she
23:14 He must not see any **s** thing among you, or he
24:1 but later discovers something about her that is **s**.
Jdg 19:23 this man is my guest, and such a thing would be **s**.
19:24 to them. But don't do such a **s** thing to this man."
20:6 men have committed this terrible and **s** crime.
20:10 Gibeah for this **s** thing they have done in Israel."
1Sa 20:34 for he was crushed by his father's **s** behavior
Job 31:11 For lust is a **s** sin, a crime that should be punished.
Ps 51:3 For I recognize my **s** deeds— / they haunt me day
119:39 Help me abandon my **s** ways; / your laws are all I
129:5 all who hate Jerusalem / be turned back in **s** defeat.
Pr 12:4 and crown; a **s** wife saps his strength.
17:2 A wise slave will rule over the master's **s** sons
25:8 You might go down before your neighbors in **s**
Hos 2:5 and became pregnant in a **s** way.
9:10 me for Baal-peor, giving themselves to that **s** idol.
Ro 1:24 and do whatever **s** things their hearts desired.
1:26 That is why God abandoned them to their **s** desires.
1:27 Men did **s** things with other men and, as a result,
1Co 11:6 And since it is **s** for a woman to have her hair cut
2Co 4:2 We reject all **s** and underhanded methods. We do
Eph 5:12 It is **s** even to talk about the things that ungodly
Php 3:19 god is their appetite, they brag about **s** things,
Col 3:5 to do with sexual sin, impurity, lust, and **s** desires.
Heb 12:2 He was willing to die a **s** death on the cross
2Pe 2:2 will follow their evil teaching and **s** immorality.
Jude 1:13 the sea, churning up the dirty foam of their **s** deeds.
Rev 21:27 no one who practices **s** idolatry and dishonesty—

SHAMEFULLY (4) [SHAME]

Mt 22:6 Others seized his messengers and treated them **s**,
Mk 12:4 but they beat him over the head and treated him **s**.
Lk 18:32 the Romans to be mocked, treated **s**, and spit upon.
20:11 he was beaten up and treated **s**, and he went away

SHAMELESS (5) [SHAME]

Eze 16:30 to do such things as these, acting like a **s** prostitute.
23:44 with Oholah and Oholibah, these **s** prostitutes,
Hos 2:5 For their mother is a **s** prostitute and became
Zep 2:1 Gather together and pray, you **s** nation.
Jude 1:12 They are **s** in the way they care only about

SHAMELESSLY (2) [SHAME]

Mk 12:40 But they **s** cheat widows out of their property,
Lk 20:47 But they **s** cheat widows out of their property,

SHAMER [KJV] See SHEMER

SHAMGAR (2)

Jdg 3:31 After Ehud, **S** son of Anath rescued Israel.
5:6 "In the days of **S** son of Anath, and in the days of

SHAMING (1) [SHAME]

1Sa 20:30 be king in your place, **s** yourself and your mother?

SHAMIR (4)

Jos 15:48 towns in the hill country: **S**, Jattir, Socoh,
Jdg 10:1 but lived in the town of **S** in the hill country of
10:2 When he died, he was buried in **S**.
1Ch 24:24 From the descendants of Micah, the leader was **S**,

SHAMMA (1)

1Ch 7:37 Bezer, Hod, **S**, Shilshah, Ithran, and Beera.

SHAMMAH (10)

Ge 36:13 sons of Reuel were Nahath, Zerah, **S**, and Mizzah.
36:17 of the clans of Nahath, Zerah, **S**, and Mizzah.
1Sa 16:9 Next Jesse summoned **S**, but Samuel said,
17:13 Jesse's three oldest sons—Eliab, Abinadab, and **S**
2Sa 23:11 Next in rank was **S** son of Agee from Harar.
23:12 but **S** held his ground in the middle of the field
23:25 **S** from Harod; / Elika from Harod;
1Ch 1:37 sons of Reuel were Nahath, Zerah, **S**, and Mizzah.
11:27 **S** from Harod; / Helez from Pelon;
27:8 **S** the Izrahite was commander of the fifth division,

SHAMMAI (5) [SHAMMAI'S]

1Ch 2:28 The sons of Onam were **S** and Jada. The sons of **S**
were Nadab and Abishur.
2:44 the father of Jorkeam. Rekem was the father of **S**.
2:45 The son of **S** was Maon. Maon was the father of
4:17 who became the mother of Miriam, **S**,

SHAMMAI'S (1) [SHAMMAI]

1Ch 2:32 **S** brother, Jada, had two sons named Jether

SHAMMUA (3)

Nu 13:4 names of the leaders: / Reuben | **S** son of Zaccur
Ne 11:17 and Abda son of **S**, son of Galal, son of Jeduthun.
12:18 **S** was leader of the family of Bilgah.

SHAMSHERAI (1)

1Ch 8:26 **S**, Shehariah, Athaliah,

SHAPE (10) [SHAPED, SHAPELY, SHAPES, SHAPING]

Ex 20:4 whether in the **s** of birds or animals or fish.
20:25 Do not chip or **s** the stones with a tool, for that
32:4 and molded and tooled it into the **s** of a calf.
Dt 4:23 You will break it if you make idols of any **s**
5:8 whether in the **s** of birds or animals or fish.
27:6 Do not **s** the stones with an iron tool. On the altar
1Ki 6:25 The two cherubim were identical in **s** and size;
Job 4:16 It stopped, but I couldn't see its **s**. There was a
38:14 For the features of the earth take **s** as the light
Eze 48:13 same size and **s** as that belonging to the priests—

SHAPED (17) [SHAPE]

Ex 25:33 Each of the six branches will hold a cup **s** like an
32:8 They have made an idol **s** like a calf, and they have
37:19 Each of the six branches held a cup **s** like an
Lev 26:1 or **s** stones to be worshiped in your land.
Jos 8:31 that are uncut and have not been **s** with iron tools."
1Ki 5:17 and **s** costly blocks of stone for the foundation of
7:19 The capitals on the columns inside the foyer were **s**
7:22 The capitals on the pillars were **s** like lilies. And
2Ki 19:18 only idols of wood and stone **s** by human hands.
2Ch 3:10 Solomon made two figures **s** like cherubim
Ne 9:18 even though they made an idol **s** like a calf
Ps 115:4 things of silver and gold, / **s** by human hands.
135:15 things of silver and gold, / **s** by human hands.
Isa 37:19 only idols of wood and stone **s** by human hands.
Hos 13:2 to worship—images **s** skillfully with human hands.
Am 4:13 For the LORD is the one who **s** the mountains,
Ac 7:41 So they made an idol **s** like a calf, and they

SHAPELY (1) [SHAPE]

Ge 29:17 in every way, with a lovely face and **s** figure.

SHAPES (1) [SHAPE]

Isa 45:9 Does the clay dispute with the one who **s** it, saying,

SHAPHAM (1)

1Ch 5:12 and **S** was second-in-command, along with Janai

SHAPHAN (26)

2Ki 22:3 King Josiah sent **S** son of Azaliah and grandson of
22:8 Hilkiah the high priest said to **S** the court secretary,
22:8 Then Hilkiah gave the scroll to **S**, and he read it.
22:9 **S** returned to the king and reported,
22:10 **S** also said to the king, "Hilkiah the priest has
given me a scroll." So **S** read it to the king.
22:12 Ahikam son of **S**, Acbor son of Micaiah, **S** the
court secretary,
22:14 So Hilkiah the priest, Ahikam, Acbor, **S**,
25:22 and grandson of **S** as governor over the people left
2Ch 34:8 and the Temple, Josiah appointed **S** son of Azaliah,
34:15 Hilkiah said to **S** the court secretary, "I have found
34:15 Then Hilkiah gave the scroll to **S**.
34:16 **S** took the scroll to the king and reported,
34:18 **S** also said to the king, "Hilkiah the priest has
given me a scroll." So **S** read it to the king.
34:20 Ahikam son of **S**, Acbor son of Micaiah, **S** the
court secretary,
Jer 26:24 Ahikam son of **S** also stood with Jeremiah
29:3 He sent the letter with Elasah son of **S**
36:10 from the Temple room of Gemariah son of **S**.
36:11 and grandson of **S** heard the messages from the
36:12 Elnathan son of Acbor, Gemariah son of **S**,
39:14 care of Gedaliah son of Ahikam and grandson of **S**,
40:5 to Gedaliah son of Ahikam and grandson of **S**.
Eze 8:11 there with Jaazaniah son of **S** in the middle.

SHAPHAT (8)

Nu 13:5 Simeon | **S** son of Hori
1Ki 19:16 and anoint Elisha son of **S** from Abel-meholah to
19:19 and found Elisha son of **S** plowing a field with a
2Ki 3:11 Joram's officers replied, "Elisha son of **S** is here.
6:31 if I don't execute Elisha son of **S** this very day,"
1Ch 3:22 his sons, Hattush, Igal, Bariah, Neariah, and **S**—
5:12 was second-in-command, along with Janai and **S**.
27:29 **S** son of Adlai was responsible for the cattle in the

SHAPHER [KJV] See SHEPHER

SHAPHIR (1)

Mic 1:11 You people of **S**, go as captives into exile—naked

SHAPING (1) [SHAPE]

Isa 44:12 a sharp tool, pounding and **s** it with all his might.

SHARAI (1)

Ezr 10:40 Macnadebai, Shashai, **S**,

SHARAIM [KJV] See SHAARAIM

SHARAR (2)
2Sa 23:33 Shagee from Harar; / Ahiam son of **S** from Harar;
1Ch 11:35 Ahiam son of **S** from Harar; / Eliphal son of Ur;

SHARE (143) [HALF-SHARE, SHARED, SHARES, SHARING]
Ge 9:27 of Japheth, / and may he **s** the prosperity of Shem;
14:24 But give a **s** of the goods to my allies—Aner,
21:10 He is not going to **s** the family inheritance with my
31:46 then sat down beside the pile of stones to **s** a meal.
Ex 12: 4 let them **s** the lamb with another family in the
12: 4 or not they **s** in this way depends on the size of
20: 5 am a jealous God who will not **s** your affection
29:28 these parts will be the regular **s** of Aaron and his
Lev 6:17 I have given it to the priests as their **s** of the
6:18 because it is their regular **s** of the offerings given
6:22 It is the LORD's regular **s**, and it must be
7:34 It is their regular **s** of the peace offerings brought
7:35 This is their **s**. It has been set apart for Aaron
7:36 regular **s** from the time of the priests' anointing.
8:29 This was Moses' **s** of the ram of ordination,
10:13 and your descendants as your regular **s** of the
10:14 and daughters as your regular **s** of the peace
22:11 his slaves have children, they also may **s** his food.
Nu 10:32 and we will **s** with you all the good things that the
14:24 His descendants will receive their full **s** of that
18: 8 offerings to you and your sons as your regular **s**.
18:11 the altar also belong to you as your regular **s**.
18:19 and daughters, to be eaten as your regular **s**.
18:20 of land or **s** of property among the people of Israel. I am your inheritance and your **s**.
18:24 to the LORD. This will be the Levites' **s**.
31:28 But first give the LORD his **s** of the captives,
31:28 one out of every five hundred as the LORD's **s**.
31:29 Give this **s** of their half to Eleazar the priest as an
31:30 Give this **s** to the Levites in charge of maintaining
31:37 of which 675 were the LORD's **s**;
31:38 36,000 cattle, of which 72 were the LORD's **s**;
31:39 30,500 donkeys, of which 61 were the LORD's **s**;
31:40 young girls, of whom 32 were the LORD's **s**.
31:41 Moses gave all the LORD's **s** to Eleazar the
31:50 offering to the LORD from our **s** of the plunder—
Dt 5: 9 am a jealous God who will not **s** your affection
10: 9 That is why the Levites have no **s** or inheritance
15:11 That is why I am commanding you to **s** your
15:14 **S** with him some of the bounty with which the
18: 3 parts the priests may claim as their **s** from the oxen
18: 4 You must also give to the priests the first **s** of the
18: 8 He may eat his **s** of the sacrifices and offerings,
28:55 He will refuse to give them a **s** of the flesh he is
33:21 for themselves; / a leader's **s** was assigned to them.
Jos 22: 8 "**S** with your relatives back home the great wealth
22: 8 **S** with them your large herds of cattle, your silver
22:19 in his Tabernacle, and we will **s** our land with you.
1Sa 30:24 We **s** and **s** alike—those who go to battle
1Ki 12:16 We have no **s** in Jesse's son! Let's go home,
1Ch 9:25 their relatives in the villages came to **s** their duties
2Ch 10:16 We have no **s** in Jesse's son! Let's go home,
Ezr 2:63 **s** of food from the sacrifices until there was a priest
Ne 7:65 **s** of food from the sacrifices until there was a priest
8:10 and **s** gifts of food with people who have nothing
8:12 and drink at a festive meal, to **s** gifts of food,
Job 31:17 my food and refused to **s** it with hungry orphans?
34:33 not mine. Go ahead, **s** your wisdom with us.
Ps 68:23 their blood, / and even your dogs will get their **s**!"
106: 5 Let me **s** in the prosperity of your chosen ones.
141: 4 Don't let me **s** in the delicacies / of those who do
145: 7 Everyone will **s** the story of your wonderful
Pr 5:15 your own well—**s** your love only with your wife.
5:17 reserve it for yourselves. Don't **s** it with strangers.
14:10 own bitterness, and no one else can fully **s** its joy.
16:19 It is better to live humbly with the poor than to **s**
17: 2 master's shameful sons and will **s** their inheritance.
Ecc 2:14 I saw that wise and foolish people **s** the same fate.
Isa 17: 3 The few left in Aram will **s** the fate of Israel's
33:23 the people of God. Even the lame will win their **s**!
42: 8 I will not **s** my praise with carved idols.
58: 7 I want you to **s** your food with the hungry and to
58:14 and give you your full **s** of the inheritance I
Eze 32:24 and **s** the humiliation of those who have gone to
45: 7 One section will **s** a border with the east side of the
45: 7 and the second section will **s** a border on the west
47:14 Otherwise each tribe will receive an equal **s**.
Hos 10:15 You will **s** that fate, Bethel, because of your great
Am 7: 1 This was after the king's **s** had been harvested
Zec 3:10 your neighbor into your home to **s** your peace
Mt 21:34 he sent his servants to collect his **s** of the crop.
21:41 will give him his **s** of the crop after each harvest."
Mk 12: 2 sent one of his servants to collect his **s** of the crop.
Lk 3:11 If you have food, **s** it with those who are hungry."
14:15 "What a privilege it would be to have a **s** in the
15:12 told his father, 'I want my **s** of your estate now,
17:22 "The time is coming when you will long to **s** in the
20:10 he sent one of his servants to collect his **s** of the
22:17 he said, "Take this and **s** it among yourselves.
Ac 1:17 was one of us, chosen to **s** in the ministry with us."
26: 7 and day, and they **s** the same hope I have.
Ro 1:11 so I can **s** a spiritual blessing with you that will
6: 8 with Christ, we know we will also **s** his new life.
8:17 since we are his children, we will **s** his treasures—
8:17 we are to **s** his glory, we must also **s** his suffering.
11:12 think how much greater a blessing the world will **s**
11:31 But someday they too will **s** in God's mercy.
12: 8 do it! If you have money, **s** it generously.
12:15 be happy with them. If they are sad, **s** their sorrow.
1Co 6: 9 do wrong will have no **s** in the Kingdom of God?
6:10 none of these will have a **s** in the Kingdom of God.
7:25 wisdom that can be trusted, and I will **s** it with you.
9: 4 the right to live in your homes and **s** your meals?
9:10 and thresh the grain expect a **s** of the harvest,
9:13 And those who serve at the altar get a **s** of the
9:22 I **s** their oppression so that I might bring them to
2Co 1: 7 We are confident that as you **s** in suffering, you will also **s** God's comfort.
4:10 these bodies of ours constantly **s** in the death of
8: 6 and encourage you to complete your **s** in this
8:14 Then at some other time they can **s** with you when
9: 8 you need and plenty left over to **s** with others.
Gal 1: 6 and mercy called you to **s** the eternal life he gives
3: 9 All who put their faith in Christ **s** the same
4:30 for the son of the slave woman will not **s** the
6: 2 **S** each other's troubles and problems, and in this
Eph 3: 6 The Gentiles have an equal **s** with the Jews in all
Php 2:17 will rejoice, and I want to **s** my joy with all of you.
4:14 you have done well to **s** with me in my present
Col 1:12 who has enabled you to **s** the inheritance that
1:27 and this is your assurance that you will **s** in his
3: 4 to the whole world, you will **s** in all his glory.
1Th 2:12 For he called you into his Kingdom to **s** his glory.
2Th 2:14 now you can **s** in the glory of our Lord Jesus
1Ti 6:18 always being ready to **s** with others whatever God
Tit 1: 4 to Titus, my true child in the faith that we **s**.
Heb 3:14 we will **s** in all that belongs to Christ.
11:25 He chose to **s** the oppression of God's people
12:10 for us because it means we will **s** in his holiness.
13: 3 **S** the sorrow of those being mistreated, as though
13:16 do good and to **s** what you have with those in need,
1Pe 4: 9 Cheerfully **s** your home with those who need a
5: 1 will **s** his glory and his honor when he returns.
5: 4 your reward will be a never-ending **s** in his glory
2Pe 1: 1 I am writing to all of you who **s** the same precious
1: 4 evil desires and that you will **s** in his divine nature.
Jude 1: 3 to write to you about the salvation we all **s**.
Rev 1: 1 so that John could **s** the revelation with God's
3:20 I will come in, and we will **s** a meal as friends.
20: 6 and holy are those who **s** in the first resurrection.
22:19 God will remove that person's **s** in the tree of life

SHARED (12) [SHARE]
Ex 24:11 In fact, they **s** a meal together in God's presence!
Lev 7:10 are to be **s** among all the priests and their sons.
Ps 41: 9 one I trusted completely, / the one who **s** my food,
Jn 17: 5 bring me into the glory we **s** before the world
Ac 2:44 met together constantly and **s** everything they had.
2:45 and **s** the proceeds with those in need.
2:46 and **s** their meals with great joy and generosity—
4:32 was not their own; they **s** everything they had.
15:38 them in Pamphylia and had not **s** in their work.
16:32 Then they **s** the word of the Lord with him and all
Php 1: 7 We have **s** together the blessings of God,
Heb 6: 4 the good things of heaven and **s** in the Holy Spirit,

SHARES (5) [SHARE]
Ps 25:14 With them he **s** the secrets of his covenant.
Eze 47:13 The tribe of Joseph will be given two **s** of land.
Mt 10:25 The student **s** the teacher's fate. The servant **s** the master's fate. And since I,
Jn 13:18 'The one who **s** my food has turned against me,'

SHAREZER (3)
2Ki 19:37 and **S** killed him with their swords.
Isa 37:38 and **S** killed him with their swords.
Zec 7: 2 The people of Bethel had sent **S**

SHARING (10) [SHARE]
2Ki 7: 9 is wonderful news, and we aren't **s** it with anyone!
Ac 2:42 **s** in the Lord's Supper and in prayer.
Ro 5: 2 and joyfully look forward to **s** God's glory.
11:17 **s** in God's rich nourishment of his special olive
1Co 10:16 aren't we **s** in the benefits of the blood of Christ?
10:16 aren't we **s** in the benefits of the body of Christ?
11:21 hurry to eat your own meal without **s** with others.
2Co 8: 4 and again for the gracious privilege of **s** in the gift
Php 3:10 what it means to suffer with him, **s** in his death,
1Pe 4:13 and afterward you will have the wonderful joy of **s**

SHARON (8)
1Ch 5:16 and its villages, and throughout the **S** Plain.
27:29 Shitrai from **S** was in charge of the cattle on the **S** Plain.
SS 2: 1 "I am the rose of **S**, the lily of the valley."
Isa 33: 9 The plain of **S** is now a wilderness. Bashan
35: 2 as Mount Carmel's pastures and the plain of **S**.
65:10 the plain of **S** will again be filled with flocks,
Ac 9:35 and **S** turned to the Lord when they saw Aeneas

SHARP (33) [SHARP-EYED, SHARPEN, SHARPENED, SHARPENING, SHARPENS, SHARPER, SHARPEST, SHARPLY]
Job 41:30 Its belly is covered with scales as **s** as glass.
Ps 45: 5 Your arrows are **s**, / piercing your enemies' hearts.
52: 2 Your tongue cuts like a **s** razor; / you're an expert
64: 3 **S** tongues are the swords they wield; / bitter words
120: 4 You will be pierced with **s** arrows / and burned
127: 4 young man / are like **s** arrows in a warrior's hands.
149: 6 be in their mouths, / and a **s** sword in their hands—
Pr 5: 4 is as bitter as poison, **s** as a double-edged sword.
25:18 with a sword, or shooting them with a **s** arrow.
30:14 They devour the poor with teeth as **s** as swords
Isa 5:28 Their arrows will be **s** and their bows ready for
21: 3 **S** pangs of horror are upon me, like the pangs of a
21:15 drawn swords and **s** arrows and the terrors of war.
41:15 be a new threshing instrument with many **s** teeth.
44:12 The blacksmith stands at his forge to make a **s** tool,
49: 2 He made my words of judgment as **s** as a sword.
49: 2 of his hand. I am like a **s** arrow in his quiver.
Eze 2: 6 Don't be afraid even though their threats are **s** as
5: 1 take a **s** sword and use it as a razor to shave your
Da 5:12 has a **s** mind and is filled with divine knowledge
Joel 1: 6 to count! Its teeth are as **s** as the teeth of lions!
Na 2: 1 and keep a **s** watch for the enemy attack to begin!
Mt 27:29 a crown of long, **s** thorns and put it on his head,
Mk 13:35 So keep a **s** lookout! For you do not know when
15:17 a crown of long, **s** thorns and put it on his head.
Jn 19: 2 a crown of long, **s** thorns and put it on his head,
Ac 15:39 over this was so **s** that they separated.
Rev 1:16 and a **s** two-edged sword came from his mouth.
2:12 This is the message from the one who has a **s**
14:14 a gold crown on his head and a **s** sickle in his hand.
14:17 the Temple in heaven, and he also had a **s** sickle.
19:15 From his mouth came a **s** sword, and with it he
19:21 Their entire army was killed by the **s** sword that

SHARP-EYED (1) [EYE, SHARP]
Job 28:21 Even the **s** birds in the sky cannot discover it.

SHARPEN (6) [SHARP]
Dt 32:41 when I **s** my flashing sword / and begin to carry
1Sa 13:20 So whenever the Israelites needed to **s** their
Ps 7:12 If a person does not repent, / God will **s** his sword;
Ecc 10:10 Since a dull ax requires great strength, **s** the blade.
Jer 46: 4 Put on your helmets, **s** your spears, and prepare
51:11 **S** the arrows! Lift up the shields! For the LORD

SHARPENED (3) [SHARP]
Eze 21: 9 from the LORD: A sword is being **s** and polished.
21:11 Yes, the sword is now being **s** and polished;
21:28 it is **s** to destroy, flashing like lightning!

SHARPENING (2) [SHARP]
1Sa 13:21 a quarter of an ounce of silver for **s** a plowshare
13:21 and an eighth of an ounce for **s** an ax, a sickle,

SHARPENS (2) [SHARP]
Pr 27:17 As iron **s** iron, a friend **s** a friend.

SHARPER (1) [SHARP]
Heb 4:12 It is **s** than the sharpest knife, cutting deep into our

SHARPEST (1) [SHARP]
Heb 4:12 It is sharper than the **s** knife, cutting deep into our

SHARPLY (5) [SHARP]
Ge 12:18 So Pharaoh called for Abram and accused him **s**.
1Sa 24: 7 So David **s** rebuked his men and did not let them
1Ki 22:16 But the king replied **s**, "How many times must I
2Ch 18:15 But the king replied **s**, "How many times must I
Ne 13:21 But I spoke **s** to them and said, "What are you

SHARPNESS [KJV] See HARSHLY

SHARUHEN (1) [SHAARAIM]
Jos 19: 6 Beth-lebaoth, and **S**—thirteen towns with their

SHASHAI (1)
Ezr 10:40 Macnadebai, **S**, Sharai,

SHASHAK (2)
1Ch 8:14 Ahio, **S**, Jeremoth,
8:25 Iphdeiah, and Penuel were the sons of **S**.

SHATTER (16) [SHATTERED, SHATTERING, SHATTERS]
Dt 7: 5 down their pagan altars and **s** their sacred pillars.
Job 7:14 you **s** me with dreams. You terrify me with visions.
Ps 3: 7 my enemies in the face! / **S** the teeth of the wicked!
110: 6 and fill them with their dead; / he will **s** heads
Jer 19:11 so I will **s** the people of Judah and Jerusalem
25:34 has arrived; you will fall and **s** like fragile pottery.
48:12 from her jar. They will pour her out, then **s** the jar!
48:18 for those who destroy Moab will **s** Dibon, too.
49:37 I myself will go with Elam's enemies to **s** it.
51:20 "With you I will **s** nations and destroy many
51:21 With you I will **s** armies, destroying the horse
51:22 With you I will **s** men and women, old people
51:23 With you I will **s** shepherds and flocks, farmers
Eze 32:12 They will **s** the pride of Egypt, and all its hordes
Da 2:44 It will **s** all these kingdoms into nothingness,
Am 3:11 He will surround them and **s** their defenses.

SHATTERED (16) [SHATTER]
Ps 30: 7 Then you turned away from me, and I was **s**.
37:17 For the strength of the wicked will be **s**,
48: 7 ships of Tarshish / being **s** by a powerful east wind.
78:47 with hail / and **s** their sycamores with sleet.
105:33 their grapevines and fig trees / and **s** all the trees.

Isa 8: 9 your best to defend yourselves, but you will be s!
30: 14 s so completely that there won't be a piece left that
30: 31 the LORD's command, the Assyrians will be s.
Jer 19: 11 As this jar lies s, so I will shatter the people of
48: 17 scepter is broken, how the beautiful staff is s!
50: 2 Her images and idols will be s. Her gods Bel
50: 23 hammer in all the earth, lies broken and s.
Eze 29: 16 Egypt's s condition will remind Israel of how
32: 9 "And when I bring your s remains to distant
Mal 1: 4 "We have been s, but we will rebuild the ruins."
Ac 16: 19 Her masters' hopes of wealth were now s, so they

SHATTERING (1) [SHATTER]
Da 12: 7 When the s of the holy people has finally come to

SHATTERS (3) [SHATTER]
Ps 29: 5 the LORD s the cedars of Lebanon.
33: 10 The LORD s the plans of the nations
Hab 3: 6 He s the everlasting mountains and levels the

SHAUL (10) [SHAUL'S, SHAULITE]
Ge 36: 37 S from the city of Rehoboth on the Euphrates
36: 38 When S died, Baal-hanan son of Acbor became
46: 10 were Jemuel, Jamin, Ohad, Jakin, Zohar, and S.
Ex 6: 15 Zohar, and S (whose mother was a Canaanite).
Nu 26: 13 The Shaulite clan, named after its ancestor S.
1Ch 1: 48 S from the city of Rehoboth on the Euphrates
1: 49 When S died, Baal-hanan son of Acbor became
4: 24 Simeon were Nemuel, Jamin, Jarib, Zerah, and S.
4: 25 The descendants of S were Shallum, Mibsam,
6: 24 Tahath, Uriel, Uzziah, and S.

SHAUL'S (1) [SHAUL]
Ge 46: 10 and Shaul. (S mother was a Canaanite woman.)

SHAULITE (1) [SHAUL]
Nu 26: 13 The S clan, named after its ancestor Shaul.

SHAVE (23) [SHAVED, SHAVING]
Ge 41: 14 After a quick s and change of clothes, he went in
Lev 13: 33 the infected person must s off all hair except the
14: 9 the seventh day, they must again s off all their hair,
21: 5 "The priests must never s their heads,
Nu 6: 9 must wait for seven days and then s their heads.
6: 18 "Then the Nazirites will s their hair at the entrance
8: 7 And have them s their entire body and wash their
Dt 14: 1 or s the hair above your foreheads for the sake of
21: 12 where she must s her head, cut her fingernails,
Jdg 16: 19 and she called in a man to s off his hair, making his
Isa 7: 20 hired to protect you—and use it to s off everything:
15: 2 They will s their heads in sorrow and cut off their
22: 12 He told you to s your heads in sorrow for your sins
Jer 7: 29 O Jerusalem, s your head in mourning, and weep
16: 6 will not cut themselves or s their heads in sadness.
48: 37 They s their heads and beards in mourning.
Eze 5: 1 and use it as a razor to s your head and beard.
7: 18 They will s their heads in sorrow and remorse.
27: 31 They s their heads in grief because of you
44: 20 let their hair grow too long nor s it off completely.
Am 8: 10 and s your heads as signs of sorrow,
Mic 1: 16 S your heads in sorrow, for the children you love
Ac 21: 23 taken a vow and are preparing to s their heads.

SHAVED (9) [SHAVE]
Nu 6: 19 After each Nazirite's head has been s, the priest
Jdg 16: 17 If my head were s, my strength would leave me,
2Sa 10: 4 and s off half of each man's beard,
1Ch 19: 4 seized David's ambassadors and s their beards,
Job 1: 20 Then he s his head and fell to the ground before
Jer 41: 5 They had s off their beards, torn their clothes,
Ac 18: 18 Paul had s his head according to Jewish custom,
21: 24 and pay for them to have their heads s.
1Co 11: 6 for a woman to have her hair cut or her head s,

SHAVEH (1) [SHAVEH KIRIATHAIM]
Ge 14: 17 came out to meet him in the valley of S (that is,

SHAVING (2) [SHAVE]
Lev 14: 8 s off all their hair, and bathing themselves in water.
1Co 11: 5 on her head, for this is the same as s her head.

SHAWLS (1)
Isa 3: 23 linen garments, head ornaments, and s.

SHE (994) [HER, HERS, HERSELF, SHE'S] See Index of Articles, Etc.

SHE'S (3) [BE, SHE] See Index of Articles, Etc.

SHEAL (1)
Ezr 10: 29 Meshullam, Malluch, Adaiah, Jashub, S,

SHEALTIEL (14)
1Ch 3: 17 was taken prisoner by the Babylonians, were S,
Ezr 3: 2 and Zerubbabel son of S with his family began to
3: 8 including Zerubbabel son of S, Jeshua son of
5: 2 Zerubbabel son of S and Jeshua son of Jehozadak
Ne 12: 1 Levites who had returned with Zerubbabel son of S
Hag 1: 1 the prophet Haggai to Zerubbabel son of S,
1: 12 Then Zerubbabel son of S, Jeshua son of
1: 14 sparked the enthusiasm of Zerubbabel son of S,
2: 2 "Say this to Zerubbabel son of S, governor of
2: 23 I will honor you, Zerubbabel son of S, my servant.
Mt 1: 12 Jehoiachin was the father of S. / S was the father
Lk 3: 27 Zerubbabel was the son of S. / S was the son of

SHEAR (1) [SHEARED, SHEARERS, SHEARING, SHEARS, SHEEP-SHEARERS, SHEEP-SHEARING, SHORN]
Dt 15: 19 and do not s the firstborn of your flocks.

SHEAR-JASHUB (1)
Isa 7: 3 "Go out to meet King Ahaz, you and your son S.

SHEARED (1) [SHEAR]
2Sa 13: 23 when Absalom's sheep were being s at Baal-hazor

SHEARERS (3) [SHEAR]
1Sa 25: 11 and water and the meat I've slaughtered for my s
Isa 53: 7 And as a sheep is silent before the s, he did not
Ac 8: 32 And as a lamb is silent before the s, / he did not

SHEARIAH (2)
1Ch 8: 38 Azrikam, Bokeru, Ishmael, S, Obadiah,
9: 44 Bokeru, Ishmael, S, Obadiah, and Hanan.

SHEARING (5) [SHEAR]
Ge 31: 19 Laban was some distance away, s his sheep.
38: 12 went to Timnah to supervise the s of his sheep.
Dt 18: 4 the new wine, the olive oil, and the wool at s time.
1Sa 25: 4 When David heard that Nabal was s his sheep,
25: 7 I am told that you are s your sheep and goats.

SHEARS (1) [SHEAR]
Isa 18: 5 LORD will cut you off as though with pruning s.

SHEATH (7)
1Sa 17: 51 he ran over and pulled Goliath's sword from its s.
2Sa 20: 8 he secretly slipped the dagger from its s.
1Ch 21: 27 to the angel, who put the sword back into its s.
Jer 47: 6 at rest again? Go back into your s; rest and be still!
Eze 21: 5 and it will not return to its s until its work is
21: 30 Should I return my sword to its s before I deal with
Jn 18: 11 said to Peter, "Put your sword back into its s.

SHEAVES (3)
Ex 22: 6 destroying the s or the standing grain,
Ru 2: 15 "Let her gather grain right among the s without
Zec 12: 6 or like a burning torch among s of grain.

SHEBA (34) [SHEBA'S]
Ge 10: 7 The descendants of Raamah were S and Dedan.
10: 28 Obal, Abimael, S,
25: 3 Jokshan's two sons were S and Dedan.
Jos 19: 2 inheritance included Beersheba, S, Moladah,
2Sa 20: 1 Then a troublemaker named S son of Bicri,
20: 2 the men of Israel deserted David and followed S.
20: 6 "That troublemaker S is going to hurt us more
20: 7 and Joab set out after S with an elite guard from
20: 10 Abishai left him lying there and continued after S.
20: 13 the way, everyone went on with Joab to capture S.
20: 14 S had traveled across Israel to mobilize his own
20: 21 All I want is a man named S son of Bicri from the
1Ki 10: 1 When the queen of S heard of Solomon's
10: 4 When the queen of S realized how wise Solomon
10: 10 so many spices brought in as those the queen of S
10: 13 King Solomon gave the queen of S whatever she
1Ch 1: 9 The descendants of Raamah were S and Dedan.
1: 22 Obal, Abimael, S,
1: 32 The sons of Jokshan were S and Dedan.
5: 13 Meshullam, S, Jorai, Jacan, Zia, and Eber.
2Ch 9: 1 When the queen of S heard of Solomon's
9: 3 When the queen of S realized how wise Solomon
9: 9 as fine as those the queen of S gave to Solomon.
9: 12 King Solomon gave the queen of S whatever she
Job 6: 19 the caravans from Tema and from S stop for water,
Ps 72: 10 The eastern kings of S and Seba / will bring him
72: 15 live the king! / May the gold of S be given to him.
Isa 60: 6 From S they will bring gold and incense for the
Jer 6: 20 is no use now in offering me sweet incense from S.
Eze 27: 22 The merchants of S and Raamah came with all
27: 23 Haran, Canneh, Eden, S, Asshur, and Kilmad came
38: 13 But S and Dedan and the merchants of Tarshish
Mt 12: 42 The queen of S will also rise up against this
Lk 11: 31 "The queen of S will rise up against this

SHEBA'S (1) [SHEBA]
2Sa 20: 22 and they cut off S head and threw it out to Joab.

SHEBAH [KJV] See OATH

SHEBAM [KJV] See SEBAM

SHEBANIAH (6)
1Ch 15: 24 S, Joshaphat, Nethanel, Amasai, Zechariah,
Ne 9: 4 Bani, Kadmiel, S, Bunni, Sherebiah, Bani,
9: 5 Bani, Hashabneiah, Sherebiah, Hodiah, S,
10: 4 Hattush, S, Malluch,
10: 10 fellow Levites: S, Hodiah, Kelita, Pelaiah, Hanan,
10: 12 Zaccur, Sherebiah, S,

SHEBER (1)
1Ch 2: 48 Maacah, gave birth to S and Tirhanah.

SHEBNA (9)
2Ki 18: 18 S the court secretary, and Joah son of Asaph,
18: 26 Then Eliakim son of Hilkiah, S, and Joah said to
18: 37 S the court secretary, and Joah son of Asaph,
19: 2 S the court secretary, and the leading priests,
Isa 22: 15 the LORD Almighty, told me to confront S,
36: 3 S the court secretary, and Joah son of Asaph,
36: 11 Then Eliakim, S, and Joah said to the king's
36: 22 S the court secretary, and Joah son of Asaph,
37: 2 S the court secretary, and the leading priests,

SHEBUEL (4)
1Ch 23: 16 The descendants of Gershom included S,
24: 20 From the descendants of Amram, the leader was S.
24: 20 From the descendants of S, the leader was
26: 24 S was a descendant of Gershom son of Moses.

SHECANIAH (11) [SHECANIAH'S]
1Ch 3: 21 Arnan's son was Obadiah. Obadiah's son was S.
24: 11 The ninth lot fell to Jeshua. / The tenth lot fell to S.
2Ch 31: 15 Miniamin, Jeshua, Shemaiah, Amariah, and S.
Ezr 8: 3 From the family of David: Hattush son of S.
8: 5 of Zattu: S son of Jahaziel and 300 other men.
10: 2 Then S son of Jehiel, a descendant of Elam,
10: 5 of Israel swear that they would do as S had said.
Ne 3: 29 and beyond him was Shemaiah son of S,
6: 18 because his father-in-law was S son of Arah
12: 3 S, Harim, Meremoth,
12: 14 of Malluch. / Joseph was leader of the family of S.

SHECANIAH'S (1) [SHECANIAH]
1Ch 3: 22 S descendants were Shemaiah and his sons,

SHECHEM (62) [SHECHEM'S, SHECHEMITES]
Ge 12: 6 they came to a place near S and set up camp beside
33: 18 Then they arrived safely at S, in Canaan, and they
34: 2 S son of Hamor the Hivite, saw her, he took her
34: 7 S had done a disgraceful thing against Jacob's
34: 8 "My son S is truly in love with your daughter,
34: 11 Then S addressed Dinah's father and brothers.
34: 13 But Dinah's brothers deceived S and Hamor
34: 13 because of what S had done to their sister.
34: 18 Hamor and S gladly agreed,
34: 19 and S lost no time in acting on this request, for he
34: 19 S was a highly respected member of his family,
34: 26 including Hamor and S. They rescued Dinah from
35: 4 and he buried them beneath the tree near S.
37: 12 brothers went to pasture their father's flocks at S.
37: 13 "Your brothers are over at S with the flocks.
37: 14 and Joseph traveled to S from his home in the
Nu 26: 31 The Shechemites, named after their ancestor S.
Jos 17: 2 Abiezer, Helek, Asriel, S, Hepher, and Shemida.
17: 7 border of Asher to Micmethath, which is east of S.
20: 7 S, in the hill country of Ephraim; and Kiriath-arba
21: 21 S (a city of refuge for those who accidentally killed
24: 1 Joshua summoned all the people of Israel to S,
24: 25 made a covenant with the people that day at S,
24: 32 with them when they left Egypt, were buried at S,
Jdg 8: 31 He also had a concubine in S, who bore him a son
9: 1 One day Gideon's son Abimelech went to S to visit
9: 2 "Ask the people of S whether they want to be
9: 3 So Abimelech's uncles spoke to all the people of S
9: 6 Then the people of S and Beth-millo called a meeting under the oak beside the pillar at S
9: 7 and shouted, "Listen to me, people of S!
9: 20 and devour the people of S and Beth-millo;
9: 20 and may fire come out from the people of S
9: 23 up trouble between Abimelech and the people of S,
9: 24 and the men of S for murdering Gideon's seventy
9: 25 The people of S set an ambush for Abimelech on
9: 26 At that time Gaal son of Ebed moved to S with his
9: 26 and gained the confidence of the people of S.
9: 27 During the annual harvest festival at S, held in the
9: 28 Gaal shouted. "He's not a true descendant of S!
9: 31 of Ebed and his brothers have come to live in S,
9: 34 into four groups, stationing themselves around S.
9: 39 then led the men of S into battle against
9: 41 and Zebul drove Gaal and his brothers out of S.
9: 42 The next day the people of S went out into the
9: 44 city gate to keep the men of S from getting back in,
9: 46 When the people who lived in the tower of S heard
9: 49 So all the people who had lived in the tower of S
9: 57 God also punished the men of S for all their evil.
21: 19 the east side of the road that goes from Bethel to S.
1Ki 12: 1 Rehoboam went to S, where all Israel had gathered
12: 25 then built up the city of S in the hill country of
1Ch 6: 67 S (a city of refuge in the hill country of Ephraim),
7: 19 sons of Shemida were Ahian, S, Likhi, and Aniam.
7: 28 and S and its surrounding villages to the north as
2Ch 10: 1 Rehoboam went to S, where all Israel had gathered
Ps 60: 6 this by his holiness: / "I will divide up S with joy.
108: 7 this by his holiness: / "I will divide up S with joy.
Jer 41: 5 eighty men arrived from S, Shiloh, and Samaria.
Hos 6: 9 of priests murder travelers along the road to S
Ac 7: 16 All of them were taken to S and buried in the tomb
7: 16 Abraham had bought from the sons of Hamor in S.

SHECHEM'S (6) [SHECHEM]
Ge 33: 19 of Hamor, S father, for a hundred pieces of silver.
34: 3 But S love for Dinah was strong, and he tried to

34: 6 Meanwhile, Hamor, **S** father, came out to discuss
34:26 They rescued Dinah from **S** house and returned to
Jdg 9:28 the men of Hamor, who are **S** true descendants.
9:40 Many of **S** warriors were killed, and the ground

SHECHEMITES (1) [SHECHEM]

Nu 26:31 The **S**, named after their ancestor Shechem.

SHED (8) [SHEDDING, SHEDS]

Ge 37:22 "Why should we **s** his blood? Let's just throw him
Lev 17: 4 Such a person has **s** blood and must be cut off from
Dt 21: 7 they must say, 'Our hands did not **s** this blood,
1Ch 22: 8 And since you have **s** so much blood before me,
28: 3 for you are a warrior and have **s** much blood.'
Ps 106:38 They **s** innocent blood, / the blood of their sons
Ro 3:25 with God when we believe that Jesus **s** his blood,
13:12 rid of your evil deeds. **S** them like dirty clothes.

SHEDDING (9) [SHED]

Ps 51:14 Forgive me for **s** blood, O God who saves;
Jer 48:10 who hold back their swords from **s** blood!
La 4:13 who defiled the city by **s** innocent blood.
Zec 9:15 drunk with wine, **s** the blood of their enemies.
1Co 11:25 between God and you, sealed by the **s** of my blood.
Heb 9:22 Without the **s** of blood, there is no forgiveness of
13:12 order to make his people holy by **s** his own blood.
1Jn 5: 6 baptism in water and by **s** his blood on the cross—
Rev 1: 5 and has freed us from our sins by **s** his blood for

SHEDEUR (5)

Nu 1: 5 chosen for the task: / Reuben | Elizur son of **S**
2:10[-11] Reuben | Elizur son of **S** | 46,500
7:30 On the fourth day Elizur son of **S**, leader of the
7:35 This was the offering brought by Elizur son of **S**.
10:18 under the leadership of Elizur son of **S**.

SHEDS (1) [SHED]

Job 15:33 like an olive tree that **s** its blossoms so the fruit

SHEEN (1)

SS 7: 5 and the **s** of your hair radiates royalty.

SHEEP (224) [SHEEP'S, SHEEP-SHEARERS, SHEEP-SHEARING, SHEEPFOLD, SHEEPFOLDS]

Ge 12:16 **s**, cattle, donkeys, male and female servants,
13: 5 was also very wealthy with **s**, cattle, and many
20:14 Then Abimelech took **s** and oxen and servants—
21:27 Then Abraham gave **s** and oxen to Abimelech,
24:35 The LORD has given him flocks of **s** and herds of
26:14 He acquired large flocks of **s** and goats, great herds
29: 2 He saw in the distance three flocks of **s** lying in an
29: 6 here comes his daughter Rachel with the **s**."
29: 9 Rachel arrived with her father's **s**, for she was a
29:10 and because the **s** were his uncle's, Jacob went
30:32 and remove all the **s** and goats that are speckled
30:32 or spotted, along with all the dark-colored **s**.
30:33 If you find in my flock any white **s** or goats that
30:35 with any white patches, and all the dark-colored **s**.
31:19 Laban was some distance away, shearing his **s**.
31:38 and all that time I cared for your **s** and goats
32: 5 donkeys, **s**, goats, and many servants, both men
38:12 went to Timnah to supervise the shearing of his **s**.
Ex 9: 3 destroy your horses, donkeys, camels, cattle, and **s**.
12: 5 either a **s** or a goat, with no physical defects.
20:24 peace offerings, your **s** and goats and your cattle.
22: 1 who steals an ox or **s** and then kills or sells it.
22: 1 For **s** the fine is four **s** for each one stolen.
22: 4 If someone steals an ox or a donkey or a **s** and it is
22: 9 donkey, **s**, article of clothing, or anything else.
22:10 ox, **s**, or any other animal, but it dies or is injured
22:30 must also give me the firstborn of your cattle and **s**.
34:19 firstborn male belongs to me—of both cattle and **s**.
Lev 1:10 bring a male **s** or goat with no physical defects.
3: 6 from the flock, you may bring either a goat or a **s**.
3: 7 If you bring a **s** as your gift, present it to the
4:32 "If any of the people bring a **s** as their sin offering,
4:35 just as is done with a **s** presented as a peace
5: 6 a female from the flock, either a **s** or a goat.
5: 7 "If any of them cannot afford to bring a **s**,
7:23 never eat fat, whether from oxen or **s** or goats.
12: 8 "If a woman cannot afford to bring a **s**, she must
27:26 or **s** because the firstborn of these animals already
Nu 15: 3 sacrifice must be an animal from your flocks of **s**
18:17 may not redeem the firstborn of cattle, **s**, or goats.
22:40 where the king sacrificed cattle and **s**. He sent
27:17 so the people of the LORD will not be like **s**
31:28 cattle, donkeys, **s**, and goats that belong to the
31:30 of every fifty of the captives, cattle, donkeys, **s**,
31:32 that the fighting men had taken totaled 675,000 **s**,
31:36 given to the fighting men totaled 337,500 **s**,
31:43 amounted to 337,500 **s**,
Dt 7:13 and olives, and great herds of cattle, **s**, and goats.
12:21 any of the cattle or **s** the LORD has given you,
14: 4 are the animals you may eat: the ox, the **s**, the goat,
14: 5 the ibex, the antelope, and the mountain **s**.
14:26 anything you want—an ox, a **s**, some wine, or beer.
17: 1 or defective ox or **s** to the LORD your God,
18: 3 the oxen and **s** that the people bring as offerings:
22: 1 you see your neighbor's ox or **s** wandering away,
28:31 Your **s** will be given to your enemies, and no one
Jos 6:21 and women, young and old, cattle, **s**, donkeys—
7:24 of gold, his sons, daughters, cattle, donkeys, **s**, tent,
Jdg 6: 4 nothing to eat, taking all the **s**, oxen, and donkeys.
1Sa 14:32 flew upon the battle plunder and butchered the **s**,
14:34 'Bring the cattle and **s** here to kill them and drain
15: 3 men, women, children, babies, cattle, **s**, camels,
15: 9 Agag's life and kept the best of the **s** and cattle,
15:14 "Then what is all the bleating of **s** and lowing of
15:15 "It's true that the army spared the best of the **s**
15:21 Then my troops brought in the best of the **s**
16:11 "But he's out in the fields watching the **s**."
17:15 and helping his father with the **s** in Bethlehem.
17:20 So David left the **s** with another shepherd and set
17:28 "What about those few **s** you're supposed to be
17:34 "I have been taking care of my father's **s**,"
22:19 and babies, and all the cattle, donkeys, and **s**.
25: 2 He had three thousand **s** and a thousand goats,
25: 4 When David heard that Nabal was shearing his **s**,
25: 7 I am told that you are shearing your **s** and goats.
25:16 they were like a wall of protection to us and the **s**.
25:18 two skins of wine, five dressed **s**, nearly a bushel
27: 9 He took the **s**, cattle, donkeys, camels, and clothing
2Sa 7: 8 a shepherd boy, tending your **s** out in the pasture.
12: 2 The rich man owned many **s** and cattle.
13:23 when Absalom's **s** were being sheared at
17:29 honey, butter, **s**, and cheese for David and those
1Ki 1: 9 where he sacrificed **s**, oxen, and fattened calves.
1:19 has sacrificed many oxen, fattened calves, and **s**,
1:25 has sacrificed many oxen, fattened calves, and **s**,
4:23 one hundred **s** or goats, as well as deer, gazelles,
8: 5 and the entire community of Israel sacrificed **s**
8:63 the LORD numbering 22,000 oxen and 120,000 **s**.
22:17 on the mountains, like **s** without a shepherd.
2Ki 3: 4 Mesha of Moab and his people were **s** breeders.
5:26 and vineyards and **s** and oxen and servants?
1Ch 5:21 250,000 **s**, 2,000 donkeys, and 100,000 captives.
12:40 cattle, and **s** were brought to the celebration.
17: 7 a shepherd boy, tending your **s** out in the pasture.
27:31 Jaziz the Hagrite was in charge of the king's **s**.
2Ch 5: 6 and the entire community of Israel sacrificed **s**
7: 5 offered a sacrifice of 22,000 oxen and 120,000 **s**.
14:15 the camps of herdsmen and captured many **s**
15:11 hundred oxen and seven thousand **s** and goats.
18: 2 They butchered great numbers of **s** and oxen for
18:16 on the mountains, like **s** without a shepherd.
29:33 hundred bulls and three thousand **s** as sacrifices.
30:24 thousand bulls and seven thousand **s** for offerings,
30:24 donated one thousand bulls and ten thousand **s**.
31: 6 brought in the tithes of their cattle and **s** and a tithe
32:28 for his cattle and folds for his flocks of **s** and goats.
Ne 3: 1 and the other priests started to rebuild at the **S**
3:32 repaired the wall from that corner to the **S** Gate.
5:18 six fat **s**, and a large number of domestic fowl.
12:39 Then we continued on to the **S** Gate and stopped at
Job 1: 3 He owned seven thousand **s**, three thousand
1:16 and burned up your **s** and all the shepherds.
21:11 Their children skip about like lambs in a flock of **s**.
24: 2 the boundary markers. They steal flocks of **s**,
42:12 For now he had fourteen thousand **s**, six thousand
Ps 8: 7 the **s** and the cattle / and all the wild animals,
44:11 You have treated us like **s** waiting to be
44:22 killed every day; / we are being slaughtered like **s**.
49:14 Like **s**, they are led to the grave, / where death will
65:13 The meadows are clothed with flocks of **s**,
74: 1 so intense against the **s** of your own pasture?
77:20 led your people along that road like a flock of **s**,
78:52 But he led his own people like a flock of **s**,
78:70 his servant David, / calling him from the **s** pens.
79:13 Then we your people, the **s** of your pasture,
95: 7 the people he watches over, / the **s** under his care.
100: 3 we are his. / We are his people, the **s** of his pasture.
107:41 and increases their families like vast flocks of **s**.
119:176 I have wandered away like a lost **s**; / come and find
Pr 27:26 your **s** will provide wool for clothing, and your
SS 1: 7 flock today? Where will you rest your **s** at noon?
4: 2 Your teeth are as white as **s**, newly shorn
Isa 7:21 will be fortunate to have a cow and two **s** left.
7:25 cover them. Cattle, **s**, and goats will graze there.
13:14 hunted deer, wandering like **s** without a shepherd.
13:20 and shepherds will not allow their **s** to stay
17: 2 **S** will graze in the streets and lie down unafraid.
31: 4 "When a lion, even a young one, kills a **s**, it pays
40:11 He will gently lead the mother **s** with their young.
49: 9 They will be my **s**, grazing in green pastures
53: 6 All of us have strayed away like **s**. We have left
53: 7 And as a **s** is silent before the shearers, he did not
Jer 5:17 your flocks of **s** and your herds of cattle.
12: 3 Drag these people away like helpless **s** to be
23: 1 the shepherds of my **s**—for they have destroyed
33:12 will once more see shepherds leading **s** and lambs.
49:19 of the Jordan, leaping on the **s** in the pasture.
50: 6 "My people have been lost **s**. Their shepherds
50:17 "The Israelites are like **s** that have been scattered
50:44 of the Jordan, leaping on the **s** in the pasture.
Eze 24: 5 Use only the best **s** from the flock and heap fuel on
25: 5 the land of the Ammonites into an enclosure for **s**.
34: 2 of your flocks. Shouldn't shepherds feed their **s**?
34: 5 So my **s** have been scattered without a shepherd.
34: 8 you didn't search for my **s** when they were lost.
34: 8 You took care of yourselves and left the **s** to starve.
34:10 their mouths; the **s** will no longer be their prey.
34:11 LORD says: I myself will search and find my **s**.
34:12 I will find my **s** and rescue them from all the places
34:15 I myself will tend my **s** and cause them to lie down
34:17 I will judge between one **s** and another, separating the **s** from the goats.
34:20 judge between the fat **s** and the scrawny **s**.
34:21 For you fat **s** push and butt and crowd my sick
34:22 And I will judge between one **s** and another.
34:31 You are my flock, the **s** of my pasture. You are my
45:15 and one **s** for every two hundred in your flocks in
Hos 12:12 to the land of Aram and earned a wife by tending **s**.
Joel 1:18 there is no pasture for them. The **s** bleat in misery.
Am 3:12 "A shepherd who tries to rescue a **s** from a lion's
Mic 2:12 I will bring you together again like **s** in a fold,
5: 8 And the other nations will be like helpless **s**,
Zep 2: 6 a place of shepherd camps and enclosures for **s**.
2:14 so proud will become a pasture for **s** and cattle.
Zec 9:16 rescue his people, just as a shepherd rescues his **s**.
10: 2 So my people are wandering like lost **s**, without a
11: 5 The buyers will slaughter their **s** without remorse.
11: 8 But I became impatient with these **s**—this nation—
11:11 Those who bought and sold **s** were watching me,
11:16 will not care for the **s** that are threatened by death,
11:16 this shepherd will eat the meat of the fattest **s**
13: 7 down the shepherd, and the **s** will be scattered,
Mt 7:15 false prophets who come disguised as harmless **s**,
9:36 go for help. They were like **s** without a shepherd.
10: 6 but only to the people of Israel—God's lost **s**.
10:16 "Look, I am sending you out as **s** among wolves.
12:11 And he answered, "If you had one **s**, and it fell
12:12 And how much more valuable is a person than a **s**!
15:24 people of Israel—God's lost **s**—not the Gentiles."
18:12 "If a shepherd has one hundred **s**, and one wanders
25:32 them as a shepherd separates the **s** from the goats.
25:33 He will place the **s** at his right hand and the goats
26:31 and the **s** of the flock will be scattered.'
Mk 6:34 because they were like **s** without a shepherd.
14:27 strike the Shepherd, / and the **s** will be scattered.'
Lk 2: 8 outside the village, guarding their flocks of **s**.
15: 4 "If you had one hundred **s**, and one of them
15: 6 to rejoice with you because your lost **s** was found.
17: 7 servant comes in from plowing or taking care of **s**,
Jn 2:14 merchants selling cattle, **s**, and doves for sacrifices;
2:15 He drove out the **s** and oxen, scattered the money
5: 2 Inside the city, near the **S** Gate, was the pool of
10: 3 for him, and the **s** hear his voice and come to him.
10: 3 He calls his own **s** by name and leads them out.
10: 7 "I assure you, I am the gate for the **s**," he said.
10: 8 and robbers. But the true **s** did not listen to them.
10:11 The good shepherd lays down his life for the **s**.
10:12 He will leave the **s** because they aren't his and he
10:13 is merely hired and has no real concern for the **s**.
10:14 I know my own **s**, and they know me,
10:15 know the Father. And I lay down my life for the **s**.
10:16 I have other **s**, too, that are not in this sheepfold.
10:27 My **s** recognize my voice; I know them, and they
21:16 I love you." "Then take care of my **s**," Jesus said.
21:17 know I love you." Jesus said, "Then feed my **s**.
Ac 8:32 "He was led as a **s** to the slaughter. / And as a
Ro 8:36 killed every day; we are being slaughtered like **s**.")
1Co 9: 7 What shepherd takes care of a flock of **s** and isn't
Heb 11:37 Some went about in skins of **s** and goats, hungry
13:20[-21] Jesus is the great Shepherd of the **s** by an
1Pe 2:25 Once you were wandering like lost **s**. But now you
Rev 18:13 fine flour, wheat, cattle, **s**, horses, chariots,

SHEEP'S (2) [SHEEP]

Lev 3: 8 then sprinkle the **s** blood against the sides of the
4:35 Those who are guilty must remove all the **s** fat,

SHEEP-SHEARERS (1) [SHEAR, SHEEP]

2Sa 13:24 went to the king and said, "My **s** are now at work.

SHEEP-SHEARING (2) [SHEAR, SHEEP]

Ge 38:13 that her father-in-law had left for the **s** at Timnah.
1Sa 25: 2 and a thousand goats, and it was **s** time.

SHEEPCOTE [KJV] See PASTURE

SHEEPDOGS (1) [DOG]

Job 30: 1 whose fathers are not worthy to run with my **s**.

SHEEPFOLD (2) [SHEEP]

Jn 10: 1 anyone who sneaks over the wall of a **s**,
10:16 I have other sheep, too, that are not in this **s**.

SHEEPFOLDS (7) [SHEEP]

Ge 49:14 is a strong beast of burden, / resting among the **s**.
Nu 32:16 "We simply want to build **s** for our flocks
32:24 build towns for your families and **s** for your flocks,
32:36 These were all fortified cities with **s** for their
Jdg 5:16 Why did you sit at home among the **s**— / to hear
1Sa 24: 3 At the place where the road passes some **s**,
Ps 68:13 Though they lived among the **s**, / now they are

SHEEPMASTER [KJV] See SHEEP (BREEDERS)

SHEERAH (1) [UZZEN-SHEERAH]

1Ch 7:24 Ephraim had a daughter named **S**. She built the

SHEET (20) [SHEETS]

Ex 26: 2 Each **s** must be forty-two feet long and six feet
26: 4 Put loops of blue yarn along the edge of the last **s**
26: 9 The sixth **s** of the second set is to be doubled over
26:10 Put fifty loops along the edge of the last **s** in each
26:12 An extra half **s** of this roof covering will be left to
36: 9 Each **s** was exactly the same size—forty-two feet
36:11 were placed along the edge of the last **s** in each set.
36:15 Each **s** was exactly the same size—forty-five feet
36:17 fifty loops along the edge of the last **s** in each set.
Nu 16:38 incense burners into a **s** as a covering for the altar,

16:39 and they were hammered out into a s of metal to
Isa 14:11 Now maggots are your s and worms your blanket.'
Mk 15:46 Joseph bought a long s of linen cloth, and taking
Ac 5:6 Then some young men wrapped him in a s
10:11 and something like a large s was let down by its
10:12 In the s were all sorts of animals, reptiles,
10:16 Then the s was pulled up again to heaven.
11:5 Something like a large s was let down by its four
11:6 When I looked inside the s, I saw all sorts of small
11:10 "This happened three times before the s and all it

SHEETS (19) [SHEET]

Ex 26:1 "Make the Tabernacle from ten s of fine linen.
26:1 These s are to be decorated with blue, purple,
26:2 feet wide. All ten s must be exactly the same size.
26:3 Join five of these s together into one set; then join the other five s into a second set.
26:6 to fasten the loops of the two sets of s together,
26:7 "Make heavy s of cloth from goat hair to cover the
26:7 the Tabernacle. There must be eleven of these s,
26:8 All eleven of these s must be exactly the same size.
36:8 The skilled weavers first made ten s from fine
36:10 Five of these s were joined together to make one
36:12 The fifty loops along the edge of the first set of s
36:14 a roof covering was made from eleven s of cloth
36:16 The craftsmen joined five of these s together to
36:16 and the six remaining s were joined to make a
36:18 so the two sets of s were firmly attached to each
39:3 made gold thread by beating gold into thin s
Pr 7:16 My bed is spread with colored s of finest linen
Jer 10:9 They bring beaten s of silver from Tarshish

SHEHARIAH (1)

1Ch 8:26 Shamsherai, S, Athaliah,

SHEKEL (6) [SHEKELS]

Lev 5:15 in silver as measured by the standard sanctuary s.
27:25 be measured in terms of the standard sanctuary s.
Nu 3:47 weighing the same as the standard sanctuary s.
18:16 weighing the same as the standard sanctuary s.
Eze 45:12 The standard unit for weight will be the silver s.
45:12 One s consists of twenty gerahs, and sixty shekels

SHEKELS (1) [SHEKEL]

Eze 45:12 of twenty gerahs, and sixty s are equal to one mina.

SHELAH (22) [SHELAH'S, SHELANITE]

Ge 10:24 Arphaxad was the father of S, and S was the father
11:12 Arphaxad was 35 years old, his son S was born.
11:13 After the birth of S, Arphaxad lived another 403
11:14 When S was 30 years old, his son Eber was born.
11:15 S lived another 403 years and had other sons
38:5 And when she had a third son, she named him S.
38:11 his youngest son, S, was old enough to marry her.
38:11 to do this because he was afraid S would also die,
38:14 Tamar was aware that S had grown up, but they
38:26 keep my promise to let her marry my son S."
46:12 sons of Judah were Er, Onan, S, Perez, and Zerah.
Nu 26:20 The Shelanite clan, named after its ancestor S.
1Ch 1:18 Arphaxad was the father of S. S was the father of
1:24 family line descended from Shem: Arphaxad, S,
2:3 Their names were Er, Onan, and S. But the oldest
4:21 S was one of Judah's sons. The descendants of S were Er (the father of
Ne 11:5 son of Joiarib, son of Zechariah, of the family of S.
Lk 3:35 Peleg was the son of Eber. / Eber was the son of S.
3:36 S was the son of Cainan. / Cainan was the son of

SHELAH'S (1) [SHELAH]

Ge 38:5 At the time of S birth, they were living at Kezib.

SHELANITE (1) [SHELAH]

Nu 26:20 The S clan, named after its ancestor Shelah.

SHELEMIAH (9)

Ezr 10:39 S, Nathan, Adaiah,
10:41 Azarel, S, Shemariah,
Ne 3:30 Next Hananiah son of S and Hanun, the sixth son
13:13 I put S the priest, Zadok the scribe, and Pedaiah,
Jer 36:14 grandson of S, and great-grandson of Cushi,
36:26 and S son of Abdeel to arrest Baruch and Jeremiah.
37:3 King Zedekiah sent Jehucal son of S
37:13 The sentry making the arrest was Irijah son of S
38:1 Gedaliah son of Pashhur, Jehucal son of S,

SHELEPH (2)

Ge 10:26 the ancestor of Almodad, S, Hazarmaveth, Jerah,
1Ch 1:20 the ancestor of Almodad, S, Hazarmaveth, Jerah,

SHELESH (1)

1Ch 7:35 brother Helem were Zophah, Imna, S, and Amal.

SHELOMI (1)

Nu 34:27 Asher | Ahihud son of S

SHELOMITH (7)

Lev 24:11 to Moses for judgment. His mother's name was S.
1Ch 3:19 and Hananiah. He also had a daughter named S.
23:18 The descendants of Izhar included S, the family
24:22 From the descendants of Izhar, the leader was S.
24:22 From the descendants of S, the leader was Jahath.
2Ch 11:20 Maacah gave birth to Abijah, Attai, Ziza, and S.
Ezr 8:10 of Bani: S son of Josiphiah and 160 other men.

SHELOMOTH (4)

1Ch 23:9 Three of the descendants of Shimei were S, Haziel,
26:25 were Rehabiah, Jeshaiah, Joram, Zicri, and S.
26:26 S and his relatives were in charge of the treasuries
26:28 S and his relatives also cared for the items

SHELTER (30) [SHELTERS]

Dt 32:38 and help you! / Let them provide you with s!
Jdg 9:15 make me your king, come and take s in my shade.
Ru 2:7 except for a few minutes' rest over there in the s."
1Ch 15:1 Ark of God and set up a special tent there to s it.
Job 27:18 as a spiderweb, as flimsy as a s made of branches.
30:7 they huddle together for s beneath the nettles.
Ps 9:9 The LORD is a s for the oppressed, / a refuge in
31:20 You hide them in the s of your presence,
31:20 You s them in your presence, / far from accusing
36:7 your unfailing love, O God! / All humanity finds s
37:40 He saves them, / and they find s in him.
61:4 your sanctuary, / safe beneath the s of your wings!
64:10 and find s in him. / And those who do what is right
73:28 I have made the Sovereign LORD my s,
91:1 Those who live in the s of the Most High
91:4 with his wings. / He will s you with his feathers.
91:9 your refuge, / if you make the Most High your s,
Isa 1:8 Jerusalem stands abandoned like a watchman's s in
4:6 It will be a s from daytime heat and a hiding place
25:4 in distress, you are a s from the rain and the heat.
32:2 He will s Israel from the storm and the wind.
Jer 4:20 tent is destroyed; in a moment, every s is crushed.
La 2:6 his Temple as though it were merely a garden s.
Eze 17:23 sort will nest in it, finding s beneath its branches.
Jnh 4:5 and made a s to sit under as he waited to see if
Mt 13:32 where birds can come and find s in its branches."
Mk 4:32 long branches where birds can come and find s."
Lk 13:19 the birds come and find s among its branches."
21:21 and those outside the city should not enter it for s.
Rev 7:15 sits on the throne will live among them and s them.

SHELTERS (27) [SHELTER]

Ge 33:17 a house and made s for his flocks and herds.
Lev 23:34 "Tell the Israelites to begin the Festival of S on
23:39 "Now, on the first day of the Festival of S,
23:42 all of you who are Israelites by birth must live in s.
23:43 in s when I rescued them from the land of Egypt.
Nu 29:12 It is the beginning of the Festival of S, a seven-day
Dt 16:13 "Another celebration, the Festival of S, must be
16:16 the Festival of Harvest, and the Festival of S.
31:10 the Year of Release, during the Festival of S,
1Ki 8:2 king at the annual Festival of S in early autumn.
8:65 and all Israel celebrated the Festival of S in the
8:65 of the altar and seven days for the Festival of S.
12:32 similar to the annual Festival of S in Judah.
2Ch 5:3 king at the annual Festival of S in early autumn.
7:8 S with huge crowds gathered from all the tribes of
7:9 for seven days and the Festival of S for seven days.
8:13 the Festival of Harvest, and the Festival of S.
Ezr 3:4 They celebrated the Festival of S as prescribed in
3:6 Fifteen days before the Festival of S began,
Ne 8:14 live in s during the festival to be held that month.
8:15 They were to use these branches to make s in
8:16 and used them to build s on the roofs of their
8:17 lived in these s for the seven days of the festival,
Eze 45:25 "During the seven days of the Festival of S,
Hos 12:9 do each year when you celebrate the Festival of S.
Zec 14:16 and to celebrate the Festival of S.
Jn 7:2 But soon it was time for the Festival of S,

SHELUMIEL (5)

Nu 1:6 Simeon | S son of Zurishaddai
2:12[-13] Simeon | S son of Zurishaddai | 59,300
7:36 On the fifth day S son of Zurishaddai, leader of the
7:41 This was the offering brought by S son of
10:19 The tribe of Simeon was led by S son of

SHEM (20) [SHEM'S]

Ge 5:32 years old, he had three sons: S, Ham, and Japheth.
6:10 Noah had three sons: S, Ham, and Japheth.
7:13 with his wife and his sons—S, Ham, and Japheth—
9:18 S, Ham, and Japheth, the three sons of Noah,
9:23 S and Japheth took a robe, held it over their
9:25 of servants / to the descendants of S and Japheth."
9:26 "May S be blessed by the LORD my God;
9:27 of Japheth, / and may he share the prosperity of S;
10:1 This is the history of the families of S, Ham,
10:21 Sons were also born to S, the older brother of
10:21 S was the ancestor of all the descendants of Eber.
10:22 The descendants of S were Elam, Asshur,
10:31 These were the descendants of S,
11:10 When S was 100 years old, his son Arphaxad was
11:11 S lived another 500 years and had other sons
1Ch 1:4 The sons of Noah were S, Ham, and Japheth.
1:17 The descendants of S were Elam, Asshur,
1:24 So this is the family line descended from S:
Lk 3:36 was the son of S. / S was the son of Noah.

SHEM'S (1) [SHEM]

Ge 11:10 This is the history of S family. When Shem was

SHEMA (6)

Jos 15:26 Amam, S, Moladah,
1Ch 2:43 of Hebron were Korah, Tappuah, Rekem, and S.
2:44 S was the father of Raham. Raham was the father
5:8 and Bela son of Azaz, son of S, son of Joel.
8:13 Beriah, and S. They were the leaders of the clans
Ne 8:4 S, Anaiah, Uriah, Hilkiah, and Maaseiah.

SHEMAAH (1)

1Ch 12:3 Their leader was Ahiezer son of S from Gibeah;

SHEMAIAH (38) [SHEMAIAH'S]

1Ki 12:22 But God said to S, the man of God,
1Ch 3:22 Shecaniah's descendants were S and his sons,
4:37 of Allon, son of Jedaiah, son of Shimri, son of S.
5:4 The descendants of Joel were S, Gog, Shimei,
9:14 The Levites who returned were S son of Hasshub,
9:16 Obadiah son of S, son of Galal, son of Jeduthun;
15:8 descendants of Elizaphan, with S as their leader.
15:11 Uriel, Asaiah, Joel, S, Eliel, and Amminadab.
24:6 S son of Nethanel, a Levite, acted as secretary
26:4 also gatekeepers, were S (the oldest),
26:6 Obed-edom's son S had sons with great ability
2Ch 11:2 But the LORD said to S, the man of God,
12:5 The prophet S then met with Rehoboam
12:5 S told them, "This is what the LORD says:
12:7 their change of heart, he gave this message to S:
12:15 are recorded in *The Record of S the Prophet*
17:8 including S, Nethaniah, Zebadiah, Asahel,
29:14 From the family of Jeduthun: S and Uzziel.
31:15 Miniamin, Jeshua, S, Amariah, and Shecaniah.
35:9 Conaniah and his brothers S and Nethanel,
Ezr 8:13 came later: Eliphelet, Jeuel, S, and 60 other men.
8:16 Ariel, S, Elnathan, Jarib, Elnathan, Nathan,
10:21 of Harim: Maaseiah, Elijah, S, Jehiel, and Uzziah.
10:31 of Harim: Eliezer, Ishijah, Malkijah, S, Shimeon,
Ne 3:29 and beyond him was S son of Shecaniah,
6:10 Later I went to visit S son of Delaiah and grandson
10:8 Maaziah, Bilgai, and S. These were the priests.
11:15 S son of Hasshub, son of Azrikam, son of
12:6 S, Joiarib, Jedaiah,
12:18 Jehonathan was leader of the family of S.
12:34 Judah, Benjamin, S, Jeremiah,
12:35 son of S, son of Mattaniah, son of Micaiah, son of
12:36 And finally came Zechariah's colleagues S,
12:42 Maaseiah, S, Eleazar, Uzzi, Jehohanan, Malkijah,
Jer 26:20 Uriah son of S from Kiriath-jearim was also
29:24 The LORD sent this message to S the Nehelamite
29:31 'This is what the LORD says concerning S the
36:12 along with Delaiah son of S, Elnathan son of

SHEMAIAH'S (1) [SHEMAIAH]

Jer 29:29 But when Zephaniah the priest received S letter,

SHEMARIAH (4)

1Ch 12:5 Eluzai, Jerimoth, Bealiah, S, and Shephatiah from
2Ch 11:19 Mahalath had three sons—Jeush, S, and Zaham.
Ezr 10:32 Benjamin, Malluch, and S.
10:41 Azarel, Shelemiah, S,

SHEMEBER (1)

Ge 14:2 King Shinab of Admah, King S of Zeboiim,

SHEMED (1)

1Ch 8:12 S (who built Ono and Lod and their villages),

SHEMER (3)

1Ki 16:24 from its owner, S, for 150 pounds of silver.
16:24 city on it and called the city Samaria in honor of S.
1Ch 6:46 Amzi, Bani, S,

SHEMIDA (3) [SHEMIDAITES]

Nu 26:32 The Shemidaites, named after their ancestor S.
Jos 17:2 Abiezer, Helek, Asriel, Shechem, Hepher, and S.
1Ch 7:19 The sons of S were Ahian, Shechem, Likhi,

SHEMIDAITES (1) [SHEMIDA]

Nu 26:32 The S, named after their ancestor Shemida.

SHEMIRAMOTH (4)

1Ch 15:18 Jaaziel, S, Jehiel, Unni, Eliab, Benaiah, Maaseiah,
15:20 Zechariah, Aziel, S, Jehiel, Unni, Eliab, Maaseiah,
16:5 then Jeiel, S, Jehiel, Mattithiah, Eliab, Benaiah,
2Ch 17:8 Nethaniah, Zebadiah, Asahel, S, Jehonathan,

SHEMUEL (2)

Nu 34:20 Simeon | S son of Ammihud
1Ch 7:2 were Uzzi, Rephaiah, Jeriel, Jahmai, Ibsam, and S.

SHENAZZAR (1)

1Ch 3:18 Malkiram, Pedaiah, S, Jekamiah, Hoshama,

SHENIR [KJV] See SENIR

SHEPHAM (2)

Nu 34:10 will start at Hazar-enan and run south to S,
1Ch 27:27 Zabdi from S was responsible for the grapes

SHEPHATIAH (13)

2Sa 3:4 The fifth was S, whose mother was Abital.
1Ch 3:3 The fifth was S, whose mother was Abital.
9:8 Meshullam son of S, son of Reuel, son of Ibnijah.

12: 5 Jerimoth, Bealiah, Shemariah, and S from Haruph;
27: 16 Eliezer son of Zicri / Simeon | S son of Maacah
2Ch 21: 2 Jehiel, Zechariah, Azariahu, Michael, and S.
Ezr 2: 4 The family of S | 372
2: 57 S, Hattil, Pokereth-hazzebaim, and Ami.
8: 8 From the family of S: Zebadiah son of Michael
Ne 7: 9 The family of S | 372
7: 59 S, Hattil, Pokereth-hazzebaim, and Ami.
11: 4 son of Zechariah, son of Amariah, son of S, son of
Jer 38: 1 Now S son of Mattan, Gedaliah son of Pashhur,

SHEPHER (2)

Nu 33: 23 They left Kehelathah and camped at Mount S.
33: 24 They left Mount S and camped at Haradah.

SHEPHERD (64) [SHEPHERD'S, SHEPHERDS, SHEPHERDS']

Ge 4: 2 When they grew up, Abel became a s, while Cain
29: 9 arrived with her father's sheep, for she was a s.
48: 15 walked, the God who has been my s all my life,
49: 24 Mighty One of Jacob, / the S, the Rock of Israel.
Nu 27: 17 of the LORD will not be like sheep without a s."
1Sa 16: 19 to Jesse to say, "Send me your son David, the s."
17: 20 So David left the sheep with another s and set out
2Sa 5: 2 told you, 'You will be the s of my people Israel.
7: 8 lead my people Israel when you were just a s boy,
1Ki 22: 17 scattered on the mountains, like sheep without a s.
1Ch 11: 2 told you, 'You will be the s of my people Israel.
17: 7 lead my people Israel when you were just a s boy,
2Ch 18: 16 scattered on the mountains, like sheep without a s.
Ps 23: 1 The LORD is my s; / I have everything I need.
28: 9 your special possession! / Lead them like a s,
49: 14 are led to the grave, / where death will be their s.
78: 71 and made him the s of Jacob's descendants—
80: 1 Please listen, O S of Israel, / you who lead Israel
Ecc 12: 11 sayings of the wise are like guidance from a s.
Isa 13: 14 like hunted deer, wandering like sheep without a s.
40: 11 He will feed his flock like a s. He will carry the
44: 28 When I say of Cyrus, 'He is my s,' he will
63: 11 Israel through the sea, with Moses as their s?
Jer 17: 16 I have not abandoned my job as a s for your
31: 10 and watch over them as a s does his flock.
43: 12 He will pick clean the land of Egypt as a s picks
Eze 34: 5 So my sheep have been scattered without a s.
34: 12 I will be like a s looking for his scattered flock.
34: 23 And I will set one s over them, even my servant
34: 23 He will feed them and be a s to them.
37: 24 will be their king, and they will have only one s.
Am 1: 1 to Amos, a s from the town of Tekoa in Judah.
3: 12 "A s who tries to rescue a sheep from a lion's
7: 14 to be one. I'm just a s, and I take care of fig trees.
Na 3: 18 There is no longer a s to gather them together.
Zep 2: 6 a place of s camps and enclosures for sheep.
Zec 9: 16 will rescue his people, just as a s rescues his sheep.
10: 2 lost sheep, without a s to protect and guide them.
11: 9 So I told them, "I won't be your s any longer.
11: 15 "Go again and play the part of a worthless s.
11: 16 This will illustrate how I will give this nation a s
11: 16 this s will eat the meat of the fattest sheep and tear
11: 17 Doom is certain for this worthless s who abandons
13: 7 "Awake, O sword, against my s, the man who is
13: 7 Strike down the s, and the sheep will be scattered,
Mt 2: 6 who will be the s for my people Israel.' "
9: 36 to go for help. They were like sheep without a s.
18: 12 "If a s has one hundred sheep, and one wanders
25: 32 and he will separate them as a s separates the sheep
26: 31 "For the Scriptures say, / 'God will strike the S,
Mk 6: 34 on them because they were like sheep without a s.
14: 27 "For the Scriptures say, / 'God will strike the S,
Jn 10: 2 For a s enters through the gate.
10: 11 "I am the good s. The good s lays down his life for the sheep.
10: 12 because they aren't his and he isn't their s.
10: 14 "I am the good s; I know my own sheep, and they
10: 16 to my voice; and there will be one flock with one s.
Ac 20: 28 Be sure that you feed and s God's flock—
1Co 9: 7 What s takes care of a flock of sheep and isn't
Heb 13: 20[-21] Jesus is the great S of the sheep by an
1Pe 2: 25 But now you have turned to your S, the Guardian
5: 4 And when the head S comes, your reward will be a
Rev 7: 17 who stands in front of the throne will be their S.

SHEPHERD'S (14) [SHEPHERD]

Ex 4: 2 there in your hand?" "A s staff," Moses replied.
4: 4 and grabbed it, and it became a s staff again.
4: 17 And be sure to take your s staff along so you can
7: 9 say to Aaron, 'Throw down your s staff,' and it
7: 15 Be sure to take along the s staff that turned into a
8: 5 "Tell Aaron to point his s staff toward all the
14: 16 Use your s staff—hold it out over the water,
17: 5 The LORD said to Moses, "Take your s staff,
1Sa 17: 40 stones from a stream and put them in his s bag.
17: 40 Then, armed only with his s staff and sling,
17: 49 Reaching into his s bag and taking out a stone,
Isa 31: 4 it pays no attention to the s shouts and noise.
38: 12 like a s tent in a storm. / It has been cut short,
Zec 11: 7 Then I took two s staffs and named one Favor

SHEPHERDS (48) [SHEPHERD]

Ge 26: 19 His s also dug in the Gerar Valley and found a
26: 20 But then the local s came and claimed the spring.
29: 4 Jacob went over to the s and asked them,
29: 8 the watering until all the flocks and s are here,"
46: 32 tell him, 'These men are s and livestock breeders.
46: 34 for s are despised in the land of Egypt."
47: 3 And they replied, "We are s like our ancestors.
Ex 2: 17 But other s would often come and chase the girls
2: 17 came to their aid, rescuing the girls from the s.
2: 19 "An Egyptian rescued us from the s," they told
Nu 14: 33 And your children will be like s, wandering in the
Jdg 5: 16 to hear the s whistle for their flocks?
1Sa 25: 7 While your s stayed among us near Carmel,
2Sa 7: 7 to Israel's leaders, the s of my people Israel.
2Ki 10: 12 Along the way, while he was at Beth-eked of the S,
1Ch 17: 6 complained to Israel's leaders, the s of my people.
Job 1: 16 and burned up your sheep and all the s.
Ps 77: 20 a flock of sheep, / with Moses and Aaron as their s.
Isa 13: 20 and s will not allow their sheep to stay overnight.
56: 10 the LORD's watchmen, his s—are blind to every
56: 11 They are stupid s, all following their own path,
Jer 6: 3 Enemy s will surround you. They will set up camp
10: 21 The s of my people have lost their senses. They no
23: 1 the s of my sheep—for they have destroyed
23: 2 the LORD, the God of Israel, says to these s:
23: 4 Then I will appoint responsible s to care for them,
25: 34 Weep and moan, you evil s! Roll in the dust,
25: 36 Listen to the frantic cries of the s, to the leaders of
31: 24 and farmers and s alike will live together in peace
33: 12 will once more see s leading sheep and lambs.
50: 6 Their s have led them astray and turned them loose
51: 23 With you I will shatter s and flocks, farmers
Eze 34: 2 "Son of man, prophesy against the s, the leaders of
34: 2 Destruction is certain for you s who feed
34: 2 of your flocks. Shouldn't s feed their sheep?
34: 7 "Therefore, you s, hear the word of the LORD:
34: 8 Though you were my s, you didn't search for my
34: 9 Therefore, you s, hear the word of the LORD.
34: 10 I now consider these s my enemies, and I will hold
Am 1: 2 Suddenly, the lush pastures of the s dry up.
Zec 10: 3 "My anger burns against your s, and I will punish
11: 3 Listen to the wailing of the s, for their wealth is
11: 5 Even the s have no compassion for them.
11: 8 I got rid of their three evil s in a single month.
Lk 2: 8 That night some s were in the fields outside the
2: 15 the s said to each other, "Come on, let's go to
2: 17 Then the s told everyone what had happened
2: 20 The s went back to their fields and flocks,

SHEPHERDS' (2) [SHEPHERD]

SS 1: 8 follow the trail of my flock to the s tents,
Lk 2: 18 All who heard the s story were astonished,

SHEPHO (2)

Ge 36: 23 Shobal were Alvan, Manahath, Ebal, S, and Onam.
1Ch 1: 40 Shobal were Alvan, Manahath, Ebal, S, and Onam.

SHEPHUPHAN (1)

1Ch 8: 5 Gera, S, and Huram.

SHERAH [KJV] See SHEERAH

SHEREBIAH (8)

Ezr 8: 18 they sent us a man named S, along with eighteen of
8: 24 the priests—S, Hashabiah, and ten other priests—
Ne 8: 7 Jeshua, Bani, S, Jamin, Akkub, Shabbethai,
9: 4 Bani, Kadmiel, Shebaniah, Bunni, S, Bani,
9: 5 Bani, Hashabneiah, S, Hodiah, Shebaniah,
10: 12 Zaccur, S, Shebaniah,
12: 8 Binnui, Kadmiel, S, Judah, and Mattaniah,
12: 24 Hashabiah, S, Jeshua, Binnui, Kadmiel, and other

SHERESH (1)

1Ch 7: 16 His brother's name was S. The sons of Peresh were

SHEREZER [KJV] See SHAREZER

SHERRIFS [KJV] See MAGISTRATES

SHESHAI (3)

Nu 13: 22 arrived at Hebron, where Ahiman, S, and Talmai—
Jos 15: 14 S, Ahiman, and Talmai—descendants of Anak.
Jdg 1: 10 defeating the forces of S, Ahiman, and Talmai.

SHESHAN (4)

1Ch 2: 31 son of Ishi was S. S had a descendant named Ahlai.
2: 34 S had no sons, though he did have daughters.
2: 35 S gave one of his daughters to be the wife of Jarha,

SHESHBAZZAR (4)

Ezr 1: 8 to count these items and present them to S,
1: 11 and silver items were turned over to S to take back
5: 14 delivered into the safekeeping of a man named S,
5: 16 So this S came and laid the foundations of the

SHETH (1)

Nu 24: 17 cracking the skulls of the people of S.

SHETHAR (1)

Est 1: 14 S, Admatha, Tarshish, Meres, Marsena,

SHETHAR-BOZENAI (4)

Ezr 5: 3 and S and their colleagues soon arrived in
5: 6 This is the letter that Tattenai the governor, S,
6: 6 to S, and to your colleagues and other officials
6: 13 and S and their colleagues complied at once with

SHEVA (2)

2Sa 20: 25 S was the court secretary. Zadok and Abiathar
1Ch 2: 49 and S (the father of Macbenah and Gibea).

SHEWBREAD [KJV] See BREAD (OF THE PRESENCE)

SHIBBOLETH (1) [SIBBOLETH]

Jdg 12: 6 they would tell him to say "S." If he was from

SHIBMAH [KJV] See SIBMAH

SHICRON [KJV] See SHIKKERON

SHIED (1)

Nu 22: 33 Three times the donkey saw me and s away;

SHIELD (32) [SHIELDED, SHIELDING, SHIELDS]

Ex 40: 21 and set up the inner curtain to s it from view,
Dt 33: 29 He is your protecting s / and your triumphant
Jdg 5: 8 the city gates. / Yet not a s or spear could be seen
1Sa 17: 7 bearer walked ahead of him carrying a huge s.
17: 41 Goliath walked out toward David with his s bearer
2Sa 1: 21 For there the s of the mighty was defiled;
1: 21 the s of Saul will no longer be anointed with oil.
22: 3 He is my s, the strength of my salvation, and my
22: 31 He is a s for all who look to him for protection.
22: 36 You have given me the s of your salvation;
1Ch 12: 8 They were expert with both s and spear, as fierce
2Ch 25: 5 and older, all trained in the use of spear and s.
Job 41: 15 The overlapping scales on its back make a s.
Ps 3: 3 But you, O LORD, are a s around me, / my glory,
5: 12 O LORD, / surrounding them with your s of love.
7: 10 God is my s, / saving those whose hearts are true
18: 2 He is my s, the strength of my salvation, and my
18: 30 He is a s for all who look to him for protection.
18: 35 You have given me the s of your salvation.
28: 7 LORD is my strength, my s from every danger.
33: 20 Only he can help us, protecting us like a s.
35: 2 Put on your armor, and take up your s.
59: 11 and bring them to their knees, / O Lord our s.
91: 4 He will s you with his wings. / He will shelter you
115: 9 trust the LORD! / He is your helper; he is your s.
115: 10 trust the LORD! / He is your helper; he is your s.
115: 11 trust the LORD! / He is your helper; he is your s.
119: 114 You are my refuge and my s; / your word is my
144: 2 He stands before me as a s, and I take refuge in
Pr 2: 7 He is their s, protecting those who walk with
Jer 46: 9 and Lydia who are skilled with the s and bow!
Eph 6: 16 In every battle you will need faith as your s to stop

SHIELDS (40) [SHIELD]

2Sa 8: 7 David brought the gold s of Hadadezer's officers
1Ki 10: 16 King Solomon made two hundred large s of
10: 17 He also made three hundred smaller s of
10: 17 The king placed these s in the Palace of the Forest
14: 26 including all the gold s Solomon had made.
14: 27 Afterward Rehoboam made bronze s as substitutes,
2Ki 11: 10 and s that had once belonged to King David
19: 32 They will not march outside its gates with their s
1Ch 5: 18 They were all skilled in combat and armed with s,
12: 24 there were 6,800 warriors armed with s and spears.
12: 34 and 37,000 warriors armed with s and spears.
18: 7 David brought the gold s of Hadadezer's officers
2Ch 9: 15 King Solomon made two hundred large s of
9: 16 He also made three hundred smaller s of
9: 16 The king placed these s in the Palace of the Forest
11: 12 He also put s and spears in these towns as a further
12: 9 the royal palace, including all of Solomon's gold s.
12: 10 King Rehoboam later replaced them with bronze s
14: 8 the tribe of Judah, armed with large s and spears.
14: 8 tribe of Benjamin, armed with small s and bows.
17: 17 were 200,000 troops equipped with bows and s.
23: 9 and s that had once belonged to King David
26: 14 Uzziah provided the entire army with s, spears,
32: 5 and manufactured large numbers of weapons and s.
32: 27 and spices, and for his s and other valuable items.
Ne 4: 16 stood guard with spears, s, bows, and coats of mail.
Job 15: 26 Holding their strong s, they defiantly charge
Ps 46: 9 snaps the spear in two; / he burns the s with fire.
76: 3 the s and swords and weapons of his foes.
SS 4: 4 of David, jeweled with the s of a thousand heroes.
Isa 21: 5 Quick! Grab your s and prepare for battle!
22: 6 drive the chariots. The men of Kir hold up the s.
37: 33 They will not march outside its gates with their s
Jer 51: 11 Sharpen the arrows! Lift up the s! For the LORD
Eze 26: 8 a ramp, and raising a roof of s against you.
27: 10 They hung their s and helmets on your walls,
27: 11 Their s hung on your walls, perfecting your
32: 27 their s covering their bodies, and their swords
39: 9 will go out and pick up your small and large s,
Na 2: 3 S flash red in the sunlight! The attack begins!

SHIFT (1) [SHIFTING, SHIFTS]

2Ch 23: 8 did not let anyone go home after their s ended.

SHIFTING (1) [SHIFT]

Jas 1: 17 Unlike them, he never changes or casts s shadows.

SHIFTS (1) [SHIFT]

1Ki 5: 14 He sent them to Lebanon in s, ten thousand every

SHIHOR (1) [SHIHOR-LIBNATH]
Jos 13: 3 This land extends from the stream of S, which is

SHIHOR-LIBNATH (1) [SHIHOR]
Jos 19:26 The boundary on the west went from Carmel to S,

SHIKKERON (1)
Jos 15:11 where it turned toward S and Mount Baalah.

SHILHI (2)
1Ki 22:42 His mother was Azubah, the daughter of S.
2Ch 20:31 His mother was Azubah, the daughter of S.

SHILHIM (1)
Jos 15:32 Lebaoth, S, Ain, and Rimmon. In all, there were

SHILLEM (3) [SHILLEMITE]
Ge 46:24 sons of Naphtali were Jahzeel, Guni, Jezer, and S.
Nu 26:49 The Shillemite clan, named after its ancestor S.
1Ch 7:13 sons of Naphtali were Jahzeel, Guni, Jezer, and S.

SHILLEMITE (1) [SHILLEM]
Nu 26:49 The S clan, named after its ancestor Shillem.

SHILOH (35) [TAANATH-SHILOH]
Jos 18: 1 the entire Israelite assembly gathered at S and set
18: 8 lots in the presence of the LORD here at S."
18: 9 Then they returned to Joshua in the camp at S.
18:10 There at S, Joshua cast sacred lots in the presence
19:51 the LORD at the entrance of the Tabernacle at S.
21: 2 They spoke to them at S in the land of Canaan,
22: 9 left the rest of Israel at S in the land of Canaan.
22:12 the whole assembly gathered at S and prepared to
Jdg 18:31 as long as the Tabernacle of God remained at S.
21:12 and they brought them to the camp at S in the land
21:19 of the annual festival of the LORD held in S,
21:21 When the women of S come out for their dances,
1Sa 1: 3 and his family would travel to S to worship
1: 9 Once when they were at S, Hannah went over to
1:24 Hannah took him to the Tabernacle in S.
2:14 All the Israelites who came to worship at S were
3:21 The LORD continued to appear at S and gave
4: 3 the Ark of the Covenant of the LORD from S.
4: 4 So they sent men to S to bring back the Ark of the
4:12 the battlefront and arrived at S later that same day.
14: 3 the priest of the LORD who had served at S.)
1Ki 2:27 had made at S concerning the descendants of Eli.
11:29 the prophet Ahijah from S met him on the road,
12:15 son of Nebat through the prophet Ahijah from S.
14: 2 Then go to the prophet Ahijah at S—the man who
14: 4 So Jeroboam's wife went to Ahijah's home at S.
15:29 Jeroboam by the prophet Ahijah from S.
2Ch 9:29 and in *The Prophecy of Ahijah from S,*
10:15 son of Nebat by the prophet Ahijah from S.
Ps 78:60 Then he abandoned his dwelling at S,
Jer 7:12 " 'Go to the place at S where I once put the
7:14 So just as I destroyed S, I will now destroy this
26: 6 then I will destroy this Temple as I destroyed S,
26: 9 name that this Temple will be destroyed like S?
41: 5 eighty men arrived from Shechem, S, and Samaria.

SHILONITE (1)
1Ch 9: 5 Others returned from the S clan, including Asaiah

SHILSHAH (1)
1Ch 7:37 Bezer, Hod, Shamma, S, Ithran, and Beera.

SHIMEA (10)
2Sa 5:14 born in Jerusalem: S, Shobab, Nathan, Solomon,
13: 3 He was the son of David's brother S.
13:32 the son of David's brother S, arrived and said,
21:21 killed by Jonathan, the son of David's brother S.
1Ch 2:13 his second was Abinadab, his third was S,
3: 5 The sons born to David in Jerusalem included S,
6:30 S, Haggiah, and Asaiah.
6:39 genealogy was traced back through Berekiah, S,
14: 4 born in Jerusalem: S, Shobab, Nathan, Solomon,
20: 7 killed by Jonathan, the son of David's brother S.

SHIMEAM (2)
1Ch 8:32 and Mikloth, who was the father of S. All these
9:38 Mikloth was the father of S. All these families

SHIMEATH (2) [SHIMEATHITES]
2Ki 12:21 The assassins were Jozacar son of S and Jehozabad
2Ch 24:26 the son of an Ammonite woman named S,

SHIMEATHITES (1) [SHIMEATH]
1Ch 2:55 living at Jabez—the Tirathites, S, and Sucathites.

SHIMEI (41) [SHIMEI'S]
Ex 6:17 The descendants of Gershon included Libni and S,
Nu 3:18 named for two of his descendants, Libni and S.
3:21 of the clans descended from Libni and S.
2Sa 16: 5 It was S son of Gera, a member of Saul's family.
16:13 and S kept pace with them on a nearby hillside,
19:16 Then S son of Gera the Benjaminite, the man from
19:18 about to cross the river, S fell down before him.
19:21 Then Abishai son of Zeruiah said, "S should die,
19:23 Then, turning to S, David vowed, "Your life will
1Ki 1: 8 son of Jehoiada, Nathan the prophet, S, Rei,
2: 8 "And remember S son of Gera, the Benjaminite
2:36 The king then sent for S and told him, "Build a
2:38 S replied, "Your sentence is fair; I will do
2:38 So S lived in Jerusalem for a long time.
2:39 Achish of Gath. When S learned where they were,
2:41 Solomon heard that S had left Jerusalem and had
2:42 So he sent for S and demanded, "Didn't I make
2:44 The king also said to S, "You surely remember all
2:46 Benaiah son of Jehoiada took S outside and killed
4:18 S son of Ela, in Benjamin.
1Ch 3:19 The sons of Pedaiah were Zerubbabel and S.
4:26 of Mishma were Hammuel, Zaccur, and S.
4:27 S had sixteen sons and six daughters, but none of
5: 4 The descendants of Joel were Shemaiah, Gog, S,
6:17 The descendants of Gershon included Libni and S.
6:29 of Merari were Mahli, Libni, S, Uzzah,
6:42 Ethan, Zimmah, S,
8:21 Adaiah, Beraiah, and Shimrath were the sons of S.
23: 7 defined by their lines of descent from Libni and S,
23: 9 Three of other descendants of S were Shelomoth,
23:10 Four other descendants of S were Jahath, Ziza,
25: 3 Gedaliah, Zeri, Jeshaiah, S, Hashabiah,
25:17 The tenth lot fell to S and twelve of his sons
27:27 S from Ramah was in charge of the king's
2Ch 29:14 From the family of Heman: Jehiel and S.
31:12 Levite was put in charge, assisted by his brother S.
Ezr 10:23 Jozabad, S, Kelaiah (also called Kelita), Pethahiah,
10:33 Zabad, Eliphelet, Jeremai, Manasseh, and S.
10:38 From the family of Binnui: S,
Est 2: 5 of Benjamin and was a descendant of Kish and S.
Zec 12:13 the family of Levi, and the family of S.

SHIMEI'S (1) [SHIMEI]
1Ki 2:39 two of S slaves escaped to King Achish of Gath.

SHIMEON (1)
Ezr 10:31 of Harim: Eliezer, Ishijah, Malkijah, Shemaiah, S,

SHIM(H)I, SHIMITES [KJV] See SHIMEI

SHIMMERING (1)
Isa 3:19 their earrings, bracelets, and veils of s gauze.

SHIMON (1)
1Ch 4:20 The sons of S were Amnon, Rinnah, Ben-hanan,

SHIMRATH (1)
1Ch 8:21 Adaiah, Beraiah, and S were the sons of Shimei.

SHIMRI (4)
1Ch 4:37 son of Allon, son of Jedaiah, son of S, son of
11:45 Jediael son of S; / Joha, his brother, from Tiz;
26:10 appointed S as the leader among his sons,
2Ch 29:13 S and Jeiel. / From the family of Asaph: Zechariah

SHIMRON (5) [SHIMRON-MERON, SHIMRONITE]
Ge 46:13 sons of Issachar were Tola, Puah, Jashub, and S.
Nu 26:24 The Shimronite clan, named after its ancestor S.
Jos 11: 1 of Madon; the king of S; the king of Acshaph;
19:15 Nahalal, S, Idalah, and Bethlehem—
1Ch 7: 1 sons of Issachar were Tola, Puah, Jashub, and S.

SHIMRON-MERON (1) [SHIMRON]
Jos 12:20 The king of S / The king of Acshaph

SHIMRONITE (1) [SHIMRON]
Nu 26:24 The S clan, named after its ancestor Shimron.

SHIMSHAI (3)
Ezr 4: 8 and S the court secretary wrote the letter,
4:17 "To Rehum the governor, S the court secretary,
4:23 S, and their colleagues, they hurried to Jerusalem

SHINAB (1)
Ge 14: 2 King Birsha of Gomorrah, King S of Admah,

SHINE (36) [SHINED, SHINES, SHINING, SHINY, SHONE]
Ge 1:15 Let their light s down upon the earth." And so it
1:16 the sun and the moon, to s down upon the earth.
Job 9: 7 the sun won't rise and the stars won't s.
22:28 and light will s on the road ahead of you.
25: 3 Does his light not s on all the earth?
25: 5 the moon and stars scarcely s compared to him.
Ps 4: 6 Let the smile of your face s on us, LORD.
31:16 Let your favor s on your servant. / In your
37: 6 and the justice of your cause will s like the
57: 5 May your glory s over all the earth.
57:11 May your glory s over all the earth.
67: 1 May his face s with favor upon us. / *Interlude*
80: 3 Make your face s down upon us. / Only then will
80: 7 Make your face s down upon us. / Only then will
80:19 Make your face s down upon us. / Only then will
108: 5 May your glory s over all the earth.
Isa 9: 2 a light that will s on all who live in the land where
13:10 No light will s from stars or sun or moon.
58:10 Then your light will s out from the darkness,
60: 1 Let your light s for all the nations to see!
60: 2 but the glory of the LORD will s over you.
60: 5 Your eyes will s, and your hearts will thrill with
Da 12: 3 Those who are wise will s as bright as the sky,
12: 3 and those who turn many to righteousness will s
Joel 2:10 and moon grow dark, and the stars no longer s.
3:15 will grow dark, and the stars will no longer s.
Zec 14: 6 On that day the sources of light will no longer s,
Mt 5:15 Instead, put it on a stand and let it s for all.
5:16 same way, let your good deeds s out for all to see,
13:43 Then the godly will s like the sun in their Father's
Mk 4:21 A lamp is placed on a stand, where its light will s.
Jn 12:35 "My light will s out for you just a little while
12:46 I have come as a light to s in this dark world,
2Co 4: 7 this light and power that now s within us—
Php 2:15 Let your lives s brightly before them.
Rev 22: 5 for lamps or sun—for the Lord God will s on them.

SHINED (1) [SHINE]
Mt 4:16 land where death casts its shadow, / a light has s."

SHINES (15) [SHINE]
Nu 8: 2 he is to place them so their light s forward."
Job 37:21 for it s brightly in the sky when the wind clears
Ps 26: 8 LORD, / the place where your glory s.
50: 2 perfection of beauty, / God s in glorious radiance.
68:34 about God's power. / His majesty s down on Israel;
72: 5 May he live as long as the sun s, / as long as the
72:17 may it continue as long as the sun s.
97:11 Light s on the godly, / and joy on those who do
139:12 To you the night s as bright as day. / Darkness
Pr 4:18 which s ever brighter until the full light of day.
Isa 62: 1 for her until her righteousness s like the dawn,
Jn 1: 5 The light s through the darkness, and the darkness
Eph 5:13 But when the light s on them, it becomes clear how
5:14 And where your light s, it will expose their evil
2Pe 1:19 and his brilliant light s in your hearts.

SHINING (13) [SHINE]
2Ki 3:22 the sun was s across the water, making it look as
Job 31:26 Have I looked at the sun s in the skies, or the moon
Ps 118:27 The LORD is God, s upon us. / Bring forward the
Isa 14:12 fallen from heaven, O s star, son of the morning!
54:12 and your gates and walls of s gems.
60: 1 to see! For the glory of the LORD is s upon you.
Eze 1:27 he looked like a burning flame, s with splendor.
1:28 glowing halo, like a rainbow s through the clouds.
Da 2:31 of a man, s brilliantly, frightening and awesome.
Lk 11:36 will be radiant, as though a floodlight is s on you."
2Co 4: 4 light of the Good News that is s upon them.
2Pe 1:19 for their words are like a light s in a dark place—
1Jn 2: 8 is disappearing and the true light is already s.

SHINY (5) [SHINE]
Lev 13: 2 or a s patch on their skin that develops into a
13:24 becoming either a s reddish white or white,
13:38 a man or woman, has s white patches on the skin,
14:56 area of skin, in a skin rash, or in a s patch of skin.
Rev 4: 6 In front of the throne was a s sea of glass,

SHION (1)
Jos 19:19 Hapharaim, S, Anaharath,

SHIP (33) [SHIP'S, SHIPOWNERS, SHIPS, SHIPWRECK, SHIPWRECKED, WARSHIPS]
Pr 30:19 slithers on a rock, / how a s navigates the ocean,
31:14 She is like a merchant's s; she brings her food
Eze 27: 5 You were like a great s built of the finest cypress
27:26 Your oarsmen are rowing your s of state into a
27:27 your s builders, merchants, and warriors.
27:34 Now you are a wrecked s, / broken at the bottom of
Jnh 1: 3 of Joppa, where he found a s leaving for Tarshish.
1: 4 But as the s was sailing along,
1: 5 and threw the cargo overboard to lighten the s.
Ac 13:13 and those with him left Paphos by s for Pamphylia,
14:26 Finally, they returned by s to Antioch of Syria,
20: 6 we boarded a s at Philippi in Macedonia and five
20:13 for us to join him, and we went on ahead by s.
20:38 Then they accompanied him down to the s.
21: 2 There we boarded a s sailing for the Syrian
21: 3 harbor of Tyre, in Syria, where the s was to unload.
21: 5 When we returned to the s at the end of the week,
27: 4 that made it difficult to keep the s on course,
27: 6 There the officer found an Egyptian s from
27:14 they called it) caught the s and blew it out to sea.
27:15 They couldn't turn the s into the wind, so they
27:17 Then we banded the s with ropes to strengthen the
27:18 as gale-force winds continued to batter the s,
27:22 lose your lives, even though the s will go down.
27:30 Then the sailors tried to abandon the s;
27:38 the crew lightened the s further by throwing the
27:39 get between the rocks and get the s safely to shore.
27:41 But the s hit a shoal and ran aground. The bow of
the s stuck fast, while the stern was
27:44 to try for it on planks and debris from the broken s.
28:11 sail on another s that had wintered at the island—
28:11 an Alexandrian s with the twin gods as its
Jas 3: 4 And a tiny rudder makes a huge s turn wherever

SHIP'S (3) [SHIP]
Ac 27: 9 in the fall, and Paul spoke to the s officers about it.
27:11 of the prisoners listened more to the s captain
27:19 The following day they even threw out the s

SHIPHI (1)
1Ch 4:37 and Ziza son of **S**, son of Allon, son of Jedaiah,

SHIPHRAH (1)
Ex 1:15 this order to the Hebrew midwives, **S** and Puah:

SHIPHTAN (1)
Nu 34:24 Ephraim son of Joseph | Kemuel son of **S**

SHIPMASTER [KJV] See CAPTAIN(S)

SHIPMEN [KJV] See SAILORS

SHIPOWNERS (1) [OWN, SHIP]
Rev 18:17 And all the **s** and captains of the merchant ships

SHIPS (31) [SHIP]
Ge 49:13 and will be a harbor for **s**; / his borders will extend
Nu 24:24 **S** will come from the coasts of Cyprus; / they will
Dt 28:68 Then the LORD will send you back to Egypt in **s**,
1Ki 9:26 Later King Solomon built a fleet of **s** at
9:27 crews of sailors to sail the **s** with Solomon's men.
10:11 (When Hiram's **s** brought gold from Ophir,
10:22 The king had a fleet of trading **s** that sailed with
10:22 Once every three years the **s** returned, loaded down
22:48 Jehoshaphat also built a fleet of trading **s** to sail to
22:48 But the **s** never set sail, for they were wrecked at
2Ch 8:18 Hiram sent him **s** commanded by his own officers
8:18 These **s** sailed to the land of Ophir with Solomon's
9:21 The king had a fleet of trading **s** manned by the
9:21 Once every three years the **s** returned, loaded down
20:36 Together they built a fleet of trading **s** at the port of
20:37 So the **s** met with disaster and never put out to sea.
Ps 48:7 or like the mighty **s** of Tarshish / being shattered
104:26 See the **s** sailing along, / and Leviathan, which you
107:23 Some went off in **s**, / plying the trade routes of the
107:26 Their **s** were tossed to the heavens / and sank again
Isa 2:16 He will destroy the great trading **s** and all the small
23:1 Weep, O **s** of Tarshish, returning home from
23:14 Wail, O **s** of Tarshish, for your home port is
43:14 will be forced to flee in those **s** they are
60:9 They are the **s** of Tarshish, reserved to bring the
Eze 27:9 **S** came with goods from every land to barter for
27:25 The **s** of Tarshish were your ocean caravans.
27:29 All the oarsmen abandon their **s**; the sailors
30:9 At that time I will send swift messengers in **s** to
Rev 8:9 And one-third of all the **s** on the sea were
18:17 all the shipowners and captains of the merchant **s**

SHIPWRECK (3) [SHIP, WRECKED]
Ac 27:10 **s**, loss of cargo, injuries, and danger to our lives."
28:11 It was three months after the **s** that we set sail on
Jude 1:12 they are like dangerous reefs that can **s** you.

SHIPWRECKED (4) [SHIP, WRECKED]
Eze 27:26 eastern gale. You are **s** in the heart of the sea!
Ac 27:26 But we will be **s** on an island."
2Co 11:25 Once I was stoned. Three times I was **s**. Once I
1Ti 1:19 their consciences; as a result, their faith has been **s**.

SHIRT (8) [NIGHTSHIRT, SHIRTS]
Ge 39:12 She came and grabbed him by his **s**, demanding,
39:12 tore himself away, but as he did, his **s** came off.
39:13 When she saw that she had his **s** and that he had
39:15 loud cries, he ran and left his **s** behind with me."
39:16 She kept the **s** with her, and when her husband
39:18 by my screams. He ran out, leaving his **s** behind!"
Mt 5:40 are ordered to court and your **s** is taken from you,
Lk 6:29 If someone demands your coat, offer your **s** also.

SHIRTS (1) [SHIRT]
Mic 2:8 You steal the **s** right off the backs of those who

SHISHA (1)
1Ki 4:3 Elihoreph and Ahijah, the sons of **S**, were court

SHISHAK (8)
1Ki 11:40 but he fled to King **S** of Egypt and stayed there
14:25 King **S** of Egypt came up and attacked Jerusalem.
2Ch 12:2 King **S** of Egypt attacked Jerusalem in the fifth
12:4 **S** conquered Judah's fortified cities and
12:5 who had all fled to Jerusalem because of **S**.
12:5 abandoned me, so I am abandoning you to **S**."
12:7 I will not use **S** to pour out my anger on Jerusalem.
12:9 So King **S** of Egypt came to Jerusalem and took

SHITRAI (1)
1Ch 27:29 **S** from Sharon was in charge of the cattle on the

SHIVERED (1) [SHIVERS]
2Co 11:27 Often I have **s** with cold, without enough clothing

SHIVERS (1) [SHIVERED]
Job 4:15 swept past my face. Its wind sent **s** up my spine.

SHIVERS [KJV] See also SMASH

SHIZA (1)
1Ch 11:42 Adina son of **S**, the Reubenite leader who had

SHOA (1)
Eze 23:23 with all the Chaldeans from Pekod and **S** and Koa.

SHOAL (1)
Ac 27:41 But the ship hit a **s** and ran aground. The bow of

SHOBAB (4)
2Sa 5:14 born in Jerusalem: Shimea, **S**, Nathan, Solomon,
1Ch 2:18 Azubah's sons were named Jesher, **S**, and Ardon.
3:5 included Shimea, **S**, Nathan, and Solomon.
14:4 born in Jerusalem: Shimea, **S**, Nathan, Solomon,

SHOBACH (4)
2Sa 10:16 troops arrived at Helam under the command of **S**,
10:18 and forty thousand horsemen, including **S**,
1Ch 19:16 These troops arrived under the command of **S**,
19:18 including **S**, the commander of their army.

SHOBAI (2)
Ezr 2:42 Ater, Talmon, Akkub, Hatita, and **S** | 139
Ne 7:45 Ater, Talmon, Akkub, Hatita, and **S** | 138

SHOBAL (8) [SHOBAL'S]
Ge 36:20 native to the land of Seir: Lotan, **S**, Zibeon, Anah,
36:23 The sons of **S** were Alvan, Manahath, Ebal,
36:29 of the Horite clans were Lotan, **S**, Zibeon, Anah,
1Ch 1:38 **S**, Zibeon, Anah, Dishon, Ezer, and Dishan.
1:40 The sons of **S** were Alvan, Manahath, Ebal,
2:50 were **S** (the father of Kiriath-jearim),
2:52 The descendants of **S** (the father of Kiriath-jearim)
4:1 of Judah were Perez, Hezron, Carmi, Hur, and **S**.

SHOBAL'S (1) [SHOBAL]
1Ch 4:2 **S** son Reaiah was the father of Jahath. Jahath was

SHOBEK (1)
Ne 10:24 Hallohesh, Pilha, **S**,

SHOBI (1)
2Sa 17:27 he was warmly greeted by **S** son of Nahash of

SHOCHOH [KJV] See SOCOH

SHOCK (2) [SHOCKED, SHOCKING]
Job 21:5 be stunned. Put your hand over your mouth in **s**.
Eze 36:34 lie empty and desolate—a **s** to all who passed by—

SHOCKED (6) [SHOCK]
Ge 34:7 They were **s** and furious that their sister had been
Lev 26:32 it will be utterly **s** at the destruction they see.
Ezr 9:3 from my head and beard, and sat down utterly **s**.
Jer 2:12 The heavens are **s** at such a thing and shrink back
Eze 16:27 and even they were **s** by your lewd conduct!
Gal 1:6 I am **s** that you are turning away so soon from

SHOCKING (4) [SHOCK]
1Sa 3:11 to Samuel, "I am about to do a **s** thing in Israel.
Jer 5:30 "A horrible and **s** thing has happened in this land—
Da 8:24 He will cause a **s** amount of destruction
12:6 "How long will it be until these **s** events happen?"

SHOC(H)O [KJV] See SOCO

SHOD [KJV] See (GAVE) SANDALS, WEAR

SHOES (1)
Eph 6:15 For **s**, put on the peace that comes from the Good

SHOE(S), SHOE'S [KJV] See SANDAL(S)

SHOELATCHET [KJV] See SANDAL THONG

SHOHAM (1)
1Ch 24:27 the leaders were Beno, **S**, Zaccur, and Ibri.

SHOMER (4)
2Ki 12:21 Jozacar son of Shimeath and Jehozabad son of **S**—
1Ch 7:32 The sons of Heber were Japhlet, **S**, and Hotham.
7:34 The sons of **S** were Ahi, Rohgah, Hubbah,
2Ch 24:26 the son of a Moabite woman named **S**.

SHONE (14) [SHINE]
Dt 33:2 us from Mount Seir; / he **s** forth from Mount Paran
2Sa 22:13 A great brightness **s** before him, / and bolts of
Eze 1:4 flashed with lightning and **s** with brilliant light.
1:7 split like calves' feet and **s** like burnished bronze.
40:3 I saw a man whose face **s** like bronze standing
43:2 and the whole landscape **s** with his glory.
Da 10:6 His arms and feet **s** like polished bronze, and his
Mt 17:2 appearance changed so that his face **s** like the sun,
28:3 His face **s** like lightning, and his clothing was as
Jn 5:35 John **s** brightly for a while, and you benefited
Ac 22:6 bright light from heaven suddenly **s** around me.
26:13 a light from heaven brighter than the sun **s** down
2Co 3:7 For his face **s** with the glory of God, even though
Rev 10:1 His face **s** like the sun, and his feet were like

SHOOK (22) [SHAKE]
Ex 19:18 and the whole mountain **s** with a violent
Jdg 5:5 Even Mount Sinai **s** in the presence of the LORD,
2Sa 22:8 and trembled; / the foundations of the heavens **s**;
1Ki 1:40 so joyous and noisy that the earth **s** with the sound.
Ne 5:13 I **s** out the fold of my robe and said, "If you fail to
Job 4:14 Fear gripped me; I trembled and **s** with terror.
Ps 18:7 and trembled; / the foundations of the mountains **s**;
77:18 lit up the world! / The earth trembled and **s**.
Isa 6:4 The glorious singing **s** the Temple to its
14:16 'Can this be the one who **s** the earth
Jer 4:24 at the mountains and hills, and they trembled and **s**.
Hos 13:1 the people **s** with fear because the other Israelite
Hab 3:16 My legs gave way beneath me, and I **s** in terror.
Mt 27:51 from top to bottom. The earth **s**, rocks split apart,
28:4 The guards **s** with fear when they saw him,
Ac 4:31 the building where they were meeting **s**,
7:32 and Jacob.' Moses **s** with terror and dared not look.
7:54 Stephen's accusation, and they **s** their fists in rage.
13:51 But they **s** off the dust of their feet against them
18:6 Paul **s** the dust from his robe and said,
28:5 But Paul **s** off the snake into the fire and was
Heb 12:26 When God spoke from Mount Sinai his voice **s** the

SHOOT (20) [OFFSHOOTS, SHOOTING, SHOOTS, SHOT]
Dt 32:23 upon them / and **s** them down with my arrows.
1Sa 20:20 and **s** three arrows to the side of the stone pile as
20:36 the boy, "so you can find the arrows as I **s** them."
2Ki 9:27 Jehu rode after him, shouting, "**S** him, too!"
13:17 and he opened it. Then he said, "**S**!" So he did.
19:32 His armies will not enter Jerusalem to **s** their
1Ch 12:2 and they could **s** arrows or sling stones with their
2Ch 26:15 designed by brilliant men to **s** arrows and hurl
Job 41:21 would kindle coals, for flames **s** from its mouth.
Ps 11:2 They **s** from the shadows at those who do right.
64:4 They **s** from ambush at the innocent,
64:7 But God himself will **s** them down. / Suddenly,
Isa 11:1 Out of the stump of David's family will grow a **s**—
13:18 The attacking armies will **s** down the young people
37:33 His armies will not enter Jerusalem to **s** their
53:2 up in the LORD's presence like a tender green **s**,
Jer 9:3 "My people bend their tongues like bows to **s** lies.
50:14 Let your archers **s** at her. Spare no arrows, for she
Eze 17:4 and plucked off its topmost **s**. Then he carried it
17:22 I will take a tender **s** from the top of a tall cedar,

SHOOTING (5) [SHOOT]
Nu 24:8 their bones in pieces, / **s** them with arrows.
1Sa 20:20 side of the stone pile as though I were **s** at a target.
2Sa 11:20 Didn't they know there would be **s** from the walls?
Pr 25:18 them with a sword, or **s** them with a sharp arrow.
26:18 Just as damaging as a mad man **s** a lethal weapon

SHOOTS (5) [SHOOT]
Ge 30:37 Now Jacob took fresh **s** from poplar, almond,
2Ki 19:26 as the grass, / as easily trampled as tender green **s**.
Pr 26:10 or a bystander is like an archer who **s** recklessly.
Isa 16:8 Her **s** once reached as far as the Dead Sea.
37:27 as the grass, / as easily trampled as tender green **s**.

SHOP (2) [SHOPS]
Jer 18:2 "Go down to the **s** where clay pots and jars are
Mt 25:9 all of us. Go to a **s** and buy some for yourselves.'

SHOPS (1) [SHOP]
Job 41:6 merchants try to buy it? Will they sell it in their **s**?

SHORE (36) [ASHORE, LAKESHORE, SEASHORE, SEASHORES, SHORELINE, SHORES]
Ex 14:2 Camp there along the **s**, opposite Baal-zephon.
14:9 as they were camped beside the **s** near Pi-hahiroth,
14:30 see the bodies of the Egyptians washed up on the **s**.
1Ki 9:26 in the land of Edom, along the **s** of the Red Sea.
2Ch 8:17 in the land of Edom, along the **s** of the Red Sea.
Ps 93:3 the mighty oceans roar as they pound the **s**.
93:4 of the seas, / mightier than the breakers on the **s**—
Isa 17:12 rush forward like waves thundering toward the **s**.
Eze 1:24 wings roared like waves crashing against the **s**,
27:29 the sailors and helmsmen come to stand on the **s**.
Mt 4:18 One day as Jesus was walking along the **s** beside
4:21 A little farther up the **s** he saw two other brothers,
13:1 Jesus left the house and went down to the **s**,
13:2 he sat and taught as the people listened on the **s**.
13:48 the net is full, they drag it up onto the **s**, sit down,
Mk 1:19 A little farther up the **s** Jesus saw Zebedee's sons,
4:1 There was such a large crowd along the **s** that he
5:21 a large crowd gathered around him on the **s**.
6:33 and people from many towns ran ahead along the **s**
Lk 5:1 One day as Jesus was preaching on the **s** of the Sea
Jn 6:16 That evening his disciples went down to the **s** to
6:22 crowds began gathering on the **s**, waiting to see
21:8 with the boat and pulled the loaded net to the **s**,
21:11 Peter went aboard and dragged the net to the **s**.
Ac 10:6 with Simon, a leatherworker who lives near the **s**.
10:32 of Simon, a leatherworker who lives near the **s**.'
21:5 and children, came down to the **s** with us.
27:13 they pulled up anchor and sailed along close to **s**.
27:29 would soon be driven against the rocks along the **s**,
27:39 get between the rocks and get the ship safely to **s**.
27:40 raised the foresail, and headed toward **s**.

28: 1 Once we were safe on s, we learned that we were
28: 2 so they built a fire on the s to welcome us
28: 7 Near the s where we landed was an estate
Rev 12:18 Then he stood waiting on the s of the sea.
20: 8 a mighty host, as numberless as sand along the s.

SHORELINE (3) [SHORE]
Jos 15:12 The western boundary was the s of the
Jer 5:22 am the one who defines the ocean's sandy s,
Eze 26: 3 like the waves of the sea crashing against your s.

SHORES (6) [SHORE]
Ge 49:13 "Zebulun will settle on the s of the sea / and will
Jos 12: 3 as far north as the western s of the Sea of Galilee
Job 38:10 For I locked it behind barred gates, limiting its s.
Eze 47:10 Fishermen will stand along the s of the Dead Sea,
47:10 The s will be covered with nets drying in the sun.
Mk 1:16 One day as Jesus was walking along the s of the

SHORN (1) [SHEAR]
SS 4: 2 teeth are as white as sheep, newly s and washed.

SHORT (27) [SHORT-LIVED, SHORT-TEMPERED, SHORTCHANGE, SHORTCUT, SHORTCUTS, SHORTENED, SHORTENING, SHORTENS, SHORTER, SHORTEST, SHORTLY, SHORTSIGHTED]
Ge 48: 7 just a s distance from Ephrath (that is, Bethlehem).
Nu 10: 6 You must sound s blasts to signal moving on.
Dt 4:26 You will live there only a s time; then you will be
Ezr 7:20 If you run s of money for anything necessary for
Job 10: 5 Is your lifetime merely human? Is your life so s
14: 1 is humanity! How s is life, and how full of trouble!
Ps 89:47 Remember how s my life is, / how empty and futile
Pr 10:27 one's life, but the years of the wicked are cut s.
24:14 a bright future, and your hopes will not be cut s.
Isa 28:20 the bed you have made is too s to lie on.
32:10 In a s time—in just a little more than a year—
38:12 like a shepherd's tent in a storm. / It has been cut s,
Eze 16:47 to you. In a very s time you far surpassed them!
17:24 down the tall tree and helps the s tree to grow tall.
Da 11:12 his enemies killed. But his success will be s lived.
11:24 of strongholds, but this will last for only a s while.
Hos 6: 2 In just a s time, he will restore us so we can live in
Jnh 4:10 to put it there. And a plant is only, at best, s lived.
Mic 6:10 by dishonestly measuring out grain in s measures.
Mk 1:25 Jesus cut him s. "Be silent! Come out of the
Lk 4:35 Jesus cut him s. "Be silent!" he told the demon.
19: 3 at Jesus, but he was too s to see over the crowds.
24:17 They stopped s, sadness written across their faces.
Ro 3:23 have sinned; all fall s of God's glorious standard.
1Co 7:29 The time that remains is very s, so husbands
16: 7 This time I don't want to make just a s visit and
1Pe 5:12 I have written this s letter to you with the help of

SHORT-LIVED (1) [LIVE, SHORT]
Job 20: 5 the triumph of the wicked has been s and the joy of

SHORT-TEMPERED (4) [SHORT, TEMPER]
Jdg 18:25 Some of us are s, and they might get angry and kill
Pr 14:17 Those who are s do foolish things, and schemers
19:19 S people must pay their own penalty. If you rescue
22:24 Keep away from angry, s people,

SHORTCHANGE (1) [SHORT]
Isa 59: 6 They cheat and s everyone. Nothing they do is

SHORTCUT (1) [SHORT]
2Sa 18:23 Then Ahimaaz took a s across the plain of the

SHORTCUTS (1) [SHORT]
Pr 21: 5 work lead to prosperity, but hasty s lead to poverty.

SHORTENED (5) [SHORT]
Job 18: 7 The confident stride of the wicked will be s.
Ps 31:10 I am dying from grief; / my years are s by sadness.
Mt 24:22 In fact, unless that time of calamity is s, the entire
24:22 But it will be s for the sake of God's chosen ones.
Mk 13:20 But for the sake of his chosen ones he has s those

SHORTENING (1) [SHORT]
Ps 102:23 He has cut me down in midlife, / s my days.

SHORTENS (1) [SHORT]
Mk 13:20 In fact, unless the Lord s that time of calamity,

SHORTER (1) [SHORT]
Da 8: 3 even though it had begun to grow later than the s

SHORTEST (1) [SHORT]
Ex 13:17 even though that was the s way from Egypt to the

SHORTLY (3) [SHORT]
1Sa 19: 8 War broke out s after that, and David led his troops
25:19 "Go on ahead. I will follow you s." But she didn't
Ac 21:15 S afterward we packed our things and left for

SHORTSIGHTED (1) [SEE, SHORT]
2Pe 1: 9 develop these virtues are blind or, at least, very s.

SHOT (18) [SHOOT]
Ge 49:23 by archers, / who s at him and harassed him.
Ex 19:13 boundary must be stoned to death or s with arrows.
Dt 4:11 Flames s into the sky, shrouded in black clouds
Jdg 13:20 As the flames from the altar s up toward the sky,
1Sa 20:36 the boy ran, and Jonathan s an arrow beyond him.
25:29 enemies will disappear like stones s from a sling!
2Sa 11:24 the archers on the wall s arrows at us. Some of our
22:15 He s his arrows and scattered his enemies;
1Ki 22:34 randomly s an arrow at the Israelite troops,
2Ki 9:24 drew his bow and s Joram between the shoulders.
9:27 So they s Ahaziah in his chariot at the Ascent of
2Ch 18:33 randomly s an arrow at the Israelite troops,
Job 41:28 Stones s from a sling are as ineffective as straw.
Ps 18:14 He s his arrows and scattered his enemies;
La 3:13 He s his arrows deep into my heart.
Mt 13: 7 Other seeds fell among thorns that s up and choked
Mk 4: 7 Other seed fell among thorns that s up and choked
Lk 8: 7 Other seed fell among thorns that s up and choked

SHOULD (526) [SHOULDN'T] See Index of Articles, Etc.

SHOULDER (17) [SHOULDERS]
Ge 24:15 named Rebekah arrived with a water jug on her s.
24:45 Rebekah coming along with her water jug on her s.
24:46 She quickly lowered the jug from her s so I could
46:29 his father and wept on his s for a long time.
49:15 pleasant the land, / he will bend his s to the task
Nu 6:19 the priest will take for each of them the boiled s of
Dt 18: 3 as offerings: the s, the cheeks, and the stomach.
Jos 4: 5 must pick up one stone and carry it out on your s—
Jdg 9:48 branches from a tree, and he put them on his s.
Job 31:22 then let my s be wrenched out of place! Let my
Ps 81: 6 "Now I will relieve your s of its burden; / I will
Eze 12: 7 went out into the darkness with my pack on my s.
24: 4 the rump and the s and all the most tender cuts.
Mt 16:24 your selfish ambition, s your cross, and follow me.
Mk 8:34 your selfish ambition, s your cross, and follow me.
Lk 9:23 selfish ambition, s your cross daily, and follow me.
Jn 20:14 She glanced over her s and saw someone standing

SHOULDER-PIECES (6) [PIECE, SHOULDER]
Ex 28: 7 and back, joined at the shoulders with two s.
28:12 Fasten the two stones on the s of the ephod as
28:25 be tied to the gold settings on the s of the ephod.
39: 4 They made two s for the ephod, which were
39: 6 two onyx stones, attached to the s of the ephod,
39:18 were tied to the gold settings on the s of the ephod.

SHOULDERS (23) [SHOULDER]
Ge 9:23 and Japheth took a robe, held it over their s,
21:14 and strapped a container of water to Hagar's s.
22: 6 placed the wood for the burnt offering on Isaac's s,
Ex 12:34 in their spare clothing and carried them on their s.
28: 7 and back, joined at the s with two shoulder-pieces.
28:14 be attached to the settings on the s of the ephod.
Nu 7: 9 the sacred objects of the Tabernacle on their s.
Jdg 16: 3 He put them on his s and carried them all the way
1Sa 9: 2 head and s taller than anyone else in the land.
10:23 and he stood head and s above anyone else.
1Ki 19:19 went over to him and threw his cloak across his s
2Ki 9:24 Jehu drew his bow and shot Joram between the s.
1Ch 15:15 Then the Levites carried the Ark of God on their s
2Ch 35: 3 do not need to carry it back and forth on your s,
Pr 30:20 shrug her s, and then say, "What's wrong with
Isa 9: 6 given to us. And the government will rest on his s.
10:27 break the yoke of slavery and lift it from their s.
46: 7 They carry it around on their s, and when they set
49:22 they will bring your daughters on their s.
Eze 12: 6 lift your pack to your s and walk away into the
29:18 rubbed bare and their s were raw and blistered.
Lk 15: 5 then you would joyfully carry it home on your s.
Ac 21:35 so violent the soldiers had to lift Paul to their s to

SHOULDN'T (40) [NOT, SHOULD] See Index of Articles, Etc.

SHOUT (107) [SHOUTED, SHOUTING, SHOUTS]
Dt 27:14 Then the Levites must s to all the people of Israel:
Jos 6: 5 on the horns, have all the people give a mighty s.
6:10 "Do not s; do not even talk," Joshua commanded.
6:10 from any of you until I tell you to s. Then s!"
6:16 on their horns, Joshua commanded the people, "S!
Jdg 7:18 the other sides of the camp blow your horns and s,
1Sa 4: 5 their s of joy was so loud that it made the ground
17:52 Then the Israelites gave a great s of triumph
2Sa 22:14 from heaven; / the Most High gave a mighty s.
1Ki 1:34 Then blow the trumpets and s, 'Long live King
18:27 "You'll have to s louder," he scoffed, "for surely
1Ch 16:32 Let the sea and everything in it s his praise!
2Ch 13:15 and the men of Judah began to s. At the sound of
20:19 the LORD, the God of Israel, with a very loud s.
Ezr 3:11 Then all the people gave a great s,
Est 6: 9 Have the prince s as they go, 'This is what
Job 30: 5 and people s after them as if they were thieves.
38:34 "Can you s to the clouds and make it rain?
39: 7 the noise of the city, and it has no driver to s at it.
39:25 of battle and the s of the captain's commands.
Ps 14: 7 Jacob will s with joy, and Israel will rejoice.
18:13 from heaven; / the Most High gave a mighty s.
20: 5 May we s for joy when we hear of your victory,
32:11 S for joy, all you whose hearts are pure!
35:21 They s that they have seen me doing wrong.
40:16 repeatedly s, "The LORD is great!"
47: 1 your hands for joy! / S to God with joyful praise!
47: 5 God has ascended with a mighty s. / The LORD
53: 6 Jacob will s with joy, and Israel will rejoice.
55: 3 My enemies s at me, / making loud and wicked
59:16 I will s with joy each morning because of your
60: 8 I will s in triumph over the Philistines."
65:13 carpeted with grain. / They all s and sing for joy!
66: 1 S joyful praises to God, all the earth!
68:11 and throngs of women s the happy news.
70: 4 love your salvation / repeatedly s, "God is great!"
71:23 I will s for joy and sing your praises, / for you have
84: 2 and soul, / I will s joyfully to the living God.
95: 1 Let us give a joyous s to the rock of our salvation!
96:11 Let the sea and everything in it s his praise!
98: 4 S to the LORD, all the earth; / break out in praise
98: 7 Let the sea and everything in it s his praise!
100: 1 S with joy to the LORD, O earth!
108: 9 I will s in triumph over the Philistines."
Pr 11:10 godly succeed; they s for joy when the godless die.
27:14 If you s a pleasant greeting to your neighbor too
Isa 9: 3 They will s with joy like warriors dividing the
10:30 S out a warning to Laishah, for the mighty army
12: 6 Let all the people of Jerusalem s his praise with
13: 4 It is the noise and the s of many nations.
21: 6 "Put a watchman on the city wall to s out what he
24:14 But all who are left will s and sing for joy.
35: 6 and those who cannot speak will s and sing!
40: 6 A voice said, "S!" I asked, "What should I s?"
40: 6 "S that people are like the grass that dies away.
40: 9 of good news, s to Zion from the mountaintops!
40: 9 S louder to Jerusalem—do not be afraid.
42: 2 be gentle—he will not s or raise his voice in public.
42:11 sing for joy; / s praises from the mountaintops!
42:13 full of fury. / He will s his thundering battle cry,
44:23 S, O earth! Break forth into song, O mountains
48:20 S to the ends of the earth that the LORD has
52: 5 Those who rule them s in exultation.
52: 8 The watchmen s and sing with joy, for before their
58: 1 "S with the voice of a trumpet blast. Tell my
Jer 2: 2 "Go and s in Jerusalem's streets: 'This is what the
4: 5 "S to Jerusalem and to all Judah! Tell them to
6: 4 They s, 'Prepare for battle and attack at noon!
7:27 S out your warnings, but do not expect them to
20: 8 violent outburst. "Violence and destruction!" I s.
22:20 Search for them in Lebanon. S for them at Bashan.
25:30 He will s against everyone on the earth,
31: 6 The day will come when watchmen will s from the
31: 7 S for the greatest of nations! S out with praise and
46:14 "S it out in Egypt! Publish it in the cities of
48:19 They s to those who flee from Moab, 'What has
50:15 S against her from every side. Look!
50:22 cry be heard in the land, a s of great destruction.
La 2: 7 They s in the LORD's Temple as though it were a
3: 8 And though I cry and s, he shuts out my prayers.
Hos 9: 7 "The prophets are crazy!" the people s.
Joel 2:11 The LORD leads them with a s! This is his
Am 2: 2 of battle, as the warriors s and the trumpets blare.
Zep 3:14 Sing, O daughter of Zion; s aloud, O Israel!
Zec 1:14 angel said to me, "S this message for all to hear:
2:10 The LORD says, "S and rejoice, O Jerusalem,
4: 7 stone of the Temple in place, and the people will s:
9: 9 S in triumph, O people of Jerusalem! Look,
9:15 They will s in battle as though drunk with wine,
Mt 6: 2 in need, don't s about it as the hypocrites do—
10:27 in the darkness, s abroad when daybreak comes.
10:27 in your ears, s from the housetops for all to hear!
12:19 He will not fight or s; / he will not raise his voice
25: 6 At midnight they were roused by the s, 'Look,
Mk 10:47 he began to s out, "Jesus, Son of David,
Lk 5: 7 A s for help brought their partners in the other
19:37 all of his followers began to s and sing as they
1Th 4:16 come down from heaven with a commanding s,
Rev 7:10 And they were shouting with a mighty s,
10: 3 And he gave a great s, like the roar of a lion.
16:17 And a mighty s came from the throne of the
18: 2 He gave a mighty s, "Babylon is fallen—that great
19: 6 Then I heard again what sounded like the s of a
21: 3 I heard a loud s from the throne, saying, "Look,

SHOUTED (130) [SHOUT]
Ge 19: 5 They s to Lot, "Where are the men who came to
19: 9 "Stand back!" they s. "Who do you think you
22:11 At that moment the angel of the LORD s to him
38:24 "Bring her out and burn her!" Judah s.
41:43 and wherever he went the command was s,
Ex 5: 4 "Who do you think you are," Pharaoh s,
10:28 "Get out of here!" Pharaoh s at Moses.
14:25 to drive. "Let's get out of here!" the Egyptians s.
32:26 he stood at the entrance to the camp and s, "All of
Lev 9:24 they s with joy and fell face down on the ground.
Nu 20:10 and gather at the rock. "Listen, you rebels!" he s.
22:29 Balaam s. "If I had a sword with me, I would kill
24:10 He angrily clapped his hands and s, "I called you
Jos 6:20 sound of the horns, they s as loud as they could.
Jdg 6:30 "Bring out your son," they s to Joash. "He must
6:31 But Joash s to the mob, "Why are you defending
7:15 Then he returned to the Israelite camp and s,
7:20 left hands and the horns in their right hands and s,
9: 7 he climbed to the top of Mount Gerizim and s,

9:28 "Who is Abimelech?" Gaal s. "He's not a true
20:32 Then the warriors of Benjamin s,
20:39 and they s, "We're defeating them as we did in the
1Sa 10:24 And all the people s, "Long live the king!"
14:11 the Philistines saw them coming, they s, "Look!
14:12 Then they s to Jonathan, "Come on up here,
14:18 Then Saul s to Ahijah, "Bring the ephod here!"
17:8 Goliath stood and s across to the Israelites,
17:45 David s in reply, "You come to me with sword,
20:37 Jonathan s, "The arrow is still ahead of you.
22:7 of Benjamin!" Saul s when he heard the news.
22:12 When they arrived, Saul s at him, "Listen to me,
22:16 along with your entire family!" the king s.
24:8 David came out and s after him, "My lord the
24:9 Then he s to Saul, "Why do you listen to the
26:14 Then he s down to Abner and Saul, "Wake up,
2Sa 2:22 Again Abner s to him, "Get away from here!
2:26 Abner s down to Joab, "Must we always solve our
3:8 he s. "After all I have done for you and your father
13:17 He s for his servant and demanded, "Throw this
16:7 you murderer, you scoundrel!" he s at David.
18:25 He s the news down to David, and the king replied,
18:26 He s down, "Here comes another one!" The king
20:1 a Benjaminite, blew a trumpet and s, "We have
20:11 One of Joab's young officers s to Amasa's troops,
1Ki 1:39 and all the people s, "Long live King Solomon!"
8:55 and s this blessing over the entire community of
12:16 they s, "Down with David and his dynasty!
13:2 at the LORD's command, he s, "O altar, altar!
13:4 So he pointed at the man and s, "Seize that man!"
18:28 So they s louder, and following their normal
18:44 Then Elijah s, "Hurry to Ahab and tell him,
22:32 after him. "There is the king of Israel!" they s.
2Ki 6:21 he s to Elisha, "My father, should I kill them?"
7:11 Then the gatekeepers s the news to the people in
9:17 and his company approaching, so he s to Joram,
9:17 if they are coming in peace," King Joram s back.
9:31 she s at him, "Have you come in peace,
9:32 Jehu looked up and saw her at the window and s,
10:14 "Take them alive!" Jehu s to his men. And they
11:12 and all the people clapped their hands and s,
11:14 she tore her clothes in despair and s, "Treason!
18:28 he stood and s in Hebrew to the people on the wall,
1Ch 16:36 And all the people s "Amen!" and praised the
2Ch 10:16 they s, "Down with David and his dynasty!
13:4 and s to Jeroboam and the Israelite army:
15:2 "Listen to me, Asa!" he s. "Listen, all you people
15:14 They s out their oath of loyalty to the LORD with
18:31 after him. "There is the king of Israel!" they s.
23:11 and everyone s, "Long live the king!"
23:13 she tore her clothes in despair and s, "Treason!
32:18 The Assyrian officials who brought the letters s
Job 38:7 stars sang together and all the angels s for joy?
Ps 74:4 There your enemies s their victorious battle cries;
Isa 36:13 he stood and s in Hebrew to the people on the wall,
Jer 26:8 at the Temple mobbed him. "Kill him!" they s.
41:13 The people Ishmael had captured s for joy when
La 4:15 "Get away!" the people s at them. "You are
Da 3:4 a herald s out, "People of all races and nations
3:25 "Look!" Nebuchadnezzar s. "I see four men,
3:26 he could to the door of the flaming furnace and s:
4:14 The messenger s, "Cut down the tree; lop off its
5:7 The king s for the enchanters, astrologers,
Jnh 1:5 the desperate sailors s to their gods for help
1:6 he s. "Get up and pray to your god! Maybe he will
3:4 the day Jonah entered the city, he s to the crowds:
Mt 14:30 and began to sink. "Save me, Lord!" he s.
20:31 but they only s louder, "Lord, Son of David,
26:66 your verdict?" "Guilty!" they s. "He must die!"
27:21 the crowd s back their reply: "Barabbas!"
27:22 the Messiah?" And they all s, "Crucify him!"
27:39 And the people passing by s abuse, shaking their
27:44 crucified with him also s the same insults at him.
27:50 Then Jesus s out again, and he gave up his spirit.
Mk 10:48 But he only s louder, "Son of David, have mercy
15:13 They s back, "Crucify him!"
15:29 And the people passing by s abuse, shaking their
Lk 12:3 doors will be s from the housetops for all to hear!
16:24 "The rich man s, 'Father Abraham, have some
18:39 but he only s louder, "Son of David, have mercy
22:70 They all s, "Then you claim you are the Son of
22:71 they s. "We ourselves heard him say it."
23:18 and with one voice they s, "Kill him, and release
23:21 But they s, "Crucify him! Crucify him!"
23:23 But the crowd s louder and louder for Jesus' death,
23:46 Then Jesus s, "Father, I entrust my spirit into your
Jn 1:15 He s to the crowds, "This is the one I was talking
7:37 Jesus stood and s to the crowds, "If you are
11:43 Then Jesus s, "Lazarus, come out!"
12:13 down the road to meet him. They s, / "Praise God!
12:44 Jesus s to the crowds, "If you trust me, you are
18:40 But they s back, "No! Not this man,
19:15 no king but Caesar," the leading priests s back.
Ac 2:14 with the eleven other apostles and s to the crowd,
14:11 they s in their local dialect, "These men are gods
16:20 city is in an uproar because of these Jews!" they s.
16:28 But Paul s to him, "Don't do it! We are all here!"
17:6 and now they are here disturbing our city," they s.
21:34 Some s one thing and some another. He couldn't
22:22 then with one voice they s, "Away with such a
23:6 so he s, "Brothers, I am a Pharisee, as were all my
23:9 "We see nothing wrong with him," they s.
24:21 except for one thing I said when I s out, 'I am on
26:24 Suddenly, Festus s, "Paul, you are insane.
Rev 5:2 And I saw a strong angel, who s with a loud voice:
7:2 And he s out to those four angels who had been
10:3 And when he s, the seven thunders answered.
11:12 Then a loud voice s from heaven, "Come up
14:7 "Fear God," he s. "Give glory to him.
14:18 the world with fire, s to the angel with the sickle,
18:21 He threw it into the ocean and s, "Babylon,

SHOUTING (65) [SHOUT]

Ex 32:17 When Joshua heard the noise of the people s below
Jdg 7:21 Midianites rushed around in a panic, s as they ran.
15:14 arrived at Lehi, the Philistines came s in triumph.
18:23 They were s as they caught up with them. The men
19:22 began beating at the door and s to the old man,
1Sa 4:6 "What's all the s about in the Hebrew camp?"
14:19 the s and confusion in the Philistine camp grew
17:23 s his challenge to the army of Israel.
2Sa 6:15 brought up the Ark of the LORD with much s
17:9 and everyone will start s that your men are being
1Ki 1:25 They are feasting and drinking with him and s,
1:40 Solomon to Jerusalem, playing flutes and s for joy.
1:41 and s just as they were finishing their banquet.
18:26 name of Baal all morning, s, "O Baal, answer us!"
2Ki 9:13 bare steps and blew a trumpet, s, "Jehu is king!"
9:23 chariot horses around and fled, s to King Ahaziah,
9:27 Jehu rode after him, s, "Shoot him, too!"
Ezr 3:12 The others, however, were s for joy.
3:13 The joyful s and weeping mingled together in a
Est 6:11 own horse, and led him through the city square, s,
Ps 65:7 pounding waves / and silenced the s of the nations.
66:4 your praises, / s your name in glorious songs."
Pr 29:6 trapped by sin, but the righteous escape, s for joy.
Isa 40:3 I hear the voice of someone s, "Make a highway
Jer 25:36 to the leaders of the flock s in despair,
48:33 with shouts of joy. There is s, yes, but not of joy.
Eze 1:24 of the Almighty, or like the s of a mighty army.
21:22 rams they will go against the gates, s for the kill.
Mt 3:3 when he said, / "He is a voice s in the wilderness:
8:25 went to him and woke him up, s, "Lord, save us!
9:27 behind him, s, "Son of David, have mercy on us!"
20:30 they began s, "Lord, Son of David, have mercy on
21:9 and the crowds all around him were s,
21:15 and heard even the little children in the Temple s,
26:65 his clothing to show his horror, s, "Blasphemy!
Mk 1:3 He is a voice s in the wilderness: / 'Prepare a
1:24 and he began s, "Why are you bothering us,
4:38 Frantically they woke him up, s, "Teacher,
11:9 and the crowds all around him were s,
Lk 3:4 when he said, / "He is a voice s in the wilderness:
4:33 a man possessed by a demon began s at Jesus,
4:41 out at his command, s, "You are the Son of God."
8:24 s, "Master, Master, we're going to drown!"
17:15 came back to Jesus, s, "Praise God, I'm healed!"
18:38 So he began s, "Jesus, Son of David, have mercy
23:10 and the teachers of religious law stood there s their
Jn 1:23 of Isaiah: / "I am a voice s in the wilderness,
19:6 the leading priests and Temple guards began s,
Ac 7:60 And he fell to his knees, s, "Lord, don't charge
12:22 s, "It is the voice of a god, not of a man!"
14:14 in dismay and ran out among the people, s,
16:17 She followed along behind us s, "These men are
19:28 At this their anger boiled, and they began s,
19:32 Inside, the people were all s, some one thing
19:34 they started s again and kept it up for two hours:
21:36 And the crowd followed behind s, "Kill him,
23:10 The s grew louder and louder, and the men were
Rev 7:10 And they were s with a mighty shout,
11:15 and there were loud voices s in heaven:
12:10 Then I heard a loud voice s across the heavens,
14:8 him through the skies, s, "Babylon is fallen—
14:9 s, "Anyone who worships the beast and his statue
16:1 Then I heard a mighty voice s from the Temple to
19:1 I heard the sound of a vast crowd in heaven s,
19:17 in the sun, s to the vultures flying high in the sky:

SHOUTS (24) [SHOUT]

1Sa 17:20 Israelite army was leaving for the battlefield with s
1Ch 15:28 the LORD's covenant to Jerusalem with s of joy,
2Ch 23:12 the people running and the s of praise to the king,
Job 8:21 mouth with laughter and your lips with s of joy.
Ps 16:9 is filled with joy, / and my mouth s his praises!
21:1 O LORD! / He s with joy because of your victory.
27:6 At his Tabernacle I will offer sacrifices with s of
29:9 forests bare. / In his Temple everyone s, "Glory!"
65:8 the sun rises to where it sets, / you inspire s of joy.
126:5 who plant in tears / will harvest with s of joy.
Pr 1:20 Wisdom s in the streets. She cries out in the public
Ecc 9:17 wise person are better than the s of a foolish king.
Isa 31:4 it pays no attention to the shepherd's s and noise.
Jer 20:16 Terrify him all day long with battle s,
48:33 No one treads the grapes with s of joy. There is
49:29 taken away. Everywhere s of panic will be heard:
51:14 and they will lift their s of triumph over you."
Eze 7:7 It will ring with s of anguish, not s of joy.
Am 1:14 There will be wild s during the battle, swirling like
Na 2:5 The king s to his officers; they stumble in their
2:8 someone s, but the people just keep on running.
Ac 2:26 is filled with joy, / and my mouth s his praises!
7:57 and drowning out his voice with their s,

SHOVELS (9)

Ex 27:3 The ash buckets, s, basins, meat hooks,
38:3 ash buckets, s, basins, meat hooks, and firepans.
Nu 4:14 the firepans, hooks, s, basins, and all the
1Ki 7:40 He also made the necessary pots, s, and basins.
7:45 the pots, the s, and the basins. All these utensils for
2Ki 25:14 also took all the pots, s, lamp snuffers, dishes,
2Ch 4:11 also made the necessary pots, s, and basins.
4:16 the pots, the s, the meat hooks, and all the related
Jer 52:18 took all the pots, s, lamp snuffers, basins, dishes,

SHOW (236) [SHOWED, SHOWING, SHOWN, SHOWS]

Ge 12:1 father's house, and go to the land that I will s you.
24:12 "Give me success and s kindness to my master,
24:49 or won't you s true kindness to my master?
31:37 Now s me what you have found that belongs to
31:39 did I s them to you and ask you to reduce the count
Ex 7:5 When I s the Egyptians my power and force them
7:9 "Pharaoh will demand that you s him a miracle to
18:20 and s them how to conduct their lives.
20:20 "for God has come in this way to s you his
25:9 exactly according to the plans I will s you.
28:2 Make special clothing for Aaron to s his separation
33:13 s me your intentions so I will understand you more
33:19 I will s kindness to anyone I choose, and I will s mercy to anyone I choose.
34:7 I s this unfailing love to many thousands by
Lev 10:3 LORD meant when he said, / 'I will s myself holy
19:3 Each of you must s respect for your mother
19:14 "S your fear of God by treating the deaf with
19:30 days of rest and s reverence toward my sanctuary,
19:32 "S your fear of God by standing up in the presence
25:17 S your fear of God by not taking advantage of each
25:36 s your fear of God by letting them live with you as
25:43 S your fear of God by treating them well;
26:2 days of rest and s reverence for my sanctuary.
Nu 6:26 May the LORD s you his favor / and give you his
10:33 moving ahead of them to s them where to stop
16:5 "Tomorrow morning the LORD will s us who
Dt 3:24 You have only begun to s me your greatness
7:2 Make no treaties with them and s them no mercy.
7:16 S them no mercy and do not worship their gods.
10:19 You, too, must s love to foreigners, for you
11:22 s love to the LORD your God by walking in his
16:19 You must never twist justice or s partiality.
19:21 You must never s pity! Your rule should be life for
Jdg 1:24 They said to him, "S us a way into the city,
4:22 and I will s you the man you are looking for."
6:17 s me a sign to prove that it is really the LORD
8:35 Nor did they s any loyalty to the family of
1Sa 4:12 his clothes and put dust on his head to s his grief.
6:5 Make these things to s honor to the God of Israel.
14:41 please s us who is guilty and who is innocent.
16:3 and I will s you which of his sons to anoint for
20:8 S me this kindness as my sworn friend—for we
2Sa 1:2 and put dirt on his head to s that he was in
6:21 So I am willing to act like a fool in order to s my
9:1 for he had promised Jonathan that he would s
9:3 I want to s God's kindness to them in any way I
9:8 "Should the king s such kindness to a dead dog
10:2 "I am going to s complete loyalty to Hanun
15:20 and may the LORD s you his unfailing love
22:26 "To the faithful you s yourself faithful; / to those with integrity you s integrity.
22:27 To the pure you s yourself pure, / but to the wicked you s yourself hostile.
22:51 your king; / you s unfailing love to your anointed,
1Ki 8:23 and s unfailing love to all who obey you
2Ki 20:13 or kingdom that Hezekiah did not s them.
1Ch 19:2 "I am going to s complete loyalty to Hanun
21:16 and the leaders of Israel put on sackcloth to s their
2Ch 6:14 and s unfailing love to all who obey you
10:7 "If you are good to the people and s them kindness
Est 3:2 Haman to s him respect whenever he passed by,
3:2 Mordecai refused to bow down or s him respect.
3:5 Mordecai would not bow down or s him respect,
4:8 of all Jews, and he asked Hathach to s it to Esther.
Job 13:23 have I done wrong? S me my rebellion and my sin.
31:35 Let the Almighty s me that I am wrong.
33:12 "In this you are not right, and I will s you why.
36:2 and I will s you the truth of what I am saying.
36:9 he takes the trouble to s them the reason. He shows
37:24 People who are truly wise s him reverence."
42:6 and I sit in dust and ashes to s my repentance."
Ps 4:6 Many people say, "Who will s us better times?"
5:8 clearly what to do, / and s me which way to turn.
16:11 You will s me the way of life, / granting me the joy
17:7 S me your unfailing love in wonderful ways.
18:25 To the faithful you s yourself faithful; / to those with integrity you s integrity.
18:26 To the pure you s yourself pure, / but to the wicked you s yourself hostile.
18:50 your king; / you s unfailing love to your anointed,
22:23 S him reverence, all you descendants of Israel!
25:4 S me the path where I should walk, O LORD;
25:12 He will s them the path they should choose.
34:9 Let the LORD's people s him reverence,
59:5 S no mercy to wicked traitors. / *Interlude*
69:11 When I dress in sackcloth to s sorrow, / they make
69:13 hoping this is the time you will s me favor.
69:20 in despair. / If only one person would s some pity;
77:7 me forever? / Will he never again s me favor?
79:10 S us your vengeance against the nations,
80:2 and Manasseh. / S us your mighty power.
85:7 S us your unfailing love, O LORD, / and grant us
90:17 And may the Lord our God s us his approval
102:14 and s favor even to the dust in her streets.
106:4 too, LORD, when you s favor to your people;
119:132 Come and s me your mercy, / as you do for all who
143:8 for I am trusting you. / S me where to walk,
Pr 12:23 Wise people don't make a s of their knowledge,
24:23 It is wrong to s favoritism when passing judgment.
Ecc 9:1 or not God will s them favor in this life.

Isa 5:19 and do something! Quick, s us what you can do.
13:13 will s my fury and fierce anger."
13:18 and will s no compassion for the children.
19: 3 and psychics to s them which way to turn.
22:12 and to wear clothes of sackcloth to s your remorse.
23: 9 and s his contempt for all human greatness.
26:11 S them your eagerness to defend your people.
27:11 the one who made them will s them no pity
29:14 I will s that human wisdom is foolish and even the
30:18 to him so he can s you his love and compassion.
33:10 "I will stand up and s my power and might.
39: 2 or kingdom that Hezekiah did not s them.
41:21 Let them come and s what they can do!"
42:21 Through it he had planned to s the world that he is
57:16 against you forever; I will not always s my anger.
58: 2 They love to make a s of coming to me and asking
61:11 The Sovereign LORD will s his justice to the
63:15 and the might you used to s on our behalf?
Jer 2:17 when he wanted to lead you and s you the way!
6:23 They are cruel and s no mercy. As they ride
16: 5 their funerals to mourn and s sympathy for them,"
16:21 "So now I will s them my power and might,"
22:30 Let the record s that this man Jehoiachin was
42: 3 Beg the LORD your God to s us what to do
50:42 They are cruel and s no mercy. As they ride
Eze 5:11 I will s you no pity at all because you have defiled
7: 4 I will turn my eyes away and s no pity,
8:13 "Come, and I will s you greater sins than these!"
8:15 "But I will s you even greater sins than these!"
9: 5 forehead is not marked. S no mercy; have no pity!
12: 3 So now put on a demonstration to s them what it
20:26 and s them that I alone am the LORD.
24: 3 Then s these rebels an illustration; give them a
24:16 Yet you must not s any sorrow. Do not weep;
35: 6 since you s no distaste for blood,
36:23 I will s how holy my great name is—the name you
38:23 Thus will I s my greatness and holiness, and I will
40: 4 Pay close attention to everything I s you.
40: 4 have been brought here so I can s you many things.
Da 2:18 He urged them to ask the God of heaven to s them
2:41 and clay s that this kingdom will be divided.
8:22 s that the Greek Empire will break into four
Hos 1: 6 for I will no longer s love to the people of Israel
1: 7 their God, will s love to the people of Judah.
2:23 I will s love to those I called 'Not loved.'
Am 5:21 "I hate all your s and pretense—the hypocrisy of
Jnh 3: 5 without food and wear sackcloth to s their sorrow.
Mic 1:10 roll in the dust to s your anguish and despair.
7:20 You will s us your faithfulness and unfailing love
Na 3: 6 with filth and s the world how vile you really are.
Hab 3: 2 S us your power to save us. And in your anger,
Zec 1: 9 horses for?" "I will s you," the angel replied.
1:12 How long will it be until you again s mercy to
1:16 I have returned to s mercy to Jerusalem.
7: 9 and s mercy and kindness to one another.
11:14 to s that the bond of unity between Judah
Mal 1: 9 of offering, why should he s you any favor at all?"
3:14 or by trying to s the LORD Almighty that we are
Mt 4:19 and I will s you how to fish for people!"
11:21 and throwing ashes on their heads to s their
12:38 we want you to s us a miraculous sign to prove that
16: 1 him to s them a miraculous sign from heaven.
22:19 Here, s me the Roman coin used for the tax."
23: 5 "Everything they do is for s. On their arms they
25:38 Or a stranger and s you hospitality? Or naked
26:65 Then the high priest tore his clothing to s his
27:43 let God s his approval by delivering him!
Mk 1: 4 be baptized to s that they had turned from their sins
1:17 and I will s you how to fish for people!"
12:15 S me a Roman coin, and I'll tell you."
13: 4 And will there be any sign ahead of time to s us
14:63 Then the high priest tore his clothing to s his
Lk 2:44 But when he didn't s up that evening, they started
3: 3 preaching that people should be baptized to s that
3:13 "S your honesty," he replied. "Make sure you
6:47 I will s you what it's like when someone comes to
10:13 and throwing ashes on their heads to s their
11:29 and this evil generation keeps asking me to s them
17:14 at them and said, "Go s yourselves to the priests."
18: 1 and to s them that they must never give up.
20:24 "S me a Roman coin. Whose picture and title are
Jn 2:18 from God, s us a miraculous sign to prove it."
6:30 "You must s us a miraculous sign if you want us
9:39 and to s those who think they see that they are
14: 8 "Lord, s us the Father and we will be satisfied."
Ac 1:24 S us which of these men you have chosen
7: 3 and come to the land that I will s you.'
9:16 And I will s him how much he must suffer for
10:34 "I see very clearly that God doesn't s partiality.
Ro 2:11 For God does not s favoritism.
2:14 they s that in their hearts they know right from
6: 1 so that God can s us more and more kindness
7:10 which was supposed to s me the way of life,
9:15 to Moses, / "I will s mercy to anyone I choose,
9:15 and I will s compassion to anyone I choose."
9:16 hard for it. God will s mercy to anyone he chooses.
15: 8 s that God is true to the promises he made to their
1Co 10:13 he will s you a way out so that you will not give in
2Co 2: 8 Now s him that you still love him.
6: 4 In everything we do we try to s that we are true
7:12 so that in the sight of God you could s how much
8:24 So s them your love, and prove to all the churches
11:30 I would rather boast about the things that s how
13: 7 not to s that our ministry to you has been
Gal 3:19 It was given to s people how guilty they are.
6:17 For I bear on my body the scars that s I belong to
Eph 3:10 God's purpose was to s his wisdom in all its rich
5: 8 light from the Lord, and your behavior should s it!
2Th 1: 5 But God will use this persecution to s his justice.
1Ti 5: 4 their first responsibility is to s godliness at home
2Ti 1: 9 to s his love and kindness to us through Christ
1:16 May the Lord s special kindness to Onesiphorus
1:18 May the Lord s him special kindness on the day of
Tit 1: 9 and s those who oppose it where they are wrong.
2:10 but they must s themselves to be entirely
3: 2 should be gentle and s true humility to everyone.
Phm 1:10 My plea is that you s kindness to Onesimus.
Heb 11: 4 God accepted Abel's offering to s that he was a
13: 2 Don't forget to s hospitality to strangers, for some
Jas 2: 4 doesn't this discrimination s that you are guided by
2:17 Faith that doesn't s itself by good deeds is no faith
2:18 but I will s you my faith through my good deeds."
1Pe 1: 7 to test your faith, to s that it is strong and pure.
2: 9 This is so you can s others the goodness of God,
2:17 S respect for everyone. Love your Christian
2:17 and sisters. Fear God. S respect for the king.
4: 8 of all, continue to s deep love for each other,
1Jn 2:15 you s that you do not have the love of the Father in
3:18 we love each other; let us really s it by our actions.
Jude 1:22 S mercy to those whose faith is wavering.
1:23 There are still others to whom you need to s mercy,
Rev 4: 1 and I will s you what must happen after these
17: 1 "and I will s you the judgment that is going to
18:19 And they will throw dust on their heads to s their
21: 9 I will s you the bride, the wife of the Lamb."

SHOWED (49) [SHOW]

Ex 15:25 LORD for help, and the LORD s him a branch.
Nu 13:26 and s them the fruit they had taken from the land.
17: 9 the LORD's presence, he s them to the people.
Dt 4:35 "He s you these things so you would realize that
34: 1 And the LORD s him the whole land,
Jdg 1:25 So he s them a way in, and they killed everyone in
Ru 2:18 it back into town and s it to her mother-in-law.
2Ki 6: 6 When he s him the place, Elisha cut a stick
11: 4 LORD's Temple; then he s them the king's son.
20:13 and s them everything in his treasure-houses—
20:13 see his armory and s them all his other treasures—
20:15 "I s them everything I own—all my treasures."
Ne 9:19 and the pillar of fire s them the way through the
Job 10:12 You gave me life and s me your unfailing love.
Isa 39: 2 and s them everything in his treasure-houses—
39: 2 see his armory and s them all his other treasures—
39: 4 "I s them everything I own—all my treasures."
47: 6 But you, Babylon, s them no mercy. You have
Jer 36:24 Neither the king nor his officials s any signs of fear
Eze 46:19 He s me a place at the extreme west end of these
Am 1:11 They s them no mercy and were unrelenting in
7: 1 The Sovereign LORD s me a vision. I saw him
7: 4 Then the Sovereign LORD s me another vision.
7: 7 Then he s me another vision. I saw the Lord
8: 1 Then the Sovereign LORD s me another vision.
Zec 1:20 Then the LORD s me four blacksmiths.
3: 1 Then the angel s me Jeshua the high priest standing
Mal 1: 2 "I s my love for you by loving your ancestor
Mt 4: 8 and s him the nations of the world and all their
21:32 John the Baptist came and s you the way to life,
Mk 7:19 he s that every kind of food is acceptable.)
Lk 5:17 (It seemed that these men s up from every village
10:37 The man replied, "The one who s him mercy."
24:40 his hands for them to see, and he s them his feet.
Jn 13: 1 He now s the disciples the full extent of his love.
20:20 his hands for them to see, and he s them his side.
Ac 9:41 all the believers, and he s them that she was alive.
Ro 5: 8 But God s his great love for us by sending Christ to
7: 7 is not sinful, but it was the law that s me my sin.
10:20 who were not looking for me. / I s myself to those
2Co 7:11 You s that you have done everything you could to
Eph 5:25 your wives with the same love Christ s the church.
2Ti 1:10 and s us the way to everlasting life through the
Tit 3: 4 But then God our Savior s us his kindness
1Jn 4: 9 God s how much he loved us by sending his only
Rev 2:14 who s Balak how to trip up the people of Israel.
21:10 and he s me the holy city, Jerusalem,
22: 1 And the angel s me a pure river with the water of
22: 8 I fell down to worship the angel who s them to me.

SHOWER (6) [SHOWERED, SHOWERING, SHOWERS]

Ps 45:12 The princes of Tyre will s you with gifts.
82: 2 How long will you s special favors on the wicked?
Eze 5:16 "I will s you with the deadly arrows of famine to
Hos 10:12 that he may come and s righteousness upon you.'
Lk 12:54 to form in the west, you say, 'Here comes a s.'
2Co 1: 5 the more God will s us with his comfort through

SHOWERED (5) [SHOWER]

Ne 9:35 they did not serve you even though you s your
Pr 10: 6 The godly are s with blessings; evil people cover
24:25 But blessings are s on those who convict the guilty.
Ac 28:10 As a result we were s with honors, and when the
Eph 1: 8 He has s his kindness on us, along with all wisdom

SHOWERING (1) [SHOWER]

Pr 22:16 or by s gifts on the rich will end in poverty.

SHOWERS (8) [SHOWER]

Dt 32: 2 on tender grass, / like gentle s on young plants.
Job 24: 8 They are soaked by mountain s, and they huddle
Ps 65:10 leveling the ridges. / You soften the earth with s
72: 6 springtime rains— / like the s that water the earth.
145: 9 to everyone. / He s compassion on all his creation.
Eze 34:26 And I will send s, s of blessings, which will
Zec 10: 1 who makes storm clouds that drop s of rain

SHOWING (14) [SHOW]

Lev 19:15 neither favoring the poor nor s deference to the
19:32 of elderly people and s respect for the aged.
Ru 2:20 "He is s his kindness to us as well as to your dead
3:10 "You are s more family loyalty now than ever by
Pr 28:21 S partiality is never good, yet some will do wrong
Hos 2:19 s you righteousness and justice, unfailing love
Mic 7:18 people forever, because you delight in s mercy.
Zec 11:10 s that I had revoked the covenant I had made with
Ac 9:39 and s him the coats and other garments Dorcas had
Ro 12: 8 And if you have a gift for s kindness to others,
1Co 10:17 we all eat from one loaf, s that we are one body.
Gal 5:15 But if instead of s love among yourselves you are
1Ti 5:21 without taking sides or s special favor to anyone.
1Jn 1:10 and s that his word has no place in our hearts.

SHOWN (58) [SHOW]

Ge 24:14 By this I will know that you have s kindness to my
32:10 and unfailing love you have s to me,
41:28 for God has s you what he is about to do.
Ex 4:17 so you can perform the miraculous signs I have s
22:13 the carcass must be s as evidence, and no payment
25:40 to the pattern I have s you here on the mountain.
26:30 to the design you were s on the mountain.
27: 8 Be careful to build it just as you were s on the
Nu 8: 4 to the exact design the LORD had s Moses.
Dt 5:24 'The LORD our God has s us his glory
Ru 2:11 and kindness you have s your mother-in-law since
1Sa 14:42 And Jonathan was s to be the guilty one.
24:19 you well for the kindness you have s me today.
2Sa 7:21 done all these great things and have s them to me.
2Ki 4:13 that we appreciate the kind concern she has s us.
8:10 But the LORD has s me that he will actually
8:13 "The LORD has s me that you are going to be the
1Ch 24: 5 of sacred lots so that no preference would be s,
2Ch 32:25 not respond appropriately to the kindness s him,
Ps 25: 6 which you have s from long ages past.
31:21 the LORD, / for he has s me his unfailing love.
78:11 the wonderful miracles he had s them,
111: 6 He has s his great power to his people / by giving
Jer 44:10 To this very hour you have s no remorse
La 2: 1 the Lord has s no mercy even to his Temple.
Eze 11:25 And I told the exiles everything the LORD had s
36: 5 because they have s utter contempt for me by
43:10 describe to the people of Israel the Temple I have s
Da 2:28 and he has s King Nebuchadnezzar what will
2:29 The revealer of mysteries has s you what is going
2:45 "The great God has s Your Majesty what will
Mal 2: 9 but have s partiality in your interpretation of the
Mt 5: 7 those who are merciful, / for they will be s mercy.
11:19 But wisdom is s to be right by what results from
Lk 7:35 But wisdom is s to be right by the lives of those
7:47 have been forgiven, so she has s me much love.
19: 9 for this man has s himself to be a son of Abraham.
Jn 15:13 the greatest love is s when people lay down their
Ac 2:28 You have s me the way of life, / and you will give
7:44 exact accordance with the plan s to Moses by God.
9:12 I have s him a vision of a man named Ananias
10:28 But God has s me that I should never think of
Ro 1: 4 And Jesus Christ our Lord was s to be the Son of
3: 9 not at all, for we have already s that all people,
3:21 But now God has s us a different way of being
1Co 1:20 and has s their wisdom to be useless nonsense.
2Co 8:22 and has s how earnest he is on many occasions.
9:14 because of the wonderful grace of God s through
Gal 3: 1 s you a signboard with a picture of Christ dying on
3:23 Until faith in Christ was s to us as the way of
Eph 2: 7 as s in all he has done for us through Christ Jesus.
1Th 4: 9 love that should be s among God's people.
1Ti 3:16 and was s to be righteous by the Spirit. / He was
Heb 6:10 and how you have s your love to him by caring for
8: 5 to the design I have s you here on the mountain."
2Pe 1:14 But the Lord Jesus Christ has s me that my days
1Jn 1: 2 This one who is life from God was s to us, and we
1: 2 He was with the Father, and then he was s to us.

SHOWS (29) [SHOW]

Dt 10:17 who s no partiality and takes no bribes.
10:18 He s love to the foreigners living among you
28:50 and heartless nation that s no respect for the old
Job 4: 8 My experience s that those who plant trouble
36: 9 He s them their sins, for they have behaved
Ps 25: 8 he s the proper path to those who go astray.
59:17 are my refuge, / the God who s me unfailing love.
Pr 3:34 mocks at mockers, but he s favor to the humble.
La 3:32 he also s compassion according to the greatness of
Da 2:43 and clay also s that these kingdoms will try to
Hos 9: 7 with sin and s only hatred for those who love God.
Mt 5:37 To strengthen your promise with a vow s that
24:28 Just as the gathering of vultures s there is a carcass
Lk 7:47 But a person who is forgiven little s only little
17:37 "Just as the gathering of vultures s there is a
Ro 1:18 But God s his anger from heaven against all sinful,
7:16 and my bad conscience s that I agree that the law is
9:18 God s mercy to some just because he wants to,
1Co 1: 6 This s that what I told you about Christ is true.
2:10 out everything and s us even God's deep secrets.
2Co 8:19 that glorifies the Lord and s our eagerness to help.
Php 3:18 that there are many whose conduct s they are really
Tit 1: 1 and to teach them to know the truth that s them
Heb 1: 4 This s that God's Son is far greater than the angels,

Jas 3:17 good deeds. It **s** no partiality and is always sincere.
4: 6 against the proud, / but he **s** favor to the humble."
1Pe 5: 5 against the proud, / but he **s** favor to the humble."
1Jn 3: 8 keep on sinning, it **s** they belong to the Devil,
4:18 and this **s** that his love has not been perfected in us.

SHRANK (1) [SHRINK]
Ac 20:20 Yet I never **s** from telling you the truth,

SHREDDED (1)
2Ki 4:39 He **s** them and put them into the kettle without

SHREWD (2) [SHREWDEST]
Lk 16: 8 had to admire the dishonest rascal for being so **s**.
16: 8 citizens of this world are more **s** than the godly are.

SHREWDEST (1) [SHREWD]
Ge 3: 1 Now the serpent was the **s** of all the creatures the

SHRIEKED (1) [SHRIEKING]
Lk 8:28 he **s** and fell to the ground before him, screaming,

SHRIEKING (2) [SHRIEKED]
Mk 3:11 they would fall down in front of him **s**, "You are
5: 7 He gave a terrible scream, **s**, "Why are you

SHRINE (14) [ENSHRINED, SHRINES]
Jdg 17: 5 Micah set up a **s**, and he made a sacred ephod
18:14 "There is a **s** here with a sacred ephod,
18:17 the five spies entered the **s** and took the carved
18:18 carrying all the sacred objects out of Micah's **s**,
1Ki 11: 7 east of Jerusalem, he even built a **s** for Chemosh,
14:24 There were even **s** prostitutes throughout the land.
15:12 He banished the **s** prostitutes from the land
22:46 He banished from the land the rest of the **s**
2Ki 23: 7 He also tore down the houses of the **s** prostitutes
23:15 the pagan **s** that Jeroboam son of Nebat had made
Eze 16:24 you built a pagan **s** and put altars to idols in every
20:29 (This idol **s** has been called Bamah—'high place'
Hos 4:14 thing, sinning with whores and **s** prostitutes.
Ac 7:43 was in your pagan gods— / the **s** of Molech,

SHRINES (65) [SHRINE]
Lev 26:30 I will destroy your pagan **s** and cut down your
Nu 33:52 and molten images and demolish all their pagan **s**.
1Ki 11: 8 Solomon built such **s** for all his foreign wives to
12:31 Jeroboam built **s** at the pagan high places
12:32 he appointed priests for the pagan **s** he had made.
13: 2 from the pagan **s** who come here to burn incense,
13:32 and against the pagan **s** in the towns of Samaria
13:33 wanted to could become a priest for the pagan **s**.
14:23 They built pagan **s** and set up sacred pillars
15:14 Although the pagan **s** were not completely
22:43 however, he failed to remove all the pagan **s**,
2Ki 12: 3 Yet even so, he did not destroy the pagan **s**,
14: 4 Amaziah did not destroy the pagan **s**,
15: 4 But he did not destroy the pagan **s**,
15:35 But he did not destroy the pagan **s**,
16: 4 and burned incense at the pagan **s** and on the hills
17: 9 They built pagan **s** for themselves in all their
17:11 They burned incense at the **s**, just like the nations
17:29 they placed their idols at the pagan **s** that the
17:32 themselves priests to offer sacrifices at the pagan **s**.
18: 4 He removed the pagan **s**, smashed the sacred
18:22 Didn't Hezekiah tear down his **s** and altars
21: 3 He rebuilt the pagan **s** his father, Hezekiah,
23: 5 for they had burned incense at the pagan **s**
23: 8 He also defiled all the pagan **s**, where they had
23: 8 He destroyed the **s** at the entrance to the gate of
23: 9 The priests who had served at the pagan **s** were not
23:13 The king also desecrated the pagan **s** east of
23:13 where King Solomon of Israel had built **s** for
23:19 buildings at the pagan **s** in the towns of Samaria,
23:20 He executed the priests of the pagan **s** on their own
2Ch 11:15 appointed his own priests to serve at the pagan **s**,
14: 3 He removed the pagan altars and the **s**,
14: 5 Asa also removed the pagan **s**, as well as the
15:17 Although the pagan **s** were not completely
17: 6 He knocked down the pagan **s** and destroyed the
20:33 however, he failed to remove all the pagan **s**,
21:11 He had built pagan **s** in the hill country of Judah
28: 4 and burned incense at the pagan **s** and on the hills
28:25 He made pagan **s** in all the towns of Judah for
31: 1 Asherah poles, and removed the pagan **s** and altars.
32:12 the very person who destroyed all the LORD's **s**
33: 3 He rebuilt the pagan **s** his father Hezekiah had
33:17 However, the people still sacrificed at the pagan **s**,
33:19 a list of the locations where he built pagan **s**
34: 3 and Jerusalem, destroying all the pagan **s**,
Isa 15: 2 people in Dibon will mourn at their temples and **s**,
36: 7 Didn't Hezekiah tear down his **s** and altars
Jer 7:31 They have built the pagan **s** of Topheth in the
17: 3 and treasures—together with your pagan **s**—
19: 5 They have built pagan **s** to Baal, and there they
32:35 They have built pagan **s** to Baal in the valley of the
48:35 "for they offer sacrifices at the pagan **s** and burn
Eze 6: 3 war upon you, and I will destroy your pagan **s**.
6: 6 I will destroy your pagan **s**, your altars, your idols,
16:16 You used the lovely things I gave you to make **s**
16:31 You build your pagan **s** on every street corner
16:39 They will knock down your pagan **s** and the altars
Hos 10: 8 And the pagan **s** of Aven, the place of Israel's sin,
Am 7: 9 The pagan **s** of your ancestors and the temples of
Mic 5:14 I will abolish your pagan **s** with their Asherah
Mt 17: 4 I'll make three **s**, one for you, one for Moses,
Mk 9: 5 "We will make three **s**—one for you, one for
Lk 9:33 We will make three **s**—one for you, one for Moses,
Ac 19:24 silver **s** of the Greek goddess Artemis.

SHRINK (4) [SHRANK, SHRINKS]
Jer 2:12 at such a thing and **s** back in horror and dismay,
Na 3: 7 All who see you will **s** back in horror and say,
Ac 20:27 for I didn't **s** from declaring all that God wants for
1Jn 2:28 full of courage and not **s** back from him in shame.

SHRINKS (2) [SHRINK]
Mt 9:16 For the patch **s** and pulls away from the old cloth,
Mk 2:21 For the new patch **s** and pulls away from the old

SHRIVEL (2) [SHRIVELED]
Zec 14:12 Their eyes will **s** in their sockets, and their tongues
Mal 3:11 Your grapes will not **s** before they are ripe,"

SHRIVELED (3) [SHRIVEL]
Ge 41: 6 but these were **s** and withered by the east wind.
41:23 came seven withered heads, **s** by the east wind.
Ps 119:83 I am **s** like a wineskin in the smoke,

SHROUDED (4) [SHROUDS]
Dt 4:11 into the sky, **s** in black clouds and deep darkness.
2Sa 22:12 He **s** himself in darkness, / veiling his approach
Job 3: 4 even to God on high, and let it be **s** in darkness.
Ps 18:11 He **s** himself in darkness, / veiling his approach

SHROUDS (1) [SHROUDED]
Job 26: 9 He **s** his throne with his clouds.

SHRUBS (2)
Job 30: 4 coarse leaves, and they burn the roots of **s** for heat.
Jer 17: 6 They are like stunted **s** in the desert, with no hope

SHRUG (1) [SHRUGGED]
Pr 30:20 **s** her shoulders, and then say, "What's wrong with

SHRUGGED (1) [SHRUG]
Jer 34:16 But now you have **s** off your oath and defiled my

SHUA (2)
Ge 38: 2 the daughter of **S**, and he married her.
1Ch 7:32 Shomer, and Hotham. They had a sister named **S**.

SHUAH (2)
Ge 25: 2 Jokshan, Medan, Midian, Ishbak, and **S**.
1Ch 1:32 Jokshan, Medan, Midian, Ishbak, and **S**.

SHUAL (2)
1Sa 13:17 One went north toward Ophrah in the land of **S**,
1Ch 7:36 of Zophah were Suah, Harnepher, **S**, Beri, Imrah,

SHUBAEL (2)
1Ch 25: 4 Uzziel, **S**, Jerimoth, Hananiah, Hanani, Eliathah,
25:20 The thirteenth lot fell to **S** and twelve of his sons

SHUDDER (2)
Job 21: 6 When I think about what I am saying, I **s**. My body
Eze 32:10 They will **s** in fear for their lives as I brandish my

SHUHAH (1)
1Ch 4:11 Kelub (the brother of **S**) was the father of Mehir.

SHUHAM (1) [SHUHAMITE]
Nu 26:42 The Shuhamite clan, named after its ancestor **S**.

SHUHAMITE (2) [SHUHAM]
Nu 26:42 The **S** clan, named after its ancestor Shuham.
26:43 All the clans of Dan were **S** clans, and the men

SHUHITE (5)
Job 2:11 Bildad the **S**, and Zophar the Naamathite.
8: 1 Then Bildad the **S** replied to Job:
18: 1 Then Bildad the **S** replied:
25: 1 Then Bildad the **S** replied:
42: 9 So Eliphaz the Temanite, Bildad the **S**, and Zophar

SHULAM (2)
SS 6:13 "Return, return to us, O maid of **S**. Come back,
6:13 do you gaze so intently at this young woman of **S**,

SHUMATHITES (1)
1Ch 2:53 the Ithrites, Puthites, **S**, and Mishraites,

SHUNEM (8)
Jos 19:18 the following towns: Jezreel, Kesulloth, **S**,
1Sa 28: 4 The Philistines set up their camp at **S**, and Saul
1Ki 1: 3 and they found Abishag from **S** and brought her to
2:17 to give me Abishag, the girl from **S**, as my wife."
2:21 marry Abishag, the girl from **S**," she replied.
2Ki 4: 8 One day Elisha went to the town of **S**. A wealthy
4:11 One day Elisha returned to **S**, and he went up to his
4:25 to Gehazi, "Look, the woman from **S** is coming.

SHUNI (2) [SHUNITE]
Ge 46:16 Haggi, **S**, Ezbon, Eri, Arodi, and Areli.
Nu 26:15 The Shunite clan, named after its ancestor **S**.

SHUNITE (1) [SHUNI]
Nu 26:15 The **S** clan, named after its ancestor Shuni.

SHUPHAM (1) [MUPPIM, SHUPHAMITE]
Nu 26:39 The Shuphamite clan, named after its ancestor **S**.

SHUPHAMITE (1) [SHUPHAM]
Nu 26:39 The **S** clan, named after its ancestor Shupham.

SHUPPIM (3)
1Ch 7:12 The sons of Ir were **S** and Huppim. Hushim was
7:15 Makir found wives for Huppim and **S**.
26:16 **S** and Hosah were assigned the west gate

SHUR (6)
Ge 16: 7 Hagar beside a desert spring along the road to **S**.
20: 1 between Kadesh and **S** at a place called Gerar.
25:18 scattered across the country from Havilah to **S**,
Ex 15:22 the Red Sea, and they moved out into the **S** Desert.
1Sa 15: 7 the Amalekites from Havilah all the way to **S**,
27: 8 people who had lived near **S**, along the road to

SHUSHAN [KJV] See SUSA

SHUT (47) [SHUTS, SHUTTING]
Ge 7:16 God had commanded. Then the LORD **s** them in.
Dt 11:17 He will **s** up the sky and hold back the rain,
Jos 2: 7 soon as the king's men had left, the city gate was **s**.
6: 1 Now the gates of Jericho were tightly **s**
1Sa 6: 7 but **s** their calves away from them in a pen.
6:10 to the cart, and their calves were **s** up in a pen.
1Ki 8:35 "If the skies are **s** up and there is no rain
2Ki 4: 4 house with your sons and **s** the door behind you.
4:21 the man of God, then **s** the door and left him there.
4:33 He went in alone and **s** the door behind him
6:32 When he arrives, **s** the door and keep him out.
2Ch 6:26 "If the skies are **s** up and there is no rain
7:13 At times I might **s** up the heavens so that no rain
28:24 He **s** the doors of the LORD's Temple so that no
29: 7 They also **s** the doors to the Temple's foyer,
Ne 6:10 inside the Temple of God and bolt the doors **s**.
7: 3 are still on duty, have them **s** and bar the doors.
13:19 then on the gates of the city should be **s** as
Job 3:10 Curse it for its failure to **s** my mother's womb,
Pr 17:28 when they keep their mouths **s**, they seem
21:13 Those who **s** their ears to the cries of the poor will
21:23 If you keep your mouth **s**, you will stay out of
Ecc 5: 1 of God, keep your ears open and your mouth **s**!
SS 8: 9 she is promiscuous, we will **s** her off from men."
Isa 6:10 Close their ears, and **s** their eyes. That way,
22:22 will open doors, and no one will be able to **s** them;
30:10 They tell the prophets, "**S** up! We don't want any
33:15 who **s** their eyes to all enticement to do wrong.
44:18 Their minds are **s**, and they cannot think.
45: 1 gates will be opened, never again to **s** against him.
Eze 3:24 to me and said, "Go, **s** yourself up in your house.
44: 2 entered here. Thus, it must always remain **s**.
46:12 he entered, and the gateway will be **s** behind him.
Da 6:22 My God sent his angel to **s** the lions' mouths
Am 2:12 your wine, and you said to my prophets, '**S** up!'
3: 5 Does a trap ever spring **s** when there's nothing
Mal 1:10 "I wish that someone among you would **s** the
Mt 6: 6 go away by yourself, **s** the door behind you,
Mk 4:21 it under a basket or under a bed to **s** out the light?
Ro 11: 8 To this very day he has **s** their eyes so they do not
Gal 4:17 They are trying to **s** you off from me so that you
Eph 4:18 the life of God because they have **s** their minds
Heb 11:33 had promised them. They **s** the mouths of lions,
Rev 3: 7 He opens doors, and no one can **s** them; he shuts
3: 8 and I have opened a door for you that no one can **s**.
11: 6 They have power to **s** the skies so that no rain will
20: 3 which he then **s** and locked so Satan could not

SHUTHELAH (3) [SHUTHELAHITE, SHUTHELAHITES]
Nu 26:35 The Shuthelahite clan, named after its ancestor **S**.
1Ch 7:20 The descendants of Ephraim were **S**, Bered,
7:21 Zabad, and **S**. / Ephraim's sons Ezer and Elead

SHUTHELAHITE (1) [SHUTHELAH]
Nu 26:35 The **S** clan, named after its ancestor Shuthelah.

SHUTHELAHITES (1) [SHUTHELAH]
Nu 26:36 This was the subclan descended from the **S**:

SHUTS (4) [SHUT]
La 3: 8 And though I cry and shout, he **s** out my prayers.
Mt 6:23 But an evil eye **s** out the light and plunges you into
Lk 11:34 But an evil eye **s** out the light and plunges you into
Rev 3: 7 shut them; he **s** doors, and no one can open them.

SHUTTING (2) [SHUT]
Ge 19: 6 outside to talk to them, **s** the door behind him.
La 3: 2 has brought me into deep darkness, **s** out all light.

SHUTTLE (4)

Jdg 16:13 fabric on your loom and tighten it with the loom s,
16:14 and tightened it with the loom s. Again she cried
16:14 But Samson woke up, pulled back the loom s,
Job 7:6 "My days are swifter than a weaver's s flying back

SIAHA (2)

Ezr 2:44 Keros, S, Padon,
Ne 7:47 Keros, S, Padon,

SIBBECAI (5)

2Sa 21:18 As they fought, S from Hushah killed Saph,
23:27 Abiezer from Anathoth; / S from Hushah;
1Ch 11:29 S from Hushah; / Zalmon from Ahoah;
20:4 As they fought, S from Hushah killed Saph,
27:11 S, a descendant of Zerah from Hushah,

SIBBOLETH (1) [SHIBBOLETH]

Jdg 12:6 If he was from Ephraim, he would say "S,"

SIBMAH (5)

Nu 32:38 Nebo, Baal-meon, and S. They changed the names
Jos 13:19 Kiriathaim, S, Zereth-shahar on the hill above the
Isa 16:8 farms of Heshbon and the vineyards at S.
16:9 and lament for Jazer and the vineyards of S.
Jer 48:32 "You people of S, rich in vineyards, I will weep

SIBRAIM (1)

Eze 47:16 then it will run to Berothah and S, which are on the

SICHEM [KJV] See SHECHEM

SICK (96) [SICKBED, SICKENING, SICKLY, SICKNESS, SICKNESSES]

Ge 27:46 "I'm s and tired of these local Hittite women.
Nu 11:20 it for a whole month until you gag and are s of it.
Dt 17:1 "Never sacrifice a s or defective ox or sheep to the
28:59 making you miserable and unbearably s.
1Sa 19:14 she told them he was s and couldn't get out of bed.
30:13 left me behind three days ago because I was s.
2Sa 12:18 "He was so broken up about the baby being s,"
13:5 what to do. Go back to bed and pretend you are s.
13:6 So Amnon pretended to be s. And when the king
1Ki 14:1 At that time Jeroboam's son Abijah became very s.
14:5 She will ask you about her son, for he is very s.
17:17 Some time later, the woman's son became s.
2Ki 8:7 the capital of Aram, where King Ben-hadad lay s.
20:12 for he had heard that Hezekiah had been very s.
2Ch 36:17 and old, men and women, healthy and s.
Ne 2:2 "Why are you so sad? You aren't s, are you?
Ps 6:3 I am s at heart. / How long, O LORD, until you
35:12 with evil for the good I do. / I am s with despair.
38:3 Because of your anger, my whole body is s;
41:3 The LORD nurses them when they are s
102:4 My heart is s, withered like grass, / and I have lost
105:37 there were no s or feeble people among them.
Pr 13:12 Hope deferred makes the heart s, but when dreams
18:14 The human spirit can endure a s body, but who can
25:16 Don't eat too much of it, or it will make you s!
SS 5:8 my beloved one, tell him that I am s with love."
Isa 1:5 Your head is injured, and your heart is s.
1:6 You are s from head to foot—covered with bruises,
1:11 "I am s of your sacrifices," says the LORD.
10:18 and they will waste away like s people in a plague.
19:10 The weavers and all the workers will be s at heart.
19:14 They cause the land of Egypt to stagger like a s
33:24 "We are s and helpless," for the LORD will
39:1 He had heard that Hezekiah had been very s
La 5:17 Our hearts are s and weary, and our eyes grow dim
Eze 16:30 "What a s heart you have, says the Sovereign
34:4 You have not tended the s or bound up the broken
34:21 For you fat sheep push and butt and crowd my s
Da 8:27 Daniel, was overcome and lay s for several days.
Hos 4:3 and all living things are becoming s and dying.
5:13 "When Israel and Judah saw how s they were,
Mal 1:13 that are stolen and mutilated, crippled and s—
Mt 4:24 so that the s were soon coming to be healed from
8:16 commanded them to leave; and he healed all the s.
9:12 people don't need a doctor—s people do."
10:8 Heal the s, raise the dead, cure those with leprosy,
12:15 followed him. He healed all the s among them,
14:14 and he had compassion on them and healed their s.
14:35 and soon people were bringing all their s to be
14:36 The s begged him to let them touch even the fringe
19:2 crowds followed him there, and he healed their s.
25:36 I was s, and you cared for me. I was in prison,
25:39 When did we ever see you s or in prison, and visit
25:43 I was s and in prison, and you didn't visit me.'
25:44 or thirsty or a stranger or naked or s or in prison,
Mk 1:30 Simon's mother-in-law was s in bed with a high
1:32 many s and demon-possessed people were brought
1:34 So Jesus healed great numbers of s people who had
2:4 Then they lowered the s man on his mat,
2:17 "Healthy people don't need a doctor—s people do.
3:10 a result, many s people were crowding around him,
6:5 them except to place his hands on a few s people
6:13 cast out many demons and healed many s people,
6:55 and began carrying s people to him on mats.
6:56 they laid the s in the market plazas and streets.
6:56 The s begged him to let them at least touch the
16:18 They will be able to place their hands on the s
Lk 4:38 where he found Simon's mother-in-law very s with
4:40 people throughout the village brought s family
5:19 and lowered the s man down into the crowd,
5:31 "Healthy people don't need a doctor—s people do.
7:2 the highly valued slave of a Roman officer was s
9:2 coming of the Kingdom of God and to heal the s.
9:6 preaching the Good News and healing the s.
10:9 and heal the s. As you heal them, say,
14:4 Jesus touched the s man and healed him and sent
Jn 4:46 in the city of Capernaum whose son was very s.
5:3 Crowds of s people—blind, lame, or paralyzed—
5:5 One of the men lying there had been s for
5:7 "I can't, sir," the s man said, "for I have no one
6:2 because they saw his miracles as he healed the s.
11:1 A man named Lazarus was s. He lived in Bethany
11:2 them with her hair. Her brother, Lazarus, was s.
11:3 telling him, "Lord, the one you love is very s."
Ac 5:15 s people were brought out into the streets on beds
5:16 bringing their s and those possessed by evil spirits,
19:12 that had touched his skin were placed on s people,
28:9 Then all the other s people on the island came
1Co 11:30 of you are weak and s and some have even died.
12:9 to someone else he gives the power to heal the s.
Gal 4:13 Surely you remember that I was s when I first
1Ti 5:23 sake of your stomach because you are s so often.
2Ti 4:20 at Corinth, and I left Trophimus s at Miletus.
Jas 5:14 Are any among you s? They should call for the
5:15 And their prayer offered in faith will heal the s,
2Pe 2:7 because he was a good man who was s of all the

SICKBED (1) [BED, SICK]

Rev 2:22 Therefore, I will throw her upon a s, and she will

SICKENING (1) [SICK]

Ecc 6:2 others get it all! This is meaningless—a s tragedy.

SICKLE (11) [SICKLES]

Dt 23:25 grain by hand, but you may not harvest it with a s.
1Sa 13:21 an ounce for sharpening an ax, a s, or an ox goad.)
Joel 3:13 Now let the s do its work, for the harvest is ripe.
Mk 4:29 the farmer comes and harvests it with a s."
Rev 14:14 a gold crown on his head and a sharp s in his hand.
14:15 "Use the s, for the time has come for you to
14:16 So the one sitting on the cloud swung his s over the
14:17 the Temple in heaven, and he also had a sharp s.
14:18 the world with fire, shouted to the angel with the s,
14:18 "Use your s now to gather the clusters of grapes
14:19 So the angel swung his s on the earth and loaded

SICKLES (1) [SICKLE]

1Sa 13:20 picks, axes, or s, they had to take them to a

SICKLY (1) [SICK]

Ps 88:15 I have been s and close to death since my youth.

SICKNESS (13) [SICK]

Dt 7:15 And the LORD will protect you from all s.
28:61 The LORD will bring against you every s
Job 33:19 Or God disciplines people with s and pain,
Isa 38:15 what could I say? / For he himself had sent this s.
Jer 6:7 Her s and sores are ever before me.
10:19 grief is great. My s is incurable, but I must bear it.
La 1:13 has made me desolate, racked with s all day long.
Eze 4:14 now I have never eaten any animal that died of s
Mt 4:23 And he healed people who had every kind of s
Lk 13:12 and said, "Woman, you are healed of your s!"
Jn 11:4 it he said, "Lazarus's s will not end in death.
Ac 12:23 an angel of the Lord struck Herod with a s,
Gal 4:14 But even though my s was revolting to you,

SICKNESSES (1) [SICK]

Mt 8:17 "He took our s and removed our diseases."

SIDDIM (1)

Ge 14:3 and mobilized their armies in S Valley (that is,

SIDE (247) [ASIDE, BESIDE, FIVE-SIDED, FOUR-SIDED, SIDED, SIDES, SIDETRACKED]

EAST SIDE (27) Ex 38:14; Lev 1:16; Nu 2:3; 10:5; 32:19, 22; 34:11,15; 35:14; Jos 1:14,15; 13:8; 14:3; 17:1; 18:7; 20:8; 22:4; 24:8; Jdg 21:19; 1Ch 9:18; 12:37; 26:32; 2Ch 5:12; Eze 42:16; 43:17; 45:7; Jnh 4:5

NORTH SIDE (18) Ex 26:20,26; 27:11; 36:25,32; 40:22; Lev 1:11; Nu 2:25; Jos 8:11; 18:18; 1Ki 7:39; 2Ki 11:11; 16:14; 2Ch 23:10; Eze 40:23,38; 42:11,17

ON EVERY SIDE (8) Jos 21:44; 1Ki 5:4; 2Ch 15:15; 20:30; Job 19:10; Ps 3:6; Eze 23:24; 2Co 4:8

OTHER SIDE (31) Ge 32:23; Ex 14:26; Nu 32:19; Dt 3:25; Jos 2:1; 4:11; 7:7; Jdg 11:18; 1Sa 31:7; 2Sa 10:16; 2Ki 2:9; 1Ch 19:16; 2Ch 7:6; Eze 41:19; Zec 5:3; Mt 8:18,28; 14:22; 16:5; Mk 4:35; 5:1,21; 6:53; 8:13; Lk 8:22,37,40; 10:31,32; Jn 1:28; 3:26

SOUTH SIDE (17) Ex 26:18,27,35; 27:9; 36:23,31; 40:24; Nu 2:10; Jos 15:7; 1Ki 6:8; 7:39; 2Ki 11:11; 2Ch 23:10; Eze 42:10,18; 47:1,2

WEST SIDE (15) Ex 26:22; 36:27,30,32; Nu 2:18; Dt 3:21; Jos 8:9,12; 12:7; 17:2; Jdg 10:9; 2Ch 32:30; Eze 42:19; 45:7; 47:20

Ge 6:16 middle, and upper—and put a door in the s.
15:10 one down the middle and laid the halves s by s.
29:12 explained that he was her cousin on her father's s,
32:23 After they were on the other s, he sent over all his
46:4 But you will die in Egypt with Joseph at your s."
Ex 14:22 sea on dry ground, with walls of water on each s!
14:26 When all the Israelites were on the other s,
17:12 Then they stood on each s, holding up his hands
25:12 attach them to its four feet, two rings on each s.
25:32 three branches going out from each s of the center
26:13 will hang down an extra eighteen inches on each s.
26:18 Twenty of these frames will support the south s of
26:20 On the north s there will also be twenty of these
26:22 On the west s there will be six frames,
26:26 five crossbars for the north s of the Tabernacle
26:27 and five for the south s. Also make five crossbars
26:35 The lampstand must be placed on the south s,
27:9 On the south s the curtains will stretch for 150 feet.
27:11 It will be the same on the north s of the courtyard
27:14 The curtain on the right s will be 22-1/2 feet long,
27:15 The curtain on the left s will also be 22-1/2 feet
32:26 "All of you who are on the LORD's s,
36:23 They made twenty frames to support the south s,
36:25 They also made twenty frames for the north s of
36:27 The west s of the Tabernacle, which was its rear,
36:30 So for the west s they made a total of eight frames,
36:31 wood to tie the frames on the south s together.
36:32 another five for the north s and five for the west s.
36:33 along each s, running from one end to the other.
37:3 were fastened to its four feet, two rings at each s.
37:18 three going out from each s of the center stem.
38:5 Four rings were cast for each s of the grating to
38:7 These poles were inserted into the rings at the s of
38:14 The courtyard entrance was on the east s,
38:14 The curtain on the right s was 22-1/2 feet long
38:15 The curtain on the left s was also 22-1/2 feet long
40:22 along the north s of the Holy Place, just outside the
40:24 from the table on the south s of the Holy Place.
Lev 1:11 Slaughter the animal on the north s of the altar in
1:16 and throw them to the east s of the altar among the
Nu 2:3[-4] the sunrise on the east s of the Tabernacle,
2:9 So the total of all the troops on Judah's s of the
2:10[-11] and Gad are to camp on the south s of the
2:16 So the total of all the troops on Reuben's s of the
2:18[-19] and Benjamin are to camp on the west s of
2:24 So the total of all the troops on Ephraim's s of the
2:25[-26] and Naphtali are to camp on the north s of the
2:31 So the total of all the troops on Dan's s of the
10:5 the tribes on the east s of the Tabernacle will break
21:13 Then they moved to the far s of the Arnon River,
32:19 But we do not want any of the land on the other s
32:19 We would rather live here on the east s where we
32:22 And the land on the east s of the Jordan will be
32:32 but our inheritance of land will be here on this s of
34:11 then down to Riblah on the east s of Ain.
34:15 on the east s of the Jordan River, across from
35:14 three on the east s of the Jordan River and three on
36:11 and Noah all married cousins on their father's s.
Dt 1:1 between Paran on one s and Tophel, Laban,
2:27 and won't turn off into the fields on either s.
3:21 to all the kingdoms on the west s of the Jordan.
3:25 the Jordan to see the wonderful land on the other s,
4:22 the land, I will die here on this s of the river.
Jos 1:14 and cattle may remain here on the east s of the
1:15 then may you settle here on the east s of the Jordan
2:1 "Spy out the land on the other s of the Jordan
4:11 And when everyone was on the other s, the priests
6:20 charged straight into the city from every s
7:7 If only we had been content to stay on the other s!
8:9 lay in ambush between Bethel and the west s of Ai.
8:11 They camped on the north s of Ai, with a valley
8:12 between Bethel and Ai, on the west s of the city.
12:7 and the Israelite armies defeated on the west s of
13:8 their inheritance on the east s of the Jordan,
14:3 and a half tribes on the east s of the Jordan River.
15:7 slopes of Adummim on the south s of the valley.
17:1 and Bashan on the east s of the Jordan had already
17:2 Land on the west s of the Jordan was allotted to the
17:9 the border of Manasseh followed the northern s of
18:7 gave them on the east s of the Jordan River."
18:18 From there it passed along the north s of the slope
20:8 On the east s of the Jordan River, across from
21:44 And the LORD gave them rest on every s, just as
22:4 gave you on the east s of the Jordan River.
22:19 land is defiled, then join us on our s of the river,
23:13 to you, a pain in your s and a thorn in your eyes,
24:8 land of the Amorites on the east s of the Jordan.
Jdg 5:6 and travelers stayed on crooked s paths.
10:9 The Ammonites also crossed to the west s of the
11:18 and camped on the other s of the Arnon River.
21:19 along the east s of the road that goes from Bethel
1Sa 20:20 and shoot three arrows to the s of the stone pile as
20:21 tell him, 'They're on this s,' then you will know,
22:8 has ever told me that my own son is on David's s.
31:7 When the Israelites on the other s of the Jezreel
2Sa 2:15 So twelve men were chosen from each s to fight
2:16 and thrust his sword into the other's s so that all of
3:21 me go and call all the people of Israel to your s.
10:16 Hadadezer from the other s of the Euphrates River.
13:34 from the Horonaim road along the s of the hill."
1Ki 2:22 the priest and Joab son of Zeruiah on his s."
5:4 LORD my God has given me peace on every s,
6:8 The entrance to the bottom floor was on the south s
6:27 Solomon placed them s by s in the inner
7:4 On each of the s walls there were three rows of
7:28 They were constructed with s panels braced with
7:30 were decorated with carvings of wreaths on each s.
7:35 and s panels were cast as one unit with the cart.
7:39 the south s of the Temple and five on the north s.

10:19 with the figure of a lion standing on each s of the
2Ki 2:9 When they came to the other s, Elijah said to
6:16 "For there are more on our s than on theirs!"
9:32 at the window and shouted, "Who is on my s?"
10:6 "If you are on my s and are going to obey me,
11:11 the south s of the Temple around to the north s
12:9 and set it on the right-hand s of the altar at the
16:14 and placed it on the north s of the new altar.
16:17 Then the king removed the s panels and basins
23:16 he noticed several tombs in the s of the hill.
1Ch 9:18 were responsible for the King's Gate on the east s.
12:18 We are on your s, son of Jesse. / Peace
12:37 From the east s of the Jordan River—
19:16 troops from the other s of the Euphrates River.
23:28 They also took care of the courtyards and s rooms,
26:32 King David sent them to the east s of the Jordan
2Ch 3:11 The total wingspan of the two cherubim standing s by s was 30 feet.
5:12 and stood at the east s of the altar playing cymbals,
7:6 On the other s of the Levites, the priests blew the
9:18 with the figure of a lion standing on each s of the
15:15 gave them rest from their enemies on every s.
20:30 at peace, for his God had given him rest on every s.
23:10 The south s of the Temple around to the north s
32:7 for there is a power far greater on our s!
32:30 through a tunnel to the west s of the City of David.
Ne 3:21 the door of Eliashib's house to the s of the house.
4:18 All the builders had a sword belted to their s.
Job 15:10 On our s are aged, gray-haired men much older
19:10 He has demolished me on every s, and I am
31:35 who would listen to me and try to see my s!
Ps 3:6 thousand enemies / who surround me on every s.
45:9 At your right s stands the queen, / wearing jewelry
56:9 enemies will retreat. / This I know: God is on my s.
91:7 Though a thousand fall at your s, / though ten
94:20 Can unjust leaders claim that God is on their s—
119:154 Argue my case; take my s! / Protect my life as you
124:1 If the LORD had not been on our s— / let Israel
124:2 if the LORD had not been on our s / when people
Pr 8:30 I was the architect at his s. I was his constant
Isa 50:9 See, the Sovereign LORD is on my s! Who will
54:15 will always be defeated because I am on your s.
Jer 50:15 Shout against her from every s. Look!
51:2 They will come from every s to rise against her in
51:31 Messengers from every s come running to the king
Eze 1:10 the face of a lion on the right s, the face of an ox on the left s,
1:11 the wings of the living beings on either s of it,
4:4 "Now lie on your left s and place the sins of Israel
4:4 sins for the number of days you lie there on your s.
4:6 turn over and lie on your right s for 40 days—
4:8 so you won't be able to turn from s to s until the
4:9 during the 390 days you will be lying on your s.
9:2 and carried a writer's case strapped to his s.
23:24 They will take up positions on every s,
40:7 There were guard alcoves on each s built into the
40:10 There were three guard alcoves on each s of the
40:21 too, there were three guard alcoves on each s,
40:23 Here on the north s, just as on the east, there was
40:38 s into a s room where the meat for sacrifices was
40:39 On each s of this foyer were two tables,
40:40 on each s of the stairs going up to the north
40:49 ten steps leading up to it, with a column on each s.
41:2 and the walls on each s were 8-3/4 feet wide.
41:3 and the walls on each s of the entrance extended
41:8 which provided a foundation for the s rooms.
41:9 The outer wall of the Temple's s rooms was 8-3/4
41:9 This left an open area between these s rooms
41:11 Two doors opened from the s rooms into the
41:19 of a man—looked toward the palm tree on one s.
41:19 looked toward the palm tree on the other s.
42:10 On the south s of the Temple there were two
42:11 just like the complex on the north s of the Temple.
42:16 He measured the east s; it was 875 feet long.
42:17 He also measured the north s and got the same
42:18 The south s was the same length,
42:19 and so was the west s.
42:20 So the area was 875 feet on each s with a wall all
43:17 measuring 24-1/2 feet on each s, with a 21-inch
43:17 There are steps going up the east s of the altar."
45:7 One section will share a border with the east s of
45:7 second section will share a border on the west s.
47:1 then passed to the right of the altar on its south s.
47:2 out through the south s of the east gateway.
47:20 "On the west s the Mediterranean itself will be
48:16 The city will measure 1-1/2 miles on each s.
48:20 is a square that measures 8-1/3 miles on each s.
Da 7:5 It was rearing up on one s, and it had three ribs in
11:32 violated the covenant and win them over to his s.
Jnh 4:5 Then Jonah went out to the east s of the city
Mic 7:10 my enemies will see that the LORD is on my s.
Zec 4:3 I see two olive trees, one on each s of the bowl."
4:11 "What are these two olive trees on each s of the
5:3 One s says that those who steal will be banished
5:3 the other s says that those who swear falsely will
Mt 8:18 he instructed his disciples to cross to the other s of
8:28 When Jesus arrived on the other s of the lake in the
14:22 and cross to the other s of the lake while he sent
14:29 So Peter went over the s of the boat and walked on
16:5 Later, after they crossed to the other s of the lake,
27:38 crucified with him, their crosses on either s of his.
Mk 4:35 "Let's cross to the other s of the lake."
5:1 So they arrived at the other s of the lake,
5:21 When Jesus went back across to the other s of the
6:53 When they arrived at Gennesaret on the other s of
8:13 left them, and he crossed to the other s of the lake.
15:27 crucified with him, their crosses on either s of his.
Lk 8:22 "Let's cross over to the other s of the lake."
8:37 and left, crossing back to the other s of the lake.
8:40 On the other s of the lake the crowds received
9:47 their thoughts, so he brought a little child to his s.
10:31 he crossed to the other s of the road and passed
10:32 lying there, but he also passed by on the other s.
23:33 the center cross, and the two criminals on either s.
Jn 3:26 the man you met on the other s of the Jordan River,
19:18 one on either s, with Jesus between them.
19:34 however, pierced his s with a spear, and blood
20:7 Jesus' head was folded up and lying to the s.
20:20 hands for them to see, and he showed them his s.
20:25 and place my hand into the wound in his s."
20:27 my hands. Put your hand into the wound in my s.
21:6 "Throw out your net on the right-hand s of the
Ac 12:7 The angel tapped him on the s to awaken him
27:7 so we sailed down to the leeward s of Crete,
Ro 12:9 Hate what is wrong. Stand on the s of the good.
2Co 4:8 We are pressed on every s by troubles, but we are
Php 1:27 I will know that you are standing s by s,
Rev 21:13 There were three gates on each s—east, north,
22:2 On each s of the river grew a tree of life,

SIDED (2) [SIDE]

2Ch 11:13 the northern tribes of Israel s with Rehoboam.
Ac 14:4 Some s with the Jews, and some with the apostles.

SIDES (53) [SIDE]

Ex 12:7 and s of the doorframe of the house where the
12:22 the hyssop against the top and s of the doorframe,
12:23 sees the blood on the top and s of the doorframe,
14:29 as the water stood up like a wall on both s.
25:14 Fit the poles into the rings at the s of the Ark to
27:7 put the poles into the rings at two s of the altar.
29:16 will be collected and sprinkled on the s of the altar.
29:20 Sprinkle the rest of the blood on the s of the altar.
30:3 Overlay the top, s, and horns of the altar with pure
30:4 Beneath the molding, on opposite s of the altar,
32:15 They were inscribed on both s, front and back.
37:5 He put the poles into the rings at the s of the Ark to
37:26 He overlaid the top, s, and horns of the altar with
37:27 Two gold rings were placed on opposite s,
Lev 1:5 will present the blood by sprinkling it against the s
1:11 will sprinkle its blood against the s of the altar.
1:15 then let its blood drain out against the s of the altar.
3:2 then sprinkle the animal's blood against the s of
3:8 then sprinkle the sheep's blood against the s of the
3:13 sprinkle the goat's blood against the s of the altar.
5:9 blood of the sin offering against the s of the altar,
7:2 and its blood sprinkled against the s of the altar.
8:19 and sprinkled it against the s of the altar.
8:24 then sprinkled the rest of the blood against the s of
9:12 and he sprinkled it against the s of the altar.
9:18 and he sprinkled it against the s of the altar.
Nu 33:55 be like splinters in your eyes and thorns in your s.
Jdg 2:3 They will be thorns in your s, and their gods will
7:18 those of you on the other s of the camp blow your
20:37 Then those who were in hiding rushed in from all s
1Sa 23:26 and David were now on opposite s of a mountain.
2Sa 2:13 facing each other from opposite s of the pool.
1Ki 6:5 all the way around the s and rear of the building.
6:10 there was a complex of rooms on three s of the
7:9 cut and trimmed to exact measure on all s.
10:19 On both s of the seat were armrests, with the figure
1Ch 9:24 The gatekeepers were stationed on all four s—
2Ch 9:18 On both s of the seat were armrests, with the figure
Job 1:19 swept in from the desert and hit the house on all s.
Jer 30:6 hands pressed against their s like women about to
52:23 There were ninety-six pomegranates on the s,
Eze 2:10 and I saw that both s were covered with funeral
30:25 while the arms of Pharaoh fall useless to his s.
41:22 Its corners, base, and s were all made of wood.
41:26 On both s of the foyer there were recessed
47:7 many trees were now growing on both s of the
47:12 All kinds of fruit trees will grow along both s of
Na 3:8 surrounded by rivers, protected by water on all s?
Zec 8:10 from the enemy, for there were enemies on all s.
Lk 3:3 Then John went from place to place on both s of
Ac 23:10 and the men were tugging at Paul from both s,
1Ti 5:21 angels to obey these instructions without taking s
Heb 9:4 which was covered with gold on all s.

SIDETRACKED (1) [SIDE]

Pr 4:27 Don't get s; keep your feet from following evil.

SIDON (38) [SIDONIANS]

Ge 10:15 Canaan's oldest son was S, the ancestor of the
10:19 Eventually the territory of Canaan spread from S to
49:13 be a harbor for ships; / his borders will extend to S.
Jos 11:8 The Israelites chased them as far as Great S
19:28 Rehob, Hammon, Kanah, and as far as Greater S
Jdg 1:31 S, Ahlab, Aczib, Helbah, Aphik, and Rehob.
10:6 the gods of Aram, S, Moab, Ammon, and Philistia.
18:7 And they lived a great distance from S and had no
18:28 for they lived a great distance from S and had no
2Sa 24:6 of Tahtim-hodshi and to Dan-jaan and around to S.
1Ki 11:1 Ammon, Edom, S, and from among the Hittites.
17:9 live in the village of Zarephath, near the city of S.
1Ch 1:13 Canaan's oldest son was S, the ancestor of the
22:4 and S had brought vast amounts of cedar to David.
Ezr 3:7 bought cedar logs from the people of Tyre and S,
Isa 23:2 you people of the coast and you merchants of S,
23:4 you are put to shame, city of S, fortress on the sea.
23:12 "Never again will you rejoice, O daughter of S.
Jer 25:22 and the kings of Tyre and S, and the kings of the
27:3 and S through their ambassadors to King Zedekiah
47:4 along with their allies from Tyre and S.
Eze 27:8 "Your oarsmen came from S and Arvad;
28:21 look toward the city of S and prophesy against it.
28:22 Give the people of S this message from the
28:22 I am your enemy, O S, and I will reveal my glory
Joel 3:4 against me, Tyre and S and you cities of Philistia?
Zec 9:2 and for the cities of Tyre and S, too, though they
Mt 11:21 I did in you had been done in wicked Tyre and S,
11:22 and S will be better off on the judgment day than
15:21 and went north to the region of Tyre and S.
Mk 3:8 and even from as far away as Tyre and S.
7:31 Jesus left Tyre and went to S, then back to the Sea
Lk 4:26 widow of Zarephath—a foreigner in the land of S.
6:17 from as far north as the seacoasts of Tyre and S.
10:13 I did in you had been done in wicked Tyre and S,
10:14 and S will be better off on the judgment day than
Ac 12:20 was very angry with the people of Tyre and S.
27:3 The next day when we docked at S, Julius was

SIDONIANS (14) [SIDON]

Ge 10:15 oldest son was Sidon, the ancestor of the S.
Dt 3:9 (Mount Hermon is called Sirion by the S;
Jos 13:4 including Mearah (which belongs to the S),
13:6 including all the land of the S.
Jdg 3:3 the five Philistine rulers), all the Canaanites, the S,
10:12 the S, the Amalekites, and the Maonites?
18:7 noticed the people living carefree lives, like the S;
1Ki 5:6 no one among us who can cut timber like you S!"
11:5 the goddess of the S, and Molech,
11:33 and worshiped Ashtoreth, the goddess of the S;
16:31 the daughter of King Ethbaal of the S,
2Ki 23:13 for Ashtoreth, the detestable goddess of the S;
1Ch 1:13 oldest son was Sidon, the ancestor of the S.
Eze 32:30 All the princes of the north and the S are there,

SIEGE (42) [BESIEGE, BESIEGED, BESIEGING]

Dt 28:52 They will lay s to your cities until all the fortified
28:53 The s will be so severe that you will eat the flesh
28:55 because he has nothing else to eat during the s that
28:57 She will have nothing else to eat during the s
2Sa 11:1 In the process they laid s to the city of Rabbah.
12:26 army were successfully ending their s of Rabbah,
1Ki 15:27 and the Israelite army were laying s to the
2Ki 18:9 and began a s on the city of Samaria.
18:27 you do not surrender, this city will be put under s.
19:30 in Judah, who have escaped the ravages of the s,
24:11 himself arrived at the city during the s.
25:1 the city and built s ramps against its walls.
25:2 Jerusalem was kept under s until the eleventh year
1Ch 20:1 In the process they laid s to the city of Rabbah
2Ch 32:1 He laid s to the fortified cities, giving orders for his
32:10 you think you can survive my s of Jerusalem?
Job 19:6 I cannot defend myself, for I am like a city under s.
Isa 1:8 harvest is over. It is as helpless as a city under s.
21:2 you Elamites and Medes, take part in the s.
23:13 They have built s ramps against its walls,
29:3 I will build s towers around it and will destroy it.
36:12 you do not surrender, this city will be put under s.
37:31 in Judah, who have escaped the ravages of the s,
Jer 10:17 and prepare to leave; the s is about to begin,"
19:9 I will see to it that your enemies lay s to the city
32:2 Jerusalem was under s from the Babylonian army,
32:24 "See how the s ramps have been built against the
33:4 the walls against the s weapons of the enemy,
37:5 about it, they withdrew from their s of Jerusalem.
52:4 the city and built s ramps against its walls.
52:5 Jerusalem was kept under s until the eleventh year
La 4:10 and eaten them in order to survive the s.
Eze 4:2 Build s ramps against the city walls. Surround it
4:7 continue your demonstration of the s of Jerusalem.
4:8 side until the days of your s have been completed.
5:2 After acting out the s, burn it there. Scatter another
17:17 when the king of Babylon lays s to Jerusalem again
21:22 They will put up s towers and build ramps against
26:8 Then he will attack you by building a s wall,
Da 11:15 and lay s to a fortified city and capture it.
Mic 5:1 your troops! The enemy is laying s to Jerusalem.
Na 3:14 Get ready for the s! Store up water!

SIEVE (1)

Am 9:9 by the other nations as grain is sifted in a s,

SIFT (2) [SIFTED, SIFTING]

Isa 30:28 He will s out the proud nations. He will bridle
Lk 22:31 has asked to have all of you, to s you like wheat.

SIFTED (1) [SIFT]

Am 9:9 by the other nations as grain is s in a sieve,

SIFTING (1) [SIFT]

2Sa 4:6 who had been s wheat, became drowsy and fell

SIGH (5) [SIGHED, SIGHING]

Ps 38:9 know what I long for, Lord; / you hear my every s.
Isa 24:7 be no wine. The merrymakers will s and mourn.
Eze 9:4 and s because of the sins they see around them."
24:17 You may s but only quietly. Let there be no
2Co 5:4 Our dying bodies make us groan and s, but it's not

SIGHED (2) [SIGH]

Mk 7:34 up to heaven, he s and commanded, "Be opened!"
8:12 When he heard this, he s deeply and said,

SIGHING (2) [SIGH]

Job 3:24 I cannot eat for s; my groans pour out like water.
Jer 45: 3 I am weary of my own s and can find no rest.'

SIGHT (144) [SEE]

Ge 6:11 Now the earth had become corrupt in God's s,
10: 9 He was a mighty hunter in the LORD's s.
10: 9 a mighty hunter in the LORD's s."
31:49 keep this treaty when we are out of each other's s.
38: 7 But Er was a wicked man in the LORD's s,
Ex 13:22 the pillar of cloud or pillar of fire from their s.
15:26 the LORD your God and do what is right in his s,
24:17 at the foot of the mountain saw an awesome s.
34: 9 "If it is true that I have found favor in your s,
Nu 22: 4 "This mob will devour everything in s, like an ox
23:21 No misfortune is in s for Jacob; / no trouble is in
Dt 4:25 This is evil in the s of the LORD your God
6:18 Do what is right and good in the LORD's s,
17: 2 has done evil in the s of the LORD your God
21: 9 and doing what is right in the LORD's s,
31:29 LORD very angry by doing what is evil in his s."
34:12 and terrifying acts in the s of all Israel.
Jdg 2:11 the Israelites did what was evil in the LORD's s
3: 7 The Israelites did what was evil in the LORD's s.
3:12 the Israelites did what was evil in the LORD's s,
4: 1 again did what was evil in the LORD's s.
6: 1 the Israelites did what was evil in the LORD's s.
10: 6 Again the Israelites did evil in the LORD's s.
13: 1 the Israelites did what was evil in the LORD's s,
1Sa 2:17 young men was very serious in the LORD's s,
14:16 Saul's lookouts in Gibeah saw a strange s—
2Sa 12:12 but I will do this to you openly in the s of all
22:25 for doing right, / because of my innocence in his s.
1Ki 9: 8 it will become an appalling s for all who pass by.
11: 6 Solomon did what was evil in the LORD's s;
11:33 my ways and done what is pleasing in my s.
14:22 of Judah did what was evil in the LORD's s,
15: 5 had done what was pleasing in the LORD's s
15:11 Asa did what was pleasing in the LORD's s,
15:26 But he did what was evil in the LORD's s
15:34 But he did what was evil in the LORD's s
16: 7 Baasha had done what was evil in the LORD's s,
16:19 had done what was evil in the LORD's s
16:25 But Omri did what was evil in the LORD's s,
16:30 But Ahab did what was evil in the LORD's s,
21:20 sold yourself to what is evil in the LORD's s.
21:25 to what was evil in the LORD's s as did Ahab,
22:43 He did what was pleasing in the LORD's s.
22:52 But he did what was evil in the LORD's s,
2Ki 2:12 And as they disappeared from s, Elisha tore his
3: 2 He did what was evil in the LORD's s, but he was
8:18 So Jehoram did what was evil in the LORD's s.
8:27 doing what was evil in the LORD's s, because he
12: 2 life Joash did what was pleasing in the LORD's s
13: 2 But he did what was evil in the LORD's s.
13:11 But he did what was evil in the LORD's s.
14: 3 Amaziah did what was pleasing in the LORD's s,
14:24 He did what was evil in the LORD's s.
15: 3 He did what was pleasing in the LORD's s,
15: 9 Zechariah did what was evil in the LORD's s,
15:18 But Menahem did what was evil in the LORD's s.
15:24 But Pekahiah did what was evil in the LORD's s.
15:28 But Pekah did what was evil in the LORD's s.
15:34 Jotham did what was pleasing in the LORD's s,
16: 2 He did not do what was pleasing in the s of the
17: 2 He did what was evil in the LORD's s, but not as
18: 3 He did what was pleasing in the LORD's s,
20: 3 faithful to you and do what is pleasing in your s."
21: 2 He did what was evil in the LORD's s,
21: 6 He did much that was evil in the LORD's s,
21:15 For they have done great evil in my s and have
21:16 leading them to do evil in the LORD's s.
21:20 He did what was evil in the LORD's s, just as his
22: 2 He did what was pleasing in the LORD's s
23:32 He did what was evil in the LORD's s, just as his
23:37 He did what was evil in the LORD's s, just as his
24: 9 Jehoiachin did what was evil in the LORD's s,
24:19 But Zedekiah did what was evil in the LORD's s,
2Ch 7:21 it will become an appalling s to all who pass by.
14: 2 and good in the s of the LORD his God.
20:32 He did what was pleasing in the LORD's s.
21: 6 So Jehoram did what was evil in the LORD's s.
22: 4 He did what was evil in the LORD's s, just as
24: 2 Joash did what was pleasing in the LORD's s
25: 2 Amaziah did what was pleasing in the LORD's s,
26: 4 He did what was pleasing in the LORD's s,
27: 2 He did what was pleasing in the LORD's s,
28: 1 He did not do what was pleasing in the s of the
28:14 and handed over the plunder in the s of all the
29: 2 He did what was pleasing in the LORD's s,
29: 6 and did what was evil in the s of the LORD our
31:20 and good in the s of the LORD his God.
33: 2 He did what was evil in the LORD's s,
33: 6 He did much that was evil in the LORD's s,
33:22 He did what was evil in the LORD's s, just as his
34: 2 He did what was pleasing in the LORD's s
36: 5 But he did what was evil in the s of the LORD his
36: 9 Jehoiachin did what was evil in the LORD's s.
36:12 He did what was evil in the s of the LORD his
Job 11: 4 teaching is pure,' and 'I am clean in the s of God.'
15:15 the heavens cannot be absolutely pure in his s.
25: 6 less are mere people, who are but worms in his s?"
Ps 18:24 because of the innocence of my hands in his s.
31: 9 My s is blurred because of my tears. / My body
32: 1 rebellion is forgiven, / whose sin is put out of s!
51: 4 have I sinned; / I have done what is evil in your s.
62: 9 greatest to the lowliest— / all are nothing in his s.
80:16 May they perish at the s of your frown.
106:39 their love of idols was adultery in the LORD's s.
147:10 how puny in his s is the strength of a man.
Pr 3:21 don't lose s of good planning and insight.
4:21 Don't lose s of my words. Let them penetrate deep
SS 1:16 "What a lovely, pleasant s you are, my love,
Isa 1:14 and sacrifices. I cannot stand the s of them!
24:23 in the s of all the leaders of his people.
38: 3 faithful to you and do what is pleasing in your s."
42:22 But what a s his people are, for they have been
Jer 15: 1 help them. Away with them! Get them out of my s!
52: 2 But Zedekiah did what was evil in the LORD's s,
Eze 27:36 of the nations / shake their heads at the s of you,
28:18 I let it burn you to ashes on the ground in the s of
Da 6:22 hurt me, for I have been found innocent in his s.
Am 7: 2 In my vision the locusts ate everything in s that
Mk 3:11 those possessed by evil spirits caught s of him,
8:25 man stared intently, his s was completely restored,
Lk 7:21 he cast out evil spirits and restored s to the blind.
16:15 What this world honors is an abomination in the s
Jn 9:39 I have come to give s to the blind and to show
Ac 9:17 has sent me so that you may get your s back
9:18 scales fell from Saul's eyes, and he regained his s.
22:13 beside me and said, 'Brother Saul, receive your s.'
Ro 1:17 News tells us how God makes us right in his s.
2:13 who obey the law will be declared right in God's s.
3:20 For no one can ever be made right in God's s by
3:21 shown us a different way of being right in his s—
3:22 We are made right in God's s when we trust in
3:26 time when he declares sinners to be right in his s
4: 7 is forgiven, / whose sins are put out of s.
4:14 and think they are "good enough" in God's s,
5: 1 since we have been made right in God's s by faith,
5: 9 And since we have been made right in God's s by
5:18 of righteousness makes all people right in God's s
5:19 many people will be made right in God's s.
2Co 7:12 so that in the s of God you could show how much
Heb 11: 7 rest of the world and was made right in God's s.
12:21 himself was so frightened at the s that he said,
Jas 1:20 Your anger can never make things right in God's s.
1:27 and lasting religion in the s of God our Father
Rev 3: 2 Your deeds are far from right in the s of God.

SIGHTED (1) [SEE]

Ac 21: 3 We s the island of Cyprus, passed it on our left,

SIGHTS (1) [SEE]

Col 3: 1 with Christ, set your s on the realities of heaven,

SIGN (77) [CO-SIGN, SIGNBOARD, SIGNED, SIGNING, SIGNPOST, SIGNS]

Ge 9:12 "I am giving you a s as evidence of my eternal
9:13 It is the s of my permanent promise to you and to
9:17 this is the s of my covenant with all the creatures
17:11 This will be a s that you and they have accepted
Ex 4: 5 "Perform this s, and they will believe you,"
4: 8 "If they do not believe the first miraculous s,
8:23 This miraculous s will happen tomorrow.' "
12:13 have smeared on your doorposts will serve as a s.
31:13 for the Sabbath is a s of the covenant between me
31:17 It is a permanent s of my covenant with them.
Dt 28:46 These horrors will serve as a s and warning among
Jdg 6:17 show me a s to prove that it is really the LORD
1Sa 1:11 and as a s that he has been dedicated to the
14:10 That will be the LORD's s that he will help us
2Sa 15:30 and his feet were bare as a s of mourning.
15:32 and put dirt on his head as a s of mourning.
1Ki 13: 3 That same day the man of God gave a s to prove
13: 3 he said, "The LORD has promised to give this s:
2Ki 4:31 but nothing happened. There was no s of life.
20: 8 "What s will the LORD give to prove that he will
20: 9 "This is the s that the LORD will give you to
2Ch 32:24 who healed him and gave him a miraculous s.
Job 31:35 my side! Look, I will s my name to my defense.
37:13 as a punishment or as a s of his unfailing love.
Ps 86:17 Send me a s of your favor. / Then those who hate
Isa 7:11 "Ask me for a s, Ahaz, to prove that I will crush
7:14 All right then, the Lord himself will choose the s.
19:20 It will be a s and a witness to the LORD
20: 3 This is a s—a symbol of the terrible troubles I will
38: 7 " 'And this is the s that the LORD will give you
38:22 "What s will prove that I will go to the Temple of
55:13 it will be an everlasting s of his power and love.
66:19 I will perform a s among them. And I will send
Eze 12: 6 All of these actions will be a s for the people of
20:12 And I gave them my Sabbath days of rest as a s
20:20 for they are a s to remind you that I am the LORD
Da 6: 8 and s this law so it cannot be changed,
6:12 "Did you not s a law that for the next thirty days
Mt 12:38 we want you to show us a miraculous s to prove
12:39 faithless generation would ask for a miraculous s;
12:39 but the only s I will give them is the s of the
16: 1 him to show them a miraculous s from heaven.
16: 4 faithless generation would ask for a miraculous s,
16: 4 but the only s I will give them is the s of the
24: 3 And will there be any s ahead of time to signal
24:30 the s of the coming of the Son of Man will appear
Mk 6:11 It is a s that you have abandoned that village to its
8:11 "Give us a miraculous s from heaven to prove
8:12 do you people keep demanding a miraculous s?
8:12 I will not give this generation any such s."
13: 4 And will there be any s ahead of time to show us
Lk 9: 5 It is a s that you have abandoned that village to its
11:16 others asked for a miraculous s from heaven to see
11:29 keeps asking me to show them a miraculous s.
11:29 But the only s I will give them is the s of the
11:30 What happened to him was a s to the people of
11:30 What happens to me will be a s that God has sent
21: 7 And will there be any s ahead of time?"
Jn 2:11 This miraculous s at Cana in Galilee was Jesus'
2:18 from God, show us a miraculous s to prove it."
4:54 This was Jesus' second miraculous s in Galilee
6:14 When the people saw this miraculous s,
6:26 I fed you, not because you saw the miraculous s.
6:30 "You must show us a miraculous s if you want us
19:19 And Pilate posted a s over him that read, "Jesus of
19:20 and the s was written in Hebrew, Latin, and Greek,
Ac 4:16 "We can't deny they have done a miraculous s,
4:22 for this miraculous s—the healing of a man who
Ro 4:11 The circumcision ceremony was a s that Abraham
1Co 1:22 because they want a s from heaven to prove it is
11:10 wear a covering on her head as a s of authority
14:22 So you see that speaking in tongues is a s, not for
2Co 4: 3 veiled from anyone, it is a s that they are perishing.
Php 1:28 This will be a s to them that they are going to be

SIGNAL (20) [SIGNALING, SIGNALS]

Nu 10: 5 "When you sound the s to move on, the tribes on
10: 6 When you sound the s a second time, the tribes on
10: 6 You must sound short blasts to s moving on.
10: 7 an assembly, blow the trumpets using a different s.
Jos 8:19 As soon as Joshua gave the s, the men in ambush
Jdg 20:39 which was the s for the Israelites to turn and attack
2Sa 5:24 That will be the s that the LORD is moving ahead
13:28 until Amnon gets drunk; then at my s, kill him!
13:29 So at Absalom's s they murdered Amnon.
1Ch 14:15 That will be the s that God is moving ahead of you
Ps 123: 2 a slave girl watches her mistress for the slightest s.
Isa 5:26 He will send a s to the nations far away. He will
49:22 "See, I will give a s to the godless nations.
Jer 4: 6 Send a s toward Jerusalem: 'Flee now! Do not
6: 1 the alarm in Tekoa! Send up a s at Beth-hakkerem!
50: 2 Raise a s flag so everyone will know that Babylon
51:27 S many nations to mobilize for war against
Mt 24: 3 And will there be any sign ahead of time to s your
26:48 Judas had given them a prearranged s: "You will
Mk 14:44 Judas had given them a prearranged s: "You will

SIGNALING (3) [SIGNAL]

Nu 10: 2 people to assemble and for s the breaking of camp.
Est 7: 8 his attendants covered Haman's face, s his doom.
Pr 6:13 s their true intentions to their friends by making

SIGNBOARD (5) [SIGN]

Isa 8: 1 "Make a large s and clearly write this name on it:
Mt 27:37 A s was fastened to the cross above Jesus' head,
Mk 15:26 A s was fastened to the cross above Jesus' head,
Lk 23:38 A s was nailed to the cross above him with these
Gal 3: 1 you a s with a picture of Christ dying on the cross.

SIGNED (12) [SIGN]

Jos 9:15 Joshua went ahead and s a peace treaty with them,
Ne 10: 1 son of Hacaliah. The priests who s were Zedekiah,
10: 9 The Levites who s were Jeshua son of Azaniah,
10:14 The leaders who s were Parosh, Pahath-moab,
Est 3:12 These letters were s in the name of King Xerxes,
Ps 83: 5 They s a treaty as allies against you—
Jer 32:10 I s and sealed the deed of purchase before
32:12 the witnesses who had s the deed, and all the men
32:44 and sold—deeds s and sealed and witnessed—
Da 6: 9 So King Darius s the law.
6:10 But when Daniel learned that the law had been s,
Heb 13:20[-21] by an everlasting covenant, s with his blood.

SIGNET (7)

Ge 41:42 Then Pharaoh placed his own s ring on Joseph's
Est 3:10 confirming his decision by removing his s ring
8: 2 The king took off his s ring—which he had taken
8: 8 you want, and seal it with the king's s ring.
8:10 and sealed the message with the king's s ring.
Jer 22:24 Even if you were the s ring on my right hand,
Hag 2:23 I will treat you like a s ring on my finger,

SIGNIFICANCE (4) [SIGNIFICANT]

Mk 6:52 They still didn't understand the s of the miracle of
Lk 9:45 Its s was hidden from them, so they could not
18:34 Its s was hidden from them, and they failed to
Rev 12: 1 Then I witnessed in heaven an event of great s.

SIGNIFICANT (2) [SIGNIFICANCE]

Rev 12: 3 Suddenly, I witnessed in heaven another s event.
15: 1 Then I saw in heaven another s event, and it was

SIGNIFICATION [KJV] See UNDERSTAND

SIGNIFY [KJV] See PUBLICLY, SPECIFYING, TELL, TOLD

SIGNING (1) [SIGN]

Da 6:14 the king was very angry with himself for s the law,

SIGNPOST (1) [SIGN]

Eze 21:19 Put a s on the road that comes out of Babylon

SIGNS (70) [SIGN]
Ge 1:14 They will be s to mark off the seasons, the days,
Ex 4: 9 if they do not believe you even after these two s,
4:17 so you can perform the miraculous s I have shown
4:28 And he told him about the miraculous s they were
4:30 and Moses performed the miraculous s as they
7: 3 so I can multiply my miraculous s and wonders in
10: 1 power by performing miraculous s among them.
Nu 14:11 even after all the miraculous s I have done among
14:22 and the miraculous s I performed both in Egypt
Dt 4:34 miraculous s, wonders, war, awesome power,
6:22 Before our eyes the LORD did miraculous s
7:19 And remember the miraculous s and wonders,
11: 3 They weren't there to see the miraculous s
13: 1 the future, and they promise you s or miracles,
13: 2 and the predicted s or miracles take place.
26: 8 and miraculous s and wonders.
29: 3 the miraculous s, and the amazing wonders.
34:11 LORD sent Moses to perform all the miraculous s
1Sa 10: 7 After these s take place, do whatever you think is
10: 9 his heart, and all Samuel's s were fulfilled that day.
Ne 9:10 You displayed miraculous s and wonders against
Ps 74: 9 We see no miraculous s / as evidence that you will
78:43 They forgot his miraculous s in Egypt,
105:27 They performed miraculous s among the
135: 9 He performed miraculous s and wonders in Egypt;
Pr 6:13 to their friends by making s with their eyes
Jer 31:21 "Set up road s; put up guideposts. Mark well the
32:20 You performed miraculous s and wonders in the
32:21 "You brought Israel out of Egypt with mighty s
36:24 Neither the king nor his officials showed any s of
Da 4: 2 "I want you all to know about the miraculous s
4: 3 How great are his s, / how powerful his wonders!
6:15 no law that the king s can be changed."
6:27 he performs miraculous s and wonders
Am 8:10 and shave your heads as s of sorrow,
Mt 16: 3 You are good at reading the weather s in the sky,
16: 3 but you can't read the obvious s of the times!
24:24 and perform great miraculous s and wonders
24:28 so these s indicate that the end is near.
Mk 13:22 and perform miraculous s and wonders so as to
16:17 These s will accompany those who believe:
16:20 confirming what they said by many miraculous s.
Lk 17:20 Kingdom of God isn't ushered in with visible s.
17:37 so these s indicate that the end is near."
21:11 and great miraculous s in the heavens.
21:25 events in the skies—s in the sun, moon, and stars.
Jn 2:23 Because of the miraculous s he did in Jerusalem at
3: 2 Your miraculous s are proof enough that God is
4:45 and had seen all his miraculous s.
4:48 "Must I do miraculous s and wonders before you
7:31 to do more miraculous s than this man has done?"
9:16 could an ordinary sinner do such miraculous s?"
11:47 "This man certainly performs many miraculous s.
12:37 But despite all the miraculous s he had done,
15:24 If I hadn't done such miraculous s among them
20:30 s besides the ones recorded in this book.
Ac 2:19 and s on the earth below— / blood and fire
2:22 wonders, and s through him, as you well know.
2:43 and the apostles performed many miraculous s
4:30 may miraculous s and wonders be done through
5:12 the apostles were performing many miraculous s
6: 8 amazing miracles and s among the people.
7:36 And by means of many miraculous s and wonders
8:13 by the great miracles and s Philip performed.
14: 3 was true by giving them power to do miraculous s
15:12 as Barnabas and Paul told about the miraculous s
Ro 15:19 by the miracles done through me as s from God—
2Co 12:12 For I patiently did many s and wonders
2Th 2: 9 of Satan with counterfeit power and s and miracles.
Heb 2: 4 and God verified the message by s and wonders

SIHON (38) [SIHON'S]
Nu 21:21 The Israelites now sent ambassadors to King S of
21:23 But King S refused to let them cross his land.
21:26 Heshbon had been the capital of King S of the
21:27 "Come to Heshbon, city of S! / May it be restored
21:28 forth from Heshbon, / a blaze from the city of S.
21:29 and his daughters as captives of S, the Amorite
21:34 You will do the same to him as you did to King S
32:33 of Joseph the territory of King S of the Amorites
Dt 1: 4 This was after he had defeated King S of the
2:24 Look, I will help you defeat S the Amorite, king of
2:26 to King S of Heshbon with this proposal of peace:
2:30 But King S refused to allow you to pass through,
2:30 because the LORD your God made S stubborn
2:31 I have begun to hand King S and his land over to
2:32 Then King S declared war on us and mobilized his
3: 2 Treat him just as you treated King S of the
3: 6 just as we had destroyed King S of Heshbon.
4:46 by the Amorites under King S of Heshbon.
29: 7 King S of Heshbon and King Og of Bashan came
31: 4 just as he destroyed S and Og, the kings of the
Jos 2:10 And we know what you did to S and Og, the two
9:10 King S of Heshbon and King Og of Bashan (who
12: 2 King S of the Amorites, who lived in Heshbon,
12: 3 S also controlled the Jordan Valley as far north as
12: 5 which was in the territory of King S of Heshbon.
12: 6 the Israelites had destroyed the people of King S
13:10 It also included all the towns of King S of the
13:21 the towns of the plain and the entire kingdom of S.
13:21 S was the Amorite king who had reigned in
13:21 princes living in the region who were allied with S.
13:27 and the rest of the kingdom of King S of Heshbon.
Jdg 11:19 "Then Israel sent messengers to King S of the
11:20 But King S didn't trust Israel to pass through his
11:21 God of Israel, gave his people victory over King S.
1Ki 4:19 including the territories of King S of the Amorites
Ne 9:22 They completely took over the land of King S of
Ps 135:11 S king of the Amorites, / Og king of Bashan,
136:19 S king of the Amorites, / His faithful love endures

SIHON'S (1) [SIHON]
Jer 48:45 fire comes from Heshbon, King S ancestral home,

SIHOR [KJV] See NILE, SHIHOR

SILAS (26)
Ac 15:22 Judas (also called Barsabbas) and S.
15:27 and S to tell you what we have decided concerning
15:32 Then Judas and S, both being prophets,
15:33 then Judas and S were sent back to Jerusalem,
15:40 Paul chose S, and the believers sent them off,
16: 1 Paul and S went first to Derbe and then on to
16: 6 and S traveled through the area of Phrygia
16:19 so they grabbed Paul and S and dragged them
16:22 A mob quickly formed against Paul and S,
16:25 Paul and S were praying and singing hymns to
16:29 to the dungeon and fell down before Paul and S.
16:36 the jailer told Paul, "You and S are free to leave.
16:38 to learn that Paul and S were Roman citizens.
16:40 Paul and S then returned to the home of Lydia,
17: 1 and S traveled through the towns of Amphipolis
17: 5 searching for Paul and S so they could drag them
17: 6 and S have turned the rest of the world upside
17:10 very night the believers sent Paul and S to Berea.
17:11 Scriptures day after day to check up on Paul and S,
17:14 the coast, while S and Timothy remained behind.
17:15 then they returned to Berea with a message for S
18: 5 And after S and Timothy came down from
2Co 1:19 S, and I preached to you, and he is the divine Yes
1Th 1: 1 This letter is from Paul, S, and Timothy. It is
2Th 1: 1 This letter is from Paul, S, and Timothy. It is
1Pe 5:12 written this short letter to you with the help of S,

SILENCE (23) [SILENCED, SILENCES, SILENT, SILENTLY]
Ge 24:21 The servant watched her in s, wondering whether
Job 29: 9 The princes stood in s and put their hands over
40: 4 I will put my hand over my mouth in s.
Ps 8: 2 to give you praise. / They s your enemies
12: 3 their flattery to an end / and s their proud tongues.
39: 2 But as I stood there in s— / not even speaking of
115:17 for they have gone into the s of the grave.
Isa 17:13 roar like breakers on a beach, God will s them.
23: 2 Mourn in s, you people of the coast and you
25: 5 of the desert. But you s the roar of foreign nations.
41: 1 "Listen in s before me, you lands beyond the sea.
47: 5 daughter of Babylonia, sit now in darkness and s.
Jer 51:55 He will s her. Waves of enemies pound against
La 2:10 The leaders of Jerusalem sit on the ground in s,
3:28 Let them sit alone in s beneath the LORD's
Eze 16:63 will remember your sins and cover your mouth in s
Am 8: 3 They will be carried out of the city in s. I,
Zep 1: 7 Stand in s in the presence of the Sovereign
Ac 19:33 He motioned for s and tried to speak in defense.
21:40 Soon a deep s enveloped the crowd, and he
22: 2 in their own language, the s was even greater.
1Pe 2:15 It is God's will that your good lives should s those
Rev 8: 1 there was s throughout heaven for about half an

SILENCED (7) [SILENCE]
Ps 31:18 May their lying lips be s— / those proud
63:11 trust in him will praise him, / while liars will be s.
65: 7 pounding waves / and s the shouting of the nations.
Jer 48: 2 The city of Madmen, too, will be s; the sword will
Mt 22:34 But when the Pharisees heard that he had s the
Lk 20:26 they were amazed by his answer, and they were s.
Tit 1:11 They must be s. By their wrong teaching,

SILENCES (1) [SILENCE]
Job 12:20 He s the trusted adviser, and he removes the

SILENT (59) [SILENCE]
Ex 15:16 of your great power, / they will be s like a stone,
Lev 10: 3 before all the people.' " And Aaron was s.
Jdg 3:19 So the king commanded his servants to be s
1Ki 18:21 follow him!" But the people were completely s.
2Ki 18:36 But the people were s and did not answer
Job 11: 3 Should I remain s while you babble on? When you
13:13 "Be s now and leave me alone. Let me speak—
13:19 prove me wrong, I would remain s until I die.
29:21 They were s as they waited for me to speak.
32:16 now that you are s? Must I also remain s?
33:33 listen to me. Keep s and I will teach you wisdom!"
Ps 4: 4 Think about it overnight and remain s.
19: 3 a sound or a word; / their voice is s in the skies;
28: 1 For if you are s, / I might as well give up and die.
30:12 that I might sing praises to you and not be s.
31:17 wicked be disgraced; / let them lie s in the grave.
35:22 you know all about this. / Do not stay s.
38:13 I am s before them as one who cannot speak.
39: 9 I am s before you; I won't say a word. / For my
46:10 "Be s, and know that I am God! / I will be honored
50:21 While you did all this, I remained s, / and you
76: 8 the earth trembled and stood s before you.
83: 1 O God, don't sit idly by, / s and inactive!
107:42 and be glad, / while the wicked are stricken s.
109: 1 O God, whom I praise, / don't stand s and aloof
Pr 11:12 a neighbor; a person with good sense remains s.
17:28 fools are thought to be wise when they keep s;
Isa 23: 7 How can this s ruin be all that is left of your once
24: 8 The melodious chords of the harp will be s.
27:10 Israel's fortified cities will be s and empty,
36:21 But the people were s and did not answer
42:14 He will say, "I have long been s; / yes, I have
50: 2 Is that why the house is s and empty when I come
53: 7 And as a sheep is s before the shearers, he did not
56:10 They are like s watchdogs that give no warning
62: 1 my heart yearns for Jerusalem, I cannot remain s.
64:12 help us? Will you continue to be s and punish us?
65: 6 I will not stand s; I will repay them in full! Yes,
Jer 8:21 of my people. I am stunned and s, mute with grief.
25:10 will fail, and all your homes will stand s and dark.
46:22 S as a serpent gliding away, Egypt flees.
La 1: 1 once bustling with people, are now s.
1: 4 The city gates are s, her priests groan, her young
Eze 27:32 a city as Tyre, / now s at the bottom of the sea?
Mic 7:16 They will stand in s awe, deaf to everything around
Hab 1:13 Should you be s while the wicked destroy people
2:20 holy Temple. Let all the earth be s before him."
Zep 3: 6 cities are now deserted; their streets are in s ruin.
Zec 2:13 Be s before the LORD, all humanity, for he is
Mt 26:63 But Jesus remained s. Then the high priest said to
27:12 their accusations against him, Jesus remained s.
Mk 1:25 Jesus cut him short. "Be s! Come out of the man."
Lk 4:35 Jesus cut him short. "Be s!" he told the demon.
4:41 he stopped them and told them to be s.
Ac 8:32 And as a lamb is s before the shearers, / he did not
18: 9 told him, "Don't be afraid! Speak out! Don't be s!
1Co 14:28 they must be s in your church meeting and speak in
14:34 Women should be s during the church meetings.

SILENTLY (2) [SILENCE]
Ge 18:12 she laughed s to herself. "How could a worn-out
Ps 10: 9 Like lions they crouch s, / waiting to pounce on the

SILK (2)
Eze 16:10 I gave you expensive clothing of linen and s,
Rev 18:12 silver, jewels, pearls, fine linen, purple dye, s,

SILLA (1)
2Ki 12:20 assassinated him at Beth-millo on the road to S.

SILLY (2)
Ecc 2: 2 "It is s to be laughing all the time," I said.
Hos 7:11 "The people of Israel have become like s,

SILLY [KJV] See also SIMPLE, VULNERABLE

SILOAH [KJV] See SHELAH

SILOAM (5)
Ne 3:15 Then he repaired the wall of the pool of S near the
Lk 13: 4 men who died when the Tower of S fell on them?
Jn 9: 7 wash in the pool of S" (S means Sent).
9:11 'Go to the pool of S and wash off the mud.'

SILVER (324) [SILVERSMITH, SILVERSMITHS]
Ge 13: 2 for Abram was very rich in livestock, s, and gold.
20:16 "I am giving your 'brother' a thousand pieces of s
23:15 "the land is worth four hundred pieces of s,
23:16 four hundred pieces of s, as was publicly agreed.
24:35 a fortune in s and gold, and many servants
24:53 Then he brought out s and gold jewelry and lovely
33:19 Shechem's father, for a hundred pieces of s.
37:28 out of the pit and sold him for twenty pieces of s,
44: 2 Then put my personal s cup at the top of the
44: 5 by stealing my master's personal s drinking cup,
44: 8 Why would we steal s or gold from your master's
45:22 changes of clothes and three hundred pieces of s!
Ex 3:22 The Israelite women will ask for s and gold
11: 2 to ask their Egyptian neighbors for articles of s
12:35 Egyptians for clothing and articles of s and gold.
20:23 you must not make or worship idols of s or gold.
21:32 the slave's owner is to be given thirty s coins in
25: 3 you may accept on my behalf: gold, s, and bronze;
26:19 They will fit into forty s bases—two bases under
26:21 with their forty s bases, two bases for each frame.
26:25 of the Tabernacle, supported by sixteen s bases—
26:32 overlaid with gold. The posts will fit into s bases.
27:10 The curtains will be held up with s hooks attached
to the s rods that are attached to the posts.
27:11 fitted into bronze bases, with s hooks and rods.
27:17 must be connected by s rods, using s hooks.
30:13 to the LORD will be one-fifth of an ounce of s.
31: 4 to create beautiful objects from gold, s, and bronze.
35: 5 these offerings to the LORD: gold, s, and bronze;
35:24 Others brought s and bronze objects as their
35:32 to create beautiful objects from gold, s, and bronze.
36:24 along with forty s bases, two for each frame.
36:26 along with forty s bases, two for each frame.
36:30 along with sixteen s bases, two for each frame.
36:36 were overlaid with gold and set into four s bases.
38:10 and there were s hooks and rods to hold up the
38:11 bronze posts and bases and with s hooks and rods.
38:12 by ten posts and bases and with s hooks and rods.
38:17 a bronze base, and all the hooks and rods were s.
38:17 The tops of the posts were overlaid with s,
38:17 and the rods to hold up the curtains were solid s.
38:19 The tops of the posts were overlaid with s,
38:19 and the hooks and rods were also made of s.
38:25 The amount of s that was given was about 7,545

38:26 It came from the tax of one-fifth of an ounce of s
38:27 the inner curtain required 7,500 pounds of s,
38:28 The rest of the s, about 45 pounds, was used to
Lev 5:15 and it must be of the proper value in s as measured
6:6 or the animal's equivalent value in s.
27:3 of twenty and sixty is valued at fifty pieces of s;
27:4 a woman of that age is valued at thirty pieces of s.
27:5 and twenty is valued at twenty pieces of s;
27:5 a girl of that age is valued at ten pieces of s.
27:6 and five years is valued at five pieces of s;
27:6 a girl of that age is valued at three pieces of s.
27:7 older than sixty is valued at fifteen pieces of s;
27:7 woman older than sixty is valued at ten pieces of s.
27:16 fifty pieces of s for an area that produces five
Nu 3:47 collect five pieces of s for each person, each piece
3:48 Give the s to Aaron and his sons as the redemption
3:50 The s collected on behalf of these firstborn sons of
7:13 The offering consisted of a s platter weighing
3-1/4 pounds and a s basin of about 1-3/4 pounds.
7:19 The offering consisted of a s platter weighing
3-1/4 pounds and a s basin of about 1-3/4 pounds.
7:25 The offering consisted of a s platter weighing
3-1/4 pounds and a s basin of about 1-3/4 pounds.
7:31 The offering consisted of a s platter weighing
3-1/4 pounds and a s basin of about 1-3/4 pounds.
7:37 The offering consisted of a s platter weighing
3-1/4 pounds and a s basin of about 1-3/4 pounds.
7:43 The offering consisted of a s platter weighing
3-1/4 pounds and a s basin of about 1-3/4 pounds.
7:49 The offering consisted of a s platter weighing
3-1/4 pounds and a s basin of about 1-3/4 pounds.
7:55 The offering consisted of a s platter weighing
3-1/4 pounds and a s basin of about 1-3/4 pounds.
7:61 The offering consisted of a s platter weighing
3-1/4 pounds and a s basin of about 1-3/4 pounds.
7:67 The offering consisted of a s platter weighing
3-1/4 pounds and a s basin of about 1-3/4 pounds.
7:73 The offering consisted of a s platter weighing
3-1/4 pounds and a s basin of about 1-3/4 pounds.
7:79 The offering consisted of a s platter weighing
3-1/4 pounds and a s basin of about 1-3/4 pounds.
7:84 twelve s platters, twelve s basins, and twelve
7:85 In all, the s objects weighed about 60 pounds,
10:2 "Make two trumpets of beaten s to be used for
18:16 The redemption price is five pieces of s, each piece
22:18 if Balak were to give me a palace filled with s
24:13 if Balak were to give me a palace filled with s
31:22 made of gold, s, bronze, iron, tin, or lead—
Dt 7:25 and do not desire the s or gold with which they are
8:13 and herds have become very large and your s
17:17 must not accumulate vast amounts of wealth in s
22:19 They will fine him one hundred pieces of s, for he
22:29 he must pay fifty pieces of s to her father. Then he
29:17 detestable idols made of wood, stone, s, and gold.
Jos 6:19 Everything made from s, gold, bronze, or iron is
6:24 Only the things made from s, gold, bronze, or iron
7:21 two hundred s coins, and a bar of gold weighing
7:21 my tent, with the s buried deeper than the rest."
7:22 Achan had said, with the s buried beneath the rest.
7:24 the s, the robe, the bar of gold, his sons, daughters,
22:8 your s and gold, your bronze and iron, and your
24:32 the sons of Hamor for one hundred pieces of s.
Jdg 9:4 They gave him seventy s coins from the temple of
16:5 of us will give you eleven hundred pieces of s."
17:2 who stole eleven hundred pieces of s from you.
17:3 "I now dedicate these s coins to the LORD.
17:4 So his mother took two hundred of the s coins to a
17:10 I will give you ten pieces of s a year, plus a change
1Sa 9:8 the servant said, "I have one small s piece.
13:21 a quarter of an ounce of s for sharpening a
2Sa 8:10 Joram presented David with many gifts of s,
8:11 along with the s and gold he had set apart from the
18:11 I would have rewarded you with ten pieces of s
18:12 "I wouldn't do it for a thousand pieces of s,"
24:24 So David paid him fifty pieces of s for the
1Ki 7:51 the s, the gold, and the other utensils—
10:21 They were not made of s because s was considered
10:22 down with gold, s, ivory, apes, and peacocks.
10:25 everyone who came to visit brought him gifts of s
10:27 The king made s as plentiful in Jerusalem as
10:29 Jerusalem could be purchased for 600 pieces of s,
10:29 and horses could be bought for 150 pieces of s.
15:15 He brought into the Temple of the LORD the s
15:18 Asa responded by taking all the s and gold that was
15:19 See, I am sending you a gift of s and gold.
16:24 from its owner, Shemer, for 150 pounds of s.
20:3 'Your s and gold are mine, and so are the best of
20:5 'I have already demanded that you give me your s,
20:7 I give him my wives and children and s and gold."
20:39 or pay a fine of seventy-five pounds of s!'
2Ki 5:5 taking as gifts 750 pounds of s, 150 pounds of
5:22 He would like 75 pounds of s and two sets of
5:23 "By all means, take 150 pounds of s,"
6:25 even a donkey's head sold for two pounds of s,
6:25 a cup of dove's dung cost about two ounces of s.
7:1 of fine flour will cost only half an ounce of s,
7:1 of barley grain will cost only half an ounce of s."
7:8 and carrying out s and gold and clothing
7:16 fine flour were sold that day for half an ounce of s,
7:16 of barley grain were sold for half an ounce of s,
7:18 quarts of fine flour will cost half an ounce of s,
7:18 quarts of barley grain will cost half an ounce of s."
12:13 to the Temple was not used for making s cups,
12:13 articles of gold or s for the Temple of the LORD.
14:14 He carried off all the gold and s and all the utensils
15:19 But Menahem paid him thirty-seven tons of s to
15:20 pay twenty ounces of s in the form of a special tax.
16:8 Then Ahaz took the s and gold from the Temple of
18:14 a settlement of more than eleven tons of s
18:15 King Hezekiah used all the s stored in the Temple
20:13 the s, the gold, the spices, and the aromatic oils.
23:33 also demanded that Judah pay 7,500 pounds of s
23:35 In order to get the s and gold demanded as tribute
25:15 and all the other utensils made of pure gold or s.
1Ch 18:10 David with many gifts of gold, s, and bronze.
18:11 along with the s and gold he had taken from the
19:6 and the Ammonites sent thirty-eight tons of s to
22:14 nearly forty thousand tons of s, and so much iron
28:14 and s should be used to make the necessary items.
28:15 and the amount of s for the s lampstands
28:16 be placed and the amount of s for other tables.
28:17 as well as the amount of s for every dish.
29:2 there is enough gold, s, bronze, iron, and wood,
29:3 treasures of gold and s to help in the construction.
29:4 and over 262 tons of refined s to be used for
29:5 other gold and s work to be done by the craftsmen.
29:7 10,000 gold coins, about 375 tons of s, about 675
2Ch 1:15 s and gold were as plentiful in Jerusalem as stones.
1:17 Jerusalem could be purchased for 600 pieces of s,
1:17 and horses could be bought for 150 pieces of s.
2:7 who can work with gold, s, bronze, and iron;
2:14 at making things from gold, s, bronze, and iron.
5:1 including all the s and gold and all the utensils.
9:14 of the land also brought gold and s to Solomon.
9:20 They were not made of s because s was considered
9:21 down with gold, s, ivory, apes, and peacocks.
9:24 everyone who came to visit brought him gifts of s
9:27 The king made s as plentiful in Jerusalem as
15:18 He brought into the Temple of God the s and gold
16:2 Asa responded by taking the s and gold from the
16:3 See, I am sending you a gift of s and gold.
17:11 of the Philistines brought him gifts and s as tribute,
21:3 father had given each of them valuable gifts of s,
24:14 and other vessels made of gold and s.
25:6 He also paid about 7,500 pounds of s to hire
25:9 "But what should I do about the s I paid to hire the
25:24 He carried off all the gold and s and all the utensils
27:5 from them an annual tribute of 7,500 pounds of s,
32:27 He had to build special treasury buildings for his s,
36:3 a tribute from Judah of 7,500 pounds of s
Ezr 1:4 toward their expenses by supplying them with s
1:6 their neighbors assisted by giving them vessels of s
1:9 s trays | 1,000 / s censers | 29
1:10 gold bowls | 30 / s bowls | 410 / other items
1:11 and s items were turned over to Sheshbazzar to
2:69 6,250 pounds of s, and 100 robes for the priests.
5:14 and s utensils that Nebuchadnezzar had taken from
6:5 And the gold and s utensils, which were taken to
7:15 We also commission you to take with you some s
7:16 "Moreover you are to take any s and gold which
7:22 You are to give him up to 7,500 pounds of s,
8:25 to be in charge of transporting the s, the gold,
8:26 24 tons of s, / 7,500 pounds of s utensils,
8:28 This s and gold is a freewill offering to the
8:33 On the fourth day after our arrival, the s, gold,
Ne 5:15 daily ration of food and wine, besides a pound of s.
7:71 and some 2,750 pounds of s for the work.
7:72 about 2,500 pounds of s, and 67 robes for the
10:32 annual Temple tax of an eighth of an ounce of s,
Est 1:6 fastened by purple ribbons to s rings embedded in
1:6 and s couches stood on a mosaic pavement of
3:9 and I will give 375 tons of s to the government
Job 3:15 princes whose palaces were filled with gold and s.
22:25 will be your treasure. He will be your precious s!
28:1 "People know how to mine s and refine gold.
28:15 "It cannot be bought for gold or s.
31:26 the skies, or the moon walking down its s pathway,
Ps 12:6 promises are pure, / like s refined in a furnace,
66:10 you have purified us like s melted in a crucible.
68:13 now they are covered with s and gold,
105:37 people safely out of Egypt, loaded with s and gold;
115:4 Their idols are merely things of s and gold,
119:72 more valuable to me / than millions in gold and s!
135:15 Their idols are merely things of s and gold,
Pr 3:14 For the profit of wisdom is better than s, and her
8:10 "Choose my instruction rather than s,
8:19 the purest gold, my wages better than sterling s!
10:20 The words of the godly are like sterling s; the heart
16:16 to get wisdom than gold, and understanding than s!
17:3 Fire tests the purity of s and gold, but the LORD
22:1 being held in high esteem is better than having s
25:4 Remove the dross from s, and the sterling will be
25:11 Timely advice is as lovely as golden apples in a s
27:21 Fire tests the purity of s and gold, but a person is
Ecc 2:8 I collected great sums of s and gold, the treasure of
12:2 and there is no s lining left among the clouds.
12:6 before the s cord of life snaps and the golden bowl
SS 1:11 will make earrings of gold for you and beads of s."
3:10 Its posts are of s, its canopy is gold, and its seat is
8:11 Each of them pays one thousand pieces of s for its
8:12 O Solomon, you can take my thousand pieces of s.
8:12 And I will give two hundred pieces of s to those
Isa 1:22 Once like pure s, you have become like worthless
2:7 Israel has vast treasures of s and gold and many
2:20 their gold and s idols to the moles and bats.
7:23 now worth as much as a thousand pieces of s,
13:17 and no amount of s or gold will buy them off.
30:22 Then you will destroy all your s idols and gold
31:7 and s images that your sinful hands have made.
39:2 the s, the gold, the spices, and the aromatic oils.
40:19 overlaid with gold, and decorated with s chains?
46:6 Some people pour out their s and gold and hire a
48:10 I have refined you but not in the way s is refined.
60:17 your iron for s, your wood for bronze, and your
Jer 6:30 I will label them 'Rejected S' because I,
10:4 They decorate it with gold and s and then fasten it
10:9 They bring beaten sheets of s from Tarshish
20:5 the precious jewels and gold and s of your kings—
32:9 paying Hanamel seventeen pieces of s for it.
32:10 before witnesses, weighed out the s, and paid him.
52:19 and all the other utensils made of pure gold or s.
Eze 16:13 so you were made beautiful with gold and s.
16:17 and gold and s ornaments I had given you
22:18 the worthless slag that remains after s is smelted.
22:22 and you will melt like s in fierce heat. Then you
27:12 trading your wares in exchange for s, iron, tin,
28:4 great wealth—gold and s for your treasuries.
38:13 will ask, 'Who are you to rob them of s and gold?
45:12 The standard unit for weight will be the s shekel.
Da 2:32 its chest and arms were of s, its belly and thighs
2:35 into a heap of iron, clay, bronze, s, and gold.
2:45 to dust the statue of iron, bronze, clay, s, and gold.
5:2 to bring in the gold and s cups that his predecessor,
5:4 made of gold, s, bronze, iron, wood, and stone.
5:23 drinking wine from them while praising gods of s,
11:8 with him, along with priceless gold and s dishes.
11:38 on him gold, s, precious stones, and costly gifts.
11:43 s, and treasures of Egypt, and the Libyans
Hos 2:8 and s she used in worshiping the god Baal were
3:2 So I bought her back for fifteen pieces of s
8:4 By making idols for themselves from their s
9:6 Briers will take over your treasures of s;
13:2 Now they keep on sinning by making s idols to
Joel 3:5 You have taken my s and gold and all my precious
Am 2:6 perverted justice by selling honest people for s
8:6 enslave poor people for a debt of one piece of s
Na 2:9 Loot the s! Plunder the gold! There seems no end
Hab 2:19 They may be overlaid with gold and s, but they are
Zep 1:18 Your s and gold will be of no use to you on that
Hag 2:8 The s is mine, and the gold is mine,
Zec 6:10 and Jedaiah will bring gifts of s and gold from the
6:11 their gifts and make a crown from the s and gold.
9:3 built a strong fortress and has piled up so much s
11:12 they counted out for my wages thirty pieces of s.
13:9 just as gold and s are refined and purified by fire.
14:14 great quantities of gold and s and fine clothing.
Mal 3:3 He will sit and judge like a refiner of s,
3:3 will purify the Levites, refining them like gold or s,
Mt 26:15 to you?" And they gave him thirty pieces of s.
27:3 So he took the thirty pieces of s back to the leading
27:9 that says, / "They took the thirty pieces of s—
Lk 7:41 five hundred pieces of s to one and fifty pieces to
10:35 next day he handed the innkeeper two pieces of s
15:8 "Or suppose a woman has ten valuable s coins
19:13 and gave them ten pounds of s to invest for him
Ac 17:29 idol designed by craftsmen from gold or s or stone.
19:24 s shrines of the Greek goddess Artemis.
1Co 3:12 may use gold, s, jewels, wood, hay, or straw.
2Ti 2:20 home some utensils are made of gold and s,
Jas 5:3 Your gold and s have become worthless. The very
1Pe 1:18 And the ransom he paid was not mere gold or s.
Rev 9:20 idols made of gold, s, bronze, stone, and wood—
18:12 s, jewels, pearls, fine linen, purple dye, silk,

SILVERSMITH (3) [SILVER, SMITHS]

Jdg 17:4 mother took two hundred of the silver coins to a s,
Pr 25:4 from silver, and the sterling will be ready for the s.
Ac 19:24 a s who had a large business manufacturing silver

SILVERSMITHS (1) [SILVER, SMITHS]

1Ch 22:16 and s and workers of bronze and iron.

SIMEON (54) [SIMEON'S]

Ge 29:33 She named him S, for she said, "The LORD
34:25 of Dinah's brothers, S and Levi, took their swords,
34:30 Afterward Jacob said to Levi and S, "You have
35:23 oldest son), S, Levi, Judah, Issachar, and Zebulun.
42:24 He then chose S from among them and had him
42:36 Joseph has disappeared, S is gone, and now you
43:14 that he might release S and return Benjamin.
43:23 Then he released S and brought him out to them.
46:10 The sons of S were Jemuel, Jamin, Ohad, Jakin,
48:5 will inherit from me just as Reuben and S will.
49:5 "S and Levi are two of a kind— / men of violence.
Ex 1:2 Reuben, S, Levi, Judah,
6:15 The descendants of S included Jemuel, Jamin,
6:15 Their descendants became the clans of S.
Nu 1:6 S | Shelumiel son of Zurishaddai
1:22[-23] S | 59,300
2:10[-11] "The divisions of Reuben, S, and Gad are to
2:12[-13] S | Shelumiel son of Zurishaddai | 59,300
7:36 leader of the tribe of S, presented his offering.
10:19 The tribe of S was led by Shelumiel son of
13:5 S | Shaphat son of Hori
25:14 of Salu, the leader of a family from the tribe of S.
26:12 were the clans descended from the sons of S:
26:14 The men from all the clans of S numbered 22,200.
34:20 S | Shemuel son of Ammihud
Dt 27:12 the tribes of S, Levi, Judah, Issachar, Joseph,
Jos 19:1 of land went to the families of the tribe of S.
19:8 was the inheritance of the families of the tribe of S.
19:9 So the tribe of S received an inheritance within the
21:4 assigned to the tribes of Judah, S, and Benjamin.
21:9 the following towns from the tribes of Judah and S
Jdg 1:3 of Judah said to their relatives from the tribe of S,
1:3 your territory." So the men of S went with Judah.
1:17 Then Judah joined with S to fight against the
1Ch 2:1 were Reuben, S, Levi, Judah, Issachar, Zebulun,
4:24 The sons of S were Nemuel, Jamin, Jarib, Zerah,

4:34 Other descendants of S included Meshobab,
4:41 the leaders of S invaded it and completely
4:42 Five hundred of these invaders from the tribe of S
6:65 of Judah, S, and Benjamin, mentioned above,
12:25 From the tribe of S, there were 7,100 warriors.
27:16 son of Zicri / S | Shephatiah son of Maacah
2Ch 15: 9 Manasseh, and S who had settled among them.
34: 6 Ephraim, and S, even as far as Naphtali.
Eze 48:24 South of Benjamin's territory lies that of S,
48:33 will have gates named for S, Issachar,
Lk 2:25 Now there was a man named S who lived in
2:28 S was there. He took the child in his arms
2:34 Then S blessed them, and he said to Mary,
2:38 She came along just as S was talking with Mary
3:30 Levi was the son of S. / S was the son of Judah.
Ac 13: 1 S (called "the black man"), Lucius (from Cyrene),
Rev 7: 7 from S | 12,000 / from Levi | 12,000

SIMEON'S (3) [SIMEON]

Jos 19: 2 S inheritance included Beersheba, Sheba,
1Ch 4:27 So S tribe never became as large as the tribe of
4:38 These were the names of some of the leaders of S

SIMILAR (12) [SIMILARLY]

Lev 6: 3 while under oath, or they commit any other s sin.
Dt 2:12 In a s way the peoples in Canaan were driven from
2:23 A s thing happened when the Caphtorites from
22:26 This case is s to that of someone who attacks
Jdg 11:17 Then they asked the king of Moab for s
1Ki 7: 8 He also built s living quarters for Pharaoh's
7:33 and were s to chariot wheels. The axles, spokes,
12:32 s to the annual Festival of Shelters in Judah.
2Ch 34:32 and the people of Benjamin to make a s pledge.
Ezr 7:20 for your God's Temple or for any s needs,
Eze 41:21 ones at the entrance of the Most Holy Place were s.
45:17 the Sabbath days, and all other s occasions.

SIMILARLY (4) [SIMILAR]

Ex 21:24 S, the payment must be hand for hand, foot for
Dt 2:22 He had s helped the descendants of Esau at Mount
Mk 7: 4 S, they eat nothing bought from the market unless
Tit 2: 3 S, teach the older women to live in a way that is

SIMON (73) [PETER, SIMON'S]

Mt 4:18 S, also called Peter, and Andrew—fishing with a
10: 2 first S (also called Peter), / then Andrew (Peter's
10: 4 S (the Zealot), / Judas Iscariot (who later betrayed
13:55 and his brothers—James, Joseph, S, and Judas.
16:16 S Peter answered, "You are the Messiah, the Son
16:17 Jesus replied, "You are blessed, S son of John,
26: 6 Meanwhile, Jesus was in Bethany at the home of S,
27:32 they came across a man named S, who was from
Mk 1:16 he saw S and his brother, Andrew, fishing with a
1:29 they went over to S and Andrew's home,
1:36 Later S and the others went out to find him.
3:16 of the twelve he chose: / S (he renamed him Peter),
3:18 (son of Alphaeus), / Thaddaeus, / S (the Zealot),
6: 3 and brother of James, Joseph, Judas, and S.
14: 3 Meanwhile, Jesus was in Bethany at the home of S,
14:37 "S!" he said to Peter. "Are you asleep?
15:21 A man named S, who was from Cyrene,
15:21 (S is the father of Alexander and Rufus.)
Lk 5: 3 Jesus asked S, its owner, to push it out into the
5: 4 he said to S, "Now go out where it is deeper
5: 5 "Master," S replied, "we worked hard all last
5: 8 When S Peter realized what had happened, he fell
5:10 also amazed. Jesus replied to S, "Don't be afraid!
6:14 S (he also called him Peter), / Andrew (Peter's
6:15 James (son of Alphaeus), / S (the Zealot),
7:40 "S," he said to the Pharisee, "I have something to
7:40 "All right, Teacher," S replied, "go ahead."
7:43 S answered, "I suppose the one for whom he
7:44 Then he turned to the woman and said to S,
22:31 "S, S, Satan has asked to have all of you,
22:32 in prayer for you, S, that your faith should not fail.
23:26 As they led Jesus away, S of Cyrene, who was
Jn 1:40 Andrew, S Peter's brother, was one of these men
1:41 Andrew did was to find his brother, S, and tell him,
1:42 Then Andrew brought S to meet Jesus.
1:42 Looking intently at S, Jesus said, "You are S, the son of John—
6: 8 Then Andrew, S Peter's brother, spoke up.
6:68 S Peter replied, "Lord, to whom would we go?
6:71 son of S Iscariot, one of the Twelve, who would
13: 2 son of S Iscariot, to carry out his plan to betray
13: 6 When he came to S Peter, Peter said to him,
13: 9 S Peter exclaimed, "Then wash my hands
13:24 S Peter motioned to him to ask who would do this
13:26 had dipped it, he gave it to Judas, son of S Iscariot.
13:36 S Peter said, "Lord, where are you going?"
18:10 Then S Peter drew a sword and slashed off the
18:15 S Peter followed along behind, as did another of
18:25 Meanwhile, as S Peter was standing by the fire,
20: 2 She ran and found S Peter and the other disciple,
20: 6 Then S Peter arrived and went inside. He also
21: 2 S Peter, Thomas (nicknamed the Twin),
21: 3 S Peter said, "I'm going fishing." "We'll come,
21: 7 When S Peter heard that it was the Lord, he put on
21:11 So S Peter went aboard and dragged the net to the
21:15 After breakfast Jesus said to S Peter, "S son of John, do you love me more than these?"
21:16 "S son of John, do you love me?" "Yes, Lord,"
21:17 he asked him, "S son of John, do you love me?"
Ac 1:13 James (son of Alphaeus), / S (the Zealot),
8: 9 A man named S had been a sorcerer there for many
8:13 Then S himself believed and was baptized.
8:18 When S saw that the Holy Spirit was given when
8:24 "Pray to the Lord for me," S exclaimed,
9:43 long time in Joppa, living with S, a leatherworker.
10: 5 men down to Joppa to find a man named S Peter.
10: 6 He is staying with S, a leatherworker who lives
10:18 They asked if this was the place where S Peter was
10:32 send some men to Joppa and summon S Peter.
10:32 He is staying in the home of S, a leatherworker
11:13 'Send messengers to Joppa to find S Peter.
2Pe 1: 1 This letter is from S Peter, a slave and apostle of

SIMON'S (3) [SIMON]

Mk 1:30 S mother-in-law was sick in bed with a high fever.
Lk 4:38 the synagogue that day, Jesus went to S home,
4:38 where he found S mother-in-law very sick with a

SIMPLE (14) [SIMPLEMINDED, SIMPLEST, SIMPLETON, SIMPLETONS, SIMPLY]

Ex 20:24 "The altars you make for me must be s altars of
2Ki 3:18 But this is only a s thing for the LORD, for he
Job 5: 2 destroys the fool, and jealousy kills the s.
11: 6 of wisdom, for true wisdom is not a s matter.
Ps 19: 7 of the LORD are trustworthy, / making wise the s.
119:130 they give light; / even the s can understand them.
Pr 9: 4 "Come home with me," she urges the s. To those
9:16 "Come home with me," she urges the s. To those
Isa 28:10 and over again, a line at a time, in very s words!"
28:13 it over and over, a line at a time, in very s words.
28:13 Yet they will stumble over this s,
Mt 5:37 Just say a s, 'Yes, I will,' or 'No, I won't.'
2Co 11: 3 led away from your pure and s devotion to Christ,
Jas 5:12 Just say a s yes or no, so that you will not sin

SIMPLEMINDED (4) [MIND, SIMPLE]

Pr 1: 4 These proverbs will make the s clever. They will
1:22 she cries. "How long will you go on being s?
7: 7 and saw a s young man who lacked common sense.
19:25 If you punish a mocker, the s will learn a lesson;

SIMPLEST (1) [SIMPLE]

Ecc 10:15 that they have no strength for even the s tasks.

SIMPLETON (4) [SIMPLE]

Pr 14:18 The s is clothed with folly, but the wise person is
21:11 A s can learn only by seeing mockers punished;
22: 3 the s goes blindly on and suffers the consequences.
27:12 The s goes blindly on and suffers the

SIMPLETONS (3) [SIMPLE]

Pr 1:22 "You s!" she cries. "How long will you go on
1:32 For they are s who turn away from me—to death.
14:15 Only s believe everything they are told!

SIMPLY (21) [SIMPLE]

Ex 23: 6 "Do not twist justice against people s because they
Lev 13:28 the skin and has faded, it is s a scar from the burn.
13:41 loses hair on his forehead, he s has a bald forehead;
Nu 21: 8 Those who are bitten will live if they s look at it!"
32:16 "We s want to build sheepfolds for our flocks
Dt 7: 8 It was s because the LORD loves you, and
1Sa 6: 9 we will know that the plague was s a coincidence
26:19 But if this is s a human scheme, then may those
1Ki 20: 9 but this last demand of yours I s cannot meet.' "
2Ki 5:13 So you should certainly obey him when he says s
Job 10: 2 I will say to God, 'Don't s condemn me—tell me
Isa 2: 9 The LORD cannot s ignore their sins!
Jer 22:21 you have been that way—you s will not listen!
Hab 1:10 They s pile ramps of earth against their walls
Lk 8:29 he s broke them and rushed out into the wilderness,
17:10 We are servants who have s done our duty.' "
19:34 And the disciples s replied, "The Lord needs it."
Jn 7:27 When the Messiah comes, he will s appear; no one
Ro 9:19 Haven't they s done what he made them do?"
Heb 5: 4 And no one can become a high priest s because he
Jude 1: 9 of blasphemy, but s said, "The Lord rebuke you."

SIMRI [KJV] See SHIMRI

SIN (473) [SIN'S, SINFUL, SINFULNESS, SINLESS, SINNED, SINNER, SINNER'S, SINNERS, SINNING, SINS]

SIN OFFERING (99) Ex 29:14; Lev 4:14,20,21,21,24,25,29,32,33; 5:6,7,8,9,11,11,12; 6:17,25,25,30; 7:7,37; 8:2,14; 9:2,3,7,8,10,15,22; 10:16,17,19,19; 14:13,19,22,31; 15:15,30; 16:3,5,6,9,11,11,15,25; 23:19; Nu 6:11,14,16; 7:16,22,28,34,40,46,52,58,64,70,76,82; 8:8,12; 15:24,25,27, 28:15,22; 29:5,11,11,16,19,22,25,28,31,34,38; 2Ch 29:21,23,24,24; Ezr 6:17; 8:35; Eze 43:19,21,22,25; 44:27; 45:19,22,23,25

SIN OFFERINGS (13) Lev 14:13; 16:27; Nu 7:87; 18:9; 2Ki 12:16; Ne 10:33; Ps 40:6; Eze 40:39; 42:13; 44:29; 45:17; 46:20; Hos 4:8

Ge 4: 7 S is waiting to attack and destroy you, and you
15:16 when the s of the Amorites has run its course."
20: 9 making me and my kingdom guilty of this great s?
26:10 and you would have made us guilty of great s."
39: 9 wicked thing? It would be a great s against God."
Ex 10:16 "I confess my s against the LORD your God
10:17 "Forgive my s only this once, and plead with the
16: 1 they left Elim and journeyed into the S Desert,
17: 1 the people of Israel left the S Desert and moved
23:33 they will infect you with their s of idol worship,
29:14 outside the camp, and burn it as a s offering.
29:36 a young bull as an offering for the atonement of s.
30:10 from the offering made for the atonement of s.
32:21 "How did they ever make you bring such terrible s
32:30 to the people, "You have committed a terrible s,
32:31 "Alas, these people have committed a terrible s.
32:32 But now, please forgive their s—and if not,
34: 7 to many thousands by forgiving every kind of s
34: 7 Even so I do not leave s unpunished, but I punish
Lev 4: 2 s unintentionally by doing anything forbidden by
4:14 When they discover their s, the leaders of the
4:14 community must bring a young bull for a s offering
4:20 following the same procedure as with the s
4:21 just as is done with the s offering for the high
4:21 This is a s offering for the entire community of
4:23 When he becomes aware of his s, he must bring as
4:24 are slaughtered. This will be his s offering.
4:25 will dip his finger into the blood of the s offering,
4:26 the priest will make atonement for the leader's s,
4:28 When they become aware of their s, they must
4:28 no physical defects. It will be offered for their s.
4:29 They are to lay a hand on the head of the s offering
4:32 "If any of the people bring a sheep as their s
4:33 They are to lay a hand on the head of the s offering
5: 5 in any of these ways, they must confess their s
5: 6 This will be a s offering to remove their s,
5: 7 or two young pigeons as the penalty for their s.
5: 7 One of the birds will be a s offering, and the other
5: 8 who will offer one of the birds as the s offering.
5: 9 Then he will sprinkle some of the blood of the s
5:11 bring two quarts of choice flour for their s offering.
5:11 Since it is a s offering, they must not mix it with
5:12 to the LORD by fire. This will be their s offering.
5:15 "If any of the people s by unintentionally defiling
5:17 "If any of them s by doing something forbidden by
6: 2 "Suppose some of the people s against the LORD
6: 3 under oath, or they commit any other similar s.
6:17 Like the s offering and the guilt offering, it is most
6:25 these further instructions regarding the s offering.
6:25 The animal given as a s offering is most holy
6:30 the blood of a s offering has been taken into the
7: 7 "For both the s offering and the guilt offering,
7:18 if you eat it, you will have to answer for your s.
7:37 the grain offering, the s offering, the guilt offering,
8: 2 the bull for the s offering, the two rams,
8:14 Then Moses brought in the bull for the s offering,
9: 2 "Take a young bull for a s offering and a ram for a
9: 3 Then tell the Israelites to take a male goat for a s
9: 7 "Approach the altar and present your s offering
9: 8 and slaughtered the calf as a s offering for himself.
9:10 and the lobe of the liver from the s offering,
9:15 people's goat and presented it as their s offering,
9:22 Then, after presenting the s offering, the whole
10:16 what had happened to the goat of the s offering,
10:17 "Why didn't you eat the s offering in the sanctuary
10:19 "Today my sons presented both their s offering
10:19 have approved if I had eaten the s offering today?"
14:13 in the sacred area at the place where s offerings
14:13 As with the s offering, the guilt offering will be
14:19 "Then the priest must offer the s offering
14:22 One of the pair must be used for a s offering
14:31 One of them is for a s offering and the other for a
15:15 one for a s offering and the other for a whole burnt
15:30 The priest will offer one for a s offering
16: 3 He must first bring a young bull for a s offering
16: 5 then bring him two male goats for a s offering
16: 6 "Aaron will present the bull as a s offering,
16: 9 LORD will be presented by Aaron as a s offering.
16:11 "Then Aaron will present the young bull as a s
16:11 After he has slaughtered this bull for the s offering,
16:15 "Then Aaron must slaughter the goat as a s
16:16 because of the defiling s and rebellion of the
16:25 He must also burn all the fat of the s offering on
16:27 "The bull and goat given as s offerings,
18:22 not practice homosexuality; it is a detestable s.
19: 8 you will answer for the s of profaning what is holy
23:19 Then you must offer one male goat as a s offering
Nu 5: 7 They must confess their s and make full restitution
5:31 but his wife will be held accountable for her s.' "
6:11 The priest will offer one of the birds for a s
6:14 a one-year-old female lamb without defect for a s
6:16 first the s offering and the burnt offering;
7:16 a male goat for a s offering;
7:22 a male goat for a s offering;
7:28 a male goat for a s offering;
7:34 a male goat for a s offering;
7:40 a male goat for a s offering;
7:46 a male goat for a s offering;
7:52 a male goat for a s offering;
7:58 a male goat for a s offering;
7:64 a male goat for a s offering;
7:70 a male goat for a s offering;
7:76 a male goat for a s offering;
7:82 a male goat for a s offering;
7:87 Twelve male goats were brought for the s
8: 8 along with a second young bull for a s offering.
8:12 One will be for a s offering and the other for a
12:11 Please don't punish us for this s we have
14:18 forgiving every kind of s and rebellion.
14:18 Even so he does not leave s unpunished, but he
15:24 and with one male goat for a s offering.
15:25 For it was an unintentional s, and they have
15:25 given to the LORD by fire and by their s offering.
15:26 for the entire population was involved in the s.

15:27 "If the unintentional s is committed by an
15:27 bring a one-year-old female goat for a s offering.
18: 9 grain offerings, s offerings, and guilt offerings—
19: 9 This ceremony is performed for the removal of s.
27: 3 against the LORD. He died because of his own s.
28:15 offer one male goat for a s offering to the LORD.
28:22 You must also offer a male goat as a s offering,
29: 5 you must sacrifice a male goat as a s offering,
29:11 You must also sacrifice one male goat for a s
29:11 This is in addition to the s offering of atonement
29:16 You must also sacrifice a male goat as a s offering,
29:19 You must also sacrifice a male goat as a s offering,
29:22 You must also sacrifice a male goat as a s offering,
29:25 You must also sacrifice a male goat as a s offering,
29:28 You must also sacrifice a male goat as a s offering,
29:31 You must also sacrifice a male goat as a s offering,
29:34 You must also sacrifice one male goat as a s
29:38 You must also sacrifice one male goat as a s
32:23 and you may be sure that your s will find you out.
33:11 They left the Red Sea and camped in the S Desert.
33:12 They left the S Desert and camped at Dophkah.
Dt 9:16 in your terrible s against the LORD your God.
9:21 I took your s—the calf you had made—and I
9:27 Overlook the stubbornness and s of these people,
15: 9 to the LORD, you will be considered guilty of s.
20:18 which would cause you to s deeply against the
23:21 all your vows. If you don't, you will be guilty of s.
23:22 it is not a s to refrain from making a vow.
24:15 and it would be counted against you as s.
Jos 22:17 Was our s at Peor not enough? We are not yet fully
22:20 was not the only one who died because of that s."
1Sa 2:17 So the s of these young men was very serious in
12:23 I will certainly not s against the LORD by ending
12:25 But if you continue to s, you and your king will be
14:34 Do not s against the LORD by eating meat with
14:38 We must find out what s was committed today.
14:41 and I guilty, or is the s among the others?"
15:23 Rebellion is as bad as the s of witchcraft,
15:25 forgive my s now and go with me to worship the
19: 4 "Please don't s against David," Jonathan pleaded.
25:39 Nabal has received the punishment for his s."
2Sa 12:13 has forgiven you, and you won't die for this s.
22:24 blameless before God; / I have kept myself from s.
1Ki 8:46 "If they s against you—and who has never
11:39 descendants of David because of Solomon's s—
12:30 This became a great s, for the people worshiped
13:34 This became a great s and resulted in the
14:16 and made all of Israel s along with him."
14:22 arousing his anger with their s, for it was even
16: 2 have aroused my anger by causing my people to s.
21:22 him very angry and have led all of Israel into s.
22:52 of Nebat, who had led Israel into the s of idolatry.
2Ki 10:29 the great s that Jeroboam son of Nebat had led
12:16 and s offerings was not brought into the LORD's
13: 6 But they continued to s, following the evil example
17:21 the LORD and made them commit a great s.
21:16 This was in addition to the s that he caused the
23:15 son of Nebat had made when he led Israel into s.
1Ch 21: 3 your servants? Why must you cause Israel to s?"
2Ch 6:36 "If they s against you—and who has never
12: 1 the LORD, and all Israel followed him in this s.
19:10 you must warn them not to s against the LORD,
24:18 against Judah and Jerusalem because of their s.
28:19 for he had encouraged his people to s and had been
29:21 and seven male goats as a s offering for the
29:23 The male goats for the s offering were
29:24 The priests then killed the goats as a s offering
29:24 and s offering should be made for all Israel.
Ezr 6:17 And twelve male goats were presented as a s
8:35 They also offered twelve goats as a s offering.
9: 7 Our whole history has been one of great s. That is
10:11 Confess your s to the LORD, the God of your
Ne 1: 8 'If you s, I will scatter you among the nations.
6:13 and make me s by following his suggestion.
9:28 all was going well, your people turned to s again,
10:33 and for the s offerings to make atonement for
13:26 exactly what led King Solomon of Israel into s?"
13:26 But even he was led into s by his foreign wives.
Job 1:22 In all of this, Job did not s by blaming God.
5:17 the chastening of the Almighty when you s.
7:21 Why not just pardon my s and take away my guilt?
10: 6 in a hurry to probe for my guilt, to search for my s?
13:23 I done wrong? Show me my rebellion and my s.
19: 5 using my humiliation as evidence of my s,
21:19 But I say that God should punish the ones who s,
31: 7 my eyes have seen, or if I am guilty of any other s,
31:11 For lust is a shameful s, a crime that should be
31:34 so that I refused to acknowledge my s and would
34:10 Everyone knows that God doesn't s!
34:31 say to God, 'I have sinned, but I will s no more'?
35: 6 If you s, what do you accomplish against him?
35: 6 Even if you s again and again, what effect will it
36:18 with wealth. Don't let yourself be bribed into s.
Ps 4: 4 Don't s by letting anger gain control over you.
5: 4 in wickedness; / you cannot tolerate the slightest s.
17: 3 for I am determined not to s in what I say.
18:23 blameless before God; / I have kept myself from s.
19:13 I will be free of guilt / and innocent of great s.
32: 1 rebellion is forgiven, / whose s is put out of sight!
32: 2 whose record the LORD has cleared of s,
32: 3 When I refused to confess my s, / I was weak
36: 1 S whispers to the wicked, deep within their hearts.
39: 1 and not s in what I say. / I will curb my tongue
40: 6 you don't require burnt offerings or s offerings.
51: 2 me clean from my guilt. / Purify me from my s.
66:18 If I had not confessed the s in my heart, / my Lord
78:17 Yet they kept on with their s, / rebelling against the
89:32 then I will punish their s with the rod, / and their
106:43 and they were finally destroyed by their s.
119:11 word in my heart, / that I might not s against you.
119:61 Evil people try to drag me into s, / but I am firmly
130: 8 He himself will free Israel / from every kind of s.
Pr 10:16 but evil people squander their money on s.
10:19 Don't talk too much, for it fosters s. Be sensible
11: 5 the wicked fall beneath their load of s.
14:21 It is s to despise one's neighbors; blessed are those
14:34 exalts a nation, but s is a disgrace to any people.
16: 6 Unfailing love and faithfulness cover s; evil is
17:19 Anyone who loves to quarrel loves s; anyone who
20: 9 cleansed my heart; I am pure and free from s"?
21: 4 a proud heart, and evil actions are all s.
28:10 Those who lead the upright into s will fall into
29: 6 Evil people are trapped by s, but the righteous
29:16 When the wicked are in authority, s increases.
29:22 person starts fights and gets into all kinds of s.
Ecc 5: 6 In such cases, your mouth is making you s.
Isa 3: 9 They s openly like the people of Sodom.
13:11 the world for its evil and the wicked for their s.
22:14 s will never be forgiven you until the day you die.
27: 9 The LORD did this to purge away Israel's s.
53:10 Yet when his life is made an offering for s, he will
59: 2 Because of your s, he has turned away and will not
59: 3 of murderers, and your fingers are filthy with s.
59: 6 do is productive; all their activity is filled with s.
64: 6 We are all infected and impure with s. When we
Jer 2: 5 "What s did your ancestors find in me that led
5: 3 You crushed them, but they refused to turn from s.
5:25 Your s has robbed you of all these good things.
6:19 It is the fruit of their own s because they refuse to
8: 6 Is anyone sorry for s? Does anyone say, "What a
8: 6 All are running down the path of s as swiftly as a
8: 9 wise teachers will be shamed by exile for their s,
16:10 What is our s against the LORD our God?'
16:17 I am watching them closely, and I see every s.
17: 3 to your enemies, for s runs rampant in your land.
18:15 of good, and they walk the muddy paths of s.
23:13 by Baal and led my people of Israel into s.
23:32 dreams are flagrant lies that lead my people into s.
32:35 an incredible evil, causing Judah to s so greatly!
50:20 "no s will be found in Israel or in Judah,
51: 5 even though their land was filled with s against the
Eze 4: 5 sins for 390 days—one day for each year of their s.
4: 6 for 40 days—one day for each year of Judah's s.
7:13 Not one person whose life is twisted by s will
7:19 for their love of money made them stumble into s.
14: 3 They have embraced things that lead them into s.
14: 4 so they fall into s and then come to a prophet
14: 7 and set up idols in their hearts so they fall into s,
14:11 not to stray from me, polluting themselves with s.
14:13 suppose the people of a country were to s against
16:22 In all your years of adultery and loathsome s,
16:31 so eager for s that you have not even demanded
20:38 purge you of all those who rebel and s against me.
21:24 out against you, for you are not ashamed of your s.
21:24 whatever you do, all your actions are filled with s.
33:12 people will not save them if they turn to s,
33:13 righteous people that they will live, but then they s,
36:26 I will take out your stony heart of s and give you a
39:23 it was punishment for s, for they acted in treachery
40:39 the burnt offerings, s offerings, and guilt offerings.
42:13 s offerings, and guilt offerings because these
43:19 are to be given a young bull for a s offering,
43:21 Then take the young bull for the s offering
43:22 sacrifice as a s offering a young male goat that has
43:25 and a ram from the flock will be sacrificed as a s
44:12 other gods, causing Israel to fall into deep s.
44:27 he must offer a s offering for himself,
44:29 the grain offerings, the s offerings, and the guilt
45:17 He will provide the s offerings, burnt offerings,
45:19 The priest will take some of the blood of this s
45:22 provide a young bull as a s offering for himself
45:23 A male goat will also be given each day for a s
45:25 provide these same sacrifices for the s offering,
46:20 and s offerings and bake the flour from the grain
Da 8:12 was restrained from destroying him for this s.
8:23 when their s is at its height, a fierce king, a master
9:11 have been poured out against us because of our s.
9:20 I went on praying and confessing my s and the sins
9:24 to bring an end to s, to atone for guilt, to bring in
Hos 4: 7 more priests there are, the more they s against me.
4: 8 "The priests get fed when the people s and bring
their s offerings to them. So the priests are glad
when the people s!
6: 9 the road to Shechem and practice every kind of s.
8:11 "Israel has built many altars to take away s,
9: 7 for the nation is burdened with s and shows only
10: 8 of Aven, the place of Israel's s, will crumble.
10: 9 in Gibeah, there has been only s and more s!
Am 2:12 "But you caused the Nazirites to s by making them
Jnh 1:14 they pleaded, "don't make us die for this man's s.
Mic 1:13 in Judah to follow Israel in the s of idol worship,
and so you led Jerusalem into s.
2:10 for you have filled it with s and ruined it
3: 8 fearlessly pointing out Israel's s and rebellion.
Hab 1: 3 Must I forever see this s and misery all around me?
1:13 But will you, who cannot allow s in any form,
Mal 2: 6 and they turned many from lives of s.
2: 8 'guidance' has caused many to stumble into s.
Mt 5:30 causes you to s, cut it off and throw it away.
6:14 "If you forgive those who s against you,
12:31 "Every s or blasphemy can be forgiven—
13:41 remove from my Kingdom everything that causes s
18: 7 it will be for anyone who causes others to s.
18: 8 So if your hand or foot causes you to s, cut it off
18: 9 And if your eye causes you to s, gouge it out
24:12 S will be rampant everywhere, and the love of
Mk 3:28 "I assure you that any s can be forgiven,
3:29 Spirit will never be forgiven. It is an eternal s."
9:43 If your hand causes you to s, cut it off. It is better
9:45 If your foot causes you to s, cut it off. It is better to
9:47 And if your eye causes you to s, gouge it out.
Lk 3:20 John in prison, adding this s to his many others.
17: 1 "There will always be temptations to s,
18:11 For I never cheat, I don't s, I don't commit
Jn 1:29 There is the Lamb of God who takes away the s of
3:20 the light because they want to s in the darkness.
7: 7 it does hate me because I accuse it of s and evil.
8:11 And Jesus said, "Neither do I. Go and s no more."
8:21 You will search for me and die in your s.
8:34 assure you that everyone who sins is a slave of s.
8:46 Which of you can truthfully accuse me of s?
9:34 "You were born in s!" they answered. "Are you
15:22 to them. But now they have no excuse for their s.
16: 8 when he comes, he will convince the world of its s,
16: 9 The world's s is unbelief in me.
19:11 the one who brought me to you has the greater s."
Ac 7:60 shouting, "Lord, don't charge them with this s!"
8:23 you are full of bitterness and held captive by s."
11:18 given the Gentiles the privilege of turning from s
13:24 the need for everyone in Israel to turn from s
19: 4 baptism was to demonstrate a desire to turn from s
20:21 the necessity of turning from s and turning to God,
Ro 1:29 s, greed, hate, envy, murder, fighting, deception,
2: 4 he has been in giving you time to turn from your s?
2: 5 your stubbornness in refusing to turn from your s.
2:12 God will punish the Gentiles when they s,
2:12 And he will punish the Jews when they s, for they
3: 8 you might as well say that the more we s the better
3: 9 whether Jews or Gentiles, are under the power of s.
4: 8 whose s is no longer counted against them by the
5:12 Adam sinned, s entered the entire human race.
5:12 Adam's s brought death, so death spread to
5:15 And what a difference between our s and God's
5:15 Adam, brought death to many through his s.
5:16 very different from the result of that one man's s.
5:16 For Adam's s led to condemnation, but we have
5:17 The s of this one man, Adam, caused death to rule
5:17 gift of righteousness will live in triumph over s
5:18 Adam's one s brought condemnation upon
5:21 So just as s ruled over all people and brought them
6: 2 Since we have died to s, how can we continue to
6: 6 so that s might lose its power in our lives. We are
no longer slaves to s.
6: 7 with Christ we were set free from the power of s.
6:10 He died once to defeat s, and now he lives for the
6:11 So you should consider yourselves dead to s
6:12 Do not let s control the way you live; do not give
6:14 S is no longer your master, for you are no longer
subject to the law, which enslaves you to s.
6:16 You can choose s, which leads to death, or you can
6:17 Once you were slaves of s, but now you have
6:18 Now you are free from s, your old master, and you
6:20 In those days, when you were slaves of s,
6:22 But now you are free from the power of s and have
6:23 For the wages of s is death, but the free gift of God
7: 7 not sinful, but it was the law that showed me my s.
7: 8 But s took advantage of this law and aroused all
7: 8 If there were no law, s would not have that power.
7:11 S took advantage of the law and fooled me; it took
7:13 S used what was good to bring about my
7:13 So we can see how terrible s really is.
7:14 I am sold into slavery, with s as my master.
7:17 because it is s inside me that makes me do these
7:20 really the one doing it; the s within me is doing it.
7:23 and makes me a slave to the s that is still within
7:24 will free me from this life that is dominated by s?
7:25 because of my sinful nature I am a slave to s.
8: 2 Jesus from the power of s that leads to death.
8:10 even though your body will die because of s,
1Co 5: 1 church who is living in s with his father's wife.
5: 9 to associate with people who indulge in sexual s.
5:10 talking about unbelievers who indulge in sexual s,
5:11 claims to be a Christian yet indulges in sexual s,
6: 9 Those who indulge in sexual s, who are idol
6:18 Run away from sexual s! No other s so clearly
affects the body as this one
6:18 For sexual immorality is a s against your own
7:22 has now set you free from the awful power of s.
7:28 But if you do get married, it is not a s. And if a
young woman gets married, it is not a s.
7:36 and time is passing, it is all right; it is not a s.
8:12 And you are sinning against Christ when you s
8:13 If what I eat is going to make another Christian s,
10:12 be careful, for you too may fall into the same s.
14:24 they will be convicted of s, and they will be
15:56 For s is the sting that results in death, and the law
gives s its power.
15:57 who gives us victory over s and death through
2Co 5:21 who never sinned, to be the offering for our s,
7:10 use sorrow in our lives to help us turn away from s
Gal 2:17 Has Christ led us into s? Of course not!
3:22 have declared that we are all prisoners of s,
5:21 drunkenness, wild parties, and other kinds of s.
6: 1 Dear friends, if a Christian is overcome by some s,
Eph 2: 2 full of s, obeying Satan, the mighty prince of the
4:26 And "don't s by letting anger gain control over
Col 3: 5 Have nothing to do with sexual s, impurity, lust,
1Th 4: 3 to be holy, so you should keep clear of all sexual s.
1Ti 2:14 who was deceived by Satan, and s was the result.
5:24 But there are others whose s will not be revealed
2Ti 3: 6 women who are burdened with the guilt of s

Tit 2:14 He gave his life to free us from every kind of **s**,
Heb 1: 3 After he died to cleanse us from the stain of **s**,
3:13 so that none of you will be deceived by **s**
4:15 all of the same temptations we do, yet he did not **s**.
7:26 because he is holy and blameless, unstained by **s**.
9:26 to remove the power of **s** forever by his sacrificial
10: 6 burned on the altar / or with other offerings for **s**.
10: 8 animals burned on the altar or other offerings for **s**,
11:25 instead of enjoying the fleeting pleasures of **s**.
12: 1 especially the **s** that so easily hinders our progress.
12: 4 not yet given your lives in your struggle against **s**.
13:11 of animals into the Holy Place as a sacrifice for **s**,
Jas 2: 9 you are committing a **s**, for you are guilty of
4:17 it is **s** to know what you ought to do and then not
5:12 so that you will not **s** and be condemned for it.
1Pe 2:24 so we can be dead to **s** and live for what is right.
2Pe 1: 9 that God has cleansed them from their old life of **s**.
2:14 They make a game of luring unstable people into **s**.
2:18 they lure back into **s** those who have just escaped
2:19 but they themselves are slaves to **s** and corruption.
2:20 Savior Jesus Christ and then get tangled up with **s**
1Jn 1: 7 blood of Jesus, his Son, cleanses us from every **s**.
1: 8 If we say we have no **s**, we are only fooling
2: 1 I am writing this to you so that you will not **s**.
2: 1 But if you do **s**, there is someone to plead for you
3: 4 Those who **s** are opposed to the law of God, for all **s** opposes the law of God.
3: 5 to take away our sins, for there is no **s** in him.
3: 6 So if we continue to live in him, we won't **s** either.
3: 9 who have been born into God's family do not **s**,
5:16 But there is a **s** that leads to death, and I am not
5:17 Every wrong is **s**, but not all **s** leads to death.
Jude 1:24 bring you into his glorious presence innocent of **s**
Rev 2:14 food offered to idols and by committing sexual **s**.
2:20 eat food offered to idols, and commit sexual **s**.

SIN'S (1) [SIN]

Ro 8: 3 God destroyed **s** control over us by giving his Son

SINAI (57)

MOUNT SINAI (43) Ex 16:1; 17:6; 19:2,11,18,20; 24:16; 31:18; 33:6; 34:2,4,32; Lev 7:38; 25:1; 26:46; 27:34; Nu 3:1; 28:6; Dt 1:2,3,6,19; 4:10,15; 5:2; 9:8; 18:16; 29:1; 33:2; Jdg 5:5; 1Ki 8:9; 19:8; 2Ch 5:10; Ne 9:13; Ps 68:17; 106:19; Mal 4:4; Ac 7:30,38; Gal 4:24,25; Heb 12:18,26

WILDERNESS OF SINAI (12) Ex 19:1; Lev 7:38; Nu 1:1,19; 3:4,14; 9:1,5; 10:12; 26:64; 33:15,16

Ex 3: 1 and he went deep into the wilderness near **S**,
16: 1 into the Sin Desert, between Elim and Mount **S**.
17: 6 I will meet you by the rock at Mount **S**.
19: 1 The Israelites arrived in the wilderness of **S** exactly
19: 2 they came to the base of Mount **S** and set up camp
19:11 for I will come down upon Mount **S** as all the
19:18 All Mount **S** was covered with smoke
19:20 The LORD came down on the top of Mount **S**
24:16 presence of the LORD rested upon Mount **S**,
31:18 finished speaking with Moses on Mount **S**,
33: 6 So from the time they left Mount **S**, the Israelites
34: 2 Be ready in the morning to come up Mount **S**
34: 4 Early in the morning he climbed Mount **S** as the
34:32 the LORD had given him on Mount **S**.
Lev 7:38 **S** when he commanded the Israelites to bring their
7:38 offerings to the LORD in the wilderness of **S**.
25: 1 While Moses was on Mount **S**, the LORD said to
26:46 gave to the Israelites through Moses on Mount **S**.
27:34 gave to the Israelites through Moses on Mount **S**.
Nu 1: 1 to Moses in the Tabernacle in the wilderness of **S**.
1:19 counted the people there in the wilderness of **S**.
3: 1 when the LORD spoke to Moses on Mount **S**:
3: 4 **S** when they burned before the LORD a different
3:14 spoke again to Moses, there in the wilderness of **S**.
9: 1 rest of the Israelites were in the wilderness of **S**:
9: 5 in the wilderness of **S** as twilight fell on the
10:12 So the Israelites set out from the wilderness of **S**
26:64 in the previous census taken in the wilderness of **S**.
28: 6 is the regular burnt offering ordained at Mount **S**,
33:15 left Rephidim and camped in the wilderness of **S**.
33:16 They left the wilderness of **S** and camped at
Dt 1: 2 days to travel from Mount **S** to Kadesh-barnea,
1: 3 But forty years after the Israelites left Mount **S**,
1: 6 "When we were at Mount **S**, the LORD our God
1:19 we left Mount **S** and traveled through the great
4:10 stood before the LORD your God at Mount **S**,
4:15 the day he spoke to you from the fire at Mount **S**.
5: 2 "While we were at Mount **S**, the LORD our God
9: 8 how angry you made the LORD at Mount **S**,
18:16 your God when you were assembled at Mount **S**.
29: 1 the covenant he had made with them at Mount **S**.
33: 2 "The LORD came from Mount **S** / and dawned
Jdg 5: 5 Even Mount **S** shook in the presence of the
1Ki 8: 9 tablets that Moses had placed there at Mount **S**,
19: 8 to travel forty days and forty nights to Mount **S**,
2Ch 5:10 tablets that Moses had placed there at Mount **S**,
Ne 9:13 "You came down on Mount **S** and spoke to them
Ps 68: 8 before you, the God of **S**, / before God, the God of
68:17 the Lord came from Mount **S** into his sanctuary.
106:19 The people made a calf at Mount **S**; / they bowed
Mal 4: 4 and regulations that I gave him on Mount **S** for all
Ac 7:30 "Forty years later, in the desert near Mount **S**,
7:38 him life-giving words on Mount **S** to pass on to us.
Gal 4:24 represents Mount **S** where people first became
4:25 And now Jerusalem is just like Mount **S** in Arabia,
Heb 12:18 as the Israelites did at Mount **S** when God gave
12:26 When God spoke from Mount **S** his voice shook

SINCE (271)

Ge 15: 2 **S** I don't have a son, Eliezer of Damascus,
16: 6 Abram replied, "**S** she is your servant, you may
18:11 And **s** Abraham and Sarah were both very old,
18:27 "**S** I have begun, let me go on and speak further to
18:31 "**S** I have dared to speak to the Lord, let me
21:31 So ever **s**, that place has been known as
23: 8 "**S** this is how you feel, be so kind as to ask
26:27 **s** you sent me from your land in a most unfriendly
29:18 **S** Jacob was in love with Rachel, he told her father,
29:34 affection for me, **s** I have given him three sons!"
35: 8 Ever **s**, the tree has been called the "Oak of
38:15 thought she was a prostitute, **s** her face was veiled.
41:39 "**S** God has revealed the meaning of the dreams to
42: 6 **S** Joseph was governor of all Egypt and in charge
44:28 by some wild animal. I have never seen him **s**.
47:16 then," Joseph replied, "**s** your money is gone,
47:26 But **s** Pharaoh had not taken over the priests' land,
Ex 4:23 worship me. But **s** you have refused, be warned!
5:19 **S** Pharaoh would not let up on his demands,
5:23 **S** I gave Pharaoh your message, he has been even
21: 8 **s** he is the one who broke the contract with her.
21:21 be punished, **s** the slave is the owner's property.
29:22 "**S** this is the ram for the ordination of Aaron
Lev 2:15 **S** it is a grain offering, put olive oil on it
5:11 **S** it is a sin offering, they must not mix it with
10:18 **S** the animal's blood was not taken into the Holy
19:20 But **s** she had not been freed at the time, the couple
20:17 **S** the man has had intercourse with his sister,
21:21 **S** he has a blemish, he may not offer food to his
25:15 be based on the number of years **s** the last jubilee.
25:20 **s** we are not allowed to plant or harvest crops that
Nu 3: 4 **S** they had no sons, this left only Eleazar
5:13 but there is no witness **s** she was not caught in the
7: 9 **s** they were required to carry the sacred objects of
11:28 who had been Moses' personal assistant **s** his
14:19 just as you have forgiven them ever **s** they left
15:31 **S** they have treated the LORD's word with
19:13 **S** the water of purification was not sprinkled on
19:20 **S** the water of purification has not been sprinkled
21: 3 and the place has been called Hormah ever **s**.
22:20 "**S** these men have come for you, get up and go
Dt 13: 5 **S** they try to keep you from following the LORD
14: 1 "**S** you are the people of the LORD your God,
22:27 **S** the man raped her out in the country, it must be
Jos 2:12 be kind to me and my family **s** I have helped you.
2:15 **s** Rahab's house was built into the city wall,
3: 4 **S** you have never traveled this way before,
7:26 place has been called the Valley of Trouble ever **s**.
10:14 or **s** has there been a day like that one,
14:10 these forty-five years **s** Moses made this promise—
17:17 of Joseph, "**S** you are so large and strong,
21:10 the tribe of Levi, **s** the sacred lot fell to them first:
Jdg 2: 3 **S** you have done this, I will no longer drive out the
4: 9 But **s** you have made this choice, you will receive
19:30 "Such a horrible crime has not been committed **s**
21: 7 **s** we have sworn by the LORD not to give them
21:16 **s** all the women of the tribe of Benjamin are dead?
21:22 And you are not guilty of breaking the vow **s** you
Ru 2: 7 She has been hard at work ever **s**, except for a few
2:11 your mother-in-law **s** the death of your husband.
1Sa 6: 4 "**S** the plague has struck both you and your five
8: 8 Ever **s** I brought them from Egypt they have
12: 2 I have served as your leader **s** I was a boy.
15:26 **S** you have rejected the LORD's command,
17:14 **S** David's three oldest brothers were in the army,
17:33 and he has been in the army **s** he was a boy!"
17:50 only a stone and sling. And **s** he had no sword,
21: 5 And **s** they stay clean even on ordinary trips,
21: 6 So, **s** there was no other food available, the priest
23:28 Ever **s** that time, the place where David was
25: 8 to us, **s** we have come at a time of celebration?
25:26 **s** the LORD has kept you from murdering
27: 8 near Shur, along the road to Egypt, **s** ancient times.
29: 3 and I've never found a single fault in him **s** he
2Sa 2:16 The place has been known ever **s** as the Field of
13:14 and **s** he was stronger than she was, he raped her.
13:20 **S** he's your brother anyway, don't worry about it."
13:32 Absalom has been plotting this ever **s** Amnon
14: 6 And **s** no one was there to stop it, one of them was
19:13 told them to tell Amasa, "**S** you are my nephew,
19:24 or clothes nor trimmed his beard **s** the day the king
1Ki 7:14 **s** his mother was a widow from the tribe of
10:12 or **s** has there been such a supply of beautiful
11:11 "**S** you have not kept my covenant and have
14: 9 And **s** you have turned your back on me,
21: 2 "**S** your vineyard is so convenient to the palace,
2Ki 1: 6 Now, **s** you have done this, you will never leave
1:16 Now, **s** you have done this, you will never leave
1:17 **S** Ahaziah did not have a son to succeed him,
2:22 The water has remained wholesome ever **s**, just as
9:15 told the men with him, "**S** you want me to be king,
10: 6 where they had been raised **s** childhood.
17:25 But **s** these foreign settlers did not worship the
21:15 and have angered me ever **s** their ancestors came
23:22 like that **s** the time when the judges ruled in Israel,
23:25 And there has never been a king like him **s**.
25: 4 But **s** the city was surrounded by the Babylonians,
1Ch 4:43 who had survived, and they have lived there ever **s**.
5: 1 But **s** he dishonored his father by sleeping with one
5: 9 And **s** they had so many cattle in the land of
9:27 the house of God, **s** it was their duty to guard it.
9:33 there **s** they were on duty at all hours.
22: 8 And **s** you have shed so much blood before me,
2Ch 8: 1 It was now twenty years **s** Solomon had become
12: 7 "**S** the people have humbled themselves, I will not
25:16 and said, "**S** when have I asked your advice?
26:23 So Uzziah died, and **s** he had leprosy, he was
30:17 **S** many of the people there had not purified
30:26 a celebration like this one **s** the days of Solomon,
31:10 "**S** the people began bringing their gifts to the
35: 3 "**S** the Ark is now in Solomon's Temple and you
35:18 Never **s** the time of the prophet Samuel had there
Ezr 4: 2 We have sacrificed to him ever **s** King Esarhaddon
4:14 "**S** we are loyal to you as your subjects and we do
5:16 The people have been working on it ever **s**,
8:18 **S** the gracious hand of our God was on us,
Ne 8:17 The Israelites had not celebrated this way **s** the
Est 3: 4 **s** Mordecai had told them he was a Jew.
3: 6 **S** he had learned that Mordecai was a Jew,
6:13 what had happened, they said, "**S** Mordecai—
Job 17: 3 O God, **s** no one else will stand up for me.
20: 4 "Don't you realize that ever **s** people were first
39:11 **S** it is so strong, can you trust it? Can you go away
41:10 And **s** no one dares to disturb the crocodile,
Ps 77: 5 I think of the good old days, long **s** ended,
88:15 I have been sickly and close to death **s** my youth.
106:31 been regarded as a righteous man / ever **s** that time.
Pr 27: 1 **s** you don't know what the day will bring.
Ecc 6: 6 And **s** he must die like everyone else—well,
10:10 **S** a dull ax requires great strength,
10:13 **S** fools base their thoughts on foolish premises,
Isa 3: 6 "**S** you have a cloak, you be our leader!
7:17 years **s** Solomon's empire was divided into Israel
28:11 **S** they refuse to listen, God will speak to them
28:17 Your refuge looks strong, but **s** it is made of lies,
28:17 **S** it is made of deception, the enemy will come like
44: 7 Let them do as I have done **s** ancient times.
46: 3 and have cared for you **s** before you were born.
47:15 those with whom you have done business **s**
64: 4 For **s** the world began, no ear has heard and no eye
Jer 3: 4 you have been my guide **s** the days of my youth.
22:21 **S** childhood you have been that way—you simply
29:31 **S** he has prophesied to you when I did not send
32:30 have done nothing but wrong **s** their earliest days.
34:17 **S** you have not obeyed me by setting your
35: 8 We have never had a drink of wine **s** then,
44:18 But ever **s** we quit burning incense to the Queen of
52: 7 But **s** the city was surrounded by the Babylonians,
Eze 5: 7 **S** you have refused to obey my laws
15: 6 **S** they are useless, I have set them aside to be
20:29 has been called Bamah—'high place'—ever **s**.)
35: 6 **s** you show no distaste for blood,
37:28 And **s** my Temple will remain among them
42: 6 **S** there were three levels and they did not have
Da 10:12 **S** the first day you began to pray for understanding
11: 1 and defense **s** the first year of the reign of Darius
12: 1 greater than any **s** nations first came into existence.
Hos 4: 6 **S** you have forgotten the laws of your God, I will
4: 9 **s** the priests are wicked, the people are wicked,
10: 9 "O Israel, ever **s** that awful night in Gibeah,
11: 5 "But **s** my people refuse to return to me, they will
Jnh 1:11 And **s** the storm was getting worse all the time,
Zec 7:13 "**S** they refused to listen when I called to them,
8: 9 LORD Almighty ever **s** the foundation was laid.
10: 5 **S** the LORD is with them as they fight, they will
Mal 2:17 favors evildoers **s** he does not punish them.
3: 7 Ever **s** the days of your ancestors, you have
Mt 10:25 And **s** I, the master of the household, have been
13:35 I will explain mysteries hidden **s** the creation of the
19: 6 **S** they are no longer two but one, let no one
22:45 **S** David called him Lord, how can he be his son at
27: 6 "**s** it's against the law to accept money paid for
Mk 3: 2 **S** it was the Sabbath, Jesus' enemies watched him
7:26 **S** she was a Gentile, born in Syrian Phoenicia,
9:21 the boy's father. He replied, "**S** he was very small.
10: 8 united into one.' **S** they are no longer two but one,
10:20 "I've obeyed all these commandments **s** I was a
11:32 **s** everyone thought that John was a prophet.
12:37 **S** David himself called him Lord, how can he be
13:19 horror than at any time **s** God created the world.
13:33 And **s** you don't know when they will happen,
Lk 1:20 And now, **s** you didn't believe what I said,
18:21 "I've obeyed all these commandments **s** I was a
20:44 **S** David called him Lord, how can he be his son at
22:22 the Son of Man, must die **s** it is part of God's plan.
24:29 to stay the night with them, **s** it was getting late.
Jn 5:47 And **s** you don't believe what he wrote, how will
8:19 Jesus answered, "**S** you don't know who I am,
8:46 And **s** I am telling you the truth, why don't you
8:47 **S** you don't, it proves you aren't God's children."
9:32 Never **s** the world began has anyone been able to
13:14 And **s** I, the Lord and Teacher, have washed your
13:29 **S** Judas was their treasurer, some thought Jesus
15:15 **s** I have told you everything the Father told me.
15:20 **S** they persecuted me, naturally they will persecute
17:10 And all of them, **s** they are mine, belong to you;
18: 8 "And **s** I am the one you want, let these others
19:42 the Passover and **s** the tomb was close at hand,
21:14 to his disciples **s** he had been raised from the dead.
Ac 4: 3 They arrested them and, **s** it was already evening,
4:14 But **s** the man who had been healed was standing
11:17 And **s** God gave these Gentiles the same gift he
13:46 But **s** you have rejected it and judged yourselves
15:38 **s** John Mark had deserted them in Pamphylia
17:24 **S** he is Lord of heaven and earth, he doesn't live in
17:29 And **s** this is true, we shouldn't think of God as an
18:15 But **s** it is merely a question of words and names
19:36 **S** this is an indisputable fact, you shouldn't be
19:40 **s** there is no cause for all this commotion.
20: 7 and **s** he was leaving the next day, he talked until
27:12 And **s** Fair Havens was an exposed harbor—
Ro 5: 1 **s** we have been made right in God's sight by faith,

5: 9 And s we have been made right in God's sight by
5:10 For s we were restored to friendship with God by
5:13 was no law to break, s it had not yet been given,
6: 2 S we have died to sin, how can we continue to live
6: 5 S we have been united with him in his death,
6: 8 And s we died with Christ, we know we will also
6:13 give yourselves completely to God s you have
6:15 So s God's grace has set us free from the law,
6:21 s now you are ashamed of the things you used to
8:10 S Christ lives within you, even though your body
8:17 And s we are his children, we will share his
8:32 S God did not spare even his own Son but gave
11:15 For s the Jews' rejection meant that God offered
11:16 And s Abraham and the other patriarchs were holy,
12: 5 And s we are all one body in Christ, we belong to
14: 6 the Lord, s they give thanks to God before eating.
15:27 S the Gentiles received the wonderful spiritual
1Co 1:21 S God in his wisdom saw to it that the world would
6: 2 And s you are going to judge the world, can't you
11: 6 And s it is shameful for a woman to have her hair
11:12 all men have been born from women ever s,
14: 2 to people, s they won't be able to understand you.
14:12 S you are so eager to have spiritual gifts, ask God
15:12 s we preach that Christ rose from the dead, why are
2Co 1:15 S I was so sure of your understanding and trust,
3:12 S this new covenant gives us such confidence,
4: 1 s God in his mercy has given us this wonderful
5:14 S we believe that Christ died for everyone, we also
8: 7 S you excel in so many ways—you have so much
11:18 And s others boast about their human
12:10 S I know it is all for Christ's good, I am quite
Gal 2:14 "S you, a Jew by birth, have discarded the Jewish
4: 7 And s you are his child, everything he has belongs
Eph 1:15 Ever s I first heard of your strong faith in the Lord
4:21 S you have heard all about him and have learned
Col 1: 5 as you have been ever s you first heard the truth of
1: 9 So we have continued praying for you ever s we
3: 1 S you have been raised to new life with Christ,
3:12 S God chose you to be the holy people whom he
1Th 4:14 For s we believe that Jesus died and was raised to
1Ti 4: 4 S everything God created is good, we should not
Heb 2:18 S he himself has gone through suffering
4: 3 place of rest has been ready s he made the world.
6:13 S there was no one greater to swear by, God took
8: 3 And s every high priest is required to offer gifts
8: 4 s there already are priests who offer the gifts
9:26 had to die again and again, ever s the world began.
10:21 And s we have a great High Priest who rules over
12: 1 s we are surrounded by such a huge crowd of
12: 9 S we respect our earthly fathers who disciplined
12:28 S we are receiving a kingdom that cannot be
1Pe 4: 1 So then, s Christ suffered physical pain, you must
2Pe 3: 4 everything has remained exactly the same s the
3:11 S everything around us is going to melt away,
1Jn 2:29 S we know that God is always right, we also know
3: 8 to the Devil, who has been sinning s the beginning.
4:11 Dear friends, s God loved us that much, we surely
5: 9 S we believe human testimony, surely we can
Rev 3:16 But s you are like lukewarm water, I will spit you

SINCERE (11) [SINCERELY, SINCERITY]

Ps 15: 2 do what is right, / speaking the truth from s hearts.
Eze 33:31 So they come pretending to be s and sit before you
Da 11:34 though many who join them will not be s.
Hos 7:14 They do not cry out to me with s hearts. Instead,
2Co 1:12 that we have been honest and s in all our dealings.
5:11 God knows we are s, and I hope you know this,
5:12 ministry rather than having a s heart before God.
6: 6 our patience, our kindness, our s love,
1Ti 1: 5 from a pure heart, a clear conscience, and s faith.
Jas 3:17 good deeds. It shows no partiality and is always s.
1Pe 1:22 Now you can have s love for each other as brothers

SINCERELY (10) [SINCERE]

1Sa 12:24 But be sure to fear the LORD and s worship him.
2Ch 11:16 those who s wanted to worship the LORD,
Ps 145:18 all who call on him, / yes, to all who call on him s.
Jer 3:10 her faithless sister Judah has never s returned to
Mk 12:14 You s teach the ways of God. Now tell us—is it
Lk 20:21 by what others think. You s teach the ways of God.
Eph 6: 5 and fear. Serve them s as you would serve Christ.
Php 1:17 They preach with selfish ambition, not s,
2Ti 1: 5 I know that you s trust the Lord, for you have the
Heb 11: 6 is a God and that he rewards those who s seek him.

SINCERITY (2) [SINCERE]

Job 33: 3 I speak with all s; I speak the truth.
2Co 2:17 We preach God's message with s and with Christ's

SINEWS (3)

Job 10:11 and flesh, and you knit my bones and s together.
40:17 a cedar. The s of its thighs are tightly knit together.
Col 2:19 we are joined together in his body by his strong s,

SINFUL (64) [SIN]

Dt 10:16 cleanse your s hearts and stop being stubborn.
Ezr 10:13 for many of us are involved in this extremely s
Ne 13:27 How could you even think of committing this s
Job 15:16 a corrupt and s person with a thirst for wickedness!
Ps 36: 4 They lie awake at night, hatching s plots.
59:12 Because of the s things they say, / because of the
Pr 24: 9 The schemes of a fool are s; everyone despises a
Ecc 3:18 that God allows people to continue in their s ways
Isa 1: 4 Oh, what a s nation they are! They are loaded
1:13 even your most pious meetings—are all s and false.
6: 5 for I am a s man and a member of a s race.
31: 7 and silver images that your s hands have made.
Jer 7:26 They have been stubborn and s—even worse than
Eze 18:13 Should such a s person live? No! He must die
18:14 "But suppose that s son, in turn, has a son who
18:24 if righteous people turn to s ways and start acting
18:26 turn from being good and start doing s things,
18:26 for it. Yes, they will die because of their s deeds.
29:16 of how s she was to trust Egypt in earlier days.
37:23 for I will save them from their s backsliding.
Hos 7: 2 Their s deeds are all around them; I see them all!
Am 9: 8 am watching this s nation of Israel, and I will
Mt 7:11 If you s people know how to give good gifts to
Mk 8:38 and my message in these adulterous and s days,
Lk 11:13 If you s people know how to give good gifts to
24: 7 of Man must be betrayed into the hands of s men
Ac 3:26 by turning each of you back from your s ways."
19:18 Many who became believers confessed their s
Ro 1:18 But God shows his anger from heaven against all s,
5:20 so that all people could see how s they were.
6: 6 Our old s selves were crucified with Christ so that
7: 5 by our old nature, s desires were at work within us,
7: 5 aroused these evil desires that produced s deeds,
7: 7 The law is not s, but it was the law that showed me
7:18 and through so far as my old s nature is concerned.
7:25 but because of my s nature I am a slave to sin.
8: 3 Moses could not save us, because of our s nature.
8: 3 in a human body like ours, except that ours are s.
8: 4 for us who no longer follow our s nature
8: 5 Those who are dominated by the s nature think
about s things,
8: 6 If your s nature controls your mind, there is death.
8: 7 For the s nature is always hostile to God. It never
8: 8 the control of their s nature can never please God.
8: 9 But you are not controlled by your s nature.
8:12 to do what your s nature urges you to do.
1Co 3: 3 for you are still controlled by your own s desires.
5: 5 so that his s nature will be destroyed and he
Gal 5:13 not freedom to satisfy your s nature, but freedom
5:16 Then you won't be doing what your s nature
5:17 The old s nature loves to do evil, which is just
5:17 that are opposite from what the s nature desires.
5:19 When you follow the desires of your s nature,
5:24 and desires of their s nature to his cross
6: 8 Those who live only to satisfy their own s desires
Col 2:11 the cutting away of your s nature.
2:13 because your s nature was not yet cut away.
2:18 but their s minds have made them proud.
3: 5 So put to death the s, earthly things lurking within
1Ti 1: 9 and rebellious, who are ungodly and s,
5:24 Remember that some people lead s lives,
Tit 2:12 to turn from godless living and s pleasures.
Heb 12: 3 Think about all he endured when s people did such

SINFULNESS (1) [SIN]

Jer 21:14 And I myself will punish you for your s,

SING (149) [SANG, SINGER, SINGERS, SINGING, SINGS, SONG, SONGS, SUNG]

Ex 15: 1 "I will s to the LORD, for he has triumphed
15:21 "I will s to the LORD, for he has triumphed
Nu 21:17 this song: / "Spring up, O well! / Yes, s about it!
21:18 S of this well, / which princes dug, / which great
Dt 31:19 Teach them to s it, so it may serve as a witness
Jdg 5: 3 you mighty rulers! / For I will s to the LORD.
5:12 Wake up, wake up, and s a song! / Arise, Barak!
1Sa 29: 5 about whom the women of Israel s in their dances,
2Sa 22:50 among the nations; / I will s joyfully to your name.
1Ch 15:16 and musicians to s joyful songs to the
16: 9 S to him; yes, s his praises. / Tell everyone
16:23 Let the whole earth s to the LORD! / Each day
23:30 and evening they stood before the LORD to s
2Ch 20:22 At the moment they began to s and give praise,
23:18 and to s and rejoice as David had instructed.
35:25 and to this day choirs still s these sad songs about
Job 21:12 They s with tambourine and harp. They make
29:13 And I caused the widows' hearts to s for joy.
Ps 5:11 in you rejoice; / let them s joyful praises forever.
7:17 I will s praise to the name of the LORD Most
9: 2 I will s praises to your name, O Most High.
9:11 S praises to the LORD who reigns in Jerusalem.
13: 6 I will s to the LORD / because he has been
18:49 among the nations; / I will s joyfully to your name.
30: 4 S to the LORD, all you godly ones! / Praise his
30:12 that I might s praises to you and not be silent.
33: 1 Let the godly s with joy to the LORD, / for it is
33: 3 S new songs of praise to him; / play skillfully on
the harp and s with joy.
40: 3 He has given me a new song to s, / a hymn of
42: 8 upon me, / and through each night I s his songs,
47: 6 S praise to God, s praises; / s praise to our King, s
praises!
51:14 then I will joyfully s of your forgiveness.
57: 7 in you, O God; / no wonder I can s your praises!
57: 9 I will s your praises among the nations.
59:16 But as for me, I will s about your power. / I will
59:17 O my Strength, to you I s praises, / for you, O God,
61: 8 Then I will always s praises to your name / as I
63: 7 I s for joy in the shadow of your protecting wings.
65:13 carpeted with grain. / They all shout and s for joy!
66: 2 S about the glory of his name! / Tell the world how
66: 4 earth will worship you; / they will s your praises,
66: 8 world bless our God / and s aloud his praises.
68: 4 S praises to God and to his name! / S loud praises
68:32 S to God, you kingdoms of the earth. / S praises to
the Lord. / *Interlude*
68:33 S to the one who rides across the ancient heavens,
69:12 of town gossip, / and all the drunkards s about me.
71:22 O God. / I will s for you with a lyre,
71:23 I will shout for joy and s your praises, / for you
75: 9 has done; / I will s praises to the God of Israel.
81: 1 S praises to God, our strength. / S to the God of
Israel.
81: 2 S! Beat the tambourine. / Play the sweet lyre
87: 7 At all the festivals, the people will s, / "The source
89: 1 I will s of the tender mercies of the LORD
90:14 so we may s for joy to the end of our lives.
92: 1 to the LORD, / to s praises to the Most High.
92: 4 I s for joy because of what you have done.
95: 1 Come, let us s to the LORD! / Let us give a
95: 2 with thanksgiving. / Let us s him psalms of praise.
96: 1 S a new song to the LORD! / Let the whole earth s
to the LORD!
96: 2 S to the LORD; bless his name. / Each day
98: 1 S a new song to the LORD, / for he has done
98: 4 all the earth; / break out in praise and s for joy!
98: 5 S your praise to the LORD with the harp,
98: 8 in glee! / Let the hills s out their songs of joy
101: 1 I will s of your love and justice. / I will praise you,
104:12 the streams / and s among the branches of the trees.
104:33 I will s to the LORD as long as I live. / I will
105: 2 S to him; yes, s his praises. / Tell everyone
107:22 and s joyfully about his glorious acts.
108: 1 in you, O God; / no wonder I can s your praises!
108: 3 I will s your praises among the nations.
115:17 The dead cannot s praises to the LORD, / for they
119:172 Let my tongue s about your word, / for all your
126: 6 but they s as they return with the harvest.
132: 9 of salvation; / may your loyal servants s for joy.
132:16 agents of salvation; / its godly people will s for joy.
137: 3 "S us one of those songs of Jerusalem!"
137: 4 But how can we s the songs of the LORD
138: 1 all my heart; / I will s your praises before the gods.
138: 5 Yes, they will s about the LORD's ways,
144: 9 I will s a new song to you, O God! / I will s your
praises with a ten-stringed harp.
145: 7 they will s with joy of your righteousness.
146: 2 I will s praises to my God even with my dying
147: 1 How good it is to s praises to our God!
147: 7 S out your thanks to the LORD; / s praises to our
God, accompanied by harps.
149: 1 Praise the LORD! / S to the LORD a new song.
149: 1 S his praises in the assembly of the faithful.
149: 5 Let them s for joy as they lie on their beds.
150: 6 Let everything that lives s praises to the LORD!
SS 6: 9 see her; even queens and concubines s her praises!
Isa 5: 1 Now I will s a song for the one I love about his
12: 1 In that day you will s: / "Praise the LORD!
12: 4 In that wonderful day you will s:
12: 5 S to the LORD, / for he has done wonderful
14: 7 land is at rest and is quiet. Finally it can s again!
14: 8 and the cedars of Lebanon—s out this joyous song:
23:15 back to life and s sweet songs like a prostitute.
23:16 will take a harp, walk the streets, and s her songs,
24:14 But all who are left will shout and s for joy.
24:16 Listen to them as they s to the LORD from the
26: 1 everyone in the land of Judah will s this song:
26:19 who sleep in the earth / will rise up and s for joy!
27: 2 "In that day we will s of the pleasant vineyard.
30:29 But the people of God will s a song of joy,
35: 6 and those who cannot speak will shout and s!
38:20 I will s his praises with instruments / every day of
42:10 S a new song to the LORD! / S his praises from the
ends of the earth! / S, all you who sail the seas,
42:11 of Kedar rejoice! / Let the people of Sela s for joy;
42:12 glorify the LORD; / let them s his praise.
44:23 S, O heavens, for the LORD has done this
49:13 S for joy, O heavens! Rejoice, O earth! Burst into
52: 8 The watchmen shout and s with joy, for before
54: 1 "S, O childless woman! Break forth into loud
65:14 in sorrow and despair, while my servants s for joy.
Jer 20:13 Now I will s out my thanks to the LORD!
31: 7 "S with joy for Israel! Shout for the greatest of
31:12 and s songs of joy on the heights of Jerusalem.
33:11 They will s, / 'Give thanks to the LORD
La 3:14 at me. All day long they s their mocking songs.
5:14 city gates; the young men no longer dance and s.
Eze 19: 1 "S this funeral song for the princes of Israel:
27: 2 "Son of man, s a funeral song for Tyre,
27:32 they wail and mourn, they s this sad funeral song:
32:16 this is the funeral song they will s for Egypt.
Hos 2:22 And the whole grand chorus will s together,
Am 6: 5 You s idle songs to the sound of the harp, and you
Zep 3:14 S, O daughter of Zion; shout aloud, O Israel!
Lk 19:37 began to shout and s as they walked along,
Ro 15: 9 the Gentiles; / I will s praises to your name."
1Co 14:15 I will s in the spirit, and I will s in words I
understand.
14:26 When you meet, one will s, another will teach,
Eph 5:19 Then you will s psalms and hymns and spiritual
Col 3:16 S psalms and hymns and spiritual songs to God
Jas 5:13 thankful should continually s praises to the Lord.

SINGED (1)

Da 3:27 Not a hair on their heads was s, and their clothing

SINGER (2) [SING]

Ezr 7:24 no priest, Levite, s, gatekeeper, Temple servant,
10:24 This is the s who was guilty: Eliashib. These are

SINGERS (27) [SING]

1Ch 15:16 leaders to appoint a choir of Levites who were **s**
15:27 the Ark, the **s**, and Kenaniah the song leader.
2Ch 5:13 and **s** performed together in unison to praise
20:21 the king appointed **s** to walk ahead of the army,
23:13 **S** with musical instruments were leading the
29:28 assembly worshiped the LORD as the **s** sang
Ezr 2:41 The **s** of the family of Asaph | 128
2:65 in addition to 7,337 servants and 200 **s**, both men
2:70 So the priests, the Levites, the **s**, the gatekeepers,
7: 7 Levites, **s**, gatekeepers, and Temple servants,
Ne 7: 1 the gatekeepers, **s**, and Levites were appointed.
7:44 The **s** of the family of Asaph | 148
7:67 in addition to 7,337 servants and 245 **s**, both men
7:73 "So the priests, the Levites, the gatekeepers, the **s**,
10:28 the priests, Levites, gatekeepers, **s**,
10:39 the ministering priests, the gatekeepers, and the **s**.
11:22 whose family served as **s** at God's Temple.
12:28 The **s** were brought together from Jerusalem
12:29 for the **s** had built their own villages around
12:42 and the **s**—Maaseiah, Shemaiah, Eleazar, Uzzi,
12:45 son Solomon, and so did the **s** and the gatekeepers.
12:47 the people brought a daily supply of food for the **s**,
13: 5 belonged to the Levites, the **s**, and the gatekeepers.
13:10 and the **s** who were to conduct the worship services
Ps 68:25 **S** are in front, musicians are behind; / with them
Ecc 2: 8 I hired wonderful **s**, both men and women, and had
Eze 40:44 there were two one-room buildings for the **s**,

SINGING (37) [SING]

Ge 31:27 with joyful **s** accompanied by tambourines
1Sa 21:11 **s**, 'Saul has killed his thousands, and David his ten
2Sa 6: 5 **s** songs and playing all kinds of musical
1Ch 13: 8 **s** and playing all kinds of musical instruments—
2Ch 7: 6 and so did the Levites who were **s**, "His faithful
7: 6 They accompanied the **s** with music from the
20:21 **s** to the LORD and praising him for his holy
Job 36:24 glorify his mighty works, **s** songs of praise.
Ps 21:13 With music and **s** we celebrate your mighty acts.
26: 7 **s** a song of thanksgiving / and telling of all your
27: 6 of joy, / **s** and praising the LORD with music.
42: 4 to the house of God, / **s** for joy and giving thanks—
67: 4 How glad the nations will be, **s** for joy,
69:30 Then I will praise God's name with **s**, / and I will
78:63 their young women died before **s** their wedding
84: 4 can live in your house, / always **s** your praises.
100: 2 with gladness. / Come before him, **s** with joy.
Pr 25:20 **S** cheerful songs to a person whose heart is heavy
SS 2:12 are springing up, and the time of **s** birds has come,
Isa 6: 4 The glorious **s** shook the Temple to its foundations,
16:10 The happy **s** in the vineyards will be heard no
24:16 Hear them **s** praises to the Righteous One! But my
35: 2 will be an abundance of flowers and **s** and joy!
35:10 will return to Jerusalem, **s** songs of everlasting joy.
48:20 Leave Babylon and the Babylonians, **s** as you go!
51:11 will return to Jerusalem, **s** songs of everlasting joy.
Jer 7:34 I will put an end to the happy **s** and laughter in the
16: 9 I will put an end to the happy **s** and laughter in this
25:10 I will take away your happy **s** and laughter.
Eze 26:17 Then they will wail for you, **s** this funeral song:
Am 5: 1 people of Israel! Listen to this funeral song I am **s**:
8: 3 In that day the riotous sounds of **s** in the Temple
Mic 2: 4 In that day your enemies will make fun of you by **s**
Zep 3:17 He will exult over you by **s** a happy song."
Ac 16:25 and Silas were praying and **s** hymns to God,
Rev 5:11 and I heard the **s** of thousands and millions of
15: 3 And they were **s** the song of Moses, the servant of

SINGLE (95) [SINGLE-MINDED, SINGLED, SINGLENESS]

Ge 11: 1 At one time the whole world spoke a **s** language
14:23 that I will not take so much as a **s** thread or sandal
31:38 In all those years I never touched a **s** ram of yours
Ex 5: 8 But don't reduce their production quotas by a **s**
8:31 to disappear. Not a **s** fly remained in the land!
9: 4 Not a **s** one of Israel's livestock will die!' "
9: 6 but the Israelites didn't lose a **s** animal from their
10:19 Not a **s** locust remained in all the land of Egypt.
12:30 There was not a **s** house where someone had not
14:28 the Israelites into the sea, not a **s** one survived.
21: 3 If he was **s** when he became your slave and
26: 6 of sheets together, making the Tabernacle a **s** unit.
26:11 In this way, the two sets will become a **s** unit.
26:24 and firmly attached at the top with a **s** ring,
forming a **s** unit.
29: 3 Place these various kinds of bread in a **s** basket,
36:29 and firmly attached at the top with a **s** ring,
forming a **s** unit from top to bottom.
Nu 16:15 from them, and I have never hurt a **s** one of them."
21:35 and his subjects; not a **s** survivor remained.
Dt 2:34 women, and children. Not a **s** person was spared.
28:31 your eyes, but you won't get a **s** bite of the meat.
Jos 6:10 "Not a **s** word from any of you until I tell you to
8:22 of them died. Not a **s** person survived or escaped.
10: 8 Not a **s** one of them will be able to stand up to
10:42 In a **s** campaign Joshua conquered all these kings
11:11 Not a **s** person was spared. And then Joshua
23:14 your God has come true. Not a **s** one has failed!
Jdg 4:16 all of Sisera's warriors. Not a **s** one was left alive.
1Sa 12: 4 and you have never taken even a **s** bribe."
17: 8 We will settle this dispute in **s** combat!
26:20 the king of Israel come out to search for a **s** flea?
29: 3 and I've never found a **s** fault in him since he
2Sa 19: 7 not a **s** one of them will remain here tonight.
23: 8 to kill eight hundred enemy warriors in a **s** battle.
23:18 to kill three hundred enemy warriors in a **s** battle.
1Ki 16:11 of Baasha, and he did not leave a **s** male child.
17:12 that I don't have a **s** piece of bread in the house.
18:40 Don't let a **s** one escape!" So the people seized
21:21 He will not let a **s** one of your male descendants,
2Ki 7:10 all in order, but there was not a **s** person around.
10:11 and priests. So Ahab was left without a **s** survivor.
10:25 and kill all of them. Don't let a **s** one escape!"
1Ch 11:11 to kill three hundred enemy warriors in a **s** battle.
11:20 to kill three hundred enemy warriors in a **s** battle.
12:38 the **s** purpose of making David the king of Israel.
23:11 Jeush and Beriah were counted as a **s** family
2Ch 20:24 could see. Not a **s** one of the enemy had escaped.
28: 6 In a **s** day Pekah son of Remaliah, Israel's king,
Est 3:13 be killed, slaughtered, and annihilated on a **s** day.
Ps 84:10 A **s** day in your courts / is better than a thousand
89:34 my covenant; / I will not take back a **s** word I said.
109:13 May his family name be blotted out in a **s**
122: 3 is a well-built city, / knit together as a **s** unit.
139:16 moment was laid out / before a **s** day had passed.
Pr 17:10 A **s** rebuke does more for a person of
Ecc 7:20 There is not a **s** person in all the earth who is
SS 4: 9 glance of your eyes, by a **s** bead of your necklace.
Isa 9:14 Therefore, in a **s** day, the LORD will destroy both
10:17 In a **s** night he will burn those thorns and briers,
34:16 He will not miss a **s** detail. Not one of these birds
43: 9 Can any of them predict something even a **s** day in
66: 8 as this? Has a nation ever been born in a **s** day?
Jer 23: 4 Not a **s** one of them will be lost or missing,"
44:22 a desolate ruin without a **s** inhabitant—as it is
46:19 will be destroyed, without a **s** person living there.
51:29 Babylon will be left desolate without a **s**
51:37 and contempt, without a **s** person living there.
Eze 22:28 when the LORD hasn't spoken a **s** word to them.
Ob 1: 8 At that time not a **s** wise person will be left in the
Mic 7: 1 or a **s** fig can be found to satisfy my hunger.
Zec 3: 9 have set before Jeshua, a **s** stone with seven facets.
3: 9 and I will remove the sins of this land in a **s** day.
11: 8 I got rid of their three evil shepherds in a **s** month.
Mt 6:27 Can all your worries add a **s** moment to your life?
18:10 "Beware that you don't despise a **s** one of these
Lk 12: 6 Yet God does not forget a **s** one of them.
12:25 Can all your worries add a **s** moment to your life?
13: 7 waited three years, and there hasn't been a **s** fig!
15:29 and never once refused to do a **s** thing you told me
19:44 Your enemies will not leave a **s** stone in place,
Jn 7:48 "Is there a **s** one of us rulers or Pharisees who
12:24 in the soil. Unless it dies it will be alone—a **s** seed.
18: 9 "I have not lost a **s** one of those you gave me."
1Co 7:11 leave him, let her remain **s** or else go back to him.
Gal 2: 5 But we refused to listen to them for a **s** moment.
Col 1:22 and blameless as you stand before him without a **s**
Heb 12:16 He traded his birthright as the oldest son for a **s**
Rev 8:13 And I heard a **s** eagle crying loudly as it flew
18: 8 and famine will overtake her in a **s** day.
18:10 In one **s** moment God's judgment came on her."
18:17 And in one **s** moment all the wealth of the city is
18:19 great wealth. And now in a **s** hour it is all gone."
18:23 Her nights will be dark, without a **s** lamp.
21:21 were made of pearls—each gate from a **s** pearl!

SINGLE-MINDED (1) [MIND, SINGLE]

2Sa 2:19 He was relentless and **s** in his pursuit.

SINGLED (6) [SINGLE]

Ge 3:14 You are **s** out from all the domestic and wild
18:19 I have **s** him out so that he will direct his sons
Jos 7:16 the LORD, and the tribe of Judah was **s** out.
7:17 came forward, and the clan of Zerah was **s** out.
7:17 the LORD, and the family of Zimri was **s** out.
7:18 forward person by person, and Achan was **s** out.

SINGLENESS (2) [SINGLE]

Eze 11:19 And I will give them **s** of heart and put a new spirit
1Co 7: 7 gift of marriage, and to others he gives the gift of **s**.

SINGS (1) [SING]

Eze 33:32 like someone who **s** love songs with a beautiful

SINITES (2)

Ge 10:17 Hivites, Arkites, **S**,
1Ch 1:15 Hivites, Arkites, **S**,

SINK (12) [SANK, SINKING, SINKS, SUNK]

Job 14:21 their sons grow up in honor or **s** to insignificance.
28: 4 They **s** a mine shaft into the earth far from where
Ps 30: 9 will you gain if I die, / if I **s** down into the grave?
69: 2 Deeper and deeper I **s** into the mire; / I can't find a
69:14 me out of the mud; / don't let me **s** any deeper!
Pr 18: 8 rumors are—but they **s** deep into one's heart.
26:22 rumors are—but they **s** deep into one's heart.
Jer 51:64 'In this same way Babylon and her people will **s**,
Eze 3:10 let all my words **s** deep into your own heart first.
26:19 You will **s** beneath the terrible waves of enemy
Am 8: 8 the Nile River at floodtime, toss about, and **s** again.
Mt 14:30 at the high waves, he was terrified and began to **s**.

SINKING (1) [SINK]

Lk 5: 7 boats were filled with fish and on the verge of **s**.

SINKS (2) [SINK]

Eze 27:27 everyone on board **s** into the depths of the sea.
Am 9: 5 like the Nile River at floodtime, and then it **s** again.

SINLESS (1) [SIN]

1Pe 1:19 lifeblood of Christ, the **s**, spotless Lamb of God.

SINNED (123) [SIN]

Ge 13:13 and **s** greatly against the LORD.
Ex 9:34 and his officials **s** yet again by stubbornly refusing
32:33 "I will blot out whoever has **s** against me.
Lev 4:22 he will be guilty even if he **s** unintentionally.
4:27 they will be guilty even if they **s** unintentionally.
6: 4 If they have **s** in any of these ways and are guilty,
Nu 14:40 "We realize that we have **s**, but now we are ready
16:38 from the burners of these men who have **s** at the
21: 7 "We have **s** by speaking against the LORD
22:34 confessed to the angel of the LORD, "I have **s**.
32:13 the whole generation that **s** against him had died.
32:23 then you will have **s** against the LORD,
Dt 1:41 you confessed, 'We have **s** against the LORD!
9:18 because you had **s** by doing what the LORD
Jos 7:11 Israel has **s** and broken my covenant! They have
7:20 Achan replied, "I have **s** against the LORD,
22:20 **s** by stealing the things set apart for the LORD?
22:31 because you have not **s** against the LORD as we
Jdg 10:10 "We have **s** against you because we have
10:15 pleaded with the LORD and said, "We have **s**.
11:27 I have not **s** against you. Rather, you have wronged
1Sa 7: 6 and confessed that they had **s** against the LORD.
12:10 'We have **s** by turning away from the LORD
15:24 Then Saul finally admitted, "Yes, I have **s**. I have
15:30 Then Saul pleaded again, "I know I have **s**.
20: 8 or kill me yourself if I have **s** against your father.
24:11 to harm you and that I have not **s** against you,
26:21 Then Saul confessed, "I have **s**. Come back home,
2Sa 12:13 to Nathan, "I have **s** against the LORD."
19:20 I know how much I **s**. That is why I have come
24:10 "I have **s** greatly and shouldn't have taken the
24:17 "I am the one who has **s** and done wrong!
1Ki 8:33 by their enemies because they have **s** against you,
8:35 is no rain because your people have **s** against you,
8:46 "If they sin against you—and who has never **s**?—
8:47 to you again in repentance and pray, 'We have **s**,
8:50 and forgive your people who have **s** against you.
14:16 He will abandon Israel because Jeroboam **s**
1Ch 21: 8 "I have **s** greatly and shouldn't have taken the
21:17 I am the one who has **s** and done wrong! But these
2Ch 6:24 by their enemies because they have **s** against you,
6:26 is no rain because your people have **s** against you,
6:36 "If they sin against you—and who has never **s**?—
6:37 to you again in repentance and pray, 'We have **s**,
6:39 and forgive your people who have **s** against you.
26:16 He **s** against the LORD his God by entering the
26:18 Get out of the sanctuary, for you have **s**.
33:23 before the LORD. Instead, Amon **s** even more.
Ezr 10:10 "You have **s**, for you have married pagan women.
Ne 1: 6 I confess that we have **s** against you. Yes, even my
own family and I have **s**!
1: 7 We have **s** terribly by not obeying the commands,
9:18 They **s** and committed terrible blasphemies.
9:33 We have **s** greatly, and you gave us only what we
Job 1: 5 "Perhaps my children have **s** and have cursed God
7:20 Have I **s**? What have I done to you, O watcher of
8: 4 Your children obviously **s** against him, so their
10:14 was to watch me, and if I **s**, you would not forgive
19: 4 And even if I have **s**, that is my concern, not yours.
32: 2 because Job refused to admit that he had **s**
33: 9 You said, 'I am pure; I am innocent; I have not **s**.
33:27 declare to his friends, 'I **s**, but it was not worth it.
34: 6 suffering is incurable, even though I have not **s**.'
34:31 say to God, 'I have **s**, but I will sin no more'?
Ps 41: 4 mercy on me. / Heal me, for I have **s** against you."
51: 4 Against you, and you alone, have I **s**; / I have done
106: 6 Both we and our ancestors have **s**. / We have done
Isa 42:24 It was the LORD whom we **s** against,
43:27 the very beginning, your ancestors **s** against me—
65:12 You deliberately **s**—before my very eyes—
66: 4 They deliberately **s**—before my very eyes—
Jer 2:35 you severely because you claim you have not **s**.
3:25 and our ancestors have always **s** against the
7:30 "The people of Judah have **s** before my very
8:14 poison to drink because we **s** against the LORD.
14: 7 We have **s** against you. So please, help us for the
14:20 of our ancestors, too. We all have **s** against you.
40: 3 For these people have **s** against the LORD
44:23 burned incense to idols and **s** against the LORD,
50: 7 for they have **s** against the LORD, their place of
50:14 Spare no arrows, for she has **s** against the LORD.
La 1: 8 Jerusalem has **s** greatly, so she has been tossed
3:42 "We have **s** and rebelled, and you have not
5: 7 It was our ancestors who **s**, but they died before the
5:16 Disaster has fallen upon us because we have **s**.
Eze 16:37 these lovers of yours with whom you have **s**,
16:47 But you have not merely **s** as they did—no,
25:12 The people of Edom have **s** greatly by avenging
28:16 great wealth filled you with violence, and you **s**.
45:20 of the new year for anyone who has **s** through error
Da 9: 5 But we have **s** and done wrong. We have rebelled
9: 8 with shame because we have **s** against you.
9:15 But we have **s** and are full of wickedness.
Hos 13: 1 But the people of Ephraim **s** by worshiping Baal
Am 1: 3 "The people of Damascus have **s** again and again,
1: 6 "The people of Gaza have **s** again and again,
1: 9 "The people of Tyre have **s** again and again,
1:11 "The people of Edom have **s** again and again,
1:13 "The people of Ammon have **s** again and again,
2: 1 "The people of Moab have **s** again and again,
2: 4 "The people of Judah have **s** again and again,
2: 6 "The people of Israel have **s** again and again,

Mic 7: 9 the LORD punishes me, for I have s against him.
Zep 1:17 "Because you have s against the LORD, I will
Mt 6:12 just as we have forgiven those who have s against
27: 4 "I have s," he declared, "for I have betrayed an
Lk 11: 4 just as we forgive those who have s against us.
15:18 "Father, I have s against both heaven and you,
15:21 'Father, I have s against both heaven and you,
Jn 8: 7 But let those who have never s throw the first
Ro 3:23 For all have s; all fall short of God's glorious
3:25 and just when he did not punish those who s in
5:12 When Adam s, sin entered the entire human race.
5:12 so death spread to everyone, for everyone s.
5:13 Yes, people s even before the law was given.
5:20 But as people s more and more, God's wonderful
2Co 5:21 For God made Christ, who never s, to be the
12:21 because many of you who s earlier have not
Heb 3:17 Wasn't it the people who s, whose bodies fell in
1Pe 2:22 He never s, and he never deceived anyone.
3:18 He never s, but he died for sinners that he might
2Pe 2: 4 For God did not spare even the angels when they s;
1Jn 1:10 If we claim we have not s, we are calling God a

SINNER (22) [SIN]

1Sa 14:39 who rescued Israel that the s will surely die,
Ps 51: 5 For I was born a s— / yes, from the moment my
Pr 11:31 the wicked and the s will get what they deserve!
Ecc 2:26 But if a s becomes wealthy, God takes the wealth
9:18 of war, but one s can destroy much that is good.
Isa 14:21 Kill the children of this s! Do not let them rise
Eze 23:10 land as a s who had received what she deserved.
Lk 5: 8 leave me—I'm too much of a s to be around you."
7:39 what kind of woman is touching him. She's a s!"
15: 7 heaven will be happier over one lost s who returns
15:10 of God's angels when even one s repents."
18:11 God, that I am not a s like everyone else,
18:13 saying, 'O God, be merciful to me, for I am a s.'
18:14 I tell you, this s, not the Pharisee, returned home
19: 7 "He has gone to be the guest of a notorious s,"
Jn 9:16 "But how could an ordinary s do such miraculous
9:24 by telling the truth, because we know Jesus is a s."
9:25 "I don't know whether he is a s," the man replied.
Ro 3: 7 and condemn me as a s if my dishonesty highlights
4: 6 describing the happiness of an undeserving s who
7: 9 I realized I had broken the law and was a s,
Jas 5:20 brings that person back will save that s from death

SINNER'S (3) [SIN]

Job 24:20 Even the s own mother will forget him.
Pr 13: 9 full of light and joy, but the s light is snuffed out.
13:22 but the s wealth passes to the godly.

SINNERS (62) [SIN]

Nu 32:14 But here you are, a brood of s, doing exactly the
1Sa 15:18 and told you, 'Go and completely destroy the s,
Job 16:11 God has handed me over to s. He has tossed me
22:30 Then even s will be rescued by your pure hands."
24:19 Death consumes s just as drought and heat
Ps 1: 1 the advice of the wicked, / or stand around with s,
1: 5 S will have no place among the godly.
15: 4 Those who despise persistent s, / and honor the
26: 9 Don't let me suffer the fate of s. / Don't condemn
51:13 Then I will teach your ways to s, / and they will
58: 3 These wicked people are born s; / even from birth
104:35 Let all s vanish from the face of the earth;
Pr 1:10 My child, if s entice you, turn your back on them!
13:21 Trouble chases s, while blessings chase the
23:17 Don't envy s, but always continue to fear the
Ecc 7:26 escape from her, but s will be caught in her snare.
9: 2 Good people receive the same treatment as s,
Isa 1:28 But all s will be completely destroyed, for they
13: 9 The land will be destroyed and all the s with it.
33:14 The s among my people shake with fear.
53:12 He was counted among those who were s. He bore
the sins of many and interceded for s.
57: 4 out your tongues? You children of s and liars!
59:12 and testify against us. Yes, we know what s we are.
64: 5 We are constant s, so your anger is heavy on us.
65:20 old at one hundred! Only s will die that young!
Eze 18:24 turn to sinful ways and start acting like other s,
Hos 6: 8 Gilead is a city of s, tracked with footprints of
12:11 But Gilead is filled with s who worship idols.
14: 9 in them. But s stumble and fall along the way.
Am 9:10 But all the s will die by the sword—all those who
Mt 9:10 fellow tax collectors and many other notorious s.
9:13 For I have come to call s, not those who think they
11:19 and a drunkard, and a friend of the worst sort of s!'
26:45 the Son of Man, am betrayed into the hands of s.
Mk 2:15 fellow tax collectors and many other notorious s.
2:17 I have come to call s, not those who think they are
14:41 the Son of Man, am betrayed into the hands of s.
Lk 5:32 I have come to call s to turn from their sins, not to
6:32 for loving those who love you? Even the s do that!
6:33 to you, is that so wonderful? Even s do that much!
6:34 Even s will lend to their own kind for a full return.
7:34 and a drunkard, and a friend of the worst sort of s!'
13: 2 "Do you think those Galileans were worse s than
13: 4 fell on them? Were they the worst s in Jerusalem?
15: 1 and other notorious s often came to listen to Jesus
Jn 9:31 Well, God doesn't listen to s, but he is ready to
Ro 3: 5 goodness when he declares us s to be innocent.
3:26 and just in this present time when he declares s to
5: 6 Christ came at just the right time and died for us s.
5: 8 sending Christ to die for us while we were still s.
5:19 one person disobeyed God, many people became s.
Gal 2:15 and I are Jews by birth, not 's' like the Gentiles.
2:17 faith in Christ and then find out that we are still s?
Col 1: 6 the truth about God's great kindness to s.
1Ti 1:15 Christ Jesus came into the world to save s—and I
1:16 of his great patience with even the worst s.
Heb 7:26 He has now been set apart from s, and he has been
Jas 4: 8 Wash your hands, you s; purify your hearts,
1Pe 3:18 but he died for s that he might bring us safely
4:18 what chance will the godless and s have?"
Jude 1:15 and of all the insults that godless s / have spoken

SINNING (37) [SIN]

Ge 20: 6 "That is why I kept you from s against me; I did
Ex 20:20 now on, let your fear of him keep you from s!"
1Sa 2:23 wicked things you are doing. Why do you keep s?
14:33 the men are s against the LORD by eating meat
2Ki 17: 7 other gods, s against the LORD their God,
Ps 78:32 But in spite of this, the people kept on s.
Isa 57:17 myself from them, but they went right on s.
59: 7 They think only about s. Wherever they go, misery
Jer 9: 5 tell lies; they wear themselves out with all their s.
26:13 But if you stop your s and begin to obey the
Eze 3:19 If you warn them and they keep on s and refuse to
Da 4:27 please listen to me. Stop s and do what is right.
Hos 4:14 same thing, s with whores and shrine prostitutes.
8:11 away sin, but these very altars became places for s!
13: 2 Now they keep on s by making silver idols to
Jn 5:14 so stop s, or something even worse may happen to
Ro 1:30 They are forever inventing new ways of s and are
2: 9 and calamity for everyone who keeps on s—
6: 1 should we keep on s so that God can show us more
6:13 become a tool of wickedness, to be used for s.
6:15 free from the law, does this mean we can go on s?
14:23 you do anything you believe is not right, you are s.
1Co 5: 6 that if even one person is allowed to go on s,
5:12 those inside the church who are s in these ways.
8:12 And you are s against Christ when you sin against
11:27 that person is guilty of s against the body
15:34 Come to your senses and stop s. For to your shame
2Co 13: 2 I have already warned those who had been s when
Tit 3:11 They are s, and they condemn themselves.
Heb 10:26 if we deliberately continue s after we have
1Pe 4: 1 to suffer for Christ, you have decided to stop s.
1Jn 3: 6 But those who keep on s have never known him
3: 8 But when people keep on s, it shows they belong
to the Devil, who has been s since the beginning.
3: 9 So they can't keep on s, because they have been
5:16 If you see any Christian s in a way that does not
5:18 part of God's family do not make a practice of s,

SINS (432) [SIN]

FORGIVE(N, -NESS, -ING, -S)...SINS (72) Ex 23:21; 34:7; Nu 14:18,19; Jos 24:19; 1Sa 3:14; 1Ki 8:34,36; 2Ch 6:25,27; 7:14; Ps 25:7,11,18; 65:3; 79:9; 85:2; 103:3; Isa 6:7; 33:24; 38:17; Jer 18:23; 31:34; 33:8,8; 36:3; Eze 16:63; Hos 14:2; Mt 6:12,15; 9:2,5,6; 18:21; 26:28; Mk 1:4; 2:5,7,9,10; 4:12; 11:25; Lk 1:77; 3:3; 5:20,21,23,24; 7:47,48,49; 11:4; 17:3; 24:47; Jn 20:23; Ac 2:38,38; 5:31,31; 10:43; 13:38; 26:18; Ro 4:7; Eph 1:7; Col 1:14; Heb 8:12; 9:22; 10:18; Jas 5:15,20; 1Jn 1:9; 2:12

Ge 44:16 God is punishing us for our s. My lord, we have all
Ex 20: 5 I do not leave unpunished the s of those who hate
20: 5 but I punish the children for the s of their parents
23:21 rebel against him, for he will not forgive your s.
32:34 I will certainly punish them for their s."
34: 7 but I punish the children for the s of their parents
34: 9 but please pardon our iniquity and our s.
Lev 4: 3 "If the high priest s, bringing guilt upon the entire
6:30 atonement in the Holy Place for the people's s,
16:21 and confess over it all the s and rebellion of the
16:21 he will lay the people's s on the head of the goat;
16:22 the goat will carry all the people's s upon itself
16:30 and you will be cleansed from all your s in the
17:11 the blood so you can make atonement for your s.
23:28 your God, and payment will be made for your s.
26:18 I will punish you for your s seven times over.
26:21 inflict you with seven more disasters for your s.
26:24 personally strike you seven times over for your s.
26:28 I will punish you seven times over for your s.
26:39 because of their s and the s of their ancestors.
26:40 "But at last my people will confess their s
26:40 and the s of their ancestors for betraying me
26:41 will be humbled, and they will pay for their s.
26:43 people will receive the due punishment for their s,
Nu 14:18 but he punishes the children for the s of their
14:19 Please pardon the s of this people because of your
14:34 for each day, suffering the consequences of your s.
16:22 angry with all the people when only one man s?"
16:26 If you do, you will be destroyed for their s."
Dt 5: 9 I do not leave unpunished the s of those who hate
5: 9 but I punish the children for the s of their parents
24:16 "Parents must not be put to death for the s of their
24:16 nor the children for the s of their parents.
31:18 s they have committed by worshiping other gods.
Jos 24:19 He will not forgive your rebellion and s.
1Sa 2:25 If someone s against another person, God can
2:25 But if someone s against the LORD, who can
3:14 So I have vowed that the s of Eli and his sons will
12:19 "For now we have added to our s by asking for a
2Sa 7:14 If he s, I will use other nations to punish him.
1Ki 8:34 then hear from heaven and forgive their s
8:35 and confess your name and turn from their s
8:36 from heaven and forgive the s of your servants,
15: 3 He committed the same s as his father before him,
15:26 continuing the s of idolatry that Jeroboam had led
15:30 by the s he had committed and the s he had led
Israel to commit.
15:34 continuing the s of idolatry that Jeroboam had led
16: 7 arousing him to anger by his s, just like the family
16:13 This happened because of the s of Baasha and his
16:13 because of all the s they led Israel to commit,
16:19 continuing the s of idolatry that Jeroboam had led
16:26 continuing the s of idolatry that Jeroboam had led
17:18 Have you come here to punish my s by killing my
2Ki 3: 3 Nevertheless he continued in the s of idolatry that
10:31 He refused to turn from the s of idolatry that
13: 2 continuing the s of idolatry that Jeroboam son of
13:11 He refused to turn from the s of idolatry that
14: 6 "Parents must not be put to death for the s of their
14: 6 nor the children for the s of their parents.
14:24 He refused to turn from the s of idolatry that
15: 9 He refused to turn from the s of idolatry that
15:18 he refused to turn from the s of idolatry that
15:24 He refused to turn from the s of idolatry that
15:28 He refused to turn from the s of idolatry that
17:22 They did not turn from these s of idolatry
21:17 and all his deeds, including the s he committed,
24: 3 his presence because of the many s of Manasseh.
2Ch 6:25 then hear from heaven and forgive the s
6:26 and confess your name and turn from their s
6:27 from heaven and forgive the s of your servants,
7:14 and will forgive their s and heal their land.
25: 4 "Parents must not be put to death for the s of their
25: 4 nor the children for the s of their parents.
28:10 What about your own s against the LORD your
28:13 "We cannot afford to add to our s and guilt.
29:24 the altar to make atonement for the s of all Israel.
30:22 and the people confessed their s to the LORD,
33:19 and an account of all his s and unfaithfulness are
Ezr 9: 6 For our s are piled higher than our heads, and our
Ne 4: 5 Do not blot out their s, for they have provoked you
9: 2 from all foreigners as they confessed their own s
and the s of their ancestors.
9: 3 three more hours they took turns confessing their s
9:30 through the prophets, warned them about their s.
9:37 kings whom you have set over us because of our s.
Job 11:11 those who are false, and he takes note of all their s.
11:14 Get rid of your s and leave all iniquity behind you.
13:26 against me and bring up all the s of my youth.
14:16 count my steps, instead of watching for my s.
14:17 My s would be sealed in a pouch, and you would
15: 5 Your s are telling your mouth what to say.
16: 8 me to skin and bones—as proof, they say, of my s.
21:28 people who came to disaster because of their s.
31:33 Have I tried to hide my s as people normally do,
34:37 and blasphemy against God to your other s."
35: 8 No, your s affect only people like yourself,
36: 9 He shows them their s, for they have behaved
Ps 5:10 Drive them away because of their many s,
19:12 How can I know all the s lurking in my heart?
19:13 Keep me from deliberate s! / Don't let them
25: 7 Forgive the rebellious s of my youth; / look instead
25:11 your name, O LORD, / forgive my many, many s.
25:18 my pain and see my trouble. / Forgive all my s.
32: 5 Finally, I confessed all my s to you / and stopped
38: 3 is sick; / my health is broken because of my s.
38: 5 wounds fester and stink / because of my foolish s.
38:18 But I confess my s; / I am deeply sorry for what I
39:11 When you discipline people for their s, / their lives
51: 1 your great compassion, / blot out the stain of my s.
51: 7 Purify me from my s, and I will be clean;
51: 9 Don't keep looking at my s. / Remove the stain of
65: 3 Though our hearts are filled with s, / you forgive
69: 5 foolish I am; / my s cannot be hidden from you.
69:27 Pile their s up high, / and don't let them go free.
78:38 Yet he was merciful and forgave their s
79: 8 Oh, do not hold us guilty for our former s!
79: 9 Oh, save us and forgive our s / for the sake of your
85: 2 your people—/ yes, you have covered all their s.
90: 8 You spread out our s before you— / our secret
s—and you see them all.
94:23 God will make the s of evil people fall back upon
94:23 He will destroy them for their s. / The LORD our
103: 3 He forgives all my s / and heals all my diseases.
103:10 He has not punished us for all our s, / nor does he
107:17 fools in their rebellion; / they suffered for their s.
109: 7 him be pronounced guilty. / Count his prayers as s.
109:14 May the LORD never forget the s of his
109:14 may his mother's s never be erased from the
109:15 May these s always remain before the LORD,
130: 3 LORD, if you kept a record of our s, / who,
Pr 5:22 An evil man is held captive by his own s; they are
14:32 The wicked are crushed by their s, but the godly
28:13 People who cover over their s will not prosper.
Ecc 7:20 in all the earth who is always good and never s.
8:12 But even though a person s a hundred times
Isa 1:18 "No matter how deep the stain of your s, I can
1:29 You will blush when you think of all the s you
2: 9 The LORD cannot simply ignore their s!
5:18 Destruction is certain for those who drag their s
6: 7 your guilt is removed, and your s are forgiven."
22:12 told you to shave your heads in sorrow for your s
24: 5 The earth suffers for the s of its people, for they
24:20 and will not rise again, for its s are very great.
26:21 heaven to punish the people of the earth for their s.
30: 1 that are not from my Spirit, thus piling up your s.
33:24 and helpless," for the LORD will forgive their s.
38:17 me from death / and have forgiven all my s.
40: 2 her sad days are gone and that her s are pardoned.
40: 2 the LORD has punished her in full for all her s."
43:24 you have burdened me with your s and wearied me
43:25 am the one who blots out your s for my own sake

44:22 I have swept away your **s** like the morning mists.
50: 1 you went away as captives because of your **s**.
50: 1 your mother, too, was taken because of your **s**.
53: 4 were a punishment from God for his own **s**!
53: 5 But he was wounded and crushed for our **s**. He was
53: 6 the LORD laid on him the guilt and **s** of us all.
53: 8 the people realized that he was dying for their **s**—
53:11 to be counted righteous, for he will bear all their **s**.
53:12 He bore the **s** of many and interceded for sinners.
58: 1 of a trumpet blast. Tell my people Israel of their **s**!
59: 2 is a problem—your **s** have cut you off from God.
59:12 For our **s** are piled up before God and testify
59:20 back those in Israel who have turned from their **s**.
64: 6 and fall. And our **s**, like the wind, sweep us away.
64: 7 turned away from us and turned us over to our **s**.
64: 9 LORD. Please don't remember our **s** forever.
65: 7 both for their own **s** and for those of their
66: 3 their own ways, delighting in their **s**, are cursed.
Jer 2:23 valley in the land! Face the awful **s** you have done.
4: 4 like an unquenchable fire because of all your **s**.
5: 6 For their rebellion is great, and their **s** are many.
11:10 They have returned to the **s** of their forefathers.
13:22 It is because of your many **s**! That is why you have
14:10 your wickedness and will punish you for your **s**."
15:13 Because of all my people's **s** against me, I will
15:17 hand was on me. I burst with indignation at their **s**.
16:18 I will punish them doubly for all their **s**,
18:23 Don't forgive their crimes and blot out their **s**.
21:12 like an unquenchable fire because of all your **s**.
23:14 evil instead of turning them away from their **s**.
25:12 the king of Babylon and his people for their **s**,
26: 3 I am ready to pour out on them because of their **s**.
26:19 they turned from their **s** and worshiped the
30:14 For your **s** are many, and your guilt is great.
30:15 because your **s** are many and your guilt is great.
31:30 All people will die for their own **s**—those who eat
31:34 and will never again remember their **s**."
31:37 not consider casting them away forever for their **s**.
32:18 though children suffer for their parents' **s**.
32:32 "The **s** of Israel and Judah—the **s** of the people of Jerusalem, the kings,
33: 8 I will cleanse away their **s** against me, and I will forgive all their **s** of rebellion.
36: 3 Then I will be able to forgive their **s**
36:31 and his family and his officials because of their **s**.
44: 9 Have you forgotten the **s** of your ancestors, the **s** of the kings and queens of Judah, and the **s** you and your wives committed in Judah
La 1: 5 LORD has punished Jerusalem for her many **s**.
1:14 "He wove my **s** into ropes to hitch me to a yoke of
1:22 as you have punished me for all my **s**.
2:14 to hold you back from exile by pointing out your **s**.
3:39 complain when we are punished for our **s**?
4:13 because of the **s** of her prophets and priests,
4:22 just beginning; soon your many **s** will be revealed.
Eze 3:18 fail to deliver the warning, they will die in their **s**.
3:19 and refuse to repent, they will die in their **s**.
3:20 of the consequences, then they will die in their **s**.
4: 4 your left side and place the **s** of Israel on yourself.
4: 4 You are to bear their **s** for the number of days you
4: 5 You will bear Israel's **s** for 390 days—one day for
7:16 will moan like doves, weeping for their **s**.
8: 6 Do you see the great **s** the people of Israel are
8: 6 and you will see even greater **s** than these!"
8:13 "Come, and I will show you greater **s** than these!"
8:15 "But I will show you even greater **s** than these!"
8:17 people of Judah that they commit these terrible **s**,
9: 4 and sigh because of the **s** they see around them."
9: 9 "The **s** of the people of Israel and Judah are very
11:12 you have copied the **s** of the nations around you."
11:21 I will repay them fully for their **s**,
13:22 them life, even though they continue in their **s**.
14:10 to want my advice—will all be punished for their **s**.
16: 2 of man, confront Jerusalem with her loathsome **s**.
16:43 I will fully repay you for all of your **s**,
16:43 For to all your disgusting **s**, you have added these
16:49 Sodom's **s** were pride, laziness, and gluttony,
16:51 "Even Samaria did not commit half your **s**.
16:52 be deeply ashamed because your **s** are so terrible.
16:54 for your **s** make them feel good in comparison.
16:58 This is your punishment for all your disgusting **s**,
16:63 You will remember your **s** and cover your mouth
18: 4 The person who **s** will be the one who dies.
18:17 Such a person will not die because of his father's **s**;
18:18 But the father will die for the many **s** he
18:19 'Doesn't the child pay for the parent's **s**?' No!
18:20 The one who **s** is the one who dies. The child will not be punished for the parent's **s**,
18:20 the parent will not be punished for the child's **s**.
18:21 But if wicked people turn away from all their **s**
18:22 All their past **s** will be forgotten, and they will live
18:24 will be forgotten, and they will die for their **s**.
18:28 thinking it over, they decided to turn from their **s**.
18:30 Turn from your **s**! Don't let them destroy you!
20:43 You will look back at all your **s** and hate
22:31 I will heap on them the full penalty for all their **s**,
24:23 but you will waste away because of your **s**.
28:18 You defiled your sanctuaries with your many **s**
33: 6 They will die in their **s**, but I will hold the
33: 8 then they will die in their **s**, but I will hold you
33: 9 and they don't repent, they will die in their **s**,
33:10 You are saying, 'Our **s** are heavy upon us; we are
33:12 nor will the **s** of evil people destroy them if they repent and turn from their **s**.
33:13 will be remembered. I will destroy them for their **s**.
33:14 but then they turn from their **s** and do what is just
33:16 None of their past **s** will be brought up again,
33:29 I have ruined the land because of their disgusting **s**,
35: 5 when I had already punished them for all their **s**.
36:31 Then you will remember your past **s** and hate
36:33 When I cleanse you from your **s**, I will bring
37:23 themselves with their detestable idols and other **s**,
39:24 them in proportion to the vileness of their **s**.
43:10 and its plan so they will be ashamed of all their **s**.
44: 6 O people of Israel, enough of your disgusting **s**!
44: 7 Thus, in addition to all your other disgusting **s**,
44:12 that they must bear the consequences for their **s**,
44:13 for they must bear the shame of all the **s** they have
Da 9:13 from the LORD our God by turning from our **s**
9:16 and your people because of our **s** and the **s** of our ancestors.
9:20 and confessing my sin and the **s** of my people,
Hos 7: 1 wanted to heal Israel, but its **s** were far too great.
8:13 I will call my people to account for their **s**, and I
9: 9 not forget. He will surely punish them for their **s**.
10:10 of the nations to punish you for your multiplied **s**.
10:13 and raised a thriving crop of **s**.
12:14 now sentence them to death in payment for their **s**.
13:12 "The **s** of Ephraim have been collected and stored
14: 1 your God, for your **s** have brought you down.
14: 2 "Forgive all our **s** and graciously receive us,
Am 3: 2 That is why I must punish you for all your **s**."
3:14 "On the very day I punish Israel for its **s**, I will
4: 4 Keep on disobeying—your **s** are mounting up!
5:12 For I know the vast number of your **s**
7: 8 this plumb line. I will no longer ignore all their **s**.
Mic 1: 5 Because of the **s** and rebellion of Israel and Judah.
6: 7 our firstborn children to pay for the **s** of our souls?
6:13 wound you! I will bring you to ruin for all your **s**.
7:18 who pardons the **s** of the survivors among his
7:19 You will trample our **s** under your feet and throw
Hab 1:12 to punish and correct us for our terrible **s**.
Zep 1:12 and punish those who sit contented in their **s**,
Zec 3: 4 to Jeshua he said, "See, I have taken away your **s**,
3: 9 and I will remove the **s** of this land in a single day.
5: 6 and it is filled with the **s** of everyone throughout
13: 1 a fountain to cleanse them from all their **s**
Mal 3:14 the LORD Almighty that we are sorry for our **s**?
Mt 1:21 for he will save his people from their **s**."
3: 2 "Turn from your **s** and turn to God,
3: 6 And when they confessed their **s**, he baptized them
3: 8 you live that you have really turned from your **s**
3:11 "I baptize with water those who turn from their **s**
4:17 to preach, "Turn from your **s** and turn to God,
6:12 and forgive us our **s**, / just as we have forgiven
6:15 forgive others, your Father will not forgive your **s**.
9: 2 "Take heart, son! Your **s** are forgiven."
9: 5 to say, 'Your **s** are forgiven' or 'Get up and walk'?
9: 6 of Man, have the authority on earth to forgive **s**."
11:20 because they hadn't turned from their **s** and turned
18: 3 unless you turn from your **s** and become as little
18:15 "If another believer **s** against you, go privately
18:21 how often should I forgive someone who **s** against
21:32 you refused to turn from your **s** and believe him.
26:28 It is poured out to forgive the **s** of many.
Mk 1: 4 baptized to show that they had turned from their **s**
1: 5 And when they confessed their **s**, he baptized them
1:15 Turn from your **s** and believe this Good News!"
2: 5 the paralyzed man, "My son, your **s** are forgiven."
2: 7 This is blasphemy! Who but God can forgive **s**!"
2: 9 'Your **s** are forgiven' or 'Get up, pick up your mat,
2:10 of Man, have the authority on earth to forgive **s**."
4:12 So they will not turn from their **s** / and be
6:12 went out, telling all they met to turn from their **s**.
11:25 so that your Father in heaven will forgive your **s**,
Lk 1:77 to find salvation / through forgiveness of their **s**.
3: 3 baptized to show that they had turned from their **s**
3: 8 you live that you have really turned from your **s**
5:20 Jesus said to the man, "Son, your **s** are forgiven."
5:21 "This is blasphemy! Who but God can forgive **s**?"
5:23 to say, 'Your **s** are forgiven' or 'Get up and walk'?
5:24 of Man, have the authority on earth to forgive **s**."
5:32 I have come to call sinners to turn from their **s**,
7:47 I tell you, her **s**—and they are many—have been
7:48 Jesus said to the woman, "Your **s** are forgiven."
7:49 this man think he is, going around forgiving **s**?"
11: 4 And forgive us our **s**— / just as we forgive those
16:30 from the dead, then they will turn from their **s**.'
17: 3 If another believer **s**, rebuke him; then if he
24:47 'There is forgiveness of **s** for all who turn to me.'
Jn 3:20 They stay away from the light for fear their **s** will
5:24 They will never be condemned for their **s**, but they
8:24 That is why I said that you will die in your **s**;
8:24 that I am who I say I am, you will die in your **s**."
8:34 "I assure you that everyone who **s** is a slave of sin.
9: 2 Was it a result of his own **s** or those of his
9: 3 "It was not because of his **s** or his parents' **s**,"
20:23 If you forgive anyone's **s**, they are forgiven.
Ac 2:38 "Each of you must turn from your **s** and turn to
2:38 name of Jesus Christ for the forgiveness of your **s**.
3:19 Now turn from your **s** and turn to God, so you can be cleansed of your **s**.
5:31 people of Israel an opportunity to turn from their **s**
5:31 and turn to God so their **s** would be forgiven.
10:43 him will have their **s** forgiven through his name."
13:38 In this man Jesus there is forgiveness for your **s**.
22:16 and be baptized, and have your **s** washed away,
26:18 Then they will receive forgiveness for their **s**
26:20 that all must turn from their **s** and turn to God—
Ro 3: 5 "But," some say, "our **s** serve a good purpose,
3:22 when we trust in Jesus Christ to take away our **s**.
3:24 who has freed us by taking away our **s**.
3:25 For God sent Jesus to take the punishment for our **s**
4: 7 is forgiven, / whose **s** are put out of sight.
4:25 He was handed over to die because of our **s**,
5:16 by God, even though we are guilty of many **s**.
8: 3 over us by giving his Son as a sacrifice for our **s**.
11:27 my covenant with them / and take away their **s**."
1Co 6:11 but now your **s** have been washed away, and you
15: 3 that Christ died for our **s**, just as the Scriptures
15:17 and you are still under condemnation for your **s**.
2Co 5:19 no longer counting people's **s** against them.
Gal 1: 4 He died for our **s**, just as God our Father planned,
Eph 1: 7 the blood of his Son, and our **s** are forgiven.
2: 1 doomed forever because of your many **s**.
2: 5 that even while we were dead because of our **s**,
5: 2 and gave himself as a sacrifice to take away your **s**.
5: 3 Such **s** have no place among God's people.
5: 6 Don't be fooled by those who try to excuse these **s**,
Col 1:14 freedom with his blood and has forgiven all our **s**.
2:13 You were dead because of your **s** and because your
2:13 made you alive with Christ. He forgave all our **s**.
1Th 2:16 By doing this, they continue to pile up their **s**.
4: 6 for the Lord avenges all such **s**, as we have
1Ti 5:20 Anyone who **s** should be rebuked in front of the
5:22 Do not participate in the **s** of others. Keep yourself
Tit 3: 5 He washed away our **s** and gave us a new life
Heb 2:17 sacrifice that would take away the **s** of the people.
5: 1 their gifts to God and offers their sacrifices for **s**.
5: 3 both for their **s** and for his own **s**.
7:27 They did this for their own **s** first and then for the **s** of the people.
8:12 and I will never again remember their **s**."
9: 7 which he offers to God to cover his own **s**
9: 7 and the **s** the people have committed in ignorance.
9:14 himself to God as a perfect sacrifice for our **s**.
9:15 the **s** they had committed under that first covenant.
9:22 the shedding of blood, there is no forgiveness of **s**.
9:28 as a sacrifice to take away the **s** of many people.
9:28 will come again but not to deal with our **s** again.
10: 3 Those yearly sacrifices reminded them of their **s**
10: 4 for the blood of bulls and goats to take away **s**.
10:11 offering sacrifices that can never take away **s**.
10:12 Priest offered himself to God as one sacrifice for **s**,
10:17 never again remember / their **s** and lawless deeds."
10:18 Now when **s** have been forgiven, there is no need
10:26 there is no other sacrifice that will cover these **s**.
Jas 5:15 And anyone who has committed **s** will be forgiven.
5:16 Confess your **s** to each other and pray for each
5:20 and bring about the forgiveness of many **s**.
1Pe 1:22 because you were cleansed from your **s** when you
2:24 He personally carried away our **s** in his own body
3:18 Christ also suffered when he died for our **s** once
4: 8 for each other, for love covers a multitude of **s**.
1Jn 1: 9 But if we confess our **s** to him, he is faithful
2: 2 He is the sacrifice for our **s**. He takes away not only our **s** but the **s** of all the world.
2:12 because your **s** have been forgiven because of
3: 5 And you know that Jesus came to take away our **s**,
4:10 and sent his Son as a sacrifice to take away our **s**.
Jude 1:23 be careful that you aren't contaminated by their **s**.
Rev 1: 5 and has freed us from our **s** by shedding his blood
2:15 follow the same teaching and commit the same **s**.
16:19 And so God remembered all of Babylon's **s**,
18: 4 Do not take part in her **s**, or you will be punished
18: 5 For her **s** are piled as high as heaven, and God is

SION [KJV] See SIRION, ZION

SIP (1)

Eze 12:19 and **s** their tiny portions of water in utter despair,

SIPHMOTH (1)

1Sa 30:28 Aroer, **S**, Eshtemoa,

SIR (52) [SIRS]

Ge 23:11 "No, **s**," he said to Abraham, "please listen to me.
24:18 "Certainly, **s**," she said, and she quickly lowered
24:46 so I could drink, and she said, 'Certainly, **s**,
42:11 We are all brothers and honest men, **s**! We are not
42:13 "**S**," they said, "there are twelve of us brothers,
43:20 They said to him, "**S**, after our first trip to Egypt to
47:25 "May it please you, **s**, to let us be Pharaoh's
Ex 1:19 "**S**," they told him, "the Hebrew women are very
32:22 "Don't get upset, **s**," Aaron replied.
Nu 31:49 and said, "**S**, we have accounted for all the men
32:27 But, **s**, all who are able to bear arms will cross over
32:31 The tribes of Gad and Reuben said again, "**S**,
36: 2 They said, "**S**, the LORD instructed you to divide
Jdg 4:18 and said to him, "Come into my tent, **s**.
6:13 "**S**," Gideon replied, "if the LORD is with us,
Ru 2:13 "I hope I continue to please you, **s**," she replied.
1Sa 1:15 "Oh no, **s**!" she replied, "I'm not drunk! But I am
1:18 "Oh, thank you, **s**!" she exclaimed. Then she went
1:26 "**S**, do you remember me?" Hannah asked. "I am
22:14 "But **s**," Ahimelech replied, "is there anyone
28:21 woman saw how distraught he was, she said, "**S**,
2Sa 9: 2 the king asked. "Yes **s**, I am," Ziba replied.
16: 4 "Thank you, **s**," Ziba replied.
1Ki 18: 9 "Oh, **s**," Obadiah protested, "what harm have I
18:14 is here'! **S**, if I do that, I'm as good as dead!"
20:31 Ben-hadad's officers said to him, "**S**, we have
20:39 prophet called out to him, "**S**, I was in the battle,
2Ki 2:16 "**S**," they said, "just say the word and fifty of our
5:13 his officers tried to reason with him and said, "**S**,
Jer 38: 4 So these officials went to the king and said, "**S**,
Mt 13:27 The farmer's servants came and told him, '**S**,
18:26 fell down before the king and begged him, 'Oh, **s**,
21:30 other son, 'You go,' and he said, 'Yes, **s**, I will.'

25:11 they stood outside, calling, 'S, open the door for
25:20 'S, you gave me five bags of gold to invest and I
25:22 with the report, 'S, you gave me two bags of gold
25:24 servant with the one bag of gold came and said, 'S,
27:63 They told him, "S, we remember what that
Jn 4:11 "But s, you don't have a rope or a bucket,"
4:15 "Please, s," the woman said, "give me some of
4:19 "S," the woman said, "you must be a prophet.
5:7 "I can't, s," the sick man said, "for I have no one
6:34 "S," they said, "give us that bread every day of
9:36 The man answered, "Who is he, s, because I
12:21 in Galilee. They said, "S, we want to meet Jesus."
20:15 "S," she said, "if you have taken him away,
Ac 9:5 "Who are you, s?" Saul asked. And the voice
10:4 "What is it, s?" he asked the angel. And the angel
22:8 " 'Who are you, s?' I asked. And he replied,
24:10 Paul said, "I know, s, that you have been a judge
26:15 " 'Who are you, s?' I asked. "And the Lord
Rev 7:14 And I said to him, "S, you are the one who

SIRAH (1)

2Sa 3:26 They found him at the pool of S and brought him

SIRION (2) [HERMON]

Dt 3:9 (Mount Hermon is called S by the Sidonians;
4:48 Aroer at the edge of the Arnon Gorge to Mount S,

SIRS (2) [SIR]

Ac 16:30 He brought them out and asked, "S, what must I
27:10 "S," he said, "I believe there is trouble ahead if

SISERA (22) [SISERA'S]

Jdg 4:2 The commander of his army was S, who lived in
4:3 S, who had nine hundred iron chariots,
4:7 I will lure S, commander of Jabin's army,
4:9 For the LORD's victory over S will be at the
4:12 When S was told that Barak son of Abinoam had
4:14 Today the LORD will give you victory over S,
4:15 the LORD threw S and all his charioteers
4:15 Then S leaped down from his chariot and escaped
4:17 Meanwhile, S ran to the tent of Jael, the wife of
4:18 Jael went out to meet S and said to him,
4:21 But when S fell asleep from exhaustion,
4:22 When Barak came looking for S, Jael went out to
4:22 her into the tent and found S lying there dead,
5:20 The stars in their orbits fought against S.
5:25 S asked for water, / and Jael gave him milk.
5:26 She hit S, crushing his head. / She pounded the tent
5:30 There are gorgeous robes for S, / and colorful,
5:31 "LORD, may all your enemies die as S did!
1Sa 12:9 so he let them be conquered by S, the general of
Ezr 2:53 Barkos, S, Temah,
Ne 7:55 Barkos, S, Temah,
Ps 83:9 or as you did to S and Jabin at the Kishon River.

SISERA'S (3) [SISERA]

Jdg 4:16 to Harosheth-haggoyim, killing all of S warriors.
5:22 the galloping, galloping of S mighty steeds.
5:28 "From the window S mother looked out.

SISMAI (2)

1Ch 2:40 Eleasah was the father of S. / S was the father of Shallum.

SISTER (94) [SISTER'S, SISTER-IN-LAW, SISTERS]

BROTHER...SISTER (6) Eze 44:25; Mt 12:50; Mk 3:35; 1Co 8:9; Jas 2:15; 1Jn 3:17

Ge 4:22 and iron. Tubal-cain had a s named Naamah.
11:29 their brother Haran. (Milcah had a s named Iscah.)
12:13 But if you say you are my s, then the Egyptians
12:19 willing to let me marry her, saying she was your s?
19:31 One day the older daughter said to her s,
19:34 morning the older daughter said to her younger s,
20:2 told people there that his wife, Sarah, was his s.
20:5 Abraham told me, 'She is my s,' and she herself
20:12 Besides, she is my s—we both have the same
20:13 have the kindness to say that you are my s.' "
24:60 "Our s, may you become / the mother of many
25:20 Aramean from Paddan-aram and the s of Laban.
26:7 asked him about Rebekah, he said, "She is my s."
26:9 your wife! Why did you say she was your s?"
28:9 She was the s of Nebaioth and the daughter of
29:16 who was the oldest, and her younger s, Rachel.
30:1 having any children, she became jealous of her s.
30:8 "I have had an intense struggle with my s,
34:7 and furious that their s had been raped.
34:13 because of what Shechem had done to their s.
34:27 the town because their s had been defiled there.
34:31 "Should he treat our s like a prostitute?"
36:3 was the daughter of Ishmael and the s of Nebaioth.
36:22 and Heman. Lotan's s was named Timna.
46:15 to Leah in Paddan-aram, along with their s, Dinah.
46:17 Ishvi, and Beriah. Their s was named Serah.
Ex 2:4 The baby's s then stood at a distance, watching to
2:7 Then the baby's s approached the princess.
6:20 Amram married his father's s Jochebed, and she
6:23 the daughter of Amminadab and s of Nahshon,
15:20 Aaron's s, took a tambourine and led all the
Lev 18:9 not have sexual intercourse with your s or half s,
18:11 of any of your father's wives; she is your half s.
18:12 have intercourse with your aunt, your father's s,
18:13 your mother's s, because she is your mother's
18:18 "Do not marry a woman and her s because they
18:18 if your wife dies, then it is all right to marry her s.
20:17 "If a man has sexual intercourse with his s,
20:17 Since the man has had intercourse with his s,
20:19 whether his mother's s or his father's s,
21:3 or virgin s who was dependent because she had no
Nu 6:7 if their own father, mother, brother, or s has died.
26:59 the parents of Aaron, Moses, and their s, Miriam.
Dt 27:22 is anyone who has sexual intercourse with his s,
Jdg 15:2 But look, her s is more beautiful than she is.
2Sa 13:1 David's son Absalom had a beautiful s named
13:4 "I am in love with Tamar, Absalom's s."
13:11 "Come to bed with me, my darling s."
13:22 because of what he had done to his s.
13:32 plotting this ever since Amnon raped his s Tamar.
17:25 of Nahash, was the s of Joab's mother, Zeruiah.)
1Ki 11:19 and he gave him a wife—the s of Queen Tahpenes.
2Ki 11:2 But Ahaziah's s Jehosheba, the daughter of King
1Ch 1:39 and Heman. Lotan's s was named Timna.
2:21 he married Gilead's s, the daughter of Makir.
4:19 Hodiah's wife was the s of Naham. One of her
7:15 and Shuppim. Makir's s was named Maacah.
7:18 Makir's s Hammoleketh gave birth to Ishhod,
7:30 Ishvi, and Beriah. They had a s named Serah.
7:32 Shomer, and Hotham. They had a s named Shua.
11:6 And Joab, the son of David's s Zeruiah,
2Ch 22:11 But Ahaziah's s Jehosheba, the daughter of King
Job 17:14 my father, and the worm my mother and my s.
Pr 7:4 Love wisdom like a s; make insight a beloved
SS 8:8 "We have a little s too young for breasts.
Jer 3:7 And though her faithless s Judah saw this,
3:10 her faithless s Judah has never sincerely returned
Eze 16:46 "Your older s was Samaria, who lived with her
16:46 Your younger s was Sodom, who lived with her
23:4 girl was named Oholah, and her s was Oholibah.
23:11 her s, she followed right in her footsteps.
23:13 she was going, defiling herself just like her older s.
23:18 disgusted with Oholibah, just as I was with her s,
23:32 will drink from the same cup of terror as your s—
23:33 of sorrow and distress, just as your s Samaria did.
23:45 But righteous people will judge these s cities for
44:25 is his father, mother, child, brother, or unmarried s.
Mt 12:50 Father in heaven is my brother and s and mother!"
Mk 3:35 does God's will is my brother and s and mother."
Lk 10:39 Her s, Mary, sat at the Lord's feet, listening to
10:40 doesn't it seem unfair to you that my s just sits
Jn 11:39 But Martha, the dead man's s, said, "Lord, by now
19:25 and his mother's s, Mary (the wife of Clopas),
Ac 25:13 A few days later King Agrippa arrived with his s,
Ro 16:1 Our s Phoebe, a deacon in the church in Cenchrea,
16:15 Julia, Nereus and his s, and to Olympas and all the
1Co 8:9 a brother or s with a weaker conscience to stumble.
Phm 1:2 and to our s Apphia and to Archippus, a fellow
Jas 2:15 you see a brother or s who needs food or clothing,
1Pe 5:13 Your s church here in Rome sends you greetings,
1Jn 3:17 sees a brother or s in need and refuses to help—
2Jn 1:13 Greetings from the children of your s, chosen by

SISTER'S (2) [SISTER]

Ge 24:30 saw the nose-ring and the bracelets on his s wrists,
Eze 23:31 Because you have followed in your s footsteps,

SISTER-IN-LAW (1) [SISTER]

Ru 1:15 "your s has gone back to her people and to her

SISTERS (94) [SISTER]

BROTHERS...SISTERS (81) Jos 2:13; Job 1:4; 42:11; Ps 22:22; Hos 2:1; Mt 13:55; 18:35; 19:29; 23:8; 25:40,45; Mk 3:32; 10:29,30; Lk 14:26; Ro 8:29; 9:3; 16:17; 1Co 1:10,26; 2:1; 3:1; 4:6; 6:8; 7:24,29; 10:1; 11:33; 12:1; 14:6,20,26,39; 15:1,50,58; 16:15; Gal 4:28; 6:10; Php 4:1; Col 1:2; 4:15; 1Th 1:4; 2:1,9,14; 4:1,13; 5:4,12,14,25; 2Th 1:3; 2:1,13,15; 3:1,6,13; 2Ti 4:21; Heb 2:11,12,17; Jas 1:2,16; 2:1,5,14; 3:1,10; 4:11; 5:7,9,12,19; 1Pe 1:22; 2:11,17; 1Jn 3:13; 4:21; Rev 12:10

Jos 2:13 with my father and mother, my brothers and s,
1Ch 2:16 Their s were named Zeruiah and Abigail.
Job 1:4 their brothers and s to join them for a celebration.
42:11 Then all his brothers, s, and former friends came
Ps 22:22 the wonder of your name to my brothers and s.
Eze 16:45 And you are exactly like your s, for they despised
16:51 far more loathsome things than your s ever did.
16:52 In comparison, you make your s seem innocent!
16:55 Yes, your s, Sodom and Samaria, and all their
16:61 I will make your s, Samaria and Sodom, to be your
22:11 their daughters-in-law or who rape their own s.
23:2 once there were two s who were daughters of the
23:40 "You s sent messengers to distant lands to get
Hos 2:1 And you will call your s Ruhamah—'The ones I
Mt 13:56 All his s live right here among us. What makes him
18:35 to forgive your brothers and s in your heart."
19:29 or brothers or s or father or mother or children
23:8 all of you are on the same level as brothers and s.
25:40 did it to one of the least of these my brothers and s,
25:45 refused to help the least of these my brothers and s,
Mk 3:32 "Your mother and your brothers and s are outside,
6:3 and Simon. And his s live right here among us."
10:29 or brothers or s or mother or father or children
10:30 houses, brothers, s, mothers, children,
Lk 14:26 and mother, wife and children, brothers and s—
Jn 11:1 He lived in Bethany with his s, Mary and Martha.
11:3 So the two s sent a message to Jesus telling him,
Ro 8:29 would be the firstborn, with many brothers and s.
9:3 for my people, my Jewish brothers and s. I would
16:17 I make one more appeal, my dear brothers and s.
1Co 1:10 Now, dear brothers and s, I appeal to you by the
1:26 Remember, dear brothers and s, that few of you
2:1 Dear brothers and s, when I first came to you I
3:1 Dear brothers and s, when I was with you I
4:6 Dear brothers and s, I have used Apollos
6:8 and cheat even your own Christian brothers and s.
7:24 So, dear brothers and s, whatever situation you
7:29 Now let me say this, dear brothers and s: The time
10:1 I don't want you to forget, dear brothers and s,
11:33 So, dear brothers and s, when you gather for the
12:1 And now, dear brothers and s, I will write about
14:6 Dear brothers and s, if I should come to you
14:20 Dear brothers and s, don't be childish in your
14:26 Well, my brothers and s, let's summarize what I
14:39 So, dear brothers and s, be eager to prophesy,
15:1 Now let me remind you, dear brothers and s,
15:50 dear brothers and s, is that flesh and blood cannot
15:58 So, my dear brothers and s, be strong and steady,
16:15 to other Christians. I urge you, dear brothers and s,
Gal 4:28 And you, dear brothers and s, are children of the
6:10 especially to our Christian brothers and s.
Php 4:1 Dear brothers and s, I love you and long to see
Col 1:2 who are faithful brothers and s in Christ.
4:15 to our Christian brothers and s at Laodicea,
1Th 1:4 We know that God loves you, dear brothers and s,
2:1 You yourselves know, dear brothers and s, that our
2:9 Don't you remember, dear brothers and s,
2:14 And then, dear brothers and s, you suffered
4:1 Finally, dear brothers and s, we urge you in the
4:13 And now, brothers and s, I want you to know what
5:4 in the dark about these things, dear brothers and s,
5:12 Dear brothers and s, honor those who are your
5:14 Brothers and s, we urge you to warn those who are
5:25 Dear brothers and s, pray for us.
2Th 1:3 Dear brothers and s, we always thank God for you,
2:1 And now, brothers and s, let us tell you about the
2:13 for you, dear brothers and s loved by the Lord.
2:15 dear brothers and s, stand firm and keep a strong
3:1 Finally, dear brothers and s, I ask you to pray for
3:6 And now, dear brothers and s, we give you this
3:13 And I say to the rest of you, dear brothers and s,
1Ti 5:2 the younger women with all purity as your own s.
2Ti 4:21 Linus, Claudia, and all the brothers and s.
Heb 2:11 is not ashamed to call them his brothers and s.
2:12 the wonder of your name to my brothers and s.
2:17 his brothers and s, so that he could be our merciful
Jas 1:2 Dear brothers and s, whenever trouble comes your
1:16 So don't be misled, my dear brothers and s.
2:1 My dear brothers and s, how can you claim that
2:5 Listen to me, dear brothers and s. Hasn't God
2:14 Dear brothers and s, what's the use of saying you
3:1 Dear brothers and s, not many of you should
3:10 Surely, my brothers and s, this is not right!
4:11 evil against each other, my dear brothers and s.
5:7 Dear brothers and s, you must be patient as you
5:9 my brothers and s, or God will judge you.
5:12 But most of all, dear brothers and s, never take an
5:19 My dear brothers and s, if anyone among you
1Pe 1:22 have sincere love for each other as brothers and s
2:11 Dear brothers and s, you are foreigners and aliens
2:17 Love your Christian brothers and s. Fear God.
1Jn 3:13 So don't be surprised, dear brothers and s,
4:21 love not only him but our Christian brothers and s,
Rev 12:10 our brothers and s before our God day and night.

SIT (97) [SAT, SITS, SITTING]

Ge 27:19 S up and eat it so you can give me your blessing."
27:31 S up and eat it so you can give me your blessing."
43:33 Joseph told each of his brothers where to s, and to
Ex 17:12 So Aaron and Hur found a stone for him to s on.
Lev 15:6 If you s where the man with the discharge has sat,
Jdg 5:10 and s on fancy saddle blankets, listen!
5:16 Why did you s at home among the sheepfolds—
Ru 4:2 from the town and asked them to s as witnesses.
1Sa 16:11 "We will not s down to eat until he arrives."
1Ki 1:13 be the next king and would s upon your throne?
1:17 be the next king and would s on your throne.
1:24 be the next king and that he will s on your throne?
1:30 will be the next king and will s on my throne,
1:35 you bring him back here, he will s on my throne.
1:48 who today has chosen someone to s on my throne
2:4 one of them will always s on the throne of Israel.'
2:45 and may one of David's descendants always s on
2Ki 7:3 "Why should we s here waiting to die?"
Job 16:15 Here I s in sackcloth. I have surrendered, and I s in the dust.
32:15 You s there baffled, with no further response.
42:6 and I s in dust and ashes to show my repentance."
Ps 7:7 before you. / S on your throne high above them.
50:20 You s around and slander a brother— / your own
83:1 O God, don't s idly by, / silent and inactive!
89:4 they will s on your throne from now until
110:1 said to my Lord, / "S in honor at my right hand
119:23 Even princes s and speak against me, / but I will
128:3 There they s around your table / as vigorous
139:2 You know when I s down or stand up. / You know
Isa 14:22 so they will never s on his throne.
21:5 They are spreading rugs for people to s on.
42:7 You will release those who s in dark dungeons.
47:1 "Come, Babylon, unconquered one, s in the dust.
47:5 of Babylonia, s now in darkness and silence.
47:14 at all. Their hearth is not a place to s for warmth.
51:21 you afflicted ones, who s in a drunken stupor,
Jer 3:2 You s like a prostitute beside the road waiting for a
3:2 You s alone like a nomad in the desert. You have
6:26 yourselves in sackcloth, and s among the ashes.

13:18 "Come down from your thrones and s in the dust,
14: 2 All the people s on the ground in mourning,
22:30 for none of his children will ever s on the throne of
36:15 "S down and read the scroll to us," the officials
36:30 He will have no heirs to s on the throne of David.
48:18 Come down from your glory and s in the dust,
La 2:10 The leaders of Jerusalem s on the ground in
3:28 Let them s alone in silence beneath the LORD's
5:14 The old men no longer s in the city gates;
Eze 26:16 They will s on the ground trembling with horror at
28: 2 I s on a divine throne in the heart of the sea.'
33:31 pretending to be sincere and s before you listening.
44: 3 Only the prince himself may s inside this gateway
Hos 7:14 Instead, they s on their couches and wail. They cut
Joel 3:12 will s to pronounce judgment on them all.
Jnh 4: 5 and made a shelter to s under as he waited to see if
Mic 7: 8 Though I s in darkness, the LORD himself will be
Zep 1:12 and punish those who s contented in their sins,
Zec 8: 4 with a cane and s together in the city squares.
Mal 3: 3 He will s and judge like a refiner of silver,
Mt 8:11 from all over the world and s down with Abraham,
13:48 s down, sort the good fish into crates, and throw
14:19 Then he told the people to s down on the grass.
15:35 So Jesus told all the people to s down on the
19:28 s upon my glorious throne in the Kingdom,
19:28 you who have been my followers will also s on
20:21 will you let my two sons s in places of honor next
20:23 "But I have no right to say who will s on the
22:44 said to my Lord, / S in honor at my right hand
23: 6 And how they love to s at the head table at
25:31 with him, then he will s upon his glorious throne.
26:36 and he said, "S here while I go on ahead to pray."
Mk 1:31 as he took her by the hand and helped her to s up,
6:39 Then Jesus told the crowd to s down in groups on
8: 6 So Jesus told all the people to s down on the
10:37 we want to s in places of honor next to you,"
10:40 but I have no right to say who will s on the thrones
12:36 said to my Lord, / S in honor at my right hand
14:32 and Jesus said, "S here while I go and pray."
Lk 1:79 to give light to those who s in darkness and in the
9:14 "Just tell them to s down on the ground in groups
12:19 And I'll s back and say to myself, My friend,
12:37 put on an apron, and serve them as they s and eat!
14: 7 dinner were trying to s near the head of the table,
14: 9 The host will say, 'Let this person s here instead.'
14:10 "Do this instead—s at the foot of the table.
17: 7 care of sheep, he doesn't just s down and eat.
20:42 said to my Lord, / S in honor at my right hand
22:30 And you will s on thrones, judging the twelve
Jn 6:10 "Tell everyone to s down," Jesus ordered. So all
Ac 2:30 would s on David's throne as the Messiah.
2:34 said to my Lord, / S in honor at my right hand
8:31 Philip to come up into the carriage and s with him.
Heb 1:13 as he did to his Son, / "S in honor at my right hand
Jas 2: 3 can stand over there, or else s on the floor"—
Rev 3:21 I will invite everyone who is victorious to s with
14: 7 For the time has come when he will s as judge.

SITE (8)

1Ki 6: 7 ax, or any other iron tool at the building s.
2Ch 3: 1 the Jebusite, the s that David had selected.
Ezr 2:68 the rebuilding of God's Temple on its original s,
3: 3 the local residents, they rebuilt the altar at its old s.
5: 8 s of the Temple of the great God in the province of
6: 3 It must be rebuilt on the s where Jews used to offer
6: 7 Let it be rebuilt on its former s, and do not hinder
Zec 14:10 the Benjamin Gate over to the s of the old gate,

SITH [KJV] See SINCE

SITHRI (1)

Ex 6:22 of Uzziel included Mishael, Elzaphan, and S.

SITS (26) [SIT]

Ex 11: 5 the oldest son of Pharaoh, who s on the throne,
Lev 15: 4 he lies and anything on which he s will be defiled.
15:20 which she lies or s during that time will be defiled.
15:22 same applies if you touch an object on which she s,
15:26 which she lies or s during that time will be defiled,
15:27 If you touch her bed or anything on which she s,
Dt 17:18 "When he s on the throne as king, he must copy
Est 6:10 Mordecai the Jew, who s at the gate of the palace.
Ps 99: 1 He s on his throne between the cherubim.
99: 2 The LORD s in majesty in Jerusalem,
Pr 9:14 She s in her doorway on the heights overlooking
31:23 for he s in the council meeting with the other civic
Isa 28: 1 It s in a rich valley, but its glorious beauty will
28: 4 It s in a fertile valley, but its glorious beauty will
40:22 It is God who s above the circle of the earth.
Jer 15: 9 She s childless now, disgraced and humiliated.
29:16 says about the king who s on David's throne
La 1: 1 broken with grief, she s alone in her mourning.
Mt 23:22 throne of God and by God, who s on the throne.
Lk 10:40 doesn't it seem unfair to you that my sister just s
22:27 Normally the master s at the table and is served by
Ac 2:33 Now he s on the throne of highest honor in heaven,
Col 3: 1 where Christ s at God's right hand in the place of
Rev 6:16 and hide us from the face of the one who s on the
7:15 And he who s on the throne will live among them
17: 1 on the great prostitute, who s on many waters.

SITTING (89) [SIT]

Ge 18: 1 as Abraham was s at the entrance to his tent,
19: 1 city of Sodom, and Lot was s there as they arrived.
23:10 Ephron was s there among the others, and he
31:34 into her camel saddle, and now she was s on them.
37:25 Then, just as they were s down to eat, they noticed
38:21 "Where can I find the prostitute who was s beside
Dt 22: 6 or eggs in it with the mother s in the nest,
Jdg 3:20 Ehud walked over to Eglon as he was s alone in a
13: 9 once again to his wife as she was s in the field.
19:17 When he saw the travelers s in the town square,
1Sa 1: 9 Eli the priest was s at his customary place beside
19: 9 But one day as Saul was s at home, the tormenting
20:25 with Jonathan s opposite him and Abner beside
22: 6 the king was s beneath a tamarisk tree on the hill at
2Sa 18:24 While David was s at the city gate, the watchman
1Ki 1:46 Solomon is now s on the royal throne as king.
13:14 the man of God and found him s under an oak tree.
13:20 Then while they were s at the table, a message
22:10 were s on thrones at the threshing floor near the
22:19 I saw the LORD s on his throne with all the
2Ki 1: 9 They found him s on top of a hill. The captain said
6:32 Elisha was s in his house at a meeting with the
7: 3 Now there were four men with leprosy s at the
9: 5 he found Jehu s in a meeting with the other army
2Ch 18: 9 were s on thrones at the threshing floor near the
18:18 I saw the LORD s on his throne with all the
Ezr 10: 9 and all the people were s in the square before the
Ne 2: 6 The king, with the queen s beside him, asked,
Est 5: 1 The king was s on his royal throne,
5: 9 But when he saw Mordecai s at the gate,
5:13 Mordecai the Jew just s there at the palace gate."
Ps 47: 8 reigns above the nations, / s on his holy throne.
Isa 6: 1 He was s on a lofty throne, and the train of his robe
Jer 13:13 from the king s on David's throne and from the
17:25 There will always be a descendant of David s on
22: 2 you king of Judah, s on David's throne.
22: 4 there will always be a descendant of David s on the
33:17 David will forever have a descendant s on the
36:22 part of the palace, s in front of a fire to keep warm.
Eze 8:14 and some women were s there, weeping for the
Zec 1: 8 I saw a man s on a red horse that was standing
5: 7 lifted off the basket, there was a woman s inside it.
Mt 4:21 and John, s in a boat with their father, Zebedee,
9: 9 he saw Matthew s at his tax-collection booth.
20:30 Two blind men were s beside the road. When they
26:64 s at God's right hand in the place of power
26:69 Meanwhile, as Peter was s outside in the courtyard,
27:19 Just then, as Pilate was s on the judgment seat,
27:61 and the other Mary were s nearby watching.
Mk 2: 6 religious law who were s there said to themselves,
2:14 he saw Levi son of Alphaeus s at his tax-collection
5:15 for he was s there fully clothed and perfectly sane.
10:46 was s beside the road as Jesus was going by.
14:18 As they were s around the table eating, Jesus said,
14:62 s at God's right hand in the place of power
Lk 2:46 was in the Temple, s among the religious teachers,
5:17 and teachers of religious law were s nearby.
5:27 he saw a tax collector named Levi s at his
8:35 been possessed by demons s quietly at Jesus' feet,
14:15 a man s at the table with Jesus exclaimed,
14:31 to war without first s down with his counselors
18:35 a blind beggar was s beside the road.
22:21 "But here at this table, s among us as a friend,
22:69 will be s at God's right hand in the place of
Jn 12:15 your King is coming, / s on a donkey's colt."
13:23 one Jesus loved, was s next to Jesus at the table.
19:29 A jar of sour wine was s there, so they soaked a
20:12 She saw two white-robed angels s at the head
Ac 20: 9 s on the windowsill, became very drowsy.
Ro 8:34 and is s at the place of highest honor next to God,
Rev 4: 2 and I saw a throne in heaven and someone s on it!
4: 3 The one s on the throne was as brilliant as
4: 9 and honor and thanks to the one s on the throne,
5: 1 the right hand of the one who was s on the throne.
5: 7 and took the scroll from the right hand of the one s
5:13 and power / belong to the one s on the throne
9:17 I saw the horses and the riders s on them.
11:16 And the twenty-four elders s on their thrones
14:14 Then I saw the Son of Man s on a white cloud.
14:15 and called out in a loud voice to the one s on the
14:16 So the one s on the cloud swung his sickle over the
17: 3 There I saw a woman s on a scarlet beast that had
17:15 "The waters where the prostitute is s represent
19: 4 and worshiped God, who was s on the throne.
19:11 And the one s on the horse was named Faithful
19:19 and their armies in order to fight against the one s
20: 4 and the people s on them had been given the
20:11 white throne, and I saw the one who was s on it.
21: 5 And the one s on the throne said, "Look, I am

SITUATED (3) [SITUATION]

Nu 24:21 the Kenites and prophesied: / "You are strongly s;
Jos 15:21 The towns of Judah s along the borders of Edom in
15:33 The following towns s in the western foothills

SITUATION (18) [SITUATED]

Ex 5:21 you for getting us into this terrible s with Pharaoh
2Sa 24:14 "This is a desperate s!" David replied to Gad.
1Ch 21:13 "This is a desperate s!" David replied to Gad.
Ezr 4: 8 telling King Artaxerxes about the s in Jerusalem.
4:22 for we must not permit the s to get out of control."
7:14 you to conduct an inquiry into the s in Judah
Ne 4:14 Then as I looked over the s, I called together the
5: 7 After thinking about the s, I spoke out against
Isa 43:26 Let us review the s together, and you can present
Da 2:14 Daniel handled the s with wisdom and discretion.
Lk 16: 5 money to his employer to come and discuss the s.
Jn 11:47 called the high council together to discuss the s.
Ac 19:33 of the Jews, who encouraged him to explain the s.
Ro 11: 7 So this is the s: Most of the Jews have not found
1Co 7:17 You must accept whatever s the Lord has put you
7:24 whatever s you were in when you became a
Php 4:12 I have learned the secret of living in every s,
2Ti 4: 5 But you should keep a clear mind in every s.

SIX (111) [SIXTH, 6]

Ge 30:20 he will honor me, for I have given him s sons."
31:41 your two daughters, and s years to get the flock.
Ex 14: 7 He took with him s hundred of Egypt's best
16:26 Gather the food for s days, but the seventh day is a
20: 9 S days a week are set apart for your daily duties
20:11 For in s days the LORD made the heavens,
21: 2 buy a Hebrew slave, he is to serve for only s years.
21: 7 she will not be freed at the end of s years as the
23:10 "Plant and harvest your crops for s years,
23:12 "Work for s days, and rest on the seventh.
24:16 Mount Sinai, and the cloud covered it for s days.
25:32 It will have s branches, three branches going out
25:33 Each of the s branches will hold a cup shaped like
26: 2 sheet must be forty-two feet long and s feet wide.
26: 8 each forty-five feet long and s feet wide.
26: 9 into one set, and join the other s into a second set.
26:22 On the west side there will be s frames,
28:10 S names will be on each stone, naming all the
31:15 Work s days only, but the seventh day must be a
31:17 For in s days the LORD made heaven and earth,
34:21 "S days are set aside for work, but on the Sabbath
35: 2 Each week, work for s days only. The seventh day
36: 9 the same size—forty-two feet long and s feet wide.
36:15 the same size—forty-five feet long and s feet wide.
36:16 and the s remaining sheets were joined to make a
36:27 which was its rear, was made from s frames,
37:18 The lampstand had s branches, three going out
37:19 Each of the s branches held a cup shaped like an
Lev 23: 3 You may work for s days each week, but on the
24: 6 arrange the loaves in two rows, with s in each row.
25: 3 For s years you may plant your fields and prune
Nu 7: 3 Together they brought s carts and twelve oxen.
35: 6 "You must give the Levites s cities of refuge,
35:13 Designate s cities of refuge for yourselves,
Dt 3:11 was more than thirteen feet long and s feet wide.
5:13 S days a week are set apart for your daily duties
15:12 becomes your servant and serves you for s years,
15:18 Remember that for s years they have given you the
16: 8 For the next s days you may not eat bread made
Jos 6: 3 is to march around the city once a day for s days.
6:14 to the camp. They followed this pattern for s days.
15:59 s towns with their surrounding villages.
15:62 s towns with their surrounding villages.
Jdg 3:31 He killed s hundred Philistines with an ox goad.
12: 7 Jephthah was Israel's judge for s years. When he
18:11 So s hundred warriors from the tribe of Dan set out
18:16 As the s hundred warriors from the tribe of Dan
20:47 leaving only s hundred men who escaped to the
Ru 3:15 He measured out s scoops of barley into the cloak
3:17 "He gave me these s scoops of barley and said,
1Sa 13: 5 s thousand horsemen, and as many warriors as the
13:15 were still with him, he found only s hundred left!
14: 2 and his s hundred men were camped on the
14:20 and his s hundred men rushed out to the battle
23:13 about s hundred of them now—left Keilah
27: 2 So David took his s hundred men and their families
30: 9 So David and his s hundred men set out, and they
2Sa 5: 5 Judah from Hebron for seven years and s months,
6:13 After the men who were carrying it had gone s
15:18 There were s hundred Gittites who had come with
15:22 So Ittai and his s hundred men and their families
21:20 a huge man with s fingers on each hand and s toes on each foot—
1Ki 7:24 There were about s gourds per foot all the way
10:19 The throne had s steps and a rounded back.
10:20 one standing on each end of each of the s steps.
11:16 Joab and the army had stayed there for s months,
16:23 He reigned twelve years in all, s of them in Tirzah.
2Ki 11: 3 for s years while Athaliah ruled over the land.
13:19 should have struck the ground five or s times!"
14:13 Then Jehoash ordered his army to demolish s
15: 8 reign in Judah. He reigned in Samaria s months.
1Ch 3: 4 These s sons were born to David in Hebron,
3:22 Igal, Bariah, Neariah, and Shaphat—s in all.
4:27 Shimei had sixteen sons and s daughters, but none
8:38 Azel had s sons: Azrikam, Bokeru, Ishmael,
9:44 Azel had s sons, and their names were Azrikam,
20: 6 a huge man with s fingers on each hand and s toes on each foot—
21:25 So David gave Araunah s hundred pieces of gold
23: 4 S thousand are to serve as officials and judges.
25: 3 Jeduthun had s sons: Gedaliah, Zeri, Jeshaiah,
26:17 S Levites were assigned each day to the east gate,
26:18 S were assigned each day to the west gate, four to
2Ch 4: 3 There were about s oxen per foot all the way
9:18 The throne had s steps, and there was a footstool of
9:19 one standing on each end of each of the s steps.
22:12 Joash remained hidden in the Temple of God for s
25:23 Then Jehoash ordered his army to demolish s
29:33 They also brought s hundred bulls and three
Ne 5:18 s fat sheep, and a large number of domestic fowl.
Est 1: 4 The celebration lasted s months—a tremendous
2:12 s months with oil of myrrh, followed by s months with special perfumes
Job 42:12 s thousand camels, one thousand teams of oxen,
Pr 6:16 There are s things the LORD hates—no,
Isa 5:10 Ten acres of vineyard will not produce even s
6: 2 him were mighty seraphim, each with s wings.
Jer 34:14 Hebrew slave must be freed after serving s years.

Eze 9: 2 S men soon appeared from the upper gate that
46: 1 will be closed during the s workdays each week,
46: 4 present to the LORD a burnt offering of s lambs
46: 6 s lambs, and one ram, all with no physical defects.
48:35 "The distance around the entire city will be s
Mt 17: 1 S days later Jesus took Peter and the two brothers,
Mk 9: 2 S days later Jesus took Peter, James, and John to
Lk 13:14 "There are s days of the week for working,"
Jn 2: 6 S stone waterpots were standing there; they were
12: 1 S days before the Passover ceremonies began,
Ac 11:12 These s brothers here accompanied me, and we
Rev 4: 8 Each of these living beings had s wings, and their

SIXTEEN (18) [SIXTEEN-YEAR-OLD, SIXTEENTH]

Ge 46:18 These s were descendants of Jacob through Zilpah,
Ex 26:25 end of the Tabernacle, supported by s silver bases
36:30 along with s silver bases, two for each frame.
Jos 15:41 s towns with their surrounding villages.
19:22 s towns with their surrounding villages.
1Ki 9:28 and brought back to Solomon some s tons of gold.
2Ki 13:10 reign in Judah. He reigned in Samaria s years.
15: 2 He was s years old when he became king, and he
15:33 became king, and he reigned in Jerusalem s years.
16: 2 became king, and he reigned in Jerusalem s years.
1Ch 4:27 Shimei had s sons and six daughters, but none of
24: 4 Eleazar's descendants were divided into s groups
2Ch 13:21 and had twenty-two sons and s daughters.
26: 3 Uzziah was s when he became king, and he
27: 1 became king, and he reigned in Jerusalem s years.
27: 8 became king, and he reigned in Jerusalem s years.
28: 1 became king, and he reigned in Jerusalem s years.
29:17 So the entire task was completed in s days.

SIXTEEN-YEAR-OLD (2) [SIXTEEN, YEAR]

2Ki 14:21 people of Judah then crowned Amaziah's s son,
2Ch 26: 1 people of Judah then crowned Amaziah's s son,

SIXTEENTH (2) [SIXTEEN]

1Ch 24:14 fifteenth lot fell to Bilgah. / The s lot fell to Immer.
25:23 The s lot fell to Hananiah and twelve of his sons

SIXTH (32) [SIX]

Ge 1:31 in every way. This all happened on the s day.
30:19 Then she became pregnant again and had a s son.
Ex 16: 5 as much as usual on the s day of each week."
16:22 On the s day, there was twice as much as usual on
16:29 That is why I give you twice as much food on the s
26: 9 The s sheet of the second set is to be doubled over
Lev 25:21 'I will order my blessing for you in the s year,
Nu 7:42 On the s day Eliasaph son of Deuel, leader of the
29:29 "On the s day of the festival, sacrifice eight young
Jos 19:32 The s allotment of land went to the families of the
2Sa 3: 5 The s was Ithream, whose mother was David's
2Ki 18:10 during the s year of King Hezekiah's reign
1Ch 2:15 his s was Ozem, and his seventh was David.
3: 3 The s was Ithream, whose mother was Eglah.
12:11 Attai was s. / Eliel was seventh.
24: 9 fifth lot fell to Malkijah. / The s lot fell to Mijamin.
25:13 The s lot fell to Bukkiah and twelve of his sons
26: 3 Elam (the fifth), Jehohanan (the s), and Eliehoenai
26: 5 Ammiel (the s), Issachar (the seventh),
27: 9 from Tekoa was commander of the s division,
27: 9 which was on duty during the s month.
Ezr 6:15 during the s year of King Darius's reign.
Ne 3:30 son of Shelemiah and Hanun, the s son of Zalaph,
Eze 8: 1 during the s year of King Jehoiachin's captivity,
Lk 1:26 In the s month of Elizabeth's pregnancy, God sent
1:36 she was barren, but she's already in her s month.
Rev 6:12 I watched as the Lamb broke the s seal, and there
9:13 Then the s angel blew his trumpet, and I heard a
9:14 And the voice spoke to the s angel who held the
16:12 Then the s angel poured out his bowl on the great
17:10 Five kings have already fallen, the s now reigns,
21:20 the fifth onyx, the s carnelian, the seventh

SIXTY (27) [60]

Ge 25:26 Isaac was s years old when the twins were born.
Lev 27: 3 of twenty and s is valued at fifty pieces of silver;
27: 7 A man older than s is valued at fifteen pieces of
27: 7 a woman older than s is valued at ten pieces of
Nu 7:88 Twenty-four young bulls, s rams, s male goats, and s one-year-old male lambs were donated for
Dt 3: 4 We conquered all s of his towns, the entire Argob
Jos 13:30 of King Og, and the s towns of Jair in Bashan.
2Sa 2:31 But three hundred and s of Abner's men, all from
1Ki 4:13 including s great fortified cities with gates barred
2Ki 25:19 was in charge of recruitment, and s other citizens.
1Ch 2:21 When Hezron was s years old, he married Gilead's
2:23 also took Kenath and its s surrounding villages.)
2Ch 11:21 In all, he had eighteen wives and s concubines,
11:21 gave birth to twenty-eight sons and s daughters.
12: 3 s thousand horsemen, and a countless army of foot
SS 3: 7 with s of Israel's mightiest men surrounding it.
6: 8 There may be s wives, all queens, and eighty
Jer 52:25 was in charge of recruitment, and s other citizens.
Eze 45:12 twenty gerahs, and s shekels are equal to one mina.
45:13 bushel of wheat or barley for every s you harvest,
Mt 13: 8 fertile soil and produced a crop that was thirty, s,
13:23 thirty, s, or even a hundred times as much as had
Mk 4: 8 fertile soil and produced a crop that was thirty, s,
4:20 thirty, s, or even a hundred times as much as had
1Ti 5: 9 must be a woman who is at least s years old

SIXTY-EIGHT (1)

1Ch 16:38 Hosah, and s other Levites as gatekeepers.

SIXTY-FIVE (1) [65]

Isa 7: 8 within s years it will be crushed and completely

SIXTY-SIX (2)

Ge 46:26 him to Egypt, not counting his sons' wives, was s.
Lev 12: 5 then wait another s days to be purified from the

SIXTY-TWO (4)

1Ch 26: 8 their sons and grandsons—s of them in all—
Da 5:31 the Mede took over the kingdom at the age of s.
9:25 Seven sets of seven plus s sets of seven will pass
9:26 "After this period of s sets of seven, the Anointed

SIZE (19)

Ex 12: 4 or not they share in this way depends on the s of
26: 2 All ten sheets must be exactly the same s.
26: 8 eleven of these sheets must be exactly the same s.
36: 9 Each sheet was exactly the same s—forty-two feet
36:15 Each sheet was exactly the same s—forty-five feet
Nu 26:54 each group's inheritance reflecting the s of its
33:54 the clans by sacred lot and in proportion to their s.
1Ki 6:25 The two cherubim were identical in shape and s;
7:37 All ten water carts were the same s and were made
18:44 "I saw a little cloud about the s of a hand rising
2Ki 10:32 LORD began to reduce the s of Israel's territory.
1Ch 28:20 Don't be afraid or discouraged by the s of the task,
Jer 49:15 "I will cut you down to s among the nations,
Eze 40:29 and foyer were the same s as those in the others.
40:33 and foyer were the same s as those of the others,
48:13 The land allotted to the Levites will be the same s
Ob 1: 2 "I will cut you down to s among the nations,
Zec 10: 8 their population will grow again to its former s.
Lk 5: 9 For he was awestruck by the s of their catch,

SKELETONS (1)

Eze 39:14 crews will be appointed to search the land for any s

SKIES (25) [SKY]

Ge 1:20 Let the s be filled with birds of every kind."
11: 4 a great city with a tower that reaches to the s—
Lev 26:19 spirit by making the s above as unyielding as iron
Dt 28:23 The s above will be as unyielding as bronze,
33:26 to help you, / across the s in majestic splendor.
Jdg 5: 4 and the cloudy s poured down rain.
1Ki 8:35 "If the s are shut up and there is no rain
2Ch 6:26 "If the s are shut up and there is no rain
Ne 9: 6 You made the s and the heavens and all the stars.
Job 31:26 Have I looked at the sun shining in the s,
37:18 he makes the s reflect the heat like a giant mirror.
Ps 19: 1 The s display his marvelous craftsmanship.
19: 3 a sound or a word; / their voice is silent in the s;
72: 5 sun shines, / as long as the moon continues in the s.
78:23 But he commanded the s to open— / he opened the
148: 1 LORD from the heavens! / Praise him from the s!
148: 4 Praise him, s above! / Praise him, vapors high
Isa 24: 4 earth dries up, the crops wither, the s refuse to rain.
50: 3 I am the one who sends darkness out across the s,
51: 6 Look up to the s above, and gaze down on the
51: 6 For the s will disappear like smoke, and the earth
Lk 21:25 "And there will be strange events in the s—
Ac 2: 2 roaring of a mighty windstorm in the s above them,
Rev 11: 6 They have power to shut the s so that no rain will
14: 8 Then another angel followed him through the s,

SKILL (17) [SKILLED, SKILLFUL, SKILLFULLY, SKILLS]

Ex 31: 3 intelligence, and s in all kinds of crafts.
31: 6 I have given special s to all the naturally talented
35:31 intelligence, and s in all kinds of crafts.
35:33 in carving wood. In fact, he has every necessary s.
36: 1 s, and intelligence will construct and furnish the
2Ki 18:20 think that mere words can substitute for military s
1Ch 15:22 was chosen as the choir leader because of his s.
2Ch 2:12 David a wise son, gifted with s and understanding,
30:22 Hezekiah encouraged the Levites for the s they
Job 26:12 By his s he crushed the great sea monster.
37:16 the clouds with wonderful perfection and s?
Ps 137: 5 let my right hand forget its s upon the harp.
144: 1 He gives me strength for war / and s for battle.
Ecc 2:19 they will control everything I have gained by my s
2:21 I do my work with wisdom, knowledge, and s,
Isa 36: 5 think that mere words can substitute for military s
Jer 48: 7 Because you have trusted in your wealth and s,

SKILLED (23) [SKILL]

Ex 31: 5 He is s in cutting and setting gemstones and in
35:25 All the women who were s in sewing and spinning
35:33 He is s in cutting and setting gemstones and in
36: 8 The s weavers first made ten sheets from fine
37:29 using the techniques of the most s incense maker.
39: 3 A s craftsman made gold thread by beating gold
1Ki 7:14 for he was a craftsman s in bronze work. He was
1Ch 5:18 There were 44,760 s warriors in the armies of
5:18 They were all s in combat and armed with shields,
7:40 They were all s warriors and prominent leaders.
8:40 The sons of Ulam were all s warriors and expert
12:33 the tribe of Zebulun, there were 50,000 s warriors.
22:15 You have many s stonemasons and carpenters
2Ch 2: 7 and a s engraver who can work with the craftsmen
34:12 Other Levites, all of whom were s musicians,
SS 3: 8 They are all s swordsmen and experienced
7: 1 thighs are like jewels, the work of a s craftsman.
Isa 3: 3 honorable citizens, advisers, s magicians,
Jer 24: 1 with the princes of Judah and all the s craftsmen,
46: 9 and Lydia who are s with the shield and bow!
Eze 21:31 I will hand you over to cruel men who are s in
27: 8 your helmsmen were s men from Tyre itself.
Mic 7: 3 How s they are at using them! Officials and judges

SKILLFUL (6) [SKILL]

Ge 25:27 As the boys grew up, Esau became a s hunter,
2Ch 2:14 He is s at making things from gold, silver, bronze,
Ps 45: 1 the king, / for my tongue is like the pen of a s poet.
78:72 them with a true heart / and led them with s hands.
Ecc 9:11 often poor, and the s are not necessarily wealthy.
Jer 10: 9 and they give these materials to s craftsmen who

SKILLFULLY (8) [SKILL]

Ex 26: 1 with figures of cherubim s embroidered into them.
26:31 with cherubim s embroidered into the cloth using
28: 6 and s embroidered with gold thread and blue,
36:35 and cherubim were s embroidered into it with blue,
Ps 33: 3 to him; / play s on the harp and sing with joy.
58: 5 of the snake charmers, / no matter how s they play.
136: 5 Give thanks to him who made the heavens so s.
Hos 13: 2 to worship—images shaped s with human hands.

SKILLS (6) [SKILL]

Ge 47: 6 And if any of them have special s, put them in
Ex 28: 3 Instruct all those who have special s as tailors to
35:26 All the women who were willing used their s to
35:34 tribe of Dan, the ability to teach their s to others.
35:35 The LORD has given them special s as jewelers,
1Ch 28:21 Others with s of every kind will volunteer,

SKIM (2)

Ps 119:119 All the wicked of the earth are the scum you s off;
Isa 1:25 I will melt you down and s off your slag.

SKIN (80) [GOATSKIN, SKIN-DEEP, SKINNED, SKINS, SMOOTH-SKINNED]

Ge 27:11 Think how hairy Esau is and how smooth my s is!
27:16 She made him a pair of gloves from the hairy s of
27:16 and she fastened a strip of the goat's s around his
Ex 29:14 Then take the carcass (including the s
Lev 13: 2 or a shiny patch on their s that develops into a contagious s disease,
13: 3 then examine the affected area of a person's s.
13: 3 than skin-deep, then it is a contagious s disease,
13: 4 "But if the affected area of the s is white but does
13: 5 affected area has not changed or spread on the s,
13: 6 The priest will examine the s again on the seventh
13: 8 for it is a contagious s disease.
13: 9 "Anyone who develops a contagious s disease
13:11 it is clearly a contagious s disease, and the priest
13:11 because it is clear that the s is defiled by the
13:12 that a rash has broken out all over someone's s,
13:13 because the s has turned completely white.
13:15 indicate the presence of a contagious s disease.
13:16 open sores heal and turn white like the rest of the s,
13:18 "If anyone has had a boil on the s that has started
13:20 It is a contagious s disease that has broken out in
13:22 during that time the affected area spreads on the s,
13:22 because it is a contagious s disease.
13:24 "If anyone has suffered a burn on the s
13:25 a contagious s disease has broken out in the burn.
13:25 for it is clearly a contagious s disease.
13:27 of that time the affected area has spread on the s,
13:27 for it is clearly a contagious s disease.
13:28 has not moved or spread on the s and has faded,
13:30 The infection is a contagious s disease of the head
13:38 or woman, has shiny white patches on the s,
13:39 patch is only a pale white, this is a harmless s rash,
13:42 the back of his head, this is a contagious s disease.
13:44 the man is infected with a contagious s disease
13:45 "Those who suffer from any contagious s disease
14: 2 seeking purification from a contagious s disease.
14: 3 that someone has been healed of the s disease,
14:10 each person cured of the s disease must bring two
14:19 ceremony for the person cured of the s disease.
14:32 who have recovered from a contagious s disease
14:54 with the various kinds of contagious s disease
14:56 in a swollen area of s, in a s rash, or in a shiny patch of s.
14:57 when dealing with any contagious s disease
19:28 mourning for the dead or mark your s with tattoos,
21:20 defective eye, or has oozing sores or scabs on his s,
22: 4 "If any of the priests have a contagious s disease
Nu 5: 2 from the camp who has a contagious s disease
Dt 24: 8 "Watch all contagious s diseases carefully
1Sa 10: 3 of bread, and the third will be carrying a s of wine.
2Sa 16: 1 hundred bunches of summer fruit, and a s of wine.
2Ki 5:10 Then your s will be restored, and you will be
5:27 he was leprous; his s was as white as snow.
6:30 he was wearing sackcloth underneath next to his s.
Job 2: 4 Satan replied to the LORD, "S for s—
2: 8 Then Job scraped his s with a piece of broken
7: 5 My s is filled with worms and scabs. My flesh
10:11 You clothed me with s and flesh, and you knit my
16: 8 You have reduced me to s and bones—as proof,
18:13 Disease eats their s; death devours their limbs.
19:20 I have been reduced to s and bones and have escaped death by the s of my teeth.

30:30 My **s** has turned dark, and my bones burn with
33:21 They waste away to **s** and bones.
Ps 102: 5 of my groaning, / I am reduced to **s** and bones.
104:15 to make them glad, / olive oil as lotion for their **s**,
109:24 are weak from fasting, / and I am **s** and bones.
SS 1: 6 complexion is so dark. The sun has burned my **s**.
Jer 13:23 Can an Ethiopian change the color of his **s**? Can a
La 3: 4 He has made my **s** and flesh grow old. He has
4: 8 Their **s** sticks to their bones; it is as dry and hard as
5:10 our **s** has been blackened as though baked in an
Eze 16: 9 your blood, and I rubbed fragrant oils into your **s**.
37: 6 put flesh and muscles on you and cover you with **s**.
37: 8 Then **s** formed to cover their bodies, but they still
Mic 3: 2 You **s** my people alive and tear the flesh off their
3: 3 cut away their **s**, and break their bones.
Ac 19:12 or cloths that had touched his **s** were placed on sick

SKIN-DEEP (10) [SKIN]

Lev 13: 3 has turned white and appears to be more than **s**,
13: 4 skin is white but does not appear to be more than **s**,
13:20 If the priest finds the disease to be more than **s**,
13:21 and if it doesn't appear to be more than **s** and has
13:25 and the problem appears to be more than **s**,
13:26 and the problem appears to be no more than **s**
13:30 If it appears to be more than **s** and fine yellow hair
13:31 examination reveals that the infection is only **s**
13:32 if the infection does not appear to be more than **s**,
13:34 it has not spread and appears to be no more than **s**,

SKINNED (1) [SKIN]

Lev 1: 6 When the animal has been **s** and cut into pieces,

SKINS (15) [SKIN]

Ge 3:21 And the LORD God made clothing from animal **s**
Ex 25: 5 tanned ram **s** and fine goatskin leather;
26:14 of these coverings place a layer of tanned ram **s**,
35: 7 tanned ram **s** and fine goatskin leather;
35:23 Some gave tanned ram **s** or fine goatskin leather.
36:19 The first was made of tanned ram **s**, and the second
39:34 the layers of tanned ram **s** and fine goatskin
Nu 6: 4 from a grapevine, not even the grape seeds or **s**.
1Sa 25:18 two **s** of wine, five dressed sheep, nearly a bushel
Mt 9:17 The old **s** would burst from the pressure, spilling the wine and ruining the **s**.
Mk 2:22 the wineskins, spilling the wine and ruining the **s**.
Lk 5:37 The new wine would burst the old **s**, spilling the wine and ruining the **s**.
Heb 11:37 Some went about in **s** of sheep and goats, hungry

SKIP (3) [SKIPPED, SKIPS]

Job 21:11 Their children **s** about like lambs in a flock of
Ps 29: 6 He makes Lebanon's mountains **s** like a calf
114: 6 Why, mountains, did you **s** like rams? / Why,

SKIPPED (1) [SKIP]

Ps 114: 4 The mountains **s** like rams, / the little hills like

SKIPS (1) [SKIP]

Job 21:17 and God **s** them when he distributes sorrows in his

SKIRTS (2)

Ex 20:26 someone might look up under the **s** of your
Na 3: 5 "And now I will lift your **s** so all the earth will see

SKULL (6) [SKULLS]

Jdg 9:53 that landed on Abimelech's head and crushed his **s**.
2Ki 9:35 they found only her **s**, her feet, and her hands.
Mt 27:33 to a place called Golgotha (which means **S** Hill).
Mk 15:22 to a place called Golgotha (which means **S** Hill).
Lk 23:33 Finally, they came to a place called The **S**.
Jn 19:17 Jesus went to the place called **S** Hill (in Hebrew,

SKULLS (2) [SKULL]

Nu 24:17 cracking the **s** of the people of Sheth.
Ps 68:21 crushing the **s** of those who love their guilty ways.

SKY (78) [SKIES]

Ge 1: 8 And God called the space "**s**." This happened on
1: 9 "Let the waters beneath the **s** be gathered into one
1:14 "Let bright lights appear in the **s** to separate the
1:26 the fish in the sea, the birds in the **s**, and all the
7:11 and the rain fell in mighty torrents from the **s**.
15: 5 LORD brought Abram outside beneath the night **s**
21:17 and the angel of God called to Hagar from the **s**,
22:17 like the stars of the **s** and the sand on the seashore.
Ex 9: 8 and have Moses toss it into the **s** while Pharaoh
9:22 said to Moses, "Lift your hand toward the **s**,
9:23 So Moses lifted his staff toward the **s**,
19:18 The smoke billowed into the **s** like smoke from a
Dt 1:28 that the walls of their towns rise high into the **s**!
4:11 Flames shot into the **s**, shrouded in black clouds
4:19 And when you look up into the **s** and see the sun,
9: 1 They live in cities with walls that reach to the **s**!
10:22 has made you as numerous as the stars in the **s**!
11:17 He will shut up the **s** and hold back the rain,
11:21 so that as long as the **s** remains above the earth,
28:24 and it will pour down from the **s** until you are
28:62 Though you are as numerous as the stars in the **s**,
Jos 8:20 smoke from the city was filling the **s**, and they had
10:13 The sun stopped in the middle of the **s**, and it did
Jdg 13:20 As the flames from the altar shot up toward the **s**,
20:40 and saw the smoke rising into the **s** from every part
2Sa 23: 4 like the sunrise bursting forth in a cloudless **s**,
1Ki 18:45 sure enough, the **s** was soon black with clouds.
Ne 9:23 their descendants as numerous as the stars in the **s**
Job 9: 9 and the constellations of the southern **s**
12: 7 Ask the birds of the **s**, and they will tell you.
26: 7 God stretches the northern **s** over empty space
28:21 Even the sharp-eyed birds in the **s** cannot discover
35: 5 Look up into the **s** and see the clouds high above
37:21 for it shines brightly in the **s** when the wind clears
Ps 8: 3 When I look at the night **s** and see the work of your
8: 8 the birds in the **s**, the fish in the sea,
68:15 mountains of Bashan / stretch high into the **s**.
68:33 his mighty voice thundering from the **s**.
77:17 their rain; / the thunder rolled and crackled in the **s**.
89:37 as the moon, / my faithful witness in the **s**!"
Pr 30:19 how an eagle glides through the **s**, / how a snake
Isa 34: 4 The stars will fall from the **s**, just as withered
51:13 the one who put the stars in the **s** and established
Jer 4:25 were gone. All the birds of the **s** had flown away.
14:22 Does it fall from the **s** by itself? No, it comes from
33:25 change my laws of night and day, of earth and **s**.
Eze 1:22 was a surface spread out above them like the **s**.
8: 3 Then the Spirit lifted me up into the **s**
Da 12: 3 Those who are wise will shine as bright as the **s**,
Hos 2:21 "I will answer the pleading of the **s** for clouds,
7:12 and bring them down like a bird from the **s**.
Zec 5: 5 "Look up! Something is appearing in the **s**."
5: 9 picked up the basket and flew with it into the **s**.
8:12 produce its crops, and the **s** will release the dew.
Mt 16: 2 'Red **s** at night means fair weather tomorrow,
16: 3 red **s** in the morning means foul weather all day.'
16: 3 You are good at reading the weather signs in the **s**,
24:27 For as the lightning lights up the entire **s**, so it will
24:29 will not give light, / the stars will fall from the **s**,
Mk 13:25 the stars will fall from the **s**, / and the powers of
Lk 12:56 to interpret the appearance of the earth and the **s**,
17:24 as evident as the lightning that flashes across the **s**.
Ac 1: 9 was taken up into the **s** while they were watching,
1:11 why are you standing here staring at the **s**?
10:11 He saw the **s** open, and something like a large
11: 5 sheet was let down by its four corners from the **s**.
Ro 1:20 have seen the earth and **s** and all that God made.
8:39 Whether we are high above the **s** or in the deepest
Heb 11:12 like the stars of the **s** and the sand on the seashore,
Rev 6:13 Then the stars of the **s** fell to the earth like green
6:14 And the **s** was rolled up like a scroll and taken
8:10 and a great flaming star fell out of the **s**,
9: 1 and I saw a star that had fallen to earth from the **s**,
9:17 armor that was fiery red and **s** blue and yellow.
16:21 pounds fell from the **s** onto the people below.
19:17 shouting to the vultures flying high in the **s**:
19:21 And all the vultures of the **s** gorged themselves on
20:11 The earth and **s** fled from his presence, but they

SLAG (4)

Isa 1:22 like pure silver, you have become like worthless **s**.
1:25 I will melt you down and skim off your **s**.
Eze 22:18 the people of Israel are the worthless **s** that remains
22:19 Because you are all worthless **s**, I will bring you to

SLAMMED (1)

Ps 77: 9 Has he **s** the door on his compassion? / *Interlude*

SLANDER (20) [SLANDERED, SLANDERERS, SLANDERING, SLANDEROUS]

Job 5:21 You will be safe from **s** and will have no fear of
Ps 15: 3 Those who refuse to **s** others / or harm their
35:15 I don't even know; / they hurl **s** at me continually.
50:20 You sit around and **s** a brother— / your own
101: 5 I will not tolerate people who **s** their neighbors.
109: 2 while the wicked **s** me / and tell lies about me.
Pr 10:18 To hide hatred is to be a liar; to **s** is to be a fool.
30:10 Never **s** a person to his employer. If you do,
Jer 6:28 Are they not the worst of rebels, full of **s**? They are
Eze 36: 3 You are the object of much mocking and **s**.
Mt 15:19 all other sexual immorality, theft, lying, and **s**.
Mk 7:22 for lustful pleasure, envy, **s**, pride, and foolishness.
Ro 3: 8 yet some **s** me by saying this is what I preach!
2Co 6: 8 or despise us, whether they **s** us or praise us.
Eph 4:31 of all bitterness, rage, anger, harsh words, and **s**,
Col 3: 8 rage, malicious behavior, **s**, and dirty language.
1Ti 6: 4 ending in jealousy, fighting, **s**, and evil suspicions.
2Ti 3: 3 they will **s** others and have no self-control;
Jas 2: 7 Aren't they the ones who **s** Jesus Christ,
Rev 2: 9 you are rich! I know the **s** of those opposing you.

SLANDERED (3) [SLANDER]

2Sa 19:27 Ziba has **s** me by saying that I refused to come.
Ac 13:45 so they **s** Paul and argued against whatever he said.
2Pe 2: 2 because of them, Christ and his true way will be **s**.

SLANDERERS (1) [SLANDER]

Ps 56: 2 My **s** hound me constantly, / and many are boldly

SLANDERING (1) [SLANDER]

Rev 13: 6 **s** his name and all who live in heaven, who are his

SLANDEROUS (3) [SLANDER]

Lev 19:16 "Do not spread **s** gossip among your people.
Isa 51: 7 Do not be afraid of people's scorn or their **s** talk.
Jer 9: 4 advantage of one another and spread their **s** lies.

SLANG [KJV] See HURLED

SLANT (3)

Ex 23: 3 And do not **s** your testimony in favor of a person
Job 13: 8 but will you **s** your testimony in his favor?
13:10 in your hearts you **s** your testimony in his favor.

SLAP (5) [SLAPPED, SLAPS]

Job 16:10 and laugh at me. They **s** my cheek in contempt.
Ps 3: 7 my God! / **S** all my enemies in the face!
Ac 23: 2 those close to Paul to **s** him on the mouth.
23: 3 But Paul said to him, "God will **s** you,
2Co 11:20 of you, put on airs, and **s** you in the face.

SLAPPED (4) [SLAP]

1Ki 22:24 walked up to Micaiah and **s** him across the face.
2Ch 18:23 walked up to Micaiah and **s** him across the face.
Mt 5:39 If you are **s** on the right cheek, turn the other,
26:67 and hit him with their fists. And some **s** him,

SLAPS (1) [SLAP]

Lk 6:29 If someone **s** you on one cheek, turn the other

SLASH (4) [SLASHED]

Jer 48:37 They **s** their hands and put on clothes made of
Eze 5: 2 third across your map and **s** at it with a sword.
21:16 O sword, **s** to the right, and **s** to the left,

SLASHED (5) [SLASH]

Jer 51: 4 land of the Babylonians, **s** to death in her streets.
Mt 26:51 and **s** off an ear of the high priest's servant.
Mk 14:47 and **s** off an ear of the high priest's servant.
Lk 22:50 And one of them **s** at the high priest's servant
Jn 18:10 drew a sword and **s** off the right ear of Malchus,

SLAUGHTER (66) [MANSLAUGHTER, SLAUGHTERED, SLAUGHTERING]

Ex 12: 6 Then each family in the community must **s** its
12:21 "Tell each of your families to **s** the lamb they have
29:11 then **s** it in the LORD's presence at the entrance
Lev 1: 5 Then **s** the animal in the LORD's presence,
1:11 **S** the animal on the north side of the altar in the
3: 2 and **s** it at the entrance of the Tabernacle.
3:13 its head, and **s** it at the entrance of the Tabernacle.
4: 4 and **s** it there in the LORD's presence.
4:15 on the bull's head and **s** it there before the LORD.
4:24 and **s** it before the LORD at the place where burnt
4:29 and **s** it at the place where burnt offerings are
4:33 and **s** it at the place where the burnt offerings are
14:13 then **s** the lamb there in the sacred area at the place
14:19 the priest will **s** the whole burnt offering
14:25 Then the priest will **s** the lamb for the guilt
14:50 He will **s** one of the birds over a clay pot that is
16:15 "Then Aaron must **s** the goat as a sin offering for
22:28 But you must never **s** a mother animal and her
26: 7 all your enemies and **s** them with your swords.
Nu 14:15 Now if you **s** all these people, the nations that have
Dt 9:28 he brought them into the wilderness to **s** them."
Jos 10:20 So Joshua and the Israelite army continued the **s**
1Sa 4:10 The **s** was great; thirty thousand Israelite men died
2Sa 18: 7 There was a great **s**, and twenty thousand men laid
1Ki 20:21 and the Arameans were killed in a great **s**.
2Ch 30:17 the Levites had to **s** their Passover lambs for them,
35: 6 **S** the Passover lambs, purify yourselves,
Est 7: 4 sold to those who would kill, **s**, and annihilate us.
8:11 They were allowed to kill, **s**, and annihilate anyone
Ps 37:14 and the oppressed, / to **s** those who do right.
Pr 7:22 like an ox going to the **s** or like a trapped stag,
Isa 22:13 you **s** sacrificial animals, feast on meat, and drink
34: 2 completely destroy them, bringing about their **s**.
34: 6 city of Bozrah. He will make a mighty **s** in Edom.
53: 7 never said a word. He was led as a lamb to the **s**.
57: 5 You **s** your children as human sacrifices down in
Jer 6:23 They are fully armed for **s**. They are cruel
7:32 valley of the son of Hinnom, but the Valley of **S**.
11:19 had been as unaware as a lamb on the way to its **s**.
19: 6 valley of the son of Hinnom, but the Valley of **S**.
19: 7 and Jerusalem and let invading armies **s** them.
21: 7 He will **s** them all without mercy, pity,
25:34 The time of your **s** has arrived; you will fall
48:15 Her most promising youth are doomed to **s**,"
50:27 it will be terrible for them, too! **S** them all!
50:42 They are fully armed for **s**. They are cruel
51:40 "I will bring them like lambs to the **s**, like rams
Eze 16:21 Must you also **s** my children by sacrificing them to
21:10 It is being prepared for terrible **s**; it will flash like
21:12 for that sword will **s** my people and their leaders—
21:15 It flashes like lightning; it is polished for **s**!
21:28 My sword is drawn for your **s**; it is sharpened to
26:15 screams of the wounded echo in the continuing **s**.
44:11 and they may still **s** the animals brought for burnt
Hos 9:16 if they give birth, I will **s** their beloved children."
Am 1: 5 and **s** its people all the way to the valley of Aven.
1: 8 I will **s** the people of Ashdod and destroy the king
2: 3 And I will destroy their king and **s** all their princes.
Ob 1: 9 the mountains of Edom will be cut down in the **s**.
Zep 1: 7 The LORD has prepared his people for a great **s**
Zec 11: 4 "Go and care for a flock that is intended for **s**.
11: 5 The buyers will **s** their sheep without remorse.
11: 7 So I cared for the flock intended for **s**—the flock
Ac 8:32 "He was led as a sheep to the **s**. / And as a lamb is
Jas 5: 5 Now your hearts are nice and fat, ready for the **s**.
Rev 6: 4 the earth. And there was war and **s** everywhere.

SLAUGHTERED (88) [SLAUGHTER]

Ge 34:25 town without opposition, and s every man there,
Ex 29:16 as it is s. Its blood will be collected and sprinkled
29:20 as it is s. Collect the blood and place some of it on
Lev 4:24 LORD at the place where burnt offerings are s.
4:29 slaughter it at the place where burnt offerings are s.
4:33 it at the place where the burnt offerings are s.
6:25 and must be s in the LORD's presence at the
6:25 at the place where the burnt offerings are s.
7: 2 The animal sacrificed as a guilt offering must be s
7: 2 be slaughtered where the burnt offerings are s,
8:15 as Moses s it. Moses took some of the blood,
8:19 as Moses s it. Then Moses took the ram's blood
8:23 as Moses s it. Then Moses took some of its blood
9: 8 the altar and s the calf as a sin offering for himself.
9:12 Next Aaron s the animal for the whole burnt
9:15 He s the people's goat and presented it as their sin
9:18 Then Aaron s the bull and the ram for the people's
14: 5 The priest will order one of the birds to be s over a
14: 6 and the hyssop branch, into the blood of the s bird.
14:13 place where sin offerings and burnt offerings are s.
14:51 and the living bird into the blood of the s bird,
16:11 After he has s this bull for the sin offering,
Nu 14:43 and Canaanites in battle, you will be s.
19: 3 be taken outside the camp and s in his presence.
21:24 But the Israelites s them and occupied their land
23:24 feasted on prey, / drinking the blood of the s!"
Dt 1:27 bringing us here from Egypt to be s by these
32:42 devour flesh—/ the blood of the s and the captives,
Jos 10:10 and the Israelites s them in great numbers at
10:30 They s everyone in the city and left no survivors.
10:32 Here, too, the entire population was s, just as at
10:41 Joshua s them from Kadesh-barnea to Gaza
11:12 Joshua s all the other kings and their people,
19:47 They captured it, s its people, and settled there.
Jdg 20:48 and s every living thing in all the towns—
1Sa 11:11 the Ammonites and s them the whole morning.
14:34 the troops brought their animals and s them there.
15: 7 Then Saul s the Amalekites from Havilah all the
23: 5 They s the Philistines and took all their livestock
25:11 and water and the meat I've s for my shearers
30:17 in among them and s them throughout that night
31: 1 Many were s on the slopes of Mount Gilboa.
2Sa 17: 9 will start shouting that your men are being s.
1Ki 19: 1 had done and that he had s the prophets of Baal.
1Ch 10: 1 Many were s on the slopes of Mount Gilboa.
2Ch 30:15 in midspring, the people s their Passover lambs.
35: 1 The Passover lambs were s at twilight of that day.
35:11 The Levites then s the Passover lambs
Ezr 6:20 So they s the Passover lamb for all the returned
Est 3:13 must be killed, s, and annihilated on a single day.
8: 6 to see my people and my family s and destroyed?"
Job 39:30 down blood, for it feeds on the carcass of the s."
Ps 44:11 You have treated us like sheep waiting to be s;
44:22 are killed every day; / we are being s like sheep.
78:64 Their priests were s, / and their widows could not
135:10 struck down great nations / and s mighty kings—
Isa 14:20 you have destroyed your nation and s your people.
30:25 In that day, when your enemies are s, there will be
Jer 6:15 even blush! Therefore, they will lie among the s.
8:12 even blush! Therefore, they will lie among the s.
9: 1 and night for all my people who have been s.
12: 3 sheep to be butchered! Set them aside to be s!
14:18 I see the bodies of people s by the enemy.
20: 4 and you will watch as they are s by the swords of
25:33 In that day those the LORD has s will fill the
41: 3 Then they went out and s all the Judean officials
La 3:43 chased us down, and s us without mercy.
Eze 5:12 A third of them will be s by the enemy outside the
11:10 You will be s all the way to the borders of Israel,
16:36 because you have s your children as sacrifices to
23:25 and any survivors will then be s by the sword.
24:21 and daughters in Judea will be s by the sword.
28:23 and your people will lie s within your walls.
30: 4 and those who are s will cover the ground.
30: 6 From Migdol to Aswan they will be s by the
30:11 They will make war against Egypt until s
32:22 of all its people, those who were s by the sword.
32:25 They have a resting place among the s,
32:25 in the pit, all of them outcasts, s by the sword.
35: 8 and your streams will be filled with people s by the
40:39 where the sacrificial animals were s for the burnt
Hos 6: 5 I have s you with my words, threatening you with
9:13 But now Israel will bring out her children to be s."
Am 4:10 killed your young men in war and s all your horses.
9: 1 Then those who survive will be s in battle. No one
Zep 2:12 "You Ethiopians will also be s by my sword,"
Ro 8:36 are killed every day; we are being s like sheep.")
Rev 18:24 She was the one who s God's people all over the

SLAUGHTERING (4) [SLAUGHTER]

Lev 3: 8 its head and s it at the entrance of the Tabernacle.
1Sa 7:11 from Mizpah to Beth-car, s them all along the way.
Jer 25:31 people of the earth, s the wicked with his sword.
La 2:21 killed them in your anger, s them without mercy.

SLAVE (97) [ENSLAVE, ENSLAVED, ENSLAVES, SLAVE'S, SLAVE-WIFE, SLAVERY, SLAVES]

Ge 39:14 "My husband has brought this Hebrew s here to
39:17 "That Hebrew s you've had around here tried to
44:10 "except that only the one who stole it will be a s.
44:17 "Only the man who stole the cup will be my s.
44:33 my lord, let me stay here as a s instead of the boy,
Ex 1:11 their slaves and put brutal s drivers over them,
3: 7 cries for deliverance from their harsh s drivers.
5: 6 That same day Pharaoh sent this order to the s
5:10 So the s drivers and foremen informed the people:
5:13 The s drivers were brutal. "Meet your daily quota
5:16 It is the fault of your s drivers for making such
11: 5 on the throne, to the oldest son of his lowliest s.
12:44 But any s who has been purchased may eat it if he
21: 2 "If you buy a Hebrew s, he is to serve for only six
21: 3 If he was single when he became your s and
21: 3 But if he was married before he became a s,
21: 4 "If his master gave him a wife while he was a s,
21: 5 But the s may plainly declare, 'I love my master,
21: 6 After that, the s will belong to his master forever.
21: 7 "When a man sells his daughter as a s, she will not
21: 9 And if the s girl's owner arranges for her to marry
21: 9 he may no longer treat her as a s girl, but he must
21:20 "If a male or female s is beaten and dies,
21:21 If the s recovers after a couple of days, however,
21:21 be punished, since the s is the owner's property.
21:26 or female s in the eye and the eye is blinded,
21:26 then the s may go free because of the eye.
21:27 owner knocks out the tooth of a male or female s,
21:27 the s should be released in payment for the tooth.
21:32 But if the bull gores a s, either male or female,
22: 3 the thief must be sold as a s to pay the debt.
Lev 19:20 "If a man has sexual intercourse with a s girl who
Dt 21:14 You may not sell her or treat her as a s, for you
24: 7 a fellow Israelite and treats him as a s or sells him,
32:36 their strength is gone / and no one is left, s or free.
Jdg 9:18 And you have chosen his s woman's son,
1Sa 8:12 of his troops, while others will be s laborers.
25:41 I am even willing to become a s to David's
30:13 an Egyptian—the s of an Amalekite," he replied.
1Ki 14:10 your dynasty and kill all your sons, s or free alike.
21:21 male descendants, s or free alike, survive in Israel!
2Ki 9: 8 wiped out—every male, s and free alike, in Israel.
Job 3:19 are there alike, and the s is free from his master.
41: 4 work for you? Can you make it be your s for life?
Ps 60: 8 my lowly servant, / and Edom will be my s.
105:17 ahead of them—/ Joseph, who was sold as a s.
108: 9 my lowly servant, / and Edom will be my s.
123: 2 as a s girl watches her mistress for the slightest
Pr 12:24 and become a leader; be lazy and become a s.
17: 2 A wise s will rule over the master's shameful sons
19:10 fool to live in luxury or for a s to rule over princes!
30:22 a s who becomes a king, / an overbearing fool who
Isa 52: 2 Remove the s bands from your neck, O captive
Jer 27: 8 I will punish any nation that refuses to be his s,
34:14 I told them that every Hebrew s must be freed after
La 1: 1 Once the queen of nations, she is now a s.
Mt 3:11 much greater that I am not even worthy to be his s.
20:27 and whoever wants to be first must become your s.
Mk 1: 7 much greater that I am not even worthy to be his s.
10:44 and whoever wants to be first must be the s of all.
Lk 3:16 much greater that I am not even worthy to be his s.
7: 2 Now the highly valued s of a Roman officer was
7: 3 Jewish leaders to ask him to come and heal his s.
7:10 to his house, they found the s completely healed.
Jn 1:27 his ministry. I am not even worthy to be his s."
8:34 "I assure you that everyone who sins is a s of sin.
8:35 A s is not a permanent member of the family,
Ac 7: 9 and they sold him to be a s in Egypt.
13:25 and I am not even worthy to be his s.'
16:16 place of prayer, we met a demon-possessed s girl.
Ro 1: 1 This letter is from Paul, Jesus Christ's s, chosen by
7:23 and makes me a s to the sin that is still within me.
7:25 but because of my sinful nature I am a s to sin.
1Co 6:12 do anything," I must not become a s to anything.
7:21 Are you a s? Don't let that worry you—but if you
7:22 if you were a s when the Lord called you, you are
now a s of Christ.
Gal 3:28 no longer Jew or Gentile, s or free, male or female.
4: 7 Now you are no longer a s but God's own child.
4:30 "Get rid of the s and her son, for the son of the s
woman will not share the
4:31 dear friends, we are not children of the s woman,
Php 2: 7 he took the humble position of a s and appeared in
Col 3:11 or uncircumcised, barbaric, uncivilized, s, or free.
4: 1 You s owners must be just and fair to your slaves.
1Ti 1:10 for homosexuals and s traders, for liars and oath
Tit 1: 1 a s of God and an apostle of Jesus Christ.
Phm 1:16 He is no longer just a s; he is a beloved brother,
1:16 to you, both as a s and as a brother in the Lord.
Jas 1: 1 a s of God and of the Lord Jesus Christ.
2Pe 1: 1 from Simon Peter, a s and apostle of Jesus Christ.
2:19 For you are a s to whatever controls you.
2:20 get tangled up with sin and become its s again,
Jude 1: 1 a s of Jesus Christ and a brother of James.
Rev 6:15 great power, and every s and every free person—
13:16 great and small, rich and poor, s and free—
19:18 of all humanity, both free and s, small and great."

SLAVE'S (1) [SLAVE]

Ex 21:32 the s owner is to be given thirty silver coins in

SLAVE-WIFE (4) [SLAVE, WIFE]

Gal 4:22 one from his s and one from his freeborn wife.
4:23 The son of the s was born in a human attempt to
4:24 Hagar, the s, represents Mount Sinai where people
4:29 was persecuted by Ishmael, the son of the s.

SLAVERY (47) [SLAVE]

Ex 1:13 and decided to make their s more bitter still.
2:23 Israelites still groaned beneath their burden of s.
6: 6 and I will free you from your s in Egypt.
6: 7 God who has rescued you from your s in Egypt.
6: 9 too discouraged by the increasing burden of their s.
13: 3 the day you left Egypt, the place of your s.
13:14 the LORD brought us out of Egypt from our s.
14:12 Our Egyptian s was far better than dying out here
20: 2 your God, who rescued you from s in Egypt.
Lev 26:13 I have lifted the yoke of s from your neck so you
Dt 5: 6 your God, who rescued you from s in Egypt.
6:12 who rescued you from s in the land of Egypt.
7: 8 power from your s under Pharaoh in Egypt.
8:14 who rescued you from s in the land of Egypt.
13: 5 who brought you out of s in the land of Egypt.
13:10 rescued you from the land of Egypt, the place of s.
Jos 5: 9 "Today I have rolled away the shame of your s in
24:17 and our ancestors from s in the land of Egypt.
Jdg 6: 8 of Israel, says: I brought you up out of s in Egypt
2Sa 7:23 have you redeemed from s to be your own people?
1Ki 6: 1 were delivered from their s in the land of Egypt.
2Ki 17: 7 who had brought them safely out of their s in
1Ch 17:21 have you redeemed from s to be your own people?
Ezr 9: 8 our eyes and granted us some relief from our s.
9: 9 unfailing love our God did not abandon us in our s.
Ne 5: 5 Yet we must sell our children into s just to get
5: 8 but you are selling them back into s again.
9:17 and appointed a leader to take them back to their s
Job 6:27 You would even send an orphan into s or sell a
Ps 2: 3 they cry, / "and free ourselves from this s."
66:11 in your net / and laid the burden of s on our backs.
Isa 10:27 He will break the yoke of s and lift it from their
14: 3 rest from sorrow and fear, from s and chains,
52:11 Go now, leave your bonds and s. Put Babylon
Jer 2:20 your yoke and tore away the chains of your s,
11: 4 ancestors when I brought them out of s in Egypt,
28:14 forcing them into s under King Nebuchadnezzar of
34:13 ago when I rescued them from their s in Egypt.
Eze 34:27 When I have broken their chains of s and rescued
Hos 12: 9 your God, who rescued you from your s in Egypt.
13: 4 your God, who rescued you from your s in Egypt.
Mic 6: 4 you out of Egypt and redeemed you from your s.
7:15 like those I did when I rescued you from s in
Ac 13:17 Then he powerfully led them out of their s.
Ro 7:14 with the law but with me, because I am sold into s,
Gal 4:25 in Arabia, because she and her children live in s.
5: 1 and don't get tied up again in s to the law.

SLAVES (109) [SLAVE]

Ge 15:13 and they will be oppressed as s for four hundred
43:18 Then he will seize us as s and take our donkeys."
44: 9 And all the rest of us will be your master's s
44:16 My lord, we have all returned to be your s—
50:18 low before him. "We are your s," they said.
Ex 1:11 So the Egyptians made the Israelites their s and put
2:11 he saw an Egyptian beating one of the Hebrew s.
6: 5 people of Israel, who are now s to the Egyptians.
14: 5 have we done, letting all these s get away?"
21:16 of their victims or have already sold them as s.
23:12 including your s and visitors, to be refreshed.
Lev 22:11 However, if the priest buys s with his own money,
22:11 And if his s have children, they also may share his
25: 6 But you, your male and female s, your hired
25:39 and sell themselves to you, do not treat them as s.
25:42 the land of Egypt, so they must never be sold as s.
25:44 or female s from among the foreigners who live
25:46 You may treat your s like this, but the people of
26:13 the land of Egypt so you would no longer be s.
Nu 14: 3 Our wives and little ones will be carried off as s!
20:15 a long time and suffered as s to the Egyptians.
Dt 5:15 Remember that you were once s in Egypt and that
6:21 must tell them, 'We were Pharaoh's s in Egypt,
15:15 Remember that you were s in the land of Egypt
16:12 Remember that you were s in Egypt, so be careful
23:15 "If s should escape from their masters and take
24:18 Always remember that you were s in Egypt
24:22 Remember that you were s in the land of Egypt.
26: 6 and humiliated us by making us their s,
28:32 as your sons and daughters are taken away as s.
28:68 will offer to sell yourselves to your enemies as s,
Jos 16:10 so the people of Gezer live as s among the people
17:13 they forced the Canaanites to work as s.
Jdg 1:28 they forced the Canaanites to work as s,
1:30 among them. But they forced them to work as s.
1:33 forced to work as s for the people of Naphtali.
1:35 they forced the Amorites to work as s.
1Sa 2:27 when the people of Israel were s in Egypt?
4: 9 we will become the Hebrews' s just as they have
8:16 He will want your male and female s and demand
8:17 a tenth of your flocks, and you will be his s.
17: 9 your man is able to kill me, then we will be your s.
But if I kill him, you will be our s!
2Sa 12:31 He also made s of the people of Rabbah and forced
1Ki 2:39 two of Shimei's s escaped to King Achish of Gath.
2Ki 4: 1 has come, threatening to take my two sons as s."
1Ch 20: 3 He also made s of the people of Rabbah and forced
2Ch 28:10 And now you are planning to make s of these
Ezr 9: 9 For we were s, but in his unfailing love our God
Ne 9:36 "So now today we are s here in the land of plenty
9:36 our ancestors! We are s among all this abundance!
Est 7: 4 If we had only been sold as s, I could remain quiet,
Ecc 2: 7 I bought s, both men and women, and others were
Isa 14:25 my mountains. My people will no longer be their s.
50: 1 LORD asks, "Did I sell you as s to my creditors?
Jer 2:14 "Why has Israel become a nation of s? Why has
34: 8 with the people, proclaiming freedom for the s.
34: 9 had ordered all the people to free their Hebrew s—
34:11 the people they had freed, making them s again.

34:15 You freed your s and made a solemn covenant with
34:16 women you had freed, making them s once again.
La 5: 8 S have now become our masters; there is no one
Eze 23:10 killed her and took away her children as their s.
27:13 Tubal, and Meshech brought s and bronze dishes.
30:17 in battle, and the women will be taken away as s.
38:12 capture vast amounts of plunder and take many s,
Joel 3: 3 lots to decide which of my people would be their s.
Am 1: 5 and the people of Aram will return to Kir as s.
1: 6 my people into exile, selling them as s in Edom.
1: 9 with Israel, selling whole villages as s to Edom.
Zec 2: 9 to crush them, and their own s will plunder them.'
Mt 8: 9 And if I say to my s, 'Do this or that,' they do it."
Lk 7: 8 And if I say to my s, 'Do this or that,' they do it."
Jn 8:33 "We have never been s to anyone on earth.
Ac 6: 9 one day some men from the Synagogue of Freed S,
7: 6 would be mistreated as s for four hundred years.
Ro 6: 6 its power in our lives. We are no longer s to sin.
6:17 Once you were s of sin, but now you have obeyed
6:18 and you have become s to your new master,
6:19 this way, using the illustration of s and masters,
6:19 you let yourselves be s of impurity
6:19 Now you must choose to be s of righteousness
6:20 In those days, when you were s of sin, you weren't
6:22 from the power of sin and have become s of God.
8:15 So you should not be like cowering, fearful s.
1Co 12:13 some are Gentiles, some are s, and some are free.
2Co 11:20 You put up with it when they make you their s,
Gal 2: 4 They wanted to force us, like s, to follow their
4: 1 those children are not much better off than s until
4: 3 We were s to the spiritual powers of this world.
4: 5 God sent him to buy freedom for us who were s to
4: 8 you were s to so-called gods that do not even exist.
4: 9 go back again and become s once more to the weak
Eph 6: 5 S, obey your earthly masters with deep respect
6: 6 As s of Christ, do the will of God with all your
6: 8 of us for the good we do, whether we are s or free.
6: 9 the same way, you masters must treat your s right.
Php 1: 1 letter is from Paul and Timothy, s of Christ Jesus.
Col 3:22 You s must obey your earthly masters in
4: 1 You slave owners must be just and fair to your s.
1Ti 6: 1 Christians who are s should give their masters full
Tit 2: 9 S must obey their masters and do their best to
3: 3 and became s to many wicked desires and evil
Heb 2:15 have lived all their lives as s to the fear of dying.
1Pe 2:16 You are not s; you are free. But your freedom is
2:16 excuse to do evil. You are free to live as God's s.
2:18 You who are s must accept the authority of your
2Pe 2:19 but they themselves are s to sin and corruption.
Rev 18:13 wheat, cattle, sheep, horses, chariots, and s—

SLAYER (13) [SLEW]

Ex 21:13 I will appoint a place where the s can run for
21:14 then the s must be dragged even from my altar
Nu 35:12 The s must not be killed before being tried by the
35:24 regulations in making a judgment between the s
35:25 They must protect the s from the avenger, and they must send the s back to live in a city of
35:26 " 'But if the s leaves the city of refuge,
35:28 The s should have stayed inside the city of refuge
35:28 high priest, the s may return to his own property.
35:32 allowing the s to return to his property before the
Dt 19: 4 the s may flee to any of these cities and be safe.
19: 5 the s could flee to one of the cities of refuge
19: 6 The s would die, even though there was no death

SLEDGE (1) [SLEDGES]

Isa 28:27 A heavy s is never used on dill; rather, it is beaten

SLEDGEHAMMERS (1) [HAMMER]

Eze 26: 9 battering rams and demolish your towers with s.

SLEDGES (1) [SLEDGE]

Am 1: 3 Gilead as grain is threshed with threshing s of iron.

SLEEK (1)

Jer 46:20 Egypt is as s as a young cow, but a gadfly from the

SLEEP (66) [ASLEEP, SLEEPER, SLEEPING, SLEEPLESS, SLEEPS, SLEPT]

Ge 2:21 the LORD God caused Adam to fall into a deep s.
15:12 the sun was going down, Abram fell into a deep s.
16: 2 Sarai said to Abram. "Go and s with my servant.
19:32 him drunk with wine, and then we will s with him.
19:34 wine again tonight, and you go in and s with him.
28:11 Jacob found a stone for a pillow and lay down to s.
30: 3 Then Rachel told him, "S with my servant, Bilhah,
30:15 "I will let him s with you tonight in exchange for
30:16 "You must s with me tonight!" she said.
38:16 So he stopped and propositioned her to s with him,
38:18 She then let him s with her, and she became
39: 7 began to desire him and invited him to s with her.
39:10 on him day after day, but he refused to s with her,
39:12 him by his shirt, demanding, "S with me!"
Ex 21:10 or clothing or fail to s with her as his wife.
Lev 14:47 All who s or eat in the house must wash their
26: 6 in the land, and you will be able to s without fear.
Dt 24:13 so your neighbor can s in it and bless you.
Jos 2: 8 Before the spies went to s that night, Rahab went
Jdg 15: 1 He intended to s with her, but her father wouldn't
16:19 Delilah lulled Samson to s with his head in her lap,
Ru 3: 7 he lay down beside the heap of grain and went to s.
1Sa 26:12 the LORD had put Saul's men into a deep s.
2Sa 11:11 I go home to wine and dine and s with my wife?
16:21 told him, "Go and s with your father's concubines,
16:22 and Absalom went into the tent to s with his
20: 3 he said, but he would no longer s with them.
1Ki 3:20 child in my arms and took mine to s beside her.
Job 7:13 and I will try to forget my misery with s,'
14:12 they will not wake up nor be roused from their s.
24:16 break into houses at night and s in the daytime.
31:10 belong to another man; may other men s with her.
33:15 in visions of the night when deep s falls on people
Ps 4: 8 I will lie down in peace and s, / for you alone,
44:23 Wake up, O Lord! Why do you s? / Get up! Do not
59:15 They scavenge for food / but go to s unsatisfied.
76: 5 They lie before us in the s of death. / No warrior
77: 4 You don't let me s. / I am too distressed even to
78:65 Then the Lord rose up as though waking from s,
121: 3 and fall; / the one who watches over you will not s.
132: 4 I will not let my eyes s / nor close my eyelids in
Pr 4:16 for evil people cannot s until they have done their
6: 9 But you, lazybones, how long will you s?
6:10 A little extra s, a little more slumber, a little
6:22 can lead you. When you s, they will protect you.
20:13 If you love s, you will end in poverty. Keep your
23:21 to poverty. Too much s clothes a person with rags.
24:33 A little extra s, a little more slumber, a little
Ecc 5:12 People who work hard s well, whether they eat
5:12 always worrying and seldom get a good night's s.
Isa 5:27 They will run without stopping for rest or s.
21: 4 The s I once enjoyed at night is now a faint
26:19 Those who s in the earth / will rise up and sing for
29:10 LORD has poured out on you a spirit of deep s.
Jer 31:26 and looked around. My s had been very sweet.
Eze 22:10 Men s with their fathers' wives and have
23:43 Then I said, 'If they really want to s with worn-out,
34:25 the wildest places and s in the woods without fear.
Da 2: 1 that disturbed him so much that he couldn't s.
6:18 usual entertainment and couldn't s at all that night.
Am 2: 7 Both father and son s with the same woman,
Jnh 1: 6 "How can you s at a time like this?" he shouted.
Zep 3:13 will live peaceful lives, lying down to s in safety;
Ac 20: 9 he sank into a deep s and fell three stories to his
Ro 11: 8 Scriptures say, / "God has put them into a deep s.
1Th 5: 7 Night is the time for s and the time when people

SLEEPER (1) [SLEEP]

Eph 5:14 This is why it is said, / "Awake, O s, / rise up from

SLEEPING (31) [SLEEP]

Ge 16: 5 though I myself gave her the privilege of s with
Nu 5:20 and defiled yourself by s with another man"—
25: 1 some of the men defiled themselves by s with the
Dt 22:13 after s with her, changes his mind about her
Jdg 19: 4 he stayed three days, eating, drinking, and s there.
1Sa 3: 3 and Samuel was s in the Tabernacle near the Ark
26: 5 were s inside a ring formed by the slumbering
2Sa 3: 7 accused Abner of s with one of his father's
17:28 They brought s mats, cooking pots, serving bowls,
1Ki 19: 5 But as he was s, an angel touched him and told
1Ch 5: 1 But since he dishonored his father by s with one of
Est 6: 1 That night the king had trouble s, so he ordered an
Pr 6:26 and s with another man's wife may cost you your
SS 5: 2 "One night as I was s, my heart awakened in a
Isa 56:10 They love to lie around, s and dreaming.
Da 2:29 "While Your Majesty was s, you dreamed about
Mt 8:24 with waves breaking into the boat. But Jesus was s.
26:43 He returned to them again and found them s,
26:45 Then he came to the disciples and said, "Still s?
28:13 disciples came during the night while we were s,
Mk 4:38 Jesus was s at the back of the boat with his head on
13:36 Don't let him find you s when he arrives without
14:40 Again he returned to them and found them s,
14:41 he returned to them the third time he said, "Still s?
Lk 5:18 Some men came carrying a paralyzed man on a s
8:23 a nap, and while he was s the wind began to rise.
22:46 "Why are you s?" he asked. "Get up and pray.
Jn 5: 8 "Stand up, pick up your s mat, and walk!"
5:10 on the Sabbath! It's illegal to carry that s mat!"
5:11 me said to me, 'Pick up your s mat and walk.' "
11:12 The disciples said, "Lord, if he is s, that means he

SLEEPLESS (3) [SLEEP]

Ge 31:40 heat of the day and through cold and s nights.
2Co 6: 5 worked to exhaustion, endured s nights,
11:27 I have lived with weariness and pain and s nights.

SLEEPS (6) [SLEEP]

Ex 22:16 who is not engaged to anyone and s with her,
Nu 5:13 Suppose she s with another man, but there is no
Ps 121: 4 who watches over Israel / never tires and never s.
Pr 6:29 So it is with the man who s with another man's
10: 5 a youth who s away the hour of opportunity brings
19:15 A lazy person s soundly—and goes hungry

SLEET (1)

Ps 78:47 with hail / and shattered their sycamores with s.

SLEIGHT [KJV] See CLEVERLY (LIED)

SLEPT (37) [SLEEP]

Ge 4: 1 Now Adam s with his wife, Eve, and she became
4:25 Adam s with his wife again, and she gave birth to
16: 4 So Abram s with Hagar, and she became pregnant.
19:33 the older daughter went in and s with her father.
19:34 her younger sister, "I s with our father last night.
19:35 and the younger daughter went in and s with him.
20: 4 But Abimelech had not s with her yet, so he said,
24:16 and she was a virgin; no man had ever s with her.
26:10 might have taken your wife and s with her,
28:12 As he s, he dreamed of a stairway that reached
29:23 Laban took Leah to Jacob, and he s with her.
29:30 So Jacob s with Rachel, too, and he loved her more
30: 4 him Bilhah to be his wife, and Jacob s with her.
30:16 roots my son has found." So Jacob s with her.
35:22 While he was there, Reuben s with Bilhah,
38:26 son Shelah." But Judah never s with Tamar again.
49: 4 first no longer. / For you s with one of my wives;
Nu 5:19 and say to her, "If no other man has s with you,
31:17 and all the women who have s with a man.
Dt 22:14 and falsely accuses her of having s with another
Jdg 16:13 So while he s, Delilah wove the seven braids of
21:12 young virgins who had never s with a man,
Ru 4:13 When he s with her, the LORD enabled her to
1Sa 1:19 When Elkanah s with Hannah, the LORD
21: 4 young men have not s with any women recently."
2Sa 11: 4 and when she came to the palace, he s with her.
11:13 to his wife. Again he s at the palace entrance.
12:24 comforted Bathsheba, his wife, and s with her.
1Ki 19: 5 Then he lay down and s under the broom tree.
21:27 He even s in sackcloth and went about in deep
1Ch 7:23 Afterward Ephraim s with his wife, and she
Job 4:13 It came in a vision at night as others s.
Ps 3: 5 I lay down and s. / I woke up in safety,
Isa 8: 3 Then I s with my wife, and she became pregnant
Eze 23:44 They s with Oholah and Oholibah, these shameless
Mt 13:25 But that night as everyone s, his enemy came
25: 5 bridegroom was delayed, they all lay down and s.

SLEW (1) [SLAYER]

Isa 51: 9 Rouse yourself as in the days of old when you s

SLIDE [KJV] See SLIP, WAVERING

SLIDING (1)

Ps 73:18 and send them s over the cliff to destruction.

SLIGHTEST (5)

1Sa 20: 9 "You know that if I had the s notion my father was
Job 6:14 but you have accused me without the s fear of the
Ps 5: 4 in wickedness; / you cannot tolerate the s sin.
123: 2 as a slave girl watches her mistress for the s signal.
Eze 16: 5 No one had the s interest in you; no one pitied you

SLIM (1)

SS 7: 7 You are tall and s like a palm tree, and your breasts

SLIME (1)

Ps 58: 8 May they be like snails that dissolve into s,

SLIMEPITS [KJV] See TAR (PITS)

SLING (9) [SLINGSHOT, SLUNG]

Jdg 20:16 each of whom could s a rock and hit a target within
1Sa 17:40 Then, armed only with his shepherd's staff and s,
17:49 he hurled it from his s and hit the Philistine in the
17:50 over the Philistine giant with only a stone and s.
25:29 enemies will disappear like stones shot from a s!
1Ch 12: 2 or s stones with their left hand as well as their
2Ch 26:14 spears, helmets, coats of mail, bows, and s stones.
Job 41:28 Stones shot from a s are as ineffective as straw.
Zec 9:15 and they will subdue their enemies with s stones.

SLINGSHOT (1) [SLING]

Pr 26: 8 Honoring a fool is as foolish as tying a stone to a s.

SLINK (2)

Ps 104:22 At dawn they s back / into their dens to rest.
112:10 in anger; / they will s away, their hopes thwarted.

SLIP (12) [SLIPPED, SLIPPERY, SLIPPING, SLIPS]

Ge 31:27 Why did you s away secretly? I would have given
Dt 32:35 In due time their feet will s. / Their day of disaster
Ps 37:31 God's law, / so they will never s from his path.
55:22 of you. / He will not permit the godly to s and fall.
Pr 10: 9 but those who follow crooked paths will s and fall.
Isa 22: 3 The people try to s away, but they are captured,
47:15 will s away and disappear, unable to help.
Jer 17: 4 I have reserved for you will s out of your hands,
20:10 old friends are watching me, waiting for a fatal s.
Da 11:21 But he will s in when least expected and take over
2Co 5: 4 We want to s into our new bodies so that these
1Pe 1:14 Don't s back into your old ways of doing evil;

SLIPPED (9) [SLIP]

Ge 14:10 and Gomorrah fled, some s into the tar pits,
1Sa 26: 5 David s over to Saul's camp one night to look
2Sa 4: 6 So Recab and Baanah s past the doorkeeper,
20: 8 he secretly s the dagger from its sheath.
Ne 2:12 I s out during the night, taking only a few others
Mk 14:54 then s inside the gates of the high priest's
Lk 4:30 but he s away through the crowd and left them.
9:10 Then he s quietly away with them toward the town
Jn 8: 9 they s away one by one, beginning with the oldest,

SLIPPERY (5) [SLIP]

2Sa 23:20 Then, despite the snow and s ground, he caught the

1Ch 11:22 Then, despite the snow and s ground, he caught the
Ps 35: 6 Make their path dark and s, / with the angel of the
73:18 Truly, you put them on a s path / and send them
Jer 23:12 "Therefore, their paths will be dark and s.

SLIPPING (7) [SLIP]

1Sa 13: 8 Saul realized that his troops were rapidly s away.
2Sa 22:37 a wide path for my feet / to keep them from s.
Ps 18:36 a wide path for my feet / to keep them from s.
56:13 me from death; / you have kept my feet from s.
73: 2 the cliff! / My feet were s, and I was almost gone.
94:18 I cried out, "I'm s!" / and your unfailing love,
Na 2: 8 The people are s away. "Stop, stop!"

SLITHER (1) [SLITHERS]

Lev 11:42 This includes all animals that s along on their

SLITHERS (1) [SLITHER]

Pr 30:19 glides through the sky, / how a snake s on a rock,

SLOPE (7) [SLOPES]

Jos 7: 5 about thirty-six who were retreating down the s.
15:10 of Kesalon on the northern s of Mount Jearim,
15:11 then proceeded to the s of the hill north of Ekron,
18:12 went north of the s of Jericho, then west through
18:16 crossing south of the s where the Jebusites lived,
18:18 From there it passed along the north side of the s
18:19 ran past the north s of Beth-hoglah, and ended at

SLOPES (20) [SLOPE]

Dt 3:17 to the Dead Sea, with the s of Pisgah on the east.
4:49 far south as the Dead Sea, below the s of Pisgah.)
Jos 10:40 the western foothills, and the mountain s.
11: 3 and the Hivites in the towns on the s of Mount
12: 3 Dead Sea, from Beth-jeshimoth to the s of Pisgah.
12: 8 the Jordan Valley, the mountain s,
13:20 Beth-peor, the s of Pisgah, and Beth-jeshimoth.
15: 7 which is across from the s of Adummim on the
15: 8 along the southern s of the Jebusites,
18:17 and on to Geliloth (which is across from the s of
Jdg 4:14 So Barak led his ten thousand warriors down the s
1Sa 31: 1 Many were slaughtered on the s of Mount Gilboa.
2Sa 1:21 let there be no dew or rain upon you or your s.
1Ch 10: 1 Many were slaughtered on the s of Mount Gilboa.
SS 4: 1 like flocks of goats frisking across the s of Gilead.
6: 5 is like a flock of goats frisking down the s of
Mt 24: 3 Later, Jesus sat on the s of the Mount of Olives.
Mk 13: 3 Jesus sat on the s of the Mount of Olives across the
Lk 6:17 When they came down the s of the mountain,
Jn 6:10 five thousand—sat down on the grassy s.

SLOTHFUL [KJV] See LAGGING, LAZY, LAZYBONES, SLOW

SLOW (14) [SLOWLY, SLOWS]

Ex 1:19 They are not s in giving birth like Egyptian
34: 6 I am s to anger and rich in unfailing love
Nu 14:18 'The LORD is s to anger and rich in unfailing
2Ki 4:24 Don't s down on my account unless I tell you to."
Ne 9:17 gracious and merciful, s to become angry, and full
Ps 86:15 are a merciful and gracious God, / s to get angry,
103: 8 he is s to get angry and full of unfailing love.
145: 8 and merciful, / s to get angry, full of unfailing love.
Jnh 4: 2 s to get angry and filled with unfailing love.
Na 1: 3 The LORD is s to get angry, but his power is
Hab 2: 3 If it seems s, wait patiently, for it will surely take
Jas 1:19 Dear friends, be quick to listen, s to speak, and s to get angry.
2Pe 3: 9 The Lord isn't really being s about his promise to

SLOWLY (2) [SLOW]

Isa 30: 6 Look at the animals moving s across the terrible
Hab 2: 3 S, steadily, surely, the time approaches when the

SLOWS (1) [SLOW]

Heb 12: 1 let us strip off every weight that s us down,

SLUMBER (3) [SLUMBERING]

Ps 132: 4 not let my eyes sleep / nor close my eyelids in s
Pr 6:10 A little extra sleep, a little more s, a little folding of
24:33 A little extra sleep, a little more s, a little folding of

SLUMBERING (1) [SLUMBER]

1Sa 26: 5 were sleeping inside a ring formed by the s

SLUNG (1) [SLING]

1Sa 17: 6 and he s a bronze javelin over his back.

SLY (1)

Pr 7:10 dressed seductively and s of heart.

SMALL (82) [SMALLER, SMALLEST]

Ge 1:24 of animal—livestock, s animals, and wildlife."
1:25 all sorts of wild animals, livestock, and s animals,
1:26 and all the livestock, wild animals, and s animals."
6:20 of bird and each kind of animal, large and s alike,
7: 8 along with all the birds and other s animals.
7:14 domestic and wild, large and s—along with birds
7:21 wild animals, all kinds of s animals,
7:23 people, animals both large and s, and birds.
9: 2 large and s, and all the birds and fish will be afraid
19:20 See, there is a s village nearby. Please let me go there instead; don't you see how s it is?
Ex 12: 4 If a family is too s to eat an entire lamb, let them
30: 1 "Then make a s altar out of acacia wood for
36:18 They also made fifty s bronze clasps to couple the
Lev 11:29 "Of the s animals that scurry or creep on the
11:31 All these s animals are unclean for you. If you
25:52 then they will repay a relatively s amount for their
Nu 11: 7 The manna looked like s coriander seeds,
16: 9 Does it seem a s thing to you that the God of Israel
Dt 33: 6 and not die out, / even though their tribe is s."
Jos 7: 3 they returned, they told Joshua, "It's a s town,
1Sa 2:19 Each year his mother made a s coat for him
9: 8 the servant said, "I have one s silver piece.
30:19 s or great, son or daughter, or anything else that
1Ki 2:20 "I have one s request to make of you," she said.
8:64 altar in the LORD's presence was too s to handle
11:17 had fled. (Hadad was a very s child at the time.)
2Ki 6: 1 this place where we meet with you is too s.
2Ch 14: 8 tribe of Benjamin, armed with s shields and bows.
24:24 Although the Arameans attacked with only a s
36:18 large and s, used in the Temple of God,
Ne 7: 4 was large and spacious, but the population was s.
Ps 104:25 teeming with life of every kind, / both great and s.
115:13 those who fear the LORD, / both great and s.
131: 2 just as a s child is quiet with its mother.
131: 2 Yes, like a s child is my soul within me.
Pr 28:21 yet some will do wrong for something as s as a
30:24 There are four things on earth that are s
Ecc 9:14 There was a s town with only a few people living
Isa 2:16 great trading ships and all the s boats in the harbor.
Jer 44:28 "Only a s number will escape death and return to
52:19 also took the s bowls, firepans, basins, pots,
Eze 39: 9 will go out and pick up your s and large shields,
Da 2:35 The pieces were crushed as s as chaff on a
7: 8 suddenly another s horn appeared among them.
8: 9 From one of the prominent horns came a s horn
Hos 9: 2 So now your harvests will be too s to feed you.
Am 6:11 homes both great and s will be smashed to pieces.
7: 2 Israel will not survive, for we are only a s nation."
7: 5 Israel will not survive, for we are only a s nation."
Ob 1: 2 the nations, Edom; you will be s and despised.
Mic 5: 2 are only a s village in Judah.
Zec 1: 8 standing among some myrtle trees in a s valley.
4:10 Do not despise these s beginnings, for the LORD
8: 6 a s and discouraged remnant of God's people.
Mt 7:14 But the gateway to life is s, and the road is narrow,
15:34 They replied, "Seven, and a few s fish."
17:20 even if you had faith as s as a mustard seed you
18: 2 Jesus called a s child over to him and put the child
25:21 You have been faithful in handling this s amount,
25:23 You have been faithful in handling this s amount,
Mk 6:37 "It would take a s fortune to buy food for all this
8: 7 A few s fish were found, too, so Jesus also blessed
9:21 the boy's father. He replied, "Since he was very s.
14: 5 "She could have sold it for a s fortune and given
Lk 6:38 Whatever measure you use in giving—large or s—
16:10 "Unless you are faithful in s matters, you won't be
17: 6 "Even if you had faith as s as a mustard seed,"
24:30 As they sat down to eat, he took a s loaf of bread,
Jn 6: 7 "It would take a s fortune to feed them!"
12: 5 "That perfume was worth a s fortune. It should
Ac 11: 6 I saw all sorts of s animals, wild animals, reptiles,
27:16 We sailed behind a s island named Cauda,
Ro 9:27 on the seashore, / only a s number will be saved.
2Co 4:17 For our present troubles are quite s and won't last
9: 6 a farmer who plants only a few seeds will get a s
Jas 3: 3 and go wherever we want by means of a s bit in its
3: 5 So also, the tongue is a s thing, but what enormous
Rev 10: 2 And in his hand was a s scroll, which he had
13:16 great and s, rich and poor, slave and free—
19:18 of all humanity, both free and slave, s and great."
20:12 I saw the dead, both great and s, standing before

SMALLER (9) [SMALL]

Ex 18:22 But they can take care of the s matters themselves.
18:26 but they judged the s matters themselves.
Nu 26:54 larger tribes more land and the s tribes less land,
26:56 by lot among the larger and s tribal groups."
33:54 and a s inheritance will be allotted to each of the s clans.
35: 8 to the Levites, while the s tribes will give fewer.
1Ki 10:17 He also made three hundred s shields of hammered
2Ch 9:16 He also made three hundred s shields of hammered

SMALLEST (14) [SMALL]

Dt 7: 7 other nations, for you were the s of all nations!
17:20 turning away from these commands in the s way.
1Sa 9:21 "But I'm only from Benjamin, the s tribe in Israel,
2Ki 17: 9 from the s outpost to the largest walled city.
18: 8 from their s outpost to their largest walled city.
Isa 42: 3 crush those who are weak or quench the s hope.
60:22 The s family will multiply into a large clan.
Mt 5:18 even the s detail of God's law will remain until its
5:19 So if you break the s commandment and teach
12:20 crush those who are weak, / or quench the s hope,
13:32 It is the s of all seeds, but it becomes the largest of
Mk 4:31 mustard seed. Though this is one of the s of seeds,
Lk 14:24 For none of those I invited first will get even the s
16:17 that the law has lost its force in even the s point.

SMART (1) [SMARTER, SMARTEST]

Pr 9: 7 Anyone who rebukes a mocker will get a s retort.

SMART [KJV] See also DANGEROUS

SMARTER (1) [SMART]

Pr 26:16 Lazy people consider themselves s than seven wise

SMARTEST (1) [SMART]

Job 13: 5 Please be quiet! That's the s thing you could do.

SMASH (14) [SMASHED, SMASHES, SMASHING]

Ex 34:13 s the sacred pillars they worship, and cut down
Dt 12: 3 Break down their altars and s their sacred pillars.
Ps 2: 9 with an iron rod / and s them like clay pots.' "
58: 6 O God! / S the jaws of these lions, O LORD!
68:21 But God will s the heads of his enemies,
Isa 45: 2 I will s down gates of bronze and cut through bars
Jer 13:14 I will s them one against the other, even parents
19:10 Jeremiah, s the jar you brought with you.
Eze 23:34 Then you will s it to pieces and beat your breast in
30:13 I will s the idols of Egypt and the images at
Da 2:40 That kingdom will s and crush all previous
Hos 10: 2 down their foreign altars and s their many idols.
Am 9: 1 S the columns so the roof will crash down on the
Rev 2:27 nations with an iron rod and s them like clay pots.

SMASHED (26) [SMASH]

Ex 34: 1 the same words that were on the tablets you s.
Lev 11:33 in the pot will be defiled, and the pot must be s.
11:35 a clay oven or cooking pot, it must be s to pieces.
Dt 9:17 them to the ground. I s them before your very eyes.
10: 2 tablets the same words that were on the ones you s.
2Ki 11:18 demolished the altars and s the idols to pieces,
18: 4 He removed the pagan shrines, s the sacred pillars,
23:12 He s them to bits and scattered the pieces in the
23:14 He s the sacred pillars and cut down the Asherah
2Ch 14: 3 He s the sacred pillars and cut down the Asherah
23:17 They demolished the altars and s the idols,
31: 1 and Manasseh, and they s the sacred pillars,
34: 4 and the cast images were s and scattered over the
Job 16:14 Again and again he s me, charging at me like a
Ps 74: 6 With axes and picks, / they s the carved paneling.
74:13 by your strength / and s the sea monster's heads.
Ecc 12: 6 Don't wait until the water jar is s at the spring
Isa 30:14 You will be s like a piece of pottery—shattered
Jer 48:38 For I have s Moab like an old, unwanted bottle.
La 2: 9 and bars are destroyed, for he has s them.
Eze 6: 4 be demolished, and your incense altars will be s.
Hos 8: 6 It is not God! Therefore, it must be s to bits.
Am 6:11 homes both great and small will be s to pieces.
Mic 1: 7 All her carved images will be s to pieces. All her
Mk 5: 4 the chains from his wrists and s the shackles.
Ac 27:41 while the stern was repeatedly s by the force of the

SMASHES (3) [SMASH]

Ps 137: 9 takes your babies / and s them against the rocks!
Jer 23:29 "Is it not like a mighty hammer that s rock to
Da 2:40 just as iron s and crushes everything it strikes.

SMASHING (2) [SMASH]

Ex 32:19 to the ground, s them at the foot of the mountain.
Da 2:34 It struck the feet of iron and clay, s them to bits.

SMEAR (3) [BLOOD-SMEARED, SMEARED, SMEARING]

Ex 12: 7 to take some of the lamb's blood and s it on the top
29:12 S some of its blood on the horns of the altar with
Eze 43:20 of its blood and s it on the four horns of the altar,

SMEARED (1) [SMEAR]

Ex 12:13 The blood you have s on your doorposts will serve

SMEARING (2) [SMEAR]

Lev 16:18 the LORD by s some of the blood from the bull
Job 13: 4 For you are s me with lies. As doctors, you are

SMELL (13) [SMELLING, SMELLS, SWEET-SMELLING]

Ge 27:27 And when Isaac caught the s of his clothes, he was
27:27 "The s of my son is the good s of the open
Ex 16:20 then it was full of maggots and had a terrible s.
Dt 4:28 gods that neither see nor hear nor eat nor s.
Ps 115: 6 cannot hear with their ears, / or s with their noses,
135:17 cannot hear with their ears / or s with their noses.
SS 2:13 How delicious they s! Yes, spring is here! Arise,
Isa 65: 5 in my nostrils, an acrid s that never goes away.
Da 3:27 was not scorched. They didn't even s of smoke!
Jn 11:39 by now the s will be terrible because he has been
1Co 12:17 were just one big ear, how could you s anything?
2Co 2:16 To those who are perishing we are a fearful s of

SMELLING (1) [SMELL]

Isa 3:24 Instead of s of sweet perfume, they will stink.

SMELLS (1) [SMELL]

SS 3: 6 Who is it that s of myrrh and frankincense

SMELT (1) [IRON-SMELTING, SMELTED]

Job 28: 2 to dig iron from the earth and s copper from stone.

SMELTED (1) [SMELT]
Eze 22:18 are the worthless slag that remains after silver is **s**.

SMILE (6) [SMILED, SMILES]
Ge 33:10 "for what a relief it is to see your friendly **s**. It is like seeing the **s** of God!
Nu 6:25 May the LORD **s** on you / and be gracious to you.
Ps 4: 6 Let the **s** of your face shine on us, LORD.
39:13 Spare me so I can **s** again / before I am gone
Da 9:17 Lord, **s** again on your desolate sanctuary.

SMILED (2) [SMILE]
Job 29:24 When they were discouraged, I **s** at them. My look
Ps 44: 3 it was because you favored them and **s** on them.

SMILES (3) [SMILE]
1Sa 15:32 Agag arrived full of **s**, for he thought,
Ps 85:11 the earth, / and righteousness **s** down from heaven.
Pr 16:15 When the king **s**, there is life; his favor refreshes

SMITHS (2) [BLACKSMITH, BLACKSMITHS, COPPERSMITH, GOLDSMITH, GOLDSMITHS, SILVERSMITH, SILVERSMITHS]
2Ki 24:14 and the best of the soldiers, craftsmen, and **s**.
24:16 the best troops and one thousand craftsmen and **s**,

SMOKE (41) [SMOKING]
Ge 19:28 and Gomorrah and saw columns of **s** and fumes,
Ex 19:18 All Mount Sinai was covered with **s**
19:18 The **s** billowed into the sky like **s** from a
20:18 and the **s** billowing from the mountain,
Jos 8:20 **s** from the city was filling the sky, and they had
8:21 had succeeded and that **s** was rising from the city,
Jdg 20:38 They sent up a large cloud of **s** from the town,
20:40 and saw the **s** rising into the sky from every part of
2Sa 22: 9 **S** poured from his nostrils; / fierce flames leaped
Job 41:20 **S** streams from its nostrils like steam from a
Ps 18: 8 **S** poured from his nostrils; / fierce flames leaped
37:20 like flowers in a field— / they will disappear like **s**.
68: 2 Drive them off like **s** blown by the wind.
102: 3 for my days disappear like **s**, / and my bones burn
119:83 I am shriveled like a wineskin in the **s**,
144: 5 Touch the mountains so they billow **s**.
Pr 10:26 They are like **s** in the eyes or vinegar that sets the
SS 3: 6 from the deserts like a cloud of **s** along the ground?
Isa 4: 5 There will be a canopy of **s** and cloud throughout
6: 4 and the entire sanctuary was filled with **s**.
9:18 too. Its burning sends up vast clouds of **s**.
30:27 burning with anger, surrounded by a thick, rising **s**.
34:10 never end; the **s** of its burning will rise forever.
51: 6 For the skies will disappear like **s**, and the earth
Da 3:27 was not scorched. They didn't even smell of **s**!
Hos 13: 3 chaff blown by the wind, like **s** from a chimney.
Joel 2:30 and on the earth—blood and fire and pillars of **s**.
Na 2:13 "Your chariots will soon go up in **s**.
Ac 2:19 the earth below— / blood and fire and clouds of **s**.
Rev 8: 4 The **s** of the incense, mixed with the prayers of the
9: 2 **s** poured out as though from a huge furnace,
9: 2 and the sunlight and air were darkened by the **s**.
9: 3 Then locusts came from the **s** and descended on the
9:17 and fire and **s** and burning sulfur billowed from
9:18 by the fire and the **s** and burning sulfur that came
14:11 The **s** of their torment rises forever and ever,
15: 8 The Temple was filled with **s** from God's glory
18: 9 as they see the **s** rising from her charred remains.
18:18 They will weep as they watch the **s** ascend,
19: 3 The **s** from that city ascends forever and forever!"

SMOKING (1) [SMOKE]
Ge 15:17 Abram saw a **s** firepot and a flaming torch pass

SMOLDERING (1) [SMOLDERS]
Isa 43:17 their lives snuffed out like a **s** candlewick.

SMOLDERS (1) [SMOLDERING]
Hos 7: 6 Their plot **s** through the night, and in the morning

SMOOTH (18) [SMOOTH-SKINNED, SMOOTH-TONGUED, SMOOTHED, SMOOTHER, SMOOTHLY]
Ge 27:11 Think how hairy Esau is and how **s** my skin is!
1Sa 17:40 He picked up five **s** stones from a stream and put
Ps 55:21 His words are as **s** as cream, / but in his heart is
Pr 6:24 from the **s** tongue of an adulterous woman.
23:31 let the sparkle and **s** taste of wine deceive you.
26:23 **S** words may hide a wicked heart, just as a pretty
SS 7: 9 **s** and sweet, flowing gently over lips and teeth."
Isa 26: 7 of justice, / and you **s** out the road ahead of them.
32: 7 The **s** tricks of evil people will be exposed,
40: 3 a straight, **s** road through the desert for our God.
40: 4 Straighten out the curves and **s** off the rough spots.
42:16 and **s** out the road ahead of them. / Yes, I will
57: 6 Your gods are the **s** stones in the valleys.
62:10 **S** out the road; pull out the boulders; raise a flag
Jer 48:11 from flask to flask, and she is now fragrant and **s**.
Lk 3: 5 Straighten the curves, / and **s** out the rough places!
Ro 16:18 By **s** talk and glowing words they deceive innocent
Rev 7: 1 in the trees, and the sea became as **s** as glass.

SMOOTH-SKINNED (2) [SKIN, SMOOTH]
Isa 18: 2 to your tall, **s** people, who are feared far and wide
18: 7 from this tall, **s** people, who are feared far

SMOOTH-TONGUED (1) [SMOOTH, TONGUE]
Jer 23:31 these **s** prophets who say, 'This prophecy is from

SMOOTHED (3) [SMOOTH]
Jn 9: 6 and **s** the mud over the blind man's eyes.
9:11 Jesus made mud and **s** it over my eyes and told me,
9:15 So he told them, "He **s** the mud over my eyes,

SMOOTHER (1) [SMOOTH]
Pr 5: 3 are as sweet as honey, and her mouth is **s** than oil.

SMOOTHLY (3) [SMOOTH]
Ge 39: 5 All his household affairs began to run **s**, and his
39:23 making everything run **s** and successfully.
Eze 32:14 and they will flow as **s** as olive oil,

SMYRNA (2)
Rev 1:11 Ephesus, **S**, Pergamum, Thyatira, Sardis,
2: 8 "Write this letter to the angel of the church in **S**.

SNAIL [KJV] See (SAND) LIZARD

SNAILS (1)
Ps 58: 8 May they be like **s** that dissolve into slime,

SNAKE (23) [SNAKEBITES, SNAKES]
Ge 49:17 He will be a **s** beside the road, / a poisonous viper
Ex 4: 3 So Moses threw it down, and it became a **s**!
7: 9 your shepherd's staff,' and it will become a **s**."
7:10 before Pharaoh and his court, and it became a **s**.
7:12 But then Aaron's **s** swallowed up their snakes.
7:15 take along the shepherd's staff that turned into a **s**.
Nu 21: 8 "Make a replica of a poisonous **s** and attach it to
21: 9 So Moses made a **s** out of bronze and attached it to
21: 9 those who were bitten looked at the bronze **s**,
Ps 58: 5 ignoring the tunes of the **s** charmers, / no matter
140: 3 Their tongues sting like a **s**; / the poison of a viper
Pr 30:19 glides through the sky, / how a **s** slithers on a rock,
Ecc 10: 8 demolish an old wall, you could be bitten by a **s**.
10:11 It does no good to charm a **s** after it has bitten you.
Isa 14:29 From that **s** a poisonous **s** will be born, a fiery
Am 5:19 against a wall in his house—and is bitten by a **s**.
Mt 7:10 Or if they ask for a fish, do you give them a **s**?
Lk 11:11 ask for a fish, do you give them a **s** instead?
Jn 3:14 And as Moses lifted up the bronze **s** on a pole in
Ac 28: 3 a poisonous **s**, driven out by the heat,
28: 5 But Paul shook off the **s** into the fire and was
Ro 3:13 "The poison of a deadly **s** drips from their lips."

SNAKEBITES (1) [BITE, SNAKE]
1Co 10: 9 the test, as some of them did and then died from **s**.

SNAKES (26) [SNAKE]
Ex 7:12 Their staffs became **s**, too! But then Aaron's snake swallowed up their **s**.
Nu 21: 6 So the LORD sent poisonous **s** among them,
21: 7 Pray that the LORD will take away the **s**."
Dt 8:15 and terrifying wilderness with poisonous **s**
32:24 wild beasts, / by poisonous **s** that glide in the dust.
32:33 Their wine is the venom of **s**, / the deadly poison
Job 20:16 He will suck the poison of **s**. The viper will kill
Ps 58: 4 They spit poison like deadly **s**; / they are like
91:13 You will trample down lions and poisonous **s**;
Isa 11: 8 Babies will crawl safely among poisonous **s**.
11: 8 a little child will put its hand in a nest of deadly **s**
30: 6 they go, where lions and poisonous **s** live.
65:25 Poisonous **s** will strike no more. In those days,
Jer 8:17 among you like poisonous **s** you cannot charm,"
Eze 8:10 and saw the walls engraved with all kinds of **s**,
Mic 7:17 Like **s** crawling from their holes, they will come
Mt 3: 7 denounced them. "You brood of **s**!" he exclaimed.
10:16 Be as wary as **s** and harmless as doves.
12:34 You brood of **s**! How could evil men like you
23:33 **S**! Sons of vipers! How will you escape the
Mk 16:18 They will be able to handle **s** with safety, and if
Lk 3: 7 "You brood of **s**! Who warned you to flee God's
10:19 and you can walk among **s** and scorpions and crush
Ro 1:23 look like mere people, or birds and animals and **s**.
Rev 9:19 For their tails had heads like **s**, with the power to

SNAP (1) [SNAPPED, SNAPS]
Jer 30: 8 break the yoke from their necks and **s** their chains.

SNAPPED (6) [SNAP]
Jdg 15:14 and he **s** the ropes on his arms as if they were burnt
16: 9 But Samson **s** the bowstrings as if they were string
16:12 But Samson **s** the ropes from his arms as if they
Ps 107:14 the darkness and deepest gloom; / he **s** their chains.
Zec 11:10 Then I took my staff called Favor and **s** it in two,
Mk 5: 4 he **s** the chains from his wrists and smashed the

SNAPS (2) [SNAP]
Ps 46: 9 He breaks the bow and **s** the spear in two;
Ecc 12: 6 before the silver cord of life **s** and the golden bowl

SNARE (15) [ENSNARE, ENSNARING, SNARES]
Dt 7:25 Do not take it or it will become a **s** to you, for it is
Jos 23:13 Instead, they will be a **s** and a trap to you, a pain in
Job 18:10 A **s** lies hidden in the ground. A rope lies coiled on
34:30 from ruling so they cannot be a **s** to the people.
Ps 35: 8 Let them be caught in the **s** they set for me!
69:22 Let the bountiful table set before them become a **s**,
Pr 7:23 He was like a bird flying into a **s**, little knowing it
Ecc 7:26 from her, but sinners will be caught in her **s**.
9:12 Like fish in a net or birds in a **s**, people are often
Isa 24:18 and those who escape the trap will step into a **s**.
Jer 48:44 and those who escape the trap will step into a **s**.
Eze 12:13 I will spread out my net and capture him in my **s**.
17:20 throw my net over him and capture him in my **s**.
Hos 5: 1 For you have led the people into a **s** by worshiping
Ro 11: 9 he said, / "Let their bountiful table become a **s**,

SNARES (8) [SNARE]
Ps 9:16 wicked have trapped themselves in their own **s**.
141: 9 have set for me, / out of the **s** of those who do evil.
141:10 Let the wicked fall into their own **s**, / but let me
Pr 13:14 those who accept it avoid the **s** of death.
14:27 it offers escape from the **s** of death.
Isa 24:17 Terror and traps and **s** will be your lot, you people
Jer 48:43 "Terror and traps and **s** will be your lot, O Moab,"
La 4:20 the very life of our nation, was caught in their **s**.

SNARL (2) [SNARLED, SNARLING]
Ps 35:16 with the worst kind of profanity, / and they **s** at me.
37:12 plot against the godly; / they **s** at them in defiance.

SNARLED (1) [SNARL]
2Sa 13:15 he had loved her. "Get out of here!" he **s** at her.

SNARLING (3) [SNARL]
Ps 59: 6 They come at night, / **s** like vicious dogs / as they
59:14 My enemies come out at night, / **s** like vicious dogs
Pr 18: 1 **s** at every sound principle of conduct.

SNATCH (8) [SNATCHED, SNATCHES, SNATCHING]
Job 9:12 If he sends death to **s** someone away, who can stop
24: 9 "The wicked **s** a widow's child from her breast;
Ps 9:13 who hate me. / **S** me back from the jaws of death.
22:21 **S** me from the lions' jaws, / and from the horns of
49:15 He will **s** me from the power of death. / *Interlude*
119:43 Do not **s** your word of truth from me, / for my only
Isa 49:24 Who can **s** the plunder of war from the hands of a
Jn 10:28 never perish. No one will **s** them away from me,

SNATCHED (10) [SNATCH]
Job 22:16 They were **s** away in the prime of life,
Ps 107:20 and they were healed— / **s** from the door of death.
Pr 22:27 pay it, even your bed will be **s** from under you.
Isa 28: 4 It will be greedily **s** up, as an early fig is hungrily
Jer 13:18 for your glorious crowns will soon be **s** from your
Am 4:11 survived were like half-burned sticks **s** from a fire.
Jnh 2: 6 have **s** me from the yawning jaws of death!
Mic 1:16 in sorrow, for the children you love will be **s** away,
Zec 3: 2 This man is like a burning stick that has been **s**
Rev 12: 5 And the child was **s** away from the dragon and was

SNATCHES (1) [SNATCH]
Mt 13:19 one comes and **s** the seed away from their hearts.

SNATCHING (1) [SNATCH]
Jude 1:23 Rescue others by **s** them from the flames of

SNEAKING (1) [SNEAKY]
Ge 31:26 "What do you mean by **s** off like this?"

SNEAKS (1) [SNEAKY]
Jn 10: 1 anyone who **s** over the wall of a sheepfold,

SNEAKY (1) [SNEAKING, SNEAKS]
2Co 12:16 But they still think I was **s** and took advantage of

SNEER (4) [SNEERED, SNEERING]
Ps 22: 7 mocks me. / They **s** and shake their heads, saying,
59: 7 fly from their lips. / "Who can hurt us?" they **s**.
Isa 3: 5 and nobodies will **s** at honorable people.
Eze 36:15 I will not allow those foreign nations to **s** at you,

SNEERED (1) [SNEER]
1Sa 25:10 "Who is this fellow David?" Nabal **s**. "Who does

SNEERING (2) [SNEER]
1Sa 17:42 **s** in contempt at this ruddy-faced boy.
Jer 33:24 They are **s** and saying that Israel is not worthy to

SNEEZED (1) [SNEEZES]
2Ki 4:35 This time the boy **s** seven times and opened his

SNEEZES (1) [SNEEZED]
Job 41:18 "When it **s**, it flashes light! Its eyes are like the red

SNIFFING (1)
Jer 2:24 are like a wild donkey, s the wind at mating time.

SNIP (1)
Isa 18:5 pruning shears. He will s your spreading branches.

SNORTING (2) [SNORTS]
Job 39:20 like a locust? Its majestic s is something to hear!
Jer 8:16 The s of the enemies' warhorses can be heard all

SNORTS (1) [SNORTING]
Job 39:25 It s at the sound of the bugle. It senses the battle

SNOUT (1)
Pr 11:22 but lacks discretion is like a gold ring in a pig's s.

SNOW (21) [SNOWSTORM]
Ex 4:6 it out again, his hand was white as s with leprosy.
Nu 12:10 Miriam suddenly became white as s with leprosy.
2Sa 23:20 Then, despite the s and slippery ground, he caught
2Ki 5:27 he was leprous; his skin was as white as s.
1Ch 11:22 Then, despite the s and slippery ground, he caught
Job 6:16 when it is swollen with ice and melting s.
24:19 sinners just as drought and heat consume s.
37:6 "He directs the s to fall on the earth and tells the
38:22 "Have you visited the treasuries of the s?
Ps 51:7 be clean; / wash me, and I will be whiter than s.
147:16 He sends the s like white wool; / he scatters frost
148:8 fire and hail, s and storm, / wind and weather that
Pr 25:13 Faithful messengers are as refreshing as s in the
26:1 Honor doesn't go with fools any more than s with
Isa 1:18 I can make you as clean as freshly fallen s.
55:10 "The rain and s come down from the heavens
Jer 18:14 Does the s ever melt high up in the mountains of
La 4:7 they were as clean as s and as elegant as jewels.
Da 7:9 His clothing was as white as s, his hair like whitest
Mt 28:3 like lightning, and his clothing was as white as s.
Rev 1:14 and his hair were white like wool, as white as s.

SNOWSTORM (1) [SNOW, STORM]
Ps 68:14 enemy kings / like a blowing s on Mount Zalmon.

SNUFFDISHES [KJV] See TRAYS

SNUFFED (6) [SNUFFERS, SNUFFING]
2Ch 29:7 to the Temple's foyer, and they s out the lamps.
Job 18:5 remains that the light of the wicked will be s out.
Pr 13:9 full of light and joy, but the sinner's light is s out.
20:20 or mother, the lamp of your life will be s out.
24:20 For the evil have no future; their light will be s out.
Isa 43:17 their lives s out like a smoldering candlewick.

SNUFFERS (8) [SNUFFED]
Ex 25:38 The lamp s and trays must also be made of pure
37:23 the lamp s, and the trays, all of pure gold.
Nu 4:9 along with its lamps, lamp s, trays, and special jars
1Ki 7:50 the cups, lamp s, basins, dishes, and firepans,
2Ki 12:13 lamp s, basins, trumpets, or other articles of gold
25:14 They also took all the pots, shovels, lamp s, dishes,
2Ch 4:22 the lamp s, basins, dishes, and firepans, all of pure
Jer 52:18 took all the pots, shovels, lamp s, basins, dishes,

SNUFFING (1) [SNUFFED]
2Sa 21:17 Why should we risk s out the light of Israel?"

SNUGLY (2)
Lk 2:7 She wrapped him s in strips of cloth and laid him
2:12 lying in a manger, wrapped s in strips of cloth!"

SO (1 of 3565) See also Index of Articles, Etc.
2Ki 17:4 by asking King S of Egypt to help him shake free

SO-CALLED (7) [CALL]
2Ch 13:9 and seven rams can become a priest of these s gods
Isa 57:12 "Now I will expose your s good deeds that you
Jer 10:11 "Your s gods, who did not make the heavens
1Co 8:5 there are many s gods and many lords, both in
Gal 2:4 had come up except for some s Christians there—
4:8 you were slaves to s gods that do not even exist.
1Ti 6:20 with those who oppose you with their s knowledge.

SOAKED (7) [SOAKS]
Lev 7:12 all made without yeast and s with olive oil.
8:26 a cake of unleavened bread s with olive oil, and a
2Ki 8:15 the next day Hazael took a blanket, s it in water,
Job 24:8 They are s by mountain showers, and they huddle
SS 5:2 My head is s with dew, my hair with the wetness
Isa 34:7 The land will be s with blood and the soil enriched
Jn 19:29 so they s a sponge in it, put it on a hyssop branch,

SOAKS (1) [SOAKED]
Heb 6:7 When the ground s up the rain that falls on it

SOAP (3)
Job 9:30 Even if I were to wash myself with s and cleanse
Jer 2:22 No amount of s or lye can make you clean.
Mal 3:2 refines metal or like a strong s that whitens clothes.

SOAR (2) [SOARING]
Job 39:26 "Are you the one who makes the hawk s
Ob 1:4 Though you s as high as eagles and build your nest

SOARING (2) [SOAR]
2Sa 22:11 mighty angel, he flew, / s on the wings of the wind.
Ps 18:10 mighty angel, he flew, / s on the wings of the wind.

SOB (1) [SOBBED, SOBBING, SOBS]
Jer 9:1 I would s day and night for all my people who

SOBBED (1) [SOB]
Ge 39:14 she s. "He tried to rape me, but I screamed.

SOBBING (2) [SOB]
2Sa 13:36 weeping and s, and the king and his officials wept
Ps 6:6 I am worn out from s. / Every night tears drench

SOBER (3)
1Sa 25:37 The next morning when he was s, she told him
Ac 26:25 Most Excellent Festus. I am speaking the s truth.
1Th 5:6 not asleep like the others. Stay alert and be s.

SOBRIETY [KJV] See MODESTY

SOBS (2) [SOB]
Ge 45:2 His s could be heard throughout the palace,
La 1:2 She s through the night; tears stream down her

SOCHO [KJV] See SOCO

SOCHOH [KJV] See SOCOH

SOCIETY (4)
Da 4:25 You will be driven from human s, and you will live
4:32 You will be driven from human s. You will live in
4:33 and Nebuchadnezzar was driven from human s.
5:21 He was driven from human s. He was given the

SOCKET (2) [SOCKETS]
Ge 32:25 Jacob's hip and knocked it out of joint at the s.
Job 31:22 out of place! Let my arm be torn from its s!

SOCKETS (2) [SOCKET]
SS 5:15 His legs are like pillars of marble set in s of the
Zec 14:12 Their eyes will shrivel in their s, and their tongues

SOCO (3)
1Ch 4:18 Heber (the father of S), and Jekuthiel (the father of
2Ch 11:7 Beth-zur, S, Adullam,
28:18 Aijalon, Gederoth, S with its villages, Timnah with

SOCOH (4)
Jos 15:35 Jarmuth, Adullam, S, Azekah,
15:48 towns in the hill country: Shamir, Jattir, S,
1Sa 17:1 and camped between S in Judah and Azekah at
1Ki 4:10 including S and all the land of Hepher.

SOD(DEN) [KJV] See BOILED, COOKING

SODI (1)
Nu 13:10 Zebulun | Gaddiel son of S

SODOM (48) [SODOM'S]
Ge 10:19 near Gaza, and to S, Gomorrah, Admah,
13:10 (This was before the LORD had destroyed S
13:12 Lot moved his tents to a place near S,
14:2 fought against King Bera of S, King Birsha of
14:3 The kings of S, Gomorrah, Admah, Zeboiim,
14:8 But now the army of the kings of S, Gomorrah,
14:10 And as the army of the kings of S and Gomorrah
14:11 then plundered S and Gomorrah
14:12 captured Lot—Abram's nephew who lived in S—
14:17 the king of S came out to meet him in the valley of
14:21 The king of S told him, "Give back my people
18:16 got up from their meal and started on toward S.
18:20 "I have heard that the people of S and Gomorrah
18:22 The two other men went on toward S,
18:26 "If I find fifty innocent people in S,
19:1 two angels came to the entrance of the city of S,
19:4 all the men of S, young and old, came from all
19:11 Then they blinded the men of S so they couldn't
19:24 and burning sulfur from the heavens on S
19:28 He looked out across the plain to S and Gomorrah
Dt 29:23 It will be just like S and Gomorrah, Admah
32:32 Their vine grows from the vine of S,
Isa 1:9 we would have been wiped out as completely as S
1:10 just like the rulers and people of S and Gomorrah.
3:9 their guilt. They sin openly like the people of S.
13:19 will be devastated like S and Gomorrah when God
Jer 23:14 These prophets are as wicked as the people of S
49:18 It will be like the destruction of S and Gomorrah
50:40 I will destroy it just as I destroyed S and Gomorrah
La 4:6 The guilt of my people is greater than that of S,
Eze 16:46 Your younger sister was S, who lived with her
16:48 S and her daughters were never as wicked as you
16:53 "But someday I will restore the fortunes of S
16:55 Yes, your sisters, S and Samaria, and all their
16:56 In your proud days you held S in contempt.
16:61 your sisters, Samaria and S, to be your daughters,
Am 4:11 of your cities, as I destroyed S and Gomorrah.
Zep 2:9 and Ammon will be destroyed as completely as S
Mt 10:15 the wicked cities of S and Gomorrah will be better
11:23 if the miracles I did for you had been done in S,
11:24 S will be better off on the judgment day than you."
Lk 10:12 even wicked S will be better off than such a town
17:29 until the morning Lot left S. Then fire and burning
Ro 9:29 wiped out / as completely as S and Gomorrah."
2Pe 2:6 he turned the cities of S and Gomorrah into heaps
2:7 God rescued Lot out of S because he was a good
Jude 1:7 And don't forget the cities of S and Gomorrah
Rev 11:8 the city which is called "S" and "Egypt," the city

SODOM'S (1) [SODOM]
Eze 16:49 S sins were pride, laziness, and gluttony,

SODOMITE(S) [KJV] See (SHRINE, TEMPLE) PROSTITUTE(S)

SOFT (4) [SOFTEN, SOFTENING, SOFTLY]
Job 41:23 Its flesh is hard and firm, not s and fat.
Pr 25:15 a prince, and s speech can crush strong opposition.
Ecc 7:26 passion is a trap, and her s hands will bind you.
SS 1:15 how beautiful! Your eyes are s like doves."

SOFTEN (1) [SOFT]
Ps 65:10 leveling the ridges. / You s the earth with showers

SOFTENING (1) [SOFT]
Ecc 8:1 Wisdom lights up a person's face, s its hardness.

SOFTLY (1) [SOFT]
Isa 28:27 on cummin; instead, it is beaten s with a flail.

SOIL (41) [SOILED]
Ge 2:5 any rain. And no one was there to cultivate the s.
2:19 So the LORD God formed from the s every kind
Nu 13:20 How is the s? Is it fertile or poor? Are there many
Dt 29:23 They will find its s turned into sulfur and salt,
1Sa 26:20 Must I die on foreign s, far from the presence of
2Ki 19:30 will take root again in your own s, and you will
2Ch 26:10 on the plains. He was also a man who loved the s.
Ne 10:35 whether it be a crop from the s or from our fruit
Job 5:6 But evil does not spring from the s, and trouble
14:19 wears away the stones and floods wash away the s,
Ps 83:10 and their decaying corpses fertilized the s.
141:7 Even as a farmer breaks up the s and brings up
Pr 8:26 the earth and fields and the first handfuls of s.
Isa 28:24 Is he forever cultivating the s and never planting
34:7 be soaked with blood and the s enriched with fat.
37:31 will take root again in your own s, and you will
Eze 17:8 this even though it was already planted in good s
17:10 It will die in the same good s where it had grown
26:4 I will scrape away its s and make it a bare rock!
Hos 14:5 it will send roots deep into the s like the cedars in
Zec 13:5 The s has been my means of livelihood from my
Mt 13:5 Other seeds fell on shallow s with underlying rock.
13:6 the roots had no nourishment in the shallow s.
13:8 But some seeds fell on fertile s and produced a
13:20 The rocky s represents those who hear the message
13:21 But like young plants in such s, their roots don't go
13:23 The good s represents the hearts of those who truly
Mk 4:5 Other seed fell on shallow s with underlying rock.
4:6 the roots had no nourishment in the shallow s.
4:8 Still other seed fell on fertile s and produced a crop
4:16 The rocky s represents those who hear the message
4:17 But like young plants in such s, their roots don't go
4:20 But the good s represents those who hear
Lk 8:6 Other seed fell on shallow s with underlying rock.
8:8 Still other seed fell on fertile s. This seed grew
8:13 The rocky s represents those who hear the message
8:13 But like young plants in such s, their roots don't go
8:15 But the good s represents honest,
14:35 Flavorless salt is good neither for the s nor for
Jn 12:24 truth is, a kernel of wheat must be planted in the s.
Eph 3:17 May your roots go down deep into the s of God's

SOILED (2) [SOIL]
SS 5:3 I have washed my feet. Should I get them s?'
Rev 3:4 "Yet even in Sardis there are some who have not s

SOJOURN(ED), SOJOURNER(S), SOJOURNETH, SOJOURNING [KJV] See ALIENS, LIVE(D), RESIDENT(S), SETTLE(D), STAY(ED, -ING), TRANSIENT

SOLACE [KJV] See ENJOY

SOLD (56) [SELL]
Ge 23:20 and the cave were s to Abraham by the Hittites as a
31:15 He s us, and what he received for us has
37:28 out of the pit and s him for twenty pieces of silver,
37:36 in Egypt, the traders s Joseph to Potiphar,
41:56 up the storehouses and s grain to the Egyptians.
45:4 am Joseph, your brother whom you s into Egypt.
47:20 All the Egyptians s him their fields
Ex 21:16 of their victims or have already s them as slaves.
22:3 the thief must be s as a slave to pay the debt.
Lev 25:23 the land must never be s on a permanent basis
25:26 but the person who s it manages to get enough

25:32 they have s within the cities belonging to them.
25:34 around each of the Levitical cities may never be s.
25:42 land of Egypt, so they must never be s as slaves.
25:51 of what they received when they s themselves.
27:20 or if the field is s to someone else by the priests,
27:28 or an inherited field—must never be s or redeemed.
Dt 32:30 thousand to flight, / unless their Rock had s them,
Jdg 2:14 He s them to their enemies all around, and they
1Ki 21:20 because you have s yourself to what is evil in the
21:25 so completely s himself to what was evil in the
2Ki 6:25 After a while even a donkey's head s for two
7:16 So it was true that five quarts of fine flour were s
7:16 and ten quarts of barley grain were s for half an
17:17 and used sorcery and s themselves to evil,
Ne 5:5 We have already s some of our daughters, and we
10:31 or grain to be s on the Sabbath or on any other holy
Est 7:4 and I have been s to those who would kill,
7:4 If we had only been s as slaves, I could remain
Ps 44:12 You s us—your precious people—for a pittance.
105:17 ahead of them— / Joseph, who was s as a slave.
Pr 27:26 and your goats will be s for the price of a field.
Isa 52:3 "When I s you into exile, I received no payment.
Jer 32:43 and s in this land about which you now say,
32:44 Yes, fields will once again be bought and s—
La 1:11 They have s their treasures for food to stay alive.
Eze 48:14 None of this special land will ever be s or traded
Hos 8:9 The people of Israel have s themselves to many
8:10 But though they have s themselves to many lands,
Joel 3:6 You have s the people of Judah and Jerusalem to
3:7 again from all these places to which you s them,
Zec 11:11 Those who bought and s sheep were watching me,
Mt 13:44 and s everything he owned to get enough money to
13:46 he s everything he owned and bought it!
18:25 and everything he had be s to pay the debt.
26:9 "She could have s it for a fortune and given the
Mk 14:5 "She could have s it for a small fortune and given
Jn 2:16 Then, going over to the people who s doves,
12:5 It should have been s and the money given to the
Ac 2:45 They s their possessions and shared the proceeds
4:34 because people who owned land or houses s them
4:37 He s a field he owned and brought the money to
5:1 with his wife, Sapphira, s some property.
7:9 and they s him to be a slave in Egypt.
Ro 7:14 the law but with me, because I am s into slavery,
1Co 10:25 You may eat any meat that is s in the marketplace.

SOLDIER (15) [SOLDIERS]

2Sa 17:8 And remember that your father is an experienced s.
1Ki 20:20 Each Israelite s killed his Aramean opponent,
22:34 An Aramean s, however, randomly shot an arrow
2Ch 17:17 were under the command of Eliada, a veteran s.
18:33 An Aramean s, however, randomly shot an arrow
Isa 14:31 of the north. Each s rushes forward ready to fight.
Mt 5:41 If a s demands that you carry his gear for a mile,
Mk 6:27 bring it to him. The s beheaded John in the prison,
Ac 10:7 two of his household servants and a devout s,
28:16 private lodging, though he was guarded by a s.
1Co 9:7 What s has to pay his own expenses? And have
Php 2:25 true brother, a faithful worker, and a courageous s.
2Ti 2:3 along with me, as a good s of Christ Jesus.
2:4 And as Christ's s, do not let yourself become tied
Phm 1:2 and to Archippus, a fellow s of the cross.

SOLDIERS (63) [SOLDIER]

Nu 11:21 "There are 600,000 foot s here with me,
Jdg 9:4 which he used to hire some s who agreed to follow
9:5 He took the s to his father's home at Ophrah,
9:29 'Get some more s, and come out and fight!' "
2Sa 8:4 hundred charioteers and twenty thousand foot s.
11:17 was killed along with several other Israelite s.
1Ki 20:10 to provide more than a handful for each of my s."
20:29 The Israelites killed 100,000 Aramean foot s in one
2Ki 1:9 Then he sent an army captain with fifty s to arrest
13:7 ten chariots, and ten thousand foot s.
24:14 including all the princes and the best of the s,
25:4 and all the s made plans to escape from the city.
1Ch 18:4 thousand charioteers, and twenty thousand foot s.
19:18 thousand charioteers and forty thousand foot s,
2Ch 12:3 and a countless army of foot s, including Libyans,
Ezr 8:22 For I was ashamed to ask the king for s
Ps 59:T regarding the time Saul sent s to watch David's
Isa 3:2 the heroes, s, judges, prophets, diviners, elders,
Jer 41:3 and Babylonian s who were with Gedaliah at
52:7 and all the s made plans to escape from the city.
Da 3:22 and killed the s as they threw the three men in!
Joel 2:7 like warriors and scale city walls like trained s.
Am 2:15 The swiftest s won't be fast enough to escape.
Na 3:10 S cast lots to see who would get the Egyptian
Mt 2:16 He sent s to kill all the boys in and around
8:9 superior officers and I have authority over my s.
27:26 then turned him over to the Roman s to crucify
27:27 Some of the governor's s took Jesus into their
27:34 The s gave him wine mixed with bitter gall,
27:35 the s gambled for his clothes by throwing dice.
27:54 and the other s at the crucifixion were terrified by
28:12 leaders was called, and they decided to bribe the s.
28:13 They told the s, "You must say, 'Jesus' disciples
Mk 6:17 For Herod had sent s to arrest and imprison John as
15:15 then turned him over to the Roman s to crucify
15:16 The s took him into their headquarters and called
Lk 3:14 asked some s. John replied, "Don't extort money,
7:8 superior officers, and I have authority over my s.
14:31 twenty thousand s who are marching against him?
23:11 Now Herod and his s began mocking
23:34 And the s gambled for his clothes by throwing
23:36 The s mocked him, too, by offering him a drink of
23:47 When the captain of the Roman s handling the
Jn 18:3 Pharisees had given Judas a battalion of Roman s
18:12 So the s, their commanding officer,
19:2 The s made a crown of long, sharp thorns and put
19:23 When the s had crucified Jesus, they divided his
19:32 So the s came and broke the legs of the two men
19:34 One of the s, however, pierced his side with a
Ac 12:4 him under the guard of four squads of four s each.
12:6 he was asleep, chained between two s, with others
12:18 there was a great commotion among the s about
21:32 He immediately called out his s and officers
21:35 so violent the s had to lift Paul to their shoulders to
22:29 The s who were about to interrogate Paul quickly
23:10 ordered his s to take him away from them
23:23 "Get two hundred s ready to leave for Caesarea at
23:31 as ordered, the s took Paul as far as Antipatris.
27:31 But Paul said to the commanding officer and the s,
27:32 The s cut the ropes and let the boat fall off.
27:42 The s wanted to kill the prisoners to make sure
1Co 14:8 how will the s know they are being called to
Php 1:13 including all the s in the palace guard,

SOLEMN (28) [SOLEMNIZE, SOLEMNLY]

Ge 24:9 So the servant took a s oath that he would follow
26:31 they each took a s oath of nonaggression.
50:10 Jordan River, they held a very great and s funeral,
Ex 6:4 And I entered into a s covenant with them.
Lev 23:36 This will be a s closing assembly, and no regular
Nu 29:1 You must call a s assembly of all the people on
Dt 4:31 or forget the s covenant he made with your
Jdg 21:5 At that time they had taken a s oath in the
21:18 because we have sworn with a s oath that anyone
1Sa 11:15 and in a s ceremony before the LORD they
2Ki 10:20 "Prepare a s assembly to worship Baal!"
Ezr 10:5 as Shecaniah had said. And they all swore a s oath.
Ne 8:18 Then on October 15 they held a s assembly,
9:34 or listen to your commands and s warnings.
9:38 we are making a s promise and putting it in
Ps 89:3 "I have made a s agreement with David,
Jer 28:7 But listen now to the s words I speak to you in the
34:15 and made a s covenant with me in my Temple.
Eze 16:59 for you have taken your s vows lightly by breaking
17:19 and despising the s oath he made in my name.
20:23 But I took a s oath against them while they were in
Da 9:11 "So now the s curses and judgments written in the
12:7 and took this s oath by the one who lives forever:
Joel 1:14 of fasting; call the people together for a s meeting.
2:15 of fasting; call the people together for a s meeting.
Am 5:21 of your religious festivals and s assemblies.
Ac 19:17 A s fear descended on the city, and the name of the
2Co 5:11 because we know this s fear of the Lord that we

SOLEMNITIES, SOLEMNITY [KJV] See WORSHIP, FESTIVAL(S)

SOLEMNIZE (1) [SOLEMN]

Jer 34:18 you walked between its halves to s your vows.

SOLEMNLY (29) [SOLEMN]

Ge 6:18 But I s swear to keep you safe in the boat,
9:11 I s promise never to send another flood to kill all
14:22 Abram replied, "I have s promised the LORD,
24:7 s promised to give this land to my offspring.
26:3 just as I s promised Abraham, your father.
47:29 swear most s that you will honor this, my last
Ex 33:1 lead them to the land I s promised Abraham,
Nu 32:11 or older will ever see the land I s promised to
Dt 1:34 he became very angry. So he s swore,
6:18 and occupy the good land that the LORD s
6:23 so he could give us this land he had s promised to
7:12 love with you, as he s promised your ancestors.
13:17 a great nation, just as he s promised your ancestors.
19:8 as he s promised your ancestors, and gives you all
26:15 and honey—just as you s promised our ancestors.'
28:9 you as his holy people as he s promised to do.
Jos 21:44 just as he had s promised their ancestors.
1Sa 8:9 but s warn them about how a king will treat them."
1Ki 2:23 Then King Solomon swore s by the LORD:
2Ki 9:26 'I s swear that I will repay him here on Naboth's
Ne 10:29 They s promised to carefully follow all the
Jer 11:7 For I s warned your ancestors when I brought them
Zec 3:6 Then the angel of the LORD spoke very s to
Mk 14:25 I s declare that I will not drink wine again until that
Gal 1:11 I s assure you that the Good News of salvation
1Th 4:6 all such sins, as we have s warned you before.
1Ti 5:21 I s command you in the presence of God
2Ti 4:1 And so I s urge you before God and before Christ
Rev 22:18 And I s declare to everyone who hears the

SOLICITING (1)

Pr 7:12 seen in the streets and markets, s at every corner.

SOLID (15) [SOLIDLY]

Ex 27:17 The posts are to be set in s bronze bases.
38:17 and the rods to hold up the curtains were s silver.
2Sa 22:32 except the LORD? / Who but our God is a s rock?
1Ki 10:21 All of King Solomon's drinking cups were s gold,
1Ch 28:17 David also designated the amount of gold for the s
2Ch 9:20 All of King Solomon's drinking cups were s gold,
Ps 18:31 except the LORD? / Who but our God is a s rock?
40:2 the mud and the mire. / He set my feet on s ground
78:69 as s and enduring as the earth itself.
114:8 of water; / yes, springs of water came from s rock.
Zec 4:2 "I see a s gold lampstand with a bowl of oil on top
Mt 7:24 is wise, like a person who builds a house on s rock.
1Co 3:2 I had to feed you with milk and not with s food,
Heb 5:12 babies who drink only milk and cannot eat s food.
5:14 S food is for those who are mature, who have

SOLIDLY (1) [SOLID]

2Ch 21:4 But when Jehoram had become s established as

SOLITARY (2)

1Ki 19:4 He sat down under a s broom tree and prayed that
Ps 102:7 I lie awake, / lonely as a s bird on the roof.

SOLOMON (268) [JEDIDIAH, SOLOMON'S]

2Sa 5:14 born in Jerusalem: Shimea, Shobab, Nathan, S,
12:24 and gave birth to a son, and they named him S.
1Ki 1:10 or the king's bodyguard, or his brother S.
1:12 to save your own life and the life of your son S,
1:13 didn't you promise me that my son S would be the
1:17 your God that my son S would be the next king
1:19 of the army. But he did not invite your servant S.
1:21 my son S and I will be treated as criminals as soon
1:26 Zadok the priest, Benaiah son of Jehoiada, nor S.
1:30 today I decree that your son S will be the next king
1:33 "Take S and my officers down to Gihon Spring. S is to ride on my personal mule.
1:34 blow the trumpets and shout, 'Long live King S!'
1:37 And may the LORD be with S as he has been
1:38 and the king's bodyguard took S down to Gihon
1:38 and S rode on King David's personal mule.
1:39 and all the people shouted, "Long live King S!"
1:40 And all the people returned with S to Jerusalem,
1:43 "Our lord King David has just declared S king!
1:46 S is now sitting on the royal throne as king.
1:50 Adonijah himself was afraid of S, so he rushed to
1:51 Word soon reached S that Adonijah had seized the
1:51 "Let S swear today that he will not kill me!"
1:52 S replied, "If he proves himself to be loyal,
1:53 So King S summoned Adonijah, and they brought
1:53 and S dismissed him, saying, "Go on home."
2:1 death approached, he gave this charge to his son S:
2:12 S succeeded him as king, replacing his father,
2:17 He replied, "Speak to King S on my behalf,
2:19 So Bathsheba went to King S to speak on
2:22 S demanded. "You might as well be asking me to
2:23 Then King S swore solemnly by the LORD:
2:25 So King S ordered Benaiah son of Jehoiada to
2:27 So S deposed Abiathar from his position as priest
2:29 When news of this reached King S, he sent
2:41 S heard that Shimei had left Jerusalem and had
3:1 S made an alliance with Pharaoh, the king of
3:3 S loved the LORD and followed all the
3:3 David, except that S, too, offered sacrifices
3:5 That night the LORD appeared to S in a dream,
3:6 S replied, "You were wonderfully kind to my
3:15 Then S woke up and realized it had been a dream.
4:1 So S was king over all Israel,
4:7 S also had twelve district governors who were over
4:21 King S ruled all the kingdoms from the Euphrates
4:21 peoples of those lands sent tribute money to S
4:25 Throughout the lifetime of S, all of Judah
4:26 S had four thousand stalls for his chariot horses
4:27 governors faithfully provided food for King S
4:29 God gave S great wisdom and understanding,
4:34 sent their ambassadors to listen to the wisdom of S.
5:1 so when he learned that David's son S was the new
5:2 Then S sent this message back to Hiram:
5:8 Then he sent this reply to S: / "I have received
5:10 So Hiram produced for S as much cedar
5:11 In return S sent him an annual payment of 100,000
5:12 So the LORD gave great wisdom to S just as he
5:12 And Hiram and S made a formal alliance of peace.
5:13 Then King S enlisted thirty thousand laborers from
5:15 S also enlisted seventy thousand common laborers,
6:2 The Temple that King S built for the LORD was
6:4 S also made narrow, recessed windows throughout
6:9 S put in a ceiling made of beams and planks of
6:11 Then the LORD gave this message to S:
6:14 So S finished building the Temple.
6:19 S prepared the inner sanctuary in the rear of the
6:20 S overlaid its walls and ceiling with pure gold.
6:23 Within the inner sanctuary S placed two cherubim
6:27 S placed them side by side in the inner sanctuary
6:31 S made double doors of olive wood with five-sided
7:1 S also built a palace for himself, and it took him
7:7 of Judgment, where S sat to hear legal matters.
7:13 King S then asked for a man named Huram to
7:14 worker from Tyre. So he came to work for King S.
7:40 So at last Huram completed everything King S had
7:45 Huram made for S were made of burnished bronze.
7:47 S did not weigh all the utensils because there were
7:48 So S made all the furnishings of the Temple of the
7:51 So King S finished all his work on the Temple of
7:51 Then S brought all the gifts his father, David,
8:1 S then summoned the leaders of all the tribes
8:5 King S and the entire community of Israel
8:12 Then S prayed, "O LORD, you have said that
8:17 Then S said, "My father, David, wanted to build
8:22 Then S stood with his hands lifted toward heaven
8:54 When S finished making these prayers
8:63 S sacrificed peace offerings to the LORD
8:65 Then S and all Israel celebrated the Festival of
8:66 the festival was over, S sent the people home.
9:1 So S finished building the Temple of the LORD,
9:2 Then the LORD appeared to S a second time,
9:10 Now at the end of the twenty years during which S

9:11 **S** gave twenty towns in the land of Galilee to King
9:12 Hiram came from Tyre to see the towns **S** had
9:14 Hiram had sent **S** nine thousand pounds of gold.
9:15 This is the account of the forced labor that **S**
9:16 his daughter as a wedding gift when she married **S**.
9:17 So **S** rebuilt the city of Gezer.) He also built up the
9:21 So **S** conscripted them for his labor force, and they
9:22 But **S** did not conscript any of the Israelites for
9:24 After **S** moved his wife, Pharaoh's daughter,
9:25 Three times each year **S** offered burnt offerings
9:26 Later King **S** built a fleet of ships at Ezion-geber,
9:28 and brought back to **S** some sixteen tons of gold.
10:2 When she met with **S**, they talked about everything
10:3 **S** answered all her questions; nothing was too hard
10:4 When the queen of Sheba realized how wise **S**
10:5 and the burnt offerings **S** made at the Temple of
10:10 brought in as those the queen of Sheba gave to **S**.
10:13 King **S** gave the queen of Sheba whatever she
10:14 Each year **S** received about twenty-five tons of
10:16 King **S** made two hundred large shields of
10:20 **S** made twelve other lion figures, one standing on
10:23 So King **S** became richer and wiser than any other
10:26 **S** built up a huge force of chariots and horses.
11:1 Now King **S** loved many foreign women.
11:2 their gods. Yet **S** insisted on loving them anyway.
11:5 **S** worshiped Ashtoreth, the goddess of the
11:6 Thus, **S** did what was evil in the LORD's sight;
11:8 **S** built such shrines for all his foreign wives to use
11:9 The LORD was very angry with **S**, for his heart
11:10 He had warned **S** specifically about worshiping
11:10 but **S** did not listen to the LORD's command.
11:14 of Edom's royal family, to be an enemy against **S**.
11:23 up Rezon son of Eliada to be an enemy against **S**.
11:27 **S** was rebuilding the Millo and repairing the walls
11:28 and when **S** saw how industrious he was,
11:31 am about to tear the kingdom from the hand of **S**,
11:33 For **S** has abandoned me and worshiped Ashtoreth,
11:34 " 'But I will not take the entire kingdom from **S** at
11:34 and laws, I will let **S** reign for the rest of his life.
11:40 **S** tried to kill Jeroboam, but he fled to King Shishak of Egypt and stayed there until **S** died.
11:41 are recorded in *The Book of the Acts of S*.
11:42 **S** ruled in Jerusalem over all Israel for forty years.
11:43 When **S** died, he was buried in the city of his
12:2 for he had fled to Egypt to escape from King **S**.
12:6 the older men who had counseled his father, **S**.
12:23 "Say to Rehoboam son of **S**, king of Judah,
14:21 Meanwhile, Rehoboam son of **S** was king in Judah.
14:26 including all the gold shields **S** had made.
2Ki 21:7 where the LORD had told David and his son **S**:
23:13 where King **S** of Israel had built shrines for
24:13 They cut apart all the gold vessels that King **S** of
25:16 for the LORD's Temple in the days of King **S**.
1Ch 3:5 included Shimea, Shobab, Nathan, and **S**.
3:10 The descendants of **S** were Rehoboam, Abijah,
6:10 the high priest at the Temple built by **S** in
6:32 **S** built the Temple of the LORD in Jerusalem.
14:4 born in Jerusalem: Shimea, Shobab, Nathan, **S**,
18:8 Later **S** melted the bronze and used it for the
22:5 "My son **S** is still young and inexperienced,
22:6 Then David sent for his son **S** and instructed him
22:9 His name will be **S**, and I will give peace and quiet
22:17 all the leaders of Israel to assist **S** in this project.
23:1 he appointed his son **S** to be king over Israel.
28:5 he chose **S** to succeed me on the throne of his
28:6 'Your son **S** will build my Temple and its
28:9 "And **S**, my son, get to know the God of your
28:11 Then David gave **S** the plans for the Temple
28:12 David also gave **S** all the plans he had in mind for
28:13 The king also gave **S** the instructions concerning
28:15 He told **S** the amount of gold needed for the gold
28:19 "Every part of this plan," David told **S**,
29:1 turned to the entire assembly and said, "My son **S**,
29:19 Give my son **S** the wholehearted desire to obey all
29:22 And again they crowned David's son **S** as their
29:23 So **S** took the throne of the LORD in place of his
29:24 of King David pledged their loyalty to King **S**.
29:25 And the LORD exalted **S** so the entire nation of
29:25 and he gave **S** even greater wealth and honor than
29:28 and honor. Then his son **S** ruled in his place.
2Ch 1:1 **S**, the son of King David, now took firm control of
1:3 Then **S** led the entire assembly to the hill at Gibeon
1:5 So **S** and the people gathered in front of it to
1:6 **S** went up to the bronze altar in the LORD's
1:7 That night God appeared to **S** in a dream and said,
1:8 **S** replied to God, "You have been so faithful
1:11 God said to **S**, "Because your greatest desire is to
1:13 Then **S** returned to Jerusalem from the Tabernacle
1:14 **S** built up a huge military force, which included
2:1 **S** now decided that the time had come to build a
2:3 **S** also sent this message to King Hiram at Tyre:
2:11 King Hiram sent this letter of reply to **S**: / "It is
2:17 **S** took a census of all foreigners in the land of
3:1 So **S** began to build the Temple of the LORD in
3:10 **S** made two figures shaped like cherubim
3:14 **S** hung a curtain made of fine linen and blue,
3:15 **S** made two pillars that were 27 feet tall,
4:1 **S** also made a bronze altar 30 feet long, 30 feet
4:7 **S** then cast ten gold lampstands according to the
4:9 **S** also built a courtyard for the priests and the large
4:11 So at last Huram-abi completed everything King **S**
4:16 of the LORD, just as King **S** had requested.
4:19 So **S** made all the furnishings for the Temple of
5:1 When **S** had finished all the work related to
5:2 **S** then summoned the leaders of all the tribes
5:6 King **S** and the entire community of Israel
6:1 Then **S** prayed, "O LORD, you have said that
6:7 Then **S** said, "My father, David, wanted to build
6:12 Then **S** stood with his hands spread out before the
7:1 When **S** finished praying, fire flashed down from
7:5 King **S** offered a sacrifice of 22,000 oxen
7:7 **S** then dedicated the central area of the courtyard
7:10 the end of the celebration, **S** sent the people home.
7:10 so good to David and **S** and to his people Israel.
7:11 So **S** finished building the Temple of the LORD,
7:12 Then one night the LORD appeared to **S** and said,
8:1 It was now twenty years since **S** had become king,
8:2 **S** now turned his attention to rebuilding the towns
8:3 that **S** fought against the city of Hamath-zobah
8:8 So **S** conscripted them for his labor force, and they
8:9 But **S** did not conscript any of the Israelites for
8:10 King **S** also appointed 250 of them to supervise the
8:11 **S** moved his wife, Pharaoh's daughter,
8:12 Then **S** sacrificed burnt offerings to the LORD on
8:14 **S** followed the regulations of his father, David.
8:15 **S** did not deviate in any way from David's
8:16 So **S** made sure that all the work related to building
8:17 Later **S** went to Ezion-geber and Elath, ports in the
8:18 and brought back to **S** almost seventeen tons of
9:2 When she met with **S**, they talked about everything
9:2 **S** answered all her questions; nothing was too hard
9:3 When the queen of Sheba realized how wise **S**
9:4 and the burnt offerings **S** made at the Temple of
9:9 as fine as those the queen of Sheba gave to **S**.
9:10 crews of Hiram and **S** brought gold from Ophir,
9:12 King **S** gave the queen of Sheba whatever she
9:13 Each year **S** received about 25 tons of gold.
9:14 of the land also brought gold and silver to **S**.
9:15 King **S** made two hundred large shields of
9:19 **S** made twelve other lion figures, one standing on
9:22 So King **S** became richer and wiser than any other
9:25 **S** had four thousand stalls for his chariot horses
9:30 **S** ruled in Jerusalem over all Israel for forty years.
10:2 for he had fled to Egypt to escape from King **S**.
10:6 the older men who had counseled his father, **S**.
11:3 "Say to Rehoboam son of **S**, king of Judah,
11:17 for three years they supported Rehoboam son of **S**
11:17 as they had done during the reigns of David and **S**.
13:6 who was a mere servant of David's son **S**,
30:26 seen a celebration like this one since the days of **S**,
33:7 place where God had told David and his son **S**:
35:4 David of Israel and the instructions of his son **S**.
Ezr 2:55 The descendants of these servants of King **S**
Ne 7:57 "The descendants of these servants of King **S**
12:45 as required by the laws of David and his son **S**,
13:26 "Wasn't this exactly what led King **S** of Israel into
Ps 72:T A psalm of **S**.
127:T A song for the ascent to Jerusalem. A psalm of **S**.
Pr 1:1 These are the proverbs of **S**, David's son, king of
10:1 The proverbs of **S**: A wise child brings joy to a
25:1 These are more proverbs of **S**, collected by the
SS 1:5 the dark tents of Kedar. Yes, even as the tents of **S**!
3:9 "King **S** has built a carriage for himself from
3:11 "Go out to look upon King **S**, O young women of
8:11 "**S** has a vineyard at Baal-hamon, which he rents
8:12 But as for my own vineyard, O **S**, you can take my
Jer 52:20 for the LORD's Temple in the days of King **S**.
Mt 1:6 David was the father of **S** (his mother was
1:7 **S** was the father of Rehoboam. / Rehoboam was
6:29 yet **S** in all his glory was not dressed as beautifully
12:42 came from a distant land to hear the wisdom of **S**.
12:42 And now someone greater than **S** is here—and you
Lk 11:31 came from a distant land to hear the wisdom of **S**.
11:31 And now someone greater than **S** is here—and you
12:27 yet **S** in all his glory was not dressed as beautifully
Ac 7:47 But it was **S** who actually built it.

SOLOMON'S (52) [SOLOMON]

1Ki 1:11 **S** mother, and asked her, "Did you realize that
1:37 and may he make **S** reign even greater than
1:39 oil from the sacred tent and poured it on **S** head.
1:47 'May your God make **S** fame even greater than
1:47 and may **S** kingdom be even greater than yours!'
2:13 was Haggith, came to see Bathsheba, **S** mother.
2:46 So the kingdom was now firmly in **S** grip.
3:10 The Lord was pleased with **S** reply and was glad
4:11 (He was married to Taphath, one of **S** daughters.)
4:15 was married to Basemath, another of **S** daughters.)
4:22 The daily food requirements for **S** palace were 150
4:24 **S** dominion extended over all the kingdoms west
5:7 When Hiram received **S** message, he was very
5:18 Men from the city of Gebal helped **S** and Hiram's
6:1 was in midspring, during the fourth year of **S** reign,
6:37 was laid in midspring of the fourth year of **S** reign.
7:2 One of **S** buildings was called the Palace of the
7:8 **S** living quarters surrounded a courtyard behind
9:27 crews of sailors to sail the ships with **S** men.
10:1 When the queen of Sheba heard of **S** reputation,
10:21 All of King **S** drinking cups were solid gold,
10:21 because silver was considered of little value in **S**
10:28 **S** horses were imported from Egypt and from
11:4 In **S** old age, they turned his heart to worship their
11:25 Rezon was Israel's bitter enemy for the rest of **S**
11:26 Jeroboam son of Nebat, one of **S** own officials.
11:39 punish the descendants of David because of **S** sin
11:41 The rest of the events in **S** reign, including his
12:2 When Jeroboam son of Nebat heard of **S** death,
2Ch 1:15 During **S** reign, silver and gold were as plentiful in
1:16 **S** horses were imported from Egypt and from
3:1 where the LORD had appeared to **S** father,
3:2 in midspring, during the fourth year of **S** reign.
8:18 These ships sailed to the land of Ophir with **S** men
9:1 When the queen of Sheba heard of **S** reputation,
9:20 All of King **S** drinking cups were solid gold,
9:20 because silver was considered of little value in **S**
9:28 **S** horses were imported from Egypt and many
9:29 The rest of the events of **S** reign, from beginning to
10:2 When Jeroboam son of Nebat heard of **S** death,
12:9 of the royal palace, including all of **S** gold shields.
13:7 defying **S** son Rehoboam when he was young
35:3 "Since the Ark is now in **S** Temple and you do not
Ezr 2:58 and the descendants of **S** servants numbered 392.
Ne 7:60 and the descendants of **S** servants numbered 392.
11:3 and descendants of **S** servants continued to live in
SS 1:1 This is **S** song of songs, more wonderful than any
3:7 Look, it is **S** carriage, with sixty of Israel's
Isa 7:17 all the years since **S** empire was divided into Israel
Jn 10:23 walking through the section known as **S**
Ac 3:11 They all rushed out to **S** Colonnade, where he was
5:12 at the Temple in the area known as **S** Colonnade.

SOLUTION (1) [SOLVE]

Ge 34:15 But here is a **s**. If every man among you will be

SOLVE (9) [SOLUTION]

Jdg 14:12 If you **s** my riddle during these seven days of the
14:13 But if you can't **s** it, then you must give me thirty
2Sa 2:26 "Must we always **s** our differences with swords?
Job 11:7 "Can you **s** the mysteries of God? Can you
Ps 49:4 and **s** riddles with inspiration from a harp.
Da 4:9 and that no mystery is too great for you to **s**.
5:12 explain riddles, and **s** difficult problems.
5:16 can give interpretations and **s** difficult problems.
Rev 13:18 Let the one who has understanding **s** the number of

SOME (703) [SOMEDAY, SOMEHOW, SOMEONE, SOMEONE'S, SOMETHING, SOMETHING'S, SOMETIMES, SOMEWHERE]

Ge 3:6 it would make her so wise! So she ate **s** of the fruit.
3:6 She also gave **s** to her husband, who was with her.
9:21 One day he became drunk on **s** wine he had made
14:10 and Gomorrah fled, **s** slipped into the tar pits,
15:11 **S** vultures came down to eat the carcasses,
18:4 while my servants get **s** water to wash your feet.
18:5 Let me prepare **s** food to refresh you. Please stay
18:6 measures of your best flour, and bake **s** bread."
18:8 he took **s** cheese curds and milk and the roasted
22:19 where Abraham lived for quite **s** time.
24:43 I will say to **s** young woman who comes to draw
25:29 One day when Jacob was cooking **s** stew,
25:30 Give me **s** of that red stew you've made."
25:34 Then Jacob gave Esau **s** bread and lentil stew.
26:8 But **s** time later, Abimelech, king of the Philistines,
27:3 the open country, and hunt **s** wild game for me.
27:17 with its rich aroma, and **s** freshly baked bread.
30:14 Reuben found **s** mandrakes growing in a field
30:14 Rachel begged Leah to give **s** of them to her.
30:16 "I have paid for you with **s** mandrake roots my son
31:19 Laban was **s** distance away, shearing his sheep.
33:13 my lord, that **s** of the children are very young,
33:15 "at least let me leave **s** of my men to guide
34:1 went to visit **s** of the young women who lived in
35:16 began while they were still **s** distance away.
37:2 But Joseph reported to his father **s** of the bad
37:11 his father gave it **s** thought and wondered what it
37:13 When they had been gone for **s** time, Jacob said to
37:29 **S** time later, Reuben returned to get Joseph out of
40:1 **S** time later, Pharaoh's chief cup-bearer and chief
40:4 They remained in prison for quite **s** time,
40:14 And please have **s** pity on me when you are back in
41:10 "**S** time ago, you were angry with the chief baker
42:2 and buy **s** for us before we all starve to death."
42:4 however, for fear **s** harm might come to him.
42:24 Returning, he talked **s** more with them. He
42:27 and one of them opened his sack to get **s** grain to
43:4 come with us, we will go down and buy **s** food.
44:28 doubtless torn to pieces by **s** wild animal.
Ex 4:9 then take **s** water from the Nile River and pour it
6:14 These are the ancestors of clans from **s** of Israel's
9:20 **S** of Pharaoh's officials believed what the LORD
12:7 They are to take **s** of the lamb's blood and smear it
16:17 this food—**s** getting more, and **s** getting less.
16:20 **s** of them didn't listen and kept **s** of it until morning
16:27 **S** of the people went out anyway to gather food,
17:5 Then call **s** of the leaders of Israel and walk on
18:2 **S** time before this, Moses had sent his wife,
18:21 But find **s** capable, honest men who fear God
21:1 "Here are **s** other instructions you must present to
24:5 Then he sent **s** of the young men to sacrifice young
29:12 Smear **s** of its blood on the horns of the altar with
29:20 and place **s** of it on the tip of the right earlobes of
29:21 Then take **s** of the blood from the altar and mix it with **s** of the anointing oil.
30:36 Beat **s** of it very fine and put **s** of it in front of the Ark of the Covenant,
32:1 they said, "make us **s** gods who can lead us.
32:23 They said to me, 'Make us **s** gods to lead us,
35:22 **S** brought to the LORD their offerings of gold—
35:23 **S** gave tanned ram skins or fine goatskin leather.
Lev 2:4 "When you present **s** kind of baked bread as a
4:5 then take **s** of the animal's blood into the
4:7 The priest will put **s** of the blood on the horns of
4:16 The priest will bring **s** of its blood into the
4:18 then put **s** of the blood on the horns of the incense
5:9 Then he will sprinkle **s** of the blood of the sin
6:2 "Suppose **s** of the people sin against the LORD

8:12 Then he poured **s** of the anointing oil on Aaron's
8:15 Moses took **s** of the blood, and with his finger he
8:20 into pieces and burned the head, **s** of its pieces,
8:23 Then Moses took **s** of its blood and put it on the
8:24 and put **s** of the blood on the lobe of their right
8:30 Next Moses took **s** of the anointing oil and **s** of the blood that was on the altar,
11:21 However, there are **s** exceptions that you may eat.
13:2 "If **s** of the people notice a swelling or a rash
13:10 If the priest sees that **s** hair has turned white
13:47 an infectious mildew contaminates **s** woolen
13:48 **s** woolen or linen fabric, the hide of an animal,
14:4 along with **s** cedarwood, a scarlet cloth, and a
14:14 then take **s** of the blood from the guilt offering
14:15 "Then the priest will pour **s** of the olive oil into the
14:17 then put **s** of the oil remaining in his left hand on
14:25 and put **s** of its blood on the tip of the person's
14:26 "The priest will also pour **s** of the olive oil into the
14:27 and sprinkle **s** of it seven times before the LORD.
14:28 then put **s** of the olive oil from his hand on the lobe
14:34 I may contaminate **s** of your houses with an
14:35 'It looks like my house has **s** kind of disease.'
14:49 **s** cedarwood, a scarlet cloth, and a hyssop branch.
16:18 LORD by smearing **s** of the blood from the bull
23:10 bring the priest **s** grain from the first portion of
24:7 Sprinkle **s** pure frankincense near each row.
25:25 go bankrupt and are forced to sell **s** inherited land,
25:47 and if **s** of your Israelite relatives go bankrupt
Nu 5:17 He must take **s** holy water in a clay jar and mix it
6:2 If **s** of the people, either men or women,
9:6 But **s** of the men had been ceremonially defiled by
11:4 to complain. "Oh, for **s** meat!" they exclaimed.
11:17 I will take **s** of the Spirit that is upon you, and I
11:25 He took **s** of the Spirit that was upon Moses
11:35 traveled to Hazeroth, where they stayed for **s** time.
13:27 with milk and honey. Here is **s** of its fruit as proof.
15:19 But you must set **s** aside as a gift to the LORD.
15:22 "But suppose **s** of you unintentionally fail to carry
15:23 And suppose **s** of your descendants in the future
19:4 Eleazar will take **s** of its blood on his finger
19:17 put **s** of the ashes from the burnt purification
21:1 the Israelites and took **s** of them as prisoners.
25:1 **s** of the men defiled themselves by sleeping with
31:3 "Choose **s** men to fight the LORD's war of
31:53 All the fighting men had taken **s** of the plunder for
32:38 They changed the names of **s** of the towns they
Dt 1:13 Choose **s** men from each tribe who have wisdom,
1:15 **S** were responsible for a thousand people, **s** for a hundred, **s** for fifty, and **s** for ten.
1:25 They picked **s** of its fruit and brought it back to us.
1:36 and his descendants **s** of the land he walked over
13:13 that **s** worthless rabble among you have led their
14:26 you want—an ox, a sheep, **s** wine, or beer.
15:11 There will always be **s** among you who are poor.
15:14 Share with him **s** of the bounty with which the
24:20 Leave **s** of the olives for the foreigners, orphans,
26:2 put **s** of the first produce from each harvest into a
27:2 set up **s** large stones and coat them with plaster.
Jos 2:2 "**S** Israelites have come here tonight to spy out the
2:12 since I have helped you. Give me **s** guarantee that
7:1 A man named Achan had stolen **s** of these things,
7:2 Joshua sent **s** of his men from Jericho to spy out
7:22 So Joshua sent **s** men to make a search. They ran to
11:22 though **s** still remained in Gaza, Gath, and Ashdod.
15:13 The LORD instructed Joshua to assign **s** of
16:9 Ephraim was also given **s** towns with surrounding
Jdg 4:19 "Please give me **s** water," he said. "I'm thirsty."
4:19 So she gave him **s** milk to drink and covered him
6:19 and with half a bushel of flour he baked **s** bread
6:37 I will put **s** wool on the threshing floor tonight.
8:5 "Will you please give my warriors **s** food?
9:4 which he used to hire **s** soldiers who agreed to
9:29 'Get **s** more soldiers, and come out and fight!' "
9:48 He took an ax and chopped **s** branches from a tree,
9:49 So each of them cut down **s** branches,
14:8 And he found that a swarm of bees had made **s**
14:9 He scooped **s** of the honey into his hands and ate it
14:9 He also gave **s** to his father and mother, and they
16:9 She had hidden **s** men in one of the rooms of her
17:5 and he made a sacred ephod and **s** household idols.
18:14 **s** household idols, a carved image, and a cast idol.
18:22 and **s** of his neighbors came chasing after them.
18:25 **S** of us are short-tempered, and they might get
19:8 to eat; then you can leave **s** time this afternoon."
19:22 **s** of the wicked men in the town surrounded the
20:5 That night **s** of the leaders of Gibeah surrounded
Ru 2:14 over here and help yourself to **s** of our food.
2:16 And pull out **s** heads of barley from the bundles
1Sa 1:24 the sacrifice and half a bushel of flour and **s** wine.
2:6 he brings **s** down to the grave but raises others up.
8:12 **S** will be commanders of his troops, while others
8:12 **S** will be forced to plow in his fields and harvest
9:11 they met **s** young women coming out to draw
10:27 But there were **s** wicked men who complained,
13:7 **S** of them crossed the Jordan River and escaped
16:15 **S** of Saul's servants suggested a remedy. "It is
17:26 David talked to **s** others standing there to verify the
17:30 He walked over to **s** others and asked them the
24:3 At the place where the road passes **s** sheepfolds,
24:10 and **s** of my men told me to kill you, but I spared
26:1 Now **s** messengers from Ziph came back to Saul at
29:6 "you are **s** of the finest men I've ever met.
30:11 **S** of David's troops found an Egyptian man in a
30:11 They gave him **s** bread to eat and **s** water to drink.
30:22 But **s** troublemakers among David's men said,
2Sa 2:12 One day Abner led **s** of Ishbosheth's troops from
3:17 "For **s** time now," he told them, "you have
3:22 and **s** of David's troops returned from a raid,
10:1 **S** time after this, King Nahash of the Ammonites
11:9 He stayed that night at the palace entrance with **s**
11:24 **S** of our men were killed, including Uriah the
13:5 him to let Tamar come and prepare **s** food for you.
13:7 and sent Tamar to Amnon's house to prepare **s**
13:8 lying down so he could watch her mix **s** dough.
13:8 Then she baked **s** special bread for him.
16:8 At last you will taste **s** of your own medicine,
17:9 He has probably already hidden in **s** pit or cave.
17:13 And if David has escaped into **s** city, you will have
18:9 Absalom came unexpectedly upon **s** of David's
18:20 You can be my messenger **s** other time, but not
23:15 how I would love **s** of that good water from the
23:16 drew **s** water from the well, and brought it back to
23:22 These are **s** of the deeds that made Benaiah almost
1Ki 3:16 **S** time later, two prostitutes came to the king to
4:32 He composed **s** 3,000 proverbs and wrote 1,005
7:10 **S** of the huge foundation stones were 15 feet long, and **s** were 12 feet long.
9:20 There were still **s** people living in the land who
9:28 and brought back to Solomon **s** sixteen tons of
10:26 in the chariot cities, and **s** near him in Jerusalem.
11:15 to bury **s** Israelites who had died in battle.
11:18 who gave them a home, food, and **s** land.
13:15 of God, "Come home with me and eat **s** food."
13:19 and the man of God ate **s** food and drank **s** water at the prophet's home.
14:3 of ten loaves of bread, **s** cakes, and a jar of honey,
15:18 He sent it with **s** of his officials to Ben-hadad son
17:17 **S** time later, the woman's son became sick.
18:5 find enough grass to save at least **s** of my horses
19:6 looked around and saw **s** bread baked on hot stones
19:7 and touched him and said, "Get up and eat **s** more,
20:17 to him, "**S** troops are coming from Samaria."
22:11 of Kenaanah, made **s** iron horns and proclaimed,
22:25 when you find yourself hiding in **s** secret room!"
2Ki 2:16 Perhaps the Spirit of the LORD has left him on **s** mountain or in **s** valley."
4:8 lived there, and she invited him to eat **s** food.
4:38 on a large kettle and make **s** stew for these men."
4:41 Elisha said, "Bring me **s** flour." Then he threw it
4:43 be plenty for all. There will even be **s** left over!"
4:44 there was plenty for all and **s** left over,
5:13 if the prophet had told you to do **s** great thing,
6:24 **S** time later, however, King Ben-hadad of Aram
7:9 **s** terrible calamity will certainly fall upon us.
8:1 "Take your family and move to **s** other place,
8:4 "Tell me **s** stories about the great things Elisha has
9:33 and **s** of her blood spattered against the wall
10:13 he met **s** relatives of King Ahaziah of Judah.
12:5 Let the priests take **s** of that money to pay for
13:15 Elisha told him, "Get a bow and **s** arrows."
13:21 Once when **s** Israelites were burying a man,
17:25 the LORD sent lions among them to kill **s** of
20:18 **S** of your own descendants will be taken away into
25:12 But the captain of the guard allowed **s** of the
1Ch 4:1 **S** of the descendants of Judah were Perez, Hezron,
4:38 These were the names of **s** of the leaders of
4:40 **S** of Ham's descendants had been living in the
9:2 With them came **s** of the priests, Levites,
9:28 **S** of the gatekeepers were assigned to care for the
9:32 And **s** members of the clan of Kohath were in
11:17 how I would love **s** of that good water from the
11:18 drew **s** water from the well, and brought it back to
11:24 These are **s** of the deeds that made Benaiah as
12:8 **S** brave and experienced warriors from the tribe of
12:19 **S** men from Manasseh defected from the Israelite
19:1 **S** time after this, King Nahash of the Ammonites
26:27 These men had dedicated **s** of the plunder they had
2Ch 1:14 in the chariot cities, and **s** near him in Jerusalem.
8:7 There were still **s** people living in the land who
9:25 in the chariot cities, and **s** near him in Jerusalem.
12:7 destroy them and will soon give them **s** relief.
13:19 Jeroboam's troops and captured **s** of his towns,
15:11 On that day they sacrificed to the LORD **s** of the
16:10 Asa also began to oppress **s** of his people.
17:11 **S** of the Philistines brought him gifts and silver as
18:10 of Kenaanah, made **s** iron horns and proclaimed,
18:24 when you find yourself hiding in **s** secret room!"
19:3 There is **s** good in you, however, for you have
19:8 Jehoshaphat appointed **s** of the Levites and priests
19:10 or **s** other violation of God's instructions,
20:1 and **s** of the Meunites declared war on
21:3 and also the ownership of **s** of Judah's fortified
21:4 all his brothers and **s** of the other leaders of Israel.
22:8 he happened to meet **s** of Judah's officials
24:4 **S** time later, Joash decided to repair and restore the
28:12 Then **s** of the leaders of Israel—Azariah son of
30:11 However, **s** from Asher, Manasseh, and Zebulun
32:21 **s** of his own sons killed him there with a sword.
36:7 Nebuchadnezzar also took **s** of the treasures from
Ezr 2:68 **s** of the family leaders gave generously toward the
2:70 and **s** of the common people settled in villages near
7:7 **S** of the people of Israel, as well as **s** of the priests,
7:15 We also commission you to take with you **s** silver
7:28 And I gathered **s** of the leaders of Israel to return
9:1 of Israel, and even **s** of the priests and Levites,
9:2 and leaders are **s** of the worst offenders."
9:8 our eyes and granted us **s** relief from our slavery.
9:13 have allowed **s** of us to survive as a remnant.
10:44 and **s** even had children by these wives.
Ne 1:2 came to visit me with **s** other men who had just
5:1 About this time **s** of the men and their wives raised
5:5 We have already sold **s** of our daughters, and we
7:3 **S** will serve at their regular posts and **s** in front of their own homes."
7:70 "**S** of the family leaders gave gifts for the work.
7:71 and **s** 2,750 pounds of silver for the work.
7:73 the Temple servants, along with **s** of the people—
9:4 **S** of the Levites were standing on the stairs,
11:4 but **s** of the people from Judah and Benjamin
11:25 **S** of the people of Judah lived in Kiriath-arba with
11:31 **S** of the people of Benjamin lived at Geba,
11:36 **S** of the Levites who lived in Judah were sent to
12:35 and **s** priests who played trumpets. Then came
13:15 One Sabbath day I saw **s** men of Judah treading
13:16 There were also **s** men from Tyre bringing in fish
13:19 I also sent **s** of my own servants to guard the gates
13:23 About the same time I realized that **s** of the men of
13:24 or **s** other people and could not speak the language
13:25 on them. I beat **s** of them and pulled out their hair.
Est 3:1 **S** time later, King Xerxes promoted Haman son of
4:14 deliverance for the Jews will arise from **s** other
Job 4:18 own angels and has charged **s** of them with folly,
26:14 "These are **s** of the minor things he does, merely a
33:7 I am not **s** great person to make you nervous
35:7 If you are good, is this **s** great gift to him?
38:3 Brace yourself, because I have **s** questions for you,
40:7 because I have **s** questions for you,
42:4 I have **s** questions for you, and you must answer
Ps 10:8 They are always searching / for **s** helpless victim.
20:7 **S** nations boast of their armies and weapons,
69:20 in despair. / If only one person would show **s** pity;
78:34 When God killed **s** of them, the rest finally sought
90:10 years are given to us! / **S** may even reach eighty.
107:4 **S** wandered in the desert, / lost and homeless.
107:10 **S** sat in darkness and deepest gloom,
107:17 **S** were fools in their rebellion; / they suffered for
107:23 **S** went off in ships, / plying the trade routes of the
Pr 12:18 **S** people make cutting remarks, but the words of
13:7 **S** who are poor pretend to be rich; others who are
19:24 **S** people are so lazy that they won't even lift a
24:23 Here are **s** further sayings of the wise: It is wrong
26:15 **S** people are so lazy that they won't lift a finger to
28:21 yet **s** will do wrong for something as small as a
30:11 **S** people curse their father and do not thank their
Ecc 6:2 God gives great wealth and honor to **s** people
7:15 including the fact that **s** good people die young and **s** wicked people live on and on.
8:15 That way they will experience **s** happiness along
SS 2:14 "My dove is hiding behind **s** rocks, behind an
8:11 at Baal-hamon, which he rents to **s** farmers there.
Isa 8:12 Do not be afraid that **s** plan conceived behind
10:28 They are storing **s** of their equipment at Micmash.
22:10 and tear **s** down to get stone to fix the walls.
39:7 **S** of your own descendants will be taken away into
44:5 **S** will proudly claim, 'I belong to the LORD.'
44:5 **S** will write the LORD's name on their hands
45:19 I do not whisper obscurities in **s** dark corner
46:6 **S** people pour out their silver and gold and hire a
56:12 they say. "We will get **s** wine and have a party.
65:8 there are **s** good grapes there!'), so I will not
66:21 "And I will appoint **s** of those who return to be my
Jer 1:10 You are to uproot **s** and tear them down, to destroy
19:1 Then ask **s** of the leaders of the people and of the
24:3 I replied, "Figs, **s** very good and **s** very bad."
26:17 Then **s** of the wise old men stood and spoke to the
33:3 and I will tell you **s** remarkable secrets about what
35:2 one of the inner rooms, and offer them **s** wine."
38:11 where he found **s** old rags and discarded clothing.
40:5 Then Nebuzaradan gave Jeremiah **s** food
52:15 then took as exiles **s** of the poorest of the people
52:16 But Nebuzaradan allowed **s** of the poorest people
Eze 3:5 I am not sending you to **s** foreign people whose
3:27 **S** of them will listen, but **s** will ignore you, for they are rebels.
4:9 "Now go and get **s** wheat, barley, beans, lentils,
8:14 and **s** women were sitting there, weeping for the
10:6 and take **s** burning coals from between the
10:7 and took **s** live coals from the fire burning among
14:1 Then **s** of the leaders of Israel visited me,
20:1 **s** of the leaders of Israel came to request a message
33:8 If I announce that **s** wicked people are sure to die
33:14 And suppose I tell **s** wicked people that they will
33:30 at the doors, saying, 'Come on, let's have **s** fun!
39:15 Whenever **s** bones are found, a marker will be set
43:20 You will take **s** of its blood and smear it on the
45:19 The priest will take **s** of the blood of this sin
Da 1:2 he took with him **s** of the sacred objects from the
1:3 to bring to the palace **s** of the young men of
1:5 then **s** of them would be made his advisers in the
2:42 **S** parts of it will be as strong as iron, and others as
3:8 But **s** of the astrologers went to the king
3:12 But there are **s** Jews—Shadrach, Meshach,
3:20 Then he ordered **s** of the strongest men of his army
6:4 and princes began searching for **s** fault in the way
8:10 throwing **s** of the heavenly beings and stars to the
11:6 "**S** years later, an alliance will be formed between
11:8 For **s** years afterward he will leave the king of the
11:35 And **s** who are wise will fall victim to persecution.
12:2 **s** to everlasting life and **s** to shame
Hos 1:2 so **s** of her children will be born to you from other
4:18 drinking bouts and off they go to find **s** prostitutes.
Am 2:11 I chose **s** of your sons to be prophets and others to
4:11 "I destroyed **s** of your cities, as I destroyed Sodom
Jnh 4:6 This eased **s** of his discomfort, and Jonah was very
Hag 2:12 and happens to brush against **s** bread or stew,
Zec 1:8 standing among **s** myrtle trees in a small valley.
Mt 2:1 About that time **s** wise men from eastern lands
9:2 **S** people brought to him a paralyzed man on a mat.
9:3 **s** of the teachers of religious law said among
9:32 **s** people brought to him a man who couldn't speak
12:1 At about that time Jesus was walking through **s**

12: 2 S Pharisees saw them do it and protested,
12:38 One day s teachers of religious law and Pharisees
13: 3 as this one: "A farmer went out to plant s seed.
13: 4 s seeds fell on a footpath, and the birds came
13: 8 But s seeds fell on fertile soil and produced a crop
14:19 he gave s of the bread and fish to each disciple,
15: 1 S Pharisees and teachers of religious law now
16:14 "Well," they replied, "s say John the Baptist,
16:14 s say Elijah, and others say Jeremiah or one of the
16:28 And I assure you that s of you standing here right
18:31 "When s of the other servants saw this, they were
19: 3 S Pharisees came and tried to trap him with this
19:12 S are born as eunuchs, s have been made that way
by others, and s choose not to marry for the sake of
19:13 S children were brought to Jesus so he could lay
20: 3 and saw s people standing around doing nothing.
20: 6 and saw s more people standing around.
22: 6 treated them shamefully, even killing s of them.
22:16 They decided to send s of their disciples,
22:23 That same day s Sadducees stepped forward—
23:34 You will kill s by crucifixion and whip others in
25: 8 'Please give us s of your oil because our lamps are
25: 9 all of us. Go to a shop and buy s for yourselves.'
25:27 my money into the bank so I could have s interest.
26:55 said to the crowd, "Am I s dangerous criminal,
26:67 and hit him with their fists. And s slapped him,
26:73 A little later s other bystanders came over to him
27: 7 After s discussion they finally decided to buy the
27:27 S of the governor's soldiers took Jesus into their
27:47 S of the bystanders misunderstood and thought he
28:11 s of the men who had been guarding the tomb went
28:17 they worshiped him—but s of them still doubted!
Mk 2: 6 But s of the teachers of religious law who were
2:16 But when s of the teachers of religious law who
2:18 One day s people came to Jesus and asked,
2:23 One Sabbath day as Jesus was walking through s
2:26 priests alone, and then gave s to his companions.
4: 3 "Listen! A farmer went out to plant s seed.
4: 4 s seed fell on a footpath, and the birds came
5: 6 When Jesus was still s distance away, the man saw
5:10 and again not to send them to s distant place.
6:14 S were saying, "This must be John the Baptist
6:36 and villages and buy themselves s food."
7: 1 One day s Pharisees and teachers of religious law
7: 2 They noticed that s of Jesus' disciples failed to
7:28 but even the dogs under the table are given s
8: 3 For s of them have come a long distance."
8:22 s people brought a blind man to Jesus, and they
8:28 they replied, "s say John the Baptist, s say Elijah,
9: 1 "I assure you that s of you standing here right now
9:14 as s teachers of religious law were arguing with
10: 2 S Pharisees came and tried to trap him with this
10:13 One day s parents brought their children to Jesus
10:48 "Be quiet!" s of the people yelled at him. But he
11: 5 s bystanders demanded, "What are you doing,
12:13 The leaders sent s Pharisees and supporters of
12:38 Here are s of the other things he taught them at this
14: 4 S of those at the table were indignant. "Why was
14:48 Jesus asked them, "Am I s dangerous criminal,
14:57 s men stood up to testify against him with this lie:
14:65 Then s of them began to spit at him, and they
14:70 A little later s other bystanders began saying to
15:35 S of the bystanders misunderstood and thought he
15:40 S women were there, watching from a distance,
Lk 2: 8 That night s shepherds were in the fields outside
3:14 asked s soldiers. John replied, "Don't extort
4:41 S were possessed by demons; and the demons
5:17 s Pharisees and teachers of religious law were
5:18 S men came carrying a paralyzed man on a
5:19 So they went up to the roof, took off s tiles,
6: 1 One Sabbath day as Jesus was walking through s
6: 2 But s Pharisees said, "You shouldn't be doing
6: 4 for the priests alone, and then gave s to his friends.
6: 7 because they were eager to find s legal charge to
7: 3 he sent s respected Jewish leaders to ask him to
7: 6 the house, the officer sent s friends to say, "Lord,
8: 2 along with s women he had healed and from whom
8: 5 "A farmer went out to plant s seed. As he scattered
8: 5 s seed fell on a footpath, where it was stepped on,
9: 7 he was worried and puzzled because s were saying,
9: 8 or s other ancient prophet risen from the dead."
9:19 they replied, "s say John the Baptist, s say Elijah,
9:27 And I assure you that s of you standing here right
11:15 but s said, "No wonder he can cast out demons.
11:49 and they will kill s and persecute the others.'
13: 1 s people from Galilee as they were sacrificing at
13:30 S who are despised now will be greatly honored
13:30 and s who are greatly honored now will be
13:31 A few minutes later s Pharisees said to him,
16:24 rich man shouted, 'Father Abraham, have s pity!
18: 9 Then Jesus told this story to s who had great
18:15 One day s parents brought their little children to
19:23 in the bank so I could at least get s interest on it?'
19:39 But s of the Pharisees among the crowd said,
20:27 Then s Sadducees stepped forward—a group of
20:39 remarked s of the teachers of religious law who
21: 5 S of his disciples began talking about the beautiful
21:16 will betray you. And s of you will be killed.
22:52 "Am I s dangerous criminal," he asked, "that you
24:22 Then s women from our group of his followers
24:24 S of our men ran out to see, and sure enough,
Jn 2: 8 "Dip s out and take it to the master of
2:15 Jesus made a whip from s ropes and chased them
4: 8 disciples had gone into the village to buy s food.
4:15 sir," the woman said, "give me s of that water!
4:51 s of his servants met him with the news that his son
6:64 But s of you don't believe me." (For Jesus knew

7:12 S said, "He's a wonderful man," while others
7:25 S of the people who lived there in Jerusalem said
7:40 s of them declared, "This man surely is the
7:44 And s wanted him arrested, but no one touched
8:37 And yet s of you are trying to kill me because my
9: 9 S said he was, and others said, "No, but he surely
9:16 S of the Pharisees said, "This man Jesus is not
10:20 S of them said, "He has a demon, or he's crazy.
11:37 But s said, "This man healed a blind man.
11:46 But s went to the Pharisees and told them what
12: 6 and he often took s for his own use.
12:20 S Greeks who had come to Jerusalem to attend the
12:29 crowd heard the voice, s thought it was thunder,
12:42 Many people, including s of the Jewish leaders,
13:29 s thought Jesus was telling him to go and pay for
the food or to give s money to the poor.
21:10 "Bring s of the fish you've just caught,"
21:12 "Now come and have s breakfast!" Jesus said.
Ac 2:15 S of you are saying these people are drunk. It isn't
3: 3 John about to enter, he asked them for s money.
4: 1 and s of the Sadducees came over to them.
5: 1 with his wife, Sapphira, sold s property.
5: 3 and you kept s of the money for yourself.
5: 6 Then s young men wrapped him in a sheet
5:15 so that Peter's shadow might fall across s of them
5:36 S time ago there was that fellow Theudas,
5:37 He got s people to follow him, but he was killed,
6: 9 But one day s men from the Synagogue of Freed
6:11 So they persuaded s men to lie about Stephen,
7:12 still grain in Egypt, so he sent his sons to buy s.
7:40 They told Aaron, 'Make us s gods who can lead us,
8: 2 (S godly people came and buried Stephen with
8:36 As they rode along, they came to s water,
8:36 and the eunuch said, "Look! There's s water!
9:19 Afterward he ate s food and was strengthened.
9:25 s of the other believers let him down in a large
9:29 He debated with s Greek-speaking Jews, but they
10: 5 Now send s men down to Joppa to find a man
10:23 accompanied by s other believers from Joppa.
10:32 Now send s men to Joppa and summon Simon
11: 2 s of the Jewish believers criticized him.
11:20 s of the believers who went to Antioch from
11:27 s prophets traveled from Jerusalem to Antioch.
12: 1 began to persecute s believers in the church.
14: 4 S sided with the Jews, and s with the apostles.
14:19 Now s Jews arrived from Antioch and Iconium
15: 1 s men from Judea arrived and began to teach the
15: 2 accompanied by s local believers, to talk to the
15: 5 then s of the men who had been Pharisees before
15: 7 you all know that God chose me from among you s
15:24 "We understand that s men from here have
15:36 After s time Paul said to Barnabas, "Let's return to
16:13 where we supposed that s people met for prayer,
16:13 and we sat down to speak with s women who had
17: 4 S who listened were persuaded and became
17: 5 so they gathered s worthless fellows from the
17: 6 out Jason and s of the other believers instead
17:12 as did s of the prominent Greek women and many
17:13 But when s Jews in Thessalonica learned that Paul
17:18 He also had a debate with s of the Epicurean
17:18 "This babbler has picked up s strange ideas."
17:18 Others said, "He's pushing s foreign religion."
17:20 "You are saying s rather startling things, and we
17:32 s laughed, but others said, "We want to hear more
17:34 but s joined him and became believers.
18:12 s Jews rose in concerted action against Paul
18:14 if this were a case involving s wrongdoing or a
18:18 Paul stayed in Corinth for s time after that and
18:23 After spending s time in Antioch, Paul went back
19: 9 But s rejected his message and publicly spoke
19:31 S of the officials of the province, friends of Paul,
19:32 were all shouting, s one thing and s another.
19:33 Alexander was thrust forward by s of the Jews,
20: 3 when he discovered a plot by s Jews against his
life,
20:30 Even s of you will distort the truth in order to draw
21:16 S believers from Caesarea accompanied us,
21:27 The seven days were almost ended when s Jews
21:34 S shouted one thing and s another. He couldn't
21:38 "Aren't you the Egyptian who led a rebellion s
22: 4 hounding s to death, binding and delivering both
23: 6 Paul realized that s members of the high council
were Sadducees and s were Pharisees,
23: 9 S of the teachers of religious law who were
23:20 "S Jews are going to ask you to bring Paul
23:20 pretending they want to get s more information.
23:27 This man was seized by s Jews, and they were
about
24: 1 arrived with s of the Jewish leaders and the lawyer
24:19 But s Jews from the province of Asia were there—
24:23 but to give him s freedom and allow his friends to
26:21 S Jews arrested me in the Temple for preaching
27:35 Then he took s bread, gave thanks to God before
28:14 There we found s believers, who invited us to stay
28:24 S believed and s didn't.
Ro 3: 3 True, s of them were unfaithful; but just
3: 5 "But," s say, "our sins serve a good purpose,
3: 5 (That is actually the way s people talk.)
3: 7 "But," s might still argue, "how can God judge
3: 8 yet s slander me by saying this is what I preach!
9:18 God shows mercy to s just because he wants to,
9:18 and he chooses to make s people refuse to listen.
11:14 and in that way I might save s of them.
11:17 But s of these branches from Abraham's tree,
11:17 s of the Jews, have been broken off.
11:25 S of the Jews have hard hearts, but this will last
14: 5 s think one day is more holy than another day,

15:15 I have been bold enough to emphasize s of these
1Co 1:11 For s members of Chloe's household have told me
1:12 S of you are saying, "I am a follower of Paul."
4:18 I know that s of you have become arrogant,
6:11 There was a time when s of you were just like that,
7: 7 God gives s the gift of marriage, and to others he
8: 5 According to s people, there are many so-called
8: 7 S are accustomed to thinking of idols as being real,
9: 7 his crop and doesn't have the right to eat s of it?
9: 7 of sheep and isn't allowed to drink s of the milk?
10: 7 or worship idols as s of them did.
10: 8 And we must not engage in sexual immorality as s
10: 9 as s of them did and then died from snakebites.
10:10 And don't grumble as s of them did, for that is why
10:19 real gods and that these sacrifices are of s value?
11:18 you meet as a church, and to s extent I believe it.
11:21 For I am told that s of you hurry to eat your own
11:21 As a result, s go hungry while others get drunk.
11:30 of you are weak and sick and s have even died.
12:13 S of us are Jews, s are Gentiles, s are slaves, and s
are free.
12:22 s of the parts that seem weakest and least important
12:28 Here is a list of s of the members that God has
14: 5 so that the whole church can get s good out of it.
14: 6 But if I bring you s revelation or s special
knowledge or s prophecy or s teaching—
14:26 another will tell s special revelation God has given,
15: 6 of whom are still alive, though s have died by now.
15:12 why are s of you saying there will be no
15:34 For to your shame I say that s of you don't even
16: 2 each of you should put aside s amount of money in
2Co 3: 1 S people need to bring letters of recommendation
8:13 I only mean that there should be s equality.
8:14 Then at s other time they can share with you when
9: 4 if s Macedonian Christians came with me, only to
10: 1 even though s of you say I am bold in my letters
10:10 For s say, "Don't worry about Paul. His letters are
12:16 S of you admit I was not a burden to you. But they
Gal 2: 4 come up except for s so-called Christians there—
2:12 when s Jewish friends of James came,
5:11 as s say I do—why would the Jews persecute me?
6: 1 Dear friends, if a Christian is overcome by s sin,
Php 1:15 S are preaching out of jealousy and rivalry.
3:15 If you disagree on s point, I believe God will make
1Th 2: 7 we certainly had a right to make s demands of you,
2:15 For s of the Jews had killed their own prophets,
and s even killed the Lord Jesus.
2:16 News to the Gentiles, for fear s might be saved.
2Th 3:11 Yet we hear that s of you are living idle lives,
1Ti 1: 6 But s teachers have missed this whole point.
1:19 For s people have deliberately violated their
4: 1 last times s will turn away from what we believe;
4: 8 Physical exercise has s value, but spiritual exercise
5:15 For I am afraid that s of them have already gone
5:24 Remember that s people lead sinful lives,
5:25 everyone knows how much good s people do,
6: 3 S false teachers may deny these things, but these
6:10 And s people, craving money, have wandered from
6:21 S people have wandered from the faith by
2Ti 2:18 and they have undermined the faith of s.
2:20 In a wealthy home s utensils are made of gold and
silver, and s are made of wood and clay.
Heb 4: 1 so we ought to tremble with fear that s of you
9: 4 Inside the Ark were a gold jar containing s manna,
10:25 as s people do, but encourage and warn each other,
11:36 S were mocked, and their backs were cut open
11:37 S died by stoning, and s were sawed in half;
11:37 S went about in skins of sheep and goats, hungry
13: 2 for s who have done this have entertained angels
Jas 2: 1 Christ if you favor s people more than others?
2:18 Now someone may argue, "S people have faith;
1Pe 5: 8 like a roaring lion, looking for s victim to devour.
2Pe 3: 9 slow about his promise to return, as s people think.
3:16 S of his comments are hard to understand,
2Jn 1: 4 How happy I was to meet s of your children
3Jn 1: 3 S of the brothers recently returned and made me
1:10 I will report s of the things he is doing
Jude 1: 4 because s godless people have wormed their way
Rev 2:10 The Devil will throw s of you into prison and put
2:14 You tolerate s among you who are like Balaam,
2:15 same way, you have s Nicolaitans among you—
3: 4 "Yet even in Sardis there are s who have not

SOMEDAY (26) [DAY, SOME]

Ge 28:15 you go. I will s bring you safely back to this land.
1Sa 26:10 Surely the LORD will strike Saul down s, or he
27: 1 thinking to himself, "S Saul is going to get me.
1Ki 2: 2 "I am going where everyone on earth must s go.
Isa 43:21 and they will s honor me before the whole world.
Jer 27:22 But s I will bring them back to Jerusalem again."
32:15 S people will again own property here in this land
32:44 For s I will restore prosperity to them. I,
Eze 16:53 "But s I will restore the fortunes of Sodom
20:40 the people of Israel will s worship me, and I will
Hos 11:10 "For s the people will follow the LORD. I will
Mic 2:12 "S, O Israel, I will gather the few of you who are
Zec 2: 4 'Jerusalem will s be so full of people that it won't
Mt 9:15 S he will be taken from them, and then they will
Mk 2:20 But s he will be taken away from them, and
Lk 5:35 S he will be taken away from them, and then they
Jn 13: 7 understand now why I am doing it; s you will."
Ac 1:11 And s, just as you saw him go, he will return!"
Ro 11:31 to you. But s they too will share in God's mercy.
1Co 6: 2 Don't you know that s we Christians are going to
6:13 though s God will do away with both of them.
15:29 Why do it unless the dead will s rise again?

15:49 the man of the earth, so we will s be like Christ,
2Co 1:13 I hope s you will fully understand us,
2Ti 3: 9 S everyone will recognize what fools they are,
4: 1 who will s judge the living and the dead when he

SOMEHOW (2) [HOW, SOME]

2Co 11: 3 But I fear that s you will be led away from your
Php 3:11 so that, s, I can experience the resurrection from

SOMEONE (256) [ONE, SOME]

Ge 10: 9 and people would speak of s as being "like
26: 9 "Because I was afraid s would kill me to get her
26:10 "S might have taken your wife and slept with her,
27:42 But s got wind of what Esau was planning
29:19 "I'd rather give her to you than to s outside the
35:22 his father's concubine, and s told Jacob about it.
38:13 S told Tamar that her father-in-law had left for the
Ex 4:13 Moses again pleaded, "Lord, please! Send s else."
12:30 There was not a single house where s had not died.
20:26 s might look up under the skirts of your clothing
21:14 if s deliberately attacks and kills another person,
21:29 If this is true and if the bull kills s, it must be
21:33 "Suppose s digs or uncovers a well and fails to
22: 4 If s steals an ox or a donkey or a sheep and it is
22: 5 and the owner lets it stray into s else's field to
22: 7 "Suppose s entrusts money or goods to a neighbor,
22:10 "Now suppose s asks a neighbor to care for a
22:14 "If s borrows an animal from a neighbor and it is
23: 5 If you see the donkey of s who hates you
30:33 or puts any of it on s who is not a priest will be cut
Lev 14: 3 If the priest finds that s has been healed of the skin
19:20 girl who is committed to become s else's wife,
22: 5 or by touching s who is ceremonially unclean for
22:12 If a priest's daughter marries s outside the priestly
27: 2 If you make a special vow to dedicate s to the
27:20 or if the field is sold to s else by the priests, it can
27:27 the priest may sell it to s else for its assessed value.
Nu 6: 9 because s suddenly falls dead beside them,
19: 9 Then s who is ceremonially clean will gather up
19:14 "This is the ritual law that applies when s dies in a
19:16 And if s outdoors touches the corpse of s
19:16 or if s touches a human bone or a grave,
19:18 Then s who is ceremonially clean must take a
27:17 Give them s who will lead them into battle,
35: 6 where a person who has accidentally killed s can
35:11 people to flee to if they have killed s accidentally.
35:15 Anyone who accidentally kills s may flee there for
35:16 " 'But if s strikes and kills another person with a
35:17 Or if s strikes and kills another person with a large
35:18 The same is true if s strikes and kills another
35:20 So if in premeditated hostility s pushes another
35:21 Or if s angrily hits another person with a fist
35:22 " 'But suppose s pushes another person without
35:23 or accidentally drops a stone on s, though they
35:31 payment for the life of s judged guilty of murder
35:32 And never accept a ransom payment from s who
Dt 4:42 where anyone who had accidentally killed s
15: 9 Do not be mean-spirited and refuse s a loan
17: 8 whether s is guilty of murder or only of
19: 3 so that anyone who has killed s can flee there for
19: 4 "If s accidentally kills a neighbor without
19: 5 suppose s goes into the forest with a neighbor to
19:11 "But suppose s hates a neighbor and deliberately
19:16 witness comes forward and accuses s of a crime,
20: 5 in the battle, and s else would dedicate your house!
20: 6 might die in battle, and s else would eat from it!
20: 7 in the battle, and s else would marry your fiancée.'
21: 1 "Suppose s is found murdered in a field in the land
21:22 "If s has committed a crime worthy of death
22: 2 If it does not belong to s nearby or you don't know
22: 8 on your household if s falls from the roof.
22:26 This case is similar to that of s who attacks
28:30 You will build a house, but s else will live in it.
Jos 2: 2 But s told the king of Jericho, "Some Israelites
21:13 city of refuge for those who accidentally killed s),
21:21 city of refuge for those who accidentally killed s),
Jdg 6:28 s discovered that the altar of Baal had been
9:25 that way. But s warned Abimelech about their plot.
9:47 S reported to Abimelech that the people were
Ru 1:13 for them to grow up and refuse to marry s else?
1Sa 2:25 If s sins against another person, God can mediate
2:25 But if s sins against the LORD, who can
3: 9 and if s calls again, say, 'Yes, LORD,
14:33 S reported to Saul, "Look, the men are sinning
15:12 S told him, "Saul went to Carmel to set up a
15:28 Israel from you today and has given it to s else—
16:17 "Find me s who plays well and bring him here."
17: 8 Choose s to fight for you, and I will represent the
19:22 "They are at Naioth in Ramah," s told him.
21:15 Why should I let s like this be my guest?"
23:21 Saul said. "At last s is concerned about me!
26:15 your master the king when s came to kill him?
2Sa 2:21 "Go fight s else!" Abner warned. "Take on one
4:10 Once before, s told me, 'Saul is dead,' thinking he
11: 3 He sent s to find out who she was, and he was told,
15:31 When s told David that his adviser Ahithophel was
1Ki 1:48 who today has chosen s to sit on my throne while I
8:31 "If s wrongs another person and is required to take
14: 5 wife will come here, pretending to be s else.
14: 6 Why are you pretending to be s else?" Then he
2Ki 3:15 Now bring me s who can play the harp."
6: 3 "Please come with us," s suggested. "I will,"
8: 7 S told the king that the man of God had come.
9:34 he said, "S go and bury this cursed woman,
1Ch 17:17 You speak as though I were s very great,
2Ch 2: 7 s who is expert at dyeing purple, scarlet, and blue
6:22 "If s wrongs another person and is required to take
Ne 2:10 they were very angry that s had come who was
6:11 "Should s in my position run away from danger?
6:11 Should s in my position enter the Temple to save
Est 6: 7 So he replied, "If the king wishes to honor s,
Job 9: 3 If s wanted to take God to court, would it be
9:12 If he sends death to snatch s away, who can stop
11: 2 "Shouldn't s answer this torrent of words? Is a
11: 3 you mock God, shouldn't s make you ashamed?
12:14 When he closes in on s, there is no escape.
16:21 Oh, that s would mediate between God and me,
22:29 If s is brought low and you say, 'Help him up,'
31: 8 then let s else harvest the crops I have planted,
31:19 Whenever I saw s who was homeless and without
31:35 "If only I had s who would listen to me and try to
Ps 39: 6 in nothing. / We heap up wealth for s else to spend.
105:17 Then he sent s to Egypt ahead of them— / Joseph,
109: 8 years be few; / let his position be given to s else.
142: 4 I look for s to come and help me, / but no one
Pr 1:11 may say, "Come and join us. Let's hide and kill s!
3:30 Don't make accusations against s who hasn't
4:16 They cannot rest unless they have caused s to
5:10 and s else will enjoy the fruit of your labor.
6: 1 or guarantee the debt of s you hardly know—
15:17 A bowl of soup with s you love is better than steak
with s you hate.
18: 9 A lazy person is as bad as s who destroys things.
18:17 Any story sounds true until s sets the record
20:16 Get a deposit if s guarantees the debt of a
20:19 so don't hang around with s who talks too much.
22:26 or put up a guarantee for s else's loan.
26:17 is as foolish as interfering in s else's argument.
26:19 is s who lies to a friend and then says, "I was only
27:13 Get a deposit if s guarantees the debt of an
28: 8 It will end up in the hands of s who is kind to the
29:20 There is more hope for a fool than for s who
SS 8: 8 for breasts. What will we do if s asks to marry her?
Isa 21:11 S from Edom keeps calling to me, "Watchman,
40: 3 I hear the voice of s shouting, "Make a highway
46: 7 And when s prays to it, there is no answer.
65: 8 found among a cluster of bad ones (and s will say,
Jer 3: 1 a man divorces a woman and she marries s else,
14: 8 Why are you like s passing through the land,
23: 9 I stagger like a drunkard, like s overcome by wine,
26:21 what he was saying, the king sent s to kill him.
29:22 so that whenever the Judean exiles want to curse s
Eze 10:13 I heard s refer to the wheels as "the whirling
22:30 "I looked for s who might rebuild the wall of
22:30 I searched for s to stand in the gap in the wall
33:32 like s who sings love songs with a beautiful voice
43: 6 And I heard s speaking to me from within the
Da 5:17 the king, "Keep your gifts or give them to s else,
7:13 I saw s who looked like a man coming with the
8:15 s who looked like a man suddenly stood in front of
10:17 How can s like me, your servant, talk to you,
Hos 4: 4 "Don't point your finger at s else and try to pass
Na 2: 8 s shouts, but the people just keep on running.
Hab 1: 5 something you wouldn't believe even if s told you
Hag 2:13 "But if s becomes ceremonially unclean by
Zec 13: 6 And if s asks, 'Then what are those scars on your
Mal 1:10 "I wish that s among you would shut the Temple
Mt 3:11 But s is coming soon who is far greater than I am
5:22 But I say, if you are angry with s, you are subject
5:22 And if you curse s, you are in danger of the fires of
5:23 and you suddenly remember that s has something
6: 2 When you give a gift to s in need, don't shout
6: 3 But when you give to s, don't tell your left hand
11: 3 waiting for, or should we keep looking for s else?"
12:41 And now s greater than Jonah is here—and you
12:42 And now s greater than Solomon is here—and you
12:47 S told Jesus, "Your mother and your brothers are
18:21 how often should I forgive s who sins against me?
19:16 S came to Jesus with this question: "Teacher,
24:26 "So if s tells you, 'Look, the Messiah is out in the
Mk 1: 7 "S is coming soon who is far greater than I am—
3:32 and s said, "Your mother and your brothers
10:11 and marries s else commits adultery against her.
14:47 But s pulled out a sword and slashed off an ear of
Lk 3:16 but s is coming soon who is greater than I am—
6:29 If s slaps you on one cheek, turn the other cheek.
6:29 If s demands your coat, offer your shirt also.
6:47 I will show you what it's like when s comes to me,
7:19 or should we keep looking for s else?"
7:20 or should we keep looking for s else?' "
8:20 S told Jesus, "Your mother and your brothers are
8:46 Jesus told him, "No, s deliberately touched me,
9:49 we saw s using your name to cast out demons.
9:57 As they were walking along s said to Jesus, "I will
11:22 until s who is stronger attacks and overpowers him,
11:31 And now s greater than Solomon is here—and you
11:32 And now s greater than Jonah is here—and you
12:13 Then s called from the crowd, "Teacher,
13:23 S asked him, "Lord, will only a few be saved?"
14: 8 What if s more respected than you has also been
16:18 his wife and marries s else commits adultery,
16:30 But if s is sent to them from the dead, then they
16:31 they won't listen even if s rises from the dead.' "
18: 3 appealing for justice against s who had harmed her.
22:58 After a while s else looked at him and said,
22:59 About an hour later s else insisted, "This must be
24: 5 "Why are you looking in a tomb for s who is
Jn 1:15 'S is coming who is far greater than I am, for he
1:26 but right here in the crowd is s you do not know,
1:33 see the Holy Spirit descending and resting upon s,
4:37 the saying, 'One person plants and s else harvests.'
5: 7 to get there, s else always gets in ahead of me."
5:32 But s else is also testifying about me, and I can
9:32 anyone been able to open the eyes of s born blind.
18:31 "Only the Romans are permitted to execute s,"
18:39 But you have a custom of asking me to release s
20:14 over her shoulder and saw s standing behind her.
Ac 1:20 And again, 'Let his position be given to s else.'
1:21 "So now we must choose s else to take Judas's
1:21 It must be s who has been with us all the time that
5:25 Then s arrived with the news that the men they had
5:36 that fellow Theudas, who pretended to be s great.
8: 9 there for many years, claiming to be s great.
8:34 "Was Isaiah talking about himself or s else?"
13:11 and he began wandering around begging for s to
13:37 No, it was a reference to s else—s whom God
raised and whose body did not decay.
13:41 wouldn't believe / even if s told you about it.' "
25:19 their religion and about s called Jesus who died,
Ro 5: 7 though s might be willing to die for a person who
10:14 And how can they hear about him unless s tells
14:14 But if s believes it is wrong, then for that person it
14:15 Don't let your eating ruin s for whom Christ died.
15:20 where a church has already been started by s else.
1Co 3:15 but like s escaping through a wall of flames.
4: 5 the Lord returns as to whether or not s is faithful.
10:27 If s who isn't a Christian asks you home for dinner,
10:28 But suppose s warns you that this meat has been
10:29 why should my freedom be limited by what s else
12: 9 and to s else he gives the power to heal the sick.
12:10 He gives s else the ability to know whether it is
14: 5 unless s interprets what you are saying so that the
14:27 and s must be ready to interpret what they are
14:30 But if s is prophesying and another person receives
15:35 But s may ask, "How will the dead be raised?
2Co 10:15 Nor do we claim credit for the work s else has
10:16 Then there will be no question about being in s
10:18 But when the Lord commends s, that's different!
Gal 6: 3 If you think you are too important to help s in
Eph 4:14 because s has told us something different or
4:14 or because s has cleverly lied to us and made the
1Ti 3: 1 It is a true saying that if s wants to be an elder,
Tit 2: 3 in a way that is appropriate for s serving the Lord.
Heb 5:12 you need s to teach you again the basic things a
6:16 they call on s greater than themselves to hold them
9:16 Now when s dies and leaves a will, no one gets
Jas 2: 2 suppose s comes into your meeting dressed in
2:11 So if you murder s, you have broken the entire law,
2:18 Now s may argue, "Some people have faith;
1Jn 2: 1 there is s to plead for you before the Father.
2: 4 If s says, "I belong to God," but doesn't obey
4: 6 That is how we know if s has the Spirit of truth
4:20 If s says, "I love God," but hates another
2Jn 1:10 If s comes to your meeting and does not teach the
Rev 4: 2 and I saw a throne in heaven and s sitting on it!

SOMEONE'S (9) [ONE, SOME]

Ge 43:12 found in your sacks, as it was probably s mistake.
Ex 21:35 "If s bull injures a neighbor's bull and the injured
Lev 13:12 that a rash has broken out all over s skin,
Dt 19:14 never steal s land by moving the boundary markers
Pr 25:20 heavy is as bad as stealing s jacket in cold weather
Eze 1:28 in the dust, and I heard s voice speaking to me.
Mic 2: 2 When you want s house, you take it by fraud
Mt 10:12 When you are invited into s home, give it your
Ac 9: 7 for they heard the sound of s voice, but they saw

SOMETHING (119) [SOME, THING]

Ge 21:26 Why didn't you say s about this before?"
Ex 5:16 as before. We are beaten for s that isn't our fault!
23: 8 for a bribe makes you ignore s that you clearly see.
32:23 for s has happened to this man Moses, who led us
Lev 4:13 "If the entire Israelite community does s forbidden
4:22 "If one of Israel's leaders does s forbidden by the
4:27 "If any of the citizens of Israel do s forbidden by
5: 1 "If any of the people are called to testify about s
5: 2 "Or if they touch s that is ceremonially unclean,
5:17 "If any of them sin by doing s forbidden by the
6: 2 or they have taken s by theft or extortion.
6: 3 and lie about it, or they deny s while under oath,
11:32 If such an animal dies and falls on s, that object,
14:57 to determine when s is ceremonially clean
Nu 35:22 or throws s that unintentionally hits another
Dt 18:22 "If the prophet predicts s in the LORD's name
24: 1 but later discovers s about her that is shameful.
Jdg 14:14 he said: / "From the one who eats came s to eat; /
out of the strong came s sweet."
19: 5 father said, "Have s to eat before you go."
19: 6 them sat down together and had s to eat and drink.
19: 8 and again the woman's father said, "Have s to eat;
19:30 Shouldn't we speak up and do s about this?"
1Sa 9: 6 But the servant said, "I've just thought of s!
18: 6 But s happened when the victorious Israelite army
20: 2 I know he wouldn't hide s like this from me.
20:26 "S must have made David ceremonially unclean.
28:22 and let me give you s to eat so you can regain your
2Sa 13: 6 come to take care of me and cook s for me to eat."
19: 5 us feel ashamed, as though we had done s wrong.
1Ki 2: 5 "And there is s else. You know that Joab son of
13: 7 "Come to the palace with me and have s to eat,
20:40 But while I was busy doing s else, the prisoner
2Ki 4:27 S is troubling her deeply, and the LORD has not
5:20 I will chase after him and get s from him."
7:13 If s happens to them, it won't be a greater loss than
Ezr 10:13 "This isn't s that can be done in a day or two,
Job 30:17 My weary nights are filled with pain as though s
39:20 like a locust? Its majestic snorting is s to hear!
Pr 25: 7 the line, publicly disgraced! Just because you see s,
27:16 to stop the wind or hold s with greased hands.

28:21 yet some will do wrong for s as small as a piece of
Ecc 5:5 It is better to say nothing than to promise s that you
9:11 I have observed s else in this world of ours.
Isa 5:19 Holy One of Israel and say, "Hurry up and do s!
41:23 and fear. Do s, whether good or bad!
43:9 Can any of them predict s even a single day in
44:20 He is trusting s that can give him no help at all.
45:19 of Israel to ask me for s I did not plan to give.
Jer 18:13 My virgin Israel has done s too terrible to
31:22 For the LORD will cause s new and different to
32:36 "Now I want to say s more about this city.
38:14 "I want to ask you s," the king said. "And don't
Da 2:9 You have conspired to tell me lies in hopes that s
11:24 and do s that none of his predecessors ever did—
Hab 1:5 For I am doing s in your own day, s you wouldn't
believe even if someone told you
2:18 How foolish to trust in s made by your own hands!
Zec 5:5 and said, "Look up! S is appearing in the sky."
Mt 5:23 and you suddenly remember that someone has s
5:37 your promise with a vow shows that s is wrong.
22:15 into saying s for which they could accuse him.
25:37 and feed you? Or thirsty and give you s to drink?
Mk 5:43 had happened, and he told them to give her s to eat.
9:22 Have mercy on us and help us. Do s if you can."
12:13 Jesus into saying s for which he could be arrested.
15:4 and Pilate asked him, "Aren't you going to say s?
Lk 7:40 he said to the Pharisee, "I have s to say to you."
8:55 stood up! Then Jesus told them to give her s to eat.
11:54 trying to trap him into saying s they could use
13:7 it down. It's taking up space we can use for s else.'
20:20 They tried to get Jesus to say s that could be
22:34 But Jesus said, "Peter, let me tell you s.
24:17 "You seem to be in a deep discussion about s,"
Jn 5:14 stop sinning, or s even worse may happen to you."
8:6 They were trying to trap him into saying s they
8:17 own law says that if two people agree about s,
Ac 9:18 Instantly s like scales fell from Saul's eyes, and he
10:11 and s like a large sheet was let down by its four
10:15 "If God says s is acceptable, don't say it isn't."
11:5 S like a large sheet was let down by its four
11:9 'If God says s is acceptable, don't say it isn't.'
13:39 right with God—s the Jewish law could never do.
13:41 doing s in your own day, / s you wouldn't believe
23:17 to the commander. He has s important to tell him."
23:18 young man to you because he has s to tell you."
23:29 I soon discovered it was s regarding their religious
25:11 If I have done s worthy of death, I don't refuse to
25:19 It was s about their religion and about someone
25:26 that after we examine him, I might have s to write.
27:34 "Please eat s now for your own good. For not a
Ro 2:25 The Jewish ceremony of circumcision is worth s
4:2 If so, he would have had s to boast about.
8:24 For if you already have s, you don't need to hope
8:25 But if we look forward to s we don't have yet,
12:20 If they are thirsty, give them s to drink,
13:4 But if you are doing s wrong, of course you should
14:16 Then you will not be condemned for doing s you
14:22 themselves by doing s they know is all right.
14:23 have doubts about whether they should eat s,
1Co 4:7 why boast as though you have accomplished s on
5:1 s so evil that even the pagans don't do it.
6:1 When you have s against another Christian,
8:12 by encouraging them to do s they believe is wrong.
9:16 For preaching the Good News is not s I can boast
12:31 let me tell you about s else that is better than any
15:2 you believed s that was never true in the first place.
2Co 8:10 and you were the first to begin doing s about it.
11:17 Such bragging is not s the Lord wants, but I am
12:5 That experience is s worth boasting about, but I am
Gal 1:15 But then s happened! For it pleased God in his
Eph 4:14 because someone has told us s different or
1Ti 5:4 care of them. This is s that pleases God very much.
Heb 11:7 who warned him about s that had never happened
1Pe 1:10 This salvation was s the prophets wanted to know
4:12 as if s strange were happening to you.
2Pe 3:16 to mean s quite different from what he meant,
Jude 1:3 But now I find that I must write about s else,

SOMETHING'S (1) [SOME, THING]

1Sa 14:38 Then Saul said to the leaders, "S wrong! I want all

SOMETIME [KJV] See (LONG) AGO, ONCE

SOMETIMES (18) [SOME, TIME]

Nu 9:20 S the cloud would stay over the Tabernacle for
9:21 S the cloud stayed only overnight and moved on
Jdg 1:33 and Beth-anath were s forced to work as slaves for
1Sa 2:15 S the servant would come even before the animal's
Job 1:5 and s they lasted several days—Job would purify
32:9 But s the elders are not wise. S the aged do not
understand justice.
Ps 34:10 Even strong young lions s go hungry, / but those
Pr 21:18 S the wicked are punished to save the godly,
Ecc 5:13 Riches are s hoarded to the harm of the saver,
Mk 2:18 John's disciples and the Pharisees s fasted.
1Co 4:9 But s I think God has put us apostles on display,
Php 1:23 S I want to live, and s I long to go and be with
Christ.
Heb 10:33 S you were exposed to public ridicule and were
10:33 and s you helped others who were suffering the
Jas 3:9 S it praises our Lord and Father, and s it breaks out
into curses against those who

SOMEWHERE (4) [SOME, WHERE]

Ge 26:16 "Go s else," he said, "for you have become too
Lev 18:9 she was brought up in the same family or s else.
Pr 4:15 Avoid their haunts. Turn away and go s else,
Heb 2:6 For s in the Scriptures it says, / "What is man that

SON (1930) [GRANDSON, GRANDSONS, GREAT-GRANDSON, SON'S, SON-IN-LAW, SONS, SONS', SONS-IN-LAW]

BELOVED SON (8) Ge 22:12,16; Mt 3:17; 17:5; Mk 1:11; 9:7; Lk 3:22; 2Pe 1:17

GOD'S SON (9) Jn 3:36; 5:28; Eph 4:13; 1Th 1:10; Heb 1:4; 5:8; 1Jn 5:6,12,18

KING'S SON (9) Jdg 8:18; 1Sa 18:1; 2Ki 11:4,12; 15:5; 2Ch 23:3,11; 28:7; Ps 72:1

MY SON (92) Ge 21:10; 22:7,8; 24:3,4,6,8,40; 27:1,8,18, 20,24,25,26,27; 30:16; 34:8; 37:35; 38:26; 42:38; 43:29; 45:28; 48:19; Jos 7:19; Jdg 8:23; 17:3; 1Sa 3:6,16; 10:2; 24:16; 26:17,21,25; 2Sa 7:14; 13:25; 14:11,15; 18:22,33,33, 33,33,33; 19:4,4,4,37; 1Ki 1:13,17,21; 3:20,21,21; 17:12,18; 22:26; 2Ki 6:28,29; 14:9; 1Ch 17:13; 22:5,10,11; 28:6,9; 29:1,19; 2Ch 18:25; 25:18; Ps 2:7; Pr 5:1,20; 6:20; 7:1; 23:26; 31:2; Jer 31:20; Hos 11:1; Mt 2:15; 17:15; 21:37; Mk 2:5; 9:17; 12:6; Lk 9:35; Ac 13:33; 1Ti 1:18; Heb 1:5,5; 5:5; 1Pe 5:13

ONLY SON (12) Ge 22:2; Jer 6:26; Am 8:10; Zec 12:10; Lk 7:12; 9:38; Jn 1:14,18; 3:16,18; Heb 11:17; 1Jn 4:9

SON OF AARON (10) Ex 6:25; 38:21; Nu 4:16,28,33; 7:8; 16:37; 26:1; Jos 24:33; Ezr 7:5

SON OF ABRAHAM (5) Ge 21:9; 25:12,19; Lk 3:34; 19:9

SON OF DAVID (16) Mt 1:20; 9:27; 12:23; 15:22; 20:30, 31; 21:9,15; 22:42; Mk 10:47,48; 12:35; Lk 3:31; 18:38,39; 20:41

SON OF GOD (41) Mt 4:3,6; 8:29; 14:33; 26:63; 27:40, 43,54; Mk 1:1; 3:11; 15:39; Lk 1:35; 3:38; 4:3,9,41; 22:70; Jn 1:34,49; 3:18; 5:25; 10:36; 11:4,27; 19:7; 20:31; Ac 9:20; Ro 1:4; 2Co 1:19; Gal 2:20; Heb 4:14; 6:6; 7:3; 10:29; 1Jn 3:8; 4:15; 5:5,10,13,20; Rev 2:18

SON OF JESSE (13) 1Sa 16:18; 20:27,31; 25:10; 2Sa 20:1; 23:1; 1Ch 10:14; 12:18; 29:26; 2Ch 11:18; Ps 72:20; Lk 3:32; Ac 13:22

SON OF MAN (176) Eze 2:1,3,6,8; 3:1,4,10,17; 4:1,16; 5:1; 6:2; 7:2; 8:5,6,8,12,17; 11:2,4,15; 12:2,9,18,22,27; 13:2, 17; 14:3,13; 15:2; 16:2; 17:2; 20:3,4,27,46; 21:2,6,9,12,14, 19,28; 22:2,18,24; 23:2,36; 24:2,16,25; 25:2; 26:2; 27:2; 28:2, 12,21; 29:2,18; 30:2,21; 31:2; 32:2,18; 33:2,7,10,12,24,30; 34:2; 35:2; 36:1,3,17; 37:3,11,16; 38:2,14; 39:1,17; 40:4; 43:7,10,18; 44:5; Da 8:17; Mt 8:20; 9:6; 10:23; 11:19; 12:8, 32,40; 13:37,41; 16:13,27,28; 17:9,12,22; 19:28; 20:18,28; 24:27,30,30,37,39,44; 25:31; 26:2,24,45,64; Mk 2:10,28; 8:31,38; 9:9,12,31; 10:33,45; 13:26,34; 14:21,41,62; Lk 5:24; 6:5,22; 7:34; 9:22,26,44,58; 11:30; 12:8,10,40; 17:22,23,24, 25,26,30; 18:8,31; 19:10; 21:27,36; 22:22,48,69; 24:7; Jn 1:51; 3:13,14; 5:27; 6:27,53,62; 8:28; 9:35; 12:23,34,34; 13:31; Ac 7:56; Heb 2:6; Rev 1:13; 14:14

Ge 4:2 Later she gave birth to a second s and named him
4:17 Cain's wife became pregnant and gave birth to a s,
4:17 Cain founded a city, he named it Enoch after his s.
4:25 his wife again, and she gave birth to another s.
4:25 "God has granted me another s in place of Abel,
4:26 Seth grew up, he had a s and named him Enosh.
5:3 Adam was 130 years old, his s Seth was born,
5:6 Seth was 105 years old, his s Enosh was born.
5:9 Enosh was 90 years old, his s Kenan was born.
5:12 Kenan was 70 years old, his s Mahalalel was born.
5:15 Mahalalel was 65 years old, his s Jared was born.
5:18 Jared was 162 years old, his s Enoch was born.
5:21 was 65 years old, his s Methuselah was born.
5:25 was 187 years old, his s Lamech was born.
5:28 Lamech was 182 years old, his s Noah was born.
5:29 Lamech named his s Noah, for he said, "He will
9:24 he learned what Ham, his youngest s, had done.
9:25 cursed the descendants of Canaan, the s of Ham:
10:15 Canaan's oldest s was Sidon, the ancestor of the
11:10 Shem was 100 years old, his s Arphaxad was born.
11:12 Arphaxad was 35 years old, his s Shelah was born.
11:14 Shelah was 30 years old, his s Eber was born.
11:16 When Eber was 34 years old, his s Peleg was born.
11:18 When Peleg was 30 years old, his s Reu was born.
11:20 When Reu was 32 years old, his s Serug was born.
11:22 Serug was 30 years old, his s Nahor was born.
11:24 Nahor was 29 years old, his s Terah was born.
11:27 Nahor, and Haran; and Haran had a s named Lot.
11:31 Terah took his s Abram, his daughter-in-law Sarai,
11:31 and his grandson Lot (his s Haran's child)
15:2 are all your blessings when I don't even have a s?
15:2 Since I don't have a s, Eliezer of Damascus,
15:4 for you will have a s of your own to inherit
16:11 "You are now pregnant and will give birth to a s.
16:12 This s of yours will be a wild one—free
16:15 So Hagar gave Abram a s, and Abram named him
17:16 And I will bless her and give you a s from her!
17:19 God replied, "Sarah, your wife, will bear you a s.
17:23 On that very day Abraham took his s Ishmael
17:25 and Ishmael his s was thirteen.
18:10 I will return, and your wife Sarah will have a s."
18:14 I told you, I will return, and Sarah will have a s."
19:37 When the older daughter gave birth to a s,
19:38 When the younger daughter gave birth to a s,
21:2 and she gave a s to Abraham in his old age.
21:3 And Abraham named his s Isaac.
21:7 Yet I have given Abraham a s in his old age!"
21:9 the s of Abraham and her Egyptian servant Hagar
21:10 and demanded, "Get rid of that servant and her s.
21:10 going to share the family inheritance with my s,
21:11 Abraham very much because Ishmael was his s.
21:12 for Isaac is the s through whom your descendants
21:13 will make a nation of the descendants of Hagar's s
because he also is your s."
21:14 He sent her away with their s, and she walked out
22:2 "Take your s, your only s—yes, Isaac,
22:3 of his servants with him, along with his s Isaac.
22:7 "Father?" "Yes, my s," Abraham replied.
22:8 will provide a lamb, my s," Abraham answered.
22:10 and lifted it up to kill his s as a sacrifice to the
22:12 You have not withheld even your beloved s from
22:13 it as a burnt offering on the altar in place of his s.
22:16 and have not withheld even your beloved s,
23:8 you feel, be so kind as to ask Ephron s of Zohar
24:3 that you will not let my s marry one of these local
24:4 my relatives, and find a wife there for my s Isaac."
24:6 "Be careful never to take my s there.
24:8 But under no circumstances are you to take my s
24:15 who was the s of Abraham's brother Nahor and his
24:36 was very old, she gave birth to my master's s,
24:38 back a young woman from here to marry his s.
24:40 you must get a wife for my s from among my
24:44 you have selected to be the wife of my master's s.'
24:47 is Bethuel, the s of Nahor and his wife, Milcah.'
24:51 Yes, let her be the wife of your master's s,
25:5 Abraham left everything he owned to his s Isaac.
25:9 in the field of Ephron s of Zohar the Hittite.
25:12 the s of Abraham through Hagar, Sarah's Egyptian
25:19 history of the family of Isaac, the s of Abraham.
25:23 the descendants of your older s will serve the
descendants of your younger s."
27:1 called for Esau, his older s, and said, "My s?"
27:4 that belongs to you, my firstborn s, before I die."
27:6 she said to her s Jacob, "I overheard your father
27:8 Now, my s, do exactly as I tell you.
27:13 "Let the curse fall on me, dear s," said Rebekah.
27:18 "Yes, my s," he answered. "Who is it—Esau
27:19 Jacob replied, "It's Esau, your older s. I've done
27:20 "How were you able to find it so quickly, my s?"
27:24 "Are you really my s Esau?" he asked. "Yes,
27:25 Then Isaac said, "Now, my s, bring me the meat.
27:26 "Come here and kiss me, my s."
27:27 he was finally convinced, and he blessed his s.
27:27 "The smell of my s is the good smell of the open
27:32 of course!" he replied. "It's Esau, your older s."
28:5 his mother's brother, the s of Bethuel the Aramean.
28:9 and the daughter of Ishmael, Abraham's s.
29:12 cousin on her father's side, her aunt Rebekah's s.
29:32 So Leah became pregnant and had a s. She named
29:33 soon became pregnant again and had another s.
29:33 that I was unloved and has given me another s."
29:34 Again she became pregnant and had a s.
29:35 Once again she became pregnant and had a s.
30:5 became pregnant and presented him with a s.
30:6 He has heard my request and given me a s."
30:7 became pregnant again and gave Jacob a second s.
30:10 Soon Zilpah presented him with another s.
30:12 Then Zilpah produced a second s,
30:16 you with some mandrake roots my s has found."
30:17 pregnant again and gave birth to her fifth s.
30:19 Then she became pregnant again and had a sixth s.
30:23 She became pregnant and gave birth to a s.
30:24 "May the LORD give me yet another s."
34:2 Shechem s of Hamor the Hivite, saw her, he took
34:8 "My s Shechem is truly in love with your
35:17 "Don't be afraid—you have another s!"
35:23 The sons of Leah were Reuben (Jacob's oldest s),
36:4 Esau and Adah had a s named Eliphaz. Esau and
Basemath had a s named Reuel.
36:10 sons were Eliphaz, the s of Esau's wife Adah;
36:10 and Reuel, the s of Esau's wife Basemath.
36:12 Eliphaz had another s named Amalek, born to
36:15 The sons of Esau's oldest s, Eliphaz,
36:16 descended from Eliphaz, the s of Esau and Adah.
36:17 The sons of Esau's s Reuel became the leaders of
36:17 from Reuel, the s of Esau and Basemath.
36:25 The s of Anah was Dishon, and Oholibamah was
36:32 Bela s of Beor, who ruled from his city of
36:33 Jobab s of Zerah from Bozrah became king.
36:35 Hadad s of Bedad became king and ruled from the
36:38 Shaul died, Baal-hanan s of Acbor became king.
37:34 He mourned deeply for his s for many days.
37:35 "I will die in mourning for my s," he would say,
38:3 She became pregnant and had a s, and Judah
38:4 Then Judah's wife had another s, and she named
38:5 And when she had a third s, she named him
38:6 When his oldest s, Er, grew up, Judah arranged his
38:8 Her first s from you will be your brother's heir."
38:11 She was to remain a widow until his youngest s,
38:26 keep my promise to let her marry my s Shelah."
41:51 Joseph named his older s Manasseh, for he said,
41:52 Joseph named his second s Ephraim, for he said,
42:38 Jacob replied, "My s will not go down with you,
43:29 me about? May God be gracious to you, my s."
44:20 old man, and a child of his old age, his youngest s.
45:9 and tell him, 'This is what your s Joseph says:
45:28 My s Joseph is alive! I will go and see him before I
46:8 with him to Egypt: Reuben was Jacob's oldest s.
46:23 The s of Dan was Hushim.
47:29 he called for his s Joseph and said to him, "If you
48:19 "I know what I'm doing, my s," he said.
49:3 "Reuben, you are my oldest s, / the child of my
50:23 three generations of descendants of his s Ephraim

50:23 and the children of Manasseh's s Makir,
Ex 2:2 The woman became pregnant and gave birth to a s.
2:10 back to the princess, who adopted him as her s.
4:22 is what the LORD says: Israel is my firstborn s.
4:23 be warned! I will kill your firstborn s!' "
4:25 his wife, took a flint knife and circumcised her s.
6:14 Israel's oldest s, included Hanoch, Pallu, Hezron,
6:25 Eleazar s of Aaron married one of the daughters of
11:5 from the oldest s of Pharaoh, who sits on the throne, to the oldest s of his lowliest slave.
12:29 from the firstborn s of Pharaoh, who sat on the
12:29 to the firstborn s of the captive in the dungeon.
13:13 However, you must redeem every firstborn s.
18:3 The name of Moses' first s was Gershom,
18:4 The name of his second s was Eliezer, for Moses
21:9 slave girl's owner arranges for her to marry his s,
31:2 "Look, I have chosen Bezalel s of Uri, grandson of
31:6 "And I have appointed Oholiab s of Ahisamach,
33:11 the young man who assisted him, Joshua s of Nun,
34:20 However, you must redeem every firstborn s.
35:30 "The LORD has chosen Bezalel s of Uri,
35:34 has given both him and Oholiab s of Ahisamach,
38:21 and Ithamar s of Aaron the priest served as
38:22 Bezalel s of Uri, grandson of Hur, of the tribe of
38:23 He was assisted by Oholiab s of Ahisamach,
Lev 12:2 a woman becomes pregnant and gives birth to a s,
12:6 the time of purification is completed for either a s
12:7 the instructions to be followed after the birth of a s
21:2 mother or father, s or daughter, brother
24:11 this s of an Israelite woman blasphemed the
Nu 1:5 chosen for the task: / Reuben | Elizur s of Shedeur
1:6 Simeon | Shelumiel s of Zurishaddai
1:7 Judah | Nahshon s of Amminadab
1:8 Issachar | Nethanel s of Zuar
1:9 Zebulun | Eliab s of Helon
1:10 Ephraim s of Joseph | Elishama s of Ammihud
1:10 Manasseh s of Joseph | Gamaliel s of Pedahzur
1:11 Benjamin | Abidan s of Gideoni
1:12 Dan | Ahiezer s of Ammishaddai
1:13 Asher | Pagiel s of Ocran
1:14 Gad | Eliasaph s of Deuel
1:15 Naphtali | Ahira s of Enan
1:32[-33] Ephraim s of Joseph | 40,500
1:34[-35] Manasseh s of Joseph | 32,200
2:3[-4] Judah | Nahshon s of Amminadab | 74,600
2:5[-6] Issachar | Nethanel s of Zuar | 54,400
2:7[-8] Zebulun | Eliab s of Helon | 57,400
2:10[-11] Reuben | Elizur s of Shedeur | 46,500
2:12[-13] Simeon | Shelumiel s of Zurishaddai | 59,300
2:14[-15] Gad | Eliasaph s of Deuel | 45,650
2:18[-19] Ephraim | Elishama s of Ammihud | 40,500
2:20[-21] Manasseh | Gamaliel s of Pedahzur | 32,200
2:22[-23] Benjamin | Abidan s of Gideoni | 35,400
2:25[-26] Dan | Ahiezer s of Ammishaddai | 62,700
2:27[-28] Asher | Pagiel s of Ocran | 41,500
2:29[-30] Naphtali | Ahira s of Enan | 53,400
3:24 The leader of the Gershonite clans was Eliasaph s
3:30 The leader of the Kohathite clans was Elizaphan s
3:32 Eleazar the priest, Aaron's s, was the chief
3:35 The leader of the Merarite clans was Zuriel s of
4:16 "Eleazar s of Aaron the priest will be responsible
4:28 They will be directly responsible to Ithamar s of
4:33 They are directly responsible to Ithamar s of Aaron
7:8 the leadership of Ithamar s of Aaron the priest.
7:12 On the first day Nahshon s of Amminadab,
7:17 This was the offering brought by Nahshon s of
7:18 On the second day Nethanel s of Zuar, leader of
7:23 This was the offering brought by Nethanel s of
7:24 On the third day Eliab s of Helon, leader of the
7:29 This was the offering brought by Eliab s of Helon.
7:30 On the fourth day Elizur s of Shedeur, leader of the
7:35 This was the offering brought by Elizur s of
7:36 On the fifth day Shelumiel s of Zurishaddai,
7:41 This was the offering brought by Shelumiel s of
7:42 On the sixth day Eliasaph s of Deuel, leader of the
7:47 This was the offering brought by Eliasaph s of
7:48 On the seventh day Elishama s of Ammihud,
7:53 This was the offering brought by Elishama s of
7:54 On the eighth day Gamaliel s of Pedahzur,
7:59 This was the offering brought by Gamaliel s of
7:60 On the ninth day Abidan s of Gideoni, leader of the
7:65 This was the offering brought by Abidan s of
7:66 On the tenth day Ahiezer s of Ammishaddai,
7:71 This was the offering brought by Ahiezer s of
7:72 On the eleventh day Pagiel s of Ocran, leader of
7:77 This was the offering brought by Pagiel s of Ocran.
7:78 On the twelfth day Ahira s of Enan, leader of the
7:83 This was the offering brought by Ahira s of Enan.
10:14 under the leadership of Nahshon s of Amminadab.
10:15 The tribe of Issachar was led by Nethanel s of
10:16 The tribe of Zebulun was led by Eliab s of Helon.
10:18 under the leadership of Elizur s of Shedeur.
10:19 The tribe of Simeon was led by Shelumiel s of
10:20 The tribe of Gad was led by Eliasaph s of Deuel.
10:22 under the leadership of Elishama s of Ammihud.
10:23 The tribe of Manasseh was led by Gamaliel s of
10:24 The tribe of Benjamin was led by Abidan s of
10:25 under the leadership of Ahiezer s of Ammishaddai.
10:26 The tribe of Asher was led by Pagiel s of Ocran.
10:27 The tribe of Naphtali was led by Ahira s of Enan.
10:29 his brother-in-law, Hobab s of Reuel the Midianite,
11:28 Joshua s of Nun, who had been Moses' personal
13:4 of the leaders: / Reuben | Shammua s of Zaccur
13:5 Simeon | Shaphat s of Hori
13:6 Judah | Caleb s of Jephunneh
13:7 Issachar | Igal s of Joseph
13:8 Ephraim | Hoshea s of Nun
13:9 Benjamin | Palti s of Raphu
13:10 Zebulun | Gaddiel s of Sodi
13:11 Manasseh s of Joseph | Gaddi s of Susi
13:12 Dan | Ammiel s of Gemalli
13:13 Asher | Sethur s of Michael
13:14 Naphtali | Nahbi s of Vophsi
13:15 Gad | Geuel s of Maki
14:6 Joshua s of Nun and Caleb s of Jephunneh,
14:30 The only exceptions will be Caleb s of Jephunneh and Joshua s of Nun.
16:1 One day Korah s of Izhar, a descendant of Kohath s of Levi, conspired with
16:1 and Abiram, the sons of Eliab, and On s of Peleth,
16:37 "Tell Eleazar s of Aaron the priest to pull all the
20:25 Now take Aaron and his s Eleazar up Mount Hor.
20:26 priestly garments and put them on Eleazar, his s.
20:28 from Aaron and put them on Eleazar, Aaron's s.
22:2 Balak s of Zippor, the Moabite king, knew what
22:5 sent messengers to Balaam s of Beor, who was
22:10 said to God, "Balak s of Zippor, king of Moab,
22:16 "This is what Balak s of Zippor says:
23:18 Balak, and listen! / Hear me, s of Zippor.
24:3 "This is the prophecy of Balaam s of Beor,
24:15 "This is the message of Balaam s of Beor,
25:7 When Phinehas s of Eleazar and grandson of
25:11 "Phinehas s of Eleazar and grandson of Aaron the
25:14 the Midianite woman was named Zimri s of Salu,
26:1 LORD said to Moses and to Eleazar s of Aaron,
26:5 the clans descended from Reuben, Jacob's oldest s:
26:29 named after its ancestor Gilead, Makir's s.
26:33 Hepher's s, Zelophehad, had no sons, but his
26:65 The only exceptions were Caleb s of Jephunneh and Joshua s of Nun.
27:1 Their father, Zelophehad, was the s of Hepher, s of Gilead, s of Makir, s of Manasseh, s of Joseph.
27:18 The LORD replied, "Take Joshua s of Nun,
31:6 and Phinehas s of Eleazar the priest led them into
31:8 They also killed Balaam s of Beor with the sword.
32:12 The only exceptions are Caleb s of Jephunneh the Kenizzite and Joshua s of Nun,
32:33 and half the tribe of Manasseh s of Joseph the
34:17 the people: Eleazar the priest and Joshua s of Nun.
34:19 of the leaders: / Judah | Caleb s of Jephunneh
34:20 Simeon | Shemuel s of Ammihud
34:21 Benjamin | Elidad s of Kislon
34:22 Dan | Bukki s of Jogli
34:23 Manasseh s of Joseph | Hanniel s of Ephod
34:24 Ephraim s of Joseph | Kemuel s of Shiphtan
34:25 Zebulun | Elizaphan s of Parnach
34:26 Issachar | Paltiel s of Azzan
34:27 Asher | Ahihud s of Shelomi
34:28 Naphtali | Pedahel s of Ammihud
36:1 of Makir, s of Manasseh, s of Joseph—
36:12 They married into the clans of Manasseh s of
Dt 1:36 except Caleb s of Jephunneh. He will see this land
1:38 Instead, your assistant, Joshua s of Nun, will lead
10:6 His s Eleazar became the high priest in his place.
13:6 "Suppose your brother, s, daughter, beloved wife,
18:10 never sacrifice your s or daughter as a burnt
21:15 And suppose the firstborn s is the son of the wife
21:15 And suppose the firstborn son is the s of the wife
21:16 not give the larger inheritance to his younger s, the s of the wife he loves.
21:17 give the customary double portion to his oldest s,
21:17 and who owns the rights of the firstborn s,
21:17 even though he is the s of the wife his father does
21:18 rebellious s who will not obey his father or mother,
21:19 and mother must take the s before the leaders of
21:20 'This s of ours is stubborn and rebellious
23:4 they tried to hire Balaam s of Beor from Pethor in
25:5 same property and one of them dies without a s,
25:6 The first s she bears to him will be counted as the s of the dead brother,
25:9 a man who refuses to raise up a s for his brother.'
28:56 husband she loves and to her own s or daughter.
31:23 Then the LORD commissioned Joshua s of Nun
32:44 So Moses came with Joshua s of Nun and recited
34:9 Now Joshua s of Nun was full of the spirit of
Jos 1:1 the LORD spoke to Joshua s of Nun,
6:26 At the cost of his firstborn s, / he will lay its
6:26 At the cost of his youngest s, / he will set up its
7:1 Achan was the s of Carmi, of the family of Zimri,
7:19 "My s, give glory to the LORD, the God of
13:22 also killed Balaam the magician, the s of Beor.
13:31 the descendants of Makir, who was Manasseh's s.
14:1 the priest, Joshua s of Nun, and the tribal leaders.
14:6 led by Caleb s of Jephunneh the Kenizzite, came to
14:13 So Joshua blessed Caleb s of Jephunneh and gave
14:14 Hebron still belongs to the descendants of Caleb s
15:6 to the stone of Bohan. (Bohan was Reuben's s.)
15:8 then passed through the valley of the s of Hinnom,
15:13 some of Judah's territory to Caleb s of Jephunneh.
15:17 Othniel, the s of Caleb's brother Kenaz,
17:1 of Manasseh, the descendants of Joseph's older s.
17:1 (Makir was Manasseh's oldest s and was the father
17:3 However, Zelophehad s of Hepher, who was a
17:4 Joshua s of Nun, and the Israelite leaders and said,
18:16 the mountain beside the valley of the s of Hinnom,
18:17 to the stone of Bohan. (Bohan was Reuben's s.)
19:51 territories that Eleazar the priest, Joshua s of Nun,
21:1 Joshua s of Nun, and the leaders of the other tribes
21:12 and the surrounding villages were given to Caleb s
22:13 they sent a delegation led by Phinehas s of Eleazar,
22:31 Phinehas s of Eleazar, the priest, replied to them,
22:32 Then Phinehas s of Eleazar, the priest, and the ten
24:3 I gave him many descendants through his s Isaac.
24:9 Then Balak s of Zippor, king of Moab, started a
24:9 He asked Balaam s of Beor to curse you,
24:29 Soon after this, Joshua s of Nun, the servant of the
24:33 Eleazar s of Aaron also died. He was buried in the
24:33 of Gibeah, which had been given to his s Phinehas.
Jdg 1:13 Othniel, the s of Caleb's younger brother Kenaz,
2:8 Then Joshua s of Nun, the servant of the LORD,
3:9 the s of Caleb's younger brother, Kenaz.
3:11 land for forty years. Then Othniel s of Kenaz died.
3:15 His name was Ehud s of Gera, of the tribe of
3:31 After Ehud, Shamgar s of Anath rescued Israel.
4:6 One day she sent for Barak s of Abinoam,
4:12 When Sisera was told that Barak s of Abinoam had
5:1 and Barak s of Abinoam sang this song:
5:6 "In the days of Shamgar s of Anath, and in the
5:12 Barak! / Lead your captives away, s of Abinoam!
6:11 Gideon s of Joash had been threshing wheat at the
6:29 they learned that it was Gideon, the s of Joash.
6:30 "Bring out your s," they shouted to Joash.
7:14 God has given Gideon s of Joash, the Israelite,
8:18 they replied. "They all had the look of a king's s."
8:20 to Jether, his oldest s, he said, "Kill them!"
8:22 You and your s and your grandson will be our
8:23 "I will not rule over you, nor will my s.
8:29 Then Gideon s of Joash returned home.
8:31 in Shechem, who bore him a s named Abimelech.
9:1 One day Gideon's s Abimelech went to Shechem
9:18 And you have chosen his slave woman's s,
9:26 At that time Gaal s of Ebed moved to Shechem
9:28 He's merely the s of Gideon, and Zebul is his
9:31 "Gaal s of Ebed and his brothers have come to live
9:57 So the curse of Jotham s of Gideon came true.
10:1 Tola, the s of Puah and descendant of Dodo,
11:1 He was the s of Gilead, but his mother was a
11:2 they said, "for you are the s of a prostitute."
11:25 Are you any better than Balak s of Zippor, king of
12:13 After Elon died, Abdon s of Hillel, from Pirathon,
13:3 will soon become pregnant and give birth to a s.
13:5 You will become pregnant and give birth to a s,
13:7 'You will become pregnant and give birth to a s.
13:7 For your s will be dedicated to God as a Nazirite
13:8 and give us more instructions about this s who is to
13:24 When her s was born, they named him Samson.
17:3 In honor of my s, I will have an image carved
18:29 Israel's s, but it had originally been called Laish.
18:30 and they appointed Jonathan s of Gershom,
20:28 and Phinehas s of Eleazar and grandson of Aaron
Ru 4:10 This way she can have a s to carry on the family
4:12 of our ancestor Perez, the s of Tamar and Judah."
4:13 her to become pregnant, and she gave birth to a s.
4:15 For he is the s of your daughter-in-law who loves
4:17 women said, "Now at last Naomi has a s again!"
1Sa 1:1 He was the s of Jeroham and grandson of Elihu,
1:11 my sorrow and answer my prayer and give me a s,
1:20 and in due time she gave birth to a s. She named
3:6 "I didn't call you, my s," Eli said. "Go on back to
3:16 But Eli called out to him, "Samuel, my s."
7:1 and ordained Eleazar, his s, to be in charge of it.
9:1 He was the s of Abiel and grandson of Zeror,
9:2 His s Saul was the most handsome man in Israel—
10:2 about you and is asking, 'Have you seen my s?'
10:11 How did the s of Kish become a prophet?"
10:21 And finally Saul s of Kish was chosen from among
13:2 The other thousand went with Saul's s Jonathan to
14:3 Ahijah was the s of Ahitub, Ichabod's brother.
14:3 Ahitub was the s of Phinehas and the grandson of
14:39 will surely die, even if it is my own s Jonathan!"
14:50 army was his cousin Abner, his uncle Ner's s.
16:8 Then Jesse told his s Abinadab to step forward
16:18 to Saul, "The s of Jesse is a talented harp player.
16:19 to say, "Send me your s David, the shepherd."
17:12 Now David was the s of a man named Jesse,
17:55 the general of his army, "Abner, whose s is he?"
18:1 talking with Saul, he met Jonathan, the king's s.
19:1 and his s Jonathan to assassinate David.
20:27 "Why hasn't the s of Jesse been here for dinner
20:30 "You stupid s of a whore!" he swore at him.
20:31 As long as that s of Jesse is alive, you'll never be
22:8 For not one of you has ever told me that my own s
22:8 My own s—encouraging David to try and kill
22:12 shouted at him, "Listen to me, you s of Ahitub!"
24:16 called back, "Is that really you, my s David?"
25:10 "Who does this s of Jesse think he is?
25:44 to a man from Gallim named Palti s of Laish.
26:5 Saul and his general, Abner s of Ner, were sleeping
26:6 Ahimelech the Hittite and Abishai s of Zeruiah,
26:17 and called out, "Is that you, my s David?"
26:21 Come back home, my s, and I will no longer try to
26:25 said to David, "Blessings on you, my s David.
30:19 small or great, s or daughter, or anything else that
2Sa 1:4 and Saul and his s Jonathan have been killed."
1:12 and fasted all day for Saul and his s Jonathan,
2:8 But Abner s of Ner, the commander of Saul's
2:8 had already gone to Mahanaim with Saul's s
2:13 Joab s of Zeruiah led David's troops from Hebron,
3:7 One day Ishbosheth, Saul's s, accused Abner of
3:14 then sent this message to Ishbosheth, Saul's s:
3:15 Michal away from her husband Palti s of Laish.
4:4 (Saul's s Jonathan had a s named Mephibosheth,
4:8 the s of your enemy Saul who tried to kill you.
7:14 I will be his father, and he will be my s. If he sins,
8:3 David also destroyed the forces of Hadadezer s of
8:10 he sent his s Joram to congratulate David on his
8:12 and from Hadadezer s of Rehob, king of Zobah.
8:16 Joab s of Zeruiah was commander of the army.
8:16 Jehoshaphat s of Ahilud was the royal historian.
8:17 Zadok s of Ahitub and Ahimelech s of Abiathar were the priests.

8:18 Benaiah s of Jehoiada was captain of the king's
9: 4 told him, "at the home of Makir s of Ammiel."
9: 6 he was Jonathan's s and Saul's grandson.
9:12 Mephibosheth had a young s named Mica.
10: 1 Ammonites died, and his s Hanun became king.
11:21 Wasn't Gideon's s Abimelech killed at Thebez by
11:27 one of his wives. Then she gave birth to a s.
12:24 She became pregnant and gave birth to a s,
13: 1 David's s Absalom had a beautiful sister named
13: 3 He was the s of David's brother Shimea.
13: 4 Why should the s of a king look so dejected
13:25 The king replied, "No, my s. If we all came,
13:32 the s of David's brother Shimea, arrived and said,
13:37 And David mourned many days for his s Amnon.
13:37 Talmai s of Ammihud, the king of Geshur.
13:39 longed to be reunited with his s Absalom.
14: 7 of the family is demanding, 'Let us have your s.
14:11 you won't let anyone take vengeance against my s.
14:13 have refused to bring home your own banished s.
14:15 "But I have come to plead with you for my s
14:33 Then at last David summoned his estranged s,
15:27 with your s Ahimaaz and Abiathar's s Jonathan.
16: 5 It was Shimei s of Gera, a member of Saul's
16: 8 and now the LORD has given it to your s
16: 9 Abishai s of Zeruiah demanded. "Let me go over
16:11 the other officers, "My own s is trying to kill me.
17:27 he was warmly greeted by Shobi s of Nahash of
17:27 and by Makir s of Ammiel of Lo-debar,
18: 2 one-third under Joab's brother Abishai s of
18:13 And if I had betrayed the king by killing his s—
18:18 he had said, "I have no s to carry on my name."
18:19 Then Zadok's s Ahimaaz said, "Let me run to the
18:20 "it wouldn't be good news to the king that his s is
18:22 let me go, too." "Why should you go, my s?"
18:27 "The first man runs like Ahimaaz s of Zadok,"
18:33 And as he went, he cried, "O my s Absalom! My s,
my s Absalom!
18:33 died instead of you! O Absalom, my s, my s."
19: 2 the troops heard of the king's deep grief for his s,
19: 4 his hands and kept on weeping, "O my s Absalom!
O Absalom, my s, my s!"
19:16 Then Shimei s of Gera the Benjaminite, the man
19:21 Then Abishai s of Zeruiah said, "Shimei should
19:37 But here is my s Kimham. Let him go with you
20: 1 Then a troublemaker named Sheba s of Bicri,
20: 1 We want no part of this s of Jesse. Come on,
20:21 All I want is a man named Sheba s of Bicri from
20:23 Benaiah s of Jehoiada was commander of the
20:24 Jehoshaphat s of Ahilud was the royal historian.
21: 7 David spared Jonathan's s Mephibosheth, who was
21: 8 the wife of Adriel s of Barzillai from Meholah.
21:12 and asked for the bones of Saul and his s Jonathan.
21:17 But Abishai s of Zeruiah came to his rescue
21:19 Elhanan s of Jair from Bethlehem killed the
21:21 by Jonathan, the s of David's brother Shimea.
23: 1 "David, the s of Jesse, speaks— / David, the man
23: 9 Next in rank among the Three was Eleazar s of
23:11 Next in rank was Shammah s of Agee from Harar.
23:18 Abishai s of Zeruiah, the brother of Joab,
23:20 There was also Benaiah s of Jehoiada, a valiant
23:24 Elhanan s of Dodo from Bethlehem;
23:26 Helez from Pelon; / Ira s of Ikkesh from Tekoa;
23:29 Heled s of Baanah from Netophah; / Ithai s of
Ribai from Gibeah (from the tribe of
23:33 Jonathan s of Shagee from Harar; / Ahiam s of
Sharar from Harar;
23:34 Eliphelet s of Ahasbai from Maacah; / Eliam s of
Ahithophel from Giloh;
23:36 Igal s of Nathan from Zobah; / Bani from Gad;
1Ki 1: 5 About that time David's s Adonijah, whose mother
1: 7 Adonijah took Joab s of Zeruiah and Abiathar the
1: 8 Benaiah s of Jehoiada, Nathan the prophet, Shimei,
1:11 "Did you realize that Haggith's s, Adonijah,
1:12 save your own life and the life of your s Solomon,
1:13 didn't you promise me that my s Solomon would
1:17 God that my s Solomon would be the next king
1:21 my s Solomon and I will be treated as criminals as
1:26 the priest, Benaiah s of Jehoiada, nor Solomon.
1:30 today I decree that your s Solomon will be the next
1:32 Nathan the prophet, and Benaiah s of Jehoiada."
1:36 "Amen!" Benaiah s of Jehoiada replied.
1:38 Nathan the prophet, Benaiah s of Jehoiada,
1:42 Jonathan s of Abiathar the priest arrived.
1:44 Nathan the prophet, and Benaiah s of Jehoiada,
2: 1 he gave this charge to his s Solomon:
2: 5 You know that Joab s of Zeruiah murdered my two
2: 5 Abner s of Ner and Amasa s of Jether.
2: 8 "And remember Shimei s of Gera, the Benjaminite
2:22 the priest and Joab s of Zeruiah on his side."
2:25 So King Solomon ordered Benaiah s of Jehoiada to
2:29 he sent Benaiah s of Jehoiada to execute him.
2:32 father was no party to the deaths of Abner s of Ner,
2:32 of the army of Israel, and Amasa s of Jether,
2:34 So Benaiah s of Jehoiada returned to the sacred
2:46 Benaiah s of Jehoiada took Shimei outside
3: 6 to him today by giving him a s to succeed him.
3:20 and took my s from beside me while I was asleep.
3:21 And in the morning when I tried to nurse my s,
3:21 the morning light, I saw that it wasn't my s at all."
3:22 "It certainly was your s, and the living child is
4: 2 high officials: / Azariah s of Zadok was the priest.
4: 3 Jehoshaphat s of Ahilud was the royal historian.
4: 4 Benaiah s of Jehoiada was commander of the
4: 5 Azariah s of Nathan presided over the district
4: 5 Zabud s of Nathan, a priest, was a trusted adviser
4: 6 Adoniram s of Abda was in charge of the labor
4:12 Baana s of Ahilud, in Taanach and Megiddo,
4:13 including the Towns of Jair (named for Jair s of
4:14 Ahinadab s of Iddo, in Mahanaim.
4:16 Baana s of Hushai, in Asher and in Aloth.
4:17 Jehoshaphat s of Paruah, in Issachar.
4:18 Shimei s of Ela, in Benjamin.
4:19 Geber s of Uri, in the land of Gilead,
5: 1 so when he learned that David's s Solomon was
5: 5 For the LORD told him, 'Your s, whom I will
5: 7 "Praise the LORD for giving David a wise s to
11:12 I will take the kingdom away from your s.
11:20 She bore him a s, Genubath, who was brought up
11:23 God also raised up Rezon s of Eliada to be an
11:26 Another rebel leader was Jeroboam s of Nebat,
11:35 But I will take the kingdom away from his s
11:36 His s will have one tribe so that the descendants of
11:43 Then his s Rehoboam became the next king.
12: 2 When Jeroboam s of Nebat heard of Solomon's
12:15 for it fulfilled the LORD's message to Jeroboam s
12:16 We have no share in Jesse's s! Let's go home,
12:23 "Say to Rehoboam s of Solomon, king of Judah,
14: 1 At that time Jeroboam's s Abijah became very
14: 5 She will ask you about her s, for he is very sick.
14:20 Jeroboam died, his s Nadab became the next king.
14:21 Rehoboam s of Solomon was king in Judah.
14:31 Then his s Abijam became the next king.
15: 4 and he gave Abijam a s to rule after him in
15: 8 of David. Then his s Asa became the next king.
15:18 He sent it with some of his officials to Ben-hadad s
15:24 Then his s Jehoshaphat became the next king.
15:25 Nadab s of Jeroboam began to rule over Israel in
15:27 Then Baasha s of Ahijah, from the tribe of
16: 1 to King Baasha by the prophet Jehu s of Hanani:
16: 3 just as I destroyed the descendants of Jeroboam s
16: 6 in Tirzah. Then his s Elah became the next king.
16: 7 and his family through the prophet Jehu s of
16: 8 Elah s of Baasha began to rule over Israel from
16:13 because of the sins of Baasha and his s Elah and
16:21 Half the people tried to make Tibni s of Ginath
16:22 defeated the supporters of Tibni s of Ginath.
16:28 in Samaria. Then his s Ahab became the next king.
16:29 Ahab s of Omri began to rule over Israel in the
16:34 he laid the foundations, his oldest s, Abiram, died.
16:34 by setting up the gates, his youngest s, Segub, died.
16:34 concerning Jericho spoken by Joshua s of Nun.
17:12 cook this last meal, and then my s and I will die."
17:13 there will still be enough food for you and your s.
17:15 and her s continued to eat from her supply of flour
17:17 Some time later, the woman's s became sick.
17:18 you come here to punish my sins by killing my s?"
17:19 But Elijah replied, "Give me your s." And he took
17:20 has opened her home to me, causing her s to die?"
17:23 to his mother. "Look, your s is alive!" he said.
19:16 Then anoint Jehu s of Nimshi to be king of Israel,
19:16 and anoint Elisha s of Shaphat from Abel-meholah
19:19 and found Elisha s of Shaphat plowing a field with
21:22 family as he did the family of Jeroboam s of Nebat
and the family of Baasha s of Ahijah,
22: 8 news for me! His name is Micaiah s of Imlah."
22: 9 "Quick! Go and get Micaiah s of Imlah."
22:11 One of them, Zedekiah s of Kenaanah, made some
22:24 Then Zedekiah s of Kenaanah walked up to
22:26 the governor of the city, and to my s Joash.
22:40 Then his s Ahaziah became the next king.
22:41 Jehoshaphat s of Asa began to rule over Judah in
22:49 At that time Ahaziah s of Ahab proposed to
22:50 Then his s Jehoram became the next king.
22:51 Ahaziah s of Ahab began to rule over Israel in the
22:52 and the example of Jeroboam s of Nebat,
2Ki 1:17 Since Ahaziah did not have a s to succeed him,
1:17 year of the reign of Jehoram s of Jehoshaphat,
3: 1 Ahab's s Joram began to rule over Israel in the
3: 3 s of Nebat had led the people of Israel to commit.
3:11 officers replied, "Elisha s of Shaphat is here.
3:27 So he took his oldest s, who would have been the
4:14 He suggested, "She doesn't have a s, and her
4:16 this time you will be holding a s in your arms!"
4:17 And at that time the following year she had a s,
4:28 "It was you, my lord, who said I would have a s.
4:36 she came in, Elisha said, "Here, take your s!"
4:37 Then she picked up her s and carried him
6:28 "This woman proposed that we eat my s one day
and her s the next.
6:29 So we cooked my s and ate him. Then the next day
I said, 'Kill your s so we can eat him,'
6:31 "May God kill me if I don't execute Elisha s of
8: 1 Elisha had told the woman whose s he had brought
8: 5 "Here is the woman now, and this is her s—
8:16 Jehoram s of King Jehoshaphat of Judah began to
8:16 Joram's reign in Israel. Joram was the s of Ahab.
8:24 Then his s Ahaziah became the next king.
8:25 Ahaziah s of Jehoram began to rule over Judah in
8:25 reign in Israel. King Joram was the s of Ahab.
9: 2 and find Jehu s of Jehoshaphat and grandson of
9: 9 as I destroyed the families of Jeroboam s of Nebat
and of Baasha s of Ahijah.
9:14 So Jehu s of Jehoshaphat and grandson of Nimshi
9:20 It must be Jehu s of Nimshi, for he is driving
10:15 Jehu left there, he met Jehonadab s of Recab,
10:23 into the temple of Baal with Jehonadab s of Recab.
10:29 the great sin that Jeroboam s of Nebat had led
10:35 Then his s Jehoahaz became the next king.
11: 1 Ahaziah of Judah, learned that her s was dead,
11: 2 of King Jehoram, took Ahaziah's infant s, Joash,
11: 4 then he showed them the king's s.
11:12 Then Jehoiada brought out Joash, the king's s,
12:21 The assassins were Jozacar s of Shimeath and
Jehozabad s of Shomer—
12:21 Then his s Amaziah became the next king.
13: 1 Jehoahaz s of Jehu began to rule over Israel in the
13: 2 He followed the example of Jeroboam s of Nebat,
13: 2 continuing the sins of idolatry that Jeroboam s of
13: 3 and his s Ben-hadad to defeat them time after time.
13: 9 Then his s Jehoash became the next king.
13:10 Jehoash s of Jehoahaz began to rule over Israel in
13:11 that Jeroboam s of Nebat had led Israel to commit.
13:13 Then his s Jeroboam II became the next king.
13:24 and his s Ben-hadad became the next king.
13:25 Then Jehoash s of Jehoahaz recaptured from
13:25 s of Hazael the towns that Hazael had taken from
14: 1 Amaziah s of Joash began to rule over Judah in the
14: 8 the s of Jehoahaz and grandson of Jehu:
14: 9 'Give your daughter in marriage to my s.' But just
14:16 Then his s Jeroboam II became the next king.
14:21 then crowned Amaziah's sixteen-year-old s,
14:23 Jeroboam II, the s of Jehoash, began to rule over
14:24 that Jeroboam s of Nebat had led Israel to commit.
14:25 of Israel, had promised through Jonah s of Amittai,
14:27 used Jeroboam II, the s of Jehoash, to save them.
14:29 Then his s Zechariah became the next king.
15: 1 Uzziah s of Amaziah began to rule over Judah in
15: 5 The king's s Jotham was put in charge of the royal
15: 7 of David. Then his s Jotham became the next king.
15: 8 Zechariah s of Jeroboam II began to rule over
15: 9 that Jeroboam s of Nebat had led Israel to commit.
15:10 Then Shallum s of Jabesh conspired against
15:13 Shallum s of Jabesh began to rule over Israel in the
15:14 Then Menahem s of Gadi went to Samaria from
15:17 Menahem s of Gadi began to rule over Israel in the
15:18 that Jeroboam s of Nebat had led Israel to commit.
15:22 his s Pekahiah became the next king.
15:23 Pekahiah s of Menahem began to rule over Israel
15:24 that Jeroboam s of Nebat had led Israel to commit.
15:25 Then Pekah s of Remaliah, the commander of
15:27 Pekah s of Remaliah began to rule over Israel in
15:28 that Jeroboam s of Nebat had led Israel to commit.
15:30 Then Hoshea s of Elah conspired against Pekah
15:30 Israel in the twentieth year of Jotham s of Uzziah.
15:32 Jotham s of Uzziah began to rule over Judah in the
15:38 of David. Then his s Ahaz became the next king.
16: 1 Ahaz s of Jotham began to rule over Judah in the
16: 3 of Israel, even sacrificing his own s in the fire.
16:20 Then his s Hezekiah became the next king.
17: 1 Hoshea s of Elah began to rule over Israel in the
17:21 they chose Jeroboam s of Nebat as their king.
18: 1 Hezekiah s of Ahaz began to rule over Judah in the
18:18 Eliakim s of Hilkiah, the palace administrator,
18:18 and Joah s of Asaph, the royal historian.
18:26 Then Eliakim s of Hilkiah, Shebna, and Joah said
18:37 Then Eliakim s of Hilkiah, the palace
18:37 and Joah s of Asaph, the royal historian, went back
19: 2 in sackcloth, to the prophet Isaiah s of Amoz.
19:20 Then Isaiah s of Amoz sent this message to
19:37 and another s, Esarhaddon, became the next king
20: 1 and the prophet Isaiah s of Amoz went to visit him.
20:12 Soon after this, Merodach-baladan s of Baladan,
20:21 his s Manasseh became the next king.
21: 6 Manasseh even sacrificed his own s in the fire.
21: 7 the LORD had told David and his s Solomon:
21:18 of Uzza. Then his s Amon became the next king.
21:24 and they made his s Josiah the next king.
21:26 of Uzza. Then his s Josiah became the next king.
22: 3 King Josiah sent Shaphan s of Azaliah
22:12 Ahikam s of Shaphan, Acbor s of Micaiah,
22:14 She was the wife of Shallum s of Tikvah
23:10 so no one could ever again use it to sacrifice a s
23:15 the pagan shrine that Jeroboam s of Nebat had
23:30 Then the people anointed his s Jehoahaz and made
24: 6 his s Jehoiachin became the next king.
25:22 Then King Nebuchadnezzar appointed Gedaliah s
25:23 These included Ishmael s of Nethaniah, Johanan s
of Kareah,
25:23 Seraiah s of Tanhumeth the Netophathite,
25:23 and Jaazaniah s of the Maacathite, and all their
25:25 Ishmael s of Nethaniah and grandson of Elishama,
1Ch 1:13 Canaan's oldest s was Sidon, the ancestor of the
1:41 The s of Anah was Dishon. The sons of Dishon
1:43 Bela s of Beor, who ruled from his city of
1:44 Jobab s of Zerah from Bozrah became king.
1:46 Hadad s of Bedad became king and ruled from the
1:49 Shaul died, Baal-hanan s of Acbor became king.
2: 3 But the oldest s, Er, was a wicked man,
2: 7 Achan s of Carmi, one of Zerah's descendants,
2: 8 The s of Ethan was Azariah.
2:13 Jesse's first s was Eliab, his second was Abinadab,
2:17 an Ishmaelite, and they had a s named Amasa.
2:18 Hezron's s Caleb had two wives named Azubah
2:19 married Ephrathah, and they had a s named Hur.
2:21 the daughter of Makir. They had a s named Segub.
2:24 his wife Abijah gave birth to a s named Ashhur
2:25 the oldest s of Hezron, were Ram (the oldest),
2:27 the oldest s of Jerahmeel, were Maaz, Jamin,
2:31 but Appaim had a s named Ishi. The s of Ishi was
Sheshan.
2:35 be the wife of Jarha, and they had a s named Attai.
2:42 The oldest s of Caleb, the brother of Jerahmeel,
2:42 Caleb's second s was Mareshah, the father of
2:45 The s of Shammai was Maon. Maon was the father
2:50 of Hur, the oldest s of Caleb's wife Ephrathah,
3:16 Jehoiakim was succeeded by his s Jehoiachin;
3:21 Jeshaiah's s was Rephaiah. Rephaiah's s was
Arnan. Arnan's s was Obadiah. Obadiah's s was
Shecaniah.
4: 2 Shobal's s Reaiah was the father of Jahath.
4: 8 and all the families of Aharhel s of Harum.

4: 15 The sons of Caleb **s** of Jephunneh were Iru, Elah, and Naam. The **s** of Elah was Kenaz.
4: 34 Jamlech, Joshah **s** of Amaziah,
4: 35 Joel, Jehu **s** of Joshibiah, **s** of Seraiah, **s** of Asiel,
4: 37 and Ziza **s** of Shiphi, **s** of Allon, **s** of Jedaiah, **s** of Shimri, **s** of Shemaiah.
5: 1 The oldest **s** of Israel was Reuben. But since he
5: 1 is not listed in the genealogy as the firstborn **s**.
5: 3 the oldest **s** of Israel, were Hanoch, Pallu, Hezron,
5: 8 and Bela **s** of Azaz, **s** of Shema, **s** of Joel.
5: 14 These were all descendants of Abihail **s** of Huri, **s** of Jaroah, **s** of Gilead, **s** of Michael, **s** of Jeshishai, **s** of Jahdo, **s** of Buz.
5: 15 Ahi **s** of Abdiel, **s** of Guni, was the leader of
6: 56 and outlying areas were given to Caleb **s** of
7: 3 The **s** of Uzzi was Izrahiah. The sons of Izrahiah
7: 10 The **s** of Jediael was Bilhan. The sons of Bilhan
7: 12 and Huppim. Hushim was the **s** of Aher.
7: 16 Maacah, gave birth to a **s** whom she named Peresh.
7: 17 The **s** of Ulam was Bedan. All these were
7: 17 descendants of Makir **s** of Manasseh.
7: 23 and she became pregnant and gave birth to a **s**.
7: 29 The descendants of Joseph **s** of Israel lived in these
8: 30 and his oldest **s** was named Abdon. Jeiel's other
9: 4 One family that returned was that of Uthai **s** of Ammihud, **s** of Omri, **s** of Imri, **s** of Bani, a descendant of Perez **s** of Judah.
9: 7 From the tribe of Benjamin came Sallu **s** of Meshullam, **s** of Hodaviah, **s** of Hassenuah;
9: 8 Ibneiah **s** of Jeroham; Elah **s** of Uzzi, **s** of Micri; Meshullam **s** of Shephatiah, **s** of Reuel, **s** of Ibnijah.
9: 11 Azariah **s** of Hilkiah, **s** of Meshullam, **s** of Zadok, **s** of Meraioth, **s** of Ahitub.
9: 12 Other returning priests were Adaiah **s** of Jeroham, **s** of Pashhur, **s** of Malkijah, and Maasai **s** of Adiel, **s** of Jahzerah, **s** of Meshullam, **s** of Meshillemith, **s** of Immer.
9: 14 The Levites who returned were Shemaiah **s** of Hasshub, **s** of Azrikam, **s** of Hashabiah, a descendant of
9: 15 Mattaniah **s** of Mica, **s** of Zicri, **s** of Asaph;
9: 16 Obadiah **s** of Shemaiah, **s** of Galal, **s** of Jeduthun; and Berekiah **s** of Asa, **s** of Elkanah, who lived
9: 19 Shallum was the **s** of Kore, a descendant of
9: 20 Phinehas **s** of Eleazar had been in charge of the
9: 21 And later Zechariah **s** of Meshelemiah had been
9: 31 a Levite and the oldest **s** of Shallum the Korahite,
9: 36 and his oldest **s** was named Abdon. Jeiel's other
9: 43 Binea's **s** was Rephaiah. / Rephaiah's **s** was Eleasah. / Eleasah's **s** was Azel.
10: 14 and turned his kingdom over to David **s** of Jesse.
11: 6 And Joab, the **s** of David's sister Zeruiah,
11: 12 Next in rank among the Three was Eleazar **s** of
11: 22 There was also Benaiah **s** of Jehoiada, a valiant
11: 26 Elhanan **s** of Dodo from Bethlehem;
11: 28 Ira **s** of Ikkesh from Tekoa; / Abiezer from
11: 30 Heled **s** of Baanah from Netophah;
11: 31 Ithai **s** of Ribai from Gibeah (from the tribe of
11: 34 from Gizon; / Jonathan **s** of Shagee from Harar;
11: 35 Ahiam **s** of Sharar from Harar; / Eliphal **s** of Ur;
11: 37 Hezro from Carmel; / Paarai **s** of Ezbai;
11: 38 Joel, the brother of Nathan; / Mibhar **s** of Hagri;
11: 41 Uriah the Hittite; / Zabad **s** of Ahlai;
11: 42 Adina **s** of Shiza, the Reubenite leader who had
11: 43 Hanan **s** of Maacah; / Joshaphat from Mithna;
11: 45 Jediael **s** of Shimri; / Joha, his brother, from Tiz;
12: 1 at Ziklag while he was hiding from Saul **s** of Kish.
12: 3 Their leader was Ahiezer **s** of Shemaah from
12: 18 We are on your side, **s** of Jesse. / Peace
15: 17 So the Levites appointed Heman **s** of Joel, Asaph **s** of Berekiah, and Ethan **s** of Kushaiah from the clan of Merari to
16: 38 This group included Obed-edom (**s** of Jeduthun),
17: 13 I will be his father, and he will be my **s**. I will not
18: 10 he sent his **s** Joram to congratulate David on his
18: 12 Abishai **s** of Zeruiah destroyed eighteen thousand
18: 15 Joab **s** of Zeruiah was commander of the army.
18: 15 Jehoshaphat **s** of Ahilud was the royal historian.
18: 16 Zadok **s** of Ahitub and Ahimelech **s** of Abiathar were the priests.
18: 17 Benaiah **s** of Jehoiada was captain of the king's
19: 1 Ammonites died, and his **s** Hanun became king.
20: 5 Elhanan **s** of Jair killed Lahmi, the brother of
20: 7 by Jonathan, the **s** of David's brother Shimea.
22: 5 "My **s** Solomon is still young and inexperienced,
22: 6 Then David sent for his **s** Solomon and instructed
22: 9 But you will have a **s** who will experience peace
22: 10 my name. He will be my **s**, and I will be his father.
22: 11 "Now, my **s**, may the LORD be with you
23: 1 he appointed his **s** Solomon to be king over Israel.
23: 17 Eliezer had only one **s**, Rehabiah, the family
24: 6 Shemaiah **s** of Nethanel, a Levite, acted as
24: 6 Zadok the priest, Ahimelech **s** of Abiathar,
26: 1 the Korahites, there was Meshelemiah **s** of Kore,
26: 6 Obed-edom's **s** Shemaiah had sons with great
26: 14 The north gate was assigned to his **s** Zechariah,
26: 24 Shebuel was a descendant of Gershom **s** of Moses.
26: 28 Saul **s** of Kish, Abner **s** of Ner, and Joab **s** of Zeruiah.
27: 2 Jashobeam **s** of Zabdiel was commander of the
27: 5 Benaiah **s** of Jehoiada the priest was commander of
27: 6 the Thirty. His **s** Ammizabad was his chief officer.
27: 7 Asahel was succeeded by his **s** Zebadiah.
27: 9 Ira **s** of Ikkesh from Tekoa was commander of the
27: 16 and their leaders: / Reuben | Eliezer **s** of Zicri / Simeon | Shephatiah **s** of Maacah
27: 17 Levi | Hashabiah **s** of Kemuel / Aaron (the priests)
27: 18 brother of David) / Issachar | Omri **s** of Michael
27: 19 Zebulun | Ishmaiah **s** of Obadiah / Naphtali | Jeremoth **s** of Azriel
27: 20 Ephraim | Hoshea **s** of Azaziah / Manasseh (west) | Joel **s** of Pedaiah
27: 21 Manasseh (east) | Iddo **s** of Zechariah / Benjamin | Jaasiel **s** of Abner
27: 22 Dan | Azarel **s** of Jeroham These were the leaders
27: 25 Azmaveth **s** of Adiel was in charge of the palace
27: 25 Jonathan **s** of Uzziah was in charge of the regional
27: 26 Ezri **s** of Kelub was in charge of the field workers
27: 29 Shaphat **s** of Adlai was responsible for the cattle in
27: 34 Ahithophel was succeeded by Jehoiada **s** of
28: 6 'Your **s** Solomon will build my Temple and its courtyards, for I have chosen him as my **s**,
28: 9 "And Solomon, my **s**, get to know the God of your
29: 1 to the entire assembly and said, "My **s** Solomon,
29: 19 Give my **s** Solomon the wholehearted desire to
29: 22 And again they crowned David's **s** Solomon as
29: 26 So David **s** of Jesse reigned over all Israel.
29: 28 and honor. Then his **s** Solomon ruled in his place.
2Ch 1: 1 Solomon, the **s** of King David, now took firm
1: 5 But the bronze altar made by Bezalel **s** of Uri
2: 12 He has given David a wise **s**, gifted with skill
2: 14 the **s** of a woman from Dan in Israel; his father is
9: 29 *of Iddo the Seer,* concerning Jeroboam **s** of Nebat.
9: 31 Then his **s** Rehoboam became the next king.
10: 2 When Jeroboam **s** of Nebat heard of Solomon's
10: 15 **s** of Nebat by the prophet Ahijah from Shiloh.
10: 16 We have no share in Jesse's **s**! Let's go home,
11: 3 "Say to Rehoboam **s** of Solomon, king of Judah,
11: 17 and for three years they supported Rehoboam **s** of
11: 18 the daughter of David's **s** Jerimoth and of Abihail,
11: 18 (Eliab was one of David's brothers, a **s** of Jesse.)
11: 22 Rehoboam made Maacah's **s** Abijah chief among
12: 16 of David. Then his **s** Abijah became the next king.
13: 6 Yet Jeroboam **s** of Nebat, who was a mere servant of David's **s** Solomon,
13: 7 defying Solomon's **s** Rehoboam when he was
14: 1 of David. Then his **s** Asa became the next king.
15: 1 Then the Spirit of God came upon Azariah **s** of
17: 1 Then Jehoshaphat, Asa's **s**, became the next king.
17: 16 Next was Amasiah **s** of Zicri, who volunteered for
18: 1 and he arranged for his **s** to marry the daughter of
18: 7 news for me! His name is Micaiah **s** of Imlah."
18: 8 "Quick! Go and get Micaiah **s** of Imlah."
18: 10 One of them, Zedekiah **s** of Kenaanah, made some
18: 23 Then Zedekiah **s** of Kenaanah walked up to
18: 25 the governor of the city, and to my **s** Joash.
19: 2 Jehu **s** of Hanani the seer went out to meet him.
19: 11 Zebadiah **s** of Ishmael, a leader from the tribe of
20: 14 His name was Jahaziel **s** of Zechariah, **s** of Benaiah, **s** of Jeiel, **s** of Mattaniah,
20: 34 are recorded in *The Record of Jehu S of Hanani,*
20: 37 Then Eliezer **s** of Dodavahu from Mareshah
21: 1 Then his **s** Jehoram became the next king.
21: 17 Only his youngest **s**, Ahaziah, was spared.
22: 1 Jehoram's youngest **s**, their next king.
22: 1 So Ahaziah **s** of Jehoram reigned as king of Judah.
22: 5 with King Joram, the **s** of King Ahab of Israel.
22: 7 went out with Joram to meet Jehu **s** of Nimshi,
22: 10 Ahaziah of Judah, learned that her **s** was dead,
22: 11 of King Jehoram, took Ahaziah's infant **s**, Joash,
23: 1 Azariah **s** of Jeroham, Ishmael **s** of Jehohanan, Azariah **s** of Obed, Maaseiah **s** of Adaiah, and Elishaphat **s** of Zicri.
23: 3 "The time has come for the king's **s** to reign!
23: 11 and his sons brought out Joash, the king's **s**,
24: 20 Then the Spirit of God came upon Zechariah **s** of
24: 22 Jehoiada for his love and loyalty—by killing his **s**.
24: 25 kill him for murdering the **s** of Jehoiada the priest.
24: 26 the **s** of an Ammonite woman named Shimeath,
24: 26 the **s** of a Moabite woman named Shomer.
24: 27 Joash died, his **s** Amaziah became the next king.
25: 17 the **s** of Jehoahaz and grandson of Jehu:
25: 18 'Give your daughter in marriage to my **s**.' But just
26: 1 then crowned Amaziah's sixteen-year-old **s**,
26: 21 His **s** Jotham was put in charge of the royal palace,
26: 22 are recorded by the prophet Isaiah **s** of Amoz.
26: 23 the kings. Then his **s** Jotham became the next king.
27: 9 of David, and his **s** Ahaz became the next king.
28: 3 He offered sacrifices in the valley of the **s** of
28: 6 In a single day Pekah **s** of Remaliah, Israel's king,
28: 7 from Ephraim, killed Maaseiah, the king's **s**;
28: 12 Azariah **s** of Jehohanan, Berekiah **s** of Meshillemoth, Jehizkiah **s** of Shallum, and Amasa **s** of Hadlai—
28: 27 Then his **s** Hezekiah became the next king.
29: 12 Mahath **s** of Amasai and Joel **s** of Azariah.
29: 12 Kish **s** of Abdi and Azariah **s** of Jehallelel.
29: 12 Joah **s** of Zimmah and Eden **s** of Joah.
30: 26 one since the days of Solomon, King David's **s**.
31: 14 Kore **s** of Imnah the Levite, who was the
32: 20 and the prophet Isaiah **s** of Amoz cried out in
32: 32 *S of Amoz,* which is included in *The Book of the*
32: 33 Then his **s** Manasseh became the next king.
33: 6 sons in the fire in the valley of the **s** of Hinnom.
33: 7 where God had told David and his **s** Solomon:
33: 20 his palace. Then his **s** Amon became the next king.
33: 25 and they made his **s** Josiah the next king.
34: 8 Josiah appointed Shaphan **s** of Azaliah,
34: 8 and Joah **s** of Joahaz, the royal historian,
34: 20 Ahikam **s** of Shaphan, Acbor **s** of Micaiah,
34: 22 She was the wife of Shallum **s** of Tikvah
35: 4 of Israel and the instructions of his **s** Solomon.
36: 1 Then the people of the land took Josiah's **s**
36: 8 Then his **s** Jehoiachin became the next
Ezr 3: 2 Then Jeshua **s** of Jehozadak with his fellow priests
3: 2 and Zerubbabel **s** of Shealtiel with his family
3: 8 including Zerubbabel **s** of Shealtiel, Jeshua **s** of Jehozadak and his fellow priests,
5: 1 and Zechariah **s** of Iddo prophesied in the name of
5: 2 Zerubbabel **s** of Shealtiel and Jeshua **s** of Jehozadak responded by beginning
6: 14 of the prophets Haggai and Zechariah **s** of Iddo.
7: 1 He was the **s** of Seraiah, **s** of Azariah, **s** of Hilkiah,
7: 2 **s** of Shallum, **s** of Zadok, **s** of Ahitub,
7: 3 **s** of Amariah, **s** of Azariah, **s** of Meraioth,
7: 4 **s** of Zerahiah, **s** of Uzzi, **s** of Bukki,
7: 5 **s** of Abishua, **s** of Phinehas, **s** of Eleazar, **s** of Aaron the high priest.
8: 3 From the family of David: Hattush **s** of Shecaniah.
8: 4 Eliehoenai **s** of Zerahiah and 200 other men.
8: 5 Shecaniah **s** of Jahaziel and 300 other men.
8: 6 of Adin: Ebed **s** of Jonathan and 50 other men.
8: 7 of Elam: Jeshaiah **s** of Athaliah and 70 other men.
8: 8 Zebadiah **s** of Michael and 80 other men.
8: 9 of Joab: Obadiah **s** of Jehiel and 218 other men.
8: 10 Shelomith **s** of Josiphiah and 160 other men.
8: 11 of Bebai: Zechariah **s** of Bebai and 28 other men.
8: 12 Johanan **s** of Hakkatan and 110 other men.
8: 18 of Mahli, who was a descendant of Levi **s** of Israel.
8: 33 and entrusted to Meremoth **s** of Uriah the priest and to Eleazar **s** of Phinehas, along with Jozabad **s** of Jeshua and Noadiah **s** of Binnui—
10: 2 Then Shecaniah **s** of Jehiel, a descendant of Elam,
10: 6 and went to the room of Jehohanan **s** of Eliashib.
10: 15 Only Jonathan **s** of Asahel and Jahzeiah **s** of Tikvah opposed this course of
10: 18 From the family of Jeshua **s** of Jehozadak and his
Ne 1: 1 These are the memoirs of Nehemiah **s** of Hacaliah.
3: 2 to them, and beyond them was Zaccur **s** of Imri.
3: 4 Meremoth **s** of Uriah and grandson of Hakkoz
3: 4 Beside him were Meshullam **s** of Berekiah
3: 4 of Meshezabel, and then Zadok **s** of Baana.
3: 6 The Old City Gate was repaired by Joiada **s** of Paseah and Meshullam **s** of Besodeiah.
3: 8 Next was Uzziel **s** of Harhaiah, a goldsmith by
3: 9 Rephaiah **s** of Hur, the leader of half the district of
3: 10 Next Jedaiah **s** of Harumaph repaired the wall
3: 10 and next to him was Hattush **s** of Hashabneiah.
3: 11 Then came Malkijah **s** of Harim and Hasshub **s** of Pahath-moab,
3: 12 Shallum **s** of Hallohesh and his daughters repaired
3: 14 The Dung Gate was repaired by Malkijah **s** of
3: 15 Shallum **s** of Col-hozeh, the leader of the Mizpah
3: 16 Next to him was Nehemiah **s** of Azbuk, the leader
3: 17 working under the supervision of Rehum **s** of Bani.
3: 18 were his countrymen led by Binnui **s** of Henadad,
3: 19 Next to them, Ezer **s** of Jeshua, the leader of
3: 20 Next to him was Baruch **s** of Zabbai, who repaired
3: 21 Meremoth **s** of Uriah and grandson of Hakkoz
3: 23 and Azariah **s** of Maaseiah and grandson of
3: 24 Next was Binnui **s** of Henadad, who rebuilt another
3: 25 Palal **s** of Uzai carried on the work from a point
3: 25 the guard. Next to him were Pedaiah **s** of Parosh
3: 29 Next Zadok **s** of Immer also rebuilt the wall next to
3: 29 and beyond him was Shemaiah **s** of Shecaniah,
3: 30 Next Hananiah **s** of Shelemiah and Hanun, the sixth **s** of Zalaph,
3: 30 while Meshullam **s** of Berekiah rebuilt the wall
6: 10 Later I went to visit Shemaiah **s** of Delaiah
6: 18 because his father-in-law was Shecaniah **s** of Arah and because his **s** Jehohanan was married to the daughter of Meshullam **s** of Berekiah.
8: 17 this way since the days of Joshua **s** of Nun.
10: 1 Nehemiah the governor, the **s** of Hacaliah.
10: 9 The Levites who signed were Jeshua **s** of Azaniah,
11: 4 Athaiah **s** of Uzziah, **s** of Zechariah, **s** of Amariah, **s** of Shephatiah, **s** of Mahalalel,
11: 5 and Maaseiah **s** of Baruch, **s** of Col-hozeh, **s** of Hazaiah, **s** of Adaiah, **s** of Joiarib, **s** of Zechariah,
11: 7 Sallu **s** of Meshullam, **s** of Joed, **s** of Pedaiah, **s** of Kolaiah, **s** of Maaseiah, **s** of Ithiel, **s** of Jeshaiah;
11: 9 Their chief officer was Joel **s** of Zicri, who was assisted by Judah **s** of Hassenuah,
11: 10 From the priests: Jedaiah **s** of Joiarib; Jakin;
11: 11 and Seraiah **s** of Hilkiah, **s** of Meshullam, **s** of Zadok, **s** of Meraioth, **s** of Ahitub,
11: 12 there was Adaiah **s** of Jeroham, **s** of Pelaliah, **s** of Amzi, **s** of Zechariah, **s** of Pashhur, **s** of Malkijah;
11: 13 There were also Amashsai **s** of Azarel, **s** of Ahzai, **s** of Meshillemoth, **s** of Immer;
11: 14 Their chief officer was Zabdiel **s** of Haggedolim.
11: 15 Shemaiah **s** of Hasshub, **s** of Azrikam, **s** of Hashabiah, **s** of Bunni;
11: 17 Mattaniah **s** of Mica, **s** of Zabdi, a descendant of Asaph,
11: 17 and Abda **s** of Shammua, **s** of Galal, **s** of Jeduthun.
11: 22 of the Levites in Jerusalem was Uzzi **s** of Bani, **s** of Hashabiah, **s** of Mattaniah, **s** of Mica,
11: 24 Pethahiah **s** of Meshezabel, a descendant of Zerah **s** of Judah,
12: 1 and Levites who had returned with Zerubbabel **s** of
12: 26 These all served in the days of Joiakim **s** of Jeshua,
12: 26 **s** of Jehozadak, and in the days of Nehemiah the
12: 35 Zechariah **s** of Jonathan, **s** of Shemaiah, **s** of Mattaniah, **s** of Micaiah, **s** of Zaccur,
12: 45 required by the laws of David and his **s** Solomon,
13: 13 And I appointed Hanan **s** of Zaccur and grandson
13: 28 One of the sons of Joiada **s** of Eliashib the high
Est 2: 5 there was a certain Jew named Mordecai **s** of Jair.
3: 1 King Xerxes promoted Haman **s** of Hammedatha

3: 10 and giving it to Haman s of Hammedatha the
9: 10 the ten sons of Haman s of Hammedatha,
9: 24 Haman s of Hammedatha the Agagite, the enemy
Job 32: 2 Then Elihu s of Barakel the Buzite, of the clan of
32: 6 Elihu s of Barakel the Buzite said, "I am young
Ps 2: 7 "The LORD said to me, 'You are my s.
2: 12 Submit to God's royal s, or he will become angry,
3: T regarding the time David fled from his s Absalom.
9: T of David, to be sung to the tune "Death of the S."
50: 20 and slander a brother— / your own mother's s.
72: 1 O God, / and righteousness to the king's s.
72: 20 (This ends the prayers of David s of Jesse.)
78: 51 He killed the oldest s in each Egyptian family,
80: 15 have planted, / this s you have raised for yourself.
80: 17 the man you love, / the s of your choice.
89: 27 I will make him my firstborn s, / the mightiest king
116: 16 I am your servant, the s of your handmaid,
Pr 1: 1 the proverbs of Solomon, David's s, king of Israel.
4: 3 For I, too, was once my father's s, tenderly loved
5: 1 My s, pay attention to my wisdom; listen carefully
5: 20 Why be captivated, my s, with an immoral woman,
6: 20 My s, obey your father's commands, and don't
7: 1 Follow my advice, my s; always treasure my
23: 26 O my s, give me your heart. May your eyes delight
30: 1 The message of Agur s of Jakeh. An oracle. I am
31: 2 O my s, O s of my womb, O s of my promises,
Ecc 1: 1 King David's s, who ruled in Jerusalem.
Isa 1: 1 and Jerusalem came to Isaiah s of Amoz during the
2: 1 This is another vision that Isaiah s of Amoz saw
7: 1 During the reign of Ahaz s of Jotham and grandson
7: 1 and King Pekah of Israel, the s of Remaliah.
7: 3 to meet King Ahaz, you and your s Shear-jashub.
7: 4 King Rezin of Aram and Pekah s of Remaliah.
7: 6 and install the s of Tabeel as Judah's king.'
7: 9 is no stronger than its king, Pekah s of Remaliah.
7: 14 She will give birth to a s and will call him
8: 2 Uriah the priest and Zechariah s of Jeberekiah,
8: 3 my wife, and she became pregnant and had a s.
9: 6 For a child is born to us, a s is given to us.
13: 1 Isaiah s of Amoz received this message concerning
14: 12 from heaven, O shining star, s of the morning!
14: 20 your people. Your s will not succeed you as king.
14: 29 his s will be worse than his father ever was.
20: 2 the LORD told Isaiah s of Amoz, "Take off all
22: 20 then I will call my servant Eliakim s of Hilkiah to
36: 3 Eliakim s of Hilkiah, the palace administrator,
36: 3 and Joah s of Asaph, the royal historian.
36: 22 Then Eliakim s of Hilkiah, the palace
36: 22 and Joah s of Asaph, the royal historian, went back
37: 2 in sackcloth, to the prophet Isaiah s of Amoz.
37: 21 Then Isaiah s of Amoz sent this message to
37: 38 and another s, Esarhaddon, became the next king
38: 1 and the prophet Isaiah s of Amoz went to visit him.
39: 1 Soon after this, Merodach-baladan s of Baladan,
66: 7 birth pains even begin, Jerusalem gives birth to a s.
Jer 1: 1 These are the words of Jeremiah s of Hilkiah,
1: 3 give messages throughout the reign of Josiah's s,
6: 26 and weep bitterly, as for the loss of an only s.
7: 31 of Topheth in the valley of the s of Hinnom,
7: 32 be called Topheth or the valley of the s of Hinnom,
15: 4 Because of the wicked things Manasseh s of
19: 2 Go out into the valley of the s of Hinnom by the
19: 6 be called Topheth or the valley of the s of Hinnom,
20: 1 Now Pashhur s of Immer, the priest in charge of
20: 15 who told my father, "Good news—you have a s!"
21: 1 when King Zedekiah sent Pashhur s of Malkijah
and Zephaniah s of Maaseiah,
22: 24 Jehoiachin s of Jehoiakim, king of Judah.
24: 1 of Babylon exiled Jehoiachin s of Jehoiakim,
25: 3 from the thirteenth year of Josiah s of Amon,
26: 1 LORD early in the reign of Jehoiakim s of Josiah,
26: 20 Uriah s of Shemaiah from Kiriath-jearim was also
26: 22 Then King Jehoiakim sent Elnathan s of Acbor to
26: 24 Ahikam s of Shaphan also stood with Jeremiah
27: 1 LORD early in the reign of Zedekiah s of Josiah,
27: 7 All the nations will serve him and his s and his
27: 20 here when he exiled Jehoiachin s of Jehoiakim,
28: 1 Hananiah s of Azzur, a prophet from Gibeon,
28: 4 And I will bring back Jehoiachin s of Jehoiakim,
29: 3 He sent the letter with Elasah s of Shaphan and
Gemariah s of Hilkiah,
29: 21 Ahab s of Kolaiah and Zedekiah s of Maaseiah—
29: 25 on your own authority to Zephaniah s of Maaseiah,
31: 20 "Is not Israel still my s, my darling child?"
32: 7 "Your cousin Hanamel s of Shallum will come
32: 12 and I handed them to Baruch s of Neriah
32: 35 shrines to Baal in the valley of the s of Hinnom,
35: 1 when Jehoiakim s of Josiah was king of Judah:
35: 3 So I went to see Jaazaniah s of Jeremiah
35: 4 room assigned to the sons of Hanan s of Igdaliah,
35: 4 directly above the room of Maaseiah s of Shallum,
35: 6 because Jehonadab s of Recab, our ancestor,
35: 19 Jehonadab s of Recab will always have
36: 1 During the fourth year that Jehoiakim s of Josiah
36: 4 So Jeremiah sent for Baruch s of Neriah, and as
36: 9 during the fifth year of the reign of Jehoiakim s of
36: 10 from the Temple room of Gemariah s of Shaphan.
36: 11 When Micaiah s of Gemariah and grandson of
36: 12 Delaiah s of Shemaiah, Elnathan s of Acbor,
Gemariah s of Shaphan, Zedekiah s of Hananiah,
36: 14 the officials sent Jehudi s of Nethaniah,
36: 26 commanded his s Jerahmeel, Seraiah s of Azriel,
and Shelemiah s of Abdeel to arrest Baruch
37: 1 Zedekiah s of Josiah succeeded Jehoiachin s of
37: 3 King Zedekiah sent Jehucal s of Shelemiah
37: 3 the priest, s of Maaseiah, to ask Jeremiah,
37: 13 The sentry making the arrest was Irijah s of
38: 1 Shephatiah s of Mattan, Gedaliah s of Pashhur,
Jehucal s of Shelemiah, and Pashhur s of Malkijah
39: 14 They put him under the care of Gedaliah s of
40: 5 then return to Gedaliah s of Ahikam and grandson
40: 6 So Jeremiah returned to Gedaliah s of Ahikam at
40: 7 s of Ahikam as governor over the poor people who
40: 8 Ishmael s of Nethaniah, Johanan and Jonathan,
sons of Kareah, Seraiah s of Tanhumeth,
40: 8 Jaazaniah s of the Maacathite, and all their men.
40: 13 Johanan s of Kareah and the other guerrilla leaders
40: 14 has sent Ishmael s of Nethaniah to assassinate
41: 1 Ishmael s of Nethaniah and grandson of Elishama,
41: 9 Ishmael s of Nethaniah filled it with corpses.
41: 11 But when Johanan s of Kareah and the rest of the
41: 16 Then Johanan s of Kareah and his officers led
42: 1 Johanan s of Kareah and Jezaniah s of Hoshaiah,
42: 8 So he called for Johanan s of Kareah and the army
43: 2 Azariah s of Hoshaiah and Johanan s of Kareah
43: 3 Baruch s of Neriah has convinced you to say this,
45: 1 The prophet Jeremiah gave a message to Baruch s
45: 1 fourth year of the reign of Jehoiakim s of Josiah,
46: 2 fourth year of the reign of Jehoiakim s of Josiah,
51: 59 Seraiah s of Neriah and grandson of Mahseiah,
Eze 1: 3 gave a message to me, Ezekiel s of Buzi, a priest,
2: 1 "Stand up, s of man," said the voice. "I want to
2: 3 "S of man," he said, "I am sending you to the
2: 6 S of man, do not fear them. Don't be afraid even
2: 8 S of man, listen to what I say to you. Do not join
3: 1 The voice said to me, "S of man, eat what I am
3: 4 Then he said, "S of man, go to the people of Israel
3: 10 Then he added, "S of man, let all my words sink
3: 17 "S of man, I have appointed you as a watchman
4: 1 "And now, s of man, take a large brick and set it
4: 16 Then he told me, "S of man, I will cause food to
5: 1 "S of man, take a sharp sword and use it as a razor
6: 2 "S of man, look over toward the mountains of
7: 2 "S of man, this is what the Sovereign LORD says
8: 5 said to me, "S of man, look toward the north."
8: 6 "S of man," he said, "do you see what they are
8: 8 He said to me, "Now, s of man, dig into the wall."
8: 11 there with Jaazaniah s of Shaphan in the middle.
8: 12 Then the LORD said to me, "S of man, have you
8: 17 "Have you seen this, s of man?" he asked. "Is it
11: 1 Jaazaniah s of Azzur and Pelatiah s of Benaiah,
11: 2 Then the Spirit said to me, "S of man, these are
11: 4 Therefore, s of man, prophesy against them loudly
11: 13 still speaking, Pelatiah s of Benaiah suddenly died.
11: 15 "S of man, the people still left in Jerusalem are
12: 2 "S of man, you live among rebels who could see
12: 9 "S of man, these rebels, the people of Israel,
12: 18 "S of man, tremble as you eat your food.
12: 22 "S of man, what is that proverb they quote in
12: 27 "S of man, the people of Israel are saying,
13: 2 "S of man, speak against the false prophets of
13: 17 "Now, s of man, also speak out against the women
14: 3 "S of man, these leaders have set up idols in their
14: 13 "S of man, suppose the people of a country were
15: 2 "S of man, how does a grapevine compare to a
16: 2 "S of man, confront Jerusalem with her loathsome
17: 2 "S of man, tell this story to the people of Israel.
18: 10 "But suppose that man has a s who grows up to be
18: 11 And suppose that s does all the evil things his
18: 14 "But suppose that sinful s, in turn, has a s who sees
18: 15 Suppose this s refuses to worship idols on the
18: 16 And suppose this s feeds the hungry,
20: 3 "S of man, give the leaders of Israel this message
20: 4 "S of man, bring judgment against them
20: 27 "Therefore, s of man, give the people of Israel this
20: 46 "S of man, look toward the south and speak out
21: 2 "S of man, look toward Jerusalem and prophesy
21: 6 "S of man, groan before the people! Groan before
21: 9 "S of man, give the people this message from the
21: 12 "S of man, cry out and wail; pound your thighs in
21: 14 "S of man, prophesy to them and clap your hands
21: 19 "S of man, make a map and trace two routes on it
21: 28 "And now, s of man, prophesy concerning the
22: 2 "S of man, are you ready to judge Jerusalem?
22: 18 "S of man, the people of Israel are the worthless
22: 24 "S of man, give the people of Israel this message:
23: 2 "S of man, once there were two sisters who were
23: 36 The LORD said to me, "S of man, you must
24: 2 "S of man, write down today's date, because on
24: 16 "S of man, I am going to take away your dearest
24: 25 Then the LORD said to me, "S of man,
25: 2 "S of man, look toward the land of Ammon
26: 2 "S of man, Tyre has rejoiced over the fall of
27: 2 "S of man, sing a funeral song for Tyre,
28: 2 "S of man, give the prince of Tyre this message
28: 12 "S of man, weep for the king of Tyre. Give him
28: 21 "S of man, look toward the city of Sidon
29: 2 "S of man, turn toward Egypt and prophesy
29: 18 "S of man, the army of King Nebuchadnezzar of
30: 2 "S of man, prophesy and give this message from
30: 21 "S of man, I have broken the arm of Pharaoh,
31: 2 "S of man, give this message to Pharaoh, king of
32: 2 "S of man, mourn for Pharaoh, king of Egypt,
32: 18 "S of man, weep for the hordes of Egypt and for
33: 2 "S of man, give your people this message: When I
33: 7 "Now, s of man, I am making you a watchman for
33: 10 "S of man, give the people of Israel this message:
33: 12 "S of man, give your people this message:
33: 24 "S of man, the scattered remnants of Judah living
33: 30 "S of man, your people are whispering behind
34: 2 "S of man, prophesy against the shepherds,
35: 2 "S of man, turn toward Mount Seir, and prophesy
36: 1 "S of man, prophesy to Israel's mountains.
36: 3 Therefore, s of man, give the mountains of Israel
36: 17 "S of man, when the people of Israel were living
37: 3 Then he asked me, "S of man, can these bones
37: 11 Then he said to me, "S of man, these bones
37: 16 "S of man, take a stick and carve on it these
38: 2 "S of man, prophesy against Gog of the land of
38: 14 "Therefore, s of man, prophesy against Gog.
39: 1 "S of man, prophesy against Gog. Give him this
39: 17 "And now, s of man, call all the birds and wild
40: 4 He said to me, "S of man, watch and listen.
43: 7 And the LORD said to me, "S of man, this is the
43: 10 "S of man, describe to the people of Israel the
43: 18 Then he said to me, "S of man, this is what the
44: 5 LORD said to me, "S of man, take careful notice;
Da 8: 17 "S of man," he said, "you must understand that
9: 1 the s of Ahasuerus, who became king of the
Hos 1: 1 The LORD gave these messages to Hosea s of
1: 1 and Jeroboam s of Jehoash was king of Israel.
1: 3 and she became pregnant and gave Hosea a s.
1: 8 became pregnant and gave birth to a second s.
11: 1 "When Israel was a child, I loved him as a s, and I
called my s out of Egypt.
Joel 1: 1 The LORD gave this message to Joel s of
Am 1: 1 king of Judah and Jeroboam II, the s of Jehoash,
2: 7 Both father and s sleep with the same woman,
8: 10 as signs of sorrow, as if your only s had died.
Jnh 1: 1 The LORD gave this message to Jonah s of
Mic 5: 3 time when the woman in labor gives birth to her s.
6: 5 and how Balaam s of Beor blessed you instead?
7: 6 For the s despises his father. The daughter defies
Zep 1: 1 when Josiah s of Amon was king of Judah.
1: 1 Zephaniah was the s of Cushi, s of Gedaliah, s of
Amariah, s of Hezekiah.
Hag 1: 1 the prophet Haggai to Zerubbabel s of Shealtiel,
1: 1 and to Jeshua s of Jehozadak, the high priest.
1: 12 Then Zerubbabel s of Shealtiel, Jeshua s of
Jehozadak, the high priest,
1: 14 the enthusiasm of Zerubbabel s of Shealtiel,
1: 14 of Judah, Jeshua s of Jehozadak, the high priest,
2: 2 "Say this to Zerubbabel s of Shealtiel, governor of
2: 2 and to Jeshua s of Jehozadak, the high priest,
2: 4 Take courage, Jeshua s of Jehozadak, the high
2: 23 honor you, Zerubbabel s of Shealtiel, my servant.
Zec 1: 1 message to the prophet Zechariah s of Berekiah
1: 7 message to the prophet Zechariah s of Berekiah
6: 10 meet them at the home of Josiah s of Zephaniah.
6: 11 Then put the crown on the head of Jeshua s of
6: 14 Tobijah, Jedaiah, and Josiah s of Zephaniah."
12: 10 have pierced and mourn for him as for an only s.
12: 10 They will grieve bitterly for him as for a firstborn s
Mal 1: 6 "A s honors his father, and a servant respects his
Mt 1: 20 "Joseph, s of David," the angel said, "do not be
1: 21 And she will have a s, and you are to name him
1: 23 will conceive a child! / She will give birth to a s,
1: 25 but she remained a virgin until her s was born.
2: 15 through the prophet: "I called my S out of Egypt."
2: 22 that the new ruler was Herod's s Archelaus,
3: 17 a voice from heaven said, "This is my beloved S,
4: 3 and said to him, "If you are the S of God,
4: 6 and said, "If you are the S of God, jump off!
8: 20 and birds have nests, but I, the S of Man, have no
8: 29 at him, "Why are you bothering us, S of God?
9: 2 Jesus said to the paralyzed man, "Take heart, s!
9: 6 I will prove that I, the S of Man, have the authority
9: 27 shouting, "S of David, have mercy on us!"
10: 2 Andrew (Peter's brother), / James (s of Zebedee),
10: 3 (the tax collector), / James (s of Alphaeus),
10: 23 I assure you that I, the S of Man, will return before
10: 37 or if you love your s or daughter more than me,
11: 19 And I, the S of Man, feast and drink, and you say,
11: 27 No one really knows the S except the Father, and
no one really knows the Father except the S and
those to whom the S chooses to reveal him."
12: 8 For I, the S of Man, am master even of the
12: 23 "Could it be that Jesus is the S of David,
12: 32 against me, the S of Man, can be forgiven,
12: 40 for three days and three nights, so I, the S of Man,
13: 37 "I, the S of Man, am the farmer who plants the
13: 41 I, the S of Man, will send my angels, and they will
13: 55 He's just a carpenter's s, and we know Mary,
14: 33 "You really are the S of God!" they exclaimed.
15: 22 "Have mercy on me, O Lord, S of David!
16: 13 "Who do people say that the S of Man is?"
16: 16 "You are the Messiah, the S of the living God."
16: 17 Jesus replied, "You are blessed, Simon s of John,
16: 27 For I, the S of Man, will come in the glory of my
16: 28 see me, the S of Man, coming in my Kingdom."
17: 5 voice from the cloud said, "This is my beloved S,
17: 9 the S of Man, have been raised from the dead."
17: 12 And soon the S of Man will also suffer at their
17: 15 "Lord, have mercy on my s, because he has
17: 22 told them, "The S of Man is going to be betrayed.
19: 28 "I assure you that when I, the S of Man,
20: 18 "the S of Man will be betrayed to the leading
20: 28 For even I, the S of Man, came here not to be
20: 30 "Lord, S of David, have mercy on us!"
20: 31 "Lord, S of David, have mercy on us!"
21: 9 were shouting, / "Praise God for the S of David!
21: 15 "Praise God for the S of David."
21: 28 'S, go out and work in the vineyard today.'
21: 29 The s answered, 'No, I won't go,' but later he
21: 30 Then the father told the other s, 'You go,' and he
21: 37 "Finally, the owner sent his s, thinking, 'Surely
they will respect my s.'
21: 38 "But when the farmers saw his s coming, they said
22: 2 king who prepared a great wedding feast for his s.
22: 42 Whose s is he?" They replied, "He is the s of
David."

22:45 him Lord, how can he be his **s** at the same time?"
23:15 then you turn him into twice the **s** of hell as you
23:35 from righteous Abel to Zechariah **s** of Barachiah,
24:27 entire sky, so it will be when the **S** of Man comes.
24:30 the sign of the coming of the **S** of Man will appear
24:30 And they will see the **S** of Man arrive on the
24:36 not even the angels in heaven or the **S** himself.
24:37 "When the **S** of Man returns, it will be like it was
24:39 That is the way it will be when the **S** of Man
24:44 For the **S** of Man will come when least expected.
25:31 "But when the **S** of Man comes in his glory,
26: 2 and I, the **S** of Man, will be betrayed
26:24 For I, the **S** of Man, must die, as the Scriptures
26:45 I, the **S** of Man, am betrayed into the hands of
26:63 us whether you are the Messiah, the **S** of God."
26:64 And in the future you will see me, the **S** of Man,
27:40 Well then, if you are the **S** of God, save yourself
27:43 For he said, 'I am the **S** of God.' "
27:54 They said, "Truly, this was the **S** of God!"
28:19 name of the Father and the **S** and the Holy Spirit.
Mk 1: 1 Good News about Jesus the Messiah, the **S** of God.
1:11 "You are my beloved **S**, and I am fully pleased
2: 5 paralyzed man, "My **s**, your sins are forgiven."
2:10 I will prove that I, the **S** of Man, have the authority
2:14 he saw Levi **s** of Alphaeus sitting at his
2:28 And I, the **S** of Man, am master even of the
3:11 in front of him shrieking, "You are the **S** of God!"
3:18 Matthew, / Thomas, / James (**s** of Alphaeus),
5: 7 you bothering me, Jesus, **S** of the Most High God?
6: 3 the **s** of Mary and brother of James, Joseph, Judas,
8:31 the **S** of Man, would suffer many terrible things
8:38 in these adulterous and sinful days, I, the **S** of Man,
9: 7 voice from the cloud said, "This is my beloved **S**.
9: 9 until he, the **S** of Man, had risen from the dead.
9:12 then is it written in the Scriptures that the **S** of Man
9:17 "Teacher, I brought my **s** for you to heal him.
9:31 to them, "The **S** of Man is going to be betrayed.
10:33 "the **S** of Man will be betrayed to the leading
10:45 For even I, the **S** of Man, came here not to be
10:46 A blind beggar named Bartimaeus (**s** of Timaeus)
10:47 "Jesus, **S** of David, have mercy on me!"
10:48 shouted louder, "**S** of David, have mercy on me!"
12: 6 was only one left—his **s** whom he loved dearly.
12: 6 sent him, thinking, 'Surely they will respect my **s**.'
12:35 law claim that the Messiah will be the **s** of David?
12:37 him Lord, how can he be his **s** at the same time?"
13:26 Then everyone will see the **S** of Man arrive on the
13:32 not even the angels in heaven or the **S** himself.
13:34 "The coming of the **S** of Man can be compared
14:21 For I, the **S** of Man, must die, as the Scriptures
14:41 I, the **S** of Man, am betrayed into the hands of
14:61 "Are you the Messiah, the **S** of the blessed God?"
14:62 "I am, and you will see me, the **S** of Man,
15:39 he exclaimed, "Truly, this was the **S** of God!"
Lk 1:13 and your wife, Elizabeth, will bear you a **s**!
1:31 You will become pregnant and have a **s**, and you
1:32 and will be called the **S** of the Most High.
1:35 will be holy, and he will be called the **S** of God.
1:76 "And you, my little **s**, / will be called the prophet
2: 7 She gave birth to her first child, a **s**. She wrapped
2:48 "**S**!" his mother said to him. "Why have you
3: 2 At this time a message from God came to John **s** of
3:22 a voice from heaven said, "You are my beloved **S**,
3:23 Jesus was known as the **s** of Joseph. / Joseph was the **s** of Heli.
3:24 Heli was the **s** of Matthat. / Matthat was the **s** of Levi. / Levi was the **s** of Melki. / Melki was the **s** of Jannai. / Jannai was the **s** of Joseph.
3:25 Joseph was the **s** of Mattathias. / Mattathias was the **s** of Amos. / Amos was the **s** of Nahum. / Nahum was the **s** of Esli. / Esli was the **s** of Naggai.
3:26 Naggai was the **s** of Maath. / Maath was the **s** of Mattathias. / Mattathias was the **s** of Semein. / Semein was the **s** of Josech. / Josech was the **s** of Joda.
3:27 Joda was the **s** of Joanan. / Joanan was the **s** of Rhesa. / Rhesa was the **s** of Zerubbabel. / Zerubbabel was the **s** of Shealtiel. / Shealtiel was the **s** of Neri.
3:28 Neri was the **s** of Melki. / Melki was the **s** of Addi. / Addi was the **s** of Cosam. / Cosam was the **s** of Elmadam. / Elmadam was the **s** of Er.
3:29 Er was the **s** of Joshua. / Joshua was the **s** of Eliezer. / Eliezer was the **s** of Jorim. / Jorim was the **s** of Matthat. / Matthat was the **s** of Levi.
3:30 Levi was the **s** of Simeon. / Simeon was the **s** of Judah. / Judah was the **s** of Joseph. / Joseph was the **s** of Jonam. / Jonam was the **s** of Eliakim.
3:31 Eliakim was the **s** of Melea. / Melea was the **s** of Menna. / Menna was the **s** of Mattatha. / Mattatha was the **s** of Nathan. / Nathan was the **s** of David.
3:32 David was the **s** of Jesse. / Jesse was the **s** of Obed. / Obed was the **s** of Boaz. / Boaz was the **s** of Salmon. / Salmon was the **s** of Nahshon
3:33 Nahshon was the **s** of Amminadab. / Amminadab was the **s** of Admin. / Admin was the **s** of Arni. / Arni was the **s** of Hezron. / Hezron was the **s** of Perez. / Perez was the **s** of Judah.
3:34 Judah was the **s** of Jacob. / Jacob was the **s** of Isaac. / Isaac was the **s** of Abraham. / Abraham was the **s** of Terah. / Terah was the **s** of Nahor.
3:35 Nahor was the **s** of Serug. / Serug was the **s** of Reu. / Reu was the **s** of Peleg. / Peleg was the **s** of Eber. / Eber was the **s** of Shelah.
3:36 Shelah was the **s** of Cainan. / Cainan was the **s** of Arphaxad. / Arphaxad was the **s** of Shem. / Shem was the **s** of Noah. / Noah was the **s** of Lamech.
3:37 Lamech was the **s** of Methuselah. / Methuselah was the **s** of Enoch. / Enoch was the **s** of Jared. / Jared was the **s** of Mahalalel. / Mahalalel was the **s** of Kenan.
3:38 Kenan was the **s** of Enosh. / Enosh was the **s** of Seth. / Seth was the **s** of Adam. / Adam was the **s** of God.
4: 3 the Devil said to him, "If you are the **S** of God,
4: 9 and said, "If you are the **S** of God, jump off!
4:22 can this be?" they asked. "Isn't this Joseph's **s**?"
4:41 his command, shouting, "You are the **S** of God."
5:20 Seeing their faith, Jesus said to the man, "**S**,
5:24 I will prove that I, the **S** of Man, have the authority
6: 5 And Jesus added, "I, the **S** of Man, am master
6:15 Matthew, / Thomas, / James (**s** of Alphaeus),
6:16 Judas (**s** of James), / Judas Iscariot (who later
6:22 because you are identified with me, the **S** of Man.
7:12 The boy who had died was the only **s** of a widow,
7:34 And I, the **S** of Man, feast and drink, and you say,
8:28 you bothering me, Jesus, **S** of the Most High God?
9:22 "For I, the **S** of Man, must suffer many terrible
9:26 ashamed of me and my message, I, the **S** of Man,
9:35 the cloud said, "This is my **S**, my Chosen One.
9:38 "Teacher, look at my boy, who is my only **s**.
9:44 what I say. The **S** of Man is going to be betrayed."
9:58 and birds have nests, but I, the **S** of Man, have no
10:22 No one really knows the **S** except the Father, and no one really knows the Father except the **S** and those to whom the **S** chooses to reveal him."
11:30 God has sent me, the **S** of Man, to these people.
12: 8 me publicly here on earth, I, the **S** of Man,
12:10 Yet those who speak against the **S** of Man may be
12:40 for the **S** of Man will come when least expected."
12:53 There will be a division between father and **s**,
14: 5 If your **s** or your cow falls into a pit, don't you
15:12 The younger **s** told his father, 'I want my share of
15:13 "A few days later this younger **s** packed all his
15:19 and I am no longer worthy of being called your **s**.
15:20 he ran to his **s**, embraced him, and kissed him.
15:21 His **s** said to him, 'Father, I have sinned against
15:21 and I am no longer worthy of being called your **s**.'
15:24 for this **s** of mine was dead and has now returned
15:25 "Meanwhile, the older **s** was in the fields working.
15:30 Yet when this **s** of yours comes back after
15:31 said to him, 'Look, dear **s**, you and I are very close,
16:25 "But Abraham said to him, '**S**, remember that
17:22 you will long to share in the days of the **S** of Man,
17:23 "Reports will reach you that the **S** of Man has
17:24 For when the **S** of Man returns, you will know it
17:25 But first the **S** of Man must suffer terribly and be
17:26 "When the **S** of Man returns, the world will be like
17:30 right up to the hour when the **S** of Man returns.
18: 8 But when I, the **S** of Man, return, how many will I
18:31 prophets concerning the **S** of Man will come true.
18:38 "Jesus, **S** of David, have mercy on me!"
18:39 shouted louder, "**S** of David, have mercy on me!"
19: 9 for this man has shown himself to be a **s** of
19:10 And I, the **S** of Man, have come to seek and save
20:13 asked himself. 'I know! I'll send my cherished **s**.
20:14 "But when the farmers saw his **s**, they said to each
20:41 "that the Messiah is said to be the **s** of David?
20:44 him Lord, how can he be his **s** at the same time?"
21:27 Then everyone will see the **S** of Man arrive on the
21:36 these horrors and stand before the **S** of Man."
22:22 For I, the **S** of Man, must die since it is part of
22:48 can you betray me, the **S** of Man, with a kiss?"
22:69 But the time is soon coming when I, the **S** of Man,
22:70 "Then you claim you are the **S** of God?"
24: 7 that the **S** of Man must be betrayed into the hands
Jn 1:14 his glory, the glory of the only **S** of the Father.
1:18 But his only **S**, who is himself God, is near to the
1:34 to Jesus, so I testify that he is the **S** of God."
1:42 Jesus said, "You are Simon, the **s** of John—
1:45 His name is Jesus, the **s** of Joseph from Nazareth."
1:47 "Here comes an honest man—a true **s** of Israel."
1:49 "Teacher, you are the **S** of God—
1:51 of God going up and down upon the **S** of Man."
3:13 For only I, the **S** of Man, have come to earth
3:14 so I, the **S** of Man, must be lifted up on a pole,
3:16 so loved the world that he gave his only **S**,
3:17 God did not send his **S** into the world to condemn
3:18 been judged for not believing in the only **S** of God.
3:35 The Father loves his **S**, and he has given him
3:36 And all who believe in God's **S** have eternal life.
3:36 Those who don't obey the **S** will never experience
4: 5 near the parcel of ground that Jacob gave to his **s**
4:46 in the city of Capernaum whose **s** was very sick.
4:47 him to come to Capernaum with him to heal his **s**,
4:50 Jesus told him, "Go back home. Your **s** will live!"
4:51 servants met him with the news that his **s** was alive
4:53 time that Jesus had told him, "Your **s** will live."
5:19 "I assure you, the **S** can do nothing by himself.
5:19 Whatever the Father does, the **S** also does.
5:20 For the Father loves the **S** and tells him everything
5:20 and the **S** will do far greater things than healing
5:22 And the Father leaves all judgment to his **S**,
5:23 so that everyone will honor the **S**, just as they
5:23 But if you refuse to honor the **S**, then you are
5:25 will hear my voice—the voice of the **S** of God.
5:26 and he has granted his **S** to have life in himself.
5:27 to judge all mankind because he is the **S** of Man.
5:28 dead in their graves will hear the voice of God's **S**,
6:27 the eternal life that I, the **S** of Man, can give you.
6:40 For it is my Father's will that all who see his **S**
6:42 They said, "This is Jesus, the **s** of Joseph.
6:53 unless you eat the flesh of the **S** of Man and drink
6:62 you see me, the **S** of Man, return to heaven again?
6:71 **s** of Simon Iscariot, one of the Twelve, who would
7:23 For if the correct time for circumcising your **s** falls
8:28 "When you have lifted up the **S** of Man on the
8:35 of the family, but a **s** is part of the family forever.
8:36 So if the **S** sets you free, you will indeed be free.
9:19 They asked them, "Is this your **s**? Was he born
9:20 "We know this is our **s** and that he was born blind,
9:35 and said, "Do you believe in the **S** of Man?"
10:36 the world by the Father says, 'I am the **S** of God'?
11: 4 I, the **S** of God, will receive glory from this."
11:27 always believed you are the Messiah, the **S** of God,
12:23 "The time has come for the **S** of Man to enter into
12:34 Why are you saying the **S** of Man will die? Who is this **S** of Man you are talking about?"
13: 2 **s** of Simon Iscariot, to carry out his plan to betray
13:26 dipped it, he gave it to Judas, **s** of Simon Iscariot.
13:31 the **S** of Man, to enter into my glory, and God will
14:13 because the work of the **S** brings glory to the
17: 1 Glorify your **S** so he can give glory back to you.
19: 7 to die because he called himself the **S** of God."
19:26 he loved, he said to her, "Woman, he is your **s**."
20:31 the **S** of God, and that by believing in him you will
21:15 "Simon **s** of John, do you love me more than
21:16 "Simon **s** of John, do you love me?" "Yes,
21:17 asked him, "Simon **s** of John, do you love me?"
Ac 1:13 Bartholomew, / Matthew, / James (**s** of Alphaeus),
1:13 Simon (the Zealot), / and Judas (**s** of James).
4:36 Barnabas (which means "**S** of Encouragement").
7: 8 And so Isaac, Abraham's **s**, was circumcised when
7:21 daughter found him and raised him as her own **s**.
7:56 and the **S** of Man standing in the place of honor at
9:20 saying, "He is indeed the **S** of God!"
13:10 "You **s** of the Devil, full of every sort of trickery
13:21 and God gave them Saul **s** of Kish, a man of the
13:22 'David **s** of Jesse is a man after my own heart,
13:33 when it says concerning Jesus, / 'You are my **S**.
20: 4 They were Sopater of Berea, the **s** of Pyrrhus;
Ro 1: 3 It is the Good News about his **S**, Jesus, who came
1: 4 And Jesus Christ our Lord was shown to be the **S**
1: 9 heart by telling others the Good News about his **S**.
5:10 the death of his **S** while we were still his enemies,
8: 3 He sent his own **S** in a human body like ours,
8: 3 God destroyed sin's control over us by giving his **S**
8:17 for everything God gives to his **S**, Christ, is ours
8:29 and he chose them to become like his **S**,
8:29 so that his **S** would be the firstborn, with many
8:32 Since God did not spare even his own **S** but gave
9: 7 "Isaac is the **s** through whom your descendants
9: 9 "Next year I will return, and Sarah will have a **s**."
9:10 This **s** was our ancestor Isaac. When he grew up,
9:12 "The descendants of your older **s** will serve the descendants of your younger **s**."
1Co 1: 9 you into this wonderful friendship with his **S**,
15:28 the **S** will present himself to God, so that God, who gave his **S** authority over all things,
2Co 1:19 because Jesus Christ, the **S** of God, never wavers
9:15 Thank God for his **S**—a gift too wonderful for
Gal 1:16 Then he revealed his **S** to me so that I could
2:20 life in this earthly body by trusting in the **S** of God,
4: 4 God sent his **S**, born of a woman, subject to the
4: 6 God has sent the Spirit of his **S** into your hearts,
4:23 The **s** of the slave-wife was born in a human
4:23 But the **s** of the freeborn wife was born as God's
4:29 was persecuted by Ishmael, the **s** of the slave-wife.
4:30 "Get rid of the slave and her **s**, for the **s** of the slave woman will not share the family inheritance with the free woman's **s**."
Eph 1: 6 out on us because we belong to his dearly loved **S**.
1: 7 purchased our freedom through the blood of his **S**,
4:13 and knowledge of God's **S** that we will be mature
Php 2:22 Like a **s** with his father, he has helped me in
Col 1:13 he has brought us into the Kingdom of his dear **S**.
1Th 1:10 forward to the coming of God's **S** from heaven—
1Ti 1:18 Timothy, my **s**, here are my instructions for you,
2Ti 1: 2 It is written to Timothy, my dear **s**. May God our
2: 1 Timothy, my dear **s**, be strong with the special
Phm 1:10 I think of him as my own **s** because he became a
Heb 1: 2 these final days, he has spoken to us through his **S**.
1: 2 God promised everything to the **S** as an
1: 2 and through the **S** he made the universe
1: 3 The **S** reflects God's own glory, and everything
1: 4 This shows that God's **S** is far greater than the
1: 5 "You are my **S**. / Today I have become your
1: 5 "I will be his Father, / and he will be my **S**."
1: 6 when he presented his honored **S** to the world,
1: 8 But to his **S** he says, / "Your throne, O God,
1:13 And God never said to an angel, as he did to his **S**,
2: 6 and the **s** of man that you should care for him?
3: 6 But Christ, the faithful **S**, was in charge of the
4:14 Priest who has gone to heaven, Jesus the **S** of God.
5: 5 chosen by God, who said to him, / "You are my **S**.
5: 8 So even though Jesus was God's **S**, he learned
6: 6 because they are nailing the **S** of God to the cross
7: 3 remains a priest forever, resembling the **S** of God.
7:28 law was given, God appointed his **S** with an oath, and his **S** has been made perfect forever.
10:29 be for those who have trampled on the **S** of God
11:17 was ready to sacrifice his only **s**, Isaac,
11:18 "Isaac is the **s** through whom your descendants
11:19 Abraham did receive his **s** back from the dead.
11:24 refused to be treated as the **s** of Pharaoh's
12:16 He traded his birthright as the oldest **s** for a single
Jas 2:21 because of what he did when he offered his **s** Isaac
1Pe 5:13 Rome sends you greetings, and so does my **s** Mark.
2Pe 1:17 called down from heaven, "This is my beloved **S**;
2:15 and followed the way of Balaam **s** of Beor,
1Jn 1: 3 our fellowship is with the Father and with his **S**,

1: 7 and the blood of Jesus, his **S**, cleanses us from
2:22 for they have denied the Father and the **S**.
2:23 Anyone who denies the **S** doesn't have the Father
2:23 But anyone who confesses the **S** has the Father
2:24 you will continue to live in fellowship with the **S**
3: 8 But the **S** of God came to destroy these works of
3:23 We must believe in the name of his **S**, Jesus Christ,
4: 9 he loved us by sending his only **S** into the world
4:10 and sent his **S** as a sacrifice to take away our sins.
4:14 and now testify that the Father sent his **S** to be the
4:15 All who proclaim that Jesus is the **S** of God have
5: 5 are the ones who believe that Jesus is the **S** of God.
5: 6 And Jesus Christ was revealed as God's **S** by his
5: 9 from God. And God has testified about his **S**.
5:10 All who believe in the **S** of God know that this is
5:10 don't believe what God has testified about his **S**.
5:11 He has given us eternal life, and this life is in his **S**.
5:12 So whoever has God's **S** has life; whoever does
not have his **S** does not have life.
5:13 I write this to you who believe in the **S** of God,
5:18 for God's **S** holds them securely, and the evil one
5:20 And we know that the **S** of God has come, and he
5:20 And now we are in God because we are in his **S**,
2Jn 1: 3 from God our Father and from Jesus Christ his **S**,
1: 9 have fellowship with both the Father and the **S**.
Rev 1:13 in the middle of the lampstands was the **S** of Man.
2:18 This is the message from the **S** of God, whose eyes
14:14 Then I saw the **S** of Man sitting on a white cloud.

SON'S (9) [SON]

Ge 24: 7 you find a young woman there to be my **s** wife.
30:15 Now will you steal my **s** mandrake roots, too?"
37:33 "Yes," he said, "it is my **s** robe. A wild animal
Lev 18:10 whether your **s** daughter or your daughter's
18:15 with your daughter-in-law; she is your **s** wife.
18:17 whether her **s** daughter or her daughter's daughter.
2Sa 14:11 "not a hair on your **s** head will be disturbed!"
14:15 my life and my **s** life have been threatened.
Pr 30: 4 What is his name—and his **s** name? Tell me if you

SON-IN-LAW (4) [SON]

1Sa 18:18 my family in Israel that I should be the king's **s**?"
18:21 "I have a way for you to become my **s** after all!"
18:22 you accept the king's offer and become his **s**?"
22:14 your servants who is as faithful as David, your **s**?

SONG (90) [SING]

Ex 15: 1 and the people of Israel sang this **s** to the LORD:
15: 2 The LORD is my strength and my **s**; / he has
15:21 And Miriam sang this **s**: / "I will sing to the
Nu 21:17 There the Israelites sang this **s**: / "Spring up,
Dt 31:19 "Now write down the words of this **s**, and teach it
31:21 and this **s** will stand as evidence against them,
31:22 that very day Moses wrote down the words of the **s**
31:30 So Moses recited this entire **s** to the assembly of
32:44 and recited all the words of this **s** to the people.
Jdg 5: 1 and Barak son of Abinoam sang this **s**:
5: 3 I will lift up my **s** to the LORD, the God of Israel.
5:12 Wake up, wake up, and sing a **s**! / Arise, Barak!
1Sa 18: 7 This was their **s**: / "Saul has killed his thousands,
2Sa 1:17 Then David composed a funeral **s** for Saul
1:18 It is known as the **S** of the Bow, and it is recorded
3:33 Then the king sang this funeral **s** for Abner:
22: 1 David sang this **s** to the LORD after the LORD
1Ch 15:27 the Ark, the singers, and Kenaniah the **s** leader.
16: 7 and his fellow Levites this **s** of thanksgiving to the
Ezr 3:11 and thanks, they sang this **s** to the LORD:
Job 30: 9 "And now their sons mock me with their vulgar **s**!
Ps 18: T He sang this **s** to the LORD on the day the
26: 7 singing a **s** of thanksgiving / and telling of all your
40: 3 He has given me a new **s** to sing, / a hymn of
45: T to be sung to the tune "Lilies." A love **s**.
46: T of Korah, to be sung by soprano voices. A **s**.
48: T A psalm of the descendants of Korah. A **s**.
57: 8 and lyre! / I will waken the dawn with my **s**.
65: T For the choir director: A psalm of David. A **s**.
66: T For the choir director: A psalm. A **s**.
67: T to be accompanied by stringed instruments. A **s**.
68: T For the choir director: A psalm of David. A **s**.
75: T to be sung to the tune "Do Not Destroy!" A **s**.
76: T to be accompanied by stringed instruments. A **s**.
83: T A psalm of Asaph. A **s**.
87: T A psalm of the descendants of Korah. A **s**.
88: T A psalm of Heman the Ezrahite. A **s**.
92: T A psalm to be sung on the LORD's Day. A **s**.
96: 1 Sing a new **s** to the LORD! / Let the whole earth
98: 1 Sing a new **s** to the LORD, / for he has done
98: 5 with the harp, / with the harp and melodious **s**,
108: T A psalm of David. A **s**.
108: 2 and lyre! / I will waken the dawn with my **s**.
118:14 The LORD is my strength and my **s**; / he has
120: T A **s** for the ascent to Jerusalem.
121: T A **s** for the ascent to Jerusalem.
122: T A **s** for the ascent to Jerusalem. A psalm of David.
123: T A **s** for the ascent to Jerusalem.
124: T A **s** for the ascent to Jerusalem. A psalm of David.
125: T A **s** for the ascent to Jerusalem.
126: T A **s** for the ascent to Jerusalem.
127: T A **s** for the ascent to Jerusalem. A psalm of
128: T A **s** for the ascent to Jerusalem.
129: T A **s** for the ascent to Jerusalem.
130: T A **s** for the ascent to Jerusalem.
131: T A **s** for the ascent to Jerusalem. A psalm of David.
132: T A **s** for the ascent to Jerusalem.
133: T A **s** for the ascent to Jerusalem. A psalm of David.
134: T A **s** for the ascent to Jerusalem.
137: 3 For there our captors demanded a **s** of us.
144: 9 I will sing a new **s** to you, O God! / I will sing your
149: 1 Praise the LORD! / Sing to the LORD a new **s**.
SS 1: 1 This is Solomon's **s** of songs, more wonderful than
Isa 5: 1 Now I will sing a **s** for the one I love about his
12: 2 The LORD GOD is my strength and my **s**;
14: 8 and the cedars of Lebanon—sing out this joyous **s**:
24: 9 Gone are the joys of wine and **s**; strong drink now
26: 1 everyone in the land of Judah will sing this **s**:
30:29 But the people of God will sing a **s** of joy,
42:10 Sing a new **s** to the LORD! / Sing his praises
44:23 Break forth into **s**, O mountains and forests
49:13 Rejoice, O earth! Burst into **s**, O mountains!
52: 9 Let the ruins of Jerusalem break into joyful **s**,
54: 1 Break forth into loud and joyful **s**, O Jerusalem,
55:12 The mountains and hills will burst into **s**,
Eze 19: 1 "Sing this funeral **s** for the princes of Israel:
19:14 This is a funeral **s**, and it is now time for the
26:17 Then they will wail for you, singing this funeral **s**:
27: 2 "Son of man, sing a funeral **s** for Tyre,
27:32 they wail and mourn, they sing this sad funeral **s**:
32:16 this is the funeral **s** they will sing for Egypt.
Am 5: 1 of Israel! Listen to this funeral **s** I am singing:
Mic 2: 4 by singing this **s** of despair about your experience:
Zep 3:17 He will exult over you by singing a happy **s**."
Gal 4:27 Break forth into loud and joyful **s**,
Rev 5: 9 And they sang a new **s** with these words:
14: 3 This great choir sang a wonderful new **s** in front of
14: 3 And no one could learn this **s** except those 144,000
15: 3 And they were singing the **s** of Moses, the servant
of God, and the **s** of the Lamb:

SONGS (53) [SING]

2Sa 6: 5 singing **s** and playing all kinds of musical
1Ki 4:32 composed some 3,000 proverbs and wrote 1,005 **s**.
1Ch 15:16 and musicians to sing joyful **s** to the
16:42 and other instruments to accompany the **s** of praise
23:30 and evening they stood before the LORD to sing **s**
2Ch 29:27 **s** of praise to the LORD were begun,
35:25 The prophet Jeremiah composed funeral **s** for
35:25 and to this day choirs still sing these sad **s** about
35:25 These **s** of sorrow have become a tradition and are
Ne 12: 8 who with his associates was in charge of the **s** of
12:27 in the joyous occasion with their **s** of thanksgiving
Job 35:10 God my Creator, the one who gives **s** in the night?
36:24 glorify his mighty works, singing **s** of praise.
Ps 28: 7 is filled with joy. / I burst out in **s** of thanksgiving.
32: 7 You surround me with **s** of victory. / *Interlude*
33: 3 Sing new **s** of praise to him; / play skillfully on the
42: 8 love upon me, / and through each night I sing his **s**,
63: 5 richest of foods. / I will praise you with **s** of joy.
66: 4 your praises, / shouting your name in glorious **s**."
77: 6 when my nights were filled with joyful **s**. / I search
78:63 young women died before singing their wedding **s**.
98: 8 hands in glee! / Let the hills sing out their **s** of joy
101: 1 and justice. / I will praise you, LORD, with **s**.
118:15 **S** of joy and victory are sung in the camp of the
137: 3 "Sing us one of those **s** of Jerusalem!"
137: 4 But how can we sing the **s** of the LORD / while in
Pr 25:20 Singing cheerful **s** to a person whose heart is heavy
SS 1: 1 This is Solomon's song of **s**, more wonderful than
Isa 23:15 come back to life and sing sweet **s** like a prostitute.
23:16 will take a harp, walk the streets, and sing her **s**,
25: 5 So the boastful **s** of ruthless people are stilled.
30:29 sing a song of joy, like the **s** at the holy festivals.
35:10 return to Jerusalem, singing **s** of everlasting joy.
51: 3 Lovely **s** of thanksgiving will fill the air.
51:11 return to Jerusalem, singing **s** of everlasting joy.
Jer 30:19 There will be joy and **s** of thanksgiving, and I will
31:12 and sing **s** of joy on the heights of Jerusalem.
33:11 along with the joyous **s** of people bringing
La 3:14 at me. All day long they sing their mocking **s**.
3:63 they constantly mock me with their **s**.
Eze 2:10 I saw that both sides were covered with funeral **s**,
26:13 I will stop the music of your **s**. No more will the
33:32 like someone who sings love **s** with a beautiful
Am 6: 5 You sing idle **s** to the sound of the harp, and you
8:10 and your **s** of joy will be turned to weeping.
Jnh 2: 9 But I will offer sacrifices to you with **s** of praise,
Mt 11:17 'We played wedding **s** and you weren't happy,
11:17 so we played funeral **s**, but you weren't sad.'
Lk 7:32 'We played wedding **s** and you weren't happy,
7:32 so we played funeral **s**, but you weren't sad.'
Eph 5:19 and hymns and spiritual **s** among yourselves,
Col 3:16 and spiritual **s** to God with thankful hearts.
Rev 18:22 heard there—no more harps, **s**, flutes, or trumpets.

SONS (735) [SON]

AARON'S SONS (13) Ex 28:4,40; 40:31; Lev 1:5,8,11; 2:2; 3:2; 6:14; 8:13,24; 10:1; Nu 3:2

KING'S SONS (7) 2Sa 13:23; 2Ki 10:2,5,6,7,8; 1Ch 27:32

SONS AND DAUGHTERS (61) Ge 5:4,7,10,13,16,19, 22,26,30; 11:11,13,15,17,19,21,23,25; 46:7; Ex 3:22; 10:9; 20:10; 32:2; Lev 10:14; 26:29; Nu 18:19; Dt 5:14; 7:3; 12:12, 31; 28:32,41,53; 32:19; 2Sa 5:13; 2Ki 17:17; 1Ch 14:3; 2Ch 24:3; 29:9; 31:18; Job 1:13,18; Ps 106:38; Isa 43:6; 56:5; Jer 3:24; 7:31; 14:16; 19:9; 32:35; 48:46; La 1:18; Eze 16:20; 23:4,47; 24:21,25; Joel 2:28; 3:8; Am 7:17; Ac 2:17; 2Co 6:18

SONS OF AARON (7) Lev 1:7; 3:5,8,13; 1Ch 6:3; 24:1; 2Ch 26:18

SONS OF ISRAEL (9) Ge 50:25; Ex 13:2,19; Nu 3:41,46, 49,50; 8:18; 1Ch 2:1

SONS OF LEVI (4) Ge 46:11; 1Ch 6:1,16; 23:6

Ge 5: 4 800 years, and he had other **s** and daughters.
5: 7 807 years, and he had other **s** and daughters.
5:10 815 years, and he had other **s** and daughters.
5:13 840 years, and he had other **s** and daughters.
5:16 lived 830 years, and he had other **s** and daughters.
5:19 800 years, and he had other **s** and daughters.
5:22 with God, and he had other **s** and daughters.
5:26 782 years, and he had other **s** and daughters.
5:30 lived 595 years, and he had other **s** and daughters.
5:32 the time Noah was 500 years old, he had three **s**:
6: 2 the **s** of God saw the beautiful women of the
6: 4 for whenever the **s** of God had intercourse with
6:10 Noah had three **s**: Shem, Ham, and Japheth.
6:18 with your wife and your **s** and their wives.
7: 7 he and his wife and his **s** and their wives.
7:13 into the boat that very day with his wife and his **s**
8:18 his wife, and his **s** and their wives left the boat.
9: 1 God blessed Noah and his **s** and told them,
9: 8 Then God told Noah and his **s**,
9:18 Shem, Ham, and Japheth, the three **s** of Noah,
9:19 From these three **s** of Noah came all the people
10: 1 of Shem, Ham, and Japheth, the three **s** of Noah.
10:21 **S** were also born to Shem, the older brother of
10:25 Eber had two **s**. The first was named Peleg—
10:32 These are the families that came from Noah's **s**,
11:11 another 500 years and had other **s** and daughters.
11:13 another 403 years and had other **s** and daughters.
11:15 another 403 years and had other **s** and daughters.
11:17 another 430 years and had other **s** and daughters.
11:19 another 209 years and had other **s** and daughters.
11:21 another 207 years and had other **s** and daughters.
11:23 another 200 years and had other **s** and daughters.
11:25 another 119 years and had other **s** and daughters.
18:19 I have singled him out so that he will direct his **s**
19:12 sons-in-law, **s**, daughters, or anyone else.
22:20 his brother Nahor's wife, had borne Nahor eight **s**.
22:24 In addition to his eight **s** from Milcah, Nahor had
25: 3 Jokshan's two **s** were Sheba and Dedan.
25: 4 Midian's **s** were Ephah, Epher, Hanoch, Abida,
25: 6 he gave gifts to the **s** of his concubines and sent
25: 9 His **s** Isaac and Ishmael buried him in the cave of
25:16 These twelve **s** of Ishmael became the founders of
25:23 "The **s** in your womb will become two rival
27:29 May all your mother's **s** bow low before you.
29:34 affection for me, since I have given him three **s**!"
30:20 he will honor me, for I have given him six **s**."
30:35 He placed them in the care of his **s**,
31: 1 But Jacob soon learned that Laban's **s** were
32:22 and eleven **s** across the Jabbok River.
34: 5 but his **s** were out in the fields herding cattle
34: 7 He arrived just as Jacob's **s** were coming in from
34: 8 Hamor told Jacob and his **s**, "My son Shechem is
34: 9 We invite you to let your daughters marry our **s**,
34:27 Then all of Jacob's **s** plundered the town
35:22 These are the names of the twelve **s** of Jacob:
35:23 The **s** of Leah were Reuben (Jacob's oldest son),
35:24 The **s** of Rachel were Joseph and Benjamin.
35:25 The **s** of Bilhah, Rachel's servant, were Dan
35:26 The **s** of Zilpah, Leah's servant, were Gad
35:26 These were the **s** born to Jacob at Paddan-aram.
35:29 in death. Then his **s**, Esau and Jacob, buried him.
36: 5 Esau and Oholibamah had **s** named Jeush, Jalam,
36: 5 All these **s** were born to Esau in the land of
36:10 Among Esau's **s** were Eliphaz, the son of Esau's
36:11 The **s** of Eliphaz were Teman, Omar, Zepho,
36:13 The **s** of Reuel were Nahath, Zerah, Shammah,
36:14 Esau also had **s** through Oholibamah, the daughter
36:15 The **s** of Esau's oldest son, Eliphaz,
36:17 The **s** of Esau's son Reuel became the leaders of
36:18 The **s** of Esau and his wife Oholibamah became the
36:22 The **s** of Lotan were Hori and Heman.
36:23 The **s** of Shobal were Alvan, Manahath, Ebal,
36:24 The **s** of Zibeon were Aiah and Anah. This is the
36:26 The **s** of Dishon were Hemdan, Eshban, Ithran,
36:27 The **s** of Ezer were Bilhan, Zaavan, and Akan.
36:28 The **s** of Dishan were Uz and Aran.
37: 2 the **s** of his father's wives Bilhah and Zilpah.
38:27 of Tamar's delivery arrived, and she had twin **s**.
41:50 two **s** were born to Joseph and his wife, Asenath,
42: 1 he said to his **s**, "Why are you standing around
42: 5 So Jacob's **s** arrived in Egypt along with others to
42:32 We are twelve brothers, **s** of one father;
42:37 "You may kill my two **s** if I don't bring Benjamin
43: 2 Jacob said to his **s**, "Go again and buy us a little
44:27 said to us, 'You know that my wife had two **s**,
45:21 So the **s** of Jacob did as they were told.
46: 5 left Beersheba, and his **s** brought him to Egypt.
46: 7 **s** and daughters, grandsons and granddaughters—
46: 9 The **s** of Reuben were Hanoch, Pallu, Hezron,
46:10 The **s** of Simeon were Jemuel, Jamin, Ohad,
46:11 The **s** of Levi were Gershon, Kohath, and Merari.
46:12 The **s** of Judah were Er, Onan, Shelah, Perez,
46:12 The **s** of Perez were Hezron and Hamul.
46:13 The **s** of Issachar were Tola, Puah, Jashub,
46:14 The **s** of Zebulun were Sered, Elon, and Jahleel.
46:15 These are the **s** of Jacob who were born to Leah in
46:16 The **s** of Gad were Zephon, Haggi, Shuni, Ezbon,
46:17 The **s** of Asher were Imnah, Ishvah, Ishvi,
46:17 named Serah. Beriah's **s** were Heber and Malkiel.
46:19 The **s** of Jacob's wife Rachel were Joseph
46:20 Joseph's **s**, born in the land of Egypt,
46:21 Benjamin's **s** were Bela, Beker, Ashbel, Gera,
46:24 The **s** of Naphtali were Jahzeel, Guni, Jezer,
46:27 Joseph also had two **s** who had been born in Egypt.
48: 1 and he took with him his two **s**, Manasseh
48: 5 Now I am adopting as my own **s** these two boys of
48: 8 at the two boys. "Are these your **s**?" he asked.

48: 9 "these are the **s** God has given me here in Egypt."
49: 1 Then Jacob called together all his **s** and said,
49: 2 "Come and listen, O **s** of Jacob; / listen to Israel,
49:28 blessings with which Jacob blessed his twelve **s**.
49:33 Then when Jacob had finished this charge to his **s**,
50:12 So Jacob's **s** did as he had commanded them.
50:25 Then Joseph made the **s** of Israel swear an oath,
Ex 1: 1 These are the **s** of Jacob who went with their father
3:22 this clothing, you will dress your **s** and daughters.
4:20 So Moses took his wife and **s**, put them on a
10: 9 "We will take our **s** and daughters and our flocks
11: 5 All the firstborn **s** will die in every family in
12:12 and kill all the firstborn **s** and firstborn male
12:29 killed all the firstborn **s** in the land of Egypt,
13: 2 "Dedicate to me all the firstborn **s** of Israel
13:12 All firstborn **s** and firstborn male animals must be
13:15 except that the firstborn **s** are always redeemed.'
13:19 for Joseph had made the **s** of Israel swear that they
18: 2 Zipporah, and his two **s** to live with Jethro,
18: 5 and he brought Moses' wife and two **s** with him.
18: 6 visit you. Your wife and your two **s** are with him."
20:10 your **s** and daughters, your male and female
21: 4 and they had **s** or daughters, then the man will be
22:29 payment for redemption of your firstborn **s**.
27:21 and his **s** will keep the lamps burning in the
28: 1 Aaron, and his **s**, Nadab, Abihu, Eleazar,
28: 4 **s** to wear when they serve as priests before me.
28:40 "Then for Aaron's **s**, make tunics, sashes,
28:41 Clothe Aaron and his **s** with these garments,
28:43 whenever Aaron and his **s** enter the Tabernacle
29: 1 for the dedication of Aaron and his **s** as priests:
29: 4 and his **s** at the entrance of the Tabernacle,
29: 8 Next present his **s**, and dress them in their tunics
29: 9 In this way, you will ordain Aaron and his **s**.
29:10 and his **s** will lay their hands on its head.
29:15 and his **s** must lay their hands on the head of one
29:19 have Aaron and his **s** lay their hands on its head
29:20 on the tip of the right earlobes of Aaron and his **s**.
29:21 Sprinkle it on Aaron and his **s** and on their clothes.
29:22 is the ram for the ordination of Aaron and his **s**,
29:24 and his **s** to be lifted up as a special gift to the
29:27 the ordination ram that belong to Aaron and his **s**.
29:32 Aaron and his **s** are to eat this meat, along with the
29:35 you will ordain Aaron and his **s** to their offices.
29:44 and I will set apart Aaron and his **s** as holy,
30:19 Aaron and his **s** will wash their hands and feet
30:30 Use this oil also to anoint Aaron and his **s**,
31:10 and the garments for his **s** to wear as they minister
32: 2 "Tell your wives and **s** and daughters to take off
32:29 him even though it meant killing your own **s**
34:16 who worship other gods, as wives for your **s**.
34:16 Then they will cause your **s** to commit adultery
35:19 and his **s** to wear while officiating as priests."
39:27 made for Aaron and his **s** from fine linen cloth.
39:41 the priest and for his **s** to wear while on duty.
40:12 and his **s** to the entrance of the Tabernacle,
40:14 Then bring his **s** and dress them in their tunics.
40:31 and Aaron and Aaron's **s** washed their hands
Lev 1: 5 the LORD's presence, and Aaron's **s**, the priests,
1: 7 the **s** of Aaron the priest will build a wood fire on
1: 8 Aaron's **s** will then put the pieces of the animal,
1:11 Aaron's **s**, the priests, will sprinkle its blood
2: 2 Bring this offering to one of Aaron's **s**, and he will
2: 3 rest of the flour will be given to Aaron and his **s**.
2:10 will be given to Aaron and his **s** as their food.
3: 2 Aaron's **s**, the priests, will then sprinkle the
3: 5 The **s** of Aaron will burn these on the altar on top
3: 8 The **s** of Aaron will then sprinkle the sheep's blood
3:13 Then the **s** of Aaron will sprinkle the goat's blood
6: 9 and his **s** the following instructions regarding the
6:14 Aaron's **s** must present this offering to the LORD
6:16 flour will belong to Aaron and his **s** for their food.
6:20 "On the day Aaron and his **s** are anointed,
6:22 As the **s** of the priests replace their fathers,
6:25 and his **s** these further instructions regarding the
7:10 are to be shared among all the priests and their **s**.
7:31 but the breast will belong to Aaron and his **s**.
8: 2 "Now bring Aaron and his **s**, along with their
8: 6 Then he presented Aaron and his **s** and washed
8:13 Next Moses presented Aaron's **s** and clothed them
8:14 and Aaron and his **s** laid their hands on its head
8:18 and Aaron and his **s** laid their hands on its head
8:22 Aaron and his **s** laid their hands on its head
8:24 Next he presented Aaron's **s** and put some of the
8:27 He gave all of these to Aaron and his **s**, and he
8:30 and his clothing and on his **s** and their clothing.
8:30 he made Aaron and his **s** and their clothing holy.
8:31 Then Moses said to Aaron and his **s**, "Boil the rest
8:36 and his **s** did everything the LORD had
9: 1 together Aaron and his **s** and the leaders of Israel.
9: 9 His **s** brought him the blood, and he dipped his
9:12 His **s** brought him the blood, and he sprinkled it
9:18 His **s** brought him the blood, and he sprinkled it
10: 1 Aaron's **s** Nadab and Abihu put coals of fire in
10: 4 Aaron's cousins, the **s** of Aaron's uncle Uzziel.
10: 6 Moses said to Aaron and his **s** Eleazar and Ithamar,
10:12 Then Moses said to Aaron and his remaining **s**,
10:14 These parts have been given to you and to your **s**
10:16 with Eleazar and Ithamar, Aaron's remaining **s**.
10:19 Then Aaron answered Moses on behalf of his **s**.
10:19 "Today my **s** presented both their sin offering
13: 2 be brought to Aaron the priest or to one of his **s**.
16: 1 spoke to Moses after the death of Aaron's two **s**,
17: 2 "Give Aaron and his **s** and all the Israelites these
21:24 to Aaron and his **s** and to all the Israelites.
22: 2 and his **s** to treat the sacred gifts that the Israelites
22:18 "Give Aaron and his **s** and all the Israelites these
26:29 You will eat the flesh of your own **s** and daughters.
Nu 3: 2 Aaron's **s** were Nadab (the firstborn), Abihu,
3: 4 Since they had no **s**, this left only Eleazar
3: 9 the Levites to Aaron and his **s** as their assistants.
3:10 and his **s** to carry out the duties of the priesthood.
3:12 for all the firstborn **s** of the people of Israel.
3:13 because all the firstborn **s** are mine. From the day I killed all the firstborn **s** of the
3:17 Levi had three **s**, who were named Gershon,
3:38 for the tents of Moses and of Aaron and his **s**,
3:40 "Now count all the firstborn **s** in Israel who are
3:41 for me as substitutes for the firstborn **s** of Israel;
3:42 So Moses counted the firstborn **s** of the people of
3:43 The total number of firstborn **s** who were one
3:45 "Take the Levites in place of the firstborn **s** of the
3:46 To redeem the 273 firstborn **s** of Israel who are in
3:48 and his **s** as the redemption price for the extra firstborn **s**."
3:49 **s** of Israel who exceeded the number of Levites.
3:50 The silver collected on behalf of these firstborn **s**
3:51 to Aaron and his **s** as the LORD had commanded.
4: 5 and his **s** must enter the Tabernacle first to take
4:11 and his **s** must also spread a dark blue cloth over
4:15 and his **s** have finished covering the sanctuary
4:19 Aaron and his **s** must always go in with them
4:27 and his **s** will direct the Gershonites regarding their
6:23 and his **s** to bless the people of Israel with this
6:27 and his **s** will designate the Israelites as my people,
8:13 have the Levites stand in front of Aaron and his **s**,
8:16 in place of all the firstborn **s** of the Israelites;
8:17 night I killed all the firstborn **s** of the Egyptians.
8:18 I claim the Levites in place of all the firstborn **s** of
8:19 I have assigned the Levites to Aaron and his **s**.
8:22 to perform their duties, helping Aaron and his **s**.
16: 1 conspired with Dathan and Abiram, the **s** of Eliab,
16:12 summoned Dathan and Abiram, the **s** of Eliab,
18: 1 "You, your **s**, and your relatives from the tribe of
18: 1 and your **s** alone will be held liable for violations
18: 2 and your **s** as you perform the sacred duties in
18: 7 But you and your **s**, the priests, must personally
18: 8 offerings to you and your **s** as your regular share.
18: 9 that portion belongs to you and your **s**.
18:15 But you must always redeem your firstborn **s**
18:19 They are for you and your **s** and daughters, to be
21:29 of Chemosh! / Chemosh has left his **s** as refugees,
21:35 and killed King Og, his **s**, and his subjects;
26:11 However, the **s** of Korah did not die that day.
26:12 These were the clans descended from the **s** of
26:15 These were the clans descended from the **s** of Gad:
26:19 Judah had two **s**, Er and Onan, who had died in the
26:20 clans descended from Judah's surviving **s**:
26:23 These were the clans descended from the **s** of
26:26 These were the clans descended from the **s** of
26:33 Hepher's son, Zelophehad, had no **s**, but his
26:35 These were the clans descended from the **s** of
26:38 These were the clans descended from the **s** of
26:42 These were the clans descended from the **s** of Dan:
26:44 These were the clans descended from the **s** of
26:48 These were the clans descended from the **s** of
27: 3 died in the wilderness without leaving any **s**,"
27: 4 of our father disappear just because he had no **s**?
27: 8 'If a man dies and has no **s**, then give his
33: 4 the Egyptians were burying all their firstborn **s**,
Dt 2:33 and we crushed him, his **s**, and all his people.
5:14 your **s** and daughters, your male and female
7: 3 and **s** marry their **s** and daughters.
11: 6 what he did to Dathan and Abiram (the **s** of Eliab,
12:12 You must celebrate there with your **s**
12:31 They have even burned their **s** and daughters as
21:15 and not the other, and both have given him **s**.
28:32 You will watch as your **s** and daughters are taken
28:41 You will have **s** and daughters, but you will not
28:53 so severe that you will eat the flesh of your own **s**
32:19 He was provoked to anger by his own **s**
33:24 "May Asher be blessed above other **s**; / may he be
Jos 5: 7 So Joshua circumcised their **s** who had not been
7:24 his **s**, daughters, cattle, donkeys, sheep, tent,
16: 4 The families of Joseph's **s**, Manasseh and Ephraim,
17: 3 of Manasseh, Makir, and Gilead, had no **s**.
24:32 the **s** of Hamor for one hundred pieces of silver.
Jdg 1:20 who were descendants of the three **s** of Anak.
3: 6 Israelite **s** married their daughters, and Israelite daughters were given in marriage to their **s**.
8:30 He had seventy **s**, for he had many wives.
9: 2 they want to be ruled by all seventy of Gideon's **s**
9:18 his descendants, killing his seventy **s** on one stone.
9:24 of Shechem for murdering Gideon's seventy **s**.
10: 4 His thirty **s** rode around on thirty donkeys,
11: 2 Gilead's wife also had several **s**, and when these
12: 9 and he had thirty **s** and thirty daughters.
12: 9 young women from outside his clan to marry his **s**.
12:14 He had forty **s** and thirty grandsons, who rode on
17: 5 Then he installed one of his **s** as the priest.
17:11 agreed to this and became like one of Micah's **s**.
Ru 1: 1 He took his wife and two **s** and went to live in the
1: 2 was Naomi. Their two **s** were Mahlon and Kilion.
1: 3 Elimelech died and Naomi was left with her two **s**.
1: 4 The two **s** married Moabite women. One married a
1: 5 This left Naomi alone, without her husband or **s**.
1:11 Can I still give birth to other **s** who could grow up
1:12 and I were to get married tonight and bear **s**,
4:15 and who has been better to you than seven **s**!"
1Sa 1: 3 of the LORD at that time were the two **s** of Eli—
1: 8 You have me—isn't that better than having ten **s**?"
2:12 Now the **s** of Eli were scoundrels who had no
2:13 Eli's **s** would send over a servant with a
2:14 that whatever it brought up be given to Eli's **s**.
2:21 And the LORD gave Hannah three **s** and two
2:22 but he was aware of what his **s** were doing to the
2:22 that his **s** were seducing the young women who
2:24 You must stop, my **s**! The reports I hear among the
2:25 But Eli's **s** wouldn't listen to their father,
2:29 Why do you honor your **s** more than me—for you
2:34 I will cause your two **s**, Hophni and Phinehas,
3:13 because his **s** are blaspheming God and he hasn't
3:14 and his **s** will never be forgiven by sacrifices
4: 4 Hophni and Phinehas, the **s** of Eli, helped carry the
4:11 and Phinehas, the two **s** of Eli, were killed.
4:17 Your two **s**, Hophni and Phinehas, were killed,
8: 1 he appointed his **s** to be judges over Israel.
8: 2 Joel and Abijah, his oldest **s**, held court in
8: 5 "you are now old, and your **s** are not like you.
8:11 "The king will draft your **s** into his army and make
12: 2 I have selected him ahead of my own **s**, and I stand
14:49 Saul's **s** included Jonathan, Ishbosheth,
14:51 Kish, were brothers; both were **s** of Abiel.
15:33 "As your sword has killed the **s** of many mothers,
16: 1 for I have selected one of his **s** to be my new
16: 3 and I will show you which of his **s** to anoint for
16: 5 rite for Jesse and his **s** and invited them,
16:10 In the same way all seven of Jesse's **s** were
16:11 Samuel asked, "Are these all the **s** you have?"
17:12 an old man at that time, and he had eight **s** in all.
17:13 Jesse's three oldest **s**—Eliab, Abinadab,
17:14 David was the youngest of Jesse's **s**. Since David's
22:20 one of the **s** of Ahimelech, escaped and fled to
28:19 and you and your **s** will be here with me.
31: 2 The Philistines closed in on Saul and his **s**, and they killed three of his **s**—
31: 6 So Saul, three of his **s**, his armor bearer, and his
31: 7 had been routed and that Saul and his **s** were dead,
31: 8 the bodies of Saul and his three **s** on Mount Gilboa.
31:12 the bodies of Saul and his **s** down from the wall.
2Sa 2:18 Joab, Abishai, and Asahel, the three **s** of Zeruiah,
3: 2 These were the **s** who were born to David in
3: 5 These **s** were all born to David in Hebron.
3:39 I am the anointed king, these two **s** of Zeruiah—
4: 2 They were **s** of Rimmon, who was a Benjaminite
4: 5 and Baanah, the **s** of Rimmon from Beeroth,
5:13 and concubines, and he had many **s** and daughters.
5:14 These are the names of David's **s** who were born in
6: 3 Uzzah and Ahio, Abinadab's **s**, were guiding the
8:18 David's **s** served as priestly leaders.
9: 3 "Yes, one of Jonathan's **s** is still alive,
9:10 You and your **s** and servants are to farm the land
9:10 Ziba, who had fifteen **s** and twenty servants,
9:11 with David, as though he were one of his own **s**.
13:23 Absalom invited all the king's **s** to come to a feast.
13:27 king until he finally agreed to let all his **s** attend,
13:29 Then the other **s** of the king jumped on their mules
13:30 "Absalom has killed all your **s**; not one is left
13:32 and said, "No, not all your **s** have been killed!
13:33 No, your **s** aren't all dead! It was only Amnon."
13:35 they are now! Your **s** are coming, just as I said."
14: 6 "My two **s** had a fight out in the field. And since
14:27 He had three **s** and one daughter. His daughter's
15:36 and they will send their **s** Ahimaaz and Jonathan to
16:10 "What am I going to do with you **s** of Zeruiah!
19: 5 "We saved your life today and the lives of your **s**,
19:17 of Saul, and Ziba's fifteen **s** and twenty servants.
19:22 "What am I going to do with you **s** of Zeruiah!"
21: 6 So let seven of Saul's **s** or grandsons be handed
21: 8 But he gave them Saul's two **s** Armoni
21: 8 He also gave them the five **s** of Saul's daughter
23:32 Eliahba from Shaalbon; / the **s** of Jashen;
1Ki 1: 9 all his brothers—the other **s** of King David—
1:19 and he has invited all your **s** and Abiathar the
1:25 and he has invited your **s** to attend the celebration.
2: 7 "Be kind to the **s** of Barzillai from Gilead.
4: 3 Elihoreph and Ahijah, the **s** of Shisha, were court
4:31 and Heman, Calcol, and Darda—the **s** of Mahol.
8:19 the one to do it. One of your **s** will build it instead.'
11:20 up in Pharaoh's palace among Pharaoh's own **s**.
13:11 and his **s** came home and told him what the man of
13:27 Then the prophet said to his **s**, "Saddle a donkey
13:31 Afterward the prophet said to his **s**, "When I die,
14:10 bring disaster on your dynasty and kill all your **s**,
21:29 It will happen to his **s**; I will destroy all his
2Ki 4: 1 has come, threatening to take my two **s** as slaves."
4: 4 Then go into your house with your **s** and shut the
4: 5 Her **s** brought many jars to her, and she filled one
4: 6 "Bring me another jar," she said to one of her **s**.
4: 7 money left over to support you and your **s**."
9:26 murder of Naboth and his **s** that I saw yesterday.'
10: 1 Now Ahab had seventy **s** living in the city of
10: 1 the people, and to the guardians of King Ahab's **s**.
10: 2 "The king's **s** are with you, and you have at your
10: 3 select the best qualified of King Ahab's **s** to be
10: 5 the other leaders and the guardians of the king's **s**,
10: 6 bring the heads of the king's **s** to me at Jezreel at
10: 6 Now the seventy **s** of the king were being cared for
10: 7 the leaders killed all seventy of the king's **s**.
10: 8 "They have brought the heads of the king's **s**."
10:13 We are going to visit the **s** of King Ahab
17:17 They even sacrificed their own **s** and daughters in
19:37 his **s** Adrammelech and Sharezer killed him with
23:34 then installed Eliakim, another of Josiah's **s**,
25: 7 made Zedekiah watch as all his **s** were killed.
1Ch 1: 4 The **s** of Noah were Shem, Ham, and Japheth.
1:19 Eber had two **s**. The first was named Peleg—
1:28 The **s** of Abraham were Isaac and Ishmael.
1:29 The **s** of Ishmael were Nebaioth (the oldest),
1:31 and Kedemah. These were the **s** of Ishmael.
1:32 The **s** of Keturah, Abraham's concubine,

1:32 The s of Jokshan were Sheba and Dedan.
1:33 The s of Midian were Ephah, Epher, Hanoch,
1:33 All these were s of Abraham by his concubine
1:34 of Isaac. The s of Isaac were Esau and Israel.
1:35 The s of Esau were Eliphaz, Reuel, Jeush, Jalam,
1:36 The s of Eliphaz were Teman, Omar, Zepho,
1:37 The s of Reuel were Nahath, Zerah, Shammah,
1:38 The s of Seir were Lotan, Shobal, Zibeon, Anah,
1:39 The s of Lotan were Hori and Heman.
1:40 The s of Shobal were Alvan, Manahath, Ebal,
1:40 and Onam. The s of Zibeon were Aiah and Anah.
1:41 The s of Dishon were Hemdan, Eshban, Ithran,
1:42 The s of Ezer were Bilhan, Zaavan, and Akan. The s of Dishan were Uz and Aran.
2: 1 The s of Israel were Reuben, Simeon, Levi, Judah,
2: 3 Judah had three s through Bathshua, a Canaanite
2: 4 Later Judah had twin s through Tamar,
2: 4 were Perez and Zerah. So Judah had five s in all.
2: 5 The s of Perez were Hezron and Hamul.
2: 6 The s of Zerah were Zimri, Ethan, Heman, Calcol,
2: 9 The s of Hezron were Jerahmeel, Ram, and Caleb.
2:16 Zeruiah had three s named Abishai, Joab,
2:18 Azubah's s were named Jesher, Shobab,
2:25 The s of Jerahmeel, the oldest son of Hezron,
2:27 The s of Ram, the oldest son of Jerahmeel,
2:28 The s of Onam were Shammai and Jada. The s of Shammai were Nadab and Abishur.
2:29 The s of Abishur and his wife Abihail were Ahban
2:30 The s of Nadab were Seled and Appaim.
2:32 Jada, had two s named Jether and Jonathan.
2:33 but Jonathan had two s named Peleth and Zaza.
2:34 Sheshan had no s, though he did have daughters.
2:43 The s of Hebron were Korah, Tappuah, Rekem,
2:47 The s of Jahdai were Regem, Jotham, Geshan,
2:50 The s of Hur, the oldest son of Caleb's wife
3: 1 These were the s who were born to David in
3: 4 These six s were born to David in Hebron,
3: 5 The s born to David in Jerusalem included Shimea,
3: 5 the daughter of Ammiel, was the mother of these s.
3: 6 David also had nine other s: Ibhar, Elishua,
3: 9 These were the s of David, not including the s of his concubines.
3:15 The s of Josiah were Johanan (the oldest),
3:17 The s of Jehoiachin, who was taken prisoner by the
3:19 The s of Pedaiah were Zerubbabel and Shimei.
3:19 The s of Zerubbabel were Meshullam
3:20 His five other s were Hashubah, Ohel, Berekiah,
3:21 The s of Hananiah were Pelatiah and Jeshaiah.
3:22 Shecaniah's descendants were Shemaiah and his s,
3:23 The s of Neariah were Elioenai, Hizkiah,
3:24 The s of Elioenai were Hodaviah, Eliashib,
4:13 The s of Kenaz were Othniel and Seraiah.
4:13 Othniel's s were Hathath and Meonothai.
4:15 The s of Caleb son of Jephunneh were Iru, Elah,
4:16 The s of Jehallelel were Ziph, Ziphah, Tiria,
4:17 The s of Ezrah were Jether, Mered, Epher,
4:19 One of her s was the father of Keilah the Garmite,
4:20 The s of Shimon were Amnon, Rinnah, Ben-hanan,
4:21 Shelah was one of Judah's s. The descendants of
4:24 The s of Simeon were Nemuel, Jamin, Jarib,
4:27 Shimei had sixteen s and six daughters, but none of
4:42 Neariah, Rephaiah, and Uzziel—all s of Ishi.
5: 1 his birthright was given to the s of his brother
5: 3 The s of Reuben, the oldest son of Israel,
6: 1 The s of Levi were Gershon, Kohath, and Merari.
6: 3 The s of Aaron were Nadab, Abihu, Eleazar,
6:16 The s of Levi were Gershon, Kohath, and Merari.
6:28 The s of Samuel were Joel (the older) and Abijah
6:33 These are the men who served, along with their s:
7: 1 The four s of Issachar were Tola, Puah, Jashub,
7: 2 The s of Tola were Uzzi, Rephaiah, Jeriel, Jahmai,
7: 3 The s of Izrahiah were Michael, Obadiah, Joel,
7: 4 for all five of them had many wives and many s.
7: 6 Three of Benjamin's s were Bela, Beker,
7: 7 The s of Bela were Ezbon, Uzzi, Uzziel, Jerimoth,
7: 8 The s of Beker were Zemirah, Joash, Eliezer,
7:10 The s of Bilhan were Jeush, Benjamin, Ehud,
7:12 The s of Ir were Shuppim and Huppim.
7:13 The s of Naphtali were Jahzeel, Guni, Jezer,
7:14 The s of Manasseh, born to his Aramean
7:16 The s of Peresh were Ulam and Rakem.
7:19 The s of Shemida were Ahian, Shechem, Likhi,
7:21 Ephraim's s Ezer and Elead were killed trying to
7:30 The s of Asher were Imnah, Ishvah, Ishvi,
7:31 The s of Beriah were Heber and Malkiel (the father
7:32 The s of Heber were Japhlet, Shomer, and Hotham.
7:33 The s of Japhlet were Pasach, Bimhal,
7:34 The s of Shomer were Ahi, Rohgah, Hubbah,
7:35 The s of his brother Helem were Zophah, Imna,
7:36 The s of Zophah were Suah, Harnepher, Shual,
7:38 The s of Jether were Jephunneh, Pispah, and Ara.
7:39 The s of Ulla were Arah, Hanniel, and Rizia.
8: 1 The s of Benjamin, in order of age, included Bela
8: 3 The s of Bela were Addar, Gera, Abihud,
8: 6 The s of Ehud, leaders of the clans living at Geba,
8: 7 Ehud's s were Naaman, Ahijah, and Gera. Gera,
8:10 These s all became the leaders of clans.
8:12 The s of Elpaal were Eber, Misham, Shemed (who
8:16 Michael, Ishpah, and Joha were the s of Beriah.
8:18 Ishmerai, Izliah, and Jobab were the s of Elpaal.
8:21 Beraiah, and Shimrath were the s of Shimei.
8:25 Iphdeiah, and Penuel were the s of Shashak.
8:27 Jaareshiah, Elijah, and Zicri were the s of Jeroham.
8:30 Jeiel's other s were Zur, Kish, Baal, Ner, Nadab,
8:38 Azel had six s: Azrikam, Bokeru, Ishmael,
8:38 Obadiah, and Hanan. These were the s of Azel.
8:39 Azel's brother Eshek had three s: Ulam (the
8:40 The s of Ulam were all skilled warriors and expert
8:40 They had many s and grandsons—150 in all.
9: 5 including Asaiah (the oldest) and his s.
9:36 Jeiel's other s were Zur, Kish, Baal, Ner, Nadab,
9:41 The s of Micah were Pithon, Melech, Tahrea,
9:44 Azel had six s, and their names were Azrikam,
9:44 Obadiah, and Hanan. These were the s of Azel.
10: 2 The Philistines closed in on Saul and his s, and they killed three of his s—
10: 6 So Saul and his three s died there together,
10: 7 had been routed and that Saul and his s were dead,
10: 8 the bodies of Saul and his s on Mount Gilboa.
10:12 the bodies of Saul and his three s back to Jabesh.
11:34 the s of Jashen from Gizon; / Jonathan son of
11:44 Shama and Jeiel, the s of Hotham, from Aroer;
11:46 Jeribai and Joshaviah, the s of Elnaam;
12: 3 Jeziel and Pelet, s of Azmaveth; / Beracah
12: 7 Joelah and Zebadiah, s of Jeroham from Gedor.
13: 3 in Jerusalem, and they had many s and daughters.
14: 4 These are the names of David's s who were born in
16:42 And the s of Jeduthun were appointed as
17:11 For when you die, I will raise up one of your s,
18:17 David's s served as the king's chief assistants.
21:20 His four s, who were with him, ran away and hid.
23: 6 after the clans descended from the three s of Levi
23: 7 descent from Libni and Shimei, the s of Gershon.
23:11 as a single family because neither had many s.
23:13 The s of Amram were Aaron and Moses. Aaron
23:14 of God, his s were included with the tribe of Levi.
23:15 The s of Moses were Gershom and Eliezer.
23:21 and Mushi. The s of Mahli were Eleazar and Kish.
23:22 Eleazar died with no s, only daughters.
23:22 His daughters married their cousins, the s of Kish.
23:23 The three s of Mushi were Mahli, Eder,
24: 1 The s of Aaron were Nadab, Abihu, Eleazar,
24: 2 died before their father did, and they had no s.
24:28 the leader was Eleazar, though he had no s.
25: 2 From the s of Asaph, there were Zaccur, Joseph,
25: 3 Jeduthun had six s: Gedaliah, Zeri, Jeshaiah,
25: 4 Heman's s were Bukkiah, Mattaniah, Uzziel,
25: 5 All these were the s of Heman, the king's seer,
25: 5 for God had honored him with fourteen s and three
25: 9 of the Asaph clan and twelve of his s and relatives.
25: 9 fell to Gedaliah and twelve of his s and relatives.
25:10 lot fell to Zaccur and twelve of his s and relatives.
25:11 lot fell to Zeri and twelve of his s and relatives.
25:12 fell to Nethaniah and twelve of his s and relatives.
25:13 fell to Bukkiah and twelve of his s and relatives.
25:14 fell to Asarelah and twelve of his s and relatives.
25:15 fell to Jeshaiah and twelve of his s and relatives.
25:16 fell to Mattaniah and twelve of his s and relatives.
25:17 lot fell to Shimei and twelve of his s and relatives.
25:18 lot fell to Uzziel and twelve of his s and relatives.
25:19 fell to Hashabiah and twelve of his s and relatives.
25:20 lot fell to Shubael and twelve of his s and relatives.
25:21 fell to Mattithiah and twelve of his s and relatives.
25:22 fell to Jerimoth and twelve of his s and relatives.
25:23 fell to Hananiah and twelve of his s and relatives.
25:24 to Joshbekashah and twelve of his s and relatives.
25:25 lot fell to Hanani and twelve of his s and relatives.
25:26 fell to Mallothi and twelve of his s and relatives.
25:27 lot fell to Eliathah and twelve of his s and relatives.
25:28 lot fell to Hothir and twelve of his s and relatives.
25:29 fell to Geddalti and twelve of his s and relatives.
25:30 fell to Mahazioth and twelve of his s and relatives.
25:31 to Romamti-ezer and twelve of his s and relatives.
26: 2 The s of Meshelemiah were Zechariah (the oldest),
26: 4 The s of Obed-edom, also gatekeepers,
26: 6 Obed-edom's son Shemaiah had s with great
26: 8 of Obed-edom, including their s and grandsons—
26: 9 Meshelemiah's eighteen s and relatives were also
26:10 appointed Shimri as the leader among his s,
26:11 His other s included Hilkiah (the second),
26:11 Hosah's s and relatives, who served as
26:15 and his s were put in charge of the storehouses.
26:22 The s of Jehiel, Zetham and his brother Joel,
26:29 and his s were appointed to serve as public
27:32 Hacmonite was responsible to teach the king's s.
28: 4 And from among my father's s, the LORD was
28: 5 And from among my s—for the LORD has given
29:24 and the s of King David pledged their loyalty to
2Ch 5:12 Heman, Jeduthun, and all their s and brothers—
6: 9 the one to do it. One of your s will build it instead.'
11:14 and his s would not allow them to serve the
11:19 Mahalath had three s—Jeush, Shemariah,
11:21 and they gave birth to twenty-eight s and sixty
11:23 also wisely gave responsibilities to his other s
13:21 and had twenty-two s and sixteen daughters.
21: 2 the other s of Jehoshaphat—were Azariah, Jehiel,
21:17 in the royal palace, including his s and his wives.
22: 1 bands of Arabs had killed all the older s.
23:11 Then Jehoiada and his s brought out Joash,
24: 3 two wives for Joash, and he had s and daughters.
24:27 The complete story about the s of Joash,
26:18 the s of Aaron who are set apart for this work.
28: 3 of Hinnom, even sacrificing his own s in the fire.
29: 9 and our s and daughters and wives are in captivity.
31:18 the little babies, the wives, and the s and daughters.
32:21 some of his own s killed him there with a sword.
33: 6 Manasseh even sacrificed his own s in the fire in
36:20 and his s until the kingdom of Persia came to
Ezr 3: 9 of God were supervised by Jeshua with his s and relatives, and Kadmiel and his s,
6:10 to the God of heaven and pray for me and my s.
7:23 anger against the realm of the king and his s?
8:18 along with eighteen of his s and brothers.
8:19 of Merari, and twenty of his s and brothers,
9: 2 and have taken them as wives for their s.
9:12 You told us not to let our daughters marry their s,
9:12 and not to let our s marry their daughters, and not
Ne 3: 3 The Fish Gate was built by the s of Hassenaah.
10:30 of the land, nor to let our s marry their daughters.
10:36 We agree to give to God our oldest s
13:28 One of the s of Joiada son of Eliashib the high
Est 9:10 the ten s of Haman son of Hammedatha, the enemy
9:12 the fortress of Susa alone and also Haman's ten s.
9:13 and have the bodies of Haman's ten s hung from
9:14 They also hung the bodies of Haman's ten s from
9:25 and Haman and his s were hanged on the gallows.
Job 1: 2 He had seven s and three daughters.
1: 4 Every year when Job's s had birthdays,
1:13 One day when Job's s and daughters were dining at
1:18 "Your s and daughters were feasting in their oldest
14:21 They never know if their s grow up in honor
24:21 of the childless who have no protecting s.
30: 9 "And now their s mock me with their vulgar song!
42:13 He also gave Job seven more s and three more
Ps 45:16 Your s will become kings like their father.
89:30 But if his s forsake my law / and fail to walk in my
106:37 They even sacrificed their s / and their daughters to
106:38 the blood of their s and daughters.
144:12 May our s flourish in their youth
Pr 5: 7 So now, my s, listen to me. Never stray from what
7:24 Listen to me, my s, and pay attention to my words.
17: 2 A wise slave will rule over the master's shameful s
19:14 Parents can provide their s with an inheritance of
Isa 23: 4 "Now I am childless; I have no s or daughters."
37:38 his s Adrammelech and Sharezer killed him with
43: 6 I will bring my s and daughters back to Israel from
49:22 They will carry your little s back to you in their
56: 5 the honor they would have received by having s
60: 4 Your s are coming from distant lands; your little
Jer 3:24 their flocks and herds, their s and daughters—
6:21 Fathers and s will both fall over them. Neighbors
7:31 where they sacrifice their little s and daughters in
14:16 Husbands, wives, s, and daughters—all will be
19: 5 and there they burn their s as sacrifices to Baal.
19: 9 those trapped inside will have to eat their own s
32:35 and there they sacrifice their s and daughters to
35: 3 of Habazziniah and all his brothers and s—
35: 4 and we went into the room assigned to the s of
35: 8 nor have our wives, our s, or our daughters.
39: 6 He made Zedekiah watch as they killed his s
40: 8 of Nethaniah, Johanan and Jonathan, s of Kareah,
40: 8 son of Tanhumeth, the s of Ephai the Netophathite,
48:46 Your s and daughters have been taken away as
52:10 made Zedekiah watch as all his s were killed;
La 1:18 for my s and daughters have been taken captive to
Eze 16:20 "Then you took your s and daughters—
23: 4 I married them, and they bore me s and daughters.
23:47 They will butcher their s and daughters and burn
24:21 Your s and daughters in Judea will be slaughtered
24:25 I will also take away their s and daughters.
46:16 If the prince gives a gift of land to one of his s,
46:17 Only the gifts given to the prince's s will be
46:18 If he gives property to his s, it must be from his
Da 11:10 the s of the king of the north will assemble a
Joel 2:28 Your s and daughters will prophesy. Your old men
3: 8 I will sell your s and daughters to the people of
Am 2:11 I chose some of your s to be prophets and others to
7:17 in this city, and your s and daughters will be killed.
Mt 20:20 the mother of James and John, the s of Zebedee, came to Jesus with her s.
20:21 will you let my two s sit in places of honor next to
21:28 A man with two s told the older boy, 'Son, go out
23:33 Snakes! S of vipers! How will you escape the
26:37 He took Peter and Zebedee's two s, James
Mk 1:19 A little farther up the shore Jesus saw Zebedee's s,
3:17 James and John (the s of Zebedee, but Jesus nicknamed them "S of Thunder"),
10:35 Then James and John, the s of Zebedee, came over
Lk 5:10 His partners, James and John, the s of Zebedee,
15:11 Jesus told them this story: "A man had two s.
15:12 father agreed to divide his wealth between his s.
Jn 4:12 water than he and his s and his cattle enjoyed?"
21: 2 the s of Zebedee, and two other disciples.
Ac 2:17 Your s and daughters will prophesy, / your young
7: 9 "These s of Jacob were very jealous of their
7:12 still grain in Egypt, so he sent his s to buy some.
7:15 Jacob went to Egypt. He died there, as did all his s.
7:16 had bought from the s of Hamor in Shechem.
7:29 in the land of Midian, where his two s were born.
13:26 you s of Abraham, and also all of you devout
19:14 Seven s of Sceva, a leading priest, were doing this.
2Co 6:18 your Father, / and you will be my s and daughters,
Gal 4:22 The Scriptures say that Abraham had two s,
Heb 11:20 It was by faith that Isaac blessed his two s, Jacob
11:21 blessed each of Joseph's s and bowed in worship
11:28 the angel of death would not kill their firstborn s.

SONS-IN-LAW (1) [SON]

Ge 19:12 of this place—s, sons, daughters, or anyone else.

SONS' (1) [SON]

Ge 46:26 to Egypt, not counting his s wives, was sixty-six.

SOON (303) [SOONER]

Ge 19:19 would catch up to me there, and I would s die.
19:31 And our father will s be too old to have children.
22:20 S after this, Abraham heard that Milcah,
26:14 S the Philistines became jealous of him,
27:30 As s as Isaac had blessed Jacob, and almost before

27:41 to himself, "My father will s be dead and gone.
29:13 As s as Laban heard about Jacob's arrival,
29:33 She s became pregnant again and had another son.
30:10 S Zilpah presented him with another son.
30:25 S after Joseph was born to Rachel, Jacob said to
31:1 But Jacob s learned that Laban's sons were
34:5 Word s reached Jacob that his daughter had been
35:8 S after this, Rebekah's old nurse, Deborah, died.
37:12 S after this, Joseph's brothers went to pasture their
39:4 Potiphar s put Joseph in charge of his entire
39:14 S all the men around the place came running.
40:10 and s there were clusters of ripe grapes.
41:5 S he fell asleep again and had a second dream.
41:32 and that he will make these events happen s.
45:16 The news s reached Pharaoh: "Joseph's brothers
46:29 As s as Joseph arrived, he embraced his father
47:17 S all the horses, flocks, herds, and donkeys of
49:29 Then Jacob told them, "S I will die. Bury me with
50:24 "S I will die," Joseph told his brothers, "but God
Ex 1:7 so quickly that they s filled the land.
1:12 The Egyptians s became alarmed
1:16 give birth, kill all the boys as s as they are born.
2:5 S after this, one of Pharaoh's daughters came down
4:31 The leaders were s convinced that the LORD had
8:29 "As s as I go," Moses said, "I will ask the
9:29 "As s as I leave the city, I will lift my hands
18:1 Word s reached Jethro, the priest of Midian
18:27 S after this, Moses said good-bye to his
34:12 If you do, you s will be following their evil ways.
Lev 5:3 they will be considered guilty as s as they become
13:15 The priest must make this pronouncement as s as
18:25 who live there, and the land will s vomit them out.
Nu 9:22 But as s as it lifted, they broke camp and moved
11:1 The people s began to complain to the LORD
25:2 and s the Israelites were feasting with them
Dt 6:10 "The LORD your God will s bring you into the
12:10 You will s cross the Jordan River and live in the
17:14 "You will s arrive in the land the LORD your
19:1 "The LORD your God will s destroy the nations
27:3 you will s cross the river to enter the land the
32:15 But Israel s became fat and unruly; / the people
Jos 2:7 And as s as the king's men had left, the city gate
3:15 But as s as the feet of the priests who were
4:18 And as s as the priests carrying the Ark of the
8:19 As s as Joshua gave the signal, the men in ambush
23:14 "S I will die, going the way of all the earth.
24:29 S after this, Joshua son of Nun, the servant of the
Jdg 1:6 but the Israelites s captured him and cut off his
6:33 S afterward the armies of Midian, Amalek,
7:18 As s as my group blows the rams' horns, those of
8:27 But s all the Israelites prostituted themselves by
8:33 As s as Gideon was dead, the Israelites prostituted
9:33 In the morning, as s as it is daylight, storm the city.
11:3 S he had a large band of rebels following him.
13:3 you will s become pregnant and give birth to a son.
16:2 Word s spread that Samson was there, so the men
20:3 (Word s reached the land of Benjamin that the
1Sa 12:9 But the people s forgot about the LORD their
13:3 S after this, Jonathan attacked and defeated the
13:17 Three raiding parties s left the camp of the
16:16 will quiet you, and you will s be well again."
17:21 S the Israelite and Philistine forces stood facing
17:24 As s as the Israelite army saw him, they began to
20:41 As s as the boy was gone, David came out from
22:1 S his brothers and other relatives joined him there.
22:6 The news of his arrival in Judah s reached Saul.
23:7 Saul s learned that David was at Keilah. "Good!"
23:13 Word s reached Saul that David had escaped,
27:4 Word s reached Saul that David had fled to Gath,
29:10 and leave with your men as s as it gets light."
30:9 men set out, and they s came to Besor Brook.
2Sa 13:36 They s arrived, weeping and sobbing, and the king
15:10 "As s as you hear the trumpets," his message
15:12 S many others also joined Absalom,
15:13 A messenger s arrived in Jerusalem to tell King
17:24 David s arrived at Mahanaim. By now,
19:1 Word s reached Joab that the king was weeping
20:10 did not need to strike again, and Amasa s died.
22:45 before me; / as s as they hear of me, they submit.
1Ki 1:21 and I will be treated as criminals as s as you are
1:51 Word s reached Solomon that Adonijah had seized
15:21 As s as Baasha of Israel heard what was
18:1 to King Ahab. Tell him that I will s send rain!"
18:12 But as s as I leave you, the Spirit of the LORD
18:45 And sure enough, the sky was s black with clouds.
20:5 S Ben-hadad's messengers returned again and said,
20:36 a lion will kill you as s as you leave me."
22:25 "You will find out s enough when you find
2Ki 1:5 he asked them, "Why have you returned so s?"
3:20 of Edom, and s there was water everywhere.
4:6 S every container was full to the brim! "Bring me
4:17 But sure enough, the woman s became pregnant.
6:20 As s as they had entered Samaria, Elisha prayed,
6:32 and keep him out. His master will s follow him."
10:2 and weapons. As s as you receive this letter,
10:25 As s as Jehu had finished sacrificing the burnt
13:21 But as s as the body touched Elisha's bones,
19:9 S afterward King Sennacherib received word that
20:12 S after this, Merodach-baladan son of Baladan,
1Ch 2:24 S after Hezron died in the town of
29:15 earth are like a shadow, gone so s without a trace.
2Ch 12:7 destroy them and will s give them some relief.
16:5 As s as Baasha of Israel heard what was
18:24 And Micaiah replied, "You will find out s enough,
18:32 As s as the charioteers realized he was not the king
Ezr 4:12 foundation for its walls and will s complete them.
5:3 and their colleagues s arrived in Jerusalem
Est 7:8 And as s as the king spoke, his attendants covered
Job 7:21 For s I will lie down in the dust and die. When you
10:9 made of dust—will you turn me back to dust so s?
16:22 For s I must go down that road from which I will
32:22 if I tried, my Creator would s do away with me.
Ps 18:44 As s as they hear of me, they submit.
37:2 For like grass, they s fade away. / Like springtime flowers, they s wither.
41:5 "How s will he die and be forgotten?" they ask.
59:11 kill them, for my people s forget such lessons;
81:14 How s my hands would be upon their foes!
90:10 and trouble; / s they disappear, and we are gone.
94:17 the LORD had helped me, / I would s have died.
106:7 They s forgot his many acts of kindness to them.
Pr 10:4 Lazy people are s poor; hard workers get rich.
12:19 Truth stands the test of time; lies are s exposed.
Ecc 1:13 I s discovered that God has dealt a tragic existence
10:18 lets the roof leak, and s the rafters begin to rot.
Isa 7:17 You will s experience greater terror than has been
9:1 land of Zebulun and Naphtali will s be humbled,
9:9 the people of Israel and Samaria will s discover it.
10:8 He will say, 'Each of my princes will s be a king,
13:22 are numbered; its time of destruction will s arrive.
21:12 "Morning is coming, but night will s follow.
29:17 S—and it will not be very long—the wilderness of
32:12 sorrow for your bountiful farms that will s be gone,
33:19 But s they will all be gone. These fierce,
34:12 Land of Nothing, and its princes s will all be gone.
37:9 S afterward King Sennacherib received word that
39:1 S after this, Merodach-baladan son of Baladan,
49:17 S your descendants will come back, and all who
49:19 land will s be crowded with your people.
50:11 from me: You will s lie down in great torment.
51:5 My mercy and justice are coming s. Your salvation
51:14 S all you captives will be released! Imprisonment,
54:3 For you will s be bursting at the seams.
56:1 is right and good, for I am coming s to rescue you.
59:15 and anyone who tries to live a godly life is s
Jer 8:13 All the good things I prepared for them will s be
13:18 for your glorious crowns will s be snatched from
22:23 but s you will cry and groan in anguish—
27:16 Do not listen to your prophets who claim that s the
28:12 S afterward the LORD gave this message to
32:25 even though the city will s belong to the
38:9 He will s die of hunger, for almost all the bread in
40:13 S after this, Johanan son of Kareah and the other
41:7 But as s as they were all inside the town, Ishmael
48:1 is certain for the city of Nebo; it will s lie in ruins.
48:12 But the time is coming s," says the LORD,
49:4 of your fertile valleys, but they will s be ruined.
50:39 "S this city of Babylon will be inhabited by
51:60 terrible disasters that would s come upon Babylon.
La 4:22 punishment will end; you will s return from exile.
4:22 just beginning; s your many sins will be revealed.
Eze 7:8 S I will pour out my fury to complete your
9:2 Six men s appeared from the upper gate that faces
11:7 you are not safe, for I will s drag you from the city.
12:11 are a demonstration of what will s happen to them,
12:23 end to this proverb, and you will s stop quoting it.
13:11 Tell these whitewashers that their wall will s fall
16:14 Your fame s spread throughout the world on
17:6 It s produced strong branches and luxuriant leaves.
19:11 It s became very tall, / towering above all the
36:7 and sworn an oath that those nations will s have
36:8 and they will be coming home again s!
Da 6:3 Daniel s proved himself more capable than all the
10:20 S I must return to fight against the spirit prince of
11:9 king of the south but will s return to his own land.
Hos 1:6 S Gomer became pregnant again and gave birth to
5:15 For as s as trouble comes, they will search for
9:7 S Israel will know this all too well. "The prophets
9:10 S they became as vile as the god they worshiped.
Joel 2:22 animals of the field! The pastures will s be green.
3:14 It is there that the day of the LORD will s arrive.
Am 7:11 'Jeroboam will s be killed and the people of Israel
Jnh 4:6 and s it spread its broad leaves over Jonah's head,
4:7 of the plant, so that it s died and withered away.
Mic 4:10 You will s be sent into exile in distant Babylon.
Na 2:10 S the city is an empty shambles, stripped of its
2:13 "Your chariots will s go up in smoke.
Hab 2:16 But s it will be your turn! Come, drink and be
Zep 3:8 the time is coming s when I will stand up
Zec 3:8 S I am going to bring my servant, the Branch.
6:10 As s as they arrive, meet them at the home of
Mt 3:11 But someone is coming s who is far greater than I
4:24 so that the sick were s coming to be healed from as
6:10 May your kingdom come s. / May your will be
13:2 where an immense crowd s gathered. He got into a
13:6 but they s wilted beneath the hot sun and died
13:21 but they wilt as s as they have problems or are
14:13 As s as Jesus heard the news, he went off by
14:35 and s people were bringing all their sick to be
17:12 And s the Son of Man will also suffer at their
25:16 immediately to invest the money and s doubled it.
Mk 1:7 "Someone is coming s who is far greater than I
1:45 such crowds s surrounded Jesus that he couldn't
2:2 S the house where he was staying was so packed
3:20 and s he and his disciples couldn't even find time
4:6 but it s wilted beneath the hot sun and died
4:17 but they wilt as s as they have problems or are
4:29 And as s as the grain is ready, the farmer comes
4:37 But s a fierce storm arose. High waves began to
5:15 A crowd s gathered around Jesus, but they were
6:14 Herod Antipas, the king, s heard about Jesus,
9:39 "No one who performs miracles in my name will s
11:2 he told them, "and as s as you enter it,
11:3 just say, 'The Lord needs it and will return it s.' "
12:21 the widow, but s he too died and left no children.
14:45 As s as they arrived, Judas walked up to Jesus.
Lk 1:24 S afterward his wife, Elizabeth, became pregnant
3:15 Everyone was expecting the Messiah to come s,
3:16 but someone is coming s who is greater than I am
4:14 S he became well known throughout the
5:7 and s both boats were filled with fish and on the
5:11 And as s as they landed, they left everything
5:29 S Levi held a banquet in his home with Jesus as the
6:12 One day s afterward Jesus went to a mountain to
7:11 S afterward Jesus went with his disciples to the
8:6 but s it withered and died for lack of moisture.
8:28 As s as he saw Jesus, he shrieked and fell to the
8:35 A crowd s gathered around Jesus, for they wanted
11:2 name be honored. / May your Kingdom come s.
16:1 but s a rumor went around that the manager was
22:10 He replied, "As s as you enter Jerusalem, a man
22:60 And as s as he said these words, the rooster
22:69 But the time is s coming when I, the Son of Man,
Jn 1:27 who will s begin his ministry. I am not even
1:30 'S a man is coming who is far greater than I am,
4:7 S a Samaritan woman came to draw water,
4:13 "People s become thirsty again after drinking this
6:5 Jesus s saw a great crowd of people climbing the
6:18 S a gale swept down upon them as they rowed,
7:2 But s it was time for the Festival of Shelters,
8:2 A crowd s gathered, and he sat down and taught
13:18 has turned against me,' and this will s come true.
13:27 As s as Judas had eaten the bread, Satan entered
13:31 As s as Judas left the room, Jesus said, "The time
13:32 And God will bring me into my glory very s.
Ac 4:23 As s as they were freed, Peter and John found the
5:5 As s as Ananias heard these words, he fell to the
5:38 things merely on their own, it will s be overthrown.
8:15 As s as they arrived, they prayed for these new
9:38 men to beg him, "Please come as s as possible!"
9:39 and as s as he arrived, they took him to the upstairs
10:7 As s as the angel was gone, Cornelius called two of
10:29 So I came as s as I was sent for. Now tell me why
11:1 S the news reached the apostles and other believers
11:12 and we s arrived at the home of the man who had
13:25 But he is coming s—and I am not even worthy to
19:5 As s as they heard this, they were baptized in the
19:29 to gather, and s the city was filled with confusion.
20:6 As s as the Passover season ended, we boarded a
21:40 S a deep silence enveloped the crowd, and he
23:29 I s discovered it was something regarding their
25:4 and he himself would be returning there s.
27:29 At this rate they were afraid we would s be driven
Ro 13:12 is almost gone; the day of salvation will s be here.
15:28 As s as I have delivered this money and completed
16:1 church in Cenchrea, will be coming to see you s.
16:20 The God of peace will s crush Satan under your
1Co 4:19 But I will come—and s—if the Lord will let me,
5:6 is allowed to go on sinning, s all will be affected?
16:11 I am looking forward to seeing him s, along with
2Co 4:18 For the troubles we see will s be over, but the joys
Gal 1:6 shocked that you are turning away so s from God,
Php 2:19 Jesus is willing, I hope to send Timothy to you s.
2:23 I hope to send him to you just as s as I find out
2:24 from the Lord that I myself will come to see you s.
4:5 in all you do. Remember, the Lord is coming s.
Col 2:22 about things that are gone as s as we use them.
1Th 3:4 we warned you that troubles would s come—
3:11 Jesus make it possible for us to come to you very s.
1Ti 3:6 because he might be proud of being chosen so s,
3:14 to you now, even though I hope to be with you s,
6:17 not to trust in their money, which will s be gone.
2Ti 4:9 Please come as s as you can.
Tit 3:12 As s as one of them arrives, do your best to meet
Phm 1:22 answer your prayers and let me return to you s.
Heb 13:19 prayers right now so that I can come back to you s.
13:23 If he comes here s, I will bring him with me to see
1Pe 4:7 The end of the world is coming s. Therefore,
2Pe 1:14 days here on earth are numbered and I am s to die.
2Jn 1:12 For I hope to visit you s and to talk with you face
3Jn 1:14 For I hope to see you s, and then we will talk face
Rev 1:1 gave him concerning the events that will happen s.
12:4 ready to devour the baby as s as it was born.
17:8 And yet he will s come up out of the bottomless pit
22:6 sent his angel to tell you what will happen s.' "
22:7 "Look, I am coming s! Blessed are those who
22:12 "See, I am coming s, and my reward is with me,
22:20 to all these things says, "Yes, I am coming s!"

SOONER (1) [SOON]

Jer 17:11 S or later they will lose their riches and, at the end

SOOT (4)

Ex 9:8 said to Moses and Aaron, "Take s from a furnace,
9:10 So they gathered s from a furnace and went to see
9:10 Pharaoh watched, Moses tossed the s into the air,
La 4:8 But now their faces are blacker than s. No one

SOOTHED (1) [SOOTHING]

Lk 10:34 the Samaritan s his wounds with medicine

SOOTHING (2) [SOOTHED]

Ps 55:21 in his heart is war. / His words are as s as lotion,
141:5 a kindness! / If they reprove me, it is s medicine.

SOP [KJV] See BREAD (DIPPED)

SOPATER (1)
Ac 20: 4 They were S of Berea, the son of Pyrrhus;

SOPE [KJV] See SOAP

SOPHERETH (2)
Ezr 2:55 Solomon returned from exile: / Sotai, S, Peruda,
Ne 7:57 Solomon returned from exile: / Sotai, S, Peruda,

SOPRANO (1)
Ps 46: T the descendants of Korah, to be sung by s voices.

SORCERER (4) [SORCERY]
Ac 8: 9 A man named Simon had been a s there for many
13: 6 where they met a Jewish s, a false prophet named
13: 8 the s (as his name means in Greek), interfered
13: 9 the Holy Spirit, looked the s in the eye and said,

SORCERERS (5) [SORCERY]
Dt 18:14 The people you are about to displace consult with s
Jer 27: 9 interpreters of dreams, mediums, and s who say,
Da 2: 2 in his magicians, enchanters, s, and astrologers,
Mal 3: 5 I will be a ready witness against all s
Rev 22:15 the s, the sexually immoral, the murderers, the idol

SORCERESS (1) [SORCERY]
Ex 22:18 "A s must not be allowed to live.

SORCERIES (1) [SORCERY]
Rev 18:23 in the world, deceived the nations with her s.

SORCERY (5) [SORCERER, SORCERERS, SORCERESS, SORCERIES]
Nu 23:23 touch Jacob; / no s has any power against Israel.
Dt 18:10 do not let your people practice fortune-telling or s,
2Ki 17:17 and used s and sold themselves to evil,
21: 6 He practiced s and divination, and he consulted
2Ch 33: 6 He practiced s, divination, and witchcraft, and he

SORE (6) [SORES]
Ge 34:25 three days later, when their wounds were still s,
Lev 13:10 and an open s appears in the affected area,
13:15 this pronouncement as soon as he sees an open s
13:29 or woman, has an open s on the head or chin,
13:43 and if he finds swelling around the reddish white s,
22:22 injured, mutilated, or that has a growth, an open s,

SOREK (1)
Jdg 16: 4 named Delilah, who lived in the valley of S.

SORELY [KJV] See GREAT, HARASSED

SORES (9) [SORE]
Lev 13:14 But if any open s appear, the infected person will
13:15 because open s indicate the presence of a
13:16 if the open s heal and turn white like the rest of the
21:20 defective eye, or has oozing s or scabs on his skin,
2Sa 3:29 generation be cursed with a man who has open s
Jer 6: 7 Her sickness and s are ever before me.
Lk 16:21 the dogs would come and lick his open s.
Rev 16: 2 malignant s broke out on everyone who had the
16:11 cursed the God of heaven for their pains and s.

SORROW (82) [SORROWING, SORROWS, SORRY]
Ge 42:38 bring my gray head down to the grave in deep s."
44:29 bring my gray head down to the grave in deep s.'
44:31 for bringing his gray head down to the grave in s.
48: 7 So with great s I buried her there beside the road to
Nu 14:39 the Israelites, there was much s among the people.
1Sa 1:11 if you will look down upon my s and answer my
1:16 I have been praying out of great anguish and s."
2Sa 1:11 and his men tore their clothes in s when they heard
13:31 His advisers also tore their clothes in horror and s.
14: 2 Act like a woman who has been in deep s for a
1Ki 8:38 people offer a prayer concerning their troubles or s,
2Ch 6:29 people offer a prayer concerning their troubles or s,
35:25 These songs of s have become a tradition and are
Est 9:22 when their s was turned into gladness and their
Ps 13: 2 anguish in my soul, / with s in my heart every day?
16: 4 who chase after other gods will be filled with s.
35:19 those who hate me without cause / gloat over my s.
69:11 When I dress in sackcloth to show s, / they make
80: 5 You have fed us with s / and made us drink tears
107:39 through oppression, trouble, and s,
116: 3 the grave overtook me. / I saw only trouble and s.
Pr 10:22 makes a person rich, and he adds no s with it.
23:29 Who has anguish? Who has s? Who is always
Ecc 1:18 my grief. To increase knowledge only increases s.
5:20 People who do this rarely look with s on the past,
7: 3 S is better than laughter, for sadness has a refining
Isa 5:30 A cloud of darkness and s will hover over Israel.
14: 3 day when the LORD gives his people rest from s
15: 2 They will shave their heads in s and cut off their
16:11 for Moab. My s for Kir-hareseth will be very great.
22:12 He told you to shave your heads in s for your sins
23: 5 hears the news about Tyre, there will be great s.
29: 2 upon you, and there will be much weeping and s.
32:12 Beat your breasts in s for your bountiful farms that
35:10 S and mourning will disappear, and they will be
49:13 and will have compassion on them in their s.
51:11 S and mourning will disappear, and they will be
65:14 You will cry in s and despair, while my servants
Jer 20:18 life has been filled with trouble, s, and shame.
31:13 comfort them and exchange their s for rejoicing.
48:38 Crying and s will be in every Moabite home
La 2: 5 He has brought unending s and tears to Jerusalem.
2:10 They throw dust on their heads in s and despair.
2:13 In all the world has there ever been such s?
3:15 He has given me a cup of deep s to drink.
3:33 does not enjoy hurting people or causing them s.
Eze 2:10 other words of s, and pronouncements of doom.
7:18 They will shave their heads in s and remorse.
23:33 reel like a drunkard beneath the awful blows of s
24:16 Yet you must not show any s. Do not weep;
Joel 1: 8 Weep with s, as a virgin weeps when her fiancé has
Am 8:10 funeral clothes and shave your heads as signs of s,
Jnh 3: 5 without food and wear sackcloth to show their s.
Mic 1: 8 walk around naked and barefoot in s and shame.
1:16 Shave your heads in s, for the children you love
Na 2: 7 like doves; watch them beat their breasts in s.
Zep 1:11 Wail in s, all you who live in the market area,
Zec 12:11 The s and mourning in Jerusalem on that day will
12:12 "All Israel will weep in profound s, each family
Mt 20:22 Are you able to drink from the bitter cup of s I am
Mk 10:38 Are you able to drink from the bitter cup of s I am
Lk 6:25 for your laughing will turn to mourning and s.
18:13 Instead, he beat his chest in s, saying, 'O God,
23:48 all that had happened, they went home in deep s.
Jn 16:22 You have s now, but I will see you again; then you
Ro 9: 2 My heart is filled with bitter s and unending grief
12:15 be happy with them. If they are sad, share their s.
1Co 5: 2 Why aren't you mourning in s and shame?
2Co 7: 9 It was the kind of s God wants his people to have,
7:10 For God can use s in our lives to help us turn away
7:10 seek salvation. We will never regret that kind of s.
7:10 But s without repentance is the kind that results in
7:11 Just see what this godly s produced in you!
Eph 4:30 And do not bring s to God's Holy Spirit by the way
Php 2:27 on me, so that I would not have such unbearable s.
1Th 4:13 so you will not be full of s like people who have no
Heb 13: 3 Share the s of those being mistreated, as though
13:17 Give them reason to do this joyfully and not with s.
Jas 4: 9 Let there be s and deep grief. Let there be sadness
Rev 18: 7 I am no helpless widow. I will not experience s.'
18:19 will throw dust on their heads to show their great s.
21: 4 there will be no more death or s or crying or pain.

SORROWING (1) [SORROW]
Jer 31:25 I have given rest to the weary and joy to the s."

SORROWS (20) [SORROW]
Ne 9: 9 saw the sufferings and s of our ancestors in Egypt,
Job 9:18 catch my breath, but fills me instead with bitter s.
21:17 and God skips them when he distributes s in his
Ps 32:10 Many s come to the wicked, / but unfailing love
56: 8 You keep track of all my s. / You have collected
119:153 Look down upon my s and rescue me, / for I have
Isa 53: 3 a man of s, acquainted with bitterest grief.
53: 4 he carried; it was our s that weighed him down.
54: 4 and the s of widowhood will be remembered no
Jer 31:12 like a watered garden, and all their s will be gone.
La 5: 1 that has happened to us. See all the s we bear!
Lk 6:24 "What s await you who are rich, / for you have
6:25 What s await you who are satisfied and prosperous
6:25 What s await you who laugh carelessly, / for your
6:26 What s await you who are praised by the crowds,
Jn 16:33 Here on earth you will have many trials and s.
1Ti 6:10 from the faith and pierced themselves with many s.
Rev 18: 7 and pleasure, so match it now with torments and s.
18: 8 the s of death and mourning and famine will
21: 4 He will remove all of their s, and there will be no

SORRY (30) [SORROW]
Ge 6: 6 So the LORD was s he had ever made them.
6: 7 and birds, too. I am s I ever made them."
Dt 19:13 Do not feel s for that murderer! Purge the guilt of
Jdg 21:15 The people felt s for Benjamin
1Sa 15:11 "I am s that I ever made Saul king, for he has not
15:35 And the LORD was s he had ever made Saul king
22: 8 You're not even s for me. Think of it! My own
2Ki 22:19 You were s and humbled yourself before the
2Ch 21:20 No one was s when he died. He was buried in the
34:27 You were s and humbled yourself before God
Ps 38:18 my sins; / I am deeply s for what I have done.
Isa 29:12 they will say, "S, we don't know how to read."
Jer 3:10 She has only pretended to be s," says the LORD.
8: 6 Is anyone s for sin? Does anyone say, "What a
15: 5 "Who will feel s for you, Jerusalem? Who will
31:19 I turned away from God, but then I was s. I kicked
42:10 For I am s for all the punishment I have had to
Jnh 4:10 Then the LORD said, "You feel s about the plant,
4:11 Shouldn't I feel s for such a great city?"
Mal 3:14 the LORD Almighty that we are s for our sins?
Mt 14: 9 The king was s, but because of his oath and
15:32 to him and said, "I feel s for these people.
20:34 Jesus felt s for them and touched their eyes.
Mk 6:26 Then the king was very s, but he was embarrassed
7:11 people to say to their parents, 'S, I can't help you.
8: 2 "I feel s for these people. They have been here
Ac 23: 5 "I'm s, brothers. I didn't realize he was the high
2Co 7: 7 and how s you were about what had happened,
7: 8 I am no longer s that I sent that letter to you,
though I was s for a time,

SORT (17) [SORTS]
Ge 1:11 "Let the land burst forth with every s of grass
1:21 and every s of fish and every kind of bird.
29:25 it was Leah! "What s of trick is this?"
Jdg 7: 4 and I will s out who will go with you and who will
1Sa 6: 4 "What s of guilt offering should we send?"
Ne 13:18 Wasn't it enough that your ancestors did this s of
Eze 17:23 Birds of every s will nest in it, finding shelter
Mt 9:35 he healed people of every s of disease and illness.
11:19 a drunkard, and a friend of the worst s of sinners!'
13:30 Then I will tell the harvesters to s out the weeds
13:48 sit down, s the good fish into crates, and throw the
Mk 1:27 "What s of new teaching is this?" they asked
Lk 7:34 a drunkard, and a friend of the worst s of sinners!'
Ac 13:10 of the Devil, full of every s of trickery and villainy,
1Co 5: 6 and yet you let this s of thing go on.
2Co 1:18 As surely as God is true, I am not that s of person.
Gal 5:21 that anyone living that s of life will not inherit the

SORTS (11) [SORT]
Ge 1:25 God made all s of wild animals, livestock,
2: 9 And the LORD God planted all s of trees in the
Ne 13:15 figs, and all s of produce to Jerusalem to sell.
Pr 24: 4 Through knowledge its rooms are filled with all s
Zep 2:14 and cattle. All s of wild animals will settle there.
Mt 23:27 with dead people's bones and all s of impurity.
Lk 22:65 And they threw all s of terrible insults at him.
Ac 10:12 In the sheet were all s of animals, reptiles,
11: 6 I saw all s of small animals, wild animals, reptiles,
14: 2 saying all s of evil things about them.
28:10 people put on board all s of things we would need

SOSIPATER (1)
Ro 16:21 and Lucius, Jason, and S, my relatives,

SOSTHENES (2)
Ac 18:17 The mob had grabbed S, the leader of the
1Co 1: 1 an apostle of Christ Jesus, and from our brother S.

SOTAI (2)
Ezr 2:55 returned from exile: / S, Sophereth, Peruda,
Ne 7:57 returned from exile: / S, Sophereth, Peruda,

SOTTISH [KJV] See SENSELESS

SOUGHT (15) [SEEK]
1Sa 13:14 for the LORD has s out a man after his own heart.
2Ch 11:17 and earnestly s to obey the LORD as they had
14: 7 land is ours because we s the LORD our God,
15: 4 the God of Israel, and s him out, you found him.
15:15 Eagerly they s after God, and they found him.
16:12 LORD's help but s help only from his physicians.
17: 4 He s his father's God and obeyed his commands
20: 3 by this news and s the LORD for guidance.
22: 9 a man who s the LORD with all his heart."
26: 5 Uzziah s God during the days of Zechariah,
26: 5 And as long as the king s the LORD, God gave
31:21 Hezekiah s his God wholeheartedly.
33:12 Manasseh s the LORD his God and cried out
Ps 78:34 God killed some of them, the rest finally s him.
Da 4:36 My advisers and officers s me out, and I was

SOUL (68) [SOULS]
Ge 49: 6 O my s, stay away from them. / May I never be a
Dt 4:29 And if you search for him with all your heart and s,
6: 5 with all your heart, all your s, and all your strength.
10:12 to love and worship him with all your heart and s,
11:13 the LORD your God with all your heart and s,
13: 3 to see if you love him with all your heart and s.
28:65 your eyesight to fail, and your s to despair.
30: 6 so that you will love him with all your heart and s,
30:10 to the LORD your God with all your heart and s.
Jos 22: 5 and serve him with all your heart and all your s."
Jdg 5:21 the Kishon. / March on, my s, with courage!
1Sa 20: 3 I swear it by the LORD and by your own s!"
1Ki 2: 4 and follow me faithfully with all their heart and s,
8:48 if they turn to you with their whole heart and s
2Ki 23: 3 regulations, and laws with all his heart and s.
23:25 to the LORD with all his heart and s and strength,
2Ch 6:38 if they turn to you with their whole heart and s
15:12 God of their ancestors, with all their heart and s.
34:31 regulations, and laws with all his heart and s.
Job 4: 3 have encouraged many a troubled s to trust in God;
10: 1 I will speak in the bitterness of my s.
24: 5 just getting enough to keep body and s together.
27: 2 by the Almighty who has embittered my s.
Ps 13: 2 How long must I struggle with anguish in my s,
16:10 For you will not leave my s among the dead
19: 7 The law of the LORD is perfect, / reviving the s.
25: 1 To you, O LORD, I lift up my s.
31: 7 and you care about the anguish of my s.
31: 9 of my tears. / My body and s are withering away.
57: 8 Wake up, my s! / Wake up, O harp and lyre!
63: 1 I earnestly search for you. / My s thirsts for you;
77: 6 I search my s and think about the difference now.
84: 2 of the LORD. / With my whole being, body and s,
108: 1 wonder I can sing your praises! / Wake up, my s!
131: 2 Yes, like a small child is my s within me.
Pr 6:32 adultery is an utter fool, for he destroys his own s.
11:17 Your own s is nourished when you are kind,
16:24 sweet to the s and healthy for the body.
18:20 Words satisfy the s as food satisfies the stomach;
22:25 you will learn to be like them and endanger your s.

24:12 He keeps watch over your s, and he knows you
24:14 In the same way, wisdom is sweet to your s.
Isa 55: 2 tell you where to get food that is good for the s!
55: 3 wide open. Listen, for the life of your s is at stake.
La 1:20 My heart is broken and my s despairs, for I have
Eze 29:11 For forty years not a s will pass that way,
Mt 6:22 for your body. A pure eye lets sunshine into your s.
10:28 can only kill your body; they cannot touch your s.
10:28 only God, who can destroy both s and body in hell.
16:26 whole world but lose your own s in the process? Is anything worth more than your s?
22:37 with all your heart, all your s, and all your mind.'
26:38 "My s is crushed with grief to the point of death.
Mk 8:36 whole world but lose your own s in the process?
8:37 Is anything worth more than your s?
12:30 all your s, all your mind, and all your strength.'
14:34 "My s is crushed with grief to the point of death.
Lk 2:35 be revealed. And a sword will pierce your very s."
9:25 but lose or forfeit your own s in the process?
10:27 all your s, all your strength, and all your mind.'
11:34 A pure eye lets sunshine into your s. But an evil
16:23 and his s went to the place of the dead. There,
Jn 12:27 Now my s is deeply troubled. Should I pray,
Ac 2:27 For you will not leave my s among the dead
23:22 "Don't let a s know you told me this,"
1Th 5:23 and may your whole spirit and s and body be kept
Phm 1:19 And I won't mention that you owe me your very s!
3Jn 1: 2 and that your body is as healthy as I know your s

SOULS (15) [SOUL]

Isa 57:16 all people would pass away—all the s I have made.
Jer 6:16 Travel its path, and you will find rest for your s.
Eze 13:18 you women who are ensnaring the s of my people,
Mic 6: 7 our firstborn children to pay for the sins of our s?
Mt 11:29 and gentle, and you will find rest for your s.
Lk 21:19 By standing firm, you will win your s.
Heb 6:19 is like a strong and trustworthy anchor for our s.
13:17 Their work is to watch over your s, and they know
Jas 1:21 your hearts, for it is strong enough to save your s.
1Pe 1: 9 for trusting him will be the salvation of your s.
2:11 evil desires because they fight against your very s.
2:25 turned to your Shepherd, the Guardian of your s.
Rev 6: 9 I saw under the altar the s of all who had been
20: 4 And I saw the s of those who had been beheaded
20: 4 And I saw the s of those who had not worshiped

SOUND (76) [FINE-SOUNDING, HIGH-SOUNDING, SOUNDED, SOUNDING, SOUNDINGS, SOUNDLY, SOUNDS]

Ex 32:18 nor a cry of defeat. It is the s of a celebration."
Lev 26:36 You will live there in such constant fear that the s
Nu 10: 5 "When you s the signal to move on, the tribes on
10: 6 When you s the signal a second time, the tribes on
10: 6 You must s short blasts to signal moving on.
10: 9 you must s the alarm with these trumpets
Jos 6:20 When the people heard the s of the horns,
Jdg 5:28 Why don't we hear the s of chariot wheels?'
1Sa 1:13 Seeing her lips moving but hearing no s,
2Sa 5:24 When you hear a s like marching feet in the tops of
1Ki 1:40 so joyous and noisy that the earth shook with the s.
1:41 When Joab heard the s of trumpets, he asked,
6: 7 so the entire structure was built without the s of
19:12 And after the fire there was the s of a gentle
1Ch 14:15 When you hear a s like marching feet in the tops of
15:19 and Ethan were chosen to s the bronze cymbals.
2Ch 13:15 At the s of their battle cry, God defeated Jeroboam
Ne 4:18 The trumpeter stayed with me to s the alarm.
Job 21:12 and harp. They make merry to the s of the flute.
30: 7 They s like animals as they howl among the
39:25 It snorts at the s of the bugle. It senses the battle
Ps 19: 3 They speak without a s or a word; / their voice is
42: 4 thanks— / it was the s of a great celebration!
81: 3 S the trumpet for a sacred feast / when the moon is
98: 6 with trumpets and the s of the ram's horn. / Make a
104: 7 At the s of your rebuke, the water fled; / at the s of your thunder, it fled away.
Pr 18: 1 snarling at every s principle of conduct.
26:24 People with hate in their hearts may s pleasant
Isa 15: 3 From every home will come the s of weeping.
21: 7 Tell him to s the alert when he sees chariots drawn
27:13 In that day the great trumpet will s. Many who
30:19 He will respond instantly to the s of your cries.
33: 3 The enemy runs at the s of your voice. When you
65:19 And the s of weeping and crying will be heard no
Jer 4: 5 Tell them to s the alarm throughout the land:
6: 1 Flee from Jerusalem! S the alarm in Tekoa!
6:17 you who said, 'Listen for the s of the trumpet!'
51:27 S the battle cry! Bring out the armies of Ararat,
51:54 the s of great destruction from the land of the
Eze 3:12 me up, and I heard a loud rumbling s behind me.
3:13 It was the s of the wings of the living beings as
23:42 From your room came the s of many men
26:13 No more will the s of harps be heard among your
26:15 The whole coastline will tremble at the s of your
31:16 I made the nations shake with fear at the s of its
33: 6 and doesn't s the alarm to warn the people,
43: 2 The s of his coming was like the roar of rushing
Da 3: 5 When you hear the s of the horn, flute, zither,
3: 7 So at the s of the musical instruments,
3:10 and worship the gold statue when they hear the s of
3:15 when you hear the s of the musical instruments,
Hos 5: 8 S the alarm in Ramah! Raise the battle cry in
8: 1 "S the alarm! The enemy descends like an eagle
Joel 2: 1 S the alarm on my holy mountain! Let everyone

Am 6: 5 You sing idle songs to the s of the harp, and you
Jnh 1: 5 And all this time Jonah was s asleep down in the
Na 2: 1 S the alarm! Man the ramparts! Muster your
Zep 1:10 And a great crashing s will come from the
Zec 9:14 The Sovereign LORD will s the trumpet; he will
Mt 7:21 "Not all people who s religious are really godly.
24:31 And he will send forth his angels with the s of a
Lk 1:41 At the s of Mary's greeting, Elizabeth's child
Jn 10:21 "This doesn't s like a man possessed by a demon!
Ac 2: 2 there was a s from heaven like the roaring of a
2: 6 When they heard this s, they came running to see
9: 7 for they heard the s of someone's voice, but they
1Co 14: 8 And if the bugler doesn't s a clear call, how will
2Co 11:23 I know I s like a madman, but I have served him
Eph 4:14 cleverly lied to us and made the lie s like the truth.
1Ti 6: 3 teachers may deny these things, but these are the s,
Rev 4: 1 spoke to me with the s of a mighty trumpet blast.
14: 2 And I heard a s from heaven like the roaring of a
14: 2 It was like the s of many harpists playing together.
18:22 Never again will the s of music be heard there—
19: 1 I heard the s of a vast crowd in heaven shouting,

SOUNDED (10) [SOUND]

Jos 6:16 as the priests s the long blast on their horns,
Jdg 3:27 the hill country of Ephraim, Ehud s a call to arms.
1Sa 13: 3 so Saul s the call to arms throughout Israel.
1Ch 16: 5 Asaph, the leader of this group, s the cymbals.
Eze 10: 5 The moving wings of the cherubim s like the voice
Lk 24:11 but the story s like nonsense, so they didn't believe
Ac 27:28 A little later they s again and found only 90 feet.
Rev 1:10 voice behind me, a voice that s like a trumpet blast.
6: 1 beings called out with a voice that s like thunder,
19: 6 Then I heard again what s like the shout of a huge

SOUNDING (5) [SOUND]

Nu 10:10 s them at your annual festivals and at the beginning
31: 6 of the sanctuary and the trumpets for s the charge.
Jos 6:13 All this time the priests were s their horns.
2Ch 15:14 to the LORD with trumpets blaring and horns s.
Ne 4:20 the blast of the trumpet, rush to wherever it is s.

SOUNDINGS (1) [SOUND]

Ac 27:28 They took s and found the water was only 120 feet

SOUNDLY (2) [SOUND]

Jos 7: 4 warriors were sent, but they were s defeated.
Pr 19:15 A lazy person sleeps s—and goes hungry.

SOUNDS (11) [SOUND]

Ex 32:17 to Moses, "It s as if there is a war in the camp!"
2Ki 7: 6 of horses and the s of a great army approaching.
Ps 115: 7 walk with their feet, / or utter s with their throats!
Pr 18:17 Any story s true until someone sets the record
Jer 6: 7 Her streets echo with the s of violence
33:11 the s of joy and laughter. The joyful voices of
Am 8: 3 In that day the riotous s of singing in the Temple
1Co 1:18 cross s to those who are on the road to destruction.
2:14 It all s foolish to them because only those who
11:17 For it s as if more harm than good is done when
15:52 For when the trumpet s, the Christians who have

SOUP (1)

Pr 15:17 A bowl of s with someone you love is better than

SOUR (13)

Job 20:14 the food he has eaten turns s within him,
Ps 69:21 for food; / they offer me s wine to satisfy my thirst.
Ecc 5:14 or they are put into risky investments that turn s,
Isa 5: 2 but the grapes that grew were wild and s.
Jer 31:29 'The parents eat s grapes, but their children's
31:30 those who eat the s grapes will be the ones whose
Eze 18: 2 'The parents have eaten s grapes, but their
Mt 27:48 One of them ran and filled a sponge with s wine,
Mk 15:36 One of them ran and filled a sponge with s wine,
Lk 23:36 too, by offering him a drink of s wine.
Jn 19:29 A jar of s wine was sitting there, so they soaked a
Rev 10: 9 you swallow it, it will make your stomach s!"
10:10 was sweet in my mouth, but it made my stomach s.

SOURCE (20) [SOURCES]

Lev 5: 3 "Or if they come into contact with any s of human
20:18 because he exposed the s of her flow, and she
Nu 16:22 "O God, the God and s of all life," they pleaded.
Dt 18: 8 and offerings, even if he has a private s of income.
Ps 42: 6 from Mount Hermon, the s of the Jordan,
43: 4 to the altar of God, / to God—the s of all my joy.
68:26 of Israel; / praise the LORD, the s of Israel's life.
87: 7 will sing, / "The s of my life is in Jerusalem!"
119:114 and my shield; / your word is my only s of hope.
Isa 45:24 "The LORD is the s of all my righteousness
65:18 a place of happiness. Her people will be a s of joy.
Eze 24:21 my Temple, the s of your security and pride.
Mic 5: 5 And he will be the s of our peace.
Na 3: 9 and the land of Egypt were the s of her strength,
Zec 8:13 and make you both a symbol and a s of blessing!
Lk 1: 2 They used as their s material the reports circulating
1Co 12: 4 but it is the same Holy Spirit who is the s of them
2Co 1: 3 He is the s of every mercy and the God who
Heb 5: 9 and he became the s of eternal salvation for all
Rev 22:16 I am both the s of David and the heir to his throne.

SOURCES (3) [SOURCE]

Ge 8: 2 The underground water s ceased their gushing,

Eze 47:11 swamps will not be purified; they will be s of salt.
Zec 14: 6 On that day the s of light will no longer shine,

SOUTH (141) [SOUTHEAST, SOUTHERN, SOUTHERNMOST, SOUTHWARD]

Ge 12: 9 Then Abram traveled s by stages toward the
20: 1 Now Abraham moved s to the Negev and settled
28:14 the land from east to west and from north to s.
Ex 26:18 Twenty of these frames will support the s side of
26:27 and five for the s side. Also make five crossbars
26:35 The lampstand must be placed on the s side,
27: 9 On the s side the curtains will stretch for 150 feet.
36:23 They made twenty frames to support the s side,
36:31 wood to tie the frames on the s side together.
38: 9 the courtyard. The s wall was 150 feet long.
40:24 from the table on the s side of the Holy Place.
Nu 2:10[-11] and Gad are to camp on the s side of the
3:29 They were assigned the area s of the Tabernacle
10: 6 a second time, the tribes on the s will follow.
34: 4 then run s past Scorpion Pass in the direction of
34:10 will start at Hazar-enan and run s to Shepham,
35: 5 east, s, west, north—with the town at the center.
Dt 4:49 bank of the Jordan Valley as far s as the Dead Sea,
11:24 the wilderness in the s to Lebanon in the north,
33:23 may you possess the west and the s."
Jos 1: 4 from the Negev Desert in the s to the Lebanon
11: 2 the kings in the Jordan Valley s of Galilee;
12: 3 of the Sea of Galilee and as far s as the Dead Sea,
13: 4 The land of the Avvites in the s also remains to be
15: 2 The southern boundary began at the s bay of the
15: 3 ran s of Scorpion Pass into the wilderness of Zin and went s of Kadesh-barnea to Hezron.
15: 7 the slopes of Adummim on the s side of the valley.
15:21 the borders of Edom in the extreme s are Kabzeel,
17: 7 Then the boundary went s from Micmethath to the
17:10 The land s of the ravine belonged to Ephraim,
18: 5 excluding Judah's territory in the s and Joseph's
18:13 From there the boundary went s to Luz (that is,
18:13 to the top of the hill s of Lower Beth-horon.
18:14 then ran s along the western edge of the hill facing
18:16 crossing s of the slope where the Jebusites lived,
19: 8 including all the villages as far s as Baalath-beer
19:34 and touched the boundary of Zebulun in the s,
Jdg 1: 9 Then they turned s to fight the Canaanites living in
1Sa 14: 5 and the one on the s was in front of Geba.
23:24 of Maon in the Arabah Valley s of Jeshimon.
27:10 "Against the s of Judah, the Jerahmeelites,
2Sa 24: 2 from Dan in the north to Beersheba in the s—
24: 5 and camped at Aroer, s of the town in the valley,
24: 7 Finally, they went s to Judah as far as Beersheba.
1Ki 4:21 of the Philistines, as far s as the border of Egypt.
6: 8 The entrance to the bottom floor was on the s side
7:21 one toward the s and one toward the north.
7:21 He named the one on the s Jakin, and the one on
7:25 Three faced north, three faced west, three faced s,
7:39 He arranged five water carts on the s side of the
7:49 five on the s and five on the north,
8:65 in the north to the brook of Egypt in the s.
2Ki 11:11 They formed a line from the s side of the Temple
23:13 of Jerusalem and s of the Mount of Corruption,
1Ch 7:28 included Bethel and its surrounding towns to the s,
9:24 stationed on all four sides—east, west, north, and s.
21: 2 from Beersheba in the s to Dan in the north—
26:15 The s gate went to Obed-edom, and his sons were
26:17 four to the north gate, four to the s gate, and two to
2Ch 3:17 one to the s of the entrance and the other to the
3:17 He named the one on the s Jakin, and the one on
4: 4 Three faced north, three faced west, three faced s,
4: 6 five to the s of the Sea and five to the north.
4: 7 Five were placed against the s wall, and five were
4: 8 five along the s wall and five along the north wall.
7: 8 in the north, to the brook of Egypt in the s.
23:10 They formed a line from the s side of the Temple
30: 5 from Beersheba in the s to Dan in the north,
Job 23: 9 he is hidden. I turn to the s, but I cannot find him.
37:17 and the s wind dies down and everything is still,
39:26 makes the hawk soar and spread its wings to the s?
Ps 78:26 and guided the s wind by his mighty power.
89:12 You created north and s. / Mount Tabor and Mount
107: 3 many lands, / from east and west, from north and s.
Ecc 1: 6 The wind blows s and north, here and there,
11: 3 When a tree falls, whether s or north, there it lies.
SS 4:16 "Awake, north wind! Come, s wind! Blow on my
Isa 43: 6 and from north and s. I will bring my sons
49:12 to the north and west, and from as far s as Egypt."
Eze 6:14 from the wilderness in the s to Riblah in the north.
7: 2 Wherever you look—east, west, north, or s—
10: 3 The cherubim were standing at the s end of the
16:46 was Sodom, who lived with her daughters in the s.
20:46 of man, look toward the s and speak out against it;
20:47 they will scorch everything from s to north.
21: 4 a clean sweep throughout the land from s to north.
29:10 to Aswan, as far s as the border of Ethiopia.
40: 2 appeared to be a city across from me toward the s.
40:24 Then the man took me around to the s gateway
40:28 Then the man took me to the s gateway leading
40:31 The foyer of the s gateway faced into the outer
40:44 one beside the north gateway, facing s,
40:44 and the other beside the s gateway, facing north.
40:46 The building beside the s inner gate is for the
41:11 feet wide. One door faced north and the other s.
42:10 On the s side of the Temple there were two blocks
42:10 just s of the inner courtyard between the Temple
42:13 overlook the Temple from the north and s are holy.
42:18 The s side was the same length,
46: 9 they must leave by the s gateway.

46: 9 And those who entered through the **s** gateway must
47: 1 then passed to the right of the altar on its **s** side.
47: 2 flowing out through the **s** side of the east gateway.
47: 17 Hamath to the north and Damascus to the **s**.
47: 18 past the Dead Sea and as far **s** as Tamar.
48: 2 Asher's territory lies **s** of Dan's and also extends
48: 3 Naphtali's land lies **s** of Asher's, also extending
48: 4 Then comes Manasseh **s** of Naphtali, and its
48: 5 **S** of Manasseh is Ephraim,
48: 8 "**S** of Judah is the land set aside for a special
48: 15 **s** of the sacred Temple area, will be allotted for
48: 23 Benjamin's territory lies just **s** of the prince's
48: 24 **S** of Benjamin's territory lies that of Simeon,
48: 27 The territory of Gad is just **s** of Zebulun with the
48: 33 The **s** wall, also 1-1/2 miles long, will have gates
Da 8: 4 to the north, and to the **s**, and no one could stand
8: 9 It extended toward the **s** and the east and toward
11: 5 "The king of the **s** will increase in power, but one
11: 6 between the king of the north and the king of the **s**.
11: 6 The daughter of the king of the **s** will be given in
11: 7 when one of her relatives becomes king of the **s**,
11: 9 the north will invade the realm of the king of the **s**
11: 11 Then the king of the **s**, in great anger, will rally
11: 12 the king of the **s** will be filled with pride and will
11: 14 will be a general uprising against the king of the **s**.
11: 15 The best troops of the **s** will not be able to stand in
11: 17 and will form an alliance with the king of the **s**.
11: 25 and raise a great army against the king of the **s**.
11: 25 The king of the **s** will go to battle with a mighty
11: 29 the appointed time he will once again invade the **s**,
11: 40 time of the end, the king of the **s** will attack him,
Am 6: 14 in the north to the Arabah Valley in the **s**."
Zec 6: 6 the chariot with dappled-gray horses is going **s**."
14: 4 will move toward the north and half toward the **s**.
14: 10 north of Judah, to Rimmon, **s** of Jerusalem,
Lk 12: 55 When the **s** wind blows, you say, 'Today will be a
Ac 8: 26 "Go **s** down the desert road that runs from
27: 13 When a light wind began blowing from the **s**,
28: 13 A day later a **s** wind began blowing,
Rev 21: 13 three gates on each side—east, north, **s**, and west.

SOUTHEAST (2) [EAST, SOUTH]

1Ki 7: 39 The Sea was placed at the **s** corner of the Temple.
2Ch 4: 10 The Sea was placed near the **s** corner of the

SOUTHERN (22) [SOUTH]

Ex 23: 31 and from the **s** deserts to the Euphrates River.
Nu 34: 3 The **s** portion of your country will extend from the
34: 3 The **s** boundary will begin on the east at the Dead
Jos 15: 2 The **s** boundary began at the south bay of the Dead
15: 4 the Mediterranean Sea. This was their **s** boundary.
15: 8 along the **s** slopes of the Jebusites, where the city
18: 15 The **s** boundary began at the outskirts of
18: 19 Dead Sea, which is the **s** end of the Jordan River.
1Sa 23: 19 hill of Hakilah, which is in the **s** part of Jeshimon.
1Ki 12: 29 He placed these calf idols at the **s** and northern
Job 9: 9 the Pleiades, and the constellations of the **s** sky.
Jer 37: 5 Hophra of Egypt appeared at the **s** border of Judah.
44: 1 and Memphis, and throughout **s** Egypt as well:
44: 15 Judeans living in Pathros, the **s** region of Egypt—
Eze 20: 47 Give the **s** wilderness this message from the
27: 6 of pine wood, brought from the **s** coasts of Cyprus.
29: 14 and bring its people back to the land of Pathros in **s**
47: 19 "The **s** border will go west from Tamar to the
47: 19 to the Mediterranean. This will be the **s** border.
47: 20 **s** border to the point where the northern border
48: 28 The **s** border of Gad runs from Tamar to the waters
Zec 9: 14 his enemies like a whirlwind from the **s** desert.

SOUTHERNMOST (2) [SOUTH, MOST]

Nu 34: 4 Its **s** point will be Kadesh-barnea, from which it
Jos 15: 1 with the wilderness of Zin being its **s** point.

SOUTHWARD (7) [SOUTH]

Ge 12: 8 Abram traveled **s** and set up camp in the hill
Jos 15: 1 the tribe of Judah reached **s** to the border of Edom,
16: 7 From Janoah it turned **s** to Ataroth and Naarah,
Ne 12: 31 One of the choirs proceeded **s** along the top of the
Eze 47: 18 and runs **s** along the Jordan River between Israel
Mt 19: 1 he left Galilee and went **s** to the region of Judea
Mk 10: 1 left Capernaum and went **s** to the region of Judea

SOUTHWEST (1) [WEST]

Ac 27: 12 Phoenix was a good harbor with only a **s**

SOVEREIGN (292) [SOVEREIGNTY]

SOVEREIGN LORD (2) Ac 4:24; Rev 6:10

SOVEREIGN LORD* (290) Ge 15:2,8; Ex 23:17; 34:23; Dt 3:24; 9:26; Jos 7:7; Jdg 6:22; 16:28; 2Sa 7:18,19,19,20,22, 28,29; 1Ki 2:26; 8:53; Ps 68:20; 69:6; 71:16; 73:28; 109:21; 140:7; 141:8; Isa 7:7; 25:8; 28:16; 30:15; 40:10; 48:16; 49:22; 50:4,5,7,9; 51:22; 52:4; 56:8; 61:1,11; 65:13,15; Jer 1:6; 2:22; 4:10; 7:20; 14:13; 32:17,25; 44:26; 50:25; Eze 2:4; 3:11,27; 4:14; 5:5,7,8,11; 6:3,3,11; 7:2,5; 8:1; 9:8; 11:7,8,13, 16,17,21; 12:10,19,23,25,28,28; 13:3,8,8,9,13,16,18,20; 14:4,6,11,14, 16,18,20,21,23; 15:6,8; 16:3,8,14,19,23,30,36, 43,48,59,63; 17:3,9,12,16,19,22; 18:3,9,23,30,32; 20:3,3,5, 27,30,31,33,36, 39,40,44,47,49; 21:7,13,24,26,28; 22:3,12,19, 28,31; 23:22, 28,32,34,35,46,49; 24:3,6,9,14,21; 25:3,3,6,8, 12,13,14,15,16; 26:3,5,7,14,15,19,21; 27:3; 28:2,6,10,12,22, 24,25; 29:3,8,13, 16,19,20; 30:2,6,10,13,22; 31:10,15,18; 32:3,8,11,14,16,31, 32; 33:11,25,27; 34:2,8,10,11,15,17,20, 30,31; 35:3,6,11,14; 36:2,3,4,5,6,7,13,14,15,22,23,32,33,37; 37:3,5,9,12,19,21; 38:3,10,14,17,18,21; 39:1,5,8,10,13,17,20, 25,29; 43:18,19, 27; 44:6,9,12,15,27; 45:9,15,18; 46:1,16; 47:13,23; 48:29; Am 1:8; 3:7,8,11; 4:2,5; 5:3; 6:8; 7:1,2,4, 5,6; 8:1,3,9,11; 9:8; Ob 1:1; Mic 1:2; Hab 3:19; Zep 1:7; Zec 9:14

Ge 15: 2 But Abram replied, "O **S** LORD, what good are
15: 8 But Abram replied, "O **S** LORD, how can I be
Ex 23: 17 every man in Israel must appear before the **S**
34: 23 men of Israel must appear before the **S** LORD,
Dt 3: 24 'O **S** LORD, I am your servant. You have only
9: 26 I prayed to the LORD and said, 'O **S** LORD,
Jos 7: 7 Then Joshua cried out, "**S** LORD, why did you
Jdg 6: 22 he cried out, "**S** LORD, I have seen the angel of
16: 28 to the LORD, "**S** LORD, remember me again.
2Sa 7: 18 the LORD and prayed, "Who am I, O **S** LORD,
7: 19 And now, **S** LORD, in addition to everything
7: 19 Do you deal with everyone this way, O **S** LORD?
7: 20 You know what I am really like, **S** LORD.
7: 22 "How great you are, O **S** LORD! There is no one
7: 28 For you are God, O **S** LORD. Your words are
7: 29 O **S** LORD, it is an eternal blessing!"
1Ki 2: 26 because you carried the Ark of the **S** LORD for
8: 53 brought our ancestors out of Egypt, O **S** LORD,
Ps 68: 20 who saves! / The **S** LORD rescues us from death.
69: 6 because of me, / O **S** LORD Almighty.
71: 16 I will praise your mighty deeds, O **S** LORD.
73: 28 near God! / I have made the **S** LORD my shelter,
109: 21 But deal well with me, O **S** LORD, / for the sake
140: 7 O **S** LORD, my strong savior, / you protected me
141: 8 I look to you for help, O **S** LORD. / You are my
Isa 7: 7 "But this is what the **S** LORD says: This invasion
25: 8 The **S** LORD will wipe away all tears. He will
28: 16 Therefore, this is what the **S** LORD says: "Look!
30: 15 The **S** LORD, the Holy One of Israel, says,
40: 10 the **S** LORD is coming in all his glorious power.
48: 16 And now the **S** LORD and his Spirit have sent me
49: 22 This is what the **S** LORD says: "See, I will give a
50: 4 The **S** LORD has given me his words of wisdom,
50: 5 The **S** LORD has spoken to me, and I have
50: 7 Because the **S** LORD helps me, I will not be
50: 9 See, the **S** LORD is on my side! Who will declare
51: 22 This is what the **S** LORD, your God
52: 4 This is what the **S** LORD says: "Long ago my
56: 8 For the **S** LORD, who brings back the outcasts of
61: 1 The Spirit of the **S** LORD is upon me,
61: 11 The **S** LORD will show his justice to the nations
65: 13 Therefore, this is what the **S** LORD says:
65: 15 for the **S** LORD will destroy you and call his true
Jer 1: 6 "O **S** LORD," I said, "I can't speak for you!
2: 22 be washed away. I, the **S** LORD, have spoken!
4: 10 Then I said, "O **S** LORD, the people have been
7: 20 So the **S** LORD says: "I will pour out my terrible
14: 13 Then I said, "O **S** LORD, their prophets are
32: 17 "O **S** LORD! You have made the heavens
32: 25 And yet, O **S** LORD, you have told me to buy the
44: 26 or use this oath: 'As surely as the **S** LORD lives!'
50: 25 will be the work of the **S** LORD Almighty.
Eze 2: 4 to say to them, 'This is what the **S** LORD says!'
3: 11 and say to them, 'This is what the **S** LORD says!'
3: 27 will say to them, 'This is what the **S** LORD says!'
4: 14 Then I said, "O **S** LORD, must I be defiled by
5: 5 "This is what the **S** LORD says: This is an
5: 7 So this is what the **S** LORD says: Since you have
5: 8 I myself, the **S** LORD, am now your enemy.
5: 11 "As surely as I live, says the **S** LORD, I will cut
6: 3 of Israel this message from the **S** LORD.
6: 3 This is what the **S** LORD says to the mountains
6: 11 "This is what the **S** LORD says: Clap your hands
7: 2 of man, this is what the **S** LORD says to Israel:
7: 5 "This is what the **S** LORD says: With one blow
8: 1 were in my home, the **S** LORD took hold of me.
9: 8 face down in the dust and cried out, "O **S** LORD!
11: 7 "Therefore, this is what the **S** LORD says:
11: 8 to the war you so greatly fear, says the **S** LORD.
11: 13 face down in the dust and cried out, "O **S** LORD,
11: 16 give the exiles this message from the **S** LORD:
11: 17 I, the **S** LORD, will gather you back from the
11: 21 them fully for their sins, says the **S** LORD."
12: 10 Say to them, 'This is what the **S** LORD says:
12: 19 Give the people this message from the **S** LORD
12: 23 Give the people this message from the **S** LORD:
12: 25 in your own lifetime, says the **S** LORD."
12: 28 give them this message from the **S** LORD:
12: 28 I have threatened! I, the **S** LORD, have spoken!"
13: 3 This is what the **S** LORD says: Destruction is
13: 8 "Therefore, this is what the **S** LORD says:
13: 8 I will stand against you, says the **S** LORD.
13: 9 Then you will know that I am the **S** LORD!
13: 13 "Therefore, this is what the **S** LORD says:
13: 16 there was no peace. I, the **S** LORD, have spoken!'
13: 18 This is what the **S** LORD says: Destruction is
13: 20 "And so the **S** LORD says: I am against all your
14: 4 Give them this message from the **S** LORD:
14: 6 give the people of Israel this message from the **S**
14: 11 and I will be their God, says the **S** LORD."
14: 14 no one but themselves, declares the **S** LORD.
14: 16 the **S** LORD swears that it would do no good—
14: 18 the **S** LORD swears that they could not save the
14: 20 the **S** LORD swears that they could not save the
14: 21 "Now this is what the **S** LORD says:
14: 23 done to Israel without cause, says the **S** LORD."
15: 6 "And this is what the **S** LORD says: The people
15: 8 have been unfaithful to me, says the **S** LORD."
16: 3 Give her this message from the **S** LORD: You are
16: 8 says the **S** LORD, and you became mine.
16: 14 on you perfected your beauty, says the **S** LORD.
16: 19 and honey I had given you, says the **S** LORD.
16: 23 "Your destruction is certain, says the **S** LORD.
16: 30 says the **S** LORD, to do such things as these,
16: 36 This is what the **S** LORD says: Because you have
16: 43 repay you for all of your sins, says the **S** LORD.
16: 48 says the **S** LORD, Sodom and her daughters were
16: 59 "Now this is what the **S** LORD says: I will give
16: 63 you of all that you have done, says the **S** LORD."
17: 3 Give them this message from the **S** LORD:
17: 9 "So now the **S** LORD asks: Should I let this vine
17: 12 I will tell you, says the **S** LORD. The king of
17: 16 For as surely as I live, says the **S** LORD, the king
17: 19 "So this is what the **S** LORD says: As surely as I
17: 22 "And the **S** LORD says: I will take a tender shoot
18: 3 As surely as I live, says the **S** LORD, you will not
18: 9 is just and will surely live, says the **S** LORD.
18: 23 "Do you think, asks the **S** LORD, that I like to
18: 30 according to your actions, says the **S** LORD.
18: 32 I don't want you to die, says the **S** LORD.
20: 3 give the leaders of Israel this message from the **S**
20: 3 tell you nothing. This is the word of the **S** LORD!
20: 5 Give them this message from the **S** LORD:
20: 27 give the people of Israel this message from the **S**
20: 30 give the people of Israel this message from the **S**
20: 31 As surely as I live, says the **S** LORD, I will not
20: 33 As surely as I live, says the **S** LORD, I will rule
20: 36 bringing them out of Egypt, says the **S** LORD.
20: 39 O people of Israel, this is what the **S** LORD says:
20: 40 For on my holy mountain, says the **S** LORD,
20: 44 in spite of your wickedness, says the **S** LORD."
20: 47 wilderness this message from the **S** LORD:
20: 49 Then I said, "O **S** LORD, they are saying of me,
21: 7 And the **S** LORD says: It is coming! It's on its
21: 13 So now the **S** LORD asks: What chance do they
21: 24 "Therefore, this is what the **S** LORD says:
21: 26 Take off your jeweled crown, says the **S** LORD.
21: 28 Give them this message from the **S** LORD:
22: 3 and give her this message from the **S** LORD:
22: 12 of me and my commands, says the **S** LORD.
22: 19 So give them this message from the **S** LORD:
22: 28 They say, 'My message is from the **S** LORD,'
22: 31 full penalty for all their sins, says the **S** LORD."
23: 22 Oholibah, this is what the **S** LORD says:
23: 28 "For this is what the **S** LORD says: I will surely
23: 32 "Yes, this is what the **S** LORD says: You will
23: 34 in anguish. For I, the **S** LORD, have spoken!
23: 35 and turned your back on me, says the **S** LORD,
23: 46 "Now this is what the **S** LORD says: Bring an
23: 49 Then you will know that I am the **S** LORD."
24: 3 give them a message from the **S** LORD.
24: 6 "Now this is what the **S** LORD says:
24: 9 "This is what the **S** LORD says: Destruction is
24: 14 of all your wicked actions, says the **S** LORD."
24: 21 This is what the **S** LORD says: I will desecrate
25: 3 Give the Ammonites this message from the **S**
25: 3 Hear the word of the **S** LORD! Because you
25: 6 "And the **S** LORD says: Because you clapped
25: 8 "And the **S** LORD says: Because the people of
25: 12 "And the **S** LORD says: The people of Edom
25: 13 Therefore, says the **S** LORD, I will raise my fist
25: 14 know it is from me. I, the **S** LORD, have spoken!
25: 15 "And the **S** LORD says: The people of Philistia
25: 16 Therefore, says the **S** LORD, I will raise my fist
26: 3 "Therefore, this is what the **S** LORD says:
26: 5 their nets, for I have spoken, says the **S** LORD.
26: 7 "For the **S** LORD says: I will bring King
26: 14 have spoken! This is the word of the **S** LORD.
26: 15 "This is what the **S** LORD says to Tyre:
26: 19 "For the **S** LORD says: I will make Tyre an
26: 21 never be found. I, the **S** LORD, have spoken!"
27: 3 Give Tyre this message from the **S** LORD:
28: 2 give the prince of Tyre this message from the **S**
28: 6 "Therefore, this is what the **S** LORD says:
28: 10 of foreigners. I, the **S** LORD, have spoken!"
28: 12 Give him this message from the **S** LORD:
28: 22 Give the people of Sidon this message from the **S**
28: 24 then they will know that I am the **S** LORD.
28: 25 "This is what the **S** LORD says: The people of
29: 3 Give them this message from the **S** LORD:
29: 8 So now the **S** LORD says: I will bring an army
29: 13 "But the **S** LORD also says: At the end of the
29: 16 Then Israel will know that I alone am the **S**
29: 19 Therefore, this is what the **S** LORD says: I will
29: 20 says the **S** LORD, because he was working for
30: 2 and give this message from the **S** LORD:
30: 6 be slaughtered by the sword, says the **S** LORD.
30: 10 "For this is what the **S** LORD says:
30: 13 "This is what the **S** LORD says: I will smash the
30: 22 Therefore, this is what the **S** LORD says: I am the
31: 10 "Therefore, this is what the **S** LORD says:
31: 15 "This is what the **S** LORD says: When Assyria
31: 18 teeming hordes. I, the **S** LORD, have spoken!"
32: 3 "Therefore, this is what the **S** LORD says:
32: 8 dark above you. I, the **S** LORD, have spoken!
32: 11 "For this is what the **S** LORD says: The sword of
32: 14 flow as smoothly as olive oil, says the **S** LORD.
32: 16 and its hordes. I, the **S** LORD, have spoken!"
32: 31 having his entire army killed, says the **S** LORD.
32: 32 died by the sword. I, the **S** LORD, have spoken!"
33: 11 As surely as I live, says the **S** LORD, I take no
33: 25 Now give these people this message from the **S**
33: 27 "Give them this message from the **S** LORD:
34: 2 Give them this message from the **S** LORD:
34: 8 As surely as I live, says the **S** LORD,
34: 10 This is what the **S** LORD says: I now consider
34: 11 "For this is what the **S** LORD says: I myself will
34: 15 them to lie down in peace, says the **S** LORD.
34: 17 my people, this is what the **S** LORD says:

34:20 "Therefore, this is what the S LORD says:
34:30 of Israel, are my people, says the S LORD.
34:31 and I am your God, says the S LORD."
35: 3 Give them this message from the S LORD:
35: 6 As surely as I live, says the S LORD, since you
35:11 Therefore, as surely as I live, says the S LORD,
35:14 "This is what the S LORD says: The whole
36: 2 This is what the S LORD says: Your enemies
36: 3 of Israel this message from the S LORD:
36: 4 of Israel, hear the word of the S LORD.
36: 5 This is what the S LORD says: My jealous anger
36: 6 Give them this message from the S LORD:
36: 7 Therefore, says the S LORD, I have raised my
36:13 "This is what the S LORD says: Now the other
36:14 or bereave your nation, says the S LORD.
36:15 or cause your nation to fall, says the S LORD."
36:22 give the people of Israel this message from the S
36:23 says the S LORD, then the nations will know that
36:32 But remember, says the S LORD, I am not doing
36:33 "This is what the S LORD says: When I cleanse
36:37 "This is what the S LORD says: I am ready to
37: 3 "O S LORD," I replied, "you alone know the
37: 5 This is what the S LORD says: Look! I am going
37: 9 'This is what the S LORD says: Come, O breath,
37:12 Now give them this message from the S LORD:
37:19 say to them, 'This is what the S LORD says:
37:21 And give them this message from the S LORD:
38: 3 Give him this message from the S LORD: Gog,
38:10 "This is what the S LORD says: At that time evil
38:14 Give him this message from the S LORD:
38:17 "This is what the S LORD says: You are the one
38:18 of Israel, says the S LORD, my fury will rise!
38:21 against you throughout Israel, says the S LORD.
39: 1 Give him this message from the S LORD: I am
39: 5 open fields, for I have spoken, says the S LORD.
39: 8 day of judgment will come, says the S LORD.
39:10 who planned to plunder them, says the S LORD.
39:13 my glory on that day, says the S LORD.
39:17 all the birds and wild animals, says the S LORD.
39:20 riders, and valiant warriors, says the S LORD.
39:25 "So now the S LORD says: I will end the
39:29 out my Spirit upon them, says the S LORD."
43:18 "Son of man, this is what the S LORD says:
43:19 a young bull for a sin offering, says the S LORD.
43:27 Then I will accept you, says the S LORD."
44: 6 people of Israel, this message from the S LORD:
44: 9 "So this is what the S LORD says: No foreigners,
44:12 the consequences for their sins, says the S LORD.
44:15 and blood of the sacrifices, says the S LORD.
44:27 offer a sin offering for himself, says the S LORD.
45: 9 For this is what the S LORD says: Enough,
45:15 for the people who bring them, says the S LORD.
45:18 "This is what the S LORD says: In early spring,
46: 1 "This is what the S LORD says: The east
46:16 "This is what the S LORD says: If the prince
47:13 This is what the S LORD says: "Follow these
47:23 they now live. I, the S LORD, have spoken!
48:29 for each tribe's inheritance, says the S LORD.
Am 1: 8 left will be killed. I, the S LORD, have spoken!"
3: 7 I, the S LORD, have now done this."
3: 8 The S LORD has spoken—I dare not refuse to
3:11 Therefore," says the S LORD, "an enemy is
4: 2 The S LORD has sworn this by his holiness:
4: 5 you Israelites love to do," says the S LORD.
5: 3 The S LORD says: "When one of your cities
6: 8 The S LORD has sworn by his own name,
7: 1 The S LORD showed me a vision. I saw him
7: 2 Then I said, "O S LORD, please forgive your
7: 4 Then the S LORD showed me another vision.
7: 5 Then I said, "O S LORD, please don't do it.
7: 6 "I won't do that either," said the S LORD.
8: 1 Then the S LORD showed me another vision.
8: 3 the city in silence. I, the S LORD, have spoken!"
8: 9 At that time," says the S LORD, "I will make
8:11 "The time is surely coming," says the S LORD,
9: 8 "I, the S LORD, am watching this sinful nation
Ob 1: 1 This is the vision that the S LORD revealed to
Mic 1: 2 The S LORD has made accusations against you;
Hab 3:19 The S LORD is my strength! He will make me as
Zep 1: 7 Stand in silence in the presence of the S LORD,
Zec 9:14 The S LORD will sound the trumpet; he will go
Ac 4:24 "O S Lord, Creator of heaven and earth, the sea,
Rev 6:10 to the Lord and said, "O S Lord, holy and true,

SOVEREIGNTY (3) [SOVEREIGN]

Da 2:37 The God of heaven has given you s, power,
5:18 the Most High God gave s, majesty, glory,
7:27 Then the s, power, and greatness of all the

SOW (3) [SOWING, SOWS]

Ps 107:37 They s their fields, plant their vineyards,
Isa 28:24 Does a farmer always plow and never s? Is he
Gal 6: 7 get away with it. You will always reap what you s!

SOWING (1) [SOW]

Mt 13:18 of the story I told about the farmer s grain:

SOWS (1) [SOW]

Pr 6:19 out lies, / a person who s discord among brothers.

SPACE (8) [SPACIOUS]

Ge 1: 6 And God said, "Let there be s between the waters,
1: 7 God made this s to separate the waters above from
1: 8 And God called the s "sky." This happened on the
Job 26: 7 God stretches the northern sky over empty s
Isa 51:16 I set all the stars in s and established the earth.
Eze 41:17 The s above the door leading into the Most Holy
42: 5 because the upper levels had to allow s for
Lk 13: 7 It's taking up s we can use for something else.'

SPACIOUS (4) [SPACE]

Ex 3: 8 them out of Egypt into their own good and s land.
Jdg 18:10 God has given us a s and fertile land, lacking in
Ne 7: 4 At that time the city was large and s,
Pr 9: 1 Wisdom has built her s house with seven pillars.

SPADE (2)

Dt 23:13 Each of you must have a s as part of your
23:13 you must dig a hole with the s and cover the

SPAIN (2)

Ro 15:24 I am planning to go to S, and when I do, I will stop
15:28 of theirs, I will come to see you on my way to S.

SPAN (1)

Ps 61: 6 life of the king! / May his years s the generations!

SPANK (1)

Pr 23:13 your children. They won't die if you s them.

SPARE (39) [SPARED, SPARES, SPARING]

Ge 12:13 of their interest in you, and they will s my life."
18:24 will you still destroy it, and not s it for their sakes?
18:26 in Sodom, I will s the entire city for their sake."
42:20 If you are, I will s you." To this they agreed.
Ex 1:22 into the Nile River. But you may s the baby girls."
12:34 They wrapped their kneading bowls in their s
Nu 11:15 than treat me like this. Please s me this misery!"
Dt 13: 8 and have no pity. Do not s or protect them.
Jos 22:22 If we have done so, do not s our lives this day.
2Sa 12:16 David begged God to s the child. He went without
2Ki 1:13 man of God, please s my life and the lives of these,
1:14 the first two groups. But now please s my life!"
2Ch 31:10 we have had enough to eat and plenty to s,
Job 2: 6 the LORD said to Satan. "But s his life."
Ps 22:20 violent death; / s my precious life from these dogs.
39:13 S me so I can smile again / before I am gone
78:50 against them; / he did not s the Egyptians' lives
119:88 In your unfailing love, s my life; / then I can
Jer 50:14 S no arrows, for she has sinned against the
50:15 The LORD has taken vengeance, so do not s her.
Eze 7: 9 I will neither s nor pity you. I will repay you for all
8:18 with them in fury. I will neither pity nor s them.
9:10 So I will not s them or have any pity on them.
12:16 But I will s a few of them from death by war,
21: 4 Yes, I will not s even the righteous! I will make a
Da 5:19 he wanted to kill and spared those he wanted to s.
Joel 2:17 weeping. Let them pray, "S your people, LORD!
Jnh 1: 6 Maybe he will have mercy on us and s our lives."
Mal 3:17 I will s them as a father spares an obedient
Lk 15:17 home even the hired men have food enough to s,
Ac 27:43 But the commanding officer wanted to s Paul,
Ro 8:32 Since God did not s even his own Son but gave
11:21 For if God did not s the branches he put there in
the first place, he won't s you either.
1Co 7:28 I am trying to s you the extra problems that come
2Co 1:23 The reason I didn't return to Corinth was to s you
13: 2 as I did before, that this next time I will not s them.
2Pe 2: 4 For God did not s even the angels when they
2: 5 And God did not s the ancient world—except for

SPARED (30) [SPARE]

Ge 32:30 seen God face to face, yet my life has been s."
Ex 12:27 he s our families and did not destroy us.' " Then
Nu 22:33 have killed you by now and s the donkey."
Dt 2:34 women, and children. Not a single person was s.
9:20 But I prayed for Aaron, and the LORD s him.
Jos 6:17 the prostitute and the others in her house will be s,
6:25 So Joshua s Rahab the prostitute and her relatives
11:11 Not a single person was s. And then Joshua burned
Jdg 21:14 who were s were given to them as wives.
1Sa 15: 9 Saul and his men s Agag's life and kept the best of
15:15 "It's true that the army s the best of the sheep
15:32 "Surely the worst is over, and I have been s!"
24:10 some of my men told me to kill you, but I s you.
2Sa 8: 2 groups to be executed for every one group to be s.
8: 2 The Moabites who were s became David's servants
15:14 and the city of Jerusalem will be s from disaster."
19:23 to Shimei, David vowed, "Your life will be s."
21: 7 David s Jonathan's son Mephibosheth, who was
1Ki 20:42 Because you have s the man I said must be
2Ch 21:17 his wives. Only his youngest son, Ahaziah, was s.
Est 7: 3 is that my life and the lives of my people will be s.
Job 10:19 Then I would have been s this miserable existence.
21:30 Evil people are s in times of calamity and are
Isa 1: 9 If the LORD Almighty had not s a few of us,
24: 2 bankers and debtors—none will be s.
27: 5 These enemies will be s only if they surrender
Jer 38:20 Your life will be s, and all will go well for you.
51: 3 No one will be s! Young and old alike will be
Da 5:19 he wanted to kill and s those he wanted to spare.
Ro 9:29 "If the Lord Almighty / had not s a few of us,

SPARES (2) [SPARE]

Isa 9:19 are fuel for the fire, and no one s anyone else.
Mal 3:17 I will spare them as a father s an obedient

SPARING (1) [SPARE]

Ac 20:29 come in among you after I leave, not s the flock.

SPARK (2) [SPARKED, SPARKS]

Isa 1:31 Your evil deeds are the s that will set the straw on
Jas 3: 5 it can do. A tiny s can set a great forest on fire.

SPARKED (1) [SPARK]

Hag 1:14 So the LORD s the enthusiasm of Zerubbabel son

SPARKLE (2) [SPARKLED, SPARKLING]

Pr 23:31 Don't let the s and smooth taste of wine deceive
Zec 9:16 They will s in his land like jewels in a crown.

SPARKLED (4) [SPARKLE]

Eze 1:16 The wheels s as if made of chrysolite. All four
1:22 spread out above them like the sky. It s like crystal.
10: 9 wheel beside him, and the wheels s like chrysolite.
Rev 21:11 with the glory of God and s like a precious gem,

SPARKLING (3) [SPARKLE]

SS 7: 4 Your eyes are like the s pools in Heshbon by the
Isa 54:12 I will make your towers of s rubies and your gates
Rev 4: 6 the throne was a shiny sea of glass, s like crystal.

SPARKS (4) [SPARK]

Job 5: 7 People are born for trouble as predictably as s fly
18: 5 be snuffed out. The s of their fire will not glow.
41:19 Fire and s leap from its mouth.
Isa 5:28 S will fly from their horses' hooves as the wheels

SPARROW (3) [SPARROWS]

Ps 84: 3 Even the s finds a home there, / and the swallow
Pr 26: 2 Like a fluttering s or a darting swallow, an unfair
Mt 10:29 Not even a s, worth only half a penny, can fall to

SPARROWS (3) [SPARROW]

Mt 10:31 are more valuable to him than a whole flock of s.
Lk 12: 6 "What is the price of five s? A couple of pennies?
12: 7 are more valuable to him than a whole flock of s.

SPATTERED (1)

2Ki 9:33 and some of her blood s against the wall and on the

SPEAK (264) [GREEK-SPEAKING, SPEAKER, SPEAKERS, SPEAKING, SPEAKS, SPOKE, SPOKEN, SPOKESMAN]

Ge 10: 9 and people would s of someone as being "like
18:27 let me go on and s further to my Lord, even though
18:30 "Let me s—suppose only thirty are found?"
18:31 "Since I have dared to s to the Lord, let me
18:32 please do not get angry; I will s but once more!
50: 4 and asked them to s to Pharaoh on his behalf.
Ex 4:11 "Who makes people so they can s or not s,
4:12 I will help you s well, and I will tell you what to
4:15 I will help both of you to s clearly, and I will tell
7: 1 Aaron, will be your prophet; he will s for you.
9:14 I will send a plague that will really s to you
19: 9 so the people themselves can hear me as I s to you.
20:19 But don't let God s directly to us. If he does,
29:42 where I will meet you and s with you.
33:11 the LORD would s to Moses face to face,
34:34 into the Tent of Meeting to s with the LORD,
34:35 on again until he returned to s with the LORD.
Nu 6: 1 "S to the people of Israel and give them these
7:89 Whenever Moses went into the Tabernacle to s
12: 8 I s to him face to face, directly and not in riddles!
22:28 Then the LORD caused the donkey to s.
22:38 I will s only the messages that God gives me."
33:51 "S to the Israelites and tell them: 'When you cross
Dt 3:26 'That's enough!' he ordered. 'S of it no more.
4:36 great fire here on earth so he could s to you from it.
18:20 or who falsely claims to s for me must die.'
20: 2 the priest will come forward to s with the troops.
31:28 your tribes so that I can s to them and call heaven
32: 1 "Listen, O heavens, and I will s! / Hear, O earth,
Jos 10:21 After that, no one dared to s a word against Israel.
Jdg 19:30 Shouldn't we s up and do something about this?"
Ru 4: 4 I felt that I should s to you about it so that you can
1Sa 2: 3 and haughty! / Don't s with such arrogance!
2Sa 3:27 Joab took him aside at the gateway as if to s with
7:19 you s of giving me a lasting dynasty!
13:13 Please, just s to the king about it, and he will let
14:12 of you!" she said. "Go ahead," he urged. "S!"
17: 6 we follow Ahithophel's advice? If not, s up."
19:43 we were the first to s of bringing him back to be
1Ki 2:17 He replied, "S to King Solomon on my behalf,
2:18 Bathsheba replied. "I will s to the king for you."
2:19 So Bathsheba went to King Solomon to s on
4:33 He could s with authority about all kinds of plants,
4:33 He could also s about animals, birds, reptiles,
12: 3 and the whole assembly of Israel went to s with
22:16 you s only the truth when you s for the LORD?"
22:22 go out and inspire all Ahab's prophets to s lies.'
22:24 "When did the Spirit of the LORD leave me to s
2Ki 3:12 "Then the LORD will s through him."
4:12 "Tell the woman I want to s to her."
6:12 tells the king of Israel even the words you s in the
18:26 "Please s to us in Aramaic, for we understand it
18:26 Don't s in Hebrew, for the people on the wall will
18:36 because Hezekiah had told them not to s.

22:13 and s to the LORD for me and for the people
1Ch 17:17 you s of giving me a lasting dynasty!
17:17 You s as though I were someone very great,
2Ch 10: 3 and all Israel went together to s with Rehoboam.
18:15 you s only the truth when you s for the LORD?"
18:21 go out and inspire all Ahab's prophets to s lies.'
18:23 "When did the Spirit of the LORD leave me to s
34:21 "Go to the Temple and s to the LORD for me
Ne 13:24 and could not s the language of Judah at all.
Job 9:35 Then I could s to him without fear, but I cannot do
10: 1 I will s in the bitterness of my soul.
11: 5 If only God would s; if only he would tell you
12: 8 S to the earth, and it will instruct you. Let the fish of the sea s to you.
13: 3 Oh, how I long to s directly to the Almighty.
13:13 Let me s—and I will face the consequences.
13:22 I will answer! Or let me s to you, and you reply.
15: 3 It isn't right to s so foolishly. What good do such
16: 3 What have I said that makes you s so endlessly?
16: 5 what I would do. I would s in a way that helps you.
16: 6 defend myself. And it does not help if I refuse to s.
18: 2 you stop talking? S sense if you want us to answer!
19:18 When I stand to s, they turn their backs on me.
21: 3 Bear with me, and let me s. After I have spoken,
27: 4 my lips will s no evil, and my tongue will s no lies.
29:21 They were silent as they waited for me to s.
29:23 They longed for me to s as they longed for rain.
32: 4 Elihu had waited for the others to s because they
32: 7 I thought, 'Those who are older should s,
32:17 I will say my piece. I will s my mind. I surely will.
32:20 I must s to find relief, so let me give my answers.
33: 2 Now that I have begun to s, let me continue.
33: 3 I s with all sincerity; I s the truth.
37:20 that I want to s? Can we s when we are confused?
42: 4 "You said, 'Listen and I will s! I have some
Ps 5: 9 My enemies cannot s one truthful word.
15: 3 or harm their neighbors / or s evil of their friends.
16: 4 their sacrifices / or even s the names of their gods.
19: 2 Day after day they continue to s; / night after night
19: 3 They s without a sound or a word; / their voice is
28: 3 those who s friendly words to their neighbors
34: 1 at all times. / I will constantly s his praises.
38:13 I am silent before them as one who cannot s.
40: 9 I have not been afraid to s out, / as you, O LORD,
50: 7 "O my people, listen as I s. / Here are my charges
73: 8 They scoff and s only evil; / in their pride they
75: 5 at the heavens / or s with rebellious arrogance.' "
78: 2 for I will s to you in a parable. / I will teach you
88:12 Can the darkness s of your miracles? / Can anyone
107: 2 Has the LORD redeemed you? Then s out!
119:23 Even princes sit and s against me, / but I will
119:46 I will s to kings about your decrees, / and I will not
120: 7 I am for peace; / but when I s, they are for war!
Pr 8: 7 for I s the truth and hate every kind of deception.
10:32 The godly s words that are helpful, but the wicked s only what is corrupt.
16:13 with righteous lips; he loves those who s honestly.
21:28 but an attentive witness will be allowed to s.
23:16 my heart will thrill when you s what is right
31: 8 S up for those who cannot s for themselves;
31: 9 Yes, s up for the poor and helpless, and see that
Ecc 3: 7 to mend. / A time to be quiet and a time to s up.
6:11 The more words you s, the less they mean. So why
Isa 3: 8 because they s out against the LORD and refuse
19:17 Just to s the name of Israel will strike deep terror in
19:18 They will even begin to s the Hebrew language.
28: 9 Why does he s to us like this? Are we little
28:11 will s to them through foreign oppressors who s an
32: 4 Those who stammer in uncertainty will s out
35: 6 and those who cannot s will shout and sing!
36:11 "Please s to us in Aramaic, for we understand it
36:11 Don't s in Hebrew, for the people on the wall will
36:21 because Hezekiah had told them not to s.
40: 2 "S tenderly to Jerusalem. Tell her that her sad
41: 1 Bring your strongest arguments. Come now and s.
44:27 When I s to the rivers and say, 'Be dry!' they will
45:19 I, the LORD, s only what is true and right.
50: 2 the reason! For I can s to the sea and make it dry!
58:13 and s of it with delight as the LORD's holy day.
Jer 1: 6 "O Sovereign LORD," I said, "I can't s for you!
5: 5 I will go and s to their leaders. Surely they will
6:10 Who will listen when I s? Their ears are closed,
10: 5 It cannot s, and it needs to be carried because it
12: 6 Do not trust them, no matter how pleasantly they s.
14:14 I did not send them or tell them to s. I did not give
14:14 They s foolishness made up in their own lying
15:19 If you s words that are worthy, you will be my
18: 2 jars are made. I will s to you while you are there."
20: 8 Whenever I s, the words come out in a violent
20: 9 say I'll never mention the LORD or s in his name,
21: 1 son of Maaseiah, the priest, to s with him.
22: 1 "Go over and s directly to the king of Judah.
23:16 everything they say. They do not s for the LORD!
23:21 not sent these prophets, yet they claim to s for me.
26:15 LORD sent me to s every word you have heard."
28: 7 But listen now to the solemn words I s to you in
38: 8 so Ebed-melech rushed from the palace to s with
Eze 2: 1 of man," said the voice. "I want to s with you."
3:27 a message, I will loosen your tongue and let you s.
13: 2 s against the false prophets of Israel who are
13:17 also s out against the women who prophesy from
20:46 of man, look toward the south and s out against it;
22:28 announce false visions and s false messages.
33:22 so I would be able to s when this man arrived the
37: 4 said to me, "S to these bones and say, 'Dry bones,
37: 9 Then he said to me, "S to the winds and say:
Da 3:29 s a word against the God of Shadrach, Meshach,
10: 9 When I heard him s, I fainted and lay there with
10:16 my lips, and I opened my mouth and began to s.
10:19 and said to him, "Now you may s, my lord,
Hos 2:14 her out into the desert and s tenderly to her there.
Hab 2:19 Can an idol s for God? They may be overlaid with
Mal 3: 5 I will s against those who cheat employees of their
Mt 9:32 some people brought to him a man who couldn't s
12:22 He healed the man so that he could both s and see.
12:34 How could evil men like you s what is good
12:36 account on judgment day of every idle word you s.
12:47 brothers are outside, and they want to s to you."
13:35 prophecy that said, / "I will s to you in parables.
15:31 Those who hadn't been able to s were talking,
17:25 But before he had a chance to s, Jesus asked him,
Mk 1:34 who he was, he refused to allow the demons to s.
7:35 the man could hear perfectly and s plainly!
9:17 He can't s because he is possessed by an evil spirit
9:39 in my name will soon be able to s evil of me.
16:17 in my name, and they will s new languages.
Lk 1:20 you won't be able to s until the child is born.
1:22 he finally did come out, he couldn't s to them.
1:64 Instantly Zechariah could s again, and he began
11:14 Jesus cast a demon out of a man who couldn't s,
12:10 Yet those who s against the Son of Man may be
20:21 we know that you s and teach what is right and are
Jn 3: 2 came to s with Jesus. "Teacher," he said, "we all
7:13 But no one had the courage to s favorably about
8:28 on my own, but I s what the Father taught me.
9:21 He is old enough to s for himself. Ask him."
9:23 why they said, "He is old enough to s for himself.
12:49 I don't s on my own authority. The Father who
Ac 4:17 We'll warn them not to s to anyone in Jesus' name
4:18 and told them never again to s or teach about Jesus.
5:40 Then they ordered them never again to s in the
8:33 no justice. / Who can s of his descendants?
13:42 and s about these things the next week.
16:13 and we sat down to s with some women who had
17:32 When they heard Paul s of the resurrection of a
18: 9 told him, "Don't be afraid! S out! Don't be silent!
19:33 He motioned for silence and tried to s in defense.
19:35 mayor was able to quiet them down enough to s.
22:14 and to see the Righteous One and hear him s.
23: 5 'Do not s evil of any one who rules over you.' "
24:10 The governor motioned for him to rise and s.
26: 1 said to Paul, "You may s in your defense."
26:26 I s frankly, for I am sure these events are all
Ro 6:19 I s this way, using the illustration of slaves
9: 1 the presence of Christ, I s with utter truthfulness—
12: 6 s out when you have faith that God is speaking
1Co 2: 6 mature Christians, I do s with words of wisdom,
2: 7 the wisdom we s of is the secret wisdom of God,
2:13 We s words given to us by the Spirit,
7:12 Now, I will s to the rest of you, though I do not
12:10 Still another person is given the ability to s in
12:28 those who s in unknown languages.
12:30 Does God give all of us the ability to s in unknown
13: 1 If I could s in any language in heaven or on earth
13: 2 so that I could s to a mountain and make it move,
14: 2 For if your gift is the ability to s in tongues,
14:11 I will not understand people who s those
14:18 I thank God that I s in tongues more than all of
14:19 But in a church meeting I would much rather s five
14:21 in the Scriptures, / "I will s to my own people
14:26 one will s in an unknown language, while another
14:27 or three should s in an unknown language.
14:27 They must s one at a time, and someone must be
14:28 church meeting and s in tongues to God privately.
14:31 In this way, all who prophesy will have a turn to s,
14:34 It is not proper for them to s. They should be
14:35 for it is improper for women to s in church
2Co 4:13 had when he said, "I believed in God, and so I s."
5:20 and God is using us to s to you.
Gal 3:23 We were kept in protective custody, so to s,
Php 2:15 so that no one can s a word of blame against you.
1Th 1:10 And they s of how you are looking forward to the
2: 4 For we s as messengers who have been approved
2Th 3:15 but s to them as you would to a Christian who
1Ti 3: 7 people outside the church must s well of him
3:11 must be respected and must not s evil of others.
5: 1 Never s harshly to an older man, but appeal to him
Tit 3: 2 They must not s evil of anyone, and they must
Heb 2: 3 It was passed on to us by those who heard him s,
Jas 1:19 Dear friends, be quick to listen, slow to s, and slow
2:12 So whenever you s, or whatever you do,
4:11 Don't s evil against each other, my dear brothers
1Pe 3: 1 Your godly lives will s to them better than any
3:16 Then if people s evil against you, they will be
4:11 Then s as though God himself were speaking
2Pe 1:21 It was the Holy Spirit who moved the prophets to s
2:11 never s out disrespectfully against the glorious
1Jn 4: 1 do not believe everyone who claims to s by the
4: 5 so they s from the world's viewpoint,
3Jn 1:12 say the same for him, and you know we s the truth.
Rev 13: 5 Then the beast was allowed to s great blasphemies
13:15 to give life to this statue so that it could s.

SPEAKER (6) [SPEAK]

Ex 4:10 with the LORD, "O Lord, I'm just not a good s.
4:14 Aaron the Levite? He is a good s. And look!
Ac 14:12 that Paul, because he was the chief s, was Hermes.
18:24 an eloquent s who knew the Scriptures well,
2Co 11: 6 I may not be a trained s, but I know what I am
1Pe 4:11 Are you called to be a s? Then speak as though

SPEAKERS (1) [SPEAK]

2Co 8: 7 you have so much faith, such gifted s,

SPEAKING (104) [SPEAK]

Ge 23:10 s publicly before all the elders of the town.
42:21 S among themselves, they said, "This has all
42:23 for he had been s to them through an interpreter.
Ex 31:18 Then as the LORD finished s with Moses on
34:33 When Moses had finished s with them, he put a
Nu 7:89 he heard the voice s to him from between the two
16:31 He had hardly finished s the words when the
21: 7 "We have sinned by s against the LORD
Dt 4:33 Has any nation ever heard the voice of God s from
5:24 Today we have seen God s to humans, and yet we
Jdg 2: 4 When the angel of the LORD finished s,
6:17 a sign to prove that it is really the LORD s to me.
15:17 When he finished s, he threw away the jawbone;
Ru 2:13 "You have comforted me by s so kindly to me,
1Ki 1:22 While she was still s with the king,
1:42 And while he was still s, Jonathan son of Abiathar
13: 4 angry with the man of God for s against the altar.
Job 1:16 While he was still s, another messenger arrived
1:17 While he was still s, a third messenger arrived with
1:18 While he was still s, another messenger arrived
4: 2 let me say a word? For who could keep from s out?
7:11 "I cannot keep from s. I must express my anguish.
27: 1 Job continued s:
29: 1 Job continued s:
36: 1 Elihu continued s:
42: 7 After the LORD had finished s to Job, he said to
Ps 12: 2 s with flattering lips and insincere hearts.
15: 2 do what is right, / s the truth from sincere hearts.
39: 2 there in silence— / not even s of good things—
Pr 15:28 The godly think before s; the wicked spout evil
Isa 9:17 For they are all hypocrites, s wickedness with lies.
Jer 11:21 They said they would kill me if I did not stop s in
Eze 1:28 in the dust, and I heard someone's voice s to me.
11:13 While I was still s, Pelatiah son of Benaiah
23: 4 I am s of Samaria and Jerusalem, for Oholah is
43: 6 And I heard someone s to me from within the
Da 4:31 While he was still s these words, a voice called
8:18 While he was s, I fainted and lay there with my
10:15 While he was s to me, I looked down at the
Hos 1: 2 When the LORD first began s to Israel through
Zec 11:11 and they knew that the LORD was s to them
Mt 7:28 After Jesus finished s, the crowds were amazed at
10:20 it will be the Spirit of your Father s through you.
12:46 As Jesus was s to the crowd, his mother
13:34 and illustrations like these when s to the crowds.
16:12 Then at last they understood that he wasn't s about
17:13 Then the disciples realized he had been s of John
19:26 looked at them intently and said, "Humanly s,
22:43 s under the inspiration of the Holy Spirit, call him
Mk 5:35 While he was still s to her, messengers arrived
10:27 looked at them intently and said, "Humanly s,
12:36 s under the inspiration of the Holy Spirit, said,
13:11 Then it is not you who will be s, but the Holy
Lk 5: 4 When he had finished s, he said to Simon,
8:49 While he was still s to her, a messenger arrived
9:31 And they were s of how he was about to fulfill
11:27 As he was s, a woman in the crowd called out,
11:37 As Jesus was s, one of the Pharisees invited him
11:53 As Jesus finished s, the Pharisees and teachers of
Jn 6:71 He was s of Judas, son of Simon Iscariot, one of
7:26 But here he is, s in public, and they say nothing to
7:39 he said "living water," he was s of the Spirit,
8: 3 As he was s, the teachers of religious law
9:37 have seen him," Jesus said, "and he is s to you!"
16:29 "At last you are s plainly and not in parables.
Ac 1:16 long ago by the Holy Spirit, s through King David.
2: 4 the Holy Spirit and began s in other languages,
2: 8 and yet we hear them s the languages of the lands
2:11 And we all hear these people s in our own
2:32 "This prophecy was s of Jesus, whom God raised
4: 1 While Peter and John were s to the people,
6:13 "This man is always s against the Temple
10:46 for they heard them s in tongues and praising God.
13:16 lifted his hand to quiet them, and started s.
20:36 When he had finished s, he knelt and prayed with
22: 2 When they heard him s in their own language,
26:25 Most Excellent Festus. I am s the sober truth.
Ro 4: 1 Abraham was, humanly s, the founder of our
12: 6 speak out when you have faith that God is s
1Co 9:10 Wasn't he also s to us? Of course he was. Just as
12: 3 No one s by the Spirit of God can curse Jesus,
12:10 is really the Spirit of God or another spirit that is s.
13: 8 but prophecy and s in unknown languages
14: 2 You will be s by the power of the Spirit, but it will
14: 5 I wish you all had the gift of s in tongues, but even
14: 5 is a greater and more useful gift than s in tongues,
14: 7 are examples of the need for s in plain language.
14:13 So anyone who has the gift of s in tongues should
14:22 So you see that s in tongues is a sign, not for
14:30 from the Lord, the one who is s must stop.
14:39 be eager to prophesy, and don't forbid s in tongues.
Gal 2:11 s strongly against what he was doing, for it was
Eph 6:20 But pray that I will keep on s boldly for him,
Tit 2: 3 They must not go around s evil of others and must
Heb 3:18 And to whom was God s when he vowed that they
3:18 of rest? He was s to those who disobeyed him.
12:19 so terrible that they begged God to stop s.
12:25 to it that you obey God, the one who is s to you.
1Pe 3:10 and good days, / keep your tongue from s evil,
4:11 Then speak as though God himself were s through
2Pe 3:16 s of these things in all of his letters. Some of his
Rev 1: 9 for preaching the word of God and s about Jesus.
1:12 When I turned to see who was s to me, I saw seven
9:13 and I heard a voice s from the four horns of the

SPEAKS (37) [SPEAK]

Ex 33:11 to Moses face to face, as a man s to his friend.
Nu 21:14 s of "the town of Waheb in the area of Suphah,
Dt 5:25 If the LORD our God s to us again, we will
1Sa 20:12 If he s favorably about you, I will let you know.
2Sa 23: 1 "David, the son of Jesse, s— / David, the man to
23: 2 "The Spirit of the LORD s through me;
1Ki 17:24 of God, and that the LORD truly s through you."
Job 26: 4 these wise sayings? Whose spirit s through you?
33:14 But God s again and again, though people do not
33:15 He s in dreams, in visions of the night when deep
34:35 'Job s without knowledge; his words lack insight.'
37: 4 He does not restrain the thunder when he s.
Ps 85: 8 for he s peace to his people, his faithful ones.
Pr 16:10 The king s with divine wisdom; he must never
17:19 loves sin; anyone who s boastfully invites disaster.
29:20 a fool than for someone who s without thinking.
31:26 When she s, her words are wise, and kindness is
Isa 49: 5 And now the LORD s—he who formed me in my
52: 6 Then at last they will recognize that it is I who s to
Jer 10:13 When he s, there is thunder in the heavens.
51:16 When he s, there is thunder in the heavens.
Eze 36: 4 He s to the hills and mountains, ravines
Mic 1: 2 against you; the Lord s from his holy Temple.
Mt 10:41 If you welcome a prophet as one who s for God,
15: 4 and 'Anyone who s evil of father or mother must
Mk 7:10 and 'Anyone who s evil of father or mother must
Lk 12:10 but anyone who s blasphemies against the Holy
Jn 3:34 He s God's words, for God's Spirit is upon him
Ac 21:28 He s against the Temple—and he even defiles it by
Ro 8:16 For his Holy Spirit s to us deep in our hearts
1Co 14: 4 A person who s in tongues is strengthened
14: 4 but one who s a word of prophecy strengthens the
2Co 13: 3 I will give you all the proof you want that Christ s
Heb 8:13 When God s of a new covenant, it means he has
11: 4 is long dead, he still s to us because of his faith.
12:25 how terrible our danger if we reject the One who s
3Jn 1:12 But everyone s highly of Demetrius, even truth

SPEAR (41) [SPEARHEAD, SPEARMEN, SPEARS]

Nu 25: 7 jumped up and left the assembly. Then he took a s
25: 8 Phinehas thrust the s all the way through the man's
Jos 8:18 "Point your s toward Ai, for I will give you the
8:26 For Joshua kept holding out his s until everyone
Jdg 5: 8 the city gates. / Yet not a shield or s could be seen
1Sa 13:22 So none of the people of Israel had a sword or s,
17: 7 The shaft of his s was as heavy and thick as a
17:45 "You come to me with sword, s, and javelin,
18:10 this happened. But Saul, who had a s in his hand,
19:10 Saul hurled his s at David in an attempt to kill him.
19:10 into the night, leaving the s stuck in the wall.
20:33 Then Saul hurled his s at Jonathan, intending to
21: 8 asked Ahimelech, "Do you have a s or sword?
22: 6 holding his s and surrounded by his officers.
26: 7 with his s stuck in the ground beside his head.
26: 8 "Let me thrust that s through him. I'll pin him to
26:11 we'll take his s and his jug of water and then get
26:12 So David took the s and jug of water that were near
26:16 Where are the king's s and the jug of water that
26:22 "Here is your s, O king," David replied. "Let one
2Sa 1: 6 I saw Saul there leaning on his s with the enemy
2:23 so Abner thrust the butt end of his s through
2:23 and the s came out through his back.
21:19 The handle of his s was as thick as a weaver's
23: 8 He once used his s to kill eight hundred enemy
23:18 He once used his s to kill three hundred enemy
23:21 a great Egyptian warrior who was armed with a s.
23:21 Benaiah wrenched the s from the Egyptian's hand
1Ch 11:11 He once used his s to kill three hundred enemy
11:20 He once used his s to kill three hundred enemy
11:23 and whose s was as thick as a weaver's beam.
11:23 Benaiah wrenched the s from the Egyptian's hand
12: 8 They were expert with both shield and s, as fierce
20: 5 The handle of Lahmi's s was as thick as a weaver's
2Ch 25: 5 and older, all trained in the use of s and shield.
Job 39:23 arrows rattle against it, and the s and javelin flash.
41:26 sword can stop it, nor s nor dart nor pointed shaft.
Ps 35: 3 Lift up your s and javelin / and block the way of
46: 9 He breaks the bow and snaps the s in two;
Hab 3:11 your arrows and the flashing of your glittering s.
Jn 19:34 however, pierced his side with a s, and blood

SPEARHEAD (2) [SPEAR]

1Sa 17: 7 tipped with an iron s that weighed fifteen pounds.
2Sa 21:16 his bronze s weighed more than seven pounds,

SPEARMEN (1) [SPEAR]

Ac 23:23 Also take two hundred s and seventy horsemen.

SPEARS (18) [SPEAR]

1Sa 13:19 they would make swords and s for the Hebrews.
2Ki 11:10 and he supplied them with the s and shields that
1Ch 12:24 were 6,800 warriors armed with shields and s.
12:34 and 37,000 warriors armed with shields and s.
2Ch 11:12 and s in these towns as a further safety measure.
14: 8 the tribe of Judah, armed with large shields and s.
23: 9 Then Jehoiada supplied the commanders with the s
26:14 s, helmets, coats of mail, bows, and sling stones.
Ne 4:13 guard by families, armed with swords, s, and bows.
4:16 worked while the other half stood guard with s,
Ps 57: 4 whose teeth pierce like s and arrows,
Isa 2: 4 into plowshares and their s into pruning hooks.
Jer 46: 4 Put on your helmets, sharpen your s, and prepare
Eze 39: 9 and large shields, bows and arrows, javelins and s,
Joel 3:10 into swords and your pruning hooks into s.
Mic 4: 3 into plowshares and their s into pruning hooks.
Na 2: 3 into position, with a forest of s waving above them.
3: 3 and glittering s in the upraised arms of the cavalry!

SPECIAL (187) [ESPECIALLY, SPECIALLY]

Ge 17:18 "Yes, may Ishmael enjoy your s blessing!"
24:42 my mission a success, please guide me in a s way.
24:67 and she was a s comfort to him after the death of
37: 3 So one day he gave Joseph a s gift—a beautiful
47: 6 And if any of them have s skills, put them in
Ex 6: 7 I will make you my own s people, and I will be
12: 6 "Take s care of these lambs until the evening of
12:14 Each year you will celebrate it as a s festival to the
12:16 all the people must gather for a time of s worship.
19: 5 you will be my own s treasure from among all the
25:30 You must always keep the s Bread of the Presence
26:31 "Across the inside of the Tabernacle hang a s
28: 2 Make s clothing for Aaron to show his separation
28: 3 Instruct all those who have s skills as tailors to
28: 4 They will also make s garments for Aaron's sons
29:24 and his sons to be lifted up as a s gift to the
29:26 and lift it up in the LORD's presence as a s gift to
31: 6 I have given s skill to all the naturally talented
31:11 anointing oil; and the s incense for the Holy Place.
33:16 How else will they know we are s and distinct
34: 9 and our sins. Accept us as your own s possession."
35:35 The LORD has given them s skills as jewelers,
Lev 6:10 after dressing in his s linen clothing
7:29 bring part of it as a s gift to the LORD.
8: 2 and his sons, along with their s clothing,
21:10 and has been ordained to wear the s priestly
25:12 and you must observe it as a s and holy time.
27: 2 If you make a s vow to dedicate someone to the
Nu 3:32 with s responsibility for the oversight of the
4: 7 spoons, bowls, cups, and the s bread on the cloth.
4: 9 lamp snuffers, trays, and s jars of olive oil.
6: 2 either men or women, take the s vow of a Nazirite,
6: 2 setting themselves apart to the LORD in a s way,
6:21 they must fulfill their s vow exactly as they have
6:23 and his sons to bless the people of Israel with this s
8:11 LORD as a s offering from the people of Israel,
8:13 and present them as a s offering to the LORD.
8:15 purified them and presented them as a s offering.
8:21 and Aaron presented them to the LORD as a s
15: 3 or a s sacrifice at any of the annual festivals,
15: 8 or a sacrifice in fulfillment of a s vow or as a peace
16:10 He has given this s ministry only to you and your
18: 6 from among the Israelites to be your s assistants.
18: 7 I am giving you the priesthood as your s gift of
25:12 So tell him that I am making my s covenant of
28:27 A s whole burnt offering will be offered that day,
28:31 These s burnt offerings, along with their drink
29: 6 These s sacrifices are in addition to your regular
29:13 That day you must present a s whole burnt offering
34: 2 which I am giving you as your s possession,
Dt 4:20 Egypt to become his own people and s possession;
4:21 your God is giving you as your s possession.
4:38 you in and give you their land as a s possession,
7: 6 your God has chosen you to be his own s treasure.
9:26 They are your s possession, redeemed from Egypt
9:29 But they are your people and your s possession,
12: 6 your sacrifices, your tithes, your s gifts,
12:10 LORD your God is giving you as a s possession.
12:11 your sacrifices, your tithes, your s gifts,
12:17 a vow, nor your freewill offerings, nor your s gifts.
14: 2 and he has chosen you to be his own s treasure
15: 4 you in the land he is giving you as a s possession.
19:10 LORD your God is giving you as a s possession,
19:14 LORD your God is giving you as a s possession,
20:16 LORD your God is giving you as a s possession,
21:23 LORD your God is giving you as a s possession.
24: 4 LORD your God is giving you as a s possession.
24: 5 into the army or given any other s responsibilities.
25:19 in the land he is giving you as a s possession,
26: 1 LORD your God is giving you as a s possession
26:12 "Every third year you must offer a s tithe of your
26:18 his own s treasure, just as he promised, and that
32: 9 belong to the LORD; / Jacob is his s possession.
33: 4 the s possession of the assembly of Israel.
Jos 11:23 He gave it to the people of Israel as their s
13: 6 So be sure to give this land to Israel as a s
14: 9 you were just walking will be your s possession
19:49 the Israelites gave a s piece of land to Joshua as his
1Sa 1: 5 But he gave Hannah a s portion because he loved
9:22 the table, honoring them above the thirty s guests.
9:27 for I have received a s message for you from
12:22 great name. He made you a s nation for himself.
13: 2 Saul selected three thousand s troops from the
18: 3 And Jonathan made a s vow to be David's friend,
24: 2 So Saul chose three thousand s troops from
2Sa 6: 1 Then David mobilized thirty thousand s troops.
6:17 The Ark of the LORD was placed inside the s tent
13: 8 some dough. Then she baked some s bread for him.
1Ki 8:36 have given to your people as their s possession.
8:51 for they are your people—your s possession—
8:53 nations of the earth to be your own s possession."
18:46 Now the LORD gave s strength to Elijah.
2Ki 15:20 pay twenty ounces of silver in the form of a s tax.
1Ch 15: 1 Ark of God and set up a s tent there to shelter it.
16: 1 So they brought the Ark of God into the s tent
16:18 you the land of Canaan / as your s possession."
2Ch 1: 4 to the s tent he had prepared for it in Jerusalem.
2: 4 spices before him, to display the s sacrificial bread,
5: 5 along with the s tent and all its sacred utensils.
6:27 have given to your people as their s possession.
32:27 He had to build s treasury buildings for his silver,
Ne 13: 5 olive oil, and the s portion set aside for the priests.
Est 1: 5 the king gave a s banquet for all the palace
2: 9 He quickly ordered a s menu for her and provided
2:12 followed by six months with s perfumes
Job 33:23 "But if a s messenger from heaven is there to
Ps 28: 9 Save your people! / Bless Israel, your s possession!
74: 2 the tribe you redeemed as your own s possession!
78:62 so angry with his own people—his s possession.
79: 1 have conquered your land, your s possession.
82: 2 How long will you shower s favors on the wicked?
94:14 he will not abandon his own s possession.
105:11 you the land of Canaan / as your s possession."
106:40 his people, / and he abhorred his own s possession.
135: 4 Jacob for himself, / Israel for his own s treasure.
135:12 an inheritance, / a s possession to his people Israel.
136:22 a s possession to his servant Israel. / His faithful
Isa 1:13 and the Sabbath day, and your s days for fasting—
14: 1 of Jacob. Israel will be his s people once again.
19:25 I have made. Blessed be Israel, my s possession!"
63:17 for we are your servants and your s possession.
Jer 10:16 that exists, / including Israel, his own s possession.
12: 7 "I have abandoned my people, my s possession.
51:19 including his people, his own s possession.
Eze 20:12 them apart to be holy, making them my s people.
39:14 s crews will be appointed to search the land for any
45: 7 "Two s sections of land will be set apart for the
46:11 "So at the s feasts and sacred festivals, the grain
48: 8 "South of Judah is the land set aside for a s
48:12 It will be their s portion when the land is
48:14 None of this s land will ever be sold or traded
Da 1:17 And God gave Daniel s ability in understanding
Mal 3:17 the day when I act, they will be my own s treasure.
Mt 12: 4 and they ate the s bread reserved for the priests
Mk 2:26 ate the s bread reserved for the priests alone,
Lk 1:66 For the hand of the Lord is surely upon him in a s
2:40 his years, and God placed his s favor upon him.
6: 4 ate the s bread reserved for the priests alone,
12:37 There will be s favor for those who are ready
12:38 there will be s favor for his servants who are
13: 8 and I'll give it s attention and plenty of fertilizer.
Jn 19:31 was the Sabbath (and a very s Sabbath at that,
Ac 4:13 they were ordinary men who had had no s training.
13: 2 and Saul for the s work I have for them."
15:11 the same way, by the s favor of the Lord Jesus."
Ro 2:17 you are relying on God's law for your s
9: 4 the people of Israel, chosen to be God's s children.
11:17 sharing in God's rich nourishment of his s olive
12: 4 have many parts and each part has a s function,
14: 6 Those who have a s day for worshiping the Lord
15:16 a s messenger from Christ Jesus to you Gentiles.
1Co 3:10 Because of God's s favor to me, I have laid the
12: 1 I will write about the s abilities the Holy Spirit
12: 8 to another he gives the gift of s knowledge.
12: 9 The Spirit gives s faith to another, and to someone
12:24 while other parts do not require this s care. So God
13: 8 and s knowledge will all disappear.
13:10 the end comes, these s gifts will all disappear.
14: 1 but also desire the s abilities the Spirit gives,
14: 6 or some s knowledge or some prophecy or some
14:26 another will tell some s revelation God has given,
15:10 because God poured out his s favor on me—
Eph 2: 5 (It is only by God's s favor that you have been
2: 8 God saved you by his s favor when you believed.
3: 2 God has given me this s ministry of announcing his
3: 7 By God's s favor and mighty power, I have been
3: 8 I was chosen for this s joy of telling the Gentiles
4: 7 he has given each one of us a s gift according to
4:16 As each part does its own s work, it helps the other
Php 1: 7 all of you, for you have a very s place in my heart.
Col 4: 8 I have sent him on this s trip to let you know how
2Th 2:16 and in his s favor gave us everlasting comfort
1Ti 5:21 without taking sides or showing s favor to anyone.
2Ti 1:16 May the Lord show s kindness to Onesiphorus
1:18 May the Lord show him s kindness on the day of
2: 1 be strong with the s favor God gives you in Christ
2:20 The expensive utensils are used for s occasions,
Heb 4: 9 So there is a s rest still waiting for the people of
12:15 so that none of you will miss out on the s favor of
13: 9 Your spiritual strength comes from God's s favor,
Jas 2: 3 If you give s attention and a good seat to the rich
2: 9 But if you pay s attention to the rich, you are
1Pe 1: 2 May you have more and more of God's s favor
1:13 Look forward to the s blessings that will come to
2Pe 1: 2 May God bless you with his s favor and wonderful
3:18 But grow in the s favor and knowledge of our Lord
Rev 14: 4 the people on the earth as a s offering to God

SPECIALLY (9) [SPECIAL]

Ex 36: 2 along with all those who were s gifted by the
Lev 27:21 it will be holy, a field s set apart for the LORD.
27:28 "However, anything s set apart by the LORD—
27:29 A person s set apart by the LORD for destruction
Nu 18:14 "Whatever is s set apart for the LORD also
Ezr 5: 8 It is being rebuilt with s prepared stones,
6: 4 Every three layers of s prepared stones will be
Est 2: 9 He also assigned her seven maids s chosen from
Hag 2:23 says the LORD, for I have s chosen you.

SPECIFIC (3) [SPECIFICALLY, SPECIFICATIONS, SPECIFIED, SPECIFYING]

Nu 4:19 and assign a s duty or load to each person.
2Ki 17:12 despite the LORD's s and repeated warnings.
Mk 7: 8 For you ignore God's s laws and substitute your

SPECIFICALLY (4) [SPECIFIC]
Ge 43: 7 “But the man s asked us about our family,”
1Ki 11:10 He had warned Solomon s about worshiping other
2Ch 29:24 The king had s commanded that this burnt offering
Ezr 7:17 These donations are to be used s for the purchase

SPECIFICATIONS (4) [SPECIFIC]
1Ch 28:13 And he gave s for the items in the LORD’s
2Ch 4: 7 then cast ten gold lampstands according to the s
Eze 43:11 describe to them all the s of its construction—
43:11 Write down all these s and directions as they watch

SPECIFIED (1) [SPECIFIC]
Ezr 3: 4 sacrificing the burnt offerings s for each day of the

SPECIFYING (1) [SPECIFIC]
Ac 25:27 to the emperor without s the charges against him!”

SPECIMEN (1)
2Sa 14:25 From head to foot, he was the perfect s of a man.

SPECK (6) [SPECKLED]
Mt 7: 3 And why worry about a s in your friend’s eye
7: 4 let me help you get rid of that s in your eye,’
7: 5 well enough to deal with the s in your friend’s eye.
Lk 6:41 “And why worry about a s in your friend’s eye
6:42 let me help you get rid of that s in your eye,’
6:42 well enough to deal with the s in your friend’s eye!

SPECKLED (9) [SPECK]
Ge 30:32 all the sheep and goats that are s or spotted,
30:33 in my flock any white sheep or goats that are not s,
30:35 and removed all the male goats that were s
30:35 the females that were s and spotted with any white
30:39 all of their offspring were streaked, s, and spotted.
31: 8 For if he said the s animals were mine, the whole flock began to produce s lambs.
31:10 mating with the flock were streaked, s, and spotted.
31:12 ‘Look, and you will see that only the streaked, s,

SPECTACLE (3)
2Ch 7:20 I will make it a s of contempt among the nations.
Am 3: 9 and witness the scandalous s of all Israel’s
1Co 4: 9 We have become a s to the entire world—to people

SPECTACULAR (1)
2Co 5:12 so you can answer those who brag about having a s

SPECULATION (1)
1Ti 1: 4 Don’t let people waste time in endless s over

SPEECH (22) [SPEECHES, SPEECHLESS]
Dt 32: 2 fall on you like rain; / my s will settle like dew.
2Ki 19: 6 Do not be disturbed by this blasphemous s against
Ps 5: 9 from an open grave. / Their s is filled with flattery.
55: 9 Destroy them, Lord, and confuse their s, / for I see
Pr 2:12 from evil people, from those whose s is corrupt.
4:24 Avoid all perverse talk; stay far from corrupt s.
7:21 So she seduced him with her pretty s. With her
8:13 I hate pride, arrogance, corruption, and perverted s.
16:23 From a wise mind comes wise s; the words of the
17: 7 Eloquent s is not fitting for a fool; even less are
20:15 Wise s is rarer and more valuable than gold
22:11 a pure heart and gracious s is the king’s friend.
25:15 a prince, and soft s can crush strong opposition.
Ecc 10:12 wise words, but the s of fools brings them to ruin.
Isa 37: 6 Do not be disturbed by this blasphemous s against
Jer 5:15 you do not know, whose s you cannot understand.
Eze 3: 6 sending you to people with strange and difficult s.
Da 7:11 because I could hear the little horn’s boastful s.
Mk 7:32 A deaf man with a s impediment was brought to
Ac 7:22 and he became mighty in both s and action.
12:21 sat on his throne, and made a s to them.
Ro 3:13 from an open grave. / Their s is filled with lies.”

SPEECHES (4) [SPEECH]
Dt 1: 3 in midwinter, Moses gave these s to the Israelites,
1Co 1:17 and not with clever s and high-sounding ideas,
2: 4 I did not use wise and persuasive s, but the Holy
2Co 10:10 but in person he is weak, and his s are really bad!”

SPEECHLESS (5) [SPEECH]
Ge 45: 3 “Is my father still alive?” But his brothers were s!
Isa 52:15 many nations. Kings will stand s in his presence.
Hab 2:19 You ask s stone images to tell you what to do.
Ac 9: 7 The men with Saul stood s with surprise, for they
1Co 12: 2 led astray and swept along in worshiping s idols.

SPEED (1) [SPEEDING]
Am 5: 9 With blinding s and power he destroys the strong,

SPEEDING (1) [SPEED]
2Ki 7: 6 army of Aram to hear the clatter of s chariots

SPELL (2) [SPELLS]
Isa 28:13 So the LORD will s out his message for them
Gal 3: 1 What magician has cast an evil s on you?

SPELLS (1) [SPELL]
Dt 18:11 or cast s, or function as mediums or psychics,

SPELT (3)
Ex 9:32 But the wheat and the s were not destroyed
Isa 28:25 cummin, wheat, barley, and s, each in its own
Eze 4: 9 some wheat, barley, beans, lentils, millet, and s,

SPEND (48) [SPENDING, SPENDS, SPENT]
Ge 19: 2 “we’ll just s the night out here in the city square.”
19: 5 “Where are the men who came to s the night with
Lev 16:29 you must s the day fasting and not do any work.
16:31 day of total rest, and you will s the day in fasting.
23:29 Anyone who does not s that day in humility will be
Jos 6:11 then everyone returned to s the night in the camp.
Jdg 19:13 We will find a place to s the night in either Gibeah
19:15 so they stopped there to s the night. They rested in
19:20 whatever you do, don’t s the night in the square.”
20: 4 a town in the land of Benjamin, to s the night.
1Sa 24:14 Should he s his time chasing one who is as
1Ch 9:27 They would s the night around the house of God,
2Ch 35: 3 s your time serving the LORD your God and his
Ne 5:16 And I required all my officials to s time working
Job 21:13 They s their days in prosperity; then they go down
24: 5 the poor must s all their time just getting enough to
Ps 26: 4 I do not s time with liars / or go along with
39: 6 We heap up wealth for someone else to s.
50:18 help him, / and you s your time with adulterers.
56: 5 they s their days plotting ways to harm me.
Pr 21:20 and luxury, but fools s whatever they get.
24: 2 For they s their days plotting violence, and their
31: 3 do not s your strength on women, on those who
Ecc 5:11 you have, the more people come to help you s it.
6: 7 All people s their lives scratching for food,
7: 2 It is better to s your time at funerals than at
SS 7:11 the fields and s the night among the wildflowers.
Isa 55: 2 Why s your money on food that does not give you
59: 4 They s their time plotting evil deeds and
59: 5 They s their time and energy spinning evil plans
Eze 6:12 by famine. So at last I will s my fury on them.
Joel 1:13 Come, s the night in sackcloth, you ministers of
Mk 9:31 in order to s more time with his disciples and teach
Lk 5:32 not to s my time with those who think they are
21:37 and each evening he returned to s the night on the
Jn 6:27 S your energy seeking the eternal life that I,
Ac 6: 2 “We apostles should s our time preaching
6: 4 Then we can s our time in prayer and preaching
17:21 to s all their time discussing the latest ideas.)
20:16 because he didn’t want to s further time in the
27:12 a poor place to s the winter—most of the crew
27:12 farther up the coast of Crete, and s the winter there.
1Co 7:32 An unmarried man can s his time doing the Lord’s
2Co 12:15 I will gladly s myself and all I have for your
1Ti 1: 6 and s their time arguing and talking foolishness.
4: 7 S your time and energy in training yourself for
5:13 and s their time gossiping from house to house,
1Pe 4: 2 And you won’t s the rest of your life chasing after

SPENDING (3) [SPEND]
2Sa 17: 8 He won’t be s the night among the troops.
Ac 18:23 After s some time in Antioch, Paul went back to
1Co 16:15 and they are s their lives in service to other

SPENDS (3) [SPEND]
Job 34: 8 of evil people. He s his time with wicked men.
Pr 23:30 It is the one who s long hours in the taverns,
1Ti 5: 5 she asks God for help and s much time in prayer.

SPENT (24) [SPEND]
Ge 27:44 Stay there with him until your brother’s fury is s.
29:20 So Jacob s the next seven years working to pay for
31:54 a feast. Afterward they s the night there in the hills.
32:21 sent on ahead, and Jacob s that night in the camp.
Jos 8:13 the city. Joshua himself s that night in the valley.
Jdg 16: 1 city of Gaza and s the night with a prostitute.
18: 2 they came to Micah’s home and s the night there.
1Sa 27: 8 and his men s their time raiding the Geshurites,
2Sa 1: 1 over the Amalekites and s two days in Ziklag.
1Ki 19: 9 There he came to a cave, where he s the night.
2Ki 12: 7 it must all be s on getting the Temple into good
Ezr 10: 6 He s the night there, but he did not eat any food
Ecc 6:12 who knows how our days can best be s?
Isa 49: 4 I have s my strength for nothing and to no purpose
Eze 5:13 Then at last my anger will be s, and I will be
16:42 “Then at last my fury against you will be s,
Da 6:14 He s the rest of the day looking for a way to get
6:18 king returned to his palace and s the night fasting.
Mk 5:26 and had s everything she had to pay them,
Lk 8:43 She had s everything she had on doctors and still
24:53 And they s all of their time in the Temple,
Ac 18: 5 Paul s his full time preaching and testifying to the
2Co 11:25 Once I s a whole night and a day adrift at sea.
Jas 5: 5 You have s your years on earth in luxury,

SPICE (4) [SPICED, SPICES]
SS 3: 6 of myrrh and frankincense and every other s?
4:14 from every incense tree, and every other lovely s.
6: 2 to his s beds, to graze and to gather the lilies.
Rev 18:13 s, incense, myrrh, frankincense, wine, olive oil,

SPICED (1) [SPICE]
SS 8: 2 I would give you s wine to drink, my sweet

SPICERY [KJV] See SPICES

SPICES (34) [SPICE]
Ge 37:25 It was a group of Ishmaelite traders taking s,
43:11 balm, honey, s, myrrh, pistachio nuts,
Ex 25: 6 s for the anointing oil and the fragrant incense;
30:23 “Collect choice s—12-1/2 pounds of pure myrrh,
30:34 “Gather sweet s—resin droplets, mollusk scent,
35: 8 s for the anointing oil and the fragrant incense;
35:28 They also brought s and olive oil for the light,
40:27 he burned the fragrant incense made from sweet s,
1Ki 10: 2 and a great caravan of camels loaded with s,
10:10 and great quantities of s and precious jewels.
10:10 so many s brought in as those the queen of Sheba
10:25 of silver and gold, clothing, weapons, s, horses,
2Ki 20:13 the silver, the gold, the s, and the aromatic oils.
1Ch 9:29 such as choice flour, wine, olive oil, incense, and s.
9:30 But it was the priests who prepared the s
2Ch 2: 4 set apart to burn incense and sweet s before him,
9: 1 and a great caravan of camels loaded with s,
9: 9 and great quantities of s and precious jewels.
9: 9 Never before had there been s as fine as those the
9:24 of silver and gold, clothing, weapons, s, horses,
16:14 He was laid on a bed perfumed with sweet s
32:27 gold, precious stones, and s, and for his shields
Ps 75: 8 his hand; / it is full of foaming wine mixed with s.
SS 4:10 perfume is more fragrant than the richest of s.
5: 1 I gather my myrrh with my s and eat my
5:13 His cheeks are like sweetly scented beds of s.
8:14 or a young deer on the mountains of s.”
Isa 39: 2 the silver, the gold, the s, and the aromatic oils.
Eze 24:10 Cook the meat well with many s. Then empty the
27:22 of Sheba and Raamah came with all kinds of s,
Mk 16: 1 and purchased burial s to put on Jesus’ body.
Lk 23:56 Then they went home and prepared s
24: 1 came to the tomb, taking the s they had prepared.
Jn 19:40 Jesus’ body in a long linen cloth with the s,

SPIDER [KJV] See LIZARDS

SPIDERWEB (2) [WEB]
Job 8:14 count on will collapse. They are leaning on a s.
27:18 The houses built by the wicked are as fragile as a s,

SPIED (1) [SPY]
2Ki 13:21 were burying a man, they s a band of these raiders.

SPIES (20) [SPY]
Ge 42: 9 He said to them, “You are s! You have come to
42:11 all brothers and honest men, sir! We are not s!”
42:14 But Joseph insisted, “As I said, you are s!
42:16 have a younger brother, then I’ll know you are s.”
42:30 roughly to us,” they told him. “He took us for s.
42:31 But we said, ‘We are honest men, not s.
42:34 I will know that you are honest men and not s.
Jos 2: 1 Then Joshua secretly sent out two s from the
2: 3 They are s sent here to discover the best way to
2: 7 So the king’s men went looking for the s along the
2: 8 Before the s went to sleep that night, Rahab went
2:22 The s went up into the hill country and stayed there
2:23 Then the two s came down from the hill country,
6:17 in her house will be spared, for she protected our s.
6:22 Then Joshua said to the two s, “Keep your
6:25 because she had hidden the s Joshua sent to
Jdg 1:23 They sent s to Bethel (formerly known as Luz),
18:17 the five s entered the shrine and took the carved
1Sa 26: 4 so he sent out s to watch his movements.
Heb 11:31 For she had given a friendly welcome to the s.

SPIKE (1)
Job 41: 2 a rope through the nose or pierce its jaw with a s?

SPIKENARD [KJV] See PERFUME

SPILL (1) [SPILLED, SPILLING]
Pr 5:16 Why s the water of your springs in public,

SPILLED (7) [SPILL]
Ge 38: 9 he s the semen on the ground to keep her from
2Sa 14:14 Our lives are like water s out on the ground,
Ps 79:10 for they have s the blood of your servants.
Jer 51:35 Babylonia be paid in full for all the blood they s,”
Eze 21:32 the fire, and your blood will be s in your own land.
28:23 against you, and blood will be s in your streets.
Rev 18:24 In her streets the blood of the prophets was s.

SPILLING (4) [SPILL]
Mt 9:17 from the pressure, s the wine and ruining the skins.
Mk 2:22 the wineskins, s the wine and ruining the skins.
Lk 5:37 the old skins, s the wine and ruining the skins.
Ac 1:18 and falling there, he burst open, s out his intestines.

SPIN (2) [SPINNING, SPINS]
Ex 35:26 the women who were willing used their skills to s
Isa 5:28 as the wheels of their chariots s like the wind.

SPINE (1)
Job 4:15 swept past my face. Its wind sent shivers up my s.

SPINNING (3) [SPIN]
Ex 35:25 who were skilled in sewing and s prepared blue,

Pr 31:19 Her hands are busy s thread, her fingers twisting
Isa 59: 5 and energy s evil plans that end up in deadly

SPINS (1) [SPIN]

Pr 31:13 She finds wool and flax and busily s it.

SPIRIT (500) [MEAN-SPIRITED, SPIRIT'S, SPIRITS, SPIRITUAL, SPIRITUALITY, SPIRITUALLY]

EVIL SPIRIT (20) Mt 12:43; Mk 1:23,26; 3:30; 5:2,8; 7:25; 9:17,18,18,20,22,25,28; Lk 8:29; 9:39,42; 11:24; 13:11; Ac 19:15

HOLY SPIRIT (155) Ps 51:11; Isa 63:10,11; Mt 1:18,20; 3:11; 4:1; 12:31,32; 22:43; 28:19; Mk 1:8,10,12; 3:29; 12:36; 13:11; Lk 1:15,35,41,67; 2:25,26; 3:16,22; 4:1; 10:21; 11:13; 12:10,12; 24:49,49; Jn 1:32,33,33; 3:6; 14:17,26; 20:22; Ac 1:2,5,8,16; 2:4,4,33,38; 4:8,25,31; 5:3,32; 6:3,5; 7:51,55; 8:15,16,17,18,19,29; 9:17,31; 10:19,38,44,45,47; 11:12,15,16, 24; 13:2,4,9,52; 15:8,28; 16:6; 19:2,2,6,21; 20:22,23,28; 21:4,11; 28:25; Ro 1:4; 5:5; 8:5,6,13,16,23,26,26; 9:1; 14:17; 15:13,16,30; 1Co 2:4; 6:19; 12:1,3,4,11; 2Co 1:22; 3:6,8; 5:5; 6:6; 13:13; Gal 3:2,2,5,14; 4:29; 5:16,17,18,22,25; Eph 1:13; 2:18; 3:5,16; 4:3,30; 5:18; 6:18; Col 1:8; 1Th 1:5,6; 4:8; 5:19; 1Ti 4:1; 2Ti 1:14; Tit 3:5; Heb 2:4; 3:7; 6:4; 9:8; 10:15,29; Jas 4:5; 1Pe 1:12; 2Pe 1:21; 1Jn 2:20,27; 3:24; Jude 1:20

SPIRIT OF GOD (24) Ge 1:2; 41:38; Ex 31:3; Nu 24:2; 1Sa 10:10; 11:6; 19:20,23; 2Ch 15:1; 24:20; Job 33:4; Eze 11:24; Mt 3:16; 12:28; Ro 8:9,11,14; 1Co 3:16; 12:3,10; 1Pe 4:14; 1Jn 4:2,2; Rev 3:1

SPIRIT OF THE LORD (5) Lk 4:18; Ac 5:9; 8:39; 2Co 3:17,18

SPIRIT OF THE LORD* (22) Jdg 3:10; 6:34; 11:29; 13:25; 14:6,19; 15:14; 1Sa 10:6; 16:13,14; 2Sa 23:2; 1Ki 18:12; 22:24; 2Ki 2:16; 2Ch 18:23; 20:14; Isa 11:2; 40:13; 63:14; Eze 11:5; 37:1; Mic 3:8

Ge 1: 2 And the S of God was hovering over its surface.
6: 3 "My S will not put up with humans for such a long
41:38 For he is a man who is obviously filled with the s
45:27 loaded with the food sent by Joseph, his s revived.
Ex 31: 3 I have filled him with the S of God, giving him
35:31 The LORD has filled Bezalel with the S of God,
Lev 26:19 I will break down your arrogant s by making the
Nu 11:17 I will take some of the S that is upon you, and I will put the S upon them also.
11:25 He took some of the S that was upon Moses
11:25 They prophesied as the S rested upon them,
11:26 were still in the camp when the S rested upon
11:29 and that the LORD would put his S upon them
24: 2 tribe by tribe. Then the S of God came upon him,
27:18 "Take Joshua son of Nun, who has the S in him,
Dt 34: 9 Now Joshua son of Nun was full of the s of
Jdg 3:10 The S of the LORD came upon him, and he
6:34 Then the S of the LORD took possession of
11:29 At that time the S of the LORD came upon
13:25 the S of the LORD began to take hold of him.
14: 6 At that moment the S of the LORD powerfully
14:19 Then the S of the LORD powerfully took control
15:14 But the S of the LORD powerfully took control of
1Sa 10: 6 At that time the S of the LORD will come upon
10:10 Then the S of God came upon Saul, and he, too,
11: 6 Then the S of God came mightily upon Saul,
16:13 And the S of the LORD came mightily upon him
16:14 Now the S of the LORD had left Saul,
16:14 and the LORD sent a tormenting s that filled him
16:15 "It is clear that a s from God is tormenting you,"
16:16 you whenever the tormenting s is bothering you.
16:23 And whenever the tormenting s from God troubled
16:23 feel better, and the tormenting s would go away.
18:10 a tormenting s from God overwhelmed Saul,
19: 9 the tormenting s from the LORD suddenly came
19:20 the S of God came upon Saul's men, and they also
19:23 But on the way to Naioth the S of God came upon
28: 8 he said. "Will you call up his s for me?"
28:11 "Well, whose s do you want me to call up?"
2Sa 23: 2 "The S of the LORD speaks through me;
1Ki 18:12 the S of the LORD will carry you away to who
22:21 until finally a s approached the LORD and said,
22:22 "And the s replied, 'I will go out and inspire all
22:23 the LORD has put a lying s in the mouths of your
22:24 "When did the S of the LORD leave me to speak
2Ki 2:16 Perhaps the S of the LORD has left him on some
5:26 "Don't you realize that I was there in s when
1Ch 12:18 Then the S came upon Amasai, who later became a
2Ch 15: 1 Then the S of God came upon Azariah son of
18:20 until finally a s approached the LORD and said,
18:21 "And the s replied, 'I will go out and inspire all
18:22 the LORD has put a lying s in the mouths of your
18:23 "When did the S of the LORD leave me to speak
20:14 the S of the LORD came upon one of the men
24:20 Then the S of God came upon Zechariah son of
Ne 9:20 You sent your good S to instruct them, and you did
9:30 You sent your S, who, through the prophets,
Job 4:15 A s swept past my face. Its wind sent shivers up
6: 4 He has sent his poisoned arrows deep within my s.
17: 1 "My s is crushed, and I am near death. The grave
20: 3 your insults, but now my s prompts me to reply.
26: 4 these wise sayings? Whose s speaks through you?
26:13 His S made the heavens beautiful, and his power
32: 8 Surely it is God's S within people, the breath of the
32:18 and full of words, and the s within me urges me on.
33: 4 For the S of God has made me, and the breath of
34:14 If God were to take back his s and withdraw his
Ps 31: 5 I entrust my s into your hand. / Rescue me,
34:18 he rescues those who are crushed in s.
51:10 a clean heart, O God. / Renew a right s within me.
51:11 and don't take your Holy S from me.
51:17 The sacrifice you want is a broken s. / A broken
73:26 My health may fail, and my s may grow weak,
76:12 For he breaks the s of princes / and is feared by the
104:30 When you send your S, new life is born
139: 7 I can never escape from your s! / I can never get
143:10 May your gracious S lead me forward / on a firm
Pr 1:23 I'll pour out the s of wisdom upon you and make
15: 4 and health; a deceitful tongue crushes the s.
15:13 makes a happy face; a broken heart crushes the s.
17:22 but a broken s saps a person's strength.
18:14 The human s can endure a sick body, but who can bear it if the s is crushed?
20:27 The LORD's searchlight penetrates the human s,
25:13 of summer. They revive the s of their employer.
Ecc 3:21 For who can prove that the human s goes upward
3:21 and the s of animals goes downward into the earth?
8: 8 None of us can hold back our s from departing.
10: 4 A quiet s can overcome even great mistakes.
12: 7 the earth, and the s will return to God who gave it.
Isa 4: 4 He will cleanse Jerusalem of its bloodstains by a s
11: 2 And the S of the LORD will rest on him—the S of wisdom and understanding, the S of counsel and might, the S of knowledge and the fear of the
19:14 The LORD has sent a s of foolishness on them,
29:10 For the LORD has poured out on you a s of deep
30: 1 You weave a web of plans that are not from my S,
32:15 until at last the S is poured down upon us from
34:16 has promised this. His S will make it all come true.
40:13 Who is able to advise the S of the LORD?
42: 1 I am pleased with him. I have put my S upon him.
44: 3 And I will pour out my S and my blessings on your
48:16 and his S have sent me with this message:
59:21 "My S will not leave them, and neither will these
61: 1 The S of the Sovereign LORD is upon me,
63:10 they rebelled against him and grieved his Holy S.
63:11 Where is the one who sent his Holy S to be among
63:14 the S of the LORD gave them rest.
Jer 9:25 those who are circumcised in body but not in s—
51:11 For the LORD has stirred up the s of the kings of
La 2:11 My heart is broken, my s poured out, as I see what
Eze 1:12 They went in whatever direction the s chose,
1:20 The s of the four living beings was in the wheels.
1:20 So wherever the s went, the wheels and the living
1:21 For the s of the living beings was in the wheels.
2: 2 The S came into me as he spoke and set me on my
3:12 Then the S lifted me up, and I heard a loud
3:14 The S lifted me up and took me away. I went in
3:24 Then the S came into me and set me on my feet.
8: 3 Then the S lifted me up into the sky
10:17 for the s of the living beings was in the wheels.
11: 1 Then the S lifted me and brought me over to the
11: 2 Then the S said to me, "Son of man, these are the
11: 5 Then the S of the LORD came upon me, and he
11:19 singleness of heart and put a new s within them.
11:24 Afterward the S of God carried me back again to
18:31 and get for yourselves a new heart and a new s.
21: 7 Every s will faint; strong knees will tremble
23: 8 she did not leave her s of prostitution behind.
36:26 and right desires, and I will put a new s in you.
36:27 And I will put my S in you so you will obey my
37: 1 and I was carried away by the S of the LORD to a
37:14 I will put my S in you, and you will live and return
39:29 for I will pour out my S upon them,
43: 5 Then the S took me up and brought me into the
Da 4: 8 after my god, and the s of the holy gods is in him.)
4: 9 I know that the s of the holy gods is in you and that
4:18 because the s of the holy gods is in you.' "
5:11 who has within him the s of the holy gods.
5:14 I have heard that you have the s of the gods within
10:13 But for twenty-one days the s prince of the
10:13 and I left him there with the s prince of the
10:20 Soon I must return to fight against the s prince of
10:20 then against the s prince of the kingdom of Greece.
10:21 (There is no one to help me against these s princes except Michael, your s prince.
Joel 2:28 rains again, I will pour out my S upon all people.
2:29 I will pour out my S even on servants, men
Mic 3: 8 I am filled with power and the S of the LORD.
Hag 2: 5 My S remains among you, just as I promised when
Zec 4: 6 but by my S, says the LORD Almighty.
6: 8 went north have vented the anger of my S there."
7:12 sent them by his S through the earlier prophets.
12: 1 of the earth, and formed the s within humans.
12:10 "Then I will pour out a s of grace and prayer on
Mal 2:15 In body and s you are his. And what does he want?
Mt 1:18 still a virgin, she became pregnant by the Holy S.
1:20 child within her has been conceived by the Holy S.
3:11 He will baptize you with the Holy S and with fire.
3:16 and he saw the S of God descending like a dove
4: 1 by the Holy S to be tempted there by the Devil.
10:20 it will be the S of your Father speaking through
12:18 very pleased with him. / I will put my S upon him,
12:28 But if I am casting out demons by the S of God,
12:31 except blasphemy against the Holy S, which can
12:32 but blasphemy against the Holy S will never be
12:43 "When an evil s leaves a person, it goes into the
12:45 Then the s finds seven other spirits more evil than
22:43 speaking under the inspiration of the Holy S,
26:41 For though the s is willing enough, the body is
27:50 Then Jesus shouted out again, and he gave up his s.
28:19 the name of the Father and the Son and the Holy S.
Mk 1: 8 but he will baptize you with the Holy S!"
1:10 and the Holy S descending like a dove on him.
1:12 Immediately the Holy S compelled Jesus to go into
1:23 A man possessed by an evil s was in the
1:26 the evil s screamed and threw the man into a
3:29 but anyone who blasphemes against the Holy S
3:30 because they were saying he had an evil s.
5: 2 a man possessed by an evil s ran out from a
5: 8 For Jesus had already said to the s, "Come out of the man, you evil s."
5: 9 And the s replied, "Legion, because there are
7:25 to him whose little girl was possessed by an evil s.
9:17 because he is possessed by an evil s that won't let
9:18 And whenever this evil s seizes him, it throws him
9:18 So I asked your disciples to cast out the evil s,
9:20 But when the evil s saw Jesus, it threw the child
9:22 The evil s often makes him fall into the fire or into
9:25 of onlookers was growing, he rebuked the evil s.
9:25 "S of deafness and muteness," he said,
9:26 Then the s screamed and threw the boy into
9:28 "Why couldn't we cast out that evil s?"
12:36 speaking under the inspiration of the Holy S,
13:11 it is not you who will be speaking, but the Holy S.
14:38 For though the s is willing enough, the body is
Lk 1:15 hard liquor, and he will be filled with the Holy S,
1:17 He will be a man with the s and power of Elijah,
1:35 angel replied, "The Holy S will come upon you,
1:41 and Elizabeth was filled with the Holy S.
1:67 was filled with the Holy S and gave this prophecy:
1:80 John grew up and became strong in s. Then he
2:25 He was filled with the Holy S, and he eagerly
2:26 The Holy S had revealed to him that he would not
2:27 That day the S led him to the Temple. So when
3:16 He will baptize you with the Holy S and with fire.
3:22 and the Holy S descended on him in the form of a
4: 1 Then Jesus, full of the Holy S, left the Jordan
4: 1 He was led by the S to go out into the wilderness,
4:18 "The S of the Lord is upon me, / for he has
8:29 For Jesus had already commanded the evil s to
8:29 This s had often taken control of the man.
9:39 An evil s keeps seizing him, making him scream.
9:40 I begged your disciples to cast the s out, but they
9:42 But Jesus rebuked the evil s and healed the boy.
10:21 Then Jesus was filled with the joy of the Holy S
11:13 Father give the Holy S to those who ask him."
11:24 "When an evil s leaves a person, it goes into the
11:26 Then the s finds seven other spirits more evil than
12:10 against the Holy S will never be forgiven.
12:12 for the Holy S will teach you what needs to be said
13:11 saw a woman who had been crippled by an evil s.
22:44 and he was in such agony of s that his sweat fell to
23:46 "Father, I entrust my s into your hands!"
24:49 "And now I will send the Holy S, just as my
24:49 But stay here in the city until the Holy S comes
Jn 1:32 "I saw the Holy S descending like a dove from
1:33 'When you see the Holy S descending and resting
1:33 He is the one who baptizes with the Holy S.'
3: 5 of God without being born of water and the S.
3: 6 but the Holy S gives new life from heaven.
3: 8 you can't explain how people are born of the S."
3:34 for God's S is upon him without measure or limit.
4:23 when true worshipers will worship the Father in s
4:24 For God is S, so those who worship him must worship in s
6:63 It is the S who gives eternal life. Human effort
6:63 And the very words I have spoken to you are s
7:39 he said "living water," he was speaking of the S,
7:39 But the S had not yet been given, because Jesus
13:21 Now Jesus was in great anguish of s, and he
14:17 He is the Holy S, who leads into all truth.
14:26 and by the Counselor I mean the Holy S—he will
15:26 "But I will send you the Counselor—the S of truth.
16:13 When the S of truth comes, he will guide you into
16:15 this is what I mean when I say that the S will
19:30 Then he bowed his head and gave up his s.
20:22 on them and said to them, "Receive the Holy S.
Ac 1: 2 apostles further instructions from the Holy S.
1: 5 a few days you will be baptized with the Holy S."
1: 8 But when the Holy S has come upon you, you will
1:16 This was predicted long ago by the Holy S,
2: 4 And everyone present was filled with the Holy S
2: 4 as the Holy S gave them this ability.
2:17 God said, / I will pour out my S upon all people.
2:18 In those days I will pour out my S / upon all my
2:33 gave him the Holy S to pour out upon us, just as
2:38 Then you will receive the gift of the Holy S.
4: 8 Then Peter, filled with the Holy S, said to them,
4:25 you spoke long ago by the Holy S through our
4:31 and they were all filled with the Holy S.
5: 3 You lied to the Holy S, and you kept some of the
5: 9 conspiring together to test the S of the Lord?
5:32 are witnesses of these things and so is the Holy S,
6: 3 and are full of the Holy S and wisdom.
6: 5 Stephen (a man full of faith and the Holy S),
6:10 against the wisdom and S by which Stephen spoke.
7:51 to the truth. Must you forever resist the Holy S?
7:55 But Stephen, full of the Holy S, gazed steadily
7:59 Stephen prayed, "Lord Jesus, receive my s."
8:15 for these new Christians to receive the Holy S.
8:16 The Holy S had not yet come upon any of them,
8:17 upon these believers, and they received the Holy S.
8:18 When Simon saw that the Holy S was given when
8:19 hands on people, they will receive the Holy S!"
8:29 The Holy S said to Philip, "Go over and walk
8:39 of the water, the S of the Lord caught Philip away.
9:17 get your sight back and be filled with the Holy S."
9:31 fear of the Lord and in the comfort of the Holy S.
10:19 puzzling over the vision, the Holy S said to him,
10:38 God anointed Jesus of Nazareth with the Holy S
10:44 the Holy S fell upon all who had heard the

10:45 the Holy S had been poured out upon the Gentiles,
10:47 now that they have received the Holy S just as we
11:12 The Holy S told me to go with them and not to
11:15 as I was getting started, the Holy S fell on them,
11:16 but you will be baptized with the Holy S.'
11:24 a good man, full of the Holy S and strong in faith.
11:28 S that a great famine was coming upon the entire
13: 2 worshiping the Lord and fasting, the Holy S said,
13: 4 Sent out by the Holy S, Saul and Barnabas went
13: 9 also known as Paul, filled with the Holy S,
13:52 believers were filled with joy and with the Holy S.
15: 8 that he accepts Gentiles by giving them the Holy S,
15:28 "For it seemed good to the Holy S and to us to lay
16: 6 because the Holy S had told them not to go into the
16: 7 but again the S of Jesus did not let them go.
19: 2 "Did you receive the Holy S when you believed?"
19: 2 We haven't even heard that there is a Holy S."
19: 6 the Holy S came on them, and they spoke in other
19:15 when they tried it on a man possessed by an evil s,
19:15 the s replied, "I know Jesus, and I know Paul.
19:21 Afterward Paul felt impelled by the Holy S to go
20:22 drawn there irresistibly by the Holy S, not knowing
20:23 except that the Holy S has told me in city after city
20:28 over whom the Holy S has appointed you as elders.
21: 4 These disciples prophesied through the Holy S that
21:11 Then he said, "The Holy S declares, 'So shall the
23: 9 "Perhaps a s or an angel spoke to him."
28:25 "The Holy S was right when he said to our
Ro 1: 4 raised him from the dead by means of the Holy S.
2:29 but a change of heart produced by God's S.
5: 5 because he has given us the Holy S to fill our
7: 6 the letter of the law, but in the new way, by the S.
8: 2 For the power of the life-giving S has freed you
8: 4 follow our sinful nature but instead follow the S.
8: 5 but those who are controlled by the Holy S think
about things that please the S.
8: 6 But if the Holy S controls your mind, there is life
8: 9 You are controlled by the S if you have the S
8: 9 (And remember that those who do not have the S
8:10 your s is alive because you have been made right
8:11 The S of God, who raised Jesus from the dead,
8:11 he will give life to your mortal body by this same S
8:13 But if through the power of the Holy S you turn
8:14 For all who are led by the S of God are children of
8:16 For his Holy S speaks to us deep in our hearts
8:23 although we have the Holy S within us as a
8:26 And the Holy S helps us in our distress. For we
8:26 But the Holy S prays for us with groanings that
8:27 who knows all hearts knows what the S is saying,
8:27 for the S pleads for us believers in harmony with
9: 1 and the Holy S confirm that what I am saying is
14:17 a life of goodness and peace and joy in the Holy S.
15:13 with hope through the power of the Holy S.
15:16 might be pure and pleasing to him by the Holy S.
15:19 as signs from God—all by the power of God's S.
15:30 of your love for me, given to you by the Holy S.
1Co 2: 4 but the Holy S was powerful among you.
2:10 because God has revealed them to us by his S,
2:10 and his S searches out everything and shows us
2:11 one can know God's thoughts except God's own S.
2:12 God has actually given us his S (not the world's s)
2:13 We speak words given to us by the S,
2:14 can't understand these truths from God's S.
2:14 because only those who have the S can understand
what the S means.
2:15 We who have the S understand these things,
3:16 temple of God and that the S of God lives in you?
5: 3 there with you in person, I am with you in the S.
5: 4 a meeting of the church, and I will be there in s,
6:11 and the S of our God have done for you.
6:17 who is joined to the Lord becomes one s with him.
6:19 know that your body is the temple of the Holy S,
7:34 can be more devoted to the Lord in body and in s,
7:40 and I think I am giving you counsel from God's S
12: 1 I will write about the special abilities the Holy S
12: 3 No one speaking by the S of God can curse Jesus,
12: 3 able to say, "Jesus is Lord," except by the Holy S.
12: 4 but it is the same Holy S who is the source of them
12: 8 To one person the S gives the ability to give wise
12: 9 The S gives special faith to another, and to
12:10 the ability to know whether it is really the S of
God or another s that is speaking.
12:11 and only Holy S who distributes these gifts.
12:13 have all been baptized into Christ's body by one S,
and we have all received the same S.
14: 1 but also desire the special abilities the S gives,
14: 2 You will be speaking by the power of the S,
14:14 For if I pray in tongues, my s is praying, but I
14:15 I will pray in the s, and I will pray in words I
14:15 I will sing in the s, and I will sing in words I
14:16 For if you praise God only in the s, how can those
14:32 that people who prophesy are in control of their s
15:45 the last Adam—that is, Christ—is a life-giving S.
2Co 1:22 S in our hearts as the first installment of everything
3: 3 with pen and ink, but with the S of the living God.
3: 6 is a covenant, not of written laws, but of the S.
3: 6 in death; in the new way, the Holy S gives life.
3: 8 far greater glory when the Holy S is giving life?
3:17 The Lord is the S, and wherever the S of the Lord
3:18 And as the S of the Lord works within us,
5: 5 and as a guarantee he has given us his Holy S.
6: 6 our sincere love, and the power of the Holy S.
7: 1 from everything that can defile our body or s.
11: 4 or a different S than the one you received, or a
12: 3 Whether my body was there or just my s, I don't
12:18 For we both have the same S and walk in each
13:13 and the fellowship of the Holy S be with you all.
Gal 3: 2 Did you receive the Holy S by keeping the law?
3: 2 for the Holy S came upon you only after you
3: 3 After starting your Christian lives in the S, why are
3: 5 does God give you the Holy S and work miracles
3:14 and we Christians receive the promised Holy S
4: 6 God has sent the S of his Son into your hearts,
4:15 Where is that joyful s we felt together then?
4:29 And we who are born of the Holy S are persecuted
5: 5 But we who live by the S eagerly wait to receive
5:16 to live according to your new life in the Holy S.
5:17 which is just opposite from what the Holy S wants.
5:17 And the S gives us desires that are opposite from
5:18 But when you are directed by the Holy S, you are
5:22 But when the Holy S controls our lives, he will
5:25 If we are living now by the Holy S, let us follow
6: 8 But those who live to please the S will harvest
everlasting life from the S.
Eph 1:13 you as his own by giving you the Holy S,
1:14 The S is God's guarantee that he will give us
2: 2 He is the s at work in the hearts of those who
2:18 may come to the Father through the same Holy S
2:22 as part of this dwelling where God lives by his S.
3: 5 but now he has revealed it by the Holy S to his
3:16 give you mighty inner strength through his Holy S.
4: 3 Always keep yourselves united in the Holy S,
4: 4 We are all one body, we have the same S, and we
4:30 And do not bring sorrow to God's Holy S by the
5:18 Instead, let the Holy S fill and control you.
6:17 and take the sword of the S, which is the Word of
6:18 and on every occasion in the power of the Holy S.
Php 1:19 pray for me and as the S of Jesus Christ helps me,
2: 1 Any fellowship together in the S? Are your hearts
3: 3 For we who worship God in the S are the only ones
4:23 the grace of the Lord Jesus Christ be with your s.
Col 1: 8 great love for others that the Holy S has given you.
1Th 1: 5 for the Holy S gave you full assurance that what
1: 6 S in spite of the severe suffering it brought you.
4: 8 but is rejecting God, who gives his Holy S to you.
5:19 Do not stifle the Holy S.
5:23 and may your whole s and soul and body be kept
2Th 2:13 a salvation that came through the S who makes you
1Ti 3:16 and was shown to be righteous by the S. / He was
4: 1 Now the Holy S tells us clearly that in the last
2Ti 1: 7 For God has not given us a s of fear and timidity,
1:14 With the help of the Holy S who lives within us,
4:22 May the Lord be with your s. Grace be with you
Tit 3: 5 our sins and gave us a new life through the Holy S.
3: 6 He generously poured out the S upon us because of
Phm 1:25 The grace of the Lord Jesus Christ be with your s.
Heb 2: 4 and by giving gifts of the Holy S whenever he
3: 7 That is why the Holy S says, / "Today you must
6: 4 good things of heaven and shared in the Holy S,
9: 8 By these regulations the Holy S revealed that the
9:14 For by the power of the eternal S, Christ offered
10:15 And the Holy S also testifies that this is so. First he
10:29 and enraged the Holy S who brings God's mercy to
Jas 2:26 Just as the body is dead without a s, so also faith is
4: 5 the Scriptures mean when they say that the Holy S,
1Pe 1: 2 chose you long ago, and the S has made you holy.
1:11 They wondered what the S of Christ within them
1:12 you in the power of the Holy S sent from heaven.
3: 4 the unfading beauty of a gentle and quiet s,
3:18 physical death, but he was raised to life in the S.
4: 6 they could still live in the s as God does.
4:14 then the glorious S of God will come upon you.
2Pe 1:21 It was the Holy S who moved the prophets to
1Jn 2:20 not like that, for the Holy S has come upon you,
2:27 But you have received the Holy S, and he lives
2:27 For the S teaches you all things, and what he
3:24 know he lives in us because the Holy S lives in us.
4: 1 not believe everyone who claims to speak by the S.
4: 1 You must test them to see if the s they have comes
4: 2 This is the way to find out if they have the S of
4: 2 a human being, that person has the S of God.
4: 3 Such a person has the s of the Antichrist.
4: 4 because the S who lives in you is greater than the s
who lives in the world.
4: 6 That is how we know if someone has the S of truth
or the s of deception.
4:13 And God has given us his S as proof that we live in
5: 6 And the S also gives us the testimony that this is
5: 8 the S, the water, and the blood—and all three
Jude 1:19 because they do not have God's S living in them.
1:20 continue to pray as you are directed by the Holy S.
Rev 1: 4 to come; from the sevenfold S before his throne;
1:10 was the Lord's Day, and I was worshiping in the S.
2: 7 who is willing to hear should listen to the S
2: 7 and understand what the S is saying to the
2:11 who is willing to hear should listen to the S
2:11 and understand what the S is saying to the
2:17 who is willing to hear should listen to the S
2:17 and understand what the S is saying to the
2:29 who is willing to hear should listen to the S
2:29 and understand what the S is saying to the
3: 1 from the one who has the sevenfold S of God
3: 6 who is willing to hear should listen to the S
3: 6 and understand what the S is saying to the
3:13 who is willing to hear should listen to the S
3:13 and understand what the S is saying to the
3:22 who is willing to hear should listen to the S
3:22 and understand what the S is saying to the
4: 2 And instantly I was in the S, and I saw a throne in
11:11 a half days, the s of life from God entered them,
14:13 Yes, says the S, they are blessed indeed, for they
17: 3 So the angel took me in s into the wilderness.
21:10 So he took me in s to a great, high mountain,
22:17 The S and the bride say, "Come." Let each one

SPIRIT'S (3) [SPIRIT]

Lk 4:14 returned to Galilee, filled with the Holy S power.
1Co 2:13 using the S words to explain spiritual truths.
Gal 5:25 let us follow the Holy S leading in every part of

SPIRITS (41) [SPIRIT]

Lev 17: 7 by offering sacrifices to evil s out in the fields.
Nu 27:16 "O LORD, the God of the s of all living things,
Dt 18:11 or psychics, or call forth the s of the dead.
Ru 3: 7 Boaz had finished his meal and was in good s,
Isa 19: 3 They will call on s, mediums, and psychics to
31: 3 not God! Their horses are puny flesh, not mighty s!
57:15 and holy place with those whose s are contrite
65: 4 the graves and secret places to worship evil s.
Zec 6: 5 "These are the four s of heaven who stand before
13: 2 false prophets and the unclean s that inspire them.
Mt 8:16 All the s fled when he commanded them to leave;
10: 1 and gave them authority to cast out evil s and to
12:45 Then the spirit finds seven other s more evil than
Mk 1:27 has such authority! Even evil s obey his orders!"
3:11 And whenever those possessed by evil s caught
5:10 Then the s begged him again and again not to send
5:12 "Send us into those pigs," the evil s begged.
5:13 So the evil s came out of the man and entered the
6: 7 out two by two, with authority to cast out evil s.
Lk 4:36 Even evil s obey him and flee at his command!"
6:18 and to be healed, and Jesus cast out many evil s.
7:21 and he cast out evil s and restored sight to the
8: 2 had healed and from whom he had cast out evil s.
10:20 But don't rejoice just because evil s obey you;
11:26 Then the spirit finds seven other s more evil than
Ac 5:16 bringing their sick and those possessed by evil s,
8: 7 Many evil s were cast out, screaming as they left
19:12 their diseases, and any evil s within them came out.
19:13 out evil s tried to use the name of the Lord Jesus.
23: 8 say there is no resurrection or angels or s,
2Co 4:16 are dying, our s are being renewed every day.
5: 3 For we will not be s without bodies, but we will
Eph 6:12 and against wicked s in the heavenly realms.
1Ti 4: 1 they will follow lying s and teachings that come
Heb 1:14 They are s sent from God to care for those who
12:23 And you have come to the s of the redeemed in
1Pe 3:19 So he went and preached to the s in prison—
Rev 4: 5 with burning flames. They are the seven s of God.
5: 6 which are the seven s of God that are sent out into
16:13 And I saw three evil s that looked like frogs leap
18: 2 She has become the hideout of demons and evil s,

SPIRITUAL (43) [SPIRIT]

Ex 34:15 They are s prostitutes, committing adultery against
Jnh 4:11 has more than 120,000 people living in s darkness,
Mt 23: 9 for only God in heaven is your s Father.
Ro 1:11 so I can share a s blessing with you that will help
4:11 So Abraham is the s father of those who have faith
4:12 And Abraham is also the s father of those who
15:27 Since the Gentiles received the wonderful s
1Co 1: 7 Now you have every s gift you need as you eagerly
2:13 using the Spirit's words to explain s truths.
4:15 teach you about Christ, you have only one s father.
9:11 We have planted good s seed among you. Is it too
12: 4 Now there are different kinds of s gifts, but it is the
12: 7 A s gift is given to each of us as a means of
14:12 Since you are so eager to have s gifts, ask God for
14:37 you claim to be a prophet or think you are very s,
15:44 but when they are raised, they will be s bodies.
15:44 there are natural bodies, so also there are s bodies.
15:46 was the natural body, then the s body comes later.
2Co 6:10 We are poor, but we give s riches to others.
12:15 gladly spend myself and all I have for your s good,
Gal 4: 3 We were slaves to the s powers of this world.
4: 9 to the weak and useless s powers of this world?
Eph 1: 3 who has blessed us with every s blessing in the
1:17 to give you s wisdom and understanding,
4:23 there must be a s renewal of your thoughts
5:19 and hymns and s songs among yourselves,
Col 1: 9 and we ask him to make you wise with s wisdom.
2:11 It was a s procedure—the cutting away of your
3:16 and s songs to God with thankful hearts.
1Ti 1: 4 in endless speculation over myths and s pedigrees.
4: 7 and energy in training yourself for s fitness.
4: 8 some value, but s exercise is much more important,
4:14 Do not neglect the s gift you received through the
2Ti 1: 6 This is why I remind you to fan into flames the s
Tit 3: 9 Do not get involved in foolish discussions about s
Heb 13: 9 Your s strength comes from God's special favor,
13:17 Obey your s leaders and do what they say.
1Pe 2: 2 You must crave pure s milk so that you can grow
2: 5 is building you, as living stones, into his s temple.
2: 5 who offer the s sacrifices that please him
4:10 to each of you from his great variety of s gifts.
1Jn 1: 6 fellowship with God but go on living in s darkness.
2:11 reject other Christians are wandering in s darkness

SPIRITUALITY (1) [SPIRIT]

1Co 5: 6 How terrible that you should boast about your s,

SPIRITUALLY (5) [SPIRIT]

Mt 8:22 Let those who are s dead care for their own dead."
Lk 9:60 "Let those who are s dead care for their own dead.
1Ti 5: 6 But the widow who lives only for pleasure is s
Heb 6:12 Then you will not become s dull and indifferent.
Rev 14: 4 For they are s undefiled, pure as virgins,

SPIT (15) [SPITS, SPITTING, SPITTLE]
Nu 12:14 said to Moses, "If her father had s in her face,
Dt 25: 9 pull his sandal from his foot, and s in his face.
Job 17: 6 of me among the people; they s in my face.
30:10 and won't come near me, except to s in my face.
Ps 58: 4 They s poison like deadly snakes; / they are like
Isa 50: 6 from shame, for they mock me and s in my face.
Jnh 2:10 Then the LORD ordered the fish to s up Jonah on
Mt 26:67 Then they s in Jesus' face and hit him with their
27:30 And they s on him and grabbed the stick and beat
Mk 10:34 They will mock him, s on him, beat him with their
14:65 Then some of them began to s at him, and they
15:19 they beat him on the head with a stick, s on him,
Lk 18:32 to be mocked, treated shamefully, and s upon.
Jn 9: 6 Then he s on the ground, made mud with the
Rev 3:16 like lukewarm water, I will s you out of my mouth!

SPITE (7) [SPITEFULLY]
Lev 26:18 "And if, in s of this, you still disobey me, I will
Ezr 10: 2 of the land. But there is hope for Israel in s of this.
Ne 9:38 "Yet in s of all this, we are making a solemn
Ps 78:32 But in s of this, the people kept on sinning.
Jer 3:10 But in s of all this, her faithless sister Judah has
Eze 20:44 by treating you mercifully in s of your wickedness,
1Th 1: 6 Spirit in s of the severe suffering it brought you.

SPITEFULLY (1) [SPITE]
Pr 24:28 Do not testify s against innocent neighbors;

SPITS (1) [SPIT]
Lev 15: 8 And if he s on you, you must undergo the same

SPITTING (2) [SPIT]
Mk 7:33 Then, s onto his own fingers, he touched the man's
8:23 Then, s on the man's eyes, he laid his hands on

SPITTLE (1) [SPIT]
Mk 7:33 he touched the man's tongue with the s.

SPLASH (1) [SPLASHED]
Eze 24: 8 So I will s her blood on a rock as an open

SPLASHED (1) [SPLASH]
Ex 24: 6 off into basins. The other half he s against the altar.

SPLATTER (1) [SPLATTERS]
Mal 2: 3 and s your faces with the dung of your festival

SPLATTERS (1) [SPLATTER]
Lev 6:27 and if the sacrificial blood s anyone's clothing,

SPLENDID (6) [SPLENDIDLY, SPLENDOR]
1Ki 10: 5 organization of his officials and their s clothing,
2Ch 9: 4 organization of his officials and their s clothing,
Ps 49:16 grow rich, / and their homes become ever more s.
Isa 62: 3 for all to see—a s crown in the hands of God.
Eze 17: 8 had plenty of water so it could grow into a s vine
2Co 8:23 They are s examples of those who bring glory to

SPLENDIDLY (1) [SPLENDID]
Lk 16:19 "There was a certain rich man who was s clothed

SPLENDOR (30) [SPLENDID]
Ex 15:11 glorious in holiness like you— / so awesome in s,
Dt 33:26 to help you, / across the skies in majestic s.
1Ch 16:29 Worship the LORD in all his holy s.
2Ch 20:21 to the LORD and praising him for his holy s.
Job 37:22 Golden s comes from the mountain of God. He is
clothed in dazzling s.
40:10 put on your robes of state, your majesty and s.
Ps 21: 5 and you have clothed him with s and majesty.
29: 2 Worship the LORD in the s of his holiness.
89:44 You have ended his s / and overturned his throne.
96: 9 Worship the LORD in all his holy s. / Let all the
145: 5 I will meditate on your majestic, glorious s
Pr 20:29 the gray hair of experience is the s of the old.
Isa 33:17 Your eyes will see the king in all his s, and you
35: 2 LORD will display his glory, the s of our God.
60: 9 the Holy One of Israel, for he will fill you with s.
La 1: 7 Jerusalem remembers her ancient s.
3:18 I cry out, "My s is gone! Everything I had hoped
Eze 1:27 he looked like a burning flame, shining with s.
16:14 because the s I bestowed on you perfected your
27:11 shields hung on your walls, perfecting your s.
28: 7 against your marvelous wisdom and defile your s!
28:17 You corrupted your wisdom for the sake of your s.
Da 4:30 and as an expression of my royal s."
11:20 who sent a tax collector to maintain the royal s,
Hab 3: 3 His brilliant s fills the heavens, and the earth is
2Th 2: 8 of his mouth and destroy by the s of his coming.
2Pe 1:16 We have seen his majestic s with our own eyes.
Rev 18: 1 and the earth grew bright with his s.
18:14 "The luxuries and s that you prized so much will

SPLINT (1)
Eze 30:21 Neither has it been bound up with a s to make it

SPLINTERED (1) [SPLINTERS]
Eze 29: 7 cracked staff, you s and stabbed her in the armpit.

SPLINTERS (1) [SPLINTERED]
Nu 33:55 those who remain will be like s in your eyes

SPLIT (20) [SPLITS]
Lev 11: 4 because they either have s hooves or chew the cud,
11: 4 though it chews the cud, it does not have s hooves.
11: 7 for though it has s hooves, it does not chew the
Nu 16:31 when the ground suddenly s open beneath them.
Dt 14: 6 "Any animal that has s hooves and chews the cud
14: 7 They chew the cud but do not have s hooves.
14: 8 for though it has s hooves, it does not chew the
Jdg 9:34 and his men went by night and s into four groups,
1Ki 13: 3 This altar will s apart, and its ashes will be poured
Ps 60: 2 You have shaken our land and s it open.
74:13 You s the sea by your strength / and smashed the
78:15 He s open the rocks in the wilderness / to give
Pr 1:14 in your lot with us; we'll s our loot with you."
Eze 1: 7 but their feet were s like calves' feet and shone
Hab 3: 9 You s open the earth with flowing rivers!
Zec 14: 4 And the Mount of Olives will s apart, making a
Mt 27:51 from top to bottom. The earth shook, rocks s apart,
Mk 1:10 he saw the heavens s open and the Holy Spirit
Lk 12:52 From now on families will be s apart, three in
Rev 16:19 The great city of Babylon s into three pieces,

SPLITS (1) [SPLIT]
Ps 29: 5 The voice of the LORD s the mighty cedars;

SPOILED (2) [SPOILING]
Jer 24: 2 while the other was filled with figs that were s
24: 8 I will treat them like s figs, too rotten to eat.

SPOILING (1) [SPOILED]
Jer 25:36 in despair, for the LORD is s their pastures.

SPOILS (2)
Nu 31:32 The plunder remaining from the s that the fighting
Dt 20:14 You may enjoy the s of your enemies that the

SPOKE (174) [SPEAK, SPOKES]
Ge 11: 1 At one time the whole world s a single language
12:14 they arrived in Egypt, everyone s of her beauty.
15: 1 Afterward the LORD s to Abram in a vision
18:27 Then Abraham s again. "Since I have begun,
34: 4 He even s to his father about it. "Get this girl for
41: 9 Then the king's cup-bearer s up. "Today I have
42:30 "The man who is ruler over the land s very
43:27 "How is your father—the old man you s about?
44: 6 and s to them in the way he had been instructed.
46: 2 During the night God s to him in a vision. "Jacob!
50:21 And he s very kindly to them, reassuring them.
Ex 16: 2 the whole community of Israel s bitterly against
16:10 And as Aaron s to the people, they looked out
19:19 As the horn blast grew louder and louder, Moses s,
33: 9 and hover at the entrance while the LORD s with
Lev 16: 1 The LORD s to Moses after the death of Aaron's
Nu 1: 1 the LORD s to Moses in the Tabernacle in the
3: 1 and Moses as it was recorded when the LORD s
3:14 The LORD s again to Moses, there in the
7:89 of the Covenant. The LORD s to him from there.
11:25 LORD came down in the cloud and s to Moses.
16: 8 Then Moses s again to Korah: "Now listen,
Dt 1: 1 This book records the words that Moses s to all the
4:12 And the LORD s to you from the fire. You heard
4:15 You did not see the LORD's form on the day he s
5: 4 The LORD s to you face to face from the heart of
5: 5 He s to me, and I passed his words on to you.
5:22 "The LORD s these words with a loud voice to
Jos 1: 1 the LORD s to Joshua son of Nun,
6: 8 After Joshua s to the people, the seven priests with
21: 2 They s to them at Shiloh in the land of Canaan,
22:33 and s no more of war against Reuben and Gad.
Jdg 9: 3 So Abimelech's uncles s to all the people of
1Sa 7:10 But the LORD s with a mighty voice of thunder
19: 4 The next morning Jonathan s with his father about
22: 9 who was standing there with Saul's men, s up.
2Sa 3:19 Abner also s with the leaders of the tribe of
13:22 And though Absalom never s to Amnon about it,
16:23 For every word Ahithophel s seemed as wise as
23: 3 The God of Israel s. / The Rock of Israel said to
1Ki 1:48 and he s these words: 'Blessed be the LORD,
12:13 But Rehoboam s harshly to them, for he rejected
2Ki 9:36 which he s through his servant Elijah from Tishbe:
10: 9 and s to the crowd that had gathered around them.
25:28 He s pleasantly to Jehoiachin and gave him
1Ch 21: 9 Then the LORD s to Gad, David's seer. This was
21:27 Then the LORD s to the angel, who put the sword
2Ch 10:13 But Rehoboam s harshly to them, for he rejected
33:10 The LORD s to Manasseh and his people,
33:18 and the words the seers s to him in the name of the
36:12 of the prophet Jeremiah, who s for the LORD.
Ne 5: 7 I s out against these nobles and officials.
9:13 down on Mount Sinai and s to them from heaven.
13:21 But I s sharply to them and said, "What are you
13:24 half their children s in the language of Ashdod
Est 3: 4 They s to him day after day, but still he refused to
3: 4 So they s to Haman about this to see if he would
7: 8 And as soon as the king s, his attendants covered
Job 3: 1 At last Job s, and he cursed the day of his birth.
6: 1 Then Job s again:
6: 3 all the sands of the sea. That is why I s so rashly.
9: 1 Then Job s again:
12: 1 Then Job s again:
16: 1 Then Job s again:
19: 1 Then Job s again:
21: 1 Then Job s again:
23: 1 Then Job s again:
26: 1 Then Job s again:
29:11 of me praised me. All who saw me s well of me.
29:22 And after I s, they had nothing to add, for my
32: 5 saw that they had no further reply, he s out angrily.
Ps 33: 6 The LORD merely s, / and the heavens were
33: 9 For when he s, the world began! / It appeared at his
66:17 For I cried out to him for help, / praising him as I s.
78:19 They even s against God himself, saying,
89:19 You once s in a vision to your prophet and said,
99: 7 He s to them from the pillar of cloud, / and they
105:31 When he s, flies descended on the Egyptians,
105:34 He s, and hordes of locusts came— / locusts
106:33 They made Moses angry, / and he s foolishly.
107:20 He s, and they were healed— / snatched from the
107:25 He s, and the winds rose, / stirring up the waves.
Isa 8: 5 Then the LORD s to me again and said,
43: 9 Who can verify that they s the truth?
48:13 the heavens above. I s, and they came into being.
65:12 you did not answer. When I s, you did not listen.
66: 4 they did not answer. When I s, they did not listen.
Jer 1:13 Then the LORD s to me again and asked,
2: 8 against me, and the prophets s in the name of Baal,
7:13 says the LORD, I s to you about it repeatedly,
11: 9 Again the LORD s to me and said, "I have
21: 1 The LORD s through Jeremiah when King
25:19 I went to Egypt and s to Pharaoh, his officials,
26: 7 and all the people listened to Jeremiah as he s in
26:12 Then Jeremiah s in his own defense. "The LORD
26:17 of the wise old men stood and s to the people there.
27:16 Then I s to the priests and the people and said,
28: 8 who preceded you and me s against many nations,
38:25 My officials may hear that I s to you. Then they
52:32 He s pleasantly to Jehoiachin and gave him
Eze 1:25 a voice s from beyond the crystal surface above
2: 2 The Spirit came into me as he s and set me on my
10: 2 Then the LORD s to the man in linen clothing
35:12 have heard every contemptuous word you s against
37: 7 So I s these words, just as he told me. Suddenly as
I s, there was a rattling noise all across
37:10 So I s as he commanded me, and the wind entered
Da 9: 6 who s your messages to our kings and princes
10:19 As he s these words, I suddenly felt stronger
Hos 12: 4 he met God face to face, and God s to him—
13: 1 In the past when the tribe of Ephraim s, the people
Jnh 3: 1 Then the LORD s to Jonah a second time:
Zec 1:13 And the LORD s kind and comforting words to
3: 6 Then the angel of the LORD s very solemnly to
Mal 3:16 Then those who feared the LORD s with each
Mt 13:34 he never s to them without using such parables.
14:27 But Jesus s to them at once. "It's all right,"
24:15 when you will see what Daniel the prophet s about:
28: 5 Then the angel s to the women. "Don't be afraid!"
Mk 4: 1 he got into a boat and sat down and s from there.
5:39 He went inside and s to the people. "Why all this
6:50 But Jesus s to them at once. "It's all right,"
9:17 One of the men in the crowd s up and said,
10:35 the sons of Zebedee, came over and s to him.
14:56 Many false witnesses s against him, but they
Lk 4:22 All who were there s well of him and were amazed
4:32 at the things he said, because he s with authority.
4:39 at her bedside, he s to the fever, rebuking it,
7:40 Then Jesus s up and answered his thoughts.
22:52 Then Jesus s to the leading priests and captains of
24:40 As he s, he held out his hands for them to see,
Jn 2: 3 so Jesus' mother s to him about the problem.
6: 8 Then Andrew, Simon Peter's brother, s up.
7:50 leader who had met with Jesus earlier, then s up.
9:29 We know God s to Moses, but as for this man,
12:28 Then a voice s from heaven, saying, "I have
18:16 Then the other disciple s to the woman watching at
20:20 As he s, he held out his hands for them to see,
20:21 He s to them again and said, "Peace be with you.
Ac 2:29 David wasn't referring to himself when he s these
3:24 every prophet s about what is happening today.
4:25 you s long ago by the Holy Spirit through our
6: 1 Those who s Greek complained against those who
s Hebrew,
6:10 against the wisdom and Spirit by which Stephen s.
8:10 to the greatest, often s of him as "the Great One—
9:10 The Lord s to him in a vision, calling, "Ananias!"
10:15 The voice s again, "If God says something is
13:46 Then Paul and Barnabas s out boldly and declared,
15:32 s extensively to the Christians, encouraging
16:18 that he turned and s to the demon within her.
17:17 and he s daily in the public square to all who
18: 9 One night the Lord s to Paul in a vision and told
19: 6 and they s in other tongues and prophesied.
19: 9 his message and publicly s against the Way,
20: 9 As Paul s on and on, a young man named
23: 9 "Perhaps a spirit or an angel s to him."
27: 9 in the fall, and Paul s to the ship's officers about it.
Ro 4: 6 King David s of this, describing the happiness of
10:20 And later Isaiah s boldly for God: / "I was found
11: 9 David s of this same thing when he said,
1Co 13:11 I s and thought and reasoned as a child does.
1Th 2:13 you didn't think of the words we s as being just our
Heb 1: 1 Long ago God s many times and in many ways to
11:22 confidently s of God's bringing the people of Israel
12: 5 forgotten the encouraging words God s to you,
12:26 When God s from Mount Sinai his voice shook the
Jas 5:10 look at the prophets who s in the name of the Lord.
Rev 4: 1 and the same voice I had heard before s to me with
9:14 And the voice s to the sixth angel who held the

10: 4 When the seven thunders s, I was about to write.
13: 6 And he s terrible words of blasphemy against God,
13: 11 of a lamb, and he s with the voice of a dragon.
17: 1 poured out the seven bowls came over and s to me.

SPOKEN (165) [SPEAK]

Ge 16: 13 who had s to her, as "the God who sees me,"
35: 13 Then God went up from the place where he had s
35: 14 pillar to mark the place where God had s to him.
35: 15 "house of God"—because God had s to him there.
Ex 4: 10 and I'm not now, even after you have s to me.
20: 22 You are witnesses that I have s to you from
34: 29 because he had s to the LORD face to face.
Nu 12: 2 "Has the LORD s only through Moses?
12: 2 Hasn't he s through us, too?" But the LORD
14: 28 very things I heard you say. I, the LORD, have s!
14: 35 I, the LORD, have s! I will do these things to
23: 19 Has he ever s and failed to act? / Has he ever
Dt 9: 10 he had s to you from the fire on the mountain.
10: 4 They were the same words the LORD had s to
18: 22 That prophet has s on his own and need not be
2Sa 2: 27 knows what would have happened if you hadn't s,
6: 22 held in honor by the girls of whom you have s!"
1Ki 16: 7 This message from the LORD had been s against
16: 34 concerning Jericho s by Joshua son of Nun.
22: 28 return safely, the LORD has not s through me!"
2Ki 10: 10 that was s concerning Ahab's family will not fail.
19: 21 This is the message that the LORD has s against
22: 15 to them, "The LORD, the God of Israel, has s!
2Ch 10: 15 for it fulfilled the prophecy of the LORD s to
18: 27 return safely, the LORD has not s through me!"
34: 23 to them, "The LORD, the God of Israel, has s!
35: 22 to whom God had indeed s, and he would not turn
36: 21 So the message of the LORD s through Jeremiah
Ne 2: 16 I had not yet s to the religious and political leaders,
6: 12 I realized that God had not s to him, but that he had
Job 21: 3 let me speak. After I have s, you may mock me.
35: 16 have protested in vain. You have s like a fool."
Ps 50: 1 The mighty God, the LORD, has s; / he has
62: 11 God has s plainly, / and I have heard it many
73: 15 If I had really s this way, / I would have been a
Isa 1: 20 by your enemies. I, the LORD, have s!"
9: 8 The Lord has s out against that braggart Israel,
14: 23 of destruction. I, the LORD Almighty, have s!"
14: 27 The LORD Almighty has s—who can change his
21: 17 I, the LORD, the God of Israel, have s!"
22: 25 it supports will fall with it. I, the LORD, have s!"
23: 11 He has s out against Phoenicia and depleted its
24: 3 completely emptied and looted. The LORD has s!
25: 8 against his land and people. The LORD has s!
37: 22 This is the message that the LORD has s against
40: 5 all people will see it together. The LORD has s!"
45: 13 for a reward! I, the LORD Almighty, have s!"
50: 5 The Sovereign LORD has s to me, and I have
54: 17 will come from me. I, the LORD, have s!
58: 14 to Jacob, your ancestor. I, the LORD, have s!"
59: 21 children's children forever. I, the LORD, have s!
65: 25 on my holy mountain. I, the LORD, have s!"
66: 2 and they are mine. I, the LORD, have s!
66: 21 be my priests and Levites. I, the LORD, have s!
Jer 1: 8 and take care of you. I, the LORD, have s!"
1: 19 and I will take care of you. I, the LORD, have s!"
2: 3 disaster fell upon them. I, the LORD, have s!' "
2: 9 in the years to come. I, the LORD, have s!
2: 19 of him. I, the Lord, the LORD Almighty, have s!
2: 22 be washed away. I, the Sovereign LORD, have s!
3: 13 refused to follow me. I, the LORD, have s!' "
8: 3 I will send them. I, the LORD Almighty, have s!
8: 13 for things will soon be gone. I, the LORD, have s!'
9: 24 that I delight in these things. I, the LORD, have s!
12: 17 and destroyed. I, the LORD, have s!"
13: 15 Listen! Do not be proud, for the LORD has s.
14: 15 for they have s in my name even though I never
15: 20 will protect and deliver you. I, the LORD, have s!
23: 9 because of the holy words the LORD has s
23: 12 time of punishment comes. I, the LORD, have s!
23: 22 they would have s my words and turned my people
25: 29 of the earth. I, the LORD Almighty, have s!'
25: 31 the wicked with his sword. The LORD has s!' "
26: 12 "The LORD gave me every word that I have s.
26: 16 for he has s to us in the name of the LORD our
27: 11 farm the land as usual. I, the LORD, have s!' "
28: 4 has put on your necks. I, the LORD, have s!"
29: 19 though I have s to them repeatedly through my
29: 32 you to rebel against me. I, the LORD, have s!' "
30: 3 and live here again. I, the LORD, have s!"
31: 14 people with my bounty. I, the LORD, have s!"
31: 37 away forever for their sins. I, the LORD, have s!
32: 42 good I have promised them. I, the LORD, have s!
32: 44 restore prosperity to them. I, the LORD, have s!"
33: 13 and all the towns of Judah. I, the LORD, have s!
35: 14 But I have s to you again and again, and you refuse
35: 19 the LORD Almighty, the God of Israel, have s!"
39: 18 and keep you safe. I, the LORD, have s!' "
44: 26 that my name will no longer be s by any of the
44: 30 of Babylon. I, the LORD, have s!"
45: 5 you wherever you go. I, the LORD, have s!"
46: 26 from the ravages of war. I, the LORD, have s!
48: 8 and in the valleys, for the LORD has s.
La 3: 46 "All our enemies have s out against us.
Eze 5: 13 the LORD, have s to them in my jealous anger.
5: 15 a nation in furious rebuke. I, the LORD, have s!
5: 17 of the enemy against you. I, the LORD, have s!"
12: 28 I, the Sovereign LORD, have s!"
13: 7 from the LORD,' when I have not even s to you?
13: 16 was no peace. I, the Sovereign LORD, have s!'
17: 21 will know that I, the LORD, have s these words.
17: 24 I, the LORD, have s! I will do what I have said."
21: 17 and I will satisfy my fury. I, the LORD, have s!"
21: 32 memory lost to history. I, the LORD, have s!"
22: 14 I, the LORD, have s! I will do what I have said.
22: 28 when the LORD hasn't s a single word to them.
23: 34 in anguish. For I, the Sovereign LORD, have s!
24: 14 I, the LORD, have s! The time has come and I
25: 14 it is from me. I, the Sovereign LORD, have s!
26: 5 their nets, for I have s, says the Sovereign LORD.
26: 14 will never be rebuilt, for I, the LORD, have s!
26: 21 never be found. I, the Sovereign LORD, have s!"
28: 10 of foreigners. I, the Sovereign LORD, have s!"
30: 12 using foreigners to do it. I, the LORD, have s!
31: 18 teeming hordes. I, the Sovereign LORD, have s!"
32: 8 dark above you. I, the Sovereign LORD, have s!
32: 16 and its hordes. I, the Sovereign LORD, have s!"
32: 32 by the sword. I, the Sovereign LORD, have s!"
34: 24 a prince among my people. I, the LORD, have s!
37: 14 just as I promised. I, the LORD, have s!"
39: 5 for I have s, says the Sovereign LORD.
47: 23 they now live. I, the Sovereign LORD, have s!
Hos 2: 17 of Baal; even their names will no longer be s.
7: 13 redeem them, but they have only s lies about me.
Joel 3: 8 a nation far away. I, the LORD, have s!"
Am 1: 5 return to Kir as slaves. I, the LORD, have s!"
1: 8 will be killed. I, the Sovereign LORD, have s!"
1: 15 will go into exile together. I, the LORD, have s!"
2: 3 slaughter all their princes. I, the LORD, have s!"
2: 16 and run for their lives. I, the LORD, have s!"
3: 1 Listen to this message that the LORD has s
3: 8 The Sovereign LORD has s—I dare not refuse to
3: 15 palaces filled with ivory. I, the LORD, have s!"
4: 3 thrown from your fortresses. I, the LORD, have s!
5: 17 and destroy them all. I, the LORD, have s!"
8: 3 city in silence. I, the Sovereign LORD, have s!"
9: 12 I, the LORD, have s, and I will do these things.
Ob 1: 4 bring you crashing down. I, the LORD, have s!
1: 18 no survivors in Edom. I, the LORD, have s!
Zep 3: 20 before their very eyes. I, the LORD, have s!"
Hag 2: 9 will bring peace. I, the LORD Almighty, have s!"
2: 23 chosen you. I, the LORD Almighty, have s!"
Zec 10: 12 they wish by my authority. I, the LORD, have s!"
Mal 3: 13 'What do you mean? How have we s against you?'
Mt 2: 15 This fulfilled what the Lord had s through the
2: 23 This fulfilled what was s by the prophets
3: 3 Isaiah had s of John when he said, / "He is a voice
Mk 12: 32 You have s the truth by saying that there is only
Lk 3: 4 Isaiah had s of John when he said, / "He is a voice
Jn 5: 18 he had s of God as his Father, thereby making
6: 63 And the very words I have s to you are spirit
12: 29 while others declared an angel had s to him.
12: 48 judged at the day of judgment by the truth I have s.
15: 22 not be guilty if I had not come and s to them.
16: 25 "I have s of these matters in parables, but the time
Ac 2: 6 hear their own languages being s by the believers.
19: 37 the temple and have not s against our goddess.
Ro 15: 21 I have been following the plan s of in the
2Co 6: 11 Corinthian friends! We have s honestly with you.
1Ti 1: 18 based on the prophetic words s about you earlier.
3: 2 For an elder must be a man whose life cannot be s
4: 14 s to you when the elders of the church laid their
Heb 1: 2 in these final days, he has s to us through his Son.
4: 8 God would not have s later about another day of
Jude 1: 15 insults that godless sinners / have s against him."

SPOKES (1) [SPOKE]

1Ki 7: 33 The axles, s, rims, and hubs were all cast from

SPOKESMAN (3) [SPEAK, MAN]

Ex 4: 16 Aaron will be your s to the people, and you will be
Jer 1: 5 and appointed you as my s to the world."
15: 19 you speak words that are worthy, you will be my s.

SPONGE (3)

Mt 27: 48 One of them ran and filled a s with sour wine,
Mk 15: 36 One of them ran and filled a s with sour wine,
Jn 19: 29 so they soaked a s in it, put it on a hyssop branch,

SPOON [KJV] See DISH(ES)

SPOONS (1)

Nu 4: 7 and place the dishes, s, bowls, cups, and the special

SPORT (1)

Ge 49: 6 murdered men, / and they crippled oxen just for s.

SPORTING [KJV] See FONDLING, REVEL

SPOT (13) [SPOTLESS, SPOTS, SPOTTED]

Ex 9: 26 The only s in all Egypt without hail that day was
Lev 13: 4 and if the hair in the s has not turned white,
13: 19 or a reddish white s remains in its place,
13: 50 After examining the affected s, the priest will put it
13: 53 and the affected s has not spread in the clothing,
13: 56 he is to cut the s from the clothing, the fabric,
13: 57 If the s reappears at a later time, however,
13: 58 But if the s disappears after the object is washed,
2Sa 2: 23 And everyone who came by that s stopped
11: 16 So Joab assigned Uriah to a s close to the city wall
15: 32 As they reached the s at the top of the Mount of
Mk 6: 32 They left by boat for a quieter s.
Eph 5: 27 her to himself as a glorious church without a s

SPOTLESS (3) [SPOT]

Hos 12: 8 one can say I got it by cheating! My record is s!"
1Pe 1: 19 lifeblood of Christ, the sinless, s Lamb of God.
Rev 15: 6 clothed in s white linen with gold belts across their

SPOTS (2) [SPOT]

Isa 40: 4 out the curves and smooth off the rough s.
Jer 13: 23 Can a leopard take away its s? Neither can you

SPOTTED (6) [SPOT]

Ge 30: 32 all the sheep and goats that are speckled or s,
30: 35 all the male goats that were speckled and s,
30: 35 that were speckled and s with any white patches,
30: 39 of their offspring were streaked, speckled, and s.
31: 10 with the flock were streaked, speckled, and s.
31: 12 and s males are mating with the females of your

SPOUSE [KJV] See BRIDE

SPOUSES (1)

Jer 29: 6 Then find s for them, and have many

SPOUT (4) [SPOUTS]

Job 16: 4 I could s off my criticisms against you and shake
Pr 15: 2 makes learning a joy; fools s only foolishness.
15: 28 think before speaking; the wicked s evil words.
Hos 10: 4 They s empty words and make promises they don't

SPOUTS (2) [SPOUT]

Jer 6: 7 She s evil like a fountain! Her streets echo with the
Zec 4: 2 seven lamps, each one having seven s with wicks.

SPRANG (2) [SPRING]

Mt 13: 5 soil with underlying rock. The plants s up quickly,
Mk 4: 5 soil with underlying rock. The plant s up quickly,

SPRAWL (1) [SPRAWLING]

Am 6: 4 How terrible it will be for you who s on ivory beds

SPRAWLING (1) [SPRAWL]

Job 30: 12 They send me s; they lay traps in my path.

SPREAD (132) [OUTSPREAD, SPREADING, SPREADS]

Ge 10: 19 Eventually the territory of Canaan s from Sidon to
Ex 9: 9 It will s like fine dust over the whole land of
9: 16 and that my fame might s throughout the earth.
25: 20 atonement cover with their wings s out above it.
40: 19 Then he s the coverings over the Tabernacle
Lev 2: 4 mixed with olive oil or wafers s with olive oil.
8: 26 with olive oil, and a thin wafer s with olive oil.
13: 5 the affected area has not changed or s on the skin,
13: 6 If the affected area has faded and not s, the priest
13: 7 But if the rash continues to s after this examination
13: 8 If the priest notices that the rash has s, then he
13: 23 But if the area grows no larger and does not s,
13: 27 If at the end of that time the affected area has s on
13: 28 area has not moved or s on the skin and has faded,
13: 32 If at the end of that time the affected area has not s
13: 34 If it has not s and appears to be no more than
13: 35 But if the infection begins to s after the person is
13: 36 If the infection has s, he must pronounce the
13: 51 If the affected area has s, the material is clearly
13: 53 and the affected spot has not s in the clothing,
13: 55 even if it did not s, the object is defiled.
14: 39 If the mildew on the walls of the house has s,
14: 44 If he sees that the affected areas have s, the walls
19: 16 "Do not s slanderous gossip among your people.
Nu 4: 7 "Next they must s a blue cloth over the table,
4: 8 They must s a scarlet cloth over that, and finally a
4: 11 and his sons must also s a dark blue cloth over the
4: 14 and a covering of fine goatskin leather must be s
6: 15 mixed with olive oil and wafers s with olive oil—
11: 32 They s the quail out all over the camp.
13: 32 So they s discouraging reports about the land
22: 11 from Egypt and has s out over the whole land.
22: 41 From there he could see the people of Israel s out
24: 6 They s before me like groves of palms,
Dt 22: 17 Then they must s the cloth before the judges.
32: 11 over her young, / so he s his wings to take them in
Jdg 8: 25 They s out a cloak, and each one threw in a gold
11: 26 s across the land from Heshbon to Aroer and in all
16: 2 Word soon s that Samson was there, so the men of
Ru 3: 9 "S the corner of your covering over me, for you
3: 15 also said to her, "Bring your cloak and s it out."
1Sa 13: 3 The news s quickly among the Philistines that
30: 16 the Amalekites were s out across the fields, eating
2Sa 5: 18 and s out across the valley of Rephaim.
5: 22 and again s out across the valley of Rephaim.
19: 8 and as the news s throughout the city that he was
21: 10 s sackcloth on a rock and stayed there the entire
1Ki 3: 28 Word of the king's decision s quickly throughout
4: 31 His fame s throughout all the surrounding nations.
8: 7 The cherubim s their wings over the Ark,
2Ki 9: 13 They quickly s out their cloaks on the bare steps
19: 14 LORD's Temple and s it out before the LORD.
19: 31 For a remnant of my people will s out from
20: 7 an ointment from figs and s it over the boil."
1Ch 5: 9 they s eastward toward the edge of the desert that
5: 11 of Gad, who were s as far east as Salecah.
5: 23 The half-tribe of Manasseh s through the land from

14:17 So David's fame **s** everywhere, and the LORD
2Ch 5: 8 The cherubim **s** their wings out over the Ark,
6:12 Then Solomon stood with his hands **s** out before
26: 8 and his fame **s** even to Egypt, for he had become
26:15 His fame **s** far and wide, for the LORD helped
Ne 4:19 and all the people, "The work is very **s** out,
Est 9: 4 and his fame **s** throughout all the provinces as he
Job 9: 8 He alone has **s** out the heavens and marches on the
15:29 and their possessions will no longer **s** across the
38:13 Have you ever told the daylight to **s** to the ends of
39:26 makes the hawk soar and **s** its wings to the south?
Ps 41: 6 and when they leave, they **s** it everywhere.
44:20 our God / or **s** our hands in prayer to foreign gods,
80:11 We **s** our branches west to the Mediterranean Sea,
90: 8 You **s** out our sins before you— / our secret sins—
105:39 The LORD **s** out a cloud above them as a
Pr 7:16 My bed is **s** with colored sheets of finest linen
8:29 so they would not **s** beyond their boundaries.
Isa 16: 8 Her tendrils **s** out as far as Jazer and trailed out into
25: 6 the LORD Almighty will **s** a wonderful feast for
32: 6 They **s** lies about the LORD; they deprive the
37:14 LORD's Temple and **s** it out before the LORD.
37:32 For a remnant of my people will **s** out from
38:21 "Make an ointment from figs and **s** it over the boil,
48:13 The palm of my right hand **s** out the heavens
54: 2 your house; build an addition; **s** out your home!
Jer 8: 2 and **s** them out on the ground before the sun,
9: 4 of one another and **s** their slanderous lies.
17:27 The fire will **s** to the palaces, and no one will be
18:18 Let's **s** rumors about him and ignore what he
43:10 have hidden. He will **s** his royal canopy over them.
49:22 as an eagle, and he will **s** his wings against Bozrah.
Eze 1:22 There was a surface **s** out above them like the sky.
5: 4 A fire will then **s** from this remnant and destroy all
12:13 Then I will **s** out my net and capture him in my
16:14 Your fame soon **s** throughout the world on account
19: 8 They **s** out their nets for him / and captured him in
23:41 and my oil on a table that was **s** before you.
26: 5 It will be a place for fishermen to **s** their nets,
26:14 a bare rock, a place for fishermen to **s** their nets.
26:17 their naval power, / once **s** fear around the world.
Hos 14: 6 Its branches will **s** out like those of beautiful olive
Jnh 4: 6 and soon it **s** its broad leaves over Jonah's head,
Mt 4:24 News about him **s** far beyond the borders of
9:31 But instead, they **s** his fame all over the region.
14:35 The news of their arrival **s** quickly throughout the
21: 8 Most of the crowd **s** their coats on the road ahead
21: 8 cut branches from the trees and **s** them on the road.
28:15 Their story **s** widely among the Jews, and they still
Mk 1:28 The news of what he had done **s** quickly through
1:45 But as the man went on his way, he **s** the news,
2: 1 and the news of his arrival **s** quickly through the
3: 8 The news about his miracles had **s** far and wide,
7:24 he couldn't. As usual, the news of his arrival **s** fast.
7:36 more he told them not to, the more they **s** the news,
11: 8 Many in the crowd **s** their coats on the road ahead
11: 8 branches in the fields and **s** them along the way.
Lk 1:58 The word **s** quickly to her neighbors and relatives
1:65 and the news of what had happened **s** throughout
4:37 The story of what he had done **s** like wildfire
5:15 the report of his power **s** even faster,
7:17 The report of what Jesus had done that day **s** all
19:36 Then the crowds **s** out their coats on the road ahead
Jn 21:23 So the rumor **s** among the community of believers
Ac 1:19 The news of his death **s** rapidly among all the
13:49 So the Lord's message **s** throughout that region.
19:17 The story of what happened **s** quickly all through
19:20 So the message about the Lord **s** widely and had a
Ro 5:12 so death **s** to everyone, for everyone sinned.
9:17 so that my fame might **s** throughout the earth."
1Co 9:23 I do all this to **s** the Good News, and in doing
2Co 2:14 and to **s** the Good News like a sweet perfume.
Php 1:12 to me here has helped to **s** the Good News.
2Th 3: 1 Pray first that the Lord's message will **s** rapidly
Rev 4: 7 of an eagle with wings **s** out as though in flight.

SPREADING (20) [SPREAD]

Lev 13:37 But if it appears that the infection has stopped **s**
13:57 at a later time, however, the mildew is clearly **s**,
Nu 14:36 LORD by **s** discouraging reports about the land
Job 8:16 in the sunshine, its branches **s** across the garden.
36:29 Can anyone really understand the **s** of the clouds
SS 1:17 shaded by cedar trees and **s** firs."
Isa 7:19 will come in vast hordes, **s** across the whole land.
16: 8 Moab was once like a **s** grapevine. Her tendrils
18: 5 with pruning shears. He will snip your **s** branches.
21: 5 They are **s** rugs for people to sit on. Everyone is
58: 9 making false accusations and **s** vicious rumors!
Jer 48:32 Your **s** vines once reached as far as the Dead Sea,
Eze 17: 6 It took root there and grew into a low, **s** vine.
Joel 2: 2 Suddenly, like dawn **s** across the mountains,
Mk 5:14 surrounding countryside, **s** the news as they ran.
Lk 8:34 surrounding countryside, **s** the news as they ran.
Ac 4:17 But perhaps we can stop them from **s** their
12:24 But God's Good News was **s** rapidly, and there
Eph 3: 7 privilege of serving him by **s** this Good News.
Php 1: 5 because you have been my partners in **s** the Good

SPREADS (5) [SPREAD]

Lev 13:22 If during that time the affected area **s** on the skin,
Job 36:30 See how he **s** the lightning around him and how it
Isa 40:22 He is the one who **s** out the heavens like a curtain
Gal 5: 9 a little yeast **s** quickly through the whole batch of
2Ti 2:17 This kind of talk **s** like cancer. Hymenaeus

SPRING (75) [MIDSPRING, SPRANG, SPRINGING, SPRINGS, SPRINGTIME, SPRINGWATER]

Ge 16: 7 Hagar beside a desert **s** along the road to Shur.
24:13 See, here I am, standing beside this **s**,
24:16 She went down to the **s**, filled her jug, and came up
24:30 and when he heard her story, he rushed out to the **s**,
24:42 "So this afternoon when I came to the **s** I prayed
24:43 Here I am, standing beside this **s**. I will say to
24:45 She went down to the **s** and drew water and filled
26:19 also dug in the Gerar Valley and found a gushing **s**.
26:20 then the local shepherds came and claimed the **s**.
Ex 13: 4 This day in early **s** will be the anniversary of your
23:15 be an annual event at the appointed time in early **s**,
34:18 at the appointed time each year in early **s**,
Lev 11:36 if the dead body of such an animal falls into a **s**
23: 5 begins at twilight on its appointed day in early **s**.
Nu 9: 1 gave these instructions to Moses in early **s**,
9: 3 at twilight on the appointed day in early **s**. Be sure
20: 1 In early **s** the people of Israel arrived in the
21:17 this song: / "**S** up, O well! / Yes, sing about it!
28:16 "On the appointed day in early **s**, you must
33: 3 after the first Passover celebration in early **s**.
Dt 16: 1 celebrate the Passover at the proper time in early **s**,
Jos 15: 9 of the mountain to the **s** at the waters of Nephtoah,
17: 7 to the people living near the **s** of Tappuah.
17: 9 From the **s** of Tappuah, the border of Manasseh
18:15 From there it ran westward to the **s** at the waters of
Jdg 7: 1 got up early and went as far as the **s** of Harod.
7: 4 Bring them down to the **s**, and I will sort out who
15:19 Then he named that place "The **S** of the One Who
1Sa 29: 1 and the Israelites camped at the **s** in Jezreel.
2Sa 11: 1 The following **s**, the time of year when kings go to
1Ki 1: 9 Adonijah went to the stone of Zoheleth near the **s**
1:33 "Take Solomon and my officers down to Gihon **S**.
1:38 king's bodyguard took Solomon down to Gihon **S**,
1:44 The king sent him down to Gihon **S** with Zadok
18: 5 "We must check every **s** and valley to see if we
20:22 for another attack by the king of Aram next **s**."
20:26 The following **s** he called up the Aramean army
2Ki 2:21 Then he went out to the **s** that supplied the town
13:20 of Moabite raiders used to invade the land each **s**.
1Ch 20: 1 The following **s**, the time of year when kings go to
2Ch 15:10 The people gathered at Jerusalem in late **s**,
29:17 The work began on a day in early **s**, and in eight
30: 3 normally celebrated one month earlier, in early **s**,
31: 7 The first of these tithes was brought in late **s**,
32:30 He blocked up the upper **s** of Gihon and brought
33:14 from west of the Gihon **S** in the Kidron Valley to
35: 1 in Jerusalem on the appointed day in early **s**.
36:10 In the **s** of the following year, Jehoiachin was
Ne 2: 1 Early the following **s**, during the twentieth year of
Job 5: 6 But evil does not **s** from the soil, and trouble does
6:15 a seasonal brook that overflows its banks in the **s**
8:19 its life, and others **s** up from the earth to replace it.
29:23 for my words were as refreshing as the **s** rain.
38:27 parched ground and makes the tender grass **s** up?
Ps 78:15 to give them plenty of water, as from a gushing **s**.
Pr 11:28 you go! But the godly flourish like leaves in **s**.
25:26 it is like polluting a fountain or muddying a **s**.
Ecc 12: 6 Don't wait until the water jar is smashed at the **s**
SS 2:13 Yes, **s** is here! Arise, my beloved, my fair one,
4:12 You are like a **s** that no one else can drink from,
6:11 the valley to see the new growth brought on by **s**.
Isa 32:20 they plant seed, bountiful crops will **s** up.
58:11 like a well-watered garden, like an ever-flowing **s**.
61:11 His righteousness will be like a garden in early **s**,
Jer 3: 3 That is why even the **s** rains have failed. For you
5:24 for he gives us rain each **s** and fall, assuring us of
15:18 a seasonal brook. It is like a **s** that has gone dry."
Eze 45:18 In early **s**, on the first day of each new year,
Hos 6: 3 arrival of dawn or the coming of rains in early **s**."
Joel 2:23 autumn rains will come, as well as the rains of **s**.
Am 3: 5 Does a trap ever **s** shut when there's nothing there
Zec 10: 1 Ask the LORD for rain in the **s**, and he will give
Jn 4:14 It becomes a perpetual **s** within them, giving them
Jas 3:11 Does a **s** of water bubble out with both fresh water
5: 7 eagerly look for the rains in the fall and in the **s**.

SPRINGING (3) [SPRING]

SS 2:12 The flowers are **s** up, and the time of singing birds
Isa 61:11 filled with young plants **s** up everywhere.
Zec 2:13 for he is **s** into action from his holy dwelling."

SPRINGS (42) [SPRING]

Ge 36:24 This is the Anah who discovered the hot **s** in the
Ex 15:27 where there were twelve **s** and seventy palm trees.
They camped there beside the **s**.
Nu 33: 9 where there are twelve **s** of water and seventy palm
Dt 8: 7 with **s** that gush forth in the valleys and hills.
Jos 15: 7 From there the border extended to the **s** at
15:19 me land in the Negev; please give me **s** as well."
So Caleb gave her the upper and lower **s**.
Jdg 1:15 me land in the Negev; please give me **s** as well."
So Caleb gave her the upper and lower **s**.
5:19 of Canaan fought at Taanach near Megiddo's **s**,
2Ki 3:19 You will cut down all their trees, stop up all their **s**,
3:25 stopped up the **s**, and cut down the good trees.
19:29 and next year you will eat what **s** up from that.
2Ch 32: 3 and they decided to stop the flow of the **s** outside
32: 4 a huge work crew to stop the flow of the **s**,
Job 38:16 "Have you explored the **s** from which the seas
Ps 74:15 You caused the **s** and streams to gush forth,
84: 6 it will become a place of refreshing **s**,
85:11 Truth **s** up from the earth, / and righteousness
90: 5 or like grass that **s** up in the morning.
104:10 You make the **s** pour water into ravines,
107:33 rivers into deserts, / and **s** of water into dry land.
107:35 into pools of water, / the dry land into flowing **s**.
114: 8 of water; / yes, **s** of water came from solid rock.
Pr 5:16 Why spill the water of your **s** in public, having sex
8:24 before the **s** bubbled forth their waters.
Isa 35: 6 **S** will gush forth in the wilderness, and streams
35: 7 a pool, and **s** of water will satisfy the thirsty land.
37:30 and next year you will eat what **s** up from that.
41:18 Rivers fed by **s** will flow across the dry,
43:20 Yes, I will make **s** in the desert, so that my chosen
Eze 31: 4 Deep **s** watered it and helped it to grow tall
Hos 10: 4 So perverted justice **s** up among them like
13:15 All their flowing **s** and wells will disappear.
Heb 12:15 for whenever it **s** up, many are corrupted by its
2Pe 2:17 These people are as useless as dried-up **s** of water
Rev 7:17 He will lead them to the **s** of life-giving water.
8:10 upon one-third of the rivers and on the **s** of water.
14: 7 and earth, the sea, and all the **s** of water."
16: 4 third angel poured out his bowl on the rivers and **s**,
21: 6 To all who are thirsty I will give the **s** of the water

SPRINGTIME (3) [SPRING]

Ge 8:22 there will be **s** and harvest, cold and heat, winter
Ps 37: 2 soon fade away. / Like **s** flowers, they soon wither.
72: 6 May his reign be as refreshing as the **s** rains—

SPRINGWATER (3) [SPRING, WATER]

Lev 14: 5 over a clay pot that is filled with fresh **s**.
14:50 the birds over a clay pot that is filled with fresh **s**.
15:13 he must wash his clothes and bathe in fresh **s**.

SPRINKLE (30) [SPRINKLED, SPRINKLES, SPRINKLING]

Ex 29:20 **S** the rest of the blood on the sides of the altar.
29:21 **S** it on Aaron and his sons and on their clothes.
40: 9 "Take the anointing oil and **s** it on the Tabernacle
40:10 **S** the anointing oil on the altar of burnt offering
Lev 1:11 will **s** its blood against the sides of the altar.
2: 1 You are to pour olive oil on it and **s** it with incense.
2:15 put olive oil on it and **s** it with incense.
3: 2 then **s** the animal's blood against the sides of the
3: 8 then **s** the sheep's blood against the sides of the
3:13 Then the sons of Aaron will **s** the goat's blood
4: 6 and **s** it seven times before the LORD in front of
4:17 and **s** it seven times before the LORD in front of
5: 9 Then he will **s** some of the blood of the sin offering
14: 7 The priest will also **s** the dead bird's blood seven
14:16 into the oil and **s** it seven times before the LORD.
14:27 and **s** some of it seven times before the LORD.
14:51 and he will **s** the house seven times.
16:14 and **s** it on the front of the atonement cover and
16:15 There he will **s** the blood on the atonement cover
16:19 into the blood and **s** it seven times over the altar.
17: 6 That way the priest will be able to **s** the blood
24: 7 **S** some pure frankincense near each row. It will
Nu 18:17 **S** their blood on the altar, and burn their fat as an
19: 4 and **s** it seven times toward the front of the
19:18 That person must **s** the water on the tent, on all the
19:19 person must **s** the water on those who are unclean.
19:21 Those who **s** the water of purification must
Eze 36:25 "Then I will **s** clean water on you, and you will be
43:24 and the priests are to **s** salt on them and offer them
Heb 11:28 and to **s** blood on the doorposts so that the angel of

SPRINKLED (26) [SPRINKLE]

Ex 24: 8 Then Moses **s** the blood from the basins over the
29:16 will be collected and **s** on the sides of the altar.
Lev 6:15 has been mixed with olive oil and **s** with incense.
7: 2 and its blood **s** against the sides of the altar.
8:11 He **s** the altar seven times, anointing it and all its
8:19 ram's blood and **s** it against the sides of the altar.
8:24 then **s** the rest of the blood against the sides of the
8:30 and he **s** them on Aaron and his clothing and on his
9:12 the blood, and he **s** it against the sides of the altar.
9:18 the blood, and he **s** it against the sides of the altar.
10: 1 fire in their incense burners and **s** incense over it.
Nu 19:13 Since the water of purification was not **s** on them,
19:20 Since the water of purification has not been **s** on
2Ki 16:13 over it, and **s** the blood of peace offerings on it.
16:15 and sacrifices should be **s** over the new altar.
2Ch 29:22 and the priests took the blood and **s** it on the altar.
29:22 they killed the rams and **s** their blood on the altar.
29:24 and **s** their blood on the altar to make atonement
30:16 blood to the priests, who then **s** it on the altar.
35:11 who **s** the blood on the altar while the Levites
Ne 9: 1 and dressed in sackcloth and **s** dust on their heads.
Da 9: 3 I wore rough sackcloth and **s** myself with ashes.
Heb 9:19 and **s** both the book of God's laws and all the
9:21 he **s** blood on the sacred tent and on everything
10:22 For our evil consciences have been **s** with Christ's
12:24 between God and people, and to the **s** blood,

SPRINKLES (2) [SPRINKLE]

Lev 7:14 then belong to the priest who **s** the altar with blood
7:33 must always be given to the priest who **s** the blood

SPRINKLING (4) [SPRINKLE]

Lev 1: 5 will present the blood by **s** it against the sides of
Nu 8: 7 Do this by **s** them with the water of purification.
Eze 43:18 and the **s** of blood when the altar is built.
Heb 9:22 nearly everything was purified by **s** with blood.

SPROUT (8) [SPROUTED, SPROUTING]
Nu 17: 5 Buds will s on the staff belonging to the man I
Job 5: 6 from the soil, and trouble does not s from the earth.
14: 7 there is hope that it will s again and grow new
14: 9 water it may bud and s again like a new seedling.
Isa 45: 8 so salvation and righteousness can s up together.
55: 13 will grow. Where briers grew, myrtles will s up.
Mt 24: 32 its buds become tender and its leaves begin to s,
Mk 13: 28 its buds become tender and its leaves begin to s,

SPROUTED (4) [SPROUT]
Ex 9: 32 because they had not yet s from the ground.
Nu 17: 8 of Levi, had s, blossomed, and produced almonds!
Mk 4: 27 the seeds s and grew without the farmer's help,
Heb 9: 4 some manna, Aaron's staff that s leaves,

SPROUTING (4) [SPROUT]
2Ki 19: 26 They are like grass s on a housetop,
Ps 72: 16 as they do in Lebanon, / s up like grass in a field.
Isa 37: 27 They are like grass s on a housetop,
53: 2 s from a root in dry and sterile ground.

SPUE(D) [KJV] See SPIT, VOMIT

SPUNGE [KJV] See SPONGE

SPUR (1)
Ecc 12: 11 A wise teacher's words s students to action

SPURNED (1)
Ac 14: 2 But the Jews who s God's message stirred up

SPY (9) [SPIED, SPIES]
Jos 2: 1 "S out the land on the other side of the Jordan
2: 2 "Some Israelites have come here tonight to s out
7: 2 Joshua sent some of his men from Jericho to s out
2Sa 3: 25 You know perfectly well that he came to s on you
10: 3 David has sent them to s out the city so that they
1Ch 19: 3 David has sent them to s out the land so that they
Ps 37: 32 Those who are evil s on the godly, / waiting for an
56: 6 They come together to s on me—/ watching my
Gal 2: 4 who came to s on us and see our freedom in Christ

SQUADS (1)
Ac 12: 4 placing him under the guard of four s of four

SQUANDER (1) [SQUANDERED, SQUANDERING]
Pr 10: 16 their lives, but evil people s their money on sin.

SQUANDERED (1) [SQUANDER]
Jer 3: 24 their sons and daughters—was s on a delusion.

SQUANDERING (1) [SQUANDER]
Lk 15: 30 Yet when this son of yours comes back after s your

SQUARE (40) [SQUARELY, SQUARES]
Ge 19: 2 "we'll just spend the night out here in the city s."
Ex 27: 1 make a s altar 7-1/2 feet wide, 7-1/2 feet long,
28: 16 two folds of cloth, forming a pouch nine inches s.
30: 2 It must be eighteen inches s and three feet high,
37: 25 It was eighteen inches s and three feet high,
38: 1 It was 7-1/2 feet s at the top and 4-1/2 feet high.
39: 9 It was doubled over to form a pouch, nine inches s.
Jdg 19: 15 They rested in the town s, but no one took them in
19: 17 When he saw the travelers sitting in the town s,
19: 20 whatever you do, don't spend the night in the s."
2Sa 21: 12 the public s of the Philistine city of Beth-shan.)
1Ki 7: 31 The panels of the carts were s, not round.
2Ch 32: 6 and asked them to assemble before him in the s at
Ezr 10: 9 and all the people were sitting in the s before the
Ne 8: 1 as one person at the s just inside the Water Gate.
8: 3 He faced the s just inside the Water Gate from
Est 4: 6 So Hathach went out to Mordecai in the s in front
6: 9 and to lead him through the city s on the king's
6: 11 and led him through the city s, shouting,
Job 30: 28 I stand in the public s and cry for help.
Pr 1: 20 shouts in the streets. She cries out in the public s.
Eze 16: 24 pagan shrine and put altars to idols in every town s.
16: 31 street corner and your altars to idols in every s.
40: 7 Each of these alcoves was 10-1/2 feet s, with a
40: 12 The alcoves themselves were 10-1/2 feet s.
40: 42 each 31-1/2 inches s and 21 inches high.
40: 47 the inner courtyard and found it to be 175 feet s.
40: 48 and found them to be 8-3/4 feet s.
41: 1 that framed its doorway. They were 10-1/2 feet s.
41: 4 The inner room was 35 feet s. "This," he told me,
41: 21 There were s columns at the entrance to the Holy
41: 22 made of wood, 3-1/2 feet s and 5-1/4 feet high.
43: 16 The top of the altar is s, measuring 21 feet by 21
43: 17 The upper ledge also forms a s, measuring 24-1/2
48: 20 is a s that measures 8-1/3 miles on each side.
Mt 11: 16 a group of children playing a game in the public s.
Lk 7: 32 a group of children playing a game in the public s.
Ac 7: 5 no inheritance here, not even one s foot of land.
17: 17 and he spoke daily in the public s to all who
Rev 21: 16 When he measured it, he found it was a s, as wide

SQUARELY (1) [SQUARE]
La 3: 12 He bent his bow and aimed it s at me.

SQUARES (7) [SQUARE]
Ne 8: 16 or in the s just inside the Water Gate
Ps 144: 14 no forced exile, / no cries of distress in our s.
SS 3: 2 the city, searching for him in all its streets and s.'
Jer 9: 21 and young men no longer gather in the s.
Am 5: 16 "There will be crying in all the public s and in
Na 2: 4 race recklessly along the streets and through the s,
Zec 8: 4 streets with a cane and sit together in the city s.

SQUASHED (1)
Jer 18: 4 so the potter s the jar into a lump of clay

SQUEEZE (1) [SQUEEZED]
Nu 22: 25 it tried to s by and crushed Balaam's foot against

SQUEEZED (2) [SQUEEZE]
Ge 40: 11 so I took the grapes and s the juice into it.
Jdg 6: 38 he s the fleece and wrung out a whole bowlful of

STAB (1) [BACK-STABBING, STABBED]
Zec 13: 3 Then his own father and mother will s him.

STABBED (5) [STAB]
Jdg 9: 54 So the young man s him with his sword, and he
2Sa 4: 6 Ishbosheth's bedroom, and s him in the stomach.
20: 10 and Joab s him in the stomach with it so that his
Ps 37: 15 But they will be s through the heart with their own
Eze 29: 7 you splintered and s her in the armpit.

STABILITY (4)
Pr 12: 3 Wickedness never brings s; only the godly have
28: 2 with wise and knowledgeable leaders, there is s.
29: 4 A just king gives s to his nation, but one who
Lk 21: 26 because the s of the very heavens will be broken

STABLE (3) [STABLES]
Dt 17: 16 The king must not build up a large s of horses for
Pr 14: 4 An empty s stays clean, but no income comes from an empty s.

STABLE [KJV] See also ESTABLISHED, PASTURE

STABLES (1) [STABLE]
1Ki 4: 28 and straw for the royal horses in the s.

STABLISH(ED), STABLISHETH [KJV] See CONFIRM, ESTABLISH(ED, -ES), FOUND, SET (UP), STRENGTHEN

STACHYS (1)
Ro 16: 9 our co-worker in Christ, and beloved S.

STACKS [KJV] See SHEAVES

STAFF (52) [STAFFS]
Ge 39: 1 a member of the personal s of Pharaoh, the king of
40: 20 gave a banquet for all his officials and household s.
47: 31 and Jacob bowed in worship as he leaned on his s.
49: 10 nor the ruler's s from his descendants,
Ex 4: 2 in your hand?" "A shepherd's s," Moses replied.
4: 4 and grabbed it, and it became a shepherd's s again.
4: 17 And be sure to take your shepherd's s along
4: 20 land of Egypt. In his hand he carried the s of God.
7: 9 say to Aaron, 'Throw down your shepherd's s,'
7: 10 Aaron threw down his s before Pharaoh and his
7: 15 Be sure to take along the shepherd's s that turned
7: 17 I will hit the water of the Nile with this s,
7: 19 "Tell Aaron to point his s toward the waters of
7: 20 Moses raised his s and hit the water of the Nile.
8: 5 "Tell Aaron to point his shepherd's s toward all
8: 16 to Moses, "Tell Aaron to strike the dust with his s.
9: 23 So Moses lifted his s toward the sky,
10: 13 So Moses raised his s, and the LORD caused an
14: 16 Use your shepherd's s—hold it out over the water,
17: 5 LORD said to Moses, "Take your shepherd's s,
17: 9 I will stand at the top of the hill with the s of God
17: 11 As long as Moses held up the s with his hands,
17: 12 became too tired to hold up the s any longer.
Nu 17: 2 and inscribe each tribal leader's name on his s.
17: 3 Inscribe Aaron's name on the s of the tribe of Levi,
17: 3 for there must be one s for the leader of each
17: 5 Buds will sprout on the s belonging to the man I
17: 6 tribal leaders, including Aaron, brought Moses a s.
17: 8 he found that Aaron's s, representing the tribe of
17: 9 them to the people. Each man claimed his own s.
17: 10 "Place Aaron's s permanently before the Ark of
20: 8 "You and Aaron must take the s and assemble the
20: 9 He took the s from the place where it was kept
20: 11 his hand and struck the rock twice with the s,
22: 27 In a fit of rage Balaam beat it again with his s.
Jdg 6: 21 touched the meat and bread with the s in his hand,
1Sa 16: 22 "Please let David join my s, for I am very pleased
17: 40 Then, armed only with his shepherd's s and sling,
2Ki 4: 29 to Gehazi, "Get ready to travel; take my s and go!
4: 29 Go quickly and lay the s on the child's face."
4: 31 hurried on ahead and laid the s on the child's face,
Est 1: 8 for the king had instructed his s to let everyone
Ps 23: 4 Your rod and your s / protect and comfort me.
Isa 10: 26 or when the LORD's s was raised to drown the
Jer 48: 17 scepter is broken, how the beautiful s is shattered!
51: 59 gave this message to Zedekiah's s officer,
Eze 29: 7 but like a cracked s, you splintered and stabbed her
Da 1: 19 So they were appointed to his regular s of advisers.
Zec 11: 10 Then I took my s called Favor and snapped it in
11: 14 Then I broke my other s, Union, to show that the
Heb 9: 4 some manna, Aaron's s that sprouted leaves,
11: 21 and bowed in worship as he leaned on his s.

STAFFS (7) [STAFF]
Ex 7: 12 Their s became snakes, too! But then Aaron's
Nu 17: 2 "Take twelve wooden s, one from each of Israel's
17: 4 Put these s in the Tabernacle in front of the Ark of
17: 7 Moses put the s in the LORD's presence in the
17: 9 When Moses brought all the s out from the
21: 18 leaders hollowed out / with their scepters and s."
Zec 11: 7 Then I took two shepherd's s and named one Favor

STAG (2)
Pr 7: 22 like an ox going to the slaughter or like a trapped s,
SS 2: 17 a gazelle or a young s on the rugged mountains."

STAGES (4)
Ge 12: 9 Then Abram traveled south by s toward the Negev.
13: 3 Then they continued traveling by s toward Bethel,
Nu 10: 12 and traveled on in s until the cloud stopped in the
33: 2 These are the s of their march, identified by the

STAGGER (15) [STAGGERED, STAGGERING, STAGGERS]
Job 12: 25 without a light. He makes them s like drunkards.
Ps 59: 11 s them with your power, and bring them to their
Pr 23: 34 You will s like a sailor tossed at sea, clinging to a
Isa 19: 14 They cause the land of Egypt to s like a sick
28: 7 and prophets reel and s from beer and wine.
29: 9 but not from wine! You s, but not from beer!
63: 6 my anger and made them s and fall to the ground."
Jer 23: 9 I s like a drunkard, like someone overcome by
25: 16 When they drink from it, they will s, crazed by the
37: 10 they would still s from their tents and burn this city
48: 26 "Let her s and fall like a drunkard, for she has
La 5: 13 and the children s under heavy loads of wood.
Am 8: 12 People will s everywhere from sea to sea,
Ob 1: 16 you nations will drink and s and disappear from
Na 3: 11 And you, Nineveh, will also s like a drunkard.

STAGGERED (3) [STAGGER]
Ps 107: 27 They reeled and s like drunkards / and were at their
Am 4: 8 People s from one town to another for a drink of
Heb 12: 20 They s back under God's command: "If even an

STAGGERING (3) [STAGGER]
1Sa 25: 31 conscience the s burden of needless bloodshed
Isa 46: 1 But look! The beasts are s under the weight!
Na 1: 10 His enemies, tangled up like thorns, s like drunks,

STAGGERS (2) [STAGGER]
Pr 5: 6 She s down a crooked trail and doesn't even realize
Isa 24: 20 The earth s like a drunkard. It trembles like a tent

STAIN (5) [STAINED, STAINING]
Ps 51: 1 your great compassion, / blot out the s of my sins.
51: 9 looking at my sins. / Remove the s of my guilt.
Isa 1: 18 "No matter how deep the s of your sins, I can
Heb 1: 3 After he died to cleanse us from the s of sin,
2Pe 2: 13 They are a disgrace and a s among you. They revel

STAINED (5) [STAIN]
Isa 1: 18 Even if you are s as red as crimson, I can make you
63: 1 from the city of Bozrah, with his clothing s red?
63: 3 my foes. It is their blood that has s my clothes.
Jer 2: 22 You are s with guilt that cannot be washed away.
2: 34 Your clothing is s with the blood of the innocent

STAINING (2) [STAIN]
Ex 12: 22 and sides of the doorframe, s it with the blood.
1Ki 2: 5 s his belt and sandals with the blood of war.

STAIRS (7) [DOWNSTAIRS, STAIRWAY, UPSTAIRS]
1Ki 6: 8 There were winding s going up to the second floor,
6: 8 and another flight of s between the second
Ne 3: 15 and he rebuilt the wall as far as the s that descend
9: 4 Some of the Levites were standing on the s,
Eze 40: 40 on each side of the s going up to the north
Ac 21: 35 As they reached the s, the mob grew so violent the
21: 40 so Paul stood on the s and motioned to the people

STAIRWAY (4) [STAIRS]
Ge 28: 12 he dreamed of a s that reached from earth to
28: 13 At the top of the s stood the LORD, and he said,
Eze 40: 26 This gateway also had a s of seven steps leading up
41: 7 A s led up from the bottom level through the

STAKE (4)
Ne 2: 20 But you have no s or claim in Jerusalem."
Isa 22: 23 for I will drive him firmly in place like a tent s.
22: 25 I will pull out the s that seemed so firm.
55: 3 wide open. Listen, for the life of your soul is at s.

STALK (9) [STALKED, STALKS]

Ge 41: 5 This time he saw seven heads of grain on one s,
41: 6 seven more heads appeared on the s,
41:22 This time there were seven heads of grain on one s,
41:23 Then out of the same s came seven withered heads,
Job 13:25 by the wind? Would you chase a dry s of grass?
38:39 "Can you s prey for a lioness and satisfy the
Isa 17: 4 Israel will be very dim, for poverty will s the land.
Eze 5:17 Disease and war will s your land, and I will bring
22:25 Your princes plot conspiracies just as lions s their

STALKED (2) [STALK]

2Ki 5:11 But Naaman became angry and s away. "I thought
Lk 4:25 for three and a half years and hunger s the land.

STALKS (3) [STALK]

Ps 91: 6 nor dread the plague that s in darkness,
Jer 4: 7 A lion s from its den, a destroyer of nations.
Hos 8: 7 The s of wheat wither, producing no grain. And if

STALL (2) [STALLS]

Job 39: 9 ox consent to being tamed? Will it stay in your s?
Da 2: 8 You are trying to s for time because you know I

STALLION (1) [STALLIONS]

Jer 50:11 about like a calf in a meadow and neigh like a s.

STALLIONS (2) [STALLION]

Isa 63:13 They were like fine s racing through the desert,
Jer 5: 8 They are well-fed, lusty s, each neighing for his

STALLS (8) [STALL]

Ge 6:14 Then construct decks and s throughout its interior.
1Ki 4:26 Solomon had four thousand s for his chariot horses
2Ch 9:25 Solomon had four thousand s for his chariot horses
32:28 and he made many s for his cattle and folds for his
Mt 21:12 money changers and the s of those selling doves.
Mk 11:15 money changers and the s of those selling doves,
Lk 13:15 your ox or your donkey from their s on the Sabbath
19:45 and began to drive out the merchants from their s.

STAMMER (1)

Isa 32: 4 Those who s in uncertainty will speak out plainly.

STAMP (2) [STAMPED]

Eze 6:11 Clap your hands in horror, and s your feet. Cry out,
30:15 of Egypt, and I will s out the people of Thebes.

STAMPED (4) [STAMP]

Eze 25: 6 Because you clapped and s and cheered with glee
Mt 22:20 he asked, "Whose picture and title are s on it?"
Mk 12:16 he asked, "Whose picture and title are s on it?"
Lk 20:24 Whose picture and title are s on it?" "Caesar's,"

STANCHED [KJV] See STOPPED

STAND (241) [LONG-STANDING, STANDING, STANDS, STANDSTILL, STOOD]

Ge 19: 9 "S back!" they shouted. "Who do you think you
24:31 Why do you s here outside the village when we
31:48 "This pile of stones will s as a witness to remind
31:52 s between us as a witness of our vows. I will not
45: 1 Joseph could s it no longer. "Out, all of you!"
Ex 7:15 to the river. S on the riverbank and meet him there.
9:11 Even the magicians were unable to s before Moses,
14:13 Just s where you are and watch the LORD rescue
17: 9 I will s at the top of the hill with the staff of God in
23: 1 with evil people by telling lies on the witness s.
23: 2 When you are on the witness s, do not be swayed
33: 8 people would get up and s in their tent entrances.
33:10 Then all the people would s and bow low at their
33:21 "S here on this rock beside me.
34:11 Then I will surely drive out all those who s in your
34:24 I will drive out the nations that s in your way
Lev 26:37 You will have no power to s before your enemies.
Nu 1:53 The Levites are responsible to s guard around the
5:18 The priest will s before her, holding the jar of bitter
8:13 Then have the Levites s in front of Aaron and his
11:16 Bring them to the Tabernacle to s there with you.
16: 9 and to s before the people to minister to them?
22:22 so he sent the angel of the LORD to s in the road
23: 3 said to Balak, "S here by your burnt offerings,
23:15 "S here by your burnt offering while I go to meet
23:24 rise up like a lioness; / like a majestic lion they s.
27:21 is needed, Joshua will s before Eleazar the priest,
30: 4 says nothing, then all her vows and pledges will s.
30: 7 the day he hears of it, her vows and pledges will s.
30:11 does nothing to stop her, her vow or pledge will s.
Dt 7:24 No one will be able to s against you, and you will
9: 2 heard the saying, 'Who can s up to the Anakites?'
11:25 No one will be able to s against you,
17:10 at the place the LORD chooses will always s.
24:11 S outside and the owner will bring it out to you.
27:12 and Benjamin must s on Mount Gerizim to
27:13 and Naphtali must s on Mount Ebal to proclaim a
28:10 by the LORD, and they will s in awe of you.
29:15 this covenant with you who s in his presence today
31:21 and this song will s as evidence against them,
Jos 1: 5 No one will be able to s their ground against you as
4: 7 These stones will s as a permanent memorial
10: 8 Not a single one of them will be able to s up to
10:12 He said, / "Let the sun s still over Gibeon,
21:44 None of their enemies could s against them,
Jdg 4:20 "S at the door of the tent," he told her.
16:16 So day after day she nagged him until he couldn't s
16:25 and made to s at the center of the temple,
1Sa 6:20 "Who is able to s in the presence of the LORD,
12: 2 own sons, and I s here, an old, gray-haired man.
12: 3 Now tell me as I s before the LORD and before
12: 7 Now s here quietly before the LORD as I remind
12:16 "Now s here and see the great thing the LORD is
14:40 and I will s over here, and all of you s over there."
2Sa 2:25 regrouped there at the top of the hill to take a s.
18:28 who has handed over the rebels who dared to s
1Ki 10: 8 What a privilege for your officials to s here day
18:15 by the LORD Almighty, in whose presence I s,
19:11 "Go out and s before me on the mountain,"
2Ki 10: 4 and said, "Two kings couldn't s against this man!
11: 6 Another third of you are to s guard at the Sur Gate.
11: 6 And the final third must s guard behind the palace
11: 7 must s guard for the king at the LORD's Temple.
2Ch 9: 7 What a privilege for your officials to s here day
13: 7 and inexperienced and could not s up to them.
13: 8 Do you really think you can s against the kingdom
17: 1 He strengthened Judah to s against any attack from
20: 6 are powerful and mighty; no one can s against you!
20: 9 we can come to s in your presence before this
20:17 then s still and watch the LORD's victory.
20:20 LORD your God, and you will be able to s firm.
29:11 The LORD has chosen you to s in his presence,
35: 5 Then s in your appointed holy places and help the
Ezr 9:15 We s before you in our guilt as nothing but an
9:15 though in such a condition none of us can s in your
Ne 4:13 I stationed the people to s guard by families,
9: 5 "S up and praise the LORD your God, for he
Est 9: 2 But no one could make a s against them,
Job 17: 3 O God, since no one else will s up for me.
19:18 When I s to speak, they turn their backs on me.
19:25 and that he will s upon the earth at last.
25: 4 How can a mere mortal s before God and claim to
30:20 I s before you, and you don't bother to look.
30:28 I s in the public square and cry for help.
33: 5 if you can; make your case and take your s.
40:12 with a glance; walk on the wicked where they s.
41:10 the crocodile, who would dare to s up to me?
Ps 1: 1 advice of the wicked, / or s around with sinners,
5: 5 the proud will not be allowed to s in your presence,
7: 6 in anger! / S up against the fury of my enemies!
10: 1 O LORD, why do you s so far away? / Why do
15: 5 the innocent. / Such people will s firm forever.
17:13 S against them and bring them to their knees!
20: 8 and collapse, / but we will rise up and s firm.
24: 3 of the LORD? / Who may s in his holy place?
26:12 I have taken a s, / and I will publicly praise the
33: 8 the LORD, / and let everyone s in awe of him.
33:11 But the LORD's plans s firm forever;
38:20 for good / and oppose me because I s for the right.
38:21 LORD. / Do not s at a distance, my God.
42: 2 living God. / When can I come and s before him?
64: 9 Then everyone will s in awe,
65: 8 at the ends of the earth / s in awe of your wonders.
69: 2 sink into the mire; / I can't find a foothold to s on.
76: 7 Who can s before you when your anger explodes?
76: 9 You s up to judge those who do evil, O God,
88:15 I s helpless and desperate before your terrors.
89: 7 The highest angelic powers s in awe of God.
94:16 Who will s up for me against evildoers?
109: 1 O God, whom I praise, / don't s silent and aloof
119:160 words are true; / all your just laws will s forever.
119:173 S ready to help me, / for I have chosen to follow
122: 5 Here s the thrones where judgment is given,
139: 2 You know when I sit down or s up. / You know my
147:17 like stones. / Who can s against his freezing cold?
Pr 12: 7 and are gone, but the children of the godly s firm.
21:30 or well advised, cannot s against the LORD.
24:11 sentenced to death; don't s back and let them die.
31:28 Her children s and bless her. Her husband praises
Ecc 4:12 but two can s back-to-back and conquer.
8: 3 and don't take a s with those who plot evil.
Isa 1:14 and sacrifices. I cannot s the sight of them!
5: 9 "Many beautiful homes will s deserted, the owners
28: 6 He will give great courage to their warriors who s
29:23 of Israel. They will s in awe of the God of Israel.
30: 8 then s until the end of time as a witness to Israel's
33: 3 of your voice. When you s up, the nations flee!
33:10 "I will s up and show my power and might.
40:20 be compared to an idol that must be placed on a s
44:11 All who worship idols will s before the LORD in
44:11 a god. Together they will s in terror and shame.
47:13 Let them s up and save you from what the future
49: 7 "Kings will s at attention when you pass by.
52:15 Kings will s speechless in his presence.
65: 6 I will not s silent; I will repay them in full! Yes,
Jer 1:10 Today I appoint you to s up against nations
1:18 or people of Judah will be able to s against you.
7:10 and s before me in my Temple and chant,
9: 3 They refuse to s up for the truth. And they only go
14: 6 The wild donkeys s on the bare hills panting like
17:19 said to me, "Go and s in the gates of Jerusalem,
23:30 "I s against these prophets who get their messages
25:10 will fail, and all your homes will s silent and dark.
26: 2 "S out in front of the Temple of the LORD,
30: 6 Then why do they s there, ashen-faced,
34: 3 You will s before the king of Babylon to be judged
46:15 They cannot s because the LORD has driven
48:19 The people of Aroer s anxiously beside the road to
51:50 Do not s and watch—flee while you can!
Eze 2: 1 "S up, son of man," said the voice. "I want to
7:27 The king and the prince will s helpless, weeping in
13: 5 They have not helped it to s firm in battle on the
13: 8 and your visions are a lie, I will s against you,
14: 9 I will s against such prophets and cut them off
22:30 I searched for someone to s in the gap in the wall
27:29 the sailors and helmsmen come to s on the shore.
44:15 They will s in my presence and offer the fat
46: 2 Then he will s by the gatepost while the priest
47:10 Fishermen will s along the shores of the Dead Sea,
Da 2:44 kingdoms into nothingness, but it will s forever.
8: 4 and no one could s against it or help its victims.
10:11 S up, for I have been sent to you." When he said
11:15 The best troops of the south will not be able to s in
Hos 4:16 She will s alone and unprotected, like a helpless
Joel 1:17 The barns and granaries s empty and abandoned.
2:17 will s between the people and the altar, weeping.
Am 2:15 The archers will fail to s their ground. The swiftest
Mic 5: 4 And he will s to lead his flock with the LORD's
5: 9 The people of Israel will s up to their foes, and all
5:14 and destroy the cities where your idol temples s.
6: 1 "S up and state your case against me.
7:16 All the nations of the world will s amazed at what
7:16 They will s in silent awe, deaf to everything
Na 1: 6 Who can s before his fierce anger? Who can
2:10 The people s aghast, their faces pale and trembling.
Hab 1:13 in any form, s idly by while they swallow us up?
2: 7 all you have, while you s trembling and helpless.
Zep 1: 7 S in silence in the presence of the Sovereign
3: 8 the time is coming soon when I will s up
Zec 4: 7 a mighty mountain, will s in Zerubbabel's way;
6: 5 "These are the four spirits of heaven who s before
14: 4 On that day his feet will s on the Mount of Olives,
Mal 3: 2 Who will be able to s and face him when he
Mt 5:15 Instead, put it on a s and let it shine for all.
9: 6 Jesus turned to the paralyzed man and said, "S up,
10:13 turns out to be a worthy home, let your blessing s;
10:18 And you must s trial before governors and kings
28:14 we'll s up for you and everything will be all
Mk 2:11 "S up, take your mat, and go on home,
3: 3 to the man, "Come and s in front of everyone."
3:26 if Satan is fighting against himself, how can he s?
4:21 A lamp is placed on a s, where its light will shine.
13:11 But when you are arrested and s trial, don't worry
Lk 1:19 "I am Gabriel! I s in the very presence of God.
5:24 Jesus turned to the paralyzed man and said, "S up,
6: 8 "Come and s here where everyone can see."
10: 6 who live there are worthy, the blessing will s;
13:11 for eighteen years and was unable to s up straight.
13:13 he touched her, and instantly she could s straight.
13:25 Then you will s outside knocking and pleading,
17:19 And Jesus said to the man, "S up and go.
21:28 s straight and look up, for your salvation is near!"
21:36 these horrors and s before the Son of Man."
Jn 5: 8 Jesus told him, "S up, pick up your sleeping mat,
Ac 6:10 None of them was able to s against the wisdom
10:26 But Peter pulled him up and said, "S up! I'm a
14:10 So Paul called to him in a loud voice, "S up!"
25: 9 to go to Jerusalem and s trial before me there?"
25:20 and I asked him whether he would be willing to s
26:16 Now s up! For I have appeared to you to appoint
27:24 Paul, for you will surely s trial before Caesar!
Ro 5: 2 this place of highest privilege where we now s,
12: 9 Hate what is wrong. S on the side of the good.
14:10 each of us will s personally before the judgment
1Co 10:13 so strong that you can't s up against it.
16:13 Be on guard. S true to what you believe.
2Co 1:21 along with you, the ability to s firm for Christ.
1:24 so you will be full of joy as you s firm in your
5:10 For we must all s before Christ to be judged.
13: 8 oppose the truth, but to s for the truth at all times.
Eph 6:11 so that you will be able to s firm against all
6:14 S your ground, putting on the sturdy belt of truth
Col 1:22 and blameless as you s before him without a single
1:23 continue to believe this truth and s in it firmly.
1Th 2:19 you will bring us much joy as we s together before
3: 1 Finally, when we could s it no longer, we decided
3:13 and holy when you s before God our Father on that
2Th 2:15 s firm and keep a strong grip on everything we
Heb 12:12 your tired hands and s firm on your shaky legs.
Jas 2: 3 "You can s over there, or else sit on the floor"—
4: 6 and more strength to s against such evil desires.
5: 3 This treasure you have accumulated will s as
1Pe 5: 9 Take a firm s against him, and be strong in your
1Jn 3:19 so we will be confident when we s before the Lord,
Rev 3:20 "Look! Here I s at the door and knock. If you hear
8: 2 And I saw the seven angels who s before God,
11: 4 and the two lampstands that s before the Lord of
18:10 They will s at a distance, terrified by her great
18:15 by selling her these things will s at a distance,
18:17 merchant ships and their crews will s at a distance.

STANDARD (12) [STANDARDS]

Lev 5:15 in silver as measured by the s sanctuary shekel.
27:25 be measured in terms of the s sanctuary shekel.
Nu 3:47 each piece weighing the same as the s sanctuary
18:16 each piece weighing the same as the s sanctuary
1Ki 10:28 traders acquired them from Cilicia at the s price.
2Ki 21:13 I will judge Jerusalem by the same s I used for
2Ch 1:16 traders acquired them from Cilicia at the s price.
Pr 16:11 fairness in every business deal; he sets the s.
Eze 45:11 The homer will be your s unit for measuring
45:12 The s unit for weight will be the silver shekel.
Ro 3:23 all have sinned; all fall short of God's glorious s.
Rev 21:17 216 feet thick (the angel used a s human measure).

STANDARDS (6) [STANDARD]

Lev 19:35 "Do not use dishonest s when measuring length,
Ps 74: 4 battle cries; / there they set up their battle s.
Pr 20:10 The LORD despises double s of every kind.
20:23 The LORD despises double s; he is not pleased
1Co 3:18 If you think you are wise by this world's s,
3:18 become a fool so you can become wise by God's s.

STANDING (164) [STAND]

Ge 7:20 s more than twenty-two feet above the highest
18: 2 he suddenly noticed three men s nearby. He got up
24:13 See, here I am, s beside this spring, and the young
24:30 where the man was still s beside his camels.
24:43 Here I am, s beside this spring. I will say to some
41: 1 Pharaoh dreamed that he was s on the bank of the
41:17 "I was s on the bank of the Nile River," he said.
42: 1 "Why are you s around looking at one another?
42:23 that Joseph understood them as he was s there,
45: 3 They were stunned to realize that Joseph was s
Ex 3: 5 off your sandals, for you are s on holy ground."
18:14 The people have been s here all day to get your
22: 6 destroying the sheaves or the s grain,
36:20 they made frames of acacia wood s on end.
Lev 19:32 "Show your fear of God by s up in the presence of
Nu 11:10 Moses heard all the families s in front of their tents
16:32 and the followers who were s with them,
22:23 s in the road with a drawn sword in his hand.
22:25 When the donkey saw the angel of the LORD s
22:31 and he saw the angel of the LORD s in the
22:34 I did not realize you were s in the road to block my
23: 6 the king was s beside his burnt offerings with all
23:17 and the officials of Moab were s beside Balak's
Dt 29:10 are s today before the LORD your God.
29:12 You are s here today to enter into a covenant with
Jos 4: 3 where the priests are s in the middle of the Jordan
4: 9 who carried the Ark of the Covenant were s.
20: 9 they could escape being killed in revenge prior to s
Jdg 6:25 to Baal, and cut down the Asherah pole s beside it.
9:35 Gaal was s at the city gates when Abimelech
Ru 4: 9 Boaz said to the leaders and to the crowd s around,
4:11 Then the leaders and all the people s there replied,
1Sa 17:26 David talked to some others s there to verify the
22: 9 who was s there with Saul's men, spoke up.
1Ki 8:14 to the entire community of Israel s before him
10:19 with the figure of a lion s on each side of the
10:20 one s on each end of each of the six steps.
13:24 the road, with the donkey and the lion s beside it.
13:25 the body lying in the road and the lion s beside it,
13:28 The donkey and lion were still s there beside it,
19:20 Elisha left the oxen s there, ran after Elijah,
22:28 Then he added to those s around, "Take note of
2Ki 11:14 And she saw the newly crowned king s in his place
1Ch 21:15 At that moment the angel of the LORD was s by
21:16 and saw the angel of the LORD s between heaven
2Ch 3:11 The total wingspan of the two cherubim s side by
6: 3 to the entire community of Israel s before him
9:18 with the figure of a lion s on each side of the
9:19 one s on each end of each of the six steps.
18:27 Then he added to those s around, "Take note of
20:14 of the LORD came upon one of the men s there.
23:13 And she saw the newly crowned king s in his place
26:19 But as he was s there with the priests before the
Ne 4: 3 the Ammonite, who was s beside him, remarked,
8: 7 instructed the people who were s there.
9: 4 Some of the Levites were s on the stairs, crying out
Est 5: 2 When he saw Queen Esther s there in the inner
5: 9 not s up or trembling nervously before him, he was
Job 33:26 receive him with joy and restore him to good s.
Ps 24: 5 and have right s with God their savior.
122: 2 And now we are s here / inside your gates,
Ecc 4:12 A person s alone can be attacked and defeated,
12: 5 You will be s at death's door. And as you near
Isa 27: 9 won't be an Asherah pole or incense altar left s.
Jer 34: 7 the only cities of Judah with their walls still s.
43:13 He will break down the sacred pillars s in the
Eze 8:11 Seventy leaders of Israel were s there with
8:16 about twenty-five men were s with their backs to
10: 3 The cherubim were s at the south end of the
40: 3 I saw a man whose face shone like bronze s beside
43: 6 (The man who had been measuring was still s
Da 3: 3 and were s before the image King Nebuchadnezzar
7: 4 and it was left s with its two hind feet on the
7:16 So I approached one of those s beside the throne
8: 2 in the province of Elam, s beside the Ulai River.
8: 3 I saw in front of me a ram with two long horns s
8: 6 two-horned ram that I had seen s beside the river.
8:17 As Gabriel approached the place where I was s,
10: 4 April 23, as I was s beside the great Tigris River,
10:16 I said to the one s in front of me, "I am terrified by
11: 1 I have been s beside Michael as his support
12: 5 and saw two others s on opposite banks of the
12: 6 dressed in linen, who was now s above the river,
12: 7 man dressed in linen, who was s above the river,
Am 7: 7 I saw the Lord s beside a wall that had been built
9: 1 Then I saw a vision of the Lord s beside the altar.
Zec 1: 8 I saw a man sitting on a red horse that was s
1:10 So the man s among the myrtle trees explained,
1:11 who was s among the myrtle trees, "We have
3: 1 Then the angel showed me Jeshua the high priest s
3: 4 So the angel said to the others s there, "Take off
3: 7 and out of my presence along with these others s
Mt 5:23 "So if you are s before the altar in the Temple,
16:28 And I assure you that some of you s here right now
20: 3 and saw some people s around doing nothing.
20: 6 in town again and saw some more people s around.
24:15 the sacrilegious object that causes desecration s in
26:71 servant girl noticed him and said to those s around,
27:11 Now Jesus was s before Pilate, the Roman
Mk 6:54 The people s there recognized him at once,
9: 1 "I assure you that some of you s here right now
11: 4 two disciples left and found the colt s in the street,
12:28 One of the teachers of religious law was s there
13:14 that causes desecration s where it should not be"—
14:69 The servant girl saw him s there and began telling
Lk 1:11 Lord appeared, s to the right of the incense altar.
4:39 S at her bedside, he spoke to the fever, rebuking it,
9:27 And I assure you that some of you s here right now
9:32 and saw Jesus' glory and the two men s with him.
12:12 you what needs to be said even as you are s there."
19:24 Then turning to the others s nearby, the king
20:39 of the teachers of religious law who were s there.
21:19 By s firm, you will win your souls.
24:36 Jesus himself was suddenly s there among them.
Jn 1:35 John was again s with two of his disciples.
2: 6 Six stone waterpots were s there; they were used
9:40 The Pharisees who were s there heard him
11:36 The people who were s nearby said, "See how
11:42 it out loud for the sake of all these people s here,
18: 5 Judas was s there with them when Jesus identified
18:18 and the household servants were s around a
18:22 One of the Temple guards s there struck Jesus on
18:25 Meanwhile, as Simon Peter was s by the fire,
19:25 S near the cross were Jesus' mother, and his
19:26 When Jesus saw his mother s there beside the
20:11 Mary was s outside the tomb crying, and as she
20:14 over her shoulder and saw someone s behind her.
20:19 Suddenly, Jesus was s there among them!
20:26 but suddenly, as before, Jesus was s among them.
21: 4 At dawn the disciples saw Jesus s on the beach,
Ac 1:11 of Galilee, why are you s here staring at the sky?
4:14 But since the man who had been healed was s right
5:23 "The jail was locked, with the guards s outside,
7:33 off your sandals, for you are s on holy ground.
7:55 and he saw Jesus s in the place of honor at God's
7:56 and the Son of Man s in the place of honor at
10:30 a man in dazzling clothes was s in front of me.
12: 6 two soldiers, with others s guard at the prison gate.
12:14 and told everyone, "Peter is s at the door!"
17:22 So Paul, s before the Council, addressed them as
22:20 witness Stephen was killed, I was s there agreeing.
22:25 down to lash him, Paul said to the officer s there,
23: 4 Those s near Paul said to him, "Is that the way to
Ro 5:21 giving us right s with God and resulting in eternal
8:30 And he gave them right s with himself, and he
8:33 He is the one who has given us right s with
1Co 10:12 If you think you are s strong, be careful, for you
Eph 6:13 so that after the battle you will still be s firm.
Php 1:27 about you, I will know that you are s side by side,
Jas 5: 9 The great Judge is coming. He is s at the door!
2Pe 1:12 you already know them and are s firm in the truth.
Rev 1:13 And s in the middle of the lampstands was the Son
4: 1 Then as I looked, I saw a door s open in heaven,
5: 6 but was now s between the throne and the four
7: 1 Then I saw four angels s at the four corners of the
7: 9 s in front of the throne and before the Lamb.
7:11 And all the angels were s around the throne
7:15 That is why they are s in front of the throne of
10: 5 Then the mighty angel s on the sea and on the land
10: 8 and take the unrolled scroll from the angel who is s
14: 1 Then I saw the Lamb s on Mount Zion, and with
19:11 saw heaven opened, and a white horse was s there.
19:17 Then I saw an angel s in the sun, shouting to the
20:12 both great and small, s before God's throne.

STANDS (40) [STAND]

Ex 40:23 the Presence on the table that s before the LORD,
Lev 1: 5 sides of the altar that s in front of the Tabernacle.
4: 7 that s in the LORD's presence in the Tabernacle.
4:18 that s in the LORD's presence in the Tabernacle.
16:12 coals from the altar that s before the LORD.
16:18 s before the LORD by smearing some of the
Jos 22:29 Only the altar of the LORD our God that s in
1Sa 6:18 still s in the field of Joshua as a reminder of what
1Ch 16:15 He always s by his covenant— / the commitment
Est 5:14 "Set up a gallows that s seventy-five feet tall,
7: 9 "Haman has set up a gallows that s seventy-five
Ps 38:11 my disease. / Even my own family s at a distance.
45: 9 At your right side s the queen, / wearing jewelry of
87: 1 On the holy mountain s the city founded by the
105: 8 He always s by his covenant— / the commitment
109:31 For he s beside the needy, / ready to save them
110: 5 The Lord s at your right hand to protect you.
119:89 Forever, O LORD, / your word s firm in heaven.
121: 5 The LORD s beside you as your protective shade.
144: 2 He s before me as a shield, and I take refuge in
Pr 8: 2 She s on the hilltop and at the crossroads.
12:19 Truth s the test of time; lies are soon exposed.
Isa 1: 8 Jerusalem s abandoned like a watchman's shelter
40: 8 flowers fade, but the word of our God s forever."
44:12 The blacksmith s at his forge to make a sharp tool,
Jer 10: 5 There s their god like a helpless scarecrow in a
20:11 But the LORD s beside me like a great warrior.
26:18 will grow on the hilltop, where the Temple now s.'
51:29 the LORD has planned against her s unchanged.
Eze 21:21 The king of Babylon now s at the fork,
41:22 "is the table that s in the LORD's presence."
Da 6:12 "Yes," the king replied, "that decision s; it is a
12: 1 the archangel who s guard over your nation,
Mic 3:12 will grow on the hilltop, where the Temple now s.
Lk 6:48 against the house, it s firm because it is well built.
2Ti 2:19 But God's truth s firm like a foundation stone with
Heb 4: 1 God's promise of entering his place of rest still s,
10:11 the priest s before the altar day after day,
Rev 7:17 For the Lamb who s in front of the throne will be
9:13 of the gold altar that s in the presence of God.

STANDSTILL (1) [STAND]

Ezr 4:24 and it remained at a s until the second year of the

STAR (15) [STARGAZERS, STARLIGHT, STARRY, STARS]

Nu 24:17 far in the distant future. / A s will rise from Jacob;
Isa 14:12 from heaven, O shining s, son of the morning!
Jer 19:13 you burned incense on the rooftops to your s gods,
Am 5:26 Sakkuth your king god and Kaiwan your s god—
Mt 2: 2 We have seen his s as it arose, and we have come
2: 7 he learned the exact time when they first saw the s.
2: 9 Once again the s appeared to them, guiding them
2:10 When they saw the s, they were filled with joy!
2:16 because the wise men had told him the s first
Ac 7:43 the shrine of Molech, / the s god Rephan,
Rev 2:28 my Father, and I will also give them the morning s!
8:10 and a great flaming s fell out of the sky,
8:11 The name of the s was Bitterness. It made
9: 1 and I saw a s that had fallen to earth from the sky,
22:16 the heir to his throne. I am the bright morning s."

STARE (6) [STARED, STARING]

2Sa 20:12 saw that a crowd was gathering around to s at him.
Job 14: 6 us a little rest, won't you? Turn away your angry s.
Ps 22:17 bone in my body. / My enemies s at me and gloat.
Isa 14:16 Everyone there will s at you and ask, 'Can this be
Eze 16:37 you naked in front of them so they can s at you.
Rev 11: 9 and nations will come to s at their bodies.

STARED (8) [STARE]

2Sa 22: 6 its ropes around me; / death itself s me in the face.
2Ki 8:11 Elisha s at Hazael with a fixed gaze until Hazael
Ps 18: 5 its ropes around me; / death itself s me in the face.
Mk 8:25 As the man s intently, his sight was completely
Lk 4:20 Everyone in the synagogue s at him intently.
Ac 6:15 At this point everyone in the council s at Stephen
10: 4 Cornelius s at him in terror. "What is it, sir?"
Rev 17: 6 witnesses for Jesus. I s at her completely amazed.

STARGAZERS (1) [STAR]

Isa 47:13 more than enough advisers, astrologers, and s.

STARING (3) [STARE]

Lk 22:56 girl noticed him in the firelight and began s at him.
Ac 1:11 of Galilee, why are you standing here s at the sky?
Rev 11:11 stood up! And terror struck all who were s at them.

STARLIGHT (1) [LIGHT, STAR]

Ps 74:16 night belong to you; / you made the s and the sun.

STARRY (1) [STAR]

Ps 104: 2 You stretch out the s curtain of the heavens;

STARS (70) [STAR]

Ge 1:16 presides through the night. He also made the s.
15: 5 up into the heavens and count the s if you can.
22:17 like the s of the sky and the sand on the seashore.
26: 4 your descendants to become as numerous as the s,
37: 9 moon, and eleven s bowed low before me!"
Ex 32:13 'I will make your descendants as numerous as the s
Dt 1:10 your God has made you as numerous as the s!
4:19 look up into the sky and see the sun, moon, and s—
10:22 God has made you as numerous as the s in the sky!
28:62 Though you are as numerous as the s in the sky,
Jdg 5:20 The s fought from heaven. / The s in their orbits
fought against Sisera.
1Ch 27:23 make the Israelites as numerous as the s in heaven.
2Ch 33: 3 He also bowed before all the s of heaven
33: 5 He put these altars for the s of heaven in both
Ne 9: 6 You made the skies and the heavens and all the s.
9:23 You made their descendants as numerous as the s
Job 3: 9 Let its morning s remain dark. Let it hope for light,
9: 7 the sun won't rise and the s won't shine.
9: 9 He made all the s—the Bear, Orion, the Pleiades,
22:12 higher than the heavens, higher than the farthest s.
25: 5 the moon and s scarcely shine compared to him.
38: 7 as the morning s sang together and all the angels
38:31 "Can you hold back the movements of the s?
Ps 8: 3 the moon and the s you have set in place—
33: 6 He breathed the word, / and all the s were born.
136: 9 and the moon and s to rule the night. / His faithful
147: 4 He counts the s / and calls them all by name.
148: 3 and moon! / Praise him, all you twinkling s!
Ecc 12: 2 of the sun and moon and s is dim to your old eyes,
Isa 13:10 No light will shine from s or sun or moon.
14:13 ascend to heaven and set my throne above God's s.
34: 4 The s will fall from the sky, just as withered leaves
40:26 Look up into the heavens. Who created all the s?
45:12 All the millions of s are at my command.
51:13 the one who put the s in the sky and established the
51:16 I set all the s in space and established the earth.
Jer 8: 2 out on the ground before the sun, moon, and s—
10: 2 other nations who try to read their future in the s.
31:35 light the day and the moon and s to light the night.
33:22 And as the s cannot be counted and the sand on the
Eze 32: 7 you out, I will veil the heavens and darken the s.
32: 8 Even the brightest s will become dark above you.
Da 8:10 and s to the ground and trampling them.

12: 3 many to righteousness will shine like **s** forever.
Joel 2: 10 and moon grow dark, and the **s** no longer shine.
3: 15 will grow dark, and the **s** will no longer shine.
Am 5: 8 It is the LORD who created the **s**, the Pleiades
Ob 1: 4 as high as eagles and build your nest among the **s**,
Na 3: 16 Merchants, as numerous as the **s**, have filled your
Zep 1: 5 up to their roofs and bow to the sun, moon, and **s**.
Mt 24: 29 will not give light, / the **s** will fall from the sky,
Mk 13: 25 the **s** will fall from the sky, / and the powers of
Lk 21: 25 events in the skies—signs in the sun, moon, and **s**.
Ac 7: 42 up to serve the sun, moon, and **s** as their gods!
27: 20 blotting out the sun and the **s**, until at last all hope
Ro 4: 18 "Your descendants will be as numerous as the **s**,"
1Co 15: 41 while the moon and **s** each have another kind.
15: 41 And even the **s** differ from each other in their
Heb 11: 12 like the **s** of the sky and the sand on the seashore,
Jude 1: 13 They are wandering **s**, heading for everlasting
Rev 1: 16 He held seven **s** in his right hand, and a sharp
1: 20 This is the meaning of the seven **s** you saw in my
1: 20 The seven **s** are the angels of the seven churches,
2: 1 the one who holds the seven **s** in his right hand,
3: 1 has the sevenfold Spirit of God and the seven **s**:
6: 13 Then the **s** of the sky fell to the earth like green
8: 12 and one-third of the **s**, and they became dark.
12: 1 her feet, and a crown of twelve **s** on her head.
12: 4 His tail dragged down one-third of the **s**, which he

START (25) [STARTED, STARTING, STARTS]

Nu 34: 10 "The eastern boundary will **s** at Hazar-enan
Dt 2: 9 the descendants of Lot, or **s** a war with them.
2: 19 the descendants of Lot, or **s** a war with them.
1Sa 9: 13 The guests won't **s** until he arrives to bless the
20: 36 "**S** running," he told the boy, "so you can find the
2Sa 17: 1 "Let me choose twelve thousand men to **s** out after
17: 9 and everyone will **s** shouting that your men are
2Ch 20: 22 and Mount Seir to **s** fighting among themselves.
Ne 2: 20 We his servants will **s** rebuilding this wall. But you
Est 1: 18 and will **s** talking to their husbands the same way.
Jer 8: 4 When they **s** down the wrong road and discover
13: 23 Neither can you **s** doing good, for you always do
49: 27 "And I will **s** a fire at the edge of Damascus that
50: 5 the way to Jerusalem and will **s** back home again.
Eze 18: 24 turn to sinful ways and **s** acting like other sinners,
18: 26 turn from being good and **s** doing sinful things,
Mk 11: 32 For they were afraid that the people would **s** a riot,
Jn 6: 13 There were only five barley loaves to **s** with,
Ac 17: 5 fellows from the streets to form a mob and **s** a riot.
Ro 1: 17 This is accomplished from **s** to finish by faith.
11: 25 so that you will not feel proud and **s** bragging.
1Co 9: 15 writing this to suggest that I would like to **s** now.
2Ti 2: 23 in foolish, ignorant arguments that only **s** fights.
Heb 6: 1 Surely we don't need to **s** all over again with the
12: 2 on whom our faith depends from **s** to finish.

STARTED (56) [START]

Ge 18: 16 got up from their meal and **s** on toward Sodom.
32: 1 As Jacob and his household **s** on their way again,
33: 16 So Esau **s** back to Seir that same day.
42: 26 up their donkeys with the grain and **s** for home.
Ex 12: 37 the people of Israel left Rameses and **s** for Succoth.
22: 6 then the one who **s** the fire must pay for the lost
Lev 13: 18 "If anyone has had a boil on the skin that has **s** to
Nu 22: 21 his donkey and **s** off with the Moabite officials.
Jos 3: 6 the people across the river." And so they **s** out.
6: 8 the seven priests with the rams' horns **s** marching
8: 10 morning Joshua roused his men and **s** toward Ai,
8: 22 came out and **s** killing the enemy from the rear.
18: 8 As the men who were mapping out the land **s** on
19: 10 The boundary of Zebulun's inheritance **s** at Sarid.
22: 9 They **s** the journey back to their own land of
24: 9 son of Zippor, king of Moab, **s** a war against Israel.
Jdg 18: 21 They **s** on their way again, placing their children,
1Sa 9: 10 So they **s** into the town where the man of God was.
10: 9 As Saul turned and **s** to leave, God changed his
17: 40 and sling, he **s** across to fight Goliath.
25: 13 Four hundred men **s** off with David, and two
2Sa 19: 15 So the king **s** back to Jerusalem. And when he
1Ki 13: 24 and the man of God **s** off again. But as he was
2Ki 5: 5 So Naaman **s** out, taking as gifts 750 pounds of
5: 19 in peace," Elisha said. So Naaman **s** home again.
8: 11 became uneasy. Then the man of God **s** weeping.
Ezr 3: 6 This was also before they had **s** to lay the
8: 31 Ahava Canal on April 19 and **s** off to Jerusalem.
Ne 3: 1 and the other priests **s** to rebuild at the Sheep Gate.
Job 8: 7 And though you **s** with little, you will end with
Isa 40: 24 They hardly get **s**, barely taking root, when he
Jer 18: 4 squashed the jar into a lump of clay and **s** again.
37: 12 Jeremiah **s** to leave the city on his way to the land
41: 10 with him, he **s** back toward the land of Ammon.
La 4: 11 He **s** a fire in Jerusalem that burned the city to its
Mt 8: 23 the boat and **s** across the lake with his disciples.
23: 32 Go ahead. Finish what they **s**.
Mk 4: 36 He was already in the boat, so they **s** out,
5: 20 So the man **s** off to visit the Ten Towns of that
6: 48 walking on the water. He **s** to go past them,
Lk 2: 43 the celebration was over, they **s** home to Nazareth,
2: 44 they **s** to look for him among their relatives
8: 22 side of the lake." So they got into a boat and **s** out.
14: 30 'There's the person who **s** that building and ran out
19: 37 As they reached the place where the road **s** down
Jn 4: 50 And the man believed Jesus' word and **s** home.
Ac 6: 9 Freed Slaves, as it was called, **s** to debate with him.
11: 15 but just as I was getting **s**, the Holy Spirit fell on
12: 10 they passed through and **s** walking down the street,
13: 16 lifted his hand to quiet them, and **s** speaking.
14: 10 And the man jumped to his feet and **s** walking.
18: 14 But just as Paul **s** to make his defense,
19: 34 they **s** shouting again and kept it up for two hours:
26: 1 So Paul, with a gesture of his hand, **s** his defense:
Ro 15: 20 rather than where a church has already been **s** by
2Co 8: 10 I suggest that you finish what you **s** a year ago,

STARTING (8) [START]

2Sa 5: 9 around the city, **s** at the Millo and working inward.
Ecc 7: 8 Finishing is better than **s**. Patience is better than
Mk 10: 17 As he was **s** out on a trip, a man came running up
Lk 9: 33 As Moses and Elijah were **s** to leave, Peter,
22: 2 But they wanted to kill him without **s** a riot,
Ac 3: 24 "**S** with Samuel, every prophet spoke about what
4: 21 didn't know how to punish them without **s** a riot.
Gal 3: 3 After **s** your Christian lives in the Spirit, why are

STARTLE (1) [STARTLED, STARTLING]

Isa 52: 15 And he will again **s** many nations. Kings will stand

STARTLED (1) [STARTLE]

Mk 16: 5 man clothed in a white robe. The women were **s**,

STARTLING (1) [STARTLE]

Ac 17: 20 "You are saying some rather **s** things, and we want

STARTS (4) [START]

Pr 15: 18 A hothead **s** fights; a cool-tempered person tries to
26: 21 A quarrelsome person **s** fights as easily as hot
29: 22 A hot-tempered person **s** fights and gets into all
Eze 47: 18 "The eastern border **s** at a point between Hauran

STARVATION (5) [STARVE]

Ge 25: 32 "Look, I'm dying of **s**!" said Esau. "What good is
43: 8 Otherwise we will all die of **s**—and not only we,
Jdg 6: 6 So Israel was reduced to **s** by the Midianites.
Isa 51: 14 Imprisonment, **s**, and death will not be your fate!
Jer 14: 18 city streets, there I see people who have died of **s**.

STARVE (18) [STARVATION, STARVED, STARVING]

Ge 41: 55 the land of Egypt the people began to **s**.
42: 2 and buy some for us before we all **s** to death."
Ex 16: 3 But now you have brought us into this desert to **s**
Dt 28: 51 your livestock and crops, and you will **s** to death.
2Ki 7: 4 "We will **s** if we stay here, and we will **s** if we go
Job 4: 11 The fierce lion will **s**, and the cubs of the lioness
27: 14 their children will die in war or **s** to death.
Pr 10: 3 The LORD will not let the godly **s** to death,
Ecc 4: 5 Foolish people refuse to work and almost **s**.
Isa 5: 13 The great and honored among them will **s**,
65: 13 "You will **s**, but my servants will eat. You will be
Jer 11: 22 die in battle, and their little boys and girls will **s**.
18: 21 So let their children **s**! Let the sword pour out their
Eze 34: 3 butcher the best animals, but you let your flocks **s**.
34: 8 You took care of yourselves and left the sheep to **s**.
Hag 1: 11 a drought to **s** both you and your cattle and to ruin
Lk 15: 14 famine swept over the land, and he began to **s**.

STARVED (2) [STARVE]

Ge 25: 30 Esau said to Jacob, "I'm **s**! Give me some of that
La 1: 19 My priests and leaders **s** to death in the city,

STARVING (6) [STARVE]

1Sa 2: 5 Those who were well fed are now **s**; / and those who were **s** are now full.
2Ki 7: 12 The Arameans know we are **s**, so they have left
Job 24: 10 forced to carry food while they themselves are **s**.
Pr 6: 30 be found for a thief who steals because he is **s**.
La 1: 6 Her princes are like **s** deer searching for pasture,

STATE (10) [OVERSTATING, STATED, STATELY, STATEMENT, STATEMENTS, STATES]

Job 40: 10 put on your robes of **s**, your majesty and splendor.
Pr 27: 23 Know the **s** of your flocks, and put your heart into
Isa 45: 21 and **s** your proofs that idol worship pays.
50: 3 across the skies, bringing it to a **s** of mourning."
Eze 27: 26 Your oarsmen are rowing your ship of **s** into a
Mic 6: 1 "Stand up and **s** your case against me.
Lk 23: 2 They began at once to **s** their case: "This man has
Jn 7: 42 For the Scriptures clearly **s** that the Messiah will be
Ac 4: 10 Let me clearly **s** to you and to all the people of
1Pe 2: 13 accept all authority—the king as head of **s**,

STATED (4) [STATE]

1Ki 6: 10 As already **s**, there was a complex of rooms on
2Ki 9: 36 When they returned and told Jehu, he **s**,
22: 16 and its people, just as I **s** in the scroll you read.
Ac 13: 34 This is **s** in the Scripture that says, 'I will give you

STATELY (5) [STATE]

Pr 30: 29 There are three **s** monarchs on the earth—no,
SS 1: 10 How **s** is your neck, accented with a long string of
4: 4 Your neck is as **s** as the tower of David,
7: 4 Your neck is as **s** as an ivory tower. Your eyes are
Isa 14: 18 "The kings of the nations lie in **s** glory in their

STATEMENT (8) [STATE]

Ne 13: 1 the people found a **s** which said that no Ammonite
Job 34: 12 There is no truer **s** than this: God will not do
Mt 19: 11 "Not everyone can accept this **s**," Jesus said.
19: 12 of Heaven. Let anyone who can, accept this **s**."
Mk 7: 17 and his disciples asked him what he meant by the **s**
Jn 3: 7 So don't be surprised at my **s** that you must be
7: 35 The Jewish leaders were puzzled by this **s**.
18: 9 He did this to fulfill his own **s**: "I have not lost a

STATEMENTS (2) [STATE]

Job 13: 12 Your **s** have about as much value as ashes.
Jn 8: 20 Jesus made these **s** while he was teaching in the

STATES (1) [STATE]

Da 3: 11 That decree also **s** that those who refuse to obey

STATION (2) [STATIONED, STATIONING]

2Sa 11: 15 "**S** Uriah on the front lines where the battle is
Jer 51: 12 Reinforce the guard and **s** the watchmen.

STATIONED (23) [STATION]

Ge 3: 24 the LORD God **s** mighty angelic beings to the
Nu 11: 24 seventy leaders and **s** them around the Tabernacle.
Jos 8: 13 So they **s** the main army north of the city
1Ki 10: 26 He **s** many of them in the chariot cities, and some
2Ki 3: 21 and old, and **s** themselves along their border.
11: 11 The guards **s** themselves around the king,
11: 18 Jehoiada the priest **s** guards at the Temple of the
1Ch 9: 24 The gatekeepers were **s** on all four sides—east,
16: 39 David **s** Zadok the priest and his fellow priests at
2Ch 1: 14 He **s** many of them in the chariot cities, and some
9: 25 He **s** many of them in the chariot cities, and some
11: 11 their defenses and **s** commanders in them.
11: 23 and **s** them in the fortified cities throughout the
17: 2 He **s** troops in all the fortified cities of Judah,
17: 13 and **s** an army of seasoned troops at Jerusalem.
17: 19 These were the troops **s** in Jerusalem to serve the
17: 19 besides those Jehoshaphat **s** in the fortified cities
23: 10 He **s** the guards around the king, with their
23: 19 He **s** gatekeepers at the gates of the LORD's
29: 25 then **s** the Levites at the Temple of the LORD
33: 14 And he **s** his military officers in all of the fortified
Ne 4: 13 I **s** the people to stand guard by families,
4: 16 The officers **s** themselves behind the people of

STATIONING (1) [STATION]

Jdg 9: 34 into four groups, **s** themselves around Shechem.

STATUE (24) [STATUES]

Ps 106: 20 their glorious God / for a **s** of a grass-eating ox!
Da 2: 31 in front of you a huge and powerful **s** of a man,
2: 32 The head of the **s** was made of fine gold, its chest
2: 35 The whole **s** collapsed into a heap of iron, clay,
2: 35 But the rock that knocked the **s** down became a
2: 45 crushing to dust the **s** of iron, bronze, clay, silver,
3: 1 King Nebuchadnezzar made a gold **s** ninety feet
3: 2 to come to the dedication of the **s** he had set up.
3: 5 ground to worship King Nebuchadnezzar's gold **s**.
3: 7 and worshiped the **s** that King Nebuchadnezzar had
3: 10 and worship the gold **s** when they hear the sound
3: 12 or to worship the gold **s** you have set up."
3: 14 my gods or to worship the gold **s** I have set up?
3: 15 and worship the **s** I have made when you hear the
3: 18 your gods or worship the gold **s** you have set up."
Rev 13: 14 of the world to make a great **s** of the first beast,
13: 15 He was permitted to give life to this **s** so that it
13: 15 Then the **s** commanded that anyone refusing to
14: 9 "Anyone who worships the beast and his **s** or who
14: 11 for they have worshiped the beast and his **s**
15: 2 and his **s** and the number representing his name.
16: 2 had the mark of the beast and who worshiped his **s**.
19: 20 the mark of the beast and who worshiped his **s**.
20: 4 of those who had not worshiped the beast or his **s**,

STATUES (3) [STATUE]

2Ki 23: 11 **s** that the former kings of Judah had dedicated to
Eze 16: 17 given you and made **s** of men and worshiped them,
Hos 10: 1 the more beautiful the **s** and idols they built.

STATURE (1)

Eph 4: 13 in the Lord, measuring up to the full **s** of Christ.

STATUS (1)

Job 12: 19 He leads priests away stripped of **s**; he overthrows

STATUTES (1)

Ps 119: 59 direction of my life, / and I turned to follow your **s**.

STAVES [KJV] See ARROWS, CLUBS, POLES, STAFF(S), STICK(S)

STAY (206) [STAYED, STAYING, STAYS]

Ge 13: 9 If you want that area over there, then I'll **s** here.
13: 9 If you want to **s** in this area, then I'll move on to
18: 5 Please **s** awhile before continuing on your
22: 5 "**S** here with the donkey," Abraham told the
24: 31 "Come and **s** with us, you who are blessed by the
24: 55 "But we want Rebekah to **s** at least ten days,"
25: 27 while Jacob was the kind of person who liked to **s**
26: 3 Do as I say, and **s** here in this land. If you do,
27: 44 **S** there with him until your brother's fury is spent.
28: 5 and he went to Paddan-aram to **s** with his uncle
33: 12 Esau said. "I will **s** with you and lead the way."

43: 5 don't let Benjamin go, we may as well s at home.
44:33 my lord, let me s here as a slave instead of the boy,
49: 6 O my soul, s away from them. / May I never be a
Ex 10:24 he said. "But let your flocks and herds s here.
16:29 On the Sabbath day you must s in your places.
19:13 The people must s away from the mountain until
22:27 Your neighbor will need it to s warm during the
24:12 S there while I give you the tablets of stone that I
24:14 "S here and wait for us until we come back.
40:37 cloud stayed, they would s until it moved again.
Lev 8:35 you must s at the entrance of the Tabernacle day
Nu 9:20 Sometimes the cloud would s over the Tabernacle
9:20 so the people would s for only a few days.
18:22 and Levites are to s away from the Tabernacle.
20:17 We will s on the king's road and never leave it
20:18 "S out of my land or I will meet you with an
20:19 Israelites answered, "We will s on the main road.
20:20 But the king of Edom replied, "S out! You may
21:22 We will s on the king's road until we have crossed
22: 8 "S here overnight," Balaam said. "In the morning
22:19 But s here one more night to see if the LORD has
31:19 or touched a dead body must s outside the camp
32: 6 "Do you mean you want to s back here while your
32:17 our families will s in the fortified cities we build
32:26 and cattle will s here in the towns of Gilead.
Dt 2:27 We will s on the main road and won't turn off into
3:19 may s behind in the towns I have given you.
5:31 But you s here with me so I can give you all my
5:33 S on the path that the LORD your God has
23: 9 your enemies, s away from everything impure.
23:10 emission must leave the camp and s away all day.
Jos 1:14 to help them conquer their territory. S with them
3: 4 S about a half mile behind them, keeping a clear
7: 7 If only we had been content to s on the other side!
20: 6 But the person who caused the death must s in that
Jdg 1:27 because the Canaanites were determined to s in
1:35 The Amorites were determined to s in Mount
5:17 And Dan, why did he s home? / Asher sat
6:18 LORD answered, "I will s here until you return."
13:15 "Please s here until we can prepare a young goat
13:16 "I will s," the angel of the LORD replied,
17:10 "S here with me," Micah said, "and you can be a
19: 4 Her father urged him to s awhile, so he stayed
19: 6 "Please s the night and enjoy yourself."
19: 7 but his father-in-law kept urging him to s, so he
19: 9 it's getting late. S the night and enjoy yourself.
19:11 late to travel; let's s in this Jebusite city tonight."
19:12 "we can't s in this foreign city where there are no
19:20 "You are welcome to s with me," the old man
Ru 1: 2 in the land of Judah. During their s in Moab,
2: 8 S right here with us when you gather grain;
2: 8 S right behind the women working in my field.
2:21 and s with his harvesters until the entire harvest is
2:22 S with his workers right through the whole harvest.
3:13 S here tonight, and in the morning I will talk to
1Sa 1:23 "S here for now, and may the LORD help you
9:12 "Yes," they replied. "S right on this road. He is at
9:27 After the servant was gone, Samuel said, "S here,
14: 9 they say to us, 'S where you are or we'll kill you,'
20: 5 and s there until the evening of the third day.
21: 5 And since they s clean even on ordinary trips,
22:23 S here with me, and I will protect you with my
23:16 and encouraged him to s strong in his faith in God.
27:12 Now he will have to s here and serve me forever!"
2Sa 10: 5 he sent messengers to tell the men to s at Jericho
11:12 "Well, s here tonight," David told him,
17:16 and urge him not to s at the shallows of the Jordan
18: 3 and it is better that you s here in the city and send
19:32 food for the king during his s in Mahanaim.
2Ki 2: 2 And Elijah said to Elisha, "S here, for the LORD
2: 4 Then Elijah said to Elisha, "S here,
2: 6 Then Elijah said to Elisha, "S here,
4:10 Then he will have a place to s whenever he comes
7: 4 "We will starve if we s here, and we will starve if
7:13 it won't be a greater loss than if they s here and die
11: 8 be killed. S right beside the king at all times."
14:10 Be content with your victory and s at home!
15:20 from attacking Israel and did not s in the land.
25:12 to s behind in Judah to care for the vineyards
1Ch 19: 5 he sent messengers to tell the men to s at Jericho
2Ch 15: 2 The LORD will s with you as long as you s
23: 5 Everyone else should s in the courtyards of the
23: 6 must obey the LORD's instructions and s outside.
23: 7 be killed. S right beside the king at all times."
25:19 conquest of Edom, but my advice is to s home.
Ezr 6: 6 west of the Euphrates: / "S away from there!
10:13 rainy season, so we cannot s out here much longer.
Job 19:13 "My relatives s far away, and my friends have
24:13 acknowledge its ways. They will not s in its paths.
39: 9 ox consent to being tamed? Will it s in your stall?
Ps 22:11 Do not s so far from me, / for trouble is near,
22:19 O LORD, do not s away! / You are my strength;
35:22 you know all about this. / Do not s silent.
38:11 My loved ones and friends s away, fearing my
49:11 is their eternal home, / where they will s forever.
71:12 O God, don't s away. / My God, please hurry to
101: 4 reject perverse ideas / and s away from every evil.
119: 9 How can a young person s pure? / By obeying your
119:148 I s awake through the night, / thinking about your
Pr 1:15 with them, my child! S far away from their paths.
2:20 men instead, and s on the paths of the righteous.
4:24 Avoid all perverse talk; s far from corrupt speech.
4:26 path for your feet; then stick to the path and s safe.
14: 7 S away from fools, for you won't find knowledge
15:12 who rebuke them, so they s away from the wise.
21:23 keep your mouth shut, you will s out of trouble.
22: 5 treacherous road; whoever values life will s away.
Ecc 11: 6 Be sure to s busy and plant a variety of crops,
Isa 13:20 and shepherds will not allow their sheep to s
16: 4 Let our outcasts s among you. Hide them from our
33:15 a profit by fraud, who s far away from bribes,
54:14 Your enemies will s far away; you will live in
55:10 the heavens and s on the ground to water the earth.
60:11 Your gates will s open around the clock to receive
Jer 7: 3 your evil ways, I will let you s in your own land.
7: 7 Then I will let you s in this land that I gave to your
17: 8 Their leaves s green, and they go right on
27:11 to s in their own country to farm the land as usual.
27:22 to Babylon and will s there until I send for them,
29: 5 "Build homes, and plan to s. Plant gardens,
29:28 should build homes and plan to s for many years.
40: 4 But if you don't want to come, you may s here.
40: 5 If you decide to s, then return to Gedaliah son of
40: 5 S there with the people he rules. But it's up to you;
40: 9 "S here, and serve the king of Babylon," he said,
40:10 I will s at Mizpah to represent you before the
42:10 'S here in this land. If you do, I will build you up
42:12 him kind, so he will let you s here in your land.'
42:13 LORD your God and say, 'We will not s here,'
43: 3 so we will s here and be killed by the Babylonians
43: 4 to obey the LORD's command to s in Judah.
51:30 They s in their barracks. Their courage is gone.
52:16 to s behind in Judah to care for the vineyards
La 1:11 They have sold their treasures for food to s alive.
4:15 among foreign nations, but none would let them s.
Eze 7:15 Those who s inside will die of famine and disease.
Hos 9: 3 You may no longer s here in this land of the
14: 8 "O Israel, s away from idols! I am the one who
Mic 7:18 You cannot s angry with your people forever,
Mt 2:13 "S there until I tell you to return, because Herod is
10:11 and s in his home until you leave for the next town.
24:43 exactly when a burglar was coming would s alert
25:13 "So s awake and be prepared, because you do not
26:38 to the point of death. S here and watch with me."
26:40 "Couldn't you s awake and watch with me even
Mk 1:45 He had to s out in the secluded places, and people
13:33 when they will happen, s alert and keep watch.
14:34 to the point of death. S here and watch with me."
14:37 Couldn't you s awake and watch with me even one
Lk 10: 7 S in one place, eating and drinking what they
24:29 but they begged him to s the night with them,
24:49 But s here in the city until the Holy Spirit comes
Jn 3:20 They s away from the light for fear their sins will
4:40 to see him, they begged him to s at their village.
4:43 At the end of the two days' s, Jesus went on into
7: 1 He wanted to s out of Judea where the Jewish
10:40 He went beyond the Jordan River to s near the
15: 7 But if you s joined to me and my words remain in
Ac 10:48 Afterward Cornelius asked him to s with them for
11:23 and he encouraged the believers to s true to the
12:19 Afterward Herod left Judea to s in Caesarea for a
16:15 to the Lord," she said, "come and s at my home."
18:20 They asked him to s longer, but he declined.
21:10 During our s of several days, a man named
21:25 and they should s away from all sexual
25:14 During their s of several days, Festus discussed
27:31 "You will all die unless the sailors s aboard."
28:14 who invited us to s with them seven days.
Ro 16:17 to what you have been taught. S away from them.
16:19 what is right and to s innocent of any wrong.
1Co 5: 7 person from among you so that you can s pure.
7: 8 to widows—it's better to s unmarried, just as I am.
7:15 or wife is not required to s with them,
7:24 s there in your new relationship with God.
16: 6 It could be that I will s awhile with you,
16: 7 I want to come and s awhile, if the Lord will let
2Co 10:13 Our goal is to s within the boundaries of God's
Gal 5: 1 Now make sure that you s free, and don't get tied
Eph 6:18 S alert and be persistent in your prayers for all
Php 2:14 you do, s away from complaining and arguing,
4: 1 So please s true to the Lord, my dear friends.
1Th 3: 1 we decided that I should s alone in Athens,
5: 6 not asleep like the others. S alert and be sober.
2Th 3: 6 S away from any Christian who lives in idleness
3:14 S away from them so they will be ashamed.
1Ti 1: 3 I urged you to s there in Ephesus and stop those
4:16 S true to what is right, and God will save you
2Ti 3: 5 You must s away from people like that.
Tit 3:12 for I have decided to s there for the winter.
Heb 13: 5 S away from the love of money; be satisfied with
Jas 2:16 s warm and eat well"—but then you don't give
4:13 are going to a certain town and will s there a year.
1Pe 4: 9 home with those who need a meal or a place to s.
Jude 1: 6 And I remind you of the angels who did not s

STAYED (99) [STAY]

Ge 13:12 So while Abram s in the land of Canaan,
24:54 the servant and the men with him s there overnight.
26: 6 So Isaac s in Gerar.
29:30 He then s and worked the additional seven years.
30:36 Meanwhile, Jacob s and cared for Laban's flock.
32:13 Jacob s where he was for the night and prepared a
35: 3 He has s with me wherever I have gone."
Ex 24:18 He s on the mountain forty days and forty nights.
33:11 son of Nun, s behind in the Tent of Meeting.
40:37 But if the cloud s, they would stay until it moved
Nu 9:18 were as long as the cloud s over the Tabernacle.
9:19 the Israelites s for a long time, just as the LORD
9:21 Sometimes the cloud s only overnight and moved
9:22 Whether the cloud s above the Tabernacle for two
9:22 the people of Israel s in camp and did not move on.
11:35 traveled to Hazeroth, where they s for some time.
22: 8 So the officials from Moab s there with Balaam.
35:28 The slayer should have s inside the city of refuge
Dt 1: 6 to us, 'You have s at this mountain long enough.
1:46 So you s there at Kadesh for a long time.
2:37 we s away from the Ammonites along the Jabbok
3:29 So we s in the valley near Beth-peor.
10:10 I s on the mountain in the LORD's presence for
Jos 2: 1 of a prostitute named Rahab and s there that night.
2:22 went up into the hill country and s there three days.
Jdg 5: 6 main roads, / and travelers s on crooked side paths.
6: 5 And they s until the land was stripped bare.
9:41 Abimelech s in Arumah, and Zebul drove Gaal
11:17 through either. So the people of Israel s in Kadesh.
16: 3 But Samson s in bed only until midnight. Then he
19: 4 so he s three days, eating, drinking, and sleeping
19: 7 him to stay, so he finally gave in and s the night.
1Sa 1:23 So she s home and nursed the baby.
3:15 Samuel s in bed until morning, then got up
13: 7 Meanwhile, Saul s at Gilgal, and his men were
17:14 in the army, they s with Saul's forces all the time.
22: 4 and David's parents s in Moab while David was
23:14 David now s in the strongholds of the wilderness
23:18 Jonathan returned home, while David s at Horesh.
25: 7 While your shepherds s among us near Carmel,
2Sa 11: 1 city of Rabbah. But David s behind in Jerusalem.
11: 9 He s that night at the palace entrance with some of
11:12 So Uriah s in Jerusalem that day and the next.
13:38 He s there in Geshur for three years.
14:32 I might as well have s there. Let me see the king;
15:29 took the Ark of God back to the city and s there.
16: 3 "He s in Jerusalem," Ziba replied. "He said,
20: 2 But the men of Judah s with their king
21:10 on a rock and s there the entire harvest season.
1Ki 11:16 Joab and the army had s there for six months,
11:40 Shishak of Egypt and s there until Solomon died.
2Ki 6:23 the Aramean raiders s away from the land of Israel.
19:36 went home to his capital of Nineveh and s there.
1Ch 20: 1 destroyed it. But David had s behind in Jerusalem.
Ne 4:18 The trumpeter s with me to sound the alarm.
11: 1 to live there, too, while the rest s where they were.
Est 7: 7 But Haman s behind to plead for his life with
Job 1: 1 He feared God and s away from evil.
23:11 "For I have s in God's paths; I have followed his
Ps 17: 5 My steps have s on your path; / I have not wavered
Isa 37:37 went home to his capital of Nineveh and s there.
Jer 39:14 So Jeremiah s in Judah among his own people.
Eze 10:16 they rose into the air, the wheels s beside them,
Mt 2:15 and they s there until Herod's death. This fulfilled
21:17 Then he returned to Bethany, where he s overnight.
Lk 1:23 He s at the Temple until his term of service was
1:56 Mary s with Elizabeth about three months and
2:37 never left the Temple but s there day and night,
2:43 home to Nazareth, but Jesus s behind in Jerusalem.
Jn 1:39 to the place, and they s there the rest of the day.
3:22 but they s in Judea for a while and baptized there.
4:40 him to stay at their village. So he s for two days,
7: 1 After this, Jesus s in Galilee, going from village to
11: 6 he s where he was for the next two days and did
11:20 she went to meet him. But Mary s at home.
11:30 Now Jesus had s outside the village, at the place
11:54 village of Ephraim, and s there with his disciples.
21: 8 The others s with the boat and pulled the loaded
Ac 9:19 Saul s with the believers in Damascus for a few
9:43 And Peter s a long time in Joppa, living with
11:26 Both of them s there with the church for a full
14: 3 The apostles s there a long time, preaching boldly
14:28 And they s there with the believers in Antioch for a
15:33 They s for a while, and then Judas and Silas were
15:35 and Barnabas s in Antioch to assist many others
16:12 and a Roman colony; we s there several days.
18: 7 After that he s with Titius Justus, a Gentile who
18:11 So Paul s there for the next year and a half,
18:18 Paul s in Corinth for some time after that and
19:22 on ahead to Macedonia while he s awhile longer in
20: 3 where he s for three months. He was preparing to
20: 6 days later arrived in Troas, where we s a week.
21: 4 found the local believers, and s with them a week.
21: 7 where we greeted the believers but s only one day.
21: 8 and s at the home of Philip the Evangelist,
28:12 Our first stop was Syracuse, where we s three days.
Gal 1:18 with Peter and s there with him for fifteen days.
2Ti 4:20 Erastus s at Corinth, and I left Trophimus sick at
1Jn 2:19 with us; otherwise they would have s with us.

STAYING (22) [STAY]

Ge 34:22 But they will consider s here only on one
Jdg 19:22 "Bring out the man who is s with you so we can
19:26 returned to the house where her husband was s.
Ru 1:14 But Ruth insisted on s with Naomi.
1Sa 13:16 and the troops with them were s at Geba,
23:22 Go and check again to be sure of where he is s
2Sa 17:17 Jonathan and Ahimaaz had been s at En-rogel
23:14 David was s in the stronghold at the time, and a
1Ch 11:16 David was s in the stronghold at the time, and a
Isa 10:29 are crossing the pass and are s overnight at Geba.
Mt 9:28 They went right into the house where he was s,
Mk 2: 2 Soon the house where he was s was so packed with
3:20 When Jesus returned to the house where he was s,
9:33 settled in the house where they would be s.
Jn 1:38 (which means Teacher), "where are you s?"
7:10 also went, though secretly, s out of public view.
Ac 1:13 the upstairs room of the house where they were s.
10: 6 He is s with Simon, a leatherworker who lives near
10:18 if this was the place where Simon Peter was s.
10:32 He is s in the home of Simon, a leatherworker who
11:11 from Caesarea arrived at the house where I was s.
1Co 16: 8 I will be s here at Ephesus until the Festival of

STAYS (10) [STAY]
Pr 1:17 When a bird sees a trap being set, it **s** away.
7:11 the brash, rebellious type who never **s** at home.
12:16 but a wise person **s** calm when insulted.
14: 4 An empty stable **s** clean, but no income comes
15:21 no sense; a sensible person **s** on the right path.
Isa 46: 7 and when they set it down, it **s** there.
Jer 21: 9 Everyone who **s** in Jerusalem will die from war,
38: 2 Everyone who **s** in Jerusalem will die from war,
Eze 18: 8 **s** away from injustice, is honest and fair when
Jn 19:22 I have written, I have written. It **s** exactly as it is."

STEADFAST (1)
Tit 1: 9 and **s** belief in the trustworthy message he was

STEADIED (2) [STEADY]
Job 4: 4 strengthened the fallen; you **s** those who wavered.
Ps 40: 2 feet on solid ground / and **s** me as I walked along.

STEADILY (5) [STEADY]
Ps 37:34 Travel **s** along his path. / He will honor you,
Hab 2: 3 Slowly, **s**, surely, the time approaches when the
Lk 8:15 cling to it, and **s** produce a huge harvest.
Ac 7:55 gazed **s** upward into heaven and saw the glory of
Jas 1:25 But if you keep looking **s** into God's perfect law—

STEADY (6) [STEADIED, STEADILY]
2Sa 6: 6 and Uzzah put out his hand to **s** the Ark of God.
1Ch 13: 9 and Uzzah put out his hand to **s** the Ark.
2Ch 24:13 renovation worked hard, and they made **s** progress.
Ps 89:21 I will **s** him, / and I will make him strong.
1Co 15:58 my dear brothers and sisters, be strong and **s**,
Jas 3:13 live a life of **s** goodness so that only good deeds

STEAK (1)
Pr 15:17 you love is better than **s** with someone you hate.

STEAL (34) [STEALING, STEALS, STOLE, STOLEN]
Ge 30:15 Now will you **s** my son's mandrake roots, too?"
44: 8 Why would we **s** silver or gold from your master's
Ex 20:15 "Do not **s**.
Lev 19:11 "Do not **s**. "Do not cheat one another. "Do not
Dt 5:19 " 'Do not **s**.
19:14 never **s** someone's land by moving the boundary
Jdg 11:15 Israel did not **s** any land from Moab or Ammon.
1Sa 17:34 a lion or a bear comes to **s** a lamb from the flock,
1Ch 7:21 and Elead were killed trying to **s** livestock from the
Job 24: 2 Evil people **s** land by moving the boundary markers. They **s** flocks of sheep,
Ps 69: 4 demanding that I give back what I didn't **s**.
80:12 our walls / so that all who pass may **s** our fruit?
Pr 22:28 Do not **s** your neighbor's property by moving the
23:10 Don't **s** the land of defenseless orphans by moving
30: 9 too poor, I may **s** and thus insult God's holy name.
Isa 9:20 They fight against their own neighbors to **s** food,
Jer 7: 9 Do you really think you can **s**, murder,
Eze 25: 4 will harvest all your fruit and **s** your livestock.
Hos 4: 2 You curse and lie and kill and **s** and commit
Am 5:11 and **s** what little they have through taxes and unfair
Mic 2: 8 You **s** the shirts right off the backs of those who
Zep 1: 9 and those who **s** and kill to fill their masters'
Zec 5: 3 One side says that those who **s** will be banished
Mt 6:19 and get rusty, and where thieves break in and **s**.
19:18 commit adultery. Do not **s**. Do not testify falsely.
Mk 10:19 Do not **s**. Do not testify falsely. Do not cheat.
Lk 12:33 no thief can **s** it and no moth can destroy it.
18:20 Do not murder. Do not **s**. Do not testify falsely.
Jn 10:10 The thief's purpose is to **s** and kill and destroy.
Ro 2:21 You tell others not to **s**, but do you **s**?
2:22 but do you **s** from pagan temples?
Tit 2:10 or **s**, but they must show themselves to be entirely

STEALING (10) [STEAL]
Ge 27:36 first taking my birthright and now **s** my blessing.
44: 5 What do you mean by **s** my master's personal
Jos 22:20 sinned by **s** the things set apart for the LORD?
1Sa 23: 1 were at Keilah **s** grain from the threshing floors.
Pr 25:20 is as bad as **s** someone's jacket in cold weather
Mt 27:64 and **s** his body and then telling everyone he came
Lk 16: 2 and said, 'What's this I hear about your **s** from me?
Ro 13: 9 against adultery and murder and **s** and coveting—
Eph 4:28 If you are a thief, stop **s**. Begin using your hands
1Pe 4:15 it must not be for murder, **s**, making trouble,

STEALS (6) [STEAL]
Ex 22: 1 "A fine must be paid by anyone who **s** an ox
22: 4 If someone **s** an ox or a donkey or a sheep and it is
Dt 27:17 'Cursed is anyone who **s** property from a neighbor
Pr 6:30 Excuses might be found for a thief who **s**
Eze 18:12 **s** from debtors by refusing to let them redeem what
Lk 8:12 but then the Devil comes and **s** it away

STEALTH [KJV] See CREPT

STEAM (1)
Job 41:20 Smoke streams from its nostrils like **s** from a

STEDFAST [KJV] See ENDURING, FIRM, SECURE, STEADFAST, VALID

STEEDS (1)
Jdg 5:22 the galloping, galloping of Sisera's mighty **s**.

STEEL [KJV] See GLITTERING

STEEP (4)
Isa 26: 7 who are righteous, / the path is not **s** and rough.
Mt 8:32 and the whole herd plunged down the **s** hillside
Mk 5:13 pigs plunged down the **s** hillside into the lake,
Lk 8:33 and the whole herd plunged down the **s** hillside

STEM (12)
Ex 25:31 the base, center **s**, lamp cups, buds, and blossoms.
25:32 branches going out from each side of the center **s**.
25:34 The center **s** of the lampstand will be decorated
25:35 of branches where they extend from the center **s**.
25:36 and branches must all be one piece with the **s**,
37:17 Its base, center **s**, lamp cups, blossoms, and buds
37:18 three going out from each side of the center **s**.
37:20 The center **s** of the lampstand was also decorated
37:21 where they extended from the center **s**.
37:22 and branches were all one piece with the **s**,
Eze 19:12 tore off its branches. / Its **s** was destroyed by fire.
Jnh 4: 7 at dawn the worm ate through the **s** of the plant,

STENCH (9) [STINK]
Ge 19:13 The **s** of the place has reached the LORD, and he
Ex 8:14 into great heaps, and a terrible **s** filled the land.
Ps 5: 9 Their talk is foul, like the **s** from an open grave.
Isa 1:13 The incense you bring me is a **s** in my nostrils!
34: 3 and the **s** of rotting bodies will fill the land.
65: 5 They are a **s** in my nostrils, an acrid smell that
Joel 2:20 The **s** of their rotting bodies will rise over the
Am 4:10 all your horses. The **s** of death filled the air!
Ro 3:13 "Their talk is foul, like the **s** from an open grave.

STEP (18) [FOOTSTEPS, STEPPED, STEPPING, STEPS]
Ge 24:49 tell me, then I'll know what my next **s** should be,
Ex 33:15 don't let us move a **s** from this place.
Dt 2: 7 and has watched your every **s** through this great
1Sa 5: 5 enters the temple of Dagon will **s** on its threshold.
16: 8 Then Jesse told his son Abinadab to **s** forward
17:39 over it, and took a **s** or two to see what it was like,
20: 3 But I swear to you that I am only a **s** away from
1Ki 2:36 But don't **s** outside the city to go anywhere else.
Job 18:11 surround the wicked and trouble them at every **s**.
31: 4 He sees everything I do and every **s** I take.
Ps 56: 6 on me— / watching my every **s**, eager to kill me.
106:30 But Phinehas had the courage to **s** in,
Isa 24:18 and those who escape the trap will **s** into a snare.
41: 2 king from the east, who meets victory at every **s**?
Jer 48:44 and those who escape the trap will **s** into a snare.
Eze 26:16 All the seaport rulers will **s** down from their
Mk 15: 1 the entire high council—met to discuss their next **s**.
1Co 9:26 I run straight to the goal with purpose in every **s**.

STEPHANAS (3)
1Co 1:16 (Oh yes, I also baptized the household of **S**. I don't
16:15 You know that **S** and his household were the first
16:17 I am so glad that **S**, Fortunatus, and Achaicus have

STEPHEN (12) [STEPHEN'S]
Ac 6: 5 **S** (a man full of faith and the Holy Spirit), Philip,
6: 8 **S**, a man full of God's grace and power,
6:10 against the wisdom and Spirit by which **S** spoke.
6:11 So they persuaded some men to lie about **S**, saying,
6:12 So they arrested **S** and brought him before the high
6:15 At this point everyone in the council stared at **S**
7: 1 Then the high priest asked **S**, "Are these
7:55 But **S**, full of the Holy Spirit, gazed steadily
7:59 **S** prayed, "Lord Jesus, receive my spirit."
8: 1 was one of the official witnesses at the killing of **S**.
8: 2 people came and buried **S** with loud weeping.)
22:20 And when your witness **S** was killed, I was

STEPHEN'S (3) [STEPHEN]
Ac 7: 2 This was **S** reply: "Brothers and honorable fathers,
7:54 The Jewish leaders were infuriated by **S**
11:19 after **S** death traveled as far as Phoenicia,

STEPPED (23) [STEP]
Ge 19: 6 Lot **s** outside to talk to them, shutting the door
44:18 Then Judah **s** forward and said, "My lord, let me
Lev 9:22 and the peace offering, he **s** down from the altar.
Nu 12: 5 and Miriam!" he called, and they **s** forward.
Jdg 19:23 The old man **s** outside to talk to them. "No,
2Sa 18:30 the king told him. So Ahimaaz **s** aside.
20: 8 As he **s** forward to greet Amasa, he secretly
2Ki 5:26 Naaman **s** down from his chariot to meet you?
14: 9 then a wild animal came by and **s** on the thistle,
2Ch 25:18 then a wild animal came by and **s** on the thistle,
Job 29: 8 The young **s** aside when they saw me, and even the
Ps 106:23 chosen one, **s** between the LORD and the people.
Isa 59:16 So he himself **s** in to save them with his mighty
Da 3:26 Meshach, and Abednego **s** out of the fire.
Jnh 3: 6 he **s** down from his throne and took off his royal
Mt 14:14 A vast crowd was there as he **s** from the boat,
22:23 That same day some Sadducees **s** forward—
Mk 6:34 A vast crowd was there as he **s** from the boat,
12:18 Then the Sadducees **s** forward—a group of Jews
Lk 8: 5 where it was **s** on, and the birds came and ate it.
20:27 Then some Sadducees **s** forward—a group of Jews
Ac 2:14 Then Peter **s** forward with the eleven other apostles
Rev 5: 7 He **s** forward and took the scroll from the right

STEPPING (3) [STEP]
Lk 5: 3 **S** into one of the boats, Jesus asked Simon,
11:44 without knowing the corruption they are **s** on."
Jn 18: 4 **S** forward to meet them, he asked, "Whom are you

STEPS (37) [STEP]
Ex 20:26 And you may not approach my altar by **s**. If you
Dt 33: 3 They follow in your **s** / and accept your instruction.
Jos 3: 8 take a few **s** into the river and stop.' "
2Sa 6:13 After the men who were carrying it had gone six **s**,
1Ki 10:19 The throne had six **s** and a rounded back. On both
10:20 one standing on each end of each of the six **s**.
2Ki 9:13 They quickly spread out their cloaks on the bare **s**
20: 9 like the shadow on the sundial to go forward ten **s** or backward ten **s**?"
20:11 and he caused the shadow to move ten **s** backward
2Ch 9:11 The king used the almug wood to make **s** for the
9:18 The throne had six **s**, and there was a footstool of
9:19 one standing on each end of each of the six **s**.
Ne 12:37 At the Fountain Gate they went straight up the **s** on
Job 14:16 For then you would count my **s**, instead of
Ps 17: 5 My **s** have stayed on your path; / I have not
37:23 The **s** of the godly are directed by the LORD.
85:13 a herald before him, / preparing the way for his **s**.
119:133 Guide my **s** by your word, / so I will not be
Pr 2:20 Follow the **s** of good men instead, and stay on the
5: 5 go down to death; her **s** lead straight to the grave.
14:15 are told! The prudent carefully consider their **s**.
16: 9 make our plans, but the LORD determines our **s**.
20:24 road we travel? It is the LORD who directs our **s**.
Isa 38: 8 I will cause the sun's shadow to move ten **s**
38: 8 the shadow on the sundial moved backward ten **s**.
Eze 40: 6 He climbed the **s** and measured the threshold of the
40:22 There were seven **s** leading up to the gateway
40:26 This gateway also had a stairway of seven **s**
40:31 and there were eight **s** leading to its entrance.
40:34 and there were eight **s** leading to its entrance.
40:37 There were eight **s** leading to its entrance.
40:49 There were ten **s** leading up to it, with a column on
43:17 There are **s** going up the east side of the altar."
2Co 12:18 have the same Spirit and walk in each other's **s**,
2Th 2: 7 the one who is holding it back **s** out of the way.
1Pe 2:21 suffered for you, is your example. Follow in his **s**.

STERILE (1)
Isa 53: 2 sprouting from a root in dry and **s** ground.

STERLING (3)
Pr 8:19 than the purest gold, my wages better than **s** silver!
10:20 The words of the godly are like **s** silver; the heart
25: 4 and the **s** will be ready for the silversmith.

STERN (4) [STERNLY]
Ex 33: 4 When the people heard these **s** words, they went
Ps 81: 8 to me, O my people, while I give you **s** warnings.
Ac 27:29 so they threw out four anchors from the **s**
27:41 while the **s** was repeatedly smashed by the force of

STERNLY (5) [STERN]
Mt 9:30 Jesus **s** warned them, "Don't tell anyone about
16:20 Then he **s** warned them not to tell anyone that he
Mk 1:43 Then Jesus sent him on his way and told him **s**,
8:33 at his disciples and then said to Peter very **s**,
Tit 1:13 So rebuke them as **s** as necessary to make them

STEW (6)
Ge 25:29 One day when Jacob was cooking some **s**,
25:30 Give me some of that red **s** you've made."
25:34 Then Jacob gave Esau some bread and lentil **s**.
2Ki 4:38 on a large kettle and make some **s** for these men."
4:40 cried out, "Man of God, there's poison in this **s**!"
Hag 2:12 and happens to brush against some bread or **s**,

STICK (33) [STICKING, STICKS, STUCK]
Ge 32:10 I left home, I owned nothing except a walking **s**,
38:18 your cord, and the walking **s** you are carrying."
38:25 and walking **s** is the father of my child.
1Sa 2:14 the servant would **s** the fork into the pot
14:27 and he dipped a **s** into a piece of honeycomb
14:43 "It was only a little bit on the end of a **s**.
17:43 roared at David, "that you come at me with a **s**?"
2Ki 6: 6 the place, Elisha cut a **s** and threw it into the water.
18:21 you will find it to be a **s** that breaks beneath your
Ps 137: 6 May my tongue **s** to the roof of my mouth / if I fail
Pr 4:26 path for your feet; then **s** to the path and stay safe.
Isa 28:27 never used on dill; rather, it is beaten with a light **s**.
36: 6 you will find it to be a **s** that breaks beneath your
La 4: 4 The parched tongues of their little ones **s** with
Eze 3:26 And I will make your tongue **s** to the roof of your
37:16 "Son of man, take a **s** and carve on it these words:
37:16 'This **s** represents Judah and its allied tribes.'
37:16 Then take another **s** and carve these words on it:
37:16 'This **s** represents the northern tribes of Israel.'
37:17 Now hold them together in your hand as one **s**.
37:19 them to Judah. I will make them one **s** in my hand.'
Hos 4:12 They think a **s** can tell them the future!
Zec 3: 2 This man is like a burning **s** that has been snatched
Mt 10:10 with an extra coat and sandals or even a walking **s**.
27:29 and they placed a **s** in his right hand as a scepter.

27:30 And they spit on him and grabbed the s and beat
27:48 holding it up to him on a s so he could drink.
Mk 6: 8 to take nothing with them except a walking s—
15:19 And they beat him on the head with a s, spit on
15:36 holding it up to him on a s so he could drink.
Lk 9: 3 "Don't even take along a walking s,"
Rev 11: 1 Then I was given a measuring s, and I was told,
21:15 in his hand a gold measuring s to measure the city,

STICKING (2) [STICK]

Isa 57: 4 you mock, making faces and s out your tongues?
Eze 29: 4 and drag you out on the land with fish s to your

STICKS (9) [STICK]

Ex 12:11 and carry your walking s in your hands.
1Ki 17:10 he saw a widow gathering s, and he asked her,
17:12 I was just gathering a few s to cook this last meal,
Ps 22:15 My tongue s to the roof of my mouth. / You have
Pr 18:24 each other, but a real friend s closer than a brother.
La 4: 8 Their skin s to their bones; it is as dry and hard as
Eze 37:20 Then hold out the s you have inscribed,
Am 4:11 Those of you who survived were like half-burned s
Ac 28: 3 As Paul gathered an armful of s and was laying

STIFFHEARTED [KJV] See STUBBORN

STIFLE (1)

1Th 5:19 Do not s the Holy Spirit.

STILL (360) [STILLBORN, STILLED, STILLNESS]

Ge 2:20 But s there was no companion suitable for him.
8: 9 no place to land because the water was s too high.
9: 4 But you must never eat animals that s have their
11:28 But while Haran was s young, he died in Ur of the
11:32 lived for 205 years and died while s at Haran.
16:14 and it can s be found between Kadesh and Bered.
18:24 will you s destroy it, and not spare it for their
19:16 When Lot s hesitated, the angels seized his hand
24:15 As he was s praying, a young woman named
24:30 where the man was s standing beside his camels.
34:25 three days later, when their wounds were s sore,
35:16 began while they were s some distance away.
41:21 but afterward they were s as ugly and gaunt as
43: 7 "He wanted to know whether our father was s
43:27 the old man you spoke about? Is he s alive?"
44:14 Joseph was s at home when Judah and his brothers
45: 3 he said to his brothers. "Is my father s alive?"
45:11 for there are s five years of famine ahead of us.
45:26 "Joseph is s alive!" they told him. "And he is
46:30 you with my own eyes and know you are s alive."
47: 9 but I am s not nearly as old as many of my
47:26 throughout the land of Egypt—and it is s the law—
48: 7 We were s on the way, just a short distance from
Ex 1:13 and decided to make their slavery more bitter s.
2:23 But the Israelites s groaned beneath their burden of
4:18 I don't even know whether they are s alive."
5:16 but we are s told to make as many bricks as before.
5:18 but you must s deliver the regular quota of
7:13 He s refused to listen, just as the LORD had
9: 7 He s refused to let the people go.
9:17 But you are s lording it over my people, and you
9:30 I know that you s do not fear the LORD God as
10:12 and eat all the crops s left after the hailstorm."
12: 1 and Aaron while they were s in the land of Egypt:
14:12 you to leave us alone while we were s in Egypt?
17: 8 While the people of Israel were s at Rephidim,
21: 4 his wife and children will s belong to his master.
22:17 the man must s pay the money for her dowry.
Lev 11:36 into a spring or a cistern, the water will s be clean.
11:37 in the field, the seed will s be considered clean.
13:40 his head becomes bald, he is s ceremonially clean.
13:41 he simply has a bald forehead; he is s clean.
14: 8 they must s remain outside their tents for seven
14:29 The oil that is s in the priest's hand will then be
22:23 it may s be offered as a freewill offering,
25:22 you will s be eating the produce of the previous
25:48 they s retain the right of redemption. They may be
25:51 If many years s remain, they will repay most of
26:18 "And if, in spite of this, you s disobey me, I will
26:27 "If after this you s refuse to listen and s remain
hostile toward me,
26:39 Those s left alive will rot away in enemy lands
Nu 5:28 be unharmed and will s be able to have children.
9:10 they may s celebrate the LORD's Passover.
9:13 yet s refuse to celebrate the Passover at the regular
11:26 were s in the camp when the Spirit rested upon
11:33 But while they were s eating the meat, the anger of
30: 3 or a pledge under oath while she is s living at her
30:16 a father and a young daughter who s lives at home.
Dt 3:11 It can s be seen in the Ammonite city of Rabbah.)
3:14 calling it the Towns of Jair, as it is s known today.)
4: 4 faithful to the LORD your God are s alive today.
7:20 to drive out the few survivors s hiding from you!
10: 5 And the tablets are s there in the Ark.
10: 8 blessings in his name. These are s their duties.
25: 8 If he s insists that he doesn't want to marry her,
29:28 them to another land, where they s live today!'
31:27 Even now, while I am s with you, you have
Jos 8:29 heap of stones over him that can s be seen today.
10:12 He said, / "Let the sun stand s over Gibeon,
10:13 and moon stood s until the Israelites had defeated
11:22 though some s remained in Gaza, Gath,
13: 2 The people s need to occupy the land of the
14:11 and I can s travel and fight as well as I could then.
14:14 Hebron s belongs to the descendants of Caleb son
22:10 But while they were s in Canaan, before they
23: 7 with the other people s remaining in the land.
Jdg 7: 4 the LORD told Gideon, "There are s too many!
10: 4 of Gilead, which are s called the Towns of Jair.
14:14 Three days later they were s trying to figure it out.
15: 5 including the grain s in piles and all that had been
15:19 Who Cried Out," and it is s in Lehi to this day.
16:15 and you s haven't told me what makes you
21:20 They told the men of Benjamin who s needed
Ru 1:11 Can I s give birth to other sons who could grow up
1Sa 2:13 While the meat of the sacrificed animal was s
6:18 s stands in the field of Joshua as a reminder of
8:19 "Even so, we s want a king," they said.
13: 8 instructed him earlier, but Samuel s didn't come.
13:15 When Saul counted the men who were s with him,
14:33 the LORD by eating meat that s has blood in it."
14:34 s in it.' " So that night all the troops brought their
16:11 "There is s the youngest," Jesse replied.
17:57 him to Saul with the Philistine's head s in his hand.
20:22 the arrows are s ahead of you,' then it will mean
20:37 Jonathan shouted, "The arrow is s ahead of you.
22:18 priests in all, all s wearing their priestly tunics.
25:22 of his household is s alive tomorrow morning!"
27: 6 So Achish gave him the town of Ziklag (which s
30:25 this a law for all of Israel, and it is s followed.
2Sa 2:23 and stood s when they saw Asahel lying there.
4: 3 fled to Gittaim, where they s live as foreigners.
6: 8 against Uzzah"). It is s called that today.
9: 1 wondering if anyone in Saul's family was s alive,
9: 3 asked him, "Is anyone s alive from Saul's family?
9: 3 "Yes, one of Jonathan's sons is s alive,
12:21 "While the baby was s living, you wept
18:14 heart as he dangled from the oak s alive.
21:19 In s another battle at Gob, Elhanan son of Jair from
1Ki 1:14 And while you are s talking with him, I will come
1:22 While she was s speaking with the king,
1:42 And while he was s speaking, Jonathan son of
1:48 to sit on my throne while I am s alive to see it.' "
8: 8 but not from outside it. They are s there to this day.
9:13 area Cabul—"worthless"—as it is s known today.
9:20 There were s some people living in the land who
11:12 David, I will not do this while you are s alive.
13:28 and lion were s standing there beside it,
17:13 Afterward there will s be enough food for you
18:29 but s there was no reply, no voice, no answer.
20:11 "A warrior s dressing for battle should not boast
20:16 and the thirty-two allied kings were s in their tents
20:32 The king of Israel responded, "Is he s alive?
22: 3 "Do you realize that the Arameans are s
22: 8 "There is s one prophet of the LORD, but I hate
22:43 and the people s offered sacrifices and burned
22:46 who s continued their practices from the days of
2Ki 2:18 Elisha was s at Jericho when they returned.
4:31 meet Elisha and told him, "The child is s dead."
6:33 While Elisha was s saying this, the messenger
12: 3 and the people s offered sacrifices and burned
12: 6 the priests s had not repaired the Temple.
13:23 And to this day he s has not completely destroyed
17:34 And this is s going on among them today.
25:19 And of the people s hiding in the city, he took an
1Ch 13:11 against Uzzah"). It is s called that today.
22: 5 "My son Solomon is s young and inexperienced,
29: 1 next king of Israel, is s young and inexperienced.
2Ch 1: 5 and grandson of Hur was s at Gibeon in front of
5: 9 but not from outside it. They are s there to this day.
8: 7 There were s some people living in the land who
12:12 And there was s goodness in the land of Judah.
18: 7 "There is s one prophet of the LORD, but I hate
20:17 then stand s and watch the LORD's victory.
20:26 It is s called the Valley of Blessing today.
32: 9 of Assyria, while s besieging the town of Lachish,
33:17 the people s sacrificed at the pagan shrines,
34: 3 the eighth year of his reign, while he was s young,
34:13 S others assisted as secretaries, officials,
35:25 and to this day choirs s sing these sad songs about
Ezr 10: 6 He was s in mourning because of the
Ne 7: 3 And while the gatekeepers are s on duty,
9:19 The pillar of cloud s led them forward by day,
9:30 them about their sins. But s they wouldn't listen!
Est 2:20 She was s following Mordecai's orders, just as she
3: 4 but s he refused to comply with the order.
6:14 While they were s talking, the king's eunuchs
Job 1:16 While he was s speaking, another messenger
1:17 While he was s speaking, a third messenger arrived
1:18 While he was s speaking, another messenger
2: 9 "Are you s trying to maintain your integrity?
8:12 While they are s flowering, not ready to be cut,
23: 2 "My complaint today is s a bitter one, and I try
29: 5 The Almighty was s with me, and my children
37:17 and the south wind dies down and everything is s,
40: 2 "Do you s want to argue with the Almighty?
Ps 11: 4 holy Temple; / the LORD s rules from heaven.
37: 7 Be s in the presence of the LORD, / and wait
55:18 against me, / even though many s oppose me.
73:23 Yet I s belong to you; / you are holding my right
76: 6 O God of Jacob, / their horses and chariots stood s.
92:14 Even in old age they will s produce fruit;
102:24 don't take my life while I am s so young!
139:18 I wake up in the morning, / you are s with me!
Ecc 2: 3 While s seeking wisdom, I clutched at foolishness.
7: 2 and you should think about it while there is s time.
8:12 person sins a hundred times and s lives a long time,
11: 8 be many. Everything s to come is meaningless.
11:10 life before it, s faces the threat of meaninglessness.
SS 6: 9 But I would s choose my dove, my perfect one,
Isa 1: 3 what I do for them, they s do not understand."
5:25 will not be satisfied. His fist is s poised to strike!
7:22 The few people s left in the land will live on curds
9:12 will not be satisfied. His fist is s poised to strike.
9:13 the people will s not repent and turn to the LORD
9:17 will not be satisfied. His fist is s poised to strike.
9:20 neighbors to steal food, but they will s be hungry.
9:21 will not be satisfied. His fist is s poised to strike.
10: 4 will not be satisfied. His fist is s poised to strike.
15: 9 red with blood, but I am s not finished with Dibon!
19:11 and wrong. Will they s boast of their wisdom?
24:16 I am discouraged, for evil s prevails, and treachery
29: 8 A hungry person dreams of eating but is s hungry.
29: 8 but is s faint from thirst when morning comes.
30:18 But the LORD s waits for you to come to him
30:20 for drink, he will s be with you to teach you.
38:11 while s in the land of the living. / Never again will
42:25 and burned, but they s refused to understand.
57:20 "But those who s reject me are like the restless
57:20 It is never s but continually churns up mire
63:16 Surely you are s our Father! Even if Abraham
63:16 disown us, LORD, you would s be our Father.
64:12 all this, LORD, must you s refuse to help us?
65: 8 destroy all Israel. For I s have true servants there.
65:24 While they are s talking to me about their needs,
Jer 2:20 of your slavery, but s you would not obey me.
2:30 but it did them no good. They s refuse to obey.
3: 1 Yet I am s calling you to come back to me.
4: 8 for the fierce anger of the LORD is s upon us.
4:19 in pain! My heart pounds within me! I cannot be s.
13:17 And if you s refuse to listen, I will weep alone
27:18 gold utensils that are s left in the LORD's Temple
29:16 and all those s living here in Jerusalem—
31:20 "Is not Israel s my son, my darling child?"
31:20 "I had to punish him, but I s love him. I long for
32:20 land of Egypt—things s remembered to this day!
33: 1 While Jeremiah was s confined in the courtyard of
33: 5 the Babylonians will s enter. The men of this city
34: 7 the only cities of Judah with their walls s standing.
37:10 they would s stagger from their tents and burn this
39:15 message to Jeremiah while he was s in prison:
40: 6 and lived in Judah with the few who were s left in
40:15 Why should the few of us who are s left be
47: 6 rest again? Go back into your sheath; rest and be s!
47: 7 But how can it be s when the LORD has sent it on
51: 5 He is s their God, even though their land was filled
52:25 And of the people s hiding in the city, he took an
La 3:21 Yet I s dare to hope when I remember this:
5:22 you utterly rejected us? Are you angry with us s?
Eze 2: 3 and they are s in revolt to this very day.
10:17 When the cherubim stood s, the wheels also
11:13 While I was s speaking, Pelatiah son of Benaiah
11:15 the people s left in Jerusalem are talking about
16: 7 and your hair grew, though you were s naked.
16:28 And after your prostitution there you s were not
16:29 land of Babylonia—but you s weren't satisfied!
20: 8 to satisfy my anger while they were s in Egypt.
23: 8 She was s as lewd as in her youth,
32:27 They brought terror to everyone while they were s
36:36 all those s left—will know that I, the LORD,
37: 8 their bodies, but they s had no breath in them.
43: 6 (The man who had been measuring was s standing
43:15 top of the altar, the hearth, rises s 7 feet higher,
44:11 They may s be Temple guards and gatemen,
44:11 and they may s slaughter the animals brought for
Da 4:31 While he was s speaking these words, a voice
6:13 He s prays to his God three times a day."
10:10 and lifted me, s trembling, to my hands and knees.
10:11 said this to me, I stood up, s trembling with fear.
11:27 for an end will s come at the appointed time.
11:35 of the end, for the appointed time is s to come.
Hos 3: 1 For the LORD s loves Israel even though the
4:10 They will eat and s be hungry. Though they do a
7: 4 hot even while the baker is s kneading the dough.
11:12 but Judah s walks with God and is faithful to the
Am 1: 8 and the few Philistines s left will be killed.
4: 6 But s you wouldn't return to me,"
4: 8 But s you wouldn't return to me,"
4: 9 But s you wouldn't return to me,"
4:10 But s you wouldn't return to me,"
4:11 But s you wouldn't return to me,"
8: 9 at noon and darken the earth while it is s day.
Mic 6:14 Your hunger pangs and emptiness will s remain.
Zep 2: 2 Gather while there is s time, before judgment
3: 5 But the LORD is s there in the city, and he does
Hag 2: 4 Take courage, all you people s left in the land,
2:19 I am giving you a promise now while the seed is s
Zec 10: 9 s they will remember me in distant lands.
14: 7 and night, for at evening time it will s be light.
Mt 1:18 But while she was s a virgin, she became pregnant
7:21 but they s won't enter the Kingdom of Heaven.
11:23 had been done in Sodom, it would s be here today.
18:17 If that person s refuses to listen, take your case to
26:45 he came to the disciples and said, "S sleeping?
26:45 S resting? Look, the time has come. I, the Son of
27: 8 That is why the field is s called the Field of Blood.
27:63 what that deceiver once said while he was s alive:
28:15 widely among the Jews, and they s tell it today.
28:17 they worshiped him—but some of them s doubted!
Mk 4: 8 S other seed fell on fertile soil and produced a crop
4:40 are you so afraid? Do you s not have faith in me?"
5: 6 When Jesus was s some distance away, the man
5:35 While he was s speaking to her,
6:15 S others thought he was a prophet like the other
6:52 They s didn't understand the significance of the
12:22 married her and died, and s there were no children.
14: 1 and the teachers of religious law were s looking for

14:41 he said, "S sleeping? S resting? Enough!
16:14 S later he appeared to the eleven disciples as they
Lk 5:19 into the crowd, s on his mat, right in front of Jesus.
8:8 S other seed fell on fertile soil. This seed grew
8:43 she had on doctors and s could find no cure.
8:49 While he was s speaking to her, a messenger
11:39 the cup and the dish, but inside you are s filthy—
14:22 done this, he reported, 'There is s room for more.'
14:32 he is not able, then while the enemy is s far away,
15:20 And while he was s a long distance away,
18:22 "There is s one thing you lack," Jesus said.
20:30 married the widow, but he also died. S no children.
24:41 S they stood there doubting, filled with joy
Jn 6:17 But as darkness fell and Jesus s hadn't come back,
7:41 is the Messiah." S others said, "But he can't be!
8:27 But they s didn't understand that he was talking to
9:5 But while I am s here in the world, I am the light
12:36 Believe in the light while there is s time; then you
14:25 I am telling you these things now while I am s with
20:1 Early Sunday morning, while it was s dark,
Ac 2:29 and was buried, and his tomb is s here among us.
7:12 Jacob heard that there was s grain in Egypt, so he
26:22 so that I am s alive today to tell these facts to
Ro 3:7 "But," some might s argue, "how can God judge
5:8 Christ to die for us while we were s sinners.
5:10 the death of his Son while we were s his enemies,
7:1 the law applies only to a person who is s living?
7:12 But s, the law itself is holy and right and good.
7:23 and makes me a slave to the sin that is s within me.
8:8 That's why those who are s under the control of
11:28 Yet the Jews are s his chosen people because of his
1Co 3:2 handle anything stronger. And you s aren't ready,
3:3 for you are s controlled by your own sinful desires.
12:2 You know that when you were s pagans you were
12:10 S another person is given the ability to speak in
15:1 You welcomed it then and s do now, for your faith
15:6 most of whom are s alive, though some have died
15:17 and you are s under condemnation for your sins.
2Co 2:8 Now show him that you s love him.
6:9 We live close to death, but here we are, s alive.
9:4 only to find that you s weren't ready after all I had
12:16 But they s think I was sneaky and took advantage
Gal 1:10 If I were s trying to please people, I would not be
1:22 And s the Christians in the churches in Judea
2:17 in Christ and then find out that we are s sinners?
5:11 if I were s preaching that you must be
5:11 The fact that I am s being persecuted proves that I
5:11 s preaching salvation through the cross of Christ
Eph 4:26 Don't let the sun go down while you are s angry,
6:13 so that after the battle you will s be standing firm.
Php 1:30 and you know that I am s in the midst of this great
3:13 No, dear friends, I am s not all I should be, but I
Col 3:7 You used to do them when your life was s part of
1Th 3:5 I sent Timothy to find out whether your faith was s
3:10 fill up anything that may s be missing in your faith.
4:15 We who are s living when the Lord returns will not
4:17 we who are s alive and remain on the earth will be
Heb 4:1 God's promise of entering his place of rest s
4:9 So there is a special rest s waiting for the people of
6:10 to him by caring for other Christians, as you s do.
9:8 and the entire system it represents were s in use.
9:17 While the person is s alive, no one can use the will
11:4 is long dead, he s speaks to us because of his faith.
Jas 2:19 Do you s think it's enough just to believe that there
1Pe 4:6 they could s live in the spirit as God does.
1Jn 2:9 but rejects another Christian is s in darkness.
3:14 But a person who doesn't love them is s dead.
Jude 1:23 There are s others to whom you need to show
Rev 1:4 one who is, who always was, and who is s to come;
1:8 who always was, and who is s to come,
4:8 who always was, who is, and who is s to come."
9:20 But the people who did not die in these plagues s

STILLBORN (3) [BEAR, STILL]

Nu 12:12 Don't let her be like a s baby, already decayed at
Job 3:16 Why was I not buried like a s child, like a baby
Ps 58:8 like a s child who will never see the sun.

STILLED (4) [STILL]

Ps 107:29 calmed the storm to a whisper / and s the waves.
131:2 But I have s and quieted myself, / just as a small
Isa 24:8 The clash of tambourines will be s; the happy cries
25:5 So the boastful songs of ruthless people are s.

STILLNESS (1) [STILL]

Ps 107:30 What a blessing was that s / as he brought them

STIMULATE (1) [STIMULATES]

2Pe 3:1 and in both of them I have tried to s your

STIMULATES (1) [STIMULATE]

2Ti 2:22 Run from anything that s youthful lust.

STING (7) [STINGING, STINGS]

Ps 140:3 Their tongues s like a snake; / the poison of a viper
Isa 7:18 you like flies. Like bees, they will s and kill.
Eze 2:6 and barbed like briers, and they s like scorpions.
1Co 15:55 where is your victory? / O death, where is your s?"
15:56 For sin is the s that results in death, and the law
Rev 9:3 and they were given power to s like scorpions.
9:10 They had tails that s like scorpions, with power to

STINGING (1) [STING]

Zep 2:9 Their land will become a place of s nettles,

STINGS (2) [STING]

Pr 23:32 it bites like a poisonous serpent; it s like a viper.
Rev 9:5 five months with agony like the pain of scorpion s.

STINGY (3)

Job 31:17 Have I been s with my food and refused to share it
Pr 11:24 but those who are s will lose everything.
23:6 Don't eat with people who are s; don't desire their

STINK (5) [STENCH]

Ge 34:30 "You have made me s among all the people of this
Ex 7:18 The fish in it will die, and the river will s.
Ps 38:5 My wounds fester and s / because of my foolish
Ecc 10:1 Dead flies will cause even a bottle of perfume to s!
Isa 3:24 Instead of smelling of sweet perfume, they will s.

STIPULATION (1) [STIPULATIONS]

Lev 25:24 "With every sale of land there must be a s that the

STIPULATIONS (5) [STIPULATION]

Dt 4:45 These are the s, laws, and regulations that Moses
6:17 your God—all the s and laws he has given you.
6:20 will ask you, 'What is the meaning of these s, laws,
1Ki 2:3 and s written in the law of Moses so that you will
Jer 44:23 obey him and follow his instructions, laws, and s."

STIR (12) [STIRRED, STIRRING, STIRS]

Jdg 6:28 next morning, as the people of the town began to s,
2Sa 15:10 part of Israel to s up a rebellion against the king.
2Ki 14:10 Why s up trouble that will bring disaster on you
2Ch 25:19 Why s up trouble that will bring disaster on you
Ps 140:2 evil in their hearts / and s up trouble all day long.
Pr 6:14 hearts plot evil. They s up trouble constantly.
15:1 turns away wrath, but harsh words s up anger.
Isa 13:17 For I will s up the Medes against Babylon, and no
Jer 32:32 the priests, and the prophets—s up my anger.
51:1 "I will s up a destroyer against Babylon
Da 11:2 he will s up everyone to war against the kingdom
11:25 "Then he will s up his courage and raise a great

STIRRED (18) [STIR]

Ex 35:21 If their hearts were s and they desired to do so,
Nu 16:19 Korah had s up the entire community against
Dt 32:16 They s up his jealousy by worshiping foreign gods;
Jdg 9:23 God s up trouble between Abimelech
Ru 1:19 the entire town was s by their arrival.
1Sa 26:19 If the LORD has s you up against me, then let
2Ch 21:16 Then the LORD s up the Philistines
Ezr 1:5 Then God s the hearts of the priests and Levites
Isa 41:2 "Who has s up this king from the east, who meets
41:25 "But I have s up a leader from the north and east.
Jer 51:11 For the LORD has s up the spirit of the kings of
Mt 21:10 The entire city of Jerusalem was s as he entered.
Mk 15:11 But at this point the leading priests s up the mob to
Jn 5:7 to help me into the pool when the water is s up.
Ac 13:50 Then the Jewish leaders s up both the influential
14:2 But the Jews who spurned God's message s up
17:13 of God in Berea, they went there and s up trouble.
2Co 9:2 it was your enthusiasm that s up many of them to

STIRRING (6) [STIR]

1Ki 20:7 said to them, "Look how this man is s up trouble!
2Ch 36:22 the LORD fulfilled Jeremiah's prophecy by s the
Ezr 1:1 the LORD fulfilled Jeremiah's prophecy by s the
Ps 107:25 He spoke, and the winds rose, / s up the waves.
Pr 24:2 and their words are always s up trouble.
Eze 32:2 in your own rivers, s up mud with your feet.

STIRS (5) [STIR]

Pr 10:12 Hatred s up quarrels, but love covers all offenses.
Isa 51:15 who s up the sea, causing its waves to roar.
Jer 31:35 the night. It is he who s the sea into roaring waves.
Am 4:13 s up the winds, and reveals his every thought.
1Ti 6:4 This s up arguments ending in jealousy, fighting,

STITCHED (2)

Ex 31:10 the beautifully s, holy garments for Aaron the
35:19 the beautifully s clothing for the priests to wear

STOCK (1)

Jer 2:21 When I planted you, I chose a vine of the purest s

STOCKED (1)

Dt 6:11 The houses will be richly s with goods you did not

STOCKS (5)

Job 13:27 You put my feet in s. You watch all my paths.
33:11 He puts my feet in the s and watches every move I
Jer 20:2 and put in s at the Benjamin Gate of the LORD's
29:26 to put anyone who claims to be a prophet in the s
Ac 16:24 the inner dungeon and clamped their feet in the s.

STOIC (1)

Ac 17:18 with some of the Epicurean and S philosophers.

STOLE (19) [STEAL]

Ge 30:15 "Wasn't it enough that you s my husband?
31:19 Rachel s her father's household gods and took
43:18 they said. "He plans to pretend that we s it.
44:10 "except that only the one who s it will be a slave.
44:15 know that a man such as I would know who s it?"
44:17 "Only the man who s the cup will be my slave.
Ex 22:8 or not it was the neighbor who s the property.
Jdg 2:14 so he handed them over to marauders who s their
11:13 they s my land from the Arnon River to the Jabbok
17:2 "I heard you curse the thief who s eleven hundred
2Sa 12:6 repay four lambs to the poor man for the one he s
15:6 Absalom s the hearts of all the people of Israel.
16:8 You s his throne, and now the LORD has given it
1Ki 14:26 the LORD and the royal palace and s everything,
2Ki 11:2 and s him away from among the rest of the king's
2Ch 22:11 and s him away from among the rest of the king's
Job 1:15 They s all the animals and killed all the farmhands.
Pr 6:31 he will be fined seven times as much as he s,
Mt 28:13 night while we were sleeping, and they s his body.'

STOLEN (33) [STEAL]

Ge 27:41 Esau hated Jacob because he had s his blessing,
30:33 you will know that I have s them from you."
31:26 of war, that you have s them away like this?
31:30 but why have you s my household gods?"
31:39 You made me pay for every animal s from the
Ex 22:1 For oxen the fine is five oxen for each one s.
22:1 For sheep the fine is four sheep for each one s.
22:3 is caught must pay in full for everything that was s.
22:7 and they are s from the neighbor's house.
22:7 is found, the fine is double the value of what was s.
22:12 But if the animal or property was s, payment must
Lev 6:2 entrusted to their safekeeping has been lost or s.
Jos 7:1 A man named Achan had s some of these things,
7:11 They have s the things that I commanded to be set
7:11 And they have not only s them; they have also lied
7:15 The one who has s what was set apart for
7:22 ran to the tent and found the s goods hidden there,
1Sa 12:3 his anointed one—whose ox or donkey have I s?
25:7 harmed them, and nothing was ever s from them.
25:15 Nothing was s from us the whole time they were
25:21 the wilderness, and nothing he owned was lost or s.
2Sa 12:9 For you have murdered Uriah and s his wife.
Job 1:17 "Three bands of Chaldean raiders have s your
5:5 Their harvests are s, and their wealth satisfies the
31:39 or if I have s its crops or murdered its owners,
Pr 9:17 "S water is refreshing; food eaten in secret tastes
20:17 S bread tastes sweet, but it turns to gravel in the
Eze 33:15 return what they have s, and obey my life-giving
Am 2:8 they lounge around in clothing s from their
2:8 they present offerings of wine purchased with s
Mal 1:13 Animals that are s and mutilated, crippled
Ac 19:37 but they have s nothing from the temple and have
Phm 1:18 harmed you in any way or s anything from you,

STOMACH (17)

Nu 25:8 through the man's body and into the woman's s.
Dt 18:3 as offerings: the shoulder, the cheeks, and the s.
2Sa 2:23 thrust the butt end of his spear through Asahel's s,
4:6 Ishbosheth's bedroom, and stabbed him in the s.
20:10 and Joab stabbed him in the s with it so that his
Job 20:14 turns sour within him, a poisonous venom in his s.
Pr 16:26 to have an appetite; an empty s drives them on.
18:20 Words satisfy the soul as food satisfies the s;
Isa 21:3 My s aches and burns with pain. Sharp pangs of
Mt 15:17 "Anything you eat passes through the s and
Mk 7:19 but only passes through the s and then comes out
1Co 6:13 You say, "Food is for the s, and the s is for food."
Php 4:12 whether it is with a full s or empty, with plenty
1Ti 5:23 ought to drink a little wine for the sake of your s
Rev 10:9 when you swallow it, it will make your s sour!"
10:10 It was sweet in my mouth, but it made my s sour.

STONE (177) [CORNERSTONE, GEMSTONES, MILLSTONE, MILLSTONES, MOONSTONE, STONE'S, STONECUTTERS, STONED, STONEMASONS, STONES, STONEWORK, STONING, STONY]

Ge 2:12 aromatic resin and onyx s are also found there.
28:11 Jacob found a s for a pillow and lay down to sleep.
28:18 He took the s he had used as a pillow and set it
29:2 But a heavy s covered the mouth of the well.
29:3 for all the flocks to arrive before removing the s.
29:3 the s would be rolled back over the mouth of the
29:8 "We don't roll away the s and begin the watering
29:10 Jacob went over to the well and rolled away the s
31:13 the place where you anointed the pillar of s
31:45 So Jacob took a s and set it up as a monument.
35:14 Jacob set up a s pillar to mark the place where God
35:20 Jacob set up a s monument over her grave, and it
Ex 7:19 wooden bowls and s pots in the people's homes."
8:26 where they can see us, they will be sure to s us.
15:5 covered them; / they sank to the bottom like a s.
15:16 of your great power, / they will be silent like a s,
17:4 I do with these people? They are about to s me!"
17:12 So Aaron and Hur found a s for him to sit on.
20:25 If you build altars from s, use only uncut stones.
21:18 and one hits the other with a s or fist,
24:12 Stay there while I give you the tablets of s that I
25:16 place inside it the s tablets inscribed with the terms
25:21 Place inside the Ark the s tablets inscribed with the

28:10 Six names will be on each s, naming all the tribes
28:21 Each s will represent one of the tribes of Israel,
31:18 he gave him the two s tablets inscribed with the
32:15 He held in his hands the two s tablets inscribed
32:16 These s tablets were God's work; the words on
32:19 terrible anger, he threw the s tablets to the ground,
34: 1 "Prepare two s tablets like the first ones.
34: 4 So Moses cut two tablets of s like the first ones.
34: 4 told him, carrying the two s tablets in his hands.
34:28 the Ten Commandments—on the s tablets.
34:29 s tablets inscribed with the terms of the covenant,
40:20 He placed inside the Ark the s tablets inscribed
Lev 24:14 Then let the entire community s him to death.
Nu 15:35 The whole community must s him outside the
35:17 and kills another person with a large s,
35:23 or accidentally drops a s on someone, though they
Dt 4:13 and wrote them on two s tablets.
4:28 you will worship idols made from wood and s,
5:22 and he wrote his words on two s tablets and gave
8: 9 It is a land where iron is as common as s,
9: 9 s inscribed with the covenant that the LORD had
9:11 the LORD handed me the two s tablets with the
9:15 holding in my hands the two s tablets of the
9:17 So I raised the s tablets and dashed them to the
10: 1 to me, 'Prepare two s tablets like the first ones,
10: 3 acacia wood and cut two s tablets like the first two,
13:10 S the guilty ones to death because they have tried
21:21 Then all the men of the town must s him to death.
22:21 and the men of the town will s her to death.
22:24 them to the gates of the town and s them to death.
28:36 in exile you will worship gods of wood and s!
28:64 ancestors have known, gods made of wood and s!
29:17 detestable idols made of wood, s, silver, and gold.
Jos 4: 5 Each of you must pick up one s and carry it out on
15: 6 then proceeded north of Beth-arabah to the s of
18:17 Then it went down to the s of Bohan. (Bohan was
24:26 he took a huge s and rolled it beneath the oak tree
24:27 "This s has heard everything the LORD said to
Jdg 3:19 But when Ehud reached the s carvings near Gilgal,
9: 5 and there, on one s, they killed all seventy of his
9:18 his descendants, killing his seventy sons on one s.
1Sa 7:12 Samuel then took a large s and placed it between
7:12 "the s of help"—for he said, "Up to this point the
14:33 Saul said. "Find a large s and roll it over here.
17:49 into his shepherd's bag and taking out a s,
17:49 The s sank in, and Goliath stumbled and fell face
17:50 triumphed over the Philistine giant with only a s
20:19 where you hid before, and wait there by the s pile.
20:20 and shoot three arrows to the side of the s pile as
20:41 out from where he had been hiding near the s pile.
2Sa 17:13 into the nearest valley until every s is torn down."
20: 8 As they arrived at the great s in Gibeon,
1Ki 1: 9 Adonijah went to the s of Zoheleth near the spring
5:17 and shaped costly blocks of s for the foundation of
5:18 builders prepare the timber and s for the Temple.
6:18 Cedar paneling completely covered the s walls
6:36 of cedar beams after every three layers of hewn s.
7: 9 costly blocks of s, cut and trimmed to exact
7:11 The costly blocks of s used in the walls were also
7:12 of cedar beams after every three layers of hewn s,
8: 9 Nothing was in the Ark except the two s tablets
21:10 the king. Then take him out and s him to death."
2Ki 12:12 and cut s for repairing the LORD's Temple,
16:17 of the bronze oxen and placed it on the s pavement.
19:18 only idols of wood and s shaped by human hands.
22: 6 and the cut s needed to repair the Temple.
1Ch 22: 2 blocks of s for building the Temple of God.
22:14 I have also gathered lumber and s for the walls,
29: 2 costly jewels, and all kinds of fine s and marble.
2Ch 5:10 Nothing was in the Ark except the two s tablets
34:11 and masons and purchased cut s for the walls
Ne 4: 3 "That s wall would collapse if even a fox walked
Job 6:12 Do I have strength as hard as s? Is my body made
28: 2 to dig iron from the earth and smelt copper from s.
28:16 of Ophir, greater than precious onyx s or sapphires.
Ps 91:12 to keep you from striking your foot on a s.
102:14 For your people love every s in her walls
118:22 The s rejected by the builders / has now become
Pr 26: 8 Honoring a fool is as foolish as tying a s to a
27: 3 A s is heavy and sand is weighty,
Isa 8:14 and Judah he will be a s that causes people to
9:10 We will replace the broken bricks with cut s,
22:10 and tear some down to get s to fix the walls.
28:16 "Look! I am placing a foundation s in Jerusalem.
37:19 only idols of wood and s shaped by human hands.
50: 7 Therefore, I have set my face like a s,
Jer 2:27 To an idol chiseled out of s they say, 'You are my
3: 9 adultery by worshiping idols made of wood and s.
5: 3 They are determined, with faces set like s;
51:63 tie it to a s, and throw it into the Euphrates River.
La 3: 9 He has blocked my path with a high s wall. He has
Eze 11:19 I will take away their hearts of s and give them
16:40 They will band together in a mob to s you and run
20:32 all around us, who serve idols of wood and s.'
23:47 For their enemies will s them and kill them with
28:13 Your clothing was adorned with every precious s—
40:17 A s pavement ran along the walls of the courtyard,
40:42 There were also four tables of hewn s for
46:23 Along the inside of these walls was a ledge of s
Da 5: 4 made of gold, silver, bronze, iron, wood, and s.
5:23 gods of silver, gold, bronze, iron, wood, and s—
6:17 A s was brought and placed over the mouth of the
6:17 The king sealed the s with his own royal seal
Hos 12:11 their altars are lined up like the heaps of s along
Am 5:11 you will never live in the beautiful s houses you
Hab 2:19 You ask speechless s images to tell you what to do.
Zec 3: 9 have set before Jeshua, a single s with seven facets.
4: 7 Then Zerubbabel will set the final s of the Temple
7:12 They made their hearts as hard as s, so they could
12: 3 On that day I will make Jerusalem a heavy s,
Mt 4: 6 to keep you from striking your foot on a s.' "
7: 9 for a loaf of bread, do you give them a s instead?
21:42 'The s rejected by the builders / has now become
21:44 Anyone who stumbles over that s will be broken to
24: 2 so completely demolished that not one s will be
27:60 Then he rolled a great s across the entrance as he
28: 2 from heaven and rolled aside the s and sat on it.
Mk 12:10 'The s rejected by the builders / has now become
13: 2 so completely demolished that not one s will be
15:46 the rock. Then he rolled a s in front of the entrance.
16: 3 roll the s away from the entrance to the tomb.
16: 4 they arrived, they looked up and saw that the s—
Lk 4: 3 the Son of God, change this s into a loaf of bread."
4:11 to keep you from striking your foot on a s.' "
19:44 Your enemies will not leave a single s in place,
20: 6 we say it was merely human, the people will s us,
20:17 'The s rejected by the builders / has now become
20:18 All who stumble over that s will be broken to
21: 6 so completely demolished that not one s will be
24: 2 They found that the s covering the entrance had
Jn 2: 6 Six s waterpots were standing there; they were
8: 5 The law of Moses says to s her. What do you
8: 7 so he stood up again and said, "All right, s her.
11:38 It was a cave with a s rolled across its entrance.
11:39 "Roll the s aside," Jesus told them. But Martha,
11:41 So they rolled the s aside. Then Jesus looked up to
19:13 platform that is called the S Pavement (in Hebrew,
20: 1 and found that the s had been rolled away from the
Ac 4:11 where it says, / 'The s that you builders rejected
7:58 dragged him out of the city and began to s him.
14: 5 with their leaders, decided to attack and s them.
17:29 idol designed by craftsmen from gold or silver or s.
Ro 9:33 "I am placing a s in Jerusalem that causes people
2Co 3: 3 It is carved not on s, but on human hearts.
3: 7 That old system of law etched in s led to death,
2Ti 2:19 But God's truth stands firm like a foundation s
Heb 9: 4 and the s tablets of the covenant with the Ten
1Pe 2: 6 express it, / "I am placing a s in Jerusalem,
2: 7 "The s that was rejected by the builders
2: 8 also say, / "He is the s that makes people stumble,
Rev 2:17 And I will give to each one a white s, and on the s
will be engraved a new name that no
9:20 idols made of gold, silver, bronze, s, and wood—
18:21 down as violently as I have thrown away this s,

STONE'S (1) [STONE]

Lk 22:41 about a s throw, and knelt down and prayed,

STONECUTTERS (5) [CUT, STONE]

1Ki 5:15 eighty thousand s in the hill country,
5:17 the s quarried and shaped costly blocks of stone for
2Ki 12:12 the masons, and the s. They also used the money to
2Ch 2: 2 eighty thousand s in the hill country, and thirty-six
2:18 80,000 as s in the hill country, and 3,600 as

STONED (21) [STONE]

Ex 19:13 or animals that cross the boundary must be s to
21:28 gores a man or woman to death, the bull must be s,
21:29 is true and if the bull kills someone, it must be s,
21:32 silver coins in payment, and the bull must be s.
Lev 20: 2 they must be s to death by people of the
24:16 be s to death by the whole community of Israel.
24:23 blasphemer outside the camp and s him to death,
Nu 15:36 took the man outside the camp and s him to death,
Dt 17: 5 be taken to the gates of the town and s to death.
Jos 7:25 And all the Israelites s Achan and his family
1Ki 12:18 to restore order, but all Israel s him to death.
21:13 So he was dragged outside the city and s to death.
21:14 word to Jezebel, "Naboth has been s to death."
2Ch 10:18 to restore order, but the Israelites s him to death.
24:21 they s him to death in the courtyard of the
Mt 21:35 his servants, beat one, killed one, and s another.
Ac 7:59 And as they s him, Stephen prayed, "Lord Jesus,
14:19 They s Paul and dragged him out of the city,
22:20 I kept the coats they laid aside as they s him.'
2Co 11:25 Once I was s. Three times I was shipwrecked.
Heb 12:20 touches the mountain, it must be s to death."

STONEMASONS (3) [MASONS, STONE]

2Sa 5:11 along with carpenters and s to build him a palace.
1Ch 14: 1 along with s and carpenters to build him a palace.
22:15 You have many skilled s and carpenters

STONES (115) [STONE]

Ge 31:46 He also told his men to gather s and pile them up
31:46 then sat down beside the pile of s to share a meal.
31:48 "This pile of s will stand as a witness to remind us
31:51 This heap of s and this pillar
Ex 20:25 If you build altars from stone, use only uncut s.
20:25 Do not chip or shape the s with a tool, for that
25: 7 onyx s, and other s to be set in the ephod
28: 9 Take two onyx s and engrave on them the names
28:11 engraves a seal. Mount the s in gold settings.
28:12 Fasten the two s on the shoulder-pieces of the
ephod as memorial s for the people of Israel.
28:20 and a jasper. All these s will be set in gold.
35: 9 onyx s, and other s to be set in the ephod
35:27 The leaders brought onyx s and the other
39: 6 The two onyx s, attached to the shoulder-pieces of
39: 6 The s were engraved with the names of the tribes
39: 7 These s served as reminders to the LORD
39:14 The s were engraved like a seal, each with the
Lev 14:40 the priest must order that the s from those areas be
14:42 Other s will be brought in to replace the ones that
14:45 It must be torn down, and all its s, timbers,
26: 1 or shaped s to be worshiped in your land.
Dt 17: 7 The witnesses must throw the first s, and then all
27: 2 set up some large s and coat them with plaster.
27: 4 set up these s at Mount Ebal and coat them with
27: 5 there to the LORD your God, using natural s.
27: 6 Do not shape the s with an iron tool. On the altar
27: 8 On the s coated with plaster, you must clearly
Jos 4: 3 Tell the men to take twelve s from where the
4: 5 twelve s in all, one for each of the twelve tribes.
4: 6 We will use these s to build a memorial.
4: 6 children will ask, 'What do these s mean to you?'
4: 7 These s will stand as a permanent memorial among
4: 8 They took twelve s from the middle of the Jordan
4: 9 Joshua also built another memorial of twelve s in
4:20 piled up the twelve s taken from the Jordan River.
4:21 your children will ask, 'What do these s mean?'
7:26 They piled a great heap of s over Achan,
8:29 They piled a great heap of s over him that can still
8:31 "Make me an altar from s that are uncut and have
8:32 Joshua copied the law of Moses onto the s of the
10:27 the opening of the cave with a large pile of s,
Jdg 6:26 your God here on this hill, laying the s carefully.
1Sa 17:40 He picked up five smooth s from a stream and put
25:29 But the lives of your enemies will disappear like s
2Sa 16: 6 He threw s at the king and the king's officers
16:13 cursing as he went and throwing s at David
18:17 pit in the forest and piled a great heap of s over it.
1Ki 6: 7 The s used in the construction of the Temple were
7:10 Some of the huge foundation s were 15 feet long,
10:27 The king made silver as plentiful in Jerusalem as s.
15:22 help to carry away the building s and timbers that
18:31 He took twelve s, one to represent each of the
18:32 and he used the s to rebuild the LORD's altar.
18:38 up the young bull, the wood, the s, and the dust.
19: 6 looked around and saw some bread baked on hot s
2Ki 3:19 their springs, and ruin all their good land with s."
3:25 covered their good land with s, stopped up the
23:15 Josiah crushed the s to dust and burned the
1Ch 12: 2 or sling s with their left hand as well as their right.
29: 2 other precious s, costly jewels, and all kinds of fine
29: 8 They also contributed numerous precious s,
2Ch 1:15 and gold were as plentiful in Jerusalem as s.
9:27 The king made silver as plentiful in Jerusalem as s.
16: 6 all the men of Judah to carry away the building s
26:14 spears, helmets, coats of mail, bows, and sling s.
26:15 and hurl s from the towers and the corners of the
32:27 gold, precious s, and spices, and for his shields
Ezr 5: 8 It is being rebuilt with specially prepared s,
6: 4 Every three layers of specially prepared s will be
Ne 4: 2 Look at those charred s they are pulling out of the
9:11 They sank like s beneath the mighty waters.
Est 1: 6 marble, mother-of-pearl, and other costly s.
Job 5:23 You will be at peace with the s of the field, and its
14:19 as water wears away the s and floods wash away
28:10 cut tunnels in the rocks and uncover precious s.
41:28 S shot from a sling are as ineffective as straw.
Ps 147:17 He hurls the hail like s. / Who can stand against his
Ecc 3: 5 A time to scatter s and a time to gather s.
10: 9 you work in a quarry, s might fall and crush you!
Isa 5: 2 He plowed the land, cleared its s, / and planted it
57: 6 Your gods are the smooth s in the valleys.
57:14 Clear away the rocks and s so my people can
60:17 your wood for bronze, and your s for iron.
Jer 43: 9 bury large rocks between the pavement s at the
43:10 I will set his throne on these s that I have hidden.
51:26 Even your s will never again be used for building.
La 3:53 They threw me into a pit and dropped s on me.
Eze 26:12 and dump your s and timbers and even your dust
28:14 mountain of God and walked among the s of fire.
28:16 from your place among the s of fire.
Da 11:38 on him gold, silver, precious s, and costly gifts.
Mic 1: 6 I will roll the s of her walls down into the valley
Na 3:10 Her babies were dashed to death against the s of
Hab 2:11 The very s in the walls of your houses cry out
Zec 5: 4 is completely destroyed—even its timbers and s."
9:15 and they will subdue their enemies with sling s.
Mt 3: 9 God can change these s here into children of
4: 3 Son of God, change these s into loaves of bread."
23:37 that kills the prophets and s God's messengers!
Mk 5: 5 in the hills, screaming and hitting himself with s.
13: 1 Look at the massive s in the walls!"
Lk 3: 8 God can change these s here into children of
13:34 that kills the prophets and s God's messengers!
19:40 the s along the road would burst into cheers!"
Jn 8: 7 let those who have never sinned throw the first s!"
8:59 At that point they picked up s to kill him. But Jesus
10:31 Once again the Jewish leaders picked up s to kill
1Pe 2: 5 building you, as living s, into his spiritual temple.
Rev 18:16 decked out with gold and precious s and pearls!
21:14 The wall of the city had twelve foundation s,
21:19 The wall of the city was built on foundation s

STONEWORK (2) [STONE]

2Ch 2:14 He also knows all about s, carpentry, and weaving.
Lk 21: 5 began talking about the beautiful s of the Temple

STONING (4) [STONE]

Lev 20:27 as mediums or psychics must be put to death by s.
Nu 14:10 But the whole community began to talk about s
1Sa 30: 6 and children, and they began to talk of s him.
Heb 11:37 Some died by s, and some were sawed in half;

STONY (2) [STONE]

Jer 17: 1 inscribed with a diamond point on their s hearts,
Eze 36:26 I will take out your s heart of sin and give you a

STOOD (184) [STAND]

Ge 19: 1 When he saw them, he s up to meet them. Then he
19:27 and hurried out to the place where he had s in the
28:13 At the top of the stairway s the LORD, and he
37: 7 My bundle s up, and then your bundles all gathered
41: 3 These cows went over and s beside the fat cows.
41:14 of clothes, he went in and s in Pharaoh's presence.
Ex 2: 4 The baby's sister then s at a distance, watching to
14:29 as the water s up like a wall on both sides.
15: 8 The surging waters s straight like a wall;
17:12 Then they s on each side, holding up his hands
19:17 with God, and they s at the foot of the mountain.
20:18 they s at a distance, trembling with fear.
20:21 As the people s in the distance, Moses entered into
32:26 he s at the entrance to the camp and shouted,
34: 5 "the LORD," as Moses s there in his presence.
Lev 9: 5 and s there in the LORD's presence.
Nu 12: 5 of cloud and s at the entrance of the Tabernacle.
13:30 But Caleb tried to encourage the people as they s
16:18 and s at the entrance of the Tabernacle with Moses
16:27 So all the people s back from the tents of Korah,
16:27 and s at the entrances of their tents with their wives
16:43 and s at the entrance of the Tabernacle,
16:48 He s between the living and the dead until the
22:24 Then the angel of the LORD s at a place where
22:26 and s in a place so narrow that the donkey could
27: 2 These women went and s before Moses,
Dt 4:10 Tell them especially about the day when you s
4:11 You came near and s at the foot of the mountain,
5: 5 I s as an intermediary between you
Jos 3:17 s on dry ground in the middle of the riverbed as the
4:10 The priests who were carrying the Ark s in the
8:33 One group s at the foot of Mount Gerizim,
8:33 and between them s the Levitical priests carrying
10:13 and moon s still until the Israelites had defeated
Jdg 4: 5 which s between Ramah and Bethel in the hill
7:21 Each man s at his position around the camp
18:16 As the six hundred warriors from the tribe of Dan s
20: 1 and s in the presence of the LORD at Mizpah.
20: 8 And all the people s up together and replied,
1Sa 1:26 "I am the woman who s here several years ago
10:23 and he s head and shoulders above anyone else.
16:13 So as David s there among his brothers,
17: 8 Goliath s and shouted across to the Israelites,
17:21 and Philistine forces s facing each other,
2Sa 2:23 and s still when they saw Asahel lying there.
7:23 drove out the nations and gods that s in their way.
18: 4 So he s at the gate of the city as all the divisions of
23: 9 and David s together against the Philistines when
1Ki 1:28 So she came back in and s before the king.
3:15 and s before the Ark of the Lord's covenant,
8:22 Then Solomon s with his hands lifted toward
8:54 he s up in front of the altar of the LORD,
8:55 He s there and shouted this blessing over the entire
18:21 Then Elijah s in front of them and said, "How long
19:11 And as Elijah s there, the LORD passed by,
19:13 and went out and s at the entrance of the cave.
2Ki 4:15 Elisha said to her as she s in the doorway,
5:15 They s before him, and Naaman said, "I know at
16:14 which had s between the entrance and the new
18:28 Then he s and shouted in Hebrew to the people on
19:11 They have crushed everyone who s in their way!
23:16 God as Jeroboam s beside the altar at the festival.
1Ch 17:21 and drove out the nations that s in their way.
23:30 and evening they s before the LORD to sing
28: 2 David rose and s before them and addressed them
29:25 so the entire nation of Israel s in awe of him,
2Ch 3:13 They both s and faced out toward the main room of
5:12 and s at the east side of the altar playing cymbals,
6:12 Then Solomon s with his hands spread out before
6:13 He s on the platform before the entire assembly,
7: 6 the priests blew the trumpets, while all Israel s.
13: 4 Abijah s on Mount Zemaraim and shouted to
15: 8 which s in front of the foyer of the LORD's
20: 5 Jehoshaphat s before the people of Judah
20:13 As all the men of Judah s before the LORD with
20:19 clans of Kohath and Korah s to praise the LORD,
24:20 He s before the people and said, "This is what God
30:27 Then the Levitical priests s and blessed the people,
33:15 altars he had built on the hill where the Temple s
Ezr 9: 5 I s up from where I had sat in mourning with my
10: 5 So Ezra s up and demanded that the leaders of the
10:10 Then Ezra the priest s and said to them:
Ne 4:16 only half my men worked while the other half s
8: 4 Ezra the scribe s on a high wooden platform that
8: 4 To his right s Mattithiah, Shema, Anaiah, Uriah,
8: 4 To his left s Pedaiah, Mishael, Malkijah, Hashum,
8: 5 Ezra s on the platform in full view of all the
12: 9 and Unni, s opposite them during the service.
12:24 who s opposite them during the ceremonies of
Est 1: 6 and silver couches s on a mosaic pavement of
4: 2 He s outside the gate of the palace, for no one was
8: 4 scepter to Esther. So she rose and s before him
Job 1:20 Job s up and tore his robe in grief. Then he shaved
29: 9 The princes s in silence and put their hands over
29:10 The highest officials of the city s quietly,
Ps 35:27 who have s with me in my defense. / Let them
39: 2 But as I s there in silence— / not even speaking of
76: 6 O God of Jacob, / their horses and chariots s still.
76: 8 the earth trembled and s silent before you.
78:13 The water s up like walls beside them!
Isa 21: 8 "Day after day I have s on the watchtower,
36:13 Then he s and shouted in Hebrew to the people on
37:11 They have crushed everyone who s in their way!
Jer 15: 1 and Samuel s before me pleading for these people,
26: 9 And all the people threatened him as he s in front
26:17 Then some of the wise old men s and spoke to the
26:24 Ahikam son of Shaphan also s with Jeremiah
28: 5 Jeremiah responded to Hananiah as they s in front
36:21 and read it to the king as all his officials s by.
Eze 1:25 As they s with their wings lowered, a voice spoke
8: 5 s the idol that had made the LORD so angry.
9: 2 the Temple courtyard and s beside the bronze altar.
10: 6 So the man went in and s beside one of the wheels.
10:17 When the cherubim s still, the wheels also stopped,
19:11 It s out because of its height / and because of its
27: 7 You s beneath blue and purple awnings made
27:11 and from Helech s on your walls as sentinels.
37:10 They all came to life and s up on their feet—
40:47 The altar s there in the courtyard in front of the
41:12 A large building s on the west, facing the Temple
42: 3 three levels high and s across from each other.
Da 2: 2 what he had dreamed. As they s before the king,
7:10 to him, and a hundred million s to attend him.
8:15 someone who looked like a man suddenly s in
10:11 he said this to me, I s up, still trembling with fear.
Ob 1:11 You s aloof, refusing to lift a finger to help when
1:14 You shouldn't have s at the crossroads,
Zec 3: 3 Jeshua's clothing was filthy as he s there before the
3: 5 in new clothes while the angel of the LORD s by.
Mal 2: 5 they greatly revered me and s in awe of my name.
Mt 8:26 Then he s up and rebuked the wind and waves,
9:25 went in and took the girl by the hand, and she s up!
25:11 they s outside, calling, 'Sir, open the door for us!'
26:62 Then the high priest s up and said to Jesus, "Well,
Mk 3:31 They s outside and sent word for him to come out
5:42 years old, immediately s up and walked around!
9:27 by the hand and helped him to his feet, and he s up.
14:57 some men s up to testify against him with this lie:
14:60 Then the high priest s up before the others
15:39 When the Roman officer who s facing him saw
Lk 1:10 was being burned, a great crowd s outside, praying.
4:16 on the Sabbath and s up to read the Scriptures.
6:17 the disciples s with Jesus on a large, level area,
8:55 her life returned, and she immediately s up!
10:25 One day an expert in religious law s up to test
17:12 he entered a village there, ten lepers s at a distance,
18:11 The proud Pharisee s by himself and prayed this
18:13 "But the tax collector s at a distance and dared not
19: 8 Zacchaeus s there and said to the Lord,
22:45 At last he s up again and returned to the disciples,
23:10 and the teachers of religious law s there shouting
23:49 him from Galilee, s at a distance watching.
24:41 Still they s there doubting, filled with joy
Jn 7:37 Jesus s and shouted to the crowds, "If you are
8: 7 so he s up again and said, "All right, stone her.
8:10 Then Jesus s up again and said to her, "Where are
18:16 Peter s outside the gate. Then the other disciple
18:18 And Peter s there with them, warming himself.
Ac 1:10 two white-robed men suddenly s there among
1:15 Peter s up and addressed them as follows:
2:12 They s there amazed and perplexed. "What can
3: 8 He jumped up, s on his feet, and began to walk!
3:11 Everyone s there in awe of the wonderful thing that
5:34 He s up and ordered that the apostles be sent
9: 7 The men with Saul s speechless with surprise,
10:17 found the house and s outside at the gate.
11:28 One of them named Agabus s up in one of the
12: 7 in the cell, and an angel of the Lord s before Peter.
13:16 So Paul s, lifted his hand to quiet them, and started
14:20 But as the believers s around him, he got up
15: 5 had been Pharisees before their conversion s up
15: 7 Peter s and addressed them as follows:
15:13 James s and said, "Brothers, listen to me.
21:40 so Paul s on the stairs and motioned to the people
22:13 He came to me and s beside me and said,
26:30 the governor, Bernice, and all the others s and left.
27:23 to whom I belong and whom I serve s beside me,
2Ti 4:17 But the Lord s with me and gave me strength,
Rev 8: 3 with a gold incense burner came and s at the altar.
10: 2 He s with his right foot on the sea and his left foot
11:11 spirit of life from God entered them, and they s up!
12: 4 He s before the woman as she was about to give
12:18 Then he s waiting on the shore of the sea.
15: 2 And on it s all the people who had been victorious

STOOPED (5) [STOOPING, STOOPS]

Hos 11: 4 the yoke from his neck, and I myself s to feed him.
Jn 8: 6 but Jesus s down and wrote in the dust with his
8: 8 Then he s down again and wrote in the dust.
20: 5 He s and looked in and saw the linen cloth lying
20:11 tomb crying, and as she wept, she s and looked in.

STOOPING (1) [STOOPED]

Lk 24:12 S, he peered in and saw the empty linen

STOOPS (1) [STOOPED]

Ps 113: 6 him are the heavens and the earth. / He s to look,

STOP (189) [STOPPED, STOPPING, STOPS]

Ge 13: 8 arguing between our herdsmen has got to s,"
18: 3 he said, "if it pleases you, s here for a while.
19:17 angels warned. "Do not s anywhere in the valley.
29: 7 "They'll be hungry if you s so early in the day."
44: 4 household manager, "Chase after them and s them.
Ex 9:29 to the LORD. Then the thunder and hail will s.
23: 5 do not walk by. Instead, s and offer to help.
40:32 they were to s and wash, just as the LORD had
Lev 17: 5 This rule will s the Israelites from sacrificing
23: 3 seventh day all work must come to a complete s.
23: 7 all the people must s their regular work and gather
23: 8 the people must again s all their regular work to
23:21 you must s all your regular work and gather for a
23:24 of complete rest. All your work must s on that day.
23:35 on the first day, and all your regular work must s.
Nu 10:33 moving ahead of them to show them where to s
11:28 protested, "Moses, my master, make them s!"
22:16 Please don't let anything s you from coming.
30:11 If her husband hears of it and does nothing to s her,
Dt 10:16 cleanse your sinful hearts and s being stubborn.
Jos 3: 8 take a few steps into the river and s.' "
22:25 And your descendants may make our descendants s
Jdg 15: 7 revenge on you, and I won't s until I'm satisfied!"
17: 8 He happened to s at Micah's house as he was
20:28 relatives from Benjamin again or should we s?"
1Sa 2: 3 "S acting so proud and haughty! / Don't speak
2:24 You must s, my sons! The reports I hear among the
6: 3 "Send a guilt offering so the plague will s. Then, if
the plague doesn't s, you will know that
6: 5 Perhaps then he will s afflicting you, your gods,
14: 9 kill you,' then we will s and not go up to them.
15:16 Then Samuel said to Saul, "S! Listen to what the
27: 1 Then Saul will s hunting for me, and I will finally
2Sa 2:29 and they did not s until they arrived at Mahanaim.
14: 6 And since no one was there to s it, one of them was
15:28 I will s at the shallows of the Jordan River and wait
16:10 has told him to curse me, who am I to s him?"
22:38 I did not s until they were conquered.
24:16 the LORD relented and said to the angel, "S!
24:21 so that the LORD will s the plague."
1Ki 18:44 If you don't hurry, the rain will s you!' "
2Ki 3:19 will cut down all their trees, s up all their springs,
4: 8 he passed that way, he would s there to eat.
1Ch 21:15 LORD relented and said to the death angel, "S!
21:22 to the LORD there, so that he will s the plague."
2Ch 20:12 O our God, won't you s them? We are powerless
32: 3 and they decided to s the flow of the springs
32: 4 They organized a huge work crew to s the flow of
34:25 against this place, and nothing will be able to s it.'
Ezr 4:21 issue orders to have these people s their work.
4:23 to Jerusalem and forced the Jews to s building.
Ne 5:10 and grain, but now let us s this business of loans.
6: 3 I cannot s to come and meet with you."
6: 9 that they could break our resolve and s the work.
9:20 and you did not s giving them bread from heaven
Est 8: 3 and begging him with tears to s Haman's evil plot
Job 4: 7 "S and think! Does the innocent person perish?
6:19 caravans from Tema and from Sheba s for water,
6:29 S assuming my guilt, for I am righteous. Don't be
9:12 death to snatch someone away, who can s him?
9:34 The mediator could make God s beating me,
11:10 he calls the court to order, who is going to s him?
16: 3 Won't you ever s your flow of foolish words?
18: 2 "How long before you s talking? Speak sense if
22:21 "S quarreling with God! If you agree with him,
34:32 evil I have done; tell me, and I will s at once'?
37:14 s and consider the wonderful miracles of God!
38:11 will you come. Here your proud waves must s!'
41:26 No sword can s it, nor spear nor dart nor pointed
42: 2 that you can do anything, and no one can s you.
Ps 12: 4 Our lips are our own—who can s us?"
18:37 I did not s until they were conquered.
30: 6 was prosperous I said, / "Nothing can s me now!"
37: 8 S your anger! / Turn from your rage! / Do not envy
55: 5 and trembling overwhelm me. / I can't s shaking.
71: 8 That is why I can never s praising you; / I declare
75: 4 "I warned the proud, 'S your boasting!' / I told the
77:12 in my thoughts. / I cannot s thinking about them.
89:33 But I will never s loving him, / nor let my promise
119:109 in the balance, / but I will not s obeying your law.
139: 3 path ahead of me / and tell me where to s and rest.
Pr 15:18 a cool-tempered person tries to s them.
19:27 If you s listening to instruction, my child, you have
27:16 Trying to s her complaints is like trying to s the
Isa 2: 4 All wars will s, and military training will come to
2:22 S putting your trust in mere humans. They are as
6:12 Do not s until the LORD has sent everyone away
7: 4 Tell him to s worrying. Tell him he doesn't need to
7:21 When they finally s plundering, a farmer will be
14:27 his plans? When his hand moves, who can s him?"
42: 4 He will not s until truth and righteousness prevail
45: 9 who shapes it, saying, 'S, you are doing it wrong!'
58: 6 and to s oppressing those who work for you.
58: 9 "S oppressing the helpless and s making false
accusations
62: 1 I will not s praying for her until her righteousness
Jer 2:25 these foreign gods, and I can't s loving them now!'
6:16 So now the LORD says, "S right where you are!
7: 5 I will be merciful only if you s your wicked
7: 6 and if you s exploiting foreigners, orphans, and
widows; and if you s your murdering;
7: 6 and if you s worshiping idols as you now do to
11:21 They said they would kill me if I did not s
14:17 I cannot s weeping, for my virgin daughter—
17:21 S carrying on your trade at Jerusalem's gates on
18:18 "Come on, let's find a way to s Jeremiah.
20: 9 And I can't s! If I say I'll never mention the
22: 3 orphans, and widows. S murdering the innocent!
23:36 But s using this phrase, 'prophecy from the
26:13 But if you s your sinning and begin to obey the
29:27 So why have you done nothing to s Jeremiah from
32:40 with them, promising not to s doing good for them.
35:15 your wicked ways and to s worshiping other gods,
38: 5 "Do as you like. I will do nothing to s you."

41:12 they took all their men and set out to s him.
La 3:49 My tears flow down endlessly. They will not s
Eze 12:23 end to this proverb, and you will soon s quoting it.
14:6 from your idols, and s all your loathsome practices.
16:41 I will see to it that you s your prostitution and end
20:39 to me. Such desecration of my holy name must s!
23:27 I will put a s to the lewdness and prostitution you
26:13 I will s the music of your songs. No more will the
37:23 They will s polluting themselves with their
45:9 S all your violence and oppression and do what is
45:9 of their land! S expelling them from their homes!
Da 4:27 please listen to me. S sinning and do what is right.
4:35 No one can s him or challenge him, / saying,
8:13 that causes desecration s the daily sacrifices?
11:16 onward unopposed; none will be able to s him.
11:31 the sanctuary, putting a s to the daily sacrifices,
Hos 2:2 suggestive clothing and to s playing the prostitute.
3:3 in my house for many days and s your prostitution.
Joel 2:8 lunge through the gaps, and no weapon can s them.
Am 7:16 against Israel. S preaching against my people.'
Jnh 1:11 "What should we do to you to s this storm?"
3:8 turn from their evil ways and s all their violence.
3:10 When God saw that they had put a s to their evil
Mic 4:3 All wars will s, and military training will come to
Na 2:8 "S, s!" someone shouts, but the people just
Hab 1:7 They do as they like, and no one can s them.
Zec 1:4 from your evil ways and s all your evil practices.'
8:17 And s this habit of swearing to things that are false.
Mt 7:1 "S judging others, and you will not be judged.
19:14 "Let the children come to me. Don't s them!
Mk 9:38 but we told him to s because he isn't one of our
9:39 "Don't s him!" Jesus said. "No one who performs
10:14 "Let the children come to me. Don't s them!
Lk 6:37 "S judging others, and you will not be judged.
6:37 S criticizing others, or it will all come back on you.
8:52 and wailing, but he said, "S the weeping!
9:49 We tried to s him because he isn't in our group."
9:50 But Jesus said, "Don't s him! Anyone who is not
10:4 And don't s to greet anyone on the road.
18:16 "Let the children come to me. Don't s them!
Jn 5:14 so s sinning, or something even worse may happen
Ac 4:17 But perhaps we can s them from spreading their
4:20 We cannot s telling about the wonderful things we
5:39 But if it is of God, you will not be able to s them.
8:38 He ordered the carriage to s, and they went down
13:10 will you never s perverting the true ways of the
15:19 so my judgment is that we should s troubling the
18:22 The next s was at the port of Caesarea. From there
21:7 The next s after leaving Tyre was Ptolemais,
28:12 Our first s was Syracuse, where we stayed three
28:31 the Lord Jesus Christ. And no one tried to s him.
Ro 11:22 But if you s trusting, you also will be cut off.
15:24 to go to Spain, and when I do, I will s off in Rome.
1Co 1:4 I can never s thanking God for all the generous
1:10 Lord Jesus Christ to s arguing among yourselves.
3:18 S fooling yourselves. If you think you are wise by
14:30 from the Lord, the one who is speaking must s.
15:34 Come to your senses and s sinning. For to your
2Co 1:16 I wanted to s and see you on my way to Macedonia
11:10 I will never s boasting about this all over Greece.
Eph 4:28 If you are a thief, s stealing. Begin using your
6:16 shield to s the fiery arrows aimed at you by Satan.
1Th 2:13 And we will never s thanking God that when we
1Ti 1:3 and s those who are teaching wrong doctrine.
2Ti 2:14 and command them in God's name to s fighting
Tit 1:14 They must s listening to Jewish myths
Heb 4:14 Let us cling to him and never s trusting him.
6:1 So let us s going over the basics of Christianity
12:19 so terrible that they begged God to s speaking.
1Pe 4:1 to suffer for Christ, you have decided to s sinning.
1Jn 2:15 S loving this evil world and all that it offers you,
3:18 let us s just saying we love each other;
Rev 5:5 of the twenty-four elders said to me, "S weeping!

STOPPED (83) [STOP]

Ge 8:2 ceased their gushing, and the torrential rains s.
11:31 But they s instead at the village of Haran
28:11 good place to set up camp and s there for the night.
29:35 the LORD!" And then she s having children.
38:16 So he s and propositioned her to sleep with him,
42:27 But when they s for the night and one of them
43:21 we s for the night and opened our sacks.
Ex 4:24 when Moses and his family had s for the night,
9:33 all at once the thunder and hail s,
12:39 Whenever they s to eat, they baked bread from the
36:6 So the people s bringing their offerings.
Lev 13:37 But if it appears that the infection has s spreading
15:3 applies whether the discharge continues or is s up.
Nu 9:18 and s wherever he told them to.
10:12 and traveled on in stages until the cloud s in the
11:2 and when he prayed to the LORD, the fire s.
16:48 the living and the dead until the plague was s.
16:50 Then because the plague had s, Aaron returned to
25:8 So the plague against the Israelites was s,
25:11 So I have s destroying all Israel as I had intended
33:2 identified by the different places they s along the
Jos 4:7 'They remind us that the Jordan River s flowing
10:13 The sun s in the middle of the sky, and it did not
Jdg 19:15 so they s there to spend the night. They rested in
Ru 1:18 made up her mind to go with her, she s urging her.
1Sa 6:14 of a man named Joshua and s beside a large rock.
27:4 David had fled to Gath, so he s hunting for him.
2Sa 2:23 And everyone who came by that spot s and stood
2:28 and his men s chasing the troops of Israel.
6:13 they s and waited so David could sacrifice an ox
12:21 you have s your mourning and are eating again."
21:10 and s wild animals from eating them at night.
24:25 LORD answered his prayer, and the plague was s.
1Ki 22:33 was not the king of Israel, and they s chasing him.
2Ki 2:7 as Elijah and Elisha s beside the Jordan River.
3:25 s up the springs, and cut down the good trees.
4:6 he told her. And then the olive oil s flowing.
18:17 The Assyrians s beside the aqueduct that feeds
19:24 I even s up the rivers of Egypt / so that my armies
2Ch 18:32 he was not the king of Israel, they s chasing him.
20:20 On the way Jehoshaphat s and said, "Listen to me,
29:7 They s burning incense and presenting burnt
Ezr 4:24 work on the Temple of God in Jerusalem had s,
Ne 12:39 on to the Sheep Gate and s at the Guard Gate.
Job 4:16 It s, but I couldn't see its shape. There was a form
Ps 32:5 and s trying to hide them. / I said to myself, "I will
106:30 had the courage to step in, / and the plague was s.
SS 3:3 The watchmen s me as they made their rounds,
Isa 36:2 The Assyrians s beside the aqueduct that feeds
37:25 I even s up the rivers of Egypt / so that my armies
Jer 19:14 and he s in front of the Temple of the LORD.
40:12 They s at Mizpah to discuss their plans with
44:18 to the Queen of Heaven and s worshiping her,
Eze 1:21 When the living beings s, the wheels s.
1:24 When they s, they let down their wings.
10:17 When the cherubim stood still, the wheels also s,
11:23 from the city and s above the mountain to the east.
Jnh 1:15 him into the raging sea, and the storm s at once!
Mt 2:9 of them and s over the place where the child was.
14:32 when they climbed back into the boat, the wind s.
20:32 Jesus s in the road and called, "What do you want
Mk 4:39 Suddenly the wind s, and there was a great calm.
5:29 Immediately the bleeding s, and she could feel that
5:37 Then Jesus s the crowd and wouldn't let anyone go
6:51 Then he climbed into the boat, and the wind s.
10:49 When Jesus heard him, he s and said, "Tell him to
11:16 and he s everyone from bringing in merchandise.
Lk 4:41 the Messiah, he s them and told them to be silent.
7:14 over to the coffin and touched it, and the bearers s.
8:24 the raging waves. The storm s and all was calm!
8:44 the fringe of his robe. Immediately, the bleeding s.
16:26 to cross over to you from here is s at its edge,
18:40 he s and ordered that the man be brought to him.
24:17 They s short, sadness written across their faces.
Jn 11:54 Jesus s his public ministry among the people
Ac 8:25 And they s in many Samaritan villages along the
15:3 and they s along the way in Phoenicia and Samaria
21:32 and the troops coming, they s beating Paul.
2Co 5:16 So we have s evaluating others by what the world
Eph 1:16 I have never s thanking God for you. I pray for you
Heb 10:2 perfect cleansing, the sacrifices would have s,
2Pe 2:16 But Balaam was s from his mad course when his

STOPPING (5) [STOP]

Ex 5:5 and you are s them from doing their work."
Ru 2:15 gather grain right among the sheaves without s her.
Isa 5:27 They will run without s for rest or sleep.
Jer 14:8 passing through the land, s only for the night?
Ac 20:16 Paul had decided against s at Ephesus this time

STOPS (11) [STOP]

Lev 15:28 "When the woman's menstrual discharge s,
2Ki 4:9 "I am sure this man who s in from time to time is a
Job 37:7 Everyone s working at such a time so they can
38:15 and it s the arm that is raised in violence.
Ps 146:4 When their breathing s, they return to the earth,
Pr 26:20 lack of fuel, and quarrels disappear when gossip s.
Isa 10:32 But the enemy s at Nob for the rest of that day.
44:19 The person who made the idol never s to reflect,
Hab 3:6 When he s, the earth shakes. When he looks,
Jn 5:17 But Jesus replied, "My Father never s working,
Ac 27:2 it was scheduled to make several s at ports along

STORAGE (3) [STORE]

Ne 13:5 had converted a large s room and placed it at
Eze 4:9 millet, and spelt, and mix them together in a s jar.
Joel 3:13 The s vats are overflowing with the wickedness of

STORE (27) [STORAGE, STORED, STOREHOUSE, STOREHOUSES, STOREROOMS, STORES, STORING]

Ge 37:24 This pit was normally used to s water, but it was
41:35 and s it away so there will be food in the cities.
Ex 16:33 Then s it in a sacred place as a reminder for all
Lev 25:5 And don't s away the crops that grow naturally
25:11 or s away any of the crops that grow naturally,
Nu 23:21 is in sight for Jacob; / no trouble is in s for Israel.
Dt 14:28 tithe of all your crops and s it in the nearest town.
2Ch 16:4 Abel-beth-maacah, and all the s cities in Naphtali.
17:12 and built fortresses and s cities throughout Judah.
Ne 10:37 We will s the produce in the storerooms of the
Job 22:22 Listen to his instructions, and s them in your heart.
27:16 and they may s away mounds of clothing.
Pr 3:1 I have taught you. S my commands in your heart,
5:2 will learn to be discreet and will s up knowledge.
30:25 aren't strong, / but they s up food for the winter.
Isa 22:9 to be repaired. You s up water in the lower pool.
33:6 providing a rich s of salvation, wisdom,
Jer 40:10 and summer fruits and olives, and s them away."
Eze 42:13 And they will use these rooms to s the grain
Na 3:14 Get ready for the siege! S up water!
Mt 6:19 "Don't s up treasures here on earth, where they
6:20 S your treasures in heaven, where they will never
22:5 their business, one to his farm, another to his s.
Lk 12:18 Then I'll have room enough to s everything.
12:21 a person is a fool to s up earthly wealth but not
12:33 in need. This will s up treasure for you in heaven!
17:2 in s for harming one of these little ones.

STORED (20) [STORE]

Ge 41:48 and s them for the government in nearby cities.
Ex 7:19 even the water s in wooden bowls and stone pots in
1Sa 17:54 but he s the Philistine's armor in his own tent.)
1Ki 7:51 and he s them in the treasuries of the LORD's
2Ki 11:10 and were s in the Temple of the LORD.
18:15 King Hezekiah used all the silver s in the Temple
20:17 all the treasures s up by your ancestors—will be
2Ch 5:1 These were s in the treasuries of the Temple of
11:11 of them, he s supplies of food, olive oil, and wine.
17:13 He s numerous supplies in Judah's towns
23:9 to King David and were s in the Temple of God.
Ezr 6:1 in the Babylonian archives, where treasures were s.
Job 38:22 Have you seen where the hail is made and s?
Ps 31:19 You have s up great blessings for those who honor
SS 7:13 as old, for I have s them up for you, my lover."
Isa 39:6 all the treasures s up by your ancestors—will be
Hos 13:12 have been collected and s away for punishment.
Mt 9:17 the skins. New wine must be s in new wineskins.
Lk 2:51 and his mother s all these things in her heart.
12:19 you have enough s away for years to come.

STOREHOUSE (2) [HOUSE, STORE]

Mal 3:10 Bring all the tithes into the s so there will be
Mt 13:52 out of the s the new teachings as well as the old."

STOREHOUSES (10) [HOUSE, STORE]

Ge 41:35 and grain of these good years into the royal s,
41:54 but in Egypt there was plenty of grain in the s.
41:56 Joseph opened up the s and sold grain to the
Dt 28:8 everything you do and will fill your s with grain.
1Ch 26:15 and his sons were put in charge of the s.
26:17 four to the south gate, and two to each of the s.
2Ch 32:28 He also constructed many s for his grain,
Ps 135:7 with the rain / and releases the wind from his s.
Jer 10:13 with the rain / and releases the wind from his s.
51:16 with the rain / and releases the wind from his s.

STOREROOMS (10) [ROOM, STORE]

1Ch 26:20 of the treasuries of the house of God and the s.
2Ch 31:11 Hezekiah decided to have s prepared in the Temple
Ezr 8:29 and the leaders of Israel at the s of the LORD's
Ne 10:37 We will store the produce in the s of the Temple of
10:38 to the Temple of our God and placed in the s.
12:25 and Akkub were the gatekeepers in charge of the s
12:44 appointed to be in charge of the s for the gifts,
13:4 who had been appointed as supervisor of the s of
13:12 of grain, new wine, and olive oil to the Temple s.
13:13 and Pedaiah, one of the Levites, in charge of the s.

STORES (2) [STORE]

Jer 41:8 go by promising to bring him their s of wheat,
Lk 16:9 your generosity s up a reward for you in heaven.

STORIES (24) [STORY]

Ex 10:2 You will be able to tell wonderful s to your
1Ki 6:6 The complex was three s high, the bottom floor
2Ki 8:4 "Tell me some s about the great things Elisha has
Ps 78:3 s we have heard and know, / s our ancestors handed down to us.
Am 9:6 The upper s of the LORD's home are in the
Mt 13:3 He told many s such as this one: "A farmer went
13:10 "Why do you always tell s when you talk to the
13:13 That is why I tell these s, because people see what
13:34 Jesus always used s and illustrations like these
13:53 When Jesus had finished telling these s, he left that
22:1 Jesus told them several other s to illustrate the
Mk 4:2 He began to teach the people by telling many s
4:10 they asked him, "What do your s mean?"
4:11 But I am using these s to conceal everything about
4:33 He used many such s and illustrations to teach the
12:1 Then Jesus began telling them s: "A man planted a
14:59 But even then they didn't get their s straight!
Lk 8:10 But I am using these s to conceal everything about
9:9 is this man about whom I hear such strange s?"
Ac 20:9 a deep sleep and fell three s to his death below.
Eph 5:4 Obscene s, foolish talk, and coarse jokes—
Heb 11:32 It would take too long to recount the s of the faith
2Pe 1:16 For we were not making up clever s when we told

STORING (7) [STORE]

Dt 32:34 " 'I am s up these things, / sealing them away
Ne 13:5 The room had previously been used for s the grain
Isa 10:28 They are s some of their equipment at Micmash.
Mt 3:12 s the grain in his barn but burning the chaff with
Lk 3:17 s the grain in his barn but burning the chaff with
Ro 2:5 So you are s up terrible punishment for yourself
1Ti 6:19 By doing this they will be s up their treasure as a

STORK (5) [STORKS]

Lev 11:19 the s, herons of all kinds, the hoopoe, and the bat.
Dt 14:18 the s, herons of all kinds, the hoopoe, and the bat.
Job 39:13 but they are no match for the feathers of the s.
Jer 8:7 The s knows the time of her migration, as do the
Zec 5:9 Their wings were like those of a s, and they picked

STORKS (1) [STORK]

Ps 104:17 their nests, / and the s make their homes in the firs.

STORM (51) [RAINSTORM, SNOWSTORM, STORM-BATTERED, STORMED, STORMS, STORMY, THUNDERSTORMS, WINDSTORM]

Ex 9:24 Never in all the history of Egypt had there been a **s**
19:16 there was a powerful thunder and lightning **s**,
Jdg 9:33 In the morning, as soon as it is daylight, **s** the city.
2Sa 22:10 came down; / dark **s** clouds were beneath his feet.
Job 21:18 Are they carried away by the **s**? Not at all!
24:20 Wicked people are broken like a tree in the **s**.
30:22 me into the whirlwind and destroy me in the **s**.
36:33 his presence; the **s** announces his indignant anger.
37:15 Do you know how God controls the **s** and causes
Ps 18:9 came down; / dark **s** clouds were beneath his feet.
50:3 in his way, / and a great **s** rages around him.
55:8 far away from this wild **s** of hatred.
57:1 shadow of your wings / until this violent **s** is past.
107:29 He calmed the **s** to a whisper / and stilled the
148:8 fire and hail, snow and **s**, / wind and weather that
Pr 1:27 when calamity overcomes you like a **s**, when you
Isa 7:2 trembled with fear, just as trees shake in a **s**.
17:13 by the wind or like dust whirling before a **s**.
24:20 It trembles like a tent in a **s**. It falls and will not
25:4 to the poor, O LORD, you are a refuge from the **s**.
25:4 ruthless people are like a **s** beating against a wall,
27:8 her land as though blown away in a **s** from the east.
29:6 with whirlwind and **s** and consuming fire.
32:2 He will shelter Israel from the **s** and the wind.
38:12 like a shepherd's tent in a **s**. / It has been cut short,
Jer 4:13 Our enemy rushes down on us like a **s** wind!
23:19 The LORD's anger bursts out like a **s**,
30:23 The LORD's anger bursts out like a **s**, a driving
49:23 hearts are troubled like a wild sea in a raging **s**.
Eze 1:4 I saw a great **s** coming toward me from the north,
13:13 I will sweep away your whitewashed wall with a **s**
38:9 will roll down on them like a **s** and cover the land
Da 7:2 saw a great **s** churning the surface of a great sea,
11:40 and the king of the north will **s** out against him
Am 1:14 the battle, swirling like a whirlwind in a mighty **s**.
Jnh 1:4 causing a violent **s** that threatened to send them to
1:7 had offended the gods and caused the terrible **s**.
1:8 "What have you done to bring this awful **s** down
1:11 And since the **s** was getting worse all the time,
1:11 "What should we do to you to stop this **s**?"
1:12 For I know that this terrible **s** is all my fault."
1:14 you have sent this **s** upon him for your own good
1:15 him into the raging sea, and the **s** stopped at once!
Na 1:3 He displays his power in the whirlwind and the **s**.
Zec 10:1 It is the LORD who makes **s** clouds that drop
Mt 8:24 Suddenly, a terrible **s** came up, with waves
Mk 4:37 But soon a fierce **s** arose. High waves began to
Lk 8:23 A fierce **s** developed that threatened to swamp
8:24 the raging waves. The **s** stopped and all was calm!
Ac 27:20 The terrible **s** raged unabated for many days,
27:27 About midnight on the fourteenth night of the **s**,

STORM-BATTERED (1) [BATTER, STORM]

Isa 54:11 "O **s** city, troubled and desolate! I will rebuild you

STORMED (1) [STORM]

Jdg 9:44 and his group **s** the city gate to keep the men of

STORMS (4) [STORM]

Job 27:20 and they are blown away in the **s** of the night.
Ps 83:15 chase them with your fierce **s**; / terrify them with
89:9 When their waves rise in fearful **s**, you subdue
Isa 4:6 daytime heat and a hiding place from **s** and rain.

STORMY (4) [STORM]

Job 37:9 The **s** wind comes from its chamber,
Jnh 1:13 But the **s** sea was too violent for them, and they
2:3 I was buried beneath your wild and **s** waves.
2Co 11:26 in the cities, in the deserts, and on the **s** seas.

STORY (56) [STORIES]

Ge 24:30 and when he heard her **s**, he rushed out to the
24:66 Then the servant told Isaac the whole **s**.
29:13 then brought him home, and Jacob told him his **s**.
39:17 she told him her **s**. "That Hebrew slave you've had
39:19 After hearing his wife's **s**, Potiphar was furious!
42:15 This is how I will test your **s**. I swear by the life of
42:16 Then we'll find out whether or not your **s** is true.
Jdg 8:28 That is the **s** of how Israel subdued Midian,
2Sa 12:1 sent Nathan the prophet to tell David this **s**:
14:3 the king and tell him the **s** I am about to tell you."
1Ki 6:10 Each **s** of the complex was 7-1/2 feet high.
11:27 This is the **s** behind his rebellion. Solomon was
22:39 events in Ahab's reign and the **s** of the ivory palace
2Ki 14:9 replied to King Amaziah of Judah with this **s**:
2Ch 24:27 The complete **s** about the sons of Joash,
25:18 replied to King Amaziah of Judah with this **s**:
Ne 6:8 are lying. There is no truth in any part of your **s**."
Est 2:23 was made and Mordecai's **s** was found to be true,
7:7 Mordecai told him the whole **s** and told him how
Ps 145:7 Everyone will share the **s** of your wonderful
Pr 18:17 Any **s** sounds true until someone sets the record
Isa 5:7 This is the **s** of the LORD's people. / They are the
24:13 Throughout the earth the **s** is the same—
Eze 17:2 "Son of man, tell this **s** to the people of Israel.
Joel 1:3 Pass the awful **s** down from generation to
Mt 13:18 "Now here is the explanation of the **s** I told about
13:24 Here is another **s** Jesus told: "The Kingdom of
13:36 "Please explain the **s** of the weeds in the field."
21:33 "Now listen to this **s**. A certain landowner planted
21:45 at them—that they were the farmers in his **s**.
22:2 **s** of a king who prepared a great wedding feast for
25:1 by the **s** of ten bridesmaids who took their lamps
25:14 the Kingdom of Heaven can be illustrated by the **s**
28:15 Their **s** spread widely among the Jews, and they
Mk 4:13 "But if you can't understand this **s**, how will you
4:30 of God? What **s** should I use to illustrate it?
12:12 at them—they were the wicked farmers in his **s**.
12:26 the writings of Moses, in the **s** of the burning bush?
Lk 2:18 All who heard the shepherds' **s** were astonished,
4:37 The **s** of what he had done spread like wildfire
7:41 Then Jesus told him this **s**: "A man loaned money
8:4 One day Jesus told this **s** to a large crowd that had
8:9 His disciples asked him what the **s** meant.
8:11 "This is the meaning of the **s**: The seed is God's
15:11 illustrate the point further, Jesus told them this **s**:
16:1 Jesus told this **s** to his disciples: "A rich man hired
18:1 One day Jesus told his disciples a **s** to illustrate
18:9 Then Jesus told this **s** to some who had great
19:11 he told a **s** to correct the impression that the
19:28 After telling this **s**, Jesus went on toward
20:9 turned to the people again and told them this **s**:
20:19 of religious law and the leading priests heard this **s**,
20:19 at them—that they were the farmers in the **s**.
24:11 but the **s** sounded like nonsense, so they didn't
24:35 Then the two from Emmaus told their **s** of how
Ac 19:17 The **s** of what happened spread quickly all through

STOUT [KJV] See ARROGANT, BOASTING, GREAT(ER), HARSH, STRONG

STRAIGHT (42) [STRAIGHTEN, STRAIGHTENS, STRAIGHTEST, STRAIGHTFORWARD]

Ge 24:27 for he has led me **s** to my master's relatives."
Ex 3:18 Then all of you must go **s** to the king of Egypt
15:8 piled up! / The surging waters stood **s** like a wall;
Jos 6:5 and the people can charge **s** into the city."
6:20 and the Israelites charged **s** into the city from every
1Sa 6:12 the cows went **s** along the road toward
2Sa 5:23 "Do not attack them **s** on," the LORD replied.
1Ki 3:23 Then the king said, "Let's get the facts **s**. Both of
1Ch 14:14 "Do not attack them **s** on," God replied. "Instead,
Ezr 10:4 duty to tell us how to proceed in setting things **s**,
Ne 12:37 At the Fountain Gate they went **s** up the steps on
Job 40:17 Its tail is as **s** as a cedar. The sinews of its thighs
Ps 107:7 He led them **s** to safety, / to a city where they could
Pr 4:11 teach you wisdom's ways and lead you in **s** paths.
4:25 Look **s** ahead, and fix your eyes on what lies
4:26 Mark out a **s** path for your feet; then stick to the
5:5 feet go down to death; her steps lead **s** to the grave.
18:17 story sounds true until someone sets the record **s**.
21:8 walk a crooked path; the innocent travel a **s** road.
Isa 40:3 Make a **s**, smooth road through the desert for our
Jer 50:9 The enemies' arrows will go **s** to the mark;
Eze 1:7 Their legs were **s** like human legs, but their feet
1:12 and they moved **s** forward in all directions without
10:11 They went **s** in the direction in which their heads
10:22 and they traveled **s** ahead, just as the others had.
Joel 2:7 **S** forward they march, never breaking rank.
Am 4:3 You will leave by going **s** through the breaks in the
7:7 was checking it with a plumb line to see if it was **s**.
Mt 3:3 the Lord's coming! / Make a **s** road for him!' "
26:49 So Judas came **s** to Jesus. "Greetings, Teacher!"
Mk 1:3 the Lord's coming! / Make a **s** road for him!' "
14:59 But even then they didn't get their stories **s**!
Lk 3:4 for the Lord's coming! / Make a **s** road for him!
13:11 for eighteen years and was unable to stand up **s**.
13:13 he touched her, and instantly she could stand **s**.
21:28 stand **s** and look up, for your salvation is near!"
Jn 1:23 'Prepare a **s** pathway for the Lord's coming!' "
Ac 9:11 The Lord said, "Go over to **S** Street, to the house
16:11 and sailed **s** across to the island of Samothrace,
21:1 Ephesian elders, we sailed **s** to the island of Cos.
1Co 9:26 So I run **s** to the goal with purpose in every step.
Heb 12:13 Mark out a **s** path for your feet. Then those who

STRAIGHTEN (3) [STRAIGHT]

Ecc 7:13 for who can **s** out what he has made crooked?
Isa 40:4 **S** out the curves and smooth off the rough spots.
Lk 3:5 and level the mountains and hills! / **S** the curves,

STRAIGHTENS (1) [STRAIGHT]

2Ti 3:16 It **s** us out and teaches us to do what is right.

STRAIGHTEST (1) [STRAIGHT]

Mic 7:4 the **s** is more crooked than a hedge of thorns.

STRAIGHTFORWARD (2) [FORWARD, STRAIGHT]

Isa 28:13 Yet they will stumble over this simple, **s** message.
2Co 1:13 My letters have been **s**, and there is nothing written

STRAIGHTWAY [KJV] See SOON, IMMEDIATELY, RIGHT (AWAY), SUDDENLY, (WITHOUT) DELAY

STRAIN (4) [STRAINING]

Ps 119:123 My eyes **s** to see your deliverance, / to see the truth
Jer 14:6 They **s** their eyes looking for grass to eat, but there
Mt 23:24 You **s** your water so you won't accidentally
Php 3:14 I **s** to reach the end of the race and receive the

STRAINING (2) [STRAIN]

Ps 119:82 My eyes are **s** to see your promises come true.
Ac 1:10 As they were **s** their eyes to see him,

STRANDED (2)

Eze 29:5 leave you and all your fish **s** in the desert to die.
32:4 I will leave you **s** on the land to die. All the birds

STRANDS (1)

Jdg 15:14 ropes on his arms as if they were burnt **s** of flax,

STRANGE (18) [ESTRANGED, STRANGELY, STRANGER, STRANGERS]

1Sa 14:16 Saul's lookouts in Gibeah saw a **s** sight—the vast
Ecc 8:10 How **s** that they were the very ones who frequented
Isa 28:21 He will come to do a **s**, unusual thing: He will
33:19 These fierce, violent people with a **s**,
45:15 our Savior, you work in **s** and mysterious ways.
66:8 has ever seen or heard of anything as **s** as this?
Jer 2:10 See if anyone has ever heard of anything as **s** as
Eze 3:6 I am not sending you to people with **s** and difficult
Da 7:6 Then the third of these **s** beasts appeared, and it
Lk 9:9 "so who is this man about whom I hear such **s**
21:25 "And there will be **s** events in the skies—signs in
21:25 perplexed by the roaring seas and **s** tides.
Jn 9:30 "Why, that's very **s**!" the man replied.
Ac 17:18 "This babbler has picked up some **s** ideas."
1Co 12:19 What a **s** thing a body would be if it had only one
2Ti 4:4 They will reject the truth and follow **s** myths.
Heb 13:9 So do not be attracted by **s**, new ideas.
1Pe 4:12 as if something **s** were happening to you.

STRANGELY (1) [STRANGE]

Lk 24:32 "Didn't our hearts feel **s** warm as he talked with us

STRANGER (16) [STRANGE]

Ge 23:4 "Here I am, a **s** in a foreign land, with no place to
42:7 them instantly, but he pretended to be a **s**.
Ex 2:22 for he said, "I have been a **s** in a foreign land."
18:3 boy was born, "I have been a **s** in a foreign land."
Job 19:15 The servant girls consider me a **s**. I am like a
31:32 I have never turned away a **s** but have opened my
Ps 69:8 they don't know me; / they treat me like a **s**.
Pr 11:15 Guaranteeing a loan for a **s** is dangerous; it is
20:16 from anyone who guarantees the debt of a **s**.
27:13 from anyone who guarantees the debt of a **s**.
Jer 14:8 in times of trouble! Why are you like a **s** to us?
Mt 25:35 I was a **s**, and you invited me into your home.
25:38 Or a **s** and show you hospitality? Or naked
25:43 I was a **s**, and you didn't invite me into your home.
25:44 or thirsty or a **s** or naked or sick or in prison,
Jn 10:5 They won't follow a **s**; they will run from him

STRANGERS (18) [STRANGE]

Ge 15:13 "You can be sure that your descendants will be **s**
Ru 2:11 and your own land to live here among complete **s**.
1Ch 16:19 were few in number, / a tiny group of **s** in Canaan.
29:15 and **s** in the land as our ancestors were before us.
Job 29:16 and made sure that even **s** received a fair trial.
Ps 54:3 For **s** are attacking me; / violent men are trying to
105:12 were few in number, / a tiny group of **s** in Canaan.
109:11 his entire estate, / and **s** take all he has earned.
Pr 5:10 **S** will obtain your wealth, and someone else will
5:17 reserve it for yourselves. Don't share it with **s**.
Jer 9:16 the world, and they will be **s** in distant lands.
La 5:2 Our inheritance has been turned over to **s**,
Eze 16:32 you are an adulterous wife who takes in **s** instead
Zec 7:14 among the distant nations where they lived as **s**.
Eph 2:19 So now you Gentiles are no longer **s**
1Ti 5:10 up her children well? Has she been kind to **s**?
Heb 13:2 Don't forget to show hospitality to **s**, for some who
3Jn 1:5 are passing through, even though they are **s** to you.

STRANGLED (3) [STRANGULATION]

Ac 15:20 consuming blood or eating the meat of **s** animals.
15:29 consuming blood or eating the meat of **s** animals,
21:25 nor consume blood, nor eat meat from **s** animals,

STRANGULATION (1) [STRANGLED]

Job 7:15 I would rather die of **s** than go on and on like this.

STRAP (1) [STRAPPED]

Ex 32:27 the God of Israel, says: **S** on your swords!

STRAPPED (8) [STRAP]

Ge 21:14 and **s** a container of water to Hagar's shoulders.
Dt 1:41 So your men **s** on their weapons, thinking it would
Jdg 3:16 and he **s** it to his right thigh, keeping it hidden
3:21 left hand, pulled out the dagger **s** to his right thigh,
1Sa 17:39 **s** the sword over it, and took a step or two to see
25:13 was David's reply as he **s** on his own.
2Sa 20:8 Joab was wearing his uniform with a dagger **s** to
Eze 9:2 in linen and carried a writer's case **s** to his side.

STRATEGIES (2)

Isa 8:10 Call your councils of war, develop your **s**,
Eph 6:11 so that you will be able to stand firm against all **s**

STRAW (23)

Ge 24:25 we have plenty of s and food for the camels,
24:32 gave him s to bed them down, fed them,
Ex 5: 7 "Do not supply the people with any more s for
5:10 "Pharaoh has ordered us not to provide s for you.
5:12 people scattered throughout the land in search of s.
5:16 "We are given no s, but we are still told to make
5:18 No s will be given to you, but you must still
15: 7 flashed forth; / it consumed them as fire burns s.
Jdg 19:19 We have s and fodder for our donkeys and plenty
1Ki 4:28 and s for the royal horses in the stables.
20:33 The men were quick to grasp at this s of hope,
Job 21:18 Are they driven before the wind like s? Are they
41:27 To the crocodile, iron is nothing but s, and bronze
41:28 Stones shot from a sling are as ineffective as s.
Isa 1:31 strongest among you will disappear like burning s.
1:31 Your evil deeds are the spark that will set the s on
5:24 Therefore, they will all disappear like burning s.
25:10 Moab will be crushed like trampled s and left to
40:24 work withers. The wind carries them off like s.
65:25 will feed together. The lion will eat s like the ox.
Na 1:10 like drunks, will be burned like dry s in a field.
Mal 4: 1 and the wicked will be burned up like s on that
1Co 3:12 may use gold, silver, jewels, wood, hay, or s.

STRAWED [KJV] See SCATTER, SCATTERED, SPREAD

STRAY (8) [ASTRAY, STRAYED, STRAYS]

Ex 22: 5 and the owner lets its s into someone else's field to
Ps 119:118 But you have rejected all who s from your
Pr 5: 7 listen to me. Never s from what I am about to say:
7:25 Don't let your hearts s away toward her.
Isa 17: 6 like the s olives left on the tree after the harvest.
24:13 like the s olives left on the tree or the few grapes
Jer 2: 5 sin did your ancestors find in me that led them to s
Eze 14:11 the people of Israel will learn not to s from me,

STRAYED (10) [STRAY]

Ex 23: 4 upon your enemy's ox or donkey that has s away,
1Sa 9: 3 One day Kish's donkeys s away, and he told Saul,
Job 31: 7 If I have s from his pathway, or if my heart has
Ps 44:18 not deserted you. / We have not s from your path.
Isa 40:26 them to see that none are lost or have s away.
53: 6 All of us have s away like sheep. We have left
Eze 34:16 I will search for my lost ones who s away, and I
44:10 s away from me to worship idols must bear the
Lk 15: 4 and one of them s away and was lost in the
15: 7 others who are righteous and haven't s away!

STRAYS (3) [STRAY]

Pr 21:16 The person who s from common sense will end up
27: 8 A person who s from home is like a bird that s

STREAKED (6) [STREAKS, WHITE-STREAKED]

Ge 30:39 all of their offspring were s, speckled, and spotted.
30:40 he turned the flocks toward the s and dark-colored
31: 8 changed his mind and said I could have the s ones,
then all the lambs were born s.
31:10 that the male goats mating with the flock were s,
31:12 'Look, and you will see that only the s, speckled,

STREAKS (2) [STREAKED]

Ge 30:37 and peeled off strips of the bark to make white s on
Lev 14:37 bright green or reddish s on the walls of the house

STREAM (20) [STREAMBEDS, STREAMING, STREAMS, UPSTREAM]

Dt 9:21 I threw the dust into the s that cascades down the
21: 4 plowed nor planted with a s running through it.
Jos 13: 3 This land extends from the s of Shihor, which is on
Jdg 7: 5 kneel down and drink with their mouths in the s."
7: 6 on their knees and drank with their mouths in the s.
1Sa 17:40 He picked up five smooth stones from a s and put
1Ki 14:15 will shake Israel like a reed whipped about in a s.
Job 40:22 give it shade among the willows beside the s.
Ps 45: 2 handsome of all. / Gracious words s from your lips.
Pr 21: 1 The king's heart is like a s of water directed by the
Isa 15: 9 The s near Dibon runs red with blood, but I am still
Jer 31: 9 Tears of joy will s down their faces, and I will lead
La 1: 2 sobs through the night; tears s down her cheeks.
Eze 16:25 to every passerby in an endless s of prostitution.
47: 1 There I saw a s flowing eastward from beneath the
47: 1 This s then passed to the right of the altar on its
47: 2 There I could see the s flowing out through the
47: 3 he led me along the s for 1,750 feet and told me to
47: 8 The waters of this s will heal the salty waters of the
Rev 14:20 and blood flowed from the winepress in a s about

STREAMBEDS (1) [STREAM]

Joel 3:18 Water will fill the dry s of Judah, and a fountain

STREAMING (1) [STREAM]

Jn 4:30 So the people came s from the village to see him.

STREAMS (27) [STREAM]

Lev 23:40 leafy branches and willows that grow by the s.
Dt 8: 7 God is bringing you into a good land of flowing s
Job 20:17 He will never again enjoy abundant s of olive oil
28:11 They dam up the trickling s and bring to light the
29: 6 and my olive groves poured out s of olive oil.
41:20 Smoke s from its nostrils like steam from a boiling
Ps 23: 2 in green meadows; / he leads me beside peaceful s.
42: 1 As the deer pants for s of water, / so I long for you,
74:15 You caused the springs and s to gush forth,
78:16 He made s pour from the rock, / making the waters
78:44 into blood, / so no one could drink from the s.
104:10 into ravines, / so s gush down from the mountains.
104:12 The birds nest beside the s / and sing among the
126: 4 our fortunes, LORD, / as s renew the desert.
SS 4:15 as refreshing as the s from the Lebanon
Isa 11:15 sending a mighty wind to divide it into seven s that
19: 6 and the s of Egypt will become foul with rotting
30:25 there will be s of water flowing down every
34: 9 The s of Edom will be filled with burning pitch,
35: 6 forth in the wilderness, and s will water the desert.
Jer 18:14 flowing s from the crags of Mount Hermon ever
31: 9 They will walk beside quiet s and not stumble.
La 3:48 S of tears flow from my eyes because of the
Eze 29: 3 you great monster, lurking in the s of the Nile.
32:13 all your flocks and herds that graze beside the s.
35: 8 and your s will be filled with people slaughtered by
Joel 1:20 The s have dried up, and fire has consumed the

STREET (23) [STREETS]

Dt 13:16 you must pile all the plunder in the middle of the s
Jos 2:19 If they go out into the s, they will be killed, and we
Ps 31:11 When they see me on the s, / they turn the other
Pr 1:21 She calls out to the crowds along the main s,
7: 8 He was crossing the s near the house of an
22:13 I might meet a lion in the s and be killed!"
Ecc 10: 3 fools just by the way they walk down the s!
Jer 5: 1 "Run up and down every s in Jerusalem,"
11:13 to your god Baal—are along every s in Jerusalem.
48:38 will be in every Moabite home and on every s.
Eze 16:25 On every s corner you defiled your beauty,
16:31 You build your pagan shrines on every s corner
26:11 His horsemen will trample every s in the city.
Am 5:16 be crying in all the public squares and in every s.
Mt 6: 5 hypocrites who love to pray publicly on s corners
22: 9 Now go out to the s corners and invite everyone
Mk 11: 4 disciples left and found the colt standing in the s,
Ac 9:11 The Lord said, "Go over to Straight S,
12:10 guard posts and came to the iron gate to the s,
12:10 passed through and started walking down the s,
Rev 11: 8 And their bodies will lie in the main s of
21:21 And the main s was pure gold, as clear as glass.
22: 2 coursing down the center of the main s. On each

STREETS (69) [STREET]

2Sa 1:20 Don't proclaim it in the s of Ashkelon,
Ps 55:11 threats and cheating are rampant in the s.
59: 6 snarling like vicious dogs / as they prowl the s.
59:14 snarling like vicious dogs / as they prowl the s.
102:14 her walls / and show favor even to the dust in her s.
Pr 1:20 Wisdom shouts in the s. She cries out in the public
7:12 She is often seen in the s and markets, soliciting at
Ecc 12: 5 the mourners will walk along the s.
SS 3: 2 the city, searching for him in all its s and squares.'
Isa 5:25 of his people are thrown as garbage into the s.
15: 3 They will wear sackcloth as they wander the s.
17: 2 Sheep will graze in the s and lie down unafraid.
23:16 she will take a harp, walk the s, and sing her songs,
24:11 Mobs gather in the s, crying out for wine. Joy has
27:10 the houses abandoned, the s covered with grass.
51:20 For your children have fainted and lie in the s,
59:14 Truth falls dead in the s, and fairness has been
Jer 2: 2 "Go and shout in Jerusalem's s: 'This is what the
6: 7 Her s echo with the sounds of violence
6:11 even on children playing in the s, on gatherings of
7:17 the towns of Judah and in the s of Jerusalem?
7:34 happy singing and laughter in the s of Jerusalem.
9:21 Children no longer play in the s, and young men no
11: 6 "Broadcast this message in the s of Jerusalem.
14:16 their bodies will be thrown out into the s of
14:18 If I walk the city s, there I see people who have
33:10 Yet in the empty s of Jerusalem and Judah's other
44: 6 on the towns of Judah and into the s of Jerusalem,
44:17 in the towns of Judah and in the s of Jerusalem.
44:21 in the towns of Judah and in the s of Jerusalem?
49:26 Her young men will fall in the s and die.
50:30 Her young men will fall in the s and die.
51: 4 land of the Babylonians, slashed to death in her s.
51:47 will be disgraced, and her dead will lie in the s.
La 1: 1 Jerusalem's s, once bustling with people, are now
1:20 In the s the sword kills, and at home there is only
2:11 and tiny babies are fainting and dying in the s.
2:19 for your children as they faint with hunger in the s.
2:21 "See them lying in the s—young and old, boys
4: 1 The sacred gemstones lie scattered in the s!
4: 5 foods now beg in the s for anything they can get.
4:14 They wandered blindly through the s, so defiled by
4:18 We couldn't go into the s without danger to our
Eze 9: 4 "Walk through the s of Jerusalem and put a mark
11: 6 murdered endlessly and filled your s with the dead.
28:23 against you, and blood will be spilled in your s.
36:38 that fill Jerusalem's s at the time of her festivals.
Da 9:25 Jerusalem will be rebuilt with s and strong
Mic 1: 6 Her s will be plowed up for planting vineyards.
2: 3 none of you will ever again walk proudly in the s."
7:10 I will see them trampled down like mud in the s.
Na 2: 4 The chariots race recklessly along the s
3: 2 chariots clatter as they bump wildly through the s.
3: 3 The dead are lying in the s—dead bodies, heaps of
3:10 were dashed to death against the stones of the s.
Zep 3: 6 cities are now deserted; their s are in silent ruin.
Zec 8: 4 and women will walk Jerusalem's s with a cane
8: 5 And the s of the city will be filled with boys
9: 3 and gold that it is as common as dust in the s!
Mt 6: 2 and s to call attention to their acts of charity!
23: 7 They enjoy the attention they get on the s, and they
Mk 6:56 they laid the sick in the market plazas and s.
Lk 10:10 refuses to welcome you, go out into its s and say,
13:26 and drank with you, and you taught in our s.'
14:21 'Go quickly into the s and alleys of the city
Ac 5:15 sick people were brought out into the s on beds
17: 5 so they gathered some worthless fellows from the s
24:12 a riot in any synagogue or on the s of the city.
Rev 18:24 In her s the blood of the prophets was spilled.

STRENGTH (179) [STRONG]

Ge 48: 2 he gathered his s and sat up in bed to greet him.
Ex 15: 2 The LORD is my s and my song; / he has become
15:13 have ransomed. / You will guide them in your s
Dt 6: 5 with all your heart, all your soul, and all your s.
8:17 so you would never think that it was your own s
9:26 from Egypt by your mighty power and glorious s.
9:29 from Egypt by your mighty power and glorious s.'
11: 8 so you may have s to go in and occupy the land
21:17 who represents the s of his father's manhood
29: 3 all the great tests of s, the miraculous signs,
32:36 about his servants, / when he sees their s is gone
33: 7 Give them s to defend their cause; / help them
33:17 Joseph has the s and majesty of a young bull;
33:25 may your s match the length of your days!"
Jdg 5:31 may those who love you rise like the sun at full s!"
6:14 "Go with the s you have and rescue Israel from the
7: 2 to me that they saved themselves by their own s.
15:18 this great victory by the s of your servant.
16: 9 in a fire. So the secret of his s was not discovered.
16:17 If my head were shaved, my s would leave me,
16:19 making his capture certain. And his s left him.
1Sa 2: 9 in darkness. / No one will succeed by s alone.
2:10 the earth. / He gives mighty s to his king;
28:22 to eat so you can regain your s for the trip back."
30: 6 But David found s in the LORD his God.
30:12 and nights. It wasn't long before his s returned.
2Sa 22: 3 He is my shield, the s of my salvation, and my
22:30 In your s I can crush an army; / with my God I can
22:40 You have armed me with s for the battle;
1Ki 18:46 Now the LORD gave special s to Elijah.
19: 8 and the food gave him enough s to travel forty
2Ki 18:20 mere words can substitute for military skill and s?
19: 3 to be born, but the mother has no s to deliver it.
23:25 to the LORD with all his heart and soul and s,
1Ch 16:11 Search for the LORD and for his s, / and keep on
16:27 surround him; / s and beauty are in his dwelling.
29:12 discretion that people are made great and given s.
Ne 6: 9 the work. So I prayed for s to continue the work.
8:10 and sad, for the joy of the LORD is your s!"
Job 6:11 But I do not have the s to endure. I do not have a
6:12 Do I have s as hard as stone? Is my body made of
9:19 As for s, he has it. As for justice, who can
9:35 him without fear, but I cannot do that in my own s.
12:16 "Yes, s and wisdom are with him; deceivers
14:10 "But when people die, they lose all s.
22: 9 without helping them and crushed the s of orphans.
26: 2 How you have saved a person who has no s!
29:20 bestowed on me, and my s is continually renewed.'
39:19 "Have you given the horse its s or clothed its neck
39:21 It paws the earth and rejoices in its s. When it
40:14 would praise you, for your own s would save you.
41:12 "I want to emphasize the tremendous s in the
41:22 "The tremendous s in its neck strikes terror
Ps 10:10 they fall beneath the s of the wicked.
17: 7 You save with your s / those who seek refuge from
18: 1 I love you, LORD; you are my s.
18: 2 He is my shield, the s of my salvation, and my
18:29 In your s I can crush an army; / with my God I can
18:32 God arms me with s; / he has made my way safe.
18:39 You have armed me with s for the battle;
21: 1 How the king rejoices in your s, O LORD!
22:15 My s has dried up like sunbaked clay. / My tongue
22:19 You are my s; come quickly to my aid!
23: 3 He renews my s. / He guides me along right paths,
28: 7 The LORD is my s, my shield from every danger.
29: 1 give honor to the LORD for his glory and s.
29:11 The LORD gives his people s. / The LORD
31:10 Misery has drained my s; / I am wasting away
32: 4 My s evaporated like water in the summer heat.
33:16 a king, / nor is great s enough to save a warrior.
33:17 give you victory— / for all its s, it cannot save you.
37:17 For the s of the wicked will be shattered,
38:10 My heart beats wildly, my s fails, / and I am going
44: 3 it was not their own s that gave them victory.
46: 1 God is our refuge and s, / always ready to help in
59: 9 You are my s; I wait for you to rescue me,
59:17 O my S, to you I sing praises, / for you, O God,
65: 6 by your power / and armed yourself with mighty s.
68:34 down on Israel; / his s is mighty in the heavens.
68:35 The God of Israel gives power and s to his people.
71: 7 because you have been my s and protection.
71: 9 Don't abandon me when my s is failing.
73:26 grow weak, / but God remains the s of my heart;
74:13 You split the sea by your s / and smashed the sea
75:10 For God says, "I will cut off the s of the wicked,
77:15 You have redeemed your people by your s,
81: 1 Sing praises to God, our s. / Sing to the God of
86:16 Give s to your servant; / yes, save me, for I am
88: 4 one who is dead, / like a strong man with no s left.
89:13 Your right hand is lifted high in glorious s.
89:17 You are their glorious s. / Our power is based on
93: 1 the LORD is robed in majesty and armed with s.

96: 6 surround him; / s and beauty are in his sanctuary.
104: 15 as lotion for their skin, / and bread to give them s.
105: 4 Search for the LORD and for his s, / and keep on
118: 14 The LORD is my s and my song; / he has become
138: 3 you encourage me by giving me the s I need.
139: 10 hand will guide me, / and your s will support me.
144: 1 who is my rock. / He gives me s for war
147: 10 The s of a horse does not impress him; / how puny in his sight is the s of a man.
Pr 8: 14 and success belong to me. Insight and s are mine.
11: 7 all perish, for they rely on their own feeble s.
12: 4 and crown; a shameful wife saps his s.
17: 22 but a broken spirit saps a person's s.
20: 29 The glory of the young is their s; the gray hair of
24: 10 If you fail under pressure, your s is not very great.
31: 3 do not spend your s on women, on those who ruin
31: 25 She is clothed with s and dignity, and she laughs
Ecc 9: 16 Then I realized that though wisdom is better than s,
10: 10 Since a dull ax requires great s, sharpen the blade.
10: 15 so exhausted by a little work that they have no s
10: 17 and whose leaders feast only to gain s for their
Isa 10: 13 By my own s I have captured many lands,
12: 2 The LORD GOD is my s and my song;
23: 11 spoken out against Phoenicia and depleted its s.
30: 15 In quietness and confidence is your s. But you
33: 2 Be our s each day and our salvation in times of
36: 5 mere words can substitute for military skill and s?
37: 3 to be born, but the mother has no s to deliver it.
40: 10 He will rule with awesome s. See, he brings his
40: 29 are tired and worn out; he offers s to the weak.
40: 31 But those who wait on the LORD will find new s.
45: 24 is the source of all my righteousness and s."
49: 4 I have spent my s for nothing and to no purpose at
49: 5 has honored me, and my God has given me s.
51: 9 Wake up, LORD! Robe yourself with s!
52: 1 wake up, O Zion! Clothe yourselves with s.
55: 2 your money on food that does not give you s?
62: 8 The LORD has sworn to Jerusalem by his own s:
63: 1 in royal robes, marching in the greatness of his s?
Jer 16: 19 LORD, you are my s and fortress, my refuge in
48: 25 "The s of Moab has ended. Her horns have been
51: 34 has eaten and crushed us and emptied out our s.
51: 53 and though she increases her s immeasurably,
La 1: 14 The Lord sapped my s and gave me to my
2: 3 All the s of Israel vanishes beneath his fury.
2: 4 His s is used against them to kill their finest youth.
Eze 21: 7 heart will melt with fear; all s will disappear.
30: 18 When I come to break the proud s of Egypt,
31: 18 which of the trees of Eden will you compare your s
Da 2: 23 for you have given me wisdom and s.
2: 37 has given you sovereignty, power, s, and honor.
10: 8 My s left me, my face grew deathly pale, and I felt
10: 17 my lord? My s is gone, and I can hardly breathe."
10: 18 a man touched me again, and I felt my s returning.
11: 5 than he and will rule his kingdom with great s.
Hos 5: 12 I will sap Judah's s as dry rot weakens wood.
7: 9 Worshiping foreign gods has sapped their s,
14: 3 Assyria cannot save us, nor can our s in battle.
Am 6: 13 "Didn't we take Karnaim by our own s
Mic 5: 4 he will stand to lead his flock with the LORD's s,
Na 3: 9 and the land of Egypt were the source of her s,
Hab 1: 11 are deeply guilty, for their own s is their god."
3: 19 The Sovereign LORD is my s! He will make me
Zec 4: 6 It is not by force nor by s, but by my Spirit,
12: 5 'The people of Jerusalem have found s in the
Mk 12: 30 all your soul, all your mind, and all your s.'
12: 33 all my heart and all my understanding and all my s,
Lk 10: 27 all your soul, all your s, and all your mind.'
16: 3 and I don't have the s to go out and dig ditches,
Ac 9: 31 and Samaria, and it grew in s and numbers.
27: 14 and a wind of typhoon s (a "northeaster,"
Ro 5: 4 And endurance develops s of character in us,
1Co 1: 25 is far stronger than the greatest of human s.
Eph 3: 16 give you mighty inner s through his Holy Spirit.
Php 4: 13 with the help of Christ who gives me the s I need.
Col 2: 19 only as we get our nourishment and s from God.
2Th 2: 17 and give you s in every good thing you do and say.
2Ti 1: 8 With the s God gives you, be ready to suffer with
4: 17 But the Lord stood with me and gave me s, that I
Heb 11: 34 Their weakness was turned to s. They became
13: 9 Your spiritual s comes from God's special favor,
Jas 4: 6 and more s to stand against such evil desires.
1Pe 4: 11 Do it with all the s and energy that God supplies.
2Pe 2: 11 far greater in power and s than these false teachers,
Rev 3: 8 You have little s, yet you obeyed my word and did
5: 12 and wisdom and s / and honor and glory
7: 12 and thanksgiving and honor and power and s

STRENGTHEN (26) [STRONG]

Ex 14: 8 The LORD continued to s Pharaoh's resolve,
Jdg 16: 28 please s me one more time so that I may pay back
2Sa 8: 3 when Hadadezer marched out to s his control along
1Ch 18: 3 when Hadadezer marched out to s his control along
2Ch 16: 9 to s those whose hearts are fully committed to him.
Ps 20: 2 from his sanctuary / and s you from Jerusalem.
80: 17 S the man you love, / the son of your choice.
SS 8: 9 If she is chaste, we will s and encourage her.
Isa 35: 3 With this news, s those who have tired hands,
41: 10 for I am your God. I will s you. I will help you.
42: 1 "Look at my servant, whom I s. He is my chosen
Jer 33: 4 and even the king's palace to get materials to s the
Eze 13: 5 They have done nothing to s the breaks in the walls
30: 24 I will s the arms of Babylon's king and put my
30: 25 I will s the arms of the king of Babylon,
34: 16 I will bind up the injured and s the weak. But I will
Da 2: 43 s themselves by forming alliances with each other
Na 3: 14 ready for the siege! Store up water! S the defenses!
Zec 10: 6 "I will s Judah and save Israel; I will reestablish
Mt 5: 37 To s your promise with a vow shows that
Lk 22: 32 turned to me again, s and build up your brothers."
Ac 15: 41 and Cilicia to s the churches there.
27: 17 Then we banded the ship with ropes to s the hull.
1Th 3: 2 We sent him to s you, to encourage you in your
1Pe 5: 10 a little while, he will restore, support, and s you,
Rev 3: 2 S what little remains, for even what is left is at the

STRENGTHENED (17) [STRONG]

Ge 49: 24 But his bow remained strong, / and his arms were s
2Ch 11: 11 Rehoboam s their defenses and stationed
11: 17 This s the kingdom of Judah, and for three years
17: 1 He s Judah to stand against any attack from Israel.
24: 13 of God according to its original design and s it.
32: 5 Then Hezekiah further s his defenses by repairing
Job 4: 4 Your words have s the fallen; you steadied those
Ps 89: 42 You have s his enemies against him / and made
Isa 57: 10 you never gave up. You s yourself and went on.
Da 10: 19 you may speak, my lord, for you have s me."
Lk 22: 43 Then an angel from heaven appeared and s him.
Ac 3: 7 the man's feet and anklebones were healed and s.
9: 19 Afterward he ate some food and was s.
14: 22 where they s the believers. They encouraged them
16: 5 So the churches were s in their faith and grew daily
1Co 14: 4 A person who speaks in tongues is s personally in
Col 1: 11 We also pray that you will be s with his glorious

STRENGTHENING (1) [STRONG]

Ac 15: 32 to the Christians, encouraging and s their faith.

STRENGTHENS (4) [STRONG]

2Sa 22: 35 me for battle; / he s me to draw a bow of bronze.
Ps 18: 34 me for battle; / he s me to draw a bow of bronze.
Ro 5: 4 and character s our confident expectation of
1Co 14: 4 but one who speaks a word of prophecy s the entire

STRENUOUSLY (1)

Jdg 14: 3 His father and mother objected s, "Isn't there one

STRESS (2)

Ps 119: 143 As pressure and s bear down on me, / I find joy in
Ro 11: 13 as the apostle to the Gentiles. I lay great s on this,

STRETCH (7) [OUTSTRETCHED, STRETCHED, STRETCHES, STRETCHING]

Ex 27: 9 On the south side the curtains will s for 150 feet.
Dt 11: 24 Your frontiers will s from the wilderness in the
Ps 21: 4 his request. / The days of his life s on forever.
68: 15 majestic mountains of Bashan / s high into the sky.
104: 2 You s out the starry curtain of the heavens;
Zec 9: 10 His realm will s from sea to sea and from the
Jn 21: 18 But when you are old, you will s out your hands,

STRETCHED (17) [STRETCH]

Ex 37: 9 and their wings were s out above the atonement
Lev 26: 26 so the bread from one oven will have to be s to
1Ki 17: 21 And he s himself out over the child three times
2Ki 4: 35 Then he s himself out again on the child.
1Ch 21: 16 earth with his sword drawn, s out over Jerusalem.
28: 18 whose wings were s out over the Ark of the
Ps 140: 5 have set a trap to catch me; / they have s out a net;
Isa 42: 5 the LORD, created the heavens and s them out.
44: 24 who made all things. I alone s out the heavens.
45: 12 to live on it. With my hands I s out the heavens.
Jer 10: 12 He has s out the heavens / by his understanding.
31: 39 A measuring line will be s out over the hill of
51: 15 He has s out the heavens / by his understanding.
Eze 1: 11 one pair s out to touch the wings of the living
1: 23 each living being s out to touch the others' wings,
Zec 12: 1 who s out the heavens, laid the foundations of the
Heb 9: 5 Their wings were s out over the Ark's cover,

STRETCHES (5) [STRETCH]

1Ch 5: 8 These Reubenites lived in the area that s from
5: 9 the edge of the desert that s to the Euphrates River.
Job 26: 7 God s the northern sky over empty space
Isa 33: 17 and you will see a land that s into the distance.
Eze 48: 18 Outside the city there will be a farming area that s

STRETCHING (4) [STRETCH]

Jos 12: 5 He ruled a territory s from Mount Hermon to
13: 4 s northward to Aphek on the border of the
Est 1: 1 who reigned over 127 provinces s from India to
8: 9 and local officials of all the 127 provinces s from

STREWN (1)

1Sa 17: 52 and wounded Philistines were s all along the road

STRICKEN (6) [STRIKE]

Ge 20: 18 For the LORD had s all the women with
2Ch 21: 15 You yourself will be s with a severe intestinal
Ps 107: 42 and be glad, / while the wicked are s silent.
Hos 9: 16 The people of Israel are s. Their roots are dried up;
Zec 14: 13 will be terrified, s by the LORD with great panic.
Ac 13: 11 and you will be s awhile with blindness."

STRICT (3) [STRICTEST, STRICTLY, STRICTNESS]

Jos 14: 5 So the distribution of the land was in s accordance
1Sa 14: 28 "Your father made the army take a s oath that
1Co 9: 25 All athletes practice s self-control. They do it to

STRICTEST (2) [STRICT]

Ac 26: 5 member of the Pharisees, the s sect of our religion.
Php 3: 5 who demand the s obedience to the Jewish law.

STRICTLY (5) [STRICT]

Lev 11: 12 not have both fins and scales is s forbidden to you.
18: 26 You must s obey all of my laws and regulations,
Dt 17: 3 of the forces of heaven, which I have s forbidden.
Da 6: 7 Majesty should make a law that will be s enforced.
Mk 3: 12 But Jesus s warned them not to say who he was.

STRICTNESS (1) [STRICT]

Jas 3: 1 who teach will be judged by God with greater s.

STRIDE (1)

Job 18: 7 The confident s of the wicked will be shortened.

STRIFE (4)

Ps 55: 9 their speech, / for I see violence and s in the city.
Pr 16: 28 A troublemaker plants seeds of s; gossip separates
17: 1 eaten in peace is better than a great feast with s.
Lk 12: 51 the earth? No, I have come to bring s and division!

STRIKE (72) [GRIEF-STRICKEN, STRICKEN, STRIKES, STRIKING, STROKE, STRUCK]

Ge 3: 15 He will crush your head, and you will s his heel."
41: 36 Otherwise disaster will surely s the land, and all
Ex 3: 20 and s at the heart of Egypt with all kinds of
8: 16 to Moses, "Tell Aaron to s the dust with his staff.
12: 13 This plague of death will not touch you when I s
12: 22 S the hyssop against the top and sides of the
12: 23 pass through the land and s down the Egyptians.
12: 23 the Destroyer to enter and s down your firstborn.
17: 6 S the rock, and water will come pouring out.
Lev 26: 24 and I will personally s you seven times over for
Nu 8: 19 so no plague will s them when they approach the
31: 16 They are the ones who caused the plague to s the
Dt 28: 22 The LORD will s you with wasting disease,
28: 28 The LORD will s you with madness, blindness,
32: 25 sword will bring death, / and inside, terror will s
33: 11 s down their foes so they never rise again."
1Sa 14: 44 May God s me dead if you are not executed for
26: 8 him to the ground, and I won't need to s twice!"
26: 10 Surely the LORD will s Saul down someday,
2Sa 5: 24 is moving ahead of you to s down the Philistines."
19: 13 may God s me dead if I do not appoint you as
20: 10 Joab did not need to s again, and Amasa soon died.
1Ki 2: 23 "May God s me dead if Adonijah has not sealed
20: 35 man, "S me!" But the man refused to s the prophet.
20: 37 prophet turned to another man and said, "S me!"
2Ki 13: 18 the other arrows and s them against the ground."
18: 23 the king of Assyria, will s a bargain with you.
1Ch 14: 15 is moving ahead of you to s down the Philistines."
2Ch 21: 14 So now the LORD is about to s you, your people,
Job 13: 11 Doesn't his majesty s terror into your heart?
38: 35 lightning appear and cause it to s as you direct it?
Ps 52: 5 But God will s you down once and for all. / He will
78: 20 Yes, he can s a rock so water gushes out, / but he
110: 5 He will s down many kings in the day of his anger.
141: 5 Let the godly s me! / It will be a kindness! / If they
Ecc 7: 14 But when hard times s, realize that both come from
Isa 5: 25 will not be satisfied. His fist is still poised to s!
9: 12 will not be satisfied. His fist is still poised to s.
9: 17 will not be satisfied. His fist is still poised to s.
9: 21 will not be satisfied. His fist is still poised to s.
10: 4 will not be satisfied. His fist is still poised to s.
10: 15 Can a whip s unless a hand is moving it? Can a
19: 17 Just to speak the name of Israel will s deep terror
19: 22 The LORD will s Egypt in a way that will bring
30: 31 be shattered. He will s them down with his rod.
31: 8 The sword of God will s them, and they will panic
36: 8 the king of Assyria, will s a bargain with you.
47: 12 Ask them to help you s terror into the hearts of
65: 25 Poisonous snakes will s no more. In those days,
Jer 4: 10 Yet the sword is even now poised to s them dead!"
50: 35 "The sword of destruction will s the
50: 35 "It will s the people of Babylon—her princes
50: 38 It will even s her water supply, causing it to dry up.
La 3: 30 Let them turn the other cheek to those who s them.
Eze 6: 12 Disease will s down those who are far away in
32: 15 everything you have and s down all your people,
Hos 6: 5 My judgment will s you as surely as day follows
Joel 3: 4 I will s swiftly and pay you back for everything
Am 9: 1 "S the tops of the Temple columns so hard that the
Mic 5: 1 With a rod they will s the leader of Israel in the
Na 1: 9 you with one blow; he won't need to s twice!
Hab 2: 17 Now terror will s you because of your murder
3: 16 day when disaster will s the people who invade us.
Zep 2: 13 And the LORD will s the lands of the north with
3: 7 listen to my warnings, so I won't need to s again.'
Zec 13: 7 S down the shepherd, and the sheep will be
14: 15 This same plague will s the horses, mules, camels,
Mal 4: 6 I will come and s the land with a curse."
Mt 26: 31 the Scriptures say, / 'God will s the Shepherd,
Mk 14: 27 the Scriptures say, / 'God will s the Shepherd,
Rev 2: 23 I will s her children dead. And all the churches will

STRIKER [KJV] See VIOLENT

STRIKES (20) [STRIKE]

Ex 21:15 "Anyone who s father or mother must be put to
Nu 35:16 " 'But if someone s and kills another person with
35:17 Or if someone s and kills another person with a
35:18 The same is true if someone s and kills another
Job 4:5 But now when trouble s, you faint and are broken.
5:18 he also bandages. He s, but his hands also heal.
34:26 He openly s them down for their wickedness.
41:22 "The tremendous strength in its neck s terror
Ps 29:7 The voice of the LORD s with lightning bolts.
86:7 I will call to you whenever trouble s, / and you will
91:6 in darkness, / nor the disaster that s at midday.
Pr 10:25 Disaster s like a cyclone, whirling the wicked
Isa 10:29 Fear s the city of Ramah. All the people of
30:32 And as the LORD s them, his people will keep
Jer 11:12 But the idols will not save them when disaster s!
50:36 And when it s her wise counselors, they will
50:36 When it s her mightiest warriors, panic will seize
50:37 When it s her horses and chariots, her allies from
50:37 When it s her treasures, they all will be plundered.
Da 2:40 just as iron smashes and crushes everything it s.

STRIKING (5) [STRIKE]

Ps 91:12 to keep you from s your foot on a stone.
Eze 7:9 know that it is I, the LORD, who is s the blow.
23:14 military officers, outfitted in s red uniforms.
Mt 4:6 to keep you from s your foot on a stone.' "
Lk 4:11 to keep you from s your foot on a stone.' "

STRING (4) [EIGHT-STRINGED, STRINGED, STRINGING, STRUNG, TEN-STRINGED]

Jdg 16:9 as if they were s that had been burned in a fire.
Ps 7:12 sharpen his sword; / he will bend and s his bow.
37:14 and s their bows / to kill the poor
SS 1:10 is your neck, accented with a long s of jewels.

STRINGED (11) [STRING]

Ps 4:T of David, to be accompanied by s instruments.
8:T of David, to be accompanied by a s instrument.
54:T is hiding." To be accompanied by s instruments.
55:T of David, to be accompanied by s instruments.
61:T of David, to be accompanied by s instruments.
67:T A psalm, to be accompanied by s instruments.
76:T of Asaph, to be accompanied by s instruments.
81:T of Asaph, to be accompanied by a s instrument.
84:T of Korah, to be accompanied by a s instrument.
150:4 praise him with s instruments and flutes!
Hab 3:19 This prayer is to be accompanied by s

STRINGING (1) [STRING]

Ps 11:2 The wicked are s their bows / and setting their

STRIP (27) [STRIPPED, STRIPPING, STRIPS]

Ge 27:16 and she fastened a s of the goat's skin around his
Lev 19:10 do not s every last bunch of grapes from the vines,
25:34 The s of pastureland around each of the Levitical
1Sa 31:8 when the Philistines went out to s the dead,
2Sa 2:21 of the younger men and s him of his weapons."
1Ch 10:8 The next day when the Philistines went out to s the
Job 41:13 Who can s off its hide, and who can penetrate its
Isa 3:18 The Lord will s away their artful beauty—
32:11 S off your pretty clothes, and wear sackcloth in
33:4 Just as locusts s the fields and vines, so Jerusalem will s the fallen army of Assyria!
47:2 the corn. Remove your veil and s off your robe.
Jer 5:10 S the branches from the vine, for they do not
49:10 But I will s bare the land of Edom, and there will
Eze 16:37 and I will s you naked in front of them so they can
16:39 They will s you and take your beautiful jewels,
23:26 They will s you of your beautiful clothes
45:2 An additional s of land 87-1/2 feet wide is to be
45:5 The s of sacred land next to it, also 8-1/3 miles
48:10 For the priests there will be a s of land measuring
48:15 "An additional s of land 8-1/3 miles long by 1-2/3
Hos 2:3 I will s her as naked as she was on the day she was
2:10 I will s her naked in public, while all her lovers
Na 3:16 of locusts, they s the land and then fly away.
Zec 9:4 But now the Lord will s away Tyre's possessions
Heb 12:1 let us s off every weight that slows us down,
Rev 17:16 They will s her naked, eat her flesh, and burn her

STRIPE(S) [KJV] See BEAT(INGS), BLOWS, BRUISES, FLOGGED, LASHES, SCOURGES, WOUNDS

STRIPPED (27) [STRIP]

Jdg 6:5 to count. And they stayed until the land was s bare.
1Sa 31:9 So they cut off Saul's head and s off his armor.
2Sa 1:27 have fallen! / S of their weapons, they lie dead.
2Ki 18:16 Hezekiah even s the gold from the doors of the
1Ch 10:9 So they s off Saul's armor and cut off his head.
Job 1:21 and I will be s of everything when I die.
12:17 He leads counselors away s of good judgment;
12:19 He leads priests away s of status; he overthrows
19:9 He has s me of my honor and removed the crown
22:6 gave you as a pledge. Yes, you s him to the bone.
Isa 17:6 Yes, Israel will be s bare of people,"
22:8 Judah's defenses have been s away. You run to the
Jer 48:32 as the Dead Sea, but the destroyer has s you bare!
La 1:8 for they have seen her s naked and humiliated.
3:17 Peace has been s away, and I have forgotten what
4:21 You, too, will be s naked in your drunkenness.
Eze 12:19 because their land will be s bare on account of
23:10 They s her and killed her and took away her
Da 5:20 down from his royal throne and s of his glory.
Hos 10:5 priests wail for it, because its glory will be s away.
Mic 2:9 and s their children of all their God-given rights.
Na 2:10 Soon the city is an empty shambles, s of its wealth.
Mt 27:28 They s him and put a scarlet robe on him.
Lk 10:30 They s him of his clothes and money, beat him up,
Jn 21:7 he put on his tunic (for he had s for work),
Ac 16:22 and the city officials ordered them s and beaten
Col 3:9 for you have s off your old evil nature and all its

STRIPPING (3) [STRIP]

Joel 1:4 the hopping locusts, and then the s locusts, too!
1:7 s their bark and leaving the branches white
2:25 "I will give you back what you lost to the s

STRIPS (6) [STRIP]

Ge 30:37 and peeled off s of the bark to make white streaks
Ex 39:3 gold into thin sheets and cutting it into fine s.
Ps 29:9 and s the forests bare. / In his Temple everyone
Lk 2:7 She wrapped him snugly in s of cloth and laid him
2:12 lying in a manger, wrapped snugly in s of cloth!"
11:22 and overpowers him, s him of his weapons,

STROKE (2) [STRIKE]

1Sa 25:37 As a result he had a s, and he lay on his bed
Ecc 10:9 chop wood, there is danger with each s of your ax!

STROKES [KJV] See DISCIPLINE

STROLL (1) [STROLLING]

2Sa 11:2 a nap and went for a s on the roof of the palace.

STROLLING (1) [STROLL]

Pr 7:8 He was s down the path by her house

STRONG (215) [STRENGTH, STRENGTHEN, STRENGTHENED, STRENGTHENING, STRENGTHENS, STRONGER, STRONGEST, STRONGLY]

Ge 29:20 her was so s that it seemed to him but a few days.
34:3 But Shechem's love for Dinah was s, and he tried
49:14 "Issachar is a s beast of burden, / resting among
49:24 But his bow remained s, / and his arms were
Ex 1:19 they told him, "the Hebrew women are very s.
10:19 The LORD responded by sending a s west wind
14:21 up a path through the water with a s east wind.
Nu 13:18 and find out whether the people living there are s
23:22 them out of Egypt; / he is like a s ox for them.
Dt 2:36 as far as Gilead. No town had walls too s for us.
9:2 They are s and tall—descendants of the famous
29:6 You had no bread or wine or other s drink, but he
31:6 Be s and courageous! Do not be afraid of them!
31:7 watched he said to him, "Be s and courageous!
31:23 of Nun with these words: "Be s and courageous!
34:7 yet his eyesight was clear, and he was as s as ever.
Jos 1:6 "Be s and courageous, for you will lead my people
1:7 Be s and very courageous. Obey all the laws
1:9 I command you—be s and courageous! Do not be
1:18 will be put to death. So be s and courageous!"
4:13 These warriors—about forty thousand s—
10:25 "Be s and courageous, for the LORD is going to
14:11 I am as s now as I was when Moses sent me on that
17:13 however, when the Israelites became s enough,
17:16 Jezreel have iron chariots—they are too s for us."
17:17 of Joseph, "Since you are so large and s,
17:18 even though they are s and have iron chariots."
23:6 "So be s! Be very careful to follow all the
Jdg 9:51 But there was a s tower inside the city,
14:14 to eat; / out of the s came something sweet."
16:5 so s and how he can be overpowered and tied up
16:6 "Please tell me what makes you so s and what it
16:15 you still haven't told me what makes you so s!"
1Sa 2:4 no more; / and those who were weak are now s.
14:52 Saul saw a young man who was brave and s,
16:18 only that; he is brave and s and has good judgment.
23:16 and encouraged him to stay s in his faith in God.
2Sa 2:7 I ask you to be my s and loyal subjects like the
3:39 Joab and Abishai—are too s for me to control.
7:12 your descendants, and I will make his kingdom s.
10:11 "If the Arameans are too s for me, then come over
10:11 "And if the Ammonites are too s for you, I will
15:3 would say, "You've really got a s case here!
22:18 from those who hated me and were too s for me.
22:33 God is my s fortress; / he has made my way safe.
2Ki 24:16 and smiths, all of whom were s and fit for war.
1Ch 16:28 recognize that the LORD is glorious and s.
17:11 one of your sons, and I will make his kingdom s.
19:12 "If the Arameans are too s for me, then come over
19:12 "And if the Ammonites are too s for you, I will
22:13 Be s and courageous; do not be afraid or lose
28:10 a Temple as his sanctuary. Be s, and do the work."
28:20 "Be s and courageous, and do the work.
2Ch 12:1 But when Rehoboam was firmly established and s,
15:7 And now, you men of Judah, be s and courageous,
30:12 giving them a s desire to unite in obeying the
32:7 "Be s and courageous! Don't be afraid of the king
Job 5:15 rescues the poor from the cutting words of the s.
8:16 The godless seem so s, like a lush plant growing in
11:15 in innocence. You will be s and free of fear.
12:21 upon princes and confiscates weapons from the s.
15:26 Holding their s shields, they defiantly charge
30:15 prosperity has vanished as a cloud before a s wind.
30:18 With a s hand, God grabs my garment. He grips
39:11 Since it is so s, can you trust it? Can you go away
40:9 Are you as s as God, and can you thunder with a
Ps 18:17 from those who hated me and were too s for me.
21:8 Your s right hand will seize all those who hate you.
24:8 The LORD, s and mighty, / the LORD,
31:24 So be s and take courage, / all you who put your
34:10 Even s young lions sometimes go hungry,
35:10 else rescues the weak and helpless from the s?
48:10 the earth. / Your s right hand is filled with victory.
60:5 Use your s right arm to save us, / and rescue your
63:8 behind you; / your s right hand holds me securely.
73:4 a painless life; / their bodies are so healthy and s.
74:11 Why do you hold back your s right hand?
84:5 Happy are those who are s in the LORD,
88:4 who is dead, / like a s man with no strength left.
89:13 Powerful is your arm! / S is your hand!
89:14 Your throne is founded on two s pillars—
89:21 I will steady him, / and I will make him s.
92:10 But you have made me as s as a wild bull.
92:12 palm trees / and grow s like the cedars of Lebanon.
96:7 recognize that the LORD is glorious and s.
108:6 Use your s right arm to save me, / and rescue your
118:15 The s right arm of the LORD has done glorious
118:16 The s right arm of the LORD is raised in triumph.
118:16 The s right arm of the LORD has done glorious
136:12 He acted with a s hand and powerful arm.
140:7 O Sovereign LORD, my s savior, / you protected
142:6 from my persecutors, / for they are too s for me.
148:14 He has made his people s, / honoring his godly
Pr 18:10 The name of the LORD is a s fortress; the godly
21:22 The wise conquer the city of the s and level the
23:11 for their Redeemer is s. He himself will bring their
24:3 by wisdom and becomes s through good sense.
24:5 A wise man is mightier than a s man, and a man of knowledge is more powerful than a s
25:15 a prince, and soft speech can crush s opposition.
30:25 Ants—they aren't s, / but they store up food for the
31:17 She is energetic and s, a hard worker.
Ecc 12:3 tremble with age, and your s legs will grow weak.
SS 5:15 of the finest gold, s as the cedars of Lebanon.
8:6 For love is as s as death, and its jealousy is as
Isa 22:17 He is going to send you into captivity, you s man!
23:12 were a lovely city, but you will never again be s.
24:9 and song; s drink now turns bitter in the mouth.
25:2 of ruins. Cities with s walls are turned to rubble.
25:3 Therefore, s nations will declare your glory;
26:1 of Judah will sing this song: / Our city is now s!
28:15 for we have built a s refuge made of lies
28:17 Your refuge looks s, but since it is made of lies,
31:8 The s young Assyrians will be taken away as
35:4 to those who are afraid, "Be s, and do not fear,
41:6 encourage one another with the words, "Be s!"
61:3 For the LORD has planted them like s
Jer 1:18 You are s like a fortified city that cannot be
18:9 a certain nation or kingdom, making it s and great,
31:11 has redeemed Israel from those too s for them.
48:17 See how the s scepter is broken, how the beautiful
50:34 But the one who redeems them is s. His name is
Eze 3:14 and turmoil, but the LORD's hold on me was s.
17:6 It soon produced s branches and luxuriant leaves.
17:9 it won't take a s arm or a large army to do it.
17:14 so Israel would not become s again and revolt.
19:3 to become a s young lion. / He learned to catch
19:5 another of her cubs / and taught him to be a s lion.
19:11 Its branches became very s, / s enough to be a ruler's scepter.
19:14 is s enough to be a ruler's scepter.' This is a
21:7 s knees will tremble and become as weak as water.
22:14 How s and courageous will you be in my day of
30:21 with a splint to make it s enough to hold a sword.
31:7 It was s and beautiful, for its roots went deep into
32:2 You think of yourself as a s young lion among the
36:35 The ruined cities now have s walls, and they are
Da 1:4 "Select only s, healthy, and good-looking young
2:40 there will be a fourth great kingdom, as s as iron.
2:42 Some parts of it will be as s as iron, and others as
4:11 The tree grew very tall and s, reaching high into
4:20 You saw a tree growing very tall and s,
4:22 For you have grown s and great; your greatness
7:2 with s winds blowing from every direction.
7:7 saw a fourth beast, terrifying, dreadful, and very s.
8:24 He will become very s, but not by his own power.
9:25 will be rebuilt with streets and s defenses,
10:19 Be at peace; take heart and be s!" As he spoke
11:23 a mere handful of followers, he will become s.
11:32 But the people who know their God will be s
Hos 7:15 "I trained them and made them s, yet now they
Joel 3:16 will be a welcoming refuge and a s fortress.
Am 2:9 Amorites were as tall as cedar trees and s as oaks,
5:9 With blinding speed and power he destroys the s,
Mic 4:7 but I will make them s again, a mighty nation.
5:8 will go out among the nations and be as s as a lion.
Na 1:7 is good. When trouble comes, he is a s refuge.
Zep 1:14 it comes—a day when s men will cry bitterly.
Zec 1:14 for Jerusalem and Mount Zion is passionate and s.
8:2 My love for Mount Zion is passionate and s;
9:3 Tyre has built a s fortress and has piled up so much
10:3 he will make them s and glorious, like a proud
10:12 I will make my people s in my power, and they
Mal 3:2 refines metal or like a s soap that whitens clothes.
Mt 12:29 You can't enter a s man's house and rob him
14:24 for a s wind had risen, and they were fighting
Mk 3:27 You can't enter a s man's house and rob him

5: 4 the shackles. No one was **s** enough to control him.
Lk 1:80 John grew up and became **s** in spirit. Then he lived
2:40 There the child grew up healthy and **s**. He was
6:48 It is like a person who builds a house on a **s**
14:31 **s** enough to defeat the twenty thousand soldiers
Ac 11:24 a good man, full of the Holy Spirit and **s** in faith.
Ro 1:11 with you that will help you grow **s** in the Lord.
16:25 God is able to make you **s**, just as the Good News
1Co 1: 8 He will keep you **s** right up to the end, and he will
10:12 If you think you are standing **s**, be careful, for you
10:13 so **s** that you can't stand up against it.
15:58 my dear brothers and sisters, be **s** and steady,
16:13 true to what you believe. Be courageous. Be **s**.
2Co 11:21 I'm ashamed to say that we were not **s** enough to
12:10 and calamities. For when I am weak, then I am **s**.
13: 9 We are glad to be weak, if you are really **s**.
Eph 1:15 Ever since I first heard of your **s** faith in the Lord
6:10 A final word: Be **s** with the Lord's mighty power.
Col 2: 2 be encouraged and knit together by **s** ties of love.
2: 5 as you should and because of your **s** faith in Christ.
2: 7 **s** and vigorous in the truth you were taught.
2:19 For we are joined together in his body by his **s**
2:23 may seem wise because they require **s** devotion,
4:12 for you, asking God to make you **s** and perfect,
1Th 3: 5 Timothy to find out whether your faith was still **s**.
3: 6 good news that your faith and love are as **s** as ever.
3: 7 because you have remained **s** in your faith.
3: 8 us new life, knowing you remain **s** in the Lord.
3:13 a result, Christ will make your hearts **s**, blameless,
4:10 your love is already **s** toward all the Christians in
2Th 2:15 and keep a **s** grip on everything we taught you both
3: 3 he will make you **s** and guard you from the evil
2Ti 2: 1 be **s** with the special favor God gives you in Christ
Tit 1: 9 He must have a **s** and steadfast belief in the
1:13 as sternly as necessary to make them **s** in the faith.
2: 2 They must have **s** faith and be filled with love
Heb 6:19 This confidence is like a **s** and trustworthy anchor
11:34 They became **s** in battle and put whole armies to
12:13 will not stumble and fall but will become **s**.
Jas 1: 4 you will be **s** in character and ready for anything.
1:21 in your hearts, for it is **s** enough to save your souls.
3: 4 pilot wants it to go, even though the winds are **s**.
1Pe 1: 7 only to test your faith, to show that it is **s** and pure.
1: 7 So if your faith remains **s** after being tried by fiery
5: 9 a firm stand against him, and be **s** in your faith.
1Jn 2:14 because you are **s** with God's word living in your
Rev 5: 2 And I saw a **s** angel, who shouted with a loud
19:18 and eat the flesh of kings, captains, and **s** warriors;

STRONGER (34) [STRONG]

Ge 25:23 One nation will be **s** than the other;
30:41 Whenever the **s** females were ready to mate,
30:42 belonged to Laban, and the **s** ones were Jacob's.
Nu 13:31 can't go up against them! They are **s** than we are!"
Dt 11:23 though they are much greater and **s** than you.
28:43 The foreigners living among you will become **s** and **s**,
Jdg 1:28 When the Israelites grew **s**, they forced the
1:35 but when the descendants of Joseph became **s**,
4:24 And from that time on Israel became **s** and **s** against King Jabin,
14:18 What is **s** than a lion?" / Samson replied, "If you
2Sa 1:23 were swifter than eagles; / they were **s** than lions.
3: 1 As time passed David became **s** and **s**,
13:14 and since he was **s** than she was, he raped her.
Job 17: 9 and those with pure hearts will become **s** and **s**.
Ps 84: 7 They will continue to grow **s**, / and each of them
Ecc 7:19 A wise person is **s** than the ten leading citizens of a
Isa 7: 8 because Aram is no **s** than its capital, Damascus.
7: 8 And Damascus is no **s** than its king, Rezin.
7: 9 Israel is no **s** than its capital, Samaria.
7: 9 And Samaria is no **s** than its king, Pekah son of
Jer 20: 7 You are **s** than I am, and you overpowered me.
Eze 21:10 Those far **s** than you have fallen beneath its power!
Da 10:19 I suddenly felt **s** and said to him, "Now you may
Mt 5:30 even if it is your **s** hand—causes you to sin, cut it
Lk 11:22 until someone who is **s** attacks and overpowers
16:17 It is **s** and more permanent than heaven and earth.
Ro 4:20 In fact, his faith grew **s**, and in this he brought
1Co 1:25 and God's weakness is far **s** than the greatest of
3: 2 solid food, because you couldn't handle anything **s**.
10:22 as Israel did? Do you think we are **s** than he is?

STRONGEST (17) [STRONG]

Jdg 3:29 and killed about ten thousand of their **s** and bravest
2Sa 1:22 Both Saul and Jonathan killed their **s** foes;
11:16 where he knew the enemy's **s** men were fighting.
2Ki 2:16 and fifty of our **s** men will search the wilderness
1Ch 12:14 regular troops, and the **s** could take on a thousand!
Ps 78:31 God rose against them, / and he killed their **s** men;
Ecc 9:11 and the **s** warrior doesn't always win the battle.
Isa 1:31 The **s** among you will disappear like burning straw.
8:11 The LORD has said to me in the **s** terms: "Do not
13: 7 arm is paralyzed with fear. Even the **s** hearts melt
34: 7 The **s** will die—veterans and young men, too.
41: 1 Bring your **s** arguments. Come now and speak.
Eze 30:15 out my fury on Pelusium, the **s** fortress of Egypt,
Da 3:20 Then he ordered some of the **s** men of his army to
11:39 foreign god's help, he will attack the **s** fortresses.
Am 2:14 not get away. The **s** among you will become weak.
Zep 1:16 Down go the walled cities and **s** battlements!

STRONGHOLD (12) [STRONGHOLDS]

1Sa 22: 4 stayed in Moab while David was living in his **s**.
22: 5 "Leave the **s** and return to the land of Judah."
24:22 But David and his men went back to their **s**.
2Sa 5:17 was told they were coming and went into the **s**.
22: 3 my shield, the strength of my salvation, and my **s**,
23:14 David was staying in the **s** at the time, and a
24: 7 Then they came to the **s** of Tyre, and all the cities
1Ch 11:16 David was staying in the **s** at the time, and a
12: 8 to David while he was at the **s** in the wilderness.
12:16 from Benjamin and Judah came to David at the **s**.
Ps 18: 2 my shield, the strength of my salvation, and my **s**.
Eze 24:25 "Son of man, on the day I take away their **s**—

STRONGHOLDS (8) [STRONGHOLD]

1Sa 23:14 David now stayed in the **s** of the wilderness and in
23:19 "He is in the **s** of Horesh on the hill of Hakilah,
23:29 David then went to live in the **s** of En-gedi.
2Sa 22:46 their courage / and come trembling from their **s**.
Ps 18:45 their courage / and come trembling from their **s**.
Jer 48:41 "Her cities will fall; her **s** will be seized.
Da 11:24 He will plot the overthrow of **s**, but this will last
2Co 10: 4 worldly weapons, to knock down the Devil's **s**.

STRONGLY (6) [STRONG]

Nu 24:21 the Kenites and prophesied: / "You are **s** situated;
2Sa 18: 3 But his men objected **s**. "You must not go,"
Lk 5:17 And the Lord's healing power was **s** with Jesus.
Ac 2:40 preaching for a long time, **s** urging all his listeners,
15:38 But Paul disagreed **s**, since John Mark had deserted
Gal 2:11 speaking **s** against what he was doing, for it was

STRUCK (55) [STRIKE]

Ge 26: 1 Now a severe famine **s** the land, as had happened
32:25 he **s** Jacob's hip and knocked it out of joint at the
Ex 9:23 sent thunder and hail, and lightning **s** the earth.
17: 5 the one you used when you **s** the water of the Nile.
Nu 14:37 were **s** dead with a plague before the LORD.
20:11 raised his hand and **s** the rock twice with the staff,
Dt 25:18 and they **s** down those who were lagging behind.
Jos 22:17 even after the plague that **s** the entire assembly of
1Sa 6: 4 "Since the plague has **s** both you and your five
14:15 And just then an earthquake **s**, and everyone was
25:38 ten days later, the LORD **s** him and he died.
2Sa 5:25 and he **s** down the Philistines all the way from
6: 7 and God **s** him dead beside the Ark of God.
22:39 I **s** them down so they could not get up;
1Ki 16:10 Zimri walked in and **s** him down and killed him.
20:37 So he **s** the prophet and wounded him.
2Ki 2: 8 folded his cloak together and **s** the water with it.
2:14 He **s** the water with the cloak and cried out,
13:18 king picked them up and **s** the ground three times.
13:19 "You should have **s** the ground five or six times!"
15: 5 The LORD **s** the king with leprosy, which lasted
1Ch 13:10 and he **s** him dead because he had laid his hand on
14:16 and he **s** down the Philistine army all the way from
2Ch 13:20 and finally the LORD **s** him down and he died.
21:18 It was after this that the LORD **s** Jehoram with
26:20 eager to get out because the LORD had **s** him.
Est 9: 5 and **s** down their enemies with the sword.
Job 2: 7 and he **s** Job with a terrible case of boils from head
6: 4 For the Almighty has **s** me down with his arrows.
19:21 have mercy, for the hand of God has **s** me.
Ps 18:38 I **s** them down so they could not get up; / they fell
38: 2 Your arrows have **s** deep, / and your blows are
78:31 he **s** down the finest of Israel's young men.
135:10 He **s** down great nations / and slaughtered mighty
136:17 Give thanks to him who **s** down mighty kings.
SS 5: 7 were making their rounds; they **s** and wounded me.
Isa 28:15 You boast that you have **s** a bargain to avoid death
Jer 4: 9 and the prophets will be **s** with horror."
5: 3 You **s** your people, but they paid no attention.
49:23 "The towns of Hamath and Arpad are **s** with fear,
La 1: 7 Her enemy **s** her down and laughed as she fell.
4: 6 where utter disaster **s** in a moment with no one to
Eze 16:27 That is why I **s** you with my fist and reduced your
32:23 These mighty men who once **s** terror in the hearts
32:26 They once **s** terror into the hearts of all people.
Da 2:34 It **s** the feet of iron and clay, smashing them to bits.
8: 7 The goat charged furiously at the ram and **s** it,
Am 4: 9 "I **s** your farms and vineyards with blight
Hab 3: 8 LORD, that you **s** the rivers and parted the sea?
Jn 18:22 One of the Temple guards standing there **s** Jesus on
Ac 12:23 an angel of the Lord **s** Herod with a sickness,
23: 3 break the law yourself by ordering me **s** like that?"
Rev 8:12 and one-third of the sun was **s**, and one-third of the
11:11 And terror **s** all who were staring at them.
19:15 a sharp sword, and with it he **s** down the nations.

STRUCTURE (9) [STRUCTURES]

1Ki 6: 7 so the entire **s** was built without the sound of
6: 9 After completing the Temple **s**, Solomon put in a
1Ch 22: 5 the Temple of the LORD must be a magnificent **s**,
Ezr 5: 3 to rebuild this Temple and restore this **s**?"
5: 9 to rebuild this Temple and restore this **s**?'
Eze 40: 9 This foyer was at the inner end of the gateway **s**,
40:16 There were also windows in the foyer **s**.
40:29 had windows along its walls and in the foyer **s**.
40:33 were windows along the walls and in the foyer **s**.

STRUCTURES (1) [STRUCTURE]

Eze 42: 2 This group of **s**, whose entrance opened toward the

STRUGGLE (10) [STRUGGLED, STRUGGLING]

Ge 3:17 All your life you will **s** to scratch a living from it.
30: 8 she said, "I have had an intense **s** with my sister,
Jdg 12: 2 "You failed to help us in our **s** against Ammon.
Job 7: 1 "Is this not the **s** of all humanity? A person's life
14:14 and through my **s** I would eagerly wait for release.
27:22 them without mercy. They **s** to flee from its power.
Ps 13: 2 How long must I **s** with anguish in my soul,
Ro 15:30 to join me in my **s** by praying to God for me.
Php 1:30 you know that I am still in the midst of this great **s**.
Heb 12: 4 you have not yet given your lives in your **s** against

STRUGGLED (4) [STRUGGLE]

Ge 25:22 But the two children **s** with each other in her
32:28 because you have **s** with both God and men
Hos 12: 3 Before Jacob was born, he **s** with his brother;
Ac 27: 8 We **s** along the coast with great difficulty

STRUGGLING (2) [STRUGGLE]

Ex 23: 5 If you see the donkey of someone who hates you **s**
Mk 6:48 rowing hard and **s** against the wind and waves.

STRUNG (2) [STRING]

Ge 3: 7 So they **s** fig leaves together around their hips to
Hab 1:15 Must we be **s** up on their hooks and dragged out in

STRUT (2) [STRUTTED, STRUTTING]

Ps 12: 8 even though the wicked **s** about, / and evil is
73: 9 and their words **s** throughout the earth.

STRUTTED (1) [STRUT]

1Sa 17:16 the Philistine giant **s** in front of the Israelite army.

STRUTTING (1) [STRUT]

Pr 30:31 the **s** rooster, / the male goat, / a king as he leads

STUBBLE (1)

Ob 1:18 will be a raging fire, and Edom, a field of dry **s**.

STUBBORN (48) [STUBBORN-HEARTED, STUBBORNLY, STUBBORNNESS]

Ex 4:21 But I will make him **s** so he will not let the people
7: 3 But I will cause Pharaoh to be **s** so I can multiply
7:13 Pharaoh's heart, however, remained hard and **s**.
7:14 the LORD said to Moses, "Pharaoh is very **s**,
7:22 So Pharaoh's heart remained hard and **s**.
8:19 But Pharaoh's heart remained hard and **s**.
9: 7 after he found it to be true, his heart remained **s**.
9:12 But the LORD made Pharaoh even more **s**,
10: 1 I have made him and his officials **s** so I can
10:20 But the LORD made Pharaoh **s** once again,
32: 9 "I have seen how **s** and rebellious these people
33: 3 along with you, for you are a **s**, unruly people.
33: 5 Moses to tell them, "You are an unruly, **s** people.
34: 9 Yes, this is an unruly and **s** people, but please
Dt 2:30 because the LORD your God made Sihon **s**
9: 6 are righteous, for you are not—you are a **s** people.
9:13 watching this people, and they are extremely **s**.
10:16 cleanse your sinful hearts and stop being **s**.
21:18 "Suppose a man has a **s**, rebellious son who will
21:20 'This son of ours is **s** and rebellious and refuses to
29:19 even though I am walking in my own **s** way.'
31:27 For I know how rebellious and **s** you are.
Jdg 2:19 refused to give up their evil practices and **s** ways.
1Sa 6: 6 Don't be **s** and rebellious as Pharaoh
2Ki 17:14 They were as **s** as their ancestors and refused to
2Ch 30: 8 Do not be **s**, as they were, but submit yourselves to
36:13 Zedekiah was a hard and **s** man, refusing to turn to
Ne 9:16 But our ancestors were a proud and **s** lot, and they
Ps 78: 8 like their ancestors— / **s**, rebellious, and unfaithful,
81:12 So I let them follow their blind and **s** way,
Pr 28:14 but the **s** are headed for serious trouble.
Isa 30: 9 For these people are **s** rebels who refuse to pay any
46:12 Listen to me, you **s**, evil people!
48: 4 "I know how **s** and obstinate you are. Your necks
63:17 Why have you given us **s** hearts so we no longer
Jer 5:23 "But my people have **s** and rebellious hearts.
7:24 following the **s** desires of their evil hearts.
7:26 They have been **s** and sinful—even worse than
La 3:65 Give them hard and **s** hearts, and then let your
Eze 2: 4 They are a hard-hearted and **s** people. But I am
3: 7 For the whole lot of them are hard-hearted and **s**.
3: 8 I have made you as hard and **s** as they are.
Hos 4:16 Israel is as **s** as a heifer, so the LORD will put her
13:13 resists being born. How **s** they are! How foolish!
Mt 17:17 Jesus replied, "You **s**, faithless people! How long
Mk 16:14 their **s** refusal to believe those who had seen him
Lk 9:41 "You **s**, faithless people," Jesus said, "how long
Ac 7:51 "You **s** people! You are heathen at heart and deaf

STUBBORNLY (13) [STUBBORN]

Ex 9:34 and his officials sinned yet again by **s** refusing to
Nu 22:32 to block your way because you are **s** resisting me.
Ne 9:29 They **s** turned their backs on you and refused to
Pr 29: 1 Whoever **s** refuses to accept criticism will
Jer 3:17 They will no longer **s** follow their own evil desires.
9:14 they have **s** followed their own desires
11: 8 Instead, they **s** followed their own evil desires.
13:10 They **s** follow their own desires and worship idols.
16:12 You **s** follow your own evil desires and refuse to
17:23 They **s** refused to pay attention and would not
19:15 because you have **s** refused to listen to me."
23:17 And to those who **s** follow their own evil desires,
Zec 7:11 They turned **s** away and put their fingers in their

STUBBORNNESS (3) [STUBBORN]
Dt 9:27 Overlook the s and sin of these people,
1Sa 15:23 of witchcraft, and s is as bad as worshiping idols.
Ro 2:5 because of your s in refusing to turn from your sin.

STUCK (3) [STICK]
1Sa 19:10 into the night, leaving the spear s in the wall.
26:7 with his spear s in the ground beside his head.
Ac 27:41 The bow of the ship s fast, while the stern was

STUDENT (5) [STUDY]
1Ch 25:8 to whether they were young or old, teacher or s.
Mt 10:24 "A s is not greater than the teacher. A servant is
10:25 The s shares the teacher's fate. The servant shares
Lk 6:40 A s is not greater than the teacher. But the s who works hard will become like the

STUDENTS (1) [STUDY]
Ecc 12:11 A wise teacher's words spur s to action

STUDIED (4) [STUDY]
Ezr 7:11 the priest and scribe who s and taught the
Ne 8:14 As they s the law, they discovered that the LORD
Jn 7:15 so much when he hasn't s everything we've s?"

STUDY (4) [STUDENT, STUDENTS, STUDIED, STUDYING]
Jos 1:8 S this Book of the Law continually. Meditate on it
Ezr 7:10 This was because Ezra had determined to s
Ps 119:15 I will s your commandments / and reflect on your
Ac 26:24 you are insane. Too much s has made you crazy!"

STUDY [KJV] See also AMBITION, STUDYING, WORK

STUDYING (2) [STUDY]
Ecc 12:12 S them can go on forever and become very
Da 9:2 I, Daniel, was s the writings of the prophets.

STUFF [KJV] See BAGGAGE, BELONGINGS, GOODS, FURNITURE, POSSESSION(S)

STUFFED (2)
Ge 31:34 and had s them into her camel saddle,
Dt 32:15 and unruly; / the people grew heavy, plump, and s!

STUMBLE (47) [STUMBLED, STUMBLES, STUMBLING]
Lev 26:37 you will s over each other in flight, as though
Job 18:12 by hunger, and calamity waits for them to s.
Ps 27:2 and foes attack me, / they will s and fall.
37:24 Though they s, they will not fall, / for the LORD
69:6 Don't let those who trust in you s because of me,
119:165 who love your law have great peace / and do not s.
121:3 He will not let you s and fall; / the one who
Pr 4:12 guided by wisdom, you won't limp or s as you run.
4:16 cannot rest unless they have caused someone to s.
24:17 fall into trouble. Don't be happy when they s.
Isa 5:27 They will not get tired or s. They will run without
8:14 and Judah he will be a stone that causes people to s
8:15 Many of them will s and fall, never to rise again.
10:4 You will s along as prisoners or lie among the
28:13 Yet they will s over this simple,
31:3 they will s and fall among those they are trying to
59:10 No wonder we grope like blind people and s along.
Jer 12:5 If you s and fall on open ground, what will you do
13:16 causing you to s and fall on the dark mountains.
20:11 Before him they will s. They cannot defeat me.
31:9 They will walk beside quiet streams and not s.
46:6 By the Euphrates River to the north they s and fall.
46:12 Your mightiest warriors will s across each other
46:16 They s and fall over each other and say among
50:32 O land of pride, you will s and fall, and no one will
Eze 7:19 for their love of money made them s into sin.
Da 11:19 take refuge in his own fortresses but will s and fall,
Hos 4:5 you will s in broad daylight, just as you might at
5:5 against her; she will s under her load of guilt.
14:9 in them. But sinners s and fall along the way.
Na 2:5 they s in their haste, rushing to the walls to set up
3:3 People s over them, scramble to their feet, and fall
Mal 2:8 Your 'guidance' has caused many to s into sin.
Lk 20:18 All who s over that stone will be broken to pieces,
Jn 12:35 you can, so you will not s when the darkness falls.
Ro 9:33 a stone in Jerusalem that causes people to s,
11:9 all is well. / Let their blessings cause them to s.
11:11 Did God's people s and fall beyond recovery?
14:20 wrong to eat anything if it makes another person s.
14:21 else if it might cause another Christian to s.
1Co 8:9 a brother or sister with a weaker conscience to s.
8:13 for I don't want to make another Christian s.
Heb 12:13 will not s and fall but will become strong.
1Pe 2:8 also say, / "He is the stone that makes people s,
2:8 They s because they do not listen to God's word
2Pe 1:10 Doing this, you will never s or fall away.
1Jn 2:10 in the light and does not cause anyone to s.

STUMBLED (6) [STUMBLE]
1Sa 17:49 and Goliath s and fell face downward to the
2Sa 2:23 his back. He s to the ground and died there.
6:6 the oxen s, and Uzzah put out his hand to steady
1Ch 13:9 the oxen s, and Uzzah put out his hand to steady
Jer 18:15 They have s off the ancient highways of good,
Ro 9:32 on faith. They s over the great rock in their path.

STUMBLES (2) [STUMBLE]
Pr 13:17 An unreliable messenger s into trouble, but a
Mt 21:44 Anyone who s over that stone will be broken to

STUMBLING (10) [STUMBLE]
Job 12:5 in trouble. They give a push to people who are s.
Ps 21:7 love of the Most High will keep him from s.
66:9 are in his hands, / and he keeps our feet from s.
116:8 from death, / my eyes from tears, / my feet from s.
Pr 3:23 you safe on your way and keep your feet from s.
4:19 Those who follow it have no idea what they are s
Isa 63:13 fine stallions racing through the desert, never s.
Jn 8:12 follow me, you won't be s through the darkness,
11:10 Only at night is there danger of s because there is
Jude 1:24 all glory to God, who is able to keep you from s,

STUMBLINGBLOCK [KJV] See CLEAR, OBSTACLE, OFFENDED, STUMBLE

STUMBLINGSTONE [KJV] See STUMBLED

STUMP (7)
Job 14:8 roots have grown old in the earth and its s decays,
Isa 6:13 Israel will remain a s, like a tree that is cut down,
6:13 but the s will be a holy seed that will grow again."
11:1 Out of the s of David's family will grow a shoot—
Da 4:15 But leave the s and the roots in the ground,
4:23 But leave the s and the roots in the ground,
4:26 But the s and the roots were left in the ground.

STUNNED (6)
Ge 45:3 They were s to realize that Joseph was standing
45:26 Jacob was s at the news—he couldn't believe it.
Job 21:5 Look at me and be s. Put your hand over your
Ps 48:5 But when they saw it, they were s; / they were
Jer 8:21 of my people. I am s and silent, mute with grief.
Mk 2:12 and pushed his way through the s onlookers.

STUNTED (3)
Lev 21:18 to me, whether he is blind or lame, s or deformed,
22:23 If the bull or lamb is deformed or s, it may still be
Jer 17:6 They are like s shrubs in the desert, with no hope

STUPID (17) [STUPIDITY]
1Sa 20:30 "You s son of a whore!" he swore at him.
Ps 119:70 Their hearts are dull and s, / but I delight in your
Pr 12:1 you must love discipline; it is s to hate correction.
28:16 Only a s prince will oppress his people, but a king
Ecc 7:25 determined to prove to myself that wickedness is s
Isa 19:11 Their best counsel to the king of Egypt is s
27:11 Israel is a foolish and s nation, for its people have
28:7 They make s mistakes as they carry out their
29:9 You are s, but not from wine! You stagger, but not
29:16 How s can you be? He is the Potter, and he is
29:16 a jar ever say, "The potter who made me is s"?
56:11 They are s shepherds, all following their own path,
Jer 10:8 The wisest of people who worship idols are s
Am 6:12 S even to ask—but that's how s you are when you
6:13 And just as s is this bragging about your conquest
Jn 11:49 high priest that year, said, "How can you be so s?

STUPIDITY (5) [STUPID]
Job 26:3 How you have enlightened my s! What wise things
Isa 44:18 Such s and ignorance! Their eyes are closed,
Jer 18:16 land will become desolate, a monument to their s.
19:8 face of the earth, making it a monument to their s.
31:19 but then I was sorry. I kicked myself for my s!

STUPOR (3)
Ge 9:24 When Noah woke up from his drunken s,
Ps 78:65 like a mighty man aroused from a drunken s.
Isa 51:21 to this, you afflicted ones, who sit in a drunken s,

STURDY (1)
Eph 6:14 putting on the s belt of truth and the body armor of

STYLE (1)
Ex 39:8 The chestpiece was made in the same s as the

SUAH (1)
1Ch 7:36 The sons of Zophah were S, Harnepher, Shual,

SUBCLAN (1) [CLAN]
Nu 26:36 This was the s descended from the Shuthelahites:

SUBCLANS (5) [CLAN]
Nu 26:21 These were the s descended from the Perezites:
26:30 These were the s descended from the Gileadites:
26:40 These were the s descended from the Belaites:
26:45 These were the s descended from the Beriites:
26:58 and the Korahites were all s of the Levites.

SUBDUE (9) [SUBDUED, SUBDUES]
Ge 1:28 and told them, "Multiply and fill the earth and s it.
4:7 to attack and destroy you, and you must s it."
Dt 9:3 He will s them so that you will quickly conquer
Jdg 4:23 So on that day Israel saw God s Jabin,
1Ch 17:10 to rule my people. And I will s all your enemies.
Ps 81:14 How quickly I would then s their enemies!
89:9 their waves rise in fearful storms, you s them.
Da 7:24 from the other ten, who will s three of them.
Zec 9:15 and they will s their enemies with sling stones.

SUBDUED (12) [SUBDUE]
Nu 32:22 then you may return when the land is finally s
Jdg 8:28 That is the story of how Israel s Midian,
11:33 as Abel-keramim. Thus Israel s the Ammonites.
1Sa 7:13 So the Philistines were s and didn't invade Israel
2Sa 8:1 David s and humbled the Philistines by conquering
8:11 he had set apart from the other nations he had s—
22:40 the battle; / you have s my enemies under my feet.
1Ch 18:1 David s and humbled the Philistines by conquering
18:11 gold he had taken from the other nations he had s—
20:4 of the giants, and so the Philistines were s.
Ne 9:24 You s whole nations before them. Even the kings
Ps 18:39 the battle; / you have s my enemies under my feet.

SUBDUES (4) [SUBDUE]
2Sa 22:48 those who harm me; / he s the nations under me
Ps 18:47 those who harm me; / he s the nations under me
47:3 He s the nations before us, / putting our enemies
144:2 I take refuge in him. / He s the nations under me.

SUBJECT (18) [SUBJECTED, SUBJECTION, SUBJECTS]
Ge 14:4 For twelve years they had all been s to King
Lev 5:1 will be held responsible and be s to punishment.
22:9 otherwise they will be s to punishment and die for
Nu 15:15 before the LORD and are s to the same laws.
35:31 judged guilty of murder and s to execution;
Jdg 3:8 And the Israelites were s to Cushan-rishathaim for
3:14 And the Israelites were s to Eglon of Moab for
1Ch 22:18 and they are now s to the LORD and his people.
Isa 45:14 Ethiopians, and Sabeans will be s to you.
Jer 28:11 now s to King Nebuchadnezzar of Babylon."
Mt 5:21 If you commit murder, you are s to judgment.'
5:22 are angry with someone, you are s to judgment!
Mk 10:10 disciples in the house, they brought up the s again.
Ro 6:14 for you are no longer s to the law, which enslaves
1Co 9:20 I do the same, even though I am not s to the law,
Gal 4:4 God sent his Son, born of a woman, s to the law.
5:18 by the Holy Spirit, you are no longer s to the law.
Heb 5:2 For he is s to the same weaknesses they have.

SUBJECTED (1) [SUBJECT]
Ro 8:20 its will, everything on earth was s to God's curse.

SUBJECTION (1) [SUBJECT]
Jdg 13:1 the Philistines, who kept them in s for forty years.

SUBJECTION [KJV] See also ACCEPT (AUTHORITY), ENSLAVE, OBEDIENCE, SUBJECT(ING), SUBMISSION, SUBMISSIVE, SUBMIT(S)

SUBJECTS (20) [SUBJECT]
Nu 16:13 and that you now treat us like your s?
21:35 and killed King Og, his sons, and his s;
2Sa 2:7 be my strong and loyal s like the people of Judah,
8:6 and the Arameans became David's s and brought
8:14 and all the Edomites became David's s.
10:19 they surrendered to them and became their s.
1Ki 12:4 imposed on us. Then we will be your loyal s."
12:7 they will always be your loyal s."
1Ch 18:2 and the Moabites became David's s and brought
18:6 and the Arameans became David's s and brought
18:13 and all the Edomites became David's s.
19:19 they surrendered to David and became his s.
2Ch 10:4 imposed on us. Then we will be your loyal s."
10:7 to please them, they will always be your loyal s."
12:8 But they will become his s, so that they can learn
Ezr 4:11 from your loyal s in the province west of the
4:14 "Since we are loyal to you as your s and we do not
Jer 22:4 and on horses, with his parade of officials and s.
22:18 he dies. His s will not even care that he is dead.
Rev 16:10 And his s ground their teeth in anguish,

SUBMERGE (1)
Isa 8:8 It will s Immanuel's land from one end to the

SUBMISSION (1) [SUBMIT]
Ps 68:31 of precious metals; / let Ethiopia bow in s to God.

SUBMISSIVE (2) [SUBMIT]
1Co 14:34 to speak. They should be s, just as the law says.
Tit 2:5 to do good, and to be s to their husbands.

SUBMISSIVELY (1) [SUBMIT]
1Ti 2:11 Women should listen and learn quietly and s.

SUBMIT (19) [SUBMISSION, SUBMISSIVE, SUBMISSIVELY, SUBMITS, SUBMITTED]
Ge 16:9 "Return to your mistress and s to her authority."
49:15 his shoulder to the task / and s to forced labor.
Ex 10:3 says: How long will you refuse to s to me?
2Sa 22:45 before me; / as soon as they hear of me, they s.

2Ch 30: 8 as they were, but s yourselves to the LORD.
Ps 2:12 S to God's royal son, or he will become angry,
18:44 As soon as they hear of me, they s;
83:16 until they s to your name, O LORD.
Jer 27: 8 So you must s to Babylon's king and serve him;
27:12 s to the king of Babylon and his people," I said.
27:13 every nation that refuses to s to Babylon's king?
La 3:27 And it is good for the young to s to the yoke of his
Da 11:39 He will honor those who s to him, appointing them
Eph 5:21 you will s to one another out of reverence for
5:22 You wives will s to your husbands as you do to the
5:24 so you wives must s to your husbands in
Col 3:18 You wives must s to your husbands, as is fitting for
Tit 3: 1 Remind your people to s to the government and its
Heb 12: 9 should we not all the more cheerfully s to the

SUBMITS (2) [SUBMIT]

Jer 27:11 But the people of any nation that s to the king of
Eph 5:24 As the church s to Christ, so you wives must

SUBMITTED (1) [SUBMIT]

La 5: 6 We s to Egypt and Assyria to get enough food to

SUBORNED [KJV] See PERSUADED

SUBSCRIBE [KJV] See SIGNED

SUBSIDE (1) [SUBSIDED]

Eze 16:42 you will be spent, and my jealous anger will s.

SUBSIDED (1) [SUBSIDE]

Eze 5:13 And when my fury against them has s, all Israel

SUBSTITUTE (5) [SUBSTITUTED, SUBSTITUTES, SUBSTITUTIONS]

Lev 1: 4 on its head so the LORD will accept it as your s,
27:10 original animal and the s will be considered holy.
2Ki 18:20 Do you think that mere words can s for military
Isa 36: 5 Do you think that mere words can s for military
Mk 7: 8 God's specific laws and s your own traditions."

SUBSTITUTED (2) [SUBSTITUTE]

Lev 27:10 should never be exchanged or s for another—
27:33 and the s one will be considered holy and cannot

SUBSTITUTES (6) [SUBSTITUTE]

Nu 3:12 s for all the firstborn sons of the people of Israel.
3:41 The Levites will be reserved for me as s for the
3:41 And the Levites' livestock are mine as s for the
3:45 And take the livestock of the Levites as s for the
8:16 of the Israelites; I have taken the Levites as their s.
1Ki 14:27 Afterward Rehoboam made bronze shields as s,

SUBSTITUTIONS (1) [SUBSTITUTE]

Lev 27:33 whether it is good or bad, and no s will be allowed.

SUBTIL [KJV] See CRAFTY, SHREWDEST, SLY

SUBTRACT (2)

Dt 4: 2 or s from these commands I am giving you from
12:32 I give you. Do not add to them or s from them.

SUBURBS [KJV] See COUNTRYSIDE, (OPEN) COUNTRY, PASTURE

SUBVERT [KJV] See PERVERTED, TURNED

SUCATHITES (1)

1Ch 2:55 at Jabez—the Tirathites, Shimeathites, and S.

SUCCEED (40) [SUCCEEDED, SUCCESS, SUCCESSFUL, SUCCESSFULLY, SUCCESSION, SUCCESSOR, SUCCESSORS]

Ex 29:29 be preserved for his descendants who will s him,
Dt 28:29 and you will not s at anything you do.
Jos 1: 8 obey all that is written in it. Only then will you s.
1Sa 2: 9 in darkness. / No one will s by strength alone.
18:14 David continued to s in everything he did,
1Ki 1:35 He will s me as king, for I have appointed him to
3: 6 to him today by giving him a son to s him.
22:22 " 'You will s,' said the LORD. 'Go ahead
2Ki 1:17 Since Ahaziah did not have a son to s him,
1Ch 28: 5 he chose Solomon to s me on the throne of his
2Ch 13:12 the God of your ancestors, for you will not s!"
18:21 " 'You will s,' said the LORD. 'Go ahead
20:20 Believe in his prophets, and you will s."
Ne 2:20 But I replied, "The God of heaven will help us s.
Est 6:13 a Jew, you will never s in your plans against him.
Job 5:12 the plans of the crafty, so their efforts will not s.
Ps 10: 5 Yet they s in everything they do. / They do not see
21:11 plot against you, / their evil schemes will never s.
37:33 But the LORD will not let the wicked s / or let the
140: 8 Do not let their evil schemes s, O God.
Pr 11:10 The whole city celebrates when the godly s;
13:13 themselves in trouble; those who respect it will s.
16: 3 to the LORD, and then your plans will s.
17: 8 magic for those who give it; they s in all they do.
20:18 Plans s through good counsel; don't go to war
28:12 When the godly s, everyone is glad.
Ecc 4:14 Such a youth could come from prison and s.
7:18 but those who fear God will s either way.
10:10 That's the value of wisdom; it helps you s.
Isa 14:20 your people. Your son will not s you as king.
48:15 I will send him on this errand and will help him s.
54:17 coming day, no weapon turned against you will s.
Jer 2:37 nations you trust. You will not s despite their help.
32: 5 fight against the Babylonians, you will never s."
Da 2:43 But this will not s, just as iron and clay do not mix.
8:24 amount of destruction and s in everything he does.
11:14 in order to fulfill the vision, but they will not s.
11:25 but to no avail, for plots against him will s.
11:36 He will s—until the time of wrath is completed.
Hab 1:17 Will they s forever in their heartless conquests?

SUCCEEDED (15) [SUCCEED]

Jos 8:21 and the other Israelites saw that the ambush had s
1Ki 2:12 Solomon s him as king, replacing his father,
1Ch 3:16 Jehoiakim was s by his son Jehoiachin; he, in turn, was s by his uncle Zedekiah.
27: 7 in his division. Asahel was s by his son Zebadiah.
27:34 Ahithophel was s by Jehoiada son of Benaiah
2Ch 32:30 City of David. And so he s in everything he did.
Ps 44: 3 It was by your mighty power that they s; / it was
Jer 22:11 who s his father, King Josiah, and was taken away
22:18 who s his father, Josiah, on the throne:
37: 1 Zedekiah son of Josiah s Jehoiachin son of
Da 8:12 was overthrown. The horn s in everything it did.
11: 2 to be s by a fourth, far richer than the others.
Ac 24:27 by in this way; then Felix was s by Porcius Festus.
Ro 9:31 to get right with God by keeping the law, never s.

SUCCESS (27) [SUCCEED]

Ge 24:12 "Give me s and show kindness to my master,
24:42 if you are planning to make my mission a s,
39: 3 was with Joseph, giving him s in everything he did.
Jos 2:22 but they finally returned to the city without s.
2Sa 8:10 sent his son Joram to congratulate David on his s.
17:20 Absalom's men looked for them without s
23: 1 the man to whom God gave such wonderful s,
23: 5 He will constantly look after my safety and s.
1Ki 22:13 Be sure that you agree with them and promise s."
1Ch 12:18 prosperity be with you, / and s to all who help you,
18:10 sent his son Joram to congratulate David on his s.
22:11 and give you s as you follow his instructions in
2Ch 18:12 Be sure that you agree with them and promise s."
26: 5 as the king sought the LORD, God gave him s.
Ezr 5: 8 The work is going forward with great energy and s.
Ne 1:11 Please grant me s now as I go to ask the king for a
Job 6:13 I am utterly helpless, without any chance of s.
Ps 21: 3 You welcomed him back with s and prosperity.
49:18 and the world loudly applauds their s.
92: 7 flourish like weeds, / and evildoers blossom with s,
118:25 please save us. / Please, LORD, please give us s.
Pr 8:14 Good advice and s belong to me. Insight
15:22 wrong for lack of advice; many counselors bring s.
Ecc 4: 4 are motivated to s by their envy of their neighbors.
Da 11:12 of his enemies killed. But his s will be short lived.
Jn 3:29 and I am filled with joy at his s.
2Co 3: 5 Our only power and s come from God.

SUCCESSFUL (18) [SUCCEED]

Ge 24:40 his angel with you and will make your mission s.
24:56 The LORD has made my mission s, and I want to
Dt 30: 9 The LORD your God will make you s in
Jos 1: 7 from them, and you will be s in everything you do.
Jdg 18: 5 "Ask God whether or not our journey will be s."
1Sa 18:16 he was so s at leading his troops into battle.
18:30 David was more s against them than all the rest of
1Ki 2: 3 so that you will be s in all you do and wherever
2Ki 18: 7 with him, and Hezekiah was s in everything he did.
1Ch 20: 1 Joab led the Israelite army in s attacks against the
22:13 gave to Israel through Moses, you will be s.
2Ch 31:21 his God wholeheartedly. As a result, he was very s.
Job 5: 3 I know that fools who turn from God may be s for
Ps 90:17 and make our efforts s. / Yes, make our efforts s!
112: 2 Their children will be s everywhere; / an entire
Ecc 9:11 And those who are educated don't always lead s
2Co 13: 7 not to show that our ministry to you has been s,

SUCCESSFULLY (4) [SUCCEED]

Ge 39:23 with him, making everything run smoothly and s.
1Sa 18: 5 Whatever Saul asked David to do, David did it s.
2Sa 12:26 and the Israelite army were s ending their siege of
Job 9: 4 and so mighty. Who has ever challenged him s?

SUCCESSION (1) [SUCCEED]

Da 11:21 man who is not directly in line for royal s.

SUCCESSOR (6) [SUCCEED]

1Ki 9: 5 'You will never fail to have a s on the throne of
2Ki 2: 9 "Please let me become your rightful s."
2:15 they exclaimed, "Elisha has become Elijah's s!"
2Ch 7:18 'You will never fail to have a s who rules over
Da 5:22 "You are his s, O Belshazzar, and you knew all
11:20 "His s will be remembered as the king who sent a

SUCCESSORS (1) [SUCCEED]

Ecc 2:19 And who can tell whether my s will be wise

SUCCOTH (15)

Ge 33:17 Jacob and his household traveled on to S.
33:17 and herds. That is why the place was named S.
Ex 12:37 the people of Israel left Rameses and started for S.
13:20 Leaving S, they camped at Etham on the edge of
Nu 33: 5 leaving Rameses, the Israelites set up camp at S.
33: 6 Then they left S and camped at Etham on the edge
Jos 13:27 valley were Beth-haram, Beth-nimrah, S, Zaphon,
Jdg 8: 5 When they reached S, Gideon asked the leaders of
8: 6 But the leaders of S replied, "You haven't caught
8:14 There he captured a young man from S
8:15 Gideon then returned to S and said to the leaders,
1Ki 7:46 cast in clay molds in the Jordan Valley between S
2Ch 4:17 cast in clay molds in the Jordan Valley between S
Ps 60: 6 with joy. / I will measure out the valley of S.
108: 7 with joy. / I will measure out the valley of S.

SUCCOTH-BENOTH (1)

2Ki 17:30 from Babylon worshiped idols of their god S.

SUCCOUR(ED), SUCCOURER [KJV] See HELP(ED)

SUCH (345)

Ge 3:13 asked the woman, "How could you do s a thing?"
6: 3 "My Spirit will not put up with humans for s a
18:25 Surely you wouldn't do s a thing,
19: 7 he begged, "don't do s a wicked thing.
19:19 saved my life, and you have granted me s mercy.
39: 9 his wife. How could I ever do s a wicked thing?
40:16 When the chief baker saw that the first dream had s
41:19 I've never seen s ugly animals in all the land of
43: 6 "Why did you have to treat me with s cruelty?"
44: 4 'Why have you repaid an act of kindness with s
44: 7 we are, that you accuse us of s a terrible thing?
44:15 "Didn't you know that a man s as I would know
Ex 5:16 It is the fault of your slave drivers for making s
9:24 with s severe hail and continuous lightning.
11: 6 there has never been s wailing before and there
15:11 so awesome in splendor, / performing s wonders?
20:24 Offer on s altars your sacrifices to me—your burnt
21:28 In s a case, however, the owner will not be held
32:11 brought from the land of Egypt with s great power
32:21 "How did they ever make you bring s terrible sin
Lev 5: 2 s as the dead body of an animal that is
6:23 All s grain offerings of the priests must be entirely
11:26 If you touch the dead body of s an animal, you will
11:27 If you touch the dead body of s an animal, you will
11:31 If you touch the dead body of s an animal, you will
11:32 If s an animal dies and falls on something,
11:33 "If s an animal dies and falls into a clay pot,
11:34 And any beverage that is in s an unclean container
11:35 Any object on which the dead body of s an animal
11:36 if the dead body of s an animal falls into a spring
11:41 along the ground; s animals may never be eaten.
11:42 All s animals are to be considered detestable.
11:43 Never defile yourselves by touching s animals.
13:11 In s cases, the person need not be quarantined for
13:13 In s cases, the priest must examine the infected
14:35 The owner of s a house must then go to the priest
17: 4 S a person has shed blood and must be cut off from
17:10 I will cut off s a person from the community,
20:14 and her mother, s an act is terribly wicked.
20:14 death to wipe out s wickedness from among you.
22:25 S animals will not be accepted on your behalf
25:31 S a house may be redeemed at any time and must
25:45 You may also purchase the children of s resident
25:47 go bankrupt and sell themselves to s a foreigner,
26:10 You will have s a surplus of crops that you will
26:36 You will live there in s constant fear that the sound
27: 8 If you desire to make s a vow but cannot afford to
27:10 But if s an exchange is in fact made, then both the
27:29 be redeemed. S a person must be put to death.
Nu 5: 4 and removed s people from the camp.
35:21 In s cases, the victim's nearest relative must
Dt 3:24 or on earth who can perform s great deeds as
7: 8 That is why the LORD rescued you with s
7:26 You must utterly detest s things, for they are set
9: 5 It is not at all because you are s righteous,
13:11 and s wickedness will never again be done among
13:14 In s cases, you must examine the facts carefully.
13:14 and can prove that s a detestable act has occurred
14: 8 not eat or even touch the dead bodies of s animals.
15:21 s as being lame or blind, or if anything else is
16: 3 as you did when you escaped from Egypt in s a
17: 1 to the LORD your God, for he detests s gifts.
17: 8 Take s cases to the place the LORD your God
17:12 be put to death. S evil must be purged from Israel.
18:14 but the LORD your God forbids you to do s
19: 5 In s cases, the slayer could flee to one of the cities
19:19 this way, you will cleanse s evil from among you.
19:20 Those who hear about it will be afraid to do s an
21: 2 In s cases, your leaders and judges must determine
21:19 In s cases, the father and mother must take the son
22:21 In s cases, the judges must take the girl to the door
22:21 S evil must be cleansed from among you.
29:20 The LORD will not pardon s people. His anger
Jos 2:11 No one has the courage to fight after hearing s
10:14 when the LORD answered s a request from a
22: 3 even though the campaign has lasted for s a long
Jdg 19:23 "No, my brothers, don't do s an evil thing. For this man is my guest, and s a thing would be shameful.
19:24 But don't do s a shameful thing to this man."
19:30 "S a horrible crime has not been committed since
Ru 1:21 me to suffer and the Almighty has sent s tragedy?"
1Sa 2: 3 and haughty! / Don't speak with s arrogance!
7:10 and the Philistines were thrown into s confusion
17:39 it was like, for he had never worn s things before.

19: 8 He attacked them with s fury that they all ran
20: 2 "I'm sure he's not planning any s thing, for he
2Sa 9: 8 "Should the king show s kindness to a dead dog
12: 5 "any man who would do s a thing deserves to die!
13: 12 You know what a serious crime it is to do s a thing
19: 43 Why did you treat us with s contempt? Remember,
23: 1 the man to whom God gave s wonderful success,
23: 18 It was by s feats that he became as famous as the
1Ki 1: 41 going on? Why is the city in s an uproar?"
3: 12 and understanding mind s as no one else has ever
8: 5 and oxen before the Ark in s numbers that no one
9: 8 'Why did the LORD do s terrible things to his
10: 12 or since has there been s a supply of beautiful
11: 8 Solomon built s shrines for all his foreign wives to
19: 11 It was s a terrible blast that the rocks were torn
2Ki 6: 8 "We will mobilize our forces at s and s a place."
8: 13 "How could a nobody like me ever accomplish s a
9: 11 "You know the way s a man babbles on,"
17: 36 who brought you out of Egypt with s mighty
19: 12 s nations as Gozan, Haran, Rezeph, and the people
19: 22 At whom did you look in s proud condescension?
19: 26 so little power / and are s easy prey for you.
21: 12 I will bring s disaster on Jerusalem and Judah that
1Ch 9: 29 and the supplies s as choice flour, wine, olive oil,
11: 20 It was by s feats that he became as famous as the
2Ch 1: 12 and honor s as no other king has ever had before
4: 18 S great quantities of bronze were used that its
5: 6 and oxen before the Ark in s numbers that no one
7: 21 'Why has the LORD done s terrible things to his
9: 11 Never before had there been s beautiful
20: 9 'Whenever we are faced with any calamity s as
35: 18 of the prophet Samuel had there been s a Passover.
Ezr 7: 28 And praise him for demonstrating s unfailing love
9: 15 though in s a condition none of us can stand in
Ne 5: 2 They were saying, "We have s large families.
8: 9 said to them, "Don't weep on s a day as this!
Est 4: 14 elevated to the palace for just s a time as this?"
Job 8: 13 S is the fate of all who forget God. The hope of the
11: 8 S knowledge is higher than the heavens—but who
13: 1 I have seen many instances s as you describe.
14: 3 Must you keep an eye on s a frail creature
15: 3 to speak so foolishly. What good do s words do?
37: 7 Everyone stops working at s a time so they can
38: 2 "Who is this that questions my wisdom with s
42: 3 'Who is this that questions my wisdom with s
Ps 15: 5 the innocent. / S people will stand firm forever.
59: 11 kill them, for my people soon forget s lessons;
71: 19 You have done s wonderful things. / Who can
72: 18 God of Israel, / who alone does s wonderful things.
73: 4 They seem to live s a painless life; / their bodies
106: 21 who had done s great things in Egypt—
106: 22 s wonderful things in that land, / s awesome deeds
112: 6 S people will not be overcome by evil
139: 6 S knowledge is too wonderful for me, / too great
Pr 1: 19 S is the fate of all who are greedy for gain. It ends
3: 32 S wicked people are an abomination to the
12: 13 by their own words, but the godly escape s trouble.
20: 30 cleanses away evil; s discipline purifies the heart.
Ecc 4: 14 S a youth could come from prison and succeed.
4: 15 Everyone is eager to help s a youth, even to help
5: 6 In s cases, your mouth is making you sin.
10: 9 with each stroke of your ax! S are the risks of life.
SS 5: 16 S, O women of Jerusalem, is my lover,
Isa 9: 5 by war. All s equipment will be burned.
24: 23 There will be s glory that the brightness of the sun
25: 1 for you are my God. You do s wonderful things!
31: 6 though you are s wicked rebels, come and return to
37: 12 s nations as Gozan, Haran, Rezeph, and the people
37: 23 At whom did you look in s proud condescension?
37: 27 so little power / and are s easy prey for you.
41: 4 Who has done s mighty deeds, directing the affairs
41: 21 "Can your idols make s claims as these? Let them
42: 25 That is why he poured out s fury on them
43: 9 Which of their idols has ever foretold s things?
43: 9 Where are the witnesses of s predictions? Who can
44: 18 S stupidity and ignorance! Their eyes are closed,
66: 3 When s people sacrifice an ox, it is no more
Jer 2: 12 The heavens are shocked at s a thing and shrink
3: 5 Surely you won't be angry about s a little thing!
5: 9 "Should I not avenge myself against a nation s as
5: 29 "Should I not avenge myself against a nation s as
7: 31 I have never commanded s a horrible deed; it
never even crossed my mind to command s a
9: 9 "Should I not avenge myself against a nation s as
10: 5 Do not be afraid of s gods, for they can neither
14: 22 the LORD our God! Only you can do s things.
16: 10 'Why has the LORD decreed s terrible things
16: 10 What have we done to deserve s treatment?
17: 8 S trees are not bothered by the heat or worried by
18: 13 LORD said, "Has anyone ever heard of s a thing,
19: 3 I will bring s a terrible disaster on this place that
19: 5 I have never commanded s a horrible deed; it
never even crossed my mind to command s a
22: 8 'Why did the LORD destroy s a great city?'
26: 15 The responsibility for s a deed will lie on you,
30: 7 In all history there has never been s a time of
32: 35 I have never commanded s a horrible deed; it
never even crossed my mind to command s a
37: 14 "I had no intention of doing any s thing."
40: 16 said to Johanan, "I forbid you to do any s thing,
50: 3 and bring s destruction that no one will live in her
La 2: 13 In all the world has there ever been s sorrow?
Eze 3: 9 their angry looks, even though they are s rebels."
12: 3 what this means, even though they are s rebels.
14: 8 I will turn against s people and make a terrible
14: 9 I will stand against s prophets and cut them off
16: 16 Unbelievable! How could s a thing ever happen?
16: 30 says the Sovereign LORD, to do s things as these,
18: 13 Should s a sinful person live? No! He must die
18: 17 S a person will not die because of his father's sins;
18: 28 to turn from their sins. S people will not die.
20: 39 to me. S desecration of my holy name must stop!
27: 32 sad funeral song: / 'Was there ever s a city as Tyre,
38: 11 and destroy these people who live in s confidence!
43: 8 They defiled my holy name by s wickedness,
44: 25 or unmarried sister. In s cases it is permitted.
44: 26 But s a priest can only return to his Temple duties
Da 2: 10 has ever asked s a thing of any magician,
2: 15 "Why has the king issued s a harsh decree?"
2: 27 or fortune-tellers who can tell the king s things.
3: 22 his anger, had demanded s a hot fire in the furnace,
5: 6 S terror gripped him that his knees knocked
Hos 4: 15 Israel is a prostitute, may Judah avoid s guilt.
9: 4 S sacrifices will be unclean, just as food touched
9: 4 All who present s sacrifices will be defiled.
Ob 1: 12 because they were suffering s misfortune.
1: 13 land of Israel when they were suffering s calamity.
Jnh 4: 11 Shouldn't I feel sorry for s a great city?"
Mic 2: 6 "Don't say s things," the people say.
2: 6 like that. S disasters will never come our way!"
2: 7 Will the LORD have patience with s behavior?
Hab 2: 18 own hands! What fools you are to believe s lies!
Mal 1: 13 Should I accept from you s offerings as these?"
3: 12 for your land will be s a delight," says the LORD
Mt 9: 4 "Why are you thinking s evil thoughts?
9: 8 They praised God for sending a man with s great
9: 11 "Why does your teacher eat with s scum?"
13: 3 He told many stories s as this one: "A farmer went
13: 21 But like young plants in s soil, their roots don't go
13: 34 he never spoke to them without using s parables.
14: 2 to life again! That is why he can do s miracles."
19: 14 For the Kingdom of Heaven belongs to s as
21: 23 from the Temple? Who gave you s authority?"
26: 10 "Why berate her for doing s a good thing to me?
Mk 1: 27 they asked excitedly. "It has s authority! Even evil
1: 45 s crowds soon surrounded Jesus that he couldn't
2: 16 to his disciples, "Why does he eat with s scum?"
4: 1 There was s a large crowd along the shore that he
4: 2 the people by telling many stories s as this one:
4: 17 But like young plants in s soil, their roots don't go
4: 33 He used many s stories and illustrations to teach
6: 2 his wisdom and the power to perform s miracles?
6: 14 to life again. That is why he can do s miracles."
7: 4 s as their ceremony of washing cups, pitchers,
7: 13 As s, you break the law of God in order to protect
8: 12 I will not give this generation any s sign."
10: 14 For the Kingdom of God belongs to s as these.
11: 28 from the Temple? Who gave you s authority?"
14: 6 Why berate her for doing s a good thing to me?
Lk 3: 18 John used many s warnings as he announced the
5: 30 "Why do you eat and drink with s scum?"
7: 6 to my home, for I am not worthy of s an honor.
8: 13 But like young plants in s soil, their roots don't go
9: 9 "so who is this man about whom I hear s strange
10: 12 even wicked Sodom will be better off than s a
12: 14 who made me a judge over you to decide s things
15: 2 that he was associating with s despicable people—
17: 23 Don't believe s reports or go out to look for him.
18: 16 For the Kingdom of God belongs to s as these.
20: 2 from the Temple? Who gave you s authority?"
20: 16 "But God forbid that s a thing should ever
21: 15 and s wisdom that none of your opponents will be
22: 23 each other which of them would ever do s a thing.
22: 44 and he was in s agony of spirit that his sweat fell to
24: 25 Jesus said to them, "You are s foolish people!
Jn 5: 12 "Who said s a thing as that?" they demanded.
7: 4 If you can do s wonderful things, prove it to the
7: 32 heard that the crowds were murmuring s things,
9: 16 "But how could an ordinary sinner do s
15: 6 S branches are gathered into a pile to be burned.
15: 24 If I hadn't done s miraculous signs among them
Ac 9: 21 Jesus' followers with s devastation in Jerusalem?"
14: 1 and preached with s power that a great number of
14: 17 s as sending you rain and good crops and giving
15: 24 but they had no s instructions from us.
18: 15 you take care of it. I refuse to judge s matters."
19: 16 and attacked them with s violence that they fled
22: 22 one voice they shouted, "Away with s a fellow!
26: 12 "One day I was on s a mission to Damascus,
Ro 2: 2 his justice, will punish anyone who does s things.
3: 8 Those who say s things deserve to be condemned,
4: 18 even though s a promise seemed utterly
8: 31 What can we say about s wonderful things as
12: 17 Do things in s a way that everyone can see you are
14: 13 Decide instead to live in s a way that you will not
15: 4 S things were written in the Scriptures long ago to
15: 26 in Jerusalem, who are going through s hard times.
16: 18 S people are not serving Christ our Lord; they are
1Co 3: 5 is Paul, that we should be the cause of s quarrels?
5: 11 or a swindler. Don't even eat with s people.
6: 4 If you have legal disputes about s matters, why do
6: 7 To have s lawsuits at all is a real defeat for you.
7: 15 In s cases the Christian husband or wife is not
9: 24 You also must run in s a way that you will win.
12: 24 So God has put the body together in s a way that
15: 33 Don't be fooled by those who say s things,
16: 16 and others like them who serve with s real
2Co 2: 16 And who is adequate for s a task as this?
3: 7 yet it began with s glory that the people of Israel
3: 12 Since this new covenant gives us s confidence,
6: 3 We try to live in s a way that no one will be
7: 11 S earnestness, s concern to clear yourselves, s
indignation, s alarm, s longing to see me, s zeal,
and s a readiness to punish the wrongdoer.
7: 15 and welcomed him with s respect and deep
8: 7 you have so much faith, s gifted speakers, s
knowledge, s enthusiasm, and s love for us—
11: 17 S bragging is not something the Lord wants,
Eph 4: 13 until we come to s unity in our faith
5: 3 S sins have no place among God's people.
Php 2: 27 so that I would not have s unbearable sorrow.
Col 2: 20 do you keep on following rules of the world, s as,
2: 22 S rules are mere human teaching about things that
3: 6 anger will come upon those who do s things.
1Th 3: 3 you know that s troubles are going to happen to us
4: 6 for the Lord avenges all s sins, as we have
2Th 3: 12 In the name of the Lord Jesus Christ we appeal to s
1Ti 5: 8 we believe. S people are worse than unbelievers.
6: 4 S a person has an unhealthy desire to quibble over
6: 21 from the faith by following s foolishness.
2Ti 2: 14 S arguments are useless, and they can ruin those
3: 7 S women are forever following new teachings,
Tit 1: 11 from the truth. S teachers only want your money.
1: 16 S people claim they know God, but they deny him
Heb 5: 4 a high priest simply because he wants s an honor.
6: 6 It is impossible to bring s people to repentance
10: 29 S people have insulted and enraged the Holy Spirit
12: 1 since we are surrounded by s a huge crowd of
12: 3 when sinful people did s terrible things to him,
13: 16 in need, for s sacrifices are very pleasing to God.
Jas 3: 15 S things are earthly, unspiritual, and motivated by
4: 6 and more strength to stand against s evil desires.
4: 16 about your own plans, and all s boasting is evil.
2Pe 2: 18 those who have just escaped from s wicked living.
1Jn 2: 18 and already many s antichrists have appeared.
2: 22 S people are antichrists, for they have denied the
4: 3 S a person has the spirit of the Antichrist.
4: 18 S love has no fear because perfect love expels all
2Jn 1: 7 S a person is a deceiver and an antichrist.
Jude 1: 4 The fate of s people was determined long ago,
1: 21 Live in s a way that God's love can bless you as
Rev 13: 4 They worshiped the dragon for giving the beast s
13: 13 s as making fire flash down to earth from heaven

SUCHATHITES [KJV] See SUCATHITES

SUCK (1) [SUCKERS]

Job 20: 16 He will s the poison of snakes. The viper will kill

SUCK(ED), SUCKING [KJV] See INFANT, NURSE(S), NURSED, NURSING

SUCKERS (1) [SUCK]

Pr 30: 15 The leech has two s that cry out, "More, more!"

SUCKLING(S) [KJV] See BABIES, INFANT(S), CHILD

SUDDEN (8) [SUDDENLY]

Lev 26: 16 You will suffer from s terrors, with wasting
Job 5: 3 for the moment, but then comes s disaster.
22: 10 is why you are surrounded by traps and s fears.
Ps 31: 22 In s fear I had cried out, / "I have been cut off
35: 8 So let s ruin overtake them! / Let them be caught in
Pr 24: 22 For you will go down with them to s disaster.
Ecc 9: 12 in a snare, people are often caught by s tragedy.
Am 7: 9 bring the dynasty of King Jeroboam to a s end."

SUDDENLY (114) [SUDDEN]

Ge 3: 7 and they s felt shame at their nakedness.
5: 24 Then s, he disappeared because God took him.
18: 2 he s noticed three men standing nearby. He got up
41: 2 healthy-looking cows s came up out of the river
41: 6 Then s, seven more heads appeared on the stalk,
41: 18 "S, seven fat, healthy-looking cows came up out
Ex 3: 2 S, the angel of the LORD appeared to him as a
7: 20 of the Nile. S, the whole river turned to blood!
8: 17 S, gnats infested the entire land,
Nu 6: 9 because someone s falls dead beside them,
12: 10 Miriam s became white as snow with leprosy.
16: 31 words when the ground s split open beneath them.
22: 23 Balaam's donkey s saw the angel of the LORD
Jos 6: 20 S, the walls of Jericho collapsed, and the Israelites
11: 7 traveled to the water near Merom and attacked s.
Jdg 7: 19 S, they blew the horns and broke their clay jars.
Ru 3: 8 Around midnight, Boaz s woke up and turned over.
1Sa 3: 4 S, the LORD called out, "Samuel! Samuel!"
4: 19 father-in-law were dead, her labor pains s began.
14: 15 S, panic broke out in the Philistine army, both in
18: 11 s hurled it at David, intending to pin him to the
19: 9 the tormenting spirit from the LORD s came upon
2Sa 13: 15 Then s Amnon's love turned to hate, and he hated
1Ki 20: 20 and s the entire Aramean army panicked and fled.
2Ki 2: 11 and talking, s a chariot of fire appeared,
3: 20 morning sacrifice was offered, water s appeared!
4: 19 S he complained, "My head hurts! My head
2Ch 26: 19 leprosy s broke out on his forehead.
Job 1: 19 S, a powerful wind swept in from the desert
9: 23 He laughs when a plague s kills the innocent.
20: 14 But s, the food he has eaten turns sour within him,
Ps 6: 10 and terrified. / May they s turn back in shame.
64: 4 at the innocent, / attacking s and fearlessly.
64: 7 shoot them down. / S, his arrows will pierce them.
Pr 6: 15 But they will be destroyed s, broken beyond all
29: 1 to accept criticism will s be broken beyond repair.
Isa 28: 1 rich valley, but its glorious beauty will s disappear.
28: 4 but its glorious beauty will s disappear.
28: 21 The LORD will come s and in anger, as he did

29: 5 "But s, your ruthless enemies will be driven away
30:13 calamity will come upon you s. It will be like a
32:10 than a year—you careless ones will s begin to care.
38:12 cuts cloth from a loom. / S, my life was over.
38:13 torn apart as though by lions. / S, my life was over.
47:11 So disaster will overtake you s, and you won't be
48: 3 Then s I took action, and all my predictions came
Jer 4:20 S, every tent is destroyed; in a moment,
6:26 For s, the destroying armies will be upon you!
10:18 "For s, I will fling you from this land and pour
15: 8 will cause anguish and terror to come upon them s.
18:22 from their homes as warriors come s upon them.
41: 2 Ishmael and his ten men s drew their swords
51: 8 But now s, Babylon, too, has fallen. Weep for her,
Eze 8: 4 S, the glory of the God of Israel was there, just as I
11:13 I was still speaking, Pelatiah son of Benaiah s died.
24:16 S she will die. Yet you must not show any sorrow.
24:27 your voice will s return so you can talk to him,
28: 7 They will s draw their swords against your
37: 7 S as I spoke, there was a rattling noise all across
43: 2 S, the glory of the God of Israel appeared from the
47: 7 S, to my surprise, many trees were now growing
Da 3:24 But s, as he was watching,
7: 8 s another small horn appeared among them.
8: 5 s a male goat appeared from the west,
8:15 someone who looked like a man s stood in front of
10: 7 but they were s terrified and ran away to hide.
10:19 I s felt stronger and said to him, "Now you may
11:45 but while he is there, his time will s run out,
Joel 2: 2 S, like dawn spreading across the mountains,
Am 1: 2 S, the lush pastures of the shepherds dry up.
6: 7 led away as captives. S, all your revelry will end.
Jnh 1: 4 s the LORD flung a powerful wind over the sea,
Hab 2: 7 S, your debtors will rise up in anger. They will turn
Mal 3: 1 Then the Lord you are seeking will s come to his
Mt 5:23 and you s remember that someone has something
8: 2 S, a man with leprosy approached Jesus. He knelt
8:24 S, a terrible storm came up, with waves breaking
8:26 rebuked the wind and waves, and s all was calm.
9:30 And s they could see! Jesus sternly warned them,
17: 3 S, Moses and Elijah appeared and began talking
26:75 S, Jesus' words flashed through Peter's mind:
28: 2 S there was a great earthquake, because an angel of
Mk 1:31 the fever s left, and she got up and prepared a meal
4:39 S the wind stopped, and there was a great calm.
9: 8 S they looked around, and Moses and Elijah were
14:72 S, Jesus' words flashed through Peter's mind:
Lk 2: 9 S, an angel of the Lord appeared among them,
2:13 S, the angel was joined by a vast host of others—
23:45 And s, the thick veil hanging in the Temple was
24: 4 S, two men appeared to them, clothed in dazzling
24:15 S, Jesus himself came along and joined them
24:31 S, their eyes were opened, and they recognized
24:36 Jesus himself was s standing there among them.
Jn 4:52 "Yesterday afternoon at one o'clock his fever s
6:19 or four miles out when s they saw Jesus walking
16:20 but your grief will s turn to wonderful joy when
20:19 S, Jesus was standing there among them!
20:26 but s, as before, Jesus was standing among them.
Ac 1:10 two white-robed men s stood there among them.
2: 2 S, there was a sound from heaven like the roaring
9: 3 a brilliant light from heaven s beamed down upon
10:30 S, a man in dazzling clothes was standing in front
12: 7 S, there was a bright light in the cell, and an angel
12:10 down the street, and then the angel s left him.
16:26 S, there was a great earthquake, and the prison was
22: 6 about noon a very bright light from heaven s shone
26:24 S, Festus shouted, "Paul, you are insane.
28: 6 people waited for him to swell up or s drop dead.
1Th 5: 3 then disaster will fall upon them as s as a woman's
Heb 11: 5 "s he disappeared because God took him."
Rev 1:10 S, I heard a loud voice behind me, a voice that
2:16 or I will come to you s and fight against them with
3: 3 Unless you do, I will come upon you s,
12: 3 S, I witnessed in heaven another significant event.

SUES (1)
1Co 6: 6 But instead, one Christian s another—right in front

SUFFER (66) [SUFFERED, SUFFERERS, SUFFERING, SUFFERINGS, SUFFERS]
Ex 15:26 then I will not make you s the diseases I sent on
Lev 13:45 "Those who s from any contagious skin disease
20:17 his sister, he will s the consequences of his guilt.
24:15 Those who blaspheme God will s the consequences
26:16 You will s from sudden terrors, with wasting
Nu 9:13 They will s the consequences of their guilt.
15:31 cut off and s the consequences of their guilt."
30:15 or pledge, he will s the consequences of her guilt."
Dt 7:15 He will not let you s from the terrible diseases you
28:33 You will s under constant oppression and harsh
Ru 1:13 because the LORD himself has caused me to s."
1:21 me Naomi when the LORD has caused me to s
2Ki 5:27 and your children's children will s from Naaman's
Job 24:11 and they tread in the winepress as they s from
36:15 means of their suffering, he rescues those who s.
Ps 9:13 See how I s at the hands of those who hate me.
26: 9 Don't let me s the fate of sinners. / Don't condemn
71:20 You have allowed me to s much hardship,
120: 5 How I s among these scoundrels of Meshech!
Pr 9:12 If you scorn wisdom, you will be the one to s.
11:15 is dangerous; it is better to refuse than to s later.
13:20 whoever walks with fools will s harm.
Isa 38:17 Yes, it was good for me to s this anguish, / for you
Jer 7: 8 because the Temple is here you will never s?
25: 7 bringing on yourselves all the disasters you now s.
32:18 though children s for their parents' sins.
44:27 You will s war and famine until all of you are
49:12 "If the innocent must s, how much more must
Eze 13:22 with your lies, when I didn't want them to s grief.
23:49 worship of idols. Yes, you will s the full penalty!
Mt 16:21 He would s at the hands of the leaders
17:12 And soon the Son of Man will also s at their
Mk 8:31 would s many terrible things and be rejected by the
9:12 in the Scriptures that the Son of Man must s
Lk 9:22 Son of Man, must s many terrible things," he said.
17:25 But first the Son of Man must s terribly and be
24:26 s all these things before entering his time of
24:46 it was written long ago that the Messiah must s
Ac 3:18 that he must s all these things.
5:41 them worthy to s dishonor for the name of Jesus.
9:16 And I will show him how much he must s for me."
26:23 that the Messiah would s and be the first to rise
Ro 8:18 Yet what we s now is nothing compared to the
1Co 3:15 the work is burned up, the builder will s great loss.
12:26 If one part suffers, all the parts s with it, and if one
2Co 1: 5 You can be sure that the more we s for Christ,
1: 6 you can patiently endure the same things we s.
4:10 so much that you s from having too little.
Php 1:30 You have seen me s for him in the past, and you
3:10 I can learn what it means to s with him, sharing in
Col 1:24 I am glad when I s for you in my body, for I am
1Ti 4:10 and s much in order that people will believe the
2Ti 1: 8 be ready to s with me for the proclamation of the
3:12 live a godly life in Christ Jesus will s persecution.
Heb 11:26 He thought it was better to s for the sake of the
13: 3 S with them as though you were there yourself.
1Pe 2:20 But if you s for doing right and are patient beneath
3:14 But even if you s for doing what is right, God will
3:17 Remember, it is better to s for doing good, if that is
what God wants, than to s for doing wrong!
4: 1 the same attitude he had, and be ready to s, too.
4: 1 For if you are willing to s for Christ, you have
4:15 If you s, however, it must not be for murder,
4:16 But it is no shame to s for being a Christian.
Rev 2:10 Don't be afraid of what you are about to s.
2:22 and she will s greatly with all who commit adultery

SUFFERED (37) [SUFFER]
Lev 13:24 "If anyone has s a burn on the skin and the burned
Nu 20:15 there a long time and s as slaves to the Egyptians.
1Sa 25:15 good to us, and we never s any harm from them.
1Ki 2:26 and you s right along with him through all his
2Ki 5: 1 Naaman was a mighty warrior, he s from leprosy.
1Ch 7:23 him Beriah because of the tragedy his family had s.
Ne 9:32 do not let all the hardships we have s be as nothing
Job 2:11 When they heard of the tragedy he had s, they got
Ps 107:17 were fools in their rebellion; / they s for their sins.
119:107 I have s much, O LORD; / restore my life again,
132: 1 LORD, remember David / and all that he s.
Isa 63: 9 In all their suffering he also s, and he personally
Jer 44:18 and have s the effects of war and famine."
La 5: 7 We have s the punishment they deserved!
Eze 16:49 while the poor and needy s outside her door.
36: 6 because you have s shame before the surrounding
Ob 1:12 You shouldn't have crowed over them as they s
Na 3:19 Where can anyone be found who has not s from
Mk 5:26 She had s a great deal from many doctors through
Lk 13: 2 from Galilee?" he asked. "Is that why they s?
Ro 1:27 s within themselves the penalty they so richly
Gal 3: 4 You have s so much for the Good News. Surely it
1Th 2: 2 before we came to you and how much we s there.
2:14 you s persecution from your own countrymen.
2:14 in Christ Jesus, s from their own people, the Jews.
2Ti 3:10 You know my faith and how long I have s.
Heb 2: 9 with glory and honor" because he s death for us.
5: 8 he learned obedience from the things he s.
10:34 You s along with those who were thrown into jail.
13:12 So also Jesus s and died outside the city gates in
1Pe 2:21 Christ, who s for you, is your example. Follow in
2:23 When he s, he did not threaten to get even. He left
3:18 Christ also s when he died for our sins once for all
3:18 He s physical death, but he was raised to life in the
4: 1 So then, since Christ s physical pain, you must arm
5:10 After you have s a little while, he will restore,
Rev 2: 3 You have patiently s for me without quitting.

SUFFERERS (1) [SUFFER]
Job 5:11 to the poor and humble, and he takes s to safety.

SUFFERING (68) [SUFFER]
Ge 3:16 "You will bear children with intense pain and s.
41:52 "God has made me fruitful in this land of my s."
Ex 3: 7 harsh slave drivers. Yes, I am aware of their s.
Lev 20:18 If a man has intercourse with a woman s from a
Nu 5:24 on the curse and cause bitter s in cases of guilt.
5:27 the water that brings the curse will cause bitter s.
14:34 year for each day, s the consequences of your sins.
Dt 16: 3 Eat this bread—the bread of s—so that you will
Jdg 2:18 who were burdened by oppression and s.
2Ki 14:26 For the LORD saw the bitter s of everyone in
Job 2:13 for they saw that his s was too great for words.
34: 6 My s is incurable, even though I have not sinned.'
36:15 But by means of their s, he rescues those who
36:21 from getting into a life of evil that God sent this s.
Ps 22:24 For he has not ignored the s of the needy. / He has
34: 6 I cried out to the LORD in my s, and he heard
44:24 Why do you ignore our s and oppression?
69:29 I am s and in pain. / Rescue me, O God, by your
88: T to be sung to the tune "The S of Affliction."
119:71 The s you sent was good for me, / for it taught me
Isa 26:18 writhe in agony, / but nothing comes of our s.
48:10 Rather, I have refined you in the furnace of s.
53: 8 for their sins—that he was s their punishment?
61: 8 I will faithfully reward my people for their s
63: 9 In all their s he also suffered, and he personally
Jer 15:15 I said, "LORD, you know I am s for your sake.
15:18 Why then does my s continue? Why is my wound
25:14 I will punish them in proportion to the s they cause
La 1:12 Look around and see if there is any s like mine,
3:19 The thought of my s and homelessness is bitter
Eze 36: 7 those nations will soon have their turn at s shame.
Ob 1:12 have rejoiced because they were s such misfortune.
1:13 the land of Israel when they were s such calamity.
Mt 26:39 let this cup of s be taken away from me.
Mk 10:38 Are you able to be baptized with the baptism of s I
14:36 Please take this cup of s away from me. Yet I want
Lk 22:15 this Passover meal with you before my s begins.
22:42 please take this cup of s away from me.
Ac 20:23 told me in city after city that jail and s lie ahead.
Ro 8:17 we are to share his glory, we must also share his s.
8:23 also groan to be released from pain and s.
2Co 1: 7 We are confident that as you share in s, you will
4:10 Through s, these bodies of ours constantly share in
Eph 3:13 It is for you that I am s, so you should feel honored
Php 1:29 in Christ but also the privilege of s for him.
1Th 1: 6 Holy Spirit in spite of the severe s it brought you.
3: 7 in all of our own crushing troubles and s,
2Th 1: 4 in all the persecutions and hardships you are s.
1: 5 you worthy of his Kingdom, for which you are s,
2Ti 1:12 And that is why I am s here in prison. But I am not
2: 3 Endure s along with me, as a good soldier of Christ
2: 9 I am s and have been chained like a criminal.
3:11 know how much persecution and s I have endured.
4: 5 Don't be afraid of s for the Lord. Work at bringing
Heb 2:10 Through the s of Jesus, God made him a perfect
2:18 Since he himself has gone through s
10:32 remained faithful even though it meant terrible s.
10:33 and sometimes you helped others who were s the
Jas 5:10 For examples of patience in s, look at the prophets
5:11 We give great honor to those who endure under s.
5:13 Are any among you s? They should keep on
1Pe 1:11 when he told them in advance about Christ's s
2:21 This s is all part of what God has called you to.
4:13 trials will make you partners with Christ in his s,
4:19 So if you are s according to God's will, keep on
5: 9 are going through the same kind of s you are.
Rev 1: 9 In Jesus we are partners in s and in the Kingdom
2: 9 "I know about your s and your poverty—but you

SUFFERINGS (4) [SUFFER]
Ne 9: 9 "You saw the s and sorrows of our ancestors in
Ac 17: 3 and proving the prophecies about the s of the
Col 1:24 for I am completing what remains of Christ's s for
1Pe 5: 1 too, am an elder and a witness to the s of Christ.

SUFFERS (5) [SUFFER]
Pr 22: 3 simpleton goes blindly on and s the consequences.
27:12 simpleton goes blindly on and s the consequences.
Isa 24: 5 The earth s for the sins of its people, for they have
Mt 17:15 on my son, because he has seizures and s terribly.
1Co 12:26 If one part s, all the parts suffer with it, and if one

SUFFICE(D), SUFFICETH [KJV] See ENOUGH, SATISFIED, SATISFIES

SUFFICIENT (1) [SELF-SUFFICIENT]
Isa 40:16 All Lebanon's forests do not contain s fuel to

SUGGEST (8) [SUGGESTED, SUGGESTING, SUGGESTION, SUGGESTIONS, SUGGESTIVE, SUGGESTS]
Ge 41: 8 but not one of them could s what they meant.
Dt 13: 7 They might s that you worship the gods of peoples
2Sa 17:11 "I s that you mobilize the entire army of Israel,
Ezr 4:15 We s that you search your ancestors' records,
Ne 6: 7 so I s that you come and talk it over with me."
Est 1:19 we s that you issue a written decree, a law of the
1Co 9:15 And I am not writing this to s that I would like to
2Co 8:10 I s that you finish what you started a year ago,

SUGGESTED (13) [SUGGEST]
Ge 4: 8 Later Cain s to his brother, Abel, "Let's go out
23:16 So Abraham paid Ephron the amount he had s,
1Sa 16:15 Some of Saul's servants s a remedy. "It is clear
2Sa 2:14 Then Abner s to Joab, "Let's have a few of our
17:15 had said and what he himself had s instead.
1Ki 20:25 will beat them." So King Ben-hadad did as they s.
2Ki 4:14 He s, "She doesn't have a son, and her husband is
6: 3 "Please come with us," someone s. "I will,"
Est 2: 2 So his attendants s, "Let us search the empire to
2:15 She asked for nothing except what he s, and she
5:14 So Haman's wife, Zeresh, and all his friends s,
6:10 Do not fail to carry out everything you have s."
Gal 2:10 The only thing they s was that we remember to

SUGGESTING (2) [SUGGEST]
Mal 2:17 You have wearied him by s that the LORD favors
Ro 7: 7 Well then, am I s that the law of God is evil?

SUGGESTION (7) [SUGGEST]
Ge 41:33 "My s is that you find the wisest man in Egypt

Ne 6:13 intimidate me and make me sin by following his s.
Est 9:23 So the Jews adopted Mordecai's s and began this
Da 1:10 But he was alarmed by Daniel's s. "My lord the
1:14 So the attendant agreed to Daniel's s and tested
Ac 21:23 "Here's our s. We have four men here who have
1Co 7:6 This is only my s. It's not meant to be an absolute

SUGGESTIONS (5) [SUGGEST]
Ge 41:37 Joseph's s were well received by Pharaoh and his
Ex 18:24 to his father-in-law's advice and followed his s.
1Ki 22:20 so that he can be killed there?' There were many s,
2Ch 18:19 so that he can be killed there?' There were many s,
Isa 19:14 of foolishness on them, so all their s are wrong.

SUGGESTIVE (1) [SUGGEST]
Hos 2:2 and s clothing and to stop playing the prostitute.

SUGGESTS (1) [SUGGEST]
1Sa 25:25 attention to him. He is a fool, just as his name s.

SUICIDE (1)
Jn 8:22 Jewish leaders asked, "Is he planning to commit s?

SUIT (1) [SUITABLE, SUITED]
Isa 61:10 I am like a bridegroom in his wedding s or a bride

SUITABLE (1) [SUIT]
Ge 2:20 But still there was no companion s for him.

SUITED (2) [SUIT]
Nu 32:1 and Gilead were ideally s for their flocks
32:4 of Israel. It is ideally s for all our flocks and herds.

SUKKITES (1)
2Ch 12:3 foot soldiers, including Libyans, S, and Ethiopians.

SULFUR (12)
Ge 19:24 and burning s from the heavens on Sodom
Dt 29:23 They will find its soil turned into s and salt,
Job 18:15 will disappear beneath a fiery barrage of burning s.
Ps 11:6 punishing them with burning s and scorching
Eze 38:22 send torrential rain, hailstones, fire, and burning s!
Lk 17:29 Then fire and burning s rained down from heaven
Rev 9:17 and burning s billowed from their mouths.
9:18 and burning s that came from the mouths of the
14:10 and burning s in the presence of the holy angels
19:20 thrown alive into the lake of fire that burns with s.
20:10 was thrown into the lake of fire that burns with s,
21:8 their doom is in the lake that burns with fire and s.

SULLEN (2)
1Ki 20:43 king of Israel went home to Samaria angry and s.
21:4 So Ahab went home angry and s because of

SUM (1) [SUMMARIZE, SUMMARY, SUMMED, SUMS]
Zec 11:13 this magnificent s at which they valued me!

SUMMARIZE (1) [SUM]
1Co 14:26 my brothers and sisters, let's s what I am saying.

SUMMARY (3) [SUM]
Nu 2:32 In s, the troops of Israel listed by their families
Mt 7:12 This is a s of all that is taught in the law
Lk 1:3 I have decided to write a careful s for you,

SUMMED (2) [SUM]
Ro 13:9 are all s up in this one commandment:
Gal 5:14 For the whole law can be s up in this one

SUMMER (25) [MIDSUMMER]
Ge 8:22 cold and heat, winter and s, day and night."
2Sa 16:1 one hundred bunches of s fruit, and a skin of wine.
16:2 the bread and s fruit are for the young men to eat.
Ps 32:4 My strength evaporated like water in the s heat.
74:17 of the earth, / and you make both s and winter.
Pr 6:8 they labor hard all s, gathering food for the winter.
10:5 A wise youth works hard all s; a youth who sleeps
25:13 are as refreshing as snow in the heat of s.
26:1 doesn't go with fools any more than snow with s
Isa 16:9 for their s fruits and harvests have all been
18:4 as quietly as the heat rises on a s day, or as the dew
18:6 to eat. The vultures will tear at corpses all s.
Jer 8:20 and the s is gone," the people cry, "yet we are not
28:1 One day in late s of that same year—the fourth
40:10 Harvest the grapes and s fruits and olives,
48:32 He has harvested your grapes and s fruits.
Am 3:15 their winter mansions and their s houses, too—
Zec 7:3 and fast each s on the anniversary of the Temple's
7:5 when you fasted and mourned in the s and at the
8:19 and times of mourning you have kept in early s,
14:8 flowing continuously both in s and in winter.
Mt 24:32 you know without being told that s is near.
Mk 13:28 you know without being told that s is near.
Lk 21:30 you know without being told that s is near.
Jn 4:35 not begin until the s ends four months from now?

SUMMIT (1)
Nu 20:28 At the s, Moses removed the priestly garments

SUMMON (12) [SUMMONED, SUMMONING]
Nu 11:16 "S before me seventy of the leaders of Israel.
Dt 4:10 where he told me, 'S the people before me, and I
25:8 town will then s him and try to reason with him.
31:28 Now s all the leaders and officials of your tribes
33:19 They s the people to the mountain / to offer proper
2Ki 6:32 of Israel when the king sent a messenger to s him.
10:19 S all the prophets and worshipers of Baal, and call
Job 13:22 Now s me, and I will answer! Or let me speak to
Ps 68:28 S your might, O God. / Display your power,
Eze 38:21 I will s the sword against you throughout Israel,
Am 5:16 and s professional mourners to wail and lament.
Ac 10:32 Now send some men to Joppa and s Simon Peter.

SUMMONED (48) [SUMMON]
Ex 8:8 Then Pharaoh s Moses and Aaron and begged,
Lev 23:2 the days when all of you will be s to worship me.
Nu 16:12 Then Moses s Dathan and Abiram, the sons of
20:10 Then he and Aaron s the people to come
23:7 "Balak s me to come from Aram;
30:1 Now Moses s the leaders of the tribes of Israel
Dt 29:2 Moses s all the Israelites and said to them,
Jos 24:1 Then Joshua s all the people of Israel to Shechem,
Jdg 12:2 "I s you at the beginning of the dispute, but you
1Sa 5:11 So the people s the rulers again and begged them,
16:9 Next Jesse s Shammah, but Samuel said,
29:6 So Achish finally s David and his men. "I swear
2Sa 7:2 David s Nathan the prophet. "Look!" David said.
9:2 He s a man named Ziba, who had been one of
9:9 Then the king s Saul's servant Ziba and said,
10:16 they were joined by additional Aramean troops s
11:10 he s him and asked, "What's the matter with you?
14:33 Then at last David s his estranged son,
21:2 So King David s the Gibeonites. They were not
1Ki 1:53 So King Solomon s Adonijah, and they brought
8:1 Solomon then s the leaders of all the tribes
18:3 So Ahab s Obadiah, who was in charge of the
18:20 So Ahab s all the people and the prophets to Mount
20:7 Then Ahab s all the leaders of the land and said to
22:6 So King Ahab s his prophets, about four hundred
2Ki 4:36 Then Elisha s Gehazi. "Call the child's mother!"
9:1 Elisha the prophet had s a member of the group of
11:4 Jehoiada the priest s the commanders, the Carite
18:18 They s King Hezekiah, but the king sent these
23:1 Then the king s all the leaders of Judah
1Ch 13:5 So David s all the people of Israel, from one end of
15:3 Then David s all the Israelites to Jerusalem to
15:11 Then David s the priests, Zadok and Abiathar,
19:16 so they s additional Aramean troops from the other
23:2 David s all the political leaders of Israel,
28:1 David s all his officials to Jerusalem—the leaders
2Ch 5:2 Solomon then s the leaders of all the tribes
18:5 So King Ahab s his prophets, four hundred of
23:2 secretly throughout Judah and s the Levites
24:5 He s the priests and Levites and gave them these
25:11 Then Amaziah s his courage and led his army to
29:4 He s the priests and Levites to meet him at the
34:29 Then the king s all the leaders of Judah
36:10 Jehoiachin was s to Babylon by King
Est 8:9 So on June 25 the king's secretaries were s.
Job 9:16 And even if I s him and he responded, he would
Ps 50:1 he has s all humanity from east to west!
Zec 6:8 Then the LORD s me and said, "Those who went

SUMMONING (3) [SUMMON]
Nu 10:2 silver to be used for s the people to assemble
Jdg 6:35 Asher, Zebulun, and Naphtali, s their warriors,
2Ki 10:21 He sent messengers throughout all Israel s those

SUMS (1) [SUM]
Ecc 2:8 I collected great s of silver and gold, the treasure of

SUN (111) [SUN'S, SUNBAKED, SUNDIAL, SUNDOWN, SUNLIGHT, SUNRISE, SUNSET, SUNSHINE]
Ge 1:16 the s and the moon, to shine down upon the earth.
1:16 The greater one, the s, presides during the day;
15:12 That evening, as the s was going down, Abram fell
15:17 As the s went down and it became dark,
19:23 The s was rising as Lot reached the village.
32:31 The s rose as he left Peniel, and he was limping
37:9 "The s, moon, and eleven stars bowed low before
Ex 14:27 So as the s began to rise, Moses raised his hand
16:21 And as the s became hot, the food they had not
Lev 22:7 When the s goes down, they will be clean again
Dt 4:19 And when you look up into the sky and see the s,
16:6 Sacrifice it there as the s goes down on the
17:3 by serving other gods or by worshiping the s,
33:14 with the riches that grow in the s, / and the bounty
Jos 10:12 He said, / "Let the s stand still over Gibeon,
10:13 So the s and moon stood still until the Israelites
10:13 The s stopped in the middle of the sky, and it did
10:27 As the s was going down, Joshua gave instructions
Jdg 5:31 But may those who love you rise like the s at full
19:14 The s was setting as they came to Gibeah, a town
2Sa 2:24 The s was just going down as they arrived at the
17:19 the top of the well with grain on it to dry in the s;
1Ki 22:36 Just as the s was setting, the cry ran through his
2Ki 3:22 the s was shining across the water, making it look
19:26 sprouting on a housetop, / easily scorched by the s.
23:5 and to the s, the moon, the constellations, and to all
23:11 the former kings of Judah had dedicated to the s.
23:11 king also burned the chariots dedicated to the s.
2Ch 18:34 Then just as the s was setting he died.
Job 9:7 the s won't rise and the stars won't shine.
31:26 Have I looked at the s shining in the skies,
37:21 We cannot look at the s, for it shines brightly in the
Ps 19:4 The s lives in the heavens / where God placed it.
19:6 The s rises at one end of the heavens / and follows
37:6 justice of your cause will shine like the noonday s.
58:8 like a stillborn child who will never see the s.
65:8 From where the s rises to where it sets,
72:5 May he live as long as the s shines, / as long as the
72:17 may it continue as long as the s shines.
74:16 belong to you; / you made the starlight and the s.
89:36 will go on forever; / his throne is as secure as the s,
104:19 the seasons / and the s that knows when to set.
119:147 I rise early, before the s is up; / I cry out for help
121:6 The s will not hurt you by day, / nor the moon at
136:8 the s to rule the day, / His faithful love endures
148:3 Praise him, s and moon! / Praise him, all you
Ecc 1:5 The s rises and sets and hurries around to rise
1:9 been done before. Nothing under the s is truly new.
1:14 Everything under the s is meaningless, like chasing
2:17 because everything done here under the s is
5:18 enjoy their work—whatever they do under the s—
6:5 and he would never have seen the s or known of its
11:7 Light is sweet; it's wonderful to see the s!
12:2 when the light of the s and moon and stars is dim
SS 1:6 complexion is so dark. The s has burned my skin.
1:6 and sent me out to tend the vineyards in the hot s.
6:10 the dawn, as fair as the moon, as bright as the s,
Isa 13:10 No light will shine from stars or s or moon.
19:18 One of these will be Heliopolis, the City of the S.
24:23 There will be such glory that the brightness of the s
30:26 The moon will be as bright as the s, and the s will be seven times brighter—
37:27 sprouting on a housetop, / easily scorched by the s.
49:10 The searing s and scorching desert winds will not
60:19 "No longer will you need the s or moon to give
60:20 The s will never set; the moon will not go down.
Jer 8:2 and spread them out on the ground before the s,
15:9 for breath; her s has gone down while it is yet day.
31:35 It is the LORD who provides the s to light the day
43:13 pillars standing in the temple of the s in Egypt,
Eze 8:16 They were facing eastward, worshiping the s!
32:7 I will cover the s with a cloud, and the moon will
47:10 shores will be covered with nets drying in the s.
Hos 13:3 like dew in the morning s, like chaff blown by the
Joel 2:10 The s and moon grow dark, and the stars no longer
2:31 The s will be turned into darkness, and the moon
3:15 The s and moon will grow dark, and the stars will
Am 8:9 "I will make the s go down at noon and darken the
Jnh 4:6 leaves over Jonah's head, shading him from the s.
4:8 And as the s grew hot, God sent a scorching east
4:8 The s beat down on his head until he grew faint
Mic 3:6 The s will set for you prophets, and your day will
Na 3:17 But like locusts that fly away when the s comes up
Hab 3:11 The s and moon began to fade, obscured by
Zep 1:5 For they go up to their roofs and bow to the s,
Mal 4:2 the S of Righteousness will rise with healing in his
Mt 13:6 but they soon wilted beneath the hot s and died
13:43 Then the godly will shine like the s in their
17:2 so that his face shone like the s,
24:29 those horrible days end, / the s will be darkened,
Mk 4:6 but it soon wilted beneath the hot s and died
13:24 those horrible days end, / the s will be darkened,
Lk 4:40 As the s went down that evening,
21:25 events in the skies—signs in the s, moon, and stars.
23:45 The light from the s was gone. And suddenly,
Ac 2:20 The s will be turned into darkness, / and the moon
7:42 away from them and gave them up to serve the s,
26:13 a light from heaven brighter than the s shone down
27:20 blotting out the s and the stars, until at last all hope
1Co 15:41 The s has one kind of glory, while the moon
Eph 4:26 Don't let the s go down while you are still angry,
Jas 1:11 The hot s rises and dries up the grass; the flower
Rev 1:16 And his face was as bright as the s in all its
6:12 The s became as dark as black cloth, and the moon
8:12 and one-third of the s was struck, and one-third of
10:1 His face shone like the s, and his feet were like
12:1 I saw a woman clothed with the s, with the moon
16:8 Then the fourth angel poured out his bowl on the s,
19:17 Then I saw an angel standing in the s, shouting to
21:23 And the city has no need of s or moon,
22:5 will be no night there—no need for lamps or s—

SUN'S (1) [SUN]
Isa 38:8 I will cause the s shadow to move ten steps

SUNBAKED (1) [BAKE, SUN]
Ps 22:15 My strength has dried up like s clay. / My tongue

SUNDAY (5)
Mt 28:1 Early on S morning, as the new day was dawning,
Mk 16:2 Very early on S morning, just at sunrise, they came
16:9 It was early on S morning when Jesus rose from
Lk 24:1 But very early on S morning the women came to
Jn 20:1 Early S morning, while it was still dark,

SUNDER [KJV] See BREAK, CRUSHED, CUT, SNAPPED, TEAR (APART)

SUNDIAL (4) [SUN]
2Ki 20:9 Would you like the shadow on the s to go forward
20:11 to move ten steps backward on the s of Ahaz!

Isa 38: 8 s of Ahaz!' " So the shadow on the s moved backward ten steps.

SUNDOWN (2) [SUN]

Ge 28:11 At s he arrived at a good place to set up camp
2Sa 3:35 "May God kill me if I eat anything before s."

SUNDRY [KJV] See MANY

SUNG (17) [SING]

Ps 9: T of David, to be s to the tune "Death of the Son."
22: T of David, to be s to the tune "Doe of the Dawn."
30: T psalm of David, s at the dedication of the Temple.
45: T descendants of Korah, to be s to the tune "Lilies."
46: T descendants of Korah, to be s by soprano voices.
56: T To be s to the tune "Dove on Distant Oaks."
57: T the cave. To be s to the tune "Do Not Destroy!"
58: T of David, to be s to the tune "Do Not Destroy!"
59: T to kill him. To be s to the tune "Do Not Destroy!"
60: T To be s to the tune "Lily of the Testimony."
69: T A psalm of David, to be s to the tune "Lilies."
75: T of Asaph, to be s to the tune "Do Not Destroy!"
80: T to be s to the tune "Lilies of the Covenant."
88: T to be s to the tune "The Suffering of Affliction."
92: T A psalm to be s on the LORD's Day. A song.
118:15 of joy and victory are s in the camp of the godly.
Hab 3: 1 This prayer was s by the prophet Habakkuk:

SUNK (1) [SINK]

La 2: 9 Jerusalem's gates have s into the ground. All their

SUNLIGHT (5) [LIGHT, SUN]

Job 30:28 I walk in gloom, without s. I stand in the public
Hos 6: 4 the morning mist and disappears like dew in the s.
Na 2: 3 Shields flash red in the s! The attack begins!
Mt 5:45 For he gives his s to both the evil and the good,
Rev 9: 2 and the s and air were darkened by the smoke.

SUNRISE (5) [SUN]

Nu 2: 3[-4] and Zebulun are to camp toward the s on the east
3:38 toward the s was reserved for the tents of Moses
2Sa 23: 4 like the s bursting forth in a cloudless sky,
Ne 4:21 We worked early and late, from s to sunset.
Mk 16: 2 Sunday morning, just at s, they came to the tomb.

SUNSET (8) [SUN]

Ex 17:12 stood on each side, holding up his hands until s.
Dt 23:11 bathe himself, and at s he may return to the camp.
24:13 Return the cloak to its owner by s so your neighbor
24:15 Pay them their wages each day before s
Jos 8:29 At s the Israelites took down the body and threw it
Jdg 14:18 So before s of the seventh day, the men of the town
Ne 4:21 We worked early and late, from sunrise to s.
Mk 1:32 That evening at s, many sick and demon-possessed

SUNSHINE (3) [SUN]

Job 8:16 so strong, like a lush plant growing in the s,
Mt 6:22 for your body. A pure eye lets s into your soul.
Lk 11:34 A pure eye lets s into your soul. But an evil eye

SUP [KJV] See ADVANCE, (SHARE A) MEAL, SUPPER

SUPER (2)

2Co 11: 5 But I don't think I am inferior to these "s
12:11 for I am not at all inferior to these "s apostles,"

SUPERB (1)

Isa 5:12 the harps, lyres, tambourines, and flutes are s!

SUPERFICIAL (2)

Jer 6:14 They offer s treatments for my people's mortal
8:11 They offer s treatments for my people's mortal

SUPERFLUITY, SUPERFLUOUS [KJV] See ALL (EVIL), DEFORMED, DEFORMITY

SUPERIOR (4)

Mt 8: 9 because I am under the authority of my s officers
Lk 7: 8 because I am under the authority of my s officers,
1Co 8:11 So because of your s knowledge, a weak Christian,
Heb 8: 6 s to the ministry of those who serve under the old

SUPERNATURAL (2)

Da 2:34 a rock was cut from a mountain by s means.
2:45 of the rock cut from the mountain by s means,

SUPERSCRIPTION [KJV] See SIGNBOARD, STAMPED

SUPERVISE (9) [SUPERVISED, SUPERVISING, SUPERVISION, SUPERVISOR, SUPERVISORS]

Ge 38:12 went to Timnah to s the shearing of his sheep.
1Ki 5:16 and thirty-six hundred foremen to s the work.
9:23 He also appointed 550 of them to s the various
2Ki 22: 5 Entrust this money to the men assigned to s the
1Ch 23: 4 "Twenty-four thousand of them will s the work at
2Ch 8:10 King Solomon also appointed 250 of them to s the
34:10 He entrusted the money to the men assigned to s
Eze 40:45 is for the priests who s the Temple maintenance.
Da 6: 2 and two others as administrators to s the princes

SUPERVISED (4) [SUPERVISE]

2Ki 25:10 Then the captain of the guard s the entire
Ezr 3: 9 The workers at the Temple of God were s by
Ne 3:17 who s the building of the wall on behalf of his own
Jer 52:14 Then the captain of the guard s the entire

SUPERVISING (1) [SUPERVISE]

1Ch 27: 1 who served the king by s the army divisions that

SUPERVISION (4) [SUPERVISE]

Nu 4:16 the s of the entire Tabernacle and everything in it
18: 3 as the Levites go about their duties under your s,
1Ch 23:32 And so, under the s of the priests, the Levites
Ne 3:17 Next was a group of Levites working under the s

SUPERVISOR (3) [SUPERVISE]

1Ki 16: 9 drunk at the home of Arza, the s of the palace.
Ne 11:11 son of Ahitub, the s of the Temple of God;
13: 4 who had been appointed as s of the storerooms of

SUPERVISORS (7) [SUPERVISE]

2Ki 12:11 Then they gave the money to the construction s,
12:15 accounting was required from the construction s,
22: 7 But there will be no need for the construction s to
22: 9 the LORD to the workers and s at the Temple."
2Ch 24:12 and Jehoiada gave the money to the construction s,
31:13 The s under them were Jehiel, Azaziah, Nahath,
34:17 the Temple of the LORD has been given to the s

SUPH (1)

Dt 1: 1 They were camped in the Jordan Valley near S,

SUPHAH (1)

Nu 21:14 speaks of "the town of Waheb in the area of S,

SUPPER (24)

Ge 24:33 Then s was served. But Abraham's servant said,
24:54 Then they had s, and the servant and the men with
Jdg 19:21 After they washed their feet, they had s together.
1Sa 1: 9 Hannah went over to the Tabernacle after s to pray
Mt 26: 7 During s, a woman came in with a beautiful jar of
26:17 do you want us to prepare the Passover s?"
26:19 Jesus told them and prepared the Passover s there.
Mk 14: 3 During s, a woman came in with a beautiful jar of
14:12 do you want us to go to prepare the Passover s?"
14:15 is the place; go ahead and prepare our s there."
14:16 had said, and they prepared the Passover s there.
Lk 17: 8 and serve him his s before eating his own.
22:12 is the place. Go ahead and prepare our s there."
22:13 had said, and they prepared the Passover s there.
22:20 After s he took another cup of wine and said,
Jn 13: 2 It was time for s, and the Devil had already enticed
21:20 the one who had leaned over to Jesus during s
Ac 2:42 sharing in the Lord's S and in prayer.
2:46 met in homes for the Lord's S, and shared their
20: 7 of the week, we gathered to observe the Lord's S.
20:11 went back upstairs and ate the Lord's S together.
1Co 11:20 It's not the Lord's S you are concerned about when
11:25 same way, he took the cup of wine after s, saying,
11:33 and sisters, when you gather for the Lord's S,

SUPPLANT [KJV] See (TAKE) ADVANTAGE

SUPPLANTS (1)

Pr 30:23 gets a husband, / a servant girl who s her mistress.

SUPPLE [KJV] See (NEVER) WASHED

SUPPLIED (13) [SUPPLY]

Ge 45:21 and he s them with provisions for the journey.
Nu 24: 7 their offspring are s with all they need.
1Ki 18: 4 in each cave and had s them with food and water.)
18:13 them in two caves and s them with food and water.
2Ki 2:21 Then he went out to the spring that s the town with
11:10 and he s them with the spears and shields that had
25:29 He s Jehoiachin with new clothes to replace his
2Ch 2: 3 "Send me cedar logs like the ones that were s to
23: 9 Then Jehoiada s the commanders with the spears
Isa 33:16 Food will be s to them, and they will have water in
Jer 52:33 He s Jehoiachin with new clothes to replace his
Ac 20:34 and I have even s the needs of those who were with
Php 4:18 I am generously s with the gifts you sent me with

SUPPLIES (11) [SUPPLY]

1Sa 17:22 David left his things with the keeper of s
1Ch 9:29 and the s such as choice flour, wine, olive oil,
12:40 Vast s of flour, fig cakes, raisins, wine, olive oil,
27:27 was responsible for the grapes and the s of wine.
27:28 Joash was responsible for the s of olive oil.
2Ch 11:11 of them, he stored s of food, olive oil, and wine.
17:13 He stored numerous s in Judah's towns
Ezr 1: 4 them with silver and gold, s for the journey,
1: 6 them vessels of silver and gold, s for the journey,
Isa 3: 1 will cut off the s of food and water from Jerusalem
1Pe 4:11 Do it with all the strength and energy that God s.

SUPPLY (26) [SUPPLIED, SUPPLIES, SUPPLYING]

Ex 1:11 of Pithom and Rameses as s centers for the king.
5: 7 "Do not s the people with any more straw for
Lev 26:26 I will completely destroy your food s, so the bread
Jdg 20:10 tribe will be chosen to s the warriors with food,
2Sa 12:27 fought against Rabbah and captured its water s.
1Ki 5: 8 I can s you with both cedar and cypress.
9:19 He built towns as s centers and constructed cities
10:12 or since has there been such a s of beautiful almug
17:15 and her son continued to eat from her s of flour
20:27 Israel then mustered its army, set up s lines,
2Ch 8: 4 and built towns in the region of Hamath as s
8: 6 also rebuilt Baalath and other s centers at this time
Ezr 7:22 550 gallons of olive oil, and an unlimited s of salt.
Ne 5:18 And every ten days we needed a large s of all kinds
12:47 the people brought a daily s of food for the singers,
13:31 I also made sure that the s of wood for the altar
Ps 104:28 When you s it, they gather it. / You open your hand
105:16 on the land of Canaan, / cutting off its food s.
130: 7 unfailing love / and an overflowing s of salvation.
Jer 31:14 I will s the priests with an abundance of offerings.
50:38 It will even strike her water s, causing it to dry up.
51:36 avenge you. I will dry up her river, her water s,
Eze 14:13 cutting off their food s and sending a famine to
Jn 2: 3 The wine s ran out during the festivities, so Jesus'
2Co 12:14 other way around; parents s food for their children.
Php 4:19 And this same God who takes care of me will s all

SUPPLYING (1) [SUPPLY]

Ezr 1: 4 toward their expenses by s them with silver

SUPPORT (30) [SUPPORTED, SUPPORTERS, SUPPORTING, SUPPORTS]

Ge 13: 6 But the land could not s both Abram and Lot with
36: 7 There was not enough land to s them both
Ex 25:27 These rings will s the poles used to carry the table.
26:18 Twenty of these frames will s the south side of the
26:29 with gold and make gold rings to s the crossbars.
27:19 including all the tent pegs used to s the Tabernacle
30: 4 attach two gold rings to s the carrying poles.
36:23 They made twenty frames to s the south side,
38: 5 for each side of the grating to s the carrying poles.
Lev 22:13 or is divorced and has no children to s her,
25:21 a bumper crop, enough to s you for three years.
25:35 relatives fall into poverty and cannot s themselves,
25:35 s them as you would a resident foreigner and allow
2Sa 16:21 of reconciliation, and they will give you their s."
1Ki 1: 8 and refused to s Adonijah were Zadok the priest,
2Ki 4: 7 and there will be enough money left over to s you
15:19 to gain his s in tightening his grip on royal power.
1Ch 19: 7 and secured the s of the king of Maacah and his
Ps 139:10 hand will guide me, / and your strength will s me.
Isa 42: 6 I will guard and s you, for I have given you to my
Da 11: 1 I have been standing beside Michael as his s
Lk 8: 3 contributing from their own resources to s Jesus
1Co 9: 6 and I who have to work to s ourselves?
9:12 If you s others who preach to you, shouldn't we
2Co 11: 9 I have never yet asked you for any s, and I never
1Ti 3:15 living God, which is the pillar and s of the truth.
5: 7 so that the widows you s will not be criticized.
5: 9 A widow who is put on the list for s must be a
1Pe 5:10 a little while, he will restore, s, and strengthen you,
3Jn 1: 8 So we ourselves should s them so that we may

SUPPORTED (23) [SUPPORT]

Ex 26:25 end of the Tabernacle, s by sixteen silver bases—
27:12 be 75 feet long, s by ten posts set into ten bases.
27:14 feet long, s by three posts set into three bases.
27:15 feet long, s by three posts set into three bases.
38:12 The walls were made from curtains s by ten posts
38:14 and was s by three posts set into three bases.
38:15 and was s by three posts set into three bases.
38:19 It was s by four posts set into four bronze bases.
38:31 the posts that s the curtains around the courtyard,
2Sa 3:19 that all the people of Israel and Benjamin s him.
19: 8 the Israelites who s Absalom had fled to their
1Ki 7: 3 It had a cedar roof s by forty-five rafters that rested
7: 6 its front, covered by a canopy that was s by pillars.
16:21 of Ginath their king, while the other half s Omri.
18:19 400 prophets of Asherah, who are s by Jezebel."
20: 1 s by the chariots and horses of thirty-two allied
2Ch 11:17 and for three years they s Rehoboam son of
Ezr 10:15 and Meshullam and Shabbethai the Levite s them.
Job 4: 3 to trust in God; you have s those who were weak.
Ps 94:18 and your unfailing love, O LORD, s me.
Na 3: 9 The nations of Put and Libya also helped and s her.
1Co 9:12 shouldn't we have an even greater right to be s?
9:14 News should be s by those who benefit from it.

SUPPORTERS (6) [SUPPORT]

1Ki 16:22 But Omri's s defeated the s of Tibni son
Da 11: 6 her father. She will be given up along with her s.
Mt 22:16 along with the s of Herod, to ask him this question:
Mk 3: 6 and met with the s of Herod to discuss plans for
12:13 and s of Herod to try to trap Jesus into saying

SUPPORTING (10) [SUPPORT]

Ex 27:18 The bases s its walls will be made of bronze.
38:27 and for the posts s the inner curtain required 7,500
Nu 3:36 for the care of the frames s the Tabernacle,
Jdg 16:25 of the temple, between the two pillars s the roof.
1Ki 7:30 At each corner of the carts were s posts for the

Ezr 8:36 who then cooperated by s the people
Ne 4:17 carried on their work with one hand s their load
Eze 40: 9 to be 14 feet deep, with columns 3-1/2 feet thick.
40:48 He measured its s columns and found them to be
42: 6 and they did not have s columns as in the

SUPPORTS (10) [SUPPORT]

1Ki 7:30 these s were decorated with carvings of wreaths on
7:34 There were s at each of the four corners of the
7:35 The s and side panels were cast as one unit with
7:36 the panels and s wherever there was room,
Job 38: 6 What s its foundations, and who laid its
Ps 18:35 Your right hand s me; / your gentleness has made
147: 6 The LORD s the humble, / but he brings the
Isa 22:25 Everything it s will fall with it. I, the LORD,
Eze 41: 6 The s for these rooms rested on ledges in the Temple wall, but the s did not extend into the wall.

SUPPOSE (78) [SUPPOSED, SUPPOSEDLY]

Ge 18:24 S you find fifty innocent people there within the
18:28 S there are only forty-five? Will you destroy the
18:29 "S there are only forty?" And the LORD replied,
18:30 "Let me speak—s only thirty are found?"
18:31 let me continue—s there are only twenty?"
18:32 but once more! S only ten are found there?"
24: 5 "But s I can't find a young woman who will travel
24:39 " 'But s I can't find a young woman willing to
Ex 21:18 "Now s two people quarrel, and one hits the other
21:22 "Now s two people are fighting, and in the
21:29 S, on the other hand, that the owner knew the bull
21:33 "S someone digs or uncovers a well and fails to
22: 7 "S someone entrusts money or goods to a
22: 9 "S there is a dispute between two people as to who
22:10 "Now s someone asks a neighbor to care for a
Lev 6: 2 "S some of the people sin against the LORD by
6: 2 Or s they have been dishonest with regard to a
6: 3 Or s they find a lost item and lie about it, or they
13:12 "Now s the priest discovers after his examination
13:47 "Now s an infectious mildew contaminates some
Nu 5:12 'S a man's wife goes astray and is unfaithful to her
5:13 S she sleeps with another man, but there is no
15:22 "But s some of you unintentionally fail to carry
15:23 And s some of your descendants in the future fail
30: 6 "Now s a young woman takes a vow or makes an
30:10 "S a woman is married and living in her husband's
35:22 " 'But s someone pushes another person without
Dt 13: 1 "S there are prophets among you, or those who
13: 6 "S your brother, son, daughter, beloved wife,
13:12 "S you hear in one of the towns the LORD your
15:16 But s your servant says, 'I will not leave you,'
17: 2 "S a man or woman among you, in one of your
17: 8 "S a case arises in a local court that is too hard for
19: 5 s someone goes into the forest with a neighbor to
19: 5 And s one of them swings an ax and the ax head
19:11 "But s someone hates a neighbor and deliberately
21: 1 "S someone is found murdered in a field in the
21:10 "S you go to war against your enemies
21:11 And s you see among the captives a beautiful
21:15 "S a man has two wives, but he loves one and not
21:15 And s the firstborn son is the son of the wife he
21:18 "S a man has a stubborn, rebellious son who will
22:13 "S a man marries a woman and, after sleeping
22:20 "But s the man's accusations are true, and her
22:23 "S a man meets a young woman, a virgin who is
24: 1 "S a man marries a woman but later discovers
25: 1 "S two people take a dispute to court,
30: 1 "S all these things happen to you—the blessings
Jer 23:33 "S one of the people or one of the prophets
23:38 But s they respond, 'This is a prophecy from the
44:19 "do you s that we were worshiping the Queen of
Eze 14:13 s the people of a country were to sin against me,
14:15 "Or s I were to send an invasion of dangerous wild
14:17 "Or s I were to bring war against the land, and I
14:19 "Or s I were to pour out my fury by sending an
18: 5 "S a certain man is just and does what is lawful
18: 6 And s he does not commit adultery or have
18: 7 S he is a merciful creditor, not keeping the items
18: 8 And s he grants loans without interest, stays away
18:10 "But s that man has a son who grows up to be a
18:11 And s that son does all the evil things his father
18:14 "But s that sinful son, in turn, has a son who sees
18:15 S this son refuses to worship idols on the
18:16 And s this son feeds the hungry, provides clothes
33:14 And s I tell some wicked people that they will
Mic 2:11 S a prophet full of lies were to say to you,
Mk 12: 9 "What do you s the owner of the vineyard will
Lk 7:42 Who do you s loved him more after that?"
7:43 "I s the one for whom he canceled the larger
11: 5 "S you went to a friend's house at midnight,
15: 8 "Or s a woman has ten valuable silver coins
20:15 "What do you s the owner of the vineyard will do
Jn 21:25 And I s that if all the other things Jesus did were
1Co 9: 9 Do you s God was thinking only about oxen when
10:28 But s someone warns you that this meat has been
12:17 S the whole body were an eye—then how would
Jas 2: 2 s someone comes into your meeting dressed in
2:15 S you see a brother or sister who needs food

SUPPOSED (10) [SUPPOSE]

Ge 4: 9 "Am I s to keep track of him wherever he goes?"
Nu 11:13 Where am I s to get meat for all these people?
1Sa 17:28 "What about those few sheep you're s to be taking
Job 15: 2 "You are s to be a wise man, and yet you give us
Mic 3: 1 of Israel! You are s to know right from wrong,
Mk 8: 4 "How are we s to find enough food for them here
Lk 17: 9 because he is merely doing what he is s to do.
Ac 16:13 where we s that some people met for prayer,
Ro 7:10 good law, which was s to show me the way of life,
1Co 11:22 the poor? What am I s to say about these things?

SUPPOSEDLY (1) [SUPPOSE]

2Th 2: 2 a revelation, or a letter s from us, don't believe

SUPREME (6) [SUPREMELY]

Jos 2:11 For the LORD your God is the s God of the
Job 21:22 "But who can teach a lesson to God, the s Judge?
Ps 83:18 you alone are the Most High, s over all the earth.
99: 2 in majesty in Jerusalem, / s above all the nations.
1Co 15:28 will be utterly s over everything everywhere.
Col 1:15 God made anything at all and is s over all creation.

SUPREMELY (1) [SUPREME]

Ex 30:10 for this is the LORD's s holy altar."

SUR (1)

2Ki 11: 6 Another third of you are to stand guard at the S

SURE (136) [SUREFOOTED, SURELY]

Ge 12:14 And s enough, when they arrived in Egypt,
15: 8 how can I be s that you will give it to me?"
15:13 "You can be s that your descendants will be
20: 7 you can be s that you and your entire household
27:21 I want to touch you to make s you really are
31:49 s that we keep this treaty when we are out of each
32:20 And be s to say, 'Your servant Jacob is right
38:17 will you give me so I can be s you will send it?"
41:47 And s enough, for the next seven years there were
Ex 2:12 After looking around to make s no one was
2:15 And s enough, when Pharaoh heard about it,
3: 7 "You can be s I have seen the misery of my people
3:16 "You can be s that I am watching over you
4:17 And be s to take your shepherd's staff along
6: 5 You can be s that I have heard the groans of the
7:15 Be s to take along the shepherd's staff that turned
8:26 where they can see us, they will be s to stone us.
13:19 led them out of Egypt—as he was s God would.
19:11 Be s they are ready on the third day, for I will
23:13 "Be s to obey all my instructions. And remember,
25:40 "Be s that you make everything according to the
34:18 "Be s to celebrate the Festival of Unleavened
Lev 10:12 Make s there is no yeast in it, and eat it beside the
Nu 9: 3 Be s to follow all my laws and regulations
16:17 Be s that each of your 250 followers brings an
18:29 Be s to set aside the best portions of the gifts given
22:20 But be s to do only what I tell you to do."
26:55 Make s you assign the land by lot, and define the
28:31 Be s that all the animals you sacrifice have no
32:23 and you may be s that your sin will find you out.
Dt 4: 9 And be s to pass them on to your children
5: 1 you today. Learn them and be s to obey them!
17:15 be s that you select as king the man the LORD
Jos 1: 8 so you may be s to obey all that is written in it.
3: 4 and the Ark. Make s you don't come any closer."
13: 6 So be s to give this land to Israel as a special
17:18 And I am s you can drive out the Canaanites from
23: 7 Make s you do not associate with the other people
Jdg 9:16 "Now make s you have acted honorably and in
13:13 "Be s your wife follows the instructions I gave
Ru 3: 4 Be s to notice where he lies down; then go
1Sa 6: 7 Make s the cows have never been yoked to a cart.
6:12 And s enough, the cows went straight along the
12:20 but make s now that you worship the LORD with
12:24 But be s to fear the LORD and sincerely worship
20: 2 "I'm s he's not planning any such thing, for he
23:22 and check again to be s of where he is staying
24:13 evil deeds.' So you can be s I will never harm you.
1Ki 11: 3 And s enough, they led his heart away from the
17:24 "Now I know for s that you are a man of God,
18:45 And s enough, the sky was soon black with clouds.
20:36 And s enough, when he had gone, a lion attacked
22:13 Be s that you agree with them and promise
2Ki 2:22 And s enough! The water has remained wholesome
3:20 And s enough, the next day at about the time when
4: 9 "I am s this man who stops in from time to time is
4:17 But s enough, the woman soon became pregnant.
4:44 And s enough, there was plenty for all and some
10:10 You can be s that the message of the LORD that
10:22 "Be s that every worshiper of Baal wears one of
10:23 "Make s that only those who worship Baal are
2Ch 8:16 So Solomon made s that all the work related to
18:12 Be s that you agree with them and promise
19:11 The Levites will assist you in making s that justice
34: 4 He also made s that the Asherah poles, the carved
Ne 6: 7 "You can be very s that this report will get back to
13:31 I also made s that the supply of wood for the altar
Job 29:16 and made s that even strangers received a fair trial.
Ps 4: 3 You can be s of this: / The LORD has set apart
69:13 O God, / answer my prayer with your s salvation.
Pr 11:21 You can be s that evil people will be punished,
18: 3 contempt, shame, and disgrace are s to follow.
20:16 Be s to get collateral from anyone who guarantees
26: 5 with fools, be s to answer their foolish arguments,
26:13 on the road! Yes, I'm s there's a lion out there!"
27:13 Be s to get collateral from anyone who guarantees
Ecc 11: 6 Be s to stay busy and plant a variety of crops,
Isa 3:11 But say to the wicked, "Your destruction is s.
33: 6 In that day he will be your s foundation,
37: 7 I myself will make s that the king will receive a
Jer 4:13 How terrible it will be! Our destruction is s!
13:27 and on the hills. Your destruction is s, Jerusalem!
22:16 He made s that justice and help were given to the
32: 8 Then I knew for s that the message I had heard was
38:27 S enough, it wasn't long before the king's officials
42:22 So you can be s that you will die from war, famine,
48:46 "O Moab, your destruction is s! The people of the
Eze 33: 8 If I announce that some wicked people are s to die
43:11 as they watch so they will be s to remember them.
Da 1: 4 "Make s they are well versed in every branch of
3:18 Your Majesty can be s that we will never serve
Zec 8: 7 You can be s that I will rescue my people from the
Mt 28:20 And be s of this: I am with you always, even to the
Mk 4:24 And be s to pay attention to what you hear.
13:29 you can be s that his return is very near, right at the
Lk 3:13 "Make s you collect no more taxes than the
8:18 So be s to pay attention to what you hear. To those
11:35 Make s that the light you think you have is not
19:33 And s enough, as they were untying it, the owners
21:31 you can be s that the Kingdom of God is near.
24:24 and s enough, Jesus' body was gone, just as the
24:39 Touch me and make s that I am not a ghost,
Jn 21:12 if he really was the Lord because they were s of it.
Ac 7:34 You can be s that I have seen the misery of my
10:36 I'm s you have heard about the Good News for the
16:23 The jailer was ordered to make s they didn't
20:28 Be s that you feed and shepherd God's flock—
26:26 for I am s these events are all familiar to him,
27:42 The soldiers wanted to kill the prisoners to make s
Ro 6: 9 We are s of this because Christ rose from the dead,
14:14 and am perfectly s on the authority of the Lord
15:29 And I am s that when I come, Christ will give me a
1Co 14:40 But be s that everything is done properly and in
2Co 1: 5 You can be s that the more we suffer for Christ,
1:15 Since I was so s of your understanding and trust,
9: 3 But I am sending these brothers just to be s that
9: 5 of me to make s the gift you promised is ready.
Gal 2: 2 I wanted to make s they did not disagree, or my
5: 1 Now make s that you stay free, and don't get tied
6: 4 Be s to do what you should, for then you will enjoy
Eph 5: 5 You can be s that no immoral, impure, or greedy
Php 1: 6 And I am s that God, who began the good work
2:29 with great joy, and be s to honor people like him.
3:16 But we must be s to obey the truth we have learned
Col 4:17 "Be s to carry out the work the Lord gave you."
2Ti 1:12 and I am s that he is able to guard what I have
4:13 be s to bring the coat I left with Carpus at Troas.
Heb 3:12 Make s that your own hearts are not evil
6:17 perfectly s that he would never change his mind.
8: 5 "Be s that you make everything according to the
11:22 so s of it that he commanded them to carry his
12:16 Make s that no one is immoral or godless like
Jas 1: 6 ask him, be s that you really expect him to answer,
5:20 you can be s that the one who brings that person
1Jn 2: 3 And how can we be s that we belong to him?
5:15 we can be s that he will give us what we ask for.

SUREFOOTED (3) [FOOT, SURE]

2Sa 22:34 He makes me as s as a deer, / leading me safely
Ps 18:33 He makes me as s as a deer, / leading me safely
Hab 3:19 He will make me as s as a deer and bring me safely

SURELY (185) [SURE]

Ge 2:17 and evil. If you eat of its fruit, you will s die."
18:25 S you wouldn't do such a thing,
18:25 guilty exactly the same! S you wouldn't do that!
28:16 woke up and said, "S the LORD is in this place,
29:34 "S now my husband will feel affection for me,
37:33 and eaten him. S Joseph has been torn in pieces!"
41:36 Otherwise disaster will s strike the land, and all the
50:24 told his brothers, "but God will s come for you,
Ex 5: 3 If we don't, we will s die by disease or the sword."
22:23 and they cry out to me, then I will s help them.
34:11 Then I will s drive out all those who stand in your
Lev 24:16 who blasphemes the LORD's name will s die.
Nu 11:18 had meat to eat! S we were better off in Egypt!"
14:21 But as s as I live, and as s as the earth is filled with the LORD's
14:28 'As s as I live, I will do to you the very things I
Dt 29:16 "S you remember how we lived in the land of
32:40 my hand to heaven / and declare, "As s as I live,
Jos 3:10 He will s drive out the Canaanites, Hittites,
23:15 But as s as the LORD your God has given you the
Jdg 8:19 "As s as the LORD lives, I wouldn't kill you if
Ru 3:13 then as s as the LORD lives, I will marry you!
1Sa 14:39 who rescued Israel that the sinner will s die,
14:45 As s as the LORD lives, not one hair on his head
15:32 for he thought, "S the worst is over, and I have
16: 6 and thought, "S this is the LORD's anointed!"
19: 6 to Jonathan and vowed, "As s as the LORD lives,
20:21 will know, as s as the LORD lives, that all is well,
22:16 "You will s die, Ahimelech, along with your entire
24:20 And now I realize that you are s going to be king,
25:26 as s as the LORD lives and you yourself live,
25:28 The LORD will s reward you with a lasting
26: 8 "God has s handed your enemy over to you this
26:10 S the LORD will strike Saul down someday,
28:10 and promised, "As s as the LORD lives,
30: 8 You will s recover everything that was taken from
2Sa 4: 9 to Recab and Baanah, "As s as the LORD lives,
12: 5 "As s as the LORD lives," he vowed, "any man
14:11 "As s as the LORD lives," he replied, "not a
1Ki 1:29 And the king vowed, "As s as the LORD lives,
2:24 So as s as the LORD lives, Adonijah will die this
2:37 day you cross the Kidron Valley, you will s die;
2:42 you not to go anywhere else, or you would s die?
2:44 "You s remember all the wicked things you did to

11:11 I will s tear the kingdom away from you and give it
13:32 shrines in the towns of Samaria will s come true."
17: 1 told King Ahab, "As s as the LORD, the God of
18:27 to shout louder," he scoffed, "for s he is a god!
22:14 But Micaiah replied, "As s as the LORD lives,
2Ki 1: 4 but you will s die.' " So Elijah went to deliver the
1: 6 bed on which you are lying, but you will s die.' "
1:16 bed on which you are lying, but you will s die."
2: 2 "As s as the LORD lives and you yourself live,
2: 4 "As s as the LORD lives and you yourself live,
2: 6 "As s as the LORD lives and you yourself live,
3:14 "As s as the LORD Almighty lives, whom I
4:30 "As s as the LORD lives and you yourself live,
5:11 "I thought he would s come out to meet me!"
5:16 "As s as the LORD lives, whom I serve,
5:20 As s as the LORD lives, I will chase after him
8:14 "He told me that you will s recover."
2Ch 18:13 But Micaiah replied, "As s as the LORD lives,
32:11 S Hezekiah is misleading you, sentencing you to
32:12 S you must realize that Hezekiah is the very person
32:13 "S you must realize what I and the other kings of
Ezr 9:14 S your anger will destroy us until even this little
Job 1:11 he has, and he will s curse you to your face!"
2: 5 his health, and he will s curse you to your face!"
5: 2 S resentment destroys the fool, and jealousy kills
22:20 will say, 'S our enemies have been destroyed.
28:23 "God s knows where it can be found,
29:18 'S I will die surrounded by my family after a long,
30:24 "S no one would turn against the needy when they
32: 8 S it is God's Spirit within people, the breath of the
32:17 I will say my piece. I will speak my mind. I s will.
Ps 10:17 S you will listen to their cries and comfort them.
23: 6 S your goodness and unfailing love will pursue me
34:21 Calamity will s overtake the wicked, / and those
44:21 God would s have known it, / for he knows the
58:11 s there is a God who judges justly here on earth."
62:12 O Lord, is yours. / S you judge all people
85: 9 S his salvation is near to those who honor him;
92: 9 Your enemies, LORD, will s perish;
115:12 LORD remembers us, / and he will s bless us.
140:12 But I know the LORD will s help those they
140:13 S the godly are praising your name, / for they will
Pr 8:17 love me. Those who search for me will s find me.
23:18 For s you have a future ahead of you; your hope
25:23 As s as a wind from the north brings rain, so a
Isa 49:18 As s as I live," says the LORD, "they will be
63: 8 S they will not be false again." And he became
63:16 S you are still our Father! Even if Abraham
66:22 "As s as my new heavens and earth will remain,
Jer 1:12 and I will s carry out my threats of punishment."
2:35 S he isn't angry with me!' Now I will punish you
3: 1 her back again, for that would s corrupt the land.
3: 5 S you won't be angry about such a little thing!
3: 5 S you can forget it!' So you talk, and keep right on
5: 2 saying, 'As s as the LORD lives,' they all tell
5: 5 S they will know the LORD's ways and what
12:16 'As s as the LORD lives' (just as they taught my
14:13 will come. The LORD will s send you peace.' "
16:14 oath will no longer say, 'As s as the LORD lives,
16:15 Instead, they will say, 'As s as the LORD lives,
22:22 S at last you will see your wickedness and be
22:24 "And as s as I live," says the LORD, "I will
23: 7 they will no longer say, 'As s as the LORD lives,
23: 8 Instead, they will say, 'As s as the LORD lives,
28: 4 I will s break the yoke that the king of Babylon has
31:20 I long for him and s will have mercy on him.
32:37 I will s bring my people back again from all the
38: 3 The city of Jerusalem will s be handed over to the
38:16 "As s as the LORD our Creator lives, I will not
43:10 I will s bring my servant Nebuchadnezzar, king of
44:26 this oath: 'As s as the Sovereign LORD lives!'
46:18 "As s as I live," says the King, whose name is the
51:47 For the time is s coming when I will punish this
Eze 5:11 "As s as I live, says the Sovereign LORD,
16:48 As s as I live, says the Sovereign LORD, Sodom
17:16 For as s as I live, says the Sovereign LORD,
17:19 As s as I live, I will punish him for breaking my
18: 3 As s as I live, says the Sovereign LORD, you will
18: 9 who does these things is just and will s live,
18:17 not die because of his father's sins; he will s live.
18:19 is right and keeps my laws, that child will s live.
18:21 what is just and right, they will s live and not die.
20: 3 for my help? As s as I live, I will tell you nothing.
20:31 As s as I live, says the Sovereign LORD, I will
20:33 As s as I live, says the Sovereign LORD, I will
21:27 Destruction! I will s destroy the kingdom.
23:28 I will s hand you over to your enemies, to those
33:11 As s as I live, says the Sovereign LORD, I take
33:14 I tell some wicked people that they will s die,
33:15 If they do this, then they will s live and not die.
33:16 done what is just and right, and they will s live.
33:24 s the land should be given to us as a possession.'
33:27 As s as I live, those living in the ruins will die by
34: 8 As s as I live, says the Sovereign LORD,
34:20 I will s judge between the fat sheep
35: 6 As s as I live, says the Sovereign LORD,
35:11 Therefore, as s as I live, says the Sovereign
Da 11:36 For what has been determined will s take place.
Hos 6: 3 Then he will respond to us as s as the arrival of
6: 5 My judgment will strike you as s as day follows
9: 9 will not forget. He will s punish them for their sins.
Joel 2:20 the land." S the LORD has done great things!
Am 8:11 "The time is s coming," says the Sovereign
Hab 1:12 S not! O LORD our Rock, you have decreed the
2: 3 Slowly, steadily, s, the time approaches when the
2: 3 seems slow, wait patiently, for it will s take place.
Zep 2: 9 Now, as s as I live," says the LORD Almighty,
3: 7 I thought, 'S they will have reverence for me now!
3: 7 S they will listen to my warnings, so I won't need
Mal 3: 1 whom you look for so eagerly, is s coming,"
Mt 6:30 and gone tomorrow, won't he more s care for you?
10:42 the least of my followers, you will s be rewarded."
18:13 he will s rejoice over it more than over the
21:37 sent his son, thinking, 'S they will respect my son.'
Mk 12: 6 sent him, thinking, 'S they will respect my son.'
Lk 1:66 For the hand of the Lord is s upon him in a special
11:51 the sanctuary. Yes, it will s be charged against you.
12:28 and gone tomorrow, won't he more s care for you?
18: 7 so don't you think God will s give justice to his
20:13 send my cherished son. S they will respect him.'
23:47 praised God and said, "S this man was innocent."
Jn 6:14 saw this miraculous sign, they exclaimed, "S,
7:40 of them declared, "This man s is the Prophet."
9: 9 and others said, "No, but he s looks like him!"
10: 1 through the gate, must s be a thief and a robber!
Ac 27:24 Paul, for you will s stand trial before Caesar!
Ro 2:16 The day will s come when God, by Jesus Christ,
14:11 Scriptures say, / " 'As s as I live,' says the Lord,
1Co 1: 9 God will s do this for you, for he always does just
6: 3 So you should s be able to resolve ordinary
2Co 1:18 As s as God is true, I am not that sort of person.
2: 3 S you know that my happiness depends on your
11:10 As s as the truth of Christ is in me, I will never
Gal 3: 4 for the Good News. S it was not in vain, was it?
4:13 S you remember that I was sick when I first
Php 2:27 And he s was ill; in fact, he almost died. But God
Heb 6: 1 S we don't need to start all over again with the
13: 4 God will s judge people who are immoral
Jas 3:10 S, my brothers and sisters, this is not right!
1Jn 4:11 loved us that much, we s ought to love each other.
5: 9 s we can believe the testimony that comes from

SURETY [KJV] See CERTAIN, GUARANTEE, INDEED, PLEDGE, SURE

SURFACE (14) [SURFACES]

Ge 1: 2 And the Spirit of God was hovering over its s.
7:18 above the ground, the boat floated safely on the s.
Ex 10:15 For the locusts covered the s of the whole country,
Lev 14:37 appears to go deeper than the wall's s,
1Ki 7:20 beside the rounded s next to the latticework.
2Ki 6: 6 Then the ax head rose to the s and floated.
Job 28: 5 but below the s the earth is melted as by fire.
38:30 ice as hard as rock, and the s of the water freezes.
Eze 1:22 There was a s spread out above them like the sky.
1:23 Beneath this s the wings of each living being
1:25 a voice spoke from beyond the crystal s above
1:26 Above the s over their heads was what looked like
10: 1 above the crystal s over the heads of the cherubim.
Da 7: 2 saw a great storm churning the s of a great sea,

SURFACES (1) [SURFACE]

Eze 40:16 The s of the dividing walls were decorated with

SURFEITING [KJV] See (LIVING IN CARELESS) EASE

SURGE (2) [SURGED, SURGING]

Ps 46: 3 Let the mountains tremble as the waters s!
Jer 48: 3 then the roar of battle will s against Horonaim,

SURGING (3) [SURGE]

Ex 14:27 swept the terrified Egyptians into the s currents.
15: 8 piled up! / The s waters stood straight like a wall;
Ps 42: 7 as your waves and s tides sweep over me.

SURMISINGS [KJV] See SUSPICIONS

SURNAME [KJV] See CALLED, NAME(D)

SURPASS (1) [SURPASSED]

Pr 31:29 capable women in the world, but you s them all!"

SURPASSED (1) [SURPASS]

Eze 16:47 nothing to you. In a very short time you far s them!

SURPLUS (3)

Lev 26:10 You will have such a s of crops that you will need
Mk 12:44 For they gave a tiny part of their s, but she, poor as
Lk 21: 4 For they have given a tiny part of their s, but she,

SURPRISE (9) [SURPRISED]

Jos 10: 9 from Gilgal and took the Amorite armies by s.
Jdg 8:11 and Jogbehah, taking the Midianite army by s.
1Sa 11:11 He launched a s attack against the Ammonites
Ps 55:15 Let death seize my enemies by s; / let the grave
Eze 47: 7 Suddenly, to my s, many trees were now growing
Mt 27:14 Jesus said nothing, much to the governor's great s.
Mk 15: 5 But Jesus said nothing, much to Pilate's s.
Lk 1:63 and to everyone's s he wrote, "His name is John!"
Ac 9: 7 The men with Saul stood speechless with s,

SURPRISED (13) [SURPRISE]

Ru 3: 8 He was s to find a woman lying at his feet!
Ecc 5: 8 being miscarried throughout the land, don't be s!
Mk 16: 6 but the angel said, "Do not be so s. You are
Jn 3: 7 So don't be s at my statement that you must be
4: 9 The woman was s, for Jews refuse to have
5:28 Don't be so s! Indeed, the time is coming when all
7:15 The Jewish leaders were s when they heard him.
Ac 21:37 "Do you know Greek?" the commander asked, s.
2Co 11:14 But I am not s! Even Satan can disguise himself as
1Th 5: 4 and you won't be s when the day of the Lord
1Pe 4: 4 your former friends are very s when you no longer
4:12 don't be s at the fiery trials you are going through,
1Jn 3:13 So don't be s, dear brothers and sisters,

SURRENDER (16) [SURRENDERED, SURRENDERS]

1Sa 23:11 Will the men of Keilah s me to him? And will Saul
2Ki 7: 4 might as well go out and s to the Aramean army.
15:16 because its citizens refused to s the town.
18:27 He wants them to know that if you do not s,
Job 24: 3 A poor widow must s her valuable ox as collateral
Isa 22: 3 All your leaders flee. They s without resistance.
27: 5 These enemies will be spared only if they s
36:12 He wants them to know that if you do not s,
Jer 21: 9 who go out and s to the Babylonians will live.
27:17 S to the king of Babylon, and you will live.
38: 2 but those who s to the Babylonians will live.
38:17 If you s to Babylon, you and your family will live,
38:18 But if you refuse to s, you will not escape!
38:19 "But I am afraid to s," the king said,
38:21 But if you refuse to s, this is what the LORD has
40: 9 it would be safe for them to s to the Babylonians.

SURRENDERED (7) [SURRENDER]

2Sa 10:19 by Israel, they s to them and became their subjects.
2Ki 24: 1 Jehoiakim s and paid him tribute for three years
24:12 and the queen mother, s to the Babylonians.
1Ch 19:19 by Israel, they s to David and became his subjects.
Job 16:15 I sit in sackcloth. I have s, and I sit in the dust.
Ps 78:61 to be captured; / he s his glory into enemy hands.
Jer 12: 7 I have s my dearest ones to their enemies.

SURRENDERS (1) [SURRENDER]

Jer 50:15 every side. Look! She s! Her walls have fallen.

SURROUND (27) [SURROUNDED, SURROUNDING, SURROUNDINGS, SURROUNDS]

Nu 4:26 for the courtyard walls that s the Tabernacle
Jos 7: 9 they will s us and wipe us off the face of the earth.
2Ki 6:14 army with many chariots and horses to s the city.
1Ch 16:27 Honor and majesty s him; / strength and beauty are
Job 18:11 "Terrors s the wicked and trouble them at every
Ps 3: 6 of ten thousand enemies / who s me on every side.
17: 9 attack me, / from murderous enemies who s me.
17:11 They track me down, s me, / and throw me to the
22: 3 you are holy. / The praises of Israel s your throne.
22:12 My enemies s me like a herd of bulls; / fierce bulls
22:16 My enemies s me like a pack of dogs; / an evil
27: 6 hold my head high, / above my enemies who s me.
32: 7 You s me with songs of victory. / *Interlude*
33:22 Let your unfailing love s us, LORD, / for our
40:12 For troubles s me— / too many to count!
89: 7 He is far more awesome than those who s his
96: 6 Honor and majesty s him; / strength and beauty are
97: 2 Clouds and darkness s him. / Righteousness
119:77 S me with your tender mercies so I may live,
125: 2 Just as the mountains s and protect Jerusalem,
Isa 60:18 Salvation will s you like city walls, and praise will
Jer 4:17 They s Jerusalem like watchmen surrounding a
6: 3 Enemy shepherds will s you. They will set up
50:29 S the city so none can escape. Do to her as she has
Eze 4: 2 S it with enemy camps and battering rams.
48:17 Open lands will s the city for 150 yards in every
Am 3:11 He will s them and shatter their defenses.

SURROUNDED (66) [SURROUND]

Ge 19: 4 came from all over the city and s the house.
Nu 3:26 the curtains of the courtyard that s the Tabernacle
Dt 5:22 the heart of the fire, s by clouds and deep darkness.
32:10 He s them and watched over them;
Jos 19: 1 Their inheritance was s by Judah's territory.
Jdg 19:22 some of the wicked men in the town s the house.
20: 5 That night some of the leaders of Gibeah s the
20:43 The Israelites s the Benjaminites and were
1Sa 22: 6 at Gibeah, holding his spear and s by his officers.
2Sa 16: 6 and all the mighty warriors who s them.
18:15 armor bearers then s Absalom and killed him.
22: 5 "The waves of death s me; / the floods of
1Ki 7: 8 Solomon's living quarters s a courtyard behind this
2Ki 8:21 The Edomites s him and his charioteers, but he
10:24 Now Jehu had s the building with eighty of his
25: 1 They s the city and built siege ramps against its
25: 4 But since the city was s by the Babylonians,
2Ch 21: 9 The Edomites s him and his charioteers, but he
Job 15:21 They are s by terrors, and even on good days they
16:13 His archers s me, and his arrows pierced me
17: 2 I am s by mockers. I watch how bitterly they taunt
22:10 That is why you are s by traps and sudden fears.
29:18 'Surely I will die s by my family after a long,
Ps 18: 4 The ropes of death s me; / the floods of destruction
31:13 the many rumors about me, / and I am s by terror.
57: 4 I am s by fierce lions / who greedily devour human
68:17 S by unnumbered thousands of chariots, / the Lord
118:10 Though hostile nations s me, / I destroyed them all
118:11 Yes, they s and attacked me, / but I destroyed them
138: 7 Though I am s by troubles, / you will preserve me
Isa 26: 1 We are s by the walls of God's salvation.

30:27 burning with anger, s by a thick, rising smoke.
Jer 42:21 go on? How long must I be s by war and death?
12: 9 And indeed, they are s by vultures. Bring on the
52: 4 They s the city and built siege ramps against its
52: 7 But since the city was s by the Babylonians,
La 3: 5 attacked me and s me with anguish and distress.
Eze 29:12 and it will be s by other desolate nations.
29:12 desolate for forty years, s by other desolate cities.
30: 7 Egypt will be desolate, s by desolate nations,
30: 7 its cities will be in ruins, s by other ruined cities.
32:22 "Assyria lies there s by the graves of all its people,
32:23 the depths of the pit, and they are s by their allies.
32:25 the slaughtered, s by the graves of all their people.
32:26 Tubal are there, s by the graves of all their hordes.
46:22 was 70 feet long and 52-1/2 feet wide, s by walls.
Da 2:22 in darkness, / though he himself is s by light.
4:15 a band of iron and bronze and s by tender grass.
4:23 a band of iron and bronze and s by tender grass.
Am 6: 4 be for you who sprawl on ivory beds s with luxury,
Na 2: 1 Nineveh, you are already s by enemy armies!
3: 8 s by rivers, protected by water on all sides?
Hab 1: 3 I am s by people who love to argue and fight.
Mt 22:41 Then, s by the Pharisees, Jesus asked them a
Mk 1:45 such crowds soon s Jesus that he couldn't enter a
Lk 2: 9 and the radiance of the Lord's glory s them.
6:17 s by many of his followers and by the crowds.
8:42 As Jesus went with him, he was s by the crowds.
21:20 "And when you see Jerusalem s by armies,
Jn 10:24 The Jewish leaders s him and asked, "How long
1Th 2: 2 even though we were s by many who opposed us.
Heb 12: 1 since we are s by such a huge crowd of witnesses
2Pe 3: 5 the earth up from the water and s it with water.
Rev 4: 4 Twenty-four thrones s him, and twenty-four elders
10: 1 s by a cloud, with a rainbow over his head.
20: 9 the earth and s God's people and the beloved city.

SURROUNDING (91) [SURROUND]

Ge 41:54 There were crop failures in all the s countries,
41:57 And people from s lands also came to Egypt to buy
Nu 21:25 including the city of Heshbon and its s villages.
32:33 the whole land with its towns and s lands.
32:42 captured the town of Kenath and its s villages,
35: 2 towns to live in, along with the s pasturelands.
35: 3 and the s lands will provide pasture for their cattle,
35: 7 forty-eight towns with the s pastureland will be
Dt 4: 6 your wisdom and intelligence to the s nations.
29:24 The s nations will ask, 'Why has the LORD done
Jos 10:37 capturing it and all of its s towns. And just as they
10:39 captured the city, its king, and all of its s villages.
14: 4 and the s pasturelands for their flocks and herds.
15:32 there were twenty-nine of these towns with their s
15:36 there were fourteen towns with their s villages.
15:41 sixteen towns with their s villages.
15:44 and Mareshah—nine towns with their s villages.
15:46 and included the towns near Ashdod with their s
15:51 and Giloh—eleven towns with their s villages.
15:54 and Zior—nine towns with their s villages.
15:57 and Timnah—ten towns with their s villages.
15:59 and Eltekon—six towns with their s villages.
15:60 and Rabbah—two towns with their s villages.
15:62 and En-gedi—six towns with their s villages.
16: 9 Ephraim was also given some towns with s
17: 8 (The land s Tappuah belonged to Manasseh,
19:15 twelve towns with their s villages.
19:22 Jordan River—sixteen towns with their s villages.
19:30 twenty-two towns with their s villages.
19:38 nineteen cities with their s villages.
21:11 hill country of Judah, along with its s pasturelands.
21:12 and the s villages were given to Caleb son of
21:17 the following towns with their s pasturelands:
21:42 Every one of these towns had pasturelands s it.
Jdg 1:18 Ashkelon, and Ekron, along with their s territories.
1:27 Dor, Ibleam, Megiddo, and their s villages,
8:34 who had rescued them from all their enemies s
1Sa 6:18 the five Philistine cities and their s villages,
1Ki 4:31 His fame spread throughout all the s nations.
5: 3 because of the many wars he waged with s nations.
2Ki 11:14 The officers and trumpeters were s him, and people
15:16 and all the s countryside as far as Tirzah,
1Ch 2:23 and also took Kenath and its sixty s villages.)
4:33 and their s villages as far away as Baalath.
6:55 included Hebron and its s pasturelands in Judah,
6:57 the following towns, each with its s pasturelands:
6:66 Ephraim these towns, each with its s pasturelands:
7:28 that included Bethel and its s towns to the south,
7:28 and its s villages to the north as far as Ayyah
7:29 Taanach, Megiddo, Dor, and their s villages.
11: 8 He extended the city from the Millo to the s area,
18: 1 the Philistines by conquering Gath and its s towns.
22: 9 I will give him peace with his enemies in all the s
22:18 "He has given you peace with the s nations.
29:30 to him and to Israel and to all the s kingdoms.
2Ch 13:19 Jeshanah, and Ephron, along with their s villages.
17:10 Then the fear of the LORD fell over all the s
20:29 When the s kingdoms heard that the LORD
23:13 The officers and trumpeters were s him, and people
32:23 became highly respected among the s nations,
36:14 They followed the pagan practices of the s nations,
Ne 3:22 Then came the priests from the s region.
6:16 When our enemies and the s nations heard about it,
11:30 and its nearby fields and Azekah with its s villages.
11:31 Micmash, Aija, and Bethel with its s villages.
12:28 and its s villages and from the villages of the
Ps 5:12 O LORD, / s them with your shield of love.
49: 5 times of trouble come, / when enemies are s me.
SS 3: 7 with sixty of Israel's mightiest men s it.

Isa 29: 3 be your enemy, s Jerusalem and attacking its walls.
45:20 and come, you fugitives from s nations.
Jer 4:16 "Warn the s nations and announce to Jerusalem:
4:17 They surround Jerusalem like watchmen s a field,
19:15 upon this city and its s towns just as I promised,
Eze 5: 6 and has been even more wicked than the s nations.
5:14 a mockery in the eyes of the s nations and to
19: 8 nations attacked him, / s him from every direction.
20: 9 That way the s nations wouldn't be able to laugh at
23:24 on every side, s you with men armed for battle.
36: 6 because you have suffered shame before the s
36:30 and never again will the s nations be able to scoff
40: 5 I could see a wall completely s the Temple area.
Joel 2:19 be an object of mockery among the s nations.
Ob 1:16 and the s nations will swallow the punishment I
Zep 1:10 And a great crashing sound will come from the s
Mt 14:35 arrival spread quickly throughout the whole s area,
Mk 5:14 fled to the nearby city and the s countryside,
9:14 they found a great crowd s the other disciples,
Lk 4:14 Soon he became well known throughout the s
8:34 they fled to the nearby city and the s countryside,
Ac 14: 6 to the cities of Lystra and Derbe and the s area,

SURROUNDINGS (2) [SURROUND]

2Ki 2:19 "This town is located in beautiful natural s,
1Ch 28:11 gave Solomon the plans for the Temple and its s,

SURROUNDS (7) [SURROUND]

Dt 33:12 live in safety beside him. / He s them continuously
Ps 27: 3 Though a mighty army s me, / my heart will know
32:10 but unfailing love s those who trust the LORD.
103: 4 and s me with love and tender mercies.
125: 2 so the LORD s and protects his people, both now
Eze 43:14 the altar rises 3-1/2 feet to a ledge that s the altar;
Hos 11:12 Israel s me with lies and deceit, but Judah still

SURVEY (2) [SURVEYED, SURVEYING]

Jos 18: 4 and I will send them out to s the unconquered
18: 8 Joshua commanded them, "Go and s the land.

SURVEYED (1) [SURVEY]

Isa 34:17 He has s and divided the land and deeded it over to

SURVEYING (1) [SURVEY]

Job 38: 5 its dimensions were determined and who did the s?

SURVIVE (42) [SURVIVED, SURVIVES, SURVIVING, SURVIVOR, SURVIVORS]

Ge 7: 3 that every kind of living creature will s the flood.
Lev 26:36 "And for those of you who s, I will demoralize
Nu 24:23 by saying: / "Alas, who can s when God does this?
Dt 4:27 among the nations, where only a few of you will s.
5:26 the living God from the heart of the fire and yet s?
1Ki 21:21 male descendants, slave or free alike, s in Israel!
2Ch 32:10 makes you think you can s my siege of Jerusalem?
Ezr 9: 8 our God has allowed a few of us to s as a remnant.
9:13 have allowed some of us to s as a remnant.
Ne 5: 2 money just so we can buy the food we need to s."
Job 27:15 Those who s will be brought down to the grave by
Ps 37:19 They will s through hard times; / even in famine
130: 3 a record of our sins, / who, O Lord, could ever s?
Pr 27: 4 but who can s the destructiveness of jealousy?
Ecc 4: 6 is better to be lazy and barely s than to work hard,
Isa 6:13 a remnant—s, it will be invaded again and burned.
10:19 Only a few from all that mighty army will s—
21:17 Only a few of its courageous archers will s. I,
66:19 And I will send those who s to be messengers to
Jer 8: 3 And the people of this evil nation who s will wish
11:23 Not one of these plotters from Anathoth will s,
44: 7 For not one of you will s—not a man, woman,
La 4:10 and eaten them in order to s the siege.
5: 6 to Egypt and Assyria to get enough food to s.
Eze 5:10 And I will punish you by scattering the few who s
7:11 None of these proud and wicked people will s.
7:13 And if any merchants should s, they will never
7:16 The few who s and escape to the mountains will
33:10 upon us; we are wasting away! How can we s?'
Hos 9:12 Even if your children do s to grow up, I will take
Am 7: 2 Unless you relent, Israel will not s, for we are only
7: 5 Unless you relent, Israel will not s, for we are only
9: 1 Then those who s will be slaughtered in battle.
Na 1: 6 Who can s his burning fury? His rage blazes forth
3:17 crowding together in the hedges to s the cold.
Zep 3:13 The people of Israel who s will do no wrong to
Zec 10: 9 they will s and come home again to Israel.
14:16 the enemies of Jerusalem who s the plague will go
Mt 12:26 against himself. His own kingdom will not s.
Mk 3:26 how can he stand? He would never s.
Lk 11:18 me to cast out his demons, how can his kingdom s?
Rev 6:17 their wrath has come, and who will be able to s?"

SURVIVED (15) [SURVIVE]

Ge 9:18 three sons of Noah, s the Flood with their father.
11:28 place of his birth. He was s by Terah, his father.
Ex 10:15 and all the fruit on the trees that had s the
14:28 chased the Israelites into the sea, not a single one s.
Dt 4:33 of God speaking from fire—as you did—and s?
Jos 8:22 all of them died. Not a single person s or escaped.
1Ch 4:43 They destroyed the few Amalekites who had s,
2Ch 30: 6 so that he will return to the few of us who have s
36:20 The few who s were taken away to Babylon,
Ne 1: 2 I asked them about the Jews who had s the
Ps 106:11 and covered their enemies; / not one of them s.

Isa 4: 3 who have s the destruction of Jerusalem, will be a
Jer 21: 7 and everyone else in the city have s war, famine,
La 2:22 of the LORD's anger, no one has escaped or s.
Am 4:11 Those of you who s were like half-burned sticks

SURVIVES (3) [SURVIVE]

Ezr 9:14 destroy us until even this little remnant no longer s.
Eze 6:12 And anyone who s will be killed by famine.
1Co 3:14 If the work s the fire, that builder will receive a

SURVIVING (7) [SURVIVE]

Nu 26:20 But the following clans descended from Judah's s
Dt 28:54 own brother, his beloved wife, and his s children.
2Ki 19:35 When the s Assyrians woke up the next morning,
2Ch 22: 9 None of the s members of Ahaziah's family was
Isa 37:36 When the s Assyrians woke up the next morning,
Zec 9: 7 All the s Philistines will worship our God and be
12:14 Each of the s families from Judah will mourn

SURVIVOR (4) [SURVIVE]

Nu 21:35 his sons, and his subjects; not a single s remained.
2Ki 10:11 and priests. So Ahab was left without a single s.
Job 18:19 nor grandchildren, nor any s in their home country.
Am 6:10 he will ask the last s, "Is there anyone else with

SURVIVORS (23) [SURVIVE]

Nu 24:19 will rise in Jacob / who will destroy the s of Ir."
Dt 7:20 hornets to drive out the few s still hiding from you!
Jos 10:30 They slaughtered everyone in the city and left no s.
10:39 And they killed everyone in it, leaving no s.
10:40 leaving no s, just as the LORD, the God of Israel,
23:12 and intermarry with the s of these nations
Jdg 20:45 The s fled into the wilderness toward the rock of
21:17 There must be heirs for the s so that an entire tribe
1Sa 4:10 died that day. The s turned and fled to their tents.
2Ki 19:31 out from Jerusalem, a group of s from Mount Zion.
Ezr 1: 4 Those who live in any place where Jewish s are
Isa 15: 9 Lions will hunt down the s, both those who try to
37:32 out from Jerusalem, a group of s from Mount Zion.
Jer 31: 2 I will care for the s as they travel through the
37:10 leaving only a handful of wounded s, they would
Eze 14:22 Yet there will be s, and they will come here to join
23:25 and any s will then be slaughtered by the sword.
Joel 2:32 These will be among the s whom the LORD has
Ob 1:14 You shouldn't have captured the s, handing them
1:18 devouring everything and leaving no s in Edom.
Mic 7:18 who pardons the sins of the s among his people?
Zep 2: 7 The few s of the tribe of Judah will pasture there.
3: 6 There are no s to even tell what happened.

SUSA (21)

Ezr 4: 9 and the people of Erech and S (that is, Elam).
Ne 1: 1 King Artaxerxes' reign, I was at the fortress of S.
Est 1: 2 his empire from his throne at the fortress of S.
1: 5 and was held at S in the courtyard of the palace
2: 3 beautiful young women into the royal harem at S.
2: 5 Now at the fortress of S there was a certain Jew
2: 8 was brought to the king's harem at the fortress of S
3:15 and it was proclaimed in the fortress of S.
3:15 down to drink, but the city of S fell into confusion.
4: 8 issued in S that called for the death of all Jews,
4:16 "Go and gather together all the Jews of S and fast
8:14 same decree was also issued at the fortress of S.
8:15 And the people of S celebrated the new decree.
9: 6 killed five hundred people in the fortress of S.
9:11 of the number of people killed in the fortress of S,
9:12 killed five hundred people in the fortress of S alone
9:13 give the Jews in S permission to do again
9:14 king agreed, and the decree was announced in S.
9:15 Then the Jews at S gathered together on March 8
9:18 But the Jews at S continued killing their enemies
Da 8: 2 This time I was at the fortress of S, in the province

SUSANCHITES [KJV] See SUSA

SUSANNA (1)

Lk 8: 3 the wife of Chuza, Herod's business manager; S;

SUSI (1)

Nu 13:11 Manasseh son of Joseph | Gaddi son of S

SUSPECT (1) [SUSPECTED, SUSPICION, SUSPICIONS, SUSPICIOUS]

Mt 6:18 Then no one will s you are fasting, except your

SUSPECTED (1) [SUSPECT]

2Sa 17:19 on it to dry in the sun; so no one s they were there.

SUSPENSE (1)

Jn 10:24 "How long are you going to keep us in s?

SUSPICION (2) [SUSPECT]

Nu 5:30 and s that his wife has been unfaithful,
2Co 8:20 By traveling together we will guard against any s,

SUSPICIONS (2) [SUSPECT]

Nu 5:18 or not her husband's s are justified.
1Ti 6: 4 ending in jealousy, fighting, slander, and evil s.

SUSPICIOUS (1) [SUSPECT]
Nu 5:14 If her husband becomes jealous and **s** of his wife,

SUSTAIN (4) [SUSTAINED, SUSTAINS]
Ps 119:116 LORD, **s** me as you promised, that I may live!
119:117 **S** me, and I will be saved; / then I will meditate on
119:175 so I can praise you, / and may your laws **s** me.
Jer 15:16 Your words are what **s** me. They bring me great

SUSTAINED (2) [SUSTAIN]
Ne 9:21 For forty years you **s** them in the wilderness.
Ps 119:92 If your law hadn't **s** me with joy, / I would have

SUSTAINS (1) [SUSTAIN]
Heb 1:3 He **s** the universe by the mighty power of his

SUSTENANCE [KJV] See EAT, FOOD

SWADDLED, SWADDLING, SWADDLINGBAND [KJV] See BORN, CLOTHED, DRESSED, STRIPS (OF CLOTH)

SWALLOW (18) [SWALLOWED, SWALLOWING, SWALLOWS]
Nu 13:32 "The land we explored will **s** up any who go to
16:34 fearing that the earth would **s** them, too.
Ps 55:15 enemies by surprise; / let the grave **s** them alive,
69:15 floods overwhelm me, / or the deep waters **s** me,
84:3 finds a home there, / and the **s** builds her nest
Pr 1:12 Let's **s** them alive as the grave swallows its
6:3 Now **s** your pride; go and beg to have your name
26:2 Like a fluttering sparrow or a darting **s**, an unfair
Isa 25:8 He will **s** up death forever! The Sovereign LORD
38:14 Delirious, I chattered like a **s** or a crane, / and
Jer 8:7 as do the turtledove, the **s**, and the crane.
Eze 26:19 waves of enemy attack. Great seas will **s** you.
Ob 1:16 and the surrounding nations will **s** the punishment I
Jnh 1:17 Now the LORD had arranged for a great fish to **s**
Hab 1:13 sin in any form, stand idly by while they **s** us up?
Mt 23:24 your water so you won't accidentally **s** a gnat, then you **s** a camel!
Rev 10:9 "At first it will taste like honey, but when you **s** it,

SWALLOWED (16) [SWALLOW]
Ge 41:7 And these thin heads **s** up the seven plump,
41:24 And the withered heads **s** up the plump ones!
Ex 7:12 too! But then Aaron's snake **s** up their snakes.
15:12 raised up your hand, / and the earth **s** our enemies.
Nu 16:32 The earth opened up and **s** the men, along with
26:10 But the earth opened up and **s** them with Korah,
Dt 11:6 when the earth opened up and **s** them, along with
Job 20:15 He will vomit the wealth he **s**. God won't let him
Ps 106:17 Because of this, the earth opened up; / it **s** Dathan
124:3 they would have **s** us alive / because of their
Isa 5:14 Her great and lowly will be **s** up, with all her
Jer 51:34 He has **s** us like a great monster and filled his belly
Hos 8:8 The people of Israel have been **s** up; they lie
Ob 1:16 Just as you **s** up my people on my holy mountain,
1Co 15:54 will come true: / "Death is **s** up in victory.
2Co 5:4 so that these dying bodies will be **s** up by

SWALLOWING (1) [SWALLOW]
Rev 12:16 and **s** the river that gushed out from the mouth of

SWALLOWS (2) [SWALLOW]
Nu 16:30 opens up and **s** them and all their belongings,
Pr 1:12 Let's swallow them alive as the grave **s** its victims.

SWAM (1) [SWIM]
Jn 21:7 for work), jumped into the water, and **s** ashore.

SWAMP (1) [SWAMPS]
Lk 8:23 A fierce storm developed that threatened to **s** them,

SWAMPS (2) [SWAMP]
Isa 14:23 a place of porcupines, filled with **s** and marshes.
Eze 47:11 But the marshes and **s** will not be purified;

SWAN [KJV] See (WHITE) OWL

SWARE [KJV] See OATH, PLEDGE(D), PROMISE(D), SWEAR(ING), SWORE, SWORN, VOW(ED)

SWARM (10) [SWARMED, SWARMING, SWARMS]
Ge 1:20 "Let the waters **s** with fish and other life.
Ex 8:3 The Nile River will **s** with them. They will come
Lev 11:46 that move through the water or **s** over the earth,
Dt 1:44 lived there came out against you like a **s** of bees.
Jdg 7:12 the east had settled in the valley like a **s** of locusts.
14:8 And he found that a **s** of bees had made some
Isa 7:18 They will **s** around you like flies. Like bees,
Joel 2:9 They **s** over the city and run along its walls.
Am 7:1 I saw him preparing to send a vast **s** of locusts over
Na 3:16 But like a **s** of locusts, they strip the land and

SWARMED (3) [SWARM]
Ex 10:14 And the locusts **s** over the land of Egypt from
Ps 105:31 on the Egyptians, / and gnats **s** across Egypt.
118:12 They **s** around me like bees; / they blazed against

SWARMING (4) [SWARM]
Lev 11:20 "You are to consider detestable all **s** insects that
11:23 But you are to consider detestable all other **s**
Joel 1:4 eating the crops, the **s** locusts took what was left!
2:25 the cutting locusts, the **s** locusts, and the hopping

SWARMS (7) [SWARM]
Ex 8:16 The dust will turn into **s** of gnats throughout the
8:21 you refuse, I will send **s** of flies throughout Egypt.
8:24 There were terrible **s** of flies in Pharaoh's palace
8:29 "I will ask the LORD to cause the **s** of flies to
8:31 did as Moses asked and caused the **s** to disappear.
Dt 28:42 **S** of insects will destroy your trees and crops.
Ps 78:45 He sent vast **s** of flies to consume them

SWAYED (1) [SWAYING]
Ex 23:2 do not be **s** in your testimony by the opinion of the

SWAYING (1) [SWAYED]
Pr 23:34 like a sailor tossed at sea, clinging to a **s** mast.

SWEAR (62) [SWEARING, SWEARS, SWORE, SWORN]
Ge 6:18 But I solemnly **s** to keep you safe in the boat,
21:23 "**S** to me in God's name that you won't deceive
21:23 so now **s** that you will be loyal to me and to this
21:24 Abraham replied, "All right, I **s** to it!"
22:16 even your beloved son, I **s** by my own self that
24:3 "**S** by the LORD, the God of heaven and earth,
24:37 And my master made me **s** that I would not let
25:33 "Well then, **s** to me right now that it is mine."
26:29 **S** that you will not harm us, just as we did not
31:32 I **s** before all these relatives of ours, I will give it
42:15 I **s** by the life of Pharaoh that you will not leave
47:29 **s** most solemnly that you will honor this, my last
47:31 "**S** that you will do it," Jacob insisted. So Joseph
50:5 "Tell Pharaoh that my father made me **s** an oath.
50:25 Then Joseph made the sons of Israel **s** an oath,
Ex 13:19 for Joseph had made the sons of Israel **s** that they
23:13 never pray to or **s** by any other gods.
Lev 19:12 "Do not use my name to **s** a falsehood and
Jos 2:12 Now **s** to me by the LORD that you will be kind
2:19 But we **s** that no one inside this house will be
23:7 their gods, much less **s** by them or worship them.
1Sa 20:3 But I **s** to you that I am only a step away from
20:3 I **s** it by the LORD and by your own soul!"
24:21 **s** to me by the LORD that when that happens you
25:34 For I **s** by the LORD, the God of Israel, who has
26:16 I **s** by the LORD that you and your men deserve
29:6 "I **s** by the LORD," he told them, "you are some
30:15 "If you **s** by God's name that you will not kill me
2Sa 11:11 I **s** that I will never be guilty of acting like that."
14:11 "Please **s** to me by the LORD your God that you
19:7 the troops, for I **s** by the LORD that if you don't,
1Ki 1:51 "Let Solomon **s** today that he will not kill me!"
2:42 "Didn't I make you **s** by the LORD and warn you
17:12 "I **s** by the LORD your God that I don't have a
18:10 For I **s** by the LORD your God that the king has
18:10 King Ahab forced the king of that nation to **s** to the
18:15 But Elijah said, "I **s** by the LORD Almighty,
2Ki 9:26 'I solemnly **s** that I will repay him here on
11:4 and made them **s** an oath of loyalty there in the
Ezr 10:5 and all the people of Israel **s** that they would do as
Ne 13:25 I made them **s** before God that they would not let
Ps 144:8 are full of lies; / they **s** to tell the truth, but they lie.
144:11 are full of lies; / they **s** to tell the truth, but they lie.
Isa 54:9 so now I **s** that I will never again pour out my
Jer 4:2 and if you will **s** by my name alone, and begin to
12:16 and if they learn to **s** by my name, saying,
12:16 as they taught my people to **s** by the name of Baal),
22:5 I **s** by my own name, says the LORD, that this
Am 8:14 those who worship and **s** by the idols of Samaria,
Zec 5:3 the other side says that those who **s** falsely will be
Mt 5:35 earth is his footstool. And don't **s**, 'By Jerusalem!'
5:36 Don't even **s**, 'By my head!' for you can't turn one
23:16 For you say that it means nothing to **s** 'by God's
23:16 then you say that it is binding to **s** 'by the gold in
23:18 but to **s** 'by the gifts on the altar' is binding!
23:20 When you **s** 'by the altar,' you are swearing by it
23:21 And when you **s** 'by the Temple,' you are swearing
23:22 And when you **s** 'by heaven,' you are swearing by
26:74 Peter said, "I **s** by God, I don't know the man."
Mk 14:71 Peter said, "I **s** by God, I don't know this man
1Co 15:31 For I **s**, dear friends, I face death daily. This is as
Heb 6:13 Since there was no one greater to **s** by, God took

SWEARING (6) [SWEAR]
Lev 6:5 or anything gained by **s** falsely. When they realize
Eze 17:18 For the king of Israel broke his treaty after **s** to
Zec 8:17 And stop this habit of **s** to things that are false.
Mt 23:20 the altar,' you are **s** by it and by everything on it.
23:21 you are **s** by it and by God, who lives in it.
23:22 you are **s** by the throne of God and by God,

SWEARS (4) [SWEAR]
Eze 14:16 the Sovereign LORD **s** that it would do no good—
14:18 the Sovereign LORD **s** that they could not save
14:20 the Sovereign LORD **s** that they could not save
Zec 5:4 and into the house of everyone who **s** falsely by

SWEAT (3)
Ge 3:19 All your life you will **s** to produce food, until your
Ex 5:9 Load them down with more work. Make them **s**!
Lk 22:44 and he was in such agony of spirit that his **s** fell to

SWEEP (21) [SWEEPING, SWEEPS, SWEPT, WINDSWEPT]
2Sa 14:14 He does not **s** away the lives of those he cares
1Ki 21:21 is going to bring disaster to you and **s** you away.
Job 20:28 A flood will **s** away his house. God's anger will
Ps 42:7 as your waves and surging tides **s** over me.
58:9 God will **s** them away, both young and old,
90:5 You **s** people away like dreams that disappear
Isa 8:8 will overflow all its channels and **s** into Judah.
14:23 I will **s** the land with the broom of destruction.
23:10 **s** over your mother Tyre like the flooding Nile,
28:17 the enemy will come like a flood to **s** it away.
64:6 and fall. And our sins, like the wind, **s** us away.
Eze 13:13 I will **s** away your whitewashed wall with a storm
21:4 I will make a clean **s** throughout the land from
Da 11:40 various lands and **s** through them like a flood.
Hos 4:19 So a mighty wind will **s** them away. They will die
Hab 1:11 They **s** past like the wind and are gone. But they
Zep 1:2 "I will **s** away everything in all your land,"
1:3 "I will **s** away both people and animals alike.
Zec 11:1 so that fire may **s** through your cedar forests.
Lk 6:49 When the floods **s** down against that house, it will
15:8 and **s** every nook and cranny until she finds it?

SWEEPING (7) [SWEEP]
1Sa 5:11 already begun, and great fear was **s** across the city.
SS 3:6 "Who is this **s** in from the deserts like a cloud of
Isa 21:1 the desert, like a whirlwind **s** in from the Negev.
30:28 out like a flood on his enemies, **s** them all away.
Joel 2:5 of chariots, like the roar of a fire **s** across a field,
Hab 1:9 from the desert, **s** captives ahead of them like sand.
Ac 8:1 began that day, **s** over the church in Jerusalem,

SWEEPS (3) [SWEEP]
Job 27:21 them away, and they are gone. It **s** them away.
Pr 13:23 may produce much food, but injustice **s** it all away.
Na 1:8 But he **s** away his enemies in an overwhelming

SWEET (44) [SWEET-SMELLING, SWEETER, SWEETLY]
Ex 30:23 6-1/4 pounds each of cinnamon and of **s** cane,
30:34 "Gather **s** spices—resin droplets, mollusk scent,
40:27 On it he burned the fragrant incense made from **s**
Jdg 9:11 'Should I quit producing my **s** fruit just to wave
14:14 to eat; / out of the strong came something **s**."
2Sa 23:1 the God of Jacob, / David, the **s** psalmist of Israel.
2Ch 2:4 set apart to burn incense and **s** spices before him,
16:14 He was laid on a bed perfumed with **s** spices
Ne 8:10 celebrate with a feast of choice foods and **s** drinks,
Job 21:33 the body is laid to rest and the earth gives **s** repose.
24:20 Worms will find him **s** to eat. No one will
Ps 81:2 Beat the tambourine. / Play the **s** lyre and the harp.
119:103 How **s** are your words to my taste; / they are
Pr 5:3 The lips of an immoral woman are as **s** as honey,
16:24 like honey—**s** to the soul and healthy for the body.
20:17 Stolen bread tastes **s**, but it turns to gravel in the
24:13 for it is good, and the honeycomb is **s** to the taste.
24:14 In the same way, wisdom is **s** to your soul. If you
27:7 is full, but even bitter food tastes **s** to the hungry.
27:9 The heartfelt counsel of a friend is as **s** as perfume
Ecc 11:7 Light is **s**; it's wonderful to see the sun!
SS 4:10 How **s** is your love, my treasure, my bride!
4:11 Your lips, my bride, are as **s** as honey. Yes, honey
5:16 His mouth is altogether **s**; he is lovely in every
7:9 smooth and **s**, flowing gently over lips and teeth."
8:2 you spiced wine to drink, my **s** pomegranate wine.
Isa 3:24 Instead of smelling of **s** perfume, they will stink.
5:2 Then he waited for a harvest of **s** grapes,
5:4 give me wild grapes / when I expected **s** ones?
5:20 and light is dark; that bitter is **s** and **s** is bitter.
23:15 come back to life and sing **s** songs like a prostitute.
Jer 6:20 There is no use now in offering me **s** incense from
6:20 Your sacrifices have no **s** fragrance for me."
31:26 and looked around. My sleep had been very **s**.
Eze 3:3 he said. And when I ate it, it tasted as **s** as honey.
Da 2:46 to offer sacrifices and burn **s** incense before him.
Joel 3:18 In that day the mountains will drip with **s** wine,
Am 6:12 and make bitter the **s** fruit of righteousness.
9:13 on the hills of Israel will drip with **s** wine!
Mal 1:11 All around the world they offer **s** incense and pure
2Co 2:14 and to spread the Good News like a **s** perfume.
Eph 5:2 because that sacrifice was like **s** perfume to him.
Rev 10:10 It was **s** in my mouth, but it made my stomach

SWEET-SMELLING (1) [SMELL, SWEET]
Php 4:18 They are a **s** sacrifice that is acceptable to God

SWEETER (4) [SWEET]
Jdg 14:18 "What is **s** than honey? / What is stronger than a
Ps 19:10 even the finest gold. / They are **s** than honey,
119:103 are your words to my taste; / they are **s** than honey.
SS 1:2 me again and again, for your love is **s** than wine.

SWEETLY (1) [SWEET]
SS 5:13 His cheeks are like s scented beds of spices.

SWEETSMELLING [KJV] See SWEET

SWELL (3) [SWELLING, SWOLLEN]
Dt 8: 4 didn't wear out, and your feet didn't blister or s.
Ne 9:21 clothes did not wear out, and their feet did not s!
Ac 28: 6 The people waited for him to s up or suddenly drop

SWELLING (4) [SWELL]
Lev 13: 2 "If some of the people notice a s or a rash or a
13:19 but a white s or a reddish white spot remains in its
13:43 and if he finds s around the reddish white sore,
Job 40:23 not even when the s Jordan rushes down upon it.

SWELTERING (1)
Job 37:17 When you are s in your clothes and the south wind

SWEPT (35) [SWEEP]
Ge 20: 8 what had happened, great fear s through the crowd.
Ex 14:27 and the LORD s the terrified Egyptians into the
Jdg 5:21 The Kishon River s them away— / that ancient
2Sa 22: 5 the floods of destruction s over me.
22:43 dust of the earth; / I s them into the gutter like dirt.
2Ki 17:18 LORD was angry, he s them from his presence.
17:23 until the LORD finally s them away, just as all his
Job 1:19 a powerful wind s in from the desert and hit the
4:15 A spirit s past my face. Its wind sent shivers up my
24:18 from the earth as quickly as foam is s down a river.
Ps 10:16 Let those who worship other gods be s from the
18: 4 the floods of destruction s over me.
18:42 by the wind. / I s them into the gutter like dirt.
73:19 an instant they are destroyed, / s away by terrors.
Ecc 5:16 for the wind, and everything will be s away.
Isa 44:22 I have s away your sins like the morning mists.
Eze 7:11 will survive. All their wealth will be s away.
Da 11:12 After the enemy army is s away, the king of the
11:22 Before him great armies will be s away,
11:26 His army will be s away, and many will be killed.
Am 8: 6 And you mix the wheat you sell with chaff s from
Mic 1:11 very foundations of their city have been s away.
Hab 3:10 and trembled. Onward s the raging waters.
Mt 9: 8 Fear s through the crowd as they saw this happen
9:26 The report of this miracle s through the entire
12:44 and finds its former home empty, s, and clean.
24:39 happen until the Flood came and s them all away.
Lk 7:16 Great fear s the crowd, and they praised God,
8:37 them alone, for a great wave of fear s over them.
11:25 and finds that its former home is all s and clean.
15:14 a great famine s over the land, and he began to
Jn 6:18 Soon a gale s down upon them as they rowed,
12:12 the news that Jesus was on the way to Jerusalem s
1Co 12: 2 and s along in worshiping speechless idols.
2Pe 2: 6 heaps of ashes and s them off the face of the earth.

SWERVED (1)
Ps 119:157 trouble me, / yet I have not s from your decrees.

SWIFT (17) [SWIFTER, SWIFTEST, SWIFTLY, SWIFTNESS]
1Ch 12: 8 as fierce as lions and as s as deer on the mountains.
Est 8:10 He sent the letters by s messengers, who rode
Job 9:26 It disappears like a s boat, like an eagle that
SS 2: 7 by the s gazelles and the deer of the wild,
2: 9 My lover is like a s gazelle or a young deer.
3: 5 by the s gazelles and the deer of the wild,
8:14 Move like a s gazelle or a young deer on the
Isa 18: 2 Go home, s messengers! Take a message to your
19: 1 is advancing against Egypt, riding on a s cloud.
27: 1 s sword and punish Leviathan, the swiftly moving
30:16 They will give us s horses for riding into battle.'
46:11 I will call a s bird of prey from the east—a leader
66:15 and his s chariots of destruction roar like a
Eze 30: 9 At that time I will send s messengers in ships to
Na 2: 4 the squares, s as lightning, flickering like torches.
Heb 1: 7 God calls his angels / "messengers s as the wind,
2Pe 2: 1 bought them. Theirs will be a s and terrible end.

SWIFTER (5) [SWIFT]
2Sa 1:23 in life and in death. / They were s than eagles;
Job 7: 6 "My days are s than a weaver's shuttle flying back
Jer 4:13 are like whirlwinds; his horses are s than eagles.
La 4:19 Our enemies were s than the eagles. If we fled to
Hab 1: 8 Their horses are s than leopards. They are a fierce

SWIFTEST (5) [SWIFT]
Est 3:15 the decree went out by the s messengers,
Job 39:18 up to run, she passes the s horse with its rider.
Jer 46: 6 The s cannot flee; the mightiest warriors cannot
Am 2:15 The s soldiers won't be fast enough to escape.
Mic 1:13 Use your s chariots and flee, you people of

SWIFTLY (12) [SWIFT]
Est 8:14 the messengers rode out s on horses bred for the
Job 9:25 "My life passes more s than a runner. It flees
Ps 102:11 My life passes as s as the evening shadows.
147:15 his orders to the world— / how s his word flies!
Isa 27: 1 the s moving serpent, the coiling, writhing serpent,
Jer 8: 6 All are running down the path of sin as s as a horse
49:22 The enemy will come as s as an eagle, and he will
Da 8: 5 the land so s that it didn't even touch the ground.
9:21 came s to me at the time of the evening sacrifice.
Joel 3: 4 I will strike s and pay you back for everything you
Mic 7: 4 But your judgment day is coming s now.
Zep 1:14 S it comes—a day when strong men will cry

SWIFTNESS (2) [SWIFT]
Isa 30:16 But the only s you are going to see is the s

SWIM (2) [SWAM, SWIMMER, SWIMMING, SWIMS]
Ac 27:42 kill the prisoners to make sure they didn't s ashore
27:43 Then he ordered all who could s to jump overboard

SWIMMER (1) [SWIM]
Isa 25:11 God will push down Moab's people as a s pushes

SWIMMING (1) [SWIM]
Eze 47: 5 and the river was too deep to cross without s.

SWIMS (1) [SWIM]
Ps 8: 8 the sea, / and everything that s the ocean currents.

SWINDLER (1) [SWINDLERS]
1Co 5:11 worships idols, or is abusive, or a drunkard, or a s.

SWINDLERS (2) [SWINDLER]
1Co 5:10 or who are greedy or are s or idol worshipers.
6:10 thieves, greedy people, drunkards, abusers, and s—

SWINE (1)
Mt 7: 6 Don't give pearls to s! They will trample the

SWINE [KJV] See also PIG(S)

SWINGING (2) [SWINGS, SWUNG]
Job 28: 4 They descend on ropes, s back and forth.
Eze 41:24 each with two s doors.

SWINGS (1) [SWINGING]
Dt 19: 5 And suppose one of them s an ax and the ax head

SWIRL (3) [SWIRLING, SWIRLS]
Job 22:14 For thick clouds s about him, and he cannot see us.
Ps 88:17 They s around me like floodwaters all day long.
Hos 11: 6 War will s through their cities; their enemies will

SWIRLING (1) [SWIRL]
Am 1:14 the battle, s like a whirlwind in a mighty storm.

SWIRLS (2) [SWIRL]
Jer 23:19 a whirlwind that s down on the heads of the
30:23 a driving wind that s down on the heads of the

SWISH (1)
Job 41:29 do no good, and it laughs at the s of the javelins.

SWITCHES (1)
1Ch 12:19 "It will cost us our lives if David s loyalties to

SWOLLEN (4) [SWELL]
Lev 14:56 in a s area of skin, in a skin rash, or in a shiny
Job 6:16 when it is s with ice and melting snow.
Ps 69: 3 is parched and dry. / My eyes are s with weeping,
Lk 14: 2 there was a man there whose arms and legs were s.

SWOON(ED) [KJV] See FAINTING

SWOOP (5) [SWOOPS]
Dt 28:49 the earth, and it will s down on you like an eagle.
Ne 4:11 we will s down on them and kill them and end their
Isa 11:14 They will join forces to s down on Philistia to the
Eze 38: 8 In the distant future you will s down on the land of
Hab 1: 8 Like eagles they s down to pounce on their prey.

SWOOPS (2) [SWOOP]
Job 9:26 a swift boat, like an eagle that s down on its prey.
Jer 48:40 "An eagle s down on the land of Moab,"

SWORD (184) [SWORDS, SWORDSMEN]
Ge 3:24 And a flaming s flashed back and forth,
27:40 and you will live by your s. You will serve your
48:22 the portion that I took from the Amorites with my s
Ex 5: 3 If we don't, we will surely die by disease or the s."
15: 9 I will unsheath my s; / my power will destroy
18: 4 he delivered me from the s of Pharaoh."
22:24 forth against you, and I will kill you with the s.
Lev 26:36 will run as though chased by a warrior with a s,
Nu 19:16 the corpse of someone who was killed with a s
22:23 standing in the road with a drawn s in his hand.
22:29 "If I had a s with me, I would kill you!"
22:31 standing in the roadway with a drawn s in his hand.
31: 8 They also killed Balaam son of Beor with the s.
Dt 32:25 Outside, the s will bring death, / and inside,
32:41 when I sharpen my flashing s / and begin to carry
32:42 drunk with blood, / and my s will devour flesh—
33:29 is your protecting shield / and your triumphant s!
Jos 5:13 and saw a man facing him with s in hand.
10:11 of the enemy than the Israelites killed with the s.
Jdg 7:20 "A s for the LORD and for Gideon!"
8:20 But Jether did not draw his s, for he was only a boy
9:54 his young armor bearer, "Draw your s and kill me!
9:54 So the young man stabbed him with his s, and he
20:25 all of whom were experienced with a s.
20:35 all of whom were experienced with a s.
1Sa 13:22 So none of the people of Israel had a s or spear,
15:33 "As your s has killed the sons of many mothers,
17:39 strapped the s over it, and took a step or two to see
17:45 "You come to me with s, spear, and javelin,
17:50 with only a stone and sling. And since he had no s,
17:51 he ran over and pulled Goliath's s from its sheath.
18: 4 pact by giving him his robe, tunic, s, bow, and belt.
21: 8 asked Ahimelech, "Do you have a spear or s?
21: 9 "I only have the s of Goliath the Philistine,
22:10 David food and the s of Goliath the Philistine."
22:13 "Why did you give him food and a s?
31: 4 "Take your s and kill me before these pagan
31: 4 not do it. So Saul took his own s and fell on it.
31: 5 he fell on his own s and died beside the king.
2Sa 1:15 So the man thrust his s into the Amalekite
2:16 and thrust his s into the other's side so that all of
3:29 or who dies by the s or who begs for food!"
11:25 David said. "The s kills one as well as another!
12:10 the s will be a constant threat to your family,
18: 8 because of the forest than were killed by the s.
21:16 seven pounds, and he was armed with a new s.
23:10 Philistines until his hand was too tired to lift his s,
1Ki 3:24 right, bring me a s." So a s was brought to the king.
2Ki 19: 7 his land, where I will have him killed with a s.' "
1Ch 10: 4 "Take your s and run me through before these
10: 4 not do it. So Saul took his own s and fell on it.
10: 5 that Saul was dead, he fell on his own s and died.
21:16 between heaven and earth with his s drawn,
21:27 to the angel, who put the s back into its sheath.
21:30 because he was terrified by the drawn s of the
2Ch 32:21 some of his own sons killed him there with a s.
Ne 4:18 All the builders had a s belted to their side.
Est 9: 5 and struck down their enemies with the s.
Job 5:20 of famine, from the power of the s in time of war.
39:22 it is unafraid. It does not run from the s.
41:26 No s can stop it, nor spear nor dart nor pointed
Ps 7:12 a person does not repent, / God will sharpen his s;
17:13 Rescue me from the wicked with your s!
44: 6 trust my bow; / I do not count on my s to save me.
45: 3 Put on your s, O mighty warrior! / You are
63:10 They will die by the s / and become the food of
76:10 your glory, / for you use it as a s of judgment.
78:62 He gave his people over to be butchered by the s,
89:43 You have made his s useless / and have refused to
144:11 Save me from the fatal s! / Rescue me from the
149: 6 be in their mouths, / and a sharp s in their hands—
Pr 5: 4 is as bitter as poison, sharp as a double-edged s.
25:18 wounding them with a s, or shooting them with a
SS 3: 8 Each one wears a s on his thigh, ready to defend
Isa 13:15 who is captured will be run through with a s.
27: 1 swift s and punish Leviathan, the swiftly moving
31: 8 The s of God will strike them, and they will panic
34: 5 And when my s has finished its work in the
34: 6 The s of the LORD is drenched with blood.
37: 7 his land, where I will have him killed with a s.' "
41: 2 He puts entire armies to the s. He scatters them in
49: 2 He made my words of judgment as sharp as a s.
65:12 I will 'destine' you to the s. All of you will bow
66:16 LORD will punish the world by fire and by his s,
Jer 4:10 Yet the s is even now poised to strike them dead!"
9:16 Their enemies will chase them with the s until I
12:12 The s of the LORD kills people from one end of
14:17 has been run through with a s and lies mortally
15: 3 "I will send the s to kill, the dogs to drag away,
18:21 their children starve! Let the s pour out their blood!
20: 4 captive to Babylon or run them through with the s.
25:31 of the earth, slaughtering the wicked with his s.
25:38 and their land will be made desolate by the s of the
26:23 The king then killed Uriah with a s and had him
43:11 he will bring the s against those destined for the s.
46:10 The s will devour until it is satisfied, yes,
46:14 for the s of destruction will devour everyone
46:16 Let's get away from the s of the enemy!'
47: 6 "Now, O s of the LORD, when will you be at rest
48: 2 will be silenced; the s will follow you there.
49:37 "Their enemies will chase them with the s until I
50:16 Let the captives escape the s of the enemy and rush
50:35 "The s of destruction will strike the Babylonians,"
51:20 "You are my battle-ax and s," says the LORD.
51:50 Go, you who escaped the s! Do not stand
La 1:20 In the streets the s kills, and at home there is only
4: 9 Those killed by the s are far better off than those
Eze 5: 1 take a sharp s and use it as a razor to shave your
5: 2 third across your map and slash at it with a s.
5: 2 to the wind, for I will scatter my people with the s.
5:12 a third to the winds and chase them with my s.
5:17 and I will bring the s of the enemy against you.
12:14 guards to the four winds and send the s after them.
21: 3 and I am about to unsheath my s to destroy your
21: 5 My s is in my hand, and it will not return to its
21: 9 the LORD: A s is being sharpened and polished.
21:11 Yes, the s is now being sharpened and polished;
21:12 for that s will slaughter my people and their
21:14 Then take the s and brandish it twice, even three
21:15 melt with terror, for the s glitters at every gate.
21:16 O s, slash to the right, and slash to the left,
21:19 and trace two routes on it for the s of Babylon's
21:28 My s is drawn for your slaughter; it is sharpened to
21:29 have given false visions and told lies about the s.

21:30 Should I return my s to its sheath before I deal with
23:25 and any survivors will then be slaughtered by the s.
24:21 daughters in Judea will be slaughtered by the s.
25:13 wipe out their people, cattle, and flocks with the s.
26: 6 its mainland villages will be destroyed by the s.
30: 4 A s will come against Egypt, and those who are
30: 6 Migdol to Aswan they will be slaughtered by the s,
30:21 with a splint to make it strong enough to hold a s.
30:22 and I will make his s clatter to the ground.
30:24 arms of Babylon's king and put my s in his hand.
30:25 And when I put my s in the hand of Babylon's king
31:18 there among the outcasts who have died by the s.
32:10 brandish my s before them on the day of your fall.
32:11 The s of the king of Babylon will come against
32:20 will fall with the many who have died by the s, for the s is drawn against them.
32:21 they lie among the outcasts, all victims of the s.'
32:22 all its people, those who were slaughtered by the s.
32:25 in the pit, all of them outcasts, slaughtered by the s.
32:26 But now they are outcasts, all victims of the s.
32:28 and broken among the outcasts, all victims of the s.
32:29 they also lie among those killed by the s,
32:30 and the Sidonians are there, all victims of the s.
32:32 there among the outcasts who have died by the s.
33:27 as I live, those living in the ruins will die by the s.
35: 8 will be filled with people slaughtered by the s.
38:21 I will summon the s against you throughout Israel,
Da 11:33 time many of these teachers will die by fire and s,
Am 9: 4 into exile, I will command the s to kill them there.
9:10 But all the sinners will die by the s—all those who
Na 3:15 the fire will devour you; the s will cut you down.
Zep 2:12 Ethiopians will also be slaughtered by my s,"
Zec 9:13 Jerusalem is my s, and like a warrior, I will
11:17 The s will cut his arm and pierce his right eye!
13: 7 "Awake, O s, against my shepherd, the man who
Mt 10:34 to bring peace to the earth! No, I came to bring a s.
26:51 One of the men with Jesus pulled out a s
26:52 "Put away your s," Jesus told him. "Those who use the s will be killed by the s.
Mk 14:47 But someone pulled out a s and slashed off an ear
Lk 2:35 be revealed. And a s will pierce your very soul."
21:24 They will be brutally killed by the s or sent away
22:36 And if you don't have a s, sell your clothes
Jn 18:10 Then Simon Peter drew a s and slashed off the
18:11 said to Peter, "Put your s back into its sheath.
Ac 12: 2 the apostle James (John's brother) killed with a s.
16:27 had escaped, so he drew his s to kill himself.
Eph 6:17 and take the s of the Spirit, which is the Word of
Heb 11:34 of fire, and escaped death by the edge of the s.
11:37 were sawed in half; others were killed with the s.
Rev 1:16 and a sharp two-edged s came from his mouth.
2:12 from the one who has a sharp two-edged s:
2:16 and fight against them with the s of my mouth.
6: 4 Its rider was given a mighty s and the authority to
6: 8 to kill with the s and famine and disease and wild
19:15 From his mouth came a sharp s, and with it he
19:21 Their entire army was killed by the sharp s that

SWORDS (54) [SWORD]

Ge 34:25 of Dinah's brothers, Simeon and Levi, took their s,
Ex 32:27 the God of Israel, says: Strap on your s!
Lev 26: 7 all your enemies and slaughter them with your s.
Jos 24:12 It was not your s or bows that brought you victory.
Jdg 7:22 in the camp to fight against each other with their s.
20: 2 tribes of Israel—400,000 warriors armed with s—
20:15 Twenty-six thousand of their warriors armed with s
20:17 Israel had 400,000 warriors armed with s,
1Sa 13:19 wouldn't allow them for fear they would make s
25:13 "Get your s!" was David's reply as he strapped on
2Sa 2:16 place has been known ever since as the Field of S.
2:26 "Must we always solve our differences with s?
1Ki 18:28 with knives and s until the blood gushed out.
2Ki 10:25 So they killed them all with their s, and the guards
19:37 and Sharezer killed him with their s.
1Ch 5:18 in combat and armed with shields, s, and bows.
Ne 4:13 guard by families, armed with s, spears, and bows.
Ps 37:14 The wicked draw their s / and string their bows
37:15 will be stabbed through the heart with their own s,
44: 3 They did not conquer the land with their s;
57: 4 and arrows, / and whose tongues cut like s.
59: 7 the piercing s that fly from their lips.
64: 3 Sharp tongues are the s they wield; / bitter words
76: 3 the shields and s and weapons of his foes.
Pr 30:14 They devour the poor with teeth as sharp as s
Isa 2: 4 All the nations will beat their s into plowshares
21:15 They have fled from drawn s and sharp arrows
31: 8 will be destroyed, but not by the s of men.
37:38 and Sharezer killed him with their s.
Jer 20: 4 and you will watch as they are slaughtered by the s
41: 2 Ishmael and his ten men suddenly drew their s
48:10 who hold back their s from shedding blood!
La 2:21 boys and girls, killed by the s of the enemy.
Eze 7:15 who leave the city walls will be killed by enemy s.
16:40 in a mob to stone you and run you through with s.
23:47 their enemies will stone them and kill them with s.
28: 7 They will suddenly draw their s against your
32:12 I will destroy you with the s of mighty warriors—
32:27 their bodies, and their s beneath their heads.
Hos 2:18 all s and bows, so you can live unafraid in peace
13:16 their pregnant women ripped open by s."
Joel 3:10 Beat your plowshares into s and your pruning
Am 1:11 chased down their relatives, the Israelites, with s.
1:13 ripping open pregnant women with their s.
Mic 4: 3 All the nations will beat their s into plowshares
5: 6 They will rule Assyria with drawn s and enter the
Na 3: 3 See the flashing s and glittering spears in the

Mt 26:47 arrived with a mob that was armed with s
26:55 that you have come armed with s and clubs to
Mk 14:43 arrived with a mob that was armed with s
14:48 that you come armed with s and clubs to arrest me?
Lk 22:38 "Lord," they replied, "we have two s among us."
22:49 "Lord, should we fight? We brought the s!"
22:52 "that you have come armed with s and clubs to

SWORDSMEN (1) [SWORD]

SS 3: 8 They are all skilled s and experienced warriors.

SWORE (43) [SWEAR]

Ge 25:33 So Esau s an oath, thereby selling all his rights as
Ex 6: 4 its terms, I s to give them the land of Canaan,
6: 8 I will bring you into the land I s to give to
13: 5 This is the land he s to give your ancestors—
13:11 into the land he s to give your ancestors long ago,
32:13 You s by your own self, 'I will make your
Nu 11:12 a baby—to the land you s to give their ancestors?
14:16 able to bring them into the land he s to give them,
14:23 They will never even see the land I s to give their
14:30 will enter the land I s to give you. The only
Dt 1: 8 for it is the land the LORD s to give to your
1:34 he became very angry. So he solemnly s,
1:35 live to see the good land I s to give your ancestors,
6:10 into the land he s to give your ancestors Abraham,
7:13 When you arrive in the land he s to give your
8: 1 and occupy the land the LORD s to give your
10:11 and lead the people into the land I s to give their
11: 9 you will enjoy a long life in the land the LORD s
11:21 in the land the LORD s to give your ancestors.
26: 3 me into the land he s to give our ancestors.'
28:11 things in the land he s to your ancestors—
29:13 and as he s to your ancestors Abraham, Isaac,
30:20 Then you will live long in the land the LORD s to
31: 7 the land that the LORD s to give their ancestors.
31:20 For I will bring them into the land I s to give their
31:21 even before they have entered the land I s to give
31:23 the people of Israel into the land I s to give them.
Jos 1: 6 to possess all the land I s to give their ancestors.
Jdg 2: 1 "I brought you out of Egypt into this land that I s
1Sa 20:30 "You stupid son of a whore!" he s at him.
1Ki 1:30 just as I s to you before the LORD, the God of
2: 8 I s by the LORD that I would not kill him.
2:23 Then King Solomon s solemnly by the LORD:
1Ch 16:16 he made with Abraham / and the oath he s to Isaac.
Ezr 10: 5 Shecaniah had said. And they all s a solemn oath.
Ps 105: 9 he made with Abraham / and the oath he s to Isaac.
106:26 Therefore, he s / that he would kill them in the
132:11 The LORD s to David / a promise he will never
Isa 54: 9 "Just as I s in the time of Noah that I would never
Eze 20: 5 in Egypt, I s that I, the LORD, would be her God.
20:15 But I s to them in the wilderness that I would not
47:14 I s that I would give this land to your ancestors,
Rev 10: 6 And he s an oath in the name of the one who lives

SWORN (28) [SWEAR]

Ge 21:31 because that was where they had s an oath.
Dt 7: 8 because he was keeping the oath he had s to your
9: 5 and to fulfill the oath he had s to your ancestors
9:28 to bring them to the land he had s to give them."
Jos 5: 6 not let them enter the land he had s to give us—
9:19 "We have s an oath in the presence of the LORD,
21:43 So the LORD gave to Israel all the land he had s
Jdg 21: 7 since we have s by the LORD not to give them
21:18 because we have s with a solemn oath that anyone
1Sa 20: 8 Show me this kindness as my s friend—for we
2Sa 21: 2 Israel had s not to kill them, but Saul, in his zeal,
21: 7 oath David and Jonathan had s before the LORD.
Ne 6:18 For many in Judah had s allegiance to him
9:15 and take possession of the land you had s to give
Ps 89: 3 my chosen servant. / I have s this oath to him:
89:35 I have s an oath to David, / and in my holiness I
Isa 14:24 The LORD Almighty has s this oath: "It will all
45:23 I have s by my own name, and I will never go back
62: 8 The LORD has s to Jerusalem by his own
Jer 5: 7 They have s by gods that are not gods at all!
44:26 I have s by my great name, says the LORD,
49:13 For I have s by my own name," says the LORD,
51:14 has taken this vow and has s to it by his own name:
Eze 17:15 Can Israel break her s treaties like that and get
36: 7 and s an oath that those nations will soon have
Am 4: 2 The Sovereign LORD has s this by his holiness:
6: 8 The Sovereign LORD has s by his own name,
8: 7 Now the LORD has s this oath by his own name,

SWUNG (3) [SWINGING]

Ge 14: 7 Then they s around to En-mishpat (now called
Rev 14:16 So the one sitting on the cloud s his sickle over the
14:19 So the angel s his sickle on the earth and loaded

SYCAMINE [KJV] See MULBERRY

SYCAMORE (5) [SYCAMORE-FIG, SYCAMORES]

1Ki 10:27 And valuable cedarwood was as common as the s
2Ch 1:15 And valuable cedarwood was as common as the s
9:27 And valuable cedarwood was as common as the s
Isa 9:10 with cut stone, the fallen s trees with cedars."
Lk 19: 4 he ran ahead and climbed a s tree beside the road,

SYCAMORE-FIG (1) [FIG, SYCAMORE]

1Ch 27:28 olive groves and s trees in the foothills of Judah.

SYCAMORES (1) [SYCAMORE]

Ps 78:47 with hail / and shattered their s with sleet.

SYCHAR (1)

Jn 4: 5 Eventually he came to the Samaritan village of S,

SYCHEM [KJV] See SHECHEM

SYCOMORE [KJV] See SYCAMORE(S)

SYMBOL (6) [SYMBOLIZE, SYMBOLIZING, SYMBOLS]

Ge 41:42 ring on Joseph's finger as a s of his authority.
Nu 6: 7 because it is the s of their separation to God.
Ps 132: 8 along with the Ark, the s of your power.
Isa 20: 3 a s of the terrible troubles I will bring upon Egypt
Eze 24:27 talk to him, and you will be a s for these people.
Zec 8:13 Now I will rescue you and make you both a s

SYMBOLIZE (1) [SYMBOL]

Eze 21:14 three times, to s the great massacre they will face!

SYMBOLIZING (1) [SYMBOL]

Ps 116:13 I will lift up a cup s his salvation; / I will praise the

SYMBOLS (2) [SYMBOL]

Zec 3: 8 other priests. You are s of the good things to come.
8:13 and Israel had become s of what it means to be

SYMPATHETIC (2) [SYMPATHY]

Eze 24:22 by eating the food brought to you by s friends.
Php 2: 1 in the Spirit? Are your hearts tender and s?

SYMPATHIZE (1) [SYMPATHY]

Isa 51:19 famine and war. And who is left to s?

SYMPATHY (4) [SYMPATHETIC, SYMPATHIZE]

2Sa 10: 2 So David sent ambassadors to express s to Hanun
1Ch 19: 2 So David sent ambassadors to express s to Hanun
Jer 16: 5 to their funerals to mourn and show s for them,"
1Pe 3: 8 should be of one mind, full of s toward each other,

SYMPHONY (1)

Ps 98: 6 Make a joyful s before the LORD, the King!

SYNAGOGUE (46) [SYNAGOGUES]

Mt 9:18 the leader of a s came and knelt down before him.
12: 9 Then he went over to the s,
13:54 When he taught there in the s, everyone was
23: 6 and in the most prominent seats in the s!
Mk 1:21 and every Sabbath day he went into the s
1:23 A man possessed by an evil spirit was in the s,
1:29 After Jesus and his disciples left the s, they went
3: 1 Jesus went into the s again and noticed a man with
5:22 A leader of the local s, whose name was Jairus,
5:38 When they came to the home of the s leader,
6: 2 The next Sabbath he began teaching in the s,
Lk 4:16 he went as usual to the s on the Sabbath and stood
4:20 sat down. Everyone in the s stared at him intently.
4:28 they heard this, the people in the s were furious.
4:31 and taught there in the s every Sabbath day.
4:33 Once when he was in the s, a man possessed by a
4:38 After leaving the s that day, Jesus went to Simon's
6: 6 a man with a deformed right hand was in the s
7: 5 "for he loves the Jews and even built a s for us."
8:41 a leader of the local s, came and fell down at
13:10 One Sabbath day as Jesus was teaching in a s,
13:14 But the leader in charge of the s was indignant that
Jn 6:59 He said these things while he was teaching in the s
9:22 was the Messiah would be expelled from the s.
9:34 to teach us?" And they threw him out of the s.
12:42 that the Pharisees would expel them from the s.
Ac 6: 9 But one day some men from the S of Freed Slaves,
13:14 On the Sabbath they went to the s for the services.
13:42 As Paul and Barnabas left the s that day, the people
13:43 to Judaism who worshiped at the s followed Paul
14: 1 Paul and Barnabas went together to the s
17: 1 came to Thessalonica, where there was a Jewish s.
17: 2 As was Paul's custom, he went to the s service,
17:10 When they arrived there, they went to the s.
17:17 He went to the s to debate with the Jews
18: 4 Each Sabbath found Paul at the s, trying to
18: 7 who worshiped God and lived next door to the s.
18: 8 Crispus, the leader of the s, and all his household
18:17 mob had grabbed Sosthenes, the leader of the s,
18:19 was there, he went to the s to debate with the Jews.
18:26 and Aquila heard him preaching boldly in the s,
19: 8 Then Paul went to the s and preached boldly for
19: 9 so Paul left the s and took the believers with him.
22:19 and beat those in every s who believed on you.
24:12 nor did I incite a riot in any s or on the streets of
Rev 2: 9 but they really aren't because theirs is a s of Satan.

SYNAGOGUES (22) [SYNAGOGUE]

Mt 4:23 Jesus traveled throughout Galilee teaching in the s,
6: 2 blowing trumpets in the s and streets to call
6: 5 and in the s where everyone can see them.
9:35 teaching in the s and announcing the Good News
10:17 be handed over to the courts and beaten in the s.

23:34 kill some by crucifixion and whip others in your **s**,
Mk 1:39 preaching in the **s** and expelling demons from
12:39 And how they love the seats of honor in the **s**
13: 9 be handed over to the courts and beaten in the **s**.
Lk 4:15 He taught in their **s** and was praised by everyone.
4:44 to travel around, preaching in **s** throughout Judea.
11:43 For how you love the seats of honor in the **s**
12:11 "And when you are brought to trial in the **s**
20:46 And how they love the seats of honor in the **s**
21:12 You will be dragged into **s** and prisons, and you
Jn 16: 2 For you will be expelled from the **s**, and the time is
18:20 because I have preached regularly in the **s**
Ac 9: 2 He requested letters addressed to the **s** in
9:20 he began preaching about Jesus in the **s**,
13: 5 they went to the Jewish **s** and preached the word of
15:21 **s** in every city on every Sabbath for many
26:11 Many times I had them whipped in the **s** to try to

SYNTYCHE (1)

Php 4: 2 to plead with those two women, Euodia and **S**.

SYRACUSE (1)

Ac 28:12 Our first stop was **S**, where we stayed three days.

SYRIA (13) [SYRIAN]

Mt 4:24 soon coming to be healed from as far away as **S**.
Lk 2: 2 census taken when Quirinius was governor of **S**.)
Ac 11:19 as far as Phoenicia, Cyprus, and Antioch of **S**.
13: 1 and teachers of the church at Antioch of **S** were
14:26 Finally, they returned by ship to Antioch of **S**,
15: 1 While Paul and Barnabas were at Antioch of **S**,
15:22 and they sent them to Antioch of **S** with Paul
15:23 to the Gentile believers in Antioch, **S**, and Cilicia.
15:41 So they traveled throughout **S** and Cilicia to
18:18 to the Christians and sailed for the coast of **S**,
20: 3 He was preparing to sail back to **S** when he
21: 3 harbor of Tyre, in **S**, where the ship was to unload.
Gal 1:21 I went north into the provinces of **S** and Cilicia.

SYRIA-DAMASCUS [KJV] See DAMASCUS

SYRIA-MAACHAH [KJV] See ARAM-MAACAH

SYRIACK [KJV] See ARAMAIC

SYRIAN (3) [SYRIA]

Mk 7:26 Since she was a Gentile, born in **S** Phoenicia,
Lk 4:27 of the prophet Elisha, who healed Naaman, a **S**,
Ac 21: 2 There we boarded a ship sailing for the **S** province

SYRIANS [KJV] See also ARAM, ARAMEAN, EDOMITES

SYROPHENICIAN [KJV] See SYRIAN (PHOENICIA)

SYRTIS (1)

Ac 27:17 across to the sandbars of **S** off the African coast,

SYSTEM (11)

2Co 3: 7 That old **s** of law etched in stone led to death,
Gal 2:18 I make myself guilty if I rebuild the old **s** I already
3:19 But this **s** of law was to last only until the coming
Eph 2:15 By his death he ended the whole **s** of Jewish law
Heb 7:23 is that there were many priests under the old **s**.
9: 8 and the entire **s** it represents were still in use.
9:10 For that old **s** deals only with food and drink
9:13 Under the old **s**, the blood of goats and bulls
10: 1 The old **s** in the law of Moses was only a shadow
10: 1 The sacrifices under the old **s** were repeated again
13:11 Under the **s** of Jewish laws, the high priest brought

---

T

TAANACH (7)

Jos 12:21 The king of **T** / The king of Megiddo
17:11 (that is, Naphoth-dor), Endor, **T**, and Megiddo,
21:25 to the priests: **T** and Gath-rimmon—two towns.
Jdg 1:27 **T**, Dor, Ibleam, Megiddo, and their surrounding
5:19 "The kings of Canaan fought at **T** near Megiddo's
1Ki 4:12 Baana son of Ahilud, in **T** and Megiddo, all of
1Ch 7:29 **T**, Megiddo, Dor, and their surrounding villages.

TAANATH-SHILOH (1) [SHILOH]

Jos 16: 6 then curved eastward past **T** to the east of Janoah.

TABBAOTH (2)

Ezr 2:43 servants returned from exile: / Ziha, Hasupha, **T**,
Ne 7:46 servants returned from exile: / Ziha, Hasupha, **T**,

TABBATH (1)

Jdg 7:22 and to the border of Abel-meholah near **T**.

TABEEL (2)

Ezr 4: 7 of Judah, led by Bishlam, Mithredath, and **T**,
Isa 7: 6 and install the son of **T** as Judah's king.'

TABERAH (2)

Nu 11: 3 After that, the area was known as **T**—"the place of
Dt 9:22 "You also made the LORD angry at **T**, Massah,

TABERING [KJV] See BEAT

TABERNACLE (266)

Ex 25: 9 You must make this **T** and its furnishings exactly
26: 1 "Make the **T** from ten sheets of fine linen.
26: 6 sets of sheets together, making the **T** a single unit.
26: 7 heavy sheets of cloth from goat hair to cover the **T**.
26:12 will be left to hang over the back of the **T**,
26:15 "The framework of the **T** will consist of frames
26:18 these frames will support the south side of the **T**.
26:25 So there will be eight frames on that end of the **T**,
26:26 five crossbars for the north side of the **T**
26:27 Also make five crossbars for the rear of the **T**,
26:28 will run all the way from one end of the **T** to the
26:30 "Set up this **T** according to the design you were
26:31 "Across the inside of the **T** hang a special curtain
27: 9 "Then make a courtyard for the **T**, enclosed with
27:19 "All the articles used in the work of the **T**,
27:19 including all the tent pegs used to support the **T**
27:21 the inner curtain of the Most Holy Place in the **T**.
28:43 be worn whenever Aaron and his sons enter the **T**
29: 3 and present them at the entrance of the **T**,
29: 4 and his sons at the entrance of the **T**,
29:10 bring the young bull to the entrance of the **T**,
29:11 in the LORD's presence at the entrance of the **T**.
29:30 seven days before beginning to minister in the **T**
29:32 with the bread in the basket, at the **T** entrance.
29:42 Offer it in the LORD's presence at the **T**
29:43 and the **T** will be sanctified by my glorious
29:44 Yes, I will make the **T** and the altar most holy,
30:16 Use this money for the care of the **T**. It will bring
30:18 Put it between the **T** and the altar, and fill it with
30:20 before they go into the **T** to appear before the
30:26 Use this scented oil to anoint the **T**, the Ark of the
30:36 the Covenant, where I will meet with you in the **T**.
31: 7 the **T** itself; the Ark of the Covenant; the Ark's
31: 7 the place of atonement; all the furnishings of the **T**;
35:11 the entire **T**, including the sacred tent and its
35:15 the curtain for the entrance of the **T**;
35:18 the tent pegs of the **T** and courtyard and their
35:21 to the LORD their offerings of materials for the **T**
36: 1 and intelligence will construct and furnish the **T**,
36:13 Thus the **T** was joined together in one piece.
36:14 Above the **T**, a roof covering was made from
36:20 For the framework of the **T**, they made frames of
36:25 made twenty frames for the north side of the **T**,
36:27 The west side of the **T**, which was its rear,
38: 8 by the women who served at the entrance of the **T**.
38:20 All the tent pegs used in the **T** and courtyard were
38:21 materials used in building the **T** of the Covenant.
38:24 all of which was used throughout the **T**.
38:30 the bases for the posts at the entrance to the **T**,
39:32 And so at last the **T** was finished. The Israelites
39:33 And they brought the entire **T** to Moses: the sacred
39:40 all the articles used in the operation of the **T**;
40: 2 "Set up the **T** on the first day of the new year.
40: 5 Set up the curtain made for the entrance of the **T**.
40: 6 Place the altar of burnt offering in front of the **T**
40: 7 Set the large washbasin between the **T** and the altar
40: 9 "Take the anointing oil and sprinkle it on the **T**
40:12 and his sons to the entrance of the **T**,
40:17 So the **T** was set up on the first day of the new
40:19 Then he spread the coverings over the **T**
40:21 he brought the Ark of the Covenant into the **T**
40:22 Next he placed the table in the **T**, along the north
40:24 He set the lampstand in the **T** across from the table
40:26 He also placed the incense altar in the **T**,
40:28 He attached the curtain at the entrance of the **T**,
40:29 and he placed the altar of burnt offering near the **T**
40:30 Next he placed the large washbasin between the **T**
40:32 Whenever they walked past the altar to enter the **T**,
40:33 the curtains forming the courtyard around the **T**
40:34 Then the cloud covered the **T**, and the glorious
40:35 Moses was no longer able to enter the **T**
40:35 and the **T** was filled with the awesome glory of the
40:36 Now whenever the cloud lifted from the **T**
40:38 The cloud of the LORD rested on the **T** during
Lev 1: 1 The LORD called to Moses from the **T** and said
1: 3 with no physical defects to the entrance of the **T**
1: 5 the sides of the altar that stands in front of the **T**.
3: 2 and slaughter it at the entrance of the **T**.
3: 8 its head and slaughtering it at the entrance of the **T**.
3:13 its head, and slaughter it at the entrance of the **T**.
4: 4 the bull to the LORD at the entrance of the **T**,
4: 5 then take some of the animal's blood into the **T**,
4: 7 altar that stands in the LORD's presence in the **T**.
4: 7 the altar of burnt offerings at the entrance of the **T**.
4:14 sin offering and present it at the entrance of the **T**.
4:16 The priest will bring some of its blood into the **T**,
4:18 altar that stands in the LORD's presence in the **T**.
4:18 the altar of burnt offerings at the entrance of the **T**.
6:16 in a sacred place within the courtyard of the **T**.
6:26 in a sacred place within the courtyard of the **T**.
6:30 **T** to make atonement in the Holy Place for the
8: 3 to the entrance of the **T**. Then call the entire
8: 4 and all the people assembled at the **T** entrance.
8:10 and anointed the **T** and everything in it,
8:31 "Boil the rest of the meat at the **T** entrance,
8:33 Do not leave the **T** entrance for seven days, for that
8:35 you must stay at the entrance of the **T** day
9: 5 brought all of these things to the entrance of the **T**,
9:23 Next Moses and Aaron went into the **T**, and when
10: 7 But you are not to leave the entrance of the **T**,
10: 9 any other alcoholic drink before going into the **T**.
12: 6 her offerings to the priest at the entrance of the **T**.
14:11 before the LORD at the entrance of the **T**.
14:23 in the LORD's presence at the **T** entrance.
15:14 himself to the LORD at the entrance of the **T**
15:29 present them to the priest at the entrance of the **T**.
15:31 so they will not die as a result of defiling my **T** that
16: 7 them to the LORD at the entrance of the **T**.
16:16 and he will do the same for the entire **T**, because of
16:17 No one else is allowed inside the **T** while Aaron
16:20 the **T**, and the altar, he must bring the living goat
16:23 "As Aaron enters the **T**, he must take off the linen
16:33 the **T**, the altar, the priests, and the entire
17: 4 and does not bring it to the entrance of the **T** to
17: 5 sacrifices to the priest at the entrance of the **T**,
17: 6 fat on the LORD's altar at the entrance of the **T**,
17: 9 and do not bring it to the entrance of the **T** to offer
19:21 present it to the LORD at the entrance of the **T**.
24: 3 the inner curtain of the Most Holy Place in the **T**
Nu 1: 1 the LORD spoke to Moses in the **T** in the
1:50 You must put the Levites in charge of the **T** of the
1:50 They must carry the **T** and its equipment as you
1:51 Whenever the **T** is moved, the Levites will take it
1:51 Anyone else who goes too near the **T** will be
1:53 But the Levites will camp around the **T** of the
1:53 are responsible to stand guard around the **T**."
2: 2 The **T** will be located at the center of these tribal
2: 3 camp toward the sunrise on the east side of the **T**,
2:10 and Gad are to camp on the south side of the **T**,
2:17 set out from the middle of the camp with the **T**.
2:18 Benjamin are to camp on the west side of the **T**,
2:25 Naphtali are to camp on the north side of the **T**,
3: 7 performing their sacred duties in and around the **T**.
3: 8 serving in the **T** on behalf of all the Israelites.
3:23 They were assigned the area to the west of the **T**
3:25 for the tent of the **T** with its layers of coverings,
3:26 the curtains of the courtyard that surrounded the **T**
3:29 They were assigned the area south of the **T** for
3:35 They were assigned the area north of the **T** for
3:36 for the care of the frames supporting the **T**,
3:38 The area in front of the **T** in the east toward the
4: 3 of thirty and fifty who qualify to work in the **T**.
4: 4 "The duties of the Kohathites at the **T** will relate
4: 5 and his sons must enter the **T** first to take down the
4:15 So these are the objects of the **T** that the
4:16 the supervision of the entire **T** and everything in it
4:23 and fifty who are eligible to serve in the **T**.
4:25 They must carry the curtains of the **T**,
4:25 the **T** itself with its coverings, the outer covering
4:25 goatskin leather, and the curtain for the **T** entrance.
4:26 curtains for the courtyard walls that surround the **T**
4:28 are the duties assigned to the Gershonites at the **T**.
4:30 and fifty who are eligible to serve in the **T**.
4:31 "Their duties at the **T** will consist of carrying
4:31 They will be required to carry the frames of the **T**,
4:33 So these are the duties of the Merarites at the **T**.
4:35 years of age who were eligible for service in the **T**,
4:37 clans who were eligible to serve at the **T**.
4:39 years of age who were eligible for service in the **T**,
4:41 clans who were eligible to serve at the **T**.
4:43 years of age who were eligible for service in the **T**,
4:47 years of age who were eligible for service in the **T**
5:17 in a clay jar and mix it with dust from the **T** floor.
6:10 pigeons to the priest at the entrance of the **T**.
6:13 they must each go to the entrance of the **T**
6:18 will shave their hair at the entrance of the **T**
7: 1 On the day Moses set up the **T**, he anointed it
7: 3 presented these to the LORD in front of the **T**.
7: 5 and use these oxen and carts for the work of the **T**.
7: 9 carry the sacred objects of the **T** on their shoulders.
7:89 Whenever Moses went into the **T** to speak with the
8: 9 and present the Levites at the entrance of the **T**.
8:15 they may go in and out of the **T** to do their work,
8:19 They will serve in the **T** on behalf of the Israelites
8:22 then on the Levites went into the **T** to perform
8:24 They must begin serving in the **T** at the age of
8:26 fellow Levites by performing guard duty at the **T**,
9:15 The **T** was set up, and on that day the cloud over
the **T** appeared to be a pillar of fire.
9:18 they were as long as the cloud stayed over the **T**.
9:19 If the cloud remained over the **T** for a long time,
9:20 Sometimes the cloud would stay over the **T** for
9:22 Whether the cloud stayed above the **T** for two
10: 3 are to gather before you at the entrance of the **T**.
10: 5 the tribes on the east side of the **T** will break camp
10:11 the cloud lifted from the **T** of the Covenant.
10:17 Then the **T** was taken down, and the Gershonite
10:17 next in the line of march, carrying the **T** with them.
10:21 the Levites, carrying the sacred objects from the **T**.
10:21 the **T** would already be set up at its new location.
11:16 Bring them to the **T** to stand there with you.
11:24 seventy leaders and stationed them around the **T**.
11:26 among the leaders but had not gone out to the **T**,
12: 4 Aaron, and Miriam and said, "Go out to the **T**,
12: 5 pillar of cloud and stood at the entrance of the **T**.
12:10 As the cloud moved from above the **T**,
14:10 appeared to all the Israelites from above the **T**.

16: 9 to be near him as you serve in the LORD's **T**
16: 18 and stood at the entrance of the **T** with Moses
16: 19 and they all assembled at the **T** entrance.
16: 42 they turned toward the **T** and saw that the cloud
16: 43 and Aaron came and stood at the entrance of the **T**,
16: 50 Aaron returned to Moses at the entrance of the **T**.
17: 4 Put these staffs in the **T** in front of the Ark of the
17: 7 in the LORD's presence in the **T** of the Covenant.
17: 8 When he went into the **T** of the Covenant the next
17: 13 Everyone who even comes close to the **T** of the
18: 2 the sacred duties in front of the **T** of the Covenant.
18: 4 for the care and maintenance of the **T**,
18: 6 are dedicated to the LORD for service in the **T**.
18: 21 I will pay them for their service in the **T** with the
18: 22 the priests and Levites are to stay away from the **T**.
18: 23 The Levites must serve at the **T**, and they will be
18: 31 for it is your compensation for serving in the **T**.
19: 4 sprinkle it seven times toward the front of the **T**.
19: 13 in the proper way defile the LORD's **T**
20: 6 from the people and went to the entrance of the **T**,
25: 6 as they were weeping at the entrance of the **T**.
27: 2 and the entire community at the entrance of the **T**.
31: 30 Levites in charge of maintaining the LORD's **T**."
31: 47 to the Levites who maintained the LORD's **T**.
31: 54 and brought the gold to the **T** as a reminder to the
Dt 31: 14 Call Joshua and take him with you to the **T**,
31: 14 Joshua went and presented themselves at the **T**.
Jos 18: 1 assembly gathered at Shiloh and set up the **T**.
19: 51 of the LORD at the entrance of the **T** at Shiloh.
22: 19 where the LORD lives among us in his **T**,
22: 29 in front of the **T** may be used for that purpose."
24: 26 and rolled it beneath the oak tree beside the **T** of
Jdg 18: 31 of Dan as long as the **T** of God remained at Shiloh.
19: 18 and we're going to the **T** of the LORD.
1Sa 1: 3 and sacrifice to the LORD Almighty at the **T**.
1: 7 would taunt Hannah as they went to the **T**.
1: 9 Hannah went over to the **T** after supper to pray to
1: 22 Then I will take him to the **T** and leave him there
1: 24 was weaned, Hannah took him to the **T** in Shiloh.
2: 22 women who assisted at the entrance of the **T**.
3: 3 and Samuel was sleeping in the **T** near the Ark of
3: 15 then got up and opened the doors of the **T** as usual.
3: 21 and gave messages to Samuel there at the **T**.
21: 6 that was placed before the LORD in the **T**.
2Sa 12: 20 Then he went to the **T** and worshiped the LORD.
15: 25 will bring me back to see the Ark and the **T** again.
1Ki 8: 4 along with the **T** and all its sacred utensils,
1Ch 6: 32 They ministered with music there at the **T** until
6: 48 were appointed to various other tasks in the **T**,
9: 19 just as their ancestors had guarded the **T** in the
9: 21 responsible for guarding the entrance to the **T**.
16: 39 and his fellow priests at the **T** of the LORD on
21: 29 the **T** of the LORD and the altar that Moses made
23: 26 Now the Levites will no longer need to carry the **T**
23: 32 the Levites watched over the **T** and the Temple
2Ch 1: 3 to the hill at Gibeon where God's **T** was located.
1: 3 This was the **T** that Moses, the LORD's servant,
1: 5 was still at Gibeon in front of the **T** of the LORD.
1: 6 There in front of the **T**, Solomon went up to the
1: 13 Then Solomon returned to Jerusalem from the **T** at
24: 6 Israel in order to maintain the **T** of the Covenant."
Ps 27: 6 At his **T** I will offer sacrifices with shouts of joy,
78: 60 the **T** where he had lived among the people.
Jer 7: 12 Shiloh where I once put the **T** to honor my name.
26: 6 the place where the **T** was located.
Ac 7: 44 "Our ancestors carried the **T** with them through
7: 45 the **T** was taken with them into their new territory.
Heb 8: 5 For when Moses was getting ready to build the **T**,
Rev 15: 5 in heaven, God's **T**, was thrown wide open!

TABITHA (2) [DORCAS]

Ac 9: 36 There was a believer in Joppa named **T** (which in
9: 40 Turning to the body he said, "Get up, **T**."

TABLE (77) [TABLES]

Ge 43: 32 and his brothers were served at a separate **t**.
43: 32 The Egyptians sat at their own **t** because Egyptians
43: 34 food was served to them from Joseph's own **t**.
Ex 25: 23 "Then make a **t** of acacia wood, 3 feet long,
25: 27 rings will support the poles used to carry the **t**.
25: 30 special Bread of the Presence on the **t** before me.
26: 35 Place the **t** and lampstand across the room from
26: 35 south side, and the **t** must be set toward the north.
30: 27 the **t** and all its utensils, the lampstand and all its
31: 8 the **t** and all its utensils; the gold lampstand with
35: 13 the **t**, its carrying poles, and all of its utensils;
37: 10 Then he made a **t** out of acacia wood, 3 feet long,
37: 12 inches wide was attached along the edges of the **t**,
37: 13 rings of gold and attached them to the four **t** legs
37: 16 dishes, bowls, and pitchers to be placed on the **t**.
39: 36 the **t** and all its utensils; the Bread of the Presence;
40: 4 Then bring in the **t**, and arrange the utensils on it.
40: 22 Next he placed the **t** in the Tabernacle,
40: 23 And he arranged the Bread of the Presence on the **t**
40: 24 from the **t** on the south side of the Holy Place.
Lev 24: 6 bread in the LORD's presence on the pure gold **t**,
Nu 3: 31 the **t**, the lampstand, the altars, the various utensils
4: 7 "Next they must spread a blue cloth over the **t**,
4: 8 Then they must insert the carrying poles into the **t**.
Jdg 1: 7 and big toes cut off, eating scraps from under my **t**.
1Sa 9: 22 the great hall and placed them at the head of the **t**,
20: 18 You will be missed when your place at the **t** is
20: 34 Jonathan left the **t** in fierce anger and refused to eat
2Sa 19: 28 honored me among those who eat at your own **t**!
1Ki 1: 49 guests jumped up in panic from the banquet **t**
7: 48 the gold **t** for the Bread of the Presence,
13: 20 Then while they were sitting at the **t**, a message
2Ki 4: 10 and furnish it with a bed, a **t**, a chair, and a lamp.
25: 29 and allowed him to dine at the king's **t** for the rest
1Ch 9: 32 the bread to be set on the **t** each Sabbath day.
23: 29 charge of the sacred bread that was set out on the **t**,
28: 16 He designated the amount of gold for the **t** on
2Ch 13: 11 They place the Bread of the Presence on the holy **t**,
29: 18 and the **t** of the Bread of the Presence with all its
Ne 5: 17 though I regularly fed 150 Jewish officials at my **t**,
Ps 69: 22 Let the bountiful **t** set before them become a snare,
128: 3 There they sit around your **t** / as vigorous
Pr 9: 2 a great banquet, mixed the wines, and set the **t**.
Jer 52: 33 and allowed him to dine at the king's **t** for the rest
Eze 23: 41 and my oil on a **t** that was spread before you.
39: 20 Feast at my banquet **t**—feast on horses, riders,
41: 22 "is the **t** that stands in the LORD's presence."
44: 16 enter my sanctuary and approach my **t** to serve me.
Da 11: 27 will plot against each other at the conference **t**,
Mal 1: 12 you are saying it's all right to defile the Lord's **t**.
Mt 15: 27 to eat crumbs that fall beneath their master's **t**."
23: 6 And how they love to sit at the head **t** at banquets
26: 20 Jesus sat down at the **t** with the twelve disciples.
Mk 7: 28 but even the dogs under the **t** are given some
14: 4 Some of those at the **t** were indignant. "Why was
14: 18 As they were sitting around the **t** eating, Jesus said,
Lk 7: 49 The men at the **t** said among themselves,
11: 37 a meal. So he went in and took his place at the **t**.
14: 7 the dinner were trying to sit near the head of the **t**,
14: 9 to take whatever seat is left at the foot of the **t**!
14: 10 "Do this instead—sit at the foot of the **t**.
14: 15 a man sitting at the **t** with Jesus exclaimed,
16: 21 lay there longing for scraps from the rich man's **t**,
22: 14 and the twelve apostles sat down together at the **t**.
22: 21 "But here at this **t**, sitting among us as a friend,
22: 27 Normally the master sits at the **t** and is served by
22: 30 to eat and drink at my **t** in that Kingdom. And you
Jn 12: 2 Martha served, and Lazarus sat at the **t** with him.
13: 4 So he got up from the **t**, took off his robe,
13: 23 one Jesus loved, was sitting next to Jesus at the **t**.
13: 28 None of the others at the **t** knew what Jesus meant.
Ro 11: 9 he said, / "Let their bountiful **t** become a snare,
1Co 10: 16 When we bless the cup at the Lord's **T**, aren't we
10: 21 cannot eat at the Lord's **T** and at the **t** of demons,
Heb 9: 2 a lampstand, a **t**, and loaves of holy bread on the **t**.

TABLES (16) [TABLE]

1Ki 2: 15 But the **t** were turned, and everything went to my
10: 5 She was also amazed at the food on his **t**,
1Ch 28: 16 be placed and the amount of silver for other **t**.
2Ch 4: 8 He also built ten **t** and placed them in the Temple,
4: 19 the gold altar; / the **t** for the Bread of the Presence;
9: 4 She was also amazed at the food on his **t**,
Isa 28: 8 Their **t** are covered with vomit; filth is everywhere.
Eze 40: 39 On each side of this foyer were two **t**,
40: 40 up to the north entrance, there were two more **t**.
40: 41 So there were eight **t** in all, four inside and four
40: 42 There were also four **t** of hewn stone for
40: 42 On these **t** were placed the butchering knives
40: 43 and set on the **t** where the sacrificial meat was to
Mt 21: 12 He knocked over the **t** of the money changers
Mk 11: 15 He knocked over the **t** of the money changers
Jn 2: 15 coins over the floor, and turned over their **t**.

TABLET (2) [TABLETS]

Hab 2: 2 clear letters on a **t**, so that a runner can read it
Lk 1: 63 He motioned for a writing **t**, and to everyone's

TABLETS (31) [TABLET]

Ex 24: 12 Stay there while I give you the **t** of stone that I
25: 16 place inside it the stone **t** inscribed with the terms
25: 21 Place inside the Ark the stone **t** inscribed with the
31: 18 he gave him the two stone **t** inscribed with the
32: 15 He held in his hands the two stone **t** inscribed with
32: 16 These stone **t** were God's work; the words on them
32: 19 terrible anger, he threw the stone **t** to the ground,
34: 1 "Prepare two stone **t** like the first ones.
34: 1 the same words that were on the **t** you smashed.
34: 4 So Moses cut two **t** of stone like the first ones.
34: 4 had told him, carrying the two stone **t** in his hands.
34: 28 the Ten Commandments—on the stone **t**.
34: 29 stone **t** inscribed with the terms of the covenant,
40: 20 He placed inside the Ark the stone **t** inscribed with
Dt 4: 13 and wrote them on two stone **t**.
5: 22 and he wrote his words on two stone **t** and gave
9: 9 **t** of stone inscribed with the covenant that the
9: 10 the **t** on which God himself had written all the
9: 11 the LORD handed me the two stone **t** with the
9: 15 holding in my hands the two stone **t** of the
9: 17 So I raised the stone **t** and dashed them to the
10: 1 said to me, 'Prepare two stone **t** like the first ones,
10: 2 and I will write on the **t** the same words that were
10: 2 Then place the **t** in the sacred chest—the Ark of
10: 3 acacia wood and cut two stone **t** like the first two,
and I took the **t** up the mountain.
10: 5 and placed the **t** in the Ark of the Covenant,
10: 5 And the **t** are still there in the Ark.
1Ki 8: 9 Nothing was in the Ark except the two stone **t** that
2Ch 5: 10 Nothing was in the Ark except the two stone **t** that
Heb 9: 4 and the stone **t** of the covenant with the Ten

TABOR (11) [AZNOTH-TABOR, KISLOTH-TABOR]

Jos 19: 22 The boundary also touched **T**, Shahazumah,
Jdg 4: 6 the tribes of Naphtali and Zebulun at Mount **T**.
4: 12 Barak son of Abinoam had gone up to Mount **T**,
4: 14 warriors down the slopes of Mount **T** into battle.
5: 13 "Down from **T** marched the remnant against the
8: 18 and Zalmunna, "The men you killed at **T**—
1Sa 10: 3 "When you get to the oak of **T**, you will see three
1Ch 6: 77 Kartah, Rimmono, and **T**, each with its
Ps 89: 12 Mount **T** and Mount Hermon praise your name.
Jer 46: 18 is coming against Egypt who is as tall as Mount **T**
Hos 5: 1 a snare by worshiping the idols at Mizpah and **T**.

TABRET(S) [KJV] See TAMBOURINE(S)

TABRIMMON (1)

1Ki 15: 18 it with some of his officials to Ben-hadad son of **T**

TACHES [KJV] See CLASP(S), HOOK(S)

TACHMONITE [KJV] See HACMONITE

TACKLE (1)

Isa 33: 23 sails hang loose on broken masts with useless **t**.

TADMOR (1)

2Ch 8: 4 He rebuilt **T** in the desert and built towns in the

TAHAN (2) [TAHANITE]

Nu 26: 35 The Tahanite clan, named after its ancestor **T**.
1Ch 7: 25 line of descent was Rephah, Resheph, Telah, **T**,

TAHANITE (1) [TAHAN]

Nu 26: 35 The **T** clan, named after its ancestor Tahan.

TAHASH (1)

Ge 22: 24 Their names were Tebah, Gaham, **T**, and Maacah.

TAHATH (6)

Nu 33: 26 They left Makheloth and camped at **T**.
33: 27 They left **T** and camped at Terah.
1Ch 6: 24 **T**, Uriel, Uzziah, and Shaul.
6: 37 **T**, Assir, Abiasaph, Korah,
7: 20 were Shuthelah, Bered, **T**, Eleadah, Tahath,
Eleadah, **T**,

TAHPANHES (8)

Jer 2: 16 marching from their cities of Memphis and **T**,
43: 7 and went to Egypt, going as far as the city of **T**.
43: 8 Then at **T**, the LORD gave another message to
43: 9 at the entrance of Pharaoh's palace here in **T**.
44: 1 **T**, and Memphis, and throughout southern Egypt
46: 14 Publish it in the cities of Migdol, Memphis, and **T**!
Eze 30: 18 strength of Egypt, it will be a dark day for **T**, too.
30: 18 A dark cloud will cover **T**, and its daughters will

TAHPENES (1)

1Ki 11: 19 and he gave him a wife—the sister of Queen **T**.

TAHREA (2)

1Ch 8: 35 was the father of Pithon, Melech, **T**, and Ahaz.
9: 41 sons of Micah were Pithon, Melech, **T**, and Ahaz.

TAHTIM-HODSHI (1)

2Sa 24: 6 then to Gilead in the land of **T** and to Dan-jaan

TAIL (12) [TAILS]

Ex 4: 4 Then the LORD told him, "Take hold of its **t**."
29: 22 including the fat **t** and the fat that covers the
Lev 3: 9 This includes the fat of the entire **t** cut off near the
7: 3 all its fat on the altar, including the fat from the **t**,
8: 25 Next he took the fat, including the fat from the **t**,
9: 19 the fat from the **t** and from around the internal
Dt 28: 13 the LORD will make you the head and not the **t**,
28: 44 They will be the head, and you will be the **t**!
Job 40: 17 Its **t** is as straight as a cedar. The sinews of its
Isa 9: 14 the LORD will destroy both the head and the **t**,
9: 15 Israel are the head, and the lying prophets are the **t**.
Rev 12: 4 His **t** dragged down one-third of the stars,

TAILOR (1) [TAILORS]

Job 34: 33 "Must God **t** his justice to your demands? But you

TAILORS (2) [TAILOR]

Ex 28: 3 Instruct all those who have special skills as **t** to
Jer 10: 9 these gods in royal purple robes made by expert **t**.

TAILS (5) [TAIL]

Jdg 15: 4 He tied their **t** together in pairs, and he fastened a
torch to each pair of **t**.
Rev 9: 10 They had **t** that sting like scorpions, with power to
9: 19 power was in their mouths, but also in their **t**.
9: 19 For their **t** had heads like snakes, with the power to

TAINTED (1)

Isa 59: 3 is full of lies, and your lips are **t** with corruption.

TAKE (667) [TAKEN, TAKES, TAKING, TOOK]

Ge 6: 21 **t** enough food for your family and for all the
7: 2 **T** along seven pairs of each animal that I have
7: 2 for sacrifice, and **t** one pair of each of the others.

11: 6 begun to **t** advantage of their common language
12:19 Here is your wife! **T** her and be gone!"
13: 9 **T** your choice of any section of the land you want,
13:17 **T** a walk in every direction and explore the new
14:23 that I will not **t** so much as a single thread
19:15 "**T** your wife and your two daughters who are
22: 2 "**T** your son, your only son—yes, Isaac,
24: 5 then **t** Isaac there to live among your relatives?"
24: 6 "Be careful never to **t** my son there.
24: 8 But under no circumstances are you to **t** my son
24:51 Here is Rebekah; **t** her and go. Yes, let her be the
27: 3 **T** your bow and a quiver full of arrows out into the
27:10 **T** the food to your father; then he can eat it
30:26 Let me **t** my wives and children, for I have earned
31:31 to myself, 'He'll **t** his daughters from me by force.'
31:50 are harsh to my daughters or if you **t** other wives,
33:11 Please **t** my gifts, for God has been very generous
34:17 Otherwise we will **t** her and be on our way."
38:20 Judah asked his friend Hirah the Adullamite to **t**
40: 4 and Potiphar assigned Joseph to **t** care of them.
40:13 Within three days Pharaoh will **t** you out of prison
42:33 and **t** grain for your families and go on home.
42:36 is gone, and now you want to **t** Benjamin, too.
43:11 **T** them to the man as gifts—balm, honey, spices,
43:12 **T** double the money that you found in your sacks,
43:13 Then **t** your brother and go back to the man.
43:16 this noon. **T** them inside and prepare a big feast."
43:18 Then he will seize us as slaves and **t** our donkeys."
44:29 If you **t** away his brother from me, too, and any
44:32 I made a pledge to my father that I would **t** care of
45:11 I will **t** care of you there, for there are still five
45:19 And tell your brothers to **t** wagons from Egypt to
47:30 **t** me out of Egypt and bury me beside my
50: 5 **t** my body back to the land of Canaan, and bury me
50:21 I myself will **t** care of you and your families."
50:25 to Canaan, you must **t** my body back with you."
Ex 2: 9 "**T** this child home and nurse him for me,"
3: 5 "**T** off your sandals, for you are standing on holy
4: 4 Then the LORD told him, "**T** hold of its tail."
4: 9 then **t** some water from the Nile River and pour it
4:17 And be sure to **t** your shepherd's staff along
5: 3 "Let us **t** a three-day trip into the wilderness
7:15 Be sure to **t** along the shepherd's staff that turned
8: 8 "Plead with the LORD to **t** the frogs away from
8:27 We must **t** a three-day trip into the wilderness to
9: 8 said to Moses and Aaron, "**T** soot from a furnace,
10: 8 "But tell me, just whom do you want to **t** along?"
10: 9 "We will **t** our sons and daughters and our flocks
10:10 to be with you if you try to **t** your little ones along!
10:17 and plead with the LORD your God to **t** away this
10:24 stay here. You can even **t** your children with you."
10:25 "we must **t** our flocks and herds for sacrifices
11: 8 And **t** all your followers with you.' Only then will
12: 6 "**T** special care of these lambs until the evening of
12: 7 They are to **t** some of the lamb's blood and smear
12:22 Then **t** a cluster of hyssop branches and dip it into
12:32 **T** your flocks and herds, and be gone. Go, but give
13:19 **t** his bones with them when God led them out of
16:32 "**T** two quarts of manna and keep it forever as a
17: 3 to complain, "Why did you ever **t** us out of Egypt?
17: 5 LORD said to Moses, "**T** your shepherd's staff,
17: 7 "Is the LORD going to **t** care of us or not?"
18:22 But they can **t** care of the smaller matters
21: 6 Then his master must **t** him to the door
22:11 then **t** an oath of innocence in the presence of the
22:26 If you **t** your neighbor's cloak as a pledge of
23: 4 that has strayed away, **t** it back to its owner.
23: 8 "**T** no bribes, for a bribe makes you ignore
28: 9 **T** two onyx stones and engrave on them the names
29: 1 **T** a young bull and two rams with no physical
29: 7 Then **t** the anointing oil and pour it over his head.
29:13 **T** all the fat that covers the internal organs,
29:14 Then **t** the carcass (including the skin
29:19 "Now **t** the other ram and have Aaron and his
29:21 Then **t** some of the blood from the altar and mix it
29:22 of Aaron and his sons, **t** the fat of the ram,
29:22 Also, **t** the long lobe of the liver, the two kidneys
29:23 Then **t** one loaf of bread, one cake mixed with
29:25 Afterward **t** the bread from their hands, and burn it
29:26 Then **t** the breast of Aaron's ordination ram,
29:31 "**T** the ram used in the ordination ceremony,
30:12 "Whenever you **t** a census of the people of Israel,
32: 2 and sons and daughters to **t** off their gold earrings,
33:12 '**T** these people up to the Promised Land.'
40: 9 "**T** the anointing oil and sprinkle it on the
Lev 1:15 The priest will **t** the bird to the altar, twist off its
2: 2 and he will **t** a handful of the flour mixed with
2: 9 The priests will **t** a token portion of the grain
2:16 The priests will **t** a token portion of the roasted
4: 5 then **t** some of the animal's blood into the
4:21 then **t** what is left of the bull outside the camp
5:12 They must **t** the flour to the priest, who will scoop
6:15 The priest on duty will **t** a handful of the choice
8:33 for that is the time it will **t** to complete the
9: 2 "**T** a young bull for a sin offering and a ram for a
9: 3 Then tell the Israelites to **t** a male goat for a sin
9: 4 Also tell them to **t** a bull and a ram for a peace
10:12 "**T** what is left of the grain offering after the
12: 6 She must **t** her offerings to the priest at the
14:12 The priest will **t** one of the lambs and the olive oil
14:14 then **t** some of the blood from the guilt offering
14:24 The priest will **t** the lamb for the guilt offering,
16:23 he must **t** off the linen garments he wore when he
24:14 "**T** the blasphemer outside the camp, and tell all
25:14 you must never **t** advantage of each other.
26:31 and I will **t** no pleasure in your offerings of
26:35 it will **t** the rest you never allowed it to **t** every
Nu 1: 2 "**T** a census of the whole community of Israel by
1:51 the Levites will **t** it down and set it up again.
3:15 "**T** a census of the tribe of Levi by its families
3:45 "**T** the Levites in place of the firstborn sons of the
3:45 And **t** the livestock of the Levites as substitutes for
4: 2 "**T** a census of the clans and families of the
4: 5 and his sons must enter the Tabernacle first to **t**
4:22 "**T** a census of the clans and families of the
4:29 "Now **t** a census of the clans and families of the
5:17 He must **t** some holy water in a clay jar and mix it
5:25 " 'Then the priest will **t** the jealousy offering
5:26 He will **t** a handful as a token portion and burn it
6: 2 or women, **t** the special vow of a Nazirite,
6:19 the priest will **t** for each of them the boiled
11:17 I will **t** some of the Spirit that is upon you, and I
13:30 "Let's go at once to **t** the land," he said. "We can
16: 6 all your followers must do this: **T** incense burners,
16:46 **t** an incense burner and place burning coals on it
17: 2 "**T** twelve wooden staffs, one from each of Israel's
19: 4 Eleazar will **t** some of its blood on his finger
19: 6 Eleazar the priest must then **t** cedarwood, a hyssop
19:18 Then someone who is ceremonially clean must **t** a
20: 8 "You and Aaron must **t** the staff and assemble the
20:25 Now **t** Aaron and his son Eleazar up Mount Hor.
21: 7 Pray that the LORD will **t** away the snakes."
23:27 "Come, I will **t** you to yet another place.
26: 2 "**T** a census of all the men of Israel who are
27:18 The LORD replied, "**T** Joshua son of Nun,
31: 2 "**T** vengeance on the Midianites for leading the
31:30 Also **t** one of every fifty of the captives, cattle,
33:53 **T** possession of the land and settle in it, because I
Dt 1:22 They will advise us on the best route to **t**
6:13 When you **t** an oath, you must use only his name.
7:25 Do not **t** it or it will become a snare to you, for it is
9:23 'Go up and **t** the land I have given you.' But you
10:11 their ancestors, so they may **t** possession of it.'
12:26 **T** your sacred gifts and your offerings given to
13: 2 and the predicted signs or miracles **t** place.
14:25 and **t** the money to the place the LORD your God
15:17 **t** an awl and push it through his earlobe into the
17: 8 **T** such cases to the place the LORD your God
17:17 The king must not **t** many wives for himself,
21:10 God hands them over to you and you **t** captives.
21:12 If this happens, you may **t** her to your home,
21:19 and mother must **t** the son before the leaders of the
22: 1 don't pretend not to see it. **T** it back to its owner.
22: 6 in the nest, do not **t** the mother with the young.
22: 7 You may **t** the young, but let the mother go,
22:21 the judges must **t** the girl to the door of her father's
22:24 you must **t** both of them to the gates of the town
23:15 escape from their masters and **t** refuge with you,
23:24 but do not **t** any away in a basket.
24: 6 "It is wrong to **t** a pair of millstones, or even just
24:14 "Never **t** advantage of poor laborers,
25: 1 "Suppose two people **t** a dispute to court,
26: 4 The priest will then **t** the basket from your hand
31: 3 living there, and you will **t** possession of their land.
31:14 Call Joshua and **t** him with you to the Tabernacle,
31:26 "**T** this Book of the Law and place it beside the
32:11 her young, / so he spread his wings to **t** them in
32:35 I will **t** vengeance; I will repay those who deserve
32:43 He will **t** vengeance on his enemies / and cleanse
32:46 "**T** to heart all the words I have given you today.
Jos 1:11 and **t** possession of the land the LORD your God
3: 8 **t** a few steps into the river and stop.' "
4: 3 Tell the men to **t** twelve stones from where the
5: 7 those who had grown up to **t** their fathers' places.
5:15 "**T** off your sandals, for this is holy ground."
6: 6 and said, "**T** up the Ark of the Covenant,
6:18 Do not **t** any of the things set apart for destruction,
7: 3 and it won't **t** more than two or three thousand of
8: 1 **T** the entire army and attack Ai, for I have given to
8: 7 up from your ambush and **t** possession of the city,
20: 9 another person could **t** refuge in one of these cities.
Jdg 2: 6 each of the tribes left to **t** possession of the land
5: 2 "When Israel's leaders **t** charge, / and the people
6:25 "**T** the second best bull from your father's herd,
9:15 me your king, come and **t** shelter in my shade.
11:35 made a vow to the LORD and cannot **t** it back."
12: 6 Then they would **t** him and kill him at the shallows
13:25 the Spirit of the LORD began to **t** hold of him.
15: 7 Samson vowed, "I will **t** my revenge on you,
16: 6 and what it would **t** to tie you up securely."
18: 9 should not hesitate to go and **t** possession of it.
19:24 **t** my virgin daughter and this man's concubine.
20:10 and the rest of us will **t** revenge on Gibeah for this
21:21 and each of you can **t** one of them home to be your
Ru 2:12 under whose wings you have come to **t** refuge,
3: 3 **t** a bath and put on perfume and dress in your
1Sa 1:22 Then I will **t** him to the Tabernacle and leave him
2:16 "**T** as much as you want, but the fat must first be
2:16 "No, give it to me now, or I'll **t** it by force."
2:20 "May the LORD give you other children to **t** the
8:13 The king will **t** your daughters from you and force
8:14 He will **t** away the best of your fields
8:15 He will **t** a tenth of your harvest and distribute it
9: 3 and he told Saul, "**T** a servant with you, and go
9:12 He has just arrived to **t** part in a public sacrifice up
10: 7 After these signs **t** place, do whatever you think is
13:20 they had to **t** them to a Philistine blacksmith.
14:24 because Saul had made them **t** an oath, saying,
14:28 "Your father made the army **t** a strict oath that
16: 2 "**T** a heifer with you," the LORD replied,
17:17 "**T** this half-bushel of roasted grain and these ten
17:35 after it with a club and **t** the lamb from its mouth.
20:29 He wanted to **t** part in a family sacrifice.
20:40 to the boy and told him to **t** them back to the city.
21: 9 **T** that if you want it, for there is nothing else
25:11 Should I **t** my bread and water and the meat I've
26:11 we'll **t** his spear and his jug of water and then get
31: 4 "**T** your sword and kill me before these pagan
2Sa 2:21 "**T** on one of the younger men and strip him of his
2:25 regrouped there at the top of the hill to **t** a stand.
13: 6 "Please let Tamar come to **t** care of me and cook
13:28 has given the command. **T** courage and do it!"
14: 9 "And I'll **t** the responsibility if you are criticized
14:11 you won't let anyone **t** vengeance against my son.
15:20 Go on back and **t** your troops with you, and may
15:25 David instructed Zadok to **t** the Ark of God back
17:13 Then we can **t** ropes and drag the walls of the city
17:17 them the message they were to **t** to King David.
19:33 king said to Barzillai. "I will **t** care of you there."
20: 6 **t** my troops and chase after him before he gets into
24: 2 "**T** a census of all the people in the land—
24: 4 But the king insisted that they **t** the census, so Joab
24:22 "**T** it, my lord, and use it as you wish,"
1Ki 1:33 "**T** Solomon and my officers down to Gihon
2: 2 earth must someday go. **T** courage and be a man.
2:35 and he installed Zadok the priest to **t** the place of
8:31 and is required to **t** an oath of innocence in front of
8:46 and **t** them captive to a foreign land far or near.
11:12 I will **t** the kingdom away from your son.
11:31 Then he said to Jeroboam, "**T** ten of these pieces,
11:34 " 'But I will not **t** the entire kingdom from
11:35 But I will **t** the kingdom away from his son
14: 3 **T** him a gift of ten loaves of bread, some cakes,
19: 2 failed to **t** your life like those whom you killed."
19: 4 "**T** my life, for I am no better than my ancestors."
20: 6 They will **t** away everything you consider
20:18 "**T** them alive," Ben-hadad commanded,
21:10 the king. Then **t** him out and stone him to death."
22:26 "Arrest Micaiah and **t** him back to Amon,
22:28 standing around, "**T** note of what I have said."
2Ki 2: 1 When the LORD was about to **t** Elijah up to
2: 3 "Did you know that the LORD is going to **t** your
2: 5 "Did you know that the LORD is going to **t** your
3: 8 Then Jehoshaphat asked, "What route will we **t**?"
4: 1 has come, threatening to **t** my two sons as slaves."
4:29 to Gehazi, "Get ready to travel; **t** my staff and go!
4:36 she came in, Elisha said, "Here, **t** your son!"
5:16 And though Naaman urged him to **t** the gifts,
5:17 from this place, and I will **t** it back home with me.
5:23 "By all means, **t** 150 pounds of silver,"
6:19 and I will **t** you to the man you are looking for."
7:12 and then they will **t** us alive and capture the city."
7:13 Let them **t** five of the remaining horses.
8: 1 "**T** your family and move to some other place,
8: 8 he said to Hazael, "**T** a gift to the man of God.
9: 1 he told him. "**T** this vial of olive oil with you,
10:14 "**T** them alive!" Jehu shouted to his men.
11:15 "**T** her out of the Temple, and kill anyone who
12: 5 Let the priests **t** some of that money to pay for
18:32 Then I will arrange to **t** you to another land like
19:30 will **t** root again in your own soil, and you will
1Ch 10: 4 "**T** your sword and run me through before these
12:14 The weakest among them could **t** on a hundred
12:14 and the strongest could **t** on a thousand!
12:32 the times and knew the best course for Israel to **t**.
17:13 I will not **t** my unfailing love from him as I took it
21: 1 and caused David to **t** a census of the Israelites.
21: 2 "**T** a census of all the people in the land—
21: 4 But the king insisted that Joab **t** the census, so Joab
21:23 "**T** it, my lord, and use it as you wish,"
21:23 And **t** the wheat for the grain offering. I will give it
21:24 I cannot **t** what is yours and give it to the LORD.
28:10 So **t** this seriously. The LORD has chosen you to
2Ch 6:22 and is required to **t** an oath of innocence in front of
6:36 and **t** them captive to a foreign land far or near.
7:18 then I will not let anyone **t** away your throne.
18:25 "Arrest Micaiah and **t** him back to Amon,
18:27 standing around, "**T** note of what I have said."
19:11 **T** courage as you fulfill your duties, and may the
20:17 **T** your positions; then stand still and watch the
23:14 "**T** her out of the Temple, and kill anyone who
35:23 He cried out to his men, "**T** me from the battle,
Ezr 1:11 **t** back to Jerusalem when the exiles returned there
7:15 We also commission you to **t** with you some silver
7:16 "Moreover you are to **t** any silver and gold which
8:23 and earnestly prayed that our God would **t** care of
10: 4 **T** courage, for it is your duty to tell us how to
Ne 9:15 and **t** possession of the land you had sworn to give
9:17 and appointed a leader to **t** them back to their
12:27 They were to **t** part in the joyous occasion with
Est 1: 8 one should be compelled to **t** more than he wanted.
2:11 Every day Mordecai would **t** a walk near the
3: 7 to determine the best day and month to **t** action.
6:14 the king's eunuchs arrived to **t** Haman to the
8:11 and wives, and to **t** the property of their enemies.
8:13 That way the Jews would be ready on that day to **t**
9:10 enemy of the Jews. But they did not **t** any plunder.
9:16 who hated them. But they did not **t** any plunder.
Job 1:11 **T** away everything he has, and he will surely
2: 5 But **t** away his health, and he will surely curse you
6:10 At least I can **t** comfort in this: Despite the pain,
7:21 Why not just pardon my sin and **t** away my guilt?
9: 3 If someone wanted to **t** God to court, would it be
9:32 so I cannot argue with him or **t** him to trial.
13:14 I will **t** my life in my hands and say what I really
16: 5 that helps you. I would try to **t** away your grief.
24: 3 and they even **t** donkeys from the poor
24: 9 her breast; they **t** the baby as a pledge for a loan.
27:10 Can they **t** delight in the Almighty? Can they call
31: 4 He sees everything I do and every step I **t**.
33: 5 if you can; make your case and **t** your stand.

34:14 If God were to **t** back his spirit and withdraw his
38:14 For the features of the earth **t** shape as the light
38:20 Can you **t** it to its home? Do you know how to get
40:15 "**T** a look at the mighty hippopotamus. I made it,
42:6 I **t** back everything I said, and I sit in dust
42:8 Now **t** seven young bulls and seven rams and go to
Ps 4:1 **T** away my distress. / Have mercy on me and hear
5:4 O God, you **t** no pleasure in wickedness;
5:11 But let all who **t** refuge in you rejoice; / let them
10:14 they cause. / You **t** note of it and punish them.
16:3 are my true heroes! / I **t** pleasure in them!
16:4 I will not **t** part in their sacrifices / or even speak
26:10 wicked schemes, / and they constantly **t** bribes.
31:13 enemies conspire against me, / plotting to **t** my life.
31:24 So be strong and **t** courage, / all you who put your
34:2 the LORD; / let all who are discouraged **t** heart.
35:2 Put on your armor, and **t** up your shield.
35:23 my defense! / **T** up my case, my God and my Lord.
37:4 **T** delight in the LORD, / and he will give you
40:6 You **t** no delight in sacrifices or offerings.
40:8 I **t** joy in doing your will, my God, / for your law is
40:14 to shame. / May those who **t** delight in my trouble
43:1 O God, **t** up my cause! / Defend me against these
45:10 to me, O royal daughter; **t** to heart what I say.
48:13 **T** note of the fortified walls, / and tour all the
51:11 and don't **t** your Holy Spirit from me.
55:22 burdens to the LORD, / and he will **t** care of you.
65:9 You **t** care of the earth and water it, / making it
69:16 Turn and **t** care of me, / for your mercy is
69:35 people will live there / and **t** possession of the land.
70:2 to shame. / May those who **t** delight in my trouble
79:12 O Lord, **t** sevenfold vengeance on our neighbors
89:34 I will not **t** back a single word I said.
90:13 long will you delay? / **T** pity on your servants!
102:24 don't **t** my life while I am still so young!
104:29 When you **t** away their breath, they die
107:43 Those who are wise will **t** all this to heart;
109:11 his entire estate, / and strangers **t** all he has earned.
119:154 Argue my case; **t** my side! / Protect my life as you
125:5 O LORD. / **T** them away with those who do evil.
132:11 swore to David / a promise he will never **t** back:
139:20 your enemies **t** your name in vain.
141:3 **T** control of what I say, O LORD, / and keep my
144:2 stands before me as a shield, and I **t** refuge in him.
Pr 4:4 My father told me, "**T** my words to heart.
6:6 **T** a lesson from the ants, you lazybones.
13:10 leads to arguments; those who **t** advice are wise.
14:2 those who **t** the wrong path despise him.
23:8 and you will have to **t** back your words of
28:12 When the wicked **t** charge, people go into hiding.
28:28 When the wicked **t** charge, people hide.
Ecc 4:15 to help such a youth, even to help him **t** the throne.
8:3 and don't **t** a stand with those who plot evil.
9:2 and people who **t** oaths are treated like people who
11:9 of it. Do everything you want to do; **t** it all in.
SS 1:4 **T** me with you. Come, let's run! Bring me into
7:8 up into the palm tree and **t** hold of its branches.'
8:12 you can **t** my thousand pieces of silver.
Isa 1:23 All of them **t** bribes and refuse to defend the
3:5 People will **t** advantage of each other—
3:6 you be our leader! **T** charge of this heap of ruins!"
5:23 They **t** bribes to pervert justice. They let the
7:20 In that day the Lord will **t** this "razor"—
15:7 The desperate refugees **t** only the possessions they
18:2 **T** a message to your land divided by rivers, to your
18:3 flag on the mountain, let all the world **t** notice.
20:2 "**T** off all your clothes, including your sandals."
20:4 For the king of Assyria will **t** away the Egyptians
21:2 you Elamites and Medes, **t** part in the siege.
23:16 she will **t** a harp, walk the streets, and sing her
26:10 and **t** no notice of the LORD's majesty.
27:1 In that day the LORD will **t** his terrible,
27:6 The time is coming when my people will **t** root.
28:17 "I will **t** the measuring line of justice
32:10 crop will fail, and the harvest will never **t** place.
36:17 Then I will arrange to **t** you to another land like
37:31 will **t** root again in your own soil, and you will
44:5 and will **t** the honored name of Israel as their own.
47:2 **T** heavy millstones and grind the corn.
47:3 I will **t** vengeance against you and will not
48:1 you who **t** oaths in the name of the LORD
54:3 Your descendants will **t** over other nations and live
54:7 but with great compassion I will **t** you back.
55:1 Come, **t** your choice of wine or milk—it's all free!
58:2 to me and asking me to **t** action on their behalf.
62:6 of his promises. **T** no rest, all you who pray.
62:8 warriors come and **t** away your grain and wine.
65:16 or **t** an oath will do so by the God of truth.
Jer 1:8 the people, for I will be with you and **t** care of you.
1:19 For I am with you, and I will **t** care of you. I,
3:1 marries someone else, he is not to **t** her back again,
6:18 all you nations. **T** note of my people's condition.
8:13 I will **t** away their rich harvests of figs and grapes.
9:4 They all **t** advantage of one another and spread
13:4 "**T** the linen belt you are wearing, and go to the
13:23 Can a leopard **t** away its spots? Neither can you
15:7 of your cities and **t** away everything you hold dear.
15:14 I will tell their enemies to **t** them as captives to a
20:4 He will **t** them captive to Babylon or run them
21:8 the LORD says: **T** your choice of life or death!
25:10 I will **t** away your happy singing and laughter.
25:15 "**T** from my hand this cup filled to the brim with
32:5 I will **t** Zedekiah to Babylon and will deal with
32:14 **T** both this sealed deed and the unsealed copy,
35:2 **T** them into one of the inner rooms, and offer them
38:10 told Ebed-melech, "**T** along thirty of my men,
39:14 of Shaphan, who was to **t** him back to his home.
40:4 Now I am going to **t** off your chains and let you
44:12 I will **t** this remnant of Judah that insisted on
49:2 will come and **t** back the land you took from her,"
49:9 came at night, even they would not **t** everything.
Eze 1:3 and I felt the hand of the LORD **t** hold of me.
4:1 **t** a large brick and set it down in front of you.
4:3 Then **t** an iron griddle and place it between you
5:1 **t** a sharp sword and use it as a razor to shave your
5:4 Then **t** a few of these hairs out and throw them into
10:2 and **t** a handful of glowing coals and scatter them
10:6 and **t** some burning coals from between the
11:19 I will **t** away their hearts of stone and give them
16:39 They will strip you and **t** your beautiful jewels,
17:9 it won't **t** a strong arm or a large army to do it.
17:13 the royal family and made him **t** an oath of loyalty.
17:22 I will **t** a tender shoot from the top of a tall cedar,
18:13 No! He must die and must **t** full blame.
20:14 I destroyed them because I couldn't **t** care of them.
21:14 Then **t** the sword and brandish it twice, even three
21:26 **T** off your jeweled crown, says the Sovereign
22:9 and people who **t** part in lewd activities.
23:24 They will **t** up positions on every side,
24:6 So **t** the meat out chunk by chunk in whatever
24:16 of man, I am going to **t** away your dearest treasure.
24:17 Do not uncover your head or **t** off your sandals.
24:25 of man, on the day I **t** away their stronghold—
24:25 I will also **t** away their sons and daughters.
26:16 and **t** off their royal robes and beautiful clothing.
33:4 Then those who hear the alarm refuse to **t**
33:11 I **t** no pleasure in the death of wicked people.
34:10 I will **t** away their right to feed the flock,
34:18 Is it not enough for you to **t** the best water for
35:10 Judah will be ours. We will **t** possession of them.
36:26 I will **t** out your stony heart of sin and give you a
37:16 "Son of man, **t** a stick and carve on it these words:
37:16 Then **t** another stick and carve these words on it:
37:19 I will **t** the northern tribes and join them to Judah.
38:7 around you mobilized, and **t** command of them.
38:12 capture vast amounts of plunder and **t** many slaves,
39:10 They will **t** plunder from those who planned to
39:12 It will **t** seven months for the people of Israel to
39:15 and **t** them to be buried in the Valley of Gog's
42:14 They must first **t** off the clothes they wore while
43:20 You will **t** some of its blood and smear it on the
43:21 Then **t** the young bull for the sin offering and burn
44:5 LORD said to me, "Son of man, **t** careful notice;
44:5 **T** careful note of who may be admitted to the
44:8 for you have hired foreigners to **t** charge of my
44:19 they must **t** off the clothes they wear while
45:19 The priest will **t** some of the blood of this sin
46:18 And the prince may never **t** anyone's property by
Da 2:24 **T** me to the king, and I will tell him the meaning of
2:39 inferior to yours, will rise to **t** your place.
7:22 Then the time arrived for the holy people to **t** over
8:14 "It will **t** twenty-three hundred evenings
8:25 He will even **t** on the Prince of princes in battle,
10:19 Be at peace; **t** heart and be strong!" As he spoke
11:19 He will **t** refuge in his own fortresses but will
11:21 and **t** over the kingdom by flattery and intrigue.
11:31 His army will **t** over the Temple fortress,
11:36 For what has been determined will surely **t** place.
Hos 2:2 Tell her to **t** off her garish makeup and suggestive
2:9 "But now I will **t** back the wine and ripened grain
2:9 I will **t** away the linen and wool clothing I gave her
4:15 Their worship is mere pretense as they **t** oaths in
8:11 "Israel has built many altars to **t** away sin,
9:6 Briers will **t** over your treasures of silver;
9:12 do survive to grow up, I will **t** them from you.
Joel 3:4 Are you trying to **t** revenge on me? If you are,
Am 3:9 "**T** your seats now on the hills around Samaria,
6:13 "Didn't we **t** Karnaim by our own strength
7:14 I'm just a shepherd, and I **t** care of fig trees.
Ob 1:5 and robbed you, they would not **t** everything.
1:19 and **t** over the fields of Ephraim and Samaria.
Mic 2:2 someone's house, you **t** it by fraud and violence.
7:9 he will **t** up my case and punish my enemies for all
Hab 2:3 wait patiently, for it will surely **t** place.
2:7 They will turn on you and **t** all you have,
Zep 2:9 who are left will plunder them and **t** their land."
Hag 1:8 Then I will **t** pleasure in it and be honored,
2:4 But now **t** courage, Zerubbabel, says the LORD.
2:4 **T** courage, Jeshua son of Jehozadak, the high
2:4 **T** courage, all you people still left in the land,
2:4 **T** courage and work, for I am with you,
Zec 3:4 others standing there, "**T** off his filthy clothes."
8:9 Almighty says: **T** heart and finish the task!
Mal 2:2 Listen to me and **t** it to heart. Honor my name,"
3:10 so great you won't have enough room to **t** it in!
Mt 2:20 "Get up and **t** the child and his mother back to the
6:1 "**T** care! Don't do your good deeds publicly,
8:4 **T** along the offering required in the law of Moses
9:2 Jesus said to the paralyzed man, "**T** heart, son!
9:6 the paralyzed man and said, "Stand up, **t** your mat,
10:9 "Don't **t** any money with you.
10:13 your blessing stand; if it is not, **t** back the blessing.
10:38 If you refuse to **t** up your cross and follow me,
11:29 **T** my yoke upon you. Let me teach you, because I
15:26 "It isn't right to **t** food from the children
17:27 a coin. **T** the coin and pay the tax for both of us."
18:16 **t** one or two others with you and go back again,
18:17 still refuses to listen, **t** your case to the church.
20:14 **T** it and go. I wanted to pay this last worker the
23:18 And you say that to **t** an oath 'by the altar' can be
24:3 and asked, "When will all this **t** place?
24:34 pass from the scene before all these things **t** place.
25:4 but the other five were wise enough to **t** along
25:28 **T** the money from this servant and give it to the
26:26 saying, "**T** it and eat it, for this is my body."
27:25 "We will **t** responsibility for his death—
27:65 "**T** guards and secure it the best you can."
Mk 1:44 **T** along the offering required in the law of Moses
2:11 "Stand up, **t** your mat, and go on home,
3:21 they tried to **t** him home with them.
6:8 He told them to **t** nothing with them except a
6:9 to wear sandals but not to **t** even an extra coat.
6:37 "It would **t** a small fortune to buy food for all this
7:27 It isn't right to **t** food from the children and throw
8:17 or understand? Are your hearts too hard to **t** it in?
9:35 "Anyone who wants to be the first must **t** last
11:6 told them to say, and they were permitted to **t** it.
13:4 "When will all this **t** place? And will there be any
14:15 He will **t** you upstairs to a large room that is
14:22 the disciples, saying, "**T** it, for this is my body."
14:36 Please **t** this cup of suffering away from me.
14:44 Then you can **t** him away under guard."
15:36 see whether Elijah will come and **t** him down!"
Lk 5:14 **T** along the offering required in the law of Moses
5:24 the paralyzed man and said, "Stand up, **t** your mat,
9:3 "Don't even **t** along a walking stick,"
10:4 Don't **t** along any money, or a traveler's bag,
10:35 pieces of silver and told him to **t** care of the man.
10:42 discovered it—and I won't **t** it away from her."
12:19 to come. Now **t** it easy! Eat, drink, and be merry!'
13:29 Then people will come from all over the world to **t**
14:9 and will have to **t** whatever seat is left at the foot
15:19 called your son. Please **t** me on as a hired man." '
16:4 then I'll have plenty of friends to **t** care of me
16:7 '**t** your bill and replace it with one for only eight
19:24 the king ordered, '**T** the money from this servant,
21:7 they asked, "when will all this **t** place?
22:12 He will **t** you upstairs to a large room that is
22:17 he said, "**T** this and share it among yourselves.
22:26 those who are the greatest should **t** the lowest rank,
22:36 he said, "**t** your money and a traveler's bag.
22:42 please **t** this cup of suffering away from me.
24:47 **t** this message of repentance to all the nations,
Jn 2:8 some out and **t** it to the master of ceremonies."
6:7 "It would **t** a small fortune to feed them!"
6:15 Jesus saw that they were ready to **t** him by force
10:18 No one can **t** my life from me. I lay down my life
10:18 when I want to and also the power to **t** it again.
10:29 than anyone else. So no one can **t** them from me.
16:33 But **t** heart, because I have overcome the world."
17:15 I'm not asking you to **t** them out of the world,
18:31 "Then **t** him away and judge him by your own
19:38 asked Pilate for permission to **t** Jesus' body down.
21:16 love you." "Then **t** care of my sheep," Jesus said.
21:18 direct you and **t** you where you don't want to go."
Ac 1:21 "So now we must choose someone else to **t**
3:1 and John went to the Temple one afternoon to **t**
5:35 **t** care what you are planning to do to these men!
7:33 "And the Lord said to him, '**T** off your sandals,
9:15 For Saul is my chosen instrument to **t** my message
9:21 and **t** them in chains to the leading priests."
11:30 and Saul to **t** to the elders of the church in
13:11 around begging for someone to **t** his hand
15:14 the Gentiles to **t** from them a people for himself.
15:37 Barnabas agreed and wanted to **t** along John Mark.
18:15 and names and your Jewish laws, you **t** care of it.
19:38 are in session and the judges can **t** the case at once.
21:20 and they all **t** the law of Moses very seriously.
22:15 You are to **t** his message everywhere,
23:10 ordered his soldiers to **t** him away from them
23:17 and said, "**T** this young man to the commander.
23:23 Also **t** two hundred spearmen and seventy
24:23 his friends to visit him and **t** care of his needs.
25:1 Three days after Festus arrived in Caesarea to **t**
27:22 But **t** courage! None of you will lose your lives,
27:25 So **t** courage! For I believe God. It will be just as
Ro 3:22 when we trust in Jesus Christ to **t** away our sins.
3:25 For God sent Jesus to **t** the punishment for our sins
11:24 For if God was willing to **t** you who were,
11:27 my covenant with them / and **t** away their sins."
12:8 leadership ability, **t** the responsibility seriously.
12:10 and **t** delight in honoring each other.
12:19 that to God. For it is written, / "I will **t** vengeance;
13:14 But let the Lord Jesus Christ **t** control of you,
15:25 I must go down to Jerusalem to **t** a gift to the
1Co 3:21 So don't **t** pride in following a particular leader.
6:15 Should a man **t** his body, which belongs to Christ,
7:21 worry you—but if you get a chance to be free, **t** it.
2Co 8:19 accompany us as we **t** the offering to Jerusalem—
9:11 And when we **t** your gifts to those who need them,
11:20 **t** everything you have, **t** advantage of you,
12:8 Three different times I begged the Lord to **t** it
12:17 Did any of the men I sent to you **t** advantage of
12:18 brother with him, did Titus **t** advantage of you?
Eph 2:8 And you can't **t** credit for this; it is a gift from
5:2 and gave himself as a sacrifice to **t** away your sins.
5:11 **T** no part in the worthless deeds of evil
6:17 and **t** the sword of the Spirit, which is the Word of
Php 3:21 He will **t** these weak mortal bodies of ours
1Th 5:14 **T** tender care of those who are weak. Be patient
2Th 3:14 **T** note of those who refuse to obey what we say in
1Ti 3:5 how can he **t** care of God's church?
5:4 have children, and **t** care of their own homes.
5:16 she must **t** care of them and not put the
6:19 for the future so that they may **t** hold of real life.
Tit 2:5 and be pure, to **t** care of their homes, to do good,
Phm 1:9 So **t** this as a request from your friend Paul, an old
Heb 2:17 then could offer a sacrifice that would **t** away the
6:16 When people **t** an oath, they call on someone
6:18 we who have fled to him for refuge can **t** new
7:23 When one priest died, another had to **t** his place.

9:28 so also Christ died only once as a sacrifice to **t**
10: 4 for the blood of bulls and goats to **t** away sins.
10:11 offering sacrifices that can never **t** away sins.
10:30 we know the one who said, / "I will **t** vengeance.
11:32 It would **t** too long to recount the stories of the
12:12 So **t** a new grip with your tired hands and stand
Jas 4: 2 so you fight and quarrel to **t** it away from them.
5: 8 And **t** courage, for the coming of the Lord is near.
5:12 never **t** an oath, by heaven or earth or anything
1Pe 5: 9 **T** a firm stand against him, and be strong in your
1Jn 3: 5 And you know that Jesus came to **t** away our sins,
4:10 and sent his Son as a sacrifice to **t** away our sins.
5:21 keep away from anything that might **t** God's place
3Jn 1: 5 you are doing a good work for God when you **t**
Rev 3:11 you have, so that no one will **t** away your crown.
5: 9 "You are worthy to **t** the scroll / and break its seals
10: 8 and **t** the unrolled scroll from the angel who is
10: 9 "Yes, **t** it and eat it," he said. "At first it will taste
16:15 "**T** note: I will come as unexpectedly as a thief!
18: 4 Do not **t** part in her sins, or you will be punished

TAKEN (216) [TAKE]

Ge 2:21 and closed up the place from which he had **t** it.
2:23 called 'woman,' because she was **t** out of a man."
12:15 the pharaoh, and she was **t** into his harem.
14:16 the goods that had been **t**, Abram's nephew Lot
20:18 to Abimelech for having **t** Abraham's wife.
21:25 servants had **t** violently from Abraham's servants.
26:10 "Someone might have **t** your wife and slept with
31:32 household gods, let the person who has **t** them die!
31:32 But Jacob didn't know that Rachel had **t** them.
31:34 Rachel had **t** the household gods and had stuffed
43:18 frightened when they saw where they were being **t**.
47:26 But since Pharaoh had not **t** over the priests' land,
Ex 25:15 These carrying poles must never be **t** from the
Lev 6: 2 or they have **t** something by theft or extortion.
6: 4 they must give back whatever they have **t** by theft
6:30 the blood of a sin offering has been **t** into the
8:26 All these were **t** from the basket of bread made
10:18 Since the animal's blood was not **t** into the Holy
11: 9 whether **t** from fresh water or salt water.
13:49 and must be **t** to the priest to be examined.
Nu 8:16 I have **t** the Levites as their substitutes.
10:17 Then the Tabernacle was **t** down,
13:26 and showed them the fruit they had **t** from the land.
14:31 " 'You said your children would be **t** captive.
15:33 He was apprehended and **t** before Moses, Aaron,
16:15 I have not **t** so much as a donkey from them,
19: 3 and it will be **t** outside the camp and slaughtered in
24:18 Edom will be **t** over, / and Seir, its enemy, will be
26:64 in the previous census **t** in the wilderness of Sinai.
31:26 are to make a list of all the plunder **t** in the battle,
31:32 that the fighting men had **t** totaled 675,000 sheep,
31:53 All the fighting men had **t** some of the plunder for
Dt 4:34 Has any other god **t** one nation for himself by
17: 5 or woman must be **t** to the gates of the town
26:13 'I have **t** the sacred gift from my house and have
28:32 as your sons and daughters are **t** away as slaves.
Jos 2: 6 (But she had **t** them up to the roof and hidden them
4:20 piled up the twelve stones **t** from the Jordan River.
8:23 Only the king of Ai was **t** alive and brought to
10:27 the bodies of the kings to be **t** down from the trees
12: 1 River who had been killed and whose land was **t**.
22: 8 the great wealth you have **t** from your enemies.
Jdg 14: 9 But he didn't tell them he had **t** the honey from the
18:24 "You've **t** away all my gods and my priest, and I
19:18 of the LORD. But no one has **t** us in for the night,
21: 5 At that time they had **t** a solemn oath in the
1Sa 7:14 the rest of the territory that the Philistines had **t**.
12: 3 Have I ever **t** a bribe? Tell me and I will make
12: 4 and you have never **t** even a single bribe."
14:26 because they all feared the oath they had **t**.
28:17 He has **t** the kingdom from you and given it to
30: 8 You will surely recover everything that was **t** from
30:16 because of the vast amount of plunder they had **t**
30:18 David got back everything the Amalekites had **t**,
30:19 or daughter, or anything else that had been **t**.
30:26 for you, **t** from the LORD's enemies," he said.
2Sa 7:15 But my unfailing love will not be **t** from him as I
16: 2 The wine is to be **t** with you into the wilderness for
24:10 But after he had **t** the census, David's conscience
24:10 sinned greatly and shouldn't have **t** the census.
1Ki 13:12 told their father which road the man of God had **t**.
16:18 When Zimri saw that the city had been **t**, he went
22:37 and his body was **t** to Samaria and buried there.
2Ki 2: 9 "What can I do for you before I am **t** away?"
2:10 "If you see me when I am **t** from you, then you
13:25 the towns that Hazael had **t** from Jehoash's father,
20:18 Some of your own descendants will be **t** away into
23:34 Jehoahaz was **t** to Egypt as a prisoner, where he
1Ch 3:17 who was **t** prisoner by the Babylonians,
5: 6 **t** into captivity by King Tiglath-pileser of Assyria.
5:21 The plunder **t** from the Hagrites included 50,000
5:22 So they lived in their land until they were **t** away
18:11 and gold he had **t** from the other nations he had
21: 8 sinned greatly and shouldn't have **t** the census.
2Ch 2:17 like the census his father had **t**, and he counted
14:14 vast quantities of plunder were **t** from these towns,
15:11 of the animals they had **t** as plunder in the battle—
25:14 he brought with him idols **t** from the people of
28:11 Listen to me and return these captives you have **t**,
28:17 of Edom had again invaded Judah and **t** captives.
29:19 We have also recovered all the utensils **t** by King
32:31 the remarkable events that had **t** place in the land,
36:10 of the LORD were **t** to Babylon at that time.
36:13 even though he had **t** an oath of loyalty in God's
36:20 The few who survived were **t** away to Babylon,
Ezr 1: 7 had **t** from the LORD's Temple in Jerusalem
2:61 Barzillai from Gilead and had **t** her family name.)
5:14 and silver utensils that Nebuchadnezzar had **t** from
5:14 These items were **t** from that temple and delivered
6: 5 which were **t** to Babylon by Nebuchadnezzar from
6: 5 will be **t** back to Jerusalem and put into God's
9: 1 They have **t** up the detestable practices of the
9: 2 and have **t** them as wives for their sons.
Ne 7:63 Barzillai from Gilead and had **t** her family name.)
Est 2:12 Before each young woman was **t** to the king's bed,
2:14 That evening she was **t** to the king's private rooms,
2:16 When Esther was **t** to King Xerxes at the royal
8: 2 which he had **t** back from Haman—and gave it to
Job 1:21 everything I had, / and the LORD has **t** it away.
24:21 For they have **t** advantage of the childless who
27: 2 vow by the living God, who has **t** away my rights,
34: 5 'I am innocent, but God has **t** away my rights.
Ps 26:12 I have **t** a stand, / and I will publicly praise the
30:11 You have **t** away my clothes of mourning
88:18 You have **t** away my companions and loved ones;
110: 4 The LORD has **t** an oath and will not break his
Pr 7:20 He has **t** a wallet full of money with him, and he
Ecc 3:14 is final. Nothing can be added to it or **t** from it.
SS 5: 3 "But I said, 'I have **t** off my robe. Should I get
Isa 3:14 You have **t** advantage of the poor, filling your
7: 1 city withstood the attack, however, and was not **t**.
31: 8 The strong young Assyrians will be **t** away as
39: 7 Some of your own descendants will be **t** away into
50: 1 And your mother, too, was **t** because of your sins.
Jer 1: 3 the people of Jerusalem were **t** away as captives.
10:20 My children have been **t** away, and I will never see
12: 2 planted them, and they have **t** root and prospered.
13:19 The people of Judah will be **t** away as captives.
16: 5 I have **t** away my unfailing love and my mercy.
22:11 King Josiah, and was **t** away as a captive:
22:22 All your friends have been **t** away as captives.
27:16 **t** from my Temple will be returned from Babylon.
28: 4 and all the other captives that were **t** to Babylon.
32: 4 and **t** to the king of Babylon to be judged
34: 3 not escape his grasp but will be **t** into captivity.
48: 7 in your wealth and skill, you will be **t** captive.
48:46 and daughters have been **t** away as captives.
49:29 their household goods and camels will be **t** away.
50:15 The LORD has **t** vengeance, so do not spare her.
50:28 **t** vengeance against those who destroyed his
51:14 The LORD Almighty has **t** this vow and has
51:44 of Babylon, and pull from his mouth what he has **t**.
52:28 The number of captives **t** to Babylon in the seventh
La 1: 5 have been captured and **t** away to distant lands.
1:18 and daughters have been **t** captive to distant lands.
Eze 8: 3 I was **t** to the north gate of the inner courtyard of
16:59 for you have **t** your solemn vows lightly by
23:25 Your children will be **t** away as captives,
24:23 remain covered, and your sandals must not be **t** off.
30:17 in battle, and the women will be **t** away as slaves.
33:22 The previous evening the LORD had **t** hold of me
34: 4 You have not **t** care of the weak. You have not
40:38 sacrifices was washed before being **t** to the altar.
44:12 and **t** an oath that they must bear the consequences
Da 5: 2 had **t** from the Temple in Jerusalem, so that he
5: 3 So they brought these gold cups **t** from the Temple
7:12 other three beasts, their authority was **t** from them,
7:26 and all his power will be **t** away and completely
9:13 All the troubles he predicted have **t** place.
12:11 "From the time the daily sacrifice is **t** away
Hos 13: 8 to pieces like a bear whose cubs have been **t** away.
Joel 3: 5 You have **t** my silver and gold and all my precious
Am 3:10 "Their fortresses are filled with wealth **t** by theft
Ob 1: 6 and looted. Every treasure will be found and **t**.
Zec 3: 4 to Jeshua he said, "See, I have **t** away your sins,
14: 2 The city will be **t**, the houses plundered,
14: 2 Half the population will be **t** away into captivity,
Mal 2: 2 because you have not **t** my warning seriously.
Mt 5:40 are ordered to court and your shirt is **t** from you,
9:15 Someday he will be **t** from them, and then they
13:12 even what they have will be **t** away from them.
21:43 What I mean is that the Kingdom of God will be **t**
24:40 together in the field; one will be **t**, the other left.
24:41 flour at the mill; one will be **t**, the other left.
25:29 even what little they have will be **t** away.
26:39 let this cup of suffering be **t** away from me.
26:42 If this cup cannot be **t** away until I drink it,
Mk 2:20 But someday he will be **t** away from them, and
4:25 even what they have will be **t** away from them."
13:30 from the scene until all these events have **t** place.
16:19 he was **t** up into heaven and sat down in the place
Lk 1:25 "He has **t** away my disgrace of having no
1:52 He has **t** princes from their thrones / and exalted
2: 1 decreed that a census should be **t** throughout the
2: 2 (This was the first census **t** when Quirinius was
5:35 Someday he will be **t** away from them, and
6:30 and when things are **t** away from you, don't try to
8:18 even what they think they have will be **t** away
8:29 This spirit had often **t** control of the man.
17:34 one will be **t** away, and the other will be left.
17:35 together at the mill; one will be **t**, the other left."
19:26 even what little they have will be **t** away.
21:32 from the scene until all these events have **t** place.
23:55 As his body was **t** away, the women from Galilee
24:51 blessing them, he left them and was **t** up to heaven.
Jn 18:28 Then he was **t** to the headquarters of the Roman
19:31 legs be broken. Then their bodies could be **t** down.
20: 2 "They have **t** the Lord's body out of the tomb,
20:13 "Because they have **t** away my Lord," she replied,
20:15 "Sir," she said, "if you have **t** him away, tell me
Ac 1: 9 It was not long after he said this that he was **t** up
1:11 Jesus has been **t** away from you into heaven.
1:22 by John until the day he was **t** from us into heaven.
7:16 All of them were **t** to Shechem and buried in the
7:45 the Tabernacle was **t** with them into their new
8:33 For his life was **t** from the earth."
18:18 according to Jewish custom, for he had **t** a vow.)
20:12 Meanwhile, the young man was **t** home unhurt,
21:23 We have four men here who have **t** a vow and are
21:29 and they assumed Paul had **t** him into the Temple.)
21:34 so he ordered Paul to be **t** to the fortress.
21:37 As Paul was about to be **t** inside, he said to the
Ro 15:26 the believers in Greece have eagerly **t** up an
2Co 3:16 anyone turns to the Lord, then the veil is **t** away.
5: 1 that when this earthly tent we live in is **t** down—
7: 2 anyone astray. We have not **t** advantage of anyone.
Gal 4:15 I know you would gladly have **t** out your own eyes
1Ti 3:16 on in the world / and was **t** up into heaven.
Heb 7: 4 by giving him a tenth of what he had **t** in battle.
7:19 and now a better hope has **t** its place.
7:21 Only to Jesus did he say, / "The Lord has **t** an oath
10:34 When all you owned was **t** from you, you accepted
11: 5 It was by faith that Enoch was **t** up to heaven
11: 5 But before he was **t** up, he was approved as
Rev 6:14 And the sky was rolled up like a scroll and **t** away.
13:10 are destined for prison will be arrested and **t** away.

TAKES (38) [TAKE]

Ge 4:24 anyone who **t** revenge against me will be punished
Ex 21:10 If he himself marries her and then **t** another wife,
Lev 24:17 "Anyone who **t** another person's life must be put
Nu 24:22 will be destroyed / when Assyria **t** you captive."
30: 6 "Now suppose a young woman **t** a vow or makes
Dt 1: 2 Normally it **t** only eleven days to travel from
10:17 who shows no partiality and **t** no bribes.
2Ki 4:13 she replied, "my family **t** good care of me."
Job 5:11 the poor and humble, and he **t** sufferers to safety.
11:11 those who are false, and he **t** note of all their sins.
12:24 He **t** away the understanding of kings, and he
27: 8 have when God cuts them off and **t** away their life?
36: 9 he **t** the trouble to show them the reason. He shows
Ps 37:17 be shattered, / but the LORD **t** care of the godly.
37:18 Day by day the LORD **t** care of the innocent,
137: 9 Happy is the one who **t** your babies / and smashes
Pr 5:21 what a man does, examining every path he **t**.
22: 3 foresees the danger ahead and **t** precautions;
27:12 foresees the danger ahead and **t** precautions.
29: 9 If a wise person **t** a fool to court, there will be
Ecc 2:26 God **t** the wealth away and gives it to those who
4: 1 Again I observed all the oppression that **t** place in
5: 4 following through, for God **t** no pleasure in fools.
Isa 3:13 The LORD **t** his place in court. He is the great
44:13 of wood, **t** the tool, and carves the figure of a man.
44:15 he **t** the rest of it and makes himself a god for
44:17 Then he **t** what's left and makes his god: a carved
Eze 16:32 you are an adulterous wife who **t** in strangers
18:12 worships idols and **t** part in loathsome practices,
Na 1: 2 He **t** revenge on all who oppose him and furiously
Zep 3: 5 his justice is more evident, but no one **t** notice—
Mk 4:15 then Satan comes at once and **t** it away from them.
Jn 1:29 There is the Lamb of God who **t** away the sin of
4:14 But the water I give them **t** away thirst altogether.
1Co 9: 7 What shepherd **t** care of a flock of sheep and isn't
Gal 5: 9 But it **t** only one wrong person among you to infect
Php 4:19 And this same God who **t** care of me will supply
1Jn 2: 2 He **t** away not only our sins but the sins of all the

TAKING (70) [TAKE]

Ge 14:11 journey home, **t** all the wealth and food with them.
24:10 **t** with him the best of everything his master
24:63 One evening as he was **t** a walk out in the fields,
27:36 first **t** my birthright and now stealing my blessing.
37:25 It was a group of Ishmaelite traders **t** spices,
38:25 But as they were **t** her out to kill her, she sent this
Lev 18: 3 or like the people of Canaan, where I am **t** you.
18:27 by the people of the land where I am **t** you,
19:14 with respect and by not **t** advantage of the blind.
25:17 Show your fear of God by not **t** advantage of each
Nu 14: 3 "Why is the LORD **t** us to this country only to
15:18 When you arrive in the land where I am **t** you,
21: 4 **t** the road to the Red Sea to go around the land of
Jos 18: 3 "How long are you going to wait before **t**
19:47 But the tribe of Dan had trouble **t** possession of
Jdg 6: 4 nothing to eat, **t** all the sheep, oxen, and donkeys.
8:11 and Jogbehah, **t** the Midianite army by surprise.
19:25 her all night, **t** turns raping her until morning.
1Sa 17:28 those few sheep you're supposed to be **t** care of?
17:34 "I have been **t** care of my father's sheep," he said.
17:49 Reaching into his shepherd's bag and **t** out a stone,
23: 6 **t** the ephod with him to get answers for David
25:26 and **t** vengeance into your own hands,
2Sa 4: 5 Ishbosheth's home around noon as he was **t** a nap.
4: 7 **T** his head with them, they fled across the Jordan
11: 2 Late one afternoon David got out of bed after **t** a
11: 2 he noticed a woman of unusual beauty **t** a bath.
12:10 because you have despised me by **t** Uriah's wife to
19:40 then went on to Gilgal, **t** Kimham with him.
24: 1 and he caused David to harm them by **t** a census.
1Ki 1:15 was very old now, and Abishag was **t** care of him.
15:18 Asa responded by **t** all the silver and gold that was
21:18 at Naboth's vineyard in Jezreel, **t** possession of it.
2Ki 5: 5 **t** as gifts 750 pounds of silver, 150 pounds of gold,
1Ch 2: 7 brought disaster on Israel by **t** plunder that had
2Ch 16: 2 Asa responded by **t** the silver and gold from the
19: 7 perverted justice, partiality, or the **t** of bribes."
Ne 2:12 out during the night, **t** only a few others with me.
Isa 40:24 They hardly get started, barely **t** root, when he

51:22 "See, I am t the terrible cup from your hands.
66: 6 It is the voice of the LORD t vengeance against
Jer 16:14 "when people who are t an oath will no longer
23: 7 says the LORD, "when people are t an oath,
34:16 and defiled my name by t back the men
41:10 T them with him, he started back toward the land
La 1:10 t everything precious that she owns.
Eze 12:12 hole in the wall, t only what he can carry with him.
36: 5 by gleefully t my land for themselves as plunder.
42:15 When the man had finished t these measurements,
Da 4:29 he was t a walk on the flat roof of the royal palace
Am 5:12 You oppress good people by t bribes and deprive
Mic 2: 4 God has confiscated our land, / t it from us.
Zec 5:10 "Where are they t the basket?" I asked the angel.
Mk 9:36 T the child in his arms, he said to them,
10:32 T the twelve disciples aside, Jesus once more
15:46 and t Jesus' body down from the cross,
Lk 1:21 to come out, wondering why he was t so long.
13: 7 It's t up space we can use for something else.'
17: 7 a servant comes in from plowing or t care of sheep,
19:21 t what isn't yours and harvesting crops you didn't
21:31 when you see the events I've described t place,
23:19 and for t part in an insurrection in Jerusalem
24: 1 came to the tomb, t the spices they had prepared.
Ac 12:25 they returned to Antioch, t John Mark with them.
18:18 the coast of Syria, t Priscilla and Aquila with him.
Ro 3:24 Christ Jesus, who has freed us by t away our sins.
1Co 6: 1 instead of t it to other Christians to decide who is
1Th 4: 6 Never cheat another Christian in this matter by t
1Ti 5: 4 at home and repay their parents by t care of them.
5:21 angels to obey these instructions without t sides

TALE [KJV] See ALL, QUOTA

TALEBEARER [KJV] See GOSSIP, RUMORS

TALENT (1) [TALENTED]

Jer 4:22 but they have no t at all for doing right!"

TALENTED (2) [TALENT]

Ex 31: 6 I have given special skill to all the naturally t
1Sa 16:18 said to Saul, "The son of Jesse is a t harp player.

TALES (1)

1Ti 4: 7 time arguing over godless ideas and old wives' t.

TALK (95) [TALKED, TALKERS, TALKING, TALKS]

Ge 11: 3 They began to t about construction projects.
19: 6 Lot stepped outside to t to them, shutting the door
31: 5 so he could t things over with them. "Your father
Ex 4:15 You will t to him, giving him the words to say.
18: 7 and then went to Moses' tent to t further.
25:22 and t to you from above the atonement cover
34:31 community leaders to come over and t with him.
Nu 11:17 I will come down and t to you there. I will take
14:10 But the whole community began to t about stoning
Dt 6: 7 T about them when you are at home and when you
11:19 T about them when you are at home and when you
Jos 2: 8 Rahab went up on the roof to t with them.
6:10 not shout; do not even t," Joshua commanded.
22:13 They crossed the river to t with the tribes of
Jdg 19:23 The old man stepped outside to t to them. "No,
Ru 3:13 here tonight, and in the morning I will t to him.
4: 1 "Come over here, friend. I want to t to you."
1Sa 19: 3 go out there with me, and I'll t to him about you.
20:12 I will t to my father and let you know at once how
25:14 "David sent men from the wilderness to t to our
25:17 so ill-tempered that no one can even t to him!"
28: 8 "I have to t to a man who has died," he said.
30: 6 and children, and they began to t of stoning him.
30:24 Do you think anyone will listen to you when you t
2Sa 20:16 to me, Joab. Come over here so I can t to you."
1Ki 22: 8 "You shouldn't t like that," Jehoshaphat said.
2Ki 4:29 my staff and go! Don't t to anyone along the way.
2Ch 18: 7 "You shouldn't t like that," Jehoshaphat said.
Ne 6: 7 so I suggest that you come and t it over with me."
Job 2:10 But Job replied, "You t like a godless woman.
15: 2 a wise man, and yet you give us all this foolish t.
23: 3 I would go to his throne and t with him there.
34: 7 as arrogant as Job, with his thirst for irreverent t?
Ps 5: 9 Their t is foul, like the stench from an open grave.
27: 8 heart has heard you say, "Come and t with me."
35:20 They don't t of peace; / they plot against innocent
88:12 Can anyone in the land of forgetfulness t about
115: 5 They cannot t, though they have mouths, / or see,
135:16 They cannot t, though they have mouths, / or see,
145:11 They will t together about the glory of your
Pr 4:24 Avoid all perverse t; stay far from corrupt speech.
10:19 Don't t too much, for it fosters sin. Be sensible
11:11 it prosper, but the t of the wicked tears it apart.
14: 3 The t of fools is a rod for their backs,
14:23 Work brings profit, but mere t leads to poverty!
17: 4 Wrongdoers listen to wicked t; liars pay attention
18:21 Those who love to t will experience the
Isa 28: 9 Are we little children, barely old enough to t?
48: 2 and t about depending on the God of Israel,
51: 7 be afraid of people's scorn or their slanderous t.
58:13 and don't follow your own desires or t idly.
Jer 3: 5 So you t, and keep right on doing all the evil you
38: 4 That kind of t will undermine the morale of the
Eze 3:22 "Go out into the valley, and I will t to you there."
13:23 But you will no longer t of seeing visions that you
24:27 voice will suddenly return so you can t to him,
33:30 They t about you in their houses and whisper about
Da 10:17 someone like me, your servant, t to you, my lord?
Mic 2: 7 Should you t that way, O family of Israel?
Mt 8: 4 examine you. Don't t to anyone along the way.
9:33 cast out the demon, and instantly the man could t.
12:22 who was both blind and unable to t, was brought to
12:46 and brothers were outside, wanting to t with him.
13:10 "Why do you always tell stories when you t to the
17:25 Then he went into the house to t to Jesus about it.
Mk 1:44 examine you. Don't t to anyone along the way.
3:31 sent word for him to come out and t with them.
9:17 is possessed by an evil spirit that won't let him t.
16: 8 to anyone because they were too frightened to t.
Lk 7:15 boy sat up and began to t to those around him!
Jn 7:46 "We have never heard anyone t like this!"
14:30 "I don't have much more time to t to you,
19:10 "You won't t to me?" Pilate demanded.
Ac 15: 2 to t to the apostles and elders about this question.
21:39 important city. Please, let me t to these people."
23: 4 to him, "Is that the way to t to God's high priest?"
Ro 3: 5 (That is actually the way some people t.)
3:13 "Their t is foul, like the stench from an open
16:18 By smooth t and glowing words they deceive
1Co 3: 1 when I was with you I couldn't t to you as I would
3: 1 I had to t as though you belonged to this world
4:20 For the Kingdom of God is not just fancy t; it is
8: 1 Now let's t about food that has been sacrificed to
14: 9 If you t to people in a language they don't
2Co 11:16 don't think that I have lost my wits to t like this.
Eph 5: 4 Obscene stories, foolish t, and coarse jokes—
5:12 It is shameful even to t about the things that
1Th 1: 3 As we t to our God and Father about you, we think
1Ti 5: 1 T to the younger men as you would to your own
2Ti 2:17 This kind of t spreads like cancer. Hymenaeus
Tit 1:10 they engage in useless t and deceive people.
2: 9 do their best to please them. They must not t back
Heb 11:14 And obviously people who t like that are looking
2Jn 1:12 to visit you soon and to t with you face to face.
3Jn 1:14 to see you soon, and then we will t face to face.

TALKED (37) [TALK]

Ge 13: 8 Then Abram t it over with Lot. "This arguing
42:24 Returning, he t some more with them. He
Ex 4:18 Moses went back home and t it over with Jethro,
Jdg 13:11 "Are you the man who t to my wife the other
14: 7 he t with the woman and was very pleased with
1Sa 17:26 David t to some others standing there to verify the
1Ki 10: 2 they t about everything she had on her mind.
2Ch 9: 2 they t about everything she had on her mind.
32:19 These officials t about the God of Jerusalem as
Job 34:36 maximum penalty for the wicked way you have t.
Ps 40:10 I have t about your faithfulness and saving power.
Jer 41: 8 The other ten had t Ishmael into letting them go by
Eze 3:24 He t to me and said, "Go, shut yourself up in your
Da 1:11 Daniel t it over with the attendant who had been
1:19 The king t with each of them, and none of them
Zec 1:13 and comforting words to the angel who t with me.
Mt 21:25 merely human?" They t it over among themselves.
26:13 this woman's deed will be t about in her
Mk 4:14 The farmer I t about is the one who brings God's
6:20 Herod was disturbed whenever he t with John,
8:32 As he t about this openly with his disciples,
11:31 They t it over among themselves. "If we say it was
14: 9 this woman's deed will be t about in her
Lk 2:38 She t about Jesus to everyone who had been
7:24 After they left, Jesus t to the crowd about John.
17:22 Later he t again about this with his disciples.
20: 5 They t it over among themselves. "If we say it was
24:32 "Didn't our hearts feel strangely warm as he t with
Jn 11:56 and as they t in the Temple, they asked each other,
Ac 1: 3 On these occasions he t to them about the
10:27 and they t together and went inside where the
18:25 and t to others with great enthusiasm and accuracy
20: 7 he was leaving the next day, he t until midnight.
24:26 so he sent for him quite often and t with him.
26:31 As they t it over they agreed, "This man hasn't
Gal 2: 2 While I was there I t privately with the leaders of
Rev 21:15 The angel who t to me held in his hand a gold

TALKERS (1) [TALK]

1Co 4:19 out whether these arrogant people are just big t

TALKING (77) [TALK]

Ge 44: 7 "What are you t about?" the brothers responded.
45:15 over them, and then they began t freely with him.
Ex 3:13 They will ask, 'Which god are you t about?
5: 8 they wouldn't be t about going into the wilderness
Dt 11: 2 I am not t now to your children, who have never
1Sa 9:21 of that tribe! Why are you t like this to me?"
14:19 But while Saul was t to the priest, the shouting
17:23 As he was t with them, he saw Goliath,
17:28 Eliab, heard David t to the men, he was angry.
18: 1 After David had finished t with Saul, he met
22: 9 he said, "I saw David t to Ahimelech the priest.
24: 4 "Today is the day the LORD was t about when
1Ki 1:14 And while you are still t with him, I will come
2Ki 2:11 As they were walking along and t, suddenly a
8: 4 As she came in, the king was t with Gehazi,
Est 1:18 and will start t to their husbands the same way.
6:14 While they were still t, the king's eunuchs arrived
7: 5 "Whom are you t about?" King Xerxes
Job 11: 2 Is a person proved innocent just by t a lot?
18: 2 "How long before you stop t? Speak sense if you
42: 3 And I was t about things I did not understand,
Isa 65:24 While they are still t to me about their needs,
Jer 5:14 "Because the people are t like this, I will give you
17:15 this 'message from the LORD' you keep t about?
38:25 'Tell us what you and the king were t about.
Eze 11:15 the people still left in Jerusalem are t about their
38:17 You are the one I was t about long ago, when I
Da 8:13 Then I heard two of the holy ones t to each other.
Zec 1: 9 I asked the angel who was t with me, "My lord,
1:19 I asked the angel who was t with me. He replied,
4: 1 Then the angel who had been t with me returned
5: 5 Then the angel who was t with me came forward
6: 4 my lord?" I asked the angel who was t with me.
Mt 10:20 For it won't be you doing the t—it will be the
11: 7 had gone, Jesus began t about him to the crowds.
15:31 Those who hadn't been able to speak were t,
16:11 How could you even think I was t about food?
17: 3 and Elijah appeared and began t with Jesus.
26:70 "I don't know what you are t about," he said.
Mk 6:14 because people everywhere were t about him.
9: 4 and Moses appeared and began t with Jesus.
14:68 "I don't know what you're t about," he said,
14:71 by God, I don't know this man you're t about."
16:19 When the Lord Jesus had finished t with them,
Lk 2:38 She came along just as Simeon was t with Mary
9:30 and Elijah, appeared and began t with Jesus.
12:42 And the Lord replied, "I'm t to any faithful,
18:34 and they failed to grasp what he was t about.
21: 5 Some of his disciples began t about the beautiful
22:60 "Man, I don't know what you are t about."
24:14 As they walked along they were t about everything
Jn 1:15 "This is the one I was t about when I said,
1:30 He is the one I was t about when I said, 'Soon a
4:27 They were astonished to find him t to a woman,
8:27 But they still didn't understand that he was t to
12:34 Who is this Son of Man you are t about?"
Ac 8:34 "Was Isaiah t about himself or someone else?"
13:33 This is what the second psalm is t about when it
19:27 I'm not just t about the loss of public respect for
20:11 And Paul continued t to them until dawn; then he
Ro 2: 1 "What terrible people you have been t about!"
1Co 5:10 But I wasn't t about unbelievers who indulge in
14: 2 you will be t to God but not to people, since they
14: 6 if I should come to you t in an unknown language,
14: 9 You might as well be t to an empty room.
14:23 and hear everyone t in an unknown language,
2Co 6:13 I am t now as I would to my own children.
11: 1 I hope you will be patient with me as I keep on t
11: 6 be a trained speaker, but I know what I am t about.
11:21 I'm t like a fool again—I can boast about it,
1Th 1: 9 for they themselves keep t about the wonderful
1Ti 1: 6 and spend their time arguing and t foolishness.
1: 7 but they don't know what they are t about,
Heb 2: 5 the future world we are t about will not be
6: 9 Dear friends, even though we are t like this,
7:13 For the one we are t about belongs to a different
1Pe 1:11 t about when he told them in advance about

TALKS (3) [TALK]

Pr 20:19 so don't hang around with someone who t too
Eze 20:49 they are saying of me, 'He only t in riddles!' "
Mt 9: 3 "Blasphemy! This man t like he is God!" some of

TALL (31) [TALLER, TALLEST]

Dt 2:10 They were as t as the Anakites, another race of
2:21 and powerful race, as t as the Anakites.
9: 2 They are strong and t—descendants of the famous
1Sa 17: 4 was a giant of a man, measuring over nine feet t!
1Ki 6:23 two cherubim made of olive wood, each 15 feet t.
6:26 each was 15 feet t.
7:15 each 27 feet t and 18 feet in circumference.
7:16 made capitals of molded bronze, each 7-1/2 feet t.
7:19 were shaped like lilies, and they were 6 feet t.
7:27 each 6 feet long, 6 feet wide, and 4-1/2 feet t.
2Ki 25:17 Each of the pillars was 27 feet t. The bronze
1Ch 11:23 Egyptian warrior who was seven and a half feet t
2Ch 3:15 Solomon made two pillars that were 27 feet t,
Est 5:14 "Set up a gallows that stands seventy-five feet t,
7: 9 that stands seventy-five feet t in his own courtyard.
SS 7: 7 You are t and slim like a palm tree, and your
Isa 2:13 He will cut down the t cedars of Lebanon
18: 2 to your t, smooth-skinned people, who are feared
18: 7 from this t, smooth-skinned people, who are feared
Jer 46:18 "one is coming against Egypt who is as t as Mount
52:21 Each of the pillars was 27 feet t and 18 feet in
Eze 1:18 The rims of the four wheels were awesomely t,
17:22 I will take a tender shoot from the top of a t cedar,
17:24 who cuts down the t tree and helps the short tree to grow t.
19:11 It soon became very t, / towering above all the
31: 4 watered it and helped it to grow t and luxuriant.
Da 3: 1 Nebuchadnezzar made a gold statue ninety feet t
4:11 The tree grew very t and strong, reaching high into
4:20 You saw a tree growing very t and strong,
Am 2: 9 The Amorites were as t as cedar trees and strong as

TALLER (4) [TALL]

Dt 1:28 They say that the people of the land are t and more
1Sa 2:26 Meanwhile, as young Samuel grew t, he also
9: 2 and shoulders t than anyone else in the land.
Eze 31: 8 This tree became t than any of the other cedars in

TALLEST (3) [TALL]

2Ki 19:23 I have cut down its t cedars / and its choicest
Isa 37:24 I have cut down its t cedars / and its choicest
Zec 11: 2 the t and most beautiful of them are fallen.

TALMAI (6)
Nu 13:22 at Hebron, where Ahiman, Sheshai, and T—
Jos 15:14 Sheshai, Ahiman, and T—descendants of Anak.
Jdg 1:10 defeating the forces of Sheshai, Ahiman, and T.
2Sa 3:3 was Maacah, the daughter of T, king of Geshur.
13:37 T son of Ammihud, the king of Geshur.
1Ch 3:2 was Maacah, the daughter of T, king of Geshur.

TALMON (5)
1Ch 9:17 Akkub, T, Ahiman, and their relatives.
Ezr 2:42 Ater, T, Akkub, Hatita, and Shobai | 139
Ne 7:45 Ater, T, Akkub, Hatita, and Shobai | 138
11:19 Akkub, T, and 172 of their associates,
12:25 Meshullam, T, and Akkub were the gatekeepers in

TAMAH [KJV] See TEMAH

TAMAR (32) [BAAL-TAMAR, HAZAZON-TAMAR, TAMAR'S]
Ge 38:6 arranged his marriage to a young woman named T.
38:8 said to Er's brother Onan, "You must marry T,
38:9 So whenever he had intercourse with T, he spilled
38:11 Then Judah told T, his daughter-in-law, not to
38:11 his two brothers.) So T went home to her parents.
38:13 Someone told T that her father-in-law had left for
38:14 T was aware that Shelah had grown up, but they
38:16 "How much will you pay me?" T asked.
38:24 word reached Judah that T, his daughter-in-law,
38:26 son Shelah." But Judah never slept with T again.
Ru 4:12 of our ancestor Perez, the son of T and Judah."
2Sa 13:1 son Absalom had a beautiful sister named T.
13:2 so obsessed with T that he became ill.
13:4 told him, "I am in love with T, Absalom's sister."
13:5 ask him to let T come and prepare some food for
13:6 "Please let T come to take care of me and cook
13:7 and sent T to Amnon's house to prepare some food
13:8 When T arrived at Amnon's house, she went to the
13:10 Then he said to T, "Now bring the food into my
13:10 and feed it to me here." So T took it to him.
13:16 "No, no!" T cried. "To reject me now is a greater
13:19 But now T tore her robe and put ashes on her head.
13:20 So T lived as a desolate woman in Absalom's
13:32 plotting this ever since Amnon raped his sister T.
14:27 His daughter's name was T, and she was very
1Ki 9:18 Baalath, and T in the desert, within his land.
1Ch 2:4 Later Judah had twin sons through T, his widowed
3:9 David also had a daughter named T.
Eze 47:18 past the Dead Sea and as far south as T.
47:19 "The southern border will go west from T to the
48:28 The southern border of Gad runs from T to the
Mt 1:3 the father of Perez and Zerah (their mother was T).

TAMAR'S (1) [TAMAR]
Ge 38:27 In due season the time of T delivery arrived,

TAMARISK (3)
Ge 21:33 Then Abraham planted a t tree at Beersheba,
1Sa 22:6 the king was sitting beneath a t tree on the hill at
31:13 and buried them beneath the t tree at Jabesh,

TAMBOURINE (7) [TAMBOURINES]
Ex 15:20 took a t and led all the women in rhythm
Jdg 11:34 to meet him, playing on a t and dancing for joy.
1Sa 10:5 They will be playing a harp, a t, a flute, and a lyre,
Job 21:12 They sing with t and harp. They make merry to the
Ps 81:2 Sing! Beat the t. / Play the sweet lyre and the harp.
149:3 name with dancing, / accompanied by t and harp.
150:4 Praise him with the t and dancing; / praise him

TAMBOURINES (9) [TAMBOURINE]
Ge 31:27 with joyful singing accompanied by t and harps.
1Sa 18:6 they sang and danced for joy with t and cymbals.
2Sa 6:5 lyres, harps, t, castanets, and cymbals.
1Ch 13:8 lyres, harps, t, cymbals, and trumpets.
Ps 68:25 with them are young women playing t.
Isa 5:12 the harps, lyres, t, and flutes are superb!
24:8 The clash of t will be stilled; the happy cries of
30:32 his people will keep time with the music of t
Jer 31:4 You will again be happy and dance merrily with t.

TAME (2) [TAMED]
Jas 3:7 People can t all kinds of animals and birds
3:8 but no one can t the tongue. It is an uncontrollable

TAMED (1) [TAME]
Job 39:9 "Will the wild ox consent to being t? Will it stay

TAMMUZ (1)
Eze 8:14 women were sitting there, weeping for the god T.

TANACH [KJV] See TAANACH

TANGLED (3)
Hos 2:12 I will let them grow into t thickets, where only
Na 1:10 His enemies, t up like thorns, staggering like
2Pe 2:20 and Savior Jesus Christ and then get t up with sin

TANHUMETH (2)
2Ki 25:23 son of Kareah, Seraiah son of T the Netophathite,
Jer 40:8 and Jonathan, sons of Kareah, Seraiah son of T,

TANK (4)
1Ki 7:23 Then Huram cast a large round t, 15 feet across
7:24 way around, and they had been cast as part of the t.
2Ch 4:2 Then he cast a large round t, 15 feet across from
4:3 way around, and they had been cast as part of the t.

TANNED (7)
Ex 25:5 t ram skins and fine goatskin leather; acacia wood;
26:14 On top of these coverings place a layer of t ram
35:7 t ram skins and fine goatskin leather; acacia wood;
35:23 Some gave t ram skins or fine goatskin leather.
36:19 The first was made of t ram skins, and the second
39:34 the layers of t ram skins and fine goatskin leather;
SS 1:5 women of Jerusalem, t as the dark tents of Kedar.

TAPE (2)
Ecc 5:8 and matters of justice only get lost in red t
Eze 40:3 He was holding in his hand a measuring t and a

TAPHATH (1)
1Ki 4:11 (He was married to T, one of Solomon's

TAPPED (1)
Ac 12:7 The angel t him on the side to awaken him

TAPPUAH (9) [BETH-TAPPUAH]
Jos 12:17 The king of T / The king of Hepher
15:34 Zanoah, En-gannim, T, Enam,
16:8 From T the border extended westward,
17:7 to the people living near the spring of T.
17:8 (The land surrounding T belonged to Manasseh,
17:8 but the town of T, on the border of Manasseh's
17:9 From the spring of T, the border of Manasseh
2Ki 15:16 At that time Menahem destroyed the town of T
1Ch 2:43 of Hebron were Korah, T, Rekem, and Shema.

TAR (4)
Ge 6:14 a boat from resinous wood and seal it with t,
14:10 As it happened, the valley was filled with t pits.
14:10 and Gomorrah fled, some slipped into the t pits,
Ex 2:3 papyrus reeds and waterproofed it with t and pitch.

TARAH [KJV] See TERAH

TARALAH (1)
Jos 18:27 Rekem, Irpeel, T,

TARE [KJV] See CONVULSION, MAULED, TORE

TARES [KJV] See WEEDS

TARGET (6)
Jdg 20:16 could sling a rock and hit a t within a hairsbreadth,
1Sa 20:20 of the stone pile as though I were shooting at a t.
Job 7:20 Why have you made me your t? Am I a burden to
16:12 dashed me to pieces. Then he set me up as his t.
36:32 hands with lightning bolts. He hurls each at its t.
Hos 7:16 are like a crooked bow that always misses its t.

TARPEL (1)
Ezr 4:9 the people of T, the Persians, the Babylonians,

TARRIED, TARRIEST, TARRIETH, TARRY, TARRYING [KJV] See CONTINUE(D), DELAY(ED), LINGERING, LIVE, REMAIN(ED), SPEND, SPENT, STAY(ED, -ING, -S), STOP(PED), SUSPENSE, WAIT(ED, -ING)

TARSHISH (18)
Ge 10:4 of Javan were Elishah, T, Kittim, and Rodanim.
1Ch 1:7 of Javan were Elishah, T, Kittim, and Rodanim.
7:10 Benjamin, Ehud, Kenaanah, Zethan, T,
Est 1:14 Shethar, Admatha, T, Meres, Marsena,
Ps 48:7 or like the mighty ships of T / being shattered by a
72:10 The western kings of T and the islands / will bring
Isa 23:1 Weep, O ships of T, returning home from distant
23:6 Flee now to T! Wail, you people who live by the
23:10 Come, T, sweep over your mother Tyre like the
23:14 Wail, O ships of T, for your home port is
60:9 They are the ships of T, reserved to bring the
66:19 to T, to the Libyans and Lydians (who are famous
Jer 10:9 They bring beaten sheets of silver from T and gold
Eze 27:12 "T was your agent, trading your wares in
27:25 The ships of T were your ocean caravans.
38:13 and Dedan and the merchants of T will ask,
Jnh 1:3 port of Joppa, where he found a ship leaving for T.
4:2 do this, LORD? That is why I ran away to T!

TARSUS (5)
Ac 9:11 of Judas. When you arrive, ask for Saul of T.
9:30 to Caesarea and sent him on to his hometown of T.
11:25 Then Barnabas went on to T to find Saul.
21:39 Paul replied, "I am a Jew from T in Cilicia,
22:3 "I am a Jew, born in T, a city in Cilicia, and I was

TARTAK (1)
2Ki 17:31 The Avvites worshiped their gods Nibhaz and T.

TARTAN [KJV] See COMMANDER-IN-CHIEF

TASK (24) [TASKS]
Ge 2:2 On the seventh day, having finished his t,
49:15 the land, / he will bend his shoulder to the t
Ex 18:22 you carry the load, making the t easier for you.
Lev 16:21 into the wilderness, led by a man chosen for this t.
Nu 1:5 and the names of the leaders chosen for the t:
4:49 Each man was assigned his t and told what to
34:18 one leader from each tribe to help them with the t.
2Sa 24:8 they completed their t in nine months and twenty
1Ch 22:2 and he assigned them the t of preparing blocks of
28:20 Don't be afraid or discouraged by the size of the t,
2Ch 29:17 So the entire t was completed in sixteen days.
36:23 the LORD's people may return to Israel for this t.
Ezr 3:9 They were helped in this t by the Levites of the
5:2 t of rebuilding the Temple of God in Jerusalem.
8:30 and the Levites accepted the t of transporting these
Job 14:6 so let us finish the t you have given us.
Ps 73:16 the wicked prosper. / But what a difficult t it is!
101:8 My daily t will be to ferret out criminals / and free
Isa 13:3 the LORD, have assigned this t to these armies,
Eze 9:6 the mark. Begin your t right here at the Temple."
Zec 8:9 Almighty says: Take heart and finish the t!
Lk 12:49 and I wish that my t were already completed!
2Co 2:16 And who is adequate for such a t as this?
5:18 And God has given us the t of reconciling people

TASKS (10) [TASK]
Ex 3:9 the Egyptians have oppressed them with heavy t.
5:4 "distracting the people from their t?
16:23 On this day we will rest from our normal daily t.
1Ch 6:48 were appointed to various other t in the
24:5 All t were assigned to the various groups by means
Ne 13:30 and assigned t to the priests and Levites,
Ps 81:6 I will free your hands from their heavy t.
Ecc 10:15 that they have no strength for even the simplest t.
Jn 9:4 All of us must quickly carry out the t assigned us
1Ti 4:15 Throw yourself into your t so that everyone will

TASSELS (6)
Nu 15:38 you must make t for the hems of your clothing
15:38 and attach the t at each corner with a blue cord.
15:39 The t will remind you of the commands of the
15:40 The t will help you remember that you must obey
Dt 22:12 "You must put t on the four corners of your
Mt 23:5 and they wear extra long t on their robes.

TASTE (13) [FORETASTE, TASTED, TASTELESS, TASTES, TASTY]
2Sa 16:8 At last you will t some of your own medicine,
Job 20:12 "He enjoyed the t of his wickedness, letting it melt
24:11 They press out olive oil without being allowed to t
Ps 28:4 Give them a t of what they have done to others.
34:8 T and see that the LORD is good. / Oh, the joys
119:103 How sweet are your words to my t; / they are
Pr 23:31 let the sparkle and smooth t of wine deceive you.
24:13 for it is good, and the honeycomb is sweet to the t.
Jer 31:29 but their children's mouths pucker at the t.'
Eze 18:2 but their children's mouths pucker at the t'?
Lk 14:24 the smallest t of what I had prepared for them.' "
1Pe 2:3 now that you have had a t of the Lord's kindness.
Rev 10:9 "At first it will t like honey, but when you

TASTED (10) [TASTE]
Ex 16:31 white like coriander seed, and it t like honey cakes.
Nu 11:8 These cakes t like they had been cooked in olive
1Sa 14:43 "I t a little honey," Jonathan admitted.
Job 21:25 dies in bitter poverty, never having t the good life.
Eze 3:3 he said. And when I ate it, it t as sweet as honey.
Mt 27:34 but when he had t it, he refused to drink it.
Jn 2:9 When the master of ceremonies t the water that
19:30 When Jesus had t it, he said, "It is finished!"
Heb 2:9 Jesus t death for everyone in all the world.
6:5 who have t the goodness of the word of God

TASTELESS (2) [TASTE]
Job 6:6 And how t is the uncooked white of an egg!
Pr 27:7 Honey seems t to a person who is full, but even

TASTES (5) [TASTE]
Job 12:11 Just as the mouth t good food, so the ear tests the
34:3 'Just as the mouth t good food, the ear tests the
Pr 9:17 is refreshing; food eaten in secret t the best!"
20:17 Stolen bread t sweet, but it turns to gravel in the
27:7 is full, but even bitter food t sweet to the hungry.

TASTY (1) [TASTE]
2Sa 19:35 Food and wine are no longer t, and I cannot hear

TATTENAI (4)
Ezr 5:3 But T, governor of the province west of the
5:6 This is the letter that T the governor,
6:6 "To T, governor of the province west of the
6:13 T, governor of the province west of the Euphrates

TATTERED (1)
Am 3:12 are rescued with only a broken chair and a t pillow.

TATTLERS [KJV] See GOSSIPING

TATTOOS (1)

Lev 19:28 in mourning for the dead or mark your skin with **t**,

TAUGHT (71) [TEACH]

Dt 31:22 the words of the song and **t** it to the Israelites.
Jdg 8:16 took the leaders of the town and **t** them a lesson,
2Sa 1:18 Later he commanded that it be **t** to all the people of
2Ki 17:28 and **t** the new residents how to worship the
Ezr 7:11 and scribe who studied and **t** the commands
Ps 8:2 You have **t** children and nursing infants / to give
71:17 you have **t** me from my earliest childhood,
119:71 for it **t** me to pay attention to your principles.
119:102 away from your laws, / for you have **t** me well.
119:130 As your words are **t**, they give light;
119:171 with praise, / for you have **t** me your principles.
Pr 3:1 My child, never forget the things I have **t** you.
31:1 of King Lemuel, an oracle that his mother **t** him.
Ecc 12:9 was wise, he **t** the people everything he knew.
12:10 Indeed, the Teacher **t** the plain truth, and he did
Jer 7:28 obey the LORD their God and who refuse to be **t**.
9:14 the images of Baal, as their ancestors **t** them.
12:16 'As surely as the LORD lives' (just as they **t** my
29:32 for my people, for he has **t** you to rebel against me.
32:33 year after year, I **t** them right from wrong,
Eze 19:5 another of her cubs / and **t** him to be a strong lion.
Hos 11:3 It was I who **t** Israel how to walk, leading him
Na 3:4 She **t** them all to worship her false gods,
Mt 5:2 This is what he **t** them:
7:12 This is a summary of all that is **t** in the law
7:29 for he **t** as one who had real authority—
13:2 he sat and **t** as the people listened on the shore.
13:54 When he **t** there in the synagogue, everyone was
21:16 'You have **t** children and infants to give you
Mk 1:21 day he went into the synagogue and **t** the people.
1:22 for he **t** as one who had real authority—
2:13 and **t** the crowds that gathered around him.
4:34 in his public teaching he **t** only with parables,
6:30 and told him all they had done and what they had **t**.
6:34 without a shepherd. So he **t** them many things.
10:1 there were the crowds, and as usual he **t** them.
11:17 He **t** them, "The Scriptures declare, 'My Temple
12:38 Here are some of the other things he **t** them at this
Lk 1:4 to reassure you of the truth of all you were **t**.
4:15 He **t** in their synagogues and was praised by
4:31 and **t** there in the synagogue every Sabbath day.
5:3 So he sat in the boat and **t** the crowds from there.
10:39 Mary, sat at the Lord's feet, listening to what he **t**.
11:1 teach us to pray, just as John **t** his disciples."
13:26 and drank with you, and you **t** in our streets.'
19:47 After that, he **t** daily in the Temple, but the leading
Jn 6:45 in the Scriptures, 'They will all be **t** by God.'
8:2 crowd soon gathered, and he sat down and **t** them.
8:28 on my own, but I speak what the Father **t** me.
Ac 7:22 Moses was **t** all the wisdom of the Egyptians,
15:1 ancient Jewish custom of circumcision **t** by Moses,
18:25 He had been **t** the way of the Lord and talked to
28:23 and **t** them about Jesus from the Scriptures—
Ro 2:18 right from wrong because you have been **t** his law.
16:17 things that are contrary to what you have been **t**.
Gal 1:12 from Jesus Christ himself. No one else **t** me.
6:6 Those who are **t** the word of God should help their
Eph 4:20 But that isn't what you were **t** when you learned
Col 2:7 strong and vigorous in the truth you were **t**.
1Th 4:1 to live in a way that pleases God, as we have **t** you.
4:2 For you remember what we **t** you in the name of
4:9 For God himself has **t** you to love one another.
2Th 2:15 and keep a strong grip on everything we **t** you both
2Ti 3:14 must remain faithful to the things you have been **t**.
3:14 for you know you can trust those who **t** you.
3:15 You have been **t** the holy Scriptures from
Tit 1:9 belief in the trustworthy message he was **t**;
Heb 13:7 Remember your leaders who first **t** you the word of
1Jn 2:24 to what you have been **t** from the beginning.
2:27 So continue in what he has **t** you, and continue to
Rev 2:14 He **t** them to worship idols by eating food offered

TAUNT (12) [TAUNTED, TAUNTING, TAUNTS]

Dt 32:27 But I feared the **t** of the enemy, / that their
1Sa 1:7 Peninnah would **t** Hannah as they went to the
Job 17:2 by mockers. I watch how bitterly they **t** me.
30:9 sons mock me with their vulgar song! They **t** me!
Ps 42:3 while my enemies continually **t** me, saying,
102:8 My enemies **t** me day after day. / They mock
119:42 Then I will have an answer for those who **t** me,
Isa 14:4 you will **t** the king of Babylon. You will say,
Jer 38:22 Then the women will **t** you, saying, 'What fine
Eze 36:13 Now the other nations **t** you, saying, 'Israel is a
Hos 9:7 So they **t**, for the nation is burdened with sin
Hab 2:6 time is coming when all their captives will **t** them,

TAUNTED (9) [TAUNT]

Ge 37:8 are going to be our king, are you?" his brothers **t**.
Jdg 8:15 you **t** me, saying, 'You haven't caught Zebah
1Sa 26:15 Abner, you're a great man, aren't you?" David **t**.
2Sa 5:6 "You'll never get in here," the Jebusites **t**.
21:21 defied and **t** Israel. But he was killed by Jonathan,
1Ch 20:7 defied and **t** Israel. But he was killed by Jonathan,
Jer 24:9 They will be disgraced and mocked, **t** and cursed,
Eze 36:2 Your enemies have **t** you, saying, 'Aha!
Mic 7:10 They will be ashamed that they **t** me, saying,

TAUNTING (1) [TAUNT]

Eze 5:15 become an object of mockery and **t** and horror.

TAUNTS (4) [TAUNT]

Ps 42:10 Their **t** pierce me like a fatal wound. / They scoff,
44:16 All we hear are the **t** of our mockers. / All we see
55:12 It is not an enemy who **t** me— / I could bear that.
Zep 2:8 "I have heard the **t** of the people of Moab

TAVERNS (2)

Pr 23:30 It is the one who spends long hours in the **t**,
Ac 28:15 Others joined us at The Three **T**. When Paul saw

TAX (33) [TAX-COLLECTING, TAX-COLLECTION, TAXES]

Ex 38:26 It came from the **t** of one-fifth of an ounce of silver
Jdg 3:15 The Israelites sent Ehud to deliver their **t** money to
3:17 He brought the **t** money to Eglon, who was very
3:18 Ehud sent home those who had carried the **t**
2Ki 15:20 twenty ounces of silver in the form of a special **t**.
23:35 Jehoiakim collected a **t** from the people of Judah,
2Ch 24:6 levied this **t** on the community of Israel in order to
24:9 telling the people to bring to the LORD the **t** that
Ne 10:32 annual Temple **t** of an eighth of an ounce of silver,
Eze 45:13 "This is the **t** you must give to the prince:
Da 11:20 sent a **t** collector to maintain the royal splendor,
Mt 5:46 is that? Even corrupt **t** collectors do that much.
9:10 along with his fellow **t** collectors and many other
10:3 Thomas, / Matthew (the **t** collector),
17:24 the **t** collectors for the Temple **t** came to Peter
17:24 "Doesn't your teacher pay the Temple **t**?"
17:25 Do kings **t** their own people or the foreigners they
17:26 "They **t** the foreigners," Peter replied. "Well,
17:27 a coin. Take the coin and pay the **t** for both of us."
18:17 treat that person as a pagan or a corrupt **t** collector.
21:31 corrupt **t** collectors and prostitutes will get into the
21:32 believe him, while **t** collectors and prostitutes did.
22:19 Here, show me the Roman coin used for the **t**."
Mk 2:15 along with his fellow **t** collectors and many other
Lk 3:12 Even corrupt **t** collectors came to be baptized
5:27 he saw a **t** collector named Levi sitting at his
5:29 Many of Levi's fellow **t** collectors and other guests
7:29 all the people, including the unjust **t** collectors,
15:1 **T** collectors and other notorious sinners often came
18:10 and the other was a dishonest **t** collector.
18:11 especially like that **t** collector over there!
18:13 "But the **t** collector stood at a distance and dared

TAX-COLLECTING (1) [COLLECT, TAX]

Lk 19:2 the most influential Jews in the Roman **t** business,

TAX-COLLECTION (3) [COLLECT, TAX]

Mt 9:9 the road, he saw Matthew sitting at his **t** booth.
Mk 2:14 he saw Levi son of Alphaeus sitting at his **t** booth.
Lk 5:27 he saw a tax collector named Levi sitting at his **t**

TAXES (16) [TAX]

1Sa 17:25 whole family will be exempted from paying **t**!"
1Ki 12:4 and heavy **t** that your father imposed on us.
2Ch 10:4 and heavy **t** that your father imposed on us.
24:6 and collect the Temple **t** from the towns of Judah
Ezr 6:8 without delay from my **t** collected in your province
7:24 of God will be required to pay **t** of any kind.'
Ne 5:4 the limit on our fields and vineyards to pay our **t**.
Am 5:11 and steal what little they have through **t** and unfair
Mt 22:17 Is it right to pay **t** to the Roman government
Mk 12:14 is it right to pay **t** to the Roman government
Lk 3:13 "Make sure you collect no more **t** than the Roman
19:8 Lord, and if I have overcharged people on their **t**,
20:22 is it right to pay **t** to the Roman government
23:2 them not to pay their **t** to the Roman government
Ro 13:6 Pay your **t**, too, for these same reasons.
13:7 Pay your **t** and import duties, and give respect

TAXING [KJV] See CENSUS

TEACH (141) [TAUGHT, TEACHER, TEACHER'S, TEACHERS, TEACHES, TEACHING, TEACHINGS]

Ex 5:9 That will **t** them to listen to these liars!"
18:16 and **t** them his laws and instructions."
18:20 **t** them God's laws and instructions,
24:12 Then you will **t** the people from them."
35:34 tribe of Dan, the ability to **t** their skills to others.
Lev 10:11 And you must **t** the Israelites all the laws that the
Dt 4:1 these laws and regulations that I am about to **t** you.
4:10 and they will be able to **t** my laws to their
5:31 You will **t** them to the people so they can obey
6:1 that the LORD your God told me to **t** you
8:3 He did it to **t** you that people need more than bread
11:19 **T** them to your children. Talk about them when
14:23 The purpose of tithing is to **t** you always to fear the
31:19 words of this song, and **t** it to the people of Israel.
31:19 **T** them to sing it, so it may serve as a witness
33:10 Now let them **t** your regulations to Jacob;
Jdg 3:2 He did this to **t** warfare to generations of Israelites
1Sa 12:23 And I will continue to **t** you what is good
14:12 "Come on up here, and we'll **t** you a lesson!"
1Ki 8:36 **T** them to do what is right, and send rain on your
2Ki 17:27 Let him **t** the new residents the religious customs
1Ch 27:32 Jehiel the Hacmonite was responsible to **t** the
2Ch 6:27 **T** them to do what is right, and send rain on your
15:3 without a priest to **t** them, and without God's law.
17:7 Jehoshaphat sent out his officials to **t** in all the
Ezr 7:10 and obey the law of the LORD and to **t** those laws
7:25 are not familiar with those laws, you must **t** them.
Job 8:10 But those who came before us will **t** you. They will **t** you from the wisdom of former
12:7 "Ask the animals, and they will **t** you.
21:22 "But who can **t** a lesson to God, the supreme
27:11 "I will **t** you about God's power. I will not conceal
33:33 listen to me. Keep silent and I will **t** you wisdom!"
37:19 so much, so **t** the rest of us what to say to God.
Ps 25:5 Lead me by your truth and **t** me, / for you are the
27:11 **T** me how to live, O LORD. / Lead me along the
34:11 listen to me, / and I will **t** you to fear the LORD.
51:6 so you can **t** me to be wise in my inmost being.
51:13 Then I will **t** your ways to sinners, / and they will
78:2 I will **t** you hidden lessons from our past—
78:5 our ancestors / to **t** them to their children,
78:6 yet born— / that they in turn might **t** their children.
86:11 **T** me your ways, O LORD, / that I may live
90:12 **T** us to make the most of our time, / so that we
94:12 LORD, / and those whom you **t** from your law.
105:22 aides as he pleased / and **t** the king's advisers.
119:12 Blessed are you, O LORD; / **t** me your principles.
119:26 and you answered. / Now **t** me your principles.
119:33 **T** me, O LORD, / to follow every one of your
119:64 full of your unfailing love; / **t** me your principles.
119:66 now **t** me good judgment and knowledge.
119:68 are good and do only good; / **t** me your principles.
119:108 accept my grateful thanks / and **t** me your laws.
119:124 me in unfailing love, / and **t** me your principles.
119:135 down on me with love; / **t** me all your principles.
132:12 and follow the decrees that I **t** them, / then your
143:10 **T** me to do your will, / for you are my God.
Pr 1:2 The purpose of these proverbs is to **t** people
4:11 I will **t** you wisdom's ways and lead you in straight
9:9 **T** the wise, and they will be wiser. **T** the righteous, and they will learn more.
22:6 **T** your children to choose the right path, and when
SS 8:2 to my childhood home, and there you would **t** me.
Isa 2:3 There he will **t** us his ways, so that we may obey
30:20 for drink, he will still be with you to **t** you.
54:13 I will **t** all your citizens, and their prosperity will
Jer 9:20 **T** your daughters to wail; **t** one another how to lament.
18:18 We don't need him to **t** the law and give us advice
31:34 And they will not need to **t** their neighbors,
31:34 nor will they need to **t** their family, saying,
Eze 22:26 And they do not **t** my people the difference
44:23 They will **t** my people the difference between what
Da 1:4 **T** these young men the language and literature of
Mic 3:11 can get; you priests **t** God's laws only for a price;
4:2 There he will **t** us his ways, so that we may obey
6:5 did everything I could to **t** you about my
Mt 5:1 with his disciples and sat down to **t** them.
5:19 and **t** others to do the same,
11:29 Let me **t** you, because I am humble and gentle,
22:16 You **t** about the way of God regardless of the
23:3 their example. For they don't practice what they **t**.
28:20 **T** these new disciples to obey all the commands I
Mk 4:2 He began to **t** the people by telling many stories
4:33 and illustrations to **t** the people as much as they
9:31 to spend more time with his disciples and **t** them.
12:14 You sincerely **t** the ways of God. Now tell us—
Lk 11:1 to him as he finished and said, "Lord, **t** us to pray,
12:12 for the Holy Spirit will **t** you what needs to be said
15:1 notorious sinners often came to listen to Jesus **t**.
20:21 we know that you speak and **t** what is right and are
20:21 others think. You sincerely **t** the ways of God.
21:37 Every day Jesus went to the Temple to **t**, and each
Jn 3:2 "we all know that God has sent you to **t** us.
7:14 Jesus went up to the Temple and began to **t**.
9:34 in sin!" they answered. "Are you trying to **t** us?"
14:26 he will **t** you everything and will remind you of
18:20 Jesus replied, "What I **t** is widely known,
18:20 and I **t** nothing in private that I have not said in
Ac 1:1 told you about everything Jesus began to do and **t**
4:18 told them never again to speak or **t** about Jesus.
5:28 "Didn't we tell you never again to **t** in this man's
5:42 they continued to **t** and preach this message:
15:1 from Judea arrived and began to **t** the Christians:
21:21 They say that you **t** people not to circumcise their
26:22 I **t** nothing except what the prophets and Moses
Ro 2:20 the ignorant and **t** children the ways of God.
2:21 Well then, if you **t** others, why don't you **t** yourself?
15:4 were written in the Scriptures long ago to **t** us.
15:14 so well that you are able to **t** others all about them.
1Co 4:15 For even if you had ten thousand others to **t** you
4:17 He will remind you of what I **t** about Christ Jesus
14:26 When you meet, one will sing, another will **t**,
2Co 10:5 rebellious ideas, and we **t** them to obey Christ.
Col 1:28 and **t** them with all the wisdom God has given us,
3:16 Use his words to **t** and counsel each other.
1Ti 2:7 and apostle to **t** the Gentiles about faith and truth.
2:12 I do not let women **t** men or have authority over
3:2 having guests in his home and must be able to **t**.
4:11 **T** these things and insist that everyone learn them.
4:12 Be an example to all believers in what you **t**,
6:2 **T** these truths, Timothy, and encourage everyone
2Ti 2:2 You have heard me **t** many things that have been
2:2 **T** these great truths to trustworthy people who are
2:24 They must be able to **t** effectively and be patient
2:25 They should gently **t** those who oppose the truth.
3:10 But you know what I **t**, Timothy, and how I live,
3:16 is inspired by God and is useful to **t** us what is true

Tit 1: 1 and to t them to know the truth that shows them
2: 2 T the older men to exercise self-control, to be
2: 3 t the older women to live in a way that is
2: 3 Instead, they should t others what is good.
2:15 You must t these things and encourage your people
Heb 5:12 you need someone to t you again the basic things a
8:11 And they will not need to t their neighbors,
8:11 nor will they need to t their family,
Jas 3: 1 for we who t will be judged by God with greater
2Pe 2: 1 They will cleverly t their destructive heresies about
1Jn 2:27 so you don't need anyone to t you what is true.
2Jn 1:10 your meeting and does not t the truth about Christ,

TEACHER (78) [TEACH]

1Ch 25: 8 to whether they were young or old, t or student.
Ezr 7:12 the priest, the t of the law of the God of heaven.
7:21 he is a priest and t of the law of the God of heaven.
Job 36:22 "Look, God is all-powerful. Who is a t like him?
Ecc 1: 1 These are the words of the T, King David's son,
1: 2 says the T, "utterly meaningless!"
1:12 I, the T, was king of Israel, and I lived in
7:27 "This is my conclusion," says the T. "I came to
12: 8 "All is meaningless," says the T,
12: 9 Because the T was wise, he taught the people
12:10 Indeed, the T taught the plain truth, and he did
Isa 28:29 The LORD Almighty is a wonderful t, and he
30:20 teach you. You will see your t with your own eyes,
40:13 Who knows enough to be his t or counselor?
Mt 8:19 "T, I will follow you no matter where you go!"
9:11 "Why does your t eat with such scum?"
10:24 "A student is not greater than the t. A servant is
12:38 and Pharisees came to Jesus and said, "T,
13:52 "Every t of religious law who has become a
17:24 asked him, "Doesn't your t pay the Temple tax?"
19:16 "T, what good things must I do to have eternal
22:16 this question: "T, we know how honest you are.
22:24 "T, Moses said, 'If a man dies without children,
22:36 "T, which is the most important commandment in
23: 8 anyone call you 'Rabbi,' for you have only one t,
26:18 Tell him, 'The T says, My time has come, and I
26:25 also asked, "T, I'm not the one, am I?"
26:49 "Greetings, T!" he exclaimed and gave him the
Mk 4:38 Frantically they woke him up, shouting, "T,
5:35 is dead. There's no use troubling the T now."
9: 5 "T, this is wonderful!" Peter exclaimed. "We will
9:17 of the men in the crowd spoke up and said, "T,
9:38 John said to Jesus, "T, we saw a man using your
10:17 up to Jesus, knelt down, and asked, "Good T,
10:20 "T," the man replied, "I've obeyed all these
10:35 "T," they said, "we want you to do us a favor."
10:51 "T," the blind man said, "I want to see!"
11:21 tree on the previous day and exclaimed, "Look, T!
12:14 "T," these men said, "we know how honest you
12:19 "T, Moses gave us a law that if a man dies,
12:32 The t of religious law replied, "Well said, T.
13: 1 one of his disciples said, "T, look at these
14:14 the house he enters, say to the owner, 'The T asks,
14:45 "T!" he exclaimed, and gave him the kiss.
Lk 3:12 tax collectors came to be baptized and asked, "T,
6:40 A student is not greater than the t. But the student
who works hard will become like the t.
7:40 "All right, T," Simon replied, "go ahead."
8:49 girl is dead. There's no use troubling the T now."
9:38 to him, "T, look at my boy, who is my only son.
10:25 "T, what must I do to receive eternal life?"
11:45 "T," said an expert in religious law, "you have
12:13 Then someone called from the crowd, "T,
18:18 "Good t, what should I do to get eternal life?"
19:39 some of the Pharisees among the crowd said, "T,
20:21 They said, "T, we know that you speak and teach
20:28 "T, Moses gave us a law that if a man dies,
20:39 "Well said, T!" remarked some of the teachers of
21: 7 "T," they asked, "when will all this take place?
22:11 say to the owner, 'The T asks, Where is the guest
24:19 He was a mighty t, highly regarded by both God
Jn 1:38 They replied, "Rabbi" (which means T),
1:49 Nathanael replied, "T, you are the Son of God—
3: 2 "T," he said, "we all know that God has sent you
3:10 Jesus replied, "You are a respected Jewish t,
3:26 John's disciples came to him and said, "T,
6:25 When they arrived and found him, they asked, "T,
8: 4 "T," they said to Jesus, "this woman was caught
9: 2 "T," his disciples asked him, "why was this man
11: 8 "T," they said, "only a few days ago the Jewish
11:28 told her, "The T is here and wants to see you."
13:13 You call me 'T' and 'Lord,' and you are right,
13:14 And since I, the Lord and T, have washed your
20:16 She turned toward him and exclaimed, "T!"
Ro 12: 7 them well. If you are a t, do a good job of teaching.
Gal 3:24 our guardian and t to lead us until Christ came.
2Ti 1:11 a preacher, an apostle, and a t of this Good News.

TEACHER'S (2) [TEACH]

Ecc 12:11 A wise t words spur students to action
Mt 10:25 The student shares the t fate. The servant shares

TEACHERS (88) [TEACH]

2Ch 35: 3 set apart to serve the LORD and were t in Israel:
Ps 119:99 Yes, I have more insight than my t, / for I am
Pr 5:13 Oh, why didn't I listen to my t? Why didn't I pay
Jer 8: 8 when your t have twisted it so badly?
8: 9 These wise t will be shamed by exile for their sin,
Da 11:33 But for a time many of these t will die by fire
Mt 2: 4 of the leading priests and t of religious law.
5:20 unless you obey God better than the t of religious
7:29 real authority—quite unlike the t of religious law.
8:19 Then one of the t of religious law said to him,
9: 3 some of the t of religious law said among
12:38 One day some t of religious law and Pharisees
15: 1 and t of religious law now arrived from Jerusalem
16:21 and the leading priests and the t of religious law.
17:10 "Why do the t of religious law insist that Elijah
20:18 to the leading priests and the t of religious law.
21:15 and the t of religious law saw these wonderful
23: 2 "The t of religious law and the Pharisees are the
23:13 "How terrible it will be for you t of religious law
23:15 how terrible it will be for you t of religious law
23:23 "How terrible it will be for you t of religious law
23:25 "How terrible it will be for you t of religious law
23:27 "How terrible it will be for you t of religious law
23:29 "How terrible it will be for you t of religious law
23:34 you prophets and wise men and t of religious law.
26:57 where the t of religious law and other leaders had
27:41 The leading priests, the t of religious law,
Mk 1:22 real authority—quite unlike the t of religious law.
2: 6 But some of the t of religious law who were sitting
2:16 But when some of the t of religious law who were
3:22 But the t of religious law who had arrived from
7: 1 and t of religious law arrived from Jerusalem to
7: 5 So the Pharisees and t of religious law asked him,
8:31 the leading priests, and the t of religious law.
9:11 "Why do the t of religious law insist that Elijah
9:14 as some t of religious law were arguing with them.
10:33 to the leading priests and the t of religious law.
11:18 and t of religious law heard what Jesus had done,
11:27 the leading priests, the t of religious law,
12:28 One of the t of religious law was standing there
12:35 "Why do the t of religious law claim that the
12:38 "Beware of these t of religious law! For they love
14: 1 and the t of religious law were still looking for an
14:43 the t of religious law, and the other leaders.
14:53 other leaders, and t of religious law had gathered.
15: 1 other leaders, and t of religious law—
15:31 and t of religious law also mocked Jesus.
Lk 2:46 was in the Temple, sitting among the religious t,
5:17 and t of religious law were sitting nearby.
5:21 and t of religious law said to each other.
5:30 and their t of religious law complained bitterly to
6: 7 The t of religious law and the Pharisees watched
9:22 the leading priests, and the t of religious law.
11:53 the Pharisees and t of religious law were furious.
15: 2 and t of religious law complain that he was
19:47 but the leading priests, the t of religious law,
20: 1 the leading priests and t of religious law and other
20:19 When the t of religious law and the leading priests
20:39 remarked some of the t of religious law who were
20:46 "Beware of these t of religious law! For they love
22: 2 and t of religious law were actively plotting Jesus'
22:66 the leading priests and the t of religious law.
23:10 and the t of religious law stood there shouting their
Jn 8: 3 the t of religious law and Pharisees brought a
Ac 4: 5 and elders and t of religious law met in Jerusalem.
6:12 the crowds, the elders, and the t of religious law.
13: 1 and t of the church at Antioch of Syria were
20:29 I know full well that false t, like vicious wolves,
23: 9 Some of the t of religious law who were Pharisees
1Co 12:28 are apostles, / second are prophets, / third are t,
12:29 course not. Is everyone a prophet? No. Are all t?
Gal 4:17 Those false t who are so anxious to win your favor
6: 6 word of God should help their t by paying them.
Eph 4:11 the prophets, the evangelists, and the pastors and t.
1Ti 1: 6 But some t have missed this whole point.
1: 7 They want to be known as t of the law of Moses,
4: 2 These t are hypocrites and liars. They pretend to be
6: 3 Some false t may deny these things, but these are
2Ti 3: 8 And these t fight the truth just as Jannes
4: 3 and will look for t who will tell them whatever
Tit 1:11 away from the truth. Such t only want your money.
Jas 3: 1 not many of you should become t in the church,
2Pe 2: 1 in Israel, just as there will be false t among you.
2:11 far greater in power and strength than these false t,
2:12 These false t are like unthinking animals,
3Jn 1: 5 care of the traveling t who are passing through,
1:10 He not only refuses to welcome the traveling t,
Jude 1: 8 Yet these false t, who claim authority from their

TEACHES (9) [TEACH]

Pr 1: 8 Listen, my child, to what your father t you.
15:33 Fear of the LORD t a person to be wise;
Isa 48:17 who t you what is good and leads you along the
Mt 5:19 and t them will be great in the Kingdom of
Ac 21:28 This is the man who t against our people and tells
1Ti 6: 4 Anyone who t anything different is both conceited
2Ti 3:16 It straightens us out and t us to do what is right.
1Jn 2:27 For the Spirit t you all things, and what he t is
true—

TEACHING (101) [TEACH]

Dt 20:18 This will keep the people of the land from t you
32: 2 My t will fall on you like rain; / my speech will
2Ch 17: 9 through all the towns of Judah, t the people.
Job 11: 4 You claim, 'My t is pure,' and 'I am clean in the
Ps 25: 9 leads the humble in what is right, / t them his way.
60: T A psalm of David useful for t, regarding the time
78: 1 O my people, listen to my t. / Open your ears to
Pr 1: 8 father teaches you. Don't neglect your mother's t.
4: 2 you good guidance. Don't turn away from my t.
6:20 and don't neglect your mother's t.
6:23 and this t are a lamp to light the way ahead of you.
6:24 and this t will keep you from the immoral woman,
22:19 I am t you today—yes, you—so you will trust in
Isa 2: 3 For in those days the LORD's t and his word will
Eze 7:26 They will receive no t from the priests and no
Mic 4: 2 For in those days the LORD's t and his word will
Mt 4:23 Jesus traveled throughout Galilee t in the
7:24 "Anyone who listens to my t and obeys me is
7:26 But anyone who hears my t and ignores it is
7:28 the crowds were amazed at his t,
9:35 t in the synagogues and announcing the Good
11: 1 he went off t and preaching in towns throughout
13:12 To those who are open to my t,
16:12 or bread but about the false t of the Pharisees
21:23 When Jesus returned to the Temple and began t,
22:33 crowds heard him, they were impressed with his t.
26:55 arrest me in the Temple? I was there t every day.
Mk 1:22 They were amazed at his t, for he taught as one
1:27 "What sort of new t is this?" they asked excitedly.
3:31 and brothers arrived at the house where he was t.
4: 1 Once again Jesus began t by the lakeshore.
4:25 To those who are open to my t,
4:34 In fact, in his public t he taught only with parables,
6: 2 The next Sabbath he began t in the synagogue,
6: 6 Then Jesus went out from village to village, t.
11:18 the people were so enthusiastic about Jesus' t.
12:35 Later, as Jesus was t the people in the Temple,
14:49 arrest me in the Temple? I was there t every day.
Lk 5:17 One day while Jesus was t, some Pharisees
6: 6 right hand was in the synagogue while Jesus was t.
6:47 comes to me, listens to my t, and then obeys me.
8:18 To those who are open to my t,
9:11 t them about the Kingdom of God and curing those
11: 5 Then, t them more about prayer, he used this
13:10 One Sabbath day as Jesus was t in a synagogue,
13:22 went through the towns and villages, t as he went,
20: 1 One day as Jesus was t and preaching the Good
Jn 6:59 He said these things while he was t in the
7:16 So Jesus told them, "I'm not t my own ideas,
7:17 will of God will know whether my t is from God
7:28 While Jesus was t in the Temple, he called out,
8:20 Jesus made these statements while he was t in the
8:51 anyone who obeys my t will never die!"
8:52 but you say that those who obey your t will never
17:17 them pure and holy by t them your words of truth.
18:19 about his followers and what he had been t them.
Ac 2:42 and devoted themselves to the apostles' t
5:21 Temple about daybreak and immediately began t.
5:25 had jailed were out in the Temple, t the people.
5:28 you have filled all Jerusalem with your t about
5:38 If they are t and doing these things merely on their
6: 2 spend our time preaching and t the word of God,
6: 4 our time in prayer and preaching and t the word."
11:26 church for a full year, t great numbers of people.
15:24 here have troubled you and upset you with their t,
15:35 stayed in Antioch to assist many others who were t
16:21 "They are t the people to do things that are against
17:11 and Silas, to see if they were really t the truth.
18:11 for the next year and a half, t the word of God.
21:21 t all the Jews living in the Gentile world to turn
28:31 with all boldness and t about the Lord Jesus Christ.
Ro 6:17 with all your heart the new t God has given you.
12: 7 them well. If you are a teacher, do a good job of t.
16:17 and upset people's faith by t things that are
1Co 11: 2 and you are following the Christian t I passed on to
14: 6 special knowledge or some prophecy or some t—
Gal 6:12 They don't want to be persecuted for t that the
Col 2:22 Such rules are mere human t about things that are
1Ti 1: 3 and stop those who are t wrong doctrine.
1:10 who do anything else that contradicts the right t
4: 6 message of faith and the true t you have followed.
4:13 the church, encouraging the believers, and t them.
4:16 Keep a close watch on yourself and on your t.
5:17 those who work hard at both preaching and t.
6: 1 that the name of God and his t will not be shamed.
2Ti 1:13 Hold on to the pattern of right t you learned from
4: 2 rebuke, and encourage your people with good t.
4: 3 when people will no longer listen to right t.
Tit 1: 9 he will be able to encourage others with right t
1:10 For there are many who rebel against right t;
1:11 By their wrong t, they have already turned whole
2: 1 promote the kind of living that reflects right t.
2: 7 do reflect the integrity and seriousness of your t.
2: 8 Let your t be so correct that it can't be criticized.
2:10 Then they will make the t about God our Savior
Heb 5:12 a long time now, and you ought to be t others.
2Pe 2: 2 Many will follow their evil t and shameful
2Jn 1: 9 For if you wander beyond the t of Christ, you will
1: 9 But if you continue in the t of Christ, you will have
Rev 2:15 people who follow the same t and commit the
2:24 who have not followed this false t ('deeper truths,'

TEACHINGS (11) [TEACH]

Ex 24: 3 When Moses had announced to the people all the t
Pr 7: 2 Guard my t as your most precious possession.
Mt 11:13 all the t of the Scriptures looked forward to this
13:52 out of the storehouse the new t as well as the old."
15: 9 God's commands with their own man-made t.' "
Mk 7: 7 God's commands with their own man-made t.'
Jn 5:36 greater witness than John—my t and my miracles.
8:31 are truly my disciples if you keep obeying my t.
1Ti 4: 1 follow lying spirits and t that come from demons.
6: 3 the sound, wholesome t of the Lord Jesus Christ,
2Ti 3: 7 Such women are forever following new t, but they

TEAM (5) [TEAMMATE, TEAMS]

1Ki 19:19 son of Shaphat plowing a field with a t of oxen.
19:19 of him, and he was plowing with the twelfth t.
Ac 19:13 A t of Jews who were traveling from town to town

1Co 3: 8 and the one who waters work as a t with the same
2Co 6:14 Don't t up with those who are unbelievers.

TEAMMATE (1) [TEAM]

Php 4: 3 And I ask you, my true t, to help these women,

TEAMS (3) [TEAM]

1Ki 19:19 There were eleven t of oxen ahead of him, and he
Job 1: 3 three thousand camels, five hundred t of oxen,
42:12 six thousand camels, one thousand t of oxen,

TEAR (57) [TEARING, TEARS, TORE, TORN]

Ex 28:32 be reinforced by a woven collar so it will not t.
39:23 reinforced with a woven collar, so it would not t.
Lev 1:17 the priest will t the bird apart, though not
13:45 any contagious skin disease must t their clothing
21:10 must never let his hair hang loose or t his clothing.
Dt 33:20 poised there like a lion / to t off an arm or a head.
Jdg 8: 7 I will return and t your flesh with the thorns
8: 9 I return in victory, I will t down this tower."
2Sa 3:31 with him, "T your clothes and put on sackcloth.
23: 6 for they t the hand that touches them.
1Ki 11:11 I will surely t the kingdom away from you
11:31 'I am about to t the kingdom from the hand of
2Ki 18:22 Didn't Hezekiah t down his shrines and altars
Job 18: 4 You may t your hair out in anger, but will that
28: 9 People know how to t apart flinty rocks
41:30 They t up the ground as it drags through the mud.
Ps 17:12 They are like hungry lions, eager to t me apart—
28: 5 So he will t them down like old buildings,
50:22 all of you who ignore me, / or I will t you apart,
124: 6 the LORD, / who did not let their teeth t us apart!
Ecc 3: 3 to heal. / A time to t down and a time to rebuild.
3: 7 A time to t and a time to mend. / A time to be quiet
Isa 5: 5 I will t down its fences / and let it be destroyed.
18: 6 to eat. The vultures will t at corpses all summer.
22:10 and t some down to get stone to fix the walls.
29:21 and tell lies to t down the innocent will be no
36: 7 Didn't Hezekiah t down his shrines and altars
41:15 You will t all your enemies apart, making chaff of
Jer 1:10 You are to uproot some and t them down,
22: 7 They will t out all your fine cedar beams
24: 6 I will build them up and not t them down. I will
42:10 If you do, I will build you up and not t you down;
48:18 too. They will t down all your towers.
Eze 13:20 I will t them from your arms, setting my people
13:21 I will t off the magic veils and save my people
22:27 leaders are like wolves, who t apart their victims.
26: 4 destroy the walls of Tyre and t down its towers.
28:24 neighbors prick and t at her like thorns and briers.
Hos 5:14 I will t at Israel and Judah as a lion rips apart its
13: 8 I will t you apart and devour you like a hungry
Joel 2:13 Don't t your clothing in your grief; instead, t your
hearts."
Mic 3: 2 skin my people alive and t the flesh off their bones.
5:11 I will t down your walls and demolish the defenses
Zec 11:16 the meat of the fattest sheep and t off their hooves.
Mt 7:15 but are really wolves that will t you apart.
24:51 He will t the servant apart and banish him with the
Lk 5: 6 this time their nets were so full they began to t!
12:18 I'll t down my barns and build bigger ones.
12:46 He will t the servant apart and banish him with the
16: 6 'T up that bill and write another one for four
Jn 19:24 "Let's not t it but throw dice to see who gets it."
Ac 23:10 the commander, fearing they would t him apart,
Ro 14:20 Don't t apart the work of God over what you eat.
2Co 10: 8 this authority is to build you up, not to t you down.
13:10 has given me to build you up, not to t you down.
2Th 2: 4 and t down every object of adoration and worship.

TEARING (4) [TEAR]

Lev 10: 6 by letting your hair hang loose or by t your clothes.
2Sa 21:10 She prevented vultures from t at their bodies
Ps 7: 2 a lion, / t me to pieces with no one to rescue me.
Jer 5: 6 their towns, t apart any who dare to venture out.

TEARS (55) [TEAR]

Ge 21:16 to watch the boy die," she said, as she burst into t.
29:11 Then Jacob kissed Rachel, and t came to his eyes.
33: 4 and kissed him. Both of them were in t.
Jdg 14:16 So Samson's wife came to him in t and said,
1Sa 1: 7 Hannah would finally be reduced to t and would
11: 4 people about their plight, everyone broke into t.
20:41 Both of them were in t as they embraced each
2Sa 18:33 up to his room over the gateway and burst into t.
2Ki 20: 5 says: I have heard your prayer and seen your t.
Est 8: 3 and begging him with t to stop Haman's evil plot
Job 16: 9 God hates me and t angrily at my flesh.
16:20 My friends scorn me, but I pour out my t to God.
Ps 6: 6 out from sobbing. / Every night t drench my bed;
31: 9 My sight is blurred because of my t. / My body
39:12 Don't ignore my t. / For I am your guest—
42: 3 Day and night, I have only t for food, / while my
56: 8 You have collected all my t in your bottle.
80: 5 with sorrow / and made us drink t by the bucketful.
88: 9 My eyes are blinded by my t. / Each day I beg for
102: 9 instead of my food. / My t run down into my drink
116: 8 He has saved me from death, / my eyes from t,
119:136 Rivers of t gush from my eyes / because people
126: 5 Those who plant in t / will harvest with shouts of
Pr 11:11 it prosper, but the talk of the wicked t it apart.
14: 1 a foolish woman t hers down with her own hands.
Ecc 4: 1 I saw the t of the oppressed, with no one to
Isa 16: 9 My t will flow for Heshbon and Elealeh, for their
25: 8 The Sovereign LORD will wipe away all t.
38: 5 says: I have heard your prayer and seen your t.
Jer 9: 1 Oh, that my eyes were a fountain of t; I would
9:18 your weeping! Let the t flow from your eyes.
13:17 My eyes will overflow with t
14:17 to them: 'Night and day my eyes overflow with t.
31: 9 T of joy will stream down their faces, and I will
La 1: 2 sobs through the night; t stream down her cheeks.
1:16 all these things I weep; t flow down my cheeks.
2: 5 has brought unending sorrow and t to Jerusalem.
2:11 I have cried until the t no longer come. My heart is
2:18 O walls of Jerusalem! Let your t flow like a river.
3:48 Streams of t flow from my eyes because of the
3:49 My t flow down endlessly. They will not stop
5:17 are sick and weary, and our eyes grow dim with t.
Eze 24:16 show any sorrow. Do not weep; let there be no t.
Mal 2:13 You cover the LORD's altar with t, weeping
Lk 5:36 "No one t a piece of cloth from a new garment
7:38 Her t fell on his feet, and she wiped them off with
7:44 but she has washed them with her t and wiped
Ac 20:19 done the Lord's work humbly—yes, and with t.
20:31 over you night and day, and my many t for you.
Php 3:18 often before, and I say it again with t in my eyes,
2Ti 1: 4 see you again, for I remember your t as we parted.
Heb 5: 7 and pleadings, with a loud cry and t,
12:17 late for repentance, even though he wept bitter t.
Jas 4: 9 Let there be t for the wrong things you have done.
Rev 7:17 And God will wipe away all their t."

TEATS [KJV] See BREASTS, FONDLED

TEBAH (3)

Ge 22:24 Their names were T, Gaham, Tahash, and Maacah.
2Sa 8: 8 amount of bronze from Hadadezer's cities of T
1Ch 18: 8 amount of bronze from Hadadezer's cities of T

TEBALIAH (1)

1Ch 26:11 T (the third), and Zechariah (the fourth).

TECHNIQUES (4)

Ex 28:36 Using the t of an engraver, inscribe it with these
30:35 Using the usual t of the incense maker, refine it to
37:29 using the t of the most skilled incense maker.
39:30 Using the t of an engraver, they inscribed it with

TEDIOUS [KJV] See BORE

TEEMING (2)

Ps 104:25 vast and wide, / t with life of every kind,
Eze 31:18 will be the fate of Pharaoh and all his t hordes.

TEETH (34) [TOOTH]

Ge 49:12 darker than wine, / and his t are whiter than milk.
Job 16: 9 He gnashes his t at me and pierces me with his
19:20 and have escaped death by the skin of my t.
41:14 Who could pry open its jaws? For its t are terrible!
Ps 3: 7 enemies in the face! / Shatter the t of the wicked!
57: 4 whose t pierce like spears and arrows,
112:10 They will grind their t in anger; / they will slink
124: 6 the LORD, / who did not let their t tear us apart!
Pr 10:26 in the eyes or vinegar that sets the t on edge.
30:14 They devour the poor with t as sharp as swords
Ecc 12: 3 Your t will be too few to do their work, and you
12: 4 And when your t are gone, keep your lips tightly
SS 4: 2 Your t are as white as sheep, newly shorn
6: 6 Your t are white like freshly washed ewes,
7: 9 smooth and sweet, flowing gently over lips and t."
Isa 41:15 be a new threshing instrument with many sharp t.
La 2:16 They scoff and grind their t and say, "We have
3:16 He has made me grind my t on gravel. He has
Da 7: 5 and it had three ribs in its mouth between its t.
7: 7 and crushed its victims with huge iron t
7:19 It devoured and crushed its victims with iron t
Joel 1: 6 to count! Its t are as sharp as the t of lions!
Mt 8:12 where there will be weeping and gnashing of t."
13:42 There will be weeping and gnashing of t.
13:50 the fire. There will be weeping and gnashing of t.
22:13 where there is weeping and gnashing of t.'
24:51 that place there will be weeping and gnashing of t.
25:30 where there will be weeping and gnashing of t.'
Mk 9:18 at the mouth and grind his t and become rigid.
Lk 13:28 there will be great weeping and gnashing of t,
Rev 9: 8 a woman, and their t were like the t of a lion.
16:10 And his subjects ground their t in anguish,

TEHINNAH (2)

1Ch 4:12 Paseah, and T. T was the father of Ir-nahash.

TEIL [KJV] See TREE

TEKEL (2)

Da 5:25 that was written: MENE, MENE, T, PARSIN.
5:27 *T* means 'weighed'—you have been weighed on

TEKOA (12)

2Sa 14: 2 So he sent for a woman from T who had a
23:26 Helez from Pelon; / Ira son of Ikkesh from T;
1Ch 2:24 gave birth to a son named Ashhur (the father of T).
4: 5 Ashhur (the father of T) had two wives,
11:28 Ira son of Ikkesh from T; / Abiezer from Anathoth;
27: 9 Ira son of Ikkesh from T was commander of the
2Ch 11: 6 He built up Bethlehem, Etam, T,
20:20 army of Judah went out into the wilderness of T.
Ne 3: 5 Next were the people from T, though their leaders
3:27 Then came the people of T, who repaired another
Jer 6: 1 Flee from Jerusalem! Sound the alarm in T!
Am 1: 1 to Amos, a shepherd from the town of T in Judah.

TEL-ABIB (1)

Eze 3:15 Then I came to the colony of Judean exiles in T,

TEL-ASSAR (2)

2Ki 19:12 Rezeph, and the people of Eden who were in T?
Isa 37:12 Rezeph, and the people of Eden who were in T?

TEL-HARSHA (2) [HARSHA]

Ezr 2:59 towns of Tel-melah, T, Kerub, Addan, and Immer.
Ne 7:61 towns of Tel-melah, T, Kerub, Addan, and Immer.

TEL-MELAH (2)

Ezr 2:59 to Jerusalem at this time from the towns of T,
Ne 7:61 to Jerusalem at this time from the towns of T,

TELAH (1)

1Ch 7:25 line of descent was Rephah, Resheph, T, Tahan,

TELAIM (1)

1Sa 15: 4 So Saul mobilized his army at T. There were

TELEM (2)

Jos 15:24 Ziph, T, Bealoth,
Ezr 10:24 gatekeepers who were guilty: Shallum, T, and Uri.

TELL (644) [TELLING, TELLS, TOLD]

Ge 12:18 "Why didn't you t me she was your wife?
13: 9 I'll t you what we'll do. Take your choice of any
19: 9 and now you are trying to t us what to do!
19:14 So Lot rushed out to t his daughters' fiancés,
24:28 The young woman ran home to t her family about
24:33 "All right," Laban said, "t us your mission."
24:49 So t me—will you or won't you show true
24:49 When you t me, then I'll know what my next step
27: 8 Now, my son, do exactly as I t you.
27:13 "Just do what I t you. Go out and get the goats."
31:28 and grandchildren and t them good-bye?
37:20 We can t our father that a wild animal has eaten
40: 8 but there is no one here to t us what they mean."
40: 8 Joseph replied. "T me what you saw."
40:18 "I'll t you what it means," Joseph told him.
41:15 "and none of these men can t me what it means.
41:16 "But God will t you what it means and will set
41:24 but not one of them could t me what they mean."
42:22 "Didn't I t you not to do it?" Reuben asked.
43: 6 "Why did you ever t him you had another
45: 9 "Hurry, return to my father and t him, 'This is
45:13 T my father how I am honored here in Egypt.
45:13 T him about everything you have seen, and bring
45:17 "T your brothers to load their pack animals
45:18 T them to bring your father and all of their
45:18 T them, 'Pharaoh will assign to you the very best
45:19 And t your brothers to take wagons from Egypt to
46:31 and t Pharaoh that you have all come from the land
46:32 And I will t him, 'These men are shepherds
46:34 t him, 'We have been livestock breeders from our
46:34 When you t him this, he will let you live here in
49: 1 and I will t you what is going to happen to you in
50: 5 "T Pharaoh that my father made me swear an
Ex 3:13 "If I go to the people of Israel and t them,
3:13 What is his name?' Then what should I t them?"
3:14 Just t them, 'I AM has sent me to you.' "
3:15 God also said, "T them, 'The LORD, the God of
3:16 T them, 'The LORD, the God of your ancestors—
3:18 must go straight to the king of Egypt and t him,
4: 1 They won't do what I t them. They'll just say,
4:12 help you speak well, and I will t you what to say."
4:15 of you to speak clearly, and I will t you what to do.
4:22 Then you will t him, 'This is what the LORD
6:11 and t him to let the people of Israel leave Egypt."
7: 2 T Aaron everything I say to you and have him
7:19 "T Aaron to point his staff toward the waters of
8: 1 "Go to Pharaoh once again and t him, 'This is
8: 5 "T Aaron to point his shepherd's staff toward all
8: 9 "T me when you want me to pray for you,
8:16 "T Aaron to strike the dust with his staff.
9: 1 "T him, 'This is what the LORD, the God of the
9:13 Go to Pharaoh and t him, 'The LORD, the God of
10: 2 You will be able to t wonderful stories to your
10: 8 "But t me, just whom do you want to take along?"
11: 2 T all the Israelite men and women to ask their
12:21 "T each of your families to slaughter the lamb
13:14 Then you will t them, 'With mighty power the
14: 2 "T the people to march toward Pi-hahiroth
14:12 Didn't we t you to leave us alone while we were
14:15 you crying out to me? T the people to get moving!
16: 5 T them to pick up twice as much as usual on the
16:12 Now t them, 'In the evening you will have meat to
18:20 You should t them God's decisions, teach them
20:19 "You t us what God says, and we will listen.
25: 2 "T the people of Israel that everyone who wants to
27:20 "T the people of Israel to bring you pure olive oil
31:13 "T the people of Israel to keep my Sabbath day,
32: 2 "T your wives and sons and daughters to take off
33: 5 For the LORD had told Moses to t them,
33:12 me by name and t me I have found favor with you.
Lev 9: 3 Then t the Israelites to take a male goat for a sin
9: 4 Also t them to take a bull and a ram for a peace

9: 4 **T** them to present all these offerings to the LORD
21: 1 "**T** the priests to avoid making themselves
21:17 "**T** Aaron that in all future generations,
22: 2 "**T** Aaron and his sons to treat the sacred gifts that
23:34 "**T** the Israelites to begin the Festival of Shelters
24:14 and **t** all those who heard him to lay their hands on
Nu 8: 2 "**T** Aaron that when he sets up the seven lamps in
9: 2 "**T** the Israelites to celebrate the Passover at the
11:18 "And **t** the people to purify themselves,
11:18 **T** them, 'The LORD has heard your whining
14:14 They will **t** this to the inhabitants of this land,
14:28 Now **t** them this: 'As surely as I live, I will do to
16:24 "Then **t** all the people to get away from the tents
16:37 "**T** Eleazar son of Aaron the priest to pull all the
16:37 are holy. Also **t** him to scatter the burning incense
19: 2 **T** the people of Israel to bring you a red heifer that
22: 8 "In the morning I will **t** you whatever the LORD
22:20 But be sure to do only what I **t** you to do."
22:35 but you may say only what I **t** you to say."
23: 3 Then I will **t** you whatever he reveals to me."
23: 5 "Go back to Balak and **t** him what I told you."
23:26 "Didn't I **t** you that I must do whatever the
24:14 But first let me **t** you what the Israelites will do to
25:12 So **t** him that I am making my special covenant of
33:51 "Speak to the Israelites and **t** them: 'When you
Dt 1:42 '**T** them not to attack, for I will not go with them.
4:10 **T** them especially about the day when you stood
5:27 Then come and **t** us everything he tells you,
5:30 Go and **t** them to return to their tents.
6:21 Then you must **t** them, 'We were Pharaoh's slaves
18:18 I will **t** that prophet what to say, and he will **t** the
people everything I command
22:16 Her father must **t** them, 'I gave my daughter to this
32: 7 Inquire of your elders, and they will **t** you.
Jos 1:11 and **t** the people to get their provisions ready.
4: 3 **T** the men to take twelve stones from where the
4: 7 Then you can **t** them, 'They remind us that the
4:22 Then you can **t** them, 'This is where the Israelites
6:10 "Not a single word from any of you until I **t** you to
7:19 your confession and **t** me what you have done.
20: 2 "Now **t** the Israelites to designate the cities of
22:32 and returned to the land of Canaan to **t** the
Jdg 7: 3 Therefore, **t** the people, 'Whoever is timid
12: 6 they would **t** him to say "Shibboleth." If he was
13: 6 where he was from, and he didn't **t** me his name.
14: 6 But he didn't **t** his father or mother about it.
14: 9 But he didn't **t** them he had taken the honey from
14:12 Samson said to them, "Let me **t** you a riddle.
14:16 or mother," he replied. "Why should I **t** you?"
16: 6 "Please **t** me what makes you so strong and what
16:10 Now please **t** me how you can be tied up
16:13 Won't you please **t** me how you can be tied up
21:22 we will **t** them, 'Please be understanding.
Ru 3: 3 Now do as I **t** you—take a bath and put on perfume
3: 4 and lie down there. He will **t** you what to do."
1Sa 2:35 priest who will serve me and do what I **t** him to do.
3:15 He was afraid to **t** Eli what the LORD had said to
3:17 did the LORD say to you? **T** me everything.
6: 2 **T** us how to return it to its own land."
9: 6 find him. Perhaps he can **t** us which way to go."
9:18 "Can you please **t** me where the seer's house is?"
9:19 In the morning I will **t** you what you want to know
9:20 And I am here to **t** you that you and your family
10: 2 They will **t** you that the donkeys have been found
10:16 But Saul didn't **t** his uncle that Samuel had
12: 3 Now **t** me as I stand before the LORD and before
12: 3 **T** me and I will make right whatever I have done
14: 1 But Jonathan did not **t** his father what he was
14:34 Then go out among the troops and **t** them,
14:39 But no one would **t** him what the trouble was.
14:43 "**T** me what you have done," Saul demanded of
17:58 "**T** me about your father, my boy," Saul said.
18:25 "**T** David that all I want for the bride price is one
19: 3 Then I'll **t** you everything I can find out."
20: 3 so he has said to himself, 'I won't **t** Jonathan—
20: 4 "**T** me what I can do!" Jonathan exclaimed.
20: 6 **t** him I asked permission to go home to Bethlehem
20: 9 was planning to kill you, I would **t** you at once."
20:21 If you hear me **t** him, 'They're on this side,'
20:22 But if I **t** him, 'Go farther—the arrows are still
21: 2 "He told me not to **t** anyone why I am here.
22:17 was running away from me, but they didn't **t** me!"
22:22 I saw Doeg there that day, I knew he would **t** Saul.
23:11 O LORD, God of Israel, please **t** me."
25: 8 your own servants, and they will **t** you this is true.
25:19 But she didn't **t** her husband what she was doing.
25:36 so she didn't **t** him anything about her meeting
26: 1 from Ziph came back to Saul at Gibeah to **t** him,
26:11 But I'll **t** you what—we'll take his spear and his
27:11 to come to Gath and **t** where he had really been.
28:15 So I have called for you to **t** me what to do."
30:22 their wives and children, and **t** them to be gone."
2Sa 1: 4 "**T** me how the battle went." The man replied,
3:19 Then he went to Hebron to **t** David that all the
4: 9 saves me from my enemies, I will **t** you the truth.
7: 5 "Go and **t** my servant David, 'This is what the
10: 5 he sent messengers to **t** the men to stay at Jericho
11:21 Then **t** him, 'Uriah the Hittite was killed, too.' "
11:25 "Well, **t** Joab not to be discouraged," David said.
12: 1 So the LORD sent Nathan the prophet to **t** David
12:18 David's advisers were afraid to **t** him. "He was
12:18 "What will he do to himself when we **t** him the
12:27 Joab sent messengers to **t** David, "I have fought
13: 5 "Well," Jonadab said, "I'll **t** you what to do.
13: 5 for you. **T** him you'll feel better if she feeds you."
13:34 He ran to **t** the king, "I see a crowd of people
14: 3 and **t** him the story I am about to **t** you."

15: 2 they were from, and they would **t** him their tribe.
15:13 A messenger soon arrived in Jerusalem to **t** King
15:34 Return to Jerusalem and **t** Absalom, 'I will now be
15:35 **T** them the plans that are being made to capture
15:36 Jonathan to find me and **t** me what is going on."
18:21 from Cush, "Go **t** the king what you have seen."
19:13 And David told them to **t** Amasa, "Since you are
21: 3 **T** me so that the LORD will bless his people
21: 4 David asked. "Just **t** me and I will do it for you."
1Ki 11:38 If you listen to what I **t** you and follow my ways
12:10 "This is what you should **t** those complainers:
18: 1 to King Ahab. **T** him that I will soon send rain!"
18: 8 "Now go and **t** your master I am here."
18:11 you say, 'Go and **t** your master that Elijah is here'!
18:14 you say, 'Go and **t** your master that Elijah is here'!
18:16 So Obadiah went to **t** Ahab that Elijah had come,
18:44 Then Elijah shouted, "Hurry to Ahab and **t** him,
22:18 "Didn't I **t** you?" the king of Israel said to
2Ki 2:18 "Didn't I **t** you not to go?" he asked.
4: 2 "**T** me, what do you have in the house?"
4:12 "**T** the woman I want to speak to her."
4:13 "**T** her that we appreciate the kind concern she has
4:24 Don't slow down on my account unless I **t** you
4:28 a son. And didn't I **t** you not to raise my hopes?"
5:22 "but my master has sent me to **t** you that two
7: 9 let's go back and **t** the people at the palace."
8: 4 "**T** me some stories about the great things Elisha
8: 8 Then **t** him to ask the LORD if I will get well
8:10 Elisha replied, "Go and **t** him, 'You will recover.'
8:14 the king asked him, "What did Elisha **t** you?"
9:12 "You're lying," they said. "**T** us." So Jehu told
10: 5 are your servants and will do anything you **t** us.
18:23 "I'll **t** you what! My master, the king of Assyria,
20: 5 **T** him, 'This is what the LORD, the God of your
22:15 has spoken! Go and **t** the man who sent you,
22:18 Judah who sent you to seek the LORD and **t** him:
1Ch 16: 9 sing his praises. / **T** everyone about his miracles.
16:24 **T** everyone about the amazing things he does.
16:31 **T** all the nations that the LORD is king.
17: 4 "Go and **t** my servant David, 'This is what the
19: 5 he sent messengers to **t** the men to stay at Jericho
2Ch 10:10 "This is what you should **t** those complainers:
18:17 "Didn't I **t** you?" the king of Israel said to
34:23 has spoken! Go and **t** the man who sent you,
34:26 Judah who sent you to seek the LORD and **t** him:
Ezr 5:10 so that we could **t** you who the leaders were.
10: 4 for it is your duty to **t** us how to proceed in setting
Est 5: 5 and said, "**T** Haman to come quickly to a banquet,
5: 6 said to Esther, "Now **t** me what you really want.
7: 2 asked her, "**T** me what you want, Queen Esther.
9:12 It will be granted to you; **t** me and I will do it."
Job 1:15 I am the only one who escaped to **t** you."
1:16 I am the only one who escaped to **t** you."
1:17 I am the only one who escaped to **t** you."
1:19 are dead. I am the only one who escaped to **t** you."
6:24 I will keep quiet. **T** me, what have I done wrong?
10: 2 **t** me the charge you are bringing against me.
11: 5 if only he would **t** you what he thinks!
11: 6 If only he would **t** you the secrets of wisdom,
12: 7 Ask the birds of the sky, and they will **t** you.
13:23 **T** me, what have I done wrong? Show me my
21:28 You will **t** me of rich and wicked people who came
21:29 But I **t** you to ask those who have been around,
and they can **t** you the truth.
31:37 For I would **t** him exactly what I have done.
32: 6 I held back and did not dare to **t** you what I think.
32:13 And don't **t** me, 'He is too wise for us. Only God
34:32 evil I have done; **t** me, and I will stop at once'?
34:34 After all, bright people will **t** me, and wise people
36:23 No one can **t** him what to do. No one can say to
38: 4 of the earth? **T** me, if you know so much.
38:18 the extent of the earth? **T** me about it if you know!
Ps 5: 6 You will destroy those who **t** lies. / The LORD
5: 8 will conquer me. / **T** me clearly what to do,
9: 1 I will **t** of all the marvelous things you have done.
9:11 **T** the world about his unforgettable deeds.
19: 1 The heavens **t** of the glory of God. / The skies
24: 4 who do not worship idols / and never **t** lies.
30: 9 the grave? / Can it **t** the world of your faithfulness?
34: 3 Come, let us **t** of the LORD's greatness; / let us
35:28 Then I will **t** everyone of your justice
66: 2 of his name! / **T** the world how glorious he is.
66:16 fear God, / and I will **t** you what he did for me.
68:34 **T** everyone about God's power. / His majesty
71:15 I will **t** everyone about your righteousness.
71:16 I will **t** everyone that you alone are just and good.
71:24 I will **t** about your righteous deeds / all day long,
73:28 and I will **t** everyone about the wonderful things
74: 9 are gone; / no one can **t** us when it will end.
75: 1 People everywhere **t** of your mighty miracles.
78: 4 but will **t** the next generation about the glorious
78: 4 We will **t** of his power and the mighty miracles he
95:10 away from me. / They refuse to do what I **t** them.'
96: 3 **T** everyone about the amazing things he does.
96:10 **T** all the nations that the LORD is king.
102:19 **T** them the LORD looked down / from his
103: 1 Praise the LORD, I **t** myself; / with my whole
103: 2 Praise the LORD, I **t** myself, / and never forget
104: 1 Praise the LORD, I **t** myself; / O LORD my
105: 2 sing his praises. / **T** everyone about his miracles.
107: 2 **T** others he has saved you from your enemies.
109: 2 while the wicked slander me / and **t** lies about me.
118:17 but I will live / to **t** what the LORD has done.
139: 3 path ahead of me / and **t** me where to stop and rest.
142: 2 complaints before him / and **t** him all my troubles.
144: 8 full of lies; / they swear to **t** the truth, but they lie.
144:11 full of lies; / they swear to **t** the truth, but they lie.

145: 4 Let each generation **t** its children / of your mighty
145:12 They will **t** about your mighty deeds / and about
146: 1 Praise the LORD! / Praise the LORD, I **t** myself.
Pr 8: 6 Listen to me! For I have excellent things to **t** you.
25: 9 matter with them privately. Don't **t** anyone else,
30: 4 his name—and his son's name? **T** me if you know!
30: 8 First, help me never to **t** a lie. Second, give me
Ecc 2:19 And who can **t** whether my successors will be wise
6:12 And who can **t** what will happen in the future after
10:14 all about the future and **t** everyone the details!
10:20 A little bird may **t** them what you have said.
SS 1: 7 "**T** me, O my love, where are you leading your
5: 8 my beloved one, **t** him that I am sick with love."
5: 9 what is it about your loved one that brings you to **t**
Isa 3:10 **T** them, "You will receive a wonderful reward!"
6: 9 And he said, "Yes, go. But **t** my people this:
7: 4 **T** him to stop worrying. **T** him he doesn't need to
12: 4 **T** the world what he has done. / Oh, how mighty
14:32 What should we **t** the enemy messengers?
14:32 **T** them that the LORD has built Jerusalem,
19:11 Will they dare **t** Pharaoh about their long line of
19:12 let them **t** you what the LORD Almighty is going
21: 7 **T** him to sound the alert when he sees chariots
29:21 and **t** lies to tear down the innocent will be no
30:10 They **t** the prophets, "Shut up! We don't want any
30:10 "Don't **t** us the truth. **T** us nice things. **T** us lies.
30:12 "Because you despise what I **t** you and trust
32: 9 Listen to me, and I will **t** you of your reward.
36: 8 "I'll **t** you what! My master, the king of Assyria,
38: 5 "Go back to Hezekiah and **t** him, 'This is what the
40: 2 **T** her that her sad days are gone and that her sins
40: 9 **T** the towns of Judah, "Your God is coming!"
41:22 "Let them try to **t** us what happened long ago
41:23 you are gods, **t** what will occur in the days ahead.
41:27 I was the first to **t** Jerusalem, 'Look! Help is on the
42: 9 I will **t** you the future before it happens."
44: 7 Who else can **t** you what is going to happen in the
44: 7 Let them **t** you if they can and thus prove their
45:19 And I did not **t** the people of Israel to ask me for
46:10 Only I can **t** you what is going to happen even
48: 6 Now I will **t** you new things I have not mentioned
48: 8 "Yes, I will **t** you of things that are entirely new,
51:18 is left alive to help you or **t** you what to do.
55: 2 and I will **t** you where to get food that is good for
58: 1 of a trumpet blast. **T** my people Israel of their sins!
58: 3 "I will **t** you why! It's because you are living for
61: 2 He has sent me to **t** those who mourn that the time
62:11 "**T** the people of Israel, 'Look, your Savior is
63: 7 I will **t** of the LORD's unfailing love. I will praise
Jer 1: 7 go wherever I send you and say whatever I **t** you.
1:17 Go out, and **t** them whatever I **t** you to say.
4: 5 **T** them to sound the alarm throughout the land:
5: 2 'As surely as the LORD lives,' they all **t** lies!"
7:27 "**T** them all this, but do not expect them to listen.
9: 5 With practiced tongues they **t** lies; they wear
13:12 "So **t** them, 'The LORD, the God of Israel,
13:12 you don't need to **t** us how prosperous we will be!'
13:13 Then **t** them, 'No, this is what the LORD means:
14:14 I did not send them or **t** them to speak. I did not
15: 2 can we go?' **t** them, 'This is what the LORD says:
15:14 I will **t** their enemies to take them as captives to a
16:10 "When you **t** the people all these things, they will
16:11 **T** them that this is the LORD's reply: It is
21: 3 "Go back to King Zedekiah and **t** him,
21: 8 "**T** all the people, 'This is what the LORD says:
23:25 And then they proceed to **t** lies in my name.
23:28 Let these false prophets **t** their dreams, but let my
25:27 "Now **t** them, 'The LORD Almighty, the God of
25:28 the cup, **t** them, 'The LORD Almighty says:
28:13 "Go and **t** Hananiah, 'This is what the LORD
29:31 **T** them, 'This is what the LORD says concerning
33: 3 and I will **t** you some remarkable secrets about
34: 2 and **t** him, 'This is what the LORD, the God of
35:15 I have sent you prophet after prophet to **t** you to
36:16 "We must **t** the king what we have heard,"
36:17 "But first, **t** us how you got these messages.
36:19 told Baruch. "Don't **t** anyone where you are!"
36:20 of Elishama the secretary and went to **t** the king.
37: 7 **T** the king of Judah, who sent you to ask me what
38:15 Jeremiah said, "If I **t** you the truth, you will kill
38:24 "Don't **t** anyone you told me this, or you will die!
38:25 '**T** us what you and the king were talking about. If
you don't **t** us, we will kill you.'
38:26 just **t** them you begged me not to send you back to
42: 4 your God, and I will **t** you everything he says.
42:20 saying, 'Just **t** us what the LORD our God says,
48:20 and wail! **T** it by the banks of the Arnon River:
50: 2 "**T** the whole world, and keep nothing back!
51:31 side come running to the king to **t** him all is lost!
Eze 9: 1 **T** them to bring their weapons with them!"
13: 2 **T** them to listen to the word of the LORD.
13:11 **T** these whitewashers that their wall will soon fall
17: 2 "Son of man, **t** this story to the people of Israel.
17:12 I will **t** you, says the Sovereign LORD. The king
20: 3 my help? As surely as I live, I will **t** you nothing.
21: 7 **t** them, 'I groan because of the terrifying news I
24:19 does all this mean? What are you trying to **t** us?"
24:26 to you in Babylon and **t** you what has happened.
33:13 When I **t** righteous people that they will live,
33:14 And suppose I **t** some wicked people that they will
33:30 Let's go hear the prophet **t** us what the LORD is
33:31 But they have no intention of doing what I **t** them.
40: 4 of Israel and **t** them everything you have seen."
43:10 **T** them its appearance and its plan so they will be
44: 5 Listen to everything I **t** you about the regulations
Da 2: 2 and he demanded that they **t** him what he had
2: 3 **T** me what I dreamed, for I must know what it

2: 4 **T** us the dream, and we will **t** you what it means."
2: 5 If you don't **t** me what my dream was and what it
2: 6 But if you **t** me what I dreamed and what the
2: 6 Just **t** me the dream and what it means!"
2: 7 **T** us the dream, and we will **t** you what it means."
2: 9 If you don't **t** me the dream, you will be
2: 9 You have conspired to **t** me lies in hopes that
2: 9 But **t** me the dream, and then I will know that you can **t** me what it means."
2:10 "There isn't a man alive who can **t** Your Majesty
2:11 No one except the gods can **t** you your dream,
2:16 so he could **t** the king what the dream meant.
2:24 and I will **t** him the meaning of his dream."
2:25 will **t** Your Majesty the meaning of your dream!"
2:26 Can you **t** me what my dream was and what it
2:27 or fortune-tellers who can **t** the king such things.
2:28 Now I will **t** you your dream and the visions you
2:36 now I will **t** Your Majesty what it means.
4: 6 so they could **t** me what my dream meant.
4: 7 the dream, but they could not **t** me what it meant.
4: 9 for you to solve. Now **t** me what my dream means.
4:18 Now **t** me what it means, for no one else can help
4:18 But you can **t** me because the spirit of the holy
5: 7 and **t** me what it means will be dressed in purple
5: 8 them could read the writing or **t** him what it meant.
5:12 and he will **t** you what the writing means."
5:16 you can read these words and **t** me their meaning,
5:17 but I will **t** you what the writing means.
8:16 "Gabriel, **t** this man the meaning of his vision."
8:19 "I am here to **t** you what will happen later in the
8:26 a long time, so do not **t** anyone about them yet."
9:23 I am here to **t** you what it was, for God loves you
10:21 I will **t** you what is written in the Book of Truth.
Hos 2: 2 **T** her to take off her garish makeup and suggestive
4:12 They are asking a piece of wood to **t** them what to
4:12 They think a stick can **t** them the future!
Joel 1: 3 **T** your children about it in the years to come.
Am 5:10 How you despise people who **t** the truth!
Jnh 3: 9 Who can **t**? Perhaps even yet God will have pity
Mic 1:10 Don't **t** our enemies in the city of Gath; don't weep
6: 3 **T** me why your patience is exhausted! Answer me!
6:12 so used to lying that their tongues can no longer **t**
Hab 2: 2 so that a runner can read it and **t** everyone else.
2:19 You ask speechless stone images to **t** you what to
Zep 3: 2 No one can **t** it anything; it refuses all correction.
3: 6 There are no survivors to even **t** what happened.
Hag 2:21 "**T** Zerubbabel, the governor of Judah, that I am
Zec 6:12 **T** him that the LORD Almighty says: Here is the
8:16 this is what you must do: **T** the truth to each other.
13: 3 his own father and mother will **t** him, 'You must
Mal 2:14 has the LORD abandoned us?" I'll **t** you why!
Mt 2: 8 come back and **t** me so that I can go and worship
2:13 "Stay there until I **t** you to return, because Herod
6: 3 don't **t** your left hand what your right hand is
6:25 "So I **t** you, don't worry about everyday life—
7:22 On judgment day many will **t** me, 'Lord, Lord,
8:10 Turning to the crowd, he said, "I **t** you the truth,
8:11 And I **t** you this, that many Gentiles will come
9:30 sternly warned them, "Don't **t** anyone about this."
10:18 This will be your opportunity to **t** them about me—
10:27 What I **t** you now in the darkness, shout abroad
11: 4 and **t** him about what you have heard and seen—
11: 6 And **t** him: 'God blesses those who are not
12: 6 I **t** you, there is one here who is even greater than
12:36 And I **t** you this, that you must give an account on
13:10 "Why do you always **t** stories when you talk to the
13:13 That is why I **t** these stories, because people see
13:30 Then I will **t** the harvesters to sort out the weeds
14:28 **t** me to come to you by walking on water."
15:23 "**T** her to leave," they said. "She is bothering us
16:20 Then he sternly warned them not to **t** anyone that
16:21 then on Jesus began to **t** his disciples plainly that
17: 9 "Don't **t** anyone what you have seen until I,
17:12 But I **t** you, he has already come, but he wasn't
18:10 For I **t** you that in heaven their angels are always in
18:18 I **t** you this: Whatever you prohibit on earth is
18:19 "I also **t** you this: If two of you agree down here
19: 9 And I **t** you this, a man who divorces his wife
19:23 Then Jesus said to his disciples, "I **t** you the truth,
21: 5 "**T** the people of Israel, / 'Look, your King is
21:24 "I'll **t** you who gave me the authority to do these
22: 4 So he sent other servants to **t** them, 'The feast has
22:17 Now **t** us what you think about this: Is it right to
22:28 So **t** us, whose wife will she be in the resurrection?
23:39 For I **t** you this, you will never see me again until
25:40 And the King will **t** them, 'I assure you, when you
26:18 **T** him, 'The Teacher says, My time has come,
26:63 "I demand in the name of the living God that you **t**
26:73 be one of them; we can **t** by your Galilean accent."
28: 7 and **t** his disciples he has been raised from the
28:10 Go **t** my brothers to leave for Galilee, and they will
28:15 widely among the Jews, and they still **t** it today.
Mk 4:13 will you understand all the others I am going to **t**?
5:19 and **t** them what wonderful things the Lord has
5:20 and began to **t** everyone about the great things
5:43 Jesus commanded them not to **t** anyone what had
7:36 Jesus told the crowd not to **t** anyone, but the more
8:30 But Jesus warned them not to **t** anyone about him.
8:31 Then Jesus began to **t** them that he, the Son of
9: 9 he told them not to **t** anyone what they had seen
9:13 But I **t** you, Elijah has already come, and he was
10:49 he stopped and said, "**T** him to come here."
11:29 "I'll **t** who gave me authority to do these things if
12: 9 "I'll **t** you—he will come and kill them all
12:14 Now **t** us—is it right to pay taxes to the Roman
12:15 Show me a Roman coin, and I'll **t** you."
12:23 So **t** us, whose wife will she be in the resurrection?
13: 9 This will be your opportunity to **t** them about me.
16:13 they rushed back to **t** the others, but no one
Lk 1:77 You will **t** his people how to find salvation
5:14 Then Jesus instructed him not to **t** anyone what had
7: 9 Turning to the crowd, he said, "I **t** you, I haven't
7:22 to John and **t** him what you have seen and heard—
7:23 And **t** him, 'God blesses those who are not
7:28 I **t** you, of all who have ever lived, none is greater
7:47 I **t** you, her sins—and they are many—have been
8:39 and **t** them all the wonderful things God has done
8:56 but Jesus insisted that they not **t** anyone what had
9: 2 Then he sent them out to **t** everyone about the
9:14 "Just **t** them to sit down on the ground in groups
9:21 Jesus warned them not to **t** anyone about this.
9:36 They didn't **t** anyone what they had seen until long
10:24 I **t** you, many prophets and kings have longed to
10:40 I do all the work? **T** her to come and help me."
11: 8 But I **t** you this—though he won't do it as a friend,
11: 9 "And so I **t** you, keep on asking, and you will be
12: 5 But I'll **t** you whom to fear. Fear God, who has the
12:13 please **t** my brother to divide our father's estate
12:22 turning to his disciples, Jesus said, "So I **t** you,
12:37 I **t** you, he himself will seat them, put on an apron,
13: 5 No, and I **t** you again that unless you repent,
13:27 And he will reply, 'I **t** you, I don't know you.
13:32 "Go **t** that fox that I will keep on casting out
16: 9 I **t** you, use your worldly resources to benefit
17: 5 "We need more faith; **t** us how to get it."
18: 8 I **t** you, he will grant justice to them quickly!
18:14 I **t** you, this sinner, not the Pharisee, returned home
20:16 "I'll **t** you—he will come and kill them all
20:22 Now **t** us—is it right to pay taxes to the Roman
20:33 So **t** us, whose wife will she be in the resurrection?
21:13 This will be your opportunity to **t** them about me.
22:16 For I **t** you now that I won't eat it again until it
22:34 But Jesus said, "Peter, let me **t** you something.
22:67 and they said, "**T** us if you are the Messiah."
22:67 But he replied, "If I **t** you, you won't believe me.
24: 9 So they rushed back to **t** his eleven disciples—
Jn 1: 7 to **t** everyone about the light so that everyone
1:22 **T** us, so we can give an answer to those who sent
1:41 did was to find his brother, Simon, and **t** him,
2:25 No one needed to **t** him about human nature.
3: 8 but can't **t** where it comes from or where it is
3:12 But if you don't even believe me when I **t** you
3:12 how can you possibly believe if I **t** you what is
4:20 So **t** me, why is it that you Jews insist that
6:10 "**T** everyone to sit down," Jesus ordered. So all of
8:25 "**T** us who you are," they demanded.
8:45 So when I **t** the truth, you just naturally don't
10:24 in suspense? If you are the Messiah, **t** us plainly."
11:40 "Didn't I **t** you that you will see God's glory if
13:19 I **t** you this now, so that when it happens you will
14: 2 for you. If this were not so, I would **t** you plainly.
15:26 to you from the Father and will **t** you all about me.
15:27 And you must also **t** others about me because you
16: 4 I didn't **t** you earlier because I was going to be
16:12 "Oh, there is so much more I want to **t** you,
16:13 what he has heard. He will **t** you about the future.
16:25 and I will **t** you plainly all about the Father.
16:30 and don't need anyone to **t** you anything.
18:34 your own question, or did others **t** you about me?"
20:15 **t** me where you have put him, and I will go and get
20:17 and **t** them that I am ascending to my Father
Ac 1: 8 and will **t** people about me everywhere—
5:28 "Didn't we **t** you never again to teach in this
8:35 then used many others to **t** him the Good News
10:29 as I was sent for. Now **t** me why you sent for me."
11:14 He will **t** you how you and all your household will
12:17 "**T** James and the other brothers what happened,"
15:20 and **t** them to abstain from eating meat sacrificed
15:27 and Silas to **t** you what we have decided
16:17 and they have come to **t** you how to be saved."
16:35 the city officials sent the police to **t** the jailer,
17:19 "Come and **t** us more about this new religion,"
17:23 who he is, and now I wish to **t** you about him.
22:27 the commander went over and asked Paul, "**T** me,
23:15 and the high council should **t** the commander to
23:17 He has something important to **t** him."
23:18 man to you because he has something to **t** you."
23:19 and asked, "What is it you want to **t** me?"
26:16 You are to **t** the world about this experience
26:22 so that I am still alive today to **t** these facts to
28:20 so I could **t** you that I am bound with this chain
Ro 1: 5 and authority to **t** Gentiles everywhere what God
2:15 accuse them or **t** them they are doing what is right.
2:21 You **t** others not to steal, but do you steal?
4: 3 For the Scriptures **t** us, "Abraham believed God,
10:11 As the Scriptures **t** us, "Anyone who believes in
10:15 how will anyone go and **t** them without being sent?
14: 4 so let him **t** him whether they are right or wrong.
1Co 2: 1 and brilliant ideas to **t** you God's message.
2:13 When we **t** you this, we do not use words of
12:31 let me **t** you about something else that is better
14:13 in order to **t** people plainly what has been said.
14:26 another will **t** some special revelation God has
15:12 But **t** me this—since we preach that Christ rose
15:45 The Scriptures **t** us, "The first man, Adam,
15:51 But let me **t** you a wonderful secret God has
2Co 1:24 But that does not mean we want to **t** you exactly
2:14 Now wherever we go he uses us to **t** others about
3: 1 Are we beginning again to **t** you how good we are?
4: 2 We **t** the truth before God, and all who are honest
5:19 This is the wonderful message he has given us to **t**
8: 1 Now I want to **t** you, dear friends, what God in his
10:12 these other men who **t** you how important they are!
11:31 who is to be praised forever, knows I **t** the truth.
12: 1 Let me **t** about the visions and revelations I
12:19 We **t** you this as Christ's servants, and we know
13: 5 If you cannot **t** that Jesus Christ is among you,
Gal 5: 2 Listen! I, Paul, **t** you this: If you are counting on
5:21 Let me **t** you again, as I have before, that anyone
Eph 4:25 all falsehood and "**t** your neighbor the truth"
6:21 will **t** you all about how I am getting along.
Php 4: 6 **T** God what you need, and thank him for all he has
Col 1:27 For it has pleased God to **t** his people that the
1:28 So everywhere we go, we **t** everyone about Christ.
4: 7 loved brother, will **t** you how I am getting along.
1Th 1: 8 faith in God. We don't need to **t** them about it,
4:15 I can **t** you this directly from the Lord: We who are
2Th 1: 4 We proudly **t** God's other churches about your
2: 1 let us **t** you about the coming again of our Lord
1Ti 6: 5 Their minds are corrupt, and they don't **t** the truth.
6:17 **T** those who are rich in this world not to be proud
6:18 **T** them to use their money to do good. They should
2Ti 1: 1 sent out to **t** others about the life he has promised
1: 8 So you must never be ashamed to **t** others about
4: 3 and will look for teachers who will **t** them
Heb 3:10 away from me. / They refuse to do what I **t** them.'
Jas 1: 5 you to do—ask him, and he will gladly **t** you.
1Pe 2:18 Do whatever they **t** you—not only if they are kind
1Jn 3:10 So now we can **t** who are children of God and who
3Jn 1:13 I have much to **t** you, but I don't want to do it in a
Jude 1:10 they do whatever their instincts **t** them,
Rev 17: 7 "I will **t** you the mystery of this woman and of the
21: 5 for what I **t** you is trustworthy and true."
22: 6 has sent his angel to **t** you what will happen

TELLING (87) [TELL]

Ge 41:25 "God was **t** you what he is about to do.
42:20 I will know whether or not you are **t** me the truth.
Ex 4:16 and you will be as God to him, **t** him what to say.
23: 1 Do not cooperate with evil people by **t** lies on the
33:12 Moses said to the LORD, "You have been **t** me,
Lev 6: 2 **t** their neighbor that an item entrusted to their
Dt 1: 3 **t** them everything the LORD had commanded
Jos 7:19 to the LORD, the God of Israel, by **t** the truth.
Jdg 7:13 Gideon crept up just as a man was **t** his friend
9:31 **t** him, "Gaal son of Ebed and his brothers have
16:13 "You have been making fun of me and **t** me lies!
2Ki 8: 5 And Gehazi was **t** the king about the time Elisha
19: 7 and the king will receive a report from Assyria **t**
2Ch 24: 9 **t** the people to bring to the LORD the tax that
Ezr 4: 8 **t** King Artaxerxes about the situation in Jerusalem.
Ne 6:19 They kept **t** me what a wonderful man Tobiah was,
8:11 too, quieted the people, **t** them, "Hush!
8:15 **t** the people to go to the hills to get branches from
Est 8: 8 **t** them whatever you want, and seal it with the
Job 15: 5 Your sins are **t** your mouth what to say.
36: 4 I am **t** you the honest truth, for I am a man of
Ps 26: 7 a song of thanksgiving / and **t** of all your miracles.
34:13 watch your tongue! / Keep your lips from **t** lies!
52: 2 cuts like a sharp razor; / you're an expert at **t** lies.
62: 4 They delight in **t** lies about me. / They are friendly
Pr 17: 9 **t** about them separates close friends.
25:18 **T** lies about others is as harmful as hitting them
Ecc 5: 6 And don't defend yourself by **t** the Temple
Isa 37: 7 from Assyria **t** him that he is needed at home.
Jer 14:13 their prophets are **t** them, 'All is well—
14:14 "These prophets are **t** lies in my name.
23:27 By **t** these false dreams, they are trying to get my
27:14 Do not listen to the false prophets who keep **t** you,
27:15 They are **t** you lies in my name, so I will drive you
29:21 son of Maaseiah—who are **t** you lies in my name:
38: 1 heard what Jeremiah had been **t** the people.
Da 2:18 to show them his mercy by **t** them the secret,
Zep 3:13 to each other, never **t** lies or deceiving one another.
Mt 8:33 **t** everyone what happened to the demon-possessed
13:53 When Jesus had finished **t** these stories, he left that
14: 4 John kept **t** Herod, "It is illegal for you to marry
20: 4 **t** them he would pay them whatever was right at
27:64 his body and then **t** everyone he came back to life!
Mk 1:45 the news, **t** everyone what had happened to him.
4: 2 He began to teach the people by **t** many stories
6:12 went out, **t** all they met to turn from their sins.
6:18 John kept **t** Herod, "It is illegal for you to marry
12: 1 Then Jesus began **t** them stories: "A man planted a
14:69 girl saw him standing there and began **t** the others,
Lk 8:39 So he went all through the city **t** about the great
19:28 After **t** this story, Jesus went on toward Jerusalem,
23: 2 "This man has been leading our people to ruin by **t**
24:36 And just as they were **t** about it, Jesus himself was
Jn 3:11 I am **t** you what we know and have seen,
8:38 I am **t** you what I saw when I was with my Father.
8:46 And since I am **t** you the truth, why don't you
9:24 and told him, "Give glory to God by **t** the truth,
11: 3 So the two sisters sent a message to Jesus **t** him,
12:17 call Lazarus back to life were **t** others all about it.
13:29 some thought Jesus was **t** him to go and pay for the
14:25 I am **t** you these things now while I am still with
16: 4 Yes, I'm **t** you these things now, so that when they
16:13 his own ideas; he will be **t** you what he has heard.
18:23 for it. Should you hit a man for **t** the truth?"
Ac 4:20 We cannot stop **t** about the wonderful things we
11:15 "Well, I began **t** them the Good News, but just as I
14:27 **t** all that God had done and how he had opened the
17: 3 "This Jesus I'm **t** you about is the Messiah."
18: 5 time preaching and testifying to the Jews, **t** them,
20:20 Yet I never shrank from **t** you the truth,
20:24 the work of **t** others the Good News about God's
22:15 **t** the whole world what you have seen and heard.
Ro 1: 9 whom I serve with all my heart by **t** others the
2Co 1:23 Now I call upon God as my witness that I am **t** the

12: 6 no fool in doing it, because I would be **t** the truth.
Gal 4:16 become your enemy because I am **t** you the truth?
Eph 3: 8 I was chosen for this special joy of **t** the Gentiles
Php 1: 7 defending the truth and **t** others the Good News.
1:14 and become more bold in **t** others about Christ.
2:19 he can cheer me up by **t** me how you are getting
3: 1 Lord give you joy. I never get tired of **t** you this.
4: 3 for they worked hard with me in **t** others the Good
Col 2: 4 I am **t** you this so that no one will be able to
1Th 1: 8 for wherever we go we find people **t** us about your
1Pe 3:10 from speaking evil, / and keep your lips from **t** lies.
1Jn 1: 3 We are **t** you about what we ourselves have
3Jn 1: 3 and made me very happy by **t** me about your

TELLS (38) [TELL]

Ge 41:55 "Go to Joseph and do whatever he **t** you."
Nu 23:12 "Can I say anything except what the LORD **t**
23:26 you that I must do whatever the LORD **t** me?"
Dt 4:30 the LORD your God and listen to what he **t** you.
5:27 Then come and tell us everything he **t** you, and we
26:17 walking in his ways and doing everything he **t** you.
1Sa 20: 2 for he always **t** me everything he's going to do,
1Ki 22:14 I will say only what the LORD **t** me to say."
2Ki 6:12 **t** the king of Israel even the words you speak in the
2Ch 18:13 I will say only what my God **t** me to say."
Ne 6: 6 "Geshem **t** me that everywhere he goes he hears
Job 37: 6 to fall on the earth and **t** the rain to pour down.
Pr 12:17 An honest witness **t** the truth; a false witness **t** lies.
20:19 A gossip **t** secrets, so don't hang around with
Isa 28:10 He **t** us everything over and over again, a line at a
54:17 And everyone who **t** lies in court will be brought to
Jer 9: 5 all fool and defraud each other; no one **t** the truth.
42: 5 us if we refuse to obey whatever he **t** us to do!
Hos 11: 9 punish you as much as my burning anger **t** me to.
Mt 24:23 "Then if anyone **t** you, 'Look, here is the
24:26 "So if someone **t** you, 'Look, the Messiah is out in
Mk 13:11 Just say what God **t** you to. Then it is not you who
13:21 "And then if anyone **t** you, 'Look, here is the
Jn 2: 5 mother told the servants, "Do whatever he **t** you."
3:32 He **t** what he has seen and heard, but how few believe what he **t** them!
5:20 loves the Son and **t** him everything he is doing,
12:50 so I say whatever the Father **t** me to say!"
Ac 3:22 Listen carefully to everything he **t** you.'
21:28 and **t** everybody to disobey the Jewish laws.
Ro 1:17 This Good News **t** us how God makes us right in
8:16 in our hearts and **t** us that we are God's children.
10:14 can they hear about him unless someone **t** them?
2Co 11: 4 You seem to believe whatever anyone **t** you,
1Ti 4: 1 Now the Holy Spirit **t** us clearly that in the last
3Jn 1:10 he also **t** others not to help them.
Rev 22: 6 who **t** his prophets what the future holds,

TEMA (5)

Ge 25:15 Hadad, **T**, Jetur, Naphish, and Kedemah.
1Ch 1:30 Mishma, Dumah, Massa, Hadad, **T**,
Job 6:19 the caravans from **T** and from Sheba stop for
Isa 21:14 O people of **T**, bring food and water to these weary
Jer 25:23 I went to Dedan, **T**, and Buz, and to the people

TEMAH (2)

Ezr 2:53 Barkos, Sisera, **T**,
Ne 7:55 Barkos, Sisera, **T**,

TEMAN (10) [TEMANITE, TEMANITES]

Ge 36:11 The sons of Eliphaz were **T**, Omar, Zepho, Gatam,
36:15 became the leaders of the clans of **T**, Omar, Zepho,
36:42 Kenaz, **T**, Mibzar,
1Ch 1:36 The sons of Eliphaz were **T**, Omar, Zepho, Gatam,
1:53 Kenaz, **T**, Mibzar,
Jer 49: 7 Almighty says: "Where are all the wise men of **T**?
49:20 the LORD's plans for Edom and the people of **T**.
Eze 25:13 I will make a wasteland of everything from **T** to
Am 1:12 So I will send down fire on **T**, and the fortresses of
Ob 1: 9 The mightiest warriors of **T** will be terrified,

TEMANITE (6) [TEMAN]

Job 2:11 Three of Job's friends were Eliphaz the **T**,
4: 1 Then Eliphaz the **T** replied to Job:
15: 1 Then Eliphaz the **T** replied:
22: 1 Then Eliphaz the **T** replied:
42: 7 finished speaking to Job, he said to Eliphaz the **T**:
42: 9 So Eliphaz the **T**, Bildad the Shuhite, and Zophar

TEMANITES (2) [TEMAN]

Ge 36:34 Husham from the land of the **T** became king.
1Ch 1:45 Husham from the land of the **T** became king.

TEMENI (1)

1Ch 4: 6 birth to Ahuzzam, Hepher, **T**, and Haahashtari.

TEMPER (3) [EVEN-TEMPERED, HOT-TEMPERED, ILL-TEMPERED, QUICK-TEMPERED, SHORT-TEMPERED]

1Sa 20: 7 But if he is angry and loses his **t**, then you will
1Ch 12:32 All these men understood the **t** of the times
Pr 14:29 those with a hasty **t** will make mistakes.

TEMPERANCE [KJV] See SELF-CONTROL

TEMPERATURE (1)

Lk 4:39 and immediately her **t** returned to normal.

TEMPERED [KJV] See MIXED, PUT, REFINE

TEMPESTS (1)

Ps 83:15 with your fierce storms; / terrify them with your **t**.

TEMPLE (879) [TEMPLE'S, TEMPLES]

HOLY TEMPLE (10) 1Ch 29:3; Ps 11:4; 65:4; 79:1; 138:2; Jnh 2:4,7; Mic 1:2; Hab 2:20; Eph 2:21

TEMPLE OF GOD (64) 1Ch 22:2; 28:21; 29:2,3,7; 2Ch 3:3; 4:11,19; 5:1,14; 7:5; 15:18; 22:12; 23:3,9; 24:7,13,27; 25:24; 28:24; 31:13,21; 34:9; 36:18,19; Ezr 1:4; 3:8,9; 4:24; 5:2,13,14,15,16; 6:3,5,7,8,16,17,18,22; 7:24; 8:17,25,36; 10:1,6,9; Ne 6:10; 11:11,16; 12:40; 13:7,11,14; Da 1:2; 5:3; Mt 26:61; 1Co 3:16; 2Th 2:4; Rev 3:12; 11:1,19

TEMPLE OF THE LORD* (120) 1Ki 3:1; 6:1; 7:40,45, 48,51; 8:10,63; 9:1,10; 10:5,12; 12:27; 14:26,28; 15:15; 2Ki 11:3,4,10,15,18,19; 12:9,13; 14:14; 15:35; 16:8,18; 18:15; 19:1; 20:5,8; 21:4; 22:3,5,9; 23:2,7; 25:9; 1Ch 6:32; 22:1,5, 11,14; 23:4; 28:13,20; 2Ch 3:1; 4:16; 5:1,13; 7:2,11; 8:16; 9:4,11; 12:9,11; 20:5,28; 23:6,14,18,20; 24:4,7,8,12,14,14,18; 26:21; 27:2; 29:3,5,15,16,17,18,20,25, 31,35; 30:1,15; 31:11; 33:4; 34:8,17,30; 35:2; 36:7,10,14; Ezr 1:3,5; 2:68; 7:27; Isa 2:2; 37:1; 38:20,22; Jer 7:4; 19:14; 20:1; 26:2; 41:5; 52:13; Eze 44:4; Joel 1:9,14; Mic 4:1; Zec 6:12,14,15; 7:3; 8:9; 11:13; 14:20,21

TEMPLE SERVANTS (15) Ezr 2:43,58,70; 7:7; 8:17,20,20; Ne 3:26,31; 7:46,60,73; 10:28; 11:3,21

Dt 23:17 or woman may ever become a **t** prostitute.
Jdg 4:21 Then she drove the tent peg through his **t** and into
4:22 lying there dead, with the tent peg through his **t**.
9: 4 They gave him seventy silver coins from the **t** of
9:27 held in the **t** of the local god, the wine flowed
9:46 they took refuge within the walls of the **t** of
9:47 that the people were gathered together in the **t**,
9:49 They piled the branches against the walls of the **t**
16:25 the prison and made to stand at the center of the **t**,
16:27 The **t** was completely filled with people.
16:29 Samson put his hands on the center pillars of the **t**
16:30 And the **t** crashed down on the Philistine leaders
1Sa 5: 2 They carried the Ark of God into the **t** of Dagon
5: 5 enters the **t** of Dagon will step on its threshold.
31: 9 the news of Saul's death in their pagan **t**
31:10 They placed his armor in the **t** of the Ashtoreths,
2Sa 7: 5 Are you the one to build me a **t** to live in?
7: 6 I have never lived in a **t**, from the day I brought the
7: 7 haven't you built me a beautiful cedar **t**?" '
7:13 one who will build a house—a **t**—for my name.
1Ki 3: 1 and the **T** of the LORD and the wall around the
3: 2 for a **t** honoring the name of the LORD had not
5: 3 was not able to build a **T** to honor the name of the
5: 5 So I am planning to build a **T** to honor the name of
5: 5 your throne, will build the **T** to honor my name.'
5:17 costly blocks of stone for the foundation of the **T**.
5:18 builders prepare the timber and stone for the **T**.
6: 1 that he began the construction of the **T** of the
6: 2 The **T** that King Solomon built for the LORD was
6: 3 The foyer at the front of the **T** was 30 feet wide, running across the entire width of the **T**.
6: 3 projected outward 15 feet from the front of the **T**.
6: 4 made narrow, recessed windows throughout the **T**.
6: 5 of rooms was built against the outer walls of the **T**,
6: 6 The rooms were connected to the walls of the **T** by
6: 7 The stones used in the construction of the **T** were
6: 8 to the bottom floor was on the south side of the **T**.
6: 9 After completing the **T** structure, Solomon put in a
6:10 attached to the **T** walls by cedar timbers.
6:12 "Concerning this **T** you are building, if you keep
6:14 So Solomon finished building the **T**.
6:16 the Most Holy Place—at the far end of the **T**.
6:17 The main room of the **T**, outside the Most Holy
6:18 covered the stone walls throughout the **T**,
6:19 prepared the inner sanctuary in the rear of the **T**,
6:22 So he finished overlaying the entire **T** with gold,
6:27 them side by side in the inner sanctuary of the **T**.
6:33 doorposts of olive wood for the entrance to the **T**.
6:37 The foundation of the LORD's **T** was laid in
6:38 of his reign. So it took seven years to build the **T**.
7:12 of the LORD's **T** with its entrance foyer.
7:21 Huram set the pillars at the entrance of the **T**,
7:39 arranged five water carts on the south side of the **T**
7:39 Sea was placed at the southeast corner of the **T**.
7:40 had assigned him to make for the **T** of the LORD:
7:45 All these utensils for the **T** of the LORD that
7:48 So Solomon made all the furnishings of the **T** of
7:50 the Most Holy Place and the main room of the **T**,
7:51 So King Solomon finished all his work on the **T** of
7:51 he stored them in the treasuries of the LORD's **T**.
8: 1 also known as Zion, to its new place in the **T**.
8: 4 all its sacred utensils, and carried them up to the **T**.
8: 6 covenant into the inner sanctuary of the **T**—
8:10 inner sanctuary, a cloud filled the **T** of the LORD.
8:11 the glorious presence of the LORD filled the **T**.
8:13 But I have built a glorious **T** for you, where you
8:16 place where a **t** should be built to honor my name.
8:17 wanted to build this **T** to honor the name of the
8:18 'It is right for you to want to build the **T** to honor
8:20 I have built this **T** to honor the name of the
8:27 contain you. How much less this **T** I have built!
8:29 May you watch over this **T** both day and night,
8:31 an oath of innocence in front of the altar at this **T**,
8:33 call on your name and pray to you here in this **T**,
8:35 and then they pray toward this **T** and confess your
8:38 or sorrow, raising their hands toward this **T**,
8:42 your power—and when they pray toward this **T**,
8:43 will know that this **T** I have built bears your name.
8:44 and toward this **T** that I have built for your name,
8:48 and toward this **T** I have built to honor your name,
8:63 and all Israel dedicated the **T** of the LORD.
8:64 area of the courtyard in front of the LORD's **T**.
9: 1 So Solomon finished building the **T** of the
9: 3 I have set apart this **T** you have built so that my
9: 7 I will reject this **T** that I have set apart to honor my
9: 8 And though this **T** is impressive now, it will
9: 8 do such terrible things to his land and to his **T**?'
9:10 during which Solomon built the **T** of the LORD
9:15 that Solomon conscripted to build the LORD's **T**,
9:25 And so he finished the work of building the **T**.
10: 5 and the burnt offerings Solomon made at the **T** of
10:12 wood to make railings for the **T** of the LORD
12:27 to offer sacrifices at the **T** of the LORD,
14:26 He ransacked the **T** of the LORD and the royal
14:28 Whenever the king went to the **T** of the LORD,
15:15 He brought into the **T** of the LORD the silver
15:18 that was left in the treasuries of the LORD's **T**
16:32 First he built a **t** and an altar for Baal in Samaria.
2Ki 1: 2 So he sent messengers to the **t** of Baal-zebub,
5:18 When my master the king goes into the **t** of the god
10:21 and filled the **t** of Baal from one end to the other.
10:23 Then Jehu went into the **t** of Baal with Jehonadab
10:24 So they were all inside the **t** to offer sacrifices
10:25 Then Jehu's men went into the fortress of the **t** of
10:27 the sacred pillar of Baal and wrecked the **t** of Baal,
11: 3 and his nurse remained hidden in the **T** of the
11: 4 and the guards to come to the **T** of the LORD.
11: 4 swear an oath of loyalty there in the LORD's **T**;
11: 7 must stand guard for the king at the LORD's **T**.
11:10 and were stored in the **T** of the LORD.
11:11 They formed a line from the south side of the **T**
11:13 she hurried to the LORD's **T** to see what was
11:15 "Take her out of the **T**, and kill anyone who tries
11:15 Do not kill her here in the **T** of the LORD."
11:18 And all the people of the land went over to the **t** of
11:18 Jehoiada the priest stationed guards at the **T** of the
11:19 land escorted the king from the **T** of the LORD.
12: 4 brought as a sacred offering to the LORD's **T**,
12: 5 to pay for whatever repairs are needed at the **T**."
12: 6 the priests still had not repaired the **T**.
12: 7 asked them, "Why haven't you repaired the **T**?
12: 7 it must all be spent on getting the **T** into good
12: 8 not to undertake the repairs of the **T** themselves.
12: 9 of the altar at the entrance of the **T** of the LORD.
12:10 money that had been brought to the LORD's **T**
12:11 it to pay the people working on the LORD's **T**—
12:12 and cut stone for repairing the LORD's **T**,
12:13 The money brought to the **T** was not used for
12:13 articles of gold or silver for the **T** of the LORD.
12:14 out to the workmen, who used it for the **T** repairs.
12:16 sin offerings was not brought into the LORD's **T**.
12:18 all the gold in the treasuries of the LORD's **T**
14:14 and all the utensils from the **T** of the LORD,
15:35 He was the one who rebuilt the upper gate of the **T**
16: 8 and gold from the **T** of the LORD and the palace
16:14 old bronze altar from the front of the LORD's **T**,
16:18 as well as the king's outer entrance to the **T** of the
18:15 King Hezekiah used all the silver stored in the **T** of
18:16 stripped the gold from the doors of the LORD's **T**
19: 1 and went into the **T** of the LORD to pray.
19:14 he went up to the LORD's **T** and spread it out
19:37 One day while he was worshiping in the **t** of his
20: 5 will get out of bed and go to the **T** of the LORD.
20: 8 and that I will go to the **T** of the LORD three
21: 4 He even built pagan altars in the **T** of the LORD,
21: 5 of heaven in both courtyards of the LORD's **T**.
21: 7 an Asherah pole he had made and set it up in the **T**,
21: 7 "My name will be honored here forever in this **T**
22: 3 the court secretary, to the **T** of the LORD.
22: 4 have collected from the people at the LORD's **T**.
22: 5 Then they can use it to pay workers to repair the **T**
22: 6 the timber and the cut stone needed to repair the **T**.
22: 8 found the Book of the Law in the LORD's **T**!"
22: 9 collected at the **T** of the LORD to the workers and supervisors at the **T**."
22:13 "Go to the **T** and speak to the LORD for me
22:14 grandson of Harhas, the keeper of the **T** wardrobe.
23: 2 And the king went up to the **T** of the LORD with
23: 2 Covenant that had been found in the LORD's **T**.
23: 4 and the **T** gatekeepers to remove from the
23: 4 **T** all the utensils that were used to worship Baal,
23: 6 removed the Asherah pole from the LORD's **T**
23: 7 prostitutes that were inside the **T** of the LORD,
23:11 He removed from the entrance of the LORD's **T**
23:12 had built in the two courtyards of the LORD's **T**.
23:24 Hilkiah the priest had found in the LORD's **T**.
23:27 and the **T** where my name was to be honored."
24:13 carried away all the treasures from the LORD's **T**
24:13 that King Solomon of Israel had placed in the **T**.
25: 9 He burned down the **T** of the LORD, the royal
25:13 and the bronze Sea that were at the LORD's **T**,
25:14 bronze utensils used for making sacrifices at the **T**.
25:16 These things had been made for the LORD's **T** in
1Ch 6:10 the high priest at the **T** built by Solomon in
6:32 Solomon built the **T** of the LORD in Jerusalem.
9: 2 came some of the priests, Levites, and **T** assistants.
9:33 all prominent Levites, lived at the **T**.
10:10 They placed his armor in the **t** of their gods,
10:10 and they fastened his head to the wall in the **t** of
17: 4 You are not the one to build me a **t** to live in.
17: 5 I have never lived in a **t**, from the day I brought the
17: 6 haven't you built me a beautiful cedar **t**?" '
17:12 He is the one who will build a house—a **t**—for me.
18: 8 Solomon melted the bronze and used it for the **T**.

18: 8 and the various bronze utensils used at the **T**.
22: 1 "This will be the location for the **T** of the LORD
22: 2 blocks of stone for building the **T** of God.
22: 5 and the **T** of the LORD must be a magnificent
22: 6 and instructed him to build a **T** for the LORD,
22: 7 "I wanted to build a **T** to honor the name of the
22: 8 you will not be the one to build a **T** to honor my
22:10 He is the one who will build a **T** to honor my
22:11 in building the **T** of the LORD your God.
22:14 materials for building the **T** of the LORD—
22:19 and the holy vessels of God into the **T** built to
23: 4 will supervise the work at the **T** of the LORD.
23:32 the Levites watched over the Tabernacle and the **T**
26:16 the west gate and the gateway leading up to the **T**.
26:18 four to the gateway leading up to the **T**, and two to
28: 2 It was my desire to build a **t** where the Ark of the
28: 3 to me, 'You must not build a **t** to honor my name,
28: 6 'Your son Solomon will build my **T** and its
28:10 The LORD has chosen you to build a **T** as his
28:11 Then David gave Solomon the plans for the **T**
28:12 had in mind for the courtyards of the LORD's **T**,
28:12 the outside rooms, the treasuries of God's **T**,
28:13 of priests and Levites in the **T** of the LORD.
28:13 the LORD's **T** which were to be used for worship
28:20 He will see to it that all the work related to the **T** of
28:21 of priests and Levites will serve in the **T** of God.
29: 1 for the **T** he will build is not just another building
29: 2 as much as I could for building the **T** of my God.
29: 3 because of my devotion to the **T** of my God,
29: 3 materials I have already collected for his holy **T**.
29: 7 For the construction of the **T** of God, they gave
29:16 build a **T** to honor your holy name come from you!
29:19 decrees, and principles, and to build this **T**,
2Ch 2: 1 that the time had come to build a **T** for the LORD
2: 4 I am about to build a **T** to honor the name of the
2: 5 "This will be a magnificent **T** because our God is
2: 6 So who am I to consider building a **T** for him,
2: 9 for the **T** I am going to build will be very large
2:12 who will build a **T** for the LORD and a royal
3: 1 So Solomon began to build the **T** of the LORD in
3: 1 The **T** was built on the threshing floor of Araunah
3: 3 The foundation for the **T** of God was ninety feet
3: 4 The foyer at the front of the **T** was thirty feet wide, running across the entire width of the **T**.
3: 5 The main room of the **T** was paneled with cypress
3: 6 The walls of the **T** were decorated with beautiful
3: 7 and thresholds throughout the **T** were overlaid with
3: 8 corresponding to the width of the **T**, and it was
3:11 was 7-1/2 feet long, and it touched the **T** wall.
3:13 and faced out toward the main room of the **T**.
3:15 For the front of the **T**, Solomon made two pillars
3:17 he set up the two pillars at the entrance of the **T**,
4: 7 that had been given and put them in the **T**.
4: 8 He also built ten tables and placed them in the **T**,
4:10 Sea was placed near the southeast corner of the **T**.
4:11 had assigned him to make for the **T** of God:
4:16 out of burnished bronze for the **T** of the LORD,
4:19 So Solomon made all the furnishings for the **T** of
4:22 the Most Holy Place and the main room of the **T**,
5: 1 the work related to building the **T** of the LORD,
5: 1 These were stored in the treasuries of the **T** of
5: 2 also known as Zion, to its new place in the **T**.
5: 5 The Levitical priests carried them all up to the **T**.
5: 7 covenant into the inner sanctuary of the **T**—
5:13 At that moment a cloud filled the **T** of the LORD.
5:14 presence of the LORD filled the **T** of God.
6: 2 But I have built a glorious **T** for you, where you
6: 5 place where a **t** should be built to honor my name.
6: 7 wanted to build this **T** to honor the name of the
6: 8 'It is right for you to want to build the **T** to honor
6:10 I have built this **T** to honor the name of the
6:18 contain you. How much less this **T** I have built!
6:20 May you watch over this **T** both day and night,
6:22 an oath of innocence in front of the altar at this **T**,
6:24 call on your name and pray to you here in this **T**,
6:26 and then they pray toward this **T** and confess your
6:29 or sorrow, raising their hands toward this **T**,
6:32 your great name and to pray toward this **T**,
6:33 will know that this **T** I have built bears your name.
6:34 and toward this **T** that I have built for your name,
6:38 and toward this **T** I have built to honor your name,
7: 1 the glorious presence of the LORD filled the **T**.
7: 2 The priests could not even enter the **T** of the
7: 3 the glorious presence of the LORD filling the **T**,
7: 5 the king and all the people dedicated the **T** of God.
7: 7 area of the courtyard in front of the LORD's **T**
7:11 So Solomon finished building the **T** of the
7:12 and have chosen this **T** as the place for making
7:16 for I have chosen this **T** and set it apart to be my
7:20 I will reject this **T** that I have set apart to honor my
7:21 And though this **T** is impressive now, it will
7:21 done such terrible things to his land and to his **T**?'
8: 1 and the great building projects of the LORD's **T**
8:12 the altar he had built in front of the foyer of the **T**
8:16 to building the **T** of the LORD was carried out,
9: 4 and the burnt offerings Solomon made at the **T** of
9:11 almug wood to make steps for the **T** of the LORD
12: 9 and took away all the treasures of the **T** of the
12:11 Whenever the king went to the **T** of the LORD,
15: 8 stood in front of the foyer of the LORD's **T**.
15:18 He brought into the **T** of God the silver and gold
16: 2 and gold from the treasuries of the LORD's **T**
20: 5 front of the new courtyard at the **T** of the LORD.
20: 8 Your people settled here and built this **T** for you.
20: 9 before this **T** where your name is honored.
20:28 and proceeded to the **T** of the LORD.
22:12 Joash remained hidden in the **T** of God for six
23: 3 They all gathered at the **T** of God, where they
23: 5 should stay in the courtyards of the LORD's **T**.
23: 6 and Levites on duty may enter the **T** of the
23: 7 Any unauthorized person who enters the **T** must be
23: 9 to King David and were stored in the **T** of God.
23:10 They formed a line from the south side of the **T**
23:12 she hurried to the LORD's **T** to see what was
23:13 place of authority by the pillar at the **T** entrance.
23:14 "Take her out of the **T**, and kill anyone who tries
23:14 Do not kill her here in the **T** of the LORD."
23:17 And all the people went over to the **t** of Baal
23:18 Levitical priests in charge of the **T** of the LORD,
23:19 **T** to keep those who were ceremonially unclean
23:20 and all the people escorted the king from the **T** of
24: 4 decided to repair and restore the **T** of the LORD.
24: 5 so that we can repair the **T** of your God.
24: 6 and collect the **T** taxes from the towns of Judah
24: 7 of wicked Athaliah had broken into the **T** of God,
24: 7 **T** of the LORD to worship the images of Baal.
24: 8 and set outside the gate leading to the **T** of the
24:11 the money and took the chest back to the **T** again.
24:12 and carpenters to restore the **T** of the LORD.
24:12 articles of iron and bronze for the LORD's **T**.
24:13 They restored the **T** of God according to its
24:14 It was used to make utensils for the **T** of the
24:14 **T** of the LORD during the lifetime of Jehoiada
24:16 so much good in Israel for God and his **T**.
24:18 They decided to abandon the **T** of the LORD,
24:21 him to death in the courtyard of the LORD's **T**.
24:27 and the record of his restoration of the **T** of God
25:24 and all the utensils from the **T** of God that had
26:16 God by entering the sanctuary of the LORD's **T**
26:19 priests before the incense altar in the LORD's **T**,
26:21 in isolation, excluded from the **T** of the LORD.
27: 2 Jotham did not enter the **T** of the LORD.
27: 3 Jotham rebuilt the Upper Gate to the LORD's **T**
28:21 Ahaz took valuable items from the LORD's **T**,
28:24 The king took the utensils from the **T** of God
28:24 He shut the doors of the LORD's **T** so that no one
29: 3 Hezekiah reopened the doors of the **T** of the
29: 4 Levites to meet him at the courtyard east of the **T**.
29: 5 Purify yourselves, and purify the **T** of the LORD,
29: 6 They abandoned the LORD and his **T**;
29:15 Then they began to purify the **T** of the LORD,
29:16 The priests went into the sanctuary of the **T** of the
29:16 and they took out to the **T** courtyard all the defiled
29:17 they had reached the foyer of the LORD's **T**.
29:17 Then they purified the **T** of the LORD itself,
29:18 "We have purified the **T** of the LORD, the altar
29:19 Ahaz when he was unfaithful and closed the **T**.
29:20 the city officials and went to the **T** of the LORD.
29:21 offering for the kingdom, for the **T**, and for Judah.
29:25 then stationed the Levites at the **T** of the LORD
29:26 then took their positions around the **T** with the
29:31 and thanksgiving offerings to the **T** of the
29:35 So the **T** of the LORD was restored to service.
30: 1 He asked everyone to come to the **T** of the LORD
30: 8 Come to his **T** which he has set apart as holy
30:15 and brought burnt offerings to the **T** of the
30:16 They took their places at the **T** according to the
31: 2 and praise to the LORD at the gates of the **T**.
31:10 began bringing their gifts to the LORD's **T**,
31:11 have storerooms prepared in the **T** of the LORD,
31:12 the gifts and tithes were faithfully brought to the **T**.
31:13 and Azariah, the chief official in the **T** of God.
31:16 who came daily to the LORD's **T** to perform their
31:21 In all that he did in the service of the **T** of God
32:12 Jerusalem to worship at only the one altar at the **T**
32:21 And when he entered the **t** of his god, some of his
33: 4 He even built pagan altars in the **T** of the LORD,
33: 5 of heaven in both courtyards of the LORD's **T**.
33: 7 a carved idol he had made and set it up in God's **T**,
33: 7 "My name will be honored here forever in this **T**
33:15 from the hills and the idol from the LORD's **T**.
33:15 the altars he had built on the hill where the **T** stood
34: 8 his reign, after he had purified the land and the **T**,
34: 8 to repair the **T** of the LORD his God.
34: 9 Levites who served as gatekeepers at the **T** of God.
34:10 to supervise the restoration of the LORD's **T**.
34:14 recording the money collected at the LORD's **T**,
34:15 found the Book of the Law in the LORD's **T**!"
34:17 The money that was collected at the **T** of the
34:21 "Go to the **T** and speak to the LORD for me
34:22 grandson of Harhas, the keeper of the **T** wardrobe.
34:30 And the king went up to the **T** of the LORD with
34:30 Covenant that had been found in the LORD's **T**.
35: 2 and encouraged them in their work at the **T** of the
35: 3 "Since the Ark is now in Solomon's **T** and you do
35: 5 to you as they bring their offerings to the **T**.
35: 8 and Jehiel, the administrators of God's **T**,
35:20 After Josiah had finished restoring the **T**,
36: 7 some of the treasures from the **T** of the LORD,
36:10 Many treasures from the **T** of the LORD were
36:14 desecrating the **T** of the LORD in Jerusalem.
36:15 for he had compassion on his people and his **T**.
36:17 young men, even chasing after them into the **T**.
36:18 large and small, used in the **T** of God,
36:18 and the treasures from both the LORD's **T**
36:19 Then his army set fire to the **T** of God, broke down
36:23 He has appointed me to build him a **T** at Jerusalem
Ezr 1: 2 He has appointed me to build him a **T** at Jerusalem
1: 3 in Judah to rebuild this **T** of the LORD,
1: 4 as well as a freewill offering for the **T** of God in
1: 5 return to Jerusalem to rebuild the **T** of the LORD.
1: 7 had taken from the LORD's **T** in Jerusalem
1: 7 and had placed in the **t** of his own gods.
2:43 The descendants of the following **T** servants
2:58 the **T** servants and the descendants of Solomon's
2:68 When they arrived at the **T** of the LORD in
2:68 the rebuilding of God's **T** on its original site,
2:70 the singers, the gatekeepers, the **T** servants,
3: 6 started to lay the foundation of the LORD's **T**.
3: 8 The construction of the **T** of God began in
3: 8 were put in charge of rebuilding the LORD's **T**.
3: 9 The workers at the **T** of God were supervised by
3:10 completed the foundation of the LORD's **T**,
3:11 because the foundation of the LORD's **T** had
3:12 Levites, and other leaders remembered the first **T**,
4: 1 that the exiles were rebuilding a **T** to the LORD,
4: 3 We alone will build the **T** for the LORD, the God
4:24 The work on the **T** of God in Jerusalem had
5: 2 the task of rebuilding the **T** of God in Jerusalem.
5: 3 "Who gave you permission to rebuild this **T**
5: 4 of all the people who were working on the **T**.
5: 8 of the **T** of the great God in the province of Judah.
5: 9 'Who gave you permission to rebuild this **T**
5:11 and we are rebuilding the **T** that was built here
5:12 who destroyed this **T** and exiled the people to
5:13 issued a decree that the **T** of God should be rebuilt.
5:14 had taken from the **T** of God in Jerusalem and had placed in the **t** of Babylon.
5:14 These items were taken from that **t** and delivered
5:15 and to rebuild the **T** of God there as it had been
5:16 and laid the foundations of the **T** of God in
5:17 issued a decree to rebuild God's **T** in Jerusalem.
6: 3 a decree was sent out concerning the **T** of God at
6: 5 Nebuchadnezzar from the **T** of God in Jerusalem,
6: 5 and put into God's **T** as they were before."
6: 7 Do not disturb the construction of the **T** of God.
6: 8 leaders of the Jews as they rebuild this **T** of God.
6:12 that violates this command and destroys this **T**.
6:14 The **T** was finally finished, as had been
6:15 The **T** was completed on March 12,
6:16 The **T** of God was then dedicated with great joy by
6:17 During the dedication ceremony for the **T** of God,
6:18 divisions to serve at the **T** of God in Jerusalem,
6:22 so that he helped them to rebuild the **T** of God,
7: 7 Levites, singers, gatekeepers, and **T** servants,
7:16 and the priests that are presented for the **T** of their
7:17 all of which will be offered on the altar of the **T** of
7:19 to you for the service of the **T** of your God,
7:20 of money for anything necessary for your God's **T**
7:23 whatever the God of heaven demands for his **T**,
7:24 no priest, Levite, singer, gatekeeper, **T** servant,
7:24 or other worker in this **T** of God will be required to
7:27 who made the king want to beautify the **T** of the
8:17 and the **T** servants to send us ministers for the **T** of God at Jerusalem.
8:20 and 220 **T** servants. The **T** servants were assistants
8:20 a group of **T** workers first instituted by King
8:25 and the people of Israel had presented for the **T** of
8:29 the storerooms of the LORD's **T** in Jerusalem."
8:30 these treasures to the **T** of our God in Jerusalem.
8:33 and other valuables were weighed at the **T** of our
8:36 by supporting the people and the **T** of God.
9: 9 so that we were able to rebuild the **T** of our God
10: 1 himself to the ground in front of the **T** of God,
10: 6 Then Ezra left the front of the **T** of God and went
10: 9 were sitting in the square before the **T** of God.
Ne 2: 8 I will need it to make beams for the gates of the **T**
3:26 and the **T** servants living on the hill of Ophel,
3:31 repaired the wall as far as the housing for the **T**
6:10 "Let us meet together inside the **T** of God and bolt
6:11 Should someone in my position enter the **T** to save
7:46 "The descendants of the following **T** servants
7:60 the **T** servants and the descendants of Solomon's
7:73 the gatekeepers, the singers, the **T** servants,
8:16 in their courtyards, in the courtyards of God's **T**,
10:28 Levites, gatekeepers, singers, **T** servants,
10:32 the annual **T** tax of an eighth of an ounce of silver,
10:32 will be enough money to care for the **T** of our God.
10:33 items necessary for the work of the **T** of our God.
10:34 **T** to be burned on the altar of the LORD our God,
10:35 the first part of every harvest to the LORD's **T**—
10:36 to the priests who minister in the **T** of our God.
10:37 the produce in the storerooms of the **T** of our God.
10:38 be delivered by the Levites to the **T** of our God
10:39 and olive oil to the **T** and place them in the sacred
10:39 "So we promise together not to neglect the **T** of
11: 3 Most of the people, priests, Levites, **T** servants,
11:11 son of Ahitub, the supervisor of the **T** of God;
11:12 with 822 of their associates, who worked at the **T**.
11:16 who were in charge of the work outside the **T** of
11:21 However, the **T** servants, whose leaders were Ziha
11:22 whose family served as singers at God's **T**.
12:40 giving thanks then proceeded to the **T** of God,
13: 4 supervisor of the storerooms of the **T** of our God
13: 5 frankincense, **T** utensils, and tithes of grain,
13: 7 with a room in the courtyards of the **T** of God—
13: 9 and I brought back the utensils for God's **T**,
13:11 "Why has the **T** of God been neglected?"
13:12 new wine, and olive oil to the **T** storerooms.
13:14 all that I have faithfully done for the **T** of my God.
Ps 5: 7 with deepest awe I will worship at your **T**.
11: 4 But the LORD is in his holy **T**; / the LORD still
27: 4 the LORD's perfections / and meditating in his **T**.
29: 9 forests bare. / In his **T** everyone shouts, "Glory!"
30: T A psalm of David, sung at the dedication of the **T**.
48: 9 on your unfailing love / as we worship in your **T**.
65: 4 What joys await us / inside your holy **T**.
66:13 Now I come to your **T** with burnt offerings
68:29 earth are bringing tribute / to your **T** in Jerusalem.
79: 1 special possession. / They have defiled your holy **T**
138: 2 I bow before your holy **T** as I worship. / I will give

Ecc 5: 6 And don't defend yourself by telling the **T**
8: 10 that they were the very ones who frequented the **T**
Isa 2: 2 the **T** of the LORD in Jerusalem will become the
2: 3 of the LORD, to the **T** of the God of Israel.
6: 1 a lofty throne, and the train of his robe filled the **T**.
6: 4 The glorious singing shook the **T** to its
37: 1 and went into the **T** of the LORD to pray.
37: 14 he went up to the LORD's **T** and spread it out
37: 38 One day while he was worshiping in the **t** of his
38: 20 every day of my life / in the **T** of the LORD.
38: 22 "What sign will prove that I will go to the **T** of the
44: 28 Jerusalem be rebuilt and that the **T** be restored."
56: 7 because my **T** will be called a house of prayer for
58: 2 They come to the **T** every day and seem delighted
60: 7 my altars. In that day I will make my **T** glorious.
60: 13 to beautify my sanctuary. My **T** will be glorious!
62: 9 Within the courtyards of the **T**, you yourselves will
64: 11 beautiful **T** where our ancestors praised you has
65: 11 and his **T** and worship the gods of Fate
66: 1 Could you ever build me a **t** as good as that?
66: 6 in the city? What is that terrible noise from the **T**?
Jer 7: 2 "Go to the entrance of the LORD's **T**, and give
7: 4 your safety because the **T** of the LORD is here.
7: 8 because the **T** is here you will never suffer?
7: 10 come here and stand before me in my **T** and chant,
7: 11 Do you think this **T**, which honors my name,
7: 14 I will now destroy this **T** that was built to honor
7: 14 this **T** that you trust for help, this place that I gave
7: 30 set up their abominable idols right in my own **T**,
11: 15 right do my beloved people have to come to my **T**,
17: 26 and thanksgiving offerings to the LORD's **T**.
19: 14 and he stopped in front of the **T** of the LORD.
20: 1 the priest in charge of the **T** of the LORD,
20: 2 in stocks at the Benjamin Gate of the LORD's **T**.
23: 11 their despicable acts right here in my own **T**,"
24: 1 placed in front of the LORD's **T** in Jerusalem.
26: 2 "Stand out in front of the **T** of the LORD,
26: 6 then I will destroy this **T** as I destroyed Shiloh,
26: 7 Jeremiah as he spoke in front of the LORD's **T**.
26: 8 and all the people at the **T** mobbed him.
26: 9 name that this **T** will be destroyed like Shiloh?
26: 9 people threatened him as he stood in front of the **T**.
26: 10 and sat down at the New Gate of the **T** to hold
26: 12 "The LORD sent me to prophesy against this **T**
26: 18 will grow on the hilltop, where the **T** now stands.'
27: 16 taken from my **T** will be returned from Babylon.
27: 18 gold utensils that are still left in the LORD's **T**
27: 19 says about the bronze pillars in front of the **T**,
27: 19 the bronze Sea in the **T** courtyard, the bronze water
27: 21 says about the precious things kept in the **T** and in
28: 1 addressed me publicly in the **T** while all the priests
28: 3 I will bring back all the **T** treasures that King
28: 5 stood in front of all the priests and people at the **T**.
28: 6 bring back from Babylon the treasures of this **T**
28: 11 of Babylon." At that, Jeremiah left the **T** area.
32: 34 set up their abominable idols right in my own **T**,
34: 15 and made a solemn covenant with me in my **T**.
35: 2 Recabites live, and invite them to the LORD's **T**.
35: 4 I took them to the **T**, and we went into the room
35: 4 of Maaseiah son of Shallum, the **T** gatekeeper.
36: 5 "I am a prisoner here and unable to go to the **T**.
36: 6 So you go to the **T** on the next day of fasting,
36: 8 messages from the LORD to the people at the **T**.
36: 9 came to attend the services at the **T** on that day.
36: 10 from the **T** room of Gemariah son of Shaphan.
36: 10 room was just off the upper courtyard of the **T**,
38: 14 meet him at the third entrance of the LORD's **T**.
41: 5 They had come to worship at the **T** of the LORD.
43: 13 sacred pillars standing in the **t** of the sun in Egypt,
50: 28 vengeance against those who destroyed his **T**.
51: 11 his vengeance against those who desecrated his **T**.
51: 51 because the LORD's **T** has been defiled by
52: 13 He burned down the **T** of the LORD, the royal
52: 17 and the bronze Sea that were at the LORD's **T**,
52: 18 bronze utensils used for making sacrifices at the **T**.
52: 20 These things had been made for the LORD's **T** in
La 1: 4 crowds on their way to celebrate the **T** festivals.
1: 10 She has seen foreigners violate her sacred **T**,
2: 1 the Lord has shown no mercy even to his **T**.
2: 6 He has broken down his **T** as though it were
2: 7 They shout in the LORD's **T** as though it were a
2: 20 and prophets die within the Lord's **T**?
Eze 5: 11 because you have defiled my **T** with idols and vile
8: 3 to the north gate of the inner courtyard of the **T**,
8: 6 people of Israel are doing to drive me from my **T**?
8: 7 Then he brought me to the door of the **T** courtyard,
8: 14 brought me to the north gate of the LORD's **T**,
8: 16 me into the inner courtyard of the LORD's **T**.
8: 16 were standing with their backs to the LORD's **T**.
9: 2 They all went into the **T** courtyard and stood
9: 3 it had rested, and moved to the entrance of the **T**.
9: 6 the mark. Begin your task right here at the **T**."
9: 7 "Defile the **T**!" the LORD commanded. "Fill its
10: 3 at the south end of the **T** when the man went in,
10: 4 the cherubim and went over to the door of the **T**.
10: 4 The **T** was filled with this cloud of glory,
10: 4 and the **T** courtyard glowed brightly with the glory
10: 18 glory of the LORD moved from the door of the **T**
10: 19 their wheels to the east gate of the LORD's **T**.
11: 1 me over to the east gateway of the LORD's **T**,
23: 38 they defiled my **T** and violated my Sabbath day!
23: 39 their idols, they boldly came into my **T** to worship!
24: 21 I will desecrate my **T**, the source of your security
25: 3 Because you scoffed when my **T** was desecrated,
37: 26 and I will put my **T** among them forever.
37: 28 And since my **T** will remain among them forever,
40: 5 I could see a wall completely surrounding the **T**
40: 9 end of the gateway structure, facing toward the **T**.
40: 17 the gateway into the outer courtyard of the **T**.
40: 45 is for the priests who supervise the **T** maintenance.
40: 47 altar stood there in the courtyard in front of the **T**.
40: 48 Then he brought me to the foyer of the **T**.
41: 1 into the Holy Place, the large main room of the **T**,
41: 5 Then he measured the wall of the **T** and found that
41: 6 for these rooms rested on ledges in the **T** wall,
41: 7 corresponding to the narrowing of the **T** wall as it
41: 8 I noticed that the **T** was built on a terrace,
41: 10 feet in width, and it went all the way around the **T**.
41: 12 building stood on the west, facing the **T** courtyard.
41: 13 Then the man measured the **T**, and he found it to
41: 14 The inner courtyard to the east of the **T** was also
41: 15 and the foyer of the **T** were all paneled with wood,
41: 16 The inner walls of the **T** were paneled with wood
41: 19 figures were carved all along the inside of the **T**,
42: 1 Then the man led me out of the **T** courtyard by
42: 8 the rooms toward the **T**—extended for 175 feet.
42: 10 On the south side of the **T** there were two blocks of
42: 10 just south of the inner courtyard between the **T**
42: 11 just like the complex on the north side of the **T**.
42: 13 "These rooms that overlook the **T** from the north
42: 15 the east gateway to measure the entire **T** area.
43: 4 And the glory of the LORD came into the **T**
43: 5 and the glory of the LORD filled the **T**.
43: 6 I heard someone speaking to me from within the **T**.
43: 10 describe to the people of Israel the **T** I have shown
43: 12 And this is the basic law of the **T**:
43: 12 The entire top of the hill where the **T** is built is
holy. Yes, this is the primary law of the **T**.
43: 21 and burn it at the appointed place outside the **T**
44: 4 me through the north gateway to the front of the **T**.
44: 4 and saw that the glory of the LORD filled the **T**
44: 5 about the regulations concerning the LORD's **T**.
44: 5 Take careful note of who may be admitted to the **T**
44: 7 you profaned my **T** even as you offered me my
44: 11 They may still be **T** guards and gatemen, and they
44: 14 They are to serve as the **T** caretakers and are
44: 15 in the **T** when Israel abandoned me for idols.
44: 17 on duty in the inner courtyard or in the **T** itself.
44: 26 But such a priest can only return to his **T** duties
44: 29 and sacrifices brought to the **T** by the people—
45: 2 875 feet by 875 feet, will be set aside for the **T**.
45: 4 for their homes, and my **T** will be located within it.
45: 5 be a living area for the Levites who work at the **T**.
45: 18 bull with no physical defects to purify the **T**.
45: 19 sin offering and put it on the doorposts of the **T**,
45: 20 In that way, you will make atonement for the **T**.
46: 24 "These are the kitchens to be used by the **T**
47: 1 the man brought me back to the entrance of the **T**.
47: 1 flowing eastward from beneath the **T** threshold.
47: 12 they are watered by the river flowing from the **T**.
48: 8 as the tribal territories, with the **T** at the center.
48: 9 "The area set aside for the LORD's **T** will be
48: 10 miles wide, with the LORD's **T** at the center.
48: 15 south of the sacred **T** area, will be allotted for
Da 1: 2 him some of the sacred objects from the **T** of God
5: 2 had taken from the **T** in Jerusalem, so that he
5: 3 So they brought these gold cups taken from the **T**
5: 23 and have had these cups from his **T** brought before
8: 11 sacrifices offered to him and by destroying his **T**.
8: 12 sacrilege was committed against the **T** ceremonies,
8: 13 How long will the **T** and heaven's armies be
8: 14 and mornings; then the **T** will be restored."
9: 26 arise whose armies will destroy the city and the **T**.
11: 31 His army will take over the **T** fortress,
Hos 3: 4 and without sacrifices, **t**, priests, or even idols!
Joel 1: 9 is no grain or wine to offer at the **T** of the LORD.
1: 13 is no grain or wine to offer at the **T** of your God.
1: 14 and all the people into the **T** of the LORD your
3: 18 a fountain will burst forth from the LORD's **T**,
Am 1: 2 "The LORD's voice roars from his **T** on Mount
8: 3 In that day the riotous sounds of singing in the **T**
9: 1 "Strike the tops of the **T** columns so hard that the
Jnh 2: 4 How will I ever again see your holy **T**?'
2: 7 my earnest prayer went out to you in your holy **T**.
Mic 1: 2 against you; the Lord speaks from his holy **T**.
3: 12 will grow on the hilltop, where the **T** now stands.
4: 1 the **T** of the LORD in Jerusalem will become the
4: 2 of the LORD, to the **T** of the God of Israel.
Hab 2: 20 But the LORD is in his holy **T**. Let all the earth
Zep 3: 4 Its priests defile the **T** by disobeying God's laws.
Hag 1: 2 come to rebuild the LORD's house—the **T**.' "
2: 3 remember this house—the **T**—as it was before?
2: 7 the treasures of all the nations will come to this **T**.
2: 9 The future glory of this **T** will be greater than its
2: 15 began to lay the foundation of the LORD's **T**.
2: 18 the day when the foundation of the LORD's **T**
Zec 1: 16 My **T** will be rebuilt, says the LORD Almighty,
3: 7 then you will be given authority over my **T** and its
4: 7 Then Zerubbabel will set the final stone of the **T** in
4: 9 is the one who laid the foundation of this **T**,
5: 11 Babylonia where they will build a **t** for the basket.
5: 11 And when the **t** is ready, they will set the basket
6: 12 out where he is and build the **T** of the LORD.
6: 13 He will build the LORD's **T**, and he will receive
6: 14 "The crown will be a memorial in the **T** of the
6: 15 Many will come from distant lands to rebuild the **T**
7: 3 and of the priests at the **T** of the LORD
8: 9 **T** of the LORD Almighty ever since the
8: 10 Before the work on the **T** began, there were no
8: 13 but instead get on with rebuilding the **T**!
9: 8 I will guard my **T** and protect it from invading
11: 13 and threw them to the potters in the **T** of the
14: 20 And the cooking pots in the **T** of the LORD will
14: 21 longer be traders in the **T** of the LORD Almighty.
Mal 1: 10 "I wish that someone among you would shut the **T**
3: 1 Lord you are seeking will suddenly come to his **T**.
3: 10 so there will be enough food in my **T**.
Mt 4: 5 him to Jerusalem, to the highest point of the **T**,
5: 23 "So if you are standing before the altar in the **T**,
12: 5 priests on duty in the **T** may work on the Sabbath?
12: 6 there is one here who is even greater than the **T**!
17: 24 the tax collectors for the **T** tax came to Peter
17: 24 asked him, "Doesn't your teacher pay the **T** tax?"
21: 12 Jesus entered the **T** and began to drive out the
21: 13 'My **T** will be called a place of prayer,'
21: 14 came to him, and he healed them there in the **T**.
21: 15 and heard even the little children in the **T** shouting,
21: 23 When Jesus returned to the **T** and began teaching,
21: 23 did you drive out the merchants from the **T**?
23: 16 say that it means nothing to swear 'by God's **T**'—
23: 16 that it is binding to swear 'by the gold in the **T**.'
23: 17 the gold, or the **T** that makes the gold sacred?
23: 21 And when you swear 'by the **T**,' you are swearing
23: 35 whom you murdered in the **T** between the altar
24: 1 As Jesus was leaving the **T** grounds, his disciples
pointed out to him the various **T**
26: 55 to arrest me? Why didn't you arrest me in the **T**?
26: 61 'I am able to destroy the **T** of God and rebuild it in
27: 5 Judas threw the money onto the floor of the **T**
27: 6 "We can't put it in the **T** treasury," they said,
27: 40 You can destroy the **T** and build it again in three
27: 51 At that moment the curtain in the **T** was torn in
Mk 11: 11 So Jesus came to Jerusalem and went into the **T**.
11: 15 Jesus entered the **T** and began to drive out the
11: 17 'My **T** will be called a place of prayer for all
11: 27 As Jesus was walking through the **T** area,
11: 28 did you drive out the merchants from the **T**?
12: 35 Later, as Jesus was teaching the people in the **T**,
12: 41 Jesus went over to the collection box in the **T**
13: 1 As Jesus was leaving the **T** that day, one of his
13: 3 the Mount of Olives across the valley from the **T**.
14: 49 Why didn't you arrest me in the **T**? I was there
14: 58 'I will destroy this **T** made with human hands,
15: 29 "You can destroy the **T** and rebuild it in three
15: 38 And the curtain in the **T** was torn in two, from top
Lk 1: 8 One day Zechariah was serving God in the **T**,
1: 22 that he must have seen a vision in the **T** sanctuary.
1: 23 He stayed at the **T** until his term of service was
2: 27 That day the Spirit led him to the **T**. So when Mary
2: 36 Anna, a prophet, was also there in the **T**. She was
2: 37 She never left the **T** but stayed there day and night,
2: 46 He was in the **T**, sitting among the religious
4: 9 to the highest point of the **T**, and said, "If you are
10: 32 A **T** assistant walked over and looked at him lying
13: 1 as they were sacrificing at the **T** in Jerusalem.
18: 10 "Two men went to the **T** to pray. One was a
19: 45 Then Jesus entered the **T** and began to drive out
19: 46 'My **T** will be a place of prayer,'
19: 47 After that, he taught daily in the **T**, but the leading
20: 1 and preaching the Good News in the **T**,
20: 2 did you drive out the merchants from the **T**?
21: 1 While Jesus was in the **T**, he watched the rich
21: 5 talking about the beautiful stonework of the **T**
21: 37 Every day Jesus went to the **T** to teach, and each
22: 4 and captains of the **T** guard to discuss the best way
22: 52 to the leading priests and captains of the **T** guard
22: 53 Why didn't you arrest me in the **T**? I was there
23: 45 the thick veil hanging in the **T** was torn apart.
24: 53 And they spent all of their time in the **T**,
Jn 1: 19 and **T** assistants from Jerusalem to ask John
2: 14 In the **T** area he saw merchants selling cattle,
2: 15 from some ropes and chased them all out of the **T**.
2: 19 "Destroy this **t**, and in three days I will raise it
2: 20 "It took forty-six years to build this **T**, and you
2: 21 But by "this **t**," Jesus meant his body.
5: 14 But afterward Jesus found him in the **T** and told
7: 14 Jesus went up to the **T** and began to teach.
7: 28 While Jesus was teaching in the **T**, he called out,
7: 31 Many among the crowds at the **T** believed in him.
7: 32 and the leading priests sent **T** guards to arrest
7: 45 The **T** guards who had been sent to arrest him
8: 2 early the next morning he was back again at the **T**.
8: 20 in the section of the **T** known as the Treasury.
8: 59 But Jesus hid himself from them and left the **T**.
10: 23 He was at the **T**, walking through the section
11: 48 will come and destroy both our **T** and our nation."
11: 56 and as they talked in the **T**, they asked each other,
18: 3 Roman soldiers and **T** guards to accompany him.
18: 12 and the **T** guards arrested Jesus and tied him up.
18: 20 preached regularly in the synagogues and the **T**.
18: 22 One of the **T** guards standing there struck Jesus on
19: 6 the leading priests and **T** guards began shouting,
Ac 1: 16 who guided the **T** police to arrest Jesus.
2: 46 They worshiped together at the **T** each day, met in
3: 1 and John went to the **T** one afternoon to take part
3: 2 As they approached the **T**, a man lame from birth
3: 2 Each day he was put beside the **T** gate, the one
3: 2 so he could beg from the people going into the **T**.
3: 8 and praising God, he went into the **T** with them.
4: 1 the leading priests, the captain of the **T** guard,
5: 12 And the believers were meeting regularly at the **T**
5: 20 "Go to the **T** and give the people this message of
5: 21 So the apostles entered the **T** about daybreak
5: 22 But when the **T** guards went to the jail, the men
5: 24 When the captain of the **T** guard and the leading
5: 25 that the men they had jailed were out in the **T**,
5: 26 The captain went with his **T** guards and arrested
5: 42 And every day, in the **T** and in their homes,
6: 13 "This man is always speaking against the **T**
6: 14 say that this Jesus of Nazareth will destroy the **T**
7: 46 of building a permanent **T** for the God of Jacob.

7:49 Could you ever build me a t as good as that?'
14:13 The t of Zeus was located on the outskirts of the
14:13 The priest of the t and the crowd brought oxen
19:27 I'm also concerned that the t of the great goddess
19:35 the official guardian of the t of the great Artemis,
19:37 but they have stolen nothing from the t and have
21:24 Go with them to the T and join them in the
21:26 purification ritual with the men and went to the T.
21:27 Jews from the province of Asia saw Paul in the T
21:28 He speaks against the T—and he even defiles it by
21:29 and they assumed Paul had taken him into the T.)
21:30 Paul was dragged out of the T, and immediately
22:17 I was praying in the T, and I fell into a trance.
24: 6 Moreover he was trying to defile the T when we
24:11 ago that I arrived in Jerusalem to worship at the T.
24:12 I didn't argue with anyone in the T, nor did I incite
24:18 My accusers saw me in the T as I was completing
25: 8 Jewish laws or the T or the Roman government."
26:21 Some Jews arrested me in the T for preaching this,
1Co 3:16 Don't you realize that all of you together are the t
3:17 God will bring ruin upon anyone who ruins this t.
3:17 For God's t is holy, and you Christians are that t.
6:19 Or don't you know that your body is the t of the
8:10 eat this food will see you eating in the t of an idol.
9:13 Don't you know that those who work in the T get
9:13 meals from the food brought to the T as offerings?
2Co 6:16 And what union can there be between God's t and
idols? For we are the t of the living God.
Eph 2:21 joined together, becoming a holy t for the Lord.
2Th 2: 4 He will position himself in the t of God,
Heb 9:24 for that was merely a copy of the real T in heaven.
13:10 We have an altar from which the priests in the T
1Pe 2: 4 to Christ, who is the living cornerstone of God's t.
2: 5 is building you, as living stones, into his spiritual t.
Rev 3:12 All who are victorious will become pillars in the T
7:15 throne of God, serving him day and night in his T.
11: 1 "Go and measure the T of God and the altar,
11:19 the T of God was opened and the Ark of his
Covenant could be seen inside the T.
13: 6 his name and all who live in heaven, who are his t.
14:15 Then an angel came from the T and called out in a
14:17 another angel came from the T in heaven,
15: 5 Then I looked and saw that the T in heaven,
15: 6 the bowls of the seven plagues came from the T,
15: 8 The T was filled with smoke from God's glory
15: 8 No one could enter the T until the seven angels
16: 1 Then I heard a mighty voice shouting from the T
16: 2 So the first angel left the T and poured out his
16:17 And a mighty shout came from the throne of the T
21:22 No t could be seen in the city, for the Lord God
Almighty and the Lamb are its t.

TEMPLE'S (13) [TEMPLE]

1Ki 6:21 Then he overlaid the rest of the T interior with
8: 8 seen from the front entrance of the T main room—
2Ki 12:12 and they paid any other expenses related to the T
22: 5 to the men assigned to supervise the T restoration.
2Ch 5: 9 seen from the front entrance of the T main room—
6:13 and had placed it at the center of the T outer
29: 7 They also shut the doors to the T foyer, and they
Ezr 3:12 and they wept aloud when they saw the new T
Eze 40:19 Then the man measured across the T outer
40:23 there was another gateway leading to the T inner
41: 9 The outer wall of the T side rooms was 8-3/4 feet
41:25 was a wooden canopy over the front of the T foyer.
Zec 7: 3 and fast each summer on the anniversary of the T

TEMPLES (13) [TEMPLE]

Lev 19:27 "Do not trim off the hair on your t or clip the
Jdg 5:26 the tent peg through his head, piercing his t.
Isa 15: 2 Your people in Dibon will mourn at their t
16:12 They will cry to the gods in their t, but no one will
Jer 43:12 He will set fire to the t of Egypt's gods, burning all
43:13 and he will burn down the t of Egypt's gods.' "
Joel 3: 5 and you have carried them off to your pagan t.
Am 7: 9 your ancestors and the t of Israel will be destroyed,
Mic 5:14 and destroy the cities where your idol t stand.
Na 1:14 I will destroy all the idols in the t of your gods.
Ac 7:48 the Most High doesn't live in t made by human
17:24 of heaven and earth, he doesn't live in man-made t,
Ro 2:22 condemn idolatry, but do you steal from pagan t?

TEMPORAL [KJV] See SOON (BE OVER)

TEMPORARY (2)

Lev 13: 6 It was only a t rash. So after washing the clothes,
Job 20: 5 and the joy of the godless has been only t?

TEMPT (1) [TEMPTATION, TEMPTATIONS, TEMPTED, TEMPTER, TEMPTING, TEMPTS]

1Co 7: 5 so that Satan won't be able to t them because of

TEMPTATION (13) [TEMPT]

Jdg 2: 3 and their gods will be a constant t to you."
Mt 6:13 And don't let us yield to t, / but deliver us from the
18: 7 T to do wrong is inevitable, but how terrible it will
26:41 and pray. Otherwise t will overpower you.
Mk 14:38 and pray. Otherwise, t will overpower you.
Lk 11: 4 sinned against us. / And don't let us yield to t."
22:40 "Pray that you will not be overcome by t."
22:46 and pray. Otherwise, t will overpower you."
1Co 10:13 He will keep the t from becoming so strong that
Gal 6: 1 And be careful not to fall into the same t yourself.
1Ti 6: 9 But people who long to be rich fall into t and are
Heb 2:18 Since he himself has gone through suffering and t,
Jas 1:14 T comes from the lure of our own evil desires.

TEMPTATIONS (3) [TEMPT]

Lk 17: 1 to his disciples, "There will always be t to sin,
1Co 10:13 But remember that the t that come into your life
Heb 4:15 for he faced all of the same t we do, yet he did not

TEMPTED (8) [TEMPT]

Ex 33: 3 I would be t to destroy you along the way."
Eze 29:16 "Then Israel will no longer be t to trust in Egypt
Mt 4: 1 by the Holy Spirit to be t there by the Devil.
Mk 1:13 He was there for forty days, being t by Satan.
Lk 4: 2 where the Devil t him for forty days. He ate
1Co 10:13 When you are t, he will show you a way out
Heb 2:18 he is able to help us when we are being t.
Jas 1:13 God is never t to do wrong, and he never tempts

TEMPTER (1) [TEMPT]

1Th 3: 5 I was afraid that the T had gotten the best of you

TEMPTING (4) [TEMPT]

Mt 18: 7 terrible it will be for the person who does the t.
Lk 4:13 When the Devil had finished t Jesus, he left him
17: 1 terrible it will be for the person who does the t.
Jas 1:13 to do wrong should ever say, "God is t me."

TEMPTS (1) [TEMPT]

Jas 1:13 to do wrong, and he never t anyone else either.

TEN (167) [ONE-TENTH, TEN-STRINGED, TENS, TENTH, TITHE, TITHES, TITHING]

Ge 8:13 t and a half months after the flood began,
16: 3 (This happened t years after Abram first arrived in
18:32 but once more! Suppose only t are found there?"
18:32 "Then, for the sake of the t, I will not destroy it."
24:10 He loaded t of Abraham's camels with gifts
24:55 "But we want Rebekah to stay at least t days,"
31:41 And you have reduced my wages t times!
32:15 forty cows, t bulls, twenty female donkeys, and t
male donkeys.
42: 3 So Joseph's t older brothers went down to Egypt to
45:23 He sent his father t donkeys loaded with the good
45:23 and t donkeys loaded with grain and all kinds of
Ex 18:21 groups of one thousand, one hundred, fifty, and t.
18:25 groups of one thousand, one hundred, fifty, and t.
26: 1 "Make the Tabernacle from t sheets of fine linen.
26: 2 All t sheets must be exactly the same size.
27:12 feet long, supported by t posts set into t bases.
34:28 the T Commandments—on the stone tablets.
36: 8 The skilled weavers first made t sheets from fine
38:12 The walls were made from curtains supported by t
Lev 26: 8 and a hundred of you will chase t thousand!
26:26 oven will have to be stretched to feed t families.
27: 5 a girl of that age is valued at t pieces of silver.
27: 7 a woman older than sixty is valued at t pieces of
Nu 11:19 just a day or two, or for five or t or even twenty.
14:36 Then the t scouts who had incited the rebellion
29: 7 "T days later, you must call another holy assembly
29:23 of the festival, sacrifice t young bulls, two rams,
Dt 1:15 some for a hundred, some for fifty, and some for t.
4:13 commanded you to keep—the T Commandments
10: 4 the T Commandments—on them and gave them to
23: 2 and their descendants for t generations may not be
23: 3 or any of their descendants for t generations,
32:30 of them, / and two people put t thousand to flight,
Jos 15:57 t towns with their surrounding villages.
17: 5 Manasseh's inheritance came to t parcels of land,
21: 5 allotted t towns from the territories of Ephraim,
21:26 So t towns with their pasturelands were given to
22:14 In this delegation were t high officials of Israel,
one from each of the t tribes,
22:32 and the t high officials left the tribes of Reuben
Jdg 1: 4 and they killed t thousand enemy warriors at the
3:29 and killed about t thousand of their strongest
4: 6 Assemble t thousand warriors from the tribes of
4:10 and t thousand warriors marched up with him.
4:14 So Barak led his t thousand warriors down the
6:27 So Gideon took t of his servants and did as the
7: 3 leaving only t thousand who were willing to fight.
12:11 became Israel's judge. He judged Israel for t years.
17:10 I will give you t pieces of silver a year, plus a
Ru 1: 4 a woman named Ruth. But about t years later,
4: 2 Then Boaz called t leaders from the town
1Sa 1: 8 have me—isn't that better than having t sons?"
17:17 and these t loaves of bread to your brothers.
17:18 And give these t cuts of cheese to their captain.
18: 7 killed his thousands, / and David his t thousands!"
18: 8 "They credit David with t thousands and me with
21:11 killed his thousands, and David his t thousands'?"
25: 5 he sent t of his young men to Carmel. He told them
25:38 About t days later, the LORD struck him and he
29: 5 killed his thousands, and David his t thousands'?"
2Sa 15:16 He left no one behind except t of his concubines to
18: 3 You are worth t thousand of us, and it is better that
18:11 I would have rewarded you with t pieces of silver
18:15 T of Joab's young armor bearers then surrounded
19:43 "But there are t tribes in Israel," the others
19:43 "So we have t times as much right to the king as
20: 3 he instructed that the t concubines he had left to
1Ki 4:23 t oxen from the fattening pens, twenty pasture-fed
5:14 them to Lebanon in shifts, t thousand every month,
7:27 Huram also made t bronze water carts, each 6 feet
7:37 All t water carts were the same size and were made
7:38 Huram also made t bronze basins, one for each
7:43 the t water carts holding the t basins,
11:31 Then he said to Jeroboam, "Take t of these pieces,
11:31 of Solomon, and I will give t of the tribes to you!
11:35 away from his son and give t of the tribes to you.
14: 3 Take him a gift of t loaves of bread, some cakes,
2Ki 5: 5 150 pounds of gold, and t sets of clothing.
7: 1 and t quarts of barley grain will cost only half an
7:16 and t quarts of barley grain were sold for half an
7:18 and t quarts of barley grain will cost half an ounce
13: 7 t chariots, and t thousand foot soldiers.
14: 7 It was Amaziah who killed t thousand Edomites in
15:17 reign in Judah. He reigned in Samaria t years.
20: 9 the shadow on the sundial to go forward t steps or
backward t steps?"
20:11 and he caused the shadow to move t steps
24:14 King Nebuchadnezzar took t thousand captives
25:25 went to Mizpah with t men and assassinated
1Ch 6:61 The remaining descendants of Kohath received t
2Ch 4: 6 He also made t basins for water to wash the
4: 7 then cast t gold lampstands according to the
4: 8 He also built t tables and placed them in the
14: 1 next king. There was peace in the land for t years,
25:11 where they killed t thousand Edomite troops from
25:12 They captured another t thousand and took them to
30:24 donated one thousand bulls and t thousand sheep.
36: 9 reigned in Jerusalem only three months and t days.
Ezr 8:24 Sherebiah, Hashabiah, and t other priests—
Ne 5:18 And every t days we needed a large supply of all
Est 9:10 the t sons of Haman son of Hammedatha,
9:12 the fortress of Susa alone and also Haman's t sons.
9:13 and have the bodies of Haman's t sons hung from
9:14 They also hung the bodies of Haman's t sons from
Job 19: 3 T times now you have meant to insult me.
Ps 3: 6 I am not afraid of t thousand enemies
91: 7 though t thousand are dying around you,
Ecc 7:19 A wise person is stronger than the t leading
SS 5:10 is dark and dazzling, better than t thousand others!
Isa 5:10 T acres of vineyard will not produce even six
5:10 T measures of seed will yield only one measure of
38: 8 I will cause the sun's shadow to move t steps
38: 8 the shadow on the sundial moved backward t steps.
Jer 41: 1 arrived in Mizpah accompanied by t men.
41: 2 Ishmael and his t men suddenly drew their swords
41: 7 Ishmael and his men killed all but t of them
41: 8 The other t had talked Ishmael into letting them go
42: 7 T days later, the LORD gave his reply to
Eze 40:49 There were t steps leading up to it, with a column
Da 1:12 "Test us for t days on a diet of vegetables
1:13 "At the end of the t days, see how we look
1:14 to Daniel's suggestion and tested them for t days.
1:15 At the end of the t days, Daniel and his three
1:20 to be t times better than that of all the magicians
7: 7 from any of the other beasts, and it had t horns.
7:20 I also asked about the t horns on the fourth beast's
7:24 Its t horns are t kings that will rule that empire.
7:24 another king will arise, different from the other t,
Am 5: 3 sends a hundred, only t will come back alive."
6: 9 If there are t men left in one house, they will all
Hag 2:16 for a twenty-bushel crop, you harvested only t.
Zec 8:23 In those days t people from nations and languages
Mt 4:25 the T Towns, Jerusalem, from all over Judea,
20:24 When the t other disciples heard what James
25: 1 by the story of t bridesmaids who took their lamps
25:28 and give it to the one with the t bags of gold.
Mk 5:20 So the man started off to visit the T Towns of that
7:31 the Sea of Galilee and the region of the T Towns.
10:41 When the t other disciples discovered what James
Lk 14:31 and discussing whether his army of t thousand is
15: 8 "Or suppose a woman has t valuable silver coins
17:12 entered a village there, t lepers stood at a distance,
17:17 Jesus asked, "Didn't I heal t men? Where are the
19:13 he called together t servants and gave them t
pounds of silver to invest for him
19:16 t times as much as the original amount!
19:17 so you will be governor of t cities as your reward.'
Ac 25: 6 Eight or t days later he returned to Caesarea,
1Co 4:15 For even if you had t thousand others to teach you
14:19 than t thousand words in an unknown language.
Eph 6: 2 This is the first of the T Commandments that ends
Heb 9: 4 and the stone tablets of the covenant with the T
Rev 2:10 you to the test. You will be persecuted for 't days.'
12: 3 a large red dragon with seven heads and t horns,
13: 1 It had seven heads and t horns, with t crowns on
17: 3 on a scarlet beast that had seven heads and t horns,
17: 7 and of the beast with seven heads and t horns.
17:12 His t horns are t kings who have not yet risen to
17:16 The scarlet beast and his t horns—which represent
t kings who will reign with him—

TEN-STRINGED (2) [STRING, TEN]

Ps 33: 2 on the lyre; / make music for him on the t harp.
144: 9 O God! / I will sing your praises with a t harp.

TENANT (3) [TENANTS]

Mt 21:33 Then he leased the vineyard to t farmers
Mk 12: 1 Then he leased the vineyard to t farmers
Lk 20: 9 man planted a vineyard, leased it out to t farmers,

TENANTS (1) [TENANT]

Lev 25:23 You are only foreigners and t living with me.

TEND (8) [TENDED, TENDING, TENDS]

Ge 2:15 God placed the man in the Garden of Eden to t
2Ki 19:29 you will t vineyards and eat their fruit.

Pr 27:18 Workers who **t** a fig tree are allowed to eat its fruit.
SS 1:6 and sent me out to **t** the vineyards in the hot sun.
Isa 27:3 will watch over it and **t** its fruitful vines.
37:30 you will **t** vineyards and eat their fruit.
61:5 and plow your fields and **t** your vineyards.
Eze 34:15 I myself will **t** my sheep and cause them to lie

TENDED (4) [TEND]

Ge 37:2 he often **t** his father's flocks with his half brothers,
Lev 24:3 and must arrange to have the lamps **t** continually,
24:4 The lamps on the pure gold lampstand must be **t**
Eze 34:4 You have not **t** the sick or bound up the broken

TENDER (34) [TENDERHEARTED, TENDERLY, TENDERNESS]

Dt 28:56 The most **t** and delicate woman among you—
32:2 like dew. / My words will fall like rain on **t** grass,
2Sa 23:4 like the refreshing rains that bring **t** grass from the
2Ki 19:26 as the grass, / as easily trampled as **t** green shoots.
Job 38:27 parched ground and makes the **t** grass spring up?
Ps 40:11 LORD, don't hold back your **t** mercies from me.
80:8 You brought us from Egypt as though we were a **t**
89:1 I will sing of the **t** mercies of the LORD forever!
103:4 and surrounds me with love and **t** mercies.
103:13 **t** and compassionate to those who fear him.
119:77 Surround me with your **t** mercies so I may live,
Pr 28:14 Blessed are those who have a **t** conscience,
Isa 15:6 banks are scorched, and the **t** plants are gone.
37:27 as the grass, / as easily trampled as **t** green shoots.
47:1 will you be the lovely princess, **t** and delicate.
53:2 up in the LORD's presence like a **t** green shoot,
Eze 11:19 their hearts of stone and give them **t** hearts instead,
17:22 I will take a **t** shoot from the top of a tall cedar,
24:4 the rump and the shoulder and all the most **t** cuts.
Da 4:15 band of iron and bronze and surrounded by **t** grass.
4:23 band of iron and bronze and surrounded by **t** grass.
Hos 10:11 Now I will put a heavy yoke on her **t** neck.
Am 6:4 eating the meat of **t** lambs and choice calves.
Na 2:11 and the young and **t** lived with nothing to fear?
Mt 13:7 thorns that shot up and choked out the **t** blades.
24:32 When its buds become **t** and its leaves begin to
Mk 4:7 and choked out the **t** blades so that it produced no
13:28 When its buds become **t** and its leaves begin to
Lk 1:78 Because of God's **t** mercy, / the light from heaven
8:7 thorns that shot up and choked out the **t** blades.
Php 1:8 and long for you with the **t** compassion of Christ
2:1 in the Spirit? Are your hearts **t** and sympathetic?
1Th 5:14 Take **t** care of those who are weak. Be patient with
1Pe 3:8 loving one another with **t** hearts and humble

TENDERHEARTED (5) [HEART, TENDER]

Dt 28:54 The most **t** man among you will have no
Ps 79:8 Let your **t** mercies quickly meet our needs,
La 4:10 **T** women have cooked their own children
Eph 4:32 Instead, be kind to each other, **t**, forgiving one
Col 3:12 you must clothe yourselves with **t** mercy, kindness,

TENDERLY (3) [TENDER]

Pr 4:3 **t** loved by my mother as an only child.
Isa 40:2 "Speak **t** to Jerusalem. Tell her that her sad days
Hos 2:14 lead her out into the desert and speak **t** to her there.

TENDERNESS (1) [TENDER]

Jas 5:11 finally ended in good, for he is full of **t** and mercy.

TENDING (5) [TEND]

Ex 3:1 One day Moses was **t** the flock of his
2Sa 7:8 a shepherd boy, **t** your sheep out in the pasture.
1Ch 17:7 a shepherd boy, **t** your sheep out in the pasture.
Ps 78:71 He took David from **t** the ewes and lambs
Hos 12:12 to the land of Aram and earned a wife by **t** sheep.

TENDRILS (1)

Isa 16:8 Her **t** spread out as far as Jazer and trailed out into

TENDS (1) [TEND]

Ex 30:8 And each evening when he **t** to the lamps, he must

TENONS [KJV] See PEGS

TENS (2) [TEN]

Ps 144:13 multiply by the thousands, / even **t** of thousands,
Mic 6:7 of rams and **t** of thousands of rivers of olive oil?

TENT (98) [TENTMAKERS, TENTS]

SACRED TENT (17) Ex 26:9,36; 35:11; 36:37; 39:33,38; Nu 3:8; 9:17; Dt 31:15; 1Ki 1:39,50; 2:28,30,34; Heb 8:2; 9:1,21

TENT OF MEETING (5) Ex 33:7,8,11,11; 34:34

Ge 9:21 on some wine he had made and lay naked in his **t**.
9:23 it over their shoulders, walked backward into the **t**,
18:1 as Abraham was sitting at the entrance to his **t**,
18:6 So Abraham ran back to the **t** and said to Sarah,
18:9 they asked him. "In the **t**," Abraham replied.
18:10 listening to this conversation from the **t** nearby.
18:33 with Abraham, and Abraham returned to his **t**.
24:67 And Isaac brought Rebekah into his mother's **t**,
31:33 Laban went first into Jacob's **t** to search there,
31:33 find the gods. Finally, he went into Rachel's **t**.
Ex 18:7 and then went to Moses' **t** to talk further.
26:9 to be doubled over at the entrance of the sacred **t**.
26:36 from fine linen for the entrance of the sacred **t**,
27:19 including all the **t** pegs used to support the
33:7 It was Moses' custom to set up the **t** known as the **T** of Meeting far outside the camp.
33:8 Whenever Moses went out to the **T** of Meeting,
33:8 people would get up and stand in their **t** entrances.
33:9 As he went into the **t**, the pillar of cloud would
33:10 would stand and bow low at their **t** entrances.
33:11 Inside the **T** of Meeting, the LORD would speak
33:11 son of Nun, stayed behind in the **T** of Meeting.
34:34 But whenever he went into the **T** of Meeting to
35:11 including the sacred **t** and its coverings, the clasps,
35:18 the **t** pegs of the Tabernacle and courtyard
36:37 another curtain for the entrance to the sacred **t**.
38:20 All the **t** pegs used in the Tabernacle and courtyard
38:31 and all the **t** pegs used to hold the curtains of the
39:33 the sacred **t** with all its furnishings, the clasps,
39:38 the curtain for the entrance of the sacred **t**;
39:40 at the courtyard entrance; the cords and **t** pegs;
40:8 set up the courtyard around the outside of the **t**,
Nu 3:8 also maintain all the furnishings of the sacred **t**,
3:25 These two clans were responsible to care for the **t**
9:17 When the cloud lifted from over the sacred **t**,
19:14 ritual law that applies when someone dies in a **t**:
19:14 Those who enter that **t**, and those who were inside
19:15 Any container in the **t** that was not covered with a
19:18 sprinkle the water on the **t**, on all the furnishings in the **t**, and on anyone who was in the **t**,
25:8 and rushed after the man into his **t**. Phinehas thrust
Dt 31:15 in a pillar of cloud at the entrance to the sacred **t**.
Jos 7:21 They are hidden in the ground beneath my **t**,
7:22 They ran to the **t** and found the stolen goods
7:23 They took the things from the **t** and brought them
7:24 his sons, daughters, cattle, donkeys, sheep, **t**,
Jdg 4:11 and pitched his **t** by the Oak of Zaanannim,
4:17 Meanwhile, Sisera ran to the **t** of Jael, the wife of
4:18 meet Sisera and said to him, "Come into my **t**, sir.
4:18 So he went into her **t**, and she covered him with a
4:20 "Stand at the door of the **t**," he told her.
4:21 quietly crept up to him with a hammer and **t** peg.
4:21 Then she drove the **t** peg through his temple
4:22 So he followed her into the **t** and found Sisera lying there dead, with the **t** peg through his temple.
5:26 Then with her left hand she reached for a **t** peg,
5:26 She pounded the **t** peg through his head,
7:13 It hit a **t**, turned it over, and knocked it flat!"
1Sa 17:54 but he stored the Philistine's armor in his own **t**.)
2Sa 6:17 inside the special **t** that David had prepared for it.
7:2 cedar palace, but the Ark of God is out in a **t**!"
7:6 My home has always been a **t**, moving from one
16:22 So they set up a **t** on the palace roof where
16:22 and Absalom went into the **t** to sleep with his
1Ki 1:39 the priest took a flask of olive oil from the sacred **t**
1:50 so he rushed to the sacred **t** and caught hold of the
2:28 he ran to the sacred **t** of the LORD and caught
2:30 Benaiah went into the sacred **t** of the LORD
2:34 So Benaiah son of Jehoiada returned to the sacred **t**
2Ki 7:8 they went into one **t** after another, eating,
1Ch 9:23 of the LORD, the house that was formerly a **t**.
15:1 Ark of God and set up a special **t** there to shelter it.
16:1 So they brought the Ark of God into the special **t**
17:1 the Ark of the LORD's covenant is out in a **t**!"
17:5 My home has always been a **t**, moving from one
2Ch 1:4 to the special **t** he had prepared for it in Jerusalem.
5:5 along with the special **t** and all its sacred utensils.
Job 4:21 Their **t** collapses; they die in ignorance.
8:22 and the **t** of the wicked will be destroyed."
18:6 The light in their **t** will grow dark. The lamp
18:14 They are torn from the security of their **t**, and they
19:12 up roads to attack me. They camp all around my **t**.
30:11 For God has cut the cords of my **t**. He has humbled
Pr 14:11 will perish, but the **t** of the godly will flourish.
Isa 22:23 for I will drive him firmly in place like a **t** stake.
24:20 It trembles like a **t** in a storm. It falls and will not
38:12 like a shepherd's **t** in a storm. / It has been cut
40:22 heavens like a curtain and makes his **t** from them.
Jer 4:20 Suddenly, every **t** is destroyed; in a moment,
Zec 10:4 the **t** peg, the battle bow, and all the rulers.
2Co 5:1 For we know that when this earthly **t** we live in is
Heb 8:2 There he ministers in the sacred **t**, the true place of
9:1 for worship and a sacred **t** here on earth.
9:2 There were two rooms in this **t**. In the first room
9:21 he sprinkled blood on the sacred **t** and on
9:23 That is why the earthly **t** and everything in it—
11:9 by faith—for he was like a foreigner, living in a **t**.

TENTH (30) [TEN]

Ge 14:20 Then Abram gave Melchizedek a **t** of all the goods
28:22 and I will give God a **t** of everything he gives
Ex 12:3 Announce to the whole community that on the **t**
Lev 27:30 "A **t** of the produce of the land, whether grain
27:31 If you want to redeem the LORD's **t** of the fruit
27:32 The LORD also owns every **t** animal counted off
27:33 The **t** animal must not be selected on the basis of
Nu 7:66 On the **t** day Ahiezer son of Ammishaddai,
18:26 the Israelites, give a **t** of the tithes you receive—
Jos 4:19 The people crossed the Jordan on the **t** day of the
Jdg 20:10 One **t** of the men from each tribe will be chosen to
1Sa 8:15 He will take a **t** of your harvest and distribute it
8:17 He will demand a **t** of your flocks, and you will be
1Ch 12:13 Jeremiah was **t**. / Macbannai was eleventh.
24:11 ninth lot fell to Jeshua. / The **t** lot fell to Shecaniah.
25:17 The **t** lot fell to Shimei and twelve of his sons
27:13 from Netophah, was commander of the **t** division,
27:13 which was on duty during the **t** month.
Ne 10:37 And we promise to bring to the Levites a **t** of
10:38 And a **t** of all that is collected as tithes will be
11:1 A **t** of the people from the other towns of Judah
Isa 6:13 Even if only a **t**—a remnant—survive, it will be
Jer 32:1 the LORD in the **t** year of the reign of Zedekiah,
Eze 29:1 during the **t** year of King Jehoiachin's captivity,
Lk 18:12 twice a week, and I give you a **t** of my income.'
Heb 7:2 Then Abraham took a **t** of all he had won in the
7:4 by giving him a **t** of what he had taken in battle.
7:6 even related to Levi, collected a **t** from Abraham.
Rev 11:13 a terrible earthquake that destroyed a **t** of the city.
21:20 the eighth beryl, the ninth topaz, the **t** chrysoprase,

TENTMAKERS (1) [TENT]

Ac 18:3 worked with them, for they were **t** just as he was.

TENTS (41) [TENT]

Ge 4:20 He became the first of the herdsmen who live in **t**.
13:5 also very wealthy with sheep, cattle, and many **t**.
13:12 Lot moved his **t** to a place near Sodom,
31:33 then he searched the **t** of the two concubines,
31:34 So although Laban searched all the **t**, he couldn't
Ex 35:20 left Moses and went to their **t** to prepare their gifts.
Lev 14:8 they must still remain outside their **t** for seven
Nu 3:38 toward the sunrise was reserved for the **t** of Moses
11:10 all the families standing in front of their **t** weeping,
16:24 "Then tell all the people to get away from the **t** of
16:25 and rushed over to the **t** of Dathan and Abiram,
16:26 "Get away from the **t** of these wicked men,
16:27 So all the people stood back from the **t** of Korah,
16:27 and stood at the entrances of their **t** with their
24:5 How beautiful are your **t**, O Jacob; / how lovely
Dt 1:27 You murmured and complained in your **t** and said,
5:30 Go and tell them to return to their **t**.
11:6 along with their households and **t** and every living
16:7 Then go back to your **t** the next morning.
33:18 the people of Issachar prosper at home in their **t**.
Jdg 5:24 May she be blessed above all women who live in **t**.
6:5 coming with their cattle and **t** as thick as locusts,
1Sa 4:10 that day. The survivors turned and fled to their **t**.
2Sa 11:11 and the armies of Israel and Judah are living in **t**,
1Ki 20:12 and the other kings as they were drinking in their **t**.
20:16 and the thirty-two allied kings were still in their **t**
2Ki 7:7 abandoning their **t**, horses, donkeys,
7:10 donkeys were tethered and the **t** were all in order,
Ps 69:25 homes become desolate / and their **t** be deserted.
78:28 to fall within their camp / and all around their **t**.
106:25 Instead, they grumbled in their **t** / and refused to
SS 1:5 of Jerusalem, tanned as the dark **t** of Kedar. Yes, even as the **t** of Solomon!
1:8 follow the trail of my flock to the shepherds' **t**,
Jer 35:7 or plant crops or vineyards, but always live in **t**.
35:10 We have lived in **t** and have fully obeyed all the
37:10 they would still stagger from their **t** and burn this
49:29 Their flocks and **t** will be captured, and their
Eze 25:4 camps among you and pitch their **t** on your land.
Da 11:45 and the sea and will pitch his royal **t** there,
Hos 12:9 And I will make you live in **t** again, as you do each

TERAH (13) [TERAH'S]

Ge 11:24 When Nahor was 29 years old, his son **T** was born.
11:25 After the birth of **T**, Nahor lived another 119 years
11:26 When **T** was 70 years old, he became the father of
11:27 **T** was the father of Abram, Nahor, and Haran;
11:28 place of his birth. He was survived by **T**, his father.
11:31 **T** took his son Abram, his daughter-in-law Sarai,
11:32 **T** lived for 205 years and died while still at Haran.
Nu 33:27 They left Tahath and camped at **T**.
33:28 They left **T** and camped at Mithcah.
Jos 24:2 Your ancestors, including **T**, the father of Abraham
1Ch 1:26 Serug, Nahor, **T**,
Lk 3:34 Abraham was the son of **T**. / **T** was the son of Nahor.

TERAH'S (1) [TERAH]

Ge 11:27 This is the history of **T** family. Terah was the

TERESH (2)

Est 2:21 two of the king's eunuchs, Bigthana and **T**—
6:2 Mordecai had exposed the plot of Bigthana and **T**,

TERM (3) [TERMS]

Nu 6:12 to the LORD for the full **t** of their vow,
1Ch 25:8 The musicians were appointed to their particular **t**
Lk 1:23 He stayed at the Temple until his **t** of service was

TERMS (39) [TERM]

Ge 17:9 told Abraham, "is to obey the **t** of the covenant.
31:44 peace treaty, you and I, and we will live by its **t**."
Ex 6:4 Under its **t**, I swore to give them the land of
25:16 place inside it the stone tablets inscribed with the **t**
25:21 stone tablets inscribed with the **t** of the covenant,
31:18 stone tablets inscribed with the **t** of the covenant.
32:15 stone tablets inscribed with the **t** of the covenant.
34:27 for they represent the **t** of my covenant with you
34:28 At that time he wrote the **t** of the covenant—
34:29 stone tablets inscribed with the **t** of the covenant,
40:20 stone tablets inscribed with the **t** of the covenant,
Lev 27:25 All the value assessments must be measured in **t** of
Dt 10:4 The LORD again wrote the **t** of the covenant—
17:19 LORD his God by obeying all the **t** of this law.
20:10 a town to attack it, first offer its people **t** for peace.
20:11 If they accept your **t** and open the gates to you,
27:3 Then write all the **t** of this law on them. I repeat,

27: 8 you must clearly write all the t of this law."
27:26 'Cursed is anyone who does not affirm the t of this
28:58 "If you refuse to obey all the t of this law that are
29: 1 These are the t of the covenant the LORD
29: 9 obey the t of this covenant so that you will prosper
31:12 your God and carefully obey all the t of this law.
Jos 2:21 "I accept your t," she replied. And she sent them
Jdg 4:17 because Heber's family was on friendly t with
1Sa 11: 3 will come to save us, we will agree to your t."
2Ki 18:31 These are the t the king of Assyria is offering:
23: 3 he confirmed all the t of the covenant that were
2Ch 34:31 He promised to obey all the t of the covenant that
Ps 132:12 If your descendants obey the t of my covenant
Isa 8:11 The LORD has said to me in the strongest t:
36:16 These are the t the king of Assyria is offering:
Jer 11: 2 and Jerusalem about the t of their covenant with
11: 3 Cursed is anyone who does not obey the t of my
32:11 which contained the t and conditions of the
34:18 Because you have refused the t of our covenant,
Eze 20:37 you carefully and hold you to the t of the covenant.
Mt 5:25 Come to t quickly with your enemy before it is too
Lk 14:32 he will send a delegation to discuss t of peace.

TERRACE (3) [TERRACED, TERRACES]

Eze 41: 8 I noticed that the Temple was built on a t,
41: 8 for the side rooms. This t was 10-1/2 feet high.
41:11 Two doors opened from the side rooms into the t

TERRACED (1) [TERRACE]

Am 9:13 Then the t vineyards on the hills of Israel will drip

TERRACES (1) [TERRACE]

2Ki 23: 4 outside Jerusalem on the t of the Kidron Valley,

TERRESTRIAL [KJV] See (ON) EARTH

TERRIBLE (193) [TERROR]

Ge 12:17 But the LORD sent a t plague upon Pharaoh's
41:31 so t that even the memory of the good years will be
43: 1 But there was no relief from the t famine
44: 7 think we are, that you accuse us of such a t thing?
Ex 5:21 you for getting us into this t situation with Pharaoh
8:14 into great heaps, and a t stench filled the land.
8:24 There were t swarms of flies in Pharaoh's palace
9:10 and t boils broke out on the people and animals
10:17 the LORD your God to take away this t plague."
16:20 then it was full of maggots and had a t smell.
32:12 Change your mind about this t disaster you are
32:19 In t anger, he threw the stone tablets to the ground,
32:21 "How did they ever make you bring such t sin
32:30 said to the people, "You have committed a t sin,
32:31 "Alas, these people have committed a t sin.
Lev 18:23 to have intercourse with it; this is a t perversion.
20:17 of either his father or his mother, it is a t disgrace.
20:23 because they do these t things that I detest them
Nu 20: 5 us leave Egypt and bring us here to this t place?
Dt 7:15 He will not let you suffer from the t diseases you
9:16 made in your t sin against the LORD your God.
28:57 and t distress that your enemy will inflict on all
31:17 T trouble will come down on them, so that they
Jos 10:11 the LORD destroyed them with a t hailstorm that
24: 5 and Aaron, and I brought t plagues on Egypt;
Jdg 20: 3 then asked how this t crime had happened.
20: 6 for these men have committed this t and shameful
20:12 saying, "What a t thing has been done among you!
1Sa 2:30 The t things you are doing cannot continue!
14:20 each other. There was t confusion everywhere.
2Sa 1: 9 of my misery, for I am in t pain and want to die.'
19:19 "Forget the t thing I did when you left Jerusalem.
1Ki 2: 8 He cursed me with a t curse as I was fleeing to
9: 8 'Why did the LORD do such t things to his land
19:11 It was such a t blast that the rocks were torn loose,
2Ki 7: 9 some t calamity will certainly fall upon us.
8:12 "I know the t things you will do to the people of
2Ch 7:21 'Why has the LORD done such t things to his
Ne 9:18 They sinned and committed t blasphemies.
9:26 return to you, and they committed t blasphemies.
Job 2: 7 and he struck Job with a t case of boils from head
41:14 Who could pry open its jaws? For its teeth are t!
Isa 3: 9 are not one bit ashamed. How t it will be for them!
7:17 "The LORD will bring a t curse on you,
13: 8 Fear grips them with t pangs, like those of a
13: 9 is coming—the t day of his fury and fierce anger.
20: 3 a symbol of the t troubles I will bring upon Egypt
22: 2 The whole city is in a t uproar. What do I see in
27: 1 In that day the LORD will take his t, swift sword
28:18 When the t enemy floods in, you will be trampled
30: 6 Look at the animals moving slowly across the t
45:10 How t it would be if a newborn baby said to its
51:22 "See, I am taking the t cup from your hands.
66: 6 in the city? What is that t noise from the Temple?
66:17 will come to a t end," says the LORD.
Jer 4: 6 For I am bringing t destruction upon you from the
4:13 How t it will be! Our destruction is sure!
7:20 "I will pour out my t fury on this place. Its people,
8: 6 Does anyone say, "What a t thing I have done"?
8:16 The whole land trembles at the approach of the t
13:16 you look for light, you will find only t darkness.
16: 4 They will die from t diseases. No one will mourn
16:10 'Why has the LORD decreed such t things
18:13 My virgin Israel has done something too t to
19: 3 I will bring such a t disaster on this place that the
21: 6 I will send a t plague upon this city, and both
25:19 and his people. They, too, drank from that t cup,
25:27 rise no more, for I am sending t wars against you.'
26:19 Then the LORD held back the t disaster he had
26:20 And he predicted the same t disaster against the
29:22 Their t fate will become proverbial, so that
29:23 For these men have done t things among my
30:12 Yours is an incurable bruise, a t wound.
32:23 That is why you have sent this t disaster upon
33: 5 for I have determined to destroy them in my t
36: 3 in writing all the t things I have planned for them.
36: 7 For the LORD's t anger has been pronounced
44:23 The very reason all these t things have happened to
50:27 Even destroy her cattle—it will be t for them, too!
51:60 Jeremiah had recorded on a scroll all the t disasters
Eze 7:12 for all of them will fall under my t anger.
7:23 for my people, for the land is bloodied by t crimes.
8:17 the people of Judah that they commit these t sins,
14: 8 against such people and make a t example of them,
14:21 How t it will be when all four of these fearsome
16:52 be deeply ashamed because your sins are so t.
20:47 The t flames will not be quenched; they will scorch
21:10 It is being prepared for t slaughter; it will flash like
22: 2 city of murderers? Denounce her t deeds in public,
23:38 Then after doing these t things, they defiled my
25:17 I will execute t vengeance against them to rebuke
26:19 You will sink beneath the t waves of enemy attack.
26:21 I will bring you to a t end, and you will be no
27:35 are appalled at your t fate. / Their kings are filled
28:19 You have come to a t end, and you are no more."
30: 3 for the t day is almost here—the day of the
33:33 But when all these t things happen to them—
Da 9:27 Then as a climax to all his t deeds, he will set up a
Hos 7:13 "How t it will be for my people who have deserted
9:12 It will be a t day when I turn away and leave you
Joel 1: 6 It is a t army, too numerous to count! Its teeth are
1:15 comes from the Almighty. How t that day will be!
2:11 The day of the LORD is an awesome, t thing.
2:14 sending you a blessing instead of this t curse.
2:31 before that great and t day of the LORD arrives.
Am 5:18 How t it will be for you who say, "If only the day
6: 1 How t it will be for you who lounge in luxury
6: 4 How t it will be for you who sprawl on ivory beds
Ob 1:14 handing them over to their enemies in that t time
Jnh 1: 7 had offended the gods and caused the t storm.
1:12 For I know that this t storm is all my fault."
Mic 2: 1 How t it will be for you who lie awake at night,
4:10 Writhe and groan in t pain, you people of
Na 3: 1 How t it will be for Nineveh, the city of murder
Hab 1:12 Babylonians to punish and correct us for our t sins.
2: 9 "How t it will be for you who get rich by unjust
2:12 "How t it will be for you who build cities with
2:15 "How t it will be for you who make your
2:19 How t it will be for you who beg lifeless wooden
Zep 1:14 "That t day of the LORD is near. Swiftly it
1:15 It is a day of t distress and anguish, a day of ruin
2: 2 and the t day of the LORD's anger begins.
2: 5 And how t it will be for you Philistines who live
3: 1 How t it will be for rebellious, polluted Jerusalem,
Mal 2: 2 "or I will bring a t curse against you.
3:13 "You have said t things about me,"
Mt 8:24 Suddenly, a t storm came up, with waves breaking
18: 7 "How t it will be for anyone who causes others to
18: 7 but how t it will be for the person who does the
23:13 "How t it will be for you teachers of religious law
23:15 how t it will be for you teachers of religious law
23:16 "Blind guides! How t it will be for you! For you
23:23 "How t it will be for you teachers of religious law
23:25 "How t it will be for you teachers of religious law
23:27 "How t it will be for you teachers of religious law
23:29 "How t it will be for you teachers of religious law
24:19 How t it will be for pregnant women and for
26:24 long ago. But how t it will be for my betrayer.
27:19 because I had a t nightmare about him last night."
Mk 5: 7 He gave a t scream, shrieking, "Why are you
8:31 would suffer many t things and be rejected by the
13:17 How t it will be for pregnant women and for
14:21 long ago. But how t it will be for my betrayer.
Lk 9:22 Son of Man, must suffer many t things," he said.
11:42 "But how t it will be for you Pharisees! For you
11:43 "How t it will be for you Pharisees! For how you
11:44 Yes, how t it will be for you. For you are like
11:46 "how t it will be for you experts in religious law!
11:47 How t it will be for you! For you build tombs for
11:52 "How t it will be for you experts in religious law!
12:50 There is a t baptism ahead of me, and I am under a
17: 1 but how t it will be for the person who does the
21:23 How t it will be for pregnant women and for
22:22 God's plan. But how t it will be for my betrayer!"
22:65 And they threw all sorts of t insults at him.
Jn 11:39 by now the smell will be t because he has been
13:24 motioned to him to ask who would do this t thing.
Ac 8:24 "that these t things won't happen to me!"
9:13 "I've heard about the t things this man has done to
27:20 The t storm raged unabated for many days,
Ro 2: 1 "What t people you have been talking about!"
2: 5 So you are storing up t punishment for yourself
7:13 So we can see how t sin really is.
1Co 5: 6 How t that you should boast about your
9:16 by God to do it. How t for me if I didn't do it!
Eph 5: 6 for the t anger of God comes upon all those who
Col 3: 6 God's t anger will come upon those who do such
Heb 10:27 forward to but the t expectation of God's judgment
10:29 Think how much more t the punishment will be for
10:31 It is a t thing to fall into the hands of the living
10:32 remained faithful even though it meant t suffering.
12: 3 when sinful people did such t things to him,
12:19 so t that they begged God to stop speaking.
12:25 how t our danger if we reject the One who speaks
Jas 5: 1 because of all the t troubles ahead of you.
1Pe 3:20 people were saved from drowning in that t flood.
4: 3 and wild parties, and their t worship of idols.
4:17 what t fate awaits those who have never believed
2Pe 2: 1 who bought them. Theirs will be a swift and t end.
3:10 Then the heavens will pass away with a t noise,
Jude 1:11 How t it will be for them! For they follow the evil
Rev 8: 5 lightning flashed, and there was a t earthquake.
11:13 And in the same hour there was a t earthquake that
13: 6 And he spoke t words of blasphemy against God,
15: 7 angels a gold bowl filled with the t wrath of God,
16:21 There was a t hailstorm, and hailstones weighing
16:21 of the hailstorm, which was a very t plague.
18:10 cry out, "How t, how t for Babylon, that great city!
18:16 "How t, how t for that great city! She was
18:19 And they will say, "How t, how t for the great city!

TERRIBLY (9) [TERROR]

Lev 20:14 a woman and her mother, such an act is t wicked.
2Ki 13: 4 The LORD could see how t the king of Aram was
Ne 1: 7 We have sinned t by not obeying the commands,
Jer 23:13 "I saw that the prophets of Samaria were t evil,
Mt 17:15 on my son, because he has seizures and suffers t.
Mk 9: 6 really know what to say, for they were all t afraid.
Lk 2: 9 glory surrounded them. They were t frightened,
17:25 But first the Son of Man must suffer t and be
24:37 But the whole group was t frightened,

TERRIFIC (1)

1Ki 18:45 A heavy wind brought a t rainstorm, and Ahab left

TERRIFIED (43) [TERROR]

Ge 32: 7 Jacob was t at the news. He divided his household,
Ex 4: 3 a snake! Moses was t, so he turned and ran away.
14:27 and the LORD swept the t Egyptians into the
15:15 The leaders of Edom will be t; / the nobles of
Nu 22: 3 Israelites there were, he and his people were t.
Dt 2:25 will make all people throughout the earth t of you.
20: 8 Then the officers will also say, 'Is anyone t?
Jos 2:24 "for all the people in the land are t of us."
Jdg 20:41 warriors realized disaster was near and became t.
1Sa 12:18 And all the people were t of the LORD and of
14:15 then an earthquake struck, and everyone was t.
17:11 heard this, they were t and deeply shaken.
1Ch 21:30 because he was t by the drawn sword of the angel
Job 23:15 No wonder I am so t in his presence. When I think
23:16 has made my heart faint; the Almighty has t me.
Ps 6:10 May all my enemies be disgraced and t. / May they
48: 5 they were stunned; / they were t and ran away.
83:17 Let them be ashamed and t forever. / Make them
Jer 10: 2 even though other nations are t by them.
47: 3 T fathers run madly, without a backward glance at
Eze 32:10 and their kings will be t because of all I do to you.
Da 4: 5 I saw visions that t me as I lay in my bed.
7:15 troubled by all I had seen, and my visions t me.
7:28 was t by my thoughts and my face was pale with
8:17 I became so t that I fell to the ground.
10: 7 but they were suddenly t and ran away to hide.
10:16 "I am t by the vision I have seen, my lord, and I
Ob 1: 9 The mightiest warriors of Teman will be t,
Jnh 1:10 The sailors were t when they heard this. "Oh,
Hab 2:17 You t the wild animals you caught in your traps.
Zec 14:13 On that day they will be t, stricken by the LORD
Mt 14:30 at the high waves, he was t and began to sink.
17: 6 The disciples were t and fell face down on the
27:54 and the other soldiers at the crucifixion were t by
Mk 6:50 They were all t when they saw him. But Jesus
Lk 24: 5 The women were t and bowed low before them.
Jn 6:19 walking on the water toward the boat. They were t,
Ac 5: 5 and died. Everyone who heard about it was t.
24:25 and the judgment to come, Felix was t.
Heb 12:21 at the sight that he said, "I am t and trembling."
Rev 11:13 And everyone who did not die was t and gave
18:10 will stand at a distance, t by her great torment.
18:15 will stand at a distance, t by her great torment.

TERRIFIES (2) [TERROR]

Job 15:24 That dark day t them. They live in distress
33:16 whispers in their ear and t them with his warning.

TERRIFY (12) [TERROR]

2Ch 32:18 trying to t them so it would be easier to capture the
Job 3: 5 black cloud overshadow it, and let the darkness t it.
5:22 and famine; wild animals will not t you.
7:14 shatter me with dreams. You t me with visions.
13:21 and don't t me with your awesome presence.
13:25 Would you t a leaf that is blown by the wind?
Ps 10:18 the oppressed, / so people can no longer t them.
83:15 your fierce storms; / t them with your tempests.
Jer 20:16 T him all day long with battle shouts,
Eze 30: 9 in ships to t the complacent Ethiopians.
Zep 2:11 The LORD will t them as he destroys all the gods
Zec 1:21 "The blacksmiths have come to t the four horns

TERRIFYING (17) [TERROR]

Ge 15:12 He saw a t vision of darkness and horror.
Ex 9:28 Please beg the LORD to end this t thunder
10:21 and t darkness will descend on the land of Egypt."
Dt 1:19 and traveled through the great and t wilderness,
4:34 wonders, war, awesome power, and t acts?
6:22 dealing t blows against Egypt and Pharaoh and all
8:15 and t wilderness with poisonous snakes
34:12 mighty power and t acts in the sight of all Israel.
Jdg 13: 6 He was like one of God's angels, t to look at.
Ps 2: 5 he rebukes them, / t them with his fierce fury.

Jer 10:22 Hear the **t** roar of great armies as they roll down
Eze 21: 7 'I groan because of the **t** news I have heard.
Da 7: 7 I saw a fourth beast, **t**, dreadful, and very strong.
7:19 the one so different from the others and so **t**.
Zep 1:18 He will make a **t** end of all the people on earth.
Lk 21:11 and there will be **t** things and great miraculous
2Pe 2:12 They laugh at the **t** powers they know so little

TERRITORIES (17) [TERRITORY]

Ge 10:20 according to their tribes, languages, **t**, and nations.
10:31 according to their tribes, languages, **t**, and nations.
48: 6 The land they inherit will be within the **t** of
Dt 12:14 the LORD will choose within one of your tribal **t**.
Jos 11:17 of Lebanon. Joshua killed all the kings of those **t**,
19:51 These are the **t** that Eleazar the priest, Joshua son
21: 5 clan were allotted ten towns from the **t** of Ephraim,
Jdg 1:18 and Ekron, along with their surrounding **t**.
1Ki 4:19 including the **t** of King Sihon of the Amorites
2Ki 14:25 Jeroboam II recovered the **t** of Israel between
1Ch 6:62 by sacred lots thirteen towns from the **t** of Issachar,
6:63 by sacred lots twelve towns from the **t** of Reuben,
6:65 The towns in the **t** of Judah, Simeon,
Ne 2: 7 travel safely through their **t** on my way to Judah.
Eze 48: 8 and will extend as far east and west as the tribal **t**,
48:22 include everything between the **t** allotted to Judah
48:23 "These are the **t** allotted to the rest of the tribes.

TERRITORY (95) [TERRITORIES]

Ge 9:27 May God enlarge the **t** of Japheth, / and may he
10:19 Eventually the **t** of Canaan spread from Sidon to
31:21 the Euphrates River, heading for the **t** of Gilead.
45:18 'Pharaoh will assign to you the very best **t** in the
Ex 13:17 them on the road that runs through Philistine **t**,
Nu 21:13 in the wilderness adjacent to the **t** of the Amorites.
21:22 on the king's road until we have crossed your **t**.
21:31 So the people of Israel occupied the **t** of the
32:33 and half the tribe of Manasseh son of Joseph the **t**
34:13 "This is the **t** you are to divide among yourselves
Dt 3:12 I gave the **t** beyond Aroer along the Arnon Gorge,
12:20 "When the LORD your God enlarges your **t** as he
19: 8 "If the LORD your God enlarges your **t**, as he
33:20 "Blessed is the one who enlarges Gad's **t**!
Jos 1:14 across the Jordan to help them conquer their **t**.
11:17 The Israelite **t** now extended all the way from
12: 1 Their **t** extended from the Arnon Gorge to Mount
12: 2 This **t** included half of the present area of Gilead,
12: 5 He ruled a **t** stretching from Mount Hermon to
12: 5 the other portion of which was in the **t** of King
13: 3 **t** that belongs to the Canaanites. This land extends
13: 7 Include all this **t** as Israel's inheritance when you
13: 9 Their **t** extended from Aroer on the edge of the
13:11 the **t** of the kingdoms of Geshur and Maacah,
13:12 and all the **t** of King Og of Bashan, who had
13:16 Their **t** extended from Aroer on the edge of the
13:25 Their **t** included Jazer, all the towns of Gilead,
13:30 Their **t** extended from Mahanaim, including all of
15:13 some of Judah's **t** to Caleb son of Jephunneh.
15:45 The **t** of the tribe of Judah also included all the
16: 2 it ran over to Ataroth in the **t** of the Arkites.
16: 3 Then it descended westward to the **t** of the
16: 5 The following **t** was given to the families of the
16: 9 villages in the **t** of the half-tribe of Manasseh.
17: 8 town of Tappuah, on the border of Manasseh's **t**,
17: 9 (Several towns in Manasseh's **t** belonged to the
17:10 North of Manasseh was the **t** of Asher, and to the
east was the **t** of Issachar.
17:11 The following towns within the **t** of Issachar
18: 4 I will send them out to survey the unconquered **t**.
18: 5 excluding Judah's **t** in the south and Joseph's **t** in
18: 9 and mapped the entire **t** into seven sections,
18:11 It lay between the **t** previously assigned to the
19: 1 Their inheritance was surrounded by Judah's **t**.
19: 9 to Judah because Judah's **t** was too large for them.
19: 9 received an inheritance within the **t** of Judah.
19:29 Sea at Hosah. The **t** also included Mehebel, Aczib,
19:35 The fortified cities included in this **t** were Ziddim,
19:46 also Rakkon along with the **t** across from Joppa.
20: 8 Ramoth in Gilead, in the **t** of the tribe of Gad;
21:41 and pasturelands within Israelite **t** given to the
22: 9 the **t** that belonged to them according to the
24:32 This land was located in the **t** allotted to the tribes
Jdg 1: 3 against the Canaanites living in the **t** allotted to us.
1: 3 Then we will help you conquer your **t**."
19:16 but he was living in Gibeah in the **t** of Benjamin.
1Sa 6: 1 The Ark of the LORD remained in Philistine **t**
7:14 along with the rest of the **t** that the Philistines had
30:14 the **t** of Judah, and the land of Caleb, and we had
1Ki 4:12 and all the **t** from Beth-shan to Abel-meholah
15:17 from entering or leaving King Asa's **t** in Judah.
2Ki 10:32 the LORD began to reduce the size of Israel's **t**.
18: 8 the Philistines as far distant as Gaza and its **t**,
1Ch 4:33 This was their **t**, and these names are recorded in
6:54 and **t** assigned by means of sacred lots to the
6:60 And from the **t** of Benjamin they were given
6:61 **t** of the half-tribe of Manasseh by means of sacred
6:66 The descendants of Kohath received from the **t** of
6:70 towns from the **t** of the half-tribe of Manasseh:
6:71 The descendants of Gershon received from the **t** of
6:72 From the **t** of Issachar, they were given Kedesh,
6:74 From the **t** of Asher, they received Mashal, Abdon,
6:76 From the **t** of Naphtali, they were given Kedesh in
6:77 from the **t** of Zebulun the towns of Jokneam,
6:78 From the **t** of Reuben, east of the Jordan River
6:80 And from the **t** of Gad, they received Ramoth in
7:28 The descendants of Ephraim lived in the **t** that
27:12 Abiezer from Anathoth in the **t** of Benjamin was
2Ch 16: 1 from entering or leaving King Asa's **t** in Judah.
30:10 and Manasseh and as far as the **t** of Zebulun.
Eze 47:23 within the **t** of the tribe with whom they now live.
48: 1 of the tribes of Israel and the **t** each is to receive.
The **t** of Dan is in the extreme north.
48: 1 Dan's **t** extends all the way across the land of
48: 2 Asher's **t** lies south of Dan's and also extends from
48: 4 and its **t** also extends from east to west.
48:12 Next to the priests' **t** will lie the land where the
48:23 Benjamin's **t** lies just south of the prince's lands,
48:24 South of Benjamin's **t** lies that of Simeon,
48:25 Next is the **t** of Issachar with the same eastern
48:26 Then comes the **t** of Zebulun, which also extends
48:27 The **t** of Gad is just south of Zebulun with the
Ac 7:45 Tabernacle was taken with them into their new **t**.
2Co 10:16 be no question about being in someone else's **t**.

TERROR (108) [TERRIBLE, TERRIBLY, TERRIFIED, TERRIFIES, TERRIFY, TERRIFYING, TERRORIZED, TERRORS]

Ge 35: 5 **t** from God came over the people in all the towns
42:21 We saw his **t** and anguish and heard his pleadings,
42:28 They were filled with **t** and said to each other,
42:35 for the grain. **T** gripped them, as it did their father.
Ex 15:16 **t** and dread will overcome them. / Because of your
23:27 "I will send my **t** upon all the people whose lands
Dt 26: 8 overwhelming **t**, and miraculous signs
28:67 because of your **t** at the awesome horrors you see
32:25 sword will bring death, / and inside, **t** will strike
Jos 2: 9 "We are all afraid of you. Everyone is living in **t**.
2Ch 14:14 and **t** from the LORD came upon the people
Job 4:14 Fear gripped me; I trembled and shook with **t**.
9:34 and I would no longer live in **t** of his punishment.
13:11 Doesn't his majesty strike **t** into your heart?
23:15 in his presence. When I think of it, **t** grips me.
27:20 **T** overwhelms them, and they are blown away in
30:15 I live in **t** now. They hold me in contempt, and my
41:22 "The tremendous strength in its neck strikes **t**
41:25 When it rises, the mighty are afraid, gripped by **t**.
Ps 14: 5 **T** will grip them, / for God is with those who obey
31:13 rumors about me, / and I am surrounded by **t**.
48: 6 They were gripped with **t**, / like a woman writhing
53: 5 But then **t** will grip them, / **t** like they have never
55: 4 is in anguish. / The **t** of death overpowers me.
78:33 their lives in failure / and gave them years of **t**.
107:26 sank again to the depths; / the sailors cringed in **t**.
Pr 1:31 They must experience the full **t** of the path they
22: 8 will harvest disaster, and their reign of **t** will end.
Isa 2:10 Hide from the **t** of the LORD and the glory of his
2:19 They will hide in caves in the rocks from the **t** of
2:21 they will try to escape the **t** of the LORD
7:17 You will soon experience greater **t** than has been
10:30 Well may you scream in **t**, you people of Gallim!
13: 6 Scream in **t**, for the LORD's time has arrived—
15: 4 bravest warriors of Moab will cry out in utter **t**.
16: 4 Hide them from our enemies until the **t** is past."
17:14 In the evening Israel waits in **t**, but by dawn its
19:17 Just to speak the name of Israel will strike deep **t** in
22: 5 What a day of confusion and **t** the Lord,
24:17 **T** and traps and snares will be your lot, you people
24:18 Those who flee in **t** will fall into a trap, and those
28:19 This message will bring **t** to your people.
31: 9 Even their generals will quake with **t** and flee
33:18 You will think back to this time of **t** when the
44:11 a god. Together they will stand in **t** and shame.
47:12 Ask them to help you strike **t** into the hearts of
51:17 You have drunk the cup of **t**, tipping out its last
54:14 you will live in peace. **T** will not come near.
Jer 1:14 "for **t** from the north will boil out on the people of
4:29 the people flee in **t** from the cities.
8:15 We hoped for a time of healing, but found only **t**.
14:19 We hoped for a time of healing but found only **t**.
15: 8 cause anguish and **t** to come upon them suddenly.
17:18 Bring shame and **t** on all who persecute me,
20: 3 on you are to be called 'The Man Who Lives in **T**.'
20: 4 I will send **t** upon you and all your friends, and you
20:10 They call me "The Man Who Lives in **T**."
30: 7 In all history there has never been such a time of **t**.
32:21 with great power and overwhelming **t**.
46: 5 But look! The Egyptian army flees in **t**.
46:15 Why have your warriors fled in **t**? They cannot
47: 2 People will scream in **t**, and everyone in the land
48: 5 while cries of **t** rise from Horonaim below.
48:34 their awful cries of **t** can be heard from Heshbon
48:43 "**T** and traps and snares will be your lot,
48:44 "Those who flee in **t** will fall into a trap, and those
49: 5 I will bring **t** upon you," says the Lord,
50:25 The **t** that falls upon the Babylonians will be the
Eze 4:17 scarce that the people will look at one another in **t**,
7:25 **T** and trembling will overcome my people.
21:15 Let their hearts melt with **t**, for the sword glitters at
23:32 You will drink from the same cup of **t** as your
23:34 In deep anguish you will drain that cup of **t** to the
27:28 by the sea tremble as your helmsmen cry out in **t**.
28: 7 against you an enemy army, the **t** of the nations.
30:16 will be torn apart; Memphis will live in constant **t**.
31:12 the **t** of the nations—cut it down and left it fallen
32:10 Yes, I will bring **t** to many lands, and their kings
32:12 swords of mighty warriors—the **t** of the nations.
32:23 These mighty men who once struck **t** in the hearts
32:26 They once struck **t** into the hearts of all people.
32:27 They brought **t** to everyone while they were still
32:30 the sword. Once a **t**, they now lie there in shame.
32:32 For I have caused my **t** to fall upon all the living.
38:20 and people—will quake in **t** at my presence.
Da 5: 6 Such **t** gripped him that his knees knocked together
Mic 4: 9 But why are you now screaming in **t**? Have you no
7:17 will fear him greatly, trembling in **t** at his presence.
Hab 2:17 Now **t** will strike you because of your murder
3: 7 the peoples of Cushan and Midian trembling in **t**.
3:16 My legs gave way beneath me, and I shook in **t**.
Zec 9: 5 Gaza will shake with **t**, and so will Ekron, for their
Mt 14:26 they screamed in **t**, thinking he was a ghost.
Mk 6:49 they screamed in **t**, thinking he was a ghost.
Lk 9:34 over them; and **t** gripped them as it covered them.
Ac 7:32 Moses shook with **t** and dared not look.
10: 4 Cornelius stared at him in **t**. "What is it, sir?"
Jas 2:19 the demons believe this, and they tremble in **t**!
Rev 8:13 "**T**, **t**, **t** to all who belong to this world because of
9:12 The first **t** is past, but look, two more terrors are
11:11 And **t** struck all who were staring at them.
11:14 The second **t** is past, but look, now the third **t** is
12:12 rejoice! But **t** will come on the earth and the sea.
18: 6 She brewed a cup of **t** for others, so give her twice

TERRORIZED (6) [TERROR]

Jer 6:25 and they are ready to kill. We are **t** at every turn!
46: 5 They are **t** at every turn, says the LORD.
49:29 of panic will be heard: 'We are **t** at every turn!'
Eze 23:46 and hand them over to be **t** and plundered.
32:24 They **t** the nations while they lived, but now they
32:25 Yes, they **t** the nations while they lived, but now

TERRORS (21) [TERROR]

Lev 26:16 You will suffer from sudden **t**, with wasting
Dt 7:19 Remember the great **t** the LORD your God sent
Job 6: 4 my spirit. All God's **t** are arrayed against me.
15:21 They are surrounded by **t**, and even on good days
18:11 "**T** surround the wicked and trouble them at every
18:14 and they are brought down to the king of **t**.
20:25 glistens with blood. The **t** of death are upon him.
24:17 They ally themselves with the **t** of the darkness.
Ps 73:19 In an instant they are destroyed, / swept away by **t**.
88:15 I stand helpless and desperate before your **t**.
88:16 has overwhelmed me. / Your **t** have cut me off.
91: 5 Do not be afraid of the **t** of the night, / nor fear the
116: 3 around my throat; / the **t** of the grave overtook me.
Isa 21:15 drawn swords and sharp arrows and the **t** of war.
Jer 25:13 I will bring upon them all the **t** I have promised in
La 2:22 "You have invited **t** from all around as though you
Eze 23:31 I will punish you with the same **t** that destroyed
Hos 10:14 Now the **t** of war will rise among your people.
13:14 O death, bring forth your **t**! O grave, bring forth
1Th 1:10 He is the one who has rescued us from the **t** of the
Rev 9:12 terror is past, but look, two more **t** are coming!

TERTIUS (1)

Ro 16:22 I, **T**, the one who is writing this letter for Paul,

TERTULLUS (3)

Ac 24: 1 with some of the Jewish leaders and the lawyer **T**,
24: 2 **T** laid charges against Paul in the following
24: 9 declaring that everything **T** said was true.

TEST (43) [TESTED, TESTER, TESTING, TESTS]

Ge 42:15 This is how I will **t** your story. I swear by the life
Ex 15:25 following conditions to **t** their faithfulness to him:
16: 4 I will **t** them in this to see whether they will follow
Dt 6:16 Do not **t** the LORD your God as you did when
8:16 this to humble you and **t** you for your own good.
33: 8 the Levites. / You put them to the **t** at Massah
Jdg 2:22 I did this to **t** Israel—to see whether or not they
3: 1 The LORD left certain nations in the land to **t**
3: 4 These people were left to **t** the Israelites—to see
1Ki 10: 1 she came to **t** him with hard questions.
2Ch 9: 1 she came to Jerusalem to **t** him with hard
32:31 God withdrew from Hezekiah in order to **t** him
Job 1:12 "All right, you may **t** him," the LORD said to
7:18 examine us every morning and **t** us every moment.
Ps 26: 2 cross-examine me. / **T** my motives and affections.
78:56 all this for them, / they continued to **t** his patience.
139:23 and know my heart; / **t** me and know my thoughts.
Pr 12:19 Truth stands the **t** of time; lies are soon exposed.
Ecc 3:18 to continue in their sinful ways so he can **t** them.
Isa 7:12 he said, "I wouldn't **t** the LORD like that."
Jer 9: 7 will melt them in a crucible and **t** them like metal.
12: 3 know my heart. You see me and **t** my thoughts.
La 3:40 Instead, let us **t** and examine our ways. Let us turn
Eze 21:13 It will put them all to the **t**! So now the Sovereign
Da 1:12 "**T** us for ten days on a diet of vegetables
5:27 weighed on the balances and have failed the **t**.
Am 7: 8 "I will **t** my people with this plumb line.
Mt 4: 7 also say, 'Do not **t** the Lord your God.' "
16: 1 and Sadducees came to **t** Jesus' claims by asking
Lk 4:12 also say, 'Do not **t** the Lord your God.' "
10:25 One day an expert in religious law stood up to **t**
11:16 Trying to **t** Jesus, others asked for a miraculous
Ac 5: 9 conspiring together to **t** the Spirit of the Lord?
1Co 10: 9 Nor should we put Christ to the **t**, as some of them
2Co 13: 5 **T** yourselves. If you cannot tell that Jesus Christ is
among you, it means you have failed the **t**.
13: 6 I hope you recognize that we have passed the **t**
1Th 5:21 but **t** everything that is said. Hold on to what is
1Ti 3:10 in the church as a **t** of their character
1Pe 1: 7 These trials are only to **t** your faith, to show that it
1Jn 4: 1 You must **t** them to see if the spirit they have
Rev 2:10 throw some of you into prison and put you to the **t**.
3:10 whole world to **t** those who belong to this world.

TESTATOR [KJV] See (WHO WROTE THE) WILL

TESTED (18) [TEST]
Ge 22: 1 Later on God t Abraham's faith and obedience.
Ex 17: 7 argued with Moses and t the LORD by saying,
Nu 14:22 but again and again they t me by refusing to listen.
Job 23:10 And when he has t me like gold in a fire, he will
Ps 17: 3 You have t my thoughts and examined my heart in
66:10 You have t us, O God; / you have purified us like
78:18 They willfully t God in their hearts,
78:41 Again and again they t God's patience
81: 7 out of the thundercloud. / I t your faith at Meribah,
105:19 fulfill his word, / the LORD t Joseph's character.
119:140 Your promises have been thoroughly t; / that is
Pr 27:21 and gold, but a person is t by being praised.
Isa 28:16 a t and precious cornerstone that is safe to build
Da 1:14 to Daniel's suggestion and t them for ten days.
2Co 8:22 them another brother who has been thoroughly t
Heb 3: 8 when they t God's patience in the wilderness.
Jas 1: 3 For when your faith is t, your endurance has a
1Pe 1: 7 It is being t as fire tests and purifies gold—

TESTER (1) [TEST]
Jer 6:27 "Jeremiah, I have made you a t of metals, that you

TESTICLES (4)
Lev 21:20 or scabs on his skin, or has damaged t.
22:24 If an animal has damaged t or is castrated, it may
Dt 23: 1 "If a man's t are crushed or his penis is cut off,
25:11 her husband by grabbing the t of the other man,

TESTIFIED (6) [TESTIFY]
Jn 5:37 And the Father himself has also t about me.
Ac 10:43 He is the one all the prophets t about, saying that
2Th 1:10 on that day, for you believed what we t about him.
1Jn 5: 9 comes from God. And God has t about his Son.
5:10 because they don't believe what God has t about
5:11 And this is what God has t: He has given us eternal

TESTIFIES (3) [TESTIFY]
Hos 5: 5 "The arrogance of Israel t against her; she will
7:10 His arrogance t against him, yet he doesn't return
Heb 10:15 And the Holy Spirit also t that this is so. First he

TESTIFY (24) [TESTIFIED, TESTIFIES, TESTIFYING, TESTIMONY]
Ex 20:16 "Do not t falsely against your neighbor.
Lev 5: 1 "If any of the people are called to t about
5: 1 but they refuse to t, they will be held responsible
Dt 5:20 " 'Do not t falsely against your neighbor.
Jos 24:27 It will be a witness to t against you if you go back
Ps 15: 5 and who refuse to accept bribes to t against the
35:11 Malicious witnesses t against me. / They accuse
Pr 24:28 Do not t spitefully against innocent neighbors;
Isa 8: 2 to t that I had written it before the child was
59:12 our sins are piled up before God and t against us.
Mt 19:18 not commit adultery. Do not steal. Do not t falsely.
Mk 10:19 Do not steal. Do not t falsely. Do not cheat.
14:55 trying to find witnesses who would t against Jesus,
14:57 some men stood up to t against him with this lie:
Lk 18:20 Do not murder. Do not steal. Do not t falsely.
Jn 1:34 happen to Jesus, so I t that he is the Son of God."
5:31 "If I were to t on my own behalf, my testimony
5:36 the Father, and they t that the Father has sent me.
Ac 10:42 and to t that Jesus is ordained of God to be the
22: 5 and the whole council of leaders can t that this is
2Co 8: 3 For I can t that they gave not only what they could
1Jn 1: 2 And now we t and announce to you that he is the
4:14 and now t that the Father sent his Son to be the
Rev 19:10 and other believers who t of their faith in Jesus.

TESTIFYING (3) [TESTIFY]
Jn 5:32 But someone else is also t about me, and I can
Ac 8:25 After t and preaching the word of the Lord in
18: 5 spent his full time preaching and t to the Jews,

TESTIMONY (31) [TESTIFY]
Ex 23: 2 do not be swayed in your t by the opinion of the
23: 3 And do not slant your t in favor of a person just
Nu 35:30 No one may be put to death on the t of only one
Dt 17: 6 But never put a person to death on the t of only
19:15 "Never convict anyone of a crime on the t of just
19:15 The facts of the case must be established by the t
Job 13: 8 but will you slant your t in his favor?
13:10 if even in your hearts you slant your t in his favor.
20:27 his guilt, and the earth will give t against him.
Ps 60: T of Salt. To be sung to the tune "Lily of the T."
Isa 8:16 I will write down all these things as a t of what the
8:20 "Check their predictions against my t,"
29:21 the innocent guilty by their false t will disappear.
Mt 26:60 to give false witness, there was no t they could use.
Jn 1: 7 so that everyone might believe because of his t.
1:19 This was the t of John when the Jewish leaders
5:31 testify on my own behalf, my t would not be valid.
5:34 But the best t about me is not from a man, though I have reminded you about John's t so you
17:20 all who will ever believe in me because of their t.
Ac 22:18 believe you when you give them your t about me.'
2Co 13: 1 of every case must be established by the t of two
1Ti 6:13 who gave a good t before Pontius Pilate,
Heb 10:28 was put to death without mercy on the t of two
1Jn 5: 6 And the Spirit also gives us the t that this is true.
5: 9 Since we believe human t, surely we can believe the t that comes from God.
Rev 1: 2 the word of God and the t of Jesus Christ—
11: 7 When they complete their t, the beast that comes
12:11 of the blood of the Lamb and because of their t.
20: 4 who had been beheaded for their t about Jesus,

TESTING (12) [TEST]
Ex 17: 2 with me? And why are you t the LORD?"
17: 7 "the place of t"—and Meribah—"the place of
Dt 8: 2 humbling you and t you to prove your character,
13: 3 The LORD your God is t you to see if you love
Ps 106:14 desires ran wild, / t God's patience in that dry land.
Mk 8:11 T him to see if he was from God, they demanded,
Lk 8:13 but they wilt when the hot winds of t blow.
Jn 6: 6 He was t Philip, for he already knew what he was
1Co 3:13 But there is going to come a time of t at the
Heb 11:17 offered Isaac as a sacrifice when God was t him.
Jas 1:12 God blesses the people who patiently endure t.
Rev 3:10 I will protect you from the great time of t that will

TESTS (7) [TEST]
Dt 29: 3 all the great t of strength, the miraculous signs,
Job 12:11 tastes good food, so the ear t the words it hears.
34: 3 tastes good food, the ear t the words it hears.'
Pr 17: 3 Fire t the purity of silver and gold, but the LORD t the heart.
27:21 Fire t the purity of silver and gold, but a person is
1Pe 1: 7 It is being tested as fire t and purifies gold—

TETHERED (1)
2Ki 7:10 The horses and donkeys were t and the tents were

THADDAEUS (2)
Mt 10: 3 (the tax collector), / James (son of Alphaeus), / T,
Mk 3:18 Thomas, / James (son of Alphaeus), / T,

THAHASH [KJV] See TAHASH

THAMAH [KJV] See TEMAH

THAMAR [KJV] See TAMAR

THAN (597)
Ge 6: 3 In the future, they will live no more t 120 years."
7:20 standing more t twenty-two feet above the highest
16:10 "I will give you more descendants t you can
19: 9 We'll treat you far worse t those other men!"
25:23 One nation will be stronger t the other;
26:12 He harvested a hundred times more grain t he
27:46 I'd rather die t see Jacob marry one of them."
28:17 It is none other t the house of God—the gateway to
29:19 "I'd rather give her to you t to someone outside
29:30 with Rachel, too, and he loved her more t Leah.
33:11 I have more t enough." Jacob continued to insist,
37: 3 Now Jacob loved Joseph more t any of his other
38:26 were his and said, "She is more in the right t I am,
39: 9 No one here has more authority t I do! He has held
41:38 Pharaoh said, "Who could do it better t Joseph?
41:40 Only I will have a rank higher t yours."
49:12 darker t wine, / and his teeth are whiter t milk.
49:26 be greater t the blessings of the eternal mountains,
Ex 9:18 a hailstorm worse t any in all of Egypt's history.
14:12 Our Egyptian slavery was far better t dying out
18:11 I know now that the LORD is greater t all other
22:20 "Anyone who sacrifices to any god other t the
36: 5 "We have more t enough materials on hand now
36: 6 You have already given more t enough."
36: 7 Their contributions were more t enough to
Lev 10: 1 him a different kind of fire t he had commanded.
13: 3 turned white and appears to be more t skin-deep,
13: 4 but does not appear to be more t skin-deep,
13:20 If the priest finds the disease to be more t
13:21 and if it doesn't appear to be more t skin-deep
13:25 and the problem appears to be more t skin-deep,
13:26 and the problem appears to be no more t skin-deep
13:30 If it appears to be more t skin-deep and fine yellow
13:32 and if the infection does not appear to be more t
13:34 not spread and appears to be no more t skin-deep,
14:37 and the contamination appears to go deeper t the
16: 1 kind of fire t the LORD had commanded.
22:13 But other t these exceptions, only members of the
27: 7 A man older t sixty is valued at fifteen pieces of
27: 7 a woman older t sixty is valued at ten pieces of
Nu 3: 4 a different kind of fire t he had commanded.
3:38 Anyone other t a priest or Levite who came too
11:15 I'd rather you killed me t treat me like this.
11:32 next day, too. No one gathered less t fifty bushels!
12: 3 Now Moses was more humble t any other person
13:31 go up against them! They are stronger t we are!"
14:12 into a nation far greater and mightier t they are!"
16: 3 t anyone else among all these people of the
18:22 Israelites other t the priests and Levites are to stay
22:15 officials t those he had sent the first time.
24: 7 Their king will be greater t Agag; / their kingdom
26:61 a different kind of fire t he had commanded.
30:15 If he waits more t a day and then tries to nullify a
35:30 but only if there is more t one witness.
Dt 1:28 of the land are taller and more powerful t we are,
3:11 His iron bed was more t thirteen feet long and six
4:38 He drove out nations far greater t you, so he could
7: 1 These seven nations are all more powerful t you.
7: 7 because you were larger or greater t other nations,
7:17 nations that are so much more powerful t we are?'
8: 3 He did it to teach you that people need more t
9: 1 to nations much greater and more powerful t you.
9:14 a nation larger and more powerful t they are.'
11:23 though they are much greater and stronger t you.
20: 1 and chariots and an army greater t your own,
25: 3 No more t forty lashes may ever be given;
25: 3 more t forty lashes would publicly humiliate your
26:19 he will make you greater t any other nation.
30: 5 more prosperous and numerous t your ancestors!
32:39 I myself am he! / There is no god other t me!
33: 9 to you / t to their parents, relatives, and children.
Jos 7: 3 and it won't take more t two or three thousand of
7:21 and a bar of gold weighing more t a pound.
7:21 my tent, with the silver buried deeper t the rest."
10: 2 as large as the royal cities and larger t Ai.
10:11 The hail killed more of the enemy t the Israelites
17:17 and strong, you will be given more t one portion.
Jdg 2:19 behaving worse t those who had lived before them.
8: 2 Aren't the last grapes of Ephraim's harvest better t
11:25 Are you any better t Balak son of Zippor, king of
12: 4 "The men of Gilead are nothing more t rejects
14:18 is sweeter t honey? / What is stronger t a lion?"
15: 2 But look, her sister is more beautiful t she is.
16:30 So he killed more people when he died t he had
18:19 of Israel t just for the household of one man?"
Ru 1:13 Things are far more bitter for me t for you,
2:14 and Boaz gave her food—more t she could eat.
3:10 "You are showing more family loyalty now t ever
3:12 man who is more closely related to you t I am.
4:15 and who has been better to you t seven sons!"
1Sa 1: 8 You have me—isn't that better t having ten sons?"
2:29 Why do you honor your sons more t me—for you
9: 2 and shoulders taller t anyone else in the land.
9: 5 By now my father will be more worried about us t
13: 4 the Philistines now hated the Israelites more t ever.
15:22 to his voice? Obedience is far better t sacrifice.
15:22 Listening to him is much better t offering the fat of
15:28 given it to someone else—one who is better t you.
18:17 and let them kill him rather t doing it myself."
18:30 David was more successful against them t all the
24:17 he said to David, "You are a better man t I am,
29: 4 with his master t by turning on us in battle?
2Sa 1:23 were swifter t eagles; / they were stronger t lions.
1:26 for me was deep, / deeper t the love of women!
6:22 and I am willing to look even more foolish t this,
13:14 and since he was stronger t she was, he raped her.
13:15 and he hated her even more t he had loved her.
13:16 "To reject me now is a greater wrong t what you
17:14 "Hushai's advice is better t Ahithophel's."
18: 8 because of the forest t were killed by the sword.
19: 7 Then you will be worse off t you have ever been."
20: 5 but it took him longer t the three days he had been
20: 6 Sheba is going to hurt us more t Absalom did.
21:16 his bronze spearhead weighed more t seven
23:23 He was more honored t the other members of the
1Ki 1:37 and may he make Solomon's reign even greater t
1:47 make Solomon's fame even greater t your own,
1:47 and may Solomon's kingdom be even greater t
2:32 two men who were more righteous and better t he.
4:31 He was wiser t anyone else, including Ethan the
10: 7 and prosperity are far greater t what I was told.
10:23 and wiser t any other king in all the earth.
12:10 'My little finger is thicker t my father's waist—
14: 9 You have done more evil t all who lived before
14:22 for it was even worse t that of their ancestors.
16:25 even more t any of the kings before him.
16:30 even more t any of the kings before him.
16:33 t any of the other kings of Israel before him.
19: 4 "Take my life, for I am no better t my ancestors."
20:10 gods bring tragedy on me, and even worse t that,
20:10 provide more t a handful for each of my soldiers."
2Ki 5:12 and Pharpar River of Damascus better t all the
6:16 "For there are more on our side t on theirs!"
7:13 it won't be a greater loss t if they stay here and die
18:14 then demanded a settlement of more t eleven tons
21: 9 and Manasseh led them to do even more evil t the
21:11 He is even more wicked t the Amorites, who lived
1Ch 4: 9 who was more distinguished t any of his brothers.
11:25 He was more honored t the other members of the
22: 3 and more bronze t they could ever weigh.
27:23 he did not count those who were younger t twenty
29: 4 I am donating more t 112 tons of gold from Ophir
29:25 even greater wealth and honor t his father.
2Ch 2: 5 our God is an awesome God, greater t any other.
9: 6 Your wisdom is far greater t what I was told.
9:12 gifts of greater value t the gifts she had given him.
9:22 and wiser t any other king in all the earth.
10:10 'My little finger is thicker t my father's waist—
11:21 Rehoboam loved Maacah more t any of his other
12: 8 better it is to serve me t to serve earthly rulers."
20:25 and other valuables—more t they could carry.
21:13 your own brothers, men who were better t you.
25: 9 "The LORD is able to give you much more t
29:34 about purifying themselves t the priests.
33: 9 and Jerusalem to do even more evil t the pagan
Ezr 9: 6 For our sins are piled higher t our heads, and our
9:13 But we have actually been punished far less t we
10:10 deeply under condemnation t we were before.
Ne 7: 2 for he was a faithful man who feared God more t
9: 5 It is far greater t we can think or say.
Est 1: 8 one should be compelled to take more t he wanted.
1:19 and that you choose another queen more worthy t
2:17 the king loved her more t any of the other young
4:11 called for me to come to him in more t a month."
6: 6 "Whom would the king wish to honor more t
Job 3:21 They search for death more eagerly t for hidden

5:14 they see no better in the daytime **t** at night.
6:3 they would be heavier **t** all the sands of the sea.
7:6 "My days are swifter **t** a weaver's shuttle flying
7:15 I would rather die of strangulation **t** go on and on
9:25 "My life passes more swiftly **t** a runner. It flees
11:6 God is doubtless punishing you far less **t** you
11:8 Such knowledge is higher **t** the heavens—but who
11:8 It is deeper **t** the underworld—what can you know
11:9 It is broader **t** the earth and wider **t** the sea.
11:12 more **t** a wild donkey can bear human offspring!
11:17 Your life will be brighter **t** the noonday.
12:3 a few things myself—and you're no better **t** I am.
13:2 know as much as you do. You are no better **t** I am.
15:10 gray-haired men much older **t** your father!
22:12 higher **t** the heavens, higher **t** the farthest stars.
28:16 Its value is greater **t** all the gold of Ophir,
28:16 greater **t** precious onyx stone or sapphires.
28:17 Wisdom is far more valuable **t** gold and crystal.
28:19 for it. Its value is greater **t** the purest gold.
30:1 now I am mocked by those who are younger **t** I,
31:23 That would be better **t** facing the judgment sent by
32:4 the others to speak because they were older **t** he.
33:12 yourself have said, 'God is greater **t** any person.'
34:12 There is no truer statement **t** this: God will not do
34:19 and he doesn't pay any more attention to the rich **t**
35:11 Where is the one who makes us wiser **t** the animals
42:12 half of his life even more **t** in the beginning.
Ps 4:7 **t** those who have abundant harvests of grain
8:1 fills the earth! / Your glory is higher **t** the heavens.
8:5 For you made us only a little lower **t** God,
19:10 They are more desirable **t** gold, / even the finest
gold. / They are sweeter **t** honey,
37:16 and have little / **t** to be evil and possess much.
37:19 even in famine they will have more **t** enough.
39:5 My life is no longer **t** the width of my hand.
40:12 They are more numerous **t** the hairs on my head.
45:7 pouring out the oil of joy on you more **t** on anyone
51:7 be clean; / wash me, and I will be whiter **t** snow.
52:3 You love evil more **t** good / and lies more **t** truth.
58:9 and old, / faster **t** a pot heats on an open flame.
62:9 them on the scales, / they are lighter **t** a puff of air.
63:3 Your unfailing love is better to me **t** life itself;
63:5 You satisfy me more **t** the richest of foods.
69:4 are more numerous **t** the hairs on my head.
69:31 For this will please the LORD more **t** sacrificing
73:25 but you? / I desire you more **t** anything on earth.
76:4 and more majestic / **t** the everlasting mountains.
84:10 your courts / is better **t** a thousand anywhere else!
84:10 **t** live the good life in the homes of the wicked.
87:2 city of Jerusalem / more **t** any other city in Israel.
89:7 He is far more awesome **t** those who surround his
93:4 But mightier **t** the violent raging of the seas, /
mightier **t** the breakers on the shore— / the LORD
above is mightier **t** these!
108:4 For your unfailing love is higher **t** the heavens.
113:4 the nations; / his glory is far greater **t** the heavens.
118:8 to trust the LORD / **t** to put confidence in people.
118:9 to trust the LORD / **t** to put confidence in princes.
119:72 more valuable to me / **t** millions in gold and silver!
119:98 Your commands make me wiser **t** my enemies,
119:99 Yes, I have more insight **t** my teachers, / for I am
119:100 I am even wiser **t** my elders, / for I have kept your
119:103 your words to my taste; / they are sweeter **t** honey.
119:127 your commands / more **t** gold, even the finest gold.
130:6 more **t** sentries long for the dawn, / yes, more **t**
sentries long for the dawn.
135:5 that our Lord is greater **t** any other god.
Pr 3:14 is better **t** silver, and her wages are better **t** gold.
3:15 Wisdom is more precious **t** rubies; nothing you
5:3 as sweet as honey, and her mouth is smoother **t** oil.
8:10 "Choose my instruction rather **t** silver,
8:11 For wisdom is far more valuable **t** rubies.
8:19 better **t** the purest gold, my wages better **t** sterling
11:15 is dangerous; it is better to refuse **t** to suffer later.
12:9 It is better to be a nobody with a servant **t** to be
15:16 It is better to have little with fear for the LORD **t**
15:17 A bowl of soup with someone you love is better **t**
16:8 is better to be poor and godly **t** rich and dishonest.
16:16 How much better to get wisdom **t** gold, and
understanding **t** silver!
16:19 It is better to live humbly with the poor **t** to share
16:32 It is better to be patient **t** powerful; it is better to
have self-control **t** to conquer a city.
17:1 A dry crust eaten in peace is better **t** a great feast
17:10 **t** a hundred lashes on the back of a fool.
17:12 It is safer to meet a bear robbed of her cubs **t** to
18:19 with an offended friend **t** to capture a fortified city.
18:24 but a real friend sticks closer **t** a brother.
19:1 to be poor and honest **t** to be a fool and dishonest.
19:22 And it is better to be poor **t** dishonest.
20:15 is rarer and more valuable **t** gold and rubies.
21:3 is just and right **t** when we give him sacrifices.
21:9 It is better to live alone in the corner of an attic **t**
21:19 It is better to live alone in the desert **t** with a
22:1 for being held in high esteem is better **t** having
22:29 They will serve kings rather **t** ordinary people.
24:5 A wise man is mightier **t** a strong man, and a man
of knowledge is more powerful **t** a
25:7 It is better to wait for an invitation **t** to be sent to
25:24 It is better to live alone in the corner of an attic **t**
26:1 Honor doesn't go with fools any more **t** snow with
26:12 There is more hope for fools **t** for people who
26:16 Lazy people consider themselves smarter **t** seven
27:3 but the resentment caused by a fool is heavier **t**
27:5 An open rebuke is better **t** hidden love!
27:6 Wounds from a friend are better **t** many kisses
27:10 It is better to go to a neighbor **t** to a relative who
28:6 is better to be poor and honest **t** rich and crooked.
28:23 people appreciate frankness more **t** flattery.
29:20 There is more hope for a fool **t** for someone who
31:10 capable wife? She is worth more **t** precious rubies.
Ecc 1:16 I am wiser **t** any of the kings who ruled in
1:16 greater wisdom and knowledge **t** any of them."
2:7 more **t** any of the kings who lived in Jerusalem
2:9 So I became greater **t** any of the kings who ruled in
2:13 Wisdom is of more value **t** foolishness, just as
light is better **t** darkness.
2:24 So I decided there is nothing better **t** to enjoy food
3:12 that there is nothing better for people **t** to be happy
3:18 they can see for themselves that they are no better **t**
3:22 So I saw that there is nothing better for people **t** to
4:2 So I concluded that the dead are better off **t** the
4:6 better to be lazy and barely survive **t** to work hard,
4:9 Two people can accomplish more **t** twice as much
4:13 is better to be a poor but wise youth **t** to be an old
5:5 It is better to say nothing **t** to promise something
6:5 Yet he would have had more peace **t** he has in
6:9 Enjoy what you have rather **t** desiring what you
7:1 A good reputation is more valuable **t** the most
7:1 the day you die is better **t** the day you are born.
7:2 It is better to spend your time at funerals **t** at
7:3 Sorrow is better **t** laughter, for sadness has a
7:5 It is better to be criticized by a wise person **t** to be
7:8 is better **t** starting. Patience is better **t** pride.
7:10 for you don't know whether they were any better **t**
7:19 A wise person is stronger **t** the ten leading citizens
7:26 that a seductive woman is more bitter **t** death.
8:15 better for people to do in this world **t** to eat,
9:4 "It is better to be a live dog **t** a dead lion!"
9:16 Then I realized that though wisdom is better **t**
9:17 the quiet words of a wise person are better **t** the
SS 1:1 song of songs, more wonderful **t** any other.
1:2 and again, for your love is sweeter **t** wine.
1:4 are for him! We praise his love even more **t** wine."
4:10 my bride! How much better it is **t** wine!
4:10 Your perfume is more fragrant **t** the richest of
5:10 is dark and dazzling, better **t** ten thousand others!
Isa 7:8 because Aram is no stronger **t** its capital,
7:8 And Damascus is no stronger **t** its king, Rezin.
7:9 Israel is no stronger **t** its capital, Samaria.
7:9 And Samaria is no stronger **t** its king, Pekah son of
7:17 You will soon experience greater terror **t** has been
9:10 in ruins now, but we will rebuild it better **t** before.
10:10 whose gods were far greater **t** those in Jerusalem
10:15 Can the ax boast greater power **t** the person who
10:15 Is the saw greater **t** the person who saws? Can a
13:12 as scarce as gold—more rare **t** the gold of Ophir.
14:29 his son will be worse **t** his father ever was.
23:17 But she will be no different **t** she was before.
29:13 to nothing more **t** human laws learned by rote.
29:16 He is the Potter, and he is certainly greater **t** you.
30:11 We have heard more **t** enough about your 'Holy
32:10 In a short time—in just a little more **t** a year—
40:17 In his eyes they are less **t** nothing—mere emptiness
41:24 You are less **t** nothing and can do nothing at all.
47:13 You have more **t** enough advisers, astrologers,
49:6 "You will do more **t** restore the people of Israel to
54:1 no children now has more **t** all the other women,"
55:9 are higher **t** the earth, so are my ways higher **t** your
ways and my thoughts higher **t** your thoughts.
56:5 and a name far greater **t** the honor they would have
57:11 Why were you more afraid of them **t** of me?
65:5 too close or you will defile me! I am holier **t** you!'
66:3 it is no more acceptable **t** a human sacrifice.
Jer 3:11 "Even faithless Israel is less guilty **t** treacherous
3:19 I wanted nothing more **t** to give you this beautiful
4:13 are like whirlwinds; his horses are swifter **t** eagles.
7:26 and sinful—even worse **t** their ancestors.
8:3 wish to die rather **t** live where I will send them.
15:8 "There will be more widows **t** the grains of sand
16:12 And you are even worse **t** your ancestors!
20:7 You are stronger **t** I am, and you overpowered me.
33:25 I would no more reject my people **t** I would change
42:21 your God any better now **t** you have in the past.
46:23 "for they are more numerous **t** grasshoppers.
48:32 I will weep for you even more **t** I did for Jazer.
La 4:6 The guilt of my people is greater **t** that of Sodom,
4:8 But now their faces are blacker **t** soot. No one even
4:9 Those killed by the sword are far better off **t** those
4:19 Our enemies were swifter **t** the eagles. If we fled to
Eze 3:7 but they won't listen to you any more **t** they listen
5:6 and has been even more wicked **t** the surrounding
5:7 and have behaved even worse **t** your neighbors,
5:9 I will punish you more severely **t** I have punished
8:6 and you will see even greater sins **t** these!"
8:13 "Come, and I will show you greater sins **t** these!"
8:15 "But I will show you even greater sins **t** these!"
16:13 and olive oil—and became more beautiful **t** ever.
16:31 You have been worse **t** a prostitute, so eager for sin
16:51 You have done far more loathsome things **t** your
21:10 Those far stronger **t** you have fallen beneath its
28:3 You regard yourself as wiser **t** Daniel and think no
31:8 This tree became taller **t** any of the other cedars in
31:14 though it be higher **t** the clouds, for all are
32:19 'O Egypt, are you lovelier **t** the other nations?
36:11 I will make you even more prosperous **t** you were
41:7 Each level was wider **t** the one below it,
42:5 levels of rooms was narrower **t** the one beneath it
Da 1:15 and better nourished **t** the young men who had
1:20 to be ten times better **t** that of all the magicians
2:30 because I am wiser **t** any living person that I know
3:19 the furnace be heated seven times hotter **t** usual.
3:28 and were willing to die rather **t** serve
4:36 of my kingdom, with even greater honor **t** before.
6:3 Daniel soon proved himself more capable **t** all the
7:20 This was the horn that seemed greater **t** the others
8:3 One of the horns was longer **t** the other,
8:3 even though it had begun to grow later **t** the shorter
11:2 to be succeeded by a fourth, far richer **t** the others.
11:5 own officials will become more powerful **t** he
11:13 a fully equipped army far greater **t** the one he lost.
11:36 and claiming to be greater **t** every god there is,
11:37 for he will boast that he is greater **t** them all.
12:1 Then there will be a time of anguish greater **t** any
Hos 2:7 because I was better off with him **t** I am now.'
4:18 Their love for shame is greater **t** their love for
6:6 know God; that's more important **t** burnt offerings.
Am 6:2 You are no better **t** they were, and look at how
9:7 you are more important to me **t** the Ethiopians?"
9:13 and grapes will grow faster **t** they can be
Jnh 4:3 I'd rather be dead **t** alive because nothing I
4:8 "Death is certainly better **t** this!" he exclaimed.
4:11 But Nineveh has more **t** 120,000 people living in
Mic 7:4 the straightest is more crooked **t** a hedge of thorns.
Na 3:8 Are you any better **t** Thebes, surrounded by rivers,
Hab 1:8 Their horses are swifter **t** leopards. They are a
fierce people, more fierce **t** wolves at dusk.
1:13 destroy people who are more righteous **t** they?
Hag 2:9 The future glory of this Temple will be greater **t** its
Zec 12:7 will not have greater honor **t** the rest of Judah.
Mt 3:11 But someone is coming soon who is far greater **t** I
4:4 'People need more **t** bread for their life;
5:20 unless you obey God better **t** the teachers of
5:29 It is better for you to lose one part of your body **t**
5:30 It is better for you to lose one part of your body **t**
6:25 Doesn't life consist of more **t** food and clothing?
6:26 And you are far more valuable to him **t** they are.
9:16 the old cloth, leaving an even bigger hole **t** before.
10:15 better off on the judgment day **t** that place will be.
10:24 "A student is not greater **t** the teacher. A servant is
not greater **t** the master.
10:31 you are more valuable to him **t** a whole flock of
10:37 love your father or mother more **t** you love me,
10:37 or if you love your son or daughter more **t** me,
11:9 for a prophet? Yes, and he is more **t** a prophet.
11:11 have ever lived, none is greater **t** John the Baptist.
11:11 person in the Kingdom of Heaven is greater **t** he is!
11:22 and Sidon will be better off on the judgment day **t**
11:24 Sodom will be better off on the judgment day **t**
12:6 there is one here who is even greater **t** the Temple!
12:12 And how much more valuable is a person **t** a
12:41 And now someone greater **t** Jonah is here—
12:42 And now someone greater **t** Solomon is here—
12:45 Then the spirit finds seven other spirits more evil **t**
12:45 live there. And so that person is worse off **t** before.
16:26 in the process? Is anything worth more **t** your soul?
18:8 or lame **t** to be thrown into the unquenchable fire
18:9 It is better to enter heaven half blind **t** to have two
18:13 he will surely rejoice over it more **t** over the
19:24 **t** for a rich person to enter the Kingdom of God!"
24:21 For that will be a time of greater horror **t** anything
27:64 we'll be worse off **t** we were at first."
Mk 1:7 "Someone is coming soon who is far greater **t** I
2:21 the old cloth, leaving an even bigger hole **t** before.
8:37 Is anything worth more **t** your soul?
9:3 far whiter **t** any earthly process could ever make it.
9:43 It is better to enter heaven with only one hand **t** to
9:45 It is better to enter heaven with only one foot **t** to
9:47 It is better to enter the Kingdom of God half blind **t**
10:25 **t** for a rich person to enter the Kingdom of God!"
12:31 No other commandment is greater **t** these."
12:33 This is more important **t** to offer all of the burnt
12:43 this poor widow has given more **t** all the others
13:19 For those will be days of greater horror **t** at any
Lk 3:13 "Make sure you collect no more taxes **t** the Roman
3:16 but someone is coming soon who is greater **t** I
4:4 'People need more **t** bread for their life.' "
4:27 rather **t** the many lepers in Israel who needed
6:40 A student is not greater **t** the teacher.
7:26 for a prophet? Yes, and he is more **t** a prophet.
7:28 of all who have ever lived, none is greater **t** John.
7:28 person in the Kingdom of God is greater **t** he is!"
10:12 even wicked Sodom will be better off **t** such a
10:14 and Sidon will be better off on the judgment day **t**
10:35 'If his bill runs higher **t** that,' he said, 'I'll pay the
11:26 Then the spirit finds seven other spirits more evil **t**
11:26 And so that person is worse off **t** before."
11:31 And now someone greater **t** Solomon is here—
11:32 And now someone greater **t** Jonah is here—
12:7 you are more valuable to him **t** a whole flock of
12:23 For life consists of far more **t** food and clothing.
12:24 And you are far more valuable to him **t** any birds!
13:2 were worse sinners **t** other people from Galilee?"
14:8 What if someone more respected **t** you has also
14:10 'Friend, we have a better place **t** this for you!'
14:26 follower you must love me more **t** your own father
14:26 brothers and sisters—yes, more **t** your own life.
15:7 to God **t** over ninety-nine others who are righteous
16:8 of this world are more shrewd **t** the godly are.
16:17 is stronger and more permanent **t** heaven and earth.
17:2 **t** to face the punishment in store for harming one
18:25 **t** for a rich person to enter the Kingdom of God!"
21:3 "this poor widow has given more **t** all the rest of
Jn 1:15 'Someone is coming who is far greater **t** I am,
1:30 'Soon a man is coming who is far greater **t** I am,
1:50 the fig tree? You will see greater things **t** this."
3:19 but they loved the darkness more **t** the light,
3:31 has come from above and is greater **t** anyone else.
4:1 is baptizing and making more disciples **t** John"
4:12 are you greater **t** our ancestor Jacob who gave us
4:12 How can you offer better water **t** he and his sons

5:20 and the Son will do far greater things **t** healing this
5:36 But I have a greater witness **t** John—my teachings
7:22 this tradition of circumcision is older **t** the law of
7:31 to do more miraculous signs **t** this man has done?"
8:53 Are you greater **t** our father Abraham, who died?
8:53 Are you greater **t** the prophets, who died?
10:1 rather **t** going through the gate, must surely be a
10:29 them to me, and he is more powerful **t** anyone else.
12:43 For they loved human praise more **t** the praise of
13:16 How true it is that a servant is not greater **t** the
13:16 Nor are messengers more important **t** the one who
14:28 now I can go to the Father, who is greater **t** I am.
15:20 'A servant is not greater **t** the master.' Since they
17:16 They are not part of this world any more **t** I am.
19:8 Pilate heard this, he was more frightened **t** ever.
21:15 son of John, do you love me more **t** these?"
Ac 4:19 "Do you think God wants us to obey you rather **t**
4:22 the healing of a man who had been lame for more **t**
5:29 "We must obey God rather **t** human authority.
15:28 and to us to lay no greater burden on you **t** these
17:11 And the people of Berea were more open-minded **t**
20:35 'It is more blessed to give **t** to receive.' "
23:13 There were more **t** forty of them.
23:21 There are more **t** forty men hiding along the way
24:11 You can quickly discover that it was no more **t**
26:13 a light from heaven brighter **t** the sun shone down
27:11 more to the ship's captain and the owner **t** to Paul.
Ro 2:25 you are no better off **t** an uncircumcised Gentile.
2:27 be much better off **t** you Jews who are circumcised
3:9 Well then, are we Jews better **t** others? No, not at
13:11 for the coming of our salvation is nearer now **t**
14:5 some think one day is more holy **t** another day,
15:20 rather **t** where a church has already been started by
1Co 1:25 This "foolish" plan of God is far wiser **t** the
1:25 and God's weakness is far stronger **t** the greatest of
2:5 so that you might trust the power of God rather **t**
3:11 For no one can lay any other foundation **t** the one
4:7 What makes you better **t** anyone else? What do
7:9 and marry. It's better to marry **t** to burn with lust.
9:12 We would rather put up with anything **t** put an
9:15 I would rather die **t** lose my distinction of
10:22 as Israel did? Do you think we are stronger **t** he is?
11:16 all I can say is that we have no other custom **t** this,
11:17 For it sounds as if more harm **t** good is done when
12:31 let me tell you about something else that is better **t**
14:5 and more useful gift **t** speaking in tongues,
14:18 I thank God that I speak in tongues more **t** all of
14:19 **t** ten thousand words in an unknown language.
14:27 No more **t** two or three should speak in an
15:6 he was seen by more **t** five hundred of his
15:10 For I have worked harder **t** all the other apostles,
2Co 2:5 trouble hurt your entire church more **t** he hurt me.
5:12 ministry rather **t** having a sincere heart before God.
7:15 Now he cares for you more **t** ever when he
11:4 even if they preach about a different Jesus **t** the
11:4 or a different Spirit **t** the one you received, or a
different kind of gospel **t** the one you believed.
12:6 I don't want anyone to think more highly of me **t**
Gal 1:8 who preaches any other message **t** the one we told
1:9 If anyone preaches any other gospel **t** the one you
4:1 those children are not much better off **t** slaves until
4:27 now has more **t** all the other women!"
Eph 3:20 he is able to accomplish infinitely more **t** we would
4:10 is the one who ascended higher **t** all the heavens,
6:7 as though you were working for the Lord rather **t**
Php 2:3 Be humble, thinking of others as better **t** yourself.
4:7 which is far more wonderful **t** the human mind can
4:16 I was in Thessalonica you sent help more **t** once.
4:18 At the moment I have all I need—more **t** I need!
Col 3:23 as though you were working for the Lord rather **t**
1Ti 5:8 we believe. Such people are worse **t** unbelievers.
2Ti 3:4 up with pride, and love pleasure rather **t** God.
Heb 1:4 This shows that God's Son is far greater **t** the
1:4 just as the name God gave him is far greater **t** their
1:9 pouring out the oil of joy on you more **t** on anyone
2:7 For a little while you made him lower **t** the angels,
2:9 who "for a little while was made lower **t** the
3:3 But Jesus deserves far more glory **t** Moses, just as
3:3 fine house deserves more praise **t** the house itself.
4:12 It is sharper **t** the sharpest knife, cutting deep into
6:16 they call on someone greater **t** themselves to hold
7:7 bless is always greater **t** the person who is blessed.
7:8 But Melchizedek is greater **t** they are, because we
9:23 with far better sacrifices **t** the blood of animals.
11:4 a more acceptable offering to God **t** Cain did.
11:13 They agreed that they were no more **t** foreigners
11:26 of the Messiah **t** to own the treasures of Egypt,
11:35 preferring to die rather **t** turn from God and be
Jas 2:1 Christ if you favor some people more **t** others?
1Pe 1:7 and your faith is far more precious to God **t** mere
3:1 Your godly lives will speak to them better **t** any
3:7 She may be weaker **t** you are, but she is your equal
3:17 is what God wants, **t** to suffer for doing wrong!
2Pe 2:11 greater in power and strength **t** these false teachers,
2:20 become its slave again, they are worse off **t** before.
2:21 had never known the right way to live **t** to know it
1Jn 3:20 For God is greater **t** our hearts, and he knows
4:4 because the Spirit who lives in you is greater **t** the
3Jn 1:4 I could have no greater joy **t** to hear that my
Rev 16:18 And there was an earthquake greater **t** ever before

THANK (45) [THANKED, THANKFUL, THANKFULNESS, THANKING, THANKS, THANKSGIVING]

1Sa 1:18 "Oh, **t** you, sir!" she exclaimed. Then she went
25:33 **T** God for your good sense! Bless you for keeping
2Sa 14:9 "Oh, **t** you, my lord," she replied. "And I'll take
16:4 Mephibosheth owns." "**T** you, sir," Ziba replied.
1Ch 16:35 among the nations, / so we can **t** your holy name
29:13 our God, we **t** you and praise your glorious name!
Ps 7:17 I will **t** the LORD because he is just; / I will sing
9:1 I will **t** you, LORD, with all my heart; / I will tell
35:18 Then I will **t** you in front of the entire
57:9 I will **t** you, Lord, in front of all the people.
75:1 We **t** you, O God! / We give thanks because you
79:13 sheep of your pasture, / will **t** you forever and ever,
106:47 among the nations, / so we can **t** your holy name
108:3 I will **t** you, LORD, in front of all the people.
111:1 the LORD! / I will **t** the LORD with all my heart
118:19 righteous enter, / and I will go in and **t** the LORD.
118:21 I **t** you for answering my prayer / and saving me!
119:7 righteous laws, / I will **t** you by living as I should!
119:62 At midnight I rise to **t** you / for your just laws.
139:14 **T** you for making me so wonderfully complex!
142:7 Bring me out of prison / so I can **t** you. / The godly
145:10 All of your works will **t** you, LORD, / and your
Pr 30:11 people curse their father and do not **t** their mother.
Isa 12:4 "**T** the LORD! / Praise his name! / Tell the world
43:20 The wild animals in the fields will **t** me, the jackals
Da 2:23 I **t** and praise you, God of my ancestors, / for you
Mt 11:25 **t** you for hiding the truth from those who think
Lk 10:21 **t** you for hiding the truth from those who think
18:11 'I **t** you, God, that I am not a sinner like everyone
Jn 11:41 to heaven and said, "Father, **t** you for hearing me.
Ro 1:8 How I **t** God through Jesus Christ for each one of
6:17 **T** God! Once you were slaves of sin, but now you
7:25 **T** God! The answer is in Jesus Christ our Lord.
1Co 1:14 I **t** God that I did not baptize any of you except
10:30 If I can **t** God for the food and enjoy it, why should
14:18 I **t** God that I speak in tongues more than all of
15:57 How we **t** God, who gives us victory over sin
2Co 9:15 **T** God for his Son—a gift too wonderful for
Php 4:6 God what you need, and **t** him for all he has done.
1Th 1:2 We always **t** God for all of you and pray for you
3:9 How we **t** God for you! Because of you we have
2Th 1:3 and sisters, we always **t** God for you, as is right,
2:13 As for us, we always **t** God for you, dear brothers
2Ti 1:3 Timothy, I **t** God for you. He is the God I serve
Phm 1:4 I always **t** God when I pray for you, Philemon,

THANKED (12) [THANK]

Jdg 7:15 heard the dream and its interpretation, he **t** God.
Ru 2:10 Ruth fell at his feet and **t** him warmly. "Why are
2Ch 20:26 because the people praised and **t** the LORD there.
31:8 they **t** the LORD and his people Israel!
Jer 5:7 But they **t** me by committing adultery and lining
Mt 15:36 took the seven loaves and the fish, **t** God for them,
Mk 8:6 **t** God for them, broke them into pieces, and gave
Lk 13:13 could stand straight. How she praised and **t** God!
17:9 And the servant is not even **t**, because he is merely
22:19 and when he had **t** God for it, he broke it in pieces
Ac 13:48 were very glad and **t** the Lord for his message;
28:15 When Paul saw them, he **t** God and took courage.

THANKFUL (12) [THANK]

Ro 16:4 I am not the only one who is **t** to them; so are all
2Co 8:16 I am **t** to God that he has given Titus the same
Col 3:15 you are all called to live in peace. And always be **t**.
3:16 and spiritual songs to God with **t** hearts.
4:2 to prayer with an alert mind and a **t** heart.
1Th 5:18 No matter what happens, always be **t**, for this is
2Th 1:3 for we are **t** that your faith is flourishing and you
2:13 We are **t** that God chose you to be among the first
1Ti 1:12 How **t** I am to Christ Jesus our Lord for
4:4 any of it. We may receive it gladly, with **t** hearts.
Heb 12:28 let us be **t** and please God by worshiping him with
Jas 5:13 And those who have reason to be **t** should

THANKFULNESS (1) [THANK]

Eph 5:4 these are not for you. Instead, let there be **t** to God.

THANKING (5) [THANK]

Lk 17:16 ground at Jesus' feet, **t** him for what he had done.
1Co 1:4 I can never stop **t** God for all the generous gifts he
Eph 1:16 I have never stopped **t** God for you. I pray for you
Col 1:12 always **t** the Father, who has enabled you to share
1Th 2:13 And we will never stop **t** God that when we

THANKS (69) [THANK]

2Sa 13:25 but the king wouldn't come, though he sent his **t**.
1Ch 16:4 and giving **t** and praise to the LORD,
16:8 Give **t** to the LORD and proclaim his greatness.
16:34 Give **t** to the LORD, for he is good! / His faithful
16:41 and the others chosen by name to give **t** to the
23:30 they stood before the LORD to sing songs of **t**
25:3 of the harp, offering **t** and praise to the LORD.
2Ch 5:13 in unison to praise and give **t** to the LORD.
20:21 This is what they sang: / "Give **t** to the LORD;
31:2 and to worship and give **t** and praise to the LORD
Ezr 3:11 With praise and **t**, they sang this song to the
Ne 12:31 the wall and organized two large choirs to give **t**.
12:40 The two choirs that were giving **t** then proceeded
12:46 and **t** to God began long ago in the days of David
Ps 30:12 O LORD my God, I will give you **t** forever!
42:4 the house of God, / singing for joy and giving **t**—
50:14 What I want instead is your true **t** to God; / I want
50:23 But giving **t** is a sacrifice that truly honors me.
56:12 O God, / and offer a sacrifice of **t** for your help.
75:1 O God! / We give **t** because you are near.
92:1 It is good to give **t** to the LORD, / to sing praises
100:4 with praise. / Give **t** to him and bless his name.
105:1 Give **t** to the LORD and proclaim his greatness.
106:1 Give **t** to the LORD, for he is good!
107:1 Give **t** to the LORD, for he is good! / His faithful
109:30 But I will give repeated **t** to the LORD,
118:1 Give **t** to the LORD, for he is good! / His faithful
118:29 Give **t** to the LORD, for he is good! / His faithful
119:108 LORD, accept my grateful **t** / and teach me your
122:4 They come to give **t** to the name of the LORD
136:1 Give **t** to the LORD, for he is good! / His faithful
136:2 Give **t** to the God of gods. / His faithful love
136:3 Give **t** to the Lord of lords. / His faithful love
136:4 Give **t** to him who alone does mighty miracles.
136:5 Give **t** to him who made the heavens so skillfully.
136:6 Give **t** to him who placed the earth on the water.
136:7 Give **t** to him who made the heavenly lights—
136:10 Give **t** to him who killed the firstborn of Egypt.
136:13 Give **t** to him who parted the Red Sea.
136:16 Give **t** to him who led his people through the
136:17 Give **t** to him who struck down mighty kings.
136:26 Give **t** to the God of heaven. / His faithful love
138:1 I give you **t**, O LORD, with all my heart; / I will
138:2 I will give **t** to your name / for your unfailing love
138:4 Every king in all the earth will give you **t**,
147:7 Sing out your **t** to the LORD; / sing praises to our
Jer 20:13 Now I will sing out my **t** to the LORD!
33:11 'Give **t** to the LORD Almighty, for the LORD is
Da 6:10 just as he had always done, giving **t** to his God.
Mt 26:27 And he took a cup of wine and gave **t** to God for it.
Mk 14:23 And he took a cup of wine and gave **t** to God for it.
Lk 22:17 and when he had given **t** for it, he said, "Take this
Jn 6:11 Then Jesus took the loaves, gave **t** to God,
Ac 27:35 gave **t** to God before them all, and broke off a
Ro 1:21 wouldn't worship him as God or even give him **t**.
14:6 the Lord, since they give **t** to God before eating.
14:6 also want to please the Lord and give **t** to God.
1Co 11:24 and when he had given **t**, he broke it and said,
14:16 How can they join you in giving **t** when they don't
14:17 You will be giving **t** very nicely, no doubt, but it
2Co 1:11 many will give **t** to God because so many people's
2:14 But **t** be to God, who made us his captives
Eph 5:20 And you will always give **t** for everything to God
Php 1:3 Every time I think of you, I give **t** to my God.
Col 1:3 and we give **t** to God the Father of our Lord Jesus
3:17 all the while giving **t** through him to God the
1Ti 2:1 plead for God's mercy upon them, and give **t**.
Rev 4:9 and honor and **t** to the one sitting on the throne,
11:17 "We give **t** to you, Lord God Almighty,

THANKSGIVING (31) [THANK]

Ex 29:28 up peace offerings or **t** offerings to the LORD,
Lev 7:12 If you present your peace offering as a **t** offering,
7:13 This peace offering of **t** must also be accompanied
22:29 When you bring a **t** offering to the LORD, it must
1Ch 16:7 and his fellow Levites this song of **t** to the
2Ch 29:31 and **t** offerings to the Temple of the LORD."
29:31 the people brought their sacrifices and **t** offerings,
33:16 and sacrificed peace offerings and **t** offerings on it.
Ne 11:17 of Asaph, who opened the **t** services with prayer;
12:8 with his associates was in charge of the songs of **t**.
12:24 them during the ceremonies of praise and **t**,
12:27 part in the joyous occasion with their songs of **t**
Ps 26:7 singing a song of **t** / and telling of all your
28:7 heart is filled with joy. / I burst out in songs of **t**.
69:30 name with singing, / and I will honor him with **t**.
95:2 Let us come before him with **t**. / Let us sing him
100:T A psalm of **t**.
100:4 Enter his gates with **t**; / go into his courts with
107:22 Let them offer sacrifices of **t** / and sing joyfully
116:17 I will offer you a sacrifice of **t** / and call on the
Isa 51:3 be found there. Lovely songs of **t** will fill the air.
Jer 17:26 incense, and **t** offerings to the LORD's Temple.
30:19 There will be joy and songs of **t**, and I will
33:11 along with the joyous songs of people bringing **t**
Am 4:5 your bread made with yeast as an offering of **t**.
2Co 4:15 and more people to Christ, there will be great **t**,
9:11 who need them, they will break out in **t** to God.
9:12 and they will joyfully express their **t** to God.
Col 2:7 Let your lives overflow with **t** for all he has done.
1Ti 4:3 But God created those foods to be eaten with **t** by
Rev 7:12 and **t** and honor and power and strength

THANKWORTHY [KJV] See PLEASED

THARA [KJV] See TERAH

THARSHISH [KJV] See TARSHISH

THAT (5637) [THAT'S] See Index of Articles, Etc.

THAT'S (42) [BE, THAT] See Index of Articles, Etc.

THAWS (1)

Ps 147:18 it all melts. / He sends his winds, and the ice **t**.

THE (52785) See Index of Articles, Etc.

THEBES (6)

Jer 46:25 "I will punish Amon, the god of **T**, and all the
Eze 30:14 I will destroy Pathros, Zoan, and **T**, and they will
30:15 of Egypt, and I will stamp out the people of **T**.

30:16 will be racked with pain; **T** will be torn apart;
Na 3:8 Are you any better than **T**, surrounded by rivers,
3:10 Yet **T** fell, and her people were led away as

THEBEZ (2)

Jdg 9:50 Then Abimelech attacked the city of **T**
2Sa 11:21 Wasn't Gideon's son Abimelech killed at **T** by a

THEFT (5) [THIEF]

Lev 6:2 or they have taken something by **t** or extortion.
6:4 they must give back whatever they have taken by **t**
Am 3:10 "Their fortresses are filled with wealth taken by **t**
Mt 15:19 all other sexual immorality, **t**, lying, and slander.
Mk 7:21 come evil thoughts, sexual immorality, **t**, murder,

THEFTS (1) [THIEF]

Rev 9:21 or their witchcraft or their immorality or their **t**.

THEIR (4131) [THEY] See Index of Articles, Etc.

THEIRS (15) [THEY] See Index of Articles, Etc.

THELASAR [KJV] See TEL-ASSAR

THEM (5038) [THEY] See Index of Articles, Etc.

THEMSELVES (257) [SELF, THEY] See Index of Articles, Etc.

THEN (3757) See Index of Articles, Etc.

THEOPHILUS (2)

Lk 1:1 Most honorable **T**: Many people have written
Ac 1:1 Dear **T**: In my first book I told you about

THERE (2016) [THERE'S] See Index of Articles, Etc.

THERE'S (13) [BE, THERE] See Index of Articles, Etc.

THEREAFTER (1)

Ge 16:13 **T**, Hagar referred to the LORD, who had spoken

THEREBY (3)

Ge 25:33 **t** selling all his rights as the firstborn to his
1Ki 2:27 **t** fulfilling the decree the LORD had made at
Jn 5:18 as his Father, **t** making himself equal with God.

THEREFORE (125)

Ge 49:7 for it is cruel. / **T**, I will scatter their descendants
Ex 6:6 "**T**, say to the Israelites: 'I am the LORD, and I
22:31 **T**, do not eat any animal that has been attacked
Lev 11:45 your God. You must **t** be holy because I am holy.
20:25 **t** make a distinction between ceremonially clean
Dt 7:9 Understand, **t**, that the LORD your God is indeed
7:11 **T**, obey all these commands, laws, and regulations
10:16 **T**, cleanse your sinful hearts and stop being
11:8 "**T**, be careful to obey every command I am giving
25:19 **T**, when the LORD your God has given you rest
29:9 "**T**, obey the terms of this covenant so that you
Jdg 7:3 **T**, tell the people, 'Whoever is timid or afraid may
1Sa 2:30 "**T**, the LORD, the God of Israel, says:
10:19 Now, **t**, present yourselves before the LORD by
2Ki 1:4 Now, **t**, this is what the LORD says: You will
Ezr 4:21 **T**, issue orders to have these people stop their
Job 20:21 gorging himself; **t**, his prosperity will not endure.
Ps 5:5 **T**, the proud will not be allowed to stand in your
12:7 **T**, LORD, we know you will protect the
32:6 **T**, let all the godly confess their rebellion to you
45:7 is wrong. / **T**, God—your God—has anointed you,
45:17 **T**, the nations will praise you forever and ever.
106:26 **T**, he swore / that he would kill them in the
Isa 1:24 **T**, the Lord, the LORD Almighty, the Mighty
5:24 **T**, they will all disappear like burning straw.
8:7 **T**, the Lord will overwhelm them with a mighty
9:14 **T**, in a single day, the LORD will destroy both
24:6 **T**, a curse consumes the earth and its people.
25:3 **T**, strong nations will declare your glory;
27:11 **T**, the one who made them will show them no pity
28:14 **T**, listen to this message from the LORD,
28:16 **T**, this is what the Sovereign LORD says: "Look!
31:6 **T**, my people, though you are such wicked rebels,
50:7 **T**, I have set my face like a stone, determined to do
64:7 **T**, you have turned away from us and turned us
65:13 **T**, this is what the Sovereign LORD says:
Jer 2:9 **T**, I will bring my case against you and will keep
3:12 **T**, go and say these words to Israel, 'This is what
5:14 **T**, this is what the LORD God Almighty says:
6:15 even blush! **T**, they will lie among the slaughtered.
6:18 "**T**, listen to this, all you nations. Take note of my
6:21 **T**, this is what the LORD says: "I will put
8:12 even blush! **T**, they will lie among the slaughtered.
9:7 **T**, the LORD Almighty says, "See, I will melt
10:21 **T**, they fail completely, and their flocks are
11:11 **T**, says the LORD, I am going to bring calamity
13:10 **T**, they will become like this linen belt—good for
14:15 **T**, says the LORD, I will punish these lying
15:6 "**T**, I will raise my clenched fists to destroy you.
18:11 "**T**, Jeremiah, go and warn all Judah
18:16 **T**, their land will become desolate, a monument to
22:18 **T**, this is the LORD's decree of punishment
23:12 "**T**, their paths will be dark and slippery. They will
23:15 **T**, this is what the LORD Almighty says
23:30 "**T**," says the LORD, "I stand against these
28:16 **T**, the LORD says you must die. Your life will
29:20 **T**, listen to this message from the LORD, all you
34:17 "**T**, this is what the LORD says: Since you have
35:17 "**T**, the LORD God Almighty, the God of Israel,
44:11 "**T**, the LORD Almighty, the God of Israel,
50:18 **T**, the LORD Almighty, the God of Israel, says:
La 2:8 **T**, the ramparts and walls have fallen down before
3:24 LORD is my inheritance; **t**, I will hope in him!"
Eze 8:18 **T**, I will deal with them in fury. I will neither pity
11:4 **T**, son of man, prophesy against them loudly
11:7 "**T**, this is what the Sovereign LORD says:
11:16 **T**, give the exiles this message from the Sovereign
12:28 **T**, give them this message from the Sovereign
13:8 "**T**, this is what the Sovereign LORD says:
13:13 "**T**, this is what the Sovereign LORD says:
14:6 "**T**, give the people of Israel this message from the
16:35 "**T**, you prostitute, listen to this message from the
17:18 treaty after swearing to obey; **t**, he will not escape.
18:30 "**T**, I will judge each of you, O people of Israel,
20:27 "**T**, son of man, give the people of Israel this
20:30 "**T**, give the people of Israel this message from the
21:24 "**T**, this is what the Sovereign LORD says:
23:22 "**T**, Oholibah, this is what the Sovereign LORD
25:13 **T**, says the Sovereign LORD, I will raise my fist
25:16 **T**, says the Sovereign LORD, I will raise my fist
26:3 "**T**, this is what the Sovereign LORD says:
28:6 "**T**, this is what the Sovereign LORD says:
29:19 **T**, this is what the Sovereign LORD says: I will
30:22 **T**, this is what the Sovereign LORD says: I am
31:10 "**T**, this is what the Sovereign LORD says:
32:3 "**T**, this is what the Sovereign LORD says:
33:7 **T**, listen to what I say and warn them for me.
34:7 "**T**, you shepherds, hear the word of the LORD:
34:9 **T**, you shepherds, hear the word of the LORD.
34:20 "**T**, this is what the Sovereign LORD says:
35:11 **T**, as surely as I live, says the Sovereign LORD,
36:3 **T**, son of man, give the mountains of Israel this
36:4 **T**, O mountains of Israel, hear the word of the
36:6 "**T**, prophesy to the hills and mountains,
36:7 **T**, says the Sovereign LORD, I have raised my
36:22 "**T**, give the people of Israel this message from the
38:14 "**T**, son of man, prophesy against Gog. Give him
39:23 **T**, I turned my back on them and let their enemies
Da 3:29 **T**, I make this decree: If any people, whatever their
Hos 8:6 It is not God! **T**, it must be smashed to bits.
8:14 **T**, I will send down fire on their palaces and burn
13:3 **T**, they will disappear like the morning mist,
Am 3:11 **T**," says the Sovereign LORD, "an enemy is
4:12 "**T**, I will bring upon you all these further disasters
5:11 **T**, you will never live in the beautiful stone houses
5:16 **T**, this is what the Lord, the LORD God
6:7 **T**, you will be the first to be led away as captives.
Mic 6:13 "**T**, I will wound you! I will bring you to ruin for
6:16 **T**, I will make an example of you, bringing you to
Zec 1:3 **T**, say to the people, 'This is what the LORD
1:16 " '**T**, this is what the LORD says: I have
Mt 18:4 **T**, anyone who becomes as humble as this little
28:19 **T**, go and make disciples of all the nations,
Lk 23:22 him to death. I will **t** flog him and let him go."
Ro 5:1 **T**, since we have been made right in God's sight
2Co 6:17 **T**, come out from them / and separate yourselves
Eph 4:1 **T** I, a prisoner for serving the Lord, beg you to
Heb 1:9 is wrong. / **T** God, your God, has anointed you,
2:17 **T**, it was necessary for Jesus to be in every respect
6:18 **T**, we who have fled to him for refuge can take
7:25 **T** he is able, once and forever, to save everyone
12:1 **T**, since we are surrounded by such a huge crowd
1Pe 4:7 **T**, be earnest and disciplined in your prayers.
Rev 2:22 **T**, I will throw her upon a sickbed, and she will
18:8 **T**, the sorrows of death and mourning and famine

THESE (1546) [THIS] See Index of Articles, Etc.

THESSALONICA (9)

Ac 17:1 of Amphipolis and Apollonia and came to **T**,
17:11 of Berea were more open-minded than those in **T**,
17:13 But when some Jews in **T** learned that Paul was
20:4 Aristarchus and Secundus, from **T**; Gaius,
27:2 And Aristarchus, a Macedonian from **T**, was also
Php 4:16 Even when I was in **T** you sent help more than
1Th 1:1 It is written to the church in **T**, you who belong to
2Th 1:1 It is written to the church in **T**, you who belong to
2Ti 4:10 he loves the things of this life and has gone to **T**.

THEUDAS (1)

Ac 5:36 Some time ago there was that fellow **T**,

THEY (7440) [THEIR, THEIRS, THEM, THEMSELVES, THEY'LL, THEY'RE] See Index of Articles, Etc.

THEY'LL (3) [THEY, WILL] See Index of Articles, Etc.

THEY'RE (2) [BE, THEY] See Index of Articles, Etc.

THICK (35) [THICKER, THICKEST]

Ex 19:9 "I am going to come to you in a **t** cloud
Jdg 6:5 coming with their cattle and tents as **t** as locusts,
1Sa 17:7 his spear was as heavy and **t** as a weaver's beam,
2Sa 18:9 but as he rode beneath the **t** branches of a great
21:15 when David and his men were in the **t** of battle,
21:19 The handle of his spear was as **t** as a weaver's
1Ki 7:26 The walls of the Sea were about three inches **t**,
8:12 you have said that you would live in **t** darkness.
1Ch 11:23 and whose spear was as **t** as a weaver's beam.
20:5 The handle of Lahmi's spear was as **t** as a
2Ch 4:5 The walls of the Sea were about three inches **t**,
6:1 you have said that you would live in **t** darkness.
Job 22:13 How can he judge through the **t** darkness?
22:14 For **t** clouds swirl about him, and he cannot see us.
23:17 **t**, impenetrable darkness is everywhere.
26:8 He wraps the rain in his **t** clouds, and the clouds do
34:22 No darkness is **t** enough to hide the wicked from
38:9 and as I clothed it with clouds and **t** darkness?
Ps 78:27 He rained down meat as **t** as dust— / birds as
Isa 30:27 with anger, surrounded by a **t**, rising smoke.
Jer 38:6 but there was a **t** layer of mud at the bottom,
52:21 They were hollow, with walls 3 inches **t**.
Eze 8:11 so there was a **t** cloud of incense above their heads.
31:3 full of **t** branches that cast deep forest shade with
31:5 It prospered and grew long **t** branches because of
40:5 and the wall was 10-1/2 feet **t** and 10-1/2 feet high.
40:9 14 feet deep, with supporting columns 3-1/2 feet **t**.
40:48 was 24-1/2 feet wide with walls 5-1/4 feet **t**.
41:3 at the entrance and found them to be 3-1/2 feet **t**.
41:5 of the Temple and found that it was 10-1/2 feet **t**.
41:9 wall of the Temple's side rooms was 8-3/4 feet **t**.
41:12 157-1/2 feet long, and its walls were 8-3/4 feet **t**.
Joel 2:2 and gloom, a day of **t** clouds and deep blackness.
Lk 23:45 the **t** veil hanging in the Temple was torn apart.
Rev 21:17 and found them to be 216 feet **t** (the angel used a

THICKER (2) [THICK]

1Ki 12:10 'My little finger is **t** than my father's waist—
2Ch 10:10 'My little finger is **t** than my father's waist—

THICKEST (1) [THICK]

Zec 11:2 of Bashan, as you watch the **t** forests being felled.

THICKET (2) [THICKETS]

Job 38:40 as they lie in their dens or crouch in the **t**?
Am 3:4 Does a lion ever roar in a **t** without first finding a

THICKETS (6) [THICKET]

Isa 17:9 largest cities will be as deserted as overgrown **t**.
Jer 12:5 what will you do in the **t** near the Jordan?
49:19 I will come like a lion from the **t** of the Jordan,
50:44 "I will come like a lion from the **t** of the Jordan,
Hos 2:12 I will let them grow into tangled **t**, where only wild
Zec 11:3 for their **t** in the Jordan Valley have been

THIEF (24) [THIEF'S, THEFT, THEFTS, THIEVES]

Ex 22:2 "If a **t** is caught in the act of breaking into a house
22:2 the person who killed the **t** is not guilty.
22:3 the one who killed the **t** is guilty of murder.
22:3 "A **t** who is caught must pay in full for everything
22:3 the **t** must be sold as a slave to pay the debt.
22:4 then the **t** must pay double the value.
22:7 If the **t** is found, the fine is double the value of
22:8 But if the **t** is not found, God will determine
Jdg 17:2 "I heard you curse the **t** who stole eleven hundred
Job 24:14 dawn to kill the poor and needy; at night he is a **t**.
Ps 50:18 When you see a **t**, you help him, / and you spend
Pr 6:30 Excuses might be found for a **t** who steals
29:24 If you assist a **t**, you are only hurting yourself.
Jer 2:26 "Like a **t**, Israel feels shame only when she gets
Zec 5:4 I am sending this curse into the house of every **t**
Lk 12:33 no **t** can steal it and no moth can destroy it.
Jn 10:1 through the gate, must surely be a **t** and a robber!
12:6 he was a **t** who was in charge of the disciples'
Eph 4:28 If you are a **t**, stop stealing. Begin using your
1Th 5:2 Lord will come unexpectedly, like a **t** in the night.
5:4 surprised when the day of the Lord comes like a **t**.
2Pe 3:10 day of the Lord will come as unexpectedly as a **t**.
Rev 3:3 will come upon you suddenly, as unexpected as a **t**.
16:15 "Take note: I will come as unexpectedly as a **t**!

THIEF'S (1) [THIEF]

Jn 10:10 The **t** purpose is to steal and kill and destroy.

THIEVES (18) [THIEF]

Job 30:5 and people shout after them as if they were **t**.
Pr 12:12 **T** are jealous of each other's loot, while the godly
Isa 1:23 Your leaders are rebels, the companions of **t**.
Jer 7:11 this Temple, which honors my name, is a den of **t**?
48:27 Was she caught in the company of **t** that you
49:9 If **t** came at night, even they would not take
Hos 5:10 "The leaders of Judah have become as bad as **t**.
7:1 Samaria is filled with liars, **t**, and bandits!
Joel 2:9 the houses, climbing like **t** through the windows.
Ob 1:5 "If **t** came at night and robbed you, they would not
Hab 2:6 all their captives will taunt them, saying: 'You **t**!
Mt 6:19 and get rusty, and where **t** break in and steal.
6:20 or rusty and where they will be safe from **t**.
21:13 of prayer,' but you have turned it into a den of **t**!"
Mk 11:17 all nations,' but you have turned it into a den of **t**."

Lk 19:46 of prayer,' but you have turned it into a den of **t**."
Jn 10: 8 "All others who came before me were **t**
1Co 6:10 **t**, greedy people, drunkards, abusers,

THIGH (15) [THIGHS]

Ex 28:42 worn next to their bodies, reaching from waist to **t**.
29:22 the two kidneys with their fat, and the right **t**.
29:27 and the **t** that were lifted up before the LORD in
Lev 7:32 You are to give the right **t** of your peace offering to
7:33 The right **t** must always be given to the priest who
7:34 designated the breast and the right **t** for the priests.
8:25 two kidneys with their fat, along with the right **t**.
10:14 and **t** that were lifted up may be eaten in any place
10:15 The **t** and breast that are lifted up must be lifted up
Nu 6:20 and **t** pieces that were lifted up before the LORD.
18:18 and right **t** that are presented by lifting them up
Jdg 3:16 and he strapped it to his right **t**, keeping it hidden
3:21 pulled out the dagger strapped to his right **t**,
SS 3: 8 Each one wears a sword on his **t**, ready to defend
Rev 19:16 On his robe and **t** was written this title: King of

THIGHS (6) [THIGH]

Lev 9:21 and right **t** as an offering to the LORD,
Job 40:17 The sinews of its **t** are tightly knit together.
SS 7: 1 Your rounded **t** are like jewels, the work of a
Eze 21:12 pound your **t** in anguish, for that sword will
Da 2:32 arms were of silver, its belly and **t** were of bronze,
2:39 represented by the bronze belly and **t**,

THIMNATHAH [KJV] See TIMNAH

THIN (10)

Ge 41: 4 Then the **t**, ugly cows ate the fat ones! At this point
41: 7 And these **t** heads swallowed up the seven plump,
41:19 They were very **t** and gaunt—in fact, I've never
41:20 These **t**, ugly cows ate up the seven fat ones that
41:27 The seven **t**, ugly cows and the seven withered
Ex 16:14 **t** flakes, white like frost, covered the ground.
29: 2 make loaves of bread, **t** cakes mixed with olive oil,
39: 3 made gold thread by beating gold into **t** sheets
Lev 8:26 with olive oil, and a **t** wafer spread with olive oil.
Da 1:10 and **t** compared to the other youths your age,

THING (171) [NOTHING, NOTHINGNESS, SOMETHING, SOMETHING'S, THINGS]

LIVING THING (10) Ge 6:17; 7:23; Dt 5:26; 11:6; 20:16; Jos 11:11; Jdg 20:48; Job 12:10; Ps 136:25; 145:16

SUCH A THING (15) Ge 3:13; 18:25; Jdg 19:23; 2Sa 12:5; 13:12; Jer 2:12; 7:31; 18:13; 19:5; 32:35; Eze 16:16; Da 2:10; Lk 20:16; 22:23; Jn 5:12

Ge 3:13 asked the woman, "How could you do such a **t**?"
6:17 earth with a flood that will destroy every living **t**.
7:23 Every living **t** on the earth was wiped out—people,
18:25 Surely you wouldn't do such a **t**,
19: 7 he begged, "don't do such a wicked **t**.
20: 9 of this great sin? This kind of **t** should not be done!
30:31 Just do one **t**, and I'll go back to work for you.
32:19 "You are all to say the same **t** to Esau when you
34: 7 Shechem had done a disgraceful **t** against Jacob's
34: 7 a **t** that should never have been done.
38:10 But the LORD considered it a wicked **t** for Onan
39: 9 are his wife. How could I ever do such a wicked **t**?
41:25 "Both dreams mean the same **t**," Joseph told
44: 5 the future? What a wicked **t** you have done!' "
44: 7 we are, that you accuse us of such a terrible **t**?
Ex 7:11 and they did the same **t** with their secret arts.
7:23 to his palace and put the whole **t** out of his mind.
8: 7 But the magicians were able to do the same **t** with
8:18 Pharaoh's magicians tried to do the same **t** with
10:15 Not one green **t** remained, neither tree nor plant,
Lev 10:19 he said. "This kind of **t** has also happened to me.
Nu 16: 9 Does it seem a small **t** to you that the God of Israel
16:40 the same **t** would happen to him as happened to
32:14 a brood of sinners, doing exactly the same **t**!
Dt 2:23 A similar **t** happened when the Caphtorites from
5:26 Can any living **t** hear the voice of the living God
11: 6 and tents and every living **t** that belonged to them.
17: 4 If it is true that this detestable **t** has been done in
19:20 about it will be afraid to do such an evil **t** again.
20:16 special possession, destroy every living **t** in them.
23:14 He must not see any shameful **t** among you,
Jos 7:15 of the LORD and has done a horrible **t** in Israel."
11:11 The Israelites completely destroyed every living **t**
Jdg 7:14 friend said, "Your dream can mean only one **t**—
11:31 I will give to the LORD the first **t** coming out of
13:19 his wife watched, the LORD did an amazing **t**.
13:23 and told us this wonderful **t** and done these
19:23 "No, my brothers, don't do such an evil **t**. For this man is my guest, and such a **t** would be shameful.
19:24 But don't do such a shameful **t** to this man."
20:10 for this shameful **t** they have done in Israel."
20:12 "What a terrible **t** has been done among you!
20:48 and slaughtered every living **t** in all the towns—
Ru 3:11 Now don't worry about a **t**, my daughter. I will do
1Sa 3:11 "I am about to do a shocking **t** in Israel.
5: 4 But the next morning the same **t** happened—
9: 7 food is gone, and we don't have a **t** to give him."
12:16 and see the great **t** the LORD is about to do.
14:24 revenge on my enemies." So no one ate a **t** all day,
17:30 and asked them the same **t** and received the same
17:32 "Don't worry about a **t**," David told Saul. "I'll go
19:21 prophesied! The same **t** happened a third time!
20: 2 "I'm sure he's not planning any such **t**, for he
24: 6 "It is a serious **t** to attack the LORD's anointed
27: 1 The best **t** for me to do is escape to the Philistines.
2Sa 2:26 Don't you realize the only **t** we will gain is
12: 5 "any man who would do such a **t** deserves to die!
13:12 You know what a serious crime it is to do such a **t**
14:12 "Please let me ask one more **t** of you!" she said.
14:18 "I want to know one **t**," the king replied. "Yes,
19:19 "Forget the terrible **t** I did when you left
24:10 forgive me, LORD, for doing this foolish **t**."
1Ki 14:13 for this child is the only good **t** that the LORD,
18:34 he said, "Do the same **t** again!" And when they
22: 3 And we haven't done a **t** about it!"
2Ki 2:10 "You have asked a difficult **t**," Elijah replied.
3:18 But this is only a simple **t** for the LORD, for he
5:13 if the prophet had told you to do some great **t**,
5:18 However, may the LORD pardon me in this one **t**.
1Ch 13: 4 for the people could see it was the right **t** to do.
21: 8 Please forgive me for doing this foolish **t**."
2Ch 25: 5 Another **t** Amaziah did was to organize the army,
34: 6 He did the same **t** in the towns of Manasseh,
Ne 3: 3 They did the whole **t**—laid the beams,
13:18 it enough that your ancestors did this sort of **t**,
Job 12:10 For the life of every living **t** is in his hand,
13: 5 Please be quiet! That's the smartest **t** you could do.
15:18 men who have heard the same **t** from their fathers,
Ps 27: 4 The one **t** I ask of the LORD— / the **t** I seek most—
34:10 trust in the LORD will never lack any good **t**.
84:11 and glory. / No good **t** will the LORD withhold
136:25 He gives food to every living **t**. / His faithful love
145:16 you satisfy the hunger and thirst of every living **t**.
148: 5 Let every created **t** give praise to the LORD,
Pr 4: 7 Getting wisdom is the most important **t** you can
15:23 it is wonderful to say the right **t** at the right time!
Ecc 5:18 Even so, I have noticed one **t**, at least, that is good.
5:19 And it is a good **t** to receive wealth from God
12:14 including every secret **t**, whether good or bad.
Isa 28:21 He will come to do a strange, unusual **t**: He will
29:16 Should the **t** that was created say to the one who
41: 7 then fasten the **t** in place so it won't fall over.
43:19 For I am about to do a brand-new **t**. See, I have
44:20 Yet he cannot bring himself to ask, "Is this **t**,
44:23 for the LORD has done this wondrous **t**.
Jer 2:12 The heavens are shocked at such a **t** and shrink
2:19 bitter **t** it is to forsake the LORD your God,
3: 5 Surely you won't be angry about such a little **t**!
5:30 and shocking **t** has happened in this land—
7:31 never even crossed my mind to command such a **t**!
8: 6 Does anyone say, "What a terrible **t** I have done"?
18:13 LORD said, "Has anyone ever heard of such a **t**,
19: 5 never even crossed my mind to command such a **t**!
32:23 They have hardly done one **t** you told them to!
32:35 never even crossed my mind to command such a **t**.
37:14 "I had no intention of doing any such **t**."
38: 9 "these men have done a very evil **t** in putting
40:16 said to Johanan, "I forbid you to do any such **t**,
Eze 16:16 Unbelievable! How could such a **t** ever happen?
Da 2:10 has ever asked such a **t** of any magician, enchanter,
2:11 This is an impossible **t** the king requires. No one
Hos 4:14 For you men are doing the same **t**, sinning with
5: 9 One **t** is certain, Israel: When your day of
6:10 Yes, I have seen a horrible **t** in Israel: My people
13:15 Every precious **t** they have will be plundered
Joel 2: 3 them is nothing but desolation; not one **t** escapes.
2:11 The day of the LORD is an awesome, terrible **t**.
Am 4: 5 This is the kind of **t** you Israelites love to do,"
Mal 2:13 Here is another **t** you do. You cover the LORD's
Mt 20: 5 and again around three o'clock he did the same **t**.
26:10 "Why berate her for doing such a good **t** to me?
Mk 10:21 "You lack only one **t**," he told him. "Go and sell
14: 6 Why berate her for doing such a good **t** to me?
Lk 2:15 Let's see this wonderful **t** that has happened,
5: 5 "we worked hard all last night and didn't catch a **t**.
8:39 telling about the great **t** Jesus had done for him.
10:42 There is really only one **t** worth being concerned
15:29 and never once refused to do a single **t** you told me
16: 4 I know just the **t**! And then I'll have plenty of
18:22 "There is still one **t** you lack," Jesus said.
18:34 But they didn't understand a **t** he said.
20:11 sent another servant, but the same **t** happened;
20:12 A third man was sent and the same **t** happened.
20:16 "But God forbid that such a **t** should ever
22:23 each other which of them would ever do such a **t**.
Jn 1:41 The first **t** Andrew did was to find his brother,
5:12 "Who said such a **t** as that?" they demanded.
8:40 to kill me. Abraham wouldn't do a **t** like that.
13:24 to him to ask who would do this terrible **t**.
Ac 3:11 Everyone stood there in awe of the wonderful **t**
5: 4 How could you do a **t** like this? You weren't lying
5: 9 "How could the two of you even think of doing a **t**
7:41 sacrificed to it and rejoiced in this **t** they had made.
19:32 were all shouting, some one **t** and some another.
21:34 Some shouted one **t** and some another. He couldn't
24:21 except for one **t** I said when I shouted out, 'I am on
28:22 for the only **t** we know about these Christians is
Ro 7:15 but I don't do it. Instead, I do the very **t** I hate.
9:20 Should the **t** that was created say to the one who
11: 9 David spoke of this same **t** when he said,
11:24 into his own good tree—a very unusual **t** to do—
1Co 5: 6 and yet you let this sort of **t** go on.
7:19 The important **t** is to keep God's commandments.
9: 8 human opinion. Doesn't God's law say the same **t**?
11: 3 But there is one **t** I want you to know: A man is
12:19 What a strange **t** a body would be if it had only one
15:11 The important **t** is that you believed what we
2Co 12:13 The only **t** I didn't do, which I do in the other
Gal 2:10 The only **t** they suggested was that we remember
Eph 6: 1 you belong to the Lord, for this is the right **t** to do.
Php 3:13 but I am focusing all my energies on this one **t**:
4: 8 let me say one more **t** as I close this letter.
Col 2:17 For these rules were only shadows of the real **t**,
2Th 2:17 and give you strength in every good **t** you do
2Ti 3:17 fully equipped for every good **t** God wants us to
Phm 1: 8 of Christ because it is the right **t** for you to do,
Heb 10:31 It is a terrible **t** to fall into the hands of the living
Jas 3: 5 So also, the tongue is a small **t**, but what enormous
2Pe 3: 3 laugh at the truth and do every evil **t** they desire.
Rev 3:17 am rich. I have everything I want. I don't need a **t**!'

THINGS (576) [THING]

ALL (OF) THESE THINGS (34) Lev 9:5; 14:43; Nu 16:28; Dt 30:1; 2Ki 23:4; 2Ch 4:16; Ps 106:29; Ecc 2:9; Isa 8:16; Jer 16:10; 25:30; 35:8; La 1:16; Eze 27:14; Da 4:28; 12:7; Zec 8:17; Mt 24:34; Lk 2:51; 21:6,28; 24:26,48; Jn 17:1; Ac 3:18; Ro 8:37; 2Co 4:15; Php 3:7; 2Th 2:15; 2Ti 2:7; Heb 9:5; Rev 2:19; 22:8,20

ALL THINGS (16) 1Ch 29:11; Ps 8:6; Isa 44:24; Ac 3:21; 1Co 15:27,27,28,28; Eph 1:11,22; 3:9; Heb 2:8,8; 1Jn 2:27; Rev 8:9; 21:5

GOOD THINGS (42) Ge 45:23; Nu 10:32; 11:4; Dt 26:11; 28:11; Jos 23:15; 1Sa 19:4; 2Sa 7:28; 19:37; 1Ch 17:26; Ne 9:25; Job 2:10; 22:18; Ps 16:2; 39:2; 81:10; 103:2,5; 107:9; 119:65; Pr 12:14; 28:10; Ecc 2:1; Jer 5:25; 8:13; 29:10,32; Zec 3:8; Mt 19:16; Lk 1:53; Ac 26:20; 2Co 9:12; Eph 2:9,10; Php 1:11; Col 3:5; 1Ti 2:10; Tit 3:5; Phm 1:6; Heb 6:4; 9:11; 10:1

GREAT THINGS (12) Jdg 2:7; 1Sa 12:7; 25:31; 2Sa 7:21; 2Ki 8:4; 1Ch 17:19; Ps 106:21; Jer 45:5; Joel 2:20,21; Mk 5:20; Lk 1:49

HOLY THINGS (5) Lev 5:16; 1Ch 23:13; Eze 22:8,26; 44:13

THINGS TO COME (2) Zec 3:8; Heb 10:1

Ge 7: 4 And I will wipe from the earth all the living **t** I
7:21 All the living **t** on earth died—birds,
8:21 destroying all living **t**, even though people's
31: 5 so he could talk **t** over with them. "Your father has
37: 2 But Joseph reported to his father some of the bad **t**
45:23 ten donkeys loaded with the good **t** of Egypt,
Ex 10: 2 and grandchildren about the marvelous **t** I am
18: 1 about all the wonderful **t** God had done for Moses
29:33 may not eat them, for these **t** are set apart and holy.
31: 6 so they can make all the **t** I have instructed you to
Lev 5:16 then make restitution for whatever holy **t** they have
9: 5 So the people brought all of these **t** to the entrance
11:46 and all the living **t** that move through the water
13:59 determine whether these **t** are ceremonially clean
14:43 "But if the mildew reappears after all these **t** have
15:31 you will keep the people of Israel separate from **t**
18:26 and you must not do any of these detestable **t**.
18:29 Whoever does any of these detestable **t** will be cut
20:23 because they do these terrible **t** that I detest them
Nu 4:15 will come and carry these **t** to the next destination.
10:32 and we will share with you all the good **t** that the
11: 4 the Israelites began to crave the good **t** of Egypt,
14:28 as I live, I will do to you the very **t** I heard you say.
14:35 I will do these **t** to every member of the
16:28 has sent me to do all these **t** that I have done—
27:16 "O LORD, the God of the spirits of all living **t**,
Dt 4: 9 Do not let these **t** escape from your mind as long as
4:35 "He showed you these **t** so you would realize that
7:26 You must utterly detest such **t**, for they are set
18:12 Anyone who does these **t** is an object of horror
18:12 because the other nations have done these **t** that the
18:14 but the LORD your God forbids you to do such **t**.
22:17 He has accused her of shameful **t**, claiming that
26:11 because of all the good **t** the LORD your God has
28:11 **t** in the land he swore to give your ancestors—
29:29 "There are secret **t** that belong to the LORD our
29:29 but the revealed **t** belong to us and our descendants
30: 1 "Suppose all these **t** happen to you—the blessings
31: 1 When Moses had finished saying these **t** to all the
32:34 " 'I am storing up these **t**, / sealing them away
Jos 2:11 one has the courage to fight after hearing such **t**.
6:18 Do not take any of the **t** set apart for destruction,
6:24 Only the **t** made from silver, gold, bronze, or iron
7: 1 But Israel was unfaithful concerning the **t** set apart
7: 1 A man named Achan had stolen some of these **t**,
7:11 They have stolen the **t** that I commanded to be set
7:11 about it and hidden the **t** among their belongings.
7:12 the **t** among you that were set apart for destruction.
7:13 O Israel, are **t** set apart for the LORD.
7:13 defeat your enemies until you remove these **t**.
7:23 They took the **t** from the tent and brought them to
22:20 sinned by stealing the **t** set apart for the LORD?
23:15 your God has given you the good **t** he promised,
24:26 Joshua recorded these **t** in the Book of the Law of
Jdg 2: 7 those who had seen all the great **t** the LORD had
2:10 or remember the mighty **t** he had done for Israel.
Ru 1:13 **T** are far more bitter for me than for you,
1Sa 2:23 from the people about the wicked **t** you are doing.
2:30 The terrible **t** you are doing cannot continue!
6: 5 Make these **t** to show honor to the God of Israel.
12: 7 you of all the great **t** the LORD has done for you
12:24 Think of all the wonderful **t** he has done for you.
17:22 David left his **t** with the keeper of supplies
17:39 it was like, for he had never worn such **t** before.
18:23 When Saul's men said these **t** to David, he replied,
19: 4 father about David, saying many good **t** about him.
20: 2 me everything he's going to do, even the little **t**.
25:31 And when the LORD has done these great **t** for
2Sa 7:21 you have done all these great **t** and have shown
7:28 and you have promised these good **t** to me,
19:37 and receive whatever good **t** you want to give

1Ki 2:44 “You surely remember all the wicked **t** you did to
9: 8 ‘Why did the LORD do such terrible **t** to his land
2Ki 8: 4 “Tell me some stories about the great **t** Elisha has
8:12 “I know the terrible **t** you will do to the people of
17: 9 The people of Israel had also secretly done many **t**
17:11 So the people of Israel had done many evil **t**,
21:11 Manasseh of Judah has done many detestable **t**.
23: 4 The king had all these **t** burned outside Jerusalem
23:16 tomb of the man of God who had predicted these **t**.
23:17 and predicted the very **t** that you have just done to
25:16 These **t** had been made for the LORD’s Temple
1Ch 16:24 Tell everyone about the amazing **t** he does.
17:19 you have done all these great **t** and have made
17:26 And you have promised these good **t** to me,
23:13 were set apart to dedicate the most holy **t**,
26:26 all the **t** dedicated to the LORD by King David,
26:30 for all matters related to the **t** of the LORD
26:32 responsible for all matters related to the **t** of God
29:11 We adore you as the one who is over all **t**.
2Ch 2: 4 He has commanded Israel to do these **t** forever.
2:14 He is skillful at making **t** from gold, silver, bronze,
4:16 Huram-abi made all these **t** out of burnished
7:21 ‘Why has the LORD done such terrible **t** to his
24: 7 and they had used all the dedicated **t** from the
29: 5 Remove all the defiled **t** from the sanctuary.
29:16 the Temple courtyard all the defiled **t** they found.
31: 6 and a tithe of the **t** that had been dedicated to the
31:14 and the **t** that had been dedicated to the LORD.
36: 8 including all the evil **t** he did and everything found
Ezr 9:12 You promised that if we avoided these **t**, we would
9:14 with people who do these detestable **t**.
10: 4 duty to tell us how to proceed in setting **t** straight,
Ne 1: 2 and about how **t** were going in Jerusalem.
1: 3 “**T** are not going well for those who returned to
6:14 all the evil **t** that Tobiah and Sanballat have done.
9:25 They took over houses full of good **t**, with cisterns
Job 2:10 Should we accept only good **t** from the hand of
10: 4 of a human? Do you see **t** as people see them?
12: 3 Well, I know a few **t** myself—and you’re no better
12: 3 Who doesn’t know these **t** you’ve been saying?
13:20 “O God, there are two **t** I beg of you, and I will be
15:13 that you turn against God and say all these evil **t**?
16: 4 I could say the same **t** if you were in my place.
20:20 Of all the **t** he dreamed about, nothing remains.
22:18 forgot that he had filled their homes with good **t**,
22:21 will have peace at last, and **t** will go well for you.
26: 3 my stupidity! What wise **t** you have said!
26:14 “These are some of the minor **t** he does, merely a
27:12 all this; yet you are saying all these useless **t** to me.
33:29 “Yes, God often does these **t** for people.
36:25 Everyone has seen these **t**, but only from a
37:13 He causes **t** to happen on earth, either as a
42: 3 And I was talking about **t** I did not understand, **t**
far too wonderful for me.
Ps 8: 6 you made, / giving us authority over all **t**—
9: 1 I will tell of all the marvelous **t** you have done.
16: 2 my Master! / All the good **t** I have are from you.”
27:12 For they accuse me of **t** I’ve never done
35:11 They accuse me of **t** I don’t even know about.
39: 2 there in silence—/ not even speaking of good **t**—
52: 4 You love to say **t** that harm others, / you liar!
59:12 Because of the sinful **t** they say, / because of the
60:12 With God’s help we will do mighty **t**, / for he will
64: 9 acts of God, / realizing all the amazing **t** he does.
71:17 told others about the wonderful **t** you do.
71:19 You have done such wonderful **t**. / Who can
72:18 God of Israel, / who alone does such wonderful **t**.
73:28 and I will tell everyone about the wonderful **t** you
74:23 Don’t overlook these **t** your enemies have said.
81:10 your mouth wide, and I will fill it with good **t**.
87: 3 O city of God, / what glorious **t** are said of you!
96: 3 Tell everyone about the amazing **t** he does.
98: 7 his praise! / Let the earth and all living **t** join in.
103: 2 and never forget the good **t** he does for me.
103: 5 He fills my life with good **t**. / My youth is renewed
104:24 O LORD, what a variety of **t** you have made!
106:21 their savior, / who had done such great **t** in Egypt
106:22 such wonderful **t** in that land, / such awesome
106:29 They angered the LORD with all these **t**, / so a
107: 9 the thirsty / and fills the hungry with good **t**.
107:42 The godly will see these **t** and be glad,
108:13 With God’s help we will do mighty **t**, / for he will
115: 4 Their idols are merely **t** of silver and gold,
118:15 right arm of the LORD has done glorious **t**!
118:16 right arm of the LORD has done glorious **t**!
119:37 Turn my eyes from worthless **t**, / and give me life
119:65 You have done many good **t** for me, LORD,
126: 2 “What amazing **t** the LORD has done for them.”
126: 3 Yes, the LORD has done amazing **t** for us!
135:15 Their idols are merely **t** of silver and gold,
141: 4 Don’t let me lust for evil **t**; / don’t let me
Pr 1:13 we’ll get! We’ll fill our houses with all kinds of **t**!
2:14 and they enjoy evil as it turns **t** upside down.
3: 1 My child, never forget the **t** I have taught you.
6:16 are six **t** the LORD hates—no, seven **t** he detests:
8: 6 Listen to me! For I have excellent **t** to tell you.
12:14 People can get many good **t** by the words they say;
14:17 Those who are short-tempered do foolish **t**,
18: 9 A lazy person is as bad as someone who destroys **t**.
23:33 will see hallucinations, and you will say crazy **t**.
25: 2 It is God’s privilege to conceal **t** and the king’s
28:10 their own trap, but the honest will inherit good **t**.
30:15 There are three other **t**—no, four!—that are never
30:18 There are three **t** that amaze me—no, four **t** I do
not understand:
30:21 There are three **t** that make the earth tremble—
30:24 There are four **t** on earth that are small

Ecc 2: 1 Let’s look for the ‘good **t**’ in life.” But I found
2: 9 so that I could evaluate all these **t**.
6: 9 Just dreaming about nice **t** is meaningless; it is like
7:13 Notice the way God does **t**; then fall into line.
7:25 to find wisdom and to understand the reason for **t**.
8: 1 to be wise, to be able to analyze and interpret **t**.
Isa 2: 8 bow down and worship these **t** they have made.
8:16 I will write down all these **t** as a testimony of what
12: 5 Sing to the LORD, / for he has done wonderful **t**.
25: 1 for you are my God. You do such wonderful **t**!
30:10 “Don’t tell us the truth. Tell us nice **t**. Tell us lies.
41:29 See, they are all foolish, worthless **t**. Your idols are
42:16 Yes, I will indeed do these **t**; / I will not forsake
43: 9 Which of their idols has ever foretold such **t**?
44:24 says: “I am the LORD, who made all **t**.
45: 7 I, the LORD, am the one who does these **t**.
45:21 worship pays. Who made these **t** known long ago?
46: 9 And do not forget the **t** I have done throughout
46:13 For I am ready to set **t** right, not in the distant
47: 9 those two **t** will come upon you in a moment:
48: 6 Now I will tell you new **t** I have not mentioned
48: 7 They are brand new, not **t** from the past. So you
48: 8 “Yes, I will tell you of **t** that are entirely new,
51:19 These two **t** have been your lot: desolation
58: 8 “If you do these **t**, your salvation will come like
64: 3 you did awesome **t** beyond our highest
64:11 burned down, and all the **t** of beauty are destroyed.
66: 4 great troubles against them—all the **t** they feared.
66:14 When you see these **t**, your heart will rejoice.
Jer 2:13 For my people have done two evil **t**: They have
5:25 Your sin has robbed you of all these good **t**.
6:15 Are they ashamed when they do these disgusting **t**?
7:13 While you were doing these wicked **t**,
8:12 Are they ashamed when they do these disgusting **t**?
8:13 All the good **t** I prepared for them will soon be
9:24 love is unfailing, and that I delight in these **t**.
10: 8 and foolish. The **t** they worship are made of wood!
11:15 where they have done so many immoral **t**?
14:22 the LORD our God! Only you can do such **t**.
15: 4 Because of the wicked **t** Manasseh son of
16:10 “When you tell the people all these **t**, they will
16:10 ‘Why has the LORD decreed such terrible **t**
25: 5 you are traveling and from the evil **t** you are doing.
25:30 “Now prophesy all these **t**, and say to them,
27: 5 I can give these **t** of mine to anyone I choose.
27:21 says about the precious **t** kept in the Temple
29:10 and do for you all the good **t** I have promised,
29:23 For these men have done terrible **t** among my
29:32 None of his descendants will see the good **t** I will
32:20 the land of Egypt—**t** still remembered to this day!
35: 8 So we have obeyed him in all these **t**. We have
36: 3 in writing all the terrible **t** I have planned for them.
44: 4 ‘Don’t do these horrible **t** that I hate so much.’
44:22 **t** you were doing that he made your land an object
44:23 The very reason all these terrible **t** have happened
45: 5 Are you seeking great **t** for yourself? Don’t do it!
52:20 These **t** had been made for the LORD’s Temple
La 1:16 “For all these **t** I weep; tears flow down my
2:14 Your “prophets” have said so many foolish **t**,
Eze 12: 7 filled with the **t** I might carry into exile.
14: 3 They have embraced **t** that lead them into sin.
14:23 you will agree that these **t** are not being done to
15: 3 Can its wood be used for making **t**, like pegs to
16:16 You used the lovely **t** I gave you to make shrines
16:30 says the Sovereign LORD, to do such **t** as these,
16:43 but have angered me by doing all these evil **t**,
16:50 She was proud and did loathsome **t**, so I wiped her
16:51 You have done far more loathsome **t** than your
18: 9 Anyone who does these **t** is just and will surely
18:11 And suppose that son does all the evil **t** his father
18:22 will live because of the righteous **t** they have done.
18:26 turn from being good and start doing sinful **t**,
22: 8 Inside your walls you despise my holy **t**
22:26 have violated my laws and defiled my holy **t**.
23:27 You will never again cast longing eyes on those **t**
23:38 Then after doing these terrible **t**, they defiled my
27:14 All these **t** were exchanged for your manufactured
33:33 But when all these terrible **t** happen to them—
36:31 and hate yourselves for all the evil **t** you did.
38:20 All living **t**—all the fish, birds, animals,
40: 4 have been brought here so I can show you many **t**.
44:13 They may not touch any of my holy **t** or the holy
Da 1: 8 chief official for permission to eat other **t** instead.
2:22 He reveals deep and mysterious **t** / and knows what
2:27 or fortune-tellers who can tell the king such **t**.
4:28 But all these **t** did happen to King
4:35 saying, ‘What do you mean by doing these **t**?’
7:28 was pale with fear, but I kept these **t** to myself.
8:26 But none of these **t** will happen for a long time,
12: 7 come to an end, all these **t** will have happened.”
Hos 2:12 and orchards, **t** she claims her lovers gave her.
4: 3 and all living **t** are becoming sick and dying.
9: 9 The **t** my people do are as depraved as what they
14: 9 Let those who are wise understand these **t**.
Joel 2:20 the land.” Surely the LORD has done great **t**!
2:21 and rejoice because the LORD has done great **t**.
Am 8: 7 “I will never forget the wicked **t** you have done!
9:12 the LORD, have spoken, and I will do these **t**.
Mic 1: 7 These **t** were bought with the money earned by her
2: 6 “Don’t say such **t**,” the people say.
Hab 1:14 but creeping **t** that have no leader to defend them
2: 3 But these **t** I plan won’t happen right away.
3: 2 and I am filled with awe by the amazing **t** you have
Hag 1: 5 Almighty says: Consider how **t** are going for you!
1: 7 Almighty says: Consider how **t** are going for you!
2:13 then brushes against any of the **t** mentioned,
2:15 consider how **t** were going for you before you

Zec 1: 6 But all the **t** I said through my servants the
3: 1 the angel’s right hand, accusing Jeshua of many **t**.
3: 8 You are symbols of the good **t** to come.
8:17 And stop this habit of swearing to **t** that are false. I
hate all these **t**, says the LORD.”
Mal 3:13 “You have said terrible **t** about me,”
Mt 6:32 pagans who are so deeply concerned about these **t**?
7:23 Go away; the **t** you did were unauthorized.’
11: 2 heard about all the **t** the Messiah was doing.
16:23 You are seeing **t** merely from a human point of
19: 1 After Jesus had finished saying these **t**, he left
19:16 what good **t** must I do to have eternal life?”
21:21 don’t doubt, you can do **t** like this and much more.
21:24 to do these **t** if you answer one question,”
23:23 but you ignore the important **t** of the law—
23:23 you should not leave undone the more important **t**.
24: 6 Yes, these **t** must come, but the end won’t follow
24:34 pass from the scene before all these **t** take place.
24:36 the day or the hour when these **t** will happen,
26: 1 When Jesus had finished saying these **t**, he said to
26:44 back to pray a third time, saying the same **t** again.
Mk 4:19 the lure of wealth, and the desire for nice **t**, so no
5:19 and tell them what wonderful **t** the Lord has done
5:20 and began to tell everyone about the great **t** Jesus
6:34 without a shepherd. So he taught them many **t**.
7:23 All these vile **t** come from within; they are what
8:31 would suffer many terrible **t** and be rejected by the
8:32 him aside and told him he shouldn’t say **t** like that.
8:33 You are seeing **t** merely from a human point of
11:29 “I’ll tell who gave me authority to do these **t** if
12:38 Here are some of the other **t** he taught them at this
13: 7 Yes, these **t** must come, but the end won’t follow
13: 9 But when these **t** begin to happen, watch out!
13:32 knows the day or hour when these **t** will happen,
14:49 But these **t** are happening to fulfill what the
Lk 1:49 is holy, / and he has done great **t** for me.
1:51 His mighty arm does tremendous **t**! / How he
1:53 He has satisfied the hungry with good **t** / and sent
2:19 but Mary quietly treasured these **t** in her heart
2:51 and his mother stored all these **t** in her heart.
3:14 and don’t accuse people of **t** you know they didn’t
4:32 too, the people were amazed at the **t** he said,
5:26 and over again, “We have seen amazing **t** today.”
6:30 and when **t** are taken away from you, don’t try to
8:39 and tell them all the wonderful **t** God has done for
9:22 Son of Man, must suffer many terrible **t**,” he said.
9:43 marveling over all the wonderful **t** he was doing,
11:42 you should not leave undone the more important **t**.
12:14 who made me a judge over you to decide such **t** as
12:26 And if worry can’t do little **t** like that, what’s the
use of worrying over bigger **t**?
12:30 These **t** dominate the thoughts of most people,
13:17 And all the people rejoiced at the wonderful **t** he
19:39 rebuke your followers for saying **t** like that!”
21: 6 “The time is coming when all these **t** will be
21: 9 Yes, these **t** must come, but the end won’t follow
21:11 and there will be terrifying **t** and great miraculous
21:28 So when all these **t** begin to happen, stand straight
23:31 For if these **t** are done when the tree is green,
24:18 the **t** that have happened there the last few days.”
24:19 “What **t**?” Jesus asked. “The **t** that happened to
24:26 all these **t** before entering his time of glory?”
24:48 You are witnesses of all these **t**.
Jn 1:50 the fig tree? You will see greater **t** than this.”
2:16 sold doves, he told them, “Get these **t** out of here.
2:18 “What right do you have to do these **t**?”
3:10 and yet you don’t understand these **t**?
3:12 when I tell you about **t** that happen here on earth,
3:31 and my understanding is limited to the **t** of earth,
5:20 and the Son will do far greater **t** than healing this
6:27 so concerned about perishable **t** like food.
6:59 He said these **t** while he was teaching in the
7: 4 If you can do such wonderful **t**, prove it to the
7:32 heard that the crowds were murmuring such **t**,
8:29 For I always do those **t** that are pleasing to him.”
8:30 Then many who heard him say these **t** believed in
8:44 the Devil, and you love to do the evil **t** he does.
8:54 But it is my Father who says these glorious **t** about
10:19 When he said these **t**, the people were again
10:32 “At my Father’s direction I have done many **t** to
12:36 After saying these **t**, Jesus went away and was
13:17 You know these **t**—now do them! That is the path
13:18 “I am not saying these **t** to all of you; I know
14:25 I am telling you these **t** now while I am still with
14:29 I have told you these **t** before they happen so that
16: 1 “I have told you these **t** so that you won’t fall
16: 4 Yes, I’m telling you these **t** now, so that when they
17: 1 When Jesus had finished saying all these **t**,
17:13 I have told them many **t** while I was with them
18: 1 After saying these **t**, Jesus crossed the Kidron
19:36 These **t** happened in fulfillment of the Scriptures
21:24 And we all know that his account of these **t** is
21:25 And I suppose that if all the other **t** Jesus did were
Ac 2:11 languages about the wonderful **t** God has done!”
3:18 that he must suffer all these **t**.
3:21 until the time for the final restoration of all **t**,
4:20 We cannot stop telling about the wonderful **t** we
5:32 We are witnesses of these **t** and so is the Holy
5:38 are teaching and doing these **t** merely on their own,
8:24 “that these terrible **t** won’t happen to me!”
9:13 “I’ve heard about the terrible **t** this man has done
9:36 She was always doing kind **t** for others and helping
10:44 Even as Peter was saying these **t**, the Holy Spirit
13:42 return again and speak about these **t** the next week.
14: 2 and Barnabas, saying all sorts of evil **t** about them.
14:15 turn from these worthless **t** to the living God,
15:18 he who made these **t** known long ago.’

16:21 "They are teaching the people to do t that are
17:20 "You are saying some rather startling t, and we
17:30 people's former ignorance about these t,
21:15 Shortly afterward we packed our t and left for
21:19 Paul gave a detailed account of the t God had
24:13 These men certainly cannot prove the t they accuse
26:20 and prove they have changed by the good t they
26:26 And King Agrippa knows about these t. I speak
28:10 people put on board all sorts of t we would need
Ro 1:10 One of the t I always pray for is the opportunity,
1:24 and do whatever shameful t their hearts desired.
1:24 did vile and degrading t with each other's bodies.
1:25 So they worshiped the t God made but not the
1:27 Men did shameful t with other men and, as a
1:28 and let them do t that should never be done.
1:32 of God's death penalty for those who do these t,
2: 1 for you do these very same t.
2: 2 in his justice, will punish anyone who does such t.
3: 8 Those who say such t deserve to be condemned,
6:21 since now you are ashamed of the t you used to do,
t that end in eternal doom.
6:22 Now you do those t that lead to holiness and result
7:17 it is sin inside me that makes me do these evil t.
8: 5 dominated by the sinful nature think about sinful t,
8: 5 the Holy Spirit think about t that please the Spirit.
8:31 What can we say about such wonderful t as these?
8:37 No, despite all these t, overwhelming victory is
9:30 Well then, what shall we say about these t?
12: 6 God has given each of us the ability to do certain t
12:17 Do t in such a way that everyone can see you are
14:20 there is nothing wrong with these t in themselves.
15: 1 We may know that these t make no difference,
15: 1 and fears of those who think these t are wrong.
15: 4 Such t were written in the Scriptures long ago to
15:14 You know these t so well that you are able to teach
16:17 and upset people's faith by teaching t that are
1Co 1:27 God deliberately chose t the world considers
1:28 God chose t despised by the world, t counted as
2:10 But we know these t because God has revealed
2:12 so we can know the wonderful t God has freely
2:15 We who have the Spirit understand these t,
2:16 But we can understand these t, for we have the
4:13 We respond gently when evil t are said about us.
4:14 I am not writing these t to shame you, but to warn
6: 2 can't you decide these little t among yourselves?
7:31 Those in frequent contact with the t of the world
10: 6 so that we would not crave evil t as they did
11:22 What am I supposed to say about these t?
13:11 But when I grew up, I put away childish t.
13:12 Now we see t imperfectly as in a poor mirror,
13:13 There are three t that will endure—faith, hope,
14:20 don't be childish in your understanding of these t.
14:23 or people who don't understand these t come into
14:24 or people who don't understand these t come into
15:27 "God has given him authority over all t."
15:27 (Of course, when it says "authority over all t,"
15:28 Then, when he has conquered all t, the Son will
15:28 so that God, who gave his Son authority over all t,
15:33 Don't be fooled by those who say such t, for "bad
2Co 1: 6 Then you can patiently endure the same t we
4:15 All of these t are for your benefit. And as God's
6:17 says the Lord. / Don't touch their filthy t,
7:11 have done everything you could to make t right.
9:12 So two good t will happen—the needs of the
11:30 I would rather boast about the t that show how
12: 4 and heard t so astounding that they cannot be told.
12:18 walk in each other's steps, doing t the same way.
Gal 4:12 with you to live as I do in freedom from these t,
5:10 to bring you back to believing as I do about these t.
6:17 now on, don't let anyone trouble me with these t.
Eph 1:11 and all t happen just as he decided long ago.
1:22 And God has put all t under the authority of Christ,
2: 9 Salvation is not a reward for the good t we have
2:10 so that we can do the good t he planned for us long
3: 9 the Creator of all t, had kept secret from the
5: 5 really an idolater who worships the t of this world.
5: 7 Don't participate in the t these people do.
5:12 It is shameful even to talk about the t that ungodly
5:13 on them, it becomes clear how evil these t are.
Php 1:11 those good t that are produced in your life by Jesus
2:30 while trying to do for me the t you couldn't do
3: 7 I once thought all these t were so very important,
3:12 mean to say that I have already achieved these t
3:15 who are mature Christians will agree on these t.
3:19 god is their appetite, they brag about shameful t,
4: 8 Think about t that are pure and lovely
4: 8 Think about t that are excellent and worthy of
Col 1:10 and you will continually do good, kind t for others.
1:16 He made the t we can see and the t we can't see—
2:22 Such rules are mere human teaching about t that
3: 2 Do not think only about t down here on earth.
3: 5 put to death the sinful, earthly t lurking within you.
3: 5 Don't be greedy for the good t of this life, for that
3: 6 terrible anger will come upon those who do such t.
1Th 5: 4 But you aren't in the dark about these t,
2Th 2:15 With all these t in mind, dear brothers and sisters,
3: 4 that you are practicing the t we commanded you,
1Ti 1: 4 For these t only cause arguments; they don't help
1: 6 They have turned away from these t and spend
2:10 make themselves attractive by the good t they do.
3:14 I am writing these t to you now, even though I
4:11 Teach these t and insist that everyone learn them.
5:13 people's business and saying t they shouldn't.
6: 3 Some false teachers may deny these t, but these are
6:11 so run from all these evil t, and follow what is
2Ti 2: 2 You have heard me teach many t that have been
2: 7 Lord will give you understanding in all these t.
2:14 Remind everyone of these t, and command them in
3:14 But you must remain faithful to the t you have
4:10 has deserted me because he loves the t of this life
Tit 2:15 You must teach these t and encourage your people
3: 5 not because of the good t we did, but because of
3: 8 These t I have told you are all true. I want you to
3: 8 These t are good and beneficial for everyone.
3: 9 These kinds of t are useless and a waste of time.
Phm 1: 6 of all the good t we can do for Christ.
Heb 2: 8 You gave him authority over all t." Now when it
says "all t," it means nothing is left
5: 8 he learned obedience from the t he suffered.
5:12 you need someone to teach you again the basic t a
6: 4 those who have experienced the good t of heaven
6: 9 We are confident that you are meant for better t, t
that come with salvation.
6:18 These two t are unchangeable because it is
9: 5 But we cannot explain all of these t now.
9: 6 When these t were all in place, the priests went in
9:11 the High Priest over all the good t that have come.
9:17 no one can use the will to get any of the t promised
9:23 in it—which were copies of t in heaven—
9:23 But the real t in heaven had to be purified with far
10: 1 law of Moses was only a shadow of the t to come,
10: 1 not the reality of the good t Christ has done for us.
10:33 you helped others who were suffering the same t.
10:34 You knew you had better t waiting for you in
11: 1 to happen. It is the evidence of t we cannot yet see.
11:40 For God had far better t in mind for us that would
12: 3 when sinful people did such terrible t to him,
12:27 This means that the t on earth will be shaken, so
that only eternal t will be left.
Jas 1:20 Your anger can never make t right in God's sight.
3:15 Such t are earthly, unspiritual, and motivated by
4: 9 Let there be tears for the wrong t you have done.
1Pe 1:12 They were told that these t would not happen
1:12 the angels are eagerly watching these t happen.
3: 9 Don't retaliate when people say unkind t about
4: 3 You have had enough in the past of the evil t that
4: 4 you no longer join them in the wicked t they do,
and they say evil t about you.
2Pe 1:12 I plan to keep on reminding you of these t—
1:13 I believe I should keep on reminding you of these t
1:15 So I will work hard to make these t clear to you.
3:14 while you are waiting for these t to happen,
3:16 speaking of these t in all of his letters. Some of his
1Jn 1: 4 We are writing these t so that our joy will be
2:26 I have written these t to you because you need to
2:27 For the Spirit teaches you all t, and what he
3:22 because we obey him and do the t that please him.
3Jn 1:10 I will report some of the t he is doing and the
wicked t he is saying about us.
Jude 1:10 and curse the t they do not understand.
1:15 He will convict the ungodly of all the evil t
Rev 1: 3 For the time is near when these t will happen.
1: 5 Jesus Christ, who is the faithful witness to these t,
1:19 the t that are now happening and the t that will
2: 2 "I know all the t you do. I have seen your hard
2:19 "I know all the t you do—your love, your faith,
2:19 I can see your constant improvement in all these t.
3: 1 "I know all the t you do, and that you have a
3: 8 "I know all the t you do, and I have opened a door
3:15 "I know all the t you do, that you are neither hot
4: 1 I will show you what must happen after these t."
8: 9 And one-third of all t living in the sea died.
18:14 "All the fancy t you loved so much are gone,"
18:15 by selling her these t will stand at a distance,
20:12 And the dead were judged according to the t
21: 5 the throne said, "Look, I am making all t new!"
22: 8 John, am the one who saw and heard all these t.
22: 8 And when I saw and heard these t, I fell down to
22:20 He who is the faithful witness to all these t says,

THINK (296) [THINKING, THINKS, THOUGHT, THOUGHT-LIFE, THOUGHTLESSLY, THOUGHTS]

Ge 11: 6 and political unity, just t of what they will do later.
19: 9 they shouted. "Who do you t you are?
25:25 so much hair that one would t he was wearing a
27:11 T how hairy Esau is and how smooth my skin is!
29:14 "Just t, my very own flesh and blood!"
44: 7 "What kind of people do you t we are, that you
Ex 2:14 "Who do you t you are?" the man replied.
5: 4 "Who do you t you are," Pharaoh shouted,
14: 3 Then Pharaoh will t, 'Those Israelites are
Nu 14:13 "But what will the Egyptians t when they hear
Dt 7:17 Perhaps you will t to yourselves, 'How can we
8:17 so you would never t that it was your own strength
17:14 Then you may begin to t, 'We ought to have a king
32: 7 the days of long ago; / t about the generations past.
Jos 3:11 T of it! The Ark of the Covenant, which belongs to
9:25 we are at your mercy—do whatever you t is right."
1Sa 1:16 Please don't t I am a wicked woman! For I have
1:23 "Whatever you t is best," Elkanah agreed.
10: 7 do whatever you t is best, for God will be with
12:24 T of all the wonderful things he has done for you.
14: 7 "Do what you t is best," the youth replied.
14:30 t how many more we could have killed!"
14:36 men replied, "We'll do whatever you t is best."
15:17 told him, "Although you may t little of yourself,
20:30 "Do you t I don't know that you want David to be
22: 8 T of it! My own son—encouraging David to try
25:10 "Who does this son of Jesse t he is?
25:17 You'd better t fast, for there is going to be trouble
29: 6 I t you should go with us, but the other Philistine
30:24 Do you t anyone will listen to you when you talk
2Sa 10: 3 "Do you really t these men are coming here to
15:15 his advisers replied. "Do what you t is best."
17: 7 "this time I t Ahithophel has made a mistake.
17:11 And I t that you should personally lead the troops.
18: 4 "If you t that's the best plan, I'll do it," the king
19:27 are like an angel of God, so do what you t is best.
24:13 T this over and let me know what answer to give
1Ki 2: 6 Do with him what you t best, but don't let him die
12: 5 "Give me three days to t this over.
12:10 if you t he was hard on you, just wait and see what
2Ki 4:14 "What do you t we can do for her?"
10: 5 not make anyone king; do whatever you t is best."
18:20 Do you t that mere words can substitute for
18:24 how can you t of challenging even the weakest
18:25 do you t we have invaded your land without the
18:35 So what makes you t that the LORD can rescue
19:22 'Whom do you t you have been insulting
1Ch 16:12 T of the wonderful works he has done,
19: 3 "Do you really t these men are coming here to
21:12 T this over and let me know what answer to give
2Ch 10:10 if you t he was hard on you, just wait and see what
13: 8 Do you really t you can stand against the kingdom
19: 6 "Always t carefully before pronouncing judgment.
32:10 What are you trusting in that makes you t you can
32:14 What makes you t your God can do any better?
Ne 4: 2 this bunch of poor, feeble Jews t they are doing?
4: 2 Do they t they can build the wall in a day if they
9: 5 It is far greater than we can t or say.
13:27 How could you even t of committing this sinful
Est 4:13 "Don't t for a moment that you will escape there
Job 4: 7 "Stop and t! Does the innocent person perish?
5:13 He catches those who t they are wise in their own
6:26 Do you t your words are convincing when you
6:30 Do you t I am lying? Don't I know the difference
7: 4 When I go to bed, I t, 'When will it be morning?'
7:13 If I t, 'My bed will comfort me, and I will try to
13: 9 Or do you t you can fool him as easily as you fool
13:14 take my life in my hands and say what I really t.
14:13 But mark your calendar to t of me again!
18: 3 Do you t we are cattle? Do you t we have no
intelligence?
21: 6 When I t about what I am saying, I shudder.
22: 8 you t the land belongs to the powerful and that
23:15 in his presence. When I t of it, terror grips me.
32: 6 so I held back and did not dare to tell you what I t.
35: 2 "Do you t it is right for you to claim, 'I am
37: 1 "My heart pounds as I t of this. It leaps within me.
37:19 "You t you know so much, so teach the rest of us
41:32 in its wake. One would t the sea had turned white.
Ps 1: 2 day and night they t about his law.
4: 4 T about it overnight and remain silent.
8: 4 what are mortals that you should t of us,
10: 4 to seek God. / They seem to t that God is dead.
10:13 How can they t, "God will never call us to
14: 4 they wouldn't t of praying to the LORD.
38:12 They t up treacherous deeds all day long.
53: 4 like bread; / they wouldn't t of praying to God.
63: 7 I t how much you have helped me; / I sing for joy
77: 3 I t of God, and I moan, / overwhelmed with
77: 5 I t of the good old days, long since ended,
77: 6 I search my soul and t about the difference now.
94: 8 T again, you fools! / When will you finally catch
105: 5 T of the wonderful works he has done,
119:97 how I love your law! / I t about it all day long.
143: 5 your great works. / I t about what you have done.
Pr 12:15 Fools t they need no advice, but the wise listen to
13:16 Wise people t before they act; fools don't and even
15:28 The godly t before speaking; the wicked spout evil
18:11 The rich t of their wealth as an impregnable
21: 2 People may t they are doing what is right,
25:27 it is not good for people to t about all the honors
26:12 There is more hope for fools than for people who t
Ecc 5:10 How absurd to t that wealth brings true happiness!
7: 2 and you should t about it while there is still time.
Isa 1:29 Shame will cover you when you t of the times you
1:29 You will blush when you t of all the sins you
5:12 But you never t about the LORD or notice what
5:21 Destruction is certain for those who t they are wise
8:11 strongest terms: "Do not t like everyone else does.
10: 7 He will merely t he is attacking my people as part
17: 7 Then at last the people will t of their Creator
22:16 "Who do you t you are, building a beautiful tomb
23: 7 T of all the colonists you sent to distant lands.
28: 9 They say, "Who does the LORD t we are?
33:18 You will t back to this time of terror when the
36: 5 Do you t that mere words can substitute for
36: 9 how can you t of challenging even the weakest
36:10 do you t we have invaded your land without the
36:20 So what makes you t that the LORD can rescue
37:23 'Whom do you t you have been insulting
38:20 T of it—the LORD has healed me! / I will sing
43:25 for my own sake and will never t of them again.
44:18 Their minds are shut, and they cannot t.
47: 7 or t about the consequences of your actions.
49:21 Then you will t to yourself, 'Who has given me all
51: 2 Yes, t about your ancestors Abraham and Sarah,
56: 3 Do not let them t that I consider them second-class
57:11 it that you don't even remember me or t about me?
58: 2 You would almost t this was a righteous nation
58: 5 Do you really t this will please the LORD?
59: 7 They t only about sinning. Wherever they go,
65:17 so wonderful that no one will even t about the old
Jer 2:10 to the land of Kedar. T about what you see there.
5:17 your fortified cities, which you t are so safe.
7: 8 " 'Do you t that because the Temple is here you
7: 9 Do you really t you can steal, murder,

7:11 Do you **t** this Temple, which honors my name,
9:17 "**T** about what is going on! Call for the mourners
23:23 "Do they **t** I cannot see what they are doing?
26:14 and in your power—do with me as you **t** best.
26:18 "**T** back to the days when Micah of Moresheth
42:14 in Egypt where you **t** you will be free from war,
44:21 "Do you **t** the LORD did not know that you
51:50 far-off land, and **t** about your home in Jerusalem."
La 2:20 "O LORD, **t** about this!" Jerusalem cries.
3:36 in the courts. Do they **t** the Lord didn't see it?
Eze 13:18 Do you **t** you can trap others without bringing
18:23 "Do you **t**, asks the Sovereign LORD, that I like
21:23 The people of Jerusalem will **t** it is a mistake,
22:12 They never even **t** of me and my commands,
28:3 than Daniel and **t** no secret is hidden from you.
28:6 Because you **t** you are as wise as a god,
32:2 You **t** of yourself as a strong young lion among the
33:25 Do you really **t** the land should be yours?
38:12 and they **t** the whole world revolves around them!'
Hos 2:7 Then she will **t**, 'I might as well return to my
4:12 They **t** a stick can tell them the future!
Am 2:9 "Yet **t** of all I did for my people! I destroyed the
6:1 and **t** you are secure in Jerusalem and Samaria!
9:7 "Do you Israelites **t** you are more important to me
Hag 2:15 So **t** about this from now on—consider how things
Zec 7:6 you don't **t** about me, but only of pleasing
8:6 But do you **t** this is impossible for me, the LORD
Mal 1:13 "**T** of it! Animals that are stolen and mutilated,
3:16 of those who feared him and loved to **t** about him.
Mt 6:7 They **t** their prayers are answered only by
6:23 If the light you **t** you have is really darkness,
7:4 How can you **t** of saying, 'Friend, let me help you
9:13 not those who **t** they are already good enough."
11:25 thank you for hiding the truth from those who **t**
16:11 How could you even **t** I was talking about food?
17:25 to speak, Jesus asked him, "What do you **t**, Peter?
21:26 because the people **t** he was a prophet."
21:28 "But what do you **t** about this? A man with two
21:40 "what do you **t** he will do to those farmers?"
22:15 Then the Pharisees met together to **t** of a way to
22:17 Now tell us what you **t** about this: Is it right to pay
22:42 "What do you **t** about the Messiah? Whose son is
25:26 You **t** I'm a hard man, do you, harvesting crops I
Mk 2:8 he said to them, "Why do you **t** this is blasphemy?
2:17 not those who **t** they are already good enough."
Lk 1:29 Mary tried to **t** what the angel could mean.
2:48 His parents didn't know what to **t**. "Son!"
4:27 Or **t** of the prophet Elisha, who healed Naaman,
5:21 "Who does this man **t** he is?" the Pharisees
5:22 he asked them, "Why do you **t** this is blasphemy?
5:32 not to spend my time with those who **t** they are
6:32 "Do you **t** you deserve credit merely for loving
6:42 How can you **t** of saying, 'Friend, let me help you
7:49 "Who does this man **t** he is, going around
8:18 even what they **t** they have will be taken away
10:21 thank you for hiding the truth from those who **t**
11:35 Make sure that the light you **t** you have is not
12:51 Do you **t** I have come to bring peace to the earth?
13:2 "Do you **t** those Galileans were worse sinners than
18:7 so don't you **t** God will surely give justice to his
19:48 But they could **t** of nothing, because all the people
20:21 is right and are not influenced by what others **t**.
24:4 trying to **t** what could have happened to it.
Jn 4:35 Do you **t** the work of harvesting will not begin
6:62 Then what will you **t** if you see me, the Son of
7:24 **T** this through and you will see that I am right."
8:53 the prophets, who died? Who do you **t** you are?"
9:17 The man replied, "I **t** he must be a prophet."
9:39 and to show those who **t** they see that they are
11:51 He didn't **t** of it himself; he was inspired to say it.
11:56 they asked each other, "What do you **t**?
16:2 who kill you will **t** they are doing God a service.
Ac 2:29 "Dear brothers, **t** about this! David wasn't
4:19 "Do you **t** God wants us to obey you rather than
5:9 "How could the two of you even **t** of doing a thing
10:28 But God has shown me that I should never **t** of
13:25 his ministry he asked, 'Do you **t** I am the Messiah?
17:29 we shouldn't **t** of God as an idol designed by
26:28 "Do you **t** you can make me a Christian
Ro 1:21 And they began to **t** up foolish ideas of what God
2:3 Do you **t** that God will judge and condemn others
2:20 You **t** you can instruct the ignorant and teach
4:14 and **t** they are "good enough" in God's sight,
8:5 Those who are dominated by the sinful nature **t**
8:5 but those who are controlled by the Holy Spirit **t**
11:9 a snare, / a trap that makes them **t** all is well.
11:12 **t** how much greater a blessing the world will share
11:20 Don't **t** highly of yourself, but fear what could
12:1 When you **t** of what he has done for you, is this too
12:2 you into a new person by changing the way you **t**.
12:16 of ordinary people. And don't **t** you know it all!
13:14 and don't **t** of ways to indulge your evil desires.
14:1 and don't argue with them about what they **t** is
14:3 Those who **t** it is all right to eat anything must not
14:5 some **t** one day is more holy than another day,
while others **t** every day is alike.
15:1 and fears of those who **t** these things are wrong.
1Co 1:27 in order to shame those who **t** they are wise.
3:18 If you **t** you are wise by this world's standards,
3:19 "God catches those who **t** they are wise
4:8 You **t** you already have everything you need!
4:9 But sometimes I **t** God has put us apostles on
7:26 present crisis, I **t** it is best to remain just as you are.
7:33 He has to **t** about his earthly responsibilities
7:40 and I **t** I am giving you counsel from God's Spirit
8:1 You **t** that everyone should agree with your perfect
8:7 they **t** of it as the worship of real gods, and their
8:10 Weak Christians who **t** it is wrong to eat this food
9:2 Even if others **t** I am not an apostle, I certainly am
10:12 If you **t** you are standing strong, be careful, for you
10:18 And **t** about the nation of Israel; all who eat the
10:22 as Israel did? Do you **t** we are stronger than he is?
10:24 Don't **t** only of your own good. **T** of other
Christians and what is best for them.
11:13 What do you **t** about this? Is it right for a woman
14:23 in an unknown language, they will **t** you are crazy.
14:36 Do you **t** that the knowledge of God's word begins
14:37 claim to be a prophet or **t** you are very spiritual,
2Co 1:8 I **t** you ought to know, dear friends,
3:5 It is not that we **t** we can do anything of lasting
5:16 a human being. How differently I **t** about him now!
10:2 those who **t** we act from purely human motives.
11:5 But I don't **t** I am inferior to these "super
11:6 I **t** you realize this by now, for we have proved it
11:16 don't **t** that I have lost my wits to talk like this.
11:19 After all, you, who **t** you are so wise,
12:6 I don't want anyone to **t** more highly of me than
12:16 But they still **t** I was sneaky and took advantage of
12:19 Perhaps you **t** we are saying all this just to defend
Gal 4:1 **T** of it this way. If a father dies and leaves great
6:3 If you **t** you are too important to help someone in
Eph 3:8 Just **t**! Though I did nothing to deserve it,
3:14 When I **t** of the wisdom and scope of God's plan,
Php 1:3 Every time I **t** of you, I give thanks to my God.
2:4 Don't **t** only about your own affairs, but be
3:19 and all they **t** about is this life here on earth.
4:8 **T** about things that are pure and lovely
4:8 **T** about things that are excellent and worthy of
Col 3:2 Do not **t** only about things down here on earth.
1Th 1:3 we **t** of your faithful work, your loving deeds,
2:13 you didn't **t** of the words we spoke as being just
5:8 But let us who live in the light **t** clearly,
5:13 **T** highly of them and give them your wholehearted
2Th 3:15 Don't **t** of them as enemies, but speak to them as
1Ti 4:12 Don't let anyone **t** less of you because you are
2Ti 2:7 **T** about what I am saying. The Lord will give you
Phm 1:10 I **t** of him as my own son because he became a
1:15 Perhaps you could **t** of it this way: Onesimus ran
Heb 2:3 What makes us **t** that we can escape if we are
2:6 it says, / "What is man that you should **t** of him,
3:1 **t** about this Jesus whom we declare to be God's
9:14 Just **t** how much more the blood of Christ will
10:24 **T** of ways to encourage one another to outbursts of
10:29 **T** how much more terrible the punishment will be
12:3 **T** about all he endured when sinful people did such
13:7 **T** of all the good that has come from their lives,
Jas 2:19 Do you still **t** it's enough just to believe that there
4:5 What do you **t** the Scriptures mean when they say
1Pe 1:13 So **t** clearly and exercise self-control.
2Pe 3:9 slow about his promise to return, as some people **t**.

THINKING (47) [THINK]

Dt 1:41 **t** it would be easy to conquer the hill country.
29:19 **t**, 'I am safe, even though I am walking in my own
1Sa 27:1 But David kept **t** to himself, "Someday Saul is
2Sa 4:10 'Saul is dead,' **t** he was bringing me good news.
2Ki 20:19 But the king was **t**, "At least there will be peace
Ne 5:7 After **t** about the situation, I spoke out against
Est 2:1 he began **t** about Vashti and what she had done
Job 21:16 so I will have nothing to do with that kind of **t**.
22:18 so I will have nothing to do with that kind of **t**.
Ps 40:17 and needy, / but the Lord is **t** about me right now.
63:6 I lie awake **t** of you, / meditating on you through
77:12 in my thoughts. / I cannot stop **t** about them.
119:99 my teachers, / for I am always **t** of your decrees.
119:148 awake through the night, / **t** about your promise.
Pr 23:7 They are always **t** about how much it costs.
29:20 for a fool than for someone who speaks without **t**.
Isa 39:8 But the king was **t**, "At least there will be peace
66:18 what they are doing, and I know what they are **t**.
Eze 18:28 They will live, because after **t** it over, they decided
Da 2:30 wanted you to understand what you were **t** about.
Mic 2:1 be for you who lie awake at night, **t** up evil plans.
Hab 3:14 out like a whirlwind, **t** Israel would be easy prey.
Zep 1:12 to the LORD, **t** he will do nothing at all to them.
Mt 9:4 Jesus knew what they were **t**, so he asked them,
"Why are you **t** such evil thoughts?
14:26 saw him, they screamed in terror, **t** he was a ghost.
16:8 Jesus knew what they were **t**, so he said,
21:37 "Finally, the owner sent his son, **t**, 'Surely they
Mk 6:49 they screamed in terror, **t** he was a ghost.
8:17 Jesus knew what they were **t**, so he said, "Why are
12:6 The owner finally sent him, **t**, 'Surely they will
Lk 5:22 Jesus knew what they were **t**, so he asked them,
24:37 was terribly frightened, **t** they were seeing a ghost!
Jn 7:35 "Maybe he is **t** of leaving the country and going to
Ac 8:20 "May your money perish with you for **t** God's gift
18:27 Apollos had been **t** about going to Achaia,
Ro 3:8 If you follow that kind of **t**, however, you might as
11:34 For who can know what the Lord is **t**? Who knows
1Co 2:11 No one can know what anyone else is really **t**
2:16 For, / "Who can know what the Lord is **t**?
4:18 become arrogant, **t** I will never visit you again.
7:32 doing the Lord's work and **t** how to please him.
8:7 Some are accustomed to **t** of idols as being real,
9:9 Do you suppose God was **t** only about oxen when
Php 2:3 Be humble, **t** of others as better than yourself.
Col 2:8 high-sounding nonsense that come from human **t**
2Pe 3:1 of them I have tried to stimulate your wholesome **t**

THINKS (13) [THINK]

Ge 24:57 "we'll call Rebekah and ask her what she **t**."
1Sa 3:18 Eli replied. "Let him do what he **t** best."
2Sa 17:5 Hushai the Arkite. Let's see what he **t** about this."
Est 8:5 Majesty is pleased with me and if he **t** it is right,
Job 11:5 would speak; if only he would tell you what he **t**!
Ecc 7:4 A wise person **t** much about death, while the fool **t**
only about having a good time
Mt 24:48 But if the servant is evil and **t**, 'My master won't
Lk 12:45 But if the servant **t**, 'My master won't be back for
1Co 4:3 it matters very little what you or anyone else **t**.
7:36 But if a man **t** he ought to marry his fiancée
10:29 my freedom be limited by what someone else **t**?
2Co 5:16 evaluating others by what the world **t** about them.

THIRD (117) [THREE]

THIRD DAY (24) Ge 1:13; 22:4; 42:18; Ex 19:11,16; Lev 7:17,18; 19:6,7,8; Nu 7:24; 29:20; Jdg 20:30; 1Sa 20:5; 2Sa 1:2; Est 9:18; Mt 16:21; 20:19; 27:64; Lk 13:32; 18:33; 24:7, 46; 1Co 15:4

THIRD OF (8) 2Ki 11:5,6; 2Ch 23:4; Eze 5:2,12,12; 46:14; Da 7:6

Ge 1:13 This all happened on the **t** day.
2:14 The **t** branch is the Tigris, which flows to the east
22:4 On the **t** day of the journey, Abraham saw the
38:5 And when she had a **t** son, she named him Shelah.
42:18 On the **t** day Joseph said to them, "I am a
Ex 19:11 Be sure they are ready on the **t** day, for I will come
19:16 On the morning of the **t** day, there was a powerful
20:5 the children for the sins of their parents to the **t**
28:19 The **t** row will contain a jacinth, an agate, and an
34:7 the children for the sins of their parents to the **t**
39:12 In the **t** row were a jacinth, an agate, and an
Lev 7:17 But anything left over until the **t** day must be
7:18 meat from this peace offering is eaten on the **t** day,
19:6 Any leftovers that remain until the **t** day must be
19:7 If any of the offering is eaten on the **t** day, it will
19:8 If you eat it on the **t** day, you will answer for the
Nu 7:24 On the **t** day Eliab son of Helon, leader of the tribe
14:18 the children for the sins of their parents to the **t**
19:12 They must purify themselves on the **t** and seventh
19:12 But if they do not do this on the **t** and seventh
19:19 On the **t** and seventh days the ceremonially clean
29:20 "On the **t** day of the festival, sacrifice eleven
31:19 and your captives on the **t** and seventh days.
Dt 5:9 the children for the sins of their parents to the **t**
14:28 "At the end of every **t** year bring the tithe of all
23:8 The **t** generation of Egyptians who came with you
26:12 "Every **t** year you must offer a special tithe of
Jos 19:10 The **t** allotment of land went to the families of the
Jdg 20:30 They went out on the **t** day and assembled at the
1Sa 3:8 So now the LORD called a **t** time, and once more
10:3 of bread, and the **t** will be carrying a skin of wine.
13:18 and the **t** moved toward the border above the
19:21 prophesied! The same thing happened a **t** time!
20:5 and stay there until the evening of the **t** day.
2Sa 1:2 On the **t** day after David's return, a man arrived
3:3 The **t** was Absalom, whose mother was Maacah,
1Ki 6:8 flight of stairs between the second and **t** floors.
15:28 Baasha killed Nadab in the **t** year of King Asa's
15:33 Baasha began to rule over Israel in the **t** year of
18:1 in the **t** year of the drought, the LORD said to
18:34 they were finished, he said, "Now do it a **t** time!"
22:2 Then during the **t** year, King Jehoshaphat of Judah
2Ki 11:5 A **t** of you who are on duty on the Sabbath are to
11:6 Another **t** of you are to stand guard at the Sur Gate.
11:6 And the final **t** must stand guard behind the palace
18:1 in the **t** year of King Hoshea's reign in Israel.
19:29 But in the **t** year you will plant crops and harvest
1Ch 2:13 his second was Abinadab, his **t** was Shimea,
3:2 The **t** was Absalom, whose mother was Maacah,
3:15 Jehoiakim (the second), Zedekiah (the **t**),
8:39 Jeush (the second), and Eliphelet (the **t**).
12:9 their leader. / Obadiah was second. / Eliab was **t**.
23:19 Amariah (the second), Jahaziel (the **t**),
24:8 The **t** lot fell to Harim. / The fourth lot fell to
24:23 Jahaziel was **t**, and Jekameam was fourth.
25:10 The **t** lot fell to Zaccur and twelve of his sons
26:2 Jediael (the second), Zebadiah (the **t**), Jathniel (the
26:4 Joah (the **t**), Sacar (the fourth), Nethanel (the fifth),
26:11 Tebaliah (the **t**), and Zechariah (the fourth).
27:5 the priest was commander of the **t** division,
27:5 which was on duty during the **t** month.
2Ch 17:7 In the **t** year of his reign, Jehoshaphat sent out his
23:4 the Sabbath, a **t** of them will serve as gatekeepers.
23:5 Another **t** will go over to the royal palace,
23:5 and the final **t** will be at the Foundation Gate.
Est 1:3 In the **t** year of his reign, he gave a banquet for all
9:18 and then rested on the **t** day, making that their day
Job 1:17 a **t** messenger arrived with this news:
42:14 the second Keziah, and the **t** Keren-happuch.
Isa 37:30 But in the **t** year you will plant crops and harvest
Jer 38:14 him at the **t** entrance of the LORD's Temple.
Eze 5:2 Place a **t** of it at the center of your map of
5:2 Scatter another **t** across your map and slash at it
5:2 Scatter the last **t** to the wind, for I will scatter my
5:12 A **t** of your people will die in the city from famine
5:12 A **t** of them will be slaughtered by the enemy
5:12 And I will scatter a **t** to the winds and chase them
10:14 was a human face, the **t** was the face of a lion,
46:14 and a half quarts of flour with a **t** of a gallon of
48:31 the second for Judah, and the **t** for Levi.
Da 1:1 During the **t** year of King Jehoiakim's reign in
2:39 that kingdom has fallen, yet a **t** great kingdom,
5:7 He will become the **t** highest ruler in the
5:16 You will become the **t** highest ruler in the
5:29 and he was proclaimed the **t** highest ruler in the
7:6 Then the **t** of these strange beasts appeared, and it

8: 1 During the **t** year of King Belshazzar's reign,
10: 1 In the **t** year of the reign of King Cyrus of Persia,
Zec 6: 3 the **t** by white horses, and the fourth by
13: 8 says the LORD. But a **t** will be left in the land.
Mt 16:21 be killed, and he would be raised on the **t** day.
20:19 But on the **t** day he will be raised from the dead."
26:44 So he went back to pray a **t** time, saying the same
27:64 So we request that you seal the tomb until the **t**
Mk 14:41 When he returned to them the **t** time he said,
Lk 13:32 and the **t** day I will accomplish my purpose.
18:33 and kill him, but on the **t** day he will rise again."
19:20 "But the **t** servant brought back only the original
20:12 A **t** man was sent and the same thing happened.
23:22 For the **t** time he demanded, "Why? What crime
24: 7 and that he would rise again the **t** day?"
24:46 and die and rise again from the dead on the **t** day.
Jn 21:14 This was the **t** time Jesus had appeared to his
21:17 Peter was grieved that Jesus asked the question a **t**
1Co 12:28 are apostles, / second are prophets, / **t** are teachers,
15: 4 and he was raised from the dead on the **t** day,
2Co 12: 2 I was caught up into the **t** heaven fourteen years
12:14 Now I am coming to you for the **t** time, and I will
13: 1 This is the **t** time I am coming to visit you.
Rev 4: 7 second looked like an ox; the **t** had a human face;
6: 5 the Lamb broke the **t** seal, I heard the **t** living being
8:10 Then the **t** angel blew his trumpet, and a great
11:14 but look, now the **t** terror is coming quickly.
14: 9 Then a **t** angel followed them, shouting,
16: 4 Then the **t** angel poured out his bowl on the rivers
21:19 second sapphire, the **t** agate, the fourth emerald,

THIRST (24) [THIRSTING, THIRSTS, THIRSTY]

Ex 17: 3 But tormented by **t**, they continued to complain,
Jdg 15:18 Must I now die of **t** and fall into the hands of these
2Ch 32:11 sentencing you to death by famine and **t**!
Ne 9:20 giving them bread from heaven or water for their **t**.
Job 5: 5 and their wealth satisfies the **t** of many others,
15:16 and sinful person with a **t** for wickedness!
24:11 they tread in the winepress as they suffer from **t**.
34: 7 as arrogant as Job, with his **t** for irreverent talk?
Ps 42: 2 I **t** for God, the living God. / When can I come
69:21 for food; / they offer me sour wine to satisfy my **t**.
104:11 the animals, / and the wild donkeys quench their **t**.
143: 6 I **t** for you as parched land thirsts for rain.
145:16 you satisfy the hunger and **t** of every living thing.
Isa 5:13 will starve, and the common people will die of **t**.
29: 8 but is still faint from **t** when morning comes.
41:17 and their tongues are parched from **t**, then I,
44: 3 I will give you abundant water to quench your **t**
49:10 They will neither hunger nor **t**. The searing sun
La 4: 4 The parched tongues of their little ones stick with **t**
Hos 2: 3 I will leave her to die of **t**, as in a desert or a dry
9: 2 The grapes you gather will not quench your **t**.
Hag 1: 6 wine to drink, but not enough to satisfy your **t**.
Jn 4:14 But the water I give them takes away **t** altogether.
6:35 Those who believe in me will never **t**.

THIRSTING (1) [THIRST]

Am 8:13 grow faint and weary, **t** for the LORD's word.

THIRSTS (2) [THIRST]

Ps 63: 1 I earnestly search for you. / My soul **t** for you;
143: 6 I thirst for you as parched land **t** for rain.

THIRSTY (40) [THIRST]

Dt 28:48 You will be left hungry, **t**, naked, and lacking in
Jdg 4:19 "Please give me some water," he said. "I'm **t**."
15:18 Now Samson was very **t**, and he cried out to the
Ru 2: 9 And when you are **t**, help yourself to the water
2Sa 17:29 and **t** after your long march through the
2Ki 18:27 so hungry and **t** that they will eat their own dung
Ne 9:15 and water from the rock when they were **t**.
Job 22: 7 You must have refused water for the **t** and food for
Ps 58: 7 May they disappear like water into **t** ground.
107: 5 Hungry and **t**, / they nearly died.
107: 9 For he satisfies the **t** / and fills the hungry with
Pr 25:21 food to eat. If they are **t**, give them water to drink.
25:25 news from far away is like cold water to the **t**.
30:16 the grave, / the barren womb, / the **t** desert,
Isa 29: 8 A **t** person dreams of drinking but is still faint from
32: 6 the hungry of food and give no water to the **t**.
35: 7 a pool, and springs of water will satisfy the **t** land.
36:12 so hungry and **t** that they will eat their own dung
44:12 His work makes him hungry and **t**, weak and faint.
48:21 They were not **t** when he led them through the
55: 1 "Is anyone **t**? Come and drink—even if you have
65:13 You will be **t**, but they will drink. You will be sad
Jer 14: 6 stand on the bare hills panting like **t** jackals.
Hos 2:22 Then the earth will answer the **t** cries of the grain,
13: 5 of you in the wilderness, in that dry and **t** land.
Mt 5: 6 God blesses those who are hungry and **t** for justice,
25:35 and you fed me. I was **t**, and you gave me a drink.
25:37 feed you? Or **t** and give you something to drink?
25:42 I was **t**, and you didn't give me anything to drink.
25:44 or **t** or a stranger or naked or sick or in prison,
Jn 4:13 "People soon become **t** again after drinking this
4:15 Then I'll never be **t** again, and I won't have to
7:37 shouted to the crowds, "If you are **t**, come to me!
19:28 and to fulfill the Scriptures he said, "I am **t**."
Ro 12:20 If they are **t**, give them something to drink,
1Co 4:11 To this very hour we go hungry and **t**,
2Co 11:27 Often I have been hungry and **t** and have gone
Rev 7:16 They will never again be hungry or **t**, and they will
21: 6 To all who are **t** I will give the springs of the water
22:17 Let the **t** ones come—anyone who wants to.

THIRTEEN (13) [THIRTEENTH]

Ge 17:25 and Ishmael his son was **t**.
Nu 29:13 It will consist of **t** young bulls, two rams,
29:14 five quarts for each of the **t** bulls, three quarts for
Dt 3:11 His iron bed was more than **t** feet long and six feet
Jos 19: 6 and Sharuhen—**t** towns with their villages.
21: 4 were given **t** towns that were originally assigned to
21: 6 The clan of Gershon received **t** towns from the
21:19 So **t** towns were given to the priests,
21:33 So **t** towns and their pasturelands were allotted to
1Ki 7: 1 and it took him **t** years to complete the
1Ch 6:60 So a total of **t** towns was given to the descendants
6:62 sacred lots **t** towns from the territories of Issachar,
26:11 who served as gatekeepers, numbered **t** in all.

THIRTEENTH (5) [THIRTEEN]

Ge 14: 4 but now in the **t** year they rebelled.
1Ch 24:13 The **t** lot fell to Huppah. / The fourteenth lot fell to
25:20 The **t** lot fell to Shubael and twelve of his sons
Jer 1: 2 during the **t** year of King Josiah's reign in Judah.
25: 3 from the **t** year of Josiah son of Amon, king of

THIRTIETH (1) [THIRTY]

Eze 1: 1 On July 31 of my **t** year, while I was with the

THIRTY (75) [THIRTIETH, 30]

Ge 18:30 "Let me speak—suppose only **t** are found?"
18:30 "I will not destroy it if there are **t**."
32:15 **t** female camels with their young, forty cows,
41:46 He was **t** years old when he entered the service of
Ex 21:32 the slave's owner is to be given **t** silver coins in
Lev 27: 4 a woman of that age is valued at **t** pieces of silver.
Nu 4: 3 Count all the men between the ages of **t** and fifty
4:23 Count all the men between the ages of **t** and fifty
4:30 Count all the men between the ages of **t** and fifty
4:35 The count included all the men between **t** and fifty
4:39 The count included all the men between **t** and fifty
4:43 The count included all the men between **t** and fifty
4:47 All the men between **t** and fifty years of age who
20:29 Aaron had died, all Israel mourned for him **t** days.
Dt 34: 8 The people of Israel mourned **t** days for Moses on
Jos 8: 3 Joshua chose **t** thousand fighting men and sent
Jdg 10: 4 His **t** sons rode around on **t** donkeys, and they
owned **t** towns in the land of Gilead,
12: 9 and he had **t** sons and **t** daughters. He married
12: 9 and brought in **t** young women from outside his
12:14 He had forty sons and **t** grandsons, who rode on
14:11 **T** young men from the town were invited to be his
14:12 will give you **t** plain linen robes and **t** fancy robes.
14:13 you must give me **t** linen robes and **t** fancy robes."
14:19 of Ashkelon, killed **t** men, took their belongings,
20:31 About **t** Israelites died in the open fields and along
20:39 Benjamin's warriors had killed about **t** Israelites,
1Sa 4:10 was great; **t** thousand Israelite men died that day.
9:22 the table, honoring them above the **t** special guests.
13: 1 Saul was **t** years old when he became king, and he
2Sa 5: 4 David was **t** years old when he began to reign,
6: 1 Then David mobilized **t** thousand special troops.
23:13 The Three (who were among the **T**—an elite group
23:18 the brother of Joab, was the leader of the **T**.
23:19 Abishai was the most famous of the **T** and was
23:23 more honored than the other members of the **T**,
23:24 Other members of the **T** included: / Asahel,
1Ki 5:13 Then King Solomon enlisted **t** thousand laborers
1Ch 11:15 The Three (who were among the **T**—an elite group
11:20 the brother of Joab, was the leader of the **T**.
11:21 Abishai was the most famous of the **T** and was
11:25 more honored than the other members of the **T**,
11:42 the Reubenite leader who had **t** men with him;
12: 4 a famous warrior and leader among the **T**;
12:18 who later became a leader among the **T**, and he
23: 3 All the Levites who were **t** years old or older were
27: 6 David's elite military group known as the **T**.
2Ch 3: 3 of God was ninety feet long and **t** feet wide.
3: 4 The foyer at the front of the Temple was **t** feet
3: 4 pure gold. The roof of the foyer was **t** feet high.
3: 8 The Most Holy Place was **t** feet wide,
3: 8 width of the Temple, and it was also **t** feet deep.
35: 7 from his personal property **t** thousand lambs
Pr 22:20 I have written **t** sayings for you, filled with advice
Jer 38:10 king told Ebed-melech, "Take along **t** of my men,
Eze 40:17 and **t** rooms were built against the walls,
41: 6 one above the other, with **t** rooms on each level.
Da 6: 7 Give orders that for the next **t** days anyone who
6:12 "Did you not sign a law that for the next **t** days
Zec 5: 2 "It appears to be about **t** feet long and fifteen feet
11:12 So they counted out for my wages **t** pieces of
11:13 So I took the **t** coins and threw them to the potters
Mt 13: 8 fell on fertile soil and produced a crop that was **t**,
13:23 **t**, sixty, or even a hundred times as much as had
26:15 to you?" And they gave him **t** pieces of silver.
27: 3 So he took the **t** pieces of silver back to the leading
27: 9 that says, / "They took the **t** pieces of silver—
Mk 4: 8 fell on fertile soil and produced a crop that was **t**,
4:20 **t**, sixty, or even a hundred times as much as had
Lk 3:23 Jesus was about **t** years old when he began his
Jn 2: 6 and held twenty to **t** gallons each.

THIRTY-EIGHT (4) [THIRTY-EIGHTH]

Dt 2:14 So **t** years passed from the time we first arrived at
1Ch 19: 6 and the Ammonites sent **t** tons of silver to hire
23: 3 were counted, and the total came to **t** thousand.
Jn 5: 5 One of the men lying there had been sick for **t**

THIRTY-EIGHTH (2) [THIRTY-EIGHT]

1Ki 16:29 Ahab son of Omri began to rule over Israel in the **t**
2Ki 15: 8 Israel in the **t** year of King Uzziah's reign in Judah.

THIRTY-FIFTH (1) [THIRTY-FIVE]

2Ch 15:19 So there was no more war until the **t** year of Asa's

THIRTY-FIRST (1)

1Ki 16:23 Omri began to rule over Israel in the **t** year of King

THIRTY-FIVE (2) [THIRTY-FIFTH, 35]

1Ki 22:42 He was **t** years old when he became king, and he
2Ch 20:31 He was **t** years old when he became king, and he

THIRTY-FOUR (1) [34]

Nu 3:50 sons of Israel came to about **t** pounds in weight.

THIRTY-NINE (1)

2Co 11:24 Five different times the Jews gave me **t** lashes.

THIRTY-NINTH (3)

2Ki 15:13 Israel in the **t** year of King Uzziah's reign in Judah.
15:17 Israel in the **t** year of King Uzziah's reign in Judah.
2Ch 16:12 In the **t** year of his reign, Asa developed a serious

THIRTY-ONE (3) [31]

Jos 12:24 In all, **t** kings and their cities were destroyed.
2Ki 22: 1 became king, and he reigned in Jerusalem **t** years.
2Ch 34: 1 became king, and he reigned in Jerusalem **t** years.

THIRTY-SECOND (2)

Ne 5:14 from the twentieth until the **t** year of the reign of
13: 6 for I had returned to the king in the **t** year of the

THIRTY-SEVEN (2) [THIRTY-SEVENTH]

2Sa 23:39 Uriah the Hittite. There were **t** in all.
2Ki 15:19 But Menahem paid him **t** tons of silver to gain his

THIRTY-SEVENTH (3) [THIRTY-SEVEN]

2Ki 13:10 Israel in the **t** year of King Joash's reign in Judah.
25:27 In the **t** year of King Jehoiachin's exile in Babylon,
Jer 52:31 In the **t** year of King Jehoiachin's exile in Babylon,

THIRTY-SIX (3) [THIRTY-SIXTH]

Jos 7: 5 and they killed about **t** who were retreating down
1Ki 5:16 and **t** hundred foremen to supervise the work.
2Ch 2: 2 in the hill country, and **t** hundred foremen.

THIRTY-SIXTH (1) [THIRTY-SIX]

2Ch 16: 1 In the **t** year of Asa's reign, King Baasha of Israel

THIRTY-THREE (6)

Ge 46:15 Jacob's descendants through Leah numbered **t**.
Lev 12: 4 Then the woman must wait for **t** days until the time
2Sa 5: 5 he reigned over all Israel and Judah for **t** years.
1Ki 2:11 seven of them in Hebron and **t** in Jerusalem.
1Ch 3: 4 to Jerusalem, where he reigned another **t** years.
29:27 years from Hebron and **t** years from Jerusalem.

THIRTY-TWO (7) [32]

1Ki 20: 1 by the chariots and horses of **t** allied kings.
20:16 and the **t** allied kings were still in their tents
22:31 Aram had issued these orders to his **t** charioteers:
2Ki 8:17 Jehoram was **t** years old when he became king,
1Ch 19: 7 They also hired **t** thousand chariots and secured the
2Ch 21: 5 Jehoram was **t** years old when he became king,
21:20 Jehoram was **t** years old when he became king,

THIS (4240) [THESE] See Index of Articles, Etc.

THISTLE (4) [THISTLES]

2Ki 14: 9 "Out in the Lebanon mountains a **t** sent a message
14: 9 then a wild animal came by and stepped on the **t**,
2Ch 25:18 a **t** sent a message to a mighty cedar tree:
25:18 then a wild animal came by and stepped on the **t**,

THISTLES (5) [THISTLE]

Ge 3:18 It will grow thorns and **t** for you, though you will
Job 31:40 then let **t** grow on that land instead of wheat
Hos 10: 8 Thorns and **t** will grow up around them.
Mt 7:16 don't pick grapes from thornbushes, or figs from **t**.
Heb 6: 8 But if a field bears **t** and thorns, it is useless.

THOMAS (11)

Mt 10: 3 Philip, / Bartholomew, / **T**, / Matthew (the tax
Mk 3:18 Andrew, / Philip, / Bartholomew, / Matthew, / **T**,
Lk 6:15 Matthew, / **T**, / James (son of Alphaeus),
Jn 11:16 **T**, nicknamed the Twin, said to his fellow
14: 5 "No, we don't know, Lord," **T** said. "We haven't
20:24 One of the disciples, **T** (nicknamed the Twin),
20:26 together again, and this time **T** was with them.
20:27 Then he said to **T**, "Put your finger here and see
20:28 "My Lord and my God!" **T** exclaimed.
21: 2 Simon Peter, **T** (nicknamed the Twin),
Ac 1:13 Peter, / John, / James, / Andrew, / Philip, / **T**,

THONG (2) [THONGS]

Ge 14:23 so much as a single thread or sandal **t** from you.

Isa 5:27 Not a belt will be loose, not a sandal **t** broken.

THONGS (1) [THONG]

Jer 27: 2 a yoke, and fasten it on your neck with leather **t**.

THORN (2) [THORNBUSH, THORNBUSHES, THORNS, THORNY]

Jos 23:13 trap to you, a pain in your side and a **t** in your eyes,
2Co 12: 7 I was given a **t** in my flesh, a messenger from

THORNBUSH (3) [THORN]

Jdg 9:14 "Then all the trees finally turned to the **t** and said,
9:15 And the **t** replied, 'If you truly want to make me
Pr 26: 9 A proverb in a fool's mouth is as dangerous as a **t**

THORNBUSHES (3) [THORN]

Hos 2: 6 "But I will fence her in with **t**. I will block the
Mt 7:16 You don't pick grapes from **t**, or figs from thistles.
Lk 6:44 Figs never grow on **t** or grapes on bramble bushes.

THORNS (34) [THORN]

Ge 3:18 It will grow **t** and thistles for you, though you will
Nu 33:55 be like splinters in your eyes and **t** in your sides.
Jdg 2: 3 They will be **t** in your sides, and their gods will be
8: 7 I will return and tear your flesh with the **t**
8:16 punishing them with **t** and briers from the
2Sa 23: 6 But the godless are like **t** to be thrown away,
Pr 24:31 I saw that it was overgrown with **t**. It was covered
Ecc 7: 6 laughter is quickly gone, like **t** crackling in a fire.
SS 2: 2 other women, my beloved is like a lily among **t**."
Isa 5: 6 I will let it be overgrown with briers and **t**.
7:23 of silver, will become patches of briers and **t**.
7:25 once grew, for briers and **t** will cover them.
9:18 It burns not only briers and **t** but the forests,
10:17 In a single night he will burn those **t** and briers,
27: 4 If I find briers and **t** bothering her, I will burn them
32:13 For your land will be overgrown with **t** and briers.
33:12 up completely, like **t** cut down and tossed in a fire.
34:13 **T** will overrun its palaces; nettles will grow in its
55:13 Where once there were **t**, cypress trees will grow.
Jer 4: 3 your hearts! Do not waste your good seed among **t**.
12:13 My people have planted wheat but are harvesting **t**.
Eze 2: 6 be afraid even though their threats are sharp as **t**
28:24 neighbors prick and tear at her like **t** and briers.
Hos 10: 8 **T** and thistles will grow up around them.
Mic 7: 4 the straightest is more crooked than a hedge of **t**.
Na 1:10 His enemies, tangled up like **t**, staggering like
Mt 13: 7 Other seeds fell among **t** that shot up and choked
27:29 a crown of long, sharp **t** and put it on his head,
Mk 4: 7 Other seed fell among **t** that shot up and choked
15:17 a crown of long, sharp **t** and put it on his head.
Lk 8: 7 Other seed fell among **t** that shot up and choked
Jn 19: 2 a crown of long, sharp **t** and put it on his head,
19: 5 Then Jesus came out wearing the crown of **t**
Heb 6: 8 But if a field bears thistles and **t**, it is useless.

THORNY (5) [THORN]

Pr 22: 5 The deceitful walk a **t**, treacherous road;
Isa 7:19 also in the desolate valleys, caves, and **t** places.
Mt 13:22 The **t** ground represents those who hear and accept
Mk 4:18 The **t** ground represents those who hear and accept
Lk 8:14 The **t** ground represents those who hear and accept

THOROUGH (3) [THOROUGHLY]

Ge 31:35 So despite his **t** search, Laban didn't find them.
Ac 12:19 Herod Agrippa ordered a **t** search for him.
26: 4 I was given a **t** Jewish training from my earliest

THOROUGHLY (11) [THOROUGH]

Lev 6:28 is used, it must be scoured and rinsed **t** with water.
14:41 inside walls of the entire house must be scraped **t**
Dt 17: 4 When you hear about it, investigate the matter **t**.
Jdg 11:33 He **t** defeated the Ammonites from Aroer to an
Job 28:27 measured it. He established it and examined it **t**.
Ps 119:140 Your promises have been **t** tested; / that is why I
Jer 20:11 defeat me. They will be shamed and **t** humiliated.
31:19 I was **t** ashamed of all I did in my younger days.'
Lk 16: 1 went around that the manager was **t** dishonest.
23:14 I have examined him **t** on this point in your
2Co 8:22 with them another brother who has been **t** tested

THOSE (1460) [THAT] See Index of Articles, Etc.

THOUGH (397) [ALTHOUGH]

Ge 3:16 And **t** your desire will be for your husband, he will
3:18 and thistles for you, **t** you will eat of its grains.
8:21 even **t** people's thoughts and actions are bent
16: 5 **t** I myself gave her the privilege of sleeping with
18:27 further to my Lord, even **t** I am but dust and ashes.
20:12 we both have the same father, **t** different mothers
28:19 **t** the name of the nearby village was Luz.
31:36 You have chased me as **t** I were a criminal.
44:18 killed in an instant, as **t** you were Pharaoh himself.
Ex 6: 3 **t** I did not reveal my name, the LORD, to them.
12:11 you eat this meal, as **t** prepared for a long journey.
12:27 And **t** he killed the Egyptians, he spared our
13:17 even **t** that was the shortest way from Egypt to the
16:27 to gather food, even **t** it was the Sabbath day.
24:11 And **t** Israel's leaders saw God, he did not destroy
28:21 that tribe will be engraved on it as **t** it were a seal.
32:29 for you obeyed him even **t** it meant killing your
Lev 1:17 the priest will tear the bird apart, **t** not completely.
7:24 be eaten, **t** it may be used for any other purpose.
11: 4 The camel may not be eaten, for **t** it chews the cud,
11: 7 for **t** it has split hooves, it does not chew the cud.
21:21 Even **t** he is a descendant of Aaron, his physical
26:36 You will run as **t** chased by a warrior with a sword,
26:37 Yes, **t** no one is chasing you, you will stumble over each other in flight, as **t** fleeing in battle.
Nu 16: 3 What right do you have to act as **t** you are greater
18:27 as **t** it were the first grain from your own threshing
18:30 it will be considered as **t** it came from your own
18:32 of the people of Israel as **t** they were common.
19: 7 **t** he will remain ceremonially unclean until
35:23 **t** they were not enemies, and the person dies.
Dt 2:20 **t** the Ammonites referred to them as
4:22 **T** you will cross the Jordan to occupy the land,
11:23 **t** they are much greater and stronger than you.
14: 8 for **t** it has split hooves, it does not chew the cud.
19: 6 even **t** there was no death sentence and the first
21:17 even **t** he is the son of the wife his father does not
21:18 his father or mother, even **t** they discipline him.
28:62 **T** you are as numerous as the stars in the sky,
29:19 even **t** I am walking in my own stubborn way.'
30: 4 **T** you are at the ends of the earth, the LORD your
33: 6 and not die out, / even **t** their tribe is small."
Jos 8:15 toward the wilderness as **t** they were badly beaten,
11:22 **t** some still remained in Gaza, Gath, and Ashdod.
17:18 even **t** they are strong and have iron chariots."
22: 3 even **t** the campaign has lasted for such a long
24:13 and olive groves for food, **t** you did not plant them.
24:20 destroy you, even **t** he has been so good to you."
Jdg 8: 4 and **t** they were exhausted, they continued to chase
13: 3 "Even **t** you have been unable to have children,
19:19 even **t** we have everything we need. We have straw
Ru 2:13 even **t** I am not as worthy as your workers."
1Sa 1: 5 even **t** the LORD had given her no children.
2:18 Now Samuel, **t** only a boy, was the LORD's
10:19 But **t** I have done so much for you, you have
12:12 even **t** the LORD your God was already your
14:25 even **t** they found honeycomb on the ground in the
20:20 of the stone pile as **t** I were shooting at a target.
24:11 even **t** you have been hunting for me to kill me.
2Sa 3:39 And even **t** I am the anointed king, these two sons
9:11 with David, as **t** he were one of his own sons.
13:22 And **t** Absalom never spoke to Amnon about it,
13:25 but the king wouldn't come, **t** he sent his thanks.
16:23 as **t** it had come directly from the mouth of God.
17:10 **t** they have the heart of a lion, will be paralyzed
19: 3 They crept back into the city as **t** they were
19: 5 feel ashamed, as **t** we had done something wrong.
20: 9 and took him by the beard with his right hand as **t**
23:19 their commander, **t** he was not one of the Three.
23:23 of the Thirty, **t** he was not one of the Three.
1Ki 9: 8 And **t** this Temple is impressive now, it will
11:39 because of Solomon's sin—**t** not forever.'"
16:31 And as **t** it were not enough to live like Jeroboam,
2Ki 5: 1 But **t** Naaman was a mighty warrior, he suffered
5:16 And **t** Naaman urged him to take the gifts,
17:33 And **t** they worshiped the LORD, they continued
1Ch 2:34 Sheshan had no sons, **t** he did have daughters.
11:21 their commander, **t** he was not one of the Three.
11:25 of the Thirty, **t** he was not one of the Three.
17:17 You speak as **t** I were someone very great,
22:14 stone for the walls, **t** you may need to add more.
24:28 of Mahli, the leader was Eleazar, **t** he had no sons.
26:10 the leader among his sons, **t** he was not the oldest.
2Ch 7:21 And **t** this Temple is impressive now, it will
30:18 even **t** this was contrary to God's laws.
30:19 even **t** they are not properly cleansed for the
32:19 of Jerusalem as **t** he were one of the pagan gods,
36:13 even **t** he had taken an oath of loyalty in God's
Ezr 3: 3 Even **t** the people were afraid of the local
5:16 working on it ever since, **t** it is not yet completed.'
9:15 **t** in such a condition none of us can stand in your
Ne 3: 5 people from Tekoa, **t** their leaders refused to help.
5:17 even **t** I regularly fed 150 Jewish officials at my
6: 1 **t** we had not yet hung the doors in the gates—
9:18 even **t** they made an idol shaped like a calf
9:35 they did not serve you even **t** you showered your
13: 2 **t** our God turned the curse into a blessing.
13: 6 **t** I later received his permission to return.
Est 4:16 And then, **t** it is against the law, I will go in to see
9:15 hundred more people, **t** again they took no plunder.
Job 2: 3 even **t** you persuaded me to harm him without
4:10 **T** they are fierce young lions, they will all be
4:12 was given me in secret, as **t** whispered in my ear.
5:14 They grope in the daylight as **t** they were blind;
5:18 For **t** he wounds, he also bandages. He strikes,
8: 7 And **t** you started with little, you will end with
9:20 **T** I am innocent, my own mouth would pronounce
9:20 **T** I am blameless, it would prove me wicked.
14: 8 **T** its roots have grown old in the earth and its
20: 6 **T** the godless man's pride reaches to the heavens and **t** his head touches the clouds,
21:14 All this, even **t** they say to God, 'Go away.
24:24 And **t** they are great now, in a moment they will be
30:17 My weary nights are filled with pain as **t**
33:14 and again, **t** people do not recognize it.
34: 6 suffering is incurable, even **t** I have not sinned.'
39:16 were not her own. She is unconcerned **t** they die,
Ps 12: 8 even **t** the wicked strut about, / and evil is praised
27: 3 **T** a mighty army surrounds me, / my heart will
35:14 I was sad, as **t** they were my friends or family,
37:10 **T** you look for them, they will be gone.
37:24 **T** they stumble, they will not fall, / for the LORD
37:36 **T** I searched for them, I could not find them!
38:19 they hate me **t** I have done nothing against them.
49:13 **t** they will be remembered as being so wise.
55:18 waged against me, / even **t** many still oppose me.
59: 3 **t** I have done them no wrong, O LORD.
65: 3 **T** our hearts are filled with sins, / you forgive them
68:13 **T** they lived among the sheepfolds, / now they are
78: 9 The warriors of Ephraim, **t** fully armed,
78:56 Yet **t** he did all this for them, / they continued to
78:65 Then the Lord rose up as **t** waking from sleep,
80: 8 You brought us from Egypt as **t** we were a tender
91: 7 **T** a thousand fall at your side, / **t** ten thousand are dying around you,
95: 9 they courted my wrath **t** they had seen my many
103:16 and we are gone— / as **t** we had never been here.
115: 5 They cannot talk, **t** they have mouths, / or see, **t** they have eyes!
118:10 **T** hostile nations surrounded me, / I destroyed
119:95 **T** the wicked hide along the way to kill me,
135:16 They cannot talk, **t** they have mouths, / or see, **t** they have eyes!
138: 6 **T** the LORD is great, he cares for the humble,
138: 7 **T** I am surrounded by troubles, / you will preserve
Pr 1:12 **T** they are in the prime of life, they will go down
1:28 Even **t** they anxiously search for me, they will not
6: 7 Even **t** they have no prince, governor, or ruler to
20: 5 **T** good advice lies deep within a person's heart,
23: 5 For riches can disappear as **t** they had the wings of
26:25 **T** they pretend to be kind, their hearts are full of all
27:22 even **t** you grind them like grain with mortar
Ecc 2:21 For **t** I do my work with wisdom, knowledge,
4:14 might even become king, **t** he was born in poverty.
8:12 But even **t** a person sins a hundred times and still
8:14 good people are often treated as **t** they were
8:14 and wicked people are often treated as **t** they were
9: 1 Even **t** the actions of godly and wise people are in
9:16 Then I realized that **t** wisdom is better than
Isa 1:15 Even **t** you offer many prayers, I will not listen.
8:17 **t** he has turned away from the people of Israel.
10:22 But **t** the people of Israel are as numerous as the
14:29 For even **t** that whip is broken, his son will be
17:13 But **t** they roar like breakers on a beach, God will
18: 5 the LORD will cut you off as **t** with pruning
27: 8 He has exiled her from her land as **t** blown away in
30: 4 For **t** his power extends to Zoan and Hanes,
30:20 **T** the Lord gave you adversity for food
31: 6 **t** you are such wicked rebels, come and return to
32:19 Even **t** the forest will be destroyed and the city torn
33: 5 **T** the LORD is very great and lives in heaven,
34: 6 It is covered with fat as **t** it had been used for
38:13 all night, / but I was torn apart as **t** by lions.
40:15 He picks up the islands as **t** they had no weight at
41: 3 on safely, **t** he is walking over unfamiliar ground.
41:14 Despised **t** you are, O Israel, don't be afraid,
43:23 **t** I have not burdened and wearied you with my
45: 5 I have prepared you, even **t** you do not know me,
48: 2 even **t** you call yourself the holy city and talk
51:21 sit in a drunken stupor, **t** not from drinking wine.
54: 1 even **t** you never gave birth to a child.
54: 6 as **t** you were a young wife abandoned by her
59:10 brightest noontime, we fall down as **t** it were dark.
60:10 For **t** I have destroyed you in my anger, I will have
60:15 "**T** you were once despised and hated and rebuffed
61: 4 **t** they have been empty for many generations.
63:19 why do you treat us as **t** we never belonged to you?
63:19 Why do you act as **t** we had never been known as
Jer 2:11 gods for another god, even **t** its gods are nothing?
2:34 You killed them even **t** they didn't break into your
3: 7 And **t** her faithless sister Judah saw this,
8: 5 refusing to turn back, even **t** I have warned them?
10: 2 even **t** other nations are terrified by them.
11:11 **T** they beg for mercy, I will not listen to their cries.
12: 8 the forest, so I have treated them as **t** I hated them.
14:15 for they have spoken in my name even **t** I never
17: 1 "My people act as **t** their evil ways are laws to be
18:20 **t** I pleaded for them and tried to protect them from
20:13 For **t** I was poor and needy, he delivered me from
23:38 the LORD," even **t** I warned you not to use it,
29:19 **t** I have spoken to them repeatedly through my
30:14 have wounded you cruelly, as **t** I were your enemy.
31:32 **t** I loved them as a husband loves his wife,"
32:18 **t** children suffer for their parents' sins.
32:25 even **t** the city will soon belong to the
33: 4 **T** you have torn down the houses of this city
33:12 **t** it is now desolate and the people and animals
34:21 And **t** Babylon's king has left this city for a while,
37: 7 to return to Egypt, **t** he came here to help you.
49:16 **T** you live among the peaks with the eagles,
51: 5 even **t** their land was filled with sin against the
51:50 the LORD, even **t** you are in a far-off land,
51:53 **T** Babylon reaches as high as the heavens,
51:53 and **t** she increases her strength immeasurably,
La 2: 4 He bends his bow against his people as **t** he were
2: 6 He has broken down his Temple as **t** it were
2: 7 They shout in the LORD's Temple as **t** it were a
2:22 "You have invited terrors from all around as **t** you
3: 8 And **t** I cry and shout, he shuts out my prayers.
3:32 **T** he brings grief, he also shows compassion
5:10 our skin has been blackened as **t** baked in an oven.
Eze 1:13 and it looked as **t** lightning was flashing back
2: 6 Don't be afraid even **t** their threats are sharp as
3: 9 their angry looks, even **t** they are such rebels."
8:18 And **t** they scream for mercy, I will not listen."
12: 3 what this means, even **t** they are such rebels.
12:13 he will never see it, and he will die there.
13: 6 the LORD,' even **t** the LORD never sent them.
13:22 them life, even **t** they continue in their sins.
16: 7 and your hair grew, **t** you were still naked.
16:61 even **t** they are not part of our covenant.

17: 8 The vine did this even **t** it was already planted in
20:13 They wouldn't obey my instructions even **t**
20:21 even **t** obeying them would have given them life.
20:31 I will not give you a message even **t** you have
23:11 "Yet even **t** Oholibah saw what had happened to
28: 2 and not a god, **t** you boast that you are like a god.
31:14 **t** it be higher than the clouds, for all are doomed.
34: 8 **T** you were my shepherds, you didn't search for
39:18 and drink the blood of princes as **t** they were rams,
Da 2:22 in darkness, / **t** he himself is surrounded by light.
5:11 and wisdom as **t** he himself were a god.
8: 3 even **t** it had begun to grow later than the shorter
8:25 but he will be broken, **t** not by human power.
9: 9 and forgiving, even **t** we have rebelled against him.
11:20 he will die, **t** neither in battle nor open conflict.
11:34 **t** many who join them will not be sincere.
Hos 3: 1 back to you and love her, even **t** she loves adultery.
3: 1 For the LORD still loves Israel even **t** the people
4:10 **T** they do a big business as prostitutes, they will
4:15 "**T** Israel is a prostitute, may Judah avoid such
6:11 **t** I wanted so much to restore the fortunes of my
8:10 But **t** they have sold themselves to many lands,
8:12 Even **t** I gave them all my laws, they act as if those
13: 9 about to be destroyed, O Israel, **t** I am your helper.
Ob 1: 4 **T** you soar as high as eagles and build your nest
1:11 You acted as **t** you were one of Israel's enemies.
1:16 from history, as **t** you had never even existed.
Jnh 4:10 about the plant, **t** you did nothing to put it there.
Mic 4: 5 Even **t** the nations around us worship idols, we will
6:14 And **t** you try to save your money, it will come to
7: 8 over me, my enemies! For **t** I fall, I will rise again.
7: 8 **T** I sit in darkness, the LORD himself will be my
Na 1:12 "Even **t** the Assyrians have many allies, they will
Hab 3:17 Even **t** the fig trees have no blossoms, and there
3:17 even **t** the olive crop fails, and the fields lie empty
3:17 even **t** the flocks die in the fields, and the cattle
Hag 1: 6 Your wages disappear as **t** you were putting them
Zec 4: 1 me returned and woke me, as **t** I had been asleep.
9: 2 cities of Tyre and Sidon, too, **t** they are so clever.
9:15 They will shout in battle as **t** drunk with wine,
10: 6 It will be as **t** I had never rejected them, for I am
10: 9 **T** I have scattered them like seeds among the
Mal 2:14 **t** she remained your faithful companion, the wife
Mt 7:25 **T** the rain comes in torrents and the floodwaters
13:33 Even **t** she used a large amount of flour, the yeast
26:41 For **t** the spirit is willing enough, the body is
26:60 But even **t** they found many who agreed to give
Mk 4:31 mustard seed. **T** this is one of the smallest of seeds,
14:38 For **t** the spirit is willing enough, the body is
Lk 11: 8 **t** he won't do it as a friend, if you keep knocking
11:36 be radiant, as **t** a floodlight is shining on you."
12:36 as **t** you were waiting for your master to return
12:47 for **t** he knew his duty, he refused to do it.
13:21 Even **t** she used a large amount of flour, the yeast
Jn 2: 9 not knowing where it had come from (**t**, of course,
4: 2 (**t** Jesus himself didn't baptize them—his disciples
5:34 **t** I have reminded you about John's testimony
5:43 even **t** you readily accept others who represent
6:36 But you haven't believed in me even **t** you have
6:58 as your ancestors did, even **t** they ate the manna."
7:10 Jesus also went, **t** secretly, staying out of public
8:14 "These claims are valid even **t** I make them about
8:50 And **t** I have no wish to glorify myself, God wants
11:25 even **t** they die like everyone else, will live again.
13:33 Then, **t** you search for me, you cannot come to
Ac 3:12 And why look at us as **t** we had made this man
5:13 to join them, **t** everyone had high regard for them.
7: 5 and his descendants—**t** he had no children yet.
7:53 **t** you received it from the hands of angels."
13:27 **t** they hear the prophets' words read every
17:27 and find him—**t** he is not far from any one of us.
27:22 will lose your lives, even **t** the ship will go down.
27:30 they lowered the lifeboat as **t** they were going to
28: 4 **T** he escaped the sea, justice will not permit him to
28:16 own private lodging, **t** he was guarded by a soldier.
28:17 even **t** I had done nothing against our people
28:19 even **t** I had no desire to press charges against my
Ro 2:12 they sin, even **t** they never had God's written law.
3: 4 **T** everyone else in the world is a liar, God is true.
4:18 even **t** such a promise seemed utterly impossible!
4:19 even **t** he knew that he was too old to be a father at
5: 7 **t** someone might be willing to die for a person who
5:13 And **t** there was no law to break, since it had not
5:14 even **t** they did not disobey an explicit
5:16 by God, even **t** we are guilty of many sins.
8:10 even **t** your body will die because of sin,
9: 7 be counted," **t** Abraham had other children, too.
9:27 "**T** the people of Israel are as numerous as the
9:30 God by faith, even **t** they were not seeking him.
1Co 2: 7 **t** he made it for our benefit before the world began.
3: 1 I had to talk as **t** you belonged to this world or as **t**
you were infants in the Christian life.
4: 7 why boast as **t** you have accomplished something
5: 3 Even **t** I am not there with you in person, I am with
6:12 And even **t** "I am allowed to do anything,"
6:13 **t** someday God will do away with both of them.
7:12 **t** I do not have a direct command from the Lord.
9:20 I do the same, even **t** I am not subject to the law,
14: 7 like the flute or the harp, **t** they are lifeless,
15: 6 of whom are still alive, **t** some have died by now.
15: 8 the others, as **t** I had been born at the wrong time.
2Co 3: 7 even **t** the brightness was already fading away.
4:16 **T** our bodies are dying, our spirits are being
5: 6 even **t** we know that as long as we live in these
5:16 that way, as **t** he were merely a human being.
5:20 as **t** Christ himself were here pleading with you,
7: 8 I sent that letter to you, **t** I was sorry for a time,
8: 2 **T** they have been going through much trouble
8: 8 do it, even **t** the other churches are eager to do it.
8: 9 **T** he was very rich, yet for your sakes he became
10: 1 even **t** some of you say I am bold in my letters
12: 7 even **t** I have received wonderful revelations from
12:11 these "super apostles," even **t** I am nothing at all.
12:15 even **t** it seems that the more I love you, the less
Gal 2: 3 Titus be circumcised, **t** he was a Gentile.
3: 1 **t** I had shown you a signboard with a picture of
4: 1 even **t** they actually own everything their father
4:14 But even **t** my sickness was revolting to you,
4:14 and cared for me as **t** I were an angel from God
4:27 even **t** you never gave birth to a child.
Eph 2:11 even **t** it affected only their bodies and not their
2:13 **T** you once were far away from God, now you
3: 8 **T** I did nothing to deserve it, and **t** I am the least
deserving Christian there is,
3:19 **t** it is so great you will never fully understand it.
5: 8 For **t** your hearts were once full of darkness,
6: 7 as **t** you were working for the Lord rather than for
Php 2: 6 **T** he was God, he did not demand and cling to his
Col 2: 5 For **t** I am far away from you, my heart is with
2:18 even **t** they say they have had visions about this.
3:23 as **t** you were working for the Lord rather than for
1Th 2: 2 even **t** we were surrounded by many who opposed
2:17 you for a little while (**t** our hearts never left you),
1Ti 1: 7 are talking about, even **t** they seem so confident.
1:13 even **t** I used to scoff at the name of Christ.
3:14 to you now, even **t** I hope to be with you soon,
5: 1 but appeal to him respectfully as **t** he were your
2Ti 1: 8 of me, either, even **t** I'm in prison for Christ.
Heb 3: 9 even **t** they saw my miracles for forty years.
3:16 rebelled against God, even **t** they heard his voice?
4: 3 'They will never enter my place of rest,' " even **t**
5: 2 with the people, **t** they are ignorant and wayward.
5: 8 So even **t** Jesus was God's Son, he learned
6: 9 Dear friends, even **t** we are talking like this,
7: 5 all the people, even **t** they are their own relatives.
10: 8 nor were you pleased with them" (**t** they are
10:32 Remember how you remained faithful even **t** it
11:11 even **t** they were too old and Sarah was barren.
11:18 **t** God had promised him, "Isaac is the son through
11:29 through the Red Sea as **t** they were on dry ground.
12:13 **t** they are weak and lame, will not stumble and fall
12:17 too late for repentance, even **t** he wept bitter tears.
13: 3 Suffer with them as **t** you were there yourself.
13: 3 as **t** you feel their pain in your own bodies.
Jas 3: 4 the pilot wants it to go, even **t** the winds are strong.
1Pe 1: 6 even **t** it is necessary for you to endure many trials
1: 8 You love him even **t** you have never seen him.
1: 8 **T** you do not see him, you trust him; and even now
1:10 even **t** they had many questions as to what it all
4:11 Then speak as **t** God himself were speaking
2Pe 1:12 even **t** you already know them and are standing
2:11 even **t** they are far greater in power and strength
3Jn 1: 5 passing through, even **t** they are strangers to you.
Jude 1: 5 that even **t** the Lord rescued the whole nation of
Rev 4: 7 of an eagle with wings spread out as **t** in flight.
9: 2 smoke poured out as **t** from a huge furnace,

THOUGHT (97) [THINK]

Ge 18:12 she **t**. "And when my master—my husband—
19:14 But the young men **t** he was only joking.
20:11 I **t**, 'They will want my wife and will kill me to get
26: 7 He **t** they would kill him to get her, because she
32: 8 He **t**, "If Esau attacks one group, perhaps the other
37:11 his father gave it some **t** and wondered what it all
38:15 her as he went by and **t** she was a prostitute,
40:23 forgot all about Joseph, never giving him another **t**.
41: 8 The next morning, as he **t** about it,
48:11 said to Joseph, "I never **t** I would see you again,
Ex 12:33 quickly as possible, for they **t**, "We will all die!"
Jos 22:31 you have not sinned against the LORD as we **t**.
Jdg 3:24 room locked. They **t** he might be using the latrine,
15: 2 "I really **t** you hated her," her father explained,
16:20 When he woke up, he **t**, "I will do as before
21:19 Then they **t** of the annual festival of the LORD
1Sa 1:13 but hearing no sound, he **t** she had been drinking.
9: 6 But the servant said, "I've just **t** of something!
15:32 for he **t**, "Surely the worst is over, and I have been
16: 6 they arrived, Samuel took one look at Eliab and **t**,
18:17 For Saul **t** to himself, "I'll send him out against
27:12 Achish believed David and **t** to himself, "By now
2Sa 5: 6 keep you out!" For the Jebusites **t** they were safe.
1Ki 12:26 Jeroboam **t** to himself, "Unless I am careful,
18:27 Perhaps he is deep in **t**, or he is relieving himself.
2Ki 5:11 "I **t** he would surely come out to meet me!"
1Ch 28: 9 and understands and knows every plan and **t**.
Est 1:21 The king and his princes **t** this made good sense,
6: 6 Haman **t** to himself, "Whom would the king wish
Job 6: 7 when I look at it; I gag at the **t** of eating it!
14:14 This **t** would give me hope, and through my
19:27 him with my own eyes. I am overwhelmed at the **t**!
29:18 "I **t**, 'Surely I will die surrounded by my family
31:21 an orphan because I **t** I could get away with it,
32: 7 I **t**, 'Those who are older should speak, for wisdom
Ps 45: 1 My heart overflows with a beautiful **t**! / I will
50:21 all this, I remained silent, / and you **t** I didn't care.
73:17 O God, / and I **t** about the destiny of the wicked.
74: 8 Then they **t**, "Let's destroy everything!" / So they
137: 1 of Babylon, we sat and wept / as we **t** of Jerusalem.
139: 2 stand up. / You know my every **t** when far away.
142: 4 and help me, / but no one gives me a passing **t**!
Pr 17:28 Even fools are **t** to be wise when they keep silent;
24:32 Then, as I looked and **t** about it, I learned this
Ecc 2: 3 After much **t**, I decided to cheer myself with wine.
3:10 I have **t** about this in connection with the various
8: 9 I have **t** deeply about all that goes on here in the
9:15 But afterward no one **t** any more about him.
Isa 47: 7 You **t**, 'I will reign forever as queen of the world!'
53: 4 And we **t** his troubles were a punishment from God
55: 7 Let them banish from their minds the very **t** of
Jer 3: 7 I **t** that after she had done all this she would return
3: 9 she **t** nothing of committing adultery by
3:16 Those days will not be missed or even **t** about,
3:19 "I **t** to myself, 'I would love to treat you as my
3:19 and I **t** you would never turn away from me again.
49: 4 in your wealth and **t** no one could ever harm you.
La 1: 9 She defiled herself with immorality with no **t** of
3:19 The **t** of my suffering and homelessness is bitter
Eze 11: 5 for I know every **t** that comes into your minds.
16:15 "But you **t** you could get along without me,
16:22 you have not once **t** of the days long ago when you
Am 4:13 stirs up the winds, and reveals his every **t**.
6: 3 You push away every **t** of coming disaster,
Zep 3: 7 I **t**, 'Surely they will have reverence for me now!
Mt 9:21 for she **t**, "If I can just touch his robe, I will be
22:34 they **t** up a fresh question of their own to ask him.
27:47 and **t** he was calling for the prophet Elijah.
Mk 5:28 For she **t** to herself, "If I can just touch his
6:15 Others **t** Jesus was the ancient prophet Elijah.
6:15 Still others **t** he was a prophet like the other great
11:32 a riot, since everyone **t** that John was a prophet.
15:35 and **t** he was calling for the prophet Elijah.
Lk 2:19 these things in her heart and **t** about them often.
16: 3 "The manager **t** to himself, 'Now what?
24:21 We had **t** he was the Messiah who had come to
Jn 11:13 They **t** Jesus meant Lazarus was having a good
12:29 the crowd heard the voice, some **t** it was thunder,
13:29 some **t** Jesus was telling him to go and pay for the
20:15 She **t** he was the gardener. "Sir," she said, "if you
Ac 9:26 They **t** he was only pretending to be a believer!
11:16 Then I **t** of the Lord's words when he said,
12: 9 the angel. But all the time he **t** it was a vision.
12:12 After a little **t**, he went to the home of Mary,
16: 2 Timothy was well **t** of by the believers in Lystra
22:12 and he was well **t** of by all the Jews of Damascus.
27:13 from the south, the sailors **t** they could make it.
1Co 1:10 you to be of one mind, united in **t** and purpose.
4:10 You are well **t** of, but we are laughed at.
13:11 a child, I spoke and **t** and reasoned as a child does.
2Co 1: 8 and we **t** we would never live through it.
5:16 Once I mistakenly **t** of Christ that way, as though
9: 5 So I **t** I should send these brothers ahead of me to
Php 2:25 I **t** I should send Epaphroditus back to you.
3: 7 I once **t** all these things were so very important,
Tit 1: 6 An elder must be well **t** of for his good life.
Heb 11:26 He **t** it was better to suffer for the sake of the

THOUGHT-LIFE (1) [LIVE, THINK]

Mk 7:20 And then he added, "It is the **t** that defiles you.

THOUGHTLESSLY (1) [THINK]

Eph 5:17 Don't act **t**, but try to understand what the Lord

THOUGHTS (58) [THINK]

Ge 6: 5 and he saw that all their **t** were consistently
8:21 even though people's **t** and actions are bent toward
1Sa 16: 7 but the LORD looks at a person's **t**
Job 21:27 "Look, I know your **t**. I know the schemes you
Ps 17: 3 You have tested my **t** and examined my heart in
19:14 May the words of my mouth and the **t** of my heart
39: 3 My **t** grew hot within me / and began to burn,
49: 3 words are wise, / and my **t** are filled with insight.
77:12 They are constantly in my **t**. / I cannot stop
92: 5 great miracles you do! / And how deep are your **t**.
94:11 The LORD knows people's **t**, / that they are
104:34 May he be pleased by all these **t** about him,
139:17 How precious are your **t** about me, O God!
139:23 and know my heart; / test me and know my **t**.
Pr 15:26 The LORD despises the **t** of the wicked, but he
16: 1 We can gather our **t**, but the LORD gives the
Ecc 7:23 I have tried my best to let wisdom guide my **t**
10:13 Since fools base their **t** on foolish premises,
10:20 Never make light of the king, even in your **t**.
Isa 26: 3 all who trust in you, / whose **t** are fixed on you!
55: 8 "My **t** are completely different from yours,"
55: 9 your ways and my **t** higher than your **t**.
65: 2 They follow their own evil paths and **t**.
Jer 4:14 be saved. How long will you harbor your evil **t**?
7: 5 I will be merciful only if you stop your wicked **t**
11:20 and you examine the deepest **t** of hearts and minds.
12: 3 you know my heart. You see me and test my **t**.
20:12 and you examine the deepest **t** of hearts and minds.
Eze 38:10 At that time evil **t** will come to your mind, and you
Da 7:28 was terrified by my **t** and my face was pale with
Jnh 2: 7 all hope, I turned my **t** once more to the LORD.
Mic 4:12 But they do not know the LORD's **t**
Mt 6:21 your treasure is, there your heart and **t** will also be.
9: 4 he asked them, "Why are you thinking such evil **t**?
12:25 Jesus knew their **t** and replied, "Any kingdom at
15:19 For from the heart come evil **t**, murder, adultery,
Mk 7:21 come evil **t**, sexual immorality, theft, murder,
Lk 2:35 the deepest **t** of many hearts will be revealed.
6: 8 But Jesus knew their **t**. He said to the man with the
7:40 Then Jesus spoke up and answered his **t**.
9:47 But Jesus knew their **t**, so he brought a little child
11:17 He knew their **t**, so he said, "Any kingdom at war
12:30 These things dominate the **t** of most people,
12:34 your treasure is, there your heart and **t** will also be.
Ac 8:22 to the Lord. Perhaps he will forgive your evil **t**,

1Co 2:11 and no one can know God's t except God's own
3:20 And again, / "The Lord knows the t of the wise,
11: 2 that you always keep me in your t and you are
14:25 As they listen, their secret t will be laid bare,
Gal 5:19 sexual immorality, impure t, eagerness for lustful
Eph 4:23 there must be a spiritual renewal of your t
Php 4: 8 Fix your t on what is true and honorable and right.
Col 1:21 separated from him by your evil t and actions,
2:23 when it comes to conquering a person's evil t
3: 2 Let heaven fill your t. Do not think only about
Heb 4:12 cutting deep into our innermost t and desires.
Rev 2:23 will know that I am the one who searches out the t

THOUSAND (205) [THOUSANDS, 1000]

Ge 20:16 "I am giving your 'brother' a t pieces of silver to
Ex 18:21 Appoint them as judges over groups of one t,
18:25 They were put in charge of groups of one t,
20: 6 and obey my commands, even for a t generations.
32:28 and about three t people died that day.
Lev 26: 8 a hundred, and a hundred of you will chase ten t!
Nu 31: 4 each tribe of Israel, send one t men into battle."
31: 5 So they chose one t men from each tribe of Israel,
a total of twelve t men armed for battle.
31: 6 Moses sent them out, a t men from each tribe,
Dt 1:11 multiply you a t times more and bless you as he
1:15 Some were responsible for a t people, some for a
5:10 and obey my commands, even for a t generations.
7: 9 God who keeps his covenant for a t generations
32:30 How could one person chase a t of them, / and two
people put ten t to flight,
Jos 4:13 These warriors—about forty t strong—were ready
7: 3 take more than two or three t of us to destroy it.
7: 4 So approximately three t warriors were sent,
8: 3 Joshua chose thirty t fighting men and sent them
8:12 That night Joshua sent five t men to lie in ambush
8:25 of Ai was wiped out that day—twelve t in all.
23:10 Each one of you will put to flight a t of the enemy,
Jdg 1: 4 and they killed ten t enemy warriors at the town of
3:29 and killed about ten t of their strongest and bravest
4: 6 Assemble ten t warriors from the tribes of Naphtali
4:10 and ten t warriors marched up with him.
4:14 So Barak led his ten t warriors down the slopes of
5: 8 could be seen / among forty t warriors in Israel!
7: 3 and go home.' " Twenty-two t of them went
7: 3 leaving only ten t who were willing to fight.
9:49 tower of Shechem died, about a t men and women.
12: 6 So forty-two t Ephraimites were killed at that time.
15:11 So three t men of Judah went down to get Samson
15:15 on the ground and killed a t Philistines with it.
15:16 the jawbone of a donkey, / I've killed a t men!"
16:27 and there were about three t on the roof who were
20:15 Twenty-six t of their warriors armed with swords
20:21 and killed twenty-two t Israelites in the field that
20:25 but the men of Benjamin killed another eighteen t
20:44 Eighteen t of Benjamin's greatest warriors died in
20:45 but Israel killed five t of them along the road.
20:45 until they had killed another two t near Gidom.
20:46 So the tribe of Benjamin lost twenty-five t brave
21:10 So they sent twelve t warriors to Jabesh-gilead
1Sa 4: 2 and defeated the army of Israel, killing four t men.
4:10 was great; thirty t Israelite men died that day.
13: 2 Saul selected three t special troops from the army
13: 2 He took two t of the chosen men with him to
13: 2 The other t went with Saul's son Jonathan to
13: 5 The Philistines mustered a mighty army of three t
13: 5 six t horsemen, and as many warriors as the grains
18:13 and appointed him commander over only a t men,
24: 2 So Saul chose three t special troops from
25: 2 He had three t sheep and a t goats, and it
26: 2 So Saul took three t of his best troops and went to
29: 2 their troops in groups of one hundred and one t,
2Sa 6: 1 Then David mobilized thirty t special troops.
8: 4 hundred charioteers and twenty t foot soldiers.
8: 5 David killed twenty-two t of them.
8:13 After his return he destroyed eighteen t Edomites
10: 6 so they hired twenty t Aramean mercenaries from
10: 6 one t from the king of Maacah, and twelve t from
the land of Tob.
10:18 seven hundred charioteers and forty t horsemen,
17: 1 "Let me choose twelve t men to start out after
18: 3 You are worth ten t of us, and it is better that you
18: 7 and twenty t men laid down their lives that day.
18:12 "I wouldn't do it for a t pieces of silver," the man
19:17 A t men from the tribe of Benjamin were with him,
24:15 Seventy t people died throughout the nation.
1Ki 3: 4 went there and sacrificed one t burnt offerings.
4:26 Solomon had four t stalls for his chariot horses and
twelve t horses.
5:13 Then King Solomon enlisted thirty t laborers from
5:14 sent them to Lebanon in shifts, ten t every month,
5:15 Solomon also enlisted seventy t common laborers,
5:15 eighty t stonecutters in the hill country,
9:14 Hiram had sent Solomon nine t pounds of gold.
10:10 Then she gave the king a gift of nine t pounds of
10:26 had fourteen hundred chariots and twelve t horses.
19:18 Yet I will preserve seven t others in Israel who
20:15 Then he called out the rest of his army of seven t
2Ki 13: 7 ten chariots, and ten t foot soldiers.
14: 7 It was Amaziah who killed ten t Edomites in the
18:23 If you can find two t horsemen in your entire army,
18:23 he will give you two t horses for them to ride on!
24:14 King Nebuchadnezzar took ten t captives from
24:16 He also took seven t of the best troops and one t
craftsmen and smiths,
1Ch 12:14 regular troops, and the strongest could take on a t!
12:20 Each commanded a t troops from the tribe of
16:15 the commitment he made to a t generations.
18: 4 David captured one t chariots, seven t charioteers,
and twenty t foot soldiers.
18: 5 David killed twenty-two t of them.
18:12 Abishai son of Zeruiah destroyed eighteen t
19: 7 They also hired thirty-two t chariots and secured
19:18 This time David's forces killed seven t charioteers
and forty t foot soldiers,
21:14 upon Israel, and seventy t people died as a result.
22:14 nearly four t tons of gold, nearly forty t tons of
silver, and so much iron
23: 3 were counted, and the total came to thirty-eight t.
23: 4 "Twenty-four t of them will supervise the work at
23: 4 Six t are to serve as officials and judges.
23: 5 Four t will work as gatekeepers, and another four t
will praise the LORD with the
27: 1 served for one month and had twenty-four t troops.
27: 2 There were twenty-four t troops in his division.
27: 4 There were twenty-four t troops in his division,
27: 5 There were twenty-four t troops in his division.
27: 7 There were twenty-four t troops in his division.
27: 8 There were twenty-four t troops in his division.
27: 9 There were twenty-four t troops in his division.
27:10 There were twenty-four t troops in his division.
27:11 There were twenty-four t troops in his division.
27:12 There were twenty-four t troops in his division.
27:13 There were twenty-four t troops in his division.
27:14 There were twenty-four t troops in his division.
27:15 There were twenty-four t troops in his division.
29:21 The next day they brought a t bulls, a t rams, and a
t male lambs as burnt offerings to the
2Ch 1: 6 and sacrificed a t burnt offerings on it.
1:14 fourteen hundred chariots and twelve t horses.
2: 2 He enlisted a force of seventy t common laborers,
2: 2 eighty t stonecutters in the hill country,
9: 9 Then she gave the king a gift of nine t pounds of
9:25 Solomon had four t stalls for his chariot horses and
twelve t horses.
12: 3 sixty t horsemen, and a countless army of foot
15:11 seven hundred oxen and seven t sheep and goats.
17:14 were 300,000 troops organized in units of one t,
25:11 where they killed ten t Edomite troops from Seir.
25:12 They captured another ten t and took them to the
25:13 killing three t people and carrying off great
29:33 six hundred bulls and three t sheep as sacrifices.
30:24 King Hezekiah gave the people one t bulls and
seven t sheep for offerings, and the officials
donated one t bulls and ten t sheep.
35: 7 from his personal property thirty t lambs
35: 7 the people's Passover offerings, and three t bulls.
35: 9 gave five t lambs and young goats and five
Est 9:16 killing seventy-five t of those who hated them.
Job 1: 3 He owned seven t sheep, three t camels, five
hundred teams of oxen,
9: 3 would it be possible to answer him even once in a t
42:12 For now he had fourteen t sheep, six t camels, one
t teams of oxen, and one t female donkeys.
Ps 3: 6 I am not afraid of ten t enemies / who surround me
50:10 forest are mine, / and I own the cattle on a t hills.
60: T and killed twelve t Edomites in the Valley of Salt.
84:10 in your courts / is better than a t anywhere else!
90: 4 For you, a t years are as yesterday! / They are like
91: 7 Though a t fall at your side, / though ten t are
dying around you,
105: 8 the commitment he made to a t generations.
Ecc 6: 6 He might live a t years twice over but not find
7:28 Just one out of every t men I interviewed can be
SS 4: 4 of David, jeweled with the shields of a t heroes.
5:10 lover is dark and dazzling, better than ten t others!
8:11 Each of them pays one t pieces of silver for its use.
8:12 O Solomon, you can take my t pieces of silver.
Isa 7:23 now worth as much as a t pieces of silver,
30:17 One of them will chase a t of you. Five of them
36: 8 If you can find two t horsemen in your entire army,
36: 8 he will give you two t horses for them to ride on!
Da 5: 1 King Belshazzar gave a great feast for a t of his
Am 5: 3 "When one of your cities sends a t men to battle,
Mt 14:21 About five t men had eaten from those five loaves,
15:38 There were four t men who were fed that day,
16: 9 Don't you remember the five t I fed with five
16:10 Don't you remember the four t I fed with seven
18:28 he went to a fellow servant who owed him a few t
Mk 5:13 and the entire herd of two t pigs plunged down the
6:44 Five t men had eaten from those five loaves!
8: 9 There were about four t people in the crowd that
8:19 What about the five t men I fed with five loaves of
8:20 "And when I fed the four t with seven loaves,
Lk 9:14 For there were about five t men there. "Just tell
14:31 and discussing whether his army of ten t is strong
14:31 twenty t soldiers who are marching against him?
16: 7 'A t bushels of wheat,' was the reply. 'Here,'
Jn 6:10 So all of them—the men alone numbered five t—
Ac 2:41 and added to the church—about three t in all.
4: 4 so that the number of believers totaled about five t
21:38 and took four t members of the Assassins out into
Ro 11: 4 I have seven t others who have never bowed down
1Co 4:15 For even if you had ten t others to teach you about
14:19 others than ten t words in an unknown language.
2Pe 3: 8 dear friends, that a day is like a t years to the Lord,
and a t years is like a day.
Rev 11:13 Seven t people died in that earthquake.
20: 2 Satan—and bound him in chains for a t years.
20: 3 the nations anymore until the t years were finished.
20: 4 and they reigned with Christ for a t years.
20: 5 not come back to life until the t years had ended.)
20: 6 and of Christ and will reign with him a t years.
20: 7 When the t years end, Satan will be let out of his

THOUSANDS (27) [THOUSAND]

Ex 34: 7 I show this unfailing love to many t by forgiving
Nu 10:36 "Return, O LORD, to the countless t of Israel!"
Dt 33:17 multitudes of Ephraim / and the t of Manasseh."
1Sa 4:17 "T of Israelite troops are dead on the battlefield.
18: 7 "Saul has killed his t, / and David his ten t!"
18: 8 "They credit David with ten t and me with only t.
21:11 'Saul has killed his t, and David his ten t'?"
29: 5 'Saul has killed his t, and David his ten t'?"
Ps 68:17 Surrounded by unnumbered t of chariots,
144:13 May the flocks in our fields multiply by the t, /
even tens of t,
Jer 32:18 You are loving and kind to t, though children
Da 11:12 and will have many t of his enemies killed.
Joel 3:14 T upon t are waiting in the valley of
Mic 6: 7 Should we offer him t of rams and tens of t of
rivers of olive oil?
Mt 26:53 Don't you realize that I could ask my Father for t
Lk 12: 1 the crowds grew until t were milling about
Ac 21:20 how many t of Jews have also believed,
Heb 12:22 and to t of angels in joyful assembly.
Jude 1:14 the Lord is coming / with t of his holy ones.
Rev 5:11 and I heard the singing of t and millions of angels

THREAD (15)

Ge 14:23 that I will not take so much as a single t or sandal
38:28 and the midwife tied a scarlet t around the wrist of
38:30 Then the baby with the scarlet t on his wrist was
Ex 28: 5 linen cloth and embroidered with gold t and blue,
28: 6 and skillfully embroidered with gold t and blue,
28: 8 fine linen cloth embroidered with gold t and blue,
28:15 fine linen cloth embroidered with gold t and blue,
39: 2 linen cloth and embroidered with gold t and blue,
39: 3 A skilled craftsman made gold t by beating gold
39: 5 and gold t, just as the LORD had commanded
39: 8 linen cloth and embroidered with gold t and blue,
Nu 19: 6 and scarlet t and throw them into the fire where the
Jdg 16:12 snapped the ropes from his arms as if they were t.
Pr 31:19 Her hands are busy spinning t, her fingers twisting
Jer 51:13 but your end has come. The t of your life is cut.

THREAT (6) [THREATEN, THREATENED, THREATENING, THREATENS, THREATS]

Ex 1: 9 "These Israelites are becoming a t to us
32:14 So the LORD withdrew his t and didn't bring
2Sa 12:10 the sword will be a constant t to your family,
Pr 16:14 The anger of the king is a deadly t; the wise do
Ecc 11:10 life before it, still faces the t of meaninglessness.
Eze 12:25 I will fulfill my t of destruction in your own

THREATEN (6) [THREAT]

Job 40:19 amazing handiwork. Only its Creator can t it.
Isa 26:11 O LORD, they do not listen when you t.
Eze 12:25 For I am the LORD! What I t always happens.
Mt 10:26 But don't be afraid of those who t you.
Eph 6: 9 Don't t them; remember, you both have the same
1Pe 2:23 When he suffered, he did not t to get even. He left

THREATENED (21) [THREAT]

Ex 32:14 bring against his people the disaster he had t.
Dt 2: 4 live in Seir. The Edomites will feel t, so be careful.
1Sa 19:17 "He t to kill me if I didn't help him."
2Sa 14:15 because my life and my son's life have been t.
2Ch 32:22 of Assyria and from all the others who t them.
Pr 13: 8 can pay a ransom, but the poor won't even get t.
Jer 15:10 I am neither a lender who has t to foreclose nor a
26: 9 And all the people t him as he stood in front of the
35:17 and Jerusalem all the disasters I have t."
39:16 says: I will do to this city everything I have t.
44:29 that all I have t will happen to you and that I will
Eze 12:28 I will now do everything I have t! I, the Sovereign
20: 8 Then I t to pour out my fury on them to satisfy my
20:13 So I t to pour out my fury on them, and I made
20:21 So again I t to pour out my fury on them in the
Jnh 1: 4 causing a violent storm that t to send them to the
3:10 and didn't carry out the destruction he had t.
Zec 11:16 who will not care for the sheep that are t by death,
Lk 8:23 A fierce storm developed that t to swamp them,
Ac 4:21 The council then t them further, but they finally let
Ro 8:35 or are hungry or cold or in danger or t with death?

THREATENING (6) [THREAT]

Ge 27:42 sent for Jacob and told him, "Esau is t to kill you.
Nu 22: 5 They cover the face of the earth and are t me.
2Ki 4: 1 has come, t to take my two sons as slaves."
2Ch 16:12 Even when the disease became life t, he did not
Ne 6:19 And Tobiah sent many t letters to intimidate me.
Hos 6: 5 slaughtered you with my words, t you with death.

THREATENS (1) [THREAT]

Jer 48:16 "Calamity is coming fast to Moab; it t ominously.

THREATS (11) [THREAT]

Lev 26:25 armies against you to carry out these covenant t.
1Sa 3:12 I am going to carry out all my t against Eli and his
Ps 10: 7 Their mouths are full of cursing, lies, and t.
38:13 But I am deaf to all their t. / I am silent before
55: 3 enemies shout at me, / making loud and wicked t.
55:11 t and cheating are rampant in the streets.
64: 1 Do not let my enemies' t overwhelm me.
Jer 1:12 and I will surely carry out my t of punishment."
Eze 2: 6 Don't be afraid even though their t are sharp as

Ac 4:29 And now, O Lord, hear their **t**, and give your
9: 1 Meanwhile, Saul was uttering **t** with every breath.

THREE (415) [THIRD, THREE-DAY, THREE-FIFTHS, THREE-PRONGED, THREE-YEAR, THREE-YEAR-OLD, TRIPLE-BRAIDED, TWO-THIRDS, 3]

THREE DAYS (75) Ge 31:22; 34:25; 40:12,13,18,19,20; 42:17; Ex 10:22; 14:5; 15:22; Nu 10:33; 33:8; Jos 1:11; 2:16,22; 3:2; 9:16,17; Jdg 14:14; 19:4; 1Sa 9:20; 30:1,12,13; 2Sa 20:4,5; 24:13,15; 1Ki 3:18; 12:5,12; 2Ki 2:17; 20:5,8; 1Ch 12:39; 21:12; 2Ch 10:5,12; 20:25; Ezr 8:15,32; 10:8,9; Ne 2:11; Est 4:16; 5:1; Isa 38:22; Am 4:4; Jnh 1:17; 3:3; Mt 12:40,40; 15:32; 17:23; 26:61; 27:40,63; Mk 8:2,31; 9:31; 10:34; 14:58; 15:29; Lk 2:46; 9:22; 24:21; Jn 2:19,20; Ac 9:9; 10:40; 25:1; 28:7,12,17

THREE MONTHS (16) Ge 38:24; Ex 2:2; 2Sa 6:11; 24:13; 2Ki 23:31; 24:8; 1Ch 13:14; 21:12; 2Ch 36:2,9; Lk 1:56; Ac 7:20; 19:8; 20:3; 28:11; Heb 11:23

THREE TIMES (26) Ex 23:17; 34:23,24; Nu 22:28,32,33; 24:10; Jdg 16:15; 1Ki 9:25; 17:21; 2Ki 13:18,19; Eze 21:14; Da 6:10,13; Mt 26:34,75; Mk 14:30,72; Lk 22:34,61; Jn 13:38; Ac 10:16; 11:10; 2Co 11:25,25

THREE YEARS (24) Lev 19:23; 25:21; Jdg 9:22; 2Sa 13:38; 21:1; 24:13; 1Ki 2:39; 10:22; 15:2; 22:1; 2Ki 17:5; 18:10; 24:1; 1Ch 21:12; 2Ch 9:21; 11:17; 13:2; 27:5; 31:16; Isa 16:14; 20:3; Lk 13:7; Ac 20:31; Gal 1:18

Ge 5:32 By the time Noah was 500 years old, he had **t** sons:
6:10 Noah had **t** sons: Shem, Ham, and Japheth.
6:16 Then put **t** decks inside the boat—bottom, middle,
9:18 Shem, Ham, and Japheth, the **t** sons of Noah,
9:19 From these **t** sons of Noah came all the people now
10: 1 of Shem, Ham, and Japheth, the **t** sons of Noah.
18: 2 he suddenly noticed **t** men standing nearby. He got
18: 6 Get **t** measures of your best flour, and bake some
29: 2 He saw in the distance **t** flocks of sheep lying in an
29:34 affection for me, since I have given him **t** sons!"
30:36 and they took them **t** days' distance from where
31:22 Laban didn't learn of their flight for **t** days.
34:25 But **t** days later, when their wounds were still sore,
38:24 About **t** months later, word reached Judah that
40:10 It had **t** branches that began to bud and blossom,
40:12 Joseph said. "The **t** branches mean **t** days.
40:13 Within **t** days Pharaoh will take you out of prison
40:16 "there were **t** baskets of pastries on my head.
40:18 Joseph told him. "The **t** baskets mean **t** days.
40:19 **T** days from now Pharaoh will cut off your head
40:20 Pharaoh's birthday came **t** days later, and he gave
42:17 So he put them all in prison for **t** days.
45:22 changes of clothes and **t** hundred pieces of silver!
50:23 He lived to see **t** generations of descendants of his
Ex 2: 2 baby he was and kept him hidden for **t** months.
10:22 was deep darkness over the entire land for **t** days.
14: 5 were not planning to return to Egypt after **t** days,
15:22 They traveled in this desert for **t** days without
21:11 If he fails in any of these **t** ways, she may leave as
23:14 "Each year you must celebrate **t** festivals in my
23:17 At these **t** times each year, every man in Israel
25:25 Put a rim about **t** inches wide around the top edge,
25:32 **t** branches going out from each side of the center
27:14 feet long, supported by **t** posts set into **t** bases.
27:15 feet long, supported by **t** posts set into **t** bases.
30: 2 It must be eighteen inches square and **t** feet high,
32:28 and about **t** thousand people died that day.
34:23 **T** times each year all the men of Israel must appear
34:24 the LORD your God those **t** times each year.
37:18 **t** going out from each side of the center stem.
37:25 It was eighteen inches square and **t** feet high,
38:14 and was supported by **t** posts set into **t** bases.
38:15 and was supported by **t** posts set into **t** bases.
Lev 19:23 leave the fruit unharvested for the first **t** years
20:14 All **t** of them must be burned to death to wipe out
23:13 A grain offering must accompany it consisting of **t**
23:17 These loaves must be baked from **t** quarts of
24: 5 choice flour, using **t** quarts of flour for each loaf.
25:21 a bumper crop, enough to support you for **t** years.
27: 6 a girl of that age is valued at **t** pieces of silver.
Nu 2: 9 These **t** tribes are to lead the way whenever the
2:16 These **t** tribes will be second in line whenever the
3:17 Levi had **t** sons, who were named Gershon,
7:86 The weight of the donated gold came to about **t**
10:33 They marched for **t** days after leaving the
11:31 were quail flying about **t** feet above the ground.
12: 4 and said, "Go out to the Tabernacle, all **t** of you!" And the **t** of them went out.
15: 6 give **t** quarts of choice flour mixed with two
20:27 The **t** of them went up Mount Hor together as the
22:28 you that deserves your beating me these **t** times?"
22:32 "Why did you beat your donkey those **t** times?"
22:33 **T** times the donkey saw me and shied away;
24:10 Instead, you have blessed them **t** times.
28: 9 They must be accompanied by a grain offering of **t**
28:12 five quarts with each bull, **t** quarts with the ram,
28:20 five quarts with each bull, **t** quarts with the ram,
28:28 five quarts with each bull, **t** quarts with the ram,
29: 3 five quarts with the bull, **t** quarts with the ram,
29: 9 with the bull, **t** quarts of choice flour with the ram,
29:14 the thirteen bulls, **t** quarts for each of the two rams,
33: 8 Then they traveled for **t** days into the Etham
35:14 **t** on the east side of the Jordan River and **t** on the west in the land of Canaan.
Dt 4:41 Then Moses set apart **t** cities of refuge east of the
16:16 every man in Israel must celebrate these **t** festivals:
17: 6 There must always be at least two or **t** witnesses.
19: 2 Then you must set apart **t** cities of refuge in the
19: 3 the LORD your God is giving you into **t** districts,
19: 7 That is why I am commanding you to set aside **t**
19: 9 you must designate **t** additional cities of refuge.
19:15 established by the testimony of two or **t** witnesses.
Jos 1:11 In **t** days you will cross the Jordan River and take
2:16 "Hide there for **t** days until the men who are
2:22 up into the hill country and stayed there **t** days.
3: 2 **T** days later, the Israelite leaders went through the
7: 3 more than two or **t** thousand of us to destroy it.
7: 4 So approximately **t** thousand warriors were sent,
9:16 **T** days later, the facts came out—these people of
9:17 to investigate and reached their towns in **t** days.
15:14 Caleb drove out the **t** Anakites—Sheshai, Ahiman,
18: 4 Select **t** men from each tribe, and I will send them
21:32 and Kartan—**t** towns with their pasturelands.
Jdg 1:20 who were descendants of the **t** sons of Anak.
7: 6 Only **t** hundred of the men drank from their hands.
7: 7 "With these **t** hundred men I will rescue you
7: 8 But he kept the **t** hundred men with him.
7:16 He divided the **t** hundred men into **t** groups
7:20 Then all **t** groups blew their horns and broke their
7:22 When the **t** hundred Israelites blew their horns,
8: 4 then crossed the Jordan River with his **t** hundred
9:22 After Abimelech had ruled over Israel for **t** years,
9:43 he divided his men into **t** groups and set an ambush
11:26 But now after **t** hundred years you make an issue
14:14 **T** days later they were still trying to figure it out.
15: 4 Then he went out and caught **t** hundred foxes.
15:11 So **t** thousand men of Judah went down to get
16:15 You've made fun of me **t** times now, and you still
16:27 and there were about **t** thousand on the roof who
19: 4 so he stayed **t** days, eating, drinking, and sleeping
1Sa 2:21 And the LORD gave Hannah **t** sons and two
9:20 about those donkeys that were lost **t** days ago,
10: 3 you will see **t** men coming toward you who are on
10: 3 One will be bringing **t** young goats, another will have **t** loaves of bread,
11:11 having divided his army into **t** detachments.
13: 2 Saul selected **t** thousand special troops from the
13: 5 The Philistines mustered a mighty army of **t**
13:17 **T** raiding parties soon left the camp of the
17:13 Jesse's **t** oldest sons—Eliab, Abinadab,
17:14 Since David's **t** oldest brothers were in the army,
20:20 and shoot **t** arrows to the side of the stone pile as
24: 2 So Saul chose **t** thousand special troops from
25: 2 He had **t** thousand sheep and a thousand goats,
26: 2 So Saul took **t** thousand of his best troops and went
30: 1 **T** days later, when David and his men arrived
30:12 had anything to eat or drink for **t** days and nights.
30:13 "My master left me behind **t** days ago because I
31: 2 on Saul and his sons, and they killed **t** of his sons—
31: 6 So Saul, **t** of his sons, his armor bearer, and his
31: 8 the bodies of Saul and his **t** sons on Mount Gilboa.
2Sa 2:18 Joab, Abishai, and Asahel, the **t** sons of Zeruiah,
2:31 But **t** hundred and sixty of Abner's men, all from
6:11 there with the family of Obed-edom for **t** months,
13:38 He stayed there in Geshur for **t** years.
14:27 He had **t** sons and one daughter. His daughter's
18:14 Then he took **t** daggers and plunged them into
20: 4 Amasa to mobilize the army of Judah within **t** days
20: 5 but it took him longer than the **t** days he had been
21: 1 famine during David's reign that lasted for **t** years,
23: 8 the Hacmonite, who was commander of the **T**—
23: 8 the **t** greatest warriors among David's men.
23: 9 Next in rank among the **T** was Eleazar son of
23:13 The **T** (who were among the Thirty—an elite
23:16 So the **T** broke through the Philistine lines,
23:17 This is an example of the exploits of the **T**.
23:18 He once used his spear to kill **t** hundred enemy
23:18 by such feats that he became as famous as the **T**.
23:19 their commander, though he was not one of the **T**.
23:22 that made Benaiah almost as famous as the **T**.
23:23 of the Thirty, though he was not one of the **T**.
24:12 is what the LORD says: I will give you **t** choices.
24:13 "Will you choose **t** years of famine throughout the land, **t** months of fleeing from your enemies, or **t** days of severe plague throughout your land?
24:15 upon Israel that morning, and it lasted for **t** days.
1Ki 2:39 But **t** years later, two of Shimei's slaves escaped to
3:18 **T** days later, she also had a baby. We were alone;
6: 6 The complex was **t** stories high, the bottom floor
6:10 there was a complex of rooms on **t** sides of the
6:36 of cedar beams after every **t** layers of hewn stone.
7: 3 by forty-five rafters that rested on **t** rows of pillars,
7: 4 On each of the side walls there were **t** rows of
7: 5 in frame; they were in sets of **t**, facing each other.
7:12 of cedar beams after every **t** layers of hewn stone,
7:25 **T** faced north, **t** faced west, **t** faced south, and **t** faced east.
7:26 The walls of the Sea were about **t** inches thick,
9:25 **T** times each year Solomon offered burnt offerings
10:17 He also made **t** hundred smaller shields of
10:22 Once every **t** years the ships returned, loaded down
11: 3 seven hundred wives and **t** hundred concubines.
12: 5 "Give me **t** days to think this over.
12:12 **T** days later, Jeroboam and all the people returned
15: 2 He reigned in Jerusalem **t** years. His mother was
17:21 And he stretched himself out over the child **t** times
18:32 the altar large enough to hold about **t** gallons.
22: 1 For **t** years there was no war between Aram
2Ki 2:17 So fifty men searched for **t** days but did not find
3: 9 and all **t** armies traveled along a roundabout route
3:10 "The LORD has brought the **t** of us here to let
3:13 For it was the LORD who called us **t** kings here
3:21 when the people of Moab heard about the **t** armies
3:23 "The **t** armies have attacked and killed each other!
9:32 And two or **t** eunuchs looked out at him.
11: 6 These **t** groups will all guard the palace.
13:18 king picked them up and struck the ground **t** times.
13:19 Now you will be victorious only **t** times."
13:25 Jehoash defeated Ben-hadad on **t** occasions,
17: 5 entire land, and for **t** years he besieged Samaria.
18:10 **T** years later, during the sixth year of King
20: 5 and **t** days from now you will get out of bed
20: 8 and that I will go to the Temple of the LORD **t**
23:31 and he reigned in Jerusalem **t** months.
24: 1 and paid him tribute for **t** years but then rebelled.
24: 8 and he reigned in Jerusalem **t** months.
25:18 assistant Zephaniah, and the **t** chief gatekeepers.
1Ch 2: 3 Judah had **t** sons through Bathshua, a Canaanite
2:16 Zeruiah had **t** sons named Abishai, Joab,
3:23 were Elioenai, Hizkiah, and Azrikam—**t** in all.
7: 6 **T** of Benjamin's sons were Bela, Beker,
8:39 Azel's brother Eshek had **t** sons: Ulam (the oldest),
10: 2 Saul and his sons, and they killed **t** of his sons—
10: 6 So Saul and his **t** sons died there together,
10:12 the bodies of Saul and his **t** sons back to Jabesh.
11:11 the Hacmonite, who was commander of the **T**—
11:11 the **t** greatest warriors among David's men.
11:11 He once used his spear to kill **t** hundred enemy
11:12 Next in rank among the **T** was Eleazar son of
11:15 The **T** (who were among the Thirty—an elite
11:18 So the **T** broke through the Philistine lines,
11:19 This is an example of the exploits of the **T**.
11:20 He once used his spear to kill **t** hundred enemy
11:20 by such feats that he became as famous as the **T**.
11:21 their commander, though he was not one of the **T**.
11:24 of the deeds that made Benaiah as famous as the **T**.
11:25 of the Thirty, though he was not one of the **T**.
12:39 They feasted and drank with David for **t** days,
13:14 there with the family of Obed-edom for **t** months,
21:10 is what the LORD says: I will give you **t** choices.
21:12 You may choose **t** years of famine, **t** months of destruction by your enemies, or **t** days of severe plague as the angel of the
23: 6 after the clans descended from the **t** sons of Levi—
23: 8 **T** of the descendants of Libni were Jehiel (the
23: 9 **T** of the descendants of Shimei were Shelomoth,
23:23 The **t** sons of Mushi were Mahli, Eder,
25: 5 honored him with fourteen sons and **t** daughters.
2Ch 4: 4 **T** faced north, **t** faced west, **t** faced south, and **t** faced east.
4: 5 The walls of the Sea were about **t** inches thick,
8:13 new moon festivals, and at the **t** annual festivals—
9:16 He also made **t** hundred smaller shields of
9:21 Once every **t** years the ships returned, loaded down
10: 5 "Come back in **t** days for my answer."
10:12 **T** days later, Jeroboam and all the people returned
11:17 and for **t** years they supported Rehoboam son of
11:19 Mahalath had **t** sons—Jeush, Shemariah,
13: 2 He reigned in Jerusalem **t** years. His mother was
14: 9 an army of a million men and **t** hundred chariots.
20:25 so much plunder that it took them **t** days just to
25:13 killing **t** thousand people and carrying off great
27: 5 For the next **t** years, he received from them an
29:33 hundred bulls and **t** thousand sheep as sacrifices.
31:16 They also distributed the gifts to all males **t** years
35: 7 people's Passover offerings, and **t** thousand bulls.
35: 8 and **t** hundred bulls as Passover offerings.
36: 2 he became king, but he reigned only **t** months.
36: 9 but he reigned in Jerusalem only **t** months and ten
Ezr 2:61 **T** families of priests—Hobaiah, Hakkoz,
6: 4 Every **t** layers of specially prepared stones will be
8:15 and we camped there for **t** days while I went over
8:32 safely in Jerusalem, where we rested for **t** days.
10: 8 Those who failed to come within **t** days would,
10: 9 Within **t** days, all the people of Judah
Ne 2:11 **T** days after my arrival at Jerusalem,
7:63 "**T** families of priests—Hobaiah, Hakkoz,
9: 3 their God was read aloud to them for about **t** hours.
9: 3 Then for **t** more hours they took turns confessing
Est 4:16 Do not eat or drink for **t** days, night or day.
5: 1 **T** days later, Esther put on her royal robes
9:15 on March 8 and killed **t** hundred more people,
Job 1: 2 He had seven sons and **t** daughters.
1: 3 **t** thousand camels, five hundred teams of oxen,
1:17 "**T** bands of Chaldean raiders have stolen your
2:11 **T** of Job's friends were Eliphaz the Temanite,
32: 1 Job's **t** friends refused to reply further to him
32: 3 He was also angry with Job's **t** friends
42:13 gave Job seven more sons and **t** more daughters.
Pr 30:15 There are **t** other things—no, four!—that are never
30:18 There are **t** things that amaze me—no, four things I
30:21 There are **t** things that make the earth tremble—
30:29 There are **t** stately monarchs on the earth—no,
Ecc 4:12 **T** are even better, for a triple-braided cord is not
Isa 16:14 the LORD says, "Within **t** years, without fail,
17: 6 Only two or **t** remain in the highest branches,
19:24 The **t** will be together, and Israel will be a blessing
20: 3 around naked and barefoot for the last **t** years.
38:22 to the Temple of the LORD **t** days from now?"
Jer 36:23 Whenever Jehudi finished reading **t** or four
52:24 assistant Zephaniah, and the **t** chief gatekeepers.
Eze 5: 1 Use a scale to weigh the hair into **t** equal parts.
14:16 Even if these **t** men were there, the Sovereign
14:16 Those **t** alone would be saved, but the land would
14:18 Even if these **t** men were in the land, the Sovereign
21:14 take the sword and brandish it twice, even **t** times,
40:10 There were **t** guard alcoves on each side of the
40:21 too, there were **t** guard alcoves on each side,
40:43 There were hooks, each **t** inches long, fastened to
41: 6 These rooms were built in **t** levels, one above the
42: 3 The two blocks were built **t** levels high and stood

42: 6 Since there were t levels and they did not have
48:31 there will be t gates, each one named after a tribe
Da 1:15 Daniel and his t friends looked healthier and better
3:22 and killed the soldiers as they threw the t men in!
3:24 "Didn't we tie up t men and throw them into the
6:10 He prayed t times a day, just as he had always
6:13 your law. He still prays to his God t times a day."
7: 5 and it had t ribs in its mouth between its teeth.
7: 8 T of the first horns were wrenched out, roots
7:12 As for the other t beasts, their authority was taken
7:20 up afterward and destroyed t of the other horns.
7:24 from the other ten, who will subdue t of them.
10: 2 I, Daniel, had been in mourning for t weeks.
11: 2 T more Persian kings will reign, to be succeeded
Am 4: 4 each morning and bring your tithes every t days!
Jnh 1:17 Jonah was inside the fish for t days and t nights.
3: 3 a city so large that it took t days to see it all.
Zec 11: 8 I got rid of their t evil shepherds in a single month.
Mt 12:40 For as Jonah was in the belly of the great fish for t days and t nights,
12:40 in the heart of the earth for t days and t nights.
14:25 About t o'clock in the morning Jesus came to
15:32 They have been here with me for t days, and they
17: 4 I'll make t shrines, one for you, one for Moses,
17:23 but t days later he will be raised from the dead."
18:16 you say may be confirmed by two or t witnesses.
18:20 For where two or t gather together because they
20: 5 and again around t o'clock he did the same thing.
26:34 the rooster crows, you will deny me t times."
26:61 the Temple of God and rebuild it in t days.' "
26:75 the rooster crows, you will deny me t times."
27:40 can destroy the Temple and build it again in t days,
27:45 darkness fell across the whole land until t o'clock.
27:46 At about t o'clock, Jesus called out with a loud
27:63 'After t days I will be raised from the dead.'
Mk 5:40 and his t disciples into the room where the girl was
6:48 About t o'clock in the morning he came to them,
8: 2 They have been here with me for t days, and they
8:31 be killed, and t days later he would rise again.
9: 5 "We will make t shrines—one for you, one for
9:31 but t days later he will rise from the dead."
10:34 and kill him, but after t days he will rise again."
14:30 rooster crows twice, you will deny me t times."
14:58 and in t days I will build another, made without
14:72 rooster crows twice, you will deny me t times."
15:29 can destroy the Temple and rebuild it in t days,
15:33 darkness fell across the whole land until t o'clock.
Lk 1:56 Mary stayed with Elizabeth about t months and
2:46 T days later they finally discovered him. He was in
4:25 when there was no rain for t and a half years
9:22 but t days later I will be raised from the dead."
9:33 We will make t shrines—one for you, one for
10:36 "Now which of these t would you say was a
11: 5 at midnight, wanting to borrow t loaves of bread.
12:52 be split apart, t in favor of me, and two against—
13: 7 he said to his gardener, 'I've waited t years,
22:34 you have denied t times that you even know me."
22:61 tomorrow morning, you will deny me t times."
23:33 All t were crucified there—Jesus on the center
23:44 and darkness fell across the whole land until t
24:21 to rescue Israel. That all happened t days ago.
Jn 2:19 this temple, and in t days I will raise it up."
2:20 to build this Temple, and you can do it in t days?"
6:19 They were t or four miles out when suddenly they
13:38 you will deny t times that you even know me.
21: 8 for they were only out about t hundred feet.
Ac 2:41 and added to the church—about t thousand in all.
3: 1 to take part in the t o'clock prayer service.
5: 7 About t hours later his wife came in, not knowing
7:20 His parents cared for him at home for t months.
9: 9 He remained there blind for t days. And all that
10: 3 One afternoon about t o'clock, he had a vision in
10:16 The same vision was repeated t times.
10:19 said to him, "T men have come looking for you.
10:30 "Four days ago I was praying in my house at t
10:40 but God raised him to life t days later. Then God
11:10 "This happened t times before the sheet and all it
11:11 then t men who had been sent from Caesarea
17: 2 and for t Sabbaths in a row he interpreted the
19: 8 and preached boldly for the next t months,
20: 3 where he stayed for t months. He was preparing to
20: 9 a deep sleep and fell t stories to his death below.
20:31 Remember the t years I was with you—
25: 1 T days after Festus arrived in Caesarea to take over
28: 7 He welcomed us courteously and fed us for t days.
28:11 It was t months after the shipwreck that we set sail
28:12 first stop was Syracuse, where we stayed t days.
28:15 Others joined us at The T Taverns. When Paul saw
28:17 T days after Paul's arrival, he called together the
1Co 13:13 There are t things that will endure—faith, hope,
14:27 or t should speak in an unknown language.
14:29 Let two or t prophesy, and let the others evaluate
2Co 11:25 T times I was beaten with rods. Once I was stoned. T times I was shipwrecked.
12: 8 T different times I begged the Lord to take it away.
13: 1 by the testimony of two or t witnesses."
Gal 1:18 It was not until t years later that I finally went to
1Ti 5:19 unless there are two or t witnesses to accuse him.
Heb 10:28 mercy on the testimony of two or t witnesses.
11:23 It was by faith that Moses' parents hid him for t
Jas 5:17 would fall, none fell for the next t and a half years!
1Jn 5: 7 So we have these t witnesses—
5: 8 the water, and the blood—and all t agree.
Rev 6: 6 wheat bread or t loaves of barley for a day's pay.
8:13 because of what will happen when the last t angels
9:18 the people on earth were killed by these t plagues
11: 9 And for t and a half days all peoples, tribes,
11:11 But after t and a half days, the spirit of life from
16:13 And I saw t evil spirits that looked like frogs leap
16:19 The great city of Babylon split into t pieces,
21:13 There were t gates on each side—east, north,

THREE-DAY (3) [DAY, THREE]

Ex 3:18 Let us go on a t journey into the wilderness to offer
5: 3 "Let us take a t trip into the wilderness so we can
8:27 We must take a t trip into the wilderness to offer

THREE-FIFTHS (2) [FIVE, THREE]

Lev 14:10 mixed with olive oil and t of a pint of olive oil.
14:21 oil as a grain offering and t of a pint of olive oil.

THREE-PRONGED (1) [THREE]

1Sa 2:13 Eli's sons would send over a servant with a t fork.

THREE-YEAR (2) [THREE, YEAR]

Da 1: 5 They were to be trained for a t period, and
1:18 When the t training period ordered by the king was

THREE-YEAR-OLD (4) [THREE, YEAR]

Ge 15: 9 LORD told him, "Bring me a t heifer, a t female goat, a t ram, a turtledove, and a young pigeon."
1Sa 1:24 They brought along a t bull for the sacrifice

THREESCORE [KJV] See SIXTY

THRESH (2) [THRESHED, THRESHES, THRESHING]

Isa 28:27 He doesn't t all his crops the same way. A heavy
1Co 9:10 and t the grain expect a share of the harvest,

THRESHED (3) [THRESH]

Dt 16:13 after the grain has been t and the grapes have been
Isa 21:10 O my people, t and winnowed, I have told you
Am 1: 3 They beat down my people in Gilead as grain is t

THRESHES (1) [THRESH]

Isa 28:28 He t it under the wheels of a cart, but he doesn't

THRESHING (43) [THRESH]

Ge 50:10 When they arrived at the t floor of Atad,
Lev 26: 5 Your t season will extend until the grape harvest,
Nu 15:20 as you do with the first grain from the t floor.
18:27 as though it were the first grain from your own t
18:30 as though it came from your own t floor
Dt 15:14 from your flock, your t floor, and your winepress.
Jdg 6:11 Gideon son of Joash had been t wheat at the
6:37 I will put some wool on the t floor tonight.
Ru 3: 2 Tonight he will be winnowing barley at the t floor.
3: 3 Then go to the t floor, but don't let Boaz see you
3: 6 So she went down to the t floor that night
3:14 must know that a woman was here at the t floor."
1Sa 23: 1 were at Keilah stealing grain from the t floors.
2Sa 6: 6 But when they arrived at the t floor of Nacon,
24:16 LORD was by the t floor of Araunah the Jebusite.
24:18 and build an altar to the LORD on the t floor of
24:21 "I have come to buy your t floor and to build an
24:22 and you can use the t tools and ox yokes for wood
24:24 So David paid him fifty pieces of silver for the t
1Ki 22:10 were sitting on thrones at the t floor near the gate
1Ch 13: 9 But when they arrived at the t floor of Nacon,
21:15 standing by the t floor of Araunah the Jebusite.
21:18 the LORD at the t floor of Araunah the Jebusite.
21:20 who was busy t wheat at the time, turned and saw
21:21 he left his t floor and bowed to the ground before
21:22 "Let me buy this t floor from you at its full price.
21:23 and you can use the t tools for wood to build a fire
21:25 hundred pieces of gold in payment for the t floor.
21:28 he offered sacrifices there at Araunah's t floor.
2Ch 3: 1 The Temple was built on the t floor of Araunah the
18: 9 were sitting on thrones at the t floor near the gate
Job 39:12 on it to return, bringing your grain to the t floor?
Isa 27:12 He will bring them to his great t floor—
28:27 A t wheel is never rolled on cummin; instead,
41:15 You will be a new t instrument with many sharp
Jer 51:33 "Babylon is like wheat on a t floor, about to be
Da 2:35 The pieces were crushed as small as chaff on a t
Hos 9: 1 offering sacrifices to other gods on every t floor.
Joel 2:24 The t floors will again be piled high with grain,
Am 1: 3 Gilead as grain is threshed with t sledges of iron.
Mic 4:12 and trampled like bundles of grain on a t floor.
Mt 3:12 Then he will clean up the t area, storing the grain
Lk 3:17 Then he will clean up the t area, storing the grain

THRESHOLD (5) [THRESHOLDS]

Jdg 19:27 She was lying face down, with her hands on the t.
1Sa 5: 5 who enters the temple of Dagon will step on its t.
Eze 40: 6 the steps and measured the t of the gateway;
40: 7 The gateway's inner t, which led to the foyer at the
47: 1 flowing eastward from beneath the Temple t.

THRESHOLDS (1) [THRESHOLD]

2Ch 3: 7 and t throughout the Temple were overlaid with

THREW (72) [THROW]

Ge 37:24 and t him into the pit. This pit was normally used
39:20 and t him into the prison where the king's
50: 1 Joseph t himself on his father and wept over him
Ex 4: 3 So Moses t it down, and it became a snake!
4:25 She t the foreskin at Moses' feet and said,
7:10 Aaron t down his staff before Pharaoh and his
10:11 And Pharaoh t them out of the palace.
14:24 of fire and cloud, and he t them into confusion.
15:25 Moses took the branch and t it into the water.
32:19 terrible anger, he t the stone tablets to the ground,
32:24 they brought them to me, I t them into the fire—
Nu 16: 4 he t himself down with his face to the ground.
Dt 9:21 I t the dust into the stream that cascades down the
Jos 7: 6 tore their clothing in dismay, t dust on their heads,
8:29 down the body and t it in front of the city gate.
10:10 The LORD t them into a panic, and the Israelites
Jdg 4:15 the LORD t Sisera and all his charioteers
8:25 and each one t in a gold earring he had gathered.
9:53 a woman on the roof t down a millstone that
14:10 Samson t a party at Timnah, as was the custom of
15:17 he finished speaking, he t away the jawbone;
2Sa 11:21 by a woman who t a millstone down on him?'
16: 6 He t stones at the king and the king's officers
18:17 They t Absalom's body into a deep pit in the forest
20:12 him off the road into a field and t a cloak over him.
20:22 and they cut off Sheba's head and t it out to Joab.
1Ki 19:19 over to him and t his cloak across his shoulders
2Ki 2:21 supplied the town with water and t the salt into it.
4:41 Then he t it into the kettle and said, "Now it's all
6: 6 the place, Elisha cut a stick and t it into the water.
9:33 So they t her out the window, and some of her
13:21 So they hastily t the body they were burying into
23: 6 pole to dust and t the dust in the public cemetery.
2Ch 16:10 so angry with Hanani for saying this that he t him
25:12 and took them to the top of a cliff and t them off,
30:14 incense altars and t them into the Kidron Valley.
Ne 9:26 They t away your law, they killed the prophets
13: 8 and t all of Tobiah's belongings from the room.
Job 2:12 and t dust into the air over their heads to
Pr 7:13 She t her arms around him and kissed him,
Jer 36:23 He then t it into the fire, section by section,
41: 7 but ten of them and t their bodies into a cistern.
La 3:53 They t me into a pit and dropped stones on me.
Eze 28:17 So I t you to the earth and exposed you to the
Da 3:21 So they tied them up and t them into the furnace,
3:22 and killed the soldiers as they t the three men in!
Jnh 1: 5 and t the cargo overboard to lighten the ship.
1:15 picked Jonah up and t him into the raging sea,
2: 3 You t me into the ocean depths, and I sank down
Zec 11:13 and t them to the potters in the Temple of the
Mt 21: 7 animals to him and t their garments over the colt,
27: 5 Then Judas t the money onto the floor of the
Mk 1:26 spirit screamed and t the man into a convulsion,
9:20 it t the child into a violent convulsion, and he fell
9:26 and t the boy into another violent convulsion
10:50 Bartimaeus t aside his coat, jumped up, and came
11: 7 the colt to Jesus and t their garments over it,
12: 8 murdered him and t his body out of the vineyard.
Lk 4:35 The demon t the man to the floor as the crowd
9:42 to the ground and t him into a violent convulsion.
19:35 and t their garments over it for him to ride on.
22:65 And they t all sorts of terrible insults at him.
Jn 9:34 to teach us?" And they t him out of the synagogue.
19:24 clothes among themselves and t dice for my robe."
Ac 22:23 They yelled, t off their coats, and tossed handfuls
27:19 The following day they even t out the ship's
27:29 so they t out four anchors from the stern
2Pe 2: 4 he t them into hell, in gloomy caves and darkness
Rev 8: 5 fire from the altar and t it down upon the earth;
12: 4 down one-third of the stars, which he t to the earth.
18:21 He t it into the ocean and shouted, "Babylon,
20: 3 The angel t him into the bottomless pit, which he

THRICE [KJV] See THREE (TIMES)

THRILL (3) [THRILLED]

Ps 92: 4 You t me, LORD, with all you have done for me!
Pr 23:16 my heart will t when you speak what is right
Isa 60: 5 eyes will shine, and your hearts will t with joy,

THRILLED (1) [THRILL]

SS 5: 4 tried to unlatch the door, and my heart t within me.

THRIVE (6) [THRIVING]

Ge 26:22 has made room for us, and we will be able to t."
Ps 102:28 children's children / will t in your presence."
Isa 44: 4 They will t like watered grass, like willows on a
Eze 16: 7 And I helped you to t like a plant in the field.
17:10 Then when the vine is transplanted, will it t?
Zec 9:17 and women will t on the abundance of grain

THRIVING (4) [THRIVE]

Ps 37:35 proud and evil people t like mighty trees.
52: 8 But I am like an olive tree, / t in the house of God.
Jer 11:16 the LORD, once called them a t olive tree,
Hos 10:13 cultivated wickedness and raised a t crop of sins.

THROAT (4) [THROATS]

Ps 69: 3 from crying for help; / my t is parched and dry.
116: 3 Death had its hands around my t; / the terrors of
Pr 23: 2 If you are a big eater, put a knife to your t,
Mt 18:28 He grabbed him by the t and demanded instant

THROATS (1) [THROAT]

Ps 115: 7 walk with their feet, / or utter sounds with their t!

THRONE (176) [ENTHRONED, THRONES]

Ex 1: 8 Then a new king came to the **t** of Egypt who knew
11: 5 from the oldest son of Pharaoh, who sits on the **t**,
12: 29 from the firstborn son of Pharaoh, who sat on the **t**,
17: 16 dared to raise their fist against the LORD's **t**,
Dt 17: 18 "When he sits on the **t** as king, he must copy these
1Sa 14: 47 Now when Saul had secured his grasp on Israel's **t**,
2Sa 7: 13 And I will establish the **t** of his kingdom forever.
7: 16 before me, and your **t** will be secure forever.' "
16: 8 You stole his **t**, and now the LORD has given it
1Ki 1: 13 would be the next king and would sit upon your **t**?
1: 17 would be the next king and would sit on your **t**.
1: 24 will be the next king and that he will sit on your **t**?
1: 30 Solomon will be the next king and will sit on my **t**,
1: 35 When you bring him back here, he will sit on my **t**.
1: 46 Solomon is now sitting on the royal **t** as king.
1: 48 who today has chosen someone to sit on my **t**
2: 4 one of them will always sit on the **t** of Israel.'
2: 12 David, and he was firmly established on the **t**.
2: 19 The king rose from his **t** to meet her, and he bowed
2: 19 When he sat down on his **t** again, he ordered that a **t** be brought for his mother,
2: 24 confirmed me and placed me on the **t** of my father,
2: 33 to David and his descendants and to his **t** forever."
2: 45 one of David's descendants always sit on this **t**."
5: 5 told him, 'Your son, whom I will place on your **t**,
7: 7 There was also the Hall of the **T**, also known as the
9: 5 then I will establish the **t** of your dynasty over
9: 5 'You will never fail to have a successor on the **t** of
10: 9 in you and has placed you on the **t** of Israel.
10: 18 Then the king made a huge ivory **t** and overlaid it
10: 19 The **t** had six steps and a rounded back. On both
10: 19 the figure of a lion standing on each side of the **t**.
10: 20 No other **t** in all the world could be compared with
11: 37 And I will place you on the **t** of Israel, and you will
22: 19 I saw the LORD sitting on his **t** with all the
2Ki 11: 19 the palace, and the king took his seat on the royal **t**.
25: 27 Evil-merodach ascended to the Babylonian **t**.
1Ch 17: 12 for me. And I will establish his **t** forever.
17: 14 for all time, and his **t** will be secure forever.' "
22: 10 And I will establish the **t** of his kingdom over
28: 5 he chose Solomon to succeed me on the **t** of his
29: 23 So Solomon took the **t** of the LORD in place of
2Ch 7: 18 then I will not let anyone take away your **t**. This is
9: 8 in you and has placed you on the **t** to rule for him.
9: 17 Then the king made a huge ivory **t** and overlaid it
9: 18 The **t** had six steps, and there was a footstool of
9: 18 the figure of a lion standing on each side of the **t**.
9: 19 No other **t** in all the world could be compared with
13: 5 and his descendants the **t** of Israel forever?
18: 18 I saw the LORD sitting on his **t** with all the
23: 20 the palace, and they seated the king on the royal **t**.
Ezr 4: 5 and lasted until King Darius of Persia took the **t**.
Est 1: 2 At that time he ruled his empire from his **t** at the
5: 1 The king was sitting on his royal **t**,
Job 23: 3 I would go to his **t** and talk with him there.
26: 9 He shrouds his **t** with his clouds.
Ps 2: 6 "I have placed my chosen king on the **t**
7: 7 before you. / Sit on your **t** high above them.
9: 4 from your **t**, you have judged with fairness.
9: 7 reigns forever, / executing judgment from his **t**.
22: 3 are holy. / The praises of Israel surround your **t**.
33: 14 From his **t** he observes / all who live on the earth.
45: 6 Your **t**, O God, endures forever and ever.
47: 8 reigns above the nations, / sitting on his holy **t**.
89: 4 they will sit on your **t** from now until eternity.' "
89: 7 far more awesome than those who surround his **t**.
89: 14 Your **t** is founded on two strong pillars—
89: 29 his **t** will be as endless as the days of heaven.
89: 36 will go on forever; / his **t** is as secure as the sun,
89: 44 have ended his splendor / and overturned his **t**.
93: 2 Your **t**, O LORD, has been established from time
97: 2 and justice are the foundation of his **t**.
99: 1 He sits on his **t** between the cherubim.
103: 19 The LORD has made the heavens his **t**;
132: 11 "I will place your descendants on your **t**.
Pr 20: 28 protect the king; his **t** is made secure through love.
Ecc 4: 15 to help such a youth, even to help him take the **t**.
Isa 6: 1 He was sitting on a lofty **t**, and the train of his robe
9: 7 and justice from the **t** of his ancestor David.
11: 10 In that day the heir to David's **t** will be a banner of
14: 13 ascend to heaven and set my **t** above God's stars.
14: 22 children's children, so they will never sit on his **t**.
16: 5 then David's **t** will be established by love.
16: 5 From that **t** a faithful king will reign, one who
24: 23 Then the LORD Almighty will mount his **t** on
66: 1 "Heaven is my **t**, and the earth is my footstool.
Jer 3: 17 In that day Jerusalem will be known as The **T** of
13: 13 from the king sitting on David's **t** and from the
14: 21 Do not disgrace yourself and the **t** of your glory.
17: 12 But we worship at your **t**—eternal, high,
17: 25 of David sitting on the **t** here in Jerusalem.
22: 2 you king of Judah, sitting on David's **t**.
22: 4 of David sitting on the **t** here in Jerusalem.
22: 18 who succeeded his father, Josiah, on the **t**:
22: 30 for none of his children will ever sit on the **t** of
23: 5 I will place a righteous Branch on King David's **t**.
29: 16 LORD says about the king who sits on David's **t**
33: 15 At that time I will bring to the **t** of David a
33: 17 forever have a descendant sitting on the **t** of Israel.
33: 21 he no longer have a descendant to reign on his **t**.
36: 30 He will have no heirs to sit on the **t** of David.
43: 10 I will set his **t** on these stones that I have hidden.
49: 38 I will set my **t** in Elam," says the LORD, "and I
52: 31 Evil-merodach ascended to the Babylonian **t**.
La 5: 19 Your **t** continues from generation to generation.
Eze 1: 26 was what looked like a **t** made of blue sapphire.
1: 26 And high above this **t** was a figure whose
10: 1 I saw what appeared to be a **t** of blue sapphire
28: 2 am a god! I sit on a divine **t** in the heart of the sea.'
43: 7 this is the place of my **t** and the place where I will
Da 2: 21 he removes kings and sets others on the **t**.
5: 20 he was brought down from his royal **t** and stripped
7: 9 He sat on a fiery **t** with wheels of blazing fire,
7: 16 So I approached one of those standing beside the **t**
Jnh 3: 6 he stepped down from his **t** and took off his royal
Mic 1: 3 He leaves his **t** in heaven and comes to earth,
Zec 6: 13 royal honor and will rule as king from his **t**.
6: 13 He will also serve as priest from his **t**, and there
Mt 5: 34 it is a sacred vow because heaven is God's **t**.
19: 28 of Man, sit upon my glorious **t** in the Kingdom,
23: 22 you are swearing by the **t** of God and by God, who sits on the **t**.
25: 31 with him, then he will sit upon his glorious **t**.
Lk 1: 32 And the Lord God will give him the **t** of his
Ac 2: 30 descendants would sit on David's **t** as the Messiah.
2: 33 Now he sits on the **t** of highest honor in heaven,
7: 18 then a new king came to the **t** of Egypt who knew
7: 49 'Heaven is my **t**, / and the earth is my footstool.
12: 21 sat on his **t**, and made a speech to them.
Ro 15: 12 Isaiah said, / "The heir to David's **t** will come,
Heb 1: 8 "Your **t**, O God, endures forever and ever.
4: 16 So let us come boldly to the **t** of our gracious God.
12: 2 place of highest honor beside God's **t** in heaven.
Rev 1: 4 still to come; from the sevenfold Spirit before his **t**;
2: 13 "I know that you live in the city where that great **t**
3: 21 everyone who is victorious to sit with me on my **t**,
3: 21 as I was victorious and sat with my Father on his **t**.
4: 2 and I saw a **t** in heaven and someone sitting on it!
4: 3 The one sitting on the **t** was as brilliant as
4: 3 And the glow of an emerald circled his **t** like a
4: 5 And from the **t** came flashes of lightning
4: 5 And in front of the **t** were seven lampstands with
4: 6 In front of the **t** was a shiny sea of glass,
4: 6 the center and around the **t** were four living beings,
4: 9 and honor and thanks to the one sitting on the **t**,
4: 10 And they lay their crowns before the **t** and say,
5: 1 the right hand of the one who was sitting on the **t**.
5: 5 tribe of Judah, the heir to David's **t**, has conquered.
5: 6 but was now standing between the **t** and the four
5: 7 from the right hand of the one sitting on the **t**.
5: 11 and millions of angels around the **t** and the living
5: 13 and power / belong to the one sitting on the **t**
6: 16 hide us from the face of the one who sits on the **t**
7: 9 standing in front of the **t** and before the Lamb.
7: 10 "Salvation comes from our God on the **t** and from
7: 11 And all the angels were standing around the **t**
7: 11 And they fell face down before the **t**
7: 15 That is why they are standing in front of the **t** of
7: 15 And he who sits on the **t** will live among them
7: 17 For the Lamb who stands in front of the **t** will be
8: 3 to be offered on the gold altar before the **t**.
12: 5 the dragon and was caught up to God and to his **t**.
13: 2 gave him his own power and **t** and great authority.
14: 3 sang a wonderful new song in front of the **t** of God
16: 10 Then the fifth angel poured out his bowl on the **t** of
16: 17 And a mighty shout came from the **t** of the Temple
18: 7 and sorrows. She boasts, 'I am queen on my **t**.
19: 4 and worshiped God, who was sitting on the **t**.
19: 5 And from the **t** came a voice that said, "Praise our
20: 11 And I saw a great white **t**, and I saw the one who
20: 12 both great and small, standing before God's **t**.
21: 3 I heard a loud shout from the **t**, saying, "Look,
21: 5 And the one sitting on the **t** said, "Look, I am
22: 1 flowing from the **t** of God and of the Lamb,
22: 3 For the **t** of God and of the Lamb will be there,
22: 16 I am both the source of David and the heir to his **t**.

THRONES (18) [THRONE]

1Ki 22: 10 were sitting on **t** at the threshing floor near the gate
2Ch 18: 9 were sitting on **t** at the threshing floor near the gate
Ps 122: 5 Here stand the **t** where judgment is given, / the **t** of the dynasty of David.
Jer 1: 15 They will set their **t** at the gates of the city.
13: 18 "Come down from your **t** and sit in the dust,
Eze 26: 16 All the seaport rulers will step down from their **t**
Da 7: 9 I watched as **t** were put in place and the Ancient
Hag 2: 22 I will overthrow royal **t**, destroying the power of
Mt 19: 28 have been my followers will also sit on twelve **t**,
20: 23 "But I have no right to say who will sit on the **t**
Mk 10: 40 but I have no right to say who will sit on the **t** next
Lk 1: 52 He has taken princes from their **t** / and exalted the
22: 30 And you will sit on **t**, judging the twelve tribes of
1Co 4: 8 I wish you really were on your **t** already, for
Rev 4: 4 Twenty-four **t** surrounded him, and twenty-four
11: 16 And the twenty-four elders sitting on their **t** before
20: 4 Then I saw **t**, and the people sitting on them had

THRONG (1) [THRONGED, THRONGS]

Ps 68: 27 Then comes a great **t** of rulers from Judah

THRONGED (1) [THRONG]

Mk 5: 24 Jesus went with him, and the crowd **t** behind.

THRONGS (1) [THRONG]

Ps 68: 11 and **t** of women shout the happy news.

THROUGH (616) [THROUGHOUT]

Ge 1: 16 the lesser one, the moon, presides **t** the night.
12: 3 All the families of the earth will be blessed **t** you."
12: 6 Traveling **t** Canaan, they came to a place near
16: 2 Perhaps I can have children **t** her." And Abram
18: 18 and all the nations of the earth will be blessed **t**
19: 32 That way we will preserve our family line **t** our
20: 8 what had happened, great fear swept **t** the crowd.
21: 12 for Isaac is the son **t** whom your descendants will
22: 18 and **t** your descendants, all the nations of the earth
24: 65 "Who is that man walking **t** the fields to meet
25: 4 These were all descendants of Abraham **t** Keturah.
25: 12 the son of Abraham **t** Hagar, Sarah's Egyptian
26: 4 And **t** your descendants all the nations of the earth
28: 14 All the families of the earth will be blessed **t** you
30: 29 "You know how faithfully I've served you **t** these
31: 37 You have searched **t** everything I own. Now show
31: 40 I worked for you **t** the scorching heat of the day and **t** cold and sleepless nights.
36: 14 Esau also had sons **t** Oholibamah, the daughter of
42: 23 for he had been speaking to them **t** an interpreter.
46: 15 Jacob's descendants **t** Leah numbered thirty-three.
46: 18 These sixteen were descendants of Jacob **t** Zilpah,
46: 25 These seven were the descendants of Jacob **t**
Ex 10: 10 ones along! I can see **t** your wicked intentions.
10: 13 an east wind to blow all that day and **t** the night.
11: 4 LORD says: About midnight I will pass **t** Egypt.
12: 12 On that night I will pass **t** the land of Egypt
12: 23 For the LORD will pass **t** the land and strike
12: 28 did just as the LORD had commanded **t** Moses
13: 17 God did not lead them on the road that runs **t**
13: 18 So God led them along a route **t** the wilderness
14: 16 and a path will open up before you **t** the sea.
14: 16 Then all the people of Israel will walk **t** on dry
14: 21 and the LORD opened up a path **t** the water with
14: 22 So the people of Israel walked **t** the sea on dry
14: 29 The people of Israel had walked **t** the middle of the
15: 19 But the people of Israel had walked **t** on dry land!
28: 24 The two gold cords will go **t** the rings on the
34: 10 the awesome power I will display **t** you.
35: 29 in the work the LORD had given them **t** Moses—
39: 17 The two gold cords were put **t** the gold rings on the
Lev 8: 36 everything the LORD had commanded **t** Moses.
10: 11 all the laws that the LORD has given **t** Moses."
11: 46 and all the living things that move **t** the water
18: 5 my laws and regulations, you will find life **t** them.
26: 46 gave to the Israelites **t** Moses on Mount Sinai.
27: 34 gave to the Israelites **t** Moses on Mount Sinai.
Nu 4: 37 just as the LORD had commanded **t** Moses.
4: 45 just as the LORD had commanded **t** Moses.
4: 49 just as the LORD had commanded **t** Moses.
9: 23 and they did whatever the LORD told them **t**
10: 13 move arrived, the LORD gave the order **t** Moses.
12: 2 They said, "Has the LORD spoken only **t** Moses?
12: 2 Hasn't he spoken **t** us, too?" But the LORD
13: 17 "Go northward **t** the Negev into the hill country.
13: 22 they passed first **t** the Negev and arrived at
15: 22 commands that the LORD has given you **t** Moses.
15: 23 everything the LORD has commanded **t** Moses.
20: 14 You know all the hardships we have been **t**,
20: 17 Please let us pass **t** your country. We will be careful not to go **t** your fields
20: 19 We only want to pass **t** your country and nothing
20: 20 "Stay out! You may not pass **t** our land."
20: 21 Because Edom refused to allow Israel to pass **t**
21: 18 left the wilderness and proceeded on **t** Mattanah,
21: 22 "Let us travel **t** your land. We will stay on the
23: 19 to act? / Has he ever promised and not carried it **t**?
25: 8 Phinehas thrust the spear all the way **t** the man's
26: 28 Two clans were descended from Joseph **t**
27: 23 just as the LORD had commanded **t** Moses.
31: 23 must be passed **t** fire in order to be made
34: 8 then to Lebo-hamath, and on **t** Zedad
36: 13 **t** Moses while they were camped on the plains of
Dt 1: 19 we left Mount Sinai and traveled **t** the great
1: 40 and go on back **t** the wilderness toward the Red
2: 4 "You will be passing **t** the country belonging to
2: 7 and has watched your every step **t** this great
2: 8 and avoided the road **t** the Arabah Valley that
2: 8 traveled northward along the desert route **t** Moab,
2: 27 'Let us pass **t** your land. We will stay on the main
2: 28 All we want is permission to pass **t** your land.
2: 29 at Mount Seir allowed us to go **t** their country,
2: 29 Let us pass **t** until we cross the Jordan into the land
2: 30 But King Sihon refused to allow you to pass **t**,
8: 2 Remember how the LORD your God led you **t**
8: 15 Do not forget that he led you **t** the great
15: 17 take an awl and push it **t** his earlobe into the door.
21: 4 plowed nor planted with a stream running **t** it.
29: 5 For forty years I led you **t** the wilderness, yet your
29: 16 and how we traveled **t** the lands of enemy nations
34: 12 And it was **t** Moses that the LORD demonstrated
Jos 1: 11 "Go **t** the camp and tell the people to get their
2: 10 path for you **t** the Red Sea when you left Egypt.
2: 15 she let them down by a rope **t** the window.
3: 2 days later, the Israelite leaders went **t** the camp
14: 2 in accordance with the LORD's command **t**
15: 7 From that point it went **t** the valley of Achor to
15: 8 then passed **t** the valley of the son of Hinnom,
16: 1 **t** the wilderness and into the hill country of Bethel.
18: 12 then west **t** the hill country and the wilderness of
22: 9 according to the LORD's command **t** Moses.
24: 3 I gave him many descendants **t** his son Isaac.
24: 17 As we traveled **t** the wilderness among our
Jdg 3: 4 the LORD had given to their ancestors **t** Moses.
3: 23 down the latrine and escaped **t** the sewage access.
4: 21 Then she drove the tent peg **t** his temple and into
4: 22 lying there dead, with the tent peg **t** his temple.
5: 26 She pounded the tent peg **t** his head, piercing his
5: 28 **T** the window she watched for his return, saying,

11:17 of Edom asking for permission to pass **t** his land.
11:17 but he wouldn't let them pass **t** either.
11:18 went around Edom and Moab **t** the wilderness.
11:19 asking for permission to cross **t** his land to get to
11:20 But King Sihon didn't trust Israel to pass **t** his
15: 5 and let the foxes run **t** the fields of the Philistines.
17: 8 to stop at Micah's house as he was traveling **t**.
Ru 2:22 Stay with his workers right **t** the whole harvest.
2:23 Then she worked with them **t** the wheat harvest,
3:18 The man won't rest until he has followed **t** on this.
1Sa 9: 4 and traveled all **t** the hill country of Ephraim,
9:14 entered the town, and as they passed **t** the gates,
19:12 So she helped him climb out **t** a window, and he
26: 8 "Let me thrust that spear **t** him. I'll pin him to the
31: 4 and kill me before these pagan Philistines run me **t**
2Sa 2:23 so Abner thrust the butt end of his spear **t** Asahel's
2:23 and the spear came out **t** his back.
2:29 and his men retreated **t** the Jordan Valley.
2:29 the Jordan River, traveling all **t** the morning,
4: 7 they fled across the Jordan Valley **t** the night.
5: 8 "Go up **t** the water tunnel into the city and destroy
5:20 "He burst **t** my enemies like a raging flood!"
5:20 (which means "the Lord who bursts **t**").
12:25 and sent word **t** Nathan the prophet that his name
15:26 But if he is **t** with me, then let him do what seems
17:29 and thirsty after your long march **t** the
23: 2 "The Spirit of the LORD speaks **t** me;
23:16 So the Three broke **t** the Philistine lines,
24: 8 Having gone **t** the entire land, they completed their
1Ki 2:26 and you suffered right along with him **t** all his
6:12 I will fulfill **t** you the promise I made to your
8:56 wonderful promises he gave **t** his servant Moses.
12:15 son of Nebat **t** the prophet Ahijah from Shiloh.
14:17 and the child died just as she walked **t** the door of
14:18 as the LORD had promised **t** the prophet Ahijah.
16: 7 and his family **t** the prophet Jehu son of Hanani.
16:12 as the LORD had promised **t** the prophet Jehu.
17:16 just as the LORD had promised **t** Elijah.
17:24 of God, and that the LORD truly speaks **t** you."
22:28 return safely, the LORD has not spoken **t** me!"
22:36 Just as the sun was setting, the cry ran **t** his troops:
2Ki 1: 2 fell **t** the latticework of an upper room at his palace
1:17 just as the LORD had promised **t** Elijah.
3: 9 a roundabout route **t** the wilderness for seven days.
3:12 "Then the LORD will speak **t** him."
3:26 to break **t** the enemy lines near the king of Edom,
5: 1 because **t** him the LORD had given Aram great
9:36 which he spoke **t** his servant Elijah from Tishbe:
10:10 The LORD declared **t** his servant Elijah that this
10:17 just as the LORD had promised **t** Elijah.
11:19 They went **t** the gate of the guards and into the
14:25 of Israel, had promised **t** Jonah son of Amittai,
17:13 and which I gave you **t** my servants the prophets."
18:12 all the laws the LORD had given **t** his servant
21: 8 the whole law that was given **t** my servant Moses
21:10 Then the LORD said **t** his servants the prophets:
23:16 This happened just as the LORD had promised **t**
24: 2 just as the LORD had promised **t** his prophets.
25: 4 and fled **t** the gate between the two walls behind
1Ch 2: 3 Judah had three sons **t** Bathshua, a Canaanite
2: 4 Later Judah had twin sons **t** Tamar, his widowed
5:23 The half-tribe of Manasseh spread **t** the land from
6:33 His genealogy was traced back **t** Joel, Samuel,
6:39 Asaph's genealogy was traced back **t** Berekiah,
6:44 Ethan's genealogy was traced back **t** Kishi, Abdi,
10: 4 and run me **t** before these pagan Philistines come
11: 3 just as the LORD had promised **t** Samuel.
11:18 So the Three broke **t** the Philistine lines,
14:11 "He used me to burst **t** my enemies like a raging
14:11 (which means "the Lord who bursts **t**").
21:19 the instructions the LORD had given him **t** Gad.
22:13 and regulations that the LORD gave to Israel **t**
24:27 From the descendants of Merari **t** Jaaziah,
26:25 His relatives **t** Eliezer were Rehabiah, Jeshaiah,
2Ch 17: 9 and traveled around **t** all the towns of Judah,
18:27 return safely, the LORD has not spoken **t** me!"
20:16 You will find them coming up **t** the ascent of Ziz at
23:20 They went **t** the Upper Gate and into the palace,
29:25 that the LORD had given to King David **t** Gad,
32: 1 giving orders for his army to break **t** their walls.
32: 4 cutting off the brook that ran **t** the fields.
32:30 and brought the water down **t** a tunnel to the west
33: 8 laws, and regulations given **t** Moses—
33:11 They put a ring **t** his nose, bound him in bronze
34:14 Law of the LORD as it had been given **t** Moses.
35: 6 Follow all the instructions that the LORD gave **t**
36:21 So the message of the LORD spoken **t** Jeremiah
Ezr 2:36 The family of Jedaiah (**t** the line of Jeshua) | 973
Ne 1: 7 and regulations that you gave us **t** your servant
2: 7 instructing them to let me travel safely **t** their
2:13 I went out **t** the Valley Gate, past the Jackal's
2:14 but my donkey couldn't get **t** the rubble.
7:39 The family of Jedaiah (**t** the line of Jeshua) | 973
8:14 they discovered that the LORD had commanded **t**
9:11 for your people so they could walk **t** on dry land!
9:14 And you commanded them, **t** Moses your servant,
9:19 and the pillar of fire showed them the way **t** the
9:30 You sent your Spirit, who, **t** the prophets,
Est 1:15 the king's orders, properly sent **t** his eunuchs?"
3: 8 "There is a certain race of people scattered **t** all
6: 9 and to lead him **t** the city square on the king's own
6:11 own horse, and led him **t** the city square, shouting,
Job 8:17 Its roots grow down **t** a pile of rocks to hold it
14:14 and **t** my struggle I would eagerly wait for release.
15:34 Their homes, enriched **t** bribery, will be consumed
22:13 am doing! How can he judge **t** the thick darkness?
26: 4 all these wise sayings? Whose spirit speaks **t** you?
29: 3 way before me and I walked safely **t** the darkness.
36:15 who suffer. For he gets their attention **t** adversity.
41: 2 Can you tie it with a rope **t** the nose or pierce its
41:30 They tear up the ground as it drags **t** the mud.
Ps 18:12 The brilliance of his presence broke **t** the clouds,
23: 4 **t** the dark valley of death, / I will not be afraid,
25: 7 look instead **t** the eyes of your unfailing love,
37:15 But they will be stabbed **t** the heart with their own
37:19 They will survive **t** hard times; / even in famine
39:12 For I am your guest— / a traveler passing **t**,
42: 8 **T** each day the LORD pours his unfailing love
upon me, / and **t** each night I sing his songs,
63: 6 thinking of you, / meditating on you **t** the night.
66: 6 He made a dry path **t** the Red Sea, / and his people
66:12 our broken bodies. / We went **t** fire and flood.
68: 7 from Egypt, / when you marched **t** the wilderness,
72:17 May all nations be blessed **t** him / and bring him
74: 3 Walk **t** the awful ruins of the city; / see how the
77:19 Your road led **t** the sea, / your pathway **t** the
78:13 For he divided the sea before them and led them **t**!
78:52 of sheep, / guiding them safely **t** the wilderness.
83:14 As a fire roars **t** a forest / and as a flame sets
84: 6 When they walk **t** the Valley of Weeping, / it will
90: 1 Lord, **t** all the generations / you have been our
105:41 to form a river **t** the dry and barren land.
107:39 **t** oppression, trouble, and sorrow,
119:37 worthless things, / and give me life **t** your word.
119:148 I stay awake **t** the night, / thinking about your
136:14 He led Israel safely **t**, / His faithful love endures
136:16 Give thanks to him who led his people **t** the
Pr 1: 3 **T** these proverbs, people will receive instruction in
13: 6 Godliness helps people all **t** life, while the evil are
15:19 A lazy person has trouble all **t** life; the path of the
20:18 Plans succeed **t** good counsel; don't go to war
20:28 protect the king; his throne is made secure **t** love.
24: 3 built by wisdom and becomes strong **t** good sense.
24: 4 **T** knowledge its rooms are filled with all sorts of
30:19 how an eagle glides **t** the sky, / how a snake
Ecc 5: 4 don't delay in following **t**, for God takes no
5: 5 to promise something that you don't follow **t** on.
5:11 except perhaps to watch it run **t** your fingers!
9: 9 Live happily with the woman you love **t** all the
SS 2: 9 Now he is looking in **t** the window, gazing into the
Isa 1:12 Why do you keep parading **t** my courts with your
11:15 The LORD will make a dry path **t** the Red Sea.
13:15 Anyone who is captured will be run **t** with a sword.
28:11 God will speak to them **t** foreign oppressors who
29:18 and blind people will see **t** the gloom and darkness.
30: 6 On **t** the wilderness they go, where lions
35: 8 And a main road will go **t** that once deserted land.
40: 3 "Make a highway for the LORD **t** the wilderness.
40: 3 a straight, smooth road **t** the desert for our God.
42:21 **T** it he had planned to show the world that he is
43: 2 When you go **t** deep waters and great trouble,
43: 2 When you go **t** rivers of difficulty, you will not
43: 2 When you walk **t** the fire of oppression, you will
43:16 I am the LORD, who opened a way **t** the waters,
making a dry path **t** the sea.
43:19 I will make a pathway **t** the wilderness for my
45: 2 smash down gates of bronze and cut **t** bars of iron.
48: 1 You don't follow **t** on any of your promises,
48: 8 from your earliest childhood, rotten **t** and **t**.
48:21 They were not thirsty when he led them **t** the
49: 9 **T** you I am saying to the prisoners of darkness,
58: 5 You humble yourselves by going **t** the motions of
60:10 in my anger, I will have mercy on you **t** my grace.
63: 9 He lifted them up and carried them **t** all the years.
63:11 "Where is the one who brought Israel **t** the sea,
63:13 Where is the one who led them **t** the bottom of the
63:13 They were like fine stallions racing **t** the desert,
Jer 2: 2 and followed me even **t** the barren wilderness.
2: 6 out of Egypt and led us **t** the barren wilderness—
6: 6 to be punished, for she is wicked **t** and **t**.
9:12 so completely that no one even dares to travel **t** it?
9:21 For death has crept in **t** our windows and has
14: 8 Why are you like someone passing **t** the land,
14:17 has been run **t** with a sword and lies mortally
17:27 **t** the gates of Jerusalem just as on other days,
20: 4 captive to Babylon or run them **t** with the sword.
21: 1 The LORD spoke **t** Jeremiah when King
22: 4 The king will ride **t** the palace gates in chariots
27: 3 and Sidon **t** their ambassadors to King Zedekiah in
29:19 though I have spoken to them repeatedly **t** my
31: 2 I will care for the survivors as they travel **t** the
32:36 'It will fall to the king of Babylon **t** war, famine,
34:12 So the LORD gave them this message **t** Jeremiah:
37: 2 land listened to what the LORD said **t** Jeremiah.
37:13 But as he was walking **t** the Benjamin Gate,
39: 2 on July 18, the Babylonians broke **t** the wall,
39: 4 They went out **t** a gate between the two walls
51:55 against her; the noise of battle rings **t** the city.
52: 7 and fled **t** the gate between the two walls behind
La 1: 2 She sobs **t** the night; tears stream down her cheeks.
4:12 would have believed an enemy could march **t** the
4:14 They wandered blindly **t** the streets, so defiled by
Eze 1:28 a glowing halo, like a rainbow shining **t** the clouds.
9: 4 "Walk **t** the streets of Jerusalem and put a mark on
9: 5 "Follow him **t** the city and kill everyone whose
12: 5 Dig a hole **t** the wall while they are watching and
carry your possessions out **t** it.
12: 7 I dug **t** the wall with my hands and went out into
12:12 "Even Zedekiah will leave Jerusalem at night **t** a
16:40 in a mob to stone you and run you **t** with swords.
26:10 and your walls will shake as the horses gallop **t**
30:10 **T** King Nebuchadnezzar of Babylon, I will destroy
33:28 so ruined that no one will even travel **t** them.
34: 6 They have wandered **t** the mountains and hills,
36:23 And when I reveal my holiness **t** you before their
38:17 when I announced **t** Israel's prophets that in future
40: 6 Then he went over to the gateway that goes **t** the
40:16 narrowed inward **t** the walls of the guard alcoves
40:17 Then the man brought me **t** the gateway into the
41: 7 A stairway led up from the bottom level **t** the
42:15 he led me out **t** the east gateway to measure the
43: 4 LORD came into the Temple **t** the east gateway.
44: 2 No man will ever pass **t** it, for the LORD,
44: 3 he may come and go only **t** the gateway's foyer."
44: 4 Then the man brought me **t** the north gateway to
44:19 by transmitting holiness to them **t** this clothing.
45:20 of the new year for anyone who has sinned **t** error
46: 8 "The prince must enter the gateway **t** the foyer,
46: 9 But when the people come in **t** the north gateway
46: 9 And those who entered **t** the south gateway must
46:19 Then the man brought me **t** the entrance beside the
46:20 avoid carrying the sacrifices **t** the outer courtyard
47: 2 The man brought me outside the wall **t** the north
47: 2 There I could see the stream flowing out **t** the
47: 8 "This river flows east **t** the desert into the Jordan
47:15 toward Hethlon, then on **t** Lebo-hamath to Zedad;
Da 2: 8 The king replied, "I can see **t** your trick! You are
2:43 forming alliances with each other **t** intermarriage.
4: 3 will last forever, / his rule **t** all generations.
9:10 for we have not followed the laws he gave us **t** his
11:40 invade various lands and sweep **t** them like a flood.
Hos 1: 2 When the LORD first began speaking to Israel **t**
5: 4 You are a prostitute **t** and **t**, and you cannot
7: 6 Their plot smolders **t** the night, and in the morning
11: 6 War will swirl **t** their cities; their enemies will
crash **t** their gates and destroy
14: 8 giving my fruit to you all **t** the year."
Joel 2: 8 They lunge **t** the gaps, and no weapon can stop
2: 9 all the houses, climbing like thieves **t** the windows.
3:20 and Jerusalem will endure **t** all future generations.
Am 2:10 from Egypt and led you **t** the desert for forty years
3: 7 first of all, I warn you **t** my servants the prophets.
4: 3 You will leave by going straight **t** the breaks in the
5: 6 If you don't, he will roar **t** Israel like a fire,
5:11 and steal what little they have **t** taxes and unfair
5:17 for I will pass **t** and destroy them all.
Jnh 4: 7 The next morning at dawn the worm ate **t** the stem
Mic 2: 3 After I am **t** with you, none of you will ever again
2:13 He will bring you **t** the gates of your cities of
5: 5 invade our land and break **t** our defenses,
6:12 The rich among you have become wealthy **t**
Na 2: 4 race recklessly along the streets and **t** the squares,
3: 2 and chariots clatter as they bump wildly **t** the
Hag 1: 1 the LORD gave a message **t** the prophet Haggai
1: 3 So the LORD sent this message **t** the prophet
2: 1 the LORD sent another message **t** the prophet
Zec 1: 6 But all the things I said **t** my servants the prophets
4:12 that pour out golden oil **t** two gold tubes?"
5: 1 I looked up again and saw a scroll flying **t** the air.
7: 7 **t** the prophets years ago when Jerusalem
7:12 had sent them by his Spirit **t** the earlier prophets.
7:14 so desolate that no one even traveled **t** it.
10:11 They will pass safely **t** the sea of distress,
11: 1 so that fire may sweep **t** your cedar forests.
11:11 the LORD was speaking to them **t** my actions.
13: 9 I will bring that group **t** the fire and make them
14: 5 You will flee **t** this valley, for it will reach across
Mal 1: 1 the LORD gave to Israel **t** the prophet Malachi.
Mt 1:22 All of this happened to fulfill the Lord's message **t**
2:15 This fulfilled what the Lord had spoken **t** the
7:13 "You can enter God's Kingdom only **t** the narrow
8:17 This fulfilled the word of the Lord **t** Isaiah,
8:28 so dangerous that no one could go **t** that area.
9: 8 Fear swept **t** the crowd as they saw this happen
9:26 The report of this miracle swept **t** the entire
9:35 Jesus traveled **t** all the cities and villages of that
10:20 it will be the Spirit of your Father speaking **t** you.
12: 1 At about that time Jesus was walking **t** some
15:17 "Anything you eat passes **t** the stomach and
19:24 it is easier for a camel to go **t** the eye of a needle
20: 3 "At nine o'clock in the morning he was passing **t**
26:75 Suddenly, Jesus' words flashed **t** Peter's mind:
Mk 1:28 The news of what he had done spread quickly **t**
2: 1 and the news of his arrival spread quickly **t** the
2: 4 They couldn't get to Jesus **t** the crowd, so they dug
t the clay roof above his head.
2:12 and pushed his way **t** the stunned onlookers.
2:23 One Sabbath day as Jesus was walking **t** some
4:28 First a leaf blade pushes **t**, then the heads of wheat
5:26 She had suffered a great deal from many doctors **t**
5:27 so she came up behind him **t** the crowd
7:19 but only passes **t** the stomach and then comes out
9:26 be dead. A murmur ran **t** the crowd, "He's dead."
9:30 Leaving that region, they traveled **t** Galilee.
10:25 It is easier for a camel to go **t** the eye of a needle
11:27 As Jesus was walking **t** the Temple area,
12:15 Jesus saw **t** their hypocrisy and said, "Who are
14:72 Suddenly, Jesus' words flashed **t** Peter's mind:
Lk 1:70 just as he promised / **t** his holy prophets long ago.
1:77 how to find salvation / **t** forgiveness of their sins.
4:30 but he slipped away **t** the crowd and left them.
5:18 They tried to push **t** the crowd to Jesus,
6: 1 One Sabbath day as Jesus was walking **t** some
8:39 So he went all **t** the city telling about the great
11:43 from everyone as you walk **t** the markets!
13:22 Jesus went **t** the towns and villages, teaching as he
16: 3 I'm **t** here, and I don't have the strength to go out
18:25 It is easier for a camel to go **t** the eye of a needle
19: 1 Jesus entered Jericho and made his way **t** the town.
20:23 He saw **t** their trickery and said,
Jn 1: 5 The light shines **t** the darkness, and the darkness

1:10 But although the world was made t him, the world
1:17 For the law was given t Moses; God's unfailing love and faithfulness came t Jesus Christ.
4:4 He had to go t Samaria on the way.
4:22 know all about him, for salvation comes t the Jews.
4:46 In the course of his journey t Galilee, he arrived at
6:31 our ancestors ate manna while they journeyed t the
7:14 Then, midway t the festival, Jesus went up to the
7:24 Think this t and you will see that I am right."
8:12 follow me, you won't be stumbling t the darkness,
10:1 rather than going t the gate, must surely be a thief
10:2 For a shepherd enters t the gate.
10:9 the gate. Those who come in t me will be saved.
10:23 walking t the section known as Solomon's
11:55 so they could go t the cleansing ceremony before
12:12 Jesus was on the way to Jerusalem swept t the city.
14:6 No one can come to the Father except t me.
14:10 but my Father who lives in me does his work t me.
Ac 1:16 ago by the Holy Spirit, speaking t King David.
2:22 wonders, and signs t him, as you well know.
3:21 as God promised long ago t his prophets.
3:25 'T your descendants all the families on earth will
4:25 you spoke long ago by the Holy Spirit t our
4:30 and wonders be done t the name of your holy
7:35 T the angel who appeared to him in the burning
7:36 t the Red Sea, and back and forth t the wilderness
7:44 "Our ancestors carried the Tabernacle with them t
9:25 in a large basket t an opening in the city wall.
9:42 The news raced t the whole town, and many
10:36 that there is peace with God t Jesus Christ, who is
10:37 You know what happened all t Judea, beginning in
10:43 in him will have their sins forgiven t his name."
12:10 So they passed t and started walking down the
13:18 He put up with them t forty years of wandering
14:22 enter into the Kingdom of God t many tribulations.
14:24 Then they traveled back t Pisidia to Pamphylia.
15:4 They reported on what God had been doing t their
15:9 and them, for he also cleansed their hearts t faith.
15:12 and wonders God had done t them among the
16:6 Next Paul and Silas traveled t the area of Phrygia
16:8 they went on t Mysia to the city of Troas.
17:1 and Silas traveled t the towns of Amphipolis
19:1 in Corinth, Paul traveled t the interior provinces.
19:17 The story of what happened spread quickly all t
19:38 take the case at once. Let them go t legal channels.
20:2 the believers in all the towns he passed t.
20:3 his life, so he decided to return t Macedonia.
21:4 These disciples prophesied t the Holy Spirit that
21:19 accomplished among the Gentiles t his ministry.
21:26 and the next day he went t the purification ritual
28:25 when he said to our ancestors t Isaiah the prophet,
Ro 1:2 This Good News was promised long ago by God t
1:5 T Christ, God has given us the privilege
1:8 How I thank God t Jesus Christ for each one of
1:17 "It is t faith that a righteous person has life."
2:28 because you have gone t the Jewish ceremony of
3:24 He has done this t Christ Jesus, who has freed us
3:28 So we are made right with God t faith and not by
5:15 one man, Adam, brought death to many t his sin.
5:15 brought forgiveness to many t God's bountiful gift.
5:17 live in triumph over sin and death t this one man,
5:21 and resulting in eternal life t Jesus Christ our Lord.
6:11 and able to live for the glory of God t Christ Jesus.
6:23 but the free gift of God is eternal life t Christ Jesus
7:18 I know I am rotten t and t so far as my old
8:2 t Christ Jesus from the power of sin that leads to
8:13 But if t the power of the Holy Spirit you turn from
8:37 overwhelming victory is ours t Christ, who loved
9:7 "Isaac is the son t whom your descendants will be
10:6 But the way of getting right with God t faith says,
12:6 when you have faith that God is speaking t you.
15:13 May you overflow with hope t the power of the
15:17 Christ Jesus has done t me in my service to God.
15:19 I have won them over by the miracles done t me as
15:26 in Jerusalem, who are going t such hard times.
16:27 alone is wise, be the glory forever t Jesus Christ.
1Co 1:21 the world would never find him t human wisdom,
3:5 only servants. T us God caused you to believe.
3:13 Everyone's work will be put t the fire to see
3:15 but like someone escaping t a wall of flames.
8:6 t whom God made everything and t whom we have been given life.
10:1 and he brought them all safely t the waters of the
12:6 but it is the same God who does the work t all of
13:7 always hopeful, and endures t every circumstance.
14:21 speak to my own people / t unknown languages / and t the lips of foreigners.
15:10 but God who was working t me by his grace.
15:21 just as death came into the world t a man, Adam,
15:21 now the resurrection from the dead has begun t
15:57 victory over sin and death t Jesus Christ our Lord!
16:5 for I am planning to travel t Macedonia.
2Co 1:5 the more God will shower us with his comfort t
1:8 about the trouble we went t in the province of
1:8 and we thought we would never live t it.
1:20 say "Amen" when we give glory to God t Christ.
3:4 all this because of our great trust in God t Christ.
4:10 T suffering, these bodies of ours constantly share
5:18 who brought us back to himself t what Christ did.
5:21 so that we could be made right with God t Christ.
8:2 Though they have been going t much trouble
8:11 Now you should carry this project t to completion
9:13 You will be glorifying God t your generous gifts.
9:14 because of the wonderful grace of God shown t
11:33 But I was lowered in a basket t a window in the
12:9 so that the power of Christ may work t me.
13:3 you all the proof you want that Christ speaks t me.
Gal 1:5 That is why all glory belongs to God t all the ages
1:6 you to share the eternal life he gives t Christ.
2:8 For the same God who worked t Peter for the
2:8 Jews worked t me for the benefit of the Gentiles.
2:17 But what if we seek to be made right with God t
3:8 when he said, "All nations will be blessed t you."
3:11 "It is t faith that a righteous person has life."
3:14 T the work of Christ Jesus, God has blessed the
3:14 Christians receive the promised Holy Spirit t faith.
3:24 So now, t faith in Christ, we are made right with
3:26 So you are all children of God t faith in Christ
4:19 I feel as if I am going t labor pains for you again,
5:5 promised to us who are right with God t faith.
5:9 a little yeast spreads quickly t the whole batch of
5:11 still preaching salvation t the cross of Christ alone.
Eph 1:5 family by bringing us to himself t Jesus Christ.
1:7 so rich in kindness that he purchased our freedom t
2:7 as shown in all he has done for us t Christ Jesus.
2:18 may come to the Father t the same Holy Spirit
2:22 T him you Gentiles are also joined together as part
3:6 and enjoy together the promise of blessings t
3:11 and it has now been carried out t Christ Jesus our
3:16 give you mighty inner strength t his Holy Spirit.
3:21 and in Christ Jesus forever and ever t endless ages.
4:6 who is over us all and in us all and living t us all.
4:22 which is rotten t and t, full of lust
4:32 one another, just as God t Christ has forgiven you.
Php 3:14 t Christ Jesus, is calling us up to heaven.
Col 1:16 Christ is the one t whom God created everything in
1:16 Everything has been created t him and for him.
1:22 He has done this t his death on the cross in his own
2:10 and you are complete t your union with Christ.
3:17 all the while giving thanks t him to God the Father.
1Th 3:3 disturbed by the troubles you were going t.
5:9 For God decided to save us t our Lord Jesus Christ,
2Th 2:13 a salvation that came t the Spirit who makes you
1Ti 2:15 But women will be saved t childbearing and by
4:14 Do not neglect the spiritual gift you received t the
2Ti 1:1 the life he has promised t faith in Christ Jesus.
1:9 to show his love and kindness to us t Christ Jesus.
1:10 and showed us the way to everlasting life t the
Tit 3:5 our sins and gave us a new life t the Holy Spirit.
Heb 1:1 and in many ways to our ancestors t the prophets.
1:2 in these final days, he has spoken to us t his Son.
1:2 and t the Son he made the universe and everything
2:2 The message God delivered t angels has always
2:10 T the suffering of Jesus, God made him a perfect
2:18 Since he himself has gone t suffering
4:7 God announced this t David a long time later in the
6:19 It leads us t the curtain of heaven into God's inner
7:9 paid a tithe to Melchizedek t their ancestor
7:25 to save everyone who comes to God t him.
10:20 life-giving way that Christ has opened up for us t
11:18 "Isaac is the son t whom your descendants will be
11:29 It was by faith that the people of Israel went right t
13:20 he produce in you, t the power of Jesus Christ,
Jas 2:18 but I will show you my faith t my good deeds."
1Pe 1:21 T Christ you have come to trust in God. And
4:10 them well so that God's generosity can flow t you.
4:11 Then speak as though God himself were speaking t
4:11 Then God will be given glory in everything t Jesus
4:12 be surprised at the fiery trials you are going t,
5:9 are going t the same kind of suffering you are.
2Pe 3:2 our Lord and Savior commanded t your apostles.
1Jn 4:9 the world so that we might have eternal life t him.
4:12 and his love has been brought to full expression t
3Jn 1:5 care of the traveling teachers who are passing t,
Jude 1:25 alone is God our Savior, t Jesus Christ our Lord.
Rev 8:13 And I heard a single eagle crying loudly as it flew t
14:6 And I saw another angel flying t the heavens,
14:8 Then another angel followed him t the skies,
22:14 so they can enter t the gates of the city and eat the

THROUGHLY [KJV] See SURELY, THOROUGHLY, TRULY

THROUGHOUT (238) [THROUGH]

Ge 1:29 I have given you the seed-bearing plants t the earth
5:24 He enjoyed a close relationship with God t his life.
6:14 Then construct decks and stalls t its interior.
41:29 be a period of great prosperity t the land of Egypt.
41:46 he made a tour of inspection t the land.
41:55 T the land of Egypt the people began to starve.
41:57 because the famine was severe t the world.
43:1 But there was no relief from the terrible famine t
45:2 His sobs could be heard t the palace, and the news
47:13 and the crops continued to fail t Egypt and Canaan.
47:26 Joseph then made it a law t the land of Egypt—
49:7 scatter their descendants / t the nation of Israel.
Ex 3:15 my name, and it will be used t all generations.
5:12 So the people scattered t the land in search of
7:21 There was blood everywhere t the land of Egypt.
8:16 The dust will turn into swarms of gnats t the land
8:21 If you refuse, I will send swarms of flies t Egypt.
9:10 boils broke out on the people and animals t Egypt.
9:16 and that my fame might spread t the earth.
9:22 and cause the hail to fall t Egypt, on the people,
10:15 neither tree nor plant, t the land of Egypt.
11:6 Then a loud wail will be heard t the land of Egypt;
12:30 and loud wailing was heard t the land of Egypt.
13:15 so the LORD killed all the firstborn males t the
36:6 and this message was sent t the camp:
38:24 all of which was used t the Tabernacle.
40:38 could see it. This continued t all their journeys.
Lev 7:36 This regulation applies t the generations to come."
25:9 blow the trumpets loud and long t the land.
Nu 6:5 "They must never cut their hair t the time of their
11:32 all that day and t the night and all the next day,
15:21 T the generations to come, you are to present this
15:38 'T the generations to come you must make tassels
28:14 offering on the first day of each month t the year.
36:8 The daughters t the tribes of Israel who are in line
Dt 2:25 Beginning today I will make all people t the earth
11:12 He watches over it day after day t the year!
16:4 Let no yeast be found in any house t your land for
16:18 They will judge the people fairly t the land.
28:40 You will grow olive trees t your land, but you will
Jos 6:27 and his name became famous t the land.
24:31 Israel served the LORD t the lifetime of Joshua
Jdg 2:7 And the Israelites served the LORD t the lifetime
2:18 and rescued the people from their enemies t the
6:35 He also sent messengers t Manasseh, Asher,
7:24 Gideon also sent messengers t the hill country of
8:28 T the rest of Gideon's lifetime—about forty years
11:29 and he went t the land of Gilead and Manasseh,
20:6 and sent the pieces t the land of Israel,
1Sa 2:10 them from heaven; / the LORD judges t the earth.
4:13 had happened, an outcry resounded t the town.
7:13 And t Samuel's lifetime, the LORD's powerful
11:3 "Give us seven days to send messengers t Israel!"
11:7 and sent the messengers to carry them t Israel with
11:9 What joy there was t the city when that message
13:3 in revolt, so Saul sounded the call to arms t Israel.
14:52 constantly with the Philistines t Saul's lifetime.
18:30 So David's name became very famous t the land.
24:2 So Saul chose three thousand special troops from t
25:28 And you have not done wrong t your entire life.
30:17 in among them and slaughtered them t that night
31:9 and to the people t the land of Philistia.
2Sa 6:23 the daughter of Saul, remained childless t her life.
7:9 Now I will make your name famous t the earth!
8:14 He placed army garrisons t Edom, and all the
15:23 There was deep sadness t the land as the king
19:8 and as the news spread t the city that he was there,
19:9 And t the tribes of Israel there was much
24:13 "Will you choose three years of famine t the land,
24:13 or three days of severe plague t your land?
24:15 Seventy thousand people died t the nation.
1Ki 1:3 So they searched t the country for a beautiful girl,
3:28 Word of the king's decision spread quickly t all
4:21 and continued to serve him t his lifetime.
4:24 to Gaza. And there was peace t the entire land.
4:25 T the lifetime of Solomon, all of Judah and Israel
4:31 His fame spread t all the surrounding nations.
6:4 also made narrow, recessed windows t the Temple.
6:18 completely covered the stone walls t the Temple,
9:19 in Jerusalem and Lebanon and t the entire realm.
14:24 There were even shrine prostitutes t the land.
15:5 and had obeyed the LORD's commands t his life,
15:6 between Abijam and Jeroboam t Abijam's reign.
15:14 Asa remained faithful to the LORD t his life.
15:22 Then King Asa sent an order t Judah,
2Ki 10:21 He sent messengers t all Israel summoning those
23:5 for they had burned incense at the pagan shrines t
23:22 t all the years of the kings of Israel and Judah.
23:24 both in Jerusalem and t the land of Judah.
1Ch 5:16 in Bashan and its villages, and t the Sharon Plain.
10:9 their idols and to the people t the land of Philistia.
12:40 There was great joy t the land of Israel.
13:2 let us send messages to all the Israelites t the land,
16:14 the LORD our God. / His rule is seen t the land.
17:8 Now I will make your name famous t the earth!
18:13 He placed army garrisons t Edom, and all the
21:4 so Joab traveled t Israel to count the people.
21:12 the LORD brings devastation t the land of Israel.
22:5 famous and glorious t the world.
26:29 serve as public administrators and judges t Israel.
27:25 in charge of the regional treasuries t the towns,
2Ch 3:7 and thresholds t the Temple were overlaid with
8:6 in Jerusalem and Lebanon and t the entire realm.
11:23 and stationed them in the fortified cities t the land
14:6 he was able to build up the fortified cities t Judah.
15:17 Asa remained fully committed to the LORD t his
17:12 and built fortresses and store cities t Judah.
17:19 Jehoshaphat stationed in the fortified cities t Judah.
19:3 for you have removed the Asherah poles t the land,
19:5 He appointed judges t the nation in all the fortified
20:3 He also gave orders that everyone t Judah should
23:2 These men traveled secretly t Judah
24:2 LORD's sight t the lifetime of Jehoiada the priest.
24:9 Then a proclamation was sent t Judah
30:5 So they sent a proclamation t all Israel,
30:6 messengers were sent t Israel and Judah.
30:10 The messengers went from town to town t
31:20 King Hezekiah handled the distribution t all Judah,
32:22 So there was peace at last t the land.
34:7 He cut down the incense altars t the land of Israel
34:33 And t the rest of his lifetime, they did not turn
36:22 into writing and to send it t his kingdom:
Ezr 1:1 into writing and to send it t his kingdom:
4:10 and t the neighboring lands of the province west of
4:17 and t the province west of the Euphrates River.
6:22 There was great joy t the land because the LORD
10:7 Then a proclamation was made t Judah
Ne 7:4 And only a few houses were scattered t the city.
8:15 He had said that a proclamation should be made t
12:27 the Levites t the land were asked to come to
Est 1:16 but also every official and citizen t your empire.
1:18 wife of every one of us, your officials t the empire,
1:18 be no end to the contempt and anger t your realm.
1:20 When this decree is published t your vast empire,
3:6 he decided to destroy all the Jews t the entire
8:5 to destroy the Jews t all the provinces of the king.

8:12 The day chosen for this event t all the provinces of
9: 2 The Jews gathered in their cities t all the king's
9: 4 and his fame spread t all the provinces as he
9:16 the other Jews t the king's provinces had gathered
9:17 T the provinces this was done on March 7.
9:20 to the Jews near and far, t all the king's provinces,
9:27 the Jews t the realm agreed to inaugurate this
9:28 and celebrated by every family t the provinces
9:30 and security were sent to the Jews t the 127
10: 1 King Xerxes imposed tribute t his empire, even to
Job 15:20 "Wicked people are in pain t their lives.
28:24 for he looks t the whole earth, under all the
36:11 then they will be blessed with prosperity t their
37:12 They do whatever he commands t the earth.
41:12 in the crocodile's limbs and t its enormous frame.
Ps 12: 8 wicked strut about, / and evil is praised t the land.
46: 9 and causes wars to end t the earth. / He breaks the
46:10 by every nation. / I will be honored t the world."
67: 2 May your ways be known t the earth, / your saving
72:16 May there be abundant crops t the land,
73: 9 the very heavens, / and their words strut t the earth.
78:51 the flower of youth t the land of Egypt.
99: 4 have acted with justice / and righteousness t Israel.
105: 7 the LORD our God. / His rule is seen t the land.
119:54 the music of my life / t the years of my pilgrimage.
135: 6 t all heaven and earth, / and on the seas and in their
Ecc 3:16 I also noticed that t the world there is evil in the
5: 8 and justice being miscarried t the land,
5:17 T their lives, they live under a cloud—frustrated,
Isa 4: 5 and cloud t the day and clouds of fire at night,
14:26 for my mighty power reaches t the world.
24:13 T the earth the story is the same—like the stray
38:15 Now I will walk humbly t my years / because of
42: 4 until truth and righteousness prevail t the earth.
45:17 be humiliated and disgraced t everlasting ages.
46: 4 I will be your God t your lifetime—until your hair
46: 9 And do not forget the things I have done t history.
59:19 and glorify the name of the LORD t the world.
62: 7 he makes Jerusalem the object of praise t the earth.
Jer 1: 3 He continued to give messages t the reign of
4: 5 all Judah! Tell them to sound the alarm t the land:
5: 1 "Look high and low; search t the city!
7:17 Do you not see what they are doing t the towns of
11: 6 Go from town to town t the land and say,
22:14 paneled t with fragrant cedar and painted a lovely
23: 5 He will do what is just and right t the land.
23:40 and your name will be infamous t the ages.' "
33:15 and he will do what is just and right t the land.
44: 1 and Memphis, and t southern Egypt as well:
51:41 is fallen—great Babylon, praised t the earth!
51:49 killed the people of Israel and others t the world,
51:52 The groans of her wounded people will be heard t
La 5:11 young girls in Jerusalem and t the towns of Judah.
Eze 9: 7 So they went t the city and did as they were told.
16:14 Your fame soon spread t the world on account of
21: 4 I will make a clean sweep t the land from south to
22: 4 I will make you an object of mockery t the world.
30:13 rulers left in Egypt; anarchy will prevail t the land!
30:23 I will scatter the Egyptians to many lands t the
36:21 which had been dishonored by my people t the
38:21 I will summon the sword against you t Israel,
Da 4: 1 of every race and nation and language t the world:
6:25 of every race and nation and language t the world:
6:26 "I decree that everyone t my kingdom should
Am 3:13 to this, and announce it t all Israel," says the Lord,
6:14 "It will oppress you bitterly t your land—
Jnh 3: 7 the king and his nobles sent this decree t the city:
Zep 1:10 and echo t the newer Mishneh section of the city.
Zec 5: 6 and it is filled with the sins of everyone t the
13: 2 I will get rid of every trace of idol worship t the
Mt 4:23 Jesus traveled t Galilee teaching in the
11: 1 off teaching and preaching in towns t the country.
14:35 The news of their arrival spread quickly t the
24:14 the Kingdom will be preached t the whole world,
26:13 wherever the Good News is preached t the world,
Mk 1:39 So he traveled t the region of Galilee, preaching in
5: 5 and t the night he would wander among the tombs
6:55 and they ran t the whole area and began carrying
14: 9 wherever the Good News is preached t the world,
Lk 1:65 and the news of what had happened spread t the
2: 1 decreed that a census should be taken t the Roman
4:14 Soon he became well known t the surrounding
4:37 had done spread like wildfire t the whole region.
4:40 people t the village brought sick family members
4:44 to travel around, preaching in synagogues t Judea.
Ac 1: 8 in Jerusalem, t Judea, in Samaria, and to the ends
9:31 The church then had peace t Judea, Galilee,
10:39 "And we apostles are witnesses of all he did t
13:49 So the Lord's message spread t that region.
15:31 And there was great joy t the church that day as
15:41 So they traveled t Syria and Cilicia to strengthen
17:26 From one man he created all the nations t the
19:10 two years, so that people t the province of Asia—
19:26 not only here in Ephesus but t the entire province!
19:27 this magnificent goddess worshiped t the province
24: 5 a man who is constantly inciting the Jews t the
26:20 then in Jerusalem and t all Judea, and also to the
Ro 1: 8 your faith in God is becoming known t the world.
9:17 and so that my fame might spread t the earth."
2Co 1: 1 in Corinth and to all the Christians t Greece.
Rev 8: 1 there was silence t heaven for about half an hour.
18: 3 and merchants t the world have grown rich as a

THROW (79) [THREW, THROWING, THROWN, THROWS]

Ge 37:20 "Come on, let's kill him and t him into a deep pit.
37:22 his blood? Let's just t him alive into this pit here.
Ex 1:22 "T all the newborn Israelite boys into the Nile
4: 3 "T it down on the ground," the LORD told him.
7: 9 say to Aaron, 'T down your shepherd's staff,'
22:31 a wild animal. T its carcass out for the dogs to eat.
Lev 1:16 and t them to the east side of the altar among the
Nu 19: 6 and t them into the fire where the heifer is burning.
Dt 7:23 He will t them into complete confusion until they
17: 7 The witnesses must t the first stones, and then all
1Sa 1:14 here drunk?" he demanded. "T away your wine!"
2Sa 13:17 for his servant and demanded, "T this woman out,
20:21 "we will t his head over the wall to you."
2Ki 9:25 "T him into the field of Naboth of Jezreel.
9:26 So t him out on Naboth's field, just as the LORD
9:33 "T her down!" Jehu yelled. So they threw her out
2Ch 20:11 For they have come to t us out of your land,
Job 22:24 for money, and t your precious gold into the river.
30:22 You t me into the whirlwind and destroy me in the
Ps 17:11 me down, surround me, / and t me to the ground.
22:18 among themselves / and t dice for my garments.
56: 7 in your anger, O God, t them to the ground.
140:10 fall down on their heads, / or t them into the fire,
Pr 1:14 Come on, t in your lot with us; we'll split our loot
16:33 We may t the dice, but the LORD determines
22:10 T out the mocker, and fighting, quarrels,
Ecc 3: 6 time to lose. / A time to keep and a time to t away.
Isa 7: 6 'We will invade Judah and t its people into panic.
30:22 You will t them out like filthy rags. "Ugh!"
31: 7 when every one of you will t away the gold idols
32:11 you women of ease; t off your unconcern.
41: 9 For I have chosen you and will not t you away.
65: 8 (and someone will say, 'Don't t them all away—
66: 5 hate you and t you out for being loyal to my name.
Jer 4: 1 "If you will t away your detestable idols and go
16:13 So I will t you out of this land and send you into a
22: 7 all your fine cedar beams and t them on the fire.
51:63 tie it to a stone, and t it into the Euphrates River.
La 2:10 They t dust on their heads in sorrow and despair.
Eze 5: 4 a few of these hairs out and t them into the fire,
7:19 "They will t away their money, tossing it out like
17:20 I will t my net over him and capture him in my
24:12 the corruption remains. So t it into the fire!
27:30 They weep bitterly as they t dust on their heads
Da 3:20 and Abednego and t them into the blazing furnace.
3:24 we tie up three men and t them into the furnace?"
Hos 7:12 I will t my net over them and bring them down like
Jnh 1:12 "T me into the sea," Jonah said, "and it will
Mic 7:19 your feet and t them into the depths of the ocean!
Zec 1:21 They will t them down and destroy them."
11:13 And the LORD said to me, "T it to the potters"—
Mt 5:29 causes you to lust, gouge it out and t it away.
5:30 causes you to sin, cut it off and t it away.
13:42 and they will t them into the furnace and burn
13:48 the good fish into crates, and t the bad ones away.
15:26 take food from the children and t it to the dogs,"
17:27 offend them, so go down to the lake and t in a line.
18: 8 or foot causes you to sin, cut it off and t it away.
18: 9 eye causes you to sin, gouge it out and t it away.
21:21 'May God lift you up and t you into the sea,'
22:13 and foot and t him out into the outer darkness,
25:30 Now t this useless servant into outer darkness,
Mk 7:27 take food from the children and t it to the dogs."
11:23 'May God lift you up and t you into the sea,'
Lk 12: 5 the power to kill people and then t them into hell.
17: 6 'May God uproot you and t you into the sea,'
22:41 about a stone's t, and knelt down and prayed,
Jn 8: 7 But let those who have never sinned t the first
19:24 "Let's not tear it but t dice to see who gets it."
21: 6 "T out your net on the right-hand side of the boat,
Ac 8: 3 out both men and women to t them into jail.
Ro 9:21 jar for decoration and another to t garbage into?
Gal 3: 4 was it? Are you now going to just t it all away?
Eph 4:22 t off your old evil nature and your former way of
1Ti 4:15 T yourself into your tasks so that everyone will see
Heb 10:35 Do not t away this confident trust in the Lord,
Rev 2:10 The Devil will t some of you into prison and put
2:22 Therefore, I will t her upon a sickbed, and she will
18:19 And they will t dust on their heads to show their

THROWING (11) [THROW]

2Sa 16:13 cursing as he went and t stones at David
Ezr 10: 1 and t himself to the ground in front of the Temple
Da 8:10 t some of the heavenly beings and stars to the
Mt 11:21 and t ashes on their heads to show their remorse.
13:50 t the wicked into the fire. There will be weeping
27:35 the soldiers gambled for his clothes by t dice.
Mk 15:24 his clothes, t dice to decide who would get them.
Lk 10:13 and t ashes on their heads to show their remorse.
23:34 And the soldiers gambled for his clothes by t dice.
Ac 27:18 the ship, the crew began t the cargo overboard.
27:38 the crew lightened the ship further by t the cargo

THROWN (78) [THROW]

Ge 49:17 that bites the horse's heels / so the rider is t off.
Ex 8:24 The whole country was t into chaos by the flies.
15: 1 he has t both horse and rider into the sea.
15: 4 and armies, / he has t into the sea.
15:21 he has t both horse and rider into the sea."
Lev 4:12 outside the camp, the place where the ashes are t.
14:40 then be t into an area outside the town designated
Jos 10:27 and t into the cave where they had been hiding.
1Sa 7:10 and the Philistines were t into such confusion that
25:36 she found that Nabal had t a big party and was
2Sa 23: 6 But the godless are like thorns to be t away,
2Ki 7:15 and equipment that the Arameans had t away in
19:18 And they have t the gods of these nations into the
Job 13:16 If I were, I would be t from his presence.
20: 7 he will perish forever, t away like his own dung.
30:11 He has humbled me, so they have t off all restraint.
30:19 He has t me into the mud. I have become as dust
41: 9 The hunter who attempts it will be t down.
Ps 36:12 They have been t down, never to rise again.
89:39 with him, / for you have t his crown in the dust.
102:10 For you have picked me up and t me out.
141: 6 When their leaders are t down from a cliff,
Isa 5:25 and the rotting bodies of his people are t as
8:22 dark despair. They will be t out into the darkness."
14:12 You have been t down to the earth, you who
14:19 but your body is t from the grave like a discarded
37:19 And they have t the gods of these nations into the
Jer 14:16 their bodies will be t out into the streets of
36:30 His dead body will be t out to lie unburied—
51:34 our riches. He has t us out of our own country.
La 1:17 Let them be t away like a filthy rag!"
2: 1 lies in the dust, t down from the heights of heaven.
Eze 19:12 and t down to the ground. / The desert wind dried
29: 7 you gave way, and her back was t out of joint.
38:20 Mountains will be t down; cliffs will crumble;
Da 3: 6 Anyone who refuses to obey will immediately be t
3:11 refuse to obey must be t into a blazing furnace.
3:15 you will be t immediately into the blazing furnace.
3:17 If we are t into the blazing furnace, the God whom
6: 7 except to Your Majesty—will be t to the lions.
6:12 except to Your Majesty—will be t to the lions?"
6:16 for Daniel to be arrested and t into the den of lions.
6:24 He had them t into the lions' den, along with their
Am 4: 3 in the wall; you will be t from your fortresses.
Mt 3:10 good fruit will be chopped down and t into the fire.
5:13 It will be t out and trampled underfoot as
5:25 into court, handed over to an officer, and t in jail.
5:29 body than for your whole body to be t into hell.
5:30 body than for your whole body to be t into hell.
7:19 good fruit is chopped down and t into the fire.
13:47 Heaven is like a fishing net that is t into the water
18: 6 it would be better for that person to be t into the
18: 8 or lame than to be t into the unquenchable fire with
18: 9 half blind than to have two eyes and be t into hell.
Mk 9:42 it would be better for that person to be t into the
9:45 only one foot than to be t into hell with two feet.
9:47 half blind than to have two eyes and be t into hell,
Lk 3: 9 fruit will be chopped down and t into the fire."
12:58 and handed over to an officer and t in jail.
13:28 within the Kingdom of God, but you will be t out.
14:35 It is t away. Anyone who is willing to hear should
17: 2 It would be better to be t into the sea with a large
Jn 15: 6 Anyone who parts from me is t away like a useless
Ac 16:23 severely beaten, and then they were t into prison.
17: 8 city officials, were t into turmoil by these reports.
Heb 10:34 You suffered along with those who were t into jail.
Rev 8: 7 and fire mixed with blood were t down upon the
8: 8 and a great mountain of fire was t into the sea.
12: 9 was t down to the earth with all his angels.
12:10 For the Accuser has been t down to earth—the one
12:13 And when the dragon realized that he had been t
15: 5 in heaven, God's Tabernacle, was t wide open!
18:21 will be t down as violently as I have t away
19:20 and his false prophet were t alive into the lake of
20:10 was t into the lake of fire that burns with sulfur,
20:14 and the grave were t into the lake of fire.
20:15 in the Book of Life was t into the lake of fire.

THROWS (4) [THROW]

Nu 35:20 or t a dangerous object and the person dies,
35:22 or t something that unintentionally hits another
Mk 9:18 it t him violently to the ground and makes him
Lk 9:39 It t him into convulsions so that he foams at the

THRUST (9) [THRUSTS]

Nu 25: 8 Phinehas t the spear all the way through the man's
1Sa 26: 8 "Let me t that spear through him. I'll pin him to
2Sa 1:15 So the man t his sword into the Amalekite
2:16 and t his sword into the other's side so that all of
2:23 so Abner t the butt end of his spear through
Job 18:18 They will be t from light into darkness,
Ps 22:10 I was t upon you at my birth. / You have been my
88: 6 You have t me down to the lowest pit,
Ac 19:33 Alexander was t forward by some of the Jews,

THRUSTS (1) [THRUST]

Dt 33:27 He t out the enemy before you; / it is he who cries,

THUMB (6) [THUMBING, THUMBS]

Lev 8:23 the t of his right hand, and the big toe of his right
8:24 the t of their right hands, and the big toe of their
14:14 on the t of the right hand, and on the big toe of the
14:17 on the t of the right hand, and on the big toe of the
14:25 on the t of the right hand, and on the big toe of the
14:28 on the t of the right hand, and on the big toe of the

THUMBING (1) [THUMB]

Eze 8:17 t their noses at me, and rousing my fury against

THUMBS (4) [THUMB]

Ex 29:20 Also put it on their right t and the big toes of their
Jdg 1: 6 soon captured him and cut off his t and big toes.
1: 7 "I once had seventy kings with t and big toes cut
La 5:12 Our princes are being hanged by their t,

THUMMIM (2)
Ex 28:30 into the pocket of the chestpiece the Urim and **T**,
Lev 8: 8 on Aaron and put the Urim and the **T** inside it.

THUNDER (35) [THUNDERCLOUD, THUNDERED, THUNDERING, THUNDERS, THUNDERSTORMS]
Ex 9:23 and the LORD sent **t** and hail, and lightning
9:28 Please beg the LORD to end this terrifying **t**
9:29 pray to the LORD. Then the **t** and hail will stop.
9:33 all at once the **t** and hail stopped,
19:16 there was a powerful **t** and lightning storm,
20:18 When the people heard the **t** and the loud blast of
1Sa 7:10 But the LORD spoke with a mighty voice of **t**
12:17 I will ask the LORD to send **t** and rain today.
12:18 to the LORD, and the LORD sent **t** and rain.
Job 26:14 Who can understand the **t** of his power?"
36:29 the clouds and the **t** that rolls forth from heaven?
36:33 The **t** announces his presence; the storm announces
37: 2 Listen carefully to the **t** of God's voice as it rolls
37: 4 Then comes the roaring of the **t**—the tremendous
37: 4 He does not restrain the **t** when he speaks.
37: 5 God's voice is glorious in the **t**. We cannot
40: 9 strong as God, and can you **t** with a voice like his?
Ps 50: 3 Our God approaches with the noise of **t**.
77:17 their rain; / the **t** rolled and crackled in the sky.
77:18 Your **t** roared from the whirlwind; / the lightning
93: 3 O LORD. / The mighty oceans roar like **t**;
104: 7 water fled; / at the sound of your **t**, it fled away.
Isa 29: 6 will come against them with **t** and earthquake
Jer 10:13 When he speaks, there is **t** in the heavens.
51:16 When he speaks, there is **t** in the heavens.
Joel 3:16 voice will roar from Zion and **t** from Jerusalem,
Mk 3:17 but Jesus nicknamed them "Sons of **T**"),
Jn 12:29 the crowd heard the voice, some thought it was **t**,
Rev 4: 5 came flashes of lightning and the rumble of **t**.
6: 1 beings called out with a voice that sounded like **t**,
8: 5 and **t** crashed, lightning flashed, and there was a
11:19 Lightning flashed, **t** crashed and roared; there was
14: 2 of a great waterfall or the rolling of mighty **t**.
16:18 Then the **t** crashed and rolled, and lightning
19: 6 roar of mighty ocean waves, or the crash of loud **t**:

THUNDERCLOUD (1) [CLOUD, THUNDER]
Ps 81: 7 and I saved you; / I answered out of the **t**.

THUNDERED (5) [THUNDER]
Ex 19:19 Moses spoke, and God **t** his reply for all to hear.
2Sa 22:14 The LORD **t** from heaven; / the Most High gave a
Ps 18:13 The LORD **t** from heaven; / the Most High gave a
Eze 9: 1 Then the LORD **t**, "Bring on the men appointed
Rev 1:15 a furnace, and his voice **t** like mighty ocean waves.

THUNDERING (3) [THUNDER]
Ps 68:33 ancient heavens, / his mighty voice **t** from the sky.
Isa 17:12 The armies rush forward like waves **t** toward the
42:13 full of fury. / He will shout his **t** battle cry,

THUNDERS (8) [THUNDER]
1Sa 2:10 He **t** against them from heaven; / the LORD
Ps 29: 3 God of glory **t**. / The LORD **t** over the mighty sea.
46: 6 kingdoms crumble! / God **t**, / and the earth melts!
Am 1: 2 his Temple on Mount Zion; he **t** from Jerusalem!
Rev 10: 3 And when he shouted, the seven **t** answered.
10: 4 When the seven **t** spoke, I was about to write.
10: 4 "Keep secret what the seven **t** said. Do not write it

THUNDERSTORMS (1) [STORM, THUNDER]
Isa 30:30 with cloudbursts, **t**, and huge hailstones,

THUS (39)
Ge 11: 9 many languages, **t** scattering them across the earth.
17:13 Your bodies will **t** bear the mark of my everlasting
30:40 **t** separating the lambs from Laban's flock.
47:21 **T**, all the people of Egypt became servants to
Ex 28:29 **T**, the LORD will be reminded of his people
28:30 **T**, Aaron will always carry the objects used to
28:38 **t** bearing the guilt connected with any errors
28:43 **T** they will not incur guilt and die. This law is
36:13 **T** the Tabernacle was joined together in one piece.
Lev 1: 4 it as your substitute, **t** making atonement for you.
8:10 and everything in it, **t** making them holy.
8:12 **t** anointing him and making him holy for his work.
12: 8 will sacrifice them, **t** making atonement for her,
14:21 **t** making atonement for the person being cleansed.
Nu 8:11 **t** dedicating them to the LORD's service.
16:40 **T**, the LORD's instructions to Moses were
36:12 **T**, their inheritance of land remained within their
Dt 9:18 what the LORD hated, **t** making him very angry.
Jdg 9:56 **T**, God punished Abimelech for the evil he had
11:33 **T** Israel subdued the Ammonites.
1Ki 11: 6 **T**, Solomon did what was evil in the LORD's
16:26 **T**, he aroused the anger of the LORD, the God of
2Ki 10:28 **T**, Jehu destroyed every trace of Baal worship
2Ch 34:11 **T**, they hired carpenters and masons and purchased
Job 38:11 I said, '**T** far and no farther will you come.
Pr 30: 9 too poor, I may steal and **t** insult God's holy name.
Isa 30: 1 that are not from my Spirit, **t** piling up your sins.
44: 7 them tell you if they can and **t** prove their power.
44:25 to give bad advice, **t** proving them to be fools.
Eze 38:23 **T** will I show my greatness and holiness, and I will
39: 7 "**T**, I will make known my holy name among my
39:21 "**T**, I will demonstrate my glory among the
43:26 for the altar, **t** setting it apart for holy use.
44: 2 entered here. **T**, it must always remain shut.
44: 7 **T**, in addition to all your other disgusting sins,
Hos 13: 1 by worshiping Baal and **t** sealed their destruction.
Zec 9: 6 **T**, I will destroy the pride of the Philistines.
Lk 2:35 **T**, the deepest thoughts of many hearts will be
Ac 27:17 the sea anchor and were **t** driven before the wind.

THWARTED (2) [THWARTS]
Job 5:13 so that their cunning schemes are **t**.
Ps 112:10 teeth in anger; / they will slink away, their hopes **t**.

THWARTS (1) [THWARTED]
Ps 33:10 the plans of the nations / and **t** all their schemes.

THYATIRA (4)
Ac 16:14 One of them was Lydia from **T**, a merchant of
Rev 1:11 Ephesus, Smyrna, Pergamum, **T**, Sardis,
2:18 "Write this letter to the angel of the church in **T**.
2:24 But I also have a message for the rest of you in **T**

THYINE [KJV] See PERFUMED

TIBERIAS (2) [GALILEE]
Jn 6: 1 the Sea of Galilee, also known as the Sea of **T**.
6:23 Several boats from **T** landed near the place where

TIBERIUS (1)
Lk 3: 1 It was now the fifteenth year of the reign of **T**,

TIBNI (3)
1Ki 16:21 Half the people tried to make **T** son of Ginath their
16:22 But Omri's supporters defeated the supporters of **T**
16:22 So **T** was killed, and Omri became the next king.

TICKET (1)
Jnh 1: 3 He bought a **t** and went on board, hoping that by

TIDAL (1)
Ge 14: 1 King Kedorlaomer of Elam, and King **T** of Goiim

TIDE (1) [TIDES]
Isa 59:19 For he will come like a flood **t** driven by the breath

TIDES (2) [TIDE]
Ps 42: 7 as your waves and surging **t** sweep over me.
Lk 21:25 perplexed by the roaring seas and strange **t**.

TIE (15) [TIED, TIES, TYING]
Ex 36:31 wood to **t** the frames on the south side together.
Lev 16: 4 He must **t** the linen sash around his waist and put
Dt 6: 8 **T** them to your hands as a reminder, and wear
11:18 **T** them to your hands as a reminder, and wear
Jdg 15:12 "We have come to **t** you up and hand you over to
15:13 "We will **t** you up and hand you over to the
16: 6 and what it would take to **t** you up securely."
Job 41: 2 Can you **t** it with a rope through the nose or pierce
Pr 6:21 always in your heart. **T** them around your neck.
7: 3 **T** them on your fingers as a reminder. Write them
Jer 51:63 **t** it to a stone, and throw it into the Euphrates
Eze 4: 8 I will **t** you up with ropes so you won't be able to
5: 3 Keep just a bit of the hair and **t** it up in your robe.
13:18 You **t** magic charms on their wrists and furnish
Da 3:24 "Didn't we **t** up three men and throw them into the

TIED (34) [TIE]
Ge 22: 9 Then he **t** Isaac up and laid him on the altar over
38:28 and the midwife **t** a scarlet thread around the wrist
42:24 and had him **t** up right before their eyes.
Ex 28:25 and the ends of the cords will be **t** to the gold
39: 4 were attached to its corners so it could be **t** down.
39:18 and the ends of the cords were **t** to the gold settings
39:31 This medallion was **t** to the turban with a blue
Lev 8: 7 embroidered tunic and **t** the sash around his waist.
Jdg 15: 4 He **t** their tails together in pairs, and he fastened a
15:13 So they **t** him up with two new ropes and led him
16: 5 and how he can be overpowered and **t** up securely.
16: 7 "If I am **t** up with seven new bowstrings that have
16: 8 new bowstrings, and she **t** Samson up with them.
16:10 Now please tell me how you can be **t** up securely."
16:11 "If I am **t** up with brand-new ropes that have never
16:12 So Delilah took new ropes and **t** him up with them.
16:13 Won't you please tell me how you can be **t** up
2Ki 5:23 two sets of clothing, **t** up the money in two bags,
Ezr 6:11 Then they will be **t** to it and flogged, and their
Ps 109:19 may they be **t** around him like a belt.
Isa 5:18 their sins behind them, **t** with cords of falsehood.
Da 3:21 So they **t** them up and threw them into the furnace,
3:23 So Shadrach, Meshach, and Abednego, securely **t**,
Mt 18: 6 the sea with a large millstone **t** around the neck.
21: 2 he said, "and you will see a donkey **t** there,
Mk 9:42 the sea with a large millstone **t** around the neck.
11: 2 you will see a colt **t** there that has never been
11: 4 the colt standing in the street, **t** outside a house.
Lk 17: 2 **t** around the neck than to face the punishment in
19:30 you will see a colt **t** there that has never been
Jn 18:12 and the Temple guards arrested Jesus and **t** him up.
Ac 22:25 As they **t** Paul down to lash him, Paul said to the
Gal 5: 1 and don't get **t** up again in slavery to the law.
2Ti 2: 4 do not let yourself become **t** up in the affairs of this

TIES (2) [TIE]
Ge 49:11 He **t** his foal to a grapevine, / the colt of his donkey
Col 2: 2 and knit together by strong **t** of love.

TIGHTEN (1) [TIGHTENED, TIGHTENING, TIGHTENS, TIGHTFISTED, TIGHTLY]
Jdg 16:13 fabric on your loom and **t** it with the loom shuttle,

TIGHTENED (1) [TIGHTEN]
Jdg 16:14 and **t** it with the loom shuttle. Again she cried out,

TIGHTENING (1) [TIGHTEN]
2Ki 15:19 to gain his support in **t** his grip on royal power.

TIGHTENS (1) [TIGHTEN]
Job 18: 9 grabs them by the heel. A noose **t** around them.

TIGHTFISTED (1) [FIST, TIGHTEN]
Dt 15: 7 do not be hard-hearted or **t** toward them.

TIGHTLY (10) [TIGHTEN]
Jos 6: 1 Now the gates of Jericho were **t** shut
Job 40:17 a cedar. The sinews of its thighs are **t** knit together.
Pr 3:18 who embrace her; happy are those who hold her **t**.
Ecc 12: 4 are gone, keep your lips **t** closed when you eat!
Ac 3:11 where he was holding **t** to Peter and John.
Php 2:16 Hold **t** to the word of life, so that when Christ
1Ti 1:19 Cling **t** to your faith in Christ, and always keep
6:12 Hold **t** to the eternal life that God has given you,
Heb 10:23 let us hold **t** to the hope we say we have,
Rev 2:25 except that you hold **t** to what you have until I

TIGLATH-PILESER (7) [PUL]
2Ki 15:19 Then King **T** of Assyria invaded the land.
15:29 his reign, King **T** of Assyria attacked Israel again,
16: 7 King Ahaz sent messengers to King **T** of Assyria
16:10 then went to Damascus to meet with King **T** of
1Ch 5: 6 were taken into captivity by King **T** of Assyria.
5:26 caused King Pul of Assyria (also known as **T**)
2Ch 28:20 So when King **T** of Assyria arrived, he oppressed

TIGRIS (3)
Ge 2:14 The third branch is the **T**, which flows to the east
Ps 89:25 the west / to the **T** and Euphrates rivers in the east.
Da 10: 4 as I was standing beside the great **T** River,

TIKVAH (3)
2Ki 22:14 She was the wife of Shallum son of **T**
2Ch 34:22 She was the wife of Shallum son of **T**
Ezr 10:15 and Jahzeiah son of **T** opposed this course of

TILES (1)
Lk 5:19 So they went up to the roof, took off some **t**,

TILGATHPILNESER [KJV] See TIGLATH-PILESER

TILL (8) [TILLED]
Ex 18:13 They were lined up in front of him from morning **t**
2Ch 35:14 because the priests had been busy from morning **t**
Job 7: 4 But the night drags on, and I toss **t** dawn.
Isa 30:24 and donkeys that **t** the ground will eat good grain,
51:13 the anger of your enemies from morning **t** night?
Zep 3: 7 they continue their evil practices from dawn **t** dusk and dusk **t** dawn."
Mal 1:11 by people of other nations from morning **t** night.

TILLAGE [KJV] See FARM, FARMED, RURAL

TILLED (1) [TILL]
Eze 36: 9 Your ground will be **t** and your crops planted.

TILON (1)
1Ch 4:20 Shimon were Amnon, Rinnah, Ben-hanan, and **T**.

TILT (1)
Job 38:37 all the clouds? Who can **t** the water jars of heaven,

TIMAEUS (1) [BARTIMEAUS]
Mk 10:46 A blind beggar named Bartimaeus (son of **T**)

TIMBER (15) [TIMBERS]
1Ki 5: 6 there is no one among us who can cut **t** like you
5: 8 and I will do as you have asked concerning the **t**.
5: 9 will break the rafts apart and deliver the **t** to you.
5:10 as much cedar and cypress **t** as he desired.
5:18 and Hiram's builders prepare the **t** and stone for
2Ki 12:12 They also used the money to buy **t** and cut stone
22: 6 Also have them buy the **t** and the cut stone needed
2Ch 2: 8 know that your men are without equal at cutting **t**.
2: 9 An immense amount of **t** will be needed,
2:16 We will cut whatever **t** you need from the Lebanon
34:11 stone for the walls and **t** for the rafters and beams.
Ezr 5: 8 prepared stones, and **t** is being laid in its walls.
6: 4 prepared stones will be topped by a layer of **t**.
Ne 2: 8 of the king's forest, instructing him to give me **t**.
Hag 1: 8 into the hills, bring down **t**, and rebuild my house.

TIMBERS (6) [TIMBER]

Lev 14:45 It must be torn down, and all its stones, t,
1Ki 6:10 attached to the Temple walls by cedar t.
15:22 and t that Baasha had been using to fortify Ramah.
2Ch 16:6 and t that Baasha had been using to fortify Ramah.
Eze 26:12 and dump your stones and t and even your dust
Zec 5:4 it is completely destroyed—even its t and stones."

TIMBREL [KJV] See TAMBOURINE

TIME (964) [MEANTIME, SOMETIMES, TIMELY, TIMES]

APPOINTED TIME (9) Ex 13:10; 23:15; 34:18; Est 9:27, 31; Da 11:27,29,35; Mt 8:29

FOR ALL TIME (11) Nu 25:13; Dt 4:40; 2Sa 7:16; 1Ch 17:14; Heb 9:12,26; 10:2,10,12; 1Pe 3:18; Jude 1:3

LONG TIME (37) Ge 6:3; 21:34; 46:29; Nu 9:19,19; 20:15; Dt 1:46; 2:1; 4:25; Jos 11:18; 22:3; 1Sa 7:2,13; 2Sa 5:2; 14:2; 1Ki 2:38; 1Ch 7:22; 11:2; 2Ch 15:3; Ecc 8:12; Jer 13:6; 32:14; Eze 12:27; 38:8; Da 8:26; Hos 3:4; Mt 25:19; Lk 8:27; 23:8; Ac 2:40; 9:43; 14:3,28; 27:21; 28:6; Heb 4:7; 5:12

TIME IS (SURELY) COMING (31) 2Ki 20:17; Isa 27:6; 39:6; Jer 4:11; 7:32; 9:25; 10:15; 16:14; 19:6; 23:5; 30:3; 31:38; 48:12; 51:18,47,52; Am 8:11; Hab 2:6; Zep 3:8; Mt 10:26; Lk 12:2; 17:22; 21:6; 22:69; Jn 4:21,23; 5:25,28; 16:2,32; 2Ti 4:3

TIME OF TROUBLE (4) Ne 9:27; Job 38:23; Jer 30:7; Ob 1:14

Ge 4:1 When the t came, she gave birth to Cain, and she
4:3 At harvest t Cain brought to the LORD a gift of
5:32 By the t Noah was 500 years old, he had three
6:3 will not put up with humans for such a long t,
6:9 the only blameless man living on earth at the t.
8:4 exactly five months from the t the flood began,
8:11 This t, toward evening, the bird returned to him
8:12 the dove again, and this t it did not come back.
11:1 At one t the whole world spoke a single language
12:6 At that t, the area was inhabited by Canaanites.
12:10 At that t there was a severe famine in the land,
13:7 At that t Canaanites and Perizzites were also living
14:1 About this t war broke out in the region.
16:16 Abram was eighty-six years old at that t.
17:21 be born to you and Sarah about this t next year."
17:24 Abraham was ninety-nine years old at that t,
18:10 of them said, "About this t next year I will return,
19:22 From that t on, that village was known as Zoar.
21:2 It all happened at the t God had said it would.
21:5 Abraham was one hundred years old at the t.
21:8 As t went by and Isaac grew and was weaned,
21:22 About this t, Abimelech came with Phicol,
21:34 Abraham lived in Philistine country for a long t.
22:19 where Abraham lived for quite some t.
25:24 And when the t came, the twins were born.
26:1 the land, as had happened before in Abraham's t.
26:8 But some t later, Abimelech, king of the
26:33 named the well "Oath," and from that t to this,
27:40 You will serve your brother for a t, but then you
29:21 Finally, the t came for him to marry her. "I have
30:40 Then at mating t, he turned the flocks toward the
31:19 At the t they left, Laban was some distance away,
31:38 and all that t I cared for your sheep and goats
34:19 and Shechem lost no t in acting on this request,
37:10 This t he told his father as well as his brothers,
37:13 When they had been gone for some t, Jacob said to
37:24 used to store water, but it was empty at the t.
37:29 Some t later, Reuben returned to get Joseph out of
38:1 About this t, Judah left home and moved to
38:5 At the t of Shelah's birth, they were living at
38:11 not to marry again at that t but to return to her
38:12 In the course of t Judah's wife died. After the t of mourning was over, Judah and his
38:27 In due season the t of Tamar's delivery arrived,
39:7 And about this t, Potiphar's wife began to desire
40:1 Some t later, Pharaoh's chief cup-bearer and chief
40:4 They remained in prison for quite some t,
41:5 This t he saw seven heads of grain on one stalk,
41:10 "Some t ago, you were angry with the chief baker
41:22 This t there were seven heads of grain on one stalk,
41:50 During this t, before the arrival of the first of the
43:10 and returned twice by this t if you had let him
46:29 his father and wept on his shoulder for a long t.
47:29 As the t of his death drew near, he called for his
Ex 1:6 In t, Joseph and each of his brothers died,
1:19 so quickly that we cannot get there in t!
2:1 During this t, a man and woman from the tribe of
2:17 This t, however, Moses came to their aid,
2:21 In t, Reuel gave Moses one of his daughters,
4:7 Moses did, and when he took it out this t, it was as
6:28 At that t, the LORD had said to them,
7:7 and Aaron was eighty-three at the t they made their
7:25 An entire week passed from the t the LORD
8:9 "You set the t!" Moses replied. "Tell me when
8:18 thing with their secret arts, but this t they failed.
9:18 So tomorrow at this t I will send a hailstorm worse
10:23 During all that t the people scarcely moved,
12:15 Anyone who eats bread made with yeast at any t
12:16 all the people must gather for a t of special
12:39 out of Egypt and had no t to wait for bread to rise.
12:47 of Israel must celebrate this festival at the same t.
13:7 within the borders of your land during this t.
13:10 "So celebrate this festival at the appointed t each
16:31 In t, the food became known as manna. It was
18:2 Some t before this, Moses had sent his wife,
21:19 the assailant must pay for t lost because of the
22:14 or killed, and if the owner was not there at the t,
23:15 an annual event at the appointed t in early spring,
23:15 Everyone must bring me a sacrifice at that t.
23:30 I will drive them out a little at a t until your
33:6 So from the t they left Mount Sinai, the Israelites
34:18 at the appointed t each year in early spring,
34:28 forty nights. In all that t he neither ate nor drank.
34:28 At that t he wrote the terms of the covenant—
Lev 5:4 not fully aware of what they were doing at the t.
7:35 t they were appointed to serve the LORD as
7:36 regular share from the t of the priests' anointing.
8:33 for that is the t it will take to complete the
12:4 t of her purification from the blood of childbirth is
12:4 During this t of purification, she must not touch
12:4 And she must not go to the sanctuary until her t of
12:6 "When the t of purification is completed for either
13:22 If during that t the affected area spreads on the
13:27 If at the end of that t the affected area has spread
13:32 If at the end of that t the affected area has not
13:57 If the spot reappears at a later t, however,
15:13 During that t, he must wash his clothes and bathe
15:19 If you touch her during that t, you will be defiled
15:20 which she lies or sits during that t will be defiled.
15:24 a man has sexual intercourse with her during this t,
15:26 which she lies or sits during that t will be defiled,
19:20 But since she had not been freed at the t,
23:4 the holy occasions to be observed at the proper t
23:6 and during that t all the bread you eat must be
23:32 This t of rest and fasting will begin the evening
25:10 a t to proclaim release for all who live there.
25:12 and you must observe it as a special and holy t.
25:24 a stipulation that the land can be redeemed at any t.
25:29 During that t, the seller retains the right to buy it
25:31 Such a house may be redeemed at any t and must
25:41 At that t they and their children will no longer be
25:54 If any Israelites have not been redeemed by the t
25:54 and their children must be set free at that t.
26:5 and your grape harvest will extend until it is t to
Nu 6:5 "They must never cut their hair throughout the t of
6:13 At the conclusion of their t of separation as
7:10 gifts for the altar at the t it was anointed.
7:84 brought by the leaders of Israel at the t it was
9:2 Israelites to celebrate the Passover at the proper t,
9:7 at the proper t with the rest of the Israelites?"
9:10 generations are ceremonially unclean at Passover t
9:11 They must eat the lamb at that t with bitter herbs
9:13 refuse to celebrate the Passover at the regular t,
9:13 to present the LORD's offering at the proper t.
9:19 cloud remained over the Tabernacle for a long t,
9:19 the Israelites stayed for a long t, just as the LORD
10:6 When you sound the signal a second t, the tribes
10:13 When the t to move arrived, the LORD gave the
11:25 upon them, but that was the only t this happened.
11:35 traveled to Hazeroth, where they stayed for some t.
13:16 By this t Moses had changed Hoshea's name to
13:24 At that t the Israelites renamed the valley Eshcol—
15:17 The LORD also said to Moses at this t,
20:15 We lived there a long t and suffered as slaves to
20:24 "The t has come for Aaron to join his ancestors in
22:15 This t he sent a larger number of even more
22:15 officials than those he had sent the first t.
22:27 This t when the donkey saw the angel, it lay down
24:17 I see him, but not in the present t. / I perceive him,
25:13 he and his descendants will be priests for all t,
26:3 At that t the entire nation of Israel was camped on
Dt 1:7 It is t to break camp and move on. Go to the hill
1:9 "At that t I told you, 'You are too great a burden
1:18 And at that t I gave you instructions about
1:46 So you stayed there at Kadesh for a long t.
2:1 and we wandered around Mount Seir for a long t.
2:14 So thirty-eight years passed from the t we first
3:5 also took many unwalled villages at the same t.
3:18 "At that t I gave this command to the tribes that
3:21 "At that t I said to Joshua, 'You have seen all that
3:23 "At that t I pleaded with the LORD and said,
4:14 It was at that t that the LORD commanded me to
4:25 and have lived in the land a long t,
4:26 You will live there only a short t; then you will be
4:32 from the t God created people on the earth until
4:40 land the LORD your God is giving you for all t."
5:22 This was all he said at that t, and he wrote his
8:11 "But that is the t to be careful! Beware that in your
8:14 that is the t to be careful. Do not become proud at that t and forget the
9:9 and all that t I ate nothing and drank no water.
10:1 "At that t the LORD said to me, 'Prepare two
10:8 At that t the LORD set apart the tribe of Levi to
10:10 for forty days and nights, as I had done the first t.
15:2 for the LORD's t of release has arrived.
16:1 always celebrate the Passover at the proper t in
16:11 It is a t to celebrate before the LORD your God at
16:14 This festival will be a happy t of rejoicing with
16:15 This festival will be a t of great joy for all.
18:4 new wine, the olive oil, and the wool at shearing t.
26:3 Go to the priest in charge at that t and say to him,
28:12 The LORD will send rain at the proper t from his
30:2 If at that t you return to the LORD your God,
31:14 said to Moses, "The t has come for you to die.
31:18 At that t I will hide my face from them on account
32:35 In due t their feet will slip. / Their day of disaster
Jos 5:2 At that t the LORD told Joshua, "Use knives of
5:12 So from that t on the Israelites ate from the crops
6:13 All this t the priests were sounding their horns.
6:15 But this t they went around the city seven times.
6:16 The seventh t around, as the priests sounded the
6:26 At that t Joshua invoked this curse:
8:2 But this t you may keep the captured goods
11:6 By this t tomorrow they will all be dead.
11:10 (Hazor had at one t been the capital of the
11:18 waging war for a long t to accomplish this.
20:6 priest who was in office at the t of the accident.
22:3 though the campaign has lasted for such a long t.
Jdg 2:15 Every t Israel went out to battle, the LORD
4:24 And from that t on Israel became stronger
6:39 This t let the fleece remain dry while the ground
8:10 By this t Zebah and Zalmunna were in Karkor with
9:8 Once upon a t the trees decided to elect a king.
9:26 At that t Gaal son of Ebed moved to Shechem with
10:17 At that t the armies of Ammon had gathered for
11:4 At about this t, the Ammonites began their war
11:26 Israel has been living here all this t, spread across
11:29 At that t the Spirit of the LORD came upon
12:6 thousand Ephraimites were killed at that t.
14:4 the Philistines, who ruled over Israel at that t.
15:3 "This t I cannot be blamed for everything I am
16:18 "Come back one more t," she said, "for he has
16:28 please strengthen me one more t so that I may pay
19:8 to eat; then you can leave some t this afternoon."
19:10 But this t the man was determined to leave. So he
20:39 By that t Benjamin's warriors had killed about
21:5 At that t they had taken a solemn oath in the
Ru 2:16 Let her pick them up, and don't give her a hard t!"
3:1 it's t that I found a permanent home for you,
1Sa 1:3 The priests of the LORD at that t were the two
1:20 and in due t she gave birth to a son. She named
2:31 the members of your family will die before their t.
3:8 So now the LORD called a third t, and once more
4:1 At that t Israel was at war with the Philistines.
4:19 was pregnant and near her t of delivery.
5:4 This t his head and hands had broken off and were
7:2 The Ark remained in Kiriath-jearim for a long t—
7:2 During that t, all Israel mourned because it seemed
7:13 and didn't invade Israel again for a long t.
9:16 "About this t tomorrow I will send you a man
9:26 up to Saul, "Get up! It's t you were on your way."
10:6 At that t the Spirit of the LORD will come upon
12:17 You know that it does not rain at this t of the year
14:18 For at that t Ahijah was wearing the ephod in front
17:12 Jesse was an old man at that t, and he had eight
17:14 the army, they stayed with Saul's forces all the t.
18:9 So from that t on Saul kept a jealous eye on David.
18:11 and escaped. This happened another t, too,
18:19 So when the t came for the wedding, Saul gave
18:26 to accept the offer. So before the t limit expired,
19:5 Have you forgotten about the t he risked his life to
19:21 prophesied! The same thing happened a third t!
20:12 the God of Israel, that by this t tomorrow,
21:8 so urgent that I didn't even have t to grab a
22:6 At the t, the king was sitting beneath a tamarisk
22:15 This was certainly not the first t I had consulted
23:28 Ever since that t, the place where David was
24:14 Should he spend his t chasing one who is as
25:2 and a thousand goats, and it was sheep-shearing t.
25:8 to us, since we have come at a t of celebration?
25:15 Nothing was stolen from us the whole t they were
25:18 Abigail lost no t. She quickly gathered two
25:39 Then David wasted no t in sending messengers to
26:8 has surely handed your enemy over to you this t!"
27:8 and his men spent their t raiding the Geshurites,
28:1 About that t the Philistines mustered their armies
2Sa 2:13 About the same t, Joab son of Zeruiah led David's
3:1 As t passed David became stronger and stronger,
3:17 "For some t now," he told them, "you have
3:18 Now is the t! For the LORD has said, 'I have
5:2 For a long t, even while Saul was our king,
7:11 from the t I appointed judges to rule my people.
7:16 and your kingdom will continue for all t before
9:11 And from that t on, Mephibosheth ate regularly
10:1 Some t after this, King Nahash of the Ammonites
10:18 This t David's forces killed seven hundred
11:1 the t of year when kings go to war, David sent
11:25 Fight harder next t, and conquer the city!"
12:10 From this t on, the sword will be a constant threat
14:2 a woman who has been in deep sorrow for a long t.
14:29 Absalom sent for him a second t, but again Joab
17:7 "this t I think Ahithophel has made a mistake.
18:20 You can be my messenger some other t, but not
20:4 Judah within three days and to report back at that t.
23:10 The rest of the army did not return until it was t to
23:11 One t the Philistines gathered at Lehi and attacked
23:14 David was staying in the stronghold at the t,
23:20 Another t he chased a lion down into a pit. Then,
23:21 Another t, armed only with a club, he killed a great
1Ki 1:5 About that t David's son Adonijah, whose mother
1:6 King David, had never disciplined him at any t,
2:1 As the t of King David's death approached,
2:5 but it was done in a t of peace, staining his belt
2:38 So Shimei lived in Jerusalem for a long t.
3:2 At that t the people of Israel sacrificed their
3:16 Some t later, two prostitutes came to the king to
9:2 Then the LORD appeared to Solomon a second t,
10:29 At that t, Egyptian chariots delivered to Jerusalem
11:17 had fled. (Hadad was a very small child at the t.)
11:34 not take the entire kingdom from Solomon at this t.
13:5 At the same t a wide crack appeared in the altar,
14:1 At that t Jeroboam's son Abijah became very sick.
17:14 and oil left in your containers until the t when the
17:17 Some t later, the woman's son became sick.
18:10 And each t when he was told, 'Elijah isn't here,'
18:13 about the t when Jezebel was trying to kill the
18:29 They raved all afternoon until the t of the evening
18:34 they were finished, he said, "Now do it a third t!"
18:36 At the customary t for offering the evening

18:44 Finally the seventh **t**, his servant told him, "I saw
19: 2 "May the gods also kill me if by this **t** tomorrow I
20: 6 But about this **t** tomorrow I will send my officials
20: 9 'I will give you everything you asked for the first **t**,
20:24 Only this **t** replace the kings with field
20:26 and marched out against Israel, this **t** at Aphek.
22:18 "He does it every **t**. He never prophesies anything
22:47 There was no king in Edom at that **t**, only a deputy.
22:49 At that **t** Ahaziah son of Ahab proposed to
2Ki 1:13 But this **t** the captain fell to his knees before Elijah.
3:20 the next day at about the **t** when the morning
4: 9 "I am sure this man who stops in from **t** to **t** is
4:16 "Next year at about this **t** you will be holding a
4:17 And at that **t** the following year she had a son,
4:35 This **t** the boy sneezed seven times and opened his
5:26 Is this the **t** to receive money and clothing
6:24 Some **t** later, however, King Ben-hadad of Aram
7: 1 By this **t** tomorrow in the markets of Samaria,
7:18 "By this **t** tomorrow in the markets of Samaria,
8: 5 And Gehazi was telling the king about the **t** Elisha
8:22 The town of Libnah revolted about that same **t**.
10: 6 sons to me at Jezreel at about this **t** tomorrow."
10:32 At about that **t** the LORD began to reduce the
12:17 About this **t** King Hazael of Aram went to war
13: 3 and his son Ben-hadad to defeat them **t** after **t**.
15:16 At that **t** Menahem destroyed the town of Tappuah
16: 6 At that **t** the king of Edom recovered the town of
18: 5 in the land of Judah, either before or after his **t**.
18:11 At that **t** the king of Assyria deported the Israelites
20: 1 About that **t** Hezekiah became deathly ill,
20:17 The **t** is coming when everything you have—
23:22 like that since the **t** when the judges ruled in Israel,
1Ch 4:31 These towns were under their control until the **t** of
7: 2 At the **t** of King David, the total number of men
7:22 Their father, Ephraim, mourned for them a long **t**,
9:18 Prior to this **t**, they were responsible for the King's
9:25 From **t** to **t**, their relatives in the villages came
11: 2 For a long **t**, even while Saul was our king,
11:16 David was staying in the stronghold at the **t**,
11:22 Another **t** he chased a lion down into a pit. Then,
11:23 Another **t**, armed with only a club, he killed an
12:29 had remained loyal to Saul until this **t**.
13: 3 It is **t** to bring back the Ark of our God, for we
15: 2 "When we transport the Ark of God this **t**, no one
15:13 you Levites did not carry the Ark the first **t**,
17:10 from the **t** I appointed judges to rule my people.
17:14 him over my dynasty and my kingdom for all **t**,
19: 1 Some **t** after this, King Nahash of the Ammonites
19:18 This **t** David's forces killed seven thousand
20: 1 the **t** of year when kings go to war,
21:20 who was busy threshing wheat at the **t**, turned
21:29 At that **t**, the Tabernacle of the LORD
2Ch 1:17 At that **t**, Egyptian chariots delivered to Jerusalem
2: 1 Solomon now decided that the **t** had come to build
8: 3 It was at this **t**, too, that Solomon fought against
8: 6 rebuilt Baalath and other supply centers at this **t**
14: 6 No one tried to make war against him at this **t**,
15: 3 For a long **t**, Israel was without the true God,
16: 7 At that **t** Hanani the seer came to King Asa
16: 8 At that **t** you relied on the LORD, and he handed
16:10 At that **t**, Asa also began to oppress some of his
18:17 "He does it every **t**. He never prophesies anything
21:10 The town of Libnah revolted about that same **t**,
21:19 In the course of **t**, at the end of two years,
23: 3 "The **t** has come for the king's son to reign!
24: 4 Some **t** later, Joash decided to repair and restore
28:16 About that **t** King Ahaz of Judah asked the king of
30: 3 but not enough priests could be purified by that **t**,
30:12 At the same **t**, God's hand was on the people in the
32:14 Name just one **t** when any god, anywhere, was able
32:24 About that **t**, Hezekiah became deathly ill.
35: 3 spend your **t** serving the LORD your God and his
35:18 Never since the **t** of the prophet Samuel had there
36:10 of the LORD were taken to Babylon at that **t**.
Ezr 2:59 Another group returned to Jerusalem at this **t** from
5: 1 At that **t** the prophets Haggai and Zechariah son of
9: 4 And I sat there utterly appalled until the **t** of the
9: 5 At the **t** of the sacrifice, I stood up from where I
10:14 wife will come at the scheduled **t** with the leaders
Ne 2: 1 never appeared sad in his presence before this **t**.
4:23 During this **t**, none of us—not I, nor my relatives,
5: 1 About this **t** some of the men and their wives
5:16 And I required all my officials to spend **t** working
5:18 the people were already having a difficult **t**.
6: 4 same message, and each **t** I gave the same reply.
6: 5 The fifth **t**, Sanballat's servant came with an open
7: 4 At that **t** the city was large and spacious,
7:61 "Another group returned to Jerusalem at this **t**
9: 1 This **t** they fasted and dressed in sackcloth
9:21 They lacked nothing in all that **t**. Their clothes did
9:27 But in their **t** of trouble they cried to you, and you
9:33 Every **t** you punished us you were being just.
11: 1 were living in Jerusalem, the holy city, at this **t**.
13: 6 I was not in Jerusalem at that **t**, for I had returned
13:21 And that was the last **t** they came on the Sabbath.
13:23 About the same **t** I realized that some of the men of
Est 1: 2 At that **t** he ruled his empire from his throne at the
1: 9 banquet for the women of the palace at the same **t**.
2:13 When the **t** came for her to go in to the king,
3: 1 Some **t** later, King Xerxes promoted Haman son of
4:14 If you keep quiet at a **t** like this, deliverance for the
4:14 elevated to the palace for just such a **t** as this?"
9:22 This would commemorate a **t** when the Jews
9:27 two prescribed days at the appointed **t** each year.
9:31 annual celebration of these days at the appointed **t**,
Job 5:20 He will save you from death in **t** of famine, from
the power of the sword in **t** of war.
5:26 You will not be harvested until the proper **t**!
10:20 I have only a little **t** left, so leave me alone—
21:17 "Yet the wicked get away with it **t** and **t** again.
24: 5 the poor must spend all their **t** just getting enough
27:10 in the Almighty? Can they call to God at any **t**?
32:11 "I have waited all this **t**, listening very carefully to
34: 8 of evil people. He spends his **t** with wicked men.
34: 9 has even said, 'Why waste **t** trying to please God?'
37: 7 Everyone stops working at such a **t** so they can
38:23 I have reserved it for the **t** of trouble, for the day of
39: 2 Are you aware of the **t** of their delivery?
Ps 1: 5 They will be condemned at the **t** of judgment.
2: 1 Why do the people waste their **t** with futile plans?
3: T regarding the **t** David fled from his son Absalom.
26: 4 I do not spend **t** with liars / or go along with
32: 6 confess their rebellion to you while there is **t**,
34: T regarding the **t** he pretended to be insane in front
39: 4 remind me how brief my **t** on earth will be.
50:18 help him, / and you spend your **t** with adulterers.
51: T regarding the **t** Nathan the prophet came to him
52: T regarding the **t** Doeg the Edomite told Saul that
54: T regarding the **t** the Ziphites came and said to Saul,
56: T regarding the **t** the Philistines seized him in Gath.
57: T regarding the **t** he fled from Saul and went into the
59: T regarding the **t** Saul sent soldiers to watch David's
60: T regarding the **t** David fought Aram-naharaim
63: T regarding a **t** when David was in the wilderness of
69:13 hoping this is the **t** you will show me favor.
72: 7 there be abundant prosperity until the end of **t**.
75: 2 God says, "At the **t** I have planned, / I will bring
78:38 destroy them all. / Many a **t** he held back his anger
89:45 You have made him old before his **t** / and publicly
90:12 Teach us to make the most of our **t**, / so that we
93: 2 has been established from **t** immemorial.
102: 2 from me / in my **t** of distress. / Bend down your ear
102:13 mercy on Jerusalem— / and now is the **t** to pity
her, / now is the **t** you promised to help.
105:19 Until the **t** came to fulfill his word, / the LORD
106:31 regarded as a righteous man / ever since that **t**.
119:126 LORD, it is **t** for you to act, / for these evil people
Pr 2: 9 how to find the right course of action every **t**.
11:26 but they bless the one who sells to them in their **t**
12:11 means prosperity; only fools idle away their **t**.
12:19 Truth stands the test of **t**; lies are soon exposed.
15:23 it is wonderful to say the right thing at the right **t**!
17:17 and a brother is born to help in **t** of need.
21:13 of the poor will be ignored in their own **t** of need.
23: 4 yourself trying to get rich. Why waste your **t**?
24:16 trip seven times, but each **t** they will rise again.
27:10 Then in your **t** of need, you won't have to ask your
Ecc 2: 2 "It is silly to be laughing all the **t**," I said.
3: 1 There is a **t** for everything, / a season for every
3: 2 A **t** to be born and a **t** to die. / A **t** to plant and a **t**
to harvest.
3: 3 A **t** to kill and a **t** to heal. / A time to **t** to tear down
and a **t** to rebuild.
3: 4 A **t** to cry and a **t** to laugh. / A **t** to grieve and a **t** to
dance.
3: 5 A **t** to scatter stones and a **t** to gather stones. / A **t**
to embrace and a **t** to turn away.
3: 6 A **t** to search and a **t** to lose. / A **t** to keep and a **t** to
throw away.
3: 7 A **t** to tear and a **t** to mend. / A **t** to be quiet and a **t**
to speak up.
3: 8 A **t** to love and a **t** to hate. / A **t** for war and a **t** for
peace.
3:11 God has made everything beautiful for its own **t**.
5: 7 Dreaming all the **t** instead of working is
7: 2 It is better to spend your **t** at funerals than at
7: 2 and you should think about it while there is still **t**.
7: 4 while the fool thinks only about having a good **t**
7:17 don't be a fool! Why should you die before your **t**?
8: 5 Those who are wise will find a **t** and a way to do
8: 6 Yes, there is a **t** and a way for everything, even as
8:12 person sins a hundred times and still lives a long **t**,
9:11 by chance, by being at the right place at the right **t**.
SS 2: 7 of the wild, not to awaken love until the **t** is right.
2:12 springing up, and the **t** of singing birds has come,
3: 5 of the wild, not to awaken love until the **t** is right."
8: 4 not to awaken love until the **t** is right."
Isa 7:15 By the **t** this child is old enough to eat curds
9: 1 that **t** of darkness and despair will not go on
9: 1 but there will be a **t** in the future when Galilee of
10:22 only a few of them will return at that **t**.
11:11 back a remnant of his people for the second **t**,
13: 6 Scream in terror, for the LORD's **t** has arrived—the
t for the Almighty to destroy.
13:22 are numbered; its **t** of destruction will soon arrive.
18: 7 But the **t** will come when the LORD Almighty
22:25 "When that **t** comes, I will pull out the stake that
27: 6 The **t** is coming when my people will take root.
27:12 Yet the **t** will come when the LORD will gather
28:10 us everything over and over again, a line at a **t**,
28:13 repeating it over and over, a line at a **t**, in very
30: 8 then stand until the end of **t** as a witness to Israel's
30:23 the LORD will bless you with rain at planting **t**.
30:32 his people will keep **t** with the music of
32:10 In a short **t**—in just a little more than a year—
33:18 You will think back to this **t** of terror when the
38: 1 About that **t** Hezekiah became deathly ill,
39: 6 The **t** is coming when everything you have—
48: 3 **T** and again I warned you about what was going to
48: 5 That is why I told you ahead of **t** what I was going
48: 7 So you cannot say, 'We knew that all the **t**!'
49: 8 "At just the right **t**, I will respond to you.
54: 9 "Just as I swore in the **t** of Noah that I would
57: 1 pass away; the godly often die before their **t**.
59: 4 They spend their **t** plotting evil deeds and
59: 5 They spend their **t** and energy spinning evil plans
60:22 the LORD, will bring it all to pass at the right **t**."
61: 2 He has sent me to tell those who mourn that the **t**
63: 4 For the **t** has come for me to avenge my people,
65:22 and will have **t** to enjoy their hard-won gains.
66: 8 But by the **t** Jerusalem's birth pains begin,
Jer 2: 8 in the name of Baal, wasting their **t** on nonsense.
2:24 like a wild donkey, sniffing the wind at mating **t**.
4:11 The **t** is coming when the LORD will say to the
6: 9 as when a harvester checks each vine a second **t** to
7:32 So beware, for the **t** is coming," says the LORD,
8: 7 The stork knows the **t** of her migration, as do the
8: 7 the crane. They all return at the proper **t** each year.
8:15 We hoped for a **t** of healing, but found only terror.
9:25 "A **t** is coming," says the LORD, "when I will
10:15 The **t** is coming when they will all be destroyed.
11:23 for I will bring disaster upon them when their **t** of
13: 6 A long **t** afterward, the LORD said to me,
14:19 We hoped for a **t** of healing but found only terror.
16:14 "But the **t** is coming," says the LORD,
19: 6 So beware, for the **t** is coming, says the LORD,
23: 5 "For the **t** is coming," says the LORD, "when I
23:12 For I will bring disaster upon them when their **t** of
25: 5 Each **t** the message was this: 'Turn from the evil
25:34 The **t** of your slaughter has arrived; you will fall
26:20 (At this **t**, Uriah son of Shemaiah from
27: 7 and his son and his grandson until his **t** is up.
30: 3 For the **t** is coming when I will restore the fortunes
30: 7 In all history there has never been such a **t** of
30: 7 It will be a **t** of trouble for my people Israel.
31:27 "The **t** will come," says the LORD, "when I will
31:38 "The **t** is coming," says the LORD, "when all
32: 6 At that **t** the LORD sent me a message. He said,
32:14 into a pottery jar to preserve them for a long **t**.
32:31 "From the **t** this city was built until now, it has
33: 6 the **t** will come when I will heal Jerusalem's
33:15 At that **t** I will bring to the throne of David a
34: 1 At that **t** this message came to Jeremiah from the
34: 7 At this **t** the Babylonian army was besieging
36: 2 message you have given, right up to the present **t**.
36:16 By the **t** Baruch had finished reading, they were
36:32 in the fire. Only this **t**, he added much more!
37: 5 At this **t** the army of Pharaoh Hophra of Egypt
38: 7 At that **t** the king was holding court at the
46:21 of great disaster for Egypt, a **t** of great punishment.
47: 4 "The **t** has come for the Philistines to be
48:12 But the **t** is coming soon," says the LORD,
48:44 for the **t** of your judgment has come,"
50:27 For the **t** has come for Babylon to be devastated.
51: 6 It is the LORD's **t** for vengeance; he will fully
51:18 The **t** is coming when they will all be destroyed.
51:46 Then there will be a **t** of violence as the leaders
51:47 For the **t** is surely coming when I will punish this
51:52 "but the **t** is coming when Babylon's idols will be
La 3:20 I will never forget this awful **t**, as I grieve over my
Eze 4:14 From the **t** I was a child until now I have never
7: 7 The **t** has come; the day of trouble is near. It will
7:12 Yes, the **t** has come; the day is here! There is no
11: 3 to the people, 'Is it not a good **t** to build houses?
11:16 I will be a sanctuary to you during your **t** in exile.
12:22 '**T** passes, making a liar of every prophet'?
12:23 'The **t** has come for every prophecy to be
12:27 'His visions won't come true for a long, long **t**.'
16:47 to you. In a very short **t** you far surpassed them!
16:55 be restored, and at that **t** you also will be restored.
19:14 is a funeral song, and it is now **t** for the funeral."
21:24 So now the **t** of your punishment has come!
23:27 those things or fondly remember your **t** in Egypt.
24:14 The **t** has come and I won't hold back; I will not
24:24 And when that **t** comes, you will know that I am
30: 9 At that **t** I will send swift messengers in ships to
36:38 that fill Jerusalem's streets at the **t** of her festivals.
38: 8 A long **t** from now you will be called into action.
38:10 At that **t** evil thoughts will come to your mind,
39:22 And from that **t** on the people of Israel will know
43:19 At that **t**, the Levitical priests of the family of
45:21 bread without yeast may be eaten during that **t**.
46:17 At that **t** the servant will be set free, and the land
47: 4 This **t** the water was up to my knees. After another
Da 1:17 for learning the literature and science of the **t**.
2: 8 You are trying to stall for **t** because you know I am
2:16 went at once to see the king and requested more **t**
4:16 For seven periods of **t**, let him have the mind of an
4:19 was overcome for a **t**, aghast at the meaning of the
4:23 the animals of the field for seven periods of **t**.'
4:25 Seven periods of **t** will pass while you live this
4:32 Seven periods of **t** will pass while you live this
4:34 "After this **t** had passed, I, Nebuchadnezzar,
7:22 Then the **t** arrived for the holy people to take over
7:25 and they will be placed under his control for a **t**,
times, and half a **t**.
8: 2 This **t** I was at the fortress of Susa, in the province
8:17 have seen in your vision relate to the **t** of the end."
8:19 to tell you what will happen later in the **t** of wrath.
8:19 What you have seen pertains to the very end of **t**.
8:26 But none of these things will happen for a long **t**,
9:21 came swiftly to me at the **t** of the evening sacrifice.
9:25 **t** the command is given to rebuild Jerusalem until
9:26 and its miseries are decreed from that **t** to the very
9:27 but after half this **t**, he will put an end to the
10: 3 All that **t** I had eaten no rich food or meat,
10:14 for this vision concerns a **t** yet to come."
11:14 At that **t** there will be a general uprising against the
11:27 for an end will still come at the appointed **t**.
11:29 "Then at the appointed **t** he will once again invade
11:29 the south, but this **t** the result will be different.

11:33 But for a **t** many of these teachers will die by fire
11:35 and cleansed and made pure until the **t** of the end,
for the appointed **t** is still to come.
11:36 He will succeed—until the **t** of wrath is completed.
11:40 "Then at the **t** of the end, the king of the south will
11:45 but while he is there, his **t** will suddenly run out,
12: 1 "At that **t** Michael, the archangel who stands
12: 1 Then there will be a **t** of anguish greater than any
12: 1 But at that **t** every one of your people whose name
12: 4 a secret; seal up the book until the **t** of the end.
12: 7 "It will go on for a **t**, times, and half a **t**.
12: 9 Daniel, for what I have said is for the **t** of the end.
12:11 "From the **t** the daily sacrifice is taken away
Hos 1:10 Yet the **t** will come when Israel will prosper
2:18 At that **t** I will make a covenant with all the wild
2:23 "At that **t** I will plant a crop of Israelites and raise
3: 3 During this **t**, you will not have sexual intercourse
3: 4 This illustrates that Israel will be a long **t** without a
6: 2 In just a short **t**, he will restore us so we can live in
9: 7 The **t** of Israel's punishment has come; the day of
10:12 for now is the **t** to seek the LORD, that he may
Joel 1:14 Announce a **t** of fasting; call the people together
2:12 LORD says, "Turn to me now, while there is **t**!
2:15 Announce a **t** of fasting; call the people together
3: 1 "At that **t**, when I restore the prosperity of Judah
Am 4: 2 "The **t** will come when you will be led away with
5:13 who are wise will keep quiet, for it is an evil **t**.
8: 9 At that **t**," says the Sovereign LORD, "I will
8:11 "The **t** is surely coming," says the Sovereign
9:13 "The **t** will come," says the LORD,
Ob 1: 8 At that **t** not a single wise person will be left in the
1:11 relatives in Israel during their **t** of greatest need.
1:14 over to their enemies in that terrible **t** of trouble.
1:18 At that **t** Israel will be a raging fire, and Edom,
Jnh 1: 5 And all this **t** Jonah was sound asleep down in the
1: 6 "How can you sleep at a **t** like this?" he shouted.
1:11 And since the storm was getting worse all the **t**,
3: 1 Then the LORD spoke to Jonah a second **t**:
3: 3 This **t** Jonah obeyed the LORD's command
Mic 5: 3 **t** when the woman in labor gives birth to her son.
5:10 "At that same **t**," says the LORD, "I will
7: 4 coming swiftly now. Your **t** of punishment is here.
Hab 2: 3 the **t** approaches when the vision will be fulfilled.
2: 6 But the **t** is coming when all their captives will
2:14 For the **t** will come when all the earth will be
3: 2 In this **t** of our deep need, begin again to help us,
Zep 2: 2 Gather while there is still **t**, before judgment
3: 3 Its judges are like ravenous wolves at evening **t**,
3: 8 the **t** is coming soon when I will stand up
Hag 1: 2 'The **t** has not yet come to rebuild the LORD's
Zec 14: 7 and night, for at evening **t** it will still be light.
Mal 3: 5 At that **t** I will put you on trial. I will be a ready
Mt 1:11 and his brothers (born at the **t** of the exile to
1:17 and fourteen from David's **t** to the Babylonian
2: 1 About that **t** some wise men from eastern lands
2: 7 At this meeting he learned the exact **t** when they
2:12 But when it was **t** to leave, they went home another
8:29 no right to torture us before God's appointed **t**!"
10:19 you will be given the right words at the right **t**.
10:26 For the **t** is coming when everything will be
11:12 And from the **t** John the Baptist began preaching
11:13 of the Scriptures looked forward to this present **t**.
12: 1 At about that **t** Jesus was walking through some
18: 1 About that **t** the disciples came to Jesus and asked,
18:29 fell down before him and begged for a little more **t**.
21:34 At the **t** of the grape harvest he sent his servants to
22: 3 he sent his servants to notify everyone that it was **t**
22:45 him Lord, how can he be his son at the same **t**?"
24: 3 And will there be any sign ahead of **t** to signal your
24:15 "The **t** will come when you will see what Daniel
24:21 For that will be a **t** of greater horror than anything
24:22 In fact, unless that **t** of calamity is shortened,
24:38 and weddings right up to the **t** Noah entered his
24:44 You also must be ready all the **t**. For the Son of
25:19 "After a long **t** their master returned from his trip
26: 3 At that same **t** the leading priests and other leaders
26:16 From that **t** on, Judas began looking for the right **t**
26:18 Tell him, 'The Teacher says, My **t** has come,
26:44 So he went back to pray a third **t**, saying the same
26:45 Look, the **t** has come. I, the Son of Man,
26:68 to us, you Messiah! Who hit you that **t**?"
26:72 Again Peter denied it, this **t** with an oath. "I don't
Mk 1:15 "At last the **t** has come!" he announced.
3:20 and his disciples couldn't even find **t** to eat.
6:31 and his apostles didn't even have **t** to eat.
8: 1 About this **t** another great crowd had gathered,
9:31 in order to spend more **t** with his disciples
11:27 By this **t** they had arrived in Jerusalem again.
12: 2 At grape-picking **t** he sent one of his servants to
12:37 him Lord, how can he be his son at the same **t**?"
12:38 some of the other things he taught them at this **t**:
13: 4 And will there be any sign ahead of **t** to show us
13:14 "The **t** will come when you will see the
13:19 horror than at any **t** since God created the world.
13:20 In fact, unless the Lord shortens that **t** of calamity,
13:24 "At that **t**, after those horrible days end, / the sun
14: 8 and has anointed my body for burial ahead of **t**.
14:11 So he began looking for the right **t** and place to
14:41 When he returned to them the third **t** he said,
14:41 The **t** has come. I, the Son of Man, am betrayed
14:65 "Who hit you that **t**, you prophet?" they jeered.
14:72 And immediately the rooster crowed the second **t**.
15: 6 to release one prisoner each year at Passover **t**—
15: 7 One of the prisoners at that **t** was Barabbas,
15:34 Then, at that **t** Jesus called out with a loud voice,
Lk 1:20 my words will certainly come true at the proper **t**."
1:57 Now it was **t** for Elizabeth's baby to be born,
2: 1 At that **t** the Roman emperor, Augustus,
2: 5 his fiancée, who was obviously pregnant by this **t**.
2: 6 they were there, the **t** came for her baby to be born.
2:22 Then it was **t** for the purification offering,
3: 2 At this **t** a message from God came to John son of
4: 2 He ate nothing all that **t** and was very hungry.
4: 5 all the kingdoms of the world in a moment of **t**.
4:19 and that the **t** of the Lord's favor has come."
4:25 widows in Israel who needed help in Elijah's **t**,
5: 6 And this **t** their nets were so full they began to
5:32 not to spend my **t** with those who think they are
6:21 for the **t** will come when you will laugh with joy.
6:25 for a **t** of awful hunger is before you.
7:21 At that very **t**, he cured many people of their
7:45 my feet again and again from the **t** I first came in.
8:27 and naked, he had lived in a cemetery for a long **t**.
9:51 As the **t** drew near for his return to heaven,
10:35 'I'll pay the difference the next **t** I am here.'
11: 7 and we are all in bed. I can't help you this **t**.'
11:53 From that **t** on they grilled him with many hostile
12: 2 The **t** is coming when everything will be revealed;
12:40 You must be ready all the **t**, for the Son of Man
13: 1 About this **t** Jesus was informed that Pilate had
14:17 to notify the guests that it was **t** for them to come.
15:14 About the **t** his money ran out, a great famine
15:29 And in all that **t** you never gave me even one
17: 4 and each **t** turns again and asks forgiveness,
17:22 "The **t** is coming when you will long to share in
17:27 and weddings right up to the **t** Noah entered his
20:10 At grape-picking **t**, he sent one of his servants to
20:44 him Lord, how can he be his son at the same **t**?"
21: 6 "The **t** is coming when all these things will be
21: 7 And will there be any sign ahead of **t**?"
21: 8 to be the Messiah and saying, 'The **t** has come!'
21:12 this occurs, there will be a **t** of great persecution.
21:20 then you will know that the **t** of its destruction has
22:14 Then at the proper **t** Jesus and the twelve apostles
22:28 You have remained true to me in my **t** of trial.
22:37 For the **t** has come for this prophecy about me to
22:53 the **t** when the power of darkness reigns."
22:64 then they hit him and asked, "Who hit you that **t**,
22:69 But the **t** is soon coming when I, the Son of Man,
23: 7 and Herod happened to be in Jerusalem at the **t**.
23: 8 and had been hoping for a long **t** to see him
23:22 For the third **t** he demanded, "Why? What crime
23:44 By this **t** it was noon, and darkness fell across the
23:56 But by the **t** they were finished it was the Sabbath,
24:26 all these things before entering his **t** of glory?"
24:28 By this **t** they were nearing Emmaus and the end of
24:53 And they spent all of their **t** in the Temple,
Jn 2: 4 and me?" Jesus asked. "My **t** has not yet come."
2:13 It was **t** for the annual Passover celebration,
3:23 At this **t** John the Baptist was baptizing at Aenon,
3:25 At that **t** a certain Jew began an argument with
4: 8 He was alone at the **t** because his disciples had
4:21 the **t** is coming when it will no longer matter
4:23 But the **t** is coming and is already here when true
4:53 Then the father realized it was the same **t** that
5:25 "And I assure you that the **t** is coming, in fact it is
5:28 the **t** is coming when all the dead in their graves
6: 4 (It was nearly **t** for the annual Passover
7: 2 But soon it was **t** for the Festival of Shelters,
7: 6 Jesus replied, "Now is not the right **t** for me to go.
7: 8 to this festival, because my **t** has not yet come."
7:23 For if the correct **t** for circumcising your son falls
7:30 laid a hand on him, because his **t** had not yet come.
8:20 was not arrested, because his **t** had not yet come.
9: 4 because there is little **t** left before the night falls
9:24 So for the second **t** they called in the man who had
10:22 and Jesus was in Jerusalem at the **t** of Hanukkah.
11:53 So from that **t** on the Jewish leaders began to plot
11:55 It was now almost **t** for the celebration of
12:16 His disciples didn't realize at the **t** that this was a
12:23 "The **t** has come for the Son of Man to enter into
12:31 The **t** of judgment for the world has come,
12:36 Believe in the light while there is still **t**; then you
13: 2 It was **t** for supper, and the Devil had already
13:31 Jesus said, "The **t** has come for me, the Son of
14: 9 I am, even after all the **t** I have been with you?
14:30 "I don't have much more **t** to talk to you,
16: 2 and the **t** is coming when those who kill you will
16:23 At that **t** you won't need to ask me for anything.
16:25 but the **t** will come when this will not be necessary,
16:32 But the **t** is coming—in fact, it is already here—
17: 1 up to heaven and said, "Father, the **t** has come.
17:12 During my **t** here, I have kept them safe. I guarded
20:26 together again, and this **t** Thomas was with them.
21:14 This was the third **t** Jesus had appeared to his
21:17 was grieved that Jesus asked the question a third **t**.
Ac 1: 3 he appeared to the apostles from **t** to **t**
1:15 During this **t**, on a day when about 120 believers
1:21 It must be someone who has been with us all the **t**
1:22 from the **t** he was baptized by John until the day he
2: 5 many nations were living in Jerusalem at that **t**.
2:40 Then Peter continued preaching for a long **t**,
3:21 For he must remain in heaven until the **t** for the
4:25 Why did the people waste their **t** with futile plans?
5:36 Some **t** ago there was that fellow Theudas,
5:37 After him, at the **t** of the census, there was Judas of
6: 2 "We apostles should spend our **t** preaching
6: 4 Then we can spend our **t** in prayer and preaching
7: 8 Abraham the covenant of circumcision at that **t**.
7:13 The second **t** they went, Joseph revealed his
7:17 "As the **t** drew near when God would fulfill his
7:20 "At that **t** Moses was born—a beautiful child in
7:45 And it was used there until the **t** of King David.
9: 9 And all that **t** he went without food and water.
9:37 About this **t** she became ill and died. Her friends
9:43 And Peter stayed a long **t** in Joppa, living with
11:27 During this **t**, some prophets traveled from
12: 1 About that **t** King Herod Agrippa began to
12: 9 the angel. But all the **t** he thought it was a vision.
13:20 judges ruled until the **t** of Samuel the prophet.
13:32 to our ancestors has come true in our own **t**,
14: 3 The apostles stayed there a long **t**,
14:28 there with the believers in Antioch for a long **t**.
15: 7 among you some **t** ago to preach to the Gentiles
15:14 Peter has told you about the **t** God first visited the
15:36 After some **t** Paul said to Barnabas, "Let's return
16: 6 them not to go into the province of Asia at that **t**.
17:21 to spend all their **t** discussing the latest ideas.)
18: 5 Paul spent his full **t** preaching and testifying to the
18:18 Paul stayed in Corinth for some **t** after that and
18:23 After spending some **t** in Antioch, Paul went back
19:23 But about that **t**, serious trouble developed in
20:16 Paul had decided against stopping at Ephesus this **t**
20:16 because he didn't want to spend further **t** in the
21:38 you the Egyptian who led a rebellion some **t** ago
27: 1 When the **t** came, we set sail for Italy. Paul
27: 9 We had lost a lot of **t**. The weather was becoming
27:21 No one had eaten for a long **t**. Finally, Paul called
28: 6 But when they had waited a long **t** and saw no
28:10 showered with honors, and when the **t** came to sail,
28:23 So a **t** was set, and on that day a large number of
Ro 1:20 From the **t** the world was created, people have seen
2: 4 Can't you see how kind he has been in giving you **t**
3:26 and just in this present **t** when he declares sinners
5: 6 Christ came at just the right **t** and died for us
8:22 in the pains of childbirth right up to the present **t**.
10:19 Yes, they did, for even in the **t** of Moses, God had
13:11 is that you know how late it is; **t** is running out.
16:25 a plan kept secret from the beginning of **t**.
1Co 3:13 But there is going to come a **t** of testing at the
6:11 There was a **t** when some of you were just like
7: 5 wife to refrain from sexual intimacy for a limited **t**,
7:29 The **t** that remains is very short, so husbands
7:32 An unmarried man can spend his **t** doing the
7:36 trouble controlling his passions and **t** is passing,
10:11 who live at the **t** when this age is drawing to a
11:26 For every **t** you eat this bread and drink this cup,
14:27 They must speak one at a **t**, and someone must be
15: 6 more than five hundred of his followers at one **t**,
15: 8 as though I had been born at the wrong **t**.
16: 7 This **t** I don't want to make just a short visit
16:12 He will be seeing you later, when the **t** is right.
2Co 2: 7 Now it is **t** to forgive him and comfort him.
6: 2 For God says, / "At just the right **t**, I heard you.
7: 8 I sent that letter to you, though I was sorry for a **t**,
8:14 Then at some other **t** they can share with you when
12: 9 Each **t** he said, "My gracious favor is all you need.
12:14 Now I am coming to you for the third **t**, and I will
13: 1 This is the third **t** I am coming to visit you.
13: 2 I did before, that this next **t** I will not spare them.
Gal 1:19 And the only other apostle I met at that **t** was
2: 1 went back to Jerusalem again, this **t** with Barnabas;
3: 8 the Scriptures looked forward to this **t** when God
4: 4 But when the right **t** came, God sent his Son,
6: 9 will reap a harvest of blessing at the appropriate **t**.
Eph 1:10 At the right **t** he will bring everything together
6:13 of God's armor to resist the enemy in the **t** of evil,
Php 1: 3 Every **t** I think of you, I give thanks to my God.
1: 5 about Christ from the **t** you first heard it until now.
Col 3: 8 But now is the **t** to get rid of anger, rage,
3:22 Try to please them all the **t**, not just when they are
1Th 5: 7 Night is the **t** for sleep and the **t** when people get
drunk.
5:10 whether we are dead or alive at the **t** of his return.
2Th 2: 6 for he can be revealed only when his **t** comes.
3:11 and wasting **t** meddling in other people's business.
1Ti 1: 4 Don't let people waste **t** in endless speculation
1: 6 and spend their **t** arguing and talking foolishness.
2: 6 message that God gave to the world at the proper **t**.
4: 7 Do not waste **t** arguing over godless ideas and old
4: 7 Spend your **t** and energy in training yourself for
5: 5 she asks God for help and spends much **t** in prayer.
5:13 and spend their **t** gossiping from house to house,
6:15 For at the right **t** Christ will be revealed from
2Ti 4: 2 Be persistent, whether the **t** is favorable or not.
4: 3 For a **t** is coming when people will no longer listen
4: 6 as an offering to God. The **t** of my death is near.
4:16 The first **t** I was brought before the judge, no one
Tit 1: 3 And now at the right **t** he has revealed this Good
3: 8 in God will be careful to do good deeds all the **t**.
3: 9 These kinds of things are useless and a waste of **t**.
Heb 4: 7 So God set another **t** for entering his place of rest,
and that **t** is today.
4: 7 God announced this through David a long **t** later in
5:12 You have been Christians a long **t** now, and you
9: 9 This is an illustration pointing to the present **t**.
9:12 Once for all **t** he took blood into that Most Holy
9:26 He came once for all **t**, at the end of the age,
9:28 This **t** he will bring salvation to all those who are
10: 2 worshipers would have been purified once for all **t**,
10:10 sacrifice of the body of Jesus Christ once for all **t**.
10:12 to God as one sacrifice for sins, good for all **t**.
1Pe 1:17 of him during your **t** as foreigners here on earth.
3:18 suffered when he died for our sins once for all **t**.
4:17 For the **t** has come for judgment, and it must begin
5: 6 power of God, and in his good **t** he will honor you.
2Pe 2: 7 But at the same **t**, God rescued Lot out of Sodom
3: 9 so he is giving more **t** for everyone to repent.
3:15 Lord is waiting so that people have **t** to be saved.
3:17 I am warning you ahead of **t**, dear friends, so that
Jude 1: 3 God gave this unchanging truth once for all **t** to his

Rev 1: 3 For the t is near when these things will happen.
2:21 I gave her t to repent, but she would not turn away
3:10 I will protect you from the great t of testing that
11:18 with you, / but now the t of your wrath has come.
11:18 It is t to judge the dead and reward your servants.
12:12 in great anger, and he knows that he has little t."
12:14 from the dragon for a t, times, and half a t.
14: 7 For the t has come when he will sit as judge.
14:15 the sickle, for the t has come for you to harvest;
19: 7 For the t has come for the wedding feast of the
22:10 prophetic words you have written, for the t is near.

TIMELY (1) [TIME]

Pr 25:11 T advice is as lovely as golden apples in a silver

TIMES (169) [TIME]

AT ALL TIMES (11) Lev 6:13; Dt 1:16; 2Ki 11:8; 1Ch 23:31; 2Ch 23:7; Ne 4:23; Ps 34:1; 62:8; 2Co 13:8; Eph 6:18; Jas 3:17

FORMER TIMES (4) Ecc 1:11; Mal 3:4; Ro 3:25; 1Co 2:7

LAST TIMES (2) 1Ti 4:1; Jude 1:18

SEVEN TIMES (31) Ge 4:15,24; 33:3; Lev 4:6,17; 8:11; 14:7,16,27,51; 16:14,19; 26:18,24,28; Nu 19:4; Jos 6:4,15; 1Ki 18:43,43; 2Ki 4:35; 5:10,14; Ps 12:6; 119:164; Pr 6:31; 24:16; Isa 30:26; Da 3:19; Mt 18:21; Lk 17:4

THREE TIMES (26) Ex 23:17; 34:23,24; Nu 22:28,32,33; 24:10; Jdg 16:15; 1Ki 9:25; 17:21; 2Ki 13:18,19; Eze 21:14; Da 6:10,13; Mt 26:34,75; Mk 14:30,72; Lk 22:34,61; Jn 13:38; Ac 10:16; 11:10; 2Co 11:25,25

Ge 4:15 for I will give seven t your punishment to anyone
4:24 If anyone who kills Cain is to be punished seven t,
4:24 against me will be punished seventy-seven t!"
26:12 He harvested a hundred t more grain than he
31:41 the flock. And you have reduced my wages ten t!
33: 3 his brother, he bowed low seven t before him.
43:34 five t as much as to any of the others.
Ex 23:17 At these three t each year, every man in Israel must
34:23 Three t each year all the men of Israel must appear
34:24 the LORD your God those three t each year.
Lev 4: 6 and sprinkle it seven t before the LORD in front
4:17 and sprinkle it seven t before the LORD in front
6:13 the fire must be kept burning on the altar at all t.
8:11 He sprinkled the altar seven t, anointing it and all
14: 7 bird's blood seven t over the person being purified,
14:16 the oil and sprinkle it seven t before the LORD.
14:27 and sprinkle some of it seven t before the LORD.
14:51 and he will sprinkle the house seven t.
16:14 and then seven t against the front of the Ark.
16:19 into the blood and sprinkle it seven t over the altar.
25: 8 seven years t seven, adding up to forty-nine years
26:18 I will punish you for your sins seven t over.
26:24 and I will personally strike you seven t over for
26:28 I will punish you seven t over for your sins.
Nu 10:10 Blow the trumpets in t of gladness, too,
19: 4 and sprinkle it seven t toward the front of the
22:28 you that deserves your beating me these three t?"
22:32 "Why did you beat your donkey those three t?"
22:33 Three t the donkey saw me and shied away;
24:10 Instead, you have blessed them three t.
28: 2 See to it that they are brought at the appointed t
Dt 1:11 multiply you a thousand t more and bless you as he
1:16 the judges, 'You must be perfectly fair at all t,
2:12 In earlier t the Horites had lived at Mount Seir,
Jos 6: 4 day you are to march around the city seven t,
6:15 But this time they went around the city seven t.
Jdg 16:15 You've made fun of me three t now, and you still
1Sa 27: 8 near Shur, along the road to Egypt, since ancient t.
2Sa 19:43 "So we have ten t as much right to the king as you
24: 3 t as many people in your kingdom as there are
1Ki 9:25 Three t each year Solomon offered burnt offerings
17:21 And he stretched himself out over the child three t
18:43 Seven t Elijah told him to go and look, and seven t he went.
22:16 "How many t must I demand that you speak only
2Ki 4:35 and walked back and forth in the room a few t.
4:35 This time the boy sneezed seven t and opened his
5:10 and wash yourself seven t in the Jordan River.
5:14 to the Jordan River and dipped himself seven t,
6:10 there to be on their guard. This happened several t.
11: 8 must be killed. Stay right beside the king at all t."
11:14 by the pillar, as was the custom at t of coronation.
13:18 king picked them up and struck the ground three t.
13:19 "You should have struck the ground five or six t!"
13:19 Now you will be victorious only three t."
1Ch 9:20 had been in charge of the gatekeepers in earlier t,
12:32 All these men understood the temper of the t
21: 3 the number of his people a hundred t over!
23:31 of Levites served in the LORD's presence at all t,
2Ch 7:13 At t I might shut up the heavens so that no rain
15: 5 During those dark t, it was not safe to travel.
18:15 "How many t must I demand that you speak only
23: 7 must be killed. Stay right beside the king at all t."
Ezr 4:19 and have indeed found that Jerusalem has in t past
Ne 4:23 We carried our weapons with us at all t, even when
6: 4 Four t they sent the same message, and each time I
10:34 at regular t each year—the families of the priests,
13:31 of wood for the altar was brought at the proper t
Est 9:31 and their descendants to establish the t of fasting
Job 9: 3 possible to answer him even once in a thousand t?
19: 3 Ten t now you have meant to insult me.
21:30 Evil people are spared in t of calamity and are
Ps 4: 6 Many people say, "Who will show us better t?"
9: 9 shelter for the oppressed, / a refuge in t of trouble.
12: 6 silver refined in a furnace, / purified seven t over.
20: 1 In t of trouble, may the LORD respond to your
33:19 from death / and keeps them alive in t of famine.
34: 1 I will praise the LORD at all t. / I will constantly
37:19 They will survive through hard t; / even in famine
37:39 saves the godly; / he is their fortress in t of trouble.
41: 1 The LORD rescues them in t of trouble.
46: 1 and strength, / always ready to help in t of trouble.
49: 5 There is no need to fear when t of trouble come,
50:15 Trust me in your t of trouble, / and I will rescue
62: 8 O my people, trust in him at all t. / Pour out your
62:11 has spoken plainly, / and I have heard it many t:
74: 2 that we are the people you chose in ancient t,
94:13 You give them relief from troubled t / until a pit is
119:164 I will praise you seven t a day / because all your
Pr 6:31 he will be fined seven t as much as he stole,
24:16 They may trip seven t, but each time they will rise
Ecc 1:11 don't remember what happened in those former t.
7:14 But when hard t strike, realize that both come from
8:12 But even though a person sins a hundred t and still
9:12 People can never predict when hard t might come.
Isa 1:29 Shame will cover you when you think of the t you
30:26 as the sun, and the sun will be seven t brighter—
33: 2 strength each day and our salvation in t of trouble.
44: 7 Let them do as I have done since ancient t.
45: 7 I am the one who sends good t and bad t.
Jer 2:27 but in t of trouble they cry out for me to save
14: 8 O Hope of Israel, our Savior in t of trouble!
15:11 will ask you to plead on their behalf in t of trouble
Eze 4:10 ounces of food for each day, and eat it at set t.
4:11 out a jar of water for each day, and drink it at set t.
21:14 take the sword and brandish it twice, even three t,
Da 1:20 men to be ten t better than that of all the magicians
3:19 He commanded that the furnace be heated seven t
6:10 He prayed three t a day, just as he had always
6:13 your law. He still prays to his God three t a day."
7:25 under his control for a time, t, and half a time.
9:25 and strong defenses, despite the perilous t.
10: 1 t of war and great hardship—and Daniel
12: 7 "It will go on for a time, t, and half a time.
Hos 2:13 I will punish her for all the t she deserted me,
Am 8:10 I will turn your celebrations into t of mourning,
Mic 3: 4 Then you beg the LORD for help in t of trouble!
Zec 8:19 and t of mourning you have kept in early summer,
14: 3 against those nations, as he has fought in t past.
Mal 3: 4 of Judah and Jerusalem, as he did in former t.
Mt 13: 8 and even a hundred t as much as had been planted.
13:23 or even a hundred t as much as had been planted."
16: 3 but you can't read the obvious signs of the t!
18:21 I forgive someone who sins against me? Seven t?"
18:22 "No!" Jesus replied, "seventy t seven!
19:29 will receive a hundred t as much in return and will
26:34 the rooster crows, you will deny me three t."
26:75 the rooster crows, you will deny me three t."
Mk 4: 8 and even a hundred t as much as had been
4:20 or even a hundred t as much as had been planted."
10:30 a hundred t over, houses, brothers, sisters, mothers,
14:30 the rooster crows twice, you will deny me three t."
14:72 the rooster crows twice, you will deny me three t."
Lk 8: 8 and produced a crop one hundred t as much as had
11:29 pressed in on Jesus, he said, "These are evil t,
12:56 and the sky, but you can't interpret these present t.
17: 4 Even if he wrongs you seven t a day and each time
18:30 will be repaid many t over in this life, as well as
19: 8 their taxes, I will give them back four t as much!"
19:16 ten t as much as the original amount!
19:18 reported a good gain—five t the original amount.
22:34 you have denied three t that you even know me."
22:61 tomorrow morning, you will deny me three t."
Jn 13:38 you will deny three t that you even know me.
18: 2 because Jesus had gone there many t with his
Ac 3:20 Then wonderful t of refreshment will come from
10:16 The same vision was repeated three t.
11:10 "This happened three t before the sheet and all it
26:11 Many t I had them whipped in the synagogues to
26:16 and about other t I will appear to you.
Ro 1:13 dear friends, that I planned many t to visit you,
3:25 he did not punish those who sinned in former t.
15:26 in Jerusalem, who are going through such hard t.
1Co 2: 7 wisdom of God, which was hidden in former t,
2Co 8: 2 have been going through much trouble and hard t,
11:23 been whipped t without number, and faced death
11:24 Five different t the Jews gave me thirty-nine
11:25 Three t I was beaten with rods. Once I was stoned. Three t I was shipwrecked.
12: 8 Three different t I begged the Lord to take it away.
13: 8 oppose the truth, but to stand for the truth at all t.
Eph 6:18 Pray at all t and on every occasion in the power of
1Ti 4: 1 last t some will turn away from what we believe;
2Ti 3: 1 that in the last days there will be very difficult t.
Heb 1: 1 Long ago God spoke many t and in many ways to
Jas 3:17 It is also peace loving, gentle at all t, and willing to
Jude 1:18 that in the last t there would be scoffers whose
Rev 12:14 from the dragon for a time, t, and half a time.

TIMID (4) [TIMIDITY]

Jdg 7: 3 'Whoever is t or afraid may leave and go
1Co 2: 3 I came to you in weakness—t and trembling.
2Co 10: 1 of you say I am bold in my letters but t in person.
1Th 5:14 Encourage those who are t. Take tender care of

TIMIDITY (1) [TIMID]

2Ti 1: 7 For God has not given us a spirit of fear and t,

TIMNA (6)

Ge 36:12 son named Amalek, born to T, his concubine.
36:22 and Heman. Lotan's sister was named T.
36:40 in the places named for them: T, Alvah, Jetheth,
1Ch 1:36 Gatam, Kenaz, and Amalek, who was born to T.
1:39 and Heman. Lotan's sister was named T.
1:51 The clan leaders of Edom were T, Alvah, Jetheth,

TIMNAH (15)

Ge 38:12 and his friend Hirah the Adullamite went to T to
38:13 father-in-law had left for the sheep-shearing at T.
38:14 to the village of Enaim, which is on the way to T.
Jos 15:10 and went down to Beth-shemesh and on to T.
15:57 Kain, Gibeah, and T—ten towns with their
19:43 Elon, T, Ekron,
Jdg 14: 1 One day when Samson was in T, he noticed a
14: 2 to marry a young Philistine woman I saw in T."
14: 5 As Samson and his parents were going down to T,
14: 5 lion attacked Samson near the vineyards of T.
14: 7 When Samson arrived in T, he talked with the
14: 8 Later, when he returned to T for the wedding,
14:10 Samson threw a party at T, as was the custom of
15: 6 "because his father-in-law from T gave Samson's
2Ch 28:18 Soco with its villages, T with its villages,

TIMNATH-SERAH (3)

Jos 19:50 He chose T in the hill country of Ephraim.
24:30 at T in the hill country of Ephraim, north of Mount
Jdg 2: 9 at T in the hill country of Ephraim, north of Mount

TIMON (1)

Ac 6: 5 Philip, Procorus, Nicanor, T, Parmenas,

TIMOTHY (35)

Ac 16: 1 There they met T, a young disciple whose mother
16: 2 T was well thought of by the believers in Lystra
16: 3 he arranged for T to be circumcised before they
17:14 on to the coast, while Silas and T remained behind.
17:15 a message for Silas and T to hurry and join him.
18: 5 And after Silas and T came down from Macedonia,
19:22 He sent his two assistants, T and Erastus, on ahead
20: 4 Gaius, from Derbe; T; and Tychicus
Ro 16:21 T, my fellow worker, and Lucius, Jason,
1Co 4:17 That is the very reason I am sending T—to help
16:10 When T comes, treat him with respect. He is doing
2Co 1: 1 of Christ Jesus, and from our dear brother T.
1:19 He is the one whom T, Silas, and I preached to
Php 1: 1 This letter is from Paul and T, slaves of Christ
2:19 Lord Jesus is willing, I hope to send T to you soon.
2:20 I have no one else like T, who genuinely cares
2:22 But you know how T has proved himself. Like a
Col 1: 1 an apostle of Christ Jesus, and from our brother T.
1Th 1: 1 This letter is from Paul, Silas, and T. It is written
3: 2 and we sent T to visit you. He is our co-worker for
3: 5 I sent T to find out whether your faith was still
3: 6 Now T has just returned, bringing the good news
2Th 1: 1 This letter is from Paul, Silas, and T. It is written
1Ti 1: 2 It is written to T, my true child in the faith.
1:18 T, my son, here are my instructions for you,
6: 2 Teach these truths, T, and encourage everyone to
6:11 But you, T, belong to God; so run from all these
6:20 T, guard what God has entrusted to you.
2Ti 1: 2 It is written to T, my dear son. May God our
1: 3 T, I thank God for you. He is the God I serve with
2: 1 T, my dear son, be strong with the special favor
3: 1 You should also know this, T, that in the last days
3:10 But you know what I teach, T, and how I live,
Phm 1: 1 News about Christ Jesus, and from our brother T.
Heb 13:23 I want you to know that our brother T is now out

TIN (4)

Nu 31:22 made of gold, silver, bronze, iron, t, or lead—
Eze 22:18 a useless mixture of copper, t, iron, and lead.
22:20 just as copper, t, iron, and lead are melted down in
27:12 your wares in exchange for silver, iron, t, and lead.

TINGLE (1)

2Ki 21:12 ears of those who hear about it will t with horror.

TINIEST (3) [TINY]

Isa 60:22 The t group will become a mighty nation. I,
Mt 23:23 For you are careful to tithe even the t part of your
Lk 11:42 For you are careful to tithe even the t part of your

TINKLE (1) [TINKLING]

Ex 28:35 and the bells will t as he goes in and out of the

TINKLING (1) [TINKLE]

Isa 3:16 noses in the air, with t ornaments on their ankles.

TINKLING [KJV] See also ANKLETS, CLANGING

TINY (17) [TINIEST]

Jos 10:20 and wiped out the five armies except for a t
1Ki 4:33 from the great cedar of Lebanon to the t hyssop
2Ki 18:24 With your t army, how can you think of
1Ch 16:19 few in number, / a t group of strangers in Canaan.
Ps 105:12 few in number, / a t group of strangers in Canaan.
Ecc 11: 5 and as mysterious as a t baby being formed in a
Isa 36: 9 With your t army, how can you think of
Jer 42: 2 we are only a t remnant compared to what we were
La 2:11 Little children and t babies are fainting and dying
Eze 12:19 and sip their t portions of water in utter despair,

Joel 2: 4 They look like **t** horses, and they run as fast.
Mk 4:31 It is like a **t** mustard seed. Though this is one of the
12:44 For they gave a **t** part of their surplus, but she,
Lk 13:19 It is like a **t** mustard seed planted in a garden;
21: 4 For they have given a **t** part of their surplus,
Jas 3: 4 And a **t** rudder makes a huge ship turn wherever
3: 5 it can do. A **t** spark can set a great forest on fire.

TIP (6) [TIPPED, TIPPING, TIPS]
Ex 29:20 and place some of it on the **t** of the right earlobes
Lev 14:14 and put it on the **t** of the healed person's right ear,
14:17 left hand on the **t** of the healed person's right ear,
14:25 and put some of its blood on the **t** of the person's
Est 5: 2 to her. So Esther approached and touched its **t**.
Lk 16:24 Send Lazarus over here to dip the **t** of his finger in

TIPHSAH (1)
1Ki 4:24 west of the Euphrates River, from **T** to Gaza.

TIPPED (1) [TIP]
1Sa 17: 7 **t** with an iron spearhead that weighed fifteen

TIPPING (2) [TIP]
Isa 51:17 have drunk the cup of terror, **t** out its last drops.
Jer 1:13 "I see a pot of boiling water, **t** from the north."

TIPS (2) [TIP]
Ps 10: 7 Trouble and evil are on the **t** of their tongues.
Isa 17: 6 four or five out on the **t** of the limbs.

TIRAS (2)
Ge 10: 2 Magog, Madai, Javan, Tubal, Meshech, and **T**.
1Ch 1: 5 Magog, Madai, Javan, Tubal, Meshech, and **T**.

TIRATHITES (1)
1Ch 2:55 at Jabez—the **T**, Shimeathites, and Sucathites.

TIRED (23) [TIRES, TIRESOME]
Ge 27:46 "I'm sick and **t** of these local Hittite women.
Ex 17:12 Moses' arms finally became too **t** to hold up the
Jdg 8: 5 They are very **t**. I am chasing Zebah
1Sa 30:21 and met the two hundred men who had been too **t**
2Sa 17:29 "You must all be very **t** and hungry and thirsty
23:10 He killed Philistines until his hand was too **t** to lift
Ne 4:10 to complain that the workers were becoming **t**.
Ps 120: 6 I am **t** of living here / among people who hate
Isa 5:27 They will not get **t** or stumble. They will run
30:11 We are **t** of listening to what he has to say."
35: 3 With this news, strengthen those who have **t** hands,
38:14 My eyes grew **t** of looking to heaven for help.
40:29 He gives power to those who are **t** and worn out;
43:22 to ask for my help. You have grown **t** of me!
Jer 12: 5 to me, "If racing against mere men makes you **t**,
15: 6 I am **t** of always giving you another chance.
Mt 27:31 When they were finally **t** of mocking him,
Mk 15:20 When they were finally **t** of mocking him,
Jn 4: 6 and Jesus, **t** from the long walk, sat wearily beside
Gal 6: 9 So don't get **t** of doing what is good. Don't get
Php 3: 1 Lord give you joy. I never get **t** of telling you this.
2Th 3:13 dear brothers and sisters, never get **t** of doing good.
Heb 12:12 So take a new grip with your **t** hands and stand

TIRES (1) [TIRED]
Ps 121: 4 who watches over Israel / never **t** and never sleeps.

TIRES [KJV] See also COVERED, CRESCENT

TIRESOME (1) [TIRED]
Ecc 1: 8 Everything is so weary and **t**! No matter how much

TIRHAKAH (2)
2Ki 19: 9 **T** of Ethiopia was leading an army to fight against
Isa 37: 9 **T** of Ethiopia was leading an army to fight against

TIRHANAH (1)
1Ch 2:48 Maacah, gave birth to Sheber and **T**.

TIRIA (1)
1Ch 4:16 of Jehallelel were Ziph, Ziphah, **T**, and Asarel.

TIRSHATHA [KJV] See GOVERNOR

TIRZAH (17)
Nu 26:33 were Mahlah, Noah, Hoglah, Milcah, and **T**.
27: 1 Mahlah, Noah, Hoglah, Milcah, and **T**.
36:11 Mahlah, **T**, Hoglah, Milcah, and Noah all married
Jos 12:24 The king of **T**. In all, thirty-one kings and their
17: 3 were Mahlah, Noah, Hoglah, Milcah, and **T**.
1Ki 14:17 So Jeroboam's wife returned to **T**, and the child
15:21 his project of fortifying Ramah and withdrew to **T**.
15:33 in Judah. Baasha reigned in **T** twenty-four years.
16: 6 When Baasha died, he was buried in **T**. Then his
16: 8 **T** in the twenty-sixth year of King Asa's reign in
16: 9 One day in **T**, Elah was getting drunk at the home
16:15 Zimri began to rule over Israel from **T** in the
16:17 army of Israel away from Gibbethon to attack **T**,
16:23 He reigned twelve years in all, six of them in **T**.
2Ki 15:14 Menahem son of Gadi went to Samaria from **T**
15:16 and all the surrounding countryside as far as **T**,
SS 6: 4 you are as beautiful as the lovely town of **T**.

TISHBE (6)
1Ki 17: 1 Now Elijah, who was from **T** in Gilead, told King
21:17 But the LORD said to Elijah, who was from **T**,
21:28 from the LORD came to Elijah, who was from **T**:
2Ki 1: 3 who was from **T**, "Go and meet the messengers of
1: 8 "It was Elijah from **T**!" the king exclaimed.
9:36 which he spoke through his servant Elijah from **T**:

TITHE (20) [TEN]
Ex 22:29 back when you give me the **t** of your crops
Nu 18:26 a **t** of the **t**—to the LORD as a gift.
18:28 You must present one-tenth of the **t** received from
Dt 12:17 neither the **t** of your grain and new wine and olive
14:22 "You must set aside a **t** of your crops—
14:23 Bring this **t** to the place the LORD your God
14:25 you may sell the **t** portion of your crops and herds
14:28 "At the end of every third year bring the **t** of all
26:12 "Every third year you must offer a special **t** of
2Ch 31: 5 of their fields. They brought a **t** of all they owned.
31: 6 and a **t** of the things that had been dedicated to the
Mt 23:23 For you are careful to **t** even the tiniest part of your
23:23 You should **t**, yes, but you should not leave undone
Lk 11:42 For you are careful to **t** even the tiniest part of your
11:42 You should **t**, yes, but you should not leave undone
Heb 7: 5 are commanded in the law of Moses to collect a **t**
7: 9 that Levi's descendants, the ones who collect the **t**,
7: 9 paid a **t** to Melchizedek through their ancestor
7:10 loins when Melchizedek collected the **t** from him.

TITHES (22) [TEN]
Nu 18:21 Tabernacle with the **t** from the entire land of Israel.
18:24 because I have given them the Israelites' **t**,
18:26 'When you receive the **t** from the Israelites, give a tenth of the **t** you receive—
18:32 **t** if you give the best portion to the priests.
Dt 12: 6 your sacrifices, your **t**, your special gifts,
12:11 your sacrifices, your **t**, your special gifts,
14:23 This applies to your **t** of grain, new wine, olive oil,
26:12 You must give these **t** to the Levites, foreigners,
2Ch 31: 6 brought in the **t** of their cattle and sheep and a tithe
31: 7 The first of these **t** was brought in late spring,
31:12 and **t** were faithfully brought to the Temple.
Ne 10:37 for it is the Levites who collect the **t** in all our rural
10:38 will be with the Levites as they receive these **t**.
10:38 And a tenth of all that is collected as **t** will be
12:44 for the gifts, the first part of the harvest, and the **t**.
13: 5 and **t** of grain, new wine, olive oil,
13:12 the people of Judah began bringing their **t** of grain,
Am 4: 4 each morning and bring your **t** every three days!
Mal 3: 8 "You have cheated me of the **t** and offerings due
3:10 Bring all the **t** into the storehouse so there will be
Heb 7: 8 of Jewish priests, **t** are paid to men who will die.

TITHING (1) [TEN]
Dt 14:23 The purpose of **t** is to teach you always to fear the

TITIUS (1) [JUSTUS]
Ac 18: 7 After that he stayed with **T** Justus, a Gentile who

TITLE (7) [TITLES]
Isa 22:21 have your royal robes, your **t**, and your authority.
Jer 10: 7 O King of nations? That **t** belongs to you alone!
Mt 22:20 "Whose picture and **t** are stamped on it?"
Mk 12:16 "Whose picture and **t** are stamped on it?"
Lk 20:24 Whose picture and **t** are stamped on it?"
Rev 19:13 dipped in blood, and his **t** was the Word of God.
19:16 On his robe and thigh was written this **t**: King of

TITLES (1) [TITLE]
Isa 9: 6 These will be his royal **t**: Wonderful Counselor,

TITTLE [KJV] See SMALLEST (DETAIL)

TITUS (14)
2Co 2:13 because my dear brother **T** hadn't yet arrived with
7: 6 are discouraged, encouraged us by the arrival of **T**.
7:13 we were especially delighted to see how happy **T**
7:14 and now my boasting to **T** has also proved true!
8: 6 So we have urged **T**, who encouraged your giving
8:16 I am thankful to God that he has given **T** the same
8:18 We are also sending another brother with **T**.
8:23 If anyone asks about **T**, say that he is my partner
12:18 When I urged **T** to visit you and sent our other
12:18 brother with him, did **T** take advantage of you?
Gal 2: 1 this time with Barnabas; and **T** came along, too.
2: 3 They did not even demand that my companion **T**
2Ti 4:10 has gone to Galatia, and **T** has gone to Dalmatia.
Tit 1: 4 This letter is written to **T**, my true child in the faith

TIZ (1)
1Ch 11:45 Jediael son of Shimri; / Joha, his brother, from **T**;

TO (20812) [TOWARD] See Index of Articles, Etc.

TOAH (1)
1Ch 6:34 Elkanah, Jeroham, Eliel, **T**,

TOASTS (1)
Da 5: 4 They drank **t** from them to honor their idols made

TOB (4)
Jdg 11: 3 fled from his brothers and lived in the land of **T**.
11: 5 of Gilead sent for Jephthah in the land of **T**.
2Sa 10: 6 and twelve thousand from the land of **T**.
10: 8 from Zobah and Rehob and the men from **T**

TOB-ADONIJAH (1)
2Ch 17: 8 Jehonathan, Adonijah, Tobijah, and **T**.

TOBIAH (14) [TOBIAH'S]
Ezr 2:60 of the families of Delaiah, **T**, and Nekoda—
Ne 2:10 and **T** the Ammonite official heard of my arrival,
2:19 But when Sanballat, **T**, and Geshem the Arab
4: 3 **T** the Ammonite, who was standing beside him,
4: 7 But when Sanballat and **T** and the Arabs,
6: 1 When Sanballat, **T**, Geshem the Arab, and the rest
6:12 against me because **T** and Sanballat had hired him.
6:14 all the evil things that **T** and Sanballat have done.
6:17 many letters went back and forth between **T**
6:19 They kept telling me what a wonderful man **T** was,
6:19 And **T** sent many threatening letters to intimidate
7:62 included the families of Delaiah, **T**, and Nekoda—
13: 4 of our God and who was also a relative of **T**,
13: 7 that he had provided **T** with a room in the

TOBIAH'S (2) [TOBIAH]
Ne 13: 5 a large storage room and placed it at **T** disposal.
13: 8 and threw all of **T** belongings from the room.

TOBIJAH (3)
2Ch 17: 8 Asahel, Shemiramoth, Jehonathan, Adonijah, **T**,
Zec 6:10 "Heldai, **T**, and Jedaiah will bring gifts of silver
6:14 Heldai, **T**, Jedaiah, and Josiah son of Zephaniah."

TODAY (203) [TODAY'S]
Ge 7: 4 One week from **t** I will begin forty days and forty
30:32 Let me go out among your flocks **t** and remove all
32:32 That is why even **t** the people of Israel don't eat
40: 7 "Why do you look so worried **t**?" he asked.
41: 9 "**T** I have been reminded of my failure," he said.
50:20 He brought me to the high position I have **t** so I
Ex 2:18 did you get the flocks watered so quickly **t**?"
5:14 you met your quotas either yesterday or **t**?"
14:13 The Egyptians that you see **t** will never be seen
16:23 So bake or boil as much as you want **t**, and set
16:25 "This is your food for **t**, for **t** is a Sabbath to the LORD. There will be no food on the ground **t**.
19:10 Purify them **t** and tomorrow, and have them wash
32:29 "**T** you have been ordained for the service of the
34:11 is to obey all the commands I am giving you **t**.
Lev 8:34 What has been done **t** was commanded by the
9: 4 because the LORD will appear to them **t**."
10:19 "**T** my sons presented both their sin offering
10:19 have approved if I had eaten the sin offering **t**?"
Dt 2:18 '**T** you will cross the border of Moab at Ar
2:25 Beginning **t** I will make all people throughout the
3:14 calling it the Towns of Jair, as it is still known **t**.)
4: 4 faithful to the LORD your God are still alive **t**.
4: 8 as fair as this body of laws that I am giving you **t**?
4:20 and special possession; that is what you are **t**.
4:26 "**T** I call heaven and earth as witnesses against
4:38 you their land as a special possession, as it is **t**.
4:40 all the laws and commands that I will give you **t**,
5: 1 to all the laws and regulations I am giving you **t**.
5: 3 our ancestors, but with all of us who are alive **t**.
5:24 **T** we have seen God speaking to humans, and yet
6: 6 to these commands I am giving you **t**.
7:11 laws, and regulations I am giving you **t**.
8: 1 to obey all the commands I am giving you **t**.
9: 1 **T** you are about to cross the Jordan River to
10:13 and laws that I am giving you **t** for your own good.
10:15 above every other nation, as is evident **t**.
11: 8 careful to obey every command I am giving you **t**,
11:13 carefully obey all the commands I am giving you **t**,
11:26 "**T** I am giving you the choice between a blessing
11:27 of the LORD your God that I am giving you **t**.
11:32 obey all the laws and regulations I am giving you **t**.
12: 8 "**T** you are doing whatever you please, but that is
13:18 and keep all the commands I am giving you **t**,
15: 5 of the LORD your God that I am giving you **t**.
20: 3 Do not be afraid as you go out to fight **t**! Do not
26:16 "**T** the LORD your God has commanded you to
26:17 You have declared **t** that the LORD is your God.
26:18 The LORD has declared **t** that you are his people,
27: 1 "Keep all these commands that I am giving you **t**.
27: 4 coat them with plaster, as I am commanding you **t**.
27: 9 **T** you have become the people of the LORD your
27:10 these commands and laws that I am giving you **t**."
28: 1 by keeping all the commands I am giving you **t**,
28:14 I am giving you **t** to follow after other gods
28:15 obey all the commands and laws I am giving you **t**,
29:10 are standing **t** before the LORD your God.
29:12 You are standing here **t** to enter into a covenant
29:12 The LORD is making this covenant with you **t**,
29:13 He wants to confirm you **t** as his people and to
29:15 this covenant with you who stand in his presence **t**
29:28 them to another land, where they still live **t**!'
30: 2 to obey all the commands I have given you **t**,
30: 8 and keep all the commands I am giving you **t**.
30:11 "This command I am giving you **t** is not too
30:15 **T** I am giving you a choice between prosperity
30:16 I have commanded you **t** to love the LORD your
30:19 "**T** I have given you the choice between life
32:46 "Take to heart all the words I have given you **t**.

Jos 3: 7 "T I will begin to make you great in the eyes of all
3:10 T you will know that the living God is among you.
5: 9 "T I have rolled away the shame of your slavery
8:29 heap of stones over him that can still be seen t.
14:10 in the wilderness. T I am eighty-five years old.
22:18 And yet t you are turning away from following the
22:18 If you rebel against the LORD t, he will be angry
22:31 "T we know the LORD is among us because you
24:15 the LORD, then choose t whom you will serve.
Jdg 4:14 T the LORD will give you victory over Sisera,
10:15 as you see fit, only rescue us t from our enemies."
11:27 who is judge, decide t which of us is right—
21: 6 "T we have lost one of the tribes from our family;
Ru 2:19 "Where did you gather all this grain t?
2:19 "The man I worked with t is named Boaz."
3:18 has followed through on this. He will settle it t."
4: 9 "You are witnesses that t I have bought from
4:10 here in his hometown. You are all witnesses t."
4:14 LORD who has given you a family redeemer t!
1Sa 9:11 and his servant asked, "Is the seer here t?"
10: 2 When you leave me t, you will see two men beside
11:13 But Saul replied, "No one will be executed t,
11:13 for t the LORD has rescued Israel!"
12:17 I will ask the LORD to send thunder and rain t.
14:28 oath that anyone who eats food t will be cursed.
14:38 We must find out what sin was committed t.
14:45 to Saul, "Should Jonathan, who saved Israel t, die?
14:45 has been used of God to do a mighty miracle t."
15:28 LORD has torn the kingdom of Israel from you t
17:46 T the LORD will conquer you, and I will kill you
20:27 Jesse been here for dinner either yesterday or t?"
24: 4 "T is the day the LORD was talking about when
24:18 Yes, you have been wonderfully kind to me t,
24:19 you well for the kindness you have shown me t.
25:32 the God of Israel, who has sent you to meet me t!
26:21 no longer try to harm you, for you valued my life t.
26:24 value my life, even as I have valued yours t.
27:10 "Where did you make your raid t?" Achish would
2Sa 3:38 great leader and a great man has fallen t in Israel?
4: 8 T the LORD has given you revenge on Saul
6: 8 "outbreak against Uzzah"). It is still called that t.
6:20 "How glorious the king of Israel looked t!
16: 3 'T I will get back the kingdom of my grandfather
18:20 can be my messenger some other time, but not t."
18:31 T the LORD has rescued you from all those who
19: 5 "We saved your life t and the lives of your sons,
19: 6 You have made it clear t that we mean nothing to
19:20 That is why I have come here t, the very first
19:35 I am eighty years old t, and I can no longer enjoy
1Ki 1:25 T he has sacrificed many oxen, fattened calves,
1:30 t I decree that your son Solomon will be the next
1:48 who t has chosen someone to sit on my throne
1:51 "Let Solomon swear t that he will not kill me!"
3: 6 to him t by giving him a son to succeed him.
8:24 and t you have fulfilled it with your own hands.
8:28 and the prayer that your servant is making to you t.
8:61 his laws and commands, just as you are doing t."
9:13 area Cabul—"worthless"—as it is still known t.
12: 7 "If you are willing to serve the people t and give
14:14 family of Jeroboam. This will happen t, even now!
18:15 I stand, that I will present myself to Ahab t."
18:36 prove t that you are God in Israel and that I am
20:13 enemy forces? T I will hand them all over to you.
2Ki 2: 3 is going to take your master away from you t?"
2: 5 is going to take your master away from you t?"
4:23 "Why t?" he asked. "It is neither a new moon
17:34 And this is still going on among them t.
1Ch 13:11 "outbreak against Uzzah"). It is still called that t.
29: 5 Who is willing to give offerings to the LORD t?"
2Ch 6:15 and t you have fulfilled it with your own hands.
20:26 It is still called the Valley of Blessing t.
35:21 king of Judah? I have no quarrel with you t!
Ezr 9: 7 captured, robbed, and disgraced, just as we are t.
Ne 8: 9 For t is a sacred day before the LORD your
9:36 "So now t we are slaves here in the land of plenty
Est 5: 4 and Haman come t to a banquet I have prepared
9:13 to do again tomorrow as they have done t,
Job 23: 2 "My complaint t is still a bitter one, and I try hard
Ps 2: 7 'You are my son. / T I have become your Father.
95: 7 his care. / Oh, that you would listen to his voice t!
119:91 Your laws remain true t, / for everything serves
Pr 22:19 I am teaching you t—yes, you—so you will trust in
Ecc 3:15 Whatever exists t and whatever will exist in the
7:10 don't know whether they were any better than t.
SS 1: 7 O my love, where are you leading your flock t?
Isa 38:19 Only the living can praise you as I do t.
51:10 Are you not the same t, the one who dried up the
Jer 1:10 T I appoint you to stand up against nations
1:18 For see, t I have made you immune to their attacks.
11: 5 the land you live in t.' " Then I replied, "So be it,
32:20 You have made your name very great, as it is t.
42:19 Don't forget this warning I have given you t.
42:21 And t I have told you exactly what he said, but you
44:22 desolate ruin without a single inhabitant—as it is t.
46:10 will receive a sacrifice t in the north country beside
Mt 6:11 Give us our food for t,
6:30 so wonderfully for flowers that are here t
6:34 its own worries. Today's trouble is enough for t.
11:23 had been done in Sodom, it would still be here t.
20: 6 asked them, 'Why haven't you been working t?'
21:28 'Son, go out and work in the vineyard t.'
28:15 widely among the Jews, and they still tell it t.
Lk 4:21 "This Scripture has come true t before your very
5:26 and over again, "We have seen amazing things t."
7:16 and "We have seen the hand of God at work t."
12:28 so wonderfully for flowers that are here t
12:55 south wind blows, you say, 'T will be a scorcher.'
13:32 and doing miracles of healing t and tomorrow;
13:33 Yes, t, tomorrow, and the next day I must proceed
19: 5 For I must be a guest in your home t."
19: 9 "Salvation has come to this home t,
19:42 "I wish that even t you would find the way of
23:43 "I assure you, t you will be with me in paradise."
Ac 2:33 to pour out upon us, just as you see and hear t.
3:24 every prophet spoke about what is happening t.
13:33 'You are my Son. / T I have become your Father.'
22: 3 God in everything I did, just as all of you are t.
24:21 'I am on trial before you t because I believe in the
26:22 so that I am still alive t to tell these facts to
28:20 I asked you to come here t so we could get
Ro 8:38 Our fears for t, our worries about tomorrow,
11: 5 It is the same t, for not all the Jews have turned
2Co 3:15 Yes, even t when they read Moses' writings,
6: 2 to help you right now. T is the day of salvation.
Heb 1: 5 are my Son. / T I have become your Father."
3: 7 Holy Spirit says, / "T you must listen to his voice.
3:13 each other every day, as long as it is called "t,"
3:15 the warning: / "T you must listen to his voice.
4: 7 for entering his place of rest, and that time is t.
4: 7 "T you must listen to his voice. / Don't harden
5: 5 are my Son. / T I have become your Father."
13: 8 Jesus Christ is the same yesterday, t, and forever.
Jas 4:13 "T or tomorrow we are going to a certain town

TODAY'S (2) [TODAY]

Eze 24: 2 "Son of man, write down t date, because on this
Mt 6:34 its own worries. T trouble is enough for today.

TOE (7) [TOES]

Lev 8:23 of his right hand, and the big t of his right foot.
8:24 of their right hands, and the big t of their right feet.
14:14 of the right hand, and on the big t of the right foot.
14:17 of the right hand, and on the big t of the right foot,
14:25 of the right hand, and on the big t of the right foot.
14:28 of the right hand, and on the big t of the right foot,
Hab 3:13 and laid bare their bones from head to t.

TOES (6) [TOE]

Ex 29:20 their right thumbs and the big t of their right feet.
Jdg 1: 6 captured him and cut off his thumbs and big t.
1: 7 had seventy kings with thumbs and big t cut off,
2Sa 21:20 six fingers on each hand and six t on each foot—
1Ch 20: 6 six fingers on each hand and six t on each foot—
Da 2:41 and t you saw that were a combination of iron

TOGARMAH (3) [BETH-TOGARMAH]

Ge 10: 3 of Gomer were Ashkenaz, Riphath, and T.
1Ch 1: 6 of Gomer were Ashkenaz, Riphath, and T.
Eze 27:14 From T came riding horses, chariot horses,

TOGETHER (294) [ALTOGETHER]

Ge 1: 5 the darkness "night." T these made up one day.
3: 7 So they strung fig leaves t around their hips to
4: 8 And while they were t there, Cain attacked
11: 4 This will bring us t and keep us from scattering all
13: 6 Lot with all their flocks and herds living so close t.
14:14 he called t the men born into his household,
22: 6 and the fire. As the two of them went on t,
22: 8 Abraham answered. And they both went on t.
49: 1 Then Jacob called t all his sons and said,
Ex 3:16 "Now go and call t all the leaders of Israel.
10: 9 We must all join t in a festival to the LORD."
12:46 All who eat the lamb must eat it t in one house.
19: 7 the mountain and called t the leaders of the people
19: 8 They all responded t, "We will certainly do
23:18 "Sacrificial blood must never be offered t with
24:11 In fact, they shared a meal t in God's presence!
26: 3 Join five of these sheets t into one set; then join the
26: 6 to fasten the loops of the two sets of sheets t,
26: 9 Join five of these t into one set, and join the other
26:11 and fasten them t with fifty bronze clasps. In this
36:10 Five of these sheets were joined t to make one set,
36:13 Thus the Tabernacle was joined t in one piece.
36:16 The craftsmen joined five of these sheets t to make
36:18 the roof covering was joined t in one piece.
36:31 acacia wood to tie the frames on the south side t.
40:18 Moses put it t by setting its frames into their bases
Lev 2: 2 t with all the incense, and burn this token portion
2:16 t with all the incense, and burn it as an offering
7:30 Bring the fat of the animal, t with the breast,
9: 1 Moses called t Aaron and his sons and the leaders
23:18 t with the accompanying grain offerings and drink
23:20 t with the loaves representing the first of your later
Nu 1:18 called t the whole community of Israel on that very
7: 3 T they brought six carts and twelve oxen.
20:27 The three of them went up Mount Hor t as the
Dt 5: 1 Moses called all the people of Israel t and said,
22:10 not plow with an ox and a donkey harnessed t.
22:11 not wear clothing made of wool and linen woven t.
25: 5 "If two brothers are living t on the same property
31:12 Call them all t—men, women, children,
32:14 from the flock, / t with the fat of lambs and goats.
32:14 and goats from Bashan, / t with the choicest wheat.
Jos 1:12 Then Joshua called t the tribes of Reuben, Gad,
4: 4 So Joshua called t the twelve men
6: 6 So Joshua called t the priests and said, "Take up
9:22 But Joshua called t the Gibeonite leaders and said,
22: 1 Then Joshua called t the tribes of Reuben, Gad,
23: 2 called t all the elders, leaders, judges, and officers
Jdg 3:13 T with the Ammonites and Amalekites,
4:10 Barak called t the tribes of Zebulun and Naphtali,
9:47 that the people were gathered t in the temple,
15: 4 He tied their tails t in pairs, and he fastened a torch
16: 2 so the men of Gaza gathered t and waited all night
18:23 Why have you called these men t and chased after
19: 6 So the two of them sat down t and had something
19:21 After they washed their feet, they had supper t.
20: 1 came t in one large assembly and stood in the
20: 8 And all the people stood up t and replied,
20:11 were united, and they gathered t to attack the town.
Ru 1:14 And again they wept t, and Orpah kissed her
4: 1 friend. I want to talk to you." So they sat down t.
1Sa 5: 8 So they called t the rulers of the five Philistine
9:19 me to the place of sacrifice, and we'll eat there t.
9:26 Saul got ready, and he and Samuel left the house t.
10:20 So Samuel called the tribal leaders t before the
11: 7 of Saul's anger, and all of them came out t as one.
11:11 so badly scattered that no two of them were left t.
20: 8 for we made a covenant t before the LORD—
20:11 Jonathan replied. And they went out there t.
31: 6 and his troops all died t that same day.
2Sa 1:23 and Jonathan! / They were t in life and in death.
21: 9 So all seven of them died t at the beginning of the
23: 9 and David stood t against the Philistines when the
1Ki 13:19 So they went back t, and the man of God ate some
21: 9 "Call the citizens t for fasting and prayer and give
2Ki 2: 2 will never leave you!" So they went on t to Bethel.
2: 4 never leave you." So they went on t to Jericho.
2: 6 I will never leave you." So they went on t.
2: 8 Then Elijah folded his cloak t and struck the water
5:12 Damascus better than all the rivers of Israel put t?
10: 5 t with the other leaders and the guardians of the
10:19 and worshipers of Baal, and call t all his priests.
1Ch 10: 6 So Saul and his three sons died there t, bringing his
11:10 T with all Israel, they determined to make David
15: 4 are the priests and Levites who were called t:
22: 2 So David gave orders to call t the foreigners living
23: 2 t with the priests and Levites, for the coronation
2Ch 1: 2 He called t all Israel—the generals and captains of
3:13 So the wingspan of both cherubim t was 30 feet.
5:13 and singers performed t in unison to praise
10: 3 and all Israel went t to speak with Rehoboam.
15: 9 Then Asa called t all the people of Judah
20:36 T they built a fleet of trading ships at the port of
29:15 These men called t their fellow Levites, and they
Ezr 3: 1 all the people assembled t as one person in
3:13 and weeping mingled t in a loud commotion that
8:19 t with Jeshaiah from the descendants of Merari,
Ne 4:14 I called t the leaders and the people and said to
6:10 "Let us meet t inside the Temple of God and bolt
7: 5 So my God gave me the idea to call t all the
8: 1 all the people assembled t as one person at the
10:39 "So we promise t not to neglect the Temple of our
11:12 t with 822 of their associates, who worked at the
12:28 The singers were brought t from Jerusalem and its
12:40 t with the group of leaders who were with me.
12:41 We went t with the trumpet-playing priests—
Est 4:16 "Go and gather t all the Jews of Susa and fast for
5:10 Then he gathered t his friends and Zeresh, his wife,
9:15 Then the Jews at Susa gathered t on March 8
9:16 provinces had gathered t to defend their lives.
Job 1: 4 On these occasions they would get t to eat
2:11 they got t and traveled from their homes to comfort
9:33 If only there were a mediator who could bring us t,
10:11 and flesh, and you knit my bones and sinews t.
17:16 with me to the grave. We will rest t in the dust!"
24: 4 are kicked aside; the needy must hide t for safety.
24: 5 time just getting enough to keep body and soul t.
30: 7 they huddle t for shelter beneath the nettles.
31:38 "If my land accuses me and all its furrows weep t,
34: 4 ourselves what is right; let us learn t what is good.
38: 7 as the morning stars sang t and all the angels
40:17 a cedar. The sinews of its thighs are tightly knit t.
41:16 They are close t so no air can get between them.
41:17 They lock t so nothing can penetrate them.
Ps 2: 2 of the earth prepare for battle; / the rulers plot t
34: 3 of the LORD's greatness; / let us exalt his name t.
35:15 I am in trouble; / they gleefully join t against me.
47: 9 The rulers of the world have gathered t. / They join
55:14 we enjoyed / as we walked t to the house of God.
56: 6 They come t to spy on me— / watching my every
71:10 against me. / They are plotting t to kill me.
85:10 Unfailing love and truth have met t.
102:22 when multitudes gather t / and kingdoms come to
122: 3 is a well-built city, / knit t as a single unit.
133: 1 how pleasant, / when brothers live t in harmony!
139:13 of my body / and knit me t in my mother's womb.
139:15 as I was woven t in the dark of the womb.
145:11 They will talk t about the glory of your kingdom;
Pr 8:12 "I, Wisdom, live t with good judgment. I know
Isa 11: 6 In that day the wolf and the lamb will live t;
11: 7 among bears. Cubs and calves will lie down t.
11:14 T they will attack and plunder the nations to the
19:24 The three will be t, and Israel will be a blessing to
27:12 gather them t one by one like handpicked grain.
31: 3 are trying to help. They will all fall down and die t.
40: 5 will be revealed, and all people will see it t.
41: 7 Carefully they join the parts t, then fasten the thing
43: 9 Gather the nations t! Which of their idols has ever
43:26 Let us review the situation t, and you can present
44:11 make a god. T they will stand in terror and shame.
45: 8 so salvation and righteousness can sprout up t.
45:20 "Gather t and come, you fugitives from
45:21 Consult t, argue your case, and state your proofs
46: 2 protect the gods. They go off into captivity t.
65:25 The wolf and lamb will feed t. The lion will eat
66:18 So I will gather all nations and peoples t, and they
Jer 3:18 and Israel will return t from exile in the north.

6:21 over them. Neighbors and friends will collapse t."
17: 3 and treasures—t with your pagan shrines—
23: 3 But I will gather t the remnant of my flock from
25: 9 I will gather t all the armies of the north under
31:10 will gather them t and watch over them as a
31:24 and farmers and shepherds alike will live t in peace
46:12 warriors will stumble across each other and fall t."
50: 4 "Then the people of Israel and Judah will join t,"
La 2: 6 Kings and priests fall t before his anger.
Eze 4: 9 millet, and spelt, and mix them t in a storage jar.
13:10 and these prophets are trying to hold it t by
16:37 I will gather t all your allies—these lovers of yours
16:40 They will band t in a mob to stone you and run you
22:21 I will gather you t and blow the fire of my anger
37: 7 The bones of each body came t and attached
37:17 Now hold them t in your hand as one stick.
39:17 Say to them: Gather t for my great sacrificial feast.
48:13 T these portions of land will measure 8-1/3 miles
Da 5: 6 Such terror gripped him that his knees knocked t
6:11 The officials went t to Daniel's house and found
6:15 In the evening the men went t to the king and said,
Hos 1:11 under one leader, and they will return from exile t.
2:22 And the whole grand chorus will sing t, 'Jezreel'—
8:10 to many lands, I will now gather them t.
Joel 1:14 of fasting; call the people t for a solemn meeting.
2:15 of fasting; call the people t for a solemn meeting.
3:11 Gather t in the valley." And now, O LORD,
Am 1:15 And their king and his princes will go into exile t.
3: 3 Can two people walk t without agreeing on the
Mic 2:12 I will bring you t again like sheep in a fold, like a
4: 6 "I will gather t my people who are lame,
4:11 True, many nations have gathered t against you,
4:12 don't know that he is gathering them t to be beaten
7: 3 pay them off, and t they scheme to twist justice.
Na 3:17 crowding t in the hedges to survive the cold.
3:18 There is no longer a shepherd to gather them t.
Zep 2: 1 Gather t and pray, you shameless nation.
3: 8 For it is my decision to gather t the kingdoms of
3: 9 everyone will be able to worship the LORD t.
3:19 I will bring t those who were chased away.
3:20 On that day I will gather you t and bring you home
Zec 8: 4 streets with a cane and sit t in the city squares.
Mt 13:30 Let both grow t until the harvest. Then I will tell
18:20 For where two or three gather t because they are
19: 6 no one separate them, for God has joined them t."
20:25 But Jesus called them t and said, "You know that
22:15 Then the Pharisees met t to think of a way to trap
23:37 How often I have wanted to gather your children t
24:31 and they will gather t his chosen ones from the
24:40 "Two men will be working t in the field; one will
25:14 He called t his servants and gave them money to
25:21 you many more responsibilities. Let's celebrate t!'
25:23 you many more responsibilities. Let's celebrate t!'
Mk 6: 7 And he called his twelve disciples t and sent them
10: 9 no one separate them, for God has joined them t."
10:42 So Jesus called them t and said, "You know that in
13:27 And he will send forth his angels to gather t his
16:14 to the eleven disciples as they were eating t.
Lk 6:13 At daybreak he called t all of his disciples
6:38 pressed down, shaken t to make room for more,
9: 1 One day Jesus called t his twelve apostles and gave
13:34 How often I have wanted to gather your children t
15: 6 you would call t your friends and neighbors to
17:35 Two women will be grinding flour t at the mill;
19:13 he called t ten servants and gave them ten pounds
22: 8 and prepare the Passover meal, so we can eat it t."
22:14 and the twelve apostles sat down t at the table.
23:13 Then Pilate called t the leading priests and other
Jn 6:22 knew that he and his disciples had come over t
11:47 and Pharisees called the high council t to discuss
11:52 but for the gathering t of all the children of God
12:22 told Andrew about it, and they went t to ask Jesus.
19:40 T they wrapped Jesus' body in a long linen cloth
20:26 Eight days later the disciples were t again, and this
Ac 1:14 They all met t continually for prayer, along with
2: 1 the believers were meeting t in one place.
2:44 And all the believers met t constantly and shared
2:46 They worshiped t at the Temple each day, met in
4:26 the earth prepared for battle; / the rulers gathered t
5: 9 conspiring t to test the Spirit of the Lord?
10:24 was waiting for him and had called t his relatives
10:27 and they talked t and went inside where the others
14: 1 Paul and Barnabas went t to the synagogue
14:27 they called the church t and reported about their
15: 6 and church elders got t to decide this question.
16:13 down to speak with some women who had come t.
19:25 He called the craftsmen t, along with others
20:11 all went back upstairs and ate the Lord's Supper t.
20:14 He joined us there and we sailed t to Mitylene.
23:12 The next morning a group of Jews got t and bound
27:21 Finally, Paul called the crew t and said, "Men,
28:17 Paul's arrival, he called t the local Jewish leaders.
Ro 8:28 to work t for the good of those who love God
15: 6 Then all of you can join t with one voice,
1Co 3: 9 We work t as partners who belong to God. You are
3:16 Don't you realize that all of you t are the temple of
7: 5 Afterward they should come t again so that Satan
11:17 if more harm than good is done when you meet t.
11:20 Supper you are concerned about when you come t.
11:34 bring judgment upon yourselves when you meet t.
12:24 So God has put the body t in such a way that extra
12:27 Now all of you t are Christ's body, and each one of
12:28 help others, / those who can get others to work t,
16: 4 for me also to go along, then we can travel t.
2Co 1:24 We want to work t with you so you will be full of
7: 3 are in our hearts forever. We live or die t with you.
8:20 By traveling t we will guard against any suspicion,
Gal 4:15 Where is that joyful spirit we felt t then? In those
Eph 1:10 At the right time he will bring everything t under
2:16 T as one body, Christ reconciled both groups to
2:21 We who believe are carefully joined t, becoming a
2:22 Through him you Gentiles are also joined t as part
3: 6 and enjoy t the promise of blessings through Christ
3:10 when Jews and Gentiles are joined t in his church.
4: 3 the Holy Spirit, and bind yourselves t with peace.
4:16 his direction, the whole body is fitted t perfectly.
Php 1: 7 We have shared t the blessings of God, both when
1:27 side by side, fighting t for the Good News.
1:30 We are in this fight t. You have seen me suffer for
2: 1 Any fellowship t in the Spirit? Are your hearts
2: 2 and working t with one heart and purpose.
Col 1:17 everything else began, and he holds all creation t.
2: 2 be encouraged and knit t by strong ties of love.
2:19 For we are joined t in his body by his strong
3:14 Love is what binds us all t in perfect harmony.
1Th 2:19 you will bring us much joy as we stand t before
4:17 Then, t with them, we who are still alive
2Th 2: 1 and how we will be gathered t to meet him.
2Ti 1: 4 And I will be filled with joy when we are t again.
Heb 2:13 I am—t with the children God has given me."
10:25 And let us not neglect our meeting t, as some
11:11 It was by faith that Sarah t with Abraham was able
1Pe 3: 7 Treat her with understanding as you live t.
Rev 14: 2 It was like the sound of many harpists playing t.
17:14 T they will wage war against the Lamb,
19:17 Gather t for the great banquet God has prepared.
20: 8 He will gather them t for battle—a mighty host,

TOHU (1)

1Sa 1: 1 from the family of T and the clan of Zuph.

TOI (4)

2Sa 8: 9 When King T of Hamath heard that David had
8:10 Hadadezer and T had long been enemies, and there
1Ch 18: 9 When King T of Hamath heard that David had
18:10 Hadadezer and T had long been enemies, and there

TOIL (2) [TOILED, TOILS]

Dt 26: 7 heard us and saw our hardship, t, and oppression.
Ecc 9: 9 God gives you is your reward for all your earthly t.

TOILED (1) [TOIL]

1Th 2: 9 Night and day we t to earn a living so that our

TOILET (1)

2Ki 10:27 the temple of Baal, converting it into a public t.

TOILS (1) [TOIL]

Rev 14:13 for they will rest from all their t and trials;

TOKEN (12)

Lev 2: 2 the incense, and burn this t portion on the altar fire.
2: 9 The priests will take a t portion of the grain
2:16 The priests will take a t portion of the roasted grain
5:12 who will scoop out a handful as a t portion.
6:15 He will burn this t portion on the altar, and it will
24: 7 It will serve as a t offering, to be burned in place of
Nu 5:26 He will take a handful as a t portion and burn it on
Dt 26:10 I have brought you a t of the first crops you have
1Ch 4:32 also lived in Etam, Ain, Rimmon, T, and Ashan—
Isa 16: 1 Jerusalem as a t of alliance with the king of Judah.
49: 8 help you. I will give you as a t and pledge to Israel.
Lk 22:20 "This wine is the t of God's new covenant to save

TOLA (6) [TOLAITE]

Ge 46:13 The sons of Issachar were T, Puah, Jashub,
Nu 26:23 The Tolaite clan, named after its ancestor T.
Jdg 10: 1 T, the son of Puah and descendant of Dodo,
10: 3 After T died, a man from Gilead named Jair
1Ch 7: 1 The four sons of Issachar were T, Puah, Jashub,
7: 2 The sons of T were Uzzi, Rephaiah, Jeriel, Jahmai,

TOLAD (1)

1Ch 4:29 Bilhah, Ezem, T,

TOLAITE (1) [TOLA]

Nu 26:23 The T clan, named after its ancestor Tola.

TOLD (873) [TELL]

Ge 1:28 God blessed them and t them, "Multiply and fill
3: 2 "Of course we may eat it," the woman t him.
3:11 "Who t you that you were naked?" the LORD
3:17 to your wife and ate the fruit I t you not to eat,
9: 1 God blessed Noah and his sons and t them,
9: 8 Then God t Noah and his sons,
9:22 was naked and went outside and t his brothers.
12: 1 Then the LORD t Abram, "Leave your country,
14:13 men who escaped came and t Abram the Hebrew,
14:21 The king of Sodom t him, "Give back my people
15: 5 Abram outside beneath the night sky and t him,
15: 7 Then the LORD t him, "I am the LORD who
15: 9 Then the LORD t him, "Bring me a
15:13 Then the LORD t Abram, "You can be sure that
17: 9 "Your part of the agreement," God t Abraham,
17:23 off their foreskins, exactly as God had t him.
18: 7 a fat calf and t a servant to hurry and butcher it.
18:14 a year from now, just as I t you, I will return,
18:20 So the LORD t Abraham, "I have heard that the
20: 2 Abraham t people there that his wife, Sarah,
20: 3 God came to Abimelech in a dream and t him,
20: 5 Abraham t me, 'She is my sister,' and she herself
20: 8 When he t them what had happened, great fear
20:13 I t her, 'Wherever we go, have the kindness to say
20:15 where you would like to live," Abimelech t him.
21:12 But God t Abraham, "Do not be upset over the
22: 3 and set out for the place where God had t him to
22: 5 here with the donkey," Abraham t the young men.
22: 9 When they arrived at the place where God had t
24:33 "I don't want to eat until I have t you why I have
24:38 I was t to bring back a young woman from here to
24:40 'You will,' he t me, 'for the LORD, in whose
24:47 she t me, 'My father is Bethuel, the son of Nahor
24:66 Then the servant t Isaac the whole story.
25:23 And the LORD t her, "The sons in your womb
26:32 servants came and t him about a well they had dug.
27:19 "It's Esau, your older son. I've done as you t me.
27:42 She sent for Jacob and t him, "Esau is threatening
29:12 So Rachel quickly ran and t her father, Laban.
29:13 then brought him home, and Jacob t him his story.
29:18 Jacob was in love with Rachel, he t her father,
30: 3 Then Rachel t him, "Sleep with my servant,
31: 5 and is not treating me like he used to," he t them.
31:16 So go ahead and do whatever God has t you."
31:20 out secretly and never t Laban they were leaving.
31:24 careful about what you say to Jacob!" he was t.
31:29 of your father appeared to me last night and t me,
31:46 He also t his men to gather stones and pile them up
32: 4 He t them, "Give this message to my master Esau:
32: 9 you t me to return to my land and to my relatives,
32:16 He t his servants to lead them on ahead,
32:19 instructions to each of the herdsmen and t them,
32:28 name will no longer be Jacob," the man t him.
34: 8 Hamor t Jacob and his sons, "My son Shechem is
35: 2 So Jacob t everyone in his household,
35:22 father's concubine, and someone t Jacob about it.
37: 9 had another dream and t his brothers about it.
37:10 This time he t his father as well as his brothers,
37:17 "Yes," the man t him, "but they are no longer
37:32 "We found this in the field," they t him.
38:11 Then Judah t Tamar, his daughter-in-law, not to
38:13 Someone t Tamar that her father-in-law had left
38:22 and t him that he couldn't find her anywhere
39: 8 "Look," he t her, "my master trusts me with
39:17 she t him her story. "That Hebrew slave you've
40: 9 The cup-bearer t his dream first. "In my dream,"
40:16 a good meaning, he t his dream to Joseph, too.
40:18 "I'll tell you what it means," Joseph t him.
41: 8 wise men of Egypt and t them about his dreams,
41:12 We t the dreams to a young Hebrew man who was
41:12 the guard. He t us what each of our dreams meant,
41:15 "I had a dream last night," Pharaoh t him,
41:17 So Pharaoh t him the dream. "I was standing on
41:24 I t these dreams to my magicians, but not one of
41:25 dreams mean the same thing," Joseph t Pharaoh.
41:55 and he t them, "Go to Joseph and do whatever he
42:29 land of Canaan and t him all that had happened.
42:30 the land spoke very roughly to us," they t him.
42:33 Then the man, the ruler of the land, t us, 'This is
43: 7 he asked us if we had another brother so we t him.
43:17 So the man did as he was t and took them to
43:23 worry about it," the household manager t them.
43:25 They were t they would be eating there, so they
43:29 your youngest brother, the one you t me about?
43:33 Joseph t each of his brothers where to sit, and to
44: 2 So the household manager did as he was t.
44:23 But you t us, 'You may not see me again unless
44:24 returned to our father and t him what you had said.
44:32 I t him, 'If I don't bring him back to you, I will
45: 1 He wanted to be alone with his brothers when he t
45:21 So the sons of Jacob did as they were t.
45:26 "Joseph is still alive!" they t him. "And he is
48: 9 "Yes," Joseph t him, "these are the sons God has
49:29 Then Jacob t them, "Soon I will die. Bury me with
50: 2 Then Joseph t his morticians to embalm the body.
50: 5 He t them, "Tell Pharaoh that my father made me
50:19 But Joseph t them, "Don't be afraid of me. Am I
50:24 "Soon I will die," Joseph t his brothers, "but God
Ex 1: 9 He t his people, "These Israelites are becoming a
1:19 "Sir," they t him, "the Hebrew women are very
2: 5 she t one of her servant girls to get it for her.
2: 9 and nurse him for me," the princess t her.
2:19 rescued us from the shepherds," they t him.
3: 5 "Do not come any closer," God t him. "Take off
3: 7 Then the LORD t him, "You can be sure I have
3:12 Then God t him, "I will be with you. And this will
4: 3 it down on the ground," the LORD t him.
4: 4 Then the LORD t him, "Take hold of its tail."
4: 5 and they will believe you," the LORD t him.
4:12 Now go, and do as I have t you. I will help you
4:28 then t Aaron everything the LORD had
4:28 And he t him about the miraculous signs they were
4:30 Aaron t them everything the LORD had t
5: 1 They t him, "This is what the LORD, the God of
5:16 but we are still t to make as many bricks as before.
6: 1 what I will do to Pharaoh," the LORD t Moses.
6: 9 So Moses t the people what the LORD had said,
7:10 the miracle just as the LORD had t them.
8:20 Next the LORD t Moses, "Get up early in the
11: 9 Now the LORD had t Moses, "Pharaoh will not
14: 4 So the Israelites camped there as they were t.
14:13 But Moses t the people, "Don't be afraid.
16: 6 a meeting of all the people of Israel and t them,
16:15 And Moses t them, "It is the food the LORD has
16:19 Then Moses t them, "Do not keep any of it
17: 6 Moses did just as he was t; and as the leaders
18: 6 Moses was t, "Jethro, your father-in-law,

18: 8 Moses **t** his father-in-law about everything the
18: 8 He also **t** him about the problems they had faced
19: 7 the people and **t** them what the LORD had said.
19: 9 Moses **t** the LORD what the people had said.
19:10 Then the LORD **t** Moses, "Go down and prepare
19:15 He **t** them, "Get ready for an important event two
19:21 Then the LORD **t** Moses, "Go back down
19:23 Moses protested. "You already **t** them not to.
19:23 You **t** me to set boundaries around the mountain
19:25 the people and **t** them what the LORD had said.
24: 3 "We will do everything the LORD has **t** us to
24:14 Moses **t** the other leaders, "Stay here and wait for
32: 7 Then the LORD **t** Moses, "Quick! Go down the
32:24 So I **t** them, 'Bring me your gold earrings.'
32:27 He **t** them, "This is what the LORD, the God of
32:29 Then Moses **t** the Levites, "Today you have been
32:34 Now go, lead the people to the place I **t** you about.
33: 1 I **t** them long ago that I would give this land to
33: 5 For the LORD had **t** Moses to tell them,
33:12 But you haven't **t** me whom you will send with
34: 1 The LORD **t** Moses, "Prepare two stone tablets
34: 4 he climbed Mount Sinai as the LORD had **t** him,
35: 1 called a meeting of all the people and **t** them,
35:30 And Moses **t** them, "The LORD has chosen
36: 2 So Moses **t** Bezalel and Oholiab to begin the work,
Lev 9: 6 Then Moses **t** them, "When you have followed
17:14 That is why I have **t** the people of Israel never to
23: 9 Then the LORD **t** Moses
23:23 The LORD **t** Moses
Nu 4:49 man was assigned his task and **t** what to carry,
9: 4 So Moses **t** the people to celebrate the Passover
9:18 and stopped wherever he **t** them to.
9:23 and they did whatever the LORD **t** them through
11:12 Is that why you have **t** me to carry them in my
15: 1 The LORD **t** Moses to give these instructions to
16:26 "Quick!" he **t** the people. "Get away from the
16:47 Aaron did as Moses **t** him and ran out among the
18:25 The LORD also **t** Moses,
20: 9 So Moses did as he was **t**. He took the staff from
21: 8 Then the LORD **t** him, "Make a replica of a
22:12 "Do not go with them," God **t** Balaam. "You are
22:13 morning Balaam got up and **t** Balak's officials,
22:20 That night God came to Balaam and **t** him,
22:35 But the angel of the LORD **t** him, "Go with these
23: 5 "Go back to Balak and tell him what I **t** you."
23:13 Then King Balak **t** him, "Come with me to
23:29 Balaam again **t** Balak, "Build me seven altars
24:12 Balaam **t** Balak, "Don't you remember what I **t**
24:13 I **t** you that I could say only what the LORD says!
30: 1 the leaders of the tribes of Israel and **t** them,
34:13 Then Moses **t** the Israelites, "This is the territory
36: 2 You were **t** by the LORD to give the inheritance
Dt 1: 9 "At that time I **t** you, 'You are too great a burden
1:41 and fight for it, as the LORD our God has **t** us.'
1:43 This is what I **t** you, but you would not listen.
2:13 "Then the LORD **t** us to cross Zered Brook,
3: 2 But the LORD **t** me, 'Do not be afraid of him,
4:10 where he **t** me, 'Summon the people before me,
5:32 So Moses **t** the people, "You must obey all the
6: 1 and regulations that the LORD your God **t** me to
10: 9 their inheritance, as the LORD your God **t** them.
17:16 for the LORD has **t** you, 'You must never return
29:25 "And they will be **t**, 'This happened
31: 2 The LORD has **t** me that I will not cross the
34: 4 and I **t** them I would give it to their descendants.
Jos 1:12 Gad, and the half-tribe of Manasseh. He **t** them,
2: 2 But someone **t** the king of Jericho,
2: 9 the LORD has given you this land," she **t** them.
2:16 "Escape to the hill country," she **t** them.
2:17 Before they left, the men **t** her, "We can
3: 5 Then Joshua **t** the people, "Purify yourselves,
3: 7 The LORD **t** Joshua, "Today I will begin to
3: 9 So Joshua **t** the Israelites, "Come and listen to
4: 5 and **t** them, "Go into the middle of the Jordan,
4: 8 So the men did as Joshua **t** them. They took twelve
5: 2 At that time the LORD **t** Joshua, "Use knives of
5:15 this is holy ground." And Joshua did as he was **t**.
7: 3 they returned, they **t** Joshua, "It's a small town,
9: 6 at Gilgal, they **t** Joshua and the men of Israel,
9:24 because we were **t** that the LORD your God
10:24 Joshua **t** the captains of his army, "Come and put
10:24 on the kings' necks." And they did as they were **t**.
10:25 ever be afraid or discouraged," Joshua **t** his men.
11:15 And Joshua did as he was **t**, carefully obeying all
18: 9 The men did as they were **t** and mapped the entire
22: 2 He **t** them, "You have done as Moses, the servant
Jdg 2: 1 He **t** them, "I brought you out of Egypt into this
4: 8 Barak **t** her, "I will go, but only if you go with
4:12 When Sisera was **t** that Barak son of Abinoam had
4:20 "Stand at the door of the tent," he **t** her.
6:10 I **t** you, 'I am the LORD your God. You must not
6:13 And where are all the miracles our ancestors **t** us
6:20 the broth over it." And Gideon did as he was **t**.
7: 4 But the LORD **t** Gideon, "There are still too
7: 5 the LORD **t** him, "Divide the men into two
7: 7 The LORD **t** Gideon, "With these three hundred
7:24 And the men of Ephraim did as they were **t**.
9:48 "Quick, do as I have done!" he **t** his men.
13: 6 The woman ran and **t** her husband, "A man of God
13: 7 But he **t** me, 'You will become pregnant and give
13:10 So she quickly ran and **t** her husband, "The man
13:18 "You wouldn't understand if I **t** you."
13:23 and **t** us this wonderful thing and done these
14: 2 he returned home, he **t** his father and mother,
14: 3 But Samson **t** his father, "Get her for me. She is
14:16 people a riddle, but you haven't **t** me the answer."
14:17 he **t** her the answer because of her persistent
15:12 But the men of Judah **t** him, "We have come to tie
16:10 said to him, "You made fun of me and **t** me a lie!
16:15 and you still haven't **t** me what makes you
16:17 Finally, Samson **t** her his secret. "My hair has
16:18 Delilah realized he had finally **t** her the truth,
16:18 she said, "for he has **t** me everything."
18: 4 He **t** them about his agreement with Micah and that
21:20 They **t** the men of Benjamin who still needed
21:23 So the men of Benjamin did as they were **t**.
Ru 1:20 "Don't call me Naomi," she **t** them. "Instead,
2:19 So Ruth **t** her mother-in-law about the man in
2:20 LORD bless him!" Naomi **t** her daughter-in-law.
2:21 Boaz even **t** me to come back and stay with his
3:16 Ruth **t** Naomi everything Boaz had done for her,
4: 5 Then Boaz **t** him, "Of course, your purchase of the
1Sa 1:22 She **t** her husband, "Wait until the baby is weaned.
3:18 So Samuel **t** Eli everything; he didn't hold
4: 6 When they were **t** it was because the Ark of the
4:13 the messenger arrived and **t** what had happened,
6: 3 God of Israel back, along with a gift," they were **t**.
6: 4 And they were **t**, "Since the plague has struck both
6:21 to the people at Kiriath-jearim and **t** them,
7: 5 Then Samuel **t** them, "Come to Mizpah, all of
8: 5 "Look," they **t** him, "you are now old, and your
8:21 So Samuel **t** the LORD what the people had said,
9: 3 and he **t** Saul, "Take a servant with you, and go
9:15 Now the LORD had **t** Samuel the previous day,
9:17 the LORD said, "That's the man I **t** you about!
9:27 Samuel **t** Saul to send his servant on ahead.
10:25 Then Samuel **t** the people what the rights
11: 4 and **t** the people about their plight,
11: 5 So they **t** him about the message from Jabesh.
11:10 The men of Jabesh then **t** their enemies,
14: 8 "All right then," Jonathan **t** him. "We will cross
15: 1 you king of Israel because the LORD **t** me to.
15:12 Someone **t** him, "Saul went to Carmel to set up a
15:16 Listen to what the LORD **t** me last night!"
15:17 And Samuel **t** him, "Although you may think little
15:18 And the LORD sent you on a mission and **t** you,
16: 8 Then Jesse **t** his son Abinadab to step forward
17:32 "Don't worry about a thing," David **t** Saul.
17:56 "Well, find out!" the king **t** him.
18:22 Then Saul **t** his men to say confidentially to David,
18:25 he **t** them, "Tell David that all I want for the bride
19: 2 **t** him what his father was planning.
19: 7 called David and **t** him what had happened.
19:11 They were **t** to kill David when he came out the
19:14 she **t** them he was sick and couldn't get out of bed.
19:18 and he **t** him all that Saul had done to him.
19:22 "They are at Naioth in Ramah," someone **t** him.
20:12 Then Jonathan **t** David, "I promise by the LORD,
20:29 demanded that he be there, so I **t** him he could go.
20:36 "Start running," he **t** the boy, "so you can find
20:40 to the boy and **t** him to take them back to the city.
21: 2 "He **t** me not to tell anyone why I am here. I have **t**
22: 5 One day the prophet Gad **t** David,
22: 8 For not one of you has ever **t** me that my own son
22:21 When he **t** David that Saul had killed the priests of
23: 2 "Yes, go and save Keilah," the LORD **t** him.
23: 9 and **t** Abiathar the priest to bring the ephod
24: 1 he was **t** that David had gone into the wilderness of
24:10 and some of my men **t** me to kill you, but I spared
25: 5 men to Carmel. He **t** them to deliver this message:
25: 7 I am **t** that you are shearing your sheep and goats.
25:12 and **t** him what Nabal had said.
25:14 one of Nabal's servants went to Abigail and **t** her,
25:35 Then David accepted her gifts and **t** her,
25:37 when he was sober, she **t** him what had happened.
25:40 the messengers arrived at Carmel, they **t** Abigail,
28: 1 King Achish **t** David, "You and your men will be
28: 2 Then Achish **t** David, "I will make you my
28:13 "Don't be afraid!" the king **t** her. "What do you
29: 3 And Achish **t** them, "This is David, the man who
29: 6 "I swear by the LORD," he **t** them, "you are
30: 8 And the LORD **t** him, "Yes, go after them.
2Sa 1:10 "So I killed him," the Amalekite **t** David, "for I
3:16 Then Abner **t** him, "Go back home!" So Palti
3:17 "For some time now," he **t** them, "you have
3:23 When Joab was **t** that Abner had just been there
4:10 Once before, someone **t** me, 'Saul is dead,'
5: 1 tribes of Israel went to David at Hebron and **t** him,
5: 2 And the LORD has **t** you, 'You will be the
5: 8 he **t** his own troops, "Go up through the water
5:17 But David was **t** they were coming and went into
6:12 Then King David was **t**, "The LORD has blessed
7:17 and **t** him everything the LORD had said.
9: 4 "In Lo-debar," Ziba **t** him, "at the home of Makir
10:11 then come over and help me," Joab **t** his brother.
11: 3 and he was **t**, "She is Bathsheba, the daughter of
11: 8 Then he **t** Uriah, "Go on home and relax."
11:12 "Well, stay here tonight," David **t** him,
11:19 He **t** his messenger, "Report all the news of the
12:21 "We don't understand you," they **t** him.
13: 4 So Amnon **t** him, "I am in love with Tamar,
13: 9 "Everyone get out of here," Amnon **t** his servants.
13:28 Absalom **t** his men, "Wait until Amnon gets
13:35 "Look!" Jonadab **t** the king. "There they are
14: 3 am about to tell you." Then Joab **t** her what to say.
14: 8 "Leave it to me," the king **t** her. "Go home,
14:19 from you. Yes, Joab sent me and **t** me what to say.
14:21 So the king sent for Joab and **t** him, "All right,
14:33 So Joab **t** the king what Absalom had said. Then at
15: 9 "All right," the king **t** him. "Go and fulfill your
15:27 Then the king **t** Zadok the priest, "Look, here is
15:31 When someone **t** David that his adviser Ahithophel
15:33 But David **t** him, "If you go with me, you will
16: 4 "In that case," the king **t** Ziba, "I give you
16:10 If the LORD has **t** him to curse me, who am I to
16:11 let him curse, for the LORD has **t** him to do it.
16:21 Ahithophel **t** him, "Go and sleep with your
17: 6 Absalom **t** him what Ahithophel had said.
17:16 "Quick!" he **t** them. "Find David and urge him
17:18 to go to David, and he **t** Absalom about it.
17:21 "Quick!" they **t** him, "cross the Jordan tonight!"
17:21 And they **t** him how Ahithophel had advised that
18: 2 The king **t** his troops, "I am going out with you."
18:10 David's men saw what had happened and **t** Joab,
18:20 "No," Joab **t** him, "it wouldn't be good news to
18:29 Ahimaaz replied, "When Joab **t** me to come,
18:30 "Wait here," the king **t** him. So Ahimaaz stepped
19:13 And David **t** them to tell Amasa, "Since you are
19:26 I **t** him, 'Saddle my donkey so that I can go with
24: 1 the people of Israel and Judah," the LORD **t** him.
1Ki 1: 2 So his advisers **t** him, "We will find a young
1:23 The king's advisers **t** him, "Nathan the prophet is
2:30 returned to the king and **t** him what Joab had said.
2:36 The king then sent for Shimei and **t** him, "Build a
5: 5 For the LORD **t** him, 'Your son, whom I will
8:16 For he **t** my father, 'From the day I brought my
8:18 But the LORD **t** him, 'It is right for you to want
8:53 you **t** your servant Moses that you had separated
10: 7 and prosperity are far greater than what I was **t**.
12:14 He **t** the people, "My father was harsh on you,
13:11 and **t** him what the man of God had done in Bethel
13:11 They also **t** him what he had said to the king.
13:12 So they **t** their father which road the man of God
13:22 and drank water where he **t** you not to eat or drink.
13:32 For the message the LORD **t** him to proclaim
14: 2 So Jeroboam **t** his wife, "Disguise yourself so that
14: 2 the man who **t** me I would become king.
14: 5 But the LORD had **t** Ahijah, "Jeroboam's wife
14: 6 Then he **t** her, "I have bad news for you.
17: 1 **t** King Ahab, "As surely as the LORD, the God
17: 5 So Elijah did as the LORD had **t** him and camped
17:24 Then the woman **t** Elijah, "Now I know for sure
18:10 And each time when he was **t**, 'Elijah isn't here,'
18:13 Has no one **t** you, my lord, about the time when
18:43 Seven times Elijah **t** him to go and look, and seven
18:44 Finally the seventh time, his servant **t** him, "I saw
19: 1 he **t** Jezebel what Elijah had done and that he had
19: 5 an angel touched him and **t** him, "Get up
19:11 before me on the mountain," the LORD **t** him.
19:15 Then the LORD **t** him, "Go back the way you
20: 9 So Ahab **t** the messengers from Ben-hadad,
20:13 Then a prophet came to see King Ahab and **t** him,
20:33 "Go and get him," the king of Israel **t** them.
20:34 Ben-hadad **t** him, "I will give back the towns my
20:36 Then the prophet **t** him, "Because you have not
20:42 And the prophet **t** him, "This is what the LORD
21: 6 or to trade it, and he refused!" Ahab **t** her.
21:23 The LORD has also **t** me that the dogs of Jezreel
22:17 So Micaiah **t** him, "In a vision I saw all Israel
2Ki 1: 3 But the angel of the LORD **t** Elijah, who was
1: 6 and **t** us to go back to the king with a message
2: 2 for the LORD has **t** me to go to Bethel."
2: 4 for the LORD has **t** me to go to Jericho."
2: 6 for the LORD has **t** me to go to the Jordan
2:19 "We have a problem, my lord," they **t** him.
4: 5 So she did as she was **t**. Her sons brought many
4: 6 he **t** her. And then the olive oil stopped flowing.
4: 7 When she **t** the man of God what had happened,
4:15 "Call her back again," Elisha **t** him.
4:26 the woman **t** Gehazi, "everything is fine."
4:27 and the LORD has not **t** me what it is."
4:31 He returned to meet Elisha and **t** him, "The child
5: 4 So Naaman **t** the king what the young girl from
5: 5 "Go and visit the prophet," the king **t** him. "I will
5:13 if the prophet had **t** you to do some great thing,
6: 1 the group of prophets came to Elisha and **t** him,
6: 2 us to meet." "All right," he **t** them, "go ahead."
6:16 "Don't be afraid!" Elisha **t** him. "For there are
6:19 Then Elisha went out and **t** them, "You have come
6:22 "Of course not!" Elisha **t** him. "Do we kill
7:10 the city and **t** the gatekeepers what had happened
7:12 of bed in the middle of the night and **t** his officers,
7:15 The scouts returned and **t** the king about it.
8: 1 Elisha had **t** the woman whose son he had brought
8: 6 the king asked her. And she **t** him that it was.
8: 7 Someone **t** the king that the man of God had come.
8:14 "He **t** me that you will surely recover."
9: 1 "Get ready to go to Ramoth-gilead," he **t** him.
9: 4 So the young prophet did as he was **t** and went to
9:12 So Jehu **t** them what the man had said and that at
9:15 So Jehu **t** the men with him, "Since you want me
9:36 When they returned and **t** Jehu, he stated,
10: 9 "You aren't to blame," he **t** them. "I am the one
11: 5 Jehoiada **t** them, "This is what you must do.
13:15 Elisha **t** him, "Get a bow and some arrows." And
the king did as he was **t**.
13:16 Then Elisha **t** the king of Israel to put his hand on
18:25 The LORD himself **t** us, 'Go and destroy it!' "
18:36 because Hezekiah had **t** them not to speak.
18:37 and **t** him what the Assyrian representative had
19: 3 They **t** him, "This is what King Hezekiah says:
21: 7 the very place where the LORD had **t** David
22: 3 to the Temple of the LORD. He **t** him,
23:17 And the people of the town **t** him, "It is the tomb
1Ch 11: 1 Then all Israel went to David at Hebron and **t** him,
11: 2 And the LORD your God has **t** you, 'You will be the
14: 8 But David was **t** they were coming, so he and his
17:15 and **t** him everything the LORD had said.
19:12 then come over and help me," Joab **t** his brother.
21:18 Then the angel of the LORD **t** Gad to instruct
22: 7 the name of the LORD my God," David **t** him.

28:15 He **t** Solomon the amount of gold needed for the
28:19 "Every part of this plan," David **t** Solomon,
2Ch 6: 4 he made to my father, David. For he **t** my father,
6: 8 But the LORD **t** him, 'It is right for you to want
9: 6 Your wisdom is far greater than what I was **t**.
10:14 He **t** the people, "My father was harsh on you,
12: 5 Shemaiah **t** them, "This is what the LORD says:
14: 7 Asa **t** the people of Judah, "Let us build towns
16: 7 time Hanani the seer came to King Asa and **t** him,
18:16 So Micaiah **t** him, "In a vision I saw all Israel
20: 2 Messengers came and **t** Jehoshaphat, "A vast army
33: 7 the very place where God had **t** David and his son
35:21 And God has **t** me to hurry! Do not interfere with
Ezr 8:22 After all, we had **t** the king, "Our God protects all
9:12 You **t** us not to let our daughters marry their sons,
Ne 1: 8 "Please remember what you **t** your servant Moses:
2:12 I had not **t** anyone about the plans God had put in
2:18 Then I **t** them about how the gracious hand of God
4:12 near the enemy came and **t** us again and again,
4:22 I also **t** everyone living outside the walls to move
5: 7 I **t** them, "You are oppressing your own relatives
6:19 Tobiah was, and then they **t** him everything I said.
Est 1:10 he **t** Mehuman, Biztha, Harbona, Bigtha, Abagtha,
2:10 Esther had not **t** anyone of her nationality
2:10 family background, for Mordecai had **t** her not to.
2:22 She then **t** the king about it and gave Mordecai
3: 4 since Mordecai had **t** them he was a Jew.
3:11 the king **t** Haman, "but go ahead and do as you
4: 4 and eunuchs came and **t** her about Mordecai,
4: 7 Mordecai **t** him the whole story and **t** him how
much money Haman had promised
4:10 Then Esther **t** Hathach to go back and relay this
4:17 So Mordecai went away and did as Esther **t** him.
6:13 When Haman **t** his wife, Zeresh, and all his friends
8: 1 for Esther had **t** the king how they were related.
9:22 He **t** them to celebrate these days with feasting
Job 29:25 I **t** them what they should do and presided over
37:20 Should God be **t** that I want to speak? Can we
38:13 Have you ever **t** the daylight to spread to the ends
Ps 22:31 His righteous acts will be **t** to those yet unborn.
40: 9 I have **t** all your people about your justice.
40:10 I have **t** everyone in the great assembly
44: 1 it with our own ears— / our ancestors have **t** us
52: T regarding the time Doeg the Edomite **t** Saul that
71:17 and I have constantly **t** others about the wonderful
75: 4 I **t** the wicked, 'Don't raise your fists!
106:34 nations in the land, / as the LORD had **t** them to.
119:26 I **t** you my plans, and you answered. / Now teach
Pr 4: 4 My father **t** me, "Take my words to heart.
14:15 Only simpletons believe everything they are **t**!
Isa 18: 4 For the LORD has **t** me this: "I will watch
20: 2 the LORD **t** Isaiah son of Amoz, "Take off all
20: 2 Isaiah did as he was **t** and walked around naked
21:10 I have **t** you everything the LORD Almighty,
22:12 He **t** you to shave your heads in sorrow for your
22:15 the LORD Almighty, **t** me to confront Shebna,
28:22 has plainly **t** me that he is determined to crush you.
31: 4 But the LORD has **t** me this: "When a lion,
36:10 The LORD himself **t** us, 'Go and destroy it!' "
36:21 because Hezekiah had **t** them not to speak.
36:22 and **t** him what the Assyrian representative had
37: 3 They **t** him, "This is what King Hezekiah says:
41:26 "Who but I have **t** you this would happen?
41:28 Not one of your idols **t** you this. Not one gave any
45:21 What idol ever **t** you they would happen? Was it
48: 5 That is why I **t** you ahead of time what I was going
48:14 "Have any of your idols ever **t** you this? Come,
48:16 I have always **t** you plainly what would happen
52:15 will see what they had not previously been **t** about;
Jer 7:23 This is what I **t** them: 'Obey me, and I will be your
11:18 Then the LORD **t** me about the plots my enemies
13: 6 and get the linen belt that I **t** you to hide there."
18: 3 So I did as he **t** me and found the potter working at
20:15 I curse the messenger who **t** my father,
26: 8 saying everything the LORD had **t** him to say,
26:18 He **t** the people of Judah, 'This is what the LORD
32:23 They have hardly done one thing you **t** them to!
32:25 you have **t** me to buy the field—
34:14 I **t** them that every Hebrew slave must be freed
35:14 because their ancestor Jehonadab **t** them not to.
36: 8 Baruch did as Jeremiah **t** him and read these
36:13 When Micaiah **t** them about the messages Baruch
36:19 Jeremiah should both hide," the officials **t** Baruch.
37:19 Where are your prophets now who **t** you the king
38:10 So the king **t** Ebed-melech, "Take along thirty of
38:24 "Don't tell anyone you **t** me this, or you will die!
39:11 King Nebuchadnezzar had **t** Nebuzaradan to find
42:19 The LORD has **t** you: 'Do not go to Egypt!'
42:21 And today I have **t** you exactly what he said,
La 3:57 Yes, you came at my despairing cry and **t** me,
Eze 3:19 your life because you did what you were **t** to do.
4:16 Then he **t** me, "Son of man, I will cause food to be
9: 7 went throughout the city and did as they were **t**.
11: 5 of the LORD came upon me, and he **t** me to say,
11:25 And I **t** the exiles everything the LORD had
12: 7 So I did as I was **t**. In broad daylight I brought my
14:17 and I **t** enemy armies to come and destroy
20:16 I **t** them this because they had rejected my laws,
20:18 and **t** them not to follow in their parents' footsteps,
20:19 'I am the LORD your God,' I **t** them. 'Follow my
21:29 have given false visions and **t** lies about the sword.
24:18 The next morning I did everything I had been **t** to
24:21 and I was **t** to give this message to the people of
37: 7 So I spoke these words, just as he **t** me.
41: 4 "This," he **t** me, "is the Most Holy Place."
41:22 "This," the man **t** me, "is the table that stands in
42:13 Then the man **t** me, "These rooms that overlook
47: 3 the stream for 1,750 feet and **t** me to go across.
47: 4 off another 1,750 feet and **t** me to go across again.
47: 6 He **t** me to keep in mind what I had seen, then he
Da 2:15 So Arioch **t** him all that had happened.
2:17 Daniel went home and **t** his friends Hananiah,
2:23 You have **t** me what we asked of you
4: 7 and fortune-tellers came in, I **t** them the dream,
4: 8 Daniel came in before me, and I **t** him the dream.
5:16 I am **t** that you can give interpretations and solve
6:13 Then they **t** the king, "That man Daniel, one of the
Hos 1:10 Then, at the place where they were **t**, 'You are not
Am 7:15 LORD called me away from my flock and **t** me,
Jnh 1:10 Then he **t** them that he was running away from the
Mic 6: 8 the LORD has already **t** you what is good,
Hab 1: 5 something you wouldn't believe even if someone **t**
Zec 11: 9 So I **t** them, "I won't be your shepherd any longer.
Mt 2: 8 Then he **t** them, "Go to Bethlehem and search
2:16 because the wise men had **t** him the star first
2:19 appeared in a dream to Joseph in Egypt and **t** him,
4: 4 But Jesus **t** him, "No! The Scriptures say,
4:10 "Get out of here, Satan," Jesus **t** him.
8:22 But Jesus **t** him, "Follow me now! Let those who
9:28 you see?" "Yes, Lord," they **t** him, "we do."
11: 4 Jesus **t** them, "Go back to John and tell him about
12:47 Someone **t** Jesus, "Your mother and your brothers
13: 3 He **t** many stories such as this one: "A farmer
13:18 "Now here is the explanation of the story I **t** about
13:24 Here is another story Jesus **t**: "The Kingdom of
13:27 The farmer's servants came and **t** him, 'Sir,
13:57 Then Jesus **t** them, "A prophet is honored
14:12 buried it. Then they **t** Jesus what had happened.
14:19 Then he **t** the people to sit down on the grass.
15:35 So Jesus **t** all the people to sit down on the ground.
16:21 and he **t** them what would happen to him there.
17:20 "You didn't have enough faith," Jesus **t** them.
17:22 Jesus **t** them, "The Son of Man is going to be
18:31 went to the king and **t** him what had happened.
19:13 for them. The disciples **t** them not to bother him.
19:21 Jesus **t** him, "If you want to be perfect, go and sell
20: 7 "The owner of the estate **t** them, 'Then go on out
20: 8 "That evening he **t** the foreman to call the workers
20:17 and **t** them what was going to happen to him.
20:22 But Jesus **t** them, "You don't know what you are
20:23 "You will indeed drink from it," he **t** them.
20:31 The crowd **t** them to be quiet, but they only
21:21 Then Jesus **t** them, "I assure you, if you have faith
21:28 A man with two sons **t** the older boy, 'Son, go out
21:30 Then the father **t** the other son, 'You go,' and he
22: 1 Jesus **t** them several other stories to illustrate the
24: 2 But he **t** them, "Do you see all these buildings?
24: 4 Jesus **t** them, "Don't let anyone mislead you.
24:32 you know without being **t** that summer is near.
26:18 "As you go into the city," he **t** them, "you will
26:19 So the disciples did as Jesus **t** them and prepared
26:25 And Jesus **t** him, "You have said it yourself."
26:31 "Tonight all of you will desert me," Jesus **t** them.
26:38 He **t** them, "My soul is crushed with grief to the
26:52 "Put away your sword," Jesus **t** him. "Those who
27:63 They **t** him, "Sir, we remember what that deceiver
28: 7 You will see him there. Remember, I have **t** you."
28:11 the leading priests and **t** them what had happened.
28:13 They **t** the soldiers, "You must say,
28:15 the bribe and said what they were **t** to say.
28:16 going to the mountain where Jesus had **t** them to
28:18 Jesus came and **t** his disciples, "I have been given
Mk 1:30 a high fever. They **t** Jesus about her right away.
1:43 Then Jesus sent him on his way and **t** him sternly,
2:17 When Jesus heard this, he **t** them, "Healthy people
3:30 He **t** them this because they were saying he had an
5:16 to the man and to the pigs **t** everyone about it,
5:20 and everyone was amazed at what he **t** them.
5:33 and fell at his feet and **t** him what she had done.
5:40 laughed at him, but he **t** them all to go outside.
5:43 and he **t** them to give her something to eat.
6: 4 Then Jesus **t** them, "A prophet is honored
6: 8 He **t** them to take nothing with them except a
6: 9 He **t** them to wear sandals but not to take even an
6:24 Her mother **t** her, "Ask for John the Baptist's
6:25 So the girl hurried back to the king and **t** him,
6:30 and **t** him all they had done and what they had
6:39 Then Jesus **t** the crowd to sit down in groups on
7:27 Jesus **t** her, "First I should help my own family,
7:36 Jesus **t** the crowd not to tell anyone, but the more
he **t** them not to, the more they spread
8: 1 of food again. Jesus called his disciples and **t** them,
8: 6 So Jesus **t** all the people to sit down on the ground.
8: 7 blessed these and **t** the disciples to pass them out.
8:32 and **t** him he shouldn't say things like that.
8:34 any of you wants to be my follower," he **t** them,
9: 9 he **t** them not to tell anyone what they had seen
9:38 but we **t** him to stop because he isn't one of our
10:11 He **t** them, "Whoever divorces his wife
10:13 but the disciples **t** them not to bother him.
10:21 "You lack only one thing," he **t** him. "Go and sell
10:33 "When we get to Jerusalem," he **t** them, "the Son
11: 2 he **t** them, "and as soon as you enter it,
11: 6 They said what Jesus had **t** them to say, and they
13:28 you know without being **t** that summer is near.
13:34 and he **t** the gatekeeper to watch for his return.
14:13 "As you go into the city," he **t** them, "a man
14:27 "All of you will desert me," Jesus **t** them.
14:34 He **t** them, "My soul is crushed with grief to the
15:45 and Pilate **t** Joseph he could have the body.
16: 7 see him there, just as he **t** you before he died!"
16:11 But when she **t** them that Jesus was alive and she
16:15 And then he **t** them, "Go into all the world
Lk 1:30 "Don't be frightened, Mary," the angel **t** her,
2:15 that has happened, which the Lord has **t** us about."
2:17 Then the shepherds **t** everyone what had happened
2:20 and praising God for what the angels had **t** them,
4: 4 But Jesus **t** him, "No! The Scriptures say,
4: 6 The Devil **t** him, "I will give you the glory of
4:35 Jesus cut him short. "Be silent!" he **t** the demon.
4:41 he stopped them and **t** them to be silent.
7:18 The disciples of John the Baptist **t** John about
7:22 Then he **t** John's disciples, "Go back to John
7:41 Then Jesus **t** him this story: "A man loaned money
8: 4 One day Jesus **t** this story to a large crowd that had
8:20 Someone **t** Jesus, "Your mother and your brothers
8:36 Then those who had seen what happened **t** the
8:46 But Jesus **t** him, "No, someone deliberately
8:55 Then Jesus **t** them to give her something to eat.
9:10 they **t** Jesus everything they had done.
9:62 But Jesus **t** him, "Anyone who puts a hand to the
10:18 "Yes," he **t** them, "I saw Satan falling from
10:28 Jesus **t** him. "Do this and you will live!"
10:35 pieces of silver and **t** him to take care of the man.
14:21 and **t** his master what they had said.
15:11 illustrate the point further, Jesus **t** them this story:
15:12 The younger son **t** his father, 'I want my share of
15:27 'Your brother is back,' he was **t**, 'and your father
15:29 and never once refused to do a single thing you **t**
16: 1 Jesus **t** this story to his disciples: "A rich man
16: 6 So the manager **t** him, 'Tear up that bill and write
18: 1 One day Jesus **t** his disciples a story to illustrate
18: 9 Then Jesus **t** this story to some who had great
18:15 but the disciples **t** them not to bother him.
18:31 Jesus **t** them, "As you know, we are going to
18:37 They **t** him that Jesus of Nazareth was going by.
19:11 he **t** a story to correct the impression that the
19:30 over there," he **t** them, "and as you enter it,
19:46 He **t** them, "The Scriptures declare, 'My Temple
20: 9 turned to the people again and **t** them this story:
21:30 you know without being **t** that summer is near.
22:25 Jesus **t** them, "In this world the kings and great
22:40 There he **t** them, "Pray that you will not be
24: 6 Don't you remember what he **t** you back in
24:10 They **t** the apostles what had happened,
24:23 and they had seen angels who **t** them Jesus is alive!
24:35 Then the two from Emmaus **t** their story of how
24:44 I **t** you that everything written about me by Moses
Jn 1:18 is near to the Father's heart; he has **t** us about him.
1:26 John **t** them, "I baptize with water, but right here
1:33 he **t** me, 'When you see the Holy Spirit descending
1:45 Philip went off to look for Nathanael and **t** him,
1:50 because I **t** you I had seen you under the fig tree?
2: 3 "They have no more wine," she **t** him.
2: 5 But his mother **t** the servants, "Do whatever he
2: 7 Jesus **t** the servants, "Fill the jars with water."
2:16 he **t** them, "Get these things out of here.
3:28 You yourselves know how plainly I **t** you that I am
4:16 "Go and get your husband," Jesus **t** her.
4:26 Then Jesus **t** her, "I am the Messiah!"
4:28 and went back to the village and **t** everyone,
4:29 and meet a man who **t** me everything I ever did!
4:39 woman had said, "He **t** me everything I ever did!"
4:42 him ourselves, not just because of what you **t** us.
4:50 Then Jesus **t** him, "Go back home. Your son will
4:53 realized it was the same time that Jesus had **t** him,
5: 8 Jesus **t** him, "Stand up, pick up your sleeping mat,
5:14 Jesus found him in the Temple and **t** him,
5:15 and **t** them it was Jesus who had healed him.
5:30 I judge as I am **t**. And my judgment is absolutely
6:12 Jesus **t** his disciples, "so that nothing is wasted."
6:29 Jesus **t** them, "This is what God wants you to do:
7:16 So Jesus **t** them, "I'm not teaching my own ideas,
7:33 But Jesus **t** them, "I will be here a little longer.
8:14 Jesus **t** them, "These claims are valid even though
8:40 I **t** you the truth I heard from God, but you are
8:42 Jesus **t** them, "If God were your Father, you would
9: 7 He **t** him, "Go and wash in the pool of Siloam"
9:11 He **t** them, "The man they call Jesus made mud
and smoothed it over my eyes and **t** me,
9:15 So he **t** them, "He smoothed the mud over my
9:24 called in the man who had been blind and **t** him,
9:27 man exclaimed. "I **t** you once. Didn't you listen?
9:39 Then Jesus **t** him, "I have come to judge the
10:25 Jesus replied, "I have already **t** you, and you don't
11:14 Then he **t** them plainly, "Lazarus is dead.
11:17 he was **t** that Lazarus had already been in his grave
11:23 Jesus **t** her, "Your brother will rise again."
11:25 Jesus **t** her, "I am the resurrection and the life.
11:27 "Yes, Lord," she **t** him. "I have always believed
11:28 called Mary aside from the mourners and **t** her,
11:34 he asked them. They **t** him, "Lord, come and see."
11:39 "Roll the stone aside," Jesus **t** them. But Martha,
11:44 Jesus **t** them, "Unwrap him and let him go!"
11:46 to the Pharisees and **t** them what Jesus had done.
12:22 Philip **t** Andrew about it, and they went together to
12:30 Then Jesus **t** them, "The voice was for your
13:27 into him. Then Jesus **t** him, "Hurry. Do it now."
13:33 cannot come to me—just as I **t** the Jewish leaders.
14: 6 Jesus **t** him, "I am the way, the truth, and the life.
14:26 and will remind you of everything I myself have **t**
14:28 Remember what I **t** you: I am going away, but I
14:29 I have **t** you these things before they happen
15:11 I have **t** you this so that you will be filled with my
15:15 since I have **t** you everything the Father **t** me.
15:20 Do you remember what I **t** you? 'A servant is not
16: 1 "I have **t** you these things so that you won't fall
16:33 I have **t** you all this so that you may have peace in
17: 4 here on earth by doing everything you **t** me to do.
17: 6 "I have **t** these men about you. They were in the
17:13 I have **t** them many things while I was with them

18: 8 "I **t** you that I am he," Jesus said. "And since I
18: 14 Caiaphas was the one who had **t** the other Jewish
18: 31 and judge him by your own laws," Pilate **t** them.
18: 38 Then he went out again to the people and **t** them,
19: 12 but the Jewish leaders **t** him, "If you release this
20: 18 Mary Magdalene found the disciples and **t** them,
20: 25 They **t** him, "We have seen the Lord!" But he
20: 29 Then Jesus **t** him, "You believe because you have
21: 15 I love you." "Then feed my lambs," Jesus **t** him.
21: 19 to glorify God. Then Jesus **t** him, "Follow me."
Ac 1: 1 In my first book I **t** you about everything Jesus
1: 4 as he was eating a meal with them, he **t** them,
1: 4 Remember, I have **t** you about this before.
4: 18 and **t** them never again to speak or teach about
4: 23 and **t** them what the leading priests and elders had
5: 19 of the jail, and brought them out. Then he **t** them,
7: 3 God **t** him, 'Leave your native land and your
7: 6 But God also **t** him that his descendants would live
7: 7 God **t** him, 'and in the end they will come out
7: 27 Moses aside and **t** him to mind his own business.
7: 37 "Moses himself **t** the people of Israel, 'God will
7: 40 They **t** Aaron, 'Make us some gods who can lead
7: 56 And he **t** them, "Look, I see the heavens opened
8: 5 and **t** the people there about the Messiah.
9: 6 the city, and you will be **t** what you are to do."
9: 24 But Saul was **t** about their plot, and that they were
9: 27 and **t** them how Saul had seen the Lord on the way
9: 27 Barnabas also **t** them what the Lord had said to
10: 8 He **t** them what had happened and sent them off to
10: 28 Peter **t** them, "You know it is against the Jewish
10: 31 He **t** me, 'Cornelius, your prayers have been heard,
11: 4 Then Peter **t** them exactly what had happened.
11: 12 The Holy Spirit **t** me to go with them and not to
11: 13 He **t** us how an angel had appeared to him in his home and had **t** him,
12: 8 Then the angel **t** him, "Get dressed and put on
12: 14 the door, she ran back inside and **t** everyone,
12: 17 them to quiet down and **t** them what had happened
13: 41 even if someone **t** you about it.' "
15: 3 They **t** them—much to everyone's joy—
15: 12 as Barnabas and Paul **t** about the miraculous signs
15: 14 Peter has **t** you about the time God first visited the
16: 6 because the Holy Spirit had **t** them not to go into
16: 36 So the jailer **t** Paul, "You and Silas are free to
17: 18 When he **t** them about Jesus and his resurrection,
18: 9 night the Lord spoke to Paul in a vision and **t** him,
19: 4 John himself **t** the people to believe in Jesus,
20: 23 except that the Holy Spirit has **t** me in city after
21: 21 **t** that you are teaching all the Jews living in the
21: 25 all we ask of them is what we already **t** them in a
22: 10 And the Lord **t** me, 'Get up and go into Damascus,
22: 10 and there you will be **t** all that you are to do.'
22: 14 "Then he **t** me, 'The God of our ancestors has
23: 11 Just as you have **t** the people about me here in
23: 14 and other leaders and **t** them what they had done.
23: 16 of their plan and went to the fortress and **t** Paul.
23: 20 Paul's nephew **t** him, "Some Jews are going to ask
23: 22 "Don't let a soul know you **t** me this,"
23: 30 I have **t** his accusers to bring their charges before
23: 35 when your accusers arrive," the governor **t** him.
24: 24 they listened as he **t** them about faith in Christ
25: 14 "There is a prisoner here," he **t** him, "whose case
27: 44 and he **t** the others to try for it on planks and debris
28: 23 He **t** them about the Kingdom of God and taught
Ro 4: 17 That is what the Scriptures mean when God **t** him,
9: 12 She was **t**, "The descendants of your older son
9: 17 For the Scriptures say that God **t** Pharaoh, "I have
9: 26 And, / "Once they were **t**, / 'You are not my
15: 21 "Those who have never been **t** about him will see,
1Co 1: 6 This shows that what I **t** you about Christ is true.
1: 11 For some members of Chloe's household have **t**
5: 1 I am **t** that you have a man in your church who is
5: 9 I **t** you not to associate with people who indulge in
10: 28 for the conscience of the one who **t** you.
11: 21 For I am **t** that some of you hurry to eat your own
2Co 7: 7 When he **t** me how much you were looking
7: 14 I had **t** him how proud I was of you—and you
7: 14 I have always **t** you the truth, and now my boasting
9: 3 as I **t** them you would be, with your money all
9: 4 that you still weren't ready after all I had **t** them!
12: 4 heard things so astounding that they cannot be **t**.
Gal 1: 8 who preaches any other message than the one we **t**
Eph 4: 14 because someone has **t** us something different
Php 3: 18 For I have **t** you often before, and I say it again
Col 1: 8 He is the one who **t** us about the great love for
2Th 2: 5 Don't you remember that I **t** you this when I was
2: 14 He called you to salvation when we **t** you the Good
Tit 3: 8 These things I have **t** you are all true. I want you to
Heb 4: 2 because they didn't believe what God **t** them.
7: 8 than they are, because we are **t** that he lives on.
Jas 2: 22 so much that he was willing to do whatever God **t**
1Pe 1: 11 when he **t** them in advance about Christ's suffering
1: 12 They were **t** that these things would not happen
2Pe 1: 16 we **t** you about the power of our Lord Jesus Christ
3Jn 1: 6 They have **t** the church here of your friendship
Jude 1: 17 what the apostles of our Lord Jesus Christ **t** you,
Rev 6: 11 And they were **t** to rest a little longer until the full
9: 4 They were **t** not to hurt the grass or plants or trees
9: 5 They were **t** not to kill them but to torture them for
11: 1 and I was **t**, "Go and measure the Temple of God

TOLERANT (1) [TOLERATE]

Ro 2: 4 Don't you realize how kind, **t**, and patient God is

TOLERATE (7) [TOLERANT]

2Ch 19: 7 for the LORD our God does not **t** perverted
Est 3: 4 about this to see if he would **t** Mordecai's conduct,
Ps 5: 4 in wickedness; / you cannot **t** the slightest sin.
101: 5 I will not **t** people who slander their neighbors.
Mic 6: 11 And how can I **t** all your merchants who use
Rev 2: 2 patient endurance. I know you don't **t** evil people.
2: 14 You **t** some among you who are like Balaam,

TOLLS (2)

Ezr 4: 13 refuse to pay their tribute, customs, and **t** to you.
4: 20 and have received vast tribute, customs, and **t**.

TOMB (40) [TOMBS]

1Sa 10: 2 you will see two men beside Rachel's **t** at Zelzah,
2Sa 4: 12 and buried it in Abner's **t** in Hebron.
21: 14 He buried them all in the **t** of Kish, Saul's father,
2Ki 13: 21 the body they were burying into the **t** of Elisha.
21: 26 He was buried in his **t** in the garden of Uzza.
23: 16 and looked up at the **t** of the man of God who had
23: 17 "It is the **t** of the man of God who came from
23: 30 Megiddo to Jerusalem and buried him in his own **t**.
2Ch 16: 14 He was buried in the **t** he had carved out for
Job 21: 32 to the grave, an honor guard keeps watch at their **t**.
Isa 22: 16 building a beautiful **t** for yourself in the rock?
Am 2: 1 They desecrated the **t** of Edom's king and burned
Mt 27: 60 He placed it in his own new **t**, which had been
27: 64 So we request that you seal the **t** until the third
27: 66 So they sealed the **t** and posted guards to protect it.
28: 1 and the other Mary went out to see the **t**.
28: 8 The women ran quickly from the **t**. They were very
28: 11 some of the men who had been guarding the **t** went
Mk 6: 29 they came for his body and buried it in a **t**.
15: 46 and laid it in a **t** that had been carved out of the
16: 2 Sunday morning, just at sunrise, they came to the **t**.
16: 3 roll the stone away from the entrance to the **t**.
16: 5 So they entered the **t**, and there on the right sat a
16: 8 The women fled from the **t**, trembling
Lk 23: 53 and laid it in a new **t** that had been carved out of
23: 55 and saw the **t** where they placed his body.
24: 1 early on Sunday morning the women came to the **t**,
24: 5 "Why are you looking in a **t** for someone who is
24: 10 The women who went to the **t** were Mary
24: 12 However, Peter ran to the **t** to look. Stooping,
24: 22 of his followers were at his **t** early this morning,
Jn 19: 41 where there was a new **t**, never used before.
19: 42 the Passover and since the **t** was close at hand,
20: 1 Mary Magdalene came to the **t** and found that the
20: 2 "They have taken the Lord's body out of the **t**,
20: 3 Peter and the other disciple ran to the **t** to see.
20: 11 Mary was standing outside the **t** crying, and as she
Ac 2: 29 and was buried, and his **t** is still here among us.
7: 16 and buried in the **t** Abraham had bought from the
13: 29 him down from the cross and placed him in a **t**.

TOMBS (9) [TOMB]

Ge 23: 6 be a privilege to have you choose the finest of our **t**
1Sa 13: 6 tried to hide in caves, holes, rocks, **t**, and cisterns.
2Ki 23: 16 he noticed several **t** in the side of the hill.
Mt 23: 27 You are like whitewashed **t**—beautiful on the
23: 29 For you build **t** for the prophets your ancestors
27: 52 and **t** opened. The bodies of many godly men
Mk 5: 3 This man lived among the **t** and could not be
5: 5 throughout the night he would wander among the **t**
Lk 11: 47 For you build **t** for the very prophets your

TOMORROW (64)

Ex 8: 10 "Do it **t**," Pharaoh said. "All right,"
8: 23 This miraculous sign will happen **t**.' "
9: 18 So **t** at this time I will send a hailstorm worse than
10: 4 For **t** I will cover the whole country with locusts.
16: 23 "The LORD has appointed **t** as a day of rest,
16: 23 as you want today, and set aside what is left for **t**."
17: 9 **T**, I will stand at the top of the hill with the staff of
19: 10 Purify them today and **t**, and have them wash their
32: 5 "**T** there will be a festival to the LORD!"
Nu 11: 18 purify themselves, for **t** they will have meat to eat.
14: 25 **T** you must set out for the wilderness in the
16: 5 "**T** morning the LORD will show us who belongs
16: 7 and burn incense in them **t** before the LORD.
16: 16 "Come here **t** and present yourself before the
Jos 3: 5 for **t** the LORD will do great wonders among
7: 13 people to purify themselves in preparation for **t**.
11: 6 By this time **t** they will all be dead. Cripple their
22: 18 the LORD today, he will be angry with all of us **t**.
Jdg 19: 9 **T** you can get up early and be on your way."
20: 28 "Go! **T** I will give you victory over them."
1Sa 9: 16 "About this time **t** I will send you a man from the
11: 9 to say, "We will rescue you by noontime **t**!"
11: 10 told their enemies, "**T** we will come out to you,
19: 2 "**T** morning," he warned him, "you must find a
20: 5 "**T** we celebrate the new moon festival.
20: 5 but **t** I'll hide in the field and stay there until the
20: 12 the LORD, the God of Israel, that by this time **t**,
20: 18 "**T** we celebrate the new moon festival.
20: 19 The day after **t**, toward evening, go to the place
25: 22 one man of his household is still alive **t** morning!"
25: 34 not one of Nabal's men would be alive **t**
28: 19 and the army of Israel over to the Philistines **t**,
2Sa 11: 12 told him, "and **t** you may return to the army."
1Ki 19: 2 "May the gods also kill me if by this time **t** I have
20: 6 But about this time **t** I will send my officials to
2Ki 7: 1 By this time **t** in the markets of Samaria,
7: 18 "By this time **t** in the markets of Samaria,
10: 6 king's sons to me at Jezreel at about this time **t**."
2Ch 20: 16 **T**, march out against them. You will find them
20: 17 Go out there **t**, for the LORD is with you!"
Est 5: 8 please come with Haman **t** to the banquet I will
5: 8 Then **t** I will explain what this is all about."
5: 12 invited me to dine with her and the king again **t**!"
9: 13 give the Jews in Susa permission to do again **t** as
Pr 3: 28 don't say, "Come back **t**, and then I'll help you."
27: 1 Don't brag about **t**, since you don't know what the
Isa 22: 13 you say. "What's the difference, for **t** we die."
56: 12 Let this go on and on, and **t** will be even better."
Mt 6: 30 for flowers that are here today and gone **t**,
6: 34 "So don't worry about **t**, for **t** will bring its own worries.
16: 2 the saying, 'Red sky at night means fair weather **t**,
Lk 12: 28 for flowers that are here today and gone **t**,
13: 32 and doing miracles of healing today and **t**;
13: 33 Yes, today, **t**, and the next day I must proceed on
22: 34 The rooster will not crow **t** morning until you have
22: 61 "Before the rooster crows **t** morning, you will
Jn 13: 38 No, before the rooster crows **t** morning, you will
Ac 23: 20 you to bring Paul before the Jewish high council **t**,
25: 22 Agrippa said. And Festus replied, "You shall—**t**!"
Ro 8: 38 Our fears for today, our worries about **t**, and even
1Co 15: 32 "Let's feast and get drunk, / for **t** we die!"
Jas 4: 13 "Today or **t** we are going to a certain town
4: 14 How do you know what will happen **t**? For your

TON (1) [TONS]

2Ki 18: 14 than eleven tons of silver and about one **t** of gold.

TONGS (3)

1Ki 7: 49 flower decorations, lamps, and **t**, all of gold,
2Ch 4: 21 flower decorations, lamps, and **t**, all of pure gold;
Isa 6: 6 and he picked up a burning coal with a pair of **t**.

TONGUE (34) [SMOOTH-TONGUED, TONGUES]

2Sa 23: 2 speaks through me; / his words are upon my **t**.
Job 20: 12 taste of his wickedness, letting it melt under his **t**.
27: 4 lips will speak no evil, and my **t** will speak no lies.
Ps 22: 15 My **t** sticks to the roof of my mouth. / You have
34: 13 Then watch your **t**! / Keep your lips from telling
39: 1 and not sin in what I say. / I will curb my **t**
45: 1 the king, / for my **t** is like the pen of a skillful poet.
52: 2 Your **t** cuts like a sharp razor; / you're an expert at
119: 172 Let my **t** sing about your word, / for all your
120: 3 O deceptive **t**, what will God do to you?
137: 6 May my **t** stick to the roof of my mouth / if I fail to
145: 6 Your awe-inspiring deeds will be on every **t**;
Pr 6: 17 haughty eyes, / a lying **t**, / hands that kill the
6: 24 from the smooth **t** of an adulterous woman.
10: 31 wise advice, but the **t** that deceives will be cut off.
13: 3 Those who control their **t** will have a long life;
15: 4 and health; a deceitful **t** crushes the spirit.
17: 20 will not prosper; the twisted **t** tumbles into trouble.
18: 21 the consequences, for the **t** can kill or nourish life.
25: 23 the north brings rain, so a gossiping **t** causes anger!
26: 28 A lying **t** hates its victims, and flattery causes ruin.
SS 4: 11 as honey. Yes, honey and cream are under your **t**.
Isa 45: 23 and every **t** will confess allegiance to my name."
Eze 3: 26 And I will make your **t** stick to the roof of your
3: 27 a message, I will loosen your **t** and let you speak.
Mk 7: 33 he touched the man's **t** with the spittle.
Lk 16: 24 to dip the tip of his finger in water and cool my **t**,
Ro 14: 11 and every **t** will confess allegiance to God.' "
Php 2: 11 and every **t** will confess that Jesus Christ is Lord,
Jas 1: 26 you claim to be religious but don't control your **t**,
3: 5 So also, the **t** is a small thing, but what enormous
3: 6 And the **t** is a flame of fire. It is full of wickedness
3: 8 but no one can tame the **t**. It is an uncontrollable
1Pe 3: 10 and good days, / keep your **t** from speaking evil,

TONGUES (32) [TONGUE]

Jdg 7: 5 in their hands and lap it up with their **t** like dogs.
Job 29: 10 of the city stood quietly, holding their **t** in respect.
Ps 10: 7 Trouble and evil are on the tips of their **t**.
12: 3 their flattery to an end / and silence their proud **t**.
31: 20 them in your presence, / far from accusing **t**.
50: 19 filled with wickedness, / and your **t** are full of lies.
57: 4 and arrows, / and whose **t** cut like swords.
64: 3 Sharp **t** are the swords they wield; / bitter words
78: 36 with their words; / they lied to him with their **t**.
140: 3 Their **t** sting like a snake; / the poison of a viper
Isa 41: 17 and their **t** are parched from thirst, then I,
57: 4 you mock, making faces and sticking out your **t**?
Jer 9: 3 "My people bend their **t** like bows to shoot lies.
9: 5 With practiced **t** they tell lies; they wear
9: 8 For their **t** aim lies like poisoned arrows.
La 4: 4 The parched **t** of their little ones stick with thirst to
Mic 6: 12 so used to lying that their **t** can no longer tell the
Zec 14: 12 their sockets, and their **t** will decay in their mouths.
Ac 2: 3 what looked like flames or **t** of fire appeared
10: 46 for they heard them speaking in **t** and praising
19: 6 on them, and they spoke in other **t** and prophesied.
1Co 14: 2 For if your gift is the ability to speak in **t**, you will
14: 4 A person who speaks in **t** is strengthened
14: 5 I wish you all had the gift of speaking in **t**,
14: 5 is a greater and more useful gift than speaking in **t**,
14: 13 So anyone who has the gift of speaking in **t** should
14: 14 For if I pray in **t**, my spirit is praying, but I don't
14: 18 I thank God that I speak in **t** more than all of you.
14: 22 So you see that speaking in **t** is a sign, not for
14: 28 church meeting and speak in **t** to God privately.
14: 39 eager to prophesy, and don't forbid speaking in **t**.
Jas 3: 2 but those who control their **t** can also control

TONIGHT (20)

Ge 19:34 Let's get him drunk with wine again **t**, and you go
30:15 "I will let him sleep with you **t** in exchange for the
30:16 meet him. "You must sleep with me **t**!" she said.
Jos 2: 2 "Some Israelites have come here **t** to spy out the
4: 3 and pile them up at the place where you camp **t**."
Jdg 6:37 I will put some wool on the threshing floor **t**.
19:11 too late to travel; let's stay in this Jebusite city **t**."
Ru 1:12 and I were to get married **t** and bear sons,
3: 2 **T** he will be winnowing barley at the threshing
3:13 Stay here **t**, and in the morning I will talk to him.
1Sa 19:11 warned him, "If you don't get away **t**,
2Sa 11:12 "Well, stay here **t**," David told him,
17: 1 twelve thousand men to start out after David **t**.
17:16 not to stay at the shallows of the Jordan River **t**.
17:21 "Quick!" they told him, "cross the Jordan **t**!"
19: 7 not a single one of them will remain here **t**.
Ne 6:10 Your enemies are coming to kill you **t**."
Mt 26:31 "**T** all of you will desert me," Jesus told them.
Lk 2:11 has been born **t** in Bethlehem, the city of David!
Ac 23:23 ready to leave for Caesarea at nine o'clock **t**.

TONS (18) [TON]

1Ki 9:28 and brought back to Solomon some sixteen **t** of
10:14 Each year Solomon received about twenty-five **t** of
2Ki 15:19 But Menahem paid him thirty-seven **t** of silver to
18:14 then demanded a settlement of more than eleven **t**
1Ch 19: 6 and the Ammonites sent thirty-eight **t** of silver to
22:14 nearly four thousand **t** of gold, nearly forty
thousand **t** of silver, and so much iron
29: 4 I am donating more than 112 **t** of gold from Ophir
29: 4 and over 262 **t** of refined silver to be used for
29: 7 they gave almost 188 **t** of gold, 10,000 gold coins,
about 375 **t** of silver, about 675 **t** of bronze, and
about 3,750 **t** of iron.
2Ch 3: 8 Its interior was overlaid with about twenty-three **t**
8:18 and brought back to Solomon almost seventeen **t**
9:13 Each year Solomon received about 25 **t** of gold.
Ezr 8:26 24 **t** of silver, / 7,500 pounds of silver utensils,
Est 3: 9 and I will give 375 **t** of silver to the government

TOO (439) See Index of Articles, Etc.

TOOK (529) [TAKE]

Ge 2:21 He **t** one of Adam's ribs and closed up the place
5:24 Then suddenly, he disappeared because God **t** him.
6: 2 human race and **t** any they wanted as their wives.
9:23 Shem and Japheth **t** a robe, held it over their
11:31 Terah **t** his son Abram, his daughter-in-law Sarai,
12: 5 He **t** his wife, Sarai, his nephew Lot, and all his
13:10 Lot **t** a long look at the fertile plains of the Jordan
14:12 who lived in Sodom—and **t** everything he owned.
15:10 Abram **t** all these and killed them. He cut each one
16: 1 So Sarai **t** her servant, an Egyptian woman named
16: 3 **t** Hagar the Egyptian servant and gave her to
17:23 On that very day Abraham **t** his son Ishmael
18: 8 he **t** some cheese curds and milk and the roasted
20: 3 are a dead man, for that woman you **t** is married."
20:14 Then Abimelech **t** sheep and oxen and servants—
21:28 But when Abraham **t** seven additional ewe lambs
22: 3 his donkey and **t** two of his servants with him,
22:10 And Abraham **t** the knife and lifted it up to kill his
22:13 So he **t** the ram and sacrificed it as a burnt offering
24: 7 who **t** me from my father's house and my native
24: 9 So the servant **t** a solemn oath that he would
26:31 they each **t** a solemn oath of nonaggression.
27:14 She **t** them and cooked a delicious meat dish,
27:15 Then she **t** Esau's best clothes, which were there in
27:25 So Jacob **t** the food over to his father, and Isaac ate
28:18 He **t** the stone he had used as a pillow and set it
29:23 when it was dark, Laban **t** Leah to Jacob,
30:36 and they **t** them three days' distance from where
30:37 Now Jacob **t** fresh shoots from poplar, almond,
31:19 her father's household gods and **t** them with her.
31:21 Jacob **t** all his possessions with him and crossed
31:39 to reduce the count of your flock? No, I **t** the loss!
31:45 So Jacob **t** a stone and set it up as a monument.
31:53 So Jacob **t** an oath before the awesome God of his
34: 2 Hamor the Hivite, saw her, he **t** her and raped her.
34:25 Dinah's brothers, Simeon and Levi, **t** their swords,
34:29 They also **t** all the women and children and wealth
36: 6 Then Esau **t** his wives, children,
37:28 and the Ishmaelite traders **t** him along to Egypt.
37:32 They **t** the beautiful robe to their father and asked
38: 7 in the LORD's sight, so the LORD **t** his life.
38:10 his dead brother. So the LORD **t** Onan's life, too.
38:19 Afterward she went home, **t** off her veil, and put
39:20 He **t** Joseph and threw him into the prison where
39:23 after that, because Joseph **t** care of everything.
40:11 so I **t** the grapes and squeezed the juice into it.
41:45 So Joseph **t** charge of the entire land of Egypt.
41:48 Joseph **t** a portion of all the crops grown in Egypt
42:30 roughly to us," they told him. "He **t** us for spies.
43:15 So they **t** Benjamin and the gifts and double the
43:17 did as he was told and **t** them to Joseph's palace.
44:11 They quickly **t** their sacks from the backs of their
47: 2 Joseph **t** five of his brothers with him
48: 1 and he **t** with him his two sons, Manasseh
48:12 Joseph **t** the boys from their grandfather's knees,
48:22 the portion that I **t** from the Amorites with my
50: 3 The embalming process **t** forty days, and there was
50: 8 Joseph also **t** his brothers and the entire household
Ex 2: 9 So the baby's mother **t** her baby home and nursed
4: 6 Moses did so, and when he **t** it out again, his hand
4: 7 Moses did, and when he **t** it out this time, it was as
4:20 So Moses **t** his wife and sons, put them on a
4:25 his wife, **t** a flint knife and circumcised her son.
12:34 The Israelites **t** with them their bread dough made
13:19 Moses **t** the bones of Joseph with him, for Joseph
14: 7 He **t** with him six hundred of Egypt's best chariots,
15:20 **t** a tambourine and led all the women in rhythm
15:25 Moses **t** the branch and threw it into the water.
24: 6 Moses **t** half the blood from these animals
24: 7 Then he **t** the Book of the Covenant and read it to
32: 4 Then Aaron **t** the gold, melted it down, and molded
32:20 He **t** the calf they had made and melted it in the
Lev 8:10 Then Moses **t** the anointing oil and anointed the
8:15 Moses **t** some of the blood, and with his finger he
8:16 He **t** all the fat around the internal organs, the lobe
8:19 Then Moses **t** the ram's blood and sprinkled it
8:23 Then Moses **t** some of its blood and put it on the
8:25 Next he **t** the fat, including the fat from the tail,
8:28 Moses then **t** all the offerings back and burned
8:29 Then Moses **t** the breast and lifted it up in the
8:30 Next Moses **t** some of the anointing oil and some
9:19 Then he **t** the fat of the bull and the ram—the fat
Nu 11:25 He **t** some of the Spirit that was upon Moses
13:23 so large that it **t** two of them to carry it on a pole
13:23 They also **t** samples of the pomegranates and figs.
15:36 So the whole community **t** the man outside the
20: 9 He **t** the staff from the place where it was kept
21: 1 the Israelites and **t** some of them as prisoners.
22: 7 and **t** money with them to pay Balaam to curse
22:41 The next morning Balak **t** Balaam up to
23:14 So Balak **t** Balaam to the plateau of Zophim on
23:28 So Balak **t** Balaam to the top of Mount Peor,
25: 7 and left the assembly. Then he **t** a spear
31:47 Moses **t** one of every fifty prisoners and animals
Dt 1:15 So I **t** the wise and respected men you had selected
2:35 We **t** all the livestock as plunder for ourselves,
3: 5 We also **t** many unwalled villages at the same
3: 7 for ourselves and **t** plunder from all the towns.
3:12 "When we **t** possession of this land, I gave the
4:49 And they **t** the eastern bank of the Jordan Valley as
9:21 I **t** your sin—the calf you had made—and I melted
10: 3 the first two, and I **t** the tablets up the mountain.
29: 8 We **t** their land and gave it to the tribes of Reuben
33:21 The people of Gad **t** the best land for themselves;
Jos 4: 8 They **t** twelve stones from the middle of the Jordan
7:21 than a pound. I wanted them so much that I **t** them.
7:23 They **t** the things from the tent and brought them to
7:24 Then Joshua and all the Israelites **t** Achan,
8:29 At sunset the Israelites **t** down the body and threw
9: 5 And they **t** along dry, moldy bread for provisions.
10: 9 from Gilgal and **t** the Amorite armies by surprise.
11:14 And the Israelites **t** all the captured goods
11:23 So Joshua **t** control of the entire land, just as the
24: 3 But I **t** your ancestor Abraham from the land
24: 8 over them, and you **t** possession of their land.
24:26 he **t** a huge stone and rolled it beneath the oak tree
Jdg 1: 7 They **t** him to Jerusalem, and he died there.
1:19 of Judah, and they **t** possession of the hill country.
2:18 For the LORD **t** pity on his people, who were
3:13 Eglon attacked Israel and **t** possession of Jericho.
3:28 And the Israelites **t** control of the shallows of the
6:27 So Gideon **t** ten of his servants and did as the
6:34 Then the Spirit of the LORD **t** possession of
7: 5 When Gideon **t** his warriors down to the water,
7:11 So Gideon **t** Purah and went down to the outposts
8:16 Then Gideon **t** the leaders of the town and taught
8:21 and **t** the royal ornaments from the necks of their
9: 5 He **t** the soldiers to his father's home at Ophrah,
9:46 they **t** refuge within the walls of the temple of
9:48 He **t** an ax and chopped some branches from a tree,
11:21 So Israel **t** control of all the land of the Amorites,
11:23 who **t** away the land from the Amorites and gave it
13:19 Then Manoah **t** a young goat and a grain offering
14: 6 Spirit of the LORD powerfully **t** control of him,
14:19 Then the Spirit of the LORD powerfully **t** control
14:19 of Ashkelon, killed thirty men, **t** their belongings,
15: 1 Samson **t** a young goat as a present to his wife.
15:14 But the Spirit of the LORD powerfully **t** control
16: 3 got up, **t** hold of the city gates with its two posts,
16:12 So Delilah **t** new ropes and tied him up with them.
16:21 They **t** him to Gaza, where he was bound with
16:31 They **t** him back home and buried him between
17: 2 Well, here they are. I was the one who **t** them."
17: 4 So his mother **t** two hundred of the silver coins to a
18: 3 they **t** him aside and asked him, "Who brought
18:17 spies entered the shrine and **t** the carved image,
18:20 so he **t** along the sacred ephod, the household
19: 3 her husband **t** a servant and an extra donkey to
19: 3 she **t** him inside, and her father welcomed him.
19:10 So he **t** his two saddled donkeys and his concubine
19:15 the town square, but no one **t** them in for the night.
19:21 So he **t** them home with him and fed their donkeys.
19:25 Then the Levite **t** his concubine and pushed her out
19:28 So he put her body on his donkey and **t** her home.
19:29 he **t** a knife and cut his concubine's body into
20: 2 **t** their positions in the assembly of the people of
20:22 But the Israelites **t** courage and assembled at the
21:23 They kidnapped the women who **t** part in the
Ru 1: 1 He **t** his wife and two sons and went to live in the
1: 7 and they **t** the road that would lead them back to
4: 1 So Boaz went to the town gate and **t** a seat there.
4:13 married Ruth and **t** her home to live with him.
4:16 Naomi **t** care of the baby and cared for him as if he
1Sa 1:24 Hannah **t** him to the Tabernacle in Shiloh.
1:25 After sacrificing the bull, they **t** the child to Eli.
5: 1 they **t** it from the battleground at Ebenezer to the
7: 1 They **t** it to the hillside home of Abinadab
7: 9 So Samuel **t** a young lamb and offered it to the
7:12 Samuel then **t** a large stone and placed it between
9: 4 So Saul **t** one of his servants and traveled all
9:25 Samuel **t** Saul up to the roof of the house
10: 1 Then Samuel **t** a flask of olive oil and poured it
11: 7 He **t** two oxen and cut them into pieces and sent
13: 2 He **t** two thousand of the chosen men with him to
16: 6 Samuel **t** one look at Eliab and thought,
16:13 Samuel **t** the olive oil he had brought and poured it
17:39 over it, and **t** a step or two to see what it was like,
17:39 "I'm not used to them." So he **t** them off again.
17:54 (David **t** Goliath's head to Jerusalem, but he stored
19: 7 Then he **t** David to see Saul, and everything was as
19:13 Then she **t** an idol and put it in his bed, covered it
19:18 Then Samuel **t** David with him to live at Naioth.
20: 3 Then David **t** an oath before Jonathan and said,
20:35 and **t** a young boy with him to gather his arrows.
23: 5 slaughtered the Philistines and **t** all their livestock
25:42 **t** along five of her servant girls as attendants,
26: 2 So Saul **t** three thousand of his best troops
26:12 So David **t** the spear and jug of water that were
27: 2 So David **t** his six hundred men and their families
27: 9 He **t** the sheep, cattle, donkeys, camels,
28:10 But Saul **t** an oath in the name of the LORD
31: 4 not do it. So Saul **t** his own sword and fell on it.
31:12 and **t** the bodies of Saul and his sons down from
31:13 Then they **t** their remains and buried them beneath
2Sa 1:10 Then I **t** his crown and one of his bracelets so I
2:32 Joab and his men **t** Asahel's body to Bethlehem
3:15 So Ishbosheth **t** Michal away from her husband
3:27 Joab **t** him aside at the gateway as if to speak with
4:12 Then they **t** Ishbosheth's head and buried it in
6:10 He **t** it instead to the home of Obed-edom of Gath.
7:15 love will not be taken from him as I **t** it from Saul,
12: 4 he **t** the poor man's lamb and killed it and served it
12:30 David **t** a vast amount of plunder from the city.
13:10 and feed it to me here." So Tamar **t** it to him.
15: 5 Instead, he **t** them by the hand and embraced them.
15:11 He **t** two hundred men from Jerusalem with him as
15:24 and the Levites **t** the Ark of the Covenant of God
15:29 and Abiathar **t** the Ark of God back to the city
18:14 Then he **t** three daggers and plunged them into
18:23 Then Ahimaaz **t** a shortcut across the plain of the
20: 5 but it **t** him longer than the three days he had been
20: 9 and **t** him by the beard with his right hand as
1Ki 1: 4 and she waited on the king and **t** care of him.
1: 7 Adonijah **t** Joab son of Zeruiah and Abiathar the
1:38 and the king's bodyguard **t** Solomon down to
1:39 There Zadok the priest **t** a flask of olive oil from
2: 7 for they **t** care of me when I fled from your brother
2:40 he had found them, he **t** them back to Jerusalem.
2:46 Benaiah son of Jehoiada **t** Shimei outside
3:20 and **t** my son from beside me while I was asleep.
3:20 child in my arms and **t** mine to sleep beside her.
6:38 his reign. So it **t** seven years to build the Temple.
7: 1 and it **t** him thirteen years to complete the
8: 4 the priests and Levites **t** the Ark of the LORD,
11:30 and Ahijah **t** the new cloak he was wearing
13:29 and **t** it back to the city to mourn over him
17:19 And he **t** the boy's body from her, carried him up
18:31 He **t** twelve stones, one to represent each of the
18:40 and Elijah **t** them down to the Kishon Valley
20:34 "I will give back the towns my father **t** from your
2Ki 1:17 This **t** place in the second year of the reign of
3:27 So he **t** his oldest son, who would have been the
4:20 So the servant **t** him home, and his mother held
5:24 Gehazi **t** the gifts from the servants and sent the
8: 2 She **t** her family and lived in the land of the
8:15 But the next day Hazael **t** a blanket, soaked it in
9:28 His officials **t** him by chariot to Jerusalem,
11: 2 of King Jehoram, **t** Ahaziah's infant son, Joash,
11: 9 The commanders **t** charge of the men reporting for
11:19 and the king **t** his seat on the royal throne.
14:14 He also **t** hostages and returned to Samaria.
15:29 and he **t** the people to Assyria as captives.
16: 8 Then Ahaz **t** the silver and gold from the Temple
17:24 So the Assyrians **t** over Samaria and the other
20:13 He also **t** them to see his armory and showed them
21: 7 Manasseh even **t** an Asherah pole he had made
22:20 place.' " So they **t** her message back to the king.
23: 3 The king **t** his place of authority beside the pillar
23: 6 and **t** it outside Jerusalem to the Kidron Valley,
23:30 Josiah's officers **t** his body back in a chariot from
24:12 Nebuchadnezzar's reign, he **t** Jehoiachin prisoner.
24:14 King Nebuchadnezzar **t** ten thousand captives from
24:16 He also **t** seven thousand of the best troops and one
25:11 then **t** as exiles those who remained in the city,
25:14 They also **t** all the pots, shovels, lamp snuffers,
25:15 captain of the guard, also **t** the firepans and basins,
25:18 The captain of the guard **t** with him as prisoners
25:19 he **t** an officer of the Judean army, five of the
25:20 Nebuzaradan the commander **t** them all to the king
1Ch 2:23 and also **t** Kenath and its sixty surrounding
4:41 who lived there and **t** the land for themselves,
10: 4 not do it. So Saul **t** his own sword and fell on it.
11:13 The battle **t** place in a field full of barley,
13:13 He **t** it instead to the home of Obed-edom of Gath.
17:13 I will not take my unfailing love from him as I **t** it
20: 2 David **t** a vast amount of plunder from the city.
23:28 They also **t** care of the courtyards and side rooms,
24: 6 of Eleazar and Ithamar **t** turns casting lots.
27:23 When David **t** his census, he did not count those
29:23 So Solomon **t** the throne of the LORD in place of
2Ch 1: 1 of King David, now **t** firm control of the kingdom,
2:17 Solomon **t** a census of all foreigners in the land of
7: 6 The priests **t** their assigned positions, and so did
12: 9 and **t** away all the treasures of the Temple of the
15: 8 he **t** courage and removed all the idols in the land

17:9 They **t** copies of the Book of the Law of the
20:25 so much plunder that it **t** them three days just to
22:11 of King Jehoram, **t** Ahaziah's infant son, Joash,
23:8 The commanders **t** charge of the men reporting for
24:11 and **t** the chest back to the Temple again.
25:5 Then he **t** a census and found that he had an army
25:12 and **t** them to the top of a cliff and threw them off,
28:8 from Judah and **t** tremendous amounts of plunder, which they **t** back to Samaria.
28:15 and **t** all the prisoners back to their own land—
28:21 Ahaz **t** valuable items from the LORD's Temple,
28:24 The king **t** the utensils from the Temple of God
29:16 and they **t** out to the Temple courtyard all the
29:17 of the LORD itself, which **t** another eight days.
29:22 and the priests **t** the blood and sprinkled it on the
29:26 then **t** their positions around the Temple with the
29:26 and the priests **t** their positions with the trumpets.
30:14 They **t** away all the incense altars and threw them
30:16 They **t** their places at the Temple according to the
33:7 Manasseh even **t** a carved idol he had made and set
33:11 the Assyrian armies, and they **t** Manasseh prisoner.
34:16 Shaphan **t** the scroll to the king and reported,
34:28 place.' " So they **t** her message back to the king.
34:31 The king **t** his place of authority beside the pillar
35:10 the priests and the Levites **t** their places,
35:14 The Levites **t** responsibility for all these
35:19 This Passover celebration **t** place in the eighteenth
36:1 Then the people of the land **t** Josiah's son Jehoahaz
36:4 Then Neco **t** Jehoahaz to Egypt as a prisoner.
36:7 Nebuchadnezzar also **t** some of the treasures from
36:18 The king also **t** home to Babylon all the utensils,
36:18 He also **t** with him all the royal princes.
Ezr 2:66 They **t** with them 736 horses, 245 mules,
3:10 and **t** their places to blow their trumpets.
4:5 and lasted until King Darius of Persia **t** the throne.
10:9 This **t** place on December 19, and all the people
Ne 2:12 We **t** no pack animals with us, except the donkey
4:23 guards who were with me—ever **t** off our clothes.
5:15 Even their assistants **t** advantage of the people.
7:68 They **t** with them 736 horses, 245 mules,
9:3 Then for three more hours they **t** turns confessing
9:22 They completely **t** over the land of King Sihon of
9:24 They went in and **t** possession of the land.
9:25 They **t** over houses full of good things,
12:40 to the Temple of God, where they **t** their places.
Est 6:11 So Haman **t** the robe and put it on Mordecai,
8:2 The king **t** off his signet ring—which he had taken
9:15 more people, though again they **t** no plunder.
Job 16:12 He **t** me by the neck and dashed me to pieces.
29:2 "I long for the years gone by when God **t** care of
29:7 and **t** my place among the honored leaders.
Ps 78:71 He **t** David from tending the ewes and lambs
80:9 ground for us, / and we **t** root and filled the land.
120:1 I **t** my troubles to the LORD; / I cried out to him,
132:2 He **t** an oath before the LORD. / He vowed to the
Ecc 2:10 Anything I wanted, I **t**. I did not restrain myself
Isa 39:2 He also **t** them to see his armory and showed them
48:3 Then suddenly I **t** action, and all my predictions
65:22 when invaders **t** the houses and confiscated the
Jer 25:17 So I **t** the cup of anger from the LORD and made
26:23 They **t** him prisoner and brought him back to King
28:10 Then Hananiah the prophet **t** the yoke off
29:29 he **t** it to Jeremiah and read it to him.
31:32 with their ancestors when I **t** them by the hand
32:11 Then I **t** the sealed deed and an unsealed copy of
34:11 They **t** back the people they had freed,
35:4 I **t** them to the Temple, and we went into the room
36:14 too. So Baruch **t** the scroll and went to them.
36:23 the king **t** his knife and cut off that section of the
36:32 Then Jeremiah **t** another scroll and dictated again
37:14 and he **t** Jeremiah before the officials.
38:6 So the officials **t** Jeremiah from his cell
38:11 So Ebed-melech **t** the men with him and went to a
39:5 They **t** him to King Nebuchadnezzar of Babylon,
41:12 they **t** all their men and set out to stop him.
41:17 They **t** them all to the village of Geruth-kimham
43:5 and his officers **t** with them all the people who had
49:2 will come and take back the land you **t** from her,"
52:15 then **t** as exiles some of the poorest of the people
52:18 They also **t** all the pots, shovels, lamp snuffers,
52:19 also **t** the small bowls, firepans, basins, pots,
52:24 The captain of the guard **t** with him as prisoners
52:25 he **t** an officer of the Judean army, seven of the
52:26 Nebuzaradan the commander **t** them all to the king
52:29 Then in Nebuchadnezzar's eighteenth year he **t**
52:30 his captain of the guard, who **t** 745 more—
Eze 3:14 The Spirit lifted me up and **t** me away. I went in
3:22 Then the LORD **t** hold of me, and he said to me,
8:1 in my home, the Sovereign LORD **t** hold of me.
8:3 out what seemed to be a hand and **t** me by the hair.
10:7 and **t** some live coals from the fire burning among
10:7 in linen clothing, and the man **t** them and went out.
16:17 You **t** the very jewels and gold and silver
16:20 "Then you **t** your sons and daughters—
17:3 He **t** hold of the highest branch of a cedar tree
17:6 It **t** root there and grew into a low, spreading vine.
17:12 **t** away her king and princes, and brought them to
19:5 for him were gone, / she **t** another of her cubs
20:23 But I **t** a solemn oath against them while they were
23:10 killed her and **t** away her children as their slaves.
27:5 They **t** a cedar from Lebanon to make a mast for
34:8 You **t** care of yourselves and left the sheep to
37:1 The LORD **t** hold of me, and I was carried away
40:1 the fall of Jerusalem—the LORD **t** hold of me.
40:2 In a vision of God he **t** me to the land of Israel
40:5 The man **t** a measuring rod that was 10-1/2 feet
40:24 Then the man **t** me around to the south gateway
40:28 Then the man **t** me to the south gateway leading
40:32 Then he **t** me to the east gateway leading to the
40:35 Then he **t** me around to the north gateway leading
43:5 Then the Spirit **t** me up and brought me into the
Da 1:2 he **t** with him some of the sacred objects from the
2:25 Then Arioch quickly **t** Daniel to the king and said,
5:31 And Darius the Mede **t** over the kingdom at the
12:7 and **t** this solemn oath by the one who lives
Hos 11:3 or even care that it was I who **t** care of him.
13:5 I **t** care of you in the wilderness, in that dry
13:11 I gave you kings, and in my fury I **t** them away.
Joel 1:4 the crops, the swarming locusts **t** what was left!
3:6 to the Greeks, who **t** them far from their homeland.
Jnh 3:3 a city so large that it **t** three days to see it all.
3:6 down from his throne and **t** off his royal robes.
Zec 11:7 Then I **t** two shepherd's staffs and named one
11:10 Then I **t** my staff called Favor and snapped it in
11:13 So I **t** the thirty coins and threw them to the potters
Mt 4:5 Then the Devil **t** him to Jerusalem, to the highest
4:8 Next the Devil **t** him to the peak of a very high
8:17 "He **t** our sicknesses and removed our diseases."
9:25 Jesus went in and **t** the girl by the hand, and she
14:11 and given to the girl, who **t** it to her mother.
14:19 And he **t** the five loaves and the fish, looked up
15:36 Then he **t** the seven loaves and the fish,
16:22 But Peter **t** him aside and corrected him.
17:1 Six days later Jesus **t** Peter and the two brothers,
20:17 he **t** the twelve disciples aside privately and told
21:39 **t** him out of the vineyard, and murdered him.
25:1 by the story of ten bridesmaids who **t** their lamps
25:3 The five who were foolish **t** no oil for their lamps,
26:26 Jesus **t** a loaf of bread and asked God's blessing on
26:27 And he **t** a cup of wine and gave thanks to God for
26:37 He **t** Peter and Zebedee's two sons, James
27:2 Then they bound him and **t** him to Pilate,
27:3 So he **t** the thirty pieces of silver back to the
27:9 that says, / "They **t** the thirty pieces of silver—
27:27 Some of the governor's soldiers **t** Jesus into their
27:31 they **t** off the robe and put his own clothes on him
27:59 Joseph **t** the body and wrapped it in a long linen
Mk 1:13 among the wild animals, and angels **t** care of him.
1:31 and as he **t** her by the hand and helped her to sit
2:12 The man jumped up, **t** the mat, and pushed his way
5:40 Then he **t** the girl's father and mother and his three
6:28 and gave it to the girl, who **t** it to her mother.
6:41 Jesus **t** the five loaves and two fish, looked up
8:6 Then he **t** the seven loaves, thanked God for them,
8:23 Jesus **t** the blind man by the hand and led him out
8:32 Peter **t** him aside and told him he shouldn't say
9:2 Six days later Jesus **t** Peter, James, and John to the
9:27 But Jesus **t** him by the hand and helped him to his
10:16 Then he **t** the children into his arms and placed his
14:22 Jesus **t** a loaf of bread and asked God's blessing on
14:23 And he **t** a cup of wine and gave thanks to God for
14:33 He **t** Peter, James, and John with him, and he
15:1 They bound Jesus and **t** him to Pilate, the Roman
15:16 The soldiers **t** him into their headquarters
15:20 they **t** off the purple robe and put his own clothes
15:25 in the morning when the crucifixion **t** place.
Lk 1:1 accounts about the events that **t** place among us.
1:48 For he **t** notice of his lowly servant girl, / and now
2:5 He **t** with him Mary, his fiancée, who was
2:22 so his parents **t** him to Jerusalem to present him to
2:28 He **t** the child in his arms and praised God, saying,
4:5 Then the Devil **t** him up and revealed to him all the
4:9 Then the Devil **t** him to Jerusalem, to the highest
4:29 and **t** him to the edge of the hill on which the city
5:19 So they went up to the roof, **t** off some tiles,
8:1 of God. He **t** his twelve disciples with him,
8:54 Then Jesus **t** her by the hand and said in a loud
9:16 Jesus **t** the five loaves and two fish, looked up
9:28 About eight days later Jesus **t** Peter, James,
10:34 the man on his own donkey and **t** him to an inn, where he **t** care of him.
11:37 a meal. So he went in and **t** his place at the table.
15:13 all his belongings and **t** a trip to a distant land,
19:6 and **t** Jesus to his house in great excitement
22:17 Then he **t** a cup of wine, and when he had given
22:19 Then he **t** a loaf of bread; and when he had thanked
22:20 After supper he **t** another cup of wine and said,
23:1 Then the entire council **t** Jesus over to Pilate,
23:53 Then he **t** the body down from the cross
24:30 As they sat down to eat, he **t** a small loaf of bread,
Jn 1:28 This incident **t** place at Bethany, a village east of
2:20 "It **t** forty-six years to build this Temple, and you
6:11 Then Jesus **t** the loaves, gave thanks to God,
9:13 Then they **t** the man to the Pharisees.
12:3 Then Mary **t** a twelve-ounce jar of expensive
12:6 and he often **t** some for his own use.
12:13 **t** palm branches and went down the road to meet
13:4 So he got up from the table, **t** off his robe,
18:13 First they **t** him to Annas, the father-in-law of
19:9 He **t** Jesus back into the headquarters again
19:16 to be crucified. / So they **t** Jesus and led him away.
19:23 They also **t** his robe, but it was seamless, woven in
19:27 And from then on this disciple **t** her into his home.
19:38 him permission, he came and **t** the body away.
Ac 3:7 Then Peter **t** the lame man by the right hand
5:6 him in a sheet and **t** him out and buried him.
7:58 The official witnesses **t** off their coats and laid
9:30 they **t** him to Caesarea and sent him on to his
9:39 soon as he arrived, they **t** him to the upstairs room.
13:20 All this **t** about 450 years. After that, judges ruled
13:29 they **t** him down from the cross and placed him in
15:23 This is the letter they **t** along with them:
15:39 Barnabas **t** John Mark with him and sailed for
16:24 So he **t** no chances but put them into the inner
17:6 and **t** them before the city council.
17:19 Then they **t** him to the Council of Philosophers.
18:26 they **t** him aside and explained the way of God
19:9 left the synagogue and **t** the believers with him.
20:10 went down, bent over him, and **t** him into his arms.
21:11 he **t** Paul's belt and bound his own feet and hands
21:16 and they **t** us to the home of Mnason, a man
21:38 and **t** four thousand members of the Assassins out
23:19 The commander **t** him by the arm, led him aside,
23:28 Then I **t** him to their high council to try to find out
23:31 as ordered, the soldiers **t** Paul as far as Antipatris.
23:32 while the horsemen **t** him on to Caesarea.
27:28 They **t** soundings and found the water was only
27:35 Then he **t** some bread, gave thanks to God before
28:15 Paul saw them, he thanked God and **t** courage.
Ro 7:8 But sin **t** advantage of this law and aroused all
7:11 Sin **t** advantage of the law and fooled me; it **t** the good law and used it to make me guilty of
1Co 11:23 he was betrayed, the Lord Jesus **t** a loaf of bread,
11:25 he **t** the cup of wine after supper, saying,
2Co 12:16 I was sneaky and **t** advantage of you by trickery.
Gal 3:13 he **t** upon himself the curse for our wrongdoing.
4:14 you **t** me in and cared for me as though I were an
Php 2:7 he **t** the humble position of a slave and appeared in
Col 2:14 He **t** it and destroyed it by nailing it to Christ's
Heb 6:13 swear by, God **t** an oath in his own name, saying:
7:2 Then Abraham **t** a tenth of all he had won in the
7:20 God **t** an oath that Christ would always be a priest,
8:9 with their ancestors / when I **t** them by the hand
9:12 Once for all time he **t** blood into that Most Holy
9:12 He **t** his own blood, and with it he secured our
9:19 he **t** the blood of calves and goats, along with
11:5 "suddenly he disappeared because God **t** him."
Jude 1:9 (This **t** place when Michael was arguing with
Rev 5:7 and **t** the scroll from the right hand of the one
5:8 And as he **t** the scroll, the four living beings
10:10 So I **t** the little scroll from the hands of the angel,
17:3 So the angel **t** me in spirit into the wilderness.
18:9 And the rulers of the world who **t** part in her
21:10 So he **t** me in spirit to a great, high mountain,

TOOL (7) [TOOLED, TOOLS]

Ex 20:25 Do not chip or shape the stones with a **t**, for that
Dt 27:6 Do not shape the stones with an iron **t**. On the altar
1Ki 6:7 ax, or any other iron **t** at the building site.
Isa 44:12 blacksmith stands at his forge to make a sharp **t**,
44:13 takes the **t**, and carves the figure of a man.
Ro 6:13 Do not let any part of your body become a **t** of
6:13 And use your whole body as a **t** to do what is right

TOOLED (1) [TOOL]

Ex 32:4 and molded and **t** it into the shape of a calf.

TOOLS (4) [TOOL]

Jos 8:31 are uncut and have not been shaped with iron **t**."
2Sa 24:22 and you can use the threshing **t** and ox yokes for
1Ch 21:23 and you can use the threshing **t** for wood to build a
Jer 22:7 who will bring out their **t** to dismantle you.

TOOTH (10) [TEETH, TOOTHACHE]

Ex 21:24 If a **t** gets knocked out, knock out the **t** of the person who did it.
21:27 And if an owner knocks out the **t** of a male
21:27 the slave should be released in payment for the **t**.
Lev 24:20 fracture for fracture, eye for eye, **t** for **t**.
Dt 19:21 eye for eye, **t** for **t**, hand for hand, foot for
Mt 5:38 If a **t** gets knocked out, knock out the **t** of the person who did it.'

TOOTHACHE (1) [ACHE, TOOTH]

Pr 25:19 in an unreliable person is like chewing with a **t**

TOP (90) [TOPMOST, TOPPED, TOPS]

Ge 28:13 At the **t** of the stairway stood the LORD, and he
40:17 In the **t** basket were all kinds of bakery goods for
42:25 return each brother's payment at the **t** of his sack.
42:35 there at the **t** of each one was the bag of money
44:2 Then put my personal silver cup at the **t** of the
Ex 12:7 take some of the lamb's blood and smear it on the **t**
12:22 Strike the hyssop against the **t** and sides of the
12:23 But when he sees the blood on the **t** and sides of
17:9 I will stand at the **t** of the hill with the staff of God
17:10 Aaron, and Hur went to the **t** of a nearby hill.
19:20 The LORD came down on the **t** of Mount Sinai
19:20 and called Moses to the **t** of the mountain.
25:21 Then put the atonement cover on **t** of the Ark.
25:25 Put a rim about three inches wide around the **t**
25:27 close to the rim around the **t**. These rings will
26:14 On **t** of these coverings place a layer of tanned ram
26:24 and firmly attached at the **t** with a single ring,
26:34 on **t** of the Ark of the Covenant inside the Most
28:23 and attach them to the **t** corners of the chestpiece.
30:3 Overlay the **t**, sides, and horns of the altar with
34:2 and present yourself to me there on the **t** of the
36:29 and firmly attached at the **t** with a single ring, forming a single unit from **t** to bottom.
37:26 He overlaid the **t**, sides, and horns of the altar with
38:1 It was 7-1/2 feet square at the **t** and 4-1/2 feet high.
39:16 and attached them to the **t** corners of the
40:20 Ark's cover—the place of atonement—on **t** of it.
Lev 1:12 the head and fat, on **t** of the wood fire on the altar.
1:17 Then he will burn it on **t** of the wood fire on the
3:5 The sons of Aaron will burn these on the altar on **t**
4:35 Then the priest will burn the fat on the altar on **t** of

6:12 then burn the fat of the peace offerings on **t** of this
8:26 On **t** of these he placed a loaf of unleavened bread,
8:28 and burned them on the altar on **t** of the burnt
9:20 He placed these fat parts on **t** of the breasts of
Nu 4: 8 and finally a covering of fine goatskin leather on **t**
20:28 Then Aaron died there on **t** of the mountain,
21: 8 of a poisonous snake and attach it to the **t** of a pole.
21: 9 out of bronze and attached it to the **t** of a pole.
23: 3 to me." So Balaam went alone to the **t** of a hill,
23:28 So Balak took Balaam to the **t** of Mount Peor,
27:12 "Climb to the **t** of the mountains east of the river,
Jos 15: 8 Then it went west to the **t** of the mountain above
15: 9 From there the border extended from the **t** of the
18:13 and proceeded down to Ataroth-addar to the **t** of
Jdg 9: 7 he climbed to the **t** of Mount Gerizim and shouted,
16: 3 and carried them all the way to the **t** of the hill
2Sa 2:25 regrouped there at the **t** of the hill to take a stand.
15:32 As they reached the spot at the **t** of the Mount of
16: 1 David was just past the **t** of the hill when Ziba,
17:19 The man's wife put a cloth over the **t** of the well
1Ki 6: 6 floor 9 feet wide, and the **t** floor 10-1/2 feet wide.
7:31 The **t** of each cart had a circular frame for the
7:31 It projected 1-1/2 feet above the cart's **t** like a
7:35 Around the **t** of each cart there was a rim 9 inches
7:41 two bowl-shaped capitals on **t** of the pillars,
7:42 were hung around the capitals on **t** of the pillars),
18:42 But Elijah climbed to the **t** of Mount Carmel
2Ki 1: 9 They found him sitting on **t** of a hill. The captain
17:10 and Asherah poles at the **t** of every hill
25:17 The bronze capital on **t** of each pillar was 7-1/2
2Ch 4:12 two bowl-shaped capitals on **t** of the pillars,
4:13 were hung around the capitals on **t** of the pillars),
25:12 and took them to the **t** of a cliff and threw them
Ne 4: 3 collapse if even a fox walked along the **t** of it!"
12:31 I led the leaders of Judah to the **t** of the wall
12:31 One of the choirs proceeded southward along the **t**
12:38 along the **t** of the wall past the Tower of the Ovens
Job 39:14 She lays her eggs on **t** of the earth, letting them be
SS 4: 8 Come down from the **t** of Mount Amana,
Jer 52:22 The bronze capital on **t** of each pillar was 7-1/2
52:23 a total of one hundred on the network around the **t**.
Eze 17:22 I will take a tender shoot from the **t** of a tall cedar,
17:22 and I will plant it on the **t** of Israel's highest
21:22 and build ramps against the walls to reach the **t**.
31: 3 deep forest shade with its **t** high among the clouds.
41: 7 level through the middle level to the **t** level.
41:20 from the floor to the **t** of the walls,
43:12 The entire **t** of the hill where the Temple is built is
43:15 The **t** of the altar, the hearth, rises still 7 feet
43:16 The **t** of the altar is square, measuring 21 feet by
Am 9: 3 Even if they hide at the very **t** of Mount Carmel,
Zec 4: 2 a solid gold lampstand with a bowl of oil on **t** of it.
Mt 24: 2 that not one stone will be left on **t** of another!"
27:51 in the Temple was torn in two, from **t** to bottom.
Mk 9: 2 took Peter, James, and John to the **t** of a mountain.
13: 2 that not one stone will be left on **t** of another."
15:38 in the Temple was torn in two, from **t** to bottom.
Lk 21: 6 that not one stone will be left on **t** of another."
Jn 19:23 but it was seamless, woven in one piece from the **t**.

TOPAZ (2)
Job 28:19 **T** from Ethiopia cannot be exchanged for it.
Rev 21:20 the eighth beryl, the ninth **t**, the tenth chrysoprase,

TOPHEL (1)
Dt 1: 1 between Paran on one side and **T**, Laban,

TOPHETH (10)
2Ki 23:10 Then the king defiled the altar of **T** in the valley of
Isa 30:33 **T**—the place of burning—has long been ready for
Jer 7:31 They have built the pagan shrines of **T** in the
7:32 "when that place will no longer be called **T**
7:32 so many bodies in **T** that there won't be room for
19: 6 when this place will no longer be called **T**
19:11 They will bury the bodies in **T** until there is no
19:12 I will cause this city to become defiled like **T**.
19:13 the palace of Judah's kings, will become like **T**—
19:14 Then Jeremiah returned from **T** where he had

TOPIC (1)
Ps 69:12 I am the favorite **t** of town gossip, / and all the

TOPMOST (1) [TOP, MOST]
Eze 17: 4 and plucked off its **t** shoot. Then he carried it away

TOPPED (2) [TOP]
2Ch 3:15 each **t** by a capital extending upward another 7-1/2
Ezr 6: 4 prepared stones will be **t** by a layer of timber.

TOPPLE (2) [TOPPLES]
Ps 62: 4 They plan to **t** me from my high position.
Eze 26:11 your people, and your famous pillars will **t**.

TOPPLES (1) [TOPPLE]
Pr 28: 2 moral rot within a nation, its government **t** easily.

TOPS (12) [TOP]
Ex 36:38 The posts with their decorated **t** and bands were
38:17 The **t** of the posts were overlaid with silver,
38:19 The **t** of the posts were overlaid with silver,
38:28 and hooks and to overlay the **t** of the posts.
Nu 23: 9 I see them from the cliff **t**; / I watch them from the
2Sa 5:24 When you hear a sound like marching feet in the **t**
1Ki 7:16 For the **t** of the pillars he made capitals of molded
1Ch 14:15 When you hear a sound like marching feet in the **t**
2Ch 3:16 and used them to decorate the **t** of the pillars.
Isa 2:21 and hide among the jagged rocks at the **t** of cliffs.
Hos 4:13 They offer sacrifices to idols on the **t** of mountains.
Am 9: 1 "Strike the **t** of the Temple columns so hard that

TORCH (7) [TORCHES]
Ge 15:17 and a flaming **t** pass between the halves of the
Dt 13:16 Put the entire town to the **t** as a burnt offering to
Jdg 7:16 each man a ram's horn and a clay jar with a **t** in it.
15: 4 in pairs, and he fastened a **t** to each pair of tails.
Isa 62: 1 the dawn, and her salvation blazes like a burning **t**.
Zec 12: 6 or like a burning **t** among sheaves of grain.
Rev 8:10 flaming star fell out of the sky, burning like a **t**.

TORCHES (6) [TORCH]
Jdg 7:20 They held the blazing **t** in their left hands
15: 5 Then he lit the **t** and let the foxes run through the
Eze 1:13 beings looked like bright coals of fire or brilliant **t**,
Da 10: 6 like lightning, and his eyes were like flaming **t**.
Na 2: 4 the squares, swift as lightning, flickering like **t**.
Jn 18: 3 Now with blazing **t**, lanterns, and weapons,

TORE (54) [TEAR]
Ge 37:29 he **t** his clothes in anguish and frustration.
37:34 Then Jacob **t** his clothes and put on sackcloth.
39:12 Joseph **t** himself away, but as he did, his shirt came
44:13 At this, they **t** their clothing in despair,
Nu 14: 6 and Caleb son of Jephunneh, **t** their clothing.
Jos 7: 6 and the leaders of Israel **t** their clothing in dismay,
Jdg 11:35 When he saw her, he **t** his clothes in anguish.
1Sa 15:27 at him to try to hold him back and **t** his robe.
19:24 He **t** off his clothes and lay on the ground all day
2Sa 1:11 and his men **t** their clothes in sorrow when they
13:19 But now Tamar **t** her robe and put ashes on her
13:31 The king jumped up, **t** his robe, and fell prostrate
13:31 His advisers also **t** their clothes in horror
1Ki 11:30 cloak he was wearing and **t** it into twelve pieces.
21:27 he **t** his clothing, dressed in sackcloth, and fasted.
2Ki 2:12 disappeared from sight, Elisha **t** his robe in two.
3: 2 He at least **t** down the sacred pillar of Baal that his
5: 7 of Israel read it, he **t** his clothes in dismay and said,
6:30 the king heard this, he **t** his clothes in despair.
11:14 she **t** her clothes in despair and shouted, "Treason!
11:18 land went over to the temple of Baal and **t** it down.
17:21 For when the LORD **t** Israel away from the
18:37 They **t** their clothes in despair, and they went in to
19: 1 he **t** his clothes and put on sackcloth and went into
22:11 in the Book of the Law, he **t** his clothes in despair.
22:19 You **t** your clothing in despair and wept before me
23: 7 He also **t** down the houses of the shrine prostitutes
23:12 Josiah **t** down the altars that the kings of Judah had
23:15 The king also **t** down the altar at Bethel, the pagan
25:10 army as they **t** down the walls of Jerusalem.
2Ch 23:13 she **t** her clothes in despair and shouted, "Treason!
23:17 went over to the temple of Baal and **t** it down.
33:15 He **t** down all the altars he had built on the hill
34:19 was written in the law, he **t** his clothes in despair.
34:27 humbled yourself and **t** your clothing in despair
Ezr 9: 3 When I heard this, I **t** my clothing, pulled hair
Est 4: 1 he **t** his clothes, put on sackcloth and ashes,
Job 1:20 Job stood up and **t** his robe in grief. Then he
2:12 they **t** their robes and threw dust into the air over
SS 5: 7 The watchman on the wall **t** off my veil.
Isa 36:22 They **t** their clothes in despair, and they went in to
37: 1 he **t** his clothes and put on sackcloth and went into
Jer 2:20 your yoke and **t** away the chains of your slavery,
31:28 In the past I uprooted and **t** down this nation.
39: 8 the palace, and **t** down the walls of the city.
52:14 army as they **t** down the walls of Jerusalem.
La 3:11 dragged me off the path and **t** me with his claws,
Eze 19:12 and **t** off its branches. / Its stem was destroyed by
Da 6:24 and **t** them apart before they even hit the floor of
Mt 26:65 Then the high priest **t** his clothing to show his
Mk 14:52 they **t** off his clothes, but he escaped and ran away
14:63 Then the high priest **t** his clothing to show his
Ac 14:14 they **t** their clothing in dismay and ran out among
Gal 2:18 guilty if I rebuild the old system I already **t** down.

TORMENT (7) [TORMENTED, TORMENTING, TORMENTORS, TORMENTS]
Isa 50:11 receive from me: You will soon lie down in great **t**.
Lk 16:23 There, in **t**, he saw Lazarus in the far distance with
16:28 and I want him to warn them about this place of **t**
2Co 12: 7 a messenger from Satan to **t** me and keep me from
Rev 14:11 The smoke of their **t** rises forever and ever,
18:10 will stand at a distance, terrified by her great **t**.
18:15 will stand at a distance, terrified by her great **t**.

TORMENTED (6) [TORMENT]
Ex 17: 3 But **t** by thirst, they continued to complain,
Pr 28:17 A murderer's **t** conscience will drive him into the
Isa 51:23 will put that cup into the hands of those who **t** you.
Rev 11:10 the death of the two prophets who had **t** them.
14:10 And they will be **t** with fire and burning sulfur in
20:10 There they will be **t** day and night forever

TORMENTING (8) [TORMENT]
1Sa 16:14 and the LORD sent a **t** spirit that filled him with
16:15 "It is clear that a spirit from God is **t** you,"
16:16 harp for you whenever the **t** spirit is bothering you.
16:23 And whenever the **t** spirit from God troubled Saul,
16:23 would feel better, and the **t** spirit would go away.
18:10 in fact, a **t** spirit from God overwhelmed Saul,
19: 9 the **t** spirit from the LORD suddenly came upon
Mt 15:22 has a demon in her, and it is severely **t** her."

TORMENTORS (2) [TORMENT]
Ps 137: 3 Our **t** requested a joyful hymn: / "Sing us one of
Isa 60:14 "The children of your **t** will come and bow before

TORMENTS (1) [TORMENT]
Rev 18: 7 and pleasure, so match it now with **t** and sorrows.

TORN (37) [TEAR]
Ge 37:33 eaten him. Surely Joseph has been **t** in pieces!"
44:28 doubtless **t** to pieces by some wild animal.
Lev 14:45 It must be **t** down, and all its stones, timbers,
22: 8 a natural death or has been **t** apart by wild animals,
1Sa 4:12 He had **t** his clothes and put dust on his head to
15:28 The LORD has **t** the kingdom of Israel from you
2Sa 1: 2 He had **t** his clothes and put dirt on his head to
15:32 Hushai had **t** his clothing and put dirt on his head
17:13 the nearest valley until every stone is **t** down."
1Ki 18:30 the altar of the LORD that had been **t** down.
19:10 **t** down your altars, and killed every one of your
19:11 It was such a terrible blast that the rocks were **t**
19:14 **t** down your altars, and killed every one of your
2Ch 34: 4 of Baal and their incense altars were **t** down.
Ezr 9: 5 where I had sat in mourning with my clothes **t**.
Ne 1: 3 The wall of Jerusalem has been **t** down,
Job 18:14 They are **t** from the security of their tent, and they
31:22 out of place! Let my arm be **t** from its socket!
Isa 23:13 **t** down its palaces, and turned it into a heap of
32:19 the forest will be destroyed and the city **t** down,
38:13 all night, / but I was **t** apart as though by lions.
Jer 9:19 because our homes have been **t** down.' "
18: 7 kingdom is to be uprooted, **t** down, and destroyed,
33: 4 Though you have **t** down the houses of this city
41: 5 off their beards, **t** their clothes, and cut themselves,
Eze 30:16 will be racked with pain; Thebes will be **t** apart;
Da 2: 5 and what it means, you will be **t** limb from limb,
3:29 and Abednego, they will be **t** limb from limb,
Hos 6: 1 He has **t** us in pieces; now he will heal us. He has
11: 8 My heart is **t** within me, and my compassion
Mt 27:51 At that moment the curtain in the Temple was **t** in
Mk 15:38 And the curtain in the Temple was **t** in two,
Lk 5:36 For then the new garment would be **t**,
23:45 the thick veil hanging in the Temple was **t** apart.
Jn 21:11 There were 153 large fish, and yet the net hadn't **t**.
Ro 11: 3 have killed your prophets and **t** down your altars.
Php 1:23 I'm **t** between two desires: Sometimes I want to

TORRENT (2) [TORRENTIAL, TORRENTS]
Job 11: 2 "Shouldn't someone answer this **t** of words?
Ps 124: 4 engulfed us; / a **t** would have overwhelmed us.

TORRENTIAL (3) [TORRENT]
Ge 8: 2 ceased their gushing, and the **t** rains stopped.
Isa 28: 2 Like a mighty hailstorm and a **t** rain, they will
Eze 38:22 I will send **t** rain, hailstones, fire, and burning

TORRENTS (4) [TORRENT]
Ge 7:11 the earth, and the rain fell in mighty **t** from the sky.
Job 20:28 his house. God's anger will descend on him in **t**.
38:25 "Who created a channel for the **t** of rain? Who laid
Mt 7:25 Though the rain comes in **t** and the floodwaters

TORTOISE [KJV] See LIZARD

TORTURE (6) [TORTURED]
Job 19: 2 "How long will you **t** me? How long will you try
Mt 8:29 You have no right to **t** us before God's appointed
Mk 5: 7 the Most High God? For God's sake, don't **t** me!"
Lk 8:28 Most High God? Please, I beg you, don't **t** me!"
Rev 9: 5 but to **t** them for five months with agony like the
9:10 that sting like scorpions, with power to **t** people.

TORTURED (1) [TORTURE]
Heb 11:35 But others trusted God and were **t**, preferring to die

TOSS (7) [TOSSED, TOSSING]
Ex 9: 8 and have Moses **t** it into the sky while Pharaoh
Job 7: 4 But the night drags on, and I **t** till dawn.
Isa 22:18 you up into a ball and **t** you away into a distant,
41:16 You will **t** them in the air, and the wind will blow
Jer 5:22 The waves may **t** and roar, but they can never pass
Am 8: 8 Nile River at floodtime, **t** about, and sink again.
Jnh 1: 7 terrible storm. When they did this, Jonah lost the **t**.

TOSSED (10) [TOSS]
Ex 9:10 As Pharaoh watched, Moses **t** the soot into the air,
Job 16:11 He has **t** me into the hands of the wicked.
Ps 43: 2 my only safe haven. / Why have you **t** me aside?
44: 9 But now you have **t** us aside in dishonor. / You no
107:26 Their ships were **t** to the heavens / and sank again
Pr 23:34 You will stagger like a sailor **t** at sea, clinging to a
Isa 33:12 up completely, like thorns cut down and **t** in a fire.
La 1: 8 so she has been **t** away like a filthy rag.
Ac 22:23 off their coats, and **t** handfuls of dust into the air.
Jas 1: 6 a wave of the sea that is driven and **t** by the wind.

TOSSING (2) [TOSS]

2Sa 16:13 throwing stones at David and **t** dust into the air.
Eze 7:19 away their money, **t** it out like worthless trash.

TOTAL (45) [TOTALED, TOTALING, TOTALLY, TOTALS]

Ge 46:26 So the **t** number of Jacob's direct descendants who
Ex 31:15 but the seventh day must be a day of **t** rest.
35:2 The seventh day is a day of **t** rest, a holy day that
36:30 So for the west side they made a **t** of eight frames,
Lev 16:31 It will be a Sabbath day of **t** rest, and you will
23:32 This will be a Sabbath day of **t** rest for you, and on
23:39 eighth day of the festival will be days of **t** rest.
25:5 unpruned vines. The land is to have a year of **t** rest.
Nu 1:46 The **t** number was 603,550.
1:47 But this **t** did not include the Levites.
2:9 So the **t** of all the troops on Judah's side of the
2:16 So the **t** of all the troops on Reuben's side of the
2:24 So the **t** of all the troops on Ephraim's side of the
2:31 So the **t** of all the troops on Dan's side of the camp
3:43 The **t** number of firstborn sons who were one
4:36 and the **t** number came to 2,750.
4:37 So this was the **t** of all those from the Kohathite
4:40 and the **t** number came to 2,630.
4:41 So this was the **t** of all those from the Gershonite
4:44 and the **t** number came to 3,200.
4:45 So this was the **t** of all those from the Merarite
26:51 So the **t** number of Israelite men counted in the
26:62 But the Levites were not included in the **t** census
31:5 a **t** of twelve thousand men armed for battle.
36:3 the **t** area of our tribal land will be reduced.
Jos 21:41 The **t** number of towns and pasturelands within
1Ch 6:60 So a **t** of thirteen towns was given to the
7:2 the **t** number of men available for military service
7:4 The **t** number of men available for military service
7:5 The **t** number of men available for military service
7:7 The **t** number of men available for military service
23:3 and the **t** came to thirty-eight thousand.
27:24 The final **t** was never recorded in King David's
2Ch 3:11 The **t** wingspan of the two cherubim standing side
Ezr 2:60 Tobiah, and Nekoda—a **t** of 652 people.
2:64 So a **t** of 42,360 people returned to Judah,
2:69 The **t** of their gifts came to 61,000 gold coins,
8:34 and the **t** weight was officially recorded.
Ne 7:62 Tobiah, and Nekoda—a **t** of 642 people.
7:66 "So a **t** of 42,360 people returned to Judah,
7:71 The other leaders gave to the treasury a **t** of 20,000
11:8 were Gabbai and Sallai, and a **t** of 928 relatives.
Jer 52:23 and a **t** of one hundred on the network around the
52:30 who took 745 more—a **t** of 4,600 captives in all.
Eze 7:5 With one blow after another I will bring **t** disaster!

TOTALED (4) [TOTAL]

Nu 2:32 the troops of Israel listed by their families **t**
31:32 that the fighting men had taken **t** 675,000 sheep,
31:36 plunder given to the fighting men **t** 337,500 sheep,
Ac 4:4 so that the number of believers **t** about five

TOTALING (1) [TOTAL]

Ex 38:24 The people brought gifts of gold **t** about 2,200

TOTALLY (4) [TOTAL]

Ge 6:5 that all their thoughts were consistently and **t** evil.
2Ki 13:23 the people of Israel, and they were not **t** destroyed.
Ezr 9:11 **t** defiled by the detestable practices of the people
Tit 2:14 own people, **t** committed to doing what is right.

TOTALS (2) [TOTAL]

1Ch 21:2 and bring me the **t** so I may know how many there
Ezr 8:26 I gave it to them and found the **t** to be as follows:

TOTTERING (1)

Ps 62:3 To them I'm just a broken-down wall / or a **t** fence.

TOUCH (67) [TOUCHED, TOUCHES, TOUCHING]

Ge 3:3 God says we must not eat it or even **t** it, or we will
20:6 from sinning against me; I did not let you **t** her.
27:21 I want to **t** you to make sure you really are Esau."
37:22 That way he will die without our having to **t** him."
Ex 12:13 This plague of death will not **t** you when I strike
19:12 not go up on the mountain or even **t** its boundaries.
Lev 5:2 "Or if they **t** something that is ceremonially
11:8 eat the meat of these animals or **t** their dead bodies.
11:11 never eat their meat or even **t** their dead bodies.
11:24 If you **t** any of their dead bodies, you will be
11:26 If you **t** the dead body of such an animal, you will
11:27 If you **t** the dead body of such an animal, you will
11:31 If you **t** the dead body of such an animal, you will
11:39 is permitted for eating dies and you **t** its carcass,
12:4 of purification, she must not **t** anything that is holy.
15:5 "So if you **t** the man's bedding, you will be
15:7 The same instructions apply if you **t** the man who
15:10 If you **t** or carry anything that was under him,
15:19 If you **t** her during that time, you will be defiled
15:21 If you **t** her bed, you must wash your clothes
15:22 The same applies if you **t** an object on which she
15:27 If you **t** her bed or anything on which she sits,
Nu 4:15 But they must not **t** the sacred objects, or they will
16:26 and don't **t** anything that belongs to them.
18:3 they must be careful not to **t** any of the sacred
19:11 "All those who **t** a dead human body will be
19:13 All those who **t** a dead body and do not purify
21:22 or **t** your vineyards or drink your well water."
23:23 No curse can **t** Jacob; / no sorcery has any power
Dt 14:8 not eat or even **t** the dead bodies of such animals.
28:56 she would not so much as **t** her feet to the ground
Jos 3:13 When their feet **t** the water, the flow of water will
9:19 the LORD, the God of Israel. We cannot **t** them.
1Sa 14:26 They didn't even **t** the honey because they all
1Ch 16:22 "Do not **t** these people I have chosen, / and do not
Est 7:5 Xerxes demanded. "Who would dare **t** you?"
Job 5:19 you again and again so that no evil can **t** you.
Ps 91:7 are dying around you, / these evils will not **t** you.
104:32 his glance; / the mountains burst into flame at his **t**.
105:15 "Do not **t** these people I have chosen, / and do not
144:5 **T** the mountains so they billow smoke.
Isa 28:15 You say, "The Assyrians can never **t** us, for we
Jer 21:13 are safe on our mountain! No one can **t** us here."
La 4:14 so defiled by blood that no one dared to **t** them.
4:15 shouted at them. "You are defiled! Don't **t** us!"
Eze 1:11 one pair stretched out to **t** the wings of the living
1:23 living being stretched out to **t** the others' wings,
9:6 little children. But do not **t** anyone with the mark.
44:13 They may not **t** any of my holy things or the holy
Da 8:5 the land so swiftly that it didn't even **t** the ground.
8:18 But Gabriel roused me with a **t** and helped me to
Mt 9:21 for she thought, "If I can just **t** his robe, I will be
10:28 can only kill your body; they cannot **t** your soul.
14:36 The sick begged him to let them **t** even the fringe
Mk 3:10 people were crowding around him, trying to **t** him.
5:28 "If I can just **t** his clothing, I will be healed."
6:56 The sick begged him to let them at least **t** the
8:22 and they begged him to **t** and heal the man.
10:13 to Jesus so he could **t** them and bless them,
12:12 But they were afraid to **t** him because of the
Lk 1:15 He must never **t** wine or hard liquor, and he will be
4:40 diseases were, the **t** of his hand healed every one.
6:19 Everyone was trying to **t** him, because healing
18:15 to Jesus so he could **t** them and bless them,
24:39 **T** me and make sure that I am not a ghost,
2Co 6:17 says the Lord. / Don't **t** their filthy things,
Col 2:21 "Don't handle, don't eat, don't **t**."

TOUCHED (61) [TOUCH]

Ge 27:22 So Jacob went over to his father, and Isaac **t** him.
31:38 In all those years I never **t** a single ram of yours for
Ex 2:6 found the baby boy. His helpless cries **t** her heart.
19:13 with arrows. They must not be **t** by human hands.'
Lev 15:12 Any clay pot **t** by the man with the discharge must
Nu 19:18 was in the tent, or anyone who has **t** a human bone,
19:18 or has **t** a person who was killed or who died naturally, or has **t** a grave.
31:19 or **t** a dead body must stay outside the camp for
Dt 26:14 I have not **t** it while I was ceremonially unclean;
Jos 3:15 carrying the Ark **t** the water at the river's edge,
16:7 turned southward to Ataroth and Naarah, **t** Jericho,
19:22 The boundary also **t** Tabor, Shahazumah,
19:34 and **t** the boundary of Zebulun in the south,
Jdg 6:21 Then the angel of the LORD **t** the meat and bread
1Sa 10:26 a band of men whose hearts God had **t** became his
14:45 LORD lives, not one hair on his head will be **t**,
1Ki 6:27 while their inner wings **t** at the center of the room.
19:5 an angel **t** him and told him, "Get up and eat!"
19:7 of the LORD came again and **t** him and said,
2Ki 13:21 But as soon as the body **t** Elisha's bones, the dead
2Ch 3:11 was 7-1/2 feet long, and it **t** the Temple wall.
3:11 feet long, **t** one of the wings of the second figure.
3:12 one wing 7-1/2 feet long that **t** the opposite wall.
3:12 also 7-1/2 feet long, **t** the wing of the first figure.
Est 5:2 scepter to her. So Esther approached and **t** its tip.
Isa 6:7 He **t** my lips with it and said, "See, this coal has **t**
Jer 1:9 Then the LORD **t** my mouth and said, "See,
Eze 1:9 The wings of each living being **t** the wings of the
Da 3:27 around them and saw that the fire had not **t** them.
10:10 Just then a hand **t** me and lifted me, still trembling,
10:16 Then the one who looked like a man **t** my lips,
10:18 Then the one who looked like a man **t** me again,
Hos 9:4 just as food **t** by a person in mourning is unclean.
Mt 8:3 Jesus **t** him. "I want to," he said. "Be healed!"
8:15 But when Jesus **t** her hand, the fever left her.
9:20 came up behind him. She **t** the fringe of his robe,
9:29 Then he **t** their eyes and said, "Because of your
14:36 the fringe of his robe, and all who **t** it were healed.
17:7 Jesus came over and **t** them. "Get up," he said,
20:34 Jesus felt sorry for them and **t** their eyes.
Mk 1:41 Moved with pity, Jesus **t** him. "I want to,"
5:27 him through the crowd and **t** the fringe of his robe.
5:30 in the crowd and asked, "Who **t** my clothes?"
5:31 around you. How can you ask, 'Who **t** me?' "
6:56 the fringe of his robe, and all who **t** it were healed.
7:33 own fingers, he **t** the man's tongue with the spittle.
Lk 5:13 Jesus reached out and **t** the man. "I want to,"
7:14 Then he walked over to the coffin and **t** it,
8:44 came up behind Jesus and **t** the fringe of his robe.
8:45 "Who **t** me?" Jesus asked. Everyone denied it,
8:46 Jesus told him, "No, someone deliberately **t** me,
8:47 The whole crowd heard her explain why she had **t**
13:13 Then he **t** her, and instantly she could stand
14:4 Jesus **t** the sick man and healed him and sent him
22:51 And he **t** the place where the man's ear had been
Jn 7:44 And some wanted him arrested, but no one **t** him.
Ac 19:12 or cloths that had **t** his skin were placed on sick
27:33 "You haven't **t** food for two weeks," he said.
1Jn 1:1 with our own eyes and **t** him with our own hands.

TOUCHES (20) [TOUCH]

Ge 27:12 What if my father **t** me? He'll see that I'm trying to
Ex 29:37 and whatever **t** it will become holy.
30:29 After this, whatever **t** them will become holy.
Lev 6:18 or anything that **t** this food will become holy."
6:27 or anyone who **t** the sacrificial meat will become
7:19 "Meat that **t** anything ceremonially unclean may
7:21 If anyone **t** anything that is unclean, whether it is
11:34 If the water used to cleanse an unclean object **t** any
15:11 If the man **t** you without first rinsing his hands,
15:12 and every wooden utensil he **t** must be rinsed with
Nu 19:16 And if someone outdoors **t** the corpse of someone
19:16 or if someone **t** a human bone or a grave,
19:21 and anyone who **t** the water of purification will
19:22 and anyone that a defiled person **t** will be
2Sa 14:8 "Go home, and I'll see to it that no one **t** him."
23:6 thrown away, / for they tear the hand that **t** them.
Job 20:6 to the heavens and though his head **t** the clouds,
Eze 47:9 Everything that **t** the water of this river will live.
Am 9:5 the LORD Almighty, **t** the land and it melts,
Heb 12:20 "If even an animal **t** the mountain, it must be

TOUCHING (13) [TOUCH]

Lev 11:43 Never defile yourselves by **t** such animals.
11:44 So do not defile yourselves by **t** any of these
21:1 ceremonially unclean by **t** a dead relative
22:4 If any of the priests become unclean by **t** a corpse,
22:5 or by **t** a creeping creature that is unclean, or by **t** someone who is ceremonially unclean for
Nu 5:2 or who has been defiled by **t** a dead person.
9:6 had been ceremonially defiled by **t** a dead person,
9:7 "We have become ceremonially unclean by **t** a
9:10 unclean at Passover time because of **t** a dead body,
Jos 19:11 it went west, going past Maralah, **t** Dabbesheth,
Hag 2:13 becomes ceremonially unclean by **t** a dead person
Lk 7:39 he would know what kind of woman is **t** him.

TOUGH (1)

Lk 19:22 If you knew so much about me and how **t** I am,

TOUR (4)

Ge 41:46 he made a **t** of inspection throughout the land.
Ps 48:13 note of the fortified walls, / and **t** all the citadels,
Mk 6:30 The apostles returned to Jesus from their ministry **t**
Lk 8:1 Not long afterward Jesus began a **t** of the nearby

TOW [KJV] See BOWSTRINGS, BURNING STRAW, CANDLEWICK

TOWARD (196) [TO]

Ge 3:8 **T** evening they heard the LORD God walking
8:11 This time, **t** evening, the bird returned to him with
8:21 and actions are bent **t** evil from childhood.
10:30 extending from Mesha **t** the eastern hills of Sephar.
12:9 Then Abram traveled south by stages **t** the Negev.
13:3 Then they continued traveling by stages **t** Bethel,
18:16 got up from their meal and started on **t** Sodom.
18:22 The two other men went on **t** Sodom,
28:10 Jacob left Beersheba and traveled **t** Haran.
30:40 he turned the flocks **t** the streaked
31:2 a considerable cooling in Laban's attitude **t** him.
35:16 they traveled on **t** Ephrath (that is, Bethlehem).
37:25 a caravan of camels in the distance coming **t** them.
Ex 7:19 "Tell Aaron to point his staff **t** the waters of
8:5 "Tell Aaron to point his shepherd's staff **t** all the
9:22 LORD said to Moses, "Lift your hand **t** the sky,
9:23 So Moses lifted his staff **t** the sky, and the LORD
10:21 "Lift your hand **t** heaven, and a deep
10:22 So Moses lifted his hand **t** heaven, and there was
13:18 along a route through the wilderness **t** the Red Sea,
14:2 "Tell the people to march **t** Pi-hahiroth between
14:10 could see them in the distance, marching **t** them.
16:10 spoke to the people, they looked out **t** the desert.
26:35 the south side, and the table must be set **t** the north.
Lev 9:22 Aaron raised his hands **t** the people and blessed
19:30 days of rest and show reverence **t** my sanctuary,
26:21 "If even then you remain hostile **t** me and refuse
26:23 a lesson from this and continue your hostility **t** me,
26:24 then I myself will be hostile **t** you, and I will
26:27 still refuse to listen and still remain hostile **t** me,
26:40 ancestors for betraying me and being hostile **t** me.
Nu 2:3 and Zebulun are to camp **t** the sunrise on the east
3:38 The area in front of the Tabernacle in the east **t** the
14:25 and don't go on **t** the land where the Amalekites
14:44 But the people pushed ahead **t** the hill country of
16:42 they turned **t** the Tabernacle and saw that the cloud
19:4 and sprinkle it seven times **t** the front of the
21:33 Then they turned and marched **t** Bashan, but King
24:1 Instead, he turned and looked out **t** the wilderness,
33:7 They left Etham and turned back **t** Pi-hahiroth,
34:5 From Azmon the boundary will turn **t** the brook of
Dt 1:19 and headed **t** the hill country of the Amorites.
1:40 and go on back through the wilderness **t** the Red
2:1 and set out across the wilderness **t** the Red Sea,
11:30 They are located **t** the west, not far from the oaks
15:7 do not be hard-hearted or tightfisted **t** them.
23:11 **T** evening he must bathe himself, and at sunset he
32:5 "But they have acted corruptly **t** him; / when they
Jos 8:10 morning Joshua roused his men and started **t** Ai,
8:15 and the Israelite army fled **t** the wilderness as
8:18 "Point your spear **t** Ai, for I will give you the
15:3 Then it went up to Addar, where it turned **t** Karka.
15:7 valley of Achor to Debir, turning north **t** Gilgal,
15:9 Then it turned **t** Baalah (that is, Kiriath-jearim).
15:11 where it turned **t** Shikkeron and Mount Baalah.
19:13 Eth-kazin, and Rimmon and turned **t** Neah.

19:27 turned east t Beth-dagon, and ran as far as Zebulun
19:29 Then the boundary turned t Ramah
Jdg 9:19 and in good faith t Gideon and his descendants,
13:20 As the flames from the altar shot up t the sky,
20:20 Then they advanced t Gibeah to attack the men of
20:42 So they ran t the wilderness, but the Israelites
20:45 The survivors fled into the wilderness t the rock of
1Sa 6:12 the cows went straight along the road t
9:11 As they were climbing a hill t the town, they met
9:14 Samuel was coming out t them to climb the hill.
10:3 you will see three men coming t you who are on
10:10 at Gibeah, they saw the prophets coming t them.
13:17 One went north t Ophrah in the land of Shual,
13:18 and the third moved t the border above the valley
17:41 Goliath walked out t David with his shield bearer
20:19 The day after tomorrow, t evening, go to the place
20:34 crushed by his father's shameful behavior t David.
25:20 she saw David and his men coming t her.
2Sa 2:26 only thing we will gain is bitterness t each other?
13:34 saw a great crowd coming t the city from the west.
15:23 Kidron Valley and then went out t the wilderness.
18:24 As he looked, he saw a lone man running t them.
18:26 the watchman saw another man running t them.
24:20 Araunah saw the king and his men coming t him,
1Ki 7:21 one t the south and one t the north.
8:22 Then Solomon stood with his hands lifted t heaven
8:29 May you always hear the prayers I make t this
8:30 and your people Israel when we pray t this place.
8:35 and then they pray t this Temple and confess your
8:38 or sorrow, raising their hands t this Temple,
8:42 your power—and when they pray t this Temple,
8:44 and if they pray to the LORD t this city that you
8:44 and t this Temple that I have built for your name,
8:48 and pray t the land you gave to their ancestors, t this city you have chosen,
8:48 and t this Temple I have built to honor your name,
8:54 where he had been kneeling with his hands raised t
18:7 was walking along, he saw Elijah coming t him.
18:43 he said to his servant, "Go and look out t the sea."
2Ki 6:18 As the Aramean army advanced t them,
1Ch 5:9 they spread eastward t the edge of the desert that
2Ch 3:13 and faced out t the main room of the Temple.
6:13 then he knelt down and lifted his hands t heaven.
6:20 May you always hear the prayers I make t this
6:21 and your people Israel when we pray t this place.
6:26 and then they pray t this Temple and confess your
6:29 or sorrow, raising their hands t this Temple,
6:32 worship your great name and to pray t this Temple,
6:34 and if they pray to you t this city that you have
6:34 and t this Temple that I have built for your name,
6:38 and pray t the land you gave to their ancestors, t this city you have chosen,
6:38 and t this Temple I have built to honor your name,
Ezr 1:4 t their expenses by supplying them with silver
2:68 some of the family leaders gave generously t the
6:22 changed the attitude of the king of Assyria t them,
Ne 3:26 who repaired the wall as far as the Water Gate t the
8:6 Amen!" as they lifted their hands t heaven.
12:37 on the ascent of the city wall t the City of David.
13:27 and acting unfaithfully t God by marrying foreign
Job 30:21 You have become cruel t me. You persecute me
39:16 She is harsh t her young, as if they were not her
Ps 28:2 for help, / as I lift my hands t your holy sanctuary.
77:2 long I pray, with hands lifted t heaven, pleading.
103:11 For his unfailing love t those who fear him
Pr 7:25 Don't let your hearts stray away t her.
Isa 5:26 of the earth, and they will come racing t Jerusalem.
17:12 The armies rush forward like waves thundering t
42:18 "Oh, how deaf and blind you are t me! Why won't
Jer 4:6 Send a signal t Jerusalem: 'Flee now! Do not
39:4 the king's garden and headed t the Jordan Valley.
41:10 with him, he started back t the land of Ammon.
Eze 1:4 I saw a great storm coming t me from the north,
4:3 Turn t it and demonstrate how the enemy will
6:2 look over t the mountains of Israel and prophesy
8:5 said to me, "Son of man, look t the north."
17:6 Its branches turned up t the eagle, and its roots
17:7 vine sent its roots and branches out t him for water.
20:46 of man, look t the south and speak out against it;
21:2 look t Jerusalem and prophesy against Israel
21:22 Then they will decide to turn t Jerusalem!
25:2 look t the land of Ammon and prophesy against its
28:21 look t the city of Sidon and prophesy against it.
29:2 turn t Egypt and prophesy against Pharaoh the king
35:2 "Son of man, turn t Mount Seir, and prophesy
39:2 turn you and drive you t the mountains of Israel,
40:2 appeared to be a city across from me t the south.
40:9 end of the gateway structure, facing t the Temple.
41:19 that of a man—looked t the palm tree on one side.
41:19 looked t the palm tree on the other side.
42:2 whose entrance opened t the north, was 175 feet
42:4 of the complex, and all the doors faced t the north.
42:8 the rooms t the Temple—extended for 175 feet.
46:19 assigned to the priests, which faced t the north.
47:15 border will run from the Mediterranean t Hethlon,
Da 6:10 upstairs room, with its windows open t Jerusalem.
8:6 headed t the two-horned ram that I had seen
8:9 It extended t the south and the east and t the glorious land of Israel.
12:7 raised both his hands t heaven and took this
Hos 7:16 by their enemies because of their insolence t me.
Zec 2:3 to meet a second angel who was coming t him.
5:9 Then I looked up and saw two women flying t us,
8:8 and I will be faithful and just t them as their God.
14:4 for half the mountain will move t the north and half t the south.
14:8 half t the Dead Sea and half t the Mediterranean,
Mt 14:19 the five loaves and two fish, looked up t heaven,
14:29 side of the boat and walked on the water t Jesus.
Mk 6:41 the five loaves and two fish, looked up t heaven,
9:15 The crowd watched Jesus in awe as he came t
15:8 The mob began to crowd in t Pilate, asking him to
Lk 9:10 Then he slipped quietly away with them t the town
9:16 the five loaves and two fish, looked up t heaven,
13:22 as he went, always pressing on t Jerusalem.
17:11 As Jesus continued on t Jerusalem, he reached the
19:28 After telling this story, Jesus went on t Jerusalem,
Jn 1:29 The next day John saw Jesus coming t him
6:17 and headed out across the lake t Capernaum.
6:19 they saw Jesus walking on the water t the boat.
13:25 Leaning t Jesus, he asked, "Lord, who is it?"
20:16 She turned t him and exclaimed, "Teacher!"
Ac 2:10 Pamphylia, Egypt, and the areas of Libya t Cyrene,
10:3 in which he saw an angel of God coming t him.
17:27 and perhaps feel their way t him and find him—
27:40 the rudders, raised the foresail, and headed t shore.
Ro 15:5 each with the attitude of Christ Jesus t the other.
2Co 1:12 we have acted t everyone, and especially t you.
7:1 And let us work t complete purity because we fear
Eph 2:7 incredible wealth of his favor and kindness t us,
2:16 and our hostility t each other was put to death.
Php 3:12 But I keep working t that day when I will finally
1Th 2:10 and honest and faultless t all of you believers.
3:12 to everyone else, just as our love overflows t you.
4:10 your love is already strong t all the Christians in all
Jas 2:13 then God's mercy t you will win out over his
1Pe 3:8 be of one mind, full of sympathy t each other,

TOWED (1)

Ac 27:16 aboard the lifeboat that was being t behind us.

TOWEL (2)

Jn 13:4 took off his robe, wrapped a t around his waist,
13:5 and to wipe them with the t he had around him.

TOWER (31) [TOWERED, TOWERING, TOWERS, WATCHTOWER, WATCHTOWERS]

Ge 11:4 Let's build a great city with a t that reaches to the
11:5 to see the city and the t the people were building.
35:21 then traveled on and camped beyond the t of Eder.
Jdg 8:9 "After I return in victory, I will tear down this t."
8:17 He also knocked down the t of Peniel and killed all
9:46 When the people who lived in the t of Shechem
9:49 So all the people who had lived in the t of
9:51 But there was a strong t inside the city,
9:51 themselves in and climbed up to the roof of the t.
9:52 Abimelech followed them to attack the t. But as he
2Sa 22:3 my high t, my savior, the one who saves me from
2Ki 9:17 The watchman on the t of Jezreel saw Jehu and his
Ne 3:1 building the wall as far as the T of the Hundred,
3:1 which they dedicated, and the T of Hananel.
3:11 of Pahath-moab, who repaired the T of the Ovens,
3:25 and the corner to the upper t that projects from the
3:26 Water Gate toward the east and the projecting t.
3:27 another section opposite the great projecting t
12:38 along the top of the wall past the T of the Ovens to
12:39 past the Fish Gate and the T of Hananel, and went on to the T of the Hundred.
Ps 144:2 and my fortress, / my t of safety, my deliverer.
SS 4:4 Your neck is as stately as the t of David,
7:4 Your neck is as stately as an ivory t. Your eyes are
7:4 Your nose is as fine as the t of Lebanon
Isa 2:15 He will break down every high t and wall.
Jer 31:38 for me, from the T of Hananel to the Corner Gate.
Zec 14:10 and from the T of Hananel to the king's
Mt 21:33 pressing out the grape juice, and built a lookout t.
Mk 12:1 pressing out the grape juice, and built a lookout t.
Lk 13:4 men who died when the T of Siloam fell on them?

TOWERED (1) [TOWER]

Eze 31:5 This great tree t above all the other trees around it.

TOWERING (3) [TOWER]

Ps 61:2 is overwhelmed. / Lead me to the t rock of safety,
78:69 There he built his t sanctuary, / as solid
Eze 19:11 It soon became very tall, / t above all the others.

TOWERS (16) [TOWER]

2Ch 14:7 and fortify them with walls, t, gates, and bars.
26:9 Uzziah built fortified t in Jerusalem at the Corner
26:15 and hurl stones from the t and the corners of the
27:4 constructed fortresses and t in the wooded areas.
Ps 48:3 God himself is in Jerusalem's t. / He reveals
48:12 of Jerusalem. / Walk around and count the many t.
148:13 very great; / his glory t over the earth and heaven!
Isa 29:3 I will build siege t around it and will destroy it.
33:18 Assyrian officers outside your walls counted your t
54:12 I will make your t of sparkling rubies and your
Jer 48:18 shatter Dibon, too. They will tear down all your t.
Eze 21:22 They will put up siege t and build ramps against
26:4 will destroy the walls of Tyre and tear down its t.
26:9 and demolish your t with sledgehammers.
27:11 Your t were manned by men from Gammad.
Zep 3:6 devastating their fortress walls and t.

TOWN (215) [HOMETOWN, TOWNS]

Ge 23:10 speaking publicly before all the elders of the t.
26:33 the t that grew up there has been called
33:18 in Canaan, and they set up camp just outside the t.
34:20 and he appeared with his father before the t leaders
34:25 took their swords, entered the t without opposition,
34:27 Then all of Jacob's sons plundered the t
34:28 both inside the t and outside in the fields.
Lev 14:40 then be thrown into an area outside the t
14:41 dumped in the unclean place outside the t.
14:45 and plaster must be carried out of t to the place
14:53 the living bird in the open fields outside the t.
Nu 13:22 (The ancient t of Hebron was founded seven years
20:16 camped at Kadesh, a t on the border of your land.
21:14 speaks of "the t of Waheb in the area of Suphah,
22:36 he went out to meet him at a Moabite t on the
32:42 a man named Nobah captured the t of Kenath
35:4 1,500 feet from the t walls in every direction.
35:5 Measure off 3,000 feet outside the t walls in every
35:5 east, south, west, north—with the t at the center.
Dt 2:36 the t in the gorge, and the whole area as far as Gilead. No t had walls too strong for us.
3:6 We destroyed all the people in every t we
11:30 who live in the Jordan Valley, near the t of Gilgal.
12:15 "But you may butcher animals for meat in any t,
13:15 you must attack that t and completely destroy all
13:16 Put the entire t to the torch as a burnt offering to
13:16 That t must remain a ruin forever; it may never be
14:28 tithe of all your crops and store it in the nearest t.
17:5 or woman must be taken to the gates of the t
18:6 so desires may come from any t in Israel,
20:10 "As you approach a t to attack it, first offer its
20:12 and prepare to fight, you must attack the t.
20:13 God hands it over to you, kill every man in the t.
20:19 "When you are besieging a t and the war drags on,
20:20 equipment you need to besiege the t until it falls.
21:2 and judges must determine which t is nearest the
21:3 Then the leaders of that t must select a young cow
21:6 "The leaders of the t nearest the body must wash
21:19 must take the son before the leaders of the t.
21:21 Then all the men of the t must stone him to death.
22:15 the proof of her virginity to the leaders of the t.
22:21 and the men of the t will stone her to death.
22:23 intercourse with her. If this happens within a t,
22:24 you must take both of them to the gates of the t
23:16 Let them live among you in whatever t they
25:7 she must go to the t gate and say to the leaders
25:8 The leaders of the t will then summon him and try
Jos 3:16 the water began piling up at a t upstream called
7:3 they returned, they told Joshua, "It's a small t,
13:9 Gorge (including the t in the middle of the gorge)
13:16 Gorge (including the t in the middle of the gorge)
13:25 as far as the t of Aroer just west of Rabbah.
15:10 passed along to the t of Kesalon on the northern
15:15 Then he fought against the people living in the t of
17:8 but the t of Tappuah, on the border of Manasseh's
19:47 of their land, so they fought against the t of Laish.
19:50 For the LORD had said he could have any t he
19:50 of Ephraim. He rebuilt the t and lived there.
24:33 in the t of Gibeah, which had been given to his son
Jdg 1:4 ten thousand enemy warriors at the t of Bezek.
1:11 in the t of Debir (formerly called Kiriath-sepher).
1:16 the people there, near the t of Arad in the Negev.
1:17 in Zephath, and they completely destroyed the t. So the t was named Hormah.
1:22 The descendants of Joseph attacked the t of Bethel,
6:27 of his father's household and the people of the t.
6:28 next morning, as the people of the t began to stir,
8:5 reached Succoth, Gideon asked the leaders of the t,
8:14 of all the seventy-seven rulers and leaders in the t.
8:16 Then Gideon took the leaders of the t and taught
8:17 the tower of Peniel and killed all the men in the t.
10:1 but lived in the t of Shamir in the hill country of
13:2 from the tribe of Dan lived in the t of Zorah.
14:11 Thirty young men from the t were invited to be his
14:18 the men of the t came to Samson with their
14:19 He went down to the t of Ashkelon, killed thirty
15:9 setting up camp in Judah and raiding the t of Lehi.
18:7 So the five men went on to the t of Laish,
18:27 his priest, the men of Dan came to the t of Laish,
18:27 killed all the people and burned the t to the ground.
18:28 There was no one to rescue the residents of the t,
18:28 Then the people of the tribe of Dan rebuilt the t
18:29 They renamed the t Dan after their ancestor,
19:14 they came to Gibeah, a t in the land of Benjamin,
19:15 They rested in the t square, but no one took them
19:17 When he saw the travelers sitting in the t square,
19:22 some of the wicked men in the t surrounded the
19:25 The men of the t abused her all night, taking turns
20:4 a t in the land of Benjamin, to spend the night.
20:11 and they gathered together to attack the t.
20:21 who were defending the t, came out and killed
20:31 out to attack, they were drawn away from the t.
20:32 along the roads and be drawn away from the t.
20:37 in from all sides and killed everyone in the t.
20:38 They sent up a large cloud of smoke from the t,
20:40 smoke rising into the sky from every part of the t,
20:48 They also burned down every t they came to.
Ru 1:19 the entire t was stirred by their arrival.
2:18 She carried it back into t and showed it to her
3:11 for everyone in t knows you are an honorable
3:15 her put it on her back. Then Boaz returned to the t.
4:1 So Boaz went to the t gate and took a seat there.
4:2 Then Boaz called ten leaders from the t and asked
4:14 And the women of the t said to Naomi,
1Sa 4:13 an outcry resounded throughout the t.
9:6 There is a man of God who lives here in this t.
9:10 So they started into the t where the man of God
9:11 As they were climbing a hill toward the t, they met
9:12 "Stay right on this road. He is at the t gates.
9:14 So they entered the t, and as they passed through

9:25 After the feast, when they had returned to the **t**,
9:27 When they reached the edge of **t**, Samuel told Saul
11:5 and when he returned to **t**, he asked,
16:4 at Bethlehem, the leaders of the **t** became afraid.
27:6 So Achish gave him the **t** of Ziklag (which still
30:1 and his men arrived home at their **t** of Ziklag,
2Sa 2:1 Then David asked, "Which **t** should I go to?"
2:3 to Judah, and they settled near the **t** of Hebron.
4:2 The **t** of Beeroth is now part of Benjamin
12:1 "There were two men in a certain **t**. One was rich,
19:37 Then let me return again to die in my own **t**,
21:14 at the **t** of Zela in the land of Benjamin.
23:14 and a Philistine detachment had occupied the **t** of
24:5 and camped at Aroer, south of the **t** in the valley,
1Ki 12:25 Later he went and built up the **t** of Peniel.
15:22 Asa used these materials to fortify the **t** of Geba in Benjamin and the **t** of Mizpah.
15:27 were laying siege to the Philistine **t** of Gibbethon.
16:15 then engaged in attacking the Philistine **t** of
19:3 He went to Beersheba, a **t** in Judah, and he left his
2Ki 2:19 Now the leaders of the **t** of Jericho visited Elisha.
2:19 "This **t** is located in beautiful natural
2:21 Then he went out to the spring that supplied the **t**
2:23 a group of boys from the **t** began mocking
4:8 One day Elisha went to the **t** of Shunem.
8:21 went with all his chariots to attack the **t** of Zair.
8:22 The **t** of Libnah revolted about that same time.
10:33 He conquered the area from the **t** of Aroer by the
14:22 Uzziah rebuilt the **t** of Elath and restored it to
15:16 At that time Menahem destroyed the **t** of Tappuah
15:16 because its citizens refused to surrender the **t**.
16:6 At that time the king of Edom recovered the **t** of
17:29 In **t** after **t** where they lived, they placed their
23:17 And the people of the **t** told him, "It is the tomb of
1Ch 2:24 Soon after Hezron died in the **t** of Caleb-ephrathah,
6:71 the **t** of Golan in Bashan with its pasturelands
6:78 they received Bezer (a desert **t**), Jahaz,
11:16 and a Philistine detachment had occupied the **t** of
2Ch 19:10 comes to you from fellow citizens in an outlying **t**,
21:10 The **t** of Libnah revolted about that same time,
26:2 Uzziah rebuilt the **t** of Elath and restored it to
30:10 The messengers went from **t** to **t** throughout
32:9 of Assyria, while still besieging the **t** of Lachish,
Ps 69:12 I am the favorite topic of **t** gossip, / and all the
Pr 29:8 Mockers can get a whole **t** agitated, but those who
Ecc 7:19 is stronger than the ten leading citizens of a **t**!
9:14 There was a small **t** with only a few people living
9:15 wise man living there who knew how to save the **t**,
SS 6:4 you are as beautiful as the lovely **t** of Tirzah.
Jer 1:1 priests from Anathoth, a **t** in the land of Benjamin.
11:6 Go from **t** to **t** throughout the land and say,
40:10 Settle in any **t** you wish, and live off the land.
41:7 But as soon as they were all inside the **t**, Ishmael
49:3 "Cry out, O Heshbon, for the **t** of Ai is destroyed.
Eze 16:24 and put altars to idols in every **t** square.
39:16 (There will be a **t** there named Hamonah—
Am 1:1 to Amos, a shepherd from the **t** of Tekoa in Judah.
4:6 brought hunger to every city and famine to every **t**.
4:7 I sent rain on one **t** but withheld it from another.
4:8 People staggered from one **t** to another for a drink
5:3 When a **t** sends a hundred, only ten will come back
Mic 1:14 The **t** of Aczib has deceived the kings of Israel,
1:15 I will bring a conqueror to capture your **t**.
Mt 2:1 Jesus was born in the **t** of Bethlehem in Judea,
2:23 So they went and lived in a **t** called Nazareth.
8:34 The entire **t** came out to meet Jesus, but they
9:1 a boat and went back across the lake to his own **t**.
10:11 and stay in his home until you leave for the next **t**.
10:23 When you are persecuted in one **t**, flee to the next.
20:6 At five o'clock that evening he was in **t** again
21:1 they came to the **t** of Bethphage on the Mount of
Mk 1:21 and his companions went to the **t** of Capernaum,
1:45 Jesus that he couldn't enter a **t** anywhere publicly.
2:1 news of his arrival spread quickly through the **t**.
10:46 Later, as Jesus and his disciples left **t**, a great
Lk 1:39 Mary hurried to the hill country of Judea, to the **t**
4:31 Then Jesus went to Capernaum, a **t** in Galilee,
5:27 Later, as Jesus left the **t**, he saw a tax collector
9:10 quietly away with them toward the **t** of Bethsaida.
10:7 When you enter a **t**, don't move around from home
10:8 "If a **t** welcomes you, eat whatever is set before
10:10 But if a **t** refuses to welcome you, go out into its
10:11 'We wipe the dust of your **t** from our feet as a
10:12 even wicked Sodom will be better off than such a **t**
17:31 to pack. A person in the field must not return to **t**.
19:1 entered Jericho and made his way through the **t**.
23:51 He was from the **t** of Arimathea in Judea, and he
Jn 4:46 he arrived at the **t** of Cana, where he had turned the
Ac 9:32 he came to the Lord's people in the **t** of Lydda.
9:42 The news raced through the whole **t**, and many
13:5 There, in the **t** of Salamis, they went to the Jewish
13:6 Afterward they preached from **t** to **t** across the
13:13 ship for Pamphylia, landing at the port **t** of Perga.
13:50 against Paul and Barnabas and ran them out of **t**.
16:4 Then they went from **t** to **t**,
16:40 and encouraged them once more before leaving **t**.
19:13 A team of Jews who were traveling from **t** to **t**
Tit 1:5 and appoint elders in each **t** as I instructed you.
Jas 4:13 "Today or tomorrow we are going to a certain **t**

TOWNCLERK [KJV] See MAYOR

TOWNS (319) [TOWN]

Ge 35:5 terror from God came over the people in all the **t** of
Nu 13:19 Do their **t** have walls or are they unprotected?
13:28 and their cities and **t** are fortified and very large.
21:2 we will completely destroy all their **t**."
21:3 Israelites completely destroyed them and their **t**,
21:25 So Israel captured all the **t** of the Amorites
21:32 they captured all the **t** in the region and drove out
31:10 They burned all the **t** and villages where the
32:24 Go ahead and build **t** for your families
32:26 flocks, and cattle will stay here in the **t** of Gilead.
32:33 the whole land with its **t** and surrounding lands.
32:34 The people of Gad built the **t** of Dibon, Ataroth,
32:37 The people of Reuben built the **t** of Heshbon,
32:38 They changed the names of some of the **t** they
32:41 captured many of the **t** in Gilead and changed the name of that region to the **T** of
35:2 the Levites from their property certain **t** to live in,
35:3 These **t** will be their homes, and the surrounding
35:4 **t** will extend 1,500 feet from the town walls in
35:5 area will serve as the larger pastureland for the **t**.
35:6 for safety. In addition, give them forty-two other **t**.
35:7 forty-eight **t** with the surrounding pastureland will
35:8 These **t** will come from the property of the people
35:8 The larger tribes will give more **t** to the Levites,
Dt 1:22 to take and decide which **t** we should capture.'
1:28 and that the walls of their **t** rise high into the sky!
2:34 We conquered all his **t** and completely destroyed
2:35 along with anything of value from the **t** we
2:37 the Jabbok River and the **t** in the hill country—
3:4 We conquered all sixty of his **t**, the entire Argob
3:7 for ourselves and took plunder from all the **t**.
3:10 and Bashan as far as the **t** of Salecah and Edrei,
3:12 plus half of the hill country of Gilead with its **t**,
3:14 calling it the **T** of Jair, as it is still known today.)
3:19 may stay behind in the **t** I have given you.
12:12 And remember the Levites who live in your **t**,
12:18 your servants, and the Levites who live in your **t**,
13:12 "Suppose you hear in one of the **t** the LORD
14:29 the orphans, and the widows in your **t**, so they can
15:7 "But if there are any poor people in your **t** when
16:5 "The Passover must not be eaten in the **t** that the
16:11 all your servants, the Levites from your **t**,
16:14 foreigners, orphans, and widows from your **t**.
16:18 and officials for each of your tribes in all the **t** the
17:2 in one of your **t** that the LORD your God is
19:1 will displace them and settle in their **t** and homes.
20:15 only to distant **t**, not to the **t** of nations nearby.
20:16 "As for the **t** of the nations the LORD your God
24:14 fellow Israelites or foreigners living in your **t**.
26:12 so that they will have enough to eat in your **t**.
28:3 You will be blessed in your **t** and in the country.
28:16 You will be cursed in your **t** and in the country.
28:52 They will attack all the **t** in the land the LORD
28:55 the siege that your enemy will inflict on all your **t**.
28:57 distress that your enemy will inflict on all your **t**.
31:12 children, and the foreigners living in your **t**—
Jos 9:17 to investigate and reached their **t** in three days.
9:17 The names of these **t** were Gibeon, Kephirah,
9:18 But the Israelites did not attack the **t**, for their
10:37 capturing it and all of its surrounding **t**. And just as
11:3 and the Hivites in the **t** on the slopes of Mount
11:21 killed them all and completely destroyed their **t**.
13:10 It also included all the **t** of King Sihon of the
13:17 It included Heshbon and the other **t** on the plain—
13:21 The land of Reuben also included all the **t** of the
13:23 The **t** and villages in this area were given as an
13:25 Their territory included Jazer, all the **t** of Gilead,
13:28 The **t** and villages in this area were given as an
13:30 of King Og, and the sixty **t** of Jair in Bashan.
14:4 only **t** to live in and the surrounding pasturelands
15:9 and from there to the **t** on Mount Ephron.
15:21 The **t** of Judah situated along the borders of Edom
15:32 there were twenty-nine of these **t** with their
15:33 The following **t** situated in the western foothills
15:36 there were fourteen **t** with their surrounding
15:41 sixteen **t** with their surrounding villages.
15:44 nine **t** with their surrounding villages.
15:45 territory of the tribe of Judah also included all the **t**
15:46 and included the **t** near Ashdod with their
15:47 It also included Ashdod with its **t** and villages
15:47 and villages and Gaza with its **t** and villages,
15:48 Judah also received the following **t** in the hill
15:51 eleven **t** with their surrounding villages.
15:52 Also included were the **t** of Arab, Dumah, Eshan,
15:54 and Zior—nine **t** with their surrounding villages.
15:57 and Timnah—ten **t** with their surrounding villages.
15:59 and Eltekon—six **t** with their surrounding villages.
15:60 and Rabbah—two **t** with their surrounding villages.
15:61 In the wilderness there were the **t** of Beth-arabah,
15:62 and En-gedi—six **t** with their surrounding villages.
16:9 Ephraim was also given some **t** with surrounding
17:9 (Several **t** in Manasseh's territory belonged to the
17:11 The following **t** within the territory of Issachar
17:12 of Manasseh were unable to occupy these **t**.
18:9 into seven sections, listing the **t** in each section.
18:14 one of the **t** belonging to the tribe of Judah.
18:21 These were the **t** given to the families of the tribe
18:24 Ophni, and Geba—twelve **t** with their villages.
18:28 and Kiriath-jearim—fourteen **t** with their villages.
19:6 and Sharuhen—thirteen **t** with their villages.
19:7 Ether, and Ashan—four **t** with their villages,
19:15 The **t** in these areas included Kattath, Nahalal,
19:15 twelve **t** with their surrounding villages.
19:18 Its boundaries included the following **t**: Jezreel,
19:22 sixteen **t** with their surrounding villages.
19:25 Its boundaries included these **t**: Helkath, Hali,
19:30 twenty-two **t** with their surrounding villages.
19:41 The **t** within Dan's inheritance included Zorah,
19:48 of the tribe of Dan—these **t** with their villages.
21:2 "The LORD instructed Moses to give us **t** to live
21:3 inheritance the following **t** with their pasturelands.
21:4 were given thirteen **t** that were originally assigned
21:5 were allotted ten **t** from the territories of Ephraim,
21:6 The clan of Gershon received thirteen **t** from the
21:8 and assigned these **t** and pasturelands to the
21:9 The Israelites gave the following **t** from the tribes
21:13 The following **t** with their pasturelands were given
21:16 and Beth-shemesh—nine **t** from these two tribes.
21:17 following **t** with their surrounding pasturelands:
21:18 Anathoth, and Almon—four **t**.
21:19 So thirteen **t** were given to the priests,
21:20 clan from the tribe of Levi was allotted these **t**
21:22 Kibzaim, and Beth-horon—four **t**.
21:23 The following **t** and pasturelands were allotted to
21:24 Aijalon, and Gath-rimmon—four **t**.
21:25 The half-tribe of Manasseh allotted the following **t**
21:25 to the priests: Taanach and Gath-rimmon—two **t**.
21:26 So ten **t** with their pasturelands were given to the
21:27 received two **t** with their pasturelands from the
21:29 and En-gannim—four **t** with their pasturelands.
21:31 Helkath, and Rehob—four **t** and their pasturelands.
21:32 and Kartan—three **t** with their pasturelands.
21:33 So thirteen **t** and their pasturelands were allotted to
21:34 were given the following **t** from the tribe of
21:35 and Nahalal—four **t** with their pasturelands.
21:37 and Mephaath—four **t** with their pasturelands.
21:39 and Jazer—four **t** with their pasturelands.
21:40 So twelve **t** were allotted to the clan of Merari.
21:41 The total number of **t** and pasturelands within
21:42 Every one of these **t** had pasturelands surrounding
Jdg 10:4 and they owned thirty **t** in the land of Gilead, which are still called the **T** of Jair.
11:26 to Aroer and in all the **t** along the Arnon River.
11:33 twenty **t**—and as far away as Abel-keramim.
12:7 he died, he was buried in one of the **t** of Gilead.
13:25 which is located between the **t** of Zorah
18:2 who lived in the **t** of Zorah and Eshtaol, to scout
20:14 they came from their **t** and gathered at Gibeah to
20:48 and slaughtered every living thing in all the **t**—
21:23 Then they rebuilt their **t** and lived in them.
1Sa 7:12 and placed it between the **t** of Mizpah
7:14 The Israelite **t** near Ekron and Gath that the
18:6 Women came out from all the **t** along the way to
27:5 we would rather live in one of the country **t** instead
30:27 The gifts were sent to the leaders of the following **t**
30:29 the **t** of the Jerahmeelites, the **t** of the Kenites,
31:7 sons were dead, they abandoned their **t** and fled.
31:7 So the Philistines moved in and occupied their **t**.
1Ki 4:13 including the **T** of Jair (named for Jair son of
8:37 people's enemies are in the land besieging their **t**—
9:11 Solomon gave twenty **t** in the land of Galilee to
9:12 Hiram came from Tyre to see the **t** Solomon had
9:13 "What kind of **t** are these, my brother?" he asked. "These **t** are worthless!"
9:17 He also built up the **t** of Lower Beth-horon,
9:19 He built **t** as supply centers and constructed cities
12:17 rule over the Israelites who lived in the **t** of Judah.
13:32 and against the pagan shrines in the **t** of Samaria
15:20 They conquered the **t** of Ijon, Dan,
20:34 "I will give back the **t** my father took from your
2Ki 13:25 the **t** that Hazael had taken from Jehoash's father,
13:25 on three occasions, and so recovered the Israelite **t**.
15:29 and he captured the **t** of Ijon, Abel-beth-maacah,
17:9 built pagan shrines for themselves in all their **t**,
17:24 and resettled them in the **t** of Samaria,
17:24 took over Samaria and the other **t** of Israel.
17:26 "The people whom you have resettled in the **t** of
23:8 the LORD, who were living in other **t** of Judah.
23:19 buildings at the pagan shrines in the **t** of Samaria,
1Ch 2:22 who ruled twenty-three **t** in the land of Gilead.
2:23 (Later Geshur and Aram captured the **T** of Jair
4:31 These **t** were under their control until the time of
4:32 in Etam, Ain, Rimmon, Token, and Ashan—five **t**
6:54 This is a record of the **t** and territory assigned by
6:57 descendants of Aaron were given the following **t**,
6:60 So a total of thirteen **t** was given to the
6:61 **t** from the territory of the half-tribe of Manasseh
6:62 lots thirteen **t** from the territories of Issachar,
6:63 sacred lots twelve **t** from the territories of Reuben,
6:64 So the people of Israel assigned all these **t**
6:65 The **t** in the territories of Judah, Simeon,
6:66 received from the territory of Ephraim these **t**,
6:70 **t** from the territory of the half-tribe of Manasseh:
6:77 from the territory of Zebulun the **t** of Jokneam,
7:24 She built the **t** of Lower and Upper Beth-horon
7:28 included Bethel and its surrounding **t** to the south,
7:28 villages to the north as far as Ayyah and its **t**.
7:29 Along the border of Manasseh were the **t** of
7:29 descendants of Joseph son of Israel lived in these **t**.
9:2 The first to return to their property in their former **t**
10:7 sons were dead, they abandoned their **t** and fled.
10:7 So the Philistines moved in and occupied their **t**.
13:2 the priests and Levites in their **t** and pasturelands.
18:1 by conquering Gath and its surrounding **t**.
19:7 troops that Hanun had recruited from his own **t**.
20:1 the Israelite army in successful attacks against the **t**
27:25 charge of the regional treasuries throughout the **t**,
2Ch 6:28 people's enemies are in the land besieging their **t**—
8:2 to rebuilding the **t** that King Hiram had given him,
8:4 and built **t** in the region of Hamath as supply
10:17 rule over the Israelites who lived in the **t** of Judah.
11:12 and spears in these **t** as a further safety measure.
13:19 Jeroboam's troops and captured some of his **t**,
14:5 as the incense altars from every one of Judah's **t**.
14:7 "Let us build **t** and fortify them with walls, towers,
14:14 were at Gerar, they attacked all the **t** in that area,
14:14 vast quantities of plunder were taken from these **t**,

15: 8 and in the t he had captured in the hill country of
16: 4 They conquered the t of Ijon, Dan,
16: 6 Asa used these materials to fortify the t of Geba
17: 2 of Judah and to the t of Ephraim that his father,
17: 7 sent out his officials to teach in all the t of Judah.
17: 9 and traveled around through all the t of Judah,
17:13 He stored numerous supplies in Judah's t
20: 4 So people from all the t of Judah came to
23: 2 and clan leaders in Judah's t to come to Jerusalem.
24: 5 "Go at once to all the t of Judah and collect the
24: 6 and collect the Temple taxes from the t of Judah
25:13 raided several of the t of Judah between Samaria
26: 6 Then he built new t in the Ashdod area and in
27: 4 He built t in the hill country of Judah
28:18 And the Philistines had raided t located in the
28:18 and the Philistines had occupied these t.
28:25 He made pagan shrines in all the t of Judah for
31: 1 the Israelites who attended went to all the t of
31: 1 the Israelites returned to their own t and homes.
31:15 the gifts among the families of priests in their t,
31:19 who were living in the open villages around the t,
32:29 He built many t and acquired vast flocks
34: 6 He did the same thing in the t of Manasseh,
Ezr 2: 1 captivity to Jerusalem and to the other t of Judah.
2:59 to Jerusalem at this time from the t of Tel-melah,
2:70 The rest of the people returned to the other t of
3: 1 when the Israelites had settled in their t,
Ne 7: 6 captivity to Jerusalem and to the other t of Judah.
7:61 to Jerusalem at this time from the t of Tel-melah,
7:73 that is to say, all Israel—settled in their own t."
7:73 when the Israelites had settled in their t,
8:15 a proclamation should be made throughout their t
10:37 the Levites who collect the tithes in all our rural t.
11: 1 A tenth of the people from the other t of Judah
11: 3 live in their own homes in the various t of Judah,
11:20 inheritance was located in any of the t of Judah.
Ps 48:11 Let the t of Judah be glad, / for your judgments are
69:35 and rebuild the t of Judah. / His people will live
Isa 32:14 the city will be deserted, and busy t will be empty.
40: 9 Tell the t of Judah, "Your God is coming!"
42:11 Join in the chorus, you desert t; / let the villages of
44:26 and the t of Judah will be lived in once again,
Jer 1:15 will attack its walls and all the other t of Judah.
2:28 as many gods as there are cities and t in Judah.
4: 7 Your t will lie in ruins, empty of people.
4:16 raising a battle cry against the t of Judah.
5: 6 A leopard will lurk near their t, tearing apart any
7:17 see what they are doing throughout the t of Judah
7:34 and brides will no longer be heard in the t of
9:11 The t of Judah will be ghost t, with no one
10:22 The t of Judah will be destroyed and will become a
11:13 you have as many gods as there are cities and t.
13:19 The t of the Negev will close their gates, and no
17:26 from the t of Judah and Benjamin,
19:15 this city and its surrounding t just as I promised,
25:18 I went to Jerusalem and the other t of Judah,
32:44 in the t of Judah and in the hill country,
33:10 the empty streets of Jerusalem and Judah's other t,
33:13 Once again their flocks will prosper in the t of the
33:13 the vicinity of Jerusalem, and all the t of Judah.
34: 1 and he fought against Jerusalem and the t of Judah.
34:22 I will see to it that all the t of Judah are destroyed
44: 2 what I did to Jerusalem and to all the t of Judah.
44: 6 fury boiled over and fell like fire on the t of Judah
44:17 and princes have always done in the t of Judah
44:21 were burning incense to idols in the t of Judah
48: 8 "All the t will be destroyed, both on the plateaus
48:15 But now Moab and her t will be destroyed.
48:28 "You people of Moab, flee from your cities and t!
49: 1 Why are you, who worship Molech, living in its t?
49: 2 and the neighboring t will be burned.
49:13 All its t and villages will be desolate forever."
49:18 of Sodom and Gomorrah and their neighboring t,"
49:23 "The t of Hamath and Arpad are struck with fear,
50:40 and Gomorrah and their neighboring t,"
La 5:11 girls in Jerusalem and throughout the t of Judah.
Eze 19: 7 and destroyed their t and cities. / Their farms were
39: 9 "Then the people in the t of Israel will go out
45: 5 It will be their possession and a place for their t.
Mic 7:12 from Assyria all the way to the t of Egypt,
Zec 1:12 have been angry with Jerusalem and the t of Judah.
1:17 The t of Israel will again overflow with prosperity,
7: 7 and the t of Judah were bustling with people,
Mt 4:25 the Ten T, Jerusalem, from all over Judea,
10:23 will return before you have reached all the t of
11: 1 and preaching in t throughout the country.
Mk 1:38 But he replied, "We must go on to other t as well,
5:20 So the man started off to visit the Ten T of that
6:33 and people from many t ran ahead along the shore
7:31 to the Sea of Galilee and the region of the Ten T.
11: 1 they came to the t of Bethphage and Bethany,
Lk 2: 3 All returned to their own t to register for this
8: 4 crowd that had gathered from many t to hear him:
10: 1 and sent them on ahead in pairs to all the t
13:22 Jesus went through the t and villages, teaching as
19:29 As they came to the t of Bethphage and Bethany,
Ac 17: 1 and Silas traveled through the t of Amphipolis
20: 2 he encouraged the believers in all the t he passed
Jude 1: 7 of Sodom and Gomorrah and their neighboring t,

TRACE (13) [TRACED]

Ex 12:15 On the very first day you must remove every t of
12:19 there must be no t of yeast in your homes.
17:14 I will blot out every t of Amalek from under
2Ki 10:28 Jehu destroyed every t of Baal worship from Israel.
1Ch 29:15 earth are like a shadow, gone so soon without a t.
Job 4:20 by evening they are dead, gone forever without a t.
13:27 You watch all my paths. You t all my footprints.
Eze 11:18 they will remove every t of their detestable idol
21:19 and t two routes on it for the sword of Babylon's
Da 2:35 and the wind blew them all away without a t.
Zep 1: 4 and destroy every last t of their Baal worship.
3: 3 who by dawn have left no t of their prey.
Zec 13: 2 I will get rid of every t of idol worship throughout

TRACED (3) [TRACE]

1Ch 6:33 His genealogy was t back through Joel, Samuel,
6:39 Asaph's genealogy was t back through Berekiah,
6:44 Ethan's genealogy was t back through Kishi,

TRACK (5) [TRACKED, TRACKLESS]

Ge 4: 9 "Am I supposed to keep t of him wherever he
41:49 that the people could not keep t of the amount.
1Sa 23:23 And if he is in the area at all, I'll t him down,
Ps 17:11 They t me down, surround me, / and throw me to
56: 8 You keep t of all my sorrows. / You have collected

TRACKED (1) [TRACK]

Hos 6: 8 is a city of sinners, t with footprints of blood.

TRACKLESS (1) [TRACK]

Ps 107:40 causing them to wander in t wastelands.

TRACONITIS (1)

Lk 3: 1 his brother Philip was ruler over Iturea and T;

TRADE (16) [TRADED, TRADEMARK, TRADER, TRADERS, TRADES, TRADESMEN, TRADING]

Ge 25:31 "All right, but t me your birthright for it."
34:10 the land is open to you! Settle here and t with us.
34:21 invite them to live here among us and ply their t.
1Ki 20:34 and you may establish places of t in Damascus,
21: 6 "I asked Naboth to sell me his vineyard or to t it,
Ne 3: 8 a goldsmith by t, who also worked on the wall.
Ps 107:23 went off in ships, / plying the t routes of the world.
Jer 17:21 Stop carrying on your t at Jerusalem's gates on the
17:24 and do not carry on your t or work on the Sabbath
Eze 26: 2 She who controlled the rich t routes to the east has
27: 9 with goods from every land to barter for your t.
27:19 Greeks from Uzal came to t for your merchandise.
27:21 and rams and goats in t for your goods.
27:24 They brought choice fabrics to t—blue cloth,
27:33 at the ends of the earth / were enriched by your t.
28:18 with your many sins and your dishonest t.

TRADED (11) [TRADE]

Ps 106:20 They t their glorious God / for a statue of a
Isa 43: 4 I t their lives for yours because you are precious to
Eze 27:16 They t turquoise, purple dyes, embroidery,
27:17 Judah and Israel t for your wares, offering wheat
27:18 Damascus t for your rich variety of goods,
27:20 Dedan t their expensive saddle blankets with you.
27:33 The merchandise you t / satisfied the needs of
48:14 land will ever be sold or t or used by others,
Joel 3: 3 They t young boys for prostitutes and little girls for
Heb 12:16 He t his birthright as the oldest son for a single
Rev 18:13 and slaves—yes, she even t in human lives.

TRADEMARK (1) [TRADE]

Isa 59: 6 their activity is filled with sin. Violence is their t.

TRADER (1) [TRADE]

Isa 23: 8 on Tyre, empire builder and chief t of the world?

TRADERS (13) [TRADE]

Ge 37:25 It was a group of Ishmaelite t taking spices, balm,
37:27 Let's sell Joseph to those Ishmaelite t. Let's not be
37:28 So when the t came by, his brothers pulled Joseph
37:28 and the Ishmaelite t took him along to Egypt.
37:36 Meanwhile, in Egypt, the t sold Joseph to Potiphar,
39: 1 Joseph arrived in Egypt with the Ishmaelite t,
1Ki 10:15 revenue he received from merchants and t,
10:28 the king's t acquired them from Cilicia at the
2Ch 1:16 the king's t acquired them from Cilicia at the
9:14 revenue he received from merchants and t.
Isa 23: 2 you merchants of Sidon. Your t crossed the sea,
Zec 14:21 And on that day there will no longer be t in the
1Ti 1:10 for homosexuals and slave t, for liars and oath

TRADES (2) [TRADE]

2Ch 34:13 were put in charge of the laborers of the various t.
Ac 19:25 along with others employed in related t,

TRADESMEN (1) [TRADE]

Ne 13:20 and t with a variety of wares camped outside

TRADING (7) [TRADE]

1Ki 10:22 The king had a fleet of t ships that sailed with
22:48 Jehoshaphat also built a fleet of t ships to sail to
2Ch 9:21 The king had a fleet of t ships manned by the
20:36 Together they built a fleet of t ships at the port of
Isa 2:16 He will destroy the great t ships and all the small
Eze 27: 3 gateway to the sea, the t center of the world.
27:12 t your wares in exchange for silver, iron, tin,

TRADITION (7) [TRADITIONAL, TRADITIONS]

2Ch 35:25 These songs of sorrow have become a t and are
Est 9:27 throughout the realm agreed to inaugurate this t
Mt 15: 2 "They ignore our t of ceremonial hand washing
15: 6 And so, by your own t, you nullify the direct
Mk 7:13 the law of God in order to protect your own t.
Jn 7:22 this t of circumcision is older than the law of
2Th 3: 6 and doesn't follow the t of hard work we gave you.

TRADITIONAL (1) [TRADITION]

Zec 8:19 The t fasts and times of mourning you have kept in

TRADITIONS (7) [TRADITION]

Mt 15: 2 "Why do your disciples disobey our age-old t?"
15: 3 Jesus replied, "And why do you, by your t,
Mk 7: 3 their cupped hands, as required by their ancient t.
7: 4 This is but one of many t they have clung to—
7: 8 God's specific laws and substitute your own t."
7: 9 God's laws in order to hold on to your own t.
Gal 1:14 and I tried as hard as possible to follow all the old t

TRAFFIC (1)

2Ki 7:17 The king appointed his officer to control the t at

TRAFFICK(ERS) [KJV] See BUY, TRADE, TRADERS

TRAGEDY (12)

Dt 28:34 You will go mad because of all the t around you.
Jdg 11:35 What a t that you came out to greet me.
Ru 1:21 me to suffer and the Almighty has sent such t?"
1Ki 17:20 why have you brought t on this widow who has
20:10 "May the gods bring t on me, and even worse than
1Ch 7:23 because of the t his family had suffered.
Ne 2:17 said to them, "You know full well the t of our city.
Job 2:11 When they heard of the t he had suffered, they got
9:25 swiftly than a runner. It flees away, filled with t.
Ecc 6: 1 There is another serious t I have seen in our world.
6: 2 get it all! This is meaningless—a sickening t.
9:12 in a snare, people are often caught by sudden t.

TRAGIC (2)

Ecc 1:13 I soon discovered that God has dealt a t existence
9: 3 It seems so t that one fate comes to all. That is why

TRAIL (3) [TRAILED, TRAILS]

2Ki 7:15 following a t of clothing and equipment that the
Pr 5: 6 She staggers down a crooked t and doesn't even
SS 1: 8 follow the t of my flock to the shepherds' tents,

TRAILED (2) [TRAIL]

Isa 16: 8 spread out as far as Jazer and t out into the desert.
Lk 23:27 Great crowds t along behind, including many

TRAILS (1) [TRAIL]

Jer 23:12 They will be chased down dark and treacherous t,

TRAIN (4) [TRAINED, TRAINING, WELL-TRAINED]

Isa 6: 1 and the t of his robe filled the Temple.
Joel 3:10 into spears. T even your weaklings to be warriors.
Tit 2: 4 These older women must t the younger women to
2Pe 2:14 They t themselves to be greedy; they are doomed

TRAINED (13) [TRAIN]

Dt 21: 3 must select a young cow that has never been t
1Ch 12:36 there were 40,000 t warriors, all prepared for
25: 7 and their families were all t in making music
2Ch 25: 5 and older, all t in the use of spear and shield.
Jer 31:18 I was like a calf that needed to be t for the yoke
Da 1: 5 They were to be t for a three-year period, and
Hos 7:15 "I t them and made them strong, yet now they plot
10:11 "Israel is like a t heifer accustomed to treading out
Joel 2: 7 like warriors and scale city walls like t soldiers.
Am 7:14 I certainly never t to be one. I'm just a shepherd,
2Co 11: 6 I may not be a t speaker, but I know what I am
Heb 5:14 who have t themselves to recognize the difference
12:11 of right living for those who are t in this way.

TRAINING (8) [TRAIN]

1Ch 26:13 without regard to age or t, for it was all decided by
Isa 2: 4 wars will stop, and military t will come to an end.
Da 1:18 When the three-year t period ordered by the king
Mic 4: 3 wars will stop, and military t will come to an end.
Ac 4:13 they were ordinary men who had had no special t.
26: 4 I was given a thorough Jewish t from my earliest
1Co 9:27 my body like an athlete, t it to do what it should.
1Ti 4: 7 and energy in t yourself for spiritual fitness.

TRAITOR (7) [TREASON]

2Ki 6:11 and demanded, "Which of you is the t?
2Ch 13: 6 of David's son Solomon, became a t to his master.
Ps 73:15 this way, / I would have been a t to your people.
Pr 14:25 witness saves lives, but a false witness is a t.
Jer 26:11 "You have heard with your own ears what a t he
38: 4 well as that of all the people, too. This man is a t!"
Ac 1:25 as an apostle to replace Judas the t in this ministry,

TRAITORS (3) [TREASON]
Ps 59: 5 Show no mercy to wicked t. / *Interlude*
119:158 I hate these t / because they care nothing for your
Isa 48: 8 are entirely new, for I know so well what t you are.

TRAMPLE (24) [TRAMPLED, TRAMPLING]
Nu 21:22 We will not t your fields or touch your vineyards
Dt 33:29 low before you, / and you will t on their backs!"
Ps 7: 5 Let them t me into the ground. / Let my honor be
36:11 Don't let the proud t me; / don't let the wicked
44: 5 only in your name can we t our foes.
60:12 will do mighty things, / for he will t down our foes.
91:13 You will t down lions and poisonous snakes;
108:13 will do mighty things, / for he will t down our foes.
Isa 5: 5 I will break down its walls / and let the animals t it.
14:25 they are in Israel; I will t them on my mountains.
26: 6 The poor and oppressed t it underfoot.
41: 2 and permits him to t their kings underfoot.
41:25 He will t them as a potter treads on clay.
Eze 26:11 His horsemen will t every street in the city.
34:18 Must you also t down the rest? Is it not enough for
Am 2: 7 They t helpless people in the dust and deny justice
5:11 You t the poor and steal what little they have
8: 4 to this, you who rob the poor and t the needy!
Mic 4:13 so you can t many nations to pieces.
6:15 You will t the grapes but get no juice to make your
7:19 You will t our sins under your feet and throw them
Na 3:14 Go into the pits to t clay, and pack it into molds!
Mt 7: 6 They will t the pearls, then turn and attack you.
Rev 11: 2 They will t the holy city for 42 months.

TRAMPLED (28) [TRAMPLE]
2Ki 7:17 and t to death as the people rushed out.
7:20 so it was, for the people t him to death at the gate!
9:33 And Jehu t her body under his horses' hooves.
19:26 as the grass, / as easily t as tender green shoots.
Isa 14:19 Like a corpse t underfoot, you will be dumped into
25:10 Moab will be crushed like t straw and left to rot.
28: 3 of Israel—will be t beneath its enemies' feet.
28:18 enemy floods in, you will be t into the ground.
37:27 as the grass, / as easily t as tender green shoots.
51:23 I will give it to those who t you into the dust
63: 3 In my anger I have t my enemies as if they were
63: 3 In my fury I have t my foes. It is their blood that
Jer 51:33 is like wheat on a threshing floor, about to be t.
La 1:15 The Lord has t his beloved city as grapes are t in a winepress.
3:34 But the leaders of his people t prisoners underfoot.
Eze 34:19 is left for my flock to eat is what you have t down.
Da 7: 7 huge iron teeth and t what was left beneath its feet.
7:19 and it t what was left beneath its feet.
8: 7 and the goat knocked it down and t it.
8:13 will the Temple and heaven's armies be t on?"
Mic 4:12 and t like bundles of grain on a threshing floor.
7:10 With my own eyes I will see them t down like mud
Hab 3:12 in awesome anger and t the nations in your fury.
3:15 You t the sea with your horses, and the mighty
Mt 5:13 It will be thrown out and t underfoot as worthless.
Lk 21:24 and t down by the Gentiles until the age of the
Heb 10:29 will be for those who have t on the Son of God

TRAMPLING (5) [TRAMPLE]
Isa 10: 6 will plunder them, t them like dirt beneath its feet.
Jer 12:10 t down the vines and turning all its beauty into a
Da 7:23 devour the whole world, t everything in its path.
8:10 and stars to the ground and t them.
Zec 10: 5 t their enemies in the mud under their feet.

TRANCE (3)
Ac 10:10 while lunch was being prepared, he fell into a t.
11: 5 I was praying, I went into a t and saw a vision.
22:17 I was praying in the Temple, and I fell into a t.

TRANSACTION (1)
Ru 4: 7 it to the other party. This publicly validated the t.

TRANSFER (2) [TRANSFERRED, TRANSFERRING]
Nu 27:20 T your authority to him so the whole community
Ac 25: 3 They asked Festus as a favor to t Paul to

TRANSFERRED (1) [TRANSFER]
Est 2:19 Even after all the young women had been t to the

TRANSFERRING (1) [TRANSFER]
Ru 4: 7 anyone t a right of purchase to remove his sandal

TRANSFORM (2) [TRANSFORMED]
Hos 2:15 and t the Valley of Trouble into a gateway of hope.
Ro 12: 2 but let God t you into a new person by changing

TRANSFORMED (5) [TRANSFORM]
1Co 15:51 to us. Not all of us will die, but we will all be t.
15:52 the Christians who have died will be raised with t
15:52 And then we who are living will be t so that we
15:53 For our perishable earthly bodies must be t into
15:54 when our perishable earthly bodies have been t

TRANSIENT (1)
Job 8: 9 so little. Our days on earth are as t as a shadow.

TRANSLATE [KJV] See GIVE...(KINGDOM)

TRANSLATED (2)
Ezr 4: 7 in the Aramaic language, and it was t for the king.
4:18 The letter you sent has been t and read to me.

TRANSLATION [KJV] See TAKEN (UP)

TRANSMITTED (1) [TRANSMITTING]
Lev 15:24 this time, her menstrual impurity will be t to him.

TRANSMITTING (2) [TRANSMITTED]
Eze 44:19 so they do not harm the people by t holiness to
46:20 and harming the people by t holiness to them."

TRANSPLANTED (3) [PLANT]
Ps 80: 8 away the pagan nations and t us into your land.
92:13 For they are t into the LORD's own house.
Eze 17:10 Then when the vine is t, will it thrive? No, it will

TRANSPORT (2) [TRANSPORTATION, TRANSPORTED, TRANSPORTING]
1Ch 15: 2 "When we t the Ark of God this time, no one
2Ch 2:16 From there you can t the logs up to Jerusalem."

TRANSPORTATION (1) [TRANSPORT]
Nu 4:47 eligible for service in the Tabernacle and for its t

TRANSPORTED (3) [TRANSPORT]
2Ki 17:24 And the king of Assyria t groups of people from
1Ch 13: 7 They t the Ark of God from the house of Abinadab
Eze 8: 3 the sky and t me in a vision of God to Jerusalem.

TRANSPORTING (3) [TRANSPORT]
Nu 4:26 The Gershonites are responsible for t all these
Ezr 8:25 to be in charge of t the silver, the gold, the gold
8:30 and the Levites accepted the task of t these

TRAP (51) [BOOBY-TRAP, TRAPPED, TRAPPING, TRAPS]
Dt 7:16 not worship their gods. If you do, they will t you.
Jos 8:22 So the men of Ai were caught in a t, and all of
23:13 Instead, they will be a snare and a t to you, a pain
Jdg 8:27 and it became a t for Gideon and his family.
1Sa 28: 9 from the land. Why are you setting a t for me?"
Job 18: 9 A t grabs them by the heel. A noose tightens
Ps 7:15 They dig a pit to t others / and then fall into it
9:15 for others. / They have been caught in their own t.
31: 4 Pull me from the t my enemies set for me, / for I
35: 7 I did them no wrong, / they laid a t for me.
57: 6 My enemies have set a t for me. / I am weary from
69:22 become a snare, / and let their security become a t.
88: 8 them all away. / I am in a t with no way of escape.
91: 3 For he will rescue you from every t / and protect
124: 7 We escaped like a bird from a hunter's t. / The t is broken, and we are free!
140: 5 The proud have set a t to catch me; / they have
Pr 1:17 When a bird sees a t being set, it stays away.
3:26 He will keep your foot from being caught in a t.
21: 6 created by lying is a vanishing mist and a deadly t.
26:27 If you set a t for others, you will get caught in it
28:10 lead the upright into sin will fall into their own t,
29: 5 To flatter people is to lay a t for their feet.
29:25 Fearing people is a dangerous t, but to trust the
Ecc 7:26 Her passion is a t, and her soft hands will bind you.
Isa 8:14 And for the people of Jerusalem he will be a t that
24:18 Those who flee in terror will fall into a t, and those who escape the t will step into a snare.
Jer 18:20 They have set a t to kill me, though I pleaded for
20:10 "He will t himself," they say, "and then we will
48:44 "Those who flee in terror will fall into a t,
48:44 and those who escape the t will step into a snare.
50:24 Listen, Babylon, for I have set a t for you. You are
La 1:13 He has placed a t in my path and turned me back.
Eze 13:18 Do you think you can t others without bringing
Hos 5: 2 You have dug a deep pit to t them at Acacia.
Am 3: 5 Does a bird ever get caught in a t that has no bait?
3: 5 Does a t ever spring shut when there's nothing
Mt 16:23 from me, Satan! You are a dangerous t to me.
19: 3 and tried to t him with this question:
22:15 t Jesus into saying something for which they could
22:35 in religious law, tried to t him with this question:
Mk 10: 2 and tried to t him with this question:
12:13 and supporters of Herod to try to t Jesus into
Lk 11:54 trying to t him into saying something they could
20:26 So they failed to t him in the presence of the
21:35 as in a t. For that day will come upon everyone
Jn 8: 6 They were trying to t him into saying something
Ro 11: 9 a snare, / a t that makes them think all is well.
1Ti 3: 7 so that he will not fall into the Devil's t and be
2Ti 2:26 come to their senses and escape from the Devil's t.

TRAPPED (15) [TRAP]
Ex 14: 3 They are t between the wilderness and the sea!'
Dt 12:30 do not be t into following their example in
1Sa 23: 7 over to me, for he has t himself in a walled city!"
Ps 9:16 The wicked have t themselves in their own snares.
Pr 6: 2 if you have t yourself by your agreement and are
7:22 like an ox going to the slaughter or like a t stag,
12:13 The wicked are t by their own words, but the godly
29: 6 Evil people are t by sin, but the righteous escape,
Isa 28:13 They will be injured, t, and captured.
42:22 have been robbed, enslaved, imprisoned, and t.
Jer 19: 9 Then those t inside will have to eat their own sons
51: 6 Save yourselves! Don't get t in her punishment!
La 3:47 filled with fear, for we are t, desolate, and ruined."
Eze 19: 4 nations heard about him, / and he was t in their pit.
1Ti 6: 9 and are t by many foolish and harmful desires that

TRAPPING (1) [TRAP]
Hos 11: 6 and destroy them, t them in their own evil plans.

TRAPS (19) [TRAP]
Job 22:10 That is why you are surrounded by t and sudden
30:12 They send me sprawling; they lay t in my path.
Ps 5:10 Let them be caught in their own t. / Drive them
25:15 for he alone can rescue me from the t of my
38:12 Meanwhile, my enemies lay t for me; / they make
64: 5 and plan how to set their t. / "Who will ever
119:110 The wicked have set their t for me along your path,
140: 5 out a net; / they have placed t all along the way.
141: 9 Keep me out of the t they have set for me, / out of
142: 3 Wherever I go, / my enemies have set t for me.
Pr 11: 6 the ambition of treacherous people t them.
Isa 24:17 Terror and t and snares will be your lot, you people
Jer 5:26 They are continually setting t for other people.
18:22 a pit for me, and they have hidden t along my path.
48:43 "Terror and t and snares will be your lot,
Hos 9: 8 yet t are laid in front of him wherever he goes.
Ob 1: 7 Your trusted friends will set t for you, and you
Mic 7: 2 all murderers, even setting t for their own brothers.
Hab 2:17 terrified the wild animals you caught in your t.

TRASH (5)
1Ki 14:10 I will burn up your royal dynasty as one burns up t
Ps 50:17 you refuse my discipline / and treat my laws like t.
Pr 15:14 is hungry for truth, while the fool feeds on t.
Eze 7:19 away their money, tossing it out like worthless t.
1Co 4:13 like the world's garbage, like everybody's t—

TRAVAIL(ED), TRAVAILEST, TRAVAILETH [KJV] See ADVERSITY, ANGUISH, BIRTH, BUSINESS, CONCEIVE, DELIVERY, HARDSHIP, LABOR, TOIL, TRIBULATION(S), WRITHE

TRAVEL (34) [TRAVELED, TRAVELER, TRAVELER'S, TRAVELERS, TRAVELING, TRAVELS]
Ge 20:13 When God sent me to t far from my father's home,
22: 5 "The boy and I will t a little farther. We will
24: 5 suppose I can't find a young woman who will t
Ex 13:21 That way they could t whether it was day or night.
33: 3 But I will not t along with you, for you are a
Nu 1:50 carry the Tabernacle and its equipment as you t,
2: 9 way whenever the Israelites t to a new campsite.
2:16 will be second in line whenever the Israelites t.
2:17 All the tribes are to t in the same order that they
21:22 "Let us t through your land. We will stay on the
Dt 1: 2 Normally it takes only eleven days to t from
Jos 14:11 and I can still t and fight as well as I could then.
Jdg 19:11 servant said to him, "It's getting too late to t;
1Sa 1: 3 and his family would t to Shiloh to worship
1Ki 19: 8 and the food gave him enough strength to t forty
19:15 you came, and t to the wilderness of Damascus.
2Ki 4:29 Then Elisha said to Gehazi, "Get ready to t;
2Ch 15: 5 During those dark times, it was not safe to t.
Ne 2: 7 instructing them to let me t safely through their
Ps 37:34 T steadily along his path. / He will honor you,
Pr 20:24 How can we understand the road we t? It is the
21: 8 walk a crooked path; the innocent t a straight road.
Isa 35: 8 of Holiness. Evil-hearted people will never t on it.
Jer 6:16 T its path, and you will find rest for your souls.
6:25 Don't go out to the fields! Don't t the roads!
9:12 so completely that no one even dares to t through
31: 2 I will care for the survivors as they t through the
Eze 33:28 so ruined that no one will even t through them.
39:11 The path of those who t there will be blocked by
Zec 8:20 and cities around the world will t to Jerusalem.
Lk 4:44 So he continued to t around, preaching in
1Co 16: 4 for me also to go along, then we can t together.
16: 5 for I am planning to t through Macedonia.
2Co 10:14 for we were the first to t all the way to you with

TRAVELED (69) [TRAVEL]
Ge 12: 8 Abram t southward and set up camp in the hill
12: 9 Then Abram t south by stages toward the Negev.
13: 1 So they left Egypt and t north into the Negev—
22:19 young men and t home again to Beersheba,
24:10 He t to Aram-naharaim and went to the village
28:10 Jacob left Beersheba and t toward Haran.
33:17 Jacob and his household t on to Succoth.
35:16 they t on toward Ephrath (that is, Bethlehem).
35:21 Jacob then t on and camped beyond the tower of
37:14 and Joseph t to Shechem from his home in the
46:29 his chariot and t to Goshen to meet his father.
Ex 4:27 So Aaron t to the mountain of God, where he
15:22 They t in this desert for three days without water.
Nu 9:18 they t at the LORD's command and stopped
9:23 So they camped or t at the LORD's command,
10:12 and t on in stages until the cloud stopped in the
11:35 From there the Israelites t to Hazeroth, where they
12:15 until she was brought back before they t again.

21:10 The Israelites t next to Oboth and camped there.
21:12 From there they t to the valley of Zered Brook
21:16 From there the Israelites t to Beer, which is the
22:1 Then the people of Israel t to the plains of Moab
33:8 Then they t for three days into the Etham
Dt 1:19 we left Mount Sinai and t through the great
2:8 "Then as we t northward along the desert route
10:6 the wells of the people of Jaakan and t to Moserah,
29:16 and how we t through the lands of enemy nations
Jos 3:4 Since you have never t this way before, they will
10:9 Joshua t all night from Gilgal and took the Amorite
11:7 and his warriors t to the water near Merom
24:17 As we t through the wilderness among our
Jdg 1:16 t with them into the wilderness of Judah.
11:18 They t along Moab's eastern border and camped
1Sa 7:16 Each year he t around, setting up his court first at
9:4 and t all through the hill country of Ephraim,
31:12 their warriors t all night to Beth-shan and took the
2Sa 2:32 Then they t all night and reached Hebron at
20:14 Sheba had t across Israel to mobilize his own clan
1Ki 11:18 Then they t to Egypt and went to Pharaoh,
2Ki 3:9 and all three armies t along a roundabout route
1Ch 4:39 who t to the region of Gedor, in the east part of the
21:4 so Joab t throughout Israel to count the people.
2Ch 17:9 and t around through all the towns of Judah,
23:2 These men t secretly throughout Judah
Ezr 7:7 t up to Jerusalem with him in the seventh year of
8:21 and protect us, our children, and our goods as we t.
Job 2:11 got together and t from their homes to comfort
Isa 57:9 You have t far, even into the world of the dead,
Eze 10:22 and they t straight ahead, just as the others had.
Zec 7:14 so desolate that no one even t through it.
Mt 4:23 Jesus t throughout Galilee teaching in the
9:35 Jesus t through all the cities and villages of that
Mk 1:5 and from all over Judea t out into the wilderness to
1:39 So he t throughout the region of Galilee,
9:30 Leaving that region, they t through Galilee.
Lk 2:4 He t there from the village of Nazareth in Galilee.
Ac 9:32 Peter t from place to place to visit the believers,
11:19 after Stephen's death t as far as Phoenicia,
11:27 some prophets t from Jerusalem to Antioch.
13:14 and Paul t inland to Antioch of Pisidia.
14:24 Then they t back through Pisidia to Pamphylia.
15:41 So they t throughout Syria and Cilicia to
16:6 Next Paul and Silas t through the area of Phrygia
17:1 and Silas t through the towns of Amphipolis
19:1 in Corinth, Paul t through the interior provinces.
20:2 he passed through. Then he t down to Greece,
1Co 10:4 For they all drank from the miraculous rock that t
2Co 11:26 I have t many weary miles. I have faced danger
Php 4:15 the Good News and then t on from Macedonia.

TRAVELER (2) [TRAVEL]

Ps 39:12 For I am your guest— / a t passing through,
Zec 8:10 No t was safe from the enemy, for there were

TRAVELER'S (6) [TRAVEL]

Mt 10:10 Don't carry a t bag with an extra coat and sandals
Mk 6:8 a walking stick—no food, no t bag, no money.
Lk 9:3 "nor a t bag, nor food, nor money.
10:4 Don't take along any money, or a t bag, or even an
22:35 a t bag, or extra clothing, did you lack anything?"
22:36 he said, "take your money and a t bag.

TRAVELERS (5) [TRAVEL]

Jdg 5:6 main roads, / and t stayed on crooked side paths.
19:17 When he saw the t sitting in the town square,
Eze 39:11 for Gog and his hordes in the Valley of the T,
Hos 6:9 Gangs of priests murder t along the road to
Lk 2:44 assumed he was with friends among the other t.

TRAVELING (26) [TRAVEL]

Ge 12:6 T through Canaan, they came to a place near
13:3 Then they continued t by stages toward Bethel,
13:5 Now Lot, who was t with Abram, was also very
35:9 he arrived at Bethel after t from Paddan-aram.
Ex 12:11 "Wear your t clothes as you eat this meal,
12:37 and children. And they were all t on foot.
Nu 11:4 Then the foreign rabble who were t with the
35:15 of Israelites, resident foreigners, and t merchants.
Jdg 17:8 He happened to stop at Micah's house as he was t
2Sa 2:29 the Jordan River, t all through the morning,
1Ki 12:30 the people worshiped them, t even as far as Dan.
13:24 But as he was t along, a lion came out and killed
19:4 Then he went on alone into the desert, t all day.
2Ki 2:1 a whirlwind, Elijah and Elisha were t from Gilgal.
2Ch 19:4 t from Beersheba to the hill country of Ephraim,
Jer 25:5 'Turn from the evil road you are t and from the
Lk 10:30 "A Jewish man was t on a trip from Jerusalem to
Jn 4:47 Jesus had come from Judea and was t in Galilee,
Ac 19:13 A team of Jews who were t from town to town
19:29 who were Paul's t companions from Macedonia.
20:4 Several men were t with him. They were Sopater
21:12 When we heard this, we who were t with him,
2Co 8:20 By t together we will guard against any suspicion,
3Jn 1:5 take care of the t teachers who are passing through,
1:7 For they are t for the Lord and accept nothing from
1:10 He not only refuses to welcome the t teachers,

TRAVELS (4) [TRAVEL]

Isa 33:8 Your roads are deserted; no one t them anymore.
Jer 2:6 and death, where no one lives or even t?'
Eze 5:14 the surrounding nations and to everyone who t by.
Ac 9:32 and in his t he came to the Lord's people in the

TRAVERSING [KJV] See RESTLESS

TRAY (5) [TRAYS]

2Sa 13:9 But when she set the serving t before him,
Mt 14:8 "I want the head of John the Baptist on a t!"
14:11 and his head was brought on a t and given to the
Mk 6:25 the head of John the Baptist, right now, on a t!"
6:28 brought his head on a t, and gave it to the girl,

TRAYS (4) [TRAY]

Ex 25:38 and t must also be made of pure gold.
37:23 the lamp snuffers, and the t, all of pure gold.
Nu 4:9 along with its lamps, lamp snuffers, t, and special
Ezr 1:9 silver t | 1,000 / silver censers | 29

TREACHEROUS (15) [TREASON]

Ps 35:19 Don't let my t enemies / rejoice over my defeat.
38:12 to ruin me. / They think up t deeds all day long.
Pr 2:22 removed from the land, and the t will be destroyed.
11:3 t people are destroyed by their dishonesty.
11:6 rescues them; the ambition of t people traps them.
12:5 of the godly are just; the advice of the wicked is t.
13:2 of their words, but those who are t crave violence.
13:15 sense is respected; a t person walks a rocky road.
21:18 to save the godly, and the t for the upright.
22:5 The deceitful walk a thorny, t road;
23:27 prostitute is a deep pit; an adulterous woman is t.
Jer 3:11 "Even faithless Israel is less guilty than t Judah!
9:2 in the desert, for they are all adulterous and t.
23:12 They will be chased down dark and t trails,
Hab 2:5 Wealth is t, and the arrogant are never at rest.

TREACHERY (7) [TREASON]

2Ki 17:4 When the king of Assyria discovered this t,
Isa 24:16 for evil still prevails, and t is everywhere.
Jer 5:11 of Israel and Judah are full of t against me,"
Eze 39:23 for sin, for they acted in t against their God.
39:26 and t against me after they come home to live in
Mal 2:11 In Judah, in Israel, and in Jerusalem there is t,
Ac 1:18 bought a field with the money he received for his t,

TREAD (3) [DOWNTRODDEN, TREADING, TREADS, TROD, TRODDEN]

Job 24:11 and they t in the winepress as they suffer from
Joel 3:13 is ripe. Come, t the winepress because it is full.
Mal 4:3 you will t upon the wicked as if they were dust

TREADING (4) [TREAD]

Ne 13:15 One Sabbath day I saw some men of Judah t their
Isa 16:10 The t out of grapes in the winepresses has ceased
63:2 so red, as if you have been t out grapes?
Hos 10:11 "Israel is like a trained heifer accustomed to t out

TREADS (6) [TREAD]

Dt 25:4 "Do not keep an ox from eating as it t out the
Isa 41:25 He will trample them as a potter t on clay.
Jer 48:33 No one t the grapes with shouts of joy. There is
Am 4:13 into darkness and t the mountains under his feet.
1Co 9:9 "Do not keep an ox from eating as it t out the
1Ti 5:18 "Do not keep an ox from eating as it t out the

TREASON (7) [TRAITOR, TRAITORS, TREACHEROUS, TREACHERY]

2Ki 9:23 shouting to King Ahaziah, "T, Ahaziah!"
11:14 she tore her clothes in despair and shouted, "T! T!"
2Ch 23:13 she tore her clothes in despair and shouted, "T! T!"
Eze 17:20 and deal with him there for this t against me.
Ac 17:7 They are all guilty of t against Caesar, for they

TREASURE (46) [TREASURE-HOUSE, TREASURE-HOUSES, TREASURED, TREASURER, TREASURERS, TREASURES, TREASURIES, TREASURY]

Ex 19:5 you will be my own special t from among all the
Dt 7:6 your God has chosen you to be his own special t.
14:2 and he has chosen you to be his own special t from
26:18 his own special t, just as he promised, and that you
1Sa 25:29 of the LORD your God, secure in his t pouch!
Ezr 8:26 I weighed the t as I gave it to them and found the
Job 3:21 search for death more eagerly than for hidden t.
22:25 Then the Almighty himself will be your t. He will
31:36 the accusation proudly. I would t it like a crown.
Ps 119:111 Your decrees are my t; / they are truly my heart's
119:162 rejoice in your word / like one who finds a great t.
135:4 Jacob for himself, / Israel for his own special t.
Pr 2:1 My child, listen to me and t my instructions.
2:4 for them as you would for lost money or hidden t.
2:7 He grants a t of good sense to the godly. He is their
7:1 my advice, my son; always t my commands.
10:14 Wise people t knowledge, but the babbling of a
15:6 There is t in the house of the godly,
15:16 for the LORD than to have great t with turmoil.
18:22 The man who finds a wife finds a t and receives
Ecc 2:8 and gold, the t of many kings and provinces.
SS 4:9 You have ravished my heart, my t, my bride.
4:10 How sweet is your love, my t, my bride!
4:12 "You are like a private garden, my t, my bride!
5:1 "I am here in my garden, my t, my bride! I gather
5:2 'Open to me, my darling, my t, my lovely dove,'
Isa 30:6 and camels loaded with t to pay for Egypt's aid.
33:6 The fear of the LORD is the key to this t.
33:23 Their t will be divided by the people of God.
Eze 24:16 of man, I am going to take away your dearest t.
24:25 and glory, their heart's desire, their dearest t—
Ob 1:6 and looted. Every t will be found and taken.
Mal 3:17 the day when I act, they will be my own special t.
Mt 2:11 Then they opened their t chests and gave him gifts
6:21 Wherever your t is, there your heart and thoughts
13:44 "The Kingdom of Heaven is like a t that a man
13:44 money to buy the field—and to get the t, too!
19:21 money to the poor, and you will have t in heaven.
Mk 10:21 money to the poor, and you will have t in heaven.
Lk 12:33 in need. This will store up t for you in heaven!
12:33 Your t will be safe—no thief can steal it and no
12:34 Wherever your t is, there your heart and thoughts
18:22 money to the poor, and you will have t in heaven.
2Co 4:7 But this precious t—this light and power that now
1Ti 6:19 By doing this they will be storing up their t as a
Jas 5:3 This t you have accumulated will stand as

TREASURE-HOUSE (2) [HOUSE, TREASURE]

Ge 47:14 for grain, and he brought the money to Pharaoh's t.
Da 1:2 and placed them in the t of his god in the land of

TREASURE-HOUSES (2) [HOUSE, TREASURE]

2Ki 20:13 and showed them everything in his t—
Isa 39:2 and showed them everything in his t—

TREASURED (5) [TREASURE]

Ex 16:32 and keep it forever as a t memorial of the
Job 23:12 his commands but have t his word in my heart.
Pr 25:12 Valid criticism is as t by the one who heeds it as
Eze 7:22 I will hide my eyes as these robbers invade my t
Lk 2:19 but Mary quietly t these things in her heart

TREASURER (4) [TREASURE]

Ezr 1:8 the t of Persia, to count these items and present
Jn 13:29 Since Judas was their t, some thought Jesus was
Ac 8:27 So he did, and he met the t of Ethiopia, a eunuch
Ro 16:23 Erastus, the city t, sends you his greetings, and

TREASURERS (1) [TREASURE]

Ezr 7:21 hereby send this decree to all the t in the province

TREASURES (51) [TREASURE]

Dt 33:19 riches of the sea / and the hidden t of the sand."
Jos 8:27 the cattle and the t of the city were not destroyed,
Jdg 5:19 but they carried off no t of battle.
8:24 Each of you can give me an earring out of the t
2Ki 20:13 to see his armory and showed them all his other t
20:15 "I showed them everything I own—all my t."
20:17 all the t stored up by your ancestors—will be
24:13 Nebuchadnezzar carried away all the t from the
1Ch 29:3 I am giving all of my own private t of gold
2Ch 12:9 and took away all the t of the Temple of the
25:24 He also seized the t of the royal palace, along with
36:7 Nebuchadnezzar also took some of the t from the
36:10 Many t from the Temple of the LORD were taken
36:18 and the t from both the LORD's Temple
Ezr 6:1 in the Babylonian archives, where t were stored.
8:28 and these t have been set apart as holy to the
8:29 Guard these t well until you present them,
8:30 these t to the Temple of our God in Jerusalem.
Job 20:26 "His t will be lost in deepest darkness. A wildfire
28:7 t that no bird of prey can see, no falcon's eye
28:8 No wild animal has ever walked upon those t;
28:11 trickling streams and bring to light the hidden t.
Isa 2:7 Israel has vast t of silver and gold and many horses
10:3 will you turn for help? Where will your t be safe?
10:13 destroyed their kings, and carried off their t.
39:2 to see his armory and showed them all his other t
39:4 "I showed them everything I own—all my t."
39:6 all the t stored up by your ancestors—will be
45:3 And I will give you t hidden in the darkness—
61:6 You will be fed with the t of the nations and will
Jer 15:13 over their wealth and t as plunder to the enemy.
17:3 So I will give all your wealth and t—together with
20:5 All the famed t of the city—the precious jewels
28:3 I will bring back all the Temple t that King
28:6 I hope he does bring back from Babylon the t of
50:37 When it strikes her t, they will all be plundered.
La 1:11 They have sold their t for food to stay alive.
Eze 22:25 innocent people, seizing t and extorting wealth.
Da 11:43 silver, and t of Egypt, and the Libyans
Hos 9:6 Briers will take over your t of silver; brambles will
Joel 3:5 taken my silver and gold and all my precious t,
Mic 1:7 to pieces. All her sacred t will be burned up.
6:10 The homes of the wicked are filled with t gained
Na 2:9 There seems no end to Nineveh's many t—its vast,
Hag 2:7 and the t of all the nations will come to this
Mt 6:19 "Don't store up t here on earth, where they can be
6:20 Store your t in heaven, where they will never
Ro 8:17 And since we are his children, we will share his t
Eph 3:8 about the endless t available to them in Christ.
Col 2:3 In him lie hidden all the t of wisdom
Heb 11:26 the sake of the Messiah than to own the t of Egypt,

TREASURIES (18) [TREASURE]

1Ki 7:51 and he stored them in the t of the LORD's
15:18 and gold that was left in the t of the LORD's
2Ki 12:18 along with all the gold in the t of the LORD's
1Ch 9:26 for the rooms and t at the house of God.

26:20 were in charge of the **t** of the house of God
26:22 were in charge of the **t** of the house of the LORD.
26:24 son of Moses. He was the chief officer of the **t**.
26:26 and his relatives were in charge of the **t** that held
27:25 son of Adiel was in charge of the palace **t**.
27:25 in charge of the regional **t** throughout the towns,
28:11 including the **t**, the upstairs rooms, the inner
28:12 the outside rooms, the **t** of God's Temple,
2Ch 5:1 These were stored in the **t** of the Temple of God.
8:15 concerning the priests and Levites and the **t**.
16:2 and gold from the **t** of the LORD's Temple
Job 38:22 "Have you visited the **t** of the snow? Have you
Pr 8:21 Those who love me inherit wealth, for I fill their **t**.
Eze 28:4 amassed great wealth—gold and silver for your **t**.

TREASURY (18) [TREASURE]

Dt 28:12 rich **t** in the heavens to bless all the work you do.
32:34 up these things, / sealing them away within my **t**.
Jos 6:19 to the LORD and must be brought into his **t**."
6:24 or iron were kept for the **t** of the LORD's house.
2Ki 14:14 of the LORD, as well as from the palace **t**.
16:8 and the palace **t** and sent it as a gift to the Assyrian
18:15 in the Temple of the LORD and in the palace **t**.
1Ch 29:8 which were deposited in the **t** of the house of the
2Ch 32:27 He had to build special **t** buildings for his silver,
Ezr 6:4 of timber. All expenses will be paid by the royal **t**.
7:20 you may requisition funds from the royal **t**.
Ne 7:70 The governor gave to the **t** 1,000 gold coins,
7:71 The other leaders gave to the **t** a total of 20,000
Est 3:9 so they can put it into the royal **t**.
4:7 pay into the royal **t** for the destruction of the Jews.
Jer 38:11 and went to a room in the palace beneath the **t**,
Mt 27:6 "We can't put it in the Temple **t**," they said,
Jn 8:20 in the section of the Temple known as the **T**.

TREAT (60) [TREATED, TREATIES, TREATING, TREATMENT, TREATMENTS, TREATS]

Ge 12:13 then the Egyptians will **t** me well because of their
16:4 she began to **t** her mistress Sarai with contempt.
19:9 We'll **t** you far worse than those other men!"
26:10 "How could you **t** us this way!"
32:9 to my relatives, and you promised to **t** me kindly.
32:12 But you promised to **t** me kindly and to multiply
34:31 "Should he **t** our sister like a prostitute?"
43:6 "Why did you have to **t** me with such cruelty?"
Ex 3:21 And I will see to it that the Egyptians **t** you well.
5:15 "Please don't **t** us like this," they begged.
21:9 he may no longer **t** her as a slave girl, but he must **t** her as his daughter.
30:32 for yourselves. It is holy, and you must **t** it as holy.
30:37 reserved for the LORD, and you must **t** it as holy.
Lev 21:8 You must **t** them as holy because they offer up
22:2 and his sons to **t** the sacred gifts that the Israelites
22:32 Do not **t** my holy name as common and ordinary.
25:39 and sell themselves to you, do not **t** them as slaves.
25:40 **T** them instead as hired servants or as resident
25:45 in your land. You may **t** them as your property,
25:46 You may **t** your slaves like this, but the people of
25:53 The foreigner must **t** them as servants hired on a
25:53 You must not allow a resident foreigner to **t** any of
Nu 10:29 Come with us and we will **t** you well,
11:15 I'd rather you killed me than **t** me like this.
16:13 and that you now **t** us like your subjects?
18:10 males may eat of it, and you must **t** it as most holy.
18:32 But be careful not to **t** the holy gifts of the people
Dt 3:2 **T** him just as you treated King Sihon of the
21:14 You may not sell her or **t** her as a slave, for you
1Sa 8:9 but solemnly warn them about how a king will **t**
8:11 "This is how a king will **t** you," Samuel said.
20:14 And may you **t** me with the faithful love of the
20:15 **t** my family with this faithful love, even when the
2Sa 16:17 "Is this the way you **t** your friend David?"
19:43 Why did you **t** us with such contempt? Remember,
Ezr 9:9 he caused the kings of Persia to **t** us favorably.
Job 42:8 I will not **t** you as you deserve, for you have not
Ps 50:17 you refuse my discipline / and **t** my laws like trash.
69:8 they don't know me; / they **t** me like a stranger.
80:6 neighboring nations. / Our enemies **t** us as a joke.
106:46 even caused their captors / to **t** them with kindness.
142:7 will crowd around me, / for you **t** me kindly."
Isa 58:6 **T** them fairly and give them what they earn.
63:19 why do you **t** us as though we never belonged to
Jer 3:19 'I would love to **t** you as my own children!'
24:8 I will **t** them like spoiled figs, too rotten to eat.
Hag 2:23 I will **t** you like a signet ring on my finger,
Zec 8:11 But now I will not **t** the remnant of my people as I
Mt 7:2 For others will **t** you as you **t** them.
18:17 **t** that person as a pagan or a corrupt tax collector.
1Co 16:10 When Timothy comes, **t** him with respect. He is
Eph 6:4 Don't make your children angry by the way you **t**
6:9 same way, you masters must **t** your slaves right.
Col 3:19 must love your wives and never **t** them harshly.
1Ti 5:2 **T** the older women as you would your mother,
5:2 and **t** the younger women with all purity as your
1Pe 3:7 **T** her with understanding as you live together.
3:7 If you don't **t** her as you should, your prayers will

TREATED (48) [TREAT]

Ge 16:6 So Sarai **t** her harshly, and Hagar ran away.
26:29 We have always **t** you well, and we sent you away
50:23 son Makir, who were **t** as if they were his own.
Ex 12:48 They will be **t** just as if they had been born among
Lev 19:34 They should be **t** like everyone else, and you must
22:32 I must be **t** as holy by the people of Israel. It is I,
25:31 will be **t** like property in the open fields.
25:46 of Israel, your relatives, must never be **t** this way.
Nu 14:23 None of those who have **t** me with contempt will
15:31 Since they have **t** the LORD's word with
Dt 3:2 Treat him just as you **t** King Sihon of the
Jdg 8:1 asked Gideon, "Why have you **t** us this way?
9:16 Have you **t** my father with the honor he deserves?
1Sa 2:14 who came to worship at Shiloh were **t** this way.
2:17 for they **t** the LORD's offerings with contempt.
1Ki 1:21 and I will be **t** as criminals as soon as you are
2Ch 30:9 and your children will be **t** mercifully by their
Est 2:9 was very impressed with Esther and **t** her kindly.
Ps 44:11 You have **t** us like sheep waiting to be slaughtered;
72:2 in the right way; / let the poor always be **t** fairly.
103:6 and justice to all who are **t** unfairly.
Ecc 8:14 good people are often **t** as though they were
8:14 and wicked people are often **t** as though they were
9:2 and people who take oaths are **t** like people who
Isa 53:7 He was oppressed and **t** harshly, yet he never said
66:12 at her breasts, carried in her arms, and **t** with love.
Jer 3:9 Israel **t** it all so lightly—she thought nothing of
12:8 the forest, so I have **t** them as though I hated them.
24:6 I will see that they are well **t**, and I will bring them
La 1:15 "The Lord has **t** my mighty men with contempt.
4:2 their weight in gold, are now **t** like pots of clay.
5:12 their thumbs, and the old men are **t** with contempt.
Eze 28:26 And when I punish the neighboring nations that **t**
Mic 6:16 You will be **t** with contempt, mocked by all who
Zec 8:11 treat the remnant of my people as I **t** them before,
Mt 22:6 seized his messengers and **t** them shamefully,
Mk 9:12 of Man must suffer and be **t** with utter contempt?
12:4 they beat him over the head and **t** him shamefully.
Lk 6:23 the ancient prophets were also **t** that way by your
18:32 Romans to be mocked, **t** shamefully, and spit upon.
20:11 he was beaten up and **t** shamefully, and he went
Ac 5:26 would kill them if they **t** the apostles roughly.
1Co 4:13 Yet we are **t** like the world's garbage,
2Co 6:9 We are well known, but we are **t** as unknown.
1Th 2:2 You know how badly we had been **t** at Philippi just
2:11 And you know that we **t** each of you as a father
Heb 10:29 and have **t** the blood of the covenant as if it were
11:24 refused to be **t** as the son of Pharaoh's daughter.

TREATIES (5) [TREAT]

Ex 23:32 "Make no **t** with them and have nothing to do with
34:12 "Be very careful never to make **t** with the people
34:15 "Do not make **t** of any kind with the people living
Dt 7:2 Make no **t** with them and show them no mercy.
Eze 17:15 Can Israel break her sworn **t** like that and get away

TREATING (9) [TREAT]

Ge 18:25 you would be **t** the innocent and the guilty exactly
31:5 turned against me and is not **t** me like he used to,"
Lev 19:14 "Show your fear of God by **t** the deaf with respect
25:43 Show your fear of God by **t** them well;
26:15 my laws and **t** my regulations with contempt,
Nu 11:11 "Why are you **t** me, your servant, so miserably?
Ne 9:10 for you knew how arrogantly the Egyptians were **t**
Eze 20:44 when I have honored my name by **t** you mercifully
Heb 12:7 remember that God is **t** you as his own children.

TREATISE [KJV] See BOOK

TREATMENT (9) [TREAT]

Ge 20:9 "What have I done to you that deserves **t** like this,
Dt 28:33 will suffer under constant oppression and harsh **t**.
1Sa 8:8 And now they are giving you the same **t**.
29:8 "What have I done to deserve this **t**?"
2Ki 25:28 and gave him preferential **t** over all the other exiled
Ecc 9:2 Good people receive the same **t** as sinners,
Jer 16:10 What have we done to deserve such **t**? What is our
52:32 and gave him preferential **t** over all the other exiled
1Pe 2:19 of your conscience, you patiently endure unfair **t**.

TREATMENTS (5) [TREAT]

Est 2:3 in charge, will see that they are all given beauty **t**.
2:9 menu for her and provided her with beauty **t**.
2:12 given the prescribed twelve months of beauty **t**—
Jer 6:14 They offer superficial **t** for my people's mortal
8:11 They offer superficial **t** for my people's mortal

TREATS (5) [TREAT]

Dt 24:7 a fellow Israelite and **t** him as a slave or sells him,
1Sa 2:8 from a pile of ashes! / He **t** them like princes,
Job 34:11 to their deeds. He **t** people according to their ways.
Gal 2:21 I am not one of those who **t** the grace of God as
1Th 2:11 treated each of you as a father **t** his own children.

TREATY (25)

Ge 21:27 and oxen to Abimelech, and they made a **t**.
26:28 So we decided we should have a **t**, a covenant
26:30 and drank in preparation for the **t** ceremony.
31:44 Come now, and we will make a peace **t**, you and I,
31:49 keep this **t** when we are out of each other's sight.
Jos 9:6 distant land to ask you to make a peace **t** with us."
9:7 For if you do, we cannot make a **t** with you."
9:15 Joshua went ahead and signed a peace **t** with them,
9:18 grumbled against their leaders because of the **t**.
1Sa 11:1 "Make a **t** with us, and we will be your servants,"
1Ki 15:19 "Let us renew the **t** that existed between your
15:19 Break your **t** with King Baasha of Israel so that he
20:34 So they made a **t**, and Ben-hadad was set free.
1Ch 16:17 to the people of Israel as a never-ending **t**:
2Ch 16:3 "Let us renew the **t** that existed between your
16:3 Break your **t** with King Baasha of Israel so that he
Ps 83:5 They signed a **t** as allies against you—
105:10 to the people of Israel as a never-ending **t**:
Eze 17:13 He made a **t** with a member of the royal family
17:14 Only by keeping her **t** with Babylon could Israel
17:16 him in power and whose **t** he despised and broke.
17:18 For the king of Israel broke his **t** after swearing to
21:23 a mistake, because of their **t** with the Babylonians.
Da 9:27 He will make a **t** with the people for a period of
Am 1:9 They broke their **t** of brotherhood with Israel,

TREE (155) [TREES]

EVERY GREEN TREE (12) Dt 12:2; 1Ki 14:23; 2Ki 16:4; 17:10; 2Ch 28:4; Isa 57:5; Jer 2:20; 3:6,13; 17:2; Eze 6:13; 20:28

EVERY TREE (5) Isa 44:23; Eze 20:47; Mt 3:10; 7:19; Lk 3:9

TREE OF LIFE (8) Ge 2:9; 3:22,24; Pr 3:18; Rev 2:7; 22:2,14,19

Ge 2:9 At the center of the garden he placed the **t** of life
2:9 and the **t** of the knowledge of good and evil.
2:17 except fruit from the **t** of the knowledge of good
3:3 "It's only the fruit from the **t** at the center of the
3:22 and evil. What if they eat the fruit of the **t** of life?
3:24 and forth, guarding the way to the **t** of life.
18:4 Rest in the shade of this **t** while my servants get
21:33 Then Abraham planted a tamarisk **t** at Beersheba,
35:4 and he buried them beneath the **t** near Shechem.
35:8 She was buried beneath the oak **t** in the valley
35:8 the **t** has been called the "Oak of Weeping."
49:22 "Joseph is a fruitful **t**, / a fruitful **t** beside a fountain.
Ex 10:15 neither **t** nor plant, throughout the land of Egypt.
Dt 12:2 up on the hills, and under every green **t**.
21:22 of death and is executed and then hanged on a **t**,
21:23 the body must never remain on the **t** overnight.
21:23 for anyone hanging on a **t** is cursed of God.
22:6 on the ground or in a **t** and there are young ones
Jos 8:29 Joshua hung the king of Ai on a **t** and left him
24:26 and rolled it beneath the oak **t** beside the
Jdg 6:11 LORD came and sat beneath the oak **t** at Ophrah,
6:19 them to the angel, who was under the oak **t**.
9:8 a king. First they said to the olive **t**, 'Be our king!'
9:10 "Then they said to the fig **t**, 'You be our king!'
9:11 But the fig **t** also refused, saying, 'Should I quit
9:48 took an ax and chopped some branches from a **t**,
1Sa 14:2 of Gibeah, around the pomegranate **t** at Migron.
22:6 the king was sitting beneath a tamarisk **t** on the hill
31:13 and buried them beneath the tamarisk **t** at Jabesh,
2Sa 18:10 and told Joab, "I saw Absalom dangling in a **t**."
1Ki 13:14 man of God and found him sitting under an oak **t**.
14:23 poles on every high hill and under every green **t**.
19:4 He sat down under a solitary broom **t** and prayed
19:5 Then he lay down and slept under the broom **t**.
2Ki 14:9 a thistle sent a message to a mighty cedar **t**:
16:4 and on the hills and under every green **t**.
17:10 at the top of every hill and under every green **t**.
1Ch 10:12 Then they buried their remains beneath the oak **t** at
2Ch 25:18 a thistle sent a message to a mighty cedar **t**:
28:4 and on the hills and under every green **t**.
Job 14:7 "If a **t** is cut down, there is hope that it will sprout
15:33 like an olive **t** that sheds its blossoms so the fruit
24:20 Wicked people are broken like a **t** in the storm.
29:19 For I am like a **t** whose roots reach the water,
Ps 52:8 But I am like an olive **t**, / thriving in the house of
Pr 3:18 Wisdom is a **t** of life to those who embrace her;
27:18 Workers who tend a fig **t** are allowed to eat its
Ecc 11:3 When a **t** falls, whether south or north, there it lies.
SS 2:3 my lover is like the finest apple **t** in the orchard.
4:14 myrrh and aloes, perfume from every incense **t**,
7:7 You are tall and slim like a palm **t**, and your
7:8 'I will climb up into the palm **t** and take hold of its
8:5 "I aroused you under the apple **t**, where your
Isa 6:13 Israel will remain a stump, like a **t** that is cut down,
10:33 LORD Almighty, will chop down the mighty **t**!
17:6 like the stray olives left on the **t** after the harvest.
24:13 like the stray olives left on the **t** or the few grapes
27:11 The people are like the dead branches of a **t**,
34:4 just as withered leaves and fruit fall from a **t**.
44:16 He burns part of the **t** to roast his meat and to keep
44:23 into song, O mountains and forests and every **t**!
57:5 idols with great passion beneath every green **t**.
Jer 1:11 And I replied, "I see a branch from an almond **t**."
2:20 On every hill and under every green **t**, you have
3:6 other gods on every hill and under every green **t**.
3:13 him by worshiping idols under every green **t**.
10:3 and foolish. They cut down a **t** and carve an idol.
11:16 the LORD, once called them a thriving olive **t**,
11:17 the LORD Almighty, who planted this olive **t**,
17:2 beneath every green **t** and on every high hill.
Eze 6:13 on every hill and mountain and under every green **t**
15:2 of man, how does a grapevine compare to a **t**?
15:2 Is a vine's wood as useful as the wood of a **t**?
17:3 He took hold of the highest branch of a cedar **t**
17:5 where it would grow as quickly as a willow **t**.
17:24 down the tall **t** and helps the short **t** to grow tall.
17:24 the green **t** wither and gives new life to the dead **t**.
20:28 every high hill and under every green **t** they saw!
20:47 you on fire, O forest, and every **t** will be burned—
31:5 This great **t** towered above all the other trees
31:8 This **t** became taller than any of the other cedars in
31:8 equal to it; no plane **t** had boughs to compare.
31:8 No **t** in the garden of God came close to it in
31:9 Because of the magnificence I gave this **t**, it was
40:22 and the palm **t** decorations were identical to those
40:26 and there were palm **t** decorations along the

40:31 It had palm **t** decorations on its columns, and there
40:34 It had palm **t** decorations on its columns, and there
40:37 and it had palm **t** decorations on the columns.
41:18 and there was a palm **t** carving between each of the
41:19 of a man—looked toward the palm **t** on one side.
41:19 looked toward the palm **t** on the other side.
Da 4:10 I saw a large **t** in the middle of the earth.
4:11 The **t** grew very tall and strong, reaching high into
4:12 in its branches. All the world was fed from this **t**.
4:14 The messenger shouted, "Cut down the **t**; lop off
4:20 You saw a **t** growing very tall and strong,
4:22 That **t**, Your Majesty, is you. For you have grown
4:23 and saying, 'Cut down the **t** and destroy it.
Hos 14:8 I am like a **t** that is always green, giving my fruit to
Hag 2:19 before the grapevine, the fig **t**, the pomegranate,
2:19 and the olive **t** have produced their crops.
Mal 4:1 They will be consumed like a **t**—roots and all.
Mt 3:10 every **t** that does not produce good fruit will be
7:16 they act, just as you can identify a **t** by its fruit.
7:17 A healthy **t** produces good fruit, and an unhealthy **t** produces bad fruit.
7:18 A good **t** can't produce bad fruit, and a bad **t** can't produce good fruit.
7:19 So every **t** that does not produce good fruit is
7:20 the way to identify a **t** or a person is by the kind of
12:33 "A **t** is identified by its fruit. Make a **t** good, and its fruit will be good. Make a **t** bad, and its fruit
13:32 and grows into a **t** where birds can come and find
21:19 and he noticed a fig **t** beside the road. He went
21:19 And immediately the fig **t** withered up.
21:20 and asked, "How did the fig **t** wither so quickly?"
24:32 "Now learn a lesson from the fig **t**. When its buds
Mk 11:13 He noticed a fig **t** a little way off that was in full
11:14 Then Jesus said to the **t**, "May no one ever eat
11:20 The next morning as they passed by the fig **t** he
11:21 Peter remembered what Jesus had said to the **t** on
11:21 Teacher! The fig **t** you cursed has withered!"
13:28 "Now, learn a lesson from the fig **t**. When its buds
Lk 3:9 every **t** that does not produce good fruit will be
6:43 "A good **t** can't produce bad fruit, and a bad **t** can't produce good fruit.
6:44 A **t** is identified by the kind of fruit it produces.
13:6 "A man planted a fig **t** in his garden and came
13:19 it grows and becomes a **t**, and the birds come
17:6 Lord answered, "you could say to this mulberry **t**,
19:4 and climbed a sycamore **t** beside the road,
21:29 "Notice the fig **t**, or any other **t**.
23:31 For if these things are done when the **t** is green,
Jn 1:48 "I could see you under the fig **t** before Philip
1:50 because I told you I had seen you under the fig **t**?
Ro 11:16 For if the roots of the **t** are holy, the branches will
11:17 But some of these branches from Abraham's **t**,
11:17 who were branches from a wild olive **t**,
11:17 in God's rich nourishment of his special olive **t**.
11:23 God will graft them back into the **t** again.
11:24 a wild olive **t** and graft you into his own good **t**—
11:24 to graft the Jews back into the **t** where they belong.
Gal 3:13 "Cursed is everyone who is hung on a **t**."
Jas 3:12 Can you pick olives from a fig **t** or figs from a
Rev 2:7 Everyone who is victorious will eat from the **t** of
22:2 On each side of the river grew a **t** of life,
22:14 gates of the city and eat the fruit from the **t** of life.
22:19 God will remove that person's share in the **t** of life

TREES (139) [TREE]

Ge 1:11 And let there be **t** that grow seed-bearing fruit.
1:11 the kinds of plants and **t** from which they came."
1:12 The land was filled with seed-bearing plants and **t**,
1:12 and their seeds produced plants and **t** of like kind.
1:29 the earth and all the fruit **t** for your food.
2:9 And the LORD God planted all sorts of **t** in the
2:9 beautiful **t** that produced delicious fruit.
3:8 in the garden, so they hid themselves among the **t**.
18:8 Abraham waited on them there beneath the **t**.
23:17 the cave that was in it, and all the **t** nearby.
30:37 and plane **t** and peeled off strips of the bark to
Ex 9:25 and crops alike. Even all the **t** were destroyed.
10:5 the hailstorm, including all the **t** in the fields.
10:15 and all the fruit on the **t** that had survived the
15:27 there were twelve springs and seventy palm **t**.
Lev 19:23 "When you enter the land and plant fruit **t**,
23:40 On the first day, gather fruit from citrus **t**,
26:4 yield its crops, and the **t** will produce their fruit.
26:20 will yield no crops, and your **t** will bear no fruit.
Nu 13:20 is the soil? Is it fertile or poor? Are there many **t**?
33:9 are twelve springs of water and seventy palm **t**.
Dt 6:11 eat from vineyards and olive **t** you did not plant.
8:8 is a land of wheat and barley, of grapevines, fig **t**,
20:19 a town and the war drags on, do not destroy the **t**. Eat the fruit, but do not cut down the **t**.
20:20 But you may cut down **t** that you know are not
24:20 When you beat the olives from your olive **t**,
28:40 You will grow olive **t** throughout your land,
28:40 for the **t** will drop the fruit before it is ripe.
28:42 Swarms of insects will destroy your **t** and crops.
Jos 10:26 five kings and hung them on five **t** until evening.
10:27 the bodies of the kings to be taken down from the **t**
Jdg 9:8 Once upon a time the **t** decided to elect a king.
9:9 and people, just to wave back and forth over the **t**?'
9:11 sweet fruit just to wave back and forth over the **t**?'
9:13 and people, just to wave back and forth over the **t**?'
9:14 "Then all the **t** finally turned to the thornbush
15:5 He also destroyed their grapevines and olive **t**.
2Sa 5:23 behind them and attack them near the balsam **t**.
5:24 like marching feet in the tops of the balsam **t**,
1Ki 6:29 carvings of cherubim, palm **t**, and open flowers.
6:32 palm **t**, and open flowers, and the doors were
6:35 palm **t**, and open flowers, and the doors were
7:36 and palm **t** decorated the panels and supports
2Ki 3:19 You will cut down all their **t**, stop up all their
3:25 stopped up the springs, and cut down the good **t**.
6:4 arrived at the Jordan, they began cutting down **t**.
18:32 and wine, bread and vineyards, olive **t** and honey
19:23 down its tallest cedars / and its choicest cypress **t**.
1Ch 14:14 behind them and attack them near the balsam **t**.
14:15 like marching feet in the tops of the balsam **t**,
16:33 Let the **t** of the forest rustle with praise before the
27:28 and sycamore-fig **t** in the foothills of Judah.
2Ch 3:5 and decorated with carvings of palm **t** and chains.
Ne 8:15 from olive, wild olive, myrtle, palm, and fig **t**.
10:35 it be a crop from the soil or from our fruit **t**.
Ps 1:3 They are like **t** planted along the riverbank,
37:35 proud and evil people thriving like mighty **t**.
72:16 May the fruit **t** flourish as they do in Lebanon,
92:12 But the godly will flourish like palm **t** / and grow
96:12 with joy! / Let the **t** of the forest rustle with praise
104:12 the streams / and sing among the branches of the **t**.
104:16 The **t** of the LORD are well cared for—
105:33 their grapevines and fig **t** / and shattered all the **t**.
128:3 as vigorous and healthy as young olive **t**.
137:2 hanging them on the branches of the willow **t**.
148:9 mountains and all hills, / fruit **t** and all cedars,
Pr 11:30 The godly are like **t** that bear life-giving fruit,
Ecc 2:5 and parks, filling them with all kinds of fruit **t**.
SS 1:17 shaded by cedar **t** and spreading firs."
2:13 The fig **t** are budding, and the grapevines are in
6:11 "I went down into the grove of nut **t** and out to the
Isa 7:2 trembled with fear, just as **t** shake in a storm.
9:10 with cut stone, the fallen sycamore **t** with cedars."
10:34 enemy as an ax cuts down the forest **t** in Lebanon.
14:8 Even the **t** of the forest—the cypress **t** and the cedars of Lebanon—sing out
37:24 down its tallest cedars / and its choicest cypress **t**.
41:19 I will plant **t**—cedar, acacia, myrtle, olive, cypress,
55:12 and the **t** of the field will clap their hands!
55:13 Where once there were thorns, cypress **t** will grow.
65:22 For my people will live as long as **t** and will have
Jer 6:6 "Cut down the **t** for battering rams.
7:20 Its people, animals, **t**, and crops will be consumed
8:13 of figs and grapes. Their fruit **t** will all die.
17:8 They are like **t** planted along a riverbank,
17:8 Such **t** are not bothered by the heat or worried by
29:28 He said we should plant fruit **t**, because we will be
46:23 They will cut down her people like **t**,"
Eze 15:6 like grapevines growing among the **t** of the forest.
17:24 And all the **t** will know that it is I, the LORD,
20:47 every tree will be burned—green and dry **t** alike.
31:4 so abundant that there was enough for all the **t**
31:5 This great tree towered above all the other **t** around
31:9 it was the envy of all the other **t** of Eden,
31:15 in black and caused the **t** of the field to wilt.
31:16 And all the other proud **t** of Eden, the most
31:18 to which of the **t** of Eden will you compare your
36:30 I will give you great harvests from your fruit **t**
40:16 dividing walls were decorated with carved palm **t**.
41:25 carved cherubim and palm **t** just as on the walls.
41:26 recessed windows decorated with carved palm **t**.
47:7 many **t** were now growing on both sides of the
47:12 All kinds of fruit **t** will grow along both sides of
47:12 The leaves of these **t** will never turn brown
Hos 2:22 the grain, the grapes, and the olive **t** for moisture.
4:13 in the pleasant shade of oaks, poplars, and other **t**.
14:6 will spread out like those of beautiful olive **t**,
Joel 1:7 They have destroyed my grapevines and fig **t**,
1:12 The grapevines and the fig **t** have all withered. The pomegranate **t**, palm **t**, and apple **t**—yes, all the fruit **t**—have dried up.
1:19 has consumed the pastures and burned up all the **t**.
2:22 The **t** will again be filled with luscious fruit;
2:22 fig **t** and grapevines will flourish once more.
Am 2:9 The Amorites were as tall as cedar **t** and strong as
4:9 Locusts devoured all your fig and olive **t**.
7:14 be one. I'm just a shepherd, and I take care of fig **t**.
Na 3:12 that fall into the mouths of those who shake the **t**.
Hab 3:17 Even though the fig **t** have no blossoms, and there
Zec 1:8 standing among some myrtle **t** in a small valley.
1:10 So the man standing among the myrtle **t** explained,
1:11 who was standing among the myrtle **t**, "We have
4:3 And I see two olive **t**, one on each side of the
4:11 "What are these two olive **t** on each side of the
11:2 Weep, you cypress **t**, for all the ruined cedars;
Mt 21:8 and others cut branches from the **t** and spread them
Mk 8:24 very clearly. They look like **t** walking around."
Jn 18:1 with his disciples and entered a grove of olive **t**.
Jude 1:12 They are like **t** without fruit at harvesttime.
Rev 6:13 green figs falling from **t** shaken by mighty winds.
7:1 Not a leaf rustled in the **t**, and the sea became as
7:3 or the **t** until we have placed the seal of God on the
8:7 One-third of the **t** were burned, and all the grass
9:4 They were told not to hurt the grass or plants or **t**
11:4 These two prophets are the two olive **t** and the two

TREMBLE (48) [TREMBLED, TREMBLES, TREMBLING]

Ge 27:33 Isaac began to **t** uncontrollably and said,
Ex 15:14 The nations will hear and **t**; / anguish will grip the
15:15 Edom will be terrified; / the nobles of Moab will **t**.
Dt 2:25 reports about you, they will **t** with dread and fear.'
28:65 And the LORD will cause your heart to **t**,
1Ch 16:30 Let all the earth **t** before him. / The world is firmly
Job 9:6 the earth from its place, and its foundations **t**.
26:5 "The dead **t** in their place beneath the waters.
26:11 The foundations of heaven **t** at his rebuke.
Ps 9:20 Make them **t** in fear, O LORD. / Let them know
27:1 protects me from danger— / so why should I **t**?
46:3 Let the mountains **t** as the waters surge!
96:9 his holy splendor. / Let all the earth **t** before him.
99:1 The LORD is king! / Let the nations **t**! / He sits
102:15 And the nations will **t** before the LORD.
102:15 The kings of the earth will **t** before his glory.
114:7 **T**, O earth, at the presence of the Lord,
119:120 I **t** in fear of you; / I fear your judgments.
Pr 30:21 There are three things that make the earth **t**—
Ecc 12:3 Your limbs will **t** with age, and your strong legs
Isa 5:25 The hills **t**, and the rotting bodies of his people are
19:1 riding on a swift cloud. The idols of Egypt **t**.
32:11 **T**, you women of ease; throw off your unconcern.
41:5 in fear. Remote lands **t** and mobilize for war.
44:8 Do not **t**; do not be afraid. Have I not proclaimed
64:2 to boil, your coming would make the nations **t**.
66:2 and contrite hearts, who **t** at my word.
66:5 this message from the LORD, and **t** at his words:
Jer 4:9 "the king and the officials will **t** in fear.
5:22 Why do you not **t** in my presence? I, the LORD,
23:9 of the false prophets, and I **t** uncontrollably.
33:9 the good I do for my people and will **t** with awe!
Eze 7:27 in despair, and the people's hands will **t** with fear.
12:18 "Son of man, **t** as you eat your food. Drink your
21:7 strong knees will **t** and become as weak as water.
26:15 The whole coastline will **t** at the sound of your fall,
26:18 Now the coastlands **t** at your fall. / The islands are
27:28 "Your cities by the sea **t** as your helmsmen cry out
Da 6:26 should **t** with fear before the God of Daniel.
Hos 10:5 The people of Samaria **t** for their calf idol at
Joel 2:1 Let everyone **t** in fear because the day of the
2:10 earth quakes as they advance, and the heavens **t**.
Am 3:8 The lion has roared—**t** in fear! The Sovereign
8:8 The earth will **t** for your deeds, and everyone will
Hab 3:6 the earth shakes. When he looks, the nations **t**.
Lk 8:47 she began to **t** and fell to her knees before him.
Heb 4:1 so we ought to **t** with fear that some of you might
Jas 2:19 even the demons believe this, and they **t** in terror!

TREMBLED (18) [TREMBLE]

Ex 19:16 loud blast from a ram's horn, and all the people **t**.
Jdg 5:4 marched across the fields of Edom, / the earth **t**
1Sa 4:13 for his heart **t** for the safety of the Ark of God.
21:1 Ahimelech **t** when he saw him. "Why are you
2Sa 22:8 "Then the earth quaked and **t**; / the foundations of
Ezr 9:4 Then all who **t** at the words of the God of Israel
Job 4:14 Fear gripped me; I **t** and shook with terror.
Ps 18:7 Then the earth quaked and **t**; / the foundations of
68:8 the earth **t**, and the heavens poured rain
76:8 the earth **t** and stood silent before you.
77:16 Red Sea saw you, O God, / its waters looked and **t**!
77:18 lightning lit up the world! / The earth **t** and shook.
Isa 7:2 So the hearts of the king and his people **t** with fear,
Jer 4:24 at the mountains and hills, and they **t** and shook.
Eze 19:7 Everyone in the land **t** in fear / when they heard
Da 5:19 and nations and languages **t** before him in fear.
Hab 3:10 The mountains watched and **t**. Onward swept the
3:16 I **t** inside when I heard all this; my lips quivered

TREMBLES (9) [TREMBLE]

Job 21:6 about what I am saying, I shudder. My body **t**.
Ps 97:4 flashes out across the world. / The earth sees and **t**.
104:32 The earth **t** at his glance; / the mountains burst into
119:161 without cause, / but my heart **t** only at your word.
Isa 24:20 It **t** like a tent in a storm. It falls and will not rise
Jer 8:16 The whole land **t** at the approach of the terrible
10:10 everlasting King! The whole earth **t** at his anger.
51:29 Babylon **t** and writhes in pain, for everything the
Na 1:5 the earth **t**, and its people are destroyed.

TREMBLING (27) [TREMBLE]

FEAR AND TREMBLING (2) Ps 55:5; Jer 30:5

Ex 20:18 the mountain, they stood at a distance, **t** with fear.
1Sa 13:7 Saul stayed at Gilgal, and his men were **t** with fear.
2Sa 22:46 their courage / and come **t** from their strongholds.
Ezr 10:9 They were **t** both because of the seriousness of the
Est 5:9 not standing up or **t** nervously before him, he was
Ps 2:11 the LORD with reverent fear, / and rejoice with **t**.
18:45 their courage / and come **t** from their strongholds.
55:5 Fear and **t** overwhelm me. / I can't stop shaking.
Isa 21:4 at night is now a faint memory. I lie awake, **t**.
Jer 30:5 heard the people crying; there is only fear and **t**.
Eze 7:25 Terror and **t** will overcome my people. They will
12:19 They will eat their food with **t** and sip their tiny
26:16 They will sit on the ground **t** with horror at what
Da 10:10 and lifted me, still **t**, to my hands and knees.
10:11 he said this to me, I stood up, still **t** with fear.
Hos 3:5 They will come **t** in awe to the LORD, and they
11:10 a lion, and my people will return **t** from the west.
Mic 7:17 will fear him greatly, **t** in terror at his presence.
Na 2:10 The people stand aghast, their faces pale and **t**.
Hab 2:7 take all you have, while you stand **t** and helpless.
3:7 I see the peoples of Cushan and Midian **t** in terror.
Mk 5:33 **t** at the realization of what had happened to her,
16:8 **t** and bewildered, saying nothing to anyone
Ac 16:29 **T** with fear, the jailer called for lights and ran to
1Co 2:3 I came to you in weakness—timid and **t**.
Heb 12:21 at the sight that he said, "I am terrified and **t**."
2Pe 2:10 to scoff at the glorious ones without so much as **t**.

TREMENDOUS (12)

Ge 26:12 That year Isaac's crops were **t**! He harvested a

Ex 9:23 The LORD sent a **t** hailstorm against all the land
2Ch 28: 8 from Judah and took **t** amounts of plunder,
Est 1: 4 a **t** display of the opulent wealth and glory of his
Job 37: 4 roaring of the thunder—the **t** voice of his majesty.
41:12 "I want to emphasize the **t** strength in the
41:22 "The **t** strength in its neck strikes terror wherever
Mt 18:32 I forgave you that **t** debt because you pleaded with
Mk 13: 1 disciples said, "Teacher, look at these **t** buildings!
Lk 1:51 His mighty arm does **t** things! / How he scatters
19:16 The first servant reported a **t** gain—ten times as
2Co 2:12 News of Christ, the Lord gave me **t** opportunities.

TRENCH (2)

1Ki 18:32 Then he dug a **t** around the altar large enough to
18:35 ran around the altar and even overflowed the **t**.

TRESSES (1)

SS 7: 5 A king is held captive in your queenly **t**.

TRIAL (26) [TRIALS]

Jos 20: 9 revenge prior to standing **t** before the community.
Job 9:32 so I cannot argue with him or take him to **t**.
29:16 and made sure that even strangers received a fair **t**.
Ps 26: 2 Put me on **t**, LORD, and cross-examine me.
109: 6 to turn on him. / Send an accuser to bring him to **t**.
143: 2 Don't bring your servant to **t**! / Compared to you,
Isa 53: 8 From prison and **t** they led him away to his death.
Mal 3: 5 At that time I will put you on **t**. I will be a ready
Mt 10:18 And you must stand **t** before governors and kings
Mk 13:11 But when you are arrested and stand **t**, don't worry
Lk 12:11 "And when you are brought to **t** in the synagogues
22:28 You have remained true to me in my time of **t**.
Jn 18:28 Jesus' **t** before Caiaphas ended in the early hours
Ac 5:21 Then they sent for the apostles to be brought for **t**.
12: 4 to bring Peter out for public **t** after the Passover.
12: 6 The night before Peter was to be placed on **t**,
16:37 "They have publicly beaten us without **t** and jailed
23: 6 And I am on **t** because my hope is in the
24:21 'I am on **t** before you today because I believe in
25: 6 and on the following day Paul's **t** began.
25: 9 to go to Jerusalem and stand **t** before me there?"
25:16 Roman law does not convict people without a **t**.
25:17 "When they came here for the **t**, I called the case
25:20 be willing to stand **t** on these charges in Jerusalem.
26: 6 Now I am on **t** because I am looking forward to the
27:24 Paul, for you will surely stand **t** before Caesar!

TRIALS (13) [TRIAL]

Dt 4:34 himself by rescuing it from another by means of **t**,
Job 42:11 because of all the **t** the LORD had brought
Da 12:10 will be purified, cleansed, and refined by these **t**.
Jn 16:33 Here on earth you will have many **t** and sorrows.
Ac 20:19 I have endured the **t** that came to me from the plots
Ro 5: 3 can rejoice, too, when we run into problems and **t**,
1Pe 1: 6 is necessary for you to endure many **t** for a while.
1: 7 These **t** are only to test your faith, to show that it is
1: 7 faith remains strong after being tried by fiery **t**,
4:12 don't be surprised at the fiery **t** you are going
4:13 because these **t** will make you partners with Christ
2Pe 2: 9 knows how to rescue godly people from their **t**,
Rev 14:13 for they will rest from all their toils and **t**;

TRIBAL (24) [TRIBE]

Nu 1:16 These **t** leaders, heads of their own families,
2: 2 will be located at the center of these **t** compounds.
7: 2 the **t** leaders who had organized the census—
10:25 They served as the rear guard for all the **t** camps.
13: 3 He sent out twelve men, all **t** leaders of Israel,
17: 2 and inscribe each **t** leader's name on his staff.
17: 6 and each of the twelve **t** leaders, including Aaron,
26:56 by lot among the larger and smaller **t** groups."
27: 2 before Moses, Eleazar the priest, the **t** leaders,
32:28 to Eleazar, Joshua, and the **t** leaders of Israel.
36: 3 the total area of our **t** land will be reduced.
Dt 5:23 blazing with fire, all your **t** leaders came to me.
12:14 will choose within one of your **t** territories.
29:10 your **t** leaders, your judges, your officers,
Jos 14: 1 the priest, Joshua son of Nun, and the **t** leaders.
19:51 and the **t** leaders gave as an inheritance to the
1Sa 10:20 So Samuel called the **t** leaders together before the
1Ch 7: 5 All of them were listed in their **t** genealogy.
7:40 among the descendants listed in their **t** genealogy.
8:28 and they were listed in their **t** genealogy.
9: 9 of clans, and they were listed in their **t** genealogy.
9:34 and were listed as prominent leaders in their **t**
Eze 45: 7 the eastern and western boundaries of the **t** areas.
48: 8 will extend as far east and west as the **t** territories,

TRIBE (286) [HALF-TRIBE, TRIBAL, TRIBE'S, TRIBES]

TRIBE OF ASHER (9) Nu 7:72; 10:26; Dt 33:24; Jos 19:24,31; 21:30; Jdg 1:31; 1Ch 12:36; Lk 2:36

TRIBE OF BENJAMIN (37) Nu 7:60; 10:24; Dt 33:12; Jos 18:11,20,21,28; 21:17; Jdg 1:21; 3:15; 20:12,46; 21:1,16; 1Sa 4:12; 9:1; 10:20,21; 2Sa 2:25,31; 3:19; 19:17; 23:29; 1Ch 9:7,9; 11:31; 12:2,29; 2Ch 14:8; Ne 11:7,36; Est 2:5; Ps 7:T; 68:27; Ac 13:21; Ro 11:1; Php 3:5

TRIBE OF DAN (21) Ex 31:6; 35:34; 38:23; Lev 24:11; Nu 7:66; 10:25; Dt 33:22; Jos 19:40,47,48; 21:23; Jdg 1:34; 13:2; 18:1,11,16,22,28,30,31; 1Ch 12:35

TRIBE OF EPHRAIM (12) Nu 7:48; Jos 16:5,8; 17:8,9; 21:20; Jdg 1:29; 12:1,5; 1Ch 12:30; Ps 78:67; Hos 13:1

TRIBE OF GAD (9) Nu 7:42; 10:20; Dt 4:43; 33:20; Jos 13:24,28; 20:8; 21:38; 1Ch 12:8

TRIBE OF ISSACHAR (9) Nu 7:18; 10:15; Jos 19:17,23; 21:28; Jdg 10:1; 1Ki 15:27; 1Ch 7:5; 12:32

TRIBE OF JOSEPH (3) Nu 36:5; Jos 14:4; Eze 47:13

TRIBE OF JUDAH (31) Ex 31:2; 35:30; 38:22; Nu 7:12; Dt 33:7; Jos 7:1,16; 14:6; 15:1,12,20,45,63; 18:14; Jdg 1:16; 2Sa 2:4,10; 1Ki 12:20; 2Ki 17:18; 1Ch 4:27; 9:6; 12:24; 28:4; 2Ch 14:8; 19:11; Ne 11:4; Ps 78:68; Da 1:6; Zep 2:7; Heb 7:14; Rev 5:5

TRIBE OF LEVI (30) Ex 2:1; Nu 1:49; 3:6,15; 4:22; 17:3,8; 18:1,2,21; Dt 10:8; 18:1,5; 33:8; Jos 13:14,33; 21:1,4,10,20, 27; Jdg 19:1; 1Sa 2:30; 6:15; 1Ki 12:31; 1Ch 12:26; 23:14; Eze 44:10; Ac 4:36; Heb 7:16

TRIBE OF MANASSEH (15) Nu 7:54; 10:23; 32:33,39, 41; 34:14; Dt 3:14; 4:43; Jos 13:8; 17:2,7; 20:8; Jdg 1:27; 6:15; 1Ch 12:20

TRIBE OF NAPHTALI (9) Nu 7:78; 10:27; Dt 33:23; Jos 19:32,39; 21:32; Jdg 1:33; 1Ki 7:14; 1Ch 12:34

TRIBE OF REUBEN (12) Nu 7:30; 16:1; Dt 4:43; 33:6,6; Jos 13:15,23,23; 20:8; 21:36; Jdg 5:15,16

TRIBE OF SIMEON (9) Nu 7:36; 10:19; 25:14; Jos 19:1,8,9; Jdg 1:3; 1Ch 4:42; 12:25

TRIBE OF ZEBULUN (7) Nu 7:24; 10:16; Jos 19:10,16; 21:34; Jdg 1:30; 1Ch 12:33

Ge 10: 5 in various lands, each **t** with its own language.
49:16 will govern his people / like any other **t** in Israel.
Ex 2: 1 a man and woman from the **t** of Levi got married.
28:21 and the name of that **t** will be engraved on it as
31: 2 son of Uri, grandson of Hur, of the **t** of Judah.
31: 6 of Ahisamach, of the **t** of Dan, to be his assistant.
35:30 son of Uri, grandson of Hur, of the **t** of Judah.
35:34 and Oholiab son of Ahisamach, of the **t** of Dan,
38:22 son of Uri, grandson of Hur, of the **t** of Judah,
38:23 of the **t** of Dan, a craftsman expert at engraving,
Lev 24:11 She was the daughter of Dibri of the **t** of Dan.
Nu 1: 4 assisted by one family leader from each **t**."
1:49 "Exempt the **t** of Levi from the census; do not
1:52 Each **t** of Israel will have a designated camping
2: 2 "Each **t** will be assigned its own area in the camp,
3: 6 "Call forward the **t** of Levi and present them to
3:15 "Take a census of the **t** of Levi by its families
4: 2 families of the Kohathite division of the Levite **t**.
4:22 and families of the Gershonite division of the **t** of
4:29 families of the Merarite division of the Levite **t**.
7:12 leader of the **t** of Judah, presented his offering.
7:18 leader of the **t** of Issachar, presented his offering.
7:24 leader of the **t** of Zebulun, presented his offering.
7:30 leader of the **t** of Reuben, presented his offering.
7:36 leader of the **t** of Simeon, presented his offering.
7:42 leader of the **t** of Gad, presented his offering.
7:48 leader of the **t** of Ephraim, presented his offering.
7:54 leader of the **t** of Manasseh, presented his offering.
7:60 leader of the **t** of Benjamin, presented his offering.
7:66 leader of the **t** of Dan, presented his offering.
7:72 leader of the **t** of Asher, presented his offering.
7:78 leader of the **t** of Naphtali, presented his offering.
10:15 The **t** of Issachar was led by Nethanel son of Zuar.
10:16 The **t** of Zebulun was led by Eliab son of Helon.
10:19 The **t** of Simeon was led by Shelumiel son of
10:20 The **t** of Gad was led by Eliasaph son of Deuel.
10:23 The **t** of Manasseh was led by Gamaliel son of
10:24 The **t** of Benjamin was led by Abidan son of
10:25 The **t** of Dan headed this group,
10:26 The **t** of Asher was led by Pagiel son of Ocran.
10:27 The **t** of Naphtali was led by Ahira son of Enan.
16: 1 and On son of Peleth, from the **t** of Reuben.
17: 3 Inscribe Aaron's name on the staff of the **t** of Levi,
17: 3 must be one staff for the leader of each ancestral **t**.
17: 8 representing the **t** of Levi, had sprouted,
18: 1 and your relatives from the **t** of Levi will be held
18: 2 "Bring your relatives of the **t** of Levi to assist you
18:21 As for the **t** of Levi, your relatives, I will pay them
24: 2 he saw the people of Israel camped, **t** by **t**.
25:14 the leader of a family from the **t** of Simeon.
26:55 and define the inheritance of each ancestral **t** by
31: 4 From each **t** of Israel, send one thousand men into
31: 5 So they chose one thousand men from each **t** of
31: 6 Moses sent them out, a thousand men from each **t**,
31:26 and the family leaders of each **t** are to make a list
32:33 and half the **t** of Manasseh son of Joseph the
32:39 Then the descendants of Makir of the **t** of
32:41 people of Jair, another clan of the **t** of Manasseh,
34:14 and half the **t** of Manasseh have already received
34:18 Also enlist one leader from each **t** to help them
35: 8 Each **t** will give in proportion to its inheritance."
36: 3 But if any of them marries a man from another **t**,
36: 3 their inheritance of land will go with them to the **t**
36: 4 of land will be added to that of the new **t**,
36: 4 causing it to be lost forever to our ancestral **t**."
36: 5 the LORD: "The men of the **t** of Joseph are right.
36: 6 as long as it is within their own ancestral **t**.
36: 7 None of the inherited land may pass from **t** to **t**,
36: 7 for the inheritance of every **t** must remain fixed as
36: 8 line to inherit property must marry within their **t**,
36: 9 No inheritance may pass from one **t** to another;
36: 9 each **t** of Israel must hold on to its allotted
36:12 of land remained within their ancestral **t**.
Dt 1:13 Choose some men from each **t** who have wisdom,
3:14 Jair, a leader from the **t** of Manasseh,
4:43 Bezer on the wilderness plateau for the **t** of
4:43 Ramoth in Gilead for the **t** of Gad; Golan in Bashan for the **t** of Manasseh.
10: 8 At that time the LORD set apart the **t** of Levi to
18: 1 and the rest of the **t** of Levi will not be given an
18: 5 For the LORD your God chose the **t** of Levi out
29:18 or **t** among you would turn away from the LORD
33: 6 Moses said this about the **t** of Reuben:
33: 6 "Let the **t** of Reuben live and not die out, / even though their **t** is small."
33: 7 Moses said this about the **t** of Judah: / "O LORD,
33: 8 Moses said this about the **t** of Levi: / "O LORD,
33:12 Moses said this about the **t** of Benjamin:
33:20 Moses said this about the **t** of Gad: / "Blessed is
33:22 Moses said this about the **t** of Dan: / "Dan is a
33:23 Moses said this about the **t** of Naphtali:
33:24 Moses said this about the **t** of Asher:
Jos 3:12 Now choose twelve men, one from each **t**.
4: 2 "Now choose twelve men, one from each **t**.
4: 8 one for each **t**, just as the LORD had commanded
7: 1 of the clan of Zerah, and of the **t** of Judah.
7:14 and the LORD will point out the **t** to which the
7:14 That **t** must come forward with its clans,
7:16 the LORD, and the **t** of Judah was singled out.
13: 8 Half the **t** of Manasseh and the tribes of Reuben
13:14 Moses did not assign any land to the **t** of Levi.
13:15 following area to the families of the **t** of Reuben.
13:23 marked the western boundary for the **t** of Reuben.
13:23 as an inheritance to the families of the **t** of Reuben.
13:24 the following area to the families of the **t** of Gad.
13:28 as an inheritance to the families of the **t** of Gad.
13:33 But Moses gave no land to the **t** of Levi,
14: 4 The **t** of Joseph had become two separate tribes—
14: 6 A delegation from the **t** of Judah, led by Caleb son
15: 1 The land assigned to the families of the **t** of Judah
15:12 These are the boundaries for the families of the **t** of
15:20 inheritance given to the families of the **t** of Judah.
15:45 The territory of the **t** of Judah also included all the
15:63 But the **t** of Judah could not drive out the Jebusites,
16: 5 families of the **t** of Ephraim as their inheritance.
16: 8 This is the inheritance given to the families of the **t**
17: 2 to the remaining families within the **t** of Manasseh:
17: 4 us an inheritance along with the men of our **t**."
17: 7 The boundary of the **t** of Manasseh extended from
17: 8 belonged to the **t** of Ephraim.)
17: 9 territory belonged to the **t** of Ephraim.)
18: 4 Select three men from each **t**, and I will send them
18: 6 to decide which section will be assigned to each **t**.
18:10 to determine which **t** should have each section.
18:11 of land went to the families of the **t** of Benjamin.
18:14 one of the towns belonging to the **t** of Judah.
18:20 This was the inheritance for the families of the **t** of
18:21 These were the towns given to the families of the **t**
18:28 given to the families of the **t** of Benjamin.
19: 1 of land went to the families of the **t** of Simeon.
19: 8 This was the inheritance of the families of the **t** of
19: 9 So the **t** of Simeon received an inheritance within
19:10 of land went to the families of the **t** of Zebulun.
19:16 This was the inheritance of the families of the **t** of
19:17 of land went to the families of the **t** of Issachar.
19:23 This was the inheritance of the families of the **t** of
19:24 of land went to the families of the **t** of Asher.
19:31 This was the inheritance of the families of the **t** of
19:32 of land went to the families of the **t** of Naphtali.
19:39 This was the inheritance of the families of the **t** of
19:40 of land went to the families of the **t** of Dan.
19:47 But the **t** of Dan had trouble taking possession of
19:48 This was the inheritance of the families of the **t** of
20: 8 Bezer, in the wilderness plain of the **t** of Reuben;
20: 8 Ramoth in Gilead, in the territory of the **t** of Gad;
20: 8 Golan in Bashan, in the land of the **t** of Manasseh.
21: 1 Then the leaders of the **t** of Levi came to consult
21: 4 of the Kohathite clan within the **t** of Levi,
21:10 of the Kohathite clan within the **t** of Levi,
21:17 From the **t** of Benjamin the priests were given the
21:20 The rest of the Kohathite clan from the **t** of Levi
21:20 and pasturelands from the **t** of Ephraim:
21:23 were allotted to the priests from the **t** of Dan:
21:27 of Gershon, another clan within the **t** of Levi,
21:28 From the **t** of Issachar they received Kishion,
21:30 From the **t** of Asher they received Mishal, Abdon,
21:32 From the **t** of Naphtali they received Kedesh in
21:34 were given the following towns from the **t** of
21:36 From the **t** of Reuben they received Bezer, Jahaz,
21:38 From the **t** of Gad they received Ramoth in Gilead
22: 7 The other half of the **t** was given land west of the
Jdg 1: 1 "Which **t** should attack the Canaanites first?"
1: 3 Judah said to their relatives from the **t** of Simeon,
1:16 When the **t** of Judah left Jericho, the Kenites,
1:21 The **t** of Benjamin, however, failed to drive out the
1:27 The **t** of Manasseh failed to drive out the people
1:29 The **t** of Ephraim also failed to drive out the
1:30 The **t** of Zebulun also failed to drive out the
1:31 The **t** of Asher also failed to drive out the residents
1:33 The **t** of Naphtali also failed to drive out the
1:34 As for the **t** of Dan, the Amorites forced them into
3:15 of the **t** of Benjamin, who was left-handed.
4:11 had moved away from the other members of his **t**
5:15 rushing into the valley. / But in the **t** of Reuben
5:16 In the **t** of Reuben / there was great indecision.
6:15 My clan is the weakest in the whole **t** of Manasseh,
10: 1 He was from the **t** of Issachar but lived in the town
12: 1 Then the **t** of Ephraim mobilized its army
12: 5 "Are you a member of the **t** of Ephraim?"
13: 2 a man named Manoah from the **t** of Dan lived in
14: 3 "Isn't there one woman in our **t** or among all the
18: 1 And the **t** of Dan was trying to find a place to
18:11 So six hundred warriors from the **t** of Dan set out
18:16 As the six hundred warriors from the **t** of Dan
18:19 Isn't it better to be a priest for an entire **t** of Israel

18:22 When the people from the **t** of Dan were quite a
18:28 Then the people of the **t** of Dan rebuilt the town
18:30 This family continued as priests for the **t** of Dan
18:31 So Micah's carved image was worshiped by the **t**
19: 1 There was a man from the **t** of Levi living in a
19:29 Then he sent one piece to each **t** of Israel.
20:10 One tenth of the men from each **t** will be chosen to
20:12 The Israelites sent messengers to the **t** of
20:18 "Which **t** should lead the attack against the people
20:46 So the **t** of Benjamin lost twenty-five thousand
21: 1 in marriage to a man from the **t** of Benjamin.
21: 5 "Was any **t** of Israel not represented when we held
21:16 since all the women of the **t** of Benjamin are dead?
21:17 so that an entire **t** of Israel will not be lost forever.
1Sa 2:30 I had promised that your branch of the **t** of Levi
4:12 A man from the **t** of Benjamin ran from the
6:15 Several men of the **t** of Levi lifted the Ark of the
9: 1 was a rich, influential man from the **t** of Benjamin.
9:21 I'm only from Benjamin, the smallest **t** in Israel,
9:21 is the least important of all the families of that **t**!
10:20 the LORD, and the **t** of Benjamin was chosen.
10:21 Then he brought each family of the **t** of Benjamin
2Sa 2: 4 and crowned him king over the **t** of Judah.
2:10 the **t** of Judah remained loyal to David.
2:25 Abner's troops from the **t** of Benjamin regrouped
2:31 all from the **t** of Benjamin, had been killed.
3:19 Abner also spoke with the leaders of the **t** of
15: 2 they were from, and they would tell him their **t**.
19:12 my relatives, my own **t**, my own flesh and blood!
19:17 A thousand men from the **t** of Benjamin were with
19:42 of Judah replied. "The king is one of our own **t**.
23:29 Ithai son of Ribai from Gibeah (from the **t** of
1Ki 7:14 since his mother was a widow from the **t** of
11:13 And even so, I will let him be king of one **t**,
11:32 But I will leave him one **t** for the sake of my
11:36 His son will have one **t** so that the descendants of
12:20 So only the **t** of Judah remained loyal to the family
12:31 those who were not from the priestly **t** of Levi.
15:27 from the **t** of Issachar, plotted against Nadab
2Ki 17:18 Only the **t** of Judah remained in the land.
1Ch 4:27 So Simeon's **t** never became as large as the **t** of
4:42 Five hundred of these invaders from the **t** of
5: 2 of Judah that became the most powerful **t**
7: 5 from all the clans of the **t** of Issachar was 87,000.
9: 6 In all, 690 families from the **t** of Judah returned.
9: 7 From the **t** of Benjamin came Sallu son of
9: 9 956 families from the **t** of Benjamin returned.
11:31 Ithai son of Ribai from Gibeah (from the **t** of
12: 2 They were all relatives of Saul from the **t** of
12: 8 and experienced warriors from the **t** of Gad also
12:20 Each commanded a thousand troops from the **t** of
12:24 From the **t** of Judah, there were 6,800 warriors
12:25 From the **t** of Simeon, there were 7,100 warriors.
12:26 From the **t** of Levi, there were 4,600 troops.
12:29 From the **t** of Benjamin, Saul's relatives,
12:30 From the **t** of Ephraim, there were 20,800 warriors,
12:32 From the **t** of Issachar, there were 200 leaders of
the **t** with their relatives.
12:33 From the **t** of Zebulun, there were 50,000 skilled
12:34 From the **t** of Naphtali, there were 1,000 officers
12:35 From the **t** of Dan, there were 28,600 warriors,
12:36 From the **t** of Asher, there were 40,000 trained
23:14 of God, his sons were included with the **t** of Levi.
28: 4 For he has chosen the **t** of Judah to rule, and from
2Ch 14: 8 an army of 300,000 warriors from the **t** of Judah,
14: 8 army of 280,000 warriors from the **t** of Benjamin,
19:11 son of Ishmael, a leader from the **t** of Judah,
Ne 11: 4 From the **t** of Judah: Athaiah son of Uzziah,
11: 7 From the **t** of Benjamin: Sallu son of Meshullam,
11:36 in Judah were sent to live with the **t** of Benjamin.
Est 2: 5 He was from the **t** of Benjamin and was a
Ps 7: T the LORD concerning Cush of the **t** of Benjamin.
68:27 Look, the little **t** of Benjamin leads the way.
74: 2 the **t** you redeemed as your own special
78:67 he did not choose the **t** of Ephraim.
78:68 He chose instead the **t** of Judah, / Mount Zion,
Eze 44:10 And the men of the **t** of Levi who abandoned me
45: 8 land to the people, giving an allotment to each **t**.
47:13 The **t** of Joseph will be given two shares of land.
47:14 Otherwise each **t** will receive an equal share.
47:23 the territory of the **t** with whom they now live.
48:31 be three gates, each one named after a **t** of Israel.
Da 1: 6 of the young men chosen, all from the **t** of Judah.
Hos 13: 1 In the past when the **t** of Ephraim spoke,
Zep 2: 7 The few survivors of the **t** of Judah will pasture
Lk 2:36 of Phanuel, of the **t** of Asher, and was very old.
Ac 4:36 He was from the **t** of Levi and came from the
13:21 a man of the **t** of Benjamin, who reigned for forty
Ro 11: 1 of Abraham and a member of the **t** of Benjamin.
Php 3: 5 Jewish family that is a branch of the **t** of Benjamin.
Heb 7:13 one we are talking about belongs to a different **t**,
7:14 I mean is, our Lord came from the **t** of Judah,
7:16 the old requirement of belonging to the **t** of Levi,
Rev 5: 5 Look, the Lion of the **t** of Judah, the heir to
5: 9 from every **t** and language and people and nation.
7: 9 from every nation and **t** and people and language,
13: 7 And he was given authority to rule over every **t**
14: 6 to every nation, **t**, language, and people.

TRIBE'S (1) [TRIBE]

Eze 48:29 that will be set aside for each **t** inheritance,

TRIBES (163) [TRIBE]

ALL THE TRIBES (14) Ex 28:10; Nu 2:17; 10:25; Dt 12:5; 29:21; Jdg 20:2; 2Sa 5:1; 1Ki 8:1; 11:32; 14:21; 2Ch 5:2; 7:8; 12:13; Rev 7:4

TRIBES OF ISRAEL (49) Ge 49:28; Ex 24:4; 28:9,21,29; 39:6,14; Nu 10:4; 30:1; 36:8; Dt 29:21; 33:5; Jos 7:16; 12:7; 14:1; 19:51; 21:1; Jdg 20:2; 21:15; 1Sa 15:17; 2Sa 5:1; 19:9; 1Ki 8:16; 11:32; 12:19; 14:21; 18:31; 2Ki 21:7; 1Ch 27:16, 22; 29:6; 2Ch 6:5; 7:8; 10:19; 11:13; 12:13; 33:7; Ezr 6:17; Ps 78:55; Eze 37:16; 45:1; 47:13,21; 48:1; Mt 19:28; Lk 22:30; Ac 26:7; Rev 7:4; 21:12

TWELVE TRIBES (11) Ge 25:16; 49:28; Ex 24:4; 39:14; Jos 4:5; Ezr 6:17; Eze 47:13; Mt 19:28; Lk 22:30; Ac 26:7; Rev 21:12

Ge 10:20 identified according to their **t**, languages,
10:31 identified according to their **t**, languages,
25:16 the founders of twelve **t** that bore their names,
36:20 These are the names of the **t** that descended from
49:28 These are the twelve **t** of Israel, and these are the
Ex 6:14 are the ancestors of clans from some of Israel's **t**:
24: 4 the altar, one for each of the twelve **t** of Israel.
28: 9 and engrave on them the names of the **t** of Israel.
28:10 naming all the **t** in the order of their ancestors'
28:21 Each stone will represent one of the **t** of Israel,
28:29 Aaron will carry the names of the **t** of Israel on the
39: 6 The stones were engraved with the names of the **t**
39:14 each with the name of one of the twelve **t** of Israel.
Nu 1: 5 These are the **t** and the names of the leaders chosen
2: 3 These are the names of the **t**, their leaders,
2: 9 These three **t** are to lead the way whenever the
2:10 These are the names of the **t**, their leaders,
2:16 These three **t** will be second in line whenever the
2:17 All the **t** are to travel in the same order that they
2:18 These are the names of the **t**, their leaders,
2:25 These are the names of the **t**, their leaders,
10: 4 then only the leaders of the **t** of Israel will come to
10: 5 the **t** on the east side of the Tabernacle will break
10: 6 signal a second time, the **t** on the south will follow.
10:14 The **t** that camped with Judah headed the march
10:18 Then the **t** that camped with Reuben set out with
10:22 Then the **t** that camped with Ephraim set out with
10:25 the **t** that camped with Dan set out under their
10:28 This was the order in which the **t** marched,
13: 2 one leader from each of the twelve ancestral **t**."
13: 4 These were the **t** and the names of the leaders:
17: 2 one from each of Israel's ancestral **t**,
26:53 "Divide the land among the **t** in proportion to their
26:54 Give the larger **t** more land and the smaller **t** less
30: 1 Now Moses summoned the leaders of the **t** of
32: 1 Now the **t** of Reuben and Gad owned vast numbers
32:31 The **t** of Gad and Reuben said again, "Sir, we will
32:33 So Moses assigned to the **t** of Gad, Reuben,
33:54 the land will be divided among your ancestral **t**.
34:13 divided up among the nine and a half remaining **t**.
34:14 The families of the **t** of Reuben, Gad, and half the
34:19 These are the **t** and the names of the leaders:
35: 8 The larger **t** will give more towns to the Levites,
while the smaller **t** will give fewer.
36: 8 The daughters throughout the **t** of Israel who are in
Dt 1:15 and respected men you had selected from your **t**
1:23 so I chose twelve scouts, one from each of your **t**.
3:12 Gilead with its towns, to the **t** of Reuben and Gad.
3:16 And to the **t** of Reuben and Gad I gave the area
3:18 "At that time I gave this command to the **t** that
10: 9 reserved for them among the other Israelite **t**.
12: 5 from among all the **t** for his name to be honored.
16:18 and officials for each of your **t** in all the towns the
18: 1 an inheritance of land like the other **t** in Israel.
18: 5 your **t** to minister in the LORD's name forever.
27:12 the **t** of Simeon, Levi, Judah, Issachar, Joseph,
27:13 And the **t** of Reuben, Gad, Asher, Zebulun, Dan,
29: 8 their land and gave it to the **t** of Reuben and Gad
29:21 The LORD will separate them from all the **t** of
31:28 and officials of your **t** so that I can speak to them
33: 5 people assembled, / when the **t** of Israel gathered."
33:13 Moses said this about the **t** of Joseph: / "May their
33:18 Moses said this about the **t** of Zebulun
Jos 1:12 Then Joshua called together the **t** of Reuben,
1:14 must lead the other **t** across the Jordan to help
4: 5 twelve stones in all, one for each of the twelve **t**.
4:12 The armed warriors from the **t** of Reuben, Gad,
7:14 In the morning you must present yourselves by **t**,
7:16 Early the next morning Joshua brought the **t** of
11:23 special possession, dividing the land among the **t**.
12: 6 And Moses gave their land to the **t** of Reuben,
12: 7 (Joshua allotted this land to the **t** of Israel as their
13: 7 when you divide the land among the nine **t**
13: 8 Half the tribe of Manasseh and the **t** of Reuben
14: 1 The remaining **t** of Israel inherited land in Canaan
14: 2 and a half **t** received their inheritance by means of
14: 3 and a half **t** on the east side of the Jordan River.
14: 4 The tribe of Joseph had become two separate **t**—
17:17 Then Joshua said to the **t** of Ephraim
18: 2 But there remained seven **t** who had not yet been
18: 7 And the **t** of Gad, Reuben, and the half-tribe of
18: 8 and I will assign the land to the **t** by casting sacred
18:11 the territory previously assigned to the **t** of Judah
19:49 After all the land was divided among the **t**,
19:51 and the tribal leaders gave as an inheritance to the **t**
21: 1 son of Nun, and the leaders of the other **t** of Israel.
21: 4 that were originally assigned to the **t** of Judah,
21: 6 received thirteen towns from the **t** of Issachar,
21: 7 Merari received twelve cities from the **t** of Reuben,
21: 9 The Israelites gave the following towns from the **t**
21:16 and Beth-shemesh—nine towns from these two **t**.
22: 1 Then Joshua called together the **t** of Reuben,
22: 3 You have not deserted the other **t**, even though the
22: 4 the LORD your God has given the other **t** rest,
22:12 and prepared to go to war against their brother **t**.
22:13 They crossed the river to talk with the **t** of Reuben,
22:14 high officials of Israel, one from each of the ten **t**,
22:15 they said to the **t** of Reuben, Gad,
22:30 and the high officials heard this from the **t** of
22:32 and the ten high officials left the **t** of Reuben
24:32 located in the territory allotted to the **t** of Ephraim
Jdg 2: 6 each of the **t** left to take possession of the land
4: 6 Assemble ten thousand warriors from the **t** of
4:10 Barak called together the **t** of Zebulun
20: 2 The leaders of all the people and all the **t** of Israel
20: 3 Benjamin that the other **t** had gone up to Mizpah.)
21: 3 has this happened? Now one of our **t** is missing!"
21: 6 "Today we have lost one of the **t** from our family;
21:15 because the LORD had left this gap in the **t** of
21:24 So the assembly of Israel departed by **t**
1Sa 10:19 present yourselves before the LORD by **t**
15:17 are you not the leader of the **t** of Israel?
2Sa 5: 1 Then all the **t** of Israel went to David at Hebron
19: 9 And throughout all the **t** of Israel there was much
19:43 "But there are ten **t** in Israel," the others replied.
1Ki 8: 1 Solomon then summoned the leaders of all the **t**
8:16 I have never chosen a city among the **t** of Israel as
11:28 he put him in charge of the labor force from the **t**
11:31 of Solomon, and I will give ten of the **t** to you!
11:32 which I have chosen out of all the **t** of Israel.
11:35 away from his son and give ten of the **t** to you.
12:19 The northern **t** of Israel have refused to be ruled by
14:21 all the **t** of Israel as the place to honor his name.
18:31 one to represent each of the **t** of Israel,
2Ki 21: 7 the city I have chosen from among all the other **t** of
1Ch 9: 3 People from the **t** of Judah, Benjamin, Ephraim,
12:37 where the **t** of Reuben and Gad and the half-tribe
21: 6 But Joab did not include the **t** of Levi
26:32 and put them in charge of the **t** of Reuben and Gad
27:16 The following were the **t** of Israel and their
27:22 Jeroham These were the leaders of the **t** of Israel.
28: 1 the leaders of the **t**, the commanders of the twelve
29: 6 the leaders of the **t** of Israel, the generals
2Ch 5: 2 Solomon then summoned the leaders of all the **t**
6: 5 I have never chosen a city among the **t** of Israel as
7: 8 with huge crowds gathered from all the **t** of Israel.
10:19 The northern **t** of Israel have refused to be ruled by
11:13 and Levites living among the northern **t** of Israel
12:13 all the **t** of Israel as the place to honor his name.
33: 7 the city I have chosen from among all the other **t** of
Ezr 1: 5 and Levites and the leaders of the **t** of Judah
6:17 as a sin offering for the twelve **t** of Israel.
Ps 78:55 by lot. / He settled the **t** of Israel into their homes.
Jer 25:24 of Arabia, the kings of the nomadic **t** of the desert,
49:31 and attack those self-sufficient nomadic **t**,"
Eze 37:16 'This stick represents Judah and its allied **t**.'
37:16 'This stick represents the northern **t** of Israel.'
37:19 I will take the northern **t** and join them to Judah.
45: 1 "When you divide the land among the **t** of Israel,
47:13 for dividing the land for the twelve **t** of Israel:
47:21 land within these boundaries among the **t** of Israel.
47:22 and they will receive an inheritance among the **t**.
48: 1 "Here is the list of the **t** of Israel and the territory
48:19 Those who come from the various **t** to work in the
48:23 are the territories allotted to the rest of the **t**.
Hos 13: 1 because the other Israelite **t** looked up to them.
Mt 19:28 on twelve thrones, judging the twelve **t** of Israel.
Lk 22:30 will sit on thrones, judging the twelve **t** of Israel.
Ac 26: 7 that is why the twelve **t** of Israel worship God
Rev 7: 4 There were 144,000 who were sealed from all the **t**
11: 9 for three and a half days all peoples, **t**, languages,
21:12 And the names of the twelve **t** of Israel were

TRIBULATION (1) [TRIBULATIONS]

Rev 7:14 "These are the ones coming out of the great **t**.

TRIBULATIONS (1) [TRIBULATION]

Ac 14:22 enter into the Kingdom of God through many **t**.

TRIBUTARIES, TRIBUTARY [KJV] See (FORCED) LABOR, VASSAL

TRIBUTE (25)

2Sa 8: 2 David's servants and brought him **t** money.
8: 6 David's subjects and brought him **t** money.
1Ki 4:21 The conquered peoples of those lands sent **t** money
2Ki 3: 4 They used to pay the king of Israel an annual **t** of
17: 3 so Israel was forced to pay heavy annual **t** to
17: 4 and by refusing to pay the annual **t** to Assyria.
18: 7 the king of Assyria and refused to pay him **t**.
18:14 I will pay whatever **t** money you demand if you
23:33 7,500 pounds of silver and 75 pounds of gold as **t**.
23:35 and gold demanded as **t** by Pharaoh Neco,
24: 1 and paid him **t** for three years but then rebelled.
1Ch 18: 2 David's subjects and brought him **t** money.
18: 6 David's subjects and brought him **t** money.
2Ch 17:11 of the Philistines brought him gifts and silver as **t**,
26: 8 The Meunites paid annual **t** to him, and his fame
27: 5 he received from them an annual **t** of 7,500 pounds
28:21 and gave them to the king of Assyria as **t**.
36: 3 who demanded a **t** from Judah of 7,500 pounds of
Ezr 4:13 for the Jews will then refuse to pay their **t**,
4:20 of the Euphrates River and have received vast **t**,
Est 10: 1 King Xerxes imposed **t** throughout his empire,
Ps 68:29 The kings of the earth are bringing **t** / to your
68:30 Humble those who demand **t** from us.
72:10 kings of Tarshish and the islands / will bring him **t**.
76:11 Let everyone bring **t** to the Awesome One.

TRICK (9) [TRICKED, TRICKERY, TRICKING, TRICKS]
Ge 27:12 He'll see that I'm trying to **t** him, and then he'll
29:25 it was Leah! "What sort of **t** is this?"
Jer 6:13 they **t** others to get what does not belong to them.
8:10 they **t** others to get what does not belong to them.
29: 8 and mediums who are there in Babylon **t** you.
Da 2: 8 The king replied, "I can see through your **t**!
Mt 22:18 "Whom are you trying to fool with your **t**
Mk 12:15 "Who are you trying to fool with your **t** questions?
2Co 4: 2 We do not try to **t** anyone, and we do not distort

TRICKED (6) [TRICK]
Ge 3:13 "The serpent **t** me," she replied. "That's why I
27:35 Isaac said, "Your brother was here, and he **t** me.
31: 7 but he has **t** me, breaking his wage agreement with
Ex 32:12 'God **t** them into coming to the mountains so he
1Sa 19:17 "Why have you **t** me and let my enemy escape?"
Jer 29:31 not send him and has **t** you into believing his lies,

TRICKERY (8) [TRICK]
Ge 29:25 years for Rachel. What do you mean by this **t**?"
Pr 26:26 While their hatred may be concealed by **t**, it will
Isa 29:21 And those who use **t** to pervert justice and tell lies
Hab 1: 4 and justice is perverted with bribes and **t**.
Lk 20:23 He saw through their **t** and said,
Ac 13:10 son of the Devil, full of every sort of **t** and villainy,
2Co 12:16 think I was sneaky and took advantage of you by **t**.
1Th 2: 3 preaching with any deceit or impure purposes or **t**.

TRICKING (1) [TRICK]
Nu 25:18 because they assaulted you with deceit by **t** you

TRICKLETH [KJV] See FLOW

TRICKLING (1)
Job 28:11 They dam up the **t** streams and bring to light the

TRICKS (2) [TRICK]
Isa 32: 7 The smooth **t** of evil people will be exposed,
Eph 6:11 stand firm against all strategies and **t** of the Devil.

TRIED (93) [TRY]
Ge 34: 3 for Dinah was strong, and he **t** to win her affection.
37:35 His family all **t** to comfort him, but it was no use.
38:23 "We **t** our best to send her the goat.
39:14 she sobbed. "He **t** to rape me, but I screamed.
39:17 "That Hebrew slave you've had around here **t** to
Ex 8:18 Pharaoh's magicians **t** to do the same thing with
Nu 13:30 But Caleb **t** to encourage the people as they stood
22:15 Then Balak **t** again. This time he sent a larger
22:25 it **t** to squeeze by and crushed Balaam's foot
35:12 The slayer must not be killed before being **t** by the
Dt 13:10 because they have **t** to draw you away from the
23: 4 they **t** to hire Balaam son of Beor from Pethor in
Jos 20: 6 and be **t** by the community and found innocent.
Jdg 12: 5 and whenever a fugitive from Ephraim **t** to go back
1Sa 4:20 but before she passed away the midwives **t** to
13: 6 they lost their nerve entirely and **t** to hide in caves,
2Sa 4: 8 the son of your enemy Saul who **t** to kill you.
15: 5 And when people **t** to bow before him,
18: 9 He **t** to escape on his mule, but as he rode beneath
21: 2 but Saul, in his zeal, had **t** to wipe them out.
1Ki 3:21 And in the morning when I **t** to nurse my son,
11:40 Solomon **t** to kill Jeroboam, but he fled to King
16:21 Half the people **t** to make Tibni son of Ginath their
18: 4 Once when Jezebel had **t** to kill all the LORD's
2Ki 5:13 But his officers **t** to reason with him and said,
20: 3 how I have always **t** to be faithful to you and do
2Ch 14: 6 No one **t** to make war against him at this time,
Ezr 4: 4 Then the local residents **t** to discourage
Ne 6:14 and all the prophets like her who have **t** to
Est 8: 7 on the gallows because he **t** to destroy the Jews.
Job 31:33 Have I **t** to hide my sins as people normally do,
32:22 And if I **t**, my Creator would soon do away with
Ps 40: 5 If I **t** to recite all your wonderful deeds, / I would
71:24 all day long, / for everyone who **t** to hurt me
73:16 So I **t** to understand why the wicked prosper.
95: 9 For there your ancestors **t** my patience;
119:10 I have **t** my best to find you— / don't let me
Ecc 2: 4 I also **t** to find meaning by building huge homes
7:23 All along I have **t** my best to let wisdom guide my
8:16 I **t** to observe everything that goes on all across the
SS 5: 4 "My lover **t** to unlatch the door, and my heart
8: 7 If a man **t** to buy love with everything he owned,
Isa 24:22 and put in prison until they are **t** and condemned.
38: 3 how I have always **t** to be faithful to you and do
Jer 7:26 people have not listened to me or even **t** to hear.
18:20 for them and **t** to protect them from your anger.
25: 4 but you have not listened or even **t** to hear.
Eze 24:13 because I **t** to cleanse you but you refused,
Da 5:15 and enchanters have **t** to read this writing on the
6:14 the law, and he **t** to find a way to save Daniel.
Ob 1:14 at the crossroads, killing those who **t** to escape.
Jnh 1:13 the sailors **t** even harder to row the boat ashore.
Mic 6: 5 how King Balak of Moab **t** to have you cursed
Mt 19: 3 and **t** to trap him with this question:
22:35 in religious law, **t** to trap him with this question:
Mk 3:21 was happening, they **t** to take him home with them.
7:24 He **t** to keep it secret that he was there, but he
9:30 through Galilee. Jesus **t** to avoid all publicity
10: 2 and **t** to trap him with this question:
14:51 in a linen nightshirt. When the mob **t** to grab him,
Lk 1:29 Mary **t** to think what the angel could mean.
5:18 They **t** to push through the crowd to Jesus,
9: 9 I hear such strange stories?" And he **t** to see him.
9:49 We **t** to stop him because he isn't in our group."
18:39 The crowds ahead of Jesus **t** to hush the man,
19: 3 He **t** to get a look at Jesus, but he was too short to
20:20 They **t** to get Jesus to say something that could be
Jn 5:18 So the Jewish leaders **t** all the more to kill him.
7:11 The Jewish leaders **t** to find him at the festival
7:30 Then the leaders **t** to arrest him; but no one laid a
10:39 Once again they **t** to arrest him, but he got away
19:12 Then Pilate **t** to release him, but the Jewish leaders
Ac 7:26 He **t** to be a peacemaker. 'Men,' he said, 'you are
9:26 he **t** to meet with the believers, but they were all
19:13 out evil spirits **t** to use the name of the Lord Jesus.
19:15 But when they **t** it on a man possessed by an evil
19:33 He motioned for silence and **t** to speak in defense.
22:25 to whip a Roman citizen who hasn't even been **t**?"
25:10 official Roman court, so I ought to be **t** right here.
26:21 Temple for preaching this, and they **t** to kill me.
27:30 Then the sailors **t** to abandon the ship;
28:18 The Romans **t** me and wanted to release me,
28:31 the Lord Jesus Christ. And no one **t** to stop him.
Ro 9:31 who **t** so hard to get right with God by keeping the
Gal 1:14 and I **t** as hard as possible to follow all the old
1:23 us now preaches the very faith he **t** to destroy!"
2:19 For when I **t** to keep the law, I realized I could
1Th 2:17 we **t** very hard to come back because of our intense
2:18 and I, Paul, **t** again and again, but Satan prevented
Heb 3: 9 There your ancestors **t** my patience, / even though
1Pe 1: 7 So if your faith remains strong after being **t** by
2Pe 3: 1 and in both of them I have **t** to stimulate your
Rev 12:15 Then the dragon **t** to drown the woman with a

TRIES (13) [TRY]
Nu 30:15 than a day and then **t** to nullify a vow or pledge,
Dt 25:11 and the wife of one **t** to rescue her husband by
Jos 6:26 who **t** to rebuild the city of Jericho. / At the cost of
2Sa 14:14 That is why God **t** to bring us back when we have
2Ki 11:15 of the Temple, and kill anyone who **t** to rescue her.
18:32 "Don't listen to Hezekiah when he **t** to mislead
2Ch 23:14 of the Temple, and kill anyone who **t** to rescue her.
Pr 15:18 starts fights; a cool-tempered person **t** to stop them.
28:22 A greedy person **t** to get rich quick, but it only
Isa 59:15 and anyone who **t** to live a godly life is soon
Am 3:12 "A shepherd who **t** to rescue a sheep from a lion's
Rev 11: 5 If anyone **t** to harm them, fire flashes from the
11: 5 This is how anyone who **t** to harm them must die.

TRIM (3) [TRIMMED, TRIMS]
Lev 19:27 "Do not **t** off the hair on your temples or clip the
21: 5 **t** the edges of their beards, or cut their bodies.
Eze 44:20 it off completely. Instead, they must **t** it regularly.

TRIMMED (2) [TRIM]
2Sa 19:24 or clothes nor **t** his beard since the day the king left
1Ki 7: 9 of stone, cut and **t** to exact measure on all sides.

TRIMS (1) [TRIM]
Ex 30: 7 "Every morning when Aaron **t** the lamps, he must

TRIP (24) [TRIPS]
Ge 27:30 left his father, Esau returned from his hunting **t**.
43:20 to him, "Sir, after our first **t** to Egypt to buy food,
Ex 5: 3 "Let us take a three-day **t** into the wilderness
8:27 We must take a three-day **t** into the wilderness to
Nu 9:13 who are ceremonially clean and not away on a **t**,
Jos 9:13 and sandals are worn out from our long, hard **t**."
1Sa 1:21 and their children went on their annual **t** to offer a
28:22 so you can regain your strength for the **t** back."
1Ki 18:27 Or maybe he is away on a **t**, or he is asleep
Pr 7:19 my husband is not home. He's away on a long **t**.
24:16 They may **t** seven times, but each time they will
Mt 25:14 be illustrated by the story of a man going on a **t**.
25:15 proportion to their abilities—and then left on his **t**.
25:19 "After a long time their master returned from his **t**
Mk 10:17 As he was starting out on a **t**, a man came running
13:34 with that of a man who left home to go on a **t**.
Lk 10:30 "A Jewish man was traveling on a **t** from
15:13 all his belongings and took a **t** to a distant land,
Ac 14:27 the church together and reported about their **t**,
28:10 board all sorts of things we would need for the **t**.
2Co 1:16 on my way to Macedonia and again on my return **t**.
Col 4: 8 I have sent him on this special **t** to let you know
Tit 3:13 to help Zenas the lawyer and Apollos with their **t**.
Rev 2:14 who showed Balak how to **t** up the people of

TRIPLE-BRAIDED (1) [THREE]
Ecc 4:12 are even better, for a **t** cord is not easily broken.

TRIPS (1) [TRIP]
1Sa 21: 5 And since they stay clean even on ordinary **t**,

TRIUMPH (21) [TRIUMPHAL, TRIUMPHANT, TRIUMPHANTLY, TRIUMPHED]
Nu 24:18 will be conquered, / while Israel continues on in **t**.
Jdg 11:31 out of my house to greet me when I return in **t**.
15:14 arrived at Lehi, the Philistines came shouting in **t**.
1Sa 17:52 Then the Israelites gave a great shout of **t**
2Sa 1:20 streets of Ashkelon, / or the pagans will laugh in **t**.
Job 17: 4 their minds to understanding, but do not let them **t**.
20: 5 the **t** of the wicked has been short-lived and the joy
Ps 30: 1 You refused to let my enemies **t** over me.
35:26 and disgraced. / May those who **t** over me
41:11 for you have not let my enemy **t** over me.
54: 7 my troubles / and help me to **t** over my enemies.
59:10 He will let me look down in **t** on all my enemies.
60: 8 my slave. / I will shout in **t** over the Philistines."
108: 9 my slave. / I will shout in **t** over the Philistines."
118: 7 help me. / I will look in **t** at those who hate me.
118:16 The strong right arm of the LORD is raised in **t**.
Isa 50: 7 determined to do his will. And I know that I will **t**.
Jer 39: 3 army came in and sat in **t** at the Middle Gate:
51:14 and they will lift their shouts of **t** over you."
Zec 9: 9 Shout in **t**, O people of Jerusalem! Look, your king
Ro 5:17 gracious gift of righteousness will live in **t** over sin

TRIUMPHAL (1) [TRIUMPH]
2Co 2:14 and leads us along in Christ's **t** procession.

TRIUMPHANT (1) [TRIUMPH]
Dt 33:29 He is your protecting shield / and your **t** sword!

TRIUMPHANTLY (2) [TRIUMPH]
Jdg 9:38 Then Zebul turned on him **t**. "Now where is that
Ps 112: 8 and fearless / and can face their foes **t**.

TRIUMPHED (7) [TRIUMPH]
Ex 15: 1 "I will sing to the LORD, for he has **t** gloriously;
15:21 "I will sing to the LORD, for he has **t** gloriously;
Dt 32:27 might misunderstand and say, / "Our power has **t**!
1Sa 17:50 So David **t** over the Philistine giant with only a
Ne 9:32 when the kings of Assyria first **t** over us until now.
Isa 10:26 as he did when Gideon **t** over the Midianites at the
La 1: 9 my deep misery," she cries. "The enemy has **t**."

TRIVIAL (1)
Est 7: 4 for that would have been a matter too **t** to warrant

TROAS (6)
Ac 16: 8 they went on through Mysia to the city of **T**.
16:11 We boarded a boat at **T** and sailed straight across
20: 5 They went ahead and waited for us at **T**.
20: 6 in Macedonia and five days later arrived in **T**,
2Co 2:12 when I came to the city of **T** to preach the Good
2Ti 4:13 be sure to bring the coat I left with Carpus at **T**.

TROD (1) [TREAD]
Rev 19:15 and he **t** the winepress of the fierce wrath of

TRODDEN (2) [TREAD]
Isa 63: 3 "I have **t** the winepress alone; no one was there to
Rev 14:20 And the grapes were **t** in the winepress outside the

TRODE, TRODDEN [KJV] See BEATEN, CONQUERING, TROD, SET (FOOT), SPURNED, TRAMPLE(D)

TROOPS (161)
Ex 14: 6 So Pharaoh called out his **t** and led the chase in his
17:13 and his **t** were able to crush the army of Amalek.
Nu 2: 3 their leaders, and the number of their available **t**:
2: 9 So the total of all the **t** on Judah's side of the camp
2:10 their leaders, and the number of their available **t**:
2:16 So the total of all the **t** on Reuben's side of the
2:18 their leaders, and the number of their available **t**:
2:24 So the total of all the **t** on Ephraim's side of the
2:25 their leaders, and the number of their available **t**:
2:31 So the total of all the **t** on Dan's side of the camp is
2:32 the **t** of Israel listed by their families totaled
32:21 and if your **t** cross the Jordan until the LORD has
Dt 20: 2 the priest will come forward to speak with the **t**.
20: 5 "Then the officers of the army will address the **t**
20: 9 the officers have finished saying this to their **t**,
Jos 10: 5 They moved all their **t** into place and attacked
1Sa 4:17 "Thousands of Israelite **t** are dead on the
8:12 Some will be commanders of his **t**, while others
13: 2 Saul selected three thousand special **t** from the
13: 6 the men of Israel saw the vast number of enemy **t**,
13: 8 Saul realized that his **t** were rapidly slipping away.
13:15 but the rest of the **t** went with Saul to meet the
13:16 and the **t** with them were staying at Geba,
14:34 Then go out among the **t** and tell them,
14:34 it.' " So that night all the **t** brought their animals
15: 4 There were 200,000 **t** in addition to 10,000 men
15:21 Then my **t** brought in the best of the sheep
17: 2 Saul countered by gathering his **t** near the valley of
18:13 but David faithfully led his **t** into battle.
18:16 he was so successful at leading his **t** into battle.
19: 8 and David led his **t** against the Philistines.
19:11 Then Saul sent **t** to watch David's house.
19:14 When the **t** came to arrest David, she told them he
19:20 he sent **t** to capture him. But when they arrived
19:21 he sent other **t**, but they, too, prophesied!
24: 2 So Saul chose three thousand special **t** from
26: 2 So Saul took three thousand of his best **t** and went
29: 2 As the Philistine rulers were leading out their **t** in
30:10 the pursuit with his four hundred remaining **t**.
30:11 Some of David's **t** found an Egyptian man in a
30:20 His **t** rounded up all the flocks and herds and drove
31: 6 and his **t** all died together that same day.
2Sa 2:12 One day Abner led some of Ishbosheth's **t** from
2:13 Joab son of Zeruiah led David's **t** from Hebron,

2:25 Abner's t from the tribe of Benjamin regrouped
2:28 and his men stopped chasing the t of Israel.
3:22 Joab and some of David's t returned from a raid,
5: 6 then led his t to Jerusalem to fight against the
5: 8 he told his own t, "Go up through the water tunnel
5:21 idols there, so David and his t confiscated them.
6: 1 Then David mobilized thirty thousand special t.
10: 8 The Ammonite t drew up their battle lines at the
10: 9 fight on two fronts, he chose the best t in his army.
10:13 When Joab and his t attacked, the Arameans began
10:16 they were joined by additional Aramean t
10:16 These t arrived at Helam under the command of
11:20 and ask, 'Why did the t go so close to the city?
15:18 to let David's t move past to lead the way.
15:20 Go on back and take your t with you, and may the
17: 2 He and his t will panic, and everyone will run
17: 8 He won't be spending the night among the t.
17: 9 of your men fall, there will be panic among your t,
17:11 And I think that you should personally lead the t.
17:24 and was leading his t across the Jordan River.
18: 1 now appointed generals and captains to lead his t.
18: 2 The king told his t, "I am going out with you."
18: 3 us die—it will make no difference to Absalom's t;
18: 4 gate of the city as all the divisions of t passed by.
18: 5 And all the t heard the king give this order to his
18: 7 and the Israelite t were beaten back by David's
19: 2 As the t heard of the king's deep grief for his son,
19: 7 Now go out there and congratulate the t, for I
20: 5 So Amasa went out to notify the t, but it took him
20: 6 take my t and chase after him before he gets into a
20:11 One of Joab's young officers shouted to Amasa's t,
20:22 the trumpet and called his t back from the attack,
1Ki 12:21 armies of Judah and Benjamin—180,000 select t—
20:14 The t of the provincial commanders will do it."
20:15 So Ahab mustered the t of the 232 provincial
20:17 the t of the provincial commanders marched out of
20:17 to him, "Some t are coming from Samaria."
22: 4 and I are brothers, and my t are yours to command.
22:34 however, randomly shot an arrow at the Israelite t,
22:36 as the sun was setting, the cry ran through his t:
2Ki 3: 7 and I are brothers, and my t are yours to command.
3: 9 The king of Edom and his t joined them, and all
6: 9 for the Arameans are planning to mobilize their t
6:13 where Elisha is, and we will send t to seize him."
6:15 and went outside, there were t, horses,
9:17 shouted to Joram, "I see a company of t coming!"
11:15 the commanders who were in charge of the t,
13: 7 Jehoahaz's army was reduced to fifty mounted t,
18:24 even the weakest contingent of my master's t,
19:35 the Assyrian camp and killed 185,000 Assyrian t.
24:16 He also took seven thousand of the best t and one
25:11 and the t who had declared their allegiance to the
1Ch 11: 6 David had said to his t, "Whoever leads the attack
12:14 among them could take on a hundred regular t,
12:18 join him, and he made them officers over his t.
12:20 Each commanded a thousand t from the tribe of
12:26 From the tribe of Levi, there were 4,600 t.
12:37 there were 120,000 t armed with every kind of
14:11 So David and his t went to Baal-perazim
19: 6 silver to hire chariots and t from Aram-naharaim,
19: 7 where they were joined by the Ammonite t that
19: 9 The Ammonite t drew up their battle lines at the
19:10 fight on two fronts, he chose the best t in his army.
19:14 When Joab and his t attacked, the Arameans began
19:16 so they summoned additional Aramean t from the
19:16 These t arrived under the command of Shobach,
19:17 and positioned his t in battle formation.
19:17 Then he engaged the enemy t in battle, and they
27: 1 for one month and had twenty-four thousand t.
27: 2 There were twenty-four thousand t in his division.
27: 4 There were twenty-four thousand t in his division,
27: 5 There were twenty-four thousand t in his division.
27: 7 There were twenty-four thousand t in his division.
27: 8 There were twenty-four thousand t in his division.
27: 9 There were twenty-four thousand t in his division.
27:10 There were twenty-four thousand t in his division.
27:11 There were twenty-four thousand t in his division.
27:12 There were twenty-four thousand t in his division.
27:13 There were twenty-four thousand t in his division.
27:14 There were twenty-four thousand t in his division.
27:15 There were twenty-four thousand t in his division.
2Ch 11: 1 armies of Judah and Benjamin—180,000 select t—
13:17 500,000 casualties among Israel's finest t that day.
13:19 Abijah and his army pursued Jeroboam's t
17: 2 He stationed t in all the fortified cities of Judah,
17:13 and stationed an army of seasoned t at Jerusalem.
17:14 there were 300,000 t organized in units of one
17:15 was Jehohanan, who commanded 280,000 t.
17:16 with 200,000 t under his command.
17:17 there were 200,000 t equipped with bows
17:19 These were the t stationed in Jerusalem to serve
18: 3 and I are brothers, and my t are yours to command.
18:33 however, randomly shot an arrow at the Israelite t,
23:14 the commanders who were in charge of the t,
25: 7 and said, "O king, do not hire t from Israel,
25: 8 If you let them go with your t into battle, you will
25:10 So Amaziah discharged the hired t and sent them
25:11 where they killed ten thousand Edomite t from
25:13 the hired t that Amaziah had sent home raided
26:13 The army consisted of 307,500 men, all elite t.
28: 6 killed 120,000 of Judah's t because they had
Job 19:12 His t advance. They build up roads to attack me.
29:25 I lived as a king among his t and as one who
Ps 56: 1 have mercy on me. / The enemy t press in on me.
60:12 You sent t to ride across our broken bodies.
Isa 10:16 will send a plague among your proud t,
36: 9 even the weakest contingent of my master's t,
37:36 the Assyrian camp and killed 185,000 Assyrian t.
Jer 8:17 "I will send these enemy t among you like
52:15 and the t who had declared their allegiance to the
Eze 38: 4 I will mobilize your t and cavalry and make you a
Da 11:15 The best t of the south will not be able to stand in
Mic 5: 1 Mobilize! Marshal your t! The enemy is laying
Na 3:13 Your t will be as weak and helpless as women.
Ac 21:32 the mob saw the commander and the t coming,
23:27 were about to kill him when I arrived with the t.
Rev 9:16 They led an army of 200 million mounted t—

TROPHIMUS (3)

Ac 20: 4 and Tychicus and T, who were from the province
21:29 that day they had seen him in the city with T,
2Ti 4:20 stayed at Corinth, and I left T sick at Miletus.

TROUBLE (168) [TROUBLED, TROUBLEMAKER, TROUBLEMAKERS, TROUBLES, TROUBLING]

DAY OF TROUBLE (5) 2Ki 19:3; Isa 37:3; Jer 16:19; 51:2; Eze 7:7

TIME OF TROUBLE (4) Ne 9:27; Job 38:23; Jer 30:7; Ob 1:14

Ge 42:21 That's why this t has come upon us."
Ex 5:19 foremen could see that they were in serious t.
Nu 23:21 is in sight for Jacob; / no t is in store for Israel.
Dt 31:17 Terrible t will come down on them, so that they
Jos 6:18 and you will bring t on all Israel.
7:25 said to Achan, "Why have you brought t on us?
7:25 The LORD will now bring t on you." And all the
7:26 place has been called the Valley of T ever since.
19:47 But the tribe of Dan had t taking possession of
Jdg 9:23 God stirred up t between Abimelech
11: 7 Why do you come to me now when you're in t?"
1Sa 14:29 "My father has made t for us all!"
14:39 But no one would tell him what the t was.
20:21 the LORD lives, that all is well, and there is no t.
22: 2 men who were in t or in debt or who were just
25:17 for there is going to be t for our master and his
28:15 "Because I am in deep t," Saul replied.
30: 6 David was now in serious t because his men were
2Sa 13: 4 One day Jonadab said to Amnon, "What's the t?
14: 5 "What's the t?" the king asked. "I am a widow,"
1Ki 2:13 "Have you come to make t?" she asked him.
8:37 the land besieging their towns—whatever the t is—
11:25 Solomon's reign, and he made t, just as Hadad did.
12:28 "It is too much t for you to worship in Jerusalem.
18:18 "I have made no t for Israel," Elijah replied.
20: 7 said to them, "Look how this man is stirring up t!
2Ki 6:33 "It is the LORD who has brought this t on us!
14:10 Why stir up t that will bring disaster on you
19: 3 This is a day of t, insult, and disgrace.
1Ch 4:10 in all that I do, and keep me from all t and pain!"
2Ch 6:28 the land besieging their towns—whatever the t is—
25:19 Why stir up t that will bring disaster on you
28:22 And when t came to King Ahaz, he became even
Ne 1: 3 They are in great t and disgrace. The wall of
9:27 But in their time of t they cried to you, and you
9:32 Great t has come upon us and upon our kings
Est 6: 1 That night the king had t sleeping, so he ordered an
Job 3:10 mother's womb, for letting me be born to all this t.
3:26 I have no rest; instead, only t comes."
4: 5 But now when t strikes, you faint and are broken.
4: 8 My experience shows that those who plant t
5: 6 from the soil, and t does not sprout from the earth.
5: 7 People are born for t as predictably as sparks fly
12: 5 People who are at ease mock those in t. They give
13:10 you will be in serious t with him if even in your
14: 1 is humanity! How short is life, and how full of t!
15:35 They conceive t and evil, and their hearts give
18:11 surround the wicked and t them at every step.
20:22 "In the midst of plenty, he will run into t,
20:23 May God give him a bellyful of t. May God rain
21:17 They rarely have t, and God skips them when he
27: 9 Will God listen to their cry when t comes upon
30:25 Did I not weep for those in t? Was I not deeply
34:29 When he is quiet, who can make t? But when he
36: 9 he takes the t to show them the reason. He shows
38:23 I have reserved it for the time of t, for the day of
Ps 7:14 wicked conceive evil; / they are pregnant with t
7:16 They make t, / but it backfires on them.
9: 9 a shelter for the oppressed, / a refuge in times of t.
10: 6 ever happen to us! / We will be free of t forever!"
10: 7 T and evil are on the tips of their tongues.
10:14 But you do see the t and grief they cause.
20: 1 In times of t, may the LORD respond to your cry.
22:11 Do not stay so far from me, / for t is near, / and no
25:18 Feel my pain and see my t. / Forgive all my sins.
32: 7 you are my hiding place; / you protect me from t.
35:15 But they are glad now that I am in t;
37:39 saves the godly; / he is their fortress in times of t.
40:14 put to shame. / May those who take delight in my t
41: 1 the poor. / The LORD rescues them in times of t.
46: 1 and strength, / always ready to help in times of t.
49: 5 There is no need to fear when times of t come,
50:15 Trust me in your times of t, / and I will rescue you,
55: 3 and wicked threats. / They bring t on me,
66:14 vows you heard me make / when I was in deep t.
69:17 answer me quickly, for I am in deep t!
70: 2 put to shame. / May those who take delight in my t
73:14 All I get is t all day long; / every morning brings
77: 2 When I was in deep t, / I searched for the Lord.
81: 7 You cried to me in t, and I saved you; / I answered
86: 7 I will call to you whenever t strikes, / and you will
90:10 the best of these years are filled with pain and t;
91:15 call on me, I will answer; / I will be with them in t.
102: T A prayer of one overwhelmed with t, pouring out
106:32 angered the LORD, / causing Moses serious t.
107: 6 "LORD, help!" they cried in their t, / and he
107:13 "LORD, help!" they cried in their t, / and he
107:19 "LORD, help!" they cried in their t, / and he
107:28 "LORD, help!" they cried in their t, / and he
107:39 through oppression, t, and sorrow,
116: 3 the grave overtook me. / I saw only t and sorrow.
119:157 Many persecute and t me, / yet I have not swerved
140: 2 plot evil in their hearts / and stir up t all day long.
Pr 1:26 So I will laugh when you are in t! I will mock you
1:27 when you are engulfed by t, and when anguish
6:14 perverted hearts plot evil. They stir up t constantly.
10:10 People who wink at wrong cause t, but a bold
10:14 but the babbling of a fool invites t.
11: 8 from danger, but he lets the wicked fall into t.
11:29 Those who bring t on their families inherit only the
12:13 by their own words, but the godly escape such t.
12:21 the godly, but the wicked have their fill of t.
13:13 who despise advice will find themselves in t;
13:17 An unreliable messenger stumbles into t, but a
13:21 T chases sinners, while blessings chase the
14: 3 but the words of the wise keep them out of t.
14:35 they are doing; he is angry with those who cause t.
15: 6 the godly, but the earnings of the wicked bring t.
15:15 For the poor, every day brings t; for the happy
15:19 A lazy person has t all through life; the path of the
17:20 will not prosper; the twisted tongue tumbles into t.
18: 7 of fools are their ruin; their lips get them into t.
21:23 If you keep your mouth shut, you will stay out of t.
24: 2 and their words are always stirring up t.
24:17 Do not rejoice when your enemies fall into t.
28:14 but the stubborn are headed for serious t.
28:20 who wants to get rich quick will only get into t.
Ecc 4:10 people who are alone when they fall are in real t.
Isa 8:22 there will be t and anguish and dark despair.
22: 5 Oh, what a day of crushing t! What a day of
33: 2 strength each day and our salvation in times of t.
33: 9 All the land of Israel is in t. Lebanon has been
37: 3 This is a day of t, insult, and disgrace.
38:14 to heaven for help. / I am in t, Lord. Help me!"
43: 2 When you go through deep waters and great t,
46: 7 no answer. It has no power to get anyone out of t.
48:16 so you would have no t understanding."
58:10 Feed the hungry and help those in t. Then your
Jer 2:27 but in times of t they cry out for me to save them!
14: 8 O Hope of Israel, our Savior in times of t! Why are
15:11 will ask you to plead on their behalf in times of t
16:19 my strength and fortress, my refuge in the day of t!
18:17 And in all their t I will turn my back on them
20:18 My entire life has been filled with t, sorrow,
30: 7 It will be a time of t for my people Israel. Yet in
44:18 we have been in great t and have suffered the
45: 3 You have said, 'I am overwhelmed with t!
51: 2 from every side to rise against her in her day of t.
Eze 7: 7 The time has come; the day of t is near. It will ring
Hos 2:15 and transform the Valley of T into a gateway of
5:15 For as soon as t comes, they will search for me."
Ob 1:14 them over to their enemies in that terrible time of t.
Jnh 2: 2 He said, "I cried out to the LORD in my great t,
Mic 3: 4 Then you beg the LORD for help in times of t!
Na 1: 7 is good. When t comes, he is a strong refuge.
Mt 6:34 its own worries. Today's t is enough for today.
14:24 the disciples were in t far away from land,
Mk 6:48 He saw that they were in serious t, rowing hard
Lk 7: 6 "Lord, don't t yourself by coming to my home,
Jn 7:13 for they were afraid of getting in t with the Jewish
Ac 17:13 of God in Berea, they went there and stirred up t.
19:23 serious t developed in Ephesus concerning the
22:30 them to try to find out what the t was all about.
27:10 he said, "I believe there is t ahead if we go on—
Ro 2: 9 There will be t and calamity for everyone who
7:14 The t is not with the law but with me, because I am
8:35 Does it mean he no longer loves us if we have t
12:12 for you. Be patient in t, and always be prayerful.
1Co 7:36 because he has t controlling his passions and time
2Co 1: 8 about the t we went through in the province of
2: 5 the t hurt your entire church more than he hurt me.
8: 2 Though they have been going through much t
10: 7 The t with you is that you make your decisions on
Gal 6:17 now on, don't let anyone t me with these things.
1Ti 5:10 Has she helped those who are in t? Has she always
6: 5 These people always cause t. Their minds are
Jas 1: 2 and sisters, whenever t comes your way,
1Pe 4:15 it must not be for murder, stealing, making t,

TROUBLED (21) [TROUBLE]

Dt 32:24 They will be t by the fangs of wild beasts,
1Sa 16:23 And whenever the tormenting spirit from God t
2Ch 15: 5 safe to travel. Problems t the nation on every hand.
Job 4: 3 "In the past you have encouraged many a t soul to
30:27 My heart is t and restless. Days of affliction have
Ps 73: 5 They aren't t like other people / or plagued with
94:13 You give them relief from t times / until a pit is
116:10 in you, so I prayed, / "I am deeply t, LORD."
Isa 54:11 "O storm-battered city, t and desolate! I will
Jer 49:23 Their hearts are t like a wild sea in a raging storm.
Da 7:15 I, Daniel, was t by all I had seen, and my visions
8:27 but I was greatly t by the vision and could not
Jn 11:33 he was moved with indignation and was deeply t.
11:38 And again Jesus was deeply t. Then they came to
12:27 Now my soul is deeply t. Should I pray, 'Father,
14: 1 "Don't be t. You trust God, now trust in me.
14:27 the peace the world gives. So don't be t or afraid.

Ac 15:24 “We understand that some men from here have **t**
17:16 he was deeply **t** by all the idols he saw everywhere
2Co 1:4 When others are **t**, we will be able to give them the
2Th 2:2 and **t** by those who say that the day of the Lord has

TROUBLEMAKER (6) [TROUBLE]

2Sa 20:1 Then a **t** named Sheba son of Bicri, a Benjaminite,
20:6 “That **t** Sheba is going to hurt us more than
1Ki 18:17 “So it's you, is it—Israel's **t**?” Ahab asked when
Pr 16:28 A **t** plants seeds of strife; gossip separates the best
24:8 person who plans evil will get a reputation as a **t**.
Ac 24:5 For we have found him to be a **t**, a man who is

TROUBLEMAKERS (4) [TROUBLE]

1Sa 30:22 But some **t** among David's men said, “They didn't
1Ki 18:18 “You and your family are the **t**, for you have
Jer 48:12 “when I will send **t** to pour her from her jar.
Gal 5:12 I only wish that those **t** who want to mutilate you

TROUBLES (52) [TROUBLE]

Ge 41:51 “God has made me forget all my **t** and the family
Ex 18:8 LORD had delivered his people from all their **t**.
1Sa 26:24 yours today. May he rescue me from all my **t**.”
1Ki 2:26 suffered right along with him through all his **t**.”
8:38 and if your people offer a prayer concerning their **t**
2Ch 6:29 and if your people offer a prayer concerning their **t**
Ne 2:2 are you? You look like a man with deep **t**.”
13:18 so that our God brought the present **t** upon us
Job 6:2 could be weighed and my **t** be put on the scales,
36:8 If **t** come upon them and they are enslaved
Ps 25:22 O God, ransom Israel / from all its **t**.
27:5 For he will conceal me there when **t** come;
31:7 of your unfailing love, / for you have seen my **t**,
34:17 to him for help. / He rescues them from all their **t**.
34:19 The righteous face many **t**, / but the LORD
35:24 Don't let my enemies laugh about me in my **t**.
35:26 May those who rejoice at my **t** / be humiliated
40:12 For **t** surround me— / too many to count!
54:7 For you will rescue me from my **t** / and help me to
55:2 and answer me, / for I am overwhelmed by my **t**.
88:3 For my life is full of **t**, / and death draws near.
119:50 promise revives me; / it comforts me in all my **t**.
120:1 I took my **t** to the LORD; / I cried out to him,
138:7 Though I am surrounded by **t**, / you will preserve
142:2 my complaints before him / and tell him all my **t**.
Pr 31:7 forget their poverty and remember their **t** no more.
Ecc 8:6 even as people's **t** lie heavily upon them.
Isa 20:3 a symbol of the terrible **t** I will bring upon Egypt
40:27 how can you say the LORD does not see your **t**?
53:4 And we thought his **t** were a punishment from God
66:4 I will send great **t** against them—all the things they
Jer 10:18 fling you from this land and pour great **t** upon you.
44:17 plenty to eat, and we were well off and had no **t**!
La 1:21 When my enemies heard of my **t**, they were happy
Da 2:3 he said, “I have had a dream that **t** me. Tell me
9:13 come true. All the **t** he predicted have taken place.
Zep 3:15 At last your **t** will be over, and you will fear
2Co 1:4 He comforts us in all our **t** so that we can comfort
1:6 So when we are weighed down with **t**, it is for your
4:8 We are pressed on every side by **t**, but we are not
4:17 For our present **t** are quite small and won't last
4:18 So we don't look at the **t** we can see right now;
4:18 For the **t** we see will soon be over, but the joys to
6:4 We patiently endure **t** and hardships and calamities
7:4 you have made me happy despite all our **t**.
Gal 6:2 Share each other's **t** and problems, and in this way
1Th 3:3 and to keep you from becoming disturbed by the **t**
3:3 you know that such **t** are going to happen to us
3:4 we warned you that **t** would soon come—
3:7 in all of our own crushing **t** and suffering,
Jas 1:27 we must care for orphans and widows in their **t**,
5:1 because of all the terrible **t** ahead of you.

TROUBLING (8) [TROUBLE]

2Ki 4:27 Something is **t** her deeply, and the LORD has not
2Ch 15:6 for God was **t** you with every kind of problem.
Est 4:5 and find out what was **t** him and why he was in
Job 3:17 For in death the wicked cease from **t**,
Mk 5:35 is dead. There's no use **t** the Teacher now.”
Lk 8:49 girl is dead. There's no use **t** the Teacher now.”
Ac 15:19 so my judgment is that we should stop **t** the
Gal 5:10 whoever it is, who has been **t** and confusing you.

TROUGH (1) [TROUGHS]

Ge 24:20 So she quickly emptied the jug into the watering **t**

TROUGHS (2) [TROUGH]

Ge 30:38 set up these peeled branches beside the watering **t**
Ex 2:16 and fill the water **t** for their father's flocks.

TRUE (240) [TRUTH]

Ge 18:15 But he said, “That is not **t**. You did laugh.”
18:21 down to see whether or not these reports are **t**.
24:49 or won't you show **t** kindness to my master?
42:16 Then we'll find out whether or not your story is **t**.
45:28 Then Jacob said, “It must be **t**! My son Joseph is
Ex 9:7 Pharaoh sent officials to see whether it was **t** that
9:7 But even after he found it to be **t**, his heart
21:29 If this is **t** and if the bull kills someone, it must be
34:9 “If it is **t** that I have found favor in your sight,
Lev 11:5 The same is **t** of the rock badger
11:32 This is **t** whether the object is made of wood,
Nu 11:23 you will see whether or not my word comes **t**!”
35:18 The same is **t** if someone strikes and kills another
Dt 13:14 If you find it is **t** and can prove that such a
16:20 Let **t** justice prevail, so you may live and occupy
17:4 If it is **t** that this detestable thing has been done in
22:20 “But suppose the man's accusations are **t**, and her
24:17 “**T** justice must be given to foreigners living
Jos 21:45 promises that the LORD had given Israel came **t**.
22:19 There is only one **t** altar of the LORD our God.
23:14 promise of the LORD your God has come **t**.
Jdg 9:28 “He's not a **t** descendant of Shechem!
9:28 men of Hamor, who are Shechem's **t** descendants.
9:57 So the curse of Jotham son of Gideon came **t**.
13:12 So Manoah asked him, “When your words come **t**,
13:17 For when all this comes **t**, we want to honor you.”
Ru 3:12 While it is **t** that I am one of your family
1Sa 2:34 And to prove that what I have said will come **t**,
9:6 all the people because everything he says comes **t**.
12:5 me of robbing you.” “Yes, it is **t**,” they replied.
15:15 “It's **t** that the army spared the best of the sheep
17:27 “What you have been hearing is **t**. That is the
20:2 “That's not **t**!” Jonathan protested. “I'm sure he's
24:10 very day you can see with your own eyes it isn't **t**.
25:8 your own servants, and they will tell you this is **t**.
2Sa 13:20 and asked, “Is it **t** that Amnon has been with you?
22:31 is perfect. / All the LORD's promises prove **t**.
1Ki 3:6 because he was honest and **t** and faithful to you.
10:6 country about your achievements and wisdom is **t**!
13:32 in the towns of Samaria will surely come **t**.”
18:12 Yet I have been a **t** servant of the LORD all my
18:24 answers by setting fire to the wood is the **t** God!”
2Ki 5:8 and he will learn that there is a **t** prophet here in
7:16 So it was **t** that five quarts of fine flour were sold
8:6 “Is this **t**?” the king asked her. And she told him
15:12 So the LORD's message to Jehu came **t**:
19:17 “It is **t**, LORD, that the kings of Assyria have
2Ch 9:5 country about your achievements and wisdom is **t**!
15:3 For a long time, Israel was without the **t** God,
34:24 written in the scroll you have read will come **t**.
Ne 9:8 you promised, for you are always **t** to your word.
9:13 that were just, and laws and commands that were **t**.
Est 2:23 was made and Mordecai's story was found to be **t**,
Job 5:27 “We have found from experience that all this is **t**.
9:2 “Yes, I know this is all **t** in principle. But how can
11:6 of wisdom, for **t** wisdom is not a simple matter.
12:13 “But **t** wisdom and power are with God; counsel
28:28 ‘The fear of the Lord is **t** wisdom; to forsake evil
Ps 1:4 But this is not **t** of the wicked. / They are like
7:10 saving those whose hearts are **t** and right.
16:3 are my **t** heroes! / I take pleasure in them!
18:30 is perfect. / All the LORD's promises prove **t**.
19:9 lasting forever. / The laws of the LORD are **t**;
33:4 For the word of the LORD holds **t**,
50:14 What I want instead is your **t** thanks to God;
78:72 He cared for them with a **t** heart / and led them
111:8 They are forever **t**, / to be obeyed faithfully
111:10 Reverence for the LORD is the foundation of **t**
119:82 My eyes are straining to see your promises come **t**.
119:91 Your laws remain **t** today, / for everything serves
119:142 justice is eternal, / and your law is perfectly **t**.
119:151 are near, O LORD, / and all your commands are **t**.
119:160 All your words are **t**; / all your just laws will stand
Pr 6:13 signaling their **t** intentions to their friends by
10:24 The fears of the wicked will all come **t**; so will the
11:31 how much more **t** that the wicked and the sinner
13:12 but when dreams come **t**, there is life and joy.
13:19 It is pleasant to see dreams come **t**, but fools will
18:4 words of **t** wisdom are as refreshing as a bubbling
18:17 Any story sounds **t** until someone sets the record
22:4 **T** humility and fear of the LORD lead to riches,
30:5 Every word of God proves **t**. He defends all who
Ecc 5:10 How absurd to think that wealth brings **t**
Isa 23:1 is gone! The rumors you heard in Cyprus are all **t**.
34:16 promised this. His Spirit will make it all come **t**.
37:18 “It is **t**, LORD, that the kings of Assyria have
42:9 Everything I prophesied has come **t**, and now I will
44:15 Then—yes, it's **t**—he takes the rest of it and makes
45:19 I, the LORD, speak only what is **t** and right.
48:3 I took action, and all my predictions came **t**.
59:8 They do not know what **t** peace is or what it means
65:8 destroy all Israel. For I still have **t** servants there.
65:15 and call his **t** servants by another name.
Jer 2:23 “You say, ‘That's not **t**! We haven't worshiped the
10:10 But the LORD is the only **t** God, the living God.
17:15 Why don't your predictions come **t**?”
23:28 but let my **t** messengers faithfully proclaim my
26:15 For it is absolutely **t** that the LORD sent me to
28:6 He said, “Amen! May your prophecies come **t**!
28:9 Only when his predictions come **t** can it be known
33:21 The same is **t** for my covenant with the Levitical
37:14 “That's not **t**!” Jeremiah protested. “I had no
44:28 came to Egypt will find out whose words are **t**,
Eze 12:27 ‘His visions won't come **t** for a long, long time.’
21:7 When it comes **t**, the boldest heart will melt with
Da 2:26 to Daniel (also known as Belteshazzar), “Is this **t**?
2:45 The dream is **t**, and its meaning is certain.”
3:14 “Is it **t**, Shadrach, Meshach, and Abednego,
4:37 All his acts are just and **t**, and he is able to humble
7:19 Then I wanted to know the **t** meaning of the fourth
8:26 twenty-three hundred evenings and mornings is **t**.
9:7 This is **t** of us all, including the people of Judah
9:13 written against us in the law of Moses has come **t**.
Hos 14:9 The paths of the LORD are **t** and right,
Am 5:15 is good; remodel your courts into **t** halls of justice.
9:9 is sifted in a sieve, yet not one **t** kernel will be lost.
Mic 4:11 **T**, many nations have gathered together against
Mt 5:45 you will be acting as **t** children of your Father in
16:25 if you give up your life for me, you will find **t** life.
Mk 7:28 She replied, “That's **t**, Lord, but even the dogs
8:35 for the sake of the Good News, you will find **t** life.
Lk 1:20 For my words will certainly come **t** at the proper
1:38 May everything you have said come **t**.” And
4:21 “This Scripture has come **t** today before your very
9:24 if you give up your life for me, you will find **t** life.
16:8 And it is **t** that the citizens of this world are more
16:11 who will trust you with the **t** riches of heaven?
18:31 prophets concerning the Son of Man will come **t**.
22:28 You have remained **t** to me in my time of trial.
22:37 written about me by the prophets will come **t**.”
24:44 the prophets and in the Psalms must all come **t**.”
Jn 1:9 The one who is the **t** light, who gives light to
1:47 “Here comes an honest man—a **t** son of Israel.”
3:33 Those who believe him discover that God is **t**.
4:23 and is already here when **t** worshipers will worship
4:37 and someone else harvests.’ And it's **t**.
5:32 assure you that everything he says about me is **t**.
6:32 And now he offers you the **t** bread from heaven.
6:33 The **t** bread of God is the one who comes down
6:55 my flesh is the **t** food, and my blood is the **t** drink.
6:58 I am the **t** bread from heaven. Anyone who eats
7:28 But I represent one you don't know, and he is **t**.
8:26 have heard from the one who sent me, and he is **t**.”
8:41 out of wedlock! Our **t** Father is God himself.”
8:55 liar as you! But it is **t**—I know him and obey him.
10:8 and robbers. But the **t** sheep did not listen to them.
10:41 all his predictions about this man have come **t**.”
12:16 they remembered that these Scriptures had come **t**
13:10 you are clean, but that isn't **t** of everyone here.”
13:13 and ‘Lord,’ and you are right, because it is **t**.
13:16 How **t** it is that a servant is not greater than the
13:18 has turned against me,’ and this will soon come **t**.
15:1 “I am the **t** vine, and my Father is the gardener.
15:8 My **t** disciples produce much fruit. This brings
17:3 to know you, the only **t** God, and Jesus Christ,
18:37 who love the truth recognize that what I say is **t**.”
Ac 2:15 are drunk. It isn't **t**! It's much too early for that.
7:1 priest asked Stephen, “Are these accusations **t**?”
11:23 and he encouraged the believers to stay **t** to the
12:11 “It's really **t**!” he said to himself. “The Lord has
13:10 will you never stop perverting the **t** ways of the
13:32 God's promise to our ancestors has come **t** in our
14:3 The Lord proved their message was **t** by giving
17:29 And since this is **t**, we shouldn't think of God as an
24:9 declaring that everything Tertullus said was **t**.
Ro 2:28 For you are not a **t** Jew just because you were born
2:29 a **t** Jew is one whose heart is right with God.
2:29 And **t** circumcision is not a cutting of the body
3:3 **T**, some of them were unfaithful; but just
3:4 everyone else in the world is a liar, God is **t**.
3:17 They do not know what **t** peace is.”
9:1 the Holy Spirit confirm that what I am saying is **t**.
13:13 We should be decent and **t** in everything we do,
15:8 God is **t** to the promises he made to their ancestors.
1Co 1:6 This shows that what I told you about Christ is **t**.
1:22 they want a sign from heaven to prove it is **t**.
6:13 This is **t**, though someday God will do away with
8:8 It's **t** that we can't win God's approval by what we
10:15 for yourselves if what I am about to say is **t**.
11:22 What? Is this really **t**? Don't you have your own
15:2 you believed something that was never **t** in the first
15:15 but that can't be **t** if there is no resurrection of the
15:54 never die—then at last the Scriptures will come **t**:
16:13 Be on guard. Stand **t** to what you believe.
2Co 1:18 As surely as God is **t**, I am not that sort of person.
6:4 In everything we do we try to show that we are **t**
7:14 and now my boasting to Titus has also proved **t**!
Gal 3:29 to Christ, you are the **t** children of Abraham.
Eph 4:24 created in God's likeness—righteous, holy, and **t**.
5:9 you produces only what is good and right and **t**.
Php 2:25 He is a **t** brother, a faithful worker, and a
4:1 So please stay **t** to the Lord, my dear friends.
4:3 And I ask you, my **t** teammate, to help these
4:8 Fix your thoughts on what is **t** and honorable
1Th 1:5 gave you full assurance that what we said was **t**.
1:9 and how you turned away from idols to serve the **t**
1Ti 1:2 It is written to Timothy, my **t** child in the faith.
1:15 This is a **t** saying, and everyone should believe it:
3:1 It is a **t** saying that if someone wants to be an elder,
4:6 of faith and the **t** teaching you have followed.
4:9 This is **t**, and everyone should accept it.
4:16 Stay **t** to what is right, and God will save you
5:5 But a woman who is a **t** widow, one who is truly
6:6 Yet **t** religion with contentment is great wealth.
2Ti 2:11 This is a **t** saying: / If we die with him, / we will
3:14 You know they are **t**, for you know you can trust
3:16 inspired by God and is useful to teach us what is **t**
Tit 1:4 to Titus, my **t** child in the faith that we share.
1:10 This is especially **t** of those who insist on
1:13 This is **t**. So rebuke them as sternly as necessary to
3:2 should be gentle and show **t** humility to everyone.
3:8 These things I have told you are all **t**. I want you to
Heb 2:2 God delivered through angels has always proved **t**,
6:11 to make certain that what you hope for will come **t**.
8:2 the **t** place of worship that was built by the Lord
10:22 presence of God, with **t** hearts fully trusting him.
13:1 Continue to love each other with **t** Christian love.
Jas 1:18 make us his own children by giving us his **t** word.
2Pe 2:2 of them, Christ and his **t** way will be slandered.
2:22 They make these proverbs come **t**: “A dog returns
1Jn 2:8 commandment is **t** in Christ and is **t** among you,
2:8 is disappearing and the **t** light is already shining.
2:27 so you don't need anyone to teach you what is **t**.
2:27 teaches you all things, and what he teaches is **t**—
5:6 the Spirit also gives us the testimony that this is **t**.
5:10 who believe in the Son of God know that this is **t**.

5:20 us understanding so that we can know the **t** God.
5:20 He is the only **t** God, and he is eternal life.
Rev 3: 7 is the message from the one who is holy and **t**.
3:14 the faithful and **t** witness, the ruler of God's
6:10 the Lord and said, "O Sovereign Lord, holy and **t**,
15: 3 Lord God Almighty. / Just and **t** are your ways,
16: 7 God Almighty, your punishments are **t** and just."
19: 2 His judgments are just and **t**. He has punished the
19: 9 "These are **t** words that come from God."
19:11 one sitting on the horse was named Faithful and **T**.
21: 5 for what I tell you is trustworthy and **t**."
22: 6 said to me, "These words are trustworthy and **t**:

TRUER (1) [TRUTH]

Job 34:12 There is no **t** statement than this: God will not do

TRULY (54) [TRUTH]

Ge 22:12 in any way, for now I know that you **t** fear God.
34: 8 "My son Shechem is **t** in love with your daughter,
Jdg 6:17 Gideon replied, "If you are **t** going to help me,
6:31 If Baal **t** is a god, let him defend himself
6:36 "If you are **t** going to use me to rescue Israel as
9:15 'If you **t** want to make me your king, come
1Ki 10: 7 **T** I had not heard the half of it! Your wisdom
17:24 and that the LORD **t** speaks through you."
2Ki 17:34 They follow their former practices instead of **t**
2Ch 9: 6 with my own eyes. **T** I had not heard the half of it!
Est 6: 6 "What should I do to honor a man who **t** pleases
Job 37:24 People who are **t** wise show him reverence."
Ps 50:23 But giving thanks is a sacrifice that **t** honors me.
58:11 "There **t** is a reward for those who live for God;
73: 1 **T** God is good to Israel, / to those whose hearts are
73:18 **T**, you put them on a slippery path / and send them
119:111 are my treasure; / they are **t** my heart's delight.
119:127 **T**, I love your commands / more than gold,
119:128 **T**, each of your commandments is right. / That is
Pr 17:27 A **t** wise person uses few words; a person with
22:29 Do you see any **t** competent workers? They will
Ecc 1: 9 been done before. Nothing under the sun is **t** new.
Isa 42:21 has magnified his law and made it **t** glorious.
45:15 **T**, O God of Israel, our Savior, you work in strange
Jer 9:24 that they **t** know me and understand that I am the
Eze 11:20 Then they will **t** be my people, and I will be their
16:45 **T** your mother must have been a Hittite and your
16:54 Then you will be **t** ashamed of everything you
37:23 Then they will **t** be my people, and I will be their
Da 2:47 The king said to Daniel, "**T**, your God is the God
Hos 11: 7 call me the Most High, but they don't **t** honor me.
Am 5:14 Then the LORD God Almighty will **t** be your
Mal 1: 5 see the destruction for yourselves, you will say, '**T**,
Mt 13:23 The good soil represents the hearts of those who **t**
27:54 They said, "**T**, this was the Son of God!"
Mk 10:18 call me good?" Jesus asked. "Only God is **t** good.
15:39 he exclaimed, "**T**, this was the Son of God!"
Lk 6:35 and you will **t** be acting as children of the Most
18:19 me good?" Jesus asked him. "Only God is **t** good.
Jn 8:31 "You are **t** my disciples if you keep obeying my
13:20 **T**, anyone who welcomes my messenger is
16:20 **T**, you will weep and mourn over what is going to
Ro 3:31 only when we have faith do we **t** fulfill the law.
9: 6 for not everyone born into a Jewish family is **t** a
9: 7 doesn't make them **t** Abraham's children.
1Co 12: 3 So I want you to know how to discern what is **t**
2Co 12:12 I certainly gave you every proof that I am **t** an
Php 2: 2 Then make me **t** happy by agreeing wholeheartedly
3: 3 the Spirit are the only ones who are **t** circumcised.
1Ti 5: 5 one who is **t** alone in this world, has placed her
5:16 Then the church can care for widows who are **t**
Jas 2: 8 it is good when you **t** obey our Lord's royal
3:13 about the good you do, then you will be **t** wise!
1Pe 1: 6 So be **t** glad! There is wonderful joy ahead,

TRUMP [KJV] See TRUMPET

TRUMPET (35) [TRUMPET-PLAYING, TRUMPETER, TRUMPETERS, TRUMPETS]

Lev 23:24 Festival of Trumpets—with loud blasts from a **t**.
2Sa 2:28 So Joab blew his **t**, and his men stopped chasing
18:16 Then Joab blew the **t**, and his men returned from
20: 1 a Benjaminite, blew a **t** and shouted, "We have
20:22 So he blew the **t** and called his troops back from
2Ki 9:13 out their cloaks on the bare steps and blew a **t**,
Ne 4:20 When you hear the blast of the **t**, rush to wherever
Job 39:24 and rushes forward into battle when the **t** blows.
Ps 81: 3 Sound the **t** for a sacred feast / when the moon is
150: 3 Praise him with a blast of the **t**; / praise him with
Isa 18: 3 all the world take notice. When I blow the **t**, listen!
27:13 In that day the great **t** will sound. Many who were
58: 1 "Shout with the voice of a **t** blast. Tell my people
Jer 6:17 over you who said, 'Listen for the sound of the **t**!'
Joel 2: 1 Blow the **t** in Jerusalem! Sound the alarm on my
2:15 Blow the **t** in Jerusalem! Announce a time of
Am 3: 6 When the war **t** blares, shouldn't the people be
Zep 1:16 **t** calls, and battle cries. Down go the walled cities
Zec 9:14 The Sovereign LORD will sound the **t**; he will go
Mt 24:31 forth his angels with the sound of a mighty **t** blast,
1Co 15:52 in the blinking of an eye, when the last **t** is blown.
15:52 For when the **t** sounds, the Christians who have
1Th 4:16 call of the archangel, and with the **t** call of God.
Heb 12:19 For they heard an awesome **t** blast and a voice with
Rev 1:10 behind me, a voice that sounded like a **t** blast.
4: 1 spoke to me with the sound of a mighty **t** blast.
8: 7 The first angel blew his **t**, and hail and fire mixed
8: 8 Then the second angel blew his **t**, and a great
8:10 Then the third angel blew his **t**, and a great flaming
8:12 Then the fourth angel blew his **t**, and one-third of
9: 1 Then the fifth angel blew his **t**, and I saw a star that
9:13 Then the sixth angel blew his **t**, and I heard a voice
9:14 the voice spoke to the sixth angel who held the **t**:
10: 7 But when the seventh angel blows his **t**,
11:15 Then the seventh angel blew his **t**, and there were

TRUMPET-PLAYING (1) [PLAY, TRUMPET]

Ne 12:41 We went together with the **t** priests—Eliakim,

TRUMPETER (1) [TRUMPET]

Ne 4:18 their side. The **t** stayed with me to sound the alarm.

TRUMPETERS (3) [TRUMPET]

2Ki 11:14 The officers and **t** were surrounding him,
2Ch 5:13 The **t** and singers performed together in unison to
23:13 The officers and **t** were surrounding him,

TRUMPETS (47) [TRUMPET]

Lev 23:24 the Festival of **T**—with loud blasts from a trumpet.
23:27 celebrated on the ninth day after the Festival of **T**.
25: 9 blow the **t** loud and long throughout the land.
Nu 10: 2 "Make two **t** of beaten silver to be used for
10: 3 When both **t** are blown, the people will know that
10: 7 to an assembly, blow the **t** using a different signal.
10: 8 Aaron's descendants, are allowed to blow the **t**.
10: 9 you must sound the alarm with these **t**
10:10 Blow the **t** in times of gladness, too,
10:10 The **t** will remind the LORD your God of his
29: 1 "The Festival of **T** will be celebrated on the
31: 6 of the sanctuary and the **t** for sounding the charge.
2Sa 6:15 the LORD with much shouting and blowing of **t**.
15:10 "As soon as you hear the **t**," his message read,
1Ki 1:34 Then blow the **t** and shout, 'Long live King
1:39 Then the **t** were blown, and all the people shouted,
1:41 When Joab heard the sound of **t**, he asked,
2Ki 11:14 all over the land were rejoicing and blowing **t**.
12:13 lamp snuffers, basins, **t**, or other articles of gold
1Ch 13: 8 lyres, harps, tambourines, cymbals, and **t**.
15:24 were chosen to blow the **t** as they marched in front
15:28 the blowing of horns and **t**, the crashing of
16: 6 played the **t** regularly before the Ark of God's
16:42 They used their **t**, cymbals, and other instruments
2Ch 5:12 were joined by 120 priests who were playing **t**.
5:13 Accompanied by **t**, cymbals, and other
7: 6 the priests blew the **t**, while all Israel stood.
13:12 His priests blow their **t** and lead us into battle
13:14 to the LORD for help. Then the priests blew the **t**,
15:14 their oath of loyalty to the LORD with **t** blaring
20:28 and **t** and proceeded to the Temple of the LORD.
23:13 all over the land were rejoicing and blowing **t**.
29:26 and the priests took their positions with the **t**.
29:27 accompanied by the **t** and other instruments of
29:28 the LORD as the singers sang and the **t** blew,
Ezr 3:10 on their robes and took their places to blow their **t**.
Ne 12:35 and some priests who played **t**. Then came
Ps 47: 5 The LORD has ascended with **t** blaring.
98: 6 with **t** and the sound of the ram's horn. / Make a
Jer 4:19 For I have heard the blast of enemy **t** and the roar
Eze 7:14 "The **t** call Israel's army to mobilize, but no one
Am 2: 2 of battle, as the warriors shout and the **t** blare.
Mt 6: 2 blowing **t** in the synagogues and streets to call
Rev 8: 2 stand before God, and they were given seven **t**.
8: 6 Then the seven angels with the seven **t** prepared to
8:13 happen when the last three angels blow their **t**."
18:22 be heard there—no more harps, songs, flutes, or **t**.

TRUNK (2)

1Sa 5: 4 the doorway. Only the **t** of his body was left intact.
Eze 31:13 The birds roosted on its fallen **t**, and the wild

TRUST (135) [ENTRUST, ENTRUSTED, ENTRUSTING, ENTRUSTS, TRUSTED, TRUSTING, TRUSTS, TRUSTWORTHY]

Ge 49:18 I **t** in you for salvation, O LORD!
Lev 19: 4 Do not put your **t** in idols or make gods of metal
Nu 20:12 "Because you did not **t** me enough to demonstrate
Dt 1:32 all he did, you refused to **t** the LORD your God,
9:23 your God and refused to **t** him or obey him.
Jdg 11:20 But King Sihon didn't **t** Israel to pass through his
2Ki 19:10 Don't let this God you **t** deceive you with promises
1Ch 9:26 all Levites, were in an office of great **t**,
2Ch 14:11 Help us, O LORD our God, for we **t** in you alone.
16: 7 "Because you have put your **t** in the king of Aram
Job 4: 3 have encouraged many a troubled soul to **t** in God;
4:18 "If God cannot **t** his own angels and has charged
4:19 how much less will he **t** those made of clay!
15:15 Why, God doesn't even **t** the angels!
15:31 Let them no longer **t** in empty riches. They are
31:24 "Have I put my **t** in money or felt secure
39:11 strong, can you **t** it? Can you go away and **t** the ox
Ps 4: 5 Offer proper sacrifices, / and **t** in the LORD.
9:10 Those who know your name **t** in you, / for you,
10:14 and punish them. / The helpless put their **t** in you.
11: 1 I **t** in the LORD for protection. / So why do you
13: 5 But I **t** in your unfailing love. / I will rejoice
22: 5 They put their **t** in you and were never
22: 9 and led me to **t** you when I was a nursing infant.
25: 2 I **t** in you, my God! / Do not let me be disgraced,
25:20 Do not let me be disgraced, for I **t** in you.
28: 7 I **t** in him with all my heart. / He helps me,
31: 6 who worship worthless idols. / I **t** in the LORD.
32:10 but unfailing love surrounds those who **t** the
33: 4 and everything he does is worthy of our **t**.
34: 8 is good. / Oh, the joys of those who **t** in him!
34:10 but those who **t** in the LORD will never lack any
37: 3 **T** in the LORD and do good. / Then you will live
37: 5 do to the LORD. / **T** him, and he will help you.
37: 9 but those who **t** in the LORD will possess the
40: 3 be astounded. / They will put their **t** in the LORD.
40: 4 Oh, the joys of those who **t** the LORD,
44: 6 I do not **t** my bow; / I do not count on my sword to
49: 6 They **t** in their wealth / and boast of great riches.
50:15 **T** me in your times of trouble, / and I will rescue
52: 7 who do not **t** in God. / They **t** their wealth instead
52: 8 I **t** in God's unfailing love / forever and ever.
56: 3 But when I am afraid, / I put my **t** in you.
56: 4 your word. / I **t** in God, so why should I be afraid?
56:11 I **t** in God, so why should I be afraid? / What can
62: 8 O my people, **t** in him at all times. / Pour out your
63:11 All who **t** in him will praise him, / while liars will
69: 6 Don't let those who **t** in you stumble because of
78:22 did not believe God / or **t** him to care for them.
84:12 LORD Almighty, / happy are those who **t** in you.
86: 2 Save me, for I serve you and **t** you. / You are my
91:14 love me. / I will protect those who **t** in my name.
111: 5 He gives food to those who **t** him; / he always
112: 7 they confidently **t** the LORD to care for them.
115: 8 them are just like them, / as are all who **t** in them.
115: 9 O Israel, **t** the LORD! / He is your helper; he is
115:10 O priests of Aaron, **t** the LORD! / He is your
115:11 All you who fear the LORD, **t** the LORD!
118: 8 It is better to **t** the LORD / than to put confidence
118: 9 It is better to **t** the LORD / than to put confidence
119:42 for those who taunt me, / for I **t** in your word.
119:138 are perfect; / they are entirely worthy of our **t**.
125: 1 Those who **t** in the LORD are as secure as Mount
135:18 them are just like them, / as are all who **t** in them.
Pr 3: 5 **T** in the LORD with all your heart; do not depend
3:29 Do not plot against your neighbors, for they **t** you.
11:28 **T** in your money and down you go! But the godly
16:20 those who **t** the LORD will be happy.
21:22 of the strong and level the fortress in which they **t**.
22:19 you today—yes, you—so you will **t** in the LORD.
29:25 dangerous trap, but to **t** the LORD means safety.
31:11 Her husband can **t** her, and she will greatly enrich
Isa 2:22 Stop putting your **t** in mere humans. They are as
10:20 those left in Israel and Judah will **t** the LORD,
12: 2 come to save me. / I will **t** in him and not be afraid.
26: 3 You will keep in perfect peace all who **t** in you,
26: 4 **T** in the LORD always, / for the LORD GOD
30: 2 You have put your **t** in Pharaoh for his protection.
30:12 what I tell you and **t** instead in oppression and lies,
37:10 Don't let this God you **t** deceive you with promises
42:17 But those who **t** in idols, / calling them their gods
49: 4 the LORD's hand; I will **t** God for my reward."
50:10 ray of light, **t** in the LORD and rely on your God.
Jer 2:37 for the LORD has rejected the nations you **t**.
7:14 this Temple that you **t** for help, this place that I
12: 6 Do not **t** them, no matter how pleasantly they
13:25 you have forgotten me and put your **t** in false gods.
17: 5 "Cursed are those who put their **t** in mere humans
17: 7 "But blessed are those who **t** in the LORD
46:25 its rulers and Pharaoh, too, and all who **t** in him.
Eze 29:16 "Then Israel will no longer be tempted to **t** in
29:16 of how sinful she was to **t** Egypt in earlier days.
Mic 7: 5 Don't **t** anyone—not your best friend or even your
Hab 2: 4 They **t** in themselves, and their lives are crooked;
2:18 How foolish to **t** in something made by your own
Zep 3: 2 It does not **t** in the LORD or draw near to its God.
3:12 for it is they who **t** in the name of the LORD.
Mk 5:36 and said to Jairus, "Don't be afraid. Just **t** me."
Lk 8:50 be afraid. Just **t** me, and she will be all right."
16:11 who will **t** you with the true riches of heaven?
Jn 2:24 But Jesus didn't **t** them, because he knew what
3:18 "There is no judgment awaiting those who **t** him.
3:18 But those who do not **t** him have already been
12:44 Jesus shouted to the crowds, "If you **t** me, you are
12:46 so that all who put their **t** in me will no longer
14: 1 "Don't be troubled. You **t** God, now **t** in me.
Ac 14:23 the care of the Lord, in whom they had come to **t**.
Ro 3:22 We are made right in God's sight when we **t** in
11:22 but kind to you as you continue to **t** in his
1Co 2: 5 so that you might **t** the power of God rather than
4: 3 I don't even **t** my own judgment on this point.
9:17 But God has chosen me and given me this sacred **t**,
15:14 preaching is useless, and your **t** in God is useless.
2Co 1:15 Since I was so sure of your understanding and **t**,
3: 4 because of our great **t** in God through Christ.
Eph 1:12 God's purpose was that we who were the first to **t**
3:17 and more at home in your hearts as you **t** in him.
Php 3: 9 ability to obey God's law, but I **t** Christ to save me.
Col 1: 4 for we have heard that you **t** in Christ Jesus
1Ti 6:17 world not to be proud and not to **t** in their money,
6:17 But their **t** should be in the living God, who richly
2Ti 1: 5 I know that you sincerely **t** the Lord, for you have
1:12 not ashamed of it, for I know the one in whom I **t**,
3:14 for you know you can **t** those who taught you.
Phm 1: 5 because I keep hearing of your **t** in the Lord Jesus
Heb 2:13 He also said, "I will put my **t** in him." And in the
10:35 Do not throw away this confident **t** in the Lord,
13: 7 come from their lives, and **t** the Lord as they do.
1Pe 1: 8 Though you do not see him, you **t** him; and even
1:21 Through Christ you have come to **t** in God. And
4:19 and **t** yourself to the God who made you, for he
1Jn 4:16 much God loves us, and we have put our **t** in him.

TRUSTED (30) [TRUST]

Dt 28:52 the walls you **t** to protect you—are knocked down.

1Ki 4: 5 son of Nathan, a priest, was a **t** adviser to the king.
2Ki 12:21 and Jehozabad son of Shomer—both **t** advisers.
18: 5 Hezekiah **t** in the LORD, the God of Israel.
1Ch 5:20 he answered their prayer because they **t** in him.
2Ch 13:18 defeated Israel because they **t** in the LORD,
Job 12:20 He silences the **t** adviser, and he removes the
Ps 22: 4 Our ancestors **t** in you, / and you rescued them.
26: 1 I have **t** in the LORD without wavering.
41: 9 Even my best friend, the one I **t** completely,
71: 5 my hope. / I've **t** you, O LORD, from childhood.
Isa 25: 9 "This is our God. We **t** in him, and he saved us.
This is the LORD, in whom we **t**.
Jer 39:18 Because you **t** me, I will preserve your life
48: 7 Because you have **t** in your wealth and skill,
49: 4 you **t** in your wealth and thought no one could ever
Eze 16:15 so you **t** instead in your fame and beauty.
Da 3:28 He sent his angel to rescue his servants who **t** in
6:23 was found on him because he had **t** in his God.
Hos 10: 6 and shamed because its people have **t** in this idol.
Ob 1: 7 Your **t** friends will set traps for you, and you won't
Mic 2: 8 the shirts right off the backs of those who **t** you,
Mt 27:43 He **t** God—let God show his approval by
Lk 16:12 why should you be **t** with money of your own?
1Co 7:25 in his kindness has given me wisdom that can be **t**,
Col 2:12 a new life because you **t** the mighty power of God,
Tit 1: 3 Savior that I have been **t** to do this work for him.
Heb 10:23 say we have, for God can be **t** to keep his promise.
11:35 But others **t** God and were tortured, preferring to
1Pe 3: 5 They **t** God and accepted the authority of their

TRUSTING (35) [TRUST]

1Ki 11: 4 their gods instead of **t** only in the LORD his God,
2Ki 18:19 What are you **t** in that makes you so confident?
18:22 you will say, 'We are **t** in the LORD our God!'
18:30 Don't let him fool you into **t** in the LORD by
2Ch 32:10 What are you **t** in that makes you think you can
Ps 31:14 But I am **t** you, O LORD, / saying, "You are my
33:21 our hearts rejoice, / for we are **t** in his holy name.
55:23 liars will die young, / but I am **t** you to save me.
91: 2 my place of safety; / he is my God, and I am **t** him.
143: 8 love to me in the morning, / for I am **t** you.
Pr 26: 6 **T** a fool to convey a message is as foolish as
28:25 causes fighting; **t** the LORD leads to prosperity.
28:26 **T** oneself is foolish, but those who walk in wisdom
Isa 30: 3 But in **t** Pharaoh, you will be humiliated
31: 1 **t** their cavalry and chariots instead of looking to
36: 4 What are you **t** in that makes you so confident?
36: 7 you will say, 'We are **t** in the LORD our God!'
36:15 Don't let him fool you into **t** in the LORD by
44:20 He is **t** something that can give him no help at all.
Hos 10:13 **t** in your military might, believing that great armies
Jn 12:44 you trust me, you are really **t** God who sent me.
Ro 10: 8 Salvation that comes from **t** Christ—which is the
11:22 But if you stop **t**, you also will be cut off.
Gal 2:20 So I live my life in this earthly body by **t** in the
5:10 I am **t** the Lord to bring you back to believing as I
Php 1:29 For you have been given not only the privilege of **t**
2Ti 3:15 the salvation that comes by **t** in Christ Jesus.
Heb 3:14 **t** God just as firmly as when we first believed,
4:14 of God. Let us cling to him and never stop **t** him.
10:22 the presence of God, with true hearts fully **t** him.
Jas 2:22 he was **t** God so much that he was willing to do
1Pe 1: 5 you receive this salvation, because you are **t** him.
1: 9 Your reward for **t** him will be the salvation of your
1Jn 5: 4 For every child of God defeats this evil world by **t**
Rev 14:12 to the end, obeying his commands and **t** in Jesus."

TRUSTS (9) [TRUST]

Ge 39: 8 "my master **t** me with everything in his entire
Ps 21: 7 For the king **t** in the LORD. / The unfailing love
25: 3 No one who **t** in you will ever be disgraced,
34:22 Everyone who **t** in him will be freely pardoned.
Isa 57:13 But whoever **t** in me will possess the land
Na 1: 7 And he knows everyone who **t** in him.
Mt 18: 6 But if anyone causes one of these little ones who **t**
Mk 9:42 one of these little ones who **t** in me to lose faith,
Tit 3: 8 so that everyone who **t** in God will be careful to do

TRUSTWORTHY (14) [TRUST]

Ps 19: 7 the soul. / The decrees of the LORD are **t**,
111: 7 and good, / and all his commandments are **t**.
119:86 All your commands are **t**. / Protect me from those
Pr 11:13 but those who are **t** can keep a confidence.
28:20 The **t** will get a rich reward. But the person who
Lk 19:17 the king exclaimed. 'You are a **t** servant.
1Co 4:17 For he is my beloved and **t** child in the Lord.
1Ti 1:12 I am to Christ Jesus our Lord for considering me **t**
2Ti 2: 2 Teach these great truths to **t** people who are able to
Tit 1: 9 and steadfast belief in the **t** message he was taught;
2:10 but they must show themselves to be entirely **t**
Heb 6:19 is like a strong and **t** anchor for our souls.
Rev 21: 5 this down, for what I tell you is **t** and true."
22: 6 the angel said to me, "These words are **t** and true:

TRUTH (205) [TRUE, TRUER, TRULY, TRUTHFUL, TRUTHFULLY, TRUTHFULNESS, TRUTHS]

Ge 42:20 I will know whether or not you are telling me the **t**.
Jos 7:19 to the LORD, the God of Israel, by telling the **t**.
Jdg 16:18 Delilah realized he had finally told her the **t**,
2Sa 4: 9 saves me from my enemies, I will tell you the **t**.
7:28 Your words are **t**, and you have promised these
1Ki 18:10 king of that nation to swear to the **t** of his claim.
22:16 speak only the **t** when you speak for the LORD?"
2Ch 18:15 speak only the **t** when you speak for the LORD?"
Ne 6: 8 are lying. There is no **t** in any part of your story."
Job 4:12 "This **t** was given me in secret, as though
17:12 is day and day is night; how they pervert the **t**!
18: 5 "The **t** remains that the light of the wicked will be
21: 7 "The **t** is that the wicked live to a good old age.
21:29 who have been around, and they can tell you the **t**.
33: 3 I speak with all sincerity; I speak the **t**.
36: 2 and I will show you the **t** of what I am saying.
36: 4 I am telling you the honest **t**, for I am a man of
Ps 15: 2 what is right, / speaking the **t** from sincere hearts.
25: 5 Lead me by your **t** and teach me, / for you are the
26: 3 and I have lived according to your **t**.
43: 3 Send out your light and your **t**; / let them guide me.
45: 4 out to victory, / defending **t**, humility, and justice.
52: 3 more than good / and lies more than **t**. / *Interlude*
85:10 Unfailing love and **t** have met together.
85:11 **T** springs up from the earth, / and righteousness
86:11 O LORD, / that I may live according to your **t**!
86:15 slow to get angry, / full of unfailing love and **t**.
89:14 Unfailing love and **t** walk before you as attendants.
96:13 with righteousness / and all the nations with his **t**.
119:43 Do not snatch your word of **t** from me, / for my
119:69 but in **t** I obey your commandments with all my
119:123 to see the **t** of your promise fulfilled.
144: 8 full of lies; / they swear to tell the **t**, but they lie.
144:11 full of lies; / they swear to tell the **t**, but they lie.
Pr 8: 7 for I speak the **t** and hate every kind of deception.
12:17 An honest witness tells the **t**; a false witness tells
12:19 **T** stands the test of time; lies are soon exposed.
15:14 A wise person is hungry for **t**, while the fool feeds
22:21 you may know the **t** and bring an accurate report to
23:23 Get the **t** and don't ever sell it; also get wisdom,
Ecc 12:10 Indeed, the Teacher taught the plain **t**, and he did
Isa 8:20 it is because there is no light or **t** in them.
11: 5 He will be clothed with fairness and **t**.
29:24 Those in error will then believe the **t**, and those
30:10 They say, "Don't tell us the **t**. Tell us nice things.
42: 4 He will not stop until **t** and righteousness prevail
43: 9 Who can verify that they spoke the **t**?
59:14 **T** falls dead in the streets, and fairness has been
59:15 Yes, **t** is gone, and anyone who tries to live a godly
65:16 or take an oath will do so by the God of **t**.
Jer 7:28 **T** has vanished from among them; it is no longer
9: 3 They refuse to stand up for the **t**. And they only go
9: 5 all fool and defraud each other; no one tells the **t**.
29:10 "The **t** is that you will be in Babylon for seventy
38:14 the king said. "And don't try to hide the **t**."
38:15 Jeremiah said, "If I tell you the **t**, you will kill me.
38:27 and they left without finding out the **t**.
Eze 12: 2 you live among rebels who could see the **t** if they
Da 8:12 the Temple ceremonies, and **t** was overthrown.
9:13 by turning from our sins and recognizing his **t**.
10:21 I will tell you what is written in the Book of **T**.
11: 2 "Now then, I will reveal the **t** to you. Three more
Am 5:10 How you despise people who tell the **t**!
Mic 6:12 to lying that their tongues can no longer tell the **t**.
Zec 8:16 this is what you must do: Tell the **t** to each other.
8:19 for the people of Judah. So love **t** and peace.
Mal 2: 6 They passed on to the people all the **t** they received
Mt 8:10 Turning to the crowd, he said, "I tell you the **t**,
11:25 thank you for hiding the **t** from those who think
19:23 Then Jesus said to his disciples, "I tell you the **t**,
26:21 While they were eating, he said, "The **t** is, one of
26:34 "Peter," Jesus replied, "the **t** is, this very night,
Mk 12:32 You have spoken the **t** by saying that there is only
14:18 Jesus said, "The **t** is, one of you will betray me,
14:30 "Peter," Jesus replied, "the **t** is, this very night,
Lk 1: 4 to reassure you of the **t** of all you were taught.
4:24 But the **t** is, no prophet is accepted in his own
10:12 The **t** is, even wicked Sodom will be better off than
10:21 thank you for hiding the **t** from those who think
Jn 1:51 Then he said, "The **t** is, you will all see heaven
3: 5 Jesus replied, "The **t** is, no one can enter the
4:23 will worship the Father in spirit and in **t**.
4:24 who worship him must worship in spirit and in **t**."
5:33 to listen to John the Baptist, and he preached the **t**.
6:26 Jesus replied, "The **t** is, you want to be with me
8:32 you will know the **t**, and the **t** will set you free."
8:40 I told you the **t** I heard from God, but you are
8:44 from the beginning and has always hated the **t**.
8:44 There is no **t** in him. When he lies, it is consistent
8:45 So when I tell the **t**, you just naturally don't
8:46 And since I am telling you the **t**, why don't you
8:58 Jesus answered, "The **t** is, I existed before
9:24 and told him, "Give glory to God by telling the **t**,
12:24 The **t** is, a kernel of wheat must be planted in the
12:48 at the day of judgment by the **t** I have spoken.
13:21 and he exclaimed, "The **t** is, one of you will betray
14: 6 Jesus told him, "I am the way, the **t**, and the life.
14:12 "The **t** is, anyone who believes in me will do the
14:17 He is the Holy Spirit, who leads into all **t**.
15:26 I will send you the Counselor—the Spirit of **t**.
16:13 the Spirit of **t** comes, he will guide you into all **t**.
16:23 The **t** is, you can go directly to the Father and ask
17:17 and holy by teaching them your words of **t**.
18:23 for it. Should you hit a man for telling the **t**?"
18:37 that purpose. And I came to bring **t** to the world.
18:37 All who love the **t** recognize that what I say is
18:38 "What is **t**?" Pilate asked. Then he went out again
21:18 The **t** is, when you were young, you were able to
Ac 7:51 You are heathen at heart and deaf to the **t**.
17:11 and Silas, to see if they were really teaching the **t**.
20:20 Yet I never shrank from telling you the **t**,
20:30 Even some of you will distort the **t** in order to draw
21:34 He couldn't find out the **t** in all the uproar
24: 8 You can find out the **t** of our accusations by
26:25 Most Excellent Festus. I am speaking the sober **t**.
Ro 1:18 wicked people who push the **t** away from
1:19 For the **t** about God is known to them instinctively.
1:25 Instead of believing what they knew was the **t**
2: 8 who refuse to obey the **t** and practice evil deeds.
2:20 in God's law you have complete knowledge and **t**.
4:23 Now this wonderful **t**—that God declared him to
7: 9 But when I learned the **t**, I realized I had broken
1Co 5: 8 but by eating the new bread of purity and **t**.
13: 6 but rejoices whenever the **t** wins out.
2Co 1:23 call upon God as my witness that I am telling the **t**.
3:14 covers their minds so they cannot understand the **t**.
4: 2 We tell the **t** before God, and all who are honest
6: 7 We have faithfully preached the **t**. God's power
7:14 I have always told you the **t**, and now my boasting
11:10 As surely as the **t** of Christ is in me, I will never
11:31 who is to be praised forever, knows I tell the **t**.
12: 6 no fool in doing it, because I would be telling the **t**.
13: 8 never to oppose the **t**, but to stand for the **t** at all
Gal 1: 7 who twist and change the **t** concerning Christ.
2: 5 We wanted to preserve the **t** of the Good News for
2:14 When I saw that they were not following the **t** of
4:16 your enemy because I am telling you the **t**?
5: 7 with you to hold you back from following the **t**?
Eph 1:13 And now you also have heard the **t**, the Good
4:14 lied to us and made the lie sound like the **t**.
4:15 Instead, we will hold to the **t** in love,
4:21 about him and have learned the **t** that is in Jesus,
4:25 away all falsehood and "tell your neighbor the **t**"
6:14 putting on the sturdy belt of **t** and the body armor
Php 1: 7 defending the **t** and telling others the Good News.
3:16 But we must be sure to obey the **t** we have learned
Col 1: 5 as you have been ever since you first heard the **t** of
1: 6 and understood the **t** about God's great kindness to
1:23 But you must continue to believe this **t** and stand
2: 7 strong and vigorous in the **t** you were taught.
1Th 1: 5 you was further proof of the **t** of our message.
2Th 2:10 because they refuse to believe the **t** that would save
2:12 they will be condemned for not believing the **t**
2:13 who makes you holy and by your belief in the **t**.
1Ti 2: 4 everyone to be saved and to understand the **t**.
2: 7 this is the absolute **t**—as a preacher and apostle to
teach the Gentiles about faith and **t**.
3:15 living God, which is the pillar and support of the **t**.
4: 3 by people who know and believe the **t**.
4:10 suffer much in order that people will believe the **t**,
6: 5 Their minds are corrupt, and they don't tell the **t**.
2Ti 2:15 and who correctly explains the word of **t**.
2:18 They have left the path of **t**, preaching the lie that
2:19 But God's **t** stands firm like a foundation stone
2:25 They should gently teach those who oppose the **t**.
2:25 those people's hearts, and they will believe the **t**.
3: 7 new teachings, but they never understand the **t**.
3: 8 And these teachers fight the **t** just as Jannes
4: 4 They will reject the **t** and follow strange myths.
Tit 1: 1 and to teach them to know the **t** that shows them
1: 2 This **t** gives them the confidence of eternal life,
1:11 already turned whole families away from the **t**.
1:14 of people who have turned their backs on the **t**.
3:11 For people like that have turned away from the **t**.
Heb 2: 1 So we must listen very carefully to the **t** we have
10:26 after we have received a full knowledge of the **t**,
Jas 5:19 if anyone among you wanders away from the **t**
1Pe 1:22 sins when you accepted the **t** of the Good News.
2Pe 1:12 already know them and are standing firm in the **t**.
3: 3 days there will be scoffers who will laugh at the **t**
1Jn 1: 6 in spiritual darkness. We are not living in the **t**.
1: 8 only fooling ourselves and refusing to accept the **t**.
2: 4 that person is a liar and does not live in the **t**.
2:20 has come upon you, and all of you know the **t**.
2:21 to you not because you don't know the **t** but
because you know the difference between **t**
3:19 by our actions that we know we are living in the **t**,
4: 6 That is how we know if someone has the Spirit of **t**
2Jn 1: 1 and to her children, whom I love in the **t**,
1: 1 as does everyone else who knows God's **t**—
1: 2 the **t** that lives in us and will be in our hearts
1: 3 Christ his Son, be with us who live in **t** and love.
1: 4 some of your children and find them living in the **t**,
1:10 your meeting and does not teach the **t** about Christ,
3Jn 1: 1 to Gaius, my dear friend, whom I love in the **t**.
1: 3 your faithfulness and that you are living in the **t**.
1: 4 joy than to hear that my children live in the **t**.
1: 8 that we may become partners with them for the **t**.
1:12 everyone speaks highly of Demetrius, even **t** itself.
1:12 the same for him, and you know we speak the **t**.
Jude 1: 3 urging you to defend the **t** of the Good News.
1: 3 God gave this unchanging **t** once for all time to his

TRUTHFUL (3) [TRUTH]

Ps 5: 9 My enemies cannot speak one **t** word.
Pr 14: 5 A **t** witness does not lie; a false witness breathes
14:25 A **t** witness saves lives, but a false witness is a

TRUTHFULLY (1) [TRUTH]

Jn 8:46 Which of you can **t** accuse me of sin? And since I

TRUTHFULNESS (2) [TRUTH]

Ro 3: 7 me as a sinner if my dishonesty highlights his **t**
9: 1 In the presence of Christ, I speak with utter **t**—

TRUTHS (10) [TRUTH]

Ps 78: 4 We will not hide these **t** from our children
119:18 Open my eyes to see / the wonderful **t** in your law.
Ecc 12:11 spur students to action and emphasize important **t**.

1Co 2:13 using the Spirit's words to explain spiritual **t**.
2:14 can't understand these **t** from God's Spirit.
1Ti 3: 9 They must be committed to the revealed **t** of the
6: 2 Teach these **t**, Timothy, and encourage everyone to
2Ti 2: 2 Teach these great **t** to trustworthy people who are
Heb 3: 5 His work was an illustration of the **t** God would
Rev 2:24 have not followed this false teaching ('deeper **t**,'

TRY (100) [TRIED, TRIES, TRYING]

Ge 4:14 All who see me will **t** to kill me!"
4:15 on Cain to warn anyone who might **t** to kill him.
Ex 10:10 be with you if you **t** to take your little ones along!
Lev 19:16 "Do not **t** to get ahead at the cost of your
Dt 13: 5 or dreamers who **t** to lead you astray must be put to
13: 5 Since they **t** to keep you from following the
23: 6 **t** to help the Ammonites or the Moabites in any
25: 8 then summon him and **t** to reason with him.
Jdg 11:25 Did he **t** to make a case against Israel for disputed
1Sa 9:10 "All right," Saul agreed, "let's **t** it!" So they
15:27 Saul grabbed at him to **t** to hold him back and tore
22: 8 own son—encouraging David to **t** and kill me!"
26:21 my son, and I will no longer **t** to harm you,
Est 9: 2 against anyone who might **t** to harm them.
Job 7:13 and I will **t** to forget my misery with sleep,'
8:15 They **t** to hold it fast, but it will not endure.
9:14 that I should **t** to answer God or even reason with
16: 5 that helps you. I would **t** to take away your grief.
17:10 "As for all of you, come back and **t** again! But I
19: 2 How long will you **t** to break me with your words?
20:24 He will **t** to escape, but God's arrow will pierce
23: 2 is still a bitter one, and I **t** hard not to groan aloud.
31:35 who would listen to me and **t** to see my side!
32:21 I won't play favorites or **t** to flatter anyone.
34:16 "Listen now and **t** to understand.
41: 6 Will merchants **t** to buy it? Will they sell it in their
41: 8 battle that follows, and you will never **t** it again!
41: 9 "No, it is useless to **t** to capture it. The hunter who
Ps 25: 3 but disgrace comes to those who **t** to deceive
40:14 May those who **t** to destroy me / be humiliated
62:10 Don't **t** to get rich / by extortion or robbery.
70: 2 May those who **t** to destroy me / be humiliated
109: 4 I love them, but they **t** to destroy me— / even as I
119:61 Evil people **t** to drag me into sin, / but I am firmly
Pr 24:12 Don't **t** to avoid responsibility by saying you
Ecc 2: 1 said to myself, "Come now, let's give pleasure a **t**.
7:18 So **t** to walk a middle course—but those who fear
8: 3 Don't **t** to avoid doing your duty, and don't take a
Isa 2:21 they will **t** to escape the terror of the LORD
15: 9 both those who **t** to run and those who remain
22: 3 The people **t** to slip away, but they are captured,
22: 4 Leave me alone to weep; do not **t** to comfort me.
29:15 Destruction is certain for those who **t** to hide their
29:15 who **t** to keep him in the dark concerning what
41:22 "Let them **t** to tell us what happened long ago
Jer 1:19 They will **t**, but they will fail. For I am with you,
10: 2 "Do not act like other nations who **t** to read their
38:14 the king said. "And don't **t** to hide the truth."
La 2:14 They did not **t** to hold you back from exile by
Eze 21:24 You don't even **t** to hide it! Wherever you go,
24: 7 rocks for all to see. She doesn't even **t** to cover it!
35: 7 killing off all who **t** to escape and any who return.
Da 2:43 and clay also shows that these kingdoms will **t** to
7:25 He will **t** to change their sacred festivals and laws,
Hos 4: 4 finger at someone else and **t** to pass the blame!
7:10 return to the LORD his God or even **t** to find him.
Mic 6:14 And though you **t** to save your money, it will come
Zec 12: 3 None of the nations who **t** to lift it will escape
13: 4 No one will wear prophet's clothes to **t** to fool the
Mal 1: 4 "They may **t** to rebuild, but I will demolish them
1: 8 **T** giving gifts like that to your governor, and see
3:10 room to take it in! **T** it! Let me prove it to you!
Mt 2:13 because Herod is going to **t** to kill the child."
6:16 who **t** to look pale and disheveled so people will
15:10 and said, "Listen to what I say and **t** to understand.
16:25 If you **t** to keep your life for yourself, you will lose
21:46 but they were afraid to **t** because the crowds
23:28 You **t** to look like upright people outwardly,
Mk 7:14 "All of you listen," he said, "and **t** to understand.
8:35 If you **t** to keep your life for yourself, you will lose
12:13 and supporters of Herod to **t** to trap Jesus into
Lk 5: 5 catch a thing. But if you say so, we'll **t** again."
6:30 are taken away from you, don't **t** to get them back.
9:24 If you **t** to keep your life for yourself, you will lose
12:58 **t** to settle the matter before it reaches the judge,
13:24 Work hard to get in, because many will **t** to enter,
14:19 bought five pair of oxen and wanted to **t** them out.
Ac 22:30 He had Paul brought in before them to **t** to find out
23:28 Then I took him to their high council to **t** to find
24:16 I always **t** to maintain a clear conscience before
26:11 in the synagogues to **t** to get them to curse Christ.
27:44 and he told the others to **t** for it on planks
Ro 4:15 But the law brings punishment on those who **t** to
7:19 And when I **t** not to do wrong, I do it anyway.
12:16 Don't **t** to act important, but enjoy the company of
14:19 harmony in the church and **t** to build each other up.
1Co 7:18 he became a believer should not **t** to reverse it.
9:22 I **t** to find common ground with everyone so that I
10:33 too. I **t** to please everyone in everything I do.
16: 2 until I get there and then **t** to collect it all at once.
2Co 4: 2 We do not **t** to trick anyone, and we do not distort
6: 3 We **t** to live in such a way that no one will be
6: 4 In everything we do we **t** to show that we are true
Eph 5: 6 Don't be fooled by those who **t** to excuse these
5:10 **T** to find out what is pleasing to the Lord.
5:17 but **t** to understand what the Lord wants you to do.
Col 3:22 **T** to please them all the time, not just when they
1Th 2: 5 Never once did we **t** to win you with flattery,
5:15 but always **t** to do good to each other and to
Heb 12:14 **T** to live in peace with everyone, and seek to live a

TRYING (93) [TRY]

Ge 19: 9 among us, and now you are **t** to tell us what to do!
27:12 He'll see that I'm **t** to trick him, and then he'll
44:15 "What were you **t** to do?" Joseph demanded.
Ex 18:14 he said, "Why are you **t** to do all this alone?
Nu 16:14 of fields and vineyards. Are you **t** to fool us?
32: 7 "Are you **t** to discourage the rest of the people of
Jdg 14:14 Three days later they were still **t** to figure it out.
18: 1 And the tribe of Dan was **t** to find a place to settle,
1Sa 24: 9 "Why do you listen to the people who say I am **t**
24:11 This proves that I am not **t** to harm you and that I
24:12 will punish you for what you are **t** to do to me,
24:14 Who is the king of Israel **t** to catch anyway?
28: 9 "Are you **t** to get me killed?" the woman
2Sa 16:11 and the other officers, "My own son is **t** to kill me.
1Ki 18:13 about the time when Jezebel was **t** to kill the
19:10 I alone am left, and now they are **t** to kill me, too."
19:14 I alone am left, and now they are **t** to kill me, too."
2Ki 5: 7 He is only **t** to find an excuse to invade us again."
1Ch 7:21 and Elead were killed **t** to steal livestock from the
2Ch 32:18 **t** to terrify them so it would be easier to capture the
Ne 6: 9 They were just **t** to intimidate us, imagining that
Job 2: 9 to him, "Are you still **t** to maintain your integrity?
9:29 I will be found guilty. So what's the use of **t**?
19: 5 You are **t** to overcome me, using my humiliation
28:18 and valuable rock crystal are worthless in **t** to get
34: 9 has even said, 'Why waste time **t** to please God?'
Ps 32: 5 and stopped **t** to hide them. / I said to myself,
35: 4 Humiliate and disgrace those **t** to kill me;
54: 3 are attacking me; / violent men are **t** to kill me.
62: 3 against one man— / all of them **t** to kill me.
86:14 rise up against me; / violent people are **t** to kill me.
Pr 23: 4 Don't wear yourself **t** to get rich. Why waste your
23:30 spends long hours in the taverns, **t** out new drinks.
27:16 **T** to stop her complaints is like **t** to stop the
Isa 8:19 So why are you **t** to find out the future by
31: 3 and fall among those they are **t** to help.
49:17 and all who are **t** to destroy you will go away.
Jer 23:27 they are **t** to get my people to forget me,
Eze 13:10 and these prophets are **t** to hold it together by
24:19 does all this mean? What are you **t** to tell us?"
Da 2: 8 You are **t** to stall for time because you know I am
8:15 was **t** to understand the meaning of this vision,
Joel 3: 4 Are you **t** to take revenge on me? If you are,
Mal 3:14 or by **t** to show the LORD Almighty that we are
Mt 2:20 because those who were **t** to kill the child are
22:18 "Whom are you **t** to fool with your trick
26:59 and the entire high council were **t** to find witnesses
Mk 3:10 people were crowding around him, **t** to touch him.
9:22 him fall into the fire or into water, **t** to kill him.
12:15 "Who are you **t** to fool with your trick questions?
14:55 and the entire high council were **t** to find witnesses
Lk 6:19 Everyone was **t** to touch him, because healing
11:16 **T** to test Jesus, others asked for a miraculous sign
11:54 **t** to trap him into saying something they could use
14: 7 the dinner were **t** to sit near the head of the table,
24: 4 **t** to think what could have happened to it.
Jn 5: 7 While I am **t** to get there, someone else always gets
7:19 the law of Moses! In fact, you are **t** to kill me."
7:20 "You're demon possessed! Who's **t** to kill you?"
7:25 "Isn't this the man they are **t** to kill?
8: 6 They were **t** to trap him into saying something they
8:37 And yet some of you are **t** to kill me because my
8:40 the truth I heard from God, but you are **t** to kill me.
9:34 in sin!" they answered. "Are you **t** to teach us?"
11: 8 ago the Jewish leaders in Judea were **t** to kill you.
11:31 When the people who were at the house **t** to
Ac 13: 8 He was **t** to turn the governor away from the
18: 4 **t** to convince the Jews and Greeks alike.
21:31 As they were **t** to kill him, word reached the
24: 6 Moreover he was **t** to defile the Temple when we
Ro 9:32 Because they were **t** to get right with God by
10: 3 way of getting right with God by **t** to keep the law.
11: 3 I alone am left, and now they are **t** to kill me, too."
14: 6 day for worshiping the Lord are **t** to honor him.
1Co 7:28 I am **t** to spare you the extra problems that come
10:19 What am I **t** to say? Am I saying that the idols to
2Co 5:12 Are we **t** to pat ourselves on the back again?
Gal 1:10 I'm not **t** to be a people pleaser! No, I am **t** to
please God. If I were still **t** to please people,
2:14 why are you **t** to make these Gentiles obey the
3: 3 why are you now **t** to become perfect by your own
3:11 can ever be right with God by **t** to keep the law.
3:17 This is what I am **t** to say: The agreement God
4:10 You are **t** to find favor with God by what you do
4:17 They are **t** to shut you off from me so that you will
5: 3 If you are **t** to find favor with God by being
5: 4 For if you are **t** to make yourselves right with God
6:12 Those who are **t** to force you to be circumcised are
Php 2:30 and he was at the point of death while **t** to do for
Col 3:21 If you do, they will become discouraged and quit **t**.
1Th 2:16 by **t** to keep us from preaching the Good News to

TRYPHENA (1)

Ro 16:12 Say hello to **T** and Tryphosa, the Lord's workers,

TRYPHOSA (1)

Ro 16:12 Say hello to Tryphena and **T**, the Lord's workers,

TUBAL (7)

Ge 10: 2 Magog, Madai, Javan, **T**, Meshech, and Tiras.
1Ch 1: 5 Magog, Madai, Javan, **T**, Meshech, and Tiras.
Isa 66:19 (who are famous as archers), to **T** and Greece,
Eze 27:13 Merchants from Greece, **T**, and Meshech brought
32:26 "Meshech and **T** are there, surrounded by the
38: 2 who rules over the nations of Meshech and **T**.
39: 1 O Gog, ruler of the nations of Meshech and **T**.

TUBAL-CAIN (2)

Ge 4:22 To Lamech's other wife, Zillah, was born **T**.
4:22 of bronze and iron. **T** had a sister named Naamah.

TUBES (2)

Job 40:18 Its bones are **t** of bronze. Its limbs are bars of iron.
Zec 4:12 that pour out golden oil through two gold **t**?"

TUCKED (1)

1Ki 18:46 He **t** his cloak into his belt and ran ahead of Ahab's

TUGGING (1)

Ac 23:10 and the men were **t** at Paul from both sides,

TUITION (1)

Pr 17:16 It is senseless to pay **t** to educate a fool who has no

TUMBLE (1) [TUMBLES, TUMBLING]

Job 15:28 live in abandoned houses that are ready to **t** down.

TUMBLES (1) [TUMBLE]

Pr 17:20 will not prosper; the twisted tongue **t** into trouble.

TUMBLING (1) [TUMBLE]

Jdg 7:13 and in my dream a loaf of barley bread came **t**

TUMORS (9)

Dt 28:27 will afflict you with the boils of Egypt and with **t**,
1Sa 5: 6 and the nearby villages with a plague of **t**.
5: 9 young and old, with a plague of **t**, and there was a
5:12 Those who didn't die were afflicted with **t**;
6: 4 five rulers, make five gold **t** and five gold rats,
6: 8 it place a chest containing the gold rats and gold **t**.
6:11 the gold rats and gold **t** were placed on the cart.
6:15 and gold **t** from the cart and placed them on the
6:17 The five gold **t** that were sent by the Philistines as

TUMULT (2)

Ps 42: 7 I hear the **t** of the raging seas / as your waves
83: 2 Don't you hear the **t** of your enemies? / Don't you

TUNE (14) [TUNELESS, TUNES]

Ps 9: T of David, to be sung to the **t** "Death of the Son."
22: T of David, to be sung to the **t** "Doe of the Dawn."
45: T descendants of Korah, to be sung to the **t** "Lilies."
56: T To be sung to the **t** "Dove on Distant Oaks."
57: T the cave. To be sung to the **t** "Do Not Destroy!"
58: T of David, to be sung to the **t** "Do Not Destroy!"
59: T to kill him. To be sung to the **t** "Do Not Destroy!"
60: T To be sung to the **t** "Lily of the Testimony."
69: T A psalm of David, to be sung to the **t** "Lilies."
75: T of Asaph, to be sung to the **t** "Do Not Destroy!"
80: T to be sung to the **t** "Lilies of the Covenant."
88: T to be sung to the **t** "The Suffering of Affliction."
125: 4 who are good, / whose hearts are in **t** with you.
Pr 2: 2 **T** your ears to wisdom, and concentrate on

TUNELESS (1) [TUNE]

Ecc 12: 4 But you yourself will be deaf and **t**, with a

TUNES (1) [TUNE]

Ps 58: 5 ignoring the **t** of the snake charmers, / no matter

TUNIC (11) [TUNICS]

Ex 28: 4 an ephod, a robe, an embroidered **t**, a turban,
28:39 "Weave Aaron's patterned **t** from fine linen cloth.
29: 5 Then put Aaron's **t** on him, along with the
Lev 8: 7 He clothed Aaron with the embroidered **t** and tied
16: 4 he must wash his entire body and put on his linen **t**
1Sa 2:18 He wore a linen **t** just like that of a priest.
18: 4 by giving him his robe, **t**, sword, bow, and belt.
2Sa 6:14 the LORD with all his might, wearing a priestly **t**.
1Ch 15:27 song leader. David was also wearing a priestly **t**.
Job 30:18 my garment. He grips me by the collar of my **t**.
Jn 21: 7 he put on his **t** (for he had stripped for work),

TUNICS (7) [TUNIC]

Ex 28:40 "Then for Aaron's sons, make **t**, sashes,
29: 8 Next present his sons, and dress them in their **t**
39:27 **T** were then made for Aaron and his sons from fine
40:14 Then bring his sons and dress them in their **t**.
Lev 8:13 and clothed them in their embroidered **t**,
10: 5 and carried them out of the camp by their **t** as
1Sa 22:18 priests in all, all still wearing their priestly **t**.

TUNNEL (3) [TUNNELS]

2Sa 5: 8 "Go up through the water **t** into the city
2Ki 20:20 built a pool and dug a **t** to bring water into the city,
2Ch 32:30 and brought the water down through a **t** to the west

TUNNELS (1) [TUNNEL]

Job 28:10 They cut **t** in the rocks and uncover precious

TURBAN (12) [TURBANS]

Ex 28: 4 a robe, an embroidered tunic, a **t**, and a sash.
28:37 to the front of Aaron's **t** by means of a blue cord.
28:39 Fashion the **t** out of this linen as well. Also make
29: 6 And place on his head the **t** with the gold
39:28 The **t**, the headdresses, and the underclothes were
39:30 of pure gold to be worn on the front of the **t**.
39:31 This medallion was tied to the **t** with a blue cord,
Lev 8: 9 He placed on Aaron's head the **t** with the gold
16: 4 around his waist and put the linen **t** on his head.
Job 29:14 covered me like a robe, and I wore justice like a **t**.
Zec 3: 5 could he also have a clean **t** on his head?"
3: 5 So they put a clean priestly **t** on his head

TURBANS (3) [TURBAN]

Lev 8:13 their sashes, and their **t**, just as the LORD had
Eze 23:15 their waists, and flowing **t** crowned their heads.
44:18 They must wear linen **t** and linen undergarments.

TURMOIL (6)

Ps 39: 2 the **t** within me grew to the bursting point.
75: 3 When the earth quakes and its people live in **t**,
Pr 15:16 for the LORD than to have great treasure with **t**.
Eze 3:14 I went in bitterness and **t**, but the LORD's hold
Lk 21:25 And down here on earth the nations will be in **t**,
Ac 17: 8 city officials, were thrown into **t** by these reports.

TURN (352) [TURNED, TURNING, TURNS]

Ge 49:19 marauding bands, / but he will **t** and plunder them.
Ex 4: 9 the dry ground. When you do, it will **t** into blood."
7:17 Nile with this staff, and the river will **t** to blood.
7:19 Everywhere in Egypt the water will **t** into blood,
8:16 The dust will **t** into swarms of gnats throughout the
32:12 face of the earth.' **T** away from your fierce anger.
Lev 13:16 open sores heal and **t** white like the rest of the skin,
17:10 "And I will **t** against anyone, whether an Israelite
20: 3 I myself will **t** against them and cut them off from
20: 5 then I myself will **t** against them and cut them off
20: 6 I will **t** against them and cut them off from the
26:17 I will **t** against you, and you will be defeated by all
Nu 14:25 Now **t** around and don't go on toward the land
20:21 their country, Israel was forced to **t** around.
25: 4 so his fierce anger will **t** away from the people of
27: 9 no daughters, **t** his inheritance over to his brothers.
32:15 If you **t** away from him like this and he abandons
34: 5 From Azmon the boundary will **t** toward the brook
Dt 1:40 **t** around now and go on back through the
2: 3 in this hill country long enough; **t** northward.
2:27 and won't **t** off into the fields on either side.
11:16 "But do not let your heart **t** away from the LORD
11:28 and **t** from his way by worshiping foreign gods.
13:17 Then the LORD will **t** from his fierce anger
23:14 thing among you, or he might **t** away from you.
28:14 You must not **t** away from any of the commands I
28:24 The LORD will **t** your rain into sand and dust,
29:18 or tribe among you would **t** away from the LORD
30:10 and if you **t** to the LORD your God with all your
31:29 and will **t** from the path I have commanded you to
Jos 1: 7 Do not **t** away from them, and you will be
7: 5 The Israelites were paralyzed with fear at this **t** of
22:16 How could you **t** away from the LORD and build
22:23 that we have not built an altar for ourselves to **t**
22:29 or **t** away from him by building our own altar for
23:12 "But if you **t** away from him and intermarry with
24:20 other gods, he will **t** against you and destroy you,
24:23 and **t** your hearts to the LORD, the God of
Jdg 20:39 which was the signal for the Israelites to **t**
Ru 1:16 "Don't ask me to leave you and **t** back.
1Sa 12:20 and that you don't **t** your back on him in any way.
2Sa 3:12 and I will help **t** the entire nation of Israel over to
18: 3 "If we have to **t** and run—and even if half of us
22:41 You made them **t** and run; / I have destroyed all
1Ki 2:16 Please don't **t** me down." "What is it?"
2:20 of you," she said. "I hope you won't **t** me down."
8:33 and if they **t** to you and call on your name and pray
8:35 and confess your name and **t** from their sins
8:47 they may **t** to you again in repentance and pray,
8:48 Then if they **t** to you with their whole heart
12:15 This **t** of events was the will of the LORD,
13:33 after this, Jeroboam did not **t** from his evil ways.
2Ki 10:31 He refused to **t** from the sins of idolatry that
13:11 He refused to **t** from the sins of idolatry that
14:24 He refused to **t** from the sins of idolatry that
15: 9 He refused to **t** from the sins of idolatry that
15:18 he refused to **t** from the sins of idolatry that
15:24 He refused to **t** from the sins of idolatry that
15:28 He refused to **t** from the sins of idolatry that
17:13 both Israel and Judah: "**T** from all your evil ways.
17:22 They did not **t** from these sins of idolatry
22: 2 He did not **t** aside from doing what was right.
1Ch 3:16 he, in **t**, was succeeded by his uncle Zedekiah.
2Ch 6:24 and if they **t** to you and call on your name and pray
6:26 and confess your name and **t** from their sins
6:37 they may **t** to you again in repentance and pray,
6:38 Then if they **t** to you with their whole heart
7:14 and seek my face and **t** from their wicked ways,
10:15 This **t** of events was the will of God, for it fulfilled
29:10 so that his fierce anger will **t** away from us.
30: 8 so that his fierce anger will **t** away from you.
30: 9 he will not continue to **t** his face from you."
34: 2 He did not **t** aside from doing what was right.
34:33 they did not **t** away from the LORD, the God of
35:22 God had indeed spoken, and he would not **t** back.
36:13 refusing to **t** to the LORD, the God of Israel.
Ne 9:35 but they refused to **t** from their wickedness.
12:47 The Levites, in **t**, gave a portion of what they
Est 2:15 When it was Esther's **t** to go to the king,
Job 5: 1 You may **t** to the angels, but they give you no help.
5: 3 I know that fools who **t** from God may be
6:18 The caravans **t** aside to be refreshed, but there is
10: 9 made of dust—will you **t** me back to dust so soon?
13:24 Why do you **t** away from me? Why do you
14: 6 a little rest, won't you? **T** away your angry stare.
15:13 that you **t** against God and say all these evil
19:18 When I stand to speak, they **t** their backs on me.
23: 9 he is hidden. I **t** to the south, but I cannot find him.
23:13 and who can **t** him from his purposes?
30:24 "Surely no one would **t** against the needy when
34:15 would cease, and humanity would **t** again to dust.
36:10 their attention and says they must **t** away from evil.
36:21 **T** back from evil, for it was to prevent you from
37:12 The clouds **t** around and around under his
Ps 5: 8 clearly what to do, / and show me which way to **t**.
6:10 and terrified. / May they suddenly **t** back in shame.
9: 3 My enemies **t** away in retreat; / they are
13: 3 **T** and answer me, O LORD my God!
18:40 You made them **t** and run; / I have destroyed all
21:12 For they will **t** and run / when they see your arrows
25:16 **T** to me and have mercy on me, / for I am alone
31:11 they see me on the street, / they **t** the other way.
34:14 **T** away from evil and do good. / Work hard at
35: 4 those trying to kill me; / **t** them back in confusion.
36: 4 never good. / They make no attempt to **t** from evil.
37: 8 Stop your anger! / **T** from your rage! / Do not envy
37:27 **T** from evil and do good, / and you will live in the
69:16 **T** and take care of me, / for your mercy is
69:20 some pity; / if only one would **t** and comfort me.
71: 2 you are just. / **T** your ear to listen and set me free.
78: 6 that they in **t** might teach their children.
80: 3 **T** us again to yourself, O God. / Make your face
80: 7 **T** us again to yourself, O God Almighty.
80:19 **T** us again to yourself, O LORD God Almighty.
85: 4 Now **t** to us again, O God of our salvation.
88:14 Why do you **t** your face away from me?
90: 3 You **t** people back to dust, saying, / "Return to
95:10 'They are a people whose hearts **t** away from me.
102: 2 Don't **t** away from me / in my time of distress.
104:29 But if you **t** away from them, they panic.
104:29 away their breath, they die / and **t** again to dust.
106:23 He begged him to **t** from his anger and not destroy
109: 6 Arrange for an evil person to **t** on him. / Send an
119:37 **T** my eyes from worthless things, / and give me
119:51 but I do not **t** away from your law.
119:110 but I will not **t** from your commandments.
125: 5 But banish those who **t** to crooked ways,
142: 3 and you alone know the way I should **t**.
143: 7 Don't **t** away from me, / or I will die.
Pr 1:10 if sinners entice you, **t** your back on them!
1:32 For they are simpletons who **t** away from me—
2:13 These people **t** from right ways to walk down dark
3: 7 Instead, fear the LORD and **t** your back on evil.
4: 2 good guidance. Don't **t** away from my teaching.
4: 5 Don't forget or **t** away from my words.
4: 6 Don't **t** your back on wisdom, for she will protect
4:15 their haunts. **T** away and go somewhere else,
10:19 for it fosters sin. Be sensible and **t** off the flow!
13:19 but fools will not **t** from evil to attain them.
24:18 with you and will **t** his anger away from them.
27:11 how happy I will be if you **t** out to be wise!
30:30 king of animals, who won't **t** aside for anything,
Ecc 3: 5 A time to embrace and a time to **t** away.
3:15 in the past. For God calls each event back in its **t**.
5:14 or they are put into risky investments that **t** sour,
Isa 1:25 I will **t** against you. I will melt you down and skim
6:10 with their hearts, and **t** to me for healing."
9:13 will still not repent and **t** to the LORD Almighty.
10: 3 To whom will you **t** for help? Where will your
10:12 he will **t** against the king of Assyria and punish
19: 3 and psychics to show them which way to **t**.
19:22 For the Egyptians will **t** to the LORD, and he will
25: 2 You **t** mighty cities into heaps of ruins. Cities with
26: 9 will people **t** from wickedness and do what is right.
30: 5 it will all **t** out to your shame. He will not help you
30:21 "This is the way; **t** around and walk here."
33:11 Your own breath will **t** to fire and kill you.
42:15 I will **t** the rivers into dry land / and will dry up all
47:10 and 'knowledge' have caused you to **t** away from
50: 2 I can **t** rivers into deserts covered with dying fish.
50: 5 and I have listened. I do not rebel or **t** away.
55: 7 Let the people **t** from their wicked deeds. Let them
t to the LORD that he may have mercy
55: 7 Yes, **t** to our God, for he will abundantly pardon.
63:17 why have you allowed us to **t** from your path?
Jer 2:25 Why do you refuse to **t** from all this running after
2:27 They **t** their backs on me, but in times of trouble
3:19 and I thought you would never **t** away from me
5: 3 You crushed them, but they refused to **t** from sin.
6:25 they are ready to kill. We are terrorized at every **t**!
8: 4 and discover their mistake, don't they **t** back?
8: 5 refusing to **t** back, even though I have warned
15: 7 because they refuse to **t** back to me from all their
17: 5 and **t** their hearts away from the LORD.
17:13 all who **t** away from you will be disgraced
18: 4 But the jar he was making did not **t** out as he had
18:11 So **t** from your evil ways, each of you, and do
18:17 And in all their trouble I will **t** my back on them
25: 5 '**T** from the evil road you are traveling and from
26: 3 Perhaps they will listen and **t** from their evil ways.
26:24 and persuaded the court not to **t** him over to the
29:21 I will **t** them over to Nebuchadnezzar for a public
31:13 I will **t** their mourning into joy. I will comfort them
31:18 **T** me again to you and restore me, for you alone
35:15 prophet to tell you to **t** from your wicked ways
36: 7 Perhaps even yet they will **t** from their evil ways
42: 6 if we obey him, everything will **t** out well for us."
44: 5 would not listen or **t** back from their wicked ways.
44:30 I will **t** Pharaoh Hophra, king of Egypt, over to his
46: 5 They are terrorized at every **t**, says the LORD.
46:21 They **t** and run, for it is a day of great disaster for
49: 8 **T** and flee! Hide in deep caves, you people of
49:24 has become feeble, and all her people **t** to flee.
49:29 panic will be heard: 'We are terrorized at every **t**!'
La 1: 3 have chased her down, and she has nowhere to **t**.
3:30 Let them **t** the other cheek to those who strike
3:40 Let us **t** again in repentance to the LORD.
Eze 1:12 in all directions without having to **t** around.
3:20 If good people **t** bad and don't listen to my
4: 3 **T** toward it and demonstrate how the enemy will
4: 6 **t** over and lie on your right side for 40 days—
4: 8 so you won't be able to **t** from side to side until the
5:14 "So I will **t** you into a ruin, a mockery in the eyes
7: 4 I will **t** my eyes away and show no pity,
13:19 You **t** my people away from me for a few handfuls
14: 6 Repent and **t** away from your idols, and stop all
14: 8 I will **t** against such people and make a terrible
18:14 "But suppose that sinful son, in **t**, has a son who
18:21 But if wicked people **t** away from all their sins
18:23 I only want them to **t** from their wicked ways
18:24 if righteous people **t** to sinful ways and start acting
18:26 When righteous people **t** from being good and start
18:27 And if wicked people **t** away from their
18:28 thinking it over, they decided to **t** from their sins.
18:30 **T** from your sins! Don't let them destroy you!
18:32 says the Sovereign LORD. **T** back and live!
20:39 but then don't **t** around and bring gifts to me.
21:22 Then they will decide to **t** toward Jerusalem!
23:25 I will **t** my jealous anger against you, and they will
25: 5 And I will **t** the city of Rabbah into a pasture for
29: 2 **t** toward Egypt and prophesy against Pharaoh the
33:11 I only want them to **t** from their wicked ways so
they can live. **T**! **T** from your wickedness,
33:12 righteous people will not save them if they **t** to sin,
33:12 destroy them if they repent and **t** from their sins.
33:14 but then they **t** from their sins and do what is just
33:18 when righteous people **t** to evil, they will die.
33:19 But if wicked people **t** from their wickedness
35: 2 "Son of man, **t** toward Mount Seir, and prophesy
35: 6 you a bloodbath of your own. Your **t** has come!
36: 7 nations will soon have their **t** at suffering shame.
38: 4 I will **t** you around and put hooks into your jaws to
38:21 Your men will **t** against each other in mortal
39: 2 I will **t** you and drive you toward the mountains of
39:29 And I will never again **t** my back on them, for I
46:12 Then he will **t** and leave the way he entered,
47:12 The leaves of these trees will never **t** brown
Da 9:16 please **t** your furious anger away from your city of
11:18 he will **t** his attention to the coastal cities
12: 3 and those who **t** many to righteousness will shine
Hos 4:13 "That is why your daughters **t** to prostitution,
9:12 It will be a terrible day when I **t** away and leave
Joel 2:12 LORD says, "**T** to me now, while there is time!
2:31 and the moon will **t** bloodred before that great
Am 1: 8 Then I will **t** to attack Ekron, and the few
6:12 but that's how stupid you are when you **t** justice
8: 3 sounds of singing in the Temple will **t** to wailing.
8:10 I will **t** your celebrations into times of mourning,
Ob 1: 7 "All your allies will **t** against you. They will help
Jnh 2: 8 Those who worship false gods **t** their backs on all
3: 8 Everyone must **t** from their evil ways and stop all
Mic 6: 3 what have I done to make you **t** from me?
Hab 2: 7 They will **t** on you and take all you have,
2:13 promised that the wealth of nations will **t** to ashes?
2:16 But soon it will be your **t**! Come, drink and be
Zec 1: 4 **T** from your evil ways and stop all your evil
11: 6 They will **t** the land into a wilderness, and I will
13: 7 will be scattered, and I will **t** against the lambs.
Mal 1:13 and you **t** up your noses at his commands,"
4: 6 His preaching will **t** the hearts of parents to their
Mt 3: 2 "**T** from your sins and **t** to God,
3:11 "I baptize with water those who **t** from their sins
and **t** to God.
4:17 to preach, "**T** from your sins and **t** to God,
5:36 my head!' for you can't **t** one hair white or black.
5:39 you are slapped on the right cheek, **t** the other, too.
5:42 and don't **t** away from those who want to borrow.
7: 6 They will trample the pearls, then **t** and attack you.
13:15 hearts cannot understand, / and they cannot **t** to me
18: 3 unless you **t** from your sins and become as little
21:32 you refused to **t** from your sins and believe him.
23:15 then you **t** him into twice the son of hell as you
24:10 And many will **t** away from me and betray
25:41 "Then the King will **t** to those on the left and say,
Mk 1:15 **T** from your sins and believe this Good News!"
4:12 So they will not **t** from their sins / and be
6:12 went out, telling all they met to **t** from their sins.
Lk 1:16 And he will persuade many Israelites to **t** to the
1:17 He will **t** the hearts of the fathers to their children,
1:66 "I wonder what this child will **t** out to be?"
5:32 I have come to call sinners to **t** from their sins,
6:25 for your laughing will **t** to mourning and sorrow.
6:29 someone slaps you on one cheek, **t** the other cheek.
13: 3 And you will also perish unless you **t** from your
evil ways and **t** to God.
16:30 from the dead, then they will **t** from their sins.'
24:47 'There is forgiveness of sins for all who **t** to me.'
Jn 2:16 Don't **t** my Father's house into a marketplace!"
12:40 hearts cannot understand, / and they cannot **t** to me
16:20 but your grief will suddenly **t** to wonderful joy
Ac 2:20 into darkness, / and the moon will **t** bloodred,

2:38 "Each of you must t from your sins and t to God,
3:19 Now t from your sins and t to God, so you can
5:31 people of Israel an opportunity to t from their sins
and t to God so their sins would be forgiven.
8:22 T from your wickedness and pray to the Lord.
13: 8 He was trying to t the governor away from the
13:24 the need for everyone in Israel to t from sin and t
to God and be baptized.
14:15 t from these worthless things to the living God,
15:19 should stop troubling the Gentiles who t to God,
17:30 but now he commands everyone everywhere to t
away from idols and t to him.
19: 4 "John's baptism was to demonstrate a desire to t
from sin and t to God.
21:21 world to t their backs on the laws of Moses.
24:10 Now it was Paul's t. The governor motioned for
25:11 neither you nor anyone else has a right to t me over
26:18 their eyes so they may t from darkness to light,
26:20 that all must t from their sins and t to God—
27:15 They couldn't t the ship into the wind, so they
28:27 hearts cannot understand, / and they cannot t to me
Ro 2: 4 he has been in giving you time to t from your sin?
2: 5 because of your stubbornness in refusing to t from
7:18 No matter which way I t, I can't make myself do
8:13 But if through the power of the Holy Spirit you t
11:23 And if the Jews t from their unbelief, God will
11:26 and he will t Israel from all ungodliness.
1Co 14:31 this way, all who prophesy will have a t to speak,
14:32 are in control of their spirit and can wait their t.
15:24 when he will t the Kingdom over to God the
2Co 1: 6 For when God comforts us, it is so that we, in t,
7:10 For God can use sorrow in our lives to help us t
9: 3 I don't want it to t out that I was wrong in my
Gal 4:14 to you, you did not reject me and t me away.
Php 1:19 helps me, this will all t out for my deliverance.
1Ti 4: 1 last times some will t away from what we believe;
2Ti 2:19 to the Lord must t away from all wickedness."
Tit 2:12 And we are instructed to t from godless living
Heb 3:10 and I said, / 'Their hearts always t away from me.
6: 6 and who then t away from God. It is impossible to
10:39 But we are not like those who t their backs on God
11:35 preferring to die rather than t from God and be
Jas 3: 3 We can make a large horse t around and go
3: 4 And a tiny rudder makes a huge ship t wherever
3: 6 It can t the entire course of your life into a blazing
1Pe 3:11 T away from evil and do good. / Work hard at
2Pe 2: 1 and even t against their Master who bought them.
Rev 2: 5 T back to me again and work as you did at first.
2:21 but she would not t away from her immorality.
2:22 unless they t away from all their evil deeds.
3: 3 believed at first; hold to it firmly and t to me again.
3:19 I love. Be diligent and t from your indifference.
9:20 plagues still refused to t from their evil deeds.
11: 6 And they have the power to t the rivers and oceans
21: 8 But cowards who t away from me,

TURNED (288) [TURN]

Ge 20:16 Then he t to Sarah. "Look," he said, "I am giving
21:10 So she t to Abraham and demanded, "Get rid of
30:40 he t the flocks toward the streaked
31: 5 "Your father has t against me and is not treating
50:20 God t into good what you meant for evil.
Ex 4: 3 a snake! Moses was terrified, so he t and ran away.
7:15 Be sure to take along the shepherd's staff that t
7:20 of the Nile. Suddenly, the whole river t to blood!
7:22 their secret arts, and they, too, t water into blood.
7:25 An entire week passed from the time the LORD t
8:17 All the dust in the land of Egypt t into gnats.
10: 6 this one!" And with that, Moses t and walked out.
14:11 Then they t against Moses and complained,
14:20 night came, the pillar of cloud t into a pillar of fire,
15:24 Then the people t against Moses. "What are we
32: 8 They have already t from the way I commanded
32:15 Then Moses t and went down the mountain.
32:21 After that, he t to Aaron. "What did the people do
Lev 13: 3 If the hair in the affected area has t white
13: 4 and if the hair in the spot has not t white,
13:10 If the priest sees that some hair has t white and an
13:13 because the skin has t completely white.
13:17 the affected areas have indeed t completely white,
13:20 and if the hair in the affected area has t white,
13:49 or the leather has t bright green or a reddish color,
Nu 16:42 they t toward the Tabernacle and saw that the
20: 6 Moses and Aaron t away from the people and went
21:33 Then they t and marched toward Bashan, but King
22:23 but Balaam beat it and t it back onto the road.
24: 1 Instead, he t and looked out toward the wilderness,
25:11 and grandson of Aaron the priest has t my anger
33: 7 They left Etham and t back toward Pi-hahiroth,
Dt 2: 1 "Then we t around and set out across the
9:12 They have already t from the way I commanded
9:16 How quickly you had t from the path the LORD
22:16 man to be his wife, and now he has t against her.
23: 5 He t the intended curse into a blessing
29:23 They will find its soil t into sulfur and salt,
29:26 They t to serve and worship other gods that were
Jos 8:20 direction of the wilderness now t on their pursuers.
8:21 from the city, they t and attacked the men of Ai.
10:38 Then they t back and attacked Debir.
11:10 Joshua then t back and captured Hazor and killed
15: 3 Then it went up to Addar, where it t toward Karka.
15: 9 Then it t toward Baalah (that is, Kiriath-jearim).
15:11 where it t toward Shikkeron and Mount Baalah.
16: 7 From Janoah it t southward to Ataroth and Naarah,
19:13 Eth-kazin, and Rimmon and t toward Neah.
19:27 t east toward Beth-dagon, and ran as far as

19:29 Then the boundary t toward Ramah
Jdg 1: 9 Then they t south to fight the Canaanites living in
2:17 How quickly they t away from the path of their
3:19 reached the stone carvings near Gilgal, he t back.
6:14 Then the LORD t to him and said, "Go with the
7:13 It hit a tent, t it over, and knocked it flat!"
9:14 "Then all the trees finally t to the thornbush
9:38 Then Zebul t on him triumphantly. "Now where is
14: 8 he t off the path to look at the carcass of the lion.
18:23 The men of Dan t around and said, "What do you
18:26 them for him to attack, he t around and went home.
20:33 reached Baal-tamar, they t and prepared to attack.
20:41 the Israelites t and attacked. At this point
Ru 3: 8 Boaz suddenly woke up and t over.
1Sa 4:10 that day. The survivors t and fled to their tents.
10: 9 As Saul t and started to leave, God changed his
14:47 And wherever he t, he was victorious.
15:27 As Samuel t to go, Saul grabbed at him to try to
17:51 saw that their champion was dead, they t and ran.
22:18 So Doeg t on them and killed them,
2Sa 1: 7 When he t and saw me, he cried out for me to
13:15 Then suddenly Amnon's love t to hate, and he
15:19 Then the king t to Ittai, the captain of the Gittites,
16:20 Then Absalom t to Ahithophel and asked him,
19: 2 the joy of that day's victory was t into deep
22:22 I have not t from my God to follow evil.
1Ki 2:15 But the tables were t, and everything went to my
8:14 Then the king t around to the entire community of
11: 4 they t his heart to worship their gods instead of
11: 9 for his heart had t away from the LORD, the God
14: 9 And since you have t your back on me,
20:37 Then the prophet t to another man and said,
22: 4 Then he t to Jehoshaphat and asked, "Will you
2Ki 2:24 Elisha t around and looked at them, and he cursed
3:24 and attacked the Moabites, who t and ran.
5:12 be healed?" So Naaman t and went away in a rage.
12:17 and captured it. Then he t to attack Jerusalem.
15:20 So the king of Assyria t from attacking Israel
20: 2 he t his face to the wall and prayed to the LORD,
23:16 Then Josiah t and looked up at the tomb of the man
23:25 who t to the LORD with all his heart and soul
1Ch 10:14 and t his kingdom over to David son of Jesse.
12:19 But as it t out, the Philistine leaders refused to let
21:20 wheat at the time, t and saw the angel there.
29: 1 Then King David t to the entire assembly and said,
2Ch 6: 3 Then the king t around to the entire community of
8: 2 Solomon now t his attention to rebuilding the
12:12 humbled himself, the LORD's anger was t aside,
15: 4 you were in distress and t to the LORD,
20:23 and Ammon t against their allies from Mount Seir
20:23 finished off the army of Seir, they t on each other.
22: 7 But this t out to be a fatal mistake, for God had
25:27 After Amaziah t away from the LORD, there was
28:11 because now the LORD's fierce anger has been t
28:13 and the LORD's fierce anger is already t against
29: 6 and his Temple; they t their backs on him.
Ezr 1:11 and silver items were t over to Sheshbazzar to take
6:21 and by the others in the land who had t from their
10:14 so that the fierce anger of our God may be t away
Ne 2:15 inspecting the wall before I t back and entered
9:28 all was going well, your people t to sin again,
9:29 They stubbornly t their backs on you and refused
13: 2 though our God t the curse into a blessing.
Est 5: 5 The king t to his attendants and said, "Tell Haman
9:22 when their sorrow was t into gladness and their
Job 3: 4 Let that day be t to darkness. Let it be lost even to
19:13 stay far away, and my friends have t against me.
19:19 friends abhor me. Those I loved have t against me.
23:11 I have followed his ways and not t aside.
30:30 My skin has t dark, and my bones burn with fever.
31:32 I have never t away a stranger but have opened my
34:27 For they t aside from following him. They have no
41:32 in its wake. One would think the sea had t white.
Ps 14: 3 But no, all have t away from God; / all have
18:21 I have not t from my God to follow evil.
22:24 He has not t and walked away. / He has listened to
30: 7 Then you t away from me, and I was shattered.
30:11 You have t my mourning into joyful dancing.
40: 1 to help me, / and he t to me and heard my cry.
40:14 take delight in my trouble / be t back in disgrace.
41: 9 the one who shared my food, / has t against me.
44:20 If we had t away from worshiping our God
53: 3 But no, all have t away from God; / all have
54: 5 May my enemies' plans for evil be t against them.
64: 8 Their own words will be t against them,
70: 2 take delight in my trouble / be t back in disgrace.
78: 9 t their backs and fled when the day of battle came.
78:34 finally sought him. / They repented and t to God.
78:44 For he t their rivers into blood, / so no one could
78:50 He t his anger against them; / he did not spare the
78:57 They t back and were as faithless as their parents
105:25 Then he t the Egyptians against the Israelites,
105:29 He t the nation's water into blood, / poisoning all
114: 3 their way! / The water of the Jordan River t away.
114: 5 What happened, Jordan River, that you t away?
114: 8 He t the rock into pools of water; / yes, springs of
119:59 of my life, / and I t to follow your statutes.
119:102 I haven't t away from your laws, / for you have
129: 5 who hate Jerusalem / be t back in shameful defeat.
Pr 19:27 my child, you have t your back on knowledge.
Ecc 2:20 So I t in despair from hard work. It was not the
7:29 but they have each t to follow their own downward
Isa 1: 2 children I raised and cared for have t against me.
1: 4 and corrupt children who have t away from the
8:17 though he has t away from the people of Israel.
17:10 Because you have t from the God who can save
23:13 torn down its palaces, and t it into a heap of rubble.

25: 2 of ruins. Cities with strong walls are t to rubble.
27:11 stupid nation, for its people have t away from God.
38: 2 he t his face to the wall and prayed to the LORD,
42:17 them their gods— / they will be t away in shame.
53: 3 We t our backs on him and looked the other way
54: 8 In a moment of anger I t my face away for a little
54:17 coming day, no weapon t against you will succeed.
59: 2 he has t away and will not listen anymore.
59:13 We have t our backs on God. We know how unfair
59:20 "to buy back those in Israel who have t from their
64: 7 you have t away from us and t us over to our sins.
Jer 2: 8 The judges ignored me, the rulers t against me,
5: 7 For even your children have t from me.
5:23 They have t against me and have chosen to
6:12 Their homes will be t over to their enemies,
12: 6 members of your own family, have t on you.
15: 6 You have forsaken me and t your back on me,"
18:15 For they have deserted me and t to worthless idols.
19: 4 and t this valley into a place of wickedness.
23:22 my words and t my people from their evil ways.
25:37 Peaceful meadows will be t into a wasteland by the
26:19 they t from their sins and worshiped the LORD.
31:19 I t away from God, but then I was sorry. I kicked
32:33 My people have t their backs on me and have
35:18 Then Jeremiah t to the Recabites and said, "This is
44:30 just as I t King Zedekiah of Judah over to King
50: 6 led them astray and t them loose in the mountains.
La 1:13 He has placed a trap in my path and t me back.
1:21 heard my groans, but no one t to comfort me.
3: 3 He has t against me. Day and night his hand is
5: 2 Our inheritance has been t over to strangers,
5:15 hearts has ended; our dancing has t to mourning.
Eze 10:11 in the direction in which their heads were t,
14: 5 and hearts of all my people who have t from me to
17: 6 Its branches t up toward the eagle, and its roots
23:19 She t to even greater prostitution, remembering her
23:22 those very nations from which you t away in
23:35 you have forgotten me and t your back on me,
39:23 I t my back on them and let their enemies destroy
39:24 I t my face away and punished them in proportion
Da 5: 6 and his face t pale with fear. Such terror gripped
5: 9 even more alarmed, and his face t ashen white.
9: 3 So I t to the Lord God and pleaded with him in
9:11 All Israel has disobeyed your law and t away,
Hos 3: 1 Israel even though the people have t to other gods,
5:13 Israel t to Assyria, to the great king there,
Joel 2:31 The sun will be t into darkness, and the moon will
Am 7: 6 Then the LORD t from this plan, too. "I won't do
8:10 and your songs of joy will be t to weeping.
Jnh 2: 7 all hope, I t my thoughts once more to the LORD.
Hab 2:16 and all your glory will be t to shame.
Zec 7:11 They t stubbornly away and put their fingers in
8:10 on all sides. I had t everyone against each other.
Mal 1: 3 I t Esau's inheritance into a desert for jackals."
2: 6 righteous lives, and they t many from lives of sin.
Mt 3: 8 Prove by the way you live that you have really t
from your sins and t to God.
9: 6 Then Jesus t to the paralyzed man and said,
9:22 Jesus t around and said to her, "Daughter,
11:20 because they hadn't t from their sins and t to God.
16:23 Jesus t to Peter and said, "Get away from me,
21:13 of prayer,' but you have t it into a den of thieves!"
27:26 then t him over to the Roman soldiers to crucify
Mk 1: 4 be baptized to show that they had t from their sins
and t to God to be forgiven.
2:10 Then Jesus t to the paralyzed man and said,
3: 4 Then he t to his critics and asked, "Is it legal to do
5:30 so he t around in the crowd and asked,
8:33 Jesus t and looked at his disciples and then said to
11:17 but you have t it into a den of thieves."
15:15 then t him over to the Roman soldiers to crucify
Lk 3: 3 be baptized to show that they had t from their sins
and t to God to be forgiven.
3: 8 Prove by the way you live that you have really t
from your sins and t to God.
5:24 Then Jesus t to the paralyzed man and said,
6:20 Then Jesus t to his disciples and said,
7:44 Then he t to the woman and said to Simon,
9:53 But they were t away. The people of the village
9:55 But Jesus t and rebuked them.
10:23 they were alone, he t to the disciples and said,
12: 1 Jesus t first to his disciples and warned them,
12:54 Then Jesus t to the crowd and said, "When you
14: 5 Then he t to them and asked, "Which of you
14:12 Then he t to his host. "When you put on a
14:25 following Jesus. He t around and said to them,
19:46 of prayer,' but you have t it into a den of thieves."
20: 9 Now Jesus t to the people again and told them this
20:45 the crowds listening, he t to his disciples and said,
22:32 So when you have repented and t to me again,
22:61 At that moment the Lord t and looked at Peter.
23: 4 Pilate t to the leading priests and to the crowd
23:28 But Jesus t and said to them, "Daughters of
Jn 1:37 Then John's two disciples t and followed Jesus.
2:15 coins over the floor, and t over their tables.
4:46 town of Cana, where he had t the water into wine.
6:66 At this point many of his disciples t away
6:67 Then Jesus t to the Twelve and asked, "Are you
13:18 'The one who shares my food has t against me,'
20:16 She t toward him and exclaimed, "Teacher!"
21:20 Peter t around and saw the disciple Jesus loved
Ac 2:20 The sun will be t into darkness, / and the moon
7:42 Then God t away from them and gave them up to
9:35 and Sharon t to the Lord when they saw Aeneas
11:21 of these Gentiles believed and t to the Lord.
13:44 The following week almost the entire city t out to
14:19 and t the crowds into a murderous mob.

16:18 so exasperated that he **t** and spoke to the demon
17: 6 and Silas have **t** the rest of the world upside down,
18:14 Gallio **t** to Paul's accusers and said, "Listen,
21:11 leaders in Jerusalem and **t** over to the Romans.' "
Ro 1:26 Even the women **t** against the natural way to have
3:12 All have **t** away from God; / all have gone wrong.
11: 5 for not all the Jews have **t** away from God.
11:12 because the Jews **t** down God's offer of salvation,
1Th 1: 9 and how you **t** away from idols to serve the true
1Ti 1: 6 They have **t** away from these things and spend
1:20 I **t** them over to Satan so they would learn not to
Tit 1:11 they have already **t** whole families away from the
1:14 and the commands of people who have **t** their
3:11 For people like that have **t** away from the truth.
Heb 8: 9 so I **t** my back on them, says the Lord.
11:34 Their weakness was **t** to strength. They became
Jas 5:18 The grass **t** green, and the crops began to grow
1Pe 2:25 But now you have **t** to your Shepherd,
2Pe 2: 6 he **t** the cities of Sodom and Gomorrah into heaps
Jude 1: 4 for they have **t** against our only Master and Lord,
Rev 1:12 When I **t** to see who was speaking to me, I saw
9:15 and year were **t** loose to kill one-third of all the
11: 2 for it has been **t** over to the nations.

TURNING (38) [TURN]

Ge 41:39 **T** to Joseph, Pharaoh said, "Since God has
Ex 14:21 wind blew all that night, **t** the seabed into dry land.
Dt 17:20 It will also prevent him from **t** away from these
Jos 15: 7 the valley of Achor to Debir, **t** north toward Gilgal,
22:18 And yet today you are **t** away from following the
Jdg 8:20 **T** to Jether, his oldest son, he said, "Kill them!"
1Sa 12:10 'We have sinned by **t** away from the LORD
29: 4 himself with his master than by **t** on us in battle?
2Sa 19:23 Then, **t** to Shimei, David vowed, "Your life will
2Ch 18:31 and God helped him by **t** the attack away from
Job 38:38 **t** the dry dust to clumps of mud?
Ps 129: 6 on a rooftop, / **t** yellow when only half grown,
Isa 1:20 But if you keep **t** away and refusing to listen,
Jer 12:10 and **t** all its beauty into a barren wilderness.
23:14 doing evil instead of **t** them away from their sins.
23:36 **t** upside down the words of our God, the living
Eze 1: 9 were able to fly in any direction without **t** around.
1:16 each wheel had a second wheel **t** crosswise within
1:17 directions they faced, without **t** as they moved.
10:10 each wheel had a second wheel **t** crosswise within
10:11 directions they faced, without **t** as they moved.
10:11 in which their heads were turned, never **t** aside.
Da 9:13 from the LORD our God by **t** from our sins
Zec 3: 4 And **t** to Jeshua he said, "See, I have taken away
Mt 8:10 **T** to the crowd, he said, "I tell you the truth,
Lk 7: 9 **T** to the crowd, he said, "I tell you, I haven't seen
12:22 Then **t** to his disciples, Jesus said, "So I tell you,
19:24 Then **t** to the others standing nearby, the king
Jn 6: 5 **T** to Philip, he asked, "Philip, where can we buy
Ac 3:26 to bless you by **t** each of you back from your sinful
9:40 **T** to the body he said, "Get up, Tabitha."
11:18 "God has also given the Gentiles the privilege of **t**
14:23 **t** them over to the care of the Lord, in whom they
20:21 the necessity of **t** from sin and **t** to God,
Gal 1: 6 I am shocked that you are **t** away so soon from
Heb 3:12 and unbelieving, **t** you away from the living God.
6: 1 with the importance of **t** away from evil deeds

TURNS (32) [TURN]

Ge 42:16 If it **t** out that you don't have a younger brother,
Lev 13:25 If the hair in the affected area **t** white
Dt 30:17 But if your heart **t** away and you refuse to listen,
Jdg 19:25 her all night, taking **t** raping her until morning.
1Sa 17:35 If the animal **t** on me, I catch it by the jaw and club
29: 4 go into the battle with us. What if he **t** against us?
2Ki 21:13 as one wipes a dish and **t** it upside down.
1Ch 12:19 David switches loyalties to Saul and **t** against us."
24: 6 of Eleazar and Ithamar took **t** casting lots.
Ne 9: 3 Then for three more hours they took **t** confessing
Job 20:14 the food he has eaten **t** sour within him,
38:30 For the water **t** to ice as hard as rock,
Ps 34:16 But the LORD **t** his face against those who do
107:34 He **t** the fruitful land into salty wastelands,
107:35 But he also **t** deserts into pools of water, / the dry
Pr 2:14 and they enjoy evil as it **t** things upside down.
15: 1 A gentle answer **t** away wrath, but harsh words stir
20:17 bread tastes sweet, but it **t** to gravel in the mouth.
21: 1 by the LORD; he **t** it wherever he pleases.
26:14 As a door **t** back and forth on its hinges, so the lazy person **t** over in bed.
Ecc 7: 7 Extortion **t** wise people into fools, and bribes
Isa 24: 9 and song; strong drink now **t** bitter in the mouth.
Jer 18:10 but then that nation **t** to evil and refuses to obey
Eze 5:15 They will see what happens when the LORD **t**
Am 4:13 He **t** the light of dawn into darkness and treads the
5: 8 It is he who **t** darkness into morning and day into
Mt 10:13 If it **t** out to be a worthy home, let your blessing
Lk 17: 4 a day and each time **t** again and asks forgiveness,
2Co 3:16 But whenever anyone **t** to the Lord, then the veil is
Heb 10:38 But I will have no pleasure in anyone who **t**
1Pe 3:12 But the Lord **t** his face / against those who do

TURQUOISE (4)

Ex 28:18 The second row will contain a **t**, a sapphire,
39:11 In the second row were a **t**, a sapphire, and a white
Eze 27:16 They traded **t**, purple dyes, embroidery, fine linen,
28:13 beryl, onyx, jasper, sapphire, **t**, and emerald—

TURTLE(S) [KJV] See DOVE, TURTLEDOVE(S)

TURTLEDOVE (4) [DOVE, TURTLEDOVES]

Ge 15: 9 a three-year-old ram, a **t**, and a young pigeon."
Lev 1:14 to the LORD, choose either a **t** or a young pigeon.
12: 6 and a young pigeon or **t** for a purification offering.
Jer 8: 7 as do the **t**, the swallow, and the crane.

TURTLEDOVES (10) [DOVE, TURTLEDOVE]

Lev 5: 7 they must bring to the LORD two young **t** or two
5:11 any of the people cannot afford to bring young **t**
12: 8 she must bring two **t** or two young pigeons.
14:22 The person being cleansed must also bring two **t**
14:30 "Then the priest will offer the two **t** or the two
15:14 On the eighth day he must bring two **t** or two
15:29 she must bring two **t** or two young pigeons
Nu 6:10 On the eighth day they must bring two **t** or two
SS 2:12 of singing birds has come, even the cooing of **t**.
Lk 2:24 "either a pair of **t** or two young pigeons."

TUSKS (1)

Eze 27:15 they brought payment in ivory **t** and ebony wood.

TUTORS [KJV] See GUARDIANS

TWAIN [KJV] See SECOND, TWO

TWELFTH (15) [TWELVE]

Nu 7:78 On the **t** day Ahira son of Enan, leader of the tribe
1Ki 19:19 ahead of him, and he was plowing with the **t** team.
2Ki 8:25 Judah in the **t** year of King Joram's reign in Israel.
17: 1 Israel in the **t** year of King Ahaz's reign in Judah.
1Ch 24:12 lot fell to Eliashib. / The **t** lot fell to Jakim.
25:19 The **t** lot fell to Hashabiah and twelve of his sons
27:15 from Netophah, was commander of the **t** division,
27:15 which was on duty during the **t** month.
2Ch 34: 3 Then in the **t** year, he began to purify Judah
Est 3: 7 of April, during the **t** year of King Xerxes' reign,
Eze 26: 1 during the **t** year of King Jehoiachin's captivity,
32: 1 during the **t** year of King Jehoiachin's captivity,
32:17 On March 17, during the **t** year, another message
33:21 On January 8, during the **t** year of our captivity,
Rev 21:20 the eleventh jacinth, the **t** amethyst.

TWELVE (168) [TWELFTH, TWELVE-OUNCE, 12, 12,000, 144,000]

TWELVE APOSTLES (5) Mt 10:2; Lk 9:1; 22:14; 1Co 15:5; Rev 21:14

TWELVE DISCIPLES (20) Mt 10:1,5; 11:1; 20:17; 26:14,20,47; Mk 4:10; 6:7; 9:35; 10:32; 11:11; 14:10,17,43; Lk 8:1; 9:12; 18:31; 22:3,47

TWELVE STONES (6) Jos 4:3,5,8,9,20; 1Ki 18:31

TWELVE TRIBES (11) Ge 25:16; 49:28; Ex 24:4; 39:14; Jos 4:5; Ezr 6:17; Eze 47:13; Mt 19:28; Lk 22:30; Ac 26:7; Rev 21:12

Ge 14: 4 For **t** years they had all been subject to King
17:20 **T** princes will be among his descendants.
25:16 These **t** sons of Ishmael became the founders of **t** tribes that bore their names,
35:22 These are the names of the **t** sons of Jacob:
42:13 "Sir," they said, "there are **t** of us brothers,
42:32 We are **t** brothers, sons of one father; one brother
49:28 These are the **t** tribes of Israel, and these are the blessings with which Jacob blessed his **t** sons.
Ex 15:27 where there were **t** springs and seventy palm trees.
24: 4 He also set up **t** pillars around the altar, one for each of the **t** tribes of Israel.
39:14 each with the name of one of the **t** tribes of Israel.
Lev 24: 5 "You must bake **t** loaves of bread from choice
Nu 1:44 by Moses and Aaron and the **t** leaders of Israel,
7: 3 Together they brought six carts and **t** oxen.
7:84 **t** silver platters, **t** silver basins, and **t** gold incense
7:87 **T** bulls, **t** rams, and **t** one-year-old male lambs
7:87 **T** male goats were brought for the sin offerings.
13: 2 Send one leader from each of the **t** ancestral
13: 3 He sent out **t** men, all tribal leaders of Israel,
14:38 Of the **t** who had explored the land, only Joshua
17: 2 "Take **t** wooden staffs, one from each of Israel's
17: 6 and each of the **t** tribal leaders, including Aaron,
29:17 sacrifice **t** young bulls, two rams, and fourteen
31: 5 a total of **t** thousand men armed for battle.
33: 9 where there are **t** springs of water and seventy
Dt 1:23 so I chose **t** scouts, one from each of your tribes.
Jos 3:12 Now choose **t** men, one from each tribe.
4: 2 "Now choose **t** men, one from each tribe.
4: 3 Tell the men to take **t** stones from where the priests
4: 4 So Joshua called together the **t** men
4: 5 **t** stones in all, one for each of the **t** tribes.
4: 8 They took **t** stones from the middle of the Jordan
4: 9 Joshua also built another memorial of **t** stones in
4:20 It was there at Gilgal that Joshua piled up the **t**
8:25 of Ai was wiped out that day—**t** thousand in all.
18:24 Ophni, and Geba—**t** towns with their villages.
19:15 **t** towns with their surrounding villages.
21: 7 The clan of Merari received **t** cities from the tribes
21:40 So **t** towns were allotted to the clan of Merari.
Jdg 19:29 a knife and cut his concubine's body into **t** pieces.
20: 6 So I cut her body into **t** pieces and sent the pieces
21:10 So they sent **t** thousand warriors to Jabesh-gilead
2Sa 2:15 So **t** men were chosen from each side to fight
10: 6 of Maacah, and **t** thousand from the land of Tob.
17: 1 "Let me choose **t** thousand men to start out after
1Ki 4: 7 Solomon also had **t** district governors who were
4: 8 These are the names of the **t** governors: / Ben-hur,
4:26 stalls for his chariot horses and **t** thousand horses.
7:25 The Sea rested on a base of **t** bronze oxen,
7:44 the Sea and the **t** oxen under it,
10:20 Solomon made **t** other lion figures, one standing on
10:26 fourteen hundred chariots and **t** thousand horses.
11:30 new cloak he was wearing and tore it into **t** pieces.
16:23 He reigned **t** years in all, six of them in Tirzah.
18:31 He took **t** stones, one to represent each of the tribes
2Ki 3: 1 reign in Judah. He reigned in Samaria **t** years.
21: 1 Manasseh was **t** years old when he became king,
1Ch 6:63 sacred lots **t** towns from the territories of Reuben,
25: 9 of the Asaph clan and **t** of his sons and relatives.
25: 9 lot fell to Gedaliah and **t** of his sons and relatives.
25:10 lot fell to Zaccur and **t** of his sons and relatives.
25:11 lot fell to Zeri and **t** of his sons and relatives.
25:12 lot fell to Nethaniah and **t** of his sons and relatives.
25:13 lot fell to Bukkiah and **t** of his sons and relatives.
25:14 lot fell to Asarelah and **t** of his sons and relatives.
25:15 lot fell to Jeshaiah and **t** of his sons and relatives.
25:16 lot fell to Mattaniah and **t** of his sons and relatives.
25:17 lot fell to Shimei and **t** of his sons and relatives.
25:18 lot fell to Uzziel and **t** of his sons and relatives.
25:19 lot fell to Hashabiah and **t** of his sons and relatives.
25:20 lot fell to Shubael and **t** of his sons and relatives.
25:21 lot fell to Mattithiah and **t** of his sons and relatives.
25:22 lot fell to Jerimoth and **t** of his sons and relatives.
25:23 lot fell to Hananiah and **t** of his sons and relatives.
25:24 fell to Joshbekashah and **t** of his sons and relatives.
25:25 lot fell to Hanani and **t** of his sons and relatives.
25:26 lot fell to Mallothi and **t** of his sons and relatives.
25:27 lot fell to Eliathah and **t** of his sons and relatives.
25:28 lot fell to Hothir and **t** of his sons and relatives.
25:29 lot fell to Geddalti and **t** of his sons and relatives.
25:30 lot fell to Mahazioth and **t** of his sons and relatives.
25:31 to Romamti-ezer and **t** of his sons and relatives.
28: 1 the commanders of the **t** army divisions, the other
2Ch 1:14 fourteen hundred chariots and **t** thousand horses.
4: 4 The Sea rested on a base of **t** bronze oxen,
4:15 the Sea and the **t** oxen under it,
9:19 Solomon made **t** other lion figures, one standing on
9:25 stalls for his chariot horses and **t** thousand horses.
12: 3 He came with **t** hundred chariots, sixty thousand
33: 1 Manasseh was **t** years old when he became king,
Ezr 6:17 And **t** male goats were presented as a sin offering for the **t** tribes of Israel.
8:24 I appointed **t** leaders of the priests—Sherebiah,
8:35 They presented **t** oxen for the people of Israel,
8:35 They also offered **t** goats as a sin offering.
Ne 5:14 I would like to mention that for the entire **t** years
Est 2:12 she was given the prescribed **t** months of beauty
Ps 60: T and killed **t** thousand Edomites in the Valley of
Jer 52:20 and the Sea with the **t** bulls beneath it was too
Eze 47:13 for dividing the land for the **t** tribes of Israel:
Da 4:29 **T** months later, he was taking a walk on the flat
Mt 9:20 a woman who had had a hemorrhage for **t** years
10: 1 Jesus called his **t** disciples to him and gave them
10: 2 Here are the names of the **t** apostles: / first Simon
10: 5 Jesus sent the **t** disciples out with these
11: 1 finished giving these instructions to his **t** disciples,
14:20 and they picked up **t** baskets of leftovers.
19:28 also sit on **t** thrones, judging the **t** tribes of Israel.
20:17 he took the **t** disciples aside privately and told
26:14 Then Judas Iscariot, one of the **t** disciples, went to
26:20 Jesus sat down at the table with the **t** disciples.
26:47 even as he said this, Judas, one of the **t** disciples,
Mk 3:14 Then he selected **t** of them to be his regular
3:16 These are the names of the **t** he chose: / Simon (he
4:10 when Jesus was alone with the **t** disciples and with
5:25 the crowd who had had a hemorrhage for **t** years.
5:42 And the girl, who was **t** years old,
6: 7 And he called his **t** disciples together and sent
6:43 and they picked up **t** baskets of leftover bread
8:19 did you pick up afterward?" "**T**," they said.
9:35 He sat down and called the **t** disciples over to him.
10:32 Taking the **t** disciples aside, Jesus once more
11:11 Then he went out to Bethany with the **t** disciples.
14:10 Then Judas Iscariot, one of the **t** disciples, went to
14:17 In the evening Jesus arrived with the **t** disciples.
14:20 He replied, "It is one of you **t**, one who is eating
14:43 as he said this, Judas, one of the **t** disciples,
Lk 2:42 When Jesus was **t** years old, they attended the
6:13 of his disciples and chose **t** of them to be apostles.
8: 1 Kingdom of God. He took his **t** disciples with him,
8:42 His only child was dying, a little girl **t** years old.
8:43 the crowd who had had a hemorrhage for **t** years.
9: 1 One day Jesus called together his **t** apostles
9:12 Late in the afternoon the **t** disciples came to him
9:17 and they picked up **t** baskets of leftovers!
18:31 Gathering the **t** disciples around him, Jesus told
22: 3 into Judas Iscariot, who was one of the **t** disciples,
22:14 and the **t** apostles sat down together at the table.
22:30 will sit on thrones, judging the **t** tribes of Israel.
22:47 led by Judas, one of his **t** disciples.
Jn 6:13 but **t** baskets were filled with the pieces of bread
6:67 Then Jesus turned to the **T** and asked, "Are you
6:70 Then Jesus said, "I chose the **t** of you, but one is a
6:71 son of Simon Iscariot, one of the **T**, who would
11: 9 "There are **t** hours of daylight every day.
Ac 6: 2 So the **T** called a meeting of all the believers.
7: 8 and Jacob was the father of the **t** patriarchs of the
19: 7 There were about **t** men in all.
24:11 **t** days ago that I arrived in Jerusalem to worship at
26: 7 that is why the **t** tribes of Israel worship God night
1Co 15: 5 He was seen by Peter and then by the **t** apostles.
Rev 12: 1 her feet, and a crown of **t** stars on her head.
21:12 and high, with **t** gates guarded by **t** angels.
21:12 And the names of the **t** tribes of Israel were written

21:14 The wall of the city had **t** foundation stones,
21:14 and on them were written the names of the **t**
21:19 was built on foundation stones inlaid with **t** gems:
21:21 The **t** gates were made of pearls—each gate from a
22: 2 bearing **t** crops of fruit, with a fresh crop each

TWELVE-OUNCE (1) [OUNCE, TWELVE]

Jn 12: 3 Then Mary took a **t** jar of expensive perfume made

TWENTIETH (8) [TWENTY]

Ex 30:14 All who have reached their **t** birthday must give
1Ki 15: 9 Asa began to rule over Judah in the **t** year of
2Ki 15:30 He began to rule over Israel in the **t** year of Jotham
1Ch 24:16 lot fell to Pethahiah. / The **t** lot fell to Jehezkel.
25:27 The **t** lot fell to Eliathah and twelve of his sons
Ne 1: 1 In late autumn of the **t** year of King Artaxerxes'
2: 1 during the **t** year of King Artaxerxes' reign,
5:14 from the **t** until the thirty-second year of the reign

TWENTY (65) [TWENTIETH, TWENTY-BUSHEL, 20]

Ge 18:31 let me continue—suppose there are only **t**?"
18:31 "Then I will not destroy it for the sake of the **t**."
31:38 "**T** years I have been with you, and all that time I
31:41 Yes, **t** years—fourteen of them earning your two
32:14 **t** male goats, two hundred ewes, **t** rams,
32:15 forty cows, ten bulls, **t** female donkeys, and ten
37:28 out of the pit and sold him for **t** pieces of silver,
Ex 26:18 **T** of these frames will support the south side of the
26:20 On the north side there will also be **t** of these
27:10 by **t** bronze posts that fit into **t** bronze bases.
27:11 150 feet of curtains held up by **t** posts fitted into
36:23 They made **t** frames to support the south side,
36:25 They also made **t** frames for the north side of the
38:10 There were **t** posts, each with its own bronze base,
38:11 with **t** bronze posts and bases and with silver hooks
38:26 This included all the men who were **t** years old
Lev 27: 3 A man between the ages of **t** and sixty is valued at
27: 5 and **t** is valued at **t** pieces of silver;
Nu 1: 3 **t** years old or older who are able to go to war.
1:18 The men of Israel **t** years old or older were
1:20[-21] This is the number of men **t** years old
1:45 all the men of Israel who were **t** years old or older
11:19 be for just a day or two, or for five or ten or even **t**.
14:29 none of you who are **t** years old or older and were
26: 2 "Take a census of all the men of Israel who are **t**
26: 4 "Count all the men of Israel **t** years old and older,
32:11 no one who is **t** years old or older will ever see the
Jdg 4: 3 ruthlessly oppressed the Israelites for **t** years.
11:33 **t** towns—and as far away as Abel-keramim.
15:20 Samson was Israel's judge for **t** years,
16:31 Samson had been Israel's judge for **t** years.
1Sa 7: 2 in Kiriath-jearim for a long time—**t** years in all.
14:14 They killed about **t** men in all, and their bodies
2Sa 3:20 When Abner came to Hebron with his **t** men,
8: 4 hundred charioteers and **t** thousand foot soldiers.
9:10 Ziba, who had fifteen sons and **t** servants, replied,
10: 6 so they hired **t** thousand Aramean mercenaries
18: 7 and **t** thousand men laid down their lives that day.
19:17 of Saul, and Ziba's fifteen sons and **t** servants.
24: 8 and **t** days and then returned to Jerusalem.
1Ki 4:23 **t** pasture-fed cattle, one hundred sheep or goats,
9:10 Now at the end of the **t** years during which
9:11 Solomon gave **t** towns in the land of Galilee to
2Ki 4:42 and **t** loaves of barley bread made from the first
15:20 demanding that each of them pay **t** ounces of silver
15:27 reign in Judah. He reigned in Samaria **t** years.
16: 2 Ahaz was **t** years old when he became king,
1Ch 18: 4 thousand charioteers, and **t** thousand foot soldiers.
23:24 Each had to be **t** years old or older to qualify for
23:27 final instructions that all the Levites **t** years old
27:23 he did not count those who were younger than **t**
2Ch 3: 9 They used gold nails that weighed about **t** ounces
8: 1 It was now **t** years since Solomon had become
25: 5 and found that he had an army of 300,000 men **t**
28: 1 Ahaz was **t** years old when he became king,
31:17 and to the Levites **t** years old or older who were
Ezr 3: 8 The Levites who were **t** years old or older were put
8:19 of Merari, and **t** of his sons and brothers,
Eze 45:12 One shekel consists of **t** gerahs, and sixty shekels
Hag 2:16 fifty gallons from the winepress, you found only **t**.
Lk 14:31 **t** thousand soldiers who are marching against him?
Jn 2: 6 and held **t** to thirty gallons each.

TWENTY-BUSHEL (1) [BUSHEL, TWENTY]

Hag 2:16 When you hoped for a **t** crop, you harvested only

TWENTY-EIGHT (2) [28]

2Ki 10:36 Jehu reigned over Israel from Samaria for **t** years.
2Ch 11:21 and they gave birth to **t** sons and sixty daughters.

TWENTY-FIFTH (1) [TWENTY-FIVE]

Eze 40: 1 On April 28, during the **t** year of our captivity—

TWENTY-FIRST (3) [TWENTY-ONE]

Ex 12:18 month until the evening of the **t** day of the month.
1Ch 24:17 The **t** lot fell to Jakin. / The twenty-second lot fell
25:28 The **t** lot fell to Hothir and twelve of his sons

TWENTY-FIVE (16) [TWENTY-FIFTH, 25]

Nu 8:24 begin serving in the Tabernacle at the age of **t**,
Jdg 20:46 So the tribe of Benjamin lost **t** thousand brave
1Ki 10:14 Each year Solomon received about **t** tons of gold.
22:42 became king, and he reigned in Jerusalem **t** years.
2Ki 14: 2 Amaziah was **t** years old when he became king,
15:33 He was **t** years old when he became king, and he
18: 2 He was **t** years old when he became king, and he
23:36 Jehoiakim was **t** years old when he became king,
2Ch 20:31 became king, and he reigned in Jerusalem **t** years.
25: 1 Amaziah was **t** years old when he became king,
27: 1 Jotham was **t** years old when he became king,
27: 8 He was **t** years old when he became king, and he
29: 1 Hezekiah was **t** years old when he became the king
36: 5 Jehoiakim was **t** years old when he became king,
Eze 8:16 about **t** men were standing with their backs to the
11: 1 where I saw **t** prominent men of the city.

TWENTY-FOUR (27) [TWENTY-FOURTH]

Nu 7:88 **T** young bulls, sixty rams, sixty male goats,
1Ki 15:33 reign in Judah. Baasha reigned in Tirzah **t** years.
1Ch 23: 4 "**T** thousand of them will supervise the work at the
27: 1 served for one month and had **t** thousand troops.
27: 2 There were **t** thousand troops in his division.
27: 4 There were **t** thousand troops in his division,
27: 5 There were **t** thousand troops in his division.
27: 7 There were **t** thousand troops in his division.
27: 8 There were **t** thousand troops in his division.
27: 9 There were **t** thousand troops in his division.
27:10 There were **t** thousand troops in his division.
27:11 There were **t** thousand troops in his division.
27:12 There were **t** thousand troops in his division.
27:13 There were **t** thousand troops in his division.
27:14 There were **t** thousand troops in his division.
27:15 There were **t** thousand troops in his division.
Rev 4: 4 **T** thrones surrounded him, and **t** elders sat on them.
4:10 the **t** elders fall down and worship the one who
5: 5 But one of the **t** elders said to me, "Stop weeping!
5: 6 and the four living beings and among the **t** elders.
5: 8 and the **t** elders fell down before the Lamb.
5:14 And the **t** elders fell down and worshiped God
7:13 Then one of the **t** elders asked me, "Who are these
11:16 And the **t** elders sitting on their thrones before God
14: 3 and before the four living beings and the **t** elders.
19: 4 Then the **t** elders and the four living beings fell

TWENTY-FOURTH (2) [TWENTY-FOUR, 24]

1Ch 24:18 lot fell to Delaiah. / The **t** lot fell to Maaziah.
25:31 The **t** lot fell to Romamti-ezer and twelve of his

TWENTY-NINE (5) [29]

Jos 15:32 there were **t** of these towns with their surrounding
2Ki 14: 2 became king, and he reigned in Jerusalem **t** years.
18: 2 became king, and he reigned in Jerusalem **t** years.
2Ch 25: 1 became king, and he reigned in Jerusalem **t** years.
29: 1 king of Judah, and he reigned in Jerusalem **t** years.

TWENTY-ONE (4) [TWENTY-FIRST, 21]

2Ki 24:18 Zedekiah was **t** years old when he became king,
2Ch 36:11 Zedekiah was **t** years old when he became king,
Jer 52: 1 Zedekiah was **t** years old when he became king,
Da 10:13 But for **t** days the spirit prince of the kingdom of

TWENTY-SECOND (2) [TWENTY-TWO]

1Ch 24:17 lot fell to Jakin. / The **t** lot fell to Gamul.
25:29 The **t** lot fell to Geddalti and twelve of his sons

TWENTY-SEVEN (1) [TWENTY-SEVENTH, 27]

1Ch 26:32 There were **t** hundred capable men among the

TWENTY-SEVENTH (4) [TWENTY-SEVEN]

1Ki 16:10 This happened in the **t** year of King Asa's reign in
16:15 Zimri began to rule over Israel from Tirzah in the **t**
2Ki 15: 1 **t** year of the reign of King Jeroboam II of Israel.
Eze 29:17 during the **t** year of King Jehoiachin's captivity,

TWENTY-SIX (3) [TWENTY-SIXTH, 26]

Jdg 20:15 **T** thousand of their warriors armed with swords
2Ch 26:12 **T** hundred clan leaders commanded these
35: 8 gave the priests **t** hundred lambs and young goats

TWENTY-SIXTH (1) [TWENTY-SIX]

1Ki 16: 8 Tirzah in the **t** year of King Asa's reign in Judah.

TWENTY-THIRD (5) [TWENTY-THREE]

2Ki 12: 6 But by the **t** year of Joash's reign, the priests still
13: 1 Israel in the **t** year of King Joash's reign in Judah.
1Ch 24:18 The **t** lot fell to Delaiah. / The twenty-fourth lot
25:30 The **t** lot fell to Mahazioth and twelve of his sons
Jer 52:30 In his **t** year he sent Nebuzaradan, his captain of

TWENTY-THREE (8) [TWENTY-THIRD, 23]

Jdg 10: 2 He was Israel's judge for **t** years. When he died,
2Ki 23:31 Jehoahaz was **t** years old when he became king,
1Ch 2:22 of Jair, who ruled **t** towns in the land of Gilead.
2Ch 3: 8 Its interior was overlaid with about **t** tons of pure
36: 2 Jehoahaz was **t** years old when he became king,
Jer 25: 3 "For the past **t** years—from the thirteenth year of
Da 8:14 "It will take **t** hundred evenings and mornings;
8:26 "This vision about the **t** hundred evenings

TWENTY-TWO (15) [TWENTY-SECOND]

Ge 7:20 standing more than **t** feet above the highest peaks.
Jos 19:30 **t** towns with their surrounding villages.
Jdg 7: 3 and go home.' " **T** thousand of them went home,
10: 3 a man from Gilead named Jair judged Israel for **t**
20:21 and killed **t** thousand Israelites in the field that day.
2Sa 8: 5 help Hadadezer, David killed **t** thousand of them.
1Ki 14:20 Jeroboam reigned in Israel **t** years.
16:29 reign in Judah. He reigned in Samaria **t** years.
2Ki 8:26 Ahaziah was **t** years old when he became king,
21:19 Amon was **t** years old when he became king,
1Ch 12:28 with **t** members of his family who were all
18: 5 help Hadadezer, David killed **t** thousand of them.
2Ch 13:21 and had **t** sons and sixteen daughters.
22: 2 Ahaziah was **t** years old when he became king,
33:21 Amon was **t** years old when he became king,

TWICE (22) [TWO]

Ge 27:36 for he has deceived me **t**, first taking my birthright
41:32 As for having the dream **t**, it means that the matter
43:10 and returned **t** by this time if you had let him come
Ex 16: 5 Tell them to pick up **t** as much as usual on the
16:22 there was **t** as much as usual on the ground—
16:29 That is why I give you **t** as much food on the sixth
Nu 20:11 raised his hand and struck the rock **t** with the staff,
Dt 24:20 from your olive trees, don't go over the boughs **t**.
1Sa 17:16 For forty days, **t** a day, morning and evening,
26: 8 him to the ground, and I won't need to strike **t**!"
1Ki 11: 9 the God of Israel, who had appeared to him **t**.
Ne 13:20 of wares camped outside Jerusalem once or **t**.
Job 42:10 In fact, the LORD gave him **t** as much as before!
Ecc 4: 9 Two people can accomplish more than **t** as much
6: 6 He might live a thousand years **t** over but not find
Eze 21:14 Then take the sword and brandish it **t**, even three
Na 1: 9 you with one blow; he won't need to strike **t**!
Mt 23:15 then you turn him into **t** the son of hell as you
Mk 14:30 truth is, this very night, before the rooster crows **t**,
14:72 "Before the rooster crows **t**, you will deny me
Lk 18:12 I fast **t** a week, and I give you a tenth of my
Rev 18: 6 for others, so give her **t** as much as she gave out.

TWIGS (1)

Isa 27:10 Cattle will graze there, chewing on **t** and branches.

TWILIGHT (7) [LIGHT]

Lev 23: 5 which begins at **t** on its appointed day in early
Nu 9: 3 at **t** on the appointed day in early spring. Be sure to
9: 5 in the wilderness of Sinai as **t** fell on the appointed
9:11 sacrifice one month later, at **t** on the appointed day.
2Ch 35: 1 The Passover lambs were slaughtered at **t** of that
Job 24:15 The adulterer waits for the **t**, for he says, 'No one
Pr 7: 9 at **t**, as the day was fading, as the dark of night set

TWIN (9) [TWINS]

Ge 25:26 Then the other **t** was born with his hand grasping
38:27 of Tamar's delivery arrived, and she had **t** sons.
1Ch 2: 4 Later Judah had **t** sons through Tamar,
SS 4: 5 Your breasts are like **t** fawns of a gazelle,
7: 3 Your breasts are like **t** fawns of a gazelle.
Jn 11:16 Thomas, nicknamed the **T**, said to his fellow
20:24 One of the disciples, Thomas (nicknamed the **T**),
21: 2 Simon Peter, Thomas (nicknamed the **T**),
Ac 28:11 an Alexandrian ship with the **t** gods as its

TWINED [KJV] See FINE

TWINKLING (1)

Ps 148: 3 sun and moon! / Praise him, all you **t** stars!

TWINS (4) [TWIN]

Ge 25:21 and his wife became pregnant with **t**.
25:24 And when the time came, the **t** were born.
25:26 Isaac was sixty years old when the **t** were born.
Ro 9:10 grew up, he married Rebekah, who gave birth to **t**.

TWIST (10) [TWISTED, TWISTING, TWISTS]

Ex 23: 6 "Do not **t** justice against people simply
Lev 1:15 **t** off its head, and burn the head on the altar.
Dt 16:19 You must never **t** justice or show partiality.
Job 8: 3 Does God **t** justice? Does the Almighty **t** what is right?
34:12 will not do wrong. The Almighty cannot **t** justice.
Am 5: 7 You **t** justice, making it a bitter pill for the poor
Mic 3: 9 of Israel! You hate justice and **t** all that is right.
7: 3 pay them off, and together they scheme to **t** justice.
Gal 1: 7 You are being fooled by those who **t** and change

TWISTED (11) [TWIST]

Dt 32: 5 They are a deceitful and **t** generation.
32:20 I will see to their end! / For they are a **t** generation,
Pr 8: 8 and good. There is nothing crooked or **t** in it.
11:20 The LORD hates people with **t** hearts, but he
17:20 will not prosper; the **t** tongue tumbles into trouble.
Isa 24: 5 for they have **t** the instructions of God, violated his
Jer 8: 8 when your teachers have **t** it so badly?
La 3: 9 He has **t** the road before me with many detours.
Eze 7:13 Not one person whose life is **t** by sin will recover.
27:35 are filled with horror / and look on with **t** faces.
2Pe 3:16 and unstable have **t** his letters around to mean

TWISTING (3) [TWIST]

Ps 56: 5 They are always **t** what I say; / they spend their
Pr 31:19 hands are busy spinning thread, her fingers **t** fiber.
Ecc 1: 6 and north, here and there, **t** back and forth,

TWISTS (1) [TWIST]

Ps 29: 9 The voice of the LORD **t** mighty oaks / and strips

TWO (644) [II, SECOND, SECOND-CLASS, SECOND-IN-COMMAND, TWICE, TWO-EDGED, TWO-HORNED, TWO-THIRDS, 2]

Ge 1:16 For God made **t** great lights, the sun and the moon,
2:24 is joined to his wife, and the **t** are united into one.
4:19 Lamech married **t** women—Adah and Zillah.
7:15 **T** by **t** they came into the boat,
8: 5 **T** and a half months later, as the waters continued
8:14 **T** more months went by, and at last the earth was
10:25 Eber had **t** sons. The first was named Peleg—
11:10 was born. This happened **t** years after the Flood.
18:22 The **t** other men went on toward Sodom,
19: 1 That evening the **t** angels came to the entrance of
19: 8 Look—I have **t** virgin daughters. Do with them as
19:10 But the **t** angels reached out and pulled Lot in
19:15 your wife and your **t** daughters who are here.
19:16 his hand and the hands of his wife and **t** daughters
19:30 in a cave in the mountains with his **t** daughters.
22: 3 his donkey and took **t** of his servants with him,
22: 6 and the fire. As the **t** of them went on together,
24:22 her nose and **t** large gold bracelets for her wrists.
25: 3 Jokshan's **t** sons were Sheba and Dedan.
25:22 But the **t** children struggled with each other in her
25:23 "The sons in your womb will become **t** rival
27: 9 out to the flocks and bring me **t** fine young goats.
27:14 his mother's instructions, bringing her the **t** goats.
29:16 Now Laban had **t** daughters: Leah, who was the
31:33 then he searched the tents of the **t** concubines,
31:41 fourteen of them earning your **t** daughters, and six
32: 7 with the flocks and herds and camels, into **t** camps.
32:10 and now my household fills **t** camps!
32:14 **t** hundred female goats, twenty male goats, **t** hundred ewes, twenty rams,
32:22 Jacob got up and sent his **t** wives, **t** concubines,
33: 2 with his **t** concubines and their children at the
34:25 **t** of Dinah's brothers, Simeon and Levi, took their
36: 2 Esau married **t** young women from Canaan:
38:11 afraid Shelah would also die, like his **t** brothers.)
41: 1 **T** years later, Pharaoh dreamed that he was
41:50 **t** sons were born to Joseph and his wife, Asenath,
42:37 "You may kill my **t** sons if I don't bring Benjamin
44:27 said to us, 'You know that my wife had **t** sons,
45: 6 These **t** years of famine will grow to seven,
46:27 Joseph also had **t** sons who had been born in
48: 1 and he took with him his **t** sons, Manasseh
48: 5 Now I am adopting as my own sons these **t** boys of
48: 8 Then Jacob looked over at the **t** boys. "Are these
49: 5 "Simeon and Levi are **t** of a kind— / men of
Ex 2:13 his people again, he saw **t** Hebrew men fighting.
4: 9 "And if they do not believe you even after these **t**
16:16 as it needs. Pick up **t** quarts for each person."
16:18 By gathering **t** quarts for each person,
16:22 four quarts for each person instead of **t**.
16:29 on the sixth day, so there will be enough for **t** days.
16:32 "Take **t** quarts of manna and keep it forever as a
16:33 "Get a container and put **t** quarts of manna into it.
16:36 manna was an omer, which held about **t** quarts.)
18: 2 Zipporah, and his **t** sons to live with Jethro,
18: 5 and he brought Moses' wife and **t** sons with him.
18: 6 Your wife and your **t** sons are with him."
19: 1 of Sinai exactly **t** months after they left Egypt.
19:15 "Get ready for an important event **t** days from
21:18 "Now suppose **t** people quarrel, and one hits the
21:22 "Now suppose **t** people are fighting, and in the
21:35 then the **t** owners must sell the live bull and divide
22: 9 "Suppose there is a dispute between **t** people as to
25:12 attach them to its four feet, **t** rings on each side.
25:18 Then use hammered gold to make **t** cherubim,
25:18 and place them at the **t** ends of the atonement
26: 6 to fasten the loops of the **t** sets of sheets together,
26:11 In this way, the **t** sets will become a single unit.
26:17 There will be **t** pegs on each frame so they can be
26:19 into forty silver bases—**t** bases under each frame.
26:21 with their forty silver bases, **t** bases for each frame.
26:25 by sixteen silver bases—**t** bases under each frame.
27: 7 put the poles into the rings at **t** sides of the altar.
27:14 will be on the east end, flanked by **t** curtains.
28: 7 It will consist of **t** pieces, front and back, joined at the shoulders with **t** shoulder-pieces.
28: 9 Take **t** onyx stones and engrave on them the names
28:12 Fasten the **t** stones on the shoulder-pieces of the
28:14 and **t** cords made of pure gold will be attached to
28:16 This chestpiece will be made of **t** folds of cloth,
28:23 Then make **t** gold rings and attach them to the top
28:24 The **t** gold cords will go through the rings on the
28:26 Then make **t** more gold rings, and attach them to the **t** lower inside corners of the
28:27 And make **t** more gold rings and attach them to the
29: 1 a young bull and **t** rams with no physical defects.
29: 3 along with the young bull and the **t** rams.
29:13 lobe of the liver and the **t** kidneys with their fat,
29:22 the **t** kidneys with their fat, and the right thigh.
29:38 on the altar. Offer **t** one-year-old lambs each day,
29:40 offer **t** quarts of fine flour mixed with one quart of
30: 4 attach **t** gold rings to support the carrying poles.
31:18 he gave him the **t** stone tablets inscribed with the
32:15 He held in his hands the **t** stone tablets inscribed
34: 1 "Prepare **t** stone tablets like the first ones.
34: 4 So Moses cut **t** tablets of stone like the first ones.
34: 4 told him, carrying the **t** stone tablets in his hands.
36:18 so the **t** sets of sheets were firmly attached to each
36:19 Then they made **t** more layers for the roof
36:22 There were **t** pegs on each frame so they could be
36:24 along with forty silver bases, **t** for each frame.
36:26 along with forty silver bases, **t** for each frame.
36:29 They made **t** of these, one for each rear corner.
36:30 along with sixteen silver bases, **t** for each frame.
37: 3 were fastened to its four feet, **t** rings at each side.
37: 7 He made **t** figures of cherubim out of hammered
37: 7 and placed them at the **t** ends of the atonement
37:27 **T** gold rings were placed on opposite sides,
38:14 entrance was on the east side, flanked by **t** curtains.
39: 4 They made **t** shoulder-pieces for the ephod,
39: 6 The **t** onyx stones, attached to the shoulder-pieces
39:16 They also made **t** gold rings and attached them to
39:17 The **t** gold cords were put through the gold rings
39:19 **T** more gold rings were attached to the lower
39:20 Then **t** gold rings were attached to the ephod near
Lev 3: 4 the **t** kidneys with the fat around them near the
3:10 the **t** kidneys with the fat around them near the
3:15 the **t** kidneys with the fat around them near the
4: 9 the **t** kidneys with the fat around them near the
5: 7 they must bring to the LORD **t** young turtledoves or **t** young pigeons as the penalty for their sin.
5:11 they must bring **t** quarts of choice flour for their
6:20 they must bring to the LORD a grain offering of **t**
7: 4 the **t** kidneys with the fat around them near the
8: 2 the bull for the sin offering, the **t** rams,
8:16 the lobe of the liver, and the **t** kidneys and their fat,
8:25 lobe of the liver, and the **t** kidneys with their fat,
12: 5 she will be ceremonially defiled for **t** weeks,
12: 8 she must bring **t** turtledoves or **t** young pigeons.
14: 4 using **t** wild birds of a kind permitted for food,
14:10 each person cured of the skin disease must bring **t**
14:21 "But anyone who cannot afford **t** lambs must
14:21 along with **t** quarts of choice flour mixed with
14:22 must also bring **t** turtledoves or **t** young pigeons,
14:30 will offer the **t** turtledoves or the **t** young pigeons,
14:49 To purify the house the priest will need **t** birds,
15:14 he must bring **t** turtledoves or **t** young pigeons
15:29 she must bring **t** turtledoves or **t** young pigeons
16: 1 spoke to Moses after the death of Aaron's **t** sons,
16: 5 then bring him **t** male goats for a sin offering
16: 7 Then he must bring the **t** male goats and present
19:19 Do not plant your field with **t** kinds of seed.
19:19 Do not wear clothing woven from **t** different kinds
23:17 bring **t** loaves of bread to be lifted up before the
23:18 and **t** rams as burnt offerings to the LORD.
23:19 and **t** one-year-old male lambs as a peace offering.
24: 6 and arrange the loaves in **t** rows, with six in each
Nu 3:18 from Gershon were named for **t** of his descendants,
3:20 The clans descended from Merari were named for **t**
3:25 These **t** clans were responsible to care for the tent
3:36 These **t** clans were responsible for the care of the
5:15 **t** quarts of barley flour to be presented on her
6:10 bring **t** turtledoves or **t** young pigeons to the priest
7: 3 There was a cart for every **t** leaders and an ox for
7: 7 He gave **t** carts and four oxen to the Gershonite
7:17 and **t** oxen, five rams, five male goats, and five
7:23 and **t** oxen, five rams, five male goats, and five
7:29 and **t** oxen, five rams, five male goats, and five
7:35 and **t** oxen, five rams, five male goats, and five
7:41 and **t** oxen, five rams, five male goats, and five
7:47 and **t** oxen, five rams, five male goats, and five
7:53 and **t** oxen, five rams, five male goats, and five
7:59 and **t** oxen, five rams, five male goats, and five
7:65 and **t** oxen, five rams, five male goats, and five
7:71 and **t** oxen, five rams, five male goats, and five
7:77 and **t** oxen, five rams, five male goats, and five
7:83 and **t** oxen, five rams, five male goats, and five
7:89 between the **t** cherubim above the Ark's cover—
9:22 the cloud stayed above the Tabernacle for **t** days,
10: 2 "Make **t** trumpets of beaten silver to be used for
11:19 And it won't be for just a day or **t**, or for five
11:26 **T** men, Eldad and Medad, were still in the camp
13:23 so large that it took **t** of them to carry it on a pole
14: 6 **T** of the men who had explored the land,
15: 4 **t** quarts of choice flour mixed with one quart of
15: 6 give three quarts of choice flour mixed with **t**
15: 7 and give **t** and a half pints of wine for a drink
15: 9 of choice flour mixed with **t** quarts of olive oil,
15:10 plus **t** quarts of wine for the drink offering.
16:41 saying, "You **t** have killed the LORD's people!"
20:24 because the **t** of you rebelled against my
22:22 As Balaam and **t** servants were riding along,
22:24 where the road narrowed between **t** vineyard walls.
23: 2 and the **t** of them sacrificed a young bull and a ram
26:19 Judah had **t** sons, Er and Onan, who had died in the
26:28 **T** clans were descended from Joseph through
28: 3 you must offer **t** one-year-old male lambs with no
28: 5 **t** quarts of choice flour mixed with one quart of
28: 9 sacrifice **t** one-year-old male lambs with no
28:11 present an extra burnt offering to the LORD of **t**
28:13 and **t** quarts with each lamb. This burnt offering
28:14 **t** quarts of wine with each bull, **t** and a half pints
28:19 as a burnt offering to the LORD **t** young bulls,
28:21 and **t** quarts with each of the seven lambs.
28:27 It will consist of **t** young bulls, one ram, and seven
28:29 and **t** quarts with each of the seven lambs.
29: 4 and **t** quarts with each of the seven lambs.
29:10 and **t** quarts of choice flour with each of the seven
29:13 It will consist of thirteen young bulls, **t** rams,
29:14 thirteen bulls, three quarts for each of the **t** rams,
29:15 and **t** quarts for each of the fourteen lambs.
29:17 sacrifice twelve young bulls, **t** rams, and fourteen
29:20 of the festival, sacrifice eleven young bulls, **t** rams,
29:23 of the festival, sacrifice ten young bulls, **t** rams,
29:26 of the festival, sacrifice nine young bulls, **t** rams,
29:29 of the festival, sacrifice eight young bulls, **t** rams,
29:32 of the festival, sacrifice seven young bulls, **t** rams,
31:27 Then divide the plunder into **t** parts, and give half
Dt 3: 8 "We now possessed all the land of the **t** Amorite
3:21 the LORD your God has done to these **t** kings.
4:13 and wrote them on **t** stone tablets.
4:47 of Bashan—the **t** Amorite kings east of the Jordan.
5:22 and he wrote his words on **t** stone tablets and gave
9:11 the LORD handed me the **t** stone tablets with the
9:15 holding in my hands the **t** stone tablets of the
10: 1 to me, 'Prepare **t** stone tablets like the first ones,
10: 3 and cut **t** stone tablets like the first **t**,
11:30 (These **t** mountains are west of the Jordan River in
17: 6 There must always be at least **t** or three witnesses.
19:15 the case must be established by the testimony of **t**
21:15 "Suppose a man has **t** wives, but he loves one
25: 1 "Suppose **t** people take a dispute to court,
25: 5 "If **t** brothers are living together on the same
25:11 "If **t** Israelite men are fighting and the wife of one
32:30 of them, / and **t** people put ten thousand to flight,
Jos 2: 1 Then Joshua secretly sent out **t** spies from the
2: 1 So the **t** men set out and came to the house of a
2: 4 Rahab, who had hidden the **t** men, replied,
2:10 the **t** Amorite kings east of the Jordan River,
2:23 Then the **t** spies came down from the hill country,
6:22 Then Joshua said to the **t** spies, "Keep your
7: 3 and it won't take more than **t** or three thousand of
7:21 **t** hundred silver coins, and a bar of gold weighing
8:33 officers, and judges, were divided into **t** groups.
9:10 We have also heard what he did to the **t** Amorite
14: 3 had already given an inheritance of land to the **t**
14: 4 The tribe of Joseph had become **t** separate tribes—
15:60 **t** towns with their surrounding villages.
21:16 and Beth-shemesh—nine towns from these **t** tribes.
21:25 to the priests: Taanach and Gath-rimmon—**t** towns.
21:27 received **t** towns with their pasturelands from the
24:12 And I sent hornets ahead of you to drive out the **t**
Jdg 5:30 goods they found— / a woman or **t** for every man.
7: 5 LORD told him, "Divide the men into **t** groups.
7:25 captured Oreb and Zeeb, the **t** Midianite generals,
8:12 Zebah and Zalmunna, the **t** Midianite kings, fled,
9:44 while Abimelech's other **t** groups cut them down
11:37 in the hills and weep with my friends for **t** months,
11:38 And he let her go away for **t** months. She and her
15:13 So they tied him up with **t** new ropes and led him
16: 3 got up, took hold of the city gates with its **t** posts,
16:25 between the **t** pillars supporting the roof.
16:26 by the hand, "Place my hands against the **t** pillars.
17: 4 So his mother took **t** hundred of the silver coins to
19: 6 So the **t** of them sat down together and had
19:10 So he took his **t** saddled donkeys and his
20:45 they had killed another **t** thousand near Gidom.
Ru 1: 1 He took his wife and **t** sons and went to live in the
1: 2 was Naomi. Their **t** sons were Mahlon and Kilion.
1: 3 Elimelech died and Naomi was left with her **t** sons.
1: 4 The **t** sons married Moabite women. One married a
1: 7 With her **t** daughters-in-law she set out from the
1: 8 on the way, Naomi said to her **t** daughters-in-law,
1:19 So the **t** of them continued on their journey.
1Sa 1: 2 Elkanah had **t** wives, Hannah and Peninnah.
1: 3 The priests of the LORD at that time were the **t**
2:21 LORD gave Hannah three sons and **t** daughters.
2:34 I will cause your **t** sons, Hophni and Phinehas,
4:11 and Phinehas, the **t** sons of Eli, were killed.
4:17 Your **t** sons, Hophni and Phinehas, were killed,
6: 7 new cart, and find **t** cows that have just had calves.
6:10 **T** cows with newborn calves were hitched to the
10: 2 you will see **t** men beside Rachel's tomb at Zelzah,
10: 4 They will greet you and offer you **t** of the loaves,
11: 7 He took **t** oxen and cut them into pieces and sent
11:11 so badly scattered that no **t** of them were left
13: 2 He took **t** thousand of the chosen men with him to
14: 4 Jonathan had to go down between **t** rocky cliffs
14:49 He also had **t** daughters: Merab, who was older,
17:39 over it, and took a step or **t** to see what it was like,
18:27 his men went out and killed **t** hundred Philistines
23:18 So the **t** of them renewed their covenant of
25:13 and **t** hundred remained behind to guard their
25:18 She quickly gathered **t** hundred loaves of bread, **t** skins of wine, five dressed sheep, nearly a bushel
25:18 one hundred raisin cakes, and **t** hundred fig cakes.
27: 3 David brought his **t** wives along with him—
28: 8 home at night, accompanied by **t** of his men.
30: 5 David's **t** wives, Ahinoam of Jezreel and Abigail,
30:10 But **t** hundred of the men were too exhausted to
30:12 gave him part of a fig cake and **t** clusters of raisins
30:18 Amalekites had taken, and he rescued his **t** wives.
30:21 and met the **t** hundred men who had been too tired
2Sa 1: 1 over the Amalekites and spent **t** days in Ziklag.
2:10 and he ruled from Mahanaim for **t** years.
2:13 The **t** groups sat down there, facing each other
2:17 The **t** armies then began to fight each other, and by
3:39 I am the anointed king, these **t** sons of Zeruiah—
4: 2 Now there were **t** brothers, Baanah and Recab,
8: 2 He measured off **t** groups to be executed for every
10: 9 When Joab saw that he would have to fight on **t**
12: 1 "There were **t** men in a certain town. One was
13:23 **T** years later, when Absalom's sheep were being
14: 6 "My **t** sons had a fight out in the field. And since
14:28 Absalom lived in Jerusalem for **t** years without
15:11 He took **t** hundred men from Jerusalem with him
16: 1 He was leading **t** donkeys loaded with **t** hundred
17:21 Then the **t** men crawled out of the well and hurried
21: 8 But he gave them Saul's **t** sons Armoni
21:10 Then Rizpah, the mother of **t** of the men,
23:20 which included killing **t** of Moab's mightiest

1Ki 2: 5 You know that Joab son of Zeruiah murdered my **t**
2:32 for the murders of **t** men who were more righteous
2:39 **t** of Shimei's slaves escaped to King Achish of
3:16 **t** prostitutes came to the king to have an argument
3:18 were alone; there were only **t** of us in the house.
3:25 "Cut the living child in **t** and give half to each of
5:14 be one month in Lebanon and **t** months at home.
6:23 Within the inner sanctuary Solomon placed **t**
6:25 The **t** cherubim were identical in shape and size;
6:28 He overlaid the **t** cherubim with gold.
6:34 There were **t** folding doors of cypress wood,
7:15 Huram cast **t** bronze pillars, each 27 feet tall
7:18 He also made **t** rows of pomegranates that
7:20 Each capital on the **t** pillars had **t** hundred
pomegranates in **t** rows around them,
7:24 The Sea was encircled just below its rim by **t** rows
7:41 **t** pillars, / **t** bowl-shaped capitals on top of the
pillars, / **t** networks of chains that decorated the
7:42 (**t** rows of pomegranates for each of the chain
8: 9 Nothing was in the Ark except the **t** stone tablets
10:16 King Solomon made **t** hundred large shields of
11:29 a new cloak. The **t** of them were alone in a field,
12:28 of his counselors, the king made **t** gold calves.
15:25 Asa's reign in Judah. He reigned in Israel **t** years.
16: 8 Asa's reign in Judah. He reigned in Israel **t** years.
16:21 But now the people of Israel were divided into **t**
18: 4 Obadiah had hidden one hundred of them in **t**
18:13 I hid a hundred of them in **t** caves and supplied
18:21 "How long are you going to waver between **t**
18:23 Now bring **t** bulls. The prophets of Baal may
20:27 But the Israelite army looked like **t** little flocks of
20:29 The **t** armies camped opposite each other for seven
21:10 Find **t** scoundrels who will accuse him of cursing
21:13 Then **t** scoundrels accused him before all the
22:51 reign in Judah. He reigned in Samaria **t** years.
2Ki 1:14 fire from heaven has destroyed the first **t** groups.
2: 8 and the **t** of them went across on dry ground!
2:12 disappeared from sight, Elisha tore his robe in **t**.
2:24 Then **t** bears came out of the woods and mauled
4: 1 has come, threatening to take my **t** sons as slaves."
4:40 after the men had eaten a bite or **t** they cried out,
5:17 but please allow me to load **t** of my mules with
5:22 "but my master has sent me to tell you that **t**
5:22 of silver and **t** sets of clothing to give to them."
5:23 gave him **t** sets of clothing, tied up the money in **t**
bags, and sent **t** of his servants to carry the gifts for
6:25 After a while even a donkey's head sold for **t**
6:25 and a cup of dove's dung cost about **t** ounces of
7:14 So **t** chariots with horses were prepared,
9:32 And **t** or three eunuchs looked out at him.
10: 4 and said, "**T** kings couldn't stand against this man!
10: 8 "Pile them in **t** heaps at the entrance of the city
11: 7 The other **t** units who are off duty on the Sabbath
14:11 The **t** armies drew up their battle lines at
15:23 reign in Judah. He reigned in Samaria **t** years.
17:16 LORD their God and made **t** calves from metal.
18:23 If you can find **t** thousand horsemen in your entire
18:23 he will give you **t** thousand horses for them to ride
21:19 became king, and he reigned in Jerusalem **t** years.
23:12 built in the **t** courtyards of the LORD's Temple.
25: 4 and fled through the gate between the **t** walls
25:16 The bronze from the **t** pillars, the water carts,
1Ch 1:19 Eber had **t** sons. The first was named Peleg—
2:18 Hezron's son Caleb had **t** wives named Azubah
2:32 Jada, had **t** sons named Jether and Jonathan.
2:33 but Jonathan had **t** sons named Peleth and Zaza.
4: 5 of Tekoa) had **t** wives, named Helah and Naarah.
11:22 which included killing **t** of Moab's mightiest
19:10 When Joab saw that he would have to fight on **t**
26:17 to the south gate, and **t** to each of the storehouses.
26:18 leading up to the Temple, and **t** to the courtyard.
2Ch 3:10 Solomon made **t** figures shaped like cherubim
3:11 The total wingspan of the **t** cherubim standing side
3:15 Solomon made **t** pillars that were 27 feet tall,
3:17 Then he set up the **t** pillars at the entrance of the
4: 3 The Sea was encircled just below its rim by **t** rows
4:12 **t** pillars, / **t** bowl-shaped capitals on top of the
pillars, / **t** networks of chains that decorated the
4:13 (**t** rows of pomegranates for each of the chain
5:10 Nothing was in the Ark except the **t** stone tablets
9:15 King Solomon made **t** hundred large shields of
21:19 In the course of time, at the end of **t** years,
24: 3 Jehoiada chose **t** wives for Joash, and he had sons
25:21 The **t** armies drew up their battle lines at
29:32 and **t** hundred lambs for burnt offerings.
33:21 became king, and he reigned in Jerusalem **t** years.
Ezr 6:17 one hundred young bulls, **t** hundred rams, and four
10:13 isn't something that can be done in a day or **t**,
Ne 12:31 and organized **t** large choirs to give thanks.
12:40 The **t** choirs that were giving thanks
Est 2:21 **t** of the king's eunuchs, Bigthana and Teresh—
2:23 to be true, the **t** men were hanged on a gallows.
6: 2 **t** of the eunuchs who guarded the door to the
9: 1 So on March 7 the **t** decrees of the king were put
9:21 to celebrate an annual festival on these **t** days.
9:27 **t** prescribed days at the appointed time each year.
Job 13:20 "O God, there are **t** things I beg of you, and I will
42: 7 "I am angry with you and with your **t** friends,
Ps 46: 9 He breaks the bow and snaps the spear in **t**;
89:14 Your throne is founded on **t** strong pillars—
Pr 30: 7 O God, I beg **t** favors from you before I die.
30:15 The leech has **t** suckers that cry out, "More,
Ecc 4: 9 **T** people can accomplish more than twice as much
4:11 **t** under the same blanket can gain warmth from
4:12 but **t** can stand back-to-back and conquer.
SS 6:13 so gracefully between **t** lines of dancers?"
8:12 And I will give **t** hundred pieces of silver to those
Isa 6: 2 With **t** wings they covered their faces, with **t** they
covered their feet, and with the remaining **t** they
flew.
7: 4 fear the fierce anger of those **t** burned-out embers,
7:16 right from wrong, the **t** kings you fear so much—
7:21 will be fortunate to have a cow and **t** sheep left.
17: 6 Only **t** or three remain in the highest branches,
36: 8 If you can find **t** thousand horsemen in your entire
36: 8 he will give you **t** thousand horses for them to ride
47: 9 those **t** things will come upon you in a moment:
51:19 These **t** things have been your lot: desolation
Jer 2:13 For my people have done **t** evil things: They have
3:14 one from here and **t** from there, from wherever you
24: 1 I saw **t** baskets of figs placed in front of the
28: 3 Within **t** years, I will bring back all the Temple
28:11 "The LORD has promised that within **t** years he
28:17 **T** months later, Hananiah died.
39: 2 **T** and a half years later, on July 18,
39: 4 They went out through a gate between the **t** walls
52: 7 and fled through the gate between the **t** walls
52:20 The bronze from the **t** pillars, the water carts,
Eze 1: 6 that each had four faces and **t** pairs of wings.
1: 9 being touched the wings of the **t** beings beside it.
1:11 Each had **t** pairs of outstretched wings—one pair
1:23 and each had **t** wings covering its body.
21:19 and trace **t** routes on it for the sword of Babylon's
21:19 out of Babylon where the road forks into **t**—
23: 2 once there were **t** sisters who were daughters of the
37:22 no longer will they be divided into **t** nations.
40:23 The distance between the **t** gateways was 175 feet.
40:27 The distance between the **t** gateways was 175 feet.
40:39 On each side of this foyer were **t** tables,
40:40 up to the north entrance, there were **t** more tables.
40:44 Inside the inner courtyard there were **t** one-room
41:11 **T** doors opened from the side rooms into the
41:15 including its **t** walls, was also 175 feet wide.
41:18 with carvings of cherubim, each with **t** faces,
41:24 each with **t** swinging doors.
42: 3 The **t** blocks were built three levels high and stood
42: 4 Between the **t** blocks of rooms ran a walkway
42: 5 Each of the **t** upper levels of rooms was narrower
42:10 On the south side of the Temple there were **t**
42:11 There was a walkway between the **t** blocks of
45: 7 "**T** special sections of land will be set apart for the
45:15 and one sheep for every **t** hundred in your flocks in
46:14 about **t** and a half quarts of flour with a third of a
47:13 The tribe of Joseph will be given **t** shares of land.
Da 6: 2 and **t** others as administrators to supervise the
7: 4 and it was left standing with its **t** hind feet on the
8: 3 I saw in front of me a ram with **t** long horns
8:13 Then I heard **t** of the holy ones talking to each
12: 5 and saw **t** others standing on opposite banks of the
Am 1: 1 He received this message in visions **t** years before
3: 3 Can **t** people walk together without agreeing on the
3:12 sheep from a lion's mouth will recover only **t** legs
Zec 4: 3 And I see **t** olive trees, one on each side of the
4:11 "What are these **t** olive trees on each side of the
4:12 and what are the **t** olive branches that pour out
golden oil through **t** gold tubes?"
4:14 "They represent the **t** anointed ones who assist the
5: 9 I looked up and saw **t** women flying toward us,
6: 1 and saw four chariots coming from between **t**
6:13 and there will be perfect harmony between the **t**.
9:12 I promise this very day that I will repay you **t**
11: 7 Then I took **t** shepherd's staffs and named one
11:10 I took my staff called Favor and snapped it in **t**,
Mt 2:16 and around Bethlehem who were **t** years old
2:16 the star first appeared to them about **t** years earlier.
4:18 beside the Sea of Galilee, he saw **t** brothers—
4:21 A little farther up the shore he saw **t** other brothers,
5:41 that you carry his gear for a mile, carry it **t** miles.
6:24 "No one can serve **t** masters. For you will hate one
8:28 **t** men who were possessed by demons met him.
9:27 **t** blind men followed along behind him, shouting,
14:17 "We have only five loaves of bread and **t** fish!"
14:19 And he took the five loaves and **t** fish, looked up
17: 1 Six days later Jesus took Peter and the **t** brothers,
18: 9 It is better to enter heaven half blind than to have **t**
18:16 take one or **t** others with you and go back again,
18:16 so that everything you say may be confirmed by **t**
18:19 If **t** of you agree down here on earth concerning
18:20 For where **t** or three gather together because they
19: 5 is joined to his wife, and the **t** are united into one.'
19: 6 Since they are no longer **t** but one, let no one
20:21 will you let my **t** sons sit in places of honor next to
20:30 **T** blind men were sitting beside the road.
21: 1 the Mount of Olives. Jesus sent **t** of them on ahead.
21: 6 The **t** disciples did as Jesus said.
21:28 A man with **t** sons told the older boy, 'Son, go out
21:31 Which of the **t** was obeying his father?"
22:40 the prophets are based on these **t** commandments."
24:40 "**T** men will be working together in the field;
24:41 **T** women will be grinding flour at the mill;
25:15 **t** bags of gold to another, and one bag of gold to
25:17 The servant with **t** bags of gold also went right to
25:22 "Next came the servant who had received the **t**
25:22 'Sir, you gave me **t** bags of gold to invest,
26: 2 the Passover celebration begins in **t** days, and I,
26:37 He took Peter and Zebedee's **t** sons, James
26:60 they could use. Finally, **t** men were found
27:21 "Which of these **t** do you want me to release to
27:38 **T** criminals were crucified with him, their crosses
27:51 moment the curtain in the Temple was torn in **t**,
Mk 5:13 and the entire herd of **t** thousand pigs plunged
6: 7 disciples together and sent them out **t** by **t**,
6:38 "We have five loaves of bread and **t** fish."
6:41 Jesus took the five loaves and **t** fish, looked up
9:43 go into the unquenchable fires of hell with **t** hands.
9:45 one foot than to be thrown into hell with **t** feet.
9:47 the Kingdom of God half blind than to have **t** eyes
10: 8 and the **t** are united into one.' Since they are no
longer **t** but one,
11: 1 the Mount of Olives. Jesus sent **t** of them on ahead.
11: 4 The **t** disciples left and found the colt standing in
12:42 Then a poor widow came and dropped in **t** pennies.
14: 1 It was now **t** days before the Passover celebration
14:13 So Jesus sent **t** of them into Jerusalem to make the
14:16 So the **t** disciples went on ahead into the city
15:27 **T** criminals were crucified with him, their crosses
15:32 Even the **t** criminals who were being crucified with
15:38 And the curtain in the Temple was torn in **t**,
16:12 Afterward he appeared to **t** who were walking
Lk 2:24 "either a pair of turtledoves or **t** young pigeons."
3:11 John replied, "If you have **t** coats, give one to the
5: 2 He noticed **t** empty boats at the water's edge,
7:18 was doing. So John called for **t** of his disciples,
7:20 John's **t** disciples found Jesus and said to him,
7:41 "A man loaned money to **t** people—five hundred
9:13 "We have only five loaves of bread and **t** fish.
9:16 Jesus took the five loaves and **t** fish, looked up
9:30 Then **t** men, Moses and Elijah, appeared and began
9:32 saw Jesus' glory and the **t** men standing with him.
10:35 The next day he handed the innkeeper **t** pieces of
12:52 be split apart, three in favor of me, and **t** against—
15:11 Jesus told them this story: "A man had **t** sons.
16:13 "No one can serve **t** masters. For you will hate one
17:34 That night **t** people will be asleep in one bed;
17:35 **T** women will be grinding flour together at the
18:10 "**T** men went to the Temple to pray. One was a
19:29 on the Mount of Olives, he sent **t** disciples ahead.
21: 2 a poor widow came by and dropped in **t** pennies.
22:38 they replied, "we have **t** swords among us."
23:32 **T** others, both criminals, were led out to be
23:33 the center cross, and the **t** criminals on either side.
24: 4 Suddenly, **t** men appeared to them, clothed in
24:13 That same day **t** of Jesus' followers were walking
24:35 Then the **t** from Emmaus told their story of how
Jn 1:35 John was again standing with **t** of his disciples.
1:37 Then John's **t** disciples turned and followed Jesus.
4:40 him to stay at their village. So he stayed for **t** days,
4:43 At the end of the **t** days' stay, Jesus went on into
6: 9 a young boy here with five barley loaves and **t** fish.
8:17 Your own law says that if **t** people agree about
11: 3 So the **t** sisters sent a message to Jesus telling him,
11: 6 he stayed where he was for the next **t** days and did
11: 7 Finally after **t** days, he said to his disciples,
19:18 There were **t** others crucified with him, one on
19:32 and broke the legs of the **t** men crucified with
20:12 She saw **t** white-robed angels sitting at the head
21: 2 the sons of Zebedee, and **t** other disciples.
Ac 1:10 **t** white-robed men suddenly stood there among
1:23 So they nominated **t** men: Joseph called Barsabbas
4: 7 They brought in the **t** disciples and demanded,
5: 9 "How could the **t** of you even think of doing a
7:26 them again and saw **t** men of Israel fighting.
7:29 in the land of Midian, where his **t** sons were born.
9:38 so they sent **t** men to beg him, "Please come as
10: 7 Cornelius called **t** of his household servants
12: 6 he was asleep, chained between **t** soldiers,
13:43 and Barnabas, and the **t** men urged them,
15:22 The men chosen were **t** of the church leaders—
19:10 This went on for the next **t** years, so that people
19:22 He sent his **t** assistants, Timothy and Erastus,
19:34 started shouting again and kept it up for **t** hours:
21:33 arrested him and ordered him bound with **t** chains.
23:23 Then the commander called **t** of his officers
23:23 "Get **t** hundred soldiers ready to leave for
23:23 Also take **t** hundred spearmen and seventy
24:27 **T** years went by in this way; then Felix was
27:33 "You haven't touched food for **t** weeks," he said.
28:30 For the next **t** years, Paul lived in his own rented
Ro 13: 5 So you must obey the government for **t** reasons:
1Co 6:16 the Scriptures say, "The **t** are united into one."
14:27 No more than **t** or three should speak in an
14:29 Let **t** or three prophesy, and let the others evaluate
2Co 9:12 So **t** good things will happen—the needs of the
13: 1 case must be established by the testimony of **t**
Gal 3:20 Now a mediator is needed if **t** people enter into an
4:22 The Scriptures say that Abraham had **t** sons,
4:24 Now these **t** women serve as an illustration of
God's **t** covenants.
5:17 These **t** forces are constantly fighting each other,
Eph 2:15 in himself one new person from the **t** groups.
5:31 is joined to his wife, and the **t** are united into one."
Php 1:23 I'm torn between **t** desires: Sometimes I want to
4: 2 And now I want to plead with those **t** women,
1Ti 1:20 Hymenaeus and Alexander are **t** examples of this.
5:19 to complaints against an elder unless there are **t**
Heb 6:18 These **t** things are unchangeable because it is
9: 2 There were **t** rooms in this tent. In the first room
10:28 put to death without mercy on the testimony of **t**
11:20 It was by faith that Isaac blessed his **t** sons, Jacob
Rev 9:12 terror is past, but look, **t** more terrors are coming!
11: 3 And I will give power to my **t** witnesses, and they
11: 4 These **t** prophets are the **t** olive trees and the **t**
lampstands that stand before the Lord of
11:10 death of the **t** prophets who had tormented them.
12:14 But she was given **t** wings like those of a great
13:11 He had **t** horns like those of a lamb, and he spoke

TWO-EDGED (2) [EDGE, TWO]

Rev 1:16 and a sharp **t** sword came from his mouth.
2:12 This is the message from the one who has a sharp **t**

TWO-HORNED (2) [HORN, TWO]
Da 8: 6 headed toward the **t** ram that I had seen standing
8:20 The **t** ram represents the kings of Media

TWO-THIRDS (1) [THREE, TWO]
Zec 13: 8 **T** of the people in the land will be cut off and die,

TYCHICUS (6)
Ac 20: 4 and **T** and Trophimus, who were from the province
Eph 6:21 **T**, a much loved brother and faithful helper in the
Col 4: 7 **T**, a much loved brother, will tell you how I am
4: 9 He and **T** will give you all the latest news.
2Ti 4:12 I sent **T** to Ephesus.
Tit 3:12 I am planning to send either Artemas or **T** to you.

TYING (4) [TIE]
Ge 37: 7 "We were out in the field **t** up bundles of grain.
Pr 26: 8 Honoring a fool is as foolish as **t** a stone to a
Mt 12:29 man's house and rob him without first **t** him up.
Mk 3:27 man's house and rob him without first **t** him up.

TYPE (1) [TYPES]
Pr 7:11 the brash, rebellious **t** who never stays at home.

TYPES (1) [TYPE]
Eph 4:31 and slander, as well as all **t** of malicious behavior.

TYPHOON (1)
Ac 27:14 and a wind of **t** strength (a "northeaster,"

TYRANNUS (1)
Ac 19: 9 he began preaching daily at the lecture hall of **T**.

TYRANNY (2) [TYRANT, TYRANT'S, TYRANTS]
2Ki 13: 5 to rescue the Israelites from the **t** of the Arameans.
Isa 14: 6 in your angry grip. Your **t** was unrestrained.

TYRANT (1) [TYRANNY]
Isa 49:24 Who can demand that a **t** let his captives go?

TYRANT'S (1) [TYRANNY]
Pr 29:16 But the godly will live to see the **t** downfall.

TYRANTS (3) [TYRANNY]
Isa 49:25 be released, and the plunder of **t** will be retrieved.
Mt 20:25 and said, "You know that in this world kings are **t**,
Mk 10:42 and said, "You know that in this world kings are **t**,

TYRE (64) [TYRE'S]
Jos 19:29 turned toward Ramah and the fortified city of **T**
2Sa 5:11 Then King Hiram of **T** sent messengers to David,
24: 7 Then they came to the stronghold of **T**, and all the
1Ki 5: 1 King Hiram of **T** had always been a loyal friend of
7:13 asked for a man named Huram to come from **T**,
7:14 and his father had been a foundry worker from **T**.
9:11 to King Hiram of **T** as payment for all the cedar
9:12 Hiram came from **T** to see the towns Solomon had
1Ch 14: 1 Now King Hiram of **T** sent messengers to David,
22: 4 for the men of **T** and Sidon had brought vast
2Ch 2: 3 also sent this message to King Hiram at **T**:
2:14 a woman from Dan in Israel; his father is from **T**.
Ezr 3: 7 and bought cedar logs from the people of **T**
Ne 13:16 There were also some men from **T** bringing in fish
Ps 45:12 The princes of **T** will shower you with gifts.
83: 7 and Amalekites, / and people from Philistia and **T**.
87: 4 also Philistia and **T**, and even distant Ethiopia.
Isa 23: 1 This message came to me concerning **T**: Weep,
23: 1 Weep for your harbor at **T** because it is gone!
23: 5 When Egypt hears the news about **T**, there will be
23: 8 Who has brought this disaster on **T**, empire builder
23:10 sweep over your mother **T** like the flooding Nile,
23:15 the length of a king's life, **T** will be forgotten.
23:17 after seventy years the LORD will revive **T**.
Jer 25:22 and the kings of **T** and Sidon, and the kings of the
27: 3 messages to the kings of Edom, Moab, Ammon, **T**,
47: 4 along with their allies from **T** and Sidon.
Eze 26: 2 **T** has rejoiced over the fall of Jerusalem, saying,
26: 3 I am your enemy, O **T**, and I will bring many
26: 4 They will destroy the walls of **T** and tear down its
26: 5 The island of **T** will become uninhabited. It will be
26: 5 **T** will become the prey of many nations,
26: 7 against **T** with his cavalry, chariots, and great
26:15 "This is what the Sovereign LORD says to **T**:
26:19 LORD says: I will make **T** an uninhabited ruin.
27: 2 "Son of man, sing a funeral song for **T**,
27: 3 Give **T** this message from the Sovereign LORD:
27: 3 You claimed, O **T**, to be perfect in beauty.
27: 8 your helmsmen were skilled men from **T** itself.
27:32 funeral song: / 'Was there ever such a city as **T**,
28: 2 give the prince of **T** this message from the
28:12 "Son of man, weep for the king of **T**. Give him
29:18 so hard against **T** that the warriors' heads were
29:20 he was working for me when he destroyed **T**.
Hos 9:13 Israel become as beautiful and pleasant as **T**.
Joel 3: 4 **T** and Sidon and you cities of Philistia?
Am 1: 9 "The people of **T** have sinned again and again,
1:10 So I will send down fire on the walls of **T**, and all
Zec 9: 2 and for the cities of **T** and Sidon, too, though they
9: 3 **T** has built a strong fortress and has piled up
9: 4 **T** will be set on fire and burned to the ground.
9: 5 The city of Ashkelon will see **T** fall and will be
Mt 11:21 miracles I did in you had been done in wicked **T**
11:22 **T** and Sidon will be better off on the judgment day
15:21 and went north to the region of **T** and Sidon.
Mk 3: 8 and even from as far away as **T** and Sidon.
7:24 left Galilee and went north to the region of **T**.
7:31 Jesus left **T** and went to Sidon, then back to the
Lk 6:17 and from as far north as the seacoasts of **T**
10:13 miracles I did in you had been done in wicked **T**
10:14 **T** and Sidon will be better off on the judgment day
Ac 12:20 Now Herod was very angry with the people of **T**
21: 3 on our left, and landed at the harbor of **T**, in Syria,
21: 7 The next stop after leaving **T** was Ptolemais,

TYRE'S (1) [TYRE]
Zec 9: 4 But now the Lord will strip away **T** possessions

U

UEL (1)
Ezr 10:34 From the family of Bani: Maadai, Amram, **U**,

UGH (1)
Isa 30:22 "**U**!" you will say to them. "Begone!"

UGLY (6)
Ge 41: 3 up from the river, but these were very **u** and gaunt.
41: 4 Then the thin, **u** cows ate the fat ones! At this point
41:19 I've never seen such **u** animals in all the land of
41:20 **u** cows ate up the seven fat ones that had come out
41:21 but afterward they were still as **u** and gaunt as
41:27 **u** cows and the seven withered heads of grain

ULAI (2)
Da 8: 2 the province of Elam, standing beside the **U** River.
8:16 And I heard a human voice calling out from the **U**

ULAM (4)
1Ch 7:16 The sons of Peresh were **U** and Rakem.
7:17 The son of **U** was Bedan. All these were
8:39 **U** (the oldest), Jeush (the second), and Eliphelet
8:40 The sons of **U** were all skilled warriors and expert

ULLA (1)
1Ch 7:39 The sons of **U** were Arah, Hanniel, and Rizia.

ULTERIOR (1)
Pr 21:27 especially when it is brought with **u** motives.

ULTIMATELY (1)
Ecc 9: 2 The same destiny **u** awaits everyone, whether they

UMBILICAL (1)
Eze 16: 4 Your **u** cord was left uncut, and you were never

UMMAH (1) [ACCO]
Jos 19:30 **U**, Aphek, and Rehob—twenty-two towns with

UNABATED (1)
Ac 27:20 The terrible storm raged **u** for many days,

UNABLE (15)
Ex 9:11 Even the magicians were **u** to stand before Moses,
Jos 17:12 But the descendants of Manasseh were **u** to occupy
Jdg 13: 2 His wife was **u** to become pregnant, and they had
13: 3 "Even though you have been **u** to have children,
2Ch 14:13 so many Ethiopians fell that they were **u** to rally.
Pr 31: 5 and be **u** to give justice to those who are
Isa 47:15 will slip away and disappear, **u** to help.
Jer 36: 5 "I am a prisoner here and **u** to go to the Temple.
48:45 people flee as far as Heshbon but are **u** to go on.
Da 10:15 I looked down at the ground, **u** to say a word.
Am 2:14 Even the mightiest warriors will be **u** to save
Mt 12:22 who was both blind and **u** to talk, was brought to
Lk 13:11 for eighteen years and was **u** to stand up straight.
Jn 8:43 what I am saying? It is because you are **u** to do so!
2Co 4: 4 so they are **u** to see the glorious light of the Good

UNACCEPTABLE (2)
Mt 15:20 could never defile you and make you **u** to God!"
Mk 7:23 they are what defile you and make you **u** to God."

UNADVISEDLY [KJV] See FOOLISHLY

UNAFRAID (5)
Job 11:19 You will lie down **u**, and many will look to you for
39:22 it is **u**. It does not run from the sword.
Pr 1:33 to me will live in peace and safety, **u** of harm."
Isa 17: 2 Sheep will graze in the streets and lie down **u**.
Hos 2:18 and bows, so you can live **u** in peace and safety.

UNAIDED (1)
Isa 63: 5 vengeance alone; **u**, I passed down judgment.

UNANIMOUS (1) [UNANIMOUSLY]
Ps 83: 5 This was their **u** decision. / They signed a treaty as

UNANIMOUSLY (3) [UNANIMOUS]
2Sa 19:14 all the leaders of Judah, and they responded **u**.
Da 6: 7 and other officials have **u** agreed that Your
Ac 15:25 good to us, having **u** agreed on our decision,

UNANNOUNCED (2)
Mt 24:50 well, the master will return **u** and unexpected.
Lk 12:46 well, the master will return **u** and unexpected.

UNANSWERED (1)
Ps 35:13 and prayed for them, / but my prayers returned **u**.

UNASHAMED (1)
Jer 3: 3 For you are a prostitute and are completely **u**.

UNAUTHORIZED (5)
Lev 22:16 by allowing **u** people to eat them. The negligent
Nu 16:40 This would warn the Israelites that no **u** man—
2Ki 11: 8 Any **u** person who approaches you must be killed.
2Ch 23: 7 Any **u** person who enters the Temple must be
Mt 7:23 knew you. Go away; the things you did were **u**.'

UNAWARE (7)
Ge 19:33 He was **u** of her lying down or getting up again.
19:35 he was **u** of her lying down or getting up again.
Lev 5: 2 and guilty, even if they are **u** of their defilement.
Nu 15:24 and the community was **u** of it,
Jer 11:19 I had been as **u** as a lamb on the way to its
Hos 7: 9 **u** of how weak and old he has become.
Lk 21:34 worries of this life. Don't let that day catch you **u**,

UNAWARES [KJV] See DECEIVED, SECRETLY, UNEXPECTED(LY), UNINTENTIONAL(LY)

UNBEARABLE (1) [UNBEARABLY]
Php 2:27 on me, so that I would not have such **u** sorrow.

UNBEARABLY (1) [UNBEARABLE]
Dt 28:59 without relief, making you miserable and **u** sick.

UNBELIEF (10) [UNBELIEVABLE, UNBELIEVER, UNBELIEVERS, UNBELIEVING]
Isa 30: 8 until the end of time as a witness to Israel's **u**.
Mt 13:58 he did only a few miracles there because of their **u**.
Mk 6: 5 And because of their **u**, he couldn't do any mighty
6: 6 And he was amazed at their **u**. / Then Jesus went
16:14 He rebuked them for their **u**—their stubborn
Jn 16: 9 The world's sin is **u** in me.
Ro 11:23 And if the Jews turn from their **u**, God will graft
1Ti 1:13 mercy on me because I did it in ignorance and **u**.
Heb 3:19 not allowed to enter his rest because of their **u**.
12:15 Watch out that no bitter root of **u** rises up among

UNBELIEVABLE (1) [UNBELIEF]
Eze 16:16 **U**! How could such a thing ever happen?

UNBELIEVER (3) [UNBELIEF]
1Co 7:12 If a Christian man has a wife who is an **u** and she
7:13 if a Christian woman has a husband who is an **u**,
2Co 6:15 How can a believer be a partner with an **u**?

UNBELIEVERS (9) [UNBELIEF]
1Co 5:10 But I wasn't talking about **u** who indulge in sexual
6: 6 one Christian sues another—right in front of **u**!
14:22 in tongues is a sign, not for believers, but for **u**;
14:22 however, is for the benefit of believers, not **u**.
14:23 if **u** or people who don't understand these things
14:24 But if all of you are prophesying and **u** or people
2Co 6:14 Don't team up with those who are **u**. How can
1Ti 5: 8 what we believe. Such people are worse than **u**.
Rev 21: 8 and **u**, and the corrupt, and murderers,

UNBELIEVING (4) [UNBELIEF]
Joel 2:17 Don't let their name become a proverb of **u**
Tit 1:15 But nothing is pure to those who are corrupt and **u**,
Heb 3:12 Make sure that your own hearts are not evil and **u**,
1Pe 2:12 Be careful how you live among your **u** neighbors.

UNBENDING (1)
Isa 48: 4 and obstinate you are. Your necks are as **u** as iron.

UNBIND (1)
Nu 5:18 he must **u** her hair and place the offering of

UNBLAMEABLE [KJV] See BLAMELESS

UNBORN (1)
Ps 22:31 His righteous acts will be told to those yet **u**.

UNBOUND (1)
Da 3:25 "I see four men, **u**, walking around in the fire.

UNBREAKABLE (2)
Nu 18:19 This is an **u** covenant between the LORD and you
2Ch 13:5 made an **u** covenant with David, giving him

UNBURIED (3)
Isa 34:3 Their dead will be left **u**, and the stench of rotting
Jer 36:30 His dead body will be thrown out to lie **u**—
Eze 29:5 You will lie **u** on the open ground, for I have given

UNCEASING (1)
Isa 14:6 You persecuted the people with **u** blows of rage

UNCERTAIN (2) [UNCERTAINTY]
Jer 15:18 Your help seems as **u** as a seasonal brook.
Eze 21:21 the fork, **u** whether to attack Jerusalem or Rabbah.

UNCERTAINTY (1) [UNCERTAIN]
Isa 32:4 Those who stammer in **u** will speak out plainly.

UNCHANGEABLE (1) [UNCHANGED]
Heb 6:18 These two things are **u** because it is impossible for

UNCHANGED (2) [UNCHANGEABLE, UNCHANGING]
Job 23:13 Nevertheless, his mind concerning me remains **u**,
Jer 51:29 the LORD has planned against her stands **u**.

UNCHANGING (2) [UNCHANGED]
Eph 1:5 His **u** plan has always been to adopt us into his
Jude 1:3 God gave this **u** truth once for all time to his holy

UNCIRCUMCISED (8)
Ex 12:48 But an **u** male may never eat of the Passover lamb.
Jer 9:26 the people of Israel also have **u** hearts."
Eze 44:7 You have brought **u** foreigners into my sanctuary
Ro 2:25 God's law, you are no better off than an **u** Gentile.
2:27 **u** Gentiles who keep God's law will be much
1Co 7:18 And the man who was **u** when he became a
Eph 2:11 You were called "the **u** ones" by the Jews,
Col 3:11 circumcised or **u**, barbaric, uncivilized, slave,

UNCIVILIZED (1)
Col 3:11 or uncircumcised, barbaric, **u**, slave, or free.

UNCLE (18) [UNCLE'S, UNCLES]
Ge 13:11 and parted company with his **u** Abram.
27:43 you should do. Flee to your **u** Laban in Haran.
28:2 and marry one of your **u** Laban's daughters.
28:5 and he went to Paddan-aram to stay with his **u**
28:9 So he visited his **u** Ishmael's family and married
32:4 I have been living with **U** Laban until recently,
Lev 10:4 Aaron's cousins, the sons of Aaron's **u** Uzziel.
18:14 And do not violate your **u**, your father's brother,
20:20 with his uncle's wife, he has violated his **u**.
25:49 an **u**, a nephew, or anyone else who is closely
1Sa 10:14 Saul's **u** asked him. "We went to look for the
10:15 "Oh? And what did he say?" his **u** asked.
10:16 But Saul didn't tell his **u** that Samuel had anointed
14:50 Saul's army was his cousin Abner, his **u** Ner's son.
2Ki 24:17 Jehoiachin's **u**, as the next king,
1Ch 3:16 he, in turn, was succeeded by his **u** Zedekiah.
27:32 Jonathan, David's **u**, was a wise counselor to the
2Ch 36:10 And Nebuchadnezzar appointed Jehoiachin's **u**,

UNCLE'S (3) [UNCLE]
Ge 29:10 and because the sheep were his **u**, Jacob went over
29:10 and rolled away the stone and watered his **u** flock.
Lev 20:20 If a man has intercourse with his **u** wife, he has

UNCLEAN (90)
CEREMONIALLY UNCLEAN (48) Lev 5:2,2,2; 7:19,20; 10:10; 11:8,24; 12:2; 13:3,8,11,14,20,22,25,27,30, 36,44,46; 14:40,45,46; 15:2,19,25; 17:15; 21:1; 22:3,4,5; 27:27; Nu 9:7,10; 19:7,10,11,14; Dt 14:3,8,10,19; 26:14; 1Sa 20:26; 2Ch 23:19; Hos 9:3; Hag 2:13

Lev 5:2 if they touch something that is ceremonially **u**,
5:2 dead body of an animal that is ceremonially **u**—
5:2 they will be considered ceremonially **u** and guilty,
7:19 "Meat that touches anything ceremonially **u** may
7:20 Anyone who is ceremonially **u** but eats meat from
7:21 If anyone touches anything that is **u**, whether it is human defilement or an **u** animal,
10:10 what is ceremonially **u** and what is clean.
11:8 their dead bodies. They are ceremonially **u** for you.
11:24 following creatures make you ceremonially **u**.
11:25 If you move the dead body of an **u** animal,
11:26 or that does not chew the cud is **u** for you.
11:27 on all fours, those that have paws are **u** for you.
11:29 or creep on the ground, these are **u** for you:
11:31 All these small animals are **u** for you. If you touch
11:32 that object, whatever its use, will be **u**.
11:34 If the water used to cleanse an **u** object touches
11:34 And any beverage that is in such an **u** container
11:47 so you can distinguish between what is **u** and may
12:2 to a son, she will be ceremonially **u** for seven days,
13:3 priest must pronounce the person ceremonially **u**.
13:8 he must pronounce this person ceremonially **u**,
13:11 priest must pronounce that person ceremonially **u**.
13:14 person will be pronounced ceremonially **u**.
13:20 priest must pronounce that person ceremonially **u**.
13:22 priest must pronounce the person ceremonially **u**,
13:25 then pronounce that person ceremonially **u**,
13:27 priest must pronounce that person ceremonially **u**,
13:30 pronounce the infected person ceremonially **u**.
13:36 pronounce the infected person ceremonially **u**,
13:44 is infected with a contagious skin disease and is **u**.
13:44 The priest must pronounce him ceremonially **u**
13:45 they must cover their mouth and call out, 'U! U!'
13:46 they will be ceremonially **u** and must live in
13:51 contaminated by an infectious mildew and is **u**.
13:59 whether these things are ceremonially clean or **u**."
14:36 so everything inside will not be pronounced **u**.
14:40 outside the town designated as ceremonially **u**.
14:41 and the scrapings dumped in the **u** place outside
14:45 of town to the place designated as ceremonially **u**.
14:46 will be considered ceremonially **u** until evening.
14:57 when something is ceremonially clean or **u**."
15:2 man who has a genital discharge is ceremonially **u**
15:3 or is stopped up. In either case the man is **u**.
15:7 if you touch the man who has the **u** discharge.
15:19 she will be ceremonially **u** for seven days.
15:25 the woman will be ceremonially **u** as long as the
17:15 Then you will remain ceremonially **u** until
20:25 between ceremonially clean and **u** animals, and between clean and **u** birds.
21:1 ceremonially **u** by touching a dead relative
22:3 **u** when they approach the sacred food presented by
22:4 kind of discharge that makes them ceremonially **u**,
22:4 If any of the priests become **u** by touching a
22:5 or by touching a creeping creature that is **u**, or by touching someone who is ceremonially **u** for
27:11 But if your vow involves an **u** animal—one that is
27:27 if it is the firstborn of a ceremonially **u** animal,
Nu 9:7 "We have become ceremonially **u** by touching a
9:10 or in future generations are ceremonially **u** at
18:15 and the firstborn males of ritually **u** animals.
19:7 though he will remain ceremonially **u** until
19:8 in water, and he, too, will remain **u** until evening.
19:10 and he will remain ceremonially **u** until evening.
19:11 human body will be ceremonially **u** for seven days.
19:12 they will continue to be **u** even after the seventh
19:14 will be ceremonially **u** for seven days.
19:16 or a grave, that person will be **u** for seven days.
19:19 person must sprinkle the water on those who are **u**.
Dt 12:15 All of you, whether ceremonially clean or **u**,
12:22 Anyone, whether ceremonially clean or **u**, may eat
14:3 must not eat animals that are ceremonially **u**.
14:8 All these animals are ceremonially **u** for you.
14:10 and scales. They are ceremonially **u** for you.
14:19 "All flying insects are ceremonially **u** for you
15:22 may eat it, whether ceremonially clean or **u**,
26:14 I have not touched it while I was ceremonially **u**;
1Sa 20:26 must have made David ceremonially **u**.
2Ch 23:19 those who were ceremonially **u** from entering.
Ecc 9:2 good or bad, ceremonially clean or **u**, religious
Isa 52:1 for **u** and godless people will no longer enter your
52:11 with everything it represents, for it is **u** to you.
Eze 22:26 between what is ceremonially clean and **u**.
44:23 what is common, what is ceremonially clean and **u**.
Hos 9:3 where you will live on food that is ceremonially **u**.
9:4 Such sacrifices will be **u**, just as food touched by a person in mourning is **u**.
Hag 2:13 "But if someone becomes ceremonially **u** by
Zec 13:2 false prophets and the **u** spirits that inspire them.

UNCLEARED (1)
Eze 22:24 you will become like an **u** wilderness or a desert

UNCLES (2) [UNCLE]
Jos 17:4 gave them an inheritance along with their **u**,
Jdg 9:3 So Abimelech's **u** spoke to all the people of

UNCOMELY [KJV] See TROUBLE (CONTROLLING)

UNCOMMON (1)
1Sa 3:1 LORD were very rare, and visions were quite **u**.

UNCONCERN (1) [UNCONCERNED]
Isa 32:11 Tremble, you women of ease; throw off your **u**.

UNCONCERNED (1) [UNCONCERN]
Job 39:16 if they were not her own. She is **u** though they die,

UNCONQUERED (4)
Jos 18:4 and I will send them out to survey the **u** territory.
23:4 as an inheritance all the land of the nations yet **u**,
Jdg 2:21 out the nations that Joshua left **u** when he died.
Isa 47:1 "Come, Babylon, **u** one, sit in the dust. For your

UNCONTROLLABLE (1) [UNCONTROLLABLY]
Jas 3:8 the tongue. It is an **u** evil, full of deadly poison.

UNCONTROLLABLY (2) [UNCONTROLLABLE]
Ge 27:33 Isaac began to tremble **u** and said, "Then who was
Jer 23:9 because of the false prophets, and I tremble **u**.

UNCOOKED (1)
Job 6:6 And how tasteless is the **u** white of an egg!

UNCORRUPTIBLE [KJV] See EVER-LIVING

UNCOUNTED (1)
Na 2:9 to Nineveh's many treasures—its vast, **u** wealth.

UNCOVER (3) [UNCOVERED, UNCOVERS]
Ru 3:4 then go and **u** his feet and lie down there.
Job 28:10 cut tunnels in the rocks and **u** precious stones.
Eze 24:17 Do not **u** your head or take off your sandals.

UNCOVERED (3) [UNCOVER]
Ru 3:7 Then Ruth came quietly, **u** his feet, and lay down.
Isa 20:4 and barefoot, both young and old, their buttocks **u**,
Eze 8:8 I dug into the wall and **u** a door to a hidden room.

UNCOVERS (1) [UNCOVER]
Ex 21:33 someone digs or **u** a well and fails to cover it,

UNCUT (3)
Ex 20:25 If you build altars from stone, use only **u** stones.
Jos 8:31 "Make me an altar from stones that are **u** and have
Eze 16:4 Your umbilical cord was left **u**, and you were

UNDECIDED (1)
Ps 119:113 I hate those who are **u** about you, / but my choice

UNDEFILED (2)
1Pe 1:4 pure and **u**, beyond the reach of change and decay.
Rev 14:4 For they are spiritually **u**, pure as virgins,

UNDEFILED [KJV] See also FAITHFUL, INTEGRITY, LASTING, LOVELY, PERFECT, UNSTAINED

UNDER (237)
Ge 12:20 then sent them out of the country **u** armed escort—
19:8 these men alone, for they are **u** my protection."
24:8 But **u** no circumstances are you to take my son
43:31 his face and came out, keeping himself **u** control.
Ex 1:11 hoping to wear them down **u** heavy burdens.
3:19 Egypt will not let you go except **u** heavy pressure.
6:4 **U** its terms, I swore to give them the land of
17:14 I will blot out every trace of Amalek from **u**
20:26 someone might look up **u** the skirts of your
21:29 in the past, yet the bull was not kept **u** control.
21:36 yet its owner failed to keep it **u** control, the money
24:10 **U** his feet there seemed to be a pavement of
26:19 fit into forty silver bases—two bases **u** each frame.
26:25 by sixteen silver bases—two bases **u** each frame.
Lev 6:3 lie about it, or they deny something while **u** oath,
10:7 **u** penalty of death, for the anointing oil of the
15:10 If you touch or carry anything that was **u** him,
Nu 2:17 each in position **u** the appropriate family banner.
2:34 and marched **u** their banners exactly as the LORD
5:19 The priest will put the woman **u** oath and say to
5:20 But if you have gone astray while **u** your
5:21 at this point the priest must put the woman **u** this
7:8 All their work was done **u** the leadership of
10:14 **u** the leadership of Nahshon son of Amminadab.
10:18 **u** the leadership of Elizur son of Shedeur.
10:22 **u** the leadership of Elishama son of Ammihud.
10:25 the tribes that camped with Dan set out **u** their
10:25 **u** the leadership of Ahiezer son of Ammishaddai.
18:3 But as the Levites go about their duties **u** your
22:27 the donkey saw the angel, it lay down **u** Balaam.
30:2 or makes a pledge **u** oath must never break it.
30:3 or a pledge **u** oath while she is still living at her
31:49 all the men who went out to battle **u** our command;
33:1 marched out of Egypt **u** the leadership of Moses
Dt 4:46 by the Amorites **u** King Sihon of Heshbon.
7:8 power from your slavery **u** Pharaoh in Egypt.
9:14 destroy them and erase their name from **u** heaven.
12:2 up on the hills, and **u** every green tree.
25:19 and erase their memory from **u** heaven.
28:33 You will suffer **u** constant oppression and harsh
29:20 and the LORD will erase their names from **u**
33:27 is your refuge, / and his everlasting arms are **u** you.
Jos 18:1 Now that the land was **u** Israelite control, the entire
Jdg 1:7 and big toes cut off, eating scraps from **u** my table.
3:3 the Philistines (those living **u** the five Philistine
3:16 to his right thigh, keeping it hidden **u** his clothing.
4:5 She would hold court **u** the Palm of Deborah,
6:19 them to the angel, who was **u** the oak tree.
9:6 and Beth-millo called a meeting **u** the oak beside
21:18 that anyone who does this will fall **u** God's curse."
Ru 2:12 **u** whose wings you have come to take refuge,
1Sa 22:3 and mother live here **u** royal protection until I
24:20 to be king, and Israel will flourish **u** your rule.
27:2 and went to live at Gath **u** the protection of King
2Sa 10:9 He placed them **u** his personal command and led
10:10 He left the rest of the army **u** the command of his
10:16 These troops arrived at Helam **u** the command of

17:25 replacing Joab, who had been commander **u** David.
18: 2 One-third were placed **u** Joab, one-third **u** Joab's brother Abishai son of Zeruiah, and one-third **u** Ittai the Gittite.
22:40 you have subdued my enemies **u** my feet.
22:48 those who harm me; / he subdues the nations **u** me
1Ki 7:32 **U** the panels were four wheels that were connected
7:44 the Sea and the twelve oxen **u** it,
13:14 man of God and found him sitting **u** an oak tree.
14:23 poles on every high hill and **u** every green tree.
19: 4 He sat down **u** a solitary broom tree and prayed
19: 5 Then he lay down and slept **u** the broom tree.
20:34 Ahab said, "I will let you go **u** these conditions."
2Ki 3:25 Kir-hareseth was left, but even that came **u** attack.
8:21 but he escaped at night **u** cover of darkness.
9:33 And Jehu trampled her body **u** his horses' hooves.
13: 7 had killed the others like they were dust **u** his feet.
16: 4 and on the hills and **u** every green tree.
17:10 at the top of every hill and **u** every green tree.
18:27 you do not surrender, this city will be put **u** siege.
25: 2 Jerusalem was kept **u** siege until the eleventh year
1Ch 4:31 These towns were **u** their control until the time of
6:15 and Jerusalem into captivity **u** Nebuchadnezzar.
12:27 family of Aaron, who had 3,700 **u** his command.
19:10 He placed them **u** his personal command and led
19:11 He left the rest of the army **u** the command of his
19:16 These troops arrived **u** the command of Shobach,
23:32 And so, **u** the supervision of the priests, the Levites
25: 2 They worked **u** the direction of their father, Asaph,
25: 3 They worked **u** the direction of their father,
25: 6 All these men were **u** the direction of their fathers
29: 8 of the house of the LORD **u** the care of Jehiel,
2Ch 4:15 the Sea and the twelve oxen **u** it,
11:12 only Judah and Benjamin remained **u** his control.
17:14 in units of one thousand, **u** the command of Adnah.
17:16 with 200,000 troops **u** his command.
17:17 They were **u** the command of Eliada, a veteran
21: 9 but he escaped at night **u** cover of darkness.
26:11 They were **u** the direction of Hananiah, one of the
28: 4 and on the hills and **u** every green tree.
31:13 The supervisors **u** them were Jehiel, Azaziah,
34:12 The workers served faithfully **u** the leadership of
Ezr 10:10 Now we are even more deeply **u** condemnation
Ne 3:17 Next was a group of Levites working **u** the
11:23 They were **u** royal orders, which determined their
12:42 and clearly **u** the direction of Jezrahiah the choir
Est 2:14 There she would be **u** the care of Shaashgaz,
Job 11:16 It will all be gone like water **u** the bridge.
19: 6 I cannot defend myself, for I am like a city **u** siege.
20:12 taste of his wickedness, letting it melt **u** his tongue.
28:24 throughout the whole earth, **u** all the heavens.
37:12 The clouds turn around and around **u** his direction.
40:21 It lies down **u** the lotus plants, hidden by the reeds.
41:11 and remain safe? Everything **u** heaven is mine.
Ps 18:39 you have subdued my enemies **u** my feet.
18:47 those who harm me; / he subdues the nations **u** me
31:21 He kept me safe when my city was **u** attack.
32: 9 that needs a bit and bridle to keep it **u** control."
61: 7 May he reign **u** God's protection forever.
91:13 will crush fierce lions and serpents **u** your feet!
95: 7 the people he watches over, / the sheep **u** his care.
106:42 and brought them **u** their cruel power.
110: 1 making them a footstool **u** your feet."
144: 2 take refuge in him. / He subdues the nations **u** me.
Pr 22:14 those living **u** the LORD's displeasure will fall
22:27 pay it, even your bed will be snatched from **u** you.
24:10 If you fail **u** pressure, your strength is not very
Ecc 1: 9 been done before. Nothing **u** the sun is truly new.
1:14 Everything **u** the sun is meaningless, like chasing
2:17 because everything done here **u** the sun is
3: 1 a season for every activity **u** heaven.
4:11 two **u** the same blanket can gain warmth from each
5: 8 For every official is **u** orders from higher up,
5:17 Throughout their lives, they live **u** a cloud—
5:18 enjoy their work—whatever they do **u** the sun—
SS 2: 6 His left hand is **u** my head, and his right hand
4:11 as honey. Yes, honey and cream are **u** your tongue.
8: 3 Your left hand would be **u** my head and your right
8: 5 "I aroused you **u** the apple tree, where your
Isa 1: 8 harvest is over. It is as helpless as a city **u** siege.
28:28 He threshes it **u** the wheels of a cart, but he doesn't
32: 1 is coming! And honest princes will rule **u** him.
36:12 you do not surrender, this city will be put **u** siege.
46: 1 But look! The beasts are staggering **u** the weight!
54:14 You will live **u** a government that is just and fair.
57: 5 down in the valleys, **u** overhanging rocks.
Jer 2:20 On every hill and **u** every green tree, you have
3: 6 other gods on every hill and **u** every green tree.
3:13 against him by worshiping idols **u** every green tree.
5: 2 Even when they are **u** oath, saying, 'As surely as
23:10 For the land is full of adultery, and it lies **u** a curse.
25: 9 I will gather together all the armies of the north **u**
27: 6 even the wild animals, **u** his control.
27: 8 and serve him; put your neck **u** Babylon's yoke!
28:14 forcing them into slavery **u** King Nebuchadnezzar
28:14 even the wild animals, **u** his control.' "
32: 2 Jerusalem was **u** siege from the Babylonian army,
38:12 "Put these rags **u** your armpits to protect you from
39:14 They put him **u** the care of Gedaliah son of
41:10 and the other people who had been left **u**
52: 5 Jerusalem was kept **u** siege until the eleventh year
La 4:20 We had foolishly boasted that **u** his protection we
5:13 and the children stagger **u** heavy loads of wood.
Eze 3:18 saying, 'You are **u** the penalty of death,'
4:17 and they will waste away **u** their punishment.
6:13 on every hill and mountain and **u** every green tree
7:12 for all of them will fall **u** my terrible anger.
10:21 and what looked like human hands **u** their wings.
20:28 on every high hill and **u** every green tree they saw!
46:23 with fireplaces **u** the ledge all the way around.
Da 2:38 has put even the animals and birds **u** your control.
7:25 and they will be placed **u** his control for a time,
7:27 and greatness of all the kingdoms **u** heaven will be
Hos 1:11 people of Judah and Israel will unite **u** one leader,
5: 5 against her; she will stumble **u** her load of guilt.
8:10 Then they will writhe **u** the burden of the great
Am 4:13 into darkness and treads the mountains **u** his feet.
Jnh 4: 5 and made a shelter to sit **u** as he waited to see if
Mic 7:19 You will trample our sins **u** your feet and throw
Zec 10: 5 trampling their enemies in the mud **u** their feet.
Mal 3: 9 You are **u** a curse, for your whole nation has been
4: 3 upon the wicked as if they were dust **u** your feet,"
Mt 2:16 around Bethlehem who were two years old and **u**,
5:15 Don't hide your light **u** a basket! Instead, put it on
8: 9 because I am **u** the authority of my superior
22:43 speaking **u** the inspiration of the Holy Spirit,
Mk 4:21 anyone light a lamp and then put it **u** a basket or **u** a bed to shut out the light?
6:20 and holy man, so he kept him **u** his protection.
7:28 but even the dogs **u** the table are given some
12:36 speaking **u** the inspiration of the Holy Spirit,
14:44 Then you can take him away **u** guard."
Lk 7: 8 because I am **u** the authority of my superior
8:16 light a lamp and then cover it up or put it **u** a bed.
8:29 the wilderness, completely **u** the demon's power.
11:33 lights a lamp and then hides it or puts it **u** a basket.
12:50 and I am **u** a heavy burden until it is accomplished.
20:43 making them a footstool **u** your feet.'
23: 7 because Galilee was **u** Herod's jurisdiction,
Jn 1:48 "I could see you **u** the fig tree before Philip found
1:50 because I told you I had seen you **u** the fig tree?
Ac 2:35 making them a footstool **u** your feet.'
8:27 a eunuch of great authority **u** the queen of
12: 4 placing him **u** the guard of four squads of four
22: 3 and educated here in Jerusalem **u** Gamaliel.
23:14 "We have bound ourselves **u** oath to neither eat
Ro 3: 9 whether Jews or Gentiles, are **u** the power of sin.
8: 8 That's why those who are still **u** the control of
16:20 The God of peace will soon crush Satan **u** your
1Co 15:17 and you are still **u** condemnation for your sins.
2Co 4:11 we live **u** constant danger of death because we
9: 5 it to be a willing gift, not one given **u** pressure.
11:12 **u** the feet of those who boast that their work is just
11:32 the governor **u** King Aretas kept guards at the city
Gal 3:10 law to make them right with God are **u** his curse,
4:21 Listen to me, you who want to live **u** the law.
Eph 1:10 everything together **u** the authority of Christ—
1:22 And God has put all things **u** the authority of
2: 3 and we were **u** God's anger just like everyone else.
4:16 **U** his direction, the whole body is fitted together
Php 2:10 will bow, in heaven and on earth and **u** the earth,
Heb 1:13 making them a footstool **u** your feet."
7:23 is that there were many priests **u** the old system.
7:28 Those who were high priests **u** the law of Moses
8: 6 to the ministry of those who serve **u** the old laws,
9:13 **U** the old system, the blood of goats and bulls
9:15 the sins they had committed **u** that first covenant.
9:18 That is why blood was required **u** the first
10: 1 The sacrifices **u** the old system were repeated
10:11 **U** the old covenant, the priest stands before the
10:13 his enemies are humbled as a footstool **u** his feet.
12:20 They staggered back **u** God's command: "If even
13:11 **U** the system of Jewish laws, the high priest
Jas 5:11 We give great honor to those who endure **u**
1Pe 5: 6 So humble yourselves **u** the mighty power of God,
1Jn 5:19 and that the world around us is **u** the power
Rev 5: 3 on earth or **u** the earth was able to open the scroll
5:13 and on earth and **u** the earth and in the sea.
6: 9 I saw **u** the altar the souls of all who had been
12: 7 and the angels **u** his command fought the dragon

UNDERCLOTHES (2) [CLOTHE]

Ex 28:42 Also make linen **u** for them, to be worn next to
39:28 and the **u** were all made of this fine linen.

UNDERFOOT (5) [FOOT]

Isa 14:19 Like a corpse trampled **u**, you will be dumped into
26: 6 The poor and oppressed trample it **u**.
41: 2 and permits him to trample their kings **u**.
La 3:34 But the leaders of his people trampled prisoners **u**.
Mt 5:13 It will be thrown out and trampled **u** as worthless.

UNDERGARMENTS (3) [GARMENT]

Lev 6:10 after dressing in his special linen clothing and **u**,
16: 4 on his linen tunic and the **u** worn next to his body.
Eze 44:18 They must wear linen turbans and linen **u**.

UNDERGIRDING [KJV] See BANDED (THE SHIP)

UNDERGO (1)

Lev 15: 8 if he spits on you, you must **u** the same procedure.

UNDERGROUND (2)

Ge 7:11 the **u** waters burst forth on the earth,
8: 2 The **u** water sources ceased their gushing,

UNDERHANDED (1)

2Co 4: 2 We reject all shameful and **u** methods. We do not

UNDERLYING (4)

Mt 13: 5 Other seeds fell on shallow soil with **u** rock.
Mk 4: 5 Other seed fell on shallow soil with **u** rock.
Lk 6:48 house on a strong foundation laid upon the **u** rock.
8: 6 Other seed fell on shallow soil with **u** rock.

UNDERMINE (2) [UNDERMINED]

Jer 38: 4 That kind of talk will **u** the morale of the few
Eze 13:11 A heavy rainstorm will **u** it; great hailstones

UNDERMINED (1) [UNDERMINE]

2Ti 2:18 and they have **u** the faith of some.

UNDERNEATH (2) [BENEATH]

2Ki 6:30 that he was wearing sackcloth **u** next to his skin.
Ps 55:21 are as soothing as lotion, / but **u** are daggers!

UNDERSETTERS [KJV] See SUPPORTS

UNDERSTAND (192) [UNDERSTANDABLE, UNDERSTANDING, UNDERSTANDS, UNDERSTOOD]

Ge 11: 7 Then they won't be able to **u** each other."
Ex 33:13 show me your intentions so I will **u** you more fully
Dt 7: 9 **U**, therefore, that the LORD your God is indeed
28:49 It is a nation whose language you do not **u**,
29: 4 day the LORD has not given you minds that **u**,
30:11 giving you today is not too difficult for you to **u**
32:29 Oh, that they were wise and could **u** this! / Oh,
Jdg 13:18 LORD replied. "You wouldn't **u** if I told you."
1Sa 20:39 He, of course, didn't **u** what Jonathan meant;
2Sa 12:21 were amazed. "We don't **u** you," they told him.
14:20 and you **u** everything that happens among us!"
2Ki 18:26 "Please speak to us in Aramaic, for we **u** it well.
Ne 8: 2 and women and all the children old enough to **u**.
8: 3 and read aloud to everyone who could **u**.
8: 8 was being read, helping the people **u** each passage.
10:28 to serve God, and who were old enough to **u**—
Job 5: 9 For he does great works too marvelous to **u**.
9:10 His great works are too marvelous to **u**.
13: 1 such as you describe. I **u** what you are saying.
15: 9 know that we don't? What do you **u** that we don't?
23: 5 would listen to his reply and **u** what he says to me.
26:14 his power. Who can **u** the thunder of his power?"
32: 9 are not wise. Sometimes the aged do not **u** justice.
34:16 "Listen now and try to **u**.
36:26 "Look, God is exalted beyond what we can **u**.
36:29 Can anyone really **u** the spreading of the clouds
37:16 Do you **u** how he balances the clouds with
42: 3 And I was talking about things I did not **u**,
Ps 40: 6 Now that you have made me listen, I finally **u**—
49:20 People who boast of their wealth don't **u** / that they
73:16 So I tried to **u** why the wicked prosper. / But what
92: 6 would not know this! / Only a fool would not **u** it.
119:27 Help me **u** the meaning of your commandments,
119:125 to me, your servant; / then I will **u** your decrees.
119:130 they give light; / even the simple can **u** them.
119:144 always fair; / help me to **u** them, that I may live.
Pr 1: 2 and discipline, and to help them **u** wise sayings.
1: 5 even wiser. And let those who **u** receive guidance
2: 5 Then you will **u** what it means to fear the LORD,
2: 9 Then you will **u** what is right, just, and fair,
20:24 How can we **u** the road we travel? It is the LORD
28: 5 Evil people don't **u** justice, but those who follow the LORD **u** completely.
30:18 things that amaze me—no, four things I do not **u**:
Ecc 7:25 to find wisdom and to **u** the reason for things.
Isa 1: 3 No matter what I do for them, they still do not **u**."
6: 9 'You will hear my words, but you will not **u**.
6:10 hear with their ears, **u** with their hearts, and turn to
36:11 "Please speak to us in Aramaic, for we **u** it well.
41:20 will see this miracle and **u** that it is the LORD,
42:20 You see and **u** what is right but refuse to act on it.
42:25 set on fire and burned, but they still refused to **u**.
43:10 believe in me, and **u** that I alone am God.
45:19 in some dark corner so no one can **u** what I mean.
52:15 they will **u** what they had not heard about.
57: 1 No one seems to **u** that God is protecting them
Jer 5: 4 They don't **u** what God expects of them.
5:15 you do not know, whose speech you cannot **u**.
9:12 Who is wise enough to **u** all this? Who has been
9:24 and **u** that I am the LORD who is just
18:13 virgin Israel has done something too terrible to **u**!
23:20 the days to come, you will **u** all this very clearly.
30:24 his plans. In the days to come, you will **u** all this.
Eze 3: 5 some foreign people whose language you cannot **u**.
17:12 Don't you **u** the meaning of this riddle of the
Da 2:30 because God wanted you to **u** what you were
4:17 **u** that the Most High rules over the kingdoms of
8:15 Daniel, was trying to **u** the meaning of this vision,
8:17 "you must **u** that the events you have seen in your
8:27 greatly troubled by the vision and could not **u** it.
9:23 so you can **u** the meaning of your vision.
9:25 Now listen and **u**! Seven sets of seven plus
12: 8 heard what he said, but I did not **u** what he meant.
12:10 in their wickedness, and none of them will **u**.
Hos 4:14 You will be destroyed, for you refuse to **u**.
14: 9 Let those who are wise **u** these things. Let those
Mic 4:12 do not know the LORD's thoughts or **u** his plan.
Mt 11:15 Anyone who is willing to hear should listen and **u**!
13: 9 who is willing to hear should listen and **u**!"
13:11 "You have been permitted to **u** the secrets of the
13:13 I say, but they don't really hear, and they don't **u**.

13:14 'You will hear my words, / but you will not **u**;
13:15 their ears cannot hear, / and their hearts cannot **u**,
13:19 the Good News about the Kingdom and don't **u** it.
13:43 Anyone who is willing to hear should listen and **u**!
13:51 Do you **u**?" "Yes," they said, "we do."
15:10 and said, "Listen to what I say and try to **u**.
15:16 "Don't you **u**?" Jesus asked him.
16: 9 Won't you ever **u**? Don't you remember the five
Mk 4: 9 who is willing to hear should listen and **u**!"
4:11 "You are permitted to **u** the secret about the
4:12 They hear my words, / but they don't **u**.
4:13 "But if you can't **u** this story, how will you **u** all the others I am going to tell?
4:23 Anyone who is willing to hear should listen and **u**!
4:24 The more you do this, the more you will **u**—
4:33 to teach the people as much as they were able to **u**.
6:52 They still didn't **u** the significance of the miracle
7:14 "All of you listen," he said, "and try to **u**.
7:18 "Don't you **u** either?" he asked. "Can't you see
8:17 about having no food? Won't you ever learn or **u**?
8:21 "Don't you **u** even yet?" he asked them.
9:32 But they didn't **u** what he was saying, and they
Lk 2:50 But they didn't **u** what he meant.
8: 8 who is willing to hear should listen and **u**!"
8:10 "You have been permitted to **u** the secrets of the
8:10 they hear what I say, / but they don't **u**.'
9:45 was hidden from them, so they could not **u** it,
14:35 who is willing to hear should listen and **u**!"
18:34 But they didn't **u** a thing he said. Its significance
24:45 Then he opened their minds to **u** these many
Jn 3:10 Jewish teacher, and yet you don't **u** these things?
6:60 Even his disciples said, "This is very hard to **u**.
8:27 But they still didn't **u** that he was talking to them
8:43 Why can't you **u** what I am saying? It is
10: 6 Those who heard Jesus use this illustration didn't **u**
12:40 their eyes cannot see, / and their hearts cannot **u**,
13: 7 "You don't **u** now why I am doing it;
13:12 sat down and asked, "Do you **u** what I was doing?
16:18 does he mean by 'a little while'? We don't **u**."
16:30 Now we **u** that you know everything and don't
17:23 and will **u** that you love them as much as you love
19: 4 you now, but I **u** clearly that I find him not guilty."
Ac 8:30 so he asked, "Do you **u** what you are reading?"
9:21 "And we **u** that he came here to arrest them
15:24 "We **u** that some men from here have troubled you
28:26 You will hear my words, / but you will not **u**;
28:27 their ears cannot hear, / and their hearts cannot **u**,
Ro 1:31 They refuse to **u**, break their promises, and are
6:19 of slaves and masters, because it is easy to **u**.
7: 9 I felt fine when I did not **u** what the law demanded.
7:15 I don't **u** myself at all, for I really want to do what
10: 3 For they don't **u** God's way of making people right
10:19 But did the people of Israel really **u**? Yes, they did,
11:25 I want you to **u** this mystery, dear friends, so that
11:33 How impossible it is for us to **u** his decisions
15:21 and those who have never heard of him will **u**."
1Co 2:14 But people who aren't Christians can't **u** these
2:14 because only those who have the Spirit can **u** what
2:15 We who have the Spirit **u** these things, but others can't **u** us at all.
2:16 But we can **u** these things, for we have the mind of
14: 2 not to people, since they won't be able to **u** you.
14: 9 If you talk to people in a language they don't **u**,
14:10 and all are excellent for those who **u** them,
14:11 I will not **u** people who speak those languages, and they will not **u** me.
14:14 spirit is praying, but I don't **u** what I am saying.
14:15 will pray in the spirit, and I will pray in words I **u**.
14:15 I will sing in the spirit, and I will sing in words I **u**.
14:16 how can those who don't **u** you praise God along
14:16 thanks when they don't **u** what you are saying?
14:23 or people who don't **u** these things come into your
14:24 or people who don't **u** these things come into your
2Co 1:13 written between the lines and nothing you can't **u**.
1:13 I hope someday you will fully **u** us,
1:14 even if you don't fully **u** us now. Then on the day
3:14 a veil covers their minds so they cannot **u** the truth.
3:15 hearts are covered with that veil, and they do not **u**.
4: 4 They don't **u** the message we preach about the
4: 6 has made us **u** that this light is the brightness of the
Gal 2: 2 I wanted them to **u** what I had been preaching to
Eph 1:18 so that you can **u** the wonderful future he has
1:19 I pray that you will begin to **u** the incredible
3: 4 you will **u** what I know about this plan regarding
3:18 And may you have the power to **u**, as all God's
3:19 though it is so great you will never fully **u** it.
5:17 but try to **u** what the Lord wants you to do.
Php 1:10 For I want you to **u** what really matters, so that you
4: 7 is far more wonderful than the human mind can **u**.
1Ti 2: 4 he wants everyone to be saved and to **u** the truth.
2Ti 3: 7 new teachings, but they never **u** the truth.
Heb 5:11 don't seem to listen, so it's hard to make you **u**.
8:10 put my laws in their minds / so they will **u** them,
10:16 put my laws in their hearts / so they will **u** them,
11: 3 By faith we **u** that the entire universe was formed
Jas 3:13 If you are wise and **u** God's ways, live a life of
2Pe 1:20 you must **u** that no prophecy in Scripture ever
3: 2 and **u** what the holy prophets said long ago
3:16 Some of his comments are hard to **u**, and those
1Jn 3: 1 know God, so they don't **u** that we are his children.
Jude 1:10 people mock and curse the things they do not **u**.
Rev 2: 7 and **u** what the Spirit is saying to the churches.
2:11 and **u** what the Spirit is saying to the churches.
2:17 and **u** what the Spirit is saying to the churches.
2:29 and **u** what the Spirit is saying to the churches.
3: 6 and **u** what the Spirit is saying to the churches.
3:13 and **u** what the Spirit is saying to the churches.
3:22 and **u** what the Spirit is saying to the churches."
13: 9 Anyone who is willing to hear should listen and **u**.
13:18 Wisdom is needed to **u** this. Let the one who has
17: 9 "And now **u** this: The seven heads of the beast

UNDERSTANDABLE (1) [UNDERSTAND]

1Co 14:19 **u** words that will help others than ten thousand

UNDERSTANDING (93) [UNDERSTAND]

Dt 1:13 **u**, and a good reputation, and I will appoint them
32:28 that lacks sense; / the people are foolish, without **u**.
Jdg 21:22 to us in protest, we will tell them, 'Please be **u**.
1Ki 3: 9 Give me an **u** mind so that I can govern your
3:12 and **u** mind such as no one else has ever had
4:29 God gave Solomon great wisdom and **u**,
1Ch 22:12 And may the LORD give you wisdom and **u**,
2Ch 2:12 has given David a wise son, gifted with skill and **u**,
Job 12:12 and **u** to those who have lived many years.
12:13 and power are with God; counsel and **u** are his.
12:24 He takes away the **u** of kings, and he leaves them
17: 4 You have closed their minds to **u**, but do not let
28:12 where to find wisdom? Where can they find **u**?
28:20 where to find wisdom? Where can they find **u**?
28:28 Lord is true wisdom; to forsake evil is real **u**.' "
34:10 "Listen to me, you who have **u**. Everyone knows
36: 5 despise anyone! He is mighty in both power and **u**.
36:12 they will perish in battle and die from lack of **u**.
39:17 deprived her of wisdom. He has given her no **u**.
Ps 14: 2 he looks to see if there is even one with real **u**,
53: 2 he looks to see if there is even one with real **u**,
119:34 Give me **u** and I will obey your law; / I will put it
119:104 Your commandments give me **u**; / no wonder I
147: 5 is absolute! / His **u** is beyond comprehension!
Pr 2: 2 Tune your ears to wisdom, and concentrate on **u**.
2: 3 Cry out for insight and **u**.
2: 6 From his mouth come knowledge and **u**.
2:11 will watch over you. **U** will keep you safe.
3: 5 with all your heart; do not depend on your own **u**.
3:13 is the person who finds wisdom and gains **u**.
3:19 founded the earth; by **u** he established the heavens.
8: 1 as wisdom calls out! Hear as **u** raises her voice!
8: 5 common sense. O foolish ones, let me give you **u**.
8: 9 My words are plain to anyone with **u**, clear to
9:10 Knowledge of the Holy One results in **u**.
10:13 Wise words come from the lips of people with **u**,
14: 6 but knowledge comes easily to those with **u**.
14:29 Those who control their anger have great **u**;
14:33 Wisdom is enshrined in an **u** heart; wisdom is not
15:32 but if you listen to correction, you grow in **u**.
16:16 better to get wisdom than gold, and **u** than silver!
16:21 The wise are known for their **u**, and instruction is
17:10 A single rebuke does more for a person of **u** than a
17:27 uses few words; a person with **u** is even-tempered.
18: 2 Fools have no interest in **u**; they only want to air
19: 8 to love oneself; people who cherish **u** will prosper.
19:14 but only the LORD can give an **u** wife.
Ecc 1:13 I devoted myself to search for **u** and to explore by
Isa 11: 2 the Spirit of wisdom and **u**, the Spirit of counsel
28:26 knows just what to do, for God has given him **u**.
29:14 and even the most brilliant people lack **u**."
32: 4 hotheads among them will be full of sense and **u**.
40:28 or weary. No one can measure the depths of his **u**.
48:16 would happen so you would have no trouble **u**."
50: 4 morning he wakens me and opens my **u** to his will.
Jer 3:15 who will guide you with knowledge and **u**.
4:22 "They are senseless children who have no **u**.
10:12 He has stretched out the heavens / by his **u**.
51:15 He has stretched out the heavens / by his **u**.
Eze 28: 4 and **u** you have amassed great wealth—
Da 1:17 And God gave Daniel special ability in **u** the
5:11 this man was found to have insight, **u**,
5:12 and is filled with divine knowledge and **u**.
5:14 and that you are filled with insight, **u**, and wisdom.
9:22 I have come here to give you insight and **u**.
10:12 Since the first day you began to pray for **u** and to
Ob 1: 8 I will destroy everyone who has wisdom and **u**.
Mt 13:12 are open to my teaching, more **u** will be given,
Mk 4:25 are open to my teaching, more **u** will be given.
12:33 with all my heart and all my **u** and all my strength,
12:34 Realizing this man's **u**, Jesus said to him,
Lk 2:47 And all who heard him were amazed at his **u**
8:18 are open to my teaching, more **u** will be given.
Jn 3:31 the earth, and my **u** is limited to the things of earth,
Ac 13: 7 a man of considerable insight and **u**.
Ro 3:11 No one has real **u**; / no one is seeking God.
1Co 14:20 don't be childish in your **u** of these things.
14:20 but be mature and wise in **u** matters of this kind.
2Co 1:15 Since I was so sure of your **u** and trust, I wanted to
6: 6 our **u**, our patience, our kindness, our sincere love,
Eph 1: 8 his kindness on us, along with all wisdom and **u**.
1:17 Jesus Christ, to give you spiritual wisdom and **u**,
Php 1: 9 will keep on growing in your knowledge and **u**.
Col 1: 9 We ask God to give you a complete **u** of what he
2: 2 because they have complete **u** of God's secret plan,
2Th 3: 5 May the Lord bring you into an ever deeper **u** of
2Ti 2: 7 The Lord will give you **u** in all these things.
Phm 1: 6 so doing you will come to an **u** of all the good
Heb 6: 1 Let us go on instead and become mature in our **u**.
6: 3 God willing, we will move forward to further **u**.
1Pe 3: 7 Treat her with **u** as you live together. She may be
1Jn 5:20 and he has given us **u** so that we can know the true
Rev 13:18 Let the one who has **u** solve the number of the

UNDERSTANDS (4) [UNDERSTAND]

1Ch 28: 9 and **u** and knows every plan and thought.
Ps 33:15 He made their hearts, / so he **u** everything they do.
103:14 For he **u** how weak we are; / he knows we are only
Heb 4:15 This High Priest of ours **u** our weaknesses, for he

UNDERSTOOD (13) [UNDERSTAND]

Ge 27:34 When Esau **u**, he let out a loud and bitter cry.
42:23 they didn't know that Joseph **u** them as he was
1Ch 12:32 All these men **u** the temper of the times and knew
Ne 8:12 because they had heard God's words and **u** them.
Pr 29:19 For the words may be **u**, but they are not heeded.
Isa 40:21 Have you never heard or **u**? Are you deaf to the
40:28 Have you never heard or **u**? Don't you know that
Da 10: 1 and Daniel **u** what the vision meant.
Mt 16:12 Then at last they **u** that he wasn't speaking about
Jn 12:34 "We **u** from Scripture that the Messiah would live
1Co 2: 8 But the rulers of this world have not **u** it; if they
Col 1: 6 and **u** the truth about God's great kindness to
1Jn 3: 6 on sinning have never known him or **u** who he is.

UNDERTAKE (1)

2Ki 12: 8 and they also agreed not to **u** the repairs of the

UNDERWORLD (2) [WORLD]

Job 11: 8 It is deeper than the **u**—what can you know in
26: 6 The **u** is naked in God's presence. There is no

UNDESERVED (3) [UNDESERVING]

Ro 11: 6 would not be what it really is—free and **u**.
Gal 1:15 call me, even before I was born! What **u** mercy!
2Th 1:12 because of the **u** favor of our God and Lord,

UNDESERVING (1) [UNDESERVED]

Ro 4: 6 describing the happiness of an **u** sinner who is

UNDILUTED (1)

Rev 14:10 It is poured out **u** into God's cup of wrath.

UNDISCIPLINED (1)

Pr 29:15 but a mother is disgraced by an **u** child.

UNDISTURBED (1)

Mic 5: 4 Then his people will live there **u**, for he will be

UNDIVIDED (1)

2Ch 19: 9 of the LORD, with integrity and with **u** hearts.

UNDOING (1) [UNDONE]

Lk 2:34 be rejected by many in Israel, and it will be their **u**.

UNDONE (2) [UNDOING]

Mt 23:23 but you should not leave **u** the more important
Lk 11:42 but you should not leave **u** the more important

UNDRESSED [KJV] See UNPRUNED

UNDYING (1)

Eph 6:24 all who love our Lord Jesus Christ with an **u** love.

UNEASY (1)

2Ki 8:11 at Hazael with a fixed gaze until Hazael became **u**.

UNEDUCATED (1)

Ro 1:14 in other cultures, to the educated and **u** alike.

UNEMPLOYED (1)

Isa 19: 8 with hooks and those who use nets will all be **u**.

UNENDING (3)

Pr 8:18 **U** riches, honor, wealth, and justice are mine to
La 2: 5 He has brought **u** sorrow and tears to Jerusalem.
Ro 9: 2 My heart is filled with bitter sorrow and **u** grief

UNEQUALED (1)

Ps 150: 2 him for his mighty works; / praise his **u** greatness!

UNEXPECTED (3) [UNEXPECTEDLY]

Mt 24:50 well, the master will return unannounced and **u**.
Lk 12:46 well, the master will return unannounced and **u**.
Rev 3: 3 I will come upon you suddenly, as **u** as a thief.

UNEXPECTEDLY (4) [UNEXPECTED]

2Sa 18: 9 Absalom came **u** upon some of David's men.
1Th 5: 2 quite well that the day of the Lord will come **u**,
2Pe 3:10 But the day of the Lord will come as **u** as a thief.
Rev 16:15 "Take note: I will come as **u** as a thief!

UNFADING (1)

1Pe 3: 4 the **u** beauty of a gentle and quiet spirit, which is

UNFAILING (113)

Ge 32:10 the faithfulness and **u** love you have shown to me,
Ex 15:13 "With **u** love you will lead / this people whom you
34: 6 slow to anger and rich in **u** love and faithfulness.
34: 7 I show this **u** love to many thousands by forgiving
Nu 14:18 'The LORD is slow to anger and rich in **u** love,
14:19 of this people because of your magnificent, **u** love,
Dt 7:12 the LORD your God will keep his covenant of **u**

2Sa 2: 6 to you in return and reward you with his **u** love!
7:15 But my **u** love will not be taken from him as I took
15:20 and may the LORD show you his **u** love
22:51 to your king; / you show **u** love to your anointed,
1Ki 8:23 and show **u** love to all who obey you
1Ch 17:13 I will not take my **u** love from him as I took it from
2Ch 6:14 and show **u** love to all who obey you
6:42 Remember your **u** love for your servant David."
Ezr 7:28 And praise him for demonstrating such **u** love to
9: 9 but in his **u** love our God did not abandon us in our
Ne 1: 5 and awesome God who keeps his covenant of **u**
9:17 to become angry, and full of **u** love and mercy.
9:32 awesome God, who keeps his covenant of **u** love,
13:22 on me according to your great and **u** love.
Job 10:12 You gave me life and showed me your **u** love.
37:13 either as a punishment or as a sign of his **u** love.
Ps 5: 7 Because of your **u** love, I can enter your house;
6: 4 and rescue me. / Save me because of your **u** love.
13: 5 But I trust in your **u** love. / I will rejoice
17: 7 Show me your **u** love in wonderful ways.
18:50 to your king; / you show **u** love to your anointed,
21: 7 The **u** love of the Most High will keep him from
23: 6 Surely your goodness and **u** love will pursue me
25: 6 O LORD, your **u** love and compassion,
25: 7 look instead through the eyes of your **u** love,
25:10 The LORD leads with **u** love and faithfulness
26: 3 For I am constantly aware of your **u** love, / and I
31: 7 I am overcome with joy because of your **u** love,
31:16 shine on your servant. / In your **u** love, save me.
31:21 the LORD, / for he has shown me his **u** love.
32:10 but **u** love surrounds those who trust the LORD.
33: 5 is just and good, / and his **u** love fills the earth.
33:18 those who fear him, / those who rely on his **u** love.
33:22 Let your **u** love surround us, LORD, / for our
36: 5 Your **u** love, O LORD, is as vast as the heavens;
36: 7 How precious is your **u** love, O God!
36:10 Pour out your **u** love on those who love you;
40:10 great assembly / of your **u** love and faithfulness.
40:11 My only hope is in your **u** love and faithfulness.
42: 8 Through each day the LORD pours his **u** love
44:26 and help us! / Save us because of your **u** love.
48: 9 O God, we meditate on your **u** love / as we
51: 1 mercy on me, O God, / because of your **u** love.
52: 8 of God. / I trust in God's **u** love / forever and ever.
57: 3 My God will send forth his **u** love and faithfulness.
57:10 For your **u** love is as high as the heavens.
59:10 In his **u** love, my God will come and help me.
59:16 with joy each morning because of your **u** love.
59:17 are my refuge, / the God who shows me **u** love.
61: 7 Appoint your **u** love and faithfulness to watch over
62:12 **u** love, O Lord, is yours. / Surely you judge all
63: 3 Your **u** love is better to me than life itself; / how I
66:20 and did not withdraw his **u** love from me.
69:13 In your **u** love, O God, / answer my prayer with
69:16 O LORD, / for your **u** love is wonderful.
77: 8 Is his **u** love gone forever? / Have his promises
85: 7 Show us your **u** love, O LORD, / and grant us
85:10 **U** love and truth have met together.
86: 5 so full of **u** love for all who ask your aid.
86:15 slow to get angry, / full of **u** love and truth.
88:11 Can those in the grave declare your **u** love?
89: 2 Your **u** love will last forever. / Your faithfulness is
89:14 **U** love and truth walk before you as attendants.
89:24 My faithfulness and **u** love will be with him,
89:49 Lord, where is your **u** love? / You promised it to
90:14 Satisfy us in the morning with your **u** love,
92: 2 It is good to proclaim your **u** love in the morning,
94:18 and your **u** love, O LORD, supported me.
100: 5 the LORD is good. / His **u** love continues forever,
103: 8 he is slow to get angry and full of **u** love.
103:11 For his **u** love toward those who fear him / is as
106:45 with them / and relented because of his **u** love.
108: 4 For your **u** love is higher than the heavens.
109:26 my God! / Save me because of your **u** love.
115: 1 goes all the glory / for your **u** love and faithfulness.
117: 2 For he loves us with **u** love; / the faithfulness of
119:41 LORD, give to me your **u** love, / the salvation
119:64 O LORD, the earth is full of your **u** love;
119:76 Now let your **u** love comfort me, / just as you
119:88 In your **u** love, spare my life; / then I can continue
119:124 I am your servant; / deal with me in **u** love,
119:159 Give back my life because of your **u** love.
130: 7 the LORD; / for with the LORD there is **u** love
138: 2 to your name / for your **u** love and faithfulness,
143: 8 Let me hear of your **u** love to me in the morning,
143:12 In your **u** love, cut off all my enemies / and destroy
145: 8 and merciful, / slow to get angry, full of **u** love.
147:11 honor him, / those who put their hope in his **u** love.
Pr 14:22 you will be granted **u** love and faithfulness.
16: 6 **U** love and faithfulness cover sin; evil is avoided
20:28 **U** love and faithfulness protect the king; his throne
21:21 pursues godliness and **u** love will find life,
Isa 55: 3 all the mercies and **u** love that I promised to David.
63: 7 I will tell of the LORD's **u** love. I will praise the
Jer 9:24 LORD who is just and righteous, whose love is **u**,
16: 5 I have taken away my **u** love and my mercy.
31: 3 With **u** love I have drawn you to myself.
La 3:22 The **u** love of the LORD never ends! By his
3:32 according to the greatness of his **u** love.
Da 9: 4 You always fulfill your promises of **u** love to those
Hos 2:19 and justice, **u** love and compassion.
Jnh 4: 2 slow to get angry and filled with **u** love.
Mic 7:20 and **u** love as you promised with an oath to our
Mk 16: S and **u** message of salvation that gives eternal life.
Jn 1:14 He was full of **u** love and faithfulness. And we
1:17 God's **u** love and faithfulness came through Jesus Christ.

UNFAIR (13) [UNFAIRLY]
Job 9:24 blinds the eyes of the judges and lets them be **u**.
31:13 "If I have been **u** to my male or female servants,
Pr 26: 2 an **u** curse will not land on its intended victim.
Ecc 2:21 to earn it. This is not only foolish but highly **u**.
Isa 10: 1 for the unjust judges, for those who issue **u** laws.
59:13 We know how **u** and oppressive we have been,
Am 5:11 steal what little they have through taxes and **u** rent.
Mt 20:13 answered one of them, 'Friend, I haven't been **u**!
Lk 10:40 doesn't it seem **u** to you that my sister just sits here
Ro 3: 5 Isn't it **u**, then, for God to punish us?" (That is
9:14 can we say? Was God being **u**? Of course not!
Heb 6:10 For God is not **u**. He will not forget how hard you
1Pe 2:19 your conscience, you patiently endure **u** treatment.

UNFAIRLY (2) [UNFAIR]
Ps 103: 6 and justice to all who are treated **u**.
Pr 16:10 speaks with divine wisdom; he must never judge **u**.

UNFAITHFUL (33) [UNFAITHFULLY, UNFAITHFULNESS]
Lev 17: 7 The people must no longer be **u** to the LORD by
20: 6 "If any among the people are **u** by consulting
Nu 5:12 a man's wife goes astray and is **u** to her husband.
5:19 and you have not defiled yourself by being **u**,
5:27 If she has defiled herself by being **u** to her
5:29 If a woman defiles herself by being **u** to her
5:30 and suspicion that his wife has been **u**,
Jos 7: 1 But Israel was **u** concerning the things set apart for
Jdg 19: 2 But she was **u** to him and returned to her father's
1Ch 5:25 But they were **u** and violated their covenant with
9: 1 to Babylon because they were **u** to the LORD.
10:13 So Saul died because he was **u** to the LORD.
2Ch 12: 2 Because they were **u** to the LORD, King Shishak
28:19 people to sin and had been utterly **u** to the LORD.
28:22 King Ahaz, he became even more **u** to the LORD.
29: 6 Our ancestors were **u** and did what was evil in the
29:19 all the utensils taken by King Ahaz when he was **u**
36:14 and the people became more and more **u**.
Ezr 10: 2 "We confess that we have been **u** to our God,
Ps 78: 8 like their ancestors— / stubborn, rebellious, and **u**,
Pr 23:28 looking for another victim who will be **u** to his
Isa 57: 7 idols there, and so you have been **u** to me.
Jer 16:11 It is because your ancestors were **u** to me.
Eze 6: 9 They will recognize how grieved I am by their **u**
15: 8 because my people have been **u** to me,
Hos 9: 1 For you have been **u** to your God,
Mt 5:32 unless she has been **u**, causes her to commit
19: 9 commits adultery—unless his wife has been **u**."
25:29 But from those who are **u**, even what little they
Lk 12:46 tear the servant apart and banish him with the **u**.
19:26 But from those who are **u**, even what little they
Ro 3: 3 True, some of them were **u**; but just because they
2Ti 2:13 If we are **u**, / he remains faithful, / for he cannot

UNFAITHFULLY (1) [UNFAITHFUL]
Ne 13:27 and acting **u** toward God by marrying foreign

UNFAITHFULNESS (4) [UNFAITHFUL]
2Ch 33:19 and **u** are recorded in *The Record of the Seers*. It
Ezr 9: 4 and sat with me because of this **u** of his people.
10: 6 because of the **u** of the returned exiles.
Eze 44:10 idols must bear the consequences of their **u**.

UNFAMILIAR (2)
Isa 41: 3 on safely, though he is walking over **u** ground.
42:16 down a new path, / guiding them along an **u** way.

UNFEIGNED [KJV] See SINCERE(LY)

UNFIT (1)
Ex 20:25 a tool, for that would make them **u** for holy use.

UNFORGETTABLE (1)
Ps 9:11 in Jerusalem. / Tell the world about his **u** deeds.

UNFORGIVEN (1) [UNFORGIVING]
Jn 20:23 If you refuse to forgive them, they are **u**."

UNFORGIVING (2) [UNFORGIVEN]
Ro 1:31 break their promises, and are heartless and **u**.
2Ti 3: 3 They will be unloving and **u**; they will slander

UNFRIENDLY (1)
Ge 26:27 since you sent me from your land in a most **u**

UNGIRDED [KJV] See UNLOADED

UNGODLINESS (2) [UNGODLY]
Ro 11:26 from Jerusalem, / and he will turn Israel from all **u**.
2Ti 2:16 foolish discussions that lead to more and more **u**.

UNGODLY (16) [UNGODLINESS]
Job 17: 8 see me. The innocent are aroused against the **u**.
Ps 7: 9 End the wickedness of the **u**, / but help all those
39: 1 will curb my tongue / when the **u** are around me."
43: 1 up my cause! / Defend me against these **u** people.
129: 4 he has cut the cords used by the **u** to bind me.
Isa 32: 5 In that day **u** fools will not be heroes.
32: 6 Everyone will recognize **u** fools for what they are.
Jer 23:11 priests are like the prophets, all **u**, wicked men.
Ac 24:15 that he will raise both the righteous and the **u**.
Eph 4:17 Live no longer as the **u** do, for they are hopelessly
5:12 It is shameful even to talk about the things that **u**
1Ti 1: 9 and rebellious, who are **u** and sinful,
2Pe 2: 5 Then God destroyed the whole world of **u** people
2: 6 them an example of what will happen to **u** people.
3: 7 on the day of judgment, when **u** people will perish.
Jude 1:15 He will convict the **u** of all the evil things

UNGRATEFUL (1)
2Ti 3: 2 scoffing at God, disobedient to their parents, and **u**.

UNHAPPY (2)
Ecc 6: 5 peace than he has in growing up to be an **u** man.
2Co 2: 1 I won't make them **u** with another painful visit."

UNHARMED (5)
Nu 5:28 she will be **u** and will still be able to have children.
2Sa 17: 3 Then all the people will remain **u** and peaceful."
Isa 11: 8 its hand in a nest of deadly snakes and pull it out **u**.
Jer 43:12 fleas from his cloak. And he himself will leave **u**.
Ac 28: 5 Paul shook off the snake into the fire and was **u**.

UNHARVESTED (1)
Lev 19:23 leave the fruit **u** for the first three years

UNHEALTHY (2)
Mt 7:17 good fruit, and an **u** tree produces bad fruit.
1Ti 6: 4 Such a person has an **u** desire to quibble over the

UNHOLY (3)
Ex 30: 9 Do not offer any **u** incense on this altar, or any
Mt 7: 6 "Don't give what is holy to **u** people. Don't give
Heb 10:29 blood of the covenant as if it were common and **u**.

UNHURT (1)
Ac 20:12 Meanwhile, the young man was taken home **u**,

UNICORN(S) [KJV] See (WILD) OX, OXEN

UNIFORM (1) [UNIFORMS]
2Sa 20: 8 Joab was wearing his **u** with a dagger strapped to

UNIFORMS (4) [UNIFORM]
Isa 9: 5 Never again will **u** be bloodstained by war.
Eze 23:12 those captains and commanders in handsome **u**—
23:14 military officers, outfitted in striking red **u**.
Na 2: 3 the sunlight! The attack begins! See their scarlet **u**!

UNIFY (1) [UNITE]
Eze 37:22 I will **u** them into one nation in the land. One king

UNIMPORTANT (1)
Eze 29:14 But Egypt will remain an **u**, minor kingdom.

UNINHABITED (3)
Eze 26: 5 The island of Tyre will become **u**. It will be a place
26:19 LORD says: I will make Tyre an **u** ruin.
29:11 neither people nor animals. It will be completely **u**.

UNINTENTIONAL (2) [UNINTENTIONALLY]
Nu 15:25 For it was an **u** sin, and they have corrected it with
15:27 "If the **u** sin is committed by an individual,

UNINTENTIONALLY (9) [UNINTENTIONAL]
Lev 4: 2 **u** by doing anything forbidden by the LORD's
4:22 his God, he will be guilty even if he sinned **u**.
4:27 they will be guilty even if they sinned **u**.
5:15 "If any of the people sin by **u** defiling the
5:17 even if it is done **u**, they will be held responsible.
Nu 15:22 "But suppose some of you **u** fail to carry out all
15:24 If the mistake was done **u**, and the community was
35:22 or throws something that **u** hits another person,
Jos 20: 3 Anyone who kills another person **u** can run to one

UNION (5) [UNITE]
Zec 11: 7 and named one Favor and the other **U**.
11:14 Then I broke my other staff, **U**, to show that the
Mal 2:15 Godly children from your **u**. So guard yourself;
2Co 6:16 And what **u** can there be between God's temple
Col 2:10 and you are complete through your **u** with Christ.

UNISON (2) [UNITE]
Ex 24: 3 the LORD had given him, they answered in **u**,
2Ch 5:13 and singers performed together in **u** to praise

UNIT (13) [UNITS]
Ex 26: 6 sheets together, making the Tabernacle a single **u**.
26:11 In this way, the two sets will become a single **u**.
26:24 at the top with a single ring, forming a single **u**.
36:29 single ring, forming a single **u** from top to bottom.
Dt 20: 9 they will announce the names of the **u**
1Ki 7:32 to axles that had been cast as one **u** with the cart.
7:34 and these, too, were cast as one **u** with the cart.
7:35 and side panels were cast as one **u** with the cart.

2Ch 26:11 ready to march into battle, **u** by **u**.
Ps 122: 3 is a well-built city, / knit together as a single **u**.
Eze 45:11 The homer will be your standard **u** for measuring
45:12 The standard **u** for weight will be the silver shekel.

UNITE (4) [REUNITED, UNIFY, UNION, UNISON, UNITED, UNITING, UNITY]

Ge 34:16 live here and **u** with you to become one people.
2Ch 30:12 giving them a strong desire to **u** in obeying the
Est 8:11 in every city authority to **u** to defend their lives.
Hos 1:11 people of Judah and Israel will **u** under one leader,

UNITED (18) [UNITE]

Ge 2:24 is joined to his wife, and the two are **u** into one.
Jos 10: 5 kings combined their armies for a **u** attack.
Jdg 7:14 victory over all the armies **u** with Midian!"
20:11 So all the Israelites were **u**, and they gathered
Mt 19: 5 is joined to his wife, and the two are **u** into one.'
Mk 10: 8 and the two are **u** into one.' Since they are no
Jn 17:11 given me—so that they will be **u** just as we are.
Ac 4:24 Then all the believers were **u** as they lifted their
4:27 and the people of Israel were all **u** against Jesus,
Ro 6: 5 Since we have been **u** with him in his death,
7: 4 And now you are **u** with the one who was raised
1Co 1:10 you to be of one mind, **u** in thought and purpose.
6:16 For the Scriptures say, "The two are **u** into one."
10:18 all who eat the sacrifices are **u** by that act.
2Co 2: 6 He was punished enough when most of you were **u**
Gal 3:27 And all who have been **u** with Christ in baptism
Eph 4: 3 Always keep yourselves **u** in the Holy Spirit,
5:31 is joined to his wife, and the two are **u** into one."

UNITING (1) [UNITE]

Jos 11: 4 their warriors and **u** to fight against Israel.

UNITS (3) [UNIT]

2Ki 11: 7 The other two **u** who are off duty on the Sabbath
1Ch 23: 7 The Gershonite family **u** were defined by their
2Ch 17:14 there were 300,000 troops organized in **u** of one

UNITY (3) [UNITE]

Ge 11: 6 of their common language and political **u**,
Zec 11:14 to show that the bond of **u** between Judah
Eph 4:13 until we come to such **u** in our faith

UNIVERSE (6)

Job 38:33 Do you know the laws of the **u** and how God rules
Eph 4:10 the heavens, so that his rule might fill the entire **u**.
Col 2:10 is the Lord over every ruler and authority in the **u**.
Heb 1: 2 and through the Son he made the **u** and everything
1: 3 He sustains the **u** by the mighty power of his
11: 3 By faith we understand that the entire **u** was

UNJUST (14) [UNJUSTLY]

Dt 27:19 'Cursed is anyone who is **u** to foreigners, orphans,
Job 6:29 my guilt, for I am righteous. Don't be so **u**.
34:18 says to kings and nobles, 'You are wicked and **u**.'
Ps 43: 1 ungodly people. / Rescue me from these **u** liars.
82: 2 "How long will you judges hand down **u**
94:20 Can **u** leaders claim that God is on their side—
Isa 10: 1 Destruction is certain for the **u** judges, for those
Jer 17:11 so are those who get their wealth by **u** means.
Eze 18:25 of Israel. Am I the one who is **u**, or is it you?
18:29 the people of Israel keep saying, 'The Lord is **u**!'
18:29 O people of Israel, it is you who are **u**, not I.
Hab 2: 9 "How terrible it will be for you who get rich by **u**
Mt 5:45 and he sends rain on the just and on the **u**, too.
Lk 7:29 all the people, including the **u** tax collectors,

UNJUSTLY (2) [UNJUST]

Pr 24:11 Rescue those who are **u** sentenced to death;
Eze 46:18 for I do not want any of my people **u** evicted from

UNKIND (1)

1Pe 3: 9 Don't retaliate when people say **u** things about

UNKNOWN (20)

Dt 8: 3 a food previously **u** to you and your ancestors.
8:16 in the wilderness, a food **u** to your ancestors.
28:36 and the king you crowned to a nation **u** to you
Ps 81: 5 Egypt to set us free. / I heard an **u** voice that said,
Isa 19:15 in Egypt, whether rich or poor, important or **u**,
28:11 foreign oppressors who speak an **u** language!
33:19 people with a strange, **u** language will disappear.
Ac 17:23 of them had this inscription on it—'To an **U** God.'
1Co 12:10 person is given the ability to speak in **u** languages,
12:28 to work together, / those who speak in **u** languages.
12:30 Does God give all of us the ability to speak in **u**
12:30 Can everyone interpret **u** languages? No!
13: 8 but prophecy and speaking in **u** languages
14: 6 if I should come to you talking in an **u** language,
14:19 others than ten thousand words in an **u** language.
14:21 will speak to my own people / through **u** languages
14:23 and hear everyone talking in an **u** language,
14:26 one will speak in an **u** language, while another will
14:27 than two or three should speak in an **u** language.
2Co 6: 9 We are well known, but we are treated as **u**.

UNLADE [KJV] See UNLOAD

UNLATCH (1)

SS 5: 4 "My lover tried to **u** the door, and my heart

UNLEARNED [KJV] See IGNORANT, OUTSIDERS, STUPID, UNEDUCATED

UNLEASH (3)

Ps 74:11 **U** your powerful fist and deliver a deathblow.
78:38 he held back his anger / and did not **u** his fury!
Eze 7: 3 hope remains, for I will **u** my anger against you.

UNLEAVENED (21)

FESTIVAL OF UNLEAVENED BREAD (14) Ex 12:17; 23:15; 34:18; Lev 23:6; Dt 16:16; 2Ch 30:13,21; 35:17; Ezr 6:22; Mt 26:17; Mk 14:1,12; Lk 22:1,7

UNLEAVENED BREAD (7) Lev 8:2,26,26; Jos 5:11; Jdg 6:20; 1Sa 28:24; 2Ki 23:9

Ex 12:17 "Celebrate this Festival of **U** Bread, for it will
23:15 The first is the Festival of **U** Bread. For seven days
34:18 "Be sure to celebrate the Festival of **U** Bread for
Lev 8: 2 the two rams, and the basket of **u** bread
8:26 On top of these he placed a loaf of **u** bread, a cake of **u** bread soaked with olive oil, and a thin
23: 6 the Festival of **U** Bread begins.
Dt 16:16 the Festival of **U** Bread, the Festival of Harvest,
Jos 5:11 The very next day they began to eat **u** bread
Jdg 6:20 "Place the meat and the **u** bread on this rock,
1Sa 28:24 killed it. She kneaded dough and baked **u** bread.
2Ki 23: 9 but they were allowed to eat **u** bread with the other
2Ch 30:13 to celebrate Passover and the Festival of **U** Bread.
30:21 Festival of **U** Bread for seven days with great joy.
35:17 and the Festival of **U** Bread for seven days.
Ezr 6:22 and celebrated the Festival of **U** Bread for seven
Mt 26:17 On the first day of the Festival of **U** Bread,
Mk 14: 1 Passover celebration and the Festival of **U** Bread.
14:12 On the first day of the Festival of **U** Bread (the day
Lk 22: 1 The Festival of **U** Bread, which begins with the
22: 7 Now the Festival of **U** Bread arrived,

UNLESS (60)

Ge 32:26 "I will not let you go **u** you bless me."
42:15 leave Egypt **u** your youngest brother comes here.
43: 3 we couldn't see him again **u** Benjamin came along.
43: 5 and see me **u** your brother is with you.' "
44:23 'You may not see me again **u** your youngest
44:26 'We can't **u** you let our youngest brother go with
44:26 of the grain **u** our youngest brother is with us.'
Lev 21: 2 **u** it is a close relative—mother or father, son
Dt 32:30 **u** their Rock had sold them, / **u** the LORD had given them up?
Jos 7:12 I will not remain with you any longer **u** you
2Sa 3:13 "but I will not negotiate with you **u** you bring
1Ki 12:26 Jeroboam thought to himself, "**U** I am careful,
17: 1 or rain during the next few years **u** I give the
2Ki 4:24 Don't slow down on my account **u** I tell you to."
4:30 yourself live, I won't go home **u** you go with me."
Est 2:14 never going to the king again **u** he had especially
4:11 to die **u** the king holds out his gold scepter.
Ps 94:17 **U** the LORD had helped me, / I would soon have
127: 1 **U** the LORD builds a house, / the work of the builders is useless. / **U** the LORD protects a city,
Pr 4:16 They cannot rest **u** they have caused someone to
Isa 10:15 Can a whip strike **u** a hand is moving it? Can a
Jer 30:21 for who would dare to come **u** invited?
Eze 44:25 in the presence of a dead person **u** it is his father,
Am 7: 2 **U** you relent, Israel will not survive, for we are
7: 5 **U** you relent, Israel will not survive, for we are
Mic 3:11 you prophets won't prophesy **u** you are paid.
Mt 5:20 **u** you obey God better than the teachers of
5:32 **u** she has been unfaithful, causes her to commit
18: 3 **u** you turn from your sins and become as little
19: 9 **u** his wife has been unfaithful."
24:22 In fact, **u** that time of calamity is shortened,
Mk 7: 4 they eat nothing bought from the market **u** they
13:20 In fact, **u** the Lord shortens that time of calamity,
Lk 13: 3 And you will also perish **u** you turn from your evil
13: 5 No, and I tell you again that **u** you repent, you will
16:10 "**U** you are faithful in small matters, you won't be
Jn 3: 3 Jesus replied, "I assure you, **u** you are born again,
6:44 For people can't come to me **u** the Father who sent
6:53 **u** you eat the flesh of the Son of Man and drink his
6:65 can't come to me **u** the Father brings them to me."
8:24 for **u** you believe that I am who I say I am,
10:37 Don't believe me **u** I carry out my Father's work.
12:24 in the soil. **U** it dies it will be alone—a single seed.
19:11 "You would have no power over me at all **u** it
20:25 "I won't believe it **u** I see the nail wounds in his
Ac 15: 1 "**U** you keep the ancient Jewish custom of
20:24 But my life is worth nothing **u** I use it for doing the
27:31 "You will all die **u** the sailors stay aboard."
Ro 10:14 But how can they call on him to save them **u** they
10:14 And how can they hear about him **u** someone tells
1Co 14: 5 **u** someone interprets what you are saying so that
14: 7 For no one will recognize the melody **u** the notes
15: 2 **u**, of course, you believed something that was
15:29 Why do it **u** the dead will someday rise again?
15:36 it doesn't grow into a plant **u** it dies first.
1Ti 5:19 Do not listen to complaints against an elder **u** there
Rev 2:22 **u** they turn away from all their evil deeds.
3: 3 **U** you do, I will come upon you suddenly,

UNLIKE (6)

Ru 2:22 You will be safe there, **u** in other fields."
2Ch 27: 2 But **u** him, Jotham did not enter the Temple of the
33:23 But **u** his father, he did not humble himself before
Mt 7:29 quite **u** the teachers of religious law.
Mk 1:22 quite **u** the teachers of religious law.
Jas 1:17 **U** them, he never changes or casts shifting

UNLIMITED (2)

Ezr 7:22 550 gallons of olive oil, and an **u** supply of salt.
Eph 3:16 **u** resources he will give you mighty inner strength

UNLOAD (1) [UNLOADED]

Ac 21: 3 harbor of Tyre, in Syria, where the ship was to **u**.

UNLOADED (1) [UNLOAD]

Ge 24:32 and Laban **u** the camels, gave him straw to bed

UNLOOSE [KJV] See (ACT AS A) SLAVE

UNLOVED (2) [UNLOVING]

Ge 29:31 But because Leah was **u**, the LORD let her have a
29:33 "The LORD heard that I was **u** and has given me

UNLOVING (1) [UNLOVED]

2Ti 3: 3 They will be **u** and unforgiving; they will slander

UNMARKED (1)

Jer 26:23 with a sword and had him buried in an **u** grave.)

UNMARRIED (4)

Eze 44:25 it is his father, mother, child, brother, or **u** sister.
Ac 21: 9 He had four **u** daughters who had the gift of
1Co 7: 8 and to widows—it's better to stay **u**, just as I am.
7:32 An **u** man can spend his time doing the Lord's

UNMOVED (1)

Jdg 5:17 did he stay home? / Asher sat **u** at the seashore,

UNNECESSARY (1)

Pr 23:29 Who has **u** bruises? Who has bloodshot eyes?

UNNI (3)

1Ch 15:18 Jehiel, **U**, Eliab, Benaiah, Maaseiah, Mattithiah,
15:20 Aziel, Shemiramoth, Jehiel, **U**, Eliab, Maaseiah,
Ne 12: 9 Their associates, Bakbukiah and **U**, stood opposite

UNNOTICED (1)

Ac 10: 4 and gifts to the poor have not gone **u** by God!

UNNUMBERED (2)

Ps 68:17 Surrounded by **u** thousands of chariots, / the Lord
SS 6: 8 eighty concubines and **u** virgins available to me.

UNOFFERED (1)

Ex 23:18 And no sacrificial fat may be left **u** until the next

UNOPPOSED (1)

Da 11:16 "The king of the north will march onward **u**;

UNPERFECT [KJV] See (BEFORE I WAS) BORN

UNPRODUCTIVE (2)

2Ki 2:19 can see. But the water is bad, and the land is **u**."
Tit 3:14 For our people should not have **u** lives. They must

UNPROTECTED (3)

Nu 13:19 or bad? Do their towns have walls or are they **u**?
Eze 38:11 'Israel is an **u** land filled with unwalled villages!
Hos 4:16 She will stand alone and **u**, like a helpless lamb in

UNPRUNED (2)

Lev 25: 5 or process the grapes that grow on your **u** vines.
25:11 and do not process the grapes that grow on your **u**

UNPUNISHED (22)

Ex 20: 5 I do not leave **u** the sins of those who hate me,
20: 7 The LORD will not let you go **u** if you misuse his
34: 7 Even so I do not leave sin **u**, but I punish the
Nu 14:18 Even so he does not leave sin **u**, but he punishes
Dt 5: 9 I do not leave **u** the sins of those who hate me,
5:11 The LORD will not let you go **u** if you misuse his
Pr 6:29 man's wife. He who embraces her will not go **u**.
19: 5 A false witness will not go **u**, nor will a liar escape.
19: 9 A false witness will not go **u**, and a liar will be
Jer 25:29 Now should I let you go **u**? No, you will not
30:11 But I must discipline you; I cannot let you go **u**.
46:28 But I must discipline you; I cannot let you go **u**."
49:12 how much more must you! You will not go **u**!
Am 1: 3 not forget it. I will not let them go **u** any longer!
1: 6 not forget it. I will not let them go **u** any longer!
1: 9 not forget it. I will not let them go **u** any longer!
1:11 not forget it. I will not let them go **u** any longer!
1:13 not forget it. I will not let them go **u** any longer!
2: 1 not forget it. I will not let them go **u** any longer!
2: 4 not forget it. I will not let them go **u** any longer!
2: 6 not forget it. I will not let them go **u** any longer!
Na 1: 3 power is great, and he never lets the guilty go **u**.

UNQUENCHABLE (5)
Jer 4: 4 or my anger will burn like an **u** fire because of all
7: 20 and crops will be consumed by the **u** fire of my
21: 12 or my anger will burn like an **u** fire because of all
Mt 18: 8 or lame than to be thrown into the **u** fire with both
Mk 9: 43 than to go into the **u** fires of hell with two hands.

UNREASONABLE (1)
Ex 5: 16 of your slave drivers for making such **u** demands."

UNREBUKEABLE [KJV] See (NO) FAULT

UNRELATED (1)
Lev 15: 25 or if she discharges blood **u** to her menstruation,

UNRELENTING (1)
Am 1: 11 showed them no mercy and were **u** in their anger.

UNRELIABLE (5)
2Ki 18: 21 your hand. The pharaoh of Egypt is completely **u**!
Job 6: 15 you have proved as **u** as a seasonal brook that
Pr 13: 17 An **u** messenger stumbles into trouble, but a
25: 19 Putting confidence in an **u** person is like chewing
Isa 36: 6 your hand. The Pharaoh of Egypt is completely **u**!

UNREPROVEABLE [KJV] See (WITHOUT) FAULT

UNRESPONSIVE (1)
Ro 11: 7 ones God has chosen—but the rest were made **u**.

UNRESTRAINED (3)
Isa 14: 6 the nations in your angry grip. Your tyranny was **u**.
Jer 31: 15 is heard in Ramah—mourning and weeping **u**.
Mt 2: 18 is heard in Ramah— / weeping and mourning **u**.

UNROLL (1) [UNROLLED]
Rev 5: 2 worthy to break the seals on this scroll and **u** it?"

UNROLLED (4) [UNROLL]
Eze 2: 10 He **u** it, and I saw that both sides were covered
Lk 4: 17 and he **u** the scroll to the place where it says:
Rev 10: 2 in his hand was a small scroll, which he had **u**.
10: 8 and take the **u** scroll from the angel who is

UNRULY (5)
Ge 49: 4 But you are as **u** as the waves of the sea, / and you
Ex 33: 3 along with you, for you are a stubborn, **u** people.
33: 5 to tell them, "You are an **u**, stubborn people.
34: 9 Yes, this is an **u** and stubborn people, but please
Dt 32: 15 But Israel soon became fat and **u**; / the people

UNSATIABLE [KJV] See (NEVER) ENOUGH

UNSATISFIED (1)
Ps 59: 15 They scavenge for food / but go to sleep **u**.

UNSAVOURY [KJV] See HOSTILE, TASTELESS

UNSCATHED (1)
Zec 12: 3 None of the nations who try to lift it will escape **u**.

UNSEAL (1) [UNSEALED]
Ps 51: 15 **U** my lips, O Lord, / that I may praise you.

UNSEALED (2) [UNSEAL]
Jer 32: 11 I took the sealed deed and an **u** copy of the deed,
32: 14 Take both this sealed deed and the **u** copy, and put

UNSEEMLY [KJV] See RUDE, SHAMEFUL

UNSEEN (2)
Eph 6: 12 the evil rulers and authorities of the **u** world,
1Ti 1: 17 He is the eternal King, the **u** one who never dies;

UNSETTLED (1)
Jas 1: 6 for a doubtful mind is as **u** as a wave of the sea that

UNSHEATH (2)
Ex 15: 9 I will **u** my sword; / my power will destroy them.'
Eze 21: 3 and I am about to **u** my sword to destroy your

UNSHRUNK (2)
Mt 9: 16 And who would patch an old garment with **u**
Mk 2: 21 And who would patch an old garment with **u**

UNSPEAKABLE (1)
Eze 8: 9 "and see the **u** wickedness going on in there!"

UNSPEAKABLE [KJV] See also (CANNOT BE) TOLD, INEXPRESSIBLE, (TOO WONDERFUL FOR) WORDS

UNSPIRITUAL (1)
Jas 3: 15 Such things are earthly, **u**, and motivated by the

UNSPLIT (1)
Lev 11: 26 "Any animal that has divided but **u** hooves or that

UNSTABLE (2)
2Pe 2: 14 They make a game of luring **u** people into sin.
3: 16 and **u** have twisted his letters around to mean

UNSTAINED (1)
Heb 7: 26 because he is holy and blameless, **u** by sin.

UNSTOP (1)
Isa 35: 5 the eyes of the blind and **u** the ears of the deaf.

UNSUCCESSFUL (1)
Mt 18: 16 But if you are **u**, take one or two others with you

UNTAMED (1)
Ge 16: 12 will be a wild one—free and **u** as a wild donkey!

UNTHANKFUL (1)
Lk 6: 35 for he is kind to the **u** and to those who are wicked.

UNTHINKING (1)
2Pe 2: 12 These false teachers are like **u** animals,

UNTIE (4) [UNTYING]
Mt 21: 2 with its colt beside it. **U** them and bring them here.
Mk 11: 2 that has never been ridden. **U** it and bring it here.
Lk 13: 15 Don't you **u** your ox or your donkey from their
19: 30 that has never been ridden. **U** it and bring it here.

UNTIL (506)
Ge 3: 19 you will sweat to produce food, **u** your dying day.
8: 7 raven that flew back and forth **u** the earth was dry.
14: 14 He chased after Kedorlaomer's army **u** he caught
19: 22 But hurry! For I can do nothing **u** you are there."
24: 19 for your camels, too, **u** they have had enough!"
24: 20 She kept carrying water to the camels **u** they had
24: 33 "I don't want to eat **u** I have told you why I have
27: 44 Stay there with him **u** your brother's fury is spent.
28: 15 I will be with you constantly **u** I have finished
29: 8 and begin the watering **u** all the flocks
29: 27 "Wait **u** the bridal week is over, and you can have
32: 4 I have been living with Uncle Laban **u** recently,
32: 12 and to multiply my descendants **u** they become as
32: 24 and a man came and wrestled with him **u** dawn.
34: 5 herding cattle so he did nothing **u** they returned.
38: 11 She was to remain a widow **u** his youngest son,
49: 10 **u** the coming of the one to whom it belongs,
Ex 7: 16 **U** now, you have refused to listen to him.
10: 26 which sacrifices he will require **u** we get there."
12: 6 "Take special care of these lambs **u** the evening of
12: 10 Do not leave any of it **u** the next day. Whatever is
12: 18 **u** the evening of the twenty-first day of the month.
12: 22 no one is allowed to leave the house **u** morning.
15: 16 like a stone, / **u** your people pass by, O LORD,
15: 16 **u** the people whom you purchased pass by.
16: 20 them didn't listen and kept some of it **u** morning.
16: 35 So the people of Israel ate manna for forty years **u**
17: 12 stood on each side, holding up his hands **u** sunset.
19: 13 The people must stay away from the mountain **u**
19: 15 And **u** then, abstain from having sexual
23: 18 And no sacrificial fat may be left unoffered **u** the
23: 30 I will drive them out a little at a time **u** your
24: 14 "Stay here and wait for us **u** we come back.
29: 34 ordination meat or bread remains **u** the morning,
33: 5 and ornaments **u** I decide what to do with you."
33: 8 They would all watch Moses **u** he disappeared
33: 22 and cover you with my hand **u** I have passed.
34: 25 lamb may be kept over **u** the following morning.
34: 34 he removed the veil **u** he came out again.
34: 35 Afterward he would put the veil on again **u** he
40: 37 the cloud stayed, they would stay **u** it moved again.
Lev 6: 9 The burnt offering must be left on the altar **u** the
7: 17 But anything left over **u** the third day must be
11: 24 of their dead bodies, you will be defiled **u** evening.
11: 25 and you will remain defiled **u** evening.
11: 26 of such an animal, you will be defiled **u** evening.
11: 27 of such an animal, you will be defiled **u** evening.
11: 28 and you will remain defiled **u** evening.
11: 31 of such an animal, you will be defiled **u** evening.
11: 32 into water, and it will remain defiled **u** evening.
11: 39 touch its carcass, you will be defiled **u** evening.
11: 40 Then you will remain defiled **u** evening.
12: 4 Then the woman must wait for thirty-three days **u**
12: 4 And she must not go to the sanctuary **u** her time of
14: 46 be considered ceremonially unclean **u** evening.
15: 5 and you will remain ceremonially defiled **u**
15: 6 in water. You will then remain defiled **u** evening.
15: 10 in water, and you will remain defiled **u** evening.
15: 11 in water, and you will remain defiled **u** evening.
15: 16 and he will remain ceremonially defiled **u** evening.
15: 17 be washed, and it will remain defiled **u** evening.
15: 18 and they will remain defiled **u** evening.
15: 19 her during that time, you will be defiled **u** evening.
15: 21 in water, and you will remain defiled **u** evening.
15: 27 in water, and you will remain defiled **u** evening.
16: 17 No one may enter **u** he comes out again after
17: 15 Then you will remain ceremonially unclean **u**
19: 6 Any leftovers that remain **u** the third day must be
22: 4 they may not eat the sacred offerings **u** they have
22: 6 they will remain defiled **u** evening. They must not eat any of the sacred offerings **u**
22: 30 Don't leave any of it **u** the second day. I am the
23: 14 or fresh kernels on that day **u** after you have
23: 16 Keep counting **u** the day after the seventh Sabbath,
23: 32 of Atonement and extend **u** evening of that day."
24: 3 from evening **u** morning, before the LORD.
24: 12 They put the man in custody **u** the LORD's will
25: 15 for the crop years left **u** the next Year of Jubilee.
25: 22 you will eat from the old crop **u** the new harvest
25: 27 on the number of years **u** the next Year of Jubilee.
25: 28 then it will belong to the new owner **u** the next
25: 40 and they will serve you only **u** the Year of Jubilee.
25: 50 number of years left **u** the next Year of Jubilee—
25: 52 If only a few years remain **u** the Year of Jubilee,
26: 5 Your threshing season will extend **u** the grape
26: 5 and your grape harvest will extend **u** it is time to
27: 18 to the years left **u** the next Year of Jubilee.
27: 23 based on the years **u** the next Year of Jubilee.
Nu 9: 8 "Wait here **u** I have received instructions for you
9: 12 They must not leave any of the lamb **u** the next
9: 15 Then from evening **u** morning the cloud over the
10: 12 and traveled on in stages **u** the cloud stopped in the
11: 20 You will eat it for a whole month **u** you gag
12: 15 and the people waited **u** she was brought back
14: 33 **u** the last of you lies dead in the wilderness.
16: 48 the living and the dead **u** the plague was stopped.
19: 7 though he will remain ceremonially unclean **u**
19: 8 and he, too, will remain unclean **u** evening.
19: 10 and he will remain ceremonially unclean **u**
19: 21 water of purification will remain defiled **u** evening.
19: 22 touches will be ceremonially defiled **u** evening."
20: 17 and never leave it **u** we have crossed the opposite
21: 22 We will stay on the king's road **u** we have crossed
23: 24 They refuse to rest / **u** they have feasted on prey,
32: 13 **u** the whole generation that sinned against him had
32: 17 and lead our fellow Israelites into battle **u** we have
32: 18 We will not return to our homes **u** all the people of
32: 21 and if your troops cross the Jordan **u** the LORD
35: 25 in a city of refuge **u** the death of the high priest.
35: 28 the city of refuge **u** the death of the high priest.
Dt 2: 14 Kadesh-barnea **u** we finally crossed Zered Brook!
2: 14 **u** all the men old enough to fight in battle had died
2: 15 The LORD had lifted his hand against them **u** all
2: 29 Let us pass through **u** we cross the Jordan into the
4: 32 from the time God created people on the earth **u**
7: 23 He will throw them into complete confusion **u** they
9: 7 From the day you left Egypt **u** now, you have
11: 5 cared for you in the wilderness **u** you arrived here.
16: 4 of the Passover lamb remain **u** the next morning.
20: 20 equipment you need to besiege the town **u** it falls.
22: 2 owner is, keep it **u** the owner comes looking for it;
28: 20 **u** at last you are completely destroyed for doing
28: 21 The LORD will send diseases among you **u** none
28: 22 These devastations will pursue you **u** you die.
28: 24 and it will pour down from the sky **u** you are
28: 45 will pursue and overtake you **u** you are destroyed.
28: 48 They will oppress you harshly **u** you are destroyed.
28: 52 They will lay siege to your cities **u** all the fortified
28: 61 in this Book of the Law, **u** you are destroyed.
28: 63 **u** you disappear from the land you are about to
34: 8 **u** the customary period of mourning was over.
Jos 1: 15 **u** the LORD gives rest to them as he has given
1: 15 and **u** they, too, possess the land the LORD your
2: 16 "Hide there for three days **u** the men who are
3: 16 flowed on to the Dead Sea **u** the riverbed was dry.
3: 17 They waited there **u** everyone had crossed the
4: 10 of the river **u** all of the LORD's instructions,
4: 23 your eyes, and he kept it dry **u** you were all across,
4: 23 just as he did at the Red Sea when he dried it up **u**
5: 6 **u** all the men who were old enough to bear arms
5: 8 they rested in the camp **u** they were healed.
6: 10 "Not a single word from any of you **u** I tell you to
7: 6 and bowed down facing the Ark of the LORD **u**
7: 13 You will never defeat your enemies **u** you remove
8: 6 We will let them chase us **u** they have all left the
8: 26 For Joshua kept holding out his spear **u** everyone
8: 29 king of Ai on a tree and left him there **u** evening.
10: 11 hailstorm that continued **u** they reached Azekah.
10: 13 and moon stood still **u** the Israelites had defeated
10: 26 five kings and hung them on five trees **u** evening.
11: 8 of Mizpah, **u** not one enemy warrior was left alive.
15: 4 to Azmon, **u** it finally reached the brook of Egypt,
20: 6 **u** the death of the high priest who was in office at
23: 8 to the LORD your God as you have done **u** now.
Jdg 4: 24 against King Jabin, **u** they finally destroyed him.
5: 7 **u** Deborah arose as a mother for Israel.
6: 5 And they stayed **u** the land was stripped bare.
6: 18 Don't go away **u** I come back and bring my
6: 18 LORD answered, "I will stay here **u** you return."
13: 7 the moment of his birth **u** the day of his death.' "
13: 15 "Please stay here **u** we can prepare a young goat
15: 7 revenge on you, and I won't stop **u** I'm satisfied!"
16: 3 But Samson stayed in bed only **u** midnight.
16: 16 So day after day she nagged him **u** he couldn't
18: 30 as priests for the tribe of Dan **u** the Exile.
19: 25 her all night, taking turns raping her **u** morning.
19: 26 at the door of the house and lay there **u** it was light.
20: 5 and they raped my concubine **u** she was dead.
20: 23 and wept in the presence of the LORD **u** evening.
20: 26 the presence of the LORD and fasted **u** evening.
20: 45 They continued the chase **u** they had killed another
21: 2 to Bethel and sat in the presence of God **u** evening,
Ru 2: 21 and stay with his harvesters **u** the entire harvest is

2:23 and gathered grain with them **u** the end of the
3: 3 but don't let Boaz see you **u** he has finished his
3:13 I will marry you! Now lie down here **u** morning."
3:14 So Ruth lay at Boaz's feet **u** the morning, but she
3:18 be patient, my daughter, **u** we hear what happens.
3:18 The man won't rest **u** he has followed through on
1Sa 1:22 She told her husband, "Wait **u** the baby is weaned.
3:15 Samuel stayed in bed **u** morning, then got up
6: 6 They wouldn't let Israel go **u** God had ravaged
9:13 The guests won't start **u** he arrives to bless the
15:18 the sinners, the Amalekites, **u** they are all dead.'
16:11 "We will not sit down to eat **u** he arrives."
20: 5 and stay there **u** the evening of the third day.
22: 2 **u** David was the leader of about four hundred men.
22: 3 and mother live here under royal protection **u** I
25:36 about her meeting with David **u** the next morning.
26:13 David climbed the hill opposite the camp **u** he was
30: 4 they wept **u** they could weep no more.
30:17 that night and the entire next day **u** evening.
2Sa 2:29 and they did not stop **u** they arrived at Mahanaim.
7: 6 from the day I brought the Israelites out of Egypt **u**
10: 5 the men to stay at Jericho **u** their beards grew out,
13:27 But Absalom kept on pressing the king **u** he finally
13:28 told his men, "Wait **u** Amnon gets drunk;
15:24 Then they offered sacrifices there **u** everyone had
17:13 the nearest valley **u** every stone is torn down."
20: 3 So each of them lived like a widow **u** she died.
22:38 I did not stop **u** they were conquered.
23:10 He killed Philistines **u** his hand was too tired to lift
23:10 The rest of the army did not return **u** it was time to
24: 3 "May the LORD your God let you live **u** there
1Ki 3: 1 He brought her to live in the City of David **u** he
5: 3 He could not build **u** the LORD gave him victory
10: 7 I didn't believe it **u** I arrived here and saw it with
11:40 Shishak of Egypt and stayed there **u** Solomon died.
14:10 royal dynasty as one burns up trash **u** it is all gone.
17:14 and oil left in your containers **u** the time when the
18:28 with knives and swords **u** the blood gushed out.
18:29 They raved all afternoon **u** the time of the evening
22:21 **u** finally a spirit approached the LORD and said,
22:27 and water **u** I return safely from the battle!' "
2Ki 2:17 But they kept urging him **u** he was embarrassed,
7: 9 If we wait **u** morning, some terrible calamity will
8:11 Elisha stared at Hazael with a fixed gaze **u** Hazael
8:15 in water, and held it over the king's face **u** he died.
10: 8 of the city gate, and leave them there **u** morning."
13:19 "Then you would have beaten Aram **u** they were
15: 5 with leprosy, which lasted **u** the day of his death;
17:20 them over to their attackers **u** they were destroyed.
17:23 **u** the LORD finally swept them away, just as all
21:16 Manasseh also murdered many innocent people **u**
22:20 disaster against this city **u** after you have died
25: 2 Jerusalem was kept under siege **u** the eleventh year
25:30 to cover his living expenses **u** the day of his death.
1Ch 4:31 These towns were under their control **u** the time of
5:22 So they lived in their land **u** they were taken away
6:32 **u** Solomon built the Temple of the LORD in
12:22 Day after day more men joined David **u** he had a
12:29 had remained loyal to Saul **u** this time.
17: 5 from the day I brought the Israelites out of Egypt **u**
19: 5 the men to stay at Jericho **u** their beards grew out,
2Ch 9: 6 I didn't believe it **u** I arrived here and saw it with
15:19 So there was no more war **u** the thirty-fifth year of
18:20 **u** finally a spirit approached the LORD and said,
18:26 and water **u** I return safely from the battle!' "
18:34 up in his chariot facing the Arameans **u** evening.
21:15 disease **u** it causes your bowels to come out."
26:15 for the LORD helped him wonderfully **u** he
26:21 So King Uzziah had leprosy **u** the day he died.
29:28 **u** all the burnt offerings were finished.
29:34 so their relatives the Levites helped them **u** the
29:34 was finished and **u** more priests had been purified.
31: 7 and the heaps continued to grow **u** early autumn.
34:28 and its people **u** after you have died and been
36:16 They scoffed at the prophets **u** the LORD's anger
36:20 and his sons **u** the kingdom of Persia came to
Ezr 2:63 **u** there was a priest who could consult the LORD
4: 5 and lasted **u** King Darius of Persia took the throne.
4:24 and it remained at a standstill **u** the second year of
5: 5 from building **u** a report was sent to Darius
8:29 Guard these treasures well **u** you present them,
9: 4 And I sat there utterly appalled **u** the time of the
9:14 Surely your anger will destroy us **u** even this little
Ne 5:14 from the twentieth **u** the thirty-second year of the
7:65 **u** there was a priest who could consult the LORD
8: 3 inside the Water Gate from early morning **u** noon
9:25 So they ate **u** they were full and grew fat
9:32 the kings of Assyria first triumphed over us **u** now.
13:19 not to be opened **u** the Sabbath ended.
Job 5:26 You will not be harvested **u** the proper time!
13:19 prove me wrong, I would remain silent **u** I die.
14:12 **U** the heavens are no more, they will not wake up
14:13 and forget me there **u** your anger has passed.
16:12 "I was living quietly **u** he broke me apart. He took
27: 5 you are right; **u** I die, I will defend my innocence.
Ps 6: 3 at heart. / How long, O LORD, **u** you restore me?
10:15 Go after them **u** the last one is destroyed!
18:37 I did not stop **u** they were conquered.
48:14 and ever, / and he will be our guide **u** we die.
57: 1 shadow of your wings / **u** this violent storm is past.
72: 7 May there be abundant prosperity **u** the end of
77: 2 pleading. / There can be no joy for me **u** he acts.
83:16 **u** they submit to your name, O LORD.
83:18 **u** they learn that you alone are called the LORD,
89: 4 they will sit on your throne from now **u**
94:13 from troubled times / **u** a pit is dug for the wicked.
104:23 they labor **u** the evening shadows fall again.
105:19 **U** the time came to fulfill his word, / the LORD
105:24 **u** they became too mighty for their enemies.
110: 1 honor at my right hand / **u** I humble your enemies,
119:67 I used to wander off **u** you disciplined me;
127: 2 so hard / from early morning **u** late at night,
132: 5 **u** I find a place to build a house for the LORD,
Pr 4:16 for evil people cannot sleep **u** they have done their
4:18 which shines ever brighter **u** the full light of day.
6: 4 Don't put it off. Do it now! Don't rest **u** you do.
7:18 Come, let's drink our fill of love **u** morning.
7:20 and he won't return **u** later in the month."
18:17 Any story sounds true **u** someone sets the record
Ecc 12: 6 Don't wait **u** the water jar is smashed at the spring
SS 2: 7 of the wild, not to awaken love **u** the time is right.
3: 4 I didn't let him go **u** I had brought him to my
3: 5 the wild, not to awaken love **u** the time is right."
8: 4 not to awaken love **u** the time is right."
Isa 6:11 And he replied, "**U** their cities are destroyed,
6:11 **U** their houses are deserted and the whole country
6:12 Do not stop **u** the LORD has sent everyone away
13:14 Everyone will run **u** exhausted, rushing back to
16: 4 Hide them from our enemies **u** the terror is past."
21:11 to me, "Watchman, how much longer **u** morning?
22:14 sin will never be forgiven you **u** the day you die.
24:22 and put in prison **u** they are tried and condemned.
26:20 Hide **u** the LORD's anger against your enemies
28:19 day and night, **u** you are carried away."
30: 8 then stand **u** the end of time as a witness to Israel's
32:15 **u** at last the Spirit is poured down upon us from
42: 4 He will not stop **u** truth and righteousness prevail
46: 4 your lifetime—**u** your hair is white with age.
62: 1 I will not stop praying for her **u** her righteousness
62: 7 Give the LORD no rest **u** he makes Jerusalem the
Jer 1: 3 **u** the eleventh year of King Zedekiah's reign in
4:20 roll over the land, **u** it lies in complete desolation.
5: 7 I fed my people **u** they were fully satisfied.
7:25 From the day your ancestors left Egypt **u** now,
9:16 Their enemies will chase them with the sword **u** I
19: 9 enemies lay siege to the city **u** all the food is gone.
19:11 They will bury the bodies in Topheth **u** there is no
23:20 The anger of the LORD will not diminish **u** it has
24:10 and disease **u** they have vanished from the land of
25: 3 of Josiah son of Amon, king of Judah, **u** now—
25:18 From that day **u** this, they have been a desolate
27: 7 and his son and his grandson **u** his time is up.
27: 8 and disease upon that nation **u** Babylon has
27:22 to Babylon and will stay there **u** I send for them,
30:24 The fierce anger of the LORD will not diminish **u**
32:31 "From the time this city was built **u** now, it has
36:23 by section, **u** the whole scroll was burned up.
38:28 of the guard **u** the day Jerusalem was captured.
44:27 will suffer war and famine **u** all of you are dead.
46:10 The sword will devour **u** it is satisfied, yes,
49:37 "Their enemies will chase them with the sword **u** I
50:10 Babylonia will be plundered **u** the attackers are
51:39 I will make them drink **u** they fall asleep,
52: 5 Jerusalem was kept under siege **u** the eleventh year
52:34 to cover his living expenses **u** the day of his death.
La 2:11 I have cried **u** the tears no longer come. My heart
3:50 **u** the LORD looks down from heaven and sees.
Eze 4: 8 so you won't be able to turn from side to side **u** the
4:14 From the time I was a child **u** now I have never
5:16 and more severe **u** every crumb of food is gone.
21: 5 and it will not return to its sheath **u** its work is
21:27 And it will not be restored **u** the one appears who
24:13 you will remain filthy **u** my fury against you has
28:15 you were created **u** the day evil was found in you.
30:11 They will make war against Egypt **u** slaughtered
34:21 and hungry flock **u** they are scattered to distant
39:19 Gorge yourselves with flesh **u** you are glutted;
drink blood **u** you are drunk.
46: 2 The gateway will not be closed **u** evening.
46:17 the servant may keep it only **u** the Year of Jubilee,
Da 1:21 Daniel remained there **u** the first year of King
4:25 **u** you learn that the Most High rules over the
4:32 **u** you learn that the Most High rules over the
4:33 He lived this way **u** his hair was as long as eagles'
5:21 **u** he learned that the Most High God rules the
7:11 I kept watching **u** the fourth beast was killed
7:22 **u** the Ancient One came and judged in favor of the
9:25 to rebuild Jerusalem **u** the Anointed One comes.
9:27 **u** the end that has been decreed is poured out on
11:35 and cleansed and made pure **u** the time of the end,
11:36 He will succeed—**u** the time of wrath is completed.
12: 4 a secret; seal up the book **u** the time of the end.
12: 6 "How long will it be **u** these shocking events
12:12 who wait and remain **u** the end of the 1,335 days!
12:13 "As for you, go your way **u** the end. You will rest,
Hos 5:15 Then I will return to my place **u** they admit their
Jnh 4: 8 The sun beat down on his head **u** he grew faint
Mic 5: 3 **u** the time when the woman in labor gives birth to
Zep 2: 5 The LORD will destroy you **u** not one of you is
Zec 1:12 How long will it be **u** you again show mercy to
5: 4 And my curse will remain in that house **u** it is
Mt 1:25 but she remained a virgin **u** her son was born.
2:13 "Stay there **u** I tell you to return, because Herod is
2:15 and they stayed there **u** Herod's death.
5:18 I assure you, **u** heaven and earth disappear,
5:18 even the smallest detail of God's law will remain **u**
5:26 I assure you that you won't be free again **u** you
10:11 and stay in his home **u** you leave for the next town.
11:12 the Baptist began preaching and baptizing **u** now,
12:20 **u** he brings full justice with his final victory.
13:30 Let both grow together **u** the harvest. Then I will
15:37 They all ate **u** they were full, and when the scraps
17: 9 "Don't tell anyone what you have seen **u** I,
17:17 How long must I be with you **u** you believe?
18:30 and jailed **u** the debt could be paid in full.
18:34 Then the angry king sent the man to prison **u** he
22:26 so on **u** she had been the wife of each of them.
22:44 **u** I humble your enemies beneath your feet.'
23:39 you this, you will never see me again **u** you say,
24:39 People didn't realize what was going to happen **u**
26:29 I will not drink wine again **u** the day I drink it new
26:42 If this cup cannot be taken away **u** I drink it,
27:45 darkness fell across the whole land **u** three o'clock.
27:64 So we request that you seal the tomb **u** the third
Mk 4:37 High waves began to break into the boat **u** it was
7: 3 do not eat **u** they have poured water over their
8: 8 They ate **u** they were full, and when the scraps
9: 9 them not to tell anyone what they had seen **u** he,
9:19 How long must I be with you **u** you believe?
12: 6 **u** there was only one left—his son whom he loved
12:22 This continued **u** all the brothers had married her
12:36 **u** I humble your enemies beneath your feet.'
13:30 this generation will not pass from the scene **u** all
14:25 **u** that day when I drink it new in the Kingdom of
15:33 darkness fell across the whole land **u** three o'clock.
Lk 1:20 you won't be able to speak **u** the child is born.
1:23 He stayed at the Temple **u** his term of service was
1:80 Then he lived out in the wilderness **u** he began his
2:26 would not die **u** he had seen the Lord's Messiah.
4:13 he left him **u** the next opportunity came.
9:36 They didn't tell anyone what they had seen **u** long
11:22 **u** someone who is stronger attacks and overpowers
12: 1 the crowds grew **u** thousands were milling about
12:50 and I am under a heavy burden **u** it is
12:59 you won't be free again **u** you have paid the last
13:35 And you will never see me again **u** you say,
14:28 "But don't begin **u** you count the cost. For who
15: 4 to go and search for the lost one **u** you found it?
15: 8 and sweep every nook and cranny **u** she finds it?
15:12 of your estate now, instead of waiting **u** you die.'
16:16 "**U** John the Baptist began to preach, the laws of
17:29 **u** the morning Lot left Sodom. Then fire
20:31 **u** each of the seven had married her and died,
20:43 **u** I humble your enemies, / making them a
21:24 and trampled down by the Gentiles **u** the age of the
21:32 this generation will not pass from the scene **u** all
22:16 For I tell you now that I won't eat it again **u** it
22:18 For I will not drink wine again **u** the Kingdom of
22:34 The rooster will not crow tomorrow morning **u** you
23:44 and darkness fell across the whole land **u** three
24:49 But stay here in the city **u** the Holy Spirit comes
Jn 2:10 But you have kept the best **u** now!"
4:35 begin **u** the summer ends four months from now?
6:11 with the fish. And they all ate **u** they were full.
8: 9 **u** only Jesus was left in the middle of the crowd
20: 9 for **u** then they hadn't realized that the Scriptures
21:22 "If I want him to remain alive **u** I return,
21:23 only said, "If I want him to remain alive **u** I return,
Ac 1: 2 **u** the day he ascended to heaven after giving his
1: 4 "Do not leave Jerusalem **u** the Father sends you
1:22 from the time he was baptized by John **u** the day
2:34 honor at my right hand / **u** I humble your enemies,
3:21 For he must remain in heaven **u** the time for the
4: 3 it was already evening, jailed them **u** morning.
7: 4 the Chaldeans and lived in Haran **u** his father died.
7:45 And it was used there **u** the time of King David.
8:40 and in every city along the way **u** he came to
13: 6 the entire island **u** finally they reached Paphos,
13:20 judges ruled **u** the time of Samuel the prophet.
16:15 and stay at my home." And she urged us **u** we did.
16:18 This went on day after day **u** Paul got
20: 7 he was leaving the next day, he talked **u** midnight.
20:11 And Paul continued talking to them **u** dawn;
20:18 the day I set foot in the province of Asia **u** now
22:22 The crowd listened **u** Paul came to that word,
23:12 oath to neither eat nor drink **u** they had killed Paul.
23:14 oath to neither eat nor drink **u** we have killed Paul.
23:21 have vowed not to eat or drink **u** they kill him.
24:22 adjourned the hearing and said, "Wait **u** Lysias,
25:21 So I ordered him back to jail **u** I could arrange to
27:20 the sun and the stars, **u** at last all hope was gone.
Ro 1:13 times to visit you, but I was prevented **u** now.
11:25 but this will last only **u** the complete number of
1Co 11:26 you are announcing the Lord's death **u** he comes
15:25 For Christ must reign **u** he humbles all his enemies
16: 2 Don't wait **u** I get there and then try to collect it all
16: 8 I will be staying here at Ephesus **u** the Festival of
Gal 1:18 It was not **u** three years later that I finally went to
3:19 But this system of law was to last only **u** the
3:23 **U** faith in Christ was shown to us as the way of
3:23 **u** we could put our faith in the coming Savior.
3:24 our guardian and teacher to lead us **u** Christ came.
4: 1 those children are not much better off than slaves **u**
4: 2 They have to obey their guardians **u** they reach
4:19 and they will continue **u** Christ is fully developed
Eph 4:13 **u** we come to such unity in our faith
Php 1: 5 about Christ from the time you first heard it **u** now.
1: 6 will continue his work **u** it is finally finished on
1:10 may live pure and blameless lives **u** Christ returns.
1Th 5:23 and body be kept blameless **u** that day when our
2Th 2: 3 For that day will not come **u** there is a great
2: 7 and it will remain secret **u** the one who is holding
1Ti 4:13 **U** I get there, focus on reading the Scriptures to the
5:24 are others whose sin will not be revealed **u** later.
5:25 others whose good deeds won't be known **u** later.
6:14 Then no one can find fault with you from now **u**
2Ti 1:12 I have entrusted to him **u** the day of his return.
1:17 to Rome, he searched everywhere **u** he found me.
Heb 1:13 honor at my right hand / **u** I humble your enemies,
9:10 external regulations that are in effect only **u** their
9:16 no one gets anything **u** it is proved that the person

10:13 There he waits **u** his enemies are humbled as a
11:40 the prize at the end of the race **u** we finish the race.
1Pe 1: 5 will protect you **u** you receive this salvation,
2Pe 1:19 **u** the day Christ appears and his brilliant light
2: 4 in gloomy caves and darkness **u** the judgment day.
2: 9 even while punishing the wicked right up **u** the day
Rev 2:25 except that you hold tightly to what you have **u** I
6:11 And they were told to rest a little longer **u** the full
7: 3 or the trees **u** we have placed the seal of God on
15: 8 No one could enter the Temple **u** the seven angels
20: 3 so Satan could not deceive the nations anymore **u**
20: 5 (The rest of the dead did not come back to life **u**

UNTIMELY [KJV] See (BORN) DEAD, GREEN, STILLBORN

UNTOWARD [KJV] See (GONE) ASTRAY

UNTRUE (1)
Hos 1: 2 This will illustrate the way my people have been **u**

UNTRUSTWORTHY (1)
Lk 16:11 And if you are **u** about worldly wealth, who will

UNTYING (4) [UNTIE]
Mk 11: 5 As they were **u** it, some bystanders demanded,
11: 5 "What are you doing, **u** that colt?"
Lk 19:33 And sure enough, as they were **u** it, the owners asked them, "Why are you **u** our colt?"

UNUSUAL (9) [UNUSUALLY]
2Sa 11: 2 he noticed a woman of **u** beauty taking a bath.
2Ki 16:10 While he was there, he noticed an **u** altar. So he
1Ch 26:14 assigned to his son Zechariah, a man of **u** wisdom.
Isa 28:21 He will come to do a strange, **u** thing: He will
Da 1:17 God gave these four young men an **u** aptitude for
Ac 7:10 God also gave Joseph **u** wisdom so that Pharaoh
19:11 God gave Paul the power to do **u** miracles,
Ro 11:24 you into his own good tree—a very **u** thing to do—
Heb 11:23 They saw that God had given them an **u** child,

UNUSUALLY (2) [UNUSUAL]
Ge 13:13 The people of this area were **u** wicked and sinned
Pr 30:24 are four things on earth that are small but **u** wise:

UNWALLED (3)
Dt 3: 5 We also took many **u** villages at the same time.
Est 9:19 rural Jews living in **u** villages celebrate an annual
Eze 38:11 'Israel is an unprotected land filled with **u** villages!

UNWANTED (2)
Jer 48:38 For I have smashed Moab like an old, **u** bottle.
Eze 16: 5 you were dumped in a field and left to die, **u**.

UNWASHED (2)
Pr 30:12 They feel pure, but they are filthy and **u**.
Mt 15:20 Eating with **u** hands could never defile you

UNWILLING (2)
Ge 24: 8 If she is **u** to come back with you, then you are free
Jos 24:15 But if you are **u** to serve the LORD, then choose

UNWORTHILY (2) [UNWORTHY]
1Co 11:27 eats this bread or drinks this cup of the Lord **u**,
11:29 For if you eat the bread or drink the cup **u**,

UNWORTHY (1) [UNWORTHILY]
Ac 13:46 rejected it and judged yourselves **u** of eternal life—

UNWRAP (1)
Jn 11:44 Jesus told them, "**U** him and let him go!"

UNYIELDING (2)
Lev 26:19 spirit by making the skies above as **u** as iron
Dt 28:23 The skies above will be as **u** as bronze,

UP (1388) [UPPER, UPWARD] See Index of Articles, Etc.

UPBRAID(ED), UPBRAIDETH [KJV] See DENOUNCE, TAUNTED, REBUKED, RESENT

UPHARSIN [KJV] See PARSIN

UPHAZ (1)
Jer 10: 9 sheets of silver from Tarshish and gold from **U**,

UPHELD (3) [UPHOLD]
2Sa 22:19 when I was weakest, / but the LORD **u** me.
Job 36:17 on the godless. Don't worry, justice will be **u**.
Ps 18:18 when I was weakest, / but the LORD **u** me.

UPHOLD (9) [UPHELD]
1Ki 8:45 hear their prayers from heaven and **u** their cause.
8:49 prayers from heaven where you live. **U** their cause
8:59 so that the LORD our God may **u** my cause
2Ch 6:35 hear their prayers from heaven and **u** their cause.
6:39 **U** their cause and forgive your people who have
Ps 82: 3 **u** the rights of the oppressed and the destitute.
Isa 41:10 I will **u** you with my victorious right hand.
Jer 4: 2 and begin to live good, honest lives and **u** justice,
Zep 2: 3 all you who are humble, all you who **u** justice.

UPHOLSTERED (1)
SS 3:10 its canopy is gold, and its seat is **u** in purple cloth.

UPON (269) See Index of Articles, Etc.

UPPER (38) [UP]
Ge 6:16 bottom, middle, and **u**—and put a door in the side.
Ex 17:11 his hands, the Amalekites gained the **u** hand.
Dt 24: 6 or even just the **u** millstone, as a pledge,
28:13 not the tail, and you will always have the **u** hand.
Jos 15:19 So Caleb gave her the **u** and lower springs.
16: 5 From there it ran to **U** Beth-horon,
Jdg 1:15 So Caleb gave her the **u** and lower springs.
1Ki 17:19 carried him up to the **u** room, where he lived,
17:23 Then Elijah brought him down from the **u** room
2Ki 1: 2 fell through the latticework of an **u** room at his
15:35 He was the one who rebuilt the **u** gate of the
18:17 the aqueduct that feeds water into the **u** pool,
23:12 built on the palace roof above the **u** room of Ahaz.
1Ch 7:24 of Lower and **U** Beth-horon and Uzzen-sheerah.
2Ch 3: 9 The walls of the **u** rooms were also overlaid with
8: 5 He fortified the cities of **U** Beth-horon and Lower
23:20 They went through the **U** Gate and into the palace,
27: 3 Jotham rebuilt the **U** Gate to the LORD's Temple
32:30 He blocked up the **u** spring of Gihon and brought
32:33 he was buried in the **u** area of the royal cemetery,
Ne 3:25 and the corner to the **u** tower that projects from the
3:31 Then he continued as far as the **u** room at the
Ps 13: 2 How long will my enemy have the **u** hand?
Isa 7: 3 of the aqueduct that feeds water into the **u** pool,
7:18 the LORD will whistle for the army of **U** Egypt
11:11 **U** Egypt, Ethiopia, Elam, Babylonia, Hamath,
36: 2 the aqueduct that feeds water into the **u** pool,
Jer 36:10 This room was just off the **u** courtyard of the
Eze 9: 2 Six men soon appeared from the **u** gate that faces
42: 5 Each of the two **u** levels of rooms was narrower
42: 5 because the **u** levels had to allow space for
42: 6 each of the **u** levels was set back from the level
43:14 From the lower ledge the altar rises 7 feet to the **u** ledge; this **u** ledge is also 21 inches wide.
43:17 The **u** ledge also forms a square, measuring 24-1/2
43:20 the four corners of the **u** ledge, and the curb that
45:19 the four corners of the **u** ledge on the altar,
Am 9: 6 The **u** stories of the LORD's home are in the

UPPERMOST [KJV] See HEAD, HIGHEST, HONOR, TOP

UPRAISED (4) [RISE]
Ps 141: 2 to you, / and my **u** hands as an evening offering.
Isa 19:16 They will cower in fear beneath the **u** fist of the
26:11 when you threaten. / They do not see your **u** fist.
Na 3: 3 and glittering spears in the **u** arms of the cavalry!

UPRIGHT (23)
Ge 28:18 used as a pillow and set it **u** as a memorial pillar.
Dt 9: 5 **u** people that you are about to occupy their land.
32: 4 God who does no wrong; / how just and **u** he is!
Job 4: 6 you believe that God will care for those who are **u**?
4: 7 When has the **u** person been destroyed?
4:17 'Can a mortal be just and **u** before God? Can a
17: 8 The **u** are astonished when they see me.
33:23 to intercede for a person, to declare that he is **u**,
Ps 94:15 and those who are **u** will have a reward.
Pr 2:21 For only the **u** will live in the land, and those who
3:33 but his blessing is on the home of the **u**.
10:29 The LORD protects the **u** but destroys the
11:11 **U** citizens bless a city and make it prosper,
15: 8 the wicked, but he delights in the prayers of the **u**.
15:19 trouble all through life; the path of the **u** is easy!
16:17 The path of the **u** leads away from evil;
21:18 to save the godly, and the treacherous for the **u**.
21:29 put up a bold front, but the **u** proceed with care.
28:10 Those who lead the **u** into sin will fall into their
29:10 hate the honest, but the **u** seek out the honest.
Ecc 7:28 thousand men I interviewed can be said to be **u**,
7:29 I discovered that God created people to be **u**,
Mt 23:28 You try to look like **u** people outwardly, but inside

UPRISING (1) [RISE]
Da 11:14 At that time there will be a general **u** against the

UPROAR (7)
1Ki 1:41 "What's going on? Why is the city in such an **u**?"
Ps 46: 6 The nations are in an **u**, / and kingdoms crumble!
74:23 have said. / Their **u** of rebellion grows ever louder.
Isa 22: 2 The whole city is in a terrible **u**. What do I see in
Ac 16:20 "The whole city is in an **u** because of these
21:31 the Roman regiment that all Jerusalem was in an **u**.
21:34 He couldn't find out the truth in all the **u**

UPROOT (10) [UPROOTED]
1Ki 9: 7 then I will **u** the people of Israel from this land I
14:15 He will **u** the people of Israel from this good land
2Ch 7:20 then I will **u** the people of Israel from this land of
Jer 1:10 You are to **u** some and tear them down, to destroy
12:14 I will **u** them from their lands just as Judah will be
24: 6 tear them down. I will plant them and not **u** them.
42:10 not tear you down; I will plant you and not **u** you.
45: 4 this nation that I built. I will **u** what I planted.
Am 9: 8 and I will **u** it and scatter its people across the
Lk 17: 6 'May God **u** you and throw you into the sea,'

UPROOTED (11) [UPROOT]
Dt 29:28 and fury the LORD **u** his people from their land
Job 8:18 But when it is **u**, it isn't even missed!
31: 8 I have planted, and let all that I have planted be **u**.
Ps 9: 6 Even the memory of their **u** cities is lost.
Jer 12:14 from their lands just as Judah will be **u** from hers.
12:17 But any nation who refuses to obey me will be **u**
18: 7 that a certain nation or kingdom is to be **u**,
31:28 In the past I **u** and tore down this nation.
Eze 19:12 But the vine was **u** in fury / and thrown down to
Da 11: 4 For his empire will be **u** and given to others.
Am 9:15 your God. "Then they will never be **u** again."

UPSET (17)
Ge 21:11 This **u** Abraham very much because Ishmael was
21:12 "Do not be **u** over the boy and your servant wife.
48:17 But Joseph was **u** when he saw that his father had
Ex 32:22 "Don't get **u**, sir," Aaron replied. "You yourself
1Sa 8: 6 Samuel was very **u** with their request and went to
29: 7 Please don't **u** them, but go back quietly."
2Sa 13:20 Well, don't be so **u**. Since he's your brother
1Ki 21: 5 has made you so **u** that you are not eating?"
2Ki 5: 8 "Why are you so **u**? Send Naaman to me, and he
6:11 The king of Aram became very **u** over this.
Ne 13: 8 I became very **u** and threw all of Tobiah's
Jer 19: 7 For I will **u** the battle plans of Judah and Jerusalem
Jnh 4: 1 This change of plans **u** Jonah, and he became very
Mt 18:31 of the other servants saw this, they were very **u**.
Lk 10:41 dear Martha, you are so **u** over all these details!
Ac 15:24 have troubled you and **u** you with their teaching,
Ro 16:17 and **u** people's faith by teaching things that are

UPSIDE (4)
2Ki 21:13 Jerusalem as one wipes a dish and turns it **u** down.
Pr 2:14 and they enjoy evil as it turns things **u** down.
Jer 23:36 turning **u** down the words of our God, the living
Ac 17: 6 and Silas have turned the rest of the world **u** down,

UPSTAIRS (12) [STAIRS]
Jdg 3:20 to Eglon as he was sitting alone in a cool **u** room
3:24 and found the doors to the **u** room locked.
1Ch 28:11 the treasuries, the **u** rooms, the inner rooms,
Da 6:10 went home and knelt down as usual in his **u** room,
Mk 14:15 He will take you **u** to a large room that is already
Lk 22:12 He will take you **u** to a large room that is already
22:39 Jesus left the **u** room and went as usual to the
Ac 1:13 Then they went to the **u** room of the house where
9:37 prepared her for burial and laid her in an **u** room.
9:39 as soon as he arrived, they took him to the **u** room.
20: 8 The **u** room where we met was lighted with many
20:11 Then they all went back **u** and ate the Lord's

UPSTREAM (2) [STREAM]
Jos 3:13 touch the water, the flow of water will be cut off **u**,
3:16 the water began piling up at a town **u** called Adam,

UPWARD (7) [UP]
Jdg 1:36 Scorpion Pass to Sela and continued **u** from there.
2Ch 3:15 each topped by a capital extending **u** another 7-1/2
Job 5: 7 trouble as predictably as sparks fly **u** from a fire.
Ecc 3:21 For who can prove that the human spirit goes **u**
Eze 1:19 When they flew **u**, the wheels went up, too.
10:15 Then the cherubim rose **u**. These were the same
Ac 7:55 gazed steadily **u** into heaven and saw the glory of

UR (5)
Ge 11:28 he died in **U** of the Chaldeans, the place of his
11:31 and left **U** of the Chaldeans to go to the land of
15: 7 "I am the LORD who brought you out of **U** of
1Ch 11:35 son of Sharar from Harar; / Eliphal son of **U**;
Ne 9: 7 and brought him from **U** of the Chaldeans

URBANUS (1)
Ro 16: 9 and **U**, our co-worker in Christ, and beloved

URGE (12) [URGED, URGES, URGING]
2Sa 17:16 and **u** him not to stay at the shallows of the Jordan
Est 4: 8 and to **u** her to go to the king to beg for mercy
Lk 14:23 behind the hedges and **u** anyone you find to come,
Ro 15:30 I **u** you in the name of our Lord Jesus Christ to join
1Co 16:15 other Christians. I **u** you, dear brothers and sisters,
2Co 5:20 We **u** you, as though Christ himself were here
1Th 4: 1 we **u** you in the name of the Lord Jesus to live in a
5:14 and sisters, we **u** you to warn those who are lazy.
1Ti 2: 1 I **u** you, first of all, to pray for all people. As you
2Ti 4: 1 And so I solemnly **u** you before God and before
Heb 13:22 I **u** you, dear friends, please listen carefully to what
2Jn 1: 5 And now I want to **u** you, dear lady, that we should

URGED (25) [URGE]
Ex 12:33 All the Egyptians **u** the people of Israel to get out
Jos 10: 4 "Come and help me destroy Gibeon," he **u** them,
15:18 she **u** him to ask her father for an additional field.
Jdg 1:14 she **u** him to ask her father for an additional field.
19: 4 Her father **u** him to stay awhile, so he stayed three

1Sa 19: 1 Saul now **u** his servants and his son Jonathan to
28:23 The men who were with him also **u** him to eat,
2Sa 14:12 of you!" she said. "Go ahead," he **u**. "Speak!"
15:14 or it will be too late!" David **u** his men. "Hurry!
17: 1 Now Ahithophel **u** Absalom, "Let me choose
18: 3 "You must not go," they **u**. "If we have to turn
2Ki 5:16 And though Naaman **u** him to take the gifts,
Est 8:14 So **u** on by the king's command, the messengers
Jer 17:16 I have not **u** you to send disaster. It is your
Da 2:18 He **u** them to ask the God of heaven to show them
Mt 15:23 a word. Then his disciples **u** him to send her away.
Jn 7: 3 and Jesus' brothers **u** him to go to Judea for the
Ac 13: 8 and **u** the governor to pay no attention to what Saul
13:43 and Barnabas, and the two men **u** them,
16:15 and stay at my home." And she **u** us until we did.
1Co 16:12 I **u** him to visit you along with the other believers,
2Co 8: 6 So we have **u** Titus, who encouraged your giving
12:18 When I **u** Titus to visit you and sent our other
1Th 2:12 and **u** you to live your lives in a way that God
1Ti 1: 3 I **u** you to stay there in Ephesus and stop those who

URGENCY (1) [URGENT]

1Co 7:37 and there is no **u** and he can control his passion,

URGENT (6) [URGENCY, URGENTLY]

Nu 22:37 "Did I not send you an **u** invitation? Why didn't
Jos 11: 1 he sent **u** messages to the following kings:
1Sa 21: 8 so **u** that I didn't even have time to grab a
23:27 an **u** message reached Saul that the Philistines
Ps 86: 6 closely to my prayer, O LORD; / hear my **u** cry.
Tit 3:14 to do good by helping others who have **u** needs.

URGENTLY (2) [URGENT]

Ex 9:27 Then Pharaoh **u** sent for Moses and Aaron.
Nu 22: 7 and **u** explained to him what Balak wanted.

URGES (4) [URGE]

Job 32:18 full of words, and the spirit within me **u** me on.
Pr 9: 4 "Come home with me," she **u** the simple.
9:16 "Come home with me," she **u** the simple.
Ro 8:12 to do what your sinful nature **u** you to do.

URGING (7) [URGE]

Jdg 19: 7 but his father-in-law kept **u** him to stay, so he
Ru 1:18 up her mind to go with her, she stopped **u** her.
2Ki 2:17 But they kept **u** him until he was embarrassed,
Mt 14: 8 At her mother's **u**, the girl asked, "I want the head
Jn 4:31 Meanwhile, the disciples were **u** Jesus to eat.
Ac 2:40 for a long time, strongly **u** all his listeners,
Jude 1: 3 **u** you to defend the truth of the Good News.

URI (8)

Ex 31: 2 "Look, I have chosen Bezalel son of **U**,
35:30 "The LORD has chosen Bezalel son of **U**,
38:22 Bezalel son of **U**, grandson of Hur, of the tribe of
1Ki 4:19 Geber son of **U**, in the land of Gilead,
1Ch 2:20 Hur was the father of **U**. **U** was the father of Bezalel.
2Ch 1: 5 But the bronze altar made by Bezalel son of **U**
Ezr 10:24 who were guilty: Shallum, Telem, and **U**.

URIAH (34) [URIAH'S]

2Sa 11: 3 daughter of Eliam and the wife of **U** the Hittite."
11: 6 David sent word to Joab: "Send me **U** the Hittite."
11: 7 When **U** arrived, David asked him how Joab
11: 8 Then he told **U**, "Go on home and relax."
11: 8 David even sent a gift to **U** after he had left the
11: 9 But **U** wouldn't go home. He stayed that night at
11:10 When David heard what **U** had done,
11:11 **U** replied, "The Ark and the armies of Israel
11:12 So **U** stayed in Jerusalem that day and the next.
11:13 then he couldn't get **U** to go home to his wife.
11:14 wrote a letter to Joab and gave it to **U** to deliver.
11:15 "Station **U** on the front lines where the battle is
11:16 So Joab assigned **U** to a spot close to the city wall
11:17 And **U** was killed along with several other Israelite
11:21 Then tell him, '**U** the Hittite was killed, too.' "
11:24 of our men were killed, including **U** the Hittite."
12: 9 For you have murdered **U** and stolen his wife.
23:39 **U** the Hittite. There were thirty-seven in all.
1Ki 15: 5 except in the affair concerning **U** the Hittite.
2Ki 16:10 So he sent a model of the altar to **U** the priest,
16:11 **U** built an altar just like it by following the king's
16:15 He said to **U** the priest, "Use the new altar for the
16:16 **U** the priest did just as King Ahaz instructed him.
1Ch 11:41 **U** the Hittite; / Zabad son of Ahlai;
Ezr 8:33 and entrusted to Meremoth son of **U** the priest
Ne 3: 4 Meremoth son of **U** and grandson of Hakkoz
3:21 Meremoth son of **U** and grandson of Hakkoz
8: 4 Shema, Anaiah, **U**, Hilkiah, and Maaseiah.
Isa 8: 2 I asked **U** the priest and Zechariah son of
Jer 26:20 **U** son of Shemaiah from Kiriath-jearim was also
26:21 But **U** heard about the plot and escaped to Egypt.
26:22 Egypt along with several other men to capture **U**.
26:23 The king then killed **U** with a sword and had him
Mt 1: 6 (his mother was Bathsheba, the widow of **U**).

URIAH'S (1) [URIAH]

2Sa 12:10 because you have despised me by taking **U** wife to

URIAS, URIJAH [KJV] See URIAH

URIEL (4)

1Ch 6:24 Tahath, **U**, Uzziah, and Shaul.
15: 5 from the clan of Kohath, with **U** as their leader.
15:11 **U**, Asaiah, Joel, Shemaiah, Eliel, and Amminadab.
2Ch 13: 2 mother was Maacah, a daughter of **U** from Gibeah.

URIM (2)

Ex 28:30 Insert into the pocket of the chestpiece the **U**
Lev 8: 8 and put the **U** and the Thummim inside it.

URINE (2)

2Ki 18:27 will eat their own dung and drink their own **u**."
Isa 36:12 will eat their own dung and drink their own **u**."

US (1594) [WE] See Index of Articles, Etc.

USE (160) [USED, USEFUL, USELESS, USES, USING]

Ge 11: 3 and collect natural asphalt to **u** as mortar.
37:35 His family all tried to comfort him, but it was no **u**.
47:24 and **u** it to plant the next year's crop and to feed
48:20 "The people of Israel will **u** your names to bless
Ex 13: 3 (Remember, you are not to **u** any yeast.)
14:16 **U** your shepherd's staff—hold it out over the
20:25 If you build altars from stone, **u** only uncut stones.
20:25 a tool, for that would make them unfit for holy **u**.
25:18 Then **u** hammered gold to make two cherubim,
28:15 **U** the same materials as you did for the ephod:
30:16 **U** this money for the care of the Tabernacle.
30:26 **U** this scented oil to anoint the Tabernacle, the Ark
30:30 **U** this oil also to anoint Aaron and his sons,
40:30 so the priests could **u** it to wash themselves.
Lev 2:11 "Do not **u** yeast in any of the grain offerings you
3: 1 offering from the herd, **u** either a bull or a cow.
11: 2 to the Israelites: The animals you may **u** for food
11:32 that object, whatever its **u**, will be unclean.
19:12 "Do not **u** my name to swear a falsehood and
19:35 "Do not **u** dishonest standards when measuring
Nu 3:26 the cords, and all the equipment related to their **u**.
3:31 and all the equipment related to their **u**.
3:36 the bases, and all the equipment related to their **u**.
4:32 accessories, and everything else related to their **u**.
6: 3 They must not **u** vinegar made from wine,
7: 5 "Receive their gifts and **u** these oxen and carts for
19: 9 They will be kept there for the people of Israel to **u**
Dt 2: 6 Pay them for whatever food or water you **u**.
6:13 When you take an oath, you must **u** only his name.
7:19 The LORD your God will **u** this same power
14:26 **u** the money to buy anything you want—
15:19 Do not **u** the firstborn of your herds to work your
15:22 Instead, **u** it for food for your family at home.
20:20 **U** them to make the equipment you need to besiege
22: 9 you are forbidden to **u** either the grapes from the
25:13 "You must **u** accurate scales when you weigh out
25:14 and you must **u** full and honest measures.
25:15 Yes, **u** honest weights and measures, so that you
28:40 but you will never **u** the olive oil, for the trees will
Jos 4: 6 We will **u** these stones to build a memorial.
5: 2 "**U** knives of flint to make the Israelites a
22:23 Nor will we **u** it for our burnt offerings or grain
Jdg 6:36 "If you are truly going to **u** me to rescue Israel as
1Sa 8:16 the finest of your cattle and donkeys for his own **u**.
2Sa 7:14 If he sins, I will **u** other nations to punish him.
24:22 "Take it, my lord, and **u** it as you wish,"
24:22 and you can **u** the threshing tools and ox yokes for
1Ki 11: 8 for all his foreign wives to **u** for burning incense
12:11 father used whips on you, but I'll **u** scorpions!' "
12:14 father used whips on you, but I'll **u** scorpions!"
21: 2 I would like to buy it to **u** as a vegetable garden.
2Ki 12: 7 Don't **u** any more gifts for your own needs.
12:16 It was given to the priests for their own **u**.
16:15 "**U** the new altar for the morning sacrifices of
16:15 old bronze altar will be only for my personal **u**."
16:18 inside the palace for **u** on the Sabbath day,
22: 5 Then they can **u** it to pay workers to repair the
23:10 so no one could ever again **u** it to sacrifice a son
1Ch 21:23 "Take it, my lord, and **u** it as you wish,"
21:23 and you can **u** the threshing tools for wood to build
2Ch 10:11 father used whips on you, but I'll **u** scorpions!' "
10:14 father used whips on you, but I'll **u** scorpions!"
12: 7 I will not **u** Shishak to pour out my anger on
25: 5 and older, all trained in the **u** of spear and shield.
29:19 the altar of the LORD, purified and ready for **u**."
Ezr 7:25 are to **u** the wisdom God has given you to appoint
Ne 8:15 They were to **u** these branches to make shelters in
Est 7: 9 He intended to **u** it to hang Mordecai, the man who
Job 6:22 Have I begged you to **u** any of your wealth on my
9:29 I will be found guilty. So what's the **u** of trying?
35: 3 also ask, 'What's the **u** of living a righteous life?
Ps 60: 5 **U** your strong right arm to save us, / and rescue
76:10 your glory, / for you **u** it as a sword of judgment.
83:12 for they said, "Let us seize for our own **u**
88:10 Of what **u** to the dead are your miracles?
104:14 You cause plants to grow for people to **u**.
108: 6 **U** your strong right arm to save me, / and rescue
Pr 12:27 but the diligent make **u** of everything they find.
Ecc 6: 6 must die like everyone else—well, what's the **u**?
6:10 So there's no **u** arguing with God about your
SS 8:11 them pays one thousand pieces of silver for its **u**.
Isa 7:20 to protect you—and **u** it to shave off everything:
19: 8 and those who **u** nets will all be unemployed.
29:21 And those who **u** trickery to pervert justice and tell
32: 7 including all the lies they **u** to oppress the poor in
48:14 He will **u** him to put an end to the empire of
Jer 6:20 There is no **u** now in offering me sweet incense
23:38 even though I warned you not to **u** it,
44:26 None of you may invoke my name or **u** this oath:
Eze 4: 9 **U** this food to make bread for yourself during the
5: 1 and **u** it as a razor to shave your head and beard.
5: 1 **U** a scale to weigh the hair into three equal parts.
13:20 which you **u** to ensnare my people like birds.
21:21 He will call his magicians to **u** divination.
24: 5 **U** only the best sheep from the flock and heap fuel
39: 9 javelins and spears, and they will **u** them for fuel.
42:13 And they will **u** these rooms to store the grain
43:26 for the altar, thus setting it apart for holy **u**.
44: 5 of man, take careful notice; **u** your eyes and ears.
45: 4 They will **u** it for their homes, and my Temple will
45:10 You must **u** only honest weights and scales,
46: 9 came in; they must always **u** the opposite gateway.
48:15 sacred Temple area, will be allotted for public **u**—
Mic 1:13 **U** your swiftest chariots and flee, you people of
6:11 And how can I tolerate all your merchants who **u**
Zep 1:18 and gold will be of no **u** to you on that day of the
Zec 14:21 All who come to worship will be free to **u** any of
Mal 3:14 "You have said, 'What's the **u** of serving God?
Mt 7: 2 Whatever measure you **u** in judging others, it will
25:29 To those who **u** well what they are given,
26:52 "Those who **u** the sword will be killed by the
26:60 false witness, there was no testimony they could **u**.
Mk 4:30 of God? What story should I **u** to illustrate it?
5:35 is dead. There's no **u** troubling the Teacher now."
Lk 6:38 Whatever measure you **u** in giving—large
8:49 is dead. There's no **u** troubling the Teacher now."
10:17 even the demons obey us when we **u** your name!"
11:54 into saying something they could **u** against him.
12:26 what's the **u** of worrying over bigger things?
13: 7 It's taking up space we can **u** for something else.'
16: 9 **u** your worldly resources to benefit others
19:26 'but to those who **u** well what they are given,
Jn 8: 6 into saying something they could **u** against him,
10: 6 Those who heard Jesus **u** this illustration didn't
12: 6 and he often took some for his own **u**.
16:23 he will grant your request because you **u** my name.
Ac 19:13 evil spirits tried to **u** the name of the Lord Jesus.
20:24 But my life is worth nothing unless I **u** it for doing
Ro 6:13 And **u** your whole body as a tool to do what is
9:21 doesn't he have a right to **u** the same lump of clay
1Co 2: 1 when I first came to you I didn't **u** lofty words
2: 4 I did not **u** wise and persuasive speeches,
2:13 tell you this, we do not **u** words of human wisdom.
3:12 Now anyone who builds on that foundation may **u**
7:31 **u** of them without becoming attached to them,
2Co 7:10 For God can **u** sorrow in our lives to help us turn
10: 1 and kindness that Christ himself would **u**,
10: 4 We **u** God's mighty weapons, not mere worldly
13: 4 God's power—the power we **u** in dealing with you.
13:10 For I want to **u** the authority the Lord has given me
Gal 6:11 Notice what large letters I **u** as I write these
Eph 4:29 Don't **u** foul or abusive language. Let everything
6:13 **U** every piece of God's armor to resist the enemy
Php 3:21 using the same mighty power that he will **u** to
Col 2:22 about things that are gone as soon as we **u** them.
3:16 **U** his words to teach and counsel each other.
2Th 1: 5 But God will **u** this persecution to show his justice.
2:10 He will **u** every kind of wicked deception to fool
1Ti 1:16 so that Christ Jesus could **u** me as a prime example
3: 6 and the Devil will **u** that pride to make him fall.
6:18 Tell them to **u** their money to do good.
2Ti 2:20 and the cheap ones are for everyday **u**.
2:21 you will be a utensil God can **u** for his purpose.
2:21 and you will be ready for the Master to **u** you for
Phm 1:11 Onesimus hasn't been of much **u** to you in the past,
Heb 9: 8 and the entire system it represents were still in **u**.
9:17 no one can **u** the will to get any of the things
Jas 2:14 what's the **u** of saying you have faith if you don't
Rev 14:15 "**U** the sickle, for the time has come for you to
14:18 "**U** your sickle now to gather the clusters of grapes

USED (203) [USE]

Ge 11: 1 spoke a single language and **u** the same words.
28:18 He took the stone he had **u** as a pillow and set it
31: 5 against me and is not treating me like he **u** to,"
37:24 This pit was normally **u** to store water, but it was
43:21 The money we had **u** to pay for the grain was there
Ex 3:15 and it will be **u** throughout all generations.
7:22 But again the magicians of Egypt **u** their secret
14: 9 chariots, and charioteers—were **u** in the chase.
16:36 (The container **u** to measure the manna was an
17: 5 the one you **u** when you struck the water of the
25:27 These rings will support the poles **u** to carry the
25:29 and bowls to be **u** in pouring out drink offerings.
27:19 "All the articles **u** in the work of the Tabernacle,
27:19 including all the tent pegs **u** to support the
28:15 make a chestpiece that will be **u** to determine
28:30 Aaron will always carry the objects **u** to determine
29:31 "Take the ram **u** in the ordination ceremony,
29:33 and bread **u** for their atonement in the ordination
35:26 All the women who were willing **u** their skills to
35:27 and the other gemstones to be **u** for the ephod
36:34 The rings **u** to hold the crossbars were made of
37:16 These utensils were to be **u** in pouring out drink
38: 3 Then he made all the bronze utensils to be **u** with
38:16 All the curtains **u** in the courtyard walls were made
38:20 All the tent pegs **u** in the Tabernacle and courtyard
38:21 Here is an inventory of the materials **u** in building
38:24 all of which was **u** throughout the Tabernacle.
38:28 was **u** to make the rods and hooks and to overlay
38:30 which was **u** for casting the bases for the posts at
38:31 Bronze was also **u** to make the bases for the posts

38:31 and all the tent pegs **u** to hold the curtains of the
39: 1 This same cloth was **u** for Aaron's sacred
39:21 Blue cords were **u** to attach the bottom rings of the
39:40 all the articles **u** in the operation of the Tabernacle;
Lev 6:28 If a clay pot is **u** to boil the sacrificial meat, it must
6:28 If a bronze kettle is **u**, it must be scoured
7:24 be eaten, though it may be **u** for any other purpose.
11:32 it will be ceremonially clean and may be **u** again.
11:34 If the water **u** to cleanse an unclean object touches
14:22 One of the pair must be **u** for a sin offering
18: 3 where you **u** to live, or like the people of Canaan,
27: 3 here is the scale of values to be **u**. A man between
Nu 3:31 the altars, the various utensils **u** in the sanctuary,
10: 2 "Make two trumpets of beaten silver to be **u** for
11: 5 "We remember all the fish we **u** to eat for free in
16:38 because they were **u** in the LORD's presence.
16:39 that had been **u** by the men who died in the fire,
Dt 3:13 (The Argob region of Bashan **u** to be known as the
7:19 and the amazing power he **u** when he brought you
Jos 22:29 of the Tabernacle may be **u** for that purpose."
Jdg 9: 4 which he **u** to hire some soldiers who agreed to
16:11 up with brand-new ropes that have never been **u**,
1Sa 2:15 it had been boiled so that it could be **u** for roasting.
9: 9 ask the seer," for prophets **u** to be called seers.)
14:45 for he has been **u** of God to do a mighty miracle
17:39 go in these," he protested. "I'm not **u** to them."
17:51 David **u** it to kill the giant and cut off his head.
20:13 May the LORD be with you as he **u** to be with
2Sa 20:18 Then she continued, "There **u** to be a saying,
23: 8 He once **u** his spear to kill eight hundred enemy
23:18 He once **u** his spear to kill three hundred enemy
1Ki 6: 7 The stones **u** in the construction of the Temple
6:15 ceilings with cedar, and he **u** cypress for the floors.
7:11 The costly blocks of stone **u** in the walls were also
cut to measure, and cedar beams were also **u**.
10:12 The king **u** the almug wood to make railings for
12:11 My father **u** whips on you, but I'll use
12:14 My father **u** whips on you, but I'll use scorpions!"
15:22 Asa **u** these materials to fortify the town of Geba
17:16 For no matter how much they **u**, there was always
18:32 and he **u** the stones to rebuild the LORD's altar.
19:21 and **u** the wood from the plow to build a fire to
2Ki 3: 4 They **u** to pay the king of Israel an annual tribute
3:11 is here. He **u** to be Elijah's personal assistant."
10:26 They dragged out the sacred pillar **u** in the worship
10:27 a public toilet. That is what it is **u** for to this day.
12:11 who **u** it to pay the people working on the
12:12 They also **u** the money to buy timber and cut stone
12:13 The money brought to the Temple was not **u** for
12:14 to the workmen, who **u** it for the Temple repairs.
13:20 Groups of Moabite raiders **u** to invade the land
14:27 he **u** Jeroboam II, the son of Jehoash, to save them.
17:17 and **u** sorcery and sold themselves to evil,
18:15 King Hezekiah **u** all the silver stored in the Temple
21:13 I will judge Jerusalem by the same standard I **u** for
21:13 and by the same measure I **u** for the family of
23: 4 all the utensils that were **u** to worship Baal,
25:14 and all the other bronze utensils **u** for making
1Ch 9:28 to care for the various utensils **u** in worship.
9:31 was entrusted with baking the bread **u** in the
11: 4 went to Jerusalem (or Jebus, as it **u** to be called),
11:11 He once **u** his spear to kill three hundred enemy
11:20 He once **u** his spear to kill three hundred enemy
14:11 "He **u** me to burst through my enemies like a
16:42 They **u** their trumpets, cymbals, and other
18: 8 melted the bronze and **u** it for the Temple.
18: 8 and the various bronze utensils **u** at the Temple.
28:13 LORD's Temple which were to be **u** for worship
28:14 and silver should be **u** to make the necessary items.
28:15 and lamps, depending on how each would be **u**.
28:17 gold meat hooks **u** to handle the sacrificial meat
29: 4 and over 262 tons of refined silver to be **u** for
2Ch 3: 9 They **u** gold nails that weighed about twenty
3:16 and **u** them to decorate the tops of the pillars.
4: 6 The priests **u** the Sea itself, and not the basins,
4:18 Such great quantities of bronze were **u** that its
9:11 The king **u** the almug wood to make steps for the
10:11 My father **u** whips on you, but I'll use
10:14 My father **u** whips on you, but I'll use scorpions!"
16: 6 Asa **u** these materials to fortify the towns of Geba
24: 7 and they had **u** all the dedicated things from the
24:14 It was **u** to make utensils for the Temple of the
36:18 large and small, **u** in the Temple of God,
Ezr 6: 3 It must be rebuilt on the site where Jews **u** to offer
7:17 These donations are to be **u** specifically for the
7:18 Any money that is left over may be **u** in whatever
Ne 8:16 and **u** them to build shelters on the roofs of their
12:36 They **u** the musical instruments prescribed by
13: 5 The room had previously been **u** for storing the
Ps 42: 4 heart is breaking / as I remember how it **u** to be:
119:67 I **u** to wander off until you disciplined me;
119:93 for you have **u** them to restore my joy and health.
129: 4 he has cut the cords **u** by the ungodly to bind me.
Isa 1:26 and wise counselors like the ones you **u** to have.
10:12 After the Lord has **u** the king of Assyria to
16: 8 The wine from those vineyards **u** to make the
23:18 not be hoarded but will be **u** to provide good food
27:11 and **u** for kindling beneath the cooking pots.
28:27 A heavy sledge is never **u** on dill; rather, it is
34: 6 It is covered with fat as though it had been **u** for
44:19 and **u** it to bake my bread and roast my meat.
63:15 and the might you **u** to show on our behalf?
Jer 23:38 Because you have **u** this phrase, "prophecy from
35: 4 This room was located next to the one **u** by the
48:14 "You **u** to boast, 'We are heroes, mighty men of
51:26 Even your stones will never again be **u** for
52:18 and all the other bronze utensils **u** for making
52:19 lampstands, dishes, bowls **u** for drink offerings,
La 2: 4 His strength is **u** against them to kill their finest
Eze 7:20 and **u** it to make vile and detestable idols.
15: 3 Can its wood be **u** for making things, like pegs to
15: 4 No, it can only be **u** for fuel, and even as fuel,
16:16 You **u** the lovely things I gave you to make shrines
16:18 You **u** the beautifully embroidered clothes I gave
16:18 Then you **u** my oil and incense to worship them.
36:34 The fields that **u** to lie empty and desolate—
46:24 "These are the kitchens to be **u** by the Temple
48:14 land will ever be sold or traded or **u** by others,
Da 10: 3 had drunk no wine, and had **u** no fragrant oils.
Hos 2: 8 and silver she **u** in worshiping the god Baal were
Am 6:12 Can oxen be **u** to plow rocks? Stupid even to ask—
Mic 6:12 so **u** to lying that their tongues can no longer tell
Zep 1: 6 And I will destroy those who **u** to worship me
Zec 9:10 and I will destroy all the weapons **u** in battle.
14:20 will be as sacred as the basins **u** beside the altar.
Mt 7: 2 it will be **u** to measure how you are judged.
13:31 Here is another illustration Jesus **u**:
13:33 Jesus also **u** this illustration: "The Kingdom of
Heaven is like yeast **u** by a
13:33 Even though she **u** a large amount of flour,
13:34 Jesus always **u** stories and illustrations like these
22:19 Here, show me the Roman coin **u** for the tax."
25:19 to give an account of how they had **u** his money.
Mk 4:33 He **u** many such stories and illustrations to teach
Lk 1: 2 They **u** as their source material the reports
1:36 People **u** to say she was barren, but she's already
3:18 John **u** many such warnings as he announced the
6:38 it will be **u** to measure what is given back to you."
11: 5 them more about prayer, he **u** this illustration:
13: 6 Then Jesus **u** this illustration: "A man planted a
13:21 It is like yeast **u** by a woman making bread.
13:21 Even though she **u** a large amount of flour,
15: 3 So Jesus **u** this illustration:
Jn 2: 6 they were **u** for Jewish ceremonial purposes
19:41 where there was a new tomb, never **u** before.
Ac 7:45 And it was **u** there until the time of King David.
8:35 then **u** many others to tell him the Good News
19:13 The incantation they **u** was this: "I command you
26: 9 "I **u** to believe that I ought to do everything I
Ro 6:13 become a tool of wickedness, to be **u** for sinning.
6:21 since now you are ashamed of the things you **u** to
7:11 the good law and **u** it to make me guilty of death.
7:13 Sin **u** what was good to bring about my
1Co 1:21 he has **u** our foolish preaching to save all who
1:28 and **u** them to bring to nothing what the world
4: 6 I have **u** Apollos and myself to illustrate what I've
9:12 to be supported? Yet we have never **u** this right.
9:15 Yet I have never **u** any of these rights. And I am
2Co 5:14 that we have all died to the old life we **u** to live.
Gal 1:23 "The one who **u** to persecute us now preaches the
3: 1 For you **u** to see the meaning of Jesus Christ's
Eph 2: 2 You **u** to live just like the rest of the world, full of
2: 3 All of us **u** to live that way, following the passions
2:11 Don't forget that you Gentiles **u** to be outsiders by
2:14 He has broken down the wall of hostility that **u** to
Col 3: 7 You **u** to do them when your life was still part of
1Ti 1: 8 We know these laws are good when they are **u** as
1:13 even though I **u** to scoff at the name of Christ.
2Ti 2:20 The expensive utensils are **u** for special occasions,
Heb 9:21 on the sacred tent and on everything **u** for worship.
2Pe 3: 6 Then he **u** the water to destroy the world with a
Rev 21:17 and found them to be 216 feet thick (the angel **u** a
22: 2 The leaves were **u** for medicine to heal the nations.

USEFUL (9) [USE]

Ps 60: T A psalm of David **u** for teaching,
Jer 4:11 It is not a gentle breeze **u** for winnowing grain.
Eze 15: 2 a tree? Is a vine's wood as **u** as the wood of a tree?
Mt 5:13 Can you make it **u** again? It will be thrown out
1Co 14: 5 a greater and more **u** gift than speaking in tongues,
14:26 But everything that is done must be **u** to all
2Ti 3:16 is inspired by God and is **u** to teach us what is true
Phm 1:11 you in the past, but now he is very **u** to both of us.
2Pe 1: 8 and **u** in your knowledge of our Lord Jesus Christ.

USELESS (44) [USE]

Dt 32:21 they have provoked my fury with **u** idols.
1Sa 12:21 that cannot help or rescue you—they really are **u**!
Job 27:12 all this; yet you are saying all these **u** things to me.
41: 9 "No, it is **u** to try to capture it. The hunter who
Ps 58: 7 Make their weapons **u** in their hands.
60:11 us against our enemies, / for all human help is **u**.
78:57 had been. / They were as **u** as a crooked bow.
89:43 You have made his sword **u** / and have refused to
108:12 us against our enemies, / for all human help is **u**.
127: 1 builds a house, / the work of the builders is **u**.
127: 2 It is **u** for you to work so hard / from early
129: 6 May they be as **u** as grass on a rooftop,
Isa 22:18 your glorious chariots will remain, broken and **u**.
33:23 sails hang loose on broken masts with **u** tackle.
47:14 But they are as **u** as dried grass burning in a fire.
49: 4 I replied, "But my work all seems so **u**! I have
Jer 13: 7 it was mildewed and falling apart. The belt was **u**.
21: 4 I will make your weapons **u** against the king of
Eze 15: 5 Vine branches are **u** both before and after being
15: 6 Since they are **u**, I have set them aside to be
22:18 a **u** mixture of copper, tin, iron, and lead.
30:25 while the arms of Pharaoh fall **u** to his sides.
Hab 1: 4 The law has become paralyzed and **u**, and there is
Zec 11:17 His arm will become **u**, and his right eye
Mt 25:30 Now throw this **u** servant into outer darkness,
Jn 15: 6 who parts from me is thrown away like a **u** branch
Ro 4:14 in God's sight, then you are saying that faith is **u**.
1Co 1:20 and has shown their wisdom to be **u** nonsense.
15:14 if Christ was not raised, then all our preaching is **u**,
and your trust in God is **u**.
15:17 if Christ has not been raised, then your faith is **u**,
15:58 know that nothing you do for the Lord is ever **u**.
Gal 2: 2 not disagree, or my ministry would have been **u**.
4: 9 to the weak and **u** spiritual powers of this world?
Php 2:16 I did not lose the race and that my work was not **u**.
1Th 3: 5 the best of you and that all our work had been **u**.
2Ti 2:14 Such arguments are **u**, and they can ruin those who
Tit 1:10 they engage in **u** talk and deceive people.
3: 9 These kinds of things are **u** and a waste of time.
Heb 6: 8 But if a field bears thistles and thorns, it is **u**.
7:18 was set aside because it was weak and **u**.
Jas 2:17 by good deeds is no faith at all—it is dead and **u**.
2:20 that faith that does not result in good deeds is **u**?
2Pe 2:17 These people are as **u** as dried-up springs of water

USES (8) [USE]

Ge 44: 5 drinking cup, which he **u** to predict the future?
Dt 24: 6 as a pledge, for the owner **u** it to make a living.
Pr 17:27 A truly wise person **u** few words; a person with
Isa 10:15 ax boast greater power than the person who **u** it?
44:15 he **u** part of the wood to make a fire to warm
Lk 5:36 a new garment and **u** it to patch an old garment.
Ro 7:13 It **u** God's good commandment for its own evil
2Co 2:14 Now wherever we go he **u** us to tell others about

USHERED (1)

Lk 17:20 "The Kingdom of God isn't **u** in with visible

USING (47) [USE]

Ge 26:18 **u** the names Abraham had given them.
Ex 26:31 skillfully embroidered into the cloth **u** blue,
26:36 designs into it, **u** blue, purple, and scarlet yarn.
27: 1 "**U** acacia wood, make a square altar 7-1/2 feet
27:17 must be connected by silver rods, **u** silver hooks.
28:36 **U** the techniques of an engraver, inscribe it with
29: 2 Then **u** fine wheat flour and no yeast, make loaves
30:35 **U** the usual techniques of the incense maker,
37:16 Next, **u** pure gold, he made the plates, dishes,
37:17 made the lampstand, again **u** pure, hammered gold.
37:29 **u** the techniques of the most skilled incense maker.
39:30 **U** the techniques of an engraver, they inscribed it
Lev 14: 4 **u** two wild birds of a kind permitted for food,
24: 5 choice flour, **u** three quarts of flour for each loaf.
Nu 10: 7 blow the trumpets **u** a different signal.
Dt 27: 5 there to the LORD your God, **u** natural stones.
Jdg 3:24 They thought he might be **u** the latrine,
6:26 **u** as fuel the wood of the Asherah pole you cut
1Sa 14:13 So they climbed up **u** both hands and feet,
1Ki 15:22 and timbers that Baasha had been **u** to fortify
1Ch 29: 2 **U** every resource at my command, I have gathered
2Ch 16: 6 and timbers that Baasha had been **u** to fortify
Ne 4: 2 they are pulling out of the rubbish and **u** again!"
Job 19: 5 **u** my humiliation as evidence of my sin,
Jer 23:36 But stop **u** this phrase, 'prophecy from the
23:36 For people are **u** it to give authority to their own
Eze 4:12 bake it over a fire **u** dried human dung as fuel
4:14 must I be defiled by **u** human dung?
30:12 of Egypt and everything in it, **u** foreigners to do it.
Da 11: 2 **U** his wealth for political advantage, he will stir up
Am 7: 7 beside a wall that had been built **u** a plumb line.
Mic 7: 3 How skilled they are at **u** them! Officials
Mt 13:34 he never spoke to them without **u** such parables.
Mk 4:11 But I am **u** these stories to conceal everything
9:38 we saw a man **u** your name to cast out demons,
12:12 The Jewish leaders wanted to arrest him for **u** this
Lk 8:10 But I am **u** these stories to conceal everything
9:49 we saw someone **u** your name to cast out demons.
Jn 15:16 will give you whatever you ask for, **u** my name.
16:24 Ask, **u** my name, and you will receive, and you
Ac 18:28 **U** the Scriptures, he explained to them,
Ro 6:19 this way, **u** the illustration of slaves and masters,
1Co 2:13 **u** the Spirit's words to explain spiritual truths.
2Co 5:20 and God is **u** us to speak to you.
Eph 4:28 Begin **u** your hands for honest work, and then give
Php 3:21 **u** the same mighty power that he will use to
Heb 9:19 **u** branches of hyssop bushes and scarlet wool.

USUAL (26) [USUALLY]

Ge 38:19 off her veil, and put on her widow's clothing as **u**.
Ex 10:23 But there was light as **u** where the people of Israel
14:27 The water roared back into its **u** place,
16: 5 Tell them to pick up twice as much as **u** on the
16:22 there was twice as much as **u** on the ground—
18:13 Moses sat as **u** to hear the people's complaints
30:35 Using the **u** techniques of the incense maker,
Lev 7:12 the **u** animal sacrifice must be accompanied by
1Sa 3:15 and opened the doors of the Tabernacle as **u**.
20:25 He sat at his **u** place against the wall,
2Ch 29:35 of burnt offerings, along with the **u** drink offerings,
Jer 27:11 to stay in their own country to farm the land as **u**.
33:20 so that they do not come on their **u** schedule,
Da 3:19 the furnace be heated seven times hotter than **u**.
6:10 and knelt down as **u** in his upstairs room,
6:18 He refused his **u** entertainment and couldn't sleep
Mt 20:13 Didn't you agree to work all day for the **u** wage?
Mk 7: 2 the **u** Jewish ritual of hand washing before eating.
7:24 As **u**, the news of his arrival spread fast.
10: 1 there were the crowds, and as **u** he taught them.
15: 8 asking him to release a prisoner as **u**.
Lk 2:42 twelve years old, they attended the festival as **u**.
4:16 he went as **u** to the synagogue on the Sabbath
17:30 it will be 'business as **u**' right up to the hour when

22:39 and went as **u** to the Mount of Olives.
Ac 13:15 After the **u** readings from the books of Moses

USUALLY (1) [USUAL]
Jn 2:10 "**U** a host serves the best wine first," he said.

USURER [KJV] See MONEYLENDER

USURP [KJV] See HAVE

UTENSIL (2) [UTENSILS]
Lev 15:12 and every wooden **u** he touches must be rinsed
2Ti 2:21 you will be a **u** God can use for his purpose.

UTENSILS (59) [UTENSIL]
Ex 30:27 the table and all its **u**, the lampstand and all its
30:28 the altar of burnt offering with all its **u**,
31: 8 the table and all its **u**; the gold lampstand with all
31: 9 the altar of burnt offering with all its **u**;
35:13 the table, its carrying poles, and all of its **u**;
35:16 grating of the altar and its carrying poles and **u**;
37:16 These **u** were to be used in pouring out drink
38: 3 Then he made all the bronze **u** to be used with the
38:30 the bronze altar with its bronze grating and altar **u**.
39:36 the table and all its **u**; the Bread of the Presence;
39:39 bronze altar; the bronze grating; its poles and **u**;
40: 4 Then bring in the table, and arrange the **u** on it.
40:10 oil on the altar of burnt offering and its **u**,
Lev 8:11 anointing it and all its **u** and the washbasin and its
Nu 3:31 the altars, the various **u** used in the sanctuary,
4:10 The lampstand with its **u** must then be covered
4:12 All the remaining **u** of the sanctuary must be
4:14 All the altar **u**—the firepans, hooks, shovels,
4:15 covering the sanctuary and all the sacred **u**,
7: 1 with all its furnishings and the altar with its **u**.
1Ki 7:45 All these **u** for the Temple of the LORD that
7:47 Solomon did not weigh all the **u** because there
7:51 the silver, the gold, and the other **u**—
8: 4 along with the Tabernacle and all its sacred **u**,
10:21 as were all the **u** in the Palace of the Forest of
15:15 and gold and the **u** that he and his father had
2Ki 14:14 and all the **u** from the Temple of the LORD,
23: 4 Temple all the **u** that were used to worship Baal,
25:14 and all the other bronze **u** used for making
25:15 and all the other **u** made of pure gold or silver.
1Ch 9:28 assigned to care for the various **u** used in worship.
18: 8 and the various bronze **u** used at the Temple.
23:26 the Tabernacle and its **u** from place to place."
2Ch 4:16 the shovels, the meat hooks, and all the related **u**.
5: 1 including all the silver and gold and all the **u**.
5: 5 along with the special tent and all its sacred **u**.
9:20 as were all the **u** in the Palace of the Forest of
15:18 and gold and the **u** that he and his father had
24:14 It was used to make **u** for the Temple of the
24:14 **u** for worship services and for burnt offerings,
25:24 and all the **u** from the Temple of God that had been
28:24 The king took the **u** from the Temple of God
29:18 the altar of burnt offering with all its **u**,
29:18 the table of the Bread of the Presence with all its **u**.
29:19 We have also recovered all the **u** taken by King
36:18 The king also took home to Babylon all the **u**,
Ezr 5:14 and silver **u** that Nebuchadnezzar had taken from
5:15 The king instructed him to return the **u** to their
6: 5 And the gold and silver **u**, which were taken to
7:19 But as for the **u** we are entrusting to you for the
8:26 24 tons of silver, / 7,500 pounds of silver **u**,
Ne 13: 5 frankincense, Temple **u**, and tithes of grain,
13: 9 and I brought back the **u** for God's Temple,
Jer 27:16 **u** taken from my Temple will be returned from
27:18 gold **u** that are still left in the LORD's Temple
52:18 and all the other bronze **u** used for making
52:19 and all the other **u** made of pure gold or silver.
2Ti 2:20 In a wealthy home some **u** are made of gold
2:20 The expensive **u** are used for special occasions,

UTHAI (2)
1Ch 9: 4 One family that returned was that of **U** son of
Ezr 8:14 the family of Bigvai: **U**, Zaccur, and 70 other men.

UTMOST (1)
Ge 49:26 reaching to the **u** bounds of the everlasting hills.

UTTER (27) [UTTERED, UTTERING, UTTERLY]
Ge 45:11 and your household will come to **u** poverty.' "
Dt 29:19 my own stubborn way.' This would lead to **u** ruin!
Job 3: 5 let the darkness and **u** gloom claim it for its own.
10:21 I leave for the land of darkness and **u** gloom,
10:22 a land of **u** gloom where confusion reigns
38:17 are located? Have you seen the gates of **u** gloom?
Ps 115: 7 with their feet, / or **u** sounds with their throats!
119:51 The proud hold me in **u** contempt, / but I do not
136:23 He remembered our **u** weakness. / His faithful love
139:15 You watched me as I was being formed in **u**
Pr 5:14 I have come to the brink of **u** ruin, and now I must
6:32 But the man who commits adultery is an **u** fool,
SS 7: 6 you are, my beloved; how pleasant for **u** delight!
Isa 6:11 and the whole country is an **u** wasteland.
10:14 flap a wing against me or **u** a peep of protest."
15: 4 The bravest warriors of Moab will cry out in **u**
66:24 All who pass by will view them with **u** horror."
Jer 18:16 and shake their heads in amazement at its **u**
19: 9 and friends. They will be driven to **u** despair.'
La 4: 6 where **u** disaster struck in a moment with no one to
Eze 12:19 and sip their tiny portions of water in **u** despair,
36: 5 because they have shown **u** contempt for me by
Na 3: 7 back in horror and say, 'Nineveh lies in **u** ruin.'
Zep 2:15 But now, look how it has become an **u** ruin,
Mk 9:12 Man must suffer and be treated with **u** contempt?
Ro 1:22 Claiming to be wise, they became **u** fools instead.
9: 1 presence of Christ, I speak with **u** truthfulness—

UTTERED (2) [UTTER]
Ne 6:12 but that he had **u** this prophecy against me
Mk 15:37 Then Jesus **u** another loud cry and breathed his

UTTERING (1) [UTTER]
Ac 9: 1 Meanwhile, Saul was **u** threats with every breath.

UTTERLY (43) [UTTER]
Ge 19:25 He **u** destroyed them, along with the other cities
Ex 23:24 you must **u** conquer them and break down their
Lev 26:32 Your enemies who come to occupy it will be **u**
26:44 I will not **u** reject or despise them while they are in
Nu 21:30 We have **u** destroyed them, / all the way from
24:24 and Eber, / but they, too, will be **u** destroyed."
Dt 4:26 only a short time; then you will be **u** destroyed.
7:26 You must **u** detest such things, for they are set
31:29 I know that after my death you will become **u**
Jdg 5:23 the angel of the LORD. / 'Let them be **u** cursed
2Sa 23: 7 them down; / they will be **u** consumed with fire."
2Ch 28:19 to sin and had been **u** unfaithful to the LORD.
Ezr 9: 3 from my head and beard, and sat down **u** shocked.
9: 4 And I sat there **u** appalled until the time of the
9: 6 I prayed, "O my God, I am **u** ashamed; I blush to
Job 6:13 No, I am **u** helpless, without any chance of
Ps 74: 7 They **u** defiled the place that bears your holy
83:16 **U** disgrace them / until they submit to your name,
Ecc 1: 2 says the Teacher, "**u** meaningless!"
2:23 at night they cannot rest. It is all **u** meaningless.
12: 8 says the Teacher, "**u** meaningless."
SS 2: 5 and your 'apples'—for I am **u** lovesick!
8: 7 he owned, his offer would be **u** despised."
Isa 2:18 Idols will be **u** abolished and destroyed.
24:19 The earth has broken down and has **u** collapsed.
Jer 2:16 have **u** destroyed Israel's glory and power.
5: 5 But the leaders, too, had **u** rejected their God.
9: 6 pile lie upon lie and **u** refuse to come to me,"
10:25 For they have **u** devoured your people Israel,
50: 2 Her gods Bel and Marduk will be **u** disgraced.
La 5:22 Or have you **u** rejected us? Are you angry with us
Eze 20:13 and I made plans to **u** consume them in the desert.
21:32 You will be **u** wiped out, your memory lost to
25:16 and **u** destroy the people who live by the sea.
29:10 I will **u** destroy the land of Egypt, from Migdol to
35: 7 I will make Mount Seir **u** desolate, killing off all
36:32 you should be **u** ashamed of all you have done!
Hos 5: 3 a prostitute leaves her husband; you are **u** defiled.
Ac 3:23 be cut off from God's people and **u** destroyed.'
Ro 4:18 even though such a promise seemed **u** impossible!
5: 6 When we were **u** helpless, Christ came at just the
1Co 15:28 will be **u** supreme over everything everywhere.
Rev 18: 8 She will be **u** consumed by fire, for the Lord God

UTTERMOST [KJV] See APPROACH, EDGE, ENDS, EXTREME, FAR, FARTHEST, LAST, MOUTH, OUTER, OUTLYING, OUTSKIRTS, SOURCES

UZ (8)
Ge 10:23 The descendants of Aram were **U**, Hul, Gether,
22:21 The oldest was named **U**, the next oldest was Buz,
36:28 The sons of Dishan were **U** and Aran.
1Ch 1:17 The descendants of Aram were **U**, Hul, Gether,
1:42 and Akan. The sons of Dishan were **U** and Aran.
Job 1: 1 was a man named Job who lived in the land of **U**.
Jer 25:20 So did all the kings of the land of **U** and the kings
La 4:21 Are you rejoicing in the land of **U**, O people of

UZAI (1)
Ne 3:25 Palal son of **U** carried on the work from a point

UZAL (3)
Ge 10:27 Hadoram, **U**, Diklah,
1Ch 1:21 Hadoram, **U**, Diklah,
Eze 27:19 Greeks from **U** came to trade for your

UZZA (5)
2Ki 21:18 was buried in the palace garden, the garden of **U**.
21:26 He was buried in his tomb in the garden of **U**.
1Ch 8: 7 Gera, the father of **U** and Ahihud, led them when
Ezr 2:49 **U**, Paseah, Besai,
Ne 7:51 Gazzam, **U**, Paseah,

UZZAH (12) [PEREZ-UZZAH]
2Sa 6: 3 **U** and Ahio, Abinadab's sons, were guiding the
6: 6 and **U** put out his hand to steady the Ark of God.
6: 7 Then the LORD's anger blazed out against **U** for
6: 8 the LORD's anger had blazed out against **U**.
6: 8 Perez-uzzah (which means "outbreak against **U**").
1Ch 6:29 of Merari were Mahli, Libni, Shimei, **U**,
13: 7 on a new cart, with **U** and Ahio guiding it.
13: 9 and **U** put out his hand to steady the Ark.
13:10 Then the LORD's anger blazed out against **U**,
13:10 on the Ark. So **U** died there in the presence of God.
13:11 the LORD's anger had blazed out against **U**.
13:11 Perez-uzzah (which means "outbreak against **U**").

UZZEN-SHEERAH (1) [SHEERAH]
1Ch 7:24 the towns of Lower and Upper Beth-horon and **U**.

UZZI (11)
1Ch 6: 5 the father of Bukki. / Bukki was the father of **U**.
6: 6 **U** was the father of Zerahiah. / Zerahiah was the
6:51 Bukki, **U**, Zerahiah,
7: 2 The sons of Tola were **U**, Rephaiah, Jeriel, Jahmai,
7: 3 The son of **U** was Izrahiah. The sons of Izrahiah
7: 7 of Bela were Ezbon, **U**, Uzziel, Jerimoth, and Iri.
9: 8 son of Jeroham; Elah son of **U**, son of Micri;
Ezr 7: 4 son of Zerahiah, son of **U**, son of Bukki,
Ne 11:22 The chief officer of the Levites in Jerusalem was **U**
12:19 of Joiarib. / **U** was leader of the family of Jedaiah.
12:42 Maaseiah, Shemaiah, Eleazar, **U**, Jehohanan,

UZZIA (1)
1Ch 11:44 **U** from Ashtaroth; / Shama and Jeiel, the sons of

UZZIAH (33) [UZZIAH'S]
2Ki 14:21 sixteen-year-old son, **U**, as their next king.
14:22 **U** rebuilt the town of Elath and restored it to Judah.
15: 1 **U** son of Amaziah began to rule over Judah in the
15: 7 When **U** died, he was buried near his ancestors in
15:30 Israel in the twentieth year of Jotham son of **U**.
15:32 Jotham son of **U** began to rule over Judah in the
15:34 the LORD's sight, just as his father **U** had done.
1Ch 3:12 Amaziah, **U**, Jotham,
6:24 Tahath, Uriel, **U**, and Shaul.
27:25 Jonathan son of **U** was in charge of the regional
2Ch 26: 1 sixteen-year-old son, **U**, as their next king.
26: 2 **U** rebuilt the town of Elath and restored it to Judah.
26: 3 **U** was sixteen when he became king, and he
26: 5 **U** sought God during the days of Zechariah,
26: 9 **U** built fortified towers in Jerusalem at the Corner
26:11 **U** had an army of well-trained warriors, ready to
26:14 **U** provided the entire army with shields, spears,
26:18 They confronted King **U** and said, "It is not for you, **U**,
26:19 **U** was furious and refused to set down the incense
26:21 So King **U** had leprosy until the day he died.
26:23 So **U** died, and since he had leprosy, he was buried
27: 2 the LORD's sight, just as his father, **U**, had done.
Ezr 10:21 Maaseiah, Elijah, Shemaiah, Jehiel, and **U**.
Ne 11: 4 Athaiah son of **U**, son of Zechariah, son of
Isa 1: 1 came to Isaiah son of Amoz during the reigns of **U**,
6: 1 In the year King **U** died, I saw the Lord. He was
7: 1 reign of Ahaz son of Jotham and grandson of **U**,
Hos 1: 1 to Hosea son of Beeri during the years when **U**,
Am 1: 1 when **U** was king of Judah and Jeroboam II,
Zec 14: 5 the earthquake in the days of King **U** of Judah.
Mt 1: 8 father of Jehoram. / Jehoram was the father of **U**.
1: 9 **U** was the father of Jotham. / Jotham was the father

UZZIAH'S (7) [UZZIAH]
2Ki 15: 6 The rest of the events in **U** reign and all his deeds
15: 8 in the thirty-eighth year of King **U** reign in Judah.
15:13 in the thirty-ninth year of King **U** reign in Judah.
15:17 in the thirty-ninth year of King **U** reign in Judah.
15:23 Israel in the fiftieth year of King **U** reign in Judah.
15:27 in the fifty-second year of King **U** reign in Judah.
2Ch 26:22 The rest of the events of **U** reign, from beginning

UZZIEL (19)
Ex 6:18 of Kohath included Amram, Izhar, Hebron, and **U**.
6:22 The descendants of **U** included Mishael, Elzaphan,
Lev 10: 4 Aaron's cousins, the sons of Aaron's uncle **U**.
Nu 3:19 of his descendants, Amram, Izhar, Hebron, and **U**.
3:27 descended from Amram, Izhar, Hebron, and **U**.
3:30 of the Kohathite clans was Elizaphan son of **U**.
1Ch 4:42 led by Pelatiah, Neariah, Rephaiah, and **U**—
6: 2 of Kohath were Amram, Izhar, Hebron, and **U**.
6:18 of Kohath included Amram, Izhar, Hebron, and **U**.
7: 7 of Bela were Ezbon, Uzzi, **U**, Jerimoth, and Iri.
15:10 There were 112 descendants of **U**,
23:12 of Kohath included Amram, Izhar, Hebron, and **U**.
23:20 The descendants of **U** included Micah (the family
24:24 From the descendants of **U**, the leader was Micah.
25: 4 **U**, Shubael, Jerimoth, Hananiah, Hanani, Eliathah,
25:18 The eleventh lot fell to **U** and twelve of his sons
26:23 descended from Amram, Izhar, Hebron, and **U**:
2Ch 29:14 From the family of Jeduthun: Shemaiah and **U**.
Ne 3: 8 Next was **U** son of Harhaiah, a goldsmith by trade,

V

VAGABOND(S) [KJV] See TRAVELING, WANDER, WANDERING

VAIL(S) [KJV] See CURTAIN(S), VEIL(S)

VAIN (15)
Lev 26:16 You will plant your crops in v because your
Job 3: 9 Let it hope for light, but in v; may it never see the
24: 1 Why must the godly wait for him in v?
35:16 Job, you have protested in v. You have spoken like
Ps 139:20 your enemies take your name in v.
Pr 10:28 but the expectations of the wicked are all in v.
SS 3: 2 all its streets and squares.' But my search was in v.
Isa 41:12 You will look for them in v. They will all be gone!
65:23 They will not work in v, and their children will not
Jer 51:58 The builders from many lands have worked in v,
La 4:17 We looked in v for our allies to come and save us,
Eze 7:26 They will look in v for a vision from the prophets.
Hab 2:13 will turn to ashes? They work so hard, but all in v!
Mk 14:55 could put him to death. But their efforts were in v.
Gal 3: 4 for the Good News. Surely it was not in v, was it?

VAIZATHA (1)
Est 9: 9 Parmashta, Arisai, Aridai, and V—

VAJEZATHA [KJV] See VAIZATHA

VALE [KJV] See VALLEY

VALIANT (3)
2Sa 23:20 son of Jehoiada, a v warrior from Kabzeel.
1Ch 11:22 son of Jehoiada, a v warrior from Kabzeel.
Eze 39:20 feast on horses, riders, and v warriors,

VALID (3)
Pr 25:12 V criticism is as treasured by the one who heeds it
Jn 5:31 on my own behalf, my testimony would not be v.
8:14 "These claims are v even though I make them

VALIDATED (1)
Ru 4: 7 it to the other party. This publicly v the transaction.

VALLEY (182) [VALLEYS]
Ge 13:10 plains of the Jordan V in the direction of Zoar.
13:11 land for himself—the Jordan V to the east of them.
14: 3 and mobilized their armies in Siddim V (that is, the v of the Dead Sea).
14: 8 prepared for battle in the v of the Dead Sea
14:10 As it happened, the v was filled with tar pits.
14:17 the king of Sodom came out to meet him in the v of Shaveh (that is, the King's V).
19:17 angels warned. "Do not stop anywhere in the v.
26:17 So Isaac moved to the Gerar V and lived there
26:19 His shepherds also dug in the Gerar V and found a
35: 8 She was buried beneath the oak tree in the v below
37:14 to Shechem from his home in the v of Hebron.
Nu 13:23 When they came to what is now known as the v of
13:24 At that time the Israelites renamed the v Eshcol—
13:29 of the Mediterranean Sea and along the Jordan V."
21:12 From there they traveled to the v of Zered Brook
21:20 Then they went to the v in Moab where Pisgah
32: 9 After they went up to the v of Eshcol and scouted
Dt 1: 1 They were camped in the Jordan V near Suph,
1: 7 the Jordan V, the hill country, the western
1:24 and came to the v of Eshcol and explored it.
2: 8 and avoided the road through the Arabah V that
3:17 They also received the Jordan V,
3:29 So we stayed in the v near Beth-peor.
4:46 and as they camped in the v near Beth-peor east of
4:49 And they took the eastern bank of the Jordan V as
11:30 land of the Canaanites who live in the Jordan V,
21: 4 They must lead it to a v that is neither plowed nor
34: 3 the Negev; the Jordan V with Jericho—the city of
34: 6 He was buried in a v near Beth-peor in Moab,
Jos 7:24 he had, and they brought them to the v of Achor.
7:26 That is why the place has been called the V of
8:11 side of Ai, with a v between them and the city.
8:13 of the city. Joshua himself spent that night in the v.
8:14 When the king of Ai saw the Israelites across the v,
8:14 the Israelites at a place overlooking the Jordan V.
10:12 and the moon over the v of Aijalon."
11: 2 the kings in the Jordan V south of Galilee;
11: 8 and eastward into the v of Mizpah,
11:16 the Jordan V, and the mountains and lowlands of
11:17 to Baal-gad at the foot of Mount Hermon in the v
12: 1 and included all the land east of the Jordan V.
12: 3 Sihon also controlled the Jordan V as far north as
12: 7 from Baal-gad in the v of Lebanon to Mount
12: 8 the Jordan V, the mountain slopes,
13:19 Sibmah, Zereth-shahar on the hill above the v,
13:27 In the v were Beth-haram, Beth-nimrah, Succoth,
15: 7 From that point it went through the v of Achor to
15: 7 the slopes of Adummim on the south side of the v.
15: 8 then passed through the v of the son of Hinnom,
15: 8 to the top of the mountain above the v of Hinnom,
15: 8 and on up to the northern end of the v of Rephaim.
17:16 and the v of Jezreel have iron chariots—
18:16 and down to the base of the mountain beside the v
18:16 at the northern end of the v of Rephaim.
18:16 From there it went down the v of Hinnom,
18:18 north side of the slope overlooking the Jordan V.
18:18 The border then went down into the v,
19:14 passed Hannathon and ended at the v of Iphtah-el.
19:27 and ran as far as Zebulun in the v of Iphtah-el,
Jdg 5:15 They followed Barak, rushing into the v.
6:33 crossed the Jordan, camping in the v of Jezreel.
7: 1 north of them in the v near the hill of Moreh.
7: 8 Now the Midianite camp was in the v just below
7:12 and the people of the east had settled in the v like a
16: 4 named Delilah, who lived in the v of Sorek.
18:28 This happened in the v near Beth-rehob.
1Sa 6:13 of Beth-shemesh were harvesting wheat in the v,
13:18 and the third moved toward the border above the v
15: 5 went to the city of Amalek and lay in wait in the v.
17: 2 Saul countered by gathering his troops near the v
17: 3 other on opposite hills, with the v between them.
17:19 with Saul and the Israelite army at the v of Elah,
21: 9 whom you killed in the v of Elah," the priest
23:24 of Maon in the Arabah V south of Jeshimon.
31: 7 the Israelites on the other side of the Jezreel V
2Sa 2:29 and his men retreated through the Jordan V.
4: 7 they fled across the Jordan V through the night.
5:18 and spread out across the v of Rephaim.
5:22 and again spread out across the v of Rephaim.
8:13 eighteen thousand Edomites in the V of Salt.
15:23 They crossed the Kidron V and then went out
17:13 and drag the walls of the city into the nearest v
18:18 had built a monument to himself in the King's V,
23:13 the Philistine army was camped in the v of
24: 5 and camped at Aroer, south of the town in the v,
1Ki 2:37 On the day you cross the Kidron V, you will surely
7:46 in clay molds in the Jordan V between Succoth
15:13 cut down the pole and burned it in the Kidron V.
18: 5 and v to see if we can find enough grass to save at
18:40 and Elijah took them down to the Kishon V
2Ki 2:16 has left him on some mountain or in some v."
3:16 This dry v will be filled with pools of water!
3:17 the LORD, but this v will be filled with water.
14: 7 who killed ten thousand Edomites in the V of Salt.
23: 4 outside Jerusalem on the terraces of the Kidron V,
23: 6 and took it outside Jerusalem to the Kidron V,
23:10 Then the king defiled the altar of Topheth in the v
23:12 to bits and scattered the pieces in the Kidron V.
25: 4 across the fields, in the direction of the Jordan V.
1Ch 4:14 the founder of the V of Craftsmen, so called
4:39 in the east part of the v, seeking pastureland for
10: 7 When the Israelites in the Jezreel V saw that their
11:15 the Philistine army was camped in the v of
14: 9 The Philistines had arrived in the v of Rephaim
14:13 the Philistines returned and raided the v again.
18:12 eighteen thousand Edomites in the V of Salt.
2Ch 4:17 in clay molds in the Jordan V between Succoth
14:10 so Asa deployed his armies for battle in the v north
15:16 broke it up, and burned it in the Kidron V.
20:16 of the v that opens into the wilderness of Jeruel.
20:26 On the fourth day they gathered in the V of
20:26 It is still called the V of Blessing today.
25:11 his courage and led his army to the V of Salt,
26: 9 at the V Gate, and at the angle in the wall.
28: 3 He offered sacrifices in the v of the son of
29:16 there the Levites carted it all out to the Kidron V.
30:14 incense altars and threw them into the Kidron V.
33: 6 own sons in the fire in the v of the son of Hinnom.
33:14 from west of the Gihon Spring in the Kidron V to
Ne 2:13 I went out through the V Gate, past the Jackal's
2:15 So I went up the Kidron V instead,
2:15 I turned back and entered again at the V Gate.
3:13 led by Hanun, rebuilt the V Gate, hung its doors,
11:30 all the way from Beersheba to the v of Hinnom.
11:35 Lod, Ono, and the V of Craftsmen.
Job 36:16 You have prospered in a wide and pleasant v.
Ps 23: 4 through the dark v of death, / I will not be afraid,
60: T and killed twelve thousand Edomites in the V of
60: 6 with joy. / I will measure out the v of Succoth.
84: 6 When they walk through the V of Weeping,
108: 7 with joy. / I will measure out the v of Succoth.
Pr 30:17 a mother will be plucked out by ravens of the v
SS 2: 1 "I am the rose of Sharon, the lily of the v."
6:11 and out to the v to see the new growth brought on
Isa 17: 5 grainfields in the v of Rephaim after the harvest.
22: 5 has brought upon the V of Vision!
28: 1 It sits in a rich v, but its glorious beauty will
28: 4 It sits in a fertile v, but its glorious beauty will
63:14 As with cattle going down into a peaceful v,
65:10 and the v of Achor will be a place to pasture herds.
Jer 2:23 can you say that? Go and look in any v in the land!
7:31 shrines of Topheth in the v of the son of Hinnom,
7:32 be called Topheth or the v of the son of Hinnom, but the V of Slaughter.
19: 2 Go out into the v of the son of Hinnom by the
19: 4 and turned this v into a place of wickedness.
19: 6 be called Topheth or the v of the son of Hinnom, but the V of Slaughter.
31:40 including the graveyard and ash dump in the v,
31:40 and all the fields out to the Kidron V on the east as
32:35 They have built pagan shrines to Baal in the v of
39: 4 the king's garden and headed toward the Jordan V.
52: 7 across the fields, in the direction of the Jordan V.
Eze 3:22 and he said to me, "Go out into the v, and I will
8: 4 was there, just as I had seen it before in the v.
37: 1 the Spirit of the LORD to a v filled with bones.
37: 2 among the old, dry bones that covered the v floor.
37: 7 I spoke, there was a rattling noise all across the v.
39:11 for Gog and his hordes in the V of the Travelers,
39:11 and they will change the name of the place to the V
39:15 and take them to be buried in the V of Gog's
47: 8 flows east through the desert into the Jordan V,
Hos 1: 5 by breaking its military power in the Jezreel V."
2:15 and transform the V of Trouble into a gateway of
Joel 3: 2 "I will gather the armies of the world into the v of
3:11 Gather together in the v." And now, O LORD,
3:12 Let them march to the v of Jehoshaphat. There I,
3:14 Thousands upon thousands are waiting in the v of
3:18 LORD's Temple, watering the arid v of acacias.
Am 1: 5 and slaughter its people all the way to the v of
6:14 from Lebo-hamath in the north to the Arabah V in
Mic 1: 6 I will roll the stones of her walls down into the v
Zec 1: 8 standing among some myrtle trees in a small v.
11: 3 for their thickets in the Jordan V have been
12:11 mourning of Hadad-rimmon in the v of Megiddo.
14: 4 making a wide v running from east to west,
14: 5 You will flee through this v, for it will reach across
Mt 3: 5 and from all over the Jordan V went out to the
Mk 13: 3 the Mount of Olives across the v from the Temple.
Jn 18: 1 Jesus crossed the Kidron V with his disciples

VALLEYS (24) [VALLEY]
Dt 8: 7 with springs that gush forth in the v and hills.
11:11 It is a land of hills and v with plenty of rain—
Jos 17:18 sure you can drive out the Canaanites from the v,
1Ch 27:29 son of Adlai was responsible for the cattle in the v.
2Ch 26:10 both on the hillsides and in the fertile v.
Ps 65:13 flocks of sheep, / and the v are carpeted with grain.
104: 8 Mountains rose and v sank / to the levels you
Isa 7:19 settle in the fertile areas and also in the desolate v,
22: 7 They fill your beautiful v and crowd against your
40: 4 Fill the v and level the hills. Straighten out the
41:18 I will give them fountains of water in the v.
49:11 for them. The highways will be raised above the v.
57: 5 your children as human sacrifices down in the v,
57: 6 Your gods are the smooth stones in the v.
Jer 48: 8 both on the plateaus and in the v, for the LORD
49: 4 You are proud of your fertile v, but they will soon
Eze 6: 3 to the mountains and hills and to the ravines and v:
31:12 across the mountains and v and ravines of the land.
32: 5 hills with your flesh and fill the v with your bones.
35: 8 Your hills, your v, and your streams will be filled
36: 4 speaks to the hills and mountains, ravines and v,
36: 6 the hills and mountains, the ravines and v of Israel.
Mic 1: 4 his feet and flow into the v like wax in a fire,
Lk 3: 5 Fill in the v, / and level the mountains and hills!

VALOUR [KJV] See ABILITY, ABLE, COURAGEOUS, FIGHTING, SOLDIERS, VALIANT, WARRIOR(S)

VALUABLE (25) [VALUE]
Ge 24:53 He also gave v presents to her mother and brother.
Dt 20:20 cut down trees that you know are not v for food.
1Ki 10:27 And v cedarwood was as common as the sycamore
20: 6 will take away everything you consider v!' "
2Ch 1:15 And v cedarwood was as common as the sycamore
9:27 And v cedarwood was as common as the sycamore
21: 3 Their father had given each of them v gifts of
28:21 Ahaz took v items from the LORD's Temple,
32:23 with v presents for King Hezekiah, too.
32:27 and spices, and for his shields and other v items.
Ezr 1: 7 King Cyrus himself brought out the v items which
Job 24: 3 A poor widow must surrender her v ox as collateral
28:17 Wisdom is far more v than gold and crystal.
28:18 and v rock crystal are worthless in trying to get it.
Ps 119:72 Your law is more v to me / than millions in gold
Pr 8:11 For wisdom is far more v than rubies. Nothing you
20:15 speech is rarer and more v than gold and rubies.
Ecc 7: 1 A good reputation is more v than the most
Da 2:48 to a high position and gave him many v gifts.
Mt 6:26 And you are far more v to him than they are.
10:31 you are more v to him than a whole flock of
12:12 And how much more v is a person than a sheep!
Lk 12: 7 you are more v to him than a whole flock of
12:24 And you are far more v to him than any birds!
15: 8 "Or suppose a woman has ten v silver coins

VALUABLES (3) [VALUE]
2Ch 20:25 vast amounts of equipment, clothing, and other v—
Ezr 8:33 and other v were weighed at the Temple of our
Pr 24: 4 are filled with all sorts of precious riches and v.

VALUE (45) [VALUABLE, VALUABLES, VALUED, VALUES]
Ex 22: 4 then the thief must pay double the v.
22: 7 the fine is double the v of what was stolen.
Lev 5:15 and it must be of the proper v in silver as measured
5:18 no physical defects, and it must be of the proper v.
6: 6 or the animal's equivalent v in silver.
7:18 It will have no v as a sacrifice, and you will
27: 2 to the LORD by paying the v of that person,
27:12 He will assess its v, and his assessment will be
27:13 you must pay the v set by the priest, plus 20
27:14 to the LORD, the priest must come to assess its v.
27:15 you must pay the v set by the priest, plus 20
27:16 its v will be assessed by the amount of seed
27:18 the priest must assess the land's v in proportion to
27:19 you must pay the land's v as assessed by the priest,
27:23 the priest must assess its v based on the years until
27:23 then give the assessed v of the land as a sacred
27:25 All the v assessments must be measured in terms
27:27 priest may sell it to someone else for its assessed v.
27:31 tenth of the fruit or grain, you must pay its v,
Dt 2:35 along with anything of v from the towns we
1Sa 26:24 Now may the LORD v my life, even as I have
1Ki 10:21 because silver was considered of little v in
2Ki 8: 6 including the v of any crops that had been
2Ch 9:12 gifts of greater v than the gifts she had given him.
9:20 because silver was considered of little v in
21:17 and carried away everything of v in the royal
36:19 and completely destroyed everything of v.
Ezr 8:27 20 gold bowls, equal in v to 1,000 gold coins,
Job 13:12 Your statements have about as much v as ashes.

28:16 Its v is greater than all the gold of Ophir,
28:19 for it. Its v is greater than the purest gold.
Pr 10: 2 Ill-gotten gain has no lasting v, but right living can
Ecc 2:13 Wisdom is of more v than foolishness, just as light
2:15 will die, so will I. So of what v is all my wisdom?
10:10 That's the v of wisdom; it helps you succeed.
Mt 13:46 When he discovered a pearl of great v, he sold
Ac 19:19 The v of the books was several million dollars.
Ro 3: 1 Is there any v in the Jewish ceremony of
12: 3 measuring your v by how much faith God has
1Co 3:13 through the fire to see whether or not it keeps its v.
10:19 real gods and that these sacrifices are of some v?
13: 3 I didn't love others, I would be of no v whatsoever.
15:32 And what v was there in fighting wild beasts—
2Co 3: 5 think we can do anything of lasting v by ourselves.
1Ti 4: 8 Physical exercise has some v, but spiritual exercise

VALUED (17) [VALUE]
Lev 27: 3 of twenty and sixty is v at fifty pieces of silver;
27: 4 a woman of that age is v at thirty pieces of silver.
27: 5 and twenty is v at twenty pieces of silver;
27: 5 a girl of that age is v at ten pieces of silver.
27: 6 and five years is v at five pieces of silver;
27: 6 a girl of that age is v at three pieces of silver.
27: 7 A man older than sixty is v at fifteen pieces of
27: 7 a woman older than sixty is v at ten pieces of
1Sa 26:21 no longer try to harm you, for you v my life today.
26:24 value my life, even as I have v yours today.
Ne 12:44 for all the people of Judah v the priests and Levites
Job 29:21 "Everyone listened to me and v my advice.
Ps 44:12 for a pittance. / You v us at nothing at all.
Isa 44: 9 These highly v objects are really worthless.
Zec 11:13 this magnificent sum at which they v me!
Mt 27: 9 the price at which he was v by the people of
Lk 7: 2 Now the highly v slave of a Roman officer was

VALUES (2) [VALUE]
Lev 27: 3 here is the scale of v to be used. A man between
Pr 22: 5 treacherous road; whoever v life will stay away.

VANIAH (1)
Ezr 10:36 V, Meremoth, Eliashib,

VANISH (7) [VANISHED, VANISHES, VANISHING]
Job 4: 9 a breath from God. They v in a blast of his anger.
20: 8 not be found. He will v like a vision in the night.
Ps 73:20 O Lord, / you will make them v from this life.
104:35 Let all sinners v from the face of the earth;
Isa 29: 7 All the nations fighting against Jerusalem will v
29: 7 Those who are attacking her walls will v like a
Jer 10:11 the heavens and earth, will v from the earth."

VANISHED (5) [VANISH]
Nu 16:33 The earth closed over them, and they all v.
Job 30:15 and my prosperity has v as a cloud before a strong
Ps 12: 1 The faithful have v from the earth!
Jer 7:28 Truth has v from among them; it is no longer heard
24:10 and disease until they have v from the land of

VANISHES (4) [VANISH]
Job 6:17 the water disappears. The brook v in the heat.
7: 9 Just as a cloud dissipates and v, those who die will
La 2: 3 All the strength of Israel v beneath his fury.
Hos 6: 4 "For your love v like the morning mist

VANISHING (1) [VANISH]
Pr 21: 6 Wealth created by lying is a v mist and a deadly

VANITIES, VANITY [KJV] See BREATH, CALAMITY, DECEIT, DELUSION, DESTRUCTION, EMPTINESS, EMPTY, EVIL, FALSE, FALSEHOOD, FUTILITY, HASTILY, IDOLS, INIQUITY, LIES, NONSENSE, NOTHING, VAIN, VAPOR, WORTHLESS

VANQUISHED (1)
La 2: 5 Yes, the Lord has v Israel like an enemy. He has

VAPOR (1) [VAPORS]
Job 36:27 He draws up the water v and then distills it into

VAPORS (1) [VAPOR]
Ps 148: 4 skies above! / Praise him, v high above the clouds!

VAPOUR [KJV] See CLOUDS, FOG, STORM, VAPOR

VARIABLENESS [KJV] See CHANGES

VARIANCE [KJV] See AGAINST, QUARRELING

VARIED (1) [VARIETY]
2Ch 8:13 The number of sacrifices v from day to day

VARIETIES (2) [VARIETY]
Lev 11:22 locusts of all v, crickets, bald locusts,
11:29 the mole, the mouse, the great lizard of all v,

VARIETY (6) [VARIED, VARIETIES, VARIOUS]
Ne 13:20 and tradesmen with a v of wares camped outside
Ps 104:24 O LORD, what a v of things you have made!
Ecc 11: 6 Be sure to stay busy and plant a v of crops, for you
Eze 27:18 Damascus traded for your rich v of goods,
Eph 3:10 to show his wisdom in all its rich v to all the rulers
1Pe 4:10 God has given gifts to each of you from his great v

VARIOUS (37) [VARIETY]
Ge 7: 8 With them were all the v kinds of animals—
8:19 And all the v kinds of animals and birds came out,
10: 5 became the seafaring peoples in v lands,
Ex 29: 3 Place these v kinds of bread in a single basket,
Lev 7:12 must be accompanied by v kinds of bread—
14:54 "These are the instructions for dealing with the v
23:37 present all the v offerings to the LORD by fire—
Nu 2: 2 and the v groups will camp beneath their family
3:31 the altars, the v utensils used in the sanctuary,
4:32 You must assign the v loads to each man by name.
1Ki 9:23 He also appointed 550 of them to supervise the v
2Ki 17:29 But these v groups of foreigners also continued to
23:19 They had been built by the v kings of Israel
1Ch 6:48 were appointed to v other tasks in the Tabernacle,
9:28 assigned to care for the v utensils used in worship.
18: 8 and the v bronze utensils used at the Temple.
24: 3 descendants into groups according to their v duties.
24: 5 All tasks were assigned to the v groups by means
24:30 These were the descendants of Levi in their v
26:13 assigned by families for guard duty at the v gates,
28:13 concerning the work of the v divisions of priests
28:21 The v divisions of priests and Levites will serve in
2Ch 8:10 appointed 250 of them to supervise the v projects.
11: 5 and fortified v cities for the defense of Judah.
34:13 were put in charge of the laborers of the v trades.
Ezr 6:18 and Levites were divided into their v divisions to
Ne 11: 3 to live in their own homes in the v towns of Judah,
Ecc 3:10 I have thought about this in connection with the v
Eze 8:10 I also saw the v idols worshiped by the people of
40:24 to the south gateway and measured its v parts,
48:19 Those who come from the v tribes to work in the
Da 11:23 deceitful promises, he will make v alliances.
11:40 He will invade v lands and sweep through them
Mt 24: 1 his disciples pointed out to him the v Temple
Lk 7:21 he cured many people of their v diseases,
Ac 5:36 he was killed, and his followers went their v ways.
Heb 2: 4 the message by signs and wonders and v miracles

VASHNI [KJV] See JOEL

VASHTI (10)
Est 1: 9 Queen V gave a banquet for the women of the
1:11 to bring Queen V to him with the royal crown on
1:12 when they conveyed the king's order to Queen V,
1:15 "What must be done to Queen V?" the king
1:16 "Queen V has wronged not only the king but also
1:17 Queen V has refused to appear before the king.
1:19 It should order that Queen V be forever banished
2: 1 he began thinking about V and what she had done
2: 4 you most will be made queen instead of V."
2:17 on her head and declared her queen instead of V.

VASSAL (1)
2Ki 16: 7 "I am your servant and your v. Come up

VAST (70)
Ex 8: 2 I will send v hordes of frogs across your entire
16:13 That evening v numbers of quail arrived
Nu 22: 5 "A v horde of people has arrived from Egypt.
22:11 'A v horde of people has come from Egypt and has
32: 1 of Reuben and Gad owned v numbers of livestock.
Dt 17:17 And he must not accumulate v amounts of wealth
Jos 11: 4 along with a v array of horses and chariots,
1Sa 13: 6 When the men of Israel saw the v number of
14:16 the v army of Philistines began to melt away in
28: 5 When Saul saw the v Philistine army, he became
30:16 because of the v amount of plunder they had taken
2Sa 12:30 David took a v amount of plunder from the city.
1Ki 4:29 and knowledge too v to be measured.
20:27 to the v Aramean forces that filled the countryside!
20:28 of the plains. So I will help you defeat this v army.
1Ch 12:40 V supplies of flour, fig cakes, raisins, wine,
20: 2 David took a v amount of plunder from the city.
22: 4 and Sidon had brought v amounts of cedar to
22: 5 So David collected v amounts of building materials
2Ch 13: 8 Your army is v indeed, but with you are those gold
14:11 It is in your name that we have come against this v
14:13 and the army of Judah carried off v quantities of
14:14 v quantities of plunder were taken from these
16: 8 to the Ethiopians and Libyans and their v army,
20: 2 "A v army from Edom is marching against you
20:25 They found v amounts of equipment, clothing,
32:29 built many towns and acquired v flocks and herds,
Ezr 4:20 of the Euphrates River and have received v tribute,
Est 1:20 When this decree is published throughout your v
Ps 33: 7 and locked the oceans in v reservoirs.
36: 5 unfailing love, O LORD, is as v as the heavens;
78:45 He sent v swarms of flies to consume them
104:25 Here is the ocean, v and wide, / teeming with life
107:41 and increases their families like v flocks of sheep.
Isa 2: 7 Israel has v treasures of silver and gold and many
7:19 They will come in v hordes, spreading across the
7:24 The entire land will be one v brier patch, a hunting
9:18 too. Its burning sends up v clouds of smoke.
10:18 Assyria's v army is like a glorious forest, yet it will
10:33 He will destroy all that v army of Assyria—
24: 1 to destroy the earth and make it a v wasteland.
60: 6 V caravans of camels will converge on you,
Eze 27:27 On that day of v ruin, everyone on board sinks into
38: 4 and cavalry and make you a v and mighty horde,
38: 9 and all your allies—a v and awesome horde—
38:12 I will capture v amounts of plunder and take many
38:15 homeland in the distant north with your v cavalry
39: 4 and all your v hordes will die on the mountains.
39:11 "And I will make a v graveyard for Gog and his
Da 10: 6 and his voice was like the roaring of a v multitude
11: 3 king will rise to power who will rule a v kingdom
11:11 will rally against the v forces assembled by the
11:40 against him with chariots, cavalry, and a v navy.
Joel 1: 6 A v army of locusts has invaded my land. It is a
Am 5:12 For I know the v number of your sins
7: 1 I saw him preparing to send a v swarm of locusts
Na 2: 9 many treasures—its v, uncounted wealth.
3:16 as the stars, have filled your city with v wealth.
Zec 14:10 south of Jerusalem, will become one v plain.
Mt 14:14 A v crowd was there as he stepped from the boat,
15:30 A v crowd brought him the lame, blind, crippled,
19: 2 V crowds followed him there, and he healed their
Mk 3: 8 and v numbers of people came to see him for
6:34 A v crowd was there as he stepped from the boat,
Lk 2:13 the angel was joined by a v host of others—
5:15 and v crowds came to hear him preach and to be
Jn 4:35 V fields are ripening all around us and are ready
2Pe 2: 5 the whole world of ungodly people with a v flood.
Rev 7: 9 After this I saw a v crowd, too great to count,
19: 1 I heard the sound of a v crowd in heaven shouting,

VATS (2)
Pr 3:10 and your v will overflow with the finest wine.
Joel 3:13 The storage v are overflowing with the wickedness

VAULT (1)
Job 22:14 He is way up there, walking on the v of heaven.'

VAUNT(ETH) [KJV] See BOAST(FUL)

VEGETABLE (2) [VEGETABLES]
Dt 11:10 irrigation ditches with your foot as in a v garden.
1Ki 21: 2 I would like to buy it to use as a v garden.

VEGETABLES (5) [VEGETABLE]
Ge 9: 3 you for food, just as I have given you grain and v.
2Ki 4:39 the young men went out into the field to gather v
Da 1:12 "Test us for ten days on a diet of v and water,"
1:16 the attendant fed them only v instead of the rich
Ro 14: 2 who has a sensitive conscience will eat only v.

VEHEMENT [KJV] See BRIGHTEST, LONGING, SCORCHING

VEIL (19) [VEILED, VEILING, VEILS]
Ge 24:65 So Rebekah covered her face with her v.
38:14 and covered herself with a v to disguise herself.
38:19 Afterward she went home, took off her v, and put
Ex 34:33 speaking with them, he put a v over his face.
34:34 he removed the v until he came out again.
34:35 Afterward he would put the v on again until he
SS 4: 1 Your eyes behind your v are like doves.
4: 3 Your cheeks behind your v are like pomegranate
5: 7 The watchman on the wall tore off my v.
6: 7 Your cheeks behind your v are like pomegranate
Isa 47: 2 the corn. Remove your v and strip off your robe.
Eze 32: 7 you out, I will v the heavens and darken the stars.
Lk 23:45 the thick v hanging in the Temple was torn apart.
2Co 3:13 who put a v over his face so the people of Israel
3:14 a v covers their minds so they cannot understand
3:14 And this v can be removed only by believing in
3:15 their hearts are covered with that v, and they do not
3:16 anyone turns to the Lord, then the v is taken away.
3:18 And all of us have had that v removed so that we

VEILED (2) [VEIL]
Ge 38:15 thought she was a prostitute, since her face was v.
2Co 4: 3 If the Good News we preach is v from anyone,

VEILING (2) [VEIL]
2Sa 22:12 v his approach with dense rain clouds.
Ps 18:11 v his approach with dense rain clouds.

VEILS (3) [VEIL]
Isa 3:19 bracelets, and v of shimmering gauze.
Eze 13:18 on their wrists and furnish them with magic v.
13:21 I will tear off the magic v and save my people from

VEIN [KJV] See MINE

VENGEANCE (37) [AVENGE, AVENGED, AVENGER, AVENGES, AVENGING, REVENGE, VENGEFUL]
Nu 31: 2 "Take v on the Midianites for leading the
31: 3 "Choose some men to fight the LORD's war of v
Dt 32:35 I will take v; I will repay those who deserve it.

32:41 to carry out justice, / I will bring **v** on my enemies
32:43 He will take **v** on his enemies / and cleanse his
1Sa 18:25 **V** on my enemies is all I really want." But what
25:26 from murdering and taking **v** into your own hands,
25:31 the staggering burden of needless bloodshed and **v**.
25:33 the man and carrying out **v** with my own hands.
2Sa 14:11 that you won't let anyone take **v** against my son.
Ps 79:10 their God?" / Show us your **v** against the nations,
79:12 O Lord, take sevenfold **v** on our neighbors
94: 1 O LORD, the God to whom **v** belongs, / O God of **v**, let your glorious justice be seen!
149: 7 to execute **v** on the nations / and punishment on the
Pr 6:34 and he will have no mercy in his day of **v**.
Isa 34: 8 For it is the day of the LORD's **v**, the year when
47: 3 I will take **v** against you and will not negotiate."
59:17 He clothed himself with the robes of **v** and godly
63: 5 So I executed **v** alone; unaided, I passed down
66: 6 It is the voice of the LORD taking **v** against his
Jer 11:20 Let me see your **v** against them, for I have
20:12 Let me see your **v** against them, for I have
46:10 the LORD Almighty, a day of **v** on his enemies.
50:15 The LORD has taken **v**, so do not spare her.
50:28 taken **v** against those who destroyed his Temple.
51: 6 It is the LORD's time for **v**; he will fully repay
51:11 This is his **v** against those who desecrated his
Eze 24: 8 an open expression of my anger and **v** against her.
25:14 They will carry out my furious **v**, and Edom will
25:17 I will execute terrible **v** against them to rebuke
Mic 5:15 I will pour out my **v** on all the nations that refuse
Na 1: 2 LORD is a jealous God, filled with **v** and wrath.
Lk 21:22 For those will be days of God's **v**,
Ro 12:19 that to God. For it is written, / "I will take **v**;
Heb 10:30 For we know the one who said, / "I will take **v**.
12:24 instead of crying out for **v** as the blood of Abel did.

VENGEFUL (1) [VENGEANCE]

Ps 44:16 of our mockers. / All we see are our **v** enemies.

VENISON [KJV] See GAME

VENOM (2)

Dt 32:33 Their wine is the **v** of snakes, / the deadly poison
Job 20:14 sour within him, a poisonous **v** in his stomach.

VENT (7) [VENTED]

Lev 26:28 then I will give full **v** to my hostility. I will punish
Job 32:19 I am like a wine cask without a **v**. My words are
40:11 Give **v** to your anger. Let it overflow against the
Pr 29:11 A fool gives full **v** to anger, but a wise person
Isa 42:14 But now I will give full **v** to my fury; / I will gasp
Jer 50:25 and brought out weapons to **v** his fury against his
Da 11:30 But he will **v** his anger against the people of the

VENTED (1) [VENT]

Zec 6: 8 "Those who went north have **v** the anger of my

VENTURE (1)

Jer 5: 6 their towns, tearing apart any who dare to **v** out.

VERDICT (6) [VERDICTS]

Dt 17:11 they have interpreted the law and reached a **v**,
17:12 Anyone arrogant enough to reject the **v** of the
2Ch 19: 6 He will be with you when you render the **v** in each
Mt 26:66 What is your **v**?" "Guilty!" they shouted.
Mk 14:64 have all heard his blasphemy. What is your **v**?"
Lk 23:14 and he announced his **v**. "You brought this man to

VERDICTS (1) [VERDICT]

Zec 8:16 Render **v** in your courts that are just and that lead

VERGE (2)

Ps 38:17 I am on the **v** of collapse, / facing constant pain.
Lk 5: 7 boats were filled with fish and on the **v** of sinking.

VERIFIED (1) [VERIFY]

Heb 2: 4 and God **v** the message by signs and wonders

VERIFY (2) [VERIFIED]

1Sa 17:26 David talked to some others standing there to **v** the
Isa 43: 9 Who can **v** that they spoke the truth?

VERILY [KJV] See CERTAINLY, INDEED, SURELY, THOUGH, TRULY, VERY, WHOLE, YES

VERITY [KJV] See TRUSTWORTHY, TRUTH

VERSED (2)

Ezr 7: 6 well **v** in the law of Moses, which the LORD,
Da 1: 4 "Make sure they are well **v** in every branch of

VERSES (1)

Mt 23: 5 extra wide prayer boxes with Scripture **v** inside,

VERY (527)

Ge 4: 5 This made Cain **v** angry and dejected.
5: 3 was born, and Seth was the **v** image of his father.
7:13 But Noah had gone into the boat that **v** day with
12:11 said to Sarai, "You are a **v** beautiful woman.
13: 2 for Abram was **v** rich in livestock, silver, and gold.
13: 5 was also **v** wealthy with sheep, cattle, and many
17:23 On that **v** day Abraham took his son Ishmael
18:11 And since Abraham and Sarah were both **v** old,
21:11 This upset Abraham **v** much because Ishmael was
24: 1 Abraham was now a **v** old man, and the LORD
24:16 Now Rebekah was **v** beautiful, and she was a
24:36 When Sarah, my master's wife, was **v** old,
24:67 He loved her **v** much, and she was a special
25:25 The first was **v** red at birth. He was covered with
26: 7 kill him to get her, because she was **v** beautiful.
26:32 That **v** day Isaac's servants came and told him
28: 8 It was now **v** clear to Esau that his father despised
28:18 The next morning he got up **v** early. He took the
29:14 "Just think, my **v** own flesh and blood!"
30:35 But that **v** day Laban went out and removed all the
30:43 and he became **v** wealthy, with many servants,
31:28 tell them good-bye? You have acted **v** foolishly!
31:36 Then Jacob became **v** angry. "What did you
33:11 take my gifts, for God has been **v** generous to me.
33:13 my lord, that some of the children are **v** young,
35:17 After a **v** hard delivery, the midwife finally
39: 6 Now Joseph was a **v** handsome and well-built
40: 2 Pharaoh became **v** angry with these officials,
41: 3 up from the river, but these were **v** ugly and gaunt.
41: 8 Pharaoh became **v** concerned as to what the
41:19 They were **v** thin and gaunt—in fact, I've never
42:30 "The man who is ruler over the land spoke **v**
44:20 and his father loves him **v** much.'
45:16 Pharaoh was **v** happy to hear this and so were his
45:18 'Pharaoh will assign to you the **v** best territory in
47: 4 our flocks in Canaan. The famine is **v** severe there.
47:19 Why should we die before your **v** eyes? Buy us
50:10 they held a **v** great and solemn funeral,
50:11 "This is a place of **v** deep mourning for these
50:21 And he spoke **v** kindly to them, reassuring them.
Ex 1:19 they told him, "the Hebrew women are **v** strong.
3:12 you will return here to worship God at this **v**
4:14 you now. And when he sees you, he will be **v** glad.
6: 8 Isaac, and Jacob. It will be your **v** own property.
7:14 the LORD said to Moses, "Pharaoh is **v** stubborn,
8:22 But it will be **v** different in the land of Goshen,
9: 5 that he would send the plague the **v** next day,
10:29 "**V** well," Moses replied. "I will never see you
11: 3 and Moses was considered a **v** great man in the
12:15 On the **v** first day you must remove every trace of
12:17 your forces out of the land of Egypt on this **v** day.
12:51 And that **v** day the LORD began to lead the
15: 4 into the sea. / The **v** best of Pharaoh's officers
16:20 terrible smell. And Moses was **v** angry with them.
22:27 to me for help, then I will hear, for I am **v** merciful.
29:18 offering to the LORD, which is **v** pleasing to him.
30:36 Beat some of it **v** fine and put some of it in front of
33:13 don't forget that this nation is your **v** own people."
34:12 "Be **v** careful never to make treaties with the
Lev 1: 9 offering made by fire, **v** pleasing to the LORD.
1:13 offering made by fire, **v** pleasing to the LORD.
1:17 offering made by fire, **v** pleasing to the LORD.
2: 2 an offering made by fire, **v** pleasing to the LORD.
2: 9 by fire, and it will be **v** pleasing to the LORD.
3: 5 an offering made by fire, **v** pleasing to the LORD.
3:16 by fire; these will be **v** pleasing to the LORD.
4:31 the altar, and it will be **v** pleasing to the LORD.
6:15 the altar, and it will be **v** pleasing to the LORD.
6:21 and it will be **v** pleasing to the LORD.
8:21 to the LORD by fire, **v** pleasing to the LORD.
8:28 to the LORD by fire, **v** pleasing to the LORD.
10:16 he became **v** angry with Eleazar and Ithamar,
17: 6 and it will be **v** pleasing to the LORD.
20:26 set you apart from all other people to be my **v** own.
22:33 you from Egypt, that I might be your **v** own God.
23:13 LORD by fire, and it will be **v** pleasing to him.
Nu 1:18 the whole community of Israel on that **v** day.
11:10 extremely angry. Moses was also **v** aggravated.
13:28 and their cities and towns are fortified and **v** large.
14:28 I will do to you the **v** things I heard you say.
15: 7 This sacrifice will be **v** pleasing to the LORD.
15:10 an offering made by fire, **v** pleasing to the LORD.
16:15 Then Moses became **v** angry and said to the
16:41 But the **v** next morning the whole community
18:17 an offering given by fire, **v** pleasing to the LORD.
28: 2 altar are my food, and they are **v** pleasing to me.
28: 6 an offering made by fire, **v** pleasing to the LORD.
28: 8 an offering made by fire, **v** pleasing to the LORD.
28:13 by fire, and it will be **v** pleasing to the LORD.
28:24 to be presented by fire, **v** pleasing to the LORD.
28:27 will be offered that day, **v** pleasing to the LORD.
29: 2 present a burnt offering, **v** pleasing to the LORD.
29: 6 to the LORD by fire and are **v** pleasing to him.
29: 8 present a burnt offering, **v** pleasing to the LORD.
29:13 burnt offering by fire, **v** pleasing to the LORD.
29:36 present a burnt offering, **v** pleasing to the LORD.
31:16 "These are the **v** ones who followed Balaam's
Dt 1:34 heard your complaining, he became **v** angry.
4: 9 Be **v** careful never to forget what you have seen
4:21 "But the LORD was **v** angry with me because of
4:34 God did for you in Egypt, right before your **v** eyes.
8:13 and herds have become **v** large and your silver
9:17 to the ground. I smashed them before your **v** eyes.
9:18 what the LORD hated, thus making him **v** angry.
11: 4 and how he has kept them devastated to this **v** day!
12:19 Be **v** careful never to forget the Levites as long as
18: 9 be **v** careful not to imitate the detestable customs
30:14 The message is **v** close at hand; it is on your lips
31:22 So that **v** day Moses wrote down the words of the
31:29 for you will make the LORD **v** angry by doing
Jos 1: 7 Be strong and **v** courageous. Obey all the laws
5:11 The **v** next day they began to eat unleavened bread
7: 1 so the LORD was **v** angry with the Israelites.
8:28 a permanent mound of ruins, desolate to this **v** day.
9: 9 They answered, "We are from a **v** distant country.
10: 2 and his people became **v** afraid when they heard all
10:27 a large pile of stones, which remains to this **v** day.
22: 5 But be **v** careful to obey all the commands
22:10 and the half-tribe of Manasseh built a **v** large altar
23: 1 from all their enemies. Joshua, who was now **v** old,
23: 6 Be **v** careful to follow all the instructions written in
23:11 So be **v** careful to love the LORD your God.
24: 7 With your **v** own eyes you saw what I did.
24:17 He performed mighty miracles before our **v** eyes.
Jdg 2:15 as he promised. And the people were **v** distressed.
3:17 He brought the tax money to Eglon, who was **v** fat.
4: 9 "**V** well," she replied, "I will go with you.
8: 5 They are **v** tired. I am chasing Zebah
8:32 Gideon died when he was **v** old, and he was buried
14: 7 talked with the woman and was **v** pleased with her.
15:18 Now Samson was **v** thirsty, and he cried out to the
18: 7 were also wealthy because their land was **v** fertile.
18: 9 We have seen the land, and it is **v** good.
Ru 1:20 for the Almighty has made life **v** bitter for me.
3: 2 and he's been **v** kind by letting you gather grain
1Sa 1: 5 a special portion because he loved her **v** much,
1:15 But I am **v** sad, and I was pouring out my heart to
2:17 So the sin of these young men was **v** serious in the
2:22 Now Eli was **v** old, but he was aware of what his
3: 1 those days messages from the LORD were **v** rare,
4:16 from the battlefront—I was there this **v** day."
4:18 broke his neck and died, for he was old and **v** fat.
8: 6 Samuel was **v** upset with their request and went to
11: 6 came mightily upon Saul, and he became **v** angry.
11:15 and Saul and all the Israelites were **v** happy.
14:33 "That is **v** wrong," Saul said. "Find a large stone
16:21 Saul liked David **v** much, and David became one
16:22 David join my staff, for I am **v** pleased with him."
18: 8 This made Saul **v** angry. "What's this?" he said.
18:10 The **v** next day, in fact, a tormenting spirit from
18:30 So David's name became **v** famous throughout the
23:22 has seen him there, for I know that he is **v** crafty.
24: 3 David and his men were hiding in that **v** cave!
24:10 This **v** day you can see with your own eyes it isn't
25:15 But David's men were **v** good to us, and we never
25:36 He was **v** drunk, so she didn't tell him anything
26:21 I have been a fool and **v**, **v** wrong."
28: 2 "**V** well!" David agreed. "Now you will see for
30: 6 because his men were **v** bitter about losing their
31: 3 The fighting grew **v** fierce around Saul,
2Sa 3:36 This pleased the people **v** much. In fact,
4:11 own bed? Should I not also demand your **v** lives?"
8:13 So David became **v** famous. After his return he
10: 5 for they were **v** embarrassed by their appearance.
11:27 But the LORD was **v** displeased with what David
13: 3 Now Amnon had a **v** crafty friend—his cousin
13:21 David heard what had happened, he was **v** angry.
14:27 name was Tamar, and she was **v** beautiful.
17:29 "You must all be **v** tired and hungry and thirsty
19:20 the **v** first person in all Israel to greet you."
19:32 He was **v** old, about eighty, and **v** wealthy.
19:43 and the men of Judah were **v** harsh in their replies.
1Ki 1: 1 Now King David was **v** old, and no matter how
1: 4 The girl was **v** beautiful, and she waited on the
1: 6 Adonijah was a **v** handsome man and had been
1:15 He was **v** old now, and Abishag was taking care of
2:24 as the LORD lives, Adonijah will die this **v** day!"
3:26 and who loved him **v** much, cried out, "Oh no,
4:20 They were **v** contented, with plenty to eat
5: 7 Solomon's message, he was **v** pleased and said,
11: 9 The LORD was **v** angry with Solomon, for his
11:17 had fled. (Hadad was a **v** small child at the time.)
11:19 Pharaoh grew **v** fond of Hadad, and he gave him a
11:28 Jeroboam was a **v** capable young man, and when
13: 4 King Jeroboam was **v** angry with the man of God
14: 1 At that time Jeroboam's son Abijah became **v** sick.
14: 5 She will ask you about her son, for he is **v** sick.
18: 2 the famine had become **v** severe in Samaria.
20:31 we have heard that the kings of Israel are **v**
21:22 for you have made him **v** angry and have led all of
2Ki 6:11 The king of Aram became **v** upset over this.
6:31 I don't execute Elisha son of Shaphat this **v** day,"
8: 5 At that **v** moment, the mother of the boy walked in
8: 5 is her son—the **v** one Elisha brought back to life!"
13: 3 So the LORD was **v** angry with Israel, and he
14:10 indeed destroyed Edom and are **v** proud about it.
20:12 for he had heard that Hezekiah had been **v** sick.
21: 7 the **v** place where the LORD had told David
22:17 and I am **v** angry with them for everything they
23:17 and predicted the **v** things that you have just done
23:19 kings of Israel and had made the LORD **v** angry.
25: 3 the famine in the city had become **v** severe,
1Ch 5:23 and Mount Hermon. They were **v** numerous.
9:13 They were heads of clans and **v** able men.
10: 3 The fighting grew **v** fierce around Saul,
14: 2 and had made his kingdom **v** great for the sake of
17:17 You speak as though I were someone **v** great,
19: 5 for they were **v** embarrassed by their appearance.
21: 7 God was **v** displeased with the census, and he
21:13 the hands of the LORD, for his mercy is **v** great.
26: 7 Elihu and Semakiah, were also **v** capable men.
26: 8 were **v** capable men, well qualified for their work.
26: 9 and relatives were also **v** capable men.
2Ch 1: 1 his God was with him and made him **v** powerful.
2: 9 for the Temple I am going to build will be **v** large
17: 5 so he became **v** wealthy and highly esteemed.
20:19 the LORD, the God of Israel, with a **v** loud shout.
20:35 King Ahaziah of Israel, who was a **v** wicked man.

24:15 Jehoiada lived to a v old age, finally dying at 130.
25:15 This made the LORD v angry, and he sent a
25:19 You may be v proud of your conquest of Edom,
26: 8 even to Egypt, for he had become v powerful.
26:15 him wonderfully until he became v powerful.
29: 3 In the v first month of the first year of his reign,
31:21 As a result, he was v successful.
32:12 Surely you must realize that Hezekiah is the v
32:27 Hezekiah was v wealthy and held in high esteem.
33: 7 the v place where God had told David and his son
33:14 around the hill of Ophel, where it was built v high.
34:25 and I am v angry with them for everything they
Ezr 8:16 for Joiarib and Elnathan, who were v wise men.
8:18 He was a v astute man and a descendant of Mahli,
Ne 2:10 they were v angry that someone had come who
4: 1 Sanballat was v angry when he learned that we
4: 6 the entire city, for the people had worked v hard.
4:19 and all the people, "The work is v spread out,
5: 6 When I heard their complaints, I was v angry.
5:11 olive groves, and homes to them this v day.
6: 7 "You can be v sure that this report will get back to
13: 8 I became v upset and threw all of Tobiah's
Est 1:11 on her beauty, for she was a v beautiful woman.
2: 4 This advice was v appealing to the king, so he put
2: 9 Hegai was v impressed with Esther and treated her
7: 8 queen right here in the palace, before my v eyes?"
10: 3 He was v great among the Jews, who held him in
Job 21:24 the v picture of good health.
32:11 this time, listening v carefully to your arguments,
33: 8 said it in my hearing. I have heard your v words.
38:21 it was all created, and you are so v experienced!
Ps 56: 9 On the v day I call to you for help, / my enemies
60: 3 You have been v hard on us, / making us drink
73: 9 They boast against the v heavens, / and their words
77:16 and trembled! / The sea quaked to its v depths.
78:59 When God heard them, he was v angry, / and he
83: 4 We will destroy the v memory of its existence."
86:13 for your love for me is v great. / You have rescued
89: 8 as you, LORD? / Faithfulness is your v character.
119:112 keep your principles, / even forever, to the v end.
119:167 obeyed your decrees, / and I love them v much.
124: 5 their fury / would have overwhelmed our v lives.
138: 5 for the glory of the LORD is v great.
140: 9 by the v evil they have planned for me.
142: 6 Hear my cry, / for I am v low. / Rescue me from
148:13 For his name is v great; / his glory towers over the
Pr 6:26 with another man's wife may cost you your v life.
8:23 in ages past, at the v first, before the earth began.
24:10 fail under pressure, your strength is not v great.
Ecc 4:16 become the leader of millions and be v popular.
5:16 And this, too, is a v serious problem. As people
6: 3 might have a hundred children and live to be v old.
7:24 Wisdom is always distant and v difficult to find.
8:10 How strange that they were the v ones who
8:10 and are praised in the v city where they committed
11: 8 When people live to be v old, let them rejoice in
12:12 them can go on forever and become v exhausting!
Isa 3: 9 The v look on their faces gives them away
10:25 It will not last v long. In a little while my anger
16:11 My sorrow for Kir-hareseth will be v great.
17: 4 "In that day the glory of Israel will be v dim,
17:11 so well that they blossom on the v morning you
24:20 and will not rise again, for its sins are v great.
28:10 over again, a line at a time, in v simple words!"
28:13 and over, a line at a time, in v simple words.
29:17 Soon—and it will not be v long—the wilderness of
33: 5 Though the LORD is v great and lives in heaven,
39: 1 He had heard that Hezekiah had been v sick
43:27 From the v beginning, your ancestors sinned
52: 8 for before their v eyes they see the LORD
55: 7 Let them banish from their minds the v thought of
63: 8 He said, "They are my v own people. Surely they
65:12 You deliberately sinned—before my v eyes—
66: 4 They deliberately sinned—before my v eyes—
Jer 2:21 I chose a vine of the purest stock—the v best.
7:30 "The people of Judah have sinned before my v
16: 9 In your own lifetime, before your v eyes, I will put
21: 5 against you with great power, for I am v angry.
23: 1 and scattered the v ones they were expected to care
23:20 to come, you will understand all this v clearly.
24: 3 I replied, "Figs, some v good and some v bad."
28:16 Your life will end this v year because you have
31:26 and looked around. My sleep had been v sweet.
32:19 You are v aware of the conduct of all people,
32:20 You have made your name v great, as it is today.
32:37 I will bring them back to this v city and let them
38: 9 "these men have done a v evil thing in putting
44:10 To this v hour you have shown no remorse
44:23 The v reason all these terrible things have
48:29 have heard of the pride of Moab, for it is v great.
52: 6 the famine in the city had become v severe,
La 4:20 the LORD's anointed, the v life of our nation,
Eze 2: 3 and they are still in revolt to this v day.
4:16 I will cause food to be v scarce in Jerusalem.
8: 3 is a large idol that has made the LORD v angry.
9: 9 sins of the people of Israel and Judah are v great.
16:17 You took the v jewels and gold and silver
16:47 to you. In a v short time you far surpassed them!
19:11 Its branches became v strong, / strong enough to be
19:11 It soon became v tall, / towering above all the
20:26 I let them pollute themselves with the v gifts I had
23:22 those v nations from which you turned away in
23:34 you will drain that cup of terror to the v bottom.
23:39 On the v day that they murdered their children in
24: 2 because on this v day the king of Babylon is
28: 5 Yes, your wisdom has made you v rich, and your riches have made you v proud.
33:32 You are v entertaining to them, like someone who
36:23 reveal my holiness through you before their v eyes,
40: 2 of Israel and set me down on a v high mountain.
Da 4:11 The tree grew v tall and strong, reaching high into
4:20 You saw a tree growing v tall and strong,
4:33 That v same hour the prophecy was fulfilled,
5: 5 At that v moment they saw the fingers of a human
5:30 That v night Belshazzar, the Babylonian king,
6:14 the king was v angry with himself for signing the
6:19 V early the next morning, the king hurried out to
7: 7 a fourth beast, terrifying, dreadful, and v strong.
8: 4 its victims. It did as it pleased and became v great.
8: 5 which had one v large horn between its eyes,
8: 8 The goat became v powerful. But at the height of
8: 9 came a small horn whose power grew v great.
8:19 What you have seen pertains to the v end of time.
8:24 He will become v strong, but not by his own
9:23 to tell you what it was, for God loves you v much.
9:26 and its miseries are decreed from that time to the v
10: 8 my face grew deathly pale, and I felt v weak.
10:16 the vision I have seen, my lord, and I am v weak.
11:20 but after a v brief reign, he will die, though neither
Hos 8:11 but these v altars became places for sinning!
Joel 1:16 We watch as our food disappears before our v
Am 3:14 "On the v day I punish Israel for its sins, I will
7:10 a plot against you right here on your v doorstep!
8:10 only son had died. How v bitter that day will be!
9: 3 Even if they hide at the v top of Mount Carmel,
Jnh 2: 5 "I sank beneath the waves, and death was v near.
2: 6 I sank down to the v roots of the mountains.
4: 1 of plans upset Jonah, and he became v angry.
4: 6 and Jonah was v grateful for the plant.
Mic 1:11 because the v foundations of their city have been
2: 8 Yet to this v hour my people rise against me!
3: 2 but you are the v ones who hate good and love
Hab 2:11 The v stones in the walls of your houses cry out
Zep 1:13 They are the v ones whose property will be
3:20 you as I restore your fortunes before their v eyes.
Zec 1: 2 the LORD, was v angry with your ancestors.
1:15 But I am v angry with the other nations that enjoy
3: 6 Then the angel of the LORD spoke v solemnly to
9:12 I promise this v day that I will repay you two
Mt 4: 2 forty nights he ate nothing and became v hungry.
4: 8 Next the Devil took him to the peak of a v high
5:12 Be happy about it! Be v glad! For a great reward
10:30 And the v hairs on your head are all numbered.
12:18 He is my Beloved, / and I am v pleased with him.
13:21 plants in such soil, their roots don't go v deep.
18:31 of the other servants saw this, they were v upset.
19:23 it is v hard for a rich person to get into the
23:36 will break upon the heads of this v generation.
24:33 you can know his return is v near, right at the door.
26:34 "Peter," Jesus replied, "the truth is, this v night,
27: 1 V early in the morning, the leading priests
27:18 (He knew v well that the Jewish leaders had
28: 8 They were v frightened but also filled with great
Mk 4:17 plants in such soil, their roots don't go v deep.
6:26 Then the king was v sorry, but he was embarrassed
8:24 "I see people, but I can't see them v clearly.
8:33 at his disciples and then said to Peter v sternly,
9:21 boy's father. He replied, "Since he was v small.
10:14 he was v displeased with his disciples.
10:24 it is v hard to get into the Kingdom of God.
13:29 you can be sure that his return is v near, right at the
14:30 "Peter," Jesus replied, "the truth is, this v night,
15: 1 V early in the morning the leading priests,
16: 2 V early on Sunday morning, just at sunrise,
16: 4 looked up and saw that the stone—a v large one—
Lk 1: 7 was barren, and now they were both v old.
1:19 "I am Gabriel! I stand in the v presence of God.
1:32 He will be v great and will be called the Son of the
1:58 and relatives that the Lord had been v kind to her,
2:25 He was a righteous man and v devout. He was
2:35 be revealed. And a sword will pierce your v soul."
2:36 of Phanuel, of the tribe of Asher, and was v old.
4: 2 He ate nothing all that time and was v hungry.
4:21 "This Scripture has come true today before your v
4:38 where he found Simon's mother-in-law v sick with
6:35 Then your reward from heaven will be v great,
7:21 At that v time, he cured many people of their
8:13 plants in such soil, their roots don't go v deep.
9:32 Peter and the others were v drowsy and had fallen
11:47 For you build tombs for the v prophets your
12: 7 And the v hairs on your head are all numbered.
12:20 said to him, 'You fool! You will die this v night.
15:31 said to him, 'Look, dear son, you and I are v close,
18:23 heard this, he became sad because he was v rich.
19: 2 tax-collecting business, and he had become v rich.
21:26 because the stability of the v heavens will be
24: 1 But v early on Sunday morning the women came
Jn 1:45 "We have found the v person Moses
4:11 or a bucket," she said, "and this is a v deep well.
4:46 in the city of Capernaum whose son was v sick.
6:18 them as they rowed, and the sea grew v rough.
6:27 For God the Father has sent me for that v
6:60 his disciples said, "This is v hard to understand.
6:63 And the v words I have spoken to you are spirit
8: 4 "this woman was caught in the v act of adultery.
9:30 "Why, that's v strange!" the man replied.
11: 3 telling him, "Lord, the one you love is v sick."
12:27 lies ahead'? But that is the v reason why I came!
13:32 And God will bring me into my glory v soon.
14:28 If you really love me, you will be v happy for me,
16: 6 Instead, you are v sad.
19:31 was the Sabbath (and a v special Sabbath at that,
Ac 3:16 name has caused this healing before your v eyes.
4: 2 They were v disturbed that Peter and John were
5:34 religious law and was v popular with the people.
7: 9 "These sons of Jacob were v jealous of their
8:11 He was v influential because of the magic he
10:17 Peter was v perplexed. What could the vision
10:34 "I see v clearly that God doesn't show partiality.
12: 5 in prison, the church prayed v earnestly for him.
12:20 Now Herod was v angry with the people of Tyre
13:48 they were v glad and thanked the Lord for his
17:10 That v night the believers sent Paul and Silas to
17:22 "Men of Athens, I notice that you are v religious,
20: 9 sitting on the windowsill, became v drowsy.
21:20 and they all take the law of Moses v seriously.
22: 3 to follow our Jewish laws and customs v carefully.
22: 3 I became v zealous to honor God in everything I
22: 6 about noon a v bright light from heaven suddenly
22:13 your sight.' And that v hour I could see him!
24: 3 And for all of this we are v grateful to you.
25:10 tried right here. You know v well I am not guilty.
25:12 with his advisers and then replied, "V well!
25:17 I called the case the v next day and ordered Paul
27: 3 Julius was v kind to Paul and let him go ashore to
28: 2 The people of the island were v kind to us. It was
Ro 1: 7 and he has called you to be his v own people.
2: 1 for you do these v same things.
5:16 And the result of God's gracious gift is v different
7:15 but I don't do it. Instead, I do the v thing I hate.
8:15 You should behave instead like God's v own
9:17 "I have appointed you for the v purpose of
9:22 but he also has the right to be v patient with those
11: 2 own people, whom he chose from the v beginning.
11: 8 To this v day he has shut their eyes so they do not
11:24 into his own good tree—a v unusual thing to do—
13: 4 The authorities are established by God for that v
14: 9 Christ died and rose again for this v purpose,
15:27 They were v glad to do this because they feel they
16: 5 He was the v first person to become a Christian in
16:13 whom the Lord picked out to be his v own;
16:19 This makes me v happy. I want you to see clearly
1Co 1:18 I know v well how foolish the message of the cross
1:18 recognize this message as the v power of God.
2: 4 And my message and my preaching were v plain.
3:10 is building on this foundation must be v careful.
4: 3 it matters v little what you or anyone else thinks.
4:11 To this v hour we go hungry and thirsty,
4:17 That is the v reason I am sending Timothy—
7:29 The time that remains is v short, so husbands
8: 2 know all the answers doesn't really know v much.
14:17 You will be giving thanks v nicely, no doubt,
14:37 claim to be a prophet or think you are v spiritual,
2Co 2: 3 I will not be made sad by the v ones who ought to
2: 4 but I wanted you to know how v much I love you.
2:11 For we are v familiar with his evil schemes.
3:12 gives us such confidence, we can be v bold.
4:17 troubles are quite small and won't last v long.
7:16 I am v happy now because I have complete
8: 9 Though he was v rich, yet for your sakes he
10: 2 but when I come I may have to be v bold with
Gal 1:23 us now preaches the v faith he tried to destroy!"
2:11 against what he was doing, for it was v wrong.
4: 5 so that he could adopt us as his v own children.
Eph 2: 4 so rich in mercy, and he loved us so v much,
Php 1: 7 of you, for you have a v special place in my heart.
2:26 and he was v distressed that you heard he was ill.
3: 7 I once thought all these things were so v important,
Col 1: 6 just as it changed yours that v first day you heard
1:22 he has brought you into the v presence of God,
1:29 I work v hard at this, as I depend on Christ's
2: 5 And I am v happy because you are living as you
1Th 2: 5 try to win you with flattery, as you v well know.
2:13 You accepted what we said as the v word of God—
2:17 we tried v hard to come back because of our
2:18 We wanted v much to come, and I, Paul,
3:11 make it possible for us to come to you v soon.
1Ti 5: 4 This is something that pleases God v much.
2Ti 3: 1 that in the last days there will be v difficult times.
Tit 2:14 to cleanse us, and to make us his v own people,
Phm 1:11 in the past, but now he is v useful to both of us.
1:19 And I won't mention that you owe me your v soul!
Heb 2: 1 So we must listen v carefully to the truth we have
5:13 And a person who is living on milk isn't v far
13:16 in need, for such sacrifices are v pleasing to God.
Jas 5: 3 The v wealth you were counting on will eat away
1Pe 2: 7 Yes, he is v precious to you who believe. But for
2: 9 of priests, God's holy nation, his v own possession.
2:11 evil desires because they fight against your v souls.
4: 4 your former friends are v surprised when you no
4:13 Instead, be v glad—because these trials will make
2Pe 1: 9 these virtues are blind or, at least, v shortsighted.
1Jn 3: 1 See how v much our heavenly Father loves us,
3Jn 1: 3 and made me v happy by telling me about your
Rev 2:26 all who are victorious, who obey me to the v end,
16:21 of the hailstorm, which was a v terrible plague.

VESSEL (1) [VESSELS]

Eze 27:26 Your mighty v flounders in the heavy eastern gale.

VESSELS (5) [VESSEL]

2Ki 24:13 They cut apart all the gold v that King Solomon of
1Ch 22:19 and the holy v of God into the Temple built to
2Ch 24:14 and other v made of gold and silver.
Ezr 1: 6 And all their neighbors assisted by giving them v
Isa 52:11 you who carry home the v of the LORD.

VESTRY [KJV] See WARDROBE

VESTURE [KJV] See CLOAKS, CLOTHES, CLOTHING, COAT, GARMENTS, ROBE

VETERAN (1) [VETERANS]
2Ch 17:17 were under the command of Eliada, a **v** soldier.

VETERANS (1) [VETERAN]
Isa 34: 7 The strongest will die—**v** and young men, too.

VEX(ED), VEXATION [KJV] See ANGUISH, BITTER, CHASING, CONQUER, DISTRESS(ED), GRIEVED, HARM, HARASS(ED), HOSTILE, OPPRESS(ED), PANIC, TERRIFY, TERROR, TORMENT(ED), TREMBLE, TROUBLE(D), TUMULT, VIOLENT, WRONG(ED)

VIAL (1)
2Ki 9: 1 he told him. "Take this **v** of olive oil with you,

VIAL(S) [KJV] See also BOWL(S)

VICINITY (2)
2Ki 23: 5 throughout Judah and even in the **v** of Jerusalem.
Jer 33:13 the land of Benjamin, the **v** of Jerusalem,

VICIOUS (4) [VICIOUSLY]
Ps 59: 6 They come at night, / snarling like **v** dogs / as they
59:14 enemies come out at night, / snarling like **v** dogs
Isa 58: 9 making false accusations and spreading **v** rumors!
Ac 20:29 I know full well that false teachers, like **v** wolves,

VICIOUSLY (2) [VICIOUS]
Ps 10: 2 Proud and wicked people **v** oppress the poor.
25:19 many enemies I have, / and how **v** they hate me!

VICTIM (8) [VICTIM'S, VICTIMS]
Jos 20: 5 If the relatives of the **v** come to avenge the killing,
2Sa 3:34 you were murdered— / the **v** of a wicked plot."
Ps 10: 8 They are always searching / for some helpless **v**.
Pr 23:28 looking for another **v** who will be unfaithful to his
26: 2 an unfair curse will not land on its intended **v**.
Da 11:35 And some who are wise will fall **v** to persecution.
Am 3: 4 lion ever roar in a thicket without first finding a **v**?
1Pe 5: 8 like a roaring lion, looking for some **v** to devour.

VICTIM'S (5) [VICTIM]
Nu 35:19 The **v** nearest relative is responsible for putting the
35:21 the **v** nearest relative must execute the murderer
35:24 the slayer and the avenger, the **v** nearest relative.
35:27 and the **v** nearest relative finds him outside the city
Mal 2:16 "It is as cruel as putting on a **v** bloodstained coat,"

VICTIMS (26) [VICTIM]
Ex 21:16 whether they are caught in possession of their **v**
Job 29:17 godless oppressors and made them release their **v**.
Ps 10: 9 Like hunters they capture their **v** / and drag them
Pr 1:12 swallow them alive as the grave swallows its **v**.
7:26 the ruin of many; numerous men have been her **v**.
26:28 A lying tongue hates its **v**, and flattery causes ruin.
Ecc 4: 1 have great power, and the **v** are helpless.
Isa 1:15 are covered with the blood of your innocent **v**.
5:30 The enemy nations will growl over their **v** like the
Jer 5:26 who lie in wait for **v** like a hunter hiding in a blind.
14:16 into the streets of Jerusalem, **v** of famine and war.
Eze 11: 7 but the **v** of your injustice are the pieces of meat.
13:21 from your grasp. They will no longer be your **v**.
22:27 leaders are like wolves, who tear apart their **v**.
32:21 they lie among the outcasts, all **v** of the sword.'
32:26 But now they are outcasts, all **v** of the sword.
32:28 and broken among the outcasts, all **v** of the sword.
32:30 and the Sidonians are there, all **v** of the sword.
Da 7: 7 It devoured and crushed its **v** with huge iron teeth
7:19 It devoured and crushed its **v** with iron teeth
8: 4 and no one could stand against it or help its **v**.
Hos 6: 9 are bands of robbers, lying in ambush for their **v**.
Zep 3: 3 leaders are like roaring lions hunting for their **v**—
Mk 1:34 he ordered many demons to come out of their **v**.
Jn 19:31 The Jewish leaders didn't want the **v** hanging there
Ac 8: 7 spirits were cast out, screaming as they left their **v**.

VICTOR'S (1) [VICTORY]
1Co 4: 9 like prisoners of war at the end of a **v** parade,

VICTORIES (6) [VICTORY]
Jdg 5:11 They recount the righteous **v** of the LORD, / and the **v** of his villagers in Israel.
2Sa 22:51 You give great **v** to your king; / you show
2Ki 5: 1 through him the LORD had given Aram great **v**.
Ps 18:50 You give great **v** to your king; / you show
44: 4 and my God. / You command **v** for your people.

VICTORIOUS (26) [VICTORY]
Ge 14:11 The **v** invaders then plundered Sodom
Ex 5:16 So, like a **v** army, they plundered the Egyptians!
Nu 21:35 And Israel was **v** and killed King Og, his sons,
1Sa 14:47 the Philistines. And wherever he turned, he was **v**.
18: 6 But something happened when the **v** Israelite army
2Sa 8:14 how the LORD made David **v** wherever he went.
1Ki 22:12 they said, "go up to Ramoth-gilead and be **v**,
2Ki 3:18 for he will make you **v** over the army of Moab!
13:19 Now you will be **v** only three times."
1Ch 18:13 how the LORD made David **v** wherever he went.
2Ch 18:11 they said, "go up to Ramoth-gilead and be **v**.
Ps 74: 4 There your enemies shouted their **v** battle cries;
110: 7 from brooks along the way. / He will be **v**.
Isa 29: 8 your enemies will dream of a **v** conquest over
41:10 help you. I will uphold you with my **v** right hand.
Zec 9: 9 He is righteous and **v**, yet he is humble, riding on a
Rev 2: 7 Everyone who is **v** will eat from the tree of life in
2:11 Whoever is **v** will not be hurt by the second death.
2:17 Everyone who is **v** will eat of the manna that has
2:26 "To all who are **v**, who obey me to the very end,
3: 5 All who are **v** will be clothed in white. I will never
3:12 All who are **v** will become pillars in the Temple of
3:21 I will invite everyone who is **v** to sit with me on
3:21 just as I was **v** and sat with my Father on his
15: 2 And on it stood all the people who had been **v** over
21: 7 All who are **v** will inherit all these blessings,

VICTORY (102) [VICTOR'S, VICTORIES, VICTORIOUS]
Ge 14:17 As Abram returned from his **v** over Kedorlaomer
Ex 15: 2 is my strength and my song; / he has become my **v**.
32:18 "No, it's neither a cry of **v** nor a cry of defeat.
Nu 21: 3 their request and gave them **v** over the Canaanites.
21:34 for I have given you **v** over Og and his entire army,
Dt 3: 2 for I have given you **v** over Og and his army,
20: 4 you against your enemies, and he will give you **v**!'
Jos 10: 8 said to Joshua, "for I will give you **v** over them.
10:12 On the day the LORD gave the Israelites **v** over
10:19 for the LORD your God has given you **v** over
11: 8 And the LORD gave them **v** over their enemies.
24: 8 fought against you, but I gave you **v** over them,
24:11 and the Jebusites. But I gave you **v** over them.
24:12 It was not your swords or bows that brought you **v**.
Jdg 1: 2 "Judah, for I have given them **v** over the land."
1: 4 the LORD gave them **v** over the Canaanites
3:10 of Aram, and the LORD gave Othniel **v** over him.
3:28 "for the LORD has given you **v** over Moab your
4: 7 Kishon River. There I will give you **v** over him."
4: 9 For the LORD's **v** over Sisera will be at the hands
4:14 Today the LORD will give you **v** over Sisera,
7: 7 will rescue you and give you **v** over the Midianites.
7: 9 Midianite camp, for I have given you **v** over them!
7:14 **v** over all the armies united with Midian!"
7:15 For the LORD has given you **v** over the
8: 3 God gave you **v** over Oreb and Zeeb, the generals
8: 7 "After the LORD gives me **v** over Zebah
8: 9 "After I return in **v**, I will tear down this tower."
11: 9 and if the LORD gives me **v** over the Ammonites,
11:21 God of Israel, gave his people **v** over King Sihon.
11:30 He said, "If you give me **v** over the Ammonites,
11:32 the Ammonites, and the LORD gave him **v**.
11:36 for the LORD has given you a great **v** over your
12: 3 and the LORD gave me **v** over the Ammonites.
15:18 "You have accomplished this great **v** by the
16:23 "Our god has given us **v** over our enemy
20:28 "Go! Tomorrow I will give you **v** over them."
1Sa 19: 5 and how the LORD brought a great **v** to Israel as
2Sa 1: 1 David returned from his **v** over the Amalekites
5:19 "Yes, go ahead. I will certainly give you the **v**."
8: 6 So the LORD gave David **v** wherever he went.
12:28 so you will get credit for the **v** instead of me."
19: 2 the joy of that day's **v** was turned into deep
22:44 "You gave me **v** over my accusers.
23:10 and the LORD gave him a great **v** that day.
23:12 So the LORD brought about a great **v**.
1Ki 5: 3 He could not build until the LORD gave him **v**
22: 6 right ahead! The Lord will give you a glorious **v**!"
22:12 be victorious, for the LORD will give you **v**!"
22:13 all the prophets are promising **v** for the king.
22:15 The LORD will give the king a glorious **v**!"
2Ki 13:17 "This is the LORD's arrow, full of **v** over Aram,
14:10 about it. Be content with your **v** and stay at home!
1Ch 11:14 the LORD saved them by giving them a great **v**.
14:10 "Yes, go ahead. I will give you the **v**."
18: 6 So the LORD gave David **v** wherever he went.
29:11 is the greatness, the power, the glory, the **v**,
2Ch 18: 5 "Go ahead, for God will give you a great **v**!"
18:11 The LORD will give you a glorious **v**!"
18:12 all the prophets are promising **v** for the king.
18:14 "Go right ahead! It will be a glorious **v**!"
20:17 then stand still and watch the LORD's **v**.
20:27 full of joy that the LORD had given them **v** over
Est 9:17 celebrating their **v** with a day of feasting
Ps 3: 8 **V** comes from you, O LORD. / May your
18:43 You gave me **v** over my accusers. / You appointed
20: 5 May we shout for joy when we hear of your **v**,
20: 9 Give **v** to our king, O LORD! / Respond to our
21: 1 O LORD! / He shouts with joy because of your **v**.
21: 5 Your **v** brings him great honor, / and you have
28: 8 his people / and gives **v** to his anointed king.
32: 7 You surround me with songs of **v**. / *Interlude*
33:17 Don't count on your warhorse to give you **v**—
44: 3 it was not their own strength that gave them **v**.
44: 7 It is you who gives us **v** over our enemies; / it is
45: 4 In your majesty, ride out to **v**, / defending truth,
48:10 the earth. / Your strong right hand is filled with **v**.
60: 9 fortified city? / Who will bring me **v** over Edom?
68:11 The Lord announces **v**, / and throngs of women
98: 1 He has won a mighty **v** / by his power
98: 2 The LORD has announced his **v** / and has
108:10 fortified city? / Who will bring me **v** over Edom?
118:14 is my strength and my song; / he has become my **v**.
118:15 of joy and **v** are sung in the camp of the godly.
144:10 For you grant **v** to kings! / You are the one who
Pr 21:31 for battle, but the **v** belongs to the LORD.
24: 6 **v** depends on having many counselors.
Isa 41: 2 this king from the east, who meets **v** at every step?
41: 2 He gives him **v** over many nations and permits him
41:25 and I will give him **v** over kings and princes.
60:11 the world will be led as captives in a **v** procession.
Eze 39:13 for it will be a glorious **v** for Israel when I
Da 1: 2 The Lord gave him **v** over King Jehoiakim of
Zec 12: 7 The LORD will give **v** to the rest of Judah first,
Mt 12:20 until he brings full justice with his final **v**.
Ro 8:37 overwhelming **v** is ours through Christ, who loved
1Co 15:54 will come true: / "Death is swallowed up in **v**.
15:55 O death, where is your **v**? / O death, where is your
15:57 who gives us **v** over sin and death through Jesus
Col 2:15 He shamed them publicly by his **v** over them on
1Jn 5: 4 this evil world by trusting Christ to give the **v**.
Rev 6: 2 He rode out to win many battles and gain the **v**.

VICTUAL(S) [KJV] See BREAD, FOOD, GRAIN, PROVISIONS

VIEW (14) [VIEWPOINT]
Ex 40:21 and set up the inner curtain to shield it from **v**,
Nu 14:14 that you have appeared in full **v** of your people in
33: 3 Israel left defiantly, in full **v** of all the Egyptians.
Dt 3:27 go to Pisgah Peak and **v** the land in every direction,
2Sa 12:11 and he will go to bed with them in public **v**.
Ne 8: 5 Ezra stood on the platform in full **v** of all the
Ps 68:24 Your procession has come into **v**, O God—
Isa 47: 2 strip off your robe. Expose yourself to public **v**.
66:24 All who pass by will **v** them with utter horror."
Da 9:16 In **v** of all your faithful mercies, Lord, please turn
Mt 16:23 are seeing things merely from a human point of **v**,
Mk 8:33 are seeing things merely from a human point of **v**,
Jn 7:10 also went, though secretly, staying out of public **v**.
Ro 4: 2 But from God's point of **v** Abraham had no basis

VIEWPOINT (1) [VIEW]
1Jn 4: 5 so they speak from the world's **v**, and the world

VIGILANT [KJV] See CAREFUL, SELF-CONTROL

VIGOR (2) [VIGOROUS, VIGOROUSLY]
Job 18:12 Their **v** is depleted by hunger, and calamity waits
Ps 110: 3 your **v** will be renewed each day like the morning

VIGOROUS (5) [VIGOR]
Ge 49: 3 you are my oldest son, / the child of my **v** youth.
Ps 128: 3 your table / as **v** and healthy as young olive trees.
Isa 59:10 are like corpses when compared to **v** young men!
66:14 your heart will rejoice. **V** health will be yours!
Col 2: 7 in faith, strong and **v** in the truth you were taught.

VIGOROUSLY (1) [VIGOR]
Eze 21:14 of man, prophesy to them and clap your hands **v**.

VILE (10) [VILENESS]
Ps 101: 3 I will refuse to look at / anything **v** and vulgar.
La 3:61 LORD, you have heard the **v** names they call me.
Eze 5:11 have defiled my Temple with idols and **v** practices.
7:20 and used it to make **v** and detestable idols.
Hos 9:10 Soon they became as **v** as the god they worshiped.
Na 3: 6 with filth and show the world how **v** you really are.
Mk 7:23 All these **v** things come from within; they are what
Ro 1:24 they did **v** and degrading things with each other's
Rev 22:11 the one who is **v**, continue to be **v**; the one who

VILENESS (1) [VILE]
Eze 39:24 and punished them in proportion to the **v** of their

VILLAGE (69) [VILLAGERS, VILLAGES]
Ge 11:31 But they stopped instead at the **v** of Haran
19:20 See, there is a small **v** nearby. Please let me go
19:21 grant your request. I will not destroy that little **v**.
19:22 From that time on, that **v** was known as Zoar.
19:23 The sun was rising as Lot reached the **v**.
24:10 and went to the **v** where Abraham's brother Nahor
24:11 camels kneel down beside a well just outside the **v**.
24:13 and the young women of the **v** are coming out to
24:31 Why do you stand here outside the **v** when we
28:19 though the name of the nearby **v** was Luz.
38:14 beside the road at the entrance to the **v** of Enaim,
38:21 sitting beside the road at the entrance to the **v**?"
38:22 and that the men of the **v** had claimed they didn't
38:23 We'd be the laughingstock of the **v** if we went
Lev 25:31 But a house in a **v**—a settlement without fortified
Jos 18:14 ending at the **v** of Kiriath-baal (that is,
Jdg 5:11 Listen to the **v** musicians gathered at the watering
1Sa 25: 2 Maon who owned property near the **v** of Carmel.
2Sa 16: 5 a man came out of the **v** cursing them.
1Ki 17: 9 "Go and live in the **v** of Zarephath, near the city of
17:10 As he arrived at the gates of the **v**, he saw a widow
Jer 41:17 They took them all to the **v** of Geruth-kimham near
Mic 5: 2 Bethlehem Ephrathah, are only a small **v** in Judah.
Mt 2: 6 of Judah, / you are not just a lowly **v** in Judah,
10:11 Whenever you enter a city or **v**, search for a
10:14 If a **v** doesn't welcome you or listen to you,
21: 2 "Go into the **v** over there," he said, "and you will

Mk 6: 6 Then Jesus went out from v to v, teaching.
6:10 "When you enter each v, be a guest in only one
6:11 "And if a v won't welcome you or listen to you,
6:11 It is a sign that you have abandoned that v to its
8:23 the blind man by the hand and led him out of the v.
8:26 "Don't go back into the v on your way home."
11: 2 "Go into that v over there," he told them, "and as
Lk 1:26 sent the angel Gabriel to Nazareth, a v in Galilee,
2: 4 He traveled there from the v of Nazareth in
2: 7 because there was no room for them in the v inn.
2: 8 some shepherds were in the fields outside the v,
2:16 They ran to the v and found Mary and Joseph.
4:16 When he came to the v of Nazareth, his boyhood
4:40 people throughout the v brought sick family
5:17 (It seemed that these men showed up from every v
7:11 Jesus went with his disciples to the v of Nain,
7:12 was coming out as he approached the v gate.
7:12 and many mourners from the v were with her.
9: 4 When you enter each v, be a guest in only one
9: 5 If the people of the v won't receive your message
9: 5 It is a sign that you have abandoned that v to its
9:52 He sent messengers ahead to a Samaritan v to
9:53 The people of the v refused to have anything to do
9:56 So they went on to another v.
10:38 they came to a v where a woman named Martha
17:12 As he entered a v there, ten lepers stood at a
19:30 "Go into that v over there," he told them, "and as
24:13 followers were walking to the v of Emmaus,
Jn 1:28 a v east of the Jordan River, where John was
2: 1 a wedding celebration in the v of Cana in Galilee.
4: 5 Eventually he came to the Samaritan v of Sychar,
4: 8 because his disciples had gone into the v to buy
4:28 the well and went back to the v and told everyone,
4:30 So the people came streaming from the v to see
4:39 Many Samaritans from the v believed in Jesus
4:40 out to see him, they begged him to stay at their v.
7: 1 Jesus stayed in Galilee, going from v to v.
7:42 in Bethlehem, the v where King David was born."
11:30 Now Jesus had stayed outside the v, at the place
11:54 to the v of Ephraim, and stayed there with his

VILLAGERS (1) [VILLAGE]

Jdg 5:11 of the LORD, / and the victories of his v in Israel.

VILLAGES (92) [VILLAGE]

Ge 19:25 along with the other cities and v of the plain,
Nu 21:25 the city of Heshbon and its surrounding v.
31:10 all the towns and v where the Midianites had lived.
32:42 captured the town of Kenath and its surrounding v,
Dt 2:23 who had lived in v in the area of Gaza.)
3: 5 We also took many unwalled v at the same time.
Jos 10:39 the city, its king, and all of its surrounding v.
13:23 and v in this area were given as an inheritance to
13:28 and v in this area were given as an inheritance to
15:32 of these towns with their surrounding v.
15:36 were fourteen towns with their surrounding v.
15:41 sixteen towns with their surrounding v.
15:44 nine towns with their surrounding v.
15:45 Judah also included all the towns and v of Ekron.
15:46 the towns near Ashdod with their surrounding v.
15:47 and v and Gaza with its towns and v,
15:51 and Giloh—eleven towns with their surrounding v.
15:54 and Zior—nine towns with their surrounding v.
15:57 and Timnah—ten towns with their surrounding v.
15:59 and Eltekon—six towns with their surrounding v.
15:60 and Rabbah—two towns with their surrounding v.
15:62 and En-gedi—six towns with their surrounding v.
16: 9 v in the territory of the half-tribe of Manasseh.
17:11 Taanach, and Megiddo, with their respective v.
18:24 Ophni, and Geba—twelve towns with their v.
18:28 and Kiriath-jearim—fourteen towns with their v.
19: 6 and Sharuhen—thirteen towns with their v.
19: 7 Ether, and Ashan—four towns with their v,
19: 8 including all the v as far south as Baalath-beer
19:15 twelve towns with their surrounding v.
19:22 sixteen towns with their surrounding v.
19:30 twenty-two towns with their surrounding v.
19:38 nineteen cities with their surrounding v.
19:48 of the tribe of Dan—these towns with their v.
21:12 and the surrounding v were given to Caleb son of
Jdg 1:27 Dor, Ibleam, Megiddo, and their surrounding v,
5: 7 There were few people left in the v of Israel—
1Sa 5: 6 and the nearby v with a plague of tumors.
6:18 the five Philistine cities and their surrounding v,
27: 9 David didn't leave one person alive in the v he
1Ch 2:23 and also took Kenath and its sixty surrounding v.)
4:33 and their surrounding v as far away as Baalath.
5:16 in Bashan and its v, and throughout the Sharon
7:28 Gezer and its v to the west, and Shechem and its
surrounding v to the north as far as Ayyah
7:29 Taanach, Megiddo, Dor, and their surrounding v.
8:12 Shemed (who built Ono and Lod and their v),
9:22 and they were listed by genealogies in their v.
9:25 their relatives in the v came to share their duties
20: 1 attacks against the towns and v of the Ammonites.
27:25 throughout the towns, v, and fortresses of Israel.
2Ch 13:19 and Ephron, along with their surrounding v.
28:18 Aijalon, Gederoth, Soco with its v, Timnah with
its v, and Gimzo with its v,
31:19 who were living in the open v around the towns,
Ezr 2:70 and some of the common people settled in v near
Ne 6: 2 to meet them at one of the v in the plain of Ono.
11:25 the people of Judah lived in Kiriath-arba with its v,
Dibon with its v, and Jekabzeel with its v.
11:27 Hazar-shual, Beersheba with its v,
11:28 Ziklag, and Meconah with its v.
11:30 Zanoah, and Adullam with their v. They were also
11:30 nearby fields and Azekah with its surrounding v.
11:31 Micmash, Aija, and Bethel with its surrounding v.
12:28 and its surrounding v and from the v of the
Netophathites.
12:29 for the singers had built their own v around
Est 9:19 rural Jews living in unwalled v celebrate an annual
Isa 42:11 you desert towns; / let the v of Kedar rejoice!
Jer 49:13 All its towns and v will be desolate forever."
Eze 26: 6 and its mainland v will be destroyed by the sword.
26: 8 First he will destroy your mainland v. Then he will
38:11 is an unprotected land filled with unwalled v!
Am 1: 9 with Israel, selling whole v as slaves to Edom.
Ob 1:20 to their homeland and resettle the v of the Negev.
Mt 9:35 traveled through all the cities and v of that area,
14:13 he was headed and followed by land from many v.
14:15 Send the crowds away so they can go to the v
Mk 6:36 and v and buy themselves some food."
6:56 he went—in v and cities and out on the farms—
8:27 and went up to the v of Caesarea Philippi.
Lk 5:12 In one of the v, Jesus met a man with an advanced
8: 1 and v to announce the Good News concerning the
9: 6 So they began their circuit of the v,
9:12 "Send the crowds away to the nearby v and farms,
10: 1 in pairs to all the towns and v he planned to visit.
13:22 Jesus went through the towns and v, teaching as he
Ac 5:16 Crowds came in from the v around Jerusalem,
8:25 And they stopped in many Samaritan v along the

VILLAINY (1)

Ac 13:10 of the Devil, full of every sort of trickery and v,

VINDICATE (1) [VINDICATED, VINDICATION]

Ps 135:14 For the LORD will v his people / and have

VINDICATED (3) [VINDICATE]

Ge 30: 6 named him Dan, for she said, "God has v me!
31:42 is why he appeared to you last night and v me."
Jer 51:10 The LORD has v us. Come, let us announce in

VINDICATION (1) [VINDICATE]

Isa 54:17 servants of the LORD; their v will come from me.

VINE (30) [VINE'S, VINES, VINEYARD, VINEYARDS]

Ge 40: 9 "In my dream," he said, "I saw a v in front of me.
49:11 a grapevine, / the colt of his donkey to a choice v.
Dt 32:32 Their v grows from the v of Sodom,
Job 15:33 They will be like a v whose grapes are harvested
Ps 80: 8 us from Egypt as though we were a tender v;
80:14 and see our plight. / Watch over and care for this v
128: 3 Your wife will be like a fruitful v,
Isa 16: 9 now the enemy has completely destroyed that v.
24:13 or the few grapes left on the v after harvest,
Jer 2:21 I planted you, I chose a v of the purest stock—
2:21 How did you grow into this corrupt wild v?
5:10 Strip the branches from the v, for they do not
6: 9 as when a harvester checks each v a second time to
Eze 15: 5 V branches are useless both before and after being
17: 6 It took root there and grew into a low, spreading v.
17: 7 So the v sent its roots and branches out toward him
17: 8 The v did this even though it was already planted
17: 8 plenty of water so it could grow into a splendid v
17: 9 Should I let this v grow and prosper? No! I will
17:10 Then when the v is transplanted, will it thrive?
19:10 'Your mother was like a v / planted by the water's
19:12 But the v was uprooted in fury / and thrown down
19:13 Now the v is growing in the wilderness,
Hos 10: 1 Israel is—a luxuriant v loaded with fruit!
Joel 1:11 Wail, all you v growers! Weep, because the wheat
Hab 3:17 no blossoms, and there are no grapes on the v;
Jn 15: 1 "I am the true v, and my Father is the gardener.
15: 4 cannot produce fruit if it is severed from the v,
15: 5 "Yes, I am the v; you are the branches. Those who

VINE'S (1) [VINE]

Eze 15: 2 a tree? Is a v wood as useful as the wood of a tree?

VINEDRESSERS [KJV] See (CARE FOR) VINEYARDS

VINEGAR (2)

Nu 6: 3 They must not use v made from wine, they must
Pr 10:26 smoke in the eyes or v that sets the teeth on edge.

VINES (15) [VINE]

Lev 19:10 do not strip every last bunch of grapes from the v,
25: 5 process the grapes that grow on your unpruned v.
25:11 process the grapes that grow on your unpruned v.
Dt 24:21 Do not glean the v after they are picked, but leave
28:39 or eat the grapes, for worms will destroy the v.
SS 7:12 Let us see whether the v have budded,
8:12 pieces of silver to those who care for its v."
Isa 5: 2 cleared its stones, / and planted it with choice v.
5: 6 I will not prune the v or hoe the ground.
27: 3 will watch over it and tend its fruitful v.
32:12 be gone, and for those fruitful v of other years.
33: 4 Just as locusts strip the fields and v, so Jerusalem
Jer 12:10 trampling down the v and turning all its beauty into
48:32 Your spreading v once reached as far as the Dead
Rev 14:18 the clusters of grapes from the v of the earth,

VINEYARD (51) [VINE]

Ge 9:20 the Flood, Noah became a farmer and planted a v.
Ex 22: 5 "If an animal is grazing in a field or v
Nu 22:24 where the road narrowed between two v walls.
Dt 20: 6 Has anyone just planted a v but not yet eaten any
22: 9 plant any other crop between the rows of your v.
22: 9 are forbidden to use either the grapes from the v
23:24 may eat your fill of grapes from your neighbor's v,
24:21 This also applies to the grapes in your v. Do not
28:30 You will plant a v, but you will never enjoy its
1Ki 21: 1 and near the palace was a v owned by a man
21: 2 "Since your v is so convenient to the palace,
21: 2 I will give you a better v in exchange, or if you
21: 6 "I asked Naboth to sell me his v or to trade it,
21: 7 and don't worry about it. I'll get you Naboth's v!"
21:15 "You know the v Naboth wouldn't sell you?
21:16 So Ahab immediately went down to the v to claim
21:18 He will be at Naboth's v in Jezreel,
Job 24:18 they own is cursed, so that no one enters their v.
Pr 24:30 field of a lazy person, the v of one lacking sense.
31:16 and buys it; with her earnings she plants a v.
SS 2:15 Catch all the little foxes before they ruin the v of
8:11 "Solomon has a v at Baal-hamon, which he rents
8:12 But as for my own v, O Solomon, you can take my
Isa 1: 8 stands abandoned like a watchman's shelter in a v
3:14 "You have ruined Israel, which is my v. You have
5: 1 I will sing a song for the one I love about his v:
5: 1 My beloved has a v / on a rich and fertile hill.
5: 4 rich harvest? / Why did my v give me wild grapes
5: 5 Now this is what I am going to do to my v:
5: 7 They are the v of the LORD Almighty. / Israel
5:10 Ten acres of v will not produce even six gallons of
27: 2 "In that day we will sing of the pleasant v.
Jer 12:10 "Many rulers have ravaged my v, trampling down
Am 5:17 There will be wailing in every v, for I will pass
Mt 20: 1 out early one morning to hire workers for his v.
20: 7 'Then go on out and join the others in my v.'
21:28 older boy, 'Son, go out and work in the v today.'
21:33 A certain landowner planted a v, built a wall
21:33 Then he leased the v to tenant farmers and moved
21:39 took him out of the v, and murdered him.
21:40 "When the owner of the v returns," Jesus asked,
21:41 and lease the v to others who will give him his
Mk 12: 1 "A man planted a v, built a wall around it, dug a
12: 1 Then he leased the v to tenant farmers and moved
12: 8 and murdered him and threw his body out of the v.
12: 9 "What do you suppose the owner of the v will
12: 9 and kill them all and lease the v to others.
Lk 20: 9 "A man planted a v, leased it out to tenant
20:15 So they dragged him out of the v and murdered
20:15 "What do you suppose the owner of the v will do
20:16 and kill them all and lease the v to others."

VINEYARDS (58) [VINE]

Ex 23:11 The same applies to your v and olive groves.
Lev 25: 3 and prune your v and harvest your crops,
25: 4 your crops or prune your v during that entire year.
Nu 16:14 or given us an inheritance of fields and v.
20:17 will be careful not to go through your fields and v.
21:22 or touch your v or drink your well water."
Dt 6:11 and you will eat from v and olive trees you did not
28:39 You will plant v and care for them, but you will
32:32 from the vine of Sodom, / from the v of Gomorrah.
Jos 24:13 I gave you v and olive groves for food, though you
Jdg 14: 5 a young lion attacked Samson near the v of
21:20 who still needed wives, "Go and hide in the v.
21:21 come out for their dances, rush out from the v,
1Sa 8:14 and v and olive groves and give them to his own
22: 7 the news. "Has David promised you fields and v?
2Ki 5:26 and v and sheep and oxen and servants?
18:32 bountiful harvests of grain and wine, bread and v,
19:29 harvest them; you will tend v and eat their fruit.
25:12 people to stay behind in Judah to care for the v
1Ch 27:27 Shimei from Ramah was in charge of the king's v.
2Ch 26:10 had many workers who cared for his farms and v,
Ne 5: 3 Others said, "We have mortgaged our fields, v,
5: 4 to the limit on our fields and v to pay our taxes.
5: 5 our fields and v are already mortgaged to others."
5:11 You must restore their fields, v, olive groves,
9:25 with cisterns already dug and v and olive groves
Job 24: 6 do not own, and they glean in the v of the wicked.
Ps 107:37 They sow their fields, plant their v, / and harvest
Ecc 2: 4 huge homes for myself and by planting beautiful v.
SS 1: 6 and sent me out to tend the v in the hot sun.
7:12 Let us get up early and go out to the v. Let us see
Isa 7:23 In that day the lush v, now worth as much as a
16: 8 abandoned farms of Heshbon and the v at Sibmah.
16: 8 The wine from those v used to make the rulers of
16: 9 So I wail and lament for Jazer and the v of Sibmah.
16:10 The happy singing in the v will be heard no more.
36:17 bountiful harvests of grain and wine, bread and v—
37:30 harvest them; you will tend v and eat their fruit.
61: 5 your flocks and plow your fields and tend your v.
65:21 houses they build and eat the fruit of their own v.
65:22 invaders took the houses and confiscated the v.
Jer 5:10 "Go down the rows of the v and destroy them,
31: 5 Again you will plant your v on the mountains of
32:15 and will buy and sell houses and v and fields."
35: 7 And do not build houses or plant crops or v,
35: 9 built houses or owned v or farms or planted crops.
39:10 and he assigned them fields and v to care for.
48:32 "You people of Sibmah, rich in v, I will weep for
52:16 people to stay behind in Judah to care for the v
Eze 28:26 in Israel and build their homes and plant their v.
Hos 2:12 I will destroy her v and orchards, things she claims
2:15 I will return her v to her and transform the Valley

Am 4: 9 "I struck your farms and v with blight and mildew.
5: 11 You will never drink wine from the lush v you are
9: 13 Then the terraced v on the hills of Israel will drip
9: 14 They will plant v and gardens; they will eat their
Mic 1: 6 Her streets will be plowed up for planting v.
Zep 1: 13 They will never drink wine from the v they have

VIOLATE (13) [VIOLATED, VIOLATES, VIOLATING, VIOLATION, VIOLATIONS]

Lev 18: 7 Do not v your father by having sexual intercourse
18: 8 of your father's wives, for this would v your father.
18: 10 or your daughter's daughter; that would v you.
18: 14 And do not v your uncle, your father's brother,
18: 16 your brother's wife; this would v your brother.
18: 19 "Do not v a woman by having sexual intercourse
Nu 15: 30 "But those who brazenly v the LORD's will,
Dt 22: 30 with his father's wife, for this would v his father.
Ezr 6: 11 "Those who v this decree in any way will have a
La 1: 10 She has seen foreigners v her sacred Temple,
Eze 22: 8 my holy things and v my Sabbath days of rest.
Mt 15: 3 v the direct commandments of God?
1Co 8: 10 but they will be encouraged to v their conscience

VIOLATED (22) [VIOLATE]

Lev 20: 19 or his father's sister, he has v a close relative.
20: 20 with his uncle's wife, he has v his uncle.
20: 21 He has v his brother, and the guilty couple will
Dt 17: 2 of the LORD your God and has v the covenant
22: 24 man must die because he v another man's wife.
22: 29 he must marry the young woman because he v her,
26: 13 I have not v or forgotten any of your commands.
27: 20 with his father's wife, for he has v his father.'
Jdg 2: 20 "Because these people have v the covenant I made
2Ki 18: 12 Instead, they had v his covenant—all the laws the
1Ch 5: 25 and v their covenant with the God of their
Ps 44: 17 our loyalty to you. / We have not v your covenant.
Isa 24: 5 v his laws, and broken his everlasting covenant.
Jer 22: 9 'Because they v their covenant with the LORD
Eze 20: 13 And they also v my Sabbath days. So I threatened
20: 16 ignored my will for them, and v my Sabbath days.
20: 21 given them life. And they also v my Sabbath days.
22: 26 Your priests have v my laws and defiled my holy
23: 38 they defiled my Temple and v my Sabbath day!
Da 11: 32 He will flatter those who have v the covenant
1Co 8: 7 of real gods, and their weak consciences are v.
1Ti 1: 19 For some people have deliberately v their

VIOLATES (1) [VIOLATE]

Ezr 6: 12 or nation that v this command and destroys this

VIOLATING (4) [VIOLATE]

Ge 17: 14 off from the covenant family for v the covenant."
Lev 22: 9 will be subject to punishment and die for v them.
Eze 20: 24 They scorned my instructions by v my Sabbath
Mal 2: 10 to each other, v the covenant of our ancestors?

VIOLATION (2) [VIOLATE]

2Ch 19: 10 murder case or some other v of God's instructions,
Heb 2: 2 and the people were punished for every v of the

VIOLATIONS (1) [VIOLATE]

Nu 18: 1 and your sons alone will be held liable for v

VIOLENCE (45) [VIOLENT]

Ge 6: 11 corrupt in God's sight, and it was filled with v.
6: 12 the world, and he saw v and depravity everywhere.
6: 13 for the earth is filled with v because of them.
49: 5 "Simeon and Levi are two of a kind— / men of v.
2Sa 22: 3 my savior, the one who saves me from v.
Job 38: 15 the wicked, and it stops the arm that is raised in v.
Ps 7: 16 but it backfires on them. / They plan v for others,
11: 5 and the wicked. / He hates everyone who loves v.
12: 5 "I have seen v done to the helpless,
27: 12 I've never done / and breathe out v against me.
55: 9 their speech, / for I see v and strife in the city.
58: 2 are crooked; / you hand out v instead of justice.
72: 14 He will save them from oppression and from v,
74: 20 for the land is full of darkness and v!
Pr 4: 17 They eat wickedness and drink v!
13: 2 their words, but those who are treacherous crave v.
21: 7 what is just, their v boomerangs and destroys them.
24: 2 For they spend their days plotting v, and their
Isa 59: 6 their activity is filled with sin. V is their trademark.
60: 18 V will disappear from your land; the desolation
Jer 6: 7 Her streets echo with the sounds of v
20: 8 in a violent outburst. "V and destruction!" I shout.
51: 35 May Babylon be repaid for all the v she did to us,"
51: 46 Then there will be a time of v as the leaders fight
Eze 7: 11 Their v will fall back on them as punishment for
7: 23 by terrible crimes. Jerusalem is filled with v.
8: 17 leading the whole nation into v, thumbing their
12: 19 land will be stripped bare on account of their v.
28: 16 Your great wealth filled you with v, and you
45: 9 Stop all your v and oppression and do what is just
Hos 4: 2 There is v everywhere, with one murder after
12: 1 They multiply lies and v; they make alliances with
Am 3: 10 are filled with wealth taken by theft and v.
Ob 1: 10 Because of the v you did to your close relatives in
Jnh 3: 8 must turn from their evil ways and stop all their v.
Mic 2: 2 want someone's house, you take it by fraud and v.
6: 12 you have become wealthy through extortion and v.
Hab 1: 2 "V!" I cry, but you do not come to save.
1: 3 Wherever I look, I see destruction and v.
1: 9 "On they come, all of them bent on v.
2: 8 You have filled the countryside with v and all the
2: 17 because of your murder and v in cities everywhere!
Zep 3: 1 polluted Jerusalem, the city of v and crime.
Ac 5: 26 Temple guards and arrested them, but without v,
19: 16 and attacked them with such v that they fled from

VIOLENT (28) [VIOLENCE, VIOLENTLY]

Ex 19: 18 and the whole mountain shook with a v
1Sa 2: 33 and grief, and their children will die a v death.
2Sa 22: 49 of my enemies; / you save me from v opponents.
Ps 18: 48 of my enemies; / you save me from v opponents.
22: 20 Rescue me from a v death; / spare my precious life
54: 3 are attacking me; / v men are trying to kill me.
57: 1 shadow of your wings / until this v storm is past.
86: 14 rise up against me; / v people are trying to kill me.
93: 4 But mightier than the v raging of the seas,
140: 1 evil people. / Preserve me from those who are v,
140: 4 Preserve me from those who are v, / for they are
140: 11 Cause disaster to fall with great force on the v.
Pr 3: 31 Do not envy v people; don't copy their ways.
11: 16 women obtain wealth, and v men get rich.
16: 29 V people deceive their companions, leading them
Isa 33: 19 These fierce, v people with a strange,
Jer 20: 8 I speak, the words come out in a v outburst.
Jnh 1: 4 causing a v storm that threatened to send them to
1: 13 But the stormy sea was too v for them, and they
Hab 1: 6 and v nation who will march across the world
Mt 11: 12 been forcefully advancing, and v people attack it.
Mk 9: 20 it threw the child into a v convulsion, and he fell to
9: 26 and threw the boy into another v convulsion
Lk 9: 42 to the ground and threw him into a v convulsion.
Ac 5: 17 who were Sadducees, reacted with v jealousy.
21: 35 so v the soldiers had to lift Paul to their shoulders
1Ti 3: 3 He must not be a heavy drinker or be v. He must
Tit 1: 7 not be a heavy drinker, v, or greedy for money.

VIOLENTLY (5) [VIOLENT]

Ge 21: 25 servants had taken v from Abraham's servants.
Mk 9: 18 it throws him v to the ground and makes him foam
Ac 26: 11 so v opposed to them that I even hounded them in
Gal 1: 13 how I v persecuted the Christians.
Rev 18: 21 will be thrown down as v as I have thrown away

VIOL(S) [KJV] See HARP(S), LYRES

VIPER (4) [VIPERS]

Ge 49: 17 beside the road, / a poisonous v along the path,
Job 20: 16 will suck the poison of snakes. The v will kill him.
Ps 140: 3 a snake; / the poison of a v drips from their lips.
Pr 23: 32 it bites like a poisonous serpent; it stings like a v.

VIPERS (2) [VIPER]

Dt 32: 33 is the venom of snakes, / the deadly poison of v.
Mt 23: 33 Snakes! Sons of v! How will you escape the

VIRGIN (33) [VIRGINITY, VIRGINS]

Ge 19: 8 Look—I have two v daughters. Do with them as
24: 16 Now Rebekah was very beautiful, and she was a v;
Ex 22: 16 "If a man seduces a v who is not engaged to
Lev 21: 3 or v sister who was dependent because she had no
21: 13 "The high priest must marry a v.
21: 14 by prostitution. She must be a v from his own clan,
Dt 22: 14 'I discovered she was not a v when I married her.'
22: 17 claiming that she was not a v when he married her.
22: 19 pieces of silver, for he falsely accused a v of Israel.
22: 23 a v who is engaged to be married, and he has
Jdg 11: 37 my friends for two months, because I will die a v."
11: 39 her father kept his vow, and she died a v.
19: 24 take my v daughter and this man's concubine.
21: 11 all the males and every woman who is not a v."
2Sa 13: 2 She was a v, and it seemed impossible that he
13: 18 as was the custom in those days for the king's v
1Ki 1: 2 "We will find a young v who will wait on you
2Ki 19: 21 'The v daughter of Zion / despises you and laughs
Isa 7: 14 Look! The v will conceive a child! She will give
37: 22 'The v daughter of Zion / despises you and laughs
Jer 14: 17 I cannot stop weeping, for my v daughter—
18: 13 My v Israel has done something too terrible to
31: 4 I will rebuild you, my v Israel. You will again be
31: 21 Come back again, my v Israel; return to your cities
46: 11 to Gilead to get ointment, O v daughter of Egypt!
La 2: 13 O v daughter of Zion, how can I comfort you?
Joel 1: 8 with sorrow, as a v weeps when her fiancé has died.
Am 5: 2 "The v Israel has fallen, / never to rise again!
Mt 1: 18 But while she was still a v, she became pregnant
1: 23 "Look! The v will conceive a child! / She will
1: 25 but she remained a v until her son was born.
Lk 1: 27 to a v named Mary. She was engaged to be married
1: 34 the angel, "But how can I have a baby? I am a v."

VIRGINITY (4) [VIRGIN]

Dt 22: 15 and mother must bring the proof of her v to the
22: 17 But here is the proof of my daughter's v.'
22: 20 accusations are true, and her v could not be proved.
Eze 23: 8 their lusts with her and robbed her of her v.

VIRGINS (6) [VIRGIN]

Nu 31: 18 Only the young girls who are v may live; you may
Jdg 21: 12 hundred young v who had never slept with a man,
Est 2: 2 the empire to find beautiful young v for the king.
SS 6: 8 and unnumbered v available to me.
Eze 44: 22 choose their wives only from among the v of Israel
Rev 14: 4 For they are spiritually undefiled, pure as v,

VIRTUE [KJV] See EXCELLENT, (MORAL) EXCELLENCE, POWER

VIRTUES (1) [VIRTUOUS]

2Pe 1: 9 But those who fail to develop these v are blind or,

VIRTUOUS (2) [VIRTUES]

Pr 31: 10 Who can find a v and capable wife? She is worth
31: 29 "There are many v and capable women in the

VISAGE [KJV] See FACE(S)

VISIBLE (4)

Ex 13: 9 This annual festival will be a v reminder to you,
13: 16 It is a v reminder that it was the LORD who
Lk 17: 20 "The Kingdom of God isn't ushered in with v
Col 1: 15 Christ is the v image of the invisible God.

VISION (78) [VISIONARIES, VISIONS]

Ge 15: 1 Afterward the LORD spoke to Abram in a v
15: 12 He saw a terrifying v of darkness and horror.
46: 2 During the night God spoke to him in a v. "Jacob!
Nu 24: 4 words of God, / who sees a v from the Almighty,
24: 16 the Most High, / who sees a v from the Almighty,
1Ki 22: 17 "In a v I saw all Israel scattered on the mountains,
2Ch 18: 16 "In a v I saw all Israel scattered on the mountains,
32: 32 and his acts of devotion are recorded in *The V of*
Job 4: 13 It came in a v at night as others slept.
15: 12 captured your reason? What has weakened your v,
20: 8 not be found. He will vanish like a v in the night.
Ps 6: 7 My v is blurred by grief; / my eyes are worn out
89: 19 You once spoke in a v to your prophet and said,
Isa 2: 1 This is another v that Isaiah son of Amoz saw
21: 2 I see an awesome v: I see you plundered
22: 5 has brought upon the Valley of V!
29: 7 attacking her walls will vanish like a v in the night.
Jer 24: 1 the skilled craftsmen, the LORD gave me this v.
Eze 3: 23 just as I had seen it in my first v by the Kebar
7: 26 They will look in vain for a v from the prophets.
8: 3 and transported me in a v of God to Jerusalem.
11: 24 And so ended the v of my visit to Jerusalem.
40: 2 In a v of God he took me to the land of Israel
43: 3 This v was just like the others I had seen, first by
Da 2: 19 That night the secret was revealed to Daniel in a v.
2: 31 in your v you saw in front of you a huge
7: 2 In my v that night, I, Daniel, saw a great storm
7: 7 Then in my v that night, I saw a fourth beast,
7: 13 As my v continued that night, I saw someone who
7: 28 That was the end of the v. I, Daniel, was terrified
8: 1 King Belshazzar's reign, I, Daniel, saw another v,
8: 13 "How long will the events of this v last?
8: 15 was trying to understand the meaning of this v,
8: 16 "Gabriel, tell this man the meaning of his v."
8: 17 have seen in your v relate to the time of the end."
8: 26 "This v about the twenty-three hundred evenings
8: 27 but I was greatly troubled by the v and could not
9: 21 Gabriel, whom I had seen in the earlier v,
9: 23 so you can understand the meaning of your v.
9: 24 to confirm the prophetic v, and to anoint the Most
10: 1 Daniel (also known as Belteshazzar) had another v.
10: 1 and Daniel understood what the v meant.
10: 2 When this v came to me, I, Daniel, had been in
10: 7 I, Daniel, am the only one who saw this v.
10: 8 I was left there all alone to watch this amazing v.
10: 14 the future, for this v concerns a time yet to come."
10: 16 "I am terrified by the v I have seen, my lord,
11: 14 own people will join them in order to fulfill the v,
Am 7: 1 The Sovereign LORD showed me a v. I saw him
7: 2 In my v the locusts ate everything in sight that was
7: 3 So the LORD relented and did not fulfill the v.
7: 4 Then the Sovereign LORD showed me another v.
7: 7 Then he showed me another v. I saw the Lord
8: 1 Then the Sovereign LORD showed me another v.
9: 1 Then I saw a v of the Lord standing beside the
Ob 1: 1 This is the v that the Sovereign LORD revealed to
Na 1: 1 This message concerning Nineveh came as a v to
Hab 1: 1 Habakkuk received from the LORD in a v.
2: 3 the time approaches when the v will be fulfilled.
Zec 1: 8 In a v during the night, I saw a man sitting on a red
Lk 1: 22 he must have seen a v in the Temple sanctuary.
Jn 12: 41 because he was given a v of the Messiah's glory.
Ac 9: 10 The Lord spoke to him in a v, calling, "Ananias!"
9: 12 I have shown him a v of a man named Ananias
10: 3 he had a v in which he saw an angel of God
10: 16 The same v was repeated three times.
10: 17 What could the v mean? Just then the men sent by
10: 19 Meanwhile, as Peter was puzzling over the v,
11: 5 I was praying, I went into a trance and saw a v.
12: 9 the angel. But all the time he thought it was a v.
16: 9 That night Paul had a v. He saw a man from
18: 9 One night the Lord spoke to Paul in a v and told
22: 18 I saw a v of Jesus saying to me, 'Hurry!
26: 19 I was not disobedient to that v from heaven.
2Th 2: 2 Even if they claim to have had a v, a revelation,
Rev 9: 17 And in my v, I saw the horses and the riders sitting
13: 1 And now in my v I saw a beast rising up out of the
17: 18 And this woman you saw in your v represents the

VISIONARIES (1) [VISION]

Isa 29: 10 He has closed the eyes of your prophets and v.

VISIONS (29) [VISION]

Nu 12: 6 I the LORD communicate by v and dreams.
1Sa 3: 1 were very rare, and v were quite uncommon.
2Ch 9:29 and also in *The V of Iddo the Seer,* concerning
Job 7:14 you shatter me with dreams. You terrify me with v.
33:15 in v of the night when deep sleep falls on people as
Isa 1: 1 These v concerning Judah and Jerusalem came to
Jer 14:14 They prophesy of v and revelations they have
La 2: 9 Her prophets receive no more v from the LORD.
Eze 1: 1 heavens were opened to me, and I saw v of God.
12:24 "Then you will see what becomes of all the false v
12:27 'His v won't come true for a long, long time.'
13: 7 Can your v be anything but false if you claim,
13: 8 Because what you say is false and your v are a lie,
13:23 But you will no longer talk of seeing v that you
21:29 and false prophets have given false v
22:28 And your prophets announce false v and speak
Da 1:17 special ability in understanding the meanings of v
2:28 and the v you saw as you lay on your bed.
4: 5 I saw v that terrified me as I lay in my bed.
7: 1 Daniel had a dream and saw v as he lay in his bed.
7:15 troubled by all I had seen, and my v terrified me.
Hos 12:10 I sent my prophets to warn you with many v
Joel 2:28 will dream dreams. Your young men will see v.
Am 1: 1 He received this message in v two years before the
Mic 1: 1 and they came to Micah in the form of v.
3: 6 night will close around you, cutting off all your v.
Ac 2:17 will prophesy, / your young men will see v,
2Co 12: 1 Let me tell about the v and revelations I received
Col 2:18 even though they say they have had v about this.

VISIT (71) [VISITED, VISITING, VISITORS, VISITS]

Ge 12: 7 an altar there to commemorate the LORD's v.
21:22 with Phicol, his army commander, to v Abraham.
26:27 "This is obviously no friendly v, since you sent
34: 1 went to v some of the young women who lived in
48: 1 So Joseph went to v him, and he took with him his
Ex 2:11 he went out to v his people, the Israelites,
2:11 During his v, he saw an Egyptian beating one of
4:18 "I would like to go back to Egypt to v my family.
18: 5 Jethro now came to v Moses, and he brought
18: 6 "Jethro, your father-in-law, has come to v you.
19:10 "Go down and prepare the people for my v.
Jdg 9: 1 went to Shechem to v his mother's brothers.
1Ki 10:24 People from every nation came to v him and to
10:25 everyone who came to v brought him gifts of silver
22: 2 King Jehoshaphat of Judah went to v King Ahab of
22: 3 During the v, Ahab said to his officials, "Do you
2Ki 4:18 her child was older, he went out to v his father,
5: 5 "Go and v the prophet," the king told him. "I will
8:29 was there, King Ahaziah of Judah went to v him.
9:16 of Judah was there, too, for he had gone to v him.
10:13 We are going to v the sons of King Ahab
20: 1 and the prophet Isaiah son of Amoz went to v him.
2Ch 9:23 Kings from every nation came to v him and to hear
9:24 everyone who came to v brought him gifts of silver
18: 2 A few years later, he went to Samaria to v Ahab,
22: 6 and King Ahaziah of Judah went to Jezreel to v
22: 7 It was during this v that Ahaziah went out with
Ne 1: 2 came to v me with some other men who had just
6:10 Later I went to v Shemaiah son of Delaiah
Job 5:24 When you v your pastures, nothing will be
Ps 41: 6 They v me as if they are my friends, / but all the
Pr 25:17 Don't v your neighbors too often, or you will wear
Isa 38: 1 and the prophet Isaiah son of Amoz went to v him.
Eze 11:24 And so ended the vision of my v to Jerusalem.
Zep 2: 7 For the LORD their God will v his people in
Mt 25:39 did we ever see you sick or in prison, and v you?'
25:43 I was sick and in prison, and you didn't v me.'
Mk 5:20 So the man started off to v the Ten Towns of that
Lk 1:43 this is, that the mother of my Lord should v me!
10: 1 pairs to all the towns and villages he planned to v.
11: 6 'A friend of mine has just arrived for a v, and I
Jn 12:21 paid a v to Philip, who was from Bethsaida in
Ac 7:23 he decided to v his relatives, the people of Israel.
7:24 During this v, he saw an Egyptian mistreating a
9:32 Peter traveled from place to place to v the
10: 6 lives near the shore. Ask him to come and v you."
13: 7 The governor invited Barnabas and Saul to v him,
15: 3 way in Phoenicia and Samaria to v the believers.
24:23 and allow his friends to v him and take care of his
27: 3 kind to Paul and let him go ashore to v with friends
Ro 1:11 For I long to v you so I can share a spiritual
1:13 dear friends, that I planned many times to v you,
15:22 my v to you has been delayed so long because I
15:23 all these long years of waiting, I am eager to v you.
1Co 4:18 become arrogant, thinking I will never v you again.
16: 5 I am coming to v you after I have been to
16: 7 This time I don't want to make just a short v
16:12 I urged him to v you along with the other believers,
2Co 2: 1 make them unhappy with another painful v."
7: 7 me how much you were looking forward to my v,
8:17 He welcomed our request that he v you again.
12:18 When I urged Titus to v you and sent our other
12:20 For I am afraid that when I come to v you I won't
13: 1 This is the third time I am coming to v you.
13: 2 been sinning when I was there on my second v.
Gal 1:18 that I finally went to Jerusalem for a v with Peter
1:21 Then after this v, I went north into the provinces of
1Th 2: 1 and sisters, that our v to you was not a failure.
3: 2 and we sent Timothy to v you. He is our co-worker
3: 6 He reports that you remember our v with joy
2Jn 1:12 For I hope to v you soon and to talk with you face

VISITATION [KJV] See CARE, JUDGE, PUNISH(MENT)

VISITED (16) [VISIT]

Ge 28: 9 So he v his uncle Ishmael's family and married one
38: 1 to Adullam, where he v a man named Hirah.
1Sa 30:31 Hebron, and all the other places they had v.
2Ki 2:19 Now the leaders of the town of Jericho v Elisha.
13:14 King Jehoash of Israel v him and wept over him.
Job 38:22 "Have you v the treasuries of the snow? Have you
Jer 32: 8 he would, Hanamel came and v me in the prison.
Eze 14: 1 Then some of the leaders of Israel v me, and while
Mt 25:36 you cared for me. I was in prison, and you v me.'
Lk 1:68 because he has v his people and redeemed them.
Ac 7:26 "The next day he v them again and saw two men
15:14 Peter has told you about the time God first v the
18:22 there he went up and v the church at Jerusalem and
21:11 When he v us, he took Paul's belt and bound his
28:30 his own rented house. He welcomed all who v him,
2Ti 1:16 and all his family because he often v

VISITING (4) [VISIT]

Ex 2:13 The next day, as Moses was out v his people again,
12:45 Hired servants and v foreigners may not eat it.
2Sa 3:23 was told that Abner had just been there v the king
Ac 18:23 back to Galatia and Phrygia, v all the believers,

VISITORS (7) [VISIT]

Ge 26:26 One day Isaac had v from Gerar. King Abimelech
Ex 23:12 including your slaves and v, to be refreshed.
1Ch 29:15 v and strangers in the land as our ancestors were
Ne 5:17 at my table, besides all the v from other lands!
Mk 2: 2 so packed with v that there wasn't room for one
Jn 12:12 through the city. A huge crowd of Passover v
Ac 2:10 v from Rome (both Jews and converts to Judaism),

VISITS (1) [VISIT]

Pr 2:19 The man who v her is doomed. He will never reach

VITAL (1) [VITALITY]

Ps 92:14 still produce fruit; / they will remain v and green.

VITALITY (1) [VITAL]

Pr 3: 8 Then you will gain renewed health and v.

VOCATION [KJV] See CALLING

VOICE (156) [VOICES]

VOICE OF THE LORD (1) Ac 7:31

VOICE OF THE LORD* (12) Ex 15:26; Dt 18:16; 1Ki 20:36; Ps 29:3,4,4,5,7,8,9; Isa 66:6; Zep 3:2

Ge 27:22 "The v is Jacob's, but the hands are Esau's,"
46: 3 "I am God," the v said, "the God of your father.
Ex 15:26 "If you will listen carefully to the v of the LORD
Nu 7:89 he heard the v speaking to him from between the
Dt 4:12 but didn't see his form; there was only a v.
4:33 Has any nation ever heard the v of God speaking
4:36 He let you hear his v from heaven so he could
5:22 "The LORD spoke these words with a loud v to
5:23 But when you heard the v from the darkness,
5:24 and we have heard his v from the heart of the fire.
5:26 Can any living thing hear the v of the living God
13: 4 his commands, listen to his v, and cling to him.
18:16 have to listen to the v of the LORD your God
30:10 your God will delight in you if you obey his v
1Sa 7:10 But the LORD spoke with a mighty v of thunder
12:14 and worship the LORD and listen to his v,
15:22 and sacrifices or your obedience to his v?
26:17 Saul recognized David's v and called out, "Is that
1Ki 18:29 but still there was no reply, no v, no answer.
19:13 And a v said, "What are you doing here, Elijah?"
20:36 "Because you have not obeyed the v of the
2Ki 19:22 Against whom did you raise your v?
Job 4:16 was a form before my eyes, and a hushed v said,
37: 2 Listen carefully to the thunder of God's v as it rolls
37: 4 of the thunder—the tremendous v of his majesty.
37: 5 God's v is glorious in the thunder. We cannot
40: 9 as God, and can you thunder with a v like his?
Ps 5: 3 Listen to my v in the morning, LORD.
19: 3 a sound or a word; / their v is silent in the skies;
22: 2 Every night you hear my v, but I find no relief.
29: 3 The v of the LORD echoes above the sea.
29: 4 The v of the LORD is powerful; / the v of the LORD is full of majesty.
29: 5 The v of the LORD splits the mighty cedars;
29: 7 The v of the LORD strikes with lightning bolts.
29: 8 The v of the LORD makes the desert quake;
29: 9 The v of the LORD twists mighty oaks
55:17 aloud in my distress, / and the LORD hears my v.
68:33 his mighty v thundering from the sky.
81: 5 to set us free. / I heard an unknown v that said,
95: 7 his care. / Oh, that you would listen to his v today!
Pr 8: 1 calls out! Hear as understanding raises her v!
8: 4 to all of you! I am raising my v to all people.
Ecc 12: 4 will be deaf and tuneless, with a quavering v.
SS 2:14 Let me see you; let me hear your v. For your v is pleasant, and you are lovely."
5: 2 awakened in a dream. I heard the v of my lover.
5: 6 but he was gone. I yearned for even his v!
8:13 that your companions can listen to your v.
Isa 14:10 With one v they all cry out, 'Now you are as weak
29: 4 Your v will whisper like a ghost from the earth
30:21 and you will hear a v say, "This is the way;
30:30 And the LORD will make his majestic v heard.
32: 3 and those who can hear will listen to his v.
33: 3 The enemy runs at the sound of your v. When you
37:23 Against whom did you raise your v?
40: 3 I hear the v of someone shouting, "Make a
40: 6 A v said, "Shout!" I asked, "What should I
42: 2 he will not shout or raise his v in public.
58: 1 "Shout with the v of a trumpet blast. Tell my
66: 6 It is the v of the LORD taking vengeance against
Eze 1:24 or like the v of the Almighty, or like the shouting
1:25 a v spoke from beyond the crystal surface above
1:28 the dust, and I heard someone's v speaking to me.
2: 1 "Stand up, son of man," said the v. "I want to
3: 1 The v said to me, "Son of man, eat what I am
10: 5 the cherubim sounded like the v of God Almighty
19: 9 in captivity, / so his v could never again be heard
24:27 your v will suddenly return so you can talk to him,
33:32 someone who sings love songs with a beautiful v
Da 4:31 a v called down from heaven, "O King
7: 5 And I heard a v saying to it, "Get up!
8:16 And I heard a human v calling out from the Ulai
9:11 and turned away, refusing to listen to your v.
10: 6 and his v was like the roaring of a vast multitude of
Joel 3:16 The LORD's v will roar from Zion and thunder
Am 1: 2 "The LORD's v roars from his Temple on Mount
Mic 6: 9 His v is calling out to everyone in Jerusalem:
Zep 3: 2 It proudly refuses to listen even to the v of the
Mt 3: 3 he said, / "He is a v shouting in the wilderness:
3:17 And a v from heaven said, "This is my beloved
12:19 not fight or shout; / he will not raise his v in public.
17: 5 and a v from the cloud said, "This is my beloved
27:46 Jesus called out with a loud v, "*Eli, Eli,*
Mk 1: 3 He is a v shouting in the wilderness: / 'Prepare a
1:11 And a v came from heaven saying, "You are my
9: 7 and a v from the cloud said, "This is my beloved
15:34 Then, at that time Jesus called out with a loud v,
Lk 1:44 my baby jumped for joy the instant I heard your v!
3: 4 he said, / "He is a v shouting in the wilderness:
3:22 And a v from heaven said, "You are my beloved
8:54 Jesus took her by the hand and said in a loud v,
9:35 Then a v from the cloud said, "This is my Son,
9:36 When the v died away, Jesus was there alone.
11:14 couldn't speak, and the man's v returned to him.
23:18 and with one v they shouted, "Kill him,
Jn 1:23 of Isaiah: / "I am a v shouting in the wilderness,
5:25 the dead will hear my v—the v of the Son of God.
5:28 dead in their graves will hear the v of God's Son,
5:37 You have never heard his v or seen him face to
10: 3 for him, and the sheep hear his v and come to him.
10: 4 and they follow him because they recognize his v.
10: 5 run from him because they don't recognize his v."
10:16 must bring them also, and they will listen to my v;
10:27 My sheep recognize my v; I know them, and they
12:28 Then a v spoke from heaven, saying, "I have
12:29 When the crowd heard the v, some thought it was
12:30 told them, "The v was for your benefit, not mine.
Ac 7:31 he went to see, the v of the Lord called out to him,
7:57 and drowning out his v with their shouts,
9: 4 He fell to the ground and heard a v saying to him,
9: 5 And the v replied, "I am Jesus, the one you are
9: 7 for they heard the sound of someone's v, but they
10:13 Then a v said to him, "Get up, Peter; kill and eat
10:15 The v spoke again, "If God says something is
11: 7 And I heard a v say, 'Get up, Peter; kill and eat
11: 9 "But the v from heaven came again, 'If God says
12:14 When she recognized Peter's v, she was
12:22 shouting, "It is the v of a god, not of a man!"
14:10 So Paul called to him in a loud v, "Stand up!"
22: 7 I fell to the ground and heard a v saying to me,
22: 9 people with me saw the light but didn't hear the v.
22:22 then with one v they shouted, "Away with such a
26:14 and I heard a v saying to me in Aramaic, 'Saul,
Ro 15: 6 Then all of you can join together with one v,
Heb 3: 7 Holy Spirit says, / "Today you must listen to his v.
3:15 the warning: / "Today you must listen to his v.
3:16 against God, even though they heard his v?
4: 7 "Today you must listen to his v. / Don't harden
12:19 an awesome trumpet blast and a v with a message
12:26 When God spoke from Mount Sinai his v shook
2Pe 1:17 majestic v called down from heaven, "This is my
1:18 We ourselves heard the v when we were there with
2:16 when his donkey rebuked him with a human v.
Rev 1:10 I heard a loud v behind me, a v that sounded like a
1:15 and his v thundered like mighty ocean waves.
4: 1 and the same v I had heard before spoke to me
4: 1 The v said, "Come up here, and I will show you
5: 2 I saw a strong angel, who shouted with a loud v:
6: 1 called out with a v that sounded like thunder,
6: 6 And a v from among the four living beings said,
9:13 and I heard a v speaking from the four horns of the
9:14 And the v spoke to the sixth angel who held the
10: 4 about to write. But a v from heaven called to me:
10: 8 Then the v from heaven called to me again: "Go
11:12 Then a loud v shouted from heaven, "Come up
12:10 Then I heard a loud v shouting across the heavens,
13:11 of a lamb, and he spoke with the v of a dragon.
14:13 And I heard a v from heaven saying, "Write this
14:15 and called out in a loud v to the one sitting on the
16: 1 Then I heard a mighty v shouting from the Temple
16: 7 And I heard a v from the altar saying, "Yes,
18: 4 Then I heard another v calling from heaven,
19: 5 And from the throne came a v that said,

VOICES (17) [VOICE]

Nu 14: 2 Their v rose in a great chorus of complaint against

Jdg 21: 2 until evening, raising their **v** and weeping bitterly.
2Ch 5: 13 they raised their **v** and praised the LORD with
Ezr 10: 12 Then the whole assembly raised their **v**
Ps 46: T the descendants of Korah, to be sung by soprano **v**.
Isa 38: 18 praise you; / they cannot raise their **v** in praise.
Jer 3: 21 **V** are heard high on the windswept mountains,
7: 34 The joyful **v** of bridegrooms and brides will no
16: 9 The joyful **v** of bridegrooms and brides will no
25: 10 The joyful **v** of bridegrooms and brides will no
33: 11 The joyful **v** of bridegrooms and brides will be
Na 2: 13 Never again will the **v** of your proud messengers
Lk 23: 23 and louder for Jesus' death, and their **v** prevailed.
Ac 4: 24 were united as they lifted their **v** in prayer:
Rev 11: 15 and there were loud **v** shouting in heaven:
18: 23 There will be no happy **v** of brides and grooms.
19: 3 Again and again their **v** rang, "Hallelujah!

VOID [KJV] See BROKEN, CLEAR, DESOLATION, EMPTY, LACKS, NULLIFIED, NULLIFIES, NULLIFY, OVERTHROW, RENOUNCED, WITHOUT

VOLCANO (1)

Isa 30: 33 of the LORD, like fire from a **v**, will set it ablaze.

VOLUME (5)

Lev 19: 35 standards when measuring length, weight, or **v**.
Job 10: 17 You pour out an ever-increasing **v** of anger upon
Eze 45: 10 honest weights and scales, honest dry **v** measures, and honest liquid **v** measures.
45: 11 homer will be your standard unit for measuring **v**.

VOLUME [KJV] See also SCRIPTURES, SCROLL

VOLUNTARILY (3) [VOLUNTEER]

Dt 15: 12 an Israelite man or woman **v** becomes your servant
23: 23 But once you have **v** made a vow, be careful to do
Jn 10: 18 can take my life from me. I lay down my life **v**.

VOLUNTARY (4) [VOLUNTEER]

2Ki 12: 4 regular assessment, a payment of vows, or a **v** gift.
Ps 54: 6 I will sacrifice a **v** offering to you; / I will praise
Eze 46: 12 Whenever the prince offers a **v** burnt offering
Am 4: 5 Then give your extra **v** offerings so you can brag

VOLUNTEER (4) [VOLUNTARILY, VOLUNTARY, VOLUNTEERED]

Ex 23: 11 Then let the poor among you harvest any **v** crop
1Sa 26: 6 "Will anyone **v** to go in there with me?"
1Ch 28: 21 Others with skills of every kind will **v**,
Ezr 7: 13 and Levites, may **v** to return to Jerusalem with you.

VOLUNTEERED (4) [VOLUNTEER]

2Ch 17: 16 son of Zicri, who **v** for the LORD's service,
Ezr 8: 15 I found that not one Levite had **v** to come along.
Ne 11: 2 And the people commended everyone who **v** to
Jer 40: 15 with Gedaliah and **v** to kill Ishmael secretly.

VOMIT (11)

Lev 18: 25 who live there, and the land will soon **v** them out.
18: 28 Do not give the land a reason to **v** you out for
18: 28 as it will **v** out the people who live there now.
20: 22 the land to which I am bringing you will **v** you out.
Job 20: 15 He will **v** the wealth he swallowed. God won't let
Pr 23: 8 You will **v** up the delicious food they serve,
26: 11 As a dog returns to its **v**, so a fool repeats his folly.
Isa 28: 8 Their tables are covered with **v**; filth is
Jer 25: 27 Get drunk and **v**, and you will fall to rise no more,
48: 26 Moab will wallow in her own **v**, ridiculed by all.
2Pe 2: 22 "A dog returns to its **v**," and "A washed pig

VOPHSI (1)

Nu 13: 14 Naphtali | Nahbi son of **V**

VOTE (1)

Ac 26: 10 And I cast my **v** against them when they were

VOW (71) [VOWED, VOWING, VOWS]

Ge 28: 20 Then Jacob made this **v**: "If God will be with me
31: 13 the pillar of stone and made a **v** to serve me.
Lev 5: 4 "Or if they make a rash **v** of any kind, whether its
7: 16 if you bring an offering to fulfill a **v** or as a
22: 18 whether to fulfill a **v** or as a freewill offering,
22: 21 whether to fulfill a **v** or as a freewill offering,
22: 23 but it may not be offered to fulfill a **v**.
27: 2 If you make a special **v** to dedicate someone to the
27: 8 If you desire to make such a **v** but cannot afford to
27: 9 "If your **v** involves giving a clean animal—
27: 11 But if your **v** involves an unclean animal—one that
Nu 6: 2 or women, take the special **v** of a Nazirite,
6: 4 As long as they are bound by their Nazirite **v**,
6: 5 never cut their hair throughout the time of their **v**,
6: 6 during the entire period of their **v** to the LORD,
6: 11 Then they must renew their **v** that day and let their
6: 12 The days of their **v** that were completed before
6: 12 to the LORD for the full term of their **v**,
6: 21 beyond what is required by their normal Nazirite **v**,
6: 21 they must fulfill their special **v** exactly as they
15: 3 a sacrifice to fulfill a **v**, a freewill offering,
15: 8 or a sacrifice in fulfillment of a special **v** or as a
21: 2 Then the people of Israel made this **v** to the
30: 2 A man who makes a **v** to the LORD or makes a
30: 3 "If a young woman makes a **v** to the LORD
30: 4 and her father hears of the **v** or pledge but says
30: 5 But if her father refuses to let her fulfill the **v**
30: 6 "Now suppose a young woman takes a **v** or makes
30: 7 If her husband learns of her **v** or pledge and raises
30: 8 But if her husband refuses to accept her **v**
30: 10 living in her husband's home when she makes a **v**
30: 11 does nothing to stop her, her **v** or pledge will stand.
30: 12 her **v** or pledge will be nullified, and the LORD
30: 15 than a day and then tries to nullify a **v** or pledge,
Dt 12: 6 your special gifts, your offerings to fulfill a **v**,
12: 11 special gifts, and your offerings to fulfill a **v**—
12: 17 your flocks and herds, nor an offering to fulfill a **v**,
12: 26 and your offerings given to fulfill a **v** to the place
23: 21 "When you make a **v** to the LORD your God,
23: 22 However, it is not a sin to refrain from making a **v**.
23: 23 But once you have voluntarily made a **v**, be careful
23: 23 for you have made a **v** to the LORD your God.
Jos 9: 18 for their leaders had made a **v** to the LORD,
Jdg 11: 30 And Jephthah made a **v** to the LORD. He said,
11: 35 For I have made a **v** to the LORD and cannot take
11: 39 her father kept his **v**, and she died a virgin.
21: 22 And you are not guilty of breaking the **v** since you
1Sa 1: 11 And she made this **v**: "O LORD Almighty,
14: 39 I **v** by the name of the LORD who rescued Israel
18: 3 And Jonathan made a special **v** to be David's
20: 17 And Jonathan made David reaffirm his **v** of
2Sa 3: 28 "I **v** by the LORD that I and my people are
3: 35 But David had made a **v**, saying, "May God kill
9: 7 can be kind to you because of my **v** to your father,
15: 7 to the LORD in fulfillment of a **v** I made to him.
15: 9 the king told him. "Go and fulfill your **v**."
15: 21 "I **v** by the LORD and by your own life that I
1Ki 14: 11 **v** that the members of your family who die in the
Ne 5: 12 and officials formally **v** to do what they had
Job 27: 2 "I make this **v** by the living God, who has taken
Ps 95: 11 So in my anger I made a **v**: / 'They will never
110: 4 LORD has taken an oath and will not break his **v**:
Jer 51: 14 The LORD Almighty has taken this **v** and has
Mt 5: 34 it is a sacred **v** because heaven is God's throne.
5: 35 it is a sacred **v** because the earth is his footstool.
5: 37 To strengthen your promise with a **v** shows that
Ac 18: 18 according to Jewish custom, for he had taken a **v**.)
21: 23 We have four men here who have taken a **v** and are
Heb 3: 11 So in my anger I made a **v**: / 'They will never
4: 3 God said, / "In my anger I made a **v**:
7: 21 and will not break his **v**: / 'You are a priest

VOWED (27) [VOW]

Ge 50: 24 He will bring you back to the land he **v** to give to
Nu 6: 21 If any Nazirites have **v** to give the LORD
32: 10 Then the LORD was furious with them, and he **v**,
Dt 2: 14 For the LORD had **v** that this could not happen
4: 21 He **v** that I would never cross the Jordan River into
Jos 5: 6 and the LORD **v** he would not let them enter the
Jdg 15: 7 "Because you did this," Samson **v**, "I will take
21: 1 The Israelites had **v** at Mizpah never to give their
1Sa 3: 14 So I have **v** that the sins of Eli and his sons will
19: 6 So Saul listened to Jonathan and **v**, "As surely as
2Sa 12: 5 "As surely as the LORD lives," he **v**, "any man
19: 23 Then, turning to Shimei, David **v**, "Your life will
1Ki 1: 17 you **v** to me by the LORD your God that my son
1: 29 And the king **v**, "As surely as the LORD lives,
2Ki 6: 31 Elisha son of Shaphat this very day," the king **v**.
25: 24 Gedaliah **v** to them that the Babylonian officials
Ezr 10: 19 They **v** to divorce their wives, and they each
Ne 10: 29 They **v** to accept the curse of God if they failed to
Ps 132: 2 the LORD. / He **v** to the Mighty One of Israel,
Ecc 8: 2 the king because you have **v** before God to do this.
Eze 20: 23 I **v** I would scatter them among all the nations
Jnh 1: 16 and they offered him a sacrifice and **v** to serve him.
Mt 26: 35 deny you!" And all the other disciples **v** the same.
Mk 7: 11 For I have **v** to give to God what I could have
14: 31 never deny you!" And all the others **v** the same.
Ac 23: 21 They have **v** not to eat or drink until they kill him.
Heb 3: 18 And to whom was God speaking when he **v** that

VOWING (1) [VOW]

Jdg 21: 5 **v** that anyone who refused to come must die.

VOWS (34) [VOW]

Ge 31: 52 stand between us as a witness of our **v**. I will not
Lev 23: 38 the offerings you make to accompany your **v**,
Nu 29: 39 and offerings you present in connection with **v**,
30: 4 says nothing, then all her **v** and pledges will stand.
30: 5 then all her **v** and pledges will become invalid.
30: 7 the day he hears of it, her **v** and pledges will stand.
30: 9 she must fulfill all her **v** and pledges no matter
30: 13 So her husband may either confirm or nullify any **v**
Dt 23: 21 God demands that you promptly fulfill all your **v**.
2Ki 12: 4 a payment of **v**, or a voluntary gift.
Ne 13: 29 and the promises and **v** of the priests and Levites.
Job 22: 27 he will hear you, and you will fulfill your **v** to him.
Ps 22: 25 I will fulfill my **v** in the presence of those who
50: 14 I want you to fulfill your **v** to the Most High.
56: 12 I will fulfill my **v** to you, O God, / and offer a
61: 5 For you have heard my **v**, O God. / You have given
61: 8 to your name / as I fulfill my **v** day after day.
65: 1 to you in Zion. / We will fulfill our **v** to you,
66: 13 burnt offerings / to fulfill the **v** I made to you—
66: 14 yes, the sacred **v** you heard me make / when I was
76: 11 Make **v** to the LORD your God, and fulfill them.
Pr 7: 14 "I've offered my sacrifices and just finished my **v**.
Jer 34: 18 walked between its halves to solemnize your **v**.
44: 25 go ahead and carry out your promises and **v** to her!
Eze 16: 8 cover your nakedness and declared my marriage **v**.
16: 59 for you have taken your solemn **v** lightly by
Jnh 2: 9 you with songs of praise, and I will fulfill all my **v**.
Na 1: 15 O people of Judah, and fulfill all your **v**,
Mal 2: 14 Because the LORD witnessed the **v** you and your
2: 14 faithful companion, the wife of your marriage **v**.
Mt 5: 33 that the law of Moses says, 'Do not break your **v**;
5: 33 you must carry out the **v** you have made to the
5: 34 But I say, don't make any **v**! If you say,
Ac 21: 26 Then he publicly announced the date when their **v**

VOYAGES (1)

Ac 27: 9 The weather was becoming dangerous for long **v**

VULGAR (2)

Job 30: 9 "And now their sons mock me with their **v** song!
Ps 101: 3 I will refuse to look at / anything vile and **v**.

VULNERABLE (3)

Ge 42: 9 You have come to see how **v** our land has
42: 12 "You have come to discover how **v** the famine has
2Ti 3: 6 and win the confidence of **v** women who are

VULTURE (5) [VULTURES]

Lev 11: 13 are detestable for you: the eagle, the **v**, the osprey,
11: 18 the white owl, the pelican, the carrion **v**,
Dt 14: 12 birds you may not eat: the eagle, the **v**, the osprey,
14: 17 the pelican, the carrion **v**, the cormorant,
Jer 12: 9 people have become as disgusting to me as a **v**.

VULTURES (19) [VULTURE]

Ge 15: 11 Some **v** came down to eat the carcasses, but Abram
2Sa 21: 10 She prevented **v** from tearing at their bodies during
1Ki 14: 11 those who die in the field will be eaten by **v**.' "
16: 4 those who die in the field will be eaten by the **v**."
21: 24 and those who die in the field will be eaten by **v**."
Pr 30: 17 plucked out by ravens of the valley and eaten by **v**.
Isa 18: 6 to eat. The **v** will tear at corpses all summer.
34: 15 And the **v** will come, each one with its mate.
Jer 7: 33 The corpses of my people will be food for the **v**
12: 9 And indeed, they are surrounded by **v**. Bring on the
15: 3 to kill, the dogs to drag away, the **v** to devour,
16: 4 and their bodies will be food for the **v** and wild
19: 7 enemy will leave the dead bodies as food for the **v**
34: 20 Your bodies will be food for the **v** and wild
Eze 39: 4 I will give you as food to the **v** and wild animals.
Mt 24: 28 Just as the gathering of **v** shows there is a carcass
Lk 17: 37 "Just as the gathering of **v** shows there is a carcass
Rev 19: 17 in the sun, shouting to the **v** flying high in the sky:
19: 21 And all the **v** of the sky gorged themselves on the

W

WAFER (3) [WAFERS]

Ex 29: 23 and one **w** from the basket of yeastless bread that
Lev 8: 26 with olive oil, and a thin **w** spread with olive oil.
Nu 6: 19 without yeast, and one **w** made without yeast,

WAFERS (5) [WAFER]

Ex 29: 2 with olive oil, and **w** with oil poured over them.
Lev 2: 4 mixed with olive oil or **w** spread with olive oil.
7: 12 loaves, **w**, and cakes—all made without yeast
Nu 6: 15 mixed with olive oil and **w** spread with olive oil—
1Ch 23: 29 the **w** made without yeast, the cakes cooked in

WAFT (1)

SS 4: 16 my garden and **w** its lovely perfume to my lover.

WAGE (8) [WAGED, WAGES, WAGING]

Ge 31: 7 breaking his **w** agreement with me again and again.
Mt 20: 2 He agreed to pay the normal daily **w** and sent them
20: 9 o'clock were paid, each received a full day's **w**.
20: 10 receive more. But they, too, were paid a day's **w**.
20: 13 Didn't you agree to work all day for the usual **w**?
2Co 10: 3 but we don't **w** war with human plans
Rev 13: 7 And the beast was allowed to **w** war against God's
17: 14 Together they will **w** war against the Lamb,

WAGED (5) [WAGE]

1Ki 5: 3 because of the many wars he **w** with surrounding
22: 45 and the wars he **w** are recorded in *The Book of*
1Ch 5: 19 They **w** war against the Hagrites, the Jeturites,
2Ch 27: 5 Jotham **w** war against the Ammonites
Ps 55: 18 and keeps me safe / from the battle **w** against me,

WAGES (19) [WAGE]

Ge 30: 31 "What **w** do you want?" Laban asked again.
30: 32 the dark-colored sheep. Give them to me as my **w**.

31: 41 the flock. And you have reduced my **w** ten times!
Dt 15: 18 the services worth double the **w** of hired workers,
24: 15 Pay them their **w** each day before sunset
1Ki 5: 6 and I will pay your men whatever **w** you ask.
Pr 3: 14 is better than silver, and her **w** are better than gold.
8: 19 the purest gold, my **w** better than sterling silver!
Jer 22: 13 By not paying **w**, he builds injustice into its walls
Zep 2: 10 They will receive the **w** of their pride, for they
Hag 1: 6 Your **w** disappear as though you were putting them
Zec 8: 10 were no jobs and no **w** for either people or animals.
11: 12 And I said to them, "If you like, give me my **w**,
11: 12 So they counted out for my **w** thirty pieces of
Mal 3: 5 against those who cheat employees of their **w**,
Jn 4: 36 The harvesters are paid good **w**, and the fruit they
Ro 4: 4 When people work, their **w** are not a gift.
6: 23 For the **w** of sin is death, but the free gift of God is
Jas 5: 4 The **w** you held back cry out against you. The cries

WAGGING [KJV] See SHAKING

WAGING (2) [WAGE]

Jos 11: 18 **w** war for a long time to accomplish this.
Da 7: 21 this horn was **w** war against the holy people

WAGON (1) [WAGONS]

Am 2: 13 "So I will make you groan as a **w** groans when it

WAGONS (6) [WAGON]

Ge 45: 19 And tell your brothers to take **w** from Egypt to
45: 21 Joseph gave them **w**, as Pharaoh had commanded,
45: 27 and when he saw the **w** loaded with the food sent
46: 5 and wives in the **w** Pharaoh had provided for them.
Isa 66: 20 in chariots and **w**, and on mules and camels,"
Eze 23: 24 **w**, and a great army fully prepared for attack.

WAHEB (1)

Nu 21: 14 speaks of "the town of **W** in the area of Suphah,

WAIL (20) [WAILED, WAILING]

Ex 11: 6 Then a loud **w** will be heard throughout the land of
Est 4: 1 out into the city, crying with a loud and bitter **w**.
Isa 16: 9 So I **w** and lament for Jazer and the vineyards of
23: 6 to Tarshish! **W**, you people who live by the sea!
23: 14 **W**, O ships of Tarshish, for your home port is
Jer 9: 10 for the mountains and **w** for the desert pastures.
9: 20 Teach your daughters to **w**; teach one another how
48: 20 comes back, 'Moab lies in ruins; weep and **w**!
48: 31 Yes, I **w** for Moab; my heart is broken for the men
49: 3 Weep and **w**, hiding in the hedges, for your god
Eze 21: 12 "Son of man, cry out and **w**; pound your thighs in
26: 17 Then they will **w** for you, singing this funeral
27: 32 As they **w** and mourn, they sing this sad funeral
Hos 7: 14 Instead, they sit on their couches and **w**. They cut
10: 5 The people mourn over it, and the priests **w** for it,
Joel 1: 11 **W**, all you vine growers! Weep, because the wheat
1: 13 **W**, you who serve before the altar! Come,
Am 5: 16 and summon professional mourners to **w**
Mic 1: 8 I will howl like a jackal and **w** like an ostrich.
Zep 1: 11 **W** in sorrow, all you who live in the market area,

WAILED (2) [WAIL]

Nu 14: 2 in Egypt, or even here in the wilderness!" they **w**.
Est 4: 3 They fasted, wept, and **w**, and many people lay in

WAILING (11) [WAIL]

Ex 11: 6 there has never been such **w** before and there never
12: 30 and loud **w** was heard throughout the land of
Job 2: 12 **W** loudly, they tore their robes and threw dust into
Jer 48: 39 How it is broken! Hear the **w**! See the shame of
Eze 24: 17 but only quietly. Let there be no **w** at her grave.
Am 5: 17 There will be **w** in every vineyard, for I will pass
8: 3 sounds of singing in the Temple will turn to **w**.
Zec 11: 3 Listen to the **w** of the shepherds, for their wealth is
Mk 5: 38 Jesus saw the commotion and the weeping and **w**.
Lk 8: 52 The house was filled with people weeping and **w**,
Jn 11: 33 her weeping and saw the other people **w** with her,

WAIST (17) [WAISTS]

Ex 28: 42 next to their bodies, reaching from **w** to thigh.
Lev 8: 7 embroidered tunic and tied the sash around his **w**.
16: 4 He must tie the linen sash around his **w** and put the
1Ki 12: 10 'My little finger is thicker than my father's **w**—
2Ki 1: 8 and he wore a leather belt around his **w**."
2Ch 10: 10 'My little finger is thicker than my father's **w**—
Job 12: 18 With ropes around their **w**, they are led away.
Jer 13: 1 and buy a linen belt and put it around your **w**,
13: 2 as the LORD directed me and put it around my **w**.
13: 11 As a belt clings to a person's **w**, so I created Judah
Eze 1: 27 From his **w** up, he looked like gleaming amber,
1: 27 And from his **w** down, he looked like a burning
8: 2 From the **w** down he looked like a burning flame.
8: 2 From the **w** up he looked like gleaming amber.
47: 4 After another 1,750 feet, it was up to my **w**.
Da 10: 5 with a belt of pure gold around his **w**.
Jn 13: 4 took off his robe, wrapped a towel around his **w**,

WAISTS (1) [WAIST]

Eze 23: 15 Handsome belts encircled their **w**, and flowing

WAIT (81) [AWAIT, AWAITED, AWAITING, AWAITS, WAITED, WAITING, WAITS]

Ge 12: 10 the land, so Abram went down to Egypt to **w** it out.
29: 3 It was the custom there to **w** for all the flocks to
29: 27 "**W** until the bridal week is over, and you can have
Ex 12: 39 out of Egypt and had no time to **w** for bread to rise.
24: 14 "Stay here and **w** for us until we come back.
Lev 12: 4 Then the woman must **w** for thirty-three days until
12: 5 then **w** another sixty-six days to be purified from
Nu 6: 9 they must **w** for seven days and then shave their
9: 8 "**W** here until I have received instructions for you
Jos 18: 3 "How long are you going to **w** before taking
Ru 1: 13 Would you **w** for them to grow up and refuse to
1Sa 1: 22 told her husband, "**W** until the baby is weaned.
10: 8 Gilgal ahead of me and **w** for me there seven days.
15: 5 to the city of Amalek and lay in **w** in the valley.
20: 19 you hid before, and **w** there by the stone pile.
20: 38 Hurry, hurry, don't **w**." So the boy quickly
2Sa 13: 28 told his men, "**W** until Amnon gets drunk;
15: 28 Jordan River and **w** there for a message from you.
18: 30 "**W** here," the king told him. So Ahimaaz stepped
1Ki 1: 2 "We will find a young virgin who will **w** on you
12: 10 was hard on you, just **w** and see what I'll be like!
2Ki 6: 33 Why should I **w** any longer for the LORD?"
7: 9 If we **w** until morning, some terrible calamity will
2Ch 10: 10 was hard on you, just **w** and see what I'll be like!
Job 13: 15 God might kill me, but I cannot **w**. I am going to
14: 14 and through my struggle I would eagerly **w** for
24: 1 Why must the godly **w** for him in vain?
32: 16 Should I continue to **w**, now that you are silent?
33: 22 are at death's door; the angels of death **w** for them.
35: 14 He will bring about justice if you will only **w**.
Ps 5: 3 I bring my requests to you and **w** expectantly.
27: 14 **W** patiently for the LORD. / Be brave and courageous. / Yes, **w** patiently for the LORD.
37: 7 of the LORD, / and **w** patiently for him to act.
52: 9 for what you have done. / I will **w** for your mercies
59: 9 You are my strength; I **w** for you to rescue me,
62: 1 I **w** quietly before God, / for my salvation comes
62: 5 I **w** quietly before God, / for my hope is in him.
106: 13 he had done! / They wouldn't **w** for his counsel!
119: 84 How long must I **w**? / When will you punish those
Pr 20: 22 **W** for the LORD to handle the matter.
24: 15 Do not lie in **w** like an outlaw at the home of the
25: 7 It is better to **w** for an invitation than to be sent to
Ecc 11: 4 If you **w** for perfect conditions, you will never get
12: 6 Don't **w** until the water jar is smashed at the spring
Isa 8: 17 I will **w** for the LORD to help us, though he has
30: 18 Blessed are those who **w** for him to help them.
40: 31 But those who **w** on the LORD will find new
42: 4 Even distant lands beyond the sea will **w** for his
49: 23 Those who **w** for me will never be put to shame."
51: 5 They will **w** for me and long for my power.
64: 4 God like you, who works for those who **w** for him!
Jer 5: 26 "Among my people are wicked men who lie in **w**
8: 14 the people will say, 'Why should we **w** here to die?
14: 22 do such things. So we will **w** for you to help us.
La 3: 25 The LORD is wonderfully good to those who **w**
3: 26 So it is good to **w** quietly for salvation from the
Eze 20: 1 They sat down in front of me to **w** for his reply.
Da 12: 12 And blessed are those who **w** and remain until the
Am 8: 5 You can't **w** for the Sabbath day to be over
Mic 1: 12 The people of Maroth anxiously **w** for relief,
7: 7 I **w** confidently for God to save me, and my God
Hab 2: 1 and **w** to see what the LORD will say to me
2: 3 If it seems slow, **w** patiently, for it will surely take
3: 16 I will **w** quietly for the coming day when disaster
Mt 18: 30 But his creditor wouldn't **w**. He had the man
Jn 6: 16 his disciples went down to the shore to **w** for him.
Ac 24: 22 adjourned the hearing and said, "**W** until Lysias,
Ro 8: 23 **w** anxiously for that day when God will give us
8: 25 have yet, we must **w** patiently and confidently.
15: 4 and encouragement as we **w** patiently for God's
1Co 1: 7 eagerly **w** for the return of our Lord Jesus Christ.
11: 33 you gather for the Lord's Supper, **w** for each other.
14: 32 are in control of their spirit and can **w** their turn.
16: 2 Don't **w** until I get there and then try to collect it
Gal 5: 5 But we who live by the Spirit eagerly **w** to receive
Jas 5: 7 you must be patient as you **w** for the Lord's return.
5: 7 They patiently **w** for the precious harvest to ripen.
Jude 1: 21 **w** for the eternal life that our Lord Jesus Christ in
Rev 7: 3 "**W**! Don't hurt the land or the sea or the trees
10: 6 everything in it. He said, "God will **w** no longer.

WAITED (30) [WAIT]

Ge 18: 8 Abraham **w** on them there beneath the trees.
Nu 12: 15 and the people **w** until she was brought back before
Jos 3: 17 They **w** there until everyone had crossed the
Jdg 3: 25 so they **w**. But when the king didn't come out after
16: 2 gathered together and **w** all night at the city gates.
1Sa 13: 8 Saul **w** there seven days for Samuel, as Samuel had
25: 9 gave this message to Nabal and **w** for his reply.
2Sa 6: 13 they stopped and **w** so David could sacrifice an ox
1Ki 1: 4 and she **w** on the king and took care of him.
20: 38 The prophet **w** for the king beside the road,
2Ki 5: 9 and chariots and **w** at the door of Elisha's house.
25: 4 they **w** for nightfall and fled through the gate
Job 29: 21 They were silent as they **w** for me to speak.
29: 23 They **w** eagerly, for my words were as refreshing
30: 26 came instead. I **w** for the light, but darkness fell.
32: 4 Elihu had **w** for the others to speak because they
32: 11 "I have **w** all this time, listening very carefully to
Ps 40: 1 I **w** patiently for the LORD to help me, / and he
Isa 5: 2 Then he **w** for a harvest of sweet grapes,
33: 2 be merciful to us, for we have **w** for you.
38: 13 I **w** patiently all night, / but I was torn apart as
Jer 52: 7 they **w** for nightfall and fled through the gate
Jnh 4: 5 and made a shelter to sit under as he **w** to see if
Mt 26: 58 and **w** to see what was going to happen to Jesus.
Lk 13: 7 he said to his gardener, 'I've **w** three years,
Ac 20: 5 They went ahead and **w** for us at Troas.
28: 6 The people **w** for him to swell up or suddenly drop
28: 6 But when they had **w** a long time and saw no harm
Heb 6: 15 Then Abraham **w** patiently, and he received what
1Pe 3: 20 those who disobeyed God long ago when God **w**

WAITING (52) [WAIT]

Ge 4: 7 Sin is **w** to attack and destroy you, and you must
29: 2 in an open field beside a well, **w** to be watered.
Ex 5: 20 and Aaron, who were **w** outside for them.
Jdg 3: 26 While the servants were **w**, Ehud escaped,
1Sa 4: 13 Eli was **w** beside the road to hear the news of the
2Sa 15: 32 David found Hushai the Arkite **w** for him.
1Ki 1: 20 all Israel is **w** for your decision as to who will
2Ki 7: 3 "Why should we sit here **w** to die?" they asked
Job 7: 2 for the day to end, like a servant **w** to be paid.
Ps 10: 9 they crouch silently, / **w** to pounce on the helpless.
17: 12 like young lions in hiding, **w** for their chance.
27: 11 of honesty, / for my enemies are **w** for me to fall.
37: 32 spy on the godly, / **w** for an excuse to kill them.
38: 15 For I am **w** for you, O LORD. / You must answer
44: 11 You have treated us like sheep **w** to be slaughtered;
59: 3 ambush for me. / Fierce enemies are out there **w**,
69: 3 swollen with weeping, / **w** for my God to help me.
119: 83 like a wineskin in the smoke, exhausted with **w**.
Pr 8: 34 me daily at my gates, **w** for me outside my home!
Isa 30: 15 in returning to me and **w** for me will you be saved.
Jer 3: 2 You sit like a prostitute beside the road **w** for a
20: 10 my old friends are watching me, **w** for a fatal slip.
La 3: 10 He hid like a bear or a lion, **w** to attack me.
4: 19 we hid in the wilderness, they were **w** for us there.
Eze 7: 6 It has finally arrived! Your final doom is **w**!
44: 26 being ritually cleansed and then **w** for seven days.
Hos 6: 11 a harvest of punishment is also **w** for you,
Joel 3: 14 Thousands upon thousands are **w** in the valley of
Mt 11: 3 "Are you really the Messiah we've been **w** for,
17: 14 of the mountain, a huge crowd was **w** for them.
Mk 15: 43 Joseph from Arimathea (who was **w** for the
Lk 1: 21 the people were **w** for Zechariah to come out,
2: 38 who had been **w** for the promised King to come
8: 40 with open arms because they had been **w** for him.
12: 36 as though you were **w** for your master to return
12: 37 favor for those who are ready and **w** for his return.
15: 12 of your estate now, instead of **w** until you die.'
23: 51 and he had been **w** for the Kingdom of God to
Jn 6: 22 began gathering on the shore, **w** to see Jesus.
Ac 10: 24 Cornelius was **w** for him and had called together
10: 33 **w** before God to hear the message the Lord has
17: 16 While Paul was **w** for them in Athens, he was
Ro 8: 19 For all creation is **w** eagerly for that future day
15: 23 and after all these long years of **w**, I am eager to
Php 3: 20 And we are eagerly **w** for him to return as our
Heb 4: 9 So there is a special rest still **w** for the people of
9: 28 salvation to all those who are eagerly **w** for him.
10: 34 You knew you had better things **w** for you in
2Pe 3: 14 while you are **w** for these things to happen,
3: 15 the Lord is **w** so that people have time to be saved.
Jude 1: 6 in prisons of darkness, **w** for the day of judgment.
Rev 12: 18 Then he stood **w** on the shore of the sea.

WAITS (8) [WAIT]

Nu 30: 15 If he **w** more than a day and then tries to nullify a
Job 18: 12 by hunger, and calamity **w** for them to stumble.
24: 15 The adulterer **w** for the twilight, for he says,
Ps 45: 13 The bride, a princess, **w** within her chamber,
Pr 23: 28 She hides and **w** like a robber, looking for another
Isa 17: 14 In the evening Israel **w** in terror, but by dawn its
30: 18 But the LORD still **w** for you to come to him
Heb 10: 13 There he **w** until his enemies are humbled as a

WAKE (30) [AWAKE, AWAKEN, AWAKENED, AWOKE, WAKEN, WAKENED, WAKENS, WAKING, WOKE]

Jdg 5: 12 "**W** up, Deborah, **w** up! / **W** up, **w** up, and sing a song! / Arise, Barak!
1Sa 26: 14 shouted down to Abner and Saul, "**W** up, Abner!"
Job 14: 12 they will not **w** up nor be roused from their sleep.
27: 19 but **w** up to find that all their wealth is gone.
41: 32 The water glistens in its **w**. One would think the
Ps 7: 6 of my enemies! / **W** up, my God, and bring justice!
35: 23 **W** up! Rise to my defense! / Take up my case,
44: 23 **W** up, O Lord! Why do you sleep? / Get up!
57: 8 **W** up, my soul! / **W** up, O harp and lyre!
108: 1 wonder I can sing your praises! / **W** up, my soul!
108: 2 **W** up, O harp and lyre! / I will waken the dawn
139: 18 And when I **w** up in the morning, / you are still
Pr 6: 9 how long will you sleep? When will you **w** up?
6: 22 When you **w** up in the morning, they will advise
23: 35 When will I **w** up so I can have another drink?"
Ecc 12: 4 Even the chirping of birds will **w** you up. But you
Isa 51: 9 **W** up, LORD! Robe yourself with strength!
51: 17 **W** up, **w** up, O Jerusalem! You have drunk
52: 1 **W** up, **w** up, O Zion! Clothe yourselves with
Jer 51: 57 "They will fall asleep and never **w** up again!"
Joel 1: 5 **W** up, you drunkards, and weep! All the grapes are
Jn 11: 11 fallen asleep, but now I will go and **w** him up."
Ro 13: 11 **W** up, for the coming of our salvation is nearer
Rev 3: 2 Now **w** up! Strengthen what little remains, for even

WAKEN (3) [WAKE]

Ps 57: 8 O harp and lyre! / I will **w** the dawn with my song.
108: 2 O harp and lyre! / I will **w** the dawn with my song.
Jer 51: 39 fall asleep, never again to **w**," says the LORD.

WAKENED (1) [WAKE]
1Ki 18:27 away on a trip, or he is asleep and needs to be **w**!"

WAKENS (1) [WAKE]
Isa 50: 4 Morning by morning he **w** me and opens my

WAKING (2) [WAKE]
1Sa 26:12 away without anyone seeing them or even **w** up,
Ps 78:65 Then the Lord rose up as though **w** from sleep,

WALK (113) [WALKED, WALKING, WALKS, WALKWAY, WALKWAYS]
Ge 13:17 Take a **w** in every direction and explore the new
24:63 One evening as he was taking a **w** out in the fields,
Ex 14:16 Then all the people of Israel will **w** through on dry
17: 5 the leaders of Israel and **w** on ahead of the people.
21:19 If the injured person is later able to **w** again,
23: 5 you struggling beneath a heavy load, do not **w** by.
Lev 11:20 all swarming insects that **w** along the ground.
11:23 detestable all other swarming insects that **w**
11:27 Of the animals that **w** on all fours, those that have
26:12 I will **w** among you; I will be your God, and you
26:13 so you can **w** free with your heads held high.
Dt 19: 9 love the LORD your God and **w** in his ways.)
25: 9 the widow must **w** over to him in the presence of
28: 9 of the LORD your God and **w** in his ways,
Jos 6: 4 Seven priests will **w** ahead of the Ark,
6: 6 and assign seven priests to **w** in front of it,
22: 5 **w** in all his ways, obey his commands, be faithful
Jdg 5:10 And you who must **w** along the road, listen!
1Sa 16: 8 to step forward and **w** in front of Samuel.
1Ki 8:40 and **w** in your ways as long as they live in the land
2Ch 6:31 and **w** in your ways as long as they live in the land
20:21 the king appointed singers to **w** ahead of the army,
Ne 5: 9 Should you not **w** in the fear of our God in order to
9:11 your people so they could **w** through on dry land!
Est 2:11 Every day Mordecai would take a **w** near the
Job 18: 8 "The wicked **w** into a net. They fall into a pit
30:28 I **w** in gloom, without sunlight. I stand in the
40:12 with a glance; **w** on the wicked where they stand.
Ps 23: 4 Even when I **w** / through the dark valley of death,
25: 4 Show me the path where I should **w**, O LORD;
48:12 **W** around and count the many towers.
56:13 So now I can **w** in your presence, O God,
74: 3 **W** through the awful ruins of the city; / see how
84: 6 When they **w** through the Valley of Weeping,
89:14 and truth **w** before you as attendants.
89:15 for they will **w** in the light of your presence,
89:30 his sons forsake my law / and fail to **w** in my ways,
115: 7 or feel with their hands, / or **w** with their feet,
116: 9 And so I **w** in the LORD's presence / as I live
119: 3 with evil, / and they **w** only in his paths.
119:35 Make me **w** along the path of your commands,
119:45 I will **w** in freedom, / for I have devoted myself to
119:101 I have refused to **w** on any path of evil, / that I may
143: 8 for I am trusting you. / Show me where to **w**,
Pr 2: 7 their shield, protecting those who **w** with integrity.
2:13 These people turn from right ways to **w** down dark
6:22 Wherever you **w**, their counsel can lead you.
6:28 Can he **w** on hot coals and not blister his feet?
8:20 I **w** in righteousness, in paths of justice.
20: 7 The godly **w** with integrity; blessed are their
21: 8 The guilty **w** a crooked path; the innocent travel a
22: 5 The deceitful **w** a thorny, treacherous road;
28:26 is foolish, but those who **w** in wisdom are safe.
Ecc 7:18 So try to **w** a middle course—but those who fear
10: 3 You can identify fools just by the way they **w**
12: 5 the mourners will **w** along the streets.
Isa 2: 5 of Israel, let us **w** in the light of the LORD!
3:16 who **w** around with their noses in the air,
9: 2 The people who **w** in darkness will see a great
10:15 unless a hand is moving it? Can a cane **w** by itself?
20: 4 He will make them **w** naked and barefoot,
23:16 will take a harp, **w** the streets, and sing her songs,
30:21 "This is the way; turn around and **w** here."
35: 8 It will be only for those who **w** in God's ways;
fools will never **w** there.
38:15 Now I will **w** humbly throughout my years
40:31 and not grow weary. They will **w** and not faint.
43: 2 When you **w** through the fire of oppression,
Jer 6:16 Look for the old, godly way, and **w** in it. Travel its
10: 5 and it needs to be carried because it cannot **w**.
14:18 If I **w** the city streets, there I see people who have
18:15 of good, and they **w** the muddy paths of sin.
31: 9 They will **w** beside quiet streams and not stumble.
Eze 9: 4 "**W** through the streets of Jerusalem and put a
12: 6 pack to your shoulders and **w** away into the night.
36:12 I will cause my people to **w** on you once again,
Da 4:29 he was taking a **w** on the flat roof of the royal
Hos 11: 3 It was I who taught Israel how to **w**, leading him
Am 3: 3 Can two people **w** together without agreeing on the
Mic 1: 8 I will **w** around naked and barefoot in sorrow
2: 3 none of you will ever again **w** proudly in the
6: 8 to love mercy, and to **w** humbly with your God.
Zep 2: 3 uphold justice. **W** humbly and do what is right.
Zec 3: 7 I will let you **w** in and out of my presence along
8: 4 and women will **w** Jerusalem's streets with a cane
8:23 And they will say, 'Please let us **w** with you,
Mt 9: 5 to say, 'Your sins are forgiven' or 'Get up and **w**'?
11: 5 the blind see, the lame **w**, the lepers are cured,
Mk 2: 9 are forgiven' or 'Get up, pick up your mat, and **w**'?
12:38 and to have everyone bow to them as they **w** in the
Lk 5:23 to say, 'Your sins are forgiven' or 'Get up and **w**'?
7:22 the blind see, the lame **w**, the lepers are cured,
10:19 and you can **w** among snakes and scorpions
11:43 from everyone as you **w** through the markets!
11:44 People **w** over them without knowing the
20:46 and to have everyone bow to them as they **w** in the
Jn 4: 6 and Jesus, tired from the long **w**, sat wearily beside
5: 8 "Stand up, pick up your sleeping mat, and **w**!"
5:11 said to me, 'Pick up your sleeping mat and **w**.' "
11: 9 As long as it is light, people can **w** safely.
12:35 **W** in it while you can, so you will not stumble
12:35 If you **w** in the darkness, you cannot see where you
Ac 3: 6 name of Jesus Christ of Nazareth, get up and **w**!"
3: 8 He jumped up, stood on his feet, and began to **w**!
3:12 though we had made this man **w** by our own power
8:29 "Go over and **w** along beside the carriage."
2Co 6:16 in them / and **w** among them. / I will be their God,
12:18 have the same Spirit and **w** in each other's steps,
Jas 1:24 You see yourself, **w** away, and forget what you
Rev 3: 4 They will **w** with me in white, for they are worthy.
9:20 and wood—idols that neither see nor hear nor **w**!
16:15 so they will not need to **w** naked and ashamed."
21:24 The nations of the earth will **w** in its light,

WALKED (56) [WALK]
Ge 9:23 it over their shoulders, **w** backward into the tent,
21:14 and she **w** out into the wilderness of Beersheba,
24:40 'for the LORD, in whose presence I have **w**,
48:15 my grandfather Abraham and my father, Isaac, **w**,
Ex 2: 5 and her servant girls **w** along the riverbank.
10: 6 this one!" And with that, Moses turned and **w** out.
14:22 So the people of Israel **w** through the sea on dry
14:29 The people of Israel had **w** through the middle of
15:19 But the people of Israel had **w** through on dry land!
40:32 Whenever they **w** past the altar to enter the
Dt 1:36 and his descendants some of the land he **w** over
Jdg 2:17 who had **w** in obedience to the LORD's
3:20 Ehud **w** over to Eglon as he was sitting alone in a
1Sa 17: 7 An armor bearer **w** ahead of him carrying a huge
17:30 He **w** over to some others and asked them the same
17:41 Goliath **w** out toward David with his shield bearer
2Sa 3:31 And King David himself **w** behind the procession
15:30 David **w** up the road that led to the Mount of
1Ki 14:17 and the child died just as she **w** through the door of
16:10 Zimri **w** in and struck him down and killed him.
18:36 Elijah the prophet **w** up to the altar and prayed,
19:19 his cloak across his shoulders and **w** away again.
22:24 Then Zedekiah son of Kenaanah **w** up to Micaiah
2Ki 4:35 Elisha got up and **w** back and forth in the room a
6:30 And as the king **w** along the wall, the people could
8: 5 the mother of the boy **w** in to make her appeal to
17:19 They **w** down the same evil paths that Israel had
2Ch 18:23 Then Zedekiah son of Kenaanah **w** up to Micaiah
Ne 4: 3 "That stone wall would collapse if even a fox **w**
Job 22:15 on the old paths where evil people have **w**?
28: 8 No wild animal has ever **w** upon those treasures;
29: 3 before me and I **w** safely through the darkness.
38:16 Have you **w** about and explored their depths?
Ps 22:24 He has not turned and **w** away. / He has listened to
40: 2 on solid ground / and steadied me as I **w** along.
42: 4 used to be: / I **w** among the crowds of worshipers,
55:14 we enjoyed / as we **w** together to the house of God.
Pr 24:30 I **w** by the field of a lazy person, the vineyard of
Isa 20: 2 as he was told and **w** around naked and barefoot.
51:23 trampled you into the dust and **w** on your backs."
Jer 34:18 you **w** between its halves to solemnize your vows.
Eze 28:14 mountain of God and **w** among the stones of fire.
Mal 2: 6 they **w** with me, living good and righteous lives,
Mt 14:29 side of the boat and **w** on the water toward Jesus.
Mk 2:14 As he **w** along, he saw Levi son of Alphaeus sitting
5:42 years old, immediately stood up and **w** around!
14:45 As soon as they arrived, Judas **w** up to Jesus.
Lk 7:14 Then he **w** over to the coffin and touched it,
10:32 A Temple assistant **w** over and looked at him lying
19:37 followers began to shout and sing as they **w** along,
22:41 He **w** away, about a stone's throw, and knelt down
22:47 Judas **w** over to Jesus and greeted him with a kiss.
24:14 As they **w** along they were talking about
Jn 1:36 As Jesus **w** by, John looked at him and
Ac 1:12 so they **w** the half mile back to Jerusalem.
14: 8 had been that way from birth, so he had never **w**.

WALKING (66) [WALK]
Ge 3: 8 Toward evening they heard the LORD God **w**
24:65 "Who is that man **w** through the fields to meet
32:10 I left home, I owned nothing except a **w** stick,
38:18 your cord, and the **w** stick you are carrying."
38:25 and **w** stick is the father of my child.
Ex 12:11 and carry your **w** sticks in your hands.
Dt 8: 6 of the LORD your God by **w** in his ways
11:22 show love to the LORD your God by **w** in his
26:17 and regulations by **w** in his ways and doing
29:19 even though I am **w** in my own stubborn way.'
30:16 laws, and regulations by **w** in his ways.
Jos 14: 9 'The land of Canaan on which you were just **w** will
2Sa 6: 4 with the Ark of God on it, with Ahio **w** in front.
1Ki 18: 7 As Obadiah was **w** along, he saw Elijah coming
2Ki 2:11 As they were **w** along and talking, suddenly a
2:23 As he was **w** along the road, a group of boys from
6:26 One day as the king of Israel was **w** along the wall
Job 22:14 He is way up there, **w** on the vault of heaven.'
31:26 the skies, or the moon **w** down its silver pathway,
Ps 81:13 that Israel would follow me, **w** in my paths!
Pr 25:19 chewing with a toothache or **w** on a broken foot.
Ecc 10: 7 riding like princes—and princes **w** like servants.
Isa 20: 3 "My servant Isaiah has been **w** around naked
41: 3 on safely, though he is **w** over unfamiliar ground.
50:10 If you are **w** in darkness, without a ray of light,
59: 9 expected light. No wonder we are **w** in the gloom.
Jer 37:13 But as he was **w** through the Benjamin Gate,
Da 3:25 "I see four men, unbound, **w** around in the fire.
Hos 14: 9 and right, and righteous people live by **w** in them.
Mic 1: 3 and comes to earth, **w** on the high places.
Zec 14:12 Their people will become like **w** corpses,
Mt 4:18 One day as Jesus was **w** along the shore beside the
10:10 with an extra coat and sandals or even a **w** stick.
12: 1 At about that time Jesus was **w** through some
14:25 in the morning Jesus came to them, **w** on the water.
14:28 really you, tell me to come to you by **w** on water."
15:31 crippled were made well, the lame were **w** around,
Mk 1:16 One day as Jesus was **w** along the shores of the Sea
2:23 One Sabbath day as Jesus was **w** through some
6: 8 He told them to take nothing with them except a **w**
6:48 in the morning he came to them, **w** on the water.
6:49 but when they saw him **w** on the water,
8:24 them very clearly. They look like trees **w** around."
8:27 As they were **w** along, he asked them, "Who do
10:32 way to Jerusalem, and Jesus was **w** ahead of them.
11:27 As Jesus was **w** through the Temple area,
16:12 Afterward he appeared to two who were **w** from
Lk 6: 1 One Sabbath day as Jesus was **w** through some
9: 3 "Don't even take along a **w** stick," he instructed
9:57 As they were **w** along someone said to Jesus,
19:28 on toward Jerusalem, **w** ahead of his disciples.
24:13 That same day two of Jesus' followers were **w** to
24:15 and joined them and began **w** beside them.
24:35 appeared to them as they were **w** along the road
Jn 5: 9 was healed! He rolled up the mat and began **w**!
6:19 or four miles out when suddenly they saw Jesus **w**
9: 1 As Jesus was **w** along, he saw a man who had been
10:23 **w** through the section known as Solomon's
Ac 3: 8 Then, **w**, leaping, and praising God, he went into
3: 9 All the people saw him **w** and heard him praising
9:31 The believers were **w** in the fear of the Lord
9:35 to the Lord when they saw Aeneas **w** around.
12:10 they passed through and started **w** down the street,
14:10 And the man jumped to his feet and started **w**.
17:23 for as I was **w** along I saw your many altars.
1Jn 2:10 But anyone who loves other Christians is **w** in the

WALKS (7) [WALK]
2Sa 3:29 or leprosy or who **w** on crutches or who dies by the
Pr 13:15 is respected; a treacherous person **w** a rocky road.
13:20 Whoever **w** with the wise will become wise;
whoever **w** with fools will suffer harm.
Hos 11:12 but Judah still **w** with God and is faithful to the
Jn 10: 4 he **w** ahead of them, and they follow him
Rev 2: 1 the one who **w** among the seven gold lampstands:

WALKWAY (3) [WALK]
Eze 42: 4 Between the two blocks of rooms ran a **w** 17-1/2
42:11 There was a **w** between the two blocks of rooms
42:12 and another on the east at the end of the interior **w**.

WALKWAYS (1) [WALK]
Eze 42: 5 because the upper levels had to allow space for **w**

WALL (184) [WALL'S, WALLED, WALLS]
Ge 49:22 beside a fountain. / His branches reach over the **w**.
Ex 14:29 as the water stood up like a **w** on both sides.
15: 8 The surging waters stood straight like a **w**;
38: 9 the courtyard. The south **w** was 150 feet long.
38:11 The north **w** was also 150 feet long, with twenty
Nu 22:25 and crushed Balaam's foot against the **w**.
Jos 2:15 since Rahab's house was built into the city **w**,
1Sa 18:11 hurled it at David, intending to pin him to the **w**.
19:10 into the night, leaving the spear stuck in the **w**.
20:25 He sat at his usual place against the **w**,
25:16 and night they were like a **w** of protection to us
31:10 and they fastened his body to the **w** of the city of
31:12 the bodies of Saul and his sons down from the **w**.
2Sa 11:16 So Joab assigned Uriah to a spot close to the city **w**
11:24 the archers on the **w** shot arrows at us. Some of our
13:34 Then the watchman on the Jerusalem **w** saw a great
18:24 climbed to the roof of the gateway by the **w**.
20:15 and built a ramp against the city **w** and began
20:21 "we will throw his head over the **w** to you."
22:30 crush an army; / with my God I can scale any **w**.
1Ki 3: 1 Temple of the LORD and the **w** around the city.
4:33 to the tiny hyssop that grows from cracks in a **w**.
6: 6 by beams resting on ledges built out from the **w**.
6:27 Their outspread wings reached from **w** to **w**,
9:15 the royal palace, the Millo, the **w** of Jerusalem,
20:30 but the **w** fell on them and killed another 27,000.
21: 4 The king went to bed with his face to the **w**
21:23 eat the body of your wife, Jezebel, at the city **w**.
2Ki 3:27 and sacrificed him as a burnt offering on the **w**.
6:26 king of Israel was walking along the **w** of the city,
6:30 And as the king walked along the **w**, the people
9:33 and some of her blood spattered against the **w**
14:13 to demolish six hundred feet of Jerusalem's **w**,
18:26 in Hebrew, for the people on the **w** will hear."
18:28 and shouted in Hebrew to the people on the **w**,
20: 2 he turned his face to the **w** and prayed to the
25: 4 Then a section of the city **w** was broken down,
1Ch 10:10 and they fastened his head to the **w** in the temple of
2Ch 3:11 was 7-1/2 feet long, and it touched the Temple **w**.
3:12 wing 7-1/2 feet long that touched the opposite **w**.
4: 7 Five were placed against the south **w**, and five
were placed against the north **w**.
4: 8 five along the south **w** and five along the north **w**.
25:23 to demolish six hundred feet of Jerusalem's **w**,
26: 9 at the Valley Gate, and at the angle in the **w**.

26:15 stones from the towers and the corners of the **w**.
27:3 and also did extensive rebuilding on the **w** at the
32:5 by repairing the **w** wherever it was broken down
32:5 and constructing a second **w** outside the first.
33:14 It was after this that Manasseh rebuilt the outer **w**
Ezr 9:9 He has given us a protective **w** in Judah
Ne 1:3 The **w** of Jerusalem has been torn down,
2:15 inspecting the **w** before I turned back and entered
2:17 Let us rebuild the **w** of Jerusalem and rid ourselves
2:18 replied at once, "Good! Let's rebuild the **w**!"
2:20 We his servants will start rebuilding this **w**.
3:1 building the **w** as far as the Tower of the Hundred,
3:4 grandson of Hakkoz repaired the next section of **w**.
3:8 a goldsmith by trade, who also worked on the **w**.
3:8 out a section of Jerusalem as far as the Broad **W**.
3:9 district of Jerusalem, was next to them on the **w**.
3:10 Next Jedaiah son of Harumaph repaired the **w**
3:11 the Ovens, in addition to another section of the **w**.
3:13 They also repaired the fifteen hundred feet of **w** to
3:15 Then he repaired the **w** of the pool of Siloam near
3:15 and he rebuilt the **w** as far as the stairs that descend
3:16 He rebuilt the **w** to a place opposite the royal
3:17 who supervised the building of the **w** on behalf of
3:19 repaired another section of **w** opposite the armory
3:21 **w** extending from a point opposite the door of
3:24 who rebuilt another section of the **w** from
3:26 who repaired the **w** as far as the Water Gate toward
3:27 great projecting tower and over to the **w** of Ophel.
3:28 The priests repaired the **w** up the hill from the
3:29 Next Zadok son of Immer also rebuilt the **w** next to
3:30 while Meshullam son of Berekiah rebuilt the **w**
3:31 repaired the **w** as far as the housing for the Temple
3:32 and merchants repaired the **w** from that corner to
4:1 when he learned that we were rebuilding the **w**.
4:2 Do they think they can build the **w** in a day if they
4:3 "That stone **w** would collapse if even a fox walked
4:6 At last the **w** was completed to half its original
4:7 and that the gaps in the **w** were being repaired,
4:13 the lowest parts of the **w** in the exposed areas.
4:15 we all returned to our work on the **w**.
4:17 who were building the **w**. The common laborers
4:19 are widely separated from each other along the **w**.
5:16 I devoted myself to working on the **w** and refused
5:16 all my officials to spend time working on the **w**.
6:1 found out that I had finished rebuilding the **w**
6:6 to rebel and that is why you are building the **w**.
6:15 So on October 2 the **w** was finally finished—
7:1 After the **w** was finished and I had hung the doors
12:27 During the dedication of the new **w** of Jerusalem,
12:30 then the people, the gates, and the **w**.
12:31 I led the leaders of Judah to the top of the **w**
12:31 southward along the top of the **w** to the Dung Gate.
12:37 the ascent of the city **w** toward the City of David.
12:38 along the top of the **w** past the Tower of the Ovens to the Broad **W**,
13:21 are you doing out here, camping around the **w**?
Ps 18:29 crush an army; / with my God I can scale any **w**.
62:3 To them I'm just a broken-down **w** / or a tottering
Pr 18:11 they imagine it is a high **w** of safety.
Ecc 10:8 When you demolish an old **w**, you could be bitten
SS 2:9 or a young deer. Look, there he is behind the **w**!
5:7 The watchman on the **w** tore off my veil.
Isa 2:15 He will break down every high tower and **w**.
21:6 "Put a watchman on the city **w** to shout out what
25:4 people are like a storm beating against a **w**,
28:17 to check the foundation **w** you have built.
30:13 It will be like a bulging **w** that bursts and falls.
36:11 in Hebrew, for the people on the **w** will hear."
36:13 and shouted in Hebrew to the people on the **w**,
38:2 he turned his face to the **w** and prayed to the
Jer 1:18 be captured, like an iron pillar or a bronze **w**.
15:20 but I will make you as secure as a fortified **w**.
39:2 on July 18, the Babylonians broke through the **w**,
51:44 and worship him. The **w** of Babylon has fallen.
52:7 Then a section of the city **w** was broken down,
La 3:9 He has blocked my path with a high stone **w**.
Eze 8:7 where I could see an opening in the **w**.
8:8 He said to me, "Now, son of man, dig into the **w**."
8:8 So I dug into the **w** and uncovered a door to a
12:5 Dig a hole through the **w** while they are watching
12:7 I dug through the **w** with my hands and went out
12:12 leave Jerusalem at night through a hole in the **w**,
13:10 It's as if the people have built a flimsy **w**,
13:11 Tell these whitewashers that their **w** will soon fall
13:12 And when the **w** falls, the people will cry out,
13:13 I will sweep away your whitewashed **w** with a
13:14 I will break down your **w** right to the foundation,
13:15 At last my anger against the **w** and those who
13:15 'The **w** and those who whitewashed it are both
22:30 "I looked for someone who might rebuild the **w** of
22:30 I searched for someone to stand in the gap in the **w**
23:14 fell in love with pictures that were painted on a **w**
26:8 Then he will attack you by building a siege **w**,
40:5 I could see a **w** completely surrounding the Temple
40:5 rod that was 10-1/2 feet long and measured the **w**,
40:5 and the **w** was 10-1/2 feet thick and 10-1/2 feet
40:6 to the gateway that goes through the eastern **w**.
40:7 between them of 8-3/4 feet along the passage **w**.
41:5 Then he measured the **w** of the Temple and found
41:5 There was a row of rooms along the outside **w**;
41:6 for these rooms rested on ledges in the Temple **w**,
41:6 but the supports did not extend into the **w**.
41:7 corresponding to the narrowing of the Temple **w** as
41:9 The outer **w** of the Temple's side rooms was 8-3/4
41:10 and the row of rooms along the outer **w** of the
41:20 the walls, including the outer **w** of the Holy Place.
42:1 and came to a group of rooms against the north **w**
42:7 There was an outer **w** that separated the rooms
42:8 This **w** added length to the outer block of rooms,
42:12 So there was an entrance in the **w** facing the doors
42:20 So the area was 875 feet on each side with a **w** all
43:8 right next to mine with only a **w** between them
44:1 me back to the east gateway in the outer **w**,
46:1 The east gateway of the inner **w** will be closed
47:2 The man brought me outside the **w** through the
48:30 the city: On the north **w**, which is 1-1/2 miles long,
48:32 On the east **w**, also 1-1/2 miles long, the gates will
48:33 The south **w**, also 1-1/2 miles long, will have gates
48:34 And on the west **w**, also 1-1/2 miles long, the gates
Da 5:5 hand writing on the plaster **w** of the king's palace,
5:15 enchanters have tried to read this writing on the **w**,
Am 4:3 leave by going straight through the breaks in the **w**;
5:19 he leans his hand against a **w** in his house—
7:7 I saw the Lord standing beside a **w** that had been
Zec 2:5 myself, will be a **w** of fire around Jerusalem,
Mt 21:33 landowner planted a vineyard, built a **w** around it,
Mk 12:1 "A man planted a vineyard, built a **w** around it,
Jn 10:1 anyone who sneaks over the **w** of a sheepfold,
Ac 9:25 in a large basket through an opening in the city **w**.
23:3 to him, "God will slap you, you whitewashed **w**!
1Co 3:15 but like someone escaping through a **w** of flames.
2Co 11:33 in a basket through a window in the city **w**,
Eph 2:14 He has broken down the **w** of hostility that used to
Rev 21:14 The **w** of the city had twelve foundation stones,
21:15 stick to measure the city, its gates, and its **w**.
21:18 The **w** was made of jasper, and the city was pure
21:19 The **w** of the city was built on foundation stones

WALL'S (1) [WALL]

Lev 14:37 appears to go deeper than the **w** surface,

WALLED (8) [WALL]

Lev 25:29 "Anyone who sells a house inside a **w** city has the
25:30 then the house within the **w** city will become the
Jos 14:12 found the Anakites living there in great, **w** cities.
1Sa 23:7 to me, for he has trapped himself in a **w** city!"
2Ki 17:9 from the smallest outpost to the largest **w** city.
18:8 from their smallest outpost to their largest **w** city.
La 3:7 He has **w** me in, and I cannot escape. He has bound
Zep 1:16 Down go the **w** cities and strongest battlements!

WALLET (1)

Pr 7:20 He has taken a **w** full of money with him, and he

WALLOW (1)

Jer 48:26 Moab will **w** in her own vomit, ridiculed by all.

WALLS (204) [WALL]

Ex 14:22 sea on dry ground, with **w** of water on each side!
27:18 and 75 feet wide, with curtain **w** 7-1/2 feet high,
27:18 The bases supporting its **w** will be made of bronze.
35:17 the curtains for the **w** of the courtyard; the posts
38:12 The **w** were made from curtains supported by ten
38:16 All the curtains used in the courtyard **w** were made
38:18 feet high, just like the curtains of the courtyard **w**.
38:27 The 100 bases for the frames of the sanctuary **w**
39:40 the curtains for the **w** of the courtyard
Lev 14:37 or reddish streaks on the **w** of the house
14:39 If the mildew on the **w** of the house has spread,
14:41 Next the inside **w** of the entire house must be
14:42 that were removed, and the **w** will be replastered.
14:44 the **w** are clearly contaminated with an infectious
25:31 in a village—a settlement without fortified **w**—
Nu 4:26 for the courtyard **w** that surround the Tabernacle
4:32 the posts for the courtyard **w** with their bases,
13:19 Do their towns have **w** or are they unprotected?
22:24 where the road narrowed between two vineyard **w**.
35:4 1,500 feet from the town **w** in every direction.
35:5 Measure off 3,000 feet outside the town **w** in every
Dt 1:28 and that the **w** of their towns rise high into the sky!
2:36 as far as Gilead. No town had **w** too strong for us.
3:5 These were all fortified cities with high **w**
9:1 They live in cities with **w** that reach to the sky!
28:52 to your cities until all the fortified **w** in your land—
28:52 the **w** you trusted to protect you—are knocked
Jos 6:5 Then the **w** of the city will collapse, and the people
6:20 Suddenly, the **w** of Jericho collapsed,
Jdg 9:46 they took refuge within the **w** of the temple of
9:49 They piled the branches against the **w** of the
2Sa 11:20 they know there would be shooting from the **w**?
17:13 and drag the **w** of the city into the nearest valley
1Ki 6:5 A complex of rooms was built against the outer **w**
6:6 The rooms were connected to the **w** of the Temple
6:6 So the beams were not inserted into the **w**
6:10 attached to the Temple **w** by cedar timbers.
6:15 He paneled the **w** and ceilings with cedar, and he
6:18 Cedar paneling completely covered the stone **w**
6:20 Solomon overlaid its **w** and ceiling with pure gold.
6:29 All the **w** of the inner sanctuary and the main room
6:36 The **w** of the inner courtyard were built so that
7:4 On each of the side **w** there were three rows of
7:11 The costly blocks of stone used in the **w** were also
7:12 The **w** of the great courtyard were built so that
7:12 just like the **w** of the inner courtyard of the
7:26 The **w** of the Sea were about three inches thick,
11:27 and repairing the **w** of the city of his father,
20:30 The rest fled behind the **w** of Aphek, but the wall
2Ki 19:32 their shields and build banks of earth against its **w**.
25:1 the city and built siege ramps against its **w**.
25:4 and fled through the gate between the two **w**
25:10 army as they tore down the **w** of Jerusalem.
1Ch 22:14 I have also gathered lumber and stone for the **w**,
29:4 to be used for overlaying the **w** of the buildings
2Ch 3:4 The inner **w** of the foyer and the ceiling were
3:6 The **w** of the Temple were decorated with beautiful
3:7 All the **w**, beams, doors, and thresholds throughout
3:7 and figures of cherubim were carved on the **w**.
3:9 The **w** of the upper rooms were also overlaid with
4:5 The **w** of the Sea were about three inches thick,
8:5 rebuilding their **w** and installing barred gates.
14:7 "Let us build towns and fortify them with **w**,
26:6 on the Philistines and broke down the **w** of Gath,
26:15 And he produced machines mounted on the **w** of
32:1 orders for his army to break through their **w**.
32:18 to the people gathered on the **w** of the city,
34:11 and masons and purchased cut stone for the **w**
36:19 broke down the **w** of Jerusalem, burned all the
Ezr 4:12 They have already laid the foundation for its **w**
4:13 that if this city is rebuilt and its **w** are completed,
4:16 that if this city is rebuilt and its **w** are completed,
5:8 prepared stones, and timber is being laid in its **w**.
Ne 2:8 for the city **w**, and for a house for myself."
2:13 and over to the Dung Gate to inspect the broken **w**
4:22 I also told everyone living outside the **w** to move
Ps 48:13 Take note of the fortified **w**, / and tour all the
51:18 on Zion and help her; / rebuild the **w** of Jerusalem.
55:10 Its **w** are patrolled day and night against invaders,
78:13 The water stood up like **w** beside them!
80:12 But now, why have you broken down our **w**
89:40 You have broken down the **w** protecting him
102:14 For your people love every stone in her **w**
122:7 O Jerusalem, may there be peace within your **w**
144:14 May there be no breached **w**, no forced exile,
Pr 24:31 covered with weeds, and its **w** were broken down.
25:28 is as defenseless as a city with broken-down **w**.
Isa 5:5 and let it be destroyed. / I will break down its **w**
14:32 that the poor of his people will find refuge in its **w**.
22:5 The **w** of Jerusalem have been broken, and cries of
22:9 You inspect the **w** of Jerusalem to see what needs
22:10 and tear some down to get stone to fix the **w**.
22:11 Between the city **w**, you build a reservoir for water
23:13 They have built siege ramps against its **w**,
25:2 of ruins. Cities with strong **w** are turned to rubble.
25:12 The high **w** of Moab will be demolished
26:1 We are surrounded by the **w** of God's salvation.
26:5 city to the dust. / Its **w** come crashing down!
29:3 surrounding Jerusalem and attacking its **w**.
29:7 Those who are attacking her **w** will vanish like a
33:18 officers outside your **w** counted your towers
37:33 their shields and build banks of earth against its **w**.
49:16 Ever before me is a picture of Jerusalem's **w** in
54:11 and make the **w** of your houses from precious
54:12 and your gates and **w** of shining gems.
56:5 in my house, within my **w**—a memorial and a
58:12 will be known as the people who rebuild their **w**
60:18 Salvation will surround you like city **w**, and praise
62:6 O Jerusalem, I have posted watchmen on your **w**;
Jer 1:15 They will attack its **w** and all the other towns of
6:6 Build ramps against the **w** of Jerusalem. This is the
22:6 you deserted, with no one living within your **w**.
22:13 he builds injustice into its **w** and oppression into its
32:24 the siege ramps have been built against the city **w**!
32:29 The Babylonians outside the **w** will come in
33:4 the **w** against the siege weapons of the enemy,
34:7 the only cities of Judah with their **w** still standing.
39:4 They went out through a gate between the two **w**
39:8 the palace, and tore down the **w** of the city.
49:31 "They live alone in the desert without **w** or gates.
50:15 Look! She surrenders! Her **w** have fallen.
50:26 Crush her **w** and houses into heaps of rubble.
51:58 "The wide **w** of Babylon will be leveled to the
52:4 the city and built siege ramps against its **w**.
52:7 and fled through the gate between the two **w**
52:14 army as they tore down the **w** of Jerusalem.
52:21 They were hollow, with **w** 3 inches thick.
La 2:2 In his anger he has broken down the fortress **w** of
2:8 The LORD was determined to destroy the **w** of
2:8 the ramparts and **w** have fallen down before him.
2:18 Cry aloud before the Lord, O **w** of Jerusalem!
Eze 4:2 Build siege ramps against the city **w**. Surround it
5:12 be slaughtered by the enemy outside the city **w**.
7:15 Any who leave the city **w** will be killed by enemy
8:10 and saw the **w** engraved with all kinds of snakes,
13:5 to strengthen the breaks in the **w** around the nation.
21:22 and build ramps against the **w** to reach the top.
22:6 "Every leader in Israel who lives within your **w** is
22:8 Inside your **w** you despise my holy things
22:11 Within your **w** live men who commit adultery with
22:28 to them. They repair cracked **w** with whitewash!
26:4 They will destroy the **w** of Tyre and tear down its
26:9 He will pound your **w** with battering rams
26:10 and your **w** will shake as the horses gallop through
26:12 and merchandise and break down your **w**.
27:10 They hung their shields and helmets on your **w**,
27:11 and from Helech stood on your **w** as sentinels.
27:11 Their shields hung on your **w**, perfecting your
28:23 and your people will lie slaughtered within your **w**.
36:35 The ruined cities now have strong **w**, and they are
38:20 cliffs will crumble; **w** will fall to the earth.
40:10 and the dividing **w** separating them were also
40:13 measuring the distance between the back **w** of
40:14 He measured the dividing **w** all along the inside of
40:16 inward through the **w** of the guard alcoves and their dividing **w**.
40:16 The surfaces of the dividing **w** were decorated with
40:17 A stone pavement ran along the **w** of the courtyard,
40:17 and thirty rooms were built against the **w**,
40:18 and extended out from the **w** into the courtyard the

40:21 alcoves on each side, with dividing w and a foyer.
40:21 and 43-3/4 feet wide between the back w of facing
40:25 It had windows along the w as the others did,
40:25 and 43-3/4 feet wide between the back w of facing
40:26 were palm tree decorations along the dividing w.
40:29 Its guard alcoves, dividing w, and foyer were the
40:29 It also had windows along its w and in the foyer
40:33 Its guard alcoves, dividing w, and foyer were the
40:33 and there were windows along the w and in the
40:36 The guard alcoves, dividing w, and foyer of this
40:43 fastened to the foyer w and set on the tables where
40:48 The entrance was 24-1/2 feet wide with w 5-1/4
41: 2 and the w on each side were 8-3/4 feet wide.
41: 3 and the w on each side of the entrance extended
41:12 157-1/2 feet long, and its w were 8-3/4 feet thick.
41:13 The courtyard around the building, including its w,
41:15 including its two w, was also 175 feet wide.
41:16 The inner w of the Temple were paneled with
41:18 All the w were decorated with carvings of
41:20 from the floor to the top of the w,
41:25 carved cherubim and palm trees just as on the w.
46:22 feet long and 52-1/2 feet wide, surrounded by w.
46:23 Along the inside of these w was a ledge of stone
Joel 2: 7 like warriors and scale city w like trained soldiers.
2: 9 They swarm over the city and run along its w.
Am 1: 7 So I will send down fire on the w of Gaza, and all
1:10 So I will send down fire on the w of Tyre, and all
1:14 So I will send down fire on the w of Rabbah,
9:11 but I will rebuild its w and restore its former glory.
Mic 1: 6 I will roll the stones of her w down into the valley
1:11 people of Zaanan dare not come outside their w.
5:11 I will tear down your w and demolish the defenses
Na 2: 5 rushing to the w to set up their defenses.
3:14 the defenses! Make bricks to repair the w!
Hab 1:10 They simply pile ramps of earth against their w
2:11 The very stones in the w of your houses cry out
Zep 3: 6 devastating their fortress w and towers.
Zec 2: 4 Many will live outside the city w, with all their
Mk 13: 1 Look at the massive stones in the w!"
Lk 19:43 your enemies will build ramparts against your w
21: 5 the Temple and the memorial decorations on the w.
Heb 11:30 seven days, and the w came crashing down.
Rev 21:12 Its w were broad and high, with twelve gates
21:17 Then he measured the w and found them to be 216

WANDER (22) [WANDERED, WANDERERS, WANDERING, WANDERS]

Nu 14:34 you must w in the wilderness for forty years—
32:13 and made them w in the wilderness for forty years
2Sa 15:20 and now should I force you to w with us?
Job 15:23 They w abroad for bread, saying, 'Where is it?'
38:41 young cry out to God as they w about in hunger?
Ps 42: 9 Why must I w in darkness, / oppressed by my
43: 2 Why must I w around in darkness, / oppressed by
107:40 causing them to w in trackless wastelands.
109:10 May his children w as beggars; / may they be
119:10 find you— / don't let me w from your commands.
119:21 cursed proud ones / who w from your commands.
119:67 I used to w off until you disciplined me; / but now
Pr 7:25 toward her. Don't w down her wayward path.
17:24 but a fool's eyes w to the ends of the earth.
SS 1: 7 For why should I w like a prostitute among the
Isa 15: 3 They will wear sackcloth as they w the streets.
Jer 14:10 "You love to w far from me and do not follow in
31:22 How long will you w, my wayward daughter?
Joel 1:18 The cattle w about confused because there is no
Mt 18:13 more than over the ninety-nine that didn't w away!
Mk 5: 5 and throughout the night he would w among the
2Jn 1: 9 For if you w beyond the teaching of Christ,

WANDERED (16) [WANDER]

Dt 2: 1 and we w around Mount Seir for a long time.
Jos 5: 6 The Israelites w in the wilderness for forty years
14:10 even while Israel w in the wilderness.
1Ch 16:20 They w back and forth between nations, / from one
Ps 105:13 They w back and forth between nations, / from one
107: 4 Some w in the desert, / lost and homeless.
119:176 I have w away like a lost sheep; / come and find
Jer 3:21 the LORD their God and w far from his ways.
La 4:14 They w blindly through the streets, so defiled by
4:15 to distant lands and w there among foreign nations,
Eze 34: 4 You have not gone looking for those who have w
34: 6 They have w through the mountains and hills,
1Ti 6:10 have w from the faith and pierced themselves with
6:21 Some people have w from the faith by following
Heb 11:38 They w over deserts and mountains, hiding in
2Pe 2:15 They have w off the right road and followed the

WANDERERS (2) [WANDER]

Isa 58: 7 and to welcome poor w into your homes.
Hos 9:17 They will be w, homeless among the nations.

WANDERING (17) [WANDER]

Ge 4:12 on the earth, constantly w from place to place."
4:14 your presence; you have made me a w fugitive.
21:14 out into the wilderness of Beersheba, w aimlessly.
37:15 a man noticed him w around the countryside.
Nu 14:33 be like shepherds, w in the wilderness forty years.
Dt 2: 3 'You have been w around in this hill country long
22: 1 "If you see your neighbor's ox or sheep w away,
26: 5 'My ancestor Jacob was a w Aramean who went to
Job 12:24 and he leaves them w in a wasteland without a
Isa 13:14 like hunted deer, w like sheep without a shepherd.
La 1: 7 And now in the midst of her sadness and w,
Zec 10: 2 So my people are w like lost sheep, without a
Ac 13:11 and he began w around begging for someone to
13:18 He put up with them through forty years of w
1Pe 2:25 Once you were w like lost sheep. But now you
1Jn 2:11 Those who reject other Christians are w in spiritual
Jude 1:13 They are w stars, heading for everlasting gloom

WANDERS (2) [WANDER]

Mt 18:12 and one w away and is lost, what will he do?
Jas 5:19 if anyone among you w away from the truth

WANT (370) [WANTED, WANTING, WANTS]

Ge 13: 9 Take your choice of any section of the land you w,
13: 9 If you w that area over there, then I'll stay here.
13: 9 If you w to stay in this area, then I'll move on to
20:11 'They will w my wife and will kill me to get her.'
21:16 "I don't w to watch the boy die," she said, as she
23: 9 I w to pay the full price, of course, whatever is
24:33 "I don't w to eat until I have told you why I have
24:55 "But we w Rebekah to stay at least ten days,"
24:56 and I w to report back to my master."
27:21 I w to touch you to make sure you really are
29:15 because we are relatives. How much do you w?"
30:25 Jacob said to Laban, "I w to go back home.
30:31 "What wages do you w?" Laban asked again.
34: 4 girl for me," he demanded. "I w to marry her."
38:18 "Well, what do you w?" he inquired. She replied,
38:18 "I w your identification seal, your cord,
42:36 is gone, and now you w to take Benjamin, too.
Ex 8: 9 "Tell me when you w me to pray for you,
10: 8 "But tell me, just whom do you w to take along?"
12:48 "If there are foreigners living among you who w
16:23 So bake or boil as much as you w today, and set
25: 8 "I w the people of Israel to build me a sacred
33:13 more fully and do exactly what you w me to do.
Lev 3: 1 "If you w to present a peace offering from the
25:18 "If you w to live securely in the land, keep my
27:13 If you w to redeem the animal, you must pay the
27:31 If you w to redeem the LORD's tenth of the fruit
Nu 9:14 And if foreigners living among you w to celebrate
15: 3 and you w to please the LORD with a burnt
15:13 If you native Israelites w to present an offering by
15:14 And if any foreigners living among you w to
20:19 We only w to pass through your country
32: 6 "Do you mean you w to stay back here while your
32:16 "We simply w to build sheepfolds for our flocks
32:19 But we do not w any of the land on the other side
35:12 dead person's relatives who w to avenge the death.
Dt 2:28 All we w is permission to pass through your land.
12:15 wherever you w, just as you do now with gazelle
12:20 has promised, you may eat meat whenever you w.
12:30 worship their gods? I w to follow their example.'
14:26 you arrive, use the money to buy anything you w—
21:11 and you are attracted to her and w to marry her.
25: 8 If he still insists that he doesn't w to marry her,
28:68 enemies as slaves, but no one will w to buy you.
31:20 they will eat all the food they w and become well
Jos 5:14 Joshua said. "What do you w your servant to do?"
Jdg 9: 2 "Ask the people of Shechem whether they w to be
9: 7 Listen to me if you w God to listen to you!
9:15 'If you truly w to make me your king, come
13:17 For when all this comes true, we w to honor you."
14: 2 "I w to marry a young Philistine woman I saw in
14: 3 his father, "Get her for me. She is the one I w."
16:26 against the two pillars. I w to rest against them."
18:23 of Dan turned around and said, "What do you w?
18:24 "What do you mean, What do I w?"
Ru 1:10 they said. "We w to go with you to your people."
4: 1 "Come over here, friend. I w to talk to you."
4: 4 If you w the land, then buy it here in the presence
4: 4 But if you don't w it, let me know right away,
1Sa 2:16 "Take as much as you w, but the fat must first be
6: 8 Then let the cows go wherever they w.
8: 7 They don't w me to be their king any longer.
8:16 He will w your male and female slaves
8:19 "Even so, we still w a king," they said.
8:20 "We w to be like the nations around us. Our king
9:19 In the morning I will tell you what you w to know
10:19 have rejected me and said, 'We w a king instead!'
14:38 I w all my army commanders to come here.
17:28 and dishonesty. You just w to see the battle!"
18:25 "Tell David that all I w for the bride price is one
18:25 Vengeance on my enemies is all I really w."
20:30 "Do you think I don't know that you w David to
21: 9 Take that if you w it, for there is nothing else
23: 3 We certainly don't w to go to Keilah to fight the
28:11 "Well, whose spirit do you w me to call up?"
2Sa 1: 9 my misery, for I am in terrible pain and w to die.'
9: 3 I w to show God's kindness to them in any way I
14:11 I w no more bloodshed." "As surely as the
14:18 "I w to know one thing," the king replied. "Yes,
16: 4 "I will always do whatever you w me to do."
19:37 and receive whatever good things you w to give
20: 1 We w no part of this son of Jesse. Come on,
20:18 to be a saying, 'If you w to settle an argument,
20:19 Why do you w to destroy what belongs to the
20:20 "Believe me, I don't w to destroy your city!
20:21 All I w is a man named Sheba son of Bicri from
21: 4 "And we don't w to see the Israelites executed in
24: 3 as there are now! But why do you w to do this?"
1Ki 1:12 If you w to save your own life and the life of your
3: 5 in a dream, and God said, "What do you w?
8:18 'It is right for you to w to build the Temple to
11:22 How have we disappointed you that you w to go
12: 9 "How should I answer these people who w me to
2Ki 3:13 "I w no part of you," Elisha said to the king of
4:12 "Tell the woman I w to speak to her."
4:13 Does she w me to put in a good word for her to the
5: 6 I w you to heal him of his leprosy."
9:11 them asked him, "What did that crazy fellow w?
9:15 the men with him, "Since you w me to be king,
19: 7 Then I will make him w to return to his land,
20:14 and asked him, "What did those men w?
1Ch 21: 3 But why, my lord, do you w to do this? Are they
29:18 make your people always w to obey you.
2Ch 1: 7 to Solomon in a dream and said, "What do you w?
6: 8 'It is right for you to w to build the Temple to
10: 9 "How should I answer these people who w me to
35:21 "What do you w with me, king of Judah? I have
35:21 I only w to fight the nation with which I am at war.
Ezr 4:14 and we do not w to see you dishonored in this way,
7:27 who made the king w to beautify the Temple of the
Est 5: 3 king asked her, "What do you w, Queen Esther?
5: 6 said to Esther, "Now tell me what you really w.
7: 2 asked her, "Tell me what you w, Queen Esther.
8: 8 telling them whatever you w, and seal it with the
9:12 But now, what more do you w? It will be granted
Job 1:12 "Do whatever you w with everything he
6:24 "All I w is a reasonable answer—then I will keep
7:16 I do not w to go on living. Oh, leave me alone for
13: 3 I w to argue my case with God himself.
18: 2 stop talking? Speak sense if you w us to answer!
21:14 We w no part of you and your ways.
24: 8 and they huddle against the rocks for w of a home.
33:32 I w to hear it, for I am anxious to see you justified.
37:20 Should God be told that I w to speak? Can we
40: 2 "Do you still w to argue with the Almighty?
41:12 "I w to emphasize the tremendous strength in the
Ps 34:12 Do any of you w to live / a life that is long
35:10 and needy from those who w to rob them?"
50: 9 But I w no more bulls from your barns; / I w no more goats from your pens.
50:14 What I w instead is your true thanks to God;
50:14 I w you to fulfill your vows to the Most High.
51:17 The sacrifice you w is a broken spirit. / A broken
71:13 and shame cover / those who w to harm me.
81:11 wouldn't listen. / Israel did not w me around.
119:39 my shameful ways; / your laws are all I w in life.
119:58 With all my heart I w your blessings. / Be merciful
142: 5 my place of refuge. / You are all I really w in life.
Pr 6: 9 will you wake up? I w you to learn this lesson:
8: 9 with understanding, clear to those who w to learn.
13: 4 Lazy people w much but get little, but those who
18: 2 they only w to air their own opinions.
Ecc 6: 2 and gives them everything they could ever w,
11: 9 of it. Do everything you w to do; take it all in.
SS 8: 4 "I w you to promise, O women of Jerusalem,
Isa 1:11 I don't w the fat from your rams or other animals.
1:11 I don't w to see the blood from your offerings of
1:13 and false. I w nothing more to do with them.
5:19 you can do. We w to see what you have planned."
7: 9 If you w me to protect you, learn to believe what I
7:11 you like, and make it as difficult as you w."
30:10 We don't w any more of your reports." They say,
37: 7 Then I will make him w to return to his land,
39: 3 and asked him, "What did those men w?
55:11 It will accomplish all I w it to, and it will prosper
58: 6 the kind of fasting I w calls you to free those who
58: 7 I w you to share your food with the hungry and to
Jer 6:10 word of the LORD. They don't w to listen at all.
6:16 But you reply, 'No, that's not the road we w!'
18:12 We will continue to live as we w to, following our
27:12 "If you w to live, submit to the king of Babylon
29:22 so that whenever the Judean exiles w to curse
32:36 "Now I w to say something more about this city.
38:14 "I w to ask you something," the king said.
38:16 or hand you over to the men who w you dead."
40: 4 If you w to come with me to Babylon, you are
40: 4 But if you don't w to come, you may stay here.
44:17 We will do whatever we w. We will burn incense
44:30 of Egypt, over to his enemies who w to kill him,
46:26 I will hand them over to those who w them killed—
La 2:12 "Mama, we w food," they cry, and then collapse
4: 9 who die of hunger, wasting away for w of food.
Eze 2: 1 of man," said the voice. "I w to speak with you."
12: 2 see the truth if they wanted to, but they don't w to.
13:22 your lies, when I didn't w them to suffer grief.
14:10 evil people who claim to w my advice—
18:23 I only w them to turn from their wicked ways
18:32 I don't w you to die, says the Sovereign LORD.
20:32 'We w to be like the nations all around us,
21:16 to the left, wherever you will, wherever you w.
23:43 I said, 'If they really w to sleep with worn-out,
33:11 I only w them to turn from their wicked ways
46:18 for I do not w any of my people unjustly evicted
Da 4: 2 "I w you all to know about the miraculous signs
Hos 6: 6 I w you to be merciful; I don't w your sacrifices. I w you to know God; that's more important than
Joel 2:26 Once again you will have all the food you w,
Am 5:24 Instead, I w to see a mighty flood of justice,
Mic 2: 2 When you w a certain piece of land, you find a
2: 2 When you w someone's house, you take it by fraud
Zec 11:12 whatever I am worth; but only if you w to."
Mal 2:15 and spirit you are his. And what does he w?
Mt 3:14 But John didn't w to baptize him. "I am the one
5:42 and don't turn away from those who w to borrow.
8: 2 "Lord," the man said, "if you w to, you can
8: 3 touched him. "I w to," he said. "Be healed!"
9:13 'I w you to be merciful; I don't w your sacrifices.'
10:28 "Don't be afraid of those who w to kill you.
12: 7 'I w you to be merciful; I don't w your sacrifices.'
12:38 we w you to show us a miraculous sign to prove
12:47 brothers are outside, and they w to speak to you."

14: 8 “I **w** the head of John the Baptist on a tray!”
14: 9 because he didn’t **w** to back down in front of his
15:32 I don’t **w** to send them away hungry, or they will
17: 4 If you **w** me to, I’ll make three shrines, one for
17:27 However, we don’t **w** to offend them, so go down
19:21 “If you **w** to be perfect, go and sell all you have
20:15 Is it against the law for me to do what I **w** with my
20:32 and called, “What do you **w** me to do for you?”
20:33 “Lord,” they said, “we **w** to see!”
26:17 “Where do you **w** us to prepare the Passover
26:39 taken away from me. Yet I **w** your will, not mine.”
27:17 “Which one do you **w** me to release to you—
27:21 “Which of these two do you **w** me to release to
Mk 1:40 “If you **w** to, you can make me well again,”
1:41 touched him. “I **w** to,” he said. “Be healed!”
6:25 “I **w** the head of John the Baptist, right now,
10:35 they said, “we **w** you to do us a favor.”
10:37 we **w** to sit in places of honor next to you,”
10:51 “What do you **w** me to do for you?” Jesus asked.
10:51 “Teacher,” the blind man said, “I **w** to see!”
14: 7 and you can help them whenever you **w** to.
14:12 “Where do you **w** us to go to prepare the Passover
14:36 away from me. Yet I **w** your will, not mine.”
Lk 5:12 “Lord,” he said, “if you **w** to, you can make me
5:13 touched the man. “I **w** to,” he said. “Be healed!”
5:39 But no one who drinks the old wine seems to **w** the
8:20 your brothers are outside, and they **w** to see you.”
11: 8 he will get up and give you what you **w** so his
12: 4 don’t be afraid of those who **w** to kill you.
13:31 “Get out of here if you **w** to live, because Herod
14:26 “If you **w** to be my follower you must love me
15:12 told his father, ‘I **w** my share of your estate now,
16:28 and I **w** him to warn them about this place of
16:29 brothers can read their writings anytime they **w** to.’
18:41 the man, “What do you **w** me to do for you?”
18:41 “Lord,” he pleaded, “I **w** to see!”
19:14 him to say they did not **w** him to be their king.
19:27 of mine who didn’t **w** me to be their king—
22: 9 “Where do you **w** us to go?” they asked him.
22:42 away from me. Yet I **w** your will, not mine.”
Jn 1:38 “What do you **w**?” he asked them. They replied,
3:20 hate the light because they **w** to sin in the darkness.
6:26 you **w** to be with me because I fed you, not
6:28 They replied, “What does God **w** us to do?”
6:30 “You must show us a miraculous sign if you **w** us
6:38 the will of God who sent me, not to do what I **w**.
9:27 Didn’t you listen? Do you **w** to hear it again?
Do you **w** to become his disciples, too?”
10:18 For I have the right to lay it down when I **w** to
12:21 in Galilee. They said, “Sir, we **w** to meet Jesus.”
12:26 All those who **w** to be my disciples must come
16:12 “Oh, there is so much more I **w** to tell you,
17:24 I **w** these whom you’ve given me to be with me,
18: 8 “And since I am the one you **w**, let these others
18:39 So if you **w** me to, I’ll release the King of the
19:31 The Jewish leaders didn’t **w** the victims hanging
21:18 direct you and take you where you don’t **w** to go.”
21:22 “If I **w** him to remain alive until I return,
21:23 “If I **w** him to remain alive until I return,
Ac 4: 9 Do you **w** to know how he was healed?
13:22 own heart, for he will do everything I **w** him to.’
16:37 So now they **w** us to leave secretly? Certainly not!
17:20 and we **w** to know what it’s all about.”
17:32 others said, “We **w** to hear more about this later.”
20:16 because he didn’t **w** to spend further time in the
23:15 “Pretend you **w** to examine his case more fully.
23:19 and asked, “What is it you **w** to tell me?”
23:20 pretending they **w** to get some more information.
28:22 But we **w** to hear what you believe, for the only
28:28 So I **w** you to realize that this salvation from God
Ro 1:12 your faith, but I also **w** to be encouraged by yours.
1:13 I **w** you to know, dear friends, that I planned many
1:13 I **w** to work among you and see good results,
7:15 for I really **w** to do what is right, but I don’t do it.
7:18 I can’t make myself do right. I **w** to, but I can’t.
7:19 When I **w** to do good, I don’t. And when I try not
7:20 But if I am doing what I don’t **w** to do, I am not
7:21 It seems to be a fact of life that when I **w** to do
7:25 In my mind I really **w** to obey God’s law, but
11:11 the Jews would be jealous and **w** it for themselves.
11:14 for I **w** to find a way to make the Jews **w** what
11:25 I **w** you to understand this mystery, dear friends,
14: 6 And those who won’t eat everything also **w** to
16:19 I **w** you to see clearly what is right and to stay
1Co 1:22 because they **w** a sign from heaven to prove it is
7:32 I **w** you to be free from the concerns of this life.
7:35 I **w** you to do whatever will help you serve the
8:13 for I don’t **w** to make another Christian stumble.
10: 1 I don’t **w** you to forget, dear brothers and sisters,
10:20 And I don’t **w** any of you to be partners with
10:27 go ahead; accept the invitation if you **w** to.
11: 3 But there is one thing I **w** you to know: A man is
11:22 Or do you really **w** to disgrace the church of God
11:22 Do you **w** me to praise you? Well, I certainly do
12: 3 So I **w** you to know how to discern what is truly
16: 7 This time I don’t **w** to make just a short visit
16: 7 I **w** to come and stay awhile, if the Lord will let
2Co 1:24 But that does not mean we **w** to tell you exactly
1:24 We **w** to work together with you so you will be full
2: 4 I didn’t **w** to hurt you, but I wanted you to know
5: 4 but it’s not that we **w** to die and have no bodies at
5: 4 We **w** to slip into our new bodies so that these
8: 1 Now I **w** to tell you, dear friends, what God in his
8: 7 now I **w** you to excel also in this gracious ministry
8:21 but we also **w** everyone else to know we are
9: 3 I don’t **w** it to turn out that I was wrong in my
9: 5 But I **w** it to be a willing gift, not one given under
12: 6 I don’t **w** anyone to think more highly of me than
12:14 I don’t **w** what you have; I **w** you. And anyway,
13: 3 I will give you all the proof you **w** that Christ
13: 7 because we **w** you to do right even if we ourselves
13:10 For I **w** to use the authority the Lord has given me
Gal 4: 9 why do you **w** to go back again and become slaves
4:21 Listen to me, you who **w** to live under the law.
4:29 are persecuted by those who **w** us to keep the law,
5:12 I only wish that those troublemakers who **w** to
6:12 They don’t **w** to be persecuted for teaching that the
6:13 They only **w** you to be circumcised so they can
Eph 1:18 I **w** you to realize what a rich and glorious
Php 1:10 For I **w** you to understand what really matters,
1:12 And I **w** you to know, dear friends, that everything
1:23 Sometimes I **w** to live, and sometimes I long to go
2:17 and I **w** to share my joy with all of you.
4: 2 And now I **w** to plead with those two women,
4:17 I don’t say this because I **w** a gift from you. What I
w is for you to receive a well-earned
Col 1:28 for we **w** to present them to God, perfect in their
2: 1 I **w** you to know how much I have agonized for
2: 2 I **w** them to have full confidence because they have
1Th 3: 6 and that you **w** to see us just as much as we **w** to
4:13 I **w** you to know what will happen to the Christians
1Ti 1: 7 They **w** to be known as teachers of the law of
2: 8 I **w** men to pray with holy hands lifted up to God,
2: 9 And I **w** women to be modest in their appearance.
5:11 their devotion to Christ and they will **w** to remarry.
2Ti 2:22 Follow anything that makes you **w** to do right.
4: 3 who will tell them whatever they **w** to hear.
Tit 1:11 from the truth. Such teachers only **w** your money.
2: 8 Then those who **w** to argue will be ashamed
3: 8 I **w** you to insist on them so that everyone who
Phm 1:14 But I didn’t **w** to do anything without your
1:14 And I didn’t **w** you to help because you were
Heb 10: 5 “You did not **w** animal sacrifices and grain
10: 8 “You did not **w** animal sacrifices or grain
13:18 and we **w** to live honorably in everything we do.
13:23 I **w** you to know that our brother Timothy is now
Jas 1: 5 if you **w** to know what God wants you to do—
3: 3 and go wherever we **w** by means of a small bit in
4: 2 You **w** what you don’t have, so you scheme
4: 2 And yet the reason you don’t have what you **w** is
4: 3 is wrong—you **w** only what will give you pleasure.
1Pe 3:10 “If you **w** a happy life and good days,
3:13 who will **w** to harm you if you are eager to do
2Pe 1:15 I **w** you to remember them long after I am gone.
3: 2 I **w** you to remember and understand what the holy
3: 3 I **w** to remind you that in the last days there will be
3: 9 He does not **w** anyone to perish, so he is giving
3:17 I don’t **w** you to lose your own secure footing.
1Jn 2:26 because you need to be aware of those who **w** to
2Jn 1: 5 And now I **w** to urge you, dear lady, that we should
1:12 to say to you, but I don’t **w** to say it in a letter.
3Jn 1:13 much to tell you, but I don’t **w** to do it in a letter.
Rev 3:17 You say, ‘I am rich. I have everything I **w**. I don’t

WANTED (105) [WANT]

Ge 6: 2 the human race and took any they **w** as their wives.
34:19 acting on this request, for he **w** Dinah desperately.
39: 6 in the world, except to decide what he **w** to eat!
43: 7 “He **w** to know whether our father was still living,
43:30 with emotion for his brother and **w** to cry.
45: 1 He **w** to be alone with his brothers when he told
Ex 4:19 to Egypt, for all those who **w** to kill you are dead.”
33: 7 Everyone who **w** to consult with the LORD
35:29 and woman who **w** to help in the work the LORD
Nu 11: 5 melons, leeks, onions, and garlic that we **w**.
22: 7 and urgently explained to him what Balak **w**.
Dt 9:20 so angry with Aaron that he **w** to destroy him.
Jos 7:21 than a pound. I **w** them so much that I took them.
19:50 the LORD had said he could have any town he **w**.
1Sa 9: 9 (In those days if people **w** a message from God,
12:12 and said that you **w** a king to reign over you,
20:29 He **w** to take part in a family sacrifice. His brother
2Sa 3:17 told them, “you have **w** to make David your king.
14:32 “Because I **w** you to ask the king why he brought
1Ki 2:15 for that is the way the LORD **w** it.
8:17 **w** to build this Temple to honor the name of the
13:33 Anyone who **w** to could become a priest for the
14: 8 his heart and always did whatever I **w** him to do.
1Ch 4:41 because they **w** its good pastureland for their
22: 7 “I **w** to build a Temple to honor the name of the
2Ch 6: 7 **w** to build this Temple to honor the name of the
11:16 those who sincerely **w** to worship the LORD,
Est 1: 8 one should be compelled to take more than he **w**.
1:11 He **w** all the men to gaze on her beauty, for she
2:13 or jewelry she **w** to enhance her beauty.
Job 9: 3 If someone **w** to take God to court, would it be
Ps 35:25 Don’t let them say, “Look! We have what we **w**!
78:29 people ate their fill. / He gave them what they **w**.
Ecc 2:10 Anything I **w**, I took. I did not restrain myself from
SS 6:11 I **w** to see whether the grapevines were budding
Jer 2:17 the LORD your God when he **w** to lead you
3:19 I **w** nothing more than to give you this beautiful
7:22 not burnt offerings and sacrifices I **w** from them.
7:24 They kept on doing whatever they **w**,
11:21 The men of Anathoth **w** me dead. They said they
Eze 12: 2 among rebels who could see the truth if they **w** to,
Da 2:30 because God **w** you to understand what you were
5:19 He killed those he **w** to kill and spared those he **w**
to spare. He honored those he **w** to honor and
disgraced those he **w** to disgrace.
7:19 Then I **w** to know the true meaning of the fourth
Hos 6:11 though I **w** so much to restore the fortunes of my
7: 1 “I **w** to heal Israel, but its sins were far too great.
7:13 I **w** to redeem them, but they have only spoken lies
Mt 14: 7 promised with an oath to give her anything she **w**.
14:20 They all ate as much as they **w**, and they picked up
20:14 and go. I **w** to pay this last worker the same as you.
21:46 They **w** to arrest him, but they were afraid to try
23:37 How often I have **w** to gather your children
27:15 during the Passover celebration—anyone they **w**.
Mk 3:13 and called the ones he **w** to go with him.
6:19 was enraged and **w** John killed in revenge,
6:42 They all ate as much as they **w**,
12:12 The Jewish leaders **w** to arrest him for using this
Lk 1:59 They **w** to name him Zechariah, after his father.
8:35 for they **w** to see for themselves what had
9:17 They all ate as much as they **w**, and they picked up
10:29 The man **w** to justify his actions, so he asked Jesus,
13:34 How often I have **w** to gather your children
14:18 said he had just bought a field and **w** to inspect it,
14:19 just bought five pair of oxen and **w** to try them out.
16:25 during your lifetime you had everything you **w**,
16:26 Anyone who **w** to cross over to you from here is
19:15 He **w** to find out what they had done with the
20:19 they **w** to arrest Jesus immediately because they
22: 2 But they **w** to kill him without starting a riot,
23:20 argued with them, because he **w** to release Jesus.
Jn 7: 1 He **w** to stay out of Judea where the Jewish leaders
7:44 And some **w** him arrested, but no one touched him.
11:56 They **w** to see Jesus, and as they talked in the
16:19 Jesus realized they **w** to ask him, so he said,
21:18 able to do as you liked and go wherever you **w** to.
Ac 7:39 ancestors rejected Moses and **w** to return to Egypt.
9: 2 He **w** to bring them—both men and women—
13: 7 Saul to visit him, for he **w** to hear the word of God.
15:37 Barnabas agreed and **w** to take along John Mark.
16: 3 so Paul **w** him to join them on their journey.
19:30 Paul **w** to go in, but the believers wouldn’t let him.
22:24 He **w** to find out why the crowd had become
24:27 because Felix **w** to gain favor with the Jewish
27:12 most of the crew **w** to go to Phoenix, farther up the
27:42 The soldiers **w** to kill the prisoners to make sure
27:43 But the commanding officer **w** to spare Paul,
28:18 The Romans tried me and **w** to release me, for they
2Co 1:15 and trust, I **w** to give you a double blessing.
1:16 I **w** to stop and see you on my way to Macedonia
2: 4 but I **w** you to know how very much I love you.
Gal 2: 2 I **w** them to understand what I had been preaching
2: 2 I **w** to make sure they did not disagree, or my
2: 4 They **w** to force us, like slaves, to follow their
2: 5 We **w** to preserve the truth of the Good News for
1Th 2:18 We **w** very much to come, and I, Paul, tried again
2Th 3: 9 but we **w** to give you an example to follow.
Phm 1:13 I really **w** to keep him here with me while I am in
1:14 you were forced to do it but because you **w** to.
Heb 12:17 And afterward, when he **w** his father’s blessing,
1Pe 1:10 This salvation was something the prophets **w** to
2Pe 1:21 or because they **w** to prophesy. It was the Holy
Rev 13: 5 And he was given authority to do what he **w** for

WANTING (4) [WANT]

1Sa 7: 3 “If you are really serious about **w** to return to the
Mt 12:46 and brothers were outside, **w** to talk with him.
Lk 11: 5 at midnight, **w** to borrow three loaves of bread.
Ac 25: 9 Then Festus, **w** to please the Jews, asked him,

WANTS (68) [WANT]

Ge 27: 7 He **w** to bless Esau in the LORD’s presence
Ex 25: 2 “Tell the people of Israel that everyone who **w** to
Dt 29:13 He **w** to confirm you today as his people and to
1Sa 20:13 But if he is angry and **w** you killed,
22:23 own life, for the same person **w** to kill us both.”
1Ki 3:27 but give the baby to the woman who **w** him to live,
2Ki 9:18 “The king **w** to know whether you are coming in
9:19 “The king **w** to know whether you come in
18:27 “My master **w** everyone in Jerusalem to hear this,
18:27 He **w** them to know that if you do not surrender,
Est 5: 8 is pleased with me and **w** to grant my request,
7: 3 is pleased with me and **w** to grant my request,
Job 23:13 from his purposes? Whatever he **w** to do, he does.
Ps 1: 2 they delight in doing everything the LORD **w**;
Pr 28:20 But the person who **w** to get rich quick will only
Isa 36:12 “My master **w** everyone in Jerusalem to hear this,
36:12 He **w** them to know that if you do not surrender,
Jer 10:21 follow the LORD or ask what he **w** of them.
39:12 after him well, and give him anything he **w**.”
Hos 8: 8 lie among the nations like an old pot that no one **w**.
Mt 16:24 the disciples, “If any of you **w** to be my follower,
20:26 Whoever **w** to be a leader among you must be your
20:27 and whoever **w** to be first must become your slave.
Mk 8:34 “If any of you **w** to be my follower,” he told
9:35 “Anyone who **w** to be the first must take last place
10:43 Whoever **w** to be a leader among you must be your
10:44 and whoever **w** to be first must be the slave of all.
Lk 1:38 and I am willing to accept whatever he **w**.
9:23 to the crowd, “If any of you **w** to be my follower,
13:31 to live, because Herod Antipas **w** to kill you!”
Jn 3:21 can see that they are doing what God **w**.”
5:21 He will even raise from the dead anyone he **w** to,
6:29 Jesus told them, “This is what God **w** you to do:
7:17 Anyone who **w** to do the will of God will know
8:50 no wish to glorify myself, God **w** to glorify me.
11:28 told her, “The Teacher is here and **w** to see you.”
Ac 4:19 “Do you think God **w** us to obey you rather than
20:27 for I didn’t shrink from declaring all that God **w**
Ro 2:18 Yes, you know what he **w**; you know right from
9:18 God shows mercy to some just because he **w** to,
12: 2 Then you will know what God **w** you to do,
1Co 7:15 with them, for God **w** his children to live in peace.)

11:16 But if anyone **w** to argue about this, all I can say is
12:18 and he has put each part just where he **w** it.
15:38 gives it a new body—just the kind he **w** it to have.
2Co 7:9 It was the kind of sorrow God **w** his people to
8:12 God **w** you to give what you have, not what you
11:17 Such bragging is not something the Lord **w**,
Gal 5:17 which is just opposite from what the Holy Spirit **w**.
Eph 5:17 but try to understand what the Lord **w** you to do.
Php 3:12 all that Christ Jesus saved me for and **w** me to be.
Col 1:9 understanding of what he **w** to do in your lives,
1Th 4:3 God **w** you to be holy, so you should keep clear of
1Ti 2:4 for he **w** everyone to be saved and to understand
3:1 It is a true saying that if someone **w** to be an elder,
2Ti 2:26 been held captive by him to do whatever he **w**.
3:12 and everyone who **w** to live a godly life in Christ
3:17 fully equipped for every good thing God **w** us to
Heb 5:4 a high priest simply because he **w** such an honor.
10:10 And what God **w** is for us to be made holy by the
11:6 Anyone who **w** to come to him must believe that
Jas 1:5 if you want to know what God **w** you to do—
1:13 no one who **w** to do wrong should ever say,
3:4 a huge ship turn wherever the pilot **w** it to go,
4:15 "If the Lord **w** us to, we will live and do this
1Pe 3:9 That is what God **w** you to do, and he will bless
3:17 if that is what God **w**, than to suffer for doing
Rev 22:17 Let the thirsty ones come—anyone who **w** to.

WAR (169) [WARFARE, WARHORSE, WARHORSES, WARRIOR, WARRIOR'S, WARRIORS, WARRIORS', WARS, WARSHIPS]

Ge 14:1 About this time **w** broke out in the region.
31:26 "Are my daughters prisoners, the plunder of **w**,
Ex 1:10 If we don't and if **w** breaks out, they will join our
17:16 so now the LORD will be at **w** with Amalek
32:17 "It sounds as if there is a **w** in the camp!"
Nu 1:3 twenty years old or older who are able to go to **w**.
1:20[-21] years old or older who were able to go to **w**,
1:45 were twenty years old or older and able to go to **w**.
10:9 your own land and go to **w** against your enemies,
31:3 "Choose some men to fight the LORD's **w** of
Dt 2:9 the descendants of Lot, or start a **w** with them.
2:19 the descendants of Lot, or start a **w** with them.
2:32 Then King Sihon declared **w** on us and mobilized
4:34 miraculous signs, wonders, **w**, awesome power,
20:19 you are besieging a town and the **w** drags on,
21:10 "Suppose you go to **w** against your enemies
23:9 "When you go to **w** against your enemies,
Jos 11:18 waging **w** for a long time to accomplish this.
11:23 the tribes. So the land finally had rest from **w**.
14:15 of the Anakites.) And the land had rest from **w**.
22:12 and prepared to go to **w** against their brother tribes.
22:33 and spoke no more of **w** against Reuben and Gad.
24:9 of Zippor, king of Moab, started a **w** against Israel.
Jdg 3:10 He went to **w** against King Cushan-rishathaim of
5:8 Israel chose new gods, / **w** erupted at the city gates.
10:17 that time the armies of Ammon had gathered for **w**
11:4 the Ammonites began their **w** against Israel.
11:25 disputed land? Did he go to **w**? No, of course not.
1Sa 4:1 At that time Israel was at **w** with the Philistines.
19:8 **W** broke out shortly after that, and David led his
28:1 mustered their armies for another **w** with Israel.
28:15 "The Philistines are at **w** with us, and God has left
2Sa 3:1 That was the beginning of a long **w** between those
3:6 As the **w** went on, Abner became a powerful leader
11:1 the time of year when kings go to **w**, David sent
11:7 were getting along and how the **w** was progressing.
21:15 Once again the Philistines were at **w** with Israel.
1Ki 2:5 He pretended that it was an act of **w**, but it was
2:5 staining his belt and sandals with the blood of **w**.
14:30 There was constant **w** between Rehoboam
15:6 There was **w** between Abijam and Jeroboam
15:7 *of Judah.* There was constant **w** between Abijam
15:16 There was constant **w** between King Asa of Judah
15:32 There was constant **w** between Asa and King
20:18 "whether they have come for peace or for **w**."
22:1 For three years there was no **w** between Aram
22:6 "Should I go to **w** against Ramoth-gilead or not?"
22:15 should we go to **w** against Ramoth-gilead or not?"
2Ki 6:8 When the king of Aram was at **w** with Israel,
6:22 "Do we kill prisoners of **w**? Give them food
8:28 Ahaziah joined King Joram of Israel in his **w**
12:17 About this time King Hazael of Aram went to **w**
13:12 his power and his **w** with King Amaziah of Judah,
14:15 his power and his **w** with King Amaziah of Judah,
16:5 and King Pekah of Israel declared **w** on Ahaz.
24:16 and smiths, all of whom were strong and fit for **w**.
1Ch 5:19 They waged **w** against the Hagrites, the Jeturites,
20:1 the time of year when kings go to **w**,
20:4 **w** broke out with the Philistines at Gezer.
2Ch 12:15 and Jeroboam were continually at **w** with each
13:2 Then **w** broke out between Abijah and Jeroboam.
14:6 No one tried to make **w** against him at this time,
15:19 So there was no more **w** until the thirty-fifth year
16:9 you have been! From now on, you will be at **w**."
17:10 so that none of them declared **w** on Jehoshaphat.
18:5 "Should we go to **w** against Ramoth-gilead
18:14 should we go to **w** against Ramoth-gilead or not?"
20:1 and some of the Meunites declared **w** on
20:9 we are faced with any calamity such as **w**,
26:6 He declared **w** on the Philistines and broke down
27:5 Jotham waged **w** against the Ammonites
35:21 only want to fight the nation with which I am at **w**.
Job 5:20 from the power of the sword in time of **w**.
27:14 their children will die in **w** or starve to death.
38:23 for the time of trouble, for the day of battle and **w**.
39:21 and rejoices in its strength. When it charges to **w**,
Ps 35:1 Declare **w** on those who are attacking me.
55:21 are as smooth as cream, / but in his heart is **w**.
68:30 from us. / Scatter the nations that delight in **w**.
120:7 I am for peace; / but when I speak, they are for **w**!
144:1 who is my rock. / He gives me strength for **w**
Pr 20:18 don't go to **w** without the advice of others.
24:6 So don't go to **w** without wise guidance;
Ecc 3:8 a time to hate. / A time for **w** and a time for peace.
9:18 A wise person can overcome weapons of **w**,
Isa 8:10 Call your councils of **w**, develop your strategies,
9:5 Never again will uniforms be bloodstained by **w**.
21:15 and sharp arrows and the terrors of **w**.
41:5 in fear. Remote lands tremble and mobilize for **w**.
49:24 Who can snatch the plunder of **w** from the hands of
51:19 desolation and destruction, famine and **w**.
60:18 the desolation and destruction of **w** will end.
Jer 4:21 How long must I be surrounded by **w** and death?
5:12 will come upon us! There will be no **w** or famine!
6:14 They give assurances of peace when all is **w**.
8:11 They give assurances of peace when all is **w**.
14:12 In return, I will give them only **w**, famine,
14:13 'All is well—no **w** or famine will come.
14:15 They say that no **w** or famine will come, but they themselves will die by **w** and famine!
14:16 the streets of Jerusalem, victims of famine and **w**.
15:2 to death; those who are destined for **w**, to **w**;
16:4 They will die from **w** and famine, and their bodies
21:7 and everyone else in the city have survived **w**,
21:9 Everyone who stays in Jerusalem will die from **w**,
24:10 I will send **w**, famine, and disease until they have
25:29 I will call for **w** against all the nations of the earth.
27:8 I will send **w**, famine, and disease upon that nation
27:13 Why should you choose **w**, famine, and disease,
28:8 always warning of **w**, famine, and disease.
29:17 "I will send **w**, famine, and disease upon them
29:18 Yes, I will pursue them with **w**, famine,
32:24 Because of **w**, famine, and disease, the city has
32:36 'It will fall to the king of Babylon through **w**,
34:4 the LORD says: 'You will not be killed in **w**
34:17 I will set you free to be destroyed by **w**, famine,
38:2 Everyone who stays in Jerusalem will die from **w**,
42:14 in Egypt where you think you will be free from **w**,
42:16 the **w** and famine you fear will follow close behind
42:17 Yes, you will die from **w**, famine, and disease.
42:22 So you can be sure that you will die from **w**,
44:12 will fall here in Egypt, killed by **w** and famine.
44:13 them in Jerusalem, by **w**, famine, and disease.
44:18 and have suffered the effects of **w** and famine."
44:27 You will suffer **w** and famine until all of you are
46:26 the land will recover from the ravages of **w**.
48:14 used to boast, 'We are heroes, mighty men of **w**.'
51:27 Signal many nations to mobilize for **w** against
Eze 5:17 Disease and **w** will stalk your land, and I will bring
6:3 I am about to bring **w** upon you, and I will destroy
6:11 Now they are going to die from **w** and famine
6:12 **W** will destroy those who are nearby. And anyone
11:8 I will expose you to the **w** you so greatly fear,
12:16 But I will spare a few of them from death by **w**,
14:17 "Or suppose I were to bring **w** against the land,
14:21 **w**, famine, beasts, and plague—destroying all her
30:5 all their other allies, will be destroyed in that **w**.
30:11 They will make **w** against Egypt until slaughtered
38:8 will be lying in peace after her recovery from **w**
Da 7:21 this horn was waging **w** against the holy people
9:26 and **w** and its miseries are decreed from that time
10:1 times of **w** and great hardship—and Daniel
11:2 he will stir up everyone to **w** against the kingdom
Hos 2:18 I will remove all weapons of **w** from the land,
10:14 Now the terrors of **w** will rise among your people.
11:6 **W** will swirl through their cities; their enemies will
Joel 3:9 Say to the nations far and wide: "Get ready for **w**!
Am 3:6 When the **w** trumpet blares, shouldn't the people
4:10 I killed your young men in **w** and slaughtered all
Mic 3:5 but you declare **w** on anyone who refuses to pay
Mt 12:25 "Any kingdom at **w** with itself is doomed.
24:7 and kingdoms will proclaim **w** against each other,
Mk 3:24 A kingdom at **w** with itself will collapse.
13:8 and kingdoms will proclaim **w** against each other,
Lk 11:17 he said, "Any kingdom at **w** with itself is doomed.
14:31 "Or what king would ever dream of going to **w**
21:10 and kingdoms will proclaim **w** against each other.
Ro 7:23 law at work within me that is at **w** with my mind.
1Co 4:9 like prisoners of **w** at the end of a victor's parade,
2Co 10:3 but we don't wage **w** with human plans
Jas 4:1 Isn't it the whole army of evil desires at **w** within
Rev 6:4 And there was **w** and slaughter everywhere.
11:7 of the bottomless pit will declare **w** against them.
12:7 Then there was **w** in heaven. Michael
12:17 and he declared **w** against the rest of her children—
13:7 And the beast was allowed to wage **w** against
17:14 Together they will wage **w** against the Lamb,
19:11 and True. For he judges fairly and then goes to **w**.

WARDROBE (3)

2Ki 10:22 And Jehu instructed the keeper of the **w**, "Be sure
22:14 grandson of Harhas, the keeper of the Temple **w**.
2Ch 34:22 grandson of Harhas, the keeper of the Temple **w**.

WAREHOUSE (1) [WARES]

Eze 27:25 Your island **w** was filled to the brim!

WARES (7) [WAREHOUSE]

Ne 13:20 and tradesmen with a variety of **w** camped outside
Eze 27:12 trading your **w** in exchange for silver, iron, tin,
27:16 "Aram sent merchants to buy your **w**. They traded
27:17 Judah and Israel traded for your **w**, offering wheat
27:19 cassia, and calamus were bartered for your **w**.
27:22 of spices, jewels, and gold in exchange for your **w**.
27:27 your riches and **w**, your sailors and helmsmen,

WARFARE (2) [WAR]

Jdg 3:2 He did this to teach **w** to generations of Israelites
Jer 25:16 crazed by the **w** I will send against them."

WARHORSE (2) [HORSE, WAR]

Ps 33:17 Don't count on your **w** to give you victory—
Zec 10:3 them strong and glorious, like a proud **w** in battle.

WARHORSES (2) [HORSE, WAR]

Jer 8:16 The snorting of the enemies' **w** can be heard all
Zec 9:10 chariots from Israel and the **w** from Jerusalem,

WARM (19) [LUKEWARM, WARMED, WARMING, WARMLY, WARMTH]

Ex 22:27 Your neighbor will need it to stay **w** during the
1Ki 1:1 many blankets covered him, he could not keep **w**.
1:2 She will lie in your arms and keep you **w**."
2Ki 4:34 And the child's body began to grow **w** again!
Job 31:20 me for providing wool clothing to keep them **w**?
Pr 31:21 her household because all of them have **w** clothes.
Ecc 4:11 from each other. But how can one be **w** alone?
Isa 44:15 he uses part of the wood to make a fire to **w**
44:16 of the tree to roast his meat and to keep himself **w**.
50:11 own light and **w** yourselves by your own fires.
Jer 36:22 of the palace, sitting in front of a fire to keep **w**.
Eze 16:4 rubbed with salt, and dressed in **w** clothing.
Na 3:17 fly away when the sun comes up to **w** the earth,
Hag 1:6 clothing to wear, but not enough to keep you **w**.
Lk 24:32 "Didn't our hearts feel strangely **w** as he talked
Ac 28:2 built a fire on the shore to welcome us and **w** us.
1Co 4:11 and thirsty, without enough clothes to keep us **w**.
2Co 11:27 with cold, without enough clothing to keep me **w**.
Jas 2:16 stay **w** and eat well"—but then you don't give that

WARMED (1) [WARM]

Job 39:14 on top of the earth, letting them be **w** in the dust.

WARMING (3) [WARM]

Mk 14:54 while he sat with the guards, **w** himself by the fire.
14:67 noticed Peter **w** himself at the fire. She looked at
Jn 18:18 And Peter stood there with them, **w** himself.

WARMLY (5) [WARM]

Ge 29:13 he rushed out to meet him and greeted him **w**.
Ex 4:27 of God, where he found Moses and greeted him **w**.
18:7 He bowed to him respectfully and greeted him **w**.
Ru 2:10 Ruth fell at his feet and thanked him **w**. "Why are
2Sa 17:27 he was **w** greeted by Shobi son of Nahash of

WARMTH (2) [WARM]

Ecc 4:11 two under the same blanket can gain **w** from each
Isa 47:14 them at all. Their hearth is not a place to sit for **w**.

WARN (42) [WARNED, WARNING, WARNINGS, WARNS]

Ge 4:15 Then the LORD put a mark on Cain to **w** anyone
Ex 19:12 **W** them, 'Be careful! Do not go up on the
19:21 and **w** the people not to cross the boundaries.
Lev 16:2 "**W** your brother Aaron not to enter the Most Holy
22:9 **W** all the priests to follow these instructions
Nu 16:40 This would **w** the Israelites that no unauthorized
Dt 30:18 then I **w** you now that you will certainly be
1Sa 8:9 but solemnly **w** them about how a king will treat
20:13 may the LORD kill me if I don't **w** you so you
1Ki 2:42 by the LORD and **w** you not to go anywhere else,
2Ki 6:9 the man of God, would **w** the king of Israel,
17:13 his prophets and seers to **w** both Israel and Judah:
2Ch 19:10 you must **w** them not to sin against the LORD,
36:15 repeatedly sent his prophets to **w** them,
Job 19:29 I **w** you, you yourselves are in danger of
Jer 4:16 "**W** the surrounding nations and announce to
6:1 **W** everyone that a powerful army is coming from
18:11 Jeremiah, go and **w** all Judah and Jerusalem.
26:5 for I sent them again and again to **w** you, but you
Eze 3:18 If I **w** the wicked, saying, 'You are under the
3:19 If you **w** them and they keep on sinning and refuse
3:20 If you did not **w** them of the consequences,
3:21 But if you **w** them and they repent, they will live,
33:3 he blows the alarm to **w** the people.
33:6 and doesn't sound the alarm to **w** the people,
33:7 Therefore, listen to what I say and **w** them for me.
33:8 and you fail to **w** them about changing their ways,
33:9 But if you **w** them to repent and they don't repent,
Hos 12:10 I sent my prophets to **w** you with many visions
Am 3:7 of all, I **w** you through my servants the prophets.
Mt 5:20 "But I **w** you—unless you obey God better than
Lk 16:28 and I want him to **w** them about this place of
Ac 4:17 We'll **w** them not to speak to anyone in Jesus'
1Co 4:14 shame you, but to **w** you as my beloved children.
10:11 They were written down to **w** us, who live at the
2Co 13:2 Now I again **w** them and all others, just as I did
Col 1:28 We **w** them and teach them with all the wisdom
1Th 5:12 among you and **w** you against all that is wrong.
5:14 and sisters, we urge you to **w** those who are lazy.
Heb 3:13 You must **w** each other every day, as long as it is

10:25 some people do, but encourage and w each other,
1Pe 2:11 So I w you to keep away from evil desires

WARNED (57) [WARN]

Ge 19:17 "Run for your lives!" the angels w. "Do not stop
24:6 "No!" Abraham w. "Be careful never to take my
28:6 and that he had w Jacob not to marry a Canaanite
43:3 "The man wasn't joking when he w that we
Ex 4:23 worship me. But since you have refused, be w!
Dt 2:9 the LORD w us, 'Do not bother the Moabites,
Jdg 9:25 But someone w Abimelech about their plot.
Ru 2:9 I have w the young men not to bother you.
1Sa 3:13 I have w him continually that judgment is coming
13:4 and he w the people that the Philistines now hated
19:2 "Tomorrow morning," he w him, "you must find
19:11 But Michal, David's wife, w him, "If you don't
2Sa 2:21 "Go fight someone else!" Abner w. "Take on one
1Ki 11:10 He had w Solomon specifically about worshiping
2Ki 10:24 building with eighty of his men and had w them,
17:23 just as all his prophets had w would happen.
1Ch 16:21 anyone oppress them. / He w kings on their behalf:
Ezr 9:11 Your servants the prophets w us that the land we
Ne 9:29 You w them to return to your law, but they became
9:30 through the prophets, w them about their sins.
Ps 2:10 act wisely! / Be w, you rulers of the earth!
75:4 "I w the proud, 'Stop your boasting!' / I told the
105:14 anyone oppress them. / He w kings on their behalf:
Ecc 12:12 But, my child, be w: There is no end of opinions
Isa 48:3 and again I w you about what was going to happen
Jer 8:5 refusing to turn back, even though I have w them?
11:7 For I solemnly w your ancestors when I brought
22:21 I w you, but you replied, 'Don't bother me.'
23:38 the LORD," even though I w you not to use it,
La 2:17 But it is the LORD who did it just as he w.
Eze 20:18 "Then I w their children and told them not to
Da 9:12 You have done exactly what you w you would do
Mt 2:12 because God had w them in a dream not to return
2:22 in another dream, he was w to go to Galilee.
3:7 "Who w you to flee God's coming judgment?
9:30 Jesus sternly w them, "Don't tell anyone about
12:16 but he w them not to say who he was.
16:6 "Watch out!" Jesus w them. "Beware of the yeast
16:20 Then he sternly w them not to tell anyone that he
24:25 See, I have w you.
Mk 3:12 But Jesus strictly w them not to say who he was.
8:15 As they were crossing the lake, Jesus w them,
8:30 But Jesus w them not to tell anyone about him.
13:23 Watch out! I have w you!
Lk 3:7 Who w you to flee God's coming judgment?
9:21 Jesus w them not to tell anyone about this.
12:1 Jesus turned first to his disciples and w them,
16:29 'Moses and the prophets have w them.
Jn 16:4 when they happen, you will remember I w you.
Ac 23:22 the commander w the young man as he sent him
Ro 9:33 God w them of this in the Scriptures when he said,
2Co 13:2 I have already w those who had been sinning when
1Th 3:4 we w you that troubles would soon come—
4:6 all such sins, as we have solemnly w you before.
2Th 3:15 as you would to a Christian who needs to be w.
Heb 11:7 who w him about something that had never
2Pe 2:5 Noah w the world of God's righteous judgment.

WARNING (43) [WARN]

Ge 2:16 But the LORD God gave him this w: "You may
20:18 w to Abimelech for having taken Abraham's wife.
Ex 8:29 But I am w you, don't change your mind again
Nu 16:38 then serve as a w to the people of Israel."
17:10 before the Ark of the Covenant as a w to rebels.
26:10 This served as a w to the entire nation of Israel.
Dt 28:46 and w among you and your descendants forever.
1Sa 8:10 So Samuel passed on the LORD's w to the
8:19 But the people refused to listen to Samuel's w.
2Ki 6:10 of God, w the people there to be on their guard.
2Ch 25:16 I have you killed!" So the prophet left with this w:
Job 9:5 "Without w, he moves the mountains,
33:16 whispers in their ear and terrifies them with his w.
Ps 19:11 They are a w to those who hear them; / there is
Isa 10:30 Shout out a w to Laishah, for the mighty army
56:10 They are like silent watchdogs that give no w when
Jer 6:8 This is your last w, Jerusalem! If you do not listen,
6:10 To whom can I give w? Who will listen when I
17:21 is what the LORD says: Listen to my w and live!
22:5 But if you refuse to pay attention to this w, I swear
23:16 This is my w to my people," says the LORD
28:8 always w of war, famine, and disease.
42:19 Don't forget this w I have given you today.
Eze 3:18 but you fail to deliver the w, they will die in their
3:20 If good people turn bad and don't listen to my w,
4:3 This will be a w to the people of Israel.
5:15 You will be a w to all the nations around you.
23:48 and my judgment will be a w to others not to
33:5 They heard the w but wouldn't listen,
33:5 If they had listened to the w, they could have saved
Da 8:25 them off guard. Without w he will destroy them.
11:24 Without w he will enter the richest areas of the
Mal 2:2 because you have not taken my w seriously.
2:4 at last you will know it was I who sent you this w
Mk 13:36 him find you sleeping when he arrives without w.
Lk 17:3 I am w you! If another believer sins, rebuke him;
Ro 12:3 As God's messenger, I give each of you this w:
1Co 10:6 These events happened as a w to us, so that we
Tit 3:10 divisions among you, give a first and second w.
Heb 3:15 But never forget the w: / "Today you must listen
8:5 to build the Tabernacle, God gave him this w:
2Pe 3:17 I am w you ahead of time, dear friends, so that you
Jude 1:7 and are a w of the eternal fire that will punish all

WARNINGS (10) [WARN]

Dt 29:19 Let none of those who hear the w of this curse
2Ki 17:12 despite the LORD's specific and repeated w.
17:15 with their ancestors, and they despised all his w.
2Ch 33:10 and his people, but they ignored all his w.
Ne 9:34 or listen to your commands and solemn w.
Ps 81:8 to me, O my people, while I give you stern w.
Jer 7:27 Shout out your w, but do not expect them to
36:31 for they would not listen to my w.' "
Zep 3:7 Surely they will listen to my w, so I won't need to
Lk 3:18 John used many such w as he announced the Good

WARNS (1) [WARN]

1Co 10:28 But suppose someone w you that this meat has

WARPED (1)

Pr 12:8 person with good sense, but a w mind is despised.

WARRANT (1)

Est 7:4 for that would have been a matter too trivial to w

WARRIOR (31) [WAR]

Ge 10:8 descendants was Nimrod, who became a heroic w.
Ex 15:3 The LORD is a w; / yes, the LORD is his name!
Lev 26:36 You will run as though chased by a w with a
Jos 11:8 of Mizpah, until not one enemy w was left alive.
17:1 to the family of Makir because he was a great w.
Jdg 11:1 Now Jephthah from Gilead was a great w. He was
1Sa 18:17 But first you must prove yourself to be a real w by
2Sa 23:20 son of Jehoiada, a valiant w from Kabzeel.
23:21 he killed a great Egyptian w who was armed with a
1Ki 20:11 "A w still dressing for battle should not boast like a w who has already won."
2Ki 5:1 But though Naaman was a mighty w, he suffered
1Ch 1:10 who was known across the earth as a heroic w.
5:24 Each of these men had a great reputation as a w
11:22 son of Jehoiada, a valiant w from Kabzeel.
11:23 he killed an Egyptian w who was seven and a half
12:4 a famous w and leader among the Thirty;
12:28 This also included Zadok, a young w,
28:3 for you are a w and have shed much blood.'
2Ch 28:7 Then Zicri, a w from Ephraim, killed Maaseiah,
Job 16:14 and again he smashed me, charging at me like a w.
Ps 33:16 a king, / nor is great strength enough to save a w.
45:3 Put on your sword, O mighty w! / You are
76:5 sleep of death. / No w could lift a hand against us.
89:19 your prophet and said, / "I have given help to a w.
Ecc 9:11 and the strongest w doesn't always win the battle.
Isa 42:13 he will come out like a w, full of fury.
49:24 snatch the plunder of war from the hands of a w?
Jer 20:11 But the LORD stands beside me like a great w.
La 2:12 Their lives ebb away like the life of a w wounded
Zec 9:13 Jerusalem is my sword, and like a w, I will

WARRIOR'S (1) [WAR]

Ps 127:4 a young man / are like sharp arrows in a w hands.

WARRIORS (152) [WAR]

Ex 17:8 the w of Amalek came to fight against them.
Jos 1:14 side of the Jordan River, but your w, fully armed,
4:12 The armed w from the tribes of Reuben, Gad,
4:13 These w—about forty thousand strong—
6:2 given you Jericho, its king, and all its mighty w.
7:4 So approximately three thousand w were sent,
10:2 than Ai. And the Gibeonite men were mighty w.
11:4 All these kings responded by mobilizing their w
11:7 and his w traveled to the water near Merom
Jdg 1:4 and they killed ten thousand enemy w at the town
3:29 ten thousand of their strongest and bravest w.
4:6 Assemble ten thousand w from the tribes of
4:7 along with his chariots and w, to the Kishon River.
4:10 and ten thousand w marched up with him.
4:13 nine hundred of his iron chariots and all of his w,
4:14 So Barak led his ten thousand w down the slopes
4:15 and all his charioteers and w into a panic.
4:16 to Harosheth-haggoyim, killing all of Sisera's w.
5:8 could be seen / among forty thousand w in Israel!
5:13 of the LORD marched down against mighty w.
5:23 to help the LORD against the mighty w.'
6:35 Zebulun, and Naphtali, summoning their w,
7:2 said to Gideon, "You have too many w with you.
7:5 When Gideon took his w down to the water,
7:8 and rams' horns of the other w and sent them
7:22 the LORD caused the w in the camp to fight
7:23 Then Gideon sent for the w of Naphtali, Asher,
8:5 the town, "Will you please give my w some food?
8:6 Catch them first, and then we will feed your w."
8:10 were in Karkor with a remnant of 15,000 w—
8:12 Gideon chased them down and captured all their w.
8:15 and then we will feed your exhausted w.' "
9:40 Many of Shechem's w were killed, and the ground
18:2 So the men of Dan chose five w from among their
18:2 When these w arrived in the hill country of
18:11 So six hundred w from the tribe of Dan set out
18:16 As the six hundred w from the tribe of Dan stood
20:2 tribes of Israel—400,000 w armed with swords—
20:10 tribe will be chosen to supply the w with food,
20:15 Twenty-six thousand of their w armed with swords
20:15 to join the seven hundred w who lived there.
20:16 Seven hundred of Benjamin's w were left-handed,
20:17 Israel had 400,000 w armed with swords, not counting Benjamin's w.
20:21 But Benjamin's w, who were defending the town,
20:24 So they went out to fight against the w of
20:31 When the w of Benjamin came out to attack,
20:32 Then the w of Benjamin shouted,
20:33 When the main group of Israelite w reached
20:35 day the Israelites killed 25,100 of Benjamin's w,
20:36 The Israelites had retreated from Benjamin's w in
20:39 for the Israelites to turn and attack Benjamin's w.
20:39 By that time Benjamin's w had killed about thirty
20:40 But when the w of Benjamin looked behind them
20:41 At this point Benjamin's w realized disaster was
20:44 Eighteen thousand of Benjamin's greatest w died
20:46 lost twenty-five thousand brave w that day,
21:10 So they sent twelve thousand w to Jabesh-gilead
1Sa 13:5 and as many w as the grains of sand along the
14:6 He can win a battle whether he has many w or only
26:5 sleeping inside a ring formed by the slumbering w.
26:7 Abner and the w were lying asleep around him.
31:12 their w traveled all night to Beth-shan and took the
2Sa 2:14 "Let's have a few of our w put on an exhibition of
16:6 and all the mighty w who surrounded them.
17:8 know your father and his men; they are mighty w.
17:10 man your father is and how courageous his w are.
21:22 of Gath, but they were killed by David and his w.
23:8 the three greatest w among David's men.
23:8 to kill eight hundred enemy w in a single battle.
23:18 to kill three hundred enemy w in a single battle.
23:20 which included killing two of Moab's mightiest w.
2Ki 3:26 he led seven hundred of his w in a desperate
1Ch 5:18 There were 44,760 skilled w in the armies of
7:7 and Iri. These five w were the leaders of clans.
7:40 They were all skilled w and prominent leaders.
8:40 The sons of Ulam were all skilled w and expert
10:12 their w went out and brought the bodies of Saul
11:11 the three greatest w among David's men.
11:11 to kill three hundred enemy w in a single battle.
11:20 to kill three hundred enemy w in a single battle.
11:22 which included killing two of Moab's mightiest w.
12:1 They were among the w who fought beside David
12:3 These were the other w: / Jeziel and Pelet, sons of
12:8 and experienced w from the tribe of Gad also
12:14 These w from Gad were army commanders.
12:21 and able w who became commanders in his army.
12:23 These are the numbers of armed w who joined
12:24 there were 6,800 w armed with shields and spears.
12:25 From the tribe of Simeon, there were 7,100 w.
12:29 of Benjamin, Saul's relatives, there were 3,000 w.
12:30 From the tribe of Ephraim, there were 20,800 w,
12:33 the tribe of Zebulun, there were 50,000 skilled w.
12:34 and 37,000 w armed with shields and spears.
12:35 there were 28,600 w, all prepared for battle.
12:36 there were 40,000 trained w, all prepared for battle.
19:8 about this, he sent Joab and all his w to fight them.
20:8 of Gath, but they were killed by David and his w.
28:1 mighty men, and all the other w in the kingdom.
2Ch 13:3 led by King Abijah, fielded 400,000 seasoned w,
14:8 King Asa had an army of 300,000 w from the tribe
14:8 He also had an army of 280,000 w from the tribe
26:11 Uzziah had an army of well-trained w, ready to
26:12 commanded these regiments of seasoned w.
28:14 So the w released the prisoners and handed over
Ne 3:16 far as the water reservoir and the House of the W.
Ps 52:7 "Look what happens to mighty w / who do not
60:7 Manasseh is mine. / Ephraim will produce my w,
78:9 The w of Ephraim, though fully armed,
108:8 Manasseh is mine. / Ephraim will produce my w,
SS 3:8 They are all skilled swordsmen and experienced w.
Isa 9:3 They will shout with joy like w dividing the
10:18 The LORD will completely destroy Assyria's w,
15:4 The bravest w of Moab will cry out in utter terror.
21:7 and w mounted on donkeys and camels."
21:9 at last—look! Here come the chariots and w!"
28:6 He will give great courage to their w who stand at
49:25 LORD says, "The captives of w will be released,
62:8 Never again will foreign w come and take away
Jer 5:16 Their weapons are deadly; their w are mighty.
18:22 Let screaming be heard from their homes as w
41:16 w, women, children, and palace officials.
46:6 swiftest cannot flee; the mightiest w cannot escape.
46:9 you horses and chariots and mighty w of Egypt!
46:12 Your mightiest w will stumble across each other
46:15 Why have your w fled in terror? They cannot stand
48:41 Even the mightiest w will be as frightened as a
49:22 Even the mightiest w will be as frightened as a
49:26 Her w will all be killed," says the LORD
49:28 against Kedar! Blot out the w from the East!
50:21 "Go up, my w, against the land of Merathaim
50:30 Her w will all be killed," says the LORD.
50:36 When it strikes her mightiest w, panic will seize
51:30 Her mightiest w no longer fight. They stay in their
51:57 wise men, rulers, captains, and w," says the King,
La 1:15 a great army has come to crush my young w.
Eze 17:21 And all the best w of Israel will be killed in battle,
27:27 your ship builders, merchants, and w.
32:12 I will destroy you with the swords of mighty w—
39:20 feast on horses, riders, and valiant w,
Hos 5:8 Lead on into battle, O w of Benjamin!
Joel 2:7 The attackers march like w and scale city walls
3:9 "Get ready for war! Call out your best w!
3:10 into spears. Train even your weaklings to be w.
3:11 the valley." And now, O LORD, call out your w!
Am 2:2 of battle, as the w shout and the trumpets blare.
2:14 Even the mightiest w will be unable to save
2:15 Even w on horses won't be able to outrun the
Ob 1:9 The mightiest w of Teman will be terrified,
Zec 10:5 They will be like mighty w in battle,
10:7 The people of Israel will become like mighty w,
Rev 19:18 and eat the flesh of kings, captains, and strong w;

WARRIORS' (1) [WAR]
Eze 29:18 so hard against Tyre that the w heads were rubbed

WARS (19) [WAR]
Nu 21:14 For this reason *The Book of the W of the*
Jdg 3: 1 who had not participated in the w of Canaan.
2Sa 8:10 and there had been many w between them.
1Ki 5: 3 because of the many w he waged with surrounding
14:19 of Jeroboam's reign, all his w and how he ruled,
22:45 and the w he waged are recorded in *The Book of*
2Ki 14:28 his deeds, including the extent of his power, his w,
1Ch 18:10 and there had been many w between them.
2Ch 26: 7 God helped him not only with his w against the
26: 7 the Arabs of Gur and in his w with the Meunites.
27: 7 including his w and other activities,
Ps 46: 9 and causes w to end throughout the earth.
Isa 2: 4 All w will stop, and military training will come to
10:13 my own power and wisdom I have won these w.
Jer 25:27 no more, for I am sending terrible w against you.'
Mic 4: 3 All w will stop, and military training will come to
Mt 24: 6 And w will break out near and far, but don't panic.
Mk 13: 7 And w will break out near and far, but don't panic.
Lk 21: 9 And when you hear of w and insurrections,

WARSHIPS (1) [SHIP, WAR]
Da 11:30 For w from western coastlands will scare him off,

WARY (1) [BEWARE]
Mt 10:16 Be as w as snakes and harmless as doves.

WAS (4748) [BE] See Index of Articles, Etc.

WASH (69) [HAND-WASHING, WASHBASIN, WASHED, WASHES, WASHING, WHITEWASH, WHITEWASHED, WHITEWASHERS]
Ge 18: 4 while my servants get some water to w your feet.
19: 2 he said, "come to my home to w your feet,
24:32 and provided water for the camel drivers to w their
35: 2 "Destroy your idols, w yourselves, and put on
43:24 led into the palace and given water to w their feet
Ex 19:10 and tomorrow, and have them w their clothing.
19:14 them for worship and had them w their clothing.
29: 4 entrance of the Tabernacle, and w them with water.
29:17 the ram and w off the internal organs and the legs.
30:19 Aaron and his sons will w their hands and feet
30:20 They must always w before ministering in these
40:12 entrance of the Tabernacle, and w them with water.
40:30 so the priests could use it to w themselves.
40:32 they were to stop and w, just as the LORD had
Lev 11:25 you must immediately w your clothes, and you will
11:28 its carcass, you must immediately w your clothes,
11:40 or carry away its carcass, you must w your clothes.
14: 9 and w their clothes and bathe themselves in water.
14:47 or eat in the house must w their clothing.
15: 5 you will be required to w your clothes and bathe in
15: 6 you will be required to w your clothes and bathe in
15:10 you will be required to w your clothes and bathe in
15:11 then you will be required to w your clothes
15:13 he must w his clothes and bathe in fresh
15:16 an emission of semen, he must w his entire body,
15:21 you must w your clothes and bathe in water,
15:27 You will be required to w your clothes and bathe
16: 4 Then he must w his entire body and put on his
16:26 the wilderness as a scapegoat must w his clothes
16:28 The man who does the burning must w his clothes
17:15 you must w your clothes and bathe yourselves in
17:16 But if you do not w your clothes and bathe,
Nu 5:23 of leather and w them off into the bitter water.
8: 7 them shave their entire body and w their clothing.
19: 7 "Then the priest must w his clothes and bathe
19: 8 The man who burns the animal must also w his
19:10 up the ashes of the heifer must also w his clothes,
19:19 day the people being cleansed must w their clothes
19:21 of purification must afterward w their clothes,
31:24 On the seventh day you must w your clothes
Dt 21: 6 "The leaders of the town nearest the body must w
2Ki 5:10 and w yourself seven times in the Jordan River.
5:12 Why shouldn't I w in them and be healed?"
5:13 when he says simply to go and w and be cured!"
2Ch 4: 6 He also made ten basins for water to w the
Job 9:30 Even if I were to w myself with soap and cleanse
14:19 wears away the stones and floods w away the soil,
Ps 26: 6 I w my hands to declare my innocence. / I come to
51: 2 W me clean from my guilt. / Purify me from my
51: 7 be clean; / w me, and I will be whiter than snow.
58:10 They will w their feet in the blood of the wicked.
68:23 You, my people, will w your feet in their blood,
Isa 1:16 W yourselves and be clean! Let me no longer see
4: 4 The Lord will w the moral filth from the women of
Jer 13: 1 and put it around your waist, but do not w it."
Mt 6:17 when you fast, comb your hair and w your face.
23:26 First w the inside of the cup, and then the outside
Lk 7:44 you didn't offer me water to w the dust from my
Jn 9: 7 and w in the pool of Siloam" (Siloam means
9:11 'Go to the pool of Siloam and w off the mud.'
13: 5 Then he began to w the disciples' feet and to wipe
13: 6 to him, "Lord, why are you going to w my feet?"
13: 8 Peter protested, "you will never w my feet!"
13: 8 Jesus replied, "But if I don't w you, you won't
13: 9 "Then w my hands and head as well, Lord,
13:10 person who has bathed all over does not need to w,
13:14 washed your feet, you ought to w each other's feet.
Jas 4: 8 W your hands, you sinners; purify your hearts,
Rev 22:14 Blessed are those who w their robes so they can

WASHBASIN (10) [BASIN, WASH]
Ex 30:18 "Make a large bronze w with a bronze pedestal.
30:28 all its utensils, and the large w with its pedestal.
31: 9 offering with all its utensils; the w and its pedestal;
35:16 and utensils; the large w with its pedestal;
38: 8 The bronze w and its bronze pedestal were cast
39:39 its poles and utensils; the large w and its pedestal;
40: 7 Set the large w between the Tabernacle
40:11 Next anoint the large w and its pedestal to make
40:30 Next he placed the large w between the Tabernacle
Lev 8:11 and all its utensils and the w and its pedestal,

WASHED (42) [WASH]
Ge 43:31 Then he w his face and came out, keeping himself
Ex 14:30 see the bodies of the Egyptians w up on the shore.
40:31 Moses and Aaron and Aaron's sons w their hands
Lev 1: 9 internal organs and legs must first be w with water.
1:13 internal organs and legs must first be w with water.
6:27 it must be w off in a sacred place.
8: 6 and his sons and w them with water.
9:14 Then he w the internal organs and the legs and also
13:54 priest will order the contaminated object to be w
13:55 area has not changed appearance after being w,
13:56 sees that the affected area has faded after being w,
13:58 But if the spot disappears after the object is w, it must be w again;
15:17 that comes in contact with the semen must be w,
Nu 8:21 Levites purified themselves and w their clothes,
Jdg 19:21 After they w their feet, they had supper together.
2Sa 12:20 w himself, put on lotions, and changed his clothes.
19:24 He had not w his feet or clothes nor trimmed his
1Ki 22:38 Then his chariot was w beside the pool of Samaria,
Job 22:16 and the foundations of their lives were w away
SS 4: 2 teeth are as white as sheep, newly shorn and w.
5: 3 I have w my feet. Should I get them soiled?'
6: 6 Your teeth are white like freshly w ewes,
Jer 2:22 You are stained with guilt that cannot be w away.
Eze 16: 4 and you were never w, rubbed with salt,
16: 9 "Then I bathed you and w off your blood, and I
36:25 Your filth will be w away, and you will no longer
40:38 for sacrifices was w before being taken to the altar.
Mt 27:24 a bowl of water and w his hands before the crowd,
Lk 7:44 but she has w them with her tears and wiped them
Jn 9: 7 So the man went and w, and came back seeing!
9:11 off the mud.' I went and w, and now I can see!"
9:15 my eyes, and when it was w away, I could see!"
13:14 since I, the Lord and Teacher, have w your feet,
Ac 16:33 That same hour the jailer w their wounds, and he
22:16 and be baptized, and have your sins w away,
1Co 6:11 but now your sins have been w away, and you have
Eph 5:26 her holy and clean, w by baptism and God's word.
Tit 3: 5 He w away our sins and gave us a new life through
Heb 10:22 and our bodies have been w with pure water.
2Pe 2:22 to its vomit," and "A w pig returns to the mud."
Rev 7:14 They w their robes in the blood of the Lamb

WASHES (1) [WASH]
Ge 49:11 He w his clothes in wine / because his harvest is

WASHING (12) [WASH]
Lev 8:21 After w the internal organs and the legs with water,
13: 6 So after w the clothes, the person will be
13:34 After w clothes, that person will be clean.
14: 8 the cleansing ceremony by w their clothes,
2Ch 4: 6 the Sea itself, and not the basins, for their own w.
Mt 15: 2 "They ignore our tradition of ceremonial hand w
Mk 7: 2 the usual Jewish ritual of hand w before eating.
7: 4 such as their ceremony of w cups, pitchers,
Lk 5: 2 the fishermen had left them and were w their nets.
11:38 the ceremonial w required by Jewish custom.
Jn 13:12 After w their feet, he put on his robe again and sat
Heb 9:10 deals only with food and drink and ritual w—

WASHPOT [KJV] See LOWLY (SERVANT)

WASN'T (30) [BE, NOT] See Index of Articles, Etc.

WASTE (18) [WASTED, WASTELAND, WASTELANDS, WASTES, WASTING]
Job 13:28 I w away like rotting wood, like a moth-eaten coat.
33:21 They w away to skin and bones.
34: 9 has even said, 'Why w time trying to please God?'
Ps 2: 1 Why do the people w their time with futile plans?
Pr 23: 4 yourself trying to get rich. Why w your time?
23: 9 Don't w your breath on fools, for they will despise
Isa 10:18 and they will w away like sick people in a plague.
Jer 2:25 But you say, 'Don't w your breath. I have fallen in
4: 3 Do not w your good seed among thorns.
18:12 But they replied, "Don't w your breath. We will
Eze 4:17 and they will w away under their punishment.
24:23 or weep, but you will w away because of your sins.
Mt 26: 8 they saw this. "What a w of money," they said.
Ac 4:25 Why did the people w their time with futile plans?
1Ti 1: 4 Don't let people w time in endless speculation over
4: 7 Do not w time arguing over godless ideas and old
Tit 3: 9 These kinds of things are useless and a w of time.
Rev 6: 6 a day's pay. And don't w the olive oil and wine."

WASTED (6) [WASTE]
1Sa 25:39 Then David w no time in sending messengers to
Pr 16:22 those who possess it, but discipline is w on fools.
29: 3 if he hangs around with prostitutes, his wealth is w.
Mk 14: 4 "Why was this expensive perfume w?"
Lk 15:13 and there he w all his money on wild living.
Jn 6:12 Jesus told his disciples, "so that nothing is w."

WASTELAND (16) [LAND, WASTE]
Nu 21:20 in Moab where Pisgah Peak overlooks the w.
23:28 to the top of Mount Peor, overlooking the w.
Dt 32:10 them in a desert land, / in an empty, howling w.
Job 12:24 and he leaves them wandering in a w without a
39: 6 have placed it in the wilderness; its home is the w.
Isa 6:11 are deserted and the whole country is an utter w.
24: 1 is about to destroy the earth and make it a vast w.
Jer 12:11 They have made it an empty w; I hear its mournful
25:11 This entire land will become a desolate w. Israel
25:12 the country of the Babylonians an everlasting w.
25:37 Peaceful meadows will be turned into a w by the
50:13 Babylon will become a deserted w.
Eze 25:13 I will make a w of everything from Teman to
29: 9 The land of Egypt will become a desolate w,
Joel 3:19 Egypt will become a w and Edom a wilderness,
Zep 2:13 Nineveh, a desolate w, parched like a desert.

WASTELANDS (4) [LAND, WASTE]
Job 30: 3 with hunger and flee to the deserts and the w,
Ps 107:34 He turns the fruitful land into salty w, / because of
107:40 causing them to wander in trackless w.
Joel 2:20 I will drive them back into the parched w,

WASTES (1) [WASTE]
Eze 36: 4 and to ruined w and long-deserted cities that have

WASTING (9) [WASTE]
Lev 26:16 with w diseases, and with burning fevers,
Dt 28:22 The LORD will strike you with w disease, fever,
32:24 I will send against them w famine, / burning fever,
Job 36:14 They die young after w their lives in immoral
Ps 31:10 drained my strength; / I am w away from within.
Jer 2: 8 in the name of Baal, w their time on nonsense.
La 4: 9 those who die of hunger, w away for want of food.
Eze 33:10 'Our sins are heavy upon us; we are w away!
2Th 3:11 and w time meddling in other people's business.

WATCH (106) [WATCHDOGS, WATCHED, WATCHER, WATCHES, WATCHING, WATCHMAN, WATCHMAN'S, WATCHMEN, WATCHTOWER, WATCHTOWERS]
Ge 4: 7 But if you refuse to respond correctly, then w out!
21:16 "I don't want to w the boy die," she said, as she
31:49 "May the LORD keep w between us to make
Ex 10: 4 If you refuse, w out! For tomorrow I will cover the
14:13 stand where you are and w the LORD rescue you.
19:11 come down upon Mount Sinai as all the people w.
33: 8 They would all w Moses until he disappeared
Nu 20: 8 As the people w, command the rock over there to
23: 9 them from the cliff tops; / I w them from the hills.
Dt 4: 9 "But w out! Be very careful never to forget what
24: 8 "W all contagious skin diseases carefully
28:32 You will w as your sons and daughters are taken
Jdg 18:25 The men of Dan said, "W what you say! Some of
1Sa 2:32 You will w with envy as I pour out prosperity on
19:11 Then Saul sent troops to w David's house.
26: 4 so he sent out spies to w his movements.
2Sa 13: 8 lying down so he could w her mix some dough.
1Ki 8:29 May you w over this Temple both day and night,
9: 3 I will always w over it and care for it.
2Ki 25: 7 The king of Babylon made Zedekiah w as all his
2Ch 6:20 May you w over this Temple both day and night,
20:17 then stand still and w the LORD's victory.
28:11 W out, because now the LORD's fierce anger has
Ne 7: 3 to act as guards, everyone on a regular w.
Job 10:14 was to w me, and if I sinned, you would not
13:27 You put my feet in stocks. You w all my paths.
17: 2 by mockers. I w how bitterly they taunt me.
21:32 to the grave, an honor guard keeps w at their tomb.
36:18 But w out, or you may be seduced with wealth.
39:29 it hunts its prey, keeping w with piercing eyes.
Ps 32: 8 for your life. / I will advise you and w over you.
34:13 Then w your tongue! / Keep your lips from telling
34:15 The eyes of the LORD w over those who do
39: 1 I said to myself, "I will w what I do / and not sin
59: T regarding the time Saul sent soldiers to w David's
61: 7 your unfailing love and faithfulness to w over him.
80:14 and see our plight. / W over and care for this vine
121: 8 The LORD keeps w over you as you come
Pr 2:11 Wise planning will w over you. Understanding will
24:12 He keeps w over your soul, and he knows you
Ecc 5:11 except perhaps to w it run through your fingers!
Isa 1: 7 As you w, foreigners plunder your fields
18: 4 "I will w quietly from my dwelling place—
22: 4 Let me cry for my people as I w them being
27: 3 will w over it and tend its fruitful vines.
27: 3 day and night I will w to keep enemies away.
34: 5 sword has finished its work in the heavens, then w.
41: 5 The lands beyond the sea w in fear. Remote lands
50:11 But w out, you who live in your own light
Jer 7:18 W how the children gather wood and the fathers
19:10 "As these men w, Jeremiah, smash the jar you

20: 4 and you will **w** as they are slaughtered by the
31:10 and **w** over them as a shepherd does his flock.
39: 6 He made Zedekiah **w** as they killed his sons
44:27 For I will **w** over you to bring you disaster and not
48:19 of Aroer stand anxiously beside the road to **w**.
51:24 "As you **w**, I will repay Babylon and the people of
51:50 Do not stand and **w**—flee while you can!
52:10 the king of Babylon made Zedekiah **w** as all his
Eze 5: 8 I will punish you publicly while all the nations **w**.
12: 4 baggage outside during the day so they can **w** you.
12: 6 As they **w**, lift your pack to your shoulders
20:41 display my holiness in you as all the nations **w**.
40: 4 He said to me, "Son of man, **w** and listen.
43:11 all these specifications and directions as they **w**
Da 6: 2 the princes and to **w** out for the king's interests.
7:11 I continued to **w** because I could hear the little
10: 8 So I was left there all alone to **w** this amazing
Joel 1:16 We **w** as our food disappears before our very eyes.
3: 4 If you are, then **w** out! I will strike swiftly and pay
Mic 5: 5 we will appoint seven rulers to **w** over us,
Na 2: 1 and keep a sharp **w** for the enemy attack to begin!
2: 3 **W** as their glittering chariots move into position,
2: 7 like doves; **w** them beat their breasts in sorrow.
Hab 1: 5 be amazed! **W** and be astounded at what I will do!
Zec 11: 2 as you **w** the thickest forests being felled.
12: 4 I will **w** over the people of Judah, but I will blind
14: 1 **W**, for the day of the LORD is coming when your
Mt 16: 6 "**W** out!" Jesus warned them. "Beware of the
26:38 to the point of death. Stay here and **w** with me."
26:40 you stay awake and **w** with me even one hour?
Mk 1:33 all over Capernaum gathered outside the door to **w**.
13: 9 But when these things begin to happen, **w** out!
13:23 **W** out! I have warned you!
13:33 when they will happen, stay alert and keep **w**.
13:34 and he told the gatekeeper to **w** for his return.
13:37 I say to you I say to everyone: **W** for his return!"
14:34 to the point of death. Stay here and **w** with me."
14:37 you stay awake and **w** with me even one hour?
Lk 19: 4 tree beside the road, so he could **w** from there.
21:34 "**W** out! Don't let me find you living in careless
21:36 Keep a constant **w**. And pray that, if possible,
Ac 20:31 **W** out! Remember the three years I was with you
20:31 my constant **w** and care over you night and day,
Ro 16:17 **W** out for people who cause divisions and upset
Gal 5:15 always biting and devouring one another, **w** out!
Php 3: 2 **W** out for those dogs, those wicked men and their
1Ti 4:16 Keep a close **w** on yourself and on your teaching.
Heb 12:15 **W** out that no bitter root of unbelief rises up
13:17 Their work is to **w** over your souls, and they know
1Pe 3:12 The eyes of the Lord **w** over those who do right,
5: 2 **W** over it willingly, not grudgingly—not for what
5: 8 **W** out for attacks from the Devil, your great
2Pe 3:17 so that you can **w** out and not be carried away by
2Jn 1: 8 **W** out, so that you do not lose the prize for which
Rev 18:18 They will weep as they **w** the smoke ascend,

WATCHDOGS (1) [DOG, WATCH]

Isa 56:10 They are like silent **w** that give no warning when

WATCHED (49) [WATCH]

Ge 24:21 The servant **w** her in silence, wondering whether
Ex 4:30 Moses performed the miraculous signs as they **w**.
7:20 As Pharaoh and all of his officials **w**, Moses raised
9:10 As Pharaoh **w**, Moses tossed the soot into the air,
Lev 26:45 I brought out of Egypt while all the nations **w**.
Nu 20:27 up Mount Hor together as the whole community **w**.
Dt 2: 7 and has **w** your every step through this great
31: 7 and as all Israel **w** he said to him, "Be strong
32:10 He surrounded them and **w** over them;
Jos 8:32 And as the Israelites **w**, Joshua copied the law of
Jdg 5:28 Through the window she **w** for his return, saying,
7:21 and **w** as all the Midianites rushed around in a
13:19 And as Manoah and his wife **w**, the LORD did an
1Sa 1:12 As she was praying to the LORD, Eli **w** her.
6:16 The five Philistine rulers **w** all this and
17:55 As Saul **w** David go out to fight Goliath, he asked
2Ki 2: 7 and **w** from a distance as Elijah and Elisha stopped
1Ch 23:32 the Levites **w** over the Tabernacle and the Temple
29:17 and I have **w** your people offer their gifts willingly
Job 39: 1 give birth? Have you **w** as the wild deer are born?
Ps 135: 9 wonders in Egypt; / Pharaoh and all his people **w**.
139:15 You **w** me as I was being formed in utter seclusion,
Ecc 9:13 me as I have **w** the way our world works.
10: 5 There is another evil I have seen as I have **w** the
Jer 3:24 From childhood we have **w** as everything our
Eze 10: 2 and scatter them over the city." He did this as I **w**.
10:19 And as I **w**, the cherubim flew with their wheels to
37: 8 Then as I **w**, muscles and flesh formed over the
Da 2:34 But as you **w**, a rock was cut from a mountain by
7: 4 As I **w**, its wings were pulled off, and it was left
7: 9 I **w** as thrones were put in place and the Ancient
7:21 As I **w**, this horn was waging war against the holy
Hos 9:13 I have **w** Israel become as beautiful and pleasant as
Hab 3:10 The mountains **w** and trembled. Onward swept the
Mt 17: 2 As the men **w**, Jesus' appearance changed so that
Mk 3: 2 it was the Sabbath, Jesus' enemies **w** him closely.
9: 2 As the men **w**, Jesus' appearance changed,
9:15 The crowd **w** Jesus in awe as he came toward
12:41 and **w** as the crowds dropped in their money.
Lk 4:35 demon threw the man to the floor as the crowd **w**,
5:25 And immediately, as everyone **w**, the man jumped
6: 7 and the Pharisees **w** closely to see whether Jesus
18:24 Jesus **w** him go and then said to his disciples,
21: 1 he **w** the rich people putting their gifts into the
23:35 The crowd **w**, and the leaders laughed and scoffed.
24:43 and he ate it as they **w**.
Rev 6: 1 As I **w**, the Lamb broke the first of the seven seals
6:12 I **w** as the Lamb broke the sixth seal, and there was
11:12 they rose to heaven in a cloud as their enemies **w**.

WATCHER (1) [WATCH]

Job 7:20 What have I done to you, O **w** of all humanity?

WATCHES (18) [WATCH]

Ex 9: 8 have Moses toss it into the sky while Pharaoh **w**.
Nu 19: 5 As Eleazar **w**, the heifer must be burned—its hide,
Dt 11:12 He **w** over it day after day throughout the year!
Job 33:11 my feet in the stocks and **w** every move I make.'
34:21 "For God carefully **w** the way people live; he sees
34:25 He **w** what they do, and in the night he overturns
Ps 1: 6 For the LORD **w** over the path of the godly,
11: 4 He **w** everything closely, / examining everyone on
33:18 But the LORD **w** over those who fear him,
66: 7 He **w** every movement of the nations; / let no rebel
95: 7 for he is our God. / We are the people he **w** over,
121: 3 and fall; / the one who **w** over you will not sleep.
121: 4 Indeed, he who **w** over Israel / never tires
121: 5 The LORD himself **w** over you! / The LORD
123: 2 as a slave girl **w** her mistress for the slightest
Pr 31:18 She **w** for bargains; her lights burn late into the
31:27 She carefully **w** all that goes on in her household
Eze 38:16 I will bring you against my land as everyone **w**,

WATCHING (54) [WATCH]

Ge 31: 4 and Leah out to the field where he was **w** the
Ex 2: 4 at a distance, **w** to see what would happen to him.
2:12 After looking around to make sure no one was **w**,
3:16 "You can be sure that I am **w** over you and have
Dt 9:13 LORD said to me, 'I have been **w** this people,
Jdg 16:27 three thousand on the roof who were **w** Samson
1Sa 16:11 "But he's out in the fields **w** the sheep."
19:24 The people who were **w** exclaimed, "What?
Ezr 5: 5 But because their God was **w** over them,
Job 1: 7 across the earth, **w** everything that's going on."
2: 2 across the earth, **w** everything that's going on."
14:16 would count my steps, instead of **w** for my sins.
24:23 to live in security, but God is always **w** them.
Ps 3: 5 up in safety, / for the LORD was **w** over me.
10:11 The wicked say to themselves, "God isn't **w**!
31:19 for protection, / blessing them before the **w** world.
56: 6 to spy on me— / **w** my every step, eager to kill me.
Pr 8:34 **w** for me daily at my gates, waiting for me outside
15: 3 The LORD is **w** everywhere, keeping his eye on
SS 8: 1 Then I could kiss you no matter who was **w**,
Jer 1:12 "That's right, and it means that I am **w**,
16:17 I am **w** them closely, and I see every sin.
20:10 Even my old friends are **w** me, waiting for a fatal
43: 9 "While the people of Judah are **w**, bury large
Eze 4:12 While all the people are **w**, bake it over a fire using
12: 4 Then as they are **w**, leave your house in the
12: 5 Dig a hole through the wall while they are **w**
28:18 ashes on the ground in the sight of all who were **w**.
28:22 everyone **w** will know that I am the LORD.
Da 3:24 But suddenly, as he was **w**,
7:11 I kept **w** until the fourth beast was killed and its
8: 5 While I was **w**, suddenly a male goat appeared
Hos 7: 2 Its people don't realize I am **w** them. Their sinful
Am 9: 8 am **w** this sinful nation of Israel, and I will uproot
Zec 9: 8 invading armies. I am closely **w** their movements.
11:11 Those who bought and sold sheep were **w** me,
Mal 3: 3 of silver, **w** closely as the dross is burned away.
Mt 27:55 with Jesus to care for him were **w** from a distance.
27:61 and the other Mary were sitting nearby **w**.
Mk 15:40 Some women were there, **w** from a distance,
Lk 14: 1 of the Pharisees. The people were **w** him closely,
20:20 **W** for their opportunity, the leaders sent secret
23:49 followed him from Galilee, stood at a distance **w**.
Jn 18:16 Then the other disciple spoke to the woman **w** at
Ac 1: 9 he was taken up into the sky while they were **w**,
9:24 and that they were **w** for him day and night at the
1Co 11:10 as a sign of authority because the angels are **w**.
2Co 2:17 And we know that the God who sent us is **w** us.
Eph 6: 6 not just to please your masters when they are **w**.
Col 3:22 them all the time, not just when they are **w** you.
1Pe 1:12 so wonderful that even the angels are eagerly **w**
3: 2 by **w** your pure, godly behavior.
Rev 13:13 down to earth from heaven while everyone was **w**.
16:15 Blessed are all who are **w** for me, who keep their

WATCHMAN (20) [WATCH]

2Sa 13:34 Then the **w** on the Jerusalem wall saw a great
18:24 the **w** climbed to the roof of the gateway by the
18:26 the **w** saw another man running toward them.
18:27 man runs like Ahimaaz son of Zadok," the **w** said.
2Ki 9:17 The **w** on the tower of Jezreel saw Jehu and his
9:18 The **w** called out to the king, "The rider has met
9:20 The **w** exclaimed, "The rider has met them,
SS 5: 7 wounded me. The **w** on the wall tore off my veil.
Isa 21: 6 "Put a **w** on the city wall to shout out what he
21: 8 Then the **w** called out, "Day after day I have stood
21: 9 Then the **w** said, "Babylon is fallen!
21:11 to me, "**W**, how much longer until morning?
21:12 The **w** replies, "Morning is coming, but night will
Eze 3:17 of man, I have appointed you as a **w** for Israel.
33: 2 a country, the people of that land choose a **w**.
33: 3 When the **w** sees the enemy coming, he blows the
33: 6 But if the **w** sees the enemy coming and doesn't
33: 6 die in their sins, but I will hold the **w** accountable.
33: 7 I am making you a **w** for the people of Israel.
Hos 9: 8 The prophet is a **w** for my God over Israel,

WATCHMAN'S (1) [WATCH]

Isa 1: 8 Jerusalem stands abandoned like a **w** shelter in a

WATCHMEN (10) [WATCH]

Ps 134: 1 you who serve as night **w** in the house of the
SS 3: 3 The **w** stopped me as they made their rounds,
5: 7 The **w** found me as they were making their rounds;
Isa 52: 8 The **w** shout and sing with joy, for before their
56:10 the LORD's **w**, his shepherds—are blind to every
62: 6 O Jerusalem, I have posted **w** on your walls;
Jer 4:17 They surround Jerusalem like **w** surrounding a
6:17 I set **w** over you who said, 'Listen for the sound of
31: 6 The day will come when **w** will shout from the hill
51:12 Reinforce the guard and station the **w**. Prepare an

WATCHTOWER (3) [TOWER, WATCH]

Isa 5: 2 it with choice vines. / In the middle he built a **w**
21: 8 "Day after day I have stood on the **w**, my lord.
Hab 2: 1 I will climb up into my **w** now and wait to see

WATCHTOWERS (1) [TOWER, WATCH]

Isa 32:14 and goats will graze on the hills where the **w** are,

WATER (459) [SPRINGWATER, WATER'S, WATERED, WATERED-DOWN, WATERFALL, WATERING, WATERLESS, WATERPOTS, WATERPROOFED, WATERS, WELL-WATERED]

FRESH WATER (3) Nu 19:17; Jas 3:11,12

LIFE-GIVING WATER (2) Pr 18:4; Rev 7:17

LIVING WATER (7) SS 4:15; Jer 2:13; 17:13; Jn 4:10,11; 7:38,39

WITH WATER (29) Ex 29:4; 30:18; 32:20; 40:7,12,30; Lev 1:9,13; 6:28; 8:6,21; 15:12; 16:24; 22:6; 1Ki 18:33; 2Ki 2:21; 3:17; Jer 51:13; Mt 3:11; Mk 1:8; Lk 3:16; Jn 1:26,31,33; 2:7; Ac 1:5; 11:16; Heb 9:19; 2Pe 3:5

Ge 1: 6 between the waters, to separate **w** from **w**."
1:10 named the dry ground "land" and the **w** "seas."
2: 6 But **w** came up out of the ground and watered all
7:19 the **w** covered even the highest mountains on the
7:24 And the **w** covered the earth for 150 days.
8: 2 The underground **w** sources ceased their gushing,
8: 9 no place to land because the **w** was still too high.
8:11 Noah now knew that the **w** was almost gone.
8:13 lifted back the cover to look. The **w** was drying up.
18: 4 while my servants get some **w** to wash your feet.
21:14 and strapped a container of **w** to Hagar's shoulders.
21:15 When the **w** was gone, she left the boy in the shade
21:19 She immediately filled her **w** container and gave
24:11 and the women were coming out to draw **w**.
24:13 women of the village are coming out to draw **w**.
24:14 'Yes, certainly, and I will **w** your camels, too!'—
24:15 a young woman named Rebekah arrived with a **w**
24:19 she said, "I'll draw **w** for your camels, too,
24:20 She kept carrying **w** to the camels until they had
24:32 and provided **w** for the camel drivers to wash their
24:43 say to some young woman who comes to draw **w**,
"Please give me a drink of **w**!"
24:44 And I'll **w** your camels, too!" LORD, let her be
24:45 I saw Rebekah coming along with her **w** jug on her
24:45 down to the spring and drew **w** and filled the jug.
24:46 'Certainly, sir, and I will **w** your camels, too!'
26:20 "This is our **w**," they said, and they argued over it
26:32 a well they had dug. "We've found **w**!" they said.
29: 7 "Why don't you **w** the flocks so they can get back
37:24 This pit was normally used to store **w**, but it was
43:24 led into the palace and given **w** to wash their feet
Ex 2:10 for she said, "I drew him out of the **w**."
2:16 who came regularly to this well to draw **w**
2:16 and fill the **w** troughs for their father's flocks.
2:17 Then he helped them draw **w** for their flocks.
2:19 "And then he drew **w** for us and watered our
4: 9 then take some **w** from the Nile River and pour it
7:17 I will hit the **w** of the Nile with this staff,
7:18 The Egyptians will not be able to drink any **w**
7:19 Everywhere in Egypt the **w** will turn into blood,
7:19 even the **w** stored in wooden bowls and stone pots
7:20 Moses raised his staff and hit the **w** of the Nile.
7:21 and the **w** became so foul that the Egyptians
7:22 their secret arts, and they, too, turned **w** into blood.
7:24 dug wells along the riverbank to get drinking **w**,
7:25 time the LORD turned the **w** of the Nile to blood.
14:16 hold it out over the **w**, and a path will open up
14:21 and the LORD opened up a path through the **w**
14:22 sea on dry ground, with walls of **w** on each side!
14:27 The **w** roared back into its usual place,
14:29 as the **w** stood up like a wall on both sides.
15:19 the LORD brought the **w** crashing down on them.
15:22 traveled in this desert for three days without **w**.
15:23 When they came to Marah, they finally found **w**.
15:25 Moses took the branch and threw it into the **w**.
This made the **w** good to drink.
17: 1 to Rephidim, but there was no **w** to be found there.
17: 2 "Give us **w** to drink!" they demanded. "Quiet!"
17: 5 the one you used when you struck the **w** of the
17: 6 Strike the rock, and **w** will come pouring out.
17: 6 and as the leaders looked on, **w** gushed out.
23:25 If you do, I will bless you with food and **w**, and I
29: 4 entrance of the Tabernacle, and wash them with **w**.
30:18 the Tabernacle and the altar, and fill it with **w**.
32:20 he ground it into powder and mixed it with **w**.

40: 7 the Tabernacle and the altar and fill it with **w**.
40: 12 entrance of the Tabernacle, and wash them with **w**.
40: 30 He filled it with **w** so the priests could use it to
Lev 1: 9 and legs must first be washed with **w**.
1: 13 and legs must first be washed with **w**.
6: 28 it must be scoured and rinsed thoroughly with **w**.
8: 6 and his sons and washed them with **w**.
8: 21 washing the internal organs and the legs with **w**,
11: 9 whether taken from fresh **w** or salt **w**.
11: 32 It must be put into **w**, and it will remain defiled
11: 34 If the **w** used to cleanse an unclean object touches
11: 36 into a spring or a cistern, the **w** will still be clean.
11: 46 and all the living things that move through the **w**
14: 8 off all their hair, and bathing themselves in **w**.
14: 9 and wash their clothes and bathe themselves in **w**.
15: 5 be required to wash your clothes and bathe in **w**,
15: 6 be required to wash your clothes and bathe in **w**.
15: 10 be required to wash your clothes and bathe in **w**,
15: 11 be required to wash your clothes and bathe in **w**,
15: 12 wooden utensil he touches must be rinsed with **w**.
15: 21 you must wash your clothes and bathe in **w**,
15: 27 be required to wash your clothes and bathe in **w**,
16: 24 Then he must bathe his entire body with **w** in a
16: 26 a scapegoat must wash his clothes and bathe in **w**.
16: 28 and bathe himself in **w** before returning to the
17: 15 must wash your clothes and bathe yourselves in **w**.
22: 6 until they have purified their bodies with **w**.
Nu 5: 17 He must take some holy **w** in a clay jar and mix it
5: 18 holding the jar of bitter **w** that brings a curse to
5: 19 the effects of this bitter **w** that causes the curse.
5: 22 Now may this **w** that brings the curse enter your
5: 23 of leather and wash them off into the bitter **w**.
5: 24 He will then make the woman drink the bitter **w**,
5: 26 Then he will require the woman to drink the **w**.
5: 27 the **w** that brings the curse will cause bitter
8: 7 Do this by sprinkling them with the **w** of
19: 7 must wash his clothes and bathe himself in **w**.
19: 8 animal must also wash his clothes and bathe in **w**,
19: 9 Israel to use in the **w** for the purification ceremony.
19: 12 and seventh days with the **w** of purification;
19: 13 Since the **w** of purification was not sprinkled on
19: 17 offering in a jar and pour fresh **w** over them.
19: 18 must take a hyssop branch and dip it into the **w**.
19: 18 That person must sprinkle the **w** on the tent,
19: 19 must sprinkle the **w** on those who are unclean.
19: 20 Since the **w** of purification has not been sprinkled
19: 21 Those who sprinkle the **w** of purification must
19: 21 and anyone who touches the **w** of purification will
20: 2 There was no **w** for the people to drink at that
20: 5 or pomegranates. And there is no **w** to drink!"
20: 8 command the rock over there to pour out its **w**.
20: 8 You will get enough **w** from the rock to satisfy all
20: 10 "Must we bring you **w** from this rock?"
20: 11 the rock twice with the staff, and **w** gushed out.
20: 17 We won't even drink **w** from your wells.
20: 19 If any of our livestock drinks your **w**, we will pay
21: 16 "Assemble the people, and I will give them **w**."
21: 22 or touch your vineyards or drink your well **w**."
24: 7 **W** will gush out in buckets; / their offspring are
31: 23 then be further purified with the **w** of purification.
31: 23 that burns must be purified by the **w** alone.
33: 9 where there are twelve springs of **w** and seventy
33: 14 where there was no **w** for the people to drink.
Dt 2: 6 Pay them for whatever food or **w** you use.
2: 28 every bite of food we eat and all the **w** we drink.
6: 11 You will draw **w** from cisterns you did not dig,
8: 7 a good land of flowing streams and pools of **w**,
8: 15 so hot and dry. He gave you **w** from the rock!
9: 9 and all that time I ate nothing and drank no **w**.
9: 18 the LORD, neither eating bread nor drinking **w**.
10: 7 from there to Jotbathah, a land with brooks of **w**.
12: 16 You must pour it out on the ground like **w**.
12: 24 Instead, pour out the blood on the ground like **w**.
15: 23 You must pour it out on the ground like **w**.
23: 4 you with food and **w** when you came out of Egypt.
29: 11 among you who chop your wood and carry your **w**.
33: 13 from the heavens, / and **w** from beneath the earth;
Jos 3: 13 When their feet touch the **w**, the flow of **w** will be cut off upstream,
3: 15 carrying the Ark touched the **w** at the river's edge,
3: 16 the **w** began piling up at a town upstream called
3: 16 And the **w** below that point flowed on to the Dead
9: 21 and carry the **w** for the entire community."
9: 23 chop wood and carry **w** for the house of my God."
9: 27 and **w** carriers for the people of Israel and for the
11: 5 They established their camp around the **w** near
11: 7 and his warriors traveled to the **w** near Merom
Jdg 4: 19 "Please give me some **w**," he said. "I'm thirsty."
5: 25 Sisera asked for **w**, / and Jael gave him milk.
6: 38 the fleece and wrung out a whole bowlful of **w**.
7: 5 When Gideon took his warriors down to the **w**,
7: 5 In one group put all those who cup **w** in their hands
15: 19 So God caused **w** to gush out of a hollow in the
Ru 2: 9 help yourself to the **w** they have drawn from the
1Sa 7: 6 drew **w** from a well and poured it out before the
9: 11 met some young women coming out to draw **w**.
25: 11 Should I take my bread and **w** and the meat I've
26: 11 we'll take his spear and his jug of **w** and then get
26: 12 the spear and jug of **w** that were near Saul's head.
26: 16 and the jug of **w** that were beside his head?"
30: 11 gave him some bread to eat and some **w** to drink.
2Sa 5: 8 "Go up through the **w** tunnel into the city
12: 27 fought against Rabbah and captured its **w** supply.
14: 14 Our lives are like **w** spilled out on the ground,
23: 15 how I would love some of that good **w** from the
23: 16 drew some **w** from the well, and brought it back to
23: 17 "This **w** is as precious as the blood of these men
1Ki 7: 26 It could hold about 11,000 gallons of **w**.
7: 27 Huram also made ten bronze **w** carts, each 6 feet
7: 37 All ten **w** carts were the same size and were made
7: 38 was 6 feet across and could hold 220 gallons of **w**.
7: 39 He arranged five **w** carts on the south side of the
7: 43 the ten **w** carts holding the ten basins,
13: 8 not eat any food or drink any **w** in this place.
13: 9 eat any food or drink any **w** while you are there,
13: 16 to eat any food or drink any **w** here in this place.
13: 17 eat any food or drink any **w** while you are there,
13: 18 and **w** to drink.' " But the old man was lying to
13: 19 and drank some **w** at the prophet's home.
13: 22 and drank **w** where he told you not to eat or drink.
17: 10 "Would you please bring me a cup of **w**?"
18: 4 each cave and had supplied them with food and **w**.)
18: 13 in two caves and supplied them with food and **w**.
18: 33 Then he said, "Fill four large jars with **w**, and pour the **w** over the offering and the wood."
18: 35 and the **w** ran around the altar and even overflowed
18: 38 the dust. It even licked up all the **w** in the ditch!
19: 6 some bread baked on hot stones and a jar of **w**!
22: 27 and **w** until I return safely from the battle!' "
2Ki 2: 8 folded his cloak together and struck the **w** with it.
2: 14 He struck the **w** with the cloak and cried out,
2: 19 But the **w** is bad, and the land is unproductive."
2: 21 out to the spring that supplied the town with **w**
2: 21 I have made this **w** wholesome. It will no longer
2: 22 The **w** has remained wholesome ever since, just as
3: 9 But there was no **w** for the men or their pack
3: 16 This dry valley will be filled with pools of **w**!
3: 17 the LORD, but this valley will be filled with **w**.
3: 20 sacrifice was offered, **w** suddenly appeared!
3: 20 of Edom, and soon there was **w** everywhere.
3: 22 the sun was shining across the **w**, making it look as
6: 6 the place, Elisha cut a stick and threw it into the **w**.
8: 15 the next day Hazael took a blanket, soaked it in **w**,
16: 17 side panels and basins from the portable **w** carts.
18: 17 the aqueduct that feeds **w** into the upper pool,
19: 24 and refreshed myself with their **w**. / I even stopped
20: 20 a pool and dug a tunnel to bring **w** into the city,
25: 13 broke up the bronze pillars, the bronze **w** carts,
25: 16 The bronze from the two pillars, the **w** carts,
1Ch 11: 17 how I would love some of that good **w** from the
11: 18 drew some **w** from the well, and brought it back to
11: 19 "This **w** is as precious as the blood of these men
2Ch 4: 5 It could hold about 16,500 gallons of **w**.
4: 6 He also made ten basins for **w** to wash the
4: 14 the **w** carts holding the basins,
18: 26 and **w** until I return safely from the battle!' "
26: 10 forts in the wilderness and dug many **w** cisterns,
32: 4 kings of Assyria come here and find plenty of **w**?"
32: 30 and brought the **w** down through a tunnel to the
Ne 3: 16 the royal cemetery as far as the **w** reservoir
3: 26 who repaired the wall as far as the **W** Gate toward
4: 23 with us at all times, even when we went for **w**.
8: 1 as one person at the square just inside the **W** Gate.
8: 3 He faced the square just inside the **W** Gate from
8: 16 or in the squares just inside the **W** Gate
9: 15 and **w** from the rock when they were thirsty.
9: 20 them bread from heaven or **w** for their thirst.
12: 37 and then proceeded to the **W** Gate on the east.
Job 3: 24 I cannot eat for sighing; my groans pour out like **w**.
5: 10 gives rain for the earth. He sends **w** for the fields.
6: 17 when the hot weather arrives, the **w** disappears.
6: 19 caravans from Tema and from Sheba stop for **w**,
8: 11 Can bulrushes flourish where there is no **w**?
11: 16 It will all be gone like **w** under the bridge.
14: 9 at the scent of **w** it may bud and sprout again like a
14: 11 As **w** evaporates from a lake and as a river
14: 19 as **w** wears away the stones and floods wash away
22: 7 You must have refused **w** for the thirsty and food
22: 11 see in the darkness, and waves of **w** cover you.
29: 19 For I am like a tree whose roots reach the **w**,
36: 27 He draws up the **w** vapor and then distills it into
37: 10 breath sends the ice, freezing wide expanses of **w**.
38: 30 For the **w** turns to ice as hard as rock, and the surface of the **w** freezes.
38: 37 all the clouds? Who can tilt the **w** jars of heaven,
41: 31 "The crocodile makes the **w** boil with its
41: 32 The **w** glistens in its wake. One would think the
Ps 22: 14 My life is poured out like **w**, / and all my bones are
32: 4 My strength evaporated like **w** in the summer heat.
42: 1 As the deer pants for streams of **w**, / so I long for
58: 7 May they disappear like **w** into thirsty ground.
63: 1 this parched and weary land / where there is no **w**.
65: 9 You take care of the earth and **w** it, / making it rich
69: 2 I am in deep **w**, / and the floods overwhelm me.
72: 6 like the showers that **w** the earth.
78: 13 The **w** stood up like walls beside them!
78: 15 to give them plenty of **w**, as from a gushing spring.
78: 20 Yes, he can strike a rock so **w** gushes out, / but he
79: 3 Blood has flowed like **w** all around Jerusalem;
81: 7 when you complained that there was no **w**.
104: 6 You clothed the earth with floods of **w**, / **w** that covered even the mountains.
104: 7 At the sound of your rebuke, the **w** fled;
104: 10 You make the springs pour **w** into ravines,
104: 11 They provide **w** for all the animals, / and the wild
105: 29 He turned the nation's **w** into blood, / poisoning all
105: 41 He opened up a rock, and **w** gushed out / to form a
106: 11 Then the **w** returned and covered their enemies;
107: 33 rivers into deserts, / and springs of **w** into dry land.
107: 35 But he also turns deserts into pools of **w**, / the dry
109: 18 part of him as his clothing, / or as the **w** he drinks,
114: 3 The **w** of the Jordan River turned away.
114: 8 He turned the rock into pools of **w**; / yes, springs of **w** came from solid rock.
136: 6 Give thanks to him who placed the earth on the **w**.
Pr 5: 15 Drink **w** from your own well—share your love
5: 16 Why spill the **w** of your springs in public,
9: 17 "Stolen **w** is refreshing; food eaten in secret tastes
18: 4 A person's words can be life-giving **w**; words of
21: 1 The king's heart is like a stream of **w** directed by
25: 21 to eat. If they are thirsty, give them **w** to drink.
25: 25 Good news from far away is like cold **w** to the
27: 19 As a face is reflected in **w**, so the heart reflects the
Ecc 1: 7 Then the **w** returns again to the rivers and flows
2: 6 I built reservoirs to collect the **w** to irrigate my
12: 6 Don't wait until the **w** jar is smashed at the spring
SS 4: 15 You are a garden fountain, a well of living **w**,
5: 12 His eyes are like doves beside brooks of **w**;
Isa 1: 30 will wither away like an oak or garden without **w**.
3: 1 supplies of food and **w** from Jerusalem and Judah.
7: 3 of the aqueduct that feeds **w** into the upper pool,
21: 14 bring food and **w** to these weary refugees.
22: 9 to be repaired. You store up **w** in the lower pool.
22: 11 you build a reservoir for **w** from the old pool.
25: 11 as a swimmer pushes down **w** with his hands.
27: 3 Each day I will **w** them; day and night I will watch
30: 14 coals from a fireplace or a little **w** from the well."
30: 25 there will be streams of **w** flowing down every
32: 6 the hungry of food and give no **w** to the thirsty.
33: 16 to them, and they will have **w** in abundance.
35: 6 in the wilderness, and streams will **w** the desert.
35: 7 and springs of **w** will satisfy the thirsty land.
36: 2 the aqueduct that feeds **w** into the upper pool,
37: 25 and refreshed myself with their **w**. / I even stopped
41: 17 "When the poor and needy search for **w** and there
41: 18 I will give them fountains of **w** in the valleys.
41: 18 In the deserts they will find pools of **w**. Rivers fed
43: 20 too, for giving them **w** in the wilderness.
44: 3 For I will give you abundant **w** to quench your
48: 21 the rock, and **w** gushed out for them to drink.
55: 10 the heavens and stay on the ground to **w** the earth.
64: 2 As fire causes wood to burn and **w** to boil,
Jer 1: 13 And I replied, "I see a pot of boiling **w**,
2: 13 They have forsaken me—the fountain of living **w**.
2: 13 cracked cisterns that can hold no **w** at all!
14: 3 The nobles send servants to get **w**, but all the wells
17: 8 a riverbank, with roots that reach deep into the **w**.
17: 13 forsaken the LORD, the fountain of living **w**.
27: 19 the bronze **w** carts, and all the other ceremonial
38: 6 There was no **w** in the cistern, but there was a thick
50: 38 It will even strike her **w** supply, causing it to dry
51: 13 You are a city rich with **w**, a great center of
51: 36 avenge you. I will dry up her river, her **w** supply,
52: 17 broke up the bronze pillars, the bronze **w** carts,
52: 20 The bronze from the two pillars, the **w** carts,
La 2: 19 cry out. Pour out your hearts like **w** to the Lord.
3: 54 The **w** flowed above my head, and I cried out,
5: 4 We have to pay for **w** to drink, and even firewood
Eze 4: 11 Then measure out a jar of **w** for each day,
4: 16 The **w** will be portioned out drop by drop,
4: 17 Food and **w** will be so scarce that the people will
7: 17 will be feeble; their knees will be as weak as **w**.
12: 18 Drink your **w** with fear, as if it were your last.
12: 19 and sip their tiny portions of **w** in utter despair,
17: 7 sent its roots and branches out toward him for **w**.
17: 8 and had plenty of **w** so it could grow into a
19: 10 green foliage / because of the abundant **w**.
21: 7 knees will tremble and become as weak as **w**.
24: 3 Put a pot of **w** on the fire to boil.
31: 4 The **w** was so abundant that there was enough for
31: 5 thick branches because of all the **w** at its roots.
31: 7 for its roots went deep into abundant **w**.
31: 16 the ones whose roots went deep into the **w**,
32: 3 to catch you in my net and haul you out of the **w**.
34: 18 Is it not enough for you to take the best **w** for
34: 19 All they have to drink is **w** that you have fouled.
36: 25 "Then I will sprinkle clean **w** on you, and you will
47: 3 go across. At that point the **w** was up to my ankles.
47: 4 This time the **w** was up to my knees. After another
47: 9 Everything that touches the **w** of this river will
47: 9 Wherever this **w** flows, everything will live.
Da 1: 12 us for ten days on a diet of vegetables and **w**,"
7: 3 Then four huge beasts came up out of the **w**,
Hos 2: 21 which will pour down **w** on the earth in answer to
Joel 1: 20 cry out to you because they have no **w** to drink.
3: 18 **W** will fill the dry streambeds of Judah, and a
Am 4: 8 from one town to another for a drink of **w**,
5: 8 It is he who draws up **w** from the oceans and pours
8: 11 not a famine of bread or **w** but of hearing the
9: 6 He draws up **w** from the oceans and pours it down
Mic 1: 4 like wax in a fire, like **w** pouring down a hill.
Na 2: 8 Nineveh is like a leaking **w** reservoir! The people
3: 8 surrounded by rivers, protected by **w** on all sides?
3: 14 Get ready for the siege! Store up **w**!
Mt 3: 11 "I baptize with **w** those who turn from their sins
3: 16 After his baptism, as Jesus came up out of the **w**,
8: 32 steep hillside into the lake and drowned in the **w**,
10: 42 And if you give even a cup of cold **w** to one of the
13: 47 is like a fishing net that is thrown into the **w**
14: 25 the morning Jesus came to them, walking on the **w**.
14: 28 tell me to come to you by walking on **w**."
14: 29 side of the boat and walked on the **w** toward Jesus.
17: 15 He often falls into the fire or into the **w**.
23: 24 You strain your **w** so you won't accidentally
27: 24 So he sent for a bowl of **w** and washed his hands
Mk 1: 8 I baptize you with **w**, but he will baptize you with
1: 10 And when Jesus came up out of the **w**, he saw the
4: 37 to break into the boat until it was nearly full of **w**.
4: 39 he rebuked the wind and said to the **w**,
6: 48 in the morning he came to them, walking on the **w**.
6: 49 but when they saw him walking on the **w**,

7: 3 do not eat until they have poured **w** over their
7: 4 unless they have immersed their hands in **w**.
9: 22 spirit often makes him fall into the fire or into **w**,
9: 41 If anyone gives you even a cup of **w** because you
14: 13 "a man carrying a pitcher of **w** will meet you.
Lk 3: 16 their questions by saying, "I baptize with **w**;
5: 3 asked Simon, its owner, to push it out into the **w**.
7: 44 you didn't offer me **w** to wash the dust from my
13: 15 their stalls on the Sabbath and lead them out for **w**?
16: 24 Lazarus over here to dip the tip of his finger in **w**
22: 10 a man carrying a pitcher of **w** will meet you.
Jn 1: 26 John told them, "I baptize with **w**, but right here in
1: 31 but I have been baptizing with **w** in order to point
1: 33 but when God sent me to baptize with **w**, he told
2: 7 Jesus told the servants, "Fill the jars with **w**."
2: 9 When the master of ceremonies tasted the **w** that
3: 5 enter the Kingdom of God without being born of **w**
3: 23 because there was plenty of **w** there and people
4: 7 Soon a Samaritan woman came to draw **w**,
4: 10 would ask me, and I would give you living **w**."
4: 11 deep well. Where would you get this living **w**?
4: 12 How can you offer better **w** than he and his sons
4: 13 soon become thirsty again after drinking this **w**.
4: 14 But the **w** I give them takes away thirst altogether.
4: 15 sir," the woman said, "give me some of that **w**!
4: 15 and I won't have to come here to haul **w**."
4: 28 The woman left her **w** jar beside the well and went
4: 46 of Cana, where he had turned the **w** into wine.
5: 7 to help me into the pool when the **w** is stirred up.
6: 19 they saw Jesus walking on the **w** toward the boat.
7: 38 For the Scriptures declare that rivers of living **w**
7: 39 (When he said "living **w**," he was speaking of the
13: 5 and poured **w** into a basin. Then he began to wash
19: 34 his side with a spear, and blood and **w** flowed out.
21: 7 for work), jumped into the **w**, and swam ashore.
Ac 1: 5 John baptized with **w**, but in just a few days you
8: 36 As they rode along, they came to some **w**,
8: 36 and the eunuch said, "Look! There's some **w**!
8: 38 and they went down into the **w**, and Philip baptized
8: 39 When they came up out of the **w**, the Spirit of the
9: 9 And all that time he went without food and **w**.
11: 16 'John baptized with **w**, but you will be baptized
27: 28 and found the **w** was only 120 feet deep.
1Co 10: 4 and all of them drank the same miraculous **w**.
1Ti 5: 23 Don't drink only **w**. You ought to drink a little
Heb 9: 19 took the blood of calves and goats, along with **w**,
10: 22 and our bodies have been washed with pure **w**.
Jas 3: 11 Does a spring of **w** bubble out with both fresh **w** and bitter **w**?
3: 12 and you can't draw fresh **w** from a salty pool.
2Pe 2: 17 people are as useless as dried-up springs of **w**
3: 5 and he brought the earth up from the **w** and surrounded it with **w**.
3: 6 Then he used the **w** to destroy the world with a
1Jn 5: 6 was revealed as God's Son by his baptism in **w**
5: 6 the cross—not by **w** only, but by **w** and blood.
5: 8 the Spirit, the **w**, and the blood—and all three
Rev 3: 16 But since you are like lukewarm **w**, I will spit you
7: 17 He will lead them to the springs of life-giving **w**.
8: 8 And one-third of the **w** in the sea became blood.
8: 10 one-third of the rivers and on the springs of **w**.
8: 11 It made one-third of the **w** bitter, and many people died because the **w** was so bitter.
12: 15 with a flood of **w** that flowed from its mouth.
14: 7 and earth, the sea, and all the springs of **w**."
16: 5 And I heard the angel who had authority over all **w**
21: 6 give the springs of the **w** of life without charge!
22: 1 And the angel showed me a pure river with the **w**
22: 17 them come and drink the **w** of life without charge.

WATER'S (2) [WATER]
Eze 19: 10 planted by the **w** edge. / It had lush, green foliage
Lk 5: 2 He noticed two empty boats at the **w** edge,

WATERED (11) [WATER]
Ge 2: 6 came up out of the ground and **w** all the land.
13: 10 The whole area was well **w** everywhere,
29: 2 in an open field beside a well, waiting to be **w**.
29: 10 and rolled away the stone and **w** his uncle's flock.
Ex 2: 18 "How did you get the flocks **w** so quickly today?"
2: 19 then he drew water for us and **w** our flocks."
Isa 44: 4 They will thrive like **w** grass, like willows on a
Jer 31: 12 Their life will be like a **w** garden, and all their
Eze 31: 4 Deep springs **w** it and helped it to grow tall
47: 12 For they are **w** by the river flowing from the
1Co 3: 6 and Apollos **w** it, but it was God, not we,

WATERED-DOWN (1) [WATER]
Isa 1: 22 Once so pure, you are now like **w** wine.

WATERFALL (2) [WATER]
Hos 5: 10 So I will pour my anger down on them like a **w**.
Rev 14: 2 a sound from heaven like the roaring of a great **w**

WATERFLOOD [KJV] See FLOOD

WATERING (9) [WATER]
Ge 2: 10 **w** the garden and then dividing into four branches.
24: 20 So she quickly emptied the jug into the **w** trough
29: 3 After **w** them, the stone would be rolled back over
29: 8 and begin the **w** until all the flocks and shepherds
30: 38 Then he set up these peeled branches beside the **w**
Jdg 5: 11 Listen to the village musicians gathered at the **w**
Isa 58: 11 **w** your life when you are dry and keeping you
Joel 3: 18 the LORD's Temple, **w** the arid valley of acacias.
1Co 3: 7 ones who do the planting or **w** aren't important,

WATERLESS (1) [WATER]
Zec 9: 11 I will free your prisoners from death in a **w**

WATERPOTS (1) [POT, WATER]
Jn 2: 6 Six stone **w** were standing there; they were used

WATERPROOFED (1) [WATER]
Ex 2: 3 made of papyrus reeds and **w** it with tar and pitch.

WATERS (73) [WATER]
Ge 1: 6 And God said, "Let there be space between the **w**,
1: 7 God made this space to separate the **w** above from the **w** below.
1: 9 "Let the **w** beneath the sky be gathered into one
1: 20 "Let the **w** swarm with fish and other life.
7: 11 the underground **w** burst forth on the earth,
7: 18 As the **w** rose higher and higher above the ground,
8: 1 He sent a wind to blow across the **w**,
8: 5 a half months later, as the **w** continued to go down,
Ex 7: 19 "Tell Aaron to point his staff toward the **w** of
14: 26 Then the **w** will rush back over the Egyptian
14: 28 The **w** covered all the chariots and charioteers—
15: 5 The deep **w** have covered them; / they sank to the
15: 8 At the blast of your breath, the **w** piled up! / The surging **w** stood straight like a wall;
15: 8 in the middle of the sea the **w** became hard.
15: 10 They sank like lead / in the mighty **w**.
Nu 20: 13 This place was known as the **w** of Meribah,
20: 24 my instructions concerning the **w** of Meribah.
24: 6 planted by the LORD, / like cedars beside the **w**.
27: 14 to demonstrate my holiness to them at the **w**."
27: 14 (These are the **w** of Meribah at Kadesh in the
Dt 32: 51 **w** of Meribah at Kadesh in the wilderness of Zin.
33: 8 and contended with them at the **w** of Meribah.
Jos 15: 9 of the mountain to the spring at the **w** of Nephtoah,
16: 1 east of the **w** of Jericho, through the wilderness
18: 15 From there it ran westward to the spring at the **w** of
2Sa 22: 17 and rescued me; / he drew me out of deep **w**.
Ne 9: 11 They sank like stones beneath the mighty **w**.
Job 12: 15 a desert. If he releases the **w**, they flood the earth.
26: 5 "The dead tremble in their place beneath the **w**.
26: 10 He created the horizon when he separated the **w**;
Ps 18: 16 and rescued me; / he drew me out of deep **w**.
46: 3 Let the mountains tremble as the **w** surge!
69: 14 who hate me, / and pull me from these deep **w**.
69: 15 floods overwhelm me, / or the deep **w** swallow me,
77: 16 Sea saw you, O God, / its **w** looked and trembled!
77: 19 the sea, / your pathway through the mighty **w**—
78: 16 the rock, / making the **w** flow down like a river!
124: 4 The **w** would have engulfed us; / a torrent would
124: 5 Yes, the raging **w** of their fury / would have
144: 7 and rescue me; / deliver me from deep **w**,
Pr 8: 24 before the springs bubbled forth their **w**.
SS 8: 7 Many **w** cannot quench love; neither can rivers
Isa 11: 9 And as the **w** fill the sea, so the earth will be filled
15: 6 Even the **w** of Nimrim are dried up! The grassy
19: 5 The **w** of the Nile will fail to rise and flood the
23: 3 sailing over deep **w**. They brought you grain from
43: 2 When you go through deep **w** and great trouble,
43: 16 am the LORD, who opened a way through the **w**,
49: 10 LORD in his mercy will lead them beside cool **w**.
Jer 2: 18 What good to you are the **w** of the Nile
5: 22 an everlasting boundary that the **w** cannot cross.
48: 34 Even the **w** of Nimrim are dried up now.
Eze 31: 15 deep places mourn, and I restrained the mighty **w**.
32: 13 or animals disturb those **w** with their feet.
32: 14 Then I will let the **w** of Egypt become calm again,
43: 2 sound of his coming was like the roar of rushing **w**,
47: 8 The **w** of this stream will heal the salty **w** of
47: 9 abound in the Dead Sea, for its **w** will be healed.
47: 19 go west from Tamar to the **w** of Meribah at Kadesh
48: 28 runs from Tamar to the **w** of Meribah at Kadesh
Jnh 2: 5 The **w** closed in around me, and seaweed wrapped
Hab 2: 14 as the **w** fill the sea, with an awareness of the glory
3: 10 and trembled. Onward swept the raging **w**.
3: 15 sea with your horses, and the mighty **w** piled high.
Zec 10: 11 And the **w** of the Nile will become dry. The pride
14: 8 On that day life-giving **w** will flow out from
1Co 3: 8 and the one who **w** work as a team with the same
10: 1 and he brought them all safely through the **w** of the
Rev 17: 1 come on the great prostitute, who sits on many **w**.
17: 15 "The **w** where the prostitute is sitting represent

WATERSPOUTS [KJV] See (RAGING) SEAS

WAVE (12) [WAVES, WAVING, WAVY]
Jdg 9: 9 just to **w** back and forth over the trees?'
9: 11 'Should I quit producing my sweet fruit just to **w**
9: 13 just to **w** back and forth over the trees?'
2Ki 5: 11 "I expected him to **w** his hand over the leprosy
Ps 88: 7 anger lies heavy on me; / **w** after **w** engulfs me.
Isa 11: 15 He will **w** his hand over the Euphrates River,
13: 2 **W** to them as they march against Babylon to
Hos 10: 7 will disappear like a chip of wood on an ocean **w**.
Lk 8: 37 them alone, for a great **w** of fear swept over them.
Ac 8: 1 A great **w** of persecution began that day,
Jas 1: 6 for a doubtful mind is as unsettled as a **w** of the sea

WAVER (2) [WAVERED, WAVERING, WAVERS]
1Ki 18: 21 "How long are you going to **w** between two
Jas 1: 8 They **w** back and forth in everything they do.

WAVERED (3) [WAVER]
Job 4: 4 strengthened the fallen; you steadied those who **w**.
Ps 17: 5 on your path; / I have not **w** from following you.
Ro 4: 20 Abraham never **w** in believing God's promise.

WAVERING (4) [WAVER]
Job 27: 6 I will maintain my innocence without **w**.
Ps 26: 1 I have trusted in the LORD without **w**.
Heb 10: 23 Without **w**, let us hold tightly to the hope we say
Jude 1: 22 Show mercy to those whose faith is **w**.

WAVERS (1) [WAVER]
2Co 1: 19 the Son of God, never **w** between yes and no.

WAVES (40) [WAVE]
Ge 49: 4 But you are as unruly as the **w** of the sea, / and you
2Sa 22: 5 "The **w** of death surrounded me; / the floods of
Job 9: 8 out the heavens and marches on the **w** of the sea.
22: 11 see in the darkness, and **w** of water cover you.
38: 11 will you come. Here your proud **w** must stop!'
Ps 42: 7 as your **w** and surging tides sweep over me.
65: 7 quieted the raging oceans / with their pounding **w**
89: 9 When their **w** rise in fearful storms, you subdue
107: 25 He spoke, and the winds rose, / stirring up the **w**.
107: 29 calmed the storm to a whisper / and stilled the **w**.
SS 4: 1 Your hair falls in **w**, like flocks of goats frisking
Isa 17: 12 The armies rush forward like **w** thundering toward
43: 17 I drew them beneath the **w**, and they drowned,
48: 18 like a gentle river and righteousness rolling like **w**.
51: 15 who stirs up the sea, causing its **w** to roar.
Jer 4: 20 **W** of destruction roll over the land, until it lies in
5: 22 The **w** may toss and roar, but they can never pass
31: 35 the night. It is he who stirs the sea into roaring **w**.
51: 42 sea has risen over Babylon; she is covered by its **w**.
51: 55 **W** of enemies pound against her; the noise of
Eze 1: 24 As they flew their wings roared like **w** crashing
26: 3 like the **w** of the sea crashing against your
26: 19 You will sink beneath the terrible **w** of enemy
Jnh 2: 3 I was buried beneath your wild and stormy **w**.
2: 5 "I sank beneath the **w**, and death was very near.
Zec 10: 11 of distress, for the **w** of the sea will be held back.
Mt 8: 24 storm came up, with **w** breaking into the boat.
8: 26 Then he stood up and rebuked the wind and **w**,
8: 27 "Even the wind and **w** obey him!"
14: 24 wind had risen, and they were fighting heavy **w**.
14: 30 But when he looked around at the high **w**, he was
Mk 4: 37 High **w** began to break into the boat until it was
4: 41 is this man, that even the wind and **w** obey him?"
6: 48 rowing hard and struggling against the wind and **w**.
Lk 8: 24 So Jesus rebuked the wind and the raging **w**.
8: 25 is this man, that even the winds and **w** obey him?"
Ac 27: 41 stern was repeatedly smashed by the force of the **w**
Jude 1: 13 They are like wild **w** of the sea, churning up the
Rev 1: 15 and his voice thundered like mighty ocean **w**.
19: 6 or the roar of mighty ocean **w**, or the crash of loud

WAVING (2) [WAVE]
Isa 13: 2 "See the flags **w** as the enemy attacks. Cheer them
Na 2: 3 into position, with a forest of spears **w** above them.

WAVY (1) [WAVE]
SS 5: 11 head is the finest gold, and his hair is **w** and black.

WAX (4)
Ps 22: 14 of joint. / My heart is like **w**, / melting within me.
68: 2 Melt them like **w** in fire. / Let the wicked perish in
97: 5 The mountains melt like **w** before the LORD,
Mic 1: 4 his feet and flow into the valleys like **w** in a fire,

WAY (680) [AWAY, GATEWAY, GATEWAY'S, GATEWAYS, MIDWAY, PATHWAY, PATHWAYS, ROADWAY, WAYS, WALKWAY, WALKWAYS]
EVIL WAY (3) Ne 13:17; Eze 36:19; Jude 1:18
IN EVERY WAY (11) Ge 1:31; 24:1; 29:17; 2Sa 19:18; SS 5:16; Ro 16:2; Eph 4:15; 1Th 5:23; 1Ti 1:13; 2Ti 3:17; Tit 2:10
WAY OF LIFE (7) Lev 18:3; Ps 16:11; 119:56,104; Ac 2:28; Ro 7:10; Eph 4:22
WAY OF THE LORD (1) Ac 18:25
WAY OF THE LORD* (1) Ge 18:19
Ge 1: 31 and he saw that it was excellent in every **w**.
3: 24 and forth, guarding the **w** to the tree of life.
4: 7 You will be accepted if you respond in the right **w**.
6: 16 Construct an opening all the **w** around the boat,
9: 23 they looked the other **w** so they wouldn't see him
11: 8 In that **w**, the LORD scattered them all over the
15: 18 all the **w** from the border of Egypt to the great
18: 16 Abraham went with them part of the **w**.
18: 19 and their families to keep the **w** of the LORD
18: 33 The LORD went on his **w** when he had finished
19: 2 as early as you like and be on your **w** again."
19: 32 That **w** we will preserve our family line through
19: 34 That **w** our family line will be preserved."

22:12 "Do not hurt the boy in any **w**, for now I know
24: 1 and the LORD had blessed him in every **w**.
24:42 mission a success, please guide me in a special **w**.
24:49 step should be, whether to move this **w** or that."
26:10 "How could you treat us this **w**!"
26:27 sent me from your land in a most unfriendly **w**."
27: 4 Prepare it just the **w** I like it so it's savory
27:14 a delicious meat dish, just the **w** Isaac liked it.
27:19 Here is the wild game, cooked the **w** you like it.
29:17 but Rachel was beautiful in every **w**, with a lovely
30:26 earned them from you, and let me be on my **w**.
31: 9 In this **w**, God has made me wealthy at your
32: 1 and his household started on their **w** again,
32: 6 the news that Esau was on his **w** to meet Jacob—
33:12 Esau said. "I will stay with you and lead the **w**."
34:17 Otherwise we will take her and be on our **w**."
35:19 and was buried on the **w** to Ephrath (that is,
37:14 So Jacob sent him on his **w**, and Joseph traveled to
37:22 That **w** he will die without our having to touch
38:14 the village of Enaim, which is on the **w** to Timnah.
39:10 and he kept out of her **w** as much as possible.
41:36 That **w** there will be enough to eat when the seven
42:20 In this **w**, I will know whether or not you are
42:33 'This is the **w** I will find out if you are honest men.
43: 8 "Send the boy with me, and we will be on our **w**.
44: 6 and spoke to them in the **w** he had been instructed.
45:24 he called after them, "Don't quarrel along the **w**!"
48: 7 We were still on the **w**, just a short distance from
48:20 as Ephraim and Manasseh.' " In this **w**,
Ex 1:10 We must find a **w** to put an end to this. If we don't
3:22 In this **w**, you will plunder the Egyptians!"
4:14 And look! He is on his **w** to meet you now.
12: 4 or not they share in this **w** depends on the size of
13:17 even though that was the shortest **w** from Egypt to
13:21 That **w** they could travel whether it was day
18: 8 him about the problems they had faced along the **w**
20:20 "for God has come in this **w** to show you his
22:21 "Do not oppress foreigners in any **w**. Remember,
23:24 gods of these other nations or serve them in any **w**,
26:11 In this **w**, the two sets will become a single unit.
26:17 next frame. All the frames must be made this **w**.
26:24 of these corner frames will be made the same **w**.
26:28 will run all the **w** from one end of the Tabernacle
28:11 Engrave these names in the same **w** a gemcutter
28:29 In this **w**, Aaron will carry the names of the tribes
28:34 and pomegranates are to alternate all the **w** around
29: 9 In this **w**, you will ordain Aaron and his sons.
29:21 In this **w**, they and their clothing will be set apart
32: 8 They have already turned from the **w** I commanded
32:34 Look! My angel will lead the **w** before you!
33: 3 I would be tempted to destroy you along the **w**."
34:11 surely drive out all those who stand in your **w**—
34:24 I will drive out the nations that stand in your **w**
36:18 In this **w**, the roof covering was joined together in
36:22 to the next frame. All the frames were made this **w**.
37: 2 and it had a molding of gold all the **w** around.
39:21 In this **w**, the chestpiece was held securely to the
Lev 4:20 In this **w**, the priest will make atonement for the
4:26 In this **w**, the priest will make atonement for the
4:31 In this **w**, the priest will make atonement for them,
4:35 In this **w**, the priest will make atonement for them,
5:10 In this **w**, the priest will make atonement for those
5:13 In this **w**, the priest will make atonement for those
5:18 In this **w**, the priest will make atonement for those
8:15 In this **w**, he set the altar apart as holy and made
8:30 In this **w**, he made Aaron and his sons and their
9:16 burnt offering and presented it in the prescribed **w**.
10: 1 In this **w**, they disobeyed the LORD by burning
11:35 It has become defiled, and it will remain that **w**.
14:18 In this **w**, the priest will make atonement before
14:20 In this **w**, the priest will make atonement for the
14:29 In this **w**, the priest will make atonement for the
14:31 In this **w**, the priest will make atonement before
14:52 After he has purified the house in this **w**,
14:53 In this **w**, the priest will make atonement for the
15:15 In this **w**, the priest will make atonement for the
15:30 In this **w**, the priest will make atonement for her
15:31 "In this **w**, you will keep the people of Israel
16:16 In this **w**, he will make atonement for the Most
16:19 In this **w**, he will cleanse it from Israel's
16:21 In this **w**, he will lay the people's sins on the head
16:24 In this **w**, he will make atonement for himself
17: 6 That **w** the priest will be able to sprinkle the blood
18: 3 taking you. You must not imitate their **w** of life.
19:25 In this **w**, its yield will be increased. I, the LORD,
25:43 exercise your power over them in a ruthless **w**.
25:46 your relatives, must never be treated this **w**.
27:28 Anything devoted in this **w** has been set apart for
Nu 2: 9 These three tribes are to lead the **w** whenever the
6: 2 themselves apart to the LORD in a special **w**,
6:11 In this **w**, he will make atonement for the guilt they
8:14 In this **w**, you will set the Levites apart from the
9:18 In this **w**, they traveled at the LORD's command
10:29 "We are on our **w** to the Promised Land
14:33 In this **w**, they will pay for your faithlessness,
19:13 and do not purify themselves in the proper **w** defile
21: 4 But the people grew impatient along the **w**,
21:30 all the **w** from Heshbon to Dibon.
22:22 of the LORD to stand in the road to block his **w**.
22:32 "I have come to block your **w** because you are
22:34 you were standing in the road to block my **w**.
22:36 When King Balak heard that Balaam was on the **w**,
25: 8 Phinehas thrust the spear all the **w** through the
33: 2 by the different places they stopped along the **w**.
33:54 In this **w**, the land will be divided among your
36: 3 In this **w**, the total area of our tribal land will be
Dt 1: 2 Sinai to Kadesh-barnea, going by **w** of Mount Seir.
1: 7 and all the **w** to the great Euphrates River.
1:44 and battered you all the **w** from Seir to Hormah.
2:12 In a similar **w** the peoples in Canaan were driven
3:14 in Bashan all the **w** to the borders of the Geshurites
3:16 all the **w** to the Jabbok River on the Ammonite
3:17 all the **w** from the Sea of Galilee down to the Dead
4:10 That **w**, they will learn to fear me as long as they
9:12 They have already turned from the **w** I commanded
11:28 and turn from his **w** by worshiping foreign gods.
12: 4 "Do not worship the LORD your God in the **w**
12:21 name to be honored is a long **w** from your home.
14:24 to be honored might be a long **w** from your home.
17: 7 In this **w**, you will purge all evil from among you.
17:11 must be fully executed; do not modify it in any **w**.
17:19 That **w** he will learn to fear the LORD his God by
17:20 away from these commands in the smallest **w**.
19:10 That **w** you will prevent the death of innocent
19:19 In this **w**, you will cleanse such evil from among
21:21 In this **w**, you will cleanse this evil from among
22: 4 donkey lying on the road, do not look the other **w**.
22: 8 That **w** you will not bring the guilt of bloodshed on
22:22 In this **w**, the evil will be cleansed from Israel.
22:24 In this **w**, you will cleanse the land of evil.
23: 6 to help the Ammonites or the Moabites in any **w**.
29:19 even though I am walking in my own stubborn **w**.'
32: 6 Is this the **w** you repay the LORD, / you foolish
Jos 2: 3 They are spies sent here to discover the best **w** to
2:16 for you have returned; then go on your **w**."
2:20 however, we are not bound by this oath in any **w**."
2:21 And she sent them on their **w**, leaving the scarlet
3: 4 Since you have never traveled this **w** before,
5: 7 been circumcised on the **w** to the Promised Land—
6: 7 and the armed men will lead the **w** in front of the
8:16 In this **w**, they were lured away from the city.
10:10 and Makkedah, killing them along the **w**.
11:17 The Israelite territory now extended all the **w** from
18: 8 who were mapping out the land started on their **w**,
20: 9 In this **w**, they could escape being killed in revenge
23: 6 Law of Moses. Do not deviate from them in any **w**.
23:14 "Soon I will die, going the **w** of all the earth.
Jdg 1:24 They said to him, "Show us a **w** into the city,
1:25 So he showed them a **w** in, and they killed
3:26 Ehud escaped, passing the idols on his **w** to Seirah.
4:16 and their chariots all the **w** to
6:37 prove it to me in this **w**. I will put some wool on
6:38 And it happened just that **w**. When Gideon got up
8: 1 asked Gideon, "Why have you treated us this **w**?
8:13 After this, Gideon returned by **w** of Heres Pass.
9:25 and robbed everyone who passed that **w**.
9:40 covered with dead bodies all the **w** to the city gate.
11:13 to the Jabbok River and all the **w** to the Jordan.
14: 9 of the honey into his hands and ate it along the **w**.
16: 3 and carried them all the **w** to the top of the hill
18:21 They started on their **w** again, placing their
18:26 So the men of Dan went on their **w**. When Micah
19: 9 you can get up early and be on your **w**."
19:18 "We are on our **w** home to a remote area in the hill
Ru 1: 8 But on the **w**, Naomi said to her two
4: 5 That **w**, she can have children who will carry on
4:10 This **w** she can have a son to carry on the family
1Sa 2:14 who came to worship at Shiloh were treated this **w**.
4:20 But she did not answer or respond in any **w**.
7:11 to Beth-car, slaughtering them all along the **w**.
9: 6 find him. Perhaps he can tell us which **w** to go."
9:19 what you want to know and send you on your **w**.
9:26 to Saul, "Get up! It's time you were on your **w**."
10: 3 you who are on their **w** to worship God at Bethel.
12: 4 "you have never cheated or oppressed us in any **w**,
12:20 and that you don't turn your back on him in any **w**.
13:15 Samuel then left Gilgal and went on his **w**,
15: 7 the Amalekites from Havilah all the **w** to Shur,
16: 7 The LORD doesn't make decisions the **w** you do!
16:10 In the same **w** all seven of Jesse's sons were
17:33 "There is no **w** you can go against this Philistine.
18: 6 Women came out from all the towns along the **w** to
18:21 "I have a **w** for you to become my son-in-law after
19: 4 He has always helped you in any **w** he could.
19:10 But David dodged out of the **w** and escaped into
19:23 But on the **w** to Naioth the Spirit of God came
23:15 David received the news that Saul was on the **w** to
24: 7 After Saul had left the cave and gone on his **w**,
25:28 Please forgive me if I have offended in any **w**.
29: 4 Is there any better **w** for him to reconcile himself
30:14 We were on our **w** back from raiding the
2Sa 3:21 So David sent Abner safely on his **w**.
5:25 and he struck down the Philistines all the **w** from
7:19 Do you deal with everyone this **w**, O Sovereign
7:23 out the nations and gods that stood in their **w**.
9: 3 I want to show God's kindness to them in any **w** I
13:30 As they were on the **w** back to Jerusalem,
15: 6 So in this **w**, Absalom stole the hearts of all the
15:18 to let David's troops move past to lead the **w**.
16:14 all who were with him grew weary along the **w**,
16:17 "Is this the **w** you treat your friend David?"
17:11 That **w** you will have an army as numerous as the
19:18 the river, helping them in every **w** they could.
20:13 With Amasa's body out of the **w**, everyone went
22:31 "As for God, his **w** is perfect. / All the LORD's
22:33 is my strong fortress; / he has made my **w** safe.
1Ki 2:15 for that is the **w** the LORD wanted it.
3: 7 but I am like a little child who doesn't know his **w**
6: 5 all the **w** around the sides and rear of the building.
7: 8 behind this hall; they were built the same **w**.
7:24 There were about six gourds per foot all the **w**
13: 9 and do not return to Judah by the same **w** you
13:10 So he left Bethel and went home another **w**.
13:12 old prophet asked them, "Which **w** did he go?"
13:17 and do not return to Judah by the same **w** you
18: 6 Ahab went one **w** by himself, and Obadiah went another **w** by himself.
18:46 and ran ahead of Ahab's chariot all the **w** to the
19:15 the LORD told him, "Go back the **w** you came,
2Ki 3: 7 On the **w**, he sent this message to King
4: 8 From then on, whenever he passed that **w**,
4:29 my staff and go! Don't talk to anyone along the **w**.
6:19 and told them, "You have come the wrong **w**!
7:15 They went all the **w** to the Jordan River,
9: 7 In this **w**, I will avenge the murder of my prophets
9:11 "You know the **w** such a man babbles on,"
10:12 Along the **w**, while he was at Beth-eked of the
10:18 Baal at all compared to the **w** I will worship him!
19:11 They have crushed everyone who stood in their **w**!
19:27 you do. / I know the **w** you have raged against me.
23: 3 In this **w**, he confirmed all the terms of the
25:17 network of bronze pomegranates all the **w** around.
1Ch 14:16 and he struck down the Philistine army all the **w**
15:13 failed to ask God how to move it in the proper **w**."
17:18 What more can I say about the **w** you have
17:21 and drove out the nations that stood in their **w**.
2Ch 3:12 In the same **w**, the second figure had one wing
4: 3 There were about six oxen per foot all the **w**
8:15 Solomon did not deviate in any **w** from David's
20:20 On the **w** Jehoshaphat stopped and said, "Listen to
22:11 In this **w**, Jehosheba, the wife of Jehoiada the
28:25 In this **w**, he aroused the anger of the LORD,
31:20 In this **w**, King Hezekiah handled the distribution
33:19 the account of the **w** God answered him,
Ezr 4:14 we do not want to see you dishonored in this **w**,
6: 9 whatever is needed in the **w** of young bulls,
6:11 "Those who violate this decree in any **w** will have
7:18 that is left over may be used in whatever **w** you
8:22 and protect us from enemies along the **w**.
8:31 saved us from enemies and bandits along the **w**.
9:12 and not to help those nations in any **w**.
Ne 2: 7 safely through their territories on my **w** to Judah.
4:22 That **w** they and their servants could go on guard
5:15 because of my fear of God, I did not act that **w**.
8:17 The Israelites had not celebrated this **w** since the
9:12 of fire at night so that they could find their **w**.
9:19 and the pillar of fire showed them the **w** through
11:30 So the people of Judah were living all the **w** from
12:38 went northward around the other **w** to meet them.
13:17 are you profaning the Sabbath in this evil **w**?
13:18 permitting the Sabbath to be desecrated in this **w**!"
Est 1:18 and will start talking to their husbands the same **w**.
5:14 you can go on your merry **w** to the banquet with
8:13 That **w** the Jews would be ready on that day to take
Job 16: 5 I would do. I would speak in a **w** that helps you.
19: 8 God has blocked my **w** and plunged my path into
22:14 He is **w** up there, walking on the vault of heaven.'
29: 3 when he lighted the **w** before me and I walked
31:29 or become excited when harm came their **w**?
34:21 "For God carefully watches the **w** people live;
34:36 penalty for the wicked **w** you have talked.
Ps 5: 8 clearly what to do, / and show me which **w** to turn.
13: 1 Forever? / How long will you look the other **w**?
16:11 You will show me the **w** of life, / granting me the
18:30 As for God, his **w** is perfect. / All the LORD's
18:32 arms me with strength; / he has made my **w** safe.
25: 9 the humble in what is right, / teaching them his **w**.
31:11 they see me on the street, / they turn the other **w**.
35: 3 and javelin / and block the **w** of my enemies.
40:12 They pile up so high / I can't see my **w** out.
44:24 Why do you look the other **w**? / Why do you
50: 3 Fire devours everything in his **w**, / and a great
58: 3 from birth they have lied and gone their own **w**.
68:27 Look, the little tribe of Benjamin leads the **w**.
72: 2 Help him judge your people in the right **w**;
73:15 If I had really spoken this **w**, / I would have been a
81:12 So I let them follow their blind and stubborn **w**,
85:13 a herald before him, / preparing the **w** for his steps.
88: 8 them all away. / I am in a trap with no **w** of escape.
110: 7 himself will be refreshed from brooks along the **w**.
114: 3 Sea saw them coming and hurried out of their **w**!
114: 5 Red Sea, that made you hurry out of their **w**?
119:56 This is my happy **w** of life: / obeying your
119:95 Though the wicked hide along the **w** to kill me,
119:104 no wonder I hate every false **w** of life.
119:128 is right. / That is why I hate every false **w**.
140: 5 out a net; / they have placed traps all along the **w**.
142: 3 and you alone know the **w** I should turn.
Pr 1:31 they must eat the bitter fruit of living their own **w**.
3:23 They keep you safe on your **w** and keep your feet
4:18 The **w** of the righteous is like the first gleam of
4:19 But the **w** of the wicked is like complete darkness.
5:12 If only I had not demanded my own **w**!
6:23 and this teaching are a lamp to light the **w** ahead of you. The correction of discipline is the **w** to life.
12:28 The **w** of the godly leads to life; their path does not
15: 9 The LORD despises the **w** of the wicked, but he
19: 2 who moves too quickly may go the wrong **w**.
20:11 Even children are known by the **w** they act,
21:17 wine and luxury are not the **w** to riches.
22:21 In this **w**, you may know the truth and bring an
23:21 for they are on their **w** to poverty. Too much sleep
24:14 In the same **w**, wisdom is sweet to your soul.
27:18 In the same **w**, workers who protect their
Ecc 2: 3 In this **w**, I hoped to experience the only happiness
3:18 That **w**, they can see for themselves that they are
7: 1 In the same **w**, the day you die is better than the
7:13 Notice the **w** God does things; then fall into line.
7:14 That **w** you will realize that nothing is certain in
7:18 but those who fear God will succeed either **w**.
8: 5 wise will find a time and a **w** to do what is right.

8: 6 Yes, there is a time and a **w** for everything, even as
8:15 That **w** they will experience some happiness along
9:13 me as I have watched the **w** our world works.
10: 3 You can identify fools just by the **w** they walk
12:10 the plain truth, and he did so in an interesting **w**.
SS 5:16 mouth is altogether sweet; he is lovely in every **w**.
Isa 2:21 In this **w**, they will try to escape the terror of the
3:11 Your well-earned punishment is on the **w**."
6:10 That **w**, they will not see with their eyes, hear with
7: 6 Then we will fight our **w** into Jerusalem and install
19: 3 and psychics to show them which **w** to turn.
19:22 The LORD will strike Egypt in a **w** that will bring
27: 7 Has the LORD punished Israel in the same **w** he
28:27 He doesn't thresh all his crops the same **w**.
29: 8 In the same **w**, your enemies will dream of a
30:21 and you will hear a voice say, "This is the **w**;
31: 4 In the same **w**, the LORD Almighty will come
37:11 They have crushed everyone who stood in their **w**!
37:28 you do. / I know the **w** you have raged against me.
41:27 first to tell Jerusalem, 'Look! Help is on the **w**!'
42:16 a new path, / guiding them along an unfamiliar **w**.
43:16 the LORD, who opened a **w** through the waters,
45:10 was I born? Why did you make me this **w**?' "
47:11 and you won't be able to buy your **w** out.
48: 5 That **w**, you could never say, 'My idols did it.
48:10 I have refined you but not in the **w** silver is refined.
48:11 That **w**, the pagan nations will not be able to claim
51: 5 Your salvation is on the **w**. I will rule the nations.
53: 3 on him and looked the other **w** when he went by.
Jer 2:17 when he wanted to lead you and show you the **w**!
5:31 iron hand. And worse yet, my people like it that **w**!
6:16 Look for the old, godly **w**, and walk in it. Travel its
8:16 heard all the **w** from the land of Dan in the north!
11:19 I had been as unaware as a lamb on the **w** to its
18:18 "Come on, let's find a **w** to stop Jeremiah.
22:21 Since childhood you have been that **w**—
23:17 they say, 'No harm will come your **w**!'
25:35 find no place to hide; there will be no **w** to escape.
37:12 Jeremiah started to leave the city on his **w** to the
46:20 young cow, but a gadfly from the north is on its **w**!
48:34 from Zoar all the **w** to Horonaim
49:21 and its cry of despair will be heard all the **w** to the
50: 5 They will ask the **w** to Jerusalem and will start
50: 6 They have lost their **w** and cannot remember how
51:64 'In this same **w** Babylon and her people will sink,
52:22 network of bronze pomegranates all the **w** around.
La 1: 4 no longer filled with crowds on their **w** to celebrate
Eze 1:28 This was the **w** the glory of the LORD appeared
11:10 You will be slaughtered all the **w** to the borders of
14:11 In this **w**, the people of Israel will learn not to stray
20: 9 That **w** the surrounding nations wouldn't be able to
20:14 That **w** the nations who saw me lead my people out
21: 7 LORD says: It is coming! It's on its **w**!' "
23:13 I saw the **w** she was going, defiling herself just like
23:27 In this **w**, I will put a stop to the lewdness
23:48 In this **w**, I will put an end to lewdness and idolatry
25:11 And in the same **w**, I will bring my judgment down
29: 7 When she put her weight on you, you gave **w**,
29:11 For forty years not a soul will pass that **w**,
32: 6 your gushing blood all the **w** to the mountains,
34:30 In this **w**, they will know that I, the LORD their
36:19 lands to punish them for the evil **w** they had lived.
41:10 in width, and it went all the **w** around the Temple.
42: 1 the Temple courtyard by **w** of the north gateway.
44: 7 In this **w**, you profaned my Temple even as you
44:14 and helping the people in a general **w**.
45:20 In that **w**, you will make atonement for the
46: 2 and then go back out the **w** he came.
46: 8 the foyer, and he must leave the same **w** he came.
46:12 Then he will turn and leave the **w** he entered,
46:23 with fireplaces under the ledge all the **w** around.
47:10 fishing all the **w** from En-gedi to En-eglaim.
48: 1 Dan's territory extends all the **w** across the land of
Da 4:25 periods of time will pass while you live this **w**,
4:32 periods of time will pass while you live this **w**,
4:33 He lived this **w** until his hair was as long as
5: 6 knocked together and his legs gave **w** beneath him.
6: 4 fault in the **w** Daniel was handling his affairs,
6:14 the law, and he tried to find a **w** to save Daniel.
6:14 He spent the rest of the day looking for a **w** to get
8: 4 The ram butted everything out of its **w** to the west,
10:13 prince of the kingdom of Persia blocked my **w**.
11:28 On the **w** he will set himself against the people of
11:35 In this **w**, they will be refined and cleansed
12:13 "As for you, go your **w** until the end. You will
Hos 1: 2 This will illustrate the **w** my people have been
2: 5 and became pregnant in a shameful **w**.
2: 6 I will block the road to make her lose her **w**.
14: 9 in them. But sinners stumble and fall along the **w**.
Joel 1:15 The day of the LORD is on the **w**, the day when
Am 1: 5 and slaughter its people all the **w** to the valley of
Ob 1: 3 'Who can ever reach us **w** up here?' you ask
Mic 2: 2 a certain piece of land, you find a **w** to seize it.
2: 6 like that. Such disasters will never come our **w**!"
2: 7 Should you talk that **w**, O family of Israel?
7:12 from Assyria all the **w** to the towns of Egypt,
7:12 and from Egypt all the **w** to the Euphrates River,
Hab 3:16 My legs gave **w** beneath me, and I shook in terror.
Zep 2:15 Everyone passing that **w** will laugh in derision
Zec 4: 7 a mighty mountain, will stand in Zerubbabel's **w**;
14:10 and will be inhabited all the **w** from the Benjamin
Mal 3: 1 and he will prepare the **w** before me.
Mt 2: 9 After this interview the wise men went their **w**.
2:12 it was time to leave, they went home another **w**,
3: 8 Prove by the **w** you live that you have really turned
5:16 In the same **w**, let your good deeds shine out for all
5:45 In that **w**, you will be acting as true children of
7:13 gate is wide for the many who choose the easy **w**.
7:16 You can detect them by the **w** they act, just as you
7:20 the **w** to identify a tree or a person is by the kind of
8: 4 examine you. Don't talk to anyone along the **w**.
9:17 That **w** both the wine and the wineskins are
11:10 and he will prepare your **w** before you.'
11:26 Yes, Father, it pleased you to do it this **w**!
13:49 That is the **w** it will be at the end of the world.
18:14 In the same **w**, it is not my heavenly Father's will
19:12 as eunuchs, some have been made that **w** by others,
20:17 As Jesus was on the **w** to Jerusalem, he took the
20:30 When they heard that Jesus was coming that **w**,
21:32 the Baptist came and showed you the **w** to life,
22:15 Then the Pharisees met together to think of a **w** to
22:16 You teach about the **w** of God regardless of the
24:39 That is the **w** it will be when the Son of Man
27:32 As they were on the **w**, they came across a man
28:11 As the women were on their **w** into the city,
Mk 1: 2 before you, / and he will prepare your **w**.
1:43 Then Jesus sent him on his **w** and told him sternly,
1:44 examine you. Don't talk to anyone along the **w**.
1:45 But as the man went on his **w**, he spread the news,
2:12 and pushed his **w** through the stunned onlookers.
3:23 them over and said to them by **w** of illustration,
8:26 "Don't go back into the village on your **w** home."
10:32 They were now on the **w** to Jerusalem, and Jesus
10:52 And Jesus said to him, "Go your **w**. Your faith has
11: 8 branches in the fields and spread them along the **w**.
11:13 He noticed a fig tree a little **w** off that was in full
16: 3 On the **w** they were discussing who would roll the
Lk 1:66 of the Lord is surely upon him in a special **w**."
1:76 because you will prepare the **w** for the Lord.
3: 8 Prove by the **w** you live that you have really turned
6:23 the ancient prophets were also treated that **w** by
7:27 and he will prepare your **w** before you.'
8:23 On the **w** across, Jesus lay down for a nap,
10:21 Yes, Father, it pleased you to do it this **w**.
10:38 and the disciples continued on their **w** to
12:52 of me, and two against—or the other **w** around.
12:58 If you are on the **w** to court and you meet your
13:33 and the next day I must proceed on my **w**.
15: 7 In the same **w**, heaven will be happier over one lost
15:10 In the same **w**, there is joy in the presence of God's
16: 9 In this **w**, your generosity stores up a reward for
16:16 and eager multitudes are forcing their **w** in.
17:10 In the same **w**, when you obey me you should say,
19: 1 entered Jericho and made his **w** through the town.
19:42 "I wish that even today you would find the **w** of
20:35 But that is not the **w** it will be in the age to come.
22: 4 guard to discuss the best **w** to betray Jesus to them.
24:33 And within the hour they were on their **w** back to
Jn 3:28 I am here to prepare the **w** for him—that is all.
4: 4 He had to go through Samaria on the **w**.
4:23 is looking for anyone who will worship him that **w**.
4:51 While he was on his **w**, some of his servants met
6:57 in the same **w**, those who partake of me will live
8:41 are obeying your real father when you act that **w**."
12:12 the news that Jesus was on the **w** to Jerusalem
14: 5 you are going, so how can we know the **w**?"
14: 6 Jesus told him, "I am the **w**, the truth, and the life.
15:12 I command you to love each other in the same **w**
16:32 each one going his own **w**, leaving me alone.
17: 3 And this is the **w** to have eternal life—to know
18:22 "Is that the **w** to answer the high priest?"
18:32 This fulfilled Jesus' prediction about the **w** he
Ac 1:26 and in this **w** Matthias was chosen and became an
2:28 You have shown me the **w** of life, / and you will
8:25 along the **w** to preach the Good News to them,
8:39 never saw him again but went on his **w** rejoicing.
8:40 and in every city along the **w** until he came to
9: 2 the arrest of any followers of the **W** he found there.
9:27 and told them how Saul had seen the Lord on the **w**
13: 3 laid their hands on them and sent them on their **w**.
14: 8 He had been that **w** from birth, so he had never
15: 3 and they stopped along the **w** in Phoenicia
15:10 Why are you now questioning God's **w** by
15:11 We believe that we are all saved the same **w**,
16:13 On the Sabbath we went a little **w** outside the city
17:27 perhaps feel their **w** toward him and find him—
18:25 He had been taught the **w** of the Lord and talked to
18:26 and explained the **w** of God more accurately.
19: 9 his message and publicly spoke against the **W**,
19:23 trouble developed in Ephesus concerning the **W**.
20: 2 Along the **w**, he encouraged the believers in all the
20:34 hands of mine have worked to pay my own **w**,
22: 4 And I persecuted the followers of the **W**,
23: 4 "Is that the **w** to talk to God's high priest?"
23:10 Paul from both sides, pulling him this **w** and that.
23:15 his case more fully. We will kill him on the **w**."
23:21 There are more than forty men hiding along the **w**
24:14 "But I admit that I follow the **W**, which they call a
24:22 Felix, who was quite familiar with the **W**,
24:27 Two years went by in this **w**; then Felix was
27:33 As the darkness gave **w** to the early morning light,
28:15 came to meet us at the Forum on the Appian **W**.
Ro 1:12 In this **w**, each of us will be a blessing to the other.
1:26 Even the women turned against the natural **w** to
3: 5 (That is actually the **w** some people talk.)
3:21 But now God has shown us a different **w** of being
3:21 but by the **w** promised in the Scriptures long ago.
3:22 And we all can be saved in this same **w**, no matter
3:30 and there is only one **w** of being accepted by him.
4:15 (The only **w** to avoid breaking the law is to have
6:12 Do not let sin control the **w** you live; do not give in
6:19 I speak this **w**, using the illustration of slaves
7: 6 not in the old **w** by obeying the letter of the law,
but in the new **w**, by the Spirit.
7:10 which was supposed to show me the **w** of life,
7:18 No matter which **w** I turn, I can't make myself do
10: 3 For they don't understand God's **w** of making
10: 3 they are clinging to their own **w** of getting right
10: 3 keep the law. They won't go along with God's **w**.
10: 5 For Moses wrote that the law's **w** of making a
10: 6 But the **w** of getting right with God through faith
11:14 for I want to find a **w** to make the Jews want what
11:14 and in that **w** I might save some of them.
11:31 And now, in the same **w**, the Jews are the rebels,
12: 2 into a new person by changing the **w** you think.
12:17 Do things in such a **w** that everyone can see you
14: 5 In the same **w**, some think one day is more holy
14:13 Decide instead to live in such a **w** that you will not
15:18 by my message and by the **w** I lived before them.
15:19 In this **w**, I have fully presented the Good News of
15:19 all the **w** from Jerusalem clear over into Illyricum.
15:24 for a little while, you can send me on my **w** again.
15:28 of theirs, I will come to see you on my **w** to Spain.
16: 2 Help her in every **w** you can, for she has helped
1Co 1:22 God's **w** seems foolish to the Jews because they
7:34 In the same **w**, a woman who is no longer married
9:12 obstacle in the **w** of the Good News about Christ.
9:14 In the same **w**, the Lord gave orders that those who
9:21 In this **w**, I gain their confidence and bring them to
9:24 You also must run in such a **w** that you will win.
10:13 he will show you a **w** out so that you will not give
11:16 and all the churches of God feel the same **w** about
11:25 In the same **w**, he took the cup of wine after
11:31 will not be examined by God and judged in this **w**.
12:24 So God has put the body together in such a **w** that
13: 5 or rude. Love does not demand its own **w**. Love is
14:31 In this **w**, all who prophesy will have a turn to
15: 9 apostle after the **w** I persecuted the church of God.
15:42 It is the same **w** for the resurrection of the dead.
16: 6 then you can send me on my **w** to the next
16:11 Send him on his **w** with your blessings when he
2Co 1:14 you will be proud of us in the same **w** we are proud
1:16 wanted to stop and see you on my **w** to Macedonia
1:16 Then you could send me on my **w** to Judea.
3: 6 The old **w** ends in death; in the new **w**, the Holy
Spirit gives life.
5:16 Once I mistakenly thought of Christ that **w**,
6: 3 We try to live in such a **w** that no one will be
hindered from finding the Lord by the **w** we act,
7: 9 to have, so you were not harmed by us in any **w**.
7:13 how happy Titus was at the **w** you welcomed him
7:15 ever when he remembers the **w** you listened to him
8: 8 to do it. This is one **w** to prove your love is real.
8:14 need it. In this **w**, everyone's needs will be met.
8:20 fault with the **w** we are handling this generous gift.
9:10 In the same **w**, he will give you many opportunities
10:14 for we were the first to travel all the **w** to you with
12:14 It's the other **w** around; parents supply food for
12:18 in each other's steps, doing things the same **w**.
Gal 1: 6 You are already following a different **w**
2: 6 (By the **w**, their reputation as great leaders made
3: 6 In the same **w**, "Abraham believed God, so God
3:12 How different from this **w** of faith is the **w** of
3:22 so the only **w** to receive God's promise is to
3:23 Until faith in Christ was shown to us as the **w** of
3:24 Let me put it another **w**. The law was our guardian
4: 1 Think of it this **w**. If a father dies and leaves great
4: 3 And that's the **w** it was with us before Christ came.
6: 2 and problems, and in this **w** obey the law of Christ.
Eph 2: 3 All of us used to live that **w**, following the passions
4:15 becoming more and more in every **w** like Christ,
4:22 off your old evil nature and your former **w** of life,
4:30 sorrow to God's Holy Spirit by the **w** you live.
5:28 In the same **w**, husbands ought to love their wives
5:32 but it is an illustration of the **w** Christ
6: 4 Don't make your children angry by the **w** you treat
6: 9 And in the same **w**, you masters must treat your
Php 3: 9 For God's **w** of making us right with himself
Col 1:10 Then the **w** you live will always honor and please
2:15 In this **w**, God disarmed the evil rulers
4:10 make Mark welcome if he comes your **w**.
1Th 1: 5 And you know that the **w** we lived among you was
1: 6 In this **w**, you imitated both us and the Lord.
2:12 and urged you to live your lives in a **w** that God
2:14 In this **w**, you imitated the believers in God's
4: 1 of the Lord Jesus to live in a **w** that pleases God,
4:12 people who are not Christians will respect the **w**
5:23 may the God of peace make you holy in every **w**,
2Th 2: 7 the one who is holding it back steps out of the **w**.
2:10 to fool those who are on their **w** to destruction
1Ti 1:13 down his people, harming them in every **w** I could.
2: 2 Pray this **w** for kings and all others who are in
2: 9 and not draw attention to themselves by the **w** they
3: 8 In the same **w**, deacons must be people who are
3:11 In the same **w**, their wives must be respected
4:12 in the **w** you live, in your love, your faith, and your
5:25 In the same **w**, everyone knows how much good
6: 5 the truth. To them religion is just a **w** to get rich.
2Ti 1:10 and showed us the **w** to everlasting life through the
3: 6 They are the kind who work their **w** into people's
3:17 It is God's **w** of preparing us in every **w**,
Tit 1:16 know God, but they deny him by the **w** they live.
2: 3 teach the older women to live in a **w** that is
2: 6 In the same **w**, encourage the young men to live
2:10 about God our Savior attractive in every **w**.
Phm 1:15 Perhaps you could think of it this **w**: Onesimus ran
1:18 If he has harmed you in any **w** or stolen anything
Heb 2:15 Only in this **w** could he deliver those who have
5: 9 In this **w**, God qualified him as a perfect High
9:21 And in the same **w**, he sprinkled blood on the
10:20 life-giving **w** that Christ has opened up for us

11:12 sand on the seashore, there is no **w** to count them.
11:15 came from, they would have found a **w** to go back.
12:11 of right living for those who are trained in this **w**.
Jas 1: 2 and sisters, whenever trouble comes your **w**,
3: 2 can also control themselves in every other **w**.
1Pe 3: 1 In the same **w**, you wives must accept the authority
3: 5 That is the **w** the holy women of old made
3: 7 In the same **w**, you husbands must give honor to
3:16 But you must do this in a gentle and respectful **w**.
2Pe 2: 2 of them, Christ and his true **w** will be slandered.
2: 3 them long ago, and their destruction is on the **w**.
2:15 and followed the **w** of Balaam son of Beor,
2:21 had never known the right **w** to live than to know it
1Jn 2: 5 That is the **w** to know whether or not we live in
4: 2 This is the **w** to find out if they have the Spirit of
5:16 If you see any Christian sinning in a **w** that does
2Jn 1:10 him into your house or encourage him in any **w**.
3Jn 1: 6 You do well to send them on their **w** in a manner
Jude 1: 4 because some godless people have wormed their **w**
1:12 They are shameless in the **w** they care only about
1:18 is to enjoy themselves in every evil **w** imaginable.
1:21 Live in such a **w** that God's love can bless you as
Rev 2:15 In the same **w**, you have some Nicolaitans among

WAYFARING [KJV] See GUEST, TRAVELER(S), TRAVELS

WAYLAY (1)

Ac 25: 3 to Jerusalem. (Their plan was to **w** and kill him.)

WAYMARKS [KJV] See GUIDEPOSTS, (ROAD) SIGNS

WAYS (131) [WAY]

EVIL WAYS (19) Ex 34:12; 1Ki 13:33; 2Ki 17:13,22; Isa 23:17; Jer 7:3; 15:7; 17:1; 18:8,11; 23:22; 26:3; 36:7; Hos 7:8,12; Jnh 3:8,10; Zec 1:4; Lk 13:3

Ex 21:11 If he fails in any of these three **w**, she may leave as
30:20 must always wash before ministering in these **w**,
34:12 If you do, you soon will be following their evil **w**.
Lev 5: 5 become aware of their guilt in any of these **w**,
6: 4 If they have sinned in any of these **w** and are
18:24 "Do not defile yourselves in any of these **w**,
Nu 15:39 following your own desires and going your own **w**,
Dt 8: 6 of the LORD your God by walking in his **w**
11:22 love to the LORD your God by walking in his **w**
19: 9 love the LORD your God and walk in his **w**.)
26:17 and regulations by walking in his **w** and doing
28: 9 of the LORD your God and walk in his **w**,
30:16 laws, and regulations by walking in his **w**.
Jos 22: 5 walk in all his **w**, obey his commands, be faithful
Jdg 2:19 judge died, the people returned to their corrupt **w**,
2:19 to give up their evil practices and stubborn **w**.
2Sa 22:22 For I have kept the **w** of the LORD; / I have not
1Ki 1:49 banquet table and quickly went their separate **w**.
2: 3 of the LORD your God and follow all his **w**.
8:40 and walk in your **w** as long as they live in the land
11:33 He has not followed my **w** and done what is
11:38 If you listen to what I tell you and follow my **w**
13:33 after this, Jeroboam did not turn from his evil **w**.
2Ki 17:13 both Israel and Judah: "Turn from all your evil **w**.
17:22 And the people of Israel persisted in all the evil **w**
17:40 not listen and continued to follow their old **w**.
21:22 and he refused to follow the LORD's **w**.
1Ch 23:28 and served in many other **w** in the house of God.
2Ch 6:31 and walk in your **w** as long as they live in the land
7:14 and seek my face and turn from their wicked **w**,
17: 6 He was committed to the **w** of the LORD.
20:32 a good king, following the **w** of his father, Asa.
27: 2 the people continued in their corrupt **w**.
Job 21:14 We want no part of you and your **w**.
23:11 I have followed his **w** and not turned aside.
24:13 They refuse to acknowledge its **w**. They will not
34:11 their deeds. He treats people according to their **w**.
34:27 They have no respect for any of his **w**.
Ps 17: 7 Show me your unfailing love in wonderful **w**.
18:21 For I have kept the **w** of the LORD; / I have not
51:13 Then I will teach your **w** to sinners, / and they will
55:19 For my enemies refuse to change their **w**;
56: 5 they spend their days plotting **w** to harm me.
67: 2 May your **w** be known throughout the earth,
68:21 the skulls of those who love their guilty **w**.
77:13 O God, your **w** are holy. / Is there any god as
85: 8 But let them not return to their foolish **w**.
86:11 Teach me your **w**, O LORD, / that I may live
89:30 his sons forsake my law / and fail to walk in my **w**,
119:15 study your commandments / and reflect on your **w**.
119:39 Help me abandon my shameful **w**; / your laws are
125: 5 But banish those who turn to crooked **w**,
128: 1 who fear the LORD— / all who follow his **w**!
138: 5 Yes, they will sing about the LORD's **w**,
Pr 2:13 These people turn from right **w** to walk down dark
2:15 What they do is crooked, and their **w** are wrong.
3:17 you down delightful paths; all her **w** are satisfying.
3:31 Do not envy violent people; don't copy their **w**.
4:11 I will teach you wisdom's **w** and lead you in
6: 6 you lazybones. Learn from their **w** and be wise!
8:32 listen to me, for happy are all who follow my **w**.
9: 6 Leave your foolish **w** behind, and begin to live;
16: 7 When the **w** of people please the LORD,
23:26 May your eyes delight in my **w** of wisdom.
Ecc 3:18 that God allows people to continue in their sinful **w**
7:13 Don't fight the **w** of God, for who can straighten
11: 5 God's **w** are as hard to discern as the pathways of
Isa 1:16 longer see your evil deeds. Give up your wicked **w**.
2: 3 There he will teach us his **w**, so that we may obey
23:17 She will return again to all her evil **w** around the
35: 8 It will be only for those who walk in God's **w**;
45:15 our Savior, you work in strange and mysterious **w**.
55: 8 "And my **w** are far beyond anything you could
55: 9 so are my **w** higher than your **w** and my
64: 5 who cheerfully do good, who follow godly **w**.
66: 3 But those who choose their own **w**, delighting in
Jer 3:21 LORD their God and wandered far from his **w**.
5: 4 They don't know the **w** of the LORD.
5: 5 Surely they will know the LORD's **w** and what
7: 3 Even now, if you quit your evil **w**, I will let you
10: 3 Their **w** are futile and foolish. They cut down a
12:16 And if these nations quickly learn the **w** of my
15: 7 they refuse to turn back to me from all their evil **w**.
17: 1 "My people act as though their evil **w** are laws to
18: 8 but then that nation renounces its evil **w**, I will not
18:11 So turn from your evil **w**, each of you, and do
23:22 my words and turned my people from their evil **w**.
26: 3 Perhaps they will listen and turn from their evil **w**.
35:15 prophet to tell you to turn from your wicked **w**
36: 7 Perhaps even yet they will turn from their evil **w**
44: 5 would not listen or turn back from their wicked **w**.
La 3:40 Instead, let us test and examine our **w**. Let us turn
Eze 18:23 I only want them to turn from their wicked **w**
18:24 if righteous people turn to sinful **w** and start acting
33: 8 and you fail to warn them about changing their **w**,
33:11 I only want them to turn from their wicked **w**
Hos 7: 8 with godless foreigners, picking up their evil **w**.
7:12 from the sky. I will punish them for all their evil **w**.
12: 2 He is about to punish Jacob for all his deceitful **w**.
Jnh 3: 8 Everyone must turn from their evil **w** and stop all
3:10 God saw that they had put a stop to their evil **w**,
Mic 4: 2 There he will teach us his **w**, so that we may obey
Zec 1: 4 Turn from your evil **w** and stop all your evil
3: 7 If you follow my **w** and obey my requirements,
Mk 12:14 You sincerely teach the **w** of God. Now tell us—
Lk 13: 3 will also perish unless you turn from your evil **w**
20:21 others think. You sincerely teach the **w** of God.
Ac 1: 3 and proved to them in many **w** that he was actually
3:26 by turning each of you back from your sinful **w**."
5:36 was killed, and his followers went their various **w**.
13:10 will you never stop perverting the true **w** of the
14:16 days he permitted all the nations to go their own **w**,
18:13 to worship God in **w** that are contrary to the law."
Ro 1:30 They are forever inventing new **w** of sinning
2:20 the ignorant and teach children the **w** of God.
13:14 and don't think of **w** to indulge your evil desires.
1Co 5:12 those inside the church who are sinning in these **w**.
12: 6 There are different **w** God works in our lives,
2Co 7: 9 caused you to have remorse and change your **w**.
8: 7 Since you excel in so many **w**—you have so much
13:11 Rejoice. Change your **w**. Encourage each other.
Eph 4:19 they have given themselves over to immoral **w**.
1Th 4: 5 the pagans do, in their ignorance of God and his **w**.
Heb 1: 1 and in many **w** to our ancestors through the
10:24 Think of **w** to encourage one another to outbursts
Jas 3:13 If you are wise and understand God's **w**, live a life
1Pe 1:14 Don't slip back into your old **w** of doing evil;
2Pe 2:20 And when people escape from the wicked **w** of the
Rev 15: 3 Lord God Almighty. / Just and true are your **w**,
16: 1 "Now go your **w** and empty out the seven bowls

WAYSIDE [KJV] See (ALONG THE) WAY, (BESIDE THE) ROAD

WAYWARD (6)

Pr 7:25 away toward her. Don't wander down her **w** path.
Jer 3:14 "Return home, you **w** children," says the LORD,
3:22 "My **w** children," says the LORD, "come back to me, and I will heal your **w** hearts."
31:22 How long will you wander, my **w** daughter?
Heb 5: 2 with the people, though they are ignorant and **w**.

WE (2351) [OUR, OURS, OURSELVES, US, WE'D, WE'LL, WE'RE, WE'VE] See Index of Articles, Etc.

WE'D (1) [BE, WE] See Index of Articles, Etc.

WE'LL (21) [BE, WE] See Index of Articles, Etc.

WE'RE (11) [BE, WE] See Index of Articles, Etc.

WE'VE (16) [HAVE, WE] See Index of Articles, Etc.

WEAK (66) [WEAKEN, WEAKENED, WEAKENS, WEAKER, WEAKEST, WEAKLINGS, WEAKNESS, WEAKNESSES]

Nu 13:18 out whether the people living there are strong or **w**,
Jdg 16: 7 not yet been dried, I will be as **w** as anyone else."
16:11 never been used, I will be as **w** as anyone else."
16:13 the loom shuttle, I will be as **w** as anyone else."
16:17 and I would become as **w** as anyone else."
1Sa 2: 4 no more; / and those who were **w** are now strong.
2Sa 21:15 the thick of battle, David became **w** and exhausted.
2Ch 28:15 They put those who were **w** on donkeys and took
Job 4: 3 in God; you have supported those who were **w**.
Ps 6: 2 Have compassion on me, LORD, for I am **w**.
32: 3 refused to confess my sin, / I was **w** and miserable,
35:10 Who else rescues the **w** and helpless from the
72:13 He feels pity for the **w** and the needy, / and he will
73:26 My health may fail, and my spirit may grow **w**,
103:14 For he understands how **w** we are; / he knows we
109:24 My knees are **w** from fasting, / and I am skin
Ecc 12: 3 with age, and your strong legs will grow **w**.
Isa 14:10 they all cry out, 'Now you are as **w** as we are!
19:16 In that day the Egyptians will be as **w** as women.
35: 3 and encourage those who have **w** knees.
40:29 are tired and worn out; he offers strength to the **w**.
42: 3 He will not crush those who are **w** or quench the
44:12 work makes him hungry and thirsty, **w** and faint.
50: 2 Was I too **w** to save you? Is that why the house is
59: 1 The LORD is not too **w** to save you, and he is not
Jer 6:24 reports about the enemy, and we are **w** with fright.
50:37 her allies from other lands will become as **w** as
50:43 reports about the enemy, and he is **w** with fright.
La 1: 6 for pasture, too **w** to run from the pursuing enemy.
Eze 7:17 will be feeble; their knees will be as **w** as water.
21: 7 knees will tremble and become as **w** as water.
34: 4 You have not taken care of the **w**. You have not
34:16 I will bind up the injured and strengthen the **w**.
Da 2:42 it will be as strong as iron, and others as **w** as clay.
10: 8 my face grew deathly pale, and I felt very **w**.
10:16 the vision I have seen, my lord, and I am very **w**.
Hos 7: 9 unaware of how **w** and old he has become.
Am 2:14 The strongest among you will become **w**.
Mic 4: 7 They are **w** and far from home, but I will make
Na 3:13 Your troops will be as **w** and helpless as women.
Zep 3:19 I will save the **w** and helpless ones; I will bring
Mt 11: 7 Did you find him **w** as a reed, moved by every
12:20 He will not crush those who are **w**, / or quench the
26:41 the spirit is willing enough, the body is **w**!"
Mk 14:38 though the spirit is willing enough, the body is **w**."
Lk 7:24 Did you find him **w** as a reed, moved by every
Ro 14: 1 Accept Christians who are **w** in faith, and don't
1Co 4:10 so wise! We are **w**, but you are so powerful!
8: 7 of real gods, and their **w** consciences are violated.
8:10 **W** Christians who think it is wrong to eat this food
8:11 a **w** Christian, for whom Christ died, will be
11:30 That is why many of you are **w** and sick and some
15:43 They are **w** now, but when they are raised,
2Co 4: 7 in perishable containers, that is, in our **w** bodies.
10:10 are demanding and forceful, but in person he is **w**,
11:29 Who is **w** without my feeling that weakness?
11:30 boast about the things that show how **w** I am.
12:10 and calamities. For when I am **w**, then I am strong.
13: 3 Christ is not **w** in his dealings with you; he is a
13: 4 We, too, are **w**, but we live in him and have God's
13: 9 We are glad to be **w**, if you are really strong.
Gal 4: 9 back again and become slaves once more to the **w**
Php 3:21 He will take these **w** mortal bodies of ours
1Th 5:14 Take tender care of those who are **w**. Be patient
Heb 7:18 was set aside because it was **w** and useless.
12:13 though they are **w** and lame, will not stumble

WEAKEN (1) [WEAK]

Ro 4:19 And Abraham's faith did not **w**, even though he

WEAKENED (1) [WEAK]

Job 15:12 has captured your reason? What has **w** your vision,

WEAKENS (1) [WEAK]

Hos 5:12 I will sap Judah's strength as dry rot **w** wood.

WEAKER (13) [WEAK]

Ge 30:42 But he didn't do this with the **w** ones,
30:42 so the **w** lambs belonged to Laban,
Dt 28:43 and stronger, while you become **w** and **w**.
2Sa 3: 1 while Saul's dynasty became **w** and **w**.
Ps 68:30 the reeds, / this herd of bulls among the **w** calves.
69:23 and let their bodies grow **w** and **w**.
Ro 11:10 and let their backs grow **w** and **w**."
1Co 8: 9 a brother or sister with a **w** conscience to stumble.
1Pe 3: 7 She may be **w** than you are, but she is your equal

WEAKEST (8) [WEAK]

Jdg 6:15 My clan is the **w** in the whole tribe of Manasseh,
2Sa 22:19 They attacked me at a moment when I was **w**,
2Ki 18:24 how can you think of challenging even the **w**
1Ch 12:14 The **w** among them could take on a hundred
Ps 18:18 They attacked me at a moment when I was **w**,
Isa 36: 9 how can you think of challenging even the **w**
Zec 12: 8 the **w** among them will be as mighty as King
1Co 12:22 some of the parts that seem **w** and least important

WEAKLINGS (1) [WEAK]

Joel 3:10 into spears. Train even your **w** to be warriors.

WEAKNESS (8) [WEAK]

Ps 136:23 He remembered our utter **w**. / His faithful love
1Co 1:25 and God's **w** is far stronger than the greatest of
2: 3 I came to you in **w**—timid and trembling.
2Co 11:29 Who is weak without my feeling that **w**? Who is
12: 9 is all you need. My power works best in your **w**."
13: 4 Although he died on the cross in **w**, he now lives
Heb 7:28 under the law of Moses were limited by human **w**.
11:34 Their **w** was turned to strength. They became

WEAKNESSES (6) [WEAK]

Isa 53: 4 Yet it was our **w** he carried; it was our sorrows that
2Co 12: 5 to do it. I am going to boast only about my **w**.
12: 9 So now I am glad to boast about my **w**, so that the
12:10 I am quite content with my **w** and with insults,

Heb 4:15 This High Priest of ours understands our **w**, for he
5: 2 For he is subject to the same **w** they have.

WEALTH (113) [WEALTHY]

Ge 12: 5 his wife, Sarai, his nephew Lot, and all his **w**—
14:11 journey home, taking all the **w** and food with them.
15: 2 a servant in my household, will inherit all my **w**.
15:14 and in the end they will come away with great **w**.
26:13 a rich man, and his **w** only continued to grow.
30:30 I came, and your **w** has increased enormously.
31: 1 "All his **w** has been gained at our father's
31:14 none of our father's **w** will come to us anyway.
34:29 all the women and children and **w** of every kind.
36: 6 all the **w** he had gained in the land of Canaan—
Nu 31: 9 their cattle and flocks and all their **w** as plunder.
Dt 17:17 And he must not accumulate vast amounts of **w** in
Jos 22: 8 "Share with your relatives back home the great **w**
2Ki 23:35 requiring them to pay in proportion to their **w**.
1Ch 29:25 and he gave Solomon even greater **w** and honor
29:28 old age, having enjoyed long life, **w**, and honor.
2Ch 1:11 and you did not ask for personal **w** and honor
1:12 And I will also give you riches, **w**, and honor such
32:29 and herds, for God had given him great **w**.
Est 1: 4 a tremendous display of the opulent **w** and glory of
5:11 and boasted to them about his great **w** and his
Job 5: 5 and their **w** satisfies the thirst of many others,
6:22 Have I begged you to use any of your **w** on my
15:29 Their **w** will not endure, and their possessions will
20:10 the poor, for he must give back his ill-gotten **w**.
20:15 He will vomit the **w** he swallowed. God won't let
20:18 will not be rewarded. His **w** will bring him no joy.
27:19 but wake up to find that all their **w** is gone.
31:25 Does my happiness depend on my **w** and all that I
36:18 But watch out, or you may be seduced with **w**.
36:19 Could all your **w** and mighty efforts keep you from
Ps 39: 6 We heap up **w** for someone else to spend.
45:12 People of great **w** will entreat your favor.
49: 6 They trust in their **w** / and boast of great riches.
49:10 and senseless, / leaving all their **w** behind.
49:11 after themselves, / but they leave their **w** to others.
49:17 Their **w** will not follow them into the grave.
49:20 People who boast of their **w** don't understand
52: 7 They trust their **w** instead / and grow more
62:10 by extortion or robbery. / And if your **w** increases,
Pr 3: 9 Honor the LORD with your **w** and with the best
5:10 Strangers will obtain your **w**, and someone else
8:18 Unending riches, honor, **w**, and justice are mine to
8:21 Those who love me inherit **w**, for I fill their
10:15 The **w** of the rich is their fortress; the poverty of
11:16 Beautiful women obtain **w**, and violent men get
13:11 **W** from get-rich-quick schemes quickly
disappears; **w** from hard work grows.
13:22 but the sinner's **w** passes to the godly.
14:24 **W** is a crown for the wise; the effort of fools yields
18:11 The rich think of their **w** as an impregnable
19: 4 **W** makes many "friends"; poverty drives them
19:14 their sons with an inheritance of houses and **w**,
21: 6 **W** created by lying is a vanishing mist and a
21:20 The wise have **w** and luxury, but fools spend
29: 3 he hangs around with prostitutes, his **w** is wasted.
Ecc 2:26 God takes the **w** away and gives it to those who
4: 8 yet who works hard to gain as much **w** as he can.
5:10 How absurd to think that **w** brings true happiness!
5:11 So what is the advantage of **w**—except perhaps to
5:15 People who live only for **w** come to the end of
5:19 And it is a good thing to receive **w** from God
6: 2 God gives great **w** and honor to some people
Isa 23:18 Her **w** will not be hoarded but will be used to
60: 5 to you. They will bring you the **w** of many lands.
60: 9 They will bring their **w** with them, and it will bring
60:11 around the clock to receive the **w** of many lands.
66:12 "The **w** of the nations will flow to her.
Jer 15:13 I will hand over their **w** and treasures as plunder to
17: 3 So I will give all your **w** and treasures—
17:11 so are those who get their **w** by unjust means.
48: 7 Because you have trusted in your **w** and skill,
48:36 and Kir-hareseth, for all their **w** has disappeared.
49: 4 you trusted in your **w** and thought no one could
Eze 7:11 will survive. All their **w** will be swept away.
7:20 That is why I will make all their **w** disgusting to
22:25 innocent people, seizing treasures and extorting **w**.
28: 4 and understanding you have amassed great **w**—
28:16 Your great **w** filled you with violence, and you
29:19 He will carry off their **w**, plundering everything
30: 4 Their **w** will be carried away and their foundations
Da 11: 2 Using his **w** for political advantage, he will stir up
11:24 among his followers the plunder and **w** of the rich.
Hos 5: 7 false religion will devour them, along with their **w**.
10: 1 But the more **w** the people got, the more they
Am 3:10 "Their fortresses are filled with **w** taken by theft
Ob 1:11 to help when foreign invaders carried off their **w**
Mic 4:13 Then you will give all the **w** they acquired as
Na 2: 9 Nineveh's many treasures—its vast, uncounted **w**.
2:10 the city is an empty shambles, stripped of its **w**.
3: 1 and lies! She is crammed with **w** to be plundered.
3:16 as the stars, have filled your city with vast **w**.
Hab 2: 5 **W** is treacherous, and the arrogant are never at
2: 9 You believe your **w** will buy security, putting your
2:13 Has not the LORD Almighty promised that the **w**
Zec 11: 3 to the wailing of the shepherds, for their **w** is gone.
14:14 The **w** of all the neighboring nations will be
Mt 13:22 out by the cares of this life and the lure of **w**,
Mk 4:19 the lure of **w**, and the desire for nice things, so no
Lk 12:21 a person is a fool to store up earthly **w** but not have
15:12 So his father agreed to divide his **w** between his
16:11 And if you are untrustworthy about worldly **w**,
19: 8 the Lord, "I will give half my **w** to the poor, Lord,
Ac 16:19 Her masters' hopes of **w** were now shattered,
19:25 you know that our **w** comes from this business.
1Co 7:30 or **w** should not keep anyone from doing God's
Gal 4: 1 and leaves great **w** for his young children,
Eph 2: 7 to us as examples of the incredible **w** of his favor
1Ti 6: 6 Yet true religion with contentment is great **w**.
Jas 5: 2 Your **w** is rotting away, and your fine clothes are
5: 3 The very **w** you were counting on will eat away
Rev 18:17 And in one single moment all the **w** of the city is
18:19 great city! She made us all rich from her great **w**.

WEALTHY (27) [WEALTH]

Ge 13: 5 was also very **w** with sheep, cattle, and many tents.
30:43 and he became very **w**, with many servants,
31: 9 God has made me **w** at your father's expense.
Dt 8:17 your own strength and energy that made you **w**.
Jdg 18: 7 The people were also **w** because their land was
Ru 2: 1 Now there was a **w** and influential man in
1Sa 25: 2 There was a **w** man from Maon who owned
2Sa 19:32 He was very old, about eighty, and very **w**. He was
2Ki 4: 8 A **w** woman lived there, and she invited him to eat
1Ch 4:38 names of some of the leaders of Simeon's **w** clans,
2Ch 17: 5 so he became very **w** and highly esteemed.
32:27 Hezekiah was very **w** and held in high esteem.
Job 3:15 I would rest with **w** princes whose palaces were
21: 7 live to a good old age. They grow old and **w**.
Ps 112: 3 They themselves will be **w**, / and their good deeds
Pr 11:24 It is possible to give freely and become more **w**,
Ecc 2:26 But if a sinner becomes **w**, God takes the wealth
9:11 often poor, and the skillful are not necessarily **w**.
Isa 32: 5 **W** cheaters will not be respected as outstanding
Eze 26: 2 Because she has been destroyed, I will become **w**!'
Am 3:15 And I will destroy the beautiful homes of the **w**—
Mic 6:12 The rich among you have become **w** through
1Co 1:26 or powerful, or **w** when God called you.
2Ti 2:20 In a **w** home some utensils are made of gold
Jas 1:11 **w** people will fade away with all of their
Rev 6:15 of the earth, the rulers, the generals, the **w** people,
18:15 The merchants who became **w** by selling her these

WEANED (4)

Ge 21: 8 As time went by and Isaac grew and was **w**,
1Sa 1:22 She told her husband, "Wait until the baby is **w**.
1:24 When the child was **w**, Hannah took him to the
Hos 1: 8 After Gomer had **w** Lo-ruhamah, she again became

WEAPON (8) [WEAPONS]

Nu 35:18 and kills another person with a wooden **w**.
1Sa 21: 8 urgent that I didn't even have time to grab a **w**!"
1Ch 12:37 were 120,000 troops armed with every kind of **w**.
Ne 4:17 supporting their load and one hand holding a **w**.
Pr 26:18 as damaging as a mad man shooting a lethal **w**
Isa 54:17 coming day, no **w** turned against you will succeed.
Joel 2: 8 lunge through the gaps, and no **w** can stop them.
2Co 6: 7 We have righteousness as our **w**, both to attack

WEAPONS (48) [WEAPON]

Lev 26: 8 enemies will fall beneath the blows of your **w**.
26:33 among the nations and attack you with my own **w**.
Dt 1:41 So your men strapped on their **w**, thinking it would
1Sa 8:12 while others will make his **w** and chariot
17:47 the LORD does not need **w** to rescue his people.
2Sa 1:27 have fallen! / Stripped of their **w**, they lie dead.
2:21 one of the younger men and strip him of his **w**."
1Ki 10:25 gifts of silver and gold, clothing, **w**, spices, horses,
2Ki 10: 2 disposal chariots, horses, a fortified city, and **w**.
11: 8 a bodyguard for the king and keep your **w** in hand.
11:11 themselves around the king, with their **w** ready.
2Ch 9:24 gifts of silver and gold, clothing, **w**, spices, horses,
23: 7 a bodyguard for the king and keep your **w** in hand.
23:10 the guards around the king, with their **w** ready.
32: 5 and manufactured large numbers of **w** and shields.
Ne 4:23 We carried our **w** with us at all times, even when
Job 12:21 upon princes and confiscates **w** from the strong.
Ps 7:13 He will prepare his deadly **w** / and ignite his
20: 7 Some nations boast of their armies and **w**, / but we
58: 7 Make their **w** useless in their hands.
76: 3 the shields and swords and **w** of his foes.
Ecc 9:18 A wise person can overcome **w** of war, but one
Isa 13: 5 They are the LORD's **w**; they carry his anger
22: 8 stripped away. You run to the armory for your **w**.
54:16 beneath the forge and makes the **w** of destruction.
Jer 5:16 Their **w** are deadly; their warriors are mighty.
21: 4 I will make your **w** useless against the king of
33: 4 the walls against the siege **w** of the enemy,
50:25 and brought out **w** to vent his fury against his
51:56 men are captured, and their **w** break in their hands.
Eze 9: 1 the city! Tell them to bring their **w** with them!"
32:27 who went down to the grave with their **w**—
38: 5 and Libya will join you, too, with all their **w**.
39: 3 I will knock your **w** from your hands and leave you
39:10 or forests, for these **w** will give them all they need.
Hos 1: 7 them from their enemies without any help from **w**
2:18 I will remove all **w** of war from the land,
Am 2:16 courageous of your fighting men will drop their **w**
Mic 5:10 says the LORD, "I will destroy all your **w**—
Hab 3: 9 You were commanding your **w** of power! You split
3:14 With their own **w**, you destroyed those who rushed
Zec 9:10 and I will destroy all the **w** used in battle.
Lk 11:22 and overpowers him, strips him of his **w**,
Jn 18: 3 Now with blazing torches, lanterns, and **w**,
2Co 10: 4 We use God's mighty **w**, not mere worldly **w**,
10: 5 With these **w** we break down every proud
10: 5 With these **w** we conquer their rebellious ideas,

WEAR (70) [WEARING, WEARS, WORE, WORN, WORN-OUT]

Ex 1:11 hoping to **w** them down under heavy burdens.
12:11 "**W** your traveling clothes as you eat this meal,
12:11 **W** your sandals, and carry your walking sticks in
18:18 "You're going to **w** yourself out—and the people,
28: 4 sons to **w** when they serve as priests before me.
28:35 Aaron will **w** this robe whenever he enters the
28:38 Aaron will **w** it on his forehead, thus bearing the
28:38 He must always **w** it so the LORD will accept the
29:30 Whoever is the next high priest after Aaron will **w**
31:10 and the garments for his sons to **w** as they minister
33: 4 and refused to **w** their jewelry and ornaments.
35:19 the beautifully stitched clothing for the priests to **w**
35:19 and his sons to **w** while officiating as priests."
39:41 the priest and for his sons to **w** while on duty.
Lev 19:19 Do not **w** clothing woven from two different kinds
21:10 and has been ordained to **w** the special priestly
Dt 6: 8 hands as a reminder, and **w** them on your forehead.
8: 4 For all these forty years your clothes didn't **w** out,
11:18 hands as a reminder, and **w** them on your forehead.
22: 5 "A woman must not **w** men's clothing, and a man
must not **w** women's clothing.
22:11 "Do not **w** clothing made of wool and linen woven
29: 5 yet your clothes and sandals did not **w** out.
1Sa 2:28 and to **w** the priestly garments as he served me.
2Sa 14: 2 **w** mourning clothes and don't bathe or **w** any
perfume.
1Ki 22:30 will recognize me, but you **w** your royal robes."
2Ch 18:29 will recognize me, but you **w** your royal robes."
28:15 They provided clothing and sandals to **w**,
Ne 9:21 Their clothes did not **w** out, and their feet did not
Job 27:17 But the righteous will **w** that clothing,
Ps 73: 6 They **w** pride like a jeweled necklace, / and their
102:26 remain forever; / they will **w** out like old clothing.
Pr 3: 3 **W** them like a necklace; write them deep within
25:17 too often, or you will **w** out your welcome.
Ecc 9: 8 **W** fine clothes, with a dash of cologne!
Isa 3:24 They will **w** ropes for sashes, and their well-set
3:24 They will **w** rough sackcloth instead of rich robes.
15: 3 They will **w** sackcloth as they wander the streets.
22:12 and to **w** clothes of sackcloth to show your
32:11 your pretty clothes, and **w** sackcloth in your grief.
51: 6 and the earth will **w** out like a piece of clothing.
Jer 9: 5 they **w** themselves out with all their sinning.
Eze 34: 3 You drink the milk, **w** the wool, and butcher the
44:17 inner courtyard, they must **w** only linen clothing.
44:17 They must **w** no wool while on duty in the inner
44:18 They must **w** linen turbans and linen
44:18 They must not **w** anything that would cause them
44:19 they must take off the clothes they **w** while
Da 5: 7 and will **w** a gold chain around his neck.
5:16 and you will **w** a gold chain around your neck.
7:25 and **w** down the holy people of the Most High.
Am 8:10 You will **w** funeral clothes and shave your heads as
Jnh 3: 5 without food and **w** sackcloth to show their sorrow.
3: 8 Everyone is required to **w** sackcloth and pray
Hag 1: 6 You have clothing to **w**, but not enough to keep
Zec 13: 4 No one will **w** prophet's clothes to try to fool the
Mt 23: 5 On their arms they **w** extra wide prayer boxes with
23: 5 and they **w** extra long tassels on their robes.
Mk 6: 9 He told them to **w** sandals but not to take even an
Lk 7:25 people who **w** beautiful clothes and live in luxury
12:22 you have enough food to eat or clothes to **w**.
1Co 11: 6 Yes, if she refuses to **w** a head covering,
11: 6 or her head shaved, then she should **w** a covering.
11: 7 A man should not **w** anything on his head when
11:10 So a woman should **w** a covering on her head as a
Col 3:14 important piece of clothing you must **w** is love.
1Ti 2: 9 They should **w** decent and appropriate clothing
Heb 1:11 remain forever. / They will **w** out like old clothing.
Rev 19: 8 She is permitted to **w** the finest white linen."

WEARIED (7) [WEARY]

Isa 43:23 and **w** you with my requests for grain offerings
43:24 me with your sins and **w** me with your faults.
Mal 2:17 You have **w** the LORD with your words.
2:17 "**W** him?" you ask. "How have we **w** him?"
2:17 You have **w** him by suggesting that the LORD
2:17 You have **w** him by asking, "Where is the God of

WEARILY (2) [WEARY]

Jn 4: 6 long walk, sat **w** beside the well about noontime.
1Co 4:12 We have worked **w** with our own hands to earn our

WEARINESS (1) [WEARY]

2Co 11:27 I have lived with **w** and pain and sleepless nights.

WEARING (22) [WEAR]

Ge 25:25 so much hair that one would think he was **w** a
1Sa 14: 3 was Ahijah the priest, who was **w** the linen ephod.
14:18 For at that time Ahijah was **w** the ephod in front of
22:18 priests in all, all still **w** their priestly tunics.
28: 8 So Saul disguised himself by **w** ordinary clothing
2Sa 6:14 the LORD with all his might, **w** a priestly tunic.
13:18 She was **w** a long, beautiful robe, as was the
20: 8 Joab was **w** his uniform with a dagger strapped to
1Ki 11:29 from Shiloh met him on the road, **w** a new cloak.
11:30 and Ahijah took the new cloak he was **w** and tore it
20:31 So let's humble ourselves by **w** sackcloth
2Ki 6:30 the people could see that he was **w** sackcloth
1Ch 15:27 the song leader. David was also **w** a priestly tunic.
Est 4: 2 for no one was allowed to enter while **w** clothes of
Ps 45: 9 the queen, / **w** jewelry of finest gold from Ophir!

Jer 13: 4 "Take the linen belt you are **w**, and go to the
Mt 22:11 he noticed a man who wasn't **w** the proper clothes
Lk 18: 5 because she is **w** me out with her constant
Jn 19: 5 Then Jesus came out **w** the crown of thorns
1Th 5: 8 and **w** as our helmet the confidence of our
1Ti 2: 9 or by **w** gold or pearls or expensive clothes.
Rev 1:13 He was **w** a long robe with a gold sash across his

WEARS (4) [WEAR]

Ex 28:35 the LORD's presence. If he **w** it, he will not die.
2Ki 10:22 "Be sure that every worshiper of Baal **w** one of
Job 14:19 as water **w** away the stones and floods wash away
SS 3: 8 Each one **w** a sword on his thigh, ready to defend

WEARY (32) [WEARIED, WEARILY, WEARINESS]

Dt 25:18 attacked you when you were exhausted and **w**,
1Sa 14:28 be cursed. That is why everyone is **w** and faint."
2Sa 16:14 and all who were with him grew **w** along the way,
17: 2 I will catch up to him while he is **w**
Job 3:17 wicked cease from troubling, and the **w** are at rest.
3:20 "Oh, why should light be given to the **w**, and life
7: 3 months of futility, long and **w** nights of misery.
30:17 My **w** nights are filled with pain as though
Ps 57: 6 have set a trap for me. / I am **w** from distress.
63: 1 in this parched and **w** land / where there is no
68: 9 O God, / to refresh the **w** Promised Land.
Pr 23: 4 Don't **w** yourself trying to get rich. Why waste
30: 1 I am **w**, O God; I am **w** and worn out, O God.
Ecc 1: 8 Everything is so **w** and tiresome! No matter how
Isa 8:21 people will be led away as captives, **w** and hungry.
21:14 of Tema, bring food and water to these **w** refugees.
32: 2 cool shadow of a large rock in a hot and **w** land.
40:28 Creator of all the earth? He never grows faint or **w**.
40:31 They will run and not grow **w**. They will walk
50: 4 so that I know what to say to all these **w** ones.
57:10 You grew **w** in your search, but you never gave up.
Jer 6:11 Yes, I am **w** of holding it in! "I will pour out my
20: 9 It's like a fire in my bones! I am **w** of holding it in!
31:25 For I have given rest to the **w** and joy to the
45: 3 I am **w** of my own sighing and can find no rest.'
La 5:17 Our hearts are sick and **w**, and our eyes grow dim
Am 8:13 and fine young men will grow faint and **w**,
Mt 11:28 all of you who are **w** and carry heavy burdens,
2Co 5: 2 We grow **w** in our present bodies, and we long for
11:26 I have traveled many **w** miles. I have faced danger
Heb 12: 3 to him, so that you don't become **w** and give up.

WEATHER (9) [WEATHERED]

Job 6:17 But when the hot **w** arrives, the water disappears.
Ps 148: 8 snow and storm, / wind and **w** that obey him,
Pr 25:20 is as bad as stealing someone's jacket in cold **w**
Zep 2:14 the cedar paneling will lie open to the wind and **w**.
Mt 16: 2 'Red sky at night means fair **w** tomorrow,
16: 3 red sky in the morning means foul **w** all day.'
16: 3 You are good at reading the **w** signs in the sky,
Ac 27: 9 The **w** was becoming dangerous for long voyages
27:14 But the **w** changed abruptly, and a wind of typhoon

WEATHERED (1) [WEATHER]

Jos 9: 4 loading their donkeys with **w** saddlebags and old

WEAVE (4) [INTERWOVEN, WEAVER, WEAVER'S, WEAVERS, WEAVING, WOVE, WOVEN]

Ex 28:39 "**W** Aaron's patterned tunic from fine linen cloth.
35:26 their skills to spin and **w** the goat hair into cloth.
Jdg 16:13 "If you **w** the seven braids of my hair into the
Isa 30: 1 You **w** a web of plans that are not from my Spirit,

WEAVER (1) [WEAVE]

Isa 38:12 cut short, / as when a **w** cuts cloth from a loom.

WEAVER'S (5) [WEAVE]

1Sa 17: 7 of his spear was as heavy and thick as a **w** beam,
2Sa 21:19 The handle of his spear was as thick as a **w** beam!
1Ch 11:23 feet tall and whose spear was as thick as a **w** beam.
20: 5 The handle of Lahmi's spear was as thick as a **w**
Job 7: 6 "My days are swifter than a **w** shuttle flying back

WEAVERS (4) [WEAVE]

Ex 35:35 designers, **w**, and embroiderers in blue, purple,
36: 8 The skilled **w** first made ten sheets from fine linen.
Isa 19: 9 The **w** will have no flax or cotton, for the crops
19:10 The **w** and all the workers will be sick at heart.

WEAVING (1) [WEAVE]

2Ch 2:14 also knows all about stonework, carpentry, and **w**

WEB (1) [SPIDERWEB]

Isa 30: 1 You weave a **w** of plans that are not from my

WEDDING (26) [WEDDINGS, WEDLOCK]

Ge 29:22 neighborhood to celebrate with Jacob at a **w** feast.
Jdg 14: 8 Later, when he returned to Timnah for the **w**,
14:20 man who had been Samson's best man at the **w**.
1Sa 18:19 So when the time came for the **w**, Saul gave Merab
1Ki 9:16 He gave the city to his daughter as a **w** gift when
Ps 19: 5 after his **w**. / It rejoices like a great athlete
78:63 their young women died before singing their **w**
SS 3:11 with which his mother crowned him on his **w** day,
Isa 61:10 I am like a bridegroom in his **w** suit or a bride with
Jer 2:32 her jewelry? Does a bride hide her **w** dress? No!
Mal 2:14 and your wife made to each other on your **w** day
Mt 9:15 "Should the **w** guests mourn while celebrating
11:17 'We played **w** songs and you weren't happy,
22: 2 of a king who prepared a great **w** feast for his son.
22: 8 And he said to his servants, 'The **w** feast is ready,
22:11 who wasn't wearing the proper clothes for a **w**.
22:12 'how is it that you are here without **w** clothes?'
Mk 2:19 "Do **w** guests fast while celebrating with the
Lk 5:34 "Do **w** guests fast while celebrating with the
7:32 'We played **w** songs and you weren't happy,
12:36 waiting for your master to return from the **w** feast.
14: 8 "If you are invited to a **w** feast, don't always head
Jn 2: 1 The next day Jesus' mother was a guest at a **w**
2:12 After the **w** he went to Capernaum for a few days
Rev 19: 7 For the time has come for the **w** feast of the Lamb,
19: 9 Blessed are those who are invited to the **w** feast of

WEDDINGS (2) [WEDDING]

Mt 24:38 and **w** right up to the time Noah entered his boat.
Lk 17:27 and **w** right up to the time Noah entered his boat

WEDLOCK (1) [WEDDING]

Jn 8:41 They replied, "We were not born out of **w**!

WEEDS (13)

Job 31:40 land instead of wheat and **w** instead of barley."
Ps 92: 7 Although the wicked flourish like **w**,
Pr 24:31 It was covered with **w**, and its walls were broken
Hos 10: 4 among them like poisonous **w** in a farmer's field.
Mt 13:25 his enemy came and planted **w** among the wheat.
13:26 began to grow and produce grain, the **w** also grew.
13:27 where you planted that good seed is full of **w**!'
13:28 " 'Shall we pull out the **w**?' they asked.
13:30 Then I will tell the harvesters to sort out the **w**
13:36 "Please explain the story of the **w** in the field."
13:38 The **w** are the people who belong to the evil one.
13:39 The enemy who planted the **w** among the wheat is
13:40 "Just as the **w** are separated out and burned,

WEEK (26) [WEEKLY, WEEKS]

Ge 7: 4 One **w** from today I will begin forty days and forty
7:10 One **w** later, the flood came and covered the earth.
8:12 A **w** later, he released the dove again, and this time
29:27 "Wait until the bridal **w** is over, and you can have
29:28 A **w** after Jacob had married Leah, Laban gave him
Ex 7:25 An entire **w** passed from the time the LORD
12:19 this **w** will be cut off from the community of Israel.
16: 5 as much as usual on the sixth day of each **w**."
20: 9 Six days a **w** are set apart for your daily duties
35: 2 Each **w**, work for six days only. The seventh day is
Lev 23: 3 You may work for six days each **w**, but on the
Dt 5:13 Six days a **w** are set apart for your daily duties
2Ch 30:23 so they celebrated joyfully for another **w**.
Isa 66:23 All humanity will come to worship me from **w** to **w**
Eze 46: 1 will be closed during the six workdays each **w**,
Lk 1: 8 in the Temple, for his order was on duty that **w**.
13:14 "There are six days of the **w** for working," he said
18:12 I fast twice a **w**, and I give you a tenth of my
Jn 20:19 That evening, on the first day of the **w**,
Ac 13:42 and speak about these things the next **w**.
13:44 The following **w** almost the entire city turned out
20: 6 days later arrived in Troas, where we stayed a **w**.
20: 7 On the first day of the **w**, we gathered to observe
21: 4 the local believers, and stayed with them a **w**.
21: 5 When we returned to the ship at the end of the **w**,

WEEKLY (1) [WEEK]

2Ch 31: 3 as well as for the **w** Sabbath festivals and monthly

WEEKS (6) [WEEK]

Lev 12: 5 she will be ceremonially defiled for two **w**,
23:15 was lifted up as an offering, count off seven **w**.
Dt 16: 9 "Count off seven **w** from the beginning of your
Da 10: 2 I, Daniel, had been in mourning for three **w**.
Ac 2: 1 day of Pentecost, seven **w** after Jesus' resurrection,
27:33 "You haven't touched food for two **w**," he said.

WEEP (79) [WEEPING, WEEPS, WEPT]

Ge 37:35 for my son," he would say, and then begin to **w**.
42:24 left the room and found a place where he could **w**.
45:14 and Benjamin also began to **w**.
Jdg 11:37 in the hills and **w** with my friends for two months,
1Sa 30: 4 they wept until they could **w** no more.
2Sa 1:24 O women of Israel, **w** for Saul, / for he dressed you
1:26 How I **w** for you, my brother Jonathan! / Oh,
Ne 8: 9 said to them, "Don't **w** on such a day as this!
8:11 quieted the people, telling them, "Hush! Don't **w**!
Job 30:25 Did I not **w** for those in trouble? Was I not deeply
30:31 sad music, and my flute accompanies those who **w**.
31:38 my land accuses me and all its furrows **w** together,
Ps 69:10 When I **w** and fast before the LORD, / they scoff
119:28 I **w** with grief; / encourage me by your word.
126: 6 They **w** as they go to plant their seed, / but they
Isa 3:26 The gates of Jerusalem will **w** and mourn. The city
14:31 **W**, you Philistine cities, for you are doomed!
16: 8 **W** for the abandoned farms of Heshbon
16:11 I will **w** for Moab. My sorrow for Kir-hareseth will
19: 8 The fishermen will **w** for lack of work. Those who
22: 4 Leave me alone to **w**; do not try to comfort me.
22:12 the LORD Almighty, called you to **w** and mourn.
23: 1 **W**, O ships of Tarshish, returning home from
23: 1 **W** for your harbor at Tyre because it is gone!
30:19 who live in Jerusalem, you will **w** no more.
33: 7 But now your ambassadors **w** in bitter
Jer 4: 8 on clothes of mourning and **w** with broken hearts,
6:26 Mourn and **w** bitterly, as for the loss of an only
7:16 Do not **w** or pray for them, and don't beg me to
7:29 head in mourning, and **w** alone on the mountains.
8:21 I **w** for the hurt of my people. I am stunned
9: 1 eyes were a fountain of tears; I would **w** forever!
9:10 I will **w** for the mountains and wail for the desert
11:14 Do not **w** or pray for them, for I will not listen to
12: 4 How long must this land **w**? Even the grass in the
13:17 to listen, I will **w** alone because of your pride.
15: 5 feel sorry for you, Jerusalem? Who will **w** for you?
22:10 Do not **w** for the dead king or mourn his loss.
22:10 Instead, **w** for the captive king being led away!
22:18 "His family will not **w** for him when he dies.
22:20 **W**, for your allies are all gone. Search for them in
25:34 **W** and moan, you evil shepherds! Roll in the dust,
31:16 "Do not **w** any longer, for I will reward you.
34: 5 They will **w** for you and say, "Alas, our king is
47: 2 scream in terror, and everyone in the land will **w**.
48:17 "You friends of Moab, **w** for her and cry! See how
48:20 reply comes back, 'Moab lies in ruins; **w** and wail!
48:32 I will **w** for you even more than I did for Jazer.
49: 3 town of Ai is destroyed. **W**, O people of Rabbah!
49: 3 **W** and wail, hiding in the hedges, for your god
51: 8 has fallen. **W** for her, and give her medicine.
La 1:16 "For all these things I **w**; tears flow down my
Eze 9: 4 and put a mark on the foreheads of all those who **w**
24:16 show any sorrow. Do not **w**; let there be no tears.
24:23 You will not mourn or **w**, but you will waste away
27:30 They **w** bitterly as they throw dust on their heads
27:31 They **w** for you with bitter anguish and deep
28:12 "Son of man, **w** for the king of Tyre. Give him this
30: 2 give this message from the Sovereign LORD: **W**,
32:18 **w** for the hordes of Egypt and for the other mighty
Joel 1: 5 Wake up, you drunkards, and **w**! All the grapes are
1: 8 **W** with sorrow, as a virgin weeps when her fiancé
1:11 **W**, because the wheat and barley—yes, all the field
Am 5:16 Call for the farmers to **w** with you, and summon
Mic 1:10 tell our enemies in the city of Gath; don't **w** at all.
1:16 **W**, you people of Judah! Shave your heads in
Zec 11: 2 **W**, you cypress trees, for all the ruined cedars;
11: 2 **W**, you oaks of Bashan, as you watch the thickest
12:12 "All Israel will **w** in profound sorrow, each family
Lk 6:21 will be satisfied. / God blesses you who **w** now,
23:28 don't **w** for me, but **w** for yourselves and for your children.
Jn 11:31 assumed she was going to Lazarus's grave to **w**.
16:20 you will **w** and mourn over what is going to
Jas 5: 1 **w** and groan with anguish because of all the
Rev 1: 7 And all the nations of the earth will **w** because of
18:11 The merchants of the world will **w** and mourn for
18:15 terrified by her great torment. They will **w** and cry.
18:18 They will **w** as they watch the smoke ascend,

WEEPING (66) [WEEP]

Ge 35: 8 the tree has been called the "Oak of **W**."
45:14 **W** with joy, he embraced Benjamin, and Benjamin
Nu 11:10 all the families standing in front of their tents **w**,
14: 1 Then all the people began **w** aloud, and they cried
25: 6 as they were **w** at the entrance of the Tabernacle.
Jdg 2: 5 So they called the place "**W**," and they offered
21: 2 until evening, raising their voices and **w** bitterly.
1Sa 5:12 afflicted with tumors; and there was **w** everywhere.
2Sa 3:16 along behind her as far as Bahurim, **w** as he went.
13:36 **w** and sobbing, and the king and his officials wept
15:30 road that led to the Mount of Olives, **w** as he went.
19: 1 Word soon reached Joab that the king was **w**
19: 4 covered his face with his hands and kept on **w**,
2Ki 8:11 became uneasy. Then the man of God started **w**.
Ezr 3:13 and **w** mingled together in a loud commotion that
10: 1 **w** and throwing himself to the ground in front of
Ne 8: 9 All the people had been **w** as they listened to the
Job 16:16 My eyes are red with **w**; darkness covers my eyes.
17: 7 My eyes are dim with **w**, and I am but a shadow of
Ps 6: 6 tears drench my bed; / my pillow is wet from **w**.
30: 5 his favor lasts a lifetime! / **W** may go on all night,
69: 3 is parched and dry. / My eyes are swollen with **w**,
84: 6 When they walk through the Valley of **W**, / it will
Isa 15: 2 and shrines, **w** for the fate of Nebo and Medeba.
15: 3 From every home will come the sound of **w**.
15: 5 **W**, they climb the road to Luhith.
15: 8 The whole land of Moab is a land of **w** from one
29: 2 upon you, and there will be much **w** and sorrow.
65:19 And the sound of **w** and crying will be heard no
Jer 3:21 the **w** and pleading of Israel's people.
8:19 Listen to the **w** of my people; it can be heard all
9:18 Quick! Begin your **w**! Let the tears flow from your
14:17 I cannot stop **w**, for my virgin daughter—
31:15 is heard in Ramah—mourning and **w** unrestrained.
41: 6 Ishmael left Mizpah to meet them, **w** as he went.
48: 5 refugees will climb the hills of Luhith, **w** bitterly,
50: 4 "**w** and seeking the LORD their God.
La 2:18 Give yourselves no rest from **w** day or night.
3:56 You listened to my pleading; you heard my **w**!
Eze 7:16 mountains will moan like doves, **w** for their sins.
7:27 and the prince will stand helpless, **w** in despair,
8:14 women were sitting there, **w** for the god Tammuz.
Joel 1: 9 Listen to the **w** of these ministers of the LORD!
2:12 your hearts. Come with fasting, **w**, and mourning.
2:17 will stand between the people and the altar, **w**.
Am 8:10 and your songs of joy will be turned to **w**.
Mal 2:13 **w** and groaning because he pays no attention to

Mt 2:18 heard in Ramah— / w and mourning unrestrained.
8:12 where there will be w and gnashing of teeth."
13:42 burn them. There will be w and gnashing of teeth.
13:50 into the fire. There will be w and gnashing of teeth.
22:13 where there is w and gnashing of teeth.'
24:51 In that place there will be w and gnashing of teeth.
25:30 where there will be w and gnashing of teeth.'
Mk 5:38 Jesus saw the commotion and the w and wailing.
5:39 "Why all this w and commotion?" he asked.
16:10 and found the disciples, who were grieving and w.
Lk 7:38 Then she knelt behind him at his feet, w. Her tears
8:52 The house was filled with people w and wailing,
but he said, "Stop the w!
13:28 "And there will be great w and gnashing of teeth,
Jn 11:33 When Jesus saw her w and saw the other people
Ac 8: 2 people came and buried Stephen with loud w.)
9:39 The room was filled with widows who were w
21:13 But he said, "Why all this w? You are breaking
Rev 5: 5 one of the twenty-four elders said to me, "Stop w!

WEEPS (6) [WEEP]

Isa 15: 5 My heart w for Moab. Its people flee to Zoar
16: 7 The entire land of Moab w. Yes, you people of
Jer 31:15 Rachel w for her children, refusing to be
La 1: 4 women are crying—how bitterly Jerusalem w!
Joel 1: 8 sorrow, as a virgin w when her fiancé has died.
Mt 2:18 Rachel w for her children, / refusing to be

WEIGH (6) [OUTWEIGH, WEIGHED, WEIGHING, WEIGHS, WEIGHT, WEIGHTS, WEIGHTY]

Dt 25:13 "You must use accurate scales when you w out
1Ki 7:47 Solomon did not w all the utensils because there
1Ch 22: 3 and more bronze than they could ever w.
Ps 62: 9 nothing in his sight. / If you w them on the scales,
Eze 5: 1 Use a scale to w the hair into three equal parts.
Am 8: 5 in false measures and w it out on dishonest scales.

WEIGHED (21) [WEIGH]

Nu 7:85 In all, the silver objects w about 60 pounds,
31:52 as a gift to the LORD w about 420 pounds.
1Sa 17: 5 and a coat of mail that w 125 pounds.
17: 7 tipped with an iron spearhead that w fifteen
2Sa 12:30 set with gems, and it w about seventy-five pounds.
14:26 When he w it out, it came to five pounds!
21:16 his bronze spearhead w more than seven pounds,
2Ki 25:16 the water carts, and the Sea was too great to be w.
1Ch 20: 2 set with gems, and it w about seventy-five pounds.
22:14 so much iron and bronze that it cannot be w.
2Ch 3: 9 They used gold nails that w about twenty ounces
Ezr 8:26 I w the treasure as I gave it to them and found the
8:33 and other valuables were w at the Temple of our
Job 6: 2 "If my sadness could be w and my troubles be put
Isa 40:12 the earth or has w out the mountains and the hills?
53: 4 he carried; it was our sorrows that w him down.
Jer 32:10 before witnesses, w out the silver, and paid him.
Eze 4:16 It will be w out with great care and eaten fearfully.
Da 5:27 *Tekel* means 'w'—you have been w on the
balances and have failed
2Co 1: 6 So when we are w down with troubles, it is for

WEIGHING (29) [WEIGH]

Ex 30:34 w out the same amounts of each.
Nu 3:47 each piece w the same as the standard sanctuary
7:13 The offering consisted of a silver platter w about
7:14 He also brought a gold container w about four
7:19 The offering consisted of a silver platter w about
7:20 He also brought a gold container w about four
7:25 The offering consisted of a silver platter w about
7:26 He also brought a gold container w about four
7:31 The offering consisted of a silver platter w about
7:32 He also brought a gold container w about four
7:37 The offering consisted of a silver platter w about
7:38 He also brought a gold container w about four
7:43 The offering consisted of a silver platter w about
7:44 He also brought a gold container w about four
7:49 The offering consisted of a silver platter w about
7:50 He also brought a gold container w about four
7:55 The offering consisted of a silver platter w about
7:56 He also brought a gold container w about four
7:61 The offering consisted of a silver platter w about
7:62 He also brought a gold container w about four
7:67 The offering consisted of a silver platter w about
7:68 He also brought a gold container w about four
7:73 The offering consisted of a silver platter w about
7:74 He also brought a gold container w about four
7:79 The offering consisted of a silver platter w about
7:80 He also brought a gold container w about four
18:16 each piece w the same as the standard sanctuary
Jos 7:21 and a bar of gold w more than a pound.
Rev 16:21 and hailstones w seventy-five pounds fell from the

WEIGHS (2) [WEIGH]

Pr 12:25 Worry w a person down; an encouraging word
20: 8 a king judges, he carefully w all the evidence,

WEIGHT (19) [WEIGH]

Lev 19:35 standards when measuring length, w, or volume.
26:26 They will ration your food by w, and even if you
Nu 3:50 of Israel came to about thirty-four pounds in w.
7:86 The w of the donated gold came to about three
Jdg 8:26 The w of the gold earrings was forty-three pounds,
1Ki 7:47 the w of the bronze could not be measured.
2Ki 18:21 will find it to be a stick that breaks beneath your w
2Ch 4:18 were used that its w could not be determined.
Ezr 8:34 Everything was accounted for by number and w,
and the total w was officially recorded.
Job 26: 8 and the clouds do not burst with the w.
Isa 36: 6 will find it to be a stick that breaks beneath your w
40:12 Who else knows the w of the earth or has weighed
40:15 He picks up the islands as though they had no w at
46: 1 But look! The beasts are staggering under the w!
La 4: 2 worth their w in gold, are now treated like pots of
Eze 29: 7 When she put her w on you, you gave way, and her
45:12 The standard unit for w will be the silver shekel.
Heb 12: 1 let us strip off every w that slows us down,

WEIGHTS (6) [WEIGH]

Lev 19:36 Your scales and w must be accurate.
Dt 25:15 Yes, use honest w and measures, so that you will
25:16 Those who cheat with dishonest w and measures
1Ch 23:29 They were also responsible to check all the w
Eze 45:10 You must use only honest w and scales, honest dry
Mic 6:11 your merchants who use dishonest scales and w?

WEIGHTY (1) [WEIGH]

Pr 27: 3 A stone is heavy and sand is w, but the resentment

WELCOME (29) [WELCOMED, WELCOMES, WELCOMING]

Dt 23: 4 These nations did not w you with food and water
Jdg 19:20 "You are w to stay with me," the old man said.
1Sa 13:10 Samuel arrived. Saul went out to meet and w him,
2Sa 19:12 Why are you the last ones to w me back?"
19:16 hurried across with the men of Judah to w King
Ps 23: 5 You w me as a guest, / anointing my head with oil.
71: 3 a protecting rock of safety, / where I am always w.
Pr 25:17 neighbors too often, or you will wear out your w.
Isa 58: 7 and to w poor wanderers into your homes.
64: 5 You w those who cheerfully do good, who follow
Jer 40: 4 you want to come with me to Babylon, you are w.
Eze 32:21 the grave mighty leaders will mockingly w Egypt
Mt 10:14 If a village doesn't w you or listen to you,
10:41 If you w a prophet as one who speaks for God,
10:41 And if you w good and godly people because of
25: 6 the bridegroom is coming! Come out and w him!'
Mk 6:11 "And if a village won't w you or listen to you,
Lk 10:10 But if a town refuses to w you, go out into its
Jn 5:43 representing my Father, and you refuse to w me,
Ac 18:27 to the believers in Achaia, asking them to w him.
28: 2 so they built a fire on the shore to w us and warm
2Co 6:17 Don't touch their filthy things, / and I will w you.
Eph 3:12 into God's presence, assured of his glad w.
Php 2:29 W him with Christian love and with great joy,
Col 4:10 make Mark w if he comes your way.
1Th 1: 9 keep talking about the wonderful w you gave us
Phm 1:17 give him the same w you would give me if I were
Heb 11:31 For she had given a friendly w to the spies.
3Jn 1:10 He not only refuses to w the traveling teachers,

WELCOMED (19) [WELCOME]

Ge 19: 1 Then he w them and bowed low to the ground.
Jdg 19: 3 she took him inside, and her father w him.
2Ki 20:13 Hezekiah w the Babylonian envoys and showed
Est 5: 2 he w her, holding out the gold scepter to her.
Ps 21: 3 You w him back with success and prosperity.
Isa 39: 2 Hezekiah w the Babylonian envoys and showed
Lk 9:11 And he w them, teaching them about the Kingdom
10:38 a woman named Martha w them into her home.
Jn 4:45 The Galileans w him, for they had been in
Ac 15: 4 Paul and Barnabas were w by the whole church,
21:17 All the believers in Jerusalem w us cordially.
28: 7 He w us courteously and fed us for three days.
28:30 in his own rented house. He w all who visited him,
1Co 15: 1 You w it then and still do now, for your faith is
2Co 7:13 to see how happy Titus was at the way you w him
7:15 and w him with such respect and deep concern.
8:17 He w our request that he visit you again. In fact,
Gal 1: 9 preaches any other gospel than the one you w,
Heb 11:13 it all from a distance and w the promises of God.

WELCOMES (15) [WELCOME]

Mt 10:40 "Anyone who w you is welcoming me, and anyone
who w me is welcoming the Father
18: 5 And anyone who w a little child like this on my
Mk 9:37 "Anyone who w a little child like this on my
behalf w me, and anyone who w me w my Father
who
Lk 9:48 "Anyone who w a little child like this on my
behalf w me, and anyone who w me w my Father
who
10: 8 "If a town w you, eat whatever is set before you
Jn 13:20 anyone who w my messenger is welcoming me,
and anyone who w me is welcoming the Father
Ro 10:16 But not everyone w the Good News, for Isaiah the

WELCOMING (7) [WELCOME]

Ge 18: 2 meet them, w them by bowing low to the ground.
Joel 3:16 the LORD will be a w refuge and a strong
Mt 10:40 "Anyone who welcomes you is w me, and anyone
who welcomes me is w the Father who
18: 5 a little child like this on my behalf is w me.
Jn 13:20 anyone who welcomes my messenger is w me, and
anyone who welcomes me is w the Father who

WELFARE (3)

Ex 2:25 on the Israelites and felt deep concern for their w.
Pr 12:10 The godly are concerned for the w of their animals,
Php 2:20 like Timothy, who genuinely cares about your w.

WELL (398) [WELLS]

Ge 12:13 then the Egyptians will treat me w because of their
13:10 The whole area was w watered everywhere,
16:14 Later that w was named Beer-lahairoi, and it can
20:11 "W," Abraham said, "I figured this to be a
21:19 Then God opened Hagar's eyes, and she saw a w.
21:25 w that Abimelech's servants had taken violently
21:30 to you as a public confirmation that I dug this w."
21:31 has been known as Beersheba—"w of the oath"—
23:14 "W," Ephron answered,
24:11 kneel down beside a w just outside the village.
24:20 the watering trough and ran down to the w again.
24:57 "W," they said, "we'll call Rebekah and ask her
25:33 So Jacob insisted, "W then, swear to me right now
26:20 So Isaac named the w "Argument," because they
26:21 Isaac's men then dug another w, but again there
26:22 Abandoning that one, he dug another w,
26:25 up his camp at that place, and his servants dug a w.
26:29 We have always treated you w, and we sent you
26:32 and told him about a w they had dug.
26:33 So Isaac named the w "Oath," and from that time
26:33 there has been called Beersheba—"w of the oath."
29: 2 flocks of sheep lying in an open field beside a w,
29: 2 But a heavy stone covered the mouth of the w.
29: 3 would be rolled back over the mouth of the w.
29: 6 "He's w and prosperous. Look, here comes his
29:10 Jacob went over to the w and rolled away the stone
33:12 "W, let's be going," Esau said. "I will stay with
33:15 "W," Esau said, "at least let me leave some of
37:10 This time he told his father as w as his brothers,
38:18 "W, what do you want?" he inquired. She replied,
41: 5 one stalk, with every kernel w formed and plump.
41:37 Joseph's suggestions were w received by Pharaoh
42: 5 buy food, for the famine had reached Canaan as w.
43: 5 don't let Benjamin go, we may as w stay at home.
43:28 "Yes," they replied. "He is alive and w."
47:16 "W, then," Joseph replied, "since your money is
Ex 2:15 Moses arrived in Midian, he sat down beside a w.
2:16 who came regularly to this w to draw water
2:20 "W, where is he then?" their father asked.
3:21 And I will see to it that the Egyptians treat you w.
4:12 I will help you speak w, and I will tell you what to
10:29 "Very w," Moses replied. "I will never see you
18:15 Moses replied, "W, the people come to me to seek
21:33 someone digs or uncovers a w and fails to cover it,
21:34 The owner of the w must pay in full for the dead
25:29 as w as pitchers and bowls to be used in pouring
26:29 Overlay the crossbars with gold as w.
28:39 Fashion the turban out of this linen as w.
Lev 6:21 and it must be w mixed and broken into pieces.
11:42 as w as those with four legs and those with many
16:29 as w as to the foreigners living among you.
17: 8 "Give them this command as w, which applies
20: 2 birth as w as to the foreigners living among you.
21: 9 defiling her father's holiness as w as herself,
22:18 birth as w as to the foreigners living among you.
25:43 Show your fear of God by treating them w;
Nu 10:29 Come with us and we will treat you w,
14:13 "They know full w the power you displayed in
14:14 who are w aware that you are with this people.
14:31 W, I will bring them safely into the land, and they
16:10 but now you are demanding the priesthood as w!
21:16 which is the w where the LORD said to Moses,
21:17 this song: / "Spring up, O w! / Yes, sing about it!
21:18 Sing of this w, / which princes dug, / which great
21:22 or touch your vineyards or drink your w water."
22:17 I will pay you w and do anything you ask of me.
Dt 4:40 all will be w with you and your children.
6: 3 Then all will go w with you, and you will have
6:18 in the LORD's sight, so all will go w with you.
12:25 then all will go w with you and your children,
12:28 so that all will go w with you and your children,
13:15 destroy all its inhabitants, as w as all the livestock.
14:29 as w as to the foreigners living among you,
15:16 and your family, and he is w off with you.
19:13 of murder from Israel so all may go w with you.
20: 7 W, go home and get married! You might die in the
31:20 all the food they want and become w nourished.
Jos 14:10 and w as he promised for all these forty-five years
14:11 and I can still travel and fight as w as I could then.
15:19 land in the Negev; please give me springs as w."
17:18 The forests of the hill country will be yours as w.
20: 9 These cities were set apart for Israelites as w as the
23: 4 as w as the land of those we have already
Jdg 1:15 land in the Negev; please give me springs as w."
4: 9 "Very w," she replied, "I will go with you.
17: 2 W, here they are. I was the one who took them."
Ru 2: 9 to the water they have drawn from the w."
2:20 "He is showing his kindness to us as w as to your
1Sa 2: 5 Those who were w fed are now starving;
7: 6 drew water from a w and poured it out before the
9: 8 "W," the servant said, "I have one small silver
12:14 follow the LORD your God, then all will be w.
16:16 will quiet you, and you will soon be w again."
16:17 "Find me someone who plays w and bring him
17:56 "W, find out!" the king told him.
19:22 went to Ramah and arrived at the great w in Secu.
20: 3 "Your father knows perfectly w about our
20: 7 If he says, 'Fine!' then you will know all is w.
20:21 LORD lives, that all is w, and there is no trouble.
23:17 I will be next to you, as my father is w aware."

24:19 May the LORD reward you w for the kindness
26:15 "W, Abner, you're a great man, aren't you?"
28: 2 "Very w!" David agreed. "Now you will see for
28:11 Finally, the woman said, "W, whose spirit do you
2Sa 3:10 I should set him up as king over Israel as w as
3:25 You know perfectly w that he came to spy on you
11:12 "W, stay here tonight," David told him,
11:25 "W, tell Joab not to be discouraged," David said.
"The sword kills one as w as another!
13: 5 "W," Jonadab said, "I'll tell you what to do.
13:20 W, don't be so upset. Since he's your brother
13:26 "W, then," Absalom said, "if you can't come,
14:32 I might as w have stayed there. Let me see the
17: 7 "W," Hushai replied, "this time I think
17:18 where a man hid them inside a w in his courtyard.
17:19 The man's wife put a cloth over the top of the w
17:21 Then the two men crawled out of the w and hurried
18:28 Then Ahimaaz cried out to the king, "All is w!"
21: 4 "W, money won't do it," the Gibeonites replied.
21:13 as w as the bones of the men the Gibeonites had
23:15 some of that good water from the w in Bethlehem,
23:16 drew some water from the w, and brought it back
1Ki 2:22 "You might as w be asking me to give him the
3: 9 so that I can govern your people w
4:23 one hundred sheep or goats, as w as deer, gazelles,
5: 4 on every side, and I have no enemies and all is w.
9: 1 Temple of the LORD, as w as the royal palace.
20:40 "W, it's your own fault," the king replied.
21:15 sell you? W, you can have it now! He's dead!"
2Ki 1: 3 god of Ekron, to ask whether the king will get w?
1: 6 god of Ekron, to ask whether the king will get w?
1:16 the god of Ekron, to ask whether you will get w?
7: 4 So we might as w go out and surrender to the
8: 8 Then tell him to ask the LORD if I will get w
10:14 of them and killed them at the w of Beth-eked.
10:30 "You have done w in following my instructions to
11: 9 as w as those who were going off duty.
14: 5 When Amaziah was w established as king,
14:14 of the LORD, as w as from the palace treasury.
16:18 as w as the king's outer entrance to the Temple of
17: 8 as w as the practices the kings of Israel had
18:26 speak to us in Aramaic, for we understand it w.
18:31 your own garden and drinking from your own w.
19:11 You know perfectly w what the kings of Assyria
19:27 'But I know you w— / your comings and goings
25:24 and all will go w for you," he promised.
25:26 as w as the army commanders, fled in panic to
1Ch 11:17 some of that good water from the w in Bethlehem,
11:18 drew some water from the w, and brought it back
12: 2 or sling stones with their left hand as w as their
26: 8 were very capable men, w qualified for their work.
28:17 as w as the amount of silver for every dish.
29: 2 iron, and wood, as w as great quantities of onyx,
2Ch 7:11 Temple of the LORD, as w as the royal palace.
14: 5 as w as the incense altars from every one of
23: 8 as w as those who were going off duty.
25: 3 When Amaziah was w established as king,
25: 8 you will be defeated no matter how w you fight.
31: 3 as w as for the weekly Sabbath festivals
34: 9 as w as from all Judah, Benjamin, and the people
Ezr 1: 4 as w as a freewill offering for the Temple of God
7: 6 w versed in the law of Moses, which the LORD,
7: 7 as w as some of the priests, Levites, singers,
7:16 as w as the freewill offerings of the people
8:29 Guard these treasures w until you present them,
8:35 as w as ninety-six rams and seventy-seven lambs.
Ne 1: 3 "Things are not going w for those who returned to
2: 4 The king asked, "W, how can I help you?"
2:13 out through the Valley Gate, past the Jackal's W,
2:17 to them, "You know full w the tragedy of our city.
4:22 on guard duty at night as w as work during the day.
5:10 I myself, as w as my brothers and my workers,
9:28 "But when all was going w, your people turned to
Est 1: 3 as w as the noblemen and provincial officials.
6: 8 as w as the king's own horse with a royal emblem
Job 8: 4 against him, so their punishment was w deserved.
12: 3 W, I know a few things myself—and you're no
21:19 " 'W,' you say, 'at least God will punish their
22:21 have peace at last, and things will go w for you.
29:11 of me praised me. All who saw me spoke w of me.
30:13 knowing full w that I have no one to help me.
33:31 Mark this w, Job. Listen to me, and let me say
Ps 28: 1 For if you are silent, / I might as w give up and die.
40: 9 afraid to speak out, / as you, O LORD, w know.
41:10 Make me w again, so I can pay them back!
76: 1 God is w known in Judah; / his name is great in
104:16 The trees of the LORD are w cared for—
109:21 But deal w with me, O Sovereign LORD,
112: 5 All goes w for those who are generous, / who lend
119:102 away from your laws, / for you have taught me w.
139:14 workmanship is marvelous—and how w I know it.
Pr 5:15 Drink water from your own w—share your love
16:21 and instruction is appreciated if it's w presented.
21:30 Human plans, no matter how wise or w advised,
23:14 Physical discipline may w save them from death.
31:23 Her husband is w known, for he sits in the council
Ecc 5:12 People who work hard sleep w, whether they eat
5:18 It is good for people to eat w, drink a good glass of
6: 6 he must die like everyone else—w, what's the use?
9:10 Whatever you do, do w. For when you go to the
10: 8 When you dig a w, you may fall in. When you
12: 6 at the spring and the pulley is broken at the w.
SS 4:15 You are a garden fountain, a w of living water,
7:13 the new as w as old, for I have stored them up for
Isa 3:10 But all will be w for those who are godly.
7:13 Then Isaiah said, "Listen w, you royal family of
7:13 You exhaust the patience of God as w!
10:30 W may you scream in terror, you people of
17:11 so w that they blossom on the very morning you
30:14 coals from a fireplace or a little water from the w."
36:11 speak to us in Aramaic, for we understand it w.
36:16 your own garden and drinking from your own w.
37:11 You know perfectly w what the kings of Assyria
37:28 'But I know you w— / your comings and goings
38: 9 When King Hezekiah was w again, he wrote this
47: 9 W, those two things will come upon you in a
48: 8 entirely new, for I know so w what traitors you are.
Jer 5:28 They are w fed and w groomed, and there is no
7:23 be my people. Only do as I say, and all will be w!'
14:13 their prophets are telling them, 'All is w—
15:11 "All will be w with you, Jeremiah.
22:16 and needy, and everything went w for him.
23:18 the LORD w enough to hear what he is saying?
24: 6 I will see that they are w treated, and I will bring
31:21 Mark w the path by which you came. Come back
38: 4 we have left, as w as that of all the people, too.
38:20 Your life will be spared, and all will go w for you.
39: 9 sent to Babylon the remnant of the population as w
39:12 "Look after him w, and give him anything he
40: 4 are welcome. I will see that you are w cared for.
40: 9 of Babylon," he said, "and all will go w for you.
42: 6 if we obey him, everything will turn out w for us."
44: 1 and throughout southern Egypt as w:
44:17 to eat, and we were w off and had no troubles!
La 3:55 on your name, LORD, from deep within the w,
Eze 17:10 in the same good soil where it had grown so w."
24:10 Cook the meat w with many spices. Then empty
33: 4 to take action—w, it is their own fault if they die.
Da 1: 4 "Make sure they are w versed in every branch of
2:48 of Babylon, as w as chief over all his wise men.
3:15 the sound of the musical instruments, all will be w.
Hos 2: 7 'I might as w return to my husband because I was
9: 7 Soon Israel will know this all too w.
Joel 2:23 autumn rains will come, as w as the rains of spring.
Zec 11: 6 as w as into the clutches of their king.
Mt 7: 5 then perhaps you will see w enough to deal with
8: 2 "if you want to, you can make me w again."
9:22 be encouraged! Your faith has made you w."
12:11 had one sheep, and it fell into a w on the Sabbath,
13:52 the storehouse the new teachings as w as the old."
15:31 the crippled were made w, the lame were walking
16:14 "W," they replied, "some say John the Baptist,
17:18 and it left him. From that moment the boy was w.
17:26 "W, then," Jesus said, "the citizens are free!
22:21 "W, then," he said, "give to Caesar what belongs
22:25 W, there were seven brothers. The oldest married
24:50 w, the master will return unannounced
25:21 of praise. 'W done, my good and faithful servant.
25:23 'W done, my good and faithful servant.
25:27 W, you should at least have put my money into the
25:29 To those who use w what they are given,
26:62 the high priest stood up and said to Jesus, "W,
27:18 (He knew very w that the Jewish leaders had
27:40 W then, if you are the Son of God, save yourself
Mk 1:38 he replied, "We must go on to other towns as w,
1:40 you want to, you can make me w again," he said.
5:34 said to her, "Daughter, your faith has made you w.
7:29 "And because you have answered so w, I have
8:28 "W," they replied, "some say John the Baptist,
10: 4 "W, he permitted it," they replied. "He said a
12:17 "W, then," Jesus said, "give to Caesar what
12:20 W, there were seven brothers. The oldest of them
12:28 He realized that Jesus had answered w, so he
12:32 teacher of religious law replied, "W said, Teacher.
14:60 stood up before the others and asked Jesus, "W,
15:30 W then, save yourself and come down from the
Lk 1:18 man now, and my wife is also w along in years."
4:14 Soon he became w known throughout the
4:22 All who were there spoke w of him and were
5:12 "if you want to, you can make me w again."
5:17 in all Galilee and Judea, as w as from Jerusalem.)
6:42 then perhaps you will see w enough to deal with
6:48 the house, it stands firm because it is w built.
8:48 he said to her, "your faith has made you w.
9:19 "W," they replied, "some say John the Baptist,
11:40 Didn't God make the inside as w as the outside?
12:35 "Be dressed for service and w prepared,
12:46 w, the master will return unannounced
14: 3 the Pharisees and experts in religious law, "W,
17:19 "Stand up and go. Your faith has made you w."
18:30 as w as receiving eternal life in the world to
19:17 'W done!' the king exclaimed. 'You are a
19:19 'W done!' the king said. 'You can be governor
19:26 'but to those who use w what they are given,
20:25 "W then," he said, "give to Caesar what belongs
20:29 W, there were seven brothers. The oldest married
20:39 "W said, Teacher!" remarked some of the
Jn 1:21 "W then, who are you?" they asked. "Are you
4: 6 Jacob's w was there; and Jesus, tired from the long
4: 6 sat wearily beside the w about noontime.
4:11 or a bucket," she said, "and this is a very deep w.
4:12 than our ancestor Jacob who gave us this w?
4:28 The woman left her water jar beside the w
4:51 him with the news that his son was alive and w.
5: 6 he asked him, "Would you like to get w?"
5:14 him in the Temple and told him, "Now you are w;
7:23 for making a man completely w on the Sabbath?
9:31 W, God doesn't listen to sinners, but he is ready to
13: 9 "Then wash my hands and head as w, Lord,
13:18 to all of you; I know so w each one of you I chose.
Ac 2:22 wonders, and signs through him, as you w know.
6: 3 and select seven men who are w respected and are
9:15 and to kings, as w as to the people of Israel.
10:20 without hesitation. All is w, for I have sent them."
10:22 God of Israel and is w respected by all the Jews.
11:15 "W, I began telling them the Good News, but just
13:46 of eternal life—w, we will offer it to Gentiles.
15:29 If you do this, you will do w. Farewell."
16: 2 Timothy was w thought of by the believers in
17: 8 The people of the city, as w as the city officials,
17:21 (It should be explained that all the Athenians as w
18:24 an eloquent speaker who knew the Scriptures w,
20:29 I know full w that false teachers, like vicious
21:12 traveling with him, as w as the local believers,
22:12 and he was w thought of by all the Jews of
25:10 tried right here. You know very w I am not guilty.
25:12 with his advisers and then replied, "Very w!
26: 4 "As the Jewish leaders are w aware, I was given a
Ro 2:17 You boast that all is w between yourself and God.
2:21 W then, if you teach others, why don't you teach
3: 8 you might as w say that the more we sin the better
3: 9 W then, are we Jews better than others? No,
3:31 W then, if we emphasize faith, does this mean that
4: 9 or is it for Gentiles, too? W, what about Abraham?
6: 1 W then, should we keep on sinning so that God
7: 7 W then, am I suggesting that the law of God is
7:16 I know perfectly w that what I am doing is wrong,
9: 6 W then, has God failed to fulfill his promise to the
9:19 W then, you might say, "Why does God blame
9:30 W then, what shall we say about these things?
11: 9 a snare, / a trap that makes them think all is w.
11:19 "W," you may say, "those branches were broken
12: 6 given each of us the ability to do certain things w.
12: 7 If your gift is that of serving others, serve them w.
13: 3 So do what they say, and you will get along w.
15:14 so w that you are able to teach others all about
1Co 1:18 I know very w how foolish the message of the
4: 3 W, it matters very little what you or anyone else
4:10 You are w thought of, but we are laughed at.
7:33 But a married man can't do that so w. He has to
7:37 he can control his passion, he does w not to marry.
7:38 So the person who marries does w, and the person
8: 4 W, we all know that an idol is not really a god
11:22 you want me to praise you? W, I certainly do not!
14: 9 You might as w be talking to an empty room.
14:15 W then, what shall I do? I will do both. I will pray
14:26 W, my brothers and sisters, let's summarize what I
14:36 ends with you Corinthians? W, you are mistaken!
16:18 You must give proper honor to all who serve so w.
2Co 2:12 W, when I came to the city of Troas to preach the
6: 9 We are w known, but we are treated as unknown.
11:26 own people, the Jews, as w as from the Gentiles.
Gal 3:19 W then, why was the law given? It was given to
3:21 W then, is there a conflict between God's law
5: 7 You were getting along so w. Who has interfered
6: 4 personal satisfaction of having done your work w,
Eph 4:31 as w as all types of malicious behavior.
Php 4:14 you have done w to share with me in my present
1Th 2: 5 try to win you with flattery, as you very w know.
3: 4 would soon come—and they did, as you w know.
5: 2 for you know quite w that the day of the Lord will
5: 3 When people are saying, "All is w; everything is
1Ti 1:18 May they give you the confidence to fight w in the
3: 4 He must manage his own family w, with children
3: 7 people outside the church must speak w of him
3:10 If they do w, then they may serve as deacons.
3:12 and he must manage his children and household w.
3:13 Those who do w as deacons will be rewarded with
5:10 She must be w respected by everyone because of
5:10 Has she brought up her children w? Has she been
5:17 Elders who do their work w should be paid w,
6:12 you have confessed so w before many witnesses.
Tit 1: 6 An elder must be w thought of for his good life.
Heb 11:32 W, how much more do I need to say? It would take
Jas 2: 3 can stand over there, or else sit on the floor"—w,
2:16 and you say, "W, good-bye and God bless you;
stay warm and eat w"—but then you don't give
2:19 W, even the demons believe this, and they tremble
5:15 will heal the sick, and the Lord will make them w.
1Pe 4:10 Manage them w so that God's generosity can flow
1Jn 3:17 But if one of you has money enough to live w
2Jn 1:12 W, I have much more to say to you, but I don't
3Jn 1: 2 I am praying that all is w with you and that your
1: 6 You do w to send them on their way in a manner
Jude 1: 5 I must remind you—and you know it w—that even
Rev 22: 9 as w as all who obey what is written in this scroll.

WELL-AGED (1) [AGE]

Isa 25: 6 of good food, with clear, w wine and choice beef.

WELL-BEING (1) [BE]

Dt 6:24 and to fear him for our own prosperity and w,

WELL-BUILT (2) [BUILD]

Ge 39: 6 Joseph was a very handsome and w young man.
Ps 122: 3 Jerusalem is a w city, / knit together as a single

WELL-EARNED (2) [EARN]

Isa 3:11 you deserve. Your w punishment is on the way."
Php 4:17 What I want is for you to receive a w reward

WELL-FED (1) [FEED]

Jer 5: 8 They are w, lusty stallions, each neighing for his

WELL-FORMED (1) [FORM]

Ge 41: 7 heads swallowed up the seven plump, w heads!

WELL-NURTURED (1)

Ps 144:12 May our sons flourish in their youth / like w plants.

WELL-ROUNDED (1) [ROUND]

Job 36: 4 the honest truth, for I am a man of w knowledge.

WELL-SET (1) [SET]

Isa 3:24 wear ropes for sashes, and their w hair will fall out.

WELL-TRAINED (1) [TRAIN]

2Ch 26:11 Uzziah had an army of w warriors, ready to march

WELL-WATERED (1) [WATER]

Isa 58:11 You will be like a w garden, like an ever-flowing

WELLBELOVED [KJV] See BELOVED, DEAR FRIEND, LOVED, LOVER

WELLPLEASING [KJV] See PLEASES, PLEASING

WELLS (10) [WELL]

Ge 26:15 and they filled up all of Isaac's w with earth.
26:15 These were the w that had been dug by the
26:18 He reopened the w his father had dug,
Ex 7:24 Then the Egyptians dug w along the riverbank to
Nu 20:17 We won't even drink water from your w.
Dt 10: 6 "The people of Israel set out from the w of the
2Ki 19:24 I have dug w in many a foreign land
Isa 37:25 I have dug w in many a foreign land
Jer 14: 3 send servants to get water, but all the w are dry.
Hos 13:15 All their flowing springs and w will disappear.

WELTS (1)

Isa 1: 6 covered with bruises, w, and infected wounds—

WEN [KJV] See GROWTH

WENCH [KJV] See SERVANT (GIRL)

WENT (895) [GO] See Index of Articles, Etc.

WEPT (39) [WEEP]

Ge 23: 2 of Canaan. There Abraham mourned and w for her.
27:38 bless me, too!" Then Esau broke down and w.
43:30 to cry. Going into his private room, he w there.
45: 2 Then he broke down and w aloud. His sobs could
45:15 kissed each of his brothers and w over them,
46:29 his father and w on his shoulder for a long time.
50: 1 on his father and w over him and kissed him.
50:17 received the message, he broke down and w.
Dt 1:45 Then you returned and w before the LORD,
Jdg 2: 4 LORD finished speaking, the Israelites w loudly.
11:38 She and her friends went into the hills and w
20:23 and w in the presence of the LORD until evening.
20:26 and w in the presence of the LORD and fasted
Ru 1: 9 them good-bye, and they all broke down and w.
1:14 And again they w together, and Orpah kissed her
1Sa 30: 4 they w until they could weep no more.
2Sa 1:12 They mourned and w and fasted all day for Saul
3:32 and the king and all the people w at his graveside.
3:34 a wicked plot." / All the people w again for Abner.
12:21 the baby was still living, you w and refused to eat.
12:22 "I fasted and w while the child was alive, for I
13:36 and the king and his officials w bitterly with them.
15:30 their heads and w as they climbed the mountain.
2Ki 13:14 King Jehoash of Israel visited him and w over him.
20: 3 in your sight." Then he broke down and w bitterly.
22:19 clothing in despair and w before me in repentance.
2Ch 34:27 clothing in despair and w before me in repentance.
Ezr 3:12 and they w aloud when they saw the new Temple's
10: 1 and children—gathered and w bitterly with him.
Ne 1: 4 When I heard this, I sat down and w. In fact,
Est 4: 3 They fasted, w, and wailed, and many people lay
Ps 137: 1 Beside the rivers of Babylon, we sat and w
Isa 38: 3 in your sight." Then he broke down and w bitterly.
Hos 12: 4 He w and pleaded for a blessing from him.
Jn 11:35 Then Jesus w.
20:11 and as she w, she stooped and looked in.
Ac 20:37 They w aloud as they embraced him in farewell,
Heb 12:17 late for repentance, even though he w bitter tears.
Rev 5: 4 Then I w because no one could be found who was

WERE (2828) [BE] See Index of Articles, Etc.

WEREN'T (17) [BE, NOT] See Index of Articles, Etc.

WEST (121) [NORTHWEST, SOUTHWEST, WESTERN, WESTWARD]

Ge 12: 8 camp in the hill country between Bethel on the w
28:14 They will cover the land from east to w and from
Ex 10:19 The LORD responded by sending a strong w
26:22 On the w side there will be six frames,
27:12 The curtains on the w end of the courtyard will be
36:27 The w side of the Tabernacle, which was its rear,
36:30 So for the w side they made a total of eight frames,
36:32 five for the north side and five for the w side.
38:12 The w end was 75 feet wide. The walls were made
Nu 2:18[-19] and Benjamin are to camp on the w side of
3:23 They were assigned the area to the w of the
35: 5 east, south, w, north—with the town at the center.
35:14 and three on the w in the land of Canaan.
Dt 3:21 He will do the same to all the kingdoms on the w
11:24 River in the east to the Mediterranean Sea in the w.
11:30 (These two mountains are w of the Jordan River in
11:30 They are located toward the w, not far from the
33:23 may you possess the w and the south."
Jos 1: 4 on the east to the Mediterranean Sea on the w,
5: 1 When all the Amorite kings w of the Jordan
8: 9 in ambush between Bethel and the w side of Ai.
8:12 between Bethel and Ai, on the w side of the city.
8:13 north of the city and the ambush w of the city.
9: 1 Now all the kings w of the Jordan heard about
11: 2 the kings of Naphoth-dor on the w;
11: 3 the kings of Canaan, both east and w; the kings of
12: 7 and the Israelite armies defeated on the w side of
13:25 as far as the town of Aroer just w of Rabbah.
15: 8 Then it went w to the top of the mountain above
15:10 The border circled w of Baalah to Mount Seir,
15:46 From Ekron the boundary extended w and included
17: 2 Land on the w side of the Jordan was allotted to
18:12 then w through the hill country and the wilderness
19:11 From there it went w, going past Maralah,
19:26 The boundary on the w went from Carmel to
19:34 the boundary of Asher on the w, and the Jordan
22: 7 The other half of the tribe was given land w of the
22:11 built the altar at Geliloth w of the Jordan River,
23: 4 Jordan River to the Mediterranean Sea in the w.
Jdg 10: 9 The Ammonites also crossed to the w side of the
18:12 They camped at a place w of Kiriath-jearim in
20:33 Then the Israelites hiding in ambush w of Gibeah
1Sa 13:18 another went w to Beth-horon, and the third moved
2Sa 13:34 a great crowd coming toward the city from the w.
1Ki 4:24 over all the kingdoms w of the Euphrates River,
7:25 Three faced north, three faced w, three faced south,
1Ch 7:28 Gezer and its villages to the w, and Shechem
9:24 on all four sides—east, w, north, and south.
12:15 in the lowlands on both the east and w banks.
12:31 From the half-tribe of Manasseh w of the Jordan,
26:16 Shuppim and Hosah were assigned the w gate
26:18 Six were assigned each day to the w gate, four to
26:30 were put in charge of the Israelite lands w of the
27:20 of Azaziah / Manasseh (w) | Joel son of Pedaiah
2Ch 4: 4 Three faced north, three faced w, three faced south,
32:30 through a tunnel to the w side of the City of David.
33:14 from w of the Gihon Spring in the Kidron Valley
Ezr 4:10 lands of the province w of the Euphrates River.
4:11 from your loyal subjects in the province w of the
4:16 the province w of the Euphrates River will be lost
4:17 and throughout the province w of the Euphrates
4:20 and the entire province w of the Euphrates River
5: 3 governor of the province w of the Euphrates,
5: 6 and the other officials of the province w of the
6: 6 governor of the province w of the Euphrates River,
6: 6 and other officials of the province w of the Euphrates:
6:13 governor of the province w of the Euphrates River,
7:21 in the province w of the Euphrates River:
7:25 people in the province w of the Euphrates River.
8:36 and the governors of the province w of the
Ne 2: 7 give me letters to the governors of the province w
2: 9 When I came to the governors of the province w of
3: 7 the headquarters of the governor of the province w
Job 18:20 People in the w are appalled at their fate; people in
23: 8 but he is not there. I go w, but I cannot find him.
Ps 50: 1 he has summoned all humanity from east to w!
75: 6 For no one on earth—from east or w, / or even
80:11 We spread our branches w to the Mediterranean
89:25 his rule from the Mediterranean Sea in the w
103:12 as far away from us as the east is from the w.
107: 3 from east and w, from north and south.
113: 3 Everywhere—from east to w— / praise the name
Isa 9:12 Arameans from the east and Philistines from the w.
11:14 join forces to swoop down on Philistia to the w.
24:14 Those in the w will praise the LORD's majesty.
27:12 River in the east to the brook of Egypt in the w.
43: 5 will gather you and your children from east and w
45: 6 so all the world from east to w will know there is
49:12 from lands to the north and w, and from as far
Jer 2:10 "Go w to the land of Cyprus; go east to the land of
Eze 7: 2 Wherever you look—east, w, north, or south—
41:12 A large building stood on the w, facing the Temple
41:15 The building to the w, including its two walls,
42:19 and so was the w side.
45: 7 and the second section will share a border on the w
46:19 He showed me a place at the extreme w end of
47:19 "The southern border will go w from Tamar to the
47:20 "On the w side the Mediterranean itself will be
48: 1 all the way across the land of Israel from east to w.
48: 2 south of Dan's and also extends from east to w.
48: 3 south of Asher's, also extending from east to w.
48: 4 and its territory also extends from east to w.
48: 7 all of whose boundaries extend from east to w.
48: 8 extend as far east and w as the tribal territories,
48:18 and 3-1/3 miles to the w along the border of the
48:21 to the east and to the w of the sacred lands
48:23 across the entire land of Israel from east to w.
48:24 also extending across the land from east to w.
48:26 which also extends across the land from east to w.
48:27 Zebulun with the same borders to the east and w.
48:34 And on the w wall, also 1-1/2 miles long, the gates
Da 8: 4 The ram butted everything out of its way to the w,
8: 5 suddenly a male goat appeared from the w,
Hos 11:10 and my people will return trembling from the w.
Jnh 1: 3 hoping that by going away to the w he could
Zec 6: 6 the chariot with white horses is going w,
8: 7 rescue my people from the east and from the w.
14: 4 making a wide valley running from east to w,
Mk 16: S sent them out from east to w with the sacred
Lk 12:54 "When you see clouds beginning to form in the w,
Rev 21:13 three gates on each side—east, north, south, and w.

WESTERN (24) [WEST]

Nu 34: 6 "Your w boundary will be the coastline of the
Dt 1: 7 the hill country, the w foothills, the Negev,
Jos 9: 1 who lived in the hill country, in the w foothills,
10:40 the Negev, the w foothills, and the mountain
11: 2 the kings in the w foothills; the kings of
11:16 the w foothills, the Jordan Valley,
12: 3 as far north as the w shores of the Sea of Galilee
12: 8 the w foothills, the Jordan Valley, the mountain
13:23 The Jordan River marked the w boundary for the
13:27 The Jordan River was the w border, extending as
15:12 The w boundary was the shoreline of the
15:33 The following towns situated in the w foothills
17:10 with the Mediterranean Sea forming Manasseh's w
18:14 then ran south along the w edge of the hill facing
18:14 to the tribe of Judah. This was the w boundary.
19:34 The w boundary ran past Aznoth-tabor, then to
Jdg 1: 9 in the hill country, the Negev, and the w foothills.
Ps 72:10 The w kings of Tarshish and the islands
Jer 17:26 from the w foothills and the hill country
Eze 45: 7 and w borders of the prince's lands will line up
45: 7 the eastern and w boundaries of the tribal areas.
48:21 directions to the eastern and w borders of Israel.
48:25 Issachar with the same eastern and w boundaries.
Da 11:30 For warships from w coastlands will scare him off,

WESTWARD (6) [WEST]

Ex 26:27 for the rear of the Tabernacle, which will face w.
Jos 12: 5 and w to the boundaries of the kingdoms of Geshur
16: 3 Then it descended w to the territory of the
16: 8 From Tappuah the border extended w,
18:15 From there it ran w to the spring at the waters of
Rev 16:12 east could march their armies w without hindrance.

WET (6) [WETNESS]

Ex 16:13 the desert all around the camp was w with dew.
Lev 11:38 But if the seed is w when the dead body falls on it,
Jdg 6:37 If the fleece is w with dew in the morning
6:39 dry while the ground around it is w with dew."
Job 16:13 without mercy. The ground is w with my blood.
Ps 6: 6 drench my bed; / my pillow is w from weeping.

WETNESS (1) [WET]

SS 5: 2 soaked with dew, my hair with the w of the night.'

WHALE(S), WHALE'S [KJV] See (GREAT) FISH, SEA (CREATURES, MONSTER)

WHAT (2460) [SOMEWHAT, WHAT'S, WHATEVER, WHATSOEVER] See Index of Articles, Etc.

WHAT'S (40) [BE, WHAT] See Index of Articles, Etc.

WHATEVER (167) [WHAT]

Ge 23: 9 the full price, of course, w is publicly agreed upon,
30:28 How much do I owe you? W it is, I'll pay it."
31:16 So go ahead and do w God has told you."
34:11 my wife," he begged. "I will give w you require.
41:55 told them, "Go to Joseph and do w he tells you."
Ex 12:10 W is not eaten that night must be burned before
12:36 and they gave the Israelites w they asked for.
21:30 of life. The owner will have to pay w is demanded.
29:37 and w touches it will become holy.
30:29 After this, w touches them will become holy.
34:34 Then he would give the people w instructions the
Lev 5:16 then make restitution for w holy things they have
6: 4 they must give back w they have taken by theft
7:16 and w is left over may be eaten on the second day.
11: 9 you may eat w has both fins and scales,
11:32 that object, w its use, will be unclean.
24:20 W anyone does to hurt another person must be
25:50 w it would cost to hire a servant for that number of
Nu 9:23 and they did w the LORD told them through
18:14 "W is specially set apart for the LORD also
22: 8 "In the morning I will tell you w the LORD
23: 3 Then I will tell you w he reveals to me."
23:26 "Didn't I tell you that I must do w the LORD
Dt 2: 6 Pay them for w food or water you use.
12: 8 "Today you are doing w you please, but that is
14: 9 you may eat w has both fins and scales.
15: 8 Instead, be generous and lend them w they need.
23:16 Let them live among you in w town they choose,
23:21 be prompt in doing w you promised him.
Jos 1:16 "We will do w you command us,
9:25 we are at your mercy—do w you think is right."
Jdg 11:10 leaders replied. "We promise to do w you say."
11:24 You keep w your god Chemosh gives you, and we will keep w the LORD our God gives us.
17: 6 so the people did w seemed right in their own eyes.
19:20 But w you do, don't spend the night in the
19:24 out to you, and you can do w you like to them.
21:25 so the people did w seemed right in their own eyes.
1Sa 1:23 "W you think is best," Elkanah agreed.
2:14 and demand that w it brought up be given to Eli's
10: 7 do w you think is best, for God will be with you.

12: 3 and I will make right **w** I have done wrong."
14: 7 "I'm with you completely, **w** you decide."
14:36 His men replied, "We'll do **w** you think is best."
18: 5 **W** Saul asked David to do, David did it
2Sa 16: 4 "I will always do **w** you want me to do."
18:22 with Joab, "**W** happens, please let me go, too."
19:37 and receive **w** good things you want to give him."
19:38 and I will do for him **w** I would have done for
1Ki 2:38 is fair; I will do **w** my lord the king commands."
5: 6 and I will pay your men **w** wages you ask.
5: 9 We will float them along the coast to **w** place you
8:37 the land besieging their towns—**w** the trouble is—
8:39 Give your people **w** they deserve, for you alone
10:13 King Solomon gave the queen of Sheba **w** she
11:38 follow my ways and do **w** I consider to be right,
14: 8 all his heart and always did **w** I wanted him to do.
2Ki 10: 5 not make anyone king; do **w** you think is best."
12: 5 to pay for **w** repairs are needed at the Temple."
18:14 I will pay **w** tribute money you demand if you will
1Ch 16:37 doing **w** needed to be done each day.
2Ch 2:16 We will cut **w** timber you need from the Lebanon
6:28 the land besieging their towns—**w** the trouble is—
6:30 Give your people **w** they deserve, for you alone
9:12 King Solomon gave the queen of Sheba **w** she
Ezr 6: 9 Give the priests in Jerusalem **w** is needed in the
7:18 Any money that is left over may be used in **w** way
7:21 'You are to give Ezra **w** he requests of you, for he
7:23 Be careful to provide **w** the God of heaven
Est 1:20 husbands everywhere, **w** their rank, will receive
2:13 she was given her choice of **w** clothing or jewelry
8: 8 telling them **w** you want, and seal it with the king's
8: 8 But remember that **w** is written in the king's name
Job 1:12 "Do **w** you want with everything he possesses,
9:29 **W** happens, I will be found guilty. So what's the
22:28 **W** you decide to do will be accomplished,
23:13 him from his purposes? **W** he wants to do, he does.
37:12 They do **w** he commands throughout the earth.
Ps 33: 5 He loves **w** is just and good, / and his unfailing
41: 8 "**W** he has, it is fatal," they say. / "He will never
135: 6 The LORD does **w** pleases him / throughout all
Pr 4: 7 can do! And **w** else you do, get good judgment.
21:20 and luxury, but fools spend **w** they get.
Ecc 3:14 And I know that **w** God does is final. Nothing can
3:15 **W** exists today and **w** will exist in the future has already existed in
5:18 and enjoy their work—**w** they do under the sun—
9: 6 **W** they did in their lifetime—loving, hating,
9:10 **W** you do, do well. For when you go to the grave,
Isa 46:10 I plan will come to pass, for I do **w** I wish.
Jer 1: 7 must go wherever I send you and say **w** I tell you.
1:17 Go out, and tell them **w** I tell you to say.
7:24 They kept on doing **w** they wanted,
11: 4 "If you obey me and do **w** I command you,
42: 5 against us if we refuse to obey **w** he tells us to do!
44:17 We will do **w** we want. We will burn incense to the
Eze 1:12 They went in **w** direction the spirit chose, and they
12: 3 Pack **w** you can carry on your back and leave your
21:24 Wherever you go, **w** you do, all your actions are
24: 6 So take the meat out chunk by chunk in **w** order it
36:27 so you will obey my laws and do **w** I command.
44:29 **W** anyone sets apart for the LORD will belong to
46: 5 and **w** amount of flour he chooses to go with each
46: 7 And with each lamb he is to bring **w** amount of
Da 3: 7 all the people, **w** their race or nation or language,
3:29 If any people, **w** their race or nation or language,
Zec 11:12 "If you like, give me my wages, **w** I am worth;
Mt 4:24 And **w** their illness and pain, or if they were
7: 2 **W** measure you use in judging others, it will be
12:34 For **w** is in your heart determines what you say.
16:19 **W** you lock on earth will be locked in heaven, and **w** you open on earth will be opened in
18:18 **W** you prohibit on earth is prohibited in heaven, and **w** you allow on earth is allowed in heaven.
20: 4 telling them he would pay them **w** was right at the
21:22 you will receive **w** you ask for in prayer."
23: 3 So practice and obey **w** they say to you, but don't
Mk 6:23 Then he promised, "I will give you **w** you ask,
Lk 1:38 and I am willing to accept **w** he wants.
6:38 **W** measure you use in giving—large or small—
6:45 **W** is in your heart determines what you say.
10: 8 "If a town welcomes you, eat **w** is set before you
12: 3 **W** you have said in the dark will be heard in the
14: 9 and will have to take **w** seat is left at the foot of the
Jn 2: 5 his mother told the servants, "Do **w** he tells you."
5:19 **W** the Father does, the Son also does.
11:22 But even now I know that God will give you **w** you
12:50 eternal life; so I say **w** the Father tells me to say!"
15:16 so that the Father will give you **w** you ask for,
16:14 He will bring me glory by revealing to you **w** he
16:15 the Spirit will reveal to you **w** he receives from me.
Ac 13:45 they slandered Paul and argued against **w** he said.
Ro 1:24 and **w** shameful things their hearts desired.
6:16 Don't you realize that **w** you choose to obey
1Co 4: 5 then God will give to everyone **w** praise is due.
7:17 You must accept **w** situation the Lord has put you
7:24 **w** situation you were in when you became a
7:35 I want you to do **w** will help you serve the Lord
10:27 Eat **w** is offered to you and don't ask any questions
10:31 **W** you eat or drink or **w** you do, you must
15:10 But **w** I am now, it is all because God poured out
15:37 dry little seed of wheat or **w** it is you are planting.
2Co 2:10 And when I forgive him (for **w** is to be forgiven),
5:10 We will each receive **w** we deserve for the good
5:14 **W** we do, it is because Christ's love controls us.
8: 5 and to us for **w** directions God might give them.
8:11 Give **w** you can according to what you have.
11: 4 You seem to believe **w** anyone tells you, even if
11:21 But **w** they dare to boast about—I'm talking like a
Gal 4: 2 guardians until they reach **w** age their father set.
Php 1:27 But **w** happens to me, you must live in a manner
3: 1 **W** happens, dear friends, may the Lord give you
Col 3:17 And **w** you do or say, let it be as a representative of
3:23 Work hard and cheerfully at **w** you do, as though
1Ti 6:18 always being ready to share with others **w** God has
2Ti 2:26 For they have been held captive by him to do **w** he
4: 3 and will look for teachers who will tell them **w**
Jas 1:17 **W** is good and perfect comes to us from God
2:12 So whenever you speak, or **w** you do,
2:22 so much that he was willing to do **w** God told him
1Pe 2:18 Do **w** they tell you—not only if they are kind
2Pe 2:19 For you are a slave to **w** controls you.
1Jn 3:22 And we will receive **w** we request because we
Jude 1:10 Like animals, they do **w** their instincts tell them,
1:16 and complainers, doing **w** evil they feel like.
Rev 2:23 And I will give to each of you **w** you deserve.

WHATSOEVER (4) [WHAT]

Hos 10: 9 and more sin! You have made no progress **w**.
Ro 1:20 So they have no excuse **w** for not knowing God.
8:12 you have no obligation **w** to do what your sinful
1Co 13: 3 if I didn't love others, I would be of no value **w**.

WHEAT (52)

Ge 30:14 One day during the **w** harvest, Reuben found some
Ex 9:32 But the **w** and the spelt were not destroyed
29: 2 Then using fine **w** flour and no yeast, make loaves
34:22 of Harvest with the first crop of the **w** harvest,
Dt 8: 8 It is a land of **w** and barley, of grapevines,
32:14 goats from Bashan, / together with the choicest **w**.
Jdg 6:11 Gideon son of Joash had been threshing **w** at the
15: 1 Later on, during the **w** harvest, Samson took a
Ru 2:23 Then she worked with them through the **w** harvest,
1Sa 6:13 The people of Beth-shemesh were harvesting **w** in
12:17 rain at this time of the year during the **w** harvest.
2Sa 4: 6 who had been sifting **w**, became drowsy and fell
17:28 **w** and barley flour, roasted grain, beans, lentils,
1Ki 5:11 payment of 100,000 bushels of **w** for his household
1Ch 21:20 who was busy threshing **w** at the time, turned
21:23 And take the **w** for the grain offering. I will give it
2Ch 2:10 I will pay your men 100,000 bushels of crushed **w**,
2:15 "Send along the **w**, barley, olive oil, and wine that
27: 5 50,000 bushels of **w**, and 50,000 bushels of barley.
Ezr 6: 9 without fail, provide them with the **w**, salt, wine,
7:22 500 bushels of **w**, 550 gallons of wine, 550 gallons
Job 31:40 then let thistles grow on that land instead of **w**
Ps 147:14 and satisfies you with plenty of the finest **w**.
Pr 20:26 A wise king finds the wicked, lays them out like **w**,
SS 7: 2 is lovely, like a heap of **w** set about with lilies.
Isa 28:25 cummin, **w**, barley, and spelt, each in its own
Jer 12:13 My people have planted **w** but are harvesting
23:28 There is a difference between chaff and **w**!
31:12 the good crops of **w**, wine, and oil, and the healthy
41: 8 go by promising to bring him their stores of **w**,
51:33 "Babylon is like **w** on a threshing floor, about to
Eze 4: 9 "Now go and get some **w**, barley, beans, lentils,
27:17 offering **w** from Minnith, early figs, honey, oil,
45:13 one bushel of **w** or barley for every sixty you
Hos 8: 7 The stalks of **w** wither, producing no grain. And if
Joel 1:11 Weep, because the **w** and barley—yes, all the field
Am 8: 6 And you mix the **w** you sell with chaff swept from
Mt 12: 1 so they began breaking off heads of **w** and eating
13:25 his enemy came and planted weeds among the **w**.
13:29 "He replied, 'No, you'll hurt the **w** if you do.
13:30 and burn them and to put the **w** in the barn.' "
13:39 The enemy who planted the weeds among the **w** is
Mk 2:23 his disciples began breaking off heads of **w**.
4:28 then the heads of **w** are formed, and finally the
Lk 6: 1 his disciples broke off heads of **w**, rubbed off the
16: 7 'A thousand bushels of **w**,' was the reply. 'Here,'
22:31 has asked to have all of you, to sift you like **w**.
Jn 12:24 truth is, a kernel of **w** must be planted in the soil.
Ac 27:38 ship further by throwing the cargo of **w** overboard.
1Co 15:37 but only a dry little seed of **w** or whatever it is you
Rev 6: 6 "A loaf of **w** bread or three loaves of barley for a
18:13 fine flour, **w**, cattle, sheep, horses, chariots,

WHEEL (9) [WHEELS]

Pr 20:26 out like wheat, then runs the crushing **w** over them.
Isa 28:27 A threshing **w** is never rolled on cummin; instead,
Jer 18: 3 he told me and found the potter working at his **w**.
Eze 1:15 the ground beneath them, one **w** belonging to each.
1:16 each **w** had a second **w** turning crosswise
10: 9 Each of the four cherubim had a **w** beside him,
10:10 each **w** had a second **w** turning crosswise

WHEELS (38) [WHEEL]

Ex 14:25 Their chariot **w** began to come off, making their
Jdg 5:28 Why don't we hear the sound of chariot **w**?'
1Ki 7:30 Each of these carts had four bronze **w** and bronze
7:32 Under the panels were four **w** that were connected
7:32 with the cart. The **w** were 2-1/4 feet in diameter
7:33 and were similar to chariot **w**. The axles, spokes,
Isa 5:28 Sparks will fly from their horses' hooves as the **w**
28:28 He threshes it under the **w** of a cart, but he doesn't
Jer 47: 3 and the rumble of **w** as the chariots rush by.
Eze 1:15 I saw four **w** on the ground beneath them,
1:16 The **w** sparkled as if made of chrysolite. All four **w** looked the same; each wheel had a
1:18 The rims of the four **w** were awesomely tall,
1:19 four living beings moved, the **w** moved with them.
1:19 When they flew upward, the **w** went up, too.
1:20 The spirit of the four living beings was in the **w**.
1:20 spirit went, the **w** and the living beings went, too.
1:21 When the living beings moved, the **w** moved.
1:21 When the living beings stopped, the **w** stopped.
1:21 the living beings flew into the air, the **w** rose up.
1:21 For the spirit of the living beings was in the **w**.
3:13 and the rumbling of their **w** beneath them.
10: 2 "Go in between the whirling **w** beneath the
10: 6 and take some burning coals from between the **w**."
10: 6 So the man went in and stood beside one of the **w**.
10: 9 beside him, and the **w** sparkled like chrysolite.
10:10 All four **w** looked the same; each wheel had a
10:12 the cherubim and the **w** were covered with eyes.
10:13 I heard someone refer to the **w** as "the whirling **w**."
10:16 the cherubim moved, the **w** moved with them.
10:16 they rose into the air, the **w** stayed beside them,
10:17 When the cherubim stood still, the **w** also stopped,
10:17 for the spirit of the living beings was in the **w**.
10:19 the cherubim flew with their **w** to the east gate of
11:22 and rose into the air with their **w** beside them,
Da 7: 9 He sat on a fiery throne with **w** of blazing fire,
Na 3: 2 **W** rumble, horses' hooves pound, and chariots

WHELP(S) [KJV] See CUB(S)

WHEN (2835) [WHENEVER] See Index of Articles, Etc.

WHENCE [KJV] See HOW, THERE, WHERE, WHICH, WHY

WHENEVER (81) [WHEN]

Ge 6: 4 for **w** the sons of God had intercourse with human
30:41 **W** the stronger females were ready to mate,
38: 9 So **w** he had intercourse with Tamar, he spilled the
Ex 12:39 **W** they stopped to eat, they baked bread from the
17:11 But **w** he lowered his hands, the Amalekites gained
28:30 will for his people **w** he goes in before the LORD.
28:35 Aaron will wear this robe **w** he enters the Holy
28:43 These must be worn **w** Aaron and his sons enter
29:28 **w** the people of Israel offer up peace offerings
30:12 "**W** you take a census of the people of Israel,
33: 8 **W** Moses went out to the Tent of Meeting,
34:34 But **w** he went into the Tent of Meeting to speak
40:32 **W** they walked past the altar to enter the
40:36 Now **w** the cloud lifted from the Tabernacle
Lev 1: 2 **W** you present offerings to the LORD, you must
15:16 "**W** a man has an emission of semen, he must
15:19 "**W** a woman has her menstrual period, she will be
16: 2 Holy Place behind the inner curtain **w** he chooses;
Nu 1:51 **W** the Tabernacle is moved, the Levites will take it
2: 9 These three tribes are to lead the way **w** the
2:16 These three tribes will be second in line **w** the
2:31 They are to bring up the rear **w** the Israelites move
7:89 **W** Moses went into the Tabernacle to speak with
10:35 And **w** the Ark set out, Moses would cry, "Arise,
21: 9 **W** those who were bitten looked at the bronze
Dt 4: 7 LORD our God is near to us **w** we call on him?
12:20 as he has promised, you may eat meat **w** you want.
23:13 **W** you relieve yourself, you must dig a hole with
Jdg 2:18 **W** the LORD placed a judge over Israel, he was
6: 3 **W** the Israelites planted their crops,
12: 5 and **w** a fugitive from Ephraim tried to go back
14:17 So she cried **w** she was with him and kept it up for
1Sa 2:13 **W** anyone offered a sacrifice, Eli's sons would
13:20 So **w** the Israelites needed to sharpen their
14:52 So **w** Saul saw a young man who was brave
16:16 for you **w** the tormenting spirit is bothering you.
16:23 And **w** the tormenting spirit from God troubled
18:10 began to play the harp, as he did **w** this happened.
18:30 **W** the Philistine army attacked, David was more
23:20 Come down **w** you're ready, O king, and we will
1Ki 8:52 Hear and answer them **w** they cry out to you.
14:28 **W** the king went to the Temple of the LORD,
2Ki 4: 8 From then on, **w** he passed that way, he would stop
4:10 Then he will have a place to stay **w** he comes by."
12:10 **W** the chest became full, the court secretary
2Ch 12:11 **W** the king went to the Temple of the LORD,
15: 2 **W** you seek him, you will find him. But if you
15: 4 But **w** you were in distress and turned to the
19:10 **W** a case comes to you from fellow citizens in an
20: 9 '**W** we are faced with any calamity such as war,
24:11 **W** the chest became full, the Levites carried it to
Ne 9:28 Yet **w** your people cried to you again for help,
Est 3: 2 before Haman to show him respect **w** he passed by,
Job 31:19 **W** I saw someone who was homeless and without
39:18 But **w** she jumps up to run, she passes the swiftest
Ps 86: 7 I will call to you **w** trouble strikes, / and you will
Jer 20: 8 **W** I speak, the words come out in a violent
29:22 so that **w** the Judean exiles want to curse someone
36:23 **W** Jehudi finished reading three or four columns,
Eze 3:17 **W** you receive a message from me, pass it on to
3:27 But **w** I give you a message, I will loosen your
39:15 **W** some bones are found, a marker will be set up
46:12 **W** the prince offers a voluntary burnt offering
Mt 10:11 **W** you enter a city or village, search for a worthy
Mk 3:11 And **w** those possessed by evil spirits caught sight
5: 4 **W** he was put into chains and shackles—as he
6:20 Herod was disturbed **w** he talked with John,
9:18 And **w** this evil spirit seizes him, it throws him
14: 7 among you, and you can help them **w** you want to.
Lk 10: 5 "**W** you enter a home, give it your blessing.
12:38 But **w** he comes, there will be special favor for his
1Co 13: 6 about injustice but rejoices **w** the truth wins out.
2Co 3:14 and even to this day **w** the old covenant is being
3:16 But **w** anyone turns to the Lord, then the veil is

Gal 6:10 W we have the opportunity, we should do good to
Heb 2:4 and by giving gifts of the Holy Spirit w he chose to
12:15 for w it springs up, many are corrupted by its
Jas 1:2 and sisters, w trouble comes your way,
2:12 So w you speak, or whatever you do,
1Jn 5:14 And we can be confident that he will listen to us w
Rev 4:9 W the living beings give glory and honor

WHERE (737) [ELSEWHERE, SOMEWHERE, WHEREVER]

Ge 2:11 around the entire land of Havilah, w gold is found.
3:9 The LORD God called to Adam, "W are you?"
4:9 the LORD asked Cain, "W is your brother? W is Abel?"
10:11 w he built Nineveh, Rehoboth-ir, Calah,
13:3 between Bethel and Ai w they had camped before.
13:4 This was the place w Abram had built the altar,
16:8 "Hagar, Sarai's servant, w have you come from, and w are you going?"
18:9 "W is Sarah, your wife?" they asked him.
19:5 "W are the men who came to spend the night with
19:27 and hurried out to the place w he had stood in the
20:15 and choose a place w you would like to live,"
21:17 God has heard the boy's cries from the place w
21:31 because that was w they had sworn an oath.
22:3 and set out for the place w God had told him to go.
22:7 said the boy, "but w is the lamb for the sacrifice?"
22:9 When they arrived at the place w God had told
22:19 w Abraham lived for quite some time.
24:10 and went to the village w Abraham's brother
24:30 w the man was still standing beside his camels.
25:10 from the Hittites, w he had buried his wife Sarah.
26:1 w Abimelech, king of the Philistines, lived.
26:24 w the LORD appeared to him on the night of his
28:4 May you own this land w we now are foreigners,
29:4 the shepherds and asked them, "W do you live?"
30:36 and they took them three days' distance from w
31:4 and Leah out to the field w he was watching the
31:13 the place w you anointed the pillar of stone
31:18 to the land of Canaan, w his father, Isaac, lived.
32:13 Jacob stayed w he was for the night and prepared a
32:17 you meet Esau, he will ask, 'W are you going?
35:3 w I will build an altar to the God who answered
35:13 Then God went up from the place w he had spoken
35:14 Jacob set up a stone pillar to mark the place w God
35:27 (now called Hebron), w Abraham had also lived.
37:1 again in the land of Canaan, w his father had lived.
38:1 to Adullam, w he visited a man named Hirah.
38:21 "W can I find the prostitute who was sitting beside
39:20 and threw him into the prison w the king's
40:3 and he put them in the prison w Joseph was,
42:7 "W are you from?" he demanded roughly.
42:24 left the room and found a place w he could weep.
43:15 to Egypt, w they presented themselves to Joseph.
43:18 They were badly frightened when they saw w they
43:33 Joseph told each of his brothers w to sit, and to
Ex 2:20 "Well, w is he then?" their father asked.
3:8 the land w the Canaanites, Hittites, Amorites,
4:27 w he found Moses and greeted him warmly.
6:4 give them the land of Canaan, w they were living.
8:22 in the land of Goshen, w the Israelites live.
8:26 If we offer them here w they can see us, they will
9:26 the land of Goshen, w the people of Israel lived.
10:23 But there was light as usual w the people of Israel
12:7 and sides of the doorframe of the house w the lamb
12:30 There was not a single house w someone had not
13:11 long ago, the land w the Canaanites are now living.
14:13 Just stand w you are and watch the LORD rescue
15:13 your strength / to the place w your holiness dwells.
15:27 w there were twelve springs and seventy palm
16:35 in the land of Canaan, w there were crops to eat.
20:21 Moses entered into the deep darkness w God was.
20:24 Build altars in the places w I remind you who I am,
21:13 I will appoint a place w the slayer can run for
25:8 me a sacred residence w I can live among them.
25:35 of branches w they extend from the center stem.
29:42 w I will meet you and speak with you.
30:36 w I will meet with you in the Tabernacle.
34:12 with the people in the land w you are going.
37:21 of branches, w they extended from the center stem.
Lev 4:12 outside the camp, the place w the ashes are thrown.
4:24 and slaughter it before the LORD at the place w
4:29 and slaughter it at the place w burnt offerings are
4:33 and slaughter it at the place w the burnt offerings
6:25 at the place w the burnt offerings are slaughtered.
7:2 slaughtered w the burnt offerings are slaughtered,
14:13 there in the sacred area at the place w sin offerings
15:6 If you sit w the man with the discharge has sat,
18:3 w you used to live, or like the people of Canaan, w I am taking you.
18:27 by the people of the land w I am taking you,
Nu 4:7 w the Bread of the Presence is displayed, and place
5:3 will not defile the camp, w I live among you."
9:18 Then they remained w they were as long as the
10:31 "You know the places in the wilderness w we
10:33 moving ahead of them to show them w to stop
11:13 W am I supposed to get meat for all these people?
11:35 traveled to Hazeroth, w they stayed for some time.
13:22 at Hebron, w Ahiman, Sheshai, and Talmai—
14:25 and don't go on toward the land w the Amalekites
15:18 When you arrive in the land w I am taking you,
17:4 of the Ark of the Covenant, w I meet with you.
19:6 and throw them into the fire w the heifer is
20:6 w they fell face down on the ground.
20:9 He took the staff from the place w it was kept
20:13 because it was w the people of Israel argued with
20:13 and w he demonstrated his holiness among them.
21:16 which is the well w the LORD said to Moses,
21:20 Then they went to the valley in Moab w Pisgah
22:24 Then the angel of the LORD stood at a place w
22:40 w the king sacrificed cattle and sheep. He sent
23:17 So Balaam returned to the place w the king
24:2 w he saw the people of Israel camped, tribe by
31:10 the towns and villages w the Midianites had lived.
32:19 We would rather live here on the east side w we
33:9 w there are twelve springs of water and seventy
33:14 w there was no water for the people to drink.
33:55 They will harass you in the land w you live.
35:6 w a person who has accidentally killed someone
35:33 This will ensure that the land w you live will not
35:34 You must not defile the land w you are going to
Dt 3:1 w King Og and his army attacked us at Edrei.
4:3 w the LORD your God destroyed everyone who
4:10 w he told me, 'Summon the people before me,
4:27 the nations, w only a few of you will survive.
4:42 w anyone who had accidentally killed someone
8:9 It is a land w food is plentiful and nothing is
8:9 It is a land w iron is as common as stone,
8:15 and scorpions, w it was so hot and dry.
9:8 at Mount Sinai, w he was ready to destroy you.
10:6 traveled to Moserah, w Aaron died and was buried.
11:10 w you planted your seed and dug out irrigation
12:2 you must destroy all the places w they worship
17:9 w the Levitical priests and the judge on duty will
21:12 w she must shave her head, cut her fingernails,
29:28 them to another land, w they still live today!'
30:3 and gather you back from all the nations w he has
31:16 the gods of the land w they are going.
32:37 Then he will ask, 'W are their gods, / the rocks
32:38 W now are those gods, / who ate the fat of their
Jos 2:4 here earlier, but I didn't know w they were from.
2:5 were about to close, and I don't know w they went.
3:1 the Jordan River, w they camped before crossing.
4:3 Tell the men to take twelve stones from w the
4:3 and pile them up at the place w you camp
4:8 They carried them to the place w they camped for
4:9 at the place w the priests who carried the Ark of
4:22 'This is w the Israelites crossed the Jordan on dry
9:8 Joshua demanded. "W do you come from?"
10:27 and thrown into the cave w they had been hiding.
15:3 w it turned up to Addar, w it turned toward Karka.
15:5 The northern boundary began at the bay w the
15:8 of the Jebusites, w the city of Jerusalem is located.
15:11 w it turned toward Shikkeron and Mount Baalah.
17:15 clear out land for yourselves in the forest w the
18:16 crossing south of the slope w the Jebusites lived,
22:19 w the LORD lives among us in his Tabernacle,
Jdg 1:26 moved to the land of the Hittites, w he built a city.
1:32 the Canaanites dominated the land w the people of
1:33 the Canaanites dominated the land w they lived.
6:2 w they made hiding places for themselves in caves
6:13 And w are all the miracles our ancestors told us
9:38 "Now w is that big mouth of yours?"
13:6 I didn't ask w he was from, and he didn't tell me
16:21 w he was bound with bronze chains and made to
16:31 and Eshtaol, w his father, Manoah, was buried.
17:9 "W are you from?" Micah asked him. And he
18:7 w they noticed the people living carefree lives,
18:15 w the young Levite lived, and greeted him kindly.
19:12 "we can't stay in this foreign city w there are no
19:17 he asked them w they were from and w they were going.
19:26 At daybreak the woman returned to the house w
20:33 west of Gibeah jumped up from w they were
20:47 the rock of Rimmon, w they lived for four months.
Ru 1:7 she set out from the place w she had been living,
1:17 I will die w you die and will be buried there.
2:19 "W did you gather all this grain today? W did you work?
3:4 Be sure to notice w he lies down; then go
1Sa 4:4 helped carry the Ark of God to w the battle was
4:21 "W is the glory?"—murmuring, "Israel's glory is
6:18 w they set the Ark of the LORD,
6:20 cried out. "W can we send the Ark from here?"
9:10 So they started into the town w the man of God
9:18 "Can you please tell me w the seer's house is?"
10:5 of God, w the garrison of the Philistines is located,
10:14 "W in the world have you been?" Saul's uncle
10:14 So we went to the prophet Samuel to ask him w
10:22 So they asked the LORD, "W is he?"
11:12 "Now w are those men who said Saul shouldn't
14:1 let's go over to w the Philistines have their
14:9 If they say to us, 'Stay w you are or we'll kill you,'
15:6 "Move away from w the Amalekites live or else
19:22 "W are Samuel and David?" he demanded.
20:6 If your father asks w I am, tell him I asked
20:19 toward evening, go to the place w you hid before,
20:41 David came out from w he had been hiding near
21:2 I am here. I have told my men w to meet me later.
22:3 w he asked the king, "Would you let my father
23:19 to him. "We know w David is hiding," they said.
23:22 and check again to be sure of w he is staying
23:28 the place w David was camped has been called the
24:3 At the place w the road passes some sheepfolds,
24:18 for when the LORD put me in a place w you
25:11 a band of outlaws who come from who knows w?"
26:3 of Hakilah, near Jeshimon, w David was hiding.
26:15 "W in all Israel is there anyone as mighty?
26:16 W are the king's spear and the jug of water that
27:10 "W did you make your raid today?"
27:11 to come to Gath and tell w he had really been.
30:13 whom do you belong, and w do you come from?"
30:27 sent to the leaders of the following towns w David
31:12 brought them to Jabesh, w they burned the bodies.
2Sa 1:3 "W have you come from?" David asked.
1:13 who had brought the news, "W are you from?"
4:3 fled to Gittaim, w they still live as foreigners.
7:10 a secure place w they will never be disturbed.
7:10 It will be their own land w wicked nations won't
9:4 "W is he?" the king asked. "In Lo-debar,"
11:15 "Station Uriah on the front lines w the battle is
11:16 w he knew the enemy's strongest men were
13:8 she went to the room w he was lying down so he
13:13 W could I go in my shame? And you would be
15:2 Absalom would ask w they were from, and they
15:20 I don't even know w we will go. Go on back
15:32 of the Mount of Olives w people worshiped God,
16:3 "And w is Mephibosheth?" the king asked him.
16:22 So they set up a tent on the palace roof w everyone
17:18 w a man hid them inside a well in his courtyard.
19:37 my own town, w my father and mother are buried.
20:6 he gets into a fortified city w we can't reach him."
1Ki 1:9 w he sacrificed sheep, oxen, and fattened calves.
2:2 "I am going w everyone on earth must someday
2:39 of Gath. When Shimei learned w they were,
3:15 w he sacrificed burnt offerings and peace
6:19 w the Ark of the LORD's covenant would be
7:7 of Judgment, w Solomon sat to hear legal matters.
8:9 w the LORD made a covenant with the people of
8:13 glorious Temple for you, w you can live forever!"
8:16 w a temple should be built to honor my name.
8:29 this place w you have said you would put your
8:30 Yes, hear us from heaven w you live, and when
8:39 then hear from heaven w you live, and forgive.
8:43 then hear from heaven w you live, and grant what
8:49 then hear their prayers from heaven w you live.
8:54 w he had been kneeling with his hands raised
9:19 and constructed cities w his chariots and horses
11:18 and went to Paran, w others joined them.
11:24 and his men fled to Damascus, w he became king.
12:1 w all Israel had gathered to make him king.
13:22 and drank water w he told you not to eat or drink.
13:25 and reported it in Bethel, w the old prophet lived.
13:31 bury me in the grave w the man of God is buried.
17:3 and hide by Kerith Brook at a place east of w it
17:19 w he lived, and laid the body on his bed.
18:12 the LORD will carry you away to who knows w.
19:9 There he came to a cave, w he spent the night.
21:8 and other leaders of the city w Naboth lived.
22:38 w the prostitutes bathed, and dogs came and licked
2Ki 2:14 with the cloak and cried out, "W is the LORD,
5:25 Elisha asked him, "W have you been, Gehazi?"
6:1 this place w we meet with you is too small.
6:2 to the Jordan River, w there are plenty of logs.
6:6 "W did it fall?" the man of God asked. When he
6:13 king commanded, "Go and find out w Elisha is,
8:7 the capital of Aram, w King Ben-hadad lay sick.
9:28 w they buried him with his ancestors in the City of
10:6 w they had been raised since childhood.
11:16 and led her out to the gate w horses enter the
14:4 w the people offered sacrifices and burned incense.
15:4 w the people offered sacrifices and burned incense.
15:35 w the people offered sacrifices and burned incense.
17:23 to the land of Assyria, w they remain to this day.
17:29 In town after town w they lived, they placed their
18:17 near the road leading to the field w cloth is
19:7 w I will have him killed with a sword.' "
20:14 W were they from?" Hezekiah replied,
21:4 the place w the LORD had said his name should
21:7 The very place w the LORD had told David
23:6 Jerusalem to the Kidron Valley, w he burned it.
23:7 w the women wove coverings for the Asherah
23:8 w they had burned incense, from Geba to
23:13 w King Solomon of Israel had built shrines for
23:27 and the Temple w my name was to be honored."
23:34 was taken to Egypt as a prisoner, w he died.
25:6 at Riblah, w sentence was passed against him.
1Ch 3:4 in Hebron, w he reigned seven and a half years.
3:4 w he reigned another thirty-three years.
5:26 and the Gozan River, w they remain to this day.
11:4 (or Jebus, as it used to be called), w the Jebusites,
12:37 w the tribes of Reuben and Gad and the half-tribe
16:39 w they continued to minister before the LORD.
17:9 a secure place w they will never be disturbed.
17:9 It will be their own land w wicked nations won't
19:7 w they were joined by the Ammonite troops that
28:2 It was my desire to build a temple w the Ark of the
28:11 and the inner sanctuary w the Ark's cover—
2Ch 1:3 the hill at Gibeon w God's Tabernacle was located.
3:1 w the LORD had appeared to Solomon's father,
6:2 glorious Temple for you, w you can live forever!"
6:5 w a temple should be built to honor my name.
6:20 this place w you have said you would put your
6:21 Yes, hear us from heaven w you live, and when
6:30 then hear from heaven w you live, and forgive.
6:33 then hear from heaven w you live, and grant what
6:39 then hear their prayers from heaven w you live.
6:41 of yours, w your magnificent Ark has been placed.
8:6 and constructed cities w his chariots and horses
10:1 w all Israel had gathered to make him king.
11:15 w they worshiped the goat and calf idols he had
11:16 w they could offer sacrifices to the LORD,
20:9 before this Temple w your name is honored.
23:3 w they made a covenant with Joash, the young
23:15 and led her out to the gate w horses enter the
25:11 w they killed ten thousand Edomite troops from
31:9 "W did all this come from?" Hezekiah asked the
33:4 the place w the LORD had said his name should
33:7 the very place w God had told David and his son
33:14 around the hill of Ophel, w it was built very high.

33:15 altars he had built on the hill **w** the Temple stood
33:19 a list of the locations **w** he built pagan shrines
35:24 they brought him back to Jerusalem, **w** he died.
Ezr 1: 4 Those who live in any place **w** Jewish survivors
4:15 **w** you will discover what a rebellious city this has
6: 1 the Babylonian archives, **w** treasures were stored.
6: 3 It must be rebuilt on the site **w** Jews used to offer
8:32 safely in Jerusalem, **w** we rested for three days.
9: 5 I stood up from **w** I had sat in mourning with my
Ne 2: 3 For the city **w** my ancestors are buried is in ruins,
2: 5 send me to Judah to rebuild the city **w** my
11: 1 live there, too, while the rest stayed **w** they were.
12:40 to the Temple of God, **w** they took their places.
Est 2:14 to the second harem, **w** the king's wives lived.
7: 8 In despair he fell on the couch **w** Queen Esther was
Job 1: 7 "**W** have you come from?" the LORD asked
2: 2 "**W** have you come from?" the LORD asked
8:11 "Can papyrus reeds grow **w** there is no marsh?
8:11 Can bulrushes flourish **w** there is no water?
10:22 a land of utter gloom **w** confusion reigns
14:10 They breathe their last, and then **w** are they?
15:23 They wander abroad for bread, saying, '**W** is it?'
17:15 But **w** then is my hope? Can anyone find it?
20: 7 Those who knew him will ask, '**W** is he?'
22:15 "Will you continue on the old paths **w** evil people
23: 3 If only I knew **w** to find God, I would go to his
23:10 But he knows **w** I am going. And when he has
26: 4 **W** have you gotten all these wise sayings?
28: 4 They sink a mine shaft into the earth far from **w**
28:12 "But do people know **w** to find wisdom? **W** can
they find understanding?
28:13 No one knows **w** to find it, for it is not found
28:20 "But do people know **w** to find wisdom? **W** can
they find understanding?
28:22 'We have heard a rumor of **w** wisdom can be
28:23 "God surely knows **w** it can be found,
35:10 Yet they don't ask, '**W** is God my Creator, the one
35:11 **W** is the one who makes us wiser than the animals
38: 4 "**W** were you when I laid the foundations of the
38:17 Do you know **w** the gates of death are located?
38:19 "**W** does the light come from, and **w** does the
darkness go?
38:22 Have you seen **w** the hail is made and stored?
38:24 **W** is the path to the origin of light? **W** is the home
of the east wind?
38:26 rain fall on barren land, in a desert **w** no one lives?
38:28 the rain have a father? **W** does dew come from?
39: 8 **w** it searches for every blade of grass.
40:12 with a glance; walk on the wicked **w** they stand.
40:20 offer it their best food, **w** all the wild animals play.
Ps 19: 4 The sun lives in the heavens / **w** God placed it.
25: 4 Show me the path **w** I should walk, O LORD;
26: 8 LORD, / the place **w** your glory shines.
31: 2 a fortress **w** my enemies cannot reach me.
39: 7 And so, Lord, **w** do I put my hope? / My only hope
42: 3 taunt me, saying, / "**W** is this God of yours?"
42:10 They scoff, "**W** is this God of yours?"
43: 3 to your holy mountain, / to the place **w** you live.
49:11 is their eternal home, / **w** they will stay forever.
49:14 led to the grave, / **w** death will be their shepherd.
54: T and said to Saul, "We know **w** David is hiding."
61: 3 a fortress **w** my enemies cannot reach me.
62: 2 my fortress **w** I will never be shaken.
62: 6 my salvation, / my fortress **w** I will not be shaken.
62: 7 He is my refuge, a rock **w** no enemy can reach me.
63: 1 this parched and weary land / **w** there is no water.
65: 8 From **w** the sun rises to **w** it sets, / you inspire
68:16 at Mount Zion, **w** God has chosen to live, / **w** the
LORD himself will live forever?
71: 3 rock of safety, / **w** I am always welcome.
74: 8 So they burned down all the places **w** God was
76: 2 Jerusalem is **w** he lives; / Mount Zion is his home.
78:60 the Tabernacle **w** he had lived among the people.
79:10 be allowed to scoff, / asking, "**W** is their God?"
84: 6 **w** pools of blessing collect after the rains!
89: 8 **W** is there anyone as mighty as you, LORD?
89:49 Lord, **w** is your unfailing love? / You promised it
94:22 my God is a mighty rock **w** I can hide.
107: 7 them straight to safety, / to a city **w** they could live.
115: 2 Why let the nations say, / "**W** is their God?"
118:19 Open for me the gates **w** the righteous enter,
119:35 for that is **w** my happiness is found.
122: 5 Here stand the thrones **w** judgment is given,
132:14 "This is my home **w** I will live forever," he said.
139: 3 path ahead of me / and tell me **w** to stop and rest. /
Every moment you know **w** I am.
143: 8 for I am trusting you. / Show me **w** to walk,
Pr 5: 6 a crooked trail and doesn't even realize **w** it leads.
8:12 I know **w** to discover knowledge and discernment.
24:15 And don't raid the house **w** the godly live.
24:22 Who knows **w** the punishment from the LORD
Ecc 8: 9 **w** people have the power to hurt each other.
8:10 and are praised in the very city **w** they committed
SS 1: 7 O my love, **w** are you leading your flock today? **W**
will you rest your sheep at noon?
3: 4 my mother's bedroom, **w** I had been conceived.
4: 8 **w** lions have their dens and panthers prowl.
6: 1 rarest of beautiful women, **w** has your lover gone?
8: 5 under the apple tree, **w** your mother gave you
birth, **w** in great pain she delivered you.
Isa 7: 3 near the road leading to the field **w** cloth is
7:25 No one will go to the fertile hillsides **w** the gardens
9: 2 a light that will shine on all who live in the land **w**
10: 3 you turn for help? **W** will your treasures be safe?
11:10 for the land **w** he lives will be a glorious place.
18: 7 in Jerusalem, the place **w** his name dwells.
29: 4 like a ghost from the earth **w** you will lie buried.
30: 6 they go, **w** lions and poisonous snakes live.
32:14 and goats will graze on the hills **w** the watchtowers
35: 7 and rushes will flourish **w** desert jackals once
36: 2 near the road leading to the field **w** cloth is
37: 7 **w** I will have him killed with a sword.' "
39: 3 **W** were they from?" Hezekiah replied,
42:24 for the people would not go **w** he sent them,
43: 9 **W** are the witnesses of such predictions? Who can
44:13 idol that cannot even move from **w** it is placed!
50: 8 me now? **W** are my enemies? Let them appear!
55: 2 and I will tell you **w** to get food that is good for the
55:13 **W** once there were thorns, cypress trees will grow.
W briers grew, myrtles will sprout up.
63:11 "**W** is the one who brought Israel through the sea,
63:11 **W** is the one who sent his Holy Spirit to be among
63:12 **W** is the one whose power divided the sea before
63:13 **W** is the one who led them through the bottom of
63:15 **W** is the passion and the might you used to show
63:15 **W** are your mercy and compassion now?
64:11 beautiful Temple **w** our ancestors praised you has
Jer 2: 6 '**W** is the LORD who brought us safely out of
2: 6 and death, **w** no one lives or even travels?'
2: 8 The priests did not ask, '**W** is the LORD?'
3: 2 Is there anywhere in the entire land **w** you have not
6:16 So now the LORD says, "Stop right **w** you are!
7:12 " 'Go to the place at Shiloh **w** I once put the
7:31 **w** they sacrifice their little sons and daughters in
8: 3 will wish to die rather than live **w** I will send them.
11:15 **w** they have done so many immoral things?
13: 7 and dug it out of the hole **w** I had hidden it.
13:20 **W** is your flock—your beautiful flock—that he
15: 2 And if they say to you, 'But **w** can we go?'
16:13 of this land and send you into a foreign land **w** you
17: 6 barren wilderness, on the salty flats **w** no one lives.
17:19 first at the gate **w** the king goes out, and then at
18: 2 "Go down to the shop **w** clay pots and jars are
19:13 all the houses **w** you burned incense on the
19:13 and **w** drink offerings were poured out to your
19:14 Then Jeremiah returned from Topheth **w** he had
23:12 down dark and treacherous trails, **w** they will fall.
25:29 the city **w** my own name is honored.
26: 6 the place **w** the Tabernacle was located.
26:18 grow on the hilltop, **w** the Temple now stands.'
29: 7 Pray to the LORD for that city **w** you are held
29:14 I will gather you out of the nations **w** I sent you
29:18 In every nation **w** I send them, I will make them an
30:11 I will completely destroy the nations **w** I have
32:29 **w** the people caused my fury to rise by offering
32:37 all the countries **w** I will scatter them in my fury.
32:43 a land **w** people and animals have all disappeared.'
35: 2 "Go to the settlement **w** the families of the
36:12 palace **w** the administrative officials were meeting.
36:19 told Baruch. "Don't tell anyone **w** you are!"
37:16 into a dungeon cell, **w** he remained for many days.
37:17 **w** the king asked him, "Do you have any messages
37:19 **W** are your prophets now who told you the king of
38:11 **w** he found some old rags and discarded clothing.
38:13 of the guard—the palace prison—**w** he remained.
41: 9 The cistern **w** Ishmael dumped the bodies of the
41:17 **w** they prepared to leave for Egypt.
42: 3 your God to show us what to do and **w** to go."
42:14 and if you insist on going to live in Egypt **w** you
42:22 and disease in Egypt, **w** you insist on going."
46:16 let's go back to our homeland **w** we were born.
49: 7 "**W** are all the wise men of Teman?
51:43 she is a dry wilderness **w** no one lives or even
52: 9 of Hamath, **w** sentence was passed against him.
La 4: 6 **w** utter disaster struck in a moment with no one to
Eze 4:13 bread in the Gentile lands, **w** I will banish them!"
6:13 and great oak **w** they offered incense to their gods,
8: 3 **w** there is a large idol that has made the LORD
8: 7 **w** I could see an opening in the wall.
9: 3 **w** it had rested, and moved to the entrance of the
11: 1 **w** I saw twenty-five prominent men of the city.
11:17 will gather you back from the nations **w** you are
13:12 will cry out, '**W** is the whitewash you applied?'
16:16 **w** you carried out your acts of prostitution.
17: 4 to a city filled with merchants, **w** he planted it.
17: 5 **w** it would grow as quickly as a willow tree.
17:10 It will die in the same good soil **w** it had grown
19:13 in the wilderness, / **w** the ground is hard and dry.
20:29 to them, 'What is this high place **w** you are going?'
20:34 and fury I will bring you out from the lands **w** you
20:38 I will bring them out of the countries **w** they are in
21:19 comes out of Babylon **w** the road forks into two—
28:25 For I will gather them from the distant lands **w** I
34:13 and by the rivers in all the places **w** people live.
37:21 land from the places **w** they have been scattered.
37:25 They will live in the land of Israel **w** their
40:25 and there was a foyer **w** the gateway passage
40:38 **w** the meat for sacrifices was washed before being
40:39 **w** the sacrificial animals were slaughtered for the
40:41 **w** the sacrifices were cut up and prepared.
40:43 and set on the tables **w** the sacrificial meat was to
43: 7 of my throne and the place **w** I will rest my feet.
43:12 The entire top of the hill **w** the Temple is built is
44:19 When they return to the outer courtyard **w** the
45: 6 This will be set aside to be a city **w** anyone in
46:20 "This is **w** the priests will cook the meat from the
47: 8 into the Jordan Valley, **w** it enters the Dead Sea.
47:20 border to the point **w** the northern border begins,
48:12 Next to the priests' territory will lie the land **w** the
Da 8:10 His power reached to the heavens **w** it attacked the
8:17 As Gabriel approached the place **w** I was standing,
Hos 1:10 Then, at the place **w** they were told, 'You are not
2:12 **w** only wild animals will eat the fruit.
9: 3 **w** you will live on food that is ceremonially
13:10 **W** now is your king? Why don't you call on him
13:10 **W** are all the leaders of the land? You asked for
Joel 2:17 foreigners who say, '**W** is the God of Israel?
2:20 back into the parched wastelands, **w** they will die.
Am 7:13 especially not here **w** the royal sanctuary is!"
Jnh 1: 3 of Joppa, **w** he found a ship leaving for Tarshish.
Mic 1: 5 **W** is the center of idolatry in Judah? In Jerusalem,
3:12 will grow on the hilltop, **w** the Temple now stands.
5:14 and destroy the cities **w** your idol temples stand.
7:10 that they taunted me, saying, "**W** is the LORD—
7:18 **W** is another God like you, who pardons the sins
Na 2:11 **W** now is that great Nineveh, lion of the nations,
2:11 **w** the old and feeble and the young and tender
3:19 **W** can anyone be found who has not suffered from
Zep 2:15 it has become an utter ruin, a place **w** animals live!
Zec 2: 2 "**W** are you going?" I asked. He replied, "I am
5:10 "**W** are they taking the basket?" I asked the angel.
5:11 "To the land of Babylonia **w** they will build a
6:12 He will branch out **w** he is and build the Temple of
7:14 the distant nations **w** they lived as strangers.
Mal 1: 6 but **w** are the honor and respect I deserve?
2:17 him by asking, "**W** is the God of justice?"
Mt 2: 2 "**W** is the newborn king of the Jews? We have
2: 4 "**W** did the prophets say the Messiah would be
2: 9 and stopped over the place **w** the child was.
2:11 They entered the house **w** the child and his mother,
4:15 in Galilee **w** so many Gentiles live—
4:16 And for those who lived in the land **w** death casts
6: 5 and in the synagogues **w** everyone can see them.
6:19 **w** they can be eaten by moths and get rusty, and **w**
thieves break in and steal.
6:20 **w** they will never become moth-eaten or rusty and
w they will be safe from thieves.
8: 8 Just say the word from **w** you are, and my servant
8:12 **w** there will be weeping and gnashing of teeth."
8:19 "Teacher, I will follow you no matter **w** you go!"
9:28 They went right into the house **w** he was staying,
9:36 so great and they didn't know **w** to go for help.
11:20 Then Jesus began to denounce the cities **w** he had
12:10 **w** he noticed a man with a deformed hand.
13: 2 **w** an immense crowd soon gathered. He got into a
13: 2 **w** he sat and taught as the people listened on the
13:27 the field **w** you planted that good seed is full of
13:32 and grows into a tree **w** birds can come and find
13:54 "**W** does he get his wisdom and his miracles?
14:13 But the crowds heard **w** he was headed
15:33 "And **w** would we get enough food out here in the
18:20 For **w** two or three gather together because they are
21:17 he returned to Bethany, **w** he stayed overnight.
22:13 **w** there is weeping and gnashing of teeth.'
25:30 **w** there will be weeping and gnashing of teeth.'
26:17 "**W** do you want us to prepare the Passover
26:57 **w** the teachers of religious law and other leaders
28: 6 would happen. Come, see **w** his body was lying.
28:16 going to the mountain **w** Jesus had told them to go.
Mk 2: 2 Soon the house **w** he was staying was so packed
3:20 When Jesus returned to the house **w** he was
3:22 That's **w** he gets the power to cast out demons."
3:31 and brothers arrived at the house **w** he was
4:21 A lamp is placed on a stand, **w** its light will shine.
4:32 with long branches **w** birds can come and find
5:13 the steep hillside into the lake, **w** they drowned.
5:40 and his three disciples into the room **w** the girl was
6: 2 "**W** did he get all his wisdom and the power to
9:33 and his disciples settled in the house **w** they would
9:48 '**w** the worm never dies and the fire never goes
13:14 causes desecration standing **w** it should not be"—
14:12 "**W** do you want us to go to prepare the Passover
14:14 **W** is the guest room **w** I can eat the Passover
14:53 Jesus was led to the high priest's home **w** the
15:47 and Mary the mother of Joseph saw **w** Jesus' body
16: 6 from the dead! Look, this is **w** they laid his body.
Lk 1:40 **w** Zechariah lived. She entered the house
4: 2 **w** the Devil tempted him for forty days. He ate
4:17 and he unrolled the scroll to the place **w** it says:
4:38 **w** he found Simon's mother-in-law very sick with
5: 4 "Now go out **w** it is deeper and let down your
6: 8 "Come and stand here **w** everyone can see."
7: 7 Just say the word from **w** you are, and my servant
8: 5 **w** it was stepped on, and the birds came and ate it.
8:16 **w** they can be seen by those entering the house.
8:25 Then he asked them, "**W** is your faith?" And they
8:33 the steep hillside into the lake, **w** they drowned.
9:11 But the crowds found out **w** he was going, and they
9:57 to Jesus, "I will follow you no matter **w** you go."
10:34 and took him to an inn, **w** he took care of him.
10:38 they came to a village **w** a woman named Martha
17:17 "Didn't I heal ten men? **W** are the other nine?
17:37 "Lord, **w** will this happen?" the disciples asked.
19:37 As they reached the place **w** the road started down
22: 9 "**W** do you want us to go?" they asked him.
22:11 **W** is the guest room **w** I can eat the Passover
22:51 And he touched the place **w** the man's ear had
23:55 and saw the tomb **w** they placed his body.
24:33 **w** the eleven disciples and the other followers of
Jn 1:28 east of the Jordan River, **w** John was baptizing.
1:38 (which means Teacher), "**w** are you staying?"
2: 9 not knowing **w** it had come from (though,
3: 8 but can't tell **w** it comes from or **w** it is going,
3:29 The bride will go **w** the bridegroom is.
4:11 very deep well. **W** would you get this living water?
4:20 at Mount Gerizim, **w** our ancestors worshiped?"
4:38 I sent you to harvest **w** you didn't plant; others had
4:46 town of Cana, **w** he had turned the water into wine.
6: 5 **w** can we buy bread to feed all these people?"
6:23 near the place **w** the Lord had blessed the bread
7: 1 He wanted to stay out of Judea **w** the Jewish

7: 3 "Go **w** your followers can see your miracles!"
7:27 could he be? For we know **w** this man comes from.
7:27 no one will know **w** he comes from."
7:28 you know me, and you know **w** I come from.
7:34 find me. And you won't be able to come **w** I am."
7:35 "**W** is he planning to go?" they asked. "Maybe he
7:36 and 'You won't be able to come **w** I am'?"
7:42 the village **w** King David was born."
8:10 up again and said to her, "**W** are your accusers?
8:14 For I know **w** I came from and **w** I am going,
8:19 "**W** is your father?" they asked. Jesus answered,
8:21 die in your sin. You cannot come **w** I am going."
8:22 does he mean, 'You cannot come **w** I am going'?"
9:12 "**W** is he now?" they asked. "I don't know,"
10:40 to stay near the place **w** John was first baptizing.
11: 6 he stayed **w** he was for the next two days and did
11:30 outside the village, at the place **w** Martha met him.
11:34 "**W** have you put him?" he asked them. They told
12:26 follow me, because my servants must be **w** I am.
12:35 in the darkness, you cannot see **w** you are going.
13:36 Simon Peter said, "Lord, **w** are you going?"
14: 3 so that you will always be with me **w** I am.
14: 4 And you know **w** I am going and how to get
14: 5 "We haven't any idea **w** you are going, so how
16: 5 and none of you has asked me **w** I am going.
19: 9 and asked him, "**W** are you from?"
19:20 The place **w** Jesus was crucified was near the city;
19:41 **w** there was a new tomb, never used before.
20: 2 the tomb, and I don't know **w** they have put him!"
20:12 and foot of the place **w** the body of Jesus had been
20:13 "and I don't know **w** they have put him."
20:15 tell me **w** you have put him, and I will go and get
21:18 direct you and take you **w** you don't want to go."
Ac 1:13 Then they went to the upstairs room of the house **w**
1:20 **w** it says, 'Let his home become desolate, with no
1:25 for he has deserted us and gone **w** he belongs."
2: 2 and it filled the house **w** they were meeting.
2: 8 the languages of the lands **w** we were born!
3:11 **w** he was holding tightly to Peter and John.
4:11 is the one referred to in the Scriptures, **w** it says,
4:31 the building **w** they were meeting shook,
5:24 were perplexed, wondering **w** it would all end.
7: 4 Then God brought him here to the land **w** you now
7: 6 **w** they would be mistreated as slaves for four
7:29 in the land of Midian, **w** his two sons were born.
10:18 They asked if this was the place **w** Simon Peter
10:27 and went inside **w** the others were assembled.
11:11 Caesarea arrived at the house **w** I was staying.
12:12 of John Mark, **w** many were gathered for prayer.
13: 6 **w** they met a Jewish sorcerer, a false prophet
14:22 **w** they strengthened the believers.
14:26 **w** their journey had begun and **w** they had been committed to the grace of
15:30 **w** they called a general meeting of the Christians
15:36 "Let's return to each city **w** we previously
16:13 **w** we supposed that some people met for prayer,
16:40 **w** they met with the believers and encouraged
17: 1 to Thessalonica, **w** there was a Jewish synagogue.
19: 1 he came to Ephesus, **w** he found several believers.
20: 3 **w** he stayed for three months. He was preparing to
20: 6 days later arrived in Troas, **w** we stayed a week.
20: 8 The upstairs room **w** we met was lighted with
20:13 to Assos, **w** he had arranged for us to join him,
21: 3 harbor of Tyre, in Syria, **w** the ship was to unload.
21: 7 **w** we greeted the believers but stayed only one
25: 2 **w** the leading priests and other Jewish leaders met
27:16 **w** with great difficulty we hoisted aboard the
28: 7 Near the shore **w** we landed was an estate
28:12 first stop was Syracuse, **w** we stayed three days.
Ro 5: 2 this place of highest privilege **w** we now stand,
11:24 to graft the Jews back into the tree **w** they belong.
15:20 News **w** the name of Christ has never been heard,
15:20 rather than **w** a church has already been started by
15:21 the plan spoken of in the Scriptures, **w** it says,
1Co 1:20 So **w** does this leave the philosophers, the scholars,
12:18 and he has put each part just **w** he wants it.
15:55 O death, **w** is your victory? / O death, **w** is your sting?"
2Co 10:16 that are far beyond you, **w** no one else is working.
Gal 4:15 **W** is that joyful spirit we felt together then?
4:24 represents Mount Sinai **w** the people first became
Eph 2:22 as part of this dwelling **w** God lives by his Spirit.
5:14 And **w** your light shines, it will expose their evil
Php 3:20 citizens of heaven, **w** the Lord Jesus Christ lives.
Col 3: 1 **w** Christ sits at God's right hand in the place of
Tit 1: 9 and show those who oppose it **w** they are wrong.
Heb 4: 8 was not the land of Canaan, **w** Joshua led them.
11: 8 He went without knowing **w** he was going.
2Pe 3: 4 Then **w** is he? Why, as far back as anyone can
3:13 a world **w** everyone is right with God.
1Jn 2:11 and don't know **w** they are going,
Jude 1: 6 God gave them but left the place **w** they belonged.
Rev 2:13 "I know that you live in the city **w** that great
7:13 who are clothed in white? **W** do they come from?"
8: 4 ascended up to God from the altar **w** the angel had
11: 8 and "Egypt," the city **w** their Lord was crucified.
12: 6 **w** God had prepared a place to give her care for
12:14 **w** she would be cared for and protected from the
17: 9 the seven hills of the city **w** this woman rules.
17:15 "The waters **w** the prostitute is sitting represent
18:18 "**W** in all the world is there another city like

WHEREVER (92) [WHERE]

Ge 4: 9 "Am I supposed to keep track of him **w** he goes?"
20:13 I told her, '**W** we go, have the kindness to say that
28:15 I will be with you, and I will protect you **w** you go.
35: 3 in distress. He has stayed with me **w** I have gone."
41:43 and **w** he went the command was shouted,
Ex 5:11 Go and get it yourselves. Find it **w** you can.
12:20 **W** you live, eat only bread that has no yeast in it."
Lev 3:17 and all your descendants, **w** they may live."
23: 3 for worship. It must be observed **w** you live.
23:14 law for you, and it must be observed **w** you live.
23:17 From **w** you live, bring two loaves of bread to be
23:21 law for you, and it must be observed **w** you live.
23:31 law for you, and it must be observed **w** you live.
Nu 9:17 And **w** the cloud settled, the people of Israel
9:18 and stopped **w** he told them to.
35:29 from generation to generation, **w** you may live.
Dt 11:24 **W** you set your feet, the land will be yours.
11:25 as he promised you, **w** you go in the whole land.
12:15 **w** you want, just as you do now with gazelle
18: 6 from **w** he is living, to the place the LORD
28: 6 You will be blessed **w** you go, both in coming
28:19 You will be cursed **w** you go, both in coming
Jos 1: 9 For the LORD your God is with you **w** you go."
1:16 you command us, and we will go **w** you send us.
9:27 **w** the LORD would choose to build it.
Ru 1:16 I will go **w** you go and live **w** you live.
1Sa 6: 8 gold tumors. Then let the cows go **w** they want.
14:47 the Philistines. And **w** he turned, he was victorious.
2Sa 7: 9 I have been with you **w** you have gone, and I have
8: 6 So the LORD gave David victory **w** he went.
8:14 the LORD made David victorious **w** he went.
15:21 and by your own life that I will go **w** you go,
1Ki 2: 3 you will be successful in all you do and **w** you go.
7:36 the panels and supports **w** there was room,
2Ki 19:11 the kings of Assyria have done **w** they have gone.
1Ch 17: 8 I have been with you **w** you have gone, and I have
18: 6 So the LORD gave David victory **w** he went.
18:13 the LORD made David victorious **w** he went.
2Ch 32: 5 by repairing the wall **w** it was broken down
Ne 4:20 the blast of the trumpet, rush to **w** it is sounding.
11:20 and the rest of the Israelites lived **w** their family
Est 8:17 and province, **w** the king's decree arrived,
Job 41:22 strength in its neck strikes terror **w** it goes.
Ps 91:11 For he orders his angels / to protect you **w** you go.
142: 3 **W** I go, / my enemies have set traps for me.
Pr 6:22 **W** you walk, their counsel can lead you. When you
21: 1 directed by the LORD; he turns it **w** he pleases.
Isa 8:22 **W** they look, there will be trouble and anguish
32:20 **W** they plant seed, bountiful crops will spring up.
37:11 the kings of Assyria have done **w** they have gone.
59: 7 **W** they go, misery and destruction follow them.
Jer 1: 7 "for you must go **w** I send you and say whatever I
3:14 and two from there, from **w** you are scattered.
23: 3 remnant of my flock from **w** I have driven them.
24: 9 and mocked, taunted and cursed, **w** I send them.
40: 4 The whole land is before you—go **w** you like.
40: 5 people he rules. But it's up to you; go **w** you like."
45: 5 all these people, but I will protect you **w** you go.
Eze 1:20 So **w** the spirit went, the wheels and the living
6: 6 **W** you live there will be desolation. I will destroy
7: 2 **W** you look—east, west, north, or south—
21:16 slash to the left, **w** you will, **w** you want.
21:24 **W** you go, whatever you do, all your actions are
47: 9 be healed. **W** this water flows, everything will live.
Da 9: 7 **w** you have driven us because of our disloyalty to
Hos 9: 8 yet traps are laid in front of him **w** he goes.
Hab 1: 3 **W** I look, I see destruction and violence.
Zec 10:12 and they will go **w** they wish by my authority.
Mt 4:25 Large crowds followed him **w** he went—
6:21 **W** your treasure is, there your heart and thoughts
9:35 And **w** he went, he healed people of every sort of
26:13 **w** the Good News is preached throughout the
Mk 6:56 **W** he went—in villages and cities and out on the
14: 9 **w** the Good News is preached throughout the
Lk 12:34 **W** your treasure is, there your heart and thoughts
Jn 6: 2 And a huge crowd kept following him **w** he went,
10: 9 be saved. **W** they go, they will find green pastures.
21:18 able to do as you liked and go **w** you wanted to.
Ac 8:13 He began following Philip **w** he went, and he was
Ro 3:16 **W** they go, destruction and misery follow them.
1Co 4:17 teach about Christ Jesus in all the churches **w** I go.
2Co 2:14 Now **w** we go he uses us to tell others about the
3:17 and **w** the Spirit of the Lord is, he gives freedom.
1Th 1: 8 for **w** we go we find people telling us about your
2Th 3: 1 will spread rapidly and be honored **w** it goes,
1Ti 2: 8 So **w** you assemble, I want men to pray with holy
Jas 3: 3 and go **w** we want by means of a small bit in its
3: 4 And a tiny rudder makes a huge ship turn **w** the
3:16 For **w** there is jealousy and selfish ambition,
Rev 14: 4 pure as virgins, following the Lamb **w** he goes.

WHETHER (162)

Ge 17:27 **w** they were born there or bought as servants.
18:21 I am going down to see **w** or not these reports are
24:21 wondering **w** or not she was the one the LORD
24:49 next step should be, **w** to move this way or that."
30:33 This will make it easy for you to see **w** or not I
31:39 from the flocks, **w** the loss was my fault or not.
42:16 Then we'll find out **w** or not your story is true.
42:20 I will know **w** or not you are telling me the truth.
43: 7 "He wanted to know **w** our father was still living,
Ex 4:18 I don't even know **w** they are still alive."
9: 7 Pharaoh sent officials to see **w** it was true that none
12: 4 **W** or not they share in this way depends on the
12:49 **w** a native-born Israelite or a foreigner who has
13:21 That way they could travel **w** it was day or night.
16: 4 I will test them in this to see **w** they will follow my
20: 4 any kind, **w** in the shape of birds or animals or fish.
21:16 **w** they are caught in possession of their victims
22: 8 God will determine **w** or not it was the neighbor
Lev 5: 2 **w** a wild animal, a domesticated animal, or an
5: 4 vow of any kind, **w** its purpose is for good or bad,
6: 4 taken by theft or extortion, **w** a security deposit,
7:10 **w** flour mixed with olive oil or dry flour,
7:21 **w** it is human defilement or an unclean animal,
7:23 must never eat fat, **w** from oxen or sheep or goats.
11: 9 and scales, **w** taken from fresh water or salt water.
11:32 This is true **w** the object is made of wood, cloth,
13:29 "If anyone, **w** a man or woman, has an open sore
13:38 "If anyone, **w** a man or woman, has shiny white
13:55 **w** it is contaminated on the inside or outside.
13:59 This is how the priest will determine **w** these
14:55 **w** in clothing, in a house,
15: 3 This defilement applies **w** the discharge continues
15:23 **w** it is her bedding or any piece of furniture.
17:10 **w** an Israelite or a foreigner living among you,
18: 9 **w** she is your father's daughter or your mother's
18: 9 **w** she was brought up in the same family
18:10 **w** your son's daughter or your daughter's daughter;
18:17 **w** her son's daughter or her daughter's daughter.
20:19 **w** his mother's sister or his father's sister, he has
21:18 to me, **w** he is blind or lame, stunted or deformed,
22:18 **w** to fulfill a vow or as a freewill offering,
22:21 or flock, **w** to fulfill a vow or as a freewill offering,
22:28 on the same day, **w** from the herd or the flock.
25:37 on anything you lend them, **w** money or food.
27:28 **w** a person, an animal, or an inherited field—
27:30 **w** grain or fruit, belongs to the LORD and must
27:33 must not be selected on the basis of **w** it is good
Nu 4:27 **w** it involves moving or doing other work.
5:18 in her hands to determine **w** or not her husband's
9:22 **W** the cloud stayed above the Tabernacle for two
11:23 Now you will see **w** or not my word comes true!"
13:18 and find out **w** the people living there are strong
15:30 **w** native Israelites or foreigners,
18:15 firstborn of every mother, **w** human or animal,
Dt 4:16 image in any form—**w** of a man or a woman,
5: 8 any kind, **w** in the shape of birds or animals or fish.
8: 2 and to find out **w** or not you would really obey his
12:15 All of you, **w** ceremonially clean or unclean,
12:22 Anyone, **w** ceremonially clean or unclean, may eat
15:22 may eat it, **w** ceremonially clean or unclean,
17: 8 **w** someone is guilty of murder or only of
18:21 'How will we know **w** the prophecy is from the
23:18 **w** a man or a woman, for both are detestable to the
23:19 **w** it is money, food, or anything else that may be
24:14 **w** fellow Israelites or foreigners living in your
27:22 **w** she is the daughter of his father or his mother.'
Jdg 2:22 to see **w** or not they would obey the LORD as
3: 4 to see **w** they would obey the commands the
9: 2 "Ask the people of Shechem **w** they want to be
18: 5 "Ask God **w** or not our journey will be
Ru 3:10 not running after a younger man, **w** rich or poor.
1Sa 14: 6 He can win a battle **w** he has many warriors
20:10 "How will I know **w** or not your father is angry?"
2Sa 15:21 matter what happens—**w** it means life or death."
1Ki 20:18 "**w** they have come for peace or for war."
2Ki 1: 2 the god of Ekron, to ask **w** he would recover.
1: 3 the god of Ekron, to ask **w** the king will get well?
1: 6 the god of Ekron, to ask **w** the king will get well?
1:16 the god of Ekron, to ask **w** you will get well?
9:18 "The king wants to know **w** you are coming in
9:19 "The king wants to know **w** you come in peace."
12: 4 **w** it is a regular assessment, a payment of vows,
1Ch 25: 8 without regard to **w** they were young or old,
2Ch 5:11 **w** or not they were on duty that day.
15:13 be put to death—**w** young or old, man or woman.
19:10 **w** a murder case or some other violation of God's
Ezr 5:17 **w** King Cyrus ever issued a decree to rebuild
Ne 10:35 **w** it be a crop from the soil or from our fruit trees.
Pr 20:11 the way they act, **w** their conduct is pure and right.
Ecc 2:19 And who can tell **w** my successors will be wise
5:12 work hard sleep well, **w** they eat little or much.
7:10 for you don't know **w** they were any better than
9: 1 no one knows **w** or not God will show them favor
9: 2 **w** they are righteous or wicked, good or bad,
11: 3 When a tree falls, **w** south or north, there it lies.
12:14 including every secret thing, **w** good or bad.
SS 6:11 I wanted to see **w** the grapevines were budding yet,
6:11 or **w** the pomegranates were blossoming.
7:12 Let us see **w** the vines have budded, **w** the blossoms have opened, and **w** the pomegranates are in flower.
Isa 19:15 in Egypt, **w** rich or poor, important or unknown,
41:23 and fear. Do something, **w** good or bad!
Jer 34:19 **w** you are officials of Judah or Jerusalem,
42: 6 **W** we like it or not, we will obey the LORD our
Eze 2: 5 And **w** they listen or not—for remember, they are
2: 7 You must give them my messages **w** they listen
3:11 Do this **w** they listen to you or not."
21:21 uncertain **w** to attack Jerusalem or Rabbah.
Da 1:13 Then you can decide **w** or not to let us continue
Mt 6:25 **w** you have enough food, drink, and clothes.
7:21 The decisive issue is **w** they obey my Father in
22:31 as to **w** there will be a resurrection of the dead—
26:63 living God that you tell us **w** you are the Messiah,
27:49 Let's see **w** Elijah will come and save him."
Mk 12:26 But now, as to **w** the dead will be raised—
15:36 Let's see **w** Elijah will come and take him down!"
Lk 3:15 and they were eager to know **w** John might be the
6: 7 and the Pharisees watched closely to see **w** Jesus
12:22 **w** you have enough food to eat or clothes to wear.
12:29 Don't worry **w** God will provide it for you.
14:31 and discussing **w** his army of ten thousand is
20:37 But now, as to **w** the dead will be raised—
Jn 1:19 to ask John **w** he claimed to be the Messiah.

4:21 the time is coming when it will no longer matter **w**
7:17 will of God will know **w** my teaching is from God
9:25 "I don't know **w** he is a sinner," the man replied.
Ac 25:20 and I asked him **w** he would be willing to stand
26:29 Paul replied, "**W** quickly or not, I pray to God that
Ro 3: 9 **w** Jews or Gentiles, are under the power of sin.
3:30 himself only by faith, **w** they are Jews or Gentiles.
4:16 to receive it, **w** or not we follow Jewish customs,
8:39 **W** we are high above the sky or in the deepest
14: 4 so let him tell them **w** they are right or wrong.
14:23 But if people have doubts about **w** they should eat
1Co 3:13 work will be put through the fire to see **w**
4: 5 to conclusions before the Lord returns as to **w**
4:19 then I'll find out **w** these arrogant people are just big talkers or **w** they really have God's power.
7:19 For it makes no difference **w** or not a man has been
10:25 Don't ask **w** or not it was offered to idols, and
12:10 He gives someone else the ability to know **w** it is
15:11 So it makes no difference **w** I preach or they
15:39 of flesh—**w** of humans, animals, birds, or fish.
2Co 5: 9 **w** we are here in this body or away from this body.
6: 8 We serve God **w** people honor us or despise us, **w** they slander us or praise us.
12: 3 **W** my body was there or just my spirit, I don't
Gal 5: 6 it makes no difference to God **w** we are
6:15 It doesn't make any difference now **w** we have
6:15 What counts is **w** we really have been changed into
Eph 6: 8 of us for the good we do, **w** we are slaves or free.
Php 1:18 But **w** or not their motives are pure, the fact
1:20 my life will always honor Christ, **w** I live or I die.
1:27 **w** I come and see you again or only hear about
4:11 for I have learned how to get along happily **w** I
4:12 **w** it is with a full stomach or empty, with plenty
1Th 3: 5 I sent Timothy to find out **w** your faith was still
5:10 **w** we are dead or alive at the time of his return.
2Ti 4: 2 Be persistent, **w** the time is favorable or not.
Jas 4:11 But you are not a judge who can decide **w** the law
1Jn 2: 5 That is the way to know **w** or not we live in him.

WHICH (433) [WHICHEVER] See Index of Articles, Etc.

WHICHEVER (3) [WHICH]

Lev 14:22 or two young pigeons, **w** the person can afford.
14:30 young pigeons, **w** the person was able to afford.
1Ki 18:23 The prophets of Baal may choose **w** one they wish

WHILE (413) [AWHILE, MEANWHILE]

Ge 4: 2 Abel became a shepherd, **w** Cain was a farmer.
4: 4 **w** Abel brought several choice lambs from the best
4: 8 And **w** they were together there, Cain attacked
11:28 But **w** Haran was still young, he died in Ur of the
11:32 Terah lived for 205 years and died **w** still at Haran.
13:12 So **w** Abram stayed in the land of Canaan,
14:10 the tar pits, **w** the rest escaped into the mountains.
18: 1 The LORD appeared again to Abraham **w** he was
18: 3 he said, "if it pleases you, stop here for a **w**.
18: 4 Rest in the shade of this tree **w** my servants get
18:22 but the LORD remained with Abraham for a **w**.
20: 1 and settled for a **w** between Kadesh and Shur at a
22: 6 **w** he himself carried the knife and the fire.
25:27 **w** Jacob was the kind of person who liked to stay
29:31 let her have a child, **w** Rachel was childless.
35:16 But Rachel's pains of childbirth began **w** they were
35:22 **W** he was there, Reuben slept with Bilhah,
36:24 wilderness **w** he was grazing his father's donkeys.
37:11 But **w** his brothers were jealous of Joseph,
Ex 9: 8 and have Moses toss it into the sky **w** Pharaoh
12: 1 and Aaron **w** they were still in the land of Egypt:
14:12 Didn't we tell you to leave us alone **w** we were still
17: 8 **W** the people of Israel were still at Rephidim,
18: 5 They arrived **w** Moses and the people were
21: 4 "If his master gave him a wife **w** he was a slave,
24:12 Stay there **w** I give you the tablets of stone that I
24:14 If there are any problems **w** I am gone,
33: 9 and hover at the entrance **w** the LORD spoke with
35:19 the priests to wear **w** ministering in the Holy Place;
35:19 and his sons to wear **w** officiating as priests."
39: 1 clothing to be worn **w** ministering in the Holy
39:41 the beautifully crafted garments to be worn **w**
39:41 the priest and for his sons to wear **w** on duty.
Lev 6: 3 lie about it, or they deny something **w** under oath,
14:46 Anyone who enters the house **w** it is closed will be
16:17 No one else is allowed inside the Tabernacle **w**
25: 1 **W** Moses was on Mount Sinai, the LORD said to
26:35 it to take every seventh year **w** you lived in it.
26:44 or despise them **w** they are in exile in the land of
26:45 whom I brought out of Egypt **w** all the nations
Nu 5:20 But if you have gone astray **w** under your
9: 1 **w** he and the rest of the Israelites were in the
11:33 But **w** they were still eating the meat, the anger of
12: 1 **W** they were at Hazeroth, Miriam and Aaron
15:32 One day **w** the people of Israel were in the
20: 1 **W** they were there, Miriam died and was buried.
20:14 **W** Moses was at Kadesh, he sent ambassadors to
23:15 "Stand here by your burnt offering **w** I go to meet
24:18 be conquered, / **w** Israel continues on in triumph.
25: 1 **W** the Israelites were camped at Acacia, some of
30: 3 or a pledge under oath **w** she is still living at her
32: 6 "Do you mean you want to stay back here **w** your
33:38 **W** they were at the foot of Mount Hor,
33:50 **W** they were camped near the Jordan River on the
35: 1 **W** Israel was camped beside the Jordan on the
35: 8 to the Levites, **w** the smaller tribes will give fewer.
36:13 **w** they were camped on the plains of Moab beside
Dt 1: 1 **w** they were in the wilderness east of the Jordan
1: 5 So Moses addressed the people of Israel **w** they
4:11 **w** the mountain was burning with fire.
5: 2 "**W** we were at Mount Sinai, the LORD our God
5:23 **w** the mountain was blazing with fire, all your
22:21 being promiscuous **w** living in her parents' home.
26:14 I have not eaten any of it **w** in mourning; I have not touched it **w** I was ceremonially
28:43 and stronger, **w** you become weaker and weaker.
29: 1 the Israelites **w** they were in the land of Moab,
31:27 Even now, **w** I am still with you, you have rebelled
33:28 of grain and wine, / **w** the heavens drop down dew.
Jos 5:10 **W** the Israelites were camped at Gilgal on the
13:32 These are the allotments Moses had made **w** he
14:10 even **w** Israel wandered in the wilderness.
22:10 But **w** they were still in Canaan, before they
24: 4 **w** Jacob and his children went down into Egypt.
Jdg 1: 5 **W** at Bezek they encountered King Adoni-bezek
3:26 **W** the servants were waiting, Ehud escaped,
6:39 This time let the fleece remain dry **w** the ground
9:44 **w** Abimelech's other two groups cut them down in
15:20 for twenty years, **w** the Philistines ruled the land.
16:13 So **w** he slept, Delilah wove the seven braids of
19:22 **W** they were enjoying themselves, some of the
Ru 2: 4 **W** she was there, Boaz arrived from Bethlehem
2:23 But all the **w** she lived with her mother-in-law.
3:12 **W** it is true that I am one of your family
1Sa 1: 2 Peninnah had children, **w** Hannah did not.
2:13 **W** the meat of the sacrificed animal was still
8:12 of his troops, **w** others will be slave laborers.
8:12 **w** others will make his weapons and chariot
14:19 But **w** Saul was talking to the priest, the shouting
22: 4 and David's parents stayed in Moab **w** David was
23:18 returned home, **w** David stayed at Horesh.
25: 7 **W** your shepherds stayed among us near Carmel,
27:11 and again **w** he was living among the Philistines.
29:11 **w** the Philistine army went on to Jezreel.
2Sa 3: 1 **w** Saul's dynasty became weaker and weaker.
5: 2 For a long time, even **w** Saul was our king,
5:22 But after a **w** the Philistines returned and again
10: 8 **w** the Arameans from Zobah and Rehob
12:21 "**W** the baby was still living, you wept and refused
12:22 "I fasted and wept **w** the child was alive, for I said,
15: 8 For **w** I was at Geshur, I promised to sacrifice to
15:10 But **w** he was there, he sent secret messengers to
15:12 **W** he was offering the sacrifices, he sent for
17: 2 I will catch up to him **w** he is weary
18:24 **W** David was sitting at the city gate, the watchman
1Ki 1:14 And **w** you are still talking with him, I will come
1:22 **W** she was still speaking with the king,
1:42 And **w** he was still speaking, Jonathan son of
1:48 to sit on my throne **w** I am still alive to see it.' "
3:17 I gave birth to a baby **w** she was with me in the
3:20 and took my son from beside me **w** I was asleep.
6:27 **w** their inner wings touched at the center of the
11:12 David, I will not do this **w** you are still alive.
11:15 **W** there, the Israelite army had killed nearly every
13: 9 eat any food or drink any water **w** you are there,
13:17 eat any food or drink any water **w** you are there,
13:20 Then **w** they were sitting at the table, a message
15:27 plotted against Nadab and assassinated him **w** he
16:21 Ginath their king, **w** the other half supported Omri.
17: 7 But after a **w** the brook dried up, for there was no
20:40 But **w** I was busy doing something else,
2Ki 3:15 **W** the harp was being played, the power of the
6:25 After a **w** even a donkey's head sold for two
6:33 **W** Elisha was still saying this, the messenger
8:29 **W** Joram was there, King Ahaziah of Judah went
10:12 the way, **w** he was at Beth-eked of the Shepherds,
11: 3 for six years **w** Athaliah ruled over the land.
16:10 **W** he was there, he noticed an unusual altar.
17:41 So **w** these new residents worshiped the LORD,
19:37 One day **w** he was worshiping in the temple of his
23:29 **W** Josiah was king, Pharaoh Neco, king of Egypt,
1Ch 11: 2 For a long time, even **w** Saul was our king,
11: 8 **w** Joab rebuilt the rest of Jerusalem.
12: 1 The following men joined David at Ziklag **w** he
12: 8 **w** he was at the stronghold in the wilderness.
14:13 But after a **w**, the Philistines returned and raided
19: 9 **w** the other kings positioned themselves to fight in
2Ch 7: 6 the priests blew the trumpets, **w** all Israel stood.
13: 3 **w** Jeroboam mustered 800,000 courageous men
14:14 **W** they were at Gerar, they attacked all the towns
22: 8 **W** Jehu was executing judgment against the family
22:12 God for six years **w** Athaliah ruled over the land.
32: 9 of Assyria, **w** still besieging the town of Lachish,
33:12 But **w** in deep distress, Manasseh sought the
34: 3 the eighth year of his reign, **w** he was still young,
35:11 who sprinkled the blood on the altar **w** the Levites
Ezr 8:15 and we camped there for three days **w** I went over
10: 1 **W** Ezra prayed and made this confession, weeping
Ne 3:30 **w** Meshullam son of Berekiah rebuilt the wall next
4:16 only half my men worked **w** the other half stood
7: 3 And **w** the gatekeepers are still on duty, have them
9:35 Even **w** they had their own kingdom, they did not
11: 1 live there, too, **w** the rest stayed where they were.
Est 4: 2 for no one was allowed to enter **w** wearing clothes
5: 6 And **w** they were drinking wine, the king said to
6:14 **W** they were still talking, the king's eunuchs
7: 2 And **w** they were drinking wine that day, the king
Job 1:16 **W** he was still speaking, another messenger
1:17 **W** he was still speaking, a third messenger arrived
1:18 **W** he was still speaking, another messenger
8:12 **W** they are still flowering, not ready to be cut,
10: 3 **w** sending joy and prosperity to the wicked?
11: 3 Should I remain silent **w** you babble on? When you
24:10 They are forced to carry food **w** they themselves
27: 3 As long as I live, **w** I have breath from God,
Ps 27:13 **w** I am here in the land of the living.
28: 3 to their neighbors / **w** planning evil in their hearts.
32: 6 let all the godly confess their rebellion to you **w**
37:10 In a little **w**, the wicked will disappear.
41: 6 are my friends, / but all the **w** they gather gossip,
42: 3 **w** my enemies continually taunt me, saying,
50:21 **W** you did all this, I remained silent, / and you
63:11 in him will praise him, / **w** liars will be silenced.
68:12 **w** the women of Israel divide the plunder.
73:12 enjoying a life of ease **w** their riches multiply.
78:30 had craved, / **w** the meat was yet in their mouths,
81: 8 to me, O my people, **w** I give you stern warnings.
89:41 along has robbed him / **w** his neighbors mock.
102:24 don't take my life **w** I am still so young!
107:42 and be glad, / **w** the wicked are stricken silent.
109: 2 **w** the wicked slander me / and tell lies about me.
137: 4 sing the songs of the LORD / **w** in a foreign land?
Pr 10:23 for a fool, **w** wise conduct is a pleasure to the wise.
11:23 to happiness, **w** the wicked can expect only wrath.
12:12 each other's loot, **w** the godly bear their own fruit.
13: 6 **w** the evil are destroyed by their wickedness.
13:21 chases sinners, **w** blessings chase the righteous!
14:20 their neighbors, **w** the rich have many "friends."
15:14 is hungry for truth, **w** the fool feeds on trash.
19:18 Discipline your children **w** there is hope. If you
21:26 always greedy for more, **w** the godly love to give!
26:26 **W** their hatred may be concealed by trickery,
29:23 Pride ends in humiliation, **w** humility brings honor.
Ecc 2: 3 **W** still seeking wisdom, I clutched at foolishness.
2:14 For the wise person sees, **w** the fool is blind.
7: 2 and you should think about it **w** there is still time.
7: 4 **w** the fool thinks only about having a good time
7:14 Enjoy prosperity **w** you can. But when hard times
12: 6 remember your Creator now **w** you are young,
SS 3: 4 A little **w** later I found him and held him. I didn't
Isa 5:23 They let the wicked go free **w** punishing the
10:25 In a little **w** my anger against you will end, and
18: 5 your attack, **w** your plans are ripening like grapes,
33: 1 to you, **w** you betray your promises to them.
37:38 One day **w** he was worshiping in the temple of his
38:11 **w** still in the land of the living. / Never again will I
54: 8 of anger I turned my face away for a little **w**.
55: 6 Seek the LORD **w** you can find him. Call on him now **w** he is near.
58: 3 because you are living for yourselves even **w** you
65:14 in sorrow and despair, **w** my servants sing for joy.
65:24 **W** they are still talking to me about their needs,
Jer 7:13 **W** you were doing these wicked things,
9: 8 They promise peace to their neighbors **w** planning
15: 9 for breath; her sun has gone down **w** it is yet day.
18: 2 are made. I will speak to you **w** you are there."
24: 2 **w** the other was filled with figs that were spoiled
28: 1 addressed me publicly in the Temple **w** all the
33: 1 **W** Jeremiah was still confined in the courtyard of
34:21 though Babylon's king has left this city for a **w**,
39:15 message to Jeremiah **w** he was still in prison:
41: 1 invited them to dinner. **W** they were eating,
43: 9 "**W** the people of Judah are watching, bury large
48: 5 **w** cries of terror rise from Horonaim below.
51:33 In just a little **w** her harvest will begin."
51:39 And **w** they lie inflamed with all their wine,
51:50 Do not stand and watch—flee **w** you can!
Eze 1: 1 **w** I was with the Judean exiles beside the Kebar
4:12 **W** all the people are watching, bake it over a fire
5: 8 I will punish you publicly **w** all the nations watch.
8: 1 **w** the leaders of Judah were in my home,
9: 8 **W** they were carrying out their orders, I was all
11:13 **W** I was still speaking, Pelatiah son of Benaiah
12: 5 Dig a hole through the wall **w** they are watching
12: 7 Then in the evening **w** the people looked on,
14: 1 leaders of Israel visited me, and **w** they were there,
16:49 **w** the poor and needy suffered outside her door.
20: 8 to satisfy my anger **w** they were still in Egypt.
20:23 But I took a solemn oath against them **w** they were
30:25 **w** the arms of Pharaoh fall useless to his sides.
32:24 They terrorized the nations **w** they lived, but now
32:25 Yes, they terrorized the nations **w** they lived,
32:27 They brought terror to everyone **w** they were still
36:22 which you dishonored **w** you were scattered among
42: 8 extended for only 87-1/2 feet, **w** the inner block—
42:14 They must first take off the clothes they wore **w**
44:17 They must wear no wool **w** on duty in the inner
44:19 they must take off the clothes they wear **w**
46: 2 Then he will stand by the gatepost **w** the priest
Da 2:29 "**W** Your Majesty was sleeping, you dreamed
2:49 of Babylon, **w** Daniel remained in the king's court.
4:10 " '**W** I was lying in my bed, this is what I
4:25 Seven periods of time will pass **w** you live this
4:31 **W** he was still speaking these words, a voice called
4:32 Seven periods of time will pass **w** you live this
5: 2 **W** Belshazzar was drinking, he gave orders to
5:23 drinking wine from them **w** praising gods of silver,
7:12 but they were allowed to live for a **w** longer.
8: 5 **W** I was watching, suddenly a male goat appeared
8:18 **W** he was speaking, I fainted and lay there with
10:15 **W** he was speaking to me, I looked down at the
11:24 of strongholds, but this will last for only a short **w**.
11:34 **W** all these persecutions are going on, a little help
11:45 but **w** he is there, his time will suddenly run out,
Hos 2:10 strip her naked in public, **w** all her lovers look on.
7: 4 They are like an oven that is kept hot even **w** the
Joel 2:12 LORD says, "Turn to me now, **w** there is time!
Am 4: 7 fell on one field, **w** another field withered away.
8: 9 down at noon and darken the earth **w** it is still day.
9: 6 are in the heavens, **w** its foundation is on the earth.
Ob 1: 7 promise you peace, **w** plotting your destruction.

Hab 1:13 in any form, stand idly by w they swallow us up?
1:13 Should you be silent w the wicked destroy people
1:15 and dragged out in their nets w they rejoice?
2:7 all you have, w you stand trembling and helpless.
Zep 2:2 Gather w there is still time, before judgment begins
Hag 1:4 "Why are you living in luxurious houses w my
1:9 w you are all busy building your own fine houses.
2:6 In just a little w I will again shake the heavens
2:19 I am giving you a promise now w the seed is still
Zec 3:5 and dressed him in new clothes w the angel of the
12:6 w the people living in Jerusalem remain secure.
Mt 1:18 But w she was still a virgin, she became pregnant
9:15 "Should the wedding guests mourn w celebrating
14:22 and cross to the other side of the lake w he sent the
14:23 by himself to pray. Night fell w he was there alone.
21:32 believe him, w tax collectors and prostitutes did.
24:48 and thinks, 'My master won't be back for a w,'
25:10 "But w they were gone to buy oil, the bridegroom
25:14 and gave them money to invest for him w he was
26:21 W they were eating, he said, "The truth is, one of
26:36 and he said, "Sit here w I go on ahead to pray."
27:63 we remember what that deceiver once said w he
28:13 'Jesus' disciples came during the night w we were
Mk 2:19 "Do wedding guests fast w celebrating with the
2:19 They can't fast w they are with the groom.
5:35 W he was still speaking to her, messengers arrived
6:31 "Let's get away from the crowds for a w
6:45 the lake to Bethsaida, w he sent the people home.
14:32 and Jesus said, "Sit here w I go and pray."
14:54 For a w he sat with the guards, warming himself by
15:41 and had cared for him w he was in Galilee.
Lk 1:10 W the incense was being burned, a great crowd
2:6 And w they were there, the time came for her baby
5:17 One day w Jesus was teaching, some Pharisees
5:34 "Do wedding guests fast w celebrating with the
6:6 hand was in the synagogue w Jesus was teaching.
8:13 They believe for a w, but they wilt when the hot
8:23 and w he was sleeping the wind began to rise.
8:49 W he was still speaking to her, a messenger
9:43 W everyone was marveling over all the wonderful
10:40 that my sister just sits here w I do all the work?
12:45 servant thinks, 'My master won't be back for a w,'
14:32 If he is not able, then w the enemy is still far away,
15:20 And w he was still a long distance away, his father
18:4 The judge ignored her for a w, but eventually she
19:13 pounds of silver to invest for him w he was gone.
21:1 W Jesus was in the Temple, he watched the rich
22:58 After a w someone else looked at him and said,
23:39 it by saving yourself—and us, too, w you're at it!"
24:51 W he was blessing them, he left them and was
Jn 3:22 but they stayed in Judea for a w and baptized there.
4:20 w we Samaritans claim it is here at Mount
4:22 one you worship, w we Jews know all about him,
4:51 W he was on his way, some of his servants met
5:7 W I am trying to get there, someone else always
5:35 John shone brightly for a w, and you benefited
6:31 our ancestors ate manna w they journeyed through
6:59 He said these things w he was teaching in the
7:12 w others said, "He's nothing but a fraud,
7:28 W Jesus was teaching in the Temple, he called out,
8:20 Jesus made these statements w he was teaching in
9:5 But w I am still here in the world, I am the light of
12:29 w others declared an angel had spoken to him.
12:35 "My light will shine out for you just a little w
12:35 Walk in it w you can, so you will not stumble
12:36 Believe in the light w there is still time; then you
14:19 In just a little w the world will not see me again,
14:25 I am telling you these things now w I am still with
16:4 because I was going to be with you for a w longer.
16:16 "In just a little w I will be gone, and you won't see
16:16 Then, just a little w after that, you will see me
16:18 And what does he mean by 'a little w'? We don't
16:19 I said in just a little w I will be gone, and you
16:19 Then, just a little w after that, you will see me
17:13 I have told them many things w I was with them
20:1 Early Sunday morning, w it was still dark,
20:7 w the cloth that had covered Jesus' head was
Ac 1:9 was taken up into the sky w they were watching,
2:47 all the w praising God and enjoying the goodwill
4:1 W Peter and John were speaking to the people,
5:34 be sent outside the council chamber for a w.
9:23 After a w the Jewish leaders decided to kill him.
10:10 But w lunch was being prepared, he fell into a
11:5 he said, "w I was praying, I went into a trance
12:5 But w Peter was in prison, the church prayed very
12:19 Herod left Judea to stay in Caesarea for a w.
14:8 W they were at Lystra, Paul and Barnabas came
15:1 W Paul and Barnabas were at Antioch of Syria,
15:33 They stayed for a w, and then Judas and Silas were
17:14 to the coast, w Silas and Timothy remained behind.
17:16 W Paul was waiting for them in Athens, he was
18:19 But w he was there, he went to the synagogue to
19:1 W Apollos was in Corinth, Paul traveled through
19:22 on ahead to Macedonia w he stayed awhile longer
23:32 w the horsemen took him on to Caesarea.
27:41 w the stern was repeatedly smashed by the force of
Ro 5:8 sending Christ to die for us w we were still sinners.
5:10 the death of his Son w we were still his enemies,
7:3 So w her husband is alive, she would be
14:5 than another day, w others think every day is alike.
14:8 W we live, we live to please the Lord. And when
15:24 after I have enjoyed your fellowship for a little w,
1Co 7:34 w the married woman must be concerned about her
8:1 W knowledge may make us feel important, it is
11:4 A man dishonors Christ if he covers his head w
11:21 As a result, some go hungry w others get drunk.
12:24 w other parts do not require this special care.
14:26 w another will interpret what is said.
15:41 w the moon and stars each have another kind.
15:47 w Christ, the second man, came from heaven.
2Co 7:8 for I know that it was painful to you for a little w.
11:16 would to a foolish person, w I also boast a little.
Gal 2:2 W I was there I talked privately with the leaders of
2:9 w they continued their work with the Jews.
Eph 2:5 that even w we were dead because of our sins,
4:26 Don't let the sun go down w you are still angry,
Php 2:30 and he was at the point of death w trying to do for
4:10 but for a w you didn't have the chance to help me.
Col 1:10 All the w, you will learn to know God better
3:17 all the w giving thanks through him to God the
1Th 2:17 after we were separated from you for a little w
3:4 Even w we were with you, we warned you that
2Th 3:10 Even w we were with you, we gave you this rule:
1Ti 3:15 so that if I can't come for a w, you will know how
Tit 2:13 w we look forward to that wonderful event when
Phm 1:13 I really wanted to keep him here with me w I am in
1:15 Onesimus ran away for a little w so you could have
Heb 2:7 For a little w you made him lower than the angels,
2:9 who "for a little w was made lower than the
5:7 W Jesus was here on earth, he offered prayers
9:17 W the person is still alive, no one can use the will
10:37 "For in just a little w, / the Coming One will come
12:11 No discipline is enjoyable w it is happening—
Jas 4:14 the morning fog—it's here a little w, then it's gone.
1Pe 1:6 is necessary for you to endure many trials for a w.
3:20 waited patiently w Noah was building his boat.
5:10 After you have suffered a little w, he will restore,
2Pe 2:9 even w punishing the wicked right up until the day
2:13 They revel in deceitfulness w they feast with you.
3:14 w you are waiting for these things to happen,
Rev 13:13 to earth from heaven w everyone was watching.
20:3 he would be released again for a little w.

WHIM (1)

Jas 5:5 years on earth in luxury, satisfying your every w.

WHINING (1)

Nu 11:18 'The LORD has heard your w and complaints:

WHIP (13) [WHIPPED, WHIPS]

Pr 26:3 Guide a horse with a w, a donkey with a bridle,
Isa 9:4 that bind his people and the w that scourges them,
10:5 is certain for Assyria, the w of my anger.
10:15 Can a w strike unless a hand is moving it? Can a
10:26 The LORD Almighty will beat them with his w,
14:29 For even though that w is broken, his son will be
Mt 23:34 by crucifixion and w others in your synagogues,
27:26 He ordered Jesus flogged with a lead-tipped w,
Mk 15:15 He ordered Jesus flogged with a lead-tipped w,
Lk 18:33 They will w him and kill him, but on the third day
Jn 2:15 Jesus made a w from some ropes and chased them
19:1 Pilate had Jesus flogged with a lead-tipped w.
Ac 22:25 "Is it legal for you to w a Roman citizen who

WHIPPED (8) [WHIP]

Ex 5:14 Then they w the Israelite foremen in charge of the
1Ki 14:15 Then the LORD will shake Israel like a reed w
Isa 53:5 might have peace. He was w, and we were healed!
Jer 20:2 So he arrested Jeremiah the prophet and had him w
Mt 20:19 to the Romans to be mocked, w, and crucified.
Ac 22:29 because he had ordered him bound and w.
26:11 Many times I had them w in the synagogues to try
2Co 11:23 been w times without number, and faced death

WHIPS (8) [WHIP]

1Ki 12:11 My father used w on you, but I'll use
12:14 My father used w on you, but I'll use scorpions!"
2Ch 10:11 My father used w on you, but I'll use
10:14 My father used w on you, but I'll use scorpions!"
Na 3:2 Hear the crack of the w as the chariots rush
Mk 10:34 spit on him, beat him with their w, and kill him,
Ac 22:24 and ordered him lashed with w to make him
Heb 11:36 and their backs were cut open with w.

WHIRLING (5) [WHIRLS, WHIRLWIND, WHIRLWINDS]

Ps 83:13 O my God, blow them away like w dust,
Pr 10:25 Disaster strikes like a cyclone, w the wicked away,
Isa 17:13 scattered by the wind or like dust w before a storm.
Eze 10:2 "Go in between the w wheels beneath the
10:13 I heard someone refer to the wheels as "the w

WHIRLS (1) [WHIRLING]

Job 27:22 It w down on them without mercy. They struggle

WHIRLWIND (19) [WHIRLS, WIND]

2Ki 2:1 was about to take Elijah up to heaven in a w,
2:11 and Elijah was carried by a w into heaven.
Job 30:22 You throw me into the w and destroy me in the
38:1 Then the LORD answered Job from the w:
40:6 Then the LORD answered Job from the w:
Ps 77:18 Your thunder roared from the w; / the lightning lit
Isa 21:1 the desert, like a w sweeping in from the Negev.
29:6 great noise, with w and storm and consuming fire.
41:16 will blow them all away; a w will scatter them.
66:15 and his swift chariots of destruction roar like a w.
Jer 23:19 a w that swirls down on the heads of the wicked.
25:32 A great w of fury is rising from the most distant
Hos 8:7 have planted the wind and will harvest the w.
Am 1:14 the battle, swirling like a w in a mighty storm.
Na 1:3 He displays his power in the w and the storm.
Hab 3:14 you destroyed those who rushed out like a w,
Zec 7:14 I scattered them as with a w among the distant
9:14 he will go out against his enemies like a w from
Heb 12:18 to a place of flaming fire, darkness, gloom, and w,

WHIRLWINDS (1) [WHIRLS, WIND]

Jer 4:13 His chariots are like w; his horses are swifter than

WHISPER (10) [WHISPERED, WHISPERING, WHISPERINGS, WHISPERS]

1Ki 19:12 after the fire there was the sound of a gentle w.
Job 26:14 the minor things he does, merely a w of his power.
Ps 41:7 All who hate me w about me, / imagining the worst
107:29 He calmed the storm to a w / and stilled the waves.
Isa 29:4 Your voice will w like a ghost from the earth
45:19 I do not w obscurities in some dark corner so no
La 3:62 the plots my enemies w and mutter against me all
Eze 33:30 you in their houses and w about you at the doors,
Am 6:10 "Hush! Don't even w the name of the LORD.
Mt 10:27 What I w in your ears, shout from the housetops

WHISPERED (4) [WHISPER]

1Sa 24:4 your opportunity!" David's men w to him.
26:8 Abishai w to David. "Let me thrust that spear
Job 4:12 was given me in secret, as though w in my ear.
Lk 12:3 and what you have w behind closed doors will be

WHISPERING (3) [WHISPER]

2Sa 12:19 But when David saw them w, he realized what had
Ps 71:10 For my enemies are w against me. / They are
Eze 33:30 "Son of man, your people are w behind your back.

WHISPERINGS (1) [WHISPER]

Isa 8:19 Do not listen to their w and mutterings.

WHISPERS (2) [WHISPER]

Job 33:16 He w in their ear and terrifies them with his
Ps 36:1 Sin w to the wicked, deep within their hearts.

WHISTLE (4)

Jdg 5:16 to hear the shepherds w for their flocks?
Isa 5:26 He will w to those at the ends of the earth, and they
7:18 In that day the LORD will w for the army of
Zec 10:8 When I w to them, they will come running, for I

WHIT [KJV] See also ALL, COMPLETELY, ENTIRELY, EVERYTHING

WHITE (74) [WHITE-HAIRED, WHITE-ROBED, WHITE-STREAKED, WHITENS, WHITER, WHITEST, WHITEWASH, WHITEWASHED, WHITEWASHERS]

Ge 30:33 If you find in my flock any w sheep or goats that
30:35 that were speckled and spotted with any w patches,
30:37 and peeled off strips of the bark to make w streaks
Ex 4:6 it out again, his hand was w as snow with leprosy.
16:14 thin flakes, w like frost, covered the ground.
16:31 It was w like coriander seed, and it tasted like
28:18 a turquoise, a sapphire, and a w moonstone.
39:11 were a turquoise, a sapphire, and a w moonstone.
Lev 11:18 the w owl, the pelican, the carrion vulture,
13:3 If the hair in the affected area has turned w
13:4 "But if the affected area of the skin is w but does
13:4 and if the hair in the spot has not turned w,
13:10 If the priest sees that some hair has turned w
13:13 because the skin has turned completely w.
13:16 open sores heal and turn w like the rest of the skin,
13:17 affected areas have indeed turned completely w,
13:19 but a w swelling or a reddish w spot remains in its place,
13:20 and if the hair in the affected area has turned w,
13:21 But if the priest sees that there is no w hair in the
13:24 becoming either a shiny reddish w or w,
13:25 If the hair in the affected area turns w
13:26 But if the priest discovers that there is no w hair in
13:38 a man or woman, has shiny w patches on the skin,
13:39 If the patch is only a pale w, this is a harmless skin
13:42 if a reddish w infection appears on the front
13:43 and if he finds swelling around the reddish w sore,
Nu 12:10 Miriam suddenly became w as snow with leprosy.
Dt 14:16 the little owl, the great owl, the w owl,
2Ki 5:27 he was leprous; his skin was as w as snow.
Est 1:6 courtyard was decorated with beautifully woven w
8:15 robe of blue and w and the great crown of gold,
Job 6:6 And how tasteless is the uncooked w of an egg!
41:32 in its wake. One would think the sea had turned w.
Ps 147:16 He sends the snow like w wool; / he scatters frost
SS 4:2 Your teeth are as w as sheep, newly shorn
6:6 Your teeth are w like freshly washed ewes,
Isa 1:18 as red as crimson, I can make you as w as wool.
46:4 your lifetime—until your hair is w with age.
Eze 27:18 wine from Helbon and w wool from Zahar.
28:13 w moonstone, beryl, onyx, jasper, sapphire,
Da 5:9 even more alarmed, and his face turned ashen w.
7:9 His clothing was as w as snow, his hair like whitest
Joel 1:7 their bark and leaving the branches w and bare.
Zec 1:8 Behind him were red, brown, and w horses,
6:3 the third by w horses, and the fourth by
6:6 the chariot with w horses is going west,

Mt 5:36 my head!' for you can't turn one hair w or black.
17: 2 like the sun, and his clothing became dazzling w.
28: 3 like lightning, and his clothing was as w as snow.
Mk 9: 3 and his clothing became dazzling w, far whiter
16: 5 on the right sat a young man clothed in a w robe.
Lk 9:29 face changed, and his clothing became dazzling w.
Rev 1:14 His head and his hair were w like wool, as w as snow.
2:17 And I will give to each one a w stone, and on the
3: 4 They will walk with me in w, for they are worthy.
3: 5 All who are victorious will be clothed in w. I will
3:18 And also buy w garments so you will not be
4: 4 They were all clothed in w and had gold crowns on
6: 2 I looked up and saw a w horse. Its rider carried a
6:11 Then a w robe was given to each of them.
7: 9 They were clothed in w and held palm branches in
7:13 asked me, "Who are these who are clothed in w?
7:14 robes in the blood of the Lamb and made them w.
14:14 Then I saw the Son of Man sitting on a w cloud.
15: 6 clothed in spotless w linen with gold belts across
19: 8 She is permitted to wear the finest w linen."
19:11 heaven opened, and a w horse was standing there.
19:14 The armies of heaven, dressed in pure w linen, followed him on w horses.
19:21 out of the mouth of the one riding the w horse.
20:11 And I saw a great w throne, and I saw the one who

WHITE-HAIRED (1) [HAIR, WHITE]

Ecc 12: 5 be afraid of heights and of falling, w and withered,

WHITE-ROBED (2) [ROBE, WHITE]

Jn 20:12 She saw two w angels sitting at the head and foot
Ac 1:10 two w men suddenly stood there among them.

WHITE-STREAKED (1) [STREAK, WHITE]

Ge 30:39 So when the flocks mated in front of the w

WHITENS (1) [WHITE]

Mal 3: 2 refines metal or like a strong soap that w clothes.

WHITER (3) [WHITE]

Ge 49:12 darker than wine, / and his teeth are w than milk.
Ps 51: 7 be clean; / wash me, and I will be w than snow.
Mk 9: 3 far w than any earthly process could ever make it.

WHITEST (1) [WHITE]

Da 7: 9 was as white as snow, his hair like w wool.

WHITEWASH (4) [WASH, WHITE]

Eze 13:10 are trying to hold it together by covering it with w!
13:12 people will cry out, 'Where is the w you applied?'
13:15 and those who covered it with w will be satisfied.
22:28 word to them. They repair cracked walls with w!

WHITEWASHED (4) [WASH, WHITE]

Eze 13:13 I will sweep away your w wall with a storm of
13:15 'The wall and those who w it are both gone.
Mt 23:27 You are like w tombs—beautiful on the outside
Ac 23: 3 Paul said to him, "God will slap you, you w wall!

WHITEWASHERS (1) [WASH, WHITE]

Eze 13:11 Tell these w that their wall will soon fall down.

WHITHER [KJV] See THAT, WHERE, WHEREVER, WHICH, WHOM

WHITHERSOEVER [KJV] See EVERYWHERE, WHATEVER, WHEREVER

WHO (4628) [WHO'S, WHOEVER, WHOM, WHOMEVER, WHOSE] See Index of Articles, Etc.

WHO'S (1) [WHO] See Index of Articles, Etc.

WHOEVER (46) [WHO]

Ex 29:30 W is the next high priest after Aaron will wear
32:33 to Moses, "I will blot out w has sinned against me.
Lev 17:14 So w eats or drinks blood must be cut off.
18:29 W does any of these detestable things will be cut
24:21 "W kills an animal must make full restitution,
24:21 but w kills another person must be put to death.
Nu 15: 4 w brings it must also give to the LORD a grain
Jdg 6:31 W pleads his case will be put to death by morning!
7: 3 'W is timid or afraid may leave and go home.' "
10:18 "W attacks the Ammonites first will become ruler
1Ch 11: 6 "W leads the attack against the Jebusites will
2Ch 13: 9 W comes to be dedicated with a young bull
Pr 8:35 For w finds me finds life and wins approval from
13:20 W walks with the wise will become wise; w walks with fools will suffer harm.
15: 5 w learns from correction is wise.
15:10 W abandons the right path will be severely punished; w hates correction will die.
16:17 leads away from evil; w follows that path is safe.
20: 1 to brawls. W is led astray by drink cannot be wise.
21:21 W pursues godliness and unfailing love will find
22: 5 treacherous road; w values life will stay away.
28:27 W gives to the poor will lack nothing. But a curse
29: 1 W stubbornly refuses to accept criticism will
29:18 they run wild. But w obeys the law is happy.
Isa 28:16 to build on. W believes need never run away again.
57:13 But w trusts in me will possess the land and inherit
Da 5: 7 "W can read this writing and tell me what it
Mt 20:26 W wants to be a leader among you must be your
20:27 and w wants to be first must become your slave.
Mk 10:11 "W divorces his wife and marries someone else
10:43 W wants to be a leader among you must be your
10:44 and w wants to be first must be the slave of all.
Lk 9:48 sent me. W is the least among you is the greatest."
17:33 W clings to this life will lose it, and w loses this life will save it.
Ac 1:22 W is chosen will join us as a witness of Jesus'
Ro 2:29 W has that kind of change seeks praise from God,
1Co 1: 2 w calls upon the name of Jesus Christ, our Lord
3:10 But w is building on this foundation must be very
Gal 5:10 w it is, who has been troubling and confusing you.
2Th 3:10 you this rule: "W does not work should not eat."
Heb 12: 7 W heard of a child who was never disciplined?
1Jn 5:12 So w has God's Son has life; w does not have his Son does not have life.
Rev 2:11 W is victorious will not be hurt by the second

WHOLE (282) [WHOLEHEARTED, WHOLEHEARTEDLY]

WHOLE ASSEMBLY (7) Jos 22:12; 1Ki 12:3; 1Ch 13:4; 29:10,20; Ezr 10:12; Ne 5:13

WHOLE BODY (9) Ps 38:3; 63:1; Mt 5:29,30; Ro 6:13; 1Co 12:17,17; Eph 4:16,16

WHOLE EARTH (25) Ge 3:14; Jos 3:11; 1Ch 16:23; 2Ch 16:9; Job 9:24; 28:24; Ps 22:27; 48:2; 72:19; 96:1; 98:3; 99:1; 110:6; Isa 6:3; 14:26; 27:6; Jer 10:10; 51:7; Eze 32:4; Da 2:35; Zec 1:11; Mt 5:5; Ac 17:26; Ro 4:13; Rev 14:16

WHOLE HEART (4) 1Ki 8:48; 1Ch 28:9; 2Ch 6:38; Ps 103:1

WHOLE LAND (22) Ex 8:6; 9:9; Nu 22:11; 32:33; Dt 11:25; 34:1; Jos 2:24; Isa 7:19; 13:5; 15:8; Jer 4:27; 8:16; 12:11; 40:4; 50:38; 51:47; La 2:3; Ob 1:8; Zep 1:18; Mt 27:45; Mk 15:33; Lk 23:44

WHOLE NATION (7) Nu 3:41; Eze 8:17; Mal 3:9; Jn 11:48,50; Heb 11:12; Jude 1:5

WHOLE WORLD (31) Ge 11:1; 1Sa 17:46; 1Ch 16:8; Est 4:11; Job 34:13; Ps 44:14; 59:13; 66:8; 67:4; 82:5; 105:1; Isa 43:21; Jer 50:2; Eze 35:14; 38:12; Da 4:17; 7:23; Mt 16:26; 24:14; Mk 8:36; Lk 9:25; Jn 12:19; 21:25; Ac 22:15; 1Co 3:22; Col 3:4; 1Pe 1:7; 2Pe 2:5; Rev 3:10; 11:15; 12:9

Ge 3:14 and wild animals of the w earth to be cursed.
11: 1 At one time the w world spoke a single language
13:10 The w area was well watered everywhere,
24:66 Then the servant told Isaac the w story.
31: 8 the w flock began to produce speckled lambs.
Ex 7:20 of the Nile. Suddenly, the w river turned to blood!
7:23 to his palace and put the w thing out of his mind.
8: 6 did so, and frogs covered the w land of Egypt!
8:24 The w country was thrown into chaos by the flies.
9: 9 It will spread like fine dust over the w land of
10: 4 For tomorrow I will cover the w country with
10:15 For the locusts covered the surface of the w
12: 3 Announce to the w community that on the tenth
12:47 The w community of Israel must celebrate this
16: 2 the w community of Israel spoke bitterly against
19:18 and the w mountain shook with a violent
36: 7 were more than enough to complete the w project.
38:22 the tribe of Judah, was in charge of the w project,
Lev 1: 3 "If your sacrifice for a w burnt offering is from the
1: 9 It is a w burnt offering made by fire, very pleasing
1:10 "If your sacrifice for a w burnt offering is from the
1:13 It is a w burnt offering made by fire, very pleasing
1:17 It is a w burnt offering made by fire, very pleasing
5:10 The priest will offer the second bird as a w burnt
6: 9 instructions regarding the w burnt offering.
6:12 and arrange the daily w burnt offering on it.
6:12 offerings on top of this daily w burnt offering.
7: 8 In the case of the w burnt offering, the hide of the
7:37 These are the instructions for the w burnt offering,
8:18 the ram to the LORD for the w burnt offering,
8:21 Moses burned the entire ram on the altar as a w
9: 2 for a sin offering and a ram for a w burnt offering,
9: 3 and a year-old lamb for a w burnt offering,
9: 5 and the w community came and stood there in the
9: 7 and your w burnt offering to make atonement for
9:12 Next Aaron slaughtered the animal for the w burnt
9:14 and also burned them on the altar as a w burnt
9:16 Then he brought the w burnt offering
9:22 the w burnt offering, and the peace offering,
9:23 of the LORD appeared to the w community.
10: 6 and the LORD will be angry with the w
12: 6 the woman must bring a year-old lamb for a w
12: 8 One will be for the w burnt offering and the other
14:19 the priest will slaughter the w burnt offering
14:22 a sin offering and the other for a w burnt offering.
14:31 a sin offering and the other for a w burnt offering,
15:15 a sin offering and the other for a w burnt offering.
15:30 a sin offering and the other for a w burnt offering.
16: 3 for a sin offering and a ram for a w burnt offering.
16: 5 for a sin offering and a ram for a w burnt offering.
16:24 and go out to sacrifice his own w burnt offering
16:24 and the w burnt offering for the people.
17: 8 If you offer a w burnt offering or a sacrifice
22:18 If you offer a w burnt offering to the LORD,
23:12 defects as a w burnt offering to the LORD.
23:18 These w burnt offerings, together with the
23:37 w burnt offerings and grain offerings,
24:16 be stoned to death by the w community of Israel.
Nu 1: 2 "Take a census of the w community of Israel by
1:18 called together the w community of Israel on that
3: 7 They will serve Aaron and the w community,
3:41 the firstborn livestock of the w nation of Israel."
8: 9 Then assemble the w community of Israel
8:20 and the w community of Israel dedicated the
11:20 You will eat it for a w month until you gag and are
11:21 and yet you promise them meat for a w month!
13:26 They reported to the w community what they had
14:10 But the w community began to talk about stoning
15: 5 For each lamb offered as a w burnt offering,
15:24 the w community must present a young bull for a
15:25 With it the priest will make atonement for the w
15:26 The w community of Israel will be forgiven,
15:35 The w community must stone him outside the
15:36 So the w community took the man outside the
16:19 of the LORD appeared to the w community,
16:41 But the very next morning the w community began
20:22 The w community of Israel left Kadesh as a group
20:27 Mount Hor together as the w community watched.
22:11 from Egypt and has spread out over the w land.
27:19 Present him to Eleazar the priest before the w
27:20 so the w community of Israel will obey him.
27:22 Joshua to Eleazar the priest and the w community.
28: 3 When you present your daily w burnt offerings to
28:10 This is the w burnt offering to be presented each
28:24 These will be offered in addition to the regular w
28:27 A special w burnt offering will be offered that day,
29:13 That day you must present a special w burnt
31:12 the priest, and to the w community of Israel,
32: 4 the LORD has conquered this w area for the
32:13 the w generation that sinned against him had died.
32:33 the w land with its towns and surrounding lands.
Dt 2:36 town in the gorge, and the w area as far as Gilead.
3:14 acquired the w Argob region in Bashan all the way
11:25 he promised you, wherever you go in the w land.
16:11 Celebrate with your w family, all your servants,
29: 2 to Pharaoh and all his servants and his w country—
33:10 and offer w burnt offerings on the altar.
34: 1 And the LORD showed him the w land,
Jos 2:24 "The LORD will certainly give us the w land,"
3:11 which belongs to the Lord of the w earth,
6:23 They moved her w family to a safe place near the
10:40 So Joshua conquered the w region—the kings
22:12 the w assembly gathered at Shiloh and prepared to
22:16 "The w community of the LORD demands to
Jdg 6:15 My clan is the weakest in the w tribe of Manasseh,
6:38 the fleece and wrung out a w bowlful of water.
Ru 2:22 Stay with his workers right through the w harvest.
1Sa 1:28 and he will belong to the LORD his w life."
7: 9 and offered it to the LORD as a w burnt offering.
11:11 and slaughtered them the w morning.
17: 8 "Do you need a w army to settle this?
17:25 and his w family will be exempted from paying
17:46 and the w world will know that there is a God in
23: 3 to go to Keilah to fight the w Philistine army!"
25:15 Nothing was stolen from us the w time they were
25:17 to be trouble for our master and his w family.
1Ki 1:45 and the w city is celebrating and rejoicing.
8:48 Then if they turn to you with their w heart and soul
12: 3 and the w assembly of Israel went to speak with
2Ki 7: 6 For the Lord had caused the w army of Aram to
17:13 which are contained in the w law that I
21: 8 the w law that was given through my servant
1Ch 13: 4 The w assembly agreed to this, for the people
16: 8 Let the w world know what he has done.
16:23 Let the w earth sing to the LORD! / Each day
28: 9 Worship and serve him with your w heart and with
29:10 the LORD in the presence of the w assembly:
29:20 Then David said to the w assembly, "Give praise
2Ch 6:38 Then if they turn to you with their w heart and soul
13: 7 Then a w gang of scoundrels joined him,
16: 9 The eyes of the LORD search the w earth in order
Ezr 9: 7 Our w history has been one of great sin. That is
10:12 Then the w assembly raised their voices
Ne 3: 3 They did the w thing—laid the beams,
5:13 The w assembly responded, "Amen," and they
9:24 You subdued w nations before them.
Est 4: 7 Mordecai told him the w story and told him how
4:11 "The w world knows that anyone who appears
Job 9:24 The w earth is in the hands of the wicked, and God
28:24 for he looks throughout the w earth, under all the
34:13 in his care? Who has set the w world in place?
Ps 22:27 The w earth will acknowledge the LORD
33:13 down from heaven / and sees the w human race.
38: 3 Because of your anger, my w body is sick;
44:14 of their jokes; / we are scorned by the w world.
48: 2 in elevation— / the w earth rejoices to see it!
51:19 and with our w burnt offerings; / and bulls will
59:13 Then the w world will know / that God reigns in
63: 1 My soul thirsts for you; / my w body longs for you
66: 8 Let the w world bless our God / and sing aloud his
67: 4 and direct the actions of the w world. / *Interlude*
72:19 Let the w earth be filled with his glory. / Amen
82: 5 are in darkness, / the w world is shaken to the core.
84: 2 of the LORD. / With my w being, body and soul,
96: 1 the LORD! / Let the w earth sing to the LORD!
98: 3 The w earth has seen the salvation of our God.
99: 1 between the cherubim. / Let the w earth quake!
103: 1 with my w heart, I will praise his holy name.
105: 1 Let the w world know what he has done.
110: 6 he will shatter heads / over the w earth.
Pr 11:10 The w city celebrates when the godly succeed;
15:27 Dishonest money brings grief to the w family,
29: 8 Mockers can get a w town agitated, but those who
30: 4 Who has created the w wide world? What is his

Ecc 3:11 people cannot see the w scope of God's work from
11:10 but remember that youth, with a w life before it,
Isa 6: 3 The w earth is filled with his glory!"
6:11 and the w country is an utter wasteland.
7:19 come in vast hordes, spreading across the w land.
13: 5 his anger with them and will destroy the w land.
14:26 I have a plan for the w earth, for my mighty power
15: 8 The w land of Moab is a land of weeping from one
22: 2 The w city is in a terrible uproar. What do I see in
27: 6 and blossom and fill the w earth with her fruit!
43:21 and they will someday honor me before the w
Jer 4:27 "The w land will be ruined, but I will not destroy
8:16 The w land trembles at the approach of the terrible
10:10 The w earth trembles at his anger.
12:11 The w land is desolate, and no one even cares.
27:17 will live. Why should this w city be destroyed?
36:23 by section, until the w scroll was burned up.
40: 4 The w land is before you—go wherever you like.
50: 2 "Tell the w world, and keep nothing back! Raise a
50:38 Because the w land is filled with idols,
51: 7 a cup from which he made the w earth drink
51:47 Her w land will be disgraced, and her dead will lie
La 2: 3 He consumes the w land of Israel like a raging fire.
Eze 3: 7 For the w lot of them are hard-hearted
8:17 leading the w nation into violence, thumbing their
26:15 The w coastline will tremble at the sound of your
32: 4 and the wild animals of the w earth will gorge
35:14 The w world will rejoice when I make you
38:12 and they think the w world revolves around them!'
43: 2 and the w landscape shone with his glory.
Da 2:35 The w statue collapsed into a heap of iron, clay,
2:35 became a great mountain that covered the w earth.
2:48 He made Daniel ruler over the w province of
4:17 The purpose of this decree is that the w world may
7:23 It will devour the w world, trampling everything in
Hos 2:22 And the w grand chorus will sing together,
Am 1: 9 with Israel, selling w villages as slaves to Edom.
Ob 1: 8 wise person will be left in the w land of Edom!"
Zep 1:18 For the w land will be devoured by the fire of his
Hag 1:12 and the w remnant of God's people obeyed the
1:14 the high priest, and the w remnant of God's people.
Zec 1:11 patrolled the earth, and the w earth is at peace."
Mal 3: 9 a curse, for your w nation has been cheating me.
Mt 5: 5 and lowly, / for the w earth will belong to them.
5:29 body than for your w body to be thrown into hell.
5:30 body than for your w body to be thrown into hell.
8:32 and the w herd plunged down the steep hillside
10:31 you are more valuable to him than a w flock of
14:35 spread quickly throughout the w surrounding area,
16:26 And how do you benefit if you gain the w world
24:14 Kingdom will be preached throughout the w world,
27:45 darkness fell across the w land until three o'clock.
Mk 6:55 and they ran throughout the w area and began
8:36 And how do you benefit if you gain the w world
15:33 darkness fell across the w land until three o'clock.
Lk 1:65 Wonder fell upon the w neighborhood,
4:37 done spread like wildfire throughout the w region.
8:33 and the w herd plunged down the steep hillside
8:35 clothed and sane. And the w crowd was afraid.
8:45 this w crowd is pressing up against you."
8:47 The w crowd heard her explain why she had
9:13 us to go and buy enough food for this w crowd?"
9:25 And how do you benefit if you gain the w world
11:36 no dark corners, then your w life will be radiant,
12: 7 you are more valuable to him than a w flock of
23:44 and darkness fell across the w land until three
24:37 But the w group was terribly frightened,
Jn 11:48 the w nation will follow him, and then the Roman
11:50 Why should the w nation be destroyed? Let this
12:19 Look, the w world has gone after him!"
21:25 the w world could not contain the books.
Ac 5:36 various ways. The w movement came to nothing.
6: 5 This idea pleased the w group, and they chose the
7: 5 that eventually the w country would belong to
9:35 Then the w population of Lydda and Sharon turned
9:42 The news raced through the w town, and many
15: 4 and Barnabas were welcomed by the w church,
15:22 and the w church in Jerusalem chose delegates,
16:20 "The w city is in an uproar because of these
17:26 he created all the nations throughout the w earth.
21:30 The w population of the city was rocked by these
22: 5 and the w council of leaders can testify that this is
22:15 telling the w world what you have seen and heard.
Ro 3: 2 the Jews were entrusted with the w revelation of
4:13 that God's promise to give the w earth to Abraham
6:13 And use your w body as a tool to do what is right
10: 4 For Christ has accomplished the w purpose of the
1Co 3:22 and Peter; the w world and life and death;
12:17 Suppose the w body were an eye—then how would
12:17 Or if your w body were just one big ear, how could
14: 5 so that the w church can get some good out of it.
14:12 ask God for those that will be of real help to the w
2Co 11:25 Once I spent a w night and a day adrift at sea.
Gal 5: 3 you must obey all of the regulations in the w law
5: 9 a little yeast spreads quickly through the w batch
5:14 For the w law can be summed up in this one
6:13 advocate circumcision don't really keep the w law.
Eph 2:15 By his death he ended the w system of Jewish law
4:16 the w body is fitted together perfectly.
4:16 so that the w body is healthy and growing and full
Col 3: 4 who is your real life, is revealed to the w world,
4:12 and perfect, fully confident of the w will of God.
1Th 5:23 and may your w spirit and soul and body be kept
1Ti 1: 6 But some teachers have missed this w point.
5:20 sins should be rebuked in front of the w church
Tit 1:11 they have already turned w families away from the
Heb 11:12 And so a w nation came from this one man,
11:34 became strong in battle and put w armies to flight.
Jas 3: 6 It is full of wickedness that can ruin your w life.
4: 1 Isn't it the w army of evil desires at war within
4: 3 you don't get it because your w motive is wrong—
1Pe 1: 7 day when Jesus Christ is revealed to the w world.
2Pe 2: 5 Then God destroyed the w world of ungodly
Jude 1: 5 that even though the Lord rescued the w nation of
Rev 3:10 the w world to test those who belong to this world.
11:15 "The w world has now become the kingdom of
12: 9 or Satan, the one deceiving the w world—
14:16 over the earth, and the w earth was harvested.

WHOLEHEARTED (2) [HEART, WHOLE]

1Ch 29:19 Give my son Solomon the w desire to obey all
1Th 5:13 Think highly of them and give them your w love

WHOLEHEARTEDLY (12) [HEART, WHOLE]

Nu 32:12 son of Nun, for they have w followed the LORD.'
Dt 6: 6 And you must commit yourselves w to these
30: 2 and your children begin w to obey all the
Jos 14: 9 because you w followed the LORD my God.'
14:14 the Kenizzite because he w followed the LORD,
24:14 "So honor the LORD and serve him w. Put away
1Ch 29: 9 for they had given freely and w to the LORD,
2Ch 25: 2 was pleasing in the LORD's sight, but not w.
31:21 and the commands, Hezekiah sought his God w.
Jer 24: 7 I will be their God, for they will return to me w.
32:41 and will faithfully and w replant them in this land.
Php 2: 2 Then make me truly happy by agreeing w with

WHOLESOME (6)

Ex 16:24 The next morning the leftover food was w
2Ki 2:21 I have made this water w. It will no longer cause
2:22 The water has remained w ever since, just as
Pr 8: 8 My advice is w and good. There is nothing
1Ti 6: 3 the sound, w teachings of the Lord Jesus Christ,
2Pe 3: 1 of them I have tried to stimulate your w thinking

WHOM (231) [WHO] See Index of Articles, Etc.

WHOMEVER (1) [WHO]

1Co 7:39 husband dies, she is free to marry w she wishes,

WHOMSOEVER [KJV] See ANY(ONE), ONE(S), WHOEVER, WHOM

WHORE (1) [WHORES]

1Sa 20:30 "You stupid son of a w!" he swore at him.

WHORE(S), WHORE'S [KJV] See also CONCUBINE, PROSTITUTE, PROSTITUTING, PROSTITUTION

WHOREDOM [KJV] See ADULTERIES, DEFILE, IDOLATRY, LUST, ORGIES, PROSTITUTED, PROSTITUTING, SEXUAL, WHORE(S)

WHOREMONGERS [KJV] See (SEXUALLY) IMMORAL

WHORES (1) [WHORE]

Hos 4:14 same thing, sinning with w and shrine prostitutes.

WHOSE (168) [WHO] See Index of Articles, Etc.

WHOSO(EVER) [KJV] See ANYONE, ONE, THOSE, WHO, WHOEVER

WHY (663)

Ge 2:24 This explains w a man leaves his father and mother
3:13 tricked me," she replied. "That's w I ate it."
4: 6 "W are you so angry?" the LORD asked him. "W
do you look so dejected?
11: 9 That is w the city was called Babel, because it was
12:18 "W didn't you tell me she was your wife?
12:19 W were you willing to let me marry her,
18:13 LORD said to Abraham, "W did Sarah laugh?
18:13 W did she say, 'Can an old woman like me have a
18:25 W, you would be treating the innocent
20: 6 "That is w I kept you from sinning against me;
20:10 W have you done this to us?"
21:26 W didn't you say something about this before?"
21:29 Abimelech asked, "W are you doing that?"
24:31 W do you stand here outside the village when we
24:33 "I don't want to eat until I have told you w I have
25:22 about it. "W is this happening to me?" she asked.
26: 9 your wife! W did you say she was your sister?"
26:27 "W have you come?" Isaac asked them. "This is
27:32 "W, it's me, of course!" he replied. "It's Esau,
27:45 for you. W should I lose both of you in one day?"
29: 7 "W don't you water the flocks so they can get
31:27 W did you slip away secretly? I would have given
31:28 W didn't you let me kiss my daughters
31:30 but w have you stolen my household gods?"
31:42 That is w he appeared to you last night
32:29 asked him. "W do you ask?" the man replied.
32:32 That is w even today the people of Israel don't eat
33:17 and herds. That is w the place was named Succoth.
37:22 "W should we shed his blood? Let's just throw
40: 7 "W do you look so worried today?" he asked.
41:15 and that is w I have called for you."
42: 1 "W are you standing around looking at one
42:21 That's w this trouble has come upon us."
43: 6 "W did you ever tell him you had another
43: 6 "W did you have to treat me with such cruelty?"
44: 4 'W have you repaid an act of kindness with such
44: 8 W would we steal silver or gold from your
47:15 they said, "but give us bread. W should we die?"
47:19 W should we die before your very eyes? Buy us
Ex 1:18 "W have you done this?" he demanded.
1:18 "W have you allowed the boys to live?"
3: 3 said to himself. "W isn't that bush burning up?
5:14 "W haven't you met your quotas either yesterday
5:22 "W have you mistreated your own people like this,
Lord? W did you send me?
6:30 I'm no orator. W should Pharaoh listen to me?"
13: 8 you must explain to your children w you are
13:15 That is w we now offer all the firstborn males to
14:11 "W did you bring us out here to die in the
14:11 graves for us in Egypt? W did you make us leave?
14:15 said to Moses, "W are you crying out to me?
15:23 (That is w the place was called Marah,
16:22 and asked Moses w this had happened.
16:29 That is w I give you twice as much food on the
17: 2 Moses replied. "W are you arguing with me? And
w are you testing the LORD?"
17: 3 "W did you ever take us out of Egypt?
17: 3 W did you bring us here? We, our children,
18:14 he said, "W are you trying to do all this alone?
20:11 That is w the LORD blessed the Sabbath day
32:11 "W are you so angry with your own people whom
Lev 10:17 "W didn't you eat the sin offering in the sanctuary
17:12 That is w I said to the Israelites: 'You
17:14 That is w I have told the people of Israel never to
18:25 That is w I am punishing the people who live there,
Nu 6: 5 That is w they must let their hair grow long.
9: 7 But w should we be excluded from presenting the
11:11 "W are you treating me, your servant,
11:12 Is that w you have told me to carry them in my
11:20 to him, "W did we ever leave Egypt?" ' "
14: 3 "W is the LORD taking us to this country only to
14:41 "W are you now disobeying the LORD's orders
18:24 That is w I said they would receive no inheritance
20: 5 W did you make us leave Egypt and bring us here
21: 5 "W have you brought us out of Egypt to die here
22:32 "W did you beat your donkey those three times?"
22:37 W didn't you come right away?" Balak asked
27: 4 W should the name of our father disappear just
31:15 "W have you let all the women live?"
Dt 5:15 That is w the LORD your God has commanded
5:25 But now, w should we die? If the LORD our God
7: 8 That is w the LORD rescued you with such
9:25 "That is w I fell down and lay before the LORD
10: 9 That is w the Levites have no share or inheritance
15:11 That is w I am commanding you to share your
15:15 That is w I am giving you this command.
19: 7 That is w I am commanding you to set aside three
24:18 That is w I have given you this command.
24:22 of Egypt. That is w I am giving you this command.
29:24 will ask, 'W has the LORD done this to his land?
W was he so angry?'
29:27 That is w the LORD's anger burned against this
Jos 7: 7 w did you bring us across the Jordan River if you
7:10 "Get up! W are you lying on your face like this?
7:12 That is w the Israelites are running from their
7:25 to Achan, "W have you brought trouble on us?
7:26 That is w the place has been called the Valley of
9:22 Gibeonite leaders and said, "W did you lie to us?
9:22 W did you say that you live in a distant land when
9:24 because of you. That is w we have done it.
17:14 "W have you given us only one portion of land
22:16 to know w you are betraying the God of Israel.
Jdg 2: 2 W, then, have you disobeyed my command?
2:23 That is w the LORD did not quickly drive the
5:16 W did you sit at home among the sheepfolds—
5:17 And Dan, w did he stay home? / Asher sat
5:28 saying, / 'W is his chariot so long in coming?
5:28 W don't we hear the sound of chariot wheels?'
6:13 LORD is with us, w has all this happened to us?
6:31 shouted to the mob, "W are you defending Baal?
8: 1 asked Gideon, "W have you treated us this way?
8: 1 W didn't you send for us when you first went out
9:28 W should we be Abimelech's servants?
9:28 true descendants. W should we serve Abimelech?
9:38 is Abimelech, and w should we be his servants?'
11: 7 W do you come to me now when you're in
11:12 demanding to know w Israel was being attacked.
11:23 gave it to Israel. W, then, should we give it to you?
11:26 W have you made no effort to recover it before
12: 1 "W didn't you call for us to help you fight against
12: 3 So w have you come to fight me?"
13:18 "W do you ask my name?" the angel of the
14: 3 W must you go to the pagan Philistines to find a
14:16 or mother," he replied. "W should I tell you?"
15:10 asked the Philistines, "W have you attacked us?"
18: 3 and what are you doing? W are you here?"
18:23 W have you called these men together and chased
21: 3 of Israel," they cried out, "w has this happened?
Ru 1:11 Naomi replied, "W should you go on with me?
1:21 W should you call me Naomi when the LORD
2:10 "W are you being so kind to me?" she asked.
1Sa 1: 8 "W aren't you eating? W be so sad just because
you have no children?

2:23 things you are doing. **W** do you keep sinning?
2:29 So **w** do you scorn my sacrifices and offerings?
2:29 **W** do you honor your sons more than me—for you
4:3 "**W** did the LORD allow us to be defeated by the
5:5 That is **w** to this day neither the priests of Dagon
9:21 of that tribe! **W** are you talking like this to me?"
11:5 "What's the matter? **W** is everyone crying?"
14:28 be cursed. That is **w** everyone is weary and faint."
15:19 **W** haven't you obeyed the LORD? **W** did you rush for the plunder and do exactly
18:22 **W** don't you accept the king's offer and become
19:5 **W** should you murder an innocent man like David?
19:17 "**W** have you tricked me and let my enemy
20:3 'I won't tell Jonathan—**w** should I hurt him?'
20:26 Yes, that must be **w** he's not here."
20:27 "**W** hasn't the son of Jesse been here for dinner
20:29 so I told him he could go. That's **w** he isn't here."
20:32 "**W** should he be put to death?"
21:1 "**W** are you alone?" he asked. "**W** is no one with you?"
21:2 "He told me not to tell anyone **w** I am here.
21:15 **W** should I let someone like this be my guest?"
22:8 Is that **w** you have conspired against me? For not
22:13 "**W** have you and David conspired against me?"
22:13 "**W** did you give him food and a sword? **W** have you inquired of God for him? **W** did you encourage him to revolt against me
22:14 **W**, he is the captain of your bodyguard and a
24:9 "**W** do you listen to the people who say I am
26:15 So **w** haven't you guarded your master the king
26:18 **W** are you chasing me? What have I done? What is
26:20 **W** has the king of Israel come out to search for a
26:20 **W** does he hunt me down like a partridge on the
28:9 from the land. **W** are you setting a trap for me?"
28:15 "**W** have you disturbed me by calling me back?"
28:16 "**W** ask me if the LORD has left you and has
29:8 "**W** can't I fight the enemies of my lord,
2Sa 7:7 "**W** haven't you built me a beautiful cedar
11:10 **W** didn't you go home last night after being away
11:20 and ask, '**W** did the troops go so close to the city?
12:9 **W**, then, have you despised the word of the
12:23 But **w** should I fast when he is dead? Can I bring
13:4 **W** should the son of a king look so dejected
13:26 Amnon instead?" "**W** Amnon?" the king asked.
14:13 "**W** don't you do as much for all the people of
14:14 That is **w** God tries to bring us back when we have
14:31 "**W** did your servants set my field on fire?"
14:32 "Because I wanted you to ask the king **w** he
15:19 and asked, "**W** are you coming with us?
16:9 "**W** should this dead dog curse my lord the king?"
16:17 Absalom asked him. "**W** aren't you with him?"
16:19 "And anyway, **w** shouldn't I serve you? I helped
18:22 let me go, too." "**W** should you go, my son?"
19:11 "**W** are you the last ones to reinstate the king?
19:12 **W** are you the last ones to welcome me back?"
19:20 That is **w** I have come here today, the very first
19:25 "**W** didn't you come with me, Mephibosheth?"
19:42 "**W** not?" the men of Judah replied. "The king is
19:42 **W** should this make you angry? We have charged
19:43 **W** did you treat us with such contempt?
20:19 **W** do you want to destroy what belongs to the
21:17 **W** should we risk snuffing out the light of Israel?"
24:3 as there are now! But **w** do you want to do this?"
24:21 "**W** have you come, my lord?" Araunah asked.
1Ki 1:13 your throne? Then **w** has Adonijah become king?'
1:41 going on? **W** is the city in such an uproar?"
2:43 Then **w** haven't you kept your oath to the LORD
8:27 **W**, even the highest heavens cannot contain you.
9:8 '**W** did the LORD do such terrible things to his
9:9 That is **w** the LORD has brought all these
11:22 "**W**?" Pharaoh asked him. "What do you lack
14:6 **W** are you pretending to be someone else?"
17:20 **w** have you brought tragedy on this widow who
20:23 gods are gods of the hills; that is **w** they won.
22:4 Jehoshaphat replied to King Ahab, "**W**, of course!
2Ki 1:3 and ask them, '**W** are you going to Baal-zebub,
1:5 he asked them, "**W** have you returned so soon?"
1:6 He said, '**W** are you going to Baal-zebub, the god
1:16 **W** did you send messengers to Baal-zebub, the god
3:7 And Jehoshaphat replied, "**W**, of course! You
4:23 "**W** today?" he asked. "It is neither a new moon
5:8 "**W** are you so upset? Send Naaman to me, and he
5:12 **W** shouldn't I wash in them and be healed?"
6:33 **W** should I wait any longer for the LORD?"
7:3 "**W** should we sit here waiting to die?" they asked
12:7 asked them, "**W** haven't you repaired the Temple?
14:10 **W** stir up trouble that will bring disaster on you
19:11 stood in their way! **W** should you be any different?
19:26 That is **w** their people have so little power / and are
1Ch 11:7 and that is **w** it is called the City of David.
17:6 "**W** haven't you built me a beautiful cedar
21:3 But **w**, my lord, do you want to do this? Are they
21:3 your servants? **W** must you cause Israel to sin?"
2Ch 6:18 **W**, even the highest heavens cannot contain you.
7:21 '**W** has the LORD done such terrible things to his
7:22 That is **w** he brought all these disasters upon
18:3 And Jehoshaphat replied, "**W**, of course! You
19:2 "**W** should you help the wicked and love those
24:6 "**W** haven't you demanded that the Levites go out
24:20 **W** do you disobey the LORD's commands
25:15 "**W** have you worshiped gods who could not even
25:19 **W** stir up trouble that will bring disaster on you
28:5 That is **w** the LORD his God allowed the king of
29:8 That is **w** the LORD's anger has fallen upon
32:4 "**W** should the kings of Assyria come here
Ezr 7:23 for **w** should we risk bringing God's anger against
9:7 That is **w** we and our kings and our priests have
Ne 2:2 So the king asked me, "**W** are you so sad?
2:3 "Long live the king! **W** shouldn't I be sad?
6:6 to rebel and that is **w** you are building the wall.
13:11 "**W** has the Temple of God been neglected?"
13:17 "**W** are you profaning the Sabbath in this evil
Est 3:3 "**W** are you disobeying the king's command?"
4:5 what was troubling him and **w** he was in mourning.
9:26 (That is **w** this celebration is called Purim,
Job 3:11 "**W** didn't I die at birth as I came from the womb?
3:12 **W** did my mother let me live? **W** did she nurse me at her breasts?
3:16 **W** was I not buried like a stillborn child, like a
3:20 "Oh, **w** should light be given to the weary, and life
3:23 **W** is life given to those with no future,
6:3 all the sands of the sea. That is **w** I spoke so rashly.
6:22 But **w**? Have I ever asked you for a gift? Have I
7:19 **W** won't you leave me alone—even for a moment?
7:20 **W** have you made me your target? Am I a burden
7:21 **W** not just pardon my sin and take away my guilt?
9:22 That is **w** I say, 'He destroys both the blameless
10:3 **W** do you reject me, the work of your own hands,
10:18 " '**W**, then, did you bring me out of my mother's womb? **W** didn't you let me die at birth?
13:24 **W** do you turn away from me? **W** do you consider me your enemy?
15:6 But **w** should I condemn you? Your own mouth
15:15 **W**, God doesn't even trust the angels!
19:22 **W** must you persecute me as God does?
19:22 **W** aren't you satisfied with my anguish?
21:15 Who is the Almighty, and **w** should we obey him?
22:10 That is **w** you are surrounded by traps and sudden
22:11 That is **w** you cannot see in the darkness,
22:13 'That's **w** God can't see what I am doing!
24:1 "**W** doesn't the Almighty open the court and bring
24:1 **W** must the godly wait for him in vain?
33:12 "In this you are not right, and I will show you **w**.
33:13 So **w** are you bringing a charge against him?
34:9 even said, '**W** waste time trying to please God?'
34:31 "**W** don't people say to God, 'I have sinned,
Ps 2:1 **W** do the nations rage? / **W** do the people waste their time with futile plans?
10:1 O LORD, **w** do you stand so far away? / **W** do you hide when I need you the most?
10:13 **W** do the wicked get away with cursing God?
11:1 So **w** do you say to me, / "Fly to the mountains for
22:1 My God, my God! **W** have you forsaken me? / **W** do you remain so distant? / **W** do you ignore my cries for help?
27:1 and my salvation— / so **w** should I be afraid?
27:1 me from danger— / so **w** should I tremble?
42:5 **W** am I discouraged? / **W** so sad? / I will put my
42:9 God my rock," I cry, / "**W** have you forsaken me?
42:9 **W** must I wander in darkness, / oppressed by my
42:11 **W** am I discouraged? / **W** so sad? / I will put my
43:2 only safe haven. / **W** have you tossed me aside?
43:2 **W** must I wander around in darkness,
43:5 **W** am I discouraged? / **W** so sad? / I will put my
44:23 Wake up, O Lord! **W** do you sleep? / Get up!
44:24 **W** do you look the other way? / **W** do you ignore our suffering and oppression?
52:1 do you? / **W** boast about this crime of yours,
56:4 I trust in God, so **w** should I be afraid?
56:11 I trust in God, so **w** should I be afraid? / What can
66:15 That is **w** I am sacrificing burnt offerings to you—
68:16 **W** do you look with envy, O rugged mountains,
71:8 That is **w** I can never stop praising you; / I declare
73:16 So I tried to understand **w** the wicked prosper.
74:1 O God, **w** have you rejected us forever? / **W** is your anger so intense against the sheep of
74:11 **W** do you hold back your strong right hand?
79:10 **W** should pagan nations be allowed to scoff,
80:12 But now, **w** have you broken down our walls
88:14 O LORD, **w** do you reject me? / **W** do you turn your face away from me?
89:38 **W** are you so angry with the one you chose as
106:40 That is **w** the LORD's anger burned against his
107:12 That is **w** he broke them with hard labor;
114:6 **W**, mountains, did you skip like rams? / **W**, little hills, like lambs?
115:2 **W** let the nations say, / "Where is their God?"
119:128 is right. / That is **w** I hate every false way.
119:140 thoroughly tested; / that is **w** I love them so much.
Pr 1:31 That is **w** they must eat the bitter fruit of living
5:13 Oh, **w** didn't I listen to my teachers? **W** didn't I pay attention to those who gave me
5:16 **W** spill the water of your springs in public,
5:20 **W** be captivated, my son, with an immoral woman,
8:13 That is **w** I hate pride, arrogance, corruption,
23:4 yourself trying to get rich. **W** waste your time?
Ecc 3:22 That is **w** they are here! No one will bring them
4:8 **W** am I giving up so much pleasure now?" It is all
6:11 you speak, the less they mean. So **w** overdo it?
7:16 don't be too good or too wise! **W** destroy yourself?
7:17 be a fool! **W** should you die before your time?
9:3 That is **w** people are not more careful to be good.
SS 1:7 For **w** should I wander like a prostitute among the
6:13 "**W** do you gaze so intently at this young woman
Isa 1:5 **W** do you continue to invite punishment?
1:12 **W** do you keep parading through my courts with
5:4 **W** did my vineyard give me wild grapes
5:25 That is **w** the anger of the LORD burns against
5:25 That is **w** he has raised his fist to crush them.
8:19 So **w** are you trying to find out the future by
8:19 out the future from the dead? **W** not ask your God?
9:17 That is **w** the Lord has no joy in the young men
17:10 **W**? Because you have turned from the God who
22:1 **W** is everyone running to the rooftops?
28:9 **W** does he speak to us like this? Are we little
29:22 That is **w** the LORD, who redeemed Abraham,
37:11 stood in their way! **W** should you be any different?
37:27 That is **w** their people have so little power / and are
42:18 **W** won't you listen? **W** do you refuse to see?
42:25 That is **w** he poured out such fury on them
43:28 That is **w** I have disgraced your priests
44:19 stops to reflect, "**W**, it's just a block of wood!
45:4 "And **w** have I called you for this work? It is for
45:10 '**W** was I born? **W** did you make me this way?' "
48:5 That is **w** I told you ahead of time what I was
50:1 Is that **w** you are not here? Is your mother gone
50:2 Is that **w** the house is silent and empty when I
51:12 So **w** are you afraid of mere humans, who wither
52:5 the LORD. "**W** are my people enslaved again?
55:2 **W** spend your money on food that does not give
55:2 **W** pay for food that does you no good? Listen,
57:1 their time. And no one seems to care or wonder **w**.
57:11 **W** were you more afraid of them than of me?
58:3 before you!' they say. '**W** aren't you impressed?
58:3 "I will tell you **w**! It's because you are living for
59:9 That is **w** God doesn't punish those who injure us.
63:2 **W** are your clothes so red, as if you have been
63:10 That is **w** he became their enemy and fought
63:17 **w** have you allowed us to turn from your path?
63:17 **W** have you given us stubborn hearts so we no
63:19 **w** do you treat us as though we never belonged to
63:19 **W** do you act as though we had never been known
Jer 2:14 "**W** has Israel become a nation of slaves? **W** has she been carried away as plunder?
2:25 **W** do you refuse to turn from all this running after
2:28 **W** don't you call on these gods you have made?
2:29 **W** do you accuse me of doing wrong? You are the
2:31 **W** then do my people say, 'At last we are free
3:3 That is **w** even the spring rains have failed. For you
4:30 **W** do you dress up in your most beautiful clothing
4:30 **W** do you brighten your eyes with mascara?
5:19 '**W** is the LORD our God doing this to us?'
5:22 **W** do you not tremble in my presence? I,
8:5 Then **w** do these people keep going along their
8:14 the people will say, '**W** should we wait here to die?
8:19 **w** have they angered me with their carved idols
8:22 **W** is there no healing for the wounds of my
9:12 **W** has the land been ruined so completely that no
12:1 **W** are the wicked so prosperous? **W** are evil people so happy?
13:22 ask yourself, "**W** is all this happening to me?"
13:22 That is **w** you have been raped and destroyed by
14:1 explaining **w** he was holding back the rain:
14:8 times of trouble! **W** are you like a stranger to us?
14:8 **W** are you like someone passing through the land,
14:19 **W** have you wounded us past all hope of healing?
15:18 **W** then does my suffering continue? **W** is my wound so incurable?
16:10 '**W** has the LORD decreed such terrible things
17:15 **W** don't your predictions come true?"
20:18 **W** was I ever born? My entire life has been filled
22:8 '**W** did the LORD destroy such a great city?'
22:15 **W** did your father, Josiah, reign so long?
22:15 in all his dealings. That is **w** God blessed him.
22:28 "**W** is this man Jehoiachin like a discarded,
22:28 **W** are he and his children to be exiled to distant
27:13 "**W** do you insist on dying—you and your people?
27:13 **W** should you choose war, famine, and disease,
27:17 will live. **W** should this whole city be destroyed?
29:27 So **w** have you done nothing to stop Jeremiah from
30:6 Then **w** do they stand there, ashen-faced,
30:15 **W** do you protest your punishment—this wound
32:23 That is **w** you have sent this terrible disaster upon
35:11 to move to Jerusalem. That is **w** we are here."
38:27 and asked him **w** the king had called for him.
40:3 and disobeyed him. That is **w** it happened.
40:15 "**W** should we let him come and murder you?"
40:15 **W** should the few of us who are still left be
44:7 asks you: **W** are you destroying yourselves?
44:8 **W** arouse my anger by burning incense to the idols
46:15 **W** have your warriors fled in terror? They cannot
49:1 **W** are you, who worship Molech, living in its
50:38 her water supply, causing it to dry up. And **w**?
La 3:39 Then **w** should we, mere humans, complain when
5:20 **W** do you continue to forget us? **W** have you forsaken us for so long?
Eze 7:20 That is **w** I will make all their wealth disgusting to
14:3 into sin. **W** should I let them ask me anything?
16:27 That is **w** I struck you with my fist and reduced
18:2 "**W** do you quote this proverb in the land of Israel:
18:31 For **w** should you die, O people of Israel?
21:7 When they ask you **w**, tell them, 'I groan
33:11 O people of Israel! **W** should you die?
39:23 then know **w** Israel was sent away to exile—
Da 2:15 "**W** has the king issued such a harsh decree?"
10:20 He replied, "Do you know **w** I have come? Soon I
Hos 4:3 That is **w** your land is not producing. It is filled
4:13 That is **w** your daughters turn to prostitution,
4:14 **W** should I punish them? For you men are doing
13:10 is your king? **W** don't you call on him for help?
Joel 2:12 That is **w** the LORD says, "Turn to me now,
Am 3:2 That is **w** I must punish you for all your sins."
Ob 1:10 "And **w**? Because of the violence you did to your
Jnh 1:10 heard this. "Oh, **w** did you do it?" they groaned.
4:2 do this, LORD? That is **w** I ran away to Tarshish!
Mic 1:5 And **w** is this happening? Because of the sins
4:9 But **w** are you now screaming in terror? Have you
6:3 Tell me **w** your patience is exhausted! Answer me!
Na 1:9 **W** are you scheming against the LORD? He will
Hag 1:4 "**W** are you living in luxurious houses while my
1:9 brought your harvest home, I blew it away. **W**?

1:10 That is w the heavens have withheld the dew
Zec 7:12 That is w the LORD Almighty was so angry with
Mal 1: 9 w should he show you any favor at all?"
2:10 Then w are we faithless to each other,
2:14 You cry out, "W has the LORD abandoned us?"
I'll tell you w!
3: 6 That is w you descendants of Jacob are not already
Mt 3:14 by you," he said, "so w are you coming to me?"
5:17 "Don't misunderstand w I have come. I did not
6:28 "And w worry about your clothes? Look at the
6:32 W be like the pagans who are so deeply concerned
7: 3 And w worry about a speck in your friend's eye
8:26 And Jesus answered, "W are you afraid?
8:29 at him, "W are you bothering us, Son of God?
9: 4 "W are you thinking such evil thoughts?
9:11 "W does your teacher eat with such scum?"
9:14 and asked him, "W do we and the Pharisees fast,
13:10 "W do you always tell stories when you talk to the
13:13 That is w I tell these stories, because people see
14: 2 to life again! That is w he can do such miracles."
14:31 much faith," Jesus said. "W did you doubt me?"
15: 2 "W do your disciples disobey our age-old
15: 3 Jesus replied, "And w do you, by your traditions,
16: 8 W are you worried about having no food?
17:10 "W do the teachers of religious law insist that
17:19 "W couldn't we cast out that demon?"
19: 5 'This explains w a man leaves his father
19: 7 "Then w did Moses say a man could merely write
19:17 "W ask me about what is good?" Jesus replied.
20: 6 asked them, 'W haven't you been working today?'
21:25 from heaven, he will ask w we didn't believe him.
22:43 Jesus responded, "Then w does David,
26:10 "W berate her for doing such a good thing to me?
26:55 arrest me? W didn't you arrest me in the Temple?
26:65 "Blasphemy! W do we need other witnesses?
27: 8 That is w the field is still called the Field of Blood.
27:23 "W?" Pilate demanded. "What crime has he
27:46 "My God, my God, w have you forsaken me?"
Mk 1:24 "W are you bothering us, Jesus of Nazareth?
1:38 preach to them, too, because that is w I came."
2: 8 said to them, "W do you think this is blasphemy?
2:16 to his disciples, "W does he eat with such scum?"
2:18 "W do John's disciples and the Pharisees fast,
4:40 And he asked them, "W are you so afraid? Do you
5: 7 shrieking, "W are you bothering me, Jesus,
5:39 "W all this weeping and commotion?" he asked.
6:14 to life again. That is w he can do such miracles."
7: 5 "W don't your disciples follow our age-old
8:12 "W do you people keep demanding a miraculous
8:17 "W are you so worried about having no food?
9:11 "W do the teachers of religious law insist that
9:12 W then is it written in the Scriptures that the Son
9:28 "W couldn't we cast out that evil spirit?"
10: 7 'This explains w a man leaves his father
10:18 "W do you call me good?" Jesus asked.
11:31 from heaven, he will ask w we didn't believe him.
12:35 "W do the teachers of religious law claim that the
14: 4 "W was this expensive perfume wasted?"
14: 6 W berate her for doing such a good thing to me?
14:11 were delighted when they heard w he had come,
14:49 W didn't you arrest me in the Temple? I was there
14:63 and said, "W do we need other witnesses?
15:14 "W?" Pilate demanded. "What crime has he
15:34 "My God, my God, w have you forsaken me?"
Lk 1:21 to come out, wondering w he was taking so long.
2:48 "W have you done this to us? Your father and I
2:49 "But w did you need to search?" he asked.
4:23 'W don't you do miracles here in your hometown
4:34 W are you bothering us, Jesus of Nazareth?
4:43 in other places, too, because that is w I was sent."
5:22 asked them, "W do you think this is blasphemy?
5:30 "W do you eat and drink with such scum?"
5:33 of the Pharisees. W are yours always feasting?"
6:41 "And w worry about a speck in your friend's eye
6:46 "So w do you call me 'Lord,' when you won't
8:28 screaming, "W are you bothering me, Jesus,
8:47 The whole crowd heard her explain w she had
12:57 "W can't you decide for yourselves what is right?
13: 2 from Galilee?" he asked. "Is that w they suffered?
16:12 w should you be trusted with money of your own?
18:19 "W do you call me good?" Jesus asked him.
19:23 w didn't you deposit the money in the bank so I
19:33 asked them, "W are you untying our colt?"
20: 5 from heaven, he will ask w we didn't believe him.
20:41 "W is it," he asked, "that the Messiah is said to
22:46 "W are you sleeping?" he asked. "Get up
22:53 W didn't you arrest me in the Temple? I was there
23:22 For the third time he demanded, "W? What crime
24: 5 "W are you looking in a tomb for someone who is
24:38 "W are you frightened?" he asked. "W do you
doubt who I am?
Jn 4: 9 W are you asking me for a drink?"
4:20 w is it that you Jews insist that Jerusalem is the
4:27 but none of them asked him w he was doing it
5:17 "My Father never stops working, so w should I?"
7:23 So w should I be condemned for making a man
7:45 and Pharisees. "W didn't you bring him in?"
8:24 That is w I said that you will die in your sins;
8:43 W can't you understand what I am saying? It is
8:46 I am telling you the truth, w don't you believe me?
9: 2 disciples asked him, "w was this man born blind?
9:23 That's w they said, "He is old enough to speak for
9:27 Didn't you listen? W do you want to hear it again?
9:30 "W, that's very strange!" the man replied.
10:20 or he's crazy. W listen to a man like that?"
10:36 w do you call it blasphemy when the Holy One
11:37 W couldn't he keep Lazarus from dying?"
11:50 W should the whole nation be destroyed? Let this
12:27 lies ahead'? But that is the very reason w I came!
12:34 W are you saying the Son of Man will die? Who is
13: 6 to him, "Lord, w are you going to wash my feet?"
13: 7 "You don't understand now w I am doing it;
13:37 "But w can't I come now, Lord?" he asked.
14: 9 seen the Father! So w are you asking to see him?
14:22 w are you going to reveal yourself only to us
18:21 W are you asking me this question? Ask those who
18:35 brought you here. W? What have you done?"
20:13 "W are you crying?" the angels asked her.
20:15 "W are you crying?" Jesus asked her. "Who are
Ac 1:11 w are you standing here staring at the sky?
3:12 And w look at us as though we had made this man
4:25 your servant, saying, / 'W did the nations rage?
4:25 W did the people waste their time with futile
5: 3 "Ananias, w has Satan filled your heart?
7:26 'you are brothers. W are you hurting each other?'
8:36 There's some water! W can't I be baptized?"
9: 4 to him, "Saul! Saul! W are you persecuting me?"
10:21 the man you are looking for. W have you come?"
10:29 as I was sent for. Now tell me w you sent for me."
14:15 "Friends, w are you doing this? We are merely
15:10 W are you now questioning God's way by
19:32 most of them didn't even know w they were there.
21:13 But he said, "W all this weeping? You are
22: 7 to me, 'Saul, Saul, w are you persecuting me?'
22:16 And now, w delay? Get up and be baptized,
22:24 He wanted to find out w the crowd had become
26: 7 that is w the twelve tribes of Israel worship God
26: 8 W does it seem incredible to any of you that God
26:14 in Aramaic, 'Saul, Saul, w are you persecuting me?
Ro 1:26 That is w God abandoned them to their shameful
2:21 if you teach others, w don't you teach yourself?
4:16 So that's w faith is the key! God's promise is given
8: 8 That's w those who are still under the control of
9:19 "W does God blame people for not listening?
9:20 who made it, "W have you made me like this?"
9:32 W not? Because they were trying to get right with
14:10 So w do you condemn another Christian? W do
you look down on another Christian?
1Co 3: 5 W, we're only servants. Through us God caused
4: 7 w boast as though you have accomplished
5: 2 W aren't you mourning in sorrow and shame?
5: 2 And w haven't you removed this man from your
6: 1 w do you file a lawsuit and ask a secular court to
6: 4 w do you go to outside judges who are not
6: 7 W not just accept the injustice and leave it at that?
W not let yourselves be cheated?
10:10 for that is w God sent his angel of death to destroy
10:29 w should my freedom be limited by what someone
10:30 enjoy it, w should I be condemned for eating it?
11:28 That is w you should examine yourself before
11:30 That is w many of you are weak and sick and some
15:12 w are some of you saying there will be no
15:29 W do it unless the dead will someday rise again?
15:30 And w should we ourselves be continually risking
2Co 1:17 You may be asking w I changed my plan. Hadn't I
1:20 That is w we say "Amen" when we give glory to
2: 3 That is w I wrote as I did in my last letter, so that
4:16 That is w we never give up. Though our bodies are
5: 7 That is w we live by believing and not by seeing.
11:11 W? Because I don't love you? God knows I do.
Gal 1: 5 That is w all glory belongs to God through all the
2:14 w are you trying to make these Gentiles obey the
3: 3 w are you now trying to become perfect by your
3:19 Well then, w was the law given? It was given to
4: 9 w do you want to go back again and become slaves
5:11 some say I do—w would the Jews persecute me?
Eph 4: 8 That is w the Scriptures say, / "When he ascended
5:14 This is w it is said, / "Awake, O sleeper, / rise up
Col 2:20 So w do you keep on following rules of the world,
4: 3 for you Gentiles. That is w I am here in chains.
1Th 3: 5 That is w, when I could bear it no longer, I sent
1Ti 1:16 But that is w God had mercy on me, so that Christ
2Ti 1: 6 This is w I remind you to fan into flames the
1:12 And that is w I am suffering here in prison. But I
Phm 1: 8 That is w I am boldly asking a favor of you.
Heb 2:11 That is w Jesus is not ashamed to call them his
3: 7 That is w the Holy Spirit says, / "Today you must
4:14 That is w we have a great High Priest who has
5: 3 That is w he has to offer sacrifices, both for their
5: 5 That is w Christ did not exalt himself to become
7:11 w did God need to send a different priest from the
9:15 That is w he is the one who mediates the new
9:18 That is w blood was required under the first
9:23 That is w the earthly tent and everything in it—
10: 5 That is w Christ, when he came into the world,
11:16 That is w God is not ashamed to be called their
13: 6 That is w we can say with confidence, / "The Lord
1Pe 4: 6 That is w the Good News was preached even to
2Pe 3: 4 W, as far back as anyone can remember,
1Jn 3:12 and killed his brother. And w did he kill him?
4: 6 to God; that is w those who know God listen to us.
Rev 7:15 That is w they are standing in front of the throne of
17: 7 "W are you so amazed?" the angel asked. "I will

WICKED (351) [WICKEDLY, WICKEDNESS]

Ge 13:13 The people of this area were unusually w
18:20 extremely evil, and that everything they do is w.
19: 7 he begged, "don't do such a w thing.
38: 7 But Er was a w man in the LORD's sight,
38:10 But the LORD considered it a w thing for Onan
39: 9 are his wife. How could I ever do such a w thing?
44: 5 the future? What a w thing you have done!' "
49: 6 May I never be a party to their w plans.
Ex 10:10 ones along! I can see through your w intentions.
32:22 know these people and what a w bunch they are.
Lev 20:14 a woman and her mother, such an act is terribly w.
Nu 14:27 "How long will this w nation complain about me?
16:26 "Get away from the tents of these w men,
Dt 1:35 'Not one of you from this entire w generation will
Jdg 19:22 some of the w men in the town surrounded the
1Sa 1:16 Please don't think I am a w woman! For I have
2: 9 his godly ones, / but the w will perish in darkness.
2:23 from the people about the w things you are doing.
10:27 But there were some w men who complained,
12:17 Then you will realize how w you have been in
25:25 I know Nabal is a w and ill-tempered man;
2Sa 3:34 you were murdered— / the victim of a w plot."
3:39 So may the LORD repay these w men for their w
deeds."
4:11 Now what reward should I give the w men who
7:10 It will be their own land where w nations won't
22:27 but to the w you show yourself hostile.
1Ki 2:44 "You surely remember all the w things you did to
2Ki 3: 2 but he was not as w as his father and mother.
8:18 of the kings of Israel and was as w as King Ahab,
21:11 He is even more w than the Amorites, who lived in
1Ch 2: 3 But the oldest son, Er, was a w man,
17: 9 It will be their own land where w nations won't
2Ch 7:14 and seek my face and turn from their w ways,
19: 2 "Why should you help the w and love those who
20:35 King Ahaziah of Israel, who was a very w man.
21: 6 of the kings of Israel and was as w as King Ahab,
24: 7 the followers of w Athaliah had broken into the
Est 7: 6 Esther replied, "This w Haman is our enemy."
Job 3:17 For in death the w cease from troubling,
5:16 poor have hope, and the fangs of the w are broken.
8:22 and the tent of the w will be destroyed."
9:20 Though I am blameless, it would prove me w.
9:22 Innocent or w, it is all the same to him. That is
9:22 'He destroys both the blameless and the w.'
9:24 The whole earth is in the hands of the w, and God
10: 3 while sending joy and prosperity to the w?
11:20 But the w will lose hope. They have no escape.
15:20 "W people are in pain throughout their lives.
15:27 "These w people are fat and rich,
16:11 He has tossed me into the hands of the w.
18: 5 "The truth remains that the light of the w will be
18: 7 The confident stride of the w will be shortened.
18: 8 "The w walk into a net. They fall into a pit that's
18:11 "Terrors surround the w and trouble them at every
18:15 The home of the w will disappear beneath a fiery
18:21 They will say, 'This was the home of a w person,
20: 5 the triumph of the w has been short-lived
20:29 This is the fate that awaits the w. It is the
21: 7 "The truth is that the w live to a good old age.
21:17 "Yet the w get away with it time and time again.
21:28 and w people who came to disaster because of their
22:19 "Now the righteous will be happy to see the w
24: 6 not own, and they glean in the vineyards of the w.
24: 9 "The w snatch a widow's child from her breast;
24:13 "W people rebel against the light. They refuse to
24:20 W people are broken like a tree in the storm.
27: 7 "May my enemy be punished like the w,
27:13 "This is what the w will receive from God; this is
27:18 The houses built by the w are as fragile as a
27:19 "The w go to bed rich but wake up to find that all
31: 3 It is calamity for the w, misfortune for those who
34: 8 of evil people. He spends his time with w men.
34:18 says to kings and nobles, 'You are w and unjust.'
34:22 No darkness is thick enough to hide the w from his
34:36 you deserve the maximum penalty for the w way
36: 6 He does not let the w live but gives justice to the
38:15 The light disturbs the haunts of the w, and it stops
40:12 with a glance; walk on the w where they stand.
Ps 1: 1 of those / who do not follow the advice of the w,
1: 4 But this is not true of the w. / They are like
1: 6 but the path of the w leads to destruction.
3: 7 enemies in the face! / Shatter the teeth of the w!
7:11 perfectly fair. / He is angry with the w every day.
7:14 The w conceive evil; / they are pregnant with
9: 5 You have rebuked the nations and destroyed the w;
9:16 The w have trapped themselves in their own
9:17 The w will go down to the grave. / This is the fate
10: 2 Proud and w people viciously oppress the poor.
10: 4 These w people are too proud to seek God.
10:10 they fall beneath the strength of the w.
10:11 The w say to themselves, "God isn't watching!
10:12 Arise, O LORD! / Punish the w, O God! / Do not
10:13 Why do the w get away with cursing God?
10:15 Break the arms of these w, evil people! / Go after
11: 2 The w are stringing their bows / and setting their
11: 5 LORD examines both the righteous and the w.
11: 6 He rains down blazing coals on the w,
12: 8 even though the w strut about, / and evil is praised
14: 6 The w frustrate the plans of the oppressed,
17: 9 Protect me from w people who attack me,
17:13 Rescue me from the w with your sword!
18:26 but to the w you show yourself hostile.
26: 5 who do evil, / and I refuse to join in with the w.
26:10 Their hands are dirty with w schemes, / and they
28: 3 Don't drag me away with the w— / with those who
31:17 I call out to you for help. / Let the w be disgraced;
32:10 Many sorrows come to the w, / but unfailing love
34:21 Calamity will surely overtake the w, / and those
36: 1 Sin whispers to the w, deep within their hearts.
36: 2 they cannot see how w they really are.
36:11 trample me; / don't let the w push me around.
37: 1 Don't worry about the w. / Don't envy those who
37: 7 people who prosper / or fret about their w schemes.
37: 9 For the w will be destroyed, / but those who trust

37:10 In a little while, the w will disappear. / Though you
37:12 The w plot against the godly; / they snarl at them
37:14 The w draw their swords / and string their bows
37:17 For the strength of the w will be shattered,
37:20 But the w will perish. / The LORD's enemies are
37:21 The w borrow and never repay, / but the godly are
37:28 safe forever, / but the children of the w will perish.
37:33 But the LORD will not let the w succeed / or let
37:34 you the land. / You will see the w destroyed.
37:38 But the w will be destroyed; / they have no future.
37:40 LORD helps them, / rescuing them from the w.
49:16 So don't be dismayed when the w grow rich,
50:16 But God says to the w: / "Recite my laws no
55: 3 enemies shout at me, / making loud and w threats.
55:23 But you, O God, will send the w / down to the pit
58: 3 These w people are born sinners; / even from birth
58:10 They will wash their feet in the blood of the w.
59: 5 Show no mercy to w traitors. / *Interlude*
64: 2 Protect me from the plots of the w,
68: 2 in fire. / Let the w perish in the presence of God.
71: 4 My God, rescue me from the power of the w,
73:16 So I tried to understand why the w prosper.
73:17 O God, / and I thought about the destiny of the w.
75: 2 I have planned, / I will bring justice against the w.
75: 4 I told the w, 'Don't raise your fists!
75: 8 wine out in judgment, / and all the w must drink it,
75:10 For God says, "I will cut off the strength of the w,
82: 2 How long will you shower special favors on the w?
84:10 than live the good life in the homes of the w.
89:22 the best of him, / nor will the w overpower him.
91: 8 your eyes; / you will see how the w are punished.
92: 7 Although the w flourish like weeds, / and evildoers
92:11 with my own ears I have heard the defeat of my w
94: 3 How long will the w be allowed to gloat?
94:13 from troubled times / until a pit is dug for the w.
94:16 Who will protect me from the w? / Who will stand
97:10 and rescues them from the power of the w.
104:35 the face of the earth; / let the w disappear forever.
106:18 upon their followers; / a flame consumed the w.
107:42 and be glad, / while the w are stricken silent.
109: 2 while the w slander me / and tell lies about me.
112:10 The w will be infuriated when they see this.
119:53 I am furious with the w, / those who reject your
119:95 Though the w hide along the way to kill me,
119:110 The w have set their traps for me along your path,
119:119 All the w of the earth are the scum you skim off;
119:155 The w are far from salvation, / for they do not
125: 3 The w will not rule the godly, / for then the godly
139:19 O God, if only you would destroy the w! / Get out
140: 4 O LORD, keep me out of the hands of the w.
141: 5 in constant prayer / against the w and their deeds.
141: 7 so the bones of the w will be scattered without a
141:10 Let the w fall into their own snares, / but let me
145:20 all those who love him, / but he destroys the w.
146: 9 and widows, / but he frustrates the plans of the w.
147: 6 but he brings the w down into the dust.
Pr 2:22 But the w will be removed from the land,
3:25 or the destruction that comes upon the w,
3:32 Such w people are an abomination to the LORD,
3:33 The curse of the LORD is on the house of the w,
4:14 Do not do as the w do or follow the path of
4:19 But the way of the w is like complete darkness.
6:12 Here is a description of worthless and w people:
9: 7 Anyone who rebukes the w will get hurt.
10: 3 but he refuses to satisfy the craving of the w.
10: 7 of the godly, but the name of a w person rots away.
10:24 The fears of the w will all come true; so will the
10:25 strikes like a cyclone, whirling the w away,
10:27 one's life, but the years of the w are cut short.
10:28 but the expectations of the w are all in vain.
10:29 LORD protects the upright but destroys the w.
10:30 but the w will be removed from the land.
10:32 are helpful, but the w speak only what is corrupt.
11: 5 their honesty; the w fall beneath their load of sin.
11: 7 When the w die, their hopes all perish, for they
11: 8 from danger, but he lets the w fall into trouble.
11:11 make it prosper, but the talk of the w tears it apart.
11:23 to happiness, while the w can expect only wrath.
11:31 how much more true that the w and the sinner will
12: 5 godly are just; the advice of the w is treacherous.
12: 6 The words of the w are like a murderous ambush,
12: 7 The w perish and are gone, but the children of the
12:10 but even the kindness of the w is cruel.
12:13 The w are trapped by their own words,
12:21 the godly, but the w have their fill of trouble.
12:26 advice to their friends; the w lead them astray.
13: 5 godly hate lies; the w come to shame and disgrace.
13:25 hearts' content, but the belly of the w goes hungry.
14:11 The house of the w will perish, but the tent of the
14:19 the w will bow at the gates of the godly.
14:32 The w are crushed by their sins, but the godly have
15: 6 the godly, but the earnings of the w bring trouble.
15: 8 The LORD hates the sacrifice of the w, but he
15: 9 The LORD despises the way of the w, but he
15:26 The LORD despises the thoughts of the w,
15:28 think before speaking; the w spout evil words.
15:29 The LORD is far from the w, but he hears the
16: 4 for his own purposes, even the w for punishment.
17: 4 Wrongdoers listen to w talk; liars pay attention to
17:23 The w accept secret bribes to pervert justice.
18: 3 When the w arrive, contempt, shame, and disgrace
19:28 of justice; the mouth of the w gulps down evil.
20:26 A wise king finds the w, lays them out like wheat,
21: 7 Because the w refuse to do what is just,
21:12 One knows what is going on in the homes of the
w; he will bring the w to disaster.
21:18 Sometimes the w are punished to save the godly,
21:29 The w put up a bold front, but the upright proceed
24:16 But one calamity is enough to lay the w low.
24:19 Do not fret because of evildoers; don't envy the w.
24:24 A judge who says to the w, "You are innocent,"
25: 5 Remove the w from the king's court, and his reign
25:26 If the godly compromise with the w, it is like
26:23 Smooth words may hide a w heart, just as a pretty
28: 1 The w run away when no one is chasing them,
28: 4 To reject the law is to praise the w; to obey the law
28:12 When the w take charge, people go into hiding.
28:15 A w ruler is as dangerous to the poor as a lion
28:28 When the w take charge, people hide.
28:28 When the w meet disaster, the godly multiply.
29: 2 But when the w are in power, they groan.
29: 7 the rights of the poor; the w don't care to know.
29:12 If a ruler honors liars, all his advisers will be w.
29:16 When the w are in authority, sin increases.
29:27 The godly despise the w; the w despise the godly.
Ecc 7:15 die young and some w people live on and on.
7:17 On the other hand, don't be too w either—don't be
8:10 I have seen w people buried with honor.
8:13 The w will never live long, good lives, for they do
8:14 people are often treated as though they were w,
8:14 and w people are often treated as though they were
9: 2 whether they are righteous or w, good or bad,
10:13 their conclusions will be w madness.
Isa 1:16 longer see your evil deeds. Give up your w ways.
3:11 But say to the w, "Your destruction is sure.
5:23 They let the w go free while punishing the
11: 4 He will rule against the w and destroy them with
13:11 punish the world for its evil and the w for their sin.
14: 5 For the LORD has crushed your w power
26:10 Your kindness to the w does not make them do
31: 2 He will rise against those who are w, and he will
31: 6 though you are such w rebels, come and return to
48:22 "But there is no peace for the w,"
55: 7 Let the people turn from their w deeds. Let them
57:21 There is no peace for the w," says my God.
Jer 5:26 "Among my people are w men who lie in wait for
5:28 and there is no limit to their w deeds.
6: 6 to be punished, for she is w through and through.
7: 5 I will be merciful only if you stop your w thoughts
7:13 While you were doing these w things,
12: 1 Why are the w so prosperous? Why are evil people
13:10 These w people refuse to listen to me.
15: 4 Because of the w things Manasseh son of
15:21 I will certainly keep you safe from these w men.
17: 9 human heart is most deceitful and desperately w.
23:11 priests are like the prophets, all ungodly, w men.
23:14 These prophets are as w as the people of Sodom
23:19 whirlwind that swirls down on the heads of the w.
25:31 of the earth, slaughtering the w with his sword.
30:23 wind that swirls down on the heads of the w.
35:15 after prophet to tell you to turn from your w ways
44: 5 would not listen or turn back from their w ways.
Eze 3:18 If I warn the w, saying, 'You are under the penalty
5: 6 and has been even more w than the surrounding
7:11 None of these proud and w people will survive.
7:21 plunder to foreigners from the most w of nations,
11: 2 these are the men who are responsible for the w
12:16 so they can confess to their captors about how w
13:22 And you have encouraged the w by promising
14:22 You will see with your own eyes how w they are,
16:48 Sodom and her daughters were never as w as you
18:20 and w people will be punished for their own
18:21 But if w people turn away from all their sins
18:23 Sovereign LORD, that I like to see w people die?
18:23 I only want them to turn from their w ways
18:27 And if w people turn away from their wickedness,
21: 3 your people—the righteous and the w alike.
21:25 "O you corrupt and w prince of Israel, your final
21:29 w for whom the day of final reckoning has come.
23:48 a warning to others not to follow their w example.
24:14 You will be judged on the basis of all your w
30:12 up the Nile River and hand the land over to w men.
33: 8 If I announce that some w people are sure to die
33:11 I take no pleasure in the death of w people.
33:11 I only want them to turn from their w ways so they
33:14 And suppose I tell some w people that they will
33:19 But if w people turn from their wickedness and do
38:10 to your mind, and you will devise a w scheme.
Da 4:27 Break from your w past by being merciful to the
12:10 But the w will continue in their wickedness,
Hos 4: 9 since the priests are w, the people are w, too.
4: 9 both priests and people for all their w deeds.
10: 9 Was it not right that the w men of Gibeah were
Am 5: 7 You w people! You twist justice, making it a bitter
8: 7 "I will never forget the w things you have done!
Jnh 1: 2 because I have seen how w its people are."
Mic 2: 1 and hurry to carry out any of the w schemes you
6:10 The homes of the w are filled with treasures gained
6:16 the only example you follow is that of w King
Hab 1: 4 The w far outnumber the righteous, and justice is
1:13 Should you be silent while the w destroy people
3:13 You crushed the heads of the w and laid bare their
Zep 1: 3 I will reduce the w to heaps of rubble, along with
3: 5 but no one takes notice—the w know no shame.
Mal 3:18 see the difference between the righteous and the w,
4: 1 and the w will be burned up like straw on that day.
4: 3 you will tread upon the w as if they were dust
Mt 10:15 the w cities of Sodom and Gomorrah will be better
11:21 For if the miracles I did in you had been done in w
13:49 and separate the w people from the godly,
13:50 throwing the w into the fire. There will be weeping
21:41 "He will put the w men to a horrible death
25:26 "But the master replied, 'You w and lazy servant!
Mk 12:12 at them—they were the w farmers in his story.
Lk 6:35 is kind to the unthankful and to those who are w.
10:12 even w Sodom will be better off than such a town
10:13 For if the miracles I did in you had been done in w
19:22 " 'You w servant!' the king roared. 'Hard, am I?
Ro 1:18 w people who push the truth away from
2: 1 When you say they are w and should be punished,
1Co 5: 7 Remove this w person from among you so that you
2Co 11:15 get every bit of punishment their w deeds deserve.
Eph 6:12 and against w spirits in the heavenly realms.
Php 3: 2 for those dogs, those w men and their evil deeds,
Col 3: 9 off your old evil nature and all its w deeds.
2Th 2:10 He will use every kind of w deception to fool those
3: 2 that we will be saved from w and evil people,
Tit 3: 3 and became slaves to many w desires and evil
1Pe 4: 4 you no longer join them in the w things they do,
2Pe 2: 9 even while punishing the w right up until the day
2:18 those who have just escaped from such w living.
2:20 And when people escape from the w ways of the
3:17 and not be carried away by the errors of these w
3Jn 1:10 he is doing and the w things he is saying about us.

WICKEDLY (3) [WICKED]

1Ki 8:47 'We have sinned, done evil, and acted w.'
2Ch 6:37 'We have sinned, done evil, and acted w.'
Ps 106: 6 We have done wrong! We have acted w!

WICKEDNESS (87) [WICKED]

Ge 6: 5 the LORD observed the extent of the people's w,
Lev 18:17 and to do this would be a horrible w.
19:29 will be filled with promiscuity and detestable w.
20:14 to death to wipe out such w from among you.
Dt 9: 4 because of the w of the other nations that he is
9: 5 nations out ahead of you only because of their w,
13:11 and such w will never again be done among you.
Ezr 9:13 because of our w and our great guilt.
Ne 9:35 fertile land, but they refused to turn from their w.
Job 15:16 is a corrupt and sinful person with a thirst for w!
20:12 "He enjoyed the taste of his w, letting it melt
22: 5 Not at all! It is because of your w! Your guilt has
34:26 He openly strikes them down for their w.
38:13 ends of the earth, to bring an end to the night's w?
Ps 5: 4 O God, you take no pleasure in w; / you cannot
7: 9 End the w of the ungodly, / but help all those who
28: 4 Measure it out in proportion to their w.
50:19 Your mouths are filled with w, / and your tongues
52: 7 and grow more and more bold in their w."
55:10 but the real danger is w within the city.
56: 7 Don't let them get away with their w; / in your
73: 3 when I saw them prosper despite their w.
107:34 because of the w of those who live there.
141: 4 evil things; / don't let me participate in acts of w.
Pr 4:17 They eat w and drink violence!
12: 2 who are good, but he condemns those who plan w.
12: 3 W never brings stability; only the godly have deep
13: 6 while the evil are destroyed by their w.
Ecc 7:25 I was determined to prove to myself that w is
8: 8 w will certainly not rescue those who practice it.
Isa 9:17 For they are all hypocrites, speaking w with lies.
9:18 This w is like a brushfire. It burns not only briers
26: 9 will people turn from w and do what is right.
47:10 "You felt secure in all your w. 'No one sees me,'
Jer 2:19 Your own w will punish you. You will see what an
3: 2 polluted the land with your prostitution and w.
5:25 Your w has deprived you of these wonderful
7:12 what I did there because of all the w of my people,
14: 7 "LORD, our w has caught up with us.
14:10 I will remember all your w and will punish you for
14:16 be gone. For I will pour out their own w on them.
14:20 we confess our w and that of our ancestors, too.
19: 4 and turned this valley into a place of w.
22:22 Surely at last you will see your w and be ashamed.
23:15 because of Jerusalem's prophets that w fills this
31:34 "And I will forgive their w and will never again
33: 5 I have abandoned them because of all their w.
44: 3 Because of all their w, my anger rose high against
Eze 6: 9 at last they will hate themselves for all their w.
7:10 The people's w and pride have reached a climax.
7:11 will fall back on them as punishment for their w.
8: 9 "and see the unspeakable w going on in there!"
16:23 Sovereign LORD. In addition to all your other w,
16:57 But now your greater w has been exposed to all the
18:14 has a son who sees his father's w but decides
18:20 wicked people will be punished for their own w.
18:27 And if wicked people turn away from their w,
20:44 name by treating you mercifully in spite of your w,
22:15 you among the nations and purge you of your w.
24: 7 for her w is evident to all. She murders boldly,
31:11 a mighty nation that destroyed it as its w deserved.
33:11 Turn! Turn from your w, O people of Israel!
33:19 But if wicked people turn from their w and do
43: 8 They defiled my holy name by such w, so I
Da 9:15 of power. But we have sinned and are full of w.
12:10 But the wicked will continue in their w, and none
Hos 7: 3 The people make the king glad with their w.
9:15 The LORD says, "All their w began at Gilgal;
10:13 "But you have cultivated w and raised a thriving
10:15 share that fate, Bethel, because of your great w.
Joel 3:13 The storage vats are overflowing with the w of
Mic 7:13 because of the w of those who live there.
Zec 5: 8 The angel said, "The woman's name is W,"
Mal 1: 4 Their country will be known as 'The Land of W,'
Mt 19: 8 divorce as a concession to your hard-hearted w,
Mk 7:22 adultery, greed, w, deceit, eagerness for lustful
10: 5 only as a concession to your hard-hearted w.
Lk 11:39 but inside you are still filthy—full of greed and w!
Ac 8:22 Turn from your w and pray to the Lord. Perhaps he

Ro 1:29 Their lives became full of every kind of w, sin,
6:13 not let any part of your body become a tool of w,
1Co 5:8 not by eating the old bread of w and evil,
2Co 6:14 How can goodness be a partner with w? How can
2Ti 2:19 belong to the Lord must turn away from all w."
Jas 3:6 of fire. It is full of w that can ruin your whole life.
2Pe 2:7 was sick of all the immorality and w around him.
2:8 righteous man who was distressed by the w he saw

WICKS (1) [CANDLEWICK]

Zec 4:2 seven lamps, each one having seven spouts with w.

WIDE (107) [EVER-WIDENING, WIDE-OPEN, WIDELY, WIDER, WIDTH]

Ge 6:15 Make it 450 feet long, 75 feet w, and 45 feet high.
Ex 25:10 3-3/4 feet long, 2-1/4 feet w, and 2-1/4 feet high.
25:17 It must be 3-3/4 feet long and 2-1/4 feet w.
25:23 3 feet long, 1-1/2 feet w, and 2-1/4 feet high.
25:25 Put a rim about three inches w around the top edge,
26:2 sheet must be forty-two feet long and six feet w.
26:8 each forty-five feet long and six feet w. All eleven
26:16 Each frame must be 15 feet high and 2-1/4 feet w.
27:1 make a square altar 7-1/2 feet w, 7-1/2 feet long,
27:18 courtyard will be 150 feet long and 75 feet w,
36:9 the same size—forty-two feet long and six feet w.
36:15 the same size—forty-five feet long and six feet w.
36:21 Each frame was 15 feet high and 2-1/4 feet w.
37:1 3-3/4 feet long, 2-1/4 feet w, and 2-1/4 feet high.
37:6 It was 3-3/4 feet long and 2-1/4 feet w.
37:10 3 feet long, 1-1/2 feet w, and 2-1/4 feet high.
37:12 A rim about 3 inches w was attached along the
38:12 The west end was 75 feet w. The walls were made
38:13 The east end was also 75 feet w.
Nu 24:4 the Almighty, / who falls down with eyes w open:
24:16 the Almighty, / who falls down with eyes w open:
Dt 3:11 was more than thirteen feet long and six feet w.
Jos 8:17 after the Israelites, and the city was left w open.
2Sa 22:37 You have made a w path for my feet / to keep them
1Ki 6:2 was 90 feet long, 30 feet w, and 45 feet high.
6:3 The foyer at the front of the Temple was 30 feet w,
6:6 the bottom floor being 7-1/2 feet w, the second floor 9 feet w, and the top floor 10-1/2 feet w.
6:20 was 30 feet long, 30 feet w, and 30 feet high.
7:2 It was 150 feet long, 75 feet w, and 45 feet high.
7:6 of Pillars, which was 75 feet long and 45 feet w.
7:27 each 6 feet long, 6 feet w, and 4-1/2 feet tall.
7:35 the top of each cart there was a rim 9 inches w.
13:5 At the same time a w crack appeared in the altar,
2Ch 3:3 of God was ninety feet long and thirty feet w.
3:4 foyer at the front of the Temple was thirty feet w,
3:8 The Most Holy Place was thirty feet w,
4:1 altar 30 feet long, 30 feet w, and 15 feet high.
6:13 7-1/2 feet w, and 4-1/2 feet high and had placed it
26:15 His fame spread far and w, for the LORD helped
Job 36:16 You have prospered in a w and pleasant valley.
37:10 breath sends the ice, freezing w expanses of water.
Ps 18:36 You have made a w path for my feet / to keep them
81:10 Open your mouth w, and I will fill it with good
104:25 Here is the ocean, vast and w, / teeming with life
Pr 8:31 he created—his w world and all the human family!
30:4 Who has created the whole w world? What is his
Isa 18:2 and w for their conquests and destruction.
18:7 and w for their conquests and destruction.
33:21 He will be like a w river of protection that no
45:8 Let the earth open w so salvation
55:3 "Come to me with your ears w open. Listen,
Jer 51:58 "The w walls of Babylon will be leveled to the
Eze 40:11 which was 17-1/2 feet w at the opening and 22-3/4 feet w in the gateway passage.
40:21 and 43-3/4 feet w between the back walls of facing
40:25 and 43-3/4 feet w between the back walls of facing
40:29 passage was 87-1/2 feet long and 43-3/4 feet w.
40:30 courtyard were 8-3/4 feet deep and 43-3/4 feet w.)
40:33 measured 87-1/2 feet long and 43-3/4 feet w.
40:36 measured 87-1/2 feet long and 43-3/4 feet w.
40:48 The entrance was 24-1/2 feet w with walls 5-1/4
41:2 The entrance was 17-1/2 feet w, and the walls on each side were 8-3/4 feet w.
41:2 Holy Place itself was 70 feet long and 35 feet w.
41:3 The entrance was 10-1/2 feet w, and the walls on
41:5 along the outside wall; each room was 7 feet w.
41:11 into the terrace yard, which was 8-3/4 feet w.
41:12 It was 122-1/2 feet w and 157-1/2 feet long,
41:14 to the east of the Temple was also 175 feet w.
41:15 including its two walls, was also 175 feet w.
42:2 the north, was 175 feet long and 87-1/2 feet w.
42:4 two blocks of rooms ran a walkway 17-1/2 feet w.
43:13 There is a gutter all around the altar 21 inches w
43:13 with a curb 9 inches w around its edge.
43:14 surrounds the altar; this lower ledge is 21 inches w.
43:14 upper ledge; this upper ledge is also 21 inches w.
45:1 of land will be 8-1/3 miles long and 6-2/3 miles w.
45:2 An additional strip of land 87-1/2 feet w is to be
45:3 portion of land 8-1/3 miles long and 3-1/3 miles w.
45:5 next to it, also 8-1/3 miles long and 3-1/3 miles w,
45:6 section of land 8-1/3 miles long and 1-2/3 miles w.
46:22 enclosures was 70 feet long and 52-1/2 feet w,
48:8 It will be 8-1/3 miles w and will extend as far east
48:9 Temple will be 8-1/3 miles long and 6-2/3 miles w.
48:10 land measuring 8-1/3 miles long by 3-1/3 miles w,
48:13 to the priests—8-1/3 miles long and 3-1/3 miles w.
48:13 will measure 8-1/3 miles long by 6-2/3 miles w.
48:15 strip of land 8-1/3 miles long by 1-2/3 miles w,
48:21 Each of these areas will be 8-1/3 miles w,
Da 3:1 made a gold statue ninety feet tall and nine feet w
Joel 3:9 Say to the nations far and w: "Get ready for war!
Na 3:13 The gates of your land will be opened w to the
Hab 2:5 They range far and w, with their mouths opened as w as death,
Zec 2:2 to see how w and how long it is."
5:2 to be about thirty feet long and fifteen feet w."
14:4 making a w valley running from east to west,
Mt 7:13 and its gate is w for the many who choose the easy
23:5 On their arms they wear extra w prayer boxes with
Mk 3:8 The news about his miracles had spread far and w,
Ac 16:27 The jailer woke up to see the prison doors w open.
Eph 3:18 God's people should, how w, how long, how high,
2Pe 1:11 And God will open w the gates of heaven for you
Rev 15:5 in heaven, God's Tabernacle, was thrown w open!
21:16 he found it was a square, as w as it was long.

WIDE-OPEN (1) [OPEN, WIDE]

1Co 16:9 for there is a w door for a great work here,

WIDELY (4) [WIDE]

Ne 4:19 and we are w separated from each other along the
Mt 28:15 Their story spread w among the Jews, and they still
Jn 18:20 Jesus replied, "What I teach is w known, because I
Ac 19:20 So the message about the Lord spread w and had a

WIDENESS [KJV] See WIDTH

WIDER (2) [WIDE]

Job 11:9 It is broader than the earth and w than the sea.
Eze 41:7 Each level was w than the one below it,

WIDOW (45) [WIDOW'S, WIDOWED, WIDOWHOOD, WIDOWS, WIDOWS']

Ge 38:11 She was to remain a w until his youngest son,
Lev 21:14 He must not marry a w, a divorced woman, or a
22:13 But if she becomes a w or is divorced and has no
Nu 30:9 If, however, a woman is a w or is divorced,
Dt 25:5 a son, his w must not marry outside the family.
25:7 if the dead man's brother refuses to marry the w,
25:9 the w must walk over to him in the presence of the
Ru 4:5 also requires that you marry Ruth, the Moabite w.
4:10 the Moabite w of Mahlon, to be my wife.
1Sa 27:3 of Jezreel and Abigail of Carmel, Nabal's w.
30:5 of Jezreel and Abigail, the w of Nabal of Carmel,
2Sa 2:2 and Abigail, the w of Nabal from Carmel.
3:3 mother was Abigail, the w of Nabal from Carmel.
14:5 the king asked. "I am a w," she replied.
20:3 So each of them lived like a w until she died.
1Ki 7:14 since his mother was a w from the tribe of
11:26 in Ephraim, and his mother was Zeruah, a w.
17:9 city of Sidon. There is a w there who will feed you.
17:10 he saw a w gathering sticks, and he asked her,
17:20 why have you brought tragedy on this w who has
2Ki 4:1 One day the w of one of Elisha's fellow prophets
Job 24:3 A poor w must surrender her valuable ox as
Ps 109:9 become fatherless, / and may his wife become a w.
Isa 47:8 to anyone! I will never be a w or lose my children.'
La 1:1 Like a w broken with grief, she sits alone in her
Mt 1:6 (his mother was Bathsheba, the w of Uriah).
22:24 his brother should marry the w and have a child
22:25 so the second brother married the w.
Mk 12:19 his brother should marry the w and have a child
12:21 So the second brother married the w, but soon he
12:42 Then a poor w came and dropped in two pennies.
12:43 this poor w has given more than all the others have
Lk 2:36 She was a w, for her husband had died when they
4:26 He was sent instead to a w of Zarephath—
7:12 The boy who had died was the only son of a w,
18:3 A w of that city came to him repeatedly,
20:28 his brother should marry the w and have a child
20:30 His brother married the w, but he also died. Still no
21:2 Then a poor w came by and dropped in two
21:3 "this poor w has given more than all the rest of
1Ti 5:3 The church should care for any w who has no one
5:5 But a woman who is a true w, one who is truly
5:6 But the w who lives only for pleasure is spiritually
5:9 A w who is put on the list for support must be a
Rev 18:7 'I am queen on my throne. I am no helpless w.

WIDOW'S (4) [WIDOW]

Ge 38:14 So she changed out of her w clothing and covered
38:19 off her veil, and put on her w clothing as usual.
Dt 24:17 and you must never accept a w garment in pledge
Job 24:9 "The wicked snatch a w child from her breast;

WIDOWED (2) [WIDOW]

1Ch 2:4 twin sons through Tamar, his w daughter-in-law.
La 5:3 are orphaned and fatherless. Our mothers are w.

WIDOWHOOD (2) [WIDOW]

Isa 47:9 w and the loss of your children. Yes,
54:4 and the sorrows of w will be remembered no more,

WIDOWS (50) [WIDOW]

Ex 22:22 "Do not exploit w or orphans.
22:24 Your wives will become w, and your children will
Dt 10:18 He gives justice to orphans and w. He shows love
14:29 the orphans, and the w in your towns, so they can
16:11 orphans, and w who live among you.
16:14 foreigners, orphans, and w from your towns.
24:19 get it. Leave it for the foreigners, orphans, and w.
24:20 of the olives for the foreigners, orphans, and w.
24:21 grapes for the foreigners, orphans, and w.
26:12 and w so that they will have enough to eat in your
26:13 foreigners, orphans, and w, just as you commanded
27:19 who is unjust to foreigners, orphans, and w.'
Job 22:9 You must have sent w away without helping them
24:21 protecting sons. They refuse to help the needy w.
31:16 or crushed the hopes of w who looked to me for
31:18 for orphans, and all my life I have cared for w.
Ps 68:5 Father to the fatherless, defender of w— / this is
78:64 and their w could not mourn their deaths.
94:6 They kill w and foreigners / and murder orphans.
146:9 He cares for the orphans and w, / but he frustrates
Pr 15:25 of the proud, but he protects the property of w.
Isa 1:17 Defend the orphan. Fight for the rights of w.
1:23 and refuse to defend the orphans and the w.
9:17 and no mercy on even the w and orphans.
10:2 They deprive the poor, the w, and the orphans of justice. Yes, they rob w and fatherless children!
Jer 7:6 if you stop exploiting foreigners, orphans, and w;
15:8 "There will be more w than the grains of sand
18:21 Let their wives become w without any children!
22:3 Do not mistreat foreigners, orphans, and w.
49:11 Your w, too, will be able to depend on me for
Eze 22:7 Orphans and w are wronged and oppressed.
22:25 They increase the number of w in the land.
44:22 among the virgins of Israel or the w of the priests.
44:22 They may not marry other w or divorced women.
Zec 7:10 Do not oppress w, orphans, foreigners, and poor
Mal 3:5 who oppress w and orphans, or who deprive the
Mk 12:40 But they shamelessly cheat w out of their property,
Lk 4:25 "Certainly there were many w in Israel who
20:47 But they shamelessly cheat w out of their property,
Ac 6:1 saying that their w were being discriminated
9:39 The room was filled with w who were weeping
9:41 Then he called in the w and all the believers,
1Co 7:8 Now I say to those who aren't married and to w—
1Ti 5:7 so that the w you support will not be criticized.
5:11 The younger w should not be on the list,
5:14 So I advise these younger w to marry again,
5:16 If a Christian woman has relatives who are w,
5:16 Then the church can care for w who are truly
Jas 1:27 we must care for orphans and w in their troubles,

WIDOWS' (1) [WIDOW]

Job 29:13 And I caused the w hearts to sing for joy.

WIDTH (11) [WIDE]

1Ki 6:3 running across the entire w of the Temple.
2Ch 3:4 running across the entire w of the Temple.
3:8 corresponding to the w of the Temple, and it was
Ezr 6:3 will be ninety feet, and its w will be ninety feet.
Ps 39:5 My life is no longer than the w of my hand.
Eze 40:13 Then he measured the entire w of the gateway,
40:49 of the foyer was 35 feet and the w was 19-1/4 feet.
41:10 This open area measured 35 feet in w, and it went
42:3 One block of rooms overlooked the 35-foot w of
42:11 rooms was the same length and w as the other one,
Rev 21:16 for its length and w and height were each 1,400

WIELD (1)

Ps 64:3 Sharp tongues are the swords they w; / bitter words

WIFE (332) [SLAVE-WIFE, WIFE'S, WIVES, WIVES']

Ge 2:24 leaves his father and mother and is joined to his w,
2:25 Now, although Adam and his w were both naked,
3:17 "Because you listened to your w and ate the fruit I
3:20 Then Adam named his w Eve, because she would
3:21 clothing from animal skins for Adam and his w.
3:23 and his w from the Garden of Eden,
4:1 Now Adam slept with his w, Eve, and she became
4:17 Then Cain's w became pregnant and gave birth to
4:22 To Lamech's other w, Zillah, was born Tubal-cain.
4:25 Adam slept with his w again, and she gave birth to
6:18 with your w and your sons and their wives.
7:7 he and his w and his sons and their wives.
7:13 had gone into the boat that very day with his w
8:18 So Noah, his w, and his sons and their wives left
12:5 He took his w, Sarai, his nephew Lot, and all his
12:12 the Egyptians see you, they will say, 'This is his w.
12:17 Pharaoh's household because of Sarai, Abram's w.
12:18 "Why didn't you tell me she was your w?
12:19 Here is your w! Take her and be gone!"
12:20 Abram and his w, with all their household
13:1 Abram with his w and Lot and all that they owned,
16:1 But Sarai, Abram's w, had no children. So Sarai
16:3 So Sarai, Abram's w, took Hagar the Egyptian servant and gave her to Abram as a w.
17:15 Then God added, "Regarding Sarai, your w—
17:19 But God replied, "Sarah, your w, will bear you a
18:9 "Where is Sarah, your w?" they asked him.
18:10 I will return, and your w Sarah will have a son."
19:15 "Take your w and your two daughters who are
19:16 his hand and the hands of his w and two daughters
19:26 But Lot's w looked back as she was following
20:2 Abraham told people there that his w, Sarah,
20:11 'They will want my w and will kill me to get her.'
20:14 to Abraham, and he returned his w, Sarah, to him.
20:17 prayed to God, and God healed Abimelech, his w,
20:18 to Abimelech for having taken Abraham's w.
21:12 "Do not be upset over the boy and your servant w.
22:20 his brother Nahor's w, had borne Nahor eight sons.
23:4 in a foreign land, with no place to bury my w.
24:4 my relatives, and find a w there for my son Isaac."

24: 7 you find a young woman there to be my son's **w**.
24:14 let her be the one you have appointed as Isaac's **w**.
24:15 the son of Abraham's brother Nahor and his **w**,
24:36 When Sarah, my master's **w**, was very old,
24:40 you must get a **w** for my son from among my
24:44 let her be the one you have selected to be the **w** of
24:47 is Bethuel, the son of Nahor and his **w**, Milcah.'
24:48 find a **w** from the family of my master's relatives.
24:51 Yes, let her be the **w** of your master's son,
24:67 into his mother's tent, and she became his **w**.
25: 1 Abraham married again. Keturah was his new **w**,
25:10 from the Hittites, where he had buried his **w** Sarah.
25:21 and his **w** became pregnant with twins.
26: 7 He was afraid to admit that she was his **w**.
26: 9 and exclaimed, "She is obviously your **w**!
26:10 "Someone might have taken your **w** and slept with
26:11 "Anyone who harms this man or his **w** will die!"
28: 6 and sent him to Paddan-aram to find a **w**,
29:18 give me Rachel, your younger daughter, as my **w**."
29:21 "Now give me my **w** so we can be married."
30: 4 So Rachel gave him Bilhah to be his **w**, and Jacob
30: 9 she gave her servant, Zilpah, to Jacob to be his **w**.
30:18 me for giving my servant to my husband as a **w**."
34: 8 your daughter, and he longs for her to be his **w**.
34:11 to me, and let me have her as my **w**," he begged.
34:12 I will pay it—only give me the girl as my **w**."
36:10 sons were Eliphaz, the son of Esau's **w** Adah;
36:10 and Reuel, the son of Esau's **w** Basemath.
36:12 These were all grandchildren of Esau's **w** Adah.
36:13 These were all grandchildren of Esau's **w**
36:18 and his **w** Oholibamah became the leaders of the
36:18 These are the clans descended from Esau's **w**
36:39 Hadad's **w** was Mehetabel, the daughter of Matred
38: 4 Then Judah's **w** had another son, and she named
38:12 In the course of time Judah's **w** died.
39: 7 Potiphar's **w** began to desire him and invited him
39: 9 from me except you, because you are his **w**.
41:45 him Zaphenath-paneah and gave him a **w**—
41:50 two sons were born to Joseph and his **w**, Asenath,
44:27 said to us, 'You know that my **w** had two sons,
46:19 The sons of Jacob's **w** Rachel were Joseph
46:22 were the descendants of Jacob and his **w** Rachel.
49:31 There Abraham and his **w** Sarah are buried.
49:31 There Isaac and his **w**, Rebekah, are buried.
Ex 2:21 Moses one of his daughters, Zipporah, to be his **w**.
4:20 So Moses took his **w** and sons, put them on a
4:25 But Zipporah, his **w**, took a flint knife
18: 2 time before this, Moses had sent his **w**, Zipporah,
18: 5 and he brought Moses' **w** and two sons with him.
18: 6 Your **w** and your two sons are with him."
20:17 Do not covet your neighbor's **w**, male or female
21: 3 became a slave, then his **w** will be freed with him.
21: 4 "If his master gave him a **w** while he was a slave,
21: 4 but his **w** and children will still belong to his
21: 5 'I love my master, my **w**, and my children.
21:10 If he himself marries her and then takes another **w**,
21:10 or clothing or fail to sleep with her as his **w**.
22:16 pay the customary dowry and accept her as his **w**.
Lev 18:14 by having sexual intercourse with his **w**;
18:15 with your daughter-in-law; she is your son's **w**.
18:16 Do not have intercourse with your brother's **w**;
18:18 But if your **w** dies, then it is all right to marry her
18:20 having sexual intercourse with your neighbor's **w**.
19:20 who is committed to become someone else's **w**,
20:10 "If a man commits adultery with another man's **w**,
20:11 If a man has intercourse with his father's **w**,
20:20 If a man has intercourse with his uncle's **w**, he has
20:21 If a man marries his brother's **w**, it is an act of
Nu 5:12 'Suppose a man's **w** goes astray and is unfaithful
5:14 husband becomes jealous and suspicious of his **w**,
5:15 the husband must bring his **w** to the priest with an
5:30 and suspicion that his **w** has been unfaithful,
5:30 the husband must present his **w** before the LORD,
5:31 but his **w** will be held accountable for her sin.' "
26:59 and Amram's **w** was named Jochebed. She also
30:16 concerning relationships between a man and his **w**,
Dt 5:21 " 'Do not covet your neighbor's **w**. Do not covet
13: 6 "Suppose your brother, son, daughter, beloved **w**,
21:15 And suppose the firstborn son is the son of the **w**
21:16 to his younger son, the son of the **w** he loves.
21:17 even though he is the son of the **w** his father does
22:16 'I gave my daughter to this man to be his **w**,
22:19 The woman will then remain the man's **w**, and he
22:22 both he and the other man's **w** must be killed.
22:24 must die because he violated another man's **w**.
22:30 man must not have intercourse with his father's **w**,
24: 5 bringing happiness to the **w** he has married.
25:11 and the **w** of one tries to rescue her husband by
27:20 who has sexual intercourse with his father's **w**,
28:54 his beloved **w**, and his surviving children.
Jos 15:17 who conquered it, so Acsah became Othniel's **w**.
Jdg 1:13 who conquered it, so Acsah became Othniel's **w**.
4: 4 Deborah, the **w** of Lappidoth, was a prophet who
4:17 ran to the tent of Jael, the **w** of Heber the Kenite,
5:24 "Most blessed is Jael, / the **w** of Heber the Kenite.
11: 2 Gilead's **w** also had several sons, and when these
13: 2 His **w** was unable to become pregnant, and they
13: 3 The angel of the LORD appeared to Manoah's **w**
13: 9 and the angel of God appeared once again to his **w**
13:11 Manoah ran back with his **w** and asked, "Are you the man who talked to my **w** the other
13:13 "Be sure your **w** follows the instructions I gave
13:19 And as Manoah and his **w** watched, the LORD
13:20 When Manoah and his **w** saw this, they fell with
13:21 angel did not appear again to Manoah and his **w**.
13:22 and he said to his **w**, "We will die, for we have
13:23 But his **w** said, "If the LORD were going to kill
14: 3 must you go to the pagan Philistines to find a **w**?"
14:15 On the fourth day they said to Samson's **w**,
14:16 So Samson's **w** came to him in tears and said,
14:20 So his **w** was given in marriage to the man who
15: 1 Samson took a young goat as a present to his **w**.
15: 6 gave Samson's **w** to be married to his best man."
21:21 of you can take one of them home to be your **w**!
Ru 1: 1 He took his **w** and two sons and went to live in the
1: 2 man's name was Elimelech, and his **w** was Naomi.
4:10 the Moabite widow of Mahlon, to be my **w**.
1Sa 2:20 Eli would bless Elkanah and his **w** and say,
4:19 the **w** of Phinehas, was pregnant and near her time
14:50 Saul's **w** was Ahinoam, the daughter of Ahimaaz.
17:25 king will give him one of his daughters for a **w**,
18:17 to give you my older daughter, Merab, as your **w**.
18:27 So Saul gave Michal to David to be his **w**.
19:11 But Michal, David's **w**, warned him, "If you don't
25: 3 and his **w**, Abigail, was a sensible and beautiful
25:39 messengers to Abigail to ask her to become his **w**.
25:42 David's messengers. And so she became his **w**.
25:44 had given his daughter Michal, David's **w**,
2Sa 3: 5 was Ithream, whose mother was David's **w** Eglah.
3:13 with you unless you bring back my **w** Michal,
3:14 "Give me back my **w** Michal, for I bought her
11: 3 daughter of Eliam and the **w** of Uriah the Hittite."
11:11 I go home to wine and dine and sleep with my **w**?
11:13 then he couldn't get Uriah to go home to his **w**.
12: 9 For you have murdered Uriah and stolen his **w**.
12:10 because you have despised me by taking Uriah's **w**
12:24 comforted Bathsheba, his **w**, and slept with her.
17:19 The man's **w** put a cloth over the top of the well
21: 8 the **w** of Adriel son of Barzillai from Meholah.
1Ki 2:17 me Abishag, the girl from Shunem, as my **w**."
9:24 After Solomon moved his **w**, Pharaoh's daughter,
11:19 grew very fond of Hadad, and he gave him a **w**—
14: 2 So Jeroboam told his **w**, "Disguise yourself
14: 4 So Jeroboam's **w** went to Ahijah's home at Shiloh.
14: 5 "Jeroboam's **w** will come here, pretending to be
14: 6 the door, he called out, "Come in, **w** of Jeroboam!
14:12 Then Ahijah said to Jeroboam's **w**, "Go on home,
14:17 So Jeroboam's **w** returned to Tirzah, and the child
21: 5 his **w**, Jezebel, asked him. "What has made you
21:23 that the dogs of Jezreel will eat the body of your **w**,
21:25 as did Ahab, for his **w**, Jezebel, influenced him.
2Ki 5: 2 girl who had been given to Naaman's **w** as a maid.
9:10 Dogs will eat Ahab's **w**, Jezebel, at the plot of land
22:14 She was the **w** of Shallum son of Tikvah
1Ch 1:50 His **w** was Mehetabel, the daughter of Matred
2:24 his **w** Abijah gave birth to a son named Ashhur
2:26 Jerahmeel had a second **w** named Atarah. She was
2:29 and his **w** Abihail were Ahban and Molid.
2:35 Sheshan gave one of his daughters to be the **w** of
2:50 of Hur, the oldest son of Caleb's **w** Ephrathah,
4:18 Mered's Egyptian **w** was named Bithiah, and she
4:19 Hodiah's **w** was the sister of Naham. One of her
7:13 They were all descendants of Jacob's **w** Bilhah.
7:16 Makir's **w**, Maacah, gave birth to a son whom she
7:23 Afterward Ephraim slept with his **w**, and she
8: 9 Hodesh, his new **w**, gave birth to Jobab, Zibia,
8:11 Shaharaim's **w** Hushim had already given birth to
2Ch 8:11 Solomon moved his **w**, Pharaoh's daughter,
8:11 "My **w** must not live in King David's palace,
22:11 this way, Jehosheba, the **w** of Jehoiada the priest,
34:22 She was the **w** of Shallum son of Tikvah
Ezr 10:14 Everyone who has a pagan **w** will come at the
10:44 Each of these men had a pagan **w**, and some even
Est 1:18 Before this day is out, the **w** of every one of us,
5:10 he gathered together his friends and Zeresh, his **w**,
5:14 So Haman's **w**, Zeresh, and all his friends
6:13 When Haman told his **w**, Zeresh, and all his friends
Job 2: 9 His **w** said to him, "Are you still trying to
19:17 My breath is repulsive to my **w**. I am loathsome to
31: 9 a woman, or if I have lusted for my neighbor's **w**,
31:10 then may my **w** belong to another man; may other
Ps 109: 9 and may his **w** become a widow.
128: 3 Your **w** will be like a fruitful vine,
Pr 5:15 your own well—share your love only with your **w**.
5:18 Let your **w** be a fountain of blessing for you. Rejoice in the **w** of your youth.
6:26 and sleeping with another man's **w** may cost you
6:29 is with the man who sleeps with another man's **w**.
12: 4 A worthy **w** is her husband's joy and crown; a shameful **w** saps his strength.
18:22 The man who finds a **w** finds a treasure
19:13 a nagging **w** annoys like a constant dripping.
19:14 but only the LORD can give an understanding **w**.
21: 9 attic than with a contentious **w** in a lovely home.
21:19 in the desert than with a crabby, complaining **w**.
23:28 for another victim who will be unfaithful to his **w**.
25:24 attic than with a contentious **w** in a lovely home.
27:15 A nagging **w** is as annoying as the constant
31:10 Who can find a virtuous and capable **w**? She is
Ecc 9: 9 The **w** God gives you is your reward for all your
Isa 8: 3 Then I slept with my **w**, and she became pregnant
54: 6 as though you were a young **w** abandoned by her
Jer 3: 6 Like a **w** who commits adultery, Israel has
3:20 You have been like a faithless **w** who leaves her
5: 8 lusty stallions, each neighing for his neighbor's **w**.
31:32 though I loved them as a husband loves his **w**,"
Eze 16:32 you are an adulterous **w** who takes in strangers
24:18 the next morning, and in the evening my **w** died.
Hos 2: 2 call Israel to account, for she is no longer my **w**,
2:19 I will make you my **w** forever, showing you
3: 1 the LORD said to me, "Go and get your **w** again.
12:12 the land of Aram and earned a **w** by tending sheep.
Am 7:17 your **w** will become a prostitute in this city,
Mic 7: 5 trust anyone—not your best friend or even your **w**!
Mal 2:14 and your **w** made to each other on your wedding
2:14 faithful companion, the **w** of your marriage vows.
2:15 Didn't the LORD make you one with your **w**?
2:15 remain loyal to the **w** of your youth.
2:16 guard yourself; always remain loyal to your **w**."
Mt 1:24 He brought Mary home to be his **w**,
5:31 'A man can divorce his **w** by merely giving her a
5:32 But I say that a man who divorces his **w**,
14: 3 and imprisoned John as a favor to his **w** Herodias (the former **w** of Herod's brother Philip).
18:25 so the king ordered that he, his **w**, his children,
19: 3 "Should a man be allowed to divorce his **w** for any
19: 5 leaves his father and mother and is joined to his **w**,
19: 9 a man who divorces his **w** and marries another
19: 9 unless his **w** has been unfaithful."
22:26 and the **w** was married to the next brother,
22:26 until she had been the **w** of each of them.
22:28 So tell us, whose **w** will she be in the resurrection?
22:28 For she was the **w** of all seven of them!"
27:19 on the judgment seat, his **w** sent him this message:
27:56 mother of James and Joseph), and Zebedee's **w**,
Mk 6:17 She had been his brother Philip's **w**, but Herod had
6:18 "It is illegal for you to marry your brother's **w**."
10: 2 "Should a man be allowed to divorce his **w**?"
10: 4 "He said a man merely has to write his **w** an
10: 7 leaves his father and mother and is joined to his **w**,
10:11 "Whoever divorces his **w** and marries someone
12:19 leaving a **w** without children, his brother should
12:23 So tell us, whose **w** will she be in the resurrection?
Lk 1: 5 His **w**, Elizabeth, was also from the priestly line of
1:13 and your **w**, Elizabeth, will bear you a son!
1:18 man now, and my **w** is also well along in years."
1:24 Soon afterward his **w**, Elizabeth, became pregnant
3:19 of Galilee, for marrying Herodias, his brother's **w**,
8: 3 Joanna, the **w** of Chuza, Herod's business
14:26 and mother, **w** and children, brothers and sisters—
16:18 "Anyone who divorces his **w** and marries someone
17:32 Remember what happened to Lot's **w**!
18:29 up house or **w** or brothers or parents or children,
20:28 leaving a **w** but no children, his brother should
20:33 So tell us, whose **w** will she be in the resurrection?
Jn 19:25 Mary (the **w** of Clopas), and Mary Magdalene.
Ac 5: 1 with his **w**, Sapphira, sold some property.
5: 2 full amount. His **w** had agreed to this deception.
5: 7 About three hours later his **w** came in, not knowing
18: 2 who had recently arrived from Italy with his **w**,
24:24 A few days later Felix came with his **w**, Drusilla,
Ro 4:19 at the age of one hundred and that Sarah, his **w**,
1Co 5: 1 church who is living in sin with his father's **w**.
7: 2 each man should have his own **w**,
7: 3 The husband should not deprive his **w** of sexual
7: 3 nor should the **w** deprive her husband.
7: 4 The **w** gives authority over her body to her
7: 4 also gives authority over his body to his **w**.
7: 5 and **w** to refrain from sexual intimacy for a limited
7:10 from the Lord. A **w** must not leave her husband.
7:11 to him. And the husband must not leave his **w**.
7:12 If a Christian man has a **w** who is an unbeliever
7:14 For the Christian **w** brings holiness to her
7:15 or **w** who isn't a Christian insists on leaving,
7:15 or **w** is not required to stay with them,
7:27 If you have a **w**, do not end the marriage. If you do not have a **w**, do not get married.
7:33 his earthly responsibilities and how to please his **w**.
7:39 A **w** is married to her husband as long as he lives.
9: 5 Don't we have the right to bring a Christian **w**
Gal 4:22 from his slave-wife and one from his freeborn **w**.
4:23 But the son of the freeborn **w** was born as God's
Eph 5:23 For a husband is the head of his **w** as Christ is the
5:28 is actually loving himself when he loves his **w**.
5:31 leaves his father and mother and is joined to his **w**,
5:33 each man must love his **w** as he loves himself, and the **w** must respect her husband.
1Th 4: 6 another Christian in this matter by taking his **w**,
1Ti 3: 2 He must be faithful to his **w**. He must exhibit
3:12 A deacon must be faithful to his **w**, and he must
Tit 1: 6 He must be faithful to his **w**, and his children must
Rev 21: 9 I will show you the bride, the **w** of the Lamb."

WIFE'S (4) [WIFE]

Ge 28: 9 His new **w** name was Mahalath. She was the sister
39:19 After hearing his **w** story, Potiphar was furious!
1Ch 8:29 lived in Gibeon. His **w** name was Maacah,
9:35 lived in Gibeon. His **w** name was Maacah,

WILD (146) [WILDERNESS, WILDEST, WILDFIRE, WILDFLOWERS, WILDLIFE, WILDLY]

Ge 1:25 God made all sorts of **w** animals, livestock,
1:26 all the livestock, **w** animals, and small animals."
2:20 names to all the livestock, birds, and **w** animals.
3:14 and **w** animals of the whole earth to be cursed.
7:14 domestic and **w**, large and small—along with birds
7:21 birds, domestic animals, **w** animals, all kinds of
9: 2 All the **w** animals, large and small, and all the
9:10 all these birds and livestock and **w** animals.
16:12 This son of yours will be a **w** one—free and untamed as a **w** donkey!
25:28 because of the **w** game he brought home,
27: 3 the open country, and hunt some **w** game for me.
27: 5 So when Esau left to hunt for the **w** game,
27: 7 to prepare him a delicious meal of **w** game.
27:19 Here is the **w** game, cooked the way you like it.
27:31 he said, "I'm back, Father, and I have the **w** game.
27:33 "Then who was it that just served me **w** game?

31:39 If any were attacked and killed by w animals,
37:20 We can tell our father that a w animal has eaten
37:33 son's robe. A w animal has attacked and eaten him.
44:28 doubtless torn to pieces by some w animal.
Ex 22:13 If it was attacked by a w animal, the carcass must
22:31 that has been attacked and killed by a w animal.
23:29 and the w animals would become too many to
Lev 5: 2 whether a w animal, a domesticated animal,
7:24 or killed by a w animal may never be eaten,
14: 4 using two w birds of a kind permitted for food,
17:15 died a natural death or was killed by a w animal,
22: 8 natural death or has been torn apart by w animals,
25: 7 and the w animals will also be allowed to eat of the
26: 6 I will remove the w animals from your land
26:22 I will release w animals that will kill your children
Nu 24: 8 up from Egypt, / drawing them along like a w ox.
Dt 7:22 the w animals would multiply too quickly for you.
14: 5 the gazelle, the roebuck, the w goat, the ibex,
28:26 bodies will be food for the birds and w animals,
32:24 They will be troubled by the fangs of w beasts,
33:17 young bull; / his power is like the horns of a w ox.
1Sa 17:44 I'll give your flesh to the birds and w animals!"
17:46 bodies of your men to the birds and w animals,
24: 2 and his men near the rocks of the w goats.
2Sa 21:10 and stopped w animals from eating them at night.
2Ki 4:39 and came back with a pocketful of w gourds.
14: 9 But just then a w animal came by and stepped on
2Ch 25:18 But just then a w animal came by and stepped on
Ne 8:15 from olive, w olive, myrtle, palm, and fig trees.
Job 5:22 and famine; w animals will not terrify you.
5:23 and its w animals will be at peace with you.
6: 5 W donkeys bray when they find no green grass,
11:12 more than a w donkey can bear human offspring!
24: 5 Like the w donkeys in the desert, the poor must
28: 8 No w animal has ever walked upon those treasures;
37: 8 The w animals hide in the rocks or in their dens.
39: 1 Have you watched as the w deer are born?
39: 5 "Who makes the w donkey w?
39: 9 "Will the w ox consent to being tamed? Will it
39:10 Can you hitch a w ox to a plow? Will it plow a
39:15 crush them or that w animals might destroy them.
40:20 it their best food, where all the w animals play.
Ps 8: 7 the sheep and the cattle / and all the w animals,
22:21 lions' jaws, / and from the horns of these w oxen.
55: 8 far away from this w storm of hatred.
68:30 these w animals lurking in the reeds,
74:19 Don't let these w beasts destroy your doves.
79: 2 godly ones / has become food for the w animals.
80:13 forest devours us, / and the w animals feed on us.
81:16 I would satisfy you with w honey from the rock."
92:10 But you have made me as strong as a w bull.
104:11 and the w donkeys quench their thirst.
104:18 High in the mountains are pastures for the w goats,
106:14 In the wilderness, their desires ran w,
147: 9 He feeds the w animals, / and the young ravens cry
148:10 w animals and all livestock, / reptiles and birds,
Pr 29:18 people do not accept divine guidance, they run w.
SS 2: 7 by the swift gazelles and the deer of the w,
3: 5 by the swift gazelles and the deer of the w,
Isa 5: 2 but the grapes that grew were w and sour.
5: 4 Why did my vineyard give me w grapes
5: 6 I will make it a w place. / I will not prune the vines
7:22 and w honey because that is all the land will
13:21 W animals of the desert will move into the ruined
13:21 the ruins, and w goats will come there to dance.
18: 6 fields for the mountain birds and w animals to eat.
18: 6 The w animals will gnaw at bones all winter.
23:13 The Assyrians have handed Babylon over to the w
34:14 W animals of the desert will mingle there with
34:14 W goats will bleat at one another among the ruins,
43:20 The w animals in the fields will thank me,
56: 9 Come, w animals of the field! Come, w animals of the forest! Come and devour
Jer 2:21 How did you grow into this corrupt w vine?
2:24 You are like a w donkey, sniffing the wind at
7:33 people will be food for the vultures and w animals,
9:10 no more; the birds and w animals all have fled.
12: 4 The w animals and birds have disappeared
12: 9 Bring on the w beasts to pick their corpses clean!
14: 6 The w donkeys stand on the bare hills panting like
15: 3 and the w animals to finish up what is left.
16: 4 bodies will be food for the vultures and w animals.
19: 7 dead bodies as food for the vultures and w animals.
27: 6 even the w animals, under his control.
28:14 even the w animals, under his control.' "
34:20 bodies will be food for the vultures and w animals.
49:23 Their hearts are troubled like a w sea in a raging
50:39 It will be a home for the w animals of the desert.
Eze 5:17 along with the famine, w animals will attack you,
14:15 of dangerous w animals to devastate the land
29: 5 for I have given you as food to the w animals
31: 6 and in its shade all the w animals gave birth to
31:13 and the w animals lay among its branches.
32: 4 and the w animals of the whole earth will gorge
33:27 Those living in the open fields will be eaten by w
34: 5 a shepherd. They are easy prey for any w animal.
34: 8 and left them to be attacked by every w animal.
34:28 and w animals will no longer attack them.
39: 4 give you as food to the vultures and w animals.
39:17 son of man, call all the birds and w animals,
Da 4:12 W animals lived in its shade, and birds nested in its
4:21 W animals lived in its shade, and birds nested in its
4:25 and you will live in the fields with the w animals.
4:32 You will live in the fields with the w animals,
5:21 of an animal, and he lived among the w donkeys.
Hos 2:12 where only w animals will eat the fruit.
2:18 At that time I will make a covenant with all the w
8: 9 Like a w donkey looking for a mate, they have
Joel 1:20 Even the w animals cry out to you because they
Am 1:14 There will be w shouts during the battle,
Jnh 2: 3 I was buried beneath your w and stormy waves.
Hab 2:17 You terrified the w animals you caught in your
Zep 2:14 and cattle. All sorts of w animals will settle there.
Mt 3: 4 a leather belt; his food was locusts and w honey.
Mk 1: 6 a leather belt; his food was locusts and w honey.
1:13 He was out among the w animals, and angels took
Lk 6:11 the enemies of Jesus were w with rage and began
15:13 and there he wasted all his money on w living.
Ac 11: 6 saw all sorts of small animals, w animals, reptiles,
Ro 11:17 who were branches from a w olive tree,
11:24 branches from a w olive tree and graft you into his
13:13 Don't participate in w parties and getting drunk,
1Co 15:32 And what value was there in fighting w beasts—
Gal 5:21 envy, drunkenness, w parties, and other kinds of
Tit 1: 6 and his children must be believers who are not w
1Pe 4: 3 their feasting and drunkenness and w parties,
Jude 1:13 They are like w waves of the sea, churning up the
Rev 6: 8 the sword and famine and disease and w animals.

WILDERNESS (246) [WILD]

Ge 14: 6 Mount Seir, as far as El-paran at the edge of the w.
21:14 and she walked out into the w of Beersheba,
21:20 And God was with the boy as he grew up in the w
36:24 in the w while he was grazing his father's donkeys.
Ex 3: 1 of Midian, and he went deep into the w near Sinai,
3:18 Let us go on a three-day journey into the w to offer
4:27 said to Aaron, "Go out into the w to meet Moses."
5: 1 for they must go out into the w to hold a religious
5: 3 "Let us take a three-day trip into the w so we can
5: 8 they wouldn't be talking about going into the w to
7:16 my people go, so they can worship me in the w."
8:25 do it here in this land. Don't go out into the w."
8:27 We must take a three-day trip into the w to offer
8:28 offer sacrifices to the LORD your God in the w.
13:18 So God led them along a route through the w
13:20 they camped at Etham on the edge of the w.
14: 3 They are trapped between the w and the sea!'
14:11 "Why did you bring us out here to die in the w?
14:12 was far better than dying out here in the w!"
16:32 in the w when he brought you out of Egypt."
19: 1 The Israelites arrived in the w of Sinai exactly two
23:29 all in one year because the land would become a w,
Lev 7:38 their offerings to the LORD in the w of Sinai.
16:10 When it is sent away into the w, it will make
16:21 then he will send it out into the w, led by a man
16:22 After the man sets it free in the w, the goat will
16:26 "The man chosen to send the goat out into the w
Nu 1: 1 spoke to Moses in the Tabernacle in the w of Sinai.
1:19 So Moses counted the people there in the w of
3: 4 and Abihu died in the LORD's presence in the w
3:14 spoke again to Moses, there in the w of Sinai.
9: 1 and the rest of the Israelites were in the w of Sinai:
9: 5 in the w of Sinai as twilight fell on the appointed
10:12 So the Israelites set out from the w of Sinai
10:12 in stages until the cloud stopped in the w of Paran.
10:31 "You know the places in the w where we should
12:16 they left Hazeroth and camped in the w of Paran.
13: 3 of Israel, from their camp in the w of Paran.
13:21 and explored the land from the w of Zin as far as
13:26 and the people of Israel at Kadesh in the w of
14: 2 wish we had died in Egypt, or even here in the w!"
14:16 he swore to give them, so he killed them in the w.'
14:22 signs I performed both in Egypt and in the w,
14:25 Tomorrow you must set out for the w in the
14:29 You will all die here in this w! Because you
14:32 But as for you, your dead bodies will fall in this w.
14:33 be like shepherds, wandering in the w forty years.
14:33 until the last of you lies dead in the w.
14:34 you must wander in the w for forty years—
14:35 against me. They will all die here in this w!"
14:41 disobeying the LORD's orders to return to the w?
15:32 One day while the people of Israel were in the w,
16:13 with milk and honey, to kill us here in this w,
20: 1 In early spring the people of Israel arrived in the w
20: 4 Did you bring the LORD's people into this w to
21: 5 you brought us out of Egypt to die here in the w?"
21:11 in the w on the eastern border of Moab.
21:13 in the w adjacent to the territory of the Amorites.
21:18 Then the Israelites left the w and proceeded on
21:23 his entire army and attacked Israel in the w,
24: 1 Instead, he turned and looked out toward the w,
26:64 in the previous census taken in the w of Sinai.
26:65 had said of them, "They will all die in the w."
27: 3 "Our father died in the w without leaving any
27:14 rebelled against my instructions in the w of Zin.
27:14 the waters of Meribah at Kadesh in the w of Zin.)
32:13 and made them wander in the w for forty years
32:15 him like this and he abandons them again in the w,
33: 6 and camped at Etham on the edge of the w.
33: 8 and crossed the Red Sea into the w beyond.
33: 8 Then they traveled for three days into the Etham w
33:15 They left Rephidim and camped in the w of Sinai.
33:16 They left the w of Sinai and camped at
33:36 and camped at Kadesh in the w of Zin.
34: 3 of your country will extend from the w of Zin,
Dt 1: 1 while they were in the w east of the Jordan River.
1:19 and traveled through the great and terrifying w,
1:31 God cared for you again and again here in the w,
1:40 and go on back through the w toward the Red Sea.'
2: 1 and set out across the w toward the Red Sea,
2: 7 has watched your every step through this great w.
2:14 men old enough to fight in battle had died in the w.
2:26 "Then from the w of Kedemoth I sent
4:43 Bezer on the w plateau for the tribe of Reuben;
8: 2 your God led you through the w for forty years,
8:15 and terrifying w with poisonous snakes
8:16 He fed you with manna in the w, a food unknown
9: 7 you made the LORD your God out in the w.
9:28 he brought them into the w to slaughter them."
11: 5 cared for you in the w until you arrived here.
11:24 Your frontiers will stretch from the w in the south
29: 5 For forty years I led you through the w, yet your
32:51 at the waters of Meribah at Kadesh in the w of Zin.
Jos 5: 4 bear arms when they left Egypt had died in the w.
5: 5 during the years in the w, had been circumcised.
5: 6 The Israelites wandered in the w for forty years
8:15 and the Israelite army fled toward the w as though
8:20 the direction of the w now turned on their pursuers.
12: 8 the mountain slopes, the Judean w, and the Negev.
14:10 this promise—even while Israel wandered in the w.
15: 1 with the w of Zin being its southernmost point.
15: 3 ran south of Scorpion Pass into the w of Zin
15:61 In the w there were the towns of Beth-arabah,
16: 1 through the w and into the hill country of Bethel.
18:12 through the hill country and the w of Beth-aven.
20: 8 Bezer, in the w plain of the tribe of Reuben;
24: 7 what I did. Then you lived in the w for many years.
24:17 As we traveled through the w among our enemies,
Jdg 1:16 traveled with them into the w of Judah.
8: 7 your flesh with the thorns and briers of the w."
8:16 punishing them with thorns and briers from the w.
11:18 they went around Edom and Moab through the w.
11:22 to the Jabbok River, and from the w to the Jordan.
20:42 So they ran toward the w, but the Israelites chased
20:45 The survivors fled into the w toward the rock of
1Sa 4: 8 Egyptians with plagues when Israel was in the w.
13:18 the border above the valley of Zeboim near the w.
23:14 David now stayed in the strongholds of the w
23:24 and his men had moved into the w of Maon in the
23:25 he went even farther into the w to the great rock,
23:25 and he remained there in the w of Maon.
24: 1 he was told that David had gone into the w of
25: 1 Then David moved down to the w of Maon.
25:14 "David sent men from the w to talk to our master,
25:21 We protected his flocks in the w, and nothing he
26: 2 and went to hunt him down in the w of Ziph.
2Sa 2:24 near Giah, along the road to the w of Gibeon.
15:23 the Kidron Valley and then went out toward the w.
15:28 in Jerusalem before I disappear into the w."
16: 2 The wine is to be taken with you into the w for
17:16 He must go across at once into the w beyond.
17:29 and thirsty after your long march through the w."
1Ki 2:34 and Joab was buried at his home in the w.
19:15 way you came, and travel to the w of Damascus.
2Ki 2:16 and fifty of our strongest men will search the w for
3: 8 "We will attack from the w of Edom,"
3: 9 a roundabout route through the w for seven days.
1Ch 12: 8 to David while he was at the stronghold in the w.
21:29 and the altar that Moses made in the w were
2Ch 1: 3 the LORD's servant, had constructed in the w.
20:16 end of the valley that opens into the w of Jeruel.
20:20 the army of Judah went out into the w of Tekoa.
20:24 army of Judah arrived at the lookout point in the w,
24: 9 of God, had required of the Israelites in the w.
26:10 He also constructed forts in the w and dug many
Ne 9:19 mercy you did not abandon them to die in the w.
9:21 For forty years you sustained them in the w.
Job 39: 6 I have placed it in the w; its home is the wasteland.
Ps 55: 7 fly far away / to the quiet of the w. / *Interlude*
63: T regarding a time when David was in the w of
65:12 The w becomes a lush pasture, / and the hillsides
68: 7 from Egypt, / when you marched through the w,
75: 6 earth—from east or west, / or even from the w—
78:15 He split open the rocks in the w / to give them
78:40 him in the desert / and grieved his heart in the w.
78:52 of sheep, / guiding them safely through the w.
79: 7 your people Israel, / making the land a desolate w.
95: 8 did at Meribah, / as they did at Massah in the w.
102: 6 owl in the desert, / like a lonely owl in a far-off w.
106:14 In the w, their desires ran wild, / testing God's
106:26 he swore / that he would kill them in the w,
136:16 thanks to him who led his people through the w.
Isa 14:17 one who destroyed the world and made it into a w?
29:17 the w of Lebanon will be a fertile field once again.
30: 6 On through the w they go, where lions
32:15 Then the w will become a fertile field,
32:16 Justice will rule in the w and righteousness in the
33: 9 The plain of Sharon is now a w. Bashan
35: 1 Even the w will rejoice in those days. The desert
35: 6 Springs will gush forth in the w, and streams will
40: 3 "Make a highway for the LORD through the w.
43:19 I will make a pathway through the w for my people
43:20 and ostriches, too, for giving them water in the w.
51: 3 Her barren w will become as beautiful as Eden—
64:10 are destroyed; even Jerusalem is a desolate w.
Jer 2: 2 and followed me even through the barren w.
2: 6 out of Egypt and led us through the barren w—
4:26 I looked, and the fertile fields had become a w.
10:25 your people Israel, making the land a desolate w.
12:10 the vines and turning all its beauty into a barren w.
17: 6 They will live in the barren w, on the salty flats
31: 2 care for the survivors as they travel through the w.
48: 6 Flee for your lives! Hide in the w!
50:12 the least of nations—a w, a dry and desolate land.
51:43 she is a dry w where no one lives or even passes
La 4:19 If we hid in the w, they were waiting for us there.
5: 9 We must hunt for food in the w at the risk of our
Eze 6:14 and make their cities desolate from the w in the
19:13 Now the vine is growing in the w,
20:10 my people out of Egypt and led them into the w.

20: 13 and they refused to obey my laws there in the **w**.
20: 15 But I swore to them in the **w** that I would not bring
20: 17 and held back from destroying them in the **w**.
20: 21 I threatened to pour out my fury on them in the **w**.
20: 23 solemn oath against them while they were in the **w**.
20: 35 I will bring you into the **w** of the nations, and there
20: 36 in the **w** after bringing them out of Egypt,
20: 47 Give the southern **w** this message from the
22: 24 you will become like an uncleared **w** or a desert
23: 42 They were lustful men and drunkards from the **w**,
36: 36 rebuilt the ruins and planted lush crops in the **w**.
Hos 2: 3 to die of thirst, as in a desert or a dry and barren **w**.
13: 5 I took care of you in the **w**, in that dry and thirsty
Joel 3: 19 Egypt will become a wasteland and Edom a **w**,
Am 5: 25 and offerings during the forty years in the **w**,
Zec 11: 6 They will turn the land into a **w**, and I will not
Mt 3: 1 John the Baptist began preaching in the Judean **w**.
3: 3 when he said, / "He is a voice shouting in the **w**:
3: 5 Valley went out to the **w** to hear him preach.
4: 1 Then Jesus was led out into the **w** by the Holy
11: 7 "Who is this man in the **w** that you went out to
11: 8 who dress like that live in palaces, not out in the **w**.
15: 33 food out here in the **w** for all of them to eat?"
Mk 1: 3 He is a voice shouting in the **w**: / 'Prepare a
1: 4 He lived in the **w** and was preaching that people
1: 5 and from all over Judea traveled out into the **w** to
1: 12 the Holy Spirit compelled Jesus to go into the **w**.
1: 35 and went out alone into the **w** to pray.
8: 4 to find enough food for them here in the **w**?"
Lk 1: 80 Then he lived out in the **w** until he began his public
3: 2 son of Zechariah, who was living out in the **w**.
3: 4 when he said, / "He is a voice shouting in the **w**:
4: 1 He was led by the Spirit to go out into the **w**,
4: 42 Early the next morning Jesus went out into the **w**.
5: 16 But Jesus often withdrew to the **w** for prayer.
7: 24 "Who is this man in the **w** that you went out to
7: 25 live in luxury are found in palaces, not in the **w**.
8: 29 he simply broke them and rushed out into the **w**,
15: 4 one of them strayed away and was lost in the **w**,
Jn 1: 23 words of Isaiah: / "I am a voice shouting in the **w**,
3: 14 lifted up the bronze snake on a pole in the **w**,
6: 31 ate manna while they journeyed through the **w**!
6: 49 Your ancestors ate manna in the **w**, but they all
11: 54 He went to a place near the **w**, to the village of
Ac 7: 36 and back and forth through the **w** for forty years.
7: 38 was with the assembly of God's people in the **w**.
7: 42 during those forty years in the **w**, Israel?
7: 44 carried the Tabernacle with them through the **w**.
13: 18 through forty years of wandering around in the **w**.
1Co 10: 1 what happened to our ancestors in the **w** long ago.
10: 5 with most of them, and he destroyed them in the **w**.
Heb 3: 8 when they tested God's patience in the **w**.
3: 17 the people who sinned, whose bodies fell in the **w**?
Rev 12: 6 And the woman fled into the **w**, where God had
12: 14 her to fly to a place prepared for her in the **w**,
17: 3 So the angel took me in spirit into the **w**. There I

WILDEST (1) [WILD]

Eze 34: 25 people will be able to camp safely in the **w** places

WILDFIRE (2) [FIRE, WILD]

Job 20: 26 A **w** will devour his goods, consuming all he has
Lk 4: 37 The story of what he had done spread like **w**

WILDFLOWERS (3) [FLOWER, WILD]

Ps 103: 15 on earth are like grass; / like **w**, we bloom and die.
SS 7: 11 into the fields and spend the night among the **w**.
1Pe 1: 24 their beauty fades as quickly as the beauty of **w**.

WILDLIFE (2) [LIVE, WILD]

Ge 1: 24 kind of animal—livestock, small animals, and **w**."
Isa 7: 24 vast brier patch, a hunting ground overrun by **w**.

WILDLY (3) [WILD]

1Ki 18: 26 Then they danced **w** around the altar they had
Ps 38: 10 My heart beats **w**, my strength fails, / and I am
Na 3: 2 and chariots clatter as they bump **w** through the

WILILY [KJV] See DECEPTION

WILL (71 of 11210) [FREEWILL, HE'LL, I'LL, THEY'LL, WE'LL, WILLFULLY, WILLING, WILLINGLY, WON'T, YOU'LL] See also Index of Articles, Etc.

GOD'S WILL (8) Ge 6:9; Ex 28:15; Mk 3:35; 1Th 5:18; 2Ti 1:1; Heb 10:36; 1Pe 2:15; 4:19

WILL OF GOD (16) Nu 22:18; 1Ch 13:2; 2Ch 10:15; Ezr 7:18; Jn 4:34; 5:30; 6:38,39; 7:17; Ac 13:36; Ro 15:32; 1Co 1:1; Eph 6:6; Col 4:12; 1Pe 4:2; 1Jn 2:17

WILL OF THE LORD (1) Ac 21:14

WILL OF THE LORD* (4) Nu 22:18; 24:13; 1Ki 12:15; 1Ch 13:2

Ge 6: 9 He consistently followed God's **w** and enjoyed a
Ex 28: 15 chestpiece that will be used to determine God's **w**.
28: 30 carry the objects used to determine the LORD's **w**
Lev 24: 12 They put the man in custody until the LORD's **w** in
Nu 15: 30 "But those who brazenly violate the LORD's **w**,
22: 18 to do anything against the **w** of the LORD my God.
24: 13 to do anything against the **w** of the LORD.'
27: 21 who will determine the LORD's **w** by means of
Dt 10: 12 you to fear him, to live according to his **w**, to love
1Sa 3: 18 "It is the LORD's **w**," Eli replied. "Let him do what
2Sa 10: 12 the cities of our God. May the LORD's **w** be done."
1Ki 8: 58 May he give us the desire to do his **w** in everything
12: 15 This turn of events was the **w** of the LORD, for it
1Ch 13: 2 "If you approve and if it is the **w** of the LORD our
19: 13 the cities of our God. May the LORD's **w** be done."
2Ch 10: 15 This turn of events was the **w** of God, for it
Ezr 7: 18 you and your colleagues feel is the **w** of your God.
Job 42: 15 And their father put them into his **w** along with
Ps 40: 8 I take joy in doing your **w**, my God, / for your law
103: 21 you armies of angels / who serve him and do his **w**!
143: 10 Teach me to do your **w**, / for you are my God.
Pr 3: 6 Seek his **w** in all you do, and he will direct your
Isa 30: 1 "You make plans that are contrary to my **w**.
50: 4 wakens me and opens my understanding to his **w**.
50: 7 set my face like a stone, determined to do his **w**.
Jer 49: 19 can challenge me? What ruler can oppose my **w**?"
50: 44 can challenge me? What ruler can oppose my **w**?"
Eze 20: 16 they had rejected my laws, ignored my **w** for them,
Mt 6: 10 May your **w** be done here on earth, / just as it is in
12: 50 Anyone who does the **w** of my Father in heaven is
18: 14 not my heavenly Father's **w** that even one of these
26: 39 away from me. Yet I want your **w**, not mine."
26: 42 be taken away until I drink it, your **w** be done."
Mk 3: 35 who does God's **w** is my brother and sister and
14: 36 away from me. Yet I want your **w**, not mine."
Lk 22: 42 away from me. Yet I want your **w**, not mine."
Jn 4: 34 "My nourishment comes from doing the **w** of God,
5: 30 because it is according to the **w** of God who sent
6: 38 have come down from heaven to do the **w** of God
6: 39 And this is the **w** of God, that I should not lose
6: 40 For it is my Father's **w** that all who see his Son
7: 17 Anyone who wants to do the **w** of God will know
9: 31 ready to hear those who worship him and do his **w**.
Ac 13: 36 served his generation according to the **w** of God,
21: 14 we gave up and said, "The **w** of the Lord be done."
22: 14 to know his **w** and to see the Righteous One and
26: 14 It is hard for you to fight against my **w**.'
Ro 8: 20 Against its **w**, everything on earth was subjected
8: 27 for us believers in harmony with God's own **w**.
12: 2 how good and pleasing and perfect his **w** really is.
15: 32 Then, by the **w** of God, I will be able to come to
1Co 1: 1 This letter is from Paul, chosen by the **w** of God to
9: 17 If I were doing this of my own free **w**, then I
2Co 8: 3 but far more. And they did it of their own free **w**.
Eph 6: 6 of Christ, do the **w** of God with all your heart.
Col 4: 12 and perfect, fully confident of the whole **w** of God.
1Th 5: 18 always be thankful, for this is God's **w** for you
2Ti 1: 1 Paul, an apostle of Christ Jesus by God's **w**, sent
Heb 9: 16 dies and leaves a **w**, no one gets anything until it is proved that the person who wrote the **w** is dead.
9: 17 The **w** goes into effect only after the death of the
9: 17 no one can use the **w** to get any of the things
10: 7 I said, 'Look, I have come to do your **w**, O God—
10: 9 Then he added, "Look, I have come to do your **w**."
10: 36 need now, so you will continue to do God's **w**.
13: 20[-21] equip you with all you need for doing his **w**.
1Pe 2: 15 It is God's **w** that your good lives should silence
4: 2 but you will be anxious to do the **w** of God.
4: 19 So if you are suffering according to God's **w**, keep
1Jn 2: 17 But if you do the **w** of God, you will live forever.
5: 14 we ask him for anything in line with his **w**.

WILLFULLY (1) [WILL]

Ps 78: 18 They **w** tested God in their hearts,

WILLING (63) [WILL]

Ge 12: 19 Why were you **w** to let me marry her, saying she
24: 39 " 'But suppose I can't find a young woman **w** to
24: 58 "Are you **w** to go with this man?" they asked her.
38: 9 But Onan was not **w** to have a child who would not
Ex 35: 22 and women came, all whose hearts were **w**.
35: 26 All the women who were **w** used their skills to spin
Jdg 7: 3 leaving only ten thousand who were **w** to fight.
Ru 3: 13 If he is **w** to redeem you, then let him marry you.
3: 13 But if he is not **w**, then as surely as the LORD
1Sa 25: 41 I am even **w** to become a slave to David's
2Sa 6: 21 So I am **w** to act like a fool in order to show my
6: 22 and I am **w** to look even more foolish than this,
1Ki 12: 7 "If you are **w** to serve the people today and give
2Ki 8: 19 But the LORD was not **w** to destroy Judah,
1Ch 19: 19 the Arameans were no longer **w** to help the
28: 9 him with your whole heart and with a **w** mind.
29: 5 Who is **w** to give offerings to the LORD today?"
2Ch 21: 7 But the LORD was not **w** to destroy David's
29: 31 and those whose hearts were **w** brought burnt
35: 8 The king's officials also made **w** contributions to
Est 4: 16 go in to see the king. If I must die, I am **w** to die."
Ps 51: 12 of your salvation, / and make me **w** to obey you.
Da 3: 28 and were **w** to die rather than serve
Mt 11: 14 And if you are **w** to accept what I say, he is Elijah,
11: 15 Anyone who is **w** to hear should listen
13: 9 Anyone who is **w** to hear should listen
13: 43 Anyone who is **w** to hear should listen
26: 41 For though the spirit is **w** enough, the body is
Mk 4: 9 "Anyone who is **w** to hear should listen
4: 23 Anyone who is **w** to hear should listen
14: 38 For though the spirit is **w** enough, the body is
Lk 1: 38 and I am **w** to accept whatever he wants.
6: 27 "But if you are **w** to listen, I say, love your
8: 8 "Anyone who is **w** to hear should listen
14: 35 Anyone who is **w** to hear should listen
22: 42 "Father, if you are **w**, please take this cup of
Ac 18: 21 he left, saying, "I will come back later, God **w**."
25: 9 "Are you **w** to go to Jerusalem and stand trial
25: 20 and I asked him whether he would be **w** to stand
Ro 1: 10 the opportunity, God **w**, to come at last to see you.
5: 7 though someone might be **w** to die for a person
9: 3 I would be **w** to be forever cursed—cut off from
11: 24 For if God was **w** to take you who were, by nature,
15: 31 Pray also that the Christians there will be **w** to
1Co 7: 12 and she is **w** to continue living with him,
7: 13 and he is **w** to continue living with her, she must
16: 12 but he was not **w** to come right now.
2Co 9: 5 But I want it to be a **w** gift, not one given under
Php 2: 19 If the Lord Jesus is **w**, I hope to send Timothy to
2Ti 2: 10 I am **w** to endure anything if it will bring salvation
Heb 6: 3 And so, God **w**, we will move forward to further
12: 2 He was **w** to die a shameful death on the cross
Jas 2: 22 so much that he was **w** to do whatever God told
3: 17 gentle at all times, and **w** to yield to others.
1Pe 4: 1 For if you are **w** to suffer for Christ, you have
Rev 2: 7 "Anyone who is **w** to hear should listen to the
2: 11 "Anyone who is **w** to hear should listen to the
2: 17 "Anyone who is **w** to hear should listen to the
2: 29 Anyone who is **w** to hear should listen to the Spirit
3: 6 Anyone who is **w** to hear should listen to the Spirit
3: 13 Anyone who is **w** to hear should listen to the Spirit
3: 22 Anyone who is **w** to hear should listen to the Spirit
13: 9 Anyone who is **w** to hear should listen

WILLINGLY (5) [WILL]

1Ch 29: 6 and the king's administrative officers all gave **w**.
29: 17 and I have watched your people offer their gifts **w**
Ps 110: 3 that day of battle, / your people will serve you **w**.
Col 3: 22 Obey them **w** because of your reverent fear of the
1Pe 5: 2 Watch over it **w**, not grudgingly—not for what you

WILLOW (2) [WILLOWS]

Ps 137: 2 hanging them on the branches of the **w** trees.
Eze 17: 5 where it would grow as quickly as a **w** tree.

WILLOWS (4) [WILLOW]

Lev 23: 40 leafy branches and **w** that grow by the streams.
Job 40: 22 The lotus plants give it shade among the **w** beside
Isa 15: 7 they can carry and flee across the Ravine of **W**.
44: 4 thrive like watered grass, like **w** on a riverbank.

WILT (5) [WILTED, WILTS]

Eze 31: 15 in black and caused the trees of the field to **w**.
Na 1: 4 Carmel fade, and the green forests of Lebanon **w**.
Mt 13: 21 but they **w** as soon as they have problems or are
Mk 4: 17 but they **w** as soon as they have problems or are
Lk 8: 13 but they **w** when the hot winds of testing blow.

WILTED (2) [WILT]

Mt 13: 6 but they soon **w** beneath the hot sun and died
Mk 4: 6 but it soon **w** beneath the hot sun and died

WILTS (1) [WILT]

Jer 14: 2 "Judah **w**; her businesses have ground to a halt.

WIN (20) [HARD-WON, WINNING, WINS, WON]

Ge 32: 25 When the man saw that he couldn't **w** the match,
34: 3 Dinah was strong, and he tried to **w** her affection.
1Sa 14: 6 He can **w** a battle whether he has many warriors
Ecc 9: 11 The fastest runner doesn't always **w** the race,
9: 11 and the strongest warrior doesn't always **w** the
Isa 33: 23 people of God. Even the lame will **w** their share!
Jer 2: 33 "How you plot and scheme to **w** your lovers.
Da 11: 32 violated the covenant and **w** them over to his side.
Hos 2: 14 "But then I will **w** her back once again. I will lead
Lk 21: 19 By standing firm, you will **w** your souls.
Ro 3: 4 in what he says, and he will **w** his case in court."
1Co 8: 8 It's true that we can't **w** God's approval by what
9: 24 You also must run in such a way that you will **w**.
9: 25 They do it to **w** a prize that will fade away, but we
Gal 4: 17 so anxious to **w** your favor are not doing it for your
1Th 2: 5 Never once did we try to **w** you with flattery,
2Ti 3: 6 and **w** the confidence of vulnerable women who
Jas 2: 13 then God's mercy toward you will **w** out over his
1Jn 5: 5 And the ones who **w** this battle against the world
Rev 6: 2 He rode out to **w** many battles and gain the victory.

WIND (122) [HEADWINDS, WINDBAG, WINDBAGS, WINDING, WINDS, WINDSTORM, WINDSWEPT, WOUND]

EAST WIND (14) Ge 41:6,23; Ex 10:13,13; 14:21; Job 27:21; 38:24; Ps 48:7; 78:26; Jer 18:17; Eze 17:10; Hos 12:1; 13:15; Jnh 4:8

SOUTH WIND (5) Job 37:17; Ps 78:26; SS 4:16; Lk 12:55; Ac 28:13

Ge 8: 1 He sent a **w** to blow across the waters,
27: 42 But someone got **w** of what Esau was planning
41: 6 these were shriveled and withered by the east **w**.
41: 23 seven withered heads, shriveled by the east **w**.
Ex 10: 13 and the LORD caused an east **w** to blow all that
10: 13 the east **w** had brought the locusts.
10: 19 The LORD responded by sending a strong west **w**
14: 21 up a path through the water with a strong east **w**.
14: 21 The **w** blew all that night, turning the seabed into
Lev 26: 36 of a leaf driven by the **w** will send you fleeing.
Nu 11: 31 Now the LORD sent a **w** that brought quail from
2Sa 22: 11 he flew, / soaring on the wings of the **w**.
1Ki 18: 45 A heavy **w** brought a terrific rainstorm, and Ahab
19: 11 were torn loose, but the LORD was not in the **w**.

19:11 After the w there was an earthquake,
2Ki 3:17 You will see neither w nor rain, says the LORD,
Job 1:19 a powerful w swept in from the desert and hit the
4:15 swept past my face. Its w sent shivers up my spine.
8: 2 you go on like this? Your words are a blustering w.
13:25 Would you terrify a leaf that is blown by the w?
21:18 Are they driven before the w like straw? Are they
27:21 The east w carries them away, and they are gone.
30:15 has vanished as a cloud before a strong w.
37: 9 The stormy w comes from its chamber,
37:17 and the south w dies down and everything is still,
37:21 for it shines brightly in the sky when the w clears
38:24 origin of light? Where is the home of the east w?
Ps 1: 4 They are like worthless chaff, scattered by the w.
18:10 he flew, / soaring on the wings of the w.
18:42 I ground them as fine as dust carried by the w.
35: 5 Blow them away like chaff in the w— / a w sent by the angel of the LORD.
48: 7 of Tarshish / being shattered by a powerful east w.
68: 2 Drive them off like smoke blown by the w.
78:26 He released the east w in the heavens / and guided the south w by his mighty power.
78:39 gone in a moment like a breath of w, never to
83:13 away like whirling dust, / like chaff before the w!
103:16 The w blows, and we are gone— / as though we
104: 3 your chariots; / you ride upon the wings of the w.
135: 7 the rain / and releases the w from his storehouses.
148: 8 snow and storm, / w and weather that obey him,
Pr 11:29 bring trouble on their families inherit only the w.
25:14 gift is like clouds and w that don't bring rain.
25:23 As surely as a w from the north brings rain, so a
27:16 to stop her complaints is like trying to stop the w
30: 4 comes back down? Who holds the w in his fists?
Ecc 1: 6 The w blows south and north, here and there,
1:14 under the sun is meaningless, like chasing the w.
1:17 now I realize that even this was like chasing the w.
2:11 was all so meaningless. It was like chasing the w.
2:17 Everything is meaningless, like chasing the w.
2:26 however, is meaningless, like chasing the w.
4: 4 But this, too, is meaningless, like chasing the w.
4:16 So again, it is all meaningless, like chasing the w.
5:16 They have been working for the w, and everything
6: 9 nice things is meaningless; it is like chasing the w.
11: 5 are as hard to discern as the pathways of the w,
SS 4:16 "Awake, north w! Come, south w! Blow on my
Isa 5:28 as the wheels of their chariots spin like the w.
11:15 sending a mighty w to divide it into seven streams
17:13 They will flee like chaff scattered by the w or like
29: 5 will be driven away like chaff before the w.
30:24 its chaff having been blown away by the w.
32: 2 He will shelter Israel from the storm and the w.
40:24 work withers. The w carries them off like straw.
41: 2 the sword. He scatters them in the w with his bow.
41:16 them in the air, and the w will blow them all away;
41:29 Your idols are all as empty as the w.
57:13 so helpless that a breath of w can knock them
58: 5 bowing your heads like a blade of grass in the w.
64: 6 and fall. And our sins, like the w, sweep us away.
Jer 2:24 like a wild donkey, sniffing the w at mating time.
4:11 "A burning w is blowing in from the desert.
4:13 Our enemy rushes down on us like a storm w!
10:13 the rain / and releases the w from his storehouses.
18:17 before their enemies as the east w scatters dust.
22:22 your allies have all disappeared with a puff of w.
30:23 a driving w that swirls down on the heads of the
51:16 the rain / and releases the w from his storehouses.
Eze 5: 2 Scatter the last third to the w, for I will scatter my
17:10 it will wither away completely when the east w
19:12 The desert w dried up its fruit / and tore off its
37:10 and the w entered the bodies, and they began to
Da 2:35 and the w blew them all away without a trace.
Hos 4:19 So a mighty w will sweep them away. They will
8: 7 "They have planted the w and will harvest the
12: 1 The people of Israel feed on the w; they chase after the east w all day long.
13: 3 like chaff blown by the w, like smoke from a
13:15 most fruitful of all his brothers, but the east w—
Jnh 1: 4 suddenly the LORD flung a powerful w over the
4: 8 God sent a scorching east w to blow on Jonah.
Hab 1: 9 Their hordes advance like a w from the desert,
1:11 They sweep past like the w and are gone. But they
Zep 2:14 and the cedar paneling will lie open to the w
Zec 5: 9 flying toward us, with wings gliding on the w.
Mt 8:26 Then he stood up and rebuked the w and waves,
8:27 "Even the w and waves obey him!"
11: 7 him weak as a reed, moved by every breath of w?
14:24 for a strong w had risen, and they were fighting
14:32 they climbed back into the boat, the w stopped.
Mk 4:39 he rebuked the w and said to the water,
4:39 Suddenly the w stopped, and there was a great
4:41 is this man, that even the w and waves obey him?"
6:48 and struggling against the w and waves.
6:51 Then he climbed into the boat, and the w stopped.
Lk 7:24 him weak as a reed, moved by every breath of w?
8:23 and while he was sleeping the w began to rise.
8:24 So Jesus rebuked the w and the raging waves.
12:55 When the south w blows, you say, 'Today will be a
Jn 3: 8 Just as you can hear the w but can't tell where it
Ac 27: 7 But the w was against us, so we sailed down to the
27:13 When a light w began blowing from the south,
27:14 and a w of typhoon strength (a "northeaster,"
27:15 They couldn't turn the ship into the w, so they
27:17 the sea anchor and were thus driven before the w.
28:13 A day later a south w began blowing,
Heb 1: 7 God calls his angels / "messengers swift as the w,
Jas 1: 6 wave of the sea that is driven and tossed by the w.
2Pe 2:17 of water or as clouds blown away by the w—

WINDBAG (1) [WIND]

Job 15: 2 us all this foolish talk. You are nothing but a w.

WINDBAGS (1) [WIND]

Jer 5:13 God's prophets are w full of words with no divine

WINDING (1) [WIND]

1Ki 6: 8 There were w stairs going up to the second floor,

WINDOW (18) [WINDOWS, WINDOWSILL]

Ge 8: 6 Noah opened the w he had made in the boat
26: 8 looked out a w and saw Isaac fondling Rebekah.
Jos 2:15 she let them down by a rope through the w.
2:18 if you leave this scarlet rope hanging from the w.
2:21 leaving the scarlet rope hanging from the w.
Jdg 5:28 "From the w Sisera's mother looked out.
5:28 Through the w she watched for his return, saying,
1Sa 19:12 So she helped him climb out through a w, and he
2Sa 6:16 the daughter of Saul, looked down from her w.
2Ki 9:30 her eyelids and fixed her hair and sat at a w.
9:32 Jehu looked up and saw her at the w and shouted,
9:33 So they threw her out the w, and some of her blood
13:17 "Open that eastern w," and he opened it.
1Ch 15:29 the daughter of Saul, looked down from her w.
Pr 7: 6 I was looking out the w of my house one day
SS 2: 9 Now he is looking in through the w, gazing into
Eze 40:36 as in the others and the same w arrangements.
2Co 11:33 But I was lowered in a basket through a w in the

WINDOWS (19) [WINDOW]

1Ki 6: 4 made narrow, recessed w throughout the Temple.
7: 4 walls there were three rows of w facing each other.
2Ki 7: 2 even if the LORD opened the w of heaven!"
7:19 even if the LORD opened the w of heaven!"
Jer 9:21 For death has crept in through our w and has
22:14 magnificent palace with huge rooms and many w,
Eze 40:16 There were recessed w that narrowed inward
40:16 There were also w in the foyer structure.
40:22 The w, the foyer, and the palm tree decorations
40:25 It had w along the walls as the others did, and there
40:29 It also had w along its walls and in the foyer
40:33 and there were w along the walls and in the foyer
41:16 as were the frames of the recessed w. The inner
41:16 were paneled with wood above and below the w.
41:26 On both sides of the foyer there were recessed w
Da 6:10 upstairs room, with its w open toward Jerusalem.
Joel 2: 9 all the houses, climbing like thieves through the w.
Zep 2:14 the ruins of its palaces, hooting from the gaping w.
Mal 3:10 "I will open the w of heaven for you.

WINDOWSILL (1) [WINDOW]

Ac 20: 9 sitting on the w, became very drowsy.

WINDS (27) [WIND]

Job 28:25 He made the w blow and determined how much
37: 9 from its chamber, and the driving w bring the cold.
Ps 11: 6 them with burning sulfur and scorching w.
104: 4 The w are your messengers; / flames of fire are
107:25 He spoke, and the w rose, / stirring up the waves.
147:18 it all melts. / He sends his w, and the ice thaws.
Isa 49:10 and scorching desert w will not reach them
Jer 13:24 just as chaff is scattered by the w blowing in from
49:32 I will scatter to the w these people who live in
49:36 and I will scatter the people of Elam to the four w.
Eze 5:12 And I will scatter a third to the w and chase them
12:14 I will scatter his servants and guards to the four w
13:11 great hailstones and mighty w will knock it down.
17:21 in the city will be scattered to the four w.
37: 9 Then he said to me, "Speak to the w and say:
37: 9 Come, O breath, from the four w! Breathe into
Da 7: 2 with strong w blowing from every direction.
Am 4:13 stirs up the w, and reveals his every thought.
Zec 2: 6 the north, for I have scattered you to the four w.
Mt 7:25 floodwaters rise and the w beat against that house,
7:27 and floods come and the w beat against that house,
Lk 8:13 but they wilt when the hot w of testing blow.
8:25 is this man, that even the w and waves obey him?"
Ac 27:18 as gale-force w continued to batter the ship,
Jas 3: 4 pilot wants it to go, even though the w are strong.
Rev 6:13 green figs falling from trees shaken by mighty w.
7: 1 holding back the four w from blowing upon the

WINDSTORM (2) [STORM, WIND]

1Ki 19:11 passed by, and a mighty w hit the mountain.
Ac 2: 2 the roaring of a mighty w in the skies above them,

WINDSWEPT (1) [SWEEP, WIND]

Jer 3:21 Voices are heard high on the w mountains,

WINDY [KJV] See WILD (STORM)

WINE (218) [WINEPRESS, WINEPRESSES, WINES, WINESKIN, WINESKINS]

Ge 9:21 One day he became drunk on some w he had made
14:18 of God Most High, brought him bread and w.
19:32 let's get him drunk with w, and then we will sleep
19:34 Let's get him drunk with w again tonight, and you
27:25 ate it. He also drank the w that Jacob served him.
27:28 for healthy crops and good harvests of grain and w.
27:37 guaranteed him an abundance of grain and w—
35:14 He then poured w over it as an offering to God
40:11 I was holding Pharaoh's w cup in my hand, so I
49:11 He washes his clothes in w / because his harvest is
49:12 His eyes are darker than w, / and his teeth are
Ex 22:29 you give me the tithe of your crops and your w.
29:40 also, offer one quart of w as a drink offering.
29:41 same offerings of flour and w as in the morning.
Lev 10: 9 "You and your descendants must never drink w
23:13 you must also offer one quart of w as a drink
Nu 6: 3 they must give up w and other alcoholic drinks.
6: 3 They must not use vinegar made from w,
6:20 this ceremony the Nazirites may again drink w.
15: 5 you must also present one quart of w for a drink
15: 7 give two and a half pints of w for a drink offering.
15:10 plus two quarts of w for the drink offering.
18:12 the LORD—the best of the olive oil, w, and grain.
18:27 threshing floor or w from your own winepress.
28:14 two quarts of w with each bull, two and a half pints
Dt 11:14 crops of grain, grapes for w, and olives for oil.
12:17 the tithe of your grain and new w and olive oil,
14:23 applies to your tithes of grain, new w, olive oil,
14:26 you want—an ox, a sheep, some w, or beer.
18: 4 the new w, the olive oil, and the wool at shearing
28:39 but you will not drink the w or eat the grapes,
28:51 you no grain, new w, olive oil, calves, or lambs,
29: 6 You had no bread or w or other strong drink,
32:14 You drank the finest w, / made from the juice of
32:33 Their w is the venom of snakes, / the deadly poison
32:38 and drank the w of their offerings? / Let those gods
33:28 Jacob in security, / in a land of grain and w,
Jdg 9:13 'Should I quit producing the w that cheers both
9:27 in the temple of the local god, the w flowed freely,
13: 4 You must not drink w or any other alcoholic drink
13: 7 You must not drink w or any other alcoholic drink
13:14 or raisins, drink w or any other alcoholic drink,
19:19 and plenty of bread and w for ourselves."
Ru 2:14 You can dip your bread in the w if you like."
1Sa 1:14 he demanded. "Throw away your w!"
1:24 the sacrifice and half a bushel of flour and some w.
10: 3 of bread, and the third will be carrying a skin of w.
16:20 and a donkey loaded down with food and w.
25:18 two skins of w, five dressed sheep, nearly a bushel
2Sa 11:11 How could I go home to w and dine and sleep with
16: 1 hundred bunches of summer fruit, and a skin of w.
16: 2 The w is to be taken with you into the wilderness
19:35 Food and w are no longer tasty, and I cannot hear
2Ki 6:27 "I have neither food nor w to give you."
7: 8 eating, drinking w, and carrying out silver and gold
18:32 a country with bountiful harvests of grain and w,
1Ch 9:29 as choice flour, w, olive oil, incense, and spices.
12:40 of flour, fig cakes, raisins, w, olive oil, cattle,
27:27 responsible for the grapes and the supplies of w.
2Ch 2:10 100,000 bushels of barley, 110,000 gallons of w,
2:15 barley, olive oil, and w that you mentioned.
11:11 he stored supplies of food, olive oil, and w.
31: 5 of their crops and grain, new w, olive oil, honey,
32:28 storehouses for his grain, new w, and olive oil;
Ezr 3: 7 and Sidon, paying them with food, w, and olive oil.
6: 9 without fail, provide them with the wheat, salt, w,
7:22 500 bushels of wheat, 550 gallons of w,
Ne 2: 1 Artaxerxes' reign, I was serving the king his w.
5:11 charged on their money, grain, w, and olive oil."
5:15 demanding a daily ration of food and w, besides a
5:18 days we needed a large supply of all kinds of w.
10:37 our fruit, and the best of our new w and olive oil.
10:39 new w, and olive oil to the Temple and place them
13: 5 and tithes of grain, new w, olive oil,
13:12 new w, and olive oil to the Temple storerooms.
13:15 And on that day they were bringing their w,
Est 1: 7 and there was an abundance of royal w, just as the
1:10 when King Xerxes was half drunk with w, he told
5: 6 And while they were drinking w, the king said to
7: 2 And while they were drinking w that day, the king
Job 32:19 I am like a w cask without a vent. My words are
Ps 4: 7 those who have abundant harvests of grain and w.
60: 3 on us, / making us drink w that sent us reeling.
69:21 they offer me sour w to satisfy my thirst.
75: 8 it is full of foaming w mixed with spices.
75: 8 He pours the w out in judgment, / and all the
104:15 w to make them glad, / olive oil as lotion for their
Pr 3:10 and your vats will overflow with the finest w.
9: 5 eat my food, and drink the w I have mixed.
20: 1 W produces mockers; liquor leads to brawls.
21:17 w and luxury are not the way to riches.
23:31 let the sparkle and smooth taste of w deceive you.
31: 4 And it is not for kings, O Lemuel, to guzzle w.
31: 6 for the dying, and w for those in deep depression.
Ecc 2: 3 much thought, I decided to cheer myself with w.
5:18 drink a good glass of w, and enjoy their work—
9: 7 Eat your food and drink your w with a happy heart,
10:19 A party gives laughter, and w gives happiness,
SS 1: 2 and again, for your love is sweeter than w.
1: 4 for him! We praise his love even more than w."
4:10 my bride! How much better it is than w!
5: 1 I drink my w with my milk." / "Oh, lover
7: 2 Your navel is as delicious as a goblet filled with w.
7: 9 May your kisses be as exciting as the best w,
8: 2 spiced w to drink, my sweet pomegranate w.
Isa 1:22 Once so pure, you are now like watered-down w.
5:10 of vineyard will not produce even six gallons of w.
5:12 furnish lovely music and w at your grand parties;
16: 8 The w from those vineyards used to make the
22:13 sacrificial animals, feast on meat, and drink w.
24: 7 The grape harvest will fail, and there will be no w.
24: 9 Gone are the joys of w and song; strong drink now
24:11 Mobs gather in the streets, crying out for w.
25: 6 with clear, well-aged w and choice beef.
28: 1 that city—the pride of a people brought low by w.

28: 7 and prophets reel and stagger from beer and **w**.
29: 9 You are stupid, but not from **w**! You stagger,
36:17 a country with bountiful harvests of grain and **w**,
51:21 in a drunken stupor, though not from drinking **w**.
55: 1 Come, take your choice of **w** or milk—it's all free!
56:12 they say. "We will get some **w** and have a party.
62: 8 warriors come and take away your grain and **w**.
62: 9 you yourselves will drink the **w** that you have
Jer 13:12 says: All your wineskins will be full of **w**.'
16: 7 No one will send a cup of **w** to console them.
23: 9 like a drunkard, like someone overcome by **w**,
31:12 **w**, and oil, and the healthy flocks and herds.
35: 2 one of the inner rooms, and offer them some **w**."
35: 5 I set cups and jugs of **w** before them and invited
35: 6 "We don't drink **w**, because Jehonadab son of
35: 6 'You and your descendants must never drink **w**.
35: 8 We have never had a drink of **w** since then,
35:14 The Recabites do not drink **w** because their
48:11 She is like **w** that has been allowed to settle.
48:33 gone from fruitful Moab. The presses yield no **w**.
51:39 And while they lie inflamed with all their **w**,
Eze 27:18 bringing **w** from Helbon and white wool from
44:21 The priests must never drink **w** before entering the
Da 1: 5 of the best food and **w** from his own kitchens.
1: 8 eating the food and **w** given to them by the king.
1:10 the king has ordered that you eat this food and **w**,"
5: 1 a thousand of his nobles and drank **w** with them.
5:23 and concubines have been drinking **w** from them
10: 3 I had eaten no rich food or meat, had drunk no **w**,
Hos 2: 8 everything she has—the grain, the **w**, the olive oil.
2: 9 "But now I will take back the **w** and ripened grain
3: 2 about five bushels of barley and a measure of **w**.
9: 4 you will not be allowed to pour out **w** as a sacrifice
Joel 1: 5 the grapes are ruined, and all your new **w** is gone!
1: 9 or **w** to offer at the Temple of the LORD.
1:10 The grain, the **w**, and the olive oil are gone.
1:13 no grain or **w** to offer at the Temple of your God.
2:14 and **w** to the LORD your God as before!
2:19 I am sending you grain and **w** and olive oil,
2:24 and the presses will overflow with **w** and olive oil.
3: 3 and little girls for enough **w** to get drunk.
3:18 In that day the mountains will drip with sweet **w**,
Am 2: 8 they present offerings of **w** purchased with stolen
2:12 the Nazirites to sin by making them drink your **w**,
5:11 You will never drink **w** from the lush vineyards
6: 6 You drink **w** by the bowlful, and you perfume
9:13 on the hills of Israel will drip with sweet **w**!
9:14 they will eat their crops and drink their **w**.
Mic 2:11 "I'll preach to you the joys of **w** and drink!"
6:15 trample the grapes but get no juice to make your **w**.
Zep 1:13 They will never drink **w** from the vineyards they
Hag 1: 6 You have **w** to drink, but not enough to satisfy
2:12 to brush against some bread or stew, **w** or oil,
Zec 9:15 They will shout in battle as though drunk with **w**,
9:17 will thrive on the abundance of grain and new **w**.
10: 7 and their hearts will be happy as if by **w**.
Mt 9:17 And no one puts new **w** into old wineskins.
9:17 spilling the **w** and ruining the skins. New **w** must be stored in new wineskins. That way both the **w** and the wineskins are
11:18 For John the Baptist didn't drink **w** and he often
26:27 And he took a cup of **w** and gave thanks to God for
26:29 I will not drink **w** again until the day I drink it new
27:34 The soldiers gave him **w** mixed with bitter gall,
27:48 One of them ran and filled a sponge with sour **w**,
Mk 2:22 And no one puts new **w** into old wineskins. The **w** would burst the wineskins, spilling the **w** and ruining the skins. New **w** needs new wineskins."
14:23 And he took a cup of **w** and gave thanks to God for
14:25 I solemnly declare that I will not drink **w** again
15:23 They offered him **w** drugged with myrrh, but he
15:36 One of them ran and filled a sponge with sour **w**,
Lk 1:15 He must never touch **w** or hard liquor, and he will
5:37 And no one puts new **w** into old wineskins. The new **w** would burst the old skins, spilling the **w** and ruining the skins.
5:38 New **w** must be put into new wineskins.
5:39 But no one who drinks the old **w** seems to want the
7:33 For John the Baptist didn't drink **w** and he often
22:17 Then he took a cup of **w**, and when he had given
22:18 For I will not drink **w** again until the Kingdom of
22:20 After supper he took another cup of **w** and said,
22:20 "This **w** is the token of God's new covenant to
23:36 too, by offering him a drink of sour **w**.
Jn 2: 3 The **w** supply ran out during the festivities,
2: 3 "They have no more **w**," she told him.
2: 9 of ceremonies tasted the water that was now **w**,
2:10 "Usually a host serves the best **w** first," he said.
4:46 of Cana, where he had turned the water into **w**.
19:29 A jar of sour **w** was sitting there, so they soaked a
Ro 14:21 Don't eat meat or drink **w** or do anything else if it
1Co 11:25 he took the cup of **w** after supper, saying,
Eph 5:18 Don't be drunk with **w**, because that will ruin your
1Ti 5:23 You ought to drink a little **w** for the sake of your
Rev 6: 6 a day's pay. And don't waste the olive oil and **w**."
14: 8 and made them drink the **w** of her passionate
14:10 must drink the **w** of God's wrath. It is poured out
16:19 cup that was filled with the **w** of his fierce wrath.
17: 2 been made drunk by the **w** of her immorality."
18: 3 For all the nations have drunk the **w** of her
18:13 **w**, olive oil, fine flour, wheat, cattle, sheep, horses,

WINEBIBBER(S) [KJV] See DRUNKARD(S)

WINEFAT [KJV] See (PIT FOR) PRESSING, (PLACE OF) TREADING

WINEPRESS (15) [WINE]

Nu 18:27 own threshing floor or wine from your own **w**.
18:30 it came from your own threshing floor or **w**.
Dt 15:14 from your flock, your threshing floor, and your **w**.
Jdg 6:11 of a **w** to hide the grain from the Midianites.
7:25 at the rock of Oreb, and Zeeb at the **w** of Zeeb.
Job 24:11 and they tread in the **w** as they suffer from thirst.
Isa 5: 2 a watchtower / and carved a **w** in the nearby rocks.
63: 3 "I have trodden the **w** alone; no one was there to
La 1:15 his beloved city as grapes are trampled in a **w**.
Joel 3:13 harvest is ripe. Come, tread the **w** because it is full.
Hag 2:16 you expected to draw fifty gallons from the **w**,
Rev 14:19 and loaded the grapes into the great **w** of God's
14:20 And the grapes were trodden in the **w** outside the
14:20 and blood flowed from the **w** in a stream about 180
19:15 and he trod the **w** of the fierce wrath of almighty

WINEPRESSES (3) [WINE]

Ne 13:15 day I saw some men of Judah treading their **w**.
Isa 16:10 The treading out of grapes in the **w** has ceased
Zec 14:10 and from the Tower of Hananel to the king's **w**.

WINES (4) [WINE]

Pr 9: 2 a great banquet, mixed the **w**, and set the table.
Da 1:16 only vegetables instead of the rich foods and **w**.
Hos 14: 7 They will be as fragrant as the **w** of Lebanon.
Jn 2:10 doesn't care, he brings out the less expensive **w**.

WINESKIN (1) [WINE]

Ps 119:83 I am shriveled like a **w** in the smoke,

WINESKINS (11) [WINE]

Jos 9: 4 with weathered saddlebags and old patched **w**.
9:13 These **w** were new when we filled them, but now
Jer 13:12 of Israel, says: All your **w** will be full of wine.'
Mt 9:17 And no one puts new wine into old **w**. The old
9:17 New wine must be stored in new **w**. That way both the wine and the **w** are preserved."
Mk 2:22 And no one puts new wine into old **w**. The wine would burst the **w**, spilling the wine and ruining the skins. New wine needs new **w**."
Lk 5:37 And no one puts new wine into old **w**. The new
5:38 New wine must be put into new **w**.

WING (7) [WINGED, WINGS, WINGSPAN]

1Ki 6:24 was 15 feet, each **w** being 7-1/2 feet long.
2Ch 3:11 One **w** of the first figure was 7-1/2 feet long,
3:11 The other **w**, also 7-1/2 feet long, touched one of
3:12 the second figure had one **w** 7-1/2 feet long that
3:12 The other **w**, also 7-1/2 feet long, touched the **w** of the first figure.
Isa 10:14 No one can even flap a **w** against me or utter a

WINGED (2) [WING]

Dt 14:20 But you may eat any **w** creature that is
Isa 18: 1 of the Nile. Its **w** sailboats glide along the river,

WINGS (71) [WING]

Ex 19: 4 you to myself and carried you on eagle's **w**.
25:20 looking down on the atonement cover with their **w**
37: 9 and their **w** were stretched out above the
Lev 1:17 Then, grasping the bird by its **w**, the priest will tear
Dt 32:11 her young, / so he spread his **w** to take them in
Ru 2:12 under whose **w** you have come to take refuge,
2Sa 22:11 he flew, / soaring on the **w** of the wind.
1Ki 6:27 Their outspread **w** reached from wall to wall,
6:27 while their inner **w** touched at the center of the
8: 6 and placed it beneath the **w** of the cherubim.
8: 7 The cherubim spread their **w** over the Ark,
1Ch 28:18 whose **w** were stretched out over the Ark of the
2Ch 3:11 touched one of the **w** of the second figure.
5: 7 and placed it beneath the **w** of the cherubim.
5: 8 The cherubim spread their **w** out over the Ark,
Job 39:13 "The ostrich flaps her **w** grandly, but they are no
39:26 makes the hawk soar and spread its **w** to the south?
Ps 17: 8 of your eye. / Hide me in the shadow of your **w**.
18:10 he flew, / soaring on the **w** of the wind.
36: 7 humanity finds shelter / in the shadow of your **w**.
55: 6 Oh, how I wish I had **w** like a dove; / then I would
57: 1 I will hide beneath the shadow of your **w**
61: 4 safe beneath the shelter of your **w**!
63: 7 I sing for joy in the shadow of your protecting **w**.
68:13 and gold, / as a dove is covered by its **w**.
91: 4 He will shield you with his **w**. / He will shelter you
104: 3 your chariots; / you ride upon the **w** of the wind.
139: 9 If I ride the **w** of the morning, / if I dwell by the
Pr 23: 5 For riches can disappear as though they had the **w**
Isa 6: 2 him were mighty seraphim, each with six **w**.
6: 2 With two **w** they covered their faces, with two they
34:15 will hatch her young and cover them with her **w**.
40:31 They will fly high on **w** like eagles. They will run
Jer 48: 9 Oh, that Moab had **w** so she could fly away,
49:22 an eagle, and he will spread his **w** against Bozrah.
Eze 1: 6 except that each had four faces and two pairs of **w**.
1: 8 Beneath each of their **w** I could see human hands.
1: 9 The **w** of each living being touched the **w** of
1:11 Each had two pairs of outstretched **w**—one pair stretched out to touch the **w** of the living
1:23 Beneath this surface the **w** of each living being stretched out to touch the others' **w**, and each had two **w** covering its body.
1:24 As they flew their **w** roared like waves crashing
1:24 When they stopped, they let down their **w**.
1:25 As they stood with their **w** lowered, a voice spoke
3:13 It was the sound of the **w** of the living beings as
10: 5 The moving **w** of the cherubim sounded like the
10: 8 looked like human hands hidden beneath their **w**.)
10:12 including their hands, their backs, and their **w**.
10:21 for each had four faces and four **w** and what looked like human hands under their **w**.
11:22 Then the cherubim lifted their **w** and rose into the
17: 3 A great eagle with broad **w** full of many-colored
17: 7 But then another great eagle with broad **w** and full
Da 7: 4 The first beast was like a lion with eagles' **w**.
7: 4 As I watched, its **w** were pulled off, and it was left
7: 6 It had four **w** like birds' **w** on its back, and it
Zec 5: 9 flying toward us, with **w** gliding on the wind.
5: 9 Their **w** were like those of a stork, and they picked
Mal 4: 2 of Righteousness will rise with healing in his **w**.
Mt 23:37 as a hen protects her chicks beneath her **w**,
Lk 13:34 as a hen protects her chicks beneath her **w**,
Heb 9: 5 Their **w** were stretched out over the Ark's cover,
Rev 4: 7 and the fourth had the form of an eagle with **w**
4: 8 Each of these living beings had six **w**, and their **w** were covered with eyes, inside and out.
9: 9 and their **w** roared like an army of chariots rushing
12:14 But she was given two **w** like those of a great

WINGSPAN (3) [WING]

1Ki 6:24 The **w** of each of the cherubim was 15 feet,
2Ch 3:11 The total **w** of the two cherubim standing side by
3:13 So the **w** of both cherubim together was 30 feet.

WINK (1)

Pr 10:10 People who **w** at wrong cause trouble, but a bold

WINNING (2) [WIN]

Ge 30: 8 an intense struggle with my sister, and I am **w**!"
Heb 7: 1 When Abraham was returning home after **w** a great

WINNOW (2) [WINNOWED, WINNOWING]

Jer 15: 7 I will **w** you like grain at the gates of your cities
51: 2 Foreigners will come and **w** her, blowing her away

WINNOWED (1) [WINNOW]

Isa 21:10 O my people, threshed and **w**, I have told you

WINNOWING (4) [WINNOW]

Ru 3: 2 Tonight he will be **w** barley at the threshing floor.
Jer 4:11 It is not a gentle breeze useful for **w** grain.
Mt 3:12 separate the chaff from the grain with his **w** fork.
Lk 3:17 separate the chaff from the grain with his **w** fork.

WINS (4) [WIN]

Pr 8:35 me finds life and **w** approval from the LORD.
Ro 7:23 This law **w** the fight and makes me a slave to the
1Co 13: 6 but rejoices whenever the truth **w** out.
2Ti 2: 5 follows the rules or is disqualified and **w** no prize.

WINTER (20) [MIDWINTER, WINTERED, WINTERIZED]

Ge 8:22 cold and heat, **w** and summer, day and night."
Est 2:16 palace in early **w** of the seventh year of his reign,
9:19 celebrate an annual festival and holiday in late **w**,
Ps 74:17 of the earth, / and you make both summer and **w**.
Pr 6: 8 labor hard all summer, gathering food for the **w**.
30:25 aren't strong, / but they store up food for the **w**.
31:21 She has no fear of **w** for her household because all
SS 2:11 For the **w** is past, and the rain is over and gone.
Isa 18: 6 The wild animals will gnaw at bones all **w**.
Am 3:15 their **w** mansions and their summer houses, too—
Zec 8:19 midsummer, autumn, and **w** are now ended.
14: 8 flowing continuously both in summer and in **w**.
Mt 24:20 And pray that your flight will not be in **w** or on the
Mk 13:18 And pray that your flight will not be in **w**.
Jn 10:22 It was now **w**, and Jesus was in Jerusalem at the
Ac 27:12 a poor place to spend the **w**—most of the crew
27:12 up the coast of Crete, and spend the **w** there.
1Co 16: 6 perhaps all **w**, and then you can send me on my
2Ti 4:21 Hurry so you can get here before **w**. Eubulus sends
Tit 3:12 you can, for I have decided to stay there for the **w**.

WINTERED (1) [WINTER]

Ac 28:11 set sail on another ship that had **w** at the island—

WINTERIZED (1) [WINTER]

Jer 36:22 and the king was in a **w** part of the palace,

WIPE (29) [WIPED, WIPES, WIPING]

Ge 6: 7 "I will completely **w** out this human race that I
6:13 Yes, I will **w** them all from the face of the earth!
7: 4 And I will **w** from the earth all the living things I
Ex 32:12 kill them and **w** them from the face of the earth.'
Lev 20:14 All three of them must be burned to death to **w** out
Dt 6:15 against you and **w** you from the face of the earth.
Jos 7: 9 will surround us and **w** us off the face of the earth.
23:15 He will completely **w** you out from this good land
2Sa 21: 2 but Saul, in his zeal, had tried to **w** them out.
2Ki 21:13 I will **w** away the people of Jerusalem as one wipes
Job 31:12 destroys to hell. It would **w** out everything I own.
Ps 21:10 You will **w** their children from the face of the
59:13 them in your anger! / **W** them out completely!
83: 4 "Come," they say, "let us **w** out Israel as a nation.

Ecc 5: 6 and he might w out everything you have achieved.
Isa 14:30 But as for you, I will w you out with famine.
25: 8 The Sovereign LORD will w away all tears.
48: 9 I will hold back my anger and not w you out.
Jer 19: 8 I will w Jerusalem from the face of the earth,
Eze 9: 8 Will your fury against Jerusalem w out everyone
25: 9 and w out their glorious frontier cities—
25:13 I will w out their people, cattle, and flocks with the
25:16 I will w out the Kerethites and utterly destroy the
32:15 I destroy Egypt and w out everything you have
Ob 1: 5 But your enemies will w you out completely!
Hab 1:12 are eternal—is your plan in all of this to w us out?
Lk 10:11 'We w the dust of your town from our feet as a
Jn 13: 5 and to w them with the towel he had around him.
Rev 7:17 And God will w away all their tears."

WIPED (23) [WIPE]

Ge 7:23 Every living thing on the earth was w out—people,
41:30 that all the prosperity will be forgotten and w out.
Ex 9:15 that would have w you from the face of the earth.
Nu 21:30 We have completely w them out / as far away as
Jos 8:25 So the entire population of Ai was w out that day
10:20 and w out the five armies except for a tiny remnant
23:13 and you will be w out from this good land the
23:16 and you will quickly be w out from the good land
Jdg 21: 6 of the tribes from our family; it is nearly w out.
2Ki 9: 8 The entire family of Ahab must be w out—
Ps 9: 5 the wicked; / you have w out their names forever.
Isa 1: 9 we would have been w out as completely as
Jer 51:26 You will be completely w out," says the LORD.
Eze 16:50 loathsome things, so I w her out, as you have seen.
21:32 You will be utterly w out, your memory lost to
35:15 You will be w out, you people of Mount Seir
Mic 5: 9 up to their foes, and all their enemies will be w out.
Zep 3: 6 "I have w out many nations, devastating their
Lk 7:38 fell on his feet, and she w them off with her hair.
7:44 them with her tears and w them with her hair.
Jn 11: 2 on the Lord's feet and w them with her hair.
12: 3 Jesus' feet with it and w his feet with her hair.
Ro 9:29 not spared a few of us, / we would have been w out

WIPES (1) [WIPE]

2Ki 21:13 I will wipe away the people of Jerusalem as one w

WIPING (1) [WIPE]

Lev 26:44 I will not cancel my covenant with them by w

WIRES [KJV] See (FINE) STRIPS

WISDOM (198) [WISE]

Ex 31: 3 giving him great w, intelligence, and skill in all
35:31 giving him great w, intelligence, and skill in all
36: 1 craftsmen whom the LORD has gifted with w,
Dt 1:13 Choose some men from each tribe who have w,
4: 6 you will display your w and intelligence to the
34: 9 Now Joshua son of Nun was full of the spirit of w,
2Sa 14: 2 from Tekoa who had a reputation for great w.
1Ki 3:10 and was glad that he had asked for w.
3:11 "Because you have asked for w in governing my
3:28 w God had given him to render decisions with
4:29 God gave Solomon great w and understanding,
4:30 his w exceeded that of all the wise men of the East
4:34 their ambassadors to listen to the w of Solomon.
5:12 So the LORD gave great w to Solomon just as he
10: 6 my country about your achievements and w is true!
10: 7 Your w and prosperity are far greater than what I
10: 8 to stand here day after day, listening to your w!
10:24 to visit him and to hear the w God had given him.
11:41 of the events in Solomon's reign, including his w,
1Ch 22:12 And may the LORD give you w
26:14 assigned to his son Zechariah, a man of unusual w.
2Ch 1:10 Give me w and knowledge to rule them properly,
1:11 but rather you asked for w and knowledge to
1:12 I will certainly give you the w and knowledge you
9: 5 my country about your achievements and w is true!
9: 6 of it! Your w is far greater than what I was told.
9: 7 to stand here day after day, listening to your w!
9:23 to visit him and to hear the w God had given him.
Ezr 7:25 are to use the w God has given you to appoint
Job 8:10 They will teach you from the w of former
11: 6 If only he would tell you the secrets of w, for true
w is not a simple matter.
12: 2 don't you? And when you die, w will die with you!
12:12 W belongs to the aged, and understanding to those
12:13 "But true w and power are with God; counsel
12:16 "Yes, strength and w are with him; deceivers
15: 8 secret council? Do you have a monopoly on w?
28:12 "But do people know where to find w? Where can
28:17 W is far more valuable than gold and crystal.
28:18 trying to get it. The price of w is far above pearls.
28:20 "But do people know where to find w? Where can
28:22 'We have heard a rumor of where w can be found.'
28:27 he had done all this, he saw w and measured it.
28:28 'The fear of the Lord is true w; to forsake evil is
32: 7 are older should speak, for w comes with age.'
33:33 listen to me. Keep silent and I will teach you w!"
34:33 is yours, not mine. Go ahead, share your w with us.
38: 2 "Who is this that questions my w with such
39:17 for God has deprived her of w. He has given her no
42: 3 'Who is this that questions my w with such
Ps 90:12 the most of our time, / so that we may grow in w.
104:24 In w you have made them all. / The earth is full of
111:10 for the LORD is the foundation of true w.
111:10 The rewards of w come to all who obey him.
Pr 1: 2 The purpose of these proverbs is to teach people w
1: 7 of knowledge. Only fools despise w and discipline.
1:20 W shouts in the streets. She cries out in the public
1:23 I'll pour out the spirit of w upon you and make you
2: 2 Tune your ears to w, and concentrate on
2: 6 For the LORD grants w! From his mouth come
2:10 For w will enter your heart, and knowledge will fill
2:12 W will save you from evil people, from those
2:16 W will save you from the immoral woman,
3: 7 Don't be impressed with your own w. Instead,
3:13 Happy is the person who finds w and gains
3:14 For the profit of w is better than silver, and her
3:15 W is more precious than rubies; nothing you desire
3:18 W is a tree of life to those who embrace her;
3:19 By w the LORD founded the earth;
4: 6 Don't turn your back on w, for she will protect
4: 7 Getting w is the most important thing you can do!
4: 8 If you prize w, she will exalt you. Embrace her
4:12 If you live a life guided by w, you won't limp
5: 1 My son, pay attention to my w; listen carefully to
7: 4 Love w like a sister; make insight a beloved
8: 1 Listen as w calls out! Hear as understanding raises
8:11 For w is far more valuable than rubies.
8:12 "I, W, live together with good judgment. I know
9: 1 W has built her spacious house with seven pillars.
9:10 Fear of the LORD is the beginning of w.
9:11 W will multiply your days and add years to your
9:12 If you scorn w, you will be the one to suffer.
11: 2 Pride leads to disgrace, but with humility comes w.
14: 6 A mocker seeks w and never finds it,
14:33 W is enshrined in an understanding heart; w is not
found among fools.
16:10 The king speaks with divine w; he must never
16:16 How much better to get w than gold,
17:16 tuition to educate a fool who has no heart for w.
17:24 Sensible people keep their eyes glued on w,
18: 4 words of true w are as refreshing as a bubbling
19: 8 To acquire w is to love oneself; people who
23:23 ever sell it; also get w, discipline, and discernment.
23:26 May your eyes delight in my ways of w.
24: 3 A house is built by w and becomes strong through
24: 7 W is too much for a fool. When the leaders gather,
24:14 In the same way, w is sweet to your soul. If you
28:26 is foolish, but those who walk in w are safe.
29: 3 The man who loves w brings joy to his father,
29:15 To discipline and reprimand a child produces w,
30: 3 I have not mastered human w, nor do I know the
Ecc 1:13 and to explore by w everything being done in the
1:16 I have greater w and knowledge than any of
1:17 So I worked hard to distinguish w from
1:18 For the greater my w, the greater my grief.
2: 3 While still seeking w, I clutched at foolishness.
2:12 So I decided to compare w and folly, and anyone
2:13 W is of more value than foolishness, just as light is
2:15 will die, so will I. So of what value is all my w?
2:21 For though I do my work with w, knowledge,
2:26 God gives w, knowledge, and joy to those who
7:12 W or money can get you almost anything, but it's
important to know that only w can save
7:23 All along I have tried my best to let w guide my
7:24 W is always distant and very difficult to find.
7:25 determined to find w and to understand the reason
8: 1 W lights up a person's face, softening its hardness.
8:16 In my search for w, I tried to observe everything
9:10 will be no work or planning or knowledge or w.
9:13 Here is another bit of w that has impressed me as I
9:16 Then I realized that though w is better than
10: 1 an ounce of foolishness can outweigh a pound of w
10:10 That's the value of w; it helps you succeed.
Isa 10:13 "By my own power and w I have won these wars.
11: 2 the Spirit of w and understanding, the Spirit of
19: 3 They will plead with their idols for w. They will
19:11 and wrong. Will they still boast of their w?
28:29 and he gives the farmer great w.
29:14 I will show that human w is foolish and even the
31: 2 In his w, the LORD will send great disaster;
33: 6 a rich store of salvation, w, and knowledge.
47:10 Your 'w' and 'knowledge' have caused you to turn
50: 4 Sovereign LORD has given me his words of w,
Jer 9:23 "Let not the wise man gloat in his w,
10:12 earth by his power, / and he preserves it by his w.
23: 5 He will be a King who rules with w. He will do
32:19 You have all w and do great and mighty miracles.
51:15 earth by his power, / and he preserves it by his w.
Eze 28: 4 With your w and understanding you have amassed
28: 5 Yes, your w has made you very rich, and your
28: 7 draw their swords against your marvelous w
28:12 You were the perfection of w and beauty.
28:17 You corrupted your w for the sake of your
Da 1:20 In all matters requiring w and balanced judgment,
2:14 Daniel handled the situation with w and discretion.
2:20 and ever, / for he alone has all w and power.
2:21 sets others on the throne. / He gives w to the wise
2:23 for you have given me w and strength.
5:11 and w as though he himself were a god.
5:14 you are filled with insight, understanding, and w.
Ob 1: 8 of Edom I will destroy everyone who has w
Mt 11:19 But w is shown to be right by what results from
12:42 because she came from a distant land to hear the w
13:54 "Where does he get his w and his miracles?
Mk 6: 2 "Where did he get all his w and the power to
Lk 1:17 will change disobedient minds to accept godly w."
2:40 He was filled with w beyond his years, and God
2:52 So Jesus grew both in height and in w, and he was
7:35 But w is shown to be right by the lives of those
11:31 because she came from a distant land to hear the w
11:49 This is what God in his w said about you: 'I will
21:15 and such w that none of your opponents will be
Ac 6: 3 and are full of the Holy Spirit and w.
6:10 None of them was able to stand against the w
7:10 God also gave Joseph unusual w so that Pharaoh
7:22 Moses was taught all the w of the Egyptians,
Ro 11:33 How great are his riches and w and knowledge!
1Co 1:19 As the Scriptures say, / "I will destroy human w
1:20 and has shown their w to be useless nonsense.
1:21 Since God in his w saw to it that the world would
never find him through human w,
1:22 they believe only what agrees with their own w.
1:24 mighty power of God and the wonderful w of God.
1:30 For our benefit God made Christ to be w itself.
2: 5 might trust the power of God rather than human w.
2: 6 mature Christians, I do speak with words of w,
2: 6 but not the kind of w that belongs to this world,
2: 7 the w we speak of is the secret w of God,
2:13 we tell you this, we do not use words of human w.
3:19 For the w of this world is foolishness to God.
7:25 But the Lord in his kindness has given me w that
2Co 1:12 on God's grace, not on our own earthly w.
Eph 1: 8 on us, along with all w and understanding.
1:17 to give you spiritual w and understanding,
3:10 God's purpose was to show his w in all its rich
3:14 When I think of the w and scope of God's plan,
Col 1: 9 and we ask him to make you wise with spiritual w.
1:28 and teach them with all the w God has given us,
2: 3 In him lie hidden all the treasures of w
2Ti 3:15 and they have given you the w to receive the
Jas 1: 5 If you need w—if you want to know what God
3:15 and selfishness are not God's kind of w.
3:17 But the w that comes from heaven is first of all
2Pe 3:15 Paul wrote to you with the w God gave him—
Rev 5:12 and w and strength / and honor and glory
7:12 They said, / "Amen! Blessing and glory and w
13:18 W is needed to understand this. Let the one who

WISDOM'S (1) [WISE]

Pr 4:11 I will teach you w ways and lead you in straight

WISE (235) [WISDOM, WISDOM'S, WISELY, WISER, WISEST]

AS WISE AS (3) 2Sa 14:20; 16:23; Eze 28:6

WISE MAN (6) 1Ki 2:9; Job 15:2; 17:10; Pr 24:5; Ecc 9:15; Jer 9:23

WISE MEN (23) Ge 41:8; Ex 7:11; 1Ki 4:30,30; Ezr 8:16; Job 15:18; 34:2; Isa 19:13; Jer 18:18; 49:7; 50:35; 51:57; Da 2:12,18,24,24,27,48; 4:6; 5:7,8,15; Mt 23:34

WISE SON (2) 1Ki 5:7; 2Ch 2:12

WISE WOMAN (2) 2Sa 20:16; Pr 14:1

WISE WOMEN (1) Jdg 5:29

Ge 3: 6 so fresh and delicious, and it would make her so w!
41: 8 and w men of Egypt and told them about his
Ex 7:11 Then Pharaoh called in his w men and magicians,
Dt 1:15 So I took the w and respected men you had
4: 6 'What other nation is as w and prudent as this!'
16:19 for bribes blind the eyes of the w and corrupt the
32:29 Oh, that they were w and could understand this!
Jdg 5:29 A reply comes from her w women, / and she
1Sa 3:19 and everything Samuel said was w and helpful.
2Sa 14:20 But you are as w as an angel of God, and you
16:23 For every word Ahithophel spoke seemed as w as
20:16 But a w woman in the city called out to Joab,
20:22 Then the woman went to the people with her w
1Ki 2: 9 You are a w man, and you will know how to
3:12 I will give you a w and understanding mind such
4:30 his wisdom exceeded that of all the w men of the
East and the w men of Egypt.
5: 7 "Praise the LORD for giving David a w son to be
10: 4 When the queen of Sheba realized how w Solomon
1Ch 27:32 David's uncle, was a w counselor to the king,
2Ch 2:12 He has given David a w son, gifted with skill
9: 3 When the queen of Sheba realized how w Solomon
Ezr 8:16 for Joiarib and Elnathan, who were very w men.
Job 5:13 He catches those who think they are w in their own
9: 4 For God is so w and so mighty. Who has ever
11:12 An empty-headed person won't become w any
15: 2 "You are supposed to be a w man, and yet you
15:18 And it is confirmed by the experience of w men
17:10 try again! But I will not find a w man among you.
22: 2 to God? Can even a w person be helpful to him?
26: 3 my stupidity! What w things you have said!
26: 4 Where have you gotten all these w sayings?
32: 9 But sometimes the elders are not w.
32:13 And don't tell me, 'He is too w for us. Only God
34: 2 "Listen to me, you w men. Pay attention, you who
34:34 people will tell me, and w people will hear me say,
37:24 People who are truly w show him reverence."
38:37 Who is w enough to count all the clouds? Who can
Ps 19: 7 LORD are trustworthy, / making w the simple.
49: 3 For my words are w, / and my thoughts are filled
49:10 Those who are w must finally die, / just like the
49:13 though they will be remembered as being so w.
51: 6 so you can teach me to be w in my inmost being.
107:43 Those who are w will take all this to heart;
119:24 Your decrees please me; / they give me w advice.
Pr 1: 2 and to help them understand w sayings.
1: 5 Let those who are w listen to these proverbs
1: 6 in these proverbs, parables, w sayings, and riddles.
1:23 the spirit of wisdom upon you and make you w.
2:11 W planning will watch over you.
3:35 The w inherit honor, but fools are put to shame!
4: 1 father's instruction. Pay attention and grow w,
4: 5 Learn to be w, and develop good judgment.

5: 1 to my wisdom; listen carefully to my w counsel.
6: 6 you lazybones. Learn from their ways and be w!
8:33 Listen to my counsel and be w. Don't ignore it.
9: 6 and begin to live; learn how to be w."
9: 8 But the w, when rebuked, will love you all the
9: 9 Teach the w, and they will be wiser.
9:12 If you become w, you will be the one to benefit.
10: 1 A w child brings joy to a father; a foolish child
10: 5 A w youth works hard all summer; a youth who
10: 8 The w are glad to be instructed, but babbling fools
10:13 W words come from the lips of people with
10:14 W people treasure knowledge, but the babbling of
10:23 a fool, while w conduct is a pleasure to the w.
10:31 The godly person gives w advice, but the tongue
11: 9 one's friends; w discernment rescues the godly.
11:14 Without w leadership, a nation falls; with many
11:29 only the wind. The fool will be a servant to the w.
11:30 life-giving fruit, and those who save lives are w.
12:15 they need no advice, but the w listen to others.
12:16 but a w person stays calm when insulted.
12:18 but the words of the w bring healing.
12:23 W people don't make a show of their knowledge,
13: 1 A w child accepts a parent's discipline; a young
13:10 leads to arguments; those who take advice are w.
13:14 The advice of the w is like a life-giving fountain;
13:16 W people think before they act; fools don't
13:20 Whoever walks with the w will become w;
14: 1 A w woman builds her house; a foolish woman
14: 3 but the words of the w keep them out of trouble.
14: 8 The w look ahead to see what is coming, but fools
14:16 The w are cautious and avoid danger; fools plunge
14:18 but the w person is crowned with knowledge.
14:24 Wealth is a crown for the w; the effort of fools
15: 2 The w person makes learning a joy; fools spout
15: 5 whoever learns from correction is w.
15: 7 Only the w can give good advice; fools cannot do
15:12 who rebuke them, so they stay away from the w.
15:14 A w person is hungry for truth, while the fool feeds
15:24 The path of the w leads to life above; they leave
15:31 you will be at home among the w.
15:33 Fear of the LORD teaches a person to be w;
16:14 deadly threat; the w do what they can to appease it.
16:21 The w are known for their understanding,
16:23 From a w mind comes w speech; the words of the
w are persuasive.
17: 2 A w slave will rule over the master's shameful
17:27 A truly w person uses few words; a person with
17:28 Even fools are thought to be w when they keep
19:20 instruction you can, and be w the rest of your life.
19:25 if you reprove the w, they will be all the wiser.
20: 1 Whoever is led astray by drink cannot be w.
20: 5 within a person's heart, the w will draw it out.
20:15 W speech is rarer and more valuable than gold
20:26 A w king finds the wicked, lays them out like
21:11 a w person learns from instruction.
21:20 The w have wealth and luxury, but fools spend
21:22 The w conquer the city of the strong and level the
21:30 Human plans, no matter how w or well advised,
22:17 Listen to the words of the w; apply your heart to
23:15 My child, how I will rejoice if you become w.
23:19 My child, listen and be w. Keep your heart on the
23:24 for joy. What a pleasure it is to have w children.
24: 5 A w man is mightier than a strong man, and a man
24: 6 So don't go to war without w guidance;
24:23 Here are some further sayings of the w: It is wrong
26: 5 or they will become w in their own estimation.
26:12 for fools than for people who think they are w.
26:16 themselves smarter than seven w counselors.
27:11 how happy I will be if you turn out to be w!
28: 2 But with w and knowledgeable leaders, there is
28: 7 Young people who obey the law are w; those who
28:11 Rich people picture themselves as w, but their real
29: 8 but those who are w will calm anger.
29: 9 If a w person takes a fool to court, there will be
29:11 vent to anger, but a w person quietly holds it back.
30:24 four things on earth that are small but unusually w:
31:26 When she speaks, her words are w, and kindness is
Ecc 2:14 For the w person sees, while the fool is blind.
2:14 Yet I saw that w and foolish people share the same
2:16 For the w person and the fool both die, and in the
2:19 And who can tell whether my successors will be w
4:13 is better to be a poor but w youth than to be an old
6: 8 do w people really have any advantage over fools?
6: 8 Do poor people gain anything by being w
7: 4 A w person thinks much about death,
7: 5 It is better to be criticized by a w person than to be
7: 7 Extortion turns w people into fools, and bribes
7:11 Being w is as good as being rich; in fact, it is
7:16 So don't be too good or too w! Why destroy
7:19 A w person is stronger than the ten leading citizens
7:23 I said to myself, "I am determined to be w."
8: 1 How wonderful to be w, to be able to analyze
8: 5 Those who are w will find a time and a way to do
9: 1 actions of godly and w people are in God's hands,
9:11 The w are often poor, and the skillful are not
9:15 w man living there who knew how to save the
9:16 those who are w will be despised if they are poor.
9:17 the quiet words of a w person are better than the
9:18 A w person can overcome weapons of war, but one
10: 2 The hearts of the w lead them to do right,
10:12 It is pleasant to listen to w words, but the speech of
12: 9 Because the Teacher was w, he taught the people
12:11 A w teacher's words spur students to action
12:11 The collected sayings of the w are like guidance
Isa 1:26 and w counselors like the ones you used to have.
5:21 is certain for those who think they are w
19:11 tell Pharaoh about their long line of w ancestors?
19:12 What has happened to your w counselors,
19:12 If they are so w, let them tell you what the LORD
19:13 The w men from Zoan are fools, and those from
44:25 I cause w people to give bad advice, thus proving
Jer 8: 8 "We are w because we have the law of the
8: 9 These w teachers will be shamed by exile for their
8: 9 the word of the LORD. Are they so w after all?
9:12 Who is w enough to understand all this? Who has
9:23 "Let not the w man gloat in his wisdom,
10: 7 Among all the w people of the earth and in all the
18:18 We have our own priests and w men and prophets.
26:17 Then some of the w old men stood and spoke to
49: 7 "Where are all the w men of Teman? Is there no
one left to give w counsel?
50:35 people of Babylon—her princes and w men, too.
50:36 And when it strikes her w counselors, they will
51:57 w men, rulers, captains, and warriors,"
Eze 27: 9 W old craftsmen from Gebal did all the caulking.
28: 6 Because you think you are as w as a god,
Da 2:12 and he sent out orders to execute all the w men of
2:18 executed along with the other w men of Babylon.
2:21 others on the throne. / He gives wisdom to the w
2:24 who had been ordered to execute the w men of
2:24 Daniel said to him, "Don't kill the w men.
2:27 "There are no w men, enchanters, magicians,
2:48 of Babylon, as well as chief over all his w men.
4: 6 So I issued an order calling in all the w men of
5: 7 He said to these w men of Babylon, "Whoever can
5: 8 But when all the king's w men came in, none of
5:15 My w men and enchanters have tried to read this
11:33 "Those who are w will give instruction to many.
11:35 And some who are w will fall victim to
12: 3 Those who are w will shine as bright as the sky,
12:10 Only those who are w will know what it means.
Hos 14: 9 Let those who are w understand these things.
Am 5:13 So those who are w will keep quiet, for it is an evil
Ob 1: 8 At that time not a single w person will be left in
Mic 4: 9 He is dead! Have you no w people to counsel you?
6: 9 Listen! Fear the LORD if you are w! His voice is
Mt 2: 1 About that time some w men from eastern lands
2: 7 Then Herod sent a private message to the w men,
2: 9 After this interview the w men went their way.
2:13 After the w men were gone, an angel of the Lord
2:16 Herod was furious when he learned that the w men
2:16 because the w men had told him the star first
7:24 who listens to my teaching and obeys me is w,
11:25 from those who think themselves so w and clever,
23:34 I will send you prophets and w men and teachers
25: 2 Five of them were foolish, and five were w.
25: 4 but the other five were w enough to take along
Lk 10:21 from those who think themselves so w and clever,
Ro 1:22 Claiming to be w, they became utter fools instead.
16:27 To God, who alone is w, be the glory forever
1Co 1:26 that few of you were w in the world's eyes,
1:27 in order to shame those who think they are w.
2: 4 I did not use w and persuasive speeches,
3:18 If you think you are w by this world's standards,
3:18 a fool so you can become w by God's standards.
3:19 "God catches those who think they are w
3:20 "The Lord knows the thoughts of the w,
4:10 Christ makes us look like fools, but you are so w!
6: 5 Isn't there anyone in all the church who is w
12: 8 To one person the Spirit gives the ability to give w
14:20 and w in understanding matters of this kind.
2Co 11:19 After all, you, who think you are so w,
Eph 5:15 how you live, not as fools but as those who are w.
Col 1: 9 and we ask him to make you w with spiritual
2:23 These rules may seem w because they require
3:16 their richness, live in your hearts and make you w.
Jas 3:13 If you are w and understand God's ways, live a life
3:13 about the good you do, then you will be truly w!
3:14 ambition in your hearts, don't brag about being w.

WISELY (9) [WISE]

2Ch 11:23 Rehoboam also w gave responsibilities to his other
Ps 2:10 Now then, you kings, act w! / Be warned,
36: 3 They refuse to act w or do what is good.
Col 4: 5 Live w among those who are not Christians,
1Ti 3: 2 live w, and have a good reputation.
Tit 1: 8 He must live w and be fair. He must live a devout
2: 2 to be worthy of respect, and to live w.
2: 5 to live w and be pure, to take care of their homes,
2: 6 encourage the young men to live w in all they do.

WISER (13) [WISE]

1Ki 4:31 He was w than anyone else, including Ethan the
10:23 and w than any other king in all the earth.
2Ch 9:22 and w than any other king in all the earth.
Job 35:11 Where is the one who makes us w than the animals
Ps 119:98 Your commands make me w than my enemies,
119:100 I am even w than my elders, / for I have kept your
Pr 1: 5 wise listen to these proverbs and become even w.
9: 9 Teach the wise, and they will be w.
19:25 if you reprove the wise, they will be all the w.
Ecc 1:16 I am w than any of the kings who ruled in
Eze 28: 3 You regard yourself as w than Daniel and think no
Da 2:30 because I am w than any living person that I know
1Co 1:25 This "foolish" plan of God is far w than the

WISEST (7) [WISE]

Ge 41:33 "My suggestion is that you find the w man in
41:39 the dreams to you, you are the w man in the land!
Pr 23: 9 breath on fools, for they will despise the w advice.
Ecc 8:17 Not even the w people know everything, even if
Jer 10: 8 The w of people who worship idols are stupid
Da 4:18 All the w men of my kingdom have failed me.
1Co 1:25 This "foolish" plan of God is far wiser than the w

WISH (46) [WISHED, WISHES, WISHING]

Ge 19: 8 Do with them as you w, but leave these men alone,
Lev 27:15 If you w to redeem the house, you must pay the
Nu 11:29 I w that all the LORD's people were prophets,
14: 2 "We w we had died in Egypt, or even here in the
18:31 your families may eat this food anywhere you w,
20: 3 "We w we had died in the LORD's presence with
Jos 17:18 Clear as much of the land as you w and live there.
Jdg 9:33 out against you, you can do with them as you w."
Ru 4: 4 to you about it so that you can redeem it if you w.
1Sa 11:10 come out to you, and you can do to us as you w."
24: 4 to do with as you w.' " Then David crept forward
2Sa 15: 4 I w I were the judge. Then people could bring their
24:22 "Take it, my lord, and use it as you w,"
1Ki 18:23 of Baal may choose whichever one they w
2Ki 5: 3 "I w my master would go to see the prophet in
1Ch 21:23 "Take it, my lord, and use it as you w,"
Ezr 4:13 But we w you to know that if this city is rebuilt
5: 8 We w to inform you that we went to the
Est 5: 7 Esther replied, "This is my request and deepest w.
6: 6 "Whom would the king w to honor more than
Job 6: 9 I w he would crush me. I w he would reach out his
hand and kill me.
14:13 "I w you would hide me with the dead and forget
Ps 55: 6 Oh, how I w I had wings like a dove; / then I
73: 7 have everything / their hearts could ever w for!
Isa 21:12 If you w to ask again, then come back and ask."
46:10 I plan will come to pass, for I do whatever I w.
Jer 3:16 "you will no longer w for 'the good old days'
8: 3 w to die rather than live where I will send them.
40:10 Settle in any town you w, and live off the land.
Da 4:19 how I w the events foreshadowed in this dream
Zec 10:12 and they will go wherever they w by my authority.
Mal 1:10 "I w that someone among you would shut the
Lk 12:49 and I w that my task were already completed!
19:42 "I w that even today you would find the way of
Jn 8:50 And though I have no w to glorify myself,
Ac 17:23 who he is, and now I w to tell you about him.
1Co 4: 8 I w you really were on your thrones already,
7: 7 I w everyone could get along without marrying,
14: 5 I w you all had the gift of speaking in tongues,
14: 5 but even more I w you were all able to prophesy.
Gal 3:12 "If you w to find life by obeying the law,
4:20 How I w I were there with you right now, so that I
5:12 I only w that those troublemakers who want to
Rev 3:15 neither hot nor cold. I w you were one or the other!
11: 6 kind of plague upon the earth as often as they w.

WISHED (4) [WISH]

Est 1: 8 But those who w could have as much as they
Jnh 4: 8 down on his head until he grew faint and w to die.
Lk 23:25 he delivered Jesus over to them to do as they w.
Ac 5: 4 property was yours to sell or not sell, as you w.

WISHES (10) [WISH]

2Ki 20:12 of Babylon, sent Hezekiah his best w and a gift,
Est 6: 7 So he replied, "If the king w to honor someone,
6: 9 'This is what happens to those the king w to
6:11 "This is what happens to those the king w to
Ps 115: 3 our God is in the heavens, / and he does as he w.
Isa 39: 1 of Babylon, sent Hezekiah his best w and a gift.
Ro 16:21 and Sosipater, my relatives, send you their good w.
1Co 1:31 the Scriptures say, / "The person who w to boast
7:39 she is free to marry whomever she w,
2Co 10:17 the Scriptures say, / "The person who w to boast

WISHING (2) [WISH]

Est 9:30 letters w peace and security were sent to the Jews
Am 5:18 But you have no idea what you are w for. That day

WIST [KJV] See KNOW(ING), REALIZE, UNINTENTIONAL(LY)

WIT [KJV] See KNOW, LEARN, SEE

WITCH [KJV] See SORCERESS, SORCERY

WITCHCRAFT (9) [WITCHES']

Lev 19:26 of its blood. "Do not practice fortune-telling or w.
Dt 18:10 or allow them to interpret omens, or engage in w,
1Sa 15:23 Rebellion is as bad as the sin of w,
2Ki 9:22 peace as long as the idolatry and w of your mother,
2Ch 33: 6 He practiced sorcery, divination, and w, and he
Isa 47: 9 will come upon you, despite all your w and magic.
Mic 5:12 I will put an end to all w; there will be no more
Rev 9:21 or their w or their immorality or their thefts.
21: 8 and the immoral, and those who practice w,

WITCHES' (1) [WITCHCRAFT]

Isa 57: 3 come here, you w children, you offspring of

WITH (5639) See Index of Articles, Etc.

WITHDRAW (4) [WITHDRAWN, WITHDREW]

Job 34:14 God were to take back his spirit and w his breath,
Ps 66:20 and did not w his unfailing love from me.
Jer 21: 2 Perhaps he will force Nebuchadnezzar to w his
Da 11:30 will scare him off, and he will w and return home.

WITHDRAWN (4) [WITHDRAW]

Ps 85: 3 You have w your fury. / You have ended your
La 2: 3 The Lord has w his protection as the enemy
Hos 5: 6 will not find him, because he has w from them,
Ro 11:29 For God's gifts and his call can never be w.

WITHDREW (10) [WITHDRAW]

Ex 32:14 So the LORD w his threat and didn't bring
1Ki 15:21 his project of fortifying Ramah and w to Tirzah.
2Ki 3:27 so they w and returned to their own land.
2Ch 24:25 The Arameans w, leaving Joash severely wounded.
32:31 God w from Hezekiah in order to test him and to
Isa 57:17 I w myself from them, but they went right on
Jer 37: 5 about it, they w from their siege of Jerusalem.
Eze 20:22 I w my judgment against them to protect the honor
Lk 5:16 But Jesus often w to the wilderness for prayer.
Ac 22:29 w when they heard he was a Roman citizen,

WITHER (18) [WITHERED, WITHERING, WITHERS]

Job 8:12 still flowering, not ready to be cut, they begin to w.
14: 2 a flower, we blossom for a moment and then w.
18:16 Their roots will dry up, and their branches will w.
Ps 1: 3 Their leaves never w, / and in all they do,
37: 2 fade away. / Like springtime flowers, they soon w.
90: 7 We w beneath your anger; / we are overwhelmed
Isa 1:30 You will w away like an oak or garden without
5:24 Their roots will rot and their flowers w, for they
19: 7 All the greenery along the riverbank will w
24: 4 The earth dries up, the crops w, the skies refuse to
51:12 mere humans, who w like the grass and disappear?
64: 6 Like autumn leaves, we w and fall. And our sins,
Eze 17: 9 I will cut off its fruit and let its leaves w and die.
17:10 it will w away completely when the east wind
17:24 It is I who makes the green tree w and gives new
Hos 8: 7 The stalks of wheat w, producing no grain. And if
Hag 1:11 a drought to w the grain and grapes and olives
Mt 21:20 and asked, "How did the fig tree w so quickly?"

WITHERED (17) [WITHER]

Ge 41: 6 but these were shriveled and w by the east wind.
41:23 Then out of the same stalk came seven w heads,
41:24 And the w heads swallowed up the plump ones!
41:27 and the seven w heads of grain represent seven
Job 24:24 will be gone like all others, w like heads of grain.
Ps 90: 6 and flourishes, / but by evening it is dry and w.
102: 4 My heart is sick, w like grass, / and I have lost my
Ecc 12: 5 of heights and of falling, white-haired and w,
Isa 34: 4 the sky, just as w leaves and fruit fall from a tree.
Jer 12: 4 Even the grass in the fields has w. The wild
Joel 1:12 The grapevines and the fig trees have all w.
Am 4: 7 Rain fell on one field, while another field w away.
Jnh 4: 7 stem of the plant, so that it soon died and w away.
Mt 21:19 fruit again!" And immediately the fig tree w up.
Mk 11:20 the disciples noticed it was w from the roots.
11:21 "Look, Teacher! The fig tree you cursed has w!"
Lk 8: 6 but soon it w and died for lack of moisture.

WITHERING (2) [WITHER]

Ps 31: 9 of my tears. / My body and soul are w away.
102:11 swiftly as the evening shadows. / I am w like grass.

WITHERS (7) [WITHER]

Isa 40: 7 The grass w, and the flowers fade beneath the
40: 8 The grass w, and the flowers fade, but the word of
40:24 when he blows on them and their work w.
Am 1: 2 All the grass on Mount Carmel w and dies."
Jn 15: 6 me is thrown away like a useless branch and w.
Jas 1:11 the grass; the flower w, and its beauty fades away.
1Pe 1:24 The grass w, / and the flowers fall away.

WITHHELD (6) [WITHHOLD]

Ge 22:12 You have not w even your beloved son from me."
22:16 obeyed me and have not w even your beloved son,
Am 4: 7 I sent rain on one town but w it from another.
Hag 1:10 That is why the heavens have w the dew and the earth has w its crops.
2Co 6:12 but because you have w your love from us.

WITHHOLD (3) [WITHHELD]

Ps 84:11 and glory. / No good thing will the LORD w
Pr 3:27 Do not w good from those who deserve it when it's
Jer 26: 3 Then I will be able to w the disaster I am ready to

WITHIN (142) [IN]

Ge 18:24 Suppose you find fifty innocent people there w the
40:13 W three days Pharaoh will take you out of prison
48: 6 The land they inherit will be w the territories of
Ex 13: 7 or anywhere w the borders of your land during this
16:10 W the guiding cloud, they could see the awesome
40: 3 and install the inner curtain to enclose the Ark w
Lev 6:16 and eaten in a sacred place w the courtyard of the
6:26 a sacred place w the courtyard of the Tabernacle.
25:30 But if it is not redeemed w a year, then the house w the walled city will become the
25:32 they have sold w the cities belonging to them.
25:33 all houses w the Levitical cities—must be returned
Nu 18: 5 "You yourselves must perform the sacred duties w
18: 7 with the altar and everything w the inner curtain.
36: 6 as long as it is w their own ancestral tribe.
36: 8 in line to inherit property must marry w their tribe,
36:12 their inheritance of land remained w their ancestral
Dt 12:14 so only at the place the LORD will choose w one
22:23 intercourse with her. If this happens w a town,
32:34 these things, / sealing them away w my treasury.
Jos 17: 2 to the remaining families w the tribe of Manasseh:
17:11 The following towns w the territory of Issachar
19: 9 So the tribe of Simeon received an inheritance w
19:41 The towns w Dan's inheritance included Zorah,
21: 4 who were members of the Kohathite clan w the
21:10 who were members of the Kohathite clan w the
21:27 of Gershon, another clan w the tribe of Levi,
21:41 and pasturelands w Israelite territory given to the
22:14 and each a leader w the family divisions of Israel.
Jdg 9:46 they took refuge w the walls of the temple of
20:16 could sling a rock and hit a target w a hairsbreadth,
2Sa 20: 4 Amasa to mobilize the army of Judah w three days
1Ki 6:23 W the inner sanctuary Solomon placed two
9:18 Baalath, and Tamar in the desert, w his land.
Ezr 10: 8 Those who failed to come w three days would,
10: 9 W three days, all the people of Judah
Job 6: 4 He has sent his poisoned arrows deep w my spirit.
20:14 the food he has eaten turns sour w him,
28: 8 for they are deep w the mines. No wild animal has
32: 8 Surely it is God's Spirit w people, the breath of the Almighty w them, that makes
32:18 and full of words, and the spirit w me urges me on.
37: 1 "My heart pounds as I think of this. It leaps w me.
Ps 7: 9 For you look deep w the mind and heart,
22:14 out of joint. / My heart is like wax, / melting w me.
31:10 drained my strength; / I am wasting away from w.
36: 1 Sin whispers to the wicked, deep w their hearts.
38: 7 A raging fever burns w me, / and my health is
39: 2 the turmoil w me grew to the bursting point.
39: 3 My thoughts grew hot w me / and began to burn,
45:13 The bride, a princess, waits w her chamber,
51:10 a clean heart, O God. / Renew a right spirit w me.
55:10 but the real danger is wickedness w the city.
55:15 them alive, / for evil makes its home w them.
69: 9 Passion for your house burns w me, / so those who
78:28 He caused the birds to fall w their camp / and all
122: 7 O Jerusalem, may there be peace w your walls
128: 3 be like a fruitful vine, / flourishing w your home.
131: 2 Yes, like a small child is my soul w me.
147:13 of your gates / and blessed your children w you.
Pr 3: 3 like a necklace; write them deep w your heart.
4:21 my words. Let them penetrate deep w your heart,
7: 3 as a reminder. Write them deep w your heart.
20: 5 Though good advice lies deep w a person's heart,
22:18 For it is good to keep these sayings deep w
28: 2 When there is moral rot w a nation, its government
SS 5: 4 to unlatch the door, and my heart thrilled w me.
Isa 7: 8 w sixty-five years it will be crushed
8: 4 This name prophesies that w a couple of years,
16:14 the LORD says, "W three years, without fail,
21:16 "But w a year," says the Lord, "all the glory of
49: 1 my birth; from w the womb he called me by name.
51:16 in your mouth and hidden you safely w my hand.
56: 5 in my house, w my walls—a memorial and a name
62: 9 W the courtyards of the Temple, you yourselves
Jer 4:19 in pain! My heart pounds w me! I cannot be still.
22: 6 you deserted, with no one living w your walls.
28: 3 W two years, I will bring back all the Temple
28:11 "The LORD has promised that w two years he
La 2:20 and prophets die w the Lord's Temple?
3:55 on your name, LORD, from deep w the well,
Eze 1:16 wheel had a second wheel turning crosswise w it.
10:10 wheel had a second wheel turning crosswise w it.
11:19 singleness of heart and put a new spirit w them.
22: 6 "Every leader in Israel who lives w your walls is
22:11 W your walls live men who commit adultery with
28:18 So I brought fire from w you, and it consumed
28:23 and your people will lie slaughtered w your walls.
43: 6 And I heard someone speaking to me from w the
45: 3 W the larger sacred area, measure out a portion of
45: 3 W it the sanctuary of the Most Holy Place will be
45: 4 their homes, and my Temple will be located w it.
47:21 "Divide the land w these boundaries among the
47:23 All these immigrants are to be given land w the
Da 5:11 There is a man in your kingdom who has w him
5:14 I have heard that you have the spirit of the gods w
11:17 in order to overthrow the kingdom from w,
Hos 11: 8 My heart is torn w me, and my compassion
Zec 12: 1 of the earth, and formed the spirit w humans.
Mt 1:20 For the child w her has been conceived by the
Mk 7:21 For from w, out of a person's heart, come evil
7:23 All these vile things come from w; they are what
Lk 1:41 of Mary's greeting, Elizabeth's child leaped w her,
13:28 and all the prophets w the Kingdom of God,
24:33 And w the hour they were on their way back to
Jn 2:17 "Passion for God's house burns w me."
4:14 It becomes a perpetual spring w them, giving them
5:42 because I know you don't have God's love w you.
6:53 his blood, you cannot have eternal life w you.
6:61 Jesus knew w himself that his disciples were
7:38 that rivers of living water will flow out from w."
Ac 16:18 that he turned and spoke to the demon w her.
19:12 and any evil spirits w them came out.
Ro 1:27 suffered w themselves the penalty they so richly
2:15 They demonstrate that God's law is written w
7: 5 by our old nature, sinful desires were at work w us,
7: 8 and aroused all kinds of forbidden desires w me!
7:20 not really the one doing it; the sin w me is doing it.
7:23 But there is another law at work w me that is at
7:23 and makes me a slave to the sin that is still w me.
8:10 Since Christ lives w you, even though your body
8:11 your mortal body by this same Spirit living w you.
8:23 although we have the Holy Spirit w us as a
10: 8 is the message we preach—is already w easy reach.
2Co 3:18 And as the Spirit of the Lord works w us,
4: 7 this light and power that now shine w us—
6: 9 We have been beaten w an inch of our lives.
10:13 Our goal is to stay w the boundaries of God's plan
Eph 3:20 By his mighty power at work w us, he is able to
5: 9 For this light w you produces only what is good
Php 1: 6 sure that God, who began the good work w you,
Col 1:29 as I depend on Christ's mighty power that works w
3: 5 to death the sinful, earthly things lurking w you.
3:10 about Christ, who created this new nature w you.
2Ti 1:14 With the help of the Holy Spirit who lives w us,
Jas 4: 1 Isn't it the whole army of evil desires at war w
4: 5 whom God has placed w us, jealously longs for us
1Pe 1:11 They wondered what the Spirit of Christ w them
3: 4 be known for the beauty that comes from w,
1Jn 2:27 have received the Holy Spirit, and he lives w you,
3:15 that murderers don't have eternal life w them.
Jude 1: 6 And I remind you of the angels who did not stay w

WITHOUT (310)

Ge 19: 3 complete with fresh bread made w yeast.
29:15 "You shouldn't work for me w pay just
31:32 relatives of ours, I will give it back w question."
31:42 you would have sent me off w a penny to my
34:25 took their swords, entered the town w opposition,
37:22 That way he will die w our having to touch him."
41:44 or a foot in the entire land of Egypt w your
43:10 by this time if you had let him come w delay."
44:30 my lord, I cannot go back to my father w the boy.
50: 5 After his burial is complete, I will return w delay."
Ex 9:26 The only spot in all Egypt w hail that day was the
12: 8 lamb with bitter herbs and bread made w yeast.
12:15 seven days, you may eat only bread made w yeast.
12:18 Only bread w yeast may be eaten from the evening
12:34 took with them their bread dough made w yeast.
12:39 It was made w yeast because the people were
13: 6 For seven days you will eat only bread w yeast.
13: 7 Eat only bread w yeast during those seven days.
15:22 They traveled in this desert for three days w water.
16:24 was wholesome and good, w maggots or odor.
21:11 she may leave as a free woman w making any
23:15 For seven days you are to eat bread made w yeast,
34:20 No one is allowed to appear before me w a gift.
Lev 2: 4 choice flour mixed with olive oil but w any yeast.
5: 8 its neck but w severing its head from the body.
6:16 be baked w yeast and eaten in a sacred place
7:12 all made w yeast and soaked with olive oil.
8:26 w yeast that was placed in the LORD's presence.
13:36 even w checking for yellow hair.
15:11 If the man touches you w first rinsing his hands,
22:14 "Anyone who eats the sacred offerings w realizing
23: 6 time all the bread you eat must be made w yeast.
25:31 house in a village—a settlement w fortified walls
26: 6 in the land, and you will be able to sleep w fear.
Nu 6:14 a one-year-old male lamb w defect for a burnt
6:14 a one-year-old female lamb w defect for a sin offering, a ram w defect for a peace offering,
6:15 a basket of bread made w yeast—cakes of choice
6:17 along with the basket of bread made w yeast.
6:19 one cake made w yeast, and one wafer made w yeast,
9:11 that time with bitter herbs and bread made w yeast.
27: 3 "Our father died in the wilderness w leaving any
27:17 the LORD will not be like sheep w a shepherd."
29: 7 the Day of Atonement, the people must go w food,
35:22 " 'But suppose someone pushes another person w
Dt 4:42 w having any previous hostility could flee for
15:10 Give freely w begrudging it, and the LORD your
16: 3 Eat it with bread made w yeast. For seven days eat only bread made w yeast,
19: 4 "If someone accidentally kills a neighbor w
25: 5 on the same property and one of them dies w a son,
25:12 her hand must be cut off w pity.
26:16 You must commit yourself to them w reservation.
28:59 These plagues will be intense and w relief,
32:12 guided them; / they lived w any foreign gods.
32:20 are a twisted generation, / children w integrity.
32:28 the people are foolish, w understanding.
Jos 2:22 but they finally returned to the city w success.
Jdg 6:19 half a bushel of flour he baked some bread w yeast.
12: 3 So I risked my life and went to battle w you,
20:16 and hit a target within a hairsbreadth, w missing.
Ru 1: 5 This left Naomi alone, w her husband or sons.
2:15 "Let her gather grain right among the sheaves w
1Sa 2:11 and Hannah returned home to Ramah w Samuel.
7: 6 They also went w food all day and confessed that
14:32 and calves, but they ate them w draining the blood.
26:12 and Abishai got away w anyone seeing them
30: 2 and everyone else but w killing anyone.
2Sa 12:16 He went w food and lay all night on the bare
14:28 Absalom lived in Jerusalem for two years w
17:20 Absalom's men looked for them w success
1Ki 1:27 Has my lord really done this w letting any of his
6: 7 so the entire structure was built w the sound of
15:22 requiring that everyone, w exception, help to carry
18:23 it on the wood of their altar, but w setting fire to it.
22:17 on the mountains, like sheep w a shepherd.
2Ki 4:39 and put them into the kettle w realizing they were
5:20 let this Aramean get away w accepting his gifts.
10:11 and priests. So Ahab was left w a single survivor.
18:25 do you think we have invaded your land w the
1Ch 2:30 were Seled and Appaim. Seled died w children,
2:32 named Jether and Jonathan. Jether died w children,
23:29 the wafers made w yeast, the cakes cooked in olive
24:31 by means of sacred lots, w regard to age or rank.
25: 8 w regard to whether they were young or old,

26:13 w regard to age or training, for it was all decided
29:15 on earth are like a shadow, gone so soon w a trace.
2Ch 2:8 for I know that your men are w equal at cutting
15:3 For a long time, Israel was w the true God, w a priest to teach them, and w God's law.
18:16 on the mountains, like sheep w a shepherd.
28:9 But you have gone too far, killing them w mercy,
Ezr 6:8 You must pay the full construction costs w delay
6:9 And w fail, provide them with the wheat, salt,
8:29 w an ounce lost, to the leading priests, the Levites,
Est 4:11 w being invited is doomed to die unless the king
Job 1:9 "Yes, Job fears God, but not w good reason!
2:3 even though you persuaded me to harm him w
4:20 by evening they are dead, gone forever w a trace.
5:9 to understand. He performs miracles w number.
6:13 I am utterly helpless, w any chance of success.
6:14 but you have accused me w the slightest fear of the
7:6 shuttle flying back and forth. They end w hope.
9:5 "W warning, he moves the mountains,
9:10 to understand. He performs miracles w number.
9:17 For he attacks me w reason, and he multiplies my wounds w cause.
9:35 Then I could speak to him w fear, but I cannot do
12:24 and he leaves them wandering in a wasteland w a
12:25 They grope in the darkness w a light. He makes
16:13 and his arrows pierced me w mercy.
21:10 to breed. Their cows bear calves w miscarriage.
22:9 You must have sent widows away w helping them
24:7 they lie naked in the cold, w clothing or covering.
24:10 The poor must go about naked, w any clothing.
24:11 They press out olive oil w being allowed to taste it,
27:6 I will maintain my innocence w wavering.
27:22 It whirls down on them w mercy. They struggle to
30:28 I walk in gloom, w sunlight. I stand in the public
31:19 I saw someone who was homeless and w clothes,
32:19 I am like a wine cask w a vent. My words are
34:20 pass away; the mighty are removed w human hand.
34:24 He brings the mighty to ruin w asking anyone,
34:35 'Job speaks w knowledge; his words lack insight.'
36:26 what we can understand. His years are w number.
Ps 1:3 the riverbank, / bearing fruit each season w fail.
7:4 a friend / or plundered my enemy w cause,
17:10 They are w pity. / Listen to their boasting.
19:3 They speak w a sound or a word; / their voice is
26:1 I have trusted in the LORD w wavering.
35:19 Don't let those who hate me w cause / gloat over
69:4 Those who hate me w cause / are more numerous
69:4 are doing so w cause. / They attack me with lies,
77:1 I cry out to God w holding back. / Oh, that God
90:2 and the world, / you are God, w beginning or end.
119:60 I will hurry, w lingering, / to obey your commands.
119:86 Protect me from those who hunt me down w cause.
119:161 Powerful people harass me w cause, / but my heart
141:7 so the bones of the wicked will be scattered w a
Pr 3:24 You can lie down w fear and enjoy pleasant
9:4 the simple. To those w good judgment, she says,
9:16 the simple. To those w good judgment, she says,
11:14 W wise leadership, a nation falls; with many
16:30 they plot evil; w a word, they plan their mischief.
19:2 Zeal w knowledge is not good; a person who
20:18 don't go to war w the advice of others.
24:6 So don't go to war w wise guidance;
25:28 A person w self-control is as defenseless as a city
29:20 a fool than for someone who speaks w thinking.
Ecc 4:8 of a man who is all alone, w a child or a brother,
12:5 and withered, dragging along w any sexual desire.
Isa 1:6 infected wounds—w any ointments or bandages.
1:30 will wither away like an oak or garden w water.
5:27 They will run w stopping for rest or sleep.
13:14 hunted deer, wandering like sheep w a shepherd.
16:14 now the LORD says, "Within three years, w fail,
22:3 All your leaders flee. They surrender w resistance.
30:2 For w consulting me, you have gone down to
36:10 do you think we have invaded your land w the
50:10 w a ray of light, trust in the LORD and rely on
52:3 Now I can redeem you w paying for you."
52:4 Now they have been oppressed w cause by
Jer 18:21 Let their wives become widows w any children!
20:16 cities of old that the LORD overthrew w mercy.
21:7 He will slaughter them all w mercy, pity,
38:27 and they left w finding out the truth.
44:19 w our husbands knowing it and helping us?
44:22 desolate ruin w a single inhabitant—as it is today.
46:5 The bravest of its fighting men run w a backward
46:19 will be destroyed, w a single person living there.
47:3 w a backward glance at their helpless children.
49:31 "They live alone in the desert w walls or gates.
51:29 Babylon will be left desolate w a single inhabitant.
51:37 and contempt, w a single person living there.
La 2:2 W mercy the Lord has destroyed every home in
2:17 He has destroyed Jerusalem w mercy and caused
2:21 them in your anger, slaughtering them w mercy.
3:37 Can anything happen w the Lord's permission?
3:43 chased us down, and slaughtered us w mercy.
4:18 We couldn't go into the streets w danger to our
Eze 1:9 were able to fly in any direction w turning around.
1:12 and they moved straight forward in all directions w
1:17 directions they faced, w turning as they moved.
10:11 directions they faced, w turning as they moved.
13:18 Do you think you can trap others w bringing
14:23 these things are not being done to Israel w cause,
16:15 "But you thought you could get along w me,
18:8 And suppose he grants loans w interest, stays away
22:24 like an uncleared wilderness or a desert w rain.
34:5 So my sheep have been scattered w a shepherd.
34:25 in the wildest places and sleep in the woods w fear.
45:21 Only bread w yeast may be eaten during that time.
45:23 seven young bulls and seven rams w any defects.
46:15 be given as a daily sacrifice every morning w fail.
47:5 and the river was too deep to cross w swimming.
47:12 There will be a new crop every month, w fail!
Da 2:35 and the wind blew them all away w a trace.
8:25 them off guard. W warning he will destroy them.
11:24 W warning he will enter the richest areas of the
Hos 1:7 I will personally free them from their enemies w
3:4 This illustrates that Israel will be a long time w a king or prince, and w sacrifices, temple, priests,
Am 3:3 Can two people walk together w agreeing on the
3:4 Does a lion ever roar in a thicket w first finding a
3:4 Does a young lion growl in its den w first catching
5:20 be a dark and hopeless day, w a ray of joy or hope.
Jnh 3:5 they decided to go w food and wear sackcloth to
Na 3:9 the source of her strength, which seemed w limit.
Zec 10:2 lost sheep, w a shepherd to protect and guide them.
11:5 The buyers will slaughter their sheep w remorse.
Mt 9:36 to go for help. They were like sheep w a shepherd.
10:29 can fall to the ground w your Father knowing it.
12:29 man's house and rob him w first tying him up.
13:34 he never spoke to them w using such parables.
22:12 'how is it that you are here w wedding clothes?'
22:24 "Teacher, Moses said, 'If a man dies w children,
22:25 The oldest married and then died w children,
22:26 This brother also died w children, and the wife was
24:32 you know w being told that summer is near.
Mk 3:27 man's house and rob him w first tying him up.
4:27 the seeds sprouted and grew w the farmer's help,
6:19 but w Herod's approval she was powerless.
6:34 because they were like sheep w a shepherd.
7:5 For they eat w first performing the hand-washing
8:3 And if I send them home w feeding them, they will
12:19 leaving a wife w children, his brother should marry
12:20 oldest of them married and then died w children.
12:21 the next brother married her and died w children.
13:28 you know w being told that summer is near.
13:36 Don't let him find you sleeping when he arrives w
14:58 I will build another, made w human hands.' "
Lk 1:74 from our enemies, / so we can serve God w fear,
4:35 then it left him w hurting him further.
6:49 is like a person who builds a house w a foundation.
11:38 w first performing the ceremonial washing
11:44 People walk over them w knowing the corruption
14:28 For who would begin construction of a building w
14:31 to war w first sitting down with his counselors
14:33 So no one can become my disciple w giving up
20:29 The oldest married and then died w children.
21:30 you know w being told that summer is near.
22:2 But they wanted to kill him w starting a riot,
Jn 3:5 no one can enter the Kingdom of God w being
3:34 for God's Spirit is upon him w measure or limit.
5:30 But I do nothing w consulting the Father. I judge
15:25 what the Scriptures said: 'They hated me w cause.'
Ac 4:21 because they didn't know how to punish them w
5:26 Temple guards and arrested them, but w violence,
9:9 And all that time he went w food and water.
10:20 Go down and go with them w hesitation. All is
14:17 but he never left himself w a witness. There were
16:37 "They have publicly beaten us w trial and jailed
17:23 You have been worshiping him w knowing who he
25:16 that Roman law does not convict people w a trial.
25:27 emperor w specifying the charges against him!"
Ro 2:19 light for people who are lost in darkness w God.
10:15 how will anyone go and tell them w being sent?
1Co 4:8 are already rich! W us you have become kings!
4:11 and thirsty, w enough clothes to keep us warm.
7:7 I wish everyone could get along w marrying,
7:31 good use of them w becoming attached to them,
9:15 die than lose my distinction of preaching w charge.
9:18 preaching the Good News w expense to anyone,
11:5 she prays or prophesies w a covering on her head,
11:13 Is it right for a woman to pray to God in public w
11:21 hurry to eat your own meal w sharing with others.
13:2 it move, w love I would be no good to anybody.
15:10 out his special favor on me—and not w results.
2Co 5:3 For we will not be spirits w bodies, but we will put
6:5 endured sleepless nights, and gone w food.
7:10 But sorrow w repentance is the kind that results in
11:7 Good News to you w expecting anything in return?
11:23 been whipped times w number, and faced death
11:27 been hungry and thirsty and have gone w food.
11:27 with cold, w enough clothing to keep me warm.
11:29 Who is weak w my feeling that weakness? Who is
Eph 1:4 us in Christ to be holy and w fault in his eyes.
2:12 You lived in this world w God and w hope.
5:27 present her to himself as a glorious church w a spot
5:27 Instead, she will be holy and w fault.
Col 1:22 and blameless as you stand before him w a single
2Th 3:8 We never accepted food from anyone w paying for
1Ti 3:16 W question, this is the great mystery of our faith:
5:21 and the holy angels to obey these instructions w
Phm 1:14 But I didn't want to do anything w your consent.
Heb 6:16 them to it. And w any question that oath is binding.
7:7 And w question, the person who has the power to
9:22 W the shedding of blood, there is no forgiveness of
10:23 W wavering, let us hold tightly to the hope we say
10:28 was put to death w mercy on the testimony of two
11:5 faith that Enoch was taken up to heaven w dying—
11:6 you see, it is impossible to please God w faith.
11:8 He went w knowing where he was going.
11:13 All these faithful ones died w receiving what God
13:2 done this have entertained angels w realizing it!
Jas 2:26 Just as the body is dead w a spirit, so also faith is dead w good deeds.
1Pe 3:6 You are her daughters when you do what is right w
2Pe 2:10 daring even to scoff at the glorious ones w
Jude 1:12 They are like clouds blowing over dry land w
1:12 They are like trees w fruit at harvesttime.
Rev 2:3 You have patiently suffered for me w quitting.
13:17 no one could buy or sell anything w that mark,
16:12 could march their armies westward w hindrance.
18:23 Her nights will be dark, w a single lamp.
21:6 will give the springs of the water of life w charge!
22:17 them come and drink the water of life w charge.

WITHS [KJV] See BOWSTRINGS

WITHSTOOD (1)

Isa 7:1 The city w the attack, however, and was not taken.

WITLESS (1) [WITS]

Hos 7:11 w doves, first calling to Egypt, then flying to

WITNESS (63) [EYEWITNESS, EYEWITNESSES, WITNESSED, WITNESSES]

FAITHFUL WITNESS (5) Ps 89:37; Jer 42:5; Rev 1:5; 2:13; 22:20

FALSE WITNESS (8) Pr 6:19; 12:17; 14:5,25; 19:5,9; 21:28; Mt 26:60

Ge 31:47 They named it "W Pile," which is
31:48 "This pile of stones will stand as a w to remind us
31:52 stand between us as a w of our vows. I will not
Ex 23:1 with evil people by telling lies on the w stand.
23:2 When you are on the w stand, do not be swayed in
Nu 5:13 but there is no w since she was not caught in the
35:30 be executed, but only if there is more than one w.
35:30 be put to death on the testimony of only one w.
Dt 17:6 a person to death on the testimony of only one w.
19:15 anyone of a crime on the testimony of just one w.
19:16 If a malicious w comes forward and accuses
30:19 call on heaven and earth to w the choice you make.
31:19 to sing it, so it may serve as a w against them.
31:26 so it may serve as a w against the people of Israel.
31:28 and call heaven and earth to w against them.
Jos 22:34 people of Reuben and Gad named the altar "W,"
22:34 "It is a w between us and them that the LORD is
24:27 It will be a w to testify against you if you go back
Jdg 11:10 "The LORD is our w," the leaders replied.
1Ch 28:8 So now, with God as our w, I give you this charge
Job 10:17 Again and again you w against me. You pour out
16:19 Even now my w is in heaven. My advocate is there
Ps 89:37 as eternal as the moon, / my faithful w in the sky!"
Pr 6:19 a false w who pours out lies, / a person who sows
12:17 An honest w tells the truth; a false w tells lies.
14:5 A truthful w does not lie; a false w breathes lies.
14:25 A truthful w saves lives, but a false w is a traitor.
19:5 A false w will not go unpunished, nor will a liar
19:9 A false w will not go unpunished, and a liar will be
19:28 A corrupt w makes a mockery of justice; the mouth
21:28 A false w will be cut off, but an attentive w will be allowed to speak.
Isa 19:20 and a w to the LORD Almighty in the land of
30:8 then stand until the end of time as a w to Israel's
55:4 He displayed my power by being my w and a
Jer 29:23 in my name. I am a w to this," says the LORD.
42:5 "May the LORD your God be a faithful w
Am 3:9 and w the scandalous spectacle of all Israel's
Mic 6:1 and hills be called to w your complaints.
Mal 3:5 I will be a ready w against all sorcerers
Mt 10:18 to tell them about me—yes, to w to the world.
26:60 they found many who agreed to give false w,
Jn 1:8 was not the light; he was only a w to the light.
5:36 But I have a greater w than John—my teachings
8:17 agree about something, their w is accepted as fact.
8:18 I am one w, and my Father who sent me is the
Ac 1:22 Whoever is chosen will join us as a w of Jesus'
4:33 And the apostles gave powerful w to the
14:17 but he never left himself without a w. There were
22:20 And when your w Stephen was killed, I was
26:16 to you to appoint you as my servant and my w.
2Co 1:23 Now I call upon God as my w that I am telling the
1Th 2:5 And God is our w that we were not just pretending
1Pe 5:1 am an elder and a w to the sufferings of Christ.
Rev 1:5 Jesus Christ, who is the faithful w to these things,
2:13 my faithful w, was martyred among you by Satan's
3:14 the faithful and true w, the ruler of God's creation:
6:9 the word of God and for being faithful in their w.
19:10 For the essence of prophecy is to give a clear w for
22:20 He who is the faithful w to all these things says,

WITNESSED (6) [WITNESS]

Lev 5:1 are called to testify about something they have w,
1Sa 20:23 our promises to each other, for he has w them."
Jer 32:44 and sold—deeds signed and sealed and w—
Mal 2:14 Because the LORD w the vows you and your
Rev 12:1 Then I w in heaven an event of great significance.
12:3 Suddenly, I w in heaven another significant event.

WITNESSES (50) [WITNESS]

Ex 20:22 You are w that I have spoken to you from heaven.
Dt 4:26 "Today I call heaven and earth as w against you.
17:6 There must always be at least two or three w.
17:7 The w must throw the first stones, and then all the
19:15 be established by the testimony of two or three w.
Ru 4:2 leaders from the town and asked them to sit as w.
4:4 then buy it here in the presence of these w.
4:9 "You are w that today I have bought from Naomi
4:10 here in his hometown. You are all w today."
4:11 all the people standing there replied, "We are w!

1Sa 12: 5 "The LORD and his anointed one are my w,"
Job 13: 8 You should be impartial w, but will you slant your
Ps 35:11 Malicious w testify against me. / They accuse me
50: 4 Heaven and earth will be his w / as he judges his
Isa 33: 8 care nothing for the promises they made before w.
43: 9 Where are the w of such predictions? Who can
43:10 "But you are my w, O Israel!" says the LORD.
43:12 You are w that I am the only God,"
44: 8 You are my w—is there any other God? No!
44: 9 They themselves are w that this is so, for their
Jer 32:10 I signed and sealed the deed of purchase before w,
32:12 the w who had signed the deed, and all the men of
32:25 paying good money for it before these w—
Mt 18:16 you say may be confirmed by two or three w.
26:59 and the entire high council were trying to find w
26:65 shouting, "Blasphemy! Why do we need other w?
Mk 14:55 and the entire high council were trying to find w
14:56 Many false w spoke against him, but they
14:63 his horror and said, "Why do we need other w?
Lk 22:71 "What need do we have for other w?"
24:48 You are w of all these things.
Ac 2:32 God raised from the dead, and we all are w of this.
3:15 God raised him to life. And we are w of this fact!
5:32 We are w of these things and so is the Holy Spirit,
6:13 The lying w said, "This man is always speaking
7:58 The official w took off their coats and laid them at
8: 1 Saul was one of the official w at the killing of
10:39 "And we apostles are w of all he did throughout
10:41 us whom God had chosen beforehand to be his w.
13:31 these are his w to the people of Israel.
2Co 13: 1 established by the testimony of two or three w."
1Th 2:10 You yourselves are our w—and so is God—
1Ti 5:19 elder unless there are two or three w to accuse him.
6:12 which you have confessed so well before many w.
2Ti 2: 2 that have been confirmed by many reliable w.
Heb 10:28 without mercy on the testimony of two or three w.
12: 1 by such a huge crowd of w to the life of faith,
1Jn 5: 7 So we have these three w—
Rev 11: 3 And I will give power to my two w, and they will
17: 6 blood of God's holy people who were w for Jesus.

WITS (1) [WITLESS, WITS']

2Co 11:16 don't think that I have lost my w to talk like this.

WITS' (1) [WITS]

Ps 107:27 staggered like drunkards / and were at their w end.

WITTY [KJV] See DISCRETION

WIVES (123) [WIFE]

Ge 4:23 said to Adah and Zillah, "Listen to me, my w.
6: 2 human race and took any they wanted as their w.
6:18 the boat, with your wife and your sons and their w.
7: 7 he and his wife and his sons and their w.
7:13 his sons—Shem, Ham, and Japheth—and their w.
8:18 his wife, and his sons and their w left the boat.
26:35 But Esau's w made life miserable for Isaac
28: 9 in addition to the w he already had.
30:26 Let me take my w and children, for I have earned
31:17 So Jacob put his w and children on camels.
31:50 are harsh to my daughters or if you take other w,
32:11 coming to kill me, along with my w and children.
32:22 during the night Jacob got up and sent his two w,
34: 9 and we will give our daughters as w for your
36: 6 Then Esau took his w, children,
37: 2 the sons of his father's w Bilhah and Zilpah.
45:19 to take wagons from Egypt to carry their w
46: 5 and w in the wagons Pharaoh had provided for
46:26 to Egypt, not counting his sons' w, was sixty-six.
49: 4 first no longer. / For you slept with one of my w;
Ex 22:24 Your w will become widows, and your children
32: 2 "Tell your w and sons and daughters to take off
34:16 who worship other gods, as w for your sons.
Lev 18: 8 sexual intercourse with any of your father's w,
18:11 with the daughter of any of your father's w;
Nu 14: 3 Our w and little ones will be carried off as slaves!
16:27 stood at the entrances of their tents with their w
32:16 and fortified cities for our w and children.
32:26 Our children, w, flocks, and cattle will stay here in
Dt 3:19 Your w, children, and numerous livestock,
17:17 The king must not take many w for himself,
21:15 "Suppose a man has two w, but he loves one
29:11 With you are your little ones, your w,
Jos 1:14 Your w, children, and cattle may remain here on
Jdg 8:30 He had seventy sons, for he had many w.
21: 7 How can we find w for the few who remain,
21:14 who were spared were given to them as w.
21:16 "How can we find w for the few who remain,
21:20 They told the men of Benjamin who still needed w,
21:22 for we didn't find enough w for them when we
1Sa 1: 2 Elkanah had two w, Hannah and Peninnah.
25:43 Ahinoam from Jezreel, making both of them his w.
27: 3 David brought his two w along with him—
30: 5 David's two w, Ahinoam of Jezreel and Abigail,
30: 6 his men were very bitter about losing their w
30:18 Amalekites had taken, and he rescued his two w.
30:22 Give them their w and children, and tell them to be
2Sa 2: 2 David's w were Ahinoam from Jezreel
2: 2 widow of Nabal from Carmel. So David and his w
5:13 David married more w and concubines, and he had
11:27 her to the palace, and she became one of his w.
12: 8 I gave you his house and his w and the kingdoms
12:11 I will give your w to another man, and he will go
19: 5 your daughters, and your w and concubines.
1Ki 7: 8 quarters for Pharaoh's daughter, one of his w.
11: 3 He had seven hundred w and three hundred
11: 8 Solomon built such shrines for all his foreign w to
20: 3 and so are the best of your w and children!' "
20: 5 that you give me your silver, gold, w, and children.
20: 7 sent the message demanding that I give him my w
2Ki 24:15 along with his w and officials, the queen mother,
1Ch 2:18 Hezron's son Caleb had two w named Azubah
4: 5 of Tekoa) had two w, named Helah and Naarah.
7: 4 for all five of them had many w and many sons.
7:15 Makir found w for Huppim and Shuppim.
8: 8 After Shaharaim divorced his w Hushim
14: 3 Then David married more w in Jerusalem, and they
2Ch 11:21 loved Maacah more than any of his other w
11:21 In all, he had eighteen w and sixty concubines,
11:23 and arranged for each of them to have several w.
13:21 He married fourteen w and had twenty-two sons
20:13 the LORD with their little ones, w, and children,
21:14 your people, your children, your w, and all that is
21:17 in the royal palace, including his sons and his w.
24: 3 Jehoiada chose two w for Joash, and he had sons
29: 9 and our sons and daughters and w are in captivity.
31:18 the little babies, the w, and the sons and daughters.
Ezr 9: 2 and have taken them as w for their sons.
10: 3 a covenant with our God to divorce our pagan w
10:17 dealing with all the men who had married pagan w.
10:18 These are the priests who had married pagan w:
10:19 They vowed to divorce their w, and they each
10:44 and some even had children by these w.
Ne 5: 1 and their w raised a cry of protest against their
13:26 But even he was led into sin by his foreign w.
Est 1:20 will receive proper respect from their w!"
2:14 to the second harem, where the king's w lived.
8:11 who might attack them or their children and w,
Job 27:15 with no one to mourn them, not even their w.
SS 6: 8 There may be sixty w, all queens, and eighty
Isa 13:16 and their w raped by the attacking hordes.
Jer 6:11 and on husbands and w and grandparents.
6:12 their enemies, and so will their fields and their w.
8:10 I will give their w and their farms to others.
14:16 Husbands, w, sons, and daughters—all will be
18:21 Let their w become widows without any children!
29:23 have committed adultery with their neighbors' w
35: 8 nor have our w, our sons, or our daughters.
38:23 All your w and children will be led out to the
44: 9 and your w committed in Judah and Jerusalem?
44:15 and all the men who knew that their w had burned
44:25 and your w have said that you will never give up
Eze 22:10 Men sleep with their fathers' w and have
22:11 men who commit adultery with their neighbors' w,
44:22 They may choose their w only from among the
Da 5: 2 in Jerusalem, so that he and his nobles, his w,
5: 3 and the king and his nobles, his w, and his
5:23 You and your nobles and your w and concubines
6:24 the lions' den, along with their w and children.
Zec 12:12 with the husbands and w in separate groups.
12:14 will mourn separately, husbands and w apart.
Ac 21: 5 the entire congregation, including w and children,
1Co 7:16 You w must remember that your husbands might
7:16 And you husbands must remember that your w
Eph 5:22 You w will submit to your husbands as you do to
5:24 so you w must submit to your husbands in
5:25 And you husbands must love your w with the same
5:28 husbands ought to love their w as they love their
Col 3:18 You w must submit to your husbands, as is fitting
3:19 And you husbands must love your w and never
1Ti 3:11 their w must be respected and must not speak evil
1Pe 3: 1 you w must accept the authority of your husbands,
3: 7 you husbands must give honor to your w.

WIVES' (1) [WIFE]

1Ti 4: 7 time arguing over godless ideas and old w tales.

WOES (1)

Zec 9:12 I will repay you two mercies for each of your w!

WOKE (23) [WAKE]

Ge 9:24 When Noah w up from his drunken stupor,
28:16 Then Jacob w up and said, "Surely the LORD is
29:25 But when Jacob w up in the morning—it was
41: 4 fat ones! At this point in the dream, Pharaoh w up.
41: 7 Then Pharaoh w up again and realized it was a
41:21 were still as ugly and gaunt as before! Then I w up.
Ex 12:30 and all the people of Egypt w up during the night,
Jdg 16:14 But Samson w up, pulled back the loom shuttle,
16:20 When he w up, he thought, "I will do as before
Ru 3: 8 Boaz suddenly w up and turned over.
1Ki 3:15 Then Solomon w up and realized it had been a
2Ki 19:35 When the surviving Assyrians w up the next
Ps 3: 5 I lay down and slept. / I w up in safety,
Isa 37:36 When the surviving Assyrians w up the next
Jer 31:26 At this, I w up and looked around. My sleep had
Zec 4: 1 who had been talking with me returned and w me,
Mt 1:24 When Joseph w up, he did what the angel of the
8:25 The disciples went to him and w him up, shouting,
Mk 4:38 Frantically they w him up, shouting, "Teacher,
4:39 When he w up, he rebuked the wind and said to the
Lk 8:24 The disciples w him up, shouting, "Master,
9:32 Now they w up and saw Jesus' glory and the two
Ac 16:27 The jailer w up to see the prison doors wide open.

WOLF (6) [WOLVES]

Ge 49:27 "Benjamin is a w that prowls. / He devours his
Isa 11: 6 In that day the w and the lamb will live together;
65:25 The w and lamb will feed together. The lion will
Jer 5: 6 a w from the desert will pounce on them.
Jn 10:12 A hired hand will run when he sees a w coming.
10:12 And so the w attacks them and scatters the flock.

WOLVES (7) [WOLF]

Eze 22:27 Your leaders are like w, who tear apart their
Hab 1: 8 are a fierce people, more fierce than w at dusk.
Zep 3: 3 Its judges are like ravenous w at evening time,
Mt 7:15 but are really w that will tear you apart.
10:16 "Look, I am sending you out as sheep among w.
Lk 10: 3 that I am sending you out as lambs among w.
Ac 20:29 I know full well that false teachers, like vicious w,

WOMAN (335) [WOMAN'S, WOMEN, WOMEN'S]

ADULTEROUS WOMAN (7) Pr 2:16; 5:20; 6:24; 7:5; 23:27; 27:13; 30:20

IMMORAL WOMAN (8) Pr 2:16; 5:3,20; 6:24; 7:5,8; 22:14; Lk 7:37

WISE WOMAN (2) 2Sa 20:16; Pr 14:1

WOMAN IN LABOR (2) Mic 4:9; 5:3

YOUNG WOMAN (25) Ge 21:21; 24:5,7,15,28,38,39, 43; 26:34; 38:6; 41:45; Nu 30:3,6; Dt 22:23,26,28,29; Ru 2:6; 4:12; Est 2:4,12; Job 31:1; SS 6:13; Jer 2:32; 1Co 7:28

Ge 2:22 Then the LORD God made a w from the rib
2:23 She will be called 'w,' because she was taken out
3: 1 "Really?" he asked the w. "Did God really say
3: 2 "Of course we may eat it," the w told him.
3: 6 The w was convinced. The fruit looked so fresh
3:12 "but it was the w you gave me who brought me
3:13 Then the LORD God asked the w, "How could
3:15 From now on, you and the w will be enemies,
3:16 Then he said to the w, "You will bear children
12:11 Abram said to Sarai, "You are a very beautiful w.
16: 1 took her servant, an Egyptian w named Hagar,
18:12 "How could a worn-out w like me have a baby?"
18:13 did she say, 'Can an old w like me have a baby?'
20: 3 are a dead man, for that w you took is married."
21:21 a marriage for him with a young w from Egypt.
24: 5 "But suppose I can't find a young w who will
24: 7 and he will see to it that you find a young w there
24:15 a young w named Rebekah arrived with a water
24:28 The young w ran home to tell her family about all
24:38 I was told to bring back a young w from here to
24:39 " 'But suppose I can't find a young w willing to
24:43 I will say to some young w who comes to draw
24:59 The w who had been Rebekah's childhood nurse
26:34 of forty, Esau married a young w named Judith,
28: 6 he had warned Jacob not to marry a Canaanite w.
38: 2 There he met a Canaanite w, the daughter of Shua,
38: 6 Judah arranged his marriage to a young w named
41:45 a young w named Asenath, the daughter of
46:10 and Shaul. (Shaul's mother was a Canaanite w.)
Ex 2: 1 a man and w from the tribe of Levi got married.
2: 2 The w became pregnant and gave birth to a son.
21:11 she may leave as a free w without making any
21:22 they hurt a pregnant w so her child is born
21:28 "If a bull gores a man or w to death, the bull must
35:29 and w who wanted to help in the work the LORD
Lev 12: 2 When a w becomes pregnant and gives birth to a
12: 4 Then the w must wait for thirty-three days until the
12: 5 If a w gives birth to a daughter, she will be
12: 6 the w must bring a year-old lamb for a whole burnt
12: 8 "If a w cannot afford to bring a sheep, she must
13:29 "If anyone, whether a man or w, has an open sore
13:38 "If anyone, whether a man or w, has shiny white
15:18 both the man and the w must bathe,
15:19 "Whenever a w has her menstrual period, she will
15:25 the w will be ceremonially unclean as long as the
15:33 for dealing with a w during her monthly menstrual
15:33 for dealing with anyone, man or w, who has had a
15:33 has had intercourse with a w during her period."
18:17 "Do not have sexual intercourse with both a w and her daughter or marry both a w and her
18:18 "Do not marry a w and her sister because they will
18:19 "Do not violate a w by having sexual intercourse
18:23 and a w must never present herself to a male
20:10 both the man and the w must be put to death.
20:11 both the man and the w must die, for they are
20:14 If a man has intercourse with both a w and her
20:16 If a w approaches a male animal to have
20:18 If a man has intercourse with a w suffering from a
20:20 and w involved are guilty of a capital offense
21:14 He must not marry a widow, a divorced w, or a w defiled by prostitution.
24:11 this son of an Israelite w blasphemed the LORD's
27: 4 a w of that age is valued at thirty pieces of silver.
27: 7 a w older than sixty is valued at ten pieces of
Nu 5:19 The priest will put the w under oath and say to her,
5:21 at this point the priest must put the w under this
5:22 And the w will be required to say, "Yes, let it be
5:24 He will then make the w drink the bitter water,
5:26 Then he will require the w to drink the water.
5:29 If a w defiles herself by being unfaithful to her
12: 1 because he had married a Cushite w.
25: 6 then one of the Israelite men brought a Midianite w
25:14 The Israelite man killed with the Midianite w was
30: 3 "If a young w makes a vow to the LORD or a
30: 6 "Now suppose a young w takes a vow or makes an
30: 9 If, however, a w is a widow or is divorced,
30:10 "Suppose a w is married and living in her
Dt 4:16 image in any form—whether of a man or a w,
15:12 or w voluntarily becomes your servant
17: 2 "Suppose a man or w among you, in one of your

17:5 or w must be taken to the gates of the town
21:11 suppose you see among the captives a beautiful w,
22:5 "A w must not wear men's clothing, and a man
22:13 "Suppose a man marries a w and, after sleeping
22:19 The w will then remain the man's wife, and he
22:23 "Suppose a man meets a young w, a virgin who is
22:24 The w is guilty because she did not scream for
22:25 "But if the man meets the engaged w out in the
22:26 Do nothing to the young w; she has committed no
22:28 "If a man is caught in the act of raping a young w
22:29 Then he must marry the young w because he
23:17 or w may ever become a temple prostitute.
23:18 whether a man or a w, for both are detestable to the
24:1 "Suppose a man marries a w but later discovers
28:30 "You will be engaged to a w, but another man will
28:56 The most tender and delicate w among you—
29:18 this covenant with you so that no man, w, family,
Jdg 4:9 victory over Sisera will be at the hands of a w."
5:30 goods they found— / a w or two for every man.
9:53 a w on the roof threw down a millstone that landed
9:54 Don't let it be said that a w killed Abimelech!"
13:6 The w ran and told her husband, "A man of God
14:1 was in Timnah, he noticed a certain Philistine w.
14:2 "I want to marry a young Philistine w I saw in
14:3 "Isn't there one w in our tribe or among all the
14:7 he talked with the w and was very pleased with
15:6 the Philistines went and got the w and her father
16:4 Later Samson fell in love with a w named Delilah,
19:1 One day he brought home a w from Bethlehem in
19:26 At daybreak the w returned to the house where her
20:4 the husband of the w who had been murdered,
21:11 all the males and every w who is not a virgin."
Ru 1:4 One married a w named Orpah, and the other a w named Ruth.
1:22 her daughter-in-law Ruth, the young Moabite w.
2:6 "She is the young w from Moab who came back
3:8 He was surprised to find a w lying at his feet!
3:11 everyone in town knows you are an honorable w.
3:14 "No one must know that a w was here at the
4:11 May the LORD make the w who is now coming
4:12 w who will be like those of our ancestor Perez,
1Sa 1:16 Please don't think I am a wicked w! For I have
1:26 "I am the w who stood here several years ago
2:5 now full. / The barren w now has seven children;
2:5 but the w with many children will have no more.
25:3 his wife, Abigail, was a sensible and beautiful w.
28:7 "Find a w who is a medium, so I can go and ask
28:9 you trying to get me killed?" the w demanded.
28:11 Finally, the w said, "Well, whose spirit do you
28:12 When the w saw Samuel, she screamed,
28:21 When the w saw how distraught he was, she said,
28:24 The w had been fattening a calf, so she hurried out
2Sa 3:7 one of his father's concubines, a w named Rizpah.
3:8 that you find fault with me about this w?
6:19 he gave a gift of food to every man and w in Israel:
11:2 he noticed a w of unusual beauty taking a bath.
11:21 by a w who threw a millstone down on him?'
13:17 for his servant and demanded, "Throw this w out,
13:20 So Tamar lived as a desolate w in Absalom's
14:2 So he sent for a w from Tekoa who had a
14:2 Act like a w who has been in deep sorrow for a
14:4 When the w approached the king, she fell with her
14:19 And the w replied, "My lord the king, how can I
20:16 But a wise w in the city called out to Joab,
20:17 As he approached, the w asked, "Are you Joab?"
20:21 "All right," the w replied, "we will throw his
20:22 Then the w went to the people with her wise
1Ki 3:17 them began, "this w and I live in the same house.
3:22 Then the other w interrupted, "It certainly was
3:22 "No," the first w said, "the dead one is yours,
3:26 Then the w who really was the mother of the living
3:26 But the other w said, "All right, he will be neither
3:27 but give the baby to the w who wants him to live,
14:21 mother was Naamah, an Ammonite w.
14:31 His mother was Naamah, an Ammonite w.
17:24 Then the w told Elijah, "Now I know for sure that
2Ki 4:8 A wealthy w lived there, and she invited him to eat
4:12 "Tell the w I want to speak to her."
4:15 When the w returned, Elisha said to her as she
4:17 But sure enough, the w soon became pregnant.
4:25 to Gehazi, "Look, the w from Shunem is coming.
4:26 the w told Gehazi, "everything is fine."
6:26 a w called to him, "Please help me, my lord the
6:28 "This w proposed that we eat my son one day
8:1 Elisha had told the w whose son he had brought
8:2 So the w did as the man of God instructed.
8:5 "Here is the w now, and this is her son—the very
9:34 he said, "Someone go and bury this cursed w,
1Ch 2:3 had three sons through Bathshua, a Canaanite w.
4:17 Mered married an Egyptian w, who became the
4:18 Mered also married a w of Judah, who became the
16:3 he gave a gift of food to every man and w in Israel:
2Ch 2:14 the son of a w from Dan in Israel; his father is
12:13 mother was Naamah, a w from Ammon.
15:13 be put to death—whether young or old, man or w.
24:26 the son of an Ammonite w named Shimeath,
24:26 the son of a Moabite w named Shomer.
Est 1:11 gaze on her beauty, for she was a very beautiful w.
2:4 the young w who pleases you most will be made
2:12 Before each young w was taken to the king's bed,
Job 2:10 But Job replied, "You talk like a godless w.
31:1 with my eyes not to look with lust upon a young w.
31:9 "If my heart has been seduced by a w, or if I have
Ps 48:6 like a w writhing in the pain of childbirth
113:9 He gives the barren w a home, / so that she
Pr 2:16 Wisdom will save you from the immoral w,
2:16 from the flattery of the adulterous w.
5:3 The lips of an immoral w are as sweet as honey,
5:20 Why be captivated, my son, with an immoral w,
5:20 or embrace the breasts of an adulterous w?
6:24 this teaching will keep you from the immoral w,
6:24 from the smooth tongue of an adulterous w.
7:5 hold you back from an affair with an immoral w,
7:5 from listening to the flattery of an adulterous w.
7:8 crossing the street near the house of an immoral w.
7:10 The w approached him, dressed seductively
9:13 The w named Folly is loud and brash. She is
11:22 A w who is beautiful but lacks discretion is like a
14:1 A wise w builds her house; a foolish w tears hers down with her own hands.
22:14 The mouth of an immoral w is a deep pit;
23:27 is a deep pit; an adulterous w is treacherous.
27:13 if someone guarantees the debt of an adulterous w.
30:19 a ship navigates the ocean, / how a man loves a w.
30:20 Equally amazing is how an adulterous w can
30:23 a bitter w who finally gets a husband, / a servant
31:30 but a w who fears the LORD will be greatly
Ecc 7:26 I discovered that a seductive w is more bitter than
7:28 can be said to be upright, but not one w!
9:9 Live happily with the w you love through all the
SS 1:8 "If you don't know, O most beautiful w,
5:9 "O w of rare beauty, what is it about your loved
6:13 do you gaze so intently at this young w of Shulam,
Isa 3:26 The city will be like a ravaged w, huddled on the
13:8 terrible pangs, like those of a w about to give birth.
21:3 are upon me, like the pangs of a w giving birth.
26:17 We were like a w about to give birth, / writhing
42:14 I will gasp and pant like a w giving birth.
54:1 "Sing, O childless w! Break forth into loud
54:1 For the w who could bear no children now has
Jer 2:32 Does a young w forget her jewelry? Does a bride
3:1 "If a man divorces a w and she marries someone
4:31 like that of a w giving birth to her first child.
6:24 gripped us, like that of a w about to give birth.
13:21 You will writhe in pain like a w giving birth!
22:23 anguish like that of a w about to give birth.
44:7 not a man, w, or child among you who has come
48:41 will be as frightened as a w about to give birth.
49:22 will be as frightened as a w about to give birth.
49:24 and pain have gripped her as they do a w giving birth.
50:43 gripped him, like that of a w about to give birth.
Eze 18:6 or have intercourse with a w during her menstrual
23:10 Her name was known to every w in the land as a
Am 2:7 Both father and son sleep with the same w,
Mic 4:9 Pain has gripped you like it does a w in labor.
5:3 the time when the w in labor gives birth to her son.
Zec 5:7 lifted off the basket, there was a w sitting inside it.
Mt 5:28 anyone who even looks at a w with lust in his eye
5:32 And anyone who marries a divorced w commits
9:20 a w who had had a hemorrhage for twelve years
9:22 you well." And the w was healed at that moment.
13:33 of Heaven is like yeast used by a w making bread.
15:22 A Gentile w who lived there came to him,
15:24 Then he said to the w, "I was sent only to help the
15:28 "W," Jesus said to her, "your faith is great.
26:7 a w came in with a beautiful jar of expensive
Mk 5:25 And there was a w in the crowd who had had a
5:33 Then the frightened w, trembling at the realization
7:25 Right away a w came to him whose little girl was
10:12 And if a w divorces her husband and remarries,
12:22 there were no children. Last of all, the w died, too.
14:3 a w came in with a beautiful jar of expensive
16:9 the w from whom he had cast out seven demons.
Lk 1:28 appeared to her and said, "Greetings, favored w!
7:37 A certain immoral w heard he was there
7:39 host saw what was happening and who the w was,
7:39 he would know what kind of w is touching him.
7:44 Then he turned to the w and said to Simon, "Look at this w kneeling here.
7:48 Then Jesus said to the w, "Your sins are
7:50 And Jesus said to the w, "Your faith has saved
8:43 And there was a w in the crowd who had had a
8:47 When the w realized that Jesus knew, she began to
10:38 they came to a village where a w named Martha
11:27 As he was speaking, a w in the crowd called out,
13:11 he saw a w who had been crippled by an evil spirit.
13:12 Jesus saw her, he called her over and said, "W,
13:16 to free this dear w from the bondage in which
13:21 It is like yeast used by a w making bread.
15:8 "Or suppose a w has ten valuable silver coins
16:18 and anyone who marries a divorced w commits
18:5 'but this w is driving me crazy. I'm going to see
20:32 Finally, the w died, too.
22:57 "W," he said, "I don't even know the man!"
Jn 4:7 Soon a Samaritan w came to draw water, and Jesus
4:9 The w was surprised, for Jews refuse to have
4:9 to Jesus, "You are a Jew, and I am a Samaritan w.
4:15 "Please, sir," the w said, "give me some of that
4:17 "I don't have a husband," the w replied.
4:19 "Sir," the w said, "you must be a prophet.
4:25 The w said, "I know the Messiah will come—
4:27 They were astonished to find him talking to a w,
4:28 The w left her water jar beside the well and went
4:39 village believed in Jesus because the w had said,
4:42 Then they said to the w, "Now we believe
8:3 and Pharisees brought a w they had caught in the
8:4 "this w was caught in the very act of adultery.
8:9 was left in the middle of the crowd with the w.
16:21 It will be like a w experiencing the pains of labor.
18:16 Then the other disciple spoke to the w watching at
18:17 The w asked Peter, "Aren't you one of Jesus'
19:26 he loved, he said to her, "W, he is your son."
Ac 17:34 of the Council, a w named Damaris, and others.
Ro 7:2 When a w marries, the law binds her to her
1Co 7:2 and each w should have her own husband.
7:3 which is her right as a married w, nor should the
7:13 And if a Christian w has a husband who is an
7:28 And if a young w gets married, it is not a sin.
7:34 a w who is no longer married or has never been
7:34 while the married w must be concerned about her
11:3 to Christ, a w is responsible to her husband,
11:5 But a w dishonors her husband if she prays
11:6 And since it is shameful for a w to have her hair
11:7 in God's own image, but w is the glory of man.
11:8 For the first man didn't come from w, but the first w came from man.
11:9 for woman's benefit, but w was made for man.
11:10 So a w should wear a covering on her head as a
11:12 For although the first w came from man, all men
11:13 Is it right for a w to pray to God in public without
Gal 4:4 God sent his Son, born of a w, subject to the law.
4:26 But Sarah, the free w, represents the heavenly
4:27 when he prophesied, / "Rejoice, O childless w!
4:27 For the w who could bear no children / now has
4:30 for the son of the slave w will not share the family
4:31 dear friends, we are not children of the slave w,
4:31 We are children of the free w, acceptable to God
1Ti 2:14 And it was the w, not Adam, who was deceived by
5:5 But a w who is a true widow, one who is truly
5:9 support must be a w who is at least sixty years old
5:16 If a Christian w has relatives who are widows,
Rev 2:20 You are permitting that w—that Jezebel who calls
9:8 Their hair was long like the hair of a w, and their
12:1 I saw a w clothed with the sun, with the moon
12:4 He stood before the w as she was about to give
12:6 And the w fled into the wilderness, where God had
12:13 he pursued the w who had given birth to the child.
12:15 Then the dragon tried to drown the w with a flood
12:17 Then the dragon became angry at the w, and he
17:3 There I saw a w sitting on a scarlet beast that had
17:4 The w wore purple and scarlet clothing
17:7 "I will tell you the mystery of this w and of the
17:9 the seven hills of the city where this w rules.
17:18 And this w you saw in your vision represents the
18:16 like a w clothed in finest purple and scarlet linens,

WOMAN'S (22) [WOMAN]

Ex 21:22 damages in the amount the w husband demands
Lev 15:28 "When the w menstrual discharge stops, she must
Nu 5:25 will take the jealousy offering from the w hand,
25:8 through the man's body and into the w stomach.
25:15 The w name was Cozbi; she was the daughter of
Dt 22:15 the w father and mother must bring the proof of
22:19 The payment will be made to the w father.
Jdg 9:18 And you have chosen his slave w son, Abimelech,
19:5 was up early, ready to leave, but the w father said,
19:6 Then the w father said, "Please stay the night
19:8 ready to leave, and again the w father said,
1Sa 28:8 Then he went to the w home at night,
1Ki 17:17 Some time later, the w son became sick. He grew
Pr 6:34 For the w husband will be furious in his jealousy,
Zec 5:8 The angel said, "The w name is Wickedness,"
Mt 26:13 this w deed will be talked about in her memory."
Mk 14:9 this w deed will be talked about in her memory."
Lk 2:23 law of the Lord says, "If a w first child is a boy,
1Co 11:9 And man was not made for w benefit, but woman
11:15 And isn't it obvious that long hair is a w pride
Gal 4:30 share the family inheritance with the free w son."
1Th 5:3 w birth pains begin when her child is about to be

WOMB (25) [WOMBS]

Ge 25:22 two children struggled with each other in her w.
25:23 "The sons in your w will become two rival
49:25 earth beneath, / and blessings of the breasts and w.
1Sa 1:6 of Hannah because the LORD had closed her w.
Job 1:21 He said, / "I came naked from my mother's w,
3:10 Curse it for its failure to shut my mother's w,
3:11 "Why didn't I die at birth as I came from the w?
10:10 guided my conception and formed me in the w.
10:18 then, did you bring me out of my mother's w?
10:19 I would have gone directly from the w to the grave.
38:8 the boundaries of the sea as it burst from the w
Ps 22:9 Yet you brought me safely from my mother's w
71:6 from my mother's w you have cared for me.
139:13 my body / and knit me together in my mother's w.
139:15 as I was woven together in the dark of the w.
Pr 30:16 the grave, / the barren w, / the thirsty desert,
31:2 O my son, O son of my w, O son of my promises,
Ecc 11:5 as a tiny baby being formed in a mother's w.
Isa 49:1 my birth; from within the w he called me by name.
49:5 he who formed me in my mother's w to be his
Jer 1:5 knew you before I formed you in your mother's w.
20:17 Oh, that I had died in my mother's w, that her body
Hos 9:11 or perish in the w or never even be conceived.
Lk 11:27 the w from which you came, and the breasts that
Jn 3:4 "How can an old man go back into his mother's w

WOMBS (2) [WOMB]

Hos 9:14 I will ask for w that don't give birth and breasts
Lk 23:29 the w that have not borne a child and the breasts

WOMEN (249) [WOMAN]

MEN AND WOMEN (29) Ge 20:14; 32:5; Ex 11:2; 35:22; Lev 20:27; Nu 5:3; Jos 6:21; Jdg 9:49; 1Sa 22:19; 2Ch 36:17; Ezr 2:65; Ne 7:67; 8:2; Ecc 2:7,8; Jer 34:9,16; 44:20; 51:22; Joel 2:29; Zec 8:4; 9:17; Mt 27:52; Ac 2:18; 5:14; 8:3,12; 9:2; 22:4

WOMEN AND CHILDREN (17) Ge 33:5; 34:29; Ex 12:37; Nu 31:9; Dt 2:34; 3:6; Jos 8:35; Jdg 21:10; 1Sa 30:2; 2Ch 28:8; Ezr 10:1; Ne 12:43; Est 3:13; Jer 43:6; Mt 14:21; 15:38; Ac 4:4

YOUNG WOMEN (21) Ge 24:13; 34:1; 36:2; Dt 32:25; Jdg 12:9; 1Sa 2:22; 9:11; Est 2:3,8,17,19; Ps 68:25; 78:63; SS 1:3; 3:10,11; 6:9; Jer 31:13; La 1:4; 2:10; 1Co 7:25

Ge 4:19 Lamech married two w—Adah and Zillah.
6:2 the sons of God saw the beautiful w of the human
6:4 the sons of God had intercourse with human w,
14:16 his possessions, and all the w and other captives.
20:14 and oxen and servants—both men and w—
20:17 his wife, and the other w of the household,
20:18 For the LORD had stricken all the w with
24:3 let my son marry one of these local Canaanite w.
24:11 and the w were coming out to draw water.
24:13 and the young w of the village are coming out to
24:37 not let Isaac marry one of the local Canaanite w.
27:46 "I'm sick and tired of these local Hittite w.
28:1 and said, "Do not marry any of these Canaanite w.
28:8 Esau that his father despised the local Canaanite w.
30:13 The other w will consider me happy indeed!"
31:15 He has reduced our rights to those of foreign w.
31:43 replied to Jacob, "These w are my daughters,
32:5 sheep, goats, and many servants, both men and w.
33:5 Then Esau looked at the w and children and asked,
34:1 went to visit some of the young w who lived in the
34:29 They also took all the w and children and wealth of
36:2 Esau married two young w from Canaan: Adah,
Ex 1:16 "When you help the Hebrew w give birth, kill all
1:19 they told him, "the Hebrew w are very strong.
1:19 are not slow in giving birth like Egyptian w."
2:7 and find one of the Hebrew w to nurse the baby for
3:22 The Israelite w will ask for silver and gold jewelry
11:2 and w to ask their Egyptian neighbors for articles
12:37 about 600,000 men, plus all the w and children.
15:20 and led all the w in rhythm and dance.
35:22 Both men and w came, all whose hearts were
35:25 All the w who were skilled in sewing and spinning
35:26 All the w who were willing used their skills to spin
38:8 w who served at the entrance of the Tabernacle.
Lev 20:27 "Men and w among you who act as mediums
21:7 "The priests must not marry w defiled by prostitution or w who have been divorced,
Nu 5:3 This applies to men and w alike. Remove them
5:6 If any of the people—men or w—
6:2 If some of the people, either men or w,
25:1 themselves by sleeping with the local Moabite w.
25:2 These w invited them to attend sacrifices to their
27:2 These w went and stood before Moses,
31:9 Then the Israelite army captured the Midianite w
31:15 "Why have you let all the w live?" he demanded.
31:17 the boys and all the w who have slept with a man.
Dt 2:34 destroyed everyone—men, w, and children.
3:6 town we conquered—men, w, and children alike.
7:14 None of your men or w will be childless, and all
20:14 But you may keep for yourselves all the w,
31:12 men, w, children, and the foreigners living in your
32:25 both young men and young w, / both infants
Jos 6:21 men and w, young and old, cattle, sheep, donkeys
8:35 including the w and children and the foreigners
17:4 These w came to Eleazar the priest, Joshua son of
Jdg 5:24 May she be blessed above all w who live in tents.
5:29 A reply comes from her wise w, / and she repeats
9:49 of Shechem died, about a thousand men and w.
11:40 for young Israelite w to go away for four days each
12:9 and brought in thirty young w from outside his
21:10 to kill everyone there, including w and children.
21:14 and the four hundred w of Jabesh-gilead who were
21:14 But there were not enough w for all of them.
21:16 since all the w of the tribe of Benjamin are dead?
21:21 When the w of Shiloh come out for their dances,
21:23 They kidnapped the w who took part in the
Ru 1:4 The two sons married Moabite w. One married a
1:19 by their arrival. "Is it really Naomi?" the w asked.
2:8 Stay right behind the w working in my field.
2:23 So Ruth worked alongside the w in Boaz's fields
4:14 And the w of the town said to Naomi,
4:17 The neighbor w said, "Now at last Naomi has a
1Sa 2:22 that his sons were seducing the young w who
9:11 they met some young w coming out to draw water.
15:3 men, w, children, babies, cattle, sheep, camels,
18:6 W came out from all the towns along the way to
21:4 young men have not slept with any w recently."
21:5 "I never allow my men to be with w when they are
22:19 men and w, children and babies, and all the cattle,
29:5 Isn't this the same David about whom the w of
30:2 They had carried off the w and children
2Sa 1:24 O w of Israel, weep for Saul, / for he dressed you
1:26 love for me was deep, / deeper than the love of w!
1Ki 3:25 child in two and give half to each of these w!"
11:1 Now King Solomon loved many foreign w.
11:1 he married w from Moab, Ammon, Edom, Sidon,
11:2 because the w they married would lead them to
2Ki 8:12 to the ground, and rip open their pregnant w!"
15:16 entire population and ripped open the pregnant w.
23:7 where the w wove coverings for the Asherah pole.
2Ch 28:8 The armies of Israel captured 200,000 w
36:17 both young and old, men and w, healthy and sick.
Ezr 2:65 to 7,337 servants and 200 singers, both men and w.
9:2 For the men of Israel have married w from these
10:1 men, w, and children—gathered and wept bitterly
10:2 for we have married these pagan w of the land.
10:10 "You have sinned, for you have married pagan w.
10:11 the people of the land and from these pagan w."
Ne 7:67 to 7,337 servants and 245 singers, both men and w.
8:2 which included the men and w and all the children
12:43 The w and children also participated in the
13:23 of the men of Judah had married w from Ashdod,
13:27 unfaithfully toward God by marrying foreign w?"
Est 1:9 Queen Vashti gave a banquet for the w of the
1:17 W everywhere will begin to despise their husbands
2:3 beautiful young w into the royal harem at Susa.
2:8 Esther, along with many other young w,
2:17 king loved her more than any of the other young w.
2:19 Even after all the young w had been transferred to
3:13 young and old, including w and children—must be
Job 42:15 In all the land there were no other w as lovely as
Ps 68:11 and throngs of w shout the happy news.
68:12 while the w of Israel divide the plunder.
68:25 with them are young w playing tambourines.
78:63 their young w died before singing their wedding
Pr 11:16 Beautiful w obtain wealth, and violent men get
31:3 do not spend your strength on w, on those who ruin
31:29 are many virtuous and capable w in the world,
Ecc 2:7 I bought slaves, both men and w, and others were
2:8 I hired wonderful singers, both men and w,
SS 1:3 your name! No wonder all the young w love you!
1:5 "I am dark and beautiful, O w of Jerusalem,
2:2 "Yes, compared to other w, my beloved is like a
2:7 "Promise me, O w of Jerusalem, by the swift
3:5 "Promise me, O w of Jerusalem, by the swift
3:10 Its interior was a gift of love from the young w of
3:11 upon King Solomon, O young w of Jerusalem.
5:8 "Make this promise to me, O w of Jerusalem!
5:16 Such, O w of Jerusalem, is my lover, my friend."
6:1 "O rarest of beautiful w, where has your lover
6:9 The young w are delighted when they see her;
8:4 "I want you to promise, O w of Jerusalem, not to
Isa 3:12 Children oppress my people, and w rule over them.
3:16 Next the LORD will judge the w of Jerusalem,
4:1 Seven w will fight over each of them and say,
4:4 The Lord will wash the moral filth from the w of
16:2 The w of Moab are left like homeless birds at the
19:16 In that day the Egyptians will be as weak as w.
32:9 Listen, you w who lie around in lazy ease.
32:11 Tremble, you w of ease; throw off your unconcern.
54:1 no children now has more than all the other w,"
Jer 7:18 See how the w knead dough and make cakes to
9:20 Listen, you w, to the words of the LORD;
30:6 hands pressed against their sides like w about to
31:8 the expectant mothers and w about to give birth.
31:13 The young w will dance for joy, and the men—
34:9 to free their Hebrew slaves—both men and w.
34:16 name by taking back the men and w you had freed,
38:22 All the w left in your palace will be brought out
38:22 Then the w will taunt you, saying, 'What fine
41:16 warriors, w, children, and palace officials.
43:6 were men, w, and children, the king's daughters,
44:15 Then all the w present and all the men who knew
44:19 "And," the w added, "do you suppose that we
44:20 men and w alike, who had given him that answer,
44:24 Then Jeremiah said to them all, including the w,
50:37 allies from other lands will become as weak as w.
51:22 With you I will shatter men and w, old people
51:30 is gone. They have become as fearful as w.
La 1:4 her priests groan, her young w are crying—
2:10 The young w of Jerusalem hang their heads in
3:51 My heart is breaking over the fate of all the w of
4:10 Tenderhearted w have cooked their own children
5:11 Our enemies rape the w and young girls in
Eze 8:14 and some w were sitting there, weeping for the god
9:6 old and young, girls and w and little children.
13:17 also speak out against the w who prophesy from
13:18 Destruction is certain for you w who are ensnaring
16:41 your homes and punish you in front of many w.
22:10 and have intercourse with w who are menstruating.
30:17 in battle, and the w will be taken away as slaves.
44:22 They may not marry other widows or divorced w.
Da 11:37 nor for the god beloved of w, nor for any other
Hos 13:16 their pregnant w ripped open by swords."
Joel 2:29 out my Spirit even on servants, men and w alike.
Am 1:13 ripping open pregnant w with their swords.
4:1 you w who oppress the poor and crush the needy
Mic 2:9 You have evicted w from their homes and stripped
Na 3:13 Your troops will be as weak and helpless as w.
Zec 5:9 Then I looked up and saw two w flying toward us,
8:4 and w will walk Jerusalem's streets with a cane
9:17 and w will thrive on the abundance of grain
14:2 be taken, the houses plundered, and the w raped.
Mal 2:11 sanctuary by marrying w who worship idols.
Mt 14:21 five loaves, in addition to all the w and children!
15:38 fed that day, in addition to all the w and children.
24:19 How terrible it will be for pregnant w and for
24:41 Two w will be grinding flour at the mill; one will
27:52 and w who had died were raised from the dead
27:55 And many w who had come from Galilee with
28:5 Then the angel spoke to the w. "Don't be afraid!"
28:8 The w ran quickly from the tomb. They were very
28:11 As the w were on their way into the city, some of
Mk 13:17 How terrible it will be for pregnant w and for
15:40 Some w were there, watching from a distance,
15:41 and many other w had come with him to
16:5 man clothed in a white robe. The w were startled,
16:8 The w fled from the tomb, trembling
Lk 1:42 "You are blessed by God above all other w,
8:2 along with some w he had healed and from whom
17:35 Two w will be grinding flour together at the mill;
21:23 How terrible it will be for pregnant w and for
23:27 along behind, including many grief-stricken w.
23:29 'Fortunate indeed are the w who are childless,
23:49 including the w who had followed him from
23:55 the w from Galilee followed and saw the tomb
24:1 But very early on Sunday morning the w came to
24:5 The w were terrified and bowed low before them.
24:10 The w who went to the tomb were Mary
24:22 Then some w from our group of his followers were
24:24 Jesus' body was gone, just as the w had said."
Ac 1:14 of Jesus, several other w, and the brothers of Jesus.
2:18 upon all my servants, men and w alike, / and they
4:4 five thousand men, not counting w and children.
5:14 brought to the Lord—crowds of both men and w.
8:3 out both men and w to throw them into jail.
8:12 As a result, many men and w were baptized.
9:2 He wanted to bring them—both men and w—
13:50 leaders stirred up both the influential religious w
16:13 and we sat down to speak with some w who had
17:4 Greek men and also many important w of the city.
17:12 as did some of the prominent Greek w and many
22:4 binding and delivering both men and w to prison.
Ro 1:26 Even the w turned against the natural way to have
1:27 of having normal sexual relationships with w,
1Co 7:25 Now, about the young w who are not yet married.
11:11 w are not independent of men, and men are not independent of w.
11:12 all men have been born from w ever since,
14:34 W should be silent during the church meetings.
14:35 for it is improper for w to speak in church
Gal 4:24 Now these two w serve as an illustration of God's
4:27 no children / now has more than all the other w!"
Php 4:2 And now I want to plead with those two w, Euodia
4:3 And I ask you, my true teammate, to help these w,
1Ti 2:9 And I want w to be modest in their appearance.
2:10 For w who claim to be devoted to God should
2:11 W should listen and learn quietly
2:12 I do not let w teach men or have authority over
2:15 But w will be saved through childbearing and by
5:2 Treat the older w as you would your mother,
5:2 and treat the younger w with all purity as your own
2Ti 3:6 and win the confidence of vulnerable w who are
3:7 Such w are forever following new teachings,
Tit 2:3 teach the older w to live in a way that is
2:4 These older w must train the younger w to
Heb 11:35 W received their loved ones back again from
1Pe 3:5 That is the way the holy w of old made themselves

WOMEN'S (1) [WOMAN]

Dt 22:5 and a man must not wear w clothing.

WOMENSERVANTS [KJV] See CONCUBINES, (WOMEN) SERVANTS

WON (15) [WIN]

Ge 32:28 struggled with both God and men and have w."
1Ki 20:11 not boast like a warrior who has already w."
20:23 gods are gods of the hills; that is why they w.
Ps 78:54 holy land, / to this land of hills he had w for them.
98:1 He has w a mighty victory / by his power
Isa 10:13 my own power and wisdom I have w these wars.
Eze 29:18 and his army w no plunder to compensate them for
Hos 12:4 Yes, he wrestled with the angel and w. He wept
Mt 18:15 and confesses it, you have w that person back.
Ro 15:19 I have w them over by the miracles done through
Heb 7:2 Then Abraham took a tenth of all he had w in the
1Pe 3:1 them better than any words. They will be w over
1Jn 2:13 because you have w your battle with Satan.
2:14 your hearts, and you have w your battle with Satan.
4:4 You have already w your fight with these false

WON'T (223) [NOT, WILL] See Index of Articles, Etc.

WONDER (36) [WONDERED, WONDERFUL, WONDERFULLY, WONDERING, WONDERS, WONDROUS]

Ge 27:36 Esau said bitterly, "No w his name is Jacob,
Dt 18:21 You may w, 'How will we know whether the
Jos 2:11 No w our hearts have melted in fear! No one has
Job 21:4 with God, not with people. No w I'm so impatient.
23:15 No w I am so terrified in his presence. When I
37:24 No w people everywhere fear him. People who are
Ps 16:9 No w my heart is filled with joy, / and my mouth
22:22 Then I will declare the w of your name to my
57:7 in you, O God; / no w I can sing your praises!
71:6 cared for me. / No w I am always praising you!
76:7 No w you are greatly feared! / Who can stand
108:1 in you, O God; / no w I can sing your praises!
119:104 no w I hate every false way of life.
119:119 you skim off; / no w I love to obey your decrees!
119:129 Your decrees are wonderful. / No w I obey them!
SS 1:3 your name! No w all the young women love you!
Isa 44:9 No w those who worship them are put to shame.
57:1 their time. And no one seems to care or w why.
59:9 No w we are in darkness when we expected light. No w we are walking in the gloom.
59:10 No w we grope like blind people and stumble
59:10 No w we are like corpses when compared to
Jer 7:18 No w I am so angry! Watch how the children
Na 3:5 "No w I am your enemy!" declares the LORD
Mt 12:24 they said, "No w he can cast out demons.
Lk 1:65 W fell upon the whole neighborhood, and the news
1:66 and asked, "I w what this child will turn out to be?
5:26 Everyone was gripped with great w and awe.
11:15 but some said, "No w he can cast out demons.
24:41 they stood there doubting, filled with joy and w.
Jn 5:44 No w you can't believe! For you gladly honor each

Ac 2: 7 They were beside themselves with w. "How can
2:26 No w my heart is filled with joy, / and my mouth
Ro 2:24 No w the Scriptures say, "The world blasphemes
2Co 11:15 So it is no w his servants can also do it by
Heb 2:12 "I will declare the w of your name to my brothers

WONDERED (7) [WONDER]

Ge 17:17 he w. "Besides, Sarah is ninety; how could she
37:11 gave it some thought and w what it all meant.
Mt 12:23 the Son of David, the Messiah?" they w out loud.
Ac 7:31 Moses saw it and w what it was. As he went to see,
27:39 and w if they could get between the rocks and get
1Pe 1:11 They w what the Spirit of Christ within them was
1:11 They w when and to whom all this would happen.

WONDERFUL (133) [WONDER]

Ex 10: 2 You will be able to tell w stories to your children
18: 1 about all the w things God had done for Moses
Nu 10:29 for the LORD has given w promises to Israel!"
14: 7 of Israel, "The land we explored is a w land!
Dt 3:25 Please let me cross the Jordan to see the w land on
Jdg 13:23 and told us this w thing and done these miracles."
Ru 2:22 "This is w!" Naomi exclaimed. "Do as he said.
1Sa 12:24 Think of all the w things he has done for you.
2Sa 23: 1 the man to whom God gave such w success,
1Ki 8:56 Not one word has failed of all the w promises he
2Ki 7: 9 This is w news, and we aren't sharing it with
1Ch 16:12 Think of the w works he has done, / the miracles,
Ne 6:19 They kept telling me what a w man Tobiah was,
9:28 In your w mercy, you rescued them repeatedly!
Job 37:14 Job; stop and consider the w miracles of God!
37:16 how he balances the clouds with w perfection
42: 3 I did not understand, things far too w for me.
Ps 16: 6 me is a pleasant land. / What a w inheritance!
17: 7 Show me your unfailing love in w ways.
37:37 for a w future lies before those who love peace.
40: 5 If I tried to recite all your w deeds, / I would never
69:16 O LORD, / for your unfailing love is w.
71:17 and I have constantly told others about the w
71:19 You have done such w things. / Who can compare
72:18 the God of Israel, / who alone does such w things.
73:28 and I will tell everyone about the w things you do.
77:11 O LORD; / I remember your w deeds of long ago.
78:11 he had done— / the w miracles he had shown them,
89:16 They rejoice all day long in your w reputation.
98: 1 song to the LORD, / for he has done w deeds.
105: 5 Think of the w works he has done, / the miracles
106:22 such w things in that land, / such awesome deeds at
107: 8 for his great love / and for all his w deeds to them.
107:15 for his great love / and for all his w deeds to them.
107:21 for his great love / and for all his w deeds to them.
107:31 for his great love / and for all his w deeds to them.
119:18 Open my eyes to see / the w truths in your law.
119:27 and I will meditate on your w miracles.
119:106 and I'll promise again: / I will obey your w laws.
119:129 Your decrees are w. / No wonder I obey them!
133: 1 How w it is, how pleasant, / when brothers live
135: 3 is good; / celebrate his w name with music.
139: 6 Such knowledge is too w for me, / too great for me
145: 5 glorious splendor / and your w miracles.
145: 7 Everyone will share the story of your w goodness;
Pr 15:23 it is w to say the right thing at the right time!
Ecc 2: 8 I hired w singers, both men and women, and had
8: 1 How w to be wise, to be able to analyze
11: 7 Light is sweet; it's w to see the sun!
11: 9 Young man, it's w to be young! Enjoy every
SS 1: 1 Solomon's song of songs, more w than any other.
8:13 how w that your companions can listen to your
Isa 3:10 Tell them, "You will receive a w reward!"
9: 6 W Counselor, Mighty God, Everlasting Father,
12: 4 In that w day you will sing: / "Thank the LORD!
12: 5 Sing to the LORD, / for he has done w things.
14: 3 In that w day when the LORD gives his people
25: 1 for you are my God. You do such w things!
25: 6 the LORD Almighty will spread a w feast for
28:29 The LORD Almighty is a w teacher, and he gives
30:23 There will be w harvests and plenty of pastureland
44:13 Now he has a w idol that cannot even move from
65:17 so w that no one will even think about the old ones
Jer 5:25 Your wickedness has deprived you of these w
17: 4 The w inheritance I have reserved for you will slip
Da 2: 6 I will give you many w gifts and honors.
Hab 3: 3 earth is filled with his praise! What a w God he is!
Zec 9:17 How w and beautiful they will be! The young men
Mt 17: 4 Peter blurted out, "Lord, this is w! If you want me
21:15 and the teachers of religious law saw these w
Mk 5:19 and tell them what w things the Lord has done for
7:37 and again they said, "Everything he does is w.
9: 5 "Teacher, this is w!" Peter exclaimed. "We will
Lk 2:15 Let's see this w thing that has happened,
6:33 only to those who do good to you, is that so w?
8:39 and tell them all the w things God has done for
9:33 he was saying, blurted out, "Master, this is w!
9:43 While everyone was marveling over all the w
13:17 And all the people rejoiced at the w things he did.
19:37 praising God for all the w miracles they had seen.
24:19 they said. "He was a prophet who did w miracles.
Jn 7: 4 If you can do such w things, prove it to the
7:12 Some said, "He's a w man," while others said,
16:20 but your grief will suddenly turn to w joy when
Ac 2:11 own languages about the w things God has done!"
2:22 endorsed Jesus of Nazareth by doing w miracles,
2:28 and you will give me w joy in your presence.'
3:11 Everyone stood there in awe of the w thing that
3:20 Then w times of refreshment will come from the
4:20 We cannot stop telling about the w things we have
20:24 others the Good News about God's w kindness
Ro 4:23 Now this w truth—that God declared him to be
5:11 So now we can rejoice in our w new relationship
5:17 death to rule over us, but all who receive God's w,
5:20 God's w kindness became more abundant.
5:21 to death, now God's w kindness rules instead,
8:31 What can we say about such w things as these?
9: 4 of worshiping him and receiving his w promises.
11: 6 God's w kindness would not be what it really is—
11:15 how much more w their acceptance will be.
11:33 Oh, what a w God we have! How great are his
15:27 Since the Gentiles received the w spiritual
1Co 1: 9 and he is the one who invited you into this w
1:24 mighty power of God and the w wisdom of God.
2:12 so we can know the w things God has freely given
15: 1 do now, for your faith is built on this w message.
15:51 But let me tell you a w secret God has revealed to
16:18 They have been a w encouragement to me, as they
2Co 4: 1 since God in his mercy has given us this w
5:19 This is the w message he has given us to tell
8: 2 their w joy and deep poverty have overflowed in
9:14 because of the w grace of God shown through you.
9:15 Thank God for his Son—a gift too w for words!
10:12 I wouldn't dare say that I am as w as these other
12: 7 even though I have received w revelations from
Gal 4:18 Now it's w if you are eager to do good,
Eph 1: 6 So we praise God for the w kindness he has poured
1:18 so that you can understand the w future he has
3: 7 I have been given the w privilege of serving him
Php 4: 7 which is far more w than the human mind can
1Th 1: 9 for they themselves keep talking about the w
Tit 2:13 while we look forward to that w event when the
Jas 5:16 a righteous person has great power and w results.
1Pe 1: 2 and more of God's special favor and w peace.
1: 3 Now we live with a w expectation because Jesus
1: 6 There is w joy ahead, even though it is necessary
1:12 so w that even the angels are eagerly watching
2: 9 for he called you out of the darkness into his w
4:13 and afterward you will have the w joy of sharing
4:16 for the privilege of being called by his w name!
2Pe 1: 2 and w peace as you come to know Jesus,
1: 4 he has given us all of his rich and w promises.
Rev 14: 3 This great choir sang a w new song in front of the

WONDERFULLY (7) [WONDER]

1Sa 24:18 Yes, you have been w kind to me today, for when
1Ki 3: 6 "You were w kind to my father, David,
2Ch 26:15 for the LORD helped him w until he became very
Ps 139:14 Thank you for making me so w complex!
La 3:25 The LORD is w good to those who wait for him
Mt 6:30 if God cares so w for flowers that are here today
Lk 12:28 if God cares so w for flowers that are here today

WONDERING (6) [WONDER]

Ge 24:21 w whether or not she was the one the LORD
2Sa 9: 1 One day David began w if anyone in Saul's family
Lk 1:21 to come out, w why he was taking so long.
24:12 then he went home again, w what had happened.
Jn 13:22 looked at each other, w whom he could mean.
Ac 5:24 they were perplexed, w where it would all end.

WONDERS (40) [WONDER]

Ex 7: 3 my miraculous signs and w in the land of Egypt.
15:11 so awesome in splendor, / performing such w?
34:10 I will perform w that have never been done before
Nu 23:23 said of Jacob, / 'What w God has done for Israel!'
Dt 4:34 miraculous signs, w, war, awesome power,
6:22 our eyes the LORD did miraculous signs and w,
7:19 And remember the miraculous signs and w,
11: 3 and w he performed in Egypt against Pharaoh
26: 8 overwhelming terror, and miraculous signs and w.
29: 3 the miraculous signs, and the amazing w.
34:11 and w in the land of Egypt against Pharaoh,
Jos 3: 5 for tomorrow the LORD will do great w among
Ne 9:10 displayed miraculous signs and w against Pharaoh,
Ps 22:30 Our children will hear about the w of the Lord.
65: 8 at the ends of the earth / stand in awe of your w.
77:14 You are the God of miracles and w!
78:43 signs in Egypt, / his w on the plain of Zoan.
111: 4 Who can forget the w he performs? / How gracious
135: 9 He performed miraculous signs and w in Egypt;
Pr 18:16 Giving a gift works w; it may bring you before
Isa 29:14 of this, I will do w among these hypocrites.
Jer 32:20 miraculous signs and w in the land of Egypt—
32:21 Israel out of Egypt with mighty signs and w,
Da 4: 2 and w the Most High God has performed for me.
4: 3 How great are his signs, / how powerful his w!
6:27 his people; / he performs miraculous signs and w
Joel 2:30 "I will cause w in the heavens and on the earth—
Mt 24:24 great miraculous signs and w so as to deceive,
Mk 13:22 perform miraculous signs and w so as to deceive,
Jn 4:48 and w before you people will believe in me?"
Ac 2:19 And I will cause w in the heavens above
2:22 w, and signs through him, as you well know.
2:43 apostles performed many miraculous signs and w.
4:30 and w be done through the name of your holy
5:12 many miraculous signs and w among the people.
7:36 miraculous signs and w he led them out of Egypt,
14: 3 giving them power to do miraculous signs and w.
15:12 and w God had done through them among the
2Co 12:12 did many signs and w and miracles among you.
Heb 2: 4 the message by signs and w and various miracles

WONDROUS (1) [WONDER]

Isa 44:23 O heavens, for the LORD has done this w thing.

WONT [KJV] See ACCUSTOMED, CUSTOM, CUSTOMARY, HABIT, SUPPOSED, USED

WOOD (129) [FIREWOOD, WOOD-CARVER, WOODCHOPPERS, WOODCUTTERS, WOODED, WOODEN, WOODPILE, WOODS, WOODSMEN]

Ge 6:14 "Make a boat from resinous w and seal it with tar,
22: 3 Then he chopped w to build a fire for a burnt
22: 6 Abraham placed the w for the burnt offering on
22: 7 "We have the w and the fire," said the boy,
22: 9 to go, he built an altar and placed the w on it.
22: 9 tied Isaac up and laid him on the altar over the w.
Ex 25: 5 ram skins and fine goatskin leather; acacia w;
25:10 "Make an Ark of acacia w—a sacred chest 3-3/4
25:13 Make poles from acacia w, and overlay them with
25:23 "Then make a table of acacia w, 3 feet long,
25:28 Make these poles from acacia w and overlay them
26:15 will consist of frames made of acacia w.
26:26 "Make crossbars of acacia w to run across the
26:32 gold hooks set into four posts made from acacia w
26:37 gold hooks set into five posts made from acacia w
27: 1 "Using acacia w, make a square altar 7-1/2 feet
27: 6 For moving the altar, make poles from acacia w,
30: 1 "Then make a small altar out of acacia w for
30: 2 carved from the same piece of w as the altar.
30: 5 The poles are to be made of acacia w and overlaid
31: 5 in cutting and setting gemstones and in carving w.
35: 7 ram skins and fine goatskin leather; acacia w;
35:24 And those who had acacia w brought it.
35:33 in cutting and setting gemstones and in carving w.
36:20 they made frames of acacia w standing on end.
36:31 Then they made five crossbars from acacia w to tie
36:36 to four gold hooks set into four posts of acacia w.
37: 1 Next Bezalel made the Ark out of acacia w. It was
37: 4 Then he made poles from acacia w and overlaid
37:10 Then he made a table out of acacia w, 3 feet long,
37:15 He made the carrying poles of acacia w
37:25 The incense altar was made of acacia w. It was
37:25 made from the same piece of w as the altar itself.
37:28 The carrying poles were made of acacia w
38: 1 animal sacrifices also was constructed of acacia w.
38: 6 carrying poles themselves were made of acacia w
Lev 1: 7 the sons of Aaron the priest will build a w fire on
1: 8 including its head and fat, on the w fire.
1:12 the head and fat, on top of the w fire on the altar.
1:17 Then he will burn it on top of the w fire on the
3: 5 the altar on top of the burnt offering on the w fire.
4:12 He will burn it all on a w fire in the ash heap.
6:12 Each morning the priest will add fresh w to the fire
11:32 This is true whether the object is made of w,
Nu 15:32 they caught a man gathering w on the Sabbath day.
31:20 and everything made of leather, goat hair, or w."
Dt 4:28 you will worship idols made from w and stone,
10: 1 and make a sacred chest of w to keep them in.
10: 3 "So I made a chest of acacia w and cut two stone
19: 5 goes into the forest with a neighbor to cut w.
28:36 Then in exile you will worship gods of w
28:64 ancestors have known, gods made of w and stone!
29:11 the foreigners living among you who chop your w
29:17 You have seen their detestable idols made of w,
Jos 9:21 But we will make them chop the w and carry the
9:23 From now on you will chop w and carry water for
Jdg 6:26 using as fuel the w of the Asherah pole you cut
1Sa 6:14 So the people broke up the w of the cart for a fire
2Sa 24:22 and ox yokes for w to build a fire on the altar.
1Ki 6:15 from floor to ceiling, was paneled with w.
6:23 Solomon placed two cherubim made of olive w,
6:31 Solomon made double doors of olive w with
6:33 Then he made four-sided doorposts of olive w for
6:34 There were two folding doors of cypress w,
10:11 they also brought rich cargoes of almug w
10:12 The king used the almug w to make railings for the
10:12 there been such a supply of beautiful almug w.)
10:27 sycamore w that grows in the foothills of Judah.
18:23 cut it into pieces and lay it on the w of their altar,
18:23 the other bull and lay it on the w on the altar,
18:24 The god who answers by setting fire to the w is the
18:25 name of your god. But do not set fire to the w."
18:33 He piled w on the altar, cut the bull into pieces,
and laid the pieces on the w.
18:33 and pour the water over the offering and the w."
18:38 up the young bull, the w, the stones, and the dust.
19:21 and used the w from the plow to build a fire to
2Ki 19:18 only idols of w and stone shaped by human hands.
1Ch 21:23 and you can use the threshing tools for w to build a
29: 2 there is enough gold, silver, bronze, iron, and w,
2Ch 1:15 sycamore w that grows in the foothills of Judah.
3: 5 room of the Temple was paneled with cypress w,
9:10 they also brought rich cargoes of almug w
9:11 The king used the almug w to make steps for the
9:27 sycamore w that grows in the foothills of Judah.
Ne 10:34 and the common people should bring w to God's
13:31 I also made sure that the supply of w for the altar
Job 13:28 I waste away like rotting w, like a moth-eaten coat.
41:27 iron is nothing but straw, and bronze is rotten w.
Pr 26:21 easily as hot embers light charcoal or fire lights w.
Ecc 10: 9 When you chop w, there is danger with each stroke
SS 3: 9 himself from w imported from Lebanon's forests.
Isa 30:33 the Assyrian king; it has been piled high with w.
37:19 only idols of w and stone shaped by human hands.
44:13 wood-carver measures and marks out a block of w,
44:15 he uses part of the w to make a fire to warm
44:19 never stops to reflect, "Why, it's just a block of w!

44:19 Should I bow down to worship a chunk of w?"
60:17 your iron for silver, your w for bronze, and your
64: 2 As fire causes w to burn and water to boil,
Jer 2:27 To an image carved from a piece of w they say,
3: 9 adultery by worshiping idols made of w
5:14 that will burn them up as if they were kindling w.
7:18 Watch how the children gather w and the fathers
10: 8 The things they worship are made of w!
La 4: 8 skin sticks to their bones; it is as dry and hard as w.
5:13 and the children stagger under heavy loads of w.
Eze 15: 2 Is a vine's w as useful as the w of a tree?
15: 3 Can its w be used for making things, like pegs to
20:32 all around us, who serve idols of w and stone.'
24:10 Yes, heap on the w! Let the fire roar to make the
27: 6 They made your deck of pine w, brought from the
27:15 they brought payment in ivory tusks and ebony w.
39:10 They won't need to cut w from the fields
41:15 the foyer of the Temple were all paneled with w,
41:16 walls of the Temple were paneled with w above
41:22 There was an altar made of w, 3-1/2 feet square
41:22 Its corners, base, and sides were all made of w.
Da 5: 4 made of gold, silver, bronze, iron, w, and stone.
5:23 gods of silver, gold, bronze, iron, w, and stone—
Hos 4:12 They are asking a piece of w to tell them what to
5:12 I will sap Judah's strength as dry rot weakens w.
10: 7 and its king will disappear like a chip of w on an
1Co 3:12 may use gold, silver, jewels, w, hay, or straw.
2Ti 2:20 and silver, and some are made of w and clay.
Rev 9:20 idols made of gold, silver, bronze, stone, and w—
18:12 every kind of perfumed w, ivory goods,
18:12 objects made of expensive w, bronze, iron,

WOOD-CARVER (1) [CARVE, WOOD]

Isa 44:13 Then the w measures and marks out a block of

WOODCHOPPERS (1) [CHOP, WOOD]

Jos 9:27 But that day he made the Gibeonites the w

WOODCUTTERS (1) [CUT, WOOD]

Ps 74: 5 chopped down the entrance / like w in a forest.

WOODED (1) [WOOD]

2Ch 27: 4 constructed fortresses and towers in the w areas.

WOODEN (13) [WOOD]

Ex 7:19 even the water stored in w bowls and stone pots in
Lev 15:12 and every w utensil he touches must be rinsed with
Nu 17: 2 "Take twelve w staffs, one from each of Israel's
35:18 and kills another person with a w weapon.
Ne 8: 4 Ezra the scribe stood on a high w platform that had
Isa 40:20 Or is a poor person's w idol better? Can God be
45:20 What fools they are who carry around their w idols
48: 5 My w image and metal god commanded it to
Jer 28:13 You have broken a w yoke, but you have replaced
Eze 41:25 And there was a w canopy over the front of the
Hab 2:19 How terrible it will be for you who beg lifeless w
Ac 16:22 ordered them stripped and beaten with w rods.
Heb 9: 4 and a w chest called the Ark of the Covenant,

WOODPILE (1) [WOOD]

Zec 12: 6 clans of Judah like a brazier that sets a w ablaze

WOODS (2) [WOOD]

2Ki 2:24 Then two bears came out of the w and mauled
Eze 34:25 the wildest places and sleep in the w without fear.

WOODSMEN (1) [WOOD, MAN]

Jer 46:22 they come against her with axes like w.

WOOL (20) [WOOLEN]

Lev 13:52 burn the linen or w clothing or the piece of leather
Dt 18: 4 new wine, the olive oil, and the w at shearing time.
22:11 "Do not wear clothing made of w and linen woven
Jdg 6:37 I will put some w on the threshing floor tonight.
2Ki 3: 4 of 100,000 lambs and the w of 100,000 rams.
Job 31:20 did they not praise me for providing w clothing to
Ps 147:16 He sends the snow like white w; / he scatters frost
Pr 27:26 your sheep will provide w for clothing, and your
31:13 She finds w and flax and busily spins it.
Isa 1:18 as red as crimson, I can make you as white as w.
51: 8 The worm will eat away at them as it eats w.
Eze 27:18 wine from Helbon and white w from Zahar.
34: 3 You drink the milk, wear the w, and butcher the
44:17 They must wear no w while on duty in the inner
Da 7: 9 was as white as snow, his hair like whitest w.
Hos 2: 5 for food and drink, for clothing of w and linen,
2: 9 and w clothing I gave her to cover her nakedness.
5:12 I will destroy Israel as a moth consumes w. I will
Heb 9:19 using branches of hyssop bushes and scarlet w.
Rev 1:14 His head and his hair were white like w, as white

WOOLEN (3) [WOOL]

Lev 13:47 an infectious mildew contaminates some w
13:48 some w or linen fabric, the hide of an animal,
13:59 for dealing with infectious mildew in w

WOOLLEN [KJV] See also WOOL, WOOLEN

WORD (214) [WORDS]

WORD OF GOD (27) Pr 30:5; Mt 4:4; Lk 5:1; 11:28; Ac 6:2; 11:1; 13:5,7; 17:13; 18:11; 2Co 4:2; Gal 6:6; Eph 6:17; 1Th 2:13; 1Ti 4:5; 2Ti 2:9; 4:2; Tit 2:5; Heb 4:12; 6:5; 13:7; 1Pe 1:23; Rev 1:2,9; 6:9; 19:13; 20:4

WORD OF THE LORD (8) Mt 8:17; Ac 8:25; 13:44; 15:35,36; 16:32; 1Th 1:8; 1Pe 1:25

WORD OF THE LORD* (21) Ex 9:21; Dt 8:3; 1Sa 15:23; 2Sa 12:9; 24:11; 2Ch 30:12; 34:21; Ps 33:4; Jer 2:4; 6:10; 8:9; 10:1; Eze 13:2; 20:47; 34:7,9; 36:1; 37:4; Da 9:2; Hos 4:1; Am 8:12

Ge 34: 5 W soon reached Jacob that his daughter had been
37: 4 They couldn't say a kind w to him.
37:14 Jacob said. "Then come back and bring me w."
38:24 w reached Judah that Tamar, his daughter-in-law,
44:18 "My lord, let me say just this one w to you.
48: 1 w came to Joseph that his father was failing
Ex 9:21 But those who had no respect for the w of the
14: 5 When w reached the king of Egypt that the
18: 1 W soon reached Jethro, the priest of Midian
18:19 Now let me give you a w of advice, and may God
22:11 The owner must accept the neighbor's w, and no
Nu 5:27 and her name will become a curse w among her
11:23 you will see whether or not my w comes true!"
15:31 Since they have treated the LORD's w with
32:20 "If you keep your w and arm yourselves for the
32:23 But if you fail to keep your w, then you will have
Dt 8: 3 real life comes by feeding on every w of the
32:46 so they will obey every w of this law.
33: 9 The Levites obeyed your w / and guarded your
Jos 1:18 Anyone who rebels against your w and does not
6:10 "Not a single w from any of you until I tell you to
10:21 After that, no one dared to speak a w against Israel.
24:27 against you if you go back on your w to God."
Jdg 12: 6 from Ephraim cannot pronounce the w correctly.
16: 2 W soon spread that Samson was there, so the men
20: 3 (W soon reached the land of Benjamin that the
1Sa 15:23 because you have rejected the w of the LORD,
16:22 Then Saul sent w to Jesse asking, "Please let
23:13 W soon reached Saul that David had escaped,
27: 4 W soon reached Saul that David had fled to Gath,
2Sa 3:11 Ishbosheth didn't dare say another w because he
11: 6 So David sent w to Joab: "Send me Uriah the
12: 9 have you despised the w of the LORD and done
12:25 and sent w through Nathan the prophet that his
16:23 For every w Ahithophel spoke seemed as wise as
19: 1 W soon reached Joab that the king was weeping
19:14 They sent w to the king, "Return to us, and bring
24:11 The next morning the w of the LORD came to the
1Ki 1:51 W soon reached Solomon that Adonijah had seized
3:28 W of the king's decision spread quickly
8:56 Not one w has failed of all the wonderful promises
13:26 The LORD has fulfilled his w by causing the lion
17: 1 during the next few years unless I give the w!"
21:14 The city officials then sent w to Jezebel,
2Ki 2:16 "just say the w and fifty of our strongest men will
4:13 Does she want me to put in a good w for her to the
6:10 So the king of Israel would send w to the place
19: 9 Soon afterward King Sennacherib received w that
2Ch 30: 1 King Hezekiah now sent w to all Israel and Judah,
30:12 who were following the w of the LORD.
34:21 because our ancestors have not obeyed the w of the
Ne 9: 8 you promised, for you are always true to your w.
Est 9:26 because it is the ancient w for casting lots.)
Job 2:13 And no one said a w, for they saw that his
4: 2 "Will you be patient and let me say a w? For who
15:11 too little for you? Is his gentle w not enough?
23:12 but have treasured his w in my heart.
Ps 5: 9 My enemies cannot speak one truthful w.
19: 3 They speak without a sound or a w; / their voice is
33: 4 For the w of the LORD holds true,
33: 6 He breathed the w, / and all the stars were born.
39: 9 I am silent before you; I won't say a w. / For my
56: 4 O God, I praise your w. / I trust in God, so why
56:10 God, I praise your w. / Yes, LORD, I praise your w.
58: 1 Justice—do you rulers know the meaning of the w?
89:34 I will not take back a single w I said.
105:19 Until the time came to fulfill his w, / the LORD
119: 9 By obeying your w and following its rules.
119:11 I have hidden your w in my heart, / that I might not
119:16 delight in your principles / and not forget your w.
119:17 to your servant, / that I may live and obey your w.
119:25 completely discouraged; / revive me by your w.
119:28 I weep with grief; / encourage me by your w.
119:37 and give me life through your w.
119:42 for those who taunt me, / for I trust in your w.
119:43 Do not snatch your w of truth from me, / for my
119:67 disciplined me; / but now I closely follow your w.
119:74 a cause for joy, / for I have put my hope in your w.
119:81 your salvation; / but I have put my hope in your w.
119:89 O LORD, / your w stands firm in heaven.
119:101 of evil, / that I may remain obedient to your w.
119:105 Your w is a lamp for my feet / and a light for my
119:114 and my shield; / your w is my only source of hope.
119:133 Guide my steps by your w, / so I will not be
119:158 because they care nothing for your w.
119:161 but my heart trembles only at your w.
119:162 I rejoice in your w / like one who finds a great
119:172 Let my tongue sing about your w, / for all your
130: 5 am counting on him. / I have put my hope in his w.
147:15 his orders to the world— / how swiftly his w flies!
Pr 12:22 The LORD hates those who don't keep their w,
12:25 an encouraging w cheers a person up.
16:30 plot evil; without a w, they plan their mischief.
30: 5 Every w of God proves true. He defends all who
Isa 2: 3 and his w will go out from Jerusalem.
5:24 They have despised the w of the Holy One of
37: 9 Soon afterward King Sennacherib received w that
40: 8 but the w of our God stands forever."
41:26 you admit that he was right? No one else said a w!
45:23 my own name, and I will never go back on my w:
53: 7 and treated harshly, yet he never said a w.
55:11 It is the same with my w. I send it out, and it
65:15 Your name will be a curse w among my people,
66: 2 and contrite hearts, who tremble at my w.
Jer 2: 4 Listen to the w of the LORD, people of Jacob—
6:10 they cannot hear. They scorn the w of the LORD.
8: 9 for they have rejected the w of the LORD.
10: 1 Hear the w of the LORD, O Israel!
20: 9 in his name, his w burns in my heart like a fire.
23:17 keep saying to these rebels who despise my w,
23:28 true messengers faithfully proclaim my every w.
23:29 Does not my w burn like fire?" asks the LORD.
26: 2 Give them my entire message; include every w.
26:12 "The LORD gave me every w that I have spoken.
26:15 sent me to speak every w you have heard."
36:18 "Jeremiah dictated them to me w by w,
Eze 13: 2 Tell them to listen to the w of the LORD.
20: 3 This is the w of the Sovereign LORD!
20:47 Hear the w of the LORD! I will set you on fire,
22:28 when the LORD hasn't spoken a single w to
25: 3 Hear the w of the Sovereign LORD! Because you
26:14 This is the w of the Sovereign LORD.
34: 7 you shepherds, hear the w of the LORD:
34: 9 you shepherds, hear the w of the LORD.
35:12 have heard every contemptuous w you spoke
36: 1 O mountains of Israel, hear the w of the LORD!
36: 4 of Israel, hear the w of the Sovereign LORD.
37: 4 and say, 'Dry bones, listen to the w of the LORD!
Da 3:29 speak a w against the God of Shadrach, Meshach,
9: 2 I learned from the w of the LORD, as recorded by
10:15 I looked down at the ground, unable to say a w.
Hos 4: 1 Hear the w of the LORD, O people of Israel!
Am 8:12 searching for the w of the LORD, running here
8:13 and weary, thirsting for the LORD's w.
Mic 4: 2 and his w will go out from Jerusalem.
Mt 4: 4 their life; / they must feed on every w of God.' "
5:37 'Yes, I will,' or 'No, I won't.' Your w is enough.
8: 8 Just say the w from where you are, and my servant
8:17 This fulfilled the w of the Lord through Isaiah,
12:36 on judgment day of every idle w you speak.
13:21 or are persecuted because they believe the w.
15:23 But Jesus gave her no reply—not even a w.
Mk 2: 2 outside the door. And he preached the w to them.
3:31 They stood outside and sent w for him to come out
4:17 or are persecuted because they believe the w.
Lk 1:58 The w spread quickly to her neighbors
5: 1 great crowds pressed in on him to listen to the w of
7: 7 Just say the w from where you are, and my servant
11:28 "But even more blessed are all who hear the w of
19:48 because all the people hung on every w he said.
Jn 1: 1 In the beginning the W already existed. He was
1:14 So the W became human and lived here on earth
4:50 And the man believed Jesus' w and started home.
11:20 When Martha got w that Jesus was coming,
17: 6 you gave them to me; and they have kept your w.
17:14 I have given them your w. And the world hates
Ac 6: 2 our time preaching and teaching the w of God,
6: 4 time in prayer and preaching and teaching the w."
8:25 and preaching the w of the Lord in Samaria,
11: 1 Judea that the Gentiles had received the w of God.
13: 5 the Jewish synagogues and preached the w of God.
13: 7 to visit him, for he wanted to hear the w of God.
13:15 if you have any w of encouragement for us, come
13:44 turned out to hear them preach the w of the Lord.
15:35 and preaching the w of the Lord there.
15:36 where we previously preached the w of the Lord,
16:32 Then they shared the w of the Lord with him
17:13 that Paul was preaching the w of God in Berea,
18:11 for the next year and a half, teaching the w of God.
20:32 now I entrust you to God and the w of his grace—
21:31 w reached the commander of the Roman regiment
21:37 to the commander, "May I have a w with you?"
22:22 The crowd listened until Paul came to that w,
28:25 they left with this final w from Paul:
1Co 14: 4 but one who speaks a w of prophecy strengthens
14:36 Do you think that the knowledge of God's w
2Co 4: 2 trick anyone, and we do not distort the w of God.
Gal 6: 6 Those who are taught the w of God should help
Eph 5:26 and clean, washed by baptism and God's w.
6: 4 And now a w to you fathers. Don't make your
6:10 A final w: Be strong with the Lord's mighty
6:17 the sword of the Spirit, which is the w of God.
Php 2:15 so that no one can speak a w of blame against you.
2:16 Hold tightly to the w of life, so that when Christ
1Th 1: 8 And now the w of the Lord is ringing out from you
2:13 You accepted what we said as the very w of God—
2:13 And this w continues to work in you who believe.
1Ti 4: 5 For we know it is made holy by the w of God
2Ti 2: 9 a criminal. But the w of God cannot be chained.
2:15 and who correctly explains the w of truth.
4: 2 Preach the w of God. Be persistent,
Tit 2: 5 Then they will not bring shame on the w of God.
Heb 4:12 For the w of God is full of living power. It is
6: 5 who have tasted the goodness of the w of God
13: 7 Remember your leaders who first taught you the w
Jas 1:18 make us his own children by giving us his true w.
1Pe 1:23 because it comes from the eternal, living w of God.
1:25 But the w of the Lord will last forever." And that
w is the Good News that was preached to
2: 8 because they do not listen to God's w or obey it,
5: 1 a w to you who are elders in the churches.
2Pe 3: 5 God made the heavens by the w of his command,
1Jn 1: 1 our own hands. He is Jesus Christ, the W of life.
1:10 and showing that his w has no place in our hearts.
2: 5 But those who obey God's w really do love him.

2:14 because you are strong with God's w living in your
Rev 1:2 John faithfully reported the w of God
1:9 to the island of Patmos for preaching the w of God
3:8 yet you obeyed my w and did not deny me.
6:9 of all who had been martyred for the w of God
19:13 dipped in blood, and his title was the W of God.
20:4 about Jesus, for proclaiming the w of God.

WORDS (294) [WORD]

ALL THE WORDS (3) Dt 9:10; 32:44,46
WORDS OF GOD (6) Nu 24:4,16; Ps 107:11; Isa 40:21; Jn 8:47; Rev 17:17
WORDS OF THE LAW (2) Dt 29:29; Ne 8:9

Ge 11:1 spoke a single language and used the same w.
24:45 "Before I had finished praying these w, I saw
Ex 4:10 after you have spoken to me. I'm clumsy with w."
4:15 You will talk to him, giving him the w to say.
28:36 techniques of an engraver, inscribe it with these w:
32:16 the w on them were written by God himself.
33:4 When the people heard these stern w, they went
34:1 I will write on them the same w that were on the
39:30 of an engraver, they inscribed it with these w:
Nu 11:24 and reported the LORD's w to the people.
14:39 When Moses reported the LORD's w to the
16:31 He had hardly finished speaking the w when the
24:4 who hears the w of God, / who sees a vision from
24:16 who hears the w of God, / who has knowledge
Dt 1:1 This book records the w that Moses spoke to all
4:12 You heard his w but didn't see his form; there was
5:5 He spoke to me, and I passed his w on to you.
5:22 "The LORD spoke these w with a loud voice to
5:22 and he wrote his w on two stone tablets and gave
9:10 w he had spoken to you from the fire on the
10:2 and I will write on the tablets the same w that were
10:4 They were the same w the LORD had spoken to
11:18 So commit yourselves completely to these w of
29:29 so that we may obey these w of the law.
31:19 "Now write down the w of this song, and teach it
31:22 So that very day Moses wrote down the w of the
31:23 commissioned Joshua son of Nun with these w:
32:1 and I will speak! / Hear, O earth, the w that I say!
32:2 like dew. / My w will fall like rain on tender grass,
32:44 and recited all the w of this song to the people.
32:45 When Moses had finished reciting these w to
32:46 "Take to heart all the w I have given you today.
32:47 These instructions are not mere w—they are your
Jdg 5:29 wise women, / and she repeats these w to herself:
13:12 So Manoah asked him, "When your w come true,
1Sa 4:1 And Samuel's w went out to all the people of
28:20 paralyzed with fright because of Samuel's w.
2Sa 7:28 Your w are truth, and you have promised these
22:2 These are the w he sang: / "The LORD is my
23:1 These are the last w of David: / "David, the son of
23:2 speaks through me; / his w are upon my tongue.
1Ki 1:48 and he spoke these w: 'Blessed be the LORD,
8:59 And may these w that I have prayed in the
2Ki 6:12 tells the king of Israel even the w you speak in the
18:20 Do you think that mere w can substitute for
19:4 the living God and will punish him for his w.
19:16 Listen to Sennacherib's w of defiance against the
22:13 Ask him about the w written in this scroll that has
22:13 because our ancestors have not obeyed the w in
2Ch 5:13 their voices and praised the LORD with these w:
13:22 of Abijah's reign, including his w and deeds,
24:22 Zechariah's last w as he died were,
32:8 for us!" These w greatly encouraged the people.
33:18 and the w the seers spoke to him in the name of the
34:21 Ask him about the w written in this scroll that has
36:16 these messengers of God and despised their w.
Ezr 9:4 Then all who trembled at the w of the God of Israel
Ne 8:9 been weeping as they listened to the w of the law.
8:12 because they had heard God's w and understood
Job 2:13 for they saw that his suffering was too great for w.
4:4 Your w have strengthened the fallen; you steadied
5:15 He rescues the poor from the cutting w of the
6:10 the pain, I have not denied the w of the Holy One.
6:25 Honest w are painful, but what do your criticisms
6:26 Do you think your w are convincing when you
8:2 you go on like this? Your w are a blustering wind.
11:2 "Shouldn't someone answer this torrent of w?
12:11 tastes good food, so the ear tests the w it hears.
15:3 to speak so foolishly. What good do such w do?
15:5 what to say. Your w are based on clever deception.
16:3 Won't you ever stop your flow of foolish w?
19:2 How long will you try to break me with your w?
19:23 "Oh, that my w could be written. Oh, that they
29:23 for my w were as refreshing as the spring rain.
31:40 and weeds instead of barley." Job's w are ended.
32:11 to your arguments, listening to you grope for w.
32:18 For I am pent up and full of w, and the spirit within
32:19 cask without a vent. My w are ready to burst out!
33:8 said it in my hearing. I have heard your very w.
34:3 tastes good food, the ear tests the w it hears.'
34:35 speaks without knowledge; his w lack insight.'
38:2 that questions my wisdom with such ignorant w?
Ps 19:4 out to all the earth, / and their w to all the world.
19:14 May the w of my mouth and the thoughts of my
28:3 those who speak friendly w to their neighbors
39:3 and began to burn, / igniting a fire of w:
45:2 of all. / Gracious w stream from your lips.
49:3 For my w are wise, / and my thoughts are filled
55:21 His w are as smooth as cream, / but in his heart is war. / His w are as soothing as lotion,
64:3 they wield; / bitter w are the arrows they aim.
64:8 Their own w will be turned against them,
73:9 and their w strut throughout the earth.
73:10 and confused, / drinking in all their w.
78:36 But they followed him only with their w;
107:11 They rebelled against the w of God,
109:3 They are all around me with their hateful w,
119:57 LORD, you are mine! / I promise to obey your w!
119:103 How sweet are your w to my taste; / they are
119:130 As your w are taught, they give light;
119:139 for my enemies have disregarded your w.
119:147 I cry out for help and put my hope in your w.
119:160 All your w are true; / all your just laws will stand
138:4 O LORD, / for all of them will hear your w.
141:6 they will listen to my w and find them pleasing.
147:19 He has revealed his w to Jacob, / his principles
Pr 4:4 My father told me, "Take my w to heart.
4:5 Don't forget or turn away from my w.
4:21 Don't lose sight of my w. Let them penetrate deep
6:21 Keep their w always in your heart. Tie them
7:24 Listen to me, my sons, and pay attention to my w.
8:9 My w are plain to anyone with understanding,
10:11 The w of the godly lead to life; evil people cover
10:13 Wise w come from the lips of people with
10:20 The w of the godly are like sterling silver; the heart
10:32 The godly speak w that are helpful, but the wicked
11:9 Evil w destroy one's friends; wise discernment
12:6 The w of the wicked are like a murderous ambush,
12:6 but the w of the godly save lives.
12:13 The wicked are trapped by their own w,
12:14 People can get many good things by the w they
12:18 but the w of the wise bring healing.
13:2 Good people enjoy the positive results of their w,
14:3 but the w of the wise keep them out of trouble.
15:1 turns away wrath, but harsh w stir up anger.
15:4 Gentle w bring life and health; a deceitful tongue
15:26 thoughts of the wicked, but he delights in pure w.
15:28 think before speaking; the wicked spout evil w.
16:23 wise speech; the w of the wise are persuasive.
16:24 Kind w are like honey—sweet to the soul
16:27 hunt for scandal; their w are a destructive blaze.
17:4 to wicked talk; liars pay attention to destructive w.
17:27 A truly wise person uses few w; a person with
18:4 A person's w can be life-giving water; w of true wisdom are as refreshing as a bubbling
18:20 W satisfy the soul as food satisfies the stomach;
18:20 the right w on a person's lips bring satisfaction.
22:17 Listen to the w of the wise; apply your heart to my
23:8 and you will have to take back your w of
23:12 attune your ears to hear w of knowledge.
24:2 and their w are always stirring up trouble.
26:23 Smooth w may hide a wicked heart, just as a pretty
29:19 For a servant, mere w are not enough—
29:19 For the w may be understood, but they are not
30:6 Do not add to his w, or he may rebuke you,
31:26 When she speaks, her w are wise, and kindness is
Ecc 1:1 These are the w of the Teacher, King David's son,
5:2 you are only here on earth. So let your w be few.
5:7 And there is ruin in a flood of empty w. Fear God
6:11 The more w you speak, the less they mean. So why
9:17 the quiet w of a wise person are better than the
10:12 It is pleasant to listen to wise w, but the speech of
12:11 A wise teacher's w spur students to action
Isa 6:9 'You will hear my w, but you will not understand.
28:10 and over again, a line at a time, in very simple w!"
28:13 it over and over, a line at a time, in very simple w.
29:18 In that day deaf people will hear w read from a
30:8 Now go and write down these w concerning Egypt.
30:27 lips are filled with fury; his w consume like fire.
34:1 Let the world and everything in it hear my w.
36:5 Do you think that mere w can substitute for
37:4 the living God and will punish him for his w.
37:17 Listen to Sennacherib's w of defiance against the
40:21 Are you deaf to the w of God—the w he gave before the world began?
41:6 They encourage one another with the w,
49:2 He made my w of judgment as sharp as a sword.
50:4 The Sovereign LORD has given me his w of
51:16 And I have put my w in your mouth and hidden
57:19 Then w of praise will be on their lips. May they
59:21 and neither will these w I have given you.
66:5 message from the LORD, and tremble at his w:
Jer 1:1 These are the w of Jeremiah son of Hilkiah, one of
1:9 and said, "See, I have put my w in your mouth!
2:31 "O my people, listen to the w of the LORD!
3:12 Therefore, go and say these w to Israel, 'This is
5:13 God's prophets are windbags full of w with no
9:20 Listen, you women, to the w of the LORD;
11:19 "Let's destroy this man and all his w," they said.
15:16 Your w are what sustain me. They bring me great
15:19 If you speak w that are worthy, you will be my
19:2 and repeat to them the w that I give you.
20:8 I speak, the w come out in a violent outburst.
23:9 because of the holy w the LORD has spoken
23:22 they would have spoken my w and turned my
23:36 turning upside down the w of our God, the living
28:7 But listen now to the solemn w I speak to you in
36:10 Baruch read Jeremiah's w to all the people from
36:18 and I wrote down his w with ink on this scroll."
44:28 who came to Egypt will find out whose w are true,
La 3:19 my suffering and homelessness is bitter beyond w.
Eze 2:2 and set me on my feet. I listened carefully to his w.
2:10 other w of sorrow, and pronouncements of doom.
3:10 let all my w sink deep into your own heart first.
17:21 will know that I, the LORD, have spoken these w.
29:21 to revive, and then at last your w will be respected.
37:7 So I spoke these w, just as he told me. Suddenly as
37:16 "Son of man, take a stick and carve on it these w:
37:16 Then take another stick and carve these w on it:
Da 4:31 While he was still speaking these w, a voice called
5:16 If you can read these w and tell me their meaning,
5:26 This is what these w mean: / *Mene* means
10:19 As he spoke these w, I suddenly felt stronger
Hos 5:1 These w of judgment are for you: You are
6:5 I have slaughtered you with my w, threatening you
10:4 They spout empty w and make promises they don't
Am 8:11 or water but of hearing the w of the LORD.
Mic 2:7 do what is right, you would find my w to be good.
Zec 1:13 and comforting w to the angel who talked with me.
14:20 bells of the horses will be inscribed with these w:
Mal 2:17 You have wearied the LORD with your w.
Mt 6:7 are answered only by repeating their w again
10:19 because you will be given the right w at the right
12:35 A good person produces good w from a good
12:35 and an evil person produces evil w from an evil
12:37 The w you say now reflect your fate then;
13:14 of Isaiah, which says: / 'You will hear my w,
15:8 'These people honor me with their w, / but their
15:18 But evil w come from an evil heart and defile the
24:35 earth will disappear, but my w will remain forever.
26:29 Mark my w—I will not drink wine again until the
26:56 But this is all happening to fulfill the w of the
26:75 Suddenly, Jesus' w flashed through Peter's mind:
Mk 4:12 They hear my w, / but they don't understand.
13:31 earth will disappear, but my w will remain forever.
14:72 Suddenly, Jesus' w flashed through Peter's mind:
Lk 1:20 For my w will certainly come true at the proper
4:22 and were amazed by the gracious w that fell from
4:36 "What authority and power this man's w possess!
21:15 for I will give you the right w and such wisdom
21:22 and the prophetic w of the Scriptures will be
21:33 earth will disappear, but my w will remain forever.
22:60 And as soon as he said these w, the rooster crowed.
23:38 was nailed to the cross above him with these w:
23:46 And with those w he breathed his last.
Jn 1:23 John replied in the w of Isaiah: / "I am a voice
3:34 He speaks God's w, for God's Spirit is upon him
6:63 And the very w I have spoken to you are spirit
6:68 we go? You alone have the w that give eternal life.
8:47 whose Father is God listens gladly to the w of God.
14:10 The w I say are not my own, but my Father who
14:24 And remember, my w are not my own.
15:7 if you stay joined to me and my w remain in you,
17:8 for I have passed on to them the w you gave me;
17:17 and holy by teaching them your w of truth.
Ac 2:29 to himself when he spoke these w I have quoted,
2:37 Peter's w convicted them deeply, and they said to
5:5 As soon as Ananias heard these w, he fell to the
7:38 and the angel who gave him life-giving w on
11:16 Then I thought of the Lord's w when he said,
13:27 though they hear the prophets' w read every
13:40 Be careful! Don't let the prophets' w apply to you.
18:15 But since it is merely a question of w and names
20:35 You should remember the w of the Lord Jesus:
28:26 and say to my people, / You will hear my w,
Ro 8:26 us with groanings that cannot be expressed in w.
9:13 In the w of the Scriptures, "I loved Jacob, but I
10:18 gone out to everyone, / and its w to all the world."
16:18 and glowing w they deceive innocent people.
1Co 2:1 when I first came to you I didn't use lofty w
2:6 mature Christians, I do speak with w of wisdom,
2:13 tell you this, we do not use w of human wisdom.
2:13 We speak w given to us by the Spirit,
2:13 using the Spirit's w to explain spiritual truths.
14:15 pray in the spirit, and I will pray in w I understand.
14:15 sing in the spirit, and I will sing in w I understand.
14:19 w that will help others than ten thousand w in an unknown language.
2Co 9:15 God for his Son—a gift too wonderful for w!
13:11 Dear friends, I close my letter with these last w:
Gal 6:11 as I write these closing w in my own handwriting.
Eph 4:29 so that your w will be an encouragement to those
4:31 of all bitterness, rage, anger, harsh w, and slander,
6:19 Ask God to give me the right w as I boldly explain
Col 3:16 Let the w of Christ, in all their richness, live in
3:16 Use his w to teach and counsel each other.
1Th 1:5 it was not only with w but also with power,
2:13 you didn't think of the w we spoke as being just
4:18 So comfort and encourage each other with these w.
1Ti 1:18 based on the prophetic w spoken about you earlier.
6:4 unhealthy desire to quibble over the meaning of w.
2Ti 2:14 them in God's name to stop fighting over w.
Heb 4:7 David a long time later in the w already quoted:
12:5 And have you entirely forgotten the encouraging w
1Pe 3:1 godly lives will speak to them better than any w.
2Pe 1:19 for their w are like a light shining in a dark place—
Rev 5:9 And they sang a new song with these w:
13:6 And he spoke terrible w of blasphemy against God,
17:17 scarlet beast, and so the w of God will be fulfilled.
19:9 "These are true w that come from God."
22:6 said to me, "These w are trustworthy and true:
22:10 "Do not seal up the prophetic w you have written,
22:18 everyone who hears the prophetic w of this book:
22:19 And if anyone removes any of the w of this

WORE (17) [WEAR]

Ex 33:6 left Mount Sinai, the Israelites w no more jewelry.
Lev 16:23 he must take off the linen garments he w when he
Jdg 8:24 being Ishmaelites, all w gold earrings.)
1Sa 2:18 He w a linen tunic just like that of a priest.
17:5 He w a bronze helmet and a coat of mail that
17:6 He also w bronze leggings, and he slung a bronze
2Ki 1:8 and he w a leather belt around his waist."
Est 8:15 and he w an outer cloak of fine linen and purple.
Job 29:14 me like a robe, and I w justice like a turban.

Eze 42:14 They must first take off the clothes they **w** while
Da 9: 3 I **w** rough sackcloth and sprinkled myself with
Mt 3: 4 woven from camel hair, and he **w** a leather belt;
Mk 1: 6 woven from camel hair, and he **w** a leather belt;
Lk 18: 4 her for a while, but eventually she **w** him out.
Rev 9: 9 They **w** armor made of iron, and their wings roared
9:17 The riders **w** armor that was fiery red and sky blue
17: 4 The woman **w** purple and scarlet clothing

WORK (388) [CO-WORKER, CO-WORKERS, HANDIWORK, HARDWORKING, MIRACLE-WORKING, STONEWORK, WORKDAYS, WORKED, WORKER, WORKERS, WORKING, WORKMAN'S, WORKMANSHIP, WORKMEN, WORKS]

Ge 2: 2 having finished his task, God rested from all his **w**.
2: 3 because it was the day when he rested from his **w**
4:12 crops for you, no matter how hard you **w**!
4:22 He was the first to **w** with metal,
29:15 "You shouldn't **w** for me without pay just
29:18 "I'll **w** for you seven years if you'll give me
29:27 if you promise to **w** another seven years for me."
29:28 So Jacob agreed to **w** seven more years. A week
30:31 Just do one thing, and I'll go back to **w** for you.
31:42 But God has seen your cruelty and my hard **w**.
39:11 no one else was around when he was doing his **w**
Ex 1:14 and mortar and to **w** long hours in the fields.
2:11 and he saw how hard they were forced to **w**.
5: 4 the people from their tasks? Get back to **w**!
5: 5 and you are stopping them from doing their **w**."
5: 9 Load them down with more **w**. Make them sweat!
5:14 the Israelite foremen in charge of the **w** crews.
5:18 Now, get back to **w**! No straw will be given to you,
12:16 No **w** of any kind may be done on these days
20: 9 are set apart for your daily duties and regular **w**,
20:10 no one in your household may do any kind of **w**.
23:12 "**W** for six days, and rest on the seventh. This will
27:19 "All the articles used in the **w** of the Tabernacle,
28: 2 beautiful garments that will lend dignity to his **w**.
31:15 **W** six days only, but the seventh day must be a day
32:16 These stone tablets were God's **w**; the words on
34:21 "Six days are set aside for **w**, but on the Sabbath
35: 2 Each week, **w** for six days only. The seventh day is
35:29 and woman who wanted to help in the **w** the
35:35 They excel in all the crafts needed for the **w**.
36: 2 So Moses told Bezalel and Oholiab to begin the **w**,
36: 4 But finally the craftsmen left their **w** to meet with
39:43 Moses inspected all their **w** and blessed them
40:33 of the courtyard. So at last Moses finished the **w**.
Lev 8:12 thus anointing him and making him holy for his **w**.
16:29 you must spend the day fasting and not do any **w**.
23: 3 You may **w** for six days each week, but on the seventh day all **w** must come to a
23: 7 all the people must stop their regular **w** and gather
23: 8 the people must again stop all their regular **w** to
23:21 you must stop all your regular **w** and gather for a
23:24 of complete rest. All your **w** must stop on that day.
23:25 You must do no regular **w** on that day. Instead,
23:28 Do no **w** during that entire day because it is the
23:30 among you who does any kind of **w** on that day.
23:31 You must do no **w** at all! This is a permanent law
23:35 on the first day, and all your regular **w** must stop.
23:36 and no regular **w** may be done that day.
26:20 All your **w** will be for nothing, for your land will
Nu 4: 3 and fifty who qualify to **w** in the Tabernacle.
4:27 whether it involves moving or doing other **w**.
7: 5 these oxen and carts for the **w** of the Tabernacle.
7: 5 the Levites according to the **w** they have to do."
7: 7 four oxen to the Gershonite division for their **w**,
7: 8 and eight oxen to the Merarite division for their **w**.
7: 8 All their **w** was done under the leadership of
8:15 may go in and out of the Tabernacle to do their **w**,
14:41 orders to return to the wilderness? It won't **w**.
28:18 None of your regular **w** may be done on that day.
28:25 None of your regular **w** may be done on that day.
28:26 None of your regular **w** may be done on that day.
29: 1 people on that day, and no regular **w** may be done.
29: 7 go without food, and no regular **w** may be done.
29:12 and on that day no regular **w** may be done.
29:35 You must do no regular **w** on that day.
Dt 5:13 are set apart for your daily duties and regular **w**,
5:14 no one in your household may do any kind of **w**.
14:29 the LORD your God will bless you in all your **w**.
15:19 Do not use the firstborn of your herds to **w** your
16: 8 your God, and no **w** may be done on that day.
16:15 you bountiful harvests and blesses all your **w**.
27:15 These idols, the **w** of craftsmen, are detestable to
28:12 treasury in the heavens to bless all the **w** you do.
32: 4 He is the Rock; his **w** is perfect. / Everything he
33:11 the Levites, O LORD, / and accept all their **w**.
Jos 17:13 they forced the Canaanites to **w** as slaves.
Jdg 1:28 they forced the Canaanites to **w** as slaves,
1:30 among them. But they forced them to **w** as slaves.
1:33 and Beth-anath were sometimes forced to **w** as
1:35 they forced the Amorites to **w** as slaves.
13:12 kind of rules should govern the boy's life and **w**?"
14: 4 and mother didn't realize the LORD was at **w** in
19:16 That evening an old man came home from his **w** in
Ru 2: 7 She has been hard at **w** ever since, except for a few
2:15 When Ruth went back to **w** again, Boaz ordered
2:19 you gather all this grain today? Where did you **w**?
2Sa 12:31 picks, and axes, and to **w** in the brick kilns.
13:24 and said, "My sheep-shearers are now at **w**.
16:18 because I **w** for the man who is chosen by the
19:41 do most of the **w** in helping him cross the Jordan.
1Ki 5: 6 Let my men **w** alongside yours, and I will pay your
5:16 and thirty-six hundred foremen to supervise the **w**.
7:14 for he was a craftsman skilled in bronze **w**. He was
7:14 from Tyre. So he came to **w** for King Solomon.
7:22 like lilies. And so the **w** on the pillars was finished.
7:51 So King Solomon finished all his **w** on the Temple
8:11 The priests could not continue their **w**
9:25 so he finished the **w** of building the Temple.
1Ch 6:32 Then they carried on their **w** there, following all
22:16 Now begin the **w**, and may the LORD be with
23: 4 will supervise the **w** at the Temple of the LORD.
23: 5 Four thousand will **w** as gatekeepers, and another
23:28 The **w** of the Levites was to assist the priests,
25: 1 Here is a list of their names and their **w**:
26: 8 were very capable men, well qualified for their **w**.
28:10 Temple as his sanctuary. Be strong, and do the **w**."
28:13 concerning the **w** of the various divisions of priests
28:20 "Be strong and courageous, and do the **w**.
28:20 He will see to it that all the **w** related to the Temple
29: 1 The **w** ahead of him is enormous, for the Temple
29: 5 and silver **w** to be done by the craftsmen.
2Ch 2: 7 "So send me a master craftsman who can **w** with
2: 7 and a skilled engraver who can **w** with the
2:14 He will **w** with your craftsmen and those appointed
5: 1 When Solomon had finished all the **w** related to
5:14 The priests could not continue their **w**
8:16 So Solomon made sure that all the **w** related to
13:10 and the Levites alone may help them in their **w**.
15: 7 and courageous, for your **w** will be rewarded."
20:37 King Ahaziah, the LORD will destroy your **w**."
26:18 That is the **w** of the priests alone, the sons of Aaron who are set apart for this **w**.
29:12 Then these Levites got right to **w**: / From the clan
29:15 to follow all the LORD's instructions in their **w**.
29:17 The **w** began on a day in early spring, and in eight
29:34 the Levites helped them until the **w** was finished
30:14 They set to **w** and removed the pagan altars from
32: 1 After Hezekiah had faithfully carried out this **w**,
32: 4 They organized a huge **w** crew to stop the flow of
35: 2 and encouraged them in their **w** at the Temple of
Ezr 3: 8 The **w** force was made up of everyone who had
4: 3 "You may have no part in this **w**, for we have
4: 4 the people of Judah to keep them from their **w**.
4: 5 They bribed agents to **w** against them and to
4:21 issue orders to have these people stop their **w**.
4:24 The **w** on the Temple of God in Jerusalem had
5: 8 The **w** is going forward with great energy
6: 7 of Judah and the leaders of the Jews in their **w**.
6: 8 so that the **w** will not be discontinued.
6:14 So the Jewish leaders continued their **w**, and they
Ne 2:18 Let's rebuild the wall!" So they began the good **w**.
3:25 Palal son of Uzai carried on the **w** from a point
4: 7 and Ashdodites heard that the **w** was going ahead
4:11 down on them and kill them and end their **w**."
4:15 we all returned to our **w** on the wall.
4:17 The common laborers carried on their **w** with one
4:19 and all the people, "The **w** is very spread out,
4:22 on guard duty at night as well as **w** during the day.
6: 3 "I am doing a great **w**! I cannot stop to come
6: 9 that they could break our resolve and stop the **w**.
6: 9 So I prayed for strength to continue the **w**.
6:16 They realized that this **w** had been done with the
7:70 "Some of the family leaders gave gifts for the **w**.
7:71 and some 2,750 pounds of silver for the **w**.
10:31 And we promise not to do any **w** every seventh
10:33 necessary for the **w** of the Temple of our God.
11:16 who were in charge of the **w** outside the Temple of
12:44 of Judah valued the priests and Levites and their **w**.
13:10 worship services had all returned to **w** their fields.
13:30 and Levites, making certain that each knew his **w**.
Job 10: 3 the **w** of your own hands, while sending joy
39:11 Can you go away and trust the ox to do your **w**?
41: 4 Will it agree to **w** for you? Can you make it be
Ps 8: 3 at the night sky and see the **w** of your fingers—
34:14 do good. / **W** hard at living in peace with others.
69:32 The humble will see their God at **w** and be glad.
90:16 let our children see your glory at **w**.
102:25 and the heavens are the **w** of your hands.
104:23 Then people go off to their **w**; / they labor until the
127: 1 builds a house, / the **w** of the builders is useless.
127: 2 It is useless for you to **w** so hard / from early
138: 8 The LORD will **w** out his plans for my life—
Pr 6: 7 have no prince, governor, or ruler to make them **w**,
12:11 Hard **w** means prosperity; only fools idle away
12:14 the **w** of their hands also gives them many benefits.
12:24 **W** hard and become a leader; be lazy and become
13: 4 but those who **w** hard will prosper and be satisfied.
13:11 quickly disappears; wealth from hard **w** grows.
14:23 **W** brings profit, but mere talk leads to poverty!
16: 3 Commit your **w** to the LORD, and then your
17: 8 A bribe seems to **w** like magic for those who give
21: 5 Good planning and hard **w** lead to prosperity,
21:25 will be their ruin, for their hands refuse to **w**.
31:15 and plan the day's **w** for her servant girls.
Ecc 1: 3 What do people get for all their hard **w**?
2:10 I even found great pleasure in hard **w**,
2:18 that I must leave the fruits of my hard **w** to others.
2:19 everything I have gained by my skill and hard **w**.
2:20 So I turned in despair from hard **w**. It was not the
2:21 For though I do my **w** with wisdom, knowledge,
2:22 So what do people get for all their hard **w**?
2:24 enjoy food and drink and to find satisfaction in **w**.
3: 9 What do people really get for all their hard **w**?
3:10 the various kinds of **w** God has given people to do.
3:11 people cannot see the whole scope of God's **w**
3:22 better for people than to be happy in their **w**.
4: 5 Foolish people refuse to **w** and almost starve.
4: 6 better to be lazy and barely survive than to **w** hard,
5:12 People who **w** hard sleep well, whether they eat
5:16 so they depart. All their hard **w** is for nothing.
5:18 drink a good glass of wine, and enjoy their **w**—
5:19 To enjoy your **w** and accept your lot in life—
7:23 am determined to be wise." But it didn't really **w**.
8:15 along with all the hard **w** God gives them.
8:17 in our world, no matter how hard they **w** at it.
9:10 there will be no **w** or planning or knowledge
10: 9 When you **w** in a quarry, stones might fall
10:15 so exhausted by a little **w** that they have no
10:17 leaders feast only to gain strength for their **w**,
12: 3 Your teeth will be too few to do their **w**, and you
SS 7: 1 thighs are like jewels, the **w** of a skilled craftsman.
Isa 13:12 Few will be left alive when I have finished my **w**.
19: 8 The fishermen will weep for lack of **w**. Those who
34: 5 And when my sword has finished its **w** in the
40:24 when he blows on them and their **w** withers.
44:12 His **w** makes him hungry and thirsty, weak
45: 4 "And why have I called you for this **w**? It is for
45:11 Do you give me orders about the **w** of my hands?
45:15 our Savior, you **w** in strange and mysterious ways.
49: 4 I replied, "But my **w** all seems so useless! I have
56: 2 honor my Sabbath days of rest by refusing to **w**.
58: 6 and to stop oppressing those who **w** for you.
65:23 They will not **w** in vain, and their children will not
Jer 14:18 The prophets and priests continue with their **w**,
17:22 Do not do your **w** on the Sabbath, but make it a
17:24 not carry on your trade or **w** on the Sabbath day,
29: 7 And **w** for the peace and prosperity of Babylon.
48:10 Cursed be those who refuse to do the **w** the
50:25 will be the **w** of the Sovereign LORD Almighty.
51:58 in vain, for their **w** will be destroyed by fire!"
La 5:13 The young men are led away to **w** at millstones,
Eze 9:11 "I have finished the **w** you gave me to do."
21: 5 and it will not return to its sheath until its **w** is
29:18 won no plunder to compensate them for all their **w**.
29:20 given him the land of Egypt as a reward for his **w**,
44:14 and are relegated to doing maintenance **w**
44:27 The first day he returns to **w** and enters the inner
45: 5 will be a living area for the Levites who **w** at the
48:19 Those who come from the various tribes to **w** in
Joel 3:13 Now let the sickle do its **w**, for the harvest is ripe.
Jnh 1: 8 "Who are you? What is your line of **w**?
Mic 5:13 so you will never again worship the **w** of your own
Hab 2:13 will turn to ashes? They **w** so hard, but all in vain!
Hag 1:14 and began their **w** on the house of the LORD
2: 4 Take courage and **w**, for I am with you,
Zec 4:10 for the LORD rejoices to see the **w** begin,
6: 5 of all the earth. They are going out to do his **w**.
8:10 Before the **w** on the Temple began, there were no
Mt 5: 9 God blesses those who **w** for peace, / for they will
6:28 they grow. They don't **w** or make their clothing,
10:10 because those who **w** deserve to be fed.
12: 2 It's against the law to **w** by harvesting grain on the
12: 5 on duty in the Temple may **w** on the Sabbath?
12:10 "Is it legal to **w** by healing on the Sabbath day?"
12:11 the Sabbath, wouldn't you get to **w** and pull it out?
20: 2 pay the normal daily wage and sent them out to **w**.
20:13 Didn't you agree to **w** all day for the usual wage?
21:28 'Son, go out and **w** in the vineyard today.'
25:17 servant with two bags of gold also went right to **w**
Mk 2:24 It's against the law to **w** by harvesting grain on the
13:34 instructions about the **w** they were to do,
Lk 6: 2 It's against the law to **w** by harvesting grain on the
7:16 and "We have seen the hand of God at **w** today."
10: 7 because those who **w** deserve their pay.
10:40 that my sister just sits here while I do all the **w**?
12:27 They don't **w** or make their clothing, yet Solomon
13:15 "You hypocrite! You **w** on the Sabbath day!
13:24 **W** hard to get in, because many will try to enter,
14: 5 "Which of you doesn't **w** on the Sabbath?
Jn 3:27 "God in heaven appoints each person's **w**.
4:34 of God, who sent me, and from finishing his **w**.
4:35 Do you think the **w** of harvesting will not begin
4:38 others had already done the **w**, and you will gather
5:10 who was cured, "You can't **w** on the Sabbath!
7:22 But you **w** on the Sabbath, too, when you obey
9: 4 before the night falls and all **w** comes to an end.
10:33 They replied, "Not for any good **w**, but for
10:37 Don't believe me unless I carry out my Father's **w**.
10:38 But if I do his **w**, believe in what I have done,
14:10 but my Father who lives in me does his **w** through
14:13 because the **w** of the Son brings glory to the
21: 7 he put on his tunic (for he had stripped for **w**),
Ac 5:15 As a result of the apostles' **w**, sick people were
13: 2 and Saul for the special **w** I have for them."
14:26 grace of God for the **w** they had now completed.
15:38 them in Pamphylia and had not shared in their **w**.
20:19 I have done the Lord's **w** humbly—yes, and with
20:24 it for doing the **w** assigned me by the Lord Jesus—
20:24 the **w** of telling others the Good News about God's
Ro 1: 9 I want to **w** among you and see good results,
1:16 It is the power of God at **w**, saving everyone who
4: 4 When people **w**, their wages are not a gift.
4: 5 because of their faith, not because of their **w**.
7: 5 our old nature, sinful desires were at **w** within us,
7:23 But there is another law at **w** within me that is at
8:28 And we know that God causes everything to **w**
12: 5 his one body, and each of us has different **w** to do.
12:11 Never be lazy in your **w**, but serve the Lord
13: 6 so they can keep on doing the **w** God intended
14:20 Don't tear apart the **w** of God over what you eat.
15:23 But now I have finished my **w** in these regions,
1Co 3: 5 to believe. Each of us did the **w** the Lord gave us.
3: 8 and the one who waters **w** as a team with the same

3: 8 according to their own hard **w**.
3: 9 We **w** together as partners who belong to God.
3:13 day to see what kind of **w** each builder has done.
3:13 Everyone's **w** will be put through the fire to see
3:14 If the **w** survives the fire, that builder will receive a
3:15 But if the **w** is burned up, the builder will suffer
7:30 should not keep anyone from doing God's **w**.
7:32 man can spend his time doing the Lord's **w**
9: 1 because of my hard **w** that you are in the Lord?
9: 6 and I who have to **w** to support ourselves?
9:13 Don't you know that those who **w** in the Temple
12: 6 but it is the same God who does the **w** through all
12:28 those who can get others to **w** together,
15:58 and steady, always enthusiastic about the Lord's **w**,
16: 9 for there is a wide-open door for a great **w** here,
16:10 He is doing the Lord's **w**, just as I am.
2Co 1:24 We want to **w** together with you so you will be full
3: 2 can read it and recognize our good **w** among you.
5:11 we know this solemn fear of the Lord that we **w**
7: 1 And let us **w** toward complete purity because we
10: 8 And I will not be put to shame by having my **w**
10:15 Nor do we claim credit for the **w** someone else has
10:15 and that our **w** among you will be greatly enlarged.
11:12 of those who boast that their **w** is just like ours.
12: 9 so that the power of Christ may **w** through me.
Gal 2: 9 while they continued their **w** with the Jews.
3: 5 you the Holy Spirit and **w** miracles among you
3:14 Through the **w** of Christ Jesus, God has blessed the
4:11 I am afraid that all my hard **w** for you was worth
6: 4 personal satisfaction of having done your **w** well,
Eph 2: 2 He is the spirit at **w** in the hearts of those who
3:20 By his mighty power at **w** within us, he is able to
4:12 responsibility is to equip God's people to do his **w**
4:16 As each part does its own special **w**, it helps the
4:28 Begin using your hands for honest **w**, and
6: 6 **W** hard, but not just to please your masters when
6: 7 **W** with enthusiasm, as though you were working
6:21 loved brother and faithful helper in the Lord's **w**,
Php 1: 6 sure that God, who began the good **w** within you, will continue his **w** until it is finally finished on
2:12 to put into action God's saving **w** in your lives,
2:16 not lose the race and that my **w** was not useless.
2:30 For he risked his life for the **w** of Christ, and he
4: 1 for you are my joy and the reward for my **w**.
4:22 too, especially those who **w** in Caesar's palace.
Col 1:29 I **w** very hard at this, as I depend on Christ's
3:23 **W** hard and cheerfully at whatever you do,
4:17 "Be sure to carry out the **w** the Lord gave you."
1Th 1: 3 we think of your faithful **w**, your loving deeds,
2:13 And this word continues to **w** in you who believe.
3: 5 the best of you and that all our **w** had been useless.
5:12 honor those who are your leaders in the Lord's **w**.
5:12 They **w** hard among you and warn you against all
5:13 them your wholehearted love because of their **w**.
2Th 2: 7 For this lawlessness is already at **w** secretly,
2: 9 This evil man will come to do the **w** of Satan with
3: 6 and doesn't follow the tradition of hard **w** we gave
3:10 this rule: "Whoever does not **w** should not eat."
3:11 refusing to **w** and wasting time meddling in other
3:12 we command them: Settle down and get to **w**.
1Ti 4:10 We **w** hard and suffer much in order that people
5:17 Elders who do their **w** well should be paid well,
5:17 especially those who **w** hard at both preaching
5:18 another place, "Those who **w** deserve their pay!"
6: 2 You should **w** all the harder because you are
2Ti 2: 5 Follow the Lord's rules for doing his **w**, just as an
2:15 **W** hard so God can approve you. Be a good
2:21 ready for the Master to use you for every good **w**.
3: 6 They are the kind who **w** their way into people's
4: 5 for the Lord. **W** at bringing others to Christ.
Tit 1: 3 that I have been trusted to do this **w** for him.
1: 5 island of Crete so you could complete our **w** there
Phm 1: 6 that you will really put your generosity to **w**,
Heb 1:10 and the heavens are the **w** of your hands.
3: 5 His **w** was an illustration of the truths God would
4: 4 "On the seventh day God rested from all his **w**."
5: 4 He has to be called by God for this **w**, just as
13:17 Their **w** is to watch over your souls, and they know
1Pe 3:11 do good. / **W** hard at living in peace with others.
2Pe 1:10 **w** hard to prove that you really are among those
1:15 So I will **w** hard to make these things clear to you.
2Jn 1:11 encourages him becomes a partner in his evil **w**.
3Jn 1: 5 you are doing a good **w** for God when you take
Rev 2: 2 I have seen your hard **w** and your patient
2: 5 Turn back to me again and **w** as you did at first.

WORKDAYS (1) [DAY, WORK]

Eze 46: 1 wall will be closed during the six **w** each week,

WORKED (53) [WORK]

Ge 29:25 Jacob raged at Laban. "I **w** seven years for Rachel.
29:30 then stayed and **w** the additional seven years.
31: 6 You know how hard I have **w** for your father,
31:40 I **w** for you through the scorching heat of the day
Dt 28:33 have never heard about will eat the crops you **w**
Jos 24:13 I gave you land you had not **w** for, and I gave you
Ru 2:19 about the man in whose field she had **w**.
2:19 "The man I **w** with today is named Boaz."
2:23 So Ruth **w** alongside the women in Boaz's fields
2:23 Then she **w** with them through the wheat harvest,
2Sa 12: 3 but a little lamb he had **w** hard to buy.
19:18 and **w** hard ferrying the king's household across
1Ch 4:23 in Netaim and Gederah. They all **w** for the king.
22:14 "I have **w** hard to provide materials for building
25: 2 They **w** under the direction of their father, Asaph,
25: 3 They **w** under the direction of their father,
2Ch 24:13 So the men in charge of the renovation **w** hard,
Ne 3: 2 People from the city of Jericho **w** next to them,
3: 8 a goldsmith by trade, who also **w** on the wall.
4: 6 the entire city, for the people had **w** very hard.
4:16 only half my men **w** while the other half stood
4:21 We **w** early and late, from sunrise to sunset.
11:12 with 822 of their associates, who **w** at the Temple.
Est 10: 3 because he **w** for the good of his people and was a
Ecc 1:17 So I **w** hard to distinguish wisdom from
2:11 But as I looked at everything I had **w** so hard to
2:21 I gain to people who haven't **w** to earn it.
Jer 3:24 have watched as everything our ancestors **w** for—
12:13 They have **w** hard, but it has done them no good.
51:58 The builders from many lands have **w** in vain,
Hag 1:11 and your cattle and to ruin everything you have **w**
Mt 20:12 'Those people **w** only one hour, and yet you've
20:12 you paid us who **w** all day in the scorching heat.'
Mk 14:66 One of the servant girls who **w** for the high priest
16:20 and preached, and the Lord **w** with them,
Lk 5: 5 "we **w** hard all last night and didn't catch a thing.
15:29 'All these years I've **w** hard for you and never
Jn 7:21 "I **w** on the Sabbath by healing a man,
Ac 18: 3 Paul lived and **w** with them, for they were
20:34 You know that these hands of mine have **w** to pay
Ro 16: 6 to Mary, who has **w** so hard for your benefit.
16:12 and to dear Persis, who has **w** so hard for the Lord.
1Co 4:12 We have **w** wearily with our own hands to earn our
15:10 For I have **w** harder than all the other apostles,
2Co 6: 5 put in jail, faced angry mobs, **w** to exhaustion,
11:23 I have **w** harder, been put in jail more often,
Gal 2: 8 For the same God who **w** through Peter for the
2: 8 Jews **w** through me for the benefit of the Gentiles.
Php 4: 3 for they **w** hard with me in telling others the Good
4: 3 And they **w** with Clement and the rest of my
1Th 2: 9 and sisters, how hard we **w** among you?
2Th 3: 8 We **w** hard day and night so that we would not be a
Heb 6:10 He will not forget how hard you have **w** for him

WORKER (8) [WORK]

1Ki 7:14 and his father had been a foundry **w** from Tyre.
Ezr 7:24 or other **w** in this Temple of God will be required
Job 7: 2 like a **w** who longs for the day to end, like a
Pr 31:17 She is energetic and strong, a hard **w**.
Mt 20:14 and go. I wanted to pay this last **w** the same as you.
Ro 16:21 Timothy, my fellow **w**, and Lucius, Jason,
Php 2:25 He is a true brother, a faithful **w**, and a courageous
2Ti 2:15 Be a good **w**, one who does not need to be

WORKERS (39) [WORK]

Lev 19:13 rob anyone. "Always pay your hired **w** promptly.
Dt 15:18 the services worth double the wages of hired **w**,
Ru 2:13 even though I am not as worthy as your **w**."
2:22 Stay with his **w** right through the whole harvest.
3: 2 very kind by letting you gather grain with his **w**.
2Ki 12:15 because they were honest and faithful **w**.
22: 5 Then they can use it to pay **w** to repair the Temple
22: 9 collected at the Temple of the LORD to the **w**
1Ch 4:21 the families of linen **w** at Beth-ashbea,
22:16 and silversmiths and **w** of bronze and iron.
27:26 Ezri son of Kelub was in charge of the field **w** who
2Ch 26:10 He had many **w** who cared for his farms
34:10 Then they paid the **w** who did the repairs
34:12 The **w** served faithfully under the leadership of
Ezr 3: 9 The **w** at the Temple of God were supervised by
8:20 a group of Temple **w** first instituted by King
Ne 4:10 began to complain that the **w** were becoming tired.
5:10 I myself, as well as my brothers and my **w**,
Pr 10: 4 Lazy people are soon poor; hard **w** get rich.
16:26 It is good for **w** to have an appetite; an empty
22:29 Do you see any truly competent **w**? They will
27:18 **W** who tend a fig tree are allowed to eat its fruit.
27:18 **w** who protect their employer's interests will be
28:19 Hard **w** have plenty of food; playing around brings
Isa 19:10 The weavers and all the **w** will be sick at heart.
58: 3 are fasting. You keep right on oppressing your **w**.
Mt 9:37 "The harvest is so great, but the **w** are so few.
9:38 ask him to send out more **w** for his fields."
20: 1 out early one morning to hire **w** for his vineyard.
20: 8 "That evening he told the foreman to call the **w** in
20: 8 and pay them, beginning with the last **w** first.
Lk 10: 2 "The harvest is so great, but the **w** are so few.
10: 2 and ask him to send out more **w** for his fields.
Ro 4: 4 wages are not a gift. **W** earn what they receive.
13: 6 For government **w** need to be paid so they can
16:12 Say hello to Tryphena and Tryphosa, the Lord's **w**,
1Co 9:10 Just as farm **w** who plow fields and thresh the
9:10 Christian **w** should be paid by those they serve.
Jas 5: 4 Hear the cries of the field **w** whom you have

WORKING (45) [WORK]

Ge 29:20 So Jacob spent the next seven years **w** to pay for
Ru 2: 3 she found herself **w** in a field that belonged to
2: 8 Stay right behind the women **w** in my field.
1Sa 17:15 But David went back and forth between **w** for Saul
2Sa 5: 9 around the city, starting at the Millo and **w** inward.
2Ki 4:18 to visit his father, who was **w** with the harvesters.
12:11 who used it to pay the people **w** on the LORD's
2Ch 2:14 blue, and scarlet cloth and in **w** with linen.
Ezr 5: 4 of all the people who were **w** on the Temple.
5:16 The people have been **w** on it ever since, though it
Ne 3:17 Next was a group of Levites **w** under the
5:16 I devoted myself to **w** on the wall and refused to
5:16 And I required all my officials to spend time **w** on
Job 37: 7 Everyone stops **w** at such a time so they can
Ps 127: 2 until late at night, / anxiously **w** for food to eat;
Ecc 4: 8 But then he asks himself, "Who am I **w** for?
5: 7 Dreaming all the time instead of **w** is foolishness.
5:16 They have been **w** for the wind, and everything
Jer 18: 3 as he told me and found the potter **w** at his wheel.
Eze 29:20 because he was **w** for me when he destroyed Tyre.
48:18 This farmland will produce food for the people **w**
Mt 12:30 and anyone who isn't **w** with me is actually **w** against me.
20: 6 He asked them, 'Why haven't you been **w** today?'
24:40 "Two men will be **w** together in the field; one will
Lk 11:23 and anyone who isn't **w** with me is actually **w** against me.
13:14 "There are six days of the week for **w**," he said to
15:25 "Meanwhile, the older son was in the fields **w**.
Jn 5:17 But Jesus replied, "My Father never stops **w**,
9:16 Jesus is not from God, for he is **w** on the Sabbath."
Ac 20:35 example of how you can help the poor by **w** hard.
Ro 9:16 We can't get it by choosing it or **w** hard for it.
1Co 15:10 but God who was **w** through me by his grace.
2Co 6: 7 preached the truth. God's power has been **w** in us.
10:13 and this plan includes our **w** there with you.
10:16 that are far beyond you, where no one else is **w**.
Eph 6: 7 as though you were **w** for the Lord rather than for
Php 2: 2 and **w** together with one heart and purpose.
2:13 For God is **w** in you, giving you the desire to obey
3:12 But I keep **w** toward that day when I will finally be
Col 3:23 as though you were **w** for the Lord rather than for
4:11 they are **w** with me here for the Kingdom of God.
1Th 4:11 your own business and **w** with your hands,
2Jn 1: 8 do not lose the prize for which we have been **w**

WORKMAN'S (1) [WORK, MAN]

Jdg 5:26 and with her right hand she reached for the **w**

WORKMANSHIP (2) [WORK]

Ex 28:15 "Then, with the most careful **w**, make a chestpiece
Ps 139:14 Your **w** is marvelous—and how well I know it.

WORKMEN (2) [WORK, MAN]

2Ki 12:14 It was paid out to the **w**, who used it for the
2Ch 34:17 LORD has been given to the supervisors and **w**."

WORKS (32) [WORK]

Ex 31:14 anyone who **w** on that day will be cut off from the
31:15 anyone who **w** on the Sabbath must be put to
35: 2 to the LORD. Anyone who **w** on that day will die.
1Ch 16:12 Think of the wonderful **w** he has done,
Job 5: 9 For he does great **w** too marvelous to understand.
9:10 His great **w** are too marvelous to understand.
36:24 Instead, glorify his mighty **w**, singing songs of
Ps 46: 8 Come, see the glorious **w** of the LORD:
105: 5 Think of the wonderful **w** he has done,
107:24 in action, / his impressive **w** on the deepest seas.
143: 5 the days of old. / I ponder all your great **w**.
145:10 All of your **w** will thank you, LORD, / and your
150: 2 Praise him for his mighty **w**; / praise his unequaled
Pr 10: 5 A wise youth **w** hard all summer; a youth who
18:16 Giving a gift **w** wonders; it may bring you before
Ecc 4: 8 yet who **w** hard to gain as much wealth as he can.
9:13 me as I have watched the way our world **w**.
Isa 25:11 He will end their pride and all their evil **w**.
64: 4 a God like you, who **w** for those who wait for him!
Eze 33:12 The good **w** of righteous people will not save them
Lk 6:40 But the student who **w** hard will become like the
Jn 14:12 anyone who believes in me will do the same **w** I
14:12 and even greater **w**, because I am going to be with
Ro 9:12 not according to our good or bad **w**.) She was told,
11: 6 by God's kindness, then it is not by their good **w**.
1Co 12: 6 There are different ways God **w** in our lives,
2Co 3:18 And as the Spirit of the Lord **w** within us,
8:23 say that he is my partner who **w** with me to help
12: 9 all you need. My power **w** best in your weakness."
Col 1:29 as I depend on Christ's mighty power that **w** within
1Ti 6:18 They should be rich in good **w** and should give
1Jn 3: 8 But the Son of God came to destroy these **w** of the

WORLD (471) [WORLD'S, WORLDLY, UNDERWORLD]

ALL THE WORLD (36) 2Sa 7:26; 1Ki 3:13; 10:20; 2Ki 5:15; 1Ch 17:24; 2Ch 9:19; Ps 19:4; 50:12; Isa 11:10; 18:3; 42:5,19; 45:6,22; 49:26; La 2:13,15; 4:12; Eze 16:57; 20:48; 21:5; 23:29,32; Da 4:11,12,20; Zep 2:15; Mt 12:21; Mk 16:15; Ro 2:5; 10:18; Heb 2:9; 1Pe 4:13; 1Jn 2:2; Rev 13:3; 18:18

WHOLE WORLD (31) Ge 11:1; 1Sa 17:46; 1Ch 16:8; Est 4:11; Job 34:13; Ps 44:14; 59:13; 66:8; 67:4; 82:5; 105:1; Isa 43:21; Jer 50:2; Eze 35:14; 38:12; Da 4:17; 7:23; Mt 16:26; 24:14; Mk 8:36; Lk 9:25; Jn 12:19; 21:25; Ac 22:15; 1Co 3:22; Col 3:4; 1Pe 1:7; 2Pe 2:5; Rev 3:10; 11:15; 12:9

Ge 6:12 God observed all this corruption in the **w**, and he
10:25 for during his lifetime the people of the **w** were
11: 1 At one time the whole **w** spoke a single language
11: 4 and keep us from scattering all over the **w**."
39: 6 With Joseph there, he didn't have a worry in the **w**,
41:57 because the famine was severe throughout the **w**.
Dt 28: 1 God will exalt you above all the nations of the **w**.
28:10 Then all the nations of the **w** will see that you are a
1Sa 2: 8 is the LORD's, / and he has set the **w** in order.
10:14 "Where in the **w** have you been?" Saul's uncle
17:46 and the whole **w** will know that there is a God in
2Sa 7:26 name be honored forever so that all the **w** will say,
1Ki 3:13 No other king in all the **w** will be compared to you
10:20 No other throne in all the **w** could be compared

21: 5 "What in the **w** is the matter?" his wife, Jezebel,
2Ki 5:15 "I know at last that there is no God in all the **w**
1Ch 1:19 for during his lifetime the people of the **w** were
16: 8 Let the whole **w** know what he has done.
16:28 O nations of the **w**, recognize the LORD,
16:30 The **w** is firmly established and cannot be shaken.
17:24 and honored forever so that all the **w** will say,
22: 5 famous and glorious throughout the **w**.
2Ch 9:19 No other throne in all the **w** could be compared
Est 4:11 "The whole **w** knows that anyone who appears
Job 18:18 thrust from light into darkness, driven from the **w**.
27:16 "Evil people may have all the money in the **w**,
34:13 Who put the **w** in his care? Who has set the whole **w** in place?
40:13 in the dust. Imprison them in the **w** of the dead.
Ps 9: 8 He will judge the **w** with justice / and rule the
9:11 Tell the **w** about his unforgettable deeds.
19: 4 out to all the earth, / and their words to all the **w**.
24: 1 in it. / The **w** and all its people belong to him.
30: 9 the grave? / Can it tell the **w** of your faithfulness?
31:19 blessing them before the watching **w**.
33: 8 Let everyone in the **w** fear the LORD, / and let
33: 9 For when he spoke, the **w** began! / It appeared at
44:14 of their jokes; / we are scorned by the whole **w**.
46: 8 See how he brings destruction upon the **w**
46:10 I will be honored throughout the **w**."
47: 9 The rulers of the **w** have gathered together.
49: 1 all you people! / Pay attention, everyone in the **w**!
49:18 and the **w** loudly applauds their success.
50:12 to you, / for all the **w** is mine and everything in it.
59:13 Then the whole **w** will know / that God reigns in
66: 2 glory of his name! / Tell the **w** how glorious he is.
66: 8 Let the whole **w** bless our God / and sing aloud his
67: 4 and direct the actions of the whole **w**. / *Interlude*
67: 7 bless us, / and people all over the **w** will fear him.
77:18 from the whirlwind; / the lightning lit up the **w**!
82: 5 are in darkness, / the whole **w** is shaken to the core.
89:11 everything in the **w** is yours—you created it all.
90: 2 before you made the earth and the **w**,
93: 1 The **w** is firmly established; / it cannot be shaken.
96: 7 O nations of the **w**, recognize the LORD;
96:10 The **w** is firmly established and cannot be shaken.
96:13 the earth. / He will judge the **w** with righteousness
97: 4 His lightning flashes out across the **w**. / The earth
98: 9 He will judge the **w** with justice, / and the nations
104: 5 You placed the **w** on its foundation / so it would
105: 1 Let the whole **w** know what he has done.
107:23 went off in ships, / plying the trade routes of the **w**.
147:15 He sends his orders to the **w**— / how swiftly his
Pr 8:31 he created—his wide **w** and all the human family!
30: 4 Who has created the whole wide **w**? What is his
31:29 are many virtuous and capable women in the **w**,
Ecc 1:13 explore by wisdom everything being done in the **w**.
2: 3 most people find during their brief life in this **w**.
3:16 I also noticed that throughout the **w** there is evil in
4: 1 all the oppression that takes place in our **w**.
4: 3 have never seen all the evil that is done in our **w**.
4: 7 yet another example of meaninglessness in our **w**.
5:13 is another serious problem I have seen in the **w**.
5:16 As people come into this **w**, so they depart.
6: 1 is another serious tragedy I have seen in our **w**.
8: 9 thought deeply about all that goes on here in the **w**,
8:14 And this is not all that is meaningless in our **w**.
8:15 nothing better for people to do in this **w** than to eat,
8:17 can discover everything God has created in our **w**,
9: 9 days of life that God has given you in this **w**.
9:11 I have observed something else in this **w** of ours.
9:13 me as I have watched the way our **w** works.
10: 5 evil I have seen as I have watched the **w** go by.
Isa 2: 2 People from all over the **w** will go there to
10: 7 my people as part of his plan to conquer the **w**.
11:10 throne will be a banner of salvation to all the **w**.
12: 4 Tell the **w** what he has done. / Oh, how mighty he
12: 5 Make known his praise around the **w**.
13:11 will punish the **w** for its evil and the wicked for
14: 2 The nations of the **w** will help the LORD's people
14: 9 **W** leaders and mighty kings long dead are there to
14:12 the earth, you who destroyed the nations of the **w**.
14:16 who shook the earth and the kingdoms of the **w**?
14:17 Is this the one who destroyed the **w** and made it
14:21 conquer the land or rebuild the cities of the **w**."
14:26 for my mighty power reaches throughout the **w**.
18: 3 flag on the mountain, let all the **w** take notice.
23: 3 the Nile. You were the merchandise mart of the **w**.
23: 8 on Tyre, empire builder and chief trader of the **w**?
23:17 will return again to all her evil ways around the **w**.
24:18 from the heavens. The **w** is shaken beneath you.
25: 6 a wonderful feast for everyone around the **w**.
26:18 We have done nothing to rescue the **w**;
34: 1 Let the **w** and everything in it hear my words.
38:11 my friends / or laugh with those who live in this **w**.
40:15 for all the nations of the **w** are nothing in
40:17 The nations of the **w** are as nothing to him. In his
40:21 of God—the words he gave before the **w** began?
40:23 He judges the great people of the **w** and brings
42: 5 He gives breath and life to everyone in all the **w**.
42:19 Who in all the **w** is as blind as my own people,
42:21 Through it he had planned to show the **w** that he is
43:21 they will someday honor me before the whole **w**.
45: 6 so all the **w** from east to west will know there is no
45:18 He made the **w** to be lived in, not to be a place of
45:22 Let all the **w** look to me for salvation! For I am
47: 7 'I will reign forever as queen of the **w**!'
47: 8 bragging as if you were the greatest in the **w**!
49:26 All the **w** will know that I, the LORD, am your
57: 9 You have traveled far, even into the **w** of the dead,
59:19 glorify the name of the LORD throughout the **w**.
60: 5 for merchants from around the **w** will come to you.
60:11 The kings of the **w** will be led as captives in a
61:11 will show his justice to the nations of the **w**.
64: 4 For since the **w** began, no ear has heard and no eye
66:16 The LORD will punish the **w** by fire and by his
Jer 1: 5 and appointed you as my spokesman to the **w**."
3:19 this beautiful land—the finest inheritance in the **w**.
4: 2 then you will be a blessing to the nations of the **w**,
9:16 I will scatter them around the **w**, and they will be
10: 7 of the earth and in all the kingdoms of the **w**,
16:19 Nations from around the **w** will come to you
25:26 one after the other—all the kingdoms of the **w**.
29:18 and disease, and I will scatter them around the **w**.
31:10 message from the LORD, you nations of the **w**;
32:20 to do great miracles in Israel and all around the **w**.
32:27 the LORD, the God of all the peoples of the **w**.
33: 9 The people of the **w** will see the good I do for my
49:36 They will be exiled to countries around the **w**.
50: 2 "Tell the whole **w**, and keep nothing back! Raise a
50:46 and her cry of despair will be heard around the **w**.
51:41 The **w** can scarcely believe its eyes at her fall!
51:49 the people of Israel and others throughout the **w**,
La 2:13 In all the **w** has there ever been such sorrow?
2:15 this the city called 'Most Beautiful in All the **W**,'
4:12 Not a king in all the earth—no one in all the **w**—
Eze 6: 8 they will be scattered among the nations of the **w**.
11:16 I have scattered you in the countries of the **w**,
16:14 Your fame soon spread throughout the **w** on
16:57 greater wickedness has been exposed to all the **w**,
20:48 And all the **w** will see that I, the LORD, have set
21: 5 All the **w** will know that I am the LORD.
22: 4 make you an object of mockery throughout the **w**.
23:29 of your prostitution will be exposed to all the **w**.
23:32 And all the **w** will mock and scorn you in your
26:17 their naval power, / once spread fear around the **w**.
26:20 like those in the pit who have entered the **w** of the
27: 3 gateway to the sea, the trading center of the **w**.
28:25 I will reveal to the nations of the **w** my holiness
30:23 the Egyptians to many lands throughout the **w**.
31: 6 All the great nations of the **w** lived in its shadow.
31:14 in the pit along with all the proud people of the **w**.
32:18 For I will send them down to the **w** below in
32:24 hordes who descended as outcasts to the **w** below.
32:24 of those who have gone to the **w** of the dead.
35:14 The whole **w** will rejoice when I make you
36:21 been dishonored by my people throughout the **w**.
38:12 and they think the whole **w** revolves around them!'
38:23 will make myself known to all the nations of the **w**.
Da 2:21 He determines the course of **w** events;
2:38 He has made you the ruler over all the inhabited **w**
2:39 the bronze belly and thighs, will rise to rule the **w**.
4: 1 and nation and language throughout the **w**:
4:11 reaching high into the heavens for all the **w** to see.
4:12 in its branches. All the **w** was fed from this tree.
4:17 The purpose of this decree is that the whole **w** may
4:17 the Most High rules over the kingdoms of the **w**
4:20 reaching high into the heavens for all the **w** to see.
4:25 the Most High rules over the kingdoms of the **w**
4:32 the Most High rules over the kingdoms of the **w**
5:21 the Most High God rules the kingdoms of the **w**
6:25 and nation and language throughout the **w**:
7:14 and royal power over all the nations of the **w**,
7:23 "This fourth beast is the fourth **w** power that will
7:23 It will devour the whole **w**, trampling everything in
Joel 3: 2 "I will gather the armies of the **w** into the valley of
Jnh 2: 2 I called to you from the **w** of the dead,
Mic 1: 2 Attention! Let all the people of the **w** listen!
4: 1 People from all over the **w** will go there to
5: 4 for he will be highly honored all around the **w**.
7:16 All the nations of the **w** will stand amazed at what
Na 3: 6 with filth and show the **w** how vile you really are.
Hab 1: 6 the Babylonians to be a new power on the **w** scene.
1: 6 and violent nation who will march across the **w**
Zep 2:11 Then people from nations around the **w** will
2:15 "In all the **w** there is no city as great as I,"
Zec 1:19 "These horns represent the **w** powers that scattered
4:10 eyes of the LORD that search all around the **w**."
8:20 and cities around the **w** will travel to Jerusalem.
8:23 and languages around the **w** will clutch at the hem
12: 3 make Jerusalem a heavy stone, a burden for the **w**.
14:17 And any nation anywhere in the **w** that refuses to
Mal 1:11 All around the **w** they offer sweet incense and pure
Mt 4: 8 and showed him the nations of the **w** and all their
5:14 You are the light of the **w**—like a city on a
8:11 that many Gentiles will come from all over the **w**
10:18 to tell them about me—yes, to witness to the **w**.
12:21 And his name will be the hope / of all the **w**."
12:32 either in this **w** or in the **w** to come.
13:35 mysteries hidden since the creation of the **w**."
13:38 The field is the **w**, and the good seed represents the
13:39 The harvest is the end of the **w**, and the harvesters
13:40 and burned, so it will be at the end of the **w**.
13:49 That is the way it will be at the end of the **w**.
16:26 And how do you benefit if you gain the whole **w**
19:25 "Then who in the **w** can be saved?" they asked.
20:25 "You know that in this **w** kings are tyrants,
24: 3 time to signal your return and the end of the **w**?"
24: 7 be famines and earthquakes in many parts of the **w**.
24: 9 You will be hated all over the **w** because of your
24:14 will be preached throughout the whole **w**,
24:21 of greater horror than anything the **w** has ever seen
25:34 prepared for you from the foundation of the **w**.
26:13 the Good News is preached throughout the **w**,
Mk 8:36 And how do you benefit if you gain the whole **w**
10:26 "Then who in the **w** can be saved?" they asked.
10:30 And in the **w** to come they will have eternal life.
10:42 "You know that in this **w** kings are tyrants,
13: 8 there will be earthquakes in many parts of the **w**,
13:19 horror than at any time since God created the **w**.
13:27 together his chosen ones from all over the **w**—
14: 9 the Good News is preached throughout the **w**,
16:15 "Go into all the **w** and preach the Good News to
Lk 4: 5 and revealed to him all the kingdoms of the **w** in a
9:25 And how do you benefit if you gain the whole **w**
11:50 of all God's prophets from the creation of the **w**—
13:29 Then people will come from all over the **w** to take
16: 8 And it is true that the citizens of this **w** are more
16:15 What this **w** honors is an abomination in the sight
17:26 the **w** will be like the people were in Noah's day.
17:28 "And the **w** will be as it was in the days of Lot.
18:26 this said, "Then who in the **w** can be saved?"
18:30 as well as receiving eternal life in the **w** to come."
21:24 or sent away as captives to all the nations of the **w**.
22:25 "In this **w** the kings and great men order their
Jn 1: 9 light to everyone, was going to come into the **w**.
1:10 But although the **w** was made through him, the **w** didn't recognize him when he came.
1:29 the Lamb of God who takes away the sin of the **w**!
3:16 so loved the **w** that he gave his only Son,
3:17 God did not send his Son into the **w** to condemn it,
3:19 The light from heaven came into the **w**, but they
4:42 you told us. He is indeed the Savior of the **w**."
6:33 comes down from heaven and gives life to the **w**."
6:51 this bread is my flesh, offered so the **w** may live."
7: 4 can do such wonderful things, prove it to the **w**!"
7: 7 The **w** can't hate you, but it does hate me because I
8:12 Jesus said to the people, "I am the light of the **w**.
8:23 I am from above. You are of this **w**; I am not.
9: 5 But while I am still here in the **w**, I am the light of the **w**."
9:32 Never since the **w** began has anyone been able to
9:39 Then Jesus told him, "I have come to judge the **w**.
10:36 One who was sent into the **w** by the Father says,
11: 9 They can see because they have the light of this **w**.
11:27 the one who has come into the **w** from God."
11:52 of all the children of God scattered around the **w**.
12:19 Look, the whole **w** has gone after him!"
12:25 Those who love their life in this **w** will lose it.
12:25 Those who despise their life in this **w** will keep it
12:31 The time of judgment for the **w** has come,
12:31 when the prince of this **w** will be cast out.
12:46 I have come as a light to shine in this dark **w**,
12:47 for I have come to save the **w** and not to judge it.
13: 1 Jesus knew that his hour had come to leave this **w**
13:35 Your love for one another will prove to the **w** that
14:17 The **w** at large cannot receive him, because it isn't
14:19 In just a little while the **w** will not see me again,
14:22 yourself only to us and not to the **w** at large?"
14:27 And the peace I give isn't like the peace the **w**
14:30 to you, because the prince of this **w** approaches.
14:31 so that the **w** will know that I love the Father.
15:18 "When the **w** hates you, remember it hated me
15:19 The **w** would love you if you belonged to it,
15:19 I chose you to come out of the **w**, and so it hates
15:21 The people of the **w** will hate you because you
16: 8 when he comes, he will convince the **w** of its sin,
16:11 because the prince of this **w** has already been
16:20 is going to happen to me, but the **w** will rejoice.
16:21 because she has brought a new person into the **w**.
16:28 Yes, I came from the Father into the **w**, and I will leave the **w** and return to the Father."
16:33 But take heart, because I have overcome the **w**."
17: 5 bring me into the glory we shared before the **w**
17: 6 They were in the **w**, but then you gave them to me.
17: 9 "My prayer is not for the **w**, but for those you
17:11 Now I am departing the **w**; I am leaving them
17:14 And the **w** hates them because they do not belong to the **w**,
17:15 I'm not asking you to take them out of the **w**,
17:16 They are not part of this **w** any more than I am.
17:18 As you sent me into the **w**, I am sending them into the **w**.
17:21 will be in us, and the **w** will believe you sent me.
17:23 Then the **w** will know that you sent me and will
17:24 because you loved me even before the **w** began!
17:25 righteous Father, the **w** doesn't know you, but I do;
18:36 Jewish leaders. But my Kingdom is not of this **w**."
18:37 that purpose. And I came to bring truth to the **w**.
21:25 the whole **w** could not contain the books.
Ac 11:28 famine was coming upon the entire Roman **w**.
17: 6 and Silas have turned the rest of the **w** upside
17:24 "He is the God who made the **w** and everything in
17:31 For he has set a day for judging the **w** with justice
19:27 the province of Asia and all around the **w**—
21:21 Gentile **w** to turn their backs on the laws of Moses.
22:15 telling the whole **w** what you have seen and heard.
24: 5 inciting the Jews throughout the **w** to riots
26:16 You are to tell the **w** about this experience
Ro 1: 8 faith in God is becoming known throughout the **w**.
1:20 From the time the **w** was created, people have seen
2: 5 of judgment when God, the just judge of all the **w**,
2:24 "The **w** blasphemes the name of God because of
3: 4 Though everyone else in the **w** is a liar, God is
3: 6 God is not just, how is he qualified to judge the **w**?
3:19 and to bring the entire **w** into judgment before
10:18 gone out to everyone, / and its words to all the **w**."
11:12 think how much greater a blessing the **w** will share
11:15 that God offered salvation to the rest of the **w**,
12: 2 Don't copy the behavior and customs of this **w**,
1Co 1:21 Since God in his wisdom saw to it that the **w**
1:27 God deliberately chose things the **w** considers
1:28 God chose things despised by the **w**,
1:28 and used them to bring to nothing what the **w**
2: 6 but not the kind of wisdom that belongs to this **w**,

2: 6 and not the kind that appeals to the rulers of this **w**,
2: 7 though he made it for our benefit before the **w**
2: 8 But the rulers of this **w** have not understood it;
3: 1 I had to talk as though you belonged to this **w**
3:19 For the wisdom of this **w** is foolishness to God.
3:22 and Peter; the whole **w** and life and death;
4: 9 We have become a spectacle to the entire **w**—
5:10 You would have to leave this **w** to avoid people
6: 2 someday we Christians are going to judge the **w**?
6: 2 And since you are going to judge the **w**, can't you
7:23 you at a high price. Don't be enslaved by the **w**.
7:31 Those in frequent contact with the things of the **w**
7:31 for this **w** and all it contains will pass away.
11:32 by the Lord, we will not be condemned with the **w**.
14:10 There are so many different languages in the **w**,
15:19 we are the most miserable people in the **w**.
15:21 just as death came into the **w** through a man,
2Co 1:17 Or am I like people of the **w** who say yes when
4: 4 Satan, the god of this evil **w**, has blinded the minds
5:16 evaluating others by what the **w** thinks about them.
5:19 God was in Christ, reconciling the **w** to himself,
Gal 1: 4 in order to rescue us from this evil **w** in which we
4: 3 We were slaves to the spiritual powers of this **w**.
4: 9 to the weak and useless spiritual powers of this **w**?
6:14 of that cross, my interest in this **w** died long ago,
Eph 1: 4 Long ago, even before he made the **w**, God loved
1:21 or power or leader or anything else in this **w** or in the **w** to come.
2: 2 You used to live just like the rest of the **w**, full of
2:12 You lived in this **w** without God and without hope.
4: 9 first came down to the lowly **w** in which we live.
5: 5 an idolater who worships the things of this **w**.
6:12 the evil rulers and authorities of the unseen **w**,
6:12 those mighty powers of darkness who rule this **w**,
Php 2:15 innocent lives as children of God in a dark **w** full
Col 1: 6 News that came to you is going out all over the **w**.
1:23 The Good News has been preached all over the **w**,
2: 8 human thinking and from the evil powers of this **w**,
2:20 he has set you free from the evil powers of this **w**.
2:20 So why do you keep on following rules of the **w**,
3: 4 who is your real life, is revealed to the whole **w**,
3: 7 to do them when your life was still part of this **w**.
1Ti 1:15 Christ Jesus came into the **w** to save sinners—
2: 6 This is the message that God gave to the **w** at the
3:16 He was believed on in the **w** / and was taken up
5: 5 one who is truly alone in this **w**, has placed her
6: 7 bring anything with us when we came into the **w**,
6:17 Tell those who are rich in this **w** not to be proud
2Ti 1: 9 because that was his plan long before the **w**
Tit 1: 2 which God promised them before the **w** began—
2:12 We should live in this evil **w** with self-control,
Heb 1: 6 when he presented his honored Son to the **w**,
2: 5 the future **w** we are talking about will not be
2: 9 Jesus tasted death for everyone in all the **w**.
4: 3 place of rest has been ready since he made the **w**.
4:10 their labors, just as God rested after creating the **w**.
9:11 by human hands and not part of this created **w**.
9:26 had to die again and again, ever since the **w** began.
10: 5 That is why Christ, when he came into the **w**, said,
11: 7 By his faith he condemned the rest of the **w**
11:38 They were too good for this **w**. They wandered
13:14 For this **w** is not our home; we are looking forward
Jas 1:27 in their troubles, and refuse to let the **w** corrupt us.
2: 5 Hasn't God chosen the poor in this **w** to be rich in
4: 4 Don't you realize that friendship with this **w** makes
4: 4 I say it again, that if your aim is to enjoy this **w**,
1Pe 1: 7 day when Jesus Christ is revealed to the whole **w**.
1:20 God chose him for this purpose long before the **w**
2:12 give honor to God when he comes to judge the **w**.
4: 7 The end of the **w** is coming soon. Therefore,
4:13 sharing his glory when it is displayed to all the **w**.
5: 9 Remember that Christians all over the **w** are going
2Pe 2: 5 And God did not spare the ancient **w**—except for
2: 5 Noah warned the **w** of God's righteous judgment.
2: 5 Then God destroyed the whole **w** of ungodly
2:20 wicked ways of the **w** by learning about our Lord
3: 4 exactly the same since the **w** was first created."
3: 6 Then he used the water to destroy the **w** with a
3:13 a **w** where everyone is right with God.
1Jn 2: 2 away not only our sins but the sins of all the **w**.
2:15 Stop loving this evil **w** and all that it offers you, for when you love the **w**,
2:16 For the **w** offers only the lust for physical pleasure,
2:16 are not from the Father. They are from this evil **w**.
2:17 And this **w** is fading away, along with everything it
2:18 From this we know that the end of the **w** has come.
3: 1 But the people who belong to this **w** don't know
3:13 dear brothers and sisters, if the **w** hates you.
4: 1 For there are many false prophets in the **w**.
4: 3 have heard that he is going to come into the **w**,
4: 4 in you is greater than the spirit who lives in the **w**.
4: 5 These people belong to this **w**, so they speak from the world's viewpoint, and the **w** listens to them.
4: 9 he loved us by sending his only Son into the **w**
4:14 the Father sent his Son to be the Savior of the **w**.
4:17 because we are like Christ here in this **w**.
5: 4 For every child of God defeats this evil **w** by
5: 5 And the ones who win this battle against the **w** are
5:19 and that the **w** around us is under the power
2Jn 1: 7 Many deceivers have gone out into the **w**. They do
Jude 1:15 He will bring the people of the **w** / to judgment.
Rev 1: 5 and the commander of all the rulers of the **w**.
3:10 the whole **w** to test those who belong to this **w**.
6:10 belong to this **w** for what they have done to us?
8:13 terror to all who belong to this **w** because of what
11:10 All the people who belong to this **w** will give
11:15 "The whole **w** has now become the kingdom of
11:19 and the **w** was shaken by a mighty earthquake.
12: 9 or Satan, the one deceiving the whole **w**—
13: 3 All the **w** marveled at this miracle and followed the
13: 8 And all the people who belong to this **w** worshiped
13: 8 the Lamb who was killed before the **w** was made.
13:12 and those who belong to this **w** to worship the first
13:14 he deceived all the people who belong to this **w**.
13:14 He ordered the people of the **w** to make a great
14: 6 to preach to the people who belong to this **w**—
14: 8 because she seduced the nations of the **w** and made
14:18 who has power to destroy the **w** with fire,
16:14 **w** to gather for battle against the Lord on that great
16:19 and cities around the **w** fell into heaps of rubble.
17: 2 The rulers of the **w** have had immoral relations
17: 2 and the people who belong to this **w** have been
17: 5 of All Prostitutes and Obscenities in the **W**."
17: 8 And the people who belong to this **w**,
17: 8 in the Book of Life from before the **w** began,
18: 3 The rulers of the **w** have committed adultery with
18: 3 and merchants throughout the **w** have grown rich
18: 9 And the rulers of the **w** who took part in her
18:11 The merchants of the **w** will weep and mourn for
18:18 "Where in all the **w** is there another city like
18:23 her merchants, who were the greatest in the **w**,
18:24 one who slaughtered God's people all over the **w**."
21: 4 For the old **w** and its evils are gone forever."
21:24 and the rulers of the **w** will come and bring their

WORLD'S (10) [WORLD]

Job 3:14 I would rest with the **w** kings and prime ministers,
Isa 14:17 Is this the king who demolished the **w** greatest
Jn 16: 9 The **w** sin is unbelief in me.
1Co 1:20 the scholars, and the **w** brilliant debaters?
1:26 that few of you were wise in the **w** eyes,
2:12 And God has actually given us his Spirit (not the **w**
3:18 If you think you are wise by this **w** standards,
4:13 Yet we are treated like the **w** garbage,
Gal 6:14 and the **w** interest in me is also long dead.
1Jn 4: 5 so they speak from the **w** viewpoint, and the world

WORLDLY (3) [WORLD]

Lk 16: 9 use your **w** resources to benefit others and make
16:11 And if you are untrustworthy about **w** wealth,
2Co 10: 4 use God's mighty weapons, not mere **w** weapons,

WORM (6) [WORMED, WORMS]

Job 17:14 my father, and the **w** my mother and my sister.
Ps 22: 6 But I am a **w** and not a man. / I am scorned
Isa 51: 8 The **w** will eat away at them as it eats wool.
Jnh 4: 7 But God also prepared a **w**! The next morning at dawn the **w** ate through the
Mk 9:48 'where the **w** never dies and the fire never goes

WORMED (1) [WORM]

Jude 1: 4 because some godless people have **w** their way in

WORMS (8) [WORM]

Dt 28:39 or eat the grapes, for **w** will destroy the vines.
Job 7: 5 My skin is filled with **w** and scabs. My flesh
21:26 buried in the same dust, both eaten by the same **w**.
24:20 **W** will find him sweet to eat. No one will
25: 6 less are mere people, who are but **w** in his sight?"
Isa 14:11 Now maggots are your sheet and **w** your blanket.'
66:24 For the **w** that devour them will never die,
Ac 12:23 to God. So he was consumed with **w** and died.

WORN (14) [WEAR]

Ex 28:42 to be **w** next to their bodies, reaching from waist to
28:43 These must be **w** whenever Aaron and his sons
39: 1 clothing to be **w** while ministering in the Holy
39:26 This robe was to be **w** when Aaron ministered to
39:30 of pure gold to be **w** on the front of the turban.
39:41 the beautifully crafted garments to be **w** while
Lev 16: 4 and the undergarments **w** next to his body.
Jos 9:13 our clothing and sandals are **w** out from our long,
1Sa 14:24 Now the men of Israel were **w** out that day,
17:39 it was like, for he had never **w** such things before.
Ps 6: 6 I am **w** out from sobbing. / Every night tears
6: 7 my eyes are **w** out because of all my enemies.
Pr 30: 1 I am weary, O God; I am weary and **w** out, O God.
Isa 40:29 He gives power to those who are tired and **w** out;

WORN-OUT (4) [WEAR]

Ge 18:12 "How could a **w** woman like me have a baby?"
Jos 9: 5 They put on ragged clothes and **w**,
Job 30: 2 A lot of good they are to me—those **w** wretches!
Eze 23:43 Then I said, 'If they really want to sleep with **w**,

WORRIED (7) [WORRY]

Ge 40: 7 "Why do you look so **w** today?" he asked.
1Sa 9: 5 By now my father will be more **w** about us than
10: 2 and that your father is **w** about you and is asking,
Jer 17: 8 by the heat or **w** by long months of drought.
Mt 16: 8 little faith! Why are you **w** about having no food?
Mk 8:17 he said, "Why are you so **w** about having no food?
Lk 9: 7 he was **w** and puzzled because some were saying,

WORRIES (7) [WORRY]

Ge 39:23 The chief jailer had no more **w** after that,
Mt 6:27 Can all your **w** add a single moment to your life?
6:34 for tomorrow will bring its own **w**.
Lk 12:25 Can all your **w** add a single moment to your life?
21:34 and drunkenness, and filled with the **w** of this life.
Ro 8:38 Our fears for today, our **w** about tomorrow,
1Pe 5: 7 Give all your **w** and cares to God, for he cares

WORRY (37) [WORRIED, WORRIES, WORRYING]

Ge 39: 6 With Joseph there, he didn't have a **w** in the world,
43:23 Don't **w** about it," the household manager told
45:20 Don't **w** about your belongings, for the best of all
Ru 3:11 Now don't **w** about a thing, my daughter. I will do
1Sa 9:20 And don't **w** about those donkeys that were lost
17:32 "Don't **w** about a thing," David told Saul. "I'll go
21: 5 "Don't **w**," David replied. "I never allow my men
2Sa 13:20 Since he's your brother anyway, don't **w** about it."
14:10 "Don't **w** about that!" the king said. "If anyone
1Ki 21: 7 "Get up and eat and don't **w** about it.
Job 36:17 on the godless. Don't **w**, justice will be upheld.
39:15 She doesn't **w** that a foot might crush them or that
Ps 37: 1 Don't **w** about the wicked. / Don't envy those who
37: 7 to act. / Don't **w** about evil people who prosper
Pr 12:25 **W** weighs a person down; an encouraging word
Jer 23:17 to these rebels who despise my word, 'Don't **w**!
Mt 6:25 "So I tell you, don't **w** about everyday life—
6:28 "And why **w** about your clothes? Look at the lilies
6:31 "So don't **w** about having enough food or drink
6:34 "So don't **w** about tomorrow, for tomorrow will
7: 3 And why **w** about a speck in your friend's eye
10:19 don't **w** about what to say in your defense,
Mk 13:11 don't **w** about what to say in your defense.
Lk 6:41 "And why **w** about a speck in your friend's eye
12:11 don't **w** about what to say in your defense,
12:22 "So I tell you, don't **w** about everyday life—
12:26 And if **w** can't do little things like that,
12:29 And don't **w** about food—what to eat and drink.
12:29 Don't **w** whether God will provide it for you.
21:14 So don't **w** about how to answer the charges
Ac 11:12 with them and not to **w** about their being Gentiles.
20:10 into his arms. "Don't **w**," he said, "he's alive!"
1Co 7:21 Don't let that **w** you—but if you get a chance to be
2Co 10:10 For some say, "Don't **w** about Paul. His letters are
10:12 Oh, don't **w**; I wouldn't dare say that I am as
Php 4: 6 Don't **w** about anything; instead, pray about
1Pe 3:14 reward you for it. So don't be afraid and don't **w**.

WORRYING (4) [WORRY]

Ecc 5:12 But the rich are always **w** and seldom get a good
Isa 7: 4 Tell him to stop **w**. Tell him he doesn't need to
Lk 10:40 But Martha was **w** over the big dinner she was
12:26 like that, what's the use of **w** over bigger things?

WORSE (31) [WORST]

Ge 19: 9 We'll treat you far **w** than those other men!"
47:13 Meanwhile, the famine became **w** and **w**,
Ex 9:18 So tomorrow at this time I will send a hailstorm **w**
Jdg 2:19 behaving **w** than those who had lived before them.
2Sa 19: 7 Then you will be **w** off than you have ever been."
1Ki 14:22 for it was even **w** than that of their ancestors.
17:17 He grew **w** and **w**, and finally he died.
20:10 gods bring tragedy on me, and even **w** than that,
Ezr 9: 2 To make matters **w**, the officials and leaders are
Ne 13:24 Even **w**, half their children spoke in the language
Ps 25:17 My problems go from bad to **w**. / Oh, save me
Isa 14:29 his son will be **w** than his father ever was.
Jer 5:31 iron hand. And **w** yet, my people like it that way!
7:26 and sinful—even **w** than their ancestors.
9: 3 And they only go from bad to **w**! They care
16:12 And you are even **w** than your ancestors!
23:14 I see that the prophets of Jerusalem are even **w**!
Eze 5: 7 and have behaved even **w** than your neighbors,
16:31 You have been **w** than a prostitute, so eager for sin
Jnh 1:11 And since the storm was getting **w** all the time,
Mt 12:45 live there. And so that person is **w** off than before.
27:64 that happens, we'll be **w** off than we were at first."
Mk 5:26 but she had gotten no better. In fact, she was **w**.
Lk 11:26 And so that person is **w** off than before."
13: 2 "Do you think those Galileans were **w** sinners than
Jn 5:14 or something even **w** may happen to you."
Ro 1:32 And, **w** yet, they encourage others to do them,
1Ti 5: 8 we believe. Such people are **w** than unbelievers.
2Pe 2:20 become its slave again, they are **w** off than before.

WORSHIP (311) [WORSHIPED, WORSHIPER, WORSHIPERS, WORSHIPING, WORSHIPS]

Ge 4:26 lifetime that people first began to **w** the LORD.
22: 5 We will **w** there, and then we will come right
35: 1 Build an altar there to **w** me—the God who
47:31 and Jacob bowed in **w** as he leaned on his staff.
Ex 3:12 you will return here to **w** God at this very
4:23 I commanded you to let him go, so he could **w** me.
7:16 people go, so they can **w** me in the wilderness."
8: 1 LORD says: Let my people go, so they can **w** me.
8:20 LORD says: Let my people go, so they can **w** me.
9: 1 says: Let my people go, so they can **w** me.
9:13 says: Let my people go, so they can **w** me.
10: 3 to me? Let my people go, so they can **w** me.
10:24 "Go and **w** the LORD," he said. "But let your
12:16 all the people must gather for a time of special **w**.
19:14 He purified them for **w** and had them wash their
20: 3 "Do not **w** any other gods besides me.
20: 5 You must never **w** or bow down to them, for I,
20:23 you must not make or **w** idols of silver or gold.
23:24 Do not **w** the gods of these other nations or serve
23:33 they will infect you with their sin of idol **w**,
24: 1 Israel's leaders. All of them must **w** at a distance.

34:13 smash the sacred pillars they w, and cut down their
34:14 You must w no other gods, but only the LORD,
34:15 they will invite you to go with them to w their
34:16 who w other gods, as wives for your sons.
Lev 23: 2 the days when all of you will be summoned to w
23: 3 day of complete rest, a holy day to assemble for w.
26:31 your cities desolate and destroy your places of w,
Nu 25: 3 Before long Israel was joining in the w of Baal of
Dt 4:19 of heaven—don't be seduced by them and w them.
4:28 you will w idols made from wood and stone,
5: 7 " 'Do not w any other gods besides me.
5: 9 You must never w or bow down to them, for I,
6:14 "You must not w any of the gods of neighboring
7: 4 your young people away from me to w other gods.
7:16 Show them no mercy and do not w their gods.
10:12 to love and w him with all your heart and soul,
10:20 the LORD your God and w him and cling to him.
11:13 God with all your heart and soul, and if you w him,
11:16 heart turn away from the LORD to w other gods.
12: 2 you must destroy all the places where they w their
12: 4 "Do not w the LORD your God in the way these
pagan peoples w their gods.
12:30 Do not say, 'How do these nations w their gods?
13: 2 'Come, let us w the gods of foreign nations,'
13: 6 to you secretly and says, 'Let us go w other gods'
13: 7 They might suggest that you w the gods of peoples
13:13 astray by encouraging them to w foreign gods.
16:22 And never set up sacred pillars for w,
20:18 you their detestable customs in the w of their gods,
26:10 produce before the LORD your God and w him.
28:14 you today to follow after other gods and w them.
28:36 Then in exile you will w gods of wood and stone!
28:64 There you will w foreign gods that neither you nor
29:18 LORD our God to w these gods of other nations,
29:26 and w other gods that were foreign to them,
30:17 if you are drawn away to serve and w other gods,
31:20 Then they will begin to w other gods; they will
32:43 O heavens, / and let all the angels of God w him,
Jos 22:24 'What right do you have to w the LORD, the God
22:27 have the right to w the LORD at his sanctuary
23: 7 of their gods, much less swear by them or w them.
24:16 would never forsake the LORD and w other gods.
Jdg 6:10 You must not w the gods of the Amorites,
1Sa 1: 3 and his family would travel to Shiloh to w
1:19 and went to w the LORD once more.
2:14 All the Israelites who came to w at Shiloh were
10: 3 you who are on their way to w God at Bethel.
12:10 But we will w you and you alone if you will rescue
12:14 "Now if you will fear and w the LORD and listen
12:20 but make sure now that you w the LORD with all
12:24 be sure to fear the LORD and sincerely w him.
15:25 my sin now and go with me to w the LORD."
15:30 and before my people by going with me to w the
26:19 live among the LORD's people and w as I should.
1Ki 1:47 Then the king bowed his head in w as he lay in his
8:41 and come from distant lands to w your great
9: 6 and laws, and if you go and w other gods,
11: 2 they married would lead them to w their gods.
11: 4 they turned his heart to w their gods instead of
12:28 "It is too much trouble for you to w in Jerusalem.
16:31 Ethbaal of the Sidonians, and he began to w Baal.
17: 1 of Israel, lives—the God whom I w and serve—
2Ki 5:18 goes into the temple of the god Rimmon to w there
10:18 Baal at all compared to the way I will w him!
10:20 "Prepare a solemn assembly to w Baal!"
10:23 "Make sure that only those who w Baal are here.
10:26 They dragged out the sacred pillar used in the w of
10:28 Jehu destroyed every trace of Baal w from Israel.
17:25 But since these foreign settlers did not w the
17:26 Israel do not know how to w the God of the land.
17:28 and taught the new residents how to w the LORD.
17:29 of foreigners also continued to w their own gods.
17:35 "Do not w any other gods or bow before them
17:36 W only the LORD, who brought you out of Egypt
17:36 You must w him and bow before him;
17:37 he wrote for you. You must not w any other gods.
17:38 I made with you, and do not w other gods.
17:39 You must w only the LORD your God. He is the
18: 4 because the people of Israel had begun to w it by
18:22 and make everyone in Judah w only at the altar
23: 4 Temple all the utensils that were used to w Baal,
23:24 and every other kind of idol w, both in Jerusalem
1Ch 9:28 assigned to care for the various utensils used in w.
16: 4 w before the Ark of the LORD by asking for his
16:29 Bring your offering and come to w him.
16:29 W the LORD in all his holy splendor.
28: 9 W and serve him with your whole heart and with a
28:13 the LORD's Temple which were to be used for w
2Ch 6:32 and they come from distant lands to w your great
7:19 I have given you, and if you go and w other gods,
11:16 those who sincerely wanted to w the LORD,
17: 3 early years and did not w the images of Baal.
21:13 led the people of Jerusalem and Judah to w idols,
24: 7 the Temple of the LORD to w the images of Baal.
24:14 utensils for w services and for burnt offerings,
28: 2 kings of Israel and cast images for the w of Baal.
28:24 LORD's Temple so that no one could w there and
29:11 and to lead the people in w and make offerings to
29:29 the king and everyone with him bowed down in w.
29:30 they offered joyous praise and bowed down in w.
30: 8 W the LORD your God so that his fierce anger
31: 2 and to w and give thanks and praise to the LORD
32:12 and Jerusalem to w at only the one altar at the
33:16 He also encouraged the people of Judah to w the
34:33 and required everyone to w the LORD their God.
Ezr 4: 2 build with you, for we w your God just as you do.
6:21 from their immoral customs to w the LORD,
8:22 the king, "Our God protects all those who w him,
Ne 9: 6 to everything, and all the angels of heaven w you.
13:10 and the singers who were to conduct the w services
Job 31:27 and been secretly enticed in my heart to w them?
Ps 5: 7 with deepest awe I will w at your Temple.
10:16 Let those who w other gods be swept from the
15: 1 Who may w in your sanctuary, LORD?
22:25 my vows in the presence of those who w you.
22:29 Let the rich of the earth feast and w. / Let all
24: 4 and hearts are pure, / who do not w idols
24: 6 and w the God of Israel. / *Interlude*
29: 2 W the LORD in the splendor of his holiness.
31: 6 I hate those who w worthless idols. / I trust in the
40: 4 confidence in the proud, / or in those who w idols.
48: 9 on your unfailing love / as we w in your Temple.
66: 4 Everything on earth will w you; / they will sing
89:15 Happy are those who hear the joyful call to w,
95: 6 Come, let us w and bow down. / Let us kneel
96: 8 Bring your offering and come to w him.
96: 9 W the LORD in all his holy splendor. / Let all the
97: 7 Those who w idols are disgraced— / all who brag
99: 9 our God / and w at his holy mountain in Jerusalem,
100: 2 W the LORD with gladness. / Come before him,
102:22 and kingdoms come to w the LORD.
106:28 Then our ancestors joined in the w of Baal at Peor;
138: 2 I bow before your holy Temple as I w. / I will give
Isa 2: 2 People from all over the world will go there to w.
2: 8 bow down and w these things they have made.
17: 8 for help or w what their own hands have made.
19:23 between their lands, and they will w the same God.
26:13 others have ruled us, / but we w you alone.
27:13 and Egypt will return to Jerusalem to w the
29:13 And their w of me amounts to nothing more than
33:20 you will see Zion as a place of w and celebration.
36: 7 and make everyone in Judah w only at the altar
44: 9 No wonder those who w them are put to shame.
44:11 All who w idols will stand before the LORD in
44:15 rest of it and makes himself a god for people to w!
44:19 Should I bow down to w a chunk of wood?"
45:21 your case, and state your proofs that idol w pays.
46: 6 make a god from it. Then they bow down and w it!
56: 6 who w him and do not desecrate the Sabbath day
57: 5 You w your idols with great passion beneath every
57: 6 You w them with drink offerings and grain
57: 8 have set up your idols and w them instead of me.
60: 6 bring gold and incense for the w of the LORD.
65: 4 the graves and secret places to w evil spirits.
65:11 his Temple and w the gods of Fate and Destiny,
66:23 "All humanity will come to w me from week to
Jer 1:16 they w idols that they themselves have made!
3:23 Our w of idols and our religious orgies on the hills
7: 2 the LORD! Listen to it, all of you who w here!
7: 9 and w Baal and all those other new gods of yours,
10: 8 The wisest of people who w idols are stupid and
foolish. The things they w are made of wood!
10:11 Say this to those who w other gods:
13:10 stubbornly follow their own desires and w idols.
13:27 and your abominable idol w out in the fields
16:13 There you can w idols all you like—and I will
17: 2 Even their children go to w at their sacred altars
17:12 But we w at your throne—eternal, high,
26: 2 who have come there to w from all over Judah.
31: 6 let us go up to Jerusalem to w the LORD our
32:39 will give them one heart and mind to w me forever,
32:40 I will put a desire in their hearts to w me, and they
41: 5 They had come to w at the Temple of the LORD.
49: 1 Why are you, who w Molech, living in its towns?
51:44 The nations will no longer come and w him.
Eze 11:18 will remove every trace of their detestable idol w.
14: 5 have turned from me to w their detestable idols.
16:18 Then you used my oil and incense to w them.
18:15 Suppose this son refuses to w idols on the
20:39 go right ahead and w your idols, but then don't
20:40 the people of Israel will someday w me, and I will
23:39 their idols, they boldly came into my Temple to w!
23:49 repaid for all your prostitution—your w of idols.
33:25 in it, you w idols, and you murder the innocent.
36:25 be washed away, and you will no longer w idols.
43: 7 any longer by their adulterous w of other gods
44:10 w idols must bear the consequences of their
44:12 But they encouraged my people to w other gods,
46: 2 He will w inside the gateway passage and then go
46: 3 The common people will w the LORD in front of
46: 9 to w the LORD during the religious festivals,
Da 3: 5 bow to the ground to w King Nebuchadnezzar's
3:10 and w the gold statue when they hear the sound of
3:12 your gods or to w the gold statue you have set up."
3:14 my gods or to w the gold statue I have set up?
3:15 and w the statue I have made when you hear the
3:18 your gods or w the gold statue you have set up."
3:28 than serve or w any god except their own God.
6:16 your God, whom you w continually, rescue you."
6:20 Was your God, whom you w continually, able to
11:38 Instead of these, he will w the god of fortresses—
Hos 4:10 for they have deserted the LORD to w other gods.
4:15 do not join with those who w me insincerely at
4:15 Their w is mere pretense as they take oaths in the
5:11 because they are determined to w idols.
8: 6 This calf you w was crafted by your own hands!
12:11 But Gilead is filled with sinners who w idols.
13: 2 they keep on sinning by making silver idols to w—
Am 5: 5 Don't go to w the idols of Bethel, Gilgal,
8:14 And those who w and swear by the idols of
Jnh 1: 9 "I am a Hebrew, and I w the LORD, the God of
2: 8 Those who w false gods turn their backs on all
Mic 1:13 city in Judah to follow Israel in the sin of idol w,
4: 1 People from all over the world will go there to w.
4: 5 Even though the nations around us w idols, we will
5:13 so you will never again w the work of your own
Na 3: 4 She taught them all to w her false gods,
Hab 1:16 Then they will w their nets and burn incense in
Zep 1: 4 my fist and destroy every last trace of their Baal w.
1: 5 follow the LORD, but then they w Molech, too.
1: 6 And I will destroy those who used to w me
1: 9 I will punish those who participate in pagan w
2:11 Then people from nations around the world will w
3: 9 so that everyone will be able to w the LORD
Zec 9: 7 All the surviving Philistines will w our God
13: 2 I will get rid of every trace of idol w throughout
14:16 will go up to Jerusalem each year to w the King,
14:17 that refuses to come to Jerusalem to w the King,
14:21 All who come to w will be free to use any of these
Mal 2:11 sanctuary by marrying women who w idols.
Mt 2: 2 his star as it arose, and we have come to w him."
2: 8 come back and tell me so that I can go and w him,
4: 9 he said, "if you will only kneel down and w me."
4:10 Scriptures say, / 'You must w the Lord your God;
15: 9 Their w is a farce, / for they replace God's
Mk 7: 7 but their hearts are far away. / Their w is a farce,
15:19 spit on him, and dropped to their knees in mock w.
Lk 4: 7 give it all to you if you will bow down and w me."
4: 8 Scriptures say, / 'You must w the Lord your God;
Jn 4:20 Jews insist that Jerusalem is the only place of w,
4:21 no longer matter whether you w the Father here
4:22 Samaritans know so little about the one you w,
4:23 and is already here when true worshipers will w
4:23 The Father is looking for anyone who will w him
4:24 so those who w him must w in spirit and in
9:31 but he is ready to hear those who w him and do his
Ac 7: 7 the end they will come out and w me in this place.'
7:43 god Rephan, / and the images you made to w them.
8:27 The eunuch had gone to Jerusalem to w,
10:25 Cornelius fell to the floor before him in w.
12:23 because he accepted the people's w instead of
18:13 They accused Paul of "persuading people to w
24:11 ago that I arrived in Jerusalem to w at the Temple.
24:14 I w the God of our ancestors, and I firmly believe
26: 7 that is why the twelve tribes of Israel w God night
Ro 1:21 but they wouldn't w him as God or even give him
1Co 8: 7 they think of it as the w of real gods, and their
10: 7 or w idols as some of them did. For the Scriptures
10:14 So, my dear friends, flee from the w of idols.
14:25 and they will fall down on their knees and w God,
Php 3: 3 For we who w God in the Spirit are the only ones
Col 2:18 And don't let anyone say you must w angels,
2Th 2: 4 and tear down every object of adoration and w.
Heb 1: 6 God said, "Let all the angels of God w him."
8: 2 the true place of w that was built by the Lord
8: 5 They serve in a place of w that is only a copy,
9: 1 there were regulations for w and a sacred tent here
9:14 that lead to death so that we can w the living God.
9:21 on the sacred tent and on everything used for w.
9:24 He did not go into the earthly place of w, for that
10: 1 provide perfect cleansing for those who came to w.
11:21 and bowed in w as he leaned on his staff.
1Pe 3:15 Instead, you must w Christ as Lord of your life.
4: 3 and wild parties, and their terrible w of idols.
Rev 2:14 He taught them to w idols by eating food offered to
2:20 She is encouraging them to w idols, eat food
4:10 and w the one who lives forever and ever.
9:20 They continued to w demons and idols made of
13:12 and those who belong to this world to w the first
13:15 commanded that anyone refusing to w it must die.
14: 7 W him who made heaven and earth, the sea,
15: 4 are holy. / All nations will come and w before you,
19:10 at his feet to w him, but he said, "No, don't w me.
19:10 who testify of their faith in Jesus. W God.
22: 3 Lamb will be there, and his servants will w him.
22: 8 I fell down to w the angel who showed them to me.
22: 9 But again he said, "No, don't w me. I am a servant
22: 9 who obey what is written in this scroll. W God!"

WORSHIPED (111) [WORSHIP]

Ge 12: 8 the east. There he built an altar and w the LORD.
13: 4 built the altar, and there he again w the LORD.
21:33 and he w the LORD, the Eternal God, at that
24:26 man fell down to the ground and w the LORD.
24:48 "Then I bowed my head and w the LORD.
24:52 servant bowed to the ground and w the LORD.
26:25 Then Isaac built an altar there and w the LORD.
Ex 4:31 for them, they all bowed their heads and w.
12:27 Then all the people bowed their heads and w.
32: 8 like a calf, and they have w and sacrificed to it.
32:35 because they had w the calf Aaron had made.
34: 8 Moses immediately fell to the ground and w.
Lev 26: 1 or shaped stones to be w in your land.
Dt 4: 3 everyone who had w the god Baal of Peor.
Jos 24: 2 the Euphrates River, and they w other gods.
24:14 Put away forever the idols your ancestors w when
Jdg 2:11 in the LORD's sight and w the images of Baal.
3: 6 to their sons. And the Israelites w their gods.
3: 7 and they w the images of Baal and the Asherah
10: 6 They w images of Baal and Ashtoreth,
18:31 So Micah's carved image was w by the tribe of
1Sa 1:28 his whole life." And they w the LORD there.
7: 4 of Baal and Ashtoreth and w only the LORD.
15:31 and went with him, and Saul w the LORD.
2Sa 12:20 Then he went to the Tabernacle and w the LORD.
15:32 top of the Mount of Olives where people w God,
1Ki 9: 9 out of Egypt, and they w other gods instead.
11: 5 Solomon w Ashtoreth, the goddess of the
11:33 For Solomon has abandoned me and w Ashtoreth,
12:30 This became a great sin, for the people w them,

18:18 the LORD and have w the images of Baal instead.
21:26 because he w idols just as the Amorites had done—
22:53 He served Baal and w him, arousing the anger of
2Ki 10:18 "Ahab hardly w Baal at all compared to the way I
10:21 all Israel summoning those who w Baal.
17: 7 nation of Israel because the people w other gods,
17:12 Yes, they w idols, despite the LORD's specific
17:15 They w worthless idols and became worthless
17:16 and w Baal and all the forces of heaven.
17:26 because they have not w him correctly."
17:30 Those from Babylon w idols of their god
17:30 Those from Cuthah w their god Nergal. And those from Hamath w Ashima.
17:31 The Avvites w their gods Nibhaz and Tartak.
17:32 These new residents w the LORD, but they
17:33 And though they w the LORD, they continued to
17:41 new residents w the LORD, they also w their idols.
21: 3 bowed before all the forces of heaven and w them.
21:21 worshiping the same idols that his father had w.
22:17 my people have abandoned me and w pagan gods,
1Ch 5:25 They w the gods of the nations that God had
2Ch 7: 3 on the ground and w and praised the LORD,
7:22 them out of Egypt, and they w other gods instead.
11:15 where they w the goat and calf idols he had made.
24:18 and they w Asherah poles and idols instead!
25:15 "Why have you w gods who could not even save
29:28 The entire assembly w the LORD as the singers
33: 3 bowed before all the stars of heaven and w them.
33:22 He w and sacrificed to all the idols his father had
34:25 of Judah have abandoned me and w pagan gods,
Ne 8: 6 and w the LORD with their faces to the ground.
Ps 74: 8 they burned down all the places where God was w.
106:36 They w their idols, / and this led to their downfall.
Isa 47:12 "Call out the demon hordes you have w all these
Jer 2: 5 They w foolish idols, only to become foolish
2:23 not true! We haven't w the images of Baal!'
3: 6 Israel has w other gods on every hill and under
8: 2 the gods my people have loved, served, and w.
9:14 their own desires and w the images of Baal,
16:11 They w other gods and served them.
16:19 ancestors were foolish, for they w worthless idols.
19: 4 idols never before w by this generation, by their
26:19 they turned from their sins and w the LORD.
44: 3 They burned incense and w other gods—gods that
Eze 8:10 I also saw the various idols w by the people of
16:17 given you and made statues of men and w them,
16:36 and because you have w detestable idols, and
18: 6 in the mountains before Israel's idols or w them.
Da 2:46 bowed to the ground before Daniel and w him,
3: 7 and w the statue that King Nebuchadnezzar had set
4:34 and I praised and w the Most High and honored the
12:11 object that causes desecration is set up to be w,
Hos 9:10 Soon they became as vile as the god they w.
Hag 1:12 had sent, and the people w the LORD in earnest.
Zec 14: 9 will be one LORD—his name alone will be w.
Mt 2:11 were, and they fell down before him and w him.
14:33 Then the disciples w him. "You really are the Son
15:25 But she came and w him and pleaded again,
28: 9 And they ran to him, held his feet, and w him.
28:17 When they saw him, they w him—but some of
Lk 24:52 They w him and then returned to Jerusalem filled
Jn 4:20 here at Mount Gerizim, where our ancestors w?"
9:38 Lord," the man said, "I believe!" And he w Jesus.
Ac 2:46 They w together at the Temple each day, met in
13:43 and godly converts to Judaism who w at the
18: 7 a Gentile who w God and lived next door to the
19:27 this magnificent goddess w throughout the
Ro 1:23 they w idols made to look like mere people,
1:25 So they w the things God made but not the Creator
Rev 5:14 elders fell down and w God and the Lamb.
7:11 they fell face down before the throne and w God.
11:16 thrones before God fell on their faces and w him.
13: 4 They w the dragon for giving the beast such power, and they w the beast.
13: 8 And all the people who belong to this world w the
14:11 for they have w the beast and his statue and have
16: 2 had the mark of the beast and who w his statue.
19: 4 and the four living beings fell down and w God,
19:20 the mark of the beast and who w his statue.
20: 4 And I saw the souls of those who had not w the

WORSHIPER (2) [WORSHIP]

2Ki 10:22 "Be sure that every w of Baal wears one of these
Ac 16:14 She was a w of God. As she listened to us,

WORSHIPERS (16) [WORSHIP]

Nu 21:29 of Moab! / You are finished, O w of Chemosh!
2Ki 10:19 Summon all the prophets and w of Baal, and call
10:19 Any of Baal's w who fail to come will be put to
10:19 But Jehu's plan was to destroy all the w of Baal.
10:23 Jehu said to the w of Baal, "Make sure that only
1Ch 16:10 in his holy name; / O w of the LORD, rejoice!
Ps 42: 4 it used to be: / I walked among the crowds of w,
105: 3 in his holy name; / O w of the LORD, rejoice!
Eze 22: 9 You are filled with idol w and people who take
Jn 4:23 and is already here when true w will worship the
1Co 5:10 or who are greedy or are swindlers or idol w.
6: 9 who are idol w, adulterers, male prostitutes,
Heb 10: 2 for the w would have been purified once for all
Rev 11: 1 of God and the altar, and count the number of w.
21: 8 who practice witchcraft, and idol w, and all liars—
22:15 the sexually immoral, the murderers, the idol w,

WORSHIPING (70) [WORSHIP]

Ge 28:22 This memorial pillar will become a place for w
Ex 34:16 to commit adultery against me by w other gods.
Lev 20: 5 along with all those who commit prostitution by w
Nu 25: 2 were feasting with them and w the gods of Moab.
25: 5 everyone who had joined in w Baal of Peor.
25:18 with deceit by tricking you into w Baal of Peor,
Dt 8:19 follow other gods, w and bowing down to them,
11:28 and turn from his way by w foreign gods.
12:30 into following their example in w their gods.
17: 3 by serving other gods or by w the sun, the moon,
31:16 are gone, these people will begin w foreign gods,
31:18 all the sins they have committed by w other gods.
32:16 They stirred up his jealousy by w foreign gods;
32:21 They have roused my jealousy by w non-gods;
Jos 22:25 may make our descendants stop w the LORD.
23:16 break the covenant of the LORD your God by w
Jdg 2:12 other gods, w the gods of the people around them.
2:19 followed other gods, w and bowing down to them.
8:27 all the Israelites prostituted themselves by w it,
8:33 the Israelites prostituted themselves by w the
1Sa 12:10 and w the images of Baal and Ashtoreth.
12:21 Don't go back to w worthless idols that cannot
15:23 and stubbornness is as bad as w idols.
1Ki 11:10 He had warned Solomon specifically about w other
14:15 for they have angered the LORD by w Asherah
2Ki 17:34 former practices instead of truly w the LORD
19:37 One day while he was w in the temple of his god
21:21 w the same idols that his father had worshiped.
2Ch 20:18 and Jerusalem did the same, w the LORD.
25:20 for God was arranging to destroy him for w the
Ne 9: 3 confessing their sins and w the LORD their God.
Ps 44:20 If we had turned away from w our God / or spread
Isa 37:38 One day while he was w in the temple of his god
44:17 He falls down in front of it, w and praying to it.
57: 7 adultery on the mountaintops by w idols there,
65: 3 All day long they insult me to my face by w idols
Jer 1:16 all their evil—for deserting me and w other gods.
3: 9 she thought nothing of committing adultery by w
3:13 and committed adultery against him by w idols
7: 6 and if you stop w idols as you now do to your own
11:10 They have refused to listen to me and are w idols.
22: 9 with the LORD their God by w other gods.' "
23:27 just as their ancestors did by w the idols of Baal.
25: 6 Do not make me angry by w the idols you have
25: 7 "You made me furious by w your idols,
35:15 from your wicked ways and to stop w other gods,
44:18 incense to the Queen of Heaven and stopped w her,
44:19 "do you suppose that we were w the Queen of
Eze 8:16 They were facing eastward, w the sun!
20:30 Do you intend to keep prostituting yourselves by w
23: 7 men of Assyria, w their idols and defiling herself.
23:37 adultery by w idols and murder by burning their
36:18 They polluted the land with murder and by w idols,
Hos 1: 2 adultery against the LORD by w other gods."
2: 8 and silver she used in w the god Baal were gifts
5: 1 For you have led the people into a snare by w the
7: 9 W foreign gods has sapped their strength, but they
13: 1 But the people of Ephraim sinned by w Baal
Hab 2:18 "What have you gained by w all your man-made
Mt 8: 2 He knelt before him, w. "Lord," the man said,
Lk 2:37 and night, w God with fasting and prayer.
Ac 13: 2 One day as these men were w the Lord and fasting,
17:23 You have been w him without knowing who he is,
Ro 1:23 And instead of w the glorious, ever-living God,
9: 4 They have the privilege of w him and receiving his
14: 6 Those who have a special day for w the Lord are
1Co 11: 7 man should not wear anything on his head when w,
12: 2 led astray and swept along in w speechless idols.
Heb 12:28 and please God by w him with holy fear and awe.
Rev 1:10 It was the Lord's Day, and I was w in the Spirit.

WORSHIPS (6) [WORSHIP]

2Ki 10:23 are here. Don't let anyone in who w the LORD!"
Eze 18:11 w idols on the mountains, commits adultery,
18:12 w idols and takes part in loathsome practices,
1Co 5:11 or is greedy, or w idols, or is abusive, or a
Eph 5: 5 For a greedy person is really an idolater who w the
Rev 14: 9 "Anyone who w the beast and his statue or who

WORST (12) [WORSE]

Ex 10:14 It was the w locust plague in Egyptian history,
1Sa 15:32 for he thought, "Surely the w is over, and I have
Ezr 9: 2 and leaders are some of the w offenders."
Ps 35:16 They mock me with the w kind of profanity,
41: 7 me whisper about me, / imagining the w for me.
Jer 6:28 Are they not the w of rebels, full of slander?
Mt 11:19 a drunkard, and a friend of the w sort of sinners!'
Lk 7:34 a drunkard, and a friend of the w sort of sinners!'
13: 4 on them? Were they the w sinners in Jerusalem?
1Ti 1:15 world to save sinners—and I was the w of them all.
1:16 of his great patience with even the w sinners.
Jas 3:14 brag about being wise. That is the w kind of lie.

WORTH (20) [WORTHLESS, WORTHWHILE, WORTHY]

Ge 23:15 "the land is w four hundred pieces of silver,
Lev 27:27 it by paying the priest's assessment of its w,
Dt 15:18 the services w double the wages of hired workers,
2Sa 18: 3 You are w ten thousand of us, and it is better that
1Ch 21:24 to Araunah, "No, I insist on paying what it is w.
Job 33:27 declare to his friends, 'I sinned, but it was not w it.
Pr 31:10 capable wife? She is w more than precious rubies.
Ecc 10: 6 and if they fail to give people of proven w their
Isa 7:23 now w as much as a thousand pieces of silver,
La 4: 2 w their weight in gold, are now treated like pots of
Zec 11:12 "If you like, give me my wages, whatever I am w;
Mt 10:29 Not even a sparrow, w only half a penny, can fall
16:26 in the process? Is anything w more than your soul?
Mk 8:37 Is anything w more than your soul?
Lk 10:42 There is really only one thing w being concerned
Jn 12: 5 "That perfume was w a small fortune. It should
Ac 20:24 But my life is w nothing unless I use it for doing
Ro 2:25 The Jewish ceremony of circumcision is w
2Co 12: 5 That experience is something w boasting about,
Gal 4:11 I am afraid that all my hard work for you was w

WORTHIES [KJV] See OFFICERS

WORTHILY [KJV] See GREAT

WORTHLESS (49) [WORTH]

Dt 13:13 that some w rabble among you have led their
21:20 and refuses to obey. He is a w drunkard.'
1Sa 12:21 Don't go back to worshiping w idols that cannot
15: 9 They destroyed only what was w or of poor
24:14 Should he spend his time chasing one who is as w
1Ki 9:13 my brother?" he asked. "These towns are w!"
9:13 that area Cabul—"w"—as it is still known today.
2Ki 17:15 They worshiped w idols and became w themselves.
Job 13: 4 me with lies. As doctors, you are w quacks.
28:18 and valuable rock crystal are w in trying to get it.
Ps 1: 4 They are like w chaff, scattered by the wind.
31: 6 I hate those who worship w idols. / I trust in the
94:11 knows people's thoughts, / that they are w!
97: 7 disgraced— / all who brag about their w gods—
119:37 Turn my eyes from w things, / and give me life
Pr 6:12 Here is a description of w and wicked people:
10:20 are like sterling silver; the heart of a fool is w.
20:14 buyer haggles over the price, saying, "It's w,"
28: 7 those who seek out w companions bring shame to
Isa 1:12 through my courts with your w sacrifices?
1:22 like pure silver, you have become like w slag.
30: 7 Egypt's promises are w! I call her the Harmless
41:29 See, they are all foolish, w things. Your idols are
44: 9 These highly valued objects are really w.
Jer 2:11 have exchanged their glorious God for w idols!
8:19 angered me with their carved idols and w gods?"
10:15 Idols are w; they are lies! / The time is coming
16:19 ancestors were foolish, for they worshiped w idols.
18:15 For they have deserted me and turned to w idols.
51:18 Idols are w; they are lies! / The time is coming
Eze 7:19 throw away their money, tossing it out like w trash.
20:25 I gave them over to w customs and laws that would
22:18 the people of Israel are the w slag that remains
22:19 Because you are all w slag, I will bring you to my
Hos 7: 8 Now they have become as w as a half-baked cake!
Zec 11:15 "Go again and play the part of a w shepherd.
11:17 Doom is certain for this w shepherd who abandons
Mal 1:10 so that these w sacrifices could not be offered!
Mt 5:13 It will be thrown out and trampled underfoot as w.
Ac 14:15 should turn from these w things to the living God,
17: 5 so they gathered some w fellows from the streets to
1Co 3:20 knows the thoughts of the wise, / that they are w."
Eph 5:11 Take no part in the w deeds of evil and darkness;
Php 3: 7 but now I consider them w because of what Christ
3: 8 everything else is w when compared with the
Tit 1:16 and disobedient, w for doing anything good.
Jas 1:26 are just fooling yourself, and your religion is w.
5: 3 Your gold and silver have become w. The very

WORTHWHILE (1) [WORTH]

Ecc 2:11 the wind. There was nothing really w anywhere.

WORTHY (66) [WORTH]

Ge 32:10 I am not w of all the faithfulness and unfailing love
Dt 10:21 He is your God, the one who is w of your praise,
21:22 "If someone has committed a crime w of death
22:26 she has committed no crime w of death.
24:16 Those w of death must be executed for their own
Ru 2:13 even though I am not as w as your workers."
2Sa 22: 4 I will call on the LORD, who is w of praise,
2Ki 14: 6 Those w of death must be executed for their own
1Ch 16:25 Great is the LORD! He is most w of praise!
2Ch 2: 6 But who can really build him a w home? Not even
25: 4 Those w of death must be executed for their own
Est 1:19 and that you choose another queen more w than
Job 30: 1 by young men whose fathers are not w to run with
Ps 18: 3 I will call on the LORD, who is w of praise,
33: 4 and everything he does is w of our trust.
51:19 Then you will be pleased with w sacrifices
96: 4 Great is the LORD! He is most w of praise!
119:138 are perfect; / they are entirely w of our trust.
145: 3 Great is the LORD! He is most w of praise!
Pr 12: 4 A w wife is her husband's joy and crown;
Isa 40:16 animals would not make an offering w of our God.
Jer 15:19 If you speak words that are w, you will be my
33:24 and saying that Israel is not w to be counted as a
Mt 3:11 so much greater that I am not even w to be his
8: 8 I am not w to have you come into my home.
10:11 search for a w man and stay in his home until you
10:13 If it turns out to be a w home, let your blessing
10:37 than you love me, you are not w of being mine;
10:37 more than me, you are not w of being mine.
10:38 and follow me, you are not w of being mine.
22: 8 and the guests I invited aren't w of the honor.
Mk 1: 7 so much greater that I am not even w to be his
Lk 3:16 so much greater that I am not even w to be his
7: 6 to my home, for I am not w of such an honor.
7: 7 I am not even w to come and meet you. Just say
10: 6 If those who live there are w, the blessing will
15:19 and I am no longer w of being called your son.

15:21 and I am no longer w of being called your son.'
17:10 obey me you should say, 'We are not w of praise.
20:35 For those w of being raised from the dead won't be
Jn 1:27 his ministry. I am not even w to be his slave."
Ac 5:41 them w to suffer dishonor for the name of Jesus.
13:25 and I am not even w to be his slave.'
23:29 certainly nothing w of imprisonment or death.
25:11 If I have done something w of death, I don't refuse
25:25 But in my opinion he has done nothing w of death.
26:31 "This man hasn't done anything w of death
Ro 9:5 rules over everything and is w of eternal praise!
16:2 her in the Lord, as one who is w of high honor.
1Co 15:9 and I am not w to be called an apostle after the
Eph 4:1 the Lord, beg you to lead a life w of your calling,
Php 1:27 you must live in a manner w of the Good News
4:8 about things that are excellent and w of praise.
1Th 2:12 your lives in a way that God would consider w.
2Th 1:5 For he will make you w of his Kingdom, for which
1:11 that our God will make you w of the life to which
1Ti 4:6 you will be doing your duty as a w servant of
Tit 2:2 to be w of respect, and to live wisely.
Rev 3:4 They will walk with me in white, for they are w.
4:11 "You are w, O Lord our God, / to receive glory
5:2 "Who is w to break the seals on this scroll
5:4 because no one could be found who was w to open
5:5 He is w to open the scroll and break its seven
5:9 "You are w to take the scroll / and break its seals
5:12 "The Lamb is w—the Lamb who was killed.
5:12 He is w to receive power and riches / and wisdom

WOT(TETH) [KJV] See CONCERN, IDEA, KNOW, TRUSTS

WOULD (859) [I'D, WE'D, WOULDN'T, YOU'D] See Index of Articles, Etc.

WOULDN'T (81) [NOT, WOULD] See Index of Articles, Etc.

WOUND (18) [DEATH-WOUND, WIND, WOUNDED, WOUNDING, WOUNDS]

Ex 21:25 burn for burn, w for w, bruise for bruise.
1Ki 22:35 The blood from his w ran down to the floor of his
Ps 42:10 Their taunts pierce me like a fatal w. / They scoff,
Pr 25:20 jacket in cold weather or rubbing salt in a w.
Jer 6:14 superficial treatments for my people's mortal w.
8:11 superficial treatments for my people's mortal w.
10:19 My w is desperate, and my grief is great.
15:18 my suffering continue? Why is my w so incurable?
30:12 Yours is an incurable bruise, a terrible w.
30:15 protest your punishment—this w that has no cure?
La 2:13 For your w is as deep as the sea. Who can heal
Mic 1:9 For my people's w is far too deep to heal. It has
6:13 "Therefore, I will w you! I will bring you to ruin
Na 3:19 There is no healing for your w; your injury is fatal.
Jn 20:25 and place my hand into the w in his side."
20:27 see my hands. Put your hand into the w in my side.
Rev 13:3 beyond recovery—but the fatal w was healed!

WOUNDED (30) [WOUND]

Ge 4:23 I have killed a youth who attacked and w me.
1Sa 17:52 and w Philistines were strewn all along the road
31:3 archers caught up with him and w him severely.
2Sa 1:4 Many men are dead and w on the battlefield,
1Ki 20:37 "Strike me!" So he struck the prophet and w him.
22:34 the driver of his chariot. "I have been badly w!"
2Ki 8:28 When King Joram was w in the battle,
9:15 But Joram had been w in the fighting and had
9:16 Jezreel to find King Joram, who was lying there w.
1Ch 10:3 archers caught up with him and w him severely.
2Ch 18:33 the driver of his chariot. "I have been badly w!"
22:5 and the Arameans w Joram in the battle.
24:25 Arameans withdrew, leaving Joash severely w.
35:23 hit King Josiah with their arrows and w him.
35:23 "Take me from the battle, for I am badly w!"
Job 24:12 the dying rise from the city, and the w cry for help,
SS 5:7 were making their rounds; they struck and w me.
Isa 53:5 But he was w and crushed for our sins. He was
Jer 14:17 with a sword and lies mortally w on the ground.
14:19 Why have you w us past all hope of healing?
30:14 I have w you cruelly, as though I were your
37:10 leaving only a handful of w survivors, they would
51:52 The groans of her w people will be heard
La 2:12 Their lives ebb away like the life of a warrior w in
Eze 26:15 as the screams of the w echo in the continuing
30:24 king of Egypt, and he will lie there mortally w,
Zec 13:6 he will say, 'I was w at the home of friends!'
Lk 20:12 thing happened. He, too, was w and chased away.
Rev 13:3 I saw that one of the heads of the beast seemed w
13:14 who was fatally w and then came back to life.

WOUNDING (1) [WOUND]

Pr 25:18 w them with a sword, or shooting them with a

WOUNDS (22) [WOUND]

Ge 34:25 But three days later, when their w were still sore,
Dt 32:39 and gives life; / I am the one who w and heals;
2Ki 8:29 he returned to Jezreel to recover from his w.
9:15 and had returned to Jezreel to recover from his w.)
2Ch 22:6 Joram returned to Jezreel to recover from his w,
28:15 and drink, and dressed their w with olive oil.
Job 5:18 For though he w, he also bandages. He strikes,
9:17 and he multiplies my w without cause.
Ps 38:5 My w fester and stink / because of my foolish sins.
147:3 He heals the brokenhearted, / binding up their w.
Pr 6:33 W and constant disgrace are his lot. His shame will
27:6 W from a friend are better than many kisses from
Isa 1:6 covered with bruises, welts, and infected w—
30:26 to heal his people and cure the w he gave them.
Jer 8:22 Why is there no healing for the w of my people?
30:17 I will give you back your health and heal your w,
Eze 28:8 home in the heart of the sea, pierced with many w.
Hos 6:1 He has injured us; now he will bandage our w.
Lk 10:34 the Samaritan soothed his w with medicine
Jn 20:25 "I won't believe it unless I see the nail w in his
Ac 16:33 That same hour the jailer washed their w, and he
1Pe 2:24 for what is right. You have been healed by his w!

WOVE (3) [WEAVE]

Jdg 16:13 Delilah w the seven braids of his hair into the
2Ki 23:7 where the women w coverings for the Asherah
La 1:14 "He w my sins into ropes to hitch me to a yoke of

WOVEN (14) [WEAVE]

Ex 28:32 The opening will be reinforced by a w collar
29:9 with their w sashes and their headdresses.
39:5 They also made an elaborate w sash of the same
39:22 The robe of the ephod was w entirely of blue yarn,
39:23 The edge of this opening was reinforced with a w
Lev 19:19 Do not wear clothing w from two different kinds of
Dt 22:11 wear clothing made of wool and linen w together.
Est 1:6 The courtyard was decorated with beautifully w
Ps 45:13 her chamber, / dressed in a gown w with gold.
73:6 and their clothing is w of cruelty.
139:15 as I was w together in the dark of the womb.
Mt 3:4 John's clothes were w from camel hair, and he
Mk 1:6 His clothes were w from camel hair, and he wore a
Jn 19:23 but it was seamless, w in one piece from the top.

WRAPPED (18) [WRAPPINGS, WRAPS]

Ex 12:34 They w their kneading bowls in their spare
Nu 4:12 of the sanctuary must be w in a dark blue cloth,
1Sa 21:9 priest replied. "It is w in a cloth behind the ephod.
28:14 "He is an old man w in a robe," she replied.
2Sa 22:6 The grave w its ropes around me; / death itself
1Ki 19:13 he w his face in his cloak and went out and stood
Ps 18:5 The grave w its ropes around me; / death itself
Eze 16:8 So I w my cloak around you to cover your
Jnh 2:5 around me, and seaweed w itself around my head.
Mt 27:59 Joseph took the body and w it in a long linen cloth.
Mk 15:46 he w it in the cloth and laid it in a tomb that had
Lk 2:7 She w him snugly in strips of cloth and laid him in
2:12 lying in a manger, w snugly in strips of cloth!"
23:53 down from the cross and w it in a long linen cloth
Jn 11:44 bound in graveclothes, his face w in a headcloth.
13:4 took off his robe, w a towel around his waist,
19:40 Together they w Jesus' body in a long linen cloth
Ac 5:6 Then some young men w him in a sheet and took

WRAPPINGS (2) [WRAPPED]

Lk 24:12 Stooping, he peered in and saw the empty linen w;
Jn 20:6 He also noticed the linen w lying there,

WRAPS (2) [WRAPPED]

Job 26:8 He w the rain in his thick clouds, and the clouds do
Pr 30:4 in his fists? Who w up the oceans in his cloak?

WRATH (31)

Ge 49:7 for it is fierce; / cursed be their w, for it is cruel.
Ne 13:18 Now you are bringing even more w upon the
Ps 78:21 The fire of his w burned against Jacob. / Yes,
79:6 Pour out your w on the nations that refuse to
85:5 Will you prolong your w to distant generations?
90:9 We live our lives beneath your w. / We end our
90:11 Your w is as awesome as the fear you deserve.
95:9 they courted my w though they had seen my many
102:10 because of your anger and w. / For you have
Pr 11:23 to happiness, while the wicked can expect only w.
15:1 A gentle answer turns away w, but harsh words stir
27:4 Anger is cruel, and w is like a flood, but who can
Jer 10:10 at his anger. The nations hide before his w.
10:25 Pour out your w on the nations that refuse to
Da 8:19 to tell you what will happen later in the time of w.
11:36 He will succeed—until the time of w is completed.
Na 1:2 is a jealous God, filled with vengeance and w.
Lk 21:23 great distress in the land and w upon this people.
Jn 3:36 eternal life, but the w of God remains upon them."
Ro 2:8 his anger and w on those who live for themselves,
Rev 6:16 who sits on the throne and from the w of the Lamb.
6:17 For the great day of their w has come, and who
11:18 with you, / but now the time of your w has come.
14:10 must drink the wine of God's w. It is poured out
undiluted into God's cup of w.
14:19 the grapes into the great winepress of God's w.
15:1 which would bring God's w to completion.
15:7 a gold bowl filled with the terrible w of God,
16:1 and empty out the seven bowls of God's w on the
16:19 cup that was filled with the wine of his fierce w.
19:15 and he trod the winepress of the fierce w of

WREATH (2) [WREATHS]

1Ki 7:29 and below the lions and oxen were w decorations.
Pr 4:9 She will place a lovely w on your head; she will

WREATHS (4) [WREATH]

1Ki 7:30 these supports were decorated with carvings of w
7:31 it was decorated on the outside with carvings of w.
7:36 there was room, and there were w all around.
Ac 14:13 and the crowd brought oxen and w of flowers,

WRECKED (3) [SHIPWRECK, SHIPWRECKED, WRECKERS]

1Ki 22:48 never set sail, for they were w at Ezion-geber.
2Ki 10:27 the sacred pillar of Baal and w the temple of Baal,
Eze 27:34 Now you are a w ship, / broken at the bottom of

WRECKERS (1) [WRECKED]

Jer 22:7 I will call for w, who will bring out their tools to

WRENCHED (4)

2Sa 23:21 Benaiah w the spear from the Egyptian's hand
1Ch 11:23 Benaiah w the spear from the Egyptian's hand
Job 31:22 then let my shoulder be w out of place! Let my arm
Da 7:8 Three of the first horns were w out, roots and all,

WREST [KJV] See SWAYED, TWIST

WRESTLED (2)

Ge 32:24 and a man came and w with him until dawn.
Hos 12:4 Yes, he w with the angel and won. He wept

WRETCHED (2) [WRETCHEDNESS, WRETCHES]

Nu 21:5 and nothing to drink. And we hate this w manna!"
Rev 3:17 And you don't realize that you are w and miserable

WRETCHEDNESS (1) [WRETCHED]

Da 9:18 hear my request. Open your eyes and see our w.

WRETCHES (1) [WRETCHED]

Job 30:2 A lot of good they are to me—those worn-out w!

WRING (1) [WRUNG]

Lev 5:8 The priest will w its neck but without severing its

WRINKLE (1)

Eph 5:27 church without a spot or w or any other blemish.

WRIST (2) [WRISTS]

Ge 38:28 and the midwife tied a scarlet thread around the w
38:30 Then the baby with the scarlet thread on his w was

WRISTS (7) [WRIST]

Ge 24:22 for her nose and two large gold bracelets for her w.
24:30 the nose-ring and the bracelets on his sister's w,
Jdg 15:14 burnt strands of flax, and they fell from his w.
Eze 13:18 You tie magic charms on their w and furnish them
23:42 who put bracelets on your w and beautiful crowns
Mk 5:4 he snapped the chains from his w and smashed the
Ac 12:7 "Quick! Get up!" And the chains fell off his w.

WRITE (68) [HANDWRITING, WRITER'S, WRITES, WRITING, WRITINGS, WRITTEN, WROTE]

Ex 17:14 "W this down as a permanent record,
34:1 I will w on them the same words that were on the
34:27 said to Moses, "W down all these instructions,
Nu 5:23 Then the priest will w these curses on a piece of
Dt 6:9 W them on the doorposts of your house and on
10:2 and I will w on the tablets the same words that
11:20 W them on the doorposts of your house and on
27:3 Then w all the terms of this law on them. I repeat,
27:8 you must clearly w all the terms of this law."
31:19 "Now w down the words of this song, and teach it
Jdg 8:14 and demanded that he w down the names of all the
Job 13:26 "You w bitter accusations against me and bring up
31:35 Let my accuser w out the charges against me.
Pr 3:3 like a necklace; w them deep within your heart.
7:3 as a reminder. W them deep within your heart.
Isa 8:1 a large signboard and clearly w this name on it:
8:16 I will w down all these things as a testimony of
30:8 and w down these words concerning Egypt.
44:5 Some will w the LORD's name on their hands
Jer 30:2 W down for the record everything I have said to
31:33 in their minds, and I will w them on their hearts.
36:2 and w down all my messages against Israel,
36:2 and w down every message you have given,
36:28 and w everything again just as you did on the
Eze 24:2 "Son of man, w down today's date, because on
43:11 W down all these specifications and directions as
Da 5:24 So God has sent this hand to w a message.
Hab 2:2 "W my answer in large, clear letters on a tablet,
Mt 19:7 "Then why did Moses say a man could merely w
Mk 10:4 "He said a man merely has to w his wife an
Lk 1:3 I have decided to w a careful summary for you,
16:6 and w another one for four hundred gallons.'
Ac 15:20 except that we should w to them and tell them to
25:26 But what shall I w the emperor? For there is no
25:26 we examine him, I might have something to w.
1Co 12:1 I will w about the special abilities the Holy Spirit
16:3 When I come I will w letters of recommendation
16:21 is my greeting, which I w with my own hand—
2Co 2:4 How painful it was to w that letter! Heartbroken,
3:1 or ask you to w letters of recommendation for
7:12 My purpose was not to w about who did the wrong

9: 1 I really don't need to w to you about this gift for
Gal 6:11 Notice what large letters I use as I w these closing
1Th 4: 9 But I don't need to w to you about the Christian
5: 1 I really don't need to w to you about how
2Th 3:17 here is my greeting, which I w with my own hand
Phm 1:19 I, Paul, w this in my own handwriting: "I will
1:21 I am confident as I w this letter that you will do
Heb 8:10 and I will w them on their hearts
10:16 and I will w them on their minds
1Jn 5:13 I w this to you who believe in the Son of God,
Jude 1: 3 I had been eagerly planning to w to you about the
1: 3 But now I find that I must w about something else,
Rev 1:11 It said, "W down what you see, and send it to the
1:19 W down what you have seen—both the things that
2: 1 "W this letter to the angel of the church in
2: 8 "W this letter to the angel of the church in
2:12 "W this letter to the angel of the church in
2:18 "W this letter to the angel of the church in
3: 1 "W this letter to the angel of the church in Sardis.
3: 7 "W this letter to the angel of the church in
3:12 And I will w my God's name on them, and they
3:14 "W this letter to the angel of the church in
10: 4 When the seven thunders spoke, I was about to w.
10: 4 what the seven thunders said. Do not w it down."
14:13 heard a voice from heaven saying, "W this down:
19: 9 And the angel said, "W this: Blessed are those
21: 5 And then he said to me, "W this down, for what I

WRITER'S (3) [WRITE]

Eze 9: 2 in linen and carried a w case strapped to his side.
9: 3 man dressed in linen who was carrying the w case.
9:11 who carried the w case, reported back and said,

WRITES (1) [WRITE]

Dt 24: 1 So he w her a letter of divorce, gives it to her,

WRITHE (5) [WRITHES, WRITHING]

Isa 26:18 we, too, w in agony, / but nothing comes of our
Jer 4:19 My heart, my heart—I w in pain! My heart pounds
13:21 You will w in pain like a woman giving birth!
Hos 8:10 Then they will w under the burden of the great
Mic 4:10 W and groan in terrible pain, you people of

WRITHES (2) [WRITHE]

Isa 24:10 The city w in chaos; every home is locked to keep
Jer 51:29 Babylon trembles and w in pain, for everything the

WRITHING (4) [WRITHE]

Ps 48: 6 like a woman w in the pain of childbirth
Isa 26:17 about to give birth, / w and crying out in pain.
27: 1 the coiling, w serpent, the dragon of the sea.
Mk 9:20 he fell to the ground, w and foaming at the mouth.

WRITING (34) [WRITE]

Dt 31:24 When Moses had finished w down this entire body
1Ch 28:19 "was given to me in w from the hand of the
2Ch 36:22 the heart of Cyrus to put this proclamation into w
Ezr 1: 1 the heart of Cyrus to put this proclamation into w
Ne 9:38 are making a solemn promise and putting it in w.
Jer 36: 3 in w all the terrible things I have planned for them.
Da 5: 5 hand w on the plaster wall of the king's palace,
5: 7 "Whoever can read this w and tell me what it
5: 8 none of them could read the w or tell him what it
5:12 and he will tell you what the w means."
5:15 and enchanters have tried to read this w on the
5:17 someone else, but I will tell you what the w means.
Lk 1:63 He motioned for a w tablet, and to everyone's
Ro 16:22 Tertius, the one who is w this letter for Paul,
1Co 1: 2 We are w to the church of God in Corinth,
4:14 I am not w these things to shame you, but to warn
9:15 And I am not w this to suggest that I would like to
2Co 1: 1 We are w to God's church in Corinth and to all the
12:11 You ought to be w commendations for me, for I
13:10 I am w this to you before I come, hoping that I
1Ti 3:14 I am w these things to you now, even though I
Phm 1: 2 I am also w to the church that meets in your house.
1Pe 1: 1 I am w to God's chosen people who are living as
5:12 My purpose in w is to encourage you and assure
2Pe 1: 1 I am w to all of you who share the same precious
1Jn 1: 4 We are w these things so that our joy will be
2: 1 I am w this to you so that you will not sin.
2: 7 Dear friends, I am not w a new commandment,
2:12 I am w to you, my dear children, because your sins
2:13 I am w to you who are mature because you know
2:13 I am w to you who are young because you have
2:21 So I am w to you not because you don't know the
Jude 1: 1 I am w to all who are called to live in the love of
Rev 5: 1 There was w on the inside and the outside of the

WRITINGS (6) [WRITE]

Da 9: 2 I, Daniel, was studying the w of the prophets.
Mt 5:17 abolish the law of Moses or the w of the prophets.
Mk 12:26 haven't you ever read about this in the w of Moses,
Lk 16:29 Your brothers can read their w anytime they want
24:27 Then Jesus quoted passages from the w of Moses
2Co 3:15 Yes, even today when they read Moses' w,

WRITTEN (125) [WRITE]

WRITTEN IN THE/THIS BOOK (15) Dt 28:58; 29:20; 30:10; Jos 8:31,34; 23:6; 2Ki 14:6; 22:11; 23:21; 2Ch 25:4; Da 10:21; 12:1; Php 4:3; Rev 13:8; 17:8

WRITTEN IN THE LAW (4) 1Ki 2:3; 1Ch 16:40; 2Ch 34:19; Da 9:11; Jn 10:34

WRITTEN IN THE/THIS SCROLL (8) 2Ki 22:13; 23:3,24; 2Ch 34:21,24,31; Rev 22:7,9

Ex 31:18 the terms of the covenant, w by the finger of God.
32:16 the words on them were w by God himself.
Nu 33: 2 Moses kept a w record of their progress.
Dt 9:10 the tablets on which God himself had w all the
28:58 all the terms of this law that are w in this book,
29:20 All the curses w in this book will come down on
30:10 the commands and laws w in this Book of the Law,
Jos 1: 8 so you may be sure to obey all that is w in it.
8:31 LORD's servant had w in the Book of the Law:
8:34 and curses Moses had w in the Book of the Law.
18: 4 They will return to me with a w report of their
18: 8 Then return to me with your w report, and I will
23: 6 Be very careful to follow all the instructions w in
1Ki 2: 3 and stipulations w in the law of Moses so that you
21:11 the instructions Jezebel had w in the letters.
2Ki 14: 6 for he obeyed the command of the LORD w in
22:11 When the king heard what was w in the Book of
22:13 Ask him about the words w in this scroll that has
23: 3 the terms of the covenant that were w in the scroll,
23:21 your God, as it is w in the Book of the Covenant."
23:24 He did this in obedience to all the laws w in the
1Ch 16:40 obeying everything w in the law of the LORD,
29:29 to end, are w in *The Record of Samuel the Seer,*
2Ch 24:27 w in *The Commentary on the Book of the Kings.*
25: 4 for he obeyed the command of the LORD w in
34:19 When the king heard what was w in the law,
34:21 Ask him about the words w in this scroll that has
34:24 All the curses w in the scroll you have read will
34:31 the terms of the covenant that were w in the scroll.
35: 4 following the w instructions of King David of
35:26 and his acts of devotion done according to the w
Ne 7: 5 first returned to Judah. This is what was w there:
Est 1:19 we suggest that you issue a w decree, a law of the
8: 8 But remember that whatever is w in the king's
8: 9 The decree was w in the scripts and languages of
9:32 of Purim, and it was all w down in the records.
Job 19:23 "Oh, that my words could be w. Oh, that they
Ps 40: 7 And this has been w about me in your scroll:
40: 8 my God, / for your law is w on my heart."
44:15 constant humiliation; / shame is w across our faces.
69: 7 for your sake; / humiliation is w all over my face.
149: 9 to execute the judgment w against them. / This is
Pr 22:20 I have w thirty sayings for you, filled with advice
Isa 4: 3 All those whose names are w down, who have
8: 2 to testify that I had w it before the child was
49:16 See, I have w your name on my hand. Ever before
65: 6 "Look, my decree is w out in front of me: I will
Jer 45: 1 after Baruch had w down everything Jeremiah had
Da 5:25 "This is the message that was w: MENE, MENE,
9:11 and judgments w in the law of Moses,
9:13 Every curse w against us in the law of Moses has
10:21 I will tell you what is w in the Book of Truth.
12: 1 whose name is w in the book will be rescued.
Mal 3:16 a scroll of remembrance was w to record the names
Mk 9:12 then is it w in the Scriptures that the Son of Man
Lk 1: 1 Many people have w accounts about the events
22:37 everything w about me by the prophets will come
24:17 They stopped short, sadness w across their faces.
24:44 I told you that everything w about me by Moses
24:46 it was w long ago that the Messiah must suffer
Jn 6:45 As it is w in the Scriptures, 'They will all be taught
10:34 "It is w in your own law that God said to certain
19:20 and the sign was w in Hebrew, Latin, and Greek,
19:22 Pilate replied, "What I have w, I have w.
20:31 But these are w so that you may believe that Jesus
21:25 that if all the other things Jesus did were w down,
Ac 7:42 as their gods! In the book of the prophets it is w,
13:27 or realize that he is the one the prophets had w
15:15 what the prophets predicted. For instance, it is w:
15:23 It is w to the Gentile believers in Antioch, Syria,
24:14 and everything w in the books of prophecy.
Ro 2:12 they sin, even though they never had God's w law.
2:14 when Gentiles, who do not have God's w law,
2:15 They demonstrate that God's law is w within them,
12:19 Leave that to God. For it is w, / "I will take
15: 4 Such things were w in the Scriptures long ago to
15:10 And in another place it is w, / "Rejoice, O you
1Co 10:11 They were w down to warn us, who live at the time
14:21 It is w in the Scriptures, / "I will speak to my own
2Co 1:13 and there is nothing w between the lines
3: 2 Your lives are a letter w in our hearts,
3: 3 It is w not with pen and ink, but with the Spirit of
3: 6 This is a covenant, not of w laws, but of the Spirit.
Gal 3:10 and obey all these commands that are w in God's
3:13 For it is w in the Scriptures, "Cursed is everyone
Eph 1: 1 It is w to God's holy people in Ephesus, who are
3: 4 As you read what I have w, you will understand
Php 1: 1 It is w to all of God's people in Philippi,
4: 3 whose names are w in the Book of Life.
Col 1: 2 It is w to God's holy people in the city of Colosse,
1Th 1: 1 It is w to the church in Thessalonica, you who
2Th 1: 1 It is w to the church in Thessalonica, you who
1Ti 1: 2 It is w to Timothy, my true child in the faith.
2Ti 1: 2 It is w to Timothy, my dear son. May God our
Tit 1: 4 This letter is w to Titus, my true child in the faith
Phm 1: 1 It is w to Philemon, our much loved co-worker,
Heb 9: 4 covenant with the Ten Commandments w on them.
10: 7 just as it is w about me in the Scriptures.' "
12:23 firstborn children, whose names are w in heaven.
Jas 1: 1 It is w to Jewish Christians scattered among the
1Pe 5:12 I have w this short letter to you with the help of
1Jn 2:14 I have w to you, children, because you have known
2:14 I have w to you who are mature because you know
2:14 I have w to you who are young because you are
2:26 I have w these things to you because you need to
2Jn 1: 1 It is w to the chosen lady and to her children,
3Jn 1: 1 It is w to Gaius, my dear friend, whom I love in the
Rev 13: 1 And w on each head were names that blasphemed
13: 8 They are the ones whose names were not w in the
14: 1 and his Father's name w on their foreheads.
17: 3 w all over with blasphemies against God.
17: 5 A mysterious name was w on her forehead:
17: 8 whose names were not w in the Book of Life from
19:12 A name was w on him, and only he knew what it
19:16 On his robe and thigh was w this title: King of
20:12 judged according to the things w in the books,
21:12 of the twelve tribes of Israel were w on the gates.
21:14 and on them were w the names of the twelve
21:27 but only those whose names are w in the Lamb's
22: 4 his face, and his name will be w on their foreheads.
22: 7 Blessed are those who obey the prophecy w in this
22: 9 as well as all who obey what is w in this scroll.
22:10 "Do not seal up the prophetic words you have w,
22:18 If anyone adds anything to what is w here,

WRONG (169) [WRONGDOER, WRONGDOERS, WRONGDOING, WRONGDOINGS, WRONGED, WRONGLY, WRONGS]

Ge 21:17 called to Hagar from the sky, "Hagar, what's w?
Ex 2:13 like that?" Moses said to the one in the w.
9:27 "The LORD is right, and my people and I are w.
Nu 5: 6 betray the LORD by doing w to another person,
Dt 15:21 being lame or blind, or if anything else is w with it,
24: 6 "It is w to take a pair of millstones, or even just
25: 1 judges declare that one is right and the other is w.
25: 2 If the person in the w is sentenced to be flogged,
32: 4 and fair. / He is a faithful God who does no w;
1Sa 12: 3 and I will make right whatever I have done w."
12:20 "You have certainly done w, but make sure now
14:33 "That is very w," Saul said. "Find a large stone
14:38 Then Saul said to the leaders, "Something's w!
16: 4 "What's w?" they asked. "Do you come in
25:28 And you have not done w throughout your entire
26:21 life today. I have been a fool and very, very w."
2Sa 13:16 "To reject me now is a greater w than what you
19: 5 feel ashamed, as though we had done something w.
24:17 "I am the one who has sinned and done w!
1Ki 3: 9 and know the difference between right and w.
11:22 "Nothing is w," he replied. "But even so, I must
2Ki 6:19 and told them, "You have come the w way!
18:14 to the king of Assyria at Lachish: "I have done w.
1Ch 21:17 I am the one who has sinned and done w! But these
2Ch 22: 3 for his mother encouraged him in doing w.
Job 2:10 anything bad?" So in all this, Job said nothing w.
6:24 I will keep quiet. Tell me, what have I done w?
6:30 Don't I know the difference between right and w?
13:19 If you could prove me w, I would remain silent
13:23 Tell me, what have I done w? Show me my
21:34 you comfort me? All your explanations are w!"
24:25 anyone claim otherwise? Who can prove me w?"
31:35 Let the Almighty show me that I am w.
34:10 that God doesn't sin! The Almighty can do no w.
34:12 God will not do w. The Almighty cannot twist
35:13 But it is w to say God doesn't listen, to say the
36:23 to do. No one can say to him, 'You have done w.'
Ps 7: 3 O LORD my God, if I have done w / or am guilty
35: 7 Although I did them no w, / they laid a trap for me.
35: 7 Although I did them no w, / they dug a pit for me.
35:21 They shout that they have seen me doing w.
37: 1 about the wicked. / Don't envy those who do w.
37:30 good counsel; / they know what is right from w.
45: 7 You love what is right and hate what is w.
59: 3 though I have done them no w, O LORD.
73:13 my heart pure / and kept myself from doing w?
99: 8 but you punished them when they went w.
106: 6 We have done w! We have acted wickedly!
114: 5 What's w, Red Sea, that made you hurry out of
125: 3 for then the godly might be forced to do w.
Pr 2:14 They rejoice in doing w, and they enjoy evil as it
2:15 What they do is crooked, and their ways are w.
6:18 a heart that plots evil, / feet that race to do w,
10:10 People who wink at w cause trouble, but a bold
10:23 Doing w is fun for a fool, while wise conduct is a
14: 2 those who take the w path despise him.
15:22 Plans go w for lack of advice; many counselors
17:26 It is w to fine the godly for being good or to punish
18: 5 It is w for a judge to favor the guilty or condemn
19: 2 a person who moves too quickly may go the w
20:22 Don't say, "I will get even for this w." Wait for
24:23 It is w to show favoritism when passing judgment.
28:21 yet some will do w for something as small as a
28:24 and then saying, "What's w with that?"
30:20 and then say, "What's w with that?"
Ecc 1:15 What is w cannot be righted. What is missing
8:11 crime is not punished, people feel it is safe to do w.
Isa 7:15 to choose what is right and reject what is w.
7:16 But before he knows right from w, the two kings
19:11 best counsel to the king of Egypt is stupid and w.
19:14 foolishness on them, so all their suggestions are w.
26:10 They keep doing w and take no notice of the
33:15 who shut their eyes to all enticement to do w.
45: 9 who shapes it, saying, 'Stop, you are doing it w!'
51: 7 you who know right from w and cherish my law in
53: 9 He had done no w, and he never deceived anyone.
55: 7 from their minds the very thought of doing w!
56: 2 are those who keep themselves from doing w.
59: 8 They continually do w, and those who follow them
Jer 2:29 Why do you accuse me of doing w? You are the

2:35 And yet you say, 'I haven't done anything **w**.
4:22 They are clever enough at doing **w**, but they have
8: 4 When they start down the **w** road and discover
32:30 have done nothing but **w** since their earliest days.
32:33 year after year, I taught them right from **w**,
51:24 and the people of Babylonia for all the **w** they have
La 3:59 You have seen the **w** they have done to me,
Eze 18:18 doing what was clearly **w** among his people.
Da 9: 5 But we have sinned and done **w**. We have rebelled
Mic 3: 1 of Israel! You are supposed to know right from **w**,
Zep 3: 5 LORD is still there in the city, and he does no **w**.
3:13 The people of Israel who survive will do no **w** to
Mal 1: 8 you give blind animals as sacrifices, isn't that **w**?
1: 8 And isn't it **w** to offer animals that are crippled
Mt 5:37 promise with a vow shows that something is **w**.
18: 7 Temptation to do **w** is inevitable, but how terrible
Lk 12:48 that they are doing **w** will be punished only lightly.
23: 4 and said, "I find nothing **w** with this man!"
23:41 evil deeds, but this man hasn't done anything **w**."
Jn 18:23 Jesus replied, "If I said anything **w**, you must give
Ac 7:27 "But the man in the **w** pushed Moses aside
23: 9 "We see nothing **w** with him," they shouted.
25: 5 If Paul has done anything **w**, you can make your
26: 7 O king, they say it is **w** for me to have this hope!
Ro 2:14 show that in their hearts they know right from **w**.
2:18 you know right from **w** because you have been
2:22 You say it is **w** to commit adultery, but do you do
3:12 All have turned away from God; / all have gone **w**.
7: 7 I would never have known that coveting is **w** if the
7:16 I know perfectly well that what I am doing is **w**,
7:19 I don't. And when I try not to do **w**, I do it anyway.
7:21 want to do what is right, I inevitably do what is **w**.
12: 9 Really love them. Hate what is **w**. Stand on the
13: 3 are doing right, but they frighten those who do **w**.
13: 4 But if you are doing something **w**, of course you
13: 4 for that very purpose, to punish those who do **w**.
13:10 Love does no **w** to anyone, so love satisfies all of
14: 1 with them about what they think is right or **w**.
14: 4 so let him tell them whether they are right or **w**.
14:14 Lord Jesus that no food, in and of itself, is **w** to eat.
14:14 believes it is **w**, then for that person it is **w**.
14:20 there is nothing **w** with these things in themselves.
14:20 But it is **w** to eat anything if it makes another
14:22 that there is nothing **w** with what you are doing,
15: 1 and fears of those who think these things are **w**.
16:19 clearly what is right and to stay innocent of any **w**.
1Co 6: 8 you yourselves are the ones who do **w** and cheat
6: 9 Don't you know that those who do **w** will have no
8:10 Weak Christians who think it is **w** to eat this food
8:10 You know there's nothing **w** with it, but they will
8:12 them to do something they believe is **w**.
15: 8 the others, as though I had been born at the **w** time.
2Co 7: 2 your hearts to us. We have not done **w** to anyone.
7:12 My purpose was not to write about who did the **w**
9: 3 I don't want it to turn out that I was **w** in my
11: 7 Did I do **w** when I humbled myself and honored
12:13 a burden to you. Please forgive me for this **w**!
13: 7 We pray to God that you will not do anything **w**.
Gal 2:11 against what he was doing, for it was very **w**.
5: 9 But it takes only one **w** person among you to infect
5:20 the feeling that everyone is **w** except those in your
Eph 4:19 They don't care anymore about right and **w**,
Col 3:25 But if you do what is **w**, you will be paid back for
the **w** you have done.
1Th 5:12 hard among you and warn you against all that is **w**.
1Ti 1: 3 and stop those who are teaching **w** doctrine.
4: 3 They will say it is **w** to be married and **w** to eat
certain foods.
2Ti 3:16 and to make us realize what is **w** in our lives.
Tit 1: 9 and show those who oppose it where they are **w**.
1:11 By their **w** teaching, they have already turned
Heb 1: 9 You love what is right and hate what is **w**.
5:14 to recognize the difference between right and **w**,
Jas 1:13 no one who wants to do **w** should ever say,
1:13 God is never tempted to do **w**, and he never tempts
2: 4 show that you are guided by **w** motives?
4: 3 you don't get it because your whole motive is **w**—
4: 9 Let there be tears for the **w** things you have done.
4:11 who can decide whether the law is right or **w**.
1Pe 2:12 Even if they accuse you of doing **w**, they will see
2:14 For the king has sent them to punish all who do **w**
2:20 for being patient if you are beaten for doing **w**.
3:17 that is what God wants, than to suffer for doing **w**!
2Pe 2:15 son of Beor, who loved to earn money by doing **w**.
1Jn 1: 9 just to forgive us and to cleanse us from every **w**.
5:17 Every **w** is sin, but not all sin leads to death.
Rev 22:11 Let the one who is doing **w** continue to do **w**;

WRONGDOER (1) [WRONG]

2Co 7:11 such zeal, and such a readiness to punish the **w**.

WRONGDOERS (1) [WRONG]

Pr 17: 4 **W** listen to wicked talk; liars pay attention to

WRONGDOING (5) [WRONG]

Pr 16:12 A king despises **w**, for his rule depends on his
Isa 61: 8 the LORD, love justice. I hate robbery and **w**.
Ac 18:14 if this were a case involving some **w** or a serious
24:20 Ask these men here what **w** the Jewish high
Gal 3:13 the cross, he took upon himself the curse for our **w**.

WRONGDOINGS (2) [WRONG]

Jer 36: 3 Then I will be able to forgive their sins and **w**."
Heb 8:12 And I will forgive their **w**, / and I will never again

WRONGED (13) [WRONG]

Nu 5: 7 and returning it to the person who was **w**.
5: 8 But if the person who was **w** is dead, and there are
Jdg 11:27 Rather, you have **w** me by attacking me.
2Sa 16:12 perhaps the LORD will see that I am being **w**
Est 1:16 "Queen Vashti has **w** not only the king but also
Job 19: 6 but it is God who has **w** me. I cannot defend
Pr 3:30 accusations against someone who hasn't **w** you.
Isa 42: 3 He will bring full justice to all who have been **w**.
Jer 50:33 "The people of Israel and Judah have been **w**.
Eze 22: 7 Orphans and widows are **w** and oppressed.
Da 6:22 in his sight. And I have not **w** you, Your Majesty."
1Co 13: 5 and it keeps no record of when it has been **w**.
2Co 7:12 to write about who did the wrong or who was **w**.

WRONGLY (1) [WRONG]

Isa 58: 6 want calls you to free those who are **w** imprisoned

WRONGS (6) [WRONG]

1Ki 8:31 "If someone **w** another person and is required to
2Ch 6:22 "If someone **w** another person and is required to
Job 35: 9 "The oppressed cry out beneath the **w** that are
Pr 19:11 their anger; they earn esteem by overlooking **w**.
Lk 3:19 brother's wife, and for many other **w** he had done.
17: 4 Even if he **w** you seven times a day and each time

WROTE (55) [WRITE]

Ex 24: 4 Then Moses carefully **w** down all the LORD's
34:28 At that time he **w** the terms of the covenant—
Nu 21:27 For this reason the ancient poets **w** this about him:
Dt 4:13 and **w** them on two stone tablets.
5:22 and he **w** his words on two stone tablets and gave
10: 4 The LORD again **w** the terms of the covenant—
31: 9 So Moses **w** down this law and gave it to the
31:22 So that very day Moses **w** down the words of the
1Sa 10:25 He **w** them down on a scroll and placed it before
2Sa 11:14 So the next morning David **w** a letter to Joab
1Ki 4:32 some 3,000 proverbs and **w** 1,005 songs.
21: 8 So she **w** letters in Ahab's name, sealed them with
2Ki 10: 1 So Jehu **w** a letter and sent copies to Samaria,
17:37 instructions, and commands that he **w** for you.
1Ch 24: 6 acted as secretary and **w** down the names
2Ch 21:12 Then Elijah the prophet **w** Jehoram this letter:
30: 1 and he **w** letters of invitation to Ephraim
32:17 He **w**, "Just as the gods of all the other nations
Ezr 4: 6 the enemies of Judah **w** him a letter of accusation
4: 8 and Shimshai the court secretary **w** the letter,
Est 8: 9 they **w** a decree to the Jews and to the princes,
8:10 Mordecai **w** in the name of King Xerxes and sealed
9:29 **w** another letter putting the queen's full authority
Isa 38: 9 well again, he **w** this poem about his experience:
Jer 29: 1 Jeremiah **w** a letter from Jerusalem to the elders,
29:25 You **w** a letter on your own authority to Zephaniah
36: 4 Baruch **w** down all the prophecies that the LORD
36:18 and I **w** down his words with ink on this scroll."
36:32 He **w** everything that had been on the scroll King
Da 5: 5 The king himself saw the hand as it **w**,
7: 1 He **w** the dream down, and this is what he saw.
Mt 2: 5 they said, "for this is what the prophet **w**:
Mk 10: 5 "He **w** those instructions only as a concession to
Lk 1:63 and to everyone's surprise he **w**, "His name is
20:37 even Moses proved this when he **w** about the
20:42 For David himself **w** in the book of Psalms:
24:25 so hard to believe all that the prophets **w** in the
Jn 1:45 the very person Moses and the prophets **w** about!
5:46 would have believed me because he **w** about me.
5:47 And since you don't believe what he **w**, how will
8: 6 stooped down and **w** in the dust with his finger.
8: 8 Then he stooped down again and **w** in the dust.
Ac 18:27 They **w** to the believers in Achaia, asking them to
23:25 Then he **w** this letter to the governor:
Ro 10: 5 For Moses **w** that the law's way of making a
15: 9 That is what the psalmist meant when he **w**:
1Co 5: 9 When I **w** to you before, I told you not to associate
2Co 2: 3 That is why I **w** as I did in my last letter, so that
2: 9 I **w** to you as I did to find out how far you would
7:12 I **w** to you so that in the sight of God you could
Col 4:16 too. And you should read the letter I **w** to them.
Heb 9:16 it is proved that the person who **w** the will is dead.
9:17 effect only after the death of the person who **w** it.
2Pe 1:19 Pay close attention to what they **w**, for their words
3:15 This is just as our beloved brother Paul **w** to you

WROUGHT (1)

Eze 27:19 **W** iron, cassia, and calamus were bartered for your

WRUNG (1) [WRING]

Jdg 6:38 the fleece and **w** out a whole bowlful of water.

X

XERXES (17) [XERXES']

Ezr 4: 6 Years later when **X** began his reign, the enemies of
Est 1: 1 This happened in the days of King **X**, who reigned
1:10 when King **X** was half drunk with wine, he told
2:16 When Esther was taken to King **X** at the royal
2:21 became angry at King **X** and plotted to assassinate
3: 1 King **X** promoted Haman son of Hammedatha the
3: 6 all the Jews throughout the entire empire of **X**.
3: 8 Then Haman approached King **X** and said,
3:12 These letters were signed in the name of King **X**,
7: 5 King **X** demanded. "Who would dare touch you?"
8: 1 On that same day King **X** gave the estate of
8: 7 Then King **X** said to Queen Esther and Mordecai
8:10 Mordecai wrote in the name of King **X** and sealed
8:12 provinces of King **X** was March 7 of the next year.
9:30 throughout the 127 provinces of the empire of **X**.
10: 1 King **X** imposed tribute throughout his empire,
10: 3 with authority next to that of King **X** himself.

XERXES' (3) [XERXES]

Est 2: 1 But after **X** anger had cooled, he began thinking
2:23 in *The Book of the History of King **X** Reign.*
3: 7 of April, during the twelfth year of King **X** reign,

Y

YANKED (1) [YANKING]

Jdg 16:14 and **y** his hair away from the loom and the fabric.

YANKING (1) [YANKED]

Pr 26:17 **Y** a dog's ears is as foolish as interfering in

YARD (2) [YARDS]

Jer 38: 6 him by ropes into an empty cistern in the prison **y**.
Eze 41:11 opened from the side rooms into the terrace **y**,

YARDS (2) [YARD]

Ge 21:16 and sat down by herself about a hundred **y** away.
Eze 48:17 Open lands will surround the city for 150 **y** in

YARN (27)

Ex 25: 4 blue, purple, and scarlet **y**; fine linen; goat hair for
26: 1 are to be decorated with blue, purple, and scarlet **y**,
26: 4 Put loops of blue **y** along the edge of the last sheet
26:31 into the cloth using blue, purple, and scarlet **y**.
26:36 designs into it, using blue, purple, and scarlet **y**.
27:16 beautiful embroidery in blue, purple, and scarlet **y**.
28: 5 with gold thread and blue, purple, and scarlet **y**.
28: 6 with gold thread and blue, purple, and scarlet **y**.
28: 8 with gold thread and blue, purple, and scarlet **y**.
28:15 with gold thread and blue, purple, and scarlet **y**.
28:33 pomegranates out of blue, purple, and scarlet **y**,
35: 6 blue, purple, and scarlet **y**; fine linen; goat hair for
35:23 brought blue, purple, and scarlet **y**, fine linen,
35:25 purple, and scarlet **y**, and fine linen cloth, and they
35:35 in blue, purple, and scarlet **y** on fine linen cloth.
36:35 embroidered into it with blue, purple, and scarlet **y**.
36:37 and embroidered with blue, purple, and scarlet **y**.
38:18 and embroidered with blue, purple, and scarlet **y**.
38:23 purple, and scarlet **y** on fine linen cloth.
39: 2 with gold thread and blue, purple, and scarlet **y**.
39: 3 it into the linen with the blue, purple, and scarlet **y**.
39: 5 fine linen cloth; blue, purple, and scarlet **y**;
39: 8 with gold thread and blue, purple, and scarlet **y**.
39:22 robe of the ephod was woven entirely of blue **y**,
39:24 were finely crafted of blue, purple, and scarlet **y**.
39:29 and embroidered with blue, purple, and scarlet **y**,
2Ch 3:14 made of fine linen and blue, purple, and scarlet **y**,

YAWNING (1)

Jnh 2: 6 have snatched me from the **y** jaws of death!

YEA [KJV] See INDEED, YES

YEAR (337) [ONE-YEAR-OLD, SIXTEEN-YEAR-OLD, YEAR-OLD, YEAR'S, YEARLING, YEARLINGS, YEARLY, YEARS]

EVERY YEAR (5) Ex 12:42; Lev 23:41; Job 1:4; Eze 45:25; Lk 2:41

FIRST YEAR (10) 2Ch 29:3; 36:22; Ezr 1:1; 5:13; 6:3; Da 1:21; 7:1; 9:1,2; 11:1

SEVENTH YEAR (20) Ex 21:2,3,4; 23:11; Lev 25:2,4,20; 26:35; Dt 15:1,12; 31:10; 2Ki 11:4; 12:1; 18:9; 2Ch 23:1; Ezr 7:7; Ne 10:31; Est 2:16; Jer 52:28; Eze 20:1

Ge 14: 4 but now in the thirteenth **y** they rebelled.
14: 5 One **y** later, Kedorlaomer and his allies arrived.
17:21 be born to you and Sarah about this time next **y**."
18:10 of them said, "About this time next **y** I will return,
18:14 About a **y** from now, just as I told you, I will
26:12 That **y** Isaac's crops were tremendous!
47:17 at least they were able to purchase food for that **y**.
47:18 The next **y** they came again and said, "Our money
Ex 12: 2 this month will be the first month of the **y** for you.

12:14 Each y you will celebrate it as a special festival to
12:41 it was on the last day of the 430th y that all the
12:42 It must be celebrated every y, from generation to
13: 8 "During these festival days each y, you must
13:10 celebrate this festival at the appointed time each y.
21: 2 Set him free in the seventh y, and he will owe you
21: 3 only he will go free in the seventh y.
21: 4 then the man will be free in the seventh y, but his
23:11 let the land rest and lie fallow during the seventh y.
23:14 "Each y you must celebrate three festivals in my
23:17 At these three times each y, every man in Israel
23:29 But I will not do this all in one y because the land
30:10 "Once a y Aaron must purify the altar by placing
34:18 at the appointed time each y in early spring,
34:23 Three times each y all the men of Israel must
34:24 the LORD your God those three times each y.
40: 2 up the Tabernacle on the first day of the new y.
40:17 was set up on the first day of the new y.
Lev 16:34 to make atonement for the Israelites once each y."
19:24 In the fourth y the entire crop will be devoted to
19:25 Finally, in the fifth y you may eat the fruit. In this
23: 4 occasions to be observed at the proper time each y.
23:41 this seven-day festival to the LORD every y.
25: 2 observe a Sabbath to the LORD every seventh y.
25: 4 but during the seventh y the land will enjoy a
Sabbath y of rest to the LORD.
25: 4 or prune your vineyards during that entire y.
25: 5 The land is to have a y of total rest.
25: 6 produce that grows naturally during the Sabbath y.
25: 9 Then on the Day of Atonement of the fiftieth y,
25:10 This y will be set apart as holy, a time to proclaim
25:10 It will be a jubilee y for you, when each of you
25:11 Yes, the fiftieth y will be a jubilee for you.
25:11 During that y, do not plant any seeds or store away
25:12 It will be a jubilee y for you, and you must observe
25:12 produce that grows naturally in the fields that y.
25:13 In the Y of Jubilee each of you must return to the
25:15 for the crop years left until the next Y of Jubilee.
25:20 might ask, 'What will we eat during the seventh y,
25:20 are not allowed to plant or harvest crops that y?'
25:21 'I will order my blessing for you in the sixth y,
25:22 As you plant the seed in the eighth y, you will still
be eating the produce of the previous y.
25:22 crop until the new harvest comes in the ninth y.'
25:27 on the number of years until the next Y of Jubilee.
25:28 to the new owner until the next Y of Jubilee.
25:28 In the jubilee y, the land will be returned to the
25:29 has the right to redeem it for a full y after its sale.
25:30 But if it is not redeemed within a y, then the house
25:30 returned to the original owner in the Y of Jubilee.
25:31 and must be returned to the original owner in the Y
25:33 must be returned in the Y of Jubilee.
25:40 and they will serve you only until the Y of Jubilee.
25:50 number of years left until the next Y of Jubilee—
25:52 If only a few years remain until the Y of Jubilee,
25:54 redeemed by the time the Y of Jubilee arrives,
26:10 the previous y to make room for each new harvest.
26:35 it to take every seventh y while you lived in it.
27:17 If the field is dedicated to the LORD in the Y of
27:18 But if the field is dedicated after the Y of Jubilee,
27:18 to the years left until the next Y of Jubilee.
27:21 When the field is released in the Y of Jubilee,
27:23 based on the years until the next Y of Jubilee.
27:24 In the Y of Jubilee the field will be released to the
Nu 1: 1 during the second y after Israel's departure from
9: 1 during the second y after Israel's departure from
9:22 a month, or a y, the people of Israel stayed in camp
10:11 during the second y after Israel's departure from
14:34 a y for each day, suffering the consequences of
15:21 LORD each y from the first of your ground flour.
28:14 on the first day of each month throughout the y.
29: 1 on the appointed day in early autumn each y.
33:38 during the fortieth y after Israel's departure from
36: 4 Then when the Y of Jubilee comes,
Dt 11:12 He watches over it day after day throughout the y!
14:22 one-tenth of all the crops you harvest each y.
14:28 "At the end of every third y bring the tithe of all
15: 1 "At the end of every seventh y you must cancel
15: 9 a loan because the y of release is close at hand.
15:12 in the seventh y you must set that servant free.
15:20 LORD your God each y at the place he chooses.
16:16 "Each y every man in Israel must celebrate these
24: 5 He must be free to be at home for one y,
26:12 "Every third y you must offer a special tithe of
31:10 "At the end of every seventh y, the Y of Release,
Jdg 10: 8 who began to oppress them that y. For eighteen
11:40 each y to lament the fate of Jephthah's daughter.
17:10 I will give you ten pieces of silver a y, plus a
1Sa 1: 3 Each y Elkanah and his family would travel to
1: 7 Y after y it was the same—Peninnah would
1:21 The next y Elkanah, Peninnah, and their children
2:19 Each y his mother made a small coat for him
7:16 Each y he traveled around, setting up his court first
12:17 You know that it does not rain at this time of the y
27: 7 and they lived there among the Philistines for a y
2Sa 11: 1 the time of y when kings go to war, David sent
14:26 He cut his hair only once a y, and then only
1Ki 4: 7 them arranged provisions for one month of the y.
6: 1 during the fourth y of Solomon's reign,
6:37 in midspring of the fourth y of Solomon's reign.
6:38 detail by midautumn of the eleventh y of his reign.
9:25 Three times each y Solomon offered burnt
10:14 Each y Solomon received about twenty-five tons of
10:25 Y after y, everyone who came to visit brought
14:25 In the fifth y of King Rehoboam's reign,
15: 1 in the eighteenth y of Jeroboam's reign in Israel.
15: 9 Asa began to rule over Judah in the twentieth y of
15:25 Israel in the second y of King Asa's reign in Judah.
15:28 Baasha killed Nadab in the third y of King Asa's
15:33 Baasha began to rule over Israel in the third y of
16: 8 in the twenty-sixth y of King Asa's reign in Judah.
16:10 This happened in the twenty-seventh y of King
16:15 the twenty-seventh y of King Asa's reign in Judah,
16:23 Omri began to rule over Israel in the thirty-first y
16:29 in the thirty-eighth y of King Asa's reign in Judah.
18: 1 in the third y of the drought, the LORD said to
22: 2 Then during the third y, King Jehoshaphat of Judah
22:41 in the fourth y of King Ahab's reign in Israel.
22:51 y of King Jehoshaphat's reign in Judah.
2Ki 1:17 This took place in the second y of the reign of
3: 1 eighteenth y of King Jehoshaphat's reign in Judah.
4:16 "Next y at about this time you will be holding a
4:17 And at that time the following y she had a son,
8:16 Judah in the fifth y of King Joram's reign in Israel.
8:25 in the twelfth y of King Joram's reign in Israel.
8:26 became king, and he reigned in Jerusalem one y.
9:29 in the eleventh y of King Joram's reign in Israel.
11: 4 In the seventh y of Athaliah's reign,
12: 1 Joash began to rule over Judah in the seventh y of
12: 6 But by the twenty-third y of Joash's reign,
13: 1 the twenty-third y of King Joash's reign in Judah.
13:10 the thirty-seventh y of King Joash's reign in Judah.
14: 1 the second y of the reign of King Jehoash of Israel.
14:23 began to rule over Israel in the fifteenth y of King
15: 1 y of the reign of King Jeroboam II of Israel.
15: 8 the thirty-eighth y of King Uzziah's reign in Judah.
15:13 the thirty-ninth y of King Uzziah's reign in Judah.
15:17 the thirty-ninth y of King Uzziah's reign in Judah.
15:23 in the fiftieth y of King Uzziah's reign in Judah.
15:27 the fifty-second y of King Uzziah's reign in Judah.
15:30 He began to rule over Israel in the twentieth y of
15:32 in the second y of King Pekah's reign in Israel.
16: 1 the seventeenth y of King Pekah's reign in Israel.
17: 1 in the twelfth y of King Ahaz's reign in Judah.
17: 6 Finally, in the ninth y of King Hoshea's reign,
18: 1 in the third y of King Hoshea's reign in Israel.
18: 9 During the fourth y of Hezekiah's reign,
18: 9 which was the seventh y of King Hoshea's reign in
18:10 during the sixth y of King Hezekiah's reign
18:10 and the ninth y of King Hoshea's reign in Israel,
18:13 In the fourteenth y of King Hezekiah's reign,
19:29 This y you will eat only what grows up by itself,
19:29 and next y you will eat what springs up from that.
19:29 But in the third y you will plant crops and harvest
22: 3 In the eighteenth y of his reign, King Josiah sent
23:23 during the eighteenth y of King Josiah's reign.
24:12 In the eighth y of Nebuchadnezzar's reign, he took
25: 1 January 15, during the ninth y of Zedekiah's reign,
25: 2 Jerusalem was kept under siege until the eleventh y
25: 3 By July 18 of Zedekiah's eleventh y, the famine in
25: 8 On August 14 of that y, which was the nineteenth
y of Nebuchadnezzar's
25:25 But in midautumn of that y, Ishmael son of
25:27 In the thirty-seventh y of King Jehoiachin's exile
25:27 and released him from prison on April 2 of that y.
1Ch 12:15 its seasonal flooding at the beginning of the y
20: 1 the time of y when kings go to war,
26:31 (In the fortieth y of David's reign, a search was
27: 1 divisions that were on duty each month of the y.
2Ch 3: 2 during the fourth y of Solomon's reign.
9:13 Each y Solomon received about 25 tons of gold.
9:24 Y after y, everyone who came to visit brought
12: 2 Jerusalem in the fifth y of King Rehoboam's reign.
13: 1 Abijah began to rule over Judah in the eighteenth y
15:10 in late spring, during the fifteenth y of Asa's reign.
15:19 So there was no more war until the thirty-fifth y of
16: 1 In the thirty-sixth y of Asa's reign, King Baasha of
16:12 In the thirty-ninth y of his reign, Asa developed a
16:13 So he died in the forty-first y of his reign.
17: 7 In the third y of his reign, Jehoshaphat sent out his
22: 2 became king, and he reigned in Jerusalem one y.
23: 1 In the seventh y of Athaliah's reign,
24:23 At the beginning of the y, the Aramean army
29: 3 In the very first month of the first y of his reign,
34: 3 During the eighth y of his reign, while he was still
34: 3 Then in the twelfth y, he began to purify Judah
34: 8 In the eighteenth y of his reign, after he had
35:19 took place in the eighteenth y of Josiah's reign.
36:10 In the spring of the following y, Jehoiachin was
36:22 In the first y of King Cyrus of Persia, the LORD
Ezr 1: 1 In the first y of King Cyrus of Persia, the LORD
3: 8 during the second y after they arrived in Jerusalem.
4:24 and it remained at a standstill until the second y of
5:13 Cyrus of Babylon, during the first y of his reign,
6: 3 "In the first y of King Cyrus's reign, a decree was
6:15 during the sixth y of King Darius's reign.
7: 7 traveled up to Jerusalem with him in the seventh y
7: 8 Ezra arrived in Jerusalem in August of that y.
10:17 By March 27 of the next y they had finished
Ne 1: 1 In late autumn of the twentieth y of King
2: 1 during the twentieth y of King Artaxerxes' reign,
5:14 from the twentieth until the thirty-second y of the
10:31 we promise not to do any work every seventh y
10:34 at regular times each y—the families of the priests,
13: 6 for I had returned to the king in the thirty-second y
Est 1: 3 In the third y of his reign, he gave a banquet for all
2:16 palace in early winter of the seventh y of his reign,
3: 7 during the twelfth y of King Xerxes' reign,
3: 7 And the day selected was March 7, nearly a y later.
3:13 This was scheduled to happen nearly a y later on
8:12 of King Xerxes was March 7 of the next y.
9:27 two prescribed days at the appointed time each y.
Job 1: 4 Every y when Job's sons had birthdays,
3: 6 never again to be counted among the days of the y,
Ps 65:11 You crown the y with a bountiful harvest;
Isa 6: 1 In the y King Uzziah died, I saw the Lord. He was
14:28 This message came to me the y King Ahaz died:
20: 1 In the y when King Sargon of Assyria captured the
21:16 "But within a y," says the Lord, "all the glory of
29: 1 Y after y you offer your many sacrifices.
32:10 In a short time—in just a little more than a y—
34: 8 the y when Edom will be paid back for all it did to
36: 1 In the fourteenth y of King Hezekiah's reign,
37:30 This y you will eat only what grows up by itself,
37:30 and next y you will eat what springs up from that.
37:30 But in the third y you will plant crops and harvest
Jer 1: 2 the thirteenth y of King Josiah's reign in Judah.
1: 3 until the eleventh y of King Zedekiah's reign in
1: 3 In August of that y, the people of Jerusalem were
8: 7 the crane. They all return at the proper time each y.
25: 1 the fourth y of Jehoiakim's reign over Judah.
25: 1 This was the y when King Nebuchadnezzar of
25: 3 from the thirteenth y of Josiah son of Amon,
28: 1 that same y—the fourth y of the reign of Zedekiah,
28:16 Your life will end this very y because you have
32: 1 the LORD in the tenth y of the reign of Zedekiah,
32: 1 This was also the eighteenth y of the reign of King
32:33 Day after day, y after y, I taught them right
36: 1 During the fourth y that Jehoiakim son of Josiah
36: 9 during the fifth y of the reign of Jehoiakim son of
39: 1 It was in January during the ninth y of King
45: 1 fourth y of the reign of Jehoiakim son of Josiah,
46: 2 fourth y of the reign of Jehoiakim son of Josiah,
51:46 For rumors will keep coming y by y.
51:59 This was during the fourth y of Zedekiah's reign.
52: 4 January 15, during the ninth y of Zedekiah's reign,
52: 5 Jerusalem was kept under siege until the eleventh y
52: 6 By July 18 of Zedekiah's eleventh y, the famine in
52:12 On August 17 of that y, which was the nineteenth
y of Nebuchadnezzar's
52:28 seventh y of Nebuchadnezzar's reign was 3,023.
52:29 Then in Nebuchadnezzar's eighteenth y he took
52:30 In his twenty-third y he sent Nebuzaradan,
52:31 In the thirty-seventh y of King Jehoiachin's exile
52:31 released him from prison on March 31 of that y.
Eze 1: 1 On July 31 of my thirtieth y, while I was with the
1: 2 This happened during the fifth y of King
4: 5 sins for 390 days—one day for each y of their sin.
4: 6 for 40 days—one day for each y of Judah's sin.
8: 1 during the sixth y of King Jehoiachin's captivity,
20: 1 during the seventh y of King Jehoiachin's
24: 1 during the ninth y of King Jehoiachin's captivity,
26: 1 during the twelfth y of King Jehoiachin's captivity,
29: 1 during the tenth y of King Jehoiachin's captivity,
29:17 during the twenty-seventh y of King Jehoiachin's
30:20 during the eleventh y of King Jehoiachin's
31: 1 during the eleventh y of King Jehoiachin's
32: 1 during the twelfth y of King Jehoiachin's captivity,
32:17 On March 17, during the twelfth y,
33:21 On January 8, during the twelfth y of our captivity,
40: 1 during the twenty-fifth y of our captivity—
45:18 In early spring, on the first day of each new y,
45:20 Do this also on the seventh day of the new y for
45:21 "On the fourteenth day of the new y, you must
45:25 of Shelters, which occurs every y in early autumn,
46:17 until the Y of Jubilee, which comes every fiftieth y.
Da 1: 1 During the third y of King Jehoiakim's reign in
1:21 Daniel remained there until the first y of King
2: 1 One night during the second y of his reign,
7: 1 during the first y of King Belshazzar's reign in
8: 1 During the third y of King Belshazzar's reign,
9: 1 It was the first y of the reign of Darius the Mede,
9: 2 During the first y of his reign, I, Daniel,
10: 1 In the third y of the reign of King Cyrus of Persia,
11: 1 and defense since the first y of the reign of Darius
Hos 12: 9 as you do each y when you celebrate the Festival
14: 8 giving my fruit to you all through the y."
Hag 1: 1 On August 29 of the second y of King Darius's
1:15 This was on September 21 of the second y of King
2: 1 Then on October 17 of that same y, the LORD
2:10 On December 18 of the second y of King Darius's
Zec 1: 1 In midautumn of the second y of King Darius's
1: 7 Then on February 15 of the second y of King
7: 1 On December 7 of the fourth y of King Darius's
14:16 go up to Jerusalem each y to worship the King,
Mt 27:15 the crowd each y during the Passover celebration—
27:16 This y there was a notorious criminal in prison,
Mk 15: 6 to release one prisoner each y at Passover time—
Lk 2:41 Every y Jesus' parents went to Jerusalem for the
3: 1 It was now the fifteenth y of the reign of Tiberius,
13: 8 Leave it another y, and I'll give it special attention
13: 9 If we get figs next y, fine. If not, you can cut it
Jn 11:49 Caiaphas, who was high priest that y, said,
18:13 father-in-law of Caiaphas, the high priest that y.
18:39 to release someone from prison each y at Passover.
Ac 11:26 of them stayed there with the church for a full y,
18:11 So Paul stayed there for the next y and a half,
Ro 9: 9 For God had promised, "Next y I will return,
2Co 8:10 I suggest that you finish what you started a y ago,
9: 2 in Greece were ready to send an offering a y ago.
Heb 9: 7 and only once a y, and always with blood,
9:25 Place y after y to offer the blood of an animal.
10: 1 system were repeated again and again, y after y,
10: 3 sacrifices reminded them of their sins y after y.
Jas 4:13 are going to a certain town and will stay there a y.
Rev 9:15 and y were turned loose to kill one-third of all the

YEAR'S (2) [YEAR]

Ge 47:24 and use it to plant the next y crop and to feed
Ex 34:26 You must bring the best of the first of each y crop

YEAR-OLD (6) [YEAR]
Lev 9: 3 a y calf and a y lamb for a whole burnt offering,
12: 6 the woman must bring a y lamb for a whole burnt
14: 10 and one female y lamb with no physical defects,
23: 12 That same day you must sacrifice a y male lamb
Eze 46: 13 "Each morning a y lamb with no physical defects

YEARLING (1) [YEAR]
Mic 6: 6 Should we bow before God with offerings of y

YEARLINGS (1) [YEAR]
Isa 11: 6 Calves and y will be safe among lions, and a little

YEARLY (2) [YEAR]
Lev 25: 53 must treat them as servants hired on a y basis.
Heb 10: 3 Those y sacrifices reminded them of their sins year

YEARN (1) [YEARNED, YEARNS]
Job 14: 15 and you would y for me, your handiwork.

YEARNED (2) [YEARN]
SS 3: 1 I y deeply for my lover, but he did not come.
5: 6 my lover, but he was gone. I y for even his voice!

YEARNS (1) [YEARN]
Isa 62: 1 I love Zion, because my heart y for Jerusalem,

YEARS (478) [YEAR]
GOOD YEARS (3) Ge 41:31,34,35
SEVEN YEARS (28) Ge 29:18,20,25,27,30; 41:26,27,29,30,36,47,49,53,54; Lev 25:8; Nu 13:22; Jdg 6:1,25; 12:9; 2Sa 5:5; 1Ki 6:38; 2Ki 8:1,2; 11:21; 1Ch 29:27; 2Ch 24:1; Eze 39:9; Lk 2:36
YEARS OF FAMINE (8) Ge 41:27,30,36,54; 45:6,11; 2Sa 24:13; 1Ch 21:12

Ge 1: 14 signs to mark off the seasons, the days, and the y.
5: 3 When Adam was 130 y old, his son Seth was born,
5: 4 Adam lived another 800 y, and he had other sons
5: 6 When Seth was 105 y old, his son Enosh was born.
5: 7 Seth lived another 807 y, and he had other sons
5: 9 When Enosh was 90 y old, his son Kenan was
5: 10 Enosh lived another 815 y, and he had other sons
5: 12 When Kenan was 70 y old, his son Mahalalel was
5: 13 Kenan lived another 840 y, and he had other sons
5: 15 When Mahalalel was 65 y old, his son Jared was
5: 16 Mahalalel lived 830 y, and he had other sons
5: 18 When Jared was 162 y old, his son Enoch was
5: 19 Jared lived another 800 y, and he had other sons
5: 21 When Enoch was 65 y old, his son Methuselah was
5: 22 Enoch lived another 300 y in close fellowship with
5: 23 Enoch lived 365 y in all.
5: 25 When Methuselah was 187 y old, his son Lamech
5: 26 Methuselah lived another 782 y, and he had other
5: 28 When Lamech was 182 y old, his son Noah was
5: 30 Lamech lived 595 y, and he had other sons
5: 32 By the time Noah was 500 y old, he had three
6: 3 In the future, they will live no more than 120 y."
7: 6 He was 600 y old when the flood came,
7: 11 When Noah was 600 y old, on the seventeenth day
8: 13 when Noah was 601 y old, ten and a half months
9: 28 Noah lived another 350 y after the Flood.
9: 29 He was 950 y old when he died.
11: 10 When Shem was 100 y old, his son Arphaxad was born. This happened two y after the Flood.
11: 11 Shem lived another 500 y and had other sons
11: 12 When Arphaxad was 35 y old, his son Shelah was
11: 13 Arphaxad lived another 403 y and had other sons
11: 14 When Shelah was 30 y old, his son Eber was born.
11: 15 Shelah lived another 403 y and had other sons
11: 16 When Eber was 34 y old, his son Peleg was born.
11: 17 Eber lived another 430 y and had other sons
11: 18 When Peleg was 30 y old, his son Reu was born.
11: 19 Peleg lived another 209 y and had other sons
11: 20 When Reu was 32 y old, his son Serug was born.
11: 21 Reu lived another 207 y and had other sons
11: 22 When Serug was 30 y old, his son Nahor was born.
11: 23 Serug lived another 200 y and had other sons
11: 24 When Nahor was 29 y old, his son Terah was born.
11: 25 Nahor lived another 119 y and had other sons
11: 26 When Terah was 70 y old, he became the father of
11: 32 Terah lived for 205 y and died while still at Haran.
12: 4 Abram was seventy-five y old when he left Haran.
14: 4 For twelve y they had all been subject to King
15: 13 will be oppressed as slaves for four hundred y.
16: 3 (This happened ten y after Abram first arrived in
16: 16 Abram was eighty-six y old at that time.
17: 1 When Abram was ninety-nine y old, the LORD
17: 24 Abraham was ninety-nine y old at that time,
21: 5 Abraham was one hundred y old at the time.
23: 1 When Sarah was 127 y old,
25: 7 Abraham lived for 175 y,
25: 20 When Isaac was forty y old, he married Rebekah,
25: 26 Isaac was sixty y old when the twins were born.
29: 18 "I'll work for you seven y if you'll give me
29: 20 So Jacob spent the next seven y working to pay for
29: 25 raged at Laban. "I worked seven y for Rachel.
29: 27 if you promise to work another seven y for me."
29: 28 So Jacob agreed to work seven more y. A week
29: 30 then stayed and worked the additional seven y.
30: 29 faithfully I've served you through these many y,
31: 38 "Twenty y I have been with you, and all that time
31: 38 In all those y I never touched a single ram of yours
31: 41 Yes, twenty y—fourteen of them earning your two daughters, and six y to get the flock.
35: 28 Isaac lived for 180 y,
37: 2 When Joseph was seventeen y old, he often tended
41: 1 Two y later, Pharaoh dreamed that he was standing
41: 26 heads of grain both represent seven y of prosperity.
41: 27 heads of grain represent seven y of famine.
41: 29 The next seven y will be a period of great
41: 30 But afterward there will be seven y of famine
41: 31 so terrible that even the memory of the good y will
41: 34 one-fifth of all the crops during the seven good y.
41: 35 and grain of these good y into the royal
41: 36 be enough to eat when the seven y of famine come.
41: 46 He was thirty y old when he entered the service of
41: 47 for the next seven y there were bumper crops
41: 48 During those y, Joseph took a portion of all the
41: 49 After seven y, the granaries were filled to
41: 50 before the arrival of the first of the famine y,
41: 53 At last the seven y of plenty came to an end.
41: 54 Then the seven y of famine began, just as Joseph
42: 9 And he remembered the dreams he had had many y
45: 6 These two y of famine will grow to seven,
45: 11 for there are still five y of famine ahead of us.
47: 9 Jacob replied, "I have lived for 130 hard y, but I
47: 28 Jacob lived for seventeen y after his arrival in Egypt, so he was 147 y old when he died.
50: 22 live in Egypt. Joseph was 110 y old when he died.
Ex 2: 11 Many y later, when Moses had grown up, he went
2: 23 Y passed, and the king of Egypt died.
6: 16 (Levi, their father, lived to be 137 y old.)
6: 18 and Uzziel. (Kohath lived to be 133 y old.)
6: 20 and Moses. (Amram lived to be 137 y old.)
7: 7 Moses was eighty y old, and Aaron was
12: 40 The people of Israel had lived in Egypt for 430 y.
16: 35 So the people of Israel ate manna for forty y until
21: 2 buy a Hebrew slave, he is to serve for only six y.
21: 7 she will not be freed at the end of six y as the men
23: 10 "Plant and harvest your crops for six y,
38: 26 This included all the men who were twenty y old
Lev 19: 23 leave the fruit unharvested for the first three y
25: 3 For six y you may plant your fields and prune your
25: 8 you must count off seven Sabbath y, seven y times seven, adding up to forty-nine y in all.
25: 15 be based on the number of y since the last jubilee.
25: 15 The seller will charge you only for the crop y left
25: 16 The more the y, the higher the price; the fewer the y, the lower the price.
25: 21 a bumper crop, enough to support you for three y.
25: 27 on the number of y until the next Year of Jubilee.
25: 50 the number of y left until the next Year of Jubilee
25: 50 it would cost to hire a servant for that number of y.
25: 51 If many y still remain, they will repay most of
25: 52 If only a few y remain until the Year of Jubilee,
26: 34 y as it lies desolate during your y of exile in the land of your enemies.
26: 43 And the land will enjoy its y of Sabbath rest as it
27: 6 and five y is valued at five pieces of silver;
27: 18 to the y left until the next Year of Jubilee.
27: 23 the priest must assess its value based on the y until
Nu 1: 3 twenty y old or older who are able to go to war.
1: 18 The men of Israel twenty y old or older were
1: 20[-21] This is the number of men twenty y old
1: 45 all the men of Israel who were twenty y old
4: 35 and fifty y of age who were eligible for service in
4: 39 and fifty y of age who were eligible for service in
4: 43 and fifty y of age who were eligible for service in
4: 47 and fifty y of age who were eligible for service in
13: 22 (The ancient town of Hebron was founded seven y
14: 29 none of you who are twenty y old or older
14: 33 wandering in the wilderness forty y.
14: 34 you must wander in the wilderness for forty y—
26: 2 of all the men of Israel who are twenty y old
26: 4 "Count all the men of Israel twenty y old
32: 11 no one who is twenty y old or older will ever see
32: 13 y until the whole generation that sinned against
33: 39 Aaron was 123 y old when he died there on Mount
Dt 1: 3 But forty y after the Israelites left Mount Sinai,
2: 7 During these forty y, the LORD your God has
2: 14 So thirty-eight y passed from the time we first
8: 2 God led you through the wilderness for forty y,
8: 4 For all these forty y your clothes didn't wear out,
15: 12 becomes your servant and serves you for six y,
15: 18 Remember that for six y they have given you the
29: 5 For forty y I led you through the wilderness,
31: 2 "I am now 120 y old and am no longer able to lead
34: 7 Moses was 120 y old when he died, yet his
Jos 5: 5 during the y in the wilderness, had been
5: 6 y until all the men who were old enough to bear
14: 7 I was forty y old when Moses, the servant of the
14: 10 and well as he promised for all these forty-five y
14: 10 in the wilderness. Today I am eighty-five y old.
23: 1 The y passed, and the LORD had given the
24: 7 Then you lived in the wilderness for many y.
Jdg 3: 8 were subject to Cushan-rishathaim for eight y.
3: 11 So there was peace in the land for forty y.
3: 14 were subject to Eglon of Moab for eighteen y.
3: 30 that day, and the land was at peace for eighty y.
4: 3 ruthlessly oppressed the Israelites for twenty y.
5: 31 Then there was peace in the land for forty y.
6: 1 handed them over to the Midianites for seven y.
6: 25 from your father's herd, the one that is seven y old.
8: 28 about forty y—the land was at peace.
9: 22 After Abimelech had ruled over Israel for three y,
10: 2 He was Israel's judge for twenty-three y. When he
10: 3 Gilead named Jair judged Israel for twenty-two y.
10: 8 For eighteen y they oppressed all the Israelites east
11: 26 But now after three hundred y you make an issue
12: 7 Jephthah was Israel's judge for six y. When he
12: 9 to marry his sons. Ibzan judged Israel for seven y.
12: 11 became Israel's judge. He judged Israel for ten y.
12: 14 seventy donkeys. He was Israel's judge for eight y.
13: 1 who kept them in subjection for forty y.
15: 20 Samson was Israel's judge for twenty y,
16: 31 Samson had been Israel's judge for twenty y.
Ru 1: 4 other a woman named Ruth. But about ten y later,
1Sa 1: 26 "I am the woman who stood here several y ago
4: 15 who was ninety-eight y old and blind.
4: 18 was old and very fat. He had led Israel for forty y.
7: 2 in Kiriath-jearim for a long time—twenty y in all.
13: 1 Saul was thirty y old when he became king, and he reigned for forty-two y.
29: 3 He's been with me for y, and I've never found a
2Sa 2: 10 Ishbosheth was forty y old when he became king, and he ruled from Mahanaim for two y.
2: 11 he ruled as king of Judah for seven and a half y.
4: 4 He was five y old when Saul and Jonathan were
5: 4 David was thirty y old when he began to reign, and he reigned forty y in all.
5: 5 had reigned over Judah from Hebron for seven y
5: 5 reigned over all Israel and Judah for thirty-three y.
13: 23 Two y later, when Absalom's sheep were being
13: 38 He stayed there in Geshur for three y.
14: 28 Absalom lived in Jerusalem for two y without
15: 7 After four y, Absalom said to the king, "Let me go
19: 35 I am eighty y old today, and I can no longer enjoy
21: 1 famine during David's reign that lasted for three y,
24: 13 "Will you choose three y of famine throughout the
1Ki 2: 11 He had reigned over Israel for forty y, seven of
2: 39 But three y later, two of Shimei's slaves escaped to
6: 1 This was 480 y after the people of Israel were
6: 38 of his reign. So it took seven y to build the Temple.
7: 1 and it took him thirteen y to complete the
9: 10 Now at the end of the twenty y during which
10: 22 Once every three y the ships returned, loaded down
11: 15 Y before, David had gone to Edom with Joab,
11: 42 ruled in Jerusalem over all Israel for forty y.
14: 20 Jeroboam reigned in Israel twenty-two y.
14: 21 He was forty-one y old when he became king, and he reigned seventeen y in Jerusalem,
15: 2 He reigned in Jerusalem three y. His mother was
15: 10 He reigned in Jerusalem forty-one y.
15: 25 Asa's reign in Judah. He reigned in Israel two y.
15: 33 in Judah. Baasha reigned in Tirzah twenty-four y.
16: 8 Asa's reign in Judah. He reigned in Israel two y.
16: 23 He reigned twelve y in all, six of them in Tirzah.
16: 29 in Judah. He reigned in Samaria twenty-two y.
17: 1 or rain during the next few y unless I give the
22: 1 For three y there was no war between Aram
22: 42 He was thirty-five y old when he became king,
22: 42 and he reigned in Jerusalem twenty-five y.
22: 51 reign in Judah. He reigned in Samaria two y.
2Ki 3: 1 reign in Judah. He reigned in Samaria twelve y.
8: 1 for a famine on Israel that will last for seven y."
8: 2 and lived in the land of the Philistines for seven y.
8: 17 Jehoram was thirty-two y old when he became king, and he reigned in Jerusalem eight y.
8: 26 Ahaziah was twenty-two y old when he became
10: 36 over Israel from Samaria for twenty-eight y.
11: 3 for six y while Athaliah ruled over the land.
11: 21 Joash was seven y old when he became king.
12: 1 He reigned in Jerusalem forty y. His mother was
13: 1 reign in Judah. He reigned in Samaria seventeen y.
13: 10 reign in Judah. He reigned in Samaria sixteen y.
14: 2 Amaziah was twenty-five y old when he became
14: 2 and he reigned in Jerusalem twenty-nine y.
14: 17 King Amaziah of Judah lived on for fifteen y after
14: 23 in Judah. Jeroboam reigned in Samaria forty-one y.
15: 2 He was sixteen y old when he became king,
15: 2 and he reigned in Jerusalem fifty-two y.
15: 17 reign in Judah. He reigned in Samaria ten y.
15: 23 reign in Judah. He reigned in Samaria two y.
15: 27 reign in Judah. He reigned in Samaria twenty y.
15: 33 He was twenty-five y old when he became king,
15: 33 and he reigned in Jerusalem sixteen y.
16: 2 Ahaz was twenty y old when he became king,
16: 2 and he reigned in Jerusalem sixteen y.
17: 1 reign in Judah. He reigned in Samaria nine y.
17: 5 entire land, and for three y he besieged Samaria.
18: 2 He was twenty-five y old when he became king,
18: 2 and he reigned in Jerusalem twenty-nine y.
18: 10 Three y later, during the sixth year of King
20: 6 I will add fifteen y to your life, and I will rescue
21: 1 Manasseh was twelve y old when he became king,
21: 1 and he reigned in Jerusalem fifty-five y.
21: 19 Amon was twenty-two y old when he became king, and he reigned in Jerusalem two y.
22: 1 Josiah was eight y old when he became king,
22: 1 and he reigned in Jerusalem thirty-one y.
23: 22 throughout all the y of the kings of Israel
23: 31 Jehoahaz was twenty-three y old when he became
23: 36 Jehoiakim was twenty-five y old when he became
23: 36 and he reigned in Jerusalem eleven y.
24: 1 and paid him tribute for three y but then rebelled.
24: 8 Jehoiachin was eighteen y old when he became
24: 18 Zedekiah was twenty-one y old when he became
24: 18 and he reigned in Jerusalem eleven y.
1Ch 2: 21 When Hezron was sixty y old, he married Gilead's
3: 4 in Hebron, where he reigned seven and a half y.
3: 4 where he reigned another thirty-three y.
21: 12 You may choose three y of famine, three months
23: 3 All the Levites who were thirty y old or older were
23: 24 Each had to be twenty y old or older to qualify for
23: 27 final instructions that all the Levites twenty y old
27: 23 those who were younger than twenty y of age,

29:27 He ruled Israel for forty y in all, seven y from Hebron and thirty-three y from Jerusalem.
2Ch 8: 1 It was now twenty y since Solomon had become
9:21 Once every three y the ships returned, loaded down
9:30 ruled in Jerusalem over all Israel for forty y.
11:17 and for three y they supported Rehoboam son of
12:13 He was forty-one y old when he became king,
12:13 and he reigned seventeen y in Jerusalem,
13: 2 He reigned in Jerusalem three y. His mother was
14: 1 next king. There was peace in the land for ten y,
14: 6 During those peaceful y, he was able to build up
17: 3 he followed the example of his father's early y
18: 2 A few y later, he went to Samaria to visit Ahab,
20:31 He was thirty-five y old when he became king,
20:31 and he reigned in Jerusalem twenty-five y.
21: 5 Jehoram was thirty-two y old when he became king, and he reigned in Jerusalem eight y.
21:19 In the course of time, at the end of two y,
21:20 Jehoram was thirty-two y old when he became king, and he reigned in Jerusalem eight y.
22: 2 Ahaziah was twenty-two y old when he became
22:12 of God for six y while Athaliah ruled over the land.
24: 1 Joash was seven y old when he became king, and he reigned in Jerusalem forty y.
24: 7 Over the y, the followers of wicked Athaliah had
25: 1 Amaziah was twenty-five y old when he became
25: 1 and he reigned in Jerusalem twenty-nine y.
25: 5 that he had an army of 300,000 men twenty y old
25:25 King Amaziah of Judah lived on for fifteen y after
26: 3 and he reigned in Jerusalem fifty-two y.
27: 1 Jotham was twenty-five y old when he became
27: 1 and he reigned in Jerusalem sixteen y.
27: 5 For the next three y, he received from them an
27: 8 He was twenty-five y old when he became king,
27: 8 and he reigned in Jerusalem sixteen y.
28: 1 Ahaz was twenty y old when he became king,
28: 1 and he reigned in Jerusalem sixteen y.
29: 1 Hezekiah was twenty-five y old when he became
29: 1 and he reigned in Jerusalem twenty-nine y.
31:16 They also distributed the gifts to all males three y
31:17 and to the Levites twenty y old or older who were
33: 1 Manasseh was twelve y old when he became king,
33: 1 and he reigned in Jerusalem fifty-five y.
33:21 Amon was twenty-two y old when he became king, and he reigned in Jerusalem two y.
34: 1 Josiah was eight y old when he became king,
34: 1 and he reigned in Jerusalem thirty-one y.
36: 2 Jehoahaz was twenty-three y old when he became
36: 5 Jehoiakim was twenty-five y old when he became
36: 5 and he reigned in Jerusalem eleven y.
36: 9 Jehoiachin was eighteen y old when he became
36:11 Zedekiah was twenty-one y old when he became
36:11 and he reigned in Jerusalem eleven y.
36:21 lying desolate for seventy y, just as the prophet had
Ezr 3: 8 The Levites who were twenty y old or older were
4: 6 Y later when Xerxes began his reign, the enemies
5:11 was built here many y ago by a great king of Israel.
7: 1 Many y later, during the reign of King Artaxerxes
Ne 5:14 I would like to mention that for the entire twelve y
9:21 For forty y you sustained them in the wilderness.
9:30 your love, you were patient with them for many y.
Job 12:12 and understanding to those who have lived many y.
29: 2 "I long for the y gone by when God took care of
29: 4 In my early y, the friendship of God was felt in my
36:11 throughout their lives. All their y will be pleasant.
36:26 we can understand. His y are without number.
42:16 Job lived 140 y after that, living to see four
Ps 31:10 dying from grief; / my y are shortened by sadness.
61: 6 Add many y to the life of the king! / May his y span the generations!
78:33 their lives in failure / and gave them y of terror.
90: 4 For you, a thousand y are as yesterday! / They are
90:10 Seventy y are given to us! / Some may even reach
90:10 But even the best of these y are filled with pain
90:15 our former misery! / Replace the evil y with good.
95:10 For forty y I was angry with them, and I said,
102:27 But you are always the same; / your y never end.
109: 8 Let his y be few; / let his position be given to
119:54 of my life / throughout the y of my pilgrimage.
Pr 9:11 will multiply your days and add y to your life.
10:27 one's life, but the y of the wicked are cut short.
Ecc 6: 6 He might live a thousand y twice over but not find
Isa 7: 8 within sixty-five y it will be crushed
7:17 y since Solomon's empire was divided into Israel
8: 4 This name prophesies that within a couple of y,
16:14 the LORD says, "Within three y, without fail,
20: 3 around naked and barefoot for the last three y.
23:15 For seventy y, the length of a king's life, Tyre will
23:17 after seventy y the LORD will revive Tyre.
32:12 be gone, and for those fruitful vines of other y.
38: 5 and seen your tears. I will add fifteen y to your life,
38:10 of the dead? / Am I to be robbed of my normal y?"
38:15 Now I will walk humbly throughout my y
47:12 the demon hordes you have worshiped all these y.
63: 9 lifted them up and carried them through all the y.
Jer 2: 9 even against your children's children in the y to
2:32 Yet for y on end my people have forgotten me.
25: 3 "For the past twenty-three y—from the thirteenth
25:11 lands will serve the king of Babylon for seventy y.
25:12 "Then, after the seventy y of captivity are over,
28: 3 Within two y, I will bring back all the Temple
28:11 "The LORD has promised that within two y he
29:10 truth is that you will be in Babylon for seventy y.
29:28 should build homes and plan to stay for many y.
29:28 because we will be here to eat the fruit for many y
34:14 Hebrew slave must be freed after serving six y.
39: 2 Two and a half y later, on July 18, the Babylonians
52: 1 Zedekiah was twenty-one y old when he became
52: 1 and he reigned in Jerusalem eleven y.
Eze 16:22 In all your y of adultery and loathsome sin,
22: 4 has come! You have reached the end of your y.
29:11 For forty y not a soul will pass that way,
29:12 Its cities will be empty and desolate for forty y,
29:13 At the end of the forty y I will bring the Egyptians
39: 9 for fuel. There will be enough to last them seven y!
40: 1 fourteen y after the fall of Jerusalem—the LORD
Da 5: 1 A number of y later, King Belshazzar gave a great
9: 2 that Jerusalem must lie desolate for seventy y.
11: 6 "Some y later, an alliance will be formed between
11: 8 For some y afterward he will leave the king of the
11:13 "A few y later, the king of the north will return
Hos 1: 1 to Hosea son of Beeri during the y when Uzziah,
Joel 1: 3 Tell your children about it in the y to come.
Am 1: 1 He received this message in visions two y before
2:10 and led you through the desert for forty y
5:25 and offerings during the forty y in the wilderness,
Mic 1: 1 to Micah of Moresheth during the y when Jotham,
Hab 3: 2 begin again to help us, as you did in y gone by.
Zec 1:12 for seventy y now you have been angry with
7: 3 as we have done for so many y?"
7: 5 'During those seventy y of exile, when you fasted
7: 7 through the prophets y ago when Jerusalem
Mt 2:16 and around Bethlehem who were two y old
2:16 the star first appeared to them about two y earlier.
9:20 a woman who had had a hemorrhage for twelve y
Mk 5:25 the crowd who had had a hemorrhage for twelve y.
5:26 a great deal from many doctors through the y
5:42 And the girl, who was twelve y old,
Lk 1:18 man now, and my wife is also well along in y."
2:36 had died when they had been married only seven y.
2:37 She was now eighty-four y old. She never left the
2:40 He was filled with wisdom beyond his y, and God
2:42 When Jesus was twelve y old, they attended the
3:23 Jesus was about thirty y old when he began his
4:25 for three and a half y and hunger stalked the land.
8:42 His only child was dying, a little girl twelve y old.
8:43 the crowd who had had a hemorrhage for twelve y.
12:19 you have enough stored away for y to come.
13: 7 he said to his gardener, 'I've waited three y,
13:11 She had been bent double for eighteen y and was
13:16 in which Satan has held her for eighteen y?"
15:29 'All these y I've worked hard for you and never
20: 9 and moved to another country to live for several y.
Jn 2:20 "It took forty-six y to build this Temple, and you
5: 5 men lying there had been sick for thirty-eight y.
8:57 The people said, "You aren't even fifty y old.
Ac 4:22 of a man who had been lame for more than forty y.
7: 6 would be mistreated as slaves for four hundred y.
7:23 "One day when he was forty y old, he decided to
7:30 "Forty y later, in the desert near Mount Sinai,
7:36 and forth through the wilderness for forty y.
7:42 during those forty y in the wilderness, Israel?
7:45 Y later, when Joshua led the battles against the
8: 9 Simon had been a sorcerer there for many y,
9:33 who had been paralyzed and bedridden for eight y.
13:18 He put up with them through forty y of wandering
13:20 All this took about 450 y. After that, judges ruled
13:21 of the tribe of Benjamin, who reigned for forty y.
19:10 This went on for the next two y, so that people
20:31 Remember the three y I was with you—
24:10 have been a judge of Jewish affairs for many y,
24:17 "After several y away, I returned to Jerusalem
24:27 Two y went by in this way; then Felix was
28:30 For the next two y, Paul lived in his own rented
Ro 15:23 and after all these long y of waiting, I am eager to
2Co 12: 2 I was caught up into the third heaven fourteen y
Gal 1:18 It was not until three y later that I finally went to
2: 1 Then fourteen y later I went back to Jerusalem
3:17 430 y later when God gave the law to Moses.
4:10 don't do on certain days or months or seasons or y.
1Ti 5: 9 must be a woman who is at least sixty y old
Heb 3: 9 even though they saw my miracles for forty y.
3:17 And who made God angry for forty y? Wasn't it
12:10 For our earthly fathers disciplined us for a few y,
Jas 5: 5 You have spent your y on earth in luxury,
5:17 would fall, none fell for the next three and a half y!
1Pe 1:12 their lifetime, but many y later, during yours.
2Pe 3: 8 that a day is like a thousand y to the Lord, and a thousand y is like a day.
Rev 20: 2 Satan—and bound him in chains for a thousand y.
20: 3 anymore until the thousand y were finished.
20: 4 and they reigned with Christ for a thousand y.
20: 5 come back to life until the thousand y had ended.)
20: 6 and of Christ and will reign with him a thousand y.
20: 7 When the thousand y end, Satan will be let out of

YEAST (57) [YEASTLESS]

Ge 19: 3 complete with fresh bread made without y.
Ex 12: 8 lamb with bitter herbs and bread made without y.
12:15 you may eat only bread made without y.
12:15 must remove every trace of y from your homes.
12:15 Anyone who eats bread made with y at any time
12:18 Only bread without y may be eaten from the
12:19 there must be no trace of y in your homes.
12:19 Anyone who eats anything made with y during this
12:20 those days you must not eat anything made with y.
12:20 you live, eat only bread that has no y in it."
12:34 took with them their bread dough made without y.
12:39 It was made without y because the people were
13: 3 (Remember, you are not to use any y.)
13: 6 For seven days you will eat only bread without y.
13: 7 Eat only bread without y during those seven days.
13: 7 there must be no y in your homes or anywhere
23:15 seven days you are to eat bread made without y.
23:18 be offered together with bread that has y in it.
29: 2 Then using fine wheat flour and no y, make loaves
34:25 "You must not offer bread made with y as a
Lev 2: 4 flour mixed with olive oil but without any y.
2: 5 choice flour and olive oil, and it must contain no y.
2:11 "Do not use y in any of the grain offerings you
2:11 because no y or honey may be burned as an
2:12 You may add y and honey to the offerings
6:16 be baked without y and eaten in a sacred place
6:17 this flour may never be prepared with y.
7:12 all made without y and soaked with olive oil.
7:13 must also be accompanied by loaves of y bread.
8:26 y that was placed in the LORD's presence.
10:12 Make sure there is no y in it, and eat it beside the
23: 6 time all the bread you eat must be made without y.
23:17 from three quarts of choice flour that contains y.
Nu 6:15 a basket of bread made without y—cakes of choice
6:17 along with the basket of bread made without y.
6:19 one cake made without y, and one wafer made without y,
9:11 time with bitter herbs and bread made without y.
28:17 will begin, but no bread made with y may be eaten.
Dt 16: 3 Eat it with bread made without y. For seven days eat only bread made without y,
16: 4 Let no y be found in any house throughout your
16: 8 next six days you may not eat bread made with y.
Jdg 6:19 a bushel of flour he baked some bread without y.
1Ch 23:29 the wafers made without y, the cakes cooked in
Eze 45:21 Only bread without y may be eaten during that
Am 4: 5 Present your bread made with y as an offering of
Mt 13:33 "The Kingdom of Heaven is like y used by a
13:33 of flour, the y permeated every part of the dough."
16: 6 "Beware of the y of the Pharisees
16:11 'Beware of the y of the Pharisees
16:12 they understood that he wasn't speaking about y
Mk 8:15 "Beware of the y of the Pharisees and of Herod."
Lk 12: 1 warned them, "Beware of the y of the Pharisees—
13:21 It is like y used by a woman making bread.
13:21 of flour, the y permeated every part of the dough."
Gal 5: 9 a little y spreads quickly through the whole batch

YEASTLESS (2) [YEAST]

Ex 12:39 they baked bread from the y dough they had
29:23 and one wafer from the basket of y bread that was

YELLED (8) [YELLING]

1Sa 17:44 flesh to the birds and wild animals!" Goliath y.
2Ki 9:33 "Throw her down!" Jehu y. So they threw her out
Ps 137: 7 "Destroy it!" they y. / "Level it to the ground!"
Mt 27:25 And all the people y back, "We will take
Mk 10:48 "Be quiet!" some of the people y at him. But he
15:29 "Ha! Look at you now!" they y at him. "You can
Jn 19:15 "Away with him," they y. "Away with him—
Ac 22:23 They y, threw off their coats, and tossed handfuls

YELLING (3) [YELLED]

Mt 27:29 Then they knelt before him in mockery, y, "Hail!
Mk 15:18 Then they saluted, y, "Hail! King of the Jews!"
Ac 21:28 y, "Men of Israel! Help! This is the man who

YELLOW (6)

Lev 13:30 and fine y hair is found in the affected area,
13:32 area has not spread and no y hair has appeared,
13:36 even without checking for y hair.
Nu 11: 7 looked like small coriander seeds, pale y in color.
Ps 129: 6 on a rooftop, / turning y when only half grown,
Rev 9:17 wore armor that was fiery red and sky blue and y.

YES (388)

Ge 3:12 "Y," Adam admitted, "but it was the woman you
6: 7 Y, and I will destroy all the animals and birds,
6:13 Y, I will wipe them all from the face of the earth!
9: 6 Y, you must execute anyone who murders another
9: 7 the earth. Y, multiply and fill the earth!"
9:17 Then God said to Noah, "Y, this is the sign of my
16:12 Y, he will live at odds with the rest of his
17: 8 Y, I will give all this land of Canaan to you and to
17:16 Y, I will bless her richly, and she will become the
17:18 And Abraham said to God, "Y, may Ishmael enjoy
20: 5 and she herself said, 'Y, he is my brother.'
20: 6 "Y, I know you are innocent," God replied.
22: 1 "Abraham!" God called. "Y," he replied.
22: 2 your only son—y, Isaac, whom you love so much
22: 7 "Father?" "Y, my son," Abraham replied.
22:11 "Abraham! Abraham!" "Y," he answered.
24:14 If she says, 'Y, certainly, and I will water your
24:25 Y, we have plenty of straw and food for the
24:40 Y, you must get a wife for my son from among my
24:51 Y, let her be the wife of your master's son,
24:58 they asked her. And she replied, "Y, I will go."
27: 1 his older son, and said, "My son?" "Y, Father?"
27:18 "Y, my son," he answered. "Who is it—Esau
27:24 he asked. "Y, of course," Jacob replied.
29: 5 grandson of Nahor?" "Y, we do," they replied.
31:11 to me, 'Jacob!' And I replied, 'Y, I'm listening!'
31:41 Y, twenty years—fourteen of them earning your
35:12 Y, I will give it to you and your descendants."
37:17 "Y," the man told him, "but they are no longer
37:33 "Y," he said, "it is my son's robe. A wild animal
42:12 "Y, you are!" he insisted. "You have come to
43:28 "Y," they replied. "He is alive and well."
44:20 We said, 'Y, we have a father, an old man, and a
45: 8 Y, it was God who sent me here, not you! And he

48: 9 "Y," Joseph told him, "these are the sons God
Ex 2: 8 "Y, do!" the princess replied. So the girl rushed
3: 7 slave drivers. Y, I am aware of their suffering.
15: 3 LORD is a warrior; / y, the LORD is his name!
16: 8 Y, your complaints are against the LORD,
29:44 Y, I will make the Tabernacle and the altar most
31: 5 in carving wood. Y, he is a master at every craft!
31:14 Y, keep the Sabbath day, for it is holy.
32:13 Y, I will give them all of this land that I have
34: 9 Y, this is an unruly and stubborn people, but please
Lev 25:11 Y, the fiftieth year will be a jubilee for you.
26:32 Y, I myself will devastate your land. Your enemies
26:37 Y, though no one is chasing you, you will stumble
Nu 5:22 woman will be required to say, "Y, let it be so."
8:18 Y, I claim the Levites in place of all the firstborn
18:19 Y, I am giving you all these holy offerings that the
21:17 this song: / "Spring up, O well! / Y, sing about it!
Dt 8: 3 Y, he humbled you by letting you go hungry
9:24 Y, you have been rebelling against the LORD as
25:15 Y, use honest weights and measures, so that you
Jos 22:22 "Y," they replied, "we are accountable."
Jdg 13:11 my wife the other day?" "Y," he replied, "I am."
Ru 2:11 "Y, I know," Boaz replied. "But I also know
1Sa 2: 8 the poor from the dust— / y, from a pile of ashes!
3: 4 the LORD called out, "Samuel! Samuel!" "Y?"
3: 9 and if someone calls again, say, 'Y, LORD,
3:10 And Samuel replied, "Y, your servant is
9:12 "Y," they replied. "Stay right on this road.
12: 5 me of robbing you." "Y, it is true," they replied.
14:44 "Y, Jonathan," Saul said, "you must die!
15:24 Then Saul finally admitted, "Y, I have sinned.
16: 5 "Y," Samuel replied. "I have come to sacrifice to
20:26 Y, that must be why he's not here."
23: 2 "Y, go and save Keilah," the LORD told him.
23:12 the LORD replied, "Y, they will betray you."
24:18 Y, you have been wonderfully kind to me today,
25:41 She bowed low to the ground and responded, "Y,
26:17 And David replied, "Y, my lord the king.
30: 8 And the LORD told him, "Y, go after them.
2Sa 2: 1 And the LORD replied, "Y." Then David asked,
2:20 "Is that you, Asahel?" "Y, it is," he replied.
5:19 over to me?" The LORD replied, "Y, go ahead.
6:22 Y, and I am willing to look even more foolish than
9: 2 the king asked. "Y sir, I am," Ziba replied.
9: 3 Ziba replied, "Y, one of Jonathan's sons is still
9:11 "Y, my lord; I will do all that you have
12:13 Nathan replied, "Y, but the LORD has forgiven
12:19 "Is the baby dead?" he asked. "Y," they replied.
14:17 Y, the king will give us peace of mind again.'
14:18 the king replied. "Y, my lord?" she asked.
14:19 Y, Joab sent me and told me what to say.
18:23 "Y, but let me go anyway," he begged.
22: 7 out to the LORD; / y, I called to my God for help.
22:29 my light; / y, LORD, you light up my darkness.
23: 5 Y, he has made an everlasting covenant with me.
1Ki 8:30 Y, hear us from heaven where you live, and when
12:11 Y, my father was harsh on you, but I'll be even
13:14 came from Judah?" "Y," he replied, "I am."
18: 8 "Y, it is," Elijah replied. "Now go and tell your
20:14 Ahab asked. "Y," the prophet answered.
20:33 and they replied, "Y, your brother Ben-hadad!"
21:20 "Y," Elijah answered, "I have come because you
22:12 "Y," they said, "go up to Ramoth-gilead and be
2Ki 4:26 with your husband, and with your child?' " "Y,"
5:22 "Y," Gehazi said, "but my master has sent me to
10:15 "Y, I am," Jehonadab replied. "If you are,"
17:12 Y, they worshiped idols, despite the LORD's
19:23 y, the remotest peaks of Lebanon.
1Ch 14:10 The LORD replied, "Y, go ahead. I will give you
16: 9 Sing to him; y, sing his praises. / Tell everyone
2Ch 6:21 Y, hear us from heaven where you live, and when
10:11 Y, my father was harsh on you, but I'll be even
18:11 "Y," they said, "go up to Ramoth-gilead and be
Ezr 10:12 their voices and answered, "Y, you are right;
Ne 1: 6 Y, even my own family and I have sinned!
Job 1: 9 Satan replied to the LORD, "Y, Job fears God,
3: 5 Y, let the darkness and utter gloom claim it for its
9: 2 "Y, I know this is all true in principle. But how
12:16 "Y, strength and wisdom are with him; deceivers
13:14 Y, I will take my life in my hands and say what I
19:27 for myself. Y, I will see him with my own eyes.
22: 6 you as a pledge. Y, you stripped him to the bone.
33:29 "Y, God often does these things for people.
34:28 God's attention. Y, he hears the cries of the needy.
41:21 Y, its breath would kindle coals, for flames shoot
Ps 18: 6 to the LORD; / y, I prayed to my God for help.
27:14 and courageous. / Y, wait patiently for the LORD.
32: 2 Y, what joy for those / whose record the LORD
51: 5 y, from the moment my mother conceived me.
56:10 praise your word. / Y, LORD, I praise your word.
64: 6 Y, the human heart and mind are cunning.
66:14 y, the sacred vows you heard me make / when I
67: 3 O God. / Y, may all the nations praise you.
67: 5 O God. / Y, may all the nations praise you.
67: 7 Y, God will bless us, / and people all over the
71: 6 Y, you have been with me from birth; / from my
72: 5 as the moon continues in the skies. / Y, forever!
78:20 Y, he can strike a rock so water gushes out,
78:21 against Jacob. / Y, his anger rose against Israel,
84: 2 I long, y, I faint with longing / to enter the courts
85: 2 your people— / y, you have covered all their sins.
85:12 Y, the LORD pours down his blessings.
86:16 to your servant; / y, save me, for I am your servant.
89:18 Y, our protection comes from the LORD,
90:17 efforts successful. / Y, make our efforts successful!
103:21 Y, praise the LORD, you armies of angels
105: 2 Sing to him; y, sing his praises. / Tell everyone
112: 1 Y, happy are those who delight in doing what he
113: 1 Y, give praise, O servants of the LORD.
114: 8 y, springs of water came from solid rock.
116:16 y, I am your servant, the son of your handmaid,
118: 7 Y, the LORD is for me; he will help me. / I will
118:11 Y, they surrounded and attacked me, / but I
119:99 Y, I have more insight than my teachers, / for I am
119:168 Y, I obey your commandments and decrees,
124: 5 Y, the raging waters of their fury / would have
126: 3 Y, the LORD has done amazing things for us!
130: 5 on the LORD; / y, I am counting on him.
130: 6 the dawn, / y, more than sentries long for the dawn.
131: 2 Y, like a small child is my soul within me.
138: 5 Y, they will sing about the LORD's ways,
139:22 Y, I hate them with complete hatred, / for your
144:15 Y, happy are those who have it like this!
145:18 call on him, / y, to all who call on him sincerely.
Pr 22:19 I am teaching you today—y, you—so you will trust
23:16 Y, my heart will thrill when you speak what is
26:13 on the road! Y, I'm sure there's a lion out there!"
31: 9 Y, speak up for the poor and helpless, and see that
Ecc 3:16 Y, even the courts of law are corrupt!
8: 6 Y, there is a time and a way for everything, even as
10: 1 Y, an ounce of foolishness can outweigh a pound
12: 6 Y, remember your Creator now while you are
SS 1: 5 tents of Kedar. Y, even as the tents of Solomon!
2: 2 "Y, compared to other women, my beloved is like
2:13 Y, spring is here! Arise, my beloved, my fair one,
4:11 Y, honey and cream are under your tongue.
5: 1 eat and drink! Y, drink deeply of this love!"
6: 4 Y, as beautiful as Jerusalem! You are as majestic
Isa 3:17 Y, the LORD will make them bald for all to see!
6: 9 And he said, "Y, go. But tell my people this:
7: 5 "Y, the kings of Aram and Israel are coming
8: 9 all you nations. Prepare for battle—and die! Y, die!
10: 2 Y, they rob widows and fatherless children!
10:10 Y, we have finished off many a kingdom whose
10:23 Y, the Lord, the LORD Almighty, has already
11: 1 y, a new Branch bearing fruit from the old root.
11: 8 Y, a little child will put its hand in a nest of deadly
14: 4 has been destroyed. Y, your insolence is ended.
16: 7 Y, you people of Moab, mourn for the delicacies of
17: 6 Y, Israel will be stripped bare of people,"
19:21 Y, they will know the LORD and will give their
22:19 "Y, I will drive you out of office,"
23:17 Y, after seventy years the LORD will revive
34: 6 Y, the LORD will offer a great sacrifice in the
35: 2 Y, there will be an abundance of flowers
37:24 y, the remotest peaks of Lebanon.
38: 6 from the king of Assyria. Y, I will defend this city.
38:17 Y, it was good for me to suffer this anguish,
40: 2 Y, the LORD has punished her in full for all her
40:10 Y, the Sovereign LORD is coming in all his
41:23 Y, that's it! If you are gods, tell what will occur in
42:14 have long been silent; / y, I have restrained myself.
42:16 Y, I will indeed do these things; / I will not forsake
43:20 Y, I will make springs in the desert, so that my
43:25 "I—y, I alone—am the one who blots out your sins
44:15 Then—y, it's true—he takes the rest of it
47: 9 Y, these calamities will come upon you, despite all
48: 8 "Y, I will tell you of things that are entirely new,
48:11 will rescue you for my sake—y, for my own sake!
51: 2 Y, think about your ancestors Abraham and Sarah,
55: 7 Y, turn to our God, for he will abundantly pardon.
58: 8 Y, your healing will come quickly. Your godliness
58: 9 will answer. 'Y, I am here,' he will quickly reply.
59:12 testify against us. Y, we know what sinners we are.
59:15 Y, truth is gone, and anyone who tries to live a
65: 6 I will repay them in full! Y, I will repay them—
Jer 1:14 "Y," the LORD said, "for terror from the north
1:16 Y, they worship idols that they themselves have
3:22 "Y, we will come," the people reply, "for you are
5:17 of cattle. Y, they will eat your grapes and figs.
6:11 Y, I am weary of holding it in! "I will pour out my
6:13 Y, even my prophets and priests are like that!
8:10 Y, even my prophets and priests are like that.
9:26 in distant places, and y, even the people of Judah.
15:21 Y, I will certainly keep you safe from these wicked
17:18 me peace. Y, bring double destruction upon them!
19:13 Y, all the houses in Jerusalem, including the palace
21: 4 Y, I will bring your enemies right into the heart of
27:21 Y, this is what the LORD Almighty, the God of
29:18 Y, I will pursue them with war, famine,
32:44 Y, fields will once again be bought and sold—
34:19 Y, I will cut you apart, whether you are officials of
37:17 "Y, I do!" said Jeremiah. "You will be defeated
42:17 Y, you will die from war, famine, and disease.
46:10 until it is satisfied, / y, drunk with your blood!
47: 4 Y, the LORD is destroying the Philistines,
48:31 Y, I wail for Moab; my heart is broken for the men
48:33 shouts of joy. There is shouting, y, but not of joy.
50:14 "Y, prepare to attack Babylon, all you nations
50:21 Y, march against Babylon, the land of rebels,
50:26 Y, come against her from distant lands. Break open
51:52 "Y," says the LORD, "but the time is coming
La 2: 5 Y, the Lord has vanquished Israel like an enemy.
3:57 Y, you came at my despairing cry and told me,
Eze 7:12 Y, the time has come; the day is here! There is no
11: 5 Y, I know it is, for I know every thought that
16:32 Y, you are an adulterous wife who takes in
16:55 Y, your sisters, Sodom and Samaria, and all their
18:26 Y, they will die because of their sinful deeds.
20:11 Y, all those who keep them will live!
21: 4 Y, I will not spare even the righteous! I will make
21:11 Y, the sword is now being sharpened and polished;
23:32 "Y, this is what the Sovereign LORD says:
23:49 of idols. Y, you will suffer the full penalty!
24:10 Y, heap on the wood! Let the fire roar to make the
25:10 Y, the Ammonites will no longer be counted
28: 5 Y, your wisdom has made you very rich, and your
29:20 Y, I have given him the land of Egypt as a reward
30:16 Y, I will set fire to all Egypt! Pelusium will be
32: 8 Y, I will bring darkness everywhere across your
32:10 Y, I will bring terror to many lands, and their kings
32:16 Y, this is the funeral song they will sing for Egypt.
32:25 Y, they terrorized the nations while they lived,
34:14 Y, I will give them good pastureland on the high
34:16 I will feed them, y—feed them justice!
43:12 is holy. Y, this is the primary law of the Temple.
Da 3:24 "Y," they said, "we did indeed, Your Majesty."
6:12 "Y," the king replied, "that decision stands;
Hos 6:10 Y, I have seen a horrible thing in Israel: My people
12: 4 Y, he wrestled with the angel and won. He wept
Joel 1:11 and barley—y, all the field crops—are ruined.
1:12 apple trees—y, all the fruit trees—have dried up.
Am 5:20 Y, the day of the LORD will be a dark
Ob 1:16 Y, you nations will drink and stagger
Jnh 4: 9 "Y," Jonah retorted, "even angry enough to die!"
Mic 2:12 Y, your land will again be filled with noisy
7:15 "Y," says the LORD, "I will do mighty miracles
Zep 1: 9 Y, I will punish those who participate in pagan
Hag 2:13 it be defiled?" And the priests answered, "Y."
Zec 3: 2 Y, the LORD, who has chosen Jerusalem,
14: 5 Y, you will flee as you did from the earthquake in
Mt 3:10 Y, every tree that does not produce good fruit will
5:37 Just say a simple, 'Y, I will,' or 'No, I won't.'
7:20 Y, the way to identify a tree or a person is by the
9:28 you see?" "Y, Lord," they told him, "we do."
10:18 to tell them about me—y, to witness to the world.
11: 9 for a prophet? Y, and he is more than a prophet.
11:26 Y, Father, it pleased you to do it this way!
12:10 (They were, of course, hoping he would say y,
12:12 a sheep! Y, it is right to do good on the Sabbath."
13:51 Do you understand?" "Y," they said, "we do."
15:27 "Y, Lord," she replied, "but even dogs are
20:22 to drink?" "Oh y," they replied, "we are able!"
21:16 "Y," Jesus replied. "Haven't you ever read the
21:30 the other son, 'You go,' and he said, 'Y, sir, I will.'
23:15 Y, how terrible it will be for you teachers of
23:23 You should tithe, y, but you should not leave
24: 6 Y, these things must come, but the end won't
26:64 Jesus replied, "Y, it is as you say. And in the
27:11 asked him. Jesus replied, "Y, it is as you say."
Mk 8:24 "Y," he said, "I see people, but I can't see them
10:39 "Oh y," they said, "we are able!" And Jesus said,
13: 7 Y, these things must come, but the end won't
15: 2 of the Jews?" Jesus replied, "Y, it is as you say."
Lk 2:11 The Savior—y, the Messiah, the Lord—has been
3: 9 Y, every tree that does not produce good fruit will
6:23 "When that happens, rejoice! Y, leap for joy!
7:26 for a prophet? Y, and he is more than a prophet.
9:61 Another said, "Y, Lord, I will follow you, but first
10:14 Y, Tyre and Sidon will be better off on the
10:18 "Y," he told them, "I saw Satan falling from
10:21 Y, Father, it pleased you to do it this way.
10:37 Then Jesus said, "Y, now go and do the same."
11:42 You should tithe, y, but you should not leave
11:44 Y, how terrible it will be for you. For you are like
11:46 "Y," said Jesus, "how terrible it will be for you
11:51 Y, it will surely be charged against you.
12:21 "Y, a person is a fool to store up earthly wealth
13:33 Y, today, tomorrow, and the next day I must
14:26 brothers and sisters—y, more than your own life.
17:30 Y, it will be 'business as usual' right up to the hour
18:29 "Y," Jesus replied, "and I assure you,
19:26 " 'Y,' the king replied, 'but to those who use well
21: 9 Y, these things must come, but the end won't
22:37 Y, everything written about me by the prophets
23: 3 of the Jews?" Jesus replied, "Y, it is as you say."
24:46 And he said, "Y, it was written long ago that the
Jn 5:45 Y, Moses, on whom you set your hopes.
6:48 Y, I am the bread of life!
7:28 he called out, "Y, you know me, and you know
8:37 Y, I realize that you are descendants of Abraham.
9:38 "Y, Lord," the man said, "I believe!" And he
10: 9 Y, I am the gate. Those who come in through me
11:24 "Y," Martha said, "when everyone else rises,
11:27 "Y, Lord," she told him. "I have always believed
14:14 Y, ask anything in my name, and I will do it!
15: 5 "Y, I am the vine; you are the branches.
15:11 be filled with my joy. Y, your joy will overflow!
16: 4 Y, I'm telling you these things now, so that when
16:28 Y, I came from the Father into the world, and I will
21:15 "Y, Lord," Peter replied, "you know I love you."
21:16 "Y, Lord," Peter said, "you know I love you."
Ac 5: 8 "Y," she replied, "that was the price."
9:10 calling, "Ananias!" "Y, Lord!" he replied.
20:19 done the Lord's work humbly—y, and with tears.
22:27 "Y, I certainly am," Paul replied.
26:17 Y, I am going to send you to the Gentiles,
Ro 1:21 Y, they knew God, but they wouldn't worship him
2:18 Y, you know what he wants; you know right from
3: 2 Y, being a Jew has many advantages. First of all,
4: 8 Y, what joy for those / whose sin is no longer
5:13 Y, people sinned even before the law was given.
5:18 Y, Adam's one sin brought condemnation upon
10:18 they actually heard the message? Y, they have:
10:19 Y, they did, for even in the time of Moses,
11:20 Y, but remember—those branches, the Jews,
14:12 Y, each of us will have to give a personal account
1Co 1:16 (Oh y, I also baptized the household of Stephanas.
7: 1 in your letter. Y, it is good to live a celibate life.
9:22 Y, I try to find common ground with everyone
11: 6 Y, if she refuses to wear a head covering,

12:14 Y, the body has many different parts, not just one
12:20 Y, there are many parts, but only one body.
2Co 1:17 Or am I like people of the world who say y when
1:18 I am not that sort of person. My y means y
1:19 the Son of God, never wavers between y and no.
1:19 and I preached to you, and he is the divine Y—
3:15 Y, even today when they read Moses' writings,
4:11 Y, we live under constant danger of death
5:8 Y, we are fully confident, and we would rather be
9:11 Y, you will be enriched so that you can give even
12:21 Y, I am afraid that when I come, God will humble
Php 3:6 Y, in fact I harshly persecuted the church.
3:8 Y, everything else is worthless when compared
1Th 2:19 Y, you will bring us much joy as we stand together
2Ti 3:12 Y, and everyone who wants to live a godly life in
4:18 Y, and the Lord will deliver me from every evil
Phm 1:20 Y, dear brother, please do me this favor for the
Heb 2:9 Y, by God's grace, Jesus tasted death for everyone
7:18 Y, the old requirement about the priesthood was
Jas 2:8 Y indeed, it is good when you truly obey our
5:12 Just say a simple y or no, so that you will not sin
1Pe 2:7 Y, he is very precious to you who believe. But for
2Pe 1:13 Y, I believe I should keep on reminding you of
2:8 Y, he was a righteous man who was distressed by
1Jn 3:2 Y, dear friends, we are already God's children,
Jude 1:25 Y, glory, majesty, power, and authority belong to
Rev 1:7 of the earth will weep because of him. Y! Amen!
10:9 "Y, take it and eat it," he said. "At first it will
14:13 Y, says the Spirit, they are blessed indeed, for they
16:7 "Y, Lord God Almighty, your punishments are
18:13 and slaves—y, she even traded in human lives.
22:20 to all these things says, "Y, I am coming soon!"

YESTERDAY (10)

Ex 2:14 you plan to kill me as you killed that Egyptian y?"
5:14 "Why haven't you met your quotas either y
1Sa 20:27 hasn't the son of Jesse been here for dinner either y
2Sa 15:20 You arrived only y, and now should I force you to
2Ki 9:26 the murder of Naboth and his sons that I saw y.'
Job 8:9 For we were born but y and know so little.
Ps 90:4 For you, a thousand years are as y! / They are like
Jn 4:52 "Y afternoon at one o'clock his fever suddenly
Ac 7:28 going to kill me as you killed that Egyptian y?'
Heb 13:8 Jesus Christ is the same y, today, and forever.

YESTERNIGHT [KJV] See (LAST) NIGHT

YET (283)

Ge 20:4 But Abimelech had not slept with her y, so he said,
21:7 Y I have given Abraham a son in his old age!"
30:24 "May the LORD give me y another son."
32:30 seen God face to face, y my life has been spared."
Ex 9:32 because they had not y sprouted from the ground.
9:34 and his officials sinned y again by stubbornly
14:17 Y I will harden the hearts of the Egyptians,
21:29 in the past, y the bull was not kept under control,
21:36 y its owner failed to keep it under control,
Lev 21:23 Y because of his physical defect, he must never go
Nu 9:13 y still refuse to celebrate the Passover at the
11:21 and y you promise them meat for a whole month!
23:27 "Come, I will take you to y another place.
29:12 you must call y another holy assembly of all the
Dt 4:34 Y that is what the LORD your God did for you in
5:24 have seen God speaking to humans, and y we live!
5:26 living God from the heart of the fire and y survive?
10:15 Y the LORD chose your ancestors as the objects
20:5 just built a new house but not y dedicated it?
20:6 planted a vineyard but not y eaten any of its fruit?
29:5 y your clothes and sandals did not wear out.
34:7 y his eyesight was clear, and he was as strong as
Jos 13:4 In the north, this area has not y been conquered:
18:2 But there remained seven tribes who had not y
22:17 We are not y fully cleansed of it, even after the
22:18 And y today you are turning away from following
23:4 all the land of the nations y unconquered,
23:9 for you, and no one has y been able to defeat you.
Jdg 2:17 Y Israel did not listen to the judges but prostituted
5:8 city gates. / Y not a shield or spear could be seen
8:6 "You haven't caught Zebah and Zalmunna y.
8:15 'You haven't caught Zebah and Zalmunna y.
10:13 Y you have abandoned me and served other gods.
16:7 seven new bowstrings that have not y been dried,
18:1 for they had not y driven out the people who lived
1Sa 3:3 The lamp of God had not y gone out, and Samuel
3:7 Samuel did not y know the LORD because he had
2Sa 19:5 Y you act like this, making us feel ashamed,
19:12 Y you are my relatives, my own tribe, my own
1Ki 3:2 the name of the LORD had not y been built.
11:2 Y Solomon insisted on loving them anyway.
18:12 Y I have been a true servant of the LORD all my
19:18 Y I will preserve seven thousand others in Israel
2Ki 12:3 Y even so, he did not destroy the pagan shrines,
1Ch 16:21 Y he did not let anyone oppress them. / He warned
28:4 "Y the LORD, the God of Israel, has chosen me
2Ch 13:6 Y Jeroboam son of Nebat, who was a mere servant
30:3 and the people had not y assembled at Jerusalem.
32:15 no god of any nation has ever y been able to rescue
Ezr 5:16 on it ever since, though it is not y completed.'
Ne 2:16 for I had not y said anything to anyone about my
2:16 I had not y spoken to the religious and political
5:5 Y we must sell our children into slavery just to get
5:18 Y I refused to claim the governor's food allowance
6:1 though we had not y hung the doors in the gates—
9:28 Y whenever your people cried to you again for
9:38 "Y in spite of all this, we are making a solemn
Job 8:21 He will y fill your mouth with laughter and your

9:11 Y when he comes near, I cannot see him. When he
10:8 you made me, and y you completely destroy me.
10:13 "'Y your real motive—I know this was your
12:4 Y my friends laugh at me. I am a man who calls on
12:4 I am a just and blameless man, y they laugh at me.
15:2 a wise man, and y you give us all this foolish talk.
16:17 Y I am innocent, and my prayer is pure.
19:26 body has decayed, y in my body I will see God!
20:7 y he will perish forever, thrown away like his own
21:17 "Y the wicked get away with it time and time
24:12 for help, y God does not respond to their moaning.
27:12 y you are saying all these useless things to me.
35:3 Y you also ask, 'What's the use of living a
35:10 Y they don't ask, 'Where is God my Creator,
36:5 "God is mighty, y he does not despise anyone!
37:23 y he is so just and merciful that he does not
Ps 10:5 Y they succeed in everything they do. / They do
19:4 y their message has gone out to all the earth,
22:3 Y you are holy. / The praises of Israel surround
22:9 Y you brought me safely from my mother's womb
22:31 His righteous acts will be told to those y unborn.
27:13 Y I am confident that I will see the LORD's
35:13 Y when they were ill, / I grieved for them. / I even
37:25 I am old. / Y I have never seen the godly forsaken,
44:19 Y you have crushed us in the desert. / You have
49:7 Y they cannot redeem themselves from death
73:23 Y I still belong to you; / you are holding my right
78:6 might know them— / even the children not y born
78:17 Y they kept on with their sin, / rebelling against the
78:30 had craved, / while the meat was y in their mouths,
78:38 Y he was merciful and forgave their sins
78:56 Y though he did all this for them, / they continued
102:18 so that a nation y to be created will praise the
105:14 Y he did not let anyone oppress them. / He warned
106:13 Y how quickly they forgot what he had done!
119:157 y I have not swerved from your decrees.
Pr 28:21 y some will do wrong for something as small as a
Ecc 2:14 Y I saw that wise and foolish people share the
2:19 And y they will control everything I have gained
4:7 I observed y another example of meaninglessness
4:8 y who works hard to gain as much wealth as he
6:5 Y he would have had more peace than he has in
SS 6:11 to see whether the grapevines were budding y,
Isa 6:5 Y I have seen the King, the LORD Almighty!"
10:18 is like a glorious forest, y it will be destroyed.
26:19 Y we have this assurance: / Those who belong to
27:12 Y the time will come when the LORD will gather
28:13 Y they will stumble over this simple,
29:2 Y I will bring disaster upon you, and there will be
44:20 Y he cannot bring himself to ask, "Is this thing,
48:6 mentioned before, secrets you have not y heard.
48:9 Y for my own sake and for the honor of my name,
48:20 Y even now, be free from your captivity!
49:4 Y I leave it all in the LORD's hand; I will trust
49:14 Y Jerusalem says, "The LORD has deserted us;
51:13 Y you have forgotten the LORD, your Creator,
53:4 Y it was our weaknesses he carried; it was our
53:6 Y the LORD laid on him the guilt and sins of us
53:7 and treated harshly, y he never said a word.
53:10 Y when his life is made an offering for sin, he will
58:2 Y they act so pious! They come to the Temple
64:7 Y no one calls on your name or pleads with you for
64:8 And y, LORD, you are our Father. We are the
65:5 Y they say to each other, 'Don't come too close
Jer 2:11 Y my people have exchanged their glorious God
2:32 Y for years on end my people have forgotten me.
2:35 And y you say, 'I haven't done anything wrong.
3:1 Y I am still calling you to come back to me.
3:4 Y you say to me, 'Father, you have been my guide
4:10 Y the sword is even now poised to strike them
5:18 "Y even in those days I will not blot you out
5:31 And worse y, my people like it that way!
8:20 is gone," the people cry, "y we are not saved!"
12:4 Y the people say, "The LORD won't do
15:9 for breath; her sun has gone down while it is y day.
15:10 who refuses to pay—y they all curse me."
20:14 Y I curse the day I was born! May the day of my
23:21 sent these prophets, y they claim to speak for me.
23:21 I have given them no message, y they prophesy.
30:7 my people Israel. Y in the end, they will be saved!
32:25 And y, O Sovereign LORD, you have told me to
33:10 Y in the streets of Jerusalem and Judah's
36:7 Perhaps even y they will turn from their evil ways
37:4 Jeremiah had not y been imprisoned, so he could
51:8 give her medicine. Perhaps she can y be healed.
La 3:21 Y I still dare to hope when I remember this:
4:13 Y it happened because of the sins of her prophets
Eze 12:3 for perhaps they will even y consider what this
13:6 And y they expect him to fulfill their prophecies!
14:22 Y there will be survivors, and they will come here
16:60 Y I will keep the covenant I made with you when
18:25 "Y you say, 'The Lord isn't being just!' Listen to
18:29 And y the people of Israel keep saying, 'The Lord
23:11 "Y even though Oholibah saw what had happened
24:16 Y you must not show any sorrow. Do not weep;
29:18 Y Nebuchadnezzar and his army won no plunder
33:24 and y he gained possession of the entire land!
34:6 of the earth, y no one has gone to search for them.
Da 2:39 that kingdom has fallen, y a third great kingdom,
5:22 knew all this, y you have not humbled yourself.
8:26 a long time, so do not tell anyone about them y."
10:14 for this vision concerns a time y to come."
Hos 1:10 Y the time will come when Israel will prosper
7:10 y he doesn't return to the LORD his God or even
7:15 made them strong, y now they plot evil against me.
9:8 y traps are laid in front of him wherever he goes.
Joel 2:14 Perhaps even y he will give you a reprieve,

3:21 my people's crimes, which I have not y pardoned;
Am 2:9 "Y think of all I did for my people! I destroyed the
5:15 Perhaps even y the LORD God Almighty will
9:8 Y I have promised that I will never completely
9:9 sifted in a sieve, y not one true kernel will be lost.
Jnh 3:9 Perhaps even y God will have pity on us and hold
Mic 2:8 Y to this very hour my people rise against me!
3:11 Y all of you claim you are depending on the
5:2 Y a ruler of Israel will come from you, one whose
Na 3:7 Y no one anywhere will regret your destruction."
3:10 Y Thebes fell, and her people were led away as
Hab 3:18 y I will rejoice in the LORD! I will be joyful in
Zep 2:3 Perhaps even y the LORD will protect you from
Hag 1:2 'The time has not y come to rebuild the LORD's
2:17 Y, even so, you refused to return to me,
Zec 2:4 with all their livestock—and y they will be safe.
9:9 He is righteous and victorious, y he is humble,
9:12 of safety, all you prisoners, for there is y hope!
14:7 y there will be continuous day! Only the LORD
Mal 1:2 your ancestor Jacob. Y Esau was Jacob's brother,
2:12 and y brings an offering to the LORD Almighty.
3:8 Y you have cheated me! "But you ask, 'What do
Mt 6:29 y Solomon in all his glory was not dressed as
11:11 Y even the most insignificant person in the
20:12 and y you've paid them just as much as you paid
26:39 away from me. Y I want your will, not mine."
Mk 8:21 "Don't you understand even y?" he asked them.
14:36 away from me. Y I want your will, not mine."
Lk 4:26 Y Elijah was not sent to any of them. He was sent
5:15 Y despite Jesus' instructions, the report of his
7:28 Y even the most insignificant person in the
12:6 Y God does not forget a single one of them.
12:10 Y those who speak against the Son of Man may be
12:27 y Solomon in all his glory was not dressed as
15:30 Y when this son of yours comes back after
22:25 and y they are called 'friends of the people.'
22:42 away from me. Y I want your will, not mine."
Jn 2:4 Jesus asked. "My time has not y come."
3:10 and y you don't understand these things?
3:11 and have seen, and y you won't believe us.
5:40 Y you refuse to come to me so that I can give you
5:45 "Y it is not I who will accuse you of this before
7:8 I am not y ready to go to this festival, because my time has not y come."
7:30 a hand on him, because his time had not y come.
7:39 But the Spirit had not y been given, because Jesus had not y entered into his glory.)
8:20 was not arrested, because his time had not y come.
8:37 And y some of you are trying to kill me
9:30 and y you don't know anything about him!
14:9 "Philip, don't you even y know who I am,
15:24 they saw all that I did and y hated both of us—
16:32 Y I am not alone because the Father is with me.
20:17 Jesus said, "for I haven't y ascended to the Father.
21:11 were 153 large fish, and y the net hadn't torn.
Ac 2:8 and y we hear them speaking the languages of the
2:34 himself never ascended into heaven, y he said,
7:5 and his descendants—though he had no children y.
8:16 The Holy Spirit had not y come upon any of them,
20:20 Y I never shrank from telling you the truth,
26:7 Y, O king, they say it is wrong for me to have this
Ro 1:32 y they go right ahead and do them anyway.
1:32 And, worse y, they encourage others to do them,
3:8 y some slander me by saying this is what I preach!
3:24 Y now God in his gracious kindness declares us
5:13 was no law to break, since it had not y been given,
5:14 between Adam and Christ, who was y to come!
8:18 Y what we suffer now is nothing compared to the
8:25 if we look forward to something we don't have y,
10:17 Y faith comes from listening to this message of
11:28 Y the Jews are still his chosen people because of
15:11 And y again, / "Praise the Lord, all you Gentiles;
1Co 2:6 Y when I am among mature Christians, I do speak
3:8 Y they will be rewarded individually, according to
4:13 Y we are treated like the world's garbage,
5:6 and y you let this sort of thing go on.
5:11 claims to be a Christian y indulges in sexual sin,
7:25 about the young women who are not y married.
9:12 to be supported? Y we have never used this right.
9:15 Y I have never used any of these rights. And I am
9:19 y I have become a servant of everyone so that I can
10:5 Y after all this, God was not pleased with most of
15:10 y it was not I but God who was working through
2Co 1:17 I changed my plan. Hadn't I made up my mind y?
2:13 because my dear brother Titus hadn't y arrived
3:7 y it began with such glory that the people of Israel
4:17 Y they produce for us an immeasurably great glory
4:18 we look forward to what we have not y seen.
6:10 We own nothing, and y we have everything.
8:9 he was very rich, y for your sakes he became poor,
11:9 I have never y asked you for any support, and I
Gal 2:16 And y we Jewish Christians know that we become
Php 1:22 Y if I live, that means fruitful service for Christ.
3:4 Y I could have confidence in myself if anyone
Col 1:22 y now he has brought you back as his friends.
2:13 because your sinful nature was not y cut away.
1Th 2:2 Y our God gave us the courage to declare his Good
2Th 3:11 Y we hear that some of you are living idle lives,
1Ti 6:6 Y true religion with contentment is great wealth.
Heb 2:8 left out. But we have not y seen all of this happen.
4:15 all of the same temptations we do, y he did not sin.
7:10 For although Levi wasn't born y, the seed from
11:1 It is the evidence of things we cannot y see.
11:39 y none of them received all that God had promised.
12:4 you have not y given your lives in your struggle
13:14 forward to our city in heaven, which is y to come.
Jas 2:6 And y, you insult the poor man! Isn't it the rich

4: 2 And y the reason you don't have what you want is
5: 17 and y when he prayed earnestly that no rain would
1Jn 2: 8 Y it is also new. This commandment is true in
Jude 1: 8 Y these false teachers, who claim authority from
Rev 2: 13 is located, and y you have remained loyal to me.
2: 14 And y I have a few complaints against you.
3: 4 "Y even in Sardis there are some who have not
3: 8 y you obeyed my word and did not deny me.
17: 8 And y he will soon come up out of the bottomless
17: 10 the sixth now reigns, and the seventh is y to come,
17: 12 His ten horns are ten kings who have not y risen to

YIELD (15) [YIELDED, YIELDS]

Ge 4: 12 No longer will it y abundant crops for you,
Lev 19: 25 In this way, its y will be increased. I, the LORD,
25: 19 Then the land will y bumper crops, and you will
26: 4 The land will then y its crops, and the trees will
26: 20 for your land will y no crops, and your trees will
Ps 67: 6 Then the earth will y its harvests, / and God,
72: 3 May the mountains y prosperity for all, / and may
85: 12 his blessings. / Our land will y its bountiful crops.
Isa 5: 7 He expected them to y a crop of justice,
5: 10 Ten measures of seed will y only one measure of
Jer 48: 33 gone from fruitful Moab. The presses y no wine.
Eze 34: 27 and fields of my people will y bumper crops,
Mt 6: 13 And don't let us y to temptation, / but deliver us
Lk 11: 4 against us. / And don't let us y to temptation."
Jas 3: 17 gentle at all times, and willing to y to others.

YIELDED (2) [YIELD]

Dt 10: 10 And once again the LORD y to my pleas
1Sa 28: 23 so he finally y and got up from the ground and sat

YIELDS (3) [YIELD]

Ge 27: 39 to him, "You will live off the land and what it y,
Pr 14: 24 crown for the wise; the effort of fools y only folly.
30: 33 As the beating of cream y butter, and a blow to the

YIRON (1)

Jos 19: 38 Y, Migdal-el, Horem, Beth-anath,

YOGURT (1)

Jdg 5: 25 In a bowl fit for kings, / she brought him y.

YOKE (21) [YOKED, YOKES]

Lev 26: 13 I have lifted the y of slavery from your neck
Isa 10: 27 He will break the y of slavery and lift it from their
Jer 2: 20 Long ago I broke your y and tore away the chains
27: 2 The LORD said to me, "Make a y, and fasten it
27: 8 and serve him; put your neck under Babylon's y!
28: 2 I will remove the y of the king of Babylon from
28: 4 I will surely break the y that the king of Babylon
28: 10 Then Hananiah the prophet took the y off
28: 11 y of oppression from all the nations now subject to
28: 13 You have broken a wooden y, but you have
replaced it with a y of iron.
28: 14 I have put a y of iron on the necks of all these
30: 8 I will break the y from their necks and snap their
31: 18 I was like a calf that needed to be trained for the y
La 1: 14 "He wove my sins into ropes to hitch me to a y of
3: 27 And it is good for the young to submit to the y of
Hos 10: 11 Now I will put a heavy y on her tender neck.
11: 4 I lifted the y from his neck, and I myself stooped to
Mt 11: 29 Take my y upon you. Let me teach you, because I
11: 30 For my y fits perfectly, and the burden I give you
Ac 15: 10 y that neither we nor our ancestors were able to

YOKED (3) [YOKE]

Nu 19: 2 no physical defects and has never been y to a plow.
Dt 21: 3 cow that has never been trained or y to a plow.
1Sa 6: 7 Make sure the cows have never been y to a cart.

YOKES (1) [YOKE]

2Sa 24: 22 and ox y for wood to build a fire on the altar.

YONDER [KJV] See BEYOND, FAR (AND WIDE), THERE

YOU (14828) [YOU'D, YOU'LL, YOU'RE, YOU'VE, YOUR, YOURS, YOURSELF, YOURSELVES] See Index of Articles, Etc.

YOU'D (1) [WOULD, YOU] See Index of Articles, Etc.

YOU'LL (8) [BE, YOU] See Index of Articles, Etc.

YOU'RE (19) [BE, YOU] See Index of Articles, Etc.

YOU'VE (11) [HAVE, YOU] See Index of Articles, Etc.

YOUNG (400) [YOUNGER, YOUNGEST, YOUNGSTER'S, YOUTH, YOUTHFUL, YOUTHS]

YOUNG MAN (31) Ge 39:6; Ex 33:11; Nu 11:27; Jdg 8:14; 9:54; 1Sa 14:1,52; 16:18; 30:15; 2Sa 1:6,13; 14:21; 18:32; 1Ki 11:28; Job 20:11; Ps 127:4; Pr 7:7; Ecc 11:9; Isa 62:5; Zec 2:4; Mt 19:20,22; Mk 14:51; 16:5; Lk 7:14; Ac 7:58; 20:9,12; 23:17,18,22

YOUNG MEN (68) Ge 14:24; 19:14; 22:5,19; 34:9; Ex 24:5; Dt 32:25; Jos 6:23; Jdg 14:11,17; Ru 2:9,15; 1Sa 2:17; 21:4; 25:5,9,27; 26:22; 30:17; 2Sa 4:12; 16:2; 1Ki 12:8,10; 2Ki 4:39; 8:12; 2Ch 10:8,10; 36:17; Job 30:1; Ps 78:31,63; 148:12; Isa 9:17; 34:7; 40:30; 59:10; Jer 6:11; 9:21; 11:22; 15:8; 18:21; 49:26; 50:30; 51:22; La 5:13,14; Eze 23:6,12,44; 30:17; Da 1:3,4,4,6,13,15,17,18,20; Joel 2:28; Am 4:10; 8:13; Zec 9:17; Ac 2:17; 5:6,9,10; Tit 2:6

YOUNG WOMAN (25) Ge 21:21; 24:5,7,15,28,38,39,43; 26:34; 38:6; 41:45; Nu 30:3,6; Dt 22:23,26,28,29; Ru 2:6; 4:12; Est 2:4,12; Job 31:1; SS 6:13; Jer 2:32; 1Co 7:28

YOUNG WOMEN (21) Ge 24:13; 34:1; 36:2; Dt 32:25; Jdg 12:9; 1Sa 2:22; 9:11; Est 2:3,8,17,19; Ps 68:25; 78:63; SS 1:3; 3:10,11; 6:9; Jer 31:13; La 1:4; 2:10; 1Co 7:25

Ge 11: 28 But while Haran was still y, he died in Ur of the
14: 24 All I'll accept is what these y men of mine have
15: 9 three-year-old ram, a turtledove, and a y pigeon."
19: 4 all the men of Sodom, y and old, came from all
19: 14 But the y men thought he was only joking.
21: 21 a marriage for him with a y woman from Egypt.
22: 5 here with the donkey," Abraham told the y men.
22: 19 Then they returned to Abraham's y men
24: 5 "But suppose I can't find a y woman who will
24: 7 and he will see to it that you find a y woman there
24: 13 and the y women of the village are coming out to
24: 15 a y woman named Rebekah arrived with a water
24: 28 The y woman ran home to tell her family about all
24: 38 I was told to bring back a y woman from here to
24: 39 " 'But suppose I can't find a y woman willing to
24: 43 I will say to some y woman who comes to draw
26: 34 of forty, Esau married a y woman named Judith,
27: 9 Go out to the flocks and bring me two fine y goats.
27: 16 a pair of gloves from the hairy skin of the y goats,
32: 15 thirty female camels with their y, forty cows,
33: 13 my lord, that some of the children are very y,
33: 13 and the flocks and herds have their y, too.
34: 1 went to visit some of the y women who lived in the
34: 9 and we will give our daughters as wives for your y
36: 2 Esau married two y women from Canaan: Adah,
38: 6 Judah arranged his marriage to a y woman named
38: 17 "I'll send you a y goat from my flock,"
38: 20 Hirah the Adullamite to take the y goat back to her
39: 6 Joseph was a very handsome and well-built y man.
41: 12 We told the dreams to a y Hebrew man who was a
41: 45 a y woman named Asenath, the daughter of
49: 9 Judah is a y lion / that has finished eating its prey.
Ex 10: 9 "Y and old, all of us will go," Moses replied.
12: 3 must choose a lamb or a y goat for a sacrifice.
23: 19 "You must not cook a y goat in its mother's milk.
24: 5 Then he sent some of the y men to sacrifice y
29: 1 Take a y bull and two rams with no physical
29: 3 along with the y bull and the two rams.
29: 10 "Then bring the y bull to the entrance of the
29: 36 Each day you must sacrifice a y bull as an offering
33: 11 but the y man who assisted him, Joshua son of
34: 26 "You must not cook a y goat in its mother's
Lev 1: 14 choose either a turtledove or a y pigeon.
4: 3 he must bring to the LORD a y bull with no
4: 14 the leaders of the community must bring a y bull
5: 7 they must bring to the LORD two y turtledoves or
two y pigeons as the penalty for their sin.
5: 11 "If any of the people cannot afford to bring y
9: 2 "Take a y bull for a sin offering and a ram for a
12: 6 and a y pigeon or turtledove for a purification
12: 8 she must bring two turtledoves or two y pigeons.
14: 22 must also bring two turtledoves or two y pigeons,
14: 30 will offer the two turtledoves or the two y pigeons,
15: 14 day he must bring two turtledoves or two y pigeons
15: 29 she must bring two turtledoves or two y pigeons
16: 3 He must first bring a y bull for a sin offering
16: 11 "Then Aaron will present the y bull as a sin
Nu 6: 10 or two y pigeons to the priest at the entrance of the
7: 15 He brought a y bull, a ram, and a one-year-old
7: 21 He brought a y bull, a ram, and a one-year-old
7: 27 He brought a y bull, a ram, and a one-year-old
7: 33 He brought a y bull, a ram, and a one-year-old
7: 39 He brought a y bull, a ram, and a one-year-old
7: 45 He brought a y bull, a ram, and a one-year-old
7: 51 He brought a y bull, a ram, and a one-year-old
7: 57 He brought a y bull, a ram, and a one-year-old
7: 63 He brought a y bull, a ram, and a one-year-old
7: 69 He brought a y bull, a ram, and a one-year-old
7: 75 He brought a y bull, a ram, and a one-year-old
7: 81 He brought a y bull, a ram, and a one-year-old
7: 88 Twenty-four y bulls, sixty rams, sixty male goats,
8: 8 Have them bring a y bull and a grain offering of
8: 8 along with a second y bull for a sin offering.
8: 12 will lay their hands on the heads of the y bulls
11: 27 A y man ran and reported to Moses, "Eldad
15: 8 "When you present a y bull as a burnt offering
15: 11 each sacrificial bull, ram, lamb, or y goat.
15: 24 the whole community must present a y bull for a
23: 1 and prepare seven y bulls and seven rams for a
23: 2 and the two of them sacrificed a y bull and a ram
23: 4 and have sacrificed a y bull and a ram on each
23: 14 and offered a y bull and a ram on each altar.
23: 29 me seven altars and prepare me seven y bulls
23: 30 and offered a y bull and a ram on each altar.
28: 11 extra burnt offering to the LORD of two y bulls,
28: 19 as a burnt offering to the LORD two y bulls,
28: 27 It will consist of two y bulls, one ram, and seven
29: 2 It will consist of one y bull, one ram, and seven
29: 8 It will consist of one y bull, one ram, and seven
29: 13 It will consist of thirteen y bulls, two rams,
29: 17 sacrifice twelve y bulls, two rams, and fourteen
29: 20 of the festival, sacrifice eleven y bulls, two rams,
29: 23 day of the festival, sacrifice ten y bulls, two rams,
29: 26 day of the festival, sacrifice nine y bulls, two rams,
29: 29 of the festival, sacrifice eight y bulls, two rams,
29: 32 of the festival, sacrifice seven y bulls, two rams,
29: 36 It will consist of one y bull, one ram, and seven
30: 3 "If a y woman makes a vow to the LORD or a
30: 6 "Now suppose a y woman takes a vow or makes
30: 16 a father and a y daughter who still lives at home.
31: 18 Only the y girls who are virgins may live; you may
31: 35 and 32,000 y girls.
31: 40 16,000 y girls, of whom 32 were the LORD's
31: 46 and 16,000 y girls.
Dt 7: 4 They will lead your y people away from me to
7: 14 will be childless, and all your livestock will bear y.
14: 21 "Do not boil a y goat in its mother's milk.
21: 3 Then the leaders of that town must select a y cow
21: 6 hands over the y cow whose neck was broken.
22: 6 nest on the ground or in a tree and there are y ones
22: 6 in the nest, do not take the mother with the y.
22: 7 You may take the y, but let the mother go, so you
22: 23 "Suppose a man meets a y woman, a virgin who is
22: 26 Do nothing to the y woman; she has committed no
22: 28 "If a man is caught in the act of raping a y woman
22: 29 Then he must marry the y woman because he
28: 50 shows no respect for the old and no pity for the y.
32: 2 on tender grass, / like gentle showers on y plants.
32: 11 that rouses her chicks / and hovers over her y,
32: 25 both y men and y women, / both infants
33: 17 Joseph has the strength and majesty of a y bull;
Jos 6: 21 and women, y and old, cattle, sheep, donkeys—
6: 23 The y men went in and brought out Rahab,
Jdg 6: 19 He cooked a y goat, and with half a bushel of flour
8: 14 There he captured a y man from Succoth
9: 54 He said to his y armor bearer, "Draw your sword
9: 54 So the y man stabbed him with his sword, and he
11: 40 for y Israelite women to go away for four days
12: 9 and brought in thirty y women from outside his
13: 15 "Please stay here until we can prepare a y goat for
13: 19 Then Manoah took a y goat and a grain offering
14: 2 "I want to marry a y Philistine woman I saw in
14: 5 a y lion attacked Samson near the vineyards of
14: 6 He did it as easily as if it were a y goat. But he
14: 11 Thirty y men from the town were invited to be his
14: 17 Then she gave the answer to the y men.
15: 1 Samson took a y goat as a present to his wife.
17: 7 One day a y Levite from Bethlehem in Judah
18: 3 Noticing the y Levite's accent, they took him aside
18: 15 where the y Levite lived, and greeted him kindly.
18: 20 The y priest was quite happy to go with them,
21: 12 hundred y virgins who had never slept with a man,
Ru 1: 22 her daughter-in-law Ruth, the y Moabite woman.
2: 6 "She is the y woman from Moab who came back
2: 9 I have warned the y men not to bother you.
2: 15 went back to work again, Boaz ordered his y men,
4: 12 y woman who will be like those of our ancestor
1Sa 2: 17 So the sin of these y men was very serious in the
2: 22 that his sons were seducing the y women who
2: 26 Meanwhile, as y Samuel grew taller, he also
5: 9 y and old, with a plague of tumors, and there was a
7: 9 So Samuel took a y lamb and offered it to the
9: 11 they met some y women coming out to draw water.
10: 3 One will be bringing three y goats, another will
14: 1 One day Jonathan said to the y man who carried
14: 52 So whenever Saul saw a y man who was brave
16: 18 He is also a fine-looking y man, and the LORD is
16: 20 along with a y goat and a donkey loaded down
20: 35 and took a y boy with him to gather his arrows.
21: 4 which I guess you can have if your y men have not
25: 5 he sent ten of his y men to Carmel. He told them to
25: 9 David's y men gave this message to Nabal
25: 27 is a present I have brought to you and your y men.
26: 22 "Let one of your y men come over and get it.
30: 15 The y man replied, "If you swear by God's name
30: 17 except four hundred y men who fled on camels.
2Sa 1: 6 The y man answered, "I happened to be on Mount
1: 13 Then David said to the y man who had brought the
4: 12 So David ordered his y men to kill them, and they
9: 12 Mephibosheth had a y son named Mica. And from
14: 21 go and bring back the y man Absalom."
16: 2 and summer fruit are for the y men to eat.
18: 5 "For my sake, deal gently with y Absalom."
18: 12 'For my sake, please don't harm y Absalom.'
18: 15 Ten of Joab's y armor bearers then surrounded
18: 29 "What about y Absalom?" the king demanded.
18: 32 "What about y Absalom?" the king demanded.
18: 32 both now and in the future, be as that y man is!"
20: 11 One of Joab's y officers shouted to Amasa's
1Ki 1: 2 "We will find a y virgin who will wait on you
11: 28 Jeroboam was a very capable y man, and when
12: 8 and instead asked the opinion of the y men who
12: 10 The y men replied, "This is what you should tell
18: 38 down from heaven and burned up the y bull,
2Ki 3: 21 mobilized every man who could fight, y and old,
4: 39 One of the y men went out into the field to gather
5: 2 and among their captives was a y girl who had
5: 4 So Naaman told the king what the y girl from
5: 14 And his flesh became as healthy as a y child's,
5: 22 "but my master has sent me to tell you that two y
8: 12 kill their y men, dash their children to the ground,
9: 4 So the y prophet did as he was told and went to
9: 6 Then the y prophet poured the oil over Jehu's head
9: 10 Then the y prophet opened the door and ran.

1Ch 12:28 This also included Zadok, a y warrior,
22: 5 "My son Solomon is still y and inexperienced,
25: 8 without regard to whether they were y or old,
29: 1 the next king of Israel, is still y and inexperienced.
2Ch 10: 8 and instead asked the opinion of the y men who
10:10 The y men replied, "This is what you should tell
13: 7 defying Solomon's son Rehoboam when he was y
13: 9 Whoever comes to be dedicated with a y bull
15:13 be put to death—whether y or old, man or woman.
23: 3 they made a covenant with Joash, the y king.
31:15 dividing the gifts fairly among y and old alike.
34: 3 the eighth year of his reign, while he was still y,
35: 7 and y goats for the people's Passover offerings,
35: 8 the priests twenty-six hundred lambs and y goats
35: 9 gave five thousand lambs and y goats and five
36:17 The Babylonians killed Judah's y men,
36:17 killing both y and old, men and women, healthy
Ezr 6: 9 whatever is needed in the way of y bulls,
6:17 one hundred y bulls, two hundred rams, and four
Est 2: 2 "Let us search the empire to find beautiful y
2: 3 beautiful y women into the royal harem at Susa.
2: 4 the y woman who pleases you most will be made
2: 7 This man had a beautiful and lovely y cousin,
2: 8 Esther, along with many other y women,
2:12 Before each y woman was taken to the king's bed,
2:17 the king loved her more than any of the other y
2:19 Even after all the y women had been transferred to
3:13 y and old, including women and children—must be
Job 4:10 Though they are fierce y lions, they will all be
19:18 Even y children despise me. When I stand to
20:11 He was just a y man, but his bones will lie in the
29: 8 The y stepped aside when they saw me, and even
30: 1 by y men whose fathers are not worthy to run with
31: 1 my eyes not to look with lust upon a y woman.
32: 6 "I am y and you are old, so I held back and did not
36:14 They die y after wasting their lives in immoral
38:39 prey for a lioness and satisfy the y lions' appetites
38:41 Who provides food for the ravens when their y cry
39: 2 you know how many months they carry their y?
39: 3 They crouch down to give birth to their y
39: 4 Their y grow up in the open fields, then leave their
39:16 She is harsh toward her y, as if they were not her
42: 8 Now take seven y bulls and seven rams and go to
Ps 17:12 like y lions in hiding, waiting for their chance.
29: 6 a calf / and Mount Hermon to leap like a y bull.
34:10 Even strong y lions sometimes go hungry,
37:25 Once I was y, and now I am old. / Yet I have never
55:23 pit of destruction. / Murderers and liars will die y,
58: 9 God will sweep them away, both y and old,
68:25 with them are y women playing tambourines.
78:31 he struck down the finest of Israel's y men.
78:63 Their y men were killed by fire; / their y women died before singing their wedding
84: 3 and raises her y— / at a place near your altar,
89: 1 Y and old will hear of your faithfulness.
102:24 don't take my life while I am still so y!
104:21 Then the y lions roar for their food, / but they are
119: 9 How can a y person stay pure? / By obeying your
127: 4 Children born to a y man / are like sharp arrows in
128: 3 as vigorous and healthy as y olive trees.
147: 9 and the y ravens cry to him for food.
148:12 y men and maidens, / old men and children.
Pr 1: 4 They will give knowledge and purpose to y people.
7: 7 and saw a simpleminded y man who lacked
13: 1 a parent's discipline; a y mocker refuses to listen.
20:29 The glory of the y is their strength; the gray hair of
28: 7 Y people who obey the law are wise; those who
Ecc 7:15 including the fact that some good people die y
11: 9 Y man, it's wonderful to be y! Enjoy every
12: 6 remember your Creator now while you are y,
SS 1: 3 your name! No wonder all the y women love you!
1: 8 the shepherds' tents, and there feed your y goats.
2: 9 My lover is like a swift gazelle or a y deer. Look,
2:17 a gazelle or a y stag on the rugged mountains."
3:10 Its interior was a gift of love from the y women of
3:11 upon King Solomon, O y women of Jerusalem.
6: 9 The y women are delighted when they see her;
6:13 do you gaze so intently at this y woman of Shulam,
8: 8 "We have a little sister too y for breasts. What will
8:14 or a y deer on the mountains of spices."
Isa 3: 5 Y people will revolt against authority,
9:17 That is why the Lord has no joy in the y men
13:18 The attacking armies will shoot down the y people
20: 4 them walk naked and barefoot, both y and old,
31: 4 "When a lion, even a y one, kills a sheep, it pays
31: 8 The strong y Assyrians will be taken away as
34: 7 The strongest will die—veterans and y men, too.
34:15 She will hatch her y and cover them with her
40:11 He will gently lead the mother sheep with their y.
40:30 will become exhausted, and y men will give up.
54: 6 as though you were a y wife abandoned by her
59:10 like corpses when compared to vigorous y men!
61:11 filled with y plants springing up everywhere.
62: 5 O Jerusalem, just as a y man cares for his bride.
65:20 old at one hundred! Only sinners will die that y!
Jer 1: 6 I said, "I can't speak for you! I'm too y!"
2: 2 eager you were to please me as a y bride long ago,
2:32 Does a y woman forget her jewelry? Does a bride
6:11 on gatherings of y men, and on husbands
9:21 and y men no longer gather in the squares.
11:22 Their y men will die in battle, and their little boys
15: 8 bring a destroyer against the mothers of y men.
18:21 in a plague, and let their y men be killed in battle!
31:13 The y women will dance for joy, and the men—old and y—
46:20 Egypt is as sleek as a y cow, but a gadfly from the
49:26 Her y men will fall in the streets and die.
50:30 Her y men will fall in the streets and die.
51: 3 Y and old alike will be completely destroyed.
51:22 old people and children, y men and maidens.
La 1: 4 her priests groan, her y women are crying—
1:15 a great army has come to crush my y warriors.
2:10 The y women of Jerusalem hang their heads in
2:21 y and old, boys and girls, killed by the swords of
3:27 And it is good for the y to submit to the yoke of his
4: 3 Even the jackals feed their y, but not my people
5:11 enemies rape the women and y girls in Jerusalem
5:13 The y men are led away to work at millstones,
5:14 the city gates; the y men no longer dance and sing.
Eze 9: 6 old and y, girls and women and little children.
13:18 the souls of my people, both y and old alike.
16:60 the covenant I made with you when you were y,
19: 2 She lay down among the y lions / and reared her
19: 3 to become a strong y lion. / He learned to catch
23: 3 Even as y girls, they allowed themselves to be
23: 6 They were all attractive y men, captains
23:12 those handsome y men on fine horses,
23:21 you celebrated your former days as a y girl in
23:23 handsome y captains, commanders,
23:44 with all the zest of lustful y men.
30:17 The y men of Heliopolis and Bubastis will die in
31: 6 its shade all the wild animals gave birth to their y.
32: 2 You think of yourself as a strong y lion among the
39:18 were rams, lambs, goats, and fat y bulls of Bashan!
41:19 The other face—that of a y lion—looked toward
43:19 are to be given a y bull for a sin offering,
43:21 Then take the y bull for the sin offering and burn it
43:22 sacrifice as a sin offering a y male goat that has no
43:22 for the altar again, just as you did with the y bull.
43:23 offer another y bull that has no defects and a
43:25 "Every day for seven days a male goat, a y bull,
45:18 sacrifice a y bull with no physical defects to purify
45:22 On the day of Passover the prince will provide a y
45:23 This daily offering will consist of seven y bulls
45:24 and a gallon of olive oil with each y bull and ram.
46: 6 he will bring one y bull, six lambs, and one ram,
46: 7 With the y bull he must bring a half bushel of flour
46:11 will be a half bushel of flour with each y bull,
Da 1: 3 to bring to the palace some of the y men of Judah's
1: 4 healthy, and good-looking y men," he said.
1: 4 Teach these y men the language and literature of
1: 6 and Azariah were four of the y men chosen,
1:13 see how we look compared to the other y men who
1:15 and better nourished than the y men who had been
1:17 God gave these four y men an unusual aptitude for
1:18 the chief official brought all the y men to King
1:20 the king found the advice of these y men to be ten
Hos 2:15 to me there, as she did long ago when she was y,
Joel 2:28 will dream dreams. Your y men will see visions.
3: 3 They traded y boys for prostitutes and little girls
Am 3: 4 Does a y lion growl in its den without first
4:10 I killed your y men in war and slaughtered all your
8:13 and fine y men will grow faint and weary,
Na 2:11 where the old and feeble and the y and tender lived
Zec 2: 4 other angel said, "Hurry, and say to that y man,
9:17 The y men and women will thrive on the
11: 3 Hear the y lions roaring, for their thickets in the
11:16 nor look after the y, nor heal the injured, nor feed
Mal 2:14 each other on your wedding day when you were y.
Mt 8: 6 "Lord, my y servant lies in bed, paralyzed
8:13 And the y servant was healed that same hour.
13:21 But like y plants in such soil, their roots don't go
19:20 all these commandments," the y man replied.
19:22 But when the y man heard this, he went sadly away
Mk 4:17 But like y plants in such soil, their roots don't go
14:51 There was a y man following along behind,
16: 5 and there on the right sat a y man clothed in a
Lk 2:24 "either a pair of turtledoves or two y pigeons."
7:14 the bearers stopped. "Y man," he said, "get up."
8:13 But like y plants in such soil, their roots don't go
15:29 And in all that time you never gave me even one y
Jn 6: 9 "There's a y boy here with five barley loaves
12:14 Jesus found a y donkey and sat on it,
21:18 The truth is, when you were y, you were able to do
Ac 2:17 will prophesy, / your y men will see visions,
5: 6 Then some y men wrapped him in a sheet and took
5: 9 Just outside that door are the y men who buried
5:10 When the y men came in and saw that she was
7:58 and laid them at the feet of a y man named Saul.
16: 1 a y disciple whose mother was a Jewish believer,
20: 9 Paul spoke on and on, a y man named Eutychus,
20:12 Meanwhile, the y man was taken home unhurt,
23:17 and said, "Take this y man to the commander.
23:18 me over and asked me to bring this y man to you
23:22 the commander warned the y man as he sent him
1Co 7:25 about the y women who are not yet married.
7:28 And if a y woman gets married, it is not a sin.
Gal 4: 1 and leaves great wealth for his y children,
1Ti 4:12 let anyone think less of you because you are y.
Tit 2: 6 encourage the y men to live wisely in all they do.
Heb 9:13 and the ashes of a y cow could cleanse people's
1Jn 2:13 I am writing to you who are y because you have
2:14 I have written to you who are y because you are

YOUNGER (33) [YOUNG]

Ge 19:34 The next morning the older daughter said to her y
19:35 and the y daughter went in and slept with him.
19:38 When the y daughter gave birth to a son,
25:23 son will serve the descendants of your y son."
25:33 thereby selling all his rights as the firstborn to his y
29:16 who was the oldest, and her y sister, Rachel.
29:18 give me Rachel, your y daughter, as my wife."
29:26 "It's not our custom to marry off a y daughter
42: 4 Jacob wouldn't let Joseph's y brother, Benjamin,
42:16 If it turns out that you don't have a y brother,
48:14 right hand was on the head of Ephraim, the y boy,
48:19 but his y brother will become even greater.
Dt 21:16 he may not give the larger inheritance to his y son,
Jdg 1:13 Othniel, the son of Caleb's y brother Kenaz,
3: 9 was Othniel, the son of Caleb's y brother, Kenaz.
Ru 3:10 loyalty now than ever by not running after a y man,
2Sa 2:21 "Take on one of the y men and strip him of his
1Ki 12:14 and followed the counsel of his y advisers. He told
1Ch 27:23 he did not count those who were y than twenty
2Ch 10:14 and followed the counsel of his y advisers. He told
Job 30: 1 "But now I am mocked by those who are y than I,
Jer 31:19 I was thoroughly ashamed of all I did in my y
Eze 16:46 Your y sister was Sodom, who lived with her
Mk 15:40 Mary (the mother of James the y and of Joseph),
Lk 15:12 The y son told his father, 'I want my share of your
15:13 "A few days later this y son packed all his
Ro 9:12 son will serve the descendants of your y son."
1Ti 5: 1 Talk to the y men as you would to your own
5: 2 and treat the y women with all purity as your own
5:11 The y widows should not be on the list,
5:14 So I advise these y widows to marry again,
Tit 2: 4 These older women must train the y women to love
1Pe 5: 5 You y men, accept the authority of the elders.

YOUNGEST (22) [YOUNG]

Ge 9:24 he learned what Ham, his y son, had done.
38:11 She was to remain a widow until his y son, Shelah,
42:13 Our y brother is there with our father, and one of
42:15 not leave Egypt unless your y brother comes here.
42:20 But bring your y brother back to me. In this way,
42:32 and the y is with our father in the land of Canaan.'
42:34 But bring your y brother back to me. Then I will
43:29 Joseph asked, "Is this your y brother, the one you
43:33 them in the order of their ages, from oldest to y.
44: 2 Then put my personal silver cup at the top of the y
44:12 brother's sack, going on down the line to the y.
44:20 an old man, and a child of his old age, his y son.
44:23 'You may not see me again unless your y brother
44:26 'We can't unless you let our y brother go with us.
44:26 charge of the grain unless our y brother is with us.'
Jos 6:26 At the cost of his y son, / he will set up its gates."
Jdg 9: 5 But the y brother, Jotham, escaped and hid.
1Sa 16:11 you have?" "There is still the y," Jesse replied.
17:14 David was the y of Jesse's sons. Since David's
1Ki 16:34 it by setting up the gates, his y son, Segub, died.
2Ch 21:17 his wives. Only his y son, Ahaziah, was spared.
22: 1 made Ahaziah, Jehoram's y son, their next king.

YOUNGSTER'S (1) [YOUNG]

Pr 22:15 A y heart is filled with foolishness, but discipline

YOUR (6301) [YOU] See Index of Articles, Etc.

YOURS (84) [YOU] See Index of Articles, Etc.

YOURSELF (178) [SELF, YOU] See Index of Articles, Etc.

YOURSELVES (175) [SELF, YOU] See Index of Articles, Etc.

YOUTH (34) [YOUNG]

Ge 4:23 I have killed a y who attacked and wounded me.
46:34 'We have been livestock breeders from our y,
49: 3 are my oldest son, / the child of my vigorous y.
Nu 11:28 had been Moses' personal assistant since his y,
Ru 4:15 May this child restore your y and care for you in
1Sa 14: 7 "Do what you think is best," the y replied.
Job 13:26 against me and bring up all the sins of my y.
Ps 25: 7 Forgive the rebellious sins of my y; / look instead
78:51 the flower of y throughout the land of Egypt.
88:15 I have been sickly and close to death since my y.
103: 5 good things. / My y is renewed like the eagle's!
129: 1 From my earliest y my enemies have persecuted
129: 2 from my earliest y my enemies have persecuted
144:12 May our sons flourish in their y
Pr 5:18 of blessing for you. Rejoice in the wife of your y.
10: 5 A wise y works hard all summer; a y who sleeps away the hour of opportunity brings
Ecc 4:13 It is better to be a poor but wise y than to be an old
4:14 Such a y could come from prison and succeed.
4:15 Everyone is eager to help such a y, even to help
11:10 So banish grief and pain, but remember that y,
12: 1 Don't let the excitement of y cause you to forget
12: 1 Honor him in your y before you grow old and no
Isa 54: 4 The shame of your y and the sorrows of
Jer 3: 4 you have been my guide since the days of my y.
9:21 our mansions. It has killed off the flower of our y:
48:15 Her most promising y are doomed to slaughter,"
La 2: 4 strength is used against them to kill their finest y.
Eze 16:43 because you have not remembered your y but have
23: 8 She was still as lewd as in her y,
23:19 remembering her y when she was a prostitute in
Na 2:13 The finest of your y will be killed in battle.
Zec 13: 5 been my means of livelihood from my earliest y.'
Mal 2:15 guard yourself; remain loyal to the wife of your y.

YOUTHFUL (2) [YOUNG]

Job 33:25 become as healthy as a child's, firm and y again.
2Ti 2:22 Run from anything that stimulates y lust.

YOUTHS (3) [YOUNG]

SS 2: 3 "And compared to other y, my lover is like the
Isa 40:30 Even y will become exhausted, and young men
Da 1:10 and thin compared to the other y your age,

Z

ZAANAIM [KJV] See ZAANANNIM

ZAANAN (1)

Mic 1:11 The people of Z dare not come outside their walls.

ZAANANNIM (2)

Jos 19:33 Its boundary ran from Heleph, from the oak at Z,
Jdg 4:11 of his tribe and pitched his tent by the Oak of Z,

ZAAVAN (2)

Ge 36:27 The sons of Ezer were Bilhan, Z, and Akan.
1Ch 1:42 The sons of Ezer were Bilhan, Z, and Akan.

ZABAD (7)

1Ch 2:36 the father of Nathan. / Nathan was the father of Z.
2:37 Z was the father of Ephlal. / Ephlal was the father
7:21 Z, and Shuthelah. / Ephraim's sons Ezer and Elead
11:41 Uriah the Hittite; / Z son of Ahlai;
Ezr 10:27 Eliashib, Mattaniah, Jeremoth, Z, and Aziza.
10:33 Mattenai, Mattattah, Z, Eliphelet, Jeremai,
10:43 Jeiel, Mattithiah, Z, Zebina, Jaddai, Joel,

ZABBAI (2)

Ezr 10:28 of Bebai: Jehohanan, Hananiah, Z, and Athlai.
Ne 3:20 Next to him was Baruch son of Z, who repaired an

ZABBUD [KJV] See ZACCUR

ZABDI (3)

1Ch 8:19 Jakim, Zicri, Z,
27:27 Z from Shepham was responsible for the grapes
Ne 11:17 son of Mica, son of Z, a descendant of Asaph,

ZABDIEL (2)

1Ch 27: 2 Jashobeam son of Z was commander of the first
Ne 11:14 Their chief officer was Z son of Haggedolim.

ZABUD (1)

1Ki 4: 5 Z son of Nathan, a priest, was a trusted adviser to

ZABULON [KJV] See ZEBULUN

ZACCAI (2)

Ezr 2: 9 The family of Z | 760
Ne 7:14 The family of Z | 760

ZACCHAEUS (5)

Lk 19: 2 There was a man there named Z. He was one of
19: 5 he looked up at Z and called him by name. "Z!" he said. "Quick, come down!
19: 6 Z quickly climbed down and took Jesus to his
19: 8 Meanwhile, Z stood there and said to the Lord,

ZACCUR (10)

Nu 13: 4 of the leaders: / Reuben | Shammua son of Z
1Ch 4:26 of Mishma were Hammuel, Z, and Shimei.
24:27 the leaders were Beno, Shoham, Z, and Ibri.
25: 2 there were Z, Joseph, Nethaniah, and Asarelah.
25:10 The third lot fell to Z and twelve of his sons
Ezr 8:14 the family of Bigvai: Uthai, Z, and 70 other men.
Ne 3: 2 next to them, and beyond them was Z son of Imri.
10:12 Z, Sherebiah, Shebaniah,
12:35 son of Mattaniah, son of Micaiah, son of Z,
13:13 And I appointed Hanan son of Z and grandson of

ZACHARIAH, ZACHARIAS, ZACHER [KJV] See ZECHARIAH

ZADOK (51) [ZADOK'S]

2Sa 8:17 Z son of Ahitub and Ahimelech son of Abiathar
15:24 Abiathar and Z and the Levites took the Ark of the
15:25 David instructed Z to take the Ark of God back
15:27 Then the king told Z the priest, "Look, here is my
15:29 So Z and Abiathar took the Ark of God back to the
15:35 Z and Abiathar, the priests, are there. Tell them the
17:15 Then Hushai reported to Z and Abiathar,
18:27 "The first man runs like Ahimaaz son of Z,"
19:11 Then King David sent Z and Abiathar, the priests,
20:25 court secretary. Z and Abiathar were the priests.
1Ki 1: 8 and refused to support Adonijah were Z the priest,
1:26 neither were Z the priest, Benaiah son of Jehoiada,
1:32 "Call Z the priest, Nathan the prophet,
1:34 There Z the priest and Nathan the prophet are to
1:38 So Z the priest, Nathan the prophet, Benaiah son of
1:39 There Z the priest took a flask of olive oil from the
1:44 The king sent him down to Gihon Spring with Z
1:45 and Z and Nathan have anointed him as the new
2:35 and he installed Z the priest to take the place of
4: 2 his high officials: / Azariah son of Z was the priest.
4: 4 of the army. / Z and Abiathar were the priests.
2Ki 15:33 His mother was Jerusha, the daughter of Z.
1Ch 6: 8 Ahitub was the father of Z. / Z was the father of Ahimaaz.
6:12 Ahitub was the father of Z. / Z was the father of Shallum.
6:53 Z, and Ahimaaz.
9:11 son of Z, son of Meraioth, son of Ahitub.
12:28 This also included Z, a young warrior,
15:11 Z and Abiathar, and these Levite leaders:
16:39 David stationed Z the priest and his fellow priests
18:16 Z son of Ahitub and Ahimelech son of Abiathar
24: 3 With the help of Z, who was a descendant of
24: 6 Z the priest, Ahimelech son of Abiathar,
24:31 Z, Ahimelech, and the family leaders of the priests
27:17 Hashabiah son of Kemuel / Aaron (the priests) | Z
29:22 as their leader, and they anointed Z as their priest.
2Ch 27: 1 His mother was Jerusha, the daughter of Z.
31:10 the high priest, from the family of Z, replied,
Ezr 7: 2 son of Shallum, son of Z, son of Ahitub,
Ne 3: 4 grandson of Meshezabel, and then Z son of Baana.
3:29 Next Z son of Immer also rebuilt the wall next to
10:21 Meshezabel, Z, Jaddua,
11:11 son of Z, son of Meraioth, son of Ahitub,
13:13 Z the scribe, and Pedaiah, one of the Levites,
Eze 40:46 the descendants of Z—for they alone of all the
43:19 that time, the Levitical priests of the family of Z,
44:15 the Levitical priests of the family of Z continued to
48:11 the descendants of Z who obeyed me and did not
Mt 1:14 Azor was the father of Z. / Z was the father of Akim.

ZADOK'S (1) [ZADOK]

2Sa 18:19 Then Z son Ahimaaz said, "Let me run to the king

ZAHAM (1)

2Ch 11:19 had three sons—Jeush, Shemariah, and Z.

ZAHAR (1)

Eze 27:18 wine from Helbon and white wool from Z.

ZAIR (1)

2Ki 8:21 went with all his chariots to attack the town of Z.

ZALAPH (1)

Ne 3:30 son of Shelemiah and Hanun, the sixth son of Z,

ZALMON (4)

Jdg 9:48 so he led his forces to Mount Z. He took an ax
2Sa 23:28 Z from Ahoah; / Maharai from Netophah;
1Ch 11:29 Sibbecai from Hushah; / Z from Ahoah;
Ps 68:14 like a blowing snowstorm on Mount Z.

ZALMONAH (2)

Nu 33:41 the Israelites left Mount Hor and camped at Z.
33:42 Then they left Z and camped at Punon.

ZALMUNNA (10)

Jdg 8: 5 I am chasing Zebah and Z, the kings of Midian."
8: 6 "You haven't caught Zebah and Z yet.
8: 7 the LORD gives me victory over Zebah and Z,
8:10 and Z were in Karkor with a remnant of 15,000
8:12 Zebah and Z, the two Midianite kings, fled,
8:15 and said to the leaders, "Here are Zebah and Z.
8:15 saying, 'You haven't caught Zebah and Z yet.
8:18 Then Gideon asked Zebah and Z, "The men you
8:21 Then Zebah and Z said to Gideon, "Don't ask a
Ps 83:11 Let all their princes die like Zebah and Z,

ZAMZUMMITES (1)

Dt 2:20 though the Ammonites referred to them as Z.

ZANOAH (5)

Jos 15:34 Z, En-gannim, Tappuah, Enam,
15:56 Jezreel, Jokdeam, Z,
1Ch 4:18 (the father of Soco), and Jekuthiel (the father of Z).
Ne 3:13 The people from Z, led by Hanun,
11:30 Z, and Adullam with their villages. They were also

ZAPHENATH-PANEAH (1)

Ge 41:45 Pharaoh renamed him Z and gave him a wife—

ZAPHON (2)

Jos 13:27 valley were Beth-haram, Beth-nimrah, Succoth, Z,
Jdg 12: 1 Ephraim mobilized its army and crossed over to Z.

ZARA(H) [KJV] See ZERAH

ZAREAH [KJV] See ZORAH

ZAREATHITES [KJV] See ZORATHITES

ZARED [KJV] See ZERED

ZAREPHATH (4)

1Ki 17: 9 "Go and live in the village of Z, near the city of
17:10 So he went to Z. As he arrived at the gates of the
Ob 1:20 and occupy the Phoenician coast as far north as Z.
Lk 4:26 He was sent instead to a widow of Z—a foreigner

ZARETHAN (4)

Jos 3:16 at a town upstream called Adam, which is near Z.
1Ki 4:12 all of Beth-shan near Z below Jezreel,
7:46 in the Jordan Valley between Succoth and Z.
2Ch 4:17 in the Jordan Valley between Succoth and Z.

ZATTU (5)

Ezr 2: 8 The family of Z | 945
8: 5 From the family of Z: Shecaniah son of Jahaziel
10:27 From the family of Z: Elioenai, Eliashib,
Ne 7:13 The family of Z | 845
10:14 signed were Parosh, Pahath-moab, Elam, Z, Bani,

ZAZA (1)

1Ch 2:33 but Jonathan had two sons named Peleth and Z.

ZEAL (5) [ZEALOT, ZEALOUS, ZEALOUSLY]

Nu 25:11 displaying passionate z among them on my behalf.
2Sa 21: 2 but Saul, in his z, had tried to wipe them out.
Pr 19: 2 Z without knowledge is not good; a person who
Ro 10: 2 they have for God, but it is misdirected z.
2Co 7:11 such alarm, such longing to see me, such z,

ZEALOT (4) [ZEAL]

Mt 10: 4 Simon (the Z), / Judas Iscariot (who later betrayed
Mk 3:18 (son of Alphaeus), / Thaddaeus, / Simon (the Z),
Lk 6:15 James (son of Alphaeus), / Simon (the Z),
Ac 1:13 James (son of Alphaeus), / Simon (the Z),

ZEALOUS (3) [ZEAL]

Nu 25:13 because he was z for his God and made atonement
Ac 22: 3 I became very z to honor God in everything I did,
Php 3: 6 And z? Yes, in fact I harshly persecuted the

ZEALOUSLY (2) [ZEAL]

1Ki 19:10 "I have z served the LORD God Almighty.
19:14 "I have z served the LORD God Almighty.

ZEBADIAH (9)

1Ch 8:15 Z, Arad, Eder,
8:17 Z, Meshullam, Hizki, Heber,
12: 7 Joelah and Z, sons of Jeroham from Gedor.
26: 2 Jediael (the second), Z (the third), Jathniel (the
27: 7 in his division. Asahel was succeeded by his son Z.
2Ch 17: 8 Nethaniah, Z, Asahel, Shemiramoth, Jehonathan,
19:11 Z son of Ishmael, a leader from the tribe of Judah,
Ezr 8: 8 of Shephatiah: Z son of Michael and 80 other men.
10:20 From the family of Immer: Hanani and Z.

ZEBAH (10)

Jdg 8: 5 I am chasing Z and Zalmunna, the kings of
8: 6 "You haven't caught Z and Zalmunna yet.
8: 7 "After the LORD gives me victory over Z
8:10 By this time Z and Zalmunna were in Karkor with
8:12 Z and Zalmunna, the two Midianite kings, fled,
8:15 said to the leaders, "Here are Z and Zalmunna.
8:15 saying, 'You haven't caught Z and Zalmunna yet.
8:18 Then Gideon asked Z and Zalmunna, "The men
8:21 Then Z and Zalmunna said to Gideon, "Don't ask
Ps 83:11 Let all their princes die like Z and Zalmunna,

ZEBAIM [KJV] See POKERETH-HAZZEBAIM

ZEBEDEE (8) [ZEBEDEE'S]

Mt 4:21 in a boat with their father, Z, mending their nets.
10: 2 then Andrew (Peter's brother), / James (son of Z),
20:20 Then the mother of James and John, the sons of Z,
Mk 1:20 Z, in the boat with the hired men and went with
3:17 James and John (the sons of Z, but Jesus
10:35 Then James and John, the sons of Z, came over
Lk 5:10 His partners, James and John, the sons of Z,
Jn 21: 2 in Galilee, the sons of Z, and two other disciples.

ZEBEDEE'S (3) [ZEBEDEE]

Mt 26:37 He took Peter and Z two sons, James and John,
27:56 (the mother of James and Joseph), and Z wife,
Mk 1:19 A little farther up the shore Jesus saw Z sons,

ZEBIDAH (1)

2Ki 23:36 His mother was Z, the daughter of Pedaiah from

ZEBINA (1)

Ezr 10:43 Jeiel, Mattithiah, Zabad, Z, Jaddai, Joel,

ZEBOIIM (6)

Ge 10:19 to Sodom, Gomorrah, Admah, and Z, near Lasha.
14: 2 King Shinab of Admah, King Shemeber of Z,
14: 3 The kings of Sodom, Gomorrah, Admah, Z,
14: 8 Gomorrah, Admah, Z, and Bela (now called Zoar)
Dt 29:23 be just like Sodom and Gomorrah, Admah and Z,
Hos 11: 8 you go? How can I destroy you like Admah and Z?

ZEBOIM (2)

1Sa 13:18 border above the valley of **Z** near the wilderness.
Ne 11:34 Hadid, **Z**, Neballat,

ZEBUDAH [KJV] See ZEBIDAH

ZEBUL (6)

Jdg 9:28 the son of Gideon, and **Z** is his administrator.
9:30 But when **Z**, the leader of the city, heard what Gaal
9:36 When Gaal saw them, he said to **Z**, "Look,
9:36 **Z** replied, "It's just the shadows of the hills that
9:38 Then **Z** turned on him triumphantly. "Now where
9:41 and **Z** drove Gaal and his brothers out of Shechem.

ZEBULUN (50) [ZEBULUN'S]

Ge 30:20 She named him **Z**, for she said, "God has given
35:23 oldest son), Simeon, Levi, Judah, Issachar, and **Z**.
46:14 The sons of **Z** were Sered, Elon, and Jahleel.
49:13 "**Z** will settle on the shores of the sea / and will be
Ex 1:3 Issachar, **Z**, Benjamin,
Nu 1:9 **Z** | Eliab son of Helon
1:30[-31] **Z** | 57,400
2:3[-4] **Z** are to camp toward the sunrise on the east
2:7[-8] **Z** | Eliab son of Helon | 57,400
7:24 leader of the tribe of **Z**, presented his offering.
10:16 The tribe of **Z** was led by Eliab son of Helon.
13:10 **Z** | Gaddiel son of Sodi
26:26 were the clans descended from the sons of **Z**:
26:27 The men from all the clans of **Z** numbered 60,500.
34:25 **Z** | Elizaphan son of Parnach
Dt 27:13 And the tribes of Reuben, Gad, Asher, **Z**, Dan,
33:18 Moses said this about the tribes of **Z** and Issachar:
33:18 "May the people of **Z** prosper in their expeditions
Jos 19:10 of land went to the families of the tribe of **Z**.
19:14 The northern boundary of **Z** passed Hannathon
19:16 the inheritance of the families of the tribe of **Z**.
19:27 and ran as far as **Z** in the valley of Iphtah-el,
19:34 and touched the boundary of **Z** in the south,
21:7 cities from the tribes of Reuben, Gad, and **Z**.
21:34 given the following towns from the tribe of **Z**:
Jdg 1:30 The tribe of **Z** also failed to drive out the
4:6 from the tribes of Naphtali and **Z** at Mount Tabor.
4:10 Barak called together the tribes of **Z** and Naphtali,
5:14 from **Z** came those who carry the rod of authority.
5:18 But **Z** risked his life, / as did Naphtali,
6:35 Asher, **Z**, and Naphtali, summoning their warriors,
12:11 After him, Elon from **Z** became Israel's judge.
12:12 When he died, he was buried at Aijalon in **Z**.
1Ch 2:1 were Reuben, Simeon, Levi, Judah, Issachar, **Z**,
6:63 towns from the territories of Reuben, Gad, and **Z**.
6:77 from the territory of **Z** the towns of Jokneam,
12:33 From the tribe of **Z**, there were 50,000 skilled
12:40 **Z**, and Naphtali brought food on donkeys, camels,
27:19 **Z** | Ishmaiah son of Obadiah / Naphtali
2Ch 30:10 and Manasseh and as far as the territory of **Z**.
30:11 and **Z** humbled themselves and went to Jerusalem.
30:18 Issachar, and **Z** had not purified themselves.
Ps 68:27 from Judah / and all the rulers of **Z** and Naphtali.
Isa 9:1 The land of **Z** and Naphtali will soon be humbled,
Eze 48:26 Then comes the territory of **Z**, which also extends
48:27 The territory of Gad is just south of **Z** with the
48:33 will have gates named for Simeon, Issachar, and **Z**.
Mt 4:13 the Sea of Galilee, in the region of **Z** and Naphtali.
4:15 "In the land of **Z** and of Naphtali, / beside the sea,
Rev 7:8 from **Z** | 12,000 / from Joseph | 12,000

ZEBULUN'S (1) [ZEBULUN]

Jos 19:10 The boundary of **Z** inheritance started at Sarid.

ZECHARIAH (63) [ZECHARIAH'S]

2Ki 14:29 of Israel. Then his son **Z** became the next king.
15:8 **Z** son of Jeroboam II began to rule over Israel in
15:9 **Z** did what was evil in the LORD's sight, as his
15:10 Then Shallum son of Jabesh conspired against **Z**,
18:2 His mother was Abijah, the daughter of **Z**.
1Ch 5:7 their genealogy by their clans: Jeiel (the leader), **Z**,
8:31 Gedor, Ahio, **Z**,
9:21 And later **Z** son of Meshelemiah had been
9:37 Gedor, Ahio, **Z**, and Mikloth.
15:18 **Z**, Jaaziel, Shemiramoth, Jehiel, Unni, Eliab,
15:20 **Z**, Aziel, Shemiramoth, Jehiel, Unni, Eliab,
15:24 Joshaphat, Nethanel, Amasai, **Z**, Benaiah,
16:5 His assistants were **Z** (the second), then Jeiel,
24:25 From the descendants of Isshiah, the leader was **Z**.
26:2 The sons of Meshelemiah were **Z** (the oldest),
26:11 Tebaliah (the third), and **Z** (the fourth).
26:14 The north gate was assigned to his son **Z**, a man of
27:21 Manasseh (east) | Iddo son of **Z** / Benjamin
2Ch 17:7 Obadiah, **Z**, Nethanel, and Micaiah.
20:14 His name was Jahaziel son of **Z**, son of Benaiah,
21:2 were Azariah, Jehiel, **Z**, Azariahu, Michael,
24:20 Then the Spirit of God came upon **Z** son of
24:21 Then the leaders plotted to kill **Z**, and by order of
26:5 Uzziah sought God during the days of **Z**,
29:1 His mother was Abijah, the daughter of **Z**.
29:13 From the family of Asaph: **Z** and Mattaniah.
34:12 of the Merarite clan, and **Z** and Meshullam,
35:8 Hilkiah, **Z**, and Jehiel, the administrators of God's
Ezr 5:1 and **Z** son of Iddo prophesied in the name of the
6:14 of the prophets Haggai and **Z** son of Iddo.
8:3 From the family of Parosh: **Z** and 150 other men.
8:11 family of Bebai: **Z** son of Bebai and 28 other men.
8:16 Shemaiah, Elnathan, Jarib, Elnathan, Nathan, **Z**,
10:26 Mattaniah, **Z**, Jehiel, Abdi, Jeremoth, and Elijah.
Ne 8:4 Mishael, Malkijah, Hashum, Hashbaddanah, **Z**,
11:4 son of **Z**, son of Amariah, son of Shephatiah,
11:5 of Hazaiah, son of Adaiah, son of Joiarib, son of **Z**,
11:12 of Pelaliah, son of Amzi, son of **Z**, son of Pashhur,
12:16 **Z** was leader of the family of Iddo.
12:35 Then came **Z** son of Jonathan, son of Shemaiah,
12:41 Maaseiah, Miniamin, Micaiah, Elioenai, **Z**,
Isa 8:2 I asked Uriah the priest and **Z** son of Jeberekiah,
Zec 1:1 the LORD gave this message to the prophet **Z** son
1:7 the LORD sent another message to the prophet **Z** son of Berekiah and grandson of Iddo. **Z** said:
7:1 another message came to **Z** from the LORD.
7:8 Then this message came to **Z** from the LORD:
Mt 23:35 people from righteous Abel to **Z** son of Barachiah,
Lk 1:5 It all begins with a Jewish priest, **Z**, who lived
1:5 **Z** was a member of the priestly order of Abijah.
1:6 **Z** and Elizabeth were righteous in God's eyes,
1:8 One day **Z** was serving God in the Temple, for his
1:11 **Z** was in the sanctuary when an angel of the Lord
1:12 **Z** was overwhelmed with fear.
1:13 But the angel said, "Don't be afraid, **Z**! For God
1:18 **Z** said to the angel, "How can I know this will
1:21 the people were waiting for **Z** to come out,
1:40 where **Z** lived. She entered the house and greeted
1:59 They wanted to name him **Z**, after his father.
1:64 Instantly **Z** could speak again, and he began
1:67 Then his father, **Z**, was filled with the Holy Spirit
3:2 time a message from God came to John son of **Z**,
11:51 from the murder of Abel to the murder of **Z**,

ZECHARIAH'S (3) [ZECHARIAH]

2Ki 15:11 The rest of the events in **Z** reign are recorded in
2Ch 24:22 **Z** last words as he died were, "May the LORD
Ne 12:36 And finally came **Z** colleagues Shemaiah, Azarel,

ZEDAD (2)

Nu 34:8 then to Lebo-hamath, and on through **Z**
Eze 47:15 then on through Lebo-hamath to **Z**;

ZEDEKIAH (59) [ZEDEKIAH'S]

1Ki 22:11 One of them, **Z** son of Kenaanah, made some iron
22:24 Then **Z** son of Kenaanah walked up to Micaiah
2Ki 24:17 next king, and he changed Mattaniah's name to **Z**.
24:18 **Z** was twenty-one years old when he became king,
24:19 But **Z** did what was evil in the LORD's sight,
24:20 Then **Z** rebelled against the king of Babylon.
25:7 The king of Babylon made **Z** watch as all his sons
1Ch 3:15 Jehoiakim (the second), **Z** (the third), and Jehoahaz
3:16 he, in turn, was succeeded by his uncle **Z**.
2Ch 18:10 One of them, **Z** son of Kenaanah, made some iron
18:23 Then **Z** son of Kenaanah walked up to Micaiah
36:10 **Z**, to be the next king in Judah and Jerusalem.
36:11 **Z** was twenty-one years old when he became king,
36:13 **Z** was a hard and stubborn man, refusing to turn to
Ne 10:1 son of Hacaliah. The priests who signed were **Z**,
Jer 21:1 The LORD spoke through Jeremiah when King **Z**
21:3 "Go back to King **Z** and tell him,
21:7 says the LORD, even after King **Z**, his officials,
24:8 "represent King **Z** of Judah, his officials,
27:1 the LORD early in the reign of **Z** son of Josiah,
27:3 and Sidon through their ambassadors to King **Z** in
27:12 Then I repeated this same message to King **Z** of
28:1 the fourth year of the reign of **Z**, king of Judah—
29:21 Ahab son of Kolaiah and **Z** son of Maaseiah—
29:22 'May the LORD make you like **Z** and Ahab,
32:1 the LORD in the tenth year of the reign of **Z**,
32:3 King **Z** had put him there because he continued to
32:4 King **Z** will be captured by the Babylonians
32:5 I will take **Z** to Babylon and will deal with him
34:2 "Go to King **Z** of Judah, and tell him, 'This is
34:4 this promise from the LORD, O **Z**, king of Judah.
34:6 prophet delivered the message to King **Z** of Judah.
34:8 after King **Z** made a covenant with the people,
34:21 I will hand over King **Z** of Judah and his officials
36:12 Gemariah son of Shaphan, **Z** son of Hananiah,
37:1 **Z** son of Josiah succeeded Jehoiachin son of
37:2 But neither King **Z** nor his officials nor the people
37:3 King **Z** sent Jehucal son of Shelemiah
37:17 Later King **Z** secretly requested that Jeremiah
37:21 So King **Z** commanded that Jeremiah not be
38:5 So King **Z** agreed. "All right," he said. "Do as
38:14 One day King **Z** sent for Jeremiah to meet him at
38:16 So King **Z** secretly promised him, "As surely as
38:17 Then Jeremiah said to **Z**, "The LORD God
38:24 Then **Z** said to Jeremiah, "Don't tell anyone you
39:4 King **Z** and his royal guard saw the Babylonians in
39:5 the king of Babylon pronounced judgment upon **Z**.
39:6 He made **Z** watch as they killed his sons and all the
44:30 just as I turned King **Z** of Judah over to King
49:34 at the beginning of the reign of King **Z** of Judah.
51:59 when he went to Babylon with King **Z** of Judah.
52:1 **Z** was twenty-one years old when he became king,
52:2 But **Z** did what was evil in the LORD's sight,
52:3 Then **Z** rebelled against the king of Babylon.
52:8 and caught King **Z** on the plains of Jericho,
52:10 the king of Babylon made **Z** watch as all his sons
52:11 **Z** remained there in prison for the rest of his life.
Eze 12:10 These actions contain a message for **Z** in
12:12 "Even **Z** will leave Jerusalem at night through a

ZEDEKIAH'S (14) [ZEDEKIAH]

2Ki 25:1 So on January 15, during the ninth year of **Z** reign,
25:2 under siege until the eleventh year of King **Z** reign.
25:3 By July 18 of **Z** eleventh year, the famine in the
25:7 Then they gouged out **Z** eyes, bound him in bronze
Jer 1:3 until the eleventh year of King **Z** reign in Judah.
29:3 when they went to Babylon as King **Z**
39:1 It was in January during the ninth year of King **Z**
39:7 Then he gouged out **Z** eyes, bound him in chains,
51:59 The prophet Jeremiah gave this message to **Z** staff
51:59 This was during the fourth year of **Z** reign.
52:4 So on January 15, during the ninth year of **Z** reign,
52:5 under siege until the eleventh year of King **Z** reign.
52:6 By July 18 of **Z** eleventh year, the famine in the
52:11 Then they gouged out **Z** eyes, bound him in bronze

ZEEB (6)

Jdg 7:25 They captured Oreb and **Z**, the two Midianite
7:25 the rock of Oreb, and **Z** at the winepress of **Z**.
7:25 brought the heads of Oreb and **Z** to Gideon,
8:3 God gave you victory over Oreb and **Z**,
Ps 83:11 Let their mighty nobles die as Oreb and **Z** did.

ZELA (2)

Jos 18:28 **Z**, Haeleph, Jebus (that is, Jerusalem), Gibeah,
2Sa 21:14 at the town of **Z** in the land of Benjamin.

ZELEK (2)

2Sa 23:37 **Z** from Ammon; / Naharai from Beeroth (Joab's
1Ch 11:39 **Z** from Ammon; / Naharai from Beeroth (Joab's

ZELOPHEHAD (9)

Nu 26:33 Hepher's son, **Z**, had no sons, but his daughters'
27:1 a petition was presented by the daughters of **Z**—
27:1 Their father, **Z**, was the son of Hepher, son of
27:7 "The daughters of **Z** are right. You must give
36:2 the inheritance of our brother **Z** to his daughters.
36:6 LORD commands concerning the daughters of **Z**:
36:10 The daughters of **Z** did as the LORD commanded
Jos 17:3 However, **Z** son of Hepher, who was a descendant
1Ch 7:15 One of his descendants was **Z**, who had only

ZELOTES [KJV] See ZEALOT

ZELZAH (1)

1Sa 10:2 you will see two men beside Rachel's tomb at **Z**,

ZEMARAIM (2)

Jos 18:22 Beth-arabah, **Z**, Bethel,
2Ch 13:4 Abijah stood on Mount **Z** and shouted to Jeroboam

ZEMARITES (2)

Ge 10:18 Arvadites, **Z**, and Hamathites.
1Ch 1:16 Arvadites, **Z**, and Hamathites.

ZEMIRAH (1)

1Ch 7:8 The sons of Beker were **Z**, Joash, Eliezer, Elioenai,

ZENAN (1)

Jos 15:37 Also included were **Z**, Hadashah, Migdal-gad,

ZENAS (1)

Tit 3:13 Do everything you can to help **Z** the lawyer

ZEPHANIAH (12)

2Ki 25:18 his assistant **Z**, and the three chief gatekeepers.
1Ch 6:36 Elkanah, Joel, Azariah, **Z**,
Jer 21:1 Pashhur son of Malkijah and **Z** son of Maaseiah,
29:25 You wrote a letter on your own authority to **Z** son
29:25 and people in Jerusalem. You said to **Z**,
29:29 But when **Z** the priest received Shemaiah's letter,
37:3 sent Jehucal son of Shelemiah and **Z** the priest,
52:24 his assistant **Z**, and the three chief gatekeepers.
Zep 1:1 The LORD gave these messages to **Z** when
1:1 **Z** was the son of Cushi, son of Gedaliah, son of
Zec 6:10 meet them at the home of Josiah son of **Z**.
6:14 Heldai, Tobijah, Jedaiah, and Josiah son of **Z**."

ZEPHATH (1)

Jdg 1:17 Simeon to fight against the Canaanites living in **Z**,

ZEPHO (3)

Ge 36:11 Eliphaz were Teman, Omar, **Z**, Gatam, and Kenaz.
36:15 the leaders of the clans of Teman, Omar, **Z**, Kenaz,
1Ch 1:36 Omar, **Z**, Gatam, Kenaz, and Amalek, who was

ZEPHON (2) [BAAL-ZEPHON, ZEPHONITE]

Ge 46:16 The sons of Gad were **Z**, Haggi, Shuni, Ezbon,
Nu 26:15 The Zephonite clan, named after its ancestor **Z**.

ZEPHONITE (1) [ZEPHON]

Nu 26:15 The **Z** clan, named after its ancestor Zephon.

ZER (1)

Jos 19:35 were Ziddim, **Z**, Hammath, Rakkath, Kinnereth,

ZERAH (23) [ZERAH'S, ZERAHITE]

Ge 36:13 of Reuel were Nahath, **Z**, Shammah, and Mizzah.
36:17 of the clans of Nahath, **Z**, Shammah, and Mizzah.
36:33 Jobab son of **Z** from Bozrah became king.
38:30 thread on his wrist was born, and he was named **Z**.
46:12 sons of Judah were Er, Onan, Shelah, Perez, and **Z**.
Nu 26:13 The Zerahite clan, named after its ancestor **Z**.
26:20 The Zerahite clan, named after its ancestor **Z**.

Jos 7: 1 of the family of Zimri, of the clan of **Z**, and of the
7: 17 came forward, and the clan of **Z** was singled out.
7: 17 Then the families of **Z** came before the LORD,
22: 20 a member of the clan of **Z**, sinned by stealing the
1Ch 1: 37 of Reuel were Nahath, **Z**, Shammah, and Mizzah.
1: 44 Jobab son of **Z** from Bozrah became king.
2: 4 Their names were Perez and **Z**. So Judah had five
2: 6 The sons of **Z** were Zimri, Ethan, Heman, Calcol,
4: 24 Simeon were Nemuel, Jamin, Jarib, **Z**, and Shaul.
6: 21 Joah, Iddo, **Z**, and Jeatherai.
6: 41 Ethni, **Z**, Adaiah,
27: 11 Sibbecai, a descendant of **Z** from Hushah,
27: 13 Maharai, a descendant of **Z** from Netophah,
2Ch 14: 9 Once an Ethiopian named **Z** attacked Judah with
Ne 11: 24 of Meshezabel, a descendant of **Z** son of Judah,
Mt 1: 3 father of Perez and **Z** (their mother was Tamar).

ZERAH'S (1) [ZERAH]
1Ch 2: 7 Achan son of Carmi, one of **Z** descendants,

ZERAHIAH (5)
1Ch 6: 6 Uzzi was the father of **Z**. / **Z** was the father of Meraioth.
6: 51 Bukki, Uzzi, **Z**,
Ezr 7: 4 son of **Z**, son of Uzzi, son of Bukki,
8: 4 Eliehoenai son of **Z** and 200 other men.

ZERAHITE (3) [ZERAH]
Nu 26: 13 The **Z** clan, named after its ancestor Zerah.
26: 20 The **Z** clan, named after its ancestor Zerah.
1Ch 9: 6 From the **Z** clan, Jeuel returned with his relatives.

ZERED (3)
Nu 21: 12 From there they traveled to the valley of **Z** Brook
Dt 2: 13 "Then the LORD told us to cross **Z** Brook,
2: 14 at Kadesh-barnea until we finally crossed **Z** Brook!

ZEREDAH (1)
1Ki 11: 26 He came from the city of **Z** in Ephraim, and his

ZERERAH (1)
Jdg 7: 22 fled to places as far away as Beth-shittah near **Z**

ZERESH (3)
Est 5: 10 Then he gathered together his friends and **Z**,
5: 14 So Haman's wife, **Z**, and all his friends suggested,
6: 13 When Haman told his wife, **Z**, and all his friends

ZERETH (1)
1Ch 4: 7 Helah gave birth to **Z**, Izhar, Ethnan,

ZERETH-SHAHAR (1)
Jos 13: 19 Kiriathaim, Sibmah, **Z** on the hill above the valley,

ZERI (2)
1Ch 25: 3 Gedaliah, **Z**, Jeshaiah, Shimei, Hashabiah,
25: 11 The fourth lot fell to **Z** and twelve of his sons

ZEROR (1)
1Sa 9: 1 He was the son of Abiel and grandson of **Z**,

ZERUAH (1)
1Ki 11: 26 in Ephraim, and his mother was **Z**, a widow.

ZERUBBABEL (25) [ZERUBBABEL'S]
1Ch 3: 19 The sons of Pedaiah were **Z** and Shimei. The sons of **Z** were Meshullam and Hananiah.
Ezr 2: 2 Their leaders were **Z**, Jeshua, Nehemiah, Seraiah,
3: 2 and **Z** son of Shealtiel with his family began to
3: 8 including **Z** son of Shealtiel, Jeshua son of
4: 2 So they approached **Z** and the other leaders
4: 3 But **Z**, Jeshua, and the other leaders of Israel
5: 2 **Z** son of Shealtiel and Jeshua son of Jehozadak
Ne 7: 7 Their leaders were **Z**, Jeshua, Nehemiah, Seraiah,
12: 1 and Levites who had returned with **Z** son of
12: 47 So now, in the days of **Z** and of Nehemiah,
Hag 1: 1 through the prophet Haggai to **Z** son of Shealtiel,
1: 12 Then **Z** son of Shealtiel, Jeshua son of Jehozadak,
1: 14 So the LORD sparked the enthusiasm of **Z** son of
2: 2 "Say this to **Z** son of Shealtiel, governor of Judah,
2: 4 But now take courage, **Z**, says the LORD.
2: 21 "Tell **Z**, the governor of Judah, that I am about to
2: 23 I will honor you, **Z** son of Shealtiel, my servant.
Zec 4: 6 he said to me, "This is what the LORD says to **Z**:
4: 7 Then **Z** will set the final stone of the Temple in
4: 9 "**Z** is the one who laid the foundation of this
Mt 1: 12 father of Shealtiel. / Shealtiel was the father of **Z**.
1: 13 **Z** was the father of Abiud. / Abiud was the father
Lk 3: 27 Rhesa was the son of **Z**. / **Z** was the son of Shealtiel.

ZERUBBABEL'S (2) [ZERUBBABEL]
Zec 4: 7 not even a mighty mountain, will stand in **Z** way;
4: 10 the work begin, to see the plumb line in **Z** hand.

ZERUIAH (22)
1Sa 26: 6 asked Ahimelech the Hittite and Abishai son of **Z**,
2Sa 2: 13 Joab son of **Z** led David's troops from Hebron,
2: 18 Joab, Abishai, and Asahel, the three sons of **Z**,
3: 39 I am the anointed king, these two sons of **Z**—
8: 16 Joab son of **Z** was commander of the army.
16: 9 Abishai son of **Z** demanded. "Let me go over
16: 10 "What am I going to do with you sons of **Z**!
17: 25 of Nahash, was the sister of Joab's mother, **Z**.)
18: 2 one-third under Joab's brother Abishai son of **Z**,
19: 21 Then Abishai son of **Z** said, "Shimei should die,
19: 22 "What am I going to do with you sons of **Z**!"
21: 17 But Abishai son of **Z** came to his rescue and killed
23: 18 Abishai son of **Z**, the brother of Joab,
1Ki 1: 7 Adonijah took Joab son of **Z** and Abiathar the
2: 5 You know that Joab son of **Z** murdered my two
2: 22 Abiathar the priest and Joab son of **Z** on his side."
1Ch 2: 16 Their sisters were named **Z** and Abigail.
2: 16 **Z** had three sons named Abishai, Joab, and Asahel.
11: 6 And Joab, the son of David's sister **Z**,
18: 12 Abishai son of **Z** destroyed eighteen thousand
18: 15 Joab son of **Z** was commander of the army.
26: 28 son of Kish, Abner son of Ner, and Joab son of **Z**.

ZEST (1)
Eze 23: 44 with all the **z** of lustful young men.

ZETHAM (2)
1Ch 23: 8 Libni were Jehiel (the family leader), **Z**, and Joel.
26: 22 The sons of Jehiel, **Z** and his brother Joel, were in

ZETHAN (1)
1Ch 7: 10 Benjamin, Ehud, Kenaanah, **Z**, Tarshish,

ZETHAR (1)
Est 1: 10 Biztha, Harbona, Bigtha, Abagtha, **Z**, and Carcas,

ZEUS (2)
Ac 14: 12 They decided that Barnabas was the Greek god **Z**
14: 13 The temple of **Z** was located on the outskirts of the

ZIA (1)
1Ch 5: 13 Meshullam, Sheba, Jorai, Jacan, **Z**, and Eber.

ZIBA (17) [ZIBA'S]
2Sa 9: 2 He summoned a man named **Z**, who had been one
9: 2 "Are you **Z**?" the king asked. "Yes sir, I am," **Z** replied.
9: 3 **Z** replied, "Yes, one of Jonathan's sons is still
9: 4 "In Lo-debar," **Z** told him, "at the home of Makir
9: 9 Then the king summoned Saul's servant **Z**
9: 10 **Z**, who had fifteen sons and twenty servants,
16: 1 David was just past the top of the hill when **Z**,
16: 2 the king asked **Z**. And **Z** replied, "The donkeys are for your people
16: 3 "He stayed in Jerusalem," **Z** replied. "He said,
16: 4 "In that case," the king told **Z**, "I give you
16: 4 "Thank you, sir," **Z** replied.
19: 17 including **Z**, the servant of Saul, and Ziba's fifteen
19: 26 "My lord the king, my servant **Z** deceived me.
19: 27 **Z** has slandered me by saying that I refused to
19: 29 and **Z** will divide your land equally between you."

ZIBA'S (2) [ZIBA]
2Sa 9: 12 all the members of **Z** household were
19: 17 of Saul, and **Z** fifteen sons and twenty servants.

ZIBEON (7)
Ge 36: 2 of Anah and granddaughter of **Z** the Hivite.
36: 14 the daughter of Anah and granddaughter of **Z**,
36: 20 native to the land of Seir: Lotan, Shobal, **Z**, Anah,
36: 24 The sons of **Z** were Aiah and Anah. This is the
36: 29 of the Horite clans were Lotan, Shobal, **Z**, Anah,
1Ch 1: 38 Shobal, **Z**, Anah, Dishon, Ezer, and Dishan.
1: 40 and Onam. The sons of **Z** were Aiah and Anah.

ZIBIA (1)
1Ch 8: 9 new wife, gave birth to Jobab, **Z**, Mesha, Malcam,

ZIBIAH (2)
2Ki 12: 1 forty years. His mother was **Z**, from Beersheba.
2Ch 24: 1 forty years. His mother was **Z**, from Beersheba.

ZICRI (12)
Ex 6: 21 of Izhar included Korah, Nepheg, and **Z**.
1Ch 8: 19 Jakim, **Z**, Zabdi,
8: 23 Abdon, **Z**, Hanan,
8: 27 Jaareshiah, Elijah, and **Z** were the sons of Jeroham.
9: 15 Mattaniah son of Mica, son of **Z**, son of Asaph;
26: 25 Jeshaiah, Joram, **Z**, and Shelomoth.
27: 16 and their leaders: / Reuben | Eliezer son of **Z**
2Ch 17: 16 Next was Amasiah son of **Z**, who volunteered for
23: 1 Maaseiah son of Adaiah, and Elishaphat son of **Z**.
28: 7 Then **Z**, a warrior from Ephraim, killed Maaseiah,
Ne 11: 9 Their chief officer was Joel son of **Z**, who was
12: 17 **Z** was leader of the family of Abijah. / There was

ZIDDIM (1)
Jos 19: 35 fortified cities included in this territory were **Z**,

ZIDKIJAH [KJV] See ZEDEKIAH

ZIDON, ZIDONIANS [KJV] See SIDONIANS

ZIF [KJV] See MIDSPRING

ZIHA (3)
Ezr 2: 43 returned from exile: / **Z**, Hasupha, Tabbaoth,
Ne 7: 46 returned from exile: / **Z**, Hasupha, Tabbaoth,
11: 21 whose leaders were **Z** and Gishpa,

ZIKLAG (13)
Jos 15: 31 **Z**, Madmannah, Sansannah,
19: 5 **Z**, Beth-marcaboth, Hazar-susah,
1Sa 27: 6 So Achish gave him the town of **Z** (which still
30: 1 and his men arrived home at their town of **Z**,
30: 1 into the Negev and had burned **Z** to the ground.
30: 14 and the land of Caleb, and we had just burned **Z**."
30: 26 When he arrived at **Z**, David sent part of the
2Sa 1: 1 over the Amalekites and spent two days in **Z**.
4: 10 good news. But I seized him and killed him at **Z**.
1Ch 4: 30 Bethuel, Hormah, **Z**,
12: 1 The following men joined David at **Z** while he was
12: 20 who defected to David as he was returning to **Z**:
Ne 11: 28 **Z**, and Meconah with its villages.

ZILLAH (3)
Ge 4: 19 Lamech married two women—Adah and **Z**.
4: 22 To Lamech's other wife, **Z**, was born Tubal-cain.
4: 23 One day Lamech said to Adah and **Z**, "Listen to

ZILLETHAI (2)
1Ch 8: 20 Elienai, **Z**, Eliel,
12: 20 Jozabad, Jediael, Michael, Jozabad, Elihu, and **Z**.

ZILPAH (7)
Ge 29: 24 And Laban gave Leah a servant, **Z**, to be her maid.
30: 9 so she gave her servant, **Z**, to Jacob to be his wife.
30: 10 Soon **Z** presented him with another son.
30: 12 Then **Z** produced a second son,
35: 26 The sons of **Z**, Leah's servant, were Gad
37: 2 the sons of his father's wives Bilhah and **Z**.
46: 18 sixteen were descendants of Jacob through **Z**,

ZIMMAH (3)
1Ch 6: 20 The descendants of Gershon were Libni, Jahath, **Z**,
6: 42 Ethan, **Z**, Shimei,
2Ch 29: 12 of Gershon: Joah son of **Z** and Eden son of Joah.

ZIMRAN (2)
Ge 25: 2 and she bore him **Z**, Jokshan, Medan, Midian,
1Ch 1: 32 were **Z**, Jokshan, Medan, Midian, Ishbak,

ZIMRI (18) [ZIMRI'S]
Nu 25: 14 the Midianite woman was named **Z** son of Salu,
Jos 7: 1 of the family of **Z**, of the clan of Zerah, and of the
7: 17 the LORD, and the family of **Z** was singled out.
1Ki 16: 9 Then **Z**, who commanded half of the royal
16: 10 **Z** walked in and struck him down and killed him.
16: 10 reign in Judah. Then **Z** became the next king.
16: 11 **Z** immediately killed the entire royal family of
16: 12 So **Z** destroyed the dynasty of Baasha as the
16: 15 **Z** began to rule over Israel from Tirzah in the
16: 16 heard that **Z** had assassinated the king, they chose
16: 18 When **Z** saw that the city had been taken, he went
2Ki 9: 31 You are just like **Z**, who murdered his master!"
1Ch 2: 6 The sons of Zerah were **Z**, Ethan, Heman, Calcol,
8: 36 was the father of Alemeth, Azmaveth, and **Z**. / **Z** was the father of Moza.
9: 42 was the father of Alemeth, Azmaveth, and **Z**. / **Z** was the father of Moza.
Jer 25: 25 and to the kings of **Z**, Elam, and Media.

ZIMRI'S (2) [ZIMRI]
Jos 7: 18 Every member of **Z** family was brought forward
1Ki 16: 20 The rest of the events of **Z** reign and his

ZIN (10)
Nu 13: 21 and explored the land from the wilderness of **Z** as
20: 1 the people of Israel arrived in the wilderness of **Z**
27: 14 against my instructions in the wilderness of **Z**.
27: 14 of Meribah at Kadesh in the wilderness of **Z**.)
33: 36 and camped at Kadesh in the wilderness of **Z**.
34: 3 your country will extend from the wilderness of **Z**,
34: 4 run south past Scorpion Pass in the direction of **Z**.
Dt 32: 51 of Meribah at Kadesh in the wilderness of **Z**.
Jos 15: 1 with the wilderness of **Z** being its southernmost
15: 3 ran south of Scorpion Pass into the wilderness of **Z**

ZION (51)
DAUGHTER OF ZION (5) 2Ki 19:21; Isa 37:22; 52:2; La 2:13; Zep 3:14

MOUNT ZION (24) 2Ki 19:31; Ps 14:7; 48:2,11; 50:2; 53:6; 68:16; 76:2; 78:68; 125:1; Isa 10:32; 24:23; 31:4; 37:32; Jer 26:18; Joel 2:32; Am 1:2; Ob 1:21; Mic 3:12; Zec 1:14; 8:2,3; Heb 12:22; Rev 14:1

2Sa 5: 7 But David captured the fortress of **Z**, now called
1Ki 8: 1 also known as **Z**, to its new place in the Temple.
2Ki 19: 21 'The virgin daughter of **Z** / despises you
19: 31 a group of survivors from Mount **Z**.
1Ch 11: 5 But David captured the fortress of **Z**, now called
2Ch 5: 2 also known as **Z**, to its new place in the Temple.
Ps 14: 7 that salvation would come from Mount **Z** to rescue
48: 2 Mount **Z**, the holy mountain, / is the city of the

48:11 Let the people on Mount **Z** rejoice. / Let the towns
50: 2 From Mount **Z**, the perfection of beauty,
51:18 Look with favor on **Z** and help her;
53: 6 that salvation would come from Mount **Z** to rescue
65: 1 What mighty praise, O God, / belongs to you in **Z**.
68:16 at Mount **Z**, where God has chosen to live,
76: 2 is where he lives; / Mount **Z** is his home.
78:68 the tribe of Judah, / Mount **Z**, which he loved.
102:21 so the LORD's fame will be celebrated in **Z**,
125: 1 who trust in the LORD are as secure as Mount **Z**;
128: 5 May the LORD continually bless you from **Z**.
133: 3 that falls on the mountains of **Z**. / And the LORD
135:21 The LORD be praised from **Z**, / for he lives here
147:12 the LORD, O Jerusalem! / Praise your God, O **Z**!
Isa 10:32 He shakes his fist at Mount **Z** in Jerusalem.
24:23 Almighty will mount his throne on Mount **Z**.
30:19 O people of **Z**, who live in Jerusalem, you will
31: 4 Almighty will come and fight on Mount **Z**.
33:20 you will see **Z** as a place of worship
37:22 'The virgin daughter of **Z** / despises you
37:32 a group of survivors from Mount **Z**.
40: 9 of good news, shout to **Z** from the mountaintops!
52: 1 Wake up, wake up, O **Z**! Clothe yourselves with
52: 2 bands from your neck, O captive daughter of **Z**.
60:14 of the LORD, and **Z** of the Holy One of Israel.
62: 1 Because I love **Z**, because my heart yearns for
Jer 26:18 Mount **Z** will be plowed like an open field;
La 2:13 O virgin daughter of **Z**, how can I comfort you?
Joel 2:32 There will be people on Mount **Z** in Jerusalem who
3:16 The LORD's voice will roar from **Z** and thunder
3:17 LORD your God, live in **Z**, my holy mountain.
Am 1: 2 voice roars from his Temple on Mount **Z**;
Ob 1:21 Deliverers will go up to Mount **Z** in Jerusalem to
Mic 3:12 of you, Mount **Z** will be plowed like an open field;
Zep 3:14 Sing, O daughter of **Z**; shout aloud, O Israel!
3:16 announcement to Jerusalem will be, "Cheer up, **Z**!
Zec 1:14 and Mount **Z** is passionate and strong.
1:17 and the LORD will again comfort **Z** and choose
8: 2 My love for Mount **Z** is passionate and strong;
8: 3 I am returning to Mount **Z**, and I will live in
9: 9 Rejoice greatly, O people of **Z**! Shout in triumph,
Heb 12:22 No, you have come to Mount **Z**, to the city of the
Rev 14: 1 Then I saw the Lamb standing on Mount **Z**,

ZIOR (1)
Jos 15:54 Humtah, Kiriath-arba (that is, Hebron), and **Z**—

ZIPH (11) [ZIPHITES]
Jos 15:24 **Z**, Telem, Bealoth,
15:55 Besides these, there were Maon, Carmel, **Z**, Juttah,
1Sa 23:14 of the wilderness and in the hill country of **Z**.
23:15 that Saul was on the way to **Z** to search for him
23:19 But now the men of **Z** went to Saul in Gibeah
23:24 So the men of **Z** returned home ahead of Saul.
26: 1 Now some messengers from **Z** came back to Saul
26: 2 and went to hunt him down in the wilderness of **Z**.
1Ch 2:42 brother of Jerahmeel, was Mesha, the father of **Z**.
4:16 The sons of Jehallelel were **Z**, Ziphah, Tiria,
2Ch 11: 8 Gath, Mareshah, **Z**,

ZIPHAH (1)
1Ch 4:16 sons of Jehallelel were Ziph, **Z**, Tiria, and Asarel.

ZIPHITES (1) [ZIPH]
Ps 54: T regarding the time the **Z** came and said to Saul,

ZIPHRON (1)
Nu 34: 9 and **Z** to Hazar-enan. This will be your northern

ZIPPOR (6)
Nu 22: 2 Balak son of **Z**, the Moabite king, knew what the
22:10 said to God, "Balak son of **Z**, king of Moab,
22:16 this message: / "This is what Balak son of **Z** says:
23:18 "Rise up, Balak, and listen! / Hear me, son of **Z**.
Jos 24: 9 Then Balak son of **Z**, king of Moab, started a war
Jdg 11:25 Are you any better than Balak son of **Z**, king of

ZIPPORAH (3)
Ex 2:21 gave Moses one of his daughters, **Z**, to be his wife.
4:25 But **Z**, his wife, took a flint knife and circumcised
18: 2 Some time before this, Moses had sent his wife, **Z**,

ZITHER (1)
Da 3: 5 flute, **z**, lyre, harp, pipes, and other instruments,

ZITHRI [KJV] See SITHRI

ZIZ (1)
2Ch 20:16 **Z** at the end of the valley that opens into the

ZIZA (4)
1Ch 4:37 and **Z** son of Shiphi, son of Allon, son of Jedaiah,
23:10 of Shimei were Jahath, **Z**, Jeush, and Beriah.
23:11 Jahath was the family leader, and **Z** was next.
2Ch 11:20 gave birth to Abijah, Attai, **Z**, and Shelomith.

ZOAN (7)
Nu 13:22 seven years before the Egyptian city of **Z**.)
Ps 78:12 did for their ancestors in Egypt, on the plain of **Z**.
78:43 signs in Egypt, / his wonders on the plain of **Z**.
Isa 19:11 What fools are the counselors of **Z**! Their best
19:13 The wise men from **Z** are fools, and those from
30: 4 For though his power extends to **Z** and Hanes,
Eze 30:14 I will destroy Pathros, **Z**, and Thebes, and they will

ZOAR (8) [BELA]
Ge 13:10 plains of the Jordan Valley in the direction of **Z**.
14: 2 of Zeboiim, and the king of Bela (now called **Z**).
14: 8 Admah, Zeboiim, and Bela (now called **Z**)
19:22 From that time on, that village was known as **Z**.
19:30 Afterward Lot left **Z** because he was afraid of the
Dt 34: 3 with Jericho—the city of palms—as far as **Z**.
Isa 15: 5 Its people flee to **Z** and Eglath-shelishiyah.
Jer 48:34 from **Z** all the way to Horonaim

ZOBAH (11) [ARAM-ZOBAH, HAMATH-ZOBAH]
1Sa 14:47 against Moab, Ammon, Edom, the kings of **Z**,
2Sa 8: 3 the forces of Hadadezer son of Rehob, king of **Z**,
8:12 and from Hadadezer son of Rehob, king of **Z**.
10: 6 mercenaries from the lands of Beth-rehob and **Z**,
10: 8 while the Arameans from **Z** and Rehob
23:36 Igal son of Nathan from **Z**; / Bani from Gad;
1Ki 11:23 had fled from his master, King Hadadezer of **Z**,
1Ch 11:47 Eliel and Obed; / Jaasiel from **Z**.
18: 3 destroyed the forces of King Hadadezer of **Z**,
18: 9 had destroyed the army of King Hadadezer of **Z**,
19: 6 troops from Aram-naharaim, Aram-maacah, and **Z**.

ZOBEBAH (1)
1Ch 4: 8 and Koz, who became the ancestor of Anub, **Z**,

ZOHAR (4)
Ge 23: 8 you feel, be so kind as to ask Ephron son of **Z**
25: 9 in the field of Ephron son of **Z** the Hittite.
46:10 were Jemuel, Jamin, Ohad, Jakin, **Z**, and Shaul.
Ex 6:15 Jamin, Ohad, Jakin, **Z**, and Shaul (whose mother

ZOHELETH (1)
1Ki 1: 9 Adonijah went to the stone of **Z** near the spring of

ZOHETH (1)
1Ch 4:20 The descendants of Ishi were **Z** and Ben-zoheth.

ZOPHAH (2)
1Ch 7:35 The sons of his brother Helem were **Z**, Imna,
7:36 The sons of **Z** were Suah, Harnepher, Shual,

ZOPHAI (1)
1Ch 6:26 Elkanah, **Z**, Nahath,

ZOPHAR (4)
Job 2:11 Bildad the Shuhite, and **Z** the Naamathite.
11: 1 Then **Z** the Naamathite replied to Job:
20: 1 Then **Z** the Naamathite replied:
42: 9 and **Z** the Naamathite did as the LORD

ZOPHIM (1)
Nu 23:14 So Balak took Balaam to the plateau of **Z** on

ZORAH (11)
Jos 15:33 were also given to Judah: Eshtaol, **Z**, Ashnah,
19:41 The towns within Dan's inheritance included **Z**,
Jdg 13: 2 from the tribe of Dan lived in the town of **Z**.
13:25 which is located between the towns of **Z**
16:31 back home and buried him between **Z** and Eshtaol,
18: 2 who lived in the towns of **Z** and Eshtaol, to scout
18: 8 When the men returned to **Z** and Eshtaol,
18:11 warriors from the tribe of Dan set out from **Z**
1Ch 2:53 from whom came the people of **Z** and Eshtaol.
2Ch 11:10 **Z**, Aijalon, and Hebron. These became the fortified
Ne 11:29 They were also in En-rimmon, **Z**, Jarmuth,

ZORATHITES (1)
1Ch 4: 2 and Lahad. These were the families of the **Z**.

ZORITES (1)
1Ch 2:54 the other half of the Manahathites, the **Z**,

ZOROBABEL [KJV] See ZERUBBABEL

ZUAR (5)
Nu 1: 8 Issachar | Nethanel son of **Z**
2: 5[-6] Issachar | Nethanel son of **Z** | 54,400
7:18 On the second day Nethanel son of **Z**, leader of the
7:23 was the offering brought by Nethanel son of **Z**.
10:15 The tribe of Issachar was led by Nethanel son of **Z**.

ZUPH (3)
1Sa 1: 1 from the family of Tohu and the clan of **Z**.
9: 5 Finally, they entered the region of **Z**, and Saul said
1Ch 6:35 **Z**, Elkanah, Mahath, Amasai,

ZUR (5) [BETH-ZUR]
Nu 25:15 she was the daughter of **Z**, the leader of a
31: 8 Evi, Rekem, **Z**, Hur, and Reba—died in the battle.
Jos 13:21 Evi, Rekem, **Z**, Hur, and Reba—princes living in
1Ch 8:30 Jeiel's other sons were **Z**, Kish, Baal, Ner, Nadab,
9:36 Jeiel's other sons were **Z**, Kish, Baal, Ner, Nadab,

ZURIEL (1)
Nu 3:35 The leader of the Merarite clans was **Z** son of

ZURISHADDAI (5)
Nu 1: 6 Simeon | Shelumiel son of **Z**
2:12[-13] Simeon | Shelumiel son of **Z** | 59,300
7:36 On the fifth day Shelumiel son of **Z**, leader of the
7:41 was the offering brought by Shelumiel son of **Z**.
10:19 tribe of Simeon was led by Shelumiel son of **Z**.

ZUZITES (1)
Ge 14: 5 the **Z** in Ham, the Emites in the plain of

NUMERALS

1-1/2 (8)
Ex 25:23 3 feet long, **1-1/2** feet wide, and 2-1/4 feet high.
37:10 3 feet long, **1-1/2** feet wide, and 2-1/4 feet high.
1Ki 7:31 It projected **1-1/2** feet above the cart's top like a
Eze 48:16 The city will measure **1-1/2** miles on each side.
48:30 city: On the north wall, which is **1-1/2** miles long,
48:32 On the east wall, also **1-1/2** miles long, the gates
48:33 The south wall, also **1-1/2** miles long, will have
48:34 on the west wall, also **1-1/2** miles long, the gates

1-2/3 (2)
Eze 45: 6 of land 8-1/3 miles long and **1-2/3** miles wide.
48:15 Additional strip of land 8-1/3 miles long by **1-2/3**

1-3/4 (13)
Nu 7:13 and a silver basin of about **1-3/4** pounds.
7:19 and a silver basin of about **1-3/4** pounds.
7:25 and a silver basin of about **1-3/4** pounds.
7:31 and a silver basin of about **1-3/4** pounds.
7:37 and a silver basin of about **1-3/4** pounds.
7:43 and a silver basin of about **1-3/4** pounds.
7:49 and a silver basin of about **1-3/4** pounds.
7:55 and a silver basin of about **1-3/4** pounds.
7:61 and a silver basin of about **1-3/4** pounds.
7:67 and a silver basin of about **1-3/4** pounds.
7:73 and a silver basin of about **1-3/4** pounds.
7:79 and a silver basin of about **1-3/4** pounds.
7:85 for each platter and **1-3/4** pounds for each basin.

2 (3) [TWO]
2Ki 25:27 and released him from prison on April **2** of that
Ezr 8:27 **2** fine articles of polished bronze, as precious as
Ne 6:15 So on October **2** the wall was finally finished—

2-1/4 (12)
Ex 25:10 feet long, **2-1/4** feet wide, and **2-1/4** feet high.
25:17 It must be 3-3/4 feet long and **2-1/4** feet wide.
25:23 3 feet long, 1-1/2 feet wide, and **2-1/4** feet high.
26:16 frame must be 15 feet high and **2-1/4** feet wide.
36:21 Each frame was 15 feet high and **2-1/4** feet wide.
37: 1 feet long, **2-1/4** feet wide, and **2-1/4** feet high.
37: 6 It was 3-3/4 feet long and **2-1/4** feet wide.
37:10 3 feet long, 1-1/2 feet wide, and **2-1/4** feet high.
1Ki 7:31 pedestal, and its opening was **2-1/4** feet across;
7:32 the cart. The wheels were **2-1/4** feet in diameter

3 (6) [THREE]
Ex 25:23 **3** feet long, 1-1/2 feet wide, and 2-1/4 feet high.
37:10 **3** feet long, 1-1/2 feet wide, and 2-1/4 feet high.
37:12 A rim about **3** inches wide was attached along the
Jer 52:21 They were hollow, with walls **3** inches thick.
Eze 26: 1 On February **3**, during the twelfth year of King
32: 1 On March **3**, during the twelfth year of King

3-1/4 (13)
Nu 7:13 of a silver platter weighing about **3-1/4** pounds
7:19 of a silver platter weighing about **3-1/4** pounds
7:25 of a silver platter weighing about **3-1/4** pounds
7:31 of a silver platter weighing about **3-1/4** pounds
7:37 of a silver platter weighing about **3-1/4** pounds
7:43 of a silver platter weighing about **3-1/4** pounds
7:49 of a silver platter weighing about **3-1/4** pounds
7:55 of a silver platter weighing about **3-1/4** pounds
7:61 of a silver platter weighing about **3-1/4** pounds
7:67 of a silver platter weighing about **3-1/4** pounds
7:73 of a silver platter weighing about **3-1/4** pounds
7:79 of a silver platter weighing about **3-1/4** pounds
7:85 about **3-1/4** pounds for each platter and 1-3/4

3-1/3 (6)
Eze 45: 3 of land 8-1/3 miles long and **3-1/3** miles wide.
45: 5 to it, also 8-1/3 miles long and **3-1/3** miles wide,
48:10 measuring 8-1/3 miles long by **3-1/3** miles wide,
48:13 the priests—8-1/3 miles long and **3-1/3** miles wide.
48:18 a farming area that stretches **3-1/3** miles to the east
48:18 and **3-1/3** miles to the west along the border of the

3-1/2 (4)
Eze 40: 9 deep, with supporting columns **3-1/2** feet thick.
41: 3 the entrance and found them to be **3-1/2** feet thick.
41: 22 of wood, **3-1/2** feet square and 5-1/4 feet high.
43: 14 From the gutter the altar rises **3-1/2** feet to a ledge

3-3/4 (4)
Ex 25: 10 a sacred chest **3-3/4** feet long, 2-1/4 feet wide,
25: 17 It must be **3-3/4** feet long and 2-1/4 feet wide.
37: 1 It was **3-3/4** feet long, 2-1/4 feet wide, and 2-1/4
37: 6 It was **3-3/4** feet long and 2-1/4 feet wide.

4 (1) [FOUR]
Ezr 7: 9 on April 8 and came to Jerusalem on August **4**,

4-1/2 (4)
Ex 27: 1 feet wide, 7-1/2 feet long, and **4-1/2** feet high.
38: 1 was 7-1/2 feet square at the top and **4-1/2** feet high.
1Ki 7: 27 each 6 feet long, 6 feet wide, and **4-1/2** feet tall.
2Ch 6: 13 and **4-1/2** feet high and had placed it at the center

5-1/4 (2)
Eze 40: 48 The entrance was 24-1/2 feet wide with walls **5-1/4**
41: 22 of wood, 3-1/2 feet square and **5-1/4** feet high.

6 (4) [SIX]
1Ki 7: 19 were shaped like lilies, and they were **6** feet tall.
7: 27 each **6** feet long, **6** feet wide, and 4-1/2 feet tall.
7: 38 Each basin was **6** feet across and could hold 220

6-1/4 (1)
Ex 30: 23 **6-1/4** pounds each of cinnamon and of sweet cane,

6-2/3 (3)
Eze 45: 1 land will be 8-1/3 miles long and **6-2/3** miles wide.
48: 9 will be 8-1/3 miles long and **6-2/3** miles wide.
48: 13 will measure 8-1/3 miles long by **6-2/3** miles wide.

7 (10) [SEVEN]
Est 3: 7 And the day selected was March **7**, nearly a year
3: 13 to happen nearly a year later on March **7**.
8: 12 of King Xerxes was March **7** of the next year.
9: 1 So on March **7** the two decrees of the king were
9: 17 the provinces this was done on March **7**.
Eze 29: 1 On January **7**, during the tenth year of King
41: 5 along the outside wall; each room was **7** feet wide.
43: 14 From the lower ledge the altar rises **7** feet to the
43: 15 top of the altar, the hearth, rises still **7** feet higher,
Zec 7: 1 On December **7** of the fourth year of King

7-1/2 (21)
Ex 27: 1 a square altar **7-1/2** feet wide, **7-1/2** feet long,
27: 18 75 feet wide, with curtain walls **7-1/2** feet high,
38: 1 was **7-1/2** feet square at the top and 4-1/2 feet high.
38: 18 It was 30 feet long and **7-1/2** feet high, just like the
1Ki 6: 6 the bottom floor being **7-1/2** feet wide, the second
6: 10 Each story of the complex was **7-1/2** feet high.
6: 24 was 15 feet, each wing being **7-1/2** feet long.
7: 16 capitals of molded bronze, each **7-1/2** feet tall.
7: 23 It was **7-1/2** feet deep and about 45 feet in
2Ki 25: 17 bronze capital on top of each pillar was **7-1/2** feet
2Ch 3: 11 One wing of the first figure was **7-1/2** feet long,
3: 11 The other wing, also **7-1/2** feet long, touched one
3: 12 the second figure had one wing **7-1/2** feet long that
3: 12 The other wing, also **7-1/2** feet long, touched the
3: 15 by a capital extending upward another **7-1/2** feet.
4: 2 It was **7-1/2** feet deep and about 45 feet in
6: 13 He had made a bronze platform **7-1/2** feet long,
6: 13 **7-1/2** feet wide, and 4-1/2 feet high and had placed
9: 16 each containing about **7-1/2** pounds of gold.
Jer 52: 22 bronze capital on top of each pillar was **7-1/2** feet

8 (4) [EIGHT]
Ezr 7: 9 He had left Babylon on April **8** and came to
Ne 8: 2 So on October **8** Ezra the priest brought the scroll
Est 9: 15 the Jews at Susa gathered together on March **8**
Eze 33: 21 On January **8**, during the twelfth year of our

8-1/3 (12)
Eze 45: 1 This piece of land will be **8-1/3** miles long and
45: 3 measure out a portion of land **8-1/3** miles long
45: 5 next to it, also **8-1/3** miles long and 3-1/3 miles
45: 6 sacred area will be a section of land **8-1/3** miles
48: 8 will be **8-1/3** miles wide and will extend as far east
48: 9 for the LORD's Temple will be **8-1/3** miles long
48: 10 land measuring **8-1/3** miles long by 3-1/3 miles
48: 13 the priests—**8-1/3** miles long and 3-1/3 miles wide.
48: 13 Together these portions of land will measure **8-1/3**
48: 15 "An additional strip of land **8-1/3** miles long by
48: 20 is a square that measures **8-1/3** miles on each side.
48: 21 Each of these areas will be **8-1/3** miles wide,

8-3/4 (7)
Eze 40: 7 with a distance between them of **8-3/4** feet along
40: 30 into the inner courtyard were **8-3/4** feet deep
40: 48 and found them to be **8-3/4** feet square.
41: 2 and the walls on each side were **8-3/4** feet wide.
41: 9 outer wall of the Temple's side rooms was **8-3/4**
41: 11 into the terrace yard, which was **8-3/4** feet wide.
41: 12 feet long, and its walls were **8-3/4** feet thick.

9 (4) [NINE]
1Ki 6: 6 the second floor **9** feet wide, and the top floor
7: 35 Around the top of each cart there was a rim **9**
Ne 8: 13 On October **9** the family leaders and the priests
Eze 43: 13 with a curb **9** inches wide around its edge.

10-1/2 (12)
1Ki 6: 6 9 feet wide, and the top floor **10-1/2** feet wide.
Eze 40: 5 man took a measuring rod that was **10-1/2** feet long
40: 5 the wall was **10-1/2** feet thick and **10-1/2** feet high.
40: 6 threshold of the gateway; it was **10-1/2** feet deep.
40: 7 Each of these alcoves was **10-1/2** feet square,
40: 7 end of the gateway passage, was **10-1/2** feet deep.
40: 12 The alcoves themselves were **10-1/2** feet square.
41: 1 framed its doorway. They were **10-1/2** feet square.
41: 3 The entrance was **10-1/2** feet wide, and the walls
41: 5 the Temple and found that it was **10-1/2** feet thick.
41: 8 the side rooms. This terrace was **10-1/2** feet high.

10-1/2-INCH (1) [INCH]
Eze 43: 17 a 21-inch gutter and a **10-1/2-inch** curb all around

12 (2) [TWELVE]
1Ki 7: 10 were 15 feet long, and some were **12** feet long.
Ezr 6: 15 The Temple was completed on March **12**,

12-1/4 (1)
Eze 41: 3 extended **12-1/4** feet to the corners of the inner

12-1/2 (2)
Ex 30: 23 **12-1/2** pounds of pure myrrh, 6-1/4 pounds each of
30: 24 **12-1/2** pounds of cassia, and one gallon of olive

14 (3) [FOURTEEN]
2Ki 25: 8 August **14** of that year, which was the nineteenth
Eze 20: 1 On August **14**, during the seventh year of King
40: 9 and found it to be **14** feet deep, with supporting

15 (16) [FIFTEEN]
Ex 26: 16 Each frame must be **15** feet high and 2-1/4 feet
36: 21 Each frame was **15** feet high and 2-1/4 feet wide.
1Ki 6: 3 It projected outward **15** feet from the front of the
6: 23 cherubim made of olive wood, each **15** feet tall.
6: 24 The wingspan of each of the cherubim was **15** feet,
6: 26 each was **15** feet tall.
7: 10 Some of the huge foundation stones were **15** feet
7: 23 a large round tank, **15** feet across from rim to rim;
2Ki 25: 1 So on January **15**, during the ninth year of
2Ch 4: 1 altar 30 feet long, 30 feet wide, and **15** feet high.
4: 2 a large round tank, **15** feet across from rim to rim;
9: 15 each containing over **15** pounds of gold.
Ne 8: 18 Then on October **15** they held a solemn assembly,
Jer 52: 4 So on January **15**, during the ninth year of
Eze 24: 1 On January **15**, during the ninth year of King
Zec 1: 7 Then on February **15** of the second year of King

17 (5) [SEVENTEEN]
Est 3: 12 On April **17** Haman called in the king's secretaries
Jer 52: 12 August **17** of that year, which was the nineteenth
Eze 8: 1 Then on September **17**, during the sixth year of
32: 17 On March **17**, during the twelfth year,
Hag 2: 1 Then on October **17** of that same year, the LORD

17-1/2 (3)
Eze 40: 11 which was **17-1/2** feet wide at the opening and
41: 2 The entrance was **17-1/2** feet wide, and the walls
42: 4 the two blocks of rooms ran a walkway **17-1/2**

18 (8) [EIGHTEEN]
Ge 6: 16 the way around the boat, **18** inches below the roof.
1Ki 7: 15 each 27 feet tall and **18** feet in circumference.
2Ki 25: 3 By July **18** of Zedekiah's eleventh year, the famine
Jer 39: 2 Two and a half years later, on July **18**,
52: 6 By July **18** of Zedekiah's eleventh year, the famine
52: 21 was 27 feet tall and **18** feet in circumference.
Hag 2: 10 On December **18** of the second year of King
2: 20 this second message to Haggai on December **18**:

19 (2) [NINETEEN]
Ezr 8: 31 We broke camp at the Ahava Canal on April **19**
10: 9 This took place on December **19**, and all the people

19-1/4 (1)
Eze 40: 49 foyer was 35 feet and the width was **19-1/4** feet.

20 (10) [TWENTY]
Lev 5: 16 for the loss, plus an added penalty of **20** percent.
6: 5 of **20** percent to the person they have harmed.
22: 14 amount eaten, plus an added penalty of **20** percent.
27: 13 pay the value set by the priest, plus **20** percent.
27: 15 pay the value set by the priest, plus **20** percent.
27: 19 value as assessed by the priest, plus **20** percent.
27: 27 priest's assessment of its worth, plus **20** percent.
27: 31 or grain, you must pay its value, plus **20** percent.
Nu 5: 7 adding a penalty of **20** percent and returning it to
Ezr 8: 27 **20** gold bowls, equal in value to 1,000 gold coins,

21 (10) [TWENTY-ONE]
Ezr 6: 19 April **21** the returned exiles celebrated Passover.
Eze 31: 1 On June **21**, during the eleventh year of King
40: 42 each 31-1/2 inches square and **21** inches high.
43: 13 There is a gutter all around the altar **21** inches wide and **21** inches deep,
43: 14 the altar; this lower ledge is **21** inches wide.
43: 14 ledge; this upper ledge is also **21** inches wide.
43: 16 of the altar is square, measuring **21** feet by **21** feet.
Hag 1: 15 This was on September **21** of the second year of

21-INCH (2) [INCH]
Eze 40: 12 of each of the guard alcoves was a **21-inch** curb.
43: 17 a **21-inch** gutter and a 10-1/2-inch curb all around

22-1/2 (4)
Ex 27: 14 curtain on the right side will be **22-1/2** feet long,
27: 15 curtain on the left side will also be **22-1/2** feet long
38: 14 The curtain on the right side was **22-1/2** feet long
38: 15 curtain on the left side was also **22-1/2** feet long

22-3/4 (1)
Eze 40: 11 and **22-3/4** feet wide in the gateway passage.

23 (1) [TWENTY-THREE]
Da 10: 4 On April **23**, as I was standing beside the great

24 (1) [TWENTY-FOUR]
Ezr 8: 26 **24** tons of silver, / 7,500 pounds of silver utensils,

24-1/2 (2)
Eze 40: 48 The entrance was **24-1/2** feet wide with walls
43: 17 measuring **24-1/2** feet on each side, with a 21-inch

25 (2) [TWENTY-FIVE]
2Ch 9: 13 Each year Solomon received about **25** tons of gold.
Est 8: 9 So on June **25** the king's secretaries were

26 (1) [TWENTY-SIX]
Eze 29: 17 On April **26**, during the twenty-seventh year of

27 (5) [TWENTY-SEVEN]
1Ki 7: 15 each **27** feet tall and 18 feet in circumference.
2Ki 25: 17 Each of the pillars was **27** feet tall. The bronze
2Ch 3: 15 Solomon made two pillars that were **27** feet tall,
Ezr 10: 17 By March **27** of the next year they had finished
Jer 52: 21 Each of the pillars was **27** feet tall and 18 feet in

28 (2) [TWENTY-EIGHT]
Ezr 8: 11 Bebai: Zechariah son of Bebai and **28** other men.
Eze 40: 1 On April **28**, during the twenty-fifth year of our

29 (5) [TWENTY-NINE]
Ge 11: 24 When Nahor was **29** years old, his son Terah was
Ezr 1: 9 silver trays | 1,000 / silver censers | **29**
10: 16 December **29**, the leaders sat down to investigate
Eze 30: 20 On April **29**, during the eleventh year of King
Hag 1: 1 On August **29** of the second year of King Darius's

30 (16) [THIRTY]
Ge 11: 14 When Shelah was **30** years old, his son Eber was
11: 18 When Peleg was **30** years old, his son Reu was
11: 22 When Serug was **30** years old, his son Nahor was
Ex 27: 16 the courtyard, make a curtain that is **30** feet long.
38: 18 It was **30** feet long and 7-1/2 feet high, just like the
1Ki 6: 2 was 90 feet long, **30** feet wide, and 45 feet high.
6: 3 The foyer at the front of the Temple was **30** feet
6: 16 It was **30** feet deep and was paneled with cedar
6: 20 This inner sanctuary was **30** feet long, **30** feet wide, and **30** feet high.
2Ch 3: 11 two cherubim standing side by side was **30** feet.
3: 13 So the wingspan of both cherubim together was **30**
4: 1 Solomon also made a bronze altar **30** feet long, **30** feet wide, and 15 feet high.
Ezr 1: 10 gold bowls | **30** / silver bowls | 410 / other items

31 (3) [THIRTY-ONE]
Ne 9: 1 On October **31** the people returned for another
Jer 52: 31 and released him from prison on March **31** of that
Eze 1: 1 On July **31** of my thirtieth year, while I was with

31-1/2 (1)
Eze 40: 42 each **31-1/2** inches square and 21 inches high.

32 (2) [THIRTY-TWO]
Ge 11: 20 When Reu was **32** years old, his son Serug was
Nu 31: 40 young girls, of whom **32** were the LORD's share.

34 (1) [THIRTY-FOUR]
Ge 11: 16 When Eber was **34** years old, his son Peleg was

35 (5) [THIRTY-FIVE]
Ge 11: 12 When Arphaxad was **35** years old, his son Shelah
Eze 40: 49 The depth of the foyer was **35** feet and the width
41: 2 Holy Place itself was 70 feet long and **35** feet wide.
41: 4 The inner room was **35** feet square. "This," he told
41: 10 This open area measured **35** feet in width, and it

35-FOOT (1)
Eze 42: 3 One block of rooms overlooked the **35-foot** width

40 (1) [FORTY]
Eze 4: 6 turn over and lie on your right side for **40** days—

42 (3) [FORTY-TWO]
Ezr 2: 24 The people of Beth-azmaveth | **42**
Ne 7: 28 The people of Beth-azmaveth | **42**
Rev 11: 2 They will trample the holy city for **42** months.

43-3/4 (7)
Eze 40: 13 facing guard alcoves; this distance was **43-3/4** feet.
40: 21 and **43-3/4** feet wide between the back walls of
40: 25 and **43-3/4** feet wide between the back walls of
40: 29 passage was 87-1/2 feet long and **43-3/4** feet wide.
40: 30 were 8-3/4 feet deep and **43-3/4** feet wide.)
40: 33 measured 87-1/2 feet long and **43-3/4** feet wide.
40: 36 measured 87-1/2 feet long and **43-3/4** feet wide.

45 (7) [FORTY-FIVE]
Ge 6: 15 it 450 feet long, 75 feet wide, and **45** feet high.
Ex 38: 28 The rest of the silver, about **45** pounds, was used to
1Ki 6: 2 was 90 feet long, 30 feet wide, and **45** feet high.
7: 2 It was 150 feet long, 75 feet wide, and **45** feet high.
7: 6 of Pillars, which was 75 feet long and **45** feet wide.
7: 23 7-1/2 feet deep and about **45** feet in circumference.
2Ch 4: 2 7-1/2 feet deep and about **45** feet in circumference.

50 (2) [FIFTY]
Ezr 8: 6 of Adin: Ebed son of Jonathan and **50** other men.
Ne 7: 70 **50** gold basins, and 530 robes for the priests.

52 (2) [FIFTY-TWO]
Ezr 2: 29 The citizens of Nebo | **52**
Ne 7: 33 The people of Nebo | **52**

52-1/2 (1)
Eze 46: 22 enclosures was 70 feet long and **52-1/2** feet wide,

56 (1)
Ezr 2: 22 The people of Netophah | **56**

60 (3) [SIXTY]
Nu 7: 85 In all, the silver objects weighed about **60** pounds,
1Ki 6: 17 outside the Most Holy Place, was **60** feet long.
Ezr 8: 13 Eliphelet, Jeuel, Shemaiah, and **60** other men.

61 (1)
Nu 31: 39 of which **61** were the LORD's share;

65 (2) [SIXTY-FIVE]
Ge 5: 15 When Mahalalel was **65** years old, his son Jared
5: 21 When Enoch was **65** years old, his son Methuselah

67 (1)
Ne 7: 72 2,500 pounds of silver, and **67** robes for the priests.

70 (6) [SEVENTY]
Ge 5: 12 When Kenan was **70** years old, his son Mahalalel
11: 26 When Terah was **70** years old, he became the
Ezr 8: 7 Elam: Jeshaiah son of Athaliah and **70** other men.
8: 14 family of Bigvai: Uthai, Zaccur, and **70** other men.
Eze 41: 2 The Holy Place itself was **70** feet long and 35 feet
46: 22 Each of these enclosures was **70** feet long

72 (1) [SEVENTY-TWO]
Nu 31: 38 36,000 cattle, of which **72** were the LORD's share;

74 (2)
Ezr 2: 40 and Kadmiel (descendants of Hodaviah) | **74**
Ne 7: 43 and Kadmiel (descendants of Hodaviah) | **74**

75 (12) [SEVENTY-FIVE]
Ge 6: 15 it 450 feet long, **75** feet wide, and 45 feet high.
Ex 27: 12 the west end of the courtyard will be **75** feet long,
27: 13 The east end will also be **75** feet long.
27: 18 courtyard will be 150 feet long and **75** feet wide,
38: 12 The west end was **75** feet wide. The walls were
38: 13 The east end was also **75** feet wide.
38: 27 pounds of silver, about **75** pounds for each base.
1Ki 7: 2 It was 150 feet long, **75** feet wide, and 45 feet high.
7: 6 of Pillars, which was **75** feet long and 45 feet wide.
2Ki 5: 22 He would like **75** pounds of silver and two sets of
23: 33 pounds of silver and **75** pounds of gold as tribute.
2Ch 36: 3 of 7,500 pounds of silver and **75** pounds of gold.

80 (2) [EIGHTY]
1Ch 15: 9 There were **80** descendants of Hebron, with Eliel
Ezr 8: 8 Zebadiah son of Michael and **80** other men.

87-1/2 (10)
Eze 40: 15 full length of the gateway passage was **87-1/2** feet
40: 21 gateway passage was **87-1/2** feet long and 43-3/4
40: 25 gateway passage was **87-1/2** feet long and 43-3/4
40: 29 gateway passage was **87-1/2** feet long and 43-3/4
40: 33 The gateway passage measured **87-1/2** feet long
40: 36 The gateway passage measured **87-1/2** feet long
42: 2 the north, was 175 feet long and **87-1/2** feet wide.
42: 7 from the outer courtyard; it was **87-1/2** feet long.
42: 8 extended for only **87-1/2** feet, while the inner
45: 2 An additional strip of land **87-1/2** feet wide is to

90 (3) [NINETY]
Ge 5: 9 When Enosh was **90** years old, his son Kenan was
1Ki 6: 2 Solomon built for the LORD was **90** feet long,
Ac 27: 28 later they sounded again and found only **90** feet.

95 (2)
Ezr 2: 20 The family of Gibbar | **95**
Ne 7: 25 The family of Gibbar | **95**

98 (2) [NINETY-EIGHT]
Ezr 2: 16 The family of Ater (descendants of Hezekiah) | **98**
Ne 7: 21 The family of Ater (descendants of Hezekiah) | **98**

100 (3) [HUNDRED]
Ge 11: 10 When Shem was **100** years old, his son Arphaxad
Ex 38: 27 The **100** bases for the frames of the sanctuary walls
Ezr 2: 69 pounds of silver, and **100** robes for the priests.

105 (2)
Ge 5: 6 When Seth was **105** years old, his son Enosh was
Eze 40: 14 to the gateway's foyer; this distance was **105** feet.

110 (5)
Ge 50: 22 in Egypt. Joseph was **110** years old when he died.
50: 26 So Joseph died at the age of **110**. They embalmed
Jos 24: 29 the servant of the LORD, died at the age of **110**.
Jdg 2: 8 the servant of the LORD, died at the age of **110**.
Ezr 8: 12 Johanan son of Hakkatan and **110** other men.

112 (4)
1Ch 15: 10 There were **112** descendants of Uzziel,
29: 4 donating more than **112** tons of gold from Ophir
Ezr 2: 18 The family of Jorah | **112**
Ne 7: 24 The family of Jorah | **112**

119 (1)
Ge 11: 25 Nahor lived another **119** years and had other sons

120 (8)
Ge 6: 3 the future, they will live no more than **120** years."
Dt 31: 2 "I am now **120** years old and am no longer able to
34: 7 Moses was **120** years old when he died, yet his
1Ch 15: 5 There were **120** from the clan of Kohath,
2Ch 5: 12 They were joined by **120** priests who were playing
Da 6: 1 decided to divide the kingdom into **120** provinces,
Ac 1: 15 on a day when about **120** believers were present,
27: 28 and found the water was only **120** feet deep.

122 (2)
Ezr 2: 27 The people of Micmash | **122**
Ne 7: 31 The people of Micmash | **122**

122-1/2 (1)
Eze 41: 12 It was **122-1/2** feet wide and 157-1/2 feet long,

123 (3)
Nu 33: 39 Aaron was **123** years old when he died there on
Ezr 2: 21 The people of Bethlehem | **123**
Ne 7: 32 The peoples of Bethel and Ai | **123**

125 (1)
1Sa 17: 5 and a coat of mail that weighed **125** pounds.

127 (4)
Ge 23: 1 When Sarah was **127** years old,
Est 1: 1 who reigned over **127** provinces stretching from
8: 9 local officials of all the **127** provinces stretching
9: 30 security were sent to the Jews throughout the **127**

128 (4)
Ezr 2: 23 The people of Anathoth | **128**
2: 41 The singers of the family of Asaph | **128**
Ne 7: 27 The people of Anathoth | **128**
11: 14 and **128** of his outstanding associates. Their chief

130 (4)
Ge 5: 3 When Adam was **130** years old, his son Seth was
47: 9 Jacob replied, "I have lived for **130** hard years,
1Ch 15: 7 There were **130** from the clan of Gershon,
2Ch 24: 15 lived to a very old age, finally dying at **130**.

133 (1)
Ex 6: 18 and Uzziel. (Kohath lived to be **133** years old.)

137 (3)
Ge 25: 17 Ishmael finally died at the age of **137** and joined
Ex 6: 16 (Levi, their father, lived to be **137** years old.)
6: 20 and Moses. (Amram lived to be **137** years old.)

138 (1)
Ne 7: 45 Ater, Talmon, Akkub, Hatita, and Shobai | **138**

139 (1)
Ezr 2: 42 Ater, Talmon, Akkub, Hatita, and Shobai | **139**

140 (1)
Job 42: 16 Job lived **140** years after that, living to see four

147 (1)
Ge 47: 28 in Egypt, so he was **147** years old when he died.

148 (1)
Ne 7: 44 The singers of the family of Asaph | **148**

150 (18)
Ge 7: 24 And the water covered the earth for **150** days.
8: 3 flood gradually began to recede. After **150** days,
Ex 27: 9 On the south side the curtains will stretch for **150**
27: 11 **150** feet of curtains held up by twenty posts fitted
27: 18 So the entire courtyard will be **150** feet long and 75
38: 9 the courtyard. The south wall was **150** feet long.
38: 11 The north wall was also **150** feet long, with twenty
1Ki 4: 22 Solomon's palace were **150** bushels of choice flour
7: 2 It was **150** feet long, 75 feet wide, and 45 feet high.
10: 29 horses could be bought for **150** pieces of silver.
16: 24 from its owner, Shemer, for **150** pounds of silver.
2Ki 5: 5 silver, **150** pounds of gold, and ten sets of clothing.
5: 23 "By all means, take **150** pounds of silver,"
1Ch 8: 40 They had many sons and grandsons—**150** in all.
2Ch 1: 17 horses could be bought for **150** pieces of silver.
Ezr 8: 3 the family of Parosh: Zechariah and **150** other men.
Ne 5: 17 even though I regularly fed **150** Jewish officials at
Eze 48: 17 Open lands will surround the city for **150** yards in

153 (1)
Jn 21: 11 were **153** large fish, and yet the net hadn't torn.

156 (1)
Ezr 2: 30 The citizens of Magbish | **156**

157-1/2 (1)
Eze 41: 12 It was 122-1/2 feet wide and **157-1/2** feet long,

160 (1)
Ezr 8: 10 Shelomith son of Josiphiah and **160** other men.

162 (1)
Ge 5: 18 When Jared was **162** years old, his son Enoch was

172 (1)
Ne 11: 19 Akkub, Talmon, and **172** of their associates,

175 (12)
Ge 25: 7 Abraham lived for **175** years,
Eze 40: 19 and inner gateways; the distance was **175** feet.
40: 23 distance between the two gateways was **175** feet.
40: 27 distance between the two gateways was **175** feet.
40: 47 inner courtyard and found it to be **175** feet square.
41: 13 the Temple, and he found it to be **175** feet long.
41: 13 its walls, was an additional **175** feet in length.
41: 14 to the east of the Temple was also **175** feet wide.
41: 15 including its two walls, was also **175** feet wide.
42: 2 the north, was **175** feet long and 87-1/2 feet wide.
42: 4 It extended the entire **175** feet of the complex,
42: 8 rooms toward the Temple—extended for **175** feet.

180 (2)
Ge 35: 28 Isaac lived for **180** years,
Rev 14: 20 the winepress in a stream about **180** miles long

182 (1)
Ge 5: 28 When Lamech was **182** years old, his son Noah

187 (1)
Ge 5: 25 When Methuselah was **187** years old, his son

188 (2)
1Ch 29: 7 gave almost **188** tons of gold, 10,000 gold coins,
Ne 7: 26 The peoples of Bethlehem and Netophah | **188**

200 (6)
Ge 11: 23 Serug lived another **200** years and had other sons
1Ch 12: 32 there were **200** leaders of the tribe with their
15: 8 There were **200** descendants of Elizaphan,
Ezr 2: 65 in addition to 7,337 servants and **200** singers,
8: 4 Eliehoenai son of Zerahiah and **200** other men.
Rev 9: 16 They led an army of **200** million mounted troops—

205 (1)
Ge 11: 32 Terah lived for **205** years and died while still at

207 (1)
Ge 11: 21 Reu lived another **207** years and had other sons

209 (1)
Ge 11: 19 Peleg lived another **209** years and had other sons

212 (1)
1Ch 9: 22 In all, there were **212** gatekeepers in those days,

216 (1)
Rev 21: 17 found them to be **216** feet thick (the angel used a

218 (1)
Ezr 8: 9 of Joab: Obadiah son of Jehiel and **218** other men.

220 (3)
1Ki 7:38 6 feet across and could hold **220** gallons of water.
1Ch 15: 6 There were **220** from the clan of Merari,
Ezr 8:20 and **220** Temple servants. The Temple servants

223 (2)
Ezr 2:19 The family of Hashum | **223**
2:28 The peoples of Bethel and Ai | **223**

232 (1)
1Ki 20:15 So Ahab mustered the troops of the **232** provincial

242 (1)
Ne 11:13 and **242** of his associates, who were heads of their

245 (3)
Ezr 2:66 They took with them 736 horses, **245** mules,
Ne 7:67 in addition to 7,337 servants and **245** singers,
7:68 They took with them 736 horses, **245** mules,

250 (6)
Nu 16: 2 involving **250** other prominent leaders,
16:17 Be sure that each of your **250** followers brings an
16:35 and burned up the **250** men who were offering
16:39 So Eleazar the priest collected the **250** bronze
26:10 and **250** of their followers were destroyed that day
2Ch 8:10 King Solomon also appointed **250** of them to

262 (1)
1Ch 29: 4 and over **262** tons of refined silver to be used for

273 (1)
Nu 3:46 To redeem the **273** firstborn sons of Israel who are

276 (1)
Ac 27:37 all **276** of us began eating—for that is the number

284 (1)
Ne 11:18 In all, there were **284** Levites in the holy city.

288 (1)
1Ch 25: 7 before the LORD, and each of them—**288** in all—

300 (3)
Ge 5:22 Enoch lived another **300** years in close fellowship
1Ki 4:22 bushels of choice flour and **300** bushels of meal,
Ezr 8: 5 Shecaniah son of Jahaziel and **300** other men.

318 (1)
Ge 14:14 the men born into his household, **318** of them in

320 (2)
Ezr 2:32 The citizens of Harim | **320**
Ne 7:35 The citizens of Harim | **320**

323 (1)
Ezr 2:17 The family of Bezai | **323**

324 (1)
Ne 7:23 The family of Bezai | **324**

328 (1)
Ne 7:22 The family of Hashum | **328**

345 (2)
Ezr 2:34 The citizens of Jericho | **345**
Ne 7:36 The citizens of Jericho | **345**

350 (1)
Ge 9:28 Noah lived another **350** years after the Flood.

365 (1)
Ge 5:23 Enoch lived **365** years in all.

372 (2)
Ezr 2: 4 The family of Shephatiah | **372**
Ne 7: 9 The family of Shephatiah | **372**

375 (2)
1Ch 29: 7 10,000 gold coins, about **375** tons of silver,
Est 3: 9 and I will give **375** tons of silver to the government

390 (2)
Eze 4: 5 You will bear Israel's sins for **390** days—one day
4: 9 during the **390** days you will be lying on your side.

392 (2)
Ezr 2:58 descendants of Solomon's servants numbered **392**.
Ne 7:60 descendants of Solomon's servants numbered **392**.

400 (1)
1Ki 18:19 prophets of Baal and the **400** prophets of Asherah,

403 (2)
Ge 11:13 Arphaxad lived another **403** years and had other
11:15 Shelah lived another **403** years and had other sons

410 (1)
Ezr 1:10 gold bowls | 30 / silver bowls | **410** / other items

420 (1)
Nu 31:52 as a gift to the LORD weighed about **420** pounds.

430 (3)
Ge 11:17 Eber lived another **430** years and had other sons
Ex 12:40 people of Israel had lived in Egypt for **430** years.
Gal 3:17 **430** years later when God gave the law to Moses.

430TH (1)
Ex 12:41 it was on the last day of the **430th** year that all the

435 (2)
Ezr 2:67 **435** camels, and 6,720 donkeys.
Ne 7:69 **435** camels, and 6,720 donkeys.

450 (4)
Ge 6:15 Make it **450** feet long, 75 feet wide, and 45 feet
1Ki 18:19 with all **450** prophets of Baal and the 400 prophets
18:22 of the LORD who is left, but Baal has **450** prophets.
Ac 13:20 All this took about **450** years. After that, judges

454 (1)
Ezr 2:15 The family of Adin | **454**

468 (1)
Ne 11: 6 There were also **468** descendants of Perez who

480 (1)
1Ki 6: 1 This was **480** years after the people of Israel were

500 (3)
Ge 5:32 By the time Noah was **500** years old, he had three
11:11 Shem lived another **500** years and had other sons
Ezr 7:22 **500** bushels of wheat, 550 gallons of wine,

530 (1)
Ne 7:70 50 gold basins, and **530** robes for the priests.

550 (3)
1Ki 9:23 He also appointed **550** of them to supervise the
Ezr 7:22 **550** gallons of wine, **550** gallons of olive oil,

595 (1)
Ge 5:30 Lamech lived **595** years, and he had other sons

600 (4)
Ge 7: 6 He was **600** years old when the flood came,
7:11 When Noah was **600** years old, on the seventeenth
1Ki 10:29 could be purchased for **600** pieces of silver,
2Ch 1:17 could be purchased for **600** pieces of silver,

601 (1)
Ge 8:13 Noah was **601** years old, ten and a half months

621 (2)
Ezr 2:26 The peoples of Ramah and Geba | **621**
Ne 7:30 The peoples of Ramah and Geba | **621**

623 (1)
Ezr 2:11 The family of Bebai | **623**

628 (1)
Ne 7:16 The family of Bebai | **628**

642 (2)
Ezr 2:10 The family of Bani | **642**
Ne 7:62 Tobiah, and Nekoda—a total of **642** people.

648 (1)
Ne 7:15 The family of Bani | **648**

652 (2)
Ezr 2:60 Tobiah, and Nekoda—a total of **652** people.
Ne 7:10 The family of Arah | **652**

655 (1)
Ne 7:20 The family of Adin | **655**

666 (2)
Ezr 2:13 The family of Adonikam | **666**
Rev 13:18 for it is the number of a man. His number is **666**.

667 (1)
Ne 7:18 The family of Adonikam | **667**

675 (2)
Nu 31:37 of which **675** were the LORD's share;
1Ch 29: 7 about 375 tons of silver, about **675** tons of bronze,

690 (1)
1Ch 9: 6 all, **690** families from the tribe of Judah returned.

721 (1)
Ne 7:37 The citizens of Lod, Hadid, and Ono | **721**

725 (1)
Ezr 2:33 The citizens of Lod, Hadid, and Ono | **725**

736 (2)
Ezr 2:66 They took with them **736** horses, 245 mules,
Ne 7:68 They took with them **736** horses, 245 mules,

743 (2)
Ezr 2:25 of Kiriath-jearim, Kephirah, and Beeroth | **743**
Ne 7:29 of Kiriath-jearim, Kephirah, and Beeroth | **743**

745 (1)
Jer 52:30 his captain of the guard, who took **745** more—

750 (1)
2Ki 5: 5 taking as gifts **750** pounds of silver, 150 pounds of

760 (2)
Ezr 2: 9 The family of Zaccai | **760**
Ne 7:14 The family of Zaccai | **760**

775 (1)
Ezr 2: 5 The family of Arah | **775**

777 (1)
Ge 5:31 He died at the age of **777**.

782 (1)
Ge 5:26 Methuselah lived another **782** years, and he had

800 (2)
Ge 5: 4 Adam lived another **800** years, and he had other
5:19 Jared lived another **800** years, and he had other

807 (1)
Ge 5: 7 Seth lived another **807** years, and he had other sons

815 (1)
Ge 5:10 Enosh lived another **815** years, and he had other sons

822 (1)
Ne 11:12 together with **822** of their associates, who worked

830 (1)
Ge 5:16 Mahalalel lived **830** years, and he had other sons

832 (1)
Jer 52:29 Nebuchadnezzar's eighteenth year he took **832**

840 (1)
Ge 5:13 Kenan lived another **840** years, and he had other

845 (1)
Ne 7:13 The family of Zattu | **845**

875 (4)
Eze 42:16 He measured the east side; it was **875** feet long.
42:20 So the area was **875** feet on each side with a wall
45: 2 of this land, measuring **875** feet by **875** feet,

895 (1)
Ge 5:17 He died at the age of **895**.

905 (1)
Ge 5:11 He died at the age of **905**.

910 (1)
Ge 5:14 He died at the age of **910**.

912 (1)
Ge 5: 8 He died at the age of **912**.

928 (1)
Ne 11: 8 Gabbai and Sallai, and a total of **928** relatives.

930 (1)
Ge 5: 5 He died at the age of **930**.

945 (1)
Ezr 2: 8 The family of Zattu | **945**

950 (1)
Ge 9:29 He was **950** years old when he died.

956 (1)
1Ch 9: 9 **956** families from the tribe of Benjamin returned.

962 (1)
Ge 5:20 He died at the age of **962**.

969 (1)
Ge 5:27 He died at the age of **969**.

973 (2)
Ezr 2:36 family of Jedaiah (through the line of Jeshua) | **973**
Ne 7:39 family of Jedaiah (through the line of Jeshua) | **973**

1,000 (5) [THOUSAND]
1Ch 12:34 there were **1,000** officers and 37,000 warriors
Ezr 1: 9 silver trays | **1,000** / silver censers | 29
1:10 bowls | 30 / silver bowls | 410 / other items | **1,000**
8:27 20 gold bowls, equal in value to **1,000** gold coins,
Ne 7:70 governor gave to the treasury **1,000** gold coins,

1,005 (1)
1Ki 4:32 some 3,000 proverbs and wrote **1,005** songs.

1,017 (2)
Ezr 2:39 The family of Harim | **1,017**
Ne 7:42 The family of Harim | **1,017**

1,052 (2)
Ezr 2:37 The family of Immer | **1,052**
Ne 7:40 The family of Immer | **1,052**

1,222 (1)
Ezr 2:12 The family of Azgad | **1,222**

1,247 (2)
Ezr 2:38 The family of Pashhur | **1,247**
Ne 7:41 The family of Pashhur | **1,247**

1,254 (4)
Ezr 2: 7 The family of Elam | **1,254**
2:31 The citizens of Elam | **1,254**
Ne 7:12 The family of Elam | **1,254**
7:34 The citizens of Elam | **1,254**

1,260 (2)
Rev 11: 3 and will prophesy during those **1,260** days."
12: 6 prepared a place to give her care for **1,260** days.

1,290 (1)
Da 12:11 is set up to be worshiped, there will be **1,290** days.

1,335 (1)
Da 12:12 wait and remain until the end of the **1,335** days!

1,400 (1)
Rev 21:16 length and width and height were each **1,400** miles.

1,500 (1)
Nu 35: 4 **1,500** feet from the town walls in every direction.

1,750 (4)
Eze 47: 3 he led me along the stream for **1,750** feet and told
47: 4 He measured off another **1,750** feet and told me to
47: 4 After another **1,750** feet, it was up to my waist.
47: 5 Then he measured another **1,750** feet, and the river

1,760 (1)
1Ch 9:13 In all, **1,760** priests returned. They were heads of

2,000 (1)
1Ch 5:21 sheep, **2,000** donkeys, and 100,000 captives.

2,056 (1)
Ezr 2:14 The family of Bigvai | **2,056**

2,067 (1)
Ne 7:19 The family of Bigvai | **2,067**

2,172 (2)
Ezr 2: 3 The family of Parosh | **2,172**
Ne 7: 8 The family of Parosh | **2,172**

2,200 (1)
Ex 38:24 people brought gifts of gold totaling about **2,200**

2,322 (1)
Ne 7:17 The family of Azgad | **2,322**

2,500 (1)
Ne 7:72 about **2,500** pounds of silver, and 67 robes for the

2,630 (1)
Nu 4:40 and the total number came to **2,630**.

2,750 (2)
Nu 4:36 and the total number came to **2,750**.
Ne 7:71 and some **2,750** pounds of silver for the work.

2,812 (1)
Ezr 2: 6 (descendants of Jeshua and Joab) | **2,812**

2,818 (1)
Ne 7:11 (descendants of Jeshua and Joab) | **2,818**

3,000 (3)
Nu 35: 5 Measure off **3,000** feet outside the town walls in
1Ki 4:32 He composed some **3,000** proverbs and wrote
1Ch 12:29 Saul's relatives, there were **3,000** warriors.

3,023 (1)
Jer 52:28 seventh year of Nebuchadnezzar's reign was **3,023**.

3,200 (1)
Nu 4:44 and the total number came to **3,200**.

3,600 (1)
2Ch 2:18 in the hill country, and **3,600** as foremen.

3,630 (1)
Ezr 2:35 The citizens of Senaah | **3,630**

3,700 (1)
1Ch 12:27 of Aaron, who had **3,700** under his command.

3,750 (1)
1Ch 29: 7 675 tons of bronze, and about **3,750** tons of iron.

3,930 (1)
Ne 7:38 The citizens of Senaah | **3,930**

4,600 (2)
1Ch 12:26 From the tribe of Levi, there were **4,600** troops.
Jer 52:30 took 745 more—a total of **4,600** captives in all.

5,310 (1)
Ex 38:29 The people also brought **5,310** pounds of bronze,

5,400 (1)
Ezr 1:11 **5,400** gold and silver items were turned over to

6,200 (1)
Nu 3:34 There were **6,200** males one month old or older

6,250 (1)
Ezr 2:69 **6,250** pounds of silver, and 100 robes for the

6,720 (2)
Ezr 2:67 435 camels, and **6,720** donkeys.
Ne 7:69 435 camels, and **6,720** donkeys.

6,800 (1)
1Ch 12:24 there were **6,800** warriors armed with shields

7,100 (1)
1Ch 12:25 the tribe of Simeon, there were **7,100** warriors.

7,337 (2)
Ezr 2:65 in addition to **7,337** servants and 200 singers,
Ne 7:67 in addition to **7,337** servants and 245 singers,

7,500 (9)
Ex 38:27 the inner curtain required **7,500** pounds of silver,
Nu 3:22 There were **7,500** males one month old or older
2Ki 23:33 He also demanded that Judah pay **7,500** pounds of
2Ch 25: 6 He also paid about **7,500** pounds of silver to hire
27: 5 he received from them an annual tribute of **7,500**
36: 3 demanded a tribute from Judah of **7,500** pounds of
Ezr 7:22 You are to give him up to **7,500** pounds of silver,
8:26 24 tons of silver, / **7,500** pounds of silver utensils, / **7,500** pounds of gold,

7,545 (1)
Ex 38:25 amount of silver that was given was about **7,545**

8,580 (1)
Nu 4:48 numbered **8,580**.

8,600 (1)
Nu 3:28 There were **8,600** males one month old or older

10,000 (2)
1Sa 15: 4 were 200,000 troops in addition to **10,000** men
1Ch 29: 7 **10,000** gold coins, about 375 tons of silver,

11,000 (1)
1Ki 7:26 It could hold about **11,000** gallons of water.

12,000 (12) [TWELVE]
Rev 7: 5 from Judah | **12,000** / from Reuben | **12,000** / from Gad | **12,000**
7: 6 from Asher | **12,000** / from Naphtali | **12,000** / from Manasseh | **12,000**
7: 7 from Simeon | **12,000** / from Levi | **12,000** / from Issachar | **12,000**
7: 8 from Zebulun | **12,000** / from Joseph | **12,000** / from Benjamin | **12,000**.

14,700 (1)
Nu 16:49 But **14,700** people died in that plague, in addition

15,000 (1)
Jdg 8:10 were in Karkor with a remnant of **15,000**

16,000 (2)
Nu 31:40 **16,000** young girls, of whom 32 were the LORD's
31:46 and **16,000** young girls.

16,500 (1)
2Ch 4: 5 It could hold about **16,500** gallons of water.

17,200 (1)
1Ch 7:11 and their descendants included **17,200** men

18,000 (1)
1Ch 12:31 **18,000** men were sent for the express purpose of

20,000 (2)
Ne 7:71 other leaders gave to the treasury a total of **20,000**
7:72 The rest of the people gave **20,000** gold coins,

20,200 (1)
1Ch 7: 9 were **20,200** men available for military service

20,800 (1)
1Ch 12:30 the tribe of Ephraim, there were **20,800** warriors,

22,000 (3)
Nu 3:39 there were **22,000** males one month old or older.
1Ki 8:63 offerings to the LORD numbering **22,000** oxen
2Ch 7: 5 King Solomon offered a sacrifice of **22,000** oxen

22,034 (1)
1Ch 7: 7 service among their descendants was **22,034**.

22,200 (1)
Nu 26:14 from all the clans of Simeon numbered **22,200**.

22,273 (1)
Nu 3:43 sons who were one month old or older was **22,273**.

22,600 (1)
1Ch 7: 2 military service from these families was **22,600**.

23,000 (2)
Nu 26:62 were one month old or older numbered **23,000**.
1Co 10: 8 them did, causing **23,000** of them to die in one day.

24,000 (1)
Nu 25: 9 but not before **24,000** people had died.

25,100 (1)
Jdg 20:35 that day the Israelites killed **25,100** of Benjamin's

26,000 (1)
1Ch 7:40 were **26,000** men available for military service

27,000 (1)
1Ki 20:30 but the wall fell on them and killed another **27,000**.

28,600 (1)
1Ch 12:35 there were **28,600** warriors, all prepared for battle.

30,000 (1)
1Sa 11: 8 men of Israel, in addition to **30,000** from Judah.

30,500 (2)
Nu 31:39 **30,500** donkeys, of which 61 were the LORD's
31:45 **30,500** donkeys,

32,000 (1)
Nu 31:35 and **32,000** young girls.

32,200 (2)
Nu 1:34[-35] Manasseh son of Joseph | **32,200**
2:20[-21] Gamaliel son of Pedahzur | **32,200**

32,500 (1)
Nu 26:37 from all the clans of Ephraim numbered **32,500**.

35,400 (2)
Nu 1:36[-37] Benjamin | **35,400**
2:22[-23] Benjamin | Abidan son of Gideoni | **35,400**

36,000 (3)
Nu 31:38 **36,000** cattle, of which 72 were the LORD's share;
31:44 **36,000** cattle,
1Ch 7: 4 service among their descendants was **36,000**,

37,000 (1)
1Ch 12:34 and **37,000** warriors armed with shields and spears.

40,000 (1)
1Ch 12:36 there were **40,000** trained warriors, all prepared for

40,500 (3)
Nu 1:32[-33] Ephraim son of Joseph | **40,500**
2:18[-19] Ephraim | Elishama son of Ammihud | **40,500**
26:18 men from all the clans of Gad numbered **40,500**.

41,500 (2)
Nu 1:40[-41] Asher | **41,500**
2:27[-28] Asher | Pagiel son of Ocran | **41,500**

42,360 (2)
Ezr 2:64 So a total of **42,360** people returned to Judah,
Ne 7:66 "So a total of **42,360** people returned to Judah,

43,730 (1)
Nu 26: 7 from all the clans of Reuben numbered **43,730**.

44,760 (1)
1Ch 5:18 There were **44,760** skilled warriors in the armies of

45,400 (1)
Nu 26:50 from all the clans of Naphtali numbered **45,400**.

45,600 (1)
Nu 26:41 from all the clans of Benjamin numbered **45,600**.

45,650 (2)
Nu 1:24[-25] Gad | **45,650**
2:14[-15] Gad | Eliasaph son of Deuel | **45,650**

46,500 (1)
Nu 2:10[-11] Reuben | Elizur son of Shedeur | **46,500**

50,000 (4)
1Ch 5:21 plunder taken from the Hagrites included **50,000**
12:33 of Zebulun, there were **50,000** skilled warriors.
2Ch 27: 5 **50,000** bushels of wheat, and **50,000** bushels of barley.

52,700 (1)
Nu 26:34 from all the clans of Manasseh numbered **52,700**.

53,400 (3)
Nu 1:42[-43] Naphtali | **53,400**
2:29[-30] Naphtali | Ahira son of Enan | **53,400**
26:47 men from all the clans of Asher numbered **53,400**.

54,400 (2)
Nu 1:28[-29] Issachar | **54,400**
2: 5[-6] Issachar | Nethanel son of Zuar | **54,400**

57,400 (2)
Nu 1:30[-31] Zebulun | **57,400**
2: 7[-8] Zebulun | Eliab son of Helon | **57,400**

59,300 (2)
Nu 1:22[-23] Simeon | **59,300**
2:12[-13] Shelumiel son of Zurishaddai | **59,300**

60,500 (1)
Nu 26:27 from all the clans of Zebulun numbered **60,500**.

61,000 (2)
Nu 31:34 **61,000** donkeys,
Ezr 2:69 The total of their gifts came to **61,000** gold coins,

62,700 (2)
Nu 1:38[-39] Dan | **62,700**
2:25[-26] Dan | Ahiezer son of Ammishaddai | **62,700**

64,300 (1)
Nu 26:25 from all the clans of Issachar numbered **64,300**.

64,400 (1)
Nu 26:43 and the men from these clans numbered **64,400**.

70,000 (1)
2Ch 2:18 He enlisted **70,000** of them as common laborers,

72,000 (1)
Nu 31:33 **72,000** cattle,

74,600 (2)
Nu 1:26[-27] Judah | **74,600**
2: 3[-4] Judah | Nahshon son of Amminadab | **74,600**

76,500 (1)
Nu 26:22 men from all the clans of Judah numbered **76,500**.

80,000 (1)
2Ch 2:18 **80,000** as stonecutters in the hill country,

87,000 (1)
1Ch 7: 5 all the clans of the tribe of Issachar was **87,000**.

100,000 (8)
1Ki 5:11 of **100,000** bushels of wheat for his household
20:29 Israelites killed **100,000** Aramean foot soldiers in
2Ki 3: 4 pay the king of Israel an annual tribute of **100,000** lambs and the wool of **100,000** rams.
1Ch 5:21 sheep, 2,000 donkeys, and **100,000** captives.
2Ch 2:10 I will pay your men **100,000** bushels of crushed wheat,
2:10 **100,000** bushels of barley, 110,000 gallons of wine,
25: 6 paid about 7,500 pounds of silver to hire **100,000**

108,100 (1)
Nu 2:24 troops on Ephraim's side of the camp is **108,100**,

110,000 (3)
1Ki 5:11 for his household and **110,000** gallons of olive oil.
2Ch 2:10 100,000 bushels of barley, **110,000** gallons of wine, and **110,000** gallons of olive oil."

120,000 (6)
Jdg 8:10 of the east—for **120,000** had already been killed.
1Ki 8:63 LORD numbering 22,000 oxen and **120,000** sheep.
1Ch 12:37 there were **120,000** troops armed with every kind
2Ch 7: 5 a sacrifice of 22,000 oxen and **120,000** sheep.
28: 6 killed **120,000** of Judah's troops because they had
Jnh 4:11 But Nineveh has more than **120,000** people living

144,000 (3) [TWELVE]
Rev 7: 4 There were **144,000** who were sealed from all the
14: 1 and with him were **144,000** who had his name and
14: 3 no one could learn this song except those **144,000**

151,450 (1)
Nu 2:16 troops on Reuben's side of the camp is **151,450**.

153,600 (1)
2Ch 2:17 his father had taken, and he counted **153,600**.

157,600 (1)
Nu 2:31 all the troops on Dan's side of the camp is **157,600**.

180,000 (3)
1Ki 12:21 armies of Judah and Benjamin—**180,000** select
2Ch 11: 1 armies of Judah and Benjamin—**180,000** select
17:18 Jehozabad, who commanded **180,000** armed men.

185,000 (2)
2Ki 19:35 to the Assyrian camp and killed **185,000** Assyrian
Isa 37:36 to the Assyrian camp and killed **185,000** Assyrian

186,400 (1)
Nu 2: 9 the troops on Judah's side of the camp is **186,400**.

200,000 (4)
1Sa 15: 4 There were **200,000** troops in addition to 10,000
2Ch 17:16 with **200,000** troops under his command.
17:17 there were **200,000** troops equipped with bows
28: 8 The armies of Israel captured **200,000** women

250,000 (1)
1Ch 5:21 **250,000** sheep, 2,000 donkeys, and 100,000

280,000 (2)
2Ch 14: 8 He also had an army of **280,000** warriors from the
17:15 was Jehohanan, who commanded **280,000** troops.

300,000 (4)
1Sa 11: 8 he found that there were **300,000** men of Israel,
2Ch 14: 8 King Asa had an army of **300,000** warriors from
17:14 there were **300,000** troops organized in units of one
25: 5 found that he had an army of **300,000** men twenty

307,500 (1)
2Ch 26:13 army consisted of **307,500** men, all elite troops.

337,500 (2)
Nu 31:36 given to the fighting men totaled **337,500** sheep,
31:43 amounted to **337,500** sheep,

400,000 (3)
Jdg 20: 2 of Israel—**400,000** warriors armed with swords—
20:17 Israel had **400,000** warriors armed with swords,
2Ch 13: 3 King Abijah, fielded **400,000** seasoned warriors,

470,000 (1)
1Ch 21: 5 of military age in Israel, and **470,000** in Judah.

500,000 (2)
2Sa 24: 9 men of military age in Israel and **500,000** in Judah.
2Ch 13:17 were **500,000** casualties among Israel's finest

600,000 (2)
Ex 12:37 There were about **600,000** men, plus all the women
Nu 11:21 "There are **600,000** foot soldiers here with me,

601,730 (1)
Nu 26:51 men counted in the census numbered **601,730**.

603,550 (3)
Ex 38:26 who were twenty years old or older, **603,550** in all.
Nu 1:46 The total number was **603,550**.
2:32 of Israel listed by their families totaled **603,550**.

675,000 (1)
Nu 31:32 the fighting men had taken totaled **675,000** sheep,

800,000 (2)
2Sa 24: 9 There were **800,000** men of military age in Israel
2Ch 13: 3 Jeroboam mustered **800,000** courageous men from

1,100,000 (1)
1Ch 21: 5 were **1,100,000** men of military age in Israel,

INDEX OF ARTICLES, CONJUNCTIONS, PARTICLES, PREPOSITIONS, PRONOUNS, AND OTHER HIGHLY FREQUENT WORDS

A (9213)

Ge 1:2; **2:**7, 7, 8, 10, 18, 19, 21, 22, 23, 24; **3:**13, 17, 17, 24; **4:**1, 2, 2, 2, 3, 12, 14, 15, 17, 17, 20, 22, 23, 26; **5:**24; **6:**3, 9, 9, 14, 16, 17, 19, 19, 19; **7:**3, 3; **8:**1, 5, 7, 8, 11, 12, 13; **9:**6, 6, 9, 12, 15, 20, 20, 23, 25; **10:**8, 9, 9; **11:**1, 2, 4, 4, 4, 27, 29; **12:**2, 2, 6, 10, 11, 17; **13:**10, 12, 15, 17; **14:**18, 20, 23, 24; **15:**1, 2, 2, 2, 4, 9, 9, 9, 9, 9, 12, 12, 13, 15, 17, 17, 18; **16:**3, 7, 11, 12, 12, 15; **17:**1, 2, 2, 4, 11, 16, 17, 17, 19, 20; **18:**3, 7, 7, 10, 12, 12, 13, 14, 14, 18, 22, 25; **19:**3, 7, 20, 26, 28, 30, 31, 37, 38; **20:**1, 1, 3, 3, 7, 8, 11, 15, 16, 18; **21:**2, 7, 7, 8, 13, 14, 15, 16, 18, 19, 19, 21, 21, 25, 27, 30, 33, 34; **22:**2, 3, 3, 5, 8, 10, 13, 13, 13, 14; **23:**4, 4, 4, 4, 6, 9, 20; **24:**1, 4, 5, 7, 9, 11, 14, 15, 15, 16, 17, 22, 25, 29, 31, 31, 35, 35, 38, 39, 40, 42, 42, 43, 45, 48, 63, 67; **25:**8, 13, 21, 25, 27, 27, 29; **26:**1, 8, 11, 12, 13, 19, 21, 24, 25, 27, 28, 28, 30, 31, 32, 34; **27:**3, 7, 14, 16, 16, 34, 40; **28:**3, 6, 6, 11, 11, 11, 12, 18, 18, 22, 22; **29:**2, 2, 5, 9, 14, 17, 20, 22, 24, 26, 28, 29, 31, 32, 34, 35; **30:**2, 5, 6, 7, 12, 14, 18, 19, 21, 22, 23, 43; **31:**2, 10, 13, 23, 24, 27, 36, 38, 42, 44, 45, 45, 46, 46, 48, 52, 54, 54; **32:**10, 13, 16, 18, 24; **33:**2, 10, 17, 19; **34:**7, 7, 14, 14, 15, 19, 31; **35:**11, 14, 17, 20, 29; **36:**4, 4, 9; **37:**3, 3, 4, 5, 15, 20, 20, 25, 25, 26, 31, 33; **38:**1, 2, 3, 5, 6, 7, 8, 9, 9, 10, 10, 11, 14, 15, 17, 21, 22, 24, 28; **39:**1, 4, 6, 6, 9, 9, 17; **40:**5, 9, 16, 19, 20, 22; **41:**5, 7, 11, 11, 12, 12, 13, 14, 15, 22, 29, 33, 38, 40, 42, 44, 44, 45, 45, 46, 48; **42:**7, 16, 18, 24; **43:**2, 16, 30, 32; **44:**5, 7, 10, 15, 18, 19, 19, 20, 20, 25, 32, 33; **45:**7, 8; **46:**2, 3, 10, 29; **47:**24, 26; **48:**4, 7, 16, 19, 19; **49:**5, 6, 9, 9, 9, 11, 11, 13, 14, 17, 17, 21, 22, 22, 22, 26, 27, 28, 30; **50:**3, 7, 9, 10, 10, 11, 13, 26; **Ex 1:**8, 9, 10; **2:**1, 2, 2, 3, 4, 15, 20, 22, 22, 22; **3:**2, 2, 8, 16, 17, 18; **4:**2, 3, 4, 10, 14, 20, 25, 25, 26, 29; **5:**1, 3, 8; **6:**4, 15, 17; **7:**4, 9, 9, 10, 15; **8:**14, 23, 27, 31; **9:**3, 4, 4, 6, 8, 10, 14, 15, 18, 23, 24; **10:**6, 9, 19, 19, 21, 26; **11:**3, 6, 7, 7; **12:**3, 3, 3, 4, 5, 5, 5, 11, 13, 14, 16, 17, 22, 22, 30, 32, 36, 49, 49; **13:**3, 5, 6, 8, 9, 9, 13, 13, 16, 16, 17, 18, 18, 21, 21; **14:**7, 14, 16, 19, 20, 21, 21, 28, 29; **15:**3, 5, 8, 10, 16, 20, 25; **16:**1, 6, 18, 18, 20, 23, 23, 25, 26, 29, 32, 33, 33, 33; **17:**10, 12, 13, 14; **18:**3, 3, 12, 12, 18, 19; **19:**6, 9, 16, 16, 16, 16, 18, 18; **20:**5, 6, 9, 10, 12, 18, 25; **21:**2, 3, 4, 4, 7, 7, 9, 11, 12, 13, 18, 19, 20, 21, 22, 24, 26, 27, 28, 28, 28, 31, 31, 32, 33, 33, 35; **22:**1, 2, 2, 3, 3, 4, 4, 5, 6, 7, 9, 9, 9, 10, 10, 13, 14, 16, 16, 18, 25, 25, 26, 31; **23:**2, 3, 5, 8, 8, 9, 12, 15, 19, 19, 29, 30, 30; **24:**1, 10, 11, 17; **25:**3, 8, 10, 11, 23, 24, 25, 25, 31, 33; **26:**3, 6, 9, 11, 14, 14, 24, 24, 31; **27:**1, 2, 4, 4, 9, 16, 21; **28:**3, 4, 4, 4, 4, 11, 11, 12, 15, 16, 17, 17, 18, 18, 18, 19, 20, 20, 21, 32, 36, 37; **29:**1, 3, 14, 18, 24, 25, 26, 31, 36, 40, 41, 42; **30:**1, 3, 10, 10, 12, 12, 18, 18, 21, 25, 33, 35; **31:**5, 13, 15, 15, 17; **32:**4, 5, 8, 10, 17, 18, 18, 18, 22, 29, 30, 31, 35; **33:**3, 3, 5, 11, 15; **34:**5, 14, 20, 20, 20, 25, 26, 33; **35:**1, 2, 2; **36:**10, 14, 16, 29, 29, 30; **37:**2, 8, 10, 11, 12, 12, 19, 26; **38:**4, 4, 17, 23; **39:**3, 6, 9, 10, 10, 11, 11, 11, 12, 13, 13, 14, 23, 31; **40:**13, 29, 29;
Lev 1:3, 3, 7, 9, 10, 10, 13, 14, 14, 14, 14, 17; **2:**1, 2, 3, 4, 5, 6, 7, 8, 9, 10, 14, 14, 15, 16; **3:**1, 1, 1, 6, 6, 6, 7, 12, 17; **4:**3, 10, 12, 12, 14, 14, 21, 23, 28, 29, 32, 32, 33, 35, 35; **5:**2, 2, 4, 6, 6, 6, 6, 7, 7, 7, 10, 11, 12, 12, 15, 16, 18, 18, 19; **6:**2, 3, 4, 4, 5, 6, 6, 11, 15, 16, 20, 21, 25, 26, 27, 28, 28, 29, 30; **7:**2, 5, 6, 6, 9, 9, 12, 14, 16, 16, 18, 20, 24, 29, 29, 32; **8:**21, 26, 26, 26; **9:**2, 2, 2, 2, 3, 3, 3, 3, 3, 4, 4, 4, 4, 8, 14, 17; **10:**1, 4, 9, 13, 16, 17; **11:**33, 35, 36, 36; **12:**2, 2, 5, 5, 6, 6, 6, 6, 6, 6, 7, 7, 8, 8; **13:**2, 2, 2, 2, 3, 3, 6, 8, 9, 11, 12, 15, 18, 19, 19, 20, 22, 24, 24, 25, 25, 27, 28, 29, 30, 38, 39, 39, 40, 41, 42, 42, 44, 49, 57; **14:**2, 3, 4, 4, 4, 4, 5, 10, 12, 13, 21, 21, 21, 22, 22, 31, 31, 32, 35, 49, 49, 50, 55, 56, 56, 56; **15:**2, 13, 15, 15, 16, 19, 24, 28, 30, 30, 31, 32, 32, 33, 33, 33, 33; **16:**1, 3, 3, 3, 3, 5, 5, 5, 6, 9, 11, 13, 15, 21, 22, 24, 26, 29, 31, 31, 34; **17:**3, 3, 3, 4, 4, 7, 8, 8, 10, 10, 15, 15; **18:**6, 17, 17, 17, 18, 19, 21, 22, 23, 23, 23, 23, 25, 28; **19:**5, 12, 18, 20, 20, 21, 21, 29; **20:**9, 10, 11, 11, 12, 12, 13, 13, 14, 14, 15, 16, 16, 16, 17, 17, 18, 18, 18, 19, 19, 19, 20, 20, 21, 24, 25, 27; **21:**1, 2, 4, 9, 9, 11, 13, 14, 14, 14, 14, 18, 19, 20, 20, 20, 21, 21; **22:**4, 4, 5, 8, 10, 10, 12, 13, 18, 18, 18, 19, 19, 19, 19, 21, 21, 21, 22, 22, 23, 23, 25, 27, 27, 27, 28, 29; **23:**3, 3, 7, 8, 12, 12, 13, 13, 14, 19, 19, 21, 21, 24, 24, 24, 27, 31, 32, 35, 36, 36, 41; **24:**3, 7, 8, 9, 9, 10, 10, 18; **25:**2, 4, 5, 10, 10, 11, 12, 12, 14, 16, 21, 23, 24, 25, 25, 29, 29, 29, 30, 31, 31, 31, 31, 35, 43, 46, 47, 47, 48, 49, 50, 52, 52, 53, 53; **26:**8, 8, 10, 23, 25, 36, 36, 36; **27:**2, 3, 4, 5, 5, 6, 6, 7, 7, 8, 9, 10, 10, 10, 10, 14, 16, 21, 22, 23, 27, 28, 29, 29, 30; **Nu 1:**2, 52; **2:**9, 31; **3:**4, 15, 38; **4:**2, 6, 7, 8, 8, 9, 10, 11, 11, 12, 13, 14, 19, 20, 22, 29; **5:**2, 2, 2, 7, 8, 9, 12, 15, 17, 18, 23, 26, 26, 27, 29, 30; **6:**2, 2, 4, 6, 11, 11, 12, 12, 14, 14, 14, 14, 14, 14, 15, 17, 20; **7:**3, 11, 13, 13, 14, 15, 15, 15, 15, 16, 16, 17, 19, 19, 20, 21, 21, 21, 21, 22, 22, 23, 25, 25, 26, 27, 27, 27, 27, 28, 28, 29, 31, 31, 32, 33, 33, 33, 33, 34, 34, 35, 37, 37, 38, 39, 39, 39, 39, 40, 40, 41, 43, 43, 44, 45, 45, 45, 45, 46, 46, 47, 49, 49, 50, 51, 51, 51, 51, 52, 52, 53, 55, 55, 56, 57, 57, 57, 57, 58, 58, 59, 61, 61, 62, 63, 63, 63, 63, 64, 64, 65, 67, 67, 68, 69, 69, 69, 69, 70, 70, 71, 73, 73, 74, 75, 75, 75, 75, 76, 76, 77, 79, 79, 80, 81, 81, 81, 81, 82, 82, 83; **8:**8, 8, 8, 8, 11, 12, 12, 13, 15, 21; **9:**6, 7, 10, 10, 13, 15, 19, 19, 20, 20, 22, 22; **10:**6, 7, 8; **11:**8, 11, 12, 12, 19, 20, 21, 27, 31, 33; **12:**1, 12; **13:**23, 23, 27, 27; **14:**2, 4, 7, 8, 12, 12, 34, 37; **15:**3, 3, 3, 3, 3, 4, 5, 5, 6, 6, 7, 7, 8, 8, 8, 8, 8, 15, 19, 20, 20, 24, 24, 24, 27, 27, 32, 38; **16:**1, 2, 9, 13, 15, 15, 29, 30, 38, 38, 38, 39, 40; **17:**6, 10; **18:**4, 10, 23, 26, 26, 26, 28; **19:**2, 2, 6, 9, 10, 11, 13, 14, 15, 16, 16, 16, 16, 17, 18, 18, 18, 18, 21, 22; **20:**15, 16, 22; **21:**8, 8, 8, 9, 9, 26, 28, 28, 35; **22:**5, 11, 15, 18, 23, 23, 24, 26, 27, 29, 29, 31, 36; **23:**1, 2, 2, 3, 4, 4, 5, 9, 10, 13, 14, 14, 16, 19, 19, 20, 22, 24, 24, 29, 30, 30; **24:**4, 8, 9, 9, 10, 13, 16, 17, 17, 19; **25:**6, 7, 14, 15, 18; **26:**2, 10, 46, 59, 61; **27:**1, 8, 11, 16, 17; **28:**5, 9, 9, 14, 14, 15, 17, 18, 19, 22, 22, 26, 27; **29:**1, 2, 5, 5, 8, 11, 12, 13, 14, 16, 16, 19, 19, 22, 22, 25, 25, 28, 28, 31, 31, 34, 36, 38; **30:**2, 2, 2, 3, 3, 3, 6, 6, 9, 9, 10, 10, 15, 15, 16, 16, 16; **31:**5, 6, 17, 19, 26, 52, 54; **32:**14, 42; **33:**2, 38, 54, 54; **34:**13; **35:**6, 12, 16, 17, 18, 20, 21, 23, 24, 25, 31, 32, 32; **36:**1, 3; **Dt 1:**3, 9, 11, 13, 14, 15, 15, 23, 25, 31, 33, 33, 44, 46; **2:**1, 9, 10, 12, 19, 21, 23, 34; **3:**14; **4:**7, 12, 16, 16, 16, 17, 18, 18, 24, 24, 25, 26, 27, 28, 37, 38, 40; **5:**2, 9, 10, 13, 14, 16, 22; **6:**2, 7, 8, 10, 15; **7:**6, 9, 13, 21, 25; **8:**3, 5, 5, 7, 8, 9, 9, 16; **9:**3, 6, 14, 14; **10:**1, 3, 7; **11:**6, 9, 9, 10, 11, 12, 18, 19, 26, 26, 28, 29, 29; **12:**6, 10, 11, 17, 21, 26; **13:**14, 16, 16, 17; **14:**21, 21, 21, 21, 22, 24, 26; **15:**4, 9, 13, 14, 18, 22; **16:**3, 10, 11, 14, 15, 16, 19; **17:**1, 2, 6, 8, 8, 8, 8, 11, 14, 15, 15, 16, 18; **18:**8, 10, 15, 18, 20; **19:**4, 5, 10, 11, 14, 15, 16, 16; **20:**5, 6, 10, 16, 19; **21:**1, 3, 3, 4, 4, 11, 13, 14, 15, 18, 18, 20, 22, 22, 23, 23; **22:**5, 5, 6, 6, 7, 8, 10, 13, 13, 14, 17, 19, 21, 22, 23, 23, 23, 23, 26, 28, 28, 30; **23:**1, 5, 10, 12, 13, 13, 17, 18, 18, 18, 19, 21, 22, 22, 23, 23, 24, 25, 25; **24:**1, 1, 1, 4, 5, 6, 6, 6, 7, 7, 12, 13, 17, 19; **25:**1, 5, 5, 9, 9, 15, 19; **26:**1, 2, 5, 5, 10, 12, 15, 19; **27:**3, 12, 13, 17, 17, 18; **28:**10, 29, 30, 30, 30, 31, 33, 36, 37, 37, 46, 49, 49, 50, 55, 68; **29:**12, 23; **30:**15, 16, 18; **31:**15, 19, 20, 24, 26; **32:**4, 5, 10, 20, 28, 30, 46, 47, 52; **33:**17, 17, 20, 20, 21, 22, 28, 29; **34:**6; **Jos 2:**1, 10, 14, 15, 19; **3:**4, 4, 8, 16; **4:**6, 7; **5:**2, 6, 13; **6:**3, 4, 5, 6, 10, 23; **7:**1, 3, 15, 21, 21, 21, 22, 26; **8:**11, 14, 17, 22, 22, 28, 29, 29; **9:**6, 6, 7, 9, 11, 15, 15, 18, 22; **10:**2, 5, 8, 10, 11, 13, 14, 14, 14, 16, 20, 21, 27, 42; **11:**4, 11, 18; **12:**2, 5, 7; **13:**6; **14:**2, 3, 6, 7, 15; **15:**19; **17:**1, 3, 5; **18:**4; **19:**49; **21:**13, 21, 27, 32, 38; **22:**3, 10, 10, 13, 14, 20, 25, 27, 28, 34; **23:**10, 13, 13, 13, 13, 14; **24:**5, 9, 19, 25, 25, 26, 26, 27;
Jdg 1:15, 24, 24, 25, 26; **2:**1, 3, 18; **3:**9, 15, 16, 19, 20, 20, 25, 25, 27, 27; **4:**2, 4, 4, 9, 11, 15, 16, 18, 21; **5:**7, 8, 12, 14, 25, 26, 29, 30; **6:**8, 11, 17, 19, 19, 19, 19, 26, 28, 28, 29, 31, 34, 34, 38; **7:**12, 13, 13, 13, 13, 16, 16, 16, 20, 21; **8:**10, 14, 16, 18, 20, 21, 21, 25, 25, 27, 27, 31, 31; **9:**6, 8, 8, 28, 48, 49, 51, 53, 53, 54; **10:**3; **11:**1, 1, 2, 3, 25, 30, 31, 34, 35, 35, 36, 36, 37, 39, 39; **12:**5, 5; **13:**2, 3, 5, 5, 6, 7, 7, 15, 16, 16, 19, 19, 19, 19; **14:**1, 2, 3, 5, 6, 8, 10, 12, 16, 18; **15:**1, 1, 4, 8, 15, 15, 16, 16, 16, 19; **16:**1, 4, 9, 10, 17, 19, 23; **17:**1, 4, 5, 5, 7, 8, 9, 9, 10, 10, 10, 13; **18:**1, 2, 7, 10, 12, 14, 14, 14, 14, 19, 19, 22, 28, 30; **19:**1, 1, 1, 3, 13, 14, 18, 23, 24, 29, 30; **20:**4, 12, 16, 16, 16, 25, 35, 38; **21:**1, 5, 11, 12, 13, 18; **Ru 1:**1, 1, 4, 4; **2:**1, 1, 3, 7, 10, 16, 17; **3:**1, 2, 3, 8, 10, 11, 14; **4:**1, 7, 10, 13, 14, 17; **1Sa 1:**1, 5, 11, 11, 16, 20, 21, 24, 24; **2:**3, 8, 13, 13, 13, 18, 18, 18, 19, 27, 31, 33, 35; **3:**7, 8, 11, 20; **4:**7, 12, 20; **5:**6, 9, 9; **6:**3, 3, 7, 7, 7, 8, 9, 10, 14, 14, 14, 14, 17, 18; **7:**2, 6, 6, 9, 9, 10, 12, 13; **8:**5, 9, 11, 15, 17, 19, 22; **9:**1, 3, 6, 7, 9, 11, 12, 16, 25, 27; **10:**1, 3, 5, 5, 5, 5, 5, 6, 11, 11, 12, 12, 19, 25, 25, 26; **11:**1, 1, 2, 11, 15; **12:**1, 2, 3, 4, 12, 17, 19, 22; **13:**5, 14, 20, 21, 21, 21, 21, 22, 23; **14:**6, 6, 12, 16, 24, 24, 27, 27, 28, 29, 33, 43, 43, 43, 45, 52; **15:**12, 18; **16:**1, 2, 2, 7, 14, 15, 15, 16, 18, 18, 20, 20; **17:**4, 4, 4, 5, 5, 6, 7, 7, 8, 10, 12, 16, 18, 25, 26, 29, 32, 33, 33, 34, 34, 34, 35, 38, 38, 39, 40, 43, 43, 46, 49, 50, 52; **18:**3, 5, 9, 10, 10, 10, 13, 17, 19, 21, 23, 23, 23; **19:**2, 5, 5, 12, 13, 16, 21, 24; **20:**3, 8, 16, 20, 21, 29, 30, 35, 42; **21:**2, 5, 8, 8, 9, 14; **22:**6, 13, 14; **23:**7, 23, 26; **24:**3, 4, 6, 11, 14, 14, 17, 18; **25:**2, 2, 3, 3, 8, 11, 16, 18, 20, 21, 25, 25, 27, 28, 29, 31, 36, 36, 37, 37, 41, 44; **26:**5, 12, 13, 15, 19, 20, 20, 21, 25; **27:**7; **28:**7, 7, 7, 8, 9, 13, 14, 24; **29:**3; **30:**1, 11, 12, 25, 26; **2Sa 1:**2, 13, 17; **2:**5, 11, 14, 18, 25; **3:**1, 6, 7, 8, 20, 21, 22, 29, 34, 35, 38, 38; **4:**2, 4, 4, 4, 5; **5:**2, 3, 11, 20, 22, 24; **6:**3, 12, 13, 14, 19, 19, 19, 19, 21; **7:**2, 5, 6, 6, 7, 8, 10, 10, 11, 11, 13, 13, 19, 23, 25, 27, 29; **8:**2, 2, 8; **9:**2, 8, 12; **11:**2, 2, 2, 2, 5, 8, 14, 16, 18, 21, 21, 22, 27; **12:**1, 3, 3, 4, 4, 5, 10, 24, 30; **13:**1, 2, 3, 4, 12, 12, 16, 18, 20, 23, 25, 34, 34; **14:**2, 2, 2, 2, 5, 6, 11, 20, 25, 26, 29; **15:**1, 2, 3, 7, 7, 10, 13, 13, 19, 19, 28, 30, 32, 33; **16:**1, 5, 5, 13, 22; **17:**3, 7, 8, 9, 10, 10, 17, 18, 18, 18, 19; **18:**7, 9, 10, 11, 12, 17, 17, 18, 21, 23, 24, 27, 29; **19:**7, 17, 22, 35; **20:**1, 1, 1, 3, 6, 8, 12, 12, 12, 15, 16, 18, 19, 21; **21:**1, 10, 12, 16, 16, 19, 20, 20; **22:**11, 13, 14, 19, 20, 31, 32, 34, 35, 37; **23:**4, 8, 9, 10, 11, 12, 14, 18, 20, 20, 20, 21, 21, 21; **24:**1, 2, 3, 14, 15, 22; **1Ki 1:**2, 3, 6, 39, 42; **2:**2, 5, 8, 9, 9, 14, 19, 36, 38; **3:**2, 5, 6, 7, 8, 11, 12, 14, 15, 15, 17, 18, 24, 24; **4:**5, 5, 33; **5:**1, 3, 5, 7, 12; **6:**5, 9, 10; **7:**1, 3, 6, 6, 8, 13, 14, 14, 14, 23, 25, 26, 26, 31, 31, 35; **8:**7, 9, 10, 13, 16, 16, 21, 37, 38, 46, 65; **9:**2, 5, 16, 26, 26; **10:**2, 2, 8, 10, 12, 18, 19, 19, 22, 26; **11:**7, 14, 17, 17, 18, 19, 20, 24, 26, 28, 29, 29; **12:**4, 7, 19, 30, 32, 32, 33, 33; **13:**1, 1, 2, 3, 5, 7, 18, 20, 24, 27, 27, 33, 34; **14:**3, 3, 13, 14, 15, 15; **15:**4, 19; **16:**11, 24, 32, 34; **17:**3, 7, 9, 10, 10, 11, 12, 12, 12, 12, 13, 24; **18:**3, 12, 13, 27, 27, 32, 34, 40, 41, 41, 42, 44, 44, 45, 45; **19:**3, 4, 6, 7, 9, 11, 11, 12, 12, 13, 19, 19, 21; **20:**10, 11, 11, 13, 20, 21, 25, 25, 28, 30, 34, 36, 36, 38, 39, 39, 39; **21:**1, 1, 1, 2, 2, 9, 12, 12, 21; **22:**3, 6, 7, 15, 17, 17, 21, 23, 43, 47, 48; **2Ki 1:**6, 6, 8, 8, 9, 10, 12, 13, 17; **2:**1, 7, 10, 11, 11, 19, 20, 23; **3:**9, 18, 26, 27, 27; **4:**1, 2, 8, 9, 10, 10, 10, 10, 10, 10, 13, 14, 16, 17, 22, 22, 23, 23, 28, 35, 38, 38, 39, 40, 42, 42; **5:**1, 2, 2, 5, 7, 8, 10, 12, 14; **6:**2, 5, 6, 8, 14, 23, 25, 25, 25, 25, 25, 26, 32, 32, 32, 32; **7:**6, 10, 13, 15; **8:**1, 5, 8, 9, 11, 13, 13, 15, 19, 26; **9:**1, 2, 5, 5, 11, 13, 14, 16, 17, 17, 18, 19, 30, 34; **10:**1, 2, 6, 8, 11, 18, 19, 20, 25, 27; **11:**2, 4, 5, 8, 11, 12, 17, 17; **12:**4, 4, 4, 4, 9, 9; **13:**5, 15, 21, 21; **14:**9, 9, 9, 9, 19, 20; **15:**5, 20; **16:**8, 10, 13, 13, 13; **17:**21, 26, 35; **18:**9, 14, 17, 21, 23, 32, 32; **19:**3, 3, 7, 7, 24, 26, 31, 31; **20:**12, 20, 20; **21:**13; **22:**10; **23:**10, 22, 25, 25, 30, 34, 35; **24:**15; **25:**4, 4, 17, 30; **1Ch 1:**10; **2:**3, 3, 10, 17, 17, 19, 21, 24, 26, 31, 31, 35, 49; **3:**4, 9, 19; **4:**9, 18; **5:**2, 24, 24; **6:**54, 57, 60, 67, 78; **7:**16, 22, 23, 24, 30, 32; **9:**4, 14, 19, 23, 31; **10:**13; **11:**2, 3, 11, 12, 13, 14, 16, 20, 22, 22, 22, 23, 23, 23; **12:**4, 14, 14, 18, 20, 20, 22, 28; **13:**7; **14:**1, 11, 13, 15; **15:**1, 1, 16, 25, 27, 27; **16:**3, 3, 3, 3, 15, 17, 17, 19; **17:**1, 4, 5, 5, 6, 7, 9, 9, 10, 10, 12, 12, 17, 21, 23, 25, 27; **18:**8; **20:**2, 4, 5, 6, 6; **21:**1, 2, 3, 13, 14, 14, 23, 24; **22:**5, 6, 7, 8, 9, 10; **23:**11; **24:**3, 3, 6; **25:**1; **26:**14, 24, 31; **27:**3, 4, 10, 11, 13, 15, 18, 32, 32, 32; **28:**2, 3, 3, 8, 9, 10; **29:**8, 15, 15, 15, 16, 21, 21, 21, 28; **2Ch 1:**6, 7, 9, 11, 14; **2:**1, 1, 2, 4, 4, 5, 6, 6, 6, 7, 7, 12, 12, 12, 13, 13, 14, 17; **3:**14, 15, 16; **4:**1, 2, 4, 5, 5, 9; **5:**8, 10, 13; **6:**2, 5, 5, 5, 13, 28, 29, 36; **7:**5, 9, 18, 20; **9:**1, 1, 7, 9, 17, 18, 18, 21; **10:**4, 19; **11:**12, 18; **12:**3, 13; **13:**2, 6, 6, 7, 9, 9, 9; **14:**5, 9, 14; **15:**3, 3, 12; **16:**3, 9, 12, 14, 14; **17:**17; **18:**2, 2, 5, 6, 11, 14, 16, 16, 20, 22; **19:**10, 10, 11; **20:**2, 3, 14, 14, 19, 24, 32, 35, 36; **21:**7, 14, 15, 19; **22:**2, 7, 9, 9, 11; **23:**1, 3, 3, 4, 7, 10, 11, 13, 16; **24:**8, 9, 11, 15, 24, 26; **25:**5, 7, 10, 12, 15, 18, 18, 18, 18, 27, 28; **26:**10, 23; **28:**6, 7, 9; **29:**10, 17, 21, 24, 35; **30:**5, 12, 13, 26; **31:**3, 5, 6, 21; **32:**4, 5, 7, 8, 21, 24, 30; **33:**7, 11, 19; **34:**18, 32; **35:**14, 18, 18, 25; **36:**3, 4, 13, 23; **Ezr 1:**2, 4; **2:**60, 63, 64; **3:**11, 13; **4:**1, 6, 7, 11, 15, 19, 19, 24; **5:**4, 5, 11, 13, 14, 17; **6:**1, 2, 3, 4, 11, 11, 17; **7:**1, 6, 11, 21; **8:**1, 18, 18, 18, 18, 20, 21, 28, 35, 35; **9:**8, 8, 8, 9, 12, 13, 15; **10:**1, 2, 3, 5, 7, 13, 14, 19, 19, 44; **Ne 1:**11; **2:**2, 4, 6, 8, 8, 12; **3:**8, 8, 8, 16, 17, 21, 25; **4:**1, 2, 3, 4, 17, 18; **5:**1, 7, 15, 15, 15, 18, 18, 18; **6:**2, 3, 7, 19; **7:**2, 3, 4, 62, 65, 66, 71; **8:**4, 9, 9, 10, 10, 11, 12, 15, 18; **9:**8, 10, 12, 12, 16, 17, 17, 18, 31, 35, 38; **10:**35, 37, 38, 38, 38; **11:**1, 3, 8, 17, 22, 24; **12:**17, 22, 35, 47, 47; **13:**1, 2, 4, 5, 7, 20, 28; **Est 1:**3, 4, 5, 6, 9, 11, 15, 19, 19; **2:**5, 5, 7, 8, 9, 11, 18, 18, 19, 20, 23; **3:**4, 6, 7, 8, 9, 13, 13, 14; **4:**1, 8, 11, 13, 14, 14; **5:**4, 5, 9, 14; **6:**6, 8, 13; **7:**4, 7, 9; **8:**5, 8, 9, 13, 17, 17; **9:**2, 17, 22, 25; **10:**3; **Job 1:**1, 1, 4, 5, 8, 14, 17, 19; **2:**3, 4, 7, 8, 10, 12, 13; **3:**5, 16, 16, 22; **4:**2, 3, 9, 9, 13, 15, 16, 16, 17, 17, 20; **5:**7, 26; **6:**5, 11, 14, 15, 22, 24, 27; **7:**1, 1, 2, 2, 6, 7, 9, 12, 12, 19, 20; **8:**2, 9, 14, 16, 17, 20; **9:**2, 3, 23, 25, 26, 31, 32, 33; **10:**4, 6, 16, 20, 20, 22, 22; **11:**2, 2, 6, 10, 12; **12:**3, 4, 4, 5, 15, 24, 24, 25; **13:**12, 25, 25, 28; **14:**2, 2, 2, 3, 5, 6, 7, 9, 11, 11, 17, 18; **15:**2, 2, 8, 14, 14, 16, 16, 24, 33; **16:**5, 10, 14, 21; **17:**6, 7, 10; **18:**4, 8, 8, 9, 9, 10, 10, 15, 21; **19:**6, 15, 15, 23; **20:**8, 8, 11, 14, 23, 26, 28; **21:**7, 11, 22, 33; **22:**2, 2, 6, 8; **23:**2, 6, 10; **24:**3, 3, 6, 8, 9, 9, 9, 14, 18, 20, 24; **25:**4; **26:**2, 14; **27:**14, 15, 18, 18; **28:**4, 22, 26; **29:**14, 14, 16, 16, 18, 19, 25; **30:**2, 15, 15, 18, 29, 29; **31:**1, 1, 9, 11, 11, 12, 32, 33, 36, 37; **32:**19, 19; **33:**10, 13, 23, 23, 24, 25; **34:**6, 7, 19, 20, 30; **35:**3, 16; **36:**4, 16, 21, 22, 25; **37:**7, 13, 13, 18; **38:**25, 26, 28, 39; **39:**10, 10, 10, 15, 19, 20, 25, 28; **40:**9, 12, 15, 17, 19, 24; **41:**1, 1, 1, 2, 2, 5, 5, 7, 8, 15, 20, 20, 24, 28; **42:**8, 11, 11, 17; **Ps 3:**T, 3; **4:**T; **5:**T; **6:**T; **7:**T, 2, 4, 11, 12, 15; **8:**T, T, 5; **9:**T, 9, 9; **11:**T; **12:**T, 6; **13:**T; **14:**T; **15:**T; **16:**T, 6, 6; **17:**T; **18:**T, 10, 13, 18, 19, 30, 31, 33, 34, 36; **19:**T, 3, 3, 5, 5, 11; **20:**T; **21:**T, 3, 9; **22:**T, 6, 6, 9, 12, 16, 20; **23:**T, 5, 5; **24:**T; **25:**T; **26:**T, 7, 12; **27:**T, 3, 5; **28:**T, 4, 9; **29:**T, 6, 6; **30:**T, 5, 5, 7; **31:**T, 2, 2, 5, 8, 12; **32:**T, 9, 9; **33:**16, 16, 20; **34:**T, 12; **35:**T, 5, 7, 7; **36:**T; **37:**T, 10, 18, 20, 26, 37; **38:**T, 4, 7, 11, 21; **39:**T, 3, 5, 5, 9, 11, 12; **40:**T, 3, 3; **41:**T; **42:**T, 4, 4, 10; **44:**T, 12; **45:**T, T, 1, 1, 1, 13, 13, 15; **46:**T, T, 4; **47:**T, 5, 7; **48:**T, T, 6, 7; **49:**T, 4, 7; **50:**T, 3, 5, 10, 18, 20, 23; **51:**T, 5, 10, 10, 16, 17, 17; **52:**T, 1, 2; **53:**T; **54:**T, 6; **55:**T, 6; **56:**T, 12; **57:**T, 6, 6; **58:**T, 8, 9, 11, 11; **59:**T, 16; **60:**T, 4, 4; **61:**T, 3; **62:**T, 3, 3, 7, 9; **63:**T, T; **64:**T; **65:**T, T, 9, 11, 12; **66:**T, T, 6, 10, 12, 15; **67:**T, T; **68:**T, T, 10, 13, 14, 18, 20, 27; **69:**T, 2, 8, 22, 22, 31; **70:**T; **71:**3, 22; **72:**T, 16; **73:**T, 4, 6, 12, 15, 16, 18, 20, 22, 24; **74:**T, 5, 11, 18; **75:**T, T, 8; **76:**T, T, 5, 10; **77:**T, 19, 20; **78:**T, 2, 14, 14, 15, 16, 20, 38, 39, 39, 49, 52, 57, 65, 65, 72; **79:**T, 1, 7; **80:**T, 1, 6, 8; **81:**T, T, 3, 4, 5, 9, 9; **82:**T; **83:**T, T, 4, 5, 14, 14, 14; **84:**T, T, 3, 3, 5, 6, 10, 10, 10; **85:**T, 13; **86:**T, 8, 15, 17; **87:**T, T, 5, 6; **88:**T, T, T, 4, 8; **89:**T, 3, 19, 19, 34, 49; **90:**T, 4, 4, 9; **91:**7, 12, 16; **92:**T, T, 6, 10; **94:**13, 15, 22; **95:**1, 3, 10, 11; **96:**1; **98:**T, 1, 1, 6; **99:**8; **100:**T; **101:**T, 2, 2, 6; **102:**T, 6, 6, 7, 18, 26; **103:**T, 13; **104:**2, 9, 18, 24; **105:**8, 10, 10, 12, 16, 17, 23, 39, 39, 39, 41, 41; **106:**9, 9, 15, 18, 19, 20, 20, 29, 31; **107:**7, 29, 30; **108:**T, T; **109:**T, 9, 13, 18, 19, 23, 23; **110:**T, 1, 4; **111:**9, 9; **113:**9, 9; **116:**13, 17; **118:**12; **119:**9, 19, 20, 74, 83, 105, 105, 122, 162, 164, 176; **120:**T; **121:**T; **122:**T, T, 3, 3; **123:**T, 2; **124:**T, T, 4, 7, 7; **125:**T; **126:**T, 1; **127:**T, T, 1, 1, 3, 3, 4, 4; **128:**T, 3; **129:**T, 3, 6; **130:**T, 3; **131:**T, T, 2, 2; **132:**T, 5, 5, 5, 11, 17, 18; **133:**T, T; **134:**T; **135:**12; **136:**12, 22; **137:**3, 3, 4; **138:**T; **139:**T, 16; **140:**T, 3, 3, 5, 5; **141:**T, 5, 6, 7, 7; **142:**T, T, 4, 4; **143:**T, 10; **144:**T, 2, 4, 4, 9, 9, 12; **145:**T; **146:**4; **147:**10, 10; **149:**1, 6; **150:**3, 5; **Pr 1:**17, 17, 27; **2:**7; **3:**2, 3, 4, 12, 12, 18, 26; **4:**9, 9, 10, 12, 13, 26; **5:**4, 6, 18, 19, 19, 21; **6:**1, 1, 5, 5, 5, 5, 6, 10, 10, 10, 11, 12, 17, 18, 19, 19, 23, 26, 27, 30; **7:**3, 4, 4, 7, 13, 19, 20, 22, 23, 23; **9:**2, 7, 7; **10:**1, 1, 1, 1, 5, 5, 7, 10, 13, 14, 18, 18, 20, 22, 23, 23, 25, 25, 26; **11:**4, 11, 12, 12, 13, 13, 14, 15, 15, 22, 22, 22, 29; **12:**4, 4, 6, 8, 8, 9, 9, 16, 16, 17, 23, 24, 24, 25, 25; **13:**1, 1, 1, 3, 3, 8, 14, 15, 15, 15, 17, 23; **14:**1, 1, 3, 5, 5, 6, 12, 13, 24, 25, 25, 25, 26, 27, 28, 28, 28, 29, 30, 32, 34, 34, 35; **15:**1, 2, 4, 5, 5, 13, 13, 13, 14, 15, 17, 18, 18, 19, 21, 23, 30, 33; **16:**12, 14, 15, 18, 22, 23, 25, 27, 28, 29, 30, 31, 31, 32; **17:**1, 1, 2, 7, 7, 8, 10, 10, 10, 10, 12, 12, 14, 14, 14, 16, 17, 17, 18, 18, 21, 21, 22, 22, 22, 24, 25, 25, 25, 27, 27; **18:**1, 4, 4, 5, 6, 9, 10, 11, 13, 14, 16, 19, 19, 20, 22, 22, 24, 24; **19:**1, 2, 5, 5, 6, 6, 9, 9, 10, 10, 12, 13, 13, 13, 13, 13, 15, 22, 24, 25, 25, 26, 28, 28; **20:**2, 3, 3, 5, 8, 14, 16, 16, 16, 19, 21, 25, 26; **21:**1, 4, 6, 6, 8, 8, 9, 9, 11, 11, 14, 14, 15, 19, 28, 29; **22:**1, 3, 5, 11, 13, 14, 15, 16, 26; **23:**1, 2, 2, 5, 18, 21, 24, 27, 27, 28, 32, 32, 34, 34; **24:**3, 5, 5, 5, 5, 7, 8, 8, 8, 9, 9, 14, 24, 30, 33, 33, 33, 34; **25:**6, 8, 11, 14, 14, 15, 18, 18, 19, 19, 20, 20, 23, 23, 24, 24, 26, 26, 28, 28; **26:**2, 2, 3, 3, 3, 3, 3, 3, 6, 6, 7, 7, 7, 8, 8, 8, 9, 9, 9, 9, 10, 10, 11, 11, 13, 13, 14, 15, 17, 18, 18, 19, 21, 23, 23, 23, 27, 27, 28; **27:**3, 3, 4, 6, 7, 8, 8, 9, 10, 10, 10, 12, 13, 13, 14, 14, 15, 15, 17, 17, 18, 19, 21, 26; **28:**2, 3, 3, 8, 9, 14, 15, 15, 16, 16, 16, 17, 20, 21, 22, 27; **29:**4, 5, 8, 9, 9, 11, 11, 12, 14, 14, 15, 15, 19, 20, 21, 21, 22, 24, 25; **30:**6, 8, 10, 17, 17, 19, 19, 19, 19, 19, 22, 22, 23, 23, 23, 31, 32, 33; **31:**10, 14, 16, 16, 17, 20, 30; **Ecc 1:**13; **2:**1, 8, 26; **3:**1, 1, 2, 2, 2, 2, 3, 3, 3, 3, 4, 4, 4, 4, 5, 5, 5, 5, 6, 6, 6, 6, 7, 7, 7, 7, 8, 8, 8, 8; **4:**8, 8, 8, 9, 11, 12, 12, 13, 14, 15; **5:**1, 3, 3, 4, 6, 7, 8, 12, 16, 17, 18, 19, 19; **6:**2, 3, 3, 3, 4, 6; **7:**1, 3, 4, 4, 5, 5, 6, 6, 17, 18, 19, 19, 20, 26, 26; **8:**1, 3, 5, 5, 6, 6, 11, 12, 12, 12; **9:**4, 4, 6, 7, 8, 12, 12, 14, 14, 14, 15, 17, 17, 18; **10:**1, 1, 4, 5, 8, 8, 9, 10, 11, 15, 16, 17, 19, 20, 20; **11:**3, 5, 5, 6, 10; **12:**4, 11, 11; **SS 1:**7, 9, 10, 13, 14, 16; **2:**2, 9, 9, 17, 17; **3:**4, 6, 8, 9, 10; **4:**3, 4, 5, 9, 12, 12, 12, 13, 15, 15; **5:**2; **6:**5; **7:**1, 2, 2, 3, 5, 7; **8:**6, 6, 7, 8, 11, 14, 14; **Isa 1:**4, 4, 8, 8, 8, 9, 13, 21; **3:**6, 6, 10, 12, 17, 26; **4:**3, 4, 5, 6, 6; **5:**1, 1, 1, 2, 2, 2, 4, 6, 7, 26, 27, 27, 30; **6:**1, 3, 5, 5, 5, 6, 6, 8, 13, 13, 13, 13, 13; **7:**2, 11, 14, 14, 17, 21, 21, 23, 24; **8:**1, 3, 4, 7, 14, 14, 14, 16; **9:**1, 2, 2, 6, 6, 14, 18; **10:**3, 5, 6, 8, 8, 10, 14, 14, 14, 15, 15, 15, 16, 16, 17, 17, 18, 18, 19, 19, 21, 22, 25, 30, 30; **11:**1, 1, 6, 8, 8, 10, 10, 11, 12, 15, 15, 16; **13:**8, 14, 15; **14:**1, 17, 19, 19, 19, 20, 23, 23, 26, 29, 29, 31; **15:**8; **16:**1, 5, 8; **17:**1, 6, 11, 13, 13; **18:**2, 4; **19:**1, 4, 4, 14, 14, 19, 20, 20, 20, 22, 23, 24; **20:**3, 3; **21:**1, 3, 4, 5, 6, 16, 17; **22:**2, 5, 5, 11, 16, 18, 18, 18, 21, 23; **23:**7, 12, 13, 15, 15, 16; **24:**1, 6, 13, 18, 18, 20, 20, 20; **25:**4, 4, 4, 4, 5, 6, 6, 11; **26:**7, 17; **27:**8, 8, 11, 11; **28:**1, 1, 2, 2, 4, 6, 10, 10, 13, 13, 15, 15, 15, 16, 16, 17, 17, 21, 24, 27, 27, 27, 27, 28, 29; **29:**4, 7, 7, 8, 8, 8, 10, 11, 16, 17, 17, 18; **30:**1, 8, 13, 14, 14, 14, 14, 17, 17, 17, 18, 21, 27, 28, 29, 29, 29, 33; **31:**4, 4, 4, 5; **32:**1, 2, 2, 2, 10, 10, 10, 15, 15; **33:**6, 9, 12, 15, 17, 19, 20, 20, 21; **34:**4, 4, 6, 6, 6, 13, 13, 16, 16; **35:**6, 7, 8; **36:**2, 6, 8, 17, 17; **37:**3, 3, 7, 7, 25, 27, 32, 32; **38:**12, 12, 12, 12, 14, 14, 14; **39:**1; **40:**3, 3, 6, 6, 11, 15, 16, 19, 20, 20, 22; **41:**15, 16, 23, 25, 25, 26; **42:**6, 10, 13, 13, 14, 15, 16, 22; **43:**3, 9, 16, 16, 17, 19, 19, 28; **44:**4, 5, 10, 11, 12, 13, 13, 13, 15, 15, 17, 19, 19, 19, 20; **45:**9, 10, 13, 18, 21, 21; **46:**6, 6, 11, 11, 11; **47:**8, 8, 9, 11, 14, 14; **48:**18; **49:**2, 2, 6, 7, 8, 15, 15, 16, 22, 24, 24; **50:**3, 7, 10; **51:**2, 4, 6, 10, 20, 21; **52:**12, 14; **53:**2, 2, 3, 4, 7, 7, 7, 9, 9, 10, 10; **54:**1, 6, 7, 8, 8, 9, 11, 14; **55:**4; **56:**5, 5, 7, 12; **57:**13; **58:**1, 2, 2, 5, 11; **59:**2, 8, 15, 19; **60:**11, 15, 22, 22; **61:**7, 9, 10, 10, 10, 11; **62:**1, 2, 3, 5, 5, 10; **63:**14, 14; **64:**4, 10; **65:**5, 8, 9, 10, 15, 16, 17, 18, 18, 20, 20; **66:**1, 1, 3, 3, 3, 3, 7, 8, 8, 8, 8, 12, 13, 15, 17, 17, 19, 22; **Jer 1:**1, 4, 11, 13, 18, 18; **2:**2, 6, 7, 12, 14, 21, 23, 23, 24, 26, 27, 30, 31, 31, 32, 32; **3:**1, 1, 2, 2, 2, 3, 5, 6, 20, 24; **4:**2, 6, 7, 7, 11, 11, 12, 13, 16, 16, 17, 18, 20, 26, 29, 31, 31; **5:**6, 6, 6, 9, 10, 15, 15, 15, 19, 26, 26, 27, 29, 30; **6:**1, 1, 7, 9, 9, 22, 22, 23, 24, 27; **7:**11, 31, 31; **8:**6, 6, 14, 15; **9:**1, 2, 7, 9, 11, 11, 25; **10:**3, 5, 5, 22, 23, 25; **11:**5, 9, 16, 19; **12:**1, 6, 8, 9, 10, 13, 16; **13:**1, 4, 6, 11, 11, 21, 23; **14:**2, 2, 8, 17, 19; **15:**8, 10, 10, 12, 12, 12, 14, 18, 18, 20; **16:**7, 7, 7, 7, 13; **17:**1, 4, 4, 8, 11, 13, 16, 22, 25; **18:**4, 7, 9, 13, 16, 18, 20, 21, 22; **19:**1, 3, 4, 5, 5, 8; **20:**8, 8, 9, 9, 10, 11, 15; **21:**2, 6, 14; **22:**4, 5, 8, 11, 12, 14, 14, 15, 15, 19, 22, 23, 23, 26, 28; **23:**4, 5, 5, 9, 10, 19, 19, 23, 28, 29, 34, 38; **25:**9, 11, 18, 32, 37, 38; **26:**11, 15, 18, 23; **27:**2, 16; **28:**1, 9, 13, 13, 14; **29:**1, 11, 11, 21, 23, 25, 26, 27, 28, 28; **30:**6, 7, 7, 12, 19, 20, 21, 23, 23; **31:**8, 10, 12, 15, 18, 31, 32, 39; **32:**6, 14, 14, 22, 35, 35, 40, 43; **33:**15, 17, 21, 24; **34:**8, 9, 13, 15, 17, 21; **35:**4, 5, 8, 13; **36:**2, 5, 22, 22; **37:**10, 13, 15, 16, 21; **38:**4, 6, 6, 9, 11, 11, 28; **39:**2, 3, 4, 10, 13; **40:**1, 11, 12, 15; **41:**1, 7; **42:**2, 5; **43:**12; **44:**6, 7, 14, 15, 22, 22, 28; **45:**1; **46:**5, 8, 10, 10, 17,

19, 20, 20, 21, 21, 22; **47:**2, 3; **48:**2, 2, 26, 36, 41, 42, 44, 44, 45; **49:**2, 9, 13, 14, 14, 16, 19, 22, 23, 23, 24, 25, 27; **50:**2, 3, 11, 11, 11, 12, 12, 13, 21, 22, 24, 29, 32, 39, 41, 41, 42, 43, 44; **51:**1, 7, 7, 13, 13, 25, 27, 27, 29, 33, 33, 34, 37, 37, 39, 43, 46, 50, 56, 60, 63; **52:**7, 7, 22, 23, 30, 34; **La 1:**1, 1, 8, 13, 14, 15, 15, 17; **2:**1, 3, 6, 7, 12, 18, 22; **3:**6, 6, 9, 10, 10, 15, 44, 52, 53; **4:**6, 11, 12; **5:**18; **Eze 1:**3, 3, 4, 4, 10, 10, 16, 22, 24, 25, 26, 26, 26, 27, 27, 28, 28; **2:**3, 4, 5, 8, 9, 9; **3:**12, 16, 17, 17, 27; **4:**1, 1, 3, 9, 11, 12, 14; **5:**1, 1, 1, 2, 2, 3, 4, 4, 12, 12, 12, 14, 14, 15, 15; **6:**1, 8; **7:**10, 26; **8:**2, 2, 2, 3, 3, 3, 8, 8, 11; **9:**2, 2, 4; **10:**1, 2, 9, 10, 14, 14; **11:**3, 16, 19; **12:**1, 3, 3, 4, 5, 6, 10, 11, 12, 16, 21, 22, 27; **13:**8, 10, 11, 13, 13, 19, 19, 20; **14:**4, 7, 8, 9, 9, 13, 13; **15:**2, 2, 2, 2; **16:**3, 3, 5, 7, 7, 8, 12, 12, 13, 15, 16, 19, 20, 22, 24, 30, 30, 31, 40, 45, 47; **17:**3, 3, 4, 5, 5, 6, 8, 9, 9, 13, 13, 15, 22, 22, 23; **18:**5, 6, 7, 10, 10, 13, 14, 17, 31, 31; **19:**2, 3, 3, 5, 6, 6, 9, 10, 11, 14, 14, 14; **20:**1, 6, 6, 6, 12, 15, 20, 23, 31; **21:**4, 6, 9, 19, 19, 23; **22:**18, 20, 23, 24, 28; **23:**10, 14, 19, 21, 24, 27, 32, 33, 41, 41, 48; **24:**3, 3, 5, 6, 8, 20, 26, 27; **25:**5, 7, 13; **26:**4, 5, 8, 8, 8, 14, 14, 20, 21; **27:**2, 5, 5, 5, 7, 26, 32, 34, 36; **28:**2, 2, 2, 2, 2, 6, 9, 9, 19, 23; **29:**6, 7, 9, 11, 20; **30:**3, 3, 4, 18, 18, 21, 21, 21; **31:**3, 3, 11, 12; **32:**2, 2, 7, 25, 30; **33:**1, 2, 2, 7, 15, 21, 24, 32, 33; **34:**5, 12, 23, 24, 25, 26, 29; **35:**1, 6; **36:**13, 17, 26, 26, 26, 34; **37:**1, 7, 10, 15, 16, 26; **38:**4, 8, 9, 9, 9, 10, 16, 19; **39:**11, 13, 15, 16; **40:**2, 2, 2, 3, 3, 3, 3, 5, 5, 7, 12, 17, 20, 21, 25, 26, 38, 38, 49; **41:**5, 7, 8, 8, 12, 18, 19, 19, 25; **42:**1, 4, 11, 20; **43:**8, 13, 13, 14, 15, 17, 17, 17, 19, 19, 22, 22, 23, 24, 25, 25, 25, 25; **44:**14, 24, 25, 25, 26, 27, 31; **45:**1, 2, 3, 4, 5, 5, 6, 6, 7, 7, 11, 18, 22, 22, 23, 23, 23, 24, 24, 24; **46:**4, 5, 5, 7, 7, 11, 12, 13, 13, 14, 14, 14, 14, 14, 15, 16, 17, 19, 23; **47:**1, 12, 18; **48:**8, 10, 15, 18, 20, 31; **Da 1:**5, 5, 12; **2:**1, 3, 10, 10, 15, 19, 28, 31, 31, 33, 34, 34, 35, 35, 35, 35, 37, 39, 40, 41, 44, 47, 48; **3:**1, 4, 6, 10, 11, 13, 22, 25, 27, 29; **4:**5, 10, 13, 13, 15, 16, 19, 20, 23, 23, 23, 25, 29, 31, 32, 33; **5:**1, 1, 1, 5, 7, 11, 11, 12, 16, 21, 24, 29; **6:**1, 7, 8, 10, 12, 12, 13, 14, 14, 17, 23; **7:**1, 2, 2, 4, 4, 4, 5, 5, 5, 6, 7, 8, 9, 10, 10, 12, 13, 20, 25, 25; **8:**3, 5, 9, 12, 15, 16, 18, 23, 23, 24, 25, 26; **9:**4, 12, 15, 23, 24, 26, 26, 27, 27, 27, 27; **10:**5, 5, 6, 6, 10, 14, 15, 16, 18; **11:**2, 3, 3, 10, 10, 13, 13, 14, 15, 17, 18, 20, 20, 21, 22, 23, 24, 25, 25, 31, 33, 34, 38, 40, 40; **12:**1, 4, 7, 7; **Hos 1:**2, 3, 6, 8, 10, 11; **2:**3, 3, 5, 5, 15, 18, 23; **3:**2, 4, 4; **4:**1, 5, 10, 12, 12, 15, 16, 16, 19; **5:**1, 2, 3, 4, 9, 10, 12, 14; **6:**2, 8, 10, 11; **7:**5, 6, 6, 8, 12, 16; **8:**9, 9; **9:**4, 4, 8, 11, 12; **10:**1, 3, 4, 6, 7, 11, 11, 12, 13; **11:**1, 1, 9, 10, 11; **12:**2, 3, 4, 11, 12, 13; **13:**3, 7, 7, 8, 8, 13, 15; **14:**5, 8; **Joel 1:**6, 6, 8, 14, 14; **2:**2, 2, 2, 5, 5, 5, 11, 14, 14, 15, 15, 17; **3:**8, 16, 16, 18, 19, 19; **Am 1:**1, 14, 14; **2:**6, 13; **3:**4, 4, 4, 4, 5, 5, 5, 6, 12, 12, 12, 12, 12, 12; **4:**2, 2, 8, 11; **5:**3, 3, 3, 3, 6, 7, 19, 19, 19, 19, 19, 20, 20, 24, 24, 27; **6:**10, 10; **7:**1, 1, 2, 4, 5, 7, 7, 7, 8, 9, 10, 10, 14, 17, 17; **8:**1, 2, 6, 6, 11, 11; **9:**1, 9, 11; **Ob** 1, 3, 5, 8, 11, 17, 17, 18, 18; **Jnh 1:**3, 3, 4, 4, 6, 9, 16, 17; **3:**1, 3, 6, 10; **4:**2, 5, 6, 7, 8, 10, 11; **Mic 1:**4, 4, 6, 8, 14, 15; **2:**2, 2, 11, 12, 12; **3:**10, 11, 12; **4:**7, 9, 12; **5:**1, 2, 2, 8; **6:**2, 14; **7:**1, 1, 4, 4; **Na 1:**1, 2, 7, 10, 14, 15, 15; **2:**1, 3, 8, 12; **3:**11, 16, 18; **Hab 1:**1, 6, 6, 8, 9; **2:**2, 2; **3:**3, 14, 19; **Zep 1:**7, 10, 10, 13, 14, 15, 15, 15, 15, 17, 17, 18; **2:**6, 6, 9, 13, 13, 14, 15, 15; **3:**17, 17, 20, 20; **Hag 1:**1, 11, 11, 11; **2:**6, 12, 13, 16, 19, 23; **Zec 1:**6, 8, 8, 8, 8, 15; **2:**1, 1, 3, 5, 8; **3:**2, 2, 5, 5, 9, 9; **4:**2, 2, 7; **5:**1, 2, 6, 7, 9, 11; **6:**11, 14; **7:**14, 14; **8:**4, 6, 13, 13; **9:**3, 7, 9, 9, 11, 13, 14, 15, 16, 16; **10:**1, 2, 3; **11:**4, 6, 8, 15, 16; **12:**3, 3, 6, 6, 6, 10, 10; **13:**1, 1, 4, 5, 5, 8; **14:**4, 12; **Mal 1:**3, 6, 6, 14, 14, 14; **2:**2, 16; **3:**2, 2, 3, 5, 9, 10, 12, 16, 17; **4:**1, 1, 6; **Mt 1:**1, 1, 18, 19, 20, 21, 23, 23, 25; **2:**4, 6, 6, 7, 12, 13, 18, 19, 23, 23; **3:**3, 3, 3, 4, 16, 17; **4:**6, 8, 16, 16, 18, 21, 21; **5:**12, 14, 14, 15, 15, 23, 28, 31, 31, 32, 32, 34, 35, 37, 37, 38, 41, 41; **6:**2, 22, 22, 27; **7:**3, 3, 9, 9, 10, 10, 12, 14, 16, 17, 18, 18, 20, 20, 24, 24, 26, 26, 27; **8:**2, 5, 14, 15, 20, 24, 28, 30; **9:**1, 2, 2, 8, 12, 18, 20, 20, 32, 32, 36; **10:**10, 10, 11, 11, 13, 14, 24, 24, 29, 29, 31, 34, 35, 35, 35, 41, 41, 41, 42; **11:**7, 8, 9, 9, 16, 16, 19, 19, 19; **12:**10, 10, 11, 12, 12, 14, 22, 25, 29, 33, 33, 33, 35, 35, 38, 39, 42, 43; **13:**2, 3, 4, 8, 8, 23, 23, 24, 31, 31, 32, 33, 33, 44, 44, 44, 45, 46, 47, 52, 52, 55, 57, 58; **14:**3, 5, 5, 6, 6, 8, 11, 13, 13, 14, 15, 24, 26; **15:**9, 14, 22, 22, 23, 29, 30, 34, 39; **16:**1, 4, 23, 23; **17:**1, 5, 5, 14, 14, 20, 25, 27, 27; **18:**2, 5, 6, 10, 12, 17, 17, 23, 28, 28, 29; **19:**3, 5, 7, 8, 9, 23, 24, 24, 24, 29; **20:**9, 10, 20, 26, 28, 29; **21:**2, 5, 5, 13, 13, 19, 26, 28, 33, 33, 33, 33, 33, 36, 41, 43, 46; **22:**2, 2, 11, 11, 15, 23, 24, 24, 31, 34, 39, 41; **23:**4, 11, 24, 24, 35, 37; **24:**17, 18, 18, 21, 28, 31, 32, 43, 43, 45, 46, 46, 48; **25:**9, 14, 14, 18, 19, 24, 26, 32, 35, 35, 38, 43, 44; **26:**5, 6, 7, 7, 8, 9, 10, 18, 26, 27, 30, 39, 44, 47, 48, 51, 69, 73; **27:**7, 16, 16, 19, 24, 24, 26, 28, 29, 29, 29, 32, 33, 37, 46, 48, 48, 55, 57, 59, 60; **28:**2, 4, 12; **Mk 1:**3, 3, 3, 6, 10, 11, 16, 19, 19, 23, 26, 30, 31, 33, 40, 45, 45; **2:**3, 3, 17; **3:**1, 1, 4, 4, 7, 9, 10, 13, 24, 25, 27, 32; **4:**1, 1, 3, 4, 8, 8, 20, 20, 21, 21, 21, 21, 21, 26, 26, 28, 29, 31, 37, 38, 39; **5:**2, 2, 3, 7, 11, 15, 21, 22, 25, 25, 26; **6:**4, 5, 8, 10, 11, 11, 15, 17, 20, 21, 22, 25, 28, 29, 31, 32, 34, 34, 35, 37, 40, 49; **7:**7, 17, 21, 25, 26, 32, 32, 33; **8:**3, 7, 10, 11, 12, 22, 33, 38; **9:**2, 7, 7, 14, 20, 23, 26, 36, 37, 38, 41, 42; **10:**2, 4, 5, 7, 12, 17, 17, 20, 25, 25, 25, 30, 35, 43, 45, 46, 46; **11:**2, 4, 13, 13, 17, 17, 25, 32, 32; **12:**1, 1, 1, 1, 1, 15, 18, 19, 19, 19, 19, 27, 42, 44; **13:**15, 16, 16, 28, 34, 34, 35; **14:**2, 3, 3, 3, 5, 6, 11, 13, 13, 15, 22, 23, 26, 35, 43, 44, 47, 51, 51, 54, 68, 70; **15:**8, 15, 17, 17, 19, 21, 22, 26, 34, 36, 36, 40, 46, 46, 46; **16:**4, 5, 5; **Lk 1:**3, 5, 5, 10, 13, 17, 22, 26, 27, 27, 27, 31, 34, 34, 39, 42, 57, 63, 66, 69; **2:**1, 4, 7, 7, 12, 12, 13, 22, 23, 23, 24, 24, 25, 25, 32, 35, 36, 36; **3:**2, 4, 4, 4, 7, 22, 22; **4:**3, 5, 11, 25, 26, 26, 27, 31, 33, 33, 38, 39; **5:**5, 7, 8, 12, 18, 18, 27, 29, 31, 36, 36; **6:**6, 6, 9, 9, 9, 12, 17, 23, 25, 34, 39, 40, 41, 41, 43, 43, 44, 45, 45, 48, 48, 48, 49, 49, 49, 49; **7:**2, 5, 11, 12, 12, 16, 24, 25, 26, 26, 32, 32, 34, 34, 34, 36, 37, 37, 39, 41, 45, 47; **8:**1, 4, 5, 5, 8, 13, 15, 16, 16, 22, 23, 23, 27, 27, 27, 32, 35, 37, 41, 41, 42, 43, 43, 49, 54; **9:**3, 3, 4, 5, 26, 28, 34, 35, 37, 38, 42, 47, 48, 52, 58, 62; **10:**4, 5, 7, 8, 10, 11, 12, 18, 30, 30, 31, 32, 33, 36, 38, 38; **11:**5, 6, 6, 8, 11, 11, 12, 14, 14, 16, 17, 24, 27, 29, 30, 30, 31, 33, 33, 33, 34, 34, 36, 37, 44, 46; **12:**6, 6, 7, 14, 16, 16, 21, 21, 21, 25, 39, 39, 43, 43, 45, 50, 50, 53, 54, 55; **13:**6, 6, 7, 10, 11, 19, 19, 19, 21, 21, 23, 31, 33, 34; **14:**1, 2, 5, 8, 10, 12, 12, 15, 15, 15, 16, 16, 18, 28, 32; **15:**8, 8, 11, 13, 13, 13, 14, 15, 19, 20, 22, 23, 27, 29, 29; **16:**1, 1, 1, 7, 9, 10, 18, 19, 20, 26; **17:**2, 4, 6, 7, 12, 12, 16, 31, 31, 37; **18:**1, 2, 2, 2, 3, 4, 6, 7, 10, 10, 11, 12, 12, 13, 13, 18, 21, 25, 25, 25, 27, 34, 35, 36; **19:**2, 3, 4, 5, 7, 9, 11, 12, 12, 14, 16, 17, 18, 21, 30, 44, 46, 46; **20:**3, 6, 9, 9, 12, 16, 19, 24, 27, 28, 28, 28, 28, 41, 43; **21:**2, 4, 12, 18, 35, 36; **22:**2, 2, 5, 10, 10, 12, 17, 19, 21, 23, 26, 29, 35, 36, 36, 41, 47, 47, 48, 55, 56, 58, 59, 68; **23:**2, 6, 8, 8, 11, 14, 18, 29, 33, 36, 38, 49, 50, 50, 53, 53; **24:**5, 17, 19, 19, 30, 37, 39, 42; **Jn 1:**8, 13, 23, 23, 28, 30, 32, 47; **2:**1, 1, 10, 12, 15, 16, 18; **3:**1, 1, 10, 14, 14, 22, 25, 29; **4:**7, 7, 9, 9, 9, 11, 11, 11, 14, 17, 17, 19, 27, 29, 44, 46; **5:**12, 34, 35, 36; **6:**2, 5, 7, 9, 18, 30, 70; **7:**4, 12, 12, 12, 21, 23, 30, 33, 48, 49, 51, 51; **8:**2, 3, 34, 35, 35, 35, 37, 40, 44, 44, 48, 52, 55; **9:**1, 2, 8, 14, 16, 17, 24, 25; **10:**1, 1, 1, 2, 5, 12, 12, 20, 20, 21, 21, 21, 33; **11:**1, 3, 8, 13, 18, 37, 38, 38, 44, 52, 54, 54; **12:**2, 3, 5, 6, 12, 14, 15, 16, 21, 24, 24, 24, 28, 35, 41, 46; **13:**4, 5, 10, 16, 34; **14:**2, 19, 27; **15:**4, 6, 6, 15, 20; **16:**2, 4, 16, 16, 18, 19, 19, 21, 21; **17:**7; **18:**1, 3, 9, 10, 18, 23, 26, 27, 30, 35, 37, 37, 39, 40; **19:**1, 2, 2, 12, 12, 12, 19, 29, 29, 29, 31, 34, 38, 40, 41, 41; **21:**9, 17; **Ac 1:**4, 5, 9, 15, 18, 22; **2:**2, 2, 30, 35, 40, 43; **3:**2, 5, 14, 22; **4:**2, 9, 9, 16, 21, 22, 37; **5:**1, 4, 6, 9, 15, 34, 34, 34; **6:**2, 2, 5, 5, 5, 8; **7:**6, 9, 11, 18, 20, 24, 26, 27, 29, 30, 35, 37, 41, 46, 49, 49, 58; **8:**1, 9, 9, 12, 27, 32, 32; **9:**3, 4, 10, 10, 12, 12, 19, 23, 25, 26, 33, 36, 43, 43; **10:**1, 1, 2, 2, 3, 5, 6, 7, 10, 11, 13, 22, 22, 22, 22, 26, 28, 30, 32; **11:**5, 5, 5, 7, 24, 26, 28; **12:**2, 7, 9, 12, 13, 18, 19, 19, 20, 21, 22, 22, 22, 23; **13:**6, 6, 7, 21, 21, 22, 22, 29, 31, 36, 37, 47, 50; **14:**1, 3, 5, 8, 10, 17, 19, 28; **15:**7, 10, 14, 30, 33; **16:**1, 1, 1, 3, 9, 9, 11, 12, 12, 13, 13, 14, 14, 16, 16, 16, 22, 26, 34; **17:**1, 2, 4, 5, 5, 12, 15, 18, 31, 32, 34, 34; **18:**2, 2, 7, 9, 11, 14, 14, 15, 18, 24; **19:**2, 4, 13, 14, 15, 17, 19, 19, 20, 24, 24, 29, 31, 34, 38, 39; **20:**3, 6, 6, 9, 9, 15, 17, 30, 35; **21:**2, 4, 10, 16, 19, 23, 25, 27, 29, 30, 37, 38, 39, 40; **22:**3, 3, 6, 7, 12, 12, 17, 18, 22, 25, 26, 27, 28, 29; **23:**6, 9, 9, 12, 22, 27, 30; **24:**4, 5, 5, 5, 10, 12, 14, 16, 18, 24; **25:**3, 11, 13, 14, 16, 27; **26:**1, 4, 5, 12, 13, 14, 18, 23, 26, 28; **27:**1, 2, 2, 9, 12, 12, 12, 13, 14, 14, 16, 21, 28, 34, 35, 39, 39, 41; **28:**2, 3, 4, 6, 6, 10, 13, 13, 16, 23, 23; **Ro 1:**3, 11, 12, 14, 17, 24, 27; **2:**5, 17, 19, 19, 28, 29, 29, 29; **3:**1, 2, 4, 5, 7, 13, 21; **4:**4, 11, 16, 18, 19; **5:**7, 7, 14, 15; **6:**13, 13; **7:**1, 2, 4, 9, 21, 23, 24, 25; **8:**3, 3, 3, 23; **9:**5, 6, 6, 9, 11, 20, 21, 21, 27, 29, 33, 33; **10:**5; **11:**1, 1, 1, 5, 5, 7, 8, 9, 9, 12, 14, 17, 18, 24, 24, 26, 33; **12:**1, 2, 4, 7, 7, 8, 14, 17; **13:**5; **14:**2, 5, 6, 12, 13, 17, 17; **15:**8, 16, 16, 20, 24, 25, 27, 29, 32; **16:**1, 5, 10, 13, 22, 23, 25; **1Co 1:**12, 22; **3:**4, 8, 13, 14, 15, 18, 21; **4:**2, 2, 9, 9; **5:**1, 4, 11, 11, 11; **6:**1, 1, 7, 10, 11, 12, 15, 15, 16, 16, 18, 20; **7:**1, 3, 5, 10, 10, 12, 12, 12, 13, 13, 14, 15, 18, 18, 18, 19, 21, 21, 22, 22, 23, 24, 25, 27, 27, 28, 28, 28, 33, 34, 36, 36, 39, 39; **8:**4, 9, 9, 11; **9:**5, 7, 7, 10, 13, 18, 19, 24, 24, 25, 26; **10:**1, 6, 11, 13, 27, 29; **11:**3, 3, 4, 5, 5, 6, 6, 6, 7, 10, 10, 10, 13, 14, 15, 15, 18, 21, 23; **12:**7, 7, 15, 15, 15, 16, 19, 19, 24, 27, 28, 29; **13:**1, 1, 2, 9, 11, 11, 12; **14:**4, 4, 5, 8, 9, 19, 22, 27, 30, 31, 33, 37, 37; **15:**20, 21, 36, 36, 36, 37, 38, 38, 45, 45, 51, 52; **16:**7, 9, 9, 18; **2Co 1:**9, 11, 12, 15, 23; **2:**13, 14, 15, 16, 16, 16; **3:**2, 3, 6, 13, 14; **4:**3; **5:**1, 5, 12, 12, 12, 16, 17; **6:**3, 12, 12, 14, 15, 15; **7:**7, 8, 8, 11; **8:**10, 15, 15, 18, 19; **9:**2, 5, 6, 6, 6, 6, 10, 15; **11:**1, 2, 4, 4, 4, 6, 16, 16, 17, 21, 23, 25, 25, 33, 33; **12:**7, 7, 11, 13, 14, 16; **13:**3; **Gal 1:**6, 10, 12, 18; **2:**3, 5, 14, 14; **3:**1, 1, 11, 13, 18, 20, 21; **4:**1, 4, 7, 23, 27; **5:**9; **6:**1, 3, 9; **Eph 1:**9, 18; **2:**8, 9, 21; **3:**1; **4:**1, 1, 7, 8, 23, 24, 24, 27, 28; **5:**2, 2, 5, 23, 27, 27, 28, 31, 32; **6:**2, 3, 4, 10, 21; **Php 1:**4, 7, 27, 28; **2:**3, 7, 8, 8, 9, 15, 15, 17, 22, 25, 25, 25; **3:**5, 5, 5, 5, 10; **4:**10, 12, 17, 17, 18; **Col 1:**9, 22, 22; **2:**9, 11, 11, 12, 23; **3:**10, 11, 11, 17; **4:**1, 2, 7, 7, 9, 11, 12; **1Th 1:**7; **2:**1, 7, 7, 9, 9, 11, 12, 17; **3:**13; **4:**1, 11, 12, 16; **5:**2, 3, 4; **2Th 2:**2, 2, 2, 3, 13, 15; **3:**8, 15; **1Ti 1:**4, 5, 5, 15, 16, 19; **2:**7; **3:**1, 2, 2, 3, 5, 6, 9, 10, 12, 15; **4:**6, 8, 16; **5:**5, 5, 9, 9, 16, 20, 22, 23; **6:**2, 3, 4, 5, 11, 13, 19; **2Ti 1:**3, 7, 9, 11, 11; **2:**3, 8, 9, 11, 15, 19, 20, 21; **3:**12; **4:**3, 5, 7; **Tit 1:**1, 7, 7, 8, 9, 12; **2:**3; **3:**5, 9, 10; **Phm 1:**2, 8, 9, 10, 10, 15, 16, 16, 16, 16, 22; **Heb 1:**13; **2:**7, 9, 10, 14, 17; **3:**3, 3, 4, 5, 11; **4:**2, 3, 7, 9, 14; **5:**1, 1, 4, 6, 7, 9, 10, 12, 12, 13; **6:**7, 8, 19; **7:**1, 1, 2, 3, 4, 5, 6, 6, 9, 11, 13, 15, 16, 16, 17, 19, 20, 21, 24; **8:**4, 5, 5, 5, 6, 6, 7, 8, 13; **9:**1, 2, 2, 3, 4, 4, 4, 7, 13, 14, 16, 18, 24, 28; **10:**1, 5, 13, 21, 26, 31, 37, 38; **11:**4, 4, 6, 9, 9, 10, 10, 11, 12, 12, 13, 14, 15, 16, 16, 16, 17, 19, 31, 35; **12:**1, 2, 7, 10, 11, 12, 13, 14, 16, 18, 18, 19, 19, 28, 29; **13:**11; **Jas 1:**1, 3, 6, 6, 10, 22, 23; **2:**3, 9, 15, 25, 26; **3:**3, 3, 4, 4, 5, 5, 5, 6, 6, 11, 12, 12, 12, 13, 18; **4:**4, 11, 13, 13, 13, 14; **5:**11, 12, 16, 17; **1Pe 1:**2, 3, 4, 6, 8, 18; **2:**2, 3, 6, 6, 9, 9, 10; **3:**4, 9, 10, 16, 16, 21, 21, 21; **4:**8, 9, 9, 11, 14, 16; **5:**1, 1, 1, 4, 8, 9, 10, 10, 12; **2Pe 1:**1, 3, 5, 5, 19, 19; **2:**1, 5, 7, 8, 13, 13, 14, 16, 19, 22, 22; **3:**6, 8, 8, 8, 8, 10, 10, 13, 14; **1Jn 1:**10; **2:**4, 7, 27; **3:**14, 15, 17; **4:**2, 2, 3, 3, 10, 19, 20; **5:**1, 10, 16, 16, 18; **2Jn** 5, 7, 7, 7, 11, 12; **3Jn** 5, 6, 9, 13; **Jude** 1, 1, 7, 21; **Rev 1:**1, 10, 10, 10, 13, 13, 15, 16; **2:**9, 12, 14, 17, 17, 20, 22, 24; **3:**1, 3, 8, 17, 20; **4:**1, 1, 2, 3, 6, 7, 7; **5:**1, 2, 2, 6, 8, 9, 12; **6:**1, 2, 2, 2, 4, 4, 5, 5, 6, 6, 6, 8, 8, 11, 11, 12, 14; **7:**1, 9, 10; **8:**3, 3, 5, 8, 10, 10, 13; **9:**1, 2, 8, 8, 13; **10:**1, 1, 2, 3, 3, 4; **11:**1, 9, 11, 12, 12, 13, 13, 19, 19; **12:**1, 1, 3, 5, 6, 10, 14, 14, 14, 14, 15; **13:**1, 2, 2, 11, 11, 14, 16, 18; **14:**2, 2, 3, 4, 9, 13, 14, 14, 14, 15, 17, 20, 20; **15:**2, 7; **16:**1, 3, 7, 15, 16, 17, 21, 21; **17:**3, 3, 4, 5, 17, 17; **18:**2, 2, 2, 3, 6, 6, 8, 10, 15, 16, 17, 19, 21, 21, 21, 23; **19:**1, 5, 6, 10, 10, 11, 12, 13, 15; **20:**1, 2, 3, 4, 6, 8, 11; **21:**1, 1, 2, 3, 10, 11, 15, 16, 16, 17, 21; **22:**1, 2, 2, 9, 15

ABOUT (1212)

Ge 3:8; **6:**17; **11:**3; **14:**1; **16:**11; **17:**21; **18:**1, 10, 14; **21:**6, 16, 22, 25, 26; **24:**28; **25:**22, 34; **26:**7, 20, 32; **29:**13, 14; **30:**30; **31:**24, 29, 50; **34:**4; **35:**18, 22; **37:**9; **38:**1, 24; **39:**7; **40:**23; **41:**8, 8, 25, 28, 42; **43:**7, 23, 27, 29; **44:**7; **45:**13, 20; **46:**33; **48:**21; **50:**5; **Ex 1:**8; **2:**15; **3:**13; **4:**14, 24, 28; **5:**8; **8:**12; **10:**2; **11:**4; **12:**26, 37; **16:**36; **17:**4; **18:**1, 1, 7, 8, 8, 9; **25:**25; **32:**5, 12, 28, 34; **34:**14; **37:**12; **38:**4, 24, 25, 27, 28; **Lev 5:**1; **6:**3; **Nu 3:**50; **7:**13, 13, 14, 19, 19, 20, 25, 25, 26, 31, 31, 32, 37, 37, 38, 43, 43, 44, 49, 49, 50, 55, 55, 56, 61, 61, 62, 67, 67, 68, 73, 73, 74, 79, 79, 80, 85, 85, 86, 86; **11:**1, 31; **13:**32; **14:**10, 13, 27, 36; **16:**11; **18:**3; **21:**17, 27; **31:**52; **Dt 1:**18; **2:**25; **4:**1, 5, 6, 10, 14; **5:**33; **6:**1, 7; **7:**1; **9:**1, 5; **11:**8, 10, 19, 31; **13:**1, 11; **17:**4, 13; **18:**14; **19:**20; **21:**21; **22:**13; **23:**20; **24:**1; **28:**21, 33, 51, 63; **30:**16; **31:**16; **32:**7, 36; **33:**6, 7, 8, 12, 13, 18, 20, 22, 23, 24; **Jos 2:**5; **3:**4; **4:**13; **7:**5, 9, 11; **9:**1; **14:**6; **Jdg 3:**7, 29; **6:**13; **7:**13; **8:**28; **9:**7, 25, 42, 49; **11:**4; **13:**8; **14:**6, 19; **16:**27; **18:**4; **19:**2, 30; **20:**7, 31, 39; **Ru 1:**4; **2:**11, 17, 19; **3:**11; **4:**4; **1Sa 2:**23; **3:**11; **4:**6, 14; **6:**2; **7:**3; **8:**9; **9:**5, 5, 16, 17, 20; **10:**2, 11; **11:**1, 4, 5; **12:**9, 16; **14:**14, 14; **16:**2; **17:**25, 28, 28, 32, 58; **18:**20; **19:**3, 4, 4, 5, 5; **20:**3, 12, 12, 26; **21:**11; **22:**2; **23:**13, 21; **24:**4; **25:**36, 38; **28:**1; **29:**5; **30:**6; **2Sa 2:**13; **3:**8, 26, 28; **4:**1; **10:**2, 7; **12:**18, 30; **13:**13, 20, 22, 26; **14:**3, 10, 14; **17:**5, 18; **18:**29, 32; **19:**18, 32; **21:**1, 16; **23:**12; **1Ki 1:**5, 11, 18, 45; **2:**28; **4:**33, 33; **7:**23, 24, 26, 26; **10:**2, 6, 14; **11:**10, 31; **14:**5, 15; **18:**13, 27, 32, 44; **20:**6, 16; **21:**7, 27; **22:**3, 6; **2Ki 2:**1; **3:**20, 21; **4:**16; **5:**8; **6:**25; **7:**15; **8:**3, 4, 5, 22; **9:**18, 19; **10:**6, 32; **11:**2; **12:**17; **14:**10; **18:**14, 34; **19:**20, 32; **20:**1; **21:**12; **22:**13; **1Ch 16:**9, 24; **17:**18; **19:**2, 8; **20:**2; **29:**7, 7, 7; **2Ch 2:**4, 14; **3:**8, 9; **4:**2, 3, 5, 5; **9:**2, 5, 13, 16; **15:**15; **20:**12; **21:**10, 14; **22:**11; **24:**27, 27; **25:**6, 9; **28:**10, 16; **29:**34; **32:**19, 24, 31; **34:**21; **35:**25; **Ezr 2:**63; **4:**8; **Ne 1:**2, 2; **2:**12, 16, 18, 18; **4:**8; **5:**1, 5, 7; **6:**7, 16; **7:**65, 72; **9:**3, 30; **13:**23; **Est 2:**1, 11, 22, 22; **3:**4; **4:**4; **5:**8, 11, 11; **7:**5; **Job 11:**7; **13:**12, 17; **20:**20; **21:**6, 11; **22:**14; **24:**10; **27:**11; **31:**14; **35:**14; **38:**16, 18, 41; **42:**3, 5, 7, 8; **Ps 1:**2; **4:**4; **9:**11; **10:**3; **12:**8; **22:**30, 31; **31:**7, 13; **35:**11, 22, 24; **37:**1, 7, 7; **40:**7, 9, 10, 17; **41:**5, 7; **50:**8; **52:**1; **59:**16; **62:**4; **66:**2; **68:**34; **69:**12; **71:**15, 17, 24; **73:**17, 28; **77:**6, 12; **78:**4, 42; **88:**12; **96:**3; **97:**7; **104:**20, 34; **105:**2; **107:**22; **109:**2; **119:**46, 69, 78, 97, 113, 148, 172; **138:**5; **139:**1, 17; **143:**5; **145:**11, 12, 12; **Pr 5:**6, 7; **13:**16; **17:**9; **20:**14; **23:**7; **24:**12, 28, 32; **25:**18, 27; **27:**1; **30:**32; **Ecc 3:**10; **6:**9, 10; **7:**2, 4, 4; **8:**9; **9:**15; **10:**14; **SS 5:**9; **7:**2; **Isa 3:**9; **5:**1, 12, 22; **13:**8; **14:**24; **16:**6, 13; **19:**11; **22:**17; **23:**5; **24:**1; **26:**17; **30:**11; **32:**6; **34:**2; **36:**19; **37:**33; **38:**1, 9; **40:**14; **43:**19; **45:**11; **47:**7, 7; **48:**2, 3; **51:**2; **52:**15, 15; **53:**2; **57:**11; **59:**4, 7; **65:**1, 1, 17, 24; **Jer 2:**10; **3:**5, 16; **5:**12; **6:**24, 24; **7:**13; **9:**17; **10:**17; **11:**2, 18, 22; **16:**3, 3; **17:**15; **18:**18, 23; **19:**3; **20:**10; **22:**11, 23; **26:**21; **27:**18, 19, 21; **29:**16, 21; **30:**6, 14; **31:**8; **32:**3, 36, 43; **33:**3; **34:**2; **35:**13; **36:**13, 30; **37:**5, 7; **38:**25; **40:**16; **41:**4; **46:**13; **48:**2, 30, 41; **49:**22; **50:**11, 14, 43, 43; **51:**33, 50; **La 2:**20; **3:**61; **Eze 6:**3; **8:**16; **11:**15; **12:**16, 24; **14:**22; **16:**4, 6, 22; **19:**4; **21:**3, 29; **23:**6; **33:**8, 30, 30; **38:**17; **43:**11; **44:**5; **46:**14; **Da 2:**5, 8, 29, 30; **4:**2; **5:**10; **6:**12; **7:**20; **8:**26, 26; **Hos 1:**4; **3:**2; **7:**3, 12, 13; **8:**4; **12:**2; **13:**9; **Joel 1:**3, 18; **Am 4:**5; **6:**13, 14; **8:**8; **Ob** 7; **Jnh 4:**2, 4, 10; **Mic 2:**4; **6:**5; **7:**3; **Na 2:**6; **Hab 1:**5; **3:**2; **Hag 2:**11, 15, 21; **Zec 5:**2; **7:**6; **8:**9; **Mal 3:**13, 16; **Mt 2:**1, 16; **4:**23, 24; **5:**11, 12; **6:**2, 5, 25, 28, 31, 32, 34; **7:**3; **9:**30, 35; **10:**18, 19; **11:**2, 4, 7; **12:**1, 24, 27; **13:**18, 19; **14:**1, 21, 25; **15:**7; **16:**8, 11, 12, 12; **17:**25; **18:**1; **19:**17; **20:**22; **21:**28; **22:**5, 16, 17, 31, 42; **24:**14, 15; **26:**13, 59, 70; **27:**19, 46; **28:**14; **Mk 1:**1, 30; **3:**8; **4:**11, 11, 14; **5:**16, 20, 23, 27; **6:**14, 14, 16, 48; **7:**6, 25; **8:**1, 9, 17, 19, 30, 32; **9:**16, 34; **10:**3, 32, 38; **11:**18; **12:**26; **13:**9, 11, 34; **14:**9, 49, 68, 71; **15:**4; **Lk 1:**1, 56, 66, 78; **2:**15, 17, 19, 33, 38; **3:**23; **6:**41; **7:**3, 18, 24; **8:**10, 39; **9:**2, 9, 11, 14, 14, 21, 28, 31, 45, 54; **10:**42; **11:**5, 19, 42, 49; **12:**1, 11, 22, 29; **13:**1, 4; **15:**14; **16:**2, 11, 28; **17:**22, 28; **18:**34; **19:**22, 27; **20:**37; **21:**5, 13, 14; **22:**37, 37, 41, 49, 59, 60; **23:**8; **24:**14, 17, 17, 18, 27, 36, 44; **Jn 1:**7, 15, 18, 22, 30, 39, 45, 48; **2:**3, 25; **3:**12; **4:**6, 22, 22, 32, 47; **5:**32, 32, 34, 34, 37, 44, 46; **6:**27, 43, 52; **7:**12, 13, 43, 49; **8:**13, 14, 14, 17, 26, 27, 54, 54; **9:**15, 29, 30; **10:**19, 41; **11:**4; **12:**17, 18, 22, 34; **15:**26, 27; **16:**13, 25; **17:**6; **18:**19, 32, 34; **19:**14, 39; **21:**8, 21; **Ac 1:**1, 3, 4, 8, 15; **2:**6, 11, 14, 25, 29, 41; **3:**3, 12, 18, 24; **4:**4, 16, 18, 20; **5:**5, 7, 21, 28, 36; **6:**11; **7:**18; **8:**4, 5, 34, 35; **9:**13, 20, 24, 30, 37; **10:**3, 9, 36, 43, 46; **11:**12, 20; **12:**1, 18; **13:**12, 20, 22, 27, 33, 41, 42; **14:**2, 3, 4, 27; **15:**2, 12, 14; **17:**3, 3, 18, 19, 20, 23, 30, 32; **18:**25, 25, 27; **19:**7, 8, 20, 23, 27, 39; **20:**24; **21:**37; **22:**6, 18, 29, 30; **23:**11, 27; **24:**24, 25; **25:**19, 19; **26:**13, 16, 16, 26; **27:**9, 27; **28:**22, 23, 23, 31; **Ro 1:**3, 9, 16, 19, 25; **2:**1, 27; **3:**31; **4:**2, 9; **7:**13; **8:**5, 5, 31, 38; **9:**30; **10:**14, 14, 17, 18; **11:**2, 2, 18, 26; **14:**1, 5, 23; **15:**14, 17, 21; **16:**25; **1Co 1:**6, 11; **4:**3, 6, 13, 15, 17; **5:**1, 6, 10; **6:**4, 13; **7:**1, 25, 33, 34; **8:**1, 4; **9:**9, 12, 16; **10:**15, 18, 27; **11:**13, 16, 16, 20, 22, 34; **12:**1, 1, 31; **13:**2, 3, 6; **15:**15, 58; **16:**1, 12; **2Co 1:**8; **2:**14; **4:**4, 5, 5; **5:**12, 16, 16; **7:**7, 12; **8:**10, 15, 23, 24; **9:**1, 3; **10:**8, 10, 16, 18; **11:**4, 6, 10, 18, 21, 21, 30; **12:**1, 5, 5, 6, 9; **Gal 1:**8, 16; **3:**2, 5; **4:**23, 30; **5:**10; **6:**13, 14; **Eph 2:**9; **3:**4, 8; **4:**14, 19, 20, 21; **5:**12; **6:**21; **Php 1:**5, 7, 14, 15, 17, 18, 26, 27, 27; **2:**4, 18, 20; **3:**3, 19, 19; **4:**6, 6, 8, 8, 10; **Col 1:**6, 8, 9, 28; **2:**18, 22; **3:**2, 10; **4:**3; **1Th 1:**3, 8, 8, 9; **4:**9; **5:**1, 3, 4; **2Th 1:**4, 10; **2:**1; **1Ti 1:**7, 18; **2:**7; **5:**22; **2Ti 1:**1, 8; **2:**7; **3:**11; **Tit 1:**12; **2:**8, 10; **3:**9, 9; **Phm 1:**1; **Heb 1:**3; **2:**5; **3:**1; **4:**8; **5:**11, 12, 13; **6:**2; **7:**13, 18; **10:**7, 32; **11:**7, 22, 37; **12:**3; **13:**3, 9; **Jas 3:**13, 14; **4:**16; **5:**9, 13, 20; **1Pe 1:**10, 10, 11, 11; **3:**3, 9, 15; **4:**4; **5:**7; **2Pe 1:**16; **2:**1, 12, 18, 20; **3:**9; **1Jn 1:**3; **3:**7; **5:**9, 10; **2Jn** 10; **3Jn** 3, 9, 10; **Jude** 3, 3, 9, 10, 12, 14; **Rev 1:**9; **2:**6, 9, 10; **8:**1; **10:**4, 11; **12:**4; **14:**20; **20:**4

AGAINST (1132)

Ge 4:24; **13:**13; **14:**2, 9, 9; **16:**12, 12; **20:**6, 16; **31:**5; **34:**7; **39:**9; **42:**36; **Ex 1:**10; **9:**23; **10:**16, 16; **12:**12, 22; **14:**11, 25, 31; **15:**7, 9, 24; **16:**2, 7, 7, 8, 8, 8; **17:**8, 16; **18:**13; **20:**16; **22:**24; **23:**6, 21; **24:**6; **32:**10, 12, 14, 33; **34:**15, 16; **Lev 1:**5, 11, 15; **3:**2, 8, 13; **5:**9, 19; **6:**2; **7:**2; **8:**19, 24; **9:**12, 18; **16:**14, 15; **17:**10; **19:**18; **20:**3, 5, 6; **26:**17, 25; **Nu 10:**9; **11:**1, 33; **13:**31; **14:**2, 9, 29, 35, 36; **16:**2, 11, 19, 41; **17:**5, 10; **18:**5, 23; **20:**2, 24; **21:**5, 7, 7; **22:**18, 25, 34; **23:**23; **24:**10, 13; **25:**3, 8; **26:**9; **27:**3, 14; **31:**3, 16; **32:**13, 23; **Dt 1:**26, 41, 43, 44; **2:**15; **4:**26; **5:**20; **6:**15, 22; **7:**4, 19, 19, 24; **9:**7, 16, 23, 24; **11:**3, 17, 25; **13:**5; **20:**4, 18; **21:**10; **22:**16; **23:**9; **24:**15, 15; **28:**20, 48, 49, 60, 61; **29:**7, 20, 22, 27; **31:**17, 19, 21, 26, 27, 28; **32:**24; **33:**7; **34:**11; **Jos 1:**5, 18; **7:**20; **9:**2, 18; **10:**6, 21; **11:**4, 5; **15:**15; **19:**47; **21:**44; **22:**12, 16, 18, 19, 22, 29, 31, 33; **23:**3, 16; **24:**8, 9, 11, 20, 27; **Jdg 1:**3, 5, 10, 11, 17; **2:**14, 15, 20; **3:**8, 10; **4:**24; **5:**13, 13, 20, 23; **6:**16, 33; **7:**22; **9:**18, 31, 33, 39, 49, 56; **10:**7, 10; **11:**4, 8, 25, 27, 29, 32; **12:**1, 2; **16:**26, 26, 29; **20:**18, 23, 23, 24, 28, 34; **1Sa 2:**10, 10, 25, 25; **3:**12; **5:**7; **7:**6, 13; **11:**1, 11; **12:**14, 15, 23; **13:**12; **14:**33, 34, 47, 47; **17:**19, 21, 33; **18:**17, 30; **19:**4, 8; **20:**8, 25; **22:**8, 13, 13, 15; **24:**11; **26:**19; **27:**10; **29:**4; **2Sa 2:**15; **3:**28; **5:**6; **6:**7, 8, 8; **11:**23; **12:**11, 13, 27; **14:**11; **15:**10, 13; **18:**28, 31; **20:**15, 21; **21:**18; **23:**9; **24:**1, 17; **1Ki 6:**5; **8:**33, 35, 46, 50; **11:**14, 23; **12:**21, 24; **13:**4, 32, 32; **15:**27; **16:**7; **20:**1, 25, 26; **22:**4, 6, 15, 20, 29; **2Ki 3:**5, 7, 21, 27; **8:**20, 28; **9:**14, 14, 25, 33; **10:**4, 9; **12:**17, 20; **13:**18; **14:**11, 19; **15:**10, 25, 30; **17:**4, 7; **18:**7, 20; **19:**6, 7, 9, 16, 21, 22, 27, 28, 32; **21:**23, 24; **22:**13, 17, 19, 20; **23:**26; **24:**2, 10, 20; **25:**1, 1, 6; **1Ch 5:**19, 22; **11:**6, 13; **12:**19, 19; **13:**10, 11, 11; **15:**13; **19:**17; **20:**1; **21:**1, 17; **27:**24; **2Ch 4:**7, 7; **6:**24, 26, 36, 39; **8:**3; **11:**1, 4, 4; **13:**8, 12, 12; **14:**6, 11, 11, 11; **15:**6, 6; **17:**1; **18:**3, 5, 14, 19, 28; **19:**2, 10, 10; **20:**2, 6, 12, 16, 23, 29, 37; **21:**8, 17; **22:**8; **24:**18, 23, 24; **25:**21, 27; **26:**7, 13, 16; **27:**5; **28:**10, 11, 13, 16; **32:**25, 25, 26; **33:**24, 25; **34:**21, 25, 27, 28; **36:**8, 13, 17; **Ezr 4:**5, 6, 15, 19; **7:**23; **8:**22; **Ne 1:**6; **2:**19; **4:**8; **5:**1, 7; **6:**12; **9:**10, 26; **Est 4:**16; **6:**13; **8:**3; **9:**2, 2; **Job 6:**4; **8:**4; **9:**13; **10:**2, 16, 17, 17; **13:**26; **15:**13, 25, 26; **16:**4, 10; **17:**8; **19:**11, 13, 19; **20:**27; **21:**27; **24:**8, 13; **30:**24; **31:**35; **33:**13; **34:**37; **35:**6, 15; **39:**23; **40:**11; **42:**11; **Ps 2:**2, 2; **3:**1; **5:**10; **7:**6; **15:**5; **17:**13; **21:**11; **27:**12; **31:**13, 20; **34:**16; **35:**11, 15, 20; **37:**12; **38:**19; **41:**4, 9; **43:**1; **48:**4; **50:**7, 21; **51:**4, 4; **54:**5; **55:**10, 18; **60:**11; **62:**3; **64:**8; **68:**18; **71:**10; **73:**9; **74:**1; **75:**2; **76:**5; **78:**17, 19, 21, 21, 31, 40, 49, 50, 56; **79:**10; **83:**3, 3, 5; **85:**4; **86:**14; **89:**42; **94:**16; **105:**25, 25; **106:**7, 40, 43; **107:**11; **108:**12; **109:**3, 20; **118:**12; **119:**11, 23; **124:**2, 3; **137:**9; **138:**7, 7; **140:**4; **141:**5; **147:**17; **149:**9; **Pr 3:**29, 30; **11:**4; **21:**30; **23:**11; **24:**28; **SS 3:**8; **Isa 1:**2, 25; **3:**5, 5, 8, 13; **5:**25; **7:**2, 5; **8:**20; **9:**8, 11, 20; **10:**12, 14, 25; **11:**4, 13; **13:**2, 17; **14:**22; **16:**3; **19:**1, 2, 2, 2, 2, 2, 17, 20; **22:**7; **23:**11, 13; **25:**4, 8;

26:20; **27:**4; **28:**2, 21, 21; **29:**6, 7; **31:**2, 3; **34:**2, 2; **36:**5; **37:**6, 9, 17, 22, 23, 28, 29, 33; **41:**25; **42:**24; **43:**14, 27; **45:**1; **47:**3; **54:**17; **57:**16; **59:**12, 13; **61:**2; **63:**10, 10; **66:**4, 6, 14, 24; **Jer 1:**10, 18; **2:**8, 9, 9, 15, 17; **3:**13, 13, 25; **4:**16, 17, 28; **5:**9, 11, 15, 23, 29; **6:**6, 22; **8:**14; **9:**9; **11:**9, 18, 20; **12:**5, 5, 6; **13:**14, 14; **14:**7, 20; **15:**3, 8, 13, 20; **16:**10, 10; **18:**11, 23; **20:**12; **21:**4, 5, 13; **22:**18; **23:**9, 30; **25:**9, 9, 13, 16, 27, 29, 30, 30, 31; **26:**11, 12, 13, 19, 20; **27:**13; **28:**8, 16; **29:**32; **30:**6; **32:**5, 24; **33:**4, 8; **34:**1, 22; **36:**2, 7; **37:**18; **40:**3; **41:**9; **42:**5; **43:**11; **44:**3, 23; **46:**18, 22; **48:**2, 3, 26, 42; **49:**14, 22, 28, 30; **50:**7, 9, 14, 15, 21, 21, 21, 24, 25, 26, 28, 41, 45; **51:**1, 2, 5, 11, 11, 12, 12, 25, 27, 28, 29, 46, 48, 55, 56; **52:**3, 4, 4, 9; **La 1:**18, 20; **2:**4, 4; **3:**3, 46, 60, 62; **4:**20; **Eze 1:**24; **2:**3, 3; **3:**13; **4:**2; **5:**6, 13, 15, 17; **6:**2; **7:**3, 14, 27; **8:**17; **9:**8; **11:**4, 9; **13:**2, 8, 9, 15, 17, 20; **14:**8, 9, 13, 17; **16:**17, 42; **17:**10, 15, 20; **18:**14; **20:**4, 8, 13, 21, 22, 23, 38, 46, 46; **21:**2, 22, 22, 24; **23:**22, 24, 25, 46; **24:**2, 8, 13; **25:**2, 7, 12, 13, 15, 16, 17; **26:**3, 3, 7, 8; **28:**7, 7, 21, 22, 23; **29:**2, 8, 18; **30:**4, 11, 25; **32:**11, 20; **33:**2; **34:**2; **35:**2, 3, 12, 13; **36:**5; **38:**2, 11, 14, 16, 17, 21, 21; **39:**1, 23, 26; **40:**17; **42:**1; **Da 3:**29; **7:**21; **8:**4, 12; **9:**5, 8, 9, 11, 12, 13, 14; **10:**20, 20, 21; **11:**2, 11, 14, 25, 25, 27, 28, 30, 40; **Hos 1:**2; **4:**1, 7; **5:**5; **6:**7; **7:**10, 13, 15; **8:**1, 5; **12:**2; **13:**15, 16, 16; **Joel 2:**25; **3:**4; **Am 3:**1; **4:**10, 10; **5:**19; **6:**14; **7:**10, 16, 16; **Ob** 7; **Jnh 1:**2; **Mic 1:**2; **2:**8; **4:**11; **6:**1, 2; **7:**9; **Na 1:**9, 11; **3:**2, 10; **Hab 1:**10; **2:**11; **Zep 1:**17; **2:**5; **3:**11; **Hag 2:**12, 13; **Zec 2:**8; **8:**10; **9:**1, 13, 14; **10:**3; **12:**9; **13:**7, 7; **14:**2, 3, 12, 13; **Mal 2:**2; **3:**5, 5, 13; **Mt 5:**23; **6:**12, 14; **7:**25, 27; **10:**21, 35, 35, 35; **12:**2, 10, 25, 26, 30, 31, 32, 32, 41, 42; **18:**15, 21; **20:**15; **24:**7; **27:**6, 12, 13, 37; **Mk 2:**24; **3:**25, 26, 29; **6:**48; **9:**40; **10:**11; **11:**25; **13:**8, 12; **14:**55, 56, 57; **15:**4, 26; **Lk 6:**2, 7, 48, 49; **8:**45; **9:**50; **11:**4, 18, 23, 31, 32, 51, 54; **12:**10, 10, 52; **14:**31; **15:**18, 21; **18:**3; **19:**43; **21:**10, 14; **23:**19; **Jn 8:**6; **13:**18; **18:**29; **19:**12; **Ac 4:**26, 26, 27; **5:**39; **6:**1, 1, 10, 13, 13; **7:**19, 45; **10:**28; **13:**45, 50, 51; **14:**2; **16:**21, 22; **17:**7; **18:**12; **19:**9, 37, 38; **20:**3, 16; **21:**27, 28, 28; **23:**7; **24:**1, 2, 4, 5, 19; **25:**2, 8, 15, 18, 26, 27; **26:**2, 10, 14; **27:**7, 29; **28:**17, 19, 21; **Ro 1:**18, 26; **3:**25; **4:**8; **8:**20, 31; **11:**30; **13:**9; **1Co 6:**1, 18; **8:**12, 12; **10:**13; **11:**27; **2Co 2:**6; **5:**19; **8:**20; **Gal 2:**11; **Eph 4:**18; **6:**11, 12, 12, 12, 12; **Php 2:**15; **Col 2:**14; **1Th 5:**12; **2Th 2:**3; **1Ti 3:**2; **5:**14, 19; **2Ti 3:**8; **4:**15, 16; **Tit 1:**10; **Heb 3:**8, 13, 15, 16; **4:**7; **7:**1; **12:**4; **Jas 2:**13; **3:**9; **4:**6, 6, 11; **5:**3, 4, 6; **1Pe 2:**11, 15; **3:**12, 16; **5:**5, 9; **2Pe 2:**1, 11; **1Jn 5:**5; **Jude** 4, 15; **Rev 2:**4, 14, 16, 20; **6:**10; **11:**7; **12:**17; **13:**4, 5, 6, 7; **14:**5; **16:**14; **17:**3, 14; **19:**19

ALL (5051)

Ge 1:13, 19, 23, 25, 26, 26, 28, 29, 30, 31, 31; **2:**2, 6, 9, 20; **3:**1, 14, 17, 19, 20; **4:**14; **5:**23; **6:**5, 7, 12, 13, 13, 16, 21; **7:**1, 1, 4, 8, 8, 21, 21, 21, 23; **8:**1, 16, 17, 19, 21; **9:**2, 2, 10, 11, 12, 13, 15, 17, 19; **10:**21; **11:**4, 8; **12:**3, 5, 5, 20; **13:**1, 6, 8, 15; **14:**4, 11, 14, 16, 20, 21, 24; **15:**2, 2, 10, 18; **16:**5; **17:**8, 9, 13, 27; **18:**5, 18, 19, 25; **19:**4, 4, 21, 25; **20:**8, 18; **21:**2, 6, 24; **22:**18, 18; **23:**10, 17; **24:**28, 31, 33, 60; **25:**4, 31, 33; **26:**3, 4, 4, 5, 15; **27:**29, 29, 29, 37; **28:**14; **29:**3, 8; **30:**31, 32, 32, 34, 35, 35, 39; **31:**1, 8, 12, 18, 21, 32, 34, 37, 38, 38, 43, 43; **32:**10, 19, 23, 24; **33:**8; **34:**23, 24, 27, 28, 29, 30, 30, 30; **35:**4, 5; **36:**5, 6, 7, 12, 13, 19; **37:**7, 8, 11, 20, 27, 35; **39:**4, 5, 14, 22; **40:**17, 20, 23; **41:**8, 19, 22, 30, 34, 35, 36, 40, 43, 48, 51, 54; **42:**2, 6, 11, 17, 21, 29; **43:**8, 23, 34; **44:**9, 16; **45:**1, 8, 9, 10, 10, 18, 20, 23, 26; **46:**1, 6, 7, 15, 28, 31, 31; **47:**1, 14, 17, 20, 20, 21, 26; **48:**15, 16; **49:**1, 8, 10; **50:**7, 14, 15; **Ex 1:**5, 16, 22, 22; **3:**15, 16, 18, 20; **4:**14, 19, 31; **6:**26; **7:**19, 20; **8:**5, 10, 11, 13, 17, 18, 25, 28, 29, 30; **9:**6, 14, 14, 15, 18, 23, 24, 25, 25, 26, 29, 31, 33; **10:**5, 6, 8, 9, 9, 12, 13, 15, 15, 19, 23, 26; **11:**2, 5, 8, 8; **12:**9, 12, 12, 16, 26, 27, 29, 30, 31, 33, 33, 37, 37, 41, 46, 48, 50; **13:**2, 9, 12, 14, 15, 15; **14:**5, 9, 9, 16, 18, 21, 23, 26, 28, 28; **15:**15, 20; **16:**6, 8, 13, 33; **17:**3; **18:**1, 8, 9, 11, 12, 14, 14, 14, 18, 22, 23, 25; **19:**5, 5, 8, 11, 16, 18, 19; **23:**13, 21, 22, 27, 29; **24:**1, 2, 3, 4, 7; **25:**11, 19, 25, 36; **26:**2, 8, 17, 28; **27:**2, 3, 17, 19, 19, 21; **28:**3, 10, 20, 34; **29:**13, 18, 24; **30:**14, 27, 27, 28; **31:**3, 6, 6, 7, 8, 8, 9, 11; **32:**3, 10, 13, 26, 26; **33:**8, 8, 10, 16, 19; **34:**10, 10, 10, 11, 11, 17, 23, 27, 28, 32; **35:**1, 4, 10, 13, 20, 22, 25, 26, 31, 35; **36:**2, 22, 34; **37:**2, 8, 11, 17, 22, 23; **38:**2, 3, 16, 17, 20, 24, 26, 26, 31; **39:**7, 21, 26, 28, 33, 36, 40, 42, 43; **40:**9, 38, 38; **Lev 2:**2, 13, 16; **3:**16, 17; **4:**8, 12, 13, 19, 26, 31, 35; **5:**10; **6:**9, 13, 23; **7:**3, 6, 10, 10, 12; **8:**4, 11, 16, 16, 21, 26, 27, 28; **9:**4, 5, 24; **10:**3, 9, 11; **11:**14, 15, 16, 19, 20, 22, 22, 23, 27, 29, 31, 34, 42, 42, 44, 46; **13:**12, 33; **14:**8, 9, 43, 45, 47; **16:**17, 21, 22, 25, 30, 34; **17:**2; **18:**4, 18, 26, 27; **19:**19, 37; **20:**5, 8, 9, 14, 22, 24, 26; **21:**6, 17, 24; **22:**7, 9, 18, 31; **23:**2, 3, 6, 7, 8, 21, 24, 31, 35, 37, 39, 41, 42; **24:**3, 14, 23; **25:**8, 10, 16, 33, 33, 33; **26:**7, 8, 17, 20, 44, 45; **27:**25; **Nu 1:**2, 16, 18, 44, 45; **2:**9, 16, 17, 24, 31; **3:**8, 8, 12, 13, 13, 13, 26, 31, 32, 36, 37, 40; **4:**3, 12, 14, 14, 15, 23, 26, 26, 30, 35, 37, 39, 41, 43, 45, 46, 47; **5:**9; **6:**19; **7:**1, 8, 85; **8:**16, 16, 17, 17, 18, 19, 20, 22; **9:**3, 12; **10:**25, 25, 32; **11:**5, 5, 10, 13, 14, 22, 22, 29, 29, 31, 32, 32, 32; **12:**4; **13:**3, 22, 32; **14:**1, 1, 10, 11, 15, 29, 35; **15:**13, 22, 40; **16:**2, 3, 3, 6, 9, 16, 19, 22, 22, 24, 27, 28, 30, 33, 34, 37; **17:**9, 13; **18:**7, 8, 9, 10, 11, 13, 19; **19:**11, 13, 18; **20:**4, 8, 11, 14, 29; **21:**2, 25, 26, 30, 32, 33, 34; **22:**26; **23:**6; **24:**7, 8; **25:**4, 6, 8, 11, 13; **26:**2, 4, 4, 7, 14, 18, 22, 25, 27, 34, 37, 37, 41, 43, 47, 50, 58, 65; **27:**16; **28:**11, 19, 31; **29:**1, 2, 7, 8, 12, 13, 17, 20, 23, 26, 29, 32, 35, 36, 40; **30:**4, 5, 9; **31:**7, 8, 9, 10, 12, 13, 14, 15, 17, 17, 19, 20, 26, 41, 47, 48, 49, 51, 51, 52, 53; **32:**4, 6, 11, 18, 27, 29, 36; **33:**3, 4, 52, 52, 52; **35:**7, 30; **36:**8, 11; **Dt 1:**1, 7, 7, 8, 8, 9, 12, 16, 32, 44; **2:**5, 14, 15, 16, 25, 28, 28, 33, 34, 35, 37; **3:**3, 3, 4, 5, 6, 7, 7, 8, 10, 10, 13, 14, 16, 17, 18, 21, 21; **4:**4, 19, 19, 29, 32, 40, 40, 40, 48; **5:**1, 1, 3, 14, 22, 22, 23, 29, 31, 32; **6:**1, 2, 3, 5, 5, 5, 17, 18, 19, 22, 24, 25; **7:**1, 6, 7, 11, 14, 14, 15, 15, 16, 18, 19, 22, 24; **8:**1, 4; **9:**5, 9, 10; **10:**12, 14; **11:**1, 3, 7, 13, 13, 22, 23, 32; **12:**2, 5, 7, 10, 12, 15, 18, 25, 28, 28, 31, 32; **13:**3, 9, 11, 15, 15, 16, 18; **14:**2, 8, 13, 14, 15, 18, 19, 22, 28, 29; **15:**18, 19; **16:**11, 12, 15, 15, 17, 18; **17:**7, 7, 19; **18:**5; **19:**8, 9, 13; **20:**3, 11, 14; **21:**5, 13, 21, 21; **23:**10, 21; **24:**8, 19; **25:**19; **26:**11, 16, 18; **27:**1, 3, 8, 9, 10, 14, 15, 16, 17, 18, 19, 20, 21, 22, 23, 24, 25, 26; **28:**1, 1, 2, 10, 12, 15, 15, 25, 34, 37, 45, 52, 52, 55, 57, 58, 60, 64; **29:**2, 2, 3, 10, 10, 15, 20, 21, 21, 27; **30:**1, 2, 3, 6, 6, 7, 8, 10; **31:**1, 7, 11, 12, 12, 18, 20, 28; **32:**22, 43, 44, 46; **33:**3, 11; **34:**2, 2, 11, 11, 12; **Jos 1:**4, 6, 7, 8; **2:**9, 13, 18, 18, 23, 24; **3:**1, 7, 13, 16; **4:**1, 5, 10, 14, 23, 23, 24; **5:**1, 1, 4, 5, 6, 8; **6:**2, 5, 13, 18, 22, 23; **7:**3, 9, 23, 24, 25; **8:**6, 14, 16, 22, 24, 25, 33, 33, 34; **9:**1, 9, 24; **10:**2, 5, 6, 9, 12, 25, 37, 39, 42; **11:**2, 4, 6, 9, 10, 12, 14, 14, 15, 17, 17, 19, 21, 21, 22; **12:**1, 5, 24; **13:**4, 5, 6, 6, 7, 10, 11, 11, 12, 21, 25, 30, 30, 31; **14:**4, 10; **15:**32, 36, 45; **19:**8, 49; **21:**43, 44, 45; **22:**5, 5, 5, 5, 18, 20, 22, 33; **23:**1, 2, 4, 5, 6, 14; **24:**1, 23, 27, 31; **Jdg 1:**8; **2:**7, 14, 23; **3:**3, 19; **4:**13, 13, 15, 16, 16; **5:**24, 31; **6:**4, 9, 13, 13, 21, 23, 35; **7:**2, 5, 5, 6, 7, 14, 20, 21; **8:**10, 12, 14, 17, 18, 24, 27, 34, 35; **9:**2, 3, 5, 14, 16, 40, 45, 45, 49, 57; **10:**6, 8, 18; **11:**8, 9, 13, 21, 26, 26; **13:**17; **14:**3, 13; **15:**5, 5, 12; **16:**2, 3, 3, 27, 29, 30; **18:**18, 19, 24, 27; **19:**25; **20:**1, 2, 2, 8, 11, 25, 26, 29, 35, 37, 48; **21:**9, 11, 14, 16; **Ru 1:**9; **2:**2, 17, 19, 23; **4:**4, 9, 10, 11, 11; **1Sa 2:**8, 14, 28, 31, 36; **3:**12, 20; **4:**1, 6, 14; **5:**7, 11; **6:**1, 3, 9, 16; **7:**2, 2, 3, 5, 6, 7, 11; **8:**5; **9:**4, 6, 10, 20, 21; **10:**9, 17, 18, 24, 24, 24; **11:**2, 2, 7, 14, 15; **12:**7, 13, 14, 18, 20, 24; **14:**8, 14, 24, 26, 29, 31, 34, 36, 38, 40, 48; **15:**7, 11, 14, 18; **16:**10, 11, 17; **17:**12, 14, 37, 52; **18:**6, 16, 21, 25, 25, 27, 30; **19:**5, 8, 18, 24, 24; **20:**7, 15, 16, 21, 34; **22:**11, 14, 18, 18, 19, 22; **23:**5, 13, 23; **25:**1, 3, 24, 26, 30; **26:**15, 16, 24; **27:**5; **28:**3, 3, 9, 20, 20; **30:**20, 20, 25, 31; **31:**6, 12; **2Sa 1:**12, 18; **2:**3, 9, 14, 16, 27, 29, 29, 31, 32; **3:**5, 8, 9, 13, 18, 19, 21, 31, 32, 34; **4:**1; **5:**1, 1, 4, 5, 17, 25; **6:**5, 5, 5, 14, 15; **7:**9, 11, 16, 21, 26; **8:**4, 11, 14, 15; **9:**7, 11, 12; **10:**16, 17; **11:**19; **12:**12, 16, 31; **13:**9, 23, 25, 27, 30, 32, 33; **14:**13, 14, 21; **15:**6, 9, 13, 22; **16:**6, 14, 21; **17:**3, 3, 3, 4, 10, 14, 22, 22, 29; **18:**4, 5, 8, 12, 23, 28, 29, 31, 32, 32; **19:**6, 11, 14, 14, 18, 20, 28, 29, 30, 36, 39, 40; **20:**1, 21, 21, 22; **21:**2, 5, 6, 9, 14; **22:**1, 23, 31, 31, 41, 46, 51; **23:**39; **24:**2, 7, 23; **1Ki 1:**9, 9, 19, 20, 39, 40, 43, 45, 47, 49; **2:**3, 3, 4, 18, 26, 44; **3:**3, 13, 15, 21, 24, 26, 28; **4:**1, 7, 10, 12, 12, 21, 24, 25, 30, 31, 33; **5:**3, 4, 13; **6:**5, 12, 12, 29; **7:**5, 9, 9, 24, 25, 33, 36, 37, 45, 47, 48, 49, 50, 51, 51; **8:**1, 2, 3, 4, 23, 23, 43, 53, 56, 58, 60, 62, 63, 65, 65, 66; **9:**8, 9, 11, 12; **10:**3, 13, 13, 15, 20, 21, 21, 23; **11:**8, 32, 37, 42; **12:**1, 12, 16, 18, 20, 23; **13:**34; **14:**8, 9, 10, 10, 13, 16, 19, 21, 26, 29; **15:**7, 12, 18, 20, 20, 29, 31; **16:**13, 14, 23, 27, 34; **18:**4, 12, 19, 19, 20, 24, 26, 29, 30, 36, 38, 40, 40, 46; **19:**4, 21; **20:**4, 4, 7, 13, 13; **21:**13, 22, 29; **22:**6, 10, 12, 13, 17, 19, 22, 35, 36, 43; **2Ki 1:**10, 12; **2:**17; **3:**9, 19, 19, 19; **4:**2, 23, 26, 41, 43, 44; **5:**12, 15, 17, 21, 23; **6:**2; **7:**10, 15; **8:**21, 23; **9:**7, 11, 22; **10:**7, 9, 11, 11, 14, 18, 18, 19, 19, 19, 21, 21, 24, 25, 25, 31, 33, 34, 36; **11:**6, 8, 9, 11, 12, 13, 14, 14, 18, 19, 20; **12:**2, 4, 7, 9, 18, 18, 18, 19; **13:**8, 12; **14:**14, 14, 28; **15:**6, 16, 21, 26, 31, 36; **17:**9, 13, 15, 16, 16, 20, 22, 23, 37, 39; **18:**6, 12, 15, 16; **19:**2, 12, 15, 17, 18, 19, 27; **20:**13, 15, 17; **21:**3, 5, 7, 17, 24, 25; **22:**13; **23:**1, 2, 2, 3, 3, 3, 3, 4, 4, 4, 5, 8, 8, 19, 21, 22, 24, 25, 25, 26, 28; **24:**5, 13, 13, 14, 15, 16; **25:**4, 5, 7, 9, 9, 13, 14, 14, 15, 17, 20, 21, 23, 23, 24, 26, 28; **1Ch 1:**23, 33; **2:**4, 6, 23, 33, 50, 55; **3:**22, 23, 24; **4:**8, 10, 10, 22, 23, 42; **5:**10, 14, 17, 18, 20; **6:**32, 49, 49, 64; **7:**4, 5, 5, 7, 13, 17, 40; **8:**10, 28, 32, 40, 40, 40; **9:**1, 6, 9, 9, 13, 22, 24, 26, 33, 33, 34, 38; **11:**1, 1, 4, 10; **12:**2, 2, 15, 18, 21, 23, 28, 32, 35, 36, 38, 38; **13:**1, 2, 5, 6, 8, 8, 8; **14:**8, 8, 16, 17; **15:**3, 12, 24, 28; **16:**25, 29, 30, 31, 36, 43; **17:**8, 10, 14, 19, 24; **18:**4, 11, 13, 14; **19:**8, 16, 17; **20:**3; **21:**2, 3, 23; **22:**9, 17, 19; **23:**2, 3, 27, 29, 31, 31, 31; **24:**5; **25:**5, 6, 7, 7; **26:**8, 8, 11, 13, 26, 28, 30, 32; **27:**3, 31; **28:**1, 1, 4, 4, 8, 8, 12, 20; **29:**2, 3, 6, 11, 16, 17, 19, 19, 23, 24, 26, 27, 29, 30; **2Ch 1:**2, 2; **2:**14, 17; **3:**7; **4:**3, 4, 16, 16, 19, 21, 22; **5:**1, 1, 1, 2, 3, 4, 5, 5, 11, 12; **6:**14, 14, 33, 40; **7:**3, 4, 5, 6, 7, 8, 10, 17, 21, 22; **8:**16; **9:**2, 12, 14, 19, 20, 20, 22, 26, 30; **10:**1, 3, 12, 16, 16; **11:**3, 13, 16, 21; **12:**1, 5, 9, 9, 13, 14; **14:**14; **15:**2, 8, 9, 12, 15, 15; **16:**4, 6, 8, 8; **17:**2, 5, 7, 9, 10; **18:**5, 9, 11, 12, 16, 18, 21, 34; **19:**5, 11, 11; **20:**4, 6, 13, 15, 18, 20, 25, 33; **21:**4, 9, 14; **22:**1, 8, 9; **23:**3, 7, 10, 13, 13, 17, 18, 20, 21; **24:**5, 7, 10, 14, 23, 23; **25:**5, 24, 24; **26:**13, 17; **28:**9, 14, 15, 23, 25, 26; **29:**5, 15, 16, 16, 18, 18, 19, 24, 24, 25, 28, 34, 36; **30:**1, 2, 4, 5, 14, 25, 25; **31:**1, 5, 5, 9, 12, 16, 18, 18, 19, 20, 21; **32:**9, 12, 13, 17, 21, 22, 33; **33:**3, 7, 8, 10, 14, 15, 15, 19, 22, 25; **34:**3, 9, 9, 12, 21, 24, 29, 30, 30, 31, 31, 31, 33; **35:**6, 14, 16, 17, 18, 18, 18, 24; **36:**8, 14, 17, 18, 18, 19, 23, 23; **Ezr 1:**2, 3, 6, 6, 11; **2:**58; **3:**1, 8, 9, 11; **4:**9; **5:**4; **6:**4, 12, 18, 20; **7:**17, 21, 25, 28; **8:**20, 21, 22, 22, 35; **9:**4, 10; **10:**5, 5, 7, 8, 9, 9, 14, 17; **Ne 4:**8, 12, 15, 18, 19, 23; **5:**8, 16, 17, 18, 19; **6:**14, 14; **7:**5, 60, 73; **8:**1, 2, 3, 5, 5, 6, 9; **9:**2, 6, 6, 10, 14, 21, 25, 26, 28, 32, 36, 38; **10:**28, 29, 29, 36, 37, 38; **11:**6, 18, 21, 24, 30; **12:**26, 44; **13:**3, 8, 10, 11, 12, 14, 15, 16, 24, 26; **Est 1:**3, 3, 5, 5, 11, 13, 22; **2:**3, 18, 19, 23; **3:**2, 6, 8, 13, 13, 14; **4:**3, 8, 13, 16; **5:**8, 11, 12, 13, 14; **6:**13; **8:**5, 9, 9, 12, 13; **9:**2, 3, 4, 16, 20, 27, 32; **10:**3; **Job 1:**8, 12, 15, 15, 16, 19, 19, 22; **2:**3, 6, 10; **3:**10; **4:**10; **5:**27; **6:**3, 4, 24; **7:**1, 20; **8:**13; **9:**2, 9, 22, 28; **11:**11, 14, 16; **12:**9, 10; **13:**26, 27, 27; **14:**10; **15:**2, 13, 32; **16:**2; **17:**10; **18:**17; **19:**12, 14; **20:**20, 26; **21:**14, 18, 34; **22:**5, 8; **23:**14, 17; **24:**5, 7, 24; **25:**3, 4; **26:**4; **27:**12, 12, 16, 17, 19; **28:**16, 21, 24, 27, 28; **29:**11, 11, 14; **30:**11, 14, 23; **31:**8, 18, 25, 38; **32:**11; **33:**3; **34:**15, 19, 20, 34; **35:**4; **36:**11, 19; **38:**7, 21, 21, 37; **40:**10, 20; **41:**34; **42:**11, 11, 15; **Ps 1:**3; **2:**12; **3:**7; **5:**5, 11, 11; **6:**7, 8, 10; **7:**9; **8:**6, 7; **9:**1, 1, 17; **10:**5; **14:**3, 3; **16:**2, 5; **18:**T, 22, 30, 30, 40, 45, 50; **19:**4, 4, 12; **20:**1, 3, 4, 5; **21:**8, 8, 13; **22:**6, 14, 22, 23, 23, 23, 25, 26, 28, 29; **23:**6; **24:**1; **25:**5, 10, 17, 18, 22; **26:**7; **27:**4; **28:**4, 7; **30:**4, 5; **31:**11, 23, 23, 24; **32:**3, 5, 5, 6, 11, 11; **33:**6, 10, 14, 17; **34:**1, 2, 4, 6, 7, 9, 17; **35:**18, 22, 28; **36:**7; **38:**12, 13; **39:**6; **40:**5, 9, 12, 16; **41:**6, 7; **43:**4; **44:**1, 2, 8, 12, 13, 16, 16, 17; **45:**2; **47:**2, 7, 9; **48:**13; **49:**1, 10, 19; **50:**1, 10, 11, 12, 21, 21, 22; **52:**2, 5; **53:**3, 3; **56:**1, 8, 8; **57:**5, 9, 11; **58:**2; **59:**8, 10; **60:**11; **62:**3, 8, 9, 12; **63:**11; **64:**8, 9; **65:**2, 3, 13; **66:**1, 16; **67:**3, 5, 7; **68:**26, 27; **69:**7, 12, 18, 19, 32, 34; **70:**4; **71:**8, 15, 18, 24; **72:**3, 7, 11, 11, 15, 17; **73:**10, 14, 14, 21; **74:**8, 9, 22; **75:**8; **77:**2, 11; **78:**25, 28, 38, 49, 56; **79:**3; **80:**12; **82:**7, 8; **83:**11, 18; **85:**2; **86:**5, 9, 12; **87:**4, 7; **88:**8, 17; **89:**5, 6, 11, 16, 42, 48; **90:**1, 8; **92:**4, 9; **95:**3; **96:**4, 9, 9, 10, 10, 13; **97:**3, 5, 7, 8, 9, 9, 12; **98:**4, 7; **99:**2; **101:**3; **103:**3, 3, 6, 10; **104:**11, 20, 24, 30, 31, 34, 35; **105:**21, 21, 29, 33, 35, 45; **106:**29, 48; **107:**8, 15, 21, 31, 43; **108:**3, 5, 12; **109:**3, 11, 13, 16, 29; **111:**1, 2, 7, 7, 10; **112:**5; **115:**1, 8, 11, 16; **116:**11, 12, 14, 18; **117:**1, 1; **118:**4, 10, 11, 12; **119:**2, 13, 34, 39, 50, 58, 69, 74, 79, 86, 97, 118, 119, 132, 135, 145, 151, 160, 160, 163, 164, 172; **120:**2; **121:**7; **122:**4, 6; **128:**1, 3; **129:**5; **132:**1; **134:**1; **135:**6, 9, 11, 18, 20; **138:**1, 2, 4, 4; **139:**13; **140:**2, 5; **142:**2, 5; **143:**4, 5, 12, 12; **145:**9, 10, 13, 13, 15, 18, 18, 20; **146:**4; **147:**4, 18; **148:**2, 2, 3, 9, 9, 10, 11, 13; **Pr 1:**13, 19, 33; **3:**5, 6, 17; **4:**23, 24; **6:**8, 15; **8:**4, 4, 13, 17, 31, 32, 36; **9:**8; **10:**5, 7, 12, 24, 28; **11:**7; **13:**6, 23; **15:**19; **17:**8; **19:**20, 25; **20:**8; **21:**4; **23:**3; **24:**4, 12, 12, 29; **25:**3, 27; **26:**25, 26; **29:**12, 22; **30:**5; **31:**12, 21, 27, 29, 31; **Ecc 1:**3, 9; **2:**2, 5, 9, 9, 10, 11, 15, 15, 22, 23; **3:**9, 17; **4:**1, 3, 3, 8, 8, 13, 16; **5:**4, 7, 16; **6:**2, 7; **7:**20, 23; **8:**9, 14, 15, 16; **9:**3, 6, 9, 9, 11; **10:**14; **11:**6, 9; **12:**8; **SS 1:**3; **2:**15, 15; **3:**2, 8; **6:**8; **Isa 1:**1, 13, 14, 23, 25, 28, 29; **2:**2, 4, 4, 16, 17; **3:**2, 10, 17; **4:**1, 3, 5; **5:**14, 22, 24; **7:**14, 17, 22; **8:**7, 8, 9, 16; **9:**2, 5, 13, 17; **10:**16, 19, 29, 31, 33; **11:**6, 9, 10, 11, 14; **12:**6; **13:**9; **14:**10, 11, 24; **15:**5; **16:**6, 9, 10; **18:**3, 6, 6; **19:**7, 7, 8, 10, 14; **20:**2; **21:**2, 9, 16; **22:**3, 11; **23:**1, 7, 7, 9, 17; **24:**7, 14, 23; **25:**8, 8, 11; **26:**2, 3, 9, 12, 21; **27:**9; **28:**27; **29:**7, 8, 11, 20; **30:**5, 6, 11, 17, 22, 28; **31:**3; **32:**7, 8; **33:**9, 11, 15, 17, 19; **34:**2, 8, 12, 16; **37:**2, 12, 16, 18, 19, 20, 28; **38:**13, 17; **39:**2, 4, 6; **40:**2, 5, 10, 15, 15, 16, 16, 23, 26, 28; **41:**11, 12, 15, 16, 24, 29, 29; **42:**3, 5, 6, 10, 10, 13, 15, 15, 19, 22; **43:**7, 17, 18, 27; **44:**11, 11, 12, 20, 24; **45:**6, 12, 13, 14, 14, 16, 22, 24, 24, 25; **46:**3; **47:**7, 9, 10, 12, 14, 15; **48:**3, 7, 14; **49:**1, 4, 4, 4, 17, 18, 21, 21, 23, 26; **50:**4, 9; **51:**1, 1, 14, 16; **52:**5, 10; **53:**6, 6, 11, 11; **54:**1, 5, 13; **55:**1, 3, 11; **56:**1, 7, 11, 11, 12; **57:**6, 16, 16, 19; **59:**6, 9; **60:**1, 2, 3, 15, 15, 18, 21, 22; **61:**3; **62:**3, 6, 10; **63:**7, 9, 9; **64:**6, 8, 9, 11, 12; **65:**2, 3, 8, 8, 8, 12, 16; **66:**4, 6, 10, 18, 19, 23, 24; **Jer 1:**15, 16; **2:**3, 4, 13, 25, 26; **3:**2, 5, 7, 9, 10, 17; **4:**2, 4, 5, 22, 25, 25, 29; **5:**2, 7, 25; **6:**10, 14, 15, 18, 19, 19, 28; **7:**2, 9, 10, 11, 12, 19, 23, 27, 32; **8:**6, 7, 9, 11, 12, 13, 13, 16, 19; **9:**1, 2, 4, 5, 5, 10, 12, 25, 26; **10:**7, 7, 14, 14, 15; **11:**8, 19; **12:**2, 10, 14, 15; **13:**12, 19, 22; **14:**2, 3, 10, 13, 16, 19, 20; **15:**4, 7, 10, 11, 13; **16:**8, 10, 13, 15, 18, 20; **17:**3, 10, 10, 13, 18, 20, 20, 26; **18:**11, 16, 17, 23; **19:**8, 9, 11, 13, 13; **20:**4, 5, 6, 6, 6, 16; **21:**7, 8, 12; **22:**7, 15, 20, 20, 22, 22; **23:**8, 11, 20, 20, 24, 32; **24:**1, 8; **25:**1, 7, 9, 9, 10, 13, 13, 15, 17, 20, 20, 26, 29, 30, 31, 31; **26:**2, 7, 8, 9; **27:**5, 7, 10, 15, 15, 16, 19, 20, 22; **28:**1, 3, 4, 5, 6, 7, 11, 14; **29:**1, 2, 4, 10, 16, 20, 31; **30:**7, 14, 16, 16, 24, 24; **31:**1, 12, 19, 30, 38, 40; **32:**12, 12, 13, 19, 19, 20, 27, 29, 30, 37, 39, 42, 42, 43; **33:**5, 8, 9, 10, 12, 13, 14; **34:**1, 9, 10, 17, 22; **35:**3, 3, 8, 10, 17, 18; **36:**2, 3, 4, 6, 9, 10, 12, 21, 31, 31; **38:**4, 5, 9, 20, 22, 23; **39:**3, 6; **40:**8, 9; **41:**3, 7, 7, 12, 14, 16, 17; **42:**1, 1, 4, 8, 10; **43:**1, 2, 4, 4, 5, 6, 12; **44:**2, 3, 8, 12, 15, 15, 15, 20, 21, 22, 23, 24, 24, 26, 27, 28, 29; **45:**5; **46:**7, 9, 25, 25; **48:**4, 8, 18, 21, 21, 24, 26, 34, 36, 39, 45; **49:**7, 10, 13, 15, 17, 21, 24, 26, 32, 36; **50:**7, 13, 14, 16, 16, 23, 27, 30, 37; **51:**12, 17, 17, 18, 24, 28, 31, 32, 35, 35, 39, 47, 56, 60; **52:**7, 8, 10, 10, 13, 13, 17, 18, 18, 19, 22, 26, 27, 30, 32; **La 1:**2, 2, 6, 8, 8, 12, 13, 16, 22, 22; **2:**2, 3, 6, 9, 13, 15, 15, 15, 16, 22, 22; **3:**2, 14, 46, 51, 61, 62, 63, 64; **4:**12, 12, 17; **5:**1; **Eze 1:**12, 16, 18, 28; **3:**3, 10; **4:**12, 15; **5:**4, 8, 11, 13, 15; **6:**4, 6, 9, 10, 11; **7:**3, 4, 8, 9, 11, 12, 14, 20; **8:**10; **9:**2, 4, 6, 8, 10; **10:**8, 10, 12; **11:**3, 10; **12:**6, 9, 10, 24; **13:**3, 9, 10, 10, 20; **14:**5, 6, 7, 10, 21, 21; **16:**22, 23, 36, 37, 43, 43, 43, 55, 57, 57, 58, 61, 63; **17:**9, 17, 21, 24; **18:**4, 11, 17, 21, 22, 24, 31; **19:**5, 11; **20:**6, 11, 23, 32, 38, 40, 41, 43, 48; **21:**5, 7, 13, 24; **22:**19, 31; **23:**6, 12, 23, 23, 24, 29, 29, 30, 30, 32, 35, 36, 44, 45, 49; **24:**4, 7, 7, 14, 19, 23; **25:**4, 5, 8; **26:**12, 16; **27:**9, 14, 22, 29, 34, 35; **28:**13, 15, 17, 18, 19; **29:**2, 5, 6, 15, 18; **30:**5, 6, 8, 16; **31:**2, 4, 5, 5, 6, 6, 9, 12, 14, 14, 16, 16, 17, 17, 18, 18; **32:**4, 6, 10, 12, 13, 15, 16, 21, 22, 25, 25, 26, 26, 26, 28, 30, 30, 30, 32; **33:**33; **34:**12, 13, 19, 19; **35:**5, 7, 11, 13, 15; **36:**3, 24, 31, 32, 34, 36, 36; **37:**7, 10, 11, 22; **38:**4, 5, 6, 7, 9, 16, 20, 20, 23; **39:**4, 6, 10, 17; **40:**14, 21, 41, 46; **41:**10, 15, 18, 19, 22; **42:**4, 20; **43:**10, 11, 11, 13, 17; **44:**7, 13, 16, 24, 30; **45:**2, 9, 16, 17; **46:**4, 6, 23; **47:**10, 12, 23; **48:**1, 7, 12; **Da 1:**6, 18, 20, 20; **2:**12, 15, 20, 35, 38, 40, 44, 48, 49; **3:**2, 3, 4, 7, 10, 15; **4:**2, 3, 6, 7, 11, 12, 12, 18, 20, 21, 28, 35, 37; **5:**8, 11, 19, 22, 23; **6:**3, 18; **7:**8, 14, 15, 16, 23, 26, 27, 27; **9:**6, 7, 7, 11, 12, 13, 16, 16, 27; **10:**3, 8; **11:**34, 37; **12:**7, 8; **Hos 2:**10, 11, 13, 18, 18, 18; **4:**3, 6, 9; **5:**1, 1, 2; **7:**2, 2, 4, 12; **8:**12, 13; **9:**4, 7, 15, 15; **10:**14; **12:**1, 2, 8; **13:**10, 15, 15; **14:**2, 8; **Joel 1:**2, 5, 5, 11, 11, 11, 12, 12, 12, 14, 19; **2:**3, 6, 9, 26, 28; **3:**5, 7, 7, 9, 11, 12, 20; **Am 1:**2, 5, 7, 10, 14; **2:**2, 3, 5, 9; **3:**2, 2, 7, 9, 11, 13, 15; **4:**7, 9, 10, 12; **5:**9, 16, 17, 18, 21, 22; **6:**6, 7, 9; **7:**8, 10; **9:**5, 10, 10, 12; **Ob** 7, 15; **Jnh 1:**5, 11, 12; **2:**7, 8, 9; **3:**3, 7, 8; **4:**11; **Mic 1:**2, 6, 7, 7, 8, 10; **2:**9; **3:**4, 6, 9, 11; **4:**1, 3, 3, 9, 13, 13; **5:**4, 9, 10, 12, 13, 15; **6:**11, 13, 16; **7:**2, 2, 9, 12, 12, 16; **Na 1:**2, 14, 15; **2:**7; **3:**4, 4, 5, 7, 8, 10, 12, 17, 19; **Hab 1:**3, 9, 10, 12; **2:**6, 7, 8, 13, 14, 16, 18, 20; **3:**2, 16; **Zep 1:**2, 4, 8, 11, 11, 12, 18; **2:**3, 3, 11, 14, 14, 15; **3:**2, 8, 9, 11, 14, 17, 19, 20; **Hag 1:**9, 11; **2:**3, 4, 7, 7, 17; **Zec 1:**4, 6, 9, 14; **2:**4, 13; **3:**8; **4:**10, 14; **6:**5, 15; **7:**5; **8:**6, 10, 17; **9:**1, 7, 10, 12; **10:**4, 7, 10; **11:**2, 10; **12:**2, 6, 9, 10, 12; **13:**1, 2; **14:**2, 5, 9, 10, 10, 12, 14, 15, 19, 21; **Mal 1:**9, 10, 11, 12; **2:**6, 9, 10, 10; **3:**5, 10, 12; **4:**1, 4, 4; **Mt 1:**17, 22; **2:**3, 16; **3:**5; **4:**8, 9, 24, 25; **5:**14, 15, 16, 20; **6:**2, 4, 5, 6, 18, 27, 29, 32, 33; **7:**12, 21; **8:**10, 11, 16, 16, 26, 32; **9:**31, 35; **10:**23, 26, 27, 30; **11:**2, 11, 13, 28; **12:**15, 21, 45; **13:**22, 32, 37, 41, 56; **14:**5, 20, 21, 27, 29, 35, 36; **15:**19, 23, 30, 33, 35, 37, 38; **16:**3, 18, 27; **18:**26; **19:**20, 21; **20:**12, 13; **21:**9; **22:**3, 28, 37, 37, 37, 40, 40; **23:**8, 27, 35, 36; **24:**2, 3, 8, 9, 14, 30, 34, 39, 44, 47; **25:**5, 7, 9, 31, 32; **26:**31, 35, 56, 56, 65; **27:**22, 25, 54; **28:**12, 14, 19, 20; **Mk 1:**5, 33; **2:**12; **3:**7; **4:**13, 19; **5:**5, 31, 39, 40; **6:**2, 12, 22, 30, 37, 42, 50, 50, 56; **7:**11, 14, 23; **8:**6, 18; **9:**6, 16, 30; **10:**20, 21, 28, 44; **11:**9, 17, 23; **12:**9, 22, 22, 23, 28, 30, 30, 30, 30, 33, 33, 33, 33, 43; **13:**4, 4, 8, 27, 30; **14:**23, 27, 31, 50, 64, 64; **15:**4, 42; **16:**15, S; **Lk 1:**3, 4, 5, 6, 42, 50, 59, 61, 71; **2:**3, 14, 18, 31, 39, 47, 51, 52; **3:**6; **4:**2, 5, 7, 22; **5:**5, 17; **6:**12, 13, 17, 19, 37; **7:**1, 9, 17, 28, 29, 40; **8:**14, 17, 21, 24, 37, 39, 39, 50, 53; **9:**1, 15, 17, 43; **10:**1, 19, 27, 27, 27, 27, 40, 41; **11:**7, 25, 26, 28, 33, 41, 50; **12:**2, 3, 7, 20, 25, 27, 31, 40, 44; **13:**3, 17, 27, 28, 29; **14:**7, 10, 17, 18; **15:**13, 13, 29, 29; **16:**14; **17:**24, 27, 29; **18:**21, 22, 31, 42, 43; **19:**37, 37, 48; **20:**16, 18, 33, 38; **21:**3, 6, 7, 12, 24, 28, 32; **22:**31, 65, 66, 70; **23:**5, 33, 48, 56; **24:**18, 19, 21, 25, 26, 27, 27, 44, 47, 47, 48, 53; **Jn 1:**12, 16, 50, 51; **2:**15, 19; **3:**2, 28, 36; **4:**22, 35, 45; **5:**18, 22, 27, 28; **6:**5, 10, 11, 31, 39, 40, 45, 49, 56; **7:**31; **8:**7, 15, 48; **9:**4, 4, 15; **10:**8, 10, 41; **11:**42, 52; **12:**9, 17, 26, 37, 46, 48; **13:**10, 11, 18, 31; **14:**9, 17, 23; **15:**24, 26; **16:**13, 15, 25, 33; **17:**1, 2, 10, 11, 20, 21, 23; **18:**4, 6, 14, 37; **19:**11; **21:**3, 3, 23, 24, 25; **Ac 1:**14, 19, 21, 24; **2:**6, 7, 11, 13, 14, 17, 18, 32, 39, 40, 41, 43, 44, 47, 47; **3:**9, 11, 13, 18, 18, 21, 25; **4:**5, 10, 12, 24, 27, 31, 32, 33; **5:**11, 16, 21, 24, 28, 37; **6:**2; **7:**10, 10, 14, 14, 15, 16, 22; **8:**1; **9:**9, 21, 26, 40, 41; **10:**12, 14, 20, 22, 36, 37, 38, 39, 42, 43, 44; **11:**6, 10, 14, 18; **12:**9, 10; **13:**10, 20, 26, 29, 39, 48; **14:**2, 16, 27; **15:**5, 7, 11, 17; **16:**26, 28, 32, 34; **17:**7, 16, 17, 20, 21, 21, 26, 27; **18:**2, 8, 23, 28; **19:**7, 17, 26, 27, 32, 40; **20:**1, 2, 11, 27, 32, 38; **21:**13, 17, 18, 20, 21, 24, 25, 25, 31, 34; **22:**3, 10, 12, 30; **23:**1, 6, 8, 9; **24:**3; **25:**18, 24, 26; **26:**2, 14, 20, 20, 26, 30; **27:**20, 21, 31, 35, 37, 43; **28:**9, 10, 30, 31; **Ro 1:**8, 9, 18, 20; **2:**5, 6, 10, 17, 26; **3:**2, 9, 9, 12, 12, 22, 23, 23, 29; **4:**2, 16; **5:**11, 14, 17, 18, 20, 21; **6:**17; **7:**8, 15, 22; **8:**9, 14, 19, 21, 22, 27, 32, 37, 39; **10:**4, 5, 12, 12, 18, 21; **11:**5, 9, 13, 26, 26, 32; **12:**5, 5, 5, 12, 16; **13:**1, 7, 8, 8, 9, 10; **14:**2, 3, 6, 16, 22; **15:**6, 11, 11, 14, 15, 17, 19, 19, 23, 33; **16:**4, 15, 16, 26; **1Co 1:**2, 4, 8, 20, 21, 23, 28; **2:**14, 15; **3:**16; **4:**7, 17; **5:**6; **6:**5, 7; **7:**7, 17, 31, 36; **8:**2, 4, 7; **9:**23, 25; **10:**1, 1, 2, 3, 4, 4, 5, 11, 17, 18, 20, 31; **11:**6, 12, 16, 16, 18; **12:**4, 6, 13, 13, 25, 26, 26, 27, 29, 30; **13:**2, 8, 10, 12; **14:**2, 5, 5, 10, 18, 24, 26, 31, 33; **15:**7, 8, 9, 10, 10, 14, 15, 18, 22, 22, 23, 24, 25, 27, 27, 28, 28, 51, 51; **16:**2, 6, 18, 19, 24; **2Co 1:**1, 3, 4, 12, 20; **2:**5; **3:**4, 10, 18; **4:**2, 2, 5, 15; **5:**4, 10, 14, 18; **7:**4; **8:**5, 18, 24; **9:**3, 4, 8; **10:**14; **11:**10, 19, 28; **12:**1, 9, 10, 11, 11, 15, 19, 19; **13:**2, 3, 8, 12, 13; **Gal 1:**2, 5, 5, 7, 14, 16, 23; **2:**14; **3:**4, 7, 8, 9, 10, 12, 22, 26, 27, 28, 29; **4:**11, 27; **5:**3, 9; **6:**16,

18; Eph 1:8, 11, 22; 2:3, 6, 7, 14, 18, 19; 3:6, 9, 10, 10, 11, 18; 4:4, 4, 6, 6, 6, 10, 19, 21, 25, 31, 31; 5:6; 6:6, 11, 11, 18, 18, 21, 24; Php 1:1, 7, 13, 19; 2:17, 21, 28, 28; 3:7, 8, 12, 13, 13, 15, 19; 4:5, 6, 9, 18, 19, 21, 22; Col 1:4, 6, 10, 11, 14, 15, 15, 17, 18, 19, 23, 25, 28; 2:3, 7, 13; 3:4, 9, 11, 11, 14, 15, 16, 17, 22; 4:9; 1Th 1:2, 7; 2:10, 19; 3:5, 7, 13; 4:3, 6, 10, 10, 14, 16; 5:1, 3, 5, 12, 27, 28; 2Th 1:3, 4, 11, 12; 2:11, 15; 3:16, 17, 18; 1Ti 1:5, 15; 2:1, 1, 2; 4:10, 12; 5:2; 6:2, 7, 10, 11, 13, 14, 17, 21; 2Ti 1:10, 15, 16; 2:7, 19; 3:11, 11, 16; 4:8, 17, 17, 21, 22; Tit 1:8, 12; 2:6, 11; 3:8, 8, 15, 15; Phm 1:5, 6; Heb 1:6; 2:8, 8, 8, 9, 12, 15, 16; 3:14; 4:4, 10, 13, 13, 15; 5:9; 6:1; 7:2, 5, 27; 9:4, 5, 6, 11, 12, 15, 19, 19, 26, 28; 10:2, 10, 12, 14, 34, 36; 11:13, 13, 29, 31, 32, 39, 39; 12:3, 4, 8, 8, 9, 23; 13:7, 20, 20, 24, 25; Jas 1:11, 17, 18, 21; 2:10, 10, 17; 3:2, 7, 17, 17; 4:16; 5:1, 12; 1Pe 1:3, 5, 10, 11, 12, 20, 22; 2:1, 13, 14, 21; 3:8, 18, 22; 4:8, 11, 11, 13; 5:5, 7, 9, 11, 14; 2Pe 1:1, 4, 4, 20; 2:7; 3:16, 18; 1Jn 1:5; 2:2, 15, 20, 27, 29; 3:3, 4; 4:15, 16, 18; 5:8, 10, 17; 3Jn 2; Jude 1, 3, 3, 7, 15, 15, 24, 25; Rev 1:3, 5, 5, 7, 16; 2:2, 19, 19, 22, 22, 23, 26, 26; 3:1, 5, 8, 12, 15; 4:4; 6:9, 14, 14, 15; 7:4, 11, 17; 8:7, 9, 9, 13; 9:4, 15, 18; 11:4, 9, 10, 11, 18, 18; 12:5, 9, 17; 13:3, 6, 8, 12, 12, 14, 14; 14:7, 13; 15:2, 2, 4; 16:5, 9, 11, 14, 15, 16, 19, 20; 17:3, 5, 13, 14, 14, 16; 18:1, 3, 6, 14, 17, 17, 18, 19, 19, 24; 19:5, 5, 18, 20, 21; 20:13; 21:4, 5, 6, 7, 7, 8, 26; 22:8, 9, 12, 15, 20, 21

ALSO (763)

Ge 1:16; 2:12; 3:6; 10:15, 21; 13:5, 7; 14:7, 12; 16:11; 17:12, 20; 18:12; 21:13; 24:53; 26:19, 26, 34; 27:25; 28:7; 31:46, 49; 34:29; 35:27; 36:1, 3, 8, 14, 19; 38:11; 41:43, 57; 42:25, 25; 43:22; 45:14; 46:27; 50:8; Ex 3:15; 14:19; 18:8; 21:29, 35; 22:30; 23:12, 16; 24:4; 25:38; 26:20, 27; 27:13, 15; 28:4, 39, 42; 29:13, 20, 22, 40; 30:30; 31:1; 35:28; 36:18, 25; 37:20, 23; 38:1, 11, 13, 15, 19, 29, 31; 39:5, 16; 40:20, 26; Lev 2:7; 7:8, 13; 9:4, 14, 17; 10:19; 11:6; 14:7, 22, 26; 16:25; 17:15; 18:14; 19:1; 22:11; 23:13; 25:7, 45, 49; 27:32; Nu 3:8, 37; 4:11, 26, 38, 42; 6:17; 7:10, 14, 20, 26, 32, 38, 44, 50, 56, 62, 68, 74, 80; 8:23; 11:4, 10, 17; 13:23, 28; 15:4, 5, 17; 16:16, 17, 37; 18:11, 12, 14, 25, 30; 19:8, 10, 15; 22:6; 26:46, 59; 28:14, 15, 22, 30; 29:11, 16, 19, 22, 25, 28, 31, 34, 38; 31:8, 20, 30; 34:18; 35:31; Dt 1:16, 37; 3:5, 17; 4:48; 8:20; 9:22; 17:20; 18:4; 20:8; 21:5; 24:3, 21; 27:7; 29:15; Jos 4:9; 7:11; 9:10; 10:1; 12:3; 13:4, 10, 21, 22, 31; 15:33, 37, 45, 47, 48, 52, 60; 16:9; 18:25; 19:7, 8, 22, 29, 46; 23:15; 24:11, 33; Jdg 1:29, 30, 31, 33; 4:10; 5:14; 6:35; 7:24; 8:17, 31; 9:11, 57; 10:9; 11:2; 14:9; 15:5; 18:7; 20:26, 48; Ru 2:11, 18; 3:15; 4:5; 1Sa 2:26; 7:6, 14; 14:49; 16:18; 17:6; 19:20; 25:43; 28:20, 23; 30:12; 2Sa 2:30; 3:19; 4:11; 5:11; 8:2, 3; 12:31; 13:31; 15:12; 18:26; 21:8; 23:20; 1Ki 1:25; 2:28, 44; 3:13, 18; 4:7, 28, 33; 5:15; 6:4, 20; 7:1, 6, 7, 7, 8, 11, 11, 18, 27, 38, 40; 8:1; 9:17, 23, 25; 10:5, 11, 17; 11:23; 12:32; 13:11; 16:7; 19:2; 21:23; 22:44, 48; 2Ki 2:7; 11:17; 12:8, 12; 14:7, 14; 15:29; 16:9, 17, 18; 17:9, 29, 41; 18:8; 20:13; 21:3, 16; 22:6, 10; 23:5, 7, 8, 11, 13, 15, 24, 33; 24:16; 25:14, 15, 30; 1Ch 1:10, 13; 2:23, 34, 49, 49; 3:6, 9, 19; 4:18, 32; 5:26; 6:48, 65; 9:27; 11:22, 26; 12:8, 28; 13:6; 14:1; 15:1, 16, 27; 16:41; 18:2; 19:7; 20:3; 22:4, 14; 23:28, 29; 26:4, 7, 9, 28, 31; 28:12, 13, 17; 29:8, 21; 2Ch 1:12; 2:3, 8, 14, 14; 3:8, 9, 11, 12, 16; 4:1, 6, 8, 9, 11; 5:2; 8:6, 10, 14; 9:4, 10, 14, 16, 29; 11:12, 23; 14:5, 8, 15; 16:10; 17:8; 20:3; 21:3; 22:3; 23:18; 24:12; 25:6, 24; 26:7, 10, 10, 16; 27:3; 28:5; 29:7, 19, 33; 31:3, 16, 18; 32:2, 5, 17, 17, 28; 33:3, 15, 16; 34:4, 18; 35:2, 8; 36:7, 13, 18, 18; Ezr 2:61; 3:5, 5, 6; 4:10; 5:4; 7:15, 24; 8:16, 19, 35; 10:23; Ne 2:7; 3:8, 13, 29; 4:22; 6:7; 7:63; 10:33; 11:6, 12, 13, 26, 29, 30, 32; 12:17, 29, 43; 13:4, 10, 15, 16, 19, 22, 31; Est 1:16; 2:7, 9; 4:8; 8:14; 9:7, 12, 14, 18; Job 5:18, 18; 32:3, 16; 35:3; 42:13; Ps 22:30; 69:9; 87:4; 94:10, 10; 99:6; 107:35; Pr 12:14; 23:23; Ecc 2:4, 7; 3:16; 7:6; 11:8; Isa 7:19; 17:3; 39:2; 55:5; 56:3, 6, 7; 63:9; 65:4, 7; Jer 9:26; 14:9; 26:20, 24; 32:1; 37:21; 38:3; 43:6; 52:10, 18, 19, 34; La 3:32; Eze 8:10; 10:17; 13:17; 16:21, 55; 17:13; 20:13, 21; 24:25; 29:13; 32:29; 34:18, 18; 36:11; 38:6; 40:8, 10, 16, 26, 29, 42; 41:14, 15, 17; 42:17; 43:14, 17; 44:30; 45:5, 20, 23; 46:14; 48:2, 3, 4, 24, 26, 32, 33, 34; Da 2:26, 43; 3:11; 4:19; 6:2; 7:20; 10:1; Hos 6:11; Jnh 4:7; Na 3:9, 11, 17; Zep 2:12; Hag 2:12; Zec 1:17; 3:5; 6:13; Mt 4:7, 18; 6:21; 10:2; 12:42; 13:26, 33; 17:12; 18:19; 19:28; 22:26, 27; 24:44; 25:17; 26:25; 27:41, 44; 28:8; Mk 4:26; 6:22; 8:7; 15:31; Lk 1:5, 18; 2:36; 3:19; 4:12; 5:10; 6:14, 23, 26, 29, 39; 10:16, 32; 11:17; 12:34; 13:3, 5, 20; 14:8; 16:22; 19:18; 20:30; Jn 2:2; 3:26; 5:19, 32, 37; 6:1; 7:10; 10:16, 18; 12:9, 39; 15:27; 17:19, 20; 19:23, 35, 39; 20:6, 8; Ac 1:23; 4:13; 5:1; 7:6, 8, 10; 9:27; 11:18; 13:9, 26; 14:23; 15:9, 22; 17:4, 18; 18:8; 19:27, 31; 21:10, 13, 20; 23:23; 24:26; 26:20; 27:2; 28:28; Ro 1:12, 16; 2:9, 10; 3:29; 4:12, 14, 18, 24; 6:4, 5, 8; 8:17, 23, 32; 9:22, 23; 11:16, 17, 22; 14:6; 15:3, 9, 31; 16:13; 1Co 1:16; 7:4; 9:10, 24; 14:1, 13; 15:3, 39, 44; 16:4; 2Co 1:7; 4:10, 14; 5:14; 7:14; 8:7, 18, 21, 22; 11:15, 16; Gal 6:14; Eph 1:13; 2:22; Php 1:29; 2:27; Col 1:11; 4:1, 3, 9, 11, 13; 1Th 1:5; 4:14; 2Th 1:7; 1Ti 3:7; 2Ti 2:11; 3:1; 4:13; Phm 1:2; Heb 2:13, 14; 6:17; 7:1, 2, 12; 9:28; 10:15, 30; 11:40; 12:26; 13:12; Jas 1:11; 2:11, 26; 3:2, 5, 17; 1Pe 2:8; 3:18; 2Pe 2:1; 3:7; 1Jn 2:8, 23, 29; 3:16; 5:6; 3Jn 10; Rev 2:24, 28; 3:18; 5:13; 8:12; 9:19; 14:17; 17:9; 18:13, 20; 21:1, 6

AM (1318)

Ge 4:9; 6:7, 17; 9:9, 12; 12:7; 13:15, 16, 17; 14:23; 15:4, 7; 16:8; 17:1, 5; 18:21, 27; 20:16; 22:1; 23:4; 24:13, 34, 43; 26:24, 24; 27:2; 28:13; 30:2, 8, 11; 31:13; 32:10, 11; 35:11; 38:26; 41:44; 42:18; 45:3, 4, 12, 13; 46:2, 3; 47:9, 30; 48:5, 21; 50:5, 19, 20; Ex 3:4, 6, 7, 10, 11, 14, 14, 16; 6:2, 6, 7, 8, 29; 7:5, 17; 8:22, 29; 10:2, 2; 12:12; 14:4, 18, 18; 15:26; 16:12; 18:16; 19:9; 20:2, 5, 24; 22:27; 23:20; 24:14; 29:46, 46, 46; 31:13; 34:6, 6, 6, 10, 11; Lev 8:5; 11:44, 44, 45, 45; 14:34; 16:2; 18:2, 3, 4, 5, 6, 21, 24, 25, 27, 30; 19:2, 3, 4, 10, 12, 14, 16, 18, 25, 28, 30, 31, 32, 34, 36, 37; 20:7, 8, 22, 24, 26; 21:8, 12, 23; 22:2, 3, 8, 9, 16, 30, 31, 33; 23:10, 22, 43; 24:22; 25:2, 17, 38, 55; 26:1, 2, 13, 44, 45; Nu 3:13, 41, 45; 10:10; 11:12, 13; 13:2; 15:2, 18, 41, 41; 18:7, 19, 20; 20:12, 24; 22:30; 24:13, 14; 25:12; 34:2; 35:34; Dt 1:8; 3:24; 4:1, 2, 8; 5:1, 6, 9, 31; 6:6; 7:11; 8:1; 10:13; 11:2, 8, 13, 26, 27, 32; 13:18; 15:5, 11, 15; 19:7; 24:22; 27:1, 4, 10; 28:1, 14, 15; 29:19, 19; 30:8, 11, 15; 31:2, 2, 27; 32:34, 39, 39, 39, 49, 52; Jos 1:2; 3:7; 5:14, 14; 7:8; 14:10, 11; 17:18; 23:2; Jdg 6:10, 14, 15; 8:5; 9:2; 13:11; 15:3; 16:7, 11; 17:9, 9; Ru 1:12; 2:10, 13; 3:9, 12, 12; 4:4; 1Sa 1:15, 16, 26, 28; 3:5, 6, 8, 11, 12, 16; 9:19, 20; 10:1; 15:11; 16:22; 17:43; 18:17, 18; 20:3, 6; 21:2; 23:10; 24:9, 11, 17; 25:7, 41; 28:15; 30:13; 2Sa 1:8, 9, 13; 3:8, 39; 6:21, 22; 7:2, 18, 20; 9:2, 6; 10:2; 13:4; 14:3, 5; 16:10, 10, 12; 18:2; 19:22, 22, 26, 30, 34, 35; 20:17, 19; 22:24; 24:17; 1Ki 1:48; 2:2; 3:7, 8; 5:5; 11:31; 12:26; 13:14, 16, 18; 15:19; 18:8, 22, 36; 19:4, 10, 14; 20:13, 28; 2Ki 1:10, 12; 2:9, 10; 4:9; 5:7; 10:9, 15, 15, 16, 19; 16:7; 19:25; 22:17, 20; 1Ch 12:17; 17:1, 16, 18; 19:2; 21:17, 17; 29:3, 4, 14; 2Ch 2:4, 6, 9, 13; 12:5; 16:3; 34:25, 28; 35:21, 23; Ezr 9:6; Ne 6:3; Est 4:16; Job 1:15, 16, 17, 19; 6:13, 29, 30; 7:12, 20; 9:14, 20, 20, 21; 10:1, 7, 9, 15, 15; 11:4; 12:3, 4, 4; 13:2, 15, 16, 17; 16:17; 17:1, 2, 7; 19:6, 10, 15, 17, 27; 20:2; 21:2, 6; 22:13; 23:10, 15; 29:19; 30:1, 14, 29; 31:7, 35; 32:6, 18, 19; 33:7, 9, 9, 32; 34:5, 6; 35:2; 36:2, 4, 4; 40:4; 42:7; Ps 3:6; 6:2, 3, 6; 7:3, 8; 17:3, 6; 18:23; 22:6, 6; 25:16; 26:3, 11; 27:8, 13, 13; 31:7, 9, 10, 10, 11, 13, 14; 35:3, 12, 15, 15; 37:25; 38:6, 8, 10, 13, 13, 15, 17, 18; 39:9, 10, 12, 13; 40:17; 41:12; 42:5, 6, 11; 43:5; 46:10; 50:7; 52:8; 55:2, 23; 56:3; 57:4, 6; 66:15; 69:2, 3, 5, 7, 12, 17, 20, 29; 70:5; 71:3, 6, 15, 18; 75:3; 77:4; 78:1; 86:2, 3, 16; 88:5, 5, 8; 91:2; 92:10; 102:5, 6, 11, 24; 109:4, 22, 23, 23, 24, 25; 116:10, 16, 16; 119:19, 20, 53, 61, 83, 94, 99, 100, 112, 124, 139, 141; 120:6, 7; 130:5, 5; 138:7; 139:3, 4; 141:1, 5; 142:3, 6; 143:4, 4, 8, 12; Pr 4:2; 5:7; 8:4; 20:9; 22:19; 30:1, 1, 2, 9; Ecc 1:16; 2:18; 4:8, 8; 7:23; SS 1:5; 2:1, 3, 5, 16; 4:9; 5:1, 8; 6:3; 7:10; 8:10, 10; Isa 1:11; 5:5; 6:5; 13:3; 15:9; 21:3; 23:4; 24:16; 28:16; 37:26; 38:10, 14; 41:4, 10, 10, 13, 13, 14, 14; 42:1, 8; 43:3, 5, 10, 11, 12, 13, 15, 16, 18, 19, 25; 44:5, 6, 24, 25; 45:3, 5, 6, 7, 7, 7, 12, 18, 22; 46:9, 9, 13, 13; 47:10; 48:12, 15, 17; 49:2, 9, 9, 23, 26; 50:3; 51:12, 15, 16, 22; 54:15; 55:3; 56:1; 58:9; 60:16; 61:10, 10; 65:1, 1, 5, 17; Jer 1:12, 15, 19; 3:1, 12, 14; 4:6; 5:22; 6:11, 11, 30; 7:18, 19; 8:21; 9:24; 11:11; 13:27; 15:6, 10, 10, 15; 16:16, 16, 17, 21; 18:11; 20:7, 7, 9; 21:5; 23:23, 24; 25:27; 26:3, 14; 29:23; 30:11; 31:9, 36, 36; 32:3, 27, 31; 34:2; 36:5; 38:19; 40:4; 42:10, 11; 45:3, 3; 46:28; 50:9, 31; 51:25, 25; La 1:11, 14; 3:1; Eze 2:3, 4; 3:1, 5, 6, 7; 5:8; 6:3, 7, 9, 10, 13, 14; 7:4, 27; 11:10, 12; 12:15, 16, 20, 25; 13:9, 14, 20, 21, 23; 14:8; 15:7; 16:37, 62; 18:25; 20:7, 19, 20, 26, 38, 42, 44; 21:3, 3, 5; 22:16; 23:4, 49; 24:16, 24, 27; 25:5, 7, 11, 17; 26:2, 3, 6; 28:2, 9, 22, 22, 23, 24, 26; 29:3, 6, 9, 10, 16, 21; 30:8, 19, 22, 25, 26; 32:15; 33:7, 29; 34:27, 30, 31; 35:3, 4, 9, 15; 36:6, 9, 11, 22, 22, 23, 32, 37, 37, 38; 37:5, 6, 13, 14; 38:3, 16, 23; 39:1, 6, 7, 22, 25, 28; 44:28; Da 1:10; 2:5, 8, 30; 5:16; 8:19; 9:23; 10:7, 14, 16, 16; Hos 1:4, 9; 2:2, 7; 7:2; 11:9, 9; 12:8, 9; 13:4, 9; 14:8, 8; Joel 2:19, 27, 27; Am 5:1; 6:14; 9:4, 8; Jnh 1:9; Mic 2:3; 3:8, 8; Na 1:14; 2:13; 3:5; Hab 1:3, 5, 6; 3:2; Hag 1:13; 2:4, 19, 21; Zec 1:15; 2:2, 10; 3:4, 8; 5:4; 8:2, 3, 12; 9:8; 10:6; 11:5, 12; Mal 1:6, 10, 14; 3:1, 6; 4:5; Mt 3:11, 11, 14, 17; 8:8, 9; 10:16; 11:10, 29; 12:8, 18, 27, 28; 13:37; 14:27; 16:15; 17:5; 18:20; 20:15, 22; 22:32; 24:5; 26:22, 25, 45, 55, 61; 27:24, 43; 28:20; Mk 1:2, 7, 7, 11; 2:28; 4:11, 13; 6:50; 8:27, 29; 10:38; 12:26; 14:19, 28, 41, 48, 62; Lk 1:19, 34, 38, 38; 3:16, 16, 22; 6:5; 7:6, 7, 8, 27; 8:10; 9:18, 20; 10:3, 35; 11:18, 19, 20; 12:50; 15:17, 19, 21; 16:24; 17:3; 18:11, 13; 19:22, 22; 22:27, 33, 52, 70; 24:38, 39; Jn 1:15, 20, 23, 27, 30; 3:11, 28, 28, 29, 29, 31; 4:9, 10, 26; 5:7, 30; 6:20, 35, 41, 48, 51, 58; 7:8, 24, 34, 36; 8:12, 14, 15, 16, 18, 19, 21, 21, 22, 23, 23, 24, 24, 25, 28, 38, 42, 43, 46, 54; 9:5, 5, 9; 10:7, 9, 11, 14, 36, 38; 11:15, 25; 12:26, 32, 47; 13:7, 18, 19, 34, 37; 14:2, 3, 4, 6, 7, 9, 10, 11, 12, 20, 20, 20, 25, 25, 27, 28, 28; 15:1, 5; 16:5, 5, 17, 32; 17:11, 11, 13, 16, 18, 20, 21; 18:5, 6, 8, 8, 17, 25, 35, 36, 37; 19:4, 21, 28; 20:17; Ac 7:32; 9:5; 13:25, 25, 41; 16:15; 18:6, 10; 19:40; 20:22; 21:13, 39; 22:3, 8, 27, 28, 28; 23:6, 6; 24:21; 25:8, 10, 11; 26:2, 6, 6, 15, 17, 22, 25, 25, 26, 29; 28:20; Ro 1:15, 16; 7:7, 14, 16, 18, 20, 20, 24, 25; 8:38; 9:1, 33; 11:1, 3, 13; 14:14; 15:14, 15, 23, 24, 29, 31; 16:4, 23; 1Co 1:12; 2:6; 3:4; 4:14, 17; 5:1, 3, 3; 6:5, 12, 12; 7:8, 28, 35, 40; 9:1, 2, 2, 2, 15, 16, 19, 20, 20, 20, 21, 22, 26; 10:15, 19, 19, 20, 23, 23; 11:2, 21, 22; 12:15, 15, 16, 16; 14:14, 26, 37; 15:9, 9, 10, 50; 16:5, 5, 10, 11, 17; 2Co 1:17, 18, 23; 2:5; 6:13; 7:8, 9, 16; 8:8, 16; 9:3; 10:1, 12; 11:2, 5, 6, 14, 17, 22, 22, 22, 30; 12:5, 5, 9, 10, 10, 10, 11, 11, 12, 14, 20, 20, 21; 13:1, 10; Gal 1:6, 10, 20, 20; 2:21; 3:17; 4:11, 16, 18, 19; 5:10, 11, 11; Eph 3:1, 8, 13; 6:20, 21, 22; Php 1:6, 13, 25, 30; 2:12, 17, 26, 28; 3:1, 5, 13, 13; 4:10, 18; Col 1:24, 24; 2:4, 5, 5; 4:3, 7, 9; 1Ti 1:12; 3:14; 5:15; 2Ti 1:12, 12, 12; 2:7, 9, 10; Tit 3:12; Phm 1:2, 6, 8, 12, 13, 21, 22; Heb 2:13; 12:21; 1Pe 1:1, 16; 2:6; 5:1; 2Pe 1:1, 14, 15, 17; 3:17; 1Jn 2:1, 7, 9, 12, 13, 13, 21; 5:16; 3Jn 2; Jude 1; Rev 1:8, 8, 9, 17, 18, 18; 2:23; 3:11, 17, 19; 18:7, 7; 19:10; 21:5, 6; 22:7, 8, 9, 12, 13, 16, 16, 20

AN (1130)

Ge 6:16; 8:20; 12:7, 8; 13:7, 18; 14:3; 16:1; 18:13; 20:4; 21:20, 31; 22:9; 23:6; 25:33; 26:25; 27:2, 33, 37; 28:17; 29:2; 30:8; 31:53; 32:6; 33:20; 35:1, 3, 7, 14; 37:36; 41:53; 42:23; 44:4, 18, 20; 48:4, 22; 50:5, 25; Ex 1:10; 2:11, 19; 5:21; 7:25; 10:13; 12:4, 48; 16:36; 17:15; 18:16; 19:15; 21:6, 13, 24, 26, 27, 33; 22:1, 4, 5, 11, 14, 19; 23:7, 15, 22; 24:4, 17; 25:2, 10, 33; 26:12, 13, 23; 28:4, 4, 17, 19, 19, 20, 32, 36, 39; 29:36, 36, 41; 30:13, 32; 32:5, 8; 33:2, 5; 34:9; 36:28; 37:19; 38:21, 26; 39:5, 10, 12, 12, 13, 23, 30; Lev 2:2, 9, 11, 12, 16; 3:3, 5, 9, 11, 14, 16; 5:2, 2, 16, 19; 6:2; 7:5, 9, 16, 18, 21, 24, 25, 30; 8:21, 28, 28; 9:21; 11:25, 26, 27, 31, 32, 33, 34, 34, 35, 36, 39; 13:9, 10, 15, 29, 47, 48, 49, 51, 52; 14:24, 34, 34, 40, 44; 15:16, 22, 32; 16:12; 17:4, 10, 13, 15; 18:23; 19:24; 20:14, 15, 21; 22:4, 8, 14, 20, 21, 22, 22, 24, 27; 23:8, 13, 15, 16, 17, 17; 24:7, 10, 10, 11, 21; 25:2, 14, 36, 49; 27:9, 10, 11, 11, 16, 28, 28; Nu 5:15, 15; 7:3; 10:7; 14:34; 15:3, 3, 10, 13, 14, 25, 27; 16:14, 17, 46; 17:5, 10; 18:17, 19; 20:16, 18, 20; 22:4, 37; 26:62; 27:7; 28:6, 7, 8, 11; 30:6; 31:29, 50; Dt 4:17; 5:5; 6:13; 9:12; 12:17; 14:26; 15:12, 17; 16:21; 18:1, 12; 19:5, 6, 6, 20; 20:1; 21:8; 22:10; 23:12; 25:4; 27:5, 6, 21, 25; 28:11, 25, 37, 49; 29:12; 32:10, 11; 33:20; Jos 6:17; 8:2, 14, 30, 31; 9:19; 13:1, 23, 28; 14:3, 13; 15:18; 17:4, 4, 6; 19:9, 51; 21:11; 22:16, 23; 23:2, 4; Jdg 1:14; 3:31; 6:24, 26, 33; 8:24; 9:25, 32, 43, 48; 11:26, 29, 33; 13:19; 14:4; 17:3, 3, 4, 4; 18:19; 19:3, 16, 23; 20:29; 21:4, 17; Ru 3:11; 1Sa 2:1, 31; 4:13; 7:17; 12:2; 13:21, 21, 21, 21, 21; 14:14, 15, 24, 35; 17:7, 7, 12, 12, 26; 18:1, 5; 19:5, 10, 13, 16; 20:3, 6, 36; 23:27; 28:10, 14; 29:9; 30:11, 13, 13; 2Sa 1:8, 13; 2:14; 3:12; 4:11; 6:13; 7:27, 29; 14:17, 20; 17:8, 11, 25, 27; 19:27; 20:7, 18; 22:30; 23:5, 13, 17; 24:18, 21, 25; 1Ki 1:41; 2:5; 3:1, 9, 16; 5:11; 6:16; 8:31; 9:7, 8; 10:9; 11:14, 23, 38; 12:20; 13:11, 14, 18; 14:4, 21, 31; 15:13, 22; 16:32, 33; 19:5, 11; 22:34, 34, 49; 2Ki 1:2, 9; 3:4; 4:14; 5:7; 7:1, 1, 16, 16, 18, 18; 11:4; 13:6; 16:10, 11; 17:16; 19:9; 20:7; 21:3, 7; 23:10, 11; 25:8, 19; 1Ch 2:17, 34; 4:17, 18; 7:2, 40; 9:26; 10:6; 11:15, 19, 23; 17:25, 27; 21:15, 18, 22, 26; 23:1; 25:7; 2Ch 2:5, 9, 14, 14; 6:22; 7:21; 12:14; 13:5; 14:8, 8, 9, 9; 15:16; 17:13; 18:33, 33; 19:10; 20:11, 35; 22:5; 24:11, 26; 25:5; 26:11; 27:5; 29:8, 31, 35; 30:7; 32:21; 33:19; 36:13; Ezr 7:14, 15, 22; 8:29; 9:12, 15; Ne 3:20; 6:5; 9:18; 10:29, 32, 32; 13:13; Est 1:7; 2:23; 6:1, 2; 8:15; 9:19, 21, 31; Job 6:6, 27; 9:26; 10:17; 11:12; 12:4; 14:3, 3; 15:24, 33; 19:11, 24; 21:32; 31:21; 38:13; 40:15; 42:17; Ps 2:9, 12; 5:9; 6:T; 12:T, 3; 17:1; 18:29; 22:16; 37:32; 38:8; 39:5; 44:13; 46:6; 52:2, 8; 54:5; 55:12; 58:9; 59:3; 61:5; 69:31; 71:7; 73:19; 79:4; 81:5; 89:29, 35; 92:6; 102:6; 105:18; 106:19; 109:6, 6, 25; 110:4; 112:2; 119:36, 42; 130:7; 132:2; 135:12; 136:21; 141:2; 145:13; 146:4; Pr 1:18; 3:32; 4:3; 5:3, 20, 20, 22; 6:11, 24, 32; 7:5, 5, 5, 8, 22; 12:17, 25; 13:17, 22; 14:4, 4, 33; 16:26, 26; 18:11, 19; 19:14, 14, 26; 20:21; 21:9, 27, 28; 22:14, 21; 23:27; 24:15, 26, 26, 34; 25:6, 7, 18, 19, 24; 26:2, 10, 10; 27:5, 6, 13; 29:15; 30:1, 19, 20, 22, 27; 31:1; Ecc 2:10; 4:13; 6:5; 10:1, 8; 11:9; 12:10; SS 2:14; 3:8; 6:4, 10; 7:4; Isa 1:30; 2:4; 6:11; 10:34; 13:4; 18:4; 19:19; 21:2, 16; 27:9; 28:4, 11; 29:2, 6; 30:13; 35:2; 37:9; 38:21; 40:16, 19, 20; 42:16; 43:14; 44:10, 15; 48:14; 53:10; 54:2; 55:3, 13; 56:5; 58:11; 60:20; 61:8; 65:5, 16; 66:3, 3, 3, 11, 20; Jer 1:11, 18; 2:19, 27, 27; 3:18; 4:4; 5:15, 22, 31; 6:26; 7:34; 10:3; 12:11; 13:11, 23; 15:4, 20; 16:9, 14; 17:1; 21:12; 23:7, 40; 24:9; 25:9, 12, 18; 26:2, 6, 15, 18, 23; 29:18, 31; 30:12, 17; 31:3, 14; 32:11, 35, 40; 38:6, 7; 42:18; 44:8, 12, 22; 47:7; 48:35, 38, 39, 39, 40; 49:13, 14, 17, 22; 50:5, 9; 51:12, 37; 52:12, 25; La 2:5; 4:12; 5:10; Eze 1:10, 10; 4:3; 5:5, 15; 8:7, 11; 10:14, 14; 11:3, 7, 11; 12:23; 14:15, 19; 16:3, 25, 32, 45, 60; 17:13; 20:33, 41; 22:4, 24; 23:46, 48; 24:3, 8, 24; 25:5; 26:19; 28:7, 10; 29:8, 14; 33:2, 28, 32; 36:7; 37:26; 38:11; 41:9, 13, 22; 42:7, 9, 12; 44:12; 45:2, 8; 46:21; 47:14, 22, 22; 48:15; Da 1:17; 2:11, 39; 4:6, 15, 16, 30; 5:21, 26; 9:24, 27; 11:6, 7, 17, 18, 27; 12:7; Hos 1:5; 2:11; 4:16; 7:4, 9; 8:1, 8; 10:7, 11; 13:16; Joel 2:11, 17, 19, 23; Am 3:11; 4:5; 5:13; 6:14; Ob 1; Mic 1:8, 16; 3:6, 12; 4:3; 5:12; 6:16; 7:20; Na 1:8; 2:10; Hab 2:14, 19; Zep 1:4; 2:15; Zec 3:9; 12:2, 10; Mal 2:12; 3:17; Mt 1:20; 2:13, 19; 5:25, 38, 39; 6:23; 7:17; 9:16, 16; 10:10; 12:35, 35, 36, 39, 43; 13:2, 12, 28; 14:7; 15:18; 16:4; 19:7; 20:1; 22:35; 23:18; 25:19, 29; 26:36, 51, 72; 27:4, 58; 28:2; Mk 1:23; 2:21, 21; 3:29, 30; 5:2; 6:9, 27; 7:25; 9:17; 10:4; 14:1, 32, 47; 15:7, 43; Lk 1:11, 18, 43; 2:9; 5:12, 36; 6:45, 45; 7:6; 9:3, 39, 46; 10:4, 25, 30, 34; 11:12, 24, 34, 45; 12:16, 37, 58; 13:11; 16:15; 21:24; 22:6, 20, 43, 59; 23:19; 24:22; Jn 1:22, 47; 3:4, 25; 8:7; 9:4, 16; 12:29; 13:15; 18:36; 19:35, 35; Ac 1:25, 26; 2:30; 5:19, 31, 34; 6:15; 7:24, 30, 41; 8:26; 9:25, 37; 10:3; 11:13; 12:7, 21, 23; 13:19; 16:20; 17:23, 29; 18:24; 19:15, 36, 40; 20:32; 21:31, 39; 23:9, 12; 24:23; 25:16, 20; 26:3; 27:1, 6, 12, 23, 26; 28:3, 7, 11; Ro 1:1; 2:25; 3:13; 4:6; 5:14; 14:13; 15:26, 32; 1Co 1:1; 3:10; 7:6, 12, 13, 32; 8:4, 10; 9:1, 2, 3, 9, 12, 12, 25, 27; 10:28; 12:16, 16, 17, 29; 14:6, 9, 19, 23, 26, 27; 15:9, 23, 48, 52; 2Co 1:1, 6; 4:17; 5:1; 6:9, 15; 9:2; 10:9; 11:14; 12:12; Gal 1:1, 8; 3:1, 15, 15, 20; 4:14, 24; Eph 1:1, 11; 2:3; 3:6; 4:29; 5:5, 32; 6:24; Col 1:1; 3:24; 4:2; 1Th 1:7; 2Th 3:5, 9; 1Ti 1:1; 3:1, 1, 2, 6; 4:12; 5:1, 18, 19, 22; 6:4; 2Ti 1:1, 11; 2:5; 4:6; Tit 1:1, 6, 7; 2:7; Phm 1:6, 9; Heb 1:2, 12, 13; 3:5; 5:4; 6:13, 16, 17; 7:20, 21, 28; 8:3; 9:9, 25; 11:7, 23; 12:19, 20; 13:10, 20; Jas 1:2; 3:8; 4:4; 5:11, 12; 1Pe 1:1; 2:16; 3:21; 5:1; 2Pe 2:6; 1Jn 2:7; 2Jn 7; Rev 1:1; 2:27; 4:3, 7, 7; 8:1; 9:9, 16, 16; 10:6; 12:1, 5; 14:15; 16:18; 19:15, 17; 20:1

AND (27934)

Ge 1:1, 2, 3, 4, 5, 6, 7, 8, 9, 9, 10, 10, 11, 11, 11, 11, 12, 12, 12, 12, 14, 14, 15, 16, 18, 18, 18, 20, 20, 21, 21, 21, 22, 22, 24, 24, 24, 25, 25, 26, 26, 27, 28, 28, 28, 28, 28, 29, 29, 30, 30, 30, 30, 31; 2:1, 1, 3, 3, 4, 4, 5, 6, 7, 7, 7, 8, 9, 9, 9, 10, 12, 15, 17, 18, 19, 19, 20, 21, 22, 23, 24, 24, 24, 25; 3:5, 6, 6, 7, 12, 14, 15, 15, 15, 15, 16, 16, 17, 17, 18, 19, 21, 21, 22, 23, 23, 24, 24; 4:1, 1, 2, 5, 7, 7, 8, 8, 14, 16, 17, 17, 19, 21, 22, 23, 23, 25, 26; 5:2, 2, 2, 3, 4, 4, 7, 7, 10, 10, 13, 13, 16, 16, 19, 19, 22, 22, 26, 26, 30, 30, 32; 6:2, 4, 5, 5, 7, 7, 7, 9, 9, 10, 11, 12, 12, 14, 14, 14, 15, 16, 16, 18, 18, 19, 20, 20, 21, 21; 7:2, 2, 3, 4, 4, 7, 7, 7, 7, 8, 8, 8, 9, 10, 11, 12, 13, 13, 13, 14, 14, 14, 16, 17, 18, 21, 22, 23, 23, 23, 24; 8:1, 1, 2, 5, 7, 7, 9, 9, 12, 13, 14, 17, 17, 18, 18, 19, 19, 20, 20, 21, 21, 21, 22, 22, 22, 22; 9:1, 1, 1, 2, 2, 2, 3, 5, 5, 7, 7, 8, 9, 10, 10, 10, 11, 12, 12, 13, 15, 15, 16, 18, 20, 21, 22, 22, 23, 23, 25, 26, 27, 27; 10:1, 2, 3, 4, 6, 7, 7, 9, 10, 12, 12, 14, 18, 19, 19, 20, 22, 23, 24, 25, 29, 31; 11:1, 2, 3, 4, 5, 6, 7, 8, 11, 11, 13, 13, 15, 15, 17, 17, 19, 19, 21, 21, 23, 23, 25, 25, 26, 27, 27, 29, 31, 31, 31, 32; 12:1, 1, 2, 2, 3, 4, 5, 5, 5, 6, 7, 7, 8, 8, 8, 13, 14, 15, 16, 16, 18, 19, 20, 20; 13:1, 1, 1, 2, 3, 4, 5, 6, 6, 7, 7, 9, 10, 11, 11, 13, 15, 16, 17; 14:1, 2, 3, 3, 5, 6, 7, 7, 8, 9, 9, 10, 10, 11, 11, 11, 12, 13, 13, 13, 15, 16, 16, 16, 17, 18, 18, 19, 20, 22, 24; 15:1, 1, 5, 5, 6, 6, 9, 10, 10, 12, 13, 14, 17, 17, 18, 21; 16:2, 2, 2, 3, 4, 5, 6, 8, 9, 11, 11, 12, 12, 14, 14, 15; 17:1, 1, 7, 7, 7, 8, 8, 9, 10, 11, 12, 16, 16, 16, 18, 19, 19, 20, 21, 22, 23, 23, 25, 27; 18:2, 6, 6, 7, 7, 7, 8, 8, 8, 10, 11, 11, 11, 12, 14, 16, 18, 18, 19, 19, 19, 20, 20, 23, 23, 24, 25, 26, 27, 27, 28, 29, 30, 31, 32, 33; 19:1, 1, 2, 2, 4, 4, 9, 9, 9, 10, 10, 13, 15, 16, 16, 16, 17, 19, 19, 19, 24, 24, 25, 25, 26, 27, 28, 28, 28, 29, 30, 31, 32, 33, 33, 34, 34, 35, 35; 20:1, 1, 2, 3, 5, 7, 7, 8, 9, 11, 12, 14, 14, 14, 14, 14, 15, 17, 17; 21:2, 3, 6, 8, 8, 9, 10, 10, 12, 14, 14, 16, 17, 18, 19, 19, 20, 21, 23, 26, 27, 27, 28, 32, 33, 34; 22:1, 2, 3, 3, 5, 5, 6, 7, 8, 9, 9, 10, 10, 13, 13, 16, 17, 18, 19, 22, 24; 23:2, 3, 7, 10, 11, 11, 13, 15, 17, 20; 24:1, 3, 4, 7, 7, 10, 10, 11, 12, 13, 14, 15, 16, 16, 18, 20, 22, 24, 25, 25, 26, 27, 30, 30, 31, 31, 32, 32, 35, 35, 35, 35, 35, 35, 36, 37, 40, 41, 44, 44, 45, 45, 46, 46, 46, 47, 47, 48, 50, 51, 52, 53, 53, 53, 54, 54, 55, 56, 57, 58, 59, 59, 61, 61, 63, 64, 65, 67, 67, 67; 25:2, 2, 3, 3, 4, 6, 8, 9, 13, 15, 16, 17, 20, 21, 23, 24, 29, 34, 34, 34; 26:2, 3, 3, 3, 4, 4, 5, 5, 7, 8, 9, 10, 10, 13, 14, 14, 15, 16, 16, 17, 19, 20, 20, 22, 22, 24, 24, 25, 25, 26, 29, 29, 30, 30, 32, 33, 35; 27:1, 1, 2, 3, 3, 4, 4, 9, 10, 11, 12, 13, 14, 15, 16, 17, 18, 19, 22, 25, 25, 26, 27, 27, 27, 28, 28, 29, 30, 31, 31, 31, 33, 33, 34, 35, 36, 37, 37, 38, 39, 40, 40, 41, 41, 42, 42, 46; 28:1, 2, 3, 3, 4, 5, 6, 6, 7, 9, 9, 10, 11, 11, 12, 12, 13, 13, 13, 14, 14, 15, 16, 16, 17, 18, 20, 20, 20, 21, 22; 29:4, 6, 8, 8, 10, 10, 10, 10, 11, 12, 13, 13, 14, 16, 17, 23, 24, 27, 29, 30, 30, 32, 32, 33, 33, 34, 35, 35; 30:3, 4, 5, 6, 7, 8, 13, 14, 17, 17, 19, 21, 22, 23, 24, 26, 26, 29, 29, 30, 31, 32, 32, 35, 35, 35, 35, 36, 36, 37, 37, 39, 40, 42, 43, 43; 31:2, 3, 3, 3, 4, 5, 7, 8, 8, 10, 10, 11, 12, 12, 13, 13, 14, 15, 16, 16, 17, 18, 19, 20, 21, 23, 27,

28, 28, 29, 30, 33, 34, 34, 38, 38, 39, 39, 40, 40, 41, 41, 42, 42, 43, 43, 43, 43, 44, 44, 44, 45, 46, 46, 47, 51, 52, 53, 54, 55, 55, 55; **32:**1, 5, 5, 5, 7, 7, 9, 9, 9, 10, 10, 11, 12, 13, 15, 19, 20, 21, 22, 22, 24, 24, 25, 28, 28, 31; **33:**2, 2, 2, 2, 4, 4, 5, 5, 6, 7, 7, 7, 8, 8, 12, 13, 13, 14, 15, 17, 17, 17, 18, 20, 20; **34:**2, 3, 7, 8, 8, 9, 10, 10, 11, 11, 13, 16, 16, 17, 18, 19, 20, 21, 21, 23, 24, 25, 25, 26, 26, 28, 28, 28, 29, 29, 30, 30, 30; **35:**1, 2, 4, 4, 5, 7, 10, 11, 12, 12, 12, 14, 19, 20, 21, 22, 23, 24, 25, 26, 29, 29; **36:**2, 2, 3, 4, 4, 5, 5, 6, 6, 7, 10, 11, 13, 14, 14, 15, 16, 16, 17, 17, 18, 18, 21, 22, 23, 24, 25, 26, 27, 28, 30, 35, 39, 39, 43; **37:**2, 5, 7, 7, 8, 8, 9, 9, 10, 10, 10, 11, 14, 14, 14, 14, 16, 17, 18, 20, 22, 24, 25, 27, 28, 28, 29, 30, 31, 32, 33, 34, 35; **38:**1, 2, 3, 3, 4, 5, 12, 14, 14, 15, 16, 18, 18, 19, 20, 22, 22, 24, 25, 26, 27, 28, 29, 29, 30; **39:**2, 3, 4, 5, 5, 6, 7, 7, 10, 12, 13, 15, 16, 20, 21, 22, 23; **40:**1, 3, 4, 5, 5, 8, 10, 10, 11, 13, 14, 14, 15, 17, 19, 19, 20, 20, 20, 20; **41:**2, 3, 3, 5, 5, 6, 7, 7, 8, 8, 10, 10, 11, 11, 13, 13, 13, 14, 14, 14, 15, 15, 16, 18, 19, 21, 22, 22, 24, 26, 27, 30, 32, 33, 34, 35, 35, 36, 37, 40, 41, 42, 43, 44, 45, 46, 47, 48, 50, 51, 55, 55, 56, 57; **42:**2, 6, 9, 11, 13, 13, 16, 21, 21, 22, 24, 24, 26, 27, 28, 29, 32, 33, 33, 34, 34, 36, 38; **43:**2, 4, 5, 7, 8, 8, 8, 10, 11, 13, 14, 14, 15, 15, 16, 17, 18, 21, 23, 24, 24, 26, 27, 28, 30, 31, 32, 32, 33, 34; **44:**1, 3, 4, 6, 9, 11, 13, 14, 14, 16, 16, 18, 20, 20, 20, 21, 24, 25, 25, 28, 28, 29, 30, 33; **45:**2, 4, 7, 8, 8, 9, 10, 10, 10, 11, 12, 13, 14, 15, 15, 16, 17, 18, 18, 19, 19, 19, 21, 22, 22, 23, 23, 24, 25, 25, 26, 27, 28; **46:**1, 4, 5, 5, 6, 6, 7, 7, 9, 10, 11, 12, 12, 12, 13, 14, 16, 17, 17, 19, 20, 21, 22, 24, 28, 28, 29, 29, 30, 31, 31, 31, 32, 32, 32, 32, 33; **47:**1, 1, 1, 1, 2, 3, 5, 6, 7, 7, 11, 12, 12, 13, 13, 13, 14, 14, 15, 17, 18, 18, 18, 19, 19, 19, 20, 22, 23, 24, 24, 24, 26, 27, 27, 29, 30, 31; **48:**1, 1, 2, 3, 4, 4, 5, 5, 6, 9, 9, 10, 10, 10, 12, 13, 14, 15, 15, 16, 16, 16, 16, 20, 21, 22, 22; **49:**1, 1, 2, 3, 4, 5, 6, 9, 12, 13, 15, 19, 23, 24, 25, 25, 27, 28, 29, 31, 31, 31, 33; **50:**1, 1, 3, 4, 5, 5, 6, 7, 8, 8, 8, 9, 10, 13, 14, 17, 18, 19, 21, 21, 22, 22, 23, 24, 25, 26; **Ex 1:**4, 6, 7, 10, 10, 11, 11, 13, 14, 14, 15, 17, 20, 20, 21; **2:**1, 2, 2, 3, 3, 3, 5, 7, 8, 9, 9, 11, 12, 14, 15, 15, 15, 16, 17, 17, 19, 19, 20, 21, 22, 23, 23, 24, 24, 25; **3:**1, 6, 8, 8, 8, 8, 9, 12, 13, 15, 15, 16, 16, 16, 17, 17, 18, 20, 21, 22, 22, 22, 22; **4:**3, 3, 4, 4, 5, 5, 6, 7, 9, 9, 10, 11, 12, 12, 14, 14, 15, 16, 17, 18, 20, 20, 21, 24, 24, 25, 25, 27, 28, 28, 29, 29, 30, 31, 31, 31, 31; **5:**1, 2, 2, 2, 3, 5, 6, 10, 11, 15, 20, 21, 22; **6:**2, 3, 4, 6, 6, 7, 7, 8, 11, 13, 13, 14, 15, 16, 17, 18, 19, 20, 20, 21, 22, 23, 23, 23, 24, 25, 26, 26; **7:**2, 3, 5, 6, 7, 8, 9, 10, 10, 10, 10, 11, 11, 13, 14, 15, 17, 18, 19, 19, 20, 20, 20, 21, 22, 22, 22, 23; **8:**1, 3, 3, 3, 4, 5, 6, 8, 8, 8, 9, 9, 12, 12, 13, 13, 14, 15, 17, 17, 18, 18, 19, 20, 21, 22, 23, 24, 24, 25, 25, 28, 29, 29, 30, 31, 31, 32; **9:**2, 3, 4, 6, 6, 8, 8, 9, 10, 10, 10, 12, 13, 14, 14, 16, 17, 19, 20, 22, 22, 23, 23, 23, 24, 25, 27, 27, 27, 28, 29, 29, 30, 31, 31, 32, 33, 33, 33, 34; **10:**1, 1, 2, 3, 3, 6, 6, 6, 6, 7, 8, 8, 9, 9, 9, 9, 11, 11, 12, 13, 13, 14, 14, 15, 16, 16, 17, 18, 20, 21, 21, 22, 24, 24, 25, 25, 26, 27; **11:**1, 2, 2, 3, 3, 6, 7, 8, 10; **12:**1, 4, 7, 7, 8, 9, 11, 12, 12, 16, 21, 22, 22, 22, 23, 23, 23, 24, 24, 27, 27, 27, 28, 29, 30, 30, 30, 31, 31, 32, 32, 34, 35, 35, 35, 35, 36, 37, 37, 37, 38, 39, 43, 45, 46, 48, 50, 51; **13:**2, 5, 5, 9, 11, 12, 14, 15, 17, 18, 21, 22; **14:**2, 3, 4, 4, 4, 5, 6, 8, 9, 10, 10, 11, 13, 16, 17, 17, 17, 18, 19, 20, 20, 21, 23, 24, 24, 26, 27, 28, 30, 31, 31; **15:**1, 1, 2, 2, 2, 4, 9, 12, 14, 16, 17, 18, 19, 20, 20, 21, 21, 22, 25, 25, 26, 26, 27; **16:**1, 1, 2, 4, 6, 6, 7, 8, 9, 10, 11, 12, 13, 15, 17, 17, 18, 20, 20, 21, 22, 23, 24, 28, 31, 32, 33; **17:**1, 2, 2, 3, 5, 6, 6, 7, 7, 9, 10, 12, 13, 14, 15; **18:**1, 1, 2, 5, 5, 5, 6, 7, 7, 8, 8, 10, 11, 12, 12, 16, 16, 18, 19, 20, 20, 21, 21, 23, 23, 24, 25, 25; **19:**2, 3, 4, 5, 6, 7, 7, 10, 10, 10, 14, 15, 16, 16, 16, 17, 18, 19, 19, 20, 21, 23, 24, 25; **20:**5, 6, 9, 10, 10, 10, 11, 11, 12, 18, 18, 18, 19, 19, 22, 24, 24, 24, 24, 24, 26, 26; **21:**2, 3, 4, 4, 5, 6, 9, 10, 13, 14, 14, 18, 19, 20, 20, 22, 26, 27, 28, 29, 29, 32, 33, 33, 35, 35; **22:**1, 2, 4, 5, 6, 7, 9, 10, 11, 13, 14, 14, 15, 16, 16, 23, 24, 24, 27, 29, 30, 31; **23:**3, 5, 10, 11, 11, 12, 12, 12, 13, 18, 21, 22, 23, 23, 23, 24, 24, 25, 25, 26, 27, 28, 29, 31, 31, 31, 32, 33; **24:**1, 1, 2, 3, 5, 6, 7, 8, 9, 11, 12, 12, 13, 14, 14, 15, 16, 16, 18; **25:**3, 4, 5, 6, 7, 7, 9, 10, 11, 11, 12, 13, 17, 18, 22, 23, 24, 25, 26, 28, 29, 29, 31, 31, 33, 34, 36, 36, 37, 38, 39; **26:**1, 2, 8, 9, 11, 13, 14, 16, 24, 27, 29, 31, 32, 35, 35, 36, 36, 37; **27:**1, 2, 2, 3, 6, 11, 16, 16, 18, 19, 21, 21; **28:**1, 1, 1, 4, 5, 5, 5, 6, 6, 6, 7, 8, 8, 8, 9, 14, 15, 15, 17, 18, 19, 20, 21, 23, 25, 26, 27, 27, 30, 33, 33, 34, 35, 35, 40, 40, 41, 41, 43, 43, 43; **29:**1, 1, 2, 2, 3, 3, 4, 4, 5, 6, 7, 8, 9, 9, 10, 10, 12, 13, 13, 14, 14, 15, 16, 17, 17, 17, 18, 19, 19, 20, 20, 20, 21, 21, 21, 21, 22, 22, 22, 23, 24, 25, 26, 27, 27, 28, 29, 30, 31, 33, 33, 35, 37, 39, 41, 42, 43, 44, 44, 44, 45, 46; **30:**2, 3, 3, 5, 8, 11, 15, 16, 17, 18, 18, 19, 19, 20, 21, 23, 24, 27, 27, 28, 30, 31, 32, 32, 34, 35, 36, 37; **31:**3, 4, 5, 5, 6, 8, 9, 10, 11, 11, 13, 17, 17; **32:**2, 2, 2, 3, 4, 4, 5, 6, 6, 6, 8, 8, 9, 10, 11, 12, 13, 13, 14, 15, 15, 19, 20, 20, 22, 24, 25, 26, 26, 26, 27, 27, 28, 29, 31, 32, 35; **33:**1, 2, 2, 3, 4, 4, 5, 8, 9, 10, 12, 13, 14, 16, 16, 17, 17, 19, 19, 20, 22, 23; **34:**2, 5, 6, 6, 6, 6, 7, 7, 8, 9, 9, 9, 10, 11, 13, 15, 16, 19, 21, 22, 22, 24, 24, 25, 27, 27, 28, 30, 30, 31, 31, 31, 32, 35; **35:**1, 5, 6, 7, 8, 9, 9, 11, 11, 12, 13, 14, 14, 15, 15, 16, 16, 17, 18, 18, 19, 20, 21, 21, 21, 22, 22, 23, 24, 24, 25, 25, 25, 26, 26, 27, 27, 28, 28, 29, 30, 31, 32, 33, 33, 34, 34, 35, 35; **36:**1, 1, 1, 2, 6, 8, 9, 10, 15, 16, 19, 21, 29, 32, 34, 35, 35, 36, 37, 37, 38; **37:**1, 2, 2, 4, 6, 7, 9, 10, 12, 13, 15, 16, 17, 19, 22, 22, 23, 25, 26, 26, 28, 29; **38:**1, 3, 6, 7, 8, 10, 10, 11, 11, 11, 12, 12, 14, 15, 17, 17, 17, 18, 18, 18, 19, 19, 20, 21, 23, 23, 27, 28, 28, 30, 30, 31; **39:**1, 2, 2, 2, 3, 3, 5, 5, 8, 8, 8, 10, 11, 13, 16, 18, 24, 26, 27, 28, 29, 29, 32, 33, 33, 34, 35, 36, 37, 37, 39, 39, 40, 40, 40, 41, 43; **40:**3, 4, 4, 4, 7, 7, 8, 9, 9, 10, 11, 12, 12, 13, 14, 18, 18, 19, 20, 21, 23, 29, 29, 30, 31, 31, 31, 32, 33, 33, 34, 35, 36, 38; **Lev 1:**1, 2, 5, 6, 8, 9, 12, 12, 13, 15, 16, 16; **2:**1, 2, 2, 3, 5, 5, 6, 7, 9, 9, 10, 12, 15, 16; **3:**2, 4, 6, 8, 10, 13, 15, 17; **4:**4, 6, 9, 11, 13, 14, 15, 17, 19, 20, 21, 24, 25, 26, 29, 30, 31, 31, 33, 34, 35; **5:**1, 2, 6, 6, 7, 9, 10, 13, 15, 16, 18, 18; **6:**1, 3, 4, 7, 9, 9, 10, 10, 11, 12, 15, 15, 16, 16, 17, 19, 20, 20, 21, 21, 21, 22, 25, 25, 27, 28; **7:**2, 4, 6, 7, 10, 12, 12, 16, 18, 19, 21, 30, 31, 33, 34, 35, 37; **8:**2, 2, 4, 6, 6, 7, 7, 8, 8, 10, 10, 11, 11, 11, 12, 13, 13, 14, 14, 15, 15, 16, 16, 16, 17, 18, 18, 19, 20, 20, 21, 22, 23, 24, 24, 25, 26, 27, 27, 28, 29, 30, 30, 30, 30, 30, 30, 30, 31, 31, 35, 36; **9:**1, 1, 2, 2, 3, 3, 4, 4, 5, 5, 7, 7, 8, 9, 9, 10, 11, 12, 13, 14, 14, 15, 16, 18, 19, 19, 19, 20, 21, 22, 22, 23, 23, 23, 24, 24, 24; **10:**1, 1, 2, 2, 3, 4, 4, 5, 6, 6, 6, 6, 9, 9, 10, 10, 11, 12, 12, 12, 13, 14, 14, 14, 15, 15, 16, 17, 19, 20; **11:**1, 3, 6, 7, 9, 10, 11, 12, 19, 22, 25, 28, 28, 30, 32, 32, 32, 33, 33, 34, 35, 39, 42, 46, 47, 47, 47; **12:**2, 4, 6, 7, 8, 8; **13:**1, 3, 3, 4, 6, 7, 10, 11, 16, 20, 21, 21, 23, 23, 24, 25, 26, 26, 28, 30, 31, 32, 32, 34, 34, 37, 39, 40, 41, 43, 44, 45, 45, 46, 49, 51, 53, 54, 57; **14:**1, 4, 6, 7, 8, 8, 9, 9, 10, 10, 12, 12, 13, 14, 14, 16, 17, 19, 20, 20, 21, 22, 24, 25, 25, 27, 28, 31, 33, 35, 36, 37, 38, 41, 42, 44, 44, 45, 45, 48, 49, 51, 51, 53, 54; **15:**1, 4, 5, 5, 6, 8, 10, 10, 11, 11, 12, 13, 14,

14, 15, 16, 17, 18, 18, 21, 21, 24, 27, 27, 29, 30, 33; **16:**2, 3, 4, 4, 4, 5, 6, 7, 8, 11, 12, 14, 14, 15, 16, 16, 17, 18, 19, 19, 20, 21, 21, 23, 24, 24, 24, 26, 27, 27, 28, 29, 29, 30, 31, 33, 33; **17:**2, 2, 4, 4, 6, 6, 8, 9, 10, 12, 13, 13, 13, 13, 15, 15, 15, 15, 16; **18:**4, 5, 14, 17, 17, 17, 18, 23, 25, 26, 26, 26, 27, 30; **19:**3, 3, 7, 8, 9, 10, 10, 12, 14, 21, 22, 23, 23, 29, 30, 31, 32, 34, 36, 37; **20:**3, 3, 4, 4, 5, 6, 6, 8, 10, 11, 12, 13, 14, 15, 16, 18, 20, 20, 21, 22, 24, 25, 25, 25, 27; **21:**6, 6, 8, 10, 22, 24, 24; **22:**2, 7, 9, 11, 13, 13, 16, 17, 18, 18, 26, 28, 32; **23:**6, 7, 10, 13, 14, 16, 18, 18, 19, 20, 21, 21, 22, 22, 27, 28, 30, 31, 32, 32, 32, 33, 35, 36, 36, 37, 37, 38, 38, 39, 40, 40, 40, 41; **24:**3, 3, 6, 9, 10, 14, 15, 22, 23; **25:**3, 3, 5, 6, 6, 7, 7, 9, 10, 11, 12, 12, 18, 19, 19, 23, 23, 25, 31, 33, 35, 35, 38, 39, 40, 41, 41, 41, 47, 47, 54; **26:**2, 3, 4, 5, 5, 6, 6, 7, 8, 9, 9, 11, 12, 15, 15, 16, 16, 17, 17, 18, 19, 20, 21, 22, 22, 23, 23, 24, 25, 26, 27, 29, 30, 30, 31, 31, 33, 33, 34, 36, 36, 38, 39, 40, 40, 41, 41, 42, 42, 43, 43, 46; **27:**3, 5, 6, 8, 10, 12, 30, 32, 33, 33, 33; **Nu 1:**2, 3, 5, 17, 17, 18, 20, 44, 45, 50, 50, 50, 50, 50; **2:**1, 2, 3, 3, 10, 10, 18, 18, 24, 25, 25, 34, 34; **3:**1, 2, 3, 4, 4, 6, 7, 7, 9, 10, 11, 13, 15, 17, 18, 19, 20, 21, 26, 26, 27, 31, 33, 36, 37, 37, 38, 38, 39, 40, 41, 45, 48, 51, 51; **4:**1, 2, 3, 5, 5, 6, 7, 7, 8, 9, 10, 11, 11, 12, 13, 14, 14, 15, 15, 15, 16, 16, 17, 19, 19, 19, 20, 21, 22, 23, 24, 25, 26, 26, 27, 29, 30, 32, 34, 34, 35, 36, 37, 38, 39, 40, 41, 42, 43, 44, 45, 46, 46, 47, 47, 49, 49; **5:**3, 4, 7, 8, 8, 11, 12, 14, 17, 18, 19, 19, 20, 22, 22, 23, 24, 25, 26, 27, 28, 28, 30, 30; **6:**1, 3, 3, 5, 6, 9, 11, 11, 12, 14, 15, 15, 16, 17, 18, 19, 19, 20, 23, 24, 25, 26, 27, 27; **7:**1, 1, 2, 3, 3, 5, 5, 6, 7, 8, 8, 13, 15, 17, 17, 19, 21, 23, 23, 25, 27, 29, 29, 31, 33, 35, 35, 37, 39, 41, 41, 43, 45, 47, 47, 49, 51, 53, 53, 55, 57, 59, 59, 61, 63, 65, 65, 67, 69, 71, 71, 73, 75, 77, 77, 79, 81, 83, 83, 84, 85, 87, 88; **8:**6, 7, 7, 8, 9, 12, 12, 13, 13, 14, 15, 15, 17, 19, 19, 19, 20, 21, 21, 22, 25; **9:**1, 3, 5, 6, 7, 10, 11, 12, 13, 14, 14, 14, 15, 17, 18, 21, 21, 22, 22, 23; **10:**2, 5, 9, 9, 10, 10, 12, 17, 17, 29, 30, 32, 33, 35, 35, 36; **11:**1, 1, 2, 4, 5, 5, 6, 8, 8, 10, 11, 13, 17, 17, 18, 18, 18, 19, 20, 20, 21, 22, 24, 24, 25, 25, 26, 27, 27, 29, 31, 31, 32, 32, 32, 33; **12:**1, 4, 4, 4, 5, 5, 5, 6, 6, 8, 9, 14, 14, 15, 16; **13:**4, 18, 20, 21, 22, 22, 23, 26, 26, 27, 27, 28, 28, 28, 29, 29, 33; **14:**1, 2, 3, 3, 4, 5, 6, 8, 8, 8, 8, 9, 10, 11, 12, 12, 14, 18, 18, 18, 21, 22, 22, 22, 24, 25, 25, 26, 29, 30, 31, 33, 38, 40, 43, 45, 45, 45; **15:**3, 3, 6, 7, 7, 14, 15, 15, 16, 16, 20, 23, 24, 24, 24, 24, 25, 25, 25, 28, 29, 30, 31, 31, 33, 33, 36, 37, 38, 39, 39, 40; **16:**1, 1, 3, 3, 3, 5, 5, 6, 7, 9, 10, 11, 12, 13, 13, 14, 14, 15, 15, 16, 16, 18, 18, 18, 19, 19, 20, 20, 22, 22, 23, 24, 25, 25, 26, 27, 27, 27, 27, 27, 28, 30, 30, 30, 30, 32, 32, 32, 33, 35, 36, 39, 40, 41, 42, 42, 42, 43, 43, 44, 45, 46, 46, 46, 47, 47, 48; **17:**2, 5, 6, 8, 10, 10; **18:**1, 1, 2, 3, 4, 5, 7, 7, 8, 9, 9, 10, 11, 12, 15, 17, 17, 18, 19, 19, 19, 20, 20, 22, 22, 23, 31; **19:**1, 2, 3, 3, 4, 5, 6, 6, 7, 8, 8, 9, 10, 10, 12, 12, 13, 13, 14, 16, 17, 18, 18, 19, 19, 19, 20, 21, 22; **20:**1, 1, 2, 3, 5, 5, 6, 6, 7, 8, 8, 8, 10, 10, 11, 11, 11, 12, 13, 15, 15, 16, 17, 17, 19, 20, 22, 23, 25, 26, 26, 28, 28, 28; **21:**1, 3, 3, 3, 5, 5, 5, 5, 6, 6, 7, 7, 8, 9, 10, 12, 13, 14, 14, 15, 16, 18, 18, 19, 23, 24, 25, 25, 26, 27, 29, 30, 32, 33, 33, 34, 35, 35, 35; **22:**1, 3, 3, 5, 6, 6, 7, 7, 7, 9, 11, 11, 13, 14, 16, 17, 18, 20, 20, 21, 22, 23, 25, 26, 31, 33, 33, 40, 40; **23:**1, 1, 2, 2, 3, 4, 4, 4, 5, 5, 7, 14, 14, 16, 16, 17, 18, 19, 19, 20, 29, 29, 30, 30; **24:**1, 3, 9, 9, 10, 13, 18, 20, 21, 24, 25; **25:**2, 2, 4, 6, 7, 7, 8, 8, 11, 13, 13, 17, 18; **26:**1, 3, 4, 9, 9, 9, 9, 10, 10, 19, 28, 33, 37, 43, 54, 55, 56, 58, 59, 59, 59, 60, 61, 63, 64, 65; **27:**1, 2, 2, 6, 8, 9, 12, 18, 19, 21, 22, 22, 23; **28:**2, 2, 4, 8, 9, 10, 11, 13, 13, 14, 14, 15, 19, 21, 24, 27, 29, 31; **29:**1, 2, 4, 6, 6, 6, 6, 7, 8, 10, 11, 11, 12, 13, 15, 16, 17, 18, 18, 19, 20, 21, 21, 22, 23, 24, 24, 25, 26, 27, 27, 28, 29, 30, 30, 31, 32, 33, 33, 34, 36, 37, 38, 39; **30:**1, 4, 4, 5, 6, 7, 7, 8, 9, 10, 11, 12, 15, 16, 16, 16; **31:**2, 6, 6, 7, 8, 9, 9, 9, 9, 10, 11, 11, 12, 12, 13, 16, 17, 19, 19, 19, 20, 24, 25, 26, 26, 26, 27, 27, 28, 30, 31, 35, 46, 47, 47, 49, 50, 51, 51, 54, 54; **32:**1, 1, 1, 2, 3, 4, 6, 6, 9, 10, 11, 12, 13, 15, 16, 16, 17, 20, 21, 22, 22, 23, 24, 24, 25, 25, 26, 28, 29, 30, 31, 33, 33, 33, 36, 38, 38, 39, 39, 40, 41, 42, 42; **33:**1, 6, 7, 7, 8, 8, 9, 9, 10, 11, 12, 13, 14, 15, 16, 17, 18, 19, 20, 21, 22, 23, 24, 25, 26, 27, 28, 29, 30, 31, 32, 33, 34, 35, 36, 37, 38, 41, 42, 43, 44, 45, 46, 47, 48, 51, 52, 52, 53, 54, 54, 55, 56; **34:**4, 5, 7, 8, 9, 10, 12, 13, 14, 16, 17, 19; **35:**3, 3, 9, 14, 15, 16, 16, 17, 17, 18, 18, 20, 21, 23, 24, 25, 27, 27, 31, 32, 33; **36:**1, 11, 13; **Dt 1:**1, 1, 4, 4, 7, 7, 7, 7, 7, 8, 8, 8, 11, 11, 12, 13, 13, 15, 15, 15, 15, 17, 17, 18, 19, 19, 19, 21, 22, 24, 24, 25, 26, 26, 27, 27, 28, 28, 31, 31, 33, 36, 37, 40, 41, 43, 44, 45; **2:**1, 1, 5, 7, 7, 8, 8, 9, 10, 11, 12, 13, 19, 19, 21, 23, 24, 24, 25, 27, 28, 29, 30, 31, 32, 33, 33, 34, 34, 36, 37; **3:**1, 2, 3, 3, 5, 6, 7, 10, 10, 10, 11, 12, 13, 14, 16, 16, 17, 18, 19, 20, 23, 24, 25, 26, 27, 28; **4:**1, 1, 1, 5, 5, 5, 6, 6, 8, 8, 9, 9, 10, 10, 11, 11, 12, 13, 13, 14, 14, 19, 19, 19, 20, 25, 25, 25, 26, 28, 29, 29, 30, 33, 34, 35, 37, 38, 39, 39, 39, 40, 40, 45, 46, 46, 46, 47, 49; **5:**1, 1, 1, 5, 5, 5, 9, 10, 13, 14, 14, 14, 14, 14, 14, 15, 15, 16, 22, 22, 22, 24, 24, 24, 25, 26, 27, 27, 27, 27, 28, 28, 29, 29, 30, 31, 33, 33; **6:**1, 1, 2, 2, 2, 2, 3, 3, 5, 5, 6, 7, 7, 7, 8, 9, 10, 11, 11, 13, 15, 17, 18, 18, 20, 22, 22, 22, 22, 24, 24, 24; **7:**1, 1, 2, 2, 3, 3, 3, 4, 5, 5, 7, 8, 9, 9, 10, 11, 12, 13, 13, 13, 13, 13, 13, 13, 14, 15, 16, 18, 19, 19, 19, 19, 20, 21, 21, 24, 24, 25; **8:**1, 1, 1, 2, 2, 3, 3, 4, 6, 7, 7, 8, 8, 9, 9, 11, 11, 12, 12, 13, 13, 13, 13, 14, 15, 15, 15, 16, 17, 18, 19, 19; **9:**1, 2, 3, 5, 5, 9, 9, 9, 11, 12, 13, 14, 14, 17, 18, 20, 21, 21, 22, 23, 23, 23, 25, 25, 26, 26, 27, 27, 29, 29; **10:**1, 2, 3, 3, 4, 5, 5, 6, 6, 7, 8, 10, 10, 10, 11, 12, 12, 12, 13, 13, 14, 14, 15, 16, 17, 17, 17, 18, 18, 18, 20, 20; **11:**1, 1, 2, 3, 3, 4, 4, 4, 6, 6, 6, 6, 6, 8, 9, 9, 10, 10, 11, 13, 13, 13, 14, 15, 17, 17, 18, 19, 19, 20, 21, 22, 23, 24, 25, 26, 28, 29, 32; **12:**1, 2, 3, 3, 6, 6, 7, 7, 10, 10, 11, 12, 12, 12, 14, 15, 17, 17, 17, 18, 21, 22, 23, 25, 26, 27, 28, 29, 29, 31; **13:**1, 2, 3, 4, 4, 6, 8, 11, 11, 14, 15, 16, 17, 17, 18; **14:**2, 5, 6, 8, 9, 10, 18, 19, 23, 23, 25, 25, 26, 27, 28, 29, 29; **15:**8, 9, 9, 10, 11, 12, 14, 15, 16, 16, 17, 18, 19, 19, 20; **16:**2, 4, 7, 8, 11, 11, 13, 14, 14, 15, 16, 18, 19, 20, 22; **17:**2, 5, 7, 9, 9, 11, 13, 14, 14, 16, 17, 17, 19, 20, 20; **18:**1, 1, 3, 3, 4, 8, 10, 12, 14, 15, 18, 22, 22; **19:**1, 1, 1, 4, 5, 5, 5, 6, 6, 8, 9, 10, 11, 11, 11, 12, 16, 17, 17, 18; **20:**1, 1, 1, 4, 5, 5, 6, 7, 7, 11, 12, 14, 17, 19; **21:**1, 2, 5, 5, 5, 9, 10, 10, 11, 11, 11, 13, 13, 14, 15, 15, 15, 17, 19, 20, 20, 21, 21, 22, 22; **22:**4, 5, 6, 7, 10, 11, 13, 14, 15, 16, 19, 20, 21, 22, 23, 24, 25, 26, 29; **23:**2, 4, 7, 10, 11, 13, 14, 15, 16, 20, 25; **24:**1, 2, 3, 7, 8, 11, 12, 13, 13, 15, 15, 17, 17, 18, 19, 19, 20, 21; **25:**1, 2, 5, 5, 7, 8, 9, 11, 14, 14, 15, 16, 18, 18, 19; **26:**1, 1, 2, 3, 4, 5, 6, 7, 7, 8, 8, 9, 9, 10, 10, 11, 11, 11, 12, 13, 13, 14, 14, 15, 15, 16, 17, 17, 18, 19, 19; **27:**1, 2, 2, 3, 4, 7, 9, 9, 10, 12, 13, 13, 15, 15, 16, 17, 18, 19, 19, 20, 21, 22, 23, 24, 25, 26; **28:**3, 4, 4, 5, 6, 8, 9, 10, 11, 13, 13, 13, 14, 15, 15, 15, 16, 17, 18, 18, 20, 21, 22, 22, 22, 23, 23, 24, 24, 26, 26, 27, 27, 28, 29, 29, 29, 31, 32, 33, 36, 36, 36, 37, 39, 41, 42, 43, 43, 44, 45, 45, 45, 46, 46, 47, 48, 49, 50, 51, 51, 53, 54, 56, 56, 57, 57, 58, 58, 59, 59, 59, 60, 61, 63, 63, 64, 65, 65, 65, 66, 67; **29:**2,

2, 2, 3, 5, 7, 8, 8, 8, 11, 11, 12, 13, 13, 13, 15, 16, 17, 18, 18, 20, 20, 22, 22, 23, 23, 23, 23, 25, 26, 28, 28, 29; **30:**1, 1, 2, 2, 3, 4, 4, 5, 5, 6, 6, 6, 7, 8, 9, 9, 10, 10, 10, 12, 12, 13, 14, 15, 15, 16, 16, 16, 16, 16, 16, 17, 17, 17, 19, 19, 19, 19, 20, 20, 20; **31:**2, 3, 3, 4, 5, 6, 7, 7, 9, 9, 12, 12, 12, 13, 14, 14, 14, 14, 15, 16, 16, 17, 19, 20, 20, 20, 21, 22, 23, 26, 27, 28, 28, 28, 29; **32:**1, 4, 4, 5, 6, 6, 7, 7, 10, 11, 11, 14, 14, 14, 15, 15, 19, 19, 22, 22, 22, 23, 24, 25, 25, 25, 27, 29, 30, 32, 35, 36, 36, 38, 38, 39, 39, 40, 41, 41, 42, 42, 42, 43, 43, 43, 44, 49, 50, 50; **33:**2, 2, 3, 6, 7, 8, 9, 9, 10, 11, 12, 13, 14, 15, 15, 16, 17, 17, 18, 19, 21, 23, 23, 25, 27, 28, 29, 29; **34:**1, 1, 2, 4, 4, 7, 9, 11, 11, 12, 12; **Jos 1:**4, 6, 7, 7, 8, 9, 11, 11, 12, 13, 14, 15, 16, 17, 18, 18; **2:**1, 1, 5, 6, 7, 10, 10, 11, 12, 13, 13, 13, 18, 18, 19, 21, 22, 23; **3:**1, 1, 4, 6, 6, 8, 9, 10, 13, 15, 16; **4:**3, 5, 5, 8, 11, 12, 13, 14, 18, 23, 24; **5:**1, 1, 3, 6, 6, 11, 12, 13, 13, 15; **6:**2, 5, 6, 6, 7, 8, 9, 11, 12, 13, 14, 15, 17, 17, 18, 19, 20, 20, 21, 21, 22, 23, 23, 24, 25, 25, 27; **7:**1, 3, 5, 5, 6, 6, 9, 9, 9, 11, 11, 11, 14, 14, 14, 15, 16, 17, 17, 18, 19, 21, 22, 23, 23, 24, 24, 24, 25, 25, 25; **8:**1, 1, 2, 2, 3, 3, 4, 5, 7, 9, 9, 10, 11, 12, 13, 14, 14, 15, 16, 17, 19, 19, 20, 21, 21, 21, 22, 22, 23, 24, 27, 29, 29, 31, 31, 32, 33, 33, 33, 34, 35, 35; **9:**1, 1, 2, 3, 4, 5, 5, 6, 9, 10, 11, 11, 11, 12, 13, 13, 13, 15, 15, 17, 17, 21, 22, 23, 24, 27, 27; **10:**1, 1, 1, 1, 2, 2, 2, 3, 4, 4, 5, 6, 7, 7, 9, 10, 10, 10, 12, 13, 13, 15, 16, 18, 19, 20, 20, 22, 23, 24, 24, 25, 26, 27, 29, 29, 30, 30, 31, 31, 32, 33, 34, 34, 35, 37, 37, 38, 39, 39, 39, 40, 40, 41, 42, 43; **11:**3, 3, 4, 4, 6, 7, 7, 8, 8, 8, 9, 10, 11, 12, 14, 14, 15, 16, 16, 20, 20, 21, 21, 21, 22; **12:**1, 2, 3, 4, 5, 5, 5, 6, 6, 6, 6, 7, 8, 8, 24; **13:**1, 2, 4, 4, 5, 6, 7, 8, 8, 10, 11, 12, 12, 12, 13, 17, 20, 21, 21, 21, 23, 25, 26, 26, 27, 28, 30, 31, 31; **14:**1, 2, 3, 4, 4, 4, 4, 6, 7, 8, 9, 10, 11, 11, 13, 15; **15:**3, 7, 8, 9, 10, 10, 11, 11, 14, 16, 19, 32, 36, 41, 44, 45, 46, 47, 47, 47, 51, 54, 57, 59, 60, 62; **16:**1, 3, 4, 7, 7; **17:**1, 2, 3, 3, 4, 4, 5, 10, 10, 11, 11, 14, 15, 16, 16, 17, 17, 18, 18, 18; **18:**1, 4, 5, 7, 7, 8, 8, 9, 11, 12, 13, 16, 16, 17, 19, 24, 28; **19:**6, 7, 11, 12, 12, 13, 13, 14, 15, 21, 22, 26, 27, 27, 28, 29, 29, 30, 33, 33, 34, 34, 38, 40, 46, 47, 50, 51; **20:**3, 4, 4, 6, 6, 7, 8; **21:**1, 2, 4, 5, 6, 7, 8, 8, 9, 12, 16, 18, 20, 22, 23, 24, 25, 27, 29, 31, 32, 33, 35, 37, 39, 41, 43, 43, 44; **22:**1, 2, 4, 5, 5, 5, 6, 8, 8, 8, 8, 9, 10, 12, 13, 14, 15, 16, 18, 19, 21, 22, 25, 25, 27, 27, 30, 30, 32, 32, 32, 33, 33, 33, 33, 34, 34; **23:**1, 2, 9, 9, 12, 13, 13, 13, 16, 16; **24:**1, 1, 2, 2, 3, 4, 4, 5, 5, 6, 7, 8, 10, 11, 11, 12, 13, 13, 14, 14, 15, 16, 17, 18, 19, 19, 20, 23, 25, 25, 26, 31, 32; **Jdg 1:**4, 4, 5, 5, 5, 6, 6, 7, 7, 8, 8, 9, 10, 12, 15, 17, 18, 19, 20, 22, 24, 25, 25, 26, 27, 29, 30, 31, 33, 33, 34, 35, 36; **2:**1, 3, 5, 7, 7, 11, 12, 13, 14, 15, 18, 18, 19, 19, 19, 20; **3:**3, 5, 6, 6, 6, 7, 7, 8, 8, 10, 10, 13, 13, 14, 16, 19, 19, 20, 21, 22, 23, 23, 23, 24, 25, 25, 28, 29, 29, 30; **4:**5, 5, 6, 7, 10, 10, 11, 13, 13, 15, 15, 15, 16, 18, 18, 19, 20, 21, 21, 21, 22, 22, 24, 24; **5:**1, 2, 4, 4, 6, 6, 9, 10, 10, 11, 12, 14, 15, 17, 25, 26, 29, 30; **6:**2, 3, 4, 4, 5, 5, 9, 9, 9, 11, 12, 13, 13, 14, 14, 15, 16, 18, 19, 19, 19, 20, 20, 20, 21, 21, 21, 24, 24, 25, 27, 27, 28, 28, 29, 29, 30, 31, 33, 33, 34, 35, 35, 38, 38; **7:**1, 1, 3, 4, 4, 5, 5, 6, 7, 8, 8, 11, 11, 12, 13, 13, 15, 15, 16, 16, 18, 18, 19, 19, 20, 20, 20, 21, 22, 23, 24, 25, 25, 25, 25; **8:**1, 3, 4, 5, 6, 6, 7, 7, 7, 8, 10, 11, 12, 12, 14, 14, 15, 15, 15, 15, 16, 16, 17, 18, 20, 21, 21, 22, 22, 25, 26, 27, 27, 27, 32; **9:**1, 2, 2, 3, 5, 5, 6, 6, 7, 9, 9, 11, 13, 13, 14, 15, 15, 15, 16, 16, 16, 17, 18, 18, 19, 19, 19, 20, 20, 20, 20, 21, 23, 23, 24, 25, 26, 27, 28, 29, 29, 31, 31, 32, 33, 34, 34, 35, 37, 38, 38, 40, 40, 41, 41, 43, 43, 43, 44, 45, 48, 48, 49, 49, 50, 51, 51, 53, 54, 54, 55; **10:**1, 4, 6, 6, 6, 6, 7, 7, 9, 9, 10, 12, 12, 13, 14, 15, 16, 16, 17; **11:**2, 3, 6, 7, 9, 11, 11, 13, 18, 18, 20, 22, 23, 24, 26, 29, 29, 29, 30, 32, 33, 34, 35, 36, 37, 37, 38, 38, 38, 39; **12:**1, 3, 3, 4, 4, 4, 5, 6, 9, 9, 9, 14, 15; **13:**2, 3, 3, 5, 5, 6, 6, 7, 8, 9, 10, 11, 12, 19, 19, 19, 20, 21, 22, 23, 23, 23, 24, 25, 25; **14:**2, 3, 4, 5, 6, 7, 8, 9, 9, 9, 12, 13, 16, 17, 19, 19, 19; **15:**4, 4, 5, 5, 5, 6, 6, 6, 7, 8, 9, 12, 13, 13, 14, 14, 15, 16, 17, 18, 18, 19, 19; **16:**1, 2, 3, 3, 3, 5, 5, 5, 6, 8, 9, 10, 12, 12, 13, 13, 14, 14, 14, 15, 17, 18, 19, 19, 20, 21, 21, 23, 25, 27, 27, 29, 30, 30, 31, 31, 31; **17:**3, 3, 4, 4, 5, 5, 9, 9, 10, 10, 10, 11, 12; **18:**1, 2, 2, 3, 3, 4, 7, 7, 7, 8, 9, 9, 10, 11, 13, 14, 15, 17, 17, 19, 19, 20, 21, 22, 23, 23, 24, 24, 25, 25, 26, 27, 27, 27, 27, 28, 28, 30; **19:**2, 3, 3, 4, 6, 6, 6, 7, 8, 9, 9, 9, 9, 10, 10, 11, 17, 18, 19, 19, 19, 21, 22, 23, 24, 24, 25, 26, 28, 29, 30; **20:**1, 1, 2, 4, 5, 6, 6, 8, 8, 10, 11, 13, 14, 16, 18, 19, 21, 22, 23, 23, 23, 26, 26, 27, 28, 28, 30, 31, 31, 31, 32, 33, 34, 35, 37, 39, 39, 40, 41, 41, 42, 43, 48; **21:**2, 2, 2, 4, 4, 6, 8, 10, 11, 12, 14, 19, 20, 21, 22, 22, 22, 23, 23, 24, 24; **Ru 1:**1, 1, 2, 2, 3, 4, 5, 6, 7, 8, 8, 9, 9, 12, 12, 13, 14, 14, 15, 16, 16, 17, 17, 21; **2:**1, 2, 3, 4, 6, 8, 9, 9, 10, 11, 11, 11, 14, 14, 16, 16, 16, 17, 18, 19, 21, 23; **3:**2, 3, 3, 4, 4, 6, 7, 7, 7, 8, 13, 15, 15, 17, 17; **4:**1, 2, 3, 5, 7, 9, 9, 10, 10, 11, 11, 11, 12, 12, 13, 13, 14, 15, 15, 16, 17, 17; **1Sa 1:**1, 1, 2, 3, 3, 3, 4, 7, 11, 11, 11, 11, 15, 16, 18, 18, 19, 20, 21, 22, 23, 23, 24, 24, 27, 28, 28; **2:**3, 3, 4, 5, 6, 7, 7, 8, 11, 11, 14, 19, 20, 20, 21, 21, 26, 27, 28, 28, 29, 29, 30, 33, 33, 34, 34, 35, 35, 36; **3:**1, 3, 5, 6, 8, 8, 9, 9, 10, 10, 10, 12, 13, 14, 15, 17, 19, 19, 21; **4:**1, 1, 2, 3, 4, 10, 10, 11, 11, 12, 12, 13, 15, 17, 17, 18, 18, 19, 19, 19, 21, 21; **5:**2, 4, 4, 6, 8, 8, 9, 9, 11, 11, 12; **6:**2, 4, 4, 4, 5, 6, 6, 7, 8, 9, 10, 11, 11, 12, 13, 14, 14, 14, 15, 15, 15, 16, 17, 18, 19, 21, 21; **7:**1, 3, 4, 4, 6, 6, 6, 7, 9, 9, 10, 12, 12, 13, 13, 14, 14, 14, 16, 17, 17; **8:**2, 3, 5, 6, 8, 8, 11, 12, 12, 13, 13, 14, 14, 14, 15, 15, 16, 16, 16, 17, 20, 22, 22, 22; **9:**1, 1, 2, 3, 3, 4, 4, 5, 7, 8, 9, 11, 13, 14, 16, 18, 19, 19, 20, 20, 20, 21, 22, 22, 24, 24, 25, 26, 26; **10:**1, 1, 2, 2, 3, 4, 5, 5, 6, 8, 8, 9, 9, 10, 10, 15, 18, 18, 19, 19, 20, 21, 22, 23, 23, 23, 24, 25, 25, 27, 27; **11:**1, 4, 5, 6, 7, 7, 7, 7, 10, 11, 11, 12, 15, 15, 15; **12:**1, 2, 3, 3, 4, 5, 6, 7, 8, 8, 9, 9, 10, 10, 10, 10, 11, 11, 12, 13, 14, 14, 14, 14, 14, 15, 16, 17, 18, 18, 18, 20, 23, 23, 24, 25; **13:**1, 2, 2, 3, 4, 4, 5, 6, 6, 7, 7, 7, 9, 9, 10, 11, 11, 12, 15, 16, 16, 18, 19, 21, 22; **14:**2, 3, 4, 5, 8, 9, 10, 12, 13, 13, 13, 14, 15, 15, 15, 15, 17, 17, 19, 19, 20, 20, 21, 21, 23, 27, 27, 28, 28, 31, 31, 32, 32, 33, 34, 34, 34, 35, 36, 40, 40, 40, 41, 41, 41, 41, 41, 42, 42, 45, 45, 46, 47, 47, 48, 49, 49, 51, 52; **15:**3, 3, 5, 6, 9, 9, 9, 9, 11, 14, 15, 17, 18, 18, 18, 19, 21, 21, 22, 23, 24, 24, 25, 27, 28, 28, 29, 30, 31, 31, 32, 33, 34, 35; **16:**1, 2, 3, 5, 5, 5, 6, 7, 8, 12, 12, 13, 13, 14, 14, 16, 17, 18, 18, 18, 20, 20, 21, 21, 23, 23; **17:**1, 1, 3, 5, 6, 7, 8, 8, 11, 11, 12, 13, 15, 15, 16, 17, 18, 18, 19, 20, 20, 21, 22, 25, 25, 26, 27, 28, 30, 30, 31, 33, 35, 35, 36, 36, 37, 37, 38, 39, 40, 40, 43, 44, 44, 45, 46, 46, 46, 46, 47, 49, 49, 49, 49, 50, 50, 51, 51, 51, 52, 52, 52, 52, 53, 58, 58; **18:**1, 2, 3, 4, 4, 5, 6, 6, 6, 6, 7, 8, 10, 11, 12, 12, 13, 16, 17, 18, 20, 22, 22, 27, 27, 27, 28, 29; **19:**1, 3, 5, 6, 7, 7, 8, 10, 12, 13, 13, 14, 15, 17, 18, 18, 20, 20, 20, 22, 22, 23, 24, 24; **20:**1, 3, 3, 5, 7, 11, 12, 13, 13, 14, 17, 19, 20, 21, 23, 24, 25, 30, 31, 34, 35, 36, 38, 39, 40, 41, 42, 42; **21:**5, 10, 11, 12, 13; **22:**1, 1, 3, 4, 5, 6, 7, 8, 10, 11, 13, 13, 13, 13, 14, 15, 17, 17, 18, 19, 19, 19, 19, 19, 20, 23; **23:**2, 2, 4, 5, 5, 5, 8, 8, 9, 9, 10, 10, 11, 11, 12, 12, 13, 13, 14, 15, 16, 17, 19, 20, 20, 22,

22, 23, 23, 24, 25, 25, 26, 26, 26, 28; **24:**2, 2, 3, 4, 7, 7, 8, 8, 10, 11, 15, 15, 17, 20, 20, 21, 22, 22; **25:**1, 2, 2, 3, 3, 3, 6, 6, 7, 7, 8, 9, 11, 11, 11, 12, 13, 14, 14, 15, 16, 16, 17, 18, 18, 20, 21, 23, 24, 25, 26, 26, 27, 27, 28, 30, 31, 31, 33, 35, 36, 37, 38, 39, 41, 42, 42; **26:**2, 5, 6, 7, 7, 7, 8, 11, 11, 12, 12, 14, 16, 16, 17, 17, 19, 21, 21, 22, 23, 23, 25, 25, 25; **27:**1, 2, 2, 3, 7, 7, 8, 8, 9, 10, 10, 11, 11, 12, 12; **28:**1, 3, 3, 3, 4, 4, 7, 9, 10, 14, 15, 15, 16, 17, 19, 19, 19, 20, 22, 23, 23, 24, 24, 25, 25; **29:**1, 2, 2, 3, 3, 5, 6, 10; **30:**1, 1, 2, 2, 3, 3, 5, 6, 6, 8, 9, 9, 11, 11, 12, 12, 13, 14, 14, 16, 16, 16, 16, 17, 17, 17, 18, 20, 20, 21, 22, 22, 23, 24, 24, 25, 27, 31; **31:**2, 2, 2, 3, 3, 4, 4, 4, 4, 5, 6, 7, 7, 7, 7, 7, 8, 9, 9, 10, 12, 12, 13, 13; **2Sa 1:**1, 2, 4, 4, 4, 5, 7, 8, 9, 9, 10, 11, 12, 12, 12, 12, 12, 13, 15, 17, 18, 19, 22, 23, 23, 23, 24, 26; **2:**1, 1, 2, 2, 3, 3, 3, 4, 5, 6, 6, 7, 7, 9, 10, 11, 11, 13, 16, 17, 17, 18, 19, 19, 20, 21, 21, 23, 23, 23, 23, 24, 28, 29, 29, 30, 31, 32, 32, 32; **3:**1, 1, 1, 8, 10, 12, 18, 19, 21, 22, 23, 25, 26, 26, 27, 28, 29, 30, 31, 31, 31, 32, 32, 35, 37, 38, 39, 39; **4:**1, 2, 4, 4, 4, 4, 5, 6, 6, 6, 8, 8, 9, 10, 11, 12, 12, 12, 12; **5:**1, 2, 3, 4, 5, 5, 5, 6, 8, 8, 8, 9, 9, 10, 10, 11, 12, 12, 13, 13, 13, 16, 17, 18, 20, 21, 22, 23, 23, 25; **6:**3, 3, 5, 5, 5, 6, 7, 9, 11, 11, 12, 12, 13, 13, 14, 15, 15, 16, 17, 17, 19, 19, 20, 21, 22; **7:**1, 3, 5, 7, 8, 9, 10, 11, 11, 12, 13, 14, 16, 16, 17, 18, 18, 18, 19, 21, 21, 23, 23, 24, 25, 25, 26, 26, 28, 29, 29; **8:**1, 2, 2, 4, 6, 6, 8, 10, 10, 10, 11, 12, 12, 14, 15, 17; **9:**5, 6, 6, 7, 9, 9, 10, 10, 10, 11, 12, 13; **10:**1, 3, 4, 4, 6, 6, 7, 8, 8, 8, 9, 11, 11, 11, 12, 13, 14, 14, 17, 17, 18, 19, 19; **11:**1, 2, 3, 3, 4, 7, 7, 8, 10, 11, 11, 11, 11, 11, 11, 12, 12, 13, 14, 17, 20, 22, 23, 25, 27, 27; **12:**1, 2, 3, 3, 4, 4, 6, 7, 8, 8, 8, 8, 9, 9, 11, 13, 14, 16, 17, 20, 20, 20, 21, 21, 22, 22, 24, 24, 24, 25, 26, 27, 28, 29, 30, 30, 30, 31, 31, 31, 31; **13:**1, 2, 5, 5, 6, 6, 7, 10, 11, 13, 13, 14, 15, 17, 17, 19, 19, 20, 22, 24, 24, 28, 29, 31, 31, 32, 36, 36, 36, 37, 39; **14:**2, 3, 4, 6, 7, 7, 8, 9, 14, 15, 16, 17, 19, 19, 20, 21, 21, 22, 22, 23, 26, 27, 27, 30, 31, 32, 33, 33, 33; **15:**1, 1, 2, 2, 4, 5, 5, 9, 12, 14, 16, 17, 17, 19, 20, 20, 20, 20, 21, 22, 22, 23, 23, 24, 24, 24, 25, 27, 27, 28, 29, 29, 30, 30, 30, 32, 34, 34, 35, 36, 36, 36; **16:**1, 2, 2, 2, 3, 5, 6, 6, 8, 8, 9, 11, 11, 12, 12, 13, 13, 13, 13, 14, 15, 18, 19, 19, 20, 21, 21, 22; **17:**2, 2, 2, 3, 3, 4, 8, 8, 9, 9, 9, 9, 10, 11, 11, 13, 13, 14, 15, 15, 16, 16, 17, 17, 18, 20, 20, 21, 21, 21, 22, 22, 23, 23, 24, 26, 27, 27, 28, 29, 29, 29, 29; **18:**1, 2, 3, 3, 3, 3, 5, 5, 5, 7, 7, 8, 9, 10, 11, 11, 12, 12, 13, 13, 14, 15, 16, 17, 17, 18, 21, 23, 25, 27, 28, 31, 32, 32, 33, 33; **19:**1, 3, 4, 5, 5, 5, 5, 6, 6, 7, 8, 8, 9, 9, 10, 11, 11, 12, 13, 14, 14, 15, 15, 17, 17, 18, 28, 29, 32, 33, 35, 35, 35, 37, 37, 38, 39, 40, 42, 43, 43; **20:**1, 2, 2, 4, 6, 7, 7, 9, 10, 10, 10, 10, 11, 11, 12, 12, 15, 15, 19, 20, 22, 22, 22, 22, 25; **21:**1, 1, 4, 4, 6, 7, 8, 10, 10, 12, 12, 12, 13, 15, 15, 15, 16, 16, 17, 20, 21, 22; **22:**1, 2, 3, 8, 10, 13, 15, 15, 16, 17, 18, 38, 41, 46, 49, 51; **23:**5, 9, 10, 11, 12, 14, 16, 19, 20, 20, 21, 23; **24:**1, 1, 1, 4, 5, 6, 6, 7, 7, 8, 8, 9, 10, 10, 12, 12, 13, 13, 15, 16, 17, 17, 18, 18, 20, 20, 21, 21, 22, 22, 22, 23, 24, 25, 25, 25, 25; **1Ki 1:**1, 2, 2, 3, 3, 4, 4, 5, 5, 6, 7, 7, 8, 8, 9, 9, 11, 11, 12, 13, 13, 14, 14, 15, 17, 18, 19, 19, 19, 19, 20, 21, 23, 24, 25, 25, 25, 25, 25, 28, 29, 30, 31, 32, 33, 34, 34, 35, 37, 37, 38, 38, 39, 39, 40, 40, 40, 41, 41, 42, 44, 45, 45, 45, 45, 47, 47, 48, 49, 50, 51, 53, 53, 53; **2:**2, 3, 3, 3, 4, 4, 5, 5, 5, 8, 9, 10, 11, 12, 15, 19, 19, 22, 22, 24, 25, 26, 28, 30, 30, 31, 31, 32, 32, 33, 33, 33, 33, 34, 34, 35, 36, 36, 40, 41, 41, 42, 42, 42, 43, 45, 46; **3:**1, 1, 1, 3, 3, 4, 5, 5, 6, 6, 6, 8, 9, 9, 10, 11, 12, 13, 13, 14, 14, 15, 15, 15, 17, 20, 20, 21, 22, 22, 22, 22, 23, 25, 26, 28; **4:**2, 3, 4, 9, 10, 12, 12, 12, 13, 16, 19, 19, 20, 20, 21, 22, 23, 24, 25, 25, 25, 25, 26, 27, 28, 29, 29, 30, 31, 31, 32, 33, 34; **5:**4, 4, 6, 7, 8, 8, 9, 9, 10, 11, 12, 12, 14, 16, 17, 18, 18; **6:**2, 5, 6, 8, 8, 9, 12, 12, 13, 15, 15, 16, 18, 18, 20, 20, 21, 25, 29, 29, 32, 32, 34, 35, 35; **7:**1, 2, 6, 9, 10, 11, 14, 15, 17, 19, 21, 21, 22, 23, 24, 25, 26, 26, 27, 29, 29, 29, 29, 30, 31, 33, 33, 34, 35, 36, 36, 36, 37, 38, 39, 40, 44, 45, 46, 49, 49, 50, 50, 51, 51; **8:**1, 4, 4, 4, 5, 5, 6, 7, 14, 20, 21, 23, 23, 24, 25, 28, 28, 29, 30, 30, 30, 31, 32, 32, 32, 33, 33, 33, 34, 34, 35, 35, 35, 35, 36, 36, 38, 39, 40, 41, 41, 42, 42, 42, 43, 43, 44, 44, 45, 46, 46, 46, 47, 47, 48, 48, 48, 50, 52, 52, 54, 55, 58, 58, 59, 59, 59, 60, 61, 61, 62, 63, 63, 63, 64, 65, 65, 66, 66, 66; **9:**3, 3, 4, 4, 4, 6, 6, 6, 6, 7, 8, 8, 8, 9, 9, 10, 11, 11, 15, 15, 16, 16, 18, 19, 19, 19, 19, 20, 21, 22, 25, 25, 28; **10:**2, 2, 4, 5, 5, 5, 6, 7, 7, 9, 9, 10, 10, 11, 12, 12, 12, 13, 13, 15, 15, 18, 19, 22, 23, 24, 25, 25, 26, 26, 26, 27, 28, 29, 29; **11:**1, 3, 3, 5, 7, 8, 11, 11, 13, 13, 16, 17, 18, 18, 18, 19, 21, 24, 24, 25, 25, 26, 27, 28, 28, 30, 30, 31, 32, 33, 33, 33, 33, 34, 34, 35, 37, 37, 38, 38, 38, 38, 38, 40; **12:**3, 4, 7, 8, 8, 10, 12, 14, 16, 18, 20, 21, 21, 23, 23, 24, 25, 25, 27, 29, 29, 31, 31, 32, 33; **13:**1, 2, 3, 3, 4, 4, 5, 6, 7, 7, 9, 10, 11, 11, 13, 14, 15, 17, 18, 18, 18, 19, 19, 21, 22, 22, 23, 24, 24, 24, 25, 25, 25, 25, 26, 28, 28, 28, 29, 29, 32, 33, 34, 34; **14:**3, 3, 4, 7, 8, 8, 8, 9, 9, 10, 11, 12, 13, 14, 15, 16, 17, 19, 21, 23, 23, 23, 25, 26, 26, 27, 28, 29, 30; **15:**3, 4, 5, 6, 7, 7, 12, 13, 15, 15, 15, 16, 17, 18, 18, 18, 19, 19, 20, 20, 21, 22, 22, 23, 26, 27, 27, 28, 30, 31, 32, 34; **16:**3, 4, 5, 7, 7, 10, 10, 11, 11, 13, 13, 14, 18, 18, 19, 20, 22, 24, 27, 31, 31, 32, 34; **17:**1, 3, 4, 5, 6, 6, 6, 9, 10, 12, 12, 12, 12, 13, 13, 14, 14, 15, 15, 15, 15, 17, 17, 19, 19, 21, 21, 22, 22, 23, 24; **18:**1, 4, 4, 5, 5, 6, 7, 8, 10, 10, 11, 11, 12, 13, 13, 14, 14, 16, 18, 18, 19, 20, 21, 23, 23, 23, 24, 24, 25, 25, 26, 27, 28, 28, 32, 33, 33, 33, 34, 35, 35, 36, 36, 36, 37, 38, 38, 39, 39, 40, 40, 41, 42, 42, 43, 43, 43, 43, 43, 44, 44, 45, 45, 46; **19:**1, 3, 3, 4, 5, 5, 5, 6, 6, 6, 6, 7, 7, 7, 8, 8, 8, 8, 10, 10, 11, 11, 11, 12, 12, 13, 13, 13, 14, 14, 15, 16, 17, 19, 19, 19, 19, 20, 20, 20, 20, 21, 21; **20:**1, 1, 3, 3, 3, 5, 5, 6, 7, 7, 7, 7, 8, 10, 12, 13, 14, 16, 20, 20, 20, 21, 21, 25, 25, 26, 27, 28, 28, 29, 30, 30, 31, 32, 32, 32, 33, 33, 33, 34, 34, 36, 36, 37, 37, 39, 41, 42, 42, 43; **21:**1, 4, 4, 6, 7, 7, 8, 8, 9, 9, 10, 10, 11, 12, 13, 13, 21, 22, 22, 24, 27, 27; **22:**1, 3, 4, 4, 4, 4, 6, 9, 9, 10, 11, 12, 13, 15, 17, 19, 20, 21, 22, 22, 22, 24, 25, 26, 26, 27, 27, 29, 30, 33, 34, 35, 35, 37, 37, 38, 38, 39, 39, 42, 43, 43, 45, 52, 52, 53; **2Ki 1:**2, 3, 3, 6, 8, 10, 10, 10, 12, 12, 12, 12, 13, 15, 16; **2:**1, 2, 2, 3, 4, 5, 6, 7, 7, 8, 8, 9, 11, 11, 12, 12, 12, 13, 14, 14, 15, 15, 16, 17, 19, 21, 21, 22, 23, 23, 24, 24, 24, 25; **3:**2, 4, 4, 6, 7, 7, 7, 9, 9, 12, 13, 16, 17, 17, 19, 20, 20, 21, 21, 23, 23, 24, 24, 25, 27, 27; **4:**1, 1, 3, 3, 4, 5, 6, 7, 7, 7, 8, 10, 10, 11, 14, 17, 20, 21, 22, 22, 24, 26, 26, 27, 27, 28, 29, 29, 30, 31, 31, 33, 33, 34, 34, 35, 35, 35, 36, 37, 38, 39, 39, 41, 41, 41, 42, 44, 44; **5:**2, 5, 5, 7, 7, 8, 9, 9, 10, 10, 11, 11, 11, 12, 12, 12, 13, 13, 13, 14, 14, 14, 15, 15, 16, 17, 18, 20, 21, 22, 23, 24, 26, 26, 26, 26, 26, 26, 27, 27; **6:**1, 6, 6, 7, 7, 8, 8, 11, 13, 13, 13, 14, 15, 15, 17, 17, 17, 18, 19, 19, 19, 20, 20, 20, 22, 22, 23, 24, 25, 28, 29, 30, 32, 33; **7:**1, 4, 4, 6, 6, 6, 7, 7, 7, 8, 8, 8, 8, 9, 9, 10, 10, 10, 10, 12, 12, 12, 12, 13, 14, 15, 15, 16, 16, 17, 18, 19, 20; **8:**1, 2, 3, 3, 5, 5, 6, 9, 10, 10, 12, 14, 15, 17, 18, 19, 20, 21, 21, 23, 26; **9:**2, 2, 3, 3, 4, 6, 6, 7, 8, 9, 10, 10, 11, 12, 13, 14, 15, 16, 17, 18, 19, 21, 22, 23, 24, 24, 25, 26, 30, 30, 32, 32, 32, 33, 33, 33, 34, 34, 34, 35, 36; **10:**1, 1, 2, 2, 3, 4, 5, 5, 5, 6, 7, 8, 8, 9, 9, 11, 11, 13, 13, 14, 14, 15, 16, 18, 19, 19,

21, 22, 24, 24, 25, 25, 25, 25, 26, 27, 29, 33, 33, 34, 34; **11:**2, 2, 3, 4, 4, 6, 8, 10, 10, 10, 11, 12, 12, 12, 12, 13, 14, 14, 14, 14, 14, 15, 16, 16, 17, 17, 17, 18, 18, 18, 18, 19, 19, 19, 20; **12:**3, 3, 7, 7, 8, 9, 10, 10, 12, 12, 12, 15, 16, 17, 18, 18, 19, 20, 21; **13:**3, 3, 4, 7, 8, 12, 12, 14, 14, 15, 15, 16, 17, 18, 18, 20, 21, 23, 23, 23, 24, 25; **14:**2, 4, 7, 8, 8, 9, 10, 10, 10, 12, 12, 13, 14, 14, 14, 15, 19, 19, 20, 22, 25, 26, 27, 28, 28, 28; **15:**2, 4, 5, 6, 10, 14, 14, 16, 16, 20, 21, 25, 26, 29, 29, 29, 29, 30, 31, 33, 35, 36, 37; **16:**2, 4, 4, 4, 5, 6, 7, 7, 7, 8, 8, 8, 9, 11, 12, 13, 13, 14, 14, 15, 15, 15, 17, 17, 19; **17:**3, 4, 4, 5, 6, 6, 10, 10, 12, 13, 13, 13, 13, 13, 14, 15, 15, 15, 16, 16, 16, 17, 17, 17, 18, 21, 22, 24, 24, 24, 24, 28, 30, 31, 31, 31, 33, 34, 34, 34, 35, 36, 36, 37, 38, 40, 41; **18:**2, 4, 6, 7, 7, 8, 9, 10, 11, 11, 13, 14, 15, 16, 16, 17, 18, 20, 21, 22, 22, 24, 25, 26, 27, 27, 28, 31, 31, 32, 32, 32, 34, 34, 34, 36, 37, 37, 37; **19:**1, 1, 2, 2, 3, 4, 7, 8, 8, 12, 13, 13, 14, 14, 15, 15, 16, 16, 18, 18, 18, 21, 21, 22, 23, 23, 24, 26, 27, 27, 28, 28, 29, 29, 29, 30, 30, 30, 32, 32, 34, 35, 36, 36, 37, 37; **20:**1, 2, 3, 3, 5, 5, 5, 6, 6, 6, 7, 7, 8, 11, 12, 13, 13, 13, 14, 19, 20, 20; **21:**1, 3, 3, 6, 6, 6, 7, 7, 7, 9, 12, 13, 13, 14, 15, 17, 19, 22, 23, 24, 25; **22:**1, 2, 3, 4, 6, 6, 8, 9, 9, 12, 13, 13, 13, 14, 14, 15, 16, 17, 17, 17, 18, 19, 19, 19, 19, 20; **23:**1, 2, 2, 2, 2, 3, 3, 3, 3, 4, 4, 4, 4, 5, 5, 5, 6, 6, 12, 13, 13, 13, 14, 15, 16, 16, 17, 17, 19, 20, 22, 24, 24, 24, 25, 25, 25, 26, 27, 27, 28, 30, 30, 31, 33, 34, 35, 36; **24:**1, 2, 4, 5, 8, 10, 12, 12, 13, 14, 14, 15, 15, 16, 16, 16, 17, 18, 20, 20; **25:**1, 4, 4, 5, 7, 9, 11, 12, 13, 13, 14, 15, 15, 16, 17, 18, 19, 19, 21, 22, 23, 23, 23, 24, 24, 25, 25, 25, 25, 27, 28, 29; **1Ch 1:**4, 4, 5, 6, 7, 8, 9, 9, 12, 16, 17, 17, 19, 23, 27, 28, 31, 32, 32, 33, 34, 35, 36, 37, 38, 39, 40, 40, 41, 42, 42, 46, 50, 50, 54; **2:**2, 3, 4, 5, 6, 9, 15, 16, 16, 17, 18, 18, 19, 23, 23, 23, 25, 27, 28, 28, 29, 29, 30, 32, 33, 35, 43, 46, 47, 48, 49, 49, 51, 53, 53, 53, 55, 55; **3:**4, 5, 8, 14, 15, 18, 19, 19, 20, 21, 22, 22, 23, 24; **4:**1, 2, 4, 5, 6, 8, 8, 10, 10, 10, 10, 12, 13, 13, 15, 16, 17, 17, 18, 18, 19, 20, 20, 22, 22, 23, 24, 25, 26, 27, 31, 32, 33, 33, 37, 40, 40, 41, 41, 41, 42, 43; **5:**2, 3, 6, 8, 8, 9, 12, 12, 13, 16, 16, 17, 18, 18, 18, 19, 20, 20, 21, 23, 24, 24, 25, 26, 26, 26; **6:**1, 2, 3, 3, 15, 16, 17, 18, 19, 21, 24, 27, 28, 30, 38, 43, 47, 49, 49, 49, 53, 54, 55, 56, 59, 60, 60, 62, 63, 64, 65, 69, 70, 71, 73, 75, 76, 77, 79, 80, 81; **7:**1, 2, 3, 4, 6, 7, 8, 10, 11, 12, 13, 14, 15, 16, 18, 19, 21, 21, 22, 23, 23, 24, 24, 27, 28, 28, 28, 28, 28, 29, 30, 31, 32, 33, 34, 35, 37, 38, 39, 40; **8:**2, 5, 6, 7, 7, 8, 10, 11, 12, 12, 13, 13, 16, 18, 21, 25, 27, 28, 30, 32, 33, 35, 36, 38, 39, 40, 40; **9:**2, 3, 3, 5, 9, 12, 13, 16, 17, 19, 20, 21, 22, 22, 23, 24, 26, 28, 29, 29, 30, 31, 32, 34, 36, 37, 39, 41, 42, 44, 44; **10:**2, 2, 2, 3, 3, 4, 4, 4, 4, 5, 6, 7, 7, 7, 7, 8, 9, 9, 10, 12, 12, 12, 13, 14; **11:**1, 2, 4, 6, 7, 9, 9, 13, 14, 14, 16, 18, 21, 22, 22, 23, 23, 23, 25, 44, 46, 47; **12:**2, 3, 3, 4, 4, 5, 6, 7, 8, 8, 8, 14, 15, 15, 16, 17, 17, 18, 18, 18, 18, 19, 19, 19, 20, 21, 24, 32, 33, 33, 34, 34, 37, 37, 39, 40, 40, 40, 40; **13:**1, 2, 2, 2, 2, 6, 7, 8, 8, 8, 9, 10, 12, 14, 14; **14:**1, 2, 2, 3, 3, 7, 8, 9, 11, 11, 13, 14, 14, 16, 17; **15:**1, 2, 4, 11, 11, 11, 12, 14, 16, 16, 17, 18, 18, 19, 20, 21, 23, 24, 24, 25, 25, 26, 26, 27, 28, 28, 28, 29; **16:**1, 1, 3, 3, 4, 4, 5, 5, 6, 7, 8, 11, 11, 12, 16, 20, 22, 27, 27, 28, 29, 30, 31, 32, 32, 35, 35, 35, 36, 36, 37, 38, 39, 40, 41, 42, 42, 43; **17:**4, 6, 7, 8, 9, 10, 10, 11, 12, 13, 14, 14, 15, 16, 16, 16, 17, 19, 19, 21, 22, 23, 23, 24, 24, 24, 26, 27, 27; **18:**1, 1, 2, 2, 4, 6, 6, 8, 8, 8, 10, 10, 10, 11, 11, 13, 14, 16; **19:**1, 3, 4, 4, 6, 6, 6, 7, 7, 8, 10, 12, 12, 13, 14, 15, 15, 17, 17, 18, 19; **20:**1, 1, 2, 2, 2, 3, 3, 3, 4, 6, 7, 8; **21:**1, 2, 2, 5, 5, 6, 7, 8, 10, 10, 11, 12, 14, 15, 15, 16, 16, 16, 16, 17, 17, 17, 20, 20, 21, 23, 23, 23, 24, 26, 26, 26, 29; **22:**1, 2, 3, 3, 4, 5, 5, 5, 6, 8, 9, 9, 9, 10, 10, 11, 12, 12, 13, 13, 14, 14, 14, 15, 15, 16, 16, 16, 16, 18, 18, 19; **23:**2, 3, 4, 5, 6, 7, 8, 9, 10, 11, 11, 12, 13, 13, 13, 15, 19, 20, 21, 21, 23, 25, 26, 28, 28, 29, 29, 30, 30, 30, 31, 32, 32, 32; **24:**1, 2, 2, 2, 3, 4, 5, 6, 6, 6, 6, 6, 23, 26, 27, 30, 31, 31; **25:**1, 1, 1, 1, 2, 3, 3, 4, 5, 6, 6, 7, 7, 9, 9, 9, 9, 10, 10, 11, 11, 12, 12, 13, 13, 14, 14, 15, 15, 16, 16, 17, 17, 18, 18, 19, 19, 20, 20, 21, 21, 22, 22, 23, 23, 24, 24, 25, 25, 26, 26, 27, 27, 28, 28, 29, 29, 30, 30, 31, 31; **26:**3, 5, 7, 7, 8, 9, 11, 11, 12, 14, 15, 16, 16, 17, 18, 19, 20, 22, 23, 25, 26, 26, 26, 26, 28, 28, 29, 29, 30, 30, 31, 32, 32, 32, 32; **27:**1, 1, 1, 3, 4, 16, 25, 27, 28, 32, 34; **28:**1, 1, 1, 2, 2, 2, 3, 4, 4, 5, 6, 6, 7, 7, 8, 9, 9, 9, 9, 9, 9, 10, 11, 11, 12, 13, 13, 13, 14, 15, 15, 15, 16, 17, 17, 18, 20, 20, 21, 21, 21; **29:**1, 1, 2, 2, 2, 3, 3, 4, 5, 5, 6, 6, 7, 9, 9, 10, 11, 11, 11, 12, 12, 12, 12, 13, 14, 14, 15, 17, 17, 17, 18, 19, 19, 20, 20, 20, 20, 21, 21, 22, 22, 22, 23, 23, 24, 25, 25, 25, 27, 28, 29, 30, 30, 30; **2Ch 1:**1, 2, 2, 2, 5, 5, 6, 7, 7, 8, 8, 10, 11, 11, 11, 12, 12, 12, 13, 14, 14, 15, 15, 16, 17, 17; **2:**1, 2, 4, 4, 4, 4, 7, 7, 7, 7, 8, 9, 10, 12, 12, 12, 14, 14, 14, 14, 14, 14, 15, 16, 17, 18; **3:**3, 4, 5, 5, 6, 7, 7, 8, 10, 11, 13, 14, 14, 16, 16, 17, 17; **4:**1, 2, 3, 4, 5, 5, 6, 6, 7, 7, 8, 8, 9, 9, 11, 15, 16, 17, 20, 21, 22, 22; **5:**1, 1, 2, 5, 6, 6, 7, 8, 12, 12, 12, 12, 12, 13, 13, 13, 13; **6:**3, 6, 10, 11, 13, 13, 13, 13, 14, 14, 14, 15, 16, 16, 19, 19, 20, 21, 21, 21, 22, 23, 23, 23, 24, 24, 24, 25, 25, 26, 26, 26, 26, 27, 27, 29, 30, 31, 32, 32, 32, 32, 33, 33, 34, 34, 35, 36, 36, 36, 37, 37, 38, 38, 38, 39, 41, 41, 41; **7:**1, 1, 1, 3, 3, 3, 4, 5, 5, 5, 6, 7, 7, 9, 10, 10, 10, 12, 12, 14, 14, 14, 14, 14, 16, 16, 17, 17, 19, 19, 19, 19, 21, 21, 22, 22; **8:**1, 1, 2, 3, 4, 5, 5, 6, 6, 6, 6, 6, 7, 8, 9, 11, 13, 13, 14, 14, 15, 15, 17, 18, 18; **9:**1, 1, 3, 4, 4, 4, 5, 6, 8, 8, 8, 9, 9, 10, 10, 11, 11, 11, 12, 12, 14, 14, 14, 17, 18, 21, 22, 23, 24, 24, 25, 25, 26, 27, 28, 29, 29; **10:**3, 3, 4, 7, 7, 8, 8, 10, 12, 14, 16, 18; **11:**1, 1, 3, 3, 4, 5, 10, 10, 11, 11, 12, 12, 13, 14, 14, 14, 14, 15, 17, 17, 17, 18, 19, 20, 21, 21, 21, 21, 23, 23, 23; **12:**1, 1, 3, 3, 4, 5, 6, 6, 7, 9, 9, 10, 11, 12, 12, 13, 13, 15, 15; **13:**2, 4, 4, 5, 7, 7, 9, 9, 9, 9, 10, 10, 11, 11, 11, 12, 14, 15, 15, 15, 15, 16, 17, 19, 19, 19, 20, 20, 21, 21, 21, 22; **14:**2, 3, 3, 4, 4, 7, 7, 7, 7, 8, 8, 9, 12, 12, 13, 13, 13, 13, 14, 15, 15; **15:**2, 2, 3, 4, 4, 6, 7, 7, 8, 8, 8, 8, 9, 9, 11, 11, 12, 14, 15, 15, 16, 18, 18, 18; **16:**1, 2, 2, 3, 3, 4, 4, 6, 6, 7, 8, 8, 8, 8, 11, 14, 14; **17:**2, 2, 3, 4, 5, 6, 7, 8, 8, 9, 11, 11, 11, 12, 12, 12, 13, 17; **18:**1, 1, 2, 2, 3, 3, 3, 5, 8, 8, 9, 10, 11, 12, 14, 16, 18, 19, 20, 21, 21, 21, 23, 24, 25, 25, 26, 26, 28, 29, 31, 33, 34; **19:**2, 3, 6, 7, 8, 8, 8, 9, 10, 10, 11; **20:**1, 2, 3, 5, 6, 7, 8, 9, 9, 10, 10, 10, 13, 15, 17, 17, 18, 18, 19, 20, 20, 20, 20, 21, 22, 22, 23, 23, 25, 25, 26, 28, 28, 31, 33, 37; **21:**2, 3, 3, 4, 5, 6, 7, 8, 9, 9, 11, 11, 13, 13, 14, 16, 17, 17, 19, 20; **22:**2, 4, 5, 6, 8, 9, 11, 11; **23:**1, 1, 2, 2, 4, 5, 6, 6, 7, 8, 9, 9, 10, 11, 11, 11, 11, 12, 13, 13, 13, 13, 13, 14, 15, 15, 16, 16, 17, 17, 17, 17, 18, 18, 20, 20, 20, 21; **24:**1, 3, 3, 4, 5, 5, 5, 6, 6, 6, 7, 8, 9, 10, 10, 10, 11, 11, 11, 12, 12, 12, 13, 13, 14, 14, 14, 14, 14, 16, 17, 17, 18, 18, 18, 20, 20, 21, 22, 22, 23, 23, 26, 27; **25:**1, 5, 5, 5, 5, 7, 10, 10, 11, 12, 12, 13, 13, 14, 15, 16, 16, 17, 17, 18, 19, 22, 22, 23, 24, 24, 24, 26, 27, 27, 28; **26:**2, 3, 5, 6, 6, 6, 7, 8, 9, 10, 10, 10, 10, 11, 11, 14, 15, 15, 15, 15, 16, 18, 19, 20, 20, 21, 23; **27:**1, 3, 4, 4, 5, 5, 7, 7, 8, 9; **28:**1, 2, 4, 4, 4, 5, 5, 7, 8, 8, 9, 9, 9, 10, 10, 11, 12, 12, 13, 13, 14, 14, 15, 15, 15, 15, 15, 17, 18, 18, 18, 18, 19, 21, 21, 22, 23, 24, 24, 26, 26; **29:**1, 3, 4, 5, 6, 6, 7, 7, 8, 8, 9, 9, 9, 11, 11, 12, 12, 12, 13, 13, 14, 14, 15, 16, 17, 18, 18, 19, 19, 20, 21, 21, 22, 22, 22,

22, 23, 24, 24, 25, 25, 26, 27, 28, 29, 30, 30, 30, 31, 31, 31, 32, 33, 34, 35, 36, 36; **30:**1, 1, 1, 2, 3, 4, 6, 6, 7, 7, 9, 9, 9, 10, 10, 10, 11, 11, 12, 13, 13, 14, 14, 15, 15, 18, 18, 20, 20, 21, 22, 24, 24, 24, 25, 27, 27; **31:**1, 1, 1, 1, 1, 2, 2, 2, 2, 2, 3, 3, 3, 4, 5, 5, 5, 6, 6, 6, 6, 7, 8, 8, 8, 9, 10, 10, 11, 12, 13, 13, 14, 15, 15, 17, 17, 17, 18, 18, 19, 20, 21, 21; **32:**3, 3, 4, 5, 5, 5, 5, 6, 7, 8, 9, 11, 12, 12, 12, 13, 16, 16, 20, 21, 21, 21, 22, 22, 23, 24, 25, 25, 25, 26, 27, 27, 27, 27, 28, 28, 28, 28, 29, 29, 30, 30, 31, 32, 32, 33, 33; **33:**1, 3, 3, 6, 6, 6, 7, 7, 7, 8, 9, 10, 11, 11, 12, 13, 13, 13, 14, 14, 15, 15, 15, 16, 16, 18, 19, 19, 19, 19, 21, 22, 24, 25; **34:**1, 2, 3, 3, 3, 4, 4, 4, 5, 5, 6, 7, 7, 7, 8, 8, 9, 9, 10, 11, 11, 11, 11, 12, 12, 12, 13, 16, 17, 20, 21, 21, 21, 22, 22, 23, 24, 25, 25, 25, 26, 27, 27, 27, 27, 28, 28, 29, 30, 30, 30, 30, 31, 31, 31, 32, 32, 33, 33; **35:**2, 3, 3, 3, 3, 4, 5, 6, 7, 7, 8, 8, 8, 8, 9, 9, 9, 9, 9, 9, 10, 11, 13, 13, 13, 14, 14, 15, 15, 17, 18, 18, 18, 20, 20, 21, 22, 23, 24, 24, 24, 25, 25, 26, 27; **36:**1, 3, 4, 4, 5, 6, 6, 6, 7, 8, 8, 9, 10, 10, 11, 12, 13, 14, 14, 15, 16, 16, 17, 17, 17, 18, 18, 18, 19, 20, 20, 22; **Ezr 1:**1, 3, 4, 4, 5, 5, 5, 6, 6, 6, 7, 8, 11; **2:**1, 2, 6, 25, 26, 28, 33, 40, 42, 54, 57, 58, 59, 60, 61, 61, 65, 65, 67, 69, 69, 70; **3:**2, 3, 5, 5, 7, 7, 7, 7, 7, 8, 8, 9, 9, 9, 10, 10, 11, 12, 12, 13; **4:**1, 2, 2, 3, 4, 5, 5, 6, 7, 7, 7, 8, 9, 9, 9, 10, 10, 10, 12, 12, 13, 13, 14, 15, 16, 17, 17, 18, 19, 19, 20, 20, 20, 23, 23, 24; **5:**1, 1, 2, 2, 2, 3, 3, 3, 3, 5, 6, 8, 8, 9, 10, 11, 11, 12, 14, 14, 14, 15, 16, 17; **6:**3, 5, 5, 5, 6, 6, 7, 7, 9, 9, 9, 10, 10, 11, 11, 12, 13, 13, 14, 14, 14, 14, 16, 17, 17, 18, 20, 20, 20, 21, 22; **7:**6, 7, 9, 10, 10, 10, 11, 11, 11, 13, 14, 14, 15, 16, 16, 17, 17, 18, 21, 22, 23, 25, 25, 26, 28, 28, 28; **8:**1, 3, 4, 5, 6, 7, 8, 9, 10, 11, 12, 13, 14, 15, 15, 16, 16, 17, 17, 18, 18, 19, 19, 20, 21, 21, 21, 21, 22, 22, 23, 23, 24, 25, 25, 26, 28, 28, 28, 29, 30, 31, 31, 31, 31, 33, 33, 33, 33, 34, 34, 35, 36, 36; **9:**1, 1, 1, 1, 2, 2, 3, 3, 4, 4, 6, 7, 7, 7, 8, 9, 9, 10, 12, 12, 12, 13, 14; **10:**1, 1, 1, 1, 3, 3, 4, 5, 5, 5, 5, 6, 7, 8, 8, 9, 9, 9, 10, 11, 11, 12, 14, 15, 15, 15, 18, 18, 19, 20, 21, 22, 23, 24, 25, 26, 27, 28, 29, 30, 32, 33, 37, 42, 43, 44; **Ne 1:**2, 3, 3, 4, 4, 5, 5, 6, 6, 6, 7, 9, 10; **2:**3, 5, 6, 8, 8, 8, 9, 10, 13, 13, 14, 15, 16, 17, 17, 18, 19; **3:**1, 1, 1, 2, 3, 3, 4, 4, 4, 6, 6, 6, 7, 7, 10, 11, 12, 13, 13, 14, 14, 15, 15, 15, 16, 21, 23, 23, 24, 25, 26, 26, 27, 29, 30, 31, 32; **4:**1, 2, 2, 4, 7, 7, 7, 7, 8, 8, 9, 9, 11, 11, 12, 12, 12, 13, 14, 14, 14, 14, 14, 15, 16, 17, 19, 19, 19, 21, 21, 22; **5:**1, 3, 4, 4, 5, 5, 5, 7, 8, 10, 10, 11, 11, 12, 12, 12, 13, 13, 13, 13, 15, 16, 16, 18, 18, 19; **6:**1, 1, 2, 3, 4, 6, 6, 6, 7, 9, 10, 10, 12, 13, 13, 14, 14, 14, 16, 16, 17, 17, 18, 19, 19; **7:**1, 1, 3, 3, 3, 4, 4, 6, 7, 11, 26, 29, 30, 32, 37, 43, 45, 56, 59, 60, 61, 62, 63, 63, 67, 67, 69, 70, 71, 72; **8:**2, 2, 3, 4, 4, 6, 6, 7, 8, 9, 9, 10, 10, 10, 10, 10, 11, 12, 12, 12, 13, 13, 15, 15, 16, 16, 16, 17; **9:**1, 1, 2, 3, 4, 5, 5, 6, 6, 6, 6, 6, 7, 7, 8, 8, 8, 9, 9, 10, 10, 11, 12, 13, 13, 13, 13, 14, 14, 15, 15, 16, 16, 17, 17, 17, 17, 17, 18, 18, 19, 20, 21, 22, 22, 22, 23, 24, 24, 25, 25, 25, 25, 25, 25, 26, 26, 27, 28, 29, 29, 29, 31, 32, 32, 32, 32, 32, 32, 32, 32, 33, 34, 34, 37, 37, 38, 38, 38; **10:**1, 8, 10, 13, 27, 28, 28, 29, 31, 31, 33, 33, 33, 34, 36, 36, 37, 37, 37, 37, 38, 38, 39, 39, 39, 39; **11:**1, 2, 3, 4, 5, 8, 8, 8, 11, 13, 14, 16, 17, 19, 20, 21, 25, 28, 30, 30, 30, 31, 35; **12:**1, 1, 7, 7, 8, 9, 22, 22, 24, 24, 25, 25, 26, 26, 26, 27, 27, 28, 28, 29, 29, 30, 30, 31, 32, 35, 36, 36, 37, 39, 39, 39, 41, 42, 42, 42, 42, 43, 43, 44, 44, 44, 44, 45, 45, 45, 45, 46, 46, 47, 47; **13:**4, 5, 5, 5, 5, 7, 8, 9, 9, 10, 11, 11, 12, 12, 13, 13, 13, 13, 14, 15, 15, 15, 16, 16, 18, 20, 21, 21, 22, 22, 23, 24, 25, 25, 26, 26, 27, 29, 29, 29, 30, 30, 31; **Est 1:**3, 3, 3, 4, 5, 5, 6, 6, 6, 7, 10, 12, 13, 14, 14, 14, 16, 16, 18, 18, 19, 19, 21, 22; **2:**1, 1, 5, 5, 6, 7, 7, 7, 8, 9, 9, 9, 9, 10, 11, 12, 14, 14, 15, 17, 18, 18, 19, 20, 21, 21, 22, 22, 23; **3:**7, 7, 8, 8, 9, 10, 11, 12, 12, 12, 13, 13, 13, 13, 14, 15, 15; **4:**1, 1, 1, 3, 3, 3, 3, 4, 4, 5, 5, 7, 8, 8, 8, 10, 11, 14, 16, 16, 16, 16, 17; **5:**1, 2, 4, 4, 5, 5, 6, 7, 8, 10, 10, 11, 11, 11, 11, 12, 12, 12, 12, 14, 14, 14; **6:**2, 6, 9, 10, 10, 10, 11, 11, 12, 13; **7:**1, 2, 3, 3, 3, 4, 4, 6, 7, 8, 10; **8:**2, 2, 3, 4, 5, 5, 6, 6, 7, 7, 8, 8, 8, 9, 9, 9, 10, 11, 11, 11, 13, 15, 15, 15, 15, 15, 16, 16, 17, 17, 17, 17, 17; **9:**3, 3, 4, 4, 5, 5, 5, 9, 12, 12, 12, 13, 13, 14, 15, 17, 18, 18, 19, 19, 20, 20, 22, 22, 22, 22, 23, 24, 24, 25, 25, 26, 27, 27, 28, 28, 28, 30, 31, 31, 31, 32; **10:**2, 2, 3; **Job 1:**1, 2, 3, 3, 4, 4, 5, 5, 5, 6, 7, 7, 8, 10, 10, 11, 13, 15, 16, 16, 17, 18, 19, 19, 20, 20, 21, 21; **2:**1, 2, 2, 3, 3, 5, 7, 9, 10, 11, 11, 11, 12, 13, 13; **3:**1, 3, 4, 5, 5, 13, 14, 15, 17, 19, 19, 20, 21; **4:**2, 5, 7, 8, 10, 11, 14, 16, 17, 18, 19; **5:**2, 5, 6, 8, 11, 11, 16, 16, 19, 21, 22, 23, 27; **6:**2, 5, 6, 9, 16, 18, 19, 21, 30; **7:**1, 3, 4, 5, 6, 7, 9, 13, 15, 18, 21, 21; **8:**5, 6, 6, 7, 9, 19, 21, 22; **9:**4, 6, 7, 8, 9, 13, 14, 16, 16, 17, 22, 24, 24, 27, 30, 31, 34; **10:**3, 8, 10, 11, 11, 11, 12, 14, 15, 15, 16, 16, 17, 17, 21, 22; **11:**4, 9, 10, 11, 13, 14, 15, 18, 19; **12:**2, 3, 4, 4, 6, 6, 7, 7, 8, 10, 12, 13, 13, 16, 16, 20, 21, 23, 23, 24; **13:**7, 13, 13, 14, 20, 21, 22, 22, 23, 26; **14:**1, 2, 3, 5, 7, 8, 9, 10, 11, 12, 13, 14, 15, 15, 17, 18, 18, 19, 20, 20, 22; **15:**2, 13, 16, 18, 21, 24, 27, 29, 30, 32, 35, 35; **16:**4, 6, 7, 8, 9, 9, 10, 12, 13, 14, 15, 17, 21; **17:**1, 7, 9, 9, 9, 10, 12, 13, 14, 14, 14; **18:**11, 12, 14, 16; **19:**4, 8, 9, 10, 13, 14, 20, 20, 24, 25, 26; **20:**5, 6, 8, 17, 19, 22, 25, 27; **21:**3, 5, 7, 8, 9, 12, 14, 15, 17, 17, 23, 28, 29, 30, 33; **22:**4, 6, 7, 8, 9, 10, 11, 14, 16, 19, 21, 22, 23, 24, 26, 27, 27, 28, 29; **23:**2, 3, 4, 5, 7, 10, 11, 13; **24:**1, 3, 3, 5, 6, 8, 11, 12, 14, 16, 19, 24; **25:**2, 4, 5; **26:**7, 8, 10, 13; **27:**4, 8, 16, 17, 20, 21, 23; **28:**1, 2, 3, 4, 6, 9, 10, 11, 17, 18, 22, 25, 26, 27, 27, 28; **29:**3, 5, 6, 7, 8, 9, 12, 13, 13, 14, 14, 15, 16, 17, 20, 21, 22, 25, 25; **30:**3, 3, 3, 4, 5, 6, 6, 9, 10, 13, 15, 16, 19, 20, 22, 23, 27, 28, 29, 30, 31; **31:**4, 8, 15, 17, 18, 19, 25, 27, 34, 34, 35, 38, 40; **32:**2, 6, 6, 10, 13, 18, 18, 22; **33:**4, 5, 6, 7, 10, 11, 12, 14, 16, 19, 20, 21, 24, 25, 26, 26, 28, 31, 33; **34:**14, 15, 16, 18, 18, 19, 24, 25, 32, 34, 37; **35:**4, 5, 6, 8, 11, 12, 12, 14; **36:**2, 5, 7, 8, 8, 10, 11, 12, 16, 19, 27, 28, 29, 30; **37:**3, 6, 9, 11, 12, 14, 15, 16, 17, 17, 23; **38:**3, 5, 6, 7, 9, 9, 11, 12, 14, 15, 16, 19, 21, 22, 23, 27, 30, 33, 34, 35, 36, 39; **39:**3, 4, 7, 11, 21, 23, 23, 24, 25, 26; **40:**7, 8, 9, 10, 16, 24; **41:**8, 10, 11, 12, 13, 19, 23, 23, 27, 29; **42:**2, 3, 4, 4, 6, 6, 7, 8, 8, 8, 8, 9, 9, 11, 11, 11, 11, 11, 11, 12, 13, 14, 15, 16; **Ps 1:**2, 3; **2:**2, 3, 8, 9, 11, 12; **3:**3, 4, 5; **4:**1, 4, 5, 7, 8; **5:**2, 3, 6, 8; **6:**4, 10; **7:**6, 9, 10, 12, 13, 14, 15; **8:**2, 3, 3, 5, 5, 7, 7, 8; **9:**3, 5, 8; **10:**2, 3, 7, 7, 9, 10, 14, 14, 16, 17, 18; **11:**2, 3, 5, 6, 7; **12:**2, 3, 5, 8; **13:**3; **14:**1, 7; **15:**2, 4, 4, 5; **16:**9, 11; **17:**3, 3, 4, 6, 11, 13, 14; **18:**T, 2, 2, 7, 9, 12, 14, 14, 15, 16, 17, 37, 40, 45, 48, 50; **19:**4, 6, 13, 14, 14; **20:**2, 3, 4, 6, 7, 8, 8; **21:**3, 4, 5, 5, 12, 13; **22:**4, 5, 5, 6, 6, 7, 9, 11, 14, 15, 16, 17, 18, 21, 22, 24, 26, 27, 29; **23:**4, 4, 6, 6; **24:**1, 1, 2, 4, 4, 5, 6, 7, 8, 9; **25:**5, 6, 8, 10, 10, 13, 16, 16, 18, 19, 21; **26:**2, 2, 3, 5, 7, 10, 12; **27:**1, 2, 2, 4, 6, 7, 8, 8, 10, 12, 14; **28:**1, 5, 7, 8, 9; **29:**1, 6, 9; **30:**2, 7, 10, 11, 12; **31:**2, 3, 7, 9, 11, 13, 18, 22, 24; **32:**3, 3, 4, 5, 5, 8, 9, 11; **33:**3, 4, 5, 5, 6, 6, 7, 8, 10, 13, 19; **34:**4, 6, 7, 8, 11, 11, 12, 14, 19, 21; **35:**2, 2, 3, 3, 4, 6, 10, 10, 13, 16, 17, 23, 26, 26, 28, 28; **36:**3, 6; **37:**3, 3, 4, 5, 6, 7, 11, 14, 14, 15, 16, 16, 18, 21, 25, 26, 27, 27, 28, 29, 35, 37, 40; **38:**2, 5, 6, 7, 8, 10, 11, 14, 20; **39:**1, 3, 4, 6, 7, 13; **40:**1, 1, 2, 2, 3, 7, 10, 10, 11, 13, 14, 16, 17, 17; **41:**2, 2, 3, 3, 5, 6, 13; **42:**2, 3, 4, 5, 7, 8, 11; **43:**3, 5; **44:**2, 3, 4, 8,

10, 13, 19, 24, 26; **45:**4, 6, 7, 8, 10, 17; **46:**1, 2, 3, 6, 6, 9, 9, 10; **47:**1; **48:**1, 4, 5, 12, 13, 14, 14; **49:**2, 2, 3, 4, 6, 9, 10, 16, 18, 19; **50:**3, 4, 10, 11, 12, 15, 15, 16, 17, 18, 19, 20, 21, 22; **51:**3, 4, 4, 7, 7, 11, 12, 13, 17, 18, 19, 19; **52:**3, 5, 5, 6, 6, 7, 7, 8; **53:**1, 6; **54:**T, 1, 5, 7; **55:**2, 3, 5, 6, 9, 9, 10, 11, 11, 13, 16, 17, 17, 18, 19, 22, 22, 23; **56:**2, 12; **57:**T, 3, 4, 4, 8; **58:**3, 9; **59:**4, 10, 11, 12; **60:**T, T, T, 1, 2, 5, 7, 7, 8; **61:**7; **62:**2, 6, 7, 10, 11; **63:**1, 2, 2, 10; **64:**4, 5, 6, 10, 10; **65:**2, 6, 7, 9, 9, 10, 10, 12, 13, 13; **66:**5, 6, 8, 9, 11, 12, 15, 15, 16, 16, 20; **67:**1, 4, 6, 7; **68:**1, 4, 6, 6, 8, 10, 11, 12, 13, 23, 24, 27, 27, 35; **69:**2, 2, 3, 7, 10, 12, 14, 16, 18, 19, 19, 20, 20, 22, 23, 23, 25, 27, 29, 30, 31, 32, 34, 34, 35, 35, 36; **70:**1, 2, 4, 5, 5; **71:**2, 3, 7, 9, 11, 13, 13, 14, 16, 17, 18, 20, 21, 23, 24; **72:**1, 3, 4, 8, 10, 10, 11, 13, 13, 14, 15, 17, 19; **73:**2, 4, 6, 8, 9, 10, 10, 13, 17, 18, 22, 26, 28; **74:**2, 6, 11, 13, 14, 15, 15, 16, 16, 17, 17, 20, 21, 22; **75:**3, 7, 8; **76:**3, 3, 4, 6, 8, 9, 11, 12; **77:**3, 6, 10, 14, 15, 16, 17, 18, 20; **78:**3, 4, 7, 8, 9, 10, 13, 14, 20, 24, 26, 28, 31, 33, 34, 38, 38, 40, 41, 42, 45, 47, 49, 56, 57, 59, 64, 66, 69, 71, 71, 72; **79:**1, 4, 9, 13; **80:**2, 4, 5, 8, 9, 9, 13, 14, 14, 16; **81:**2, 7, 10, 12; **82:**3, 3, 4, 5, 6, 8; **83:**1, 6, 6, 7, 7, 7, 8, 9, 10, 11, 11, 14, 17; **84:**2, 3, 3, 3, 7, 11, 11; **85:**7, 10, 10, 11; **86:**1, 2, 7, 9, 9, 9, 10, 14, 15, 15, 16, 17; **87:**4, 4, 4, 5, 5; **88:**1, 3, 5, 10, 15, 15, 18; **89:**1, 11, 12, 12, 14, 14, 18, 19, 21, 23, 24, 24, 25, 26, 26, 28, 30, 31, 32, 35, 40, 42, 43, 44, 45, 47, 52; **90:**2, 6, 6, 8, 10, 10, 17, 17; **91:**2, 3, 4, 13, 13, 15, 16; **92:**3, 3, 5, 7, 12, 14; **93:**1; **94:**6, 6, 7, 12, 15, 18, 19, 21; **95:**4, 6, 10; **96:**6, 6, 7, 8, 10, 11, 11, 12, 13; **97:**2, 2, 3, 4, 8, 8, 10, 11, 12; **98:**1, 2, 3, 4, 5, 6, 7, 7, 9; **99:**3, 4, 6, 6, 7, 7, 9; **100:**3, 4, 5; **101:**1, 3, 4, 5, 7, 8; **102:**2, 3, 4, 5, 8, 10, 10, 13, 13, 14, 15, 21, 22, 25, 26; **103:**2, 3, 4, 4, 6, 7, 8, 8, 13, 15, 16, 21; **104:**1, 8, 11, 12, 13, 15, 17, 18, 19, 20, 25, 25, 26, 28, 29; **105:**1, 4, 4, 5, 9, 13, 15, 18, 20, 22, 24, 25, 27, 31, 32, 33, 33, 34, 36, 37, 39, 40, 41, 41, 44, 45; **106:**3, 6, 8, 9, 10, 11, 16, 17, 17, 23, 23, 25, 30, 33, 35, 36, 37, 38, 39, 40, 41, 42, 43, 43, 44, 45, 46, 47, 47; **107:**3, 3, 4, 5, 6, 8, 9, 10, 12, 13, 14, 15, 18, 19, 20, 21, 22, 25, 26, 27, 27, 28, 29, 31, 32, 33, 36, 37, 38, 39, 39, 41, 42; **108:**2, 6, 8, 8, 9; **109:**1, 2, 3, 5, 9, 11, 16, 16, 19, 21, 22, 22, 24, 24; **110:**4, 6; **111:**3, 4, 7, 7, 8; **112:**3, 4, 5, 8, 8, 9; **113:**2, 6, 7, 7; **114:**2, 3; **115:**1, 3, 4, 8, 12, 12, 13, 14, 15, 18; **116:**1, 2, 3, 6, 9, 16, 17; **118:**5, 5, 11, 14, 15, 19, 19, 20, 21, 23, 24, 27, 28, 28; **119:**2, 3, 9, 15, 16, 17, 22, 23, 26, 27, 34, 37, 44, 46, 48, 55, 59, 66, 68, 70, 72, 79, 83, 93, 105, 106, 108, 114, 117, 121, 124, 132, 137, 141, 142, 143, 147, 151, 153, 157, 163, 165, 167, 168, 174, 175, 176; **120:**1, 2, 4; **121:**2, 3, 4, 7, 8, 8; **122:**2, 7, 8; **123:**4; **124:**7, 8; **125:**2, 2, 2, 5, 5; **126:**2, 2; **128:**3, 3, 6, 6; **129:**8; **130:**7; **131:**2, 3; **132:**1, 8, 12, 15; **133:**2, 3; **134:**2, 3; **135:**6, 6, 7, 8, 9, 9, 10, 11, 14, 15, 18; **136:**9, 9, 12, 15, 20; **137:**1, 9; **138:**2; **139:**1, 3, 3, 5, 10, 11, 12, 13, 14, 18, 23, 23, 24; **140:**2; **141:**2, 3, 5, 6, 7; **142:**2, 3, 4; **143:**1, 7, 12; **144:**1, 2, 2, 5, 6, 6, 7, 14; **145:**1, 1, 1, 2, 5, 8, 10, 12, 12, 14, 16, 19, 21, 21; **146:**4, 6, 6, 7, 9; **147:**1, 2, 4, 8, 9, 13, 14, 18, 19; **148:**3, 5, 6, 8, 8, 8, 9, 9, 10, 10, 11, 11, 12, 12, 13; **149:**3, 6, 7, 8; **150:**3, 4, 4; **Pr 1:**2, 2, 3, 3, 4, 5, 5, 6, 7, 9, 11, 11, 13, 21, 23, 23, 25, 27, 27, 29, 30, 32, 33; **2:**1, 2, 3, 5, 6, 8, 9, 9, 10, 13, 14, 15, 17, 20, 21, 22; **3:**2, 3, 4, 4, 6, 7, 8, 9, 10, 11, 13, 14, 16, 16, 20, 21, 22, 22, 23, 24, 28; **4:**1, 4, 5, 6, 7, 8, 10, 10, 11, 15, 17, 22, 25, 26; **5:**2, 3, 6, 9, 10, 12, 14, 22; **6:**2, 3, 6, 11, 12, 13, 13, 20, 23, 24, 26, 27, 28, 33, 34; **7:**2, 7, 10, 12, 13, 13, 14, 15, 17, 20, 24; **8:**2, 7, 8, 10, 12, 13, 14, 14, 15, 16, 18, 25, 26, 26, 29, 31, 31, 32, 33, 35; **9:**2, 5, 6, 9, 9, 11, 13, 13; **10:**9, 19, 22; **11:**11, 16, 24, 25, 28, 30, 31; **12:**4, 7, 24, 24; **13:**4, 5, 9, 12, 16, 18; **14:**6, 9, 10, 16, 17, 22; **15:**3, 4, 11; **16:**3, 6, 8, 8, 16, 18, 21, 24; **17:**2, 3, 15, 17, 25; **18:**3, 10, 18, 22; **19:**1, 1, 3, 9, 14, 15, 16, 17, 20, 20, 22, 23, 26, 29; **20:**9, 11, 12, 13, 15, 15, 28; **21:**3, 4, 5, 6, 7, 17, 18, 20, 21, 21, 22, 24; **22:**2, 3, 3, 4, 4, 6, 8, 10, 10, 11, 13, 20, 21, 25; **23:**3, 7, 8, 16, 19, 20, 22, 23, 23, 28, 31, 33, 35; **24:**2, 3, 4, 5, 11, 12, 12, 12, 13, 14, 15, 18, 21, 21, 22, 24, 29, 31, 32, 34; **25:**2, 4, 5, 14, 15, 22; **26:**3, 14, 19, 20, 27, 28; **27:**3, 4, 9, 12, 12, 20, 21, 22, 23, 24, 25, 26, 27, 27; **28:**2, 6, 6, 13, 16, 24; **29:**9, 13, 15, 17, 17, 22; **30:**1, 2, 4, 4, 6, 9, 9, 9, 10, 11, 12, 13, 17, 17, 20, 33; **31:**4, 5, 6, 7, 9, 9, 10, 11, 13, 13, 15, 16, 17, 20, 24, 25, 25, 26, 27, 28, 29, 30; **Ecc 1:**4, 5, 5, 6, 6, 6, 7, 8, 11, 12, 13, 16; **2:**4, 5, 7, 7, 7, 8, 8, 8, 8, 9, 12, 12, 14, 16, 16, 19, 19, 21, 23, 24, 24, 26, 26; **3:**2, 2, 3, 3, 4, 4, 5, 5, 6, 6, 7, 7, 8, 8, 12, 13, 13, 13, 14, 15, 17, 19, 19, 20, 21; **4:**1, 3, 5, 6, 8, 10, 11, 12, 12, 13, 14, 16, 16; **5:**1, 2, 2, 6, 6, 7, 8, 8, 8, 12, 14, 15, 16, 16, 17, 18, 19, 19, 19; **6:**2, 2, 2, 3, 3, 4, 5, 5, 6, 8, 12; **7:**2, 7, 15, 15, 20, 23, 24, 25, 25, 26; **8:**1, 3, 5, 6, 8, 10, 12, 14, 14, 15, 16; **9:**1, 2, 7, 11, 11, 11, 14, 14, 15; **10:**1, 2, 5, 6, 7, 9, 14, 16, 17, 18, 19, 19, 20; **11:**5, 6, 10; **12:**1, 2, 2, 2, 3, 3, 4, 4, 5, 5, 5, 6, 6, 7, 9, 10, 11, 12, 13; **SS 1:**2, 3, 5, 6, 8, 11, 17; **2:**3, 3, 5, 6, 7, 8, 10, 11, 11, 12, 13, 13, 14, 16, 17; **3:**2, 2, 3, 4, 5, 6, 6, 8, 10; **4:**2, 3, 6, 6, 8, 8, 11, 11, 14, 14, 14, 14, 16, 16; **5:**1, 1, 1, 4, 7, 10, 11, 11; **6:**2, 3, 6, 7, 8, 8, 9, 11; **7:**5, 7, 7, 8, 8, 9, 9, 11, 12, 12, 12, 13; **8:**1, 2, 3, 6, 9, 10, 10, 12; **Isa 1:**1, 1, 2, 3, 3, 4, 5, 6, 7, 7, 9, 10, 10, 11, 11, 13, 13, 13, 14, 16, 19, 20, 21, 23, 23, 25, 26, 26, 27, 31; **2:**1, 3, 3, 4, 4, 6, 7, 7, 8, 9, 10, 11, 13, 14, 15, 16, 18, 19, 20, 20, 21, 21; **3:**1, 1, 3, 4, 5, 8, 8, 9, 12, 14, 18, 19, 20, 22, 23, 24, 26; **4:**1, 1, 2, 2, 5, 5, 5, 6, 6; **5:**1, 2, 2, 2, 3, 5, 5, 6, 7, 12, 12, 13, 13, 14, 17, 19, 19, 20, 20, 20, 21, 24, 25, 26, 26, 28, 29, 29, 30; **6:**1, 2, 4, 5, 6, 7, 7, 8, 9, 10, 10, 10, 11, 11, 12, 13; **7:**1, 1, 1, 2, 3, 4, 5, 6, 6, 8, 8, 9, 11, 14, 15, 15, 16, 17, 17, 18, 18, 19, 19, 20, 20, 21, 22, 23, 25, 25; **8:**1, 2, 3, 3, 3, 4, 4, 5, 6, 6, 7, 8, 9, 10, 14, 14, 14, 15, 18, 19, 19, 21, 21, 21, 21, 21, 22, 22; **9:**1, 1, 1, 3, 4, 6, 7, 9, 9, 9, 12, 13, 14, 14, 15, 17, 17, 18, 19, 21; **10:**2, 2, 9, 10, 11, 12, 12, 13, 13, 14, 16, 17, 17, 18, 20, 25, 27, 29, 31, 33; **11:**2, 2, 2, 2, 4, 4, 5, 6, 6, 6, 6, 7, 7, 8, 9, 11, 13, 14, 14; **12:**2, 2; **13:**2, 3, 4, 5, 8, 9, 9, 11, 11, 13, 13, 16, 17, 18, 19, 20, 20, 21, 22; **14:**1, 1, 1, 2, 2, 3, 3, 5, 6, 7, 8, 9, 11, 11, 13, 14, 16, 16, 17, 17, 20, 21, 22, 23, 30, 32; **15:**1, 2, 2, 2, 4, 5, 6, 7, 9; **16:**4, 4, 5, 6, 8, 8, 9, 9, 9, 9, 14; **17:**2, 3, 7, 11, 11, 14; **18:**2, 2, 2, 6, 7, 7; **19:**3, 3, 5, 5, 6, 6, 7, 7, 8, 10, 11, 13, 19, 20, 21, 21, 21, 22, 22, 23, 23, 23, 24, 24; **20:**2, 2, 3, 3, 4, 4, 4, 5; **21:**2, 2, 2, 3, 5, 5, 7, 7, 9, 10, 12, 14, 15, 15; **22:**2, 5, 5, 7, 10, 12, 12, 13, 13, 13, 15, 17, 18, 18, 18, 20, 21, 21, 21, 22, 22, 24, 25; **23:**2, 3, 8, 9, 11, 13, 15, 16, 18; **24:**1, 2, 2, 2, 2, 2, 2, 3, 5, 6, 7, 7, 9, 14, 16, 17, 17, 18, 19, 19, 20, 21, 22, 23, 23, 23; **25:**1, 2, 4, 6, 8, 8, 9, 10, 10, 11, 12; **26:**5, 6, 7, 7, 9, 10, 14, 14, 14, 17, 19, 20; **27:**1, 3, 3, 4, 5, 5, 6, 6, 10, 10, 11, 11, 13; **28:**1, 2, 2, 3, 4, 5, 7, 7, 7, 10, 13, 13, 15, 15, 16, 17, 18, 19, 19, 21, 21, 24, 24, 25, 29; **29:**2, 2, 3, 3, 6, 6, 6, 6, 9, 9, 10, 13, 13, 14, 16, 17, 17, 18, 18, 20, 20, 21, 21, 23, 24; **30:**3, 4, 6, 6, 6, 8, 12, 12, 13, 13, 15, 15, 18, 20, 21, 21, 22, 23, 24, 25, 26, 26, 26, 28, 30, 30, 32, 32; **31:**1, 2, 3, 3, 4, 5, 5, 6, 7, 8, 8, 9; **32:**1, 2, 2, 2, 3, 4, 6, 8, 9, 10, 10, 11, 12, 13, 13, 14, 14, 14, 15, 15, 16, 17, 17, 19, 20; **33:**1, 2, 4, 5, 5, 6, 8, 9, 10, 10, 11, 12, 13, 15, 16, 17, 18, 20, 20, 22, 22, 24; **34:**1, 1, 3, 4, 5, 5, 6, 6, 7, 7, 9, 11, 11, 12, 13, 14, 15, 15, 15, 16, 16, 16, 17, 17; **35:**2, 2, 2, 3, 4, 5, 5, 6, 6, 6, 7, 7, 7, 8, 9, 10, 10, 10; **36:**1, 3, 5, 6, 7, 7, 9, 10, 11, 12, 12, 13, 16, 16, 17, 17, 19, 19, 21, 22, 22, 22; **37:**1, 1, 2, 2, 3, 4, 8, 8, 12, 13, 13, 14, 14, 15, 16, 17, 17, 19, 19, 19, 22, 22, 23, 24, 24, 25, 27, 28, 28, 29, 29, 30, 30, 30, 31, 31, 31, 33, 33, 35, 36, 37, 37, 38, 38; **38:**1, 2, 3, 3, 5, 5, 6, 6, 7, 14, 16, 16, 17, 21, 21, 22; **39:**1, 1, 2, 2, 2, 3, 8; **40:**2, 4, 4, 5, 7, 7, 8, 12, 17, 19, 22, 23, 24, 26, 29, 30, 31, 31; **41:**1, 2, 3, 4, 5, 7, 9, 11, 13, 16, 16, 17, 17, 17, 19, 20, 21, 23, 24, 25, 25, 25, 25; **42:**1, 4, 5, 5, 5, 5, 6, 6, 7, 9, 13, 14, 15, 15, 15, 16, 18, 20, 21, 22, 22, 23, 24, 25, 25; **43:**2, 3, 4, 5, 5, 6, 6, 6, 10, 10, 10, 11, 12, 14, 15, 17, 17, 20, 21, 23, 23, 24, 25, 25, 26, 28, 28; **44:**2, 3, 3, 3, 5, 6, 6, 7, 11, 12, 12, 12, 13, 13, 14, 15, 15, 15, 15, 15, 16, 17, 17, 18, 18, 19, 19, 21, 23, 23, 23, 24, 24, 26, 27, 28; **45:**2, 2, 3, 4, 6, 7, 7, 8, 8, 10, 11, 12, 13, 13, 13, 14, 14, 14, 14, 15, 16, 17, 18, 18, 18, 19, 19, 20, 20, 21, 21, 23, 23, 24, 24, 24, 25; **46:**1, 2, 2, 3, 4, 4, 6, 6, 6, 7, 7, 9, 9, 11, 11, 13; **47:**1, 1, 2, 2, 3, 3, 5, 6, 8, 8, 9, 10, 10, 11, 11, 13, 13, 15, 15; **48:**1, 1, 2, 3, 3, 4, 5, 6, 6, 8, 9, 9, 12, 13, 14, 15, 16, 16, 16, 17, 18, 20, 21; **49:**3, 4, 5, 5, 6, 7, 7, 8, 8, 9, 10, 11, 12, 12, 13, 17, 18, 20, 21, 23, 23, 25, 25, 26; **50:**1, 1, 2, 2, 4, 5, 6, 6, 7, 10, 10, 11; **51:**2, 3, 3, 4, 5, 5, 6, 6, 7, 11, 11, 11, 12, 13, 14, 16, 16, 16, 19, 19, 19, 20, 22, 23; **52:**1, 5, 6, 7, 8, 11, 12, 14, 15; **53:**2, 3, 3, 3, 4, 5, 5, 6, 7, 7, 8, 9, 10, 10, 11, 12, 12; **54:**1, 3, 4, 9, 10, 11, 11, 11, 12, 13, 14, 16, 16, 17; **55:**1, 2, 3, 4, 5, 8, 9, 10, 10, 10, 11, 11, 12, 12, 12, 13; **56:**1, 1, 2, 3, 3, 4, 5, 5, 6, 6, 6, 6, 7, 7, 9, 10, 11, 12, 12, 12; **57:**1, 3, 4, 4, 6, 7, 8, 9, 10, 13, 14, 15, 15, 15, 15, 17, 18, 19, 20; **58:**2, 3, 4, 5, 6, 6, 7, 7, 8, 9, 9, 10, 10, 11, 12, 13, 13, 14; **59:**1, 2, 3, 3, 4, 4, 5, 6, 7, 7, 8, 8, 10, 12, 13, 14, 14, 15, 15, 16, 17, 17, 19, 21, 21, 21, 21; **60:**4, 5, 6, 6, 7, 8, 9, 10, 13, 14, 14, 15, 15, 16, 16, 17, 17, 18, 18, 19; **61:**1, 1, 2, 3, 5, 5, 6, 7, 7, 8, 8, 9, 10; **62:**1, 2, 4, 4, 6, 8, 8, 9, 12, 12, 12; **63:**5, 6, 6, 7, 8, 9, 9, 9, 10, 10, 14, 15, 15, 15, 16, 17, 17, 18; **64:**1, 2, 3, 4, 6, 6, 6, 7, 8, 8, 9, 11, 12; **65:**2, 4, 4, 7, 7, 8, 9, 9, 10, 11, 11, 11, 12, 13, 14, 15, 16, 17, 18, 19, 19, 21, 22, 22, 23, 23, 24, 25; **66:**1, 2, 2, 2, 4, 5, 5, 9, 10, 12, 12, 14, 15, 15, 16, 16, 17, 17, 18, 18, 18, 19, 19, 19, 19, 20, 20, 20, 21, 21, 22, 23, 24, 24; **Jer 1:**5, 7, 8, 8, 9, 10, 10, 10, 10, 11, 12, 12, 12, 13, 13, 15, 16, 17, 17, 19; **2:**2, 2, 3, 6, 6, 6, 7, 7, 7, 8, 9, 12, 12, 13, 15, 16, 16, 17, 17, 18, 18, 20, 20, 23, 25, 26, 28, 33, 34, 35; **3:**1, 2, 3, 5, 6, 7, 8, 8, 9, 12, 13, 14, 15, 15, 16, 16, 18, 19, 21, 21, 22, 23, 23, 24, 24, 25, 25; **4:**1, 2, 2, 2, 2, 2, 3, 4, 5, 7, 8, 9, 9, 15, 16, 19, 21, 22, 23, 23, 23, 24, 24, 24, 25, 26, 28, 29, 30, 30, 30; **5:**1, 1, 1, 4, 5, 5, 6, 7, 10, 11, 12, 17, 17, 17, 17, 19, 19, 20, 21, 22, 23, 23, 24, 27, 27, 28, 28, 28, 30, 31, 31; **6:**2, 3, 4, 4, 5, 6, 7, 7, 10, 11, 11, 11, 12, 12, 13, 16, 16, 21, 21, 23, 24, 24, 25, 26, 26, 28, 29; **7:**2, 5, 5, 6, 6, 6, 6, 9, 9, 10, 10, 14, 15, 16, 17, 18, 18, 18, 20, 21, 22, 22, 23, 23, 25, 26, 28, 29, 29, 31, 33, 33, 34, 34; **8:**1, 1, 1, 2, 2, 2, 3, 4, 6, 7, 10, 10, 13, 14, 16, 16, 17, 19, 20, 21; **9:**1, 2, 2, 2, 3, 4, 5, 6, 7, 10, 10, 10, 12, 14, 15, 16, 21, 21, 22, 24, 24, 24, 26; **10:**3, 3, 4, 4, 4, 5, 6, 7, 8, 9, 9, 11, 12, 13, 14, 17, 18, 19, 20, 20, 21, 22; **11:**2, 4, 4, 5, 6, 6, 7, 8, 9, 10, 10, 11, 11, 12, 12, 13, 16, 16, 17, 19, 20, 20, 22, 22; **12:**2, 2, 3, 4, 5, 9, 10, 11, 15, 16, 16, 17; **13:**1, 1, 2, 4, 5, 6, 7, 7, 9, 10, 11, 12, 13, 13, 16, 17, 18, 18, 19, 22, 25, 27, 27, 27; **14:**2, 3, 4, 10, 10, 12, 12, 14, 15, 16, 16, 17, 17, 18, 20, 21; **15:**1, 2, 3, 6, 7, 8, 9, 9, 9, 11, 13, 14, 15, 16, 20; **16:**3, 3, 4, 4, 4, 5, 5, 5, 6, 8, 8, 8, 9, 11, 12, 12, 13, 13, 13, 15, 16, 17, 18, 19, 19, 21; **17:**2, 2, 3, 4, 5, 7, 7, 8, 9, 10, 11, 12, 13, 13, 15, 18, 19, 19, 20, 20, 21, 23, 24, 24, 25, 25, 25, 26, 26, 26, 26, 26, 26, 27, 27, 27; **18:**2, 3, 4, 7, 9, 9, 9, 10, 11, 11, 11, 15, 15, 16, 17, 17, 18, 18, 18, 18, 20, 21, 22, 23; **19:**1, 1, 2, 3, 4, 4, 5, 7, 7, 8, 9, 9, 11, 12, 13, 14, 15; **20:**2, 2, 4, 4, 5, 5, 5, 6, 6, 6, 7, 7, 8, 9, 10, 10, 11, 12, 12, 13, 18; **21:**1, 2, 3, 4, 6, 6, 7, 7, 7, 9, 10, 10, 14; **22:**1, 2, 3, 3, 4, 4, 6, 6, 7, 8, 9, 11, 12, 13, 13, 14, 14, 15, 16, 16, 16, 17, 17, 19, 22, 22, 23, 24, 25, 26, 26, 28; **23:**1, 2, 3, 3, 4, 5, 6, 6, 8, 9, 10, 10, 12, 12, 13, 14, 14, 15, 17, 22, 24, 25, 28, 32, 39, 40, 40; **24:**1, 2, 3, 6, 6, 6, 7, 8, 9, 9, 9, 10, 10; **25:**2, 4, 5, 5, 8, 9, 9, 9, 9, 9, 10, 10, 10, 10, 11, 12, 14, 15, 17, 18, 18, 18, 18, 19, 19, 20, 20, 21, 22, 22, 22, 23, 23, 25, 25, 26, 26, 26, 27, 27, 28, 30, 34, 34, 38, 38; **26:**2, 3, 4, 5, 5, 6, 7, 8, 8, 9, 10, 11, 11, 12, 13, 14, 15, 16, 17, 19, 19, 20, 20, 21, 21, 21, 23, 23, 24; **27:**2, 3, 5, 5, 7, 7, 7, 7, 8, 8, 9, 10, 10, 12, 13, 15, 16, 16, 17, 18, 18, 19, 20, 21, 22; **28:**1, 4, 4, 5, 6, 8, 8, 10, 11, 13; **29:**1, 2, 3, 5, 5, 6, 6, 7, 7, 8, 10, 10, 11, 11, 14, 14, 16, 17, 17, 18, 18, 19, 21, 22, 23, 25, 25, 26, 28, 29, 31, 32; **30:**3, 3, 3, 4, 5, 8, 9, 10, 10, 10, 10, 11, 14, 14, 15, 16, 16, 17, 18, 19, 19, 19, 19, 20, 20, 21, 22; **31:**1, 4, 5, 7, 8, 8, 8, 9, 9, 9, 10, 12, 12, 12, 12, 12, 13, 13, 13, 15, 18, 20, 22, 23, 24, 24, 24, 24, 25, 26, 27, 27, 28, 28, 28, 31, 32, 33, 33, 34, 34, 34, 35, 35, 35, 37, 39, 40, 40, 40; **32:**2, 4, 4, 5, 7, 8, 10, 10, 11, 12, 12, 12, 14, 14, 15, 15, 15, 17, 18, 18, 19, 19, 19, 20, 20, 20, 21, 21, 22, 23, 23, 24, 25, 28, 28, 29, 29, 30, 32, 32, 33, 35, 35, 36, 37, 37, 38, 39, 39, 39, 40, 40, 41, 41, 43, 43, 44, 44, 44, 44, 44, 44; **33:**2, 3, 4, 6, 6, 7, 7, 8, 9, 9, 10, 10, 10, 11, 11, 12, 12, 12, 13, 14, 15, 15, 16, 16, 18, 18, 18, 20, 22, 22, 22, 24, 24, 24, 25, 25, 26, 26; **34:**1, 1, 2, 2, 3, 5, 7, 9, 10, 15, 15, 16, 16, 17, 20, 20, 21, 21, 22, 22, 22; **35:**2, 2, 3, 3, 3, 4, 5, 5, 6, 7, 10, 11, 13, 13, 13, 14, 14, 15, 15, 17, 18; **36:**2, 2, 2, 3, 4, 5, 6, 7, 8, 11, 12, 14, 14, 14, 15, 15, 18, 19, 20, 21, 22, 23, 25, 26, 26, 28, 29, 30, 31, 31, 31, 31, 32; **37:**3, 4, 8, 8, 10, 13, 13, 14, 15, 15; **38:**1, 4, 6, 6, 10, 11, 11, 11, 14, 15, 17, 17, 18, 19, 20, 22, 22, 23, 23, 23, 25, 27, 27, 27, 28; **39:**1, 2, 2, 3, 3, 3, 3, 4, 4, 5, 6, 7, 8, 10, 10, 12, 13, 13, 13, 14, 18; **40:**1, 2, 3, 4, 5, 5, 6, 7, 8, 8, 9, 9, 10, 10, 10, 10, 11, 11, 12, 12, 13, 15, 15, 15; **41:**1, 2, 2, 3, 3, 5, 5, 5, 5, 6, 7, 7, 8, 10, 11, 12, 13, 14, 14, 15, 16, 16; **42:**1, 1, 3, 4, 8, 8, 9, 10, 11, 11, 13, 14, 14, 16, 16, 17, 18, 18, 18, 20, 21, 22; **43:**2, 2, 3, 4, 4, 5, 6, 6, 6, 7, 11, 12, 12, 13; **44:**1, 1, 2, 2, 3, 4, 6, 6, 6, 7, 8, 8, 9, 9, 9, 9, 10, 10, 12, 12, 12, 13, 15, 17, 17, 17, 17, 17, 17, 17, 18, 18, 19, 19, 19, 20, 21, 21, 21, 21, 23, 23, 23, 25, 25, 25, 25, 27, 27, 28, 29, 29; **45:**3, 3; **46:**2, 3, 4, 4, 6, 9, 9, 9, 9, 12, 14, 16, 16, 21, 25, 25, 25, 26, 27, 27, 27, 27; **47:**2, 2, 2, 3, 4, 5, 6, 7; **48:**1, 3, 7, 7, 8, 11, 11, 15, 17, 18, 20, 20, 21, 21, 22, 22, 22, 23, 23, 24, 24, 24, 25, 26, 28, 29, 32, 33, 34, 34, 35, 36, 37, 37, 38, 38, 43, 43, 44, 46; **49:**2, 2, 3, 3, 4, 5, 8, 10, 10, 10, 12, 13, 13, 13, 14, 16, 16, 17, 18, 18, 19, 19, 20, 20, 21, 22, 23, 24, 24, 26, 27, 28, 29, 29, 30, 31, 32, 33, 36, 38, 38; **50:**1, 2, 2, 2, 3, 3, 4, 4, 5, 6, 6, 9, 11, 11, 12, 12, 13, 16, 18, 19, 19, 19, 19, 21, 21, 23, 25, 26, 26, 30, 32, 32, 33, 33, 33, 34, 35, 36, 37, 38, 38, 39, 40, 40, 41, 42, 43, 43, 44, 44, 45, 45, 46; **51:**1, 2, 3, 5, 7, 8, 11, 12, 14, 14, 15, 16, 17, 20, 20, 21, 21, 22, 22, 22, 23, 23, 23, 24, 27, 27, 28, 28, 29, 30, 32, 34, 34, 34, 36, 37, 37, 39, 40, 44, 44, 44, 47, 47, 48, 49, 50, 50, 51, 53, 56, 56, 57, 57, 58, 59, 62, 63, 64; **52:**1, 3, 3, 4, 7, 7, 8, 11, 13, 15, 15, 16, 17, 17, 18, 19, 20, 21, 22, 23, 24, 25, 25, 27, 31, 32, 33; **La 1:**3, 3, 3, 5, 5, 6, 7, 7, 7, 7, 8, 8, 11, 12, 13, 14, 18, 18, 18, 19, 20, 20, 22; **2:**2, 5, 5, 6, 6, 8, 8, 9, 9, 10, 11, 11, 12, 15, 15, 16, 16, 16, 17, 17, 19, 20, 21, 21, 22; **3:**3, 4, 5, 5, 7, 8, 8, 11, 11, 12, 17, 19, 25, 27, 38, 40, 41, 41, 42, 42, 43, 45, 47, 50, 53, 54, 56, 57, 59, 62, 65, 65; **4:**7, 8, 10, 13, 15, 16, 16, 16, 17; **5:**3, 4, 6, 11, 12, 13, 14, 17, 17, 18, 21; **Eze 1:**1, 3, 4, 6, 7, 10, 11, 12, 13, 13, 14, 18, 20, 23, 26, 27, 28; **2:**2, 3, 4, 5, 6, 6, 8, 9, 9, 10, 10; **3:**1, 2, 3, 6, 7, 8, 11, 12, 13, 14, 14, 18, 19, 20, 20, 21, 21, 22, 22, 23, 23, 24, 24, 26, 27; **4:**1, 1, 2, 3, 3, 3, 4, 6, 7, 9, 9, 10, 11, 12, 14, 16, 16, 17, 17; **5:**1, 1, 2, 3, 4, 4, 6, 7, 7, 10, 10, 11, 12, 12, 13, 13, 14, 15, 15, 16, 17, 17, 17; **6:**2, 3, 3, 3, 3, 4, 5, 6, 8, 9, 10, 11, 11, 11, 12, 13, 13, 13, 13, 14; **7:**4, 10, 11, 13, 15, 16, 18, 18, 20, 20, 21, 22, 24, 25, 26, 27, 27, 27; **8:**3, 3, 5, 6, 8, 9, 10, 10, 13, 14, 16, 17, 18; **9:**2, 2, 3, 3, 4, 4, 5, 6, 6, 6, 7, 8, 9, 11; **10:**2, 2, 2, 3, 4, 4, 5, 5, 6, 6, 7, 7, 7, 9, 12, 12, 14, 18, 19, 19, 21, 21, 22; **11:**1, 1, 4, 5, 6, 7, 9, 10, 11, 12, 13, 17, 19, 19, 19, 20, 20, 22, 22, 23, 24, 25; **12:**3, 5, 6, 6, 7, 10, 11, 12, 13, 13, 14, 14, 15, 19, 19, 20, 23, 24; **13:**3, 6, 6, 8, 9, 9, 10, 11, 12, 13, 14, 15, 15, 18, 18, 19, 20, 21, 22; **14:**1, 4, 5, 6, 6, 7, 7, 7, 8, 9, 9, 9, 10, 11, 13, 13, 14, 15, 17, 17, 19, 19, 20, 21, 21, 22, 22, 23; **15:**3, 4, 5, 6, 7, 8; **16:**3, 4, 4, 5, 6, 7, 7, 7, 8, 8, 8, 8, 9, 9, 10, 10, 11, 12, 12, 13, 13, 13, 13, 13, 15, 17, 17, 17, 18, 19, 19, 20, 20, 22, 24, 27, 27, 28, 31, 36, 36, 37, 37, 38, 39, 39, 39, 39, 40, 41, 41, 42, 42, 45, 45, 45, 45, 48, 48, 49, 49, 50, 53, 55, 55, 55, 57, 57, 57, 60, 61, 62, 62, 63, 63; **17:**4, 6, 6, 6, 7, 7, 8, 8, 8, 9, 9, 9, 9, 12, 12, 13, 14, 15, 15, 16, 16, 17, 17, 19, 20, 20, 21, 21, 22, 22, 23, 24, 24, 24; **18:**4, 4, 5, 5, 6, 6, 7, 7, 8, 8, 9, 9, 9, 10, 11, 12, 12, 13, 13, 13, 16, 16, 16, 17, 17, 18, 19, 20, 20, 21, 21, 21, 21, 22, 23, 24, 24, 26, 27, 27, 27, 29, 31, 31, 32; **19:**2, 3, 3, 4, 5, 6, 6, 6, 7, 7, 7, 8, 9, 11, 12, 12, 13, 14, 14; **20:**4, 5, 6, 6, 6, 8, 10, 12, 12, 13, 13, 13, 15, 16, 17, 18, 20, 21, 21, 24, 25, 26, 26, 27, 28, 28, 28, 28, 31, 32, 33, 34, 35, 37, 38, 38, 39, 39, 40, 40, 40, 41, 43, 46, 47, 47, 48; **21:**2, 2, 3, 3, 5, 6, 7, 7, 9, 11, 12, 12, 14, 14, 16, 17, 19, 20, 20, 20, 22, 23, 24, 25, 26, 27, 28, 28, 29, 29, 29, 31, 32; **22:**3, 3, 3, 4, 5, 7, 7, 7, 8, 9, 9, 10, 12, 12, 13, 14, 15, 16, 18, 20, 21, 22, 25, 26, 26, 26, 26, 28, 28, 29; **23:**3, 4, 4, 4, 4, 4, 5, 6, 7, 7, 8, 9, 10, 10, 11, 11, 12, 15, 17, 17, 18, 20, 21, 21, 23, 23, 23, 23, 24, 24, 25, 25, 25, 25, 26, 27, 29, 29, 32, 32, 32, 33, 34, 35, 35, 35, 36, 37, 37, 38, 39, 40, 41, 41, 42, 42, 44, 44, 45, 46, 46, 47, 47, 47, 48, 48; **24:**4, 4, 5, 5, 8, 10, 11, 13, 13, 13, 14, 18, 21, 21, 21, 23, 24, 25, 25, 26, 26, 27, 27; **25:**2, 3, 4, 4, 5, 5, 6, 6, 6, 7, 8, 9, 9, 10, 11, 12, 13, 14, 15, 15, 16, 17; **26:**2, 3, 4, 4, 6, 7, 8, 9, 10, 11, 12, 12, 12, 12, 12, 16, 16, 21; **27:**7, 7, 8, 10, 10, 11, 12, 13, 13, 14, 15, 16, 16, 17, 17, 18, 19, 21, 21, 22, 22, 23, 24, 24, 27, 27, 27, 29, 30, 31, 31, 32, 34, 35, 36; **28:**2, 3, 4, 4, 5, 7, 8, 12, 13, 13, 14, 14, 16, 17, 18, 18, 19, 21, 22, 22, 23, 23, 24, 24, 26, 26, 26; **29:**2, 2, 4, 5, 5, 7, 7, 8, 8, 9, 10, 12, 12, 14, 18, 18, 18, 21, 21; **30:**2, 3, 4, 4, 5, 6, 7, 8, 8, 11, 12, 12, 13, 14, 14, 15, 17, 17, 18, 19, 19, 22, 24, 24, 25, 25; **31:**2, 3, 4, 4, 5, 6, 7, 10, 10, 12, 12, 12, 12, 13, 15, 15, 16, 16, 17, 18, 18; **32:**2, 3, 4, 4, 5, 7, 7, 9, 10, 12, 13, 14, 15, 15, 15, 16, 18, 19, 21, 23, 24, 26, 27, 28, 29, 30, 32, 32; **33:**6, 7, 8, 9, 12, 14, 14, 14, 15, 15, 16, 16, 19, 19, 21, 22, 24, 25, 27, 28, 30, 31; **34:**3, 4, 4, 6, 8, 8, 10, 11, 12, 12, 13, 13, 14, 15, 16, 16, 16, 17, 17, 20, 21, 21, 21, 22, 22, 22, 22, 23, 23, 24, 24, 25, 25, 26, 26, 27, 27, 27, 28, 28, 29, 30, 31; **35:**2, 3, 4, 4, 7, 8, 10, 11, 11, 13, 15; **36:**3, 3, 4, 4, 4, 4, 4, 6, 6, 7, 8, 9, 9, 10, 10, 11, 12, 15, 18, 20, 23, 24, 25, 25, 26, 26, 26, 27, 27, 28, 28, 29, 30, 30, 31, 33, 34, 35, 35, 36, 36, 37, 38; **37:**1, 4, 5, 6, 6, 6, 7, 8, 9, 10, 10, 10, 12, 14, 14, 16, 16, 16, 19, 21, 23, 23, 24, 24, 25, 25, 25, 26, 26, 26, 27, 28; **38:**2, 4, 4, 4, 4, 5, 6, 6, 7, 8, 9, 9, 9, 10, 11, 12, 12, 13, 13, 13, 13, 13, 15, 16, 16, 19, 20, 22, 22, 22, 23, 23; **39:**1, 2, 3, 4, 4, 6, 6, 7, 7, 9, 9, 9, 9, 9, 11, 11, 11, 14, 15, 16, 17, 17, 17, 17, 17, 18, 18, 20, 21, 22, 23, 24, 26, 26, 26, 28, 29; **40:**2, 3, 4, 4, 5, 5, 5, 6, 9, 10, 11, 16, 17, 18, 19, 20, 21, 21, 22, 22, 24, 24, 25, 25, 25, 26, 27, 28, 29, 29, 29, 29, 30, 31, 32, 33, 33, 33, 33, 34, 35, 36, 36, 36, 37, 39, 41, 41, 42, 42, 43, 44, 45, 47, 48, 49; **41:**1, 2, 2, 3, 3, 5, 10, 10, 11, 12, 12, 13, 15, 16, 18, 21, 22, 22, 23, 25, 25; **42:**1, 2, 3, 4, 6, 10, 11, 11, 11, 12, 13, 13, 13, 17, 19; **43:**2, 3, 3, 4, 5, 5, 6, 7, 7, 7, 8, 9, 9, 10, 10, 11, 11, 11, 12, 13, 13, 17, 18, 20, 20, 21, 22, 23, 24, 24, 25, 26, 27, 27; **44:**2, 3, 4, 4, 5, 5, 5, 6, 7, 9, 10, 11, 11, 11, 12, 14, 14, 15, 15, 16, 18, 19, 23, 24, 24, 24, 26, 27, 27, 29, 29, 30, 30; **45:**1, 3, 4, 5, 5, 6, 6, 7, 7, 7, 7, 8, 9, 9, 9, 10, 10, 11, 12, 15, 15, 17, 17, 19, 22, 23, 24, 24, 25; **46:**1, 2, 2, 3, 4, 5, 6, 7, 8, 9, 10, 11, 11, 12, 12, 14, 15, 16, 17, 18, 19, 20, 20, 20, 21, 22; **47:**2, 3, 4, 5, 8, 8, 11, 12, 12, 14, 16, 16, 17, 18, 18, 18, 19, 22, 22, 22; **48:**1, 2, 4, 6, 7, 8, 8, 9, 11, 11, 13, 13, 15, 18, 20, 21, 21, 21, 22, 22, 23, 25, 27, 28, 31, 32, 33, 34, 34, 35; **Da 1:**1, 2, 3, 4, 4, 4, 4, 5, 5, 6, 8, 10, 10, 11, 12, 14, 15, 15, 16, 17, 17, 17, 19, 19, 20, 20; **2:**2, 2, 4, 5, 5, 6, 6, 6, 7, 9, 10, 10, 11, 12, 13, 13, 13, 14, 16, 17, 17, 20, 20, 21, 21, 22, 22, 23, 23, 24, 25, 26, 28, 28, 30, 31, 31, 32, 32, 33, 33, 34, 35, 35, 37, 38, 38, 39, 40, 40, 41, 41, 42, 43, 43, 45, 45, 46, 46, 46, 48, 49; **3:**1, 1, 2, 3, 4, 4, 5, 7, 8, 10, 12, 13, 13, 14, 15, 16, 19, 20, 20, 21, 22, 22, 23, 24, 24, 25, 26, 26, 26, 27, 27, 27, 28, 28, 29, 29, 30; **4:**1, 1, 2, 4, 7, 8, 8, 9, 11, 12, 12, 14, 14, 15, 15, 15, 15, 17, 19, 19, 20, 21, 21, 22, 22, 23, 23, 23, 23, 23, 24, 25, 25, 25, 26, 27, 30, 32, 32, 33, 33, 33, 34, 34, 34, 34, 35, 36, 36, 36, 36, 37, 37, 37, 37; **5:**1, 2, 2, 2, 3, 3, 3, 4, 6, 6, 7, 7, 7, 9, 10, 11, 11, 12, 12, 12, 12, 14, 14, 15, 16, 16, 18, 19, 19, 19, 19, 20, 20, 21, 21, 21, 22, 23, 23, 23, 23, 23, 26, 27, 28, 28, 29, 31; **6:**1, 2, 2, 3, 4, 4, 4, 6, 6, 7, 8, 8, 8, 10, 11, 11, 12, 12, 14, 15, 15, 16, 17, 17, 18, 18, 22, 23, 24, 24, 25, 25, 25, 26, 26, 27, 27, 27, 28; **7:**1, 1, 4, 4, 5, 5, 5, 6, 6, 7, 7, 7, 7, 8, 8, 9, 10, 10, 10, 11, 13, 14, 14, 14, 15, 16, 18, 18, 19, 19, 19, 19, 20, 20, 20, 20, 21, 22, 25, 25, 25, 26, 26, 27, 27, 27, 28; **8:**4, 4, 4, 7, 7, 9, 9, 10, 10, 11, 12, 13, 14, 16, 18, 18, 20, 21, 24, 24, 26, 27, 27, 27; **9:**3, 3, 3, 4, 4, 4, 5, 5, 5, 6, 6, 6, 7, 7, 7, 8, 8, 9, 11, 11, 12, 13, 14, 15, 16, 16, 18, 18, 19, 20, 20, 22, 24, 24, 25, 25, 26, 26, 26, 26, 27; **10:**1, 3, 5, 6, 6, 6, 7, 8, 9, 10, 10, 11, 12, 12, 13, 16, 16, 16, 17, 18, 19, 19, 20; **11:**1, 3, 4, 4, 5, 6, 6, 7, 7, 8, 10, 11, 12, 15, 15, 17, 18, 18, 19, 19, 20, 21, 21, 24, 24, 25, 26, 30, 30, 30, 31, 31, 32, 33, 33, 35, 35, 35, 36, 38, 38, 39, 40, 40, 40, 41, 41, 42, 43, 43, 43, 44, 44, 45, 45, 45; **12:**2, 2, 2, 3, 4, 4, 5, 7, 7, 10, 10, 11, 12, 12, 13; **Hos 1:**1, 1, 2, 3, 3, 4, 6, 6, 8, 9, 9, 10, 11, 11; **2:**1, 2, 2, 2, 2, 3, 4, 5, 5, 5, 5, 5, 8, 9, 9, 11, 12, 13, 13, 14, 15, 18, 18, 18, 18, 19, 19, 20, 20, 22, 22, 23, 23; **3:**1, 1, 2, 2, 3, 4, 5, 5; **4:**2, 2, 2, 2, 3, 3, 3, 4, 5, 5, 8, 9, 10, 11, 12, 13, 13, 14, 15, 16, 18; **5:**1, 1, 4, 4, 6, 6, 11, 13, 14, 14, 15; **6:**4, 4, 7, 9; **7:**1, 5, 6, 7, 9, 12, 14, 14, 15; **8:**1, 3, 4, 4, 7, 7, 13, 14, 14; **9:**3, 7, 12, 13, 14, 16; **10:**1, 2, 2, 4, 5, 6, 7, 8, 8, 8, 9, 10, 11, 12, 12, 13, 14; **11:**1, 2, 4, 4, 5, 6, 8, 8, 9, 9, 10, 11, 12, 12; **12:**1, 1, 4, 4, 4, 6, 6, 8, 9, 10, 11, 12, 13; **13:**1, 2, 2, 6, 6, 8, 11, 12, 15, 15; **14:**2, 2, 4, 4, 7, 8, 9, 9, 9; **Joel 1:**4, 5, 5, 7, 7, 7, 10, 10, 11, 12, 12, 14, 14, 17, 17, 17, 19, 20; **2:**2, 2, 2, 2, 3, 4, 7, 8, 9, 10, 10, 10, 11, 12, 13, 13, 14, 16, 16, 17, 18, 19, 19, 20, 21, 22, 24, 24, 25, 26, 27, 28, 29, 30, 30,

30, 31, 31, 32; **3:**1, 2, 3, 4, 4, 4, 5, 5, 5, 6, 7, 8, 8, 9, 10, 11, 15, 15,
16, 16, 16, 16, 17, 18, 18, 19, 19, 20, 21; **Am 1:**1, 2, 2, 3, 3, 4, 5, 5,
6, 6, 7, 8, 8, 9, 9, 10, 11, 11, 11, 12, 13, 13, 14, 15, 15; **2:**1, 1, 1, 2, 2,
3, 3, 4, 4, 5, 6, 6, 6, 7, 7, 9, 9, 10, 11, 12, 16; **3:**1, 9, 9, 10, 11, 12, 12,
13, 14, 15, 15; **4:**1, 1, 4, 4, 4, 6, 9, 9, 9, 10, 11, 13, 13; **5:**4, 5, 6, 7, 7,
8, 8, 8, 9, 11, 11, 12, 12, 14, 15, 16, 16, 16, 17, 18, 18, 19, 20, 21,
21, 22, 25, 26; **6:**1, 1, 1, 2, 2, 2, 4, 5, 6, 8, 8, 8, 8, 10, 10, 11, 12, 13,
13; **7:**1, 3, 4, 8, 8, 9, 9, 11, 12, 14, 15, 15, 17, 17, 17, 17; **8:**4, 5, 5, 6,
8, 8, 9, 10, 10, 12, 13, 13, 14, 14, 14; **9:**2, 3, 3, 4, 5, 5, 5, 6, 7, 8, 8,
11, 12, 12, 12, 13, 14, 14, 14, 14; **Ob** 1, 2, 3, 4, 5, 6, 6, 6, 7, 8, 9, 10,
10, 11, 13, 16, 16, 16, 17, 18, 18, 19, 19, 19, 20, 20, 21; **Jnh 1:**2, 3,
3, 5, 5, 6, 6, 7, 9, 9, 9, 11, 12, 13, 14, 15, 15, 16, 16, 17, 17; **2:**2, 2, 3,
3, 5, 5, 6, 7, 9, 10; **3:**2, 2, 3, 5, 5, 6, 6, 7, 8, 8, 9, 10; **4:**1, 2, 2, 5, 6, 6,
6, 7, 8, 8, 10; **Mic 1:**1, 1, 1, 3, 4, 5, 5, 5, 7, 8, 8, 8, 8, 10, 11, 13, 13,
15, 16; **2:**1, 2, 5, 9, 10, 10, 11, 13; **3:**2, 2, 3, 6, 7, 7, 8, 8, 8, 9, 10;
4:2, 2, 3, 3, 4, 5, 7, 8, 10, 12, 13, 13; **5:**4, 5, 5, 6, 8, 8, 9, 10, 11, 13,
14; **6:**1, 1, 2, 4, 4, 5, 5, 7, 8, 8, 11, 11, 12, 14, 14; **7:**3, 3, 3, 7, 9, 9,
11, 12, 12, 12, 12, 13, 14, 14, 14, 19, 20, 20; **Na 1:**2, 2, 3, 3, 4, 4, 4,
5, 5, 6, 7, 12, 12, 13, 14, 14, 15; **2:**1, 2, 2, 4, 7, 10, 10, 11, 11, 11, 11,
12, 12, 12; **3:**1, 2, 3, 3, 4, 5, 5, 6, 7, 9, 9, 9, 10, 11, 13, 13, 13, 14, 16,
17, 17; **Hab 1:**3, 3, 3, 4, 4, 4, 4, 5, 5, 6, 6, 7, 10, 10, 10, 11, 12, 14,
15, 16; **2:**1, 1, 2, 4, 5, 5, 5, 6, 7, 7, 8, 10, 11, 12, 15, 16, 16, 17, 19;
3:2, 2, 3, 3, 6, 7, 8, 10, 11, 11, 12, 13, 15, 16, 17, 17, 17, 17, 19;
Zep 1:3, 3, 4, 4, 5, 5, 6, 7, 8, 8, 9, 9, 10, 10, 11, 12, 15, 15, 15, 16,
16, 17, 18; **2:**1, 2, 2, 3, 4, 5, 5, 6, 7, 8, 8, 9, 9, 9, 9, 13, 13, 14, 14,
14; **3:**1, 5, 6, 7, 8, 8, 8, 11, 11, 12, 14, 15, 15, 15, 19, 19, 19, 19, 20;
Hag 1:1, 8, 8, 9, 10, 11, 11, 11, 11, 11, 11, 12, 12, 14, 14; **2:**2, 2, 4,
6, 6, 7, 8, 9, 12, 13, 13, 14, 14, 17, 17, 19, 19, 21, 22, 22; **Zec 1:**1, 3,
4, 5, 6, 7, 8, 11, 12, 13, 13, 14, 14, 15, 16, 17, 17, 18, 19, 21, 21; **2:**2,
4, 4, 5, 9, 10, 11, 11, 12; **3:**2, 4, 4, 5, 6, 7, 7, 7, 8, 9, 10, 10; **4:**1, 3, 7,
9, 12; **5:**1, 2, 4, 4, 4, 4, 5, 6, 8, 8, 9, 9, 9, 11; **6:**1, 3, 4, 6, 7, 7, 7, 8,
10, 10, 11, 11, 12, 13, 13, 13, 14, 15; **7:**2, 3, 3, 5, 5, 5, 6, 7, 7, 7, 9, 9,
9, 10, 10, 11; **8:**2, 3, 3, 4, 4, 5, 5, 6, 7, 8, 8, 9, 10, 12, 12, 12, 13, 13,
13, 14, 15, 16, 17, 19, 19, 19, 19, 20, 21, 22, 23, 23; **9:**1, 2, 2, 3, 3, 4,
4, 5, 5, 5, 5, 7, 7, 8, 9, 10, 10, 10, 13, 13, 15, 17, 17, 17; **10:**1, 2, 2, 3,
3, 4, 6, 7, 7, 9, 10, 10, 10, 11, 11, 12; **11:**2, 4, 6, 6, 7, 7, 8, 9, 10, 11,
11, 12, 13, 13, 14, 15, 16, 17, 17; **12:**1, 2, 4, 5, 6, 7, 8, 10, 10, 10, 11,
12, 13, 14; **13:**1, 1, 2, 2, 3, 3, 6, 7, 7, 8, 9, 9, 9, 9, 9; **14:**2, 2, 4, 4, 5,
7, 8, 8, 9, 10, 10, 11, 11, 12, 12, 14, 14, 15, 16, 17, 18, 19, 20, 21,
21; **Mal 1:**2, 3, 3, 4, 4, 6, 6, 6, 8, 8, 8, 10, 11, 13, 13, 13, 14; **2:**2, 3,
3, 5, 5, 5, 5, 6, 6, 7, 9, 11, 12, 13, 13, 14, 15, 15; **3:**1, 2, 3, 4, 5, 5, 5,
6, 7, 7, 8, 11, 15, 16, 16, 17, 18, 18; **4:**1, 1, 2, 4, 5, 6, 6; **Mt 1:**1, 2, 3,
11, 17, 17, 20, 21, 21, 23, 25; **2:**2, 4, 8, 8, 8, 8, 9, 11, 11, 11, 11, 11,
13, 13, 14, 15, 16, 16, 18, 19, 20, 20, 21, 23; **3:**2, 4, 4, 5, 5, 6, 7, 8,
10, 11, 11, 16, 16, 17, 17; **4:**2, 2, 3, 6, 6, 8, 8, 9, 11, 11, 12, 13, 15,
16, 17, 18, 19, 20, 20, 21, 21, 22, 23, 23, 24, 24, 25; **5:**1, 5, 6, 11, 11,
12, 13, 15, 18, 19, 19, 20, 22, 23, 24, 24, 25, 25, 29, 30, 30, 32, 35,
35, 40, 42, 43, 45, 45, 45; **6:**2, 4, 5, 5, 6, 7, 7, 12, 13, 16, 16, 17, 18,
19, 19, 19, 20, 21, 23, 24, 24, 24, 25, 25, 26, 28, 28, 30, 30, 33, 33;
7:1, 3, 6, 7, 7, 7, 8, 12, 13, 14, 14, 17, 18, 19, 22, 22, 24, 25, 25, 26,
27, 27; **8:**3, 4, 5, 6, 7, 8, 9, 9, 9, 9, 11, 11, 11, 12, 13, 15, 16, 17, 20,
21, 23, 25, 26, 26, 26, 26, 27, 28, 32, 32, 32, 34; **9:**1, 5, 6, 6, 7, 7, 9,
10, 10, 13, 14, 14, 15, 16, 16, 17, 17, 17, 18, 18, 19, 22, 22, 23, 25,
25, 28, 29, 30, 33, 35, 35, 35, 35, 36; **10:**1, 1, 1, 7, 8, 10, 11, 15, 16,
17, 18, 18, 21, 21, 22, 25, 28, 30, 35, 35, 38, 40, 41, 41, 42; **11:**1, 4,
4, 5, 6, 9, 10, 12, 12, 12, 14, 15, 17, 18, 18, 19, 19, 19, 19, 19, 20,
21, 21, 21, 22, 23, 25, 25, 25, 27, 27, 28, 28, 29, 29, 30; **12:**1, 2, 3, 4,
5, 11, 11, 11, 12, 13, 14, 15, 18, 18, 21, 22, 22, 25, 26, 27, 29, 30,
33, 33, 34, 35, 36, 38, 38, 40, 40, 41, 41, 41, 42, 42, 42, 44, 44, 45,
45, 45, 46, 47, 47, 49, 49, 50, 50; **13:**1, 2, 4, 4, 6, 7, 8, 8, 9, 10, 12,
13, 15, 15, 15, 15, 15, 15, 16, 17, 17, 17, 19, 19, 20, 22, 22, 23, 25,
26, 27, 30, 30, 32, 32, 34, 38, 39, 40, 41, 41, 42, 42, 42, 43, 44, 44,
46, 47, 48, 49, 50, 54, 54, 55, 55, 55, 57, 57, 57, 58; **14:**3, 9, 11, 11,
12, 13, 14, 14, 15, 15, 15, 17, 19, 19, 19, 19, 19, 20, 21, 22, 24, 29,
30, 31, 32, 35, 36; **15:**1, 3, 4, 4, 6, 10, 10, 11, 12, 14, 17, 18, 19, 20,
21, 21, 22, 25, 25, 26, 28, 29, 29, 30, 30, 30, 31, 31, 32, 32, 33, 34,
36, 36, 37, 38, 39, 39; **16:**1, 4, 6, 9, 11, 12, 14, 18, 18, 19, 19, 21, 21,
21, 21, 22, 23, 23, 24, 26, 27, 28; **17:**1, 1, 1, 2, 3, 3, 4, 5, 5, 6, 7, 8,
12, 12, 14, 14, 15, 18, 20, 23, 24, 27, 27, 27; **18:**1, 2, 3, 5, 8, 8, 9, 9,
9, 12, 12, 12, 13, 15, 15, 16, 18, 21, 25, 26, 26, 27, 27, 28, 29, 29,
30, 31, 32, 35; **19:**1, 1, 2, 3, 4, 5, 5, 5, 5, 7, 9, 9, 12, 13, 15, 15, 18,
19, 21, 21, 21, 26, 28, 29, 29, 30; **20:**2, 3, 5, 6, 7, 8, 12, 14, 16, 16,
17, 18, 19, 20, 21, 24, 25, 25, 27, 28, 29, 32, 34; **21:**1, 2, 2, 3, 7, 7, 8,
8, 9, 11, 12, 12, 12, 14, 14, 15, 15, 16, 16, 19, 19, 20, 21, 21, 21, 21,
23, 23, 27, 28, 29, 30, 31, 32, 32, 32, 32, 32, 33, 33, 35, 38, 39, 41,
42, 43, 44, 45; **22:**3, 4, 5, 6, 7, 8, 8, 9, 10, 10, 12, 13, 13, 13, 16, 20,
22, 24, 25, 26, 26, 27, 29, 31, 32, 37, 38, 40, 46; **23:**1, 2, 3, 4, 5, 6, 6,
7, 8, 8, 9, 10, 12, 13, 13, 15, 15, 15, 18, 20, 21, 21, 22, 22, 23, 23,
25, 25, 25, 26, 27, 27, 28, 29, 29, 34, 34, 34, 35, 37, 38, 38; **24:**3, 3,
3, 6, 6, 7, 7, 7, 9, 10, 10, 10, 11, 11, 12, 14, 14, 19, 20, 24, 24, 24,
26, 29, 30, 30, 30, 30, 31, 31, 31, 32, 35, 38, 38, 39, 43, 45, 46, 48,
49, 49, 50, 51, 51; **25:**1, 2, 5, 6, 7, 9, 10, 10, 13, 14, 15, 15, 16, 17,
18, 19, 20, 21, 22, 23, 24, 24, 25, 26, 26, 28, 29, 30, 31, 32, 33, 35,
35, 35, 36, 36, 36, 37, 37, 38, 38, 39, 40, 40, 41, 41, 42, 42, 43, 43,
43, 43, 44, 45, 45, 46; **26:**2, 2, 3, 4, 7, 9, 15, 15, 16, 17, 18, 19, 25,
26, 26, 26, 27, 27, 27, 28, 30, 31, 32, 35, 36, 37, 37, 37, 37, 38, 39,
40, 40, 41, 42, 43, 45, 47, 47, 47, 48, 49, 50, 50, 51, 53, 55, 56, 57,
58, 58, 59, 61, 62, 64, 64, 67, 67, 69, 71, 73, 74, 75; **27:**1, 2, 3, 5, 5,
7, 10, 12, 20, 20, 22, 24, 24, 25, 25, 27, 28, 29, 29, 30, 30, 30, 31,
32, 36, 39, 40, 40, 41, 42, 44, 47, 48, 49, 50, 52, 52, 53, 54, 54, 55,
56, 56, 56, 58, 58, 59, 61, 62, 64, 64, 65, 66; **28:**1, 2, 2, 3, 4, 7, 7, 7,
8, 9, 9, 9, 10, 11, 12, 13, 14, 15, 15, 18, 18, 19, 19, 19, 20; **Mk 1:**2,
4, 4, 5, 5, 5, 6, 6, 9, 10, 10, 11, 11, 13, 15, 16, 17, 18, 18, 19, 20, 20,
21, 21, 21, 24, 26, 27, 29, 29, 29, 29, 31, 31, 31, 31, 32, 33, 34, 35,
36, 38, 39, 40, 43, 44, 45; **2:**1, 2, 9, 10, 11, 12, 13, 14, 15, 15, 18, 18,
18, 20, 21, 21, 22, 22, 25, 26, 27, 28; **3:**1, 3, 4, 5, 6, 7, 8, 8, 8, 8, 9,
11, 13, 13, 15, 17, 20, 20, 23, 26, 27, 31, 31, 31, 32, 32, 32, 34, 34,
35, 35; **4:**1, 1, 4, 4, 6, 7, 8, 8, 9, 10, 12, 15, 16, 18, 19, 20, 20, 21, 23,
24, 24, 27, 27, 28, 29, 29, 32, 33, 39, 39, 40, 41, 41, 41; **5:**3, 4, 4, 5,
5, 5, 6, 9, 10, 13, 13, 14, 15, 16, 17, 17, 19, 19, 20, 20, 22, 23, 24,
25, 26, 27, 29, 30, 33, 33, 34, 36, 37, 37, 37, 38, 38, 39, 39, 40, 40,
42, 42, 43; **6:**1, 2, 2, 3, 3, 3, 3, 4, 4, 5, 5, 6, 7, 7, 11, 13, 13, 17, 19,
20, 20, 21, 21, 22, 22, 24, 25, 27, 28, 29, 30, 30, 31, 31, 31, 33, 33,
34, 35, 35, 36, 36, 38, 38, 38, 41, 41, 41, 43, 43, 45, 47, 48, 48, 51,
52, 54, 55, 55, 56, 56, 56, 56; **7:**1, 4, 5, 8, 10, 10, 13, 14, 14, 15, 17,
19, 20, 22, 23, 24, 25, 25, 27, 29, 30, 30, 31, 31, 32, 34, 34, 35, 37,
37; **8:**1, 1, 2, 3, 6, 7, 8, 9, 10, 12, 13, 13, 15, 20, 22, 22, 23, 23, 25,
27, 27, 28, 31, 31, 31, 32, 33, 33, 34, 34, 34, 35, 36, 38, 38; **9:**2, 3, 4,
4, 5, 7, 8, 8, 8, 12, 13, 15, 17, 18, 18, 18, 18, 20, 20, 22, 25, 25, 26,
26, 26, 27, 27, 31, 32, 33, 35, 35, 37, 47, 47, 48, 50; **10:**1, 1, 1, 2, 4,
6, 7, 7, 8, 11, 12, 12, 13, 16, 16, 17, 19, 21, 21, 21, 22, 23, 27, 28,
29, 29, 30, 30, 31, 32, 32, 33, 33, 34, 35, 35, 37, 39, 39, 41, 42, 42,
44, 45, 46, 46, 49, 50, 52, 52; **11:**1, 1, 2, 2, 3, 4, 6, 7, 7, 8, 8, 9, 11,
11, 14, 15, 15, 15, 16, 18, 19, 21, 23, 23, 23, 24, 27, 33; **12:**1, 1, 3, 4,
7, 8, 8, 9, 9, 11, 12, 13, 14, 15, 15, 16, 19, 20, 21, 21, 22, 22, 24, 26,
26, 29, 30, 30, 32, 33, 33, 33, 33, 33, 34, 37, 38, 39, 39, 40, 41, 41,
42, 43; **13:**3, 3, 4, 7, 7, 8, 8, 8, 9, 9, 10, 11, 12, 12, 13, 17, 18, 19, 21,
22, 22, 22, 25, 26, 27, 27, 28, 31, 33, 33, 34; **14:**1, 1, 1, 3, 5, 5, 7, 8,
11, 11, 15, 16, 16, 22, 22, 23, 23, 23, 24, 24, 26, 27, 28, 31, 32, 32,
32, 33, 33, 33, 34, 35, 37, 37, 38, 39, 40, 40, 43, 43, 43, 44, 45, 46,
47, 48, 50, 52, 53, 54, 55, 58, 60, 62, 62, 63, 64, 65, 65, 65, 67, 68,
69, 72, 72, 72; **15:**1, 1, 4, 16, 17, 17, 19, 19, 20, 21, 21, 22, 29, 29,
30, 31, 32, 35, 36, 36, 37, 38, 40, 40, 41, 41, 43, 44, 45, 46, 46, 47;
16:1, 1, 1, 4, 5, 7, 8, 9, 10, 10, 11, 15, 15, 16, 17, 18, 18, 19, 20, 20,
20, S, S; **Lk 1:**2, 6, 6, 7, 9, 13, 13, 14, 14, 15, 16, 17, 17, 18, 20, 23,
24, 28, 29, 31, 31, 32, 32, 33, 35, 35, 38, 38, 40, 41, 42, 42, 44, 48,
49, 51, 52, 53, 54, 55, 56, 57, 58, 58, 59, 63, 64, 65, 66, 67, 68, 71,
75, 76, 79, 79, 80; **2:**4, 6, 7, 9, 12, 14, 16, 16, 16, 17, 19, 20, 20, 20,
25, 25, 25, 27, 28, 32, 33, 34, 34, 35, 36, 37, 37, 38, 38, 38, 40, 40,
44, 47, 47, 48, 51, 51, 52, 52, 52; **3:**1, 2, 3, 5, 5, 5, 6, 8, 9, 12, 14, 14,
15, 16, 19, 22, 22, 22; **4:**2, 5, 6, 7, 9, 10, 11, 15, 16, 17, 19, 20, 22,
25, 25, 29, 30, 31, 36, 36, 39, 39, 41, 41, 42; **5:**2, 3, 4, 4, 5, 6, 7, 7, 8,
10, 11, 11, 13, 13, 14, 15, 15, 17, 17, 17, 19, 21, 23, 24, 24, 25, 25,
26, 26, 26, 28, 29, 30, 30, 33, 33, 35, 36, 36, 37, 37, 39; **6:**1, 3, 4, 5,
7, 8, 10, 10, 11, 12, 13, 17, 17, 17, 17, 18, 18, 19, 20, 22, 22, 22, 23,
25, 25, 30, 33, 34, 35, 35, 35, 37, 38, 39, 41, 43, 45, 47, 48, 49; **7:**2,
3, 4, 5, 7, 7, 8, 8, 8, 8, 10, 12, 14, 14, 15, 15, 16, 16, 17, 19, 20, 21,
21, 22, 22, 22, 23, 25, 26, 27, 30, 32, 33, 33, 34, 34, 34, 34, 34, 36,
37, 38, 38, 39, 40, 41, 44, 44, 45, 47, 50; **8:**1, 2, 3, 3, 5, 5, 6, 7, 8, 8,
12, 12, 12, 14, 14, 14, 14, 15, 16, 17, 19, 20, 20, 21, 21, 22, 23, 23,
24, 24, 25, 25, 25, 27, 28, 29, 32, 33, 33, 34, 35, 35, 35, 37, 37, 37,
39, 41, 41, 43, 43, 44, 45, 47, 47, 50, 51, 51, 52, 54, 55, 55; **9:**1, 1, 1,
2, 6, 7, 9, 11, 11, 11, 12, 12, 12, 13, 13, 16, 16, 16, 17, 18, 19, 22,
23, 25, 26, 26, 26, 27, 28, 29, 29, 30, 30, 31, 32, 32, 32, 32, 33, 33,
34, 39, 41, 42, 42, 44, 45, 48, 54, 55, 58, 59, 60, 62; **10:**1, 1, 2, 3, 4,
7, 9, 10, 11, 13, 13, 13, 14, 15, 16, 16, 19, 19, 19, 19, 21, 21, 21, 21,
22, 22, 23, 24, 24, 24, 27, 27, 28, 29, 30, 30, 30, 31, 32, 33, 34, 34,
35, 37, 38, 40, 40, 42; **11:**1, 4, 4, 6, 7, 8, 9, 9, 9, 9, 10, 14, 19, 22, 22,
23, 25, 25, 26, 26, 26, 27, 28, 29, 31, 31, 31, 32, 32, 32, 33, 34, 37,
39, 39, 41, 42, 43, 46, 49, 49, 49, 50, 51, 52, 53; **12:**1, 1, 3, 5, 7, 8,
11, 11, 11, 16, 18, 19, 19, 19, 23, 24, 26, 27, 28, 28, 29, 29, 33, 33,
33, 34, 35, 36, 36, 37, 37, 37, 42, 42, 43, 45, 45, 46, 46, 48, 49, 50,
51, 52, 53, 53, 53, 54, 54, 55, 56, 58, 58, 58, 59; **13:**3, 3, 4, 5, 6, 6, 7,
8, 8, 11, 12, 13, 13, 15, 17, 19, 19, 19, 22, 25, 26, 26, 27, 28, 28, 28,
30, 30, 32, 32, 32, 33, 34, 35, 35; **14:**2, 3, 4, 4, 5, 9, 10, 12, 13, 16,
18, 19, 21, 21, 21, 21, 21, 23, 23, 25, 26, 26, 26, 27, 27, 28, 29, 30,
31, 35; **15:**1, 2, 4, 4, 4, 5, 6, 7, 8, 8, 8, 8, 9, 9, 13, 13, 14, 17, 18, 18,
19, 20, 20, 20, 21, 21, 22, 22, 23, 24, 25, 26, 27, 27, 28, 28, 29, 29,
31, 31, 32; **16:**2, 3, 3, 3, 4, 5, 6, 7, 7, 8, 9, 11, 12, 13, 13, 13, 16, 16,
17, 17, 18, 18, 19, 21, 22, 22, 23, 24, 25, 25, 26, 26, 28, 29, 31; **17:**4,
4, 6, 6, 7, 8, 9, 11, 14, 14, 19, 19, 23, 25, 27, 27, 27, 28, 28, 28, 28,
29, 29, 33, 34; **18:**1, 7, 9, 10, 11, 12, 13, 15, 16, 20, 22, 22, 24, 28,
29, 31, 32, 33, 34, 40, 42, 43, 43; **19:**1, 2, 4, 5, 6, 6, 8, 8, 10, 10, 11,
12, 13, 14, 15, 20, 20, 21, 22, 24, 27, 27, 29, 30, 30, 32, 33, 34, 35,
37, 38, 41, 42, 43, 43, 44, 45, 47; **20:**1, 1, 1, 8, 9, 9, 10, 11, 11, 12,
12, 14, 15, 16, 16, 17, 18, 19, 21, 21, 23, 24, 26, 28, 29, 31, 31, 36,
37, 37, 40, 45, 46, 46, 46, 47; **21:**2, 5, 7, 8, 9, 9, 10, 11, 11, 11, 11,
12, 12, 12, 15, 16, 16, 17, 20, 21, 22, 23, 23, 24, 24, 25, 25, 25, 25,
27, 28, 33, 34, 34, 36, 36, 37; **22:**2, 4, 4, 5, 8, 8, 8, 12, 13, 13, 14, 17,
17, 19, 19, 20, 24, 25, 25, 26, 27, 29, 30, 30, 32, 32, 33, 35, 36, 36,
36, 39, 41, 41, 43, 44, 45, 46, 47, 50, 50, 51, 51, 52, 52, 52, 54, 54,
55, 55, 56, 58, 60, 61, 62, 63, 64, 65, 66, 67, 68, 70; **23:**2, 4, 4, 7, 8,
10, 11, 11, 11, 12, 13, 14, 14, 15, 18, 18, 19, 22, 23, 23, 25, 26, 28,
28, 29, 30, 33, 34, 35, 35, 39, 43, 44, 45, 46, 47, 48, 50, 51, 51, 52,
53, 53, 55, 56, 56; **24:**5, 7, 7, 9, 10, 12, 15, 15, 19, 20, 20, 20, 22, 23,
24, 27, 28, 31, 31, 32, 33, 33, 35, 36, 39, 40, 41, 43, 44, 44, 46, 46,
46, 49, 49, 50, 51, 52, 53; **Jn 1:**1, 4, 5, 11, 12, 14, 14, 14, 17, 19, 29,
32, 33, 36, 37, 38, 39, 39, 40, 41, 43, 44, 45, 45, 46, 48, 51, 51; **2:**2,
4, 6, 8, 10, 11, 12, 13, 14, 14, 15, 15, 15, 19, 20, 22, 22; **3:**4, 5, 10,
11, 11, 13, 14, 20, 22, 22, 23, 26, 26, 29, 30, 30, 30, 31, 31, 32, 35,
36; **4:**1, 6, 7, 9, 10, 10, 11, 12, 12, 12, 15, 16, 18, 23, 23, 24, 28, 28,
29, 34, 35, 36, 36, 37, 37, 38, 41, 45, 47, 47, 48, 50, 50, 51, 52, 53,
53; **5:**6, 8, 9, 11, 14, 15, 20, 20, 22, 24, 25, 25, 26, 27, 29, 29, 30, 32,
33, 35, 35, 36, 36, 37, 38, 43, 47; **6:**2, 3, 9, 11, 11, 15, 17, 17, 18, 21,
22, 22, 23, 24, 25, 32, 33, 37, 39, 40, 42, 44, 45, 53, 54, 54, 55, 56,
56, 58, 63, 63, 64, 66, 67, 69; **7:**3, 6, 7, 11, 14, 18, 21, 23, 24, 26, 28,
28, 29, 32, 34, 35, 36, 37, 38, 44, 45, 52, 53; **8:**2, 2, 3, 6, 7, 8, 10, 11,
11, 14, 16, 18, 21, 26, 26, 28, 29, 32, 32, 37, 44, 44, 44, 46, 49, 50,
52, 55, 56, 59; **9:**4, 6, 7, 7, 7, 8, 9, 9, 11, 11, 11, 11, 11, 15, 17, 20,
24, 25, 28, 30, 31, 34, 35, 37, 38, 39, 40; **10:**1, 3, 3, 3, 4, 8, 10, 10,
12, 12, 12, 13, 14, 15, 15, 16, 16, 18, 22, 24, 25, 27, 28, 29, 30, 35,
38, 39, 41, 42; **11:**1, 2, 5, 6, 11, 15, 16, 19, 19, 19, 25, 26, 28, 28, 28,
32, 32, 33, 33, 34, 38, 41, 44, 44, 46, 47, 48, 48, 48, 49, 54, 54, 55,
56, 57; **12:**2, 3, 3, 3, 5, 6, 9, 11, 13, 14, 22, 26, 26, 28, 32, 36, 40, 40,
40, 40, 47, 47, 48, 50; **13:**1, 2, 3, 3, 5, 5, 9, 10, 12, 12, 13, 13, 14, 14,
18, 20, 21, 26, 29, 31, 32, 33, 36; **14:**2, 3, 4, 4, 6, 7, 8, 10, 11, 12, 13,
14, 16, 16, 17, 17, 19, 20, 20, 21, 21, 21, 22, 23, 23, 24, 26, 26, 27,
27; **15:**1, 2, 4, 4, 5, 6, 7, 7, 10, 13, 16, 19, 20, 22, 24, 24, 26, 27;
16:2, 5, 8, 8, 8, 10, 16, 17, 17, 18, 19, 20, 22, 23, 23, 24, 24, 25, 27,
28, 28, 29, 30, 33; **17:**1, 3, 3, 5, 6, 6, 8, 8, 8, 10, 10, 11, 11, 13, 14,
17, 19, 21, 21, 21, 23, 23, 25, 26, 26, 26; **18:**1, 3, 3, 3, 6, 7, 8, 10, 12,
12, 16, 18, 18, 19, 20, 20, 24, 27, 28, 29, 31, 33, 35, 37, 37, 38; **19:**2,
2, 3, 4, 5, 5, 6, 9, 14, 16, 19, 20, 20, 24, 25, 25, 27, 27, 28, 29, 30,
31, 32, 34, 34, 37, 38, 39, 42, 42; **20:**1, 2, 2, 2, 3, 4, 5, 5, 6, 7, 8, 8,
11, 11, 12, 13, 14, 15, 15, 16, 17, 17, 17, 18, 20, 21, 22, 25, 26, 27,
28, 29, 31; **21:**2, 6, 6, 7, 8, 9, 9, 11, 11, 12, 12, 13, 18, 18, 18, 20, 20,
24, 24, 25; **Ac 1:**1, 3, 6, 7, 8, 8, 9, 11, 13, 14, 15, 18, 19, 20, 23, 25,
26, 26; **2:**2, 3, 4, 4, 6, 8, 10, 10, 11, 11, 12, 14, 14, 17, 17, 18, 18, 19,
19, 19, 19, 20, 20, 21, 22, 23, 24, 26, 28, 29, 29, 30, 31, 31, 32, 33,
33, 36, 37, 37, 38, 38, 39, 39, 41, 42, 42, 42, 43, 43, 44, 44, 45, 46,
46, 47, 47; **3:**1, 3, 4, 4, 6, 7, 7, 7, 7, 8, 8, 9, 11, 12, 12, 12, 13, 14, 15,
16, 17, 19, 20, 23, 25; **4:**1, 1, 2, 3, 4, 5, 5, 6, 7, 8, 10, 10, 13, 15, 15,
16, 18, 19, 20, 23, 23, 23, 24, 24, 26, 27, 28, 29, 29, 30, 31, 31, 32,
32, 33, 33, 35, 36, 37; **5:**3, 4, 5, 6, 6, 8, 9, 9, 10, 10, 10, 11, 12, 12,
14, 14, 14, 14, 15, 16, 16, 17, 18, 19, 20, 21, 21, 22, 24, 26, 28, 29,
31, 31, 32, 33, 34, 34, 36, 37, 38, 40, 40, 42, 42, 42, 42; **6:**2, 3, 3, 3, 4, 4,
5, 5, 5, 7, 8, 8, 9, 10, 11, 12, 12, 13, 14; **7:**2, 3, 3, 4, 5, 7, 7, 8, 8, 9,
10, 10, 10, 11, 13, 14, 16, 19, 21, 22, 22, 24, 26, 27, 27, 29, 31, 32,
32, 33, 35, 35, 35, 36, 36, 36, 36, 38, 39, 41, 41, 42, 42, 43, 45, 46,
49, 50, 51, 51, 52, 54, 55, 55, 56, 56, 57, 58, 58, 59, 60, 60; **8:**1, 1, 2,
3, 5, 7, 12, 12, 13, 13, 13, 14, 17, 17, 22, 23, 25, 25, 25, 27, 28, 29,
30, 31, 31, 32, 33, 35, 36, 38, 38, 40; **9:**2, 4, 5, 6, 6, 9, 9, 12, 14, 15,
15, 16, 17, 17, 17, 18, 18, 19, 20, 21, 21, 22, 22, 24, 24, 27, 27, 28,
30, 31, 31, 31, 31, 32, 33, 34, 34, 35, 36, 37, 37, 39, 39, 39, 40, 40,
41, 41, 41, 42, 43; **10:**2, 4, 4, 6, 7, 8, 10, 11, 12, 13, 17, 20, 21, 22,
22, 24, 24, 26, 27, 27, 31, 32, 33, 35, 38, 38, 38, 39, 39, 41, 42, 42,
42, 46, 46; **11:**1, 3, 5, 5, 6, 7, 7, 10, 12, 12, 13, 14, 17, 18, 18, 19, 20,
21, 21, 23, 23, 24, 24, 30; **12:**4, 7, 7, 7, 8, 8, 8, 10, 10, 10, 10, 10, 11,
11, 13, 14, 16, 17, 17, 17, 17, 19, 20, 21, 21, 23, 24, 25; **13:**1, 1, 2, 2,
3, 3, 4, 4, 5, 7, 7, 8, 8, 9, 10, 11, 11, 11, 11, 11, 12, 13, 13, 14, 15,
15, 16, 16, 17, 19, 21, 22, 23, 24, 24, 25, 26, 27, 29, 31, 32, 32, 36,
36, 37, 39, 41, 42, 42, 43, 43, 43, 45, 46, 46, 46, 48, 48, 50, 50, 50,
50, 51, 52, 52; **14:**1, 1, 1, 2, 3, 4, 5, 5, 6, 6, 7, 8, 9, 9, 10, 10, 12, 13,
13, 13, 14, 14, 15, 15, 17, 17, 17, 18, 19, 19, 19, 20, 21, 21, 21, 23,
23, 26, 27, 27, 28; **15:**1, 1, 2, 2, 2, 2, 3, 3, 4, 4, 5, 5, 6, 7, 7, 9, 12, 12,
12, 13, 15, 16, 16, 19, 20, 20, 22, 22, 22, 22, 22, 23, 23, 24, 25, 27,
28, 29, 30, 31, 32, 32, 33, 33, 35, 35, 37, 38, 39, 40, 41; **16:**1, 1, 2, 4,
5, 6, 6, 9, 11, 11, 12, 13, 14, 15, 15, 15, 17, 18, 18, 19, 19, 22, 22,
22, 23, 24, 25, 25, 25, 26, 26, 29, 29, 29, 30, 31, 32, 33, 33, 34, 34,
36, 37, 37, 38, 39, 39, 40, 40; **17:**1, 1, 1, 2, 3, 3, 4, 4, 5, 5, 6, 6, 6, 6,
7, 9, 10, 11, 11, 11, 12, 13, 14, 15, 15, 17, 17, 18, 18, 19, 20, 23, 23,
24, 24, 25, 25, 25, 26, 26, 27, 27, 28, 28, 29, 30, 31, 34, 34; **18:**1, 3,
4, 5, 5, 5, 6, 6, 7, 8, 8, 9, 10, 11, 12, 14, 15, 15, 16, 17, 18, 18, 18,
22, 22, 23, 23, 25, 25, 26, 26, 27; **19:**3, 4, 6, 6, 8, 9, 9, 10, 12, 15, 16,
16, 16, 17, 17, 19, 20, 21, 21, 22, 25, 26, 26, 27, 27, 28, 29, 29, 32,
33, 34, 37, 38, 38, 39, 40, 41; **20:**1, 1, 4, 4, 4, 5, 6, 7, 9, 9, 10, 11, 11,
12, 13, 14, 15, 19, 21, 21, 21, 22, 23, 24, 25, 28, 28, 31, 31, 31, 32,
32, 32, 34, 35, 36; **21:**1, 3, 4, 5, 6, 6, 8, 11, 11, 11, 14, 15, 16, 16, 18,
20, 23, 24, 24, 24, 25, 26, 26, 26, 27, 28, 28, 29, 30, 30, 32, 32, 32,
33, 33, 34, 34, 36, 38, 40, 40; **22:**1, 3, 3, 3, 4, 4, 4, 5, 7, 8, 10, 10, 10,
11, 12, 13, 13, 13, 14, 14, 15, 16, 16, 16, 17, 19, 20, 23, 24, 26, 27,
28, 29, 29, 30; **23:**6, 6, 10, 10, 10, 10, 11, 12, 14, 14, 15, 16, 16, 17,
18, 19, 21, 23, 23, 24, 27, 33, 34; **24:**1, 2, 3, 5, 10, 10, 14, 14, 15, 16,
17, 18, 19, 22, 23, 23, 25, 25, 26, 27; **25:**2, 2, 3, 4, 6, 7, 9, 12, 12, 15,
15, 17, 19, 20, 22, 23, 23, 24, 24, 25, 26; **26:**3, 4, 7, 7, 10, 12, 13, 14,
15, 16, 16, 17, 17, 18, 18, 19, 20, 20, 20, 20, 21, 22, 23, 23, 26, 29,
30, 30, 32; **27:**1, 2, 3, 4, 5, 6, 7, 8, 9, 10, 11, 12, 12, 12, 13, 14, 14,
15, 17, 19, 20, 21, 21, 21, 23, 24, 28, 28, 29, 31, 32, 35, 35, 37, 39,
39, 40, 40, 41, 41, 42, 43, 44, 44; **28:**2, 2, 3, 4, 5, 6, 6, 7, 8, 8, 8, 9,
10, 14, 15, 15, 17, 18, 20, 23, 23, 23, 23, 24, 25, 26, 27, 27, 27, 27,
27, 27, 28, 31, 31; **Ro 1:**1, 4, 5, 5, 7, 7, 7, 9, 9, 13, 14, 14, 16, 20, 20,
20, 21, 21, 23, 23, 23, 24, 24, 26, 27, 27, 28, 29, 30, 30, 31, 31, 32,
32; **2:**1, 1, 2, 3, 3, 4, 7, 7, 8, 8, 9, 9, 10, 10, 10, 12, 17, 19, 20, 20, 26,
26, 27, 29; **3:**4, 7, 7, 14, 16, 19, 22, 25, 25, 26, 26, 28, 30; **4:**10, 11,
11, 12, 13, 14, 14, 16, 17, 19, 19, 20, 22, 25; **5:**2, 2, 3, 4, 4, 5, 6, 9,
13, 14, 15, 15, 16, 17, 18, 20, 21, 21; **6:**1, 1, 3, 4, 4, 8, 9, 10, 11, 13,
16, 18, 19, 19, 21, 22, 22; **7:**3, 4, 5, 6, 8, 9, 11, 11, 12, 12, 16, 18, 19,
23; **8:**6, 7, 9, 11, 13, 16, 17, 21, 23, 23, 25, 26, 27, 28, 28, 29, 29, 30,
30, 30, 34, 34, 38, 38, 38, 38; **9:**1, 1, 2, 3, 4, 4, 5, 5, 5, 9, 15, 17, 18,
21, 22, 22, 24, 25, 26, 28, 29, 29, 32, 33; **10:**1, 6, 7, 8, 9, 10, 12, 14,
14, 15, 15, 18, 20, 21; **11:**1, 2, 3, 3, 4, 6, 6, 8, 10, 10, 11, 11, 11, 14,
16, 16, 17, 17, 20, 22, 23, 24, 25, 26, 26, 27, 27, 28, 29, 31, 31, 33,
33, 33, 35, 36; **12:**1, 1, 2, 2, 2, 2, 4, 5, 5, 5, 8, 10, 12, 13, 16, 20;
13:2, 3, 5, 7, 7, 7, 9, 9, 9, 9, 13, 13, 13, 13, 14; **14:**1, 3, 6, 6, 8, 8, 9,
9, 11, 14, 14, 15, 17, 17, 18, 19, 22; **15:**1, 1, 4, 5, 6, 9, 10, 11, 12, 12,
13, 16, 16, 18, 21, 23, 24, 24, 28, 29, 32, 33; **16:**3, 7, 7, 9, 9, 10, 12,
12, 13, 14, 14, 15, 15, 15, 17, 17, 17, 18, 19, 21, 21, 23, 23, 25, 26,
26; **1Co 1:**1, 2, 3, 3, 5, 8, 9, 10, 10, 14, 17, 17, 19, 20, 20, 22, 23, 24,
24, 25, 26, 27, 28, 30, 30; **2:**1, 1, 2, 3, 4, 4, 4, 6, 9, 10, 10, 11, 12;
3:1, 2, 2, 3, 4, 5, 6, 8, 16, 17, 20, 22, 22, 22, 22, 22, 23, 23; **4:**1, 4, 5,
5, 6, 6, 7, 9, 11, 11, 16, 17, 19, 19, 21, 21; **5:**2, 2, 2, 4, 4, 5, 5, 6, 8,
8; **6:**1, 2, 7, 8, 8, 10, 11, 11, 12, 13, 13, 14, 15, 16, 19; **7:**2, 4, 5, 7, 8,
9, 11, 12, 13, 13, 14, 16, 17, 18, 22, 22, 24, 25, 28, 29, 31, 32, 33,
34, 34, 36, 37, 37, 38, 40; **8:**3, 4, 4, 5, 5, 6, 6, 6, 7, 8, 12; **9:**4, 5, 5, 6,
7, 7, 7, 8, 10, 11, 13, 15, 17, 17, 21, 23; **10:**1, 1, 2, 3, 4, 4, 5, 7, 7, 8,
9, 10, 13, 16, 17, 18, 19, 20, 21, 21, 24, 25, 26, 27, 30; **11:**1, 2, 3, 6,
9, 11, 12, 15, 15, 16, 18, 22, 22, 23, 24, 24, 25, 26, 27, 28, 29, 30,
30, 31, 32, 33; **12:**1, 1, 2, 3, 9, 10, 10, 11, 13, 13, 16, 16, 18, 22, 23,
24, 26, 27, 27, 31; **13:**2, 2, 2, 2, 3, 4, 5, 7, 8, 8, 9, 11, 11, 12, 13, 13;
14:3, 5, 6, 8, 9, 10, 11, 15, 15, 20, 20, 21, 23, 24, 24, 25, 25, 26, 26,
27, 28, 29, 30, 31, 32, 36, 39, 39, 40; **15:**1, 1, 2, 3, 4, 5, 7, 9, 10, 14,
14, 15, 17, 17, 19, 26, 30, 32, 32, 34, 37, 39, 39, 40, 41, 41, 41, 42,
50, 50, 52, 56, 57, 58, 58; **16:**2, 2, 4, 6, 7, 7, 9, 14, 15, 15, 15, 16, 17,
19, 19; **2Co 1:**1, 1, 2, 2, 3, 3, 6, 8, 8, 10, 10, 12, 12, 12, 13, 13, 15,
16, 16, 19, 19, 19, 22; **2:**2, 7, 10, 13, 14, 14, 15, 16, 16, 17, 17, 17;
3:2, 2, 3, 5, 14, 14, 15, 17, 18, 18, 18, 18; **4:**1, 2, 2, 2, 7, 7, 8, 8, 9,
13, 14, 15, 15, 15, 15, 17; **5:**1, 1, 2, 4, 4, 5, 7, 8, 11, 13, 15, 18, 20;
6:3, 4, 4, 5, 6, 7, 10, 15, 16, 16, 16, 16, 17, 17, 18, 18, 18; **7:**1, 4, 5,
7, 7, 9, 10, 11, 13, 14, 14, 15, 15; **8:**2, 2, 3, 4, 5, 6, 7, 9, 10, 14, 15,
17, 19, 22, 22, 23, 24; **9:**2, 4, 8, 8, 10, 10, 11, 12, 14; **10:**1, 3, 5, 6, 6,
8, 10, 10, 11, 12, 13, 15, 16; **11:**3, 6, 7, 9, 9, 9, 18, 20, 22, 22, 23, 23,
25, 26, 26, 26, 27, 27, 27, 27, 29, 33; **12:**1, 4, 6, 6, 7, 10, 10, 12, 12,
14, 14, 15, 16, 18, 18, 19, 20, 20, 21, 21; **13:**2, 4, 6, 11, 11, 13;
Gal 1:1, 3, 3, 6, 7, 8, 14, 15, 17, 18, 19, 21, 22, 24; **2:**1, 3, 4, 6, 9, 9,
9, 10, 13, 14, 15, 16, 16, 17, 20; **3:**5, 9, 10, 14, 16, 16, 16, 19, 19, 21,
24, 27, 29, 29; **4:**1, 3, 6, 6, 7, 9, 9, 9, 14, 14, 15, 18, 19, 22, 25, 25,
26, 27, 28, 28, 29, 30; **5:**1, 10, 15, 17, 17, 21, 23, 24, 24; **6:**1, 1, 2, 2,
4, 7, 8, 9, 10, 13, 13, 14, 15, 16; **Eph 1:**2, 2, 4, 4, 5, 7, 8, 10, 10, 11,
13, 13, 14, 15, 17, 18, 20, 22, 22, 23; **2:**3, 3, 4, 6, 7, 7, 8, 11, 12, 12,
14, 15, 16, 17, 18, 19, 20, 20; **3:**5, 6, 6, 6, 7, 8, 10, 10, 11, 12, 13, 14,
14, 15, 17, 17, 18, 18, 19, 21, 21; **4:**2, 3, 4, 6, 6, 6, 6, 8, 11, 11, 12,
13, 13, 14, 15, 16, 16, 18, 19, 19, 19, 21, 22, 22, 22, 23, 24, 25, 26,
28, 29, 30, 31; **5:**2, 2, 4, 5, 8, 9, 9, 11, 11, 14, 14, 18, 19, 19, 20, 21,
25, 26, 26, 27, 30, 31, 31, 31, 32, 33; **6:**2, 3, 3, 4, 4, 5, 9, 9, 11, 12,
12, 12, 14, 17, 18, 18, 19, 21, 22, 23, 23; **Php 1:**1, 1, 1, 2, 2, 4, 6, 7,
7, 8, 9, 9, 9, 10, 11, 12, 14, 14, 15, 18, 19, 20, 20, 21, 23, 23, 25, 27,
30; **2:**1, 2, 2, 4, 6, 7, 8, 9, 10, 10, 11, 12, 12, 13, 14, 15, 16, 17, 18,
18, 21, 24, 25, 25, 26, 27, 27, 28, 29, 29, 30; **3:**2, 6, 6, 9, 10, 12, 13,
14, 17, 18, 19, 20, 21; **4:**1, 1, 1, 2, 2, 3, 3, 3, 6, 7, 8, 8, 8, 8, 8, 8, 9,
9, 9, 10, 15, 18, 19, 20, 22; **Col 1:**1, 2, 2, 3, 4, 6, 7, 9, 10, 10, 10, 11,
13, 14, 15, 16, 16, 16, 16, 17, 20, 20, 21, 22, 22, 23, 23, 26, 27, 27,

28; **2:**1, 1, 2, 3, 5, 5, 6, 7, 7, 8, 8, 8, 10, 10, 12, 13, 14, 15, 18, 19, 19, 20, 23, 23; **3:**1, 3, 4, 5, 8, 9, 10, 11, 12, 13, 14, 15, 15, 16, 16, 16, 16, 17, 19, 19, 21, 23, 24; **4:**1, 2, 5, 6, 8, 9, 9, 10, 10, 11, 12, 13, 13, 14, 15, 15, 15, 16, 17; **1Th 1:**1, 1, 1, 2, 3, 3, 4, 4, 5, 6, 8, 9, 9, 10; **2:**1, 2, 5, 7, 9, 9, 10, 10, 10, 11, 12, 13, 13, 14, 14, 15, 15, 15, 18, 18, 19, 19, 19, 20; **3:**2, 2, 3, 4, 5, 6, 6, 7, 10, 11, 12, 12, 12, 13; **4:**1, 1, 1, 4, 4, 5, 10, 11, 12, 13, 13, 14, 16, 17, 17, 18; **5:**1, 3, 3, 4, 4, 5, 5, 6, 7, 8, 8, 11, 12, 12, 13, 13, 14, 15, 23, 23, 23, 25, 28; **2Th 1:**1, 1, 2, 2, 3, 3, 4, 4, 6, 7, 7, 8, 9, 10, 10, 11, 11, 11, 12, 12; **2:**1, 1, 1, 2, 3, 4, 4, 4, 6, 7, 8, 9, 9, 11, 12, 13, 13, 15, 15, 15, 16, 16, 16, 17, 17; **3:**1, 1, 2, 3, 4, 4, 5, 6, 6, 6, 8, 11, 12, 13, 13; **1Ti 1:**1, 2, 2, 3, 4, 5, 6, 6, 9, 9, 9, 10, 10, 10, 12, 13, 14, 14, 15, 15, 16, 17, 17, 19, 20; **2:**1, 2, 2, 2, 3, 4, 5, 5, 7, 7, 7, 8, 9, 9, 9, 11, 11, 13, 14, 14, 15, 15; **3:**2, 2, 3, 4, 6, 7, 8, 8, 9, 10, 11, 11, 12, 12, 13, 15, 16, 16, 16; **4:**1, 2, 3, 3, 5, 6, 7, 7, 8, 9, 10, 10, 11, 12, 13, 16, 16, 16; **5:**2, 4, 5, 5, 9, 11, 13, 13, 14, 15, 16, 17, 18, 21, 21, 24; **6:**1, 2, 3, 4, 4, 5, 7, 8, 9, 9, 9, 10, 10, 11, 11, 11, 13, 13, 15, 15, 16, 16, 17, 18; **2Ti 1:**2, 2, 3, 4, 5, 7, 7, 8, 9, 9, 10, 10, 11, 11, 12, 12, 13, 13, 15, 16, 16, 18; **2:**4, 5, 8, 9, 9, 10, 14, 14, 15, 16, 17, 18, 19, 20, 20, 20, 20, 21, 22, 22, 22, 24, 25, 26; **3:**2, 2, 2, 3, 3, 3, 4, 6, 6, 8, 8, 8, 9, 10, 10, 10, 10, 11, 11, 12, 13, 13, 15, 16, 16, 16; **4:**1, 1, 1, 2, 3, 4, 7, 8, 8, 10, 10, 13, 17, 17, 18, 18, 18, 19, 19, 20, 21, 21, 21; **Tit 1:**1, 1, 2, 3, 3, 4, 4, 5, 6, 8, 8, 8, 9, 9, 10, 12, 14, 15, 15, 16; **2:**2, 2, 2, 3, 4, 5, 5, 7, 7, 9, 10, 12, 12, 12, 13, 14, 15; **3:**1, 2, 2, 3, 3, 3, 3, 3, 4, 5, 7, 8, 9, 9, 10, 11, 13; **Phm 1:**1, 2, 2, 3, 3, 5, 6, 7, 12, 13, 14, 16, 19, 21, 22, 24; **Heb 1:**1, 2, 2, 3, 5, 5, 6, 7, 8, 9, 10, 10, 13; **2:**2, 2, 4, 4, 4, 4, 5, 6, 7, 7, 9, 9, 10, 10, 11, 11, 12, 13, 14, 14, 14, 17, 17, 18; **3:**1, 1, 1, 2, 6, 6, 10, 12, 13, 16, 17, 18; **4:**7, 12, 13, 14, 16; **5:**1, 2, 2, 3, 4, 6, 7, 7, 7, 9, 10, 12, 12, 13, 13, 14, 14; **6:**1, 1, 1, 2, 3, 4, 5, 6, 7, 8, 8, 10, 12, 12, 14, 15, 16, 18, 19; **7:**1, 1, 2, 6, 7, 11, 11, 11, 12, 14, 17, 18, 19, 19, 21, 25, 26, 26, 27, 28; **8:**2, 3, 3, 8, 9, 10, 10, 11, 12, 12, 13; **9:**1, 1, 2, 3, 4, 4, 6, 7, 7, 7, 8, 9, 10, 10, 11, 12, 12, 13, 13, 15, 16, 19, 19, 19, 19, 21, 21, 23, 25, 26, 27, 27; **10:**1, 2, 4, 5, 10, 15, 16, 17, 19, 21, 22, 24, 25, 25, 27, 29, 29, 29, 33, 33, 37, 38, 39; **11:**4, 6, 7, 8, 9, 9, 9, 10, 11, 12, 12, 13, 13, 14, 19, 20, 21, 21, 22, 23, 28, 30, 32, 33, 34, 34, 35, 35, 36, 37, 37, 37, 37, 38, 38; **12:**1, 3, 5, 5, 6, 8, 9, 10, 12, 13, 13, 14, 14, 17, 18, 19, 21, 22, 23, 24, 24, 28, 28; **13:**4, 4, 7, 8, 12, 13, 16, 17, 17, 17, 18, 20, 20, 24; **Jas 1:**1, 2, 4, 5, 6, 8, 10, 11, 11, 13, 13, 15, 16, 17, 18, 19, 21, 21, 22, 23, 24, 25, 25, 26, 27, 27, 27; **2:**1, 2, 2, 2, 3, 5, 6, 6, 10, 14, 16, 16, 16, 17, 19, 23, 25; **3:**1, 3, 4, 6, 7, 7, 7, 9, 9, 10, 10, 10, 11, 12, 13, 13, 14, 15, 15, 16, 16, 17, 17, 17, 18, 18; **4:**1, 2, 2, 2, 2, 3, 6, 7, 8, 9, 9, 10, 10, 11, 11, 11, 13, 13, 15, 16, 17; **5:**1, 2, 3, 5, 6, 7, 7, 8, 9, 11, 12, 12, 13, 14, 15, 15, 15, 16, 16, 17, 17, 18, 18, 19, 19, 20; **1Pe 1:**1, 2, 2, 2, 2, 3, 4, 4, 5, 7, 7, 7, 7, 7, 8, 11, 11, 12, 13, 17, 18, 20, 21, 21, 21, 22, 24, 25; **2:**1, 1, 1, 5, 6, 8, 8, 11, 11, 12, 12, 14, 14, 17, 18, 20, 22, 24; **3:**4, 5, 8, 9, 10, 10, 11, 12, 14, 15, 16, 19, 21, 22, 22, 22; **4:**1, 2, 3, 3, 3, 3, 4, 5, 7, 11, 11, 11, 13, 17, 17, 18, 18, 19; **5:**1, 1, 1, 1, 4, 4, 5, 6, 7, 9, 10, 10, 11, 12, 13; **2Pe 1:**1, 1, 2, 2, 2, 3, 4, 4, 4, 6, 7, 8, 10, 11, 11, 12, 14, 16, 17, 17, 19; **2:**1, 1, 2, 2, 2, 3, 4, 5, 5, 6, 6, 7, 8, 10, 10, 11, 12, 12, 13, 14, 14, 15, 17, 19, 20, 20, 20, 20, 21, 22; **3:**1, 1, 2, 2, 2, 3, 5, 5, 7, 7, 8, 10, 10, 10, 12, 12, 13, 14, 14, 14, 15, 16, 16, 16, 17, 18, 18, 18, 18; **1Jn 1:**1, 1, 2, 2, 2, 2, 3, 3, 3, 5, 7, 8, 9, 9, 10; **2:**3, 4, 8, 8, 10, 11, 14, 15, 16, 17, 18, 20, 21, 22, 22, 24, 25, 27, 27, 27, 28, 28; **3:**1, 2, 3, 5, 10, 10, 12, 12, 12, 13, 15, 16, 17, 17, 20, 22, 22, 23, 23, 24, 24; **4:**3, 5, 7, 10, 12, 13, 13, 14, 15, 16, 16, 16, 17, 18, 21, 21; **5:**1, 2, 3, 5, 6, 6, 6, 6, 8, 8, 9, 11, 11, 14, 15, 16, 16, 18, 19, 19, 20, 20, 20, 20; **2Jn** 1, 2, 3, 3, 3, 4, 5, 6, 7, 9, 10, 12; **3Jn** 2, 3, 3, 6, 7, 10, 10, 11, 12, 14; **Jude** 1, 1, 2, 2, 4, 5, 6, 7, 7, 7, 7, 7, 8, 10, 10, 11, 13, 15, 16, 16, 19, 20, 24, 24, 24, 25, 25; **Rev 1:**2, 3, 3, 4, 4, 5, 5, 5, 6, 6, 7, 7, 8, 8, 8, 9, 9, 9, 10, 11, 11, 13, 14, 14, 15, 16, 16, 17, 17, 18, 18, 18, 19, 20, 20; **2:**2, 5, 5, 7, 8, 8, 9, 10, 10, 11, 13, 13, 14, 14, 15, 16, 17, 17, 17, 19, 19, 20, 22, 23, 23, 23, 27, 28, 29; **3:**1, 1, 3, 3, 5, 6, 7, 7, 7, 8, 8, 9, 12, 12, 12, 12, 13, 14, 17, 17, 17, 17, 17, 18, 18, 19, 19, 20, 20, 20, 21, 22; **4:**1, 1, 2, 2, 2, 3, 3, 4, 4, 5, 5, 5, 6, 6, 7, 8, 8, 8, 8, 9, 9, 9, 10, 10, 10, 10, 11, 11, 11, 11; **5:**1, 1, 1, 2, 2, 3, 4, 5, 6, 6, 6, 6, 7, 8, 8, 8, 9, 9, 9, 9, 9, 9, 9, 10, 10, 10, 11, 11, 11, 11, 12, 12, 12, 12, 12, 12, 12, 13, 13, 13, 13, 13, 13, 13, 13, 13, 14, 14, 14, 14; **6:**2, 2, 2, 4, 4, 4, 4, 5, 5, 5, 6, 6, 6, 7, 8, 8, 8, 8, 8, 8, 9, 9, 10, 10, 11, 12, 12, 14, 14, 14, 14, 15, 15, 15, 16, 16, 16, 16, 17; **7:**1, 2, 2, 2, 4, 9, 9, 9, 9, 9, 10, 10, 11, 11, 11, 11, 11, 12, 12, 12, 12, 12, 12, 12, 14, 14, 15, 15, 15, 16, 17; **8:**2, 2, 3, 3, 5, 5, 5, 7, 7, 7, 7, 8, 8, 9, 9, 10, 10, 11, 12, 12, 12, 12, 12, 12, 13; **9:**1, 1, 2, 2, 3, 3, 7, 8, 9, 11, 13, 14, 15, 15, 15, 15, 17, 17, 17, 17, 17, 17, 17, 18, 18, 20, 20, 21; **10:**1, 2, 2, 3, 3, 5, 6, 6, 6, 6, 6, 6, 8, 8, 9, 9, 10, 11; **11:**1, 1, 1, 1, 3, 3, 3, 4, 5, 6, 6, 6, 7, 8, 8, 9, 9, 9, 11, 11, 11, 12, 13, 13, 13, 15, 15, 15, 15, 16, 16, 17, 17, 17, 18, 18, 18, 19, 19, 19; **12:**1, 2, 3, 5, 5, 5, 6, 7, 7, 8, 8, 10, 10, 10, 10, 10, 11, 11, 11, 12, 12, 12, 13, 14, 14, 16, 17, 17; **13:**1, 1, 1, 2, 2, 2, 2, 3, 4, 5, 6, 6, 7, 7, 7, 7, 7, 7, 8, 9, 10, 10, 11, 12, 12, 14, 14, 16, 16, 16, 17; **14:**1, 1, 2, 3, 3, 3, 4, 6, 6, 7, 7, 8, 9, 10, 10, 10, 11, 11, 11, 11, 12, 12, 13, 13, 14, 15, 16, 17, 19, 20, 20, 20; **15:**1, 1, 2, 2, 2, 3, 3, 3, 3, 4, 4, 5, 7, 7, 8; **16:**1, 2, 2, 2, 3, 3, 4, 4, 5, 5, 6, 6, 7, 7, 9, 9, 10, 10, 11, 11, 12, 13, 13, 15, 16, 16, 17, 18, 18, 18, 19, 19, 19, 20, 20, 21; **17:**1, 1, 2, 3, 4, 4, 4, 4, 4, 5, 7, 7, 8, 8, 8, 9, 10, 11, 11, 13, 14, 14, 14, 14, 15, 15, 16, 16, 17, 18; **18:**1, 2, 2, 3, 5, 7, 7, 8, 8, 9, 9, 11, 12, 13, 14, 15, 16, 16, 16, 17, 17, 17, 17, 18, 19, 19, 19, 20, 20, 20, 21, 21, 22, 23; **19:**1, 2, 2, 3, 3, 4, 4, 5, 7, 7, 7, 9, 9, 10, 11, 11, 11, 11, 12, 12, 13, 15, 15, 16, 16, 18, 18, 18, 18, 18, 18, 19, 19, 20, 20, 20, 20, 21; **20:**1, 2, 3, 4, 4, 4, 4, 6, 6, 6, 8, 9, 9, 9, 9, 10, 10, 10, 11, 11, 11, 12, 12, 12, 13, 13, 14, 14, 15; **21:**1, 1, 1, 2, 3, 4, 4, 5, 5, 5, 6, 6, 6, 7, 7, 8, 8, 8, 8, 8, 8, 8, 8, 9, 10, 11, 12, 12, 13, 14, 15, 16, 16, 17, 18, 21, 22, 23, 23, 24, 24, 26, 26, 27; **22:**1, 1, 3, 3, 4, 4, 5, 5, 5, 6, 8, 8, 8, 9, 11, 12, 13, 13, 13, 14, 15, 16, 17, 17, 18, 19, 19

ARE (4398)

Ge 2:12, 24; **3:**3, 9, 14, 22; **4:**6, 11; **6:**3; **8:**21; **10:**32; **12:**11, 13; **13:**8; **15:**2; **16:**8, 11, 11; **18:**20, 21, 28, 29, 29, 30, 30, 31, 32; **19:**5, 8, 9, 9, 15, 22; **20:**3, 6, 13; **21:**23, 29, 30; **23:**6; **24:**8, 8, 13, 23, 24, 31, 42, 58; **27:**21, 22, 24, 29, 29, 32; **28:**4, 13; **29:**8, 15; **30:**27, 32, 33; **31:**12, 16, 26, 43, 43, 43, 49, 50; **32:**17, 17, 17, 18, 19; **33:**5, 5, 8, 13, 13; **34:**10, 15, 21, 22, 30; **35:**3, 22; **36:**18, 19, 20, 30, 31, 40, 43; **37:**8, 8, 13, 14, 15, 17; **38:**18; **39:**9; **40:**14; **41:**39; **42:**1, 7, 9, 11, 11, 12, 13, 14, 16, 19, 20, 20, 22, 31, 32, 33, 34; **44:**7, 7; **45:**11; **46:**8, 15, 30, 32, 34; **47:**1, 1, 3, 8, 18, 29; **48:**8, 9; **49:**3, 3, 4, 5, 12, 12, 28, 28, 31, 31; **50:**18; **Ex 1:**1, 9, 9, 16, 19, 19; **2:**13, 14; **3:**5, 13; **4:**18, 19, 25; **5:**4, 5, 5, 16, 16, 16; **6:**5, 14, 16, 19, 25, 26, 27; **7:**17; **9:**17, 27; **12:**7, 24, 43, 43, 48; **13:**2, 3, 8, 11, 15, 17; **14:**3, 3, 13, 15; **15:**24; **16:**7, 8; **17:**2, 2, 4; **18:**6, 14; **19:**11; **20:**9, 22; **21:**1, 7, 16, 22; **22:**7, 31; **23:**2, 6, 15, 16, 22; **24:**2, 2, 14, 14; **25:**15; **26:**1, 5; **27:**2, 10, 17; **28:**4, 13, 34; **29:**32, 33, 38; **30:**5; **32:**4, 8, 8, 9, 11, 12, 22, 26, 32; **33:**3, 5, 16, 17; **34:**12, 15, 15, 21; **35:**10; **39:**6; **40:**15; **Lev 2:**1; **4:**12, 24, 29, 29, 31, 33, 33, 35; **5:**1, 2, 10, 13, 18; **6:**4, 14, 20, 22, 25; **7:**1, 2, 10, 11, 19, 32, 37; **10:**3, 7, 10, 13, 15; **11:**8, 10, 13, 13, 20, 21, 23, 27, 29, 31, 42, 46; **12:**7; **13:**59, 59; **14:**13, 32, 44, 54; **15:**32; **16:**4, 29; **18:**17, 26, 27; **20:**2, 6, 9, 11, 12, 13, 16, 19, 20, 27; **21:**6; **22:**3, 4, 13, 18, 25; **23:**20, 24, 25, 37, 42; **25:**20, 23, 25, 33, 42, 55; **26:**3, 44, 46; **27:**32, 34; **Nu 1:**3, 3, 5, 53; **2:**3, 3, 9, 10, 10, 17, 18, 18, 25, 25, 31; **3:**12, 13, 13, 40, 41, 46; **4:**11, 14, 15, 23, 26, 26, 27, 28, 30, 33, 33; **5:**6, 8, 18, 18; **6:**4, 4, 5, 8, 20; **8:**16, 17; **9:**10, 10, 13; **10:**3, 3, 8, 29; **11:**6, 11, 12, 20, 21, 27, 29; **13:**16, 18, 19, 20, 28, 28, 28, 31, 31; **14:**9, 12, 14, 14, 29, 40, 41; **15:**11, 15, 15, 21, 39, 39; **16:**3, 5, 7, 10, 11, 11, 14, 37; **17:**12, 12, 13; **18:**6, 8, 9, 16, 17, 18, 19, 22; **19:**19; **20:**16; **21:**8, 29; **22:**5, 6, 6, 9, 12, 32, 34; **24:**5, 5, 6, 7, 21; **26:**2, 2, 9, 63; **27:**7, 14; **28:**2, 2, 2, 31; **29:**6, 6, 6, 39; **30:**16; **31:**16, 16, 18, 26, 50; **32:**7, 12, 14, 14, 25, 27, 29; **33:**2, 9; **34:**12, 13, 17, 17, 19, 29; **35:**15, 29, 34; **36:**5, 8, 13; **Dt 1:**9, 17, 17, 17, 28, 28; **2:**11; **4:**4, 5, 14, 20, 26, 45; **5:**3, 13, 28, 33; **6:**1, 1, 7, 7, 7, 7, 25; **7:**1, 1, 6, 17, 17, 23, 25, 26; **9:**1, 2, 4, 5, 5, 6, 6, 6, 13, 14, 26, 29; **10:**5, 8; **11:**8, 10, 19, 19, 19, 19, 23, 30, 30, 31, 31; **12:**1, 8, 16; **13:**1; **14:**1, 3, 4, 8, 10, 12, 19, 21; **15:**7, 11; **16:**17; **18:**3, 7, 14; **19:**17; **20:**8, 19, 19, 20; **21:**5, 11; **22:**6, 9, 20; **23:**1, 7, 18, 20; **24:**15, 15, 19, 21; **25:**5, 11, 16, 19; **26:**18; **27:**15; **28:**10, 20, 21, 21, 24, 32, 45, 48, 52, 58, 61, 62, 63; **29:**1, 10, 11, 12, 14, 29; **30:**1, 4, 16, 17, 18; **31:**7, 13, 16, 16, 16, 21, 27; **32:**5, 5, 20, 28, 32, 32, 37, 38, 47, 47, 47; **33:**3, 12, 23, 27, 29; **Jos 2:**3, 9, 16, 20, 24; **3:**8; **4:**3; **5:**13; **6:**4; **7:**7, 10, 12, 13, 21; **8:**6, 31; **9:**8, 9, 13, 13, 25; **12:**1, 8; **13:**1, 32; **15:**12, 21; **17:**16, 17, 18; **18:**3; **19:**51; **22:**16, 17, 18; **24:**13, 15, 19, 21, 22, 22; **Jdg 4:**22; **5:**30, 30; **6:**13, 17, 31, 36, 37; **7:**4, 10, 11; **8:**5, 15; **9:**28, 31, 33, 36, 37, 38; **10:**4; **11:**2, 25; **12:**1, 4, 5; **13:**11; **15:**11; **17:**2, 9; **18:**3, 3, 18, 25; **19:**12, 18, 20; **21:**11, 16, 22; **Ru 1:**13; **2:**9, 9, 10; **3:**9, 9, 10, 11; **4:**9, 10, 11; **1Sa 2:**4, 4, 5, 5, 23, 24, 30, 33; **3:**13; **4:**8, 17; **5:**10; **7:**3; **8:**5, 5, 7, 8, 18; **9:**20, 21; **10:**3, 4; **11:**12; **12:**5, 21; **13:**11, 12; **14:**9, 11, 33, 41, 44; **15:**15, 17, 18; **16:**11; **17:**18, 28, 33; **19:**22, 22; **20:**22; **21:**1, 5; **22:**17; **23:**17; **24:**12, 17, 20; **25:**7, 10, 28, 29, 29; **26:**16, 18, 23; **28:**9, 9, 12, 15; **29:**3, 6, 9; **2Sa 1:**4, 5, 8, 13; **3:**25, 28, 29, 39; **5:**1, 14; **7:**5, 22, 28, 28; **9:**2, 10; **10:**3, 11, 11; **11:**11, 11; **12:**7, 21; **13:**5, 24, 35, 35; **14:**2, 9, 14, 17, 20; **15:**15, 19, 19, 35, 35; **16:**2, 2, 2; **17:**8, 8, 9, 10; **18:**3; **19:**11, 11, 12, 12, 13, 14, 27, 35, 37, 43; **20:**9, 11, 17, 19; **21:**1, 17; **22:**2, 23, 28, 28, 29; **23:**1, 2, 6, 8, 22; **24:**2, 3, 3, 17, 22; **1Ki 1:**6, 14, 21, 25, 34, 42; **2:**9; **3:**8; **4:**8; **6:**12; **8:**8, 23, 33, 35, 37, 51, 61; **9:**13, 13; **10:**7; **11:**12, 41; **12:**7, 28; **13:**9, 14, 17, 18; **14:**6, 19, 29; **15:**7, 23, 31; **16:**5, 14, 20, 27; **17:**24; **18:**9, 18, 19, 21, 25, 36, 37; **19:**9, 10, 13, 14; **20:**3, 3, 17, 23, 31; **21:**5, 7; **22:**3, 4, 4, 4, 13, 39, 45; **2Ki 1:**3, 4, 6, 6, 16, 18; **3:**7, 7, 7; **4:**4; **5:**8; **6:**2, 9, 16, 19; **7:**12, 12; **8:**13, 23; **9:**7, 17, 18, 22, 31; **10:**2, 5, 6, 6, 13, 13, 13, 15, 15, 23, 34; **11:**5, 5, 6, 7; **12:**5, 19; **13:**8, 12; **14:**10, 15, 18, 28; **15:**6, 11, 15, 21, 26, 31, 36; **16:**19; **17:**13; **18:**19, 22, 31; **19:**4, 15, 15, 19, 26, 26, 26, 30; **20:**1, 20; **21:**14, 17, 25; **22:**7; **23:**28; **24:**5; **1Ch 1:**43; **4:**33; **5:**7; **6:**33; **11:**1, 10, 24; **12:**17, 18, 18, 23; **14:**4; **15:**4, 12; **16:**26, 27; **17:**4, 26; **19:**3, 12, 12; **21:**2, 3, 11, 17, 23; **22:**16, 18; **23:**4; **26:**1, 23; **28:**3, 21; **29:**12, 12, 14, 15, 15, 29; **2Ch 2:**8; **5:**9; **6:**14, 24, 26, 28; **7:**14; **9:**29; **10:**7; **12:**15, 15; **13:**8, 11, 22; **14:**11; **16:**9, 11; **18:**3, 3, 12; **20:**2, 6, 6, 6, 9, 10, 12, 12, 34; **23:**6; **24:**22, 27; **25:**26; **26:**18, 22; **27:**7; **28:**10, 11, 26; **29:**9, 19; **30:**19; **32:**8, 10, 32; **33:**18, 19; **34:**16; **35:**25, 27; **36:**8, 23; **Ezr 1:**3, 4; **2:**36, 40; **4:**12, 13, 14, 16, 19; **5:**11, 11; **6:**8; **7:**15, 16, 16, 17, 19, 21, 22, 25, 25; **9:**2, 6, 7, 13, 14, 15; **10:**10, 12, 13, 18, 23, 24, 25; **Ne 1:**1, 3, 3, 9, 10; **2:**2, 2, 3, 5, 5, 17, 19; **4:**2, 2, 4, 19; **5:**5, 5, 5, 7, 8, 8, 9; **6:**6, 6, 8, 10; **7:**3, 39, 43; **9:**6, 7, 8, 17, 31, 36, 36, 37, 38, 38; **13:**17, 18, 21; **Est 2:**3; **3:**3, 8; **4:**13; **7:**5; **10:**2; **Job 1:**19; **2:**9; **3:**8, 8, 17, 18, 19; **4:**5, 6, 10, 19, 20, 20; **5:**4, 5, 7, 13, 13, 16; **6:**4, 20, 21, 25, 26; **7:**6, 10, 17; **8:**2, 6, 9, 12, 14; **9:**10, 12, 13; **10:**2, 4, 6; **11:**8, 11; **12:**5, 5, 6, 13, 13, 16, 16, 18; **13:**1, 2, 4, 4, 7, 9, 20; **14:**5, 6, 10, 12, 22; **15:**2, 2, 5, 5, 10, 20, 21, 27, 28, 31, 33, 33, 34; **16:**2, 16; **17:**7, 8, 8, 11, 11; **18:**3, 14, 14, 20, 20; **19:**5, 14, 29; **20:**25; **21:**9, 18, 18, 21, 26, 30, 30, 32, 34; **22:**3, 8, 10; **24:**4, 8, 10, 10, 16, 20, 24; **25:**6, 6; **26:**14; **27:**5, 12, 18, 20, 21; **28:**8, 18; **29:**19, 20; **30:**1, 1, 2, 3, 5, 8, 17, 23; **31:**40; **32:**6, 7, 9, 16, 19; **33:**6, 12, 13, 22; **34:**17, 18, 20; **35:**7, 9; **36:**8, 13, 17, 26; **37:**17, 19, 20, 24; **38:**17, 21, 31; **39:**1, 2, 8, 13, 26; **40:**2, 8, 8, 9, 17, 18, 18; **41:**14, 16, 18, 25, 28; **Ps 1:**3, 4; **2:**7; **3:**1, 2, 3; **6:**7; **7:**10, 14; **8:**4; **9:**3, 6, 20; **10:**4, 7, 7, 8, 10, 14; **11:**2; **12:**1, 4, 6; **14:**1, 1; **16:**2, 2, 3, 5; **17:**10, 12; **18:**1, 22, 27; **19:**7, 8, 8, 9, 10, 10, 11; **22:**3, 14, 19; **23:**4; **24:**4; **25:**5, 7, 12, 15; **26:**10; **27:**11; **28:**1, 1; **31:**3, 5, 9, 10, 11, 14, 23, 23; **32:**2, 7, 11; **33:**21; **34:**2, 15, 18; **35:**1, 15, 20; **36:**2, 9; **37:**11, 20, 21, 23, 26, 32, 33, 37; **38:**2, 6, 19; **39:**1, 4, 6; **40:**5, 12, 17; **41:**1, 3, 6, 11; **43:**2; **44:**4, 13, 14, 16, 16, 22, 22; **45:**2, 3, 5, 8, 8, 9; **46:**6; **48:**11; **49:**3, 3, 5, 10, 14; **50:**7, 10, 19, 19; **53:**1, 1; **54:**3, 3; **55:**10, 11, 11, 21, 21, 21; **56:**2, 5; **57:**3; **58:**2, 3, 4; **59:**3, 9, 9, 17; **61:**3; **62:**4, 9, 9; **63:**1; **64:**3, 3, 6; **65:**3, 5, 13, 13; **66:**3, 9; **68:**13, 25, 25, 25, 29; **69:**1, 3, 4, 4, 9, 33; **70:**5; **71:**1, 2, 3, 5, 10, 10, 16, 22; **72:**14; **73:**1, 4, 10, 19, 23; **74:**2, 9, 12; **75:**1; **76:**4, 7; **77:**12, 13, 14; **79:**4, 8; **80:**16; **82:**5, 5, 6, 7; **83:**2, 18, 18; **84:**4, 5, 5, 12; **86:**2, 5, 8, 10, 10, 14, 15; **87:**3; **88:**9, 10; **89:**9, 10, 11, 15, 17, 26, 38, 50; **90:**2, 4, 4, 7, 10, 10, 10; **91:**4, 7, 8; **92:**5, 8, 13; **93:**2; **94:**10, 11, 12, 15; **95:**4, 7, 10; **96:**5, 6; **97:**2, 7, 8, 9, 9, 12; **100:**3, 3; **101:**6; **102:**25, 27; **103:**6, 14, 14, 15, 16, 18; **104:**1, 1, 2, 4, 4, 16, 18, 21, 28; **106:**3, 5; **107:**42, 43; **109:**3, 20, 21, 24; **110:**4; **111:**2, 7, 8; **112:**1, 1, 4, 5, 6, 8; **113:**6; **115:**4, 8, 8; **116:**11, 15; **118:**15, 28, 28; **119:**1, 2, 12, 39, 55, 57, 68, 70, 75, 82, 86, 98, 103, 103, 111, 111, 113, 114, 118, 119, 122, 129, 130, 137, 137, 138, 138, 144, 150, 151, 151, 155, 160, 164, 172; **120:**7; **122:**2; **124:**7; **125:**1, 4, 4; **127:**3, 3, 4; **128:**1; **131:**1; **135:**15, 18, 18; **138:**2; **139:**8, 8, 12, 17, 17, 18, 22; **140:**1, 4, 4, 6, 13; **141:**6, 8; **142:**5, 5, 6; **143:**1, 10; **144:**3, 4, 4, 8, 10, 11, 15, 15; **146:**5; **148:**14; **Pr 1:**1, 5, 12, 19, 26, 27, 32, 32; **2:**8, 15; **3:**14, 17, 18, 32, 35; **4:**19; **5:**3, 22; **6:**2, 12, 16, 23, 33; **7:**15; **8:**5, 9, 14, 18, 19, 32, 34; **9:**15, 18; **10:**4, 6, 8, 17, 20, 21, 26, 26, 27, 28, 32; **11:**3, 3, 5, 13, 17, 17, 24, 25, 30, 30, 31; **12:**2, 5, 6, 7, 10, 12, 13, 19, 20, 20; **13:**2, 5, 6, 7, 7, 10; **14:**15, 16, 17, 17, 20, 21, 26, 32, 35; **15:**11; **16:**21, 23, 24, 27; **17:**6, 6, 7, 28; **18:**3, 4, 6, 7, 8, 10, 15, 24; **19:**3, 7, 17, 24, 26; **20:**4, 6, 7, 11, 12; **21:**2, 4, 17, 18, 24, 26, 31; **22:**6, 9, 9, 22; **23:**2, 6, 7, 21; **24:**2, 4, 9, 11, 23, 24, 25; **25:**1, 13, 21, 21; **26:**4, 12, 15, 22, 25; **27:**6, 18, 20, 25; **28:**1, 7, 9, 14, 14, 18, 26; **29:**2, 2, 6, 8, 16, 19, 19, 24; **30:**12, 13, 15, 15, 18, 21, 24, 24, 28, 28, 29; **31:**1, 5, 8, 19, 26, 29; **Ecc 1:**1, 8, 8, 11; **2:**23; **3:**13, 16, 18, 22; **4:**1, 2, 3, 4, 10, 10, 12; **5:**1, 2, 12, 13, 14; **6:**12; **7:**1, 2; **8:**5, 10, 14, 14; **9:**1, 2, 2, 3, 5, 11, 11, 11, 12, 16, 16, 17; **10:**9, 15; **11:**3, 5; **12:**4, 6, 11; **SS 1:**4, 7, 9, 10, 15, 15, 16; **2:**12, 13, 13, 14, 15; **3:**8, 10; **4:**1, 1, 2, 2, 3, 3, 5, 7, 11, 11, 12, 12, 13, 15; **5:**12, 12, 13, 13, 14, 15; **6:**4, 4, 6, 7, 9; **7:**1, 1, 3, 4, 6, 7, 7, 12, 13; **Isa 1:**4, 4, 4, 6, 7, 13, 15, 18, 22, 23, 31; **2:**22; **3:**9, 10, 12, 12; **4:**3; **5:**7, 7, 8, 12, 21, 22, 25; **6:**7, 11, 11; **7:**5, 5; **8:**6, 19, 20, 21; **9:**15, 15, 17, 19; **10:**6, 22, 28, 28, 28, 29, 29, 29, 31; **13:**5, 8, 22; **14:**9, 10, 10, 11, 11, 12, 25, 31; **15:**6, 6, 6; **16:**2, 6; **17:**14; **18:**2, 2, 5, 7; **19:**11, 12, 13, 13, 14; **21:**3, 5, 5, 5; **22:**2, 3, 6, 11, 16, 18; **23:**1, 4, 13; **24:**6, 9, 14, 20, 22; **25:**1, 2, 4, 4, 4, 5; **26:**1, 2, 3, 7, 7, 14, 14, 17; **27:**11; **28:**8, 9, 9, 19, 20; **29:**7, 9, 9, 11, 13, 13, 16, 19; **30:**1, 1, 7, 9, 11, 16, 18, 25, 27; **31:**2, 3, 3, 3, 6; **32:**6, 14; **33:**8, 13, 15, 15, 16, 24; **35:**4; **36:**3, 4, 7, 16; **37:**4, 16, 16, 20, 27, 27, 27, 31; **38:**1; **40:**2, 2, 6, 15, 15, 17, 17, 21, 21, 26, 29; **41:**14, 17, 23, 24, 29, 29; **42:**3, 18, 22, 22; **43:**1, 4, 4, 8, 8, 9, 10, 10, 12, 14; **44:**8, 8, 9, 9, 9, 9, 17, 18, 18, 21, 25; **45:**9, 12, 20; **46:**1, 1, 2, 3; **47:**8, 14; **48:**1, 4, 4, 4, 7, 8, 8; **49:**3, 17; **50:**1, 8, 10; **51:**5, 10, 12, 16; **52:**5, 7, 11; **54:**17; **55:**8, 8, 9, 9; **56:**2, 2, 2, 2, 3, 3, 3, 10, 10, 11, 11; **57:**6, 6, 8, 13, 15, 20; **58:**3, 3, 6, 11; **59:**3, 3, 3, 4, 9, 9, 10, 12, 12, 14; **60:**4, 9; **61:**9; **63:**2, 8, 15, 16, 16, 17; **64:**5, 5, 6, 6, 8, 8, 8, 8, 9, 10, 11; **65:**1, 5, 8, 8, 23, 24; **66:**2, 3, 18, 18, 19; **Jer 1:**1, 10, 10, 18; **2:**11, 12, 15, 18, 22, 23, 24, 26, 27, 27, 28, 29, 31; **3:**3, 3, 14, 21, 22, 23; **4:**13, 13, 22, 22, 22, 30; **5:**2, 3, 3, 6, 7, 8, 11, 13, 14, 16, 16, 17, 26, 26, 27, 27, 28; **6:**2, 4, 7, 10, 13, 15, 16, 23, 23, 23, 24, 25, 25, 28, 28; **7:**5, 10, 17, 19; **8:**6, 8, 9, 10, 12, 12, 20; **9:**2, 10, 19, 25; **10:**2, 3, 6, 8, 8, 14, 14, 15, 15, 21; **11:**10, 13, 13, 20; **12:**1, 1, 9, 13; **13:**4, 27; **14:**3, 4, 8, 8, 9, 9, 9, 9, 13, 14, 18; **15:**2, 2, 2, 2, 5, 9, 16, 16, 19, 19; **16:**12, 14, 19, 20; **17:**1, 5, 6, 7, 8, 8, 11, 14, 17; **18:**2, 2, 6, 19; **20:**3, 4, 7, 10, 12; **21:**4, 13; **22:**6, 17, 20, 20, 25, 28; **23:**7, 10, 11, 14, 14, 14, 16, 23, 26, 26, 27, 32, 33, 36; **24:**6; **25:**5, 5, 12; **27:**10, 14, 15, 18, 18; **29:**7, 8, 11, 19, 21, 26; **30:**13, 14, 15, 17; **31:**15, 18; **32:**18, 18, 19; **33:**5, 24, 24; **34:**19, 22; **35:**11; **36:**6, 19; **37:**9, 13, 19; **40:**4, 4, 8, 15, 16; **42:**2; **43:**9; **44:**6, 7, 27, 28; **45:**5; **46:**5, 9, 23; **48:**14, 15, 30, 33, 34, 45, 46; **49:**1, 1, 1, 4, 7, 16, 16, 23, 23, 29; **50:**7, 10, 11, 17, 24, 38, 41, 42, 42, 42; **51:**13, 17, 17, 18, 18, 20, 32, 32, 50, 51, 51, 56; **La 1:**1, 2, 4, 4, 4, 6, 6, 15, 16, 22; **2:**9, 11, 20; **3:**39, 47, 47, 58; **4:**2, 8, 9, 15, 16, 21; **5:**3, 3, 5, 5, 5, 12, 12, 13, 17, 22; **Eze 2:**3, 4, 5, 6, 6, 7; **3:**7, 8, 9, 18, 26, 27; **4:**4, 12; **6:**9, 11, 12, 12; **8:**6, 6, 12, 12; **9:**9, 9; **11:**2, 2, 5, 7, 7, 13, 15, 15, 17; **12:**2, 3, 4, 5, 11, 27; **13:**2, 3, 4, 8, 10, 15, 18; **14:**22, 23; **15:**5, 6, 6; **16:**3, 32, 34, 45, 52, 57, 61; **18:**4, 29; **20:**20, 29, 34, 38, 49; **21:**24, 24, 26, 26, 31, 32; **22:**2, 2, 4, 7, 7, 7, 9, 10, 12, 18, 18, 19, 20, 27; **23:**45; **24:**19; **26:**18; **27:**26, 26, 34, 35, 35; **28:**2, 2, 6, 19, 19; **30:**4; **31:**3, 14; **32:**2, 19, 23, 23, 23, 26, 26, 27, 30; **33:**8, 10, 10, 10, 17, 17, 20, 24, 30, 32; **34:**4, 5, 16, 21, 26, 30, 31, 31; **36:**3, 3, 20, 35; **37:**11; **38:**12, 12, 13, 13, 14, 17; **39:**15, 19, 19; **42:**13, 13, 14; **43:**11, 13, 17, 19, 24, 24; **44:**14, 14, 16, 16, 19; **45:**12, 17; **46:**24; **47:**12, 16, 22, 23; **48:**23, 29; **Da 1:**4, 4, 13; **2:**8, 27, 37, 38; **3:**12, 17; **4:**3, 31, 35, 37, 37; **5:**13, 14, 22; **7:**24; **9:**4, 7, 7, 8, 15, 18, 26; **10:**19; **11:**33, 34, 35; **12:**3, 10, 12; **Hos 1:**10, 10; **2:**4, 23, 23; **4:**3, 6, 7, 8, 9, 9, 12, 14; **5:**1, 1, 3, 3, 4, 6, 11; **6:**9; **7:**2, 4, 4, 5, 16; **8:**2, 13; **9:**7, 7, 8, 9, 15, 16, 16; **10:**2, 2, 11; **11:**7; **12:**7, 11; **13:**9, 10, 13, 13; **14:**9, 9, 9; **Joel 1:**5, 6, 9, 9, 10, 10, 11, 16; **2:**2, 23; **3:**4, 4, 13, 14; **Am 2:**7; **3:**10, 12; **4:**1, 4; **5:**7, 11, 11, 13, 18, 23; **6:**1, 1, 2, 9, 12; **7:**2, 5; **9:**4, 6, 7; **Ob** 3; **Jnh 1:**2, 8, 8; **Mic 2:**4, 12; **3:**1, 2, 5, 10, 11, 11; **4:**6, 7, 9, 9; **5:**2, 2; **6:**9, 9, 10, 12, 16; **7:**2, 3, 17; **Na 1:**3, 5, 9, 14; **2:**1, 6, 8; **3:**3, 6, 8, 17, 18; **Hab 1:**6, 7, 8, 8, 11, 11, 12, 13, 13, 14, 14, 16; **2:**4, 5, 5, 18, 19; **3:**17, 17; **Zep 1:**13; **2:**3, 9; **3:**3, 3, 4, 6, 6, 6, 12; **Hag 1:**2, 4, 5, 7, 9; **Zec 1:**5, 9, 10, 19, 21; **2:**2, 7; **3:**8; **4:**2, 4, 11, 12; **5:**10; **6:**4, 5, 5; **8:**16, 17, 19, 21; **9:**1, 2; **10:**2, 8; **11:**2, 9, 9, 16; **13:**6, 9, 9; **Mal 1:**6, 8, 12, 13; **2:**7, 10, 10, 10, 15; **3:**1, 6, 9, 11, 14, 15; **Mt 1:**21; **2:**6, 18, 20; **3:**14; **4:**3, 6; **5:**5, 6, 7, 8, 10, 11, 11, 13, 14, 21, 22, 22, 22, 22, 23, 25, 39, 40, 47, 47, 48; **6:**7, 18, 26, 26, 29, 30, 32; **7:**2, 15, 21; **8:**8, 22, 26, 29; **9:**2, 4, 5, 6, 13, 17, 37; **10:**2, 12, 18, 19, 23, 30, 31, 37, 37, 38; **11:**3, 5, 5, 6, 14, 16, 28; **12:**20, 38, 47, 48, 49; **13:**12, 12, 15, 16, 21, 38, 39, 40; **14:**33; **15:**8, 11, 11, 14, 20, 27; **16:**3, 8, 16, 17, 18, 23, 23; **17:**26; **18:**10, 16, 17, 20; **19:**5, 6, 12, 30; **20:**16, 16, 22, 22, 22, 25; **21:**3, 16; **22:**12, 14, 14, 16, 16, 18, 20, 40; **23:**2, 8, 15, 20, 21, 22, 23, 25, 25, 27, 28, 31; **25:**8, 24, 29, 29, 34; **26:**63, 70; **27:**11, 40; **28:**5; **Mk 1:**11, 24, 24; **2:**5, 9, 11, 17, 19; **3:**11, 16, 32, 33, 34; **4:**11, 17, 25, 25, 28, 38, 40; **5:**7, 9; **7:**7, 13, 15, 15, 23, 28, 37; **8:**4, 17, 17, 28, 29, 33; **10:**8, 8, 31, 38, 38, 38, 39, 42; **11:**3, 5, 25, 25; **12:**14, 14, 15, 16, 34, 38, 40; **13:**11; **14:**37, 49, 61, 70; **15:**2; **16:**6; **Lk 1:**13, 31, 42, 45; **3:**11, 22; **4:**3, 6, 9, 34, 34, 41; **5:**20, 23, 24, 32, 33; **6:**13, 20, 21, 22, 22, 24, 25, 26, 27, 30, 35; **7:**7, 19, 20, 22, 22, 23, 25, 32, 47, 48; **8:**16, 18, 18, 20, 21, 28; **9:**13, 19, 20, 60; **10:**2, 6, 6, 20, 23, 41; **11:**7, 28, 29, 36, 39, 39, 42, 44, 44; **12:**7, 7, 11, 12, 24, 27, 28, 37, 38, 48, 48, 54, 58; **13:**12, 14, 30, 30; **14:**8, 31; **15:**7, 27, 31; **16:**2, 8, 8, 10, 11, 12, 16, 25; **17:**10, 10, 17; **18:**31; **19:**10, 17, 21, 26, 26, 31, 33; **20:**6, 21, 24, 36, 36, 38, 47; **22:**25, 26, 42, 46, 60, 67, 70, 70; **23:**3, 29, 29, 29, 31, 34, 37, 39, 40; **24:**5, 17, 25, 38, 48; **Jn 1:**13, 21, 21, 21, 22, 33, 38, 42, 49; **3:**2, 3, 8, 10, 21; **4:**9, 9, 12, 35, 35, 36; **5:**14, 23; **6:**63, 67, 69; **7:**18, 18, 19, 25, 37, 52; **8:**10, 13, 14, 23, 23, 25, 29, 31, 33, 37, 37, 38, 40, 41, 43, 44, 52, 53, 53, 53; **9:**28, 28, 34, 39, 40, 40; **10:**16, 24, 24, 26, 30, 32, 34; **11:**8, 9, 26, 27, 47; **12:**34, 34, 35, 44, 45; **13:**6, 10, 11, 13, 16, 33, 35, 36; **14:**2, 5, 9, 10, 20, 21, 22, 24; **15:**5, 6, 14, 15; **16:**2, 6, 19, 29; **17:**10, 10, 11, 16, 21, 21, 22; **18:**4, 7, 21, 31, 33, 37, 37; **19:**9, 12; **20:**13, 15, 15, 23, 23, 29, 31; **21:**18; **Ac 1:**6, 7, 11; **2:**7, 9, 15, 15, 32; **3:**15, 25, 25; **4:**9; **5:**9, 32, 35, 38, 42; **6:**3, 3; **7:**1, 26, 26, 28, 33, 51; **8:**23, 30; **9:**4, 5, 5, 6; **10:**21, 33, 39; **11:**6; **13:**31, 32, 33; **14:**11, 15, 15; **15:**10, 11, 27, 36; **16:**17, 21, 21, 28, 36, 37; **17:**6, 7, 20, 22, 28; **18:**5, 13, 28; **19:**15, 38, 39, 40; **21:**13, 21, 23, 24; **22:**3, 7, 8, 8, 10, 15, 26, 27; **23:**3, 20, 21, 21; **24:**3; **25:**9, 16; **26:**2, 3, 4, 14, 15, 15, 16, 18, 24, 26; **28:**22, 27; **Ro 1:**6, 30, 30, 30, 31, 32; **2:**1, 1, 1, 5, 15, 17, 17, 19, 19, 19, 20, 23, 25, 27, 28; **3:**9, 9, 14, 15, 22, 22, 25, 28, 30; **4:**4, 5, 7, 11, 14, 14, 16; **5:**3, 16; **6:**6, 9, 14, 14, 18, 21, 22; **7:**1, 4, 6; **8:**3, 5, 5, 8, 9, 9, 9, 14, 14, 16, 17, 17, 19, 24, 28, 35, 35, 36, 36, 39; **9:**4, 7, 8, 8, 20, 22, 22, 26, 26, 27; **10:**3, 4, 10, 10, 12, 15; **11:**3, 4, 5, 6, 7, 16, 18, 20, 28, 28, 31, 33; **12:**5, 5, 7, 13, 14, 15, 15, 17, 20, 20; **13:**2, 3, 4, 4, 4, 9; **14:**1, 4, 4, 4, 6, 7, 9, 15, 22, 22, 23; **15:**1, 3, 14, 14, 26; **16:**4, 7, 7, 14, 15, 17, 18, 18, 19; **1Co 1:**2, 12, 12, 18, 18, 23, 27, 27, 27; **2:**6; **3:**3, 3, 3, 3, 4, 9, 10, 16, 17, 18, 19, 20; **4:**8, 10, 10, 10, 10, 10, 12, 13, 13, 19; **5:**2, 4, 10, 10, 11, 12; **6:**2, 2, 4, 8, 9, 15, 16; **7:**7, 10, 14, 21, 22, 25, 26, 34; **8:**5, 7, 7, 12; **9:**1, 2, 22; **10:**12, 13, 13, 15, 17, 18, 19, 19, 20, 22; **11:**2, 10, 11, 11, 18, 19, 20, 26, 29, 30, 32, 34; **12:**4, 5, 5, 6, 13, 13, 13, 13, 20, 22, 23, 24, 26, 27, 28, 28, 28, 29; **13:**13; **14:**5, 7, 7, 7, 8,

10, 10, 12, 16, 23, 24, 27, 32, 36, 37; **15:**6, 12, 17, 19, 22, 22, 29, 37, 39, 39, 40, 40, 42, 43, 43, 43, 44, 44, 44, 44, 49, 50, 52; **16:**9, 9, 15; **2Co 1:**1, 4, 6, 7, 10, 11, 14; **2:**11, 15, 16, 16, 16, 16, 17, 17; **3:**1, 1, 2, 3, 4, 13, 15; **4:**2, 3, 4, 5, 8, 8, 8, 9, 15, 16, 16, 17; **5:**6, 6, 8, 9, 11, 12, 12, 13, 13, 17, 20; **6:**4, 8, 9, 9, 9, 10, 11, 14, 16; **7:**3, 6; **8:**8, 12, 12, 18, 20, 20, 21, 21, 22, 23, 23; **9:**2, 3, 13; **10:**3, 10, 10, 11, 12, 12, 14, 16; **11:**13, 19, 22, 22, 22, 26, 28; **12:**19; **13:**4, 6, 9, 9; **Gal 1:**6, 6, 7; **2:**14, 14, 15, 17; **3:**3, 4, 7, 10, 10, 19, 22, 24, 26, 28, 28, 29, 29; **4:**1, 7, 7, 10, 17, 17, 17, 18, 28, 29, 29, 31, 31; **5:**2, 3, 4, 5, 6, 15, 17, 17, 17, 18, 18, 25; **6:**1, 3, 3, 3, 5, 6, 12, 12, 16; **Eph 1:**1, 7; **2:**6, 6, 10, 19, 19, 19, 20, 21, 22; **3:**6, 10, 13; **4:**4, 17, 18, 18, 19, 24, 26, 28; **5:**1, 4, 8, 13, 15, 30, 31, 32; **6:**6, 8, 12, 22; **Php 1:**11, 15, 18, 27, 28, 28, 30; **2:**1, 4, 15, 19; **3:**3, 3, 15, 18, 18, 20, 20; **4:**1, 3, 5, 8, 8, 10, 18, 21; **Col 1:**2, 5, 22, 27; **2:**5, 10, 19, 19, 22, 22; **3:**11, 15, 22, 24; **4:**5, 8, 11, 11; **1Th 1:**10; **2:**10, 20; **3:**3, 6; **4:**1, 12, 15, 15, 17; **5:**3, 5, 10, 11, 12, 14, 14, 14; **2Th 1:**3, 3, 4, 5, 7; **2:**10, 13; **3:**4, 4, 11, 17; **1Ti 1:**3, 7, 8, 8, 9, 9, 9, 10, 10, 18, 20; **2:**2; **3:**8, 10; **4:**2, 2, 12; **5:**8, 10, 13, 16, 16, 19, 23, 24, 25; **6:**1, 2, 3, 3, 5, 9, 17; **2Ti 1:**4, 15; **2:**2, 6, 13, 14, 17, 19, 20, 20, 20, 20; **3:**5, 6, 6, 7, 8, 9, 14; **Tit 1:**6, 9, 10, 12, 12, 15, 15, 15, 16; **2:**12; **3:**8, 8, 9, 11, 13; **Phm 1:**6; **Heb 1:**5, 10, 12, 14, 14; **2:**3, 5, 14, 18; **3:**1, 6, 12, 14; **4:**12; **5:**2, 5, 6, 12, 14; **6:**6, 9, 9, 9, 12, 18; **7:**5, 5, 5, 8, 8, 8, 13, 17, 21; **8:**4; **9:**9, 10, 15, 28; **10:**8, 13, 39; **11:**14; **12:**1, 8, 8, 11, 13, 14, 15, 23, 28; **13:**4, 14, 16, 17; **Jas 1:**9, 10, 22, 26; **2:**4, 9, 9, 24; **3:**4, 13, 14, 15, 15, 18; **4:**2, 11, 11, 13; **5:**2, 5, 13, 14, 17; **1Pe 1:**1, 2, 5, 7, 8, 12, 14, 24; **2:**5, 9, 9, 9, 10, 11, 16, 16, 16, 18, 18, 18, 20, 20; **3:**6, 7, 12, 13, 15, 22; **4:**1, 4, 11, 11, 12, 14, 18, 19; **5:**1, 2, 9, 9, 14; **2Pe 1:**9, 10, 12, 14, 19; **2:**10, 11, 12, 12, 13, 14, 17, 17, 19, 19, 20; **3:**13, 14, 16, 16; **1Jn 1:**3, 4, 6, 6, 7, 8, 10; **2:**11, 11, 13, 13, 14, 14, 14, 16, 16, 20, 22, 29; **3:**1, 1, 2, 4, 7, 10, 10, 19; **4:**1, 17, 18; **5:**5, 10, 19, 20, 20; **3Jn** 3, 5, 5, 5, 7, 7, 11; **Jude** 1, 7, 7, 12, 12, 12, 12, 12, 13, 13, 16, 16, 19, 19, 19, 20, 23; **Rev 1:**9, 19, 20, 20; **2:**2, 2, 2, 9, 9, 10, 14, 18, 18, 20, 26; **3:**1, 2, 4, 4, 5, 5, 9, 9, 9, 12, 15, 16, 17; **4:**5, 11; **5:**6, 6, 9; **7:**13, 13, 14, 14, 15; **9:**12, 14; **11:**4; **13:**6, 8, 10, 10; **14:**4, 5, 13, 13, 18; **15:**3, 3, 4; **16:**5, 7, 15, 15; **17:**7, 12, 14; **18:**5, 14, 14; **19:**2, 9, 9, 9; **20:**6, 8; **21:**4, 6, 7, 22, 27; **22:**6, 7, 14, 15, 19

AREN'T (51)

Ge 34:14; **Nu 23:**25; **Jdg 8:**2; **11:**7; **1Sa 1:**8; **26:**15; **2Sa 13:**33; **16:**17; **2Ki 4:**6; **5:**12; **7:**9; **10:**9; **Ne 2:**2; **Job 19:**22; **Ps 73:**5; **Pr 30:**25, 26; **Isa 7:**13; **58:**3; **Jer 37:**9; **Da 3:**25; **Hos 5:**7; **Mt 12:**7; **15:**15; **22:**8; **26:**62; **Mk 14:**60; **15:**4; **Jn 1:**25; **4:**18; **8:**47, 57; **10:**12; **18:**17, 25; **Ac 19: 26; 21:**38; **Ro 3:**20; **1Co 2:**14; **3:**2, 4, 7; **5:**2; **7:**8; **10:**16, 16; **1Th 5:**4; **Jas 2:**5, 7; **Jude 1:**23; **Rev 2:**9

AS (4872)

Ge 3:14, 14, 22; **6:**2, 22; **7:**5, 9, 16, 18; **8:**5, 22, 22; **9:**3, 12, 23; **10:**9; **11:**2, 3; **12:**4, 11; **13:**14, 14, 15; **14:**6, 6, 10, 10, 17, 23; **15:**12, 13, 17; **16:**3, 6, 12, 13; **17:**5, 20, 20, 23, 27; **18:**1, 5, 8, 14; **19:**1, 2, 2, 4, 8, 22, 23, 26, 28, 35, 37, 38; **20:**18; **21:**4, 8, 12, 16, 20, 30, 31; **22:**2, 6, 10, 13; **23:**8, 10, 13, 16, 20; **24:**14, 15, 51, 60, 63; **25:**27, 33; **26:**1, 3, 3, 4, 4, 29; **27:**8, 19, 30, 30; **28:**12, 14, 14, 18, 18; **29:**9, 13, 13, 18; **30:**16, 18, 32, 34, 38, 43; **31:**25, 32, 36, 45, 48, 52; **32:**1, 12, 12, 31; **33:**3, 8; **34:**7, 9, 11, 12, 22; **35:**14; **36:**1, 8, 19; **37:**10, 10, 25; **38:**8, 15, 19, 24, 25, 28; **39:**2, 10, 10, 12, 12; **40:**13, 22; **41:**8, 8, 13, 13, 21, 21, 28, 32, 38, 42, 54; **42:**5, 14, 18, 23, 34, 34, 35, 35; **43:**5, 11, 12, 14, 17, 18, 19, 21, 34, 34; **44:**1, 1, 2, 15, 18, 33; **45:**21, 21, 24; **46:**29, 29, 34; **47:**9, 9, 11, 29, 31; **48:**4, 5, 5, 7, 14, 20, 20; **49:**4, 4; **50:**6, 12, 20, 20, 23; **Ex 1:**11, 16, 16; **2:**6, 10, 13, 14; **3:**2, 12; **4:**6, 7, 7, 12, 16, 30; **5:**11, 11, 13, 16, 16, 20; **6:**3; **7:**6, 10, 13, 15, 20, 20, 22; **8:**10, 10, 10, 13, 15, 17, 19, 20, 24, 27, 29, 29, 31; **9:**6, 10, 12, 29, 29, 30, 30, 33, 34, 35; **10:**23; **12:**11, 11, 13, 14, 19, 28, 31, 32, 33, 33, 35, 48; **13:**19; **14:**4, 9, 10, 20, 27, 29; **15:**7, 17; **16:**4, 4, 5, 5, 10, 16, 16, 21, 22, 22, 23, 23, 23, 29, 29, 31, 32, 33, 34; **17:**6, 6, 11, 11, 13, 14; **18:**9, 12, 13, 21; **19:**9, 11, 19; **20:**1, 11, 21; **21:**7, 7, 9, 9, 10, 11, 16; **22:**3, 9, 13, 16, 26; **23:**15, 19; **24:**5, 10, 10, 18; **25:**29, 29; **26:**29; **27:**8; **28:**3, 3, 4, 12, 12, 15, 21, 35, 36, 39, 41, 41; **29:**1, 14, 16, 20, 21, 24, 25, 26, 27, 36, 40, 41, 44; **30:**2, 12, 30, 32, 37; **31:**10, 10, 18; **32:**13, 13, 17; **33:**7, 9, 11, 22; **34:**4, 5, 9, 16, 18, 25; **35:**19, 24, 35; **36:**1; **37:**9, 25; **38:**21, 22; **39:**1, 5, 6, 7, 7, 8, 21, 26, 29, 30, 31, 32, 43; **40:**13, 15, 15, 16, 19, 21, 23, 25, 27, 29, 32; **Lev 1:**4, 14; **2:**4, 9, 10, 11, 12, 16; **3:**3, 7, 9, 11, 12, 14, 16; **4:**10, 10, 20, 21, 23, 26, 28, 31, 32, 35, 35; **5:**2, 3, 3, 6, 7, 8, 10, 12, 13, 15, 15, 16, 18; **6:**4, 17, 22, 25; **7:**2, 5, 12, 14, 16, 18, 18, 19, 29, 30, 32, 35, 36; **8:**9, 13, 15, 15, 17, 19, 21, 21, 23, 28, 29, 31; **9:**5, 7, 8, 10, 14, 15, 15, 21, 21; **10:**5, 7, 13, 14, 15, 16, 18; **11:**9, 42, 42; **12:**2, 5; **13:**15, 15, 45, 46, 46; **14:**12, 13, 21, 24, 34, 40, 45; **15:**25, 25, 26, 31; **16:**6, 9, 11, 15, 15, 23, 26, 27, 29, 29; **17:**4, 5, 8; **18:**21, 25, 28; **19:**18, 21, 24, 34; **20:**2, 2, 2, 27; **21:**4, 6, 7, 8, 9, 9; **22:**18, 18, 18, 21, 23, 25, 27, 32, 32; **23:**12, 13, 15, 17, 18, 19, 19; **24:**7, 7, 8, 23; **25:**2, 10, 12, 22, 35, 36, 39, 40, 40, 42, 45, 46, 53; **26:**19, 19, 19, 19, 34, 35, 36, 37, 43; **27:**9, 11, 19, 23, 28, 30, 32; **Nu 1:**19, 50, 54; **2:**34, 34; **3:**1, 3, 4, 6, 9, 12, 16, 41, 41, 42, 45, 47, 48, 51; **4:**37, 41, 45, 49, 49; **5:**4, 26; **6:**4, 4, 8, 8, 13, 21, 27; **7:**1, 15, 21, 27, 33, 39, 45, 51, 57, 63, 69, 75, 81; **8:**3, 11, 13, 15, 16, 21; **9:**5, 5, 18, 18, 19, 22, 22; **10:**25, 34; **11:**3, 25; **12:**8, 10, 10; **13:**3, 17, 21, 21, 23, 27, 30; **14:**3, 17, 17, 19, 20, 21, 21, 21, 21, 28, 28, 32, 45, 45; **15:**5, 8, 8, 19, 20, 20, 36, 39; **16:**3, 7, 9, 10, 15, 34, 38, 38, 40, 42, 47; **17:**10, 11, 12, 12; **18:**2, 3, 7, 8, 10, 10, 11, 12, 16, 17, 19, 21, 24, 26, 27, 28, 29, 30, 32; **19:**5; **20:**8, 9, 13, 15, 22, 27, 27; **21:**1, 15, 15, 24, 24, 26, 26, 29, 29, 30, 30, 34; **22:**22; **23:**10, 10, 30; **24:**1; **25:**6, 11; **26:**4, 10, 53, 63; **27:**11, 11, 13, 22, 23; **28:**7, 19, 22; **29:**5, 16, 19, 22, 25, 28, 31, 34, 38, 39, 40; **31:**7, 9, 28, 29, 31, 41, 47, 50, 52, 54; **32:**5, 27, 29, 31; **33:**1, 49, 49; **34:**2; **35:**5; **36:**6, 6, 7, 10; **Dt 1:**5, 10, 10, 11, 13, 15, 19, 21, 30, 31, 38, 40, 41; **2:**1, 5, 8, 9, 10, 10, 11, 19, 20, 21, 21, 30, 35, 36, 36; **3:**2, 6, 10, 10, 13, 14, 18, 20, 24; **4:**6, 6, 7, 7, 8, 8, 9, 9, 10, 10, 21, 26, 32, 32, 33, 38, 38, 46, 46, 49, 49; **5:**5, 12, 14, 16, 31; **6:**2, 2, 3, 8, 16, 19, 24; **7:**12; **8:**5, 9, 9, 20; **9:**3, 24, 24; **10:**4, 5, 9, 10, 10, 15, 15, 22, 22; **11:**4, 10, 18, 21, 21, 25; **12:**1, 1, 10, 12, 15, 15, 15, 19, 19, 20, 21, 22, 31; **13:**15, 15, 16, 17; **14:**2, 9, 21, 27, 29, 29; **15:**4, 6, 21, 22; **16:**3, 3, 3, 6, 17; **17:**15, 18, 19, 19, 20; **18:**2, 3, 3, 10, 11, 17; **19:**8, 10, 14; **20:**3, 10, 16, 16, 17; **21:**14, 23; **23:**6, 6, 7, 13, 23; **24:**4, 6, 7, 9, 12, 13, 15; **25:**4, 6, 10, 17, 19; **26:**1, 13, 15, 18, 19; **27:**1, 3, 4, 9; **28:**9, 9, 23, 23, 23, 23, 32, 32, 32, 46, 56, 62, 62, 63, 68; **29:**8, 13, 13, 13, 16; **30:**1, 9; **31:**3, 4, 5, 7, 7, 13, 13, 19, 21, 26; **32:**10, 31, 40, 40, 46, 49, 50; **34:**1, 1, 3, 3, 5, 7, 7, 9; **Jos 1:**5, 5, 5, 15, 17, 17; **2:**5, 7, 7, 14; **3:**7, 15, 15, 17; **4:**7, 8, 8, 12, 14, 14, 18, 18, 18, 23; **5:**13, 15; **6:**8, 15, 16, 17, 20, 20; **7:**5, 5, 22; **8:**2, 5, 6, 8, 15, 18, 19, 19, 27, 32; **9:**1, 1, 12; **10:**1, 2, 2, 11, 13, 24, 27, 28, 30, 32, 35, 37, 39, 40; **11:**8, 8, 9, 12, 15, 15, 20, 23, 23; **12:**2, 3, 3, 3, 3, 7; **13:**6, 6, 7, 9, 9, 10, 10, 11, 11, 14, 23, 25, 25, 27, 27, 28; **14:**1, 10, 10, 11, 11, 11, 11, 12, 12, 13; **15:**18, 19, 47, 47; **16:**3, 3, 5, 10; **17:**4, 5, 13, 18, 18, 18; **18:**7, 8, 9; **19:**8, 8, 8, 27, 27, 28, 28, 33, 33, 49, 51; **20:**2, 7, 8, 9, 9; **21:**3, 44; **22:**2, 4, 7, 25, 27, 31; **23:**4, 4, 4, 5, 8, 10, 15, 15; **24:**5, 15, 17, 26; **Jdg 1:**14, 15, 20, 23, 28, 30, 33, 34, 35; **2:**15, 22; **3:**20, 20; **5:**7, 18, 31; **6:**4, 4, 5, 5, 16, 20, 26, 26, 27, 28, 34, 36, 37, 40; **7:**1, 1, 13, 17, 18, 18, 21, 21, 22, 22, 24; **8:**19, 19, 33, 33; **9:**33, 33, 33, 48, 52; **10:**10, 15; **11:**31, 33, 33; **13:**5, 7, 9, 16, 19, 19, 20, 24; **14:**5, 6, 6, 10, 10; **15:**1, 14, 14, 19; **16:**7, 7, 9, 11, 11, 12, 12, 13, 13, 17, 17, 17, 20; **17:**5, 8, 12, 13; **18:**16, 23, 30, 30, 31, 31; **19:**9, 14; **20:**30, 31, 32, 39; **21:**14, 23; **Ru 2:**3, 13, 13, 20, 20, 22; **3:**3, 13, 13; **4:**2, 8, 16; **1Sa 1:**7, 10, 11, 12; **2:**1, 13, 16, 16, 26, 28, 31, 32; **3:**10, 15, 19, 20; **4:**9, 9; **6:**6, 12, 12, 12, 14, 17, 18; **7:**9, 10, 15; **8:**1, 7, 9, 22; **9:**11, 14; **10:**9, 24; **11:**2, 7, 10; **12:**1, 2, 3, 7, 15, 15, 23; **13:**5, 5, 8, 10, 21; **14:**13, 31, 41, 45, 45; **15:**23, 23, 23, 23, 27, 33; **16:**1, 4, 13; **17:**7, 7, 20, 23, 24, 24, 27, 48, 52, 52, 52, 52, 55; **18:**10, 17; **19:**5, 6, 6, 7, 9, 9, 15; **20:**8, 13, 14, 14, 17, 17, 20, 21, 21, 31, 31, 35, 36, 41, 41, 41; **22:**11, 14, 14; **23:**11, 17, 26; **24:**3, 4, 13, 14, 14; **25:**13, 20, 25, 26, 26, 26, 26, 37, 42; **26:**15, 19, 24; **28:**10, 10, 17; **29:**2, 9, 9, 9, 9, 10, 10; **30:**20; **2Sa 1:**18; **2:**7, 11, 16, 24; **3:**1, 6, 10, 10, 10, 16, 16, 16, 27, 33; **4:**3, 4, 4, 4, 5, 7, 9, 9; **6:**16, 21; **7:**10, 15, 25, 25; **8:**18; **9:**11; **11:**2, 23, 25, 25; **12:**5, 5; **13:**11, 18, 20, 30, 35; **14:**11, 11, 13, 13, 20, 20, 25, 25, 30, 32; **15:**10, 10, 11, 23, 30, 30, 30, 32, 32, 34, 37; **16:**5, 13, 23, 23, 23; **17:**3, 8, 8, 11, 11, 11, 11, 17, 25; **18:**4, 9, 14, 18, 24, 25, 32, 33; **19:**2, 3, 5, 8, 13, 18, 26, 35, 43, 43; **20:**8, 8, 9, 17; **21:**13, 13, 18, 19, 19; **22:**31, 34, 34, 43, 43, 44, 45, 45; **23:**17, 17, 18, 18, 22, 22; **24:**3, 3, 7, 7, 16, 22; **1Ki 1:**20, 21, 21, 21, 29, 29, 30, 35, 37, 41, 45, 46, 47; **2:**1, 4, 8, 12, 15, 17, 22, 24, 24, 24, 27, 31, 42; **3:**12, 14, 28; **4:**20, 20, 21, 21, 23, 23; **5:**5, 6, 8, 10, 10, 12; **6:**10; **7:**7, 24, 32, 34, 35; **8:**1, 9, 10, 16, 25, 36, 40, 40, 43, 56, 57, 61, 65, 65, 66; **9:**1, 1, 2, 4, 4, 11, 13, 16, 19, 22; **10:**10, 21, 27, 27, 27, 27; **11:**4, 6, 25, 29, 33, 38, 38; **12:**12, 24, 30, 30; **13:**1, 5, 11, 18, 24; **14:**2, 10, 17, 18, 21, 27; **15:**3, 3, 11, 13, 21, 21, 29; **16:**3, 12, 16, 24, 31; **17:**1, 1, 5, 10, 11, 15, 16; **18:**7, 12, 12, 14, 14, 30, 34; **19:**5, 11, 16, 21; **20:**12, 16, 17, 25, 34, 36, 36, 39, 41; **21:**2, 19, 22, 25, 26; **22:**14, 14, 30, 35, 36, 38, 53; **2Ki 1:**17; **2:**2, 2, 4, 4, 6, 6, 7, 11, 12, 19, 22, 23; **3:**2, 2, 14, 14, 22, 22, 24, 27, 27; **4:**1, 3, 3, 4, 5, 15, 17, 25, 30, 30, 38, 44; **5:**2, 5, 14, 14, 14, 16, 16, 20, 20, 27, 27; **6:**1, 5, 18, 18, 20, 20, 25, 26, 30; **7:**4, 16, 17, 17; **8:**2, 4, 9, 18, 18; **9:**4, 9, 22, 22, 26, 27, 27; **10:**2, 2, 15, 15, 17, 25, 25, 33, 33; **11:**9, 9, 9, 14; **12:**4; **13:**5, 15, 21, 21; **14:**5, 7, 14, 14, 21, 25; **15:**3, 9, 16, 16, 29, 34; **16:**2, 6, 8, 9, 16, 18, 18; **17:**2, 2, 8, 8, 14, 14, 21, 23, 31; **18:**3, 8, 8; **19:**12, 17, 21, 26, 26, 26, 26; **20:**9; **21:**3, 13, 14, 20; **22:**16; **23:**8, 10, 16, 16, 16, 19, 21, 27, 32, 33, 34, 35, 37; **24:**2, 9, 13, 15, 17, 19; **25:**7, 10, 11, 18, 22, 23, 26, 26; **1Ch 1:**10, 27; **4:**27, 27, 33, 33; **5:**1, 11, 11, 24, 26, 26; **6:**49; **7:**28, 28; **9:**18, 19, 29, 34; **11:**3, 4, 10, 19, 19, 20, 20, 23, 23, 24, 24; **12:**2, 2, 8, 8, 8, 8, 19, 20, 23, 40, 40; **13:**2; **15:**5, 6, 7, 8, 9, 10, 15, 18, 22, 24, 26, 27, 29; **16:**17, 17, 18, 38, 42; **17:**9, 13, 17, 23; **18:**3, 3, 17; **20:**4, 5, 5; **21:**12, 14, 15, 23; **22:**11, 12; **23:**4, 5, 11, 14, 28; **24:**2, 6; **25:**6; **26:**10, 11, 29; **27:**6, 23, 23; **28:**2, 6, 7, 8, 8, 10, 17, 17; **29:**2, 2, 2, 2, 11, 15, 21, 22, 22, 22; **2Ch 1:**9, 9, 12, 15, 15, 15, 15; **2:**6, 18, 18, 18; **4:**3, 16, 20; **5:**2; **6:**5, 6, 6, 16, 27, 31, 31, 33; **7:**8, 8, 11, 11, 12, 17, 17; **8:**4, 9; **9:**9, 9, 20, 27, 27, 27, 27; **10:**12; **11:**12, 14, 17; **12:**13; **13:**8, 10, 10; **14:**5, 5, 13, 13, 14; **15:**2, 2, 2, 11, 16; **16:**5, 5; **17:**11; **18:**13, 13, 29, 32, 32, 34; **19:**8, 11; **20:**9, 11, 13, 24, 24; **21:**4, 6, 6, 13, 13, 13, 19; **22:**1, 4; **23:**4, 6, 8, 8, 8, 18, 18; **24:**22, 25; **25:**3, 14; **26:**1, 4, 5, 5, 19; **27:**2; **28:**1, 21; **29:**2, 8, 15, 21, 24, 27, 28, 33; **30:**5, 7, 8, 8, 10, 10, 22; **31:**3, 3, 3, 19, 21; **32:**17, 19; **33:**22; **34:**6, 6, 9, 9, 9, 13, 14, 14, 32; **35:**5, 8, 13, 16, 18; **36:**4, 4, 21; **Ezr 1:**4, 4; **2:**62, 69, 69; **3:**1, 2, 4, 10; **4:**2, 3, 14; **5:**14, 15; **6:**5, 8, 12, 14, 17; **7:**7, 7, 15, 16, 16, 19; **8:**21, 26, 26, 27, 27, 28, 35, 35, 35, 35; **9:**2, 7, 8, 12, 13, 15; **10:**5, 12, 19; **Ne 1:**11; **3:**1, 1, 8, 8, 15, 15, 16, 16, 26, 26, 31, 31, 31, 31; **4:**14, 22, 22; **5:**10, 10, 12, 13; **7:**3, 64; **8:**1, 6, 9, 9, 14, 15, 18; **9:**2, 23, 23, 24, 32; **10:**29, 34, 36, 38, 38; **11:**22; **12:**12, 24, 44, 45; **13:**1, 4, 13, 19; **Est 1:**3, 3, 7, 8, 8; **2:**7, 8, 20, 21; **3:**11; **4:**3, 5, 14, 17; **5:**5, 9, 13, 13; **6:**4, 8, 8, 9, 10; **7:**4, 8, 8, 8; **8:**9, 13; **9:**4, 5, 13, 31; **Job 2:**6, 8; **3:**11; **4:**12, 13, 19, 19; **5:**7, 7, 14, 25, 25; **6:**12, 12, 15, 15; **7:**9; **8:**9, 9; **9:**19, 19; **10:**4, 22, 22, 22, 22; **11:**17, 17; **12:**11; **13:**1, 2, 2, 4, 9, 9, 12, 12, 12, 12; **14:**11, 11, 18, 18, 19; **16:**6, 8, 12, 21; **17:**10; **19:**5, 11, 22, 25; **21:**33; **22:**6; **24:**3, 9, 11, 18, 18, 19; **27:**3, 3, 6, 6, 18, 18, 18, 18; **28:**3, 5; **29:**15, 21, 23, 23, 23, 25, 25, 25; **30:**5, 7, 15, 17, 19; **31:**33; **33:**12, 15, 25, 25; **34:**3, 7, 7; **37:**1, 2, 13, 13; **38:**7, 8, 9, 14, 30, 30, 35, 40, 41; **39:**1, 16; **40:**9, 9, 15, 17, 17; **41:**24, 24, 24, 24, 28, 28, 30, 30, 30; **42:**7, 8, 8, 9, 10, 10, 15, 15; **Ps 2:**8, 8; **5:**1; **12:**5; **17:**6, 8; **18:**30, 33, 33, 42, 42, 43, 44, 44; **21:**9; **23:**5; **28:**1, 2, 2; **29:**10; **30:**7, 7; **31:**12, 12; **35:**14, 14; **36:**5, 5; **37:**6, 6; **38:**13; **39:**2, 11, 11, 12; **40:**2, 9, 17; **41:**6; **42:**1, 4, 7; **45:**15; **46:**3; **47:**4; **48:**3, 9, 10; **49:**13, 15; **50:**4, 7; **54:**5; **55:**14, 20, 21, 21, 21, 21; **57:**10, 10; **59:**6, 14, 16; **61:**8; **63:**4, 4; **64:**6; **66:**15, 17; **68:**13, 24, 28; **72:**5, 5, 5, 5, 6, 6, 16, 17, 17; **73:**2, 28; **74:**2, 9; **75:**9; **76:**10; **77:**13, 13, 20; **78:**15, 27, 27, 27, 27, 57, 57, 57, 57, 65, 69, 69; **79:**2; **80:**6, 8; **82:**7; **83:**4, 5, 9, 9, 11, 14, 14; **85:**13; **88:**4, 5, 5; **89:**2, 2, 4, 8, 8, 14, 29, 29, 36, 36, 37, 37, 38, 51; **90:**4, 11, 11; **92:**10, 10; **93:**3; **95:**8, 8; **102:**7, 11, 11; **103:**10, 11, 11, 12, 12, 16, 22; **104:**15, 27, 33, 33, 35; **105:**10, 10, 11, 17, 22, 23, 39; **106:**9, 9, 31, 34; **107:**30; **109:**4, 7, 10, 18, 18, 18; **111:**1; **115:**3, 8; **116:**2, 2, 9; **119:**7, 14, 14, 58, 65, 76, 90, 90, 107, 116, 130, 132, 143, 154, 170; **120:**7; **121:**5, 8; **122:**3, 4; **123:**2, 2; **125:**1, 1, 2; **126:**4, 6, 6; **128:**3, 3, 5, 5; **129:**3, 6, 6; **131:**2; **132:**13; **133:**2, 2, 3, 3; **134:**1; **135:**12, 18; **136:**21; **137:**1; **138:**2; **139:**12, 12, 15, 15; **141:**2, 2, 7; **143:**6; **144:**2; **145:**15; **146:**2, 2, 5; **149:**5; **Pr 1:**12; **2:**4, 14; **3:**12; **4:**3, 10, 12, 14; **5:**3, 3, 4, 4, 4; **6:**31, 31; **7:**2, 3, 9, 9; **8:**1, 1; **18:**4, 4, 9, 9, 11, 20; **22:**7; **23:**5; **24:**8, 32; **25:**11, 11, 12, 12, 13, 13, 18, 18, 20, 20, 23, 23, 27, 28, 28; **26:**4, 4, 6, 6, 7, 7, 8, 8, 9, 9, 11, 14, 17, 17, 18, 18, 21, 21, 23; **27:**9, 9, 14, 15, 15, 17, 19, 20; **28:**1, 1, 11, 15, 15, 21, 21, 24, 24; **30:**14, 14, 31, 33; **Ecc 2:**11, 13, 15; **3:**12, 12; **4:**8, 8, 9, 9; **5:**1, 3, 15, 15, 16; **7:**11, 11; **8:**6, 14, 14; **9:**2, 4, 13; **10:**5; **11:**5, 5, 5, 5; **12:**5; **SS 1:**5, 5, 16; **3:**1, 3; **4:**2, 2, 4, 4, 11, 11, 15, 15; **5:**2, 5, 7, 15; **6:**4, 4, 4, 4, 4, 4, 5, 10, 10, 10, 10, 10, 10, 13; **7:**2, 2, 4, 4, 4, 4, 5, 5, 9, 9, 13, 13; **8:**6, 6, 6, 6, 12; **Isa 1:**7, 8, 8, 9, 9, 18, 18, 18, 18, 18, 18; **2:**21, 22, 22; **4:**1; **5:**25, 28; **6:**8; **7:**2, 6, 8, 11, 11, 11, 13, 23, 23; **8:**2, 16, 21; **9:**3, 4; **10:**4, 7, 9, 9, 9, 14, 22, 22, 24, 26, 34; **11:**7, 9, 16; **13:**2, 2, 4, 8, 12, 12; **14:**10, 10, 20, 24, 30; **15:**3; **16:**1, 8, 8, 8, 8; **17:**9, 9; **18:**4, 4, 4, 5; **19:**16, 16; **20:**2, 4; **22:**4; **24:**16; **25:**11; **27:**8; **28:**4, 7, 21, 23; **29:**2; **30:**8, 26, 26, 29, 32; **31:**5, 8; **32:**2, 2, 5; **33:**4, 20; **34:**4, 6; **35:**2, 2, 2, 2; **37:**12, 18, 22, 27, 27, 27, 27; **38:**7, 12, 13, 19; **40:**6, 6, 10, 15, 17; **41:**4, 8, 21, 25, 29, 29; **42:**6, 19, 19, 19, 19, 19, 19; **43:**3, 7; **44:**5, 7, 25, 28; **45:**14; **47:**5, 7, 8, 14, 14; **48:**4, 4, 4, 4, 14, 19, 19, 20; **49:**2, 2, 8, 12, 12, 18, 18; **50:**1, 1; **51:**3, 3, 8, 8, 9, 20; **52:**4; **53:**7, 7; **54:**6, 9; **55:**9; **56:**3, 3, 11, 11; **57:**5, 9; **58:**10, 10, 12, 13; **59:**10, 17; **60:**2, 2, 11; **62:**4, 5, 5, 11, 12; **63:**2, 3, 11, 14, 19, 19, 19; **64:**2; **65:**8, 18, 22, 22; **66:**1, 1, 3, 3, 3, 8, 8, 11, 13, 19, 20, 22, 22, 24; **Jer 1:**3, 5; **2:**2, 10, 10, 14, 28, 28, 30, 36; **3:**17, 18, 19, 24; **5:**2, 2, 9, 14, 29; **6:**9, 23, 26, 28, 28, 28, 28; **7:**6, 14, 15, 23; **8:**6, 6, 7; **9:**9, 14; **10:**22; **11:**13, 13, 19, 19; **12:**3, 8, 9, 9, 14, 14, 16, 16, 16; **13:**2, 5, 11, 19, 21, 24; **14:**9, 10, 16; **15:**13, 14, 18, 18, 20, 20; **16:**14, 14, 15, 15; **17:**1, 3, 4, 16, 27; **18:**3, 4, 6, 6, 8, 10, 12, 17, 22; **19:**5, 7, 10, 11, 15; **20:**4, 6, 6; **21:**2; **22:**6, 6, 11, 22, 24, 24; **23:**7, 7, 8, 8, 14, 14, 27; **24:**7; **25:**9, 14, 30; **26:**6, 7, 9, 14, 14, 20; **27:**11; **28:**5; **29:**3, 26; **30:**14, 18, 20, 20; **31:**2, 10, 32, 36, 36, 37, 40, 40; **32:**8, 13, 20, 24, 42; **33:**5, 5, 22, 24; **34:**5, 18; **36:**4, 8, 15, 21, 28; **37:**1, 4, 13, 21, 21; **38:**4, 4, 5, 16, 16; **39:**6, 9, 9; **40:**3, 7, 10; **41:**6, 7, 7; **42:**2, 18; **43:**7, 7, 12, 12; **44:**1, 13, 17, 17, 17, 17, 22, 26, 26, 30; **46:**18, 18, 18, 18, 20, 20, 22; **47:**3; **48:**13, 27, 32, 32, 41, 41, 45, 45, 46; **49:**5, 22, 22, 22, 22, 24; **50:**15, 18, 21, 28, 29, 37, 37, 40, 42; **51:**2, 24, 30, 30, 46, 49, 53, 53; **52:**2, 10, 14, 15, 24; **La 1:**7, 11, 15, 19, 21, 22; **2:**3, 4, 6, 7, 11, 13, 13, 17, 19, 22; **3:**20, 45; **4:**7, 7, 7, 7, 8, 8; **5:**10; **Eze 1:**4, 13, 15, 16, 17, 24, 25; **2:**2, 6; **3:**3, 3, 8, 8, 9, 9, 13, 17, 23; **4:**12, 12; **5:**1, 11, 11; **7:**11, 17, 17, 21, 22; **8:**4; **9:**7; **10:**1, 2, 11, 13, 16, 19, 22; **11:**21; **12:**4, 4, 6, 7, 18, 18; **13:**10; **14:**22; **15:**2, 2, 4; **16:**6, 15, 19, 30, 36, 47, 48, 48, 48, 48, 50; **17:**5, 5, 16, 16, 19, 19; **18:**3, 3; **20:**3, 3, 12, 26, 28, 30, 31, 31, 31, 33, 33, 36, 39, 41, 41, 41; **21:**7, 7; **22:**20, 25; **23:**3, 8, 8, 10, 10, 18, 21, 24, 25, 32, 33, 37; **24:**8, 22, 24; **25:**3, 7, 10; **26:**10, 15, 18; **27:**7, 11, 28, 30, 32, 32; **28:**3, 6, 6, 14; **29:**5, 10, 10, 20; **30:**17, 18; **31:**3, 11; **32:**2, 10, 14, 14, 24, 29, 30; **33:**11, 11, 24, 27, 27, 33; **34:**8, 8, 17; **35:**6, 6, 11, 11, 12; **36:**5, 17, 17; **37:**7, 7, 7, 8, 10, 14, 17; **38:**16; **39:**4, 8, 18; **40:**3, 18, 23, 24, 25, 28, 29, 32, 33, 35, 36; **41:**7, 16, 25; **42:**6, 11; **43:**11, 22, 22, 24, 25; **44:**7, 13, 14, 15, 24, 24, 28; **45:**1, 22, 24; **46:**11, 11, 12, 13, 15; **47:**3, 10, 14, 18, 18, 22; **48:**8, 8, 13, 14; **Da 1:**3, 19, 19; **2:**2, 26, 28, 34, 35, 35, 40, 40, 40, 42, 42, 42, 42, 43, 48, 48; **3:**22, 24, 26, 26; **4:**5, 13, 19, 30, 30, 30, 33, 33, 35, 36; **5:**5, 11; **6:**2, 10, 10; **7:**1, 4, 8, 9, 9, 9, 12, 13, 21; **8:**3, 4, 12, 15, 17, 22, 22; **9:**2, 7, 17, 21, 27; **10:**1, 4, 19; **11:**1, 10, 10, 20, 36, 39, 44; **12:**3, 3, 13; **Hos 2:**3, 3, 3, 4, 7, 15, 20; **4:**5, 5, 6, 10, 15, 16, 16; **5:**3, 10, 10, 12, 12, 14, 15, 15; **6:**3, 3, 5, 5; **7:**8, 8, 12; **8:**12; **9:**1, 4, 4, 9, 9, 10, 10, 13, 13; **10:**6, 14; **11:**1, 9, 9; **12:**9; **14:**6, 6, 7, 7; **Joel 1:**6, 6, 8, 16; **2:**3, 3, 4, 5, 10, 14, 23, 23, 32; **Am 1:**3, 5, 6, 9; **2:**2, 9, 9, 9, 13; **4:**5, 11, 12; **5:**8, 14; **6:**5, 7, 13; **7:**1; **8:**10, 10; **9:**6, 7, 9; **Ob** 4, 4, 11, 12, 15, 16, 16, 20, 20; **Jnh 1:**4; **4:**5, 8; **Mic 1:**11, 12, 16, 16; **2:**8, 8; **3:**8; **4:**7, 8, 13; **5:**8, 8; **7:**7, 9, 14, 20; **Na 1:**1; **2:**3, 4; **3:**2, 2, 10, 10, 13, 13, 16, 16; **Hab 1:**7; **2:**5, 5, 14; **3:**2, 19, 19; **Zep 1:**17, 17; **2:**9, 9, 9, 9, 11, 15, 15; **3:**20; **Hag 1:**6; **2:**3, 5; **Zec 1:**6, 6, 17; **3:**3; **4:**1; **6:**10, 10, 13, 13; **7:**3, 12, 12, 14, 14; **8:**8, 11; **9:**3, 3, 7, 7, 15, 16; **10:**5, 6, 7; **11:**2, 6, 6; **12:**8, 8, 10, 10; **13:**9; **14:**3, 5, 20, 20, 20, 21; **Mal 1:**4, 8, 13, 13; **2:**16, 16; **3:**3, 4, 17; **4:**3; **Mt 1:**19, 20; **2:**2, 3; **3:**16; **4:**18, 24, 24; **5:**1, 13, 45, 48; **6:**2, 7, 10, 12, 16, 29, 29; **7:**2, 15, 16, 21, 29; **8:**1; **9:**8, 9, 18, 19; **10:**8, 8, 14, 16, 16, 16, 16, 41; **11:**7; **12:**40, 46; **13:**2, 3, 4, 8, 8, 21, 21, 23, 23, 25, 40, 52, 52; **14:**3, 13, 13, 14, 20, 20; **17:**2, 5, 9, 20, 20; **18:**3, 4, 4, 17, 33; **19:**8, 12, 14, 19, 29; **20:**12, 12, 14, 17, 28, 29; **21:**1, 6, 10, 18; **22:**31, 39; **23:**8, 9, 15, 35, 37; **24:**1, 24, 27, 28; **25:**32; **26:**2, 18, 19, 24, 26, 47, 56, 64, 69; **27:**10, 11, 17, 19, 29, 32, 36, 57, 60; **28:**1, 3, 3, 6, 9, 11; **Mk 1:**16, 22, 31, 38, 45, 45; **2:**14, 23; **3:**8, 8, 10; **4:**2, 4, 8, 8, 17, 17, 20, 20, 27, 29, 29, 33, 33, 35; **5:**2, 4, 14; **6:**11, 17, 33, 34, 42, 42; **7:**3, 4, 13, 24; **8:**15, 25, 27, 32; **9:**2, 9, 13, 14, 15; **10:**1, 1, 5, 14, 17, 19, 21, 45, 46, 46; **11:**1, 2, 2, 5, 12, 20, 27; **12:**26, 31, 33, 35, 38, 41, 44; **13:**1, 22; **14:**13, 16, 18, 21, 22, 43, 45, 45, 65; **15:**2, 8, 42; **16:**7, 14; **Lk 1:**2, 9, 70; **2:**20, 22, 27, 29, 38, 42; **3:**18, 21, 23; **4:**16, 35, 40; **5:**1, 9, 11, 11, 17, 17, 25, 27, 29; **6:**1, 17, 17, 31, 35, 36; **7:**12, 24; **8:**5, 8, 8, 27, 28, 28, 34, 42; **9:**5, 17, 17, 18, 29, 33, 34, 34, 42, 43, 46, 51, 57; **10:**3, 9, 11, 18, 20, 27, 38; **11:**1, 1, 4, 8, 27, 29, 36, 37, 40, 40, 43, 53; **12:**12, 14, 27, 27, 36, 37; **13:**1, 10, 22, 34; **15:**19; **16:**21; **17:**6, 6, 11, 12, 14, 24, 24, 28, 30, 37; **18:**13, 16, 20, 30, 30, 31, 35; **19:**8, 16, 16, 17, 29, 30, 32, 33, 37, 37, 41; **20:**1, 37, 37, 46; **21:**4, 24, 35; **22:**10, 10, 13, 21, 24, 29, 39, 47, 60, 60; **23:**3, 24, 25, 25, 26, 55, 56; **24:**14, 24, 30, 32, 35, 35, 36, 39, 40, 43, 49; **Jn 1:**36, 47; **3:**8, 14; **5:**12, 18, 21, 23, 30; **6:**1, 2, 17, 18, 31, 45, 58; **7:**23; **8:**3, 17, 20, 55, 55, 56; **9:**1, 8, 14, 29; **10:**15, 23; **11:**9, 9, 51, 54, 56; **12:**39, 46, 49; **13:**9, 15, 27, 27, 31, 31, 33, 34; **14:**18, 26; **15:**9, 10, 24; **17:**11, 12, 14, 18, 21, 21, 22, 23, 23; **18:**6, 15, 25; **19:**22, 40; **20:**11, 20, 21, 26; **21:**18; **Ac 1:**4, 10, 11, 15, 22, 23, 25; **2:**4, 22, 30, 33, 33; **3:**2, 7, 12, 21; **4:**13, 23, 23, 24; **5:**4, 5, 5, 12, 15, 15, 31, 35; **6:**1, 6, 9, 15, 15; **7:**6, 11, 15, 17, 21, 28, 29, 31, 42, 48, 49, 49, 59; **8:**7, 10, 12, 15, 15, 26, 32, 32, 36; **9:**3, 8, 15, 15, 38, 38, 39, 39; **10:**2, 7, 7, 9, 19, 25, 28, 29, 29, 44, 47; **11:**15, 15, 19, 19, 29, 29; **13:**2, 5, 8, 9, 19, 25, 42, 47; **14:**9, 17, 20; **15:**7, 8, 12, 31; **16:**4, 14, 16; **17:**2, 8, 8, 12, 12, 21, 21, 22, 23, 28, 29; **18:**2, 3, 14; **19:**5, 5, 25, 26; **20:**6, 6, 9, 28, 37; **21:**12, 12, 25, 31, 35, 37; **22:**1, 3, 6, 20, 25; **23:**6, 11, 22, 31, 31, 31; **24:**4, 5, 10, 15, 18, 24, 25; **25:**3, 20; **26:**4, 16, 23, 29, 31; **27:**18, 25, 27, 30, 33; **28:**3, 8, 10, 11; **Ro 1:**3, 13, 17, 21, 24, 27; **2:**1; **3:**4, 7, 8, 10; **4:**16, 18, 18; **5:**14, 20, 21; **6:**4, 5, 13; **7:**2, 2, 4, 14, 18; **8:**3, 11, 22, 23, 23, 31; **9:**5, 5, 27, 27, 29, 29; **10:**11; **11:**5, 8, 13, 22; **12:**3, 4, 18, 18; **13:**9, 12; **14:**4, 11, 11; **15:**3, 4, 7, 8, 13, 16, 19, 28, 28; **16:**2, 8, 22, 25, 26, 26; **1Co 1:**2, 7, 18, 19, 28, 31; **3:**1, 1, 1, 8, 9, 19; **4:**1, 2, 5, 7, 14, 16; **5:**4, 13; **6:**14, 18; **7:**3, 7, 8, 17, 20, 26, 35, 35, 39, 39; **8:**7, 7, 13, 13; **9:**1, 1, 3, 5, 9, 10, 13, 18, 21, 21; **10:**2, 6, 6, 7, 8, 9, 10, 11, 22; **11:**1, 5, 10, 15, 17, 18, 21, 23, 25, 25; **12:**7, 23; **13:**11, 12, 12; **14:**9, 20, 25, 33, 34; **15:**3, 4, 8, 21, 31, 31, 39, 44, 49; **16:**10, 18; **2Co 1:**7, 9, 11, 18, 18, 22, 22, 23, 24; **2:**3, 9, 16; **3:**18; **4:**15; **5:**5, 6, 6, 16, 20; **6:**1, 7, 9, 13, 16; **8:**11, 11, 18, 19; **9:**3, 7, 9; **10:**7, 7, 11, 11, 12, 12, 17; **11:**1, 2, 3, 10, 10, 13, 14, 16, 26, 26; **12:**19; **13:**1, 2; **Gal 1:**4, 14, 14; **2:**6, 7, 9, 9, 21; **3:**1, 1, 15, 16, 18, 23, 25; **4:**5, 12, 14, 19, 23, 24, 29; **5:**10, 11, 14, 21; **6:**11, 13, 14; **Eph 1:**11, 13; **2:**7, 7, 16, 22; **3:**2, 3, 4, 17, 18; **4:**16, 17, 30, 31, 31, 32; **5:**2, 15, 15, 22, 23, 24, 27, 28, 29, 31, 33; **6:**5, 6, 7, 16, 17, 19, 20, 20; **Php 1:**7, 17, 19, 19, 20, 27; **2:**3, 6, 15, 23, 23; **3:**8, 10, 20; **4:**7, 8, 15; **Col 1:**5, 6, 22, 22, 22, 29; **2:**5, 6, 6, 19, 20, 22, 22; **3:**10, 15, 17, 18, 23, 24; **4:**4, 4, 10; **1Th 1:**3, 7; **2:**4, 5, 6, 7, 7,

7, 9, 11, 13, 13, 19; 3:4, 6, 6, 6, 6, 12, 13; 4:1, 5, 6, 11, 12; 5:3, 3, 8, 11; 2Th 1:3; 2:13; 3:1, 15, 15; 1Ti 1:7, 8, 16, 19; 2:1, 7; 3:10, 10, 10, 13; 4:6; 5:1, 1, 2, 2, 18; 6:19; 2Ti 1:3, 4, 15; 2:3, 4, 5; 3:5, 8, 9; 4:6, 6, 9, 9; Tit 1:5, 13, 13; 2:1; 3:12, 12, 12, 12; Phm 1:9, 10, 10, 16, 16, 21; Heb 1:2, 4, 7, 13; 2:14, 15; 3:2, 3, 5, 8, 13, 13, 14, 14, 15; 4:2, 3, 10, 11; 5:4, 9; 6:10, 11, 11; 9:6, 8, 8, 14, 18, 24, 27, 28; 10:7, 12, 13, 25, 29; 11:5, 8, 17, 21, 24, 29; 12:6, 7, 7, 8, 16, 18, 24; 13:3, 3, 7, 11; Jas 1:6, 6; 2:8, 10, 10, 23, 26; 4:6; 5:3, 7, 17, 17; 1Pe 1:1, 2, 7, 10, 15, 17, 22, 24, 24, 24; 2:2, 5, 6, 13, 16; 3:7, 7, 15; 4:6, 11, 12; 5:1; 2Pe 1:2, 3, 13, 13; 2:1, 10, 17, 17, 17, 18; 3:4, 4, 9, 10, 10, 15, 16; 1Jn 1:7; 2:6; 3:2, 3, 7, 23; 4:10, 13, 17, 19; 5:6; 2Jn 1, 4, 6; 3Jn 2, 2; Jude 20, 21; Rev 1:14, 14, 15, 15, 16, 16, 17; 2:4, 5, 6, 24; 3:3, 3, 20, 21; 4:1, 3, 3, 7; 5:8; 6:1, 12, 12, 12, 12, 12; 7:1, 1; 8:13; 9:2; 10:7; 11:6, 6, 6, 6, 12; 12:2, 4, 4, 4; 13:4, 4, 13; 14:4, 4, 7, 20, 20; 16:15, 15; 18:3, 5, 5, 6, 6, 6, 9, 18, 21, 21, 21, 21; 20:8, 8, 9; 21:16, 16, 18, 18, 21, 21; 22:1, 9, 9

AT (2475)

Ge 2:9, 23; 3:3, 7, 7; 4:3; 5:5, 8, 11, 14, 17, 20, 27, 31; 6:9; 8:14; 11:1, 31, 32; 12:5, 6, 6, 10; 13:7, 10, 18; 14:6, 13; 15:15; 16:12, 16; 17:3, 17, 24; 18:1; 19:3, 9, 15; 20:1, 2; 21:2, 5, 33, 33; 22:9, 11; 23:2, 9, 17, 18, 19; 24:22, 52, 55; 25:8, 17, 25, 27; 26:22, 25, 34; 28:2, 11, 11, 13; 29:4, 22, 25; 30:31, 40; 31:1, 9, 13, 18, 19; 32:7, 25; 33:2, 5, 14, 14, 15, 18; 35:6, 7, 9, 26, 29; 37:12, 13, 24, 33; 38:5, 5, 11, 13, 14, 21; 40:19; 41:4, 14, 16, 53; 42:1, 25, 35; 43:5, 11, 19, 25, 29, 32, 32; 44:2, 3, 13, 14; 45:26; 46:4; 47:17; 48:3, 8, 13, 13; 49:23; 50:10, 26; Ex 2:4; 3:6, 12, 20, 20; 4:25; 6:28; 7:7; 9:18, 28, 33; 10:28; 12:15, 29, 47; 13:10, 20, 21; 14:4, 17; 15:8, 25; 16:3; 17:1, 6, 8, 9, 16; 18:4; 19:2, 13, 17; 20:18; 21:7; 22:14; 23:15, 15, 16, 17, 30; 24:1, 2, 4, 17; 25:14, 18, 26; 26:9, 23, 24, 24; 27:2, 4, 7; 28:7; 29:3, 4, 11, 12, 32, 42; 30:2; 31:5; 32:19, 26; 33:9, 10, 20; 34:17, 18, 22, 28; 36:28, 29, 29; 37:3, 5, 7; 38:1, 2, 7, 8, 23, 30, 31; 39:32, 40; 40:28, 33, 33, 38; Lev 2:8, 12; 3:2, 8, 13; 4:4, 7, 7, 14, 18, 18, 24, 25, 29, 30, 33, 34; 5:4, 9; 6:13, 25; 8:4, 9, 15, 31, 35; 9:9; 12:6, 7; 13:27, 32, 57; 14:3, 7, 11, 13, 23; 15:14, 29; 16:7; 17:5, 6; 19:6, 16, 20, 21; 23:4, 5, 31; 25:24, 31, 41, 54; 26:32, 34, 40, 41, 43; 27:3, 4, 5, 5, 6, 6, 7, 7; Nu 2:2; 3:26, 39; 4:4, 20, 28, 31, 33, 37, 41; 5:21; 6:10, 13, 18; 7:10, 84; 8:9, 24, 25, 26; 9:2, 3, 7, 10, 10, 11, 11, 13, 13, 16, 18, 20, 23; 10:3, 10, 10, 21, 21; 12:1, 5, 12; 13:22, 24, 26, 30; 15:3, 17, 38; 16:18, 19, 27, 38, 43, 50; 18:5, 23; 20:1, 2, 10, 14, 16, 22, 23, 28; 21:8, 9, 23, 33; 22:11, 24, 26, 36, 36; 23:13, 25; 24:20, 21; 25:1, 6, 18; 26:3; 27:2, 14, 14; 28:2, 6; 29:39; 30:3, 16; 31:16; 33:2, 5, 6, 8, 9, 12, 13, 14, 16, 17, 18, 19, 20, 21, 22, 23, 24, 25, 26, 27, 28, 29, 30, 31, 32, 33, 34, 35, 36, 37, 37, 38, 41, 42, 43, 44, 45, 46; 34:3, 5, 7, 10; 35:5; Dt 1:6, 6, 9, 16, 18, 19, 33, 46; 2:2, 12, 14, 18, 22, 29, 32; 3:1, 5, 18, 21, 23; 4:3, 10, 11, 14, 15, 48; 5:2, 22; 6:7, 16; 7:22; 8:14; 9:5, 8, 11, 22, 23; 10:1, 8; 11:19; 12:5, 14, 17, 18, 21; 14:28; 15:1, 9, 20, 22; 16:1, 2, 6, 11, 13, 15, 16; 17:6, 10; 18:4, 16; 23:11; 24:5; 26:3; 27:4; 28:12, 20, 29, 67; 29:1; 30:2, 4, 14; 31:10, 11, 14, 15, 18; 32:51, 51; 33:2, 8, 8, 18; Jos 2:1, 5; 3:1, 15, 16; 4:3, 9, 19, 20, 23; 5:2, 3, 10, 14, 14; 6:15, 26, 26, 26; 7:5; 8:3, 14, 29, 33, 33; 9:6, 6, 17, 25; 10:6, 10, 10, 15, 16, 18, 21, 32, 35, 37, 43; 11:10, 17; 12:4; 14:4, 6, 6; 15:2, 5, 7, 9, 11; 16:5, 6, 7; 18:1, 8, 9, 10, 12, 14, 15, 15, 16, 19; 19:10, 14, 22, 29, 33, 33, 51, 51; 20:4, 6; 21:2; 22:9, 10, 11, 12, 17, 27, 28; 24:6, 25, 29, 30, 32; Jdg 1:4, 5; 2:8, 9; 3:30; 4:6, 9, 10, 20; 5:5, 8, 11, 16, 17, 19, 27, 31; 6:11, 11, 27; 7:21, 24, 24, 25, 25; 8:18, 28, 32; 9:5, 6, 26, 27, 35; 10:6, 17, 17; 11:4, 11, 16, 20, 29; 12:2, 6, 6, 10, 12, 15; 13:6; 14:4, 4, 6, 8, 10, 17, 20; 15:11, 14, 19; 16:2, 25; 17:8; 18:12, 31; 19:3, 22, 25, 26, 26; 20:1, 14, 22, 30, 41; 21:1, 5, 5, 8, 12, 13; Ru 1:22; 2:7, 10, 14; 3:2, 8, 14, 14; 4:17; 1Sa 1:3, 3, 9, 9; 2:14, 22; 3:21, 21; 4:1, 1, 1, 12; 5:1, 9; 6:9, 18, 21; 7:6, 7, 16, 16, 16, 16, 17, 17; 8:4; 9:8, 12, 18, 22, 26; 10:2, 3, 5, 6, 10, 17, 26; 11:8; 12:17; 13:3, 4, 4, 5, 7, 11, 16, 16, 23; 14:2, 3, 18; 15:4, 27, 30, 33, 34; 16:4, 6, 7, 11; 17:1, 12, 19, 20, 42, 43, 43; 18:2, 11, 16; 19:5, 9, 10, 13, 16, 18, 19, 22, 22; 20:9, 12, 12, 18, 20, 25, 30, 30, 33, 33, 42; 22:6, 6, 9, 11, 12; 23:1, 7, 18, 21, 23; 24:3, 10, 11; 25:1, 8, 24, 40; 26:1, 13, 16; 27:2; 28:4, 4, 7, 8, 15, 21; 29:1, 1, 2; 30:1, 26; 31:13; 2Sa 2:13, 24, 25, 29, 32; 3:26, 27, 27, 30, 32; 4:1, 4, 8, 10; 5:1, 3, 9; 6:6; 9:4, 7, 10, 13; 10:4, 5, 8, 16; 11:9, 13, 21, 24; 12:4; 13:8, 15, 23, 24, 28, 29; 14:22, 33; 15:8, 14, 16, 17, 28, 32; 16:6, 7, 8, 13, 15; 17:13, 16, 16, 17, 24, 27; 18:4, 24; 19:8, 15, 28; 20:3, 4, 8, 12, 14, 18, 22; 21:5, 6, 9, 10, 10, 14, 15, 18, 19, 20; 22:16, 16, 19; 23:11, 13, 14; 24:5, 16; 1Ki 1:6, 13, 43; 2:8, 19, 27, 34, 46; 3:2, 2, 3, 4, 21; 5:14, 17; 6:3, 7, 7, 16, 27; 7:6, 21, 30, 34, 39, 40; 8:2, 9, 31, 44; 9:2, 10, 12, 26; 10:5, 5, 28, 29; 11:17, 34; 12:21, 27, 29, 31, 32, 32, 33; 13:1, 2, 4, 5, 19, 20; 14:1, 2, 4, 6; 16:9; 17:3, 10; 18:5, 7, 9, 36, 36; 19:13; 20:26, 33; 21:12, 18, 23; 22:4, 10, 34, 47, 48, 49; 2Ki 1:2; 2:18, 24; 3:2, 7, 20, 24; 4:2, 16, 17, 25, 27, 37; 5:9, 15, 24; 6:4, 8, 8, 13, 32; 7:3, 8, 9, 17, 20; 8:5, 11, 21, 28; 9:10, 12, 14, 21, 27, 30, 31, 32, 32, 36; 10:2, 6, 6, 7, 8, 12, 14, 18, 29, 32; 11:6, 7, 8, 14, 18, 20; 12:5, 9, 20; 13:17; 14:10, 11, 13; 15:16, 25; 16:4, 6; 17:10, 11, 29, 32; 18:11, 14, 22; 19:7, 18, 21, 22; 20:19; 22:4, 9, 9; 23:5, 8, 9, 9, 15, 16, 16, 16, 17, 19, 19, 29, 33; 24:11; 25:6, 13, 14, 20, 21, 23, 29; 1Ch 2:55; 4:21; 6:10, 31, 32; 7:2; 8:6; 9:13, 26, 33, 33; 10:12; 11:1, 3, 13, 15, 16; 12:1, 8, 15, 16, 23; 13:9; 16:39; 18:8; 19:4, 5, 7, 9; 20:2, 4, 6; 21:6, 15, 18, 20, 22, 28, 29, 29; 23:4, 28, 31, 31, 31, 32; 25:6, 6; 26:12, 13, 31; 28:21; 29:2, 12, 28; 2Ch 1:3, 5, 13, 16, 17; 2:3, 4, 4, 7, 8, 14; 3:4, 17; 4:11; 5:3, 10, 12, 13; 6:13, 22, 34; 7:10, 13; 8:3, 6, 13; 9:4, 4; 11:1, 15; 12:15; 13:15; 14:6, 14; 15:10; 16:7, 8, 9, 10, 14; 17:13; 18:9, 33; 20:2, 5, 16, 22, 24, 30, 36; 21:9, 19, 19; 22:5; 23:3, 5, 7, 13, 19; 24:5, 15, 23; 25:21, 23; 26:9, 9, 9; 27:3; 28:4; 29:4, 7, 25; 30:1, 3, 6, 10, 12, 13, 16; 31:2, 14; 32:6, 12, 12, 22, 23, 33; 33:17, 20, 24; 34:9, 14, 17; 35:1, 2, 20, 21; 36:10, 16, 23; Ezr 1:2; 2:59, 68; 3:3, 9; 4:21, 24; 5:1; 6:2, 2, 3, 13, 18; 8:15, 17, 17, 29, 31, 32, 33; 9:4, 5, 7; 10:14; Ne 1:1; 2:11, 15, 18; 3:1, 31; 4:2, 6, 22, 23; 5:8, 17, 18; 6:2; 7:3, 4, 61; 8:1, 12; 9:12, 37; 10:34; 11:1, 12, 22, 31; 12:25, 37, 39; 13:5, 6, 16, 24, 31; Est 1:2, 2, 5, 9; 2:3, 5, 8, 16, 21, 21, 21; 3:3, 15; 4:14; 5:9, 13; 6:10; 8:3, 14; 9:15, 18, 27, 31; 10:3; Job 1:13, 14; 3:1, 8, 11, 12, 13, 13, 13, 17, 18; 4:13; 5:14, 16, 22, 23, 23; 6:7, 7, 10, 28; 10:18; 12:4, 4, 5; 14:9; 15:8; 16:4, 9, 9, 10, 14; 18:11, 20; 19:25, 27; 21:5, 18, 19, 32; 22:5, 21; 24:14, 16; 26:11; 27:10, 23; 29:8, 24; 30:14, 17; 31:26; 33:22; 34:20, 32; 36:32; 37:7, 21; 39:7, 25, 25, 25, 27; 40:15; 41:29; Ps 1:5; 2:4; 5:7; 6:3; 8:3; 9:13, 14; 11:2; 13:4; 16:7; 18:15, 15, 18; 19:6; 21:12; 22:10, 13, 17; 27:6; 30:T; 33:9; 34:1, 14; 35:15, 16, 26; 36:4; 37:12, 37; 38:11, 16, 21; 44:12, 12; 45:9; 46:5; 51:9; 52:2; 55:3; 58:11; 59:6, 8, 8, 14; 62:8; 64:4; 65:8; 68:16; 69:10, 26, 32; 73:12; 74:18; 75:2, 5; 78:14, 60; 79:12; 80:16; 81:7; 83:9, 10; 84:3; 87:7; 90:16; 91:6, 7; 95:8, 8; 99:9; 101:3; 104:7, 7, 22, 32, 32; 106:7, 12, 19, 22, 28, 32; 107:27; 109:23; 110:1, 5; 114:7, 7; 118:7; 119:55, 62, 161; 121:6; 127:2, 5; 128:3; 147:18; Pr 3:34; 6:3; 7:9, 11, 12, 22; 8:2, 3, 3, 23, 30, 34; 10:10; 14:19; 15:23, 31; 16:7; 17:5; 18:1; 19:3; 20:4; 23:34; 24:15; Ecc 2:3, 11, 23; 5:18; 7:2, 2, 21, 22; 8:17; 9:5, 11, 11; 12:5, 6, 6; SS 1:7; 5:2; 6:13; 7:13; 8:1, 11; Isa 2:21; 3:5; 4:5; 5:12, 26; 7:3; 8:21; 9:3; 10:20, 22, 26, 28, 28, 28, 29, 32, 32; 11:6, 13; 13:8; 14:7, 7, 16; 15:2; 16:1, 2, 8; 17:7; 18:1, 6, 6; 19:10, 19; 21:4, 8, 9; 23:1, 13; 28:5, 6, 10, 13, 21, 21; 30:6, 23, 29, 31; 32:15, 18, 18; 33:3; 34:14; 36:7; 37:7, 19, 22, 23; 39:8; 40:15; 41:2, 7, 24; 42:1; 44:12, 20; 45:12; 47:7, 8, 14; 49:4, 7, 8; 51:8, 22; 52:6; 54:3; 55:3; 59:10, 19; 60:16, 22; 63:5; 64:9; 65:4, 20; 66:2, 5, 11, 12; Jer 1:15; 2:12, 13, 24, 31; 4:22, 22, 23, 23, 24, 29; 5:7, 7; 6:1, 4, 10, 15, 25; 7:12; 8:7, 12, 16; 10:10, 14, 18; 12:2, 8; 13:5; 15:7, 8, 10, 17; 16:8, 20, 21; 17:2, 11, 12, 15, 19, 19, 21; 18:3, 16; 19:8; 20:2, 17; 22:20, 22; 23:32; 26:8, 10, 20; 28:5, 11; 31:26, 29; 32:6, 7, 8, 9; 33:15; 34:1, 7; 36:8, 9, 24; 37:5, 5; 38:6, 7, 7, 14; 39:3, 5; 40:1, 6, 8, 10, 12, 13; 41:3, 5, 12; 43:8, 9; 46:5, 7; 47:3, 6; 48:13, 13, 35; 49:9, 17, 27, 29, 34; 50:13, 14; 51:17, 41; 52:9, 10, 17, 18, 26, 27, 33; La 1:15, 20, 22; 2:15, 16; 3:12, 14, 29, 57, 63; 4:15, 17; 5:5, 9, 13; Eze 1:10, 15; 2:5; 3:16; 4:10, 11, 17; 5:2, 2, 5, 11, 13; 6:9, 12; 8:16, 17; 9:6; 10:3, 22; 12:12; 13:3, 10, 15; 16:37, 42, 55; 18:2, 13, 17; 20:9, 43; 21:15, 21; 24:17; 25:3, 6; 26:15, 16, 18; 27:32, 33, 34, 35, 36; 28:10, 19, 24; 29:13, 21; 30:9, 13; 31:5, 16; 32:23; 33:30; 35:15, 15; 36:7, 15, 30, 38; 38:10, 20; 39:14, 20; 40:7, 9, 11, 22; 41:3, 3, 21, 21; 42:12; 43:19, 21; 44:24; 45:5, 17, 19; 46:6, 11, 17, 19; 47:3, 18, 19; 48:8, 10, 15, 28; Da 1:13, 15; 2:16, 49; 3:7; 4:8, 19, 30; 5:5, 23, 29, 31; 6:16, 18; 7:8; 8:2, 7, 8, 23, 23; 9:21; 10:15, 19; 11:4, 14, 27, 27, 29, 40; 12:1, 1, 13; Hos 1:4, 10; 2:18, 23; 4:4, 5, 15, 15; 5:1, 2, 6, 14; 7:16; 9:11, 15; 10:5, 6; 12:4; Joel 1:9, 13; 2:5, 20; 3:1; Am 2:8; 3:14; 4:4; 6:2, 6; 8:8, 9, 9; 9:3, 3, 5; Ob 5, 8, 13, 14, 18; Jnh 1:6, 15; 3:7; 4:7, 10; Mic 1:10; 2:1, 1; 3:4; 5:3, 10; 7:3, 16, 17; Na 1:4; Hab 1:5, 5, 8, 10; 2:4, 5, 6; Zep 1:12; 2:10; 3:3, 15; Hag 2:3; Zec 1:11; 3:1, 9; 6:7, 10; 7:3, 5; 8:5, 23; 11:13; 13:6; 14:7, 11, 14; Mal 1:9, 10, 13; 2:4; 3:5; Mt 1:11; 2:7; 4:20; 5:20, 28; 6:26, 28; 7:28; 8:11, 14, 29; 9:9, 22, 23, 24; 10:19; 12:1, 18, 25, 41; 13:21, 40, 49; 14:6, 8, 27, 30, 34; 16:2, 3, 12, 21; 17:12, 14; 19:26; 20:3, 4, 5, 6, 9, 21, 21; 21:34, 45; 22:44, 45; 23:6, 6; 24:30, 33, 41; 25:6, 27, 33, 33; 26:3, 3, 6, 18, 20, 56, 64; 27:9, 44, 45, 46, 51, 54, 64; Mk 1:15, 18, 22, 26, 32; 2:14; 3:5, 6, 24, 31, 34; 4:15, 17, 38; 5:1, 20, 30, 33, 33, 40; 6:6, 50, 51, 53, 54, 56; 7:25; 8:18, 22, 33; 9:14, 18, 20, 33; 10:21, 22, 27, 37, 37, 48; 11:11; 12:2, 12, 36, 37, 38, 39; 13:1, 1, 19, 24, 29, 35; 14:3, 4, 14, 62, 65, 67, 67; 15:6, 7, 11, 29, 29, 33, 34; 16:2, 12, 19; Lk 1:14, 20, 23, 41; 2:1, 33, 43, 47; 3:2; 4:20, 32, 33, 36, 39, 39, 41; 5:2, 27; 6:10, 11, 13; 7:6, 16, 21, 38, 44, 49; 8:35, 41, 51, 53, 55; 9:38, 39; 10:32, 39; 11:5, 17, 32, 37; 12:24, 27; 13:1, 3, 17; 14:5, 9, 10, 14, 15, 29; 15:17; 16:14, 20, 26; 17:12, 14, 16, 35; 18:13; 19:3, 5, 23; 20:10, 17, 19, 42, 44, 46; 22:10, 14, 14, 21, 27, 30, 45, 50, 56, 58, 61, 61, 65, 66, 69; 23:2, 7, 8, 39, 49; 24:22, 31, 39, 39; Jn 1:28, 36, 42; 2:1, 11, 23; 3:7, 23, 23, 25, 29; 4:8, 20, 40, 43, 45, 46, 52; 5:20; 6:21, 39, 40, 44, 54, 66; 7:11, 31; 8:2, 59; 10:22, 23, 32; 11:10, 17, 20, 30, 31, 32; 12:2, 16, 48; 13:22, 23, 28, 30; 14:11, 17, 22; 16:23, 29; 18:3, 16, 39; 19:11, 31, 39, 42; 20:12; 21:4, 23; Ac 1:11, 12; 2:5, 33, 34, 46; 3:4, 4, 5, 10, 12; 5:12, 19, 31, 33, 37; 6:15, 15; 7:8, 20, 20, 21, 51, 55, 56, 57, 58; 8:1, 40; 9:24, 38; 10:4, 17, 30, 33; 11:11, 12, 15, 22, 26; 12:6, 13, 14, 18; 13:1, 12, 13, 43; 14:8, 13; 15:1, 2, 7, 30; 16:6, 10, 11, 11, 15, 19; 17:14; 18:4, 18, 19, 22, 22; 19:9, 19, 26, 28, 35, 38; 20:5, 6, 15, 16, 17, 17; 21:3, 5, 8, 13, 21; 22:3; 23:1, 10, 23, 35; 24:11; 25:4, 18, 23; 27:2, 3, 5, 8, 20, 29; 28:11, 15, 15; Ro 1:10, 16; 3:9; 4:2, 19; 5:6; 7:5, 15, 23, 23; 8:9, 34; 10:8; 1Co 1:28; 2:15; 3:13; 4:1, 6, 9, 10; 6:7, 7; 7:23; 9:13; 10:11, 16, 20, 21, 21; 11:34; 14:27, 35; 15:6, 8, 54; 16:2, 8; 2Co 3:7, 10; 4:18; 5:4, 6, 8; 6:2; 7:13, 13; 8:14; 11:8, 25, 32; 12:11, 11, 19; 13:8; Gal 1:7, 19; 4:20; 6:9; Eph 1:10, 20; 2:2; 3:17, 20; 6:16, 18; Php 2:10, 30; 4:18; Col 1:15, 29; 2:1; 3:1, 23; 4:15, 16; 1Th 2:2, 16; 5:10, 20; 2Th 2:7; 3:17; 1Ti 1:13; 2:6; 5:4, 9, 17; 6:10, 15; 2Ti 1:18; 3:2; 4:5, 13, 19, 20, 20; Tit 1:3; 3:12; Heb 1:3, 13; 7:13; 8:1; 9:26; 10:12, 12; 11:3, 40; 12:18, 21; Jas 1:23; 2:17; 3:17; 4:1; 5:9, 10; 1Pe 1:13; 3:11; 4:12; 2Pe 1:9; 2:7, 10, 12; 3:3, 14; 1Jn 1:5; 3:15; Jude 8, 12; Rev 1:17; 2:4, 5; 3:2, 3, 9, 20; 7:1; 8:3; 9:14; 10:9; 11:9, 11; 12:10, 17; 13:3; 17:6, 8; 18:10, 15, 17, 20; 19:10; 21:25

BE (5584)

Ge 1:3, 6, 9, 11, 14, 20, 26, 26, 28; 2:18, 23; 3:5, 14, 14, 15, 15, 16, 16, 20; 4:7, 12, 24, 24; 6:20; 7:1, 3; 8:22; 9:2, 5, 14, 15, 25, 26, 26, 27; 11:6, 7; 12:3, 19; 13:16; 14:19, 20; 15:1, 1, 3, 4, 5, 8, 13, 13, 13; 16:12, 12, 12, 14; 17:5, 5, 5, 6, 7, 8, 10, 11, 11, 12, 13, 14, 14, 15, 16, 20, 21; 18:18, 25, 30; 19:2, 2, 15, 20, 31, 34; 20:7, 9, 11; 21:12, 12, 17, 23; 22:14, 18; 23:6, 8; 24:6, 7, 14, 27, 41, 44, 44, 49, 51; 25:23; 26:3, 4, 22, 24; 27:2, 11, 29, 37, 40, 41; 28:14, 14, 15, 15, 20; 29:2, 3, 7, 21, 24, 29; 30:4, 9, 26, 34; 31:3, 24, 29; 32:5, 20, 20, 28; 33:12, 15; 34:8, 11, 14, 15, 17, 22, 30; 35:10, 11, 17, 20; 37:8, 27; 38:8, 9, 17, 23, 29; 39:9; 40:22; 41:29, 30, 30, 31, 31, 35, 36, 38; 42:7, 34, 37; 43:5, 8, 11, 14, 25, 29; 44:9, 10, 16, 17, 18, 26, 31; 45:1, 2, 5, 6, 10, 23, 28; 46:3; 47:6, 19, 25; 48:6, 6, 21; 49:4, 6, 7, 7, 13, 17, 19, 26; 50:19, 21; Ex 2:6, 14, 21; 3:7, 12, 15, 15, 16; 4:14, 16, 16, 17, 19, 23; 5:8, 17, 18; 6:1, 5, 7, 8, 16, 18, 20; 7:1, 2, 3, 15, 18; 8:3, 4, 5, 9, 10, 11, 21, 21, 22, 22, 26; 9:7; 10:2, 5, 5, 10, 26; 11:1, 6, 6, 7; 12:2, 5, 7, 9, 10, 15, 16, 17, 17, 18, 19, 19, 24, 32, 42, 48, 48; 13:4, 7, 9, 12, 13, 13, 16; 14:13, 13; 15:15, 16; 16:12, 25, 26, 27, 29, 32; 17:1, 6, 16; 18:10, 19, 19, 19, 22, 23; 19:5, 6, 11, 12, 13, 13; 20:20, 24; 21:3, 4, 7, 8, 12, 14, 15, 16, 17, 19, 20, 21, 23, 23, 24, 27, 28, 28, 28, 29, 29, 32, 32, 36; 22:1, 3, 11, 12, 13, 13, 18, 19, 20, 25; 23:2, 9, 12, 13, 15, 18, 18, 19, 22, 26, 33; 24:10; 25:7, 15, 15, 17, 29, 31, 34, 35, 36, 36, 38, 40; 26:1, 2, 2, 7, 8, 9, 12, 16, 17, 17, 17, 20, 22, 24, 24, 25, 35, 35; 27:3, 8, 8, 10, 10, 11, 12, 13, 14, 14, 15, 16, 17, 17, 18, 18, 19, 20, 21, 21; 28:1, 1, 5, 6, 8, 10, 13, 14, 15, 16, 17, 20, 21, 25, 29, 30, 32, 37, 42, 43; 29:9, 16, 21, 24, 25, 28, 29, 29, 34, 34, 37, 41, 42, 43, 44, 45; 30:2, 5, 8, 10, 12, 13, 21, 31, 32, 33, 38; 31:6, 14, 15, 15; 32:5, 30; 33:3, 14, 23; 34:2, 12, 12, 18, 20, 25; 35:9, 27; 36:22; 37:16, 16; 38:3; 39:1, 4, 26, 30, 41; Lev 1:3, 9, 13; 2:3, 3, 4, 4, 5, 7, 9, 10, 10, 11, 12; 3:3, 4, 6, 9, 10, 14, 15, 16; 4:7, 12, 13, 18, 20, 22, 24, 26, 27, 28, 31, 31, 32, 35; 5:1, 1, 2, 3, 4, 6, 7, 7, 9, 10, 12, 13, 15, 16, 17, 18, 18; 6:6, 7, 9, 9, 12, 13, 15, 16, 17, 20, 20, 21, 21, 21, 22, 22, 23, 23, 25, 27, 28, 28, 30, 30; 7:2, 4, 6, 10, 11, 12, 13, 14, 15, 15, 16, 16, 17, 18, 18, 19, 19, 19, 19, 20, 21, 24, 24, 25, 27, 33; 8:32; 10:3, 6, 9, 13, 14, 15; 11:4, 6, 7, 11, 22, 24, 26, 27, 31, 32, 32, 32, 32, 33, 33, 34, 34, 35, 35, 36, 36, 37, 37, 38, 39, 41, 42, 44, 45, 45, 47, 47; 12:2, 3, 5, 5, 7, 7, 8, 8; 13:2, 3, 4, 6, 7, 11, 14, 19, 20, 21, 25, 26, 30, 32, 34, 34, 46, 49, 49, 52, 54, 55, 57, 58, 58; 14:2, 2, 5, 7, 8, 9, 13, 18, 20, 21, 22, 23, 29, 31, 36, 40, 40, 41, 42, 42, 45, 45, 46, 53, 57; 15:4, 5, 6, 9, 10, 11, 12, 12, 13, 17, 19, 19, 20, 24, 24, 25, 26, 26, 27, 27, 28; 16:8, 8, 9, 9, 10, 10, 27, 27, 30, 30, 31, 32; 17:4, 4, 6, 6, 7, 7, 9, 14, 15, 16; 18:4, 17, 18, 29, 30; 19:2, 5, 6, 7, 8, 17, 20, 20, 22, 24, 25, 29, 31, 34, 36, 36, 37; 20:2, 7, 9, 10, 12, 14, 15, 15, 16, 17, 18, 26, 26, 27; 21:6, 7, 9, 14; 22:3, 7, 9, 19, 19, 20, 22, 23, 23, 24, 25, 25, 27, 27, 29, 29, 32, 33; 23:2, 3, 4, 6, 11, 13, 13, 14, 17, 17, 17, 18, 18, 21, 27, 28, 28, 29, 31, 32, 36, 36, 38, 38, 39, 41; 24:2, 3, 4, 7, 8, 15, 16, 17, 19, 20, 21; 25:7, 10, 10, 11, 12, 15, 22, 23, 24, 24, 27, 28, 30, 31, 31, 31, 33, 33, 34, 38, 41, 42, 46, 48, 50, 54; 26:1, 6, 12, 12, 13, 17, 20, 22, 24, 25, 26, 26, 32, 38, 41; 27:3, 9, 10, 10, 12, 14, 16, 20, 21, 24, 25, 28, 29, 29, 30, 33, 33, 33, 33; Nu 1:51; 2:2, 2, 16; 3:10, 38, 41, 45; 4:10, 10, 12, 13, 13, 14, 14, 14, 16, 16, 18, 24, 28, 31; 5:8, 8, 15, 19, 22, 22, 28, 28, 31, 31; 6:9, 25; 8:7, 12; 9:3, 7, 10, 13, 15; 10:2, 8, 21, 32, 35; 11:19, 22; 12:8, 12; 13:20; 14:3, 9, 9, 17, 30, 31, 33, 42, 43; 15:3, 7, 10, 24, 24, 25, 26, 28, 30, 31, 35, 40, 41; 16:9, 16, 17, 22, 26; 17:3; 18:1, 1, 3, 6, 7, 15, 18, 19, 22, 23, 24, 27, 29, 30, 32, 32; 19:3, 5, 9, 11, 12, 12, 13, 14, 16, 19, 20, 22; 20:17; 21:27, 34; 22:6, 11, 18, 20; 23:23; 24:7, 7, 18, 18, 22, 24; 25:13; 26:56; 27:17; 28:4, 9, 10, 12, 13, 13, 17, 18, 20, 24, 24, 25, 26, 27, 28, 31; 29:1, 1, 3, 6, 7, 9, 12, 14, 18, 21, 24, 27, 30, 33, 37; 30:12; 31:23, 23, 23, 23, 24; 32:15, 17, 22, 23, 32; 33:54, 54, 54, 55; 34:2, 4, 6, 9, 13; 35:3, 7, 12, 12, 16, 16, 16, 17, 18, 18, 18, 27, 30, 30, 31, 33, 33; 36:3, 4, 4; Dt 1:16, 17, 17, 21, 21, 27, 29, 39, 39, 41, 42; 2:4, 4; 3:2, 11, 13, 22; 4:9, 9, 10, 15, 19, 23, 26, 40; 5:1, 25; 6:3, 11, 12; 7:6, 14, 14, 18, 21, 24, 26; 8:1, 11, 14, 19, 20; 10:20; 11:8, 22, 24, 25, 27, 32; 12:5, 8, 11, 13, 17, 19, 21, 25, 27, 28, 28, 30; 13:5, 9, 11, 11, 16, 17, 18; 14:2, 6, 7, 8, 19, 23, 24, 24, 29; 15:2, 4, 7, 8, 9, 9, 11, 17; 16:2, 2, 2, 4, 5, 6, 6, 8, 11, 12, 13, 14, 15; 17:5, 6, 11, 12, 12, 13, 15; 18:1, 9, 13, 22; 19:4, 5, 6, 10, 12, 15, 18, 18, 20, 21; 20:1, 3, 5, 19; 21:8, 21; 22:16, 19, 20, 21, 22, 22, 23, 27, 29; 23:1, 2, 3, 14, 19, 21, 21, 23; 24:4, 5, 5, 5, 15, 16, 16, 17; 25:2, 2, 3, 6, 6, 10, 12; 26:2, 19; 27:9; 28:3, 4, 4, 5, 6, 16, 17, 18, 18, 19, 23, 23, 25, 25, 26, 26, 27, 29, 30, 31, 31, 31, 31, 31, 41, 44, 44, 48, 53, 56, 59, 62; 29:23, 25; 30:18; 31:6, 6, 7, 8, 8, 17, 21, 23, 23, 27; 32:24; 33:13, 24, 24, 25; Jos 1:3, 5, 5, 6, 7, 7, 8, 9, 9, 17, 18, 18; 2:12, 18, 19, 19, 19, 19; 3:13, 13; 6:17, 17, 18, 19; 7:11, 15; 8:1, 4, 29; 9:8, 11, 20, 23; 10:8, 8, 25, 25, 27; 11:6, 6; 13:1, 4, 6, 33; 14:9; 17:17, 18; 18:6; 20:3, 6; 22:5, 5, 18, 27, 29, 29; 23:5, 6, 6, 8, 11, 13, 13, 16; 24:15, 27; Jdg 2:3, 3; 3:19, 24; 4:9, 18; 5:8, 23, 23, 24; 6:16, 23, 31, 39; 7:11, 11; 8:22, 22; 9:2, 8, 10, 12, 14, 18, 28, 38, 54; 11:6; 13:5, 5, 7, 8, 13; 14:11; 15:3, 6; 16:5, 7, 10, 11, 13, 13; 17:10; 18:5, 19, 19, 19; 19:1, 9, 23; 20:7, 10, 32; 21:17, 17, 21, 22; Ru 1:11, 16, 16, 17; 2:4, 22; 3:1, 2, 4, 18; 4:10, 11, 12, 14; 1Sa 1:7, 8, 11, 11; 2:10, 14, 15, 16, 28, 30, 35; 3:14; 4:3, 20; 5:7; 6:6; 7:1; 8:1, 7, 12, 12, 12, 17, 20; 9:5, 9, 16; 10:1, 3, 3, 5, 5, 6, 7, 16; 11:1, 13; 12:9, 14, 15, 20, 24, 25; 13:14; 14:10, 28, 42, 45; 15:33; 16:1, 16; 17:9, 9, 25, 28, 33, 37; 18:3, 8, 17, 18, 25, 27; 19:6, 11; 20:13, 13, 18, 26, 29, 30, 31, 32; 21:5, 13, 15; 23:14, 17, 17, 17, 22; 24:13, 20; 25:8, 17, 26, 31, 34; 26:19, 25; 27:1; 28:1, 13, 19; 30:22, 23; 2Sa 1:6, 18, 21, 21; 2:6, 7, 22; 3:8, 21, 29; 5:2, 2, 24; 6:22; 7:10, 10, 14, 14, 15, 16, 23, 26, 26; 8:2, 2; 9:7, 7; 10:12, 12; 11:11, 15, 20, 25; 12:10, 10, 22, 25; 13:6, 12, 13, 20, 25, 28, 39; 14:11, 14, 17; 15:14, 14, 33, 34; 16:2; 17:8, 9, 10, 17, 21, 29; 18:3, 13, 20, 20, 22, 28, 32; 19:6, 7, 10, 23, 35, 43; 20:3, 3, 18; 21:6; 22:16, 47, 47; 23:6, 7, 7; 1Ki 1:2, 13, 17, 21, 24, 27, 30, 35, 36, 37, 47, 48, 52, 52; 2:2, 3, 7, 15, 19, 22, 33, 37; 3:13, 26; 4:29; 5:6, 7, 14; 6:19; 7:47; 8:8, 15, 16, 16, 19, 52, 53, 57, 59, 61; 9:3, 9, 19; 10:8, 20, 29, 29; 11:13, 14, 23, 36, 38, 38; 12:4, 7, 10, 11, 14, 19; 13:2, 2, 3, 22; 14:5, 6, 11, 11; 16:4, 4; 17:1, 13, 13, 14; 18:27; 19:15, 16, 17, 17; 20:42; 21:18, 24, 24; 22:12, 13, 20; 2Ki 1:15; 3:11, 13, 16, 17; 4:7, 16, 43, 43; 5:10, 10, 12, 13; 6:10, 16; 7:2, 13, 19; 8:13; 9:3, 8, 15, 20, 22, 37, 37; 10:3, 10, 19, 22, 30; 11:2, 8, 17; 12:7; 13:19; 14:6, 6, 10; 15:12; 16:15, 15; 17:37; 18:21, 27, 29, 30; 19:3, 6, 10, 11; 20:3, 17, 17, 18, 19; 21:4, 7; 22:7, 17, 19; 23:16, 27; 25:16; 1Ch 2:35; 4:10; 9:32; 11:2, 2, 4; 12:18, 38; 14:15; 16:25, 30, 31, 36, 37; 17:9, 9, 13, 13, 14, 21, 22, 23, 24, 24; 19:13, 13; 22:1, 3, 5, 8, 9, 10, 10, 11, 13, 13, 13, 14, 16; 23:1, 24; 24:5; 28:4, 6, 8, 10, 11, 13, 14, 15, 16, 20, 20; 29:1, 4, 5, 10; 2Ch 1:17, 17; 2:4, 5, 9, 9, 12; 4:18; 5:9; 6:4, 5, 9, 40, 41; 7:16, 16, 22; 8:6; 9:7, 19; 10:4, 7, 10, 11, 14, 19; 11:22; 13:9; 15:7, 7, 13; 16:9; 18:11, 12, 14, 19; 19:6, 10, 11; 20:15, 15, 17, 20; 21:15; 22:7, 11; 23:3, 5, 7, 16; 24:8; 25:4, 4, 8, 16, 19; 29:24, 27; 30:3, 7, 8, 9, 9; 32:7, 7, 18; 33:4, 7; 34:25, 25; 35:1; 36:10, 16, 23; Ezr 1:3; 3:13; 4:12, 13, 16, 19, 21; 5:13; 6:1, 3, 3, 3, 4, 4, 5, 7, 8, 10, 11, 11, 12; 7:17, 17, 18, 23, 24, 26; 8:25, 26; 10:8, 13, 14; Ne 1:9, 11; 2:3, 6; 4:10, 14; 6:6, 7, 13; 8:10, 14, 15; 9:32; 10:31, 32, 34, 35, 38, 38; 12:43, 44; 13:1, 9, 18, 19, 19, 19; Est 1:8, 15, 18, 19, 19, 22; 2:4, 14, 23; 3:9, 13, 13, 14, 14; 6:1, 13; 7:3; 8:2, 8, 13, 13; 9:12, 28, 28; Job 1:21; 3:3, 3, 4, 4, 4, 6, 6, 7, 10, 13, 20, 25; 4:2, 10, 11, 17, 17; 5:3, 21, 23, 23, 24, 25, 25, 26; 6:2, 2, 3, 14, 18, 21, 29; 7:2, 4, 8, 8, 10, 21; 8:12, 22, 22; 9:2, 3, 24, 27, 29, 31; 11:15, 16, 17, 17, 18; 12:14; 13:5, 8, 9, 10, 13, 16, 18, 20; 14:12, 17; 15:2, 14, 14, 15, 22, 28, 29, 31, 32, 33, 34; 18:4, 5, 6, 7, 7, 18; 19:3, 23, 23; 20:8, 18, 26; 21:5; 22:2, 2, 3, 19, 23, 25, 25, 28, 30; 23:7; 24:23, 24; 25:4; 27:7, 15; 28:15, 17, 19, 22, 23; 31:8, 11, 22, 22, 23, 28; 33:7, 10, 24, 26; 34:19, 30; 36:11, 11, 17, 18, 18, 20, 21; 37:20; 39:14; 41:4, 7, 9; Ps 1:5; 2:10, 12; 4:T, 3; 5:T, 5, 10, 11; 6:T, 10; 7:5; 8:T; 9:T, 2, 18, 18, 19; 10:2, 6, 16; 12:T; 16:4, 8; 17:15; 18:15, 46, 46; 19:13, 14; 22:T, 26, 31; 23:4; 25:2, 3, 20; 27:1, 7, 14; 28:5; 30:12; 31:1, 2, 17, 17, 18, 24; 32:9, 11; 33:11; 34:T, 5, 20, 21, 22; 35:8, 9, 26, 26; 37:7, 9, 10, 15, 15, 16, 16, 17, 33, 34, 38; 39:4, 11; 40:3, 14, 14, 15, 16; 41:5; 42:4; 44:11; 45:T; 46:T, 5, 10, 10, 10; 48:10, 11, 14; 49:13, 14, 16; 50:4, 6; 51:4, 6, 7, 7, 16, 19, 19; 52:6; 54:T, 5; 55:T; 56:T, 4, 11; 57:T, 5, 11; 58:T, 8; 59:T, 12; 60:T, 8; 61:T; 62:2, 6; 63:11; 64:8; 67:T, 1, 2, 4; 68:3, 3, 35; 69:T, 5, 6, 25, 28, 32; 70:2, 2, 3, 4; 71:1, 3; 72:2, 3, 6, 7, 15, 16, 17, 19; 73:28; 74:21; 75:T; 76:T; 77:2, 9; 78:8, 61, 62; 79:5, 10; 80:T, 3, 4, 7, 19; 81:T, 14; 83:17; 84:T, 10; 85:5, 9; 86:3, 17; 87:5;

88:T; 89:19, 24, 28, 29, 52; 91:5, 15; 92:T, 9; 93:1, 5; 94:1, 3; 96:4, 10, 11; 97:1, 12; 98:3; 101:2, 6, 7, 8; 102:18, 18, 21; 104:5, 34; 106:48; 107:42; 108:5, 9; 109:7, 8, 8, 10, 12, 13, 14, 15, 19, 28; 110:3, 7, 7; 111:8; 112:2, 2, 3, 3, 6, 6, 9, 10; 113:2, 5; 115:15; 118:6, 24; 119:6, 17, 30, 31, 46, 58, 79, 80, 80, 116, 117, 133; 120:4; 122:7, 8; 124:6; 125:1, 3; 127:5; 128:2, 3; 129:5, 6, 8; 132:9, 17, 18; 135:21; 137:8; 140:9; 141:5, 7; 144:12, 13, 14, 14; 145:6; 148:6; 149:6; Pr 2:22, 22; 3:7, 11, 25; 4:5; 5:2, 18, 19, 20, 23; 6:6, 15, 27, 30, 31, 33, 34; 8:11, 33; 9:6, 9, 12, 12; 10:8, 13, 18, 18, 19, 30, 30, 31; 11:21, 21, 25, 29; 12:9, 9, 24; 13:4, 7, 7, 18, 24; 14:22, 22, 26; 15:10, 31, 33; 16:2, 5, 5, 8, 20, 32; 17:5, 11, 21, 28; 18:4; 19:1, 1, 9, 20, 22, 25, 29, 29; 20:1, 13, 16, 20; 21:13, 25, 28, 28; 22:13, 25, 27; 23:3, 18, 19, 25, 28; 24:14, 17, 18, 20, 24; 25:4, 5, 7, 8; 26:5, 13, 25, 26; 27:11, 11, 11, 13, 14, 18, 24, 26; 28:6, 18, 18; 29:1, 9, 12, 19, 24, 24; 30:2, 6, 17; 31:5, 30; Ecc 1:15, 15; 2:2, 16, 19; 3:2, 7, 12, 14, 22; 4:6, 11, 12, 13, 13, 16; 5:1, 2, 8, 16; 6:3, 5, 10, 12; 7:5, 5, 9, 16, 17, 17, 23, 26, 28, 28, 29; 8:1, 1, 5, 12; 9:3, 4, 10, 16, 16; 10:8, 13; 11:6, 8, 8, 9; 12:2, 3, 3, 4, 5, 5, 12, 12; SS 6:8; 7:8, 9; 8:3, 7; Isa 1:16, 20, 26, 27, 28, 31; 2:9, 11, 11, 17, 17, 18, 22; 3:6, 9, 10, 14, 20, 24, 24, 26; 4:1, 1, 1, 2, 2, 3, 5, 6; 5:3, 5, 6, 8, 14, 15, 15, 21, 25, 27, 28, 29; 6:13, 13; 7:8, 16, 21, 24; 8:9, 12, 12, 14, 14, 15, 21, 22, 22; 9:1, 1, 1, 3, 5, 5, 5, 6, 12, 17, 20, 21; 10:3, 4, 8, 17, 18, 24; 11:5, 6, 6, 9, 10, 10, 15; 12:2; 13:9, 10, 12, 12, 15, 16, 16, 19, 20, 21; 14:1, 2, 14, 15, 16, 19, 20, 25, 29, 29, 31; 15:1, 4, 5; 16:5, 10, 11, 14, 14; 17:2, 2, 3, 4, 5, 6, 6, 9, 11; 18:6; 19:5, 8, 10, 16, 18, 19, 19, 20, 23, 24, 24, 24, 25, 25, 25; 20:5; 21:11; 22:9, 13, 14, 21, 22, 22, 24; 23:5, 7, 12, 15, 16, 17, 18, 18; 24:2, 3, 6, 7, 7, 8, 8, 8, 17, 22, 23; 25:2, 6, 10, 12; 26:11, 21; 27:4, 5, 9, 9, 10; 28:3, 4, 5, 5, 13, 18, 22; 29:2, 3, 5, 9, 16, 17, 17, 19, 20, 20, 21, 22; 30:3, 13, 14, 14, 15, 17, 19, 20, 23, 25, 26, 26, 26, 29, 31; 31:4, 8, 8; 32:3, 4, 5, 5, 7, 8, 8, 12, 13, 13, 14, 14, 18, 19; 33:1, 2, 2, 6, 12, 16, 16, 19, 21, 21, 23; 34:3, 7, 8, 9, 9, 11, 12, 12, 16; 35:2, 4, 8, 8, 9, 10; 36:6, 12, 14, 15; 37:3, 6, 10, 11; 38:3, 10; 39:6, 6, 7, 8; 40:5, 9, 13, 19, 20, 20; 41:6, 10, 10, 12, 13, 14, 15; 42:2, 6, 17, 24; 43:1, 2, 2, 5, 10, 14, 20; 44:2, 8, 9, 14, 19, 25, 26, 26, 26, 27, 27, 28, 28; 45:1, 1, 9, 10, 14, 14, 16, 17, 18, 18, 24, 25; 46:4; 47:1, 3, 5, 8, 11, 11; 48:11, 20; 49:5, 9, 11, 18, 19, 19, 23, 25, 25, 26; 50:7, 9; 51:3, 4, 7, 11, 14, 14; 52:13; 53:11, 11; 54:3, 4, 5, 10, 13, 15, 15, 17; 55:13; 56:1, 7, 12; 57:19; 58:10, 11, 12, 14; 59:8, 11, 11, 14, 21; 60:4, 7, 7, 11, 12, 12, 13, 13, 15, 15, 17, 18, 19, 19, 20, 21; 61:1, 1, 5, 6, 6, 9, 11; 62:2, 4, 4, 12, 12; 63:8, 11, 16; 64:5, 9, 12; 65:10, 10, 13, 13, 15, 18, 18, 19, 20, 22, 23, 23, 25; 66:3, 5, 5, 5, 8, 10, 12, 14, 16, 19, 21, 22; Jer 1:8, 8, 17, 18, 18; 2:22, 37; 3:5, 10, 12, 16, 16, 17; 4:2, 9, 13, 14, 19, 21, 27, 28; 5:12; 6:6, 9, 12, 15, 26; 7:4, 5, 20, 23, 23, 23, 28, 32, 32, 33, 33, 34; 8:2, 2, 9, 12, 13, 16, 19; 9:11, 11, 16, 22, 22; 10:2, 5, 5, 15, 22, 24; 11:4, 4, 5, 19; 12:3, 3, 14, 16, 17; 13:11, 12, 12, 15, 17, 18, 19, 19, 19, 27; 14:6, 16, 16, 16; 15:8, 9, 11, 15, 19; 16:4, 9; 17:1, 13, 13, 25, 27; 18:7, 15, 16, 21, 22; 19:6, 8, 9; 20:3, 5, 6, 6, 7, 11, 11, 14, 16; 21:2, 10; 22:3, 4, 9, 19, 22, 23, 28; 23:3, 4, 4, 5, 6, 12, 12, 40; 24:2, 7, 7, 9; 25:10, 33, 35, 37, 38; 26:3, 9, 9, 15, 18, 18, 24; 27:8, 11, 16, 17, 18, 22; 28:9; 29:10, 14, 26, 27, 28, 28; 30:7, 7, 8, 10, 10, 16, 16, 16, 16, 18, 18, 19, 21, 22, 22; 31:1, 1, 4, 12, 12, 12, 15, 18, 30, 32, 33, 33, 37, 37, 38, 39, 40, 40; 32:4, 4, 38, 38, 43, 44; 33:10, 11, 16, 16, 18, 21, 22, 22, 24; 34:3, 3, 3, 4, 14, 17, 17, 20; 36:3, 6, 30; 37:17, 18, 21, 21; 38:3, 17, 18, 20, 20, 22, 23, 23, 23; 40:9, 15; 42:5, 12, 14, 18, 22; 43:3, 3; 44:12, 26; 45:5; 46:19, 24, 24, 27, 27; 47:4, 5, 6, 6, 7, 7; 48:1, 1, 2, 7, 7, 8, 9, 10, 13, 15, 34, 38, 41, 41, 42, 43; 49:2, 3, 4, 10, 10, 10, 11, 13, 13, 15, 17, 17, 18, 20, 20, 21, 22, 25, 26, 29, 29, 29, 32, 33, 33, 36; 50:2, 2, 3, 5, 9, 10, 12, 13, 19, 20, 22, 25, 27, 27, 30, 34, 37, 39, 39, 45, 45, 46; 51:3, 3, 8, 9, 9, 14, 18, 25, 26, 26, 26, 29, 33, 35, 35, 36, 37, 40, 46, 47, 49, 52, 52, 58, 58, 58; 52:20; La 1:17, 17; 3:59; 4:21, 22; Eze 2:6, 6; 3:9, 12, 25, 26; 4:3, 8, 9, 14, 16, 16, 16, 17; 5:12, 13, 13, 15; 6:4, 4, 6, 8, 12; 7:11, 13, 15, 17, 17; 8:2, 3; 10:1, 5; 11:3, 10, 11, 11, 16, 20, 20; 12:3, 6, 11, 19, 20, 23, 25; 13:7, 9, 15, 21; 14:10, 11, 11, 16, 16, 18, 20, 21, 22; 15:3, 4, 6; 16:8, 20, 42, 42, 42, 52, 54, 55, 55, 61; 17:21, 21; 18:4, 10, 20, 20, 20, 20, 22, 24, 24; 19:5, 9, 11, 14; 20:5, 9, 12, 14, 31, 32, 41, 47, 47, 48; 21:27, 32, 32; 22:5, 14; 23:3, 21, 25, 25, 25, 29, 46, 48, 49; 24:14, 16, 17, 21, 23, 27; 25:10; 26:5, 6, 13, 14, 20, 21, 21, 21; 27:3, 36; 28:9, 23; 29:11, 12, 12, 15, 16, 21; 30:4, 4, 5, 6, 7, 7, 13, 16, 16, 17, 18, 18; 31:14, 18, 18; 32:10, 12, 20, 31; 33:9, 13, 16, 22, 24, 25, 27, 28, 31; 34:8, 10, 12, 22, 23, 24, 24, 25, 26, 28, 29; 35:8, 9, 10, 15; 36:8, 9, 10, 12, 15, 25, 25, 28, 28, 30, 32, 33, 34, 38; 37:22, 23, 23, 24, 25, 27, 27, 28; 38:7, 8, 8, 16, 20; 39:7, 9, 11, 13, 14, 14, 15, 15, 16, 16, 27; 40:2, 9, 43, 47, 48; 41:3, 13; 43:10, 11, 18, 19, 25; 44:2, 5, 5, 11, 11, 24, 30; 45:1, 1, 2, 2, 3, 4, 4, 5, 5, 6, 6, 6, 7, 8, 11, 12, 15, 17, 21, 23; 46:1, 1, 2, 11, 11, 12, 12, 13, 14, 14, 15, 17, 17, 18, 24; 47:9, 10, 11, 11, 12, 12, 12, 13, 18, 19, 20, 22, 23; 48:8, 9, 10, 12, 13, 14, 15, 18, 21, 29, 30, 31, 31, 32, 34, 35, 35; Da 1:5, 5, 20; 2:5, 5, 9, 18, 40, 41, 42, 44, 49; 3:6, 11, 13, 15, 15, 15, 18, 19, 29, 29; 4:15, 19, 23, 25, 25, 32; 5:7, 7, 10, 16; 6:5, 7, 7, 8, 8, 12, 12, 15, 16, 23, 26; 7:14, 18, 23, 25, 26, 27; 8:13, 14, 25, 25; 9:25, 26; 10:12, 19, 19, 19; 11:2, 4, 4, 4, 6, 6, 6, 12, 12, 14, 15, 16, 19, 20, 21, 22, 26, 26, 29, 32, 33, 34, 35, 36, 43, 45; 12:1, 1, 6, 10, 11, 11; Hos 1:2, 10, 10, 11; 2:7, 10, 17, 20; 3:4; 4:10, 14; 5:6, 11, 14; 6:6; 7:13, 16; 8:5, 6; 9:2, 3, 4, 4, 4, 6, 11, 12, 13, 17; 10:2, 5, 6, 6, 7, 15; 11:5; 13:9, 15, 16; 14:4, 5, 7; Joel 1:15; 2:2, 14, 17, 18, 19, 21, 21, 22, 22, 22, 24, 26, 27, 31, 32, 32, 32; 3:3, 10, 12, 16, 17; Am 1:4, 7, 8, 10, 12, 14, 14; 2:2, 5, 11, 11, 14, 15, 15; 3:6, 12, 14; 4:2, 2, 3; 5:5, 6, 14, 16, 17, 18, 19, 20; 6:1, 4, 5, 7, 7, 11, 12; 7:9, 11, 11, 14, 17, 17; 8:3, 3, 5, 10, 10; 9:1, 9, 9, 12, 13, 15; Ob 2, 6, 6, 8, 9, 9, 10, 15, 17, 18, 21; Jnh 3:4; 4:3, 4, 9; Mic 1:6, 7, 7, 7, 16, 16; 2:1, 3, 7, 12; 3:7, 12, 12; 4:4, 8, 10, 12; 5:3, 4, 5, 7, 8, 8, 9, 12; 6:1, 10, 16; 7:1, 6, 8, 9, 10, 11, 11, 16; Na 1:10, 12; 2:13, 13; 3:1, 1, 12, 13, 13, 15, 19; Hab 1:5, 5, 6, 13, 14, 15; 2:3, 3, 9, 12, 14, 15, 16, 16, 16, 17, 19, 19, 20; 3:14, 18, 19; Zep 1:13, 13, 15, 17, 18, 18; 2:4, 5, 9, 12; 3:1, 8, 8, 9, 11, 11, 11, 12, 13, 14, 15, 16, 16, 18; Hag 1:8; 2:5, 9, 13; Zec 1:4, 12, 16, 16; 2:4, 4, 5, 5, 11, 12, 12, 13; 3:7; 5:2, 3, 3; 6:7, 13, 14; 8:3, 3, 5, 7, 8, 8, 12, 13, 13, 15; 9:4, 5, 5, 5, 5, 7, 15, 17; 10:5, 6, 7, 7, 10, 11, 11; 11:9; 12:8, 8, 11; 13:1, 2, 4, 7, 8, 8; 14:1, 2, 2, 2, 7, 7, 7, 9, 9, 9, 10, 10, 11, 11, 13, 14, 14, 19, 20, 20, 21, 21, 21; Mal 1:4, 4, 9, 10; 3:2, 2, 2, 5, 10, 11, 12, 17, 17; 4:1, 1; Mt 1:18, 20, 23, 24; 2:4, 6, 18, 23; 3:7, 10, 11, 13, 14, 15; 4:1, 19, 24; 5:4, 7, 9, 12, 12, 13, 19, 19, 24, 26, 29, 30, 45, 48; 6:1, 5, 8, 9, 10, 19, 20, 21, 23, 24, 32; 7:1, 2, 7, 7; 8:3, 8, 12, 12; 9:9, 10, 13, 15, 17, 21, 22; 10:10, 13, 15, 15, 16, 17, 18, 19, 20, 20, 21, 22, 26, 26, 26, 28, 31, 36, 41, 42; 11:19, 22, 23, 23, 23, 24; 12:2, 7, 21, 23, 29, 31, 31, 32, 32, 33, 33, 37, 37, 40, 45; 13:12, 12, 40, 42, 49, 50; 14:2, 13, 27, 35; 15:4, 13; 16:19, 19, 21, 21, 24; 17:7, 17, 20, 22, 23, 23; 18:6, 6, 7, 7, 8, 9, 16, 23, 25, 26, 29, 30; 19:3, 21, 25, 30, 30, 30; 20:15, 16, 16, 18, 19, 19, 26, 26, 26, 27, 28, 31; 21:13, 26, 43, 44, 46; 22:2, 21, 24, 28, 30, 30, 31, 45; 23:11, 12, 12, 13, 15, 16, 18, 23, 25, 27, 29; 24:2, 2, 3, 7, 8, 9, 9, 12, 13, 14, 19, 20, 21, 22, 22, 27, 29, 29, 30, 37, 39, 40, 40, 41, 41, 42, 43, 44, 46, 48, 51; 25:1, 13, 14, 29, 29, 30, 32; 26:2, 5, 11, 13, 24, 31, 37, 39, 42, 42, 46, 52, 54, 73; 27:20, 20, 31, 63, 64; 28:5, 10, 14, 20; Mk 1:4, 4, 7, 17, 25, 40, 41; 2:14, 15, 20, 24; 3:14, 27, 28, 29; 4:12, 12, 22, 24, 25, 25; 5:3, 11, 28, 36; 6:10, 14, 50; 7:10, 34; 8:31, 31, 34, 38; 9:12, 19, 26, 29, 31, 31, 33, 35, 35, 39, 41, 42, 42, 45, 47, 49; 10:2, 26, 31, 31, 31, 33, 38, 38, 39, 43, 43, 43, 44, 44, 45, 48; 11:17, 23; 12:13, 17, 19, 23, 25, 25, 26, 35, 37, 40; 13:2, 2, 4, 4, 6, 8, 8, 9, 9, 9, 10, 11, 12, 13, 14, 17, 18, 19, 20, 24, 25, 29, 34; 14:2, 7, 9, 21, 27, 33, 42, 70; 15:20; 16:6, 16, 16, 18, 18; Lk 1:13, 15, 15, 17, 20, 27, 30, 32, 32, 35, 35, 54, 55, 57, 66, 71, 76; 2:1, 6, 10, 23, 34, 34, 34, 35, 49; 3:3, 3, 9, 12, 14, 15, 16; 4:18, 18, 22, 35, 41; 5:8, 10, 10, 12, 13, 15, 27, 35, 36, 38; 6:2, 13, 18, 21, 35, 35, 35, 36, 37, 37, 38; 7:7, 35; 8:10, 16, 17, 18, 18, 18, 50, 50; 9:4, 22, 22, 22, 23, 26, 41, 44, 46, 59; 10:12, 14, 15, 15; 11:2, 8, 9, 9, 30, 36, 41, 42, 43, 44, 46, 47, 50, 51, 52; 12:2, 2, 3, 3, 4, 7, 10, 10, 12, 15, 19, 32, 33, 34, 35, 36, 37, 38, 39, 40, 43, 45, 47, 48, 52, 53, 55, 58, 59; 13:14, 23, 25, 28, 28, 30, 30, 33; 14:9, 10, 11, 11, 15, 18, 23, 26, 26, 27; 15:7; 16:2, 10, 10, 12, 13, 22; 17:1, 1, 2, 2, 21, 22, 24, 25, 26, 28, 30, 34, 34, 34, 35, 35; 18:13, 14, 14, 26, 30, 32, 32, 40; 19:5, 7, 9, 12, 14, 17, 19, 26, 26, 27, 46; 20:18, 19, 20, 20, 25, 28, 33, 35, 35, 37, 41, 44, 47; 21:6, 6, 7, 8, 11, 11, 11, 12, 12, 12, 13, 15, 16, 22, 22, 23, 23, 24, 24, 25, 25, 26, 31; 22:22, 24, 26, 37, 40, 58, 59, 69; 23:7, 32, 43; 24:7, 7, 17, 18, 20, 36; Jn 1:19, 27, 42, 43; 3:4, 7, 7, 14, 20, 20; 4:15, 19, 29; 5:20, 24, 28, 31, 34; 6:20, 26, 27, 35, 45; 7:23, 26, 27, 33, 34, 36, 39, 41, 42; 8:12, 16, 25, 36, 50, 55; 9:3, 17, 22, 41; 10:1, 9, 16, 35; 11:39, 49, 50, 52; 12:8, 15, 24, 24, 26, 26, 31, 48; 13:10; 14:1, 3, 8, 12, 17, 27, 28, 31; 15:4, 6, 7, 11, 22, 24; 16:2, 4, 13, 13, 16, 19, 21, 25, 32; 17:11, 13, 19, 21, 21, 22, 24, 26; 18:28, 33; 19:16, 31, 31, 36; 20:19, 21, 26, 27; Ac 1:5, 16, 20, 21, 24; 2:7, 20, 21, 25, 31, 36, 36, 38; 3:17, 19, 23, 25; 4:30; 5:21, 31, 34, 36, 38, 39; 7:6, 9, 26, 34, 35; 8:9, 20, 36; 9:6, 17, 26; 10:23, 41, 42, 46, 48; 11:14, 16; 12:6, 15, 19; 13:11, 24, 25, 40, 41, 46; 14:9; 15:1, 5, 5, 17; 16:3, 4, 15, 17, 30, 31; 17:17, 21; 18:6, 9, 9, 14, 27; 19:27, 36, 39; 20:26, 28; 21:11, 13, 14, 22, 26, 34, 37, 40; 22:5, 10, 11, 16; 23:11; 24:5, 19; 25:4, 10, 20, 23; 26:10, 18, 23, 32; 27:24, 25, 26, 29; Ro 1:1, 4, 7, 7, 12, 12, 22, 25, 28; 2:1, 1, 9, 10, 13, 27; 3:4, 5, 8, 20, 22, 26, 27; 4:3, 6, 11, 18, 19, 22, 23, 24; 5:7, 10, 19; 6:5, 13, 19, 19; 7:3, 13, 21; 8:4, 15, 23, 26, 29, 31, 39; 9:3, 3, 4, 7, 8, 22, 23, 27, 33; 10:1, 9, 11, 13; 11:6, 11, 15, 15, 16, 16, 18, 22, 24, 26, 29, 34, 36; 12:1, 3, 11, 12, 12, 12, 13, 15, 20; 13:4, 4, 6, 12, 13; 14:8, 9, 16, 23; 15:1, 7, 16, 17, 31, 31, 32, 32, 33; 16:1, 13, 20, 27; 1Co 1:1, 2, 10, 10, 10, 13, 20, 30, 30; 3:5, 8, 10, 13, 15; 4:2, 5, 8; 5:4, 4, 5, 5, 6, 11; 6:3, 7; 7:5, 5, 6, 16, 16, 18, 21, 23, 25, 29, 32, 34, 34, 39, 40; 8:9, 10, 11; 9:10, 12, 14, 27; 10:12, 20, 25, 27, 29, 29, 30, 33; 11:19, 19, 31, 32; 12:19, 23; 13:1, 2, 2, 3; 14:1, 2, 2, 2, 2, 9, 12, 17, 20, 20, 20, 24, 24, 25, 26, 27, 28, 31, 34, 34, 37, 38, 39, 40; 15:9, 12, 15, 15, 20, 22, 23, 26, 28, 29, 30, 32, 33, 35, 42, 43, 43, 44, 48, 49, 51, 52, 52, 53, 58; 16:6, 8, 12, 13, 13, 13, 14, 23; 2Co 1:1, 4, 5, 6, 14, 17, 24; 2:3, 7, 10, 14; 3:12, 14, 18; 4:6, 10, 11, 15, 18; 5:3, 4, 8, 8, 10, 12, 20, 21, 21; 6:3, 14, 15, 15, 16, 16, 16, 18, 18; 8:13, 14, 21; 9:3, 3, 4, 5, 9, 11, 12, 13; 10:2, 2, 8, 8, 11, 15, 16, 16; 11:1, 3, 6, 15, 26, 31; 12:4, 6, 6, 11, 14; 13:1, 9, 11, 13; Gal 1:3, 7, 8, 10, 10; 2:3, 16, 16, 17, 21; 3:8, 11, 17, 17, 18, 18; 4:20; 5:11, 14, 16, 26; 6:1, 4, 7, 12, 12, 13, 16, 18; Eph 1:1, 2, 4, 14, 18; 2:11; 3:17, 19, 20, 21; 4:2, 2, 13, 14, 23, 29, 29, 30, 32; 5:3, 4, 5, 6, 15, 18, 23, 27; 6:10, 11, 13, 15, 18, 24; Php 1:11, 20, 23, 23, 28, 28, 28, 28; 2:3, 3, 4, 5, 12, 16, 17, 18, 28, 29; 3:2, 2, 12, 12, 13, 16; 4:4, 9, 20, 23; Col 1:1, 11, 11; 2:2, 4, 18; 3:5, 12, 15, 17, 25; 4:1, 6, 17, 18; 1Th 1:1, 4; 2:4, 5, 9, 16; 3:10; 4:3, 7, 9, 11, 13, 17; 5:3, 3, 4, 6, 6, 14, 16, 18, 23, 28; 2Th 1:9, 10, 12; 2:1, 2, 3, 6, 8, 12, 13; 3:1, 2, 8, 14, 15, 16, 18; 1Ti 1:5, 7; 2:4, 9, 10, 15; 3:1, 2, 2, 2, 2, 3, 3, 3, 6, 6, 7, 8, 8, 8, 9, 10, 11, 11, 12, 13, 14, 16; 4:2, 3, 3, 6, 12; 5:7, 9, 10, 11, 12, 14, 17, 20, 22, 24, 24, 25; 6:1, 8, 9, 15, 16, 17, 17, 17, 18, 19, 21; 2Ti 1:4, 8, 8, 8, 11; 2:1, 9, 15, 15, 21, 21, 21, 24, 24, 24; 3:1, 2, 3, 3, 4, 4, 13; 4:2, 5, 11, 13, 15, 16, 18, 22, 22; Tit 1:6, 6, 6, 7, 7, 8, 9, 11; 2:2, 2, 3, 5, 5, 7, 8, 8, 8, 10, 13; 3:1, 2, 8, 15; Phm 1:25; Heb 1:5, 5; 2:5, 17, 17; 3:1, 12, 13; 5:4, 10, 12; 6:17; 7:12, 16, 20; 8:4, 5, 9, 10, 10, 13; 9:10, 23, 23; 10:10, 23, 27, 29; 11:3, 16, 18, 24, 35; 12:2, 5, 11, 20, 27, 27, 28, 28; 13:5, 6, 9, 17, 20, 25; Jas 1:2, 4, 6, 9, 10, 16, 19, 26; 2:5, 12, 13, 23; 3:1, 13; 4:4, 5, 9, 9, 9, 16; 5:7, 8, 12, 13, 15, 16, 20; 1Pe 1:5, 6, 9, 15, 15, 16, 21; 2:1, 1, 6, 12, 24; 3:1, 3, 4, 7, 7, 8, 14, 15, 16; 4:1, 2, 7, 11, 11, 12, 13, 14, 15, 17; 5:4, 8, 9, 14; 2Pe 2:1, 1, 2, 12, 12, 14, 21; 3:3, 4, 7, 10, 11, 14, 15, 17, 18; 1Jn 1:4; 2:3, 26, 28; 3:1, 2, 2, 12, 13, 17, 19; 4:14, 17; 5:14, 15; 2Jn 2, 3, 8, 12; 3Jn 9, 15; Jude 11, 18, 23; Rev 1:17; 2:10, 10, 11, 17; 3:5, 12, 18, 18, 18, 19; 5:4; 6:10, 17; 7:16, 16, 17; 8:3; 10:7; 11:3, 9, 19; 12:14; 13:10, 10, 10, 16; 14:5, 10; 15:2; 17:8, 10, 12, 17; 18:4, 8, 14, 21, 22, 22, 23, 23; 19:7; 20:3, 6, 7, 10; 21:3, 3, 4, 7, 7, 17, 22, 27; 22:3, 3, 4, 5, 11, 21

BECAUSE (1291)

Ge 2:3, 23; 3:10, 14, 17, 20; 5:24; 6:13; 8:9; 11:9; 12:13, 16, 17; 15:6; 19:30; 21:11, 13, 31; 22:16, 18; 24:48; 25:21, 28; 26:5, 7, 9, 20, 24; 27:20, 23, 41; 29:10, 10, 15, 31; 30:27; 31:31; 32:28, 31; 34:13, 14, 27; 35:7, 15; 36:7; 37:3, 4; 38:11, 26; 39:9, 23; 41:57; 42:21, 22; 43:18, 30, 32; 47:20; 48:10; 49:11; Ex 1:9, 17, 21; 2:14; 3:2, 6; 9:11, 31, 32; 12:39; 15:16, 23; 17:7; 18:11; 19:18; 21:19, 26; 22:15; 23:3, 6, 29; 31:15; 32:29, 35; 34:29; 39:43; 40:35; Lev 2:11; 6:18; 9:4; 11:4, 13, 44, 45; 13:11, 13, 15, 22, 44, 52; 14:48; 15:2; 16:16; 18:12, 13, 18, 24; 19:2; 20:3, 18, 23, 26; 21:3, 8, 8, 12, 15, 23; 22:20, 25; 23:28; 25:23; 26:16, 39; 27:26; Nu 3:13; 6:7, 9; 8:15; 9:10; 11:3, 34; 12:1; 13:24; 14:19, 29, 34, 42, 43; 15:34; 16:38, 50; 18:24; 20:12, 13, 21, 24; 21:24; 22:6, 29, 32; 25:13, 18, 18; 26:62; 27:3, 4; 30:5; 33:53; Dt 1:36, 37; 2:30; 3:26; 4:21, 37; 7:7, 8, 8; 9:4, 4, 5, 5, 6, 12, 18, 28, 28; 12:7, 25, 28; 13:10; 15:9, 16; 17:17; 18:12; 22:24, 24, 29; 23:5, 7, 10; 24:15; 26:11; 28:34, 47, 55, 62, 67; 29:25; 31:17; Jos 5:4; 6:1, 25; 9:18, 24, 24; 10:2; 14:9, 14; 17:1, 6; 19:9; 20:6; 22:19, 20, 24, 31; Jdg 1:19, 27, 32; 2:20; 4:17; 5:23; 6:7, 27, 32; 9:3, 18, 21; 10:10; 11:8, 37, 38; 12:6; 14:17; 15:6, 7; 17:13; 18:7; 21:15, 18; Ru 1:1, 13; 4:4, 6; 1Sa 1:5, 6, 8; 3:7, 13; 4:6, 21, 21; 6:19, 19; 7:2; 9:6; 10:1; 14:24, 26; 15:1, 23; 18:12, 16; 19:1; 23:10; 24:5; 26:12, 16; 28:15, 18, 20; 30:6, 12, 13, 16; 2Sa 1:12; 3:11, 30; 4:3; 5:10; 6:8, 12; 7:27; 9:7; 10:2; 12:10, 11, 25; 13:22; 14:13, 15, 26, 32; 16:12, 18; 18:8; 21:1, 7; 22:8, 20, 21, 25; 1Ki 2:26; 3:6, 11; 5:3; 7:47; 8:11, 33, 35, 35, 64, 66; 9:9; 10:9, 21; 11:2, 39; 13:22; 14:16; 15:13, 30; 16:7, 7, 13, 13; 20:36, 42; 21:4, 19, 20, 26, 29; 2Ki 5:1, 27; 8:27; 10:30; 11:20; 12:2, 15; 13:23; 14:27; 15:16; 17:7, 18, 26; 18:4, 36; 19:28; 22:13; 23:26; 24:3; 1Ch 4:9, 14, 41; 5:20, 22; 7:23; 9:1, 22; 10:13; 11:9; 13:10, 11; 15:13, 22, 26; 17:25; 19:2; 21:6, 30; 23:11; 27:23, 24; 29:3; 2Ch 1:11; 2:5, 11; 5:14; 6:24, 26, 26; 7:2, 7, 10, 22; 9:8, 20; 11:14; 12:2, 5, 12; 13:18; 14:7; 15:16; 16:7; 17:3; 20:26, 37; 21:3, 10; 22:9; 23:21; 24:16, 18; 25:16; 26:10, 20; 27:6; 28:6, 11, 19; 29:36; 34:21; 35:14; Ezr 3:11; 4:15; 5:5, 12; 6:22; 7:6, 10, 28; 9:4, 13; 10:6, 9, 9; Ne 2:8; 5:15, 18; 6:12, 18, 18; 8:12; 9:37; Est 8:7; 9:26, 26, 26; 10:3; Job 2:4; 11:18; 20:2; 21:28; 22:4, 5; 31:21, 24; 32:1, 2, 3, 4; 35:12, 15; 38:3; 40:7; 42:11; Ps 5:7, 10; 6:4, 7; 7:17; 9:2; 13:5, 6; 17:6, 15; 18:7, 19, 20, 24; 21:1; 31:7, 9; 35:9; 38:3, 3, 5, 20; 41:12; 44:3, 26; 51:1, 1; 59:12, 12, 16; 67:4; 69:6; 71:7, 22; 72:3; 75:1; 78:62; 82:5; 89:24; 92:4; 97:8; 102:5, 10; 106:17, 45; 107:34; 109:21, 26; 116:1, 2; 119:55, 75, 136, 158, 159, 164, 168; 124:3; 138:2; 143:1; Pr 5:23; 6:30; 8:15; 21:7; 22:9, 22; 24:19; 25:7; 26:13; 31:21; Ecc 2:17; 8:2, 15; 12:9; SS 1:6; Isa 1:27; 2:6; 3:8; 5:13; 7:8, 22; 8:20, 21; 10:16; 17:10; 22:11; 23:1; 29:11, 14; 30:12; 36:21; 37:29; 38:15; 43:4; 49:7; 50:1, 1, 1, 2, 7; 53:11, 12; 54:15, 15; 55:5; 56:7; 57:11; 58:3; 59:2, 9; 61:1; 62:1, 1; 65:11; Jer 2:35; 4:4, 28; 5:14; 6:19, 29, 30; 7:4, 8, 12; 8:8, 14; 9:13, 19; 10:5; 11:8; 12:4; 13:17, 17, 22, 25; 14:5; 15:4, 7, 13, 17; 16:11, 18; 19:15; 21:12; 22:9, 15; 23:9, 9, 15, 38; 25:8; 26:3; 28:16; 29:9, 28; 30:15; 31:12; 32:3, 24; 33:5; 34:18; 35:6, 14, 17, 19; 36:29, 31; 37:11; 39:18; 44:3, 22, 23; 46:15; 48:7; 49:16; 50:13, 38; 51:51, 64; La 3:48; 4:13; 5:10, 16; Eze 3:19; 5:9, 11; 6:11; 9:4; 12:2, 19; 13:8; 14:9; 15:8; 16:14, 36, 36, 36, 43, 52; 18:17, 22, 26, 28; 19:10, 11, 11; 20:14, 16, 24, 43; 21:7, 23; 22:19; 23:18, 31, 35; 24:2, 13, 23; 25:3, 6, 8; 26:2; 27:31; 28:6, 17; 29:9, 20; 31:5, 9, 10, 10; 32:10; 33:29; 36:5, 6, 22, 32; 42:5, 13, 14; Da 2:8, 13, 30, 30; 3:22; 4:18; 6:3, 23; 7:11; 9:7, 8, 11, 16, 18, 18; Hos 2:4, 7; 4:6, 17, 19; 5:6, 11; 7:16; 9:15, 15, 17; 10:3, 5, 6, 15; 13:1, 16; Joel 1:9, 11, 18, 20; 2:1, 21; 3:13, 19; Am 3:6; 7:17; Ob 3, 10, 12; Jnh 1:2, 14; 4:3, 9; Mic 1:5, 8, 11; 3:12; 7:13, 18; Na 1:14; 3:4; Hab 2:17; Zep 1:17; Hag 1:9; Zec 9:11; 10:6; Mal 2:2, 13, 14; Mt 2:12, 13, 16, 20; 3:2, 15; 4:17; 5:10, 11, 34, 35; 6:1, 8, 26; 7:25; 8:9; 9:6, 29, 32, 34, 36; 10:10, 18, 19, 22, 41; 11:20, 29; 12:41, 42; 13:6, 13, 16, 16, 21, 58; 14:5, 9, 9; 16:7, 17; 17:15; 18:20, 32; 19:22; 20:7, 15; 21:26, 46; 24:9, 42; 25:8, 13; 27:19; 28:2; Mk 1:34, 38; 2:11; 3:5, 30; 4:6, 17, 28; 5:9; 6:5, 14, 34; 7:29; 8:16; 9:17, 34, 38, 41; 10:22; 11:11, 13, 18; 12:12, 12, 40; 13:6, 13; 14:70; 16:8, 12; Lk 1:7, 45, 68, 76, 78; 2:4, 7, 20, 44; 4:6, 32, 41, 43; 5:24; 6:7, 19, 22, 48; 7:8; 8:19, 40, 53; 9:7, 49, 53; 10:7, 20, 20; 11:31, 32; 12:24; 13:24, 31; 14:2; 15:6, 9, 27; 16:2, 24; 17:9; 18:5, 23; 19:11, 21, 44, 48; 20:6, 19, 47; 21:17, 26, 26; 22:59; 23:7, 8, 20, 34; 24:16, 39; Jn 1:7, 50; 2:23, 24; 3:20, 23; 4:8, 39, 42, 42; 5:27, 30, 38, 39, 42, 46; 6:2, 26, 26, 41, 57; 7:7, 8, 29, 30, 39; 8:12, 16, 20, 37, 42, 43; 9:3, 4, 22, 24, 36, 41; 10:4, 5, 12, 13, 17, 26, 33; 11:9, 10, 15, 39; 12:11, 18, 26, 41, 42; 13:13, 31; 14:11, 12, 13, 17, 17, 21, 28, 30; 15:15, 21, 27; 16:3, 4, 7, 7, 10, 11, 21, 23, 27, 32, 33; 17:9, 14, 20, 24; 18:2, 18, 20, 28; 19:7, 31, 38, 42; 20:13, 19, 29; 21:6, 12; Ac 4:9, 21, 34; 6:15; 8:6, 11; 12:20, 23; 14:12; 16:6, 20, 34; 18:10; 20:16, 38; 22:29; 23:6, 18; 24:16, 21, 27; 26:6; 27:9; 28:20; Ro 2:5, 18, 24, 28, 28; 3:3, 26, 27; 4:2, 5, 5, 9, 17, 22, 25; 5:1, 2, 5, 11, 19, 19; 6:9, 19; 7:4, 14, 17, 25; 8:3, 10, 10; 9:18, 32; 11:12, 20, 20, 28; 12:14; 15:22, 27, 30; 1Co 1:22, 22; 2:10, 14; 3:2, 7, 10; 6:11; 7:2, 5, 16, 16, 26, 36; 8:11; 9:1, 19; 11:10; 12:15, 16; 15:10, 22; 2Co 1:11, 11, 19; 2:13; 3:4; 4:5, 11, 13; 5:11, 14; 6:12, 12; 7:1, 1, 9, 9, 16; 8:22; 9:14; 11:11; 12:6, 21, 21; 13:7; Gal 1:24; 2:2, 12, 16, 16; 3:5, 5, 6, 9; 4:6, 16, 25, 31; 6:14; Eph 1:3, 6, 11; 2:1, 5, 6, 13, 18; 3:1, 12, 13; 4:2, 14, 14, 18, 24, 25; 5:1, 2, 18; 6:1; Php 1:5, 13, 14, 16; 2:9, 30; 3:7; 4:2, 17, 17; Col 1:5; 2:2, 5, 5, 12, 13, 13, 23; 3:22; 1Th 2:14, 17; 3:7, 9; 5:13; 2Th 1:12, 12; 2:10; 1Ti 1:13; 3:6; 4:12; 5:10, 11, 23; 6:2; 2Ti 1:9, 9, 16, 16; 2:9; 4:10; Tit 1:7, 15; 2:8; 3:5, 5, 6, 7; Phm 1:5, 6, 7, 8, 9, 10, 14, 14; Heb 2:9, 14; 3:19; 4:2, 4, 6; 5:2, 4, 7; 6:6, 12, 18; 7:2, 8, 18, 22, 26; 10:19; 11:2, 4, 5, 10, 27, 39; 12:2, 10; Jas 2:21; 4:3; 5:1; 1Pe 1:3, 5, 14, 16, 21, 22, 23, 23; 2:5, 8, 11; 3:16; 4:13; 5:2; 2Pe 1:19, 21; 2:2, 7; 1Jn 2:8, 12, 12, 13, 13, 14, 14, 14, 19, 21, 21, 26; 3:7, 9, 9, 12, 16, 22, 24; 4:4, 17, 18; 5:10, 20; Jude 4, 11, 19; Rev 1:7; 2:9; 3:10; 5:4; 8:11, 13; 12:11, 11; 14:8; 16:21; 17:14; 18:23; 21:25

BEEN (1007)

Ge 3:23; 8:20; 14:4, 14, 16; 19:19; 21:23, 31; 24:27, 59; 26:15, 33; 29:14; 30:33; 31:1, 5, 38; 32:4, 30; 33:11; 34:5, 7, 7, 27; 35:8; 37:3, 13, 33; 41:9, 32; 42:23; 43:27; 44:6; 46:27, 34, 34; 48:15; 49:23; Ex 2:22; 3:15; 4:10; 5:23; 9:24; 10:6, 14; 11:6; 12:19, 42, 44, 44, 48; 14:19; 15:4; 16:3; 18:3, 14; 22:31; 32:29; 33:12; 34:10; 39:43; Lev 1:6; 2:8, 14; 5:3, 10, 19; 6:2, 2, 15, 30; 7:9, 35; 8:34; 10:12, 13, 13, 14, 16; 13:52; 14:2, 3, 43; 15:32; 19:20, 26; 21:7, 10, 12; 22:4, 7, 8; 25:45, 54; 27:28; Nu 5:2, 30; 6:19; 9:6; 11:8, 28; 12:14; 14:27; 16:3, 39; 18:17, 24; 19:2, 20; 20:14; 21:3, 26; 23:21; 26:64; 27:7; Dt 2:3, 7; 4:46; 9:13, 24; 13:17; 14:2; 16:13, 13; 17:4; 19:6; 21:3; 24:4; 34:10; Jos 5:5, 5, 7, 8, 9; 7:7, 12, 26; 8:31; 10:14, 17, 27; 11:10; 12:1; 13:4; 14:15, 15; 15:13, 19; 17:1; 18:2; 19:9; 22:3; 23:9; 24:20, 33; Jdg 1:15; 6:11, 28, 28; 8:10; 11:26; 13:3; 14:20; 15:5; 16:7, 9, 11, 13, 17, 31; 18:29; 19:18, 30; 20:4, 12; Ru 1:7; 2:7; 3:2; 4:15; 1Sa 1:11, 13, 16; 2:15, 15, 23; 4:9, 17, 17, 19, 21, 22; 6:7; 9:20, 23; 10:2, 14, 16; 12:17; 13:4, 23; 14:30, 45; 15:11, 32; 17:27, 33, 34; 19:7; 20:27, 41; 21:6; 23:28; 24:11, 18; 25:21; 26:21; 27:11; 28:24; 29:3; 30:19, 21, 27; 31:7; 2Sa 1:4; 2:16, 17, 31; 3:1, 23, 23; 4:6; 5:17; 7:6, 9, 27; 8:10, 10; 9:2; 10:19; 12:8; 13:20, 32, 32; 14:2, 14, 15; 15:10; 17:8, 17, 17, 25; 19:3, 7; 20:5; 1Ki 1:6, 37; 3:2, 15; 5:1; 7:14, 24, 32; 8:54, 66; 10:12; 14:8; 15:3, 22; 16:7, 18; 18:12, 30; 21:14; 22:17, 34; 2Ki 3:27; 5:2, 25, 25; 6:11; 8:6, 22; 9:12, 14, 15; 10:6; 11:20; 12:10; 16:18; 17:28; 18:35; 19:22; 20:12; 22:13, 13, 20; 23:2, 5, 19, 22, 25, 25; 25:16; 1Ch 2:7; 4:9, 40; 9:20, 20, 21; 10:7; 12:39; 14:8; 17:5, 8, 25; 18:10, 10; 19:19; 23:31; 2Ch 1:8; 4:3, 7; 6:41; 7:10; 8:11; 9:9, 11; 16:6, 9; 18:16, 33; 21:10, 13; 23:21; 25:24; 26:11; 28:11, 19; 29:9, 34, 34, 36; 30:5; 31:6, 14,

18; 32:15; 34:9, 14, 17, 21, 21, 21, 28, 30; 35:3, 14, 18; Ezr 2:1; 3:11; 4:15, 18, 19; 5:15, 16; 6:14; 8:28; 9:7, 7, 7, 8, 13; 10:2; Ne 1:3, 3; 2:3, 16, 18; 5:10; 6:16; 7:6; 8:4, 9; 9:10; 13:2, 4, 5, 10, 11; Est 2:6, 19; 4:1, 5, 14; 5:11; 6:3; 7:4, 4, 4; 8:7; 9:4; Job 1:7; 2:2; 4:7; 7:3; 10:19; 12:3; 18:8; 19:20; 20:5, 5; 21:29; 22:20, 20; 31:9, 13, 17, 27; 32:14; 34:7; 42:7, 8; Ps 9:15; 13:6; 22:10; 27:9; 31:12, 22; 36:12; 40:7, 9; 59:16; 60:1, 3; 71:6, 7, 24; 73:15, 21; 76:5; 78:57; 88:4, 15; 90:1; 93:2; 103:16; 106:31; 116:7; 119:54, 140; 124:1, 2; 129:2; Pr 7:26, 26; 30:32; Ecc 1:9; 5:16; 6:3, 4, 10; SS 3:4; 5:2; Isa 1:9; 7:17; 14:4, 12; 16:9; 20:3; 22:5, 8; 24:11; 26:18, 21; 30:24, 33, 33; 33:9, 9; 34:6; 35:10; 36:20; 37:23; 38:12, 12; 39:1; 42:3, 14, 22; 43:10, 10; 48:8, 19; 50:9; 51:11, 19; 52:4, 15; 57:7; 59:13, 14; 61:4; 63:2, 19; 64:11; 66:8; Jer 2:14, 15, 31, 31; 3:2, 4, 9, 20; 4:10, 15, 29, 30; 7:26; 9:1, 12, 12, 19; 10:20; 11:19; 13:22; 14:17; 16:13; 20:17, 18; 21:12; 22:3, 21, 22; 25:3, 18; 29:1, 2; 30:7; 31:26; 32:24, 24, 36, 43; 33:10; 36:7, 32; 37:4, 15; 38:1; 40:5; 41:10; 44:18; 48:2, 11, 11, 20, 21, 25, 25, 46; 50:6, 17, 33; 51:7, 51; 52:20; La 1:3, 5, 8, 18; 2:9, 13; 3:17, 22; 4:11; 5:2, 10; Eze 4:8, 14; 5:6; 12:16; 15:8; 16:31, 45, 57; 20:29; 22:16; 24:13, 18; 26:2, 2, 17; 29:13; 30:11, 21, 21; 33:33; 34:5; 35:12, 12; 36:4, 21; 37:7, 21; 40:4; 43:6; 44:9; Da 1:3, 11, 15; 2:24, 47; 4:17; 5:23, 27, 28; 6:10, 22; 9:11, 12, 24, 27; 10:2, 11, 12; 11:1, 36; Hos 1:2; 8:8; 9:1; 10:9; 13:8, 12, 13; Joel 2:2; Am 2:4; 7:1, 7; Mic 1:11; 4:6; Na 1:15; 2:7; Zep 3:19; Hag 1:12; Zec 1:12; 3:2; 4:1, 1; 6:15; 7:14; 8:9; 11:3; 13:5; Mal 1:4; 2:14; 3:9; Mt 1:20; 4:12; 5:32; 8:4; 10:25; 11:3, 12, 21, 23; 13:8, 11, 23; 15:31, 31, 32; 17:9, 13; 19:9, 12, 28; 20:6, 13; 22:4, 4, 26; 25:21, 23; 26:24, 32, 47; 27:3, 60; 28:6, 7, 11, 18; Mk 1:44; 3:10; 4:8, 20; 5:15, 18, 19, 29, 34; 6:17; 8:2; 9:21, 34; 11:2; 14:21, 43; 15:41, 46; 16:4, 6; Lk 1:58, 72, 74; 2:11, 36, 38, 48; 5:14; 7:19, 20, 29, 47; 8:8, 10, 35, 36, 38, 40, 47; 10:13; 11:1; 13:7, 11, 11; 14:8, 20; 15:23; 19:17, 30; 22:51; 23:2, 8, 12, 51, 53; 24:2; Jn 1:31; 2:7; 3:18; 4:27, 45; 5:5, 6, 36; 6:14; 7:39, 45, 47; 8:33; 9:1, 17, 18, 24, 32; 11:17, 21, 32, 39; 12:5; 14:9; 15:3, 27; 16:11; 18:19, 20; 19:38; 20:1, 12; 21:14; Ac 1:11, 21; 2:39; 4:13, 14, 22; 8:7, 9, 16, 32; 9:33; 10:31, 31, 45; 11:11; 14:8, 26; 15:4, 5, 21; 17:23, 32; 18:2, 25, 27; 19:19; 20:26, 35; 21:8, 21; 22:25; 24:10; 26:5; Ro 1:6; 2:1, 4, 18; 4:9, 10, 11, 12, 19; 5:1, 9, 13; 6:5, 13; 7:6; 8:10, 22; 9:29, 30; 11:17, 28; 13:1; 15:15, 20, 20, 20, 21, 21, 22, 22; 16:3, 13, 17; 1Co 1:2; 4:1, 3, 6; 5:7; 6:11, 11, 11; 7:19, 34; 8:1, 4, 6, 7, 10; 10:28; 11:12, 15; 12:13; 13:5; 14:13; 15:3, 8, 13, 16, 17, 20, 54; 16:5, 17, 18, 18; 2Co 1:11, 12, 13, 20; 3:11; 6:5, 5, 7, 9; 7:13; 8:2, 22; 9:2; 11:23, 23, 27; 13:2, 7; Gal 2:2, 2, 10, 19; 3:21, 27, 27; 4:15; 5:4, 10, 13; 6:15, 15; Eph 1:5, 9; 2:5, 13; 3:7, 11; 4:1, 4; Php 1:5, 20, 29; 2:26; 3:5; 4:10, 19; Col 1:5, 16, 23, 23, 26; 3:1; 4:11; 1Th 2:2, 4; 3:5, 7; 1Ti 1:19; 2:7; 5:10, 10; 2Ti 1:14; 2:2, 9, 26; 3:14, 15; 4:6; Tit 1:1, 3; 2:11; Phm 1:11; Heb 4:2, 3, 8; 5:12; 7:26, 26, 28; 8:6, 7, 7; 9:26; 10:2, 18, 22, 22; 12:23; Jas 2:13, 13; 3:9; 1Pe 1:12, 23; 2:8, 24; 1Jn 2:12, 24; 3:8, 9, 9, 12, 12; 4:12, 18; 2Jn 4, 8; Jude 3, 12; Rev 2:17; 3:18; 5:6; 6:9, 11; 7:2; 9:15; 11:2; 12:10, 13; 13:12; 14:3, 4; 15:2, 4; 16:6; 17:2; 20:4, 4

BEFORE (1022)

Ge 13:3, 10; 18:5; 19:3, 35; 21:26; 23:7, 10; 24:45; 25:6; 26:1; 27:4, 7, 10, 29, 30, 33; 29:3; 30:30; 31:32, 37, 53; 32:20; 33:3, 6; 34:20; 36:31; 37:7, 9, 10; 39:22; 41:21, 50; 42:2, 6, 9, 24; 43:14, 26, 28; 44:14; 45:28; 47:10, 19, 27; 48:5, 15; 49:8; 50:16, 18; Ex 3:11; 4:19; 5:11, 13, 16; 7:10; 9:11; 11:6; 12:10; 14:16; 15:25; 18:2, 19; 19:3; 21:3, 6; 22:9; 23:15, 17, 20, 23, 27; 25:30; 28:4, 12, 30; 29:23, 27, 30; 30:20, 20, 20, 20, 30; 32:34; 33:2, 19; 34:10, 20, 23, 24; 40:23; Lev 2:8; 4:6, 15, 17, 24; 6:6, 7; 7:30; 8:27; 10:1, 2, 3, 9, 17; 14:11, 12, 16, 18, 24, 27, 31, 36; 15:15, 30; 16:12, 18, 28; 19:22; 20:23; 23:11, 17, 20, 28, 32, 40; 24:3, 8; 26:37; Nu 3:4; 5:16, 18, 18, 25, 30; 6:12, 16, 20, 20; 7:10; 8:10; 10:3, 35; 11:16; 12:15; 13:22, 30; 14:5, 14, 37; 15:15, 28, 33; 16:7, 9, 16, 17; 17:10; 18:11, 18; 20:9; 22:30, 31; 24:6; 25:3, 4, 6, 9; 26:61; 27:2, 5, 19, 21; 31:50; 32:22; 33:4; 35:12, 32; Dt 1:30, 33, 45; 3:28; 4:10, 10, 32, 34; 6:22; 9:17, 18, 25; 10:8, 10; 16:8, 11, 16; 18:13; 19:17, 17; 20:2, 8; 21:5, 19; 22:17; 24:15; 26:4, 10; 27:7; 28:31, 40; 29:10; 31:8, 11, 21; 32:17; 33:1, 10, 27, 29; Jos 2:8, 17; 3:1, 4; 4:18, 23; 6:15; 7:16, 17; 8:5, 6; 10:14; 18:3; 20:4, 9; 22:10; 24:17; Jdg 2:19; 8:15; 9:45; 11:26; 14:18; 16:12, 20, 22; 19:5; 20:18, 30, 31; Ru 3:14; 1Sa 2:15, 15, 20, 31, 36; 3:7, 10; 4:7, 9, 20; 5:4; 7:6; 8:11; 9:13, 24, 24; 10:17, 19, 20, 21, 25; 11:11, 15; 12:3, 3, 7; 13:12; 14:24, 24; 15:30, 30, 33; 17:27, 39; 18:26; 19:7; 20:3, 8, 19; 21:6; 23:18; 24:8; 25:23; 27:9; 28:14; 30:12; 31:4; 2Sa 1:2; 3:35; 4:7, 10; 5:3; 6:5, 14, 16, 21; 7:15, 16, 18, 29; 9:8; 13:9; 14:20, 22, 33; 15:5, 14, 28; 17:22; 19:18; 20:6; 21:6, 7, 9; 22:13, 23, 24, 45; 23:16; 24:20; 1Ki 1:16, 23, 28, 30, 31, 53; 2:19; 3:15, 22; 8:2, 5, 14, 22, 59; 9:2; 10:12; 11:15; 14:9; 15:3; 16:25, 30, 33; 18:2, 7; 19:11; 21:12, 13, 29; 22:15; 2Ki 1:13; 2:9, 15; 4:27, 38; 5:15; 6:32; 17:2, 8, 35, 36; 18:5; 19:9, 14, 15; 20:4; 21:3, 11; 22:19, 19; 23:25; 1Ch 1:43; 10:4, 9; 11:3, 18; 13:8; 15:2; 16:1, 4, 6, 30, 33, 37, 39; 17:13, 16, 27; 21:21; 22:5, 8; 23:30; 24:2; 25:7; 28:2; 29:15, 20, 22; 2Ch 1:12; 2:4; 5:3, 6; 6:3, 12, 13; 9:9, 11; 13:15; 14:15; 18:14; 19:6, 6; 20:5, 9, 13; 24:17, 20; 25:16; 26:19; 29:23; 32:6, 13; 33:3, 19, 23; 34:27, 27; Ezr 3:6, 6; 5:15; 6:5; 7:28; 8:21; 9:15; 10:9, 10; Ne 2:1, 15; 4:11; 8:2, 9, 10; 9:24; 13:4, 25; Est 1:17, 18; 2:12; 3:2; 4:11; 5:9; 7:6, 8; 8:1, 3, 4; 9:25; Job 1:6, 20; 2:1; 4:16, 17, 17; 8:10; 10:21; 15:7, 19, 33; 16:2; 18:2; 21:18; 25:4; 29:3; 30:15, 20; 31:37; 33:6; 34:23; 35:2; 38:21; 42:5, 10; Ps 7:7; 9:3; 18:22, 23, 44; 22:27; 31:19; 35:18; 37:33, 37; 38:13; 39:9, 12, 13; 42:2; 45:5; 47:3; 49:19; 53:5; 60:2; 62:1, 5; 66:3; 68:8, 8; 69:10, 22; 72:9, 9, 11; 76:5, 7, 8; 78:13, 30, 55, 63; 81:9, 15; 83:13; 84:7; 85:13; 86:9; 88:15; 89:14, 23, 45; 90:2, 2, 8; 95:2, 6; 96:9, 13; 97:3, 5, 5; 98:6, 9; 99:5; 100:2; 102:T, 15, 15; 106:19; 107:32, 32; 109:15; 119:147; 132:2, 7; 138:1, 2; 139:4, 16, 16; 142:2; 144:2; Pr 2:17; 4:25; 8:22, 23, 24, 24, 25, 26; 13:16; 14:12, 19; 15:28; 16:18, 18, 25; 17:14; 18:12, 13, 16; 20:25; 23:1; 24:27; 25:8; 30:7; 31:15; Ecc 1:9, 16; 2:7, 9; 7:17; 8:2; 11:10; 12:1, 6; SS 2:15, 17; 4:6; 6:12; Isa 7:16; 8:2, 4; 9:10; 10:9; 13:16; 17:13; 18:5; 23:17; 26:14; 29:5; 33:8; 37:9, 14, 15; 40:21; 41:1; 42:9, 16; 43:12, 21; 44:11; 45:1, 2; 46:3, 10; 48:6; 49:1, 16, 23; 52:8, 10; 53:7; 57:1; 58:3; 59:12; 60:14; 63:12; 65:1, 12, 12, 20, 24; 66:4, 7; Jer 1:5, 5; 2:36; 4:4, 31; 6:7; 7:10, 30; 8:2; 10:10; 11:12; 12:1; 13:16, 16, 27; 15:1; 16:9; 18:17, 23; 19:4; 20:11; 30:18, 20; 32:7, 8, 10, 22, 25; 33:9, 21, 22; 34:3; 35:5; 36:7; 37:14; 38:10, 27; 40:4, 10; 41:4; 42:2; 44:10, 17; 47:1; La 2:6, 8, 18; 3:9; 5:7; Eze 1:4; 4:14; 5:9; 8:4; 15:5; 16:19; 18:6; 19:9; 21:6, 6, 30; 23:18, 41; 32:10; 33:31; 36:6, 11, 23; 37:7; 40:38; 42:14; 43:3, 19; 44:21; Da 2:2, 46, 46; 3:3, 13, 16; 4:8, 36; 5:7, 13, 19, 23; 6:24, 26; 10:12, 21; 11:22, 28; Hos 12:3; Joel 1:2, 13, 16; 2:2, 14, 31; Am 1:1; 2:9; Jnh 4:2; Mic 6:6; Na 1:6; Hab 2:20; 3:5; Zep 2:2, 2; 3:20; Hag 2:3, 15, 19, 19; Zec 2:13; 3:1, 3, 9; 4:7; 6:5; 8:10, 11; 12:7, 8; Mal 3:1, 11; 4:5; Mt 2:11; 5:22, 23, 25; 6:8; 8:2, 29; 9:8, 16, 18; 10:18, 23, 32, 33; 11:10, 10, 13; 12:45; 15:2, 30; 16:28; 17:10, 14, 25; 18:26, 29; 19:15; 21:31; 24:34, 38; 26:34, 75; 27:11, 17, 24, 29; Mk 1:2, 35; 2:12, 21; 5:6, 22; 7:2; 9:1, 11; 13:9; 14:1, 30, 60, 72; 15:42; 16:7; Lk 1:15; 2:21; 4:21; 5:8; 6:25; 7:6, 27, 27; 8:28, 47; 9:27; 10:8; 11:26; 12:9, 11, 38, 58; 14:29, 30; 17:8, 27; 18:14; 19:13, 43; 21:12, 12, 36; 22:15, 61, 66; 23:12; 24:5, 26, 44; Jn 1:15, 30, 48; 3:24; 4:48, 49; 5:45; 7:51; 8:58; 9:4; 10:8; 11:55; 12:1, 16; 13:1, 33, 38; 14:29; 15:18; 16:24; 17:5, 24; 18:28; 19:41, 42; 20:26; Ac 1:4; 2:20; 3:13, 16, 16; 5:27; 6:12; 7:2, 10; 8:21, 32; 10:25, 33; 11:10; 12:6, 7; 13:24; 15:5; 16:3, 19, 29, 34, 40; 17:6, 22; 18:12; 19:21; 22:30; 23:1, 20, 30; 24:16, 21; 25:9, 26; 27:15, 17, 24, 35; Ro 3:19; 4:10, 11, 12, 17; 5:13; 6:19; 9:11, 11, 25; 14:6, 10, 23; 15:18, 25; 16:7; 1Co 2:7; 4:5; 5:9; 7:18; 11:28; 15:1; 2Co 4:2; 5:10, 12; 7:3; 8:21; 13:2, 10; Gal 1:15, 17, 20; 4:3, 8; 5:21; Eph 1:4; Php 2:15; 3:18; Col 1:15, 17, 22; 4:10; 1Th 2:2, 19; 3:13; 4:6, 11; 1Ti 3:10; 6:12, 13, 13, 13; 2Ti 1:9; 4:1, 1, 16, 21; Tit 1:2; Heb 2:17; 4:13; 9:24; 10:11; 11:5, 7; 12:1; Jas 4:7, 10; 1Pe 1:20; 3:22; 2Pe 2:20; 1Jn 2:1, 7; 3:19; Rev 1:4, 6; 3:5; 4:1, 10; 5:8; 6:10; 7:9, 11; 8:2, 3; 11:4, 16; 12:4, 10; 13:8; 14:3; 15:2, 4; 16:18; 17:8; 20:12

BUT (4392)

Ge 2:6, 16, 20; 3:12; 4:5, 7, 10; 6:8, 18; 7:13; 8:1, 9; 9:4; 11:5, 28, 31; 12:13, 17; 13:6; 14:4, 8, 15, 21, 24; 15:2, 8, 11, 14, 15; 16:1; 17:4, 12, 17, 19, 21; 18:15, 22, 27, 32; 19:3, 8, 10, 14, 19, 22, 26, 29; 20:3, 4, 7; 21:9, 12, 13, 28; 22:7; 23:15; 24:5, 8, 33, 39, 41, 54, 55, 56; 25:6, 22, 28, 31; 26:8, 20, 21, 35; 27:5, 11, 22, 23, 32, 35, 40, 42; 29:2, 17, 20, 20, 25, 31; 30:15, 30, 35, 42; 31:1, 5, 7, 7, 23, 24, 29, 30, 32, 32, 33, 42, 43, 50; 32:12, 22, 26; 33:13; 34:2, 3, 5, 13, 15, 22, 23, 25; 35:16, 18; 37:2, 4, 11, 17, 21, 24, 35; 38:7, 9, 10, 11, 11, 14, 20, 25, 26, 29; 39:8, 10, 12, 14, 21; 40:8, 15, 17, 22; 41:3, 6, 8, 15, 16, 19, 21, 24, 30, 44, 54; 42:7, 8, 14, 20, 21, 22, 25, 27, 31, 34, 38; 43:1, 3, 5, 7, 8; 44:4, 22, 23; 45:3, 5, 22, 27; 46:4, 12; 47:9, 15, 17, 18, 26; 48:6, 11, 14, 17, 19, 19, 21; 49:4, 19, 24; 50:8, 15, 19, 24; Ex 1:7, 12, 17, 22; 2:3, 15, 17, 23; 3:2, 11, 13, 19; 4:1, 10, 13, 21, 23, 25; 5:3, 8, 11, 16, 17, 18; 6:9, 12, 13; 7:3, 12, 22; 8:7, 15, 18, 19, 22, 25, 26, 28, 29, 32; 9:4, 6, 7, 12, 16, 17, 21, 30, 32; 10:8, 20, 23, 24; 11:7, 9; 12:23, 32, 44, 48; 13:13; 14:13, 20, 24; 15:10, 19, 23; 16:3, 20, 26, 27; 17:1, 3, 11; 18:21, 22, 26; 19:23, 24; 20:5, 6, 10, 19; 21:3, 4, 5, 8, 9, 13, 18, 23, 32, 34, 36, 36; 22:3, 8, 10, 12, 15, 17; 23:11, 22, 29; 31:15, 17; 32:11, 18, 30, 32, 34; 33:3, 11, 12, 20, 23; 34:7, 9, 14, 20, 21, 31, 34; 36:4; 40:37; Lev 1:9; 2:4, 12; 4:11; 5:1, 8; 7:17, 20, 31; 10:7, 14; 11:4, 23, 26, 36, 38; 13:4, 4, 7, 14, 19, 21, 23, 26, 28, 35, 37, 53, 56, 58; 14:21, 32, 43, 48; 17:16; 18:18; 19:18, 20; 20:24; 22:13, 13, 23, 28; 23:3; 24:21; 25:4, 6, 20, 26, 28, 30, 31, 46; 26:40, 44; 27:8, 10, 11, 18, 20, 22; Nu 1:47, 53; 3:4; 4:15; 5:8, 13, 20, 28, 31; 7:9; 8:26; 9:6, 7, 13, 21, 22; 10:4, 7, 30; 11:6, 6, 21, 25, 26, 29, 33; 12:2, 7; 13:28, 30, 31; 14:9, 10, 13, 18, 21, 22, 24, 32, 40, 41, 44; 15:19, 22, 30; 16:10, 12, 22, 30, 41, 45, 47, 49; 18:1, 3, 4, 7, 15, 23, 32; 19:12, 20; 20:12, 16, 18, 20; 21:4, 23, 24, 33; 22:18, 19, 20, 22, 23, 30, 35, 35, 38; 23:8, 12, 26; 24:11, 14, 17, 17, 20, 22, 24; 25:9; 26:10, 20, 33, 61, 62; 27:3, 11; 28:17; 30:4, 5, 8, 12, 14; 31:14, 23, 28; 32:14, 16, 19, 23, 24, 27, 30, 32; 33:55; 35:16, 22, 26, 28, 30; 36:3; Dt 1:3, 12, 16, 22, 26, 29, 32, 39, 42, 43, 44, 45; 2:11, 12, 19, 21, 30, 33; 3:2, 7, 26, 27, 28; 4:4, 9, 12, 15, 21; 5:3, 9, 10, 14, 23, 25, 31; 6:21; 7:10, 15, 18, 23; 8:11, 19; 9:3, 19, 20, 23, 27, 29; 10:11, 22; 11:7, 16; 12:8, 15, 17, 27; 14:7, 7, 20, 21; 15:6, 6, 7, 16, 21, 23; 17:6; 18:14, 20; 19:11; 20:5, 6, 12, 14, 15, 19, 20; 21:14, 15; 22:7, 17, 20, 25, 27; 23:5, 20, 23, 24, 25; 24:1, 21; 25:7; 26:5; 28:7, 12, 15, 25, 30, 30, 30, 31, 32, 38, 39, 40, 41, 68; 29:4, 6, 7, 14, 29; 30:17; 31:3; 32:5, 15, 27, 31, 52; 34:4, 6; Jos 1:14; 2:2, 4, 6, 19, 22; 3:15; 5:5; 6:2, 15; 7:1, 4, 10; 8:2, 9, 14; 9:3, 8, 12, 13, 14, 18, 19, 21, 22, 27; 10:33; 11:14; 13:13, 33; 14:8, 12; 15:63; 17:8, 12, 13; 18:2; 19:47; 20:6; 21:12; 22:5, 10, 19, 22, 27; 23:8, 12, 15; 24:3, 6, 8, 10, 11, 15, 15, 21; Jdg 1:6, 19, 28, 30, 35; 2:17, 19; 3:9, 15, 19, 25; 4:8, 9, 21; 5:15, 18, 19, 31; 6:10, 13, 15, 27, 31, 37, 39, 40; 7:4, 8, 10; 8:2, 6, 8, 12, 20, 23, 27; 9:5, 9, 11, 13, 18, 20, 25, 30, 37, 40, 51, 52; 10:1, 6, 15; 11:1, 7, 17, 17, 18, 20, 21, 26, 28, 37; 12:2; 13:7, 9, 16, 23; 14:3, 6, 9, 13, 16, 19; 15:1, 2, 11, 12, 12, 14; 16:3, 9, 12, 14, 20, 22; 18:29; 19:2, 5, 7, 10, 15, 16, 18, 20, 24, 25, 28; 20:13, 21, 22, 25, 32, 40, 42, 45; 21:14, 18; Ru 1:4, 8, 11, 14, 16, 17, 21; 2:11, 23; 3:3, 12, 13, 14; 4:4; 1Sa 1:5, 6, 13, 15, 22; 2:5, 6, 9, 16, 22, 25, 25, 30, 32; 3:16; 4:20, 20; 5:3, 4, 9, 10; 6:7, 19; 7:10; 8:3, 9, 18, 19; 9:4, 6, 7, 21; 10:12, 14, 16, 19, 21, 27, 27; 11:1, 2, 11, 13; 12:9, 10, 12, 15, 20, 24, 25; 13:8, 11, 14, 15; 14:1, 10, 19, 27, 28, 31, 32, 36, 37, 39, 45; 15:8, 15, 20, 20, 22, 26, 30, 33, 35; 16:2, 7, 7, 8, 9, 10, 11; 17:9, 15, 28, 34, 45, 54; 18:6, 10, 11, 13, 16, 17, 21, 25; 19:1, 9, 10, 11, 16, 20, 21, 23; 20:3, 5, 7, 8, 13, 14, 22, 25, 27, 32; 21:4, 11; 22:14, 17, 17; 23:3, 9, 14, 19, 25; 24:3, 5, 10, 11, 12, 22; 25:3, 15, 19, 21, 25, 29; 26:3, 11, 11, 19, 19; 27:1; 28:6, 10, 16, 23; 29:3, 4, 6, 7, 9, 9; 30:2, 6, 10, 22, 23; 31:4, 11; 2Sa 2:8, 21, 23, 31; 3:13, 22, 26, 27, 35; 4:4, 7, 9, 10; 5:7, 17, 22; 6:6, 16, 22; 7:2, 4, 15; 8:4; 9:3, 7, 10; 10:2, 18; 11:1, 9, 13, 20, 27; 12:3, 4, 12, 13, 14, 17, 19, 21, 23, 23; 13:9, 11, 14, 16, 19, 25, 27, 32; 14:7, 15, 20, 24, 24, 29, 29; 15:10, 11, 21, 26, 33; 17:5, 18, 20; 18:3, 9, 20, 22, 23, 29; 19:9, 22, 27, 28, 37, 41, 43; 20:2, 3, 5, 12, 16, 19; 21:2, 2, 8, 17, 21, 22; 22:7, 19, 27, 28, 32, 42, 42; 23:6, 12, 16; 24:3, 3, 4, 10, 14, 16, 17, 24; 1Ki 1:4, 8, 10, 18, 19, 26, 52; 2:5, 6, 9, 15, 26, 30, 36, 39, 45; 3:7, 19, 21, 26, 27; 5:4; 8:8, 13, 16, 18, 19, 27, 47; 9:6, 12, 22; 11:10, 12, 17, 22, 32, 34, 35, 39, 40; 12:8, 11, 11, 13, 14, 14, 17, 18, 22; 13:4, 8, 18, 18, 24, 33; 14:5, 8; 15:4, 26, 34; 16:2, 15, 21, 22, 25, 30; 17:7, 12, 13, 13, 19; 18:12, 15, 21, 21, 22, 23, 23, 25, 26, 29, 42, 43; 19:5, 9, 10, 11, 11, 12, 14, 20; 20:6, 9, 19, 20, 23, 27, 30, 35, 40; 21:3, 17; 22:5, 7, 8, 8, 14, 16, 18, 27, 28, 30, 32, 48, 49, 52; 2Ki 1:3, 4, 6, 10, 13, 14, 16; 2:2, 4, 6, 10, 17, 17, 19; 3:2, 5, 9, 11, 13, 17, 18, 22, 25, 26; 4:1, 17, 20, 23, 27, 27, 30, 31, 38, 40, 43; 5:1, 8, 10, 11, 13, 16, 17, 20, 22, 24, 26; 6:5, 9, 28, 29, 32; 7:2, 2, 4, 5, 10, 17, 19; 8:10, 13, 15, 18, 19, 21; 9:15, 18, 20, 27, 35; 10:4, 9, 19, 31; 11:2; 12:6, 20; 13:2, 6, 11, 19, 21, 23; 14:3, 9, 9, 11, 19; 15:4, 18, 19, 24, 28, 35; 16:5; 17:2, 14, 19, 25, 29, 32, 40; 18:18, 22, 22, 27, 36; 19:3, 4, 18, 25, 27, 29; 20:4, 19; 21:9, 24; 22:7, 18; 23:9, 29; 24:1, 19; 25:4, 5, 12, 25; 1Ch 2:3, 31, 33; 4:27, 41; 5:1, 2, 25; 6:56; 9:30; 10:4, 11; 11:5, 14, 18; 12:17, 19; 13:9; 14:8, 13; 15:29; 16:26; 17:1, 3; 18:4; 19:2, 18; 20:1, 7, 8; 21:3, 3, 4, 6, 13, 15, 17, 17, 24, 30; 22:8, 9; 24:2; 27:24; 28:3, 9; 29:14; 2Ch 1:5, 11; 2:6; 5:9; 6:2, 6, 8, 9, 18, 37; 7:19; 8:9; 10:8, 11, 11, 13, 14, 14, 17, 18; 11:2, 13; 12:1, 8, 14; 13:8, 10, 11; 14:11; 15:2, 4; 16:12; 18:4, 6, 7, 7, 13, 15, 17, 26, 27, 29, 31; 19:4, 6; 20:12, 15, 17, 35; 21:4, 6, 7, 9, 20; 22:7, 11; 24:5, 17, 19, 25, 25; 25:2, 7, 9, 16, 18, 18, 19, 20, 27; 26:7, 16, 19; 27:2; 28:9, 9, 21, 23, 27; 29:10, 34; 30:3, 8, 10, 18; 32:8, 25; 33:9, 10, 12, 17, 23, 25; 34:26; 35:21, 22, 23; 36:2, 5, 9, 16; Ezr 2:62; 4:3, 13; 5:3, 5, 12; 6:2; 7:19; 8:22; 9:1, 8, 9, 13, 14, 15; 10:2, 6; Ne 1:9; 2:3, 10, 14, 17, 19, 20, 20; 4:7, 9, 16; 5:8, 10, 15; 6:2, 11, 12; 7:4, 64; 9:16, 17, 19, 26, 27, 28, 29, 30, 31, 35; 11:4; 13:21, 26; Est 1:8, 12, 16; 2:1, 22; 3:2, 4, 11, 15; 4:4, 14, 14; 5:9, 13; 6:12; 7:7; 8:8; 9:1, 2, 5, 10, 12, 16, 18, 25; Job 1:9, 11, 12; 2:5, 6, 10; 3:9; 4:5, 16, 20; 5:1, 1, 3, 6, 17, 18; 6:11, 14, 17, 18, 20, 22, 25; 7:4, 7, 8, 8; 8:5, 9, 10, 15, 15, 18, 20; 9:2, 18, 21, 33, 35; 11:8, 20; 12:6, 13; 13:8, 15, 16; 14:10, 13, 18; 15:2, 6, 28; 16:5, 6, 20; 17:4, 7, 10, 15; 18:4; 19:6, 7, 7, 16, 25; 20:3, 11, 14, 20, 24; 21:16, 19, 22, 29; 22:13, 18; 23:8, 8, 9, 10, 12; 24:18, 22, 23; 25:6; 27:12, 17, 19, 23; 28:5, 12, 20, 22; 30:1, 20, 26, 26, 29; 31:32; 32:5, 9, 12; 33:14, 23, 27, 32, 33; 34:5, 6, 29, 31, 33; 35:13, 15; 36:6, 7, 12, 15, 17, 18, 25; 38:21; 39:13, 18; 40:2; 41:27; 42:5; Ps 1:2, 4, 6; 2:4, 12; 3:3; 5:2, 11; 7:9, 16, 16; 9:7; 10:14; 11:4; 13:5; 14:3, 6; 17:15; 18:6, 18, 26, 27, 31, 41, 41; 20:7, 8; 22:2, 2, 6; 25:3; 26:11; 30:5, 5; 31:8, 14, 22, 23; 32:10; 33:11, 18; 34:10, 16, 19, 22; 35:13, 15, 27; 37:9, 13, 15, 17, 20, 21, 22, 28, 33, 36, 38; 38:13, 18; 39:2, 5; 40:16, 17; 41:5, 5, 6; 42:6; 44:9; 48:5, 8; 49:11, 15, 19; 50:9, 16, 21, 23; 51:6; 52:5, 8; 53:3, 5; 54:4; 55:10, 16, 21, 21, 23, 23; 56:3; 57:6; 59:8, 15, 16; 60:4, 9; 62:4; 63:9, 11; 64:7; 66:12, 19; 68:3, 6, 21; 69:13, 21; 70:4, 5; 71:14, 20; 73:2, 16, 25, 26, 27, 28; 75:9, 10; 78:4, 20, 23, 30, 32, 36, 50, 52, 53, 67; 80:12; 81:11, 13, 16; 82:5, 7; 85:8; 86:15; 89:30, 33, 38; 90:6, 10; 91:8; 92:8, 10, 12, 15; 93:4; 94:22; 96:5; 99:8; 102:12, 24, 26, 27; 103:17; 104:21, 29; 105:26, 37; 106:15, 23, 30, 43; 107:35, 41; 108:10; 109:4, 15, 21, 28, 28, 30; 110:7; 115:1, 16, 18; 118:11, 12, 13, 17, 18; 119:19, 23, 51, 61, 67, 69, 70, 81, 83, 87, 96, 109, 110, 113, 118, 141, 151, 161, 163; 120:7; 125:1, 5; 126:6; 129:2, 4; 130:4; 131:2; 132:18; 136:15; 137:4; 138:6; 139:12; 140:12; 141:5, 10; 142:4; 144:8, 11; 145:20; 146:5, 9; 147:6; Pr 1:18, 24, 24, 33; 2:22; 3:32, 33, 34, 35; 4:19; 5:4; 6:9, 15, 31, 32; 8:36; 9:8, 18; 10:2, 3, 7, 8, 9, 10, 12, 13, 14, 16, 17, 21, 25, 27, 28, 29, 30, 31, 32; 11:1, 2, 4, 8, 11, 13, 17, 18, 20, 21, 22, 24, 26, 27, 28; 12:2, 6, 7, 8, 9, 10, 13, 15, 16, 18, 21, 22, 23, 27; 13:2, 4, 4, 8, 9, 12, 17, 19, 22, 23, 25; 14:3, 4, 6, 8, 9, 11, 12, 18, 22, 23, 25, 31, 32, 34; 15:1, 6, 8, 9, 25, 26, 27, 29, 32; 16:1, 2, 9, 22, 25, 33; 17:3, 11, 22, 24; 18:8, 14, 24; 19:7, 12, 14, 21; 20:6, 17; 21:2, 5, 15, 20, 28, 29, 31; 22:12, 15; 23:7, 17, 35; 24:16, 16, 25; 26:22, 24; 27:3, 4, 7, 21; 28:1, 2, 5, 10, 11, 13, 14, 16, 18, 20, 22, 26, 27; 29:2, 3, 4, 6, 8, 9, 10, 11, 15, 16, 18, 19, 24, 25, 26; 30:4, 12, 24, 25, 26, 27, 28; 31:12, 29, 30; Ecc 1:4, 7, 17; 2:1, 11, 21, 26; 3:11; 4:4, 8, 10, 11, 12, 13, 16; 5:12; 6:2, 3, 6, 7; 7:12, 14, 18, 23, 26, 28, 29; 8:12; 9:3, 5, 15, 17, 18; 10:12, 14; 11:8, 9, 10; 12:4, 12; SS 3:1, 2; 5:3, 6, 6, 6; 6:9; 8:9, 12; Isa 1:3, 20, 28; 3:10, 11; 4:2; 5:2, 7, 7, 9, 12, 16, 25; 6:9, 9, 9, 13; 7:7, 12, 16; 8:9, 14; 9:1, 10, 12, 17, 18, 20, 21; 10:4, 7, 22, 32, 33; 12:1; 13:20; 14:1, 7, 15, 19, 30; 15:9; 16:9, 12, 12, 14; 17:11, 13, 14; 18:7; 21:12, 16; 22:3, 11, 13; 23:4, 12, 15, 17, 18, 18; 24:14, 16; 25:4, 5; 26:7, 13, 18; 27:8; 28:1, 4, 12, 17, 28; 29:5, 8, 8, 8, 9, 9, 13; 30:3, 15, 16, 18, 29; 31:4, 8; 32:8; 33:1, 2, 7, 10, 19; 36:7, 7, 12, 21; 37:3, 4, 19, 26, 28, 30; 38:13, 15; 39:8; 40:8, 15, 31; 41:2, 8, 24, 25, 26; 42:14, 17, 20, 20, 22, 25; 43:1, 8, 8, 10, 18, 22; 44:1, 10, 26; 45:17, 21; 46:1, 13; 47:6, 14; 48:6, 10, 22; 49:4, 15, 25; 50:11; 51:2, 6, 8, 21, 23; 52:6; 53:5, 8, 9, 10; 54:7, 8, 10, 17; 57:3, 10, 13, 17, 18, 20, 20; 58:13; 59:2, 11, 11; 60:2; 63:5, 10; 64:5, 6; 65:2, 8, 11, 13, 13, 13; 66:3, 5, 8; Jer 1:19; 2:20, 23, 25, 27, 30, 36; 3:1, 7, 8, 10, 20; 4:22, 27; 5:3, 3, 4, 5, 7, 10, 21, 21, 22, 23, 31; 6:2, 4, 16, 17, 29; 7:4, 13, 13, 24, 26, 27, 27, 32; 8:2, 7, 15, 15; 9:25; 10:10, 12, 14, 16, 19, 24; 11:8, 12, 16; 12:2, 3, 13, 13, 15, 17; 13:1, 7, 11; 14:3, 6, 15, 18, 19, 19; 15:2, 20; 16:14, 16; 17:7, 10, 12, 18, 22, 23, 24, 27; 18:4, 8, 10, 12, 15; 19:6; 20:11; 21:9; 22:5, 6, 15, 17, 21, 23; 23:3, 14, 18, 28, 36, 38; 24:8; 25:3, 4, 7; 26:5, 8, 13, 15, 19, 21; 27:7, 11, 22; 28:7, 13, 15; 29:10, 16, 29; 30:11, 11, 16, 18; 31:16, 18, 19, 20, 28, 29, 33; 32:23, 30, 31, 33, 36; 33:25; 34:3, 4, 5, 11, 14, 16; 35:6, 7, 11, 14, 15, 16; 36:17, 26; 37:2, 13, 14; 38:2, 6, 7, 18, 19, 21, 27; 39:5, 10, 17; 40:4, 5, 14, 16; 41:1, 7, 7, 11; 42:13, 21; 44:5, 18, 26; 45:5, 5; 46:5, 11, 20, 26, 27, 28, 28; 47:7; 48:12, 15, 30, 32, 33, 45, 47; 49:4, 5, 6, 10, 11, 16, 39; 50:8, 12, 34, 34; 51:8, 9, 13, 17, 19, 25, 46, 52; 52:2, 7, 8, 16; La 1:7, 17, 19, 21; 2:17; 3:34, 55; 4:3, 4, 8, 11, 15, 17, 21, 22; 5:5, 7, 19; Eze 1:7; 2:4, 7; 3:7, 8, 14, 18, 19, 21, 27, 27; 5:6; 6:8; 7:14, 25; 8:6, 15; 9:6; 11:7, 21; 12:2, 2, 16; 13:7, 23; 14:14, 16; 16:3, 6, 15, 29, 33, 43, 43, 47, 53, 57; 17:7; 18:2, 7, 10, 14, 14, 16, 18, 21; 19:12; 20:8, 9, 13, 14, 15, 21, 23, 32, 38, 39; 21:23; 22:13, 30; 23:17, 19, 45; 24:12, 13, 17, 23; 26:21; 27:26; 28:2, 9; 29:7, 13, 14; 30:24; 32:2, 24, 25, 26; 33:5, 6, 6, 8, 9, 9, 13, 14, 17, 19, 20, 31, 31, 32, 33; 34:3, 16; 36:8, 11, 14, 20, 22, 32; 37:8; 38:13, 18; 41:6; 44:1, 3, 12, 26; 46:1, 9, 17; 47:11; Da 1:8, 10; 2:5, 6, 9, 28, 30, 34, 35, 39, 43, 44; 3:8, 12, 15, 18, 24; 4:5, 7, 15, 18, 23, 26, 28; 5:8, 10, 15, 17, 20, 23; 6:4, 10; 7:12, 18, 26, 28; 8:8, 12, 18, 24, 25, 26, 27; 9:5, 7, 9, 13, 15, 18, 27; 10:7, 13, 21; 11:4, 5, 6, 7, 9, 12, 14, 17, 18, 19, 20, 21, 24, 25, 27, 27, 29, 30, 32, 33, 41, 44, 45; 12:1, 4, 8, 9, 10; Hos 1:7; 2:2, 6, 7, 9, 14; 3:5; 5:2, 6, 13; 6:7; 7:1, 9, 12, 13; 8:3, 4, 10, 11, 13, 14; 9:4, 10, 13; 10:1, 3, 13; 11:2, 3, 5, 7, 12; 12:7, 11, 14; 13:1, 4, 6, 13, 15; 14:9; Joel 2:3; 3:7, 16, 20; Am 2:9, 12; 3:7; 4:6, 7, 8, 8, 9, 10, 11; 5:18, 18; 6:3, 12; 7:10, 14, 15, 17; 8:11, 12; 9:7, 10, 11; Ob 5, 17; Jnh 1:3, 4, 13; 2:6, 9; 4:7, 11; Mic 1:12; 2:3; 3:2, 5, 8; 4:7, 9, 10, 12; 5:2; 6:14, 14, 15, 15, 15; 7:4, 9, 13; Na 1:3, 8; 2:2, 6, 8; 3:15, 16, 17; Hab 1:2, 2, 11, 13, 14, 14; 2:3, 4, 5, 6, 10, 13, 16, 19, 20; 3:6; Zep 1:5, 6; 2:15; 3:5, 5, 7; Hag 1:6, 6, 6, 6, 9; 2:4, 13, 23; Zec 1:6, 15, 15; 4:6; 7:6; 8:6, 11, 13, 13, 16; 9:4; 11:8, 12; 12:4; 13:8; 14:10; Mal 1:2, 4, 4, 4, 6, 6, 9, 11, 12, 14; 2:8, 9, 14; 3:2, 7, 8, 13; 4:2; Mt 1:18, 25; 2:12, 22; 3:7, 11, 12, 14, 15; 4:4, 13; 5:13, 19, 20, 22, 28, 32, 34, 39, 44, 48; 6:3, 6, 13, 15, 17, 23; 7:14, 15, 21, 23, 26; 8:12, 15, 20, 20, 22, 24, 34; 9:14, 18, 24, 31, 34, 37; 10:6, 17, 22, 26, 33, 39; 11:17, 19; 12:3, 7, 15, 16, 24, 28, 32, 39, 39, 43;

13:6, 8, 11, 12, 13, 13, 14, 14, 16, 17, 21, 21, 22, 25, 32; 14:5, 6, 9, 13, 16, 27, 30; 15:5, 8, 18, 23, 25, 27; 16:3, 4, 12, 22, 25, 26; 17:5, 12, 12, 16, 23, 25; 18:6, 7, 16, 17, 26, 28, 30; 19:6, 8, 14, 17, 22, 26, 30; 20:10, 19, 22, 23, 25, 26, 28, 31; 21:13, 15, 19, 26, 28, 29, 30, 35, 36, 38, 46; 22:3, 5, 11, 14, 18, 21, 31, 34; 23:3, 12, 16, 18, 23, 23, 25, 27, 28, 37; 24:2, 6, 6, 8, 13, 22, 35, 48; 25:4, 9, 10, 12, 18, 26, 29, 31, 46; 26:5, 10, 11, 24, 32, 54, 56, 60, 63, 70; 27:12, 14, 22, 23, 34, 42, 49; 28:8, 17; Mk 1:8, 26, 34, 38, 45; 2:6, 7, 16, 18, 20, 24, 25; 3:4, 12, 17, 22, 29; 4:6, 11, 12, 12, 13, 15, 17, 17, 19, 20, 25, 34, 37; 5:15, 19, 26, 32, 36, 40; 6:9, 17, 19, 20, 26, 33, 37, 49, 50; 7:4, 7, 11, 19, 24, 28, 36; 8:14, 24, 30, 35, 36; 9:10, 13, 18, 20, 24, 27, 31, 32, 34, 38, 42, 50; 10:5, 6, 8, 13, 14, 19, 24, 27, 31, 34, 38, 40, 43, 45, 48; 11:13, 17, 18, 25, 32; 12:3, 4, 7, 12, 17, 21, 26, 40, 44; 13:7, 7, 8, 9, 11, 11, 13, 20, 31; 14:2, 6, 7, 21, 28, 47, 49, 52, 55, 56, 59; 15:5, 11, 12, 14, 23, 31; 16:4, 6, 11, 12, 13, 16; Lk 1:13, 34, 36, 60; 2:10, 19, 34, 37, 43, 44, 49, 50; 3:16, 17; 4:4, 24, 30, 41, 43; 5:5, 16, 19, 21, 30, 39; 6:2, 8, 27, 40, 49; 7:6, 30, 32, 35, 42, 44, 45, 46, 47; 8:6, 10, 10, 10, 12, 13, 13, 14, 15, 18, 38, 46, 50, 52, 53, 56; 9:11, 13, 22, 24, 25, 34, 40, 42, 45, 47, 50, 53, 55, 58, 58, 59, 61, 62; 10:2, 10, 20, 24, 31, 32, 40, 41; 11:8, 15, 18, 20, 24, 28, 29, 34, 39, 42, 42, 42; 12:5, 9, 10, 20, 21, 30, 38, 45, 48, 56; 13:6, 14, 15, 25, 25, 26, 28, 34; 14:11, 18, 28, 34; 15:16, 22, 24, 29, 32; 16:1, 15, 16, 17, 25, 29, 30, 31; 17:1, 22, 25; 18:4, 5, 8, 13, 14, 15, 20, 23, 33, 34, 39; 19:3, 7, 14, 20, 25, 26, 26, 39, 41, 42, 46, 47, 48; 20:6, 10, 11, 14, 16, 19, 25, 28, 30, 35, 37, 47; 21:4, 5, 8, 9, 12, 18, 33; 22:2, 21, 22, 26, 27, 32, 34, 36, 47, 48, 51, 53, 60, 67, 69; 23:5, 9, 16, 21, 23, 25, 28, 40, 41, 49, 51, 56; 24:1, 3, 11, 16, 20, 29, 37, 49; Jn 1:10, 12, 18, 26, 31, 33, 42; 2:5, 10, 21, 24; 3:6, 8, 12, 16, 17, 18, 19, 21, 22, 31, 32, 36; 4:11, 14, 23, 27; 5:9, 14, 17, 23, 24, 30, 32, 34, 36, 39, 44, 46; 6:9, 13, 17, 20, 27, 36, 39, 43, 49, 54, 64, 70; 7:2, 6, 7, 10, 12, 13, 16, 18, 22, 26, 27, 28, 30, 33, 34, 36, 39, 41, 44, 49; 8:2, 6, 7, 14, 15, 20, 26, 27, 28, 33, 35, 38, 40, 42, 52, 54, 55, 55, 59; 9:5, 9, 16, 21, 25, 26, 28, 29, 31, 41; 10:8, 26, 33, 38, 39, 41; 11:4, 8, 11, 13, 20, 22, 37, 39, 42, 46, 52; 12:4, 8, 16, 24, 27, 37, 39, 42, 48; 13:8, 10, 36, 37; 14:10, 17, 19, 22, 26, 28, 31; 15:7, 19, 22, 24, 26; 16:5, 7, 12, 20, 20, 22, 25, 32, 33; 17:6, 9, 15, 20, 25; 18:11, 26, 36, 39, 40, 40; 19:4, 9, 12, 15, 23, 24, 33; 20:5, 14, 17, 25, 26, 31; 21:3, 4, 18, 23; Ac 1:5, 8; 2:13, 23, 30; 3:6, 15, 18; 4:4, 10, 14, 17, 19, 21; 5:2, 4, 19, 22, 23, 26, 29, 34, 36, 37, 39; 6:1, 9; 7:5, 6, 7, 9, 11, 18, 25, 27, 39, 47, 51, 55; 8:4, 12, 20, 39; 9:7, 13, 15, 24, 26, 29, 38, 40; 10:10, 26, 28, 40, 41; 11:2, 9, 15, 16, 19; 12:5, 9, 24; 13:8, 14, 22, 24, 25, 28, 30, 45, 46, 51; 14:2, 4, 14, 17, 18, 20; 15:5, 24, 38; 16:1, 7, 24, 28, 37; 17:5, 9, 13, 30, 32, 34; 18:6, 12, 14, 15, 17, 19, 20; 19:9, 15, 15, 23, 26, 30, 34, 37; 20:17, 24; 21:7, 13, 13, 20; 22:9, 19, 21, 28; 23:3, 8, 16, 21, 30; 24:4, 14, 19, 23; 25:4, 10, 11, 18, 19, 21, 25, 26; 26:22, 25; 27:7, 11, 14, 22, 26, 31, 39, 41, 43; 28:5, 6, 19, 22, 25, 26, 26; Ro 1:12, 13, 18, 21, 25; 2:1, 5, 8, 10, 21, 22, 22, 23, 25, 27, 29; 3:3, 5, 7, 21, 21; 4:2, 5, 10, 11, 12, 13, 15; 5:8, 15, 16, 17, 18, 19, 20; 6:17, 22, 23; 7:2, 3, 6, 6, 7, 8, 9, 12, 13, 14, 15, 17, 18, 20, 23, 25; 8:3, 4, 5, 6, 9, 13, 17, 25, 26, 32; 9:11, 13, 22, 26, 31, 33; 10:2, 6, 14, 16, 18, 19, 21, 21; 11:7, 17, 18, 20, 20, 22, 22, 25, 28, 30, 31; 12:2, 11, 16, 21; 13:3, 4, 14; 14:2, 14, 17, 20, 22, 23; 15:1, 23, 25; 16:19, 26; 1Co 1:17, 18, 24; 2:4, 6, 8, 10, 14, 15, 16; 3:6, 7, 10, 13, 15, 15; 4:4, 9, 10, 10, 10, 14, 19; 5:8, 10, 12, 13; 6:6, 8, 11, 12, 13, 17; 7:2, 7, 9, 10, 11, 14, 15, 21, 25, 28, 33, 36, 37, 39, 40; 8:3, 6, 9, 10; 9:17, 21, 24, 25; 10:13, 23, 23, 28, 29, 33; 11:3, 5, 7, 8, 9, 11, 16, 17, 19, 31, 32; 12:4, 5, 6, 12, 13, 18, 20; 13:1, 2, 3, 6, 8, 10, 11, 12, 12; 14:1, 2, 2, 3, 4, 5, 6, 11, 14, 17, 19, 20, 21, 22, 24, 26, 28, 30, 33, 38, 40; 15:10, 10, 12, 15, 20, 22, 23, 35, 37, 43, 43, 44, 45, 48, 51, 51; 16:9, 12; 2Co 1:9, 9, 24; 2:4, 13, 14, 15, 16; 3:2, 3, 3, 6, 14, 16; 4:7, 8, 8, 9, 9, 12, 13, 18; 5:3, 4; 6:8, 9, 9, 10, 10, 12; 7:6, 7, 9, 10; 8:3, 21; 9:3, 5, 6; 10:1, 2, 3, 8, 10, 12, 13, 18; 11:3, 5, 6, 12, 14, 16, 17, 21, 23, 26, 33; 12:1, 4, 5, 6, 7, 16, 17; 13:4, 7, 8; Gal 1:7, 15; 2:5, 11, 12, 16, 17, 20; 3:10, 13, 16, 18, 19, 20, 22, 25; 4:4, 7, 14, 19, 20, 23, 26, 30; 5:5, 9, 13, 15, 18, 22; 6:8; Eph 2:4, 13; 3:5; 4:20; 5:13, 15, 17, 29, 32; 6:6, 12, 20; Php 1:15, 18, 20, 24, 27, 28, 29; 2:4, 17, 22, 27; 3:7, 9, 12, 13, 16, 20; 4:10, 14; Col 1:23, 26; 2:11, 18, 19, 23; 3:8, 25; 1Th 1:5; 2:7, 8, 16, 18; 3:3; 4:8, 9; 5:4, 8, 15, 21; 2Th 1:5; 3:3, 9, 15; 1Ti 1:6, 7, 9, 13, 16; 2:15; 4:2, 3, 8; 5:1, 4, 5, 6, 8, 24, 25; 6:3, 9, 11, 17; 2Ti 1:7, 9, 12; 2:9, 19, 24; 3:5, 7, 9, 10, 11, 13, 14; 4:5, 8, 14, 17; Tit 1:15, 16; 2:1, 10; 3:4, 5; Phm 1:9, 11, 14, 14; Heb 1:2, 8, 11, 12, 14; 2:8; 3:3, 4, 5, 6, 15; 4:2, 5, 6; 5:11; 6:8; 7:6, 8, 16, 20, 24, 27, 28; 8:6, 8, 10; 9:5, 7, 12, 23, 26, 28; 10:1, 3, 5, 12, 25, 27, 38, 39; 11:5, 13, 16, 29, 35; 12:10, 11, 13, 26, 26; 13:11; Jas 1:6, 23, 25, 26; 2:3, 9, 13, 16, 18; 3:2, 5, 8, 14, 17; 4:6, 11; 5:12; 1Pe 1:12, 15, 20, 23, 25; 2:4, 7, 9, 16, 18, 20, 25; 3:7, 12, 14, 16, 18, 18; 4:2, 5, 16; 5:2, 3, 5; 2Pe 1:9, 14; 2:1, 3, 7, 11, 16, 19; 3:8, 10, 13, 18; 1Jn 1:6, 7, 9; 2:1, 2, 4, 5, 9, 10, 17, 20, 21, 23, 27; 3:1, 2, 6, 8, 8, 14, 17; 4:4, 6, 8, 10, 12, 17, 20, 21; 5:6, 16, 17; 2Jn 5, 9, 12; 3Jn 9, 12, 13; Jude 3, 6, 9, 9, 10, 12, 12, 17, 20, 23; Rev 1:17; 2:2, 4, 6, 9, 9, 20, 21, 24; 3:1, 5, 9, 16; 5:3, 5, 6; 9:4, 5, 6, 6, 12, 19, 20; 10:4, 7, 9, 10; 11:2, 11, 14, 18; 12:12, 14, 16; 13:2, 3, 10; 16:11; 17:8, 10, 14; 18:20; 19:10; 20:6, 9, 11; 21:8, 27; 22:9

BY (2544)

Ge 5:32; 7:15; 8:14, 19; 9:26; 10:32; 11:9, 28; 12:6, 9; 13:3, 18; 14:19; 15:10; 17:2; 18:2; 19:36; 21:8, 16, 28; 22:13, 16, 21; 23:18, 20; 24:3, 14, 31; 25:13, 13; 26:15; 27:40; 29:25; 30:22, 27; 31:26, 27, 31, 39, 44; 32:16, 16; 37:26, 28; 38:15; 39:1, 12, 18; 41:6, 23, 32, 37; 42:15; 43:10, 32; 44:5, 28; 45:27; 46:18, 25; 49:19, 23, 24; Ex 3:17; 5:3, 8; 6:9, 26; 8:4, 24; 9:15, 34; 10:1, 19; 11:3; 12:24, 42, 51; 13:3, 13, 13, 21; 15:16, 16; 16:18, 20, 21, 32; 17:3, 6, 7; 18:18; 19:13; 20:8, 26; 22:1, 13, 15, 26, 31; 23:1, 2, 5, 13; 25:26; 26:25; 27:10, 11, 12, 14, 14, 15, 17, 21; 28:32, 37; 29:36, 36, 41, 43; 30:10; 31:18; 32:13, 16; 33:12, 22; 34:7, 15, 16, 20, 20; 36:2, 3, 38; 38:8, 12, 14, 14, 15, 19, 23; 39:3; 40:18; Lev 1:3, 5, 9, 13, 17, 17; 2:2, 3, 9, 10, 11, 16; 3:3, 5, 8, 9, 11, 14, 16; 4:2, 2, 13, 22, 27, 35; 5:12, 15, 15, 16, 17, 17; 6:2, 2, 4, 5, 17, 18, 22; 7:5, 12, 13, 18, 18, 19, 24, 25, 30, 30, 34, 35; 8:21, 27, 28, 34; 9:13; 10:1, 5, 6, 6, 6, 9, 12, 13, 14, 15; 11:43, 44; 13:7, 11, 51, 52, 52; 14:2, 8, 12, 21; 15:12, 32; 16:9, 18, 21, 29, 32; 17:7, 15; 18:7, 14, 19, 20, 23, 26, 27, 30; 19:14, 14, 29, 31, 32; 20:2, 2, 3, 5, 6, 23, 25, 27; 21:1, 6, 7, 11, 12, 12, 14, 21; 22:3, 4, 4, 5, 5, 8, 15, 16, 18, 22, 27, 31, 32; 23:8, 13, 18, 25, 27, 36, 36, 37, 37, 40, 41, 42; 24:3, 7, 9, 16, 22; 25:17, 33, 36, 43, 48, 54; 26:15, 17, 19, 25, 26, 36, 36, 44; 27:2, 8, 13, 15, 16, 19, 20, 27, 28, 29; Nu 1:2, 4, 18, 18, 44, 45; 2:32, 33; 3:15, 39; 4:32, 34, 38, 42, 46; 5:2, 6, 19, 20, 27, 29; 6:4, 21; 7:17, 23, 29, 35, 41, 47, 53, 59, 65, 71, 77, 83, 84; 8:7, 26; 9:6, 7; 10:15, 16, 19, 20, 23, 24, 26, 27, 28; 11:8, 14; 12:6; 13:16; 14:14, 14, 22, 36, 42; 15:3, 10, 13, 14, 25, 25, 27; 16:3, 25, 28, 39; 18:8, 11, 11, 12, 17, 18; 19:2; 21:7; 22:25, 26, 33; 23:3, 9, 15; 24:1, 2, 6, 6, 23; 25:1, 11, 18; 26:10, 53, 55, 55, 56, 63; 27:1, 21; 28:2, 6, 8, 9, 12, 13, 20, 24, 28; 29:3, 6, 9, 13, 14, 18, 21, 24, 27, 30, 33, 37; 31:23; 32:17; 33:2, 38, 54; 34:13; 35:12, 33; 36:2, 2; Dt 1:2, 9, 12, 27, 33, 33, 42; 2:12; 3:9; 4:16, 19, 25, 34, 34, 46, 46; 5:12, 22, 25; 7:22; 8:3, 3, 6; 9:18, 26, 29; 11:22, 28; 13:13; 16:1, 17; 17:3, 3, 19; 18:1; 19:14, 15, 21; 21:9; 22:21; 23:25; 24:13; 25:11; 26:6, 17; 27:10, 17, 26; 28:1, 10, 25; 30:16; 31:18, 21, 29; 32:16, 19, 21, 21, 21, 24, 24, 47; 33:12, 13, 24, 29; Jos 2:12, 15, 20; 3:17; 7:14, 14, 18, 19; 8:10; 10:9; 11:4, 6; 13:21; 14:1, 2, 6; 18:8; 19:1, 51; 20:6; 21:3, 8; 22:13, 19, 20, 29, 31; 23:7, 16; Jdg 1:26; 2:18; 3:30; 4:11; 6:6, 31; 7:2, 25; 8:10, 11, 11, 13, 27, 33; 9:2, 2, 16, 16, 32, 34, 56; 10:16; 11:27; 15:9, 18; 16:25, 26; 18:31; 20:39; 21:7, 24; Ru 1:6, 19, 22; 2:13; 3:2, 10; 4:1, 12; 1Sa 2:9, 16; 3:1, 2, 14; 4:3; 6:9, 15, 17, 18; 9:5, 6; 10:19; 11:9; 12:9, 9, 10, 19, 23; 13:23; 14:33, 34, 39; 15:30; 16:7, 7, 20; 17:2, 35, 43; 18:4, 5, 17, 21; 19:11; 20:3, 3, 12, 12, 19, 34; 22:6; 24:21; 25:29, 34; 26:5, 16, 19; 27:12; 28:6, 6, 6, 8, 8, 15, 15; 29:4, 6; 30:15; 2Sa 2:16, 17, 17, 23; 3:8, 24, 28, 29; 6:22; 8:1; 10:5, 16, 16, 19; 11:21; 12:10; 14:11; 15:5, 21, 21, 23, 24; 16:15, 18, 18; 17:24, 27, 27, 27; 18:4, 7, 8, 13, 24; 19:7, 27; 20:9; 21:21, 22; 23:1, 15, 18; 24:1, 16; 1Ki 1:6, 17, 44; 2:8, 23, 42; 3:6, 9; 6:6, 10, 27, 38; 7:3, 6, 6, 24; 8:33; 9:8; 12:9, 19; 13:9, 17, 25, 26; 14:11, 11, 15; 15:18, 29, 30; 16:1, 2, 4, 4, 7, 34, 34; 17:3, 12, 18; 18:6, 6, 10, 15, 19, 24; 19:2, 11, 17, 17; 20:1, 19, 22, 31, 39; 21:1, 3, 24, 24; 2Ki 2:11, 11; 3:13; 4:10; 5:23; 6:10; 7:1, 18; 8:27; 9:7, 28; 10:6, 33; 11:13, 14; 12:6; 14:9, 12; 15:5; 16:11; 17:4, 4, 20; 18:4, 22, 30, 32; 19:6, 10, 18, 23, 26, 28, 29, 33; 20:17; 21:13, 13; 23:3, 5, 14, 19, 35; 24:7; 25:3, 4, 5; 1Ch 1:33; 2:7; 3:16, 16, 17; 4:42; 5:1, 6, 7; 6:10, 49, 54, 61, 62, 63, 65; 9:22, 23; 11:14, 17, 20; 12:39; 16:4, 15, 41; 18:1; 19:5, 7, 19; 20:7, 8; 21:12, 15, 26, 30; 23:7, 24, 24; 24:5, 19, 31; 25:2, 8; 26:13, 13, 20, 26, 28; 27:1, 7, 34, 34; 28:20; 29:5; 2Ch 1:5; 2:7, 14; 3:11, 15; 4:3; 5:1, 12, 13; 6:24; 7:14, 21; 8:14, 18, 18; 9:21, 21; 10:9, 15, 19; 13:3, 8, 21; 14:13; 16:2; 18:31; 20:3, 15; 23:13, 18, 18; 24:21, 22; 25:18, 22; 26:11, 11, 15, 16, 22; 28:15; 29:19, 27; 30:3, 9, 21; 31:12, 13, 15, 16, 17; 32:5, 5, 11, 19; 33:13; 34:9, 9, 31; 35:10, 12, 15, 15; 36:3, 10, 22; Ezr 1:1, 4, 6; 2:1, 63; 3:5, 9, 9; 4:7; 5:2, 11; 6:4, 4, 5, 14, 14, 14, 16, 21, 21; 7:26, 28; 8:20, 20, 21, 34, 36; 9:2, 11; 10:3, 3, 16, 17, 19, 44; Ne 1:7, 10; 3:3, 6, 8, 13, 14, 18, 19; 4:10, 13; 5:7, 9; 6:3, 13; 7:6, 65; 9:12, 19, 29; 10:29, 31, 38; 11:1, 9, 12:24, 36, 44, 45; 13:18, 26, 27; Est 1:6; 2:6, 12, 14, 15; 3:2, 10, 13, 15; 8:10, 14; 9:22, 24, 28, 31; Job 1:22; 3:23; 4:9, 20; 5:17; 10:3, 12; 11:2; 13:7, 25; 15:18, 21, 34; 16:12; 17:2; 18:9, 12; 19:20; 20:29; 21:2, 18, 26; 22:10, 30; 23:7; 24:2, 8; 26:12, 12; 27:2, 2, 15, 18, 28; 29:2, 18; 30:1, 1, 18; 31:9, 23, 28; 32:3; 36:15, 31; 40:21, 23; 41:7, 7, 25; Ps 1:4; 4:T, 4; 5:T; 6:T, 7; 8:T; 10:8; 12:T; 17:14; 18:42; 20:6; 22:6; 25:5; 31:10, 11, 11, 13; 35:5, 15; 36:9; 37:18, 22, 22, 23, 24; 39:10; 40:15; 42:9; 43:2; 44:3, 5, 14; 45:8, 14; 46:T, 10; 48:7; 49:7; 50:5; 54:T; 55:T, 2, 15; 57:4; 59:12; 60:6; 61:T; 62:10; 63:10; 65:6; 66:7; 67:T; 68:2, 13, 17; 69:29; 70:3; 71:15; 73:19, 21; 74:13; 76:T, 12; 77:15, 15; 78:10, 14, 14, 26, 46, 55, 58, 62, 63; 79:4, 11; 80:5, 16; 81:T, 4; 83:1; 84:T; 87:1; 88:9, 13; 90:6, 7; 92:3, 10; 94:20; 98:1; 104:34; 105:8; 106:7, 38, 39, 43; 108:7; 111:6; 112:6; 115:4, 15; 118:22; 119:7, 9, 25, 28, 30, 133, 133; 121:6; 129:4, 7, 7, 8; 135:15; 138:2, 3, 7; 139:9; 140:9; 144:13; 147:4, 7; 149:3; Pr 1:6, 27; 3:19, 19, 20; 4:3, 12; 5:19, 22; 6:2, 2, 13; 7:8; 9:15; 10:21; 11:3, 3, 5; 12:13, 14; 13:6; 14:20, 32; 15:11; 16:6, 31; 19:3, 11; 20:1, 11, 23; 21:1, 6, 11; 22:16, 16, 28, 28; 23:10; 24:3, 12, 24, 24, 30; 25:1, 5, 12; 26:9, 26; 27:3, 21; 28:8; 29:6, 15; 30:17, 17, 32; Ecc 1:13; 2:4, 4, 19; 4:4; 5:6, 8; 6:8; 7:5, 5; 8:4; 9:11, 11, 12; 10:3, 5, 8, 15; SS 1:12, 17; 2:7; 3:5; 4:9, 9; 6:11; 7:4; Isa 1:20; 4:1, 4; 5:16, 16; 7:1, 15, 24; 8:19; 9:5, 11, 19; 10:13, 13, 14, 15; 11:3; 13:16, 21; 16:5; 17:13, 14; 18:2, 7; 19:23; 21:7; 22:2; 23:6; 24:6; 26:1; 27:12; 28:1, 7; 29:13, 21; 30:24, 27; 31:8; 33:11, 15, 23; 34:11; 35:10; 36:7, 15, 18; 37:6, 10, 19, 24, 27, 29, 30, 34; 38:13; 39:6; 40:26; 41:4, 13, 18; 43:1; 44:14, 24, 25; 45:3, 4, 23; 47:6; 48:1; 49:1, 7, 7; 50:4, 9, 11; 51:11; 52:4; 53:1, 11; 54:6, 17; 55:4; 56:2, 5; 57:7; 58:5; 59:19; 60:15; 62:2, 8, 12; 64:8; 65:1, 3, 15, 16, 23; 66:8, 13, 16, 16, 16, 24; Jer 2:17, 18, 20; 3:2, 9, 13; 4:2, 10, 12, 21, 26; 5:7, 7; 6:5; 7:4, 20; 8:9; 9:11, 12; 10:2, 9, 12, 12, 12; 11:17; 12:9, 16, 16; 13:22, 24; 14:15, 18, 22; 17:8, 8, 11; 18:16; 19:2, 4, 4, 4, 8; 20:4, 7; 21:10; 22:5, 8, 9, 13; 23:9, 13, 27, 27; 25:6, 7, 13, 16, 37, 38; 27:5; 29:1, 14; 31:21, 32; 32:4, 7, 8, 17, 29, 29, 43; 34:16, 17, 17, 17; 35:4; 36:16, 18, 21, 23; 37:1, 17; 38:6, 23; 40:5; 41:1, 8, 9, 10, 18; 42:12; 43:3; 44:8, 12, 13, 25, 26, 26; 46:2, 6, 18; 47:1, 3; 48:20, 26; 49:2, 13, 15, 17, 28, 33; 50:13, 17, 39; 51:14, 15, 15, 15, 37, 42, 43, 46, 51, 58; 52:6, 7, 8; La 1:12; 2:14, 15, 21; 3:22; 4:9, 13, 14; 5:12, 18; Eze 2:6; 3:23; 4:14, 16; 5:10, 12, 14; 6:9, 12; 7:13, 15, 23; 8:3, 10; 9:6; 10:20; 12:16; 13:10, 10, 19, 22; 14:19, 20; 16:6, 8, 21, 27, 29, 43, 57, 57, 59; 17:14; 18:7, 12; 19:10, 12; 20:11, 24, 30, 44; 21:21; 22:5; 23:25, 30, 37, 37; 24:6, 17, 21, 22, 22; 25:12, 14, 16; 26:6, 8; 27:11, 28, 33; 28:22; 29:12, 12; 30:6, 7, 7, 14; 31:18; 32:20, 22, 22, 23, 25, 25, 26, 29, 32; 33:27, 27; 34:8, 13, 29; 35:8, 11; 36:3, 4, 5, 15, 17, 18, 21, 34; 37:1; 38:16; 39:11, 12; 42:1; 43:3, 7, 7, 8, 16; 44:19, 25, 29, 31; 45:2; 46:2, 9, 9, 18, 20, 22, 24, 24; 47:12; 48:10, 13, 14, 15; Da 1:8, 8, 10, 11, 15, 18; 2:18, 22, 34, 39, 43, 45; 3:12, 25; 4:15, 17, 17, 19, 23, 27, 30, 35; 5:13; 7:11, 15, 28; 8:11, 11, 24, 25, 25, 27; 9:2, 13, 15; 10:16, 19; 11:2, 4, 11, 21, 23, 33; 12:7, 10; Hos 1:2, 5; 5:1, 11; 6:10; 7:16; 8:4, 6; 9:4, 6; 11:3; 12:8, 8, 12, 13; 13:1, 2, 3, 16, 16; 14:9; Am 2:4, 6, 12; 3:10; 4:2, 3; 5:12, 19; 6:8, 8, 13; 8:7, 14; 9:9, 10; Jnh 1:3, 16; Mic 1:7; 2:2, 4; 5:7; 6:10, 10, 16; Na 2:1; 3:8, 8; Hab 1:3, 13; 2:4, 9, 10, 12, 18, 18; 3:1, 2, 2, 11, 19; Zep 1:13, 18; 2:12; 3:3, 4, 5, 8, 17; Hag 1:12; 2:13; Zec 3:5; 4:6, 6, 6; 5:4; 6:2, 2, 3, 3; 7:12; 10:7, 12; 11:16; 12:12; 13:9; 14:13; Mal 1:2, 7, 7, 11, 12; 2:10, 11, 17, 17; 3:4, 14, 14; Mt 1:18, 20; 2:3, 23; 3:8, 13, 14; 4:1, 1, 24; 5:31, 34, 35, 35, 36; 6:6, 7, 19; 7:16, 16, 20; 8:28; 9:25, 32, 34; 11:6, 7, 19; 12:2, 10, 27, 28, 33, 37; 13:22, 33; 14:13, 13, 23, 28; 15:3, 5, 6, 11, 11, 12, 13, 15; 16:1; 18:16, 28; 19:12; 21:23, 42; 22:2, 41; 23:16, 16, 18, 18, 20, 20, 20, 21, 21, 21, 22, 22, 22, 34; 25:1, 6, 14, 34; 26:22, 47, 52, 71, 73, 74; 27:9, 35, 39, 43, 54; Mk 1:9, 13, 14, 23, 31; 2:24; 3:5, 7, 11, 22, 23; 4:1, 2, 19, 27; 5:2; 6:7, 32, 46; 7:3, 15, 15, 17, 19, 25; 8:23, 31; 9:10, 17, 27, 29; 10:46; 11:20, 27, 28; 12:10, 32; 14:19, 35, 43, 54, 71; 15:10, 29; 16:20; Lk 1:9, 42, 61, 62, 72; 2:5, 13, 21, 22, 34, 52, 52; 3:8, 16; 4:1, 15, 22, 33, 41; 5:9; 6:2, 10, 17, 17, 23, 26, 44; 7:6, 23, 24, 29, 35; 8:14, 16, 27, 35, 42, 54; 9:22, 31; 10:25, 30, 31, 31, 32, 36; 11:3, 18, 18, 19, 20, 38; 12:15; 13:11, 21; 14:12; 15:30; 16:22; 17:25; 18:11, 37; 19:5, 5; 20:2, 17, 21, 26; 21:2, 19, 20, 24, 24, 25; 22:27, 37, 39, 40, 47; 23:2, 2, 34, 36, 39, 44, 56, 56; 24:19, 26, 28, 44; Jn 1:24, 36; 2:21; 3:34; 5:19, 36; 6:15, 45, 57; 7:21, 35; 8:9, 48, 52; 9:4, 24; 10:3, 21, 36; 11:39; 12:48; 14:26; 15:3; 16:14, 18; 17:4, 17; 18:20, 25, 31, 36; 19:7, 17, 31; 20:31; Ac 1:16, 22; 2:6, 15, 16, 22, 36, 39; 3:7, 12, 13, 26; 4:7, 25; 5:15, 16, 30, 32; 6:10; 7:35, 36, 44, 48, 54; 8:13, 23; 9:9, 14; 10:4, 11, 14, 17, 22, 22, 23, 31, 38, 39; 11:5, 8, 28; 12:10; 13:4, 13, 27, 43; 14:3, 26; 15:1, 2, 4, 8, 10, 11; 16:2, 4; 17:8, 16, 29, 31, 31; 18:27; 19:13, 15, 21, 31, 33, 40; 20:3, 13, 13, 22, 24, 35; 21:11, 28, 30; 22:11, 11, 12, 28; 23:3, 19, 27; 24:8, 27, 27; 25:14, 23, 24, 24; 26:2, 10, 18, 20; 27:9, 38, 41; 28:3, 16; Ro 1:1, 2, 4, 9, 12, 17; 2:16, 23, 29; 3:8, 20, 21, 21, 24, 27, 28, 30, 30; 4:1, 8, 9, 11, 13; 5:1, 8, 9, 10, 10, 16; 6:4, 4, 14; 7:5, 6, 6, 24; 8:3, 5, 5, 9, 9, 11; 9:16, 30, 31, 32, 32; 10:3, 10, 10, 19, 19, 20; 11:6, 6, 24, 36; 12:2, 3, 21; 13:1, 4, 4; 14:15, 22; 15:15, 16, 18, 18, 19, 19, 20, 30, 30, 32; 16:17, 18; 1Co 1:1, 2, 2, 10, 24, 28; 2:10, 13; 3:3, 3, 18, 18; 4:20; 5:8; 6:4, 14, 19; 7:23; 8:8, 10, 12; 9:10, 14, 16; 10:1, 18, 27, 29; 11:25, 31, 32; 12:3, 3, 13; 14:2, 24; 15:5, 5, 6, 6, 7, 7, 10, 30, 33; 2Co 1:1, 11, 22; 2:3, 15, 15, 15; 3:3, 5, 14; 4:8; 5:1, 1, 4, 7, 7, 16; 6:3, 6; 7:6, 9, 13; 8:9, 19, 20; 10:8, 8, 9, 12; 11:3, 6, 7, 8, 13, 15; 12:12, 16; 13:1, 4, 6; Gal 1:1, 1, 7, 12; 2:6, 14, 15, 16, 16, 16, 16, 20, 21; 3:2, 3, 11, 12, 13, 18, 21, 23; 4:10, 29, 29; 5:3, 4, 5, 12, 18, 25; 6:1, 6, 16; Eph 1:1, 5, 13, 23; 2:5, 8, 11, 11, 14, 15, 15, 16, 22; 3:5, 6, 7, 7, 20; 4:1, 26, 30; 5:6, 26; 6:4, 4, 16; Php 1:11, 27, 28, 28; 2:2, 8, 19; Col 1:1, 20, 20, 21, 23, 25; 2:2, 11, 14, 15, 18, 19; 1Th 2:2, 4, 16, 16; 3:3; 4:6, 8; 5:8; 2Th 1:11; 2:2, 3, 8, 13, 13, 15; 1Ti 1:1, 1, 11; 2:9, 9, 10, 14, 15; 3:16, 16; 4:3, 5, 6; 5:4, 10; 6:2, 9, 15, 19, 21; 2Ti 1:1, 10; 2:2, 26; 3:6, 15, 16; Tit 1:3, 11, 16; 2:7; 3:3, 14; Heb 1:3; 2:3, 3, 4, 4, 5, 9, 14, 14; 3:13; 5:4, 5; 6:6, 10, 13; 7:4, 16, 16, 26, 28; 8:2, 2, 4, 9; 9:8, 11, 14, 22, 23, 26; 10:8, 10, 14, 20, 38; 11:3, 4, 5, 7, 7, 8, 9, 10, 11, 17, 20, 21, 22, 23, 24, 27, 28, 29, 30, 31, 33, 34, 37; 12:1, 2, 15, 28; 13:9, 12, 15, 20; Jas 1:6, 12, 14, 17, 22, 22, 24, 24, 25, 25; 3:1, 3, 6, 15; 5:12; 1Pe 1:2, 3, 7, 12; 2:4, 7, 24; 3:2, 21; 4:16; 5:3, 10; 2Pe 1:1, 4, 4, 19; 2:8, 15, 17, 20; 3:5, 7, 17; 1Jn 2:3; 3:18, 19; 4:1, 9; 5:4, 6, 6, 6, 6; 2Jn 4, 13; 3Jn 3; Jude 7, 12, 19, 20, 23; Rev 1:5; 2:11, 13, 14, 14; 3:18, 18; 6:8, 13; 9:2, 18, 18; 10:1; 11:19; 12:16; 16:9; 17:2; 18:8, 10, 15, 15; 19:8, 21; 21:12

CAME (861)

Ge 1:11; 2:6; 3:19; 4:1; 7:1, 6, 9, 10, 15; 8:4, 19; 9:19; 10:14, 32; 11:5; 12:6; 14:13, 17; 15:11; 19:1, 4, 5; 20:3; 21:22; 24:16, 42; 25:24; 26:20, 32; 27:33; 29:11, 21; 30:30, 38; 31:33; 32:1, 24; 33:6, 7, 7, 8; 34:6; 35:5, 27; 37:21, 28; 38:28; 39:12, 12, 14, 16; 40:17, 20; 41:2, 3, 18, 19, 23, 53, 57; 42:6, 29; 43:3, 26, 31; 45:4; 46:1; 47:1, 15, 18; 48:1; 50:18; Ex 1:8; 2:5, 16, 17; 10:7; 14:20; 15:23, 27; 16:22; 17:1, 8; 18:5, 12; 19:2, 16, 20; 32:19, 24, 26; 34:5, 29, 32, 34; 35:22; 38:26; Lev 9:5, 23; 10:5; Nu 3:38, 50; 4:36, 40, 44; 7:2, 86; 9:6; 10:21; 11:9, 25; 13:23; 14:45; 16:18, 27, 43; 18:30; 21:7; 22:9, 20; 24:2; 26:4; 31:48; 32:2; 36:1; Dt 1:24, 44; 4:11, 46; 5:23; 9:15; 10:5; 11:10; 23:4, 8; 25:17; 29:7, 7; 32:44; 33:2, 2; Jos 2:1, 23; 4:18; 7:17, 17; 8:22; 9:16; 13:14; 14:6; 17:4, 5, 14; 19:9, 29; 21:1, 41, 45; 24:1, 11; Jdg 3:10, 19; 4:5, 22; 5:14, 14; 6:11, 34; 7:13; 9:35, 57; 10:1; 11:13, 29, 35; 14:14, 14, 16, 18; 15:14; 18:2, 13, 22, 27; 19:14, 16; 20:1, 4, 14, 21, 31, 48; Ru 1:19; 2:6, 17; 3:7; 4:1, 3; 1Sa 2:14, 19, 27; 3:10; 6:14; 7:1; 10:10; 11:4, 6, 7; 12:12; 13:12; 15:2, 6; 16:13; 17:4; 18:6, 19; 19:9, 11, 14, 16, 20, 23; 20:41; 23:1; 24:8; 26:1, 15; 30:9; 2Sa 2:4, 23, 23; 3:20, 25; 6:20; 9:6; 11:4, 23; 13:6, 25; 14:26, 31, 33; 16:5; 18:9, 25; 19:15; 21:17; 22:10, 42; 24:7, 11, 13, 18, 20; 1Ki 1:28, 32, 53; 2:8, 13; 3:16; 7:14; 8:10; 9:12; 10:1, 24, 25; 11:26; 13:9, 11, 14, 17, 20, 22, 24, 25; 14:25; 17:22; 19:7, 9, 15; 20:13; 21:28; 22:38; 2Ki 1:6; 2:3, 5, 9, 24; 3:15, 25; 4:1, 27, 36, 39; 6:1, 13; 7:17; 8:4; 10:21; 14:9; 15:12; 17:7, 33; 18:13, 37; 19:33; 20:4, 14; 21:15; 23:17; 24:10; 1Ch 1:12; 2:53; 7:22; 9:2, 3, 7, 25; 12:16, 18, 38; 21:11; 23:3; 26:29, 30, 31; 2Ch 7:8; 9:1, 23, 24; 12:3, 9; 14:14; 15:1; 16:7; 20:2, 4, 14, 29; 24:17, 20; 25:7, 18; 28:15, 22; 30:18, 25, 25; 31:8, 16; 32:25; 36:6, 20; Ezr 2:69; 4:12; 5:16; 7:6, 9; 8:1, 13; 9:1, 4; Ne 1:2; 2:9; 3:11, 17, 22, 27; 4:12; 6:5; 9:13; 11:3; 12:29, 35, 36; 13:21; Est 2:13; 4:4; 6:6; 8:3; 9:25; Job 1:6, 6, 21; 2:1, 1; 3:11; 4:13; 8:10; 21:28; 30:26; 31:29, 29; 42:11; Ps 18:9, 41; 51:T; 54:T; 68:17; 73:2; 78:9; 105:19, 34; 114:8; 148:5; Pr 7:15; Ecc 3:20; 7:27; 9:14; Isa 1:1; 13:5; 14:28; 15:1; 17:1, 9; 19:1; 21:1, 11, 13; 22:1; 23:1; 36:1; 37:29, 34; 38:4; 39:3; 48:3, 13; 51:2; 63:5; 64:3; Jer 8:15; 14:1, 19; 25:1; 26:1; 27:1; 31:21; 32:1, 8, 23, 26; 33:19; 34:1, 1, 8; 36:9; 37:7; 38:27; 39:3; 40:8, 8, 13; 44:28; 49:9, 34; La 3:57; Eze 1:5; 2:2; 3:15, 24; 6:1; 7:1; 11:5, 14; 12:1, 8, 17, 21, 26; 13:1; 14:2, 12; 15:1; 16:1, 6, 15; 17:1, 3, 7, 11, 12; 18:1; 20:1, 2, 45; 21:1, 18; 22:1, 17, 23; 23:1, 17, 39, 39, 42; 24:1, 15, 20; 25:1; 26:1; 27:1, 8, 9, 14, 15, 19, 22, 23; 28:1, 11, 20; 29:1, 14, 17; 30:1, 20; 31:1, 8; 32:1, 17; 33:1, 21, 23; 34:1; 35:1; 36:16; 37:7, 10, 15; 38:1; 42:1; 43:3, 4; 46:2, 8, 9; 47:1, 8; 48:1; Da 1:1; 2:14; 3:26; 4:7, 8; 5:8; 7:3, 20, 22; 8:9; 9:21; 10:2, 6, 13; 12:1; Joel 1:4; Ob 5; Mic 1:1; Na 1:1; Hag 1:14; 2:5; Zec 4:8; 5:5; 7:1, 8; 8:1, 18; 12:1; Mt 3:16; 4:3, 11; 5:17; 8:1, 5, 24, 32, 34; 9:14, 18, 20, 36; 10:34, 34; 11:13; 12:38, 42, 44; 13:4, 10, 25, 27; 14:12, 15, 25; 15:12, 22, 25; 16:1, 13; 17:5, 7, 14, 24; 18:1, 21; 19:3, 16; 20:10, 20, 28; 21:1, 14, 23, 32; 22:11; 24:3, 39; 25:10, 22, 24; 26:7, 17, 45, 49, 58, 69, 73; 27:32, 64; 28:2, 13, 18; Mk 1:9, 10, 11, 38, 40, 45; 2:18; 3:8, 13; 4:4, 35; 5:13, 22, 27, 33, 38; 6:21, 22, 29, 35, 38, 48; 7:25, 25; 8:11; 9:7, 15; 10:2, 17, 35; 11:4, 15, 27; 12:42; 13:3; 14:3, 32; 16:2; Lk 1:44, 59; 2:6, 27, 38; 3:2, 7, 12; 4:13, 16, 41; 5:15, 18; 6:8, 17; 7:45; 8:5, 19, 27, 33, 41, 44; 9:12, 18, 34, 42; 10:31, 33, 38, 40; 11:1, 24, 27, 31; 13:6; 15:1, 17, 28; 17:15, 27; 18:3; 19:5, 29, 41; 20:1; 21:2; 23:15, 33, 48; 24:1, 15, 22; Jn 1:10, 17; 3:2, 19, 26; 4:5, 7, 30, 40; 6:42, 51; 8:14; 9:7; 10:8; 11:38, 44, 51; 12:27; 13:6; 16:27, 28, 30; 17:8; 18:37; 19:5, 32, 33, 38, 39; 20:1, 24; Ac 2:6, 43; 4:1, 36; 5:7, 10, 16, 19, 36; 7:11, 18, 24; 8:2, 36, 39, 40; 9:21, 32; 10:29, 45; 11:5, 9; 12:10, 13; 13:24; 14:8; 16:39; 17:1; 18:5; 19:1, 6, 12; 20:19; 21:5; 22:13, 22; 24:24; 25:17; 27:1; 28:9, 10, 14, 15, 23; Ro 1:3; 5:6; 15:8, 9; 1Co 2:1, 3; 11:8, 12; 15:21, 46, 47;

2Co 2:12; 9:4; 11:9; Gal 1:12; 2:1, 4, 11, 12; 3:2, 24; 4:3, 4; Eph 4:9, 10; Col 1:6; 2:11; 1Th 2:2; 2Th 2:13; 3:1; 1Ti 1:15; 6:7; 2Ti 1:15, 17; Heb 2:16; 7:10, 14; 9:26; 10:1, 5; 11:12, 15, 30; 2Pe 1:20; 1Jn 3:5, 8; 2Jn 7; Rev 1:16; 4:5; 8:3; 9:3, 18; 13:14; 14:15, 17; 15:6; 16:17; 17:1; 18:10; 19:5, 15, 21; 20:4, 9; 21:9

CAN (1177)

Ge 8:17; 11:6; 12:12; 13:14; 15:5, 8, 13; 16:2, 10, 14; 18:13; 19:5, 22; 20:7; 23:6, 13; 24:50, 55; 26:28; 27:10, 19, 31; 29:7, 21, 27; 31:43; 32:8; 33:13; 34:21; 35:20; 37:20, 26, 30; 38:17, 21; 41:15, 15; 44:1, 16, 16, 16, 21, 34; 45:10, 12, 12; 47:23; Ex 3:7, 11, 16; 4:11, 17; 5:3, 11, 17; 6:5, 12; 7:3, 16; 8:1, 8, 20, 26; 9:1, 13; 10:1, 3, 10, 24, 26; 12:4; 16:4; 18:22, 22, 22; 19:9; 21:13; 25:8; 26:17; 27:20; 28:41; 29:29; 30:30; 31:6; 32:1, 10; Lev 11:47; 14:7, 22; 17:5, 11; 24:2; 25:24, 33, 49; 26:13; 27:20; Nu 5:8; 13:30; 16:17, 45; 23:8, 8, 10, 10, 12, 23; 24:23; 35:6, 33; Dt 1:12, 28; 3:11, 24, 27; 5:26, 31, 31; 7:17; 9:2; 11:14; 13:14; 14:29; 19:3; 24:13; 28:57; 30:12, 13, 14; 31:28; Jos 2:5, 17; 4:7, 22; 6:5; 8:29; 9:12; 14:10, 11; 15:18; 17:18; 20:3; 22:28; Jdg 1:14; 6:15; 7:14; 8:24; 9:33; 13:15; 16:5, 10, 13, 15, 25; 17:10; 19:8, 9, 22, 24; 20:13; 21:7, 16, 21; Ru 1:11; 2:14; 4:4, 5, 10; 1Sa 2:25, 25; 4:8; 6:20; 9:6, 8, 18; 10:12, 27; 11:10; 12:5; 14:6, 6; 16:2; 17:33; 18:23; 19:3, 15; 20:4, 13, 31, 36; 21:4; 24:10, 13; 25:17; 26:9, 19; 28:2, 7, 22; 2Sa 1:7; 6:9; 7:20; 9:3, 7; 10:3; 12:23; 14:10, 17, 19, 19; 15:34; 17:12, 13; 18:20; 19:26, 28, 35; 20:16; 21:3, 4; 22:30, 30; 24:22; 1Ki 1:16; 2:22; 3:9; 5:6, 8, 9; 8:13; 10:9; 18:5; 20:23; 21:15; 22:20, 20, 21; 2Ki 2:9, 19; 3:11, 15; 4:2, 3, 13, 14, 22, 42, 43; 5:7; 6:1, 2, 27, 29; 9:22; 10:4, 10; 18:20, 23, 24, 35; 22:5; 1Ch 13:12; 15:12; 16:35; 17:18; 19:3; 21:23; 22:19; 2Ch 2:6, 6, 7, 7, 14, 16; 6:2; 9:8; 12:8; 13:8, 9; 14:11; 18:19, 19, 20; 20:6, 9, 9; 24:5; 29:8; 30:7; 32:10, 14; Ezr 9:10, 15; 10:13; Ne 2:4; 4:2; 5:2, 8; 6:7; 9:5; Est 3:9; 4:14; 5:14; 8:6, 8; Job 4:17, 17; 5:19; 6:10; 8:11, 11; 9:2, 12, 19; 10:7; 11:7, 7, 8, 12; 13:9, 19; 14:4, 14; 15:14, 14; 17:15; 21:2, 22, 29, 34; 22:2, 2, 13, 17; 23:7, 13; 24:25, 25; 25:4; 26:14; 27:10, 10; 28:7, 12, 20, 22, 23; 30:13; 32:13; 33:5; 34:10, 29, 29; 36:23, 23, 26, 29; 37:7, 18, 20; 38:20, 31, 32, 34, 35, 37, 39; 39:10, 11, 11, 12; 40:8, 9, 19, 24; 41:1, 2, 4, 5, 13, 13, 16, 17, 26; 42:2, 2; Ps 2:12; 4:3; 5:7; 6:5; 9:14, 14; 10:13, 18; 11:3; 12:4; 18:29, 29; 19:6, 12; 22:11, 17; 25:15; 30:6, 9, 9; 33:11, 20; 35:10; 39:11, 13; 41:10; 42:2; 44:5, 5; 49:8; 51:6; 56:4, 11, 13; 57:7; 59:7; 62:7; 71:8, 19; 74:9; 75:6; 76:7; 77:2; 78:7, 20; 80:18; 84:4; 85:6; 88:11, 11, 12, 12; 89:6, 48, 48; 90:11; 94:20, 22; 106:2, 2, 47; 108:1; 111:4; 112:8; 113:5; 115:18; 116:7, 12; 118:6; 119:9, 88, 130, 134, 175; 137:4; 139:7, 7; 142:7; 147:17; Pr 3:15, 24, 28; 4:7; 6:3, 22, 27, 28; 8:11; 10:2; 11:13, 21, 23, 23; 12:14; 13:3, 8; 14:10, 13; 15:7; 16:1, 9, 14; 18:4, 14, 14, 18, 21; 19:14, 14, 20, 21; 20:6, 9, 24; 21:11; 23:5, 35; 24:29; 25:3, 15, 15; 27:4; 29:8; 30:20; 31:10, 11; Ecc 1:10; 2:19, 25; 3:12, 14, 18, 18, 21; 4:8, 9, 10, 11, 11, 12, 12; 6:12, 12; 7:12, 12, 13, 14, 28; 8:4, 7, 8, 17; 9:12, 18, 18; 10:1, 3, 4, 14; 12:12; SS 2:4; 4:12; 5:15; 8:7, 12, 13; Isa 1:18, 18, 18; 2:22; 5:8, 19, 22; 8:19; 10:14, 15, 15, 15; 11:15; 14:7, 16, 27, 27; 15:5, 7; 17:10, 10; 19:15; 20:6; 23:7; 28:15; 29:11, 16; 30:18; 32:3, 3; 33:14, 15, 21; 36:5, 8, 9, 20; 38:18, 19, 19; 40:18, 19, 20, 27, 27, 28; 41:9, 21, 21, 24; 43:9, 9, 13, 13, 20, 26; 44:7, 7, 11, 19, 20; 45:8, 9, 19; 46:10; 49:15, 15, 24, 24; 50:2, 2; 52:3; 55:6; 57:13, 13, 14; 59:1; 64:5; 66:18; Jer 2:13, 22, 23, 24, 28; 3:5, 5; 5:1, 4, 7, 22; 6:10; 7:9; 8:8, 16, 19; 9:7, 12; 10:5; 11:15; 13:23, 23, 23; 14:22, 22; 15:2, 12, 19; 16:13, 20; 17:14, 14; 18:6, 15; 21:13; 23:18, 24; 27:5; 28:9; 33:20; 42:22; 45:3; 47:7; 48:34; 49:19, 19; 50:29, 44, 44; 51:8, 9, 41, 50; La 1:8; 2:13, 13, 13; 3:37; 4:5; Eze 12:3, 3, 4, 12, 16; 13:7, 18; 15:3, 4; 16:28, 37; 17:15; 23:24; 24:27; 33:10, 11; 37:3, 20; 40:4; 44:26; 45:6; Da 1:13; 2:8, 9, 10, 11, 26, 27; 3:18, 29; 4:18, 18, 35; 5:7, 12, 16, 16; 6:15; 9:23; 10:17, 17; Hos 2:18; 4:12; 6:2; 11:8, 8, 8; 12:8; 14:3; Joel 2:8, 11; Am 2:11; 3:3; 4:5; 6:12, 12; 8:5; 9:13; Ob 3; Jnh 1:6; 3:9; Mic 3:11, 11; 4:13; 5:7; 6:6, 11, 12; 7:1, 1; Na 1:6, 6; 3:19; Hab 1:7; 2:2, 15, 19; Zep 3:2, 3; Hag 2:3; Zec 8:7; Mal 3:7; Mt 2:8; 3:9; 5:13, 31; 6:5, 19, 24, 27; 7:4, 13, 16, 16; 8:2; 9:18, 21, 28, 34; 10:28, 28, 29; 12:24, 29, 31, 31, 32; 13:32; 14:2, 15; 18:23; 19:11, 12, 17, 25; 21:21, 21; 22:2, 45; 23:16, 18; 24:33, 45; 25:1, 14; 26:73; 27:40, 40, 65; Mk 1:40; 2:7; 3:23, 26, 27, 28; 4:30, 32; 5:23, 28, 31; 6:14, 36; 8:23; 9:22, 23, 29; 10:26; 11:23, 24; 12:37; 13:29, 34; 14:7, 14, 44; 15:29, 29, 32; Lk 1:18, 34, 74; 2:29; 3:8; 4:22; 5:12, 21; 6:8, 34, 42; 8:16; 9:12; 10:19; 11:15, 18; 12:4, 25, 33, 33; 13:7, 9, 18; 14:33; 16:13, 26, 29; 18:26, 42; 19:19; 20:44; 21:31; 22:8, 11, 48; 24:39; Jn 1:5, 22, 46; 2:20; 3:3, 4, 5, 6, 8, 12, 21; 4:12, 29; 5:19, 32, 40; 6:5, 27, 42, 52, 60; 7:3, 4, 6, 26; 8:46, 57; 9:11, 19, 21, 25, 41; 10:18, 21, 29; 11:9, 9, 49; 12:35; 14:5, 6, 13, 28; 15:5; 16:22, 23; 17:1, 24; 19:35; Ac 2:7, 12; 3:17, 19; 4:17; 6:4; 7:34, 40; 8:20, 21, 23, 31, 33; 9:12; 10:22, 47; 19:38, 39; 20:26, 35; 21:22; 22:5; 24:8, 11; 25:5, 5; 26:8, 28; Ro 1:11, 20; 2:20; 3:7, 20, 22, 27, 31; 5:3, 11; 6:1, 2, 15, 16; 7:4, 6, 13, 13; 8:8, 31, 31, 35, 38; 9:14; 10:14, 14, 14; 11:29, 34; 12:17; 13:6, 8, 13; 15:6, 24, 27; 16:2; 1Co 1:4, 13, 15, 29; 2:11, 11, 12, 14, 16, 16, 16; 3:11, 18; 5:1, 7; 7:5, 25, 32, 34, 37; 8:10; 9:16, 19, 20, 20, 21; 10:30; 11:16; 12:3, 21, 28, 28, 30; 14:5, 16, 16, 28, 32; 16:4, 6; 2Co 1:4, 5, 6, 6, 9, 12; 3:2, 5, 12, 14, 18; 4:7, 18; 5:12; 6:3, 14, 14, 15, 15, 16; 7:1, 10; 8:3, 11, 14, 14; 9:11; 11:14, 15, 21; 12:6; Gal 3:11, 15; 4:6; 5:14; 6:12, 13; Eph 1:18; 2:7, 9, 10; 3:12; 5:5; Php 2:15, 19; 3:10, 10, 11; 4:7, 13; Col 1:16; 3:25; 4:13, 16; 1Th 2:3; 4:15; 5:10; 2Th 2:6, 14; 1Ti 1:16; 2:2, 5; 3:5; 5:16; 6:14, 16, 16; 2Ti 2:14, 15, 21; 3:14; 4:9, 21; Tit 3:12, 13; Phm 1:6; Heb 2:3; 4:3, 13; 5:4; 6:18, 18; 9:10, 14, 15, 17, 22; 10:11, 19, 23; 11:3, 14; 13:6, 6, 19; Jas 1:20; 2:1, 3; 3:2, 3, 5, 5, 6, 6, 7, 8, 12; 4:11, 12; 5:20; 1Pe 1:21, 22; 2:2, 9, 24; 4:10; 2Pe 3:4, 17; 1Jn 2:3; 3:10, 17, 21; 4:17, 20, 20; 5:9, 14, 15, 20; 3Jn 12; Jude 12, 21; Rev 2:19; 3:7, 7, 8; 14:5; 22:14

CAN'T (114)

Ge 24:5, 39; 43:11; 44:26; Ex 6:30; Nu 11:14; 13:31; Jdg 14:13; 19:12; Ru 4:6; 1Sa 5:7; 17:39; 29:4, 8; 30:22; 2Sa 13:26; 20:6; Job 10:15; 22:13; Ps 40:12; 44:15; 55:5; 69:2; 78:19, 20; 139:18; 140:10; Pr 22:27; 26:13; Isa 3:7, 12; 29:11, 15; Jer 1:6; 2:25; 20:9; Am 8:5; Mt 5:20, 36; 7:4, 18, 18; 12:29; 16:3; 27:6, 42; Mk 2:19; 3:27; 4:13; 7:11, 18; 8:18, 18, 24; 9:17; 15:31; Lk 6:42, 43, 43; 11:7; 12:26, 56, 57; Jn 3:8, 8; 5:7, 10, 44; 6:44, 65; 7:4, 7, 41; 8:43; 13:36, 37; 16:12; Ac 4:16; 8:36; 17:25; Ro 2:4; 7:17, 18, 18; 8:38, 38, 38, 38, 38; 9:16; 1Co 2:14, 15; 6:2; 7:9, 33; 8:8; 10:13; 12:21; 15:15; 2Co 1:13; Gal 6:7; Eph 2:8; Col 1:16; 1Ti 3:15; Tit 2:8; Heb 11:40; Jas 1:8; 2:14, 18; 3:12; 4:2, 4; 1Jn 3:2, 9

CANNOT (221)

Ge 13:16; 19:19; 44:22, 30, 34; Ex 1:19; 19:23; Lev 5:7, 11; 12:8; 14:21, 32; 25:28, 35; 27:8, 29, 33; Nu 9:10; 23:20; Dt 28:27; Jos 2:19; 9:7, 19; Jdg 11:35; 12:6; 15:3; 21:18; Ru 4:6; 1Sa 2:30; 12:21; 2Sa 12:23; 14:14; 19:35; 24:24; 1Ki 8:27; 13:16; 18:12; 20:9; 1Ch 16:30; 21:24; 22:14; 2Ch 6:18; 24:20; 28:13; Ezr 10:13; Ne 6:3; Est 1:19; Job 3:24; 4:18; 7:11; 9:11, 32, 35; 12:14; 13:15; 15:15, 33; 19:6; 22:11, 14; 23:8, 9; 28:15, 17, 19, 21; 34:12, 30; 37:5, 21, 23; 41:28; Ps 5:4, 9; 31:2; 33:16, 17; 36:2; 38:13; 46:5; 49:7; 61:3; 69:5, 23; 77:12; 89:35; 93:1, 5; 96:10; 115:5, 6, 17; 135:16, 17; 139:12; Pr 4:16, 16; 15:7; 20:1; 21:30; 27:22; 30:21; 31:8; Ecc 1:15, 15; 2:23; 3:11; SS 8:7; Isa 1:14; 2:9; 29:12; 35:6; 38:18, 18; 44:10, 13, 18, 18, 20; 45:20; 46:2, 2, 7; 47:14; 48:7; 59:8; 62:1; Jer 1:18; 2:22; 4:19; 5:15, 22; 6:10, 20; 8:17; 10:5, 5; 14:17; 16:17; 20:11; 23:23; 25:28; 30:11; 31:37, 37; 33:22, 22; 46:6, 6, 15, 28; 50:6; 51:9; La 3:7, 44; Eze 3:5, 25; Da 5:15; 6:8, 8, 12; Hos 5:4; 14:3; Mic 7:18; Hab 1:13; Mt 6:24; 10:28; 13:15, 15, 15, 15, 15; 26:42; Lk 12:4; 14:26, 27; 16:13; Jn 6:53; 8:21, 22; 10:35; 12:35, 40, 40, 40; 13:33; 14:17; 15:4, 4; Ac 4:20; 15:1; 24:13; 28:27, 27, 27, 27, 27; Ro 8:26; 11:10; 15:1; 1Co 10:21, 21; 11:17; 15:50; 2Co 3:14; 12:4; 13:5; Gal 5:2; 1Ti 3:2, 5; 6:7; 2Ti 2:4, 9, 13; Tit 1:2; Heb 5:12; 7:16; 9:5; 11:1; 12:28; 1Jn 5:18

COME (1275)

Ge 6:20; 8:12; 11:3, 7; 15:14; 16:8; 19:2, 32; 22:5; 24:8, 31, 33, 38, 39, 41; 26:27; 27:21, 26; 31:14, 44; 34:23, 30; 37:10, 14, 20; 38:14; 40:19; 41:20, 36; 42:4, 7, 9, 10, 12, 21, 34; 43:4, 5, 10; 45:4, 9, 11, 16, 18; 46:31; 47:4; 49:1, 2; 50:24; Ex 2:17; 3:5, 8; 8:3, 7; 9:19; 11:8; 12:48; 14:25; 16:9; 17:6; 18:6, 15; 19:9, 11, 21, 22, 23, 24; 20:20, 24; 22:9; 23:4, 11, 24; 24:1, 2, 2, 12, 14; 32:1, 26; 33:9; 34:2, 3, 30, 31; 35:10; Lev 5:3; 7:36; 10:4; 21:18, 23; 23:3; 26:32; 27:14; Nu 4:15; 10:4, 29, 32; 11:17; 15:21, 38; 16:12, 14, 16; 18:22; 20:10, 24; 21:27; 22:5, 6, 11, 11, 14, 17, 20, 32, 37, 38; 23:7, 7, 7, 13, 27; 24:24; 34:2; 35:8; Dt 4:30; 5:27; 13:2, 7; 18:6; 20:2; 28:15, 29; 29:20, 22, 22; 31:14, 17, 17, 21, 29, 29; Jos 2:2, 3; 3:4, 9; 4:16; 7:14, 14, 14; 8:5; 9:6, 8; 10:4, 6, 6, 24; 20:5; 23:14; Jdg 1:34; 3:25; 4:18, 18, 22; 5:23; 6:18; 7:17, 24; 9:14, 15, 15, 20, 20, 29, 31, 32, 33; 11:6, 7, 9; 12:2, 3; 13:8, 12; 15:10, 10, 12; 16:9, 12, 14, 18, 20; 18:19; 19:3; 21:5, 21, 22; Ru 2:12, 14, 21; 4:1; 1Sa 1:14; 2:15, 34; 4:7, 16; 6:21; 7:5; 10:6; 11:3, 10, 14; 13:8; 14:1, 10, 12, 12, 38; 16:2, 4, 5, 5; 17:23, 43, 44, 45, 45; 20:11, 20; 22:13; 23:10, 11, 11, 20, 23; 24:13; 25:8, 11; 26:20, 21, 22; 27:11; 30:13; 2Sa 1:3, 7, 9; 3:13; 9:7; 10:3, 11, 11; 13:5, 6, 11, 23, 24, 25, 26; 14:15, 24, 29, 29; 15:18, 22; 16:23; 18:29; 19:10, 20, 25, 27, 33; 20:1, 11, 16; 21:1; 22:46; 24:21, 21; 1Ki 1:14, 42; 2:13, 13, 30; 7:13; 8:41, 43; 12:5; 13:2, 7, 15, 32; 14:5, 6; 17:18; 18:16, 30; 20:18; 21:20; 2Ki 1:9, 10, 11, 12; 4:1, 22; 5:11; 6:3, 19; 7:9; 8:7; 9:19, 22, 30, 31; 10:16, 19; 11:4; 14:8; 16:7; 18:31; 1Ch 4:22; 10:4; 12:17, 17; 13:2; 16:29; 19:3, 12; 29:12, 14, 16; 2Ch 2:1; 6:32, 33; 10:5; 14:11; 19:10; 20:9, 11; 21:15, 19; 23:2, 3, 4; 25:17; 29:31; 30:1, 5, 8; 31:9; 32:4, 26; 34:24; 35:6; Ezr 2:70; 8:15; 10:7, 8, 14; Ne 2:10; 4:8, 12; 6:3, 7; 9:32; 12:27; Est 1:12; 4:11; 5:4, 5, 8; Job 1:7; 2:2; 3:21, 25; 7:9; 17:10; 19:16; 30:10, 14, 27; 31:37; 34:23; 36:8; 38:11, 16, 19, 28; Ps 7:1; 14:7; 16:1; 18:45; 22:13, 19; 26:6; 27:2, 5, 8; 31:1, 11, 19; 32:10; 34:3, 11; 35:2; 38:8, 22; 40:5, 7, 13; 42:2; 44:26; 46:2, 8; 47:1; 49:5, 8; 53:6; 54:1; 56:6; 59:1, 6, 10, 14; 62:7; 63:9; 65:2; 66:5, 6, 13, 16; 68:24, 31; 69:18; 70:1; 71:18; 80:2, 14; 83:4; 86:9; 90:13; 91:10; 94:15; 95:1, 2, 6; 96:8; 100:2; 101:2; 102:22; 106:4; 111:10; 112:4; 119:82, 132, 176; 121:1, 8; 122:4; 142:4; 143:7, 8; 144:5; 146:4; Pr 1:11, 14, 23, 24; 2:6; 3:28; 5:14; 7:18; 9:3, 4, 5, 16; 10:13, 24; 13:5, 12, 19; 26:26; 28:27; 30:5; Ecc 1:4; 2:1, 12, 16; 4:14; 5:11, 15, 16; 7:14; 9:12; 11:3, 8; SS 1:4; 2:10, 12, 13, 17; 3:1; 4:8, 8, 16, 16; 6:13, 13; 7:11; 8:14; Isa 1:18, 28; 2:3, 3, 4, 5; 5:26; 7:2, 17, 19; 12:2; 13:20, 21; 14:1, 2, 8, 24; 15:3; 16:12; 18:7; 21:9, 12; 22:25; 23:10, 15; 26:5, 9; 27:12; 28:17, 19, 21, 21; 29:6; 30:13, 13, 18; 31:4, 6, 7; 34:1, 14, 15, 16; 36:16; 41:1, 21, 25; 42:9, 13; 43:7, 19; 45:14, 20, 24; 46:10, 11; 47:1, 9, 9; 48:14, 16; 49:9, 17, 18; 50:2; 52:6; 54:14, 17; 55:1, 1, 3, 5, 10; 56:9, 9, 9, 12; 57:1, 3; 58:2, 8, 8; 59:19, 20; 60:3, 3, 5, 10, 14, 20; 61:2; 62:8; 63:4; 64:1; 65:5; 66:8, 8, 17, 23; Jer 1:15; 2:9, 24; 3:1, 7, 12, 17, 22, 22; 4:1, 2, 5; 5:12; 7:10; 8:14; 9:6, 17, 19; 11:15; 13:18; 14:13, 15; 15:8; 16:19; 17:15, 26; 18:18, 22; 20:8; 23:17, 20; 26:2; 28:6, 9; 29:10, 28; 30:21, 24; 31:2, 6, 6, 12, 16, 17, 21, 27, 31; 32:7, 29; 33:6, 14, 20; 35:13; 36:14, 17; 37:4, 8, 17; 40:4, 4, 10, 15; 41:5, 6; 44:7; 46:9, 9, 16, 22; 47:4; 48:2, 18, 44; 49:2, 19, 22; 50:26, 27, 29, 44; 51:2, 2, 10, 13, 31, 44, 48, 56, 60; La 1:15; 2:11; 3:1; 4:17; Eze 7:6, 7, 12; 8:6, 13; 12:23, 27; 13:16; 14:4, 7, 17, 22; 16:33; 19:14; 20:3, 31; 21:24, 29; 22:4; 23:16, 23, 23, 24; 24:14, 26; 27:29, 36; 28:19, 23; 29:21; 30:4, 9, 18; 32:11, 21; 33:28, 30, 31; 34:26; 35:6; 36:9; 37:6, 9; 38:10, 15; 39:8, 17, 26; 44:3, 29; 45:6; 46:9; 47:14; 48:19; Da 3:2, 26, 26; 9:13, 22, 26; 10:12, 14, 20; 11:15, 17, 21, 27, 35; 12:7; Hos 1:10; 3:5; 5:6; 6:1; 9:7; 10:12; 11:9, 11; 12:6; Joel 1:3, 3; 2:12, 23; 3:11, 13; Am 4:2; 5:3, 4, 5, 6; 9:13; Ob 17; Mic 1:11; 2:6, 8; 3:6, 11; 4:2, 2, 3, 8; 5:2; 6:14; 7:12, 14, 17, 17; Hab 1:2, 9; 2:14, 16; Zep 1:7, 10, 10; 3:10; Hag 1:2; 2:7; Zec 1:21; 2:6, 7; 3:8; 6:15; 8:22; 9:12; 10:4, 8, 9; 12:9; 14:5, 17, 21; Mal 3:1; 4:6; Mt 2:2, 6, 7, 8; 4:19, 21; 5:17, 17, 24, 25; 6:10; 7:15, 27; 8:7, 8, 9, 9, 11; 9:9, 13, 18; 10:35; 11:14, 28; 12:32; 13:32, 49; 14:2, 28, 29; 15:18, 19; 16:27; 17:12; 19:14, 21; 21:25, 38; 22:3; 24:5, 6, 8, 14, 15, 44; 25:6, 34; 26:18, 45, 50, 55; 27:40, 42, 49, 55; 28:6; Mk 1:15, 17, 24, 25, 34; 2:14, 17; 3:3, 31; 4:32; 5:8, 23; 6:14, 16; 7:14, 19, 21, 23; 8:3, 34; 9:13, 25; 10:14, 21, 30, 49, 49; 11:30; 12:9; 13:6, 7, 8, 14; 14:11, 41, 48; 15:30, 32, 36, 41, 43; Lk 1:20, 21, 22, 35, 38; 2:15, 25, 38; 3:15; 4:19, 21, 34, 35; 5:27, 32; 6:8, 18, 21, 37; 7:3, 4, 7, 8, 8, 36; 8:29, 41; 9:7, 37, 59; 10:40; 11:2; 12:19, 38, 40, 49, 51, 51; 13:14, 19, 29; 14:7, 10, 17, 20, 23; 15:32; 16:5, 21, 28; 17:20; 18:16, 22, 30, 31; 19:5, 9, 10; 20:4, 16, 35; 21:8, 8, 9, 30, 35; 22:18, 37, 37, 52; 23:42, 51; 24:21, 44; Jn 1:9, 39, 43, 46, 46; 2:4, 9; 3:13, 21, 31, 31; 4:15, 25, 29, 47, 47, 49; 5:40, 43; 6:17, 22, 37, 38, 44, 65; 7:8, 28, 29, 30, 34, 36, 37, 38, 41; 8:20, 21, 22, 42; 9:39, 39; 10:3, 9, 41; 11:15, 19, 27, 34, 43, 48, 56; 12:16, 20, 23, 26, 31, 46, 47; 13:1, 3, 18, 31, 33, 37; 14:3, 6, 18, 23, 28, 31; 15:19, 22, 26; 16:7, 7, 11, 25; 17:1; 19:39; 21:3, 12; Ac 1:8; 3:20; 7:3, 7, 14, 34; 8:16, 31; 9:38; 10:6, 19, 21, 28, 33; 13:15, 32; 14:15, 23; 16:9, 13, 15, 17, 18, 37; 17:19; 18:21; 19:4, 13; 20:17, 29; 21:22; 24:25; 28:6, 20, 20; Ro 1:10, 15; 2:5, 16; 5:14; 8:30; 11:26, 31; 15:12, 25, 28, 29, 32; 1Co 3:13; 4:19, 21, 21; 7:5, 28; 10:13; 11:8, 20; 14:6, 23, 24; 15:24, 34, 54; 16:3, 7, 12, 17, 22; 2Co 2:3; 3:5; 4:18; 6:17; 10:2; 12:20, 21; 13:10, 10; Gal 2:4; 3:25; Eph 1:21; 2:18; 3:12; 4:13; Php 1:27; 2:24; Col 2:8; 3:6; 1Th 2:17, 18; 3:4, 11; 4:16; 5:2; 2Th 1:7; 2:3, 9; 1Ti 3:15; 4:1; 2Ti 2:26; 4:9, 11, 13; Phm 1:6; Heb 4:16; 6:5, 9, 11; 7:15; 8:8; 9:11, 28; 10:1, 7, 9, 37; 11:3, 6; 12:18, 22, 23, 23, 23, 24; 13:7, 14, 19; Jas 3:10; 1Pe 1:13, 21, 23; 2:4; 4:14, 17; 2Pe 1:2; 2:22; 3:4, 10; 1Jn 2:18, 20; 3:21; 4:3; 5:20; 2Jn 3; 3Jn 10; Rev 1:4, 8; 2:5, 16, 25; 3:3, 9, 10, 20; 4:1, 6:1, 3, 5, 7, 17; 7:13; 11:9, 12, 18; 12:12, 12; 13:11; 14:7, 15; 15:4; 16:15; 17:1, 1, 8, 10; 18:1, 4; 19:7, 9, 17, 18; 20:1, 5; 21:9, 24; 22:17, 17, 17, 17, 20

COMES (219)

Ge 24:43; 29:6; 37:19; 42:15; 44:29; 50:25; Lev 15:17; 16:17; 23:5; 25:22; Nu 3:10; 6:4; 11:23; 17:13; 18:7; 36:4; Dt 2:8; 8:3; 13:6; 19:16; 22:2; Jdg 4:20; 5:29; 13:17; 16:2; 1Sa 8:18; 9:6; 17:25, 34; 2Sa 13:5; 17:9; 18:26, 27; 1Ki 18:12; 2Ki 4:10; 10:19; 2Ch 13:9; 19:6, 10; Job 3:26; 5:3, 21; 8:13; 9:11; 11:10; 27:9; 28:5; 32:7; 37:4, 9, 22; Ps 3:8; 17:1; 25:3; 30:5; 59:7; 62:1; 68:27; 89:18, 41; 118:26; 121:2; Pr 3:25; 11:2; 14:4, 6; 16:23; 29:26; 30:4; Ecc 9:3; SS 2:8, 17; 4:6; Isa 5:22; 10:30; 22:25; 26:18; 29:8; 35:5; 40:10; 54:15; 56:10; 62:11; 63:1; Jer 2:28; 5:31; 11:23; 14:22; 23:12; 43:11; 48:20, 45; Eze 11:5; 21:7, 19; 24:6, 24; 46:17; 48:4, 26; Da 2:39; 9:25; Hos 5:9, 15; Joel 1:15; Am 3:6; 4:2; Jnh 2:9; Mic 1:3; Na 1:7; 3:17; Zep 1:14; Mal 3:2; Mt 7:25; 10:27; 13:19; 17:10; 21:9, 38; 23:39; 24:27, 39; 25:31; Mk 4:15, 29; 7:19; 9:11; 11:9; 12:7; Lk 6:47; 8:12; 12:38, 54; 13:35; 15:30; 17:7; 19:38; 20:14; 21:24; 22:16; 24:49; Jn 1:13, 47; 3:8; 4:22, 25, 34; 5:44; 6:33, 35, 45; 7:27, 27, 27, 52; 9:4; 12:13; 16:8, 13; Ac 19:25; Ro 4:13; 10:8, 17; 11:25, 36; 1Co 4:5; 7:10; 11:12, 26; 13:10; 14:20; 15:23, 46; 16:10; 2Co 1:14; Gal 1:8; Eph 3:19; 5:6; 6:15; Php 1:6; 2:19; Col 2:23; 3:15; 4:10; 1Th 2:19; 3:13; 4:14; 5:4, 23; 2Th 1:10; 2:6; 3:5; 1Ti 1:5, 11; 2Ti 3:15; Phm 1:12; Heb 7:25; 9:27; 13:9, 23; Jas 1:2, 14, 17; 2:2, 2; 3:17; 1Pe 1:23; 2:12; 3:4; 5:4; 1Jn 3:2; 4:1, 7; 5:9; 2Jn 10; Rev 1:7; 3:12; 7:10; 11:7

COMING (259)

Ge 24:11, 13, 45, 63; 30:16; 32:5, 11, 18; 33:1; 34:7; 37:18, 25; 49:10; Ex 32:12; Nu 22:16; Dt 24:9; 28:6, 19; Jdg 1:24; 5:5, 28; 6:5; 9:36, 37, 37, 43; 11:31; Ru 1:8; 4:11; 1Sa 3:13; 4:5; 5:10; 9:11, 14; 10:3, 5, 10; 14:11; 22:2; 25:20; 28:13; 2Sa 2:20; 5:17; 10:3; 13:34, 34, 35; 15:19; 20:8; 24:20; 1Ki 18:7, 41; 20:17; 2Ki 4:25; 9:17, 17, 18; 10:15; 20:17; 1Ch 14:8; 16:33; 19:3; 2Ch 7:3; 20:16; Ne 6:10; Job 29:8; Ps 27:8; 37:13; 96:13, 13; 98:9; 114:3; 119:150; Pr 14:8; SS 8:5; Isa 2:11; 7:5; 10:28; 13:9; 14:31; 21:12; 26:21; 27:6; 30:27; 32:1; 35:4, 4; 39:6; 40:9, 10; 41:7; 51:5; 54:17; 56:1; 58:2; 60:4, 4; 62:11; 64:2; 66:15; Jer 4:11, 16; 6:1; 7:32; 8:16; 9:25; 10:15; 16:14; 19:6; 23:5; 30:3, 16, 31:38; 44:12; 46:18; 47:2; 48:12, 16; 51:18, 46, 47, 52; Eze 1:4; 21:7; 33:3, 6; 36:8; 43:2; Da 2:29; 4:13, 23; 7:13; Hos 2:16; 6:3; Am 3:11; 6:3; 7:1; 8:11; Mic 1:3; 4:6; 6:9; 7:4; Na 1:15; Hab 2:6; 3:16; Zep 3:8; Zec 1:21; 2:3, 10; 6:1; 9:9; 14:1; Mal 3:1; 4:1; Mt 3:5, 7, 7, 11, 14; 4:24; 10:26; 16:28; 17:11; 20:30; 21:5, 38; 24:30, 42, 43; 25:6; 26:64; 27:64; Mk 1:3, 7; 6:31; 9:12; 11:10; 13:34; 14:62; 15:21; Lk 1:17; 3:4, 7, 16; 7:6, 12; 9:2, 60; 12:2, 39; 15:20; 17:22; 21:6, 26; 22:24, 69; 23:26, 29; Jn 1:15, 23, 29, 30; 3:23, 26; 4:21, 23, 54; 5:25, 28; 8:56; 10:12; 11:20; 12:15; 16:2, 8, 32; 17:11, 13; Ac 7:52; 9:12; 10:3; 11:28; 13:25; 16:7; 21:32; 28:15; Ro 13:11; 16:1; 1Co 16:5; 2Co 12:14; 13:1; Gal 3:19, 23; Php 4:5; 1Th 1:10, 10; 2Th 2:1, 8; 2Ti 1:10; 4:3; Phm 1:17; Heb 10:25, 37; Jas 5:8, 9; 1Pe 4:7; 2Pe 1:16; 1Jn 2:18; Jude 14; Rev 3:11; 7:2, 14; 9:12; 10:1; 11:14; 21:2; 22:7, 12, 20

COULD (449)

Ge 3:13; 8:8; 13:6; 16:2; 17:17, 17; 18:12; 20:17; 24:46; 26:10; 31:5, 8, 29; 34:28; 39:9; 41:8, 24, 38, 49; 42:24; 43:7, 10; 44:18; 45:1, 2; 48:10; 50:20; Ex 2:3; 4:23; 5:19; 9:15, 15; 10:23; 13:21; 14:10, 30; 16:10; 29:46; 32:12; 36:22; 39:4; 40:30, 38; Nu 9:6; 22:26, 41; 24:13; Dt 2:14, 21, 22, 30; 4:36, 36, 38, 42; 6:23; 9:16; 19:5; 22:20; 32:29, 30; Jos 5:1; 6:20; 14:11; 15:63; 17:12; 19:50; 20:9, 9; 21:44; 22:16; Jdg 5:8; 14:3; 20:16; Ru 1:11; 2:7, 14; 1Sa 2:15; 14:30; 19:4; 20:28, 29; 24:18; 30:4; 2Sa 1:10; 2:18; 5:6; 6:13; 11:11; 13:2, 8, 13; 15:4; 16:22; 17:14; 18:33; 19:18, 28; 22:16, 39; 1Ki 1:1; 3:1; 4:33, 33; 5:3; 7:26, 38, 47; 8:5, 8, 11; 9:19; 10:20, 29, 29; 13:33; 14:4; 2Ki 3:21; 6:30; 8:13; 13:4; 19:18, 24; 23:10; 1Ch 12:2, 14, 14; 13:4; 22:3; 28:2; 29:2, 14; 2Ch 1:17, 17; 4:5, 18; 5:6, 9, 14; 7:2, 7, 7; 8:6; 9:19; 11:16; 13:7; 20:24, 25; 22:11; 25:15; 28:24; 30:3; 31:4; 35:12, 13; 36:16; Ezr 2:59, 63, 69; 3:2, 13; 5:10; Ne 4:10, 22; 6:9; 7:61, 65; 8:3; 9:11, 12, 24; 12:43; 13:19, 24, 26, 27; Est 1:8; 6:1; 7:4; 9:2; Job 4:2; 6:2; 9:15, 33, 34, 35; 13:5, 19; 16:4, 4; 19:23, 23; 31:14, 14, 21; 34:17; 35:7; 36:19; 40:4; 41:14; Ps 18:15, 38; 37:36; 55:12, 12; 73:7; 76:5; 78:25, 44, 64; 105:22; 107:7; 130:3; 139:11; Ecc 2:8, 9; 4:14; 6:2; 10:8; SS 8:1; Isa 5:4; 10:19; 28:12; 37:19, 25; 38:15; 48:5; 54:1; 55:8; 66:1, 1; Jer 2:21, 33; 9:2; 11:5; 24:2; 37:4; 44:22; 48:9; 49:4; 51:9; La 4:12, 17, 20; Eze 1:8, 17; 8:7; 10:5, 11; 12:2, 2; 14:18, 20; 16:15, 16; 17:8, 14; 19:9; 20:11; 33:5; 40:2, 5; 47:2; Da 2:16; 3:26; 4:6, 7; 5:8; 6:17; 7:11; 8:4, 7, 27; Hos 5:13; 10:3, 13; Am 2:10; Jnh 1:3; 4:2; Mic 1:14; 6:5; Zec 3:5; 7:12; 14:7; Mal 1:10; Mt 8:28; 9:30, 33; 12:10, 22, 23, 34; 13:17; 15:20, 31; 16:11; 17:20; 18:30; 19:7, 13; 20:34; 22:10, 15, 46; 25:27; 26:9, 53, 59, 60; 27:48; Mk 5:3, 29; 7:11, 35; 8:25; 9:3; 10:13, 52; 11:13; 12:13; 14:5, 8, 55; 15:36, 45; Lk 1:29, 64; 7:42; 8:43; 9:45; 10:24; 11:54; 13:13; 14:14; 17:6; 18:15, 43; 19:4, 23, 48; 20:20; 22:6; 24:4; Jn 1:48; 7:27; 8:6; 9:3, 15, 16; 11:55, 57; 13:22; 15:24; 19:20, 31; 21:25; Ac 2:24; 3:2; 4:13; 5:4, 9; 7:49, 49; 9:24; 10:17, 46; 11:29; 13:39; 14:18; 15:7; 16:10; 17:5; 22:13; 25:21; 26:9, 32; 27:3, 13,

19, 39, 43; 28:20, 20; Ro 5:20; 8:3; 11:20, 32, 35; 1Co 2:16; 7:7; 12:17; 13:1, 2, 3; 16:6; 2Co 1:16; 3:7; 5:21; 7:11, 12; 8:3, 9; 11:8; Gal 1:16; 2:19, 21; 3:17, 18, 21, 21, 23; 4:5, 20, 27; Php 3:4, 4; 1Th 3:1, 5; 1Ti 1:13, 16; 2Ti 3:5; Tit 1:5; Phm 1:8, 15, 15; Heb 2:14, 14, 15, 17, 17; 5:7; 6:17; 7:11; 9:13; 10:2; 1Pe 1:10; 4:6; 3Jn 4; Rev 1:1; 5:4; 11:19; 13:15, 17; 14:3; 15:8; 16:12; 17:6; 20:3; 21:22

COULDN'T (72)

Ge 19:11; 31:34; 32:25; 34:14; 37:4; 38:20, 22; 43:3; 45:26; Ex 7:21, 24; 14:20; 15:23; Jdg 16:16; 1Sa 9:4; 10:14; 19:14; 2Sa 1:10; 11:13; 1Ki 13:4; 2Ki 7:2, 19; 10:4; Ne 2:14; Job 4:16; SS 5:6; La 4:18; Eze 20:14; 36:20; Da 2:1; 6:4, 18; Jnh 1:13; Mt 9:32; 17:16, 19; 18:25; 26:40, 43; Mk 1:45; 2:4; 3:20; 6:5; 7:24; 9:18, 28; 14:37, 40, 15:44; Lk 1:22; 2:45; 5:19; 8:19; 9:40; 11:14; 14:20; 24:3; Jn 9:33; 11:37; 12:39; 21:4, 6; Ac 9:22; 12:19; 21:14, 34; 25:7; 27:15; 1Co 3:1, 2; 2Co 2:13; Php 2:30

DID (889)

Ge 3:1; 4:5; 6:22; 7:5; 8:12; 9:23; 15:10; 18:13, 13, 15; 20:6; 21:1; 24:46; 26:9, 29; 27:23; 31:23, 27, 36, 39; 34:5; 38:29; 39:3, 12; 40:15; 42:21, 35; 43:6, 6, 17; 44:2; 45:5, 5, 21; 50:12, 15, 17; Ex 2:18, 20; 4:6, 7; 5:8, 13, 17, 22; 6:3; 7:6, 11, 20; 8:6, 13, 17, 24, 31; 9:6; 10:20; 11:10; 12:27, 28, 35; 13:8, 17, 22; 14:11, 11; 16:34; 17:3, 3, 6, 10; 19:4; 21:24, 24; 24:11; 28:15; 32:21, 21; 33:3; 40:15; Lev 8:36; 10:7; 13:55; 16:15; Nu 1:47, 54; 2:34; 5:4; 8:3; 9:22, 23; 11:11, 20; 13:3; 15:34; 16:40, 47; 17:11; 20:4, 5, 9, 12, 27; 21:34; 22:32, 34, 37; 23:17, 30; 24:1, 1; 26:11; 27:13, 22; 31:31; 32:8; 36:10; Dt 1:32; 2:13, 29; 4:3, 15, 33, 34; 5:3, 5, 29; 6:10, 11, 11, 11, 16, 22; 7:7, 18, 22; 8:3, 16, 17; 9:18; 11:4, 6; 16:3; 18:22; 21:7, 7; 22:3, 24; 23:4; 24:9; 25:17; 29:2, 5; 32:27; 34:9; Jos 2:10; 4:8, 23, 24; 5:15; 7:7; 8:5, 6, 17, 18; 9:9, 10, 14, 18, 22, 22, 24, 26; 10:13, 24; 11:13, 15; 13:14; 16:10; 17:13; 18:9; 24:7, 13, 13; Jdg 1:7, 28, 32; 2:10, 11, 17, 22, 22, 23; 3:2, 7, 12; 4:1; 5:16, 17, 18, 23, 31; 6:1, 20, 27, 27, 29, 40; 7:24; 8:20, 35; 10:6, 11; 11:15, 25, 25; 13:1, 19, 21; 14:6, 15; 15:6, 7, 10, 11; 17:6; 18:8; 20:32, 39; 21:22, 23, 25; Ru 2:19, 19; 1Sa 1:2, 22; 3:5, 7, 17; 4:3, 20; 10:11, 15; 14:1, 48; 15:19, 20, 24; 16:4; 18:5, 10, 14; 22:13, 13; 24:7; 25:21; 27:10; 28:18; 2Sa 1:22; 2:29; 3:36; 4:12; 5:25; 7:10; 11:20; 12:12; 14:19, 20, 24, 31; 18:13; 19:19, 43; 20:6, 10; 22:38; 23:10, 17, 20; 1Ki 1:10, 11, 19; 2:44; 3:13, 14; 7:47; 9:4, 8, 22; 10:15; 11:6, 10, 25, 33, 38, 38; 13:12, 33; 14:8, 22; 15:11, 26, 34; 16:11, 25, 30, 33; 17:5, 15; 18:34; 20:25, 34; 21:22, 25; 22:24, 43, 52; 2Ki 1:7, 16, 17; 2:3, 5, 17; 3:2; 4:5, 41; 6:6, 18, 20; 8:2, 14, 18; 9:4, 11; 10:20, 29, 31; 11:9; 12:2, 3; 13:2, 11, 15, 17; 14:3, 4, 6, 24; 15:3, 4, 9, 18, 20, 24, 28, 34, 35; 16:2, 5, 16; 17:2, 22, 25; 18:3, 7, 34, 36; 19:22, 22; 20:7, 13, 14, 15; 21:2, 6, 20; 22:2, 2; 23:5, 18, 24, 26, 32, 37; 24:9, 19; 1Ch 2:34; 11:19, 22; 14:16; 15:13; 16:21; 17:9; 21:6; 24:2; 27:23; 2Ch 1:11; 7:6, 7, 17; 8:9, 15; 9:14; 11:4; 12:12, 14; 14:2; 16:12; 17:3; 18:23; 20:7, 7, 10, 18, 32; 21:6, 13, 19; 22:4; 23:8, 8; 24:2, 5; 25:2, 4, 5; 26:4; 27:2, 2, 3; 28:1, 21; 29:2, 6, 22; 31:9, 21; 32:25, 26, 30; 33:2, 6, 22, 23; 34:2, 2, 6, 10, 32, 33; 35:12, 15, 18; 36:5, 8, 9, 12; Ezr 3:3; 9:9; 10:6; Ne 2:16; 3:3; 5:13, 15; 9:17, 17, 19, 20, 21, 21, 29, 31, 34, 35; 12:40, 45; 13:18; Est 1:18; 2:20; 4:17; 6:3; 9:5, 10, 16; Job 1:22; 3:12, 12; 10:18; 29:14; 30:25; 31:20; 32:6; 38:5; 39:20; 42:3, 9; Ps 18:37; 35:7, 7; 44:1, 3; 50:21; 66:16, 19, 20, 20; 78:4, 10, 12, 22, 37, 38, 50, 56, 67; 81:11; 83:9, 9, 11; 95:8, 8; 105:14; 114:6; 118:13; 124:6; 137:7; Ecc 2:10, 12; 9:6; 12:10; SS 3:1; Isa 5:4; 9:4; 10:9, 9, 9, 24, 26; 11:16; 20:2; 27:9; 28:21; 34:8; 36:19, 21; 37:23, 23; 39:2, 3, 4; 41:20; 43:12; 45:4, 10, 19, 19; 47:7; 48:5; 50:1; 53:3, 7; 57:16; 64:3; 65:12, 12; 66:4, 4; Jer 2:5, 6, 8, 21, 30, 36; 3:7; 7:12, 15; 10:11; 11:8, 21; 14:14, 14, 15:4; 16:11; 17:23; 18:3, 4; 20:17; 22:8, 15; 23:27, 32; 25:20; 26:19, 20, 29:31; 30:20; 31:19; 32:12; 34:5, 15; 36:8, 15, 17, 28; 40:14; 44:2, 17, 21; 48:27, 32; 51:35; 52:2; La 2:8, 14, 17; Eze 3:6, 19, 20; 9:7; 10:2; 12:7; 16:47, 50, 51, 51; 17:8; 20:8, 24, 30, 36; 23:8, 33, 44; 24:18; 27:9; 28:15; 36:31; 40:25; 41:6; 42:6; 43:22; 48:11, 11; Da 3:24; 4:28, 36; 6:12; 8:4, 12; 9:14; 11:24; 12:8; Hos 2:15; 9:9; 10:14; Am 2:9; 7:3; Ob 10; Jnh 1:7, 10; 2:10; 4:10; Mic 6:5; 7:14, 15; Hab 3:2; Zec 8:14; 9:7; 14:5; Mal 2:6; 3:4, 8; Mt 1:24; 2:4; 5:17, 38, 38; 7:23; 11:7, 21, 23; 12:3; 13:58; 14:31; 16:17; 19:7; 20:5; 21:6, 20, 23, 25, 32; 25:37, 39, 40, 44; 26:19, 54; Mk 2:25; 3:2; 6:2, 52; 8:19, 20; 10:3; 11:28, 30; Lk 1:22; 2:49; 4:23; 6:3; 7:24; 10:13; 11:48; 13:17; 19:14; 20:2, 4; 22:35, 35; 24:19; Jn 1:15, 30, 41; 2:23; 3:17; 4:2, 29, 39; 6:11, 13, 25, 32, 58; 8:16; 9:26, 26; 10:8; 11:6; 12:7, 37; 15:24; 18:9, 15, 34; 19:25; 21:6, 25; Ac 3:7, 17; 4:25, 25, 28; 5:31; 7:5, 15, 51; 8:6, 27, 32; 10:2, 39, 47; 11:30; 12:8; 13:37; 16:7, 15; 17:12; 19:2, 3; 22:3; 23:18; 24:12; Ro 1:24, 27; 3:25; 4:10, 19; 5:14, 14; 7:9, 13; 8:4, 7, 32; 9:25; 10:19, 19; 11:11, 21; 16:7; 1Co 1:2, 14; 2:4, 5; 3:5; 10:6, 7, 8, 9, 10, 22; 2Co 1:10; 2:3, 9; 5:18; 7:12; 8:3; 11:7, 9; 12:12, 17, 18; 13:2; Gal 1:13, 16, 17; 2:2, 3, 3; 3:2; 4:12, 14; Eph 2:12; 3:5, 8; 5:27; Php 2:6, 16; 4:15; 1Th 2:5; 3:4; 1Ti 1:13; 2Ti 1:3, 9; Tit 3:5, 6; Heb 1:13; 3:8, 15; 4:2, 11, 15; 5:5; 7:11, 20, 21, 27, 27; 8:9; 9:24, 25; 10:5, 8; 11:3, 4, 9, 10, 19, 31; 12:3, 18, 24, 25; Jas 2:21, 22; 1Pe 1:20, 23; 2:23, 23; 2Pe 2:4, 5; 3:4; 1Jn 2:6; 3:12; Jude 5, 6, 9; Rev 2:4, 5; 3:8; 9:4, 20, 21; 11:13; 13:13; 16:9; 19:20; 20:5

DIDN'T (251)

Ge 12:18; 21:26; 30:42; 31:22, 28, 32, 33, 35; 38:11, 22, 26; 39:6; 42:8, 22, 23; 44:8, 15; 47:22, 22; Ex 3:2; 9:6; 14:12; 16:20; 32:14; Lev 10:17; Nu 22:37, 37; 23:26; Dt 4:12; 8:4, 4; 10:10; 11:4, 5; Jos 2:4; 8:14; 22:20; Jdg 3:25; 6:13; 8:1; 11:20; 12:1; 13:6, 6, 16; 14:4, 6, 9; 16:20; 20:34; 21:22; 1Sa 2:27; 3:5, 6, 18; 5:12; 6:3; 7:13; 10:16; 13:8, 11; 14:26; 19:17; 20:26, 39; 21:8; 22:17; 23:13, 14; 24:11, 18; 25:19, 36; 27:9; 30:22; 2Sa 3:11; 11:10, 20; 14:32; 18:11, 29; 19:25; 20:10; 1Ki 1:13; 2:42; 10:7; 18:43; 22:18; 2Ki 2:18; 4:28; 18:22; 2Ch 9:6; 18:17; Job 3:11; 10:18; Ps 50:21; 69:4; 78:38; Pr 1:24; 5:13, 13; 23:35, 35; 24:12; Ecc 1:10; 7:23; SS 3:4; Isa 29:16; 36:7; Jer 2:34; La 3:36; Eze 13:22; 20:9; 23:19; 34:8; Da 3:24, 27; 8:5; Hos 10:3; Am 6:13; Jnh 3:10; 4:2; Mal 2:15; Mt 3:14; 9:36; 11:18; 14:9; 17:20; 18:13; 20:13; 21:25, 30, 32, 42; 24:39; 25:24, 24, 26, 26, 42, 42, 43, 43; 26:55; Mk 6:31, 52; 9:6, 32, 34; 11:31; 12:10; 14:40, 49, 59; 16:11, 12; Lk 1:20; 2:43, 44, 48, 50; 3:14; 5:5; 7:33, 44, 45; 9:36, 45; 11:40; 17:17; 18:34; 19:21, 23, 27; 20:5; 22:53; 24:11, 16, 32; Jn 1:3, 10, 31, 33; 2:24; 4:2, 38; 5:13; 6:32, 64; 7:5, 45; 8:10, 27, 48; 9:27; 10:6, 41; 11:40, 51; 12:16; 15:16; 16:4; 18:26, 28; 19:31, 33; 20:5, 14; Ac 4:21; 5:28; 7:25, 50, 52; 12:9; 13:27; 16:23; 19:32; 20:16, 27; 22:9; 23:5; 24:12; 27:39, 42, 43; 28:24; Ro 4:17; 11:20; 15:3; 1Co 1:17; 2:1; 9:16; 11:8; 13:1, 2, 3; 2Co 1:23; 2:4; 7:14; 11:9; 12:13; Gal 1:22; Php 4:10; 1Th 2:13; 2Th 3:9; 1Ti 6:7; Phm 1:14, 14; Heb 4:2, 3; 1Pe 1:14

DO (2229)

Ge 3:13; 4:6; 11:6; 13:9; 15:1; 18:5, 19, 19, 20, 25, 25, 25, 32; 19:7, 8, 9, 9, 12, 17, 22; 21:12, 12, 17, 22; 22:12; 24:31; 26:2, 3, 3, 5, 24, 24; 27:8, 13, 43; 28:1; 29:4, 5, 5, 15, 25; 30:28, 30, 31, 31, 42; 31:7, 16, 26, 43; 32:29; 34:23; 37:10, 30; 38:11, 18, 25; 39:9, 9; 40:7; 41:16, 25, 28, 38, 55; 42:18, 22; 43:11; 44:5, 7, 15, 34; 46:3; 47:29, 31; Ex 2:8, 14, 14; 3:5; 4:1, 2, 8, 9, 9, 12, 15, 19, 21, 28; 5:4, 7, 8, 17; 6:1, 30; 8:7, 10, 18, 25, 26; 9:30, 34; 10:8, 28; 11:9; 12:10; 15:26; 16:19, 29, 29; 17:4; 18:14, 23; 19:8, 12, 12, 21, 24, 24; 20:3, 4, 5, 7, 10, 13, 14, 15, 16, 17, 17, 25, 26; 22:21, 22, 23, 25, 27, 28, 29, 31; 23:1, 1, 2, 2, 2, 3, 5, 6, 9, 13, 21, 24, 25, 29, 32, 33, 33; 24:3, 3, 7; 30:9; 32:11, 21; 33:5, 13, 13, 17; 34:3, 7, 12, 15, 15; 35:3, 21; 36:5; 40:16; Lev 2:11; 4:27; 8:5, 33; 10:6, 6, 9; 11:10, 44; 13:36; 16:16, 29; 17:9, 16; 18:3, 7, 8, 9, 10, 11, 12, 13, 14, 15, 16, 17, 17, 18, 19, 20, 21, 22, 24, 26, 28, 30, 30; 19:4, 9, 9, 10, 10, 11, 11, 11, 12, 13, 16, 16, 17, 19, 19, 19, 26, 27, 29, 31, 33, 35; 20:18, 23, 23; 22:2, 20, 32; 23:14, 22, 22, 25, 28, 31; 25:4, 11, 11, 36, 37, 39; 26:1, 14; 27:27; Nu 1:49; 4:19; 5:15; 7:5; 8:7, 15; 11:11; 13:19, 19; 14:9, 28, 35, 42; 15:12, 20, 23, 34, 39; 16:3, 6, 15, 26, 28; 18:3, 32; 19:12, 12, 13, 20; 21:34, 34; 22:12, 17, 18, 20, 20; 23:26; 24:13, 14; 25:11; 27:21; 29:35; 30:2, 2; 31:23; 32:6, 6, 19, 24, 31; 33:56, 56; Dt 1:18, 30, 42; 2:9, 19; 3:2, 21, 22; 4:2, 9, 9, 16, 25; 5:7, 8, 9, 11, 14, 14, 17, 18, 19, 20, 21, 21; 6:16, 18; 7:3, 16, 16, 21, 25, 25, 26; 8:11, 14, 15; 9:26; 11:16, 17; 12:4, 14, 14, 15, 18, 22, 25, 30, 30, 30, 31, 32; 13:3, 8, 8, 8; 14:7, 10, 21, 21, 21, 27, 27; 15:7, 9, 10, 13, 17, 18, 18, 19, 19, 23; 16:4; 17:9, 10, 11; 18:10, 14, 17; 19:13, 20; 20:1, 3, 3, 19, 19; 21:8, 14, 23; 22:3, 4, 5, 6, 9, 9, 10, 11, 26; 23:7, 15, 16, 18, 19, 20, 23, 24; 24:10, 12, 19, 21; 25:4; 26:19; 27:6; 28:8, 9, 12, 15, 20, 29, 32, 49, 58; 29:9; 30:9, 16; 31:6, 8, 13, 13; Jos 1:7, 7, 9, 16; 3:5; 4:6, 21; 5:14, 14; 6:10, 10, 18; 8:1; 9:7, 7, 8, 25; 10:8, 25; 11:6; 15:18; 22:19, 22, 24; 23:6, 7, 7; Jdg 1:14; 6:23; 7:17, 17; 8:21, 21; 9:33, 48; 11:7, 10, 36; 13:18; 15:3; 16:20; 18:14, 23, 24, 24; 19:20, 23, 24, 24, 30; 21:11; Ru 1:15; 2:2, 22; 3:3, 4, 5, 11; 4:6; 1Sa 1:26; 2:23, 29, 29, 35, 35; 3:5, 6, 8, 11, 18; 5:8; 6:2; 8:7, 9, 22; 10:7; 11:10; 12:14, 16; 14:7, 34, 36, 45; 15:19, 19; 16:2, 4, 7; 17:8, 36; 18:5, 22; 20:2, 4, 30; 21:8, 12; 22:3, 10, 18; 23:9; 24:4, 9, 12, 18; 26:25; 27:1; 28:2, 6, 7, 11, 13, 15, 22; 30:13, 13, 24; 31:4; 2Sa 1:5; 3:11, 24, 38; 5:23, 23; 6:20; 7:3, 19, 25; 9:11; 10:3; 12:5, 12, 18; 13:5, 12, 12, 28; 14:7, 13, 13; 15:15, 26; 16:4, 4, 10, 11, 11, 20; 18:4, 12; 19:13, 22, 27, 38, 41, 43; 20:1, 19; 21:3, 4, 4, 4, 6; 24:3, 3, 12, 14, 19; 1Ki 1:16, 18, 21; 2:3, 4, 6, 17, 31, 38, 42; 3:5, 26, 27; 5:5, 8; 8:19, 23, 36, 43, 58; 9:1, 8; 11:12, 22, 38; 12:24; 13:9, 17; 14:8; 18:14, 25, 34, 34; 20:13, 14, 14; 21:29, 29; 22:3, 21, 21, 22; 2Ki 2:9; 3:10, 11; 4:2, 2, 13, 14, 14; 5:13; 6:9, 15, 22, 27; 8:12; 9:18, 19, 22, 25; 10:4, 5, 5; 11:5, 15; 16:2, 6; 17:26, 35, 38, 38, 41; 18:20, 25, 27; 19:6, 22, 27; 20:3, 6, 9, 11; 21:9, 16; 22:13; 25:24; 1Ch 4:10; 10:4; 13:4; 14:14, 14; 16:22, 22; 17:23; 19:3; 21:3, 3, 6, 10, 13, 17; 22:13; 28:10, 20; 2Ch 1:7; 2:4; 6:9, 14, 27, 33, 42; 7:11; 10:7; 11:4; 13:8, 12; 14:11; 18:20, 20, 21; 19:6, 10, 11; 20:12, 12, 15, 17; 23:4, 14; 24:5, 20; 25:7, 9; 28:1; 29:11; 30:7, 8; 32:14; 33:9; 34:16, 21; 35:3, 20, 21, 21; Ezr 4:2, 14, 22; 6:7, 7; 9:14; 10:5, 11, 12; Ne 4:2, 5, 5; 5:5, 12, 12; 6:11; 7:3; 9:32; 10:31; 13:14, 21; Est 3:11, 14; 4:16, 16; 5:3; 6:6, 10, 10; 8:17; 9:12, 12, 13; Job 1:8, 12; 2:3, 6; 5:17; 6:11, 11, 12, 25, 26, 30; 7:16; 9:11, 35; 10:3, 3, 4; 13:2, 5, 9, 24, 24; 14:12; 15:3, 3, 8, 9, 9; 16:5, 18; 17:4; 18:3, 3; 21:15, 16; 22:17, 18, 28; 23:9, 13, 14; 24:6; 26:8; 27:8; 28:12, 20; 29:25; 30:13; 31:3, 4, 33; 32:9, 22; 33:14, 20, 24; 34:10, 12, 21, 25; 35:2, 6, 12, 15; 36:20, 23; 37:12, 15, 16, 18; 38:5, 17, 18, 20, 33; 39:1, 2, 11; 40:2, 2; 41:29; 42:2; Ps 1:1, 3; 2:1, 1; 5:5, 8; 6:1, 8; 9:19; 10:1, 1, 5, 5, 12, 13, 14; 11:1, 2, 3, 7; 12:5; 14:4; 15:2, 5; 17:2; 22:1, 1, 2, 11, 19; 24:4; 25:2, 20; 26:4, 5, 11; 27:9, 9, 12; 28:3; 31:1; 32:9; 33:15; 34:12, 14, 15, 16; 35:12, 17, 21, 22; 36:3; 37:1, 3, 5, 8, 14, 27; 38:21, 21; 39:1, 7; 40:17; 44:6, 6, 23, 23, 24, 24; 51:11; 52:1, 7; 53:4; 54:5; 55:1, 19; 56:4, 11; 57:T; 58:T, 1, 1; 59:T; 60:12; 64:1, 2, 5, 10; 68:16; 70:5; 71:17, 18; 72:16; 73:28; 74:11; 75:T; 76:9; 79:6, 8; 83:9, 17; 84:11; 88:10, 14, 14; 89:31; 91:5; 92:5; 95:10; 97:11; 101:3; 103:21; 105:15, 15; 106:3; 108:13; 112:7; 118:6; 119:3, 36, 43, 51, 68, 116, 132, 155, 165, 168; 120:3; 125:3, 4, 5; 127:1; 132:10; 140:8, 8; 141:4, 9; 143:10; 147:20; Pr 2:15; 3:5, 6, 27, 29, 31; 4:7, 7, 10, 14, 14, 14, 23; 5:9; 6:4, 4, 18; 12:22; 14:17; 15:7; 16:14; 17:8; 19:19; 21:3, 7; 22:22, 26, 28, 29; 23:20; 24:15, 17, 19, 28; 25:16; 27:2; 28:21; 29:18; 30:3, 6, 10, 11, 18; 31:3; Ecc 1:3, 10; 2:2, 21, 22; 3:9, 10; 5:18, 20; 6:8, 8; 8:2, 5, 11, 13, 15, 17; 9:10, 10; 10:2, 2; 11:2, 9, 9, 9; 12:3, 14; SS 6:13; 8:8; Isa 1:3, 3, 5, 12, 13, 17; 5:5, 13, 19, 19; 6:9, 11, 12; 7:9; 8:9, 11, 12, 13, 16, 19; 10:3, 24; 11:7; 14:21, 29; 16:3, 12; 19:12; 20:6; 22:2, 4, 16; 25:1; 26:9, 10, 11, 11; 28:21, 26; 29:9, 14, 15; 32:8; 33:15; 34:16; 35:4; 36:5, 10, 12; 37:6, 23, 28; 38:3, 7, 19; 40:9, 16; 41:10, 13, 21, 23, 24; 42:16, 18; 43:1, 5, 12, 13, 18, 19, 19; 44:2, 2, 7, 8, 8, 28; 45:3, 5, 11, 11, 11, 19; 46:8, 9, 10, 11, 11; 48:5; 49:6; 50:5, 6, 7; 51:7, 18; 56:1, 2, 3, 4, 6; 57:4, 13, 18; 58:5, 7, 8, 13, 13; 59:6, 7, 8, 8; 60:8; 63:19, 19; 64:5; 65:12, 16; 66:4; Jer 1:11, 13, 17; 2:24, 25, 29, 31, 31; 4:3, 6, 22, 30, 30, 30; 5:10, 15, 21, 21, 22, 22, 24, 31; 6:8, 15; 7:4, 6, 8, 9, 11, 16, 17, 23, 27, 27; 8:5, 6, 7, 7, 12, 17; 9:7; 10:2, 2, 5, 5, 24, 25; 11:4, 6, 14, 15; 12:4, 5, 6; 13:1, 15, 23; 14:10, 11, 18, 19, 21, 21, 22; 15:19; 16:2, 5, 8, 8; 17:17, 22, 22, 24, 27; 18:6, 11, 14, 19; 19:12; 21:2, 12; 22:3, 3, 10; 23:5, 10, 16, 16, 23; 24:3; 25:6, 30; 26:9, 9, 14; 27:9, 13, 14, 16, 17; 29:6, 8, 8, 10, 32; 30:6, 6, 10, 10, 14, 15; 31:16, 36; 32:19, 20, 42; 33:9, 14, 15, 20; 35:7, 14; 37:9, 17, 17; 38:5, 5, 19; 39:16; 40:16; 41:18; 42:3, 5, 10, 11, 19, 20; 44:4, 17, 19, 21; 45:5; 46:27, 27; 48:10, 27, 44; 49:24; 50:15, 15, 29; 51:46, 50; La 1:8; 3:36, 57; 5:20; Eze 2:6, 6, 8; 3:11, 19; 8:6, 6; 9:6, 11; 12:4, 28; 13:18; 14:5, 16; 16:30, 37, 45; 17:9, 24; 18:2, 10, 11, 21, 23, 27; 20:7, 9, 30, 30; 21:13, 24; 22:14, 26; 23:24; 24:16, 17, 17, 18, 22, 24; 30:12; 32:10; 33:14, 15, 19, 25, 32; 35:10, 11; 36:27, 36; 43:26; 44:9, 19; 45:9, 20; 46:18, 20; Da 2:11, 43; 3:16; 4:27, 35, 35; 8:26; 9:12, 18, 19; 10:20, 21; 11:3, 24, 36; Hos 4:10, 12, 15; 6:4; 7:14; 9:1, 1, 5, 5, 9, 12; 10:3; 12:9; 14:3; Joel 3:4, 13; Am 3:10; 4:5; 5:14; 7:3, 5, 6, 8, 12; 8:2; 9:7, 12; Jnh 1:10, 11; 4:2; Mic 2:7; 3:4; 4:12; 6:8; 7:8, 15, 16; Na 1:12; Hab 1:2, 2, 5, 7; 2:19; Zep 1:6, 12; 2:3; 3:13; Hag 2:5, 14; Zec 1:4, 6, 21; 4:2, 4, 10; 5:2; 6:5; 7:10, 10; 8:6, 16, 17; Mal 2:13; 3:5, 6, 8, 10, 13, 15, 18; Mt 1:20; 3:15; 4:7; 5:19, 20, 21, 27, 33, 46, 47; 6:1, 2, 7, 16, 18; 7:9, 10, 12, 12; 8:9, 9; 9:12, 14, 28, 28; 11:26; 12:2, 12; 13:10, 13, 14, 29, 41, 51, 51; 14:2; 15:2, 3, 11, 12, 34; 16:13, 15, 26; 17:10, 25, 25; 18:7, 12, 19, 35; 19:16, 18, 18, 18, 18, 20; 20:15, 32, 32; 21:16, 21, 24, 28, 31, 40, 40; 22:42; 23:5; 24:2; 25:13, 26; 26:17, 50, 62, 65; 27:4, 17, 21, 22; Mk 2:8, 17, 18, 19; 3:4; 4:10, 12, 24, 40; 6:5, 14, 38; 7:3, 15; 8:5, 12, 27, 29, 36; 9:11, 18, 22, 23, 24, 50; 10:17, 18, 19, 19, 19, 19, 19, 35, 51, 51; 11:23, 29, 32; 12:9, 9, 35; 13:34, 35; 14:12, 60, 63; 15:12; 16:6; Lk 1:45; 3:10, 12, 14, 14; 4:12, 23; 5:22, 30, 31, 33, 34; 6:9, 11, 27, 31, 31, 32, 32, 33, 33, 33, 35, 46; 7:8, 8, 42; 8:10; 9:18, 20, 25, 40, 53; 10:21, 25, 26, 28, 37, 40; 11:8, 11, 12; 12:4, 26, 47, 51; 13:2, 25, 27, 33; 14:10, 27, 34; 15:29; 16:5, 7; 17:9; 18:18, 19, 20, 20, 20, 20, 41, 41; 20:13, 15, 15, 17; 22:9, 19, 23, 71; 23:25; 24:38, 39, 41; Jn 1:22, 25, 26, 38, 48, 50; 2:5, 18, 18, 20; 3:4, 9, 18, 21; 4:9, 35, 48; 5:19, 20, 30, 38, 38; 6:6, 28, 29, 30, 38, 38; 7:4, 17, 23, 31, 49, 49; 8:5, 11, 28, 29, 33, 40, 43, 44, 53, 55; 9:16, 17, 26, 27, 27, 31, 33, 35; 10:25, 36, 38, 41; 11:26, 47, 56; 12:28; 13:12, 15, 17, 24, 27; 14:11, 12, 13, 14, 17, 23, 24, 29, 31; 15:2, 5, 20, 24; 16:7, 31; 17:4, 14, 14, 25, 26; 20:30; 21:15, 16, 17, 18; Ac 1:1, 4; 2:37; 4:9, 16, 19; 5:4, 35; 7:51; 8:30; 9:6, 15; 10:35; 12:11; 13:22, 25, 39; 14:3; 15:29; 16:21, 28, 30; 19:11, 36; 21:37; 22:10, 10; 23:5, 21; 24:15; 26:9, 20, 27, 27, 28; 28:26; Ro 1:24, 28, 32, 32, 32; 2:1, 3, 3, 10, 12, 14, 21, 22, 22, 22; 3:17, 31; 4:21; 6:12, 12, 13, 13, 21, 22; 7:7, 15, 15, 15, 17, 18, 19, 19, 19, 20, 21, 21; 8:9, 12, 12; 9:1, 19; 11:2, 4, 8, 8, 20, 23, 24, 26; 12:2, 5, 6, 7, 8, 8, 17, 18, 20; 13:3, 3, 3, 4, 6, 13; 14:3, 4, 6, 10, 10, 21, 22, 23; 15:1, 2, 24, 27, 27, 30; 1Co 1:9; 2:6, 13; 3:7; 4:7, 16, 16, 17, 21; 5:1; 6:1, 4, 8, 9, 12, 12, 13, 19; 7:5, 7, 12, 25, 27, 27, 27, 28, 32, 33, 35; 8:8, 9, 12; 9:1, 5, 9, 9, 16, 16, 20, 21, 21, 23, 25, 25, 27; 10:22, 22, 23, 23, 25, 31, 31, 33, 33; 11:13, 22, 22, 22, 24, 25; 12:24, 28, 29; 14:15, 15, 36, 38; 15:1, 29, 58; 16:14; 2Co 2:1, 3, 10; 3:5, 15; 4:2, 2; 5:14; 6:4; 7:12; 8:8, 8, 15; 9:10; 10:13, 15; 11:7, 11, 15, 16, 21, 22, 29; 12:4, 5, 6, 13, 13, 19; 13:7, 7, 10; Gal 2:10; 4:8, 9, 10, 10, 12, 18, 20, 21, 30; 5:10, 11, 17; 6:4, 10; Eph 2:10; 4:12, 17, 30; 5:1, 7, 12, 17, 22; 6:1, 6, 8; Php 1:7, 17, 20; 2:13, 14, 30, 30; 4:5, 7, 13; Col 1:5, 9, 10; 2:20; 3:2, 5, 6, 7, 17, 21, 22, 23, 25; 1Th 4:1, 5; 5:15, 19, 20, 24; 2Th 2:9, 12, 17; 3:17; 1Ti 1:9, 10; 2:10, 12; 3:10, 11, 13; 4:7, 14; 5:10, 17, 18, 19, 22, 25; 6:18; 2Ti 2:4, 22, 26; 3:16, 17; 4:21; Tit 1:3; 2:5, 6, 7, 9, 15, 15; 3:1, 8, 9, 10, 12, 13, 14; Phm 1:6, 8, 14, 14, 20, 21, 24; Heb 2:4, 9; 3:10; 4:11, 15; 5:14; 6:10; 7:13; 10:7, 9, 25, 35, 36; 11:20, 23, 32; 12:2; 13:6, 7, 9, 16, 17, 17, 18; Jas 1:5, 8, 13, 13, 25; 2:11, 11, 11, 12, 16, 19, 22, 22, 24; 3:5, 13; 4:3, 5, 12, 13, 14, 15, 17, 17; 1Pe 1:8, 15, 17, 22; 2:8, 14, 14, 16, 18; 3:6, 6, 9, 11, 12, 12, 13, 16; 4:2, 4, 11; 2Pe 3:3, 16; 1Jn 2:1, 5, 15, 17, 19, 24, 29; 3:2, 7, 9, 22; 4:1, 6, 6; 5:18; 2Jn 7, 8; 3Jn 6, 10, 11, 11, 11, 13; Jude 10, 11, 19; Rev 2:6, 19; 3:1, 3, 8, 15; 7:13; 10:4; 11:2; 13:5, 10; 18:4, 6; 22:10, 11, 11

DOES (289)

Ge 4:15; Ex 12:26; 13:14; 20:19; 21:6, 8; Lev 4:13, 22; 11:4, 7, 12, 26; 13:4, 13, 23, 32; 16:28; 17:4; 18:29; 23:29, 30; 24:20; Nu 10:32; 14:18; 16:9; 24:23; 30:11; Dt 7:10; 8:18; 10:12; 14:8; 18:12, 22; 21:15, 17; 22:2, 15; 27:26; 32:4, 4; Jos 1:18; Jdg 21:18; 1Sa 12:17; 14:43; 17:47; 25:10; 26:20; 28:14; 2Sa 14:14; 1Ki 1:52; 2:9; 22:18; 2Ki 4:13; 1Ch 16:24; 28:7; 2Ch 18:17; 19:7; Ne 4:2; Est 1:15; Job 1:10; 4:6, 7; 5:6, 6, 9; 8:3, 3; 9:13; 13:11; 15:6; 16:6; 19:22; 21:9; 23:13; 24:12; 25:3; 26:14; 31:25; 33:13, 29; 35:12, 15; 36:5, 6; 37:4, 23; 38:19, 19, 28, 28; 39:22; Ps 7:12; 9:12; 14:1, 3; 25:8; 33:4; 49:8; 53:1, 3; 64:9; 66:5; 69:33; 72:3, 18; 73:11; 96:3; 103:2, 10; 111:3, 7; 115:3; 121:1; 135:6; 136:4; 145:13, 17; 147:10; Pr 5:6, 21; 12:28; 14:5; 15:11; 17:10; 31:27, 30; Ecc 2:2; 3:14; 6:3; 7:13; 10:11; Isa 8:11; 16:5; 26:10; 28:9, 9, 24, 25; 29:16; 40:14, 27; 45:7, 9, 9, 9; 55:2, 2; 57:6; Jer 2:32, 32; 3:6; 6:13; 8:6, 10; 11:3; 14:22; 15:18; 18:14; 22:15; 23:29; 26:16; 28:6, 6; 31:10; La 3:31, 33; Eze 15:2; 18:5, 6, 7, 9, 11, 15, 16, 16, 17, 19; 24:19; 46:12; Da 8:24; 9:14; Joel 2:26; Am 3:4, 4, 5, 5; Mic 4:9; Zep 3:2, 5; Hag 2:3; Mal 2:15, 17; Mt 3:10; 7:19; 9:11; 12:50; 13:54; 17:25; 18:7; 22:43; Mk 2:16; 3:35; 7:37; Lk 1:51; 3:9; 5:21; 7:49; 10:26; 12:6; 17:1, 18; Jn 2:4; 5:19, 19, 19, 20, 21; 6:28, 61; 7:7, 15, 36; 8:22, 37, 44; 13:10; 14:10; 16:17, 17, 18; Ac 25:16; 26:8; Ro 2:2, 11; 3:3, 12, 31; 6:15; 7:3; 8:35; 9:19; 13:10; 16:23; 1Co 1:9, 20; 6:18; 7:11, 37, 38, 38; 12:6, 15, 29, 30, 30; 13:5, 11; 15:27; 16:22; 2Co 1:24; Gal 3:5, 10; Eph 4:16; Col 4:10, 14; 2Th 3:10; 2Ti 2:15; Heb 7:27; 12:8; Jas 2:16, 20; 3:11; 1Pe 4:6; 5:13; 2Pe 3:9; 1Jn 2:4, 10; 3:10, 10, 10; 4:3, 8, 8; 5:12, 12, 16; 2Jn 1, 10; 3Jn 9

DOESN'T (99)

Lev 13:21; Dt 14:7; 25:8; 1Sa 6:3; 10:12; 16:7; 2Sa 14:7; 15:3; 1Ki 1:11; 3:7; 2Ki 4:14; 6:27; Job 12:3; 13:9, 11; 15:15; 19:16; 24:1; 34:10, 19, 19; 35:13, 14; 39:15; Ps 94:7, 10; Pr 5:6; 9:13; 25:14; 26:1; Ecc 5:1; 6:2; 9:11, 11; Isa 7:4; 28:27, 28, 28; 29:15; 59:9; Eze 8:12; 9:9; 18:19; 24:7; 33:6; Da 3:18; Hos 2:3, 8; 7:10; 11:3; Mal 2:13; Mt 6:25; 10:14; 17:24; Mk 7:19; 10:15; Lk 6:49; 10:40; 14:5; 16:17; 17:7; 18:17; Jn 2:10; 8:54; 9:31; 10:21; 12:47; 14:17, 24; 15:2, 15; 17:25; Ac 7:48; 10:34; 17:24; 25:27; Ro 9:7, 21; 1Co 3:3; 7:38, 40; 8:2; 9:7, 8; 14:8, 17; 15:36; 2Co 10:18; Gal 3:16; 6:15; Col 3:11; 2Th 3:6; Heb 5:13; 12:8; Jas 2:4, 17; 1Jn 2:4, 23; 3:14

DOING (261)

Ge 16:5; 21:29; 37:2; 39:11; 48:19; Ex 2:13; 5:5; 10:2; 16:32; 18:12, 14; Lev 4:2; 5:4, 17; 8:35; 18:30; Nu 4:27; 5:6; 32:14; Dt 9:4, 18; 12:8, 25, 28; 13:18; 21:9; 23:21; 26:17; 28:20; 31:29; Jdg 15:11; 18:3, 18; 1Sa 2:22, 23, 30; 10:1; 14:1; 17:28; 18:17; 25:19, 39; 26:23; 28:10; 29:3; 2Sa 3:25; 6:7; 22:21, 25; 24:10; 1Ki 1:6; 8:61; 12:24; 19:9, 13; 20:40; 2Ki 8:27; 22:2, 13, 19; 1Ch 16:37; 21:8; 2Ch 11:4; 12:6; 20:10; 22:3; 24:22; 31:20; 34:2,

16, 21; Ne 2:16, 19; 3:28; 4:2; 5:8, 9; 6:3; 13:21; Job 9:12; 13:9; 21:16; 22:13; Ps 1:2; 18:20, 24; 35:21; 40:8; 69:4; 73:13; 83:2; 94:10; 109:27; 112:1; 118:23; Pr 1:3; 2:14; 10:23; 14:35; 21:2; Ecc 1:11; 8:3; Isa 5:12; 26:10; 45:9; 55:7; 56:2; 59:4; 66:18; Jer 2:29; 3:5; 4:22, 22, 30; 5:19; 7:13, 17, 24; 11:15; 13:23; 14:18; 23:14, 23; 25:5; 32:40, 41; 37:14; 44:22; 49:1; La 2:20; Eze 8:6, 6, 12; 16:43; 18:18, 26; 23:38; 33:15, 31; 36:22, 32; 44:14; Da 4:35; 11:28; Hos 4:14; Hab 1:5; Mt 6:3; 10:20; 11:2; 12:2; 20:3; 21:3, 42; 25:40; 26:10; Mk 2:24; 3:4; 11:3, 5; 12:11; 14:6; Lk 6:2, 9; 7:18; 9:43; 12:48; 13:32; 17:9; 19:31; 23:34; Jn 3:21; 4:27, 34; 5:19, 20; 13:7, 12; 16:2; 17:4; Ac 2:22; 3:13; 5:9, 38; 9:36; 10:38; 13:41; 14:15; 15:4; 19:14; 20:24; 22:26; 24:13; Ro 2:3, 7, 15; 3:20; 6:20; 7:16, 20, 20, 20; 12:21; 13:3, 4, 6; 14:16, 22, 22; 1Co 7:30, 32; 9:17, 23; 16:10; 2Co 8:10; 11:12; 12:6, 18; Gal 2:11, 16; 4:17; 5:16; 6:9, 12; Eph 3:13; 5:16; Php 2:4; 3:1; 4:9; Col 4:8; 1Th 2:16; 4:1; 5:11; 2Th 3:13; 1Ti 4:6; 6:19; 2Ti 2:5; Tit 1:16; 2:7, 14; Phm 1:6; Heb 5:13; 12:10; 13:20; Jas 1:23, 25; 1Pe 1:14; 2:12, 20, 20; 3:14, 17, 17; 4:19; 2Pe 1:10; 2:15; 1Jn 3:12, 12; 2Jn 6; 3Jn 5, 10; Jude 16; Rev 22:11

DON'T (1038)

Ge 4:9; 15:2, 2; 18:30; 19:7, 17, 20; 20:7; 21:16; 24:33, 56; 29:7, 8; 30:27, 31; 32:32; 35:17; 42:16, 37; 43:5, 9, 23; 44:32; 45:5, 20, 24; 50:19, 21; Ex 1:10; 4:18; 5:2, 3, 8, 8, 15, 17; 8:25, 28, 29; 9:14; 10:7, 28; 14:13; 20:19, 20; 32:1, 22; 33:13, 15, 15, 16; Lev 5:3; 22:30; 25:5; Nu 4:18; 10:31; 12:11, 12; 14:9, 9, 25; 16:26; 22:16; 23:25; 24:12; Dt 1:17, 21, 21, 29; 2:5; 4:19; 7:3, 18; 9:4; 21:1; 22:1, 2, 3; 23:21; 24:19, 20; Jos 2:5, 14; 3:4; 7:19; 9:7; 10:6, 19, 25; Jdg 4:18; 5:28; 6:18, 39; 8:21; 9:54; 14:16; 15:11; 16:15; 19:20, 23, 24; Ru 1:16, 20; 2:8, 16; 3:3, 11, 17; 4:4; 1Sa 1:16; 2:3; 4:9, 20; 6:6, 9; 8:7; 9:7, 7, 20; 12:20, 20, 21; 16:7; 17:32, 33, 55; 18:22; 19:4, 11; 20:8, 13, 30, 38; 21:4, 5; 22:15; 23:3, 17; 25:25, 31; 26:9; 28:13; 29:7; 30:23; 2Sa 1:20, 20; 2:26; 3:9; 9:7; 12:21; 13:12, 12, 20, 20, 28; 14:2, 10, 13; 15:20; 18:12; 19:7; 20:20; 21:4; 22:44; 1Ki 2:6, 16, 36; 17:12, 13; 18:40, 44; 20:8; 21:7; 2Ki 1:15; 2:16; 4:16, 24, 29; 5:26; 6:16, 31; 9:15; 10:23, 25; 12:7; 18:26, 29, 30, 31, 32; 19:10; 23:18; 1Ch 28:20; 2Ch 13:5; 16:8; 20:15; 32:7, 15, 15; Ne 4:14; 8:9, 10, 11; Est 4:13; Job 1:12; 6:5, 29, 30; 10:2; 12:2; 13:21; 15:9, 9; 20:4; 27:12; 30:20, 20; 32:13; 33:7; 34:31, 32; 35:10; 36:17, 18; Ps 4:4; 7:2; 13:4, 4; 18:43; 19:13; 26:9, 9; 27:9, 9; 28:1, 3; 31:1, 17; 33:17; 35:11, 15, 19, 19, 20, 22, 24, 25; 36:11, 11; 37:1, 1, 7, 34; 38:1, 1, 16; 39:10, 12; 40:6, 11; 49:16, 20; 50:13, 13, 16; 51:9, 11; 56:7; 59:11; 62:10, 10; 69:6, 6, 8, 14, 15, 17, 27, 28; 71:9, 9, 12; 74:19, 19, 21, 23; 75:4, 5; 77:4; 83:1, 2, 2; 95:8; 102:2, 24; 109:1, 17; 119:8, 10, 19, 22, 31, 121, 122, 141; 131:1; 137:6; 138:8; 140:11; 141:4, 4, 4, 5, 8; 143:2, 7; 146:3; Pr 1:8, 15; 3:7, 11, 11, 21, 28, 30, 31; 4:2, 5, 6, 13, 21, 27; 5:8, 17; 6:4, 4, 20, 25, 25; 7:25, 25; 8:33; 9:8, 18; 10:19; 12:22, 23, 27; 13:16, 24; 15:12; 19:18; 20:18, 19, 22; 23:3, 4, 6, 6, 7, 9, 10, 13, 17, 22, 23, 31; 24:1, 1, 6, 11, 12, 15, 17, 19, 21, 28, 29; 25:6, 8, 9, 14, 16, 17; 26:4, 24; 27:1, 1, 2, 24; 28:5, 17; 29:7, 24; 30:32; Ecc 1:11; 5:1, 2, 4, 5, 6, 8; 6:9; 7:9, 10, 10, 13, 16, 17, 17, 21; 8:3, 3, 7; 9:2, 11; 10:4, 20; 12:1, 6; SS 1:6, 8; Isa 1:11, 11, 11; 3:7, 7; 29:12; 30:10, 10; 36:11, 14, 15, 16, 18; 37:10; 40:28; 41:10, 14; 42:20; 48:1; 57:11; 58:3, 13, 13; 64:9, 9; 65:5, 8; Jer 1:7, 8; 2:25, 28; 5:4, 4; 6:10, 15, 25, 25; 7:8, 16; 8:4, 4, 12; 13:12; 14:9, 21; 15:15; 17:15; 18:12, 18, 23; 22:21; 23:17; 35:6; 36:19; 37:20; 38:14, 24, 25; 40:4; 42:19; 44:4; 45:5, 5; 49:16; 51:3, 6; La 4:15; Eze 2:6; 3:9, 20; 12:2, 6; 17:12; 18:30, 32; 20:39; 21:24; 33:9, 32; Da 2:5, 9, 24; 4:19; 5:10; 10:12, 19; Hos 4:4, 6; 6:6; 7:2, 9; 8:12; 9:14; 10:4; 11:7; 13:10; Joel 2:13, 17, 17, 21, 22; Am 5:5, 6; 6:10; 7:5, 13, 16; Ob 3; Jnh 1:14, 14; Mic 1:10, 10; 2:6, 6; 4:12; 6:5; 7:5; Na 1:14; Zep 3:16; Zec 4:5, 13; 7:6; 8:13, 15; 14:19; Mt 3:9; 5:15, 17, 34, 35, 36, 39, 42; 6:1, 2, 3, 5, 7, 8, 13, 16, 19, 25, 26, 28, 31, 34; 7:6, 6, 16; 8:4; 9:12, 13, 14, 30; 10:5, 9, 10, 10, 19, 26, 28, 31, 34; 12:7; 13:13, 13, 13, 19, 21; 14:27, 31; 15:5, 16, 32; 16:9, 10; 17:7, 9, 27; 18:10; 19:14; 20:22; 21:21, 27; 22:16, 29, 29; 23:3, 3, 8, 9, 10; 24:4, 6, 23, 26, 26, 42; 25:9, 12; 26:53, 70, 72, 74; 27:13; 28:5, 10; Mk 1:44; 2:17, 18; 4:12, 12, 17, 38; 5:7, 36; 6:50; 7:5, 18; 8:18, 21, 26; 9:39; 10:14, 38; 11:33; 12:14, 24, 24; 13:5, 7, 11, 21, 33, 36; 14:68, 71; Lk 1:13, 30; 2:10; 3:8, 14, 14; 4:23; 5:10, 31; 6:30, 35; 7:6, 13; 8:10, 10, 13, 28, 50; 9:3, 50; 10:4, 4, 7, 7, 11, 20; 11:4, 7, 52; 12:4, 7, 11, 15, 15, 22, 24, 27, 29, 29, 32; 13:15, 27; 14:5, 8, 12, 28; 16:3; 17:23; 18:7, 11, 11, 16; 20:7; 21:8, 8, 9, 14, 34, 34; 22:36, 51, 57, 60; 23:28, 34, 40; 24:6, 39; Jn 2:16; 3:7, 10, 12, 36; 4:11, 17, 17, 32; 5:28, 42, 44, 47; 6:20, 43, 64; 7:28; 8:14, 19, 19, 45, 46, 47; 9:12, 21, 25, 29, 30; 10:5, 25, 26, 37, 38; 12:15, 49; 13:7, 8; 14:1, 5, 9, 10, 27, 30; 15:19, 21; 16:7, 18, 30; 19:10; 20:2, 13, 17, 27; 21:18; Ac 2:15; 3:6; 7:40, 60; 10:15; 11:9; 13:40; 16:28; 18:9, 9; 19:2, 36; 20:10; 23:21, 22; 25:11; 27:24; Ro 2:4, 4, 21, 25, 27; 6:16; 7:1, 15, 15, 19, 20; 8:24, 25, 26; 9:20; 10:3, 6, 7; 11:20; 12:2, 9, 14, 16, 16, 21; 13:12, 13, 14; 14:1, 13, 15, 20, 21; 1Co 1:16; 3:3, 16, 21; 4:3; 5:1, 6, 11; 6:2, 3, 9, 9, 15, 16, 19; 7:21, 23; 8:8, 8, 8, 13; 9:4, 5, 13; 10:1, 10, 20, 24, 25, 27, 28, 32, 33; 11:22; 12:21, 21; 14:9, 14, 16, 16, 20, 23, 24, 39; 15:33, 34; 16:2, 7, 11; 2Co 1:14; 4:4, 4, 5, 8, 18; 6:14, 17; 8:12, 13; 9:1, 3, 7; 10:3, 10, 12; 11:5, 11, 16; 12:3, 6, 14, 14; Gal 2:12; 4:10, 20; 5:1; 6:7, 9, 9, 12, 13, 17; Eph 2:11; 3:13; 4:19, 26, 26, 29; 5:6, 7, 17, 18; 6:4, 9; Php 1:22, 28; 2:3, 3, 4; 3:12; 4:6, 17; Col 1:23; 2:8, 16, 18, 18, 21, 21, 21; 3:5, 9, 21; 4:3; 1Th 1:8; 2:9; 4:9; 5:1, 5; 2Th 1:8; 2:2, 2, 3, 5; 3:15; 1Ti 1:4, 4, 7; 4:12; 5:23; 6:5; 2Ti 1:8; 2:23; 4:5; Tit 2:15; Heb 3:8, 15; 4:7; 5:11; 6:1, 2, 9; 10:32; 12:3, 5, 5; 13:2, 3, 9, 16; Jas 1:16, 22, 23, 25, 26; 2:14, 16, 18, 21; 3:13, 14; 4:2, 2, 2, 3, 4, 11; 5:9; 1Pe 1:14; 2:1; 3:3, 7, 9, 9, 14, 14; 4:12; 5:3; 2Pe 3:17; 1Jn 2:11, 21, 27; 3:1, 1, 7, 13, 15; 4:20; 5:10, 10; 2Jn 10, 12; 3Jn 11, 13; Jude 7; Rev 1:17; 2:2, 4, 5, 10; 3:17, 17; 6:6; 7:3; 19:10; 22:9

DONE (530)

Ge 3:14; 4:10; 9:24; 12:18; 20:9, 9, 9, 10; 27:19, 45; 31:12; 34:7, 7, 13; 42:28; 44:5; Ex 1:8, 18; 2:14; 12:16; 14:5; 18:1, 8, 9; 30:8; 34:10; 39:7, 21, 32, 43; Lev 4:10, 21, 26, 31, 35; 5:17; 8:21, 34; 9:15; 14:43; 23:36; Nu 5:7; 7:8; 14:11; 15:24; 16:28, 28; 22:2, 28, 30; 23:11, 23; 28:18, 25, 26; 29:1, 7, 12; 31:47; Dt 2:7, 30; 3:21; 9:4; 10:10, 21; 13:11; 15:2; 16:8; 17:2, 4; 18:12; 26:14; 29:24; Jos 6:15; 7:15, 19; 8:33; 9:24; 10:37; 22:2, 22; 23:3, 8; 24:31; Jdg 2:3, 7, 10; 6:27; 8:2, 3, 35; 9:16, 48, 56; 13:23; 20:7, 10, 12, 31; Ru 3:16; 1Sa 2:3; 6:19; 10:19; 12:1, 3, 7, 20, 24; 13:11; 14:43; 17:29, 36; 19:4, 18; 20:1, 32; 24:6; 25:28, 30, 31; 26:18; 28:17, 18; 29:8; 31:11; 2Sa 2:6; 3:8, 24; 5:20; 7:21; 10:12; 11:10, 27; 12:9, 11; 13:16, 22; 16:23; 19:5, 38; 21:11; 24:17, 17; 1Ki 1:27; 2:5; 8:20, 25, 47; 9:2; 11:4, 6, 33; 13:11; 14:9; 15:5, 11, 30; 16:7, 19; 17:18; 18:9, 33, 36; 19:1, 20; 21:19, 26, 29; 22:3, 53; 2Ki 1:6, 16; 5:13, 27; 8:4; 9:15; 10:30; 15:3, 9, 34; 16:2; 17:9, 11; 18:3, 14; 19:11; 21:3, 11, 15, 20; 22:17; 23:17, 19, 32, 37; 24:9, 19; 1Ch 10:11; 14:11; 16:8, 12, 37; 17:19; 19:13; 21:17, 17; 24:31; 29:5, 17; 2Ch 6:10, 16, 37; 7:21; 11:17; 19:2; 21:19; 22:4; 24:16; 25:16; 26:4; 27:2; 28:1; 29:2, 36; 31:11; 32:13; 33:22; 34:25; 35:26; Ezr 10:13; Ne 4:10; 5:19; 6:14, 16; 9:8, 17; 13:14; Est 1:15; 2:1; 4:1; 5:14; 6:3; 9:12, 13, 17; Job 6:24; 7:20; 12:9; 13:23; 21:31; 28:27; 31:37; 34:32; 35:9; 36:23; Ps 7:3; 9:1; 12:5; 17:15; 22:31; 27:12; 28:4, 5; 31:19; 38:18, 19; 40:3, 5; 51:4; 52:9; 59:3; 62:12; 66:5; 71:15, 19; 75:9; 77:11; 78:11; 92:4, 4; 98:1; 105:1, 5; 106:6, 13, 21; 109:27; 116:12; 118:15, 16, 17; 119:65, 121; 126:2, 3; 137:8; 143:5; 147:20; Pr 4:16; 24:12; 31:31; Ecc 1:9, 13; 2:17; 4:3; 11:4; SS 1:6; Isa 5:4; 12:4, 5; 23:9; 26:18; 33:13; 37:11; 41:4; 43:12; 44:7, 23, 26; 46:9; 47:15; 53:9; 58:3; 63:7; Jer 2:13, 23, 35; 3:7; 8:6; 11:15, 17; 12:13; 16:10; 18:6, 13; 21:2; 23:2; 29:23, 27; 32:23, 30, 31; 34:14; 37:18; 38:9; 41:11; 44:17; 50:15, 29; 51:10, 24; 52:2; La 1:21; 3:59, 64; Eze 6:11; 7:27; 9:10; 13:5; 14:22, 23; 16:51, 54, 61, 63; 18:22; 20:43; 24:22, 23, 24; 25:17; 33:16; 36:32; 37:14; 43:11; Da 6:10; 9:5, 12; Hos 5:2; Joel 2:20, 21; 3:4, 7; Am 3:7; 8:7; 9:7; Ob 12, 15, 15; Jnh 1:8; Mic 3:4; 6:3, 6; 7:9; Hab 3:2; Zec 1:6; 7:3; Mal 2:12; Mt 3:15; 6:10; 11:20, 21, 23; 13:28; 21:4; 24:46; 25:21, 23; 26:42; Mk 1:28; 5:19, 20, 32, 33; 6:30; 11:18; 14:8; Lk 1:2, 49; 2:48; 3:19; 4:37; 7:17; 8:39, 39; 9:10; 10:13; 11:48; 12:43; 14:22; 17:10, 16; 19:15, 17, 19; 23:15, 31, 41, 54; Jn 4:38; 5:29; 7:31; 10:32, 38; 11:46; 12:37; 13:15; 14:12; 15:24; 16:24; 18:35; Ac 2:11; 3:17; 4:7, 9, 16, 30; 9:13; 14:11, 27; 15:12; 20:19; 21:14, 22, 33; 23:14, 28; 25:5, 11, 25; 26:26, 31; 28:17; Ro 1:5, 13, 28; 2:6; 3:22, 24, 27; 5:1, 11; 9:11, 19; 12:1, 20; 15:17, 19; 1Co 1:31; 3:13; 5:3; 6:11; 11:17; 14:26, 40; 15:31; 16:14; 2Co 4:5; 5:10; 7:2, 11; 8:1; 10:15, 17; Gal 6:4; Eph 2:7, 9, 18; Php 1:26; 3:3, 7; 4:6, 14; Col 1:22; 2:7; 3:25; 1Ti 5:10; 2Ti 4:14, 14; Heb 4:13; 10:1; 13:2; Jas 4:9; 1Pe 2:1; 2Pe 2:13; Jude 15; Rev 6:10; 18:6; 19:8; 20:12

DOWN (1034)

Ge 1:15, 16; 8:5; 11:5, 7; 12:10; 15:10, 11, 12, 17; 17:3, 17; 18:21; 19:9, 24, 33, 35; 21:16; 22:12; 23:9; 24:11, 16, 20, 26, 32, 45; 27:38; 28:11, 12; 31:46; 33:7; 37:25; 41:43; 42:2, 3, 38, 38; 43:4; 44:12, 29, 31; 45:2, 9; 46:3, 4; 49:9; 50:17; Ex 1:5, 11; 2:5, 15, 21, 25; 3:21; 4:3, 3; 5:9; 7:9, 10, 15; 8:20; 12:23, 23; 14:24; 15:19; 16:4; 17:14; 19:10, 11, 14, 16, 20, 21, 24, 25; 20:5; 23:24; 24:4; 25:20; 26:13; 27:5; 32:1, 4, 7, 15; 33:9; 34:5, 13, 13, 27, 29; 37:9; 38:4; 39:4; 40:35; Lev 9:22, 24; 14:45; 22:7; 26:7, 19, 30; Nu 1:51; 4:5; 10:17, 36; 11:9, 17, 25; 13:23; 14:5, 45; 16:4, 22, 30, 33, 45; 20:6, 15, 28; 22:26, 27, 31; 24:4, 9, 16; 34:11, 11; Dt 3:17; 4:44; 5:9; 6:7; 7:5, 5; 8:19; 9:12, 15, 21, 25; 10:5; 11:19; 12:3, 3; 16:6; 19:6; 20:19, 20; 25:2, 18; 26:15; 28:24, 49, 52; 29:20, 27; 30:12; 31:9, 17, 19, 21, 22, 24, 29; 32:23; 33:11, 28; Jos 2:15, 23; 7:5, 6; 8:29; 10:11, 19, 27, 27; 15:10, 18; 18:13, 16, 16, 16, 17, 18; 24:4, 7; Jdg 1:14, 34; 2:17, 19; 3:23, 27; 4:14, 15; 5:4, 11, 13, 13, 14, 14; 6:25, 25, 26, 28, 30, 31, 32; 7:4, 5, 5, 6, 9, 10, 11, 13, 24; 8:9, 12, 14, 17; 9:36, 37, 37, 44, 49, 53; 12:1; 14:5, 15, 19; 15:11; 16:30, 31; 19:6, 27; 20:43, 48; Ru 1:9; 3:4, 4, 6, 7, 7, 13; 4:1; 1Sa 1:11; 2:6, 7; 3:9; 5:4; 9:16; 10:5, 8, 25; 14:4; 16:11, 20; 20:24; 21:13; 23:4, 20, 23; 25:1; 26:2, 10, 14, 20; 28:19; 31:12; 2Sa 2:13, 24, 26; 5:24, 25; 6:16; 8:2; 11:21; 13:8; 14:4; 15:24; 17:13; 18:7, 25, 26; 19:17, 18; 20:15; 22:10, 17, 39; 23:7, 13, 20; 1Ki 1:33, 38, 44, 53; 2:8, 16, 19, 19, 20; 9:16; 10:22; 12:16; 15:13; 16:10, 18; 17:23; 18:30, 38, 40; 19:4, 5, 6, 10, 14; 21:3, 16, 18; 22:35; 2Ki 1:10, 11, 12; 2:15; 3:2, 19, 25; 4:24, 34; 5:14, 21, 26; 6:2, 4; 7:17; 8:9; 9:24, 33; 10:27, 30; 11:18; 15:12; 17:19; 18:4, 22; 19:23; 20:3; 21:13; 23:7, 12, 14, 15; 25:4, 9, 10; 1Ch 6:32; 11:15, 22; 12:21; 14:15, 16; 15:29; 16:12; 21:16; 24:6; 2Ch 2:16; 6:13; 7:1, 3, 3; 9:21; 10:16; 13:20; 14:3; 15:16; 17:6; 20:18; 21:17; 23:17; 25:14; 26:6, 19; 29:29, 30; 31:1; 32:5, 30; 33:15; 34:4, 7; 36:19; Ezr 3:7; 9:3; 10:16; Ne 1:3, 4, 6; 2:3; 3:18; 4:11; 8:6; 9:13; 12:23; 13:25; Est 3:2, 2, 5, 15; 8:3; 9:5, 32; Job 6:4; 7:21; 8:17; 9:26; 11:19; 14:7, 12; 15:28, 32; 16:7, 22; 17:16; 18:14; 20:15, 23; 21:13; 24:18; 27:15, 22; 30:14; 31:26; 34:26; 36:28; 37:6, 17; 39:3, 30; 40:21, 23; 41:9; Ps 3:5; 4:8; 9:17; 11:6; 14:2; 17:6, 11; 18:9, 12, 16, 38; 20:8; 22:27, 29; 28:5; 30:9; 31:2, 15; 33:13; 36:12; 44:25; 45:5; 52:5; 53:2; 55:3, 23; 59:10; 60:12; 63:9; 64:7; 68:22, 34; 74:5, 8; 77:17; 78:3, 16, 24, 27, 31; 80:3, 7, 12, 14, 19; 81:9; 82:2; 85:11, 12; 86:1, 16; 88:6; 89:23, 40; 91:13; 95:6; 102:2, 9, 19, 23; 104:10; 105:5; 107:16; 108:13; 110:5; 116:2; 119:86, 135, 143, 153; 133:2; 135:10; 136:17; 139:2, 8; 140:10; 141:6; 144:5, 5, 7, 14; 147:6; Pr 1:12; 2:13, 14; 3:17, 20, 24; 5:5, 6; 7:8, 25; 11:28; 12:25; 14:1; 16:29; 19:28; 24:22, 31; 25:8; 26:27; 30:4; Ecc 3:3; 10:3; 11:3; SS 1:6; 4:8; 6:2, 5, 11; Isa 1:4, 25; 2:8, 12, 13, 15; 3:12; 4:3; 5:5, 5, 15; 6:13; 8:16, 16; 9:16; 10:33, 34, 34; 11:7, 14; 13:18; 14:8, 12, 15, 15, 30; 15:9; 17:2, 8; 18:2; 21:1; 22:10, 19, 24; 23:13; 24:12, 19; 25:11, 11; 26:5; 28:17; 29:21; 30:2, 8, 13, 25, 30, 31; 31:3; 32:15, 19; 33:12; 36:7; 37:24; 38:3, 18; 40:20; 42:16; 44:14, 15, 17, 19; 45:2; 46:2, 6, 7; 50:11; 51:6; 53:4; 55:10; 57:5, 13; 59:10; 60:20; 63:5, 14, 15; 64:1, 3, 11; Jer 1:10; 2:20, 36; 3:25; 4:13; 5:1, 10; 6:6; 8:4, 4, 6; 9:19; 10:3, 22; 12:10; 13:13, 18, 20; 15:9; 18:2, 7; 23:12, 19, 36; 24:6; 26:10; 30:2, 23; 31:9, 28; 32:29; 33:4; 36:2, 2, 4, 12, 15, 18; 38:6, 12; 39:8; 42:10; 43:13, 13; 45:1; 46:23; 48:1, 18, 18, 40; 49:15, 16; 51:25, 30; 52:7, 13, 14; La 1:2, 3, 7, 16; 2:1, 2, 6, 8; 3:29, 43, 49, 50, 66; Eze 1:24, 27, 28; 3:23; 4:1; 6:12; 7:24; 8:2; 9:8; 11:13; 13:11, 11, 14; 16:39; 17:6, 24; 19:2, 12; 20:1; 22:20, 20; 24:2; 25:11; 26:4, 12, 16; 28:8; 31:12, 15, 16, 17, 18; 32:15, 18, 19, 21, 21, 27, 29; 34:14, 15, 18, 19; 38:8, 9, 20; 39:6; 40:2; 43:3, 11; Da 2:35; 3:10, 15, 23; 4:13, 14, 23, 23, 31; 5:20; 6:10; 7:1, 9, 25; 8:7; 9:24; 10:15; Hos 2:21; 5:10; 7:12; 8:13, 14; 10:2; 14:1; Joel 1:3; Am 1:3, 4, 5, 7, 10, 11, 12, 14; 2:2, 5, 13; 5:8; 6:2; 8:9, 14; 9:1, 2, 2, 2, 6; Ob 2, 4, 9; Jnh 1:3, 5, 6, 8; 2:3, 6; 3:6; 4:8; Mic 1:4, 6; 5:11; 7:10; Na 3:15; Hab 1:8; 2:17, 17; Zep 1:16; 2:7; 3:13; Hag 1:8; Zec 1:21; 13:7; Mt 2:11; 3:10; 4:9; 5:1; 7:19; 8:1, 11, 32; 9:9, 18; 11:23; 13:1, 48; 14:9, 19; 15:29, 35; 17:6, 27; 18:19, 26, 29; 25:5; 26:20, 39; 27:40, 42; 28:2; Mk 2:4; 3:11; 4:1, 39; 5:6, 13, 22; 6:39; 8:6; 9:35; 10:17, 52; 14:35, 72; 15:30, 32, 36, 46; 16:19; Lk 3:9; 4:7, 20, 40; 5:4, 12, 19; 6:17, 38, 39, 49; 7:36; 8:23, 33, 41; 9:14, 15, 37, 54; 10:15; 11:38; 12:18; 13:7, 9; 14:31; 17:7, 16, 29; 19:5, 6, 37; 21:24, 25; 22:14, 41; 23:53; 24:30; Jn 1:51; 6:3, 10, 10, 16, 18, 33, 38, 42, 51; 8:2, 6, 8; 10:11, 15, 17, 18, 18; 11:18, 32; 12:13; 13:12; 15:13; 19:13, 31, 38; 21:25; Ac 6:14; 8:26, 38; 9:3, 25; 10:5, 11, 20, 21; 11:5, 5; 12:10, 17; 13:4, 29; 16:13, 16, 29; 17:6; 18:5; 19:35, 35; 20:2, 10, 17, 38; 21:5, 32; 22:25; 26:13, 14; 27:7, 22; Ro 10:6; 11:3, 4, 12; 14:3, 10; 15:25; 1Co 10:11; 14:25; 15:24; 2Co 1:6; 4:9, 9; 5:1; 10:4, 5, 8; 13:10; Gal 2:18; Eph 2:14; 3:17; 4:9, 10, 26; Col 2:7; 3:2; 1Th 4:16; 2Th 2:4; 3:12; 1Ti 1:13; Heb 1:3; 8:1; 10:12; 11:30; 12:1; Jas 4:10; 5:18; 2Pe 1:17; Rev 1:11, 19; 3:9, 12; 4:10; 5:8, 14; 7:11; 8:5, 7; 10:1, 4; 12:4, 9, 10, 12, 13; 13:13; 14:13; 18:1, 21; 19:4, 10, 15; 20:1, 9; 21:2, 5; 22:2, 8

EVEN (1068)

Ge 3:3; 6:4; 7:19; 8:21; 15:2; 18:27; 22:12, 16; 27:36; 28:16; 32:32; 34:4; 35:11; 37:5; 41:31; 48:19; Ex 4:9, 10, 18; 5:23, 23; 7:4, 19; 8:3, 3, 22; 9:7, 11, 12, 25; 10:24; 11:5, 7, 9; 12:29; 13:17; 16:27; 19:12, 22; 20:6; 21:14, 19; 23:13, 33; 32:27, 29; 33:5; 34:3, 7, 21; 35:3; Lev 4:22, 27; 5:2, 3, 4, 17; 7:26; 11:11; 13:36, 55; 21:11, 21; 22:10; 26:17, 21, 26, 36; Nu 4:20; 5:14; 6:4, 7; 11:19, 22, 22; 12:6; 13:33; 14:2, 11, 18, 23; 17:13; 19:12; 20:17; 22:15, 18; 23:10; 24:13; 32:14; Dt 1:28, 32; 5:10; 12:31; 14:8; 18:8; 19:6; 21:17, 18; 24:6; 28:61; 29:19, 23; 30:5; 31:21, 27; 32:26, 31; 33:6; Jos 6:10; 14:10; 17:18; 22:3, 17; 23:7; 24:20; Jdg 5:5; 13:3; 14:16; 19:19; Ru 1:12; 2:13, 21; 1Sa 1:5, 7; 2:15; 8:19; 9:7, 24; 12:4, 12; 13:12; 14:15, 21, 23, 25, 26, 39; 18:15, 29; 20:2, 15; 21:5, 8; 22:8; 23:3, 23, 25; 24:11; 25:17, 22, 25, 29, 41; 26:12, 23, 24; 2Sa 3:39; 5:2, 6; 6:22; 7:22; 11:8, 13; 13:15; 15:20; 16:11; 17:10; 18:3; 19:42; 22:44; 1Ki 1:6, 11, 18, 37, 47, 47; 8:27; 11:7, 13, 22; 12:11, 14, 30; 13:8, 33; 14:14, 22, 24; 15:13; 16:11, 25, 30; 18:35, 38; 20:10; 21:27; 22:4; 2Ki 3:7, 19, 25; 4:43; 6:12, 25; 7:2, 19; 12:3; 13:6; 16:3; 17:17, 19, 31; 18:16, 24, 24; 19:24; 21:4, 6, 7, 9, 11, 14; 23:5, 26; 1Ch 10:13; 11:2; 17:20; 29:16, 25; 2Ch 1:11; 2:6; 6:18; 7:2; 10:11, 14; 11:14; 15:16; 16:12; 20:17; 21:13; 25:15; 26:8; 28:3, 21, 22; 30:18, 19; 33:4, 6, 7, 9, 23; 34:6; 36:13, 17; Ezr 2:63; 3:3; 4:7; 9:1, 14; 10:10, 44; Ne 1:6, 9; 4:3, 23; 5:15, 17; 7:65; 9:18, 24, 35, 35; 13:18, 24, 26, 27; Est 2:19; 3:8; 5:3, 6; 7:2, 8; 10:1; Job 2:3; 3:4, 18; 6:27; 7:19; 8:18; 9:3, 14, 15, 16, 30; 10:15; 12:6; 13:10; 15:15, 15, 21; 16:19; 19:4, 16, 18; 21:14; 22:2, 30; 24:3, 20; 25:5; 27:15; 28:21; 29:8, 16; 33:20; 34:6, 9; 35:6, 14; 36:13; 39:25; 40:14, 23; 42:12; Ps 9:6; 12:8; 14:2, 3; 15:4; 16:4, 7; 18:43; 19:10, 10; 23:4; 27:3, 10; 31:11; 34:10; 35:11, 13, 15; 37:19; 38:11; 39:2, 8; 41:9; 46:2; 53:2, 3; 55:18; 58:3; 65:5, 11; 68:18, 23; 69:8; 71:21; 72:16; 73:11; 75:6; 77:4; 78:6, 19; 84:3; 87:4; 90:10, 10; 92:14; 95:4; 102:14, 26; 104:6; 105:30; 106:8, 28, 37, 44, 46; 109:4; 113:8; 119:23, 96, 100, 112, 127, 130; 133:3; 139:4, 10, 12, 18; 141:7; 144:13; 146:2; Pr 1:5, 28; 5:6; 6:7, 31; 9:13; 12:10, 27; 13:8, 16; 14:20; 15:11; 16:4, 7; 17:7, 28; 19:24; 20:11, 22; 22:27; 23:35; 24:29; 27:7, 22; 30:28; Ecc 1:17; 2:10, 23, 26; 3:11, 16; 4:12, 14, 15; 5:9, 18; 6:3, 4; 8:6, 12, 17, 17; 9:1, 17; 10:1, 4, 7, 15, 20; 12:4; SS 1:4, 5; 2:12; 5:6; 6:9; Isa 1:3, 13, 15, 18; 5:10, 19, 25; 6:13; 9:12, 17, 17, 20, 21; 10:4, 14; 13:7; 14:8, 29; 15:4, 6; 18:5; 19:18; 22:24; 23:12; 28:22; 29:14; 30:5; 31:4, 9; 32:4, 19; 33:23; 35:1; 36:9, 9; 37:25; 40:30; 42:4, 23; 43:9; 44:13; 45:5; 46:7, 10; 47:6, 14; 48:2, 20; 49:15, 19; 51:12; 54:1, 10; 55:1; 56:12; 57:9, 11; 58:3, 3; 59:10; 63:16; 64:10; 65:17, 24; 66:7, 11; Jer 2:2, 6, 9, 11, 24, 34; 3:3, 11, 16; 4:10; 5:1, 2, 7, 18; 6:9, 11, 13, 15; 7:3, 26, 26, 31; 8:5, 10, 12; 9:12, 26; 10:2; 11:8; 12:4, 6, 11; 13:14; 14:15; 15:1, 5; 16:7, 12; 17:2; 18:13; 19:5; 20:10; 21:7; 22:18, 24; 23:14, 18, 18, 38; 25:4; 27:6; 28:14; 32:25, 35; 33:4; 36:7, 25; 37:10; 44:7; 48:32, 34, 41; 49:9, 20, 22; 50:27, 38, 45; 51:5, 26, 43, 50; La 1:19; 2:1; 4:1, 3, 8; 5:4; Eze 2:6; 3:9; 5:6, 7; 8:6, 15; 11:11; 12:3, 3, 12; 13:6, 7, 22; 14:14, 16, 18, 20; 15:4; 16:27, 31, 51, 61; 17:8; 20:13, 21, 31; 21:4, 14, 24, 29; 22:12, 29; 23:3, 11, 11, 14, 19; 24:7; 26:12; 32:8; 33:28; 34:23; 36:11; 44:7; Da 2:38; 3:18, 25, 27, 30; 4:17, 36; 5:9; 6:24; 8:3, 5, 11, 25; 9:9; 11:36; Hos 2:8, 17; 3:1, 1, 3, 4; 4:3; 7:4, 9, 10; 8:12; 9:6, 8, 11, 12; 10:14; 11:3; 12:3; Joel 1:20; 2:14, 16, 29; 3:10; Am 2:14, 15; 5:15, 22; 6:10. 12; 9:2, 2, 3, 3, 4; Ob 7, 16; Jnh 1:13; 3:7, 9; 4:9; Mic 1:9, 12; 3:4; 4:5; 7:2, 4, 5; Na 1:12; 3:15; Hab 1:5; 3:17, 17, 17; Zep 1:3, 4; 2:3; 3:2, 6; Hag 2:17; Zec 4:7; 5:4; 7:6, 14; 8:22; 9:9; 10:5; 11:5; 13:2; 14:20; Mal 2:2; Mt 3:10, 11; 5:18, 28, 29, 30, 36, 46, 47, 48; 6:8; 8:20, 27; 9:16; 10:10, 29, 42; 11:11; 12:6, 8; 13:8, 12, 23, 33; 14:36; 15:23, 27; 16:11; 17:5, 20; 18:14; 20:28; 21:5, 15, 21, 32; 22:6; 23:23; 24:18, 24, 36; 25:29, 29; 26:33, 35, 40, 47, 60, 72; 28:20; Mk 1:7, 27; 2:2, 21, 28; 3:8, 20; 4:8, 20, 24, 25, 38, 41; 5:3; 6:9, 20, 31; 7:28, 37; 8:21; 9:41; 10:45; 13:16, 22, 32; 14:29, 31, 37, 59, 65; 15:32; Lk 1:15; 2:21; 3:9, 12, 16; 4:36; 5:15, 36; 6:5, 32, 33, 34; 7:5, 7, 17, 28; 8:18, 25, 29; 9:3, 3, 33, 34, 58; 10:4, 12, 17; 11:28, 42; 12:12; 13:16, 21; 14:24; 15:2, 10, 16, 17, 29; 16:10, 17, 31; 17:4, 6, 9; 18:7, 13; 19:26, 26, 42; 20:37; 21:16; 22:33, 34, 47, 57; 23:40; Jn 1:11, 27; 3:12; 4:18; 5:14, 21, 43; 6:36, 39, 58, 60; 7:5, 35; 8:10, 14, 52, 55, 57, 58; 10:38; 11:22, 25; 13:38; 14:9, 9, 12; 15:2, 9; 17:24; Ac 2:39; 5:9, 39; 6:11; 7:5, 52; 10:44; 11:3; 13:25, 41; 14:18; 19:2, 12, 32; 20:30, 34; 21:28; 22:2, 25; 26:11; 27:19, 22; 28:17, 19; Ro 1:21, 26; 2:12, 14; 3:10, 12; 4:11, 18, 19; 5:13, 14, 16; 8:10, 23, 26, 32, 36, 38; 9:24, 30; 10:19; 15:3, 15; 1Co 2:10; 4:3, 15; 5:1, 3, 6, 11; 6:8, 12; 7:38; 9:2, 12, 20; 11:30; 13:3, 9; 14:5, 7, 21, 23; 15:34, 41; 2Co 1:14; 3:7, 14, 15, 18; 5:6; 8:8, 22; 9:11; 10:1; 11:4, 14, 16; 12:7, 11, 15; 13:7; Gal 1:8, 15; 2:3, 4, 13; 4:1, 8, 14, 14, 27; 6:13; Eph 1:4; 2:5, 11; 5:12; Php 1:21, 26, 28; 2:8, 12, 17; 3:4; 4:14, 16; Col 2:18; 1Th 1:8; 2:2, 15; 3:4; 4:10; 2Th 2:2; 3:10; 1Ti 1:7, 13, 16; 3:14; 2Ti 1:8, 15; Phm 1:21; Heb 1:11; 3:9, 16; 4:3; 5:8; 6:9; 7:4, 5, 6, 9, 15; 8:4; 10:32; 11:9, 11, 12, 17, 20; Jas 2:11, 19, 23; 3:4; 4:3; 1Pe 1:6, 8, 8, 10, 12; 2:12, 18, 23; 3:1, 14; 4:6, 17; 2Pe 1:12, 19; 2:1, 4, 9, 10, 11; 1Jn 3:2, 7, 20; 3Jn 5, 12; Jude 5, 9; Rev 1:7; 2:10, 13; 3:2, 4; 18:13

FOR (8187)

Ge 1:16, 29, 30; 2:5, 15, 18, 19, 20; 3:16, 18, 19, 21; 4:12, 13, 15,

25; **5:**29; **6:**3, 3, 4, 13, 21, 21; **7:**1, 2, 2, 8, 12, 17, 24; **8:**20; **9:**3, 6; **10:**10, 25; **11:**6, 32; **12:**18; **13:**2, 6, 11; **14:**4, 8, 21; **15:**1, 4, 13; **16:**5, 11, 13; **17:**5, 14, 20; **18:**3, 14, 18, 19, 22, 24, 26, 28, 31, 32; **19:**2, 4, 8, 13, 16, 17, 22, 31; **20:**1, 2, 3, 7, 7, 9, 16, 18, 18; **21:**7, 12, 14, 18, 21, 34; **22:**3, 3, 6, 7, 12, 19; **23:**2, 4, 6, 9, 13; **24:**4, 7, 14, 18, 19, 22, 22, 23, 25, 25, 27, 31, 31, 32, 40, 40, 53; **25:**7, 31; **26:**9, 12, 16, 16, 22, 22, 24, 30, 30, 35; **27:**1, 3, 4, 5, 28, 36, 36, 38, 40, 42, 45; **28:**1, 4, 11, 11, 22; **29:**3, 9, 15, 18, 20, 20, 21, 25, 27, 32, 33, 34, 34, 35; **30:**3, 6, 8, 11, 13, 15, 16, 18, 18, 20, 20, 24, 26, 26, 27, 30, 31, 33, 36, 38; **31:**6, 8, 12, 14, 15, 21, 22, 30, 32, 37, 38, 38, 39, 40, 42, 49; **32:**13, 13, 18, 26, 30; **33:**10, 11, 15, 17, 19; **34:**3, 4, 8, 9, 14, 19, 21; **35:**28; **36:**40; **37:**8, 13, 15, 16, 27, 28, 34, 34, 35; **38:**10, 13; **39:**5; **40:**4, 15, 17, 20, 20; **41:**8, 14, 15, 28, 32, 38, 38, 47, 48, 51, 52, 55; **42:**2, 4, 5, 17, 19, 23, 25, 26, 27, 30, 33, 35, 37, 38; **43:**10, 21, 21, 24, 25, 30; **44:**16, 18, 18, 22, 31, 34; **45:**5, 11, 12, 20, 21; **46:**1, 3, 5, 29, 30, 33, 34, 34; **47:**4, 4, 6, 9, 14, 15, 17, 17, 19, 20, 22, 23, 24, 28, 29; **49:**4, 6, 6, 7, 7, 13, 18, 20, 30; **50:**3, 10, 11, 11, 13, 15, 17, 20, 24; **Ex 1:**11, 18; **2:**2, 5, 7, 9, 9, 10, 16, 17, 19, 20, 22, 23, 23, 25; **3:**5, 7, 10, 22; **4:**19, 24, 31; **5:**1, 7, 10, 16, 16, 20, 21; **7:**1, 24; **8:**9, 25, 28; **9:**16, 21, 27, 30; **10:**4, 11, 15, 16, 22, 23, 24, 25, 26; **11:**2; **12:**2, 3, 11, 11, 12, 15, 16, 17, 17, 21, 21, 23, 27, 31, 33, 35, 36, 37, 39, 40, 43; **13:**3, 6, 8, 19; **14:**10, 11, 14, 25; **15:**1, 21, 22, 25, 26; **16:**4, 4, 8, 16, 18, 22, 23, 25, 25, 26, 26, 29, 33, 34, 35; **17:**12; **18:**1, 3, 4, 9, 10, 14, 18, 22; **19:**5, 10, 11, 14, 15, 19, 21; **20:**5, 5, 6, 9, 11, 20, 24, 25, 25; **21:**2, 2, 9, 13, 19, 19, 24, 24, 25, 25, 25, 27, 30, 34, 36; **22:**1, 1, 1, 1, 3, 6, 9, 10, 14, 17, 27, 27, 29, 30, 31; **23:**8, 10, 11, 12, 15, 15, 20, 21, 23, 33; **24:**4, 14, 16; **25:**4, 6, 6, 12, 22, 37, 39; **26:**21, 26, 27, 27, 36; **27:**6, 9, 9, 16, 20, 21; **28:**2, 4, 12, 15, 30, 32, 40, 42, 43; **29:**1, 22, 26, 29, 30, 33, 33, 34, 35, 36, 36, 37, 37; **30:**1, 10, 10, 12, 15, 16, 16, 21, 32, 37, 37, 38; **31:**10, 10, 11, 13, 14, 17; **32:**23, 29, 29, 30, 31, 34; **33:**3, 5, 5, 14, 17, 20; **34:**7, 14, 16, 17, 18, 18, 21, 27; **35:**2, 6, 8, 8, 14, 15, 17, 17, 19, 19, 21, 21, 23, 27, 28, 35; **36:**3, 19, 20, 24, 25, 26, 29, 30, 30, 32, 32, 37; **37:**29; **38:**1, 5, 27, 27, 27, 30, 30, 30, 31, 31; **39:**1, 1, 4, 23, 27, 37, 38, 40, 41, 41; **40:**5, 8, 15; **Lev 1:**3, 4, 10; **3:**17; **4:**2, 14, 20, 20, 21, 21, 26, 28, 31, 35; **5:**4, 6, 7, 10, 11, 13, 16, 16, 16, 18, 19; **6:**7, 16, 29, 30; **7:**1, 6, 7, 15, 18, 18, 19, 24, 34, 34, 35, 37; **8:**2, 12, 14, 15, 18, 33, 33, 34, 35; **9:**2, 2, 3, 3, 3, 4, 4, 7, 7, 8, 12, 15, 15, 18; **10:**4, 6, 7, 9, 12, 13, 17, 17, 17; **11:**2, 4, 7, 8, 9, 13, 26, 27, 29, 31, 39; **12:**2, 4, 5, 6, 6, 6, 7, 8, 8, 8; **13:**4, 5, 8, 9, 11, 21, 25, 26, 27, 31, 33, 36, 50, 54, 59; **14:**4, 8, 11, 18, 19, 20, 21, 21, 22, 22, 23, 24, 25, 29, 31, 31, 31, 32, 32, 38, 39, 48, 53, 54; **15:**15, 15, 15, 15, 19, 24, 25, 30, 30, 30, 30, 32, 33, 33, 33; **16:**2, 2, 3, 3, 5, 5, 6, 10, 11, 11, 15, 16, 16, 17, 18, 20, 21, 24, 24, 24, 27, 29, 30, 31, 33, 34, 34; **17:**7, 11, 11, 13, 14; **18:**4, 6, 8, 21, 28, 30; **19:**3, 3, 4, 8, 10, 10, 16, 17, 17, 22, 23, 28, 28, 30, 31, 32, 36, 37; **20:**7, 8, 11, 13, 16; **21:**7, 23; **22:**2, 5, 7, 8, 9, 14, 27, 31; **23:**3, 3, 6, 7, 14, 21, 21, 22, 27, 28, 28, 31, 32, 34, 36, 40, 41; **24:**2, 3, 5, 9, 11, 18, 20, 20, 20; **25:**3, 10, 10, 11, 12, 15, 21, 21, 25, 29, 33, 50, 52, 55; **26:**2, 10, 18, 20, 20, 21, 24, 28, 34, 36, 40, 41, 43, 43; **27:**10, 10, 10, 16, 21, 27, 28, 29; **Nu 1:**5, 48, 50; **3:**12, 13, 18, 19, 20, 23, 25, 28, 29, 31, 32, 35, 36, 37, 38, 38, 41, 41, 41, 45, 47, 48, 49; **4:**16, 20, 25, 26, 26, 32, 35, 39, 43, 45, 47, 47; **5:**7, 8, 15, 29, 31; **6:**5, 9, 11, 11, 11, 12, 12, 14, 14, 14, 17, 19, 20; **7:**3, 3, 5, 7, 8, 10, 11, 16, 17, 22, 23, 28, 29, 34, 35, 40, 41, 46, 47, 52, 53, 58, 59, 64, 65, 70, 71, 76, 77, 82, 83, 84, 85, 85, 86, 87, 87, 88, 88; **8:**8, 12, 12, 16, 16, 17, 17, 19; **9:**8, 13, 19, 19, 20, 20, 22; **10:**2, 2, 25, 29, 32, 33; **11:**2, 4, 5, 13, 18, 19, 19, 20, 20, 21, 29, 31, 35; **12:**11, 14, 14, 15; **13:**20, 25; **14:**17, 18, 25, 32, 33, 34, 34, 34, 34, 40; **15:**5, 5, 7, 10, 11, 15, 24, 24, 25, 25, 26, 27, 28, 38; **16:**26, 28, 37, 38, 38, 46, 47; **17:**3, 3; **18:**1, 1, 4, 6, 14, 17, 19, 21, 21, 23, 31, 32; **19:**9, 9, 10, 11, 14, 16, 20; **20:**2, 19, 24, 29; **21:**7, 14, 27, 34; **22:**6, 12, 17, 20; **23:**1, 5, 7, 21, 21, 21, 22, 23, 23, 29; **25:**13, 13, 13; **26:**57, 65; **27:**14, 16; **28:**14, 14, 15, 22, 30; **29:**5, 11, 14, 14, 15; **31:**2, 5, 6, 18, 19, 49, 50, 53; **32:**1, 4, 4, 11, 12, 13, 15, 16, 16, 20, 24, 24, 27, 32, 36; **33:**8, 14; **35:**3, 5, 6, 11, 13, 15, 15, 19, 29, 31, 33, 33, 34; **36:**7; **Dt 1:**8, 9, 15, 15, 15, 15, 17, 17, 22, 30, 31, 31, 33, 40, 41, 42, 46; **2:**1, 5, 6, 7, 14, 22, 28, 35, 36; **3:**1, 2, 7, 22, 22, 28; **4:**7, 9, 19, 23, 27, 29, 29, 31, 34, 34, 40, 42, 43, 43, 43; **5:**5, 9, 9, 10, 13; **6:**15, 24, 25; **7:**6, 7, 9, 21, 22, 22, 25, 26, 26, 26, 26; **8:**2, 3, 4, 7, 10, 12, 16, 20; **9:**4, 6, 9, 12, 18, 19, 19, 20, 25; **10:**9, 10, 13, 19; **11:**5, 10, 12, 14, 14, 15, 25, 31; **12:**5, 11, 12, 15, 21, 23; **13:**5, 17; **14:**1, 8, 8, 9, 10, 19, 21, 23, 24, 27; **15:**2, 4, 12, 17, 17, 18, 19, 22, 22; **16:**1, 2, 3, 4, 6, 8, 11, 13, 15, 15, 15, 18, 19, 22, 22; **17:**1, 8, 8, 16, 16, 17, 17, 18, 20; **18:**1, 5, 10, 15, 16, 16, 20; **19:**3, 5, 10, 13, 19, 21, 21, 21, 21, 21; **20:**4, 4, 10, 14, 16, 20; **21:**5, 13, 13, 14, 23; **22:**2, 19, 24, 30; **23:**2, 3, 12, 14, 18, 21, 23; **24:**4, 5, 6, 16, 16, 16, 19, 20, 21, 21; **25:**9; **26:**2; **27:**20; **28:**20, 26, 32, 38, 39, 39, 40, 41, 47, 50, 50, 54, 64; **29:**5, 26; **30:**9, 11, 20; **31:**7, 7, 8, 14, 20, 21, 27, 29; **32:**9, 20, 22, 37, 43, 51; **33:**17, 21, 21; **34:**8, 9; **Jos 1:**5, 6, 9; **2:**7, 10, 10, 11, 14, 16, 16, 24; **3:**5; **4:**5, 8, 8, 13, 14, 23; **5:**6, 6, 15; **6:**3, 14, 16, 17, 18, 24; **7:**1, 3, 9, 11, 12, 12, 12, 13, 13, 13, 15, 15, 21; **8:**1, 2, 4, 6, 7, 18, 20, 26, 27, 27, 33; **9:**5, 7, 11, 11, 18, 20, 21, 23, 24, 27, 27; **10:**4, 5, 6, 8, 14, 19, 20, 25, 27, 42, 42; **11:**14, 18, 20, 20; **12:**2; **13:**6, 8, 12, 23, 33; **14:**4, 8, 10; **15:**12, 18, 18; **17:**15, 15, 16, 16; **18:**7, 20; **19:**9, 50; **20:**3, 5, 9; **21:**2, 13, 21, 44; **22:**3, 19, 20, 23, 23, 23, 26, 28, 29, 29, 34; **23:**3, 3, 5, 9, 9, 10, 10, 13; **24:**7, 13, 13, 15, 17, 18, 19, 22, 31, 32; **Jdg 1:**2, 7, 14, 14, 25, 33, 34; **2:**1, 2, 7, 10, 18; **3:**8, 9, 11, 14, 15, 19, 20, 28, 30; **4:**3, 3, 6, 9, 13, 14, 22, 22; **5:**3, 7, 16, 25, 25, 26, 26, 28, 30, 30, 30, 31; **6:**1, 2, 6, 30, 30; **7:**9, 15, 18, 18, 20, 20, 23; **8:**1, 8, 10, 20, 22, 27, 30, 35; **9:**17, 17, 22, 24, 25, 56, 57; **10:**2, 3, 8, 17; **11:**2, 5, 17, 17, 19, 25, 34, 35, 36, 37, 38, 40, 40; **12:**1, 7, 9, 11, 14; **13:**1, 5, 7, 15, 17, 22; **14:**3, 8, 10, 17; **15:**3, 10, 11, 20; **16:**17, 18, 18, 25, 28, 31; **17:**2, 8, 9; **18:**1, 2, 6, 19, 19, 26, 28, 30; **19:**15, 18, 19, 19, 23; **20:**6, 10, 23, 39, 47; **21:**6, 7, 9, 14, 15, 16, 17, 21, 22, 22; **Ru 1:**8, 12, 13, 13, 13, 20, 20; **2:**7, 16; **3:**1, 1, 9, 11, 14, 14, 16; **4:**7, 15, 15, 16; **1Sa 1:**11, 16, 20, 20, 23, 24; **2:**1, 3, 8, 11, 12, 13, 15, 17, 19, 19, 22, 25, 25, 29, 36; **3:**13; **4:**13, 13, 18, 18, 22; **5:**11; **6:**14; **7:**2, 5, 10, 12, 13, 15; **8:**3, 3, 6, 7, 13, 16, 18; **9:**3, 9, 16, 20, 23, 24, 25, 27, 27; **10:**7, 8, 14, 19, 21; **11:**1, 13; **12:**7, 13, 17, 19, 19, 19, 22, 22, 23, 23, 24; **13:**1, 8, 11, 12, 14, 14, 19, 19, 21, 21, 22; **14:**6, 12, 18, 29, 44, 45; **15:**2, 6, 11, 19, 24, 29, 32, 35; **16:**1, 1, 3, 5, 7, 11, 12, 16, 22; **17:**1, 8, 15, 16, 20, 25, 26, 27, 31, 36, 39; **18:**6, 6, 12, 14, 17, 19, 21, 23, 25, 29; **19:**5, 9; **20:**2, 6, 8, 17, 22, 23, 26, 27, 34, 42; **21:**7, 9; **22:**3, 8, 8, 11, 13, 15, 15, 17, 23; **23:**4, 6, 7, 15, 22, 25; **24:**2, 6, 10, 10, 11, 12, 17, 17, 18, 19; **25:**1, 9, 11, 17, 17, 21, 28, 31, 33, 33, 34, 39; **26:**9, 19, 20, 21, 23, 23, 23; **27:**1, 1, 4, 7; **28:**1, 2, 2, 3, 8, 9, 10, 15, 20, 22; **29:**3, 4; **30:**12, 25, 26; **31:**13; **2Sa 1:**7, 9, 10, 12, 12, 16, 17, 21, 24, 24, 26, 26; **2:**5, 6, 10, 11, 27; **3:**8, 14, 17, 18, 27, 29, 31, 33, 34, 37, 39, 39; **4:**10; **5:**2, 5, 5, 6, 11, 12; **6:**7, 11, 16, 17; **7:**3, 10, 11, 12, 13, 16, 21, 23, 27, 28, 29; **8:**2; **9:**1, 5, 10, 10; **10:**5, 11, 11, 15; **11:**2, 4, 10, 26, 27; **12:**4, 6, 6, 9, 13, 22, 28; **13:**2, 5, 6, 7, 8, 17, 18, 37, 38; **14:**2, 2, 7, 9, 13, 13, 15, 21, 22, 28, 29, 29, 29; **15:**2, 8, 12, 19, 28, 32; **16:**2, 2, 2, 8, 11, 18, 21, 23; **17:**10, 14, 17, 20, 29, 29; **18:**3, 5, 12, 18, 22, 31; **19:**1, 2, 7, 11, 21, 22, 22, 26, 32, 34, 38, 38; **20:**3, 11; **21:**1, 3, 4, 12; **22:**4, 7, 18, 21, 22, 23, 25, 31, 31, 31, 32, 35, 37, 40, 42, 50; **23:**6; **24:**10, 14, 15, 22, 24, 24; **1Ki 1:**3, 16, 20, 35, 40, 42; **2:**7, 9, 11, 15, 17, 18, 19, 26, 32, 32, 36, 38, 40, 42, 44; **3:**2, 9, 10, 11, 11, 11, 12, 13, 13, 27; **4:**7, 7, 7, 13, 22, 26, 27, 28; **5:**5, 6, 7, 9, 10, 11, 17, 18; **6:**2, 15, 31, 33; **7:**1, 8, 13, 14, 14, 16, 30, 31, 37, 38, 40, 42, 45, 45, 48, 50; **8:**13, 16, 18, 20, 21, 25, 39, 42, 44, 51, 53, 65, 65, 65; **9:**3, 4, 5, 8, 11, 11, 21, 22, 24; **10:**3, 8, 12, 12, 13, 29, 29; **11:**7, 7, 8, 8, 9, 12, 13, 13, 16, 25, 31, 32, 32, 33, 34, 34, 36, 38, 38, 42; **12:**2, 3, 5, 13, 15, 16, 24, 28, 30, 32, 33; **13:**4, 9, 13, 17, 23, 27, 28, 32, 33; **14:**5, 6, 13, 13, 15, 18, 22; **15:**4, 5; **16:**19, 24, 32; **17:**4, 7, 13, 14, 15, 16, 24; **18:**10, 18, 18, 25, 27, 36, 41, 45; **19:**3, 4, 7; **20:**9, 10, 11, 18, 18, 22, 29, 38, 39; **21:**2, 9, 12, 22, 25; **22:**1, 8, 12, 13, 16, 18, 23, 23, 48, 48; **2Ki 2:**2, 4, 6, 9, 16, 17; **3:**9, 9, 13, 14, 14, 17, 17, 18, 18; **4:**10, 13, 13, 14, 38, 43, 43, 44; **5:**1, 5, 23; **6:**2, 9, 16, 19, 23, 25, 33; **7:**6, 7, 16, 16, 20; **8:**1, 1, 1, 2, 9, 18, 19; **9:**3, 5, 5, 5, 16, 20, 26, 34; **10:**3, 6, 12, 19, 24, 27, 36; **11:**3, 7, 8, 9; **12:**5, 7, 7, 12, 13, 13, 14, 16, 16; **13:**4, 17; **14:**6, 6, 6, 6, 12, 17, 26, 28; **16:**6, 11, 15, 15, 18; **17:**4, 5, 9, 21, 35, 37; **18:**12, 20, 23, 26, 26; **19:**4, 4, 10, 26, 28, 31, 34, 34; **20:**1, 6, 12; **21:**3, 5, 13, 13, 14, 15; **22:**7, 7, 13, 13, 13, 17, 17; **23:**5, 7, 13, 13, 13, 27; **24:**1, 7, 16; **25:**4, 5, 12, 14, 16, 24, 26, 29; **1Ch 1:**19; **2:**7; **4:**23, 39, 41, 41; **5:**1, 2; **6:**49; **7:**2, 4, 4, 5, 7, 9, 11, 15, 22, 40; **9:**13, 18, 18, 19, 21, 23, 25, 26, 26, 28, 29; **10:**12, 14; **11:**2; **12:**18, 19, 21, 31, 32, 33, 35, 36, 39, 39, 39; **13:**3, 4, 14; **14:**1, 2; **15:**1, 1, 3, 12, 29, 29; **16:**1, 4, 11, 11, 33, 34, 37, 40, 41; **17:**2, 9, 10, 11, 12, 14, 19, 21, 25, 26, 27; **18:**8; **19:**5, 12, 12, 16; **21:**7, 8, 13, 17, 23, 23, 23, 25; **22:**1, 1, 2, 3, 3, 3, 4, 5, 6, 6, 13, 14, 14; **23:**2, 14, 24, 25, 27, 29; **24:**1, 4, 5; **25:**5; **26:**8, 12, 13, 13, 14, 28, 30, 32; **27:**1, 3, 27, 28, 29; **28:**2, 3, 4, 5, 6, 8, 9, 11, 12, 12, 13, 13, 15, 15, 16, 16, 17, 17, 17, 18, 18, 20; **29:**1, 1, 2, 3, 4, 5, 7, 9, 12, 15, 18, 19, 27; **2Ch 1:**1, 4, 9, 10, 11, 11, 17, 17; **2:**1, 1, 6, 8, 9, 12, 12; **3:**3, 15; **4:**6, 6, 9, 11, 13, 16, 19, 19, 22; **6:**2, 4, 8, 10, 16, 30, 34, 42; **7:**6, 8, 9, 9, 9, 12, 16, 17; **8:**8, 9, 11, 11; **9:**2, 7, 8, 11, 11, 12, 25, 30; **10:**2, 3, 5, 13, 15, 16; **11:**4, 5, 17, 23; **12:**14; **13:**10, 12, 14; **14:**1, 2, 6, 10, 11; **15:**3, 6, 7, 15; **16:**10, 14; **17:**16; **18:**1, 2, 2, 5, 7, 12, 15, 17, 22, 22; **19:**3, 7, 8; **20:**2, 3, 8, 11, 12, 15, 17, 21, 24, 30; **21:**6, 7, 19; **22:**3, 7, 9, 12; **23:**3, 6, 7, 8; **24:**3, 6, 8, 12, 14, 14, 14, 16, 22, 25; **25:**4, 4, 4, 4, 7, 8, 20, 20, 22, 25; **26:**8, 10, 15, 18, 18, 18, 18; **27:**5; **28:**2, 11, 16, 19, 23, 25; **29:**19, 21, 21, 21, 23, 24, 24, 32, 34, 36, 36; **30:**4, 9, 9, 17, 18, 18, 19, 21, 22, 22, 23, 24, 26; **31:**3, 3, 3, 10, 18, 19; **32:**1, 4, 7, 8, 9, 23, 23, 27, 27, 28, 28, 28, 29; **33:**3, 5, 13; **34:**4, 11, 11, 21, 21, 25, 25; **35:**4, 7, 9, 10, 14, 14, 14, 15, 16, 17, 23, 24, 25; **36:**12, 15, 21, 23; **Ezr 1:**4, 4, 6; **2:**69; **3:**4, 5, 7, 7, 11, 12; **4:**2, 3, 3, 7, 9, 12, 13, 22; **5:**4; **6:**9, 10, 17, 17, 20, 20, 20, 22; **7:**6, 9, 16, 17, 19, 19, 20, 20, 20, 21, 23, 23, 28; **8:**15, 16, 16, 17, 21, 22, 22, 25, 32, 34, 35; **9:**2, 2, 6, 8, 9, 10, 13; **10:**2, 2, 4, 10, 13; **Ne 1:**3, 4, 6, 9, 11; **2:**3, 6, 8, 8, 8, 8, 12, 16; **3:**31; **4:**4, 5, 6, 14, 20, 23; **5:**5, 14, 17, 18, 19, 19; **6:**9, 18; **7:**2, 5, 70, 70, 71, 72; **8:**1, 4, 9, 9, 10, 11, 17; **9:**1, 3, 3, 5, 8, 10, 11, 17, 20, 21, 28, 30; **10:**32, 33, 33, 33, 33, 33, 33, 33, 33, 37; **12:**29, 43, 43, 44, 44, 44, 47; **13:**2, 5, 5, 6, 9, 14, 15, 29, 31, 31; **Est 1:**3, 5, 5, 8, 8, 9, 11, 13, 15; **2:**2, 9, 10, 13, 14, 15, 18, 18, 22; **3:**2; **4:**2, 5, 7, 8, 8, 8, 11, 13, 14, 14, 16, 16; **5:**4, 8, 12; **6:**3, 10; **7:**4, 4, 7, 10; **8:**1, 6, 10, 12, 14, 17; **9:**2, 3, 4, 12, 26, 31; **10:**3, 3; **Job 1:**4, 5, 5; **2:**4, 13, 13, 13; **3:**5, 9, 10, 10, 13, 14, 17, 21, 21, 24; **4:**2, 6, 6; **5:**1, 3, 7, 9, 10, 10, 18; **6:**4, 19, 22, 29; **7:**2, 8, 16, 18, 19, 21, 21; **8:**9, 15; **9:**4, 15, 17, 19, 19, 28; **10:**6, 6, 15, 21; **11:**6, 11, 19; **12:**10; **13:**4, 8; **14:**2, 14, 15, 16, 16; **15:**4, 11, 16, 22, 23, 24, 25, 31, 34; **16:**22; **17:**3, 5, 10; **18:**12; **19:**6, 7, 21, 25, 27, 29; **20:**10, 19; **21:**21, 31; **22:**4, 6, 7, 7, 14, 17, 17, 21, 24; **23:**9, 11, 14; **24:**1, 3, 4, 5, 5, 8, 9, 12, 15, 15, 21; **26:**6, 10; **27:**6, 8, 12; **28:**3, 8, 13, 15, 19, 21, 24, 26; **29:**2, 12, 13, 15, 15, 19, 21, 22, 23, 23, 23; **30:**4, 7, 11, 24, 25, 25, 26, 26, 28; **31:**2, 3, 3, 6, 7, 9, 11, 15, 16, 18, 18, 20, 23, 28, 30, 37; **32:**4, 7, 11, 13, 18; **33:**4, 20, 22, 23, 24, 24, 29, 32; **34:**4, 5, 7, 18, 21, 23, 26, 27, 27, 36, 37; **35:**2; **36:**2, 4, 9, 13, 13, 15, 20, 20, 21; **37:**21; **38:**3, 7, 10, 14, 21, 23, 23, 25, 25, 30, 39, 41; **39:**8, 10, 13, 17, 30; **40:**7, 14; **41:**3, 3, 4, 4, 14, 21; **42:**3, 4, 7, 8, 8, 8, 10, 12; **Ps 1:**6; **2:**2, 6, 12, 12; **3:**5; **4:**T, 3, 8; **5:**T, 2, 2, 5, 10, 12; **6:**T, 2, 2, 5, 8; **7:**1, 8, 9, 16; **8:**T, 4, 5; **9:**T, 4, 9, 10, 10, 12, 12, 12, 15, 16, 18; **10:**2, 3, 8; **11:**T, 1, 1, 7; **12:**T, 1, 5; **13:**T; **14:**T, 2, 5, 7; **16:**1, 1, 8, 10; **17:**1, 1, 1, 2, 3, 12, 15; **18:**T, 3, 6, 17, 20, 21, 22, 24, 30, 30, 30, 31, 34, 36, 39, 41, 49; **19:**T, 9, 11; **20:**T, 5, 9; **21:**T, 2, 7, 12, 13; **22:**T, 1, 5, 11, 15, 18, 24, 24, 28; **23:**4, 5; **24:**2; **25:**4, 5, 7, 11, 14, 15, 15, 16, 20, 21; **26:**1, 3; **27:**5, 11, 11, 12, 14, 14; **28:**1, 2, 2, 4, 5, 5, 6, 6; **29:**1, 2; **30:**1, 2, 5, 8; **31:**T, 1, 1, 2, 3, 4, 4, 5, 7, 9, 17, 17, 19, 19, 19, 21, 22, 22, 23; **32:**1, 2, 7, 8, 11; **33:**1, 2, 4, 9, 12, 12, 17, 21, 22; **34:**5, 7, 9, 15, 17, 20; **35:**2, 7, 7, 8, 8, 12, 13, 13, 14, 24; **36:**T, 6, 9; **37:**2, 7, 9, 10, 13, 17, 24, 25, 28, 32, 34, 36, 37; **38:**9, 12, 15, 15, 15, 18, 20, 20; **39:**T, 6, 8, 9, 11, 12, 12; **40:**T, 1, 5, 5, 8, 12, 15, 16, 17; **41:**T, 4, 7, 11; **42:**T, 1, 1, 2, 3, 4; **43:**2; **44:**T, 4, 12, 21, 22; **45:**T, 1, 11, 11; **46:**T; **47:**T, 1, 2, 7, 9; **48:**11, 14; **49:**T, 3, 8, 15, 17; **50:**6, 10, 12, 17; **51:**T, 3, 5, 14; **52:**T, 5, 9, 9; **53:**T, 2, 5, 6; **54:**T, 3, 3, 5, 6, 7; **55:**T, 1, 2, 9, 15, 19, 20; **56:**T, 9, 12, 13; **57:**T, 1, 2, 6, 10; **58:**T, 11, 11; **59:**T, 3, 9, 9, 11, 15, 16, 16, 17; **60:**T, 4, 11, 12; **61:**T, 2, 2, 3, 5, 5; **62:**T, 1, 5, 8; **63:**1, 1, 1, 7; **64:**T; **65:**T, 2, 4, 9, 13; **66:**T, 5, 7, 16, 17, 17; **67:**T, 4; **68:**T, 1, 6, 10, 19; **69:**T, 1, 3, 3, 7, 7, 9, 16, 16, 17, 21, 31, 33, 35; **70:**T, 3, 4; **71:**2, 3, 6, 10, 11, 14, 15, 15, 22, 23, 23, 24; **72:**3, 13, 14, 15; **73:**2, 3, 7, 13, 27, 28; **74:**20; **75:**T, 6, 8, 9, 10; **76:**T, 10, 12; **77:**T, 2, 2, 3; **78:**2, 5, 12, 13, 22, 22, 24, 39, 44, 54, 56, 72; **79:**2, 2, 7, 8, 8, 9, 9, 10, 12; **80:**T, 9, 14, 15, 16; **81:**T, 3, 4, 5, 10; **82:**7, 8; **83:**12, 12; **84:**T, 11; **85:**T, 8, 13; **86:**1, 2, 2, 3, 4, 5, 10, 13, 13, 16, 17; **88:**T, 3, 9, 9; **89:**5, 6, 15, 29, 39; **90:**4, 14; **91:**3, 11; **92:**4, 4, 13; **94:**13, 15, 16, 23; **95:**3, 5, 7, 9, 10; **96:**13; **97:**7, 9; **98:**1, 4, 9; **99:**5, 6, 9; **100:**5; **102:**3, 10, 14, 16, 18; **103:**2, 10, 11, 14, 20, 22; **104:**9, 11, 14, 14, 15, 16, 18, 18, 21, 34, 35; **105:**4, 4, 16, 20, 24, 28, 38, 40, 42; **106:**1, 13, 15, 20, 24, 24; **107:**1, 3, 8, 8, 9, 15, 15, 16, 17, 21, 21, 31, 31; **108:**4, 12, 13; **109:**T, 3, 4, 5, 5, 6, 7, 16, 20, 21, 22, 31; **111:**9, 10; **112:**5, 7; **113:**4; **115:**1, 3, 17; **116:**7, 12, 12, 13; **117:**2; **118:**1, 6, 7, 19, 21, 29; **119:**2, 20, 22, 35, 36, 36, 38, 42, 42, 43, 45, 49, 62, 65, 71, 71, 74, 74, 77, 81, 85, 91, 93, 94, 98, 99, 100, 102, 105, 105, 110, 115, 121, 122, 126, 126, 131, 132, 139, 147, 153, 155, 158, 166, 171, 172, 173, 174, 176; **120:**T, 7, 7, 7; **121:**T; **122:**T, 6, 8, 9, 9; **123:**T, 2, 2, 3; **124:**T; **125:**T, 3; **126:**T, 2, 2, 3; **127:**T, 2, 2, 2; **128:**T, 4; **129:**T; **130:**T, 1, 6, 6, 6, 7; **131:**T, 1; **132:**T, 5, 5, 9, 10, 10, 13, 14, 16, 17; **133:**T, 2, 3; **134:**T; **135:**3, 4, 4, 4, 14, 21; **136:**1; **137:**3, 8; **138:**2, 4, 5, 6, 8, 8, 8; **139:**T, 6, 6, 14, 22; **140:**T, 4, 6, 9, 13; **141:**1, 4, 8, 9; **142:**1, 3, 3, 4, 6, 6, 6, 7; **143:**6, 6, 6, 7, 8, 8, 10, 11, 12; **144:**1, 1, 3, 4, 10; **145:**13, 15, 19; **146:**3, 9; **147:**8, 9, 13; **148:**5, 13; **149:**4, 5; **150:**2; **Pr 1:**18, 19, 28, 28, 29, 32; **2:**3, 4, 4, 6, 10, 21; **3:**2, 12, 14, 22, 26, 29; **4:**2, 3, 6, 13, 16, 16, 22, 23, 26; **5:**6, 17, 18, 21, 23; **6:**1, 8, 23, 25, 26, 30, 32, 34; **7:**15, 19, 26; **8:**6, 7, 11, 17, 21, 32, 34, 34, 35; **10:**19, 23; **11:**7, 10, 15, 18, 26, 27, 27; **12:**10; **14:**3, 7, 24, 26; **15:**14, 15, 15, 16, 22, 30; **16:**4, 4, 12, 21, 24, 26, 27; **17:**7, 7, 8, 10, 13, 16, 18, 21, 26, 26; **18:**5, 6, 15, 21, 23; **19:**10, 10; **20:**22, 22; **21:**18, 25, 26, 31; **22:**1, 18, 20, 23, 26; **23:**5, 8, 9, 11, 18, 21, 24, 28, 32; **24:**2, 7, 12, 13, 18, 20, 22, 29; **25:**4, 6, 7, 27; **26:**12, 12, 20, 26, 27; **27:**10, 23, 24, 24, 26, 26, 27; **28:**14, 21; **29:**5, 6, 19, 19, 20, 20; **30:**5, 9, 10, 25, 30; **31:**4, 5, 6, 6, 8, 8, 8, 9, 15, 15, 18, 21, 23, 31; **Ecc 1:**3, 13, 18; **2:**1, 4, 10, 14, 16, 20, 21, 22, 25; **3:**1, 1, 8, 8, 9, 11, 12, 13, 15, 17, 18, 19, 21, 22; **4:**3, 8, 9, 12; **5:**2, 4, 8, 9, 15, 16, 16, 18, 18, 20, 20; **6:**7; **7:**2, 3, 9, 10, 10, 13, 22, 25; **8:**3, 6, 13, 15, 16; **9:**3, 4, 4, 7, 9, 10, 16; **10:**15, 16, 17; **11:**1, 2, 4, 6, 9; **12:**7, 13, 14; **SS 1:**2, 4, 7, 11; **2:**5, 11, 14, 15; **3:**1, 2, 9; **5:**2, 6, 6; **6:**5; **7:**6, 13, 13; **8:**6, 8, 11, 12, 12; **Isa 1:**2, 3, 13, 15, 17, 28; **2:**3; **3:**9, 10, 17, 24; **4:**5; **5:**1, 2, 8, 11, 18, 20, 21, 22, 24, 27, 28; **6:**5, 8, 10; **7:**8, 11, 11, 18, 18, 25; **8:**9, 10, 14, 17, 18; **9:**4, 6, 13, 16, 17, 19; **10:**1, 1, 3, 5, 12, 29, 30, 32; **11:**10, 11, 12, 16, 16; **12:**5, 6; **13:**6, 6, 9, 11, 11, 13, 17, 18; **14:**5, 13, 20, 26, 26, 29, 30, 31, 31; **15:**2, 5; **16:**7, 8, 9, 9, 9, 11, 11; **17:**4, 7, 8; **18:**1, 2, 4, 6, 7; **19:**3, 8, 9, 17, 20, 22, 25; **20:**3, 4, 6; **21:**5, 5; **22:**4, 8, 11, 11, 12, 13, 16, 17, 23; **23:**1, 4, 9, 10, 14, 15, 18; **24:**5, 5, 11, 14, 16, 20; **25:**1, 4, 6, 10; **26:**4, 7, 9, 9, 9, 12, 16, 19, 19, 21, 21; **27:**5, 7, 11, 11; **28:**1, 1, 2, 6, 13, 15, 20, 22, 25, 26; **29:**1, 2, 10, 15, 23; **30:**1, 2, 2, 4, 6, 9, 15, 16, 18, 18, 18, 19, 20, 20, 23, 33; **31:**1, 1, 3; **32:**3, 6, 8, 10, 12, 12, 13; **33:**1, 2, 2, 7, 8, 8, 22, 22, 24; **34:**2, 6, 6, 8, 8, 11, 13, 13, 16; **35:**4, 8; **36:**5, 8, 11, 11; **37:**4, 4, 10, 27, 29, 32, 35, 35; **38:**1, 14, 15, 16, 17, 17, 18; **40:**2, 3, 3, 15; **41:**1, 5, 8, 9, 10, 10, 12, 14, 17, 18; **42:**4, 6, 11, 22, 22, 24; **43:**1, 3, 3, 4, 5, 7, 7, 14, 19, 19, 19, 20, 21, 22, 23, 23, 25; **44:**3, 8, 9, 15, 19, 21, 22, 23, 23; **45:**4, 4, 9, 13, 18, 19, 21, 22, 22; **46:**3, 4, 9, 10, 13; **47:**1, 6, 14; **48:**8, 9, 9, 11, 11, 19, 21, 22; **49:**4, 4, 10, 11, 13, 13, 15, 18, 18, 21, 21, 23, 23, 25; **50:**2, 6; **51:**1, 4, 5, 5, 6, 8, 15, 20; **52:**1, 3, 3, 8, 9, 11, 12, 12, 15; **53:**4, 5, 8, 10, 11, 11, 12; **54:**1, 3, 5, 6, 7, 8, 10; **55:**2, 2, 3, 7, 9, 10, 10; **56:**1, 3, 3, 4, 5, 7, 8, 10; **57:**2, 8, 13, 13, 16, 19, 21; **58:**3, 6; **59:**11, 12, 18, 19; **60:**1, 4, 5, 6, 7, 9, 10, 12, 15, 17, 17, 17, 17, 19, 20, 21; **61:**3, 3, 3, 4, 8, 8, 10; **62:**1, 1, 3, 4, 5, 5, 6, 10, 10; **63:**4, 4, 7, 17; **64:**2, 4, 4, 4, 7; **65:**1, 7, 7, 7, 8, 8, 10, 10, 12, 14, 15, 16, 22, 23; **66:**1, 4, 5, 10, 24; **Jer 1:**6, 7, 8, 14, 16, 16, 18, 19; **2:**11, 11, 13, 13, 23, 24, 27, 28, 32, 36, 37; **3:**1, 2, 3, 12, 14, 16, 21, 22, 24, 25; **4:**5, 6, 7, 8, 10, 10, 11, 17, 19, 22, 29, 31, 31; **5:**3, 6, 7, 8, 9, 10, 22, 24, 26, 26, 29; **6:**1, 3, 4, 6, 6, 12, 14, 16, 16, 17, 20, 23, 26, 26; **7:**14, 16, 16, 16, 29, 32, 32, 33; **8:**6, 9, 9, 11, 13, 14, 15, 15, 16, 21, 22; **9:**1, 2, 3, 3, 8, 9, 10, 10, 10, 17, 21; **10:**5, 6, 14, 18, 22, 24, 25; **11:**4, 7, 11, 13, 14, 14, 14, 17, 20, 23; **12:**3, 13, 14, 14; **13:**10, 15, 16, 16, 18, 20, 23, 25; **14:**4, 6, 7, 8, 10, 11, 15, 16, 16, 17, 19, 19, 21, 22; **15:**1, 2, 2, 2, 2, 5, 5, 9, 14, 15, 16, 20; **16:**3, 4, 4, 5, 5, 6, 7, 7, 9, 15, 15, 16, 16, 18, 19; **17:**3, 4, 4, 6, 13, 14, 16; **18:**15, 20, 20, 22, 22; **19:**4, 6, 7, 7; **20:**4, 6, 10, 12, 13, 17; **21:**5, 10, 14; **22:**7, 10, 10, 10, 11, 13, 16, 18, 20, 20, 20, 20, 30; **23:**1, 1, 2, 4, 5, 10, 10, 12, 13, 15, 16, 21, 32, 36; **24:**6, 7; **25:**1, 3, 11, 12, 27, 29, 31, 33, 36; **26:**5, 11, 14, 15, 15, 16, 19, 20; **27:**4, 19, 22; **29:**6, 7, 7, 10, 10, 11, 11, 11, 11, 13, 15, 19, 21, 23, 28, 28, 32, 32; **30:**2, 3, 7, 8, 9, 9, 10, 11, 14, 17, 21; **31:**2, 7, 7, 8, 9, 11, 11, 13, 13, 15, 15, 16, 17, 18, 18, 19, 20, 22, 25, 30, 34, 37, 38; **32:**8, 8, 9, 14, 15, 17, 18, 25, 27, 39, 39, 40, 44; **33:**4, 5, 9, 11, 11, 14, 17, 21; **34:**5, 5, 8, 19, 20, 21; **36:**3, 4, 7, 20, 31; **37:**3, 9, 16, 20; **38:**9, 14, 19, 20, 26, 27; **39:**10; **40:**2, 3, 4, 9, 9, 10, 16; **41:**13, 17; **42:**2, 6, 6, 8, 8, 10, 10, 11, 18, 20, 20; **43:**11, 11, 11; **44:**7, 8, 17, 27; **45:**5; **46:**10, 14, 14, 19, 21, 21, 23, 27, 28; **47:**4, 7; **48:**1, 2, 4, 6, 8, 9, 17, 18, 26, 29, 31, 31, 32, 32, 35, 36, 36, 38, 42, 44, 45; **49:**2, 3, 3, 8, 9, 11, 13, 14, 19, 20, 23, 30, 30; **50:**3, 7, 9, 14, 20, 24, 24, 24, 27, 27, 27, 29, 29, 32, 34, 39, 42, 44; **51:**5, 6, 8, 9, 11, 12, 17, 24, 26, 27, 29, 33, 35, 35, 39, 46, 47, 48, 55, 56, 58; **52:**7, 8, 11, 16, 18, 19, 20, 33; **La 1:**5, 5, 6, 8, 11, 11, 16, 16, 17, 18, 18, 19, 19, 20, 22; **2:**8, 9, 13, 19; **3:**18, 25, 26, 27, 29, 31, 33, 39, 47, 58, 64; **4:**4, 5, 5, 9, 17, 19; **5:**4, 9, 18, 20; **Eze 1:**21; **2:**5, 6, 7; **3:**7, 10, 15, 17, 18, 20, 26, 26, 27; **4:**4, 5, 5, 6, 6, 9, 10, 11, 13, 14; **5:**2; **6:**9, 9; **7:**3, 3, 4, 8, 9, 11, 12, 12, 12, 13, 14, 16, 19, 23, 25, 26; **8:**14, 18; **9:**10; **10:**17, 21; **11:**2, 5, 7, 11, 12, 21, 21, 21; **12:**3, 6, 10, 11, 11, 23, 25, 27; **13:**3, 18, 19, 23; **14:**4, 7, 10; **15:**3, 4; **16:**5, 12, 12, 12, 15, 16, 31, 31, 33, 38, 43, 43, 45, 45, 54, 58, 59; **17:**7, 16, 18, 19, 20; **18:**4, 7, 16, 18, 18, 19, 19, 20, 20, 20, 20, 24, 26, 31, 31; **19:**1, 5, 8, 14; **20:**1, 3, 6, 7, 9, 16, 20, 24, 28, 31, 39, 40; **21:**10, 11, 12, 15, 15, 19, 22, 24, 28, 29, 32; **22:**7, 27, 30, 30, 31; **23:**4, 8, 23, 24, 24, 28, 34, 40, 45, 47, 49; **24:**6, 7, 7, 9, 23, 24, 27; **25:**5, 5, 17; **26:**5, 5, 7, 14, 14, 17, 19, 21; **27:**2, 5, 6, 9, 12, 14, 17, 18, 19, 19, 21, 22, 31, 36; **28:**4, 12, 13, 17, 24, 25; **29:**3, 3, 5, 6, 6, 11, 12, 16, 18, 20, 20; **30:**3, 3, 6, 10, 18; **31:**4, 7, 14, 16; **32:**2, 10, 11, 16, 16, 18, 18, 18, 20, 32; **33:**6, 7, 7, 8, 13, 15, 16, 18; **34:**2, 4, 5, 6, 8, 10, 11, 12, 16, 17, 18, 18, 18, 19, 21, 28, 29; **35:**5, 5, 6, 10, 11, 12; **36:**5, 5, 8, 9, 19, 20, 21, 24, 30, 31, 36, 37; **37:**23, 28; **38:**12, 19; **39:**5, 9, 10, 10, 11, 12, 13, 13, 14, 17, 19, 23, 23, 25, 25, 26, 28, 28, 29; **40:**38, 39, 42, 44, 45, 46, 46; **41:**6, 8; **42:**5, 8, 8; **43:**18, 19, 20, 21, 22, 25, 26, 26, 26; **44:**2, 7, 8, 11, 12, 13, 15, 26, 27, 28, 29; **45:**1, 2, 4, 4, 5, 5, 7, 9, 11, 12, 13, 15, 15, 17, 20, 20, 21, 22, 23, 25; **46:**5, 7, 12, 14, 18; **47:**3, 9, 12, 12, 12, 13, 13, 22, 22; **48:**8, 9, 10, 11, 14, 15, 17, 18, 22, 22, 29, 31, 31, 31, 32, 33, 34; **Da 1:**5, 8, 9, 10, 12, 14, 17; **2:**3, 8, 20, 23, 47; **4:**2, 9, 11, 12, 16, 17, 18, 19, 20, 21, 22, 23, 31, 34; **5:**1, 7, 12, 23; **6:**2, 4, 5, 7, 11, 12, 14, 14, 16, 22, 26; **7:**8, 12, 12, 22, 25; **8:**12, 26, 27, 27; **9:**2, 10, 14, 17, 18, 19, 19, 20, 23, 24, 24, 27; **10:**2, 11, 12, 13, 14, 19, 19; **11:**2, 4, 8, 21, 24, 25, 27, 30, 33, 35, 36, 37, 37, 37, 37; **12:**7, 9, 9, 13, 13; **Hos 1:**4, 6, 9; **2:**2, 5, 5, 5, 5, 7, 13, 13, 21, 21, 22, 23; **3:**1, 2, 3; **4:**5, 6, 7, 9, 10, 14, 14, 18, 18; **5:**1, 1, 2, 7, 15, 15, 15; **6:**4, 9, 11; **7:**7, 12, 13, 13, 14; **8:**1, 2, 4, 9, 11, 13; **9:**1, 7, 7, 8, 9, 10, 11, 14, 14; **10:**3, 5, 5, 10, 10, 12; **11:**7, 9, 10; **12:**2, 4, 14; **13:**4, 10, 10, 12, 14; **14:**1, 4, 8; **Joel 1:**14, 18; **2:**13, 15, 18, 23, 26; **3:**2, 2, 3, 3, 4, 7, 9, 9, 13; **Am 2:**6, 6, 9, 10, 16; **3:**2, 14; **4:**1, 8, 13; **5:**5, 7, 12, 13, 16, 17, 18, 18, 18; **6:**1, 1, 4, 10; **7:**2, 5; **8:**2, 5, 6, 8, 12, 13; **9:**7, 9; **Ob** 5, 7, 8, 11, 17; **Jnh 1:**3, 5, 5, 12, 13, 14, 14, 14, 17, 17; **2:**9; **4:**2, 4, 6, 6, 9, 11; **Mic 1:**5, 6, 9, 12, 14, 16, 16; **2:**1, 10; **3:**3, 4, 5, 6, 6, 8, 11, 11,

11; **4:**2, 4, 8, 10, 11, 13; **5:**4; **6:**4, 6, 7, 13; **7:**2, 6, 7, 7, 7, 8, 9, 9, 15, 16; **Na 1:**14, 15; **2:**1, 2; **3:**1, 11, 14, 19, 19; **Hab 1:**2, 5, 7, 11, 12; **2:**3, 6, 9, 12, 14, 15, 19, 19; **3:**16, 19; **Zep 1:**5, 6, 7, 7, 11, 17, 18; **2:**5, 5, 6, 7, 10, 14; **3:**1, 3, 3, 7, 8, 11, 12, 15, 17, 18; **Hag 1:**5, 7, 9, 11; **2:**4, 6, 15, 16, 23; **Zec 1:**9, 12, 14, 14, 16; **2:**4, 5, 6, 8, 10, 13; **4:**10, 10; **5:**6, 11; **7:**3, 5; **8:**2, 2, 6, 10, 10, 12, 14, 19, 23; **9:**1, 2, 2, 5, 12, 12; **10:**1, 3, 6, 8, 10, 11; **11:**2, 3, 3, 4, 4, 5, 7, 7, 12, 16, 17; **12:**3, 9, 10, 10, 10, 10; **13:**1, 1, 3; **14:**1, 4, 5, 7; **Mal 1:**2, 3, 5, 11, 14; **2:**1, 5, 7, 7, 9, 11, 16; **3:**1, 2, 5, 9, 10, 11, 12, 14, 15; **4:**2, 4; **Mt 1:**20, 21; **2:**5, 6, 6, 8, 14, 18, 18; **3:**3, 3; **4:**2, 4, 6, 10, 11, 16, 18, 19; **5:**3, 3, 4, 5, 6, 6, 7, 8, 9, 9, 10, 10, 12, 14, 15, 16, 29, 29, 30, 30, 35, 36, 41, 44, 45; **6:**11, 16, 22, 24, 30, 30, 33, 34, 34; **7:**2, 7, 8, 9, 10, 12, 12, 13, 29; **8:**4, 12, 15, 22; **9:**8, 13, 16, 20, 21, 24, 36, 36, 38; **10:**11, 11, 17, 20, 26, 27, 39, 41; **11:**3, 3, 9, 13, 18, 21, 23, 23, 25, 25, 29, 30; **12:**4, 8, 14, 27, 34, 39, 40, 40, 40; **13:**15, 45; **14:**3, 4, 6, 12, 15, 24; **15:**4, 5, 9, 19, 22, 32, 32, 33, 36; **16:**4, 25, 25, 27; **17:**4, 4, 4, 14, 24, 27; **18:**6, 7, 7, 10, 12, 19, 20, 23, 27, 29; **19:**3, 6, 12, 13, 14, 23, 24, 24, 29; **20:**1, 1, 13, 15, 23, 28, 28, 32, 34; **21:**9, 15, 16, 22, 32, 33, 36, 38; **22:**2, 11, 14, 15, 19, 28, 30, 43; **23:**3, 5, 8, 9, 10, 13, 13, 15, 15, 16, 16, 19, 23, 23, 25, 27, 29, 29, 29, 39; **24:**5, 19, 19, 21, 22, 24, 27, 44, 48; **25:**3, 9, 9, 11, 14, 18, 34, 35, 36, 41, 42; **26:**9, 10, 12, 16, 24, 24, 24, 26, 27, 28, 31, 41, 43, 50, 53, 62; **27:**4, 6, 7, 20, 20, 24, 25, 35, 43, 47, 55, 58; **28:**5, 10, 14, 16; **Mk 1:**3, 3, 13, 16, 17, 22, 31, 37, 44; **2:**2, 21, 26; **3:**4, 6, 8, 31, 32; **4:**19; **5:**7, 8, 14, 15, 19, 20, 25, 28; **6:**17, 18, 21, 22, 24, 24, 29, 31, 32, 37, 52; **7:**5, 7, 8, 10, 11, 11, 21, 22, 37; **8:**2, 2, 3, 4, 6, 35, 35, 35; **9:**5, 5, 5, 6, 17, 40, 42, 49, 50; **10:**6, 9, 14, 19, 21, 23, 25, 25, 29, 29, 40, 45, 45, 51; **11:**13, 17, 24, 32; **12:**1, 7, 12, 13, 23, 25, 36, 38, 44; **13:**17, 17, 19, 20, 22, 34, 35, 37; **14:**1, 5, 6, 8, 11, 21, 21, 21, 22, 23, 24, 27, 36, 38, 40, 54, 60, 66; **15:**7, 10, 24, 35, 41, 43, 43, 44; **16:**6, 14; **Lk 1:**3, 8, 13, 15, 17, 20, 21, 24, 30, 37, 44, 48, 49, 49, 55, 57, 59, 63, 66, 76; **2:**3, 6, 7, 10, 20, 22, 36, 38, 41, 44, 45, 48; **3:**4, 4, 7, 19, 19; **4:**2, 4, 10, 18, 25, 39, 42; **5:**2, 7, 9, 10, 14, 16, 36; **6:**4, 9, 9, 20, 21, 21, 23, 23, 24, 25, 25, 26, 28, 28, 30, 31, 31, 32, 34, 35, 38, 39; **7:**5, 5, 6, 18, 19, 20, 26, 29, 30, 30, 33, 36, 43; **8:**6, 13, 17, 23, 27, 29, 30, 35, 35, 37, 39, 39, 40, 43, 46; **9:**12, 13, 14, 22, 24, 24, 33, 33, 33, 50, 51, 51, 52, 60, 62; **10:**2, 13, 21, 21; **11:**6, 6, 7, 9, 10, 11, 12, 16, 19, 21, 24, 34, 37, 42, 42, 43, 43, 44, 44, 46, 46, 47, 47, 47, 50, 52, 52; **12:**3, 12, 15, 19, 23, 28, 28, 29, 32, 33, 35, 36, 37, 37, 38, 40, 41, 41, 45, 47, 57; **13:**7, 11, 14, 15, 16, 16, 25, 28, 33, 33; **14:**8, 10, 11, 12, 14, 17, 22, 24, 24, 28, 33, 34, 35, 35; **15:**4, 22, 22, 24, 29, 29, 32; **16:**6, 7, 8, 9, 13, 21, 28; **17:**1, 2, 16, 21, 23, 24; **18:**1, 2, 3, 4, 11, 13, 14, 16, 16, 20, 24, 25, 25, 29, 41; **19:**5, 9, 13, 35, 37, 39; **20:**9, 14, 20, 33, 34, 35, 42, 46; **21:**4, 8, 15, 21, 22, 23, 23, 23, 28, 35; **22:**6, 16, 17, 18, 19, 19, 20, 22, 22, 27, 32, 37, 37, 71; **23:**8, 15, 19, 19, 22, 23, 25, 28, 28, 28, 29, 31, 34, 41, 51, 52, 54; **24:**5, 40, 47; **Jn 1:**15, 17, 23, 30, 33, 45, 46; **2:**6, 12, 13, 14, 17; **3:**13, 16, 18, 19, 20, 22, 23, 28, 34, 34; **4:**9, 9, 10, 18, 22, 23, 24, 35, 40, 41, 45; **5:**1, 5, 7, 13, 16, 20, 24, 35, 43, 44; **6:**4, 5, 6, 16, 22, 24, 27, 27, 30, 38, 40, 44, 55, 64; **7:**2, 3, 5, 6, 10, 13, 18, 18, 23, 23, 23, 27, 34, 36, 38, 42, 52; **8:**14, 21, 24, 26, 29, 39, 44, 44, 49; **9:**16, 21, 23, 24, 29; **10:**2, 3, 7, 11, 13, 15, 18, 18, 29, 32, 33, 33; **11:**4, 6, 15, 17, 26, 39, 41, 42, 50, 51, 52, 52, 55, 56; **12:**6, 6, 7, 11, 23, 25, 30, 31, 35, 39, 43, 45, 47; **13:**2, 10, 11, 29, 31, 33, 35, 37, 38; **14:**2, 13, 17, 19, 28; **15:**3, 4, 5, 13, 16, 21, 22; **16:**2, 4, 7, 23, 27; **17:**2, 8, 9, 9, 11, 12, 20, 20, 21, 26; **18:**4, 7, 14, 23, 23, 33, 37; **19:**14, 24, 38; **20:**9, 15, 17, 20; **21:**7, 7, 8; **Ac 1:**7, 14, 16, 18, 24, 25; **2:**15, 24, 25, 27, 29, 34, 38, 40, 46; **3:**3, 6, 13, 21, 21, 25; **4:**9, 11, 12, 13, 21, 22, 22, 26, 27, 36, 37; **5:**3, 8, 13, 21, 21, 26, 28, 34, 41, 42; **6:**6; **7:**6, 11, 14, 20, 20, 33, 34, 36, 40, 46, 46, 49; **8:**5, 9, 15, 16, 20, 21, 23, 24, 26, 33; **9:**7, 9, 11, 15, 16, 19, 24, 33, 36, 37, 39; **10:**19, 20, 21, 22, 23, 24, 28, 29, 29, 33, 36, 38, 46, 48, 48; **11:**12, 26; **12:**4, 5, 12, 17, 19, 19, 20; **13:**2, 2, 4, 7, 11, 13, 14, 15, 21, 21, 22, 24, 26, 34, 36, 38, 40, 41, 47, 48; **14:**6, 20, 23, 26, 28; **15:**9, 14, 15, 21, 21, 26, 28, 33, 39; **16:**3, 3, 7, 10, 10, 13, 16, 29; **17:**2, 5, 7, 15, 16, 23, 25, 28, 31, 31; **18:**3, 5, 10, 11, 12, 18, 18, 18, 28; **19:**8, 10, 27, 33, 34, 40; **20:**1, 1, 3, 5, 13, 16, 21, 24, 27, 27, 31, 32; **21:**2, 13, 13, 15, 22, 24, 25, 26, 29; **22:**5, 18, 21, 25; **23:**5, 8, 23, 24; **24:**2, 3, 4, 5, 10, 10, 21, 24, 25, 25, 26; **25:**1, 14, 17, 26, 27; **26:**3, 7, 14, 16, 18, 21, 26, 26, 29; **27:**1, 3, 6, 9, 20, 21, 23, 24, 25, 29, 33, 34, 34, 37, 43, 44; **28:**6, 7, 8, 10, 18, 18, 22, 27, 30; **Ro 1:**5, 8, 9, 10, 11, 14, 16, 19, 20, 27, 32; **2:**1, 3, 5, 5, 8, 9, 9, 9, 10, 10, 10, 11, 12, 13, 15, 17, 19, 19, 20, 28; **3:**5, 5, 9, 19, 20, 20, 23, 25, 25, 25; **4:**2, 3, 7, 8, 9, 9, 14, 16, 23, 24; **5:**1, 3, 3, 5, 6, 7, 7, 8, 8, 10, 11, 12, 15, 16; **6:**4, 7, 10, 11, 13, 13, 14, 23; **7:**4, 6, 13, 15; **8:**1, 2, 3, 4, 7, 13, 14, 16, 17, 19, 19, 22, 23, 24, 24, 26, 26, 26, 27, 27, 28, 28, 29, 31, 32, 33, 34, 34, 34, 34, 36, 38; **9:**3, 6, 7, 9, 15, 16, 17, 17, 19, 21, 22, 28; **10:**2, 3, 4, 5, 9, 10, 12, 13, 16, 19, 20, 20, 20; **11:**5, 6, 7, 11, 13, 14, 15, 15, 16, 19, 21, 24, 28, 29, 32, 33, 34, 36, 36; **12:**1, 8, 12, 12, 13, 13, 17, 19; **13:**1, 3, 4, 4, 5, 6, 6, 8, 9, 11, 11; **14:**2, 3, 6, 7, 9, 11, 14, 15, 16, 17, 19, 23; **15:**3, 4, 9, 15, 17, 24, 26, 26, 29, 30, 30; **16:**2, 3, 4, 6, 12, 17, 22, 25; **1Co 1:**4, 7, 9, 9, 11, 13, 15, 17, 17, 30, 30; **2:**2, 7, 9, 16, 16; **3:**3, 11, 17, 19; **4:**8, 15, 15, 17, 20; **5:**7; **6:**7, 11, 11, 12, 13, 13, 13, 13, 16, 18, 20; **7:**5, 10, 14, 14, 15, 17, 18, 19, 25, 31, 35, 40; **8:**3, 6, 11, 13; **9:**2, 9, 11, 16, 16, 25; **10:**4, 7, 10, 11, 12, 15, 24, 26, 27, 28, 29, 29, 30, 30, 31, 33, 33; **11:**5, 6, 7, 8, 9, 9, 12, 13, 14, 15, 17, 21, 22, 23, 24, 26, 29, 33, 33; **12:**1, 25, 25; **14:**2, 5, 7, 7, 9, 10, 12, 13, 14, 16, 22, 22, 22, 33, 34, 35, 35; **15:**1, 3, 9, 10, 13, 15, 17, 19, 25, 27, 29, 31, 32, 33, 34, 42, 42, 44, 52, 53, 56, 58, 58; **16:**1, 2, 3, 4, 5, 9, 9, 17, 19, 20; **2Co 1:**5, 6, 6, 11, 11, 20, 21; **2:**2, 10, 10, 11, 16; **3:**1, 7; **4:**5, 6, 12, 15, 17, 17, 18; **5:**1, 1, 2, 3, 5, 8, 10, 10, 13, 14, 15, 15, 17, 19, 21, 21; **6:**2, 16; **7:**3, 5, 7, 8, 8, 8, 10, 12, 15; **8:**1, 3, 4, 4, 5, 5, 7, 9, 10, 16, 20; **9:**1, 2, 7, 10, 13, 14, 15, 15; **10:**10, 13, 14, 15, 18; **11:**2, 2, 6, 9, 9; **12:**10, 10, 11, 11, 12, 13, 14, 14, 14, 15, 18, 19, 20, 21; **13:**8, 9, 10; **Gal 1:**4, 12, 15, 18, 18, 20; **2:**4, 5, 5, 6, 8, 8, 8, 11, 16, 19, 19, 20, 21, 21; **3:**1, 2, 4, 10, 11, 13, 13, 18, 28; **4:**1, 5, 11, 11, 12, 14, 17, 19, 27, 30; **5:**4, 6, 8, 13, 14, 19; **6:**4, 5, 5, 9, 12, 12, 14, 17; **Eph 1:**6, 11, 14, 15, 16, 16, 19, 22; **2:**6, 7, 8, 9, 10, 10, 14, 18, 21; **3:**8, 13; **4:**1, 1, 2, 17, 27, 28; **5:**2, 4, 5, 6, 8, 9, 16, 20, 21, 23, 25, 28, 29, 29; **6:**1, 7, 7, 8, 12, 15, 18, 19, 19, 20, 20, 22; **Php 1:**4, 7, 8, 9, 10, 11, 13, 16, 19, 19, 19, 20, 20, 21, 21, 22, 23, 24, 26, 27, 29, 29, 30; **2:**13, 17, 21, 21, 26, 28, 30, 30, 30; **3:**1, 2, 3, 3, 4, 5, 9, 12, 14, 18, 20; **4:**1, 1, 3, 6, 10, 10, 11, 13, 17; **Col 1:**3, 4, 8, 9, 10, 13, 16, 19, 24, 24, 24, 26, 27, 27, 27, 28; **2:**1, 1, 1, 5, 7, 9, 12, 16, 16, 17, 19; **3:**3, 5, 5, 9, 13, 15, 18, 20, 23, 23, 25, 25; **4:**3, 3, 6, 11, 12, 13, 13; **1Th 1:**2, 2, 5, 5, 8, 9; **2:**4, 6, 6, 7, 12, 15, 16, 17, 20; **3:**2, 9, 10, 11; **4:**2, 6, 9, 14, 16; **5:**2, 5, 7, 9, 10, 15, 18, 18, 25; **2Th 1:**3, 3, 3, 5, 5, 7, 7, 10, 11; **2:**3, 6, 7, 12, 12, 13, 13; **3:**1, 2, 7, 8; **1Ti 1:**3, 4, 9, 9, 10, 10, 10, 10, 12, 18, 19; **2:**1, 1, 2, 4, 5, 6, 10, 13; **3:**2, 5, 8, 15; **4:**5, 7, 8, 10; **5:**3, 3, 5, 6, 8, 9, 15, 16, 18, 23; **6:**2, 3, 10, 12, 15, 17, 19; **2Ti 1:**3, 4, 5, 7, 8, 8, 12; **2:**4, 5, 13, 20, 20, 21, 21, 21, 26; **3:**2, 9, 14, 17; **4:**3, 3, 5, 6, 8, 8, 11, 14, 15, 17; **Tit 1:**3, 6, 7, 10, 10, 16; **2:**1, 3, 11; **3:**8, 11, 12, 12, 14; **Phm 1:**1, 4, 5, 6, 6, 8, 9, 13, 15, 18, 20, 22, 22; **Heb 1:**5, 14; **2:**2, 6, 6, 7, 9, 9, 9, 10, 12, 14, 17; **3:**1, 2, 4, 9, 14, 17; **4:**2, 3, 3, 6, 7, 9, 10, 11, 12, 12, 15; **5:**1, 2, 3, 3, 4, 7, 9, 14; **6:**4, 7, 9, 10, 10, 10, 11, 13, 18, 18, 18, 19, 20; **7:**10, 13, 19, 20, 27, 27, 27; **8:**5, 6, 6, 7, 11; **9:**1, 9, 10, 12, 14, 14, 15, 19, 21, 24, 24, 26, 26, 28; **10:**1, 1, 2, 2, 4, 4, 6, 8, 10, 10, 12, 12, 14, 20, 20, 22, 23, 29, 30, 34, 37; **11:**1, 9, 16, 16, 16, 23, 26, 26, 31, 38, 40, 40, 40; **12:**6, 10, 10, 10, 11, 13, 14, 15, 16, 17, 19, 24, 25, 29; **13:**2, 5, 11, 14, 16, 17, 18, 18, 20; **Jas 1:**2, 3, 4, 4, 6, 9, 10, 21, 23, 25, 27; **2:**2, 9, 11, 13, 13; **3:**1, 6, 15, 16; **4:**2, 2, 5, 9, 14; **5:**4, 5, 7, 7, 7, 8, 9, 10, 11, 12, 14, 16, 17, 18; **1Pe 1:**3, 4, 4, 4, 5, 6, 6, 9, 10, 16, 18, 19, 20, 20, 20, 22, 23; **2:**2, 2, 7, 8, 9, 9, 13, 14, 17, 17, 19, 19, 20, 20, 20, 21, 24; **3:**4, 6, 9, 9, 10, 14, 14, 17, 17, 18, 18, 18; **4:**1, 1, 8, 8, 14, 14, 15, 16, 16, 17, 17, 19; **5:**2, 2, 5, 7, 8, 8; **2Pe 1:**3, 7, 7, 11, 16, 19; **2:**4, 5, 13, 19; **3:**9, 9, 14, 16; **1Jn 2:**1, 2, 7, 11, 15, 16, 16, 16, 20, 22, 27; **3:**1, 2, 4, 5, 16, 16, 20; **4:**1, 7, 8, 18, 20; **5:**4, 14, 15, 16, 18; **2Jn** 8, 9, 12; **3Jn** 5, 7, 7, 8, 12, 14; **Jude** 3, 4, 6, 11, 11, 11, 12, 13, 21; **Rev 1:**3, 5, 9; **2:**3, 10, 24; **3:**1, 2, 4, 8, 18; **4:**11, 11; **5:**9, 9; **6:**6, 9, 9, 10, 17; **7:**17; **8:**1; **9:**5, 7, 10, 15, 19; **11:**2, 2, 6, 9, 17; **12:**6, 10, 12, 14, 14, 14; **13:**4, 5, 10, 10, 10, 18; **14:**4, 7, 11, 13, 13, 15, 15, 18, 18; **15:**4, 4; **16:**6, 11, 14, 15; **17:**6, 12, 17; **18:**2, 2, 3, 5, 5, 6, 6, 8, 9, 10, 11, 11, 16, 19, 20; **19:**6, 7, 7, 10, 10, 10, 11, 17; **20:**2, 3, 4, 4, 4, 6, 8; **21:**1, 2, 4, 5, 16, 22, 23; **22:**2, 3, 5, 5, 10, 16

FROM (5218)

Ge 1:4, 6, 7, 11, 14, 18; **2:**2, 3, 7, 10, 17, 19, 21, 22; **3:**3, 14, 15, 17, 19, 19, 21, 23, 23, 24; **4:**4, 10, 11, 12, 12, 14, 14; **5:**29; **6:**13, 14; **7:**4, 4, 11; **8:**4, 21; **9:**19, 24; **10:**11, 14, 19, 30, 32; **11:**4; **14:**15, 17, 23; **15:**18; **16:**2, 8, 8; **17:**14, 15, 16; **18:**10, 14, 16, 17; **19:**4, 22, 24, 28, 28, 29; **20:**6, 13; **21:**17, 17, 18, 21, 25; **22:**11, 12, 15, 24, 24; **23:**13; **24:**5, 7, 8, 38, 40, 40, 41, 46, 48, 62; **25:**6, 10, 18, 18, 20, 29; **26:**9, 23, 26, 27, 29, 33; **27:**9, 16, 30, 40; **28:**12, 14, 14; **30:**16, 26, 30, 33, 36, 37, 40, 40; **31:**13, 16, 25, 31, 39; **32:**4, 11, 32; **33:**19; **34:**7, 26; **35:**1, 5, 7, 9, 13; **36:**2, 6, 16, 17, 18, 19, 20, 32, 33, 34, 35, 36, 37, 39; **37:**14, 25; **38:**8, 9, 17; **39:**5, 9, 12; **40:**15, 19, 20; **41:**3, 14, 19, 57, 57; **42:**7, 7, 24; **43:**1, 2, 33, 34; **44:**8, 11, 29; **45:**19; **46:**31, 34; **47:**1, 22, 26; **48:**5, 7, 7, 12, 16, 22; **49:**6, 10, 10, 30, 32; **Ex 1:**10; **2:**1, 15, 17, 19; **3:**4, 7, 8, 17, 22; **4:**9; **5:**4, 5; **6:**6, 7, 14, 27; **7:**18, 24, 25; **8:**2, 8, 29; **9:**6, 8, 10, 15, 19, 20, 32; **10:**14, 26; **11:**5; **12:**2, 15, 15, 17, 18, 19, 29, 39, 39, 42, 42; **13:**9, 13, 14, 17, 22; **14:**9, 24, 30; **15:**22; **16:**4, 23, 29, 32; **17:**1, 14; **18:**4, 8, 8, 10, 10, 10, 11, 13, 25; **19:**3, 5, 7, 13, 13, 15, 15, 16, 17, 18; **20:**2, 18, 20, 20, 22, 25; **21:**14, 30, 36; **22:**7, 14; **23:**7, 15, 31, 31; **24:**6, 8, 12, 16; **25:**13, 15, 22, 22, 28, 32, 35, 36; **26:**1, 7, 28, 32, 33, 35, 36, 37; **27:**6, 8, 9, 16, 18; **28:**1, 3, 39, 42; **29:**21, 23, 25, 42; **30:**2, 8, 10, 10, 21, 33, 38; **31:**4, 14; **32:**1, 7, 8, 11, 12, 12, 27; **33:**6, 15, 16, 23; **34:**20; **35:**1, 22, 32; **36:**8, 14, 14, 27, 29, 31, 33, 38; **37:**4, 6, 18, 21, 22, 24, 25; **38:**7, 8, 12, 26, 26; **39:**2, 8, 27; **40:**15, 21, 24, 27, 36; **Lev 1:**1, 2, 3, 10; **2:**14; **3:**1, 6; **5:**6, 8, 15, 18; **6:**18, 29; **7:**3, 6, 14, 18, 20, 20, 21, 21, 23, 25, 25, 27, 35, 35, 36; **8:**25, 26; **9:**6, 10, 19, 19, 22, 24; **10:**2, 4; **11:**9, 45; **12:**4, 5; **13:**12, 23, 28, 45, 45, 56; **14:**2, 14, 28, 32, 40; **15:**31; **16:**12, 18, 19, 30; **17:**2, 4, 5, 9, 10, 15; **18:**24, 29; **19:**8, 10, 19; **20:**3, 5, 6, 14, 17, 18, 18, 24, 26; **21:**14, 21, 22; **22:**3, 21, 25, 27, 28, 33; **23:**10, 15, 17, 17, 17, 24, 29, 40, 43; **24:**3, 5; **25:**15, 22, 27, 44; **26:**6, 6, 10, 13, 13, 16, 23, 26; **27:**24, 32; **Nu 1:**1, 4, 16, 49, 53; **2:**17, 33; **3:**12, 13, 18, 19, 20, 21, 27, 33; **4:**13, 18, 37, 41, 45; **5:**2, 4, 17, 19, 25; **6:**3, 4, 9, 11; **7:**89, 89; **8:**4, 6, 11, 14, 22; **9:**1, 7, 8, 13, 15, 17; **10:**8, 9, 11, 11, 12, 21; **11:**1, 3, 8, 31, 31, 34, 35; **12:**10, 14, 15; **13:**2, 3, 21, 26; **14:**10, 13, 24; **15:**3, 3, 19, 20, 20, 21, 30; **16:**1, 9, 15, 21, 24, 26, 27, 35, 37, 38, 45, 46; **17:**2, 9; **18:**1, 6, 9, 9, 21, 22, 22, 26, 27, 27, 28, 28, 30; **19:**13, 17, 20; **20:**6, 8, 9, 10, 14, 17, 28; **21:**4, 12, 16, 24, 28, 28, 30; **22:**1, 5, 6, 8, 11, 11, 16, 41; **23:**7, 7, 9, 9, 9, 27; **24:**4, 8, 11, 16, 16, 17, 17, 24; **25:**4, 11, 14; **26:**3, 5, 7, 10, 12, 14, 15, 18, 20, 21, 22, 23, 25, 26, 27, 28, 29, 30, 34, 35, 36, 37, 38, 40, 41, 42, 43, 44, 45, 47, 48, 50, 62, 63; **27:**21; **31:**4, 5, 6, 12, 14, 32, 42, 47, 50, 51, 54; **32:**7, 8, 9, 11, 15, 17, 22; **33:**3, 38, 48, 49; **34:**3, 4, 5, 11, 15, 18; **35:**1, 2, 4, 8, 12, 25, 29, 32; **36:**3, 5, 7, 9, 13; **Dt 1:**2, 13, 15, 23, 27, 35, 44; **2:**8, 12, 14, 23, 26, 35, 37; **3:**7, 8, 14, 16, 17; **4:**2, 2, 9, 12, 15, 20, 26, 28, 29, 32, 32, 33, 34, 36, 36, 46, 48; **5:**4, 6, 22, 23, 24, 26; **6:**11, 11, 12, 15; **7:**4, 8, 15, 15, 20, 24; **8:**14, 15; **9:**7, 10, 12, 12, 14, 15, 16, 26, 29; **10:**4, 6, 7; **11:**10, 16, 24, 24, 28, 29, 29, 30; **12:**3, 5, 10, 21, 32; **13:**5, 5, 7, 10, 10, 17; **14:**2, 24; **15:**2, 3, 14, 19; **16:**2, 3, 3, 6, 9, 10, 11, 14; **17:**7, 12, 17, 20, 20, 20; **18:**1, 3, 6, 6, 15, 18, 20, 21; **19:**12, 13, 19; **20:**6, 18; **21:**9, 21; **22:**8, 9, 21, 22; **23:**4, 8, 9, 14, 15, 18, 22, 24; **24:**7, 9, 19, 20; **25:**4, 9, 17, 19, 19; **26:**2, 4, 10, 13, 15; **27:**17; **28:**7, 7, 12, 12, 14, 24, 25, 25, 27, 35, 49, 57, 63, 64; **29:**18, 20, 21, 22, 28; **30:**3; **31:**17, 18, 29; **32:**13, 13, 14, 14, 14, 14, 32, 32, 39, 49, 52; **33:**2, 2, 2, 2, 12, 13, 13, 15, 19, 22; **34:**1, 1, 1; **Jos 1:**4, 4, 7; **2:**1, 4, 18, 21, 23; **3:**12; **4:**2, 3, 8, 12, 19, 20; **5:**10, 11, 12, 12; **6:**10, 19, 20, 24; **7:**2, 5, 8, 12, 19, 21, 23; **8:**5, 6, 7, 16, 20, 21, 22, 31; **9:**6, 8, 9, 12, 13, 23; **10:**9, 11, 14, 19, 27, 31, 41, 41; **11:**17, 23; **12:**1, 2, 3, 5, 7; **13:**3, 5, 6, 9, 14, 16, 26, 26, 30; **14:**6, 7, 7, 8, 15; **15:**4, 7, 7, 7, 9, 9, 9, 46; **16:**1, 2, 5, 7, 8; **17:**7, 7, 9, 18; **18:**4, 13, 15, 16, 17, 17, 18; **19:**9, 11, 12, 12, 26, 33, 33, 46; **20:**3, 8; **21:**5, 6, 7, 9, 16, 17, 20, 20, 23, 27, 28, 30, 32, 34, 36, 38; **22:**8, 14, 16, 18, 23, 29, 29, 30, 31; **23:**1, 4, 6, 12, 13, 13, 15, 16; **24:**3, 10, 17, 32; **Jdg 1:**3, 7, 11, 36, 36; **2:**1, 16, 17, 18; **3:**3, 20, 20, 27, 28, 28; **4:**6, 11, 13, 15, 21, 24; **5:**4, 13, 14, 14, 14, 20, 28, 29; **6:**3, 9, 9, 11, 14, 21, 25, 32; **7:**6; **8:**8, 14, 16, 21, 22, 24, 27, 34; **9:**4, 15, 17, 20, 20, 36, 37, 43, 44, 48; **10:**1, 3, 11, 15; **11:**1, 3, 7, 13, 15, 16, 19, 22, 22, 23, 26, 33; **12:**4, 5, 6, 6, 9, 11, 13; **13:**2, 5, 5, 6, 7, 20; **14:**9, 11, 14, 15; **15:**6, 13, 14; **16:**3, 5, 12, 14, 17, 25; **17:**2, 7, 9, 9; **18:**2, 7, 11, 11, 16, 22, 22, 28; **19:**1, 1, 16, 16, 17; **20:**1, 1, 10, 13, 14, 23, 27, 28, 31, 32, 33, 34, 36, 37, 38, 40; **21:**1, 6, 8, 9, 19, 21; **Ru 1:**1, 2, 7, 22; **2:**4, 6, 9, 16, 18; **4:**2, 3, 5, 9, 11; **1Sa 1:**1; **2:**8, 8, 10, 23, 27, 28, 29; **3:**1, 7, 17, 20; **4:**3, 3, 8, 12, 12, 16, 18, 22; **5:**1, 11; **6:**7, 15, 17, 19, 20; **7:**3, 6, 8, 10, 11; **8:**8, 13, 18; **9:**1, 1, 9, 16, 16, 21, 27; **10:**5, 18, 18, 18, 18, 21; **11:**5, 8; **12:**8, 10, 10; **13:**2, 11, 15; **14:**30, 31, 45, 46, 48; **15:**1, 2, 4, 6, 6, 7, 23, 26, 28; **16:**13, 15, 23; **17:**4, 12, 18, 23, 23, 25, 34, 35, 37, 37, 40, 49, 51, 52; **18:**2, 6, 9, 10, 13, 19, 23; **19:**9; **20:**1, 2, 3, 41; **21:**10; **22:**17; **23:**1, 6; **24:**1, 2, 13, 15; **25:**2, 7, 10, 11, 14, 15, 15, 26, 29, 33, 34, 39, 43, 44; **26:**1, 19, 20, 24; **28:**3, 9, 17, 23; **29:**3; **30:**8, 13, 14, 16, 25, 26; **31:**12; **2Sa 1:**1, 2, 3, 3, 13, 22; **2:**2, 2, 10, 12, 13, 13, 15, 22, 25, 26, 31; **3:**3, 10, 15, 18, 18, 22; **4:**2, 5, 9; **5:**5, 5, 8, 13, 25; **6:**3, 16; **7:**6, 6, 11, 11, 15, 15, 23, 23; **8:**5, 8, 11, 12; **9:**3, 5, 11, 12; **10:**6, 6, 6, 8, 8, 14, 16, 18; **11:**20; **12:**3, 3, 4, 7, 10, 20, 30, 30; **13:**34, 34; **14:**2, 7, 14, 16, 16, 17, 19, 25, 32; **15:**2, 11, 14, 18, 28; **16:**23; **17:**11, 27; **18:**14, 16, 19, 21, 23, 31, 31; **19:**9, 16, 17, 24, 28, 31; **20:**2, 7, 8, 8, 21, 22; **21:**5, 8, 10, 10, 12, 18, 19, 22; **22:**1, 1, 3, 4, 7, 9, 9, 9, 14, 17, 18, 18, 22, 24, 37, 46, 49, 49; **23:**4, 11, 15, 16, 20, 21, 24, 25, 25, 26, 26, 27, 27, 28, 28, 29, 29, 29, 30, 30, 31, 32, 33, 33, 34, 34, 35, 35, 36, 36, 37, 37, 38, 38; **24:**2, 13; **1Ki 1:**3, 29, 39, 49, 53; **2:**7, 7, 8, 17, 19, 21, 27, 31, 31; **3:**20; **4:**7, 12, 21, 23, 24, 25, 33, 33, 34; **5:**6, 9, 13, 18; **6:**1, 3, 6, 15, 16, 27; **7:**7, 9, 13, 14, 14, 23, 33, 37, 42; **8:**1, 8, 8, 16, 30, 30, 32, 34, 35, 36, 39, 41, 43, 45, 49, 53, 65; **9:**7, 12, 24; **10:**11, 15, 24, 28, 28, 28; **11:**1, 1, 3, 9, 11, 12, 18, 23, 26, 28, 29, 31, 34, 35; **12:**2, 2, 15, 20, 31, 31; **13:**1, 2, 5, 14, 18, 20, 21, 33, 33; **14:**7, 7, 8, 15, 21, 24; **15:**12, 13, 17, 27, 29; **16:**1, 7, 8, 15, 17, 24, 34, 34; **17:**1, 4, 6, 15, 19, 23; **18:**10, 38, 44; **19:**16, 17, 21; **20:**9, 10, 17, 34, 41; **21:**17, 26, 28, 28; **22:**27, 27, 35, 46, 46; **2Ki 1:**1, 3, 6, 8, 10, 10, 12, 12, 14; **2:**1, 3, 3, 5, 5, 7, 7, 10, 12, 15, 23, 25; **3:**6, 8, 20; **4:**3, 4, 8, 9, 25, 42, 42; **5:**1, 4, 17, 17, 20, 21, 22, 24, 26, 27; **6:**23; **7:**1; **8:**22, 29; **9:**2, 15, 36, 36; **10:**17, 21, 28, 31, 33, 36; **11:**2, 2, 11, 14, 19; **12:**1, 7, 8, 15; **13:**5, 11, 23, 25, 25; **14:**2, 13, 14, 14, 24, 25; **15:**2, 9, 14, 18, 20, 20, 24, 25, 28; **16:**3, 7, 8, 11, 14, 15, 17, 17; **17:**8, 9, 11, 13, 16, 18, 21, 21, 22, 24, 27, 28, 30, 30, 30, 31, 32, 33, 39; **18:**8, 16, 16, 17, 28, 29, 31, 31, 33, 34, 35; **19:**6, 7, 19, 29, 29, 31, 31; **20:**1, 4, 5, 6, 7, 8, 14, 14, 16, 19; **21:**2, 7, 8, 16, 19; **22:**1, 2, 4; **23:**2, 4, 6, 8, 11, 17, 18, 26, 27, 30, 31, 33, 33, 35, 36; **24:**3, 7, 8, 13, 14, 18, 20; **25:**4, 16, 21, 26, 27; **1Ch 1:**12, 24, 43, 44, 45, 46, 47, 48, 50; **2:**53, 55; **3:**1; **4:**10, 22, 42; **5:**8, 11, 21, 23; **6:**33, 39, 44, 54, 60, 61, 62, 62, 63, 66, 70, 71, 72, 74, 76, 77, 78, 80; **7:**2, 5, 21; **9:**3, 5, 6, 6, 7, 9, 19, 25, 33; **11:**8, 17, 18, 22, 23, 26, 27, 27, 28, 28, 29, 29, 30, 30, 31, 31, 31, 32, 33, 33, 34, 34, 35, 36, 36, 37, 39, 39, 40, 40, 43, 44, 44, 45, 46, 46, 47; **12:**1, 2, 3, 3, 4, 4, 5, 7, 8, 14, 16, 19, 19, 20, 20, 24, 25, 26, 29, 30, 31, 32, 33, 34, 35, 36, 37, 40; **13:**5, 5, 7; **14:**16; **15:**5, 6, 7, 17, 29; **16:**20, 35, 36; **17:**5, 5, 10, 13, 13, 21, 21; **18:**5, 8, 11; **19:**6, 7, 15, 16, 18; **20:**2, 2, 4; **21:**2, 22, 26; **23:**6, 7, 26; **24:**5, 20, 20, 20, 21, 22, 22, 23, 24, 24, 25, 26, 26, 27, 28, 29, 30; **25:**1, 2; **26:**1, 19, 21, 23, 24, 29, 30, 31, 31; **27:**9, 10, 11, 12, 13, 14, 15, 27, 27, 28, 29, 30; **28:**4, 4, 4, 5, 19; **29:**4, 12, 14, 16, 27, 27, 29; **2Ch 1:**4, 13, 16, 16, 16; **2:**8, 14, 14, 14, 16, 16; **3:**6; **4:**2, 13; **5:**2, 9, 9; **6:**5, 21, 21, 23, 25, 26, 27, 30, 32, 33, 35, 39; **7:**1, 6, 7, 8, 8, 14, 14, 20; **8:**11, 13, 15, 16; **9:**10, 14, 23, 26, 28, 29, 29; **10:**2, 2, 15; **11:**16; **12:**13, 13, 15; **13:**2, 3, 14, 16; **14:**5, 6, 7, 8, 8, 14, 14; **15:**2, 8, 15, 16, 17; **16:**1, 2, 2, 9, 11, 12; **17:**1, 14, 17; **18:**26, 26, 31; **19:**4, 10, 11; **20:**2, 2, 4, 19, 23, 34, 37; **21:**10; **22:**6, 11; **23:**10, 13, 19, 20; **24:**1, 6, 6, 7; **25:**1, 5, 6, 7, 11, 14, 14, 15, 23, 24, 26, 27; **26:**3, 15, 21, 22; **27:**5; **28:**3, 7, 8, 10, 12, 15, 21, 21, 24, 26; **29:**5, 10, 12, 12, 12, 13, 13, 14, 14, 16, 35; **30:**5, 8, 9, 10, 11, 14, 18, 25, 27; **31:**6, 9, 10; **32:**11, 13, 14, 15, 15, 17, 22, 22, 23, 31, 31; **33:**2, 7, 8, 14, 15, 15; **34:**2, 9, 9, 9, 30, 33, 33; **35:**7, 14, 18, 20, 23, 27; **36:**3, 7, 10, 18; **Ezr 1:**7, 11; **2:**1, 2, 36, 40, 43, 55, 59, 61, 63, 70; **3:**7, 7, 8; **4:**4, 10, 11, 12, 23; **5:**5, 14, 14; **6:**5, 6, 8, 11, 16, 21, 21; **7:**6, 12, 16, 20; **8:**1, 2, 2, 3, 3, 4, 5, 6, 7, 8, 9, 10, 11, 12, 13, 14, 19, 22, 31, 35; **9:**1, 2, 3, 5, 8, 11; **10:**1, 8, 11, 11, 14, 18, 20, 21, 22, 25, 26, 27, 28, 29, 30, 31, 33, 34, 38, 43; **Ne 1:**2; **3:**2, 5, 7, 7, 7, 13, 15, 20, 21, 22, 24, 25, 25, 28, 32; **4:**12, 16, 19, 21; **5:**12, 13, 13, 14, 17; **6:**11; **7:**6, 7, 39, 43, 46, 57, 61, 63, 65; **8:**3, 8, 15, 17, 18; **9:**2, 5, 7, 9, 13, 15, 15, 20, 27, 27, 28, 32, 35; **10:**9, 28, 35, 35; **11:**1, 4, 4, 7, 10, 15, 19, 30; **12:**28, 28, 29, 44; **13:**3, 8, 16, 19, 23, 26, 28; **Est 1:**1, 2, 5, 19, 20; **2:**5, 6, 9; **3:**8, 10; **4:**14; **5:**1; **6:**4; **7:**8, 9; **8:**2, 9; **9:**13, 14, 16, 22, 28; **Job 1:**1, 7, 10, 16, 19, 21; **2:**2, 7, 10, 11, 12; **3:**11, 17, 19; **4:**2, 9; **5:**3, 3, 4, 6, 6, 7, 15, 15, 20, 20, 21, 27; **6:**19, 19, 23, 23; **7:**10, 11; **8:**10, 19; **9:**6; **10:**7, 19; **12:**21; **13:**16, 21, 24; **14:**3, 11, 12, 18, 20; **15:**17, 18; **16:**22; **18:**4, 14, 17, 18, 18; **19:**9; **20:**10, 25; **21:**9; **23:**12, 13; **24:**3, 9, 11, 12, 18; **27:**3, 13, 13, 22; **28:**2, 2, 4, 5, 19, 21; **30:**5, 14; **31:**2, 7, 18, 22; **33:**6, 17, 18, 18, 23, 28, 30; **34:**22, 27, 30; **36:**10, 12, 16, 19, 21, 21, 25, 28, 28, 29; **37:**2, 9, 15, 22; **38:**1, 8, 16, 19, 28, 29; **39:**22, 29; **40:**6; **41:**19, 20, 20, 21, 28; **Ps 2:**3; **3:**T, 4, 8; **5:**9; **6:**5, 6, 6; **7:**1; **9:**4, 7, 13; **10:**16; **11:**2, 4; **12:**1, 7; **14:**2, 3, 7; **15:**2; **16:**2; **17:**1, 4, 5, 7, 9, 9, 13, 14; **18:**T, T, 3, 6, 8, 8, 8, 13, 16, 17, 17, 21, 23, 36, 45, 48, 48; **19:**6, 10, 12, 13; **20:**1, 2, 2, 6; **21:**7, 10; **22:**9, 10, 11, 20, 20, 21, 21, 27; **25:**6, 15, 17, 17, 20, 22; **27:**1, 9; **28:**7; **30:**3, 3, 7, 9; **31:**4, 10, 10, 15, 20, 20, 22; **32:**7; **33:**13, 14, 19; **34:**4, 6, 13, 14, 16, 17, 19, 20; **35:**10, 10, 10, 17, 17; **36:**4, 8, 8; **37:**8, 27, 30, 31, 40; **38:**8; **39:**8, 9, 10; **40:**11; **41:**2, 13; **42:**6, 6; **43:**1; **44:**10, 18, 20; **45:**2, 9; **49:**4, 7, 14, 15; **50:**1, 2, 9, 9; **51:**2, 2, 5, 6, 7, 11, 11; **52:**5, 5; **53:**2, 3, 6; **54:**7; **55:**8, 12, 18; **56:**13, 13; **57:**T, 3, 3, 6; **58:**3; **59:**1, 1, 2, 2, 7, 7; **61:**2; **62:**1, 4, 7, 9; **64:**2, 2, 4; **65:**8; **66:**9, 20; **68:**7, 17, 18, 18, 20, 22, 22, 27, 30, 33; **69:**3, 5, 14, 14, 17, 18, 28; **71:**2, 4, 4, 5, 6, 6, 17, 20; **72:**8, 8, 14, 14; **73:**13, 20; **74:**12; **75:**6, 6; **76:**8; **77:**18; **78:**2, 4, 15, 16, 24, 42, 44, 65, 65, 70, 71; **79:**13; **80:**8, 13, 14; **81:**6, 10, 16; **82:**4; **83:**7; **84:**11; **85:**11, 11; **86:**13; **88:**5, 14; **89:**4, 18, 19, 25; **91:**3, 3, 12; **93:**2, 2; **94:**12, 13, 16; **95:**10; **97:**10; **99:**7; **101:**4, 8; **102:**2, 19, 19; **103:**4, 12, 12, 19; **104:**10, 13, 14, 29, 35; **105:**13, 40; **106:**10, 10, 23, 47, 48; **107:**2, 3, 3, 3, 6, 13, 14, 19, 20, 28, 41; **109:**10, 14, 15, 24, 31; **110:**2, 7; **113:**3, 7, 7; **114:**1, 8; **116:**8, 8, 8, 16; **118:**26; **119:**10, 19, 21, 29, 37, 43, 51, 86, 102, 110, 118, 134, 136, 150, 152, 155, 157; **120:**2, 2, 5; **121:**1, 2, 7; **124:**7, 8; **127:**2, 3, 3; **128:**5; **129:**1, 2; **130:**1, 8; **133:**3; **134:**3; **135:**7, 21; **136:**24; **138:**6; **139:**7, 7, 12; **140:**1, 1, 3, 4, 10; **141:**6; **142:**6; **143:**7, 9; **144:**7, 7, 7, 11, 11; **148:**1, 1, 7; **Pr 1:**9, 15, 32; **2:**6, 12, 12, 13, 16, 16, 22; **3:**3, 23, 26, 27; **4:**2, 5, 24, 27; **5:**7, 8, 15; **6:**5, 5, 6, 6, 24, 24; **7:**5, 5, 16; **8:**22, 35; **9:**3; **10:**13, 30; **11:**8; **13:**11, 11, 19; **14:**4, 7, 27; **15:**5, 12, 29; **16:**17, 23; **18:**22; **19:**6, 23; **20:**8, 9, 12, 16; **21:**10, 11, 16; **22:**24, 27; **23:**14; **24:**18, 22; **25:**4, 5, 12, 23, 25; **27:**6, 6, 8, 8, 13, 22; **28:**18; **29:**21, 26; **30:**7, 14; **31:**14; **Ecc 1:**17; **2:**10, 20, 24, 25; **3:**11, 13, 14, 20, 22; **4:**11, 14; **5:**8, 19, 19; **7:**14, 26, 27; **8:**8; **12:**11; **SS 3:**6, 9, 9, 10; **4:**8, 8, 8, 12, 14, 15; **8:**5, 9; **Isa 1:**4, 4, 6, 11, 11, 15; **2:**2, 3, 6, 10, 19; **3:**1, 14; **4:**4, 6, 6; **5:**28; **7:**16; **8:**7, 8, 17, 19, 20; **9:**7, 12, 12; **10:**3, 19, 27; **11:**1, 11, 12, 16, 16; **12:**3; **13:**5, 10, 13; **14:**1, 3, 3, 12, 19, 29; **15:**3, 4, 8, 8; **16:**3, 4, 5, 8; **17:**10, 11; **18:**4, 7, 7; **19:**13, 13; **20:**6; **21:**1, 1, 11, 13, 15; **22:**5, 11, 19; **23:**1, 3, 3, 16; **24:**11, 16, 18; **25:**4, 4; **26:**9, 12, 21; **27:**8, 8, 11, 12; **28:**7, 14; **29:**4, 8, 9, 9, 15, 18, 19; **30:**1, 14, 14, 16, 27, 33; **32:**2, 15; **33:**15, 18; **34:**4, 4, 10, 17; **36:**2, 13, 16, 16, 18, 19, 20; **37:**6, 7, 20, 30, 30, 32, 32; **38:**1, 4, 6, 12, 17, 21, 22; **39:**3, 3, 5, 8; **40:**9, 22; **41:**2, 8, 9, 17, 25; **42:**7, 10, 11, 23; **43:**5, 6, 6, 13, 24, 27; **44:**8, 13; **45:**6, 20; **46:**6, 11,

11; 47:10, 13, 14; 48:7, 8, 20; 49:1, 12, 12, 12, 23, 24; 50:6, 11; 51:1, 1, 2, 7, 8, 13, 17, 21, 22; 52:2, 2, 12; 53:2, 4, 8; 54:6, 11, 17; 55:7, 7, 8, 10; 56:2; 57:1, 14, 17; 58:7, 8, 10; 59:2, 9, 11, 20; 60:4, 5, 6, 18; 63:1, 1, 4, 15, 15, 16, 17; 64:1, 7; 66:5, 6, 9, 20, 23, 23; Jer 1:1, 11, 13, 14; 2:16, 25, 27, 31, 33, 36; 3:14, 14, 14, 18, 19, 21, 24; 4:6, 7, 11, 15, 16, 29; 5:3, 4, 6, 6, 7, 10, 24; 6:1, 1, 13, 20, 22, 22; 7:2, 22, 25, 28; 8:10, 16; 9:3, 18; 10:9, 9, 11, 13, 18, 22; 11:6, 23; 12:12, 14, 14; 13:8, 13, 13, 14, 18, 18, 20, 24; 14:1, 2, 10, 22, 22; 15:7, 12, 21, 21; 16:4, 4, 5, 14, 15, 15, 17, 19; 17:5, 13, 15, 20, 26, 26, 26; 18:11, 14, 20, 22; 19:3, 8, 14; 20:3, 8, 13; 21:9, 11, 12; 22:2, 3, 8, 23, 26, 29; 23:3, 7, 8, 8, 14, 22, 24, 25, 30, 31, 34, 36, 38, 38, 39; 24:5, 10; 25:1, 3, 5, 5, 15, 15, 16, 17, 17, 18, 18, 19, 26, 27, 28, 30, 30, 32, 33; 26:1, 2, 3, 10, 19, 20; 27:1, 10, 15, 16, 16; 28:1, 2, 6, 9, 11; 29:1, 2, 4, 20, 27; 30:8, 10, 10, 18; 31:5, 6, 8, 8, 10, 11, 16, 19, 34, 38; 32:1, 2, 8, 26, 31, 33, 37; 33:19; 34:1, 1, 4, 8, 13; 35:15; 36:6, 6, 7, 8, 9, 10, 11, 17, 21; 37:5, 10, 17; 38:2, 6, 8, 12; 39:17; 40:12; 41:5, 14, 15; 42:1, 4, 8, 11, 14, 17, 17, 22; 43:1, 5, 12; 44:5, 7, 12, 16, 24, 26, 28; 46:1, 9, 16, 20, 24, 26, 27, 27; 47:2, 4, 4; 48:2, 5, 10, 11, 11, 12, 18, 19, 28, 33, 34, 34, 45; 49:2, 5, 14, 19, 19, 28, 32, 34, 36; 50:3, 8, 9, 15, 16, 26, 28, 37, 41, 41, 44, 44; 51:2, 6, 7, 16, 25, 31, 44, 45, 45, 54, 58; 52:1, 3, 7, 20, 27, 31; La 1:6, 13; 2:1, 9, 14, 18, 22; 3:1, 18, 22, 26, 48, 50, 55, 66; 4:21, 22; 5:16, 19; Eze 1:4, 5, 25, 27, 27; 2:3; 3:17; 4:8, 14; 5:4, 12; 6:1, 3, 11, 14; 7:1, 21, 26, 26, 26; 8:2, 2, 6; 9:2, 3; 10:4, 6, 7, 18; 11:3, 7, 14, 15, 16, 17, 23; 12:1, 8, 11, 16, 17, 19, 21, 23, 26, 28; 13:1, 6, 7, 9, 9, 17, 19, 20, 20, 21, 23; 14:2, 4, 5, 6, 6, 9, 11, 12, 16; 15:1, 7; 16:1, 3, 35; 17:1, 3, 11, 22; 18:1, 8, 12, 21, 23, 26, 27, 28, 30; 19:8, 14; 20:1, 2, 3, 5, 17, 27, 30, 34, 41, 45, 47, 47; 21:1, 3, 4, 9, 18, 21, 28; 22:1, 3, 17, 19, 23, 28; 23:1, 15, 22, 23, 24, 27, 32, 42, 42; 24:1, 3, 5, 15, 20, 26; 25:1, 3, 4, 7, 10, 13, 14; 26:1, 7, 16; 27:1, 3, 5, 5, 6, 6, 7, 8, 8, 9, 9, 10, 11, 11, 11, 13, 14, 15, 17, 18, 18, 19; 28:1, 2, 3, 11, 12, 15, 16, 16, 18, 20, 22, 23, 25; 29:1, 3, 10, 13, 14, 17; 30:1, 2, 6, 20; 31:1; 32:1, 17; 33:1, 11, 11, 12, 14, 19, 21, 23, 25, 27; 34:1, 2, 10, 12, 13, 17, 25, 27; 35:1, 3; 36:3, 3, 6, 16, 22, 24, 30, 33; 37:9, 12, 15, 21, 21, 21, 23; 38:1, 3, 6, 8, 8, 8, 12, 14, 15; 39:1, 2, 3, 10, 10, 17, 22, 27; 40:2, 2, 15, 18, 38; 41:7, 11, 20; 42:3, 6, 7, 9, 9, 13, 20; 43:2, 6, 14, 14, 15, 23, 25; 44:5, 6, 10, 22, 29, 31; 45:9; 46:2, 18, 18, 20, 20; 47:1, 10, 12, 15, 17, 19, 20; 48:1, 2, 3, 4, 7, 19, 23, 24, 26, 28, 35; Da 1:2, 5, 6; 2:5, 25, 34, 45; 3:15, 17, 29; 4:12, 13, 14, 14, 23, 25, 27, 31, 32, 33; 5:2, 2, 3, 3, 4, 13, 20, 21, 23, 23; 6:13, 17, 20, 23, 27; 7:2, 3, 7, 10, 12, 17, 19, 23, 24; 8:5, 7, 9, 12, 16; 9:2, 13, 13, 15, 16, 25, 26; 10:6; 11:17, 18, 30, 44; 12:11; Hos 1:2, 7, 7, 11; 2:8, 10, 15, 18; 5:6; 7:12; 8:4; 9:4, 6, 12, 15; 11:4, 10, 11, 11; 12:4, 7, 9; 13:3, 4, 14, 14, 15; 14:5, 8; Joel 1:3, 15; 2:16, 16, 20; 3:6, 7, 16, 16, 18; Am 1:1, 2, 2; 2:8, 10; 3:1, 2, 12; 4:3, 7, 7, 8, 11; 5:8, 11, 14, 18, 19; 6:14; 7:1, 6, 15, 16, 17; 8:6, 12; 9:6, 7, 14; Ob 1, 7, 16, 20; Jnh 1:3, 3, 8, 10; 2:1, 2, 4, 6, 9; 3:4, 5, 6, 8, 9; 4:6; Mic 1:2; 2:4, 8, 9; 3:1, 7; 4:1, 2, 7, 7, 10; 5:2, 2, 3, 6; 6:3, 4, 5; 7:12, 12, 12, 12, 15, 17; Na 1:13, 15; 2:13; 3:19; Hab 1:1, 8, 9, 14; 2:16; 3:3, 4, 11, 13; Zep 1:10, 10, 13; 2:3, 11, 14; 3:7, 11; Hag 1:12, 13; 2:15, 16, 19; Zec 1:4, 6; 2:6, 13; 3:2; 4:8; 5:3, 3; 6:1, 9, 10, 11, 13, 13, 15, 15; 7:1, 8, 11; 8:1, 7, 7, 10, 18, 20, 22, 23; 9:1, 8, 10, 10, 10, 10, 11, 14; 10:4, 8, 10; 12:1, 1, 14; 13:1, 2, 5; 14:4, 5, 8, 10, 10, 10; Mal 1:11, 13, 14; 2:5, 6, 6, 12, 15; 3:11, 15; Mt 1:17, 17, 17, 21; 2:1, 6; 3:2, 4, 5, 5, 5, 8, 11, 12, 13, 17; 4:6, 17, 17, 24, 25, 25, 25; 5:40, 42, 47; 6:1, 13, 20, 33; 7:5, 16, 16; 8:8, 11; 9:15, 16, 17; 10:14, 27; 11:12, 19, 20, 25; 12:24, 35, 35, 38, 42, 44; 13:12, 19, 41, 49; 14:13, 14, 21, 24; 15:1, 18, 19, 26; 16:1, 17, 21, 23, 23, 23; 17:5, 9, 18, 20, 23; 18:3, 23; 19:4; 20:19, 22, 23; 21:8, 11, 23, 25, 25, 32, 43; 23:34, 35; 24:10, 29, 31, 32, 34; 25:19, 28, 29, 32, 34; 26:16, 27, 32, 39; 27:32, 40, 42, 51, 52, 55, 55, 57, 63, 64; 28:2, 6, 7, 8; Mk 1:4, 5, 5, 6, 9, 11, 15, 24, 33, 39, 45; 2:20, 21; 3:7, 8, 8, 22; 4:1, 11, 12, 15, 25; 5:2, 2, 4, 26, 30, 35; 6:6, 11, 12, 16, 30, 31, 33, 34, 44; 7:1, 4, 10, 17, 21, 23, 26, 27, 28, 33; 8:11, 11, 33, 33, 33; 9:7, 9, 10, 31; 10:6, 38, 39, 47; 11:16, 20, 28, 30, 31; 12:34; 13:3, 25, 27, 27, 28, 30; 14:23, 28, 36, 70; 15:21, 21, 30, 32, 38, 40, 43, 46; 16:3, 6, 8, 9, 9, 12, S; Lk 1:2, 3, 5, 22, 50, 52, 69, 71, 71, 74, 78; 2:4; 3:2, 3, 3, 6, 8, 17, 22; 4:11, 18, 22, 34; 5:3, 10, 17, 17, 32, 35, 36; 6:17, 17, 17, 19, 30, 35, 42, 45, 45; 7:7, 12, 44, 45; 8:2, 2, 3, 4, 10, 12, 18, 26, 46, 49; 9:5, 8, 19, 20, 22, 35, 45, 54; 10:7, 11, 18, 21, 30, 42; 11:7, 15, 16, 16, 24, 27, 31, 43, 50, 51, 52, 52, 53; 12:3, 13, 31, 36, 48, 48, 52; 13:1, 2, 3, 15, 16, 29; 16:2, 21, 26, 30, 30, 31; 17:7, 29; 18:6, 27, 34; 19:4, 24, 26, 37, 42, 45; 20:2, 4, 5, 35; 21:32; 22:42, 43, 45; 23:5, 18, 26, 45, 49, 51, 53, 55; 24:6, 16, 19, 22, 27, 35, 46, 49; Jn 1:13, 13, 16, 19, 32, 44, 45, 46; 2:9, 15, 17, 18, 22; 3:6, 8, 19, 20, 31, 31; 4:6, 30, 34, 34, 35, 39, 47, 54; 5:21, 24, 34, 44; 6:23, 31, 32, 32, 33, 38, 41, 42, 44, 45, 46, 50, 58, 64; 7:1, 17, 27, 27, 28, 29, 38, 41, 52, 52; 8:14, 23, 23, 26, 40, 42, 44, 59; 9:1, 16, 22, 33; 10:5, 18, 28, 29; 11:4, 18, 27, 28, 37, 51, 53, 55; 12:1, 3, 9, 21, 27, 28, 34, 36, 42; 13:3, 4; 14:7, 24; 15:4, 4, 5, 6, 26, 27; 16:2, 14, 15, 27, 28, 30, 30; 17:7, 8, 15; 18:11, 39; 19:9, 11, 21, 23, 27, 35, 39; 20:1, 9; 21:2, 14; Ac 1:2, 3, 11, 22, 22; 2:2, 5, 7, 9, 10, 24, 32, 38, 40; 3:2, 2, 19, 20, 22, 23, 26; 4:10, 10, 17, 36, 36; 5:16, 30, 31; 6:9, 9; 7:10, 16, 37, 42, 53; 8:3, 10, 22, 26, 28, 30, 33; 9:3, 18, 32; 10:23, 41; 11:5, 9, 11, 18, 19, 20, 27; 12:11, 11; 13:1, 6, 8, 15, 15, 22, 24, 29, 30, 31, 34, 39, 46; 14:8, 15, 18, 19; 15:1, 7, 14, 16, 20, 20, 20, 23, 24, 24, 29, 29, 29; 16:4, 9, 12, 14; 17:3, 5, 26, 27, 29, 30, 31; 18:2, 2, 2, 5, 6, 6, 21, 22, 24; 19:4, 13, 16, 25, 29, 35, 37; 20:4, 4, 4, 18, 19, 20, 21, 27; 21:10, 16, 16, 25, 25, 27, 29, 39; 22:5, 5, 6, 30; 23:10, 10, 26, 34; 24:19; 25:7; 26:4, 13, 17, 18, 18, 19, 20, 22, 23; 27:2, 4, 6, 13, 29, 30, 44; 28:13, 21, 21, 23, 23, 25, 28; Ro 1:1, 4, 7, 17, 18, 18, 20; 2:4, 5, 10, 14, 18, 22, 29, 29; 3:12, 13, 13, 19; 4:2, 24, 25; 5:9, 10, 16; 6:4, 7, 9, 15, 18, 22; 7:3, 4, 6, 24; 8:2, 11, 11, 13, 21, 23, 35, 38, 39; 9:3, 11, 24, 24; 10:8, 9, 17; 11:2, 5, 17, 17, 23, 24, 26, 26, 36; 13:5; 15:15, 16, 19, 19, 27, 31; 16:17, 25; 1Co 1:1, 1, 8, 22; 2:14; 4:7; 5:2, 7, 13; 6:14, 14, 18; 7:5, 10, 10, 12, 22, 25, 30, 32, 40; 9:9, 13, 14, 18; 10:4, 9, 13, 13, 14, 17, 21, 21; 11:8, 8, 12, 12, 12, 28; 12:3, 23; 14:30, 37; 15:4, 12, 15, 20, 21, 32, 38, 40, 41, 47, 47, 49; 2Co 1:1, 1, 10, 23; 2:13; 3:3, 5; 4:3, 7; 5:8, 9, 18; 6:3, 12, 17, 17; 7:1, 5, 7, 10; 8:13; 10:2, 5; 11:3, 9, 12, 26, 26, 26, 26, 26; 12:1, 7, 7, 7, 7; Gal 1:1, 1, 1, 1, 3, 3, 4, 6, 8, 12; 3:12, 13, 15; 4:12, 12, 14, 17, 22, 22; 5:4, 4, 7, 17, 17, 17; 6:8, 17; Eph 1:1, 2, 11, 11, 20; 2:5, 6, 8, 12, 12, 13, 15, 17; 3:9, 11, 16, 19; 4:18; 5:8, 14; 6:15, 23; Php 1:1, 5; 2:1, 1, 14, 24; 3:10, 11, 17; 4:9, 9, 15, 17, 19; Col 1:1, 1, 13, 18, 21, 21, 23; 2:5, 7, 8, 8, 8, 12, 19, 20; 3:15; 4:12; 1Th 1:1, 6, 8, 9, 10, 10, 10; 2:6, 14, 14, 16, 17; 3:3; 4:15, 16, 16; 5:22; 2Th 1:1, 7, 9, 9, 10; 2:2; 3:2, 3, 5, 6, 8, 14, 17; 1Ti 1:1, 5, 6, 11; 2:8; 3:13; 4:1, 1; 5:13, 18; 6:10, 11, 14, 15, 21; 2Ti 1:1, 13, 15; 2:8, 19, 22, 26; 3:5, 11, 15; 4:17, 18; Tit 1:1, 11, 12; 2:12, 14; 3:11; Phm 1:1, 1, 7, 9, 18; Heb 1:3, 14; 2:1; 3:10, 12; 4:4, 10, 13; 5:8; 6:1, 6; 7:5, 6, 10, 10, 11, 11, 14, 15, 26; 8:11; 9:13, 14, 15; 10:34; 11:3, 7, 12, 13, 15, 19, 35, 35; 12:2, 25, 26; 13:5, 7, 9, 9, 10, 20, 24; Jas 1:1, 7, 14, 17; 3:12, 12, 12, 17; 4:2, 7; 5:11, 19, 20; 1Pe 1:1, 3, 12, 18, 18, 21, 22, 23, 23; 2:11; 3:4, 10, 10, 11, 20, 21, 21; 4:10; 5:8; 2Pe 1:1, 9, 17, 17, 20, 21; 2:9, 16, 18, 20; 3:5, 16; 1Jn 1:1, 2, 7, 9; 2:7, 13, 14, 16, 16, 18, 24, 28; 3:11, 14; 4:1, 3, 5, 7; 5:9, 21; 2Jn 1, 3, 3, 5, 6, 13; 3Jn 1, 7; Jude 1, 5, 8, 23, 24; Rev 1:1, 4, 4, 4, 5, 5, 5, 16; 2:1, 5, 5, 7, 8, 12, 18, 21, 22, 28; 3:1, 2, 5, 7, 10, 12, 12, 14, 18, 19; 4:5; 5:7, 9; 6:4, 6, 13, 16, 16; 7:1, 2, 4, 5, 5, 5, 6, 6, 6, 7, 7, 7, 8, 8, 8, 9, 10, 10, 13, 16; 8:4, 5; 9:1, 2, 3, 11, 13, 17, 18, 20; 10:1, 4, 8, 8, 10; 11:5, 11, 12, 18; 12:5, 14, 15, 16; 13:13; 14:2, 3, 4, 13, 13, 13, 15, 17, 18, 20; 15:6, 8; 16:1, 7, 12, 13, 17, 21; 17:8; 18:1, 4, 4, 9, 19; 19:1, 3, 5, 5, 9, 15; 20:1, 8, 9, 11; 21:2, 3, 8, 10, 21; 22:1, 14

GAVE (684)

Ge 2:16, 20; 3:6, 12; 4:1, 2, 17, 20, 25; 6:4; 12:16; 14:20; 16:2, 3, 5, 15; 19:37, 38; 20:14; 21:2, 8, 19, 27; 24:22, 32, 36, 47, 53; 25:6, 34; 27:17; 28:4; 29:24, 28, 29; 30:4, 7, 9, 17, 21, 23; 32:17, 19; 35:4, 12; 37:3, 11; 38:18; 39:6; 40:20; 41:43, 45; 42:25, 25; 43:26, 34; 44:1; 45:21, 22, 22; 47:17, 31; Ex 1:15, 21, 22; 2:2, 15, 21; 5:23; 12:1, 36; 14:1; 16:32; 18:12; 21:4; 31:12, 18; 34:32; 35:23; 36:3, 6; Lev 7:38; 8:27; 21:24; 23:44; 24:23; 26:46; 27:34; Nu 2:1; 3:51; 5:1; 7:7, 9; 8:22; 9:1; 10:13; 13:17; 17:6; 18:8; 21:3; 22:16; 23:5, 16; 29:40; 30:16; 31:41, 47; 32:28, 40; 36:5, 13; Dt 1:3, 18; 3:12, 13, 15, 16, 18; 4:5, 45; 5:22; 8:15; 9:10; 10:4; 22:16; 26:9; 27:11; 29:6, 8; 31:9, 10, 25; 32:14; 33:1; Jos 1:7, 15; 4:17; 6:7; 8:19; 10:12, 27, 30, 32; 11:8, 23; 12:6; 13:33; 14:7, 13; 15:19; 17:4; 18:7; 19:49, 51; 21:9, 43, 44; 22:4, 5; 24:3, 4, 4, 8, 11, 13, 13, 13; Jdg 1:4, 15; 3:10, 12; 4:19; 5:25; 6:9; 7:16; 8:3; 9:4; 11:21, 23, 32; 12:3; 13:13; 14:9, 17, 19; 15:2, 6; 19:7; Ru 2:14, 18; 3:17; 4:13; 1Sa 1:5, 20; 2:20, 21, 27; 3:21; 10:18; 15:20; 17:38, 52; 18:19, 27; 20:40; 21:6; 22:10; 25:9; 27:6; 30:11, 12; 2Sa 4:10; 6:19; 8:6; 11:14, 22, 27; 12:8, 24; 14:24; 18:5; 21:8, 8; 22:14, 44; 23:1, 10; 1Ki 2:1; 3:17; 4:29; 5:3, 12; 6:11; 8:14, 34, 40, 48, 56, 58; 9:11, 16; 10:10, 10, 13; 11:18, 19; 13:3, 8, 9, 17, 18, 21; 14:8, 15; 15:4; 17:23; 18:46; 19:8; 2Ki 5:23; 12:11; 17:13, 34; 18:16; 20:1; 21:8; 22:8, 12; 25:28, 30; 1Ch 2:24, 35, 46, 48, 49; 4:6, 7; 7:16, 18, 23; 8:9; 14:12; 16:3, 7; 18:6; 21:2, 25; 22:2, 13; 28:11, 12, 13, 13, 14; 29:6, 7, 25; 2Ch 6:3, 25, 31, 38; 7:18; 9:9, 9, 12; 11:20, 21, 23; 12:7; 15:15; 19:6; 20:3, 11; 24:5, 8, 12; 26:5; 28:15, 21; 29:18; 30:24; 32:24; 33:8; 34:9, 15, 20; 35:6, 8, 9; Ezr 1:6; 2:68, 69; 3:11; 5:3, 9; 7:6; 8:21, 26; Ne 1:7; 6:4; 7:2, 5, 70, 70, 71, 72; 9:13, 15, 33, 35, 36; 12:47; Est 1:3, 5, 9; 2:18, 22; 4:8, 12; 8:1, 2, 11; Job 1:21; 10:12; 22:6; 42:10, 13; Ps 18:13, 43; 33:7; 44:2, 3; 78:5, 24, 25, 29, 33, 46, 55, 62; 94:19; 99:7; 105:39, 40, 44; 106:15; 135:12; 136:21; Pr 5:13; 23:22, 25; Ecc 12:7; SS 8:5; Isa 30:20, 26; 38:1; 40:21; 41:28; 43:3; 54:1; 57:10; 63:14; Jer 1:2, 4; 2:1; 3:18; 5:19; 7:1, 7, 14; 9:13; 11:1; 12:14; 13:3, 20; 16:1, 15; 17:22; 18:1, 5; 23:39; 24:1, 4, 10; 25:5; 26:12; 28:12; 29:30; 30:1, 3, 4; 32:22; 33:1, 23; 34:12; 35:1, 6, 12, 15; 36:1, 27; 37:6; 40:1, 5; 42:7; 43:8; 44:10; 45:1; 46:13; 50:1; 51:59; 52:32, 34; La 1:14; Eze 1:3; 3:16; 5:6; 9:11; 16:10, 11, 15, 16, 18; 20:11, 12, 25; 23:5, 18; 28:25; 29:7; 31:6, 9; 36:28; 37:25; 44:8; Da 1:2, 17, 17; 2:48; 5:1, 2, 6, 18; 6:16, 24; 9:10; Hos 1:1, 3, 6, 8; 2:8, 9, 12; 8:12; 13:11; Joel 1:1; Jnh 1:1; Mic 1:1; Hab 3:16; Zep 1:1; Hag 1:1, 13; Zec 1:1; 6:14; Mal 1:1; 2:5; 4:4; Mt 2:11; 10:1; 14:19, 19; 15:23, 36; 21:23, 24; 25:14, 15, 20, 22, 35, 36, 43; 26:15, 26, 27, 27, 49; 27:34, 50; Mk 2:26; 3:15; 5:7, 13; 6:21, 28; 7:10; 8:6; 11:28, 29; 12:19, 44; 13:34; 14:22, 23, 23, 45; Lk 1:42, 67, 73; 2:7; 5:36; 6:4, 39; 7:15; 8:32; 9:1, 42; 12:16; 14:7; 15:16, 29; 19:13; 20:2, 28; 21:29; 22:19; 24:30, 42; Jn 1:12; 3:16; 4:5, 12; 6:11, 31; 12:49; 13:26; 17:6, 6, 8, 22, 24; 18:9; 19:9, 16, 30, 38; 20:18; Ac 1:19; 2:4, 33; 4:33; 7:5, 8, 10, 10, 38, 42; 9:41; 10:2, 48; 11:17, 17; 12:22; 13:19, 21; 15:8; 19:11; 21:14, 19; 27:15, 33, 35; Ro 7:10; 8:30, 32, 32; 9:4, 10; 1Co 1:30; 3:5; 9:14; 13:3; 15:27, 28; 16:1; 2Co 2:12; 8:3; 11:24; 12:12; Gal 1:24; 2:20; 3:16, 17, 18, 19, 29; 4:27; Eph 1:5, 22; 2:5; 4:8, 11; 5:2, 23, 25; Php 2:9; 4:15; Col 4:17; 1Th 1:5, 9; 2:2, 8; 2Th 2:16; 3:6, 10; 1Ti 2:6, 6; 6:13; 2Ti 1:6; 4:17; Tit 2:14; 3:5; Heb 1:4; 2:8; 7:2; 8:5; 11:2, 9; 12:18; 1Pe 1:21, 23; 2Pe 3:15; 1Jn 3:16; Jude 3, 6; Rev 1:1; 2:21; 10:3; 11:13; 12:5; 13:2; 18:2, 6; 20:13, 13

GIVE (1106)

Ge 4:15; 11:7; 12:7; 13:15, 16; 14:21, 24; 15:7, 8; 16:10, 11; 17:6, 8, 16; 23:11, 11; 24:7, 12, 17, 43, 45; 25:21, 30; 26:3, 4, 24; 27:19, 25, 28, 31, 37; 28:3, 13, 20, 22; 29:18, 19, 21; 30:1, 2, 14, 24, 31, 32; 31:32; 32:4; 34:9, 11, 12; 35:12; 37:26; 38:17; 42:34; 43:14; 47:6, 15, 16, 16, 19; 48:4, 22; 50:24; Ex 1:16; 6:4, 8, 29; 11:9; 12:25, 32; 13:5, 11; 16:8, 29; 17:2; 18:19; 19:3, 6; 20:12; 22:29, 30, 30; 23:12, 26; 24:12; 25:16, 21, 22; 28:40; 30:14, 15, 15; 32:13, 29; 33:1, 14; 34:34; Lev 1:2; 4:2; 5:16; 6:4, 9, 25; 7:23, 29, 32, 36; 11:2; 12:1; 15:2, 14; 17:2, 8; 18:21, 28; 20:2; 22:18; 23:2, 10, 24; 25:2, 38; 26:6, 28; 27:2, 23; Nu 3:48; 5:6; 6:1, 3, 21, 26; 11:12, 13, 18; 14:8, 8, 16, 23, 30; 15:1, 2, 4, 6, 7, 18; 18:12, 26, 32; 19:3; 21:16; 22:18; 23:16; 24:13; 26:54; 27:4, 7, 8, 10, 17; 28:1, 14; 31:27, 28, 29, 30; 32:29; 34:2; 35:2, 6, 6, 8, 8, 8; 36:2; Dt 1:8, 35, 36, 39; 2:4, 5, 9, 19, 24; 3:28; 4:38, 40; 5:16, 31; 6:10, 18, 23, 23; 7:13, 13, 13; 8:1; 9:28; 10:11; 11:9, 15, 21, 22; 12:32; 13:8; 14:21, 29; 15:10, 14; 16:17; 18:4, 20, 22; 19:9; 20:4; 21:16, 17; 24:12; 26:3, 12; 28:11, 11, 55; 30:9, 20; 31:7, 20, 21, 23; 33:7, 10; 34:4; Jos 1:6; 2:12, 24; 3:8; 5:6; 6:5, 5; 7:19; 8:7, 18; 10:8; 13:6; 14:12; 15:16, 19, 19, 19; 17:4; 21:2, 43; Jdg 1:12, 15, 15, 15; 2:1, 19; 4:7, 14, 19; 7:7; 8:5, 24; 11:13, 23, 30, 31; 13:3, 5, 7, 8; 14:12, 13; 16:5; 17:10; 19:20; 20:13, 28, 36; 21:1, 7, 18, 22; Ru 1:11; 2:16; 4:12; 1Sa 1:4, 11, 11, 27; 2:16, 20, 36; 8:5, 14, 22; 9:7; 10:8; 11:3; 17:18, 25, 44, 46, 47; 18:17; 21:3, 9; 22:13; 25:8, 11; 28:22; 30:15, 22; 2Sa 2:23; 3:10, 14; 4:11; 5:19; 9:7; 12:11; 14:17; 15:4, 31; 16:4, 21; 18:5; 19:30, 37; 22:51; 24:12, 13, 23; 1Ki 2:17, 22, 22; 3:5, 9, 12, 12, 13, 14, 25, 26, 27; 8:39, 58; 11:11, 31, 35, 38; 12:5, 7, 27; 13:3, 7, 18; 14:5, 5, 7; 17:1, 19; 20:5, 7, 8, 9, 25, 34; 21:2, 3, 9, 19; 22:6, 12, 15, 27; 2Ki 4:42, 43; 5:7, 22; 6:22, 27; 10:15; 14:9; 18:20, 23; 20:8, 9; 1Ch 14:10; 16:8, 18, 29, 34, 41; 21:10, 12, 23, 24; 22:9, 9, 11, 12; 28:8; 29:5, 14, 14, 19, 20; 2Ch 1:7, 10, 12, 12; 5:13; 6:30; 12:7; 18:5, 11, 26; 20:7, 21, 22; 21:11; 25:9, 18; 31:2; Ezr 6:9; 7:21, 22; 8:21; Ne 2:7, 8; 5:12; 9:6, 8, 15; 10:36; 12:31; Est 3:9; 5:3, 6; 6:3; 7:2; 9:13; Job 2:4; 4:6; 5:1; 12:5; 14:6, 14; 15:2, 35; 20:10, 23, 27; 22:24; 23:6; 32:20; 35:7; 36:3; 39:1, 3, 20; 40:11, 22; 41:5; Ps 2:8; 7:14; 8:2; 18:50; 20:9; 28:1, 4, 4; 29:1, 1, 2; 30:12; 33:17; 35:24, 27; 36:10; 37:4, 26; 44:8; 50:15; 51:8; 55:22; 69:4, 21; 71:3; 72:1; 74:21; 75:1; 78:8, 15, 19, 20; 81:8; 82:3; 86:4, 12, 16; 90:15; 91:16; 92:1; 94:13; 95:1; 96:8; 100:4; 104:15, 27; 105:1, 11; 106:1; 107:1; 109:30; 112:9; 113:1; 118:1, 25, 29; 119:8, 24, 29, 34, 36, 37, 41, 73, 104, 125, 130, 156, 159, 169; 122:4; 129:8; 136:1, 2, 3, 4, 5, 6, 7, 10, 13, 16, 17, 26; 138:1, 2, 4; 140:8; 145:15; 148:5; Pr 1:4; 3:2; 8:5, 5; 10:21; 11:24; 12:26; 15:7; 17:8; 18:13; 19:14; 21:3, 26; 23:25, 26; 25:14, 21, 21; 29:17; 30:8, 8; 31:5; Ecc 2:1; 6:2; 10:6, 6; 11:1, 9; SS 7:12, 13; 8:2, 12; Isa 1:16, 26; 5:4; 7:14; 13:8; 19:21; 22:15, 22; 23:18; 24:15; 26:17; 28:6, 6; 29:11, 12; 30:6, 16; 32:6; 36:5, 8; 38:7; 40:30; 41:18, 25; 42:8, 14; 44:3, 20, 25; 45:3, 11, 19; 46:13; 49:8, 22; 50:6; 51:23; 53:12; 55:2, 3; 56:5, 5, 10; 57:15; 58:6, 7, 14, 14; 60:19; 61:3; 62:2, 7; Jer 1:3; 3:15, 19; 5:14, 31; 6:10, 14, 24; 7:2, 18; 8:10, 11; 9:15; 10:9; 11:5; 12:1, 2; 13:16; 14:12, 14; 15:15; 17:3, 10, 18; 18:18; 19:2; 21:12; 22:23; 23:15, 36; 24:7; 26:2; 27:4, 5, 6; 29:11; 30:6, 6, 17; 31:2, 8; 32:3, 39; 33:6, 11; 34:20; 38:15; 39:12; 44:25, 29; 48:41; 49:7, 22; 50:34, 43; 51:8; La 2:18; 3:65; 4:4; 5:21; Eze 2:7, 8; 3:1, 27; 6:3; 7:21; 11:16, 17, 19, 19; 12:19, 23, 23, 28; 14:4, 6; 16:3, 33, 39, 59; 17:3; 20:3, 5, 26, 27, 30, 31, 31, 47; 21:3, 9, 28; 22:3, 19, 24; 23:16; 24:3, 21; 25:3, 7; 27:3; 28:2, 12, 22; 29:3, 19; 30:2; 31:2; 32:2, 7; 33:2, 10, 12, 15, 25, 27; 34:2, 14, 29; 35:3, 6; 36:1, 3, 6, 22, 26, 26, 29, 30; 37:12, 21, 26; 38:3, 14; 39:1, 4, 10; 44:6; 45:13; 46:7, 11; 47:14; Da 2:6; 3:15; 5:16, 17; 6:7; 9:22; 11:17, 33; Hos 2:15; 9:14, 14, 16; 11:8; Joel 2:12, 14, 14, 25; Am 4:5; 6:8; Mic 1:14; 3:5; 4:13, 13; 6:14; Zep 3:19, 20; Zec 10:1, 2; 11:12, 16; 12:7; Mal 1:8, 14; Mt 1:23; 4:9; 5:40, 42; 6:2, 3, 4, 11, 33; 7:6, 6, 9, 10, 11, 11; 10:8, 12, 39, 42; 11:28, 30; 12:36, 39; 14:7; 15:5; 16:4, 19, 25; 19:21; 20:28; 21:16, 41; 22:21; 24:29, 45; 25:8, 19, 21, 23, 28, 37, 38, 42; 26:48, 60; 28:8; Mk 5:43; 6:22, 23, 41; 7:11; 8:11, 12, 35; 10:21, 45; 12:17; 13:24; 14:44; 15:9; 16:7; Lk 1:32, 79; 3:11; 4:6, 6, 7; 6:30, 38; 7:45; 8:55; 9:16, 24; 10:5; 11:3, 8, 11, 12, 13, 13, 29, 33, 41; 12:31, 32, 33; 13:8, 8; 17:18; 18:1, 7, 12, 22; 19:8, 8, 24; 20:25; 21:15; Jn 1:22; 4:7, 10, 14, 15; 5:39, 40; 6:27, 32, 34, 52, 68; 9:24, 39; 10:10, 28; 11:15, 22; 13:26, 29; 14:16, 27; 15:16; 17:1, 19; 18:23; Ac 2:28; 3:6; 4:29, 35; 5:4, 20, 31; 10:22; 13:15, 34; 20:32, 35; 22:18; 24:4, 23; Ro 1:21; 2:7, 26; 4:13; 6:12, 13; 8:11, 18, 23, 32; 11:35; 12:1, 3, 20; 13:7, 7; 14:6, 6, 12; 15:4, 9, 29; 16:5, 6, 7, 10, 10, 14, 15; 1Co 1:3; 2:16; 4:5; 7:5; 10:13, 32; 11:34; 12:8, 30; 16:17, 18; 2Co 1:2, 4, 11, 15, 20, 22; 2:3; 4:1, 8, 16; 6:10; 8:5, 11, 12, 12, 12, 13; 9:7, 7, 9, 10, 11; 13:3; Gal 3:5, 19; 6:9; Eph 1:14, 17; 3:16; 4:28; 5:14, 20; 6:19, 23; Php 1:2, 3; 3:1; 4:21; Col 1:2, 3, 9; 3:24; 4:3, 9, 15; 1Th 2:5; 5:13; 2Th 1:2, 12; 2:17; 3:6, 9, 16; 1Ti 1:2, 18; 2:1; 4:15; 5:7; 6:1, 18; 2Ti 1:2; 2:7; 4:8, 19; Tit 1:4; 3:10, 15; Phm 1:3, 17, 17, 20; Heb 11:8, 26; 12:3; 13:4, 17, 24; Jas 2:3, 16; 4:3, 10; 5:11; 1Pe 2:12; 3:7; 5:7; 1Jn 3:16; 5:4, 15, 16; 3Jn 15; Jude 21; Rev 1:6; 2:10, 17, 23, 26, 28; 4:9; 10:9; 11:3, 10, 17; 12:4, 6; 13:15; 14:7; 16:9; 17:13, 17; 18:6, 6; 19:10; 21:6; 22:16

GIVEN (630)

Ge 1:29, 30; 9:3, 3; 15:3, 18; 21:7; 24:35, 36; 25:34; 26:18; 29:33, 34; 30:6, 20, 20; 31:16, 27; 33:5; 38:20; 43:24; 45:27; 46:18, 25; 48:9, 22; Ex 5:16, 18, 21; 6:29; 16:15, 29; 21:32; 24:3; 29:42; 30:15; 31:6, 11; 34:32, 34; 35:29, 34, 35; 36:5, 6; 38:25; Lev 2:3, 3, 10, 10, 16; 3:11; 4:35; 5:12; 6:17, 18, 25; 7:25, 30, 33, 35; 8:21, 28; 10:11, 13, 13, 13, 14, 15, 17; 14:13; 16:27, 34; 17:11; 22:27; 23:13, 18, 38; 24:7, 9; 26:41; Nu 5:8; 10:29; 15:3, 22, 25; 16:10, 14; 18:8, 17, 24, 29; 21:34; 26:62; 27:7, 12; 29:6, 6; 31:21, 36, 47; 32:7; 33:53; 35:7; Dt 1:25; 2:5, 9, 19, 29; 3:2, 18, 19, 20, 20; 6:17, 20, 25; 8:10; 9:4, 23; 12:21, 26; 15:18; 16:17; 18:1, 1; 19:9; 20:14; 21:15; 24:5, 8, 17, 18; 25:3, 19; 26:10, 11, 13, 15; 28:31, 45, 52, 53; 29:4; 30:2, 19; 32:18, 30, 46; 33:8; Jos 1:3, 11, 13, 15; 2:9; 4:10; 6:2, 16; 8:1, 33, 35; 10:19; 13:23, 28, 31; 14:3, 4; 15:13, 20, 33; 16:5, 8, 9; 17:1, 1, 6, 11, 14, 14, 17; 18:3, 21, 28; 19:9; 21:3, 4, 12, 13, 17, 19, 26, 34, 41, 45; 22:2, 4, 7, 7; 23:1, 13, 15, 15, 16; 24:33; Jdg 1:2, 20; 3:4, 6, 28; 7:9, 14, 15; 11:36; 14:16, 16, 20; 16:23; 18:10; 21:14; Ru 4:14; 1Sa 1:5, 27; 2:14; 12:1; 15:28; 25:44; 28:17; 30:23; 2Sa 4:8; 9:9; 12:8, 14; 13:28; 16:8; 19:42; 20:5; 22:36; 1Ki 3:28; 5:4; 8:36, 56; 9:7, 12; 10:13, 24; 17:9; 2Ki 5:1, 2; 10:22; 12:16; 18:6, 12; 20:19; 21:8; 22:9, 10; 1Ch 5:1; 6:49, 56, 57, 60, 60, 72, 76; 8:11; 16:40; 21:11, 19; 22:18; 23:25, 31; 28:5, 19; 29:9, 12, 14; 2Ch 2:12, 14; 4:7; 6:27; 7:19, 20; 8:2, 13; 9:12, 23; 14:7; 20:27, 30; 21:3; 22:9; 23:18; 29:25; 31:18; 32:29; 33:8; 34:14, 17, 18; 35:15; 36:23; Ezr 1:2; 3:7; 7:6, 25; 8:35; 9:8, 8, 9; 10:3; Ne 8:1; 12:43; 13:10; Est 2:3, 12, 13; 3:13; 5:11; 8:7; Job 3:20, 23; 4:12; 14:5, 6; 15:19; 39:17, 19; Ps 4:7; 16:6; 18:35; 21:2, 6; 40:3; 52:T; 61:5; 72:15; 89:18, 19; 90:10; 109:8; 115:16; 119:13; 122:5; Ecc 3:10; 5:20; 9:9; Isa 8:18; 9:6; 14:20; 28:26; 39:8; 42:6; 49:5, 21; 50:4; 57:9; 59:21; 60:7; 63:17; Jer 3:8; 8:14; 12:16; 17:16; 22:16; 23:21; 26:4; 31:12, 25; 32:16; 36:2, 4; 37:21; 38:22; 39:15; 42:19; 44:20; 46:1, 2; 48:1, 10; 49:1, 7, 23, 28; La 2:7; 3:15; 5:5; Eze 11:2, 15; 16:17, 19; 18:7, 12; 20:13, 15, 16, 21, 26; 21:29; 26:20; 28:13; 29:5, 20; 33:24; 35:12; 43:19; 44:30; 45:17, 23; 46:11, 14, 15, 17; 47:13, 23; Da 1:8, 9; 2:23, 37; 5:21, 28; 7:4, 6, 14, 18, 27; 9:23, 25; 11:4, 6, 6; Am 1:1; 9:15; Jnh 3:2; Mic 2:4; Hab 1:4; Zec 3:7; Mt 5:3; 7:7; 10:19, 41; 11:27; 13:12; 14:11; 19:27, 29; 21:43; 22:21; 25:29, 29; 26:9, 48; 28:18, 20; Mk 4:25; 7:11, 28; 10:28, 29; 12:17, 43, 43, 44; 14:5, 44; Lk 2:21, 31; 6:20, 38; 8:18; 10:19, 22; 11:9; 12:48, 48; 18:29; 19:15, 26, 26; 20:25; 21:3, 4, 4; 22:17, 19; Jn 1:17; 3:35; 5:27; 6:37, 39; 7:39, 39, 51; 10:18, 29; 11:26; 12:5, 41; 13:3, 15; 15:3; 17:2, 2, 9, 10, 11, 14, 22, 24; 18:3, 11; 19:11; Ac 1:20; 5:32; 8:18; 10:33; 11:18; 13:46; 24:2; 25:16; 26:4, 18; Ro 1:5; 3:19; 4:16; 5:5, 13, 13, 20; 6:13, 17; 8:33; 11:28; 12:3, 6, 6, 8; 15:30; 1Co 1:4; 2:12, 12, 13; 4:7; 6:19; 7:25; 8:6; 9:17; 11:15, 24, 24; 12:7, 10, 10, 24; 14:26; 15:22, 27; 2Co 1:4; 4:1; 5:5, 18, 19; 8:16; 9:5; 10:8; 12:7; 13:10; Gal 2:7, 7, 9; 3:19, 19, 21; 4:15; Eph 1:18; 3:2, 7, 21; 4:7, 19; Php 1:29; 4:19; Col 1:8, 25, 28; 1Ti 3:10; 6:12, 18; 2Ti 1:7; 3:15; 4:5; Tit 3:13; Heb 2:13; 6:18; 7:26, 28; 8:6; 9:19; 10:5; 11:23, 31; 12:4; 1Pe 1:3; 4:10, 11; 2Pe 1:1, 4; 2:21; 1Jn 1:5;

4:13; 5:11, 20; Rev 6:4, 8, 11; 7:2; 8:2, 3; 9:1, 3, 10; 11:1; 12:13, 14; 13:5, 7, 16; 15:2; 16:6; 20:4

GIVES (147)

Ge 28:22; Lev 12:2, 5; Nu 22:38; Dt 8:18; 10:18, 18; 12:10, 15; 16:15; 19:8; 24:1; 32:39; Jos 1:15; 2:14; Jdg 8:7; 11:9, 24, 24; 1Sa 2:10; 26:23; Job 5:10, 11; 21:33; 33:4; 35:10; 36:6; 38:29, 36; Ps 28:8; 29:11; 41:2; 42:8; 44:7; 68:6, 35; 84:11; 103:6; 111:5; 113:9; 127:2; 136:25; 142:4; 144:1; 146:7; Pr 10:31; 12:14; 16:1; 19:6, 23; 28:27; 29:4, 11, 13; 31:26; Ecc 2:26, 26; 5:3; 6:2, 2; 8:15; 9:9; 10:19, 19, 19; Isa 3:9; 14:3; 28:29; 40:29; 41:2; 42:5; 50:8; 66:7; Jer 5:24; 51:56; Eze 14:9; 17:24; 18:7; 46:16, 17, 18; Da 2:21; 4:17, 25, 32; 5:23; Am 6:11; Mic 5:3; Mt 5:45; Mk 9:41; 16:S; Lk 12:32, 42; Jn 1:4, 9; 3:6; 6:33, 50, 63; 14:27; 16:21; 17:2; Ac 17:25; 24:10; Ro 5:18; 8:17; 10:12; 15:5, 13, 33; 1Co 7:4, 4, 7, 7; 12:1, 8, 8, 9, 9, 10, 10; 13:7; 14:1; 15:38, 56, 57; 2Co 1:21; 3:6, 12, 17; 9:7, 10; Gal 1:6; 5:17; Eph 4:27; Php 4:13; 1Th 2:19; 3:8; 4:8; 1Ti 6:13, 17; 2Ti 1:8; 2:1; Tit 1:2; Jas 4:6; 2Pe 1:3; 1Jn 5:6

GIVING (190)

Ge 9:12; 11:9; 13:17; 15:4; 20:16; 28:15; 30:18, 22; 36:43; 39:3; 40:23; Ex 1:19; 4:15; 24:8; 31:3; 34:11; 35:31; Lev 14:34; 20:3; 23:10; 25:2; 27:9; Nu 13:2; 18:7, 19; 20:12, 24; 21:34; 32:5, 9; 34:2; Dt 1:8, 20; 3:2, 20; 4:1, 2, 8, 21, 40; 5:1, 31; 6:6; 7:11; 8:1; 9:6; 10:13; 11:8, 13, 17, 26, 27, 31, 32; 12:1, 9, 10; 13:12, 18; 15:4, 5, 7, 15; 16:5, 18, 20; 17:2, 14; 18:9; 19:1, 2, 3, 10, 14; 20:16; 21:1, 23; 24:4, 22; 25:15, 19; 26:1; 27:1, 2, 3, 10; 28:1, 8, 14, 15; 30:8, 11, 15; 32:49, 52; Jos 1:2, 13, 15; 3:3; Ru 1:6; 1Sa 1:28; 8:8; 18:4; 2Sa 2:5; 7:19; 1Ki 3:6; 5:7; 1Ch 11:14; 16:4; 17:17; 29:3; 2Ch 13:5; 14:6; 30:12; 32:1; Ezr 1:6; Ne 9:20; 12:40; Est 2:18; 3:10; 9:22; Job 36:16, 31; Ps 8:6; 19:8; 37:34; 42:4; 50:5, 23; 111:6; 138:3; Pr 4:2; 18:16; Ecc 4:8; Isa 21:3; 42:14; 43:20; 49:9; Jer 4:31; 13:21; 15:6; 25:3; 43:1; 49:24; 51:56; Eze 3:1; 27:10; 45:8; Da 6:10; Hos 9:10; 14:8; Hag 2:19; Zec 3:4; Mal 1:8; Mt 5:31; 11:1; Mk 6:41; Lk 6:38; 9:16; 14:33; Jn 4:14; 13:34; 19:35; Ac 1:2; 11:29; 12:23; 14:3, 17; 15:8; Ro 2:4; 5:21; 8:3; 15:6; 1Co 7:40; 14:16, 17; 2Co 3:8; 5:12; 8:6, 6, 7; Eph 1:13; Php 2:13; Col 3:17; Heb 2:4; 7:4; Jas 1:18; 2Pe 3:9; Jude 12; Rev 13:4

GO (1158)

Ge 4:8; 7:1; 8:5; 11:7, 31; 12:1; 16:2; 18:27; 19:19, 20, 34; 20:13; 21:18; 22:2, 3, 9; 23:11, 15; 24:4, 41, 51, 55, 58, 58; 26:2, 16; 27:9, 13; 28:2, 15; 30:25, 31, 32; 31:16, 30; 32:26, 26; 33:14; 37:13, 14; 41:55; 42:2, 4, 16, 19, 33, 38; 43:2, 4, 5, 13, 14; 44:10, 17, 25, 26, 30; 45:28; 46:3, 4, 31; 50:5, 6; Ex 2:7, 20; 3:3, 10, 13, 16, 18, 18, 19, 20; 4:12, 18, 18, 21, 21, 23, 27; 5:1, 1, 2, 2, 11, 17; 6:1, 11; 7:5, 14, 15, 16; 8:1, 1, 8, 20, 25, 25, 28, 28, 28, 29, 29, 32; 9:1, 1, 2, 7, 13, 13, 17, 28; 10:3, 7, 7, 8, 9, 11, 20, 24, 26, 27; 11:1, 8; 12:31, 31, 32; 13:15, 17; 16:4; 18:23; 19:10, 12, 21, 24; 20:7; 21:3, 5, 26; 23:7, 23; 28:24; 29:35; 30:20; 32:7, 27, 34; 33:7, 14, 15, 16; 34:9, 15, 24; Lev 6:12, 13; 12:4; 13:9, 19, 45; 14:35, 36, 37; 16:18, 24; 17:13; 21:23; 25:25, 39, 47; 27:8; Nu 1:3, 20, 45; 4:19; 6:6, 13; 8:15; 10:9, 30; 12:4; 13:17, 30, 31, 32; 14:4, 14, 25, 40, 42; 16:30; 18:3; 20:17; 21:4; 22:12, 13, 13, 20, 34, 35; 23:3, 5, 15, 16; 24:11; 29:7; 32:6, 24; 33:38; 34:4; 36:3; Dt 1:7, 7, 8, 21, 26, 28, 40, 41, 42; 2:29; 3:27; 5:11, 27, 30; 6:3, 18; 8:3; 9:12, 23; 11:8, 25; 12:25, 28; 13:6; 16:7; 19:13; 20:1, 2, 3, 5, 6, 7, 8; 21:5, 10, 14; 22:4, 7; 23:9; 24:19, 20; 25:7; 26:3, 11; 28:6, 19, 34; 30:4, 12; 31:3, 6; 32:49; Jos 1:3, 9, 11, 16; 2:16, 19; 4:5; 6:1, 22; 7:3; 8:20; 9:11; 18:8; 22:4, 12; 24:27; Jdg 4:8, 8, 9; 6:14, 18; 7:3, 4, 9, 10; 9:38; 10:14; 11:25, 37, 38, 38, 40; 12:5; 14:3; 18:6, 6, 9, 20; 19:5, 12, 25, 28; 20:18, 23, 28; 21:20; Ru 1:8, 10, 11, 16, 16, 18; 2:2, 2, 8; 3:3, 4, 17; 1Sa 1:22; 3:5, 6, 9; 6:6, 8, 9; 9:3, 5, 6, 6, 9, 19, 24; 10:8; 11:14; 12:21; 14:1, 4, 6, 9, 10, 34, 37; 15:3, 18, 25, 27; 16:1, 23; 17:32, 33, 35, 37, 39, 55; 19:3; 20:6, 19, 22, 28, 29, 31, 42; 23:2, 2, 3, 4, 13, 22, 23; 25:19; 26:6, 6; 28:7; 29:4, 6, 7; 30:8, 21, 22, 24; 2Sa 2:1, 21; 3:10, 16, 21, 31; 5:8, 19, 19; 7:3, 5, 8; 11:1, 8, 9, 10, 11, 13, 20; 12:11, 23; 13:5, 13; 14:3, 8, 12, 21, 24, 30; 15:7, 9, 19, 20, 20, 21, 21, 33; 16:9, 21; 17:16, 18; 18:3, 21, 22, 22, 23, 23; 19:7, 26, 36, 37, 38; 20:1; 24:1, 12, 18; 1Ki 1:13, 53; 2:2, 3, 26, 36, 42; 8:44; 9:6; 11:22; 12:16, 24, 27; 13:8, 12; 14:2, 12; 17:3, 9, 13; 18:1, 8, 11, 14, 25, 41, 43, 43, 44; 19:11, 15, 20, 20, 20; 20:33, 34; 21:18; 22:6, 6, 9, 12, 15, 15, 20, 22, 22, 30; 2Ki 1:3, 6, 15; 2:2, 4, 6, 18, 23, 23; 3:13, 23; 4:4, 29, 29, 30, 30, 41; 5:3, 5, 10, 13, 19; 6:2, 2, 9, 13; 7:4, 4, 9; 8:10; 9:1, 27, 34; 10:25; 18:14, 25; 19:24; 20:5, 5, 8, 9, 10; 22:4, 13, 15, 18; 25:24; 1Ch 12:19; 14:10, 10; 17:2, 4, 7; 20:1; 21:10, 30; 2Ch 6:34; 7:19; 10:16; 11:4; 18:5, 5, 8, 11, 14, 14, 19, 21, 21, 29; 20:17; 23:5, 8; 24:5, 6; 25:8; 34:21, 23, 26; Ne 1:11; 4:22; 8:10, 13, 15; 9:15; Est 2:13, 15; 3:11; 4:5, 8, 10, 16, 16; 5:14; 6:9; 8:8; Job 5:8; 7:4, 15, 16; 8:2; 9:11; 15:22; 16:22; 17:13, 16; 19:28; 21:13, 14; 22:21; 23:3, 8, 8; 24:5, 10; 27:19; 31:31, 34; 33:32; 34:33; 36:2; 38:19; 39:11; 42:8; Ps 6:8; 9:17; 10:15; 25:8, 17; 26:4; 30:5; 34:10; 43:4; 45:4; 48:12; 59:15; 63:9; 69:23, 27; 71:11; 89:36, 46; 91:11; 100:4; 104:23; 105:28; 109:28; 118:19; 121:8; 122:1; 126:6; 132:3, 7; 139:8, 8; 142:3; Pr 1:12, 15, 22; 4:15; 5:5, 8; 6:3, 29; 11:21, 28; 15:22; 19:2, 5, 9; 20:18; 22:13; 24:6, 22; 25:8, 8; 26:1, 13; 27:10; 28:12; Ecc 1:4; 3:20; 9:7, 10; 10:5; 12:12; SS 3:4, 11; 4:6; 7:11, 12; Isa 2:2, 3, 3; 5:23; 6:8, 8, 9; 7:3, 25; 9:1; 10:31; 13:20; 18:2; 21:2; 26:20; 29:9; 30:6, 8; 35:8; 36:10; 37:25; 38:5, 18, 22; 42:24; 43:2, 2; 45:2, 23; 46:2; 48:20; 49:17, 24; 52:11, 12; 56:12; 59:7; 60:20; 62:10; 65:4, 24, 66:24, 24, Jer 1:7, 17; 2:2, 10, 10, 23; 3:12; 4:1, 21; 5:5, 10; 6:25; 7:2, 10, 12; 8:14; 9:2, 3; 11:6; 13:1, 4, 6; 14:18; 15:2, 10; 16:5, 8; 17:2, 8, 19; 18:2, 11; 19:1, 2; 20:6; 21:3, 9; 22:1; 23:26; 25:29; 28:13; 30:11; 31:6; 34:2; 35:2, 13; 36:5, 6; 37:4; 38:20; 40:4, 4, 5, 5, 9; 41:8; 42:3, 19; 43:2; 44:25; 45:5; 46:11, 16, 28; 47:6; 48:45; 49:12, 31, 37; 50:9, 21, 33; 51:7, 9, 50; La 4:18; Eze 3:1, 4, 11, 22, 24, 25; 4:9; 8:9; 9:7; 10:2, 6; 12:3, 3; 20:39; 21:22, 24; 32:19; 33:30; 34:29; 38:12; 39:9; 42:14; 44:3, 30; 46:2, 5, 5; 47:3, 4, 19; 48:11; Da 11:25; 12:7, 9, 13; Hos 1:2; 3:1; 4:13, 18; 8:13; 10:6; 11:5, 8; Joel 2:20, 20; Am 1:3, 6, 9, 11, 13, 15; 2:1, 4, 6; 4:4; 5:5; 6:1, 2, 2; 7:12, 15; 8:9; Ob 21; Jnh 1:2; 3:2, 5; Mic 1:11, 15; 4:1, 2, 2; 5:7, 8; 7:3; Na 1:3; 2:13; 3:14; Zep 1:5, 16; Hag 1:8; Zec 6:7; 8:21, 21; 9:14; 10:12; 11:4, 15; 14:3, 16, 18, 19; Mal 1:9; 2:7; 3:15; 4:2; Mt 1:20; 2:8, 8, 22; 5:24; 6:6; 7:23; 8:4, 9, 9, 13, 19, 28, 32, 34; 9:6, 13, 24, 36; 10:5, 7; 11:4; 13:21; 14:15; 16:21; 17:27; 18:12, 15, 16; 19:21, 24; 20:7, 14; 21:2, 28, 29, 30, 30; 22:9; 23:13, 32; 24:17, 26; 25:9, 46, 46; 26:18, 32, 36, 48, 50; 28:7, 10, 16, 19; Mk 1:12, 38, 44; 2:11; 3:13; 4:17; 5:17, 18, 19, 34, 37, 40; 6:36, 38, 48; 8:26; 9:43; 10:21, 25, 52; 11:2; 13:15, 34; 14:12, 13, 15, 28, 32, 44; 16:7, 15; Lk 2:4, 15; 4:1, 34; 5:4, 14, 24; 7:8, 8, 22, 40, 50; 8:13, 37, 38, 39, 46, 48, 51; 9:13, 53, 57, 60; 10:3, 10, 37; 13:27, 32; 14:21, 23; 15:4, 18, 28; 16:3; 17:14, 19, 23, 31; 18:24, 25; 19:30; 22:8, 9, 12, 33; 23:22; Jn 1:43; 3:4, 29; 4:4, 16, 50; 6:68; 7:3, 3, 6, 6, 8, 8, 23, 35; 8:11; 9:7, 11; 10:9; 11:6, 7, 11, 15, 16, 44, 55; 13:29, 33, 36; 14:28; 15:16; 16:7, 7, 10, 23; 18:8, 28; 20:5, 15, 17; 21:18, 18; Ac 1:11; 4:21; 5:20, 40; 7:34; 8:26, 29; 9:6, 11, 15; 10:20, 20, 22; 11:12; 14:16; 16:6, 7, 35, 36; 18:6; 19:21, 21, 30, 38; 21:4, 12, 24; 22:10; 24:25; 25:9, 12; 27:3, 10, 12, 22; 28:26; Ro 1:24, 32; 3:16; 6:15; 10:3, 6, 7, 15; 11:10; 14:8; 15:1, 24, 25; 1Co 4:11, 17; 5:6, 6; 6:4; 7:9, 11, 15; 10:27; 11:21; 16:4, 7; 2Co 2:9, 14; 4:5; 8:17; 10:16; 12:1; Gal 1:17; 2:2; 4:9; Eph 3:17; 4:26; Php 1:23; Col 1:28; 1Th 1:8; 2Ti 3:13; Tit 2:3; Heb 6:1; 9:24; 10:22; 11:8, 15; 13:13; Jas 3:3, 4; 1Jn 1:6; Rev 3:3; 10:8; 11:1; 16:1; 17:8, 11; 20:8

GOES (65)

Ge 4:9; Ex 7:15; 8:20; 22:6; 28:29, 30, 30, 35; Lev 16:17; 22:7; Nu 1:51; 5:12; Dt 1:33; 16:6; 19:5; 31:8; Jdg 5:9; 21:19; 1Sa 9:13; 2Ki 5:18; Ne 6:6; Job 21:33; 41:22; Ps 68:24; 85:13; 97:3; 112:5; 115:1; Pr 11:13; 13:25; 16:18; 18:12; 19:15; 22:3; 25:3; 26:20; 27:12; 30:4; 31:16, 27; Ecc 3:21, 21; 8:9, 16; Isa 31:4; 41:3; 65:5; Jer 17:19; Eze 40:6; Da 11:44; Hos 9:8; Am 6:10; Zec 12:8; Mt 12:43; 15:17; Mk 9:48; Lk 1:50; 11:24; 23:5; Jn 7:22; 2Th 3:1; Heb 9:7, 17; Rev 14:4; 19:11

GOING (309)

Ge 12:7; 13:15, 16; 15:12; 16:8; 18:21; 19:14; 21:10; 28:12; 29:9; 32:17; 33:12; 35:3; 37:8, 13, 17; 42:22, 36; 43:30; 44:12; 49:1; Ex 5:8; 7:17; 15:24; 16:4; 17:7; 18:18; 19:9; 25:32; 34:10, 12; 37:18; Lev 8:5; 10:9; 21:11; Nu 13:22; 15:2, 39; 22:22, 34; 23:25; 32:7; 35:34; Dt 1:2, 30; 20:4; 28:6, 19; 31:16; Jos 7:7; 10:25, 27; 18:3; 19:11; 23:14; Jdg 6:17, 36, 37; 12:1; 13:23; 14:5; 15:3; 19:17, 18; 1Sa 3:12; 4:6; 14:19; 15:15, 30; 20:2; 22:3; 23:17; 24:20; 25:17; 27:1; 2Sa 2:24; 10:2; 15:36; 16:10; 18:2, 9; 19:9, 22; 20:6; 21:17; 1Ki 1:41; 2:2; 6:8; 17:11; 18:21; 21:21, 22; 2Ki 1:3, 6; 2:3, 5; 8:13; 10:6, 13, 19; 11:9; 17:34; 20:1; 22:20; 1Ch 19:2; 2Ch 2:9; 23:8; 34:28; Ezr 5:8; Ne 1:2, 3; 4:7; 9:28; Est 2:14; Job 1:7, 7; 2:2, 2; 11:10; 13:15; 23:10; 34:17; 35:14; 40:8; Ps 17:4; 38:10; 73:11; 139:4; Pr 7:22; 9:15; 21:12; Ecc 7:2; 8:7; 10:14; Isa 5:5; 19:12; 22:17; 29:15; 30:16; 38:1; 43:18; 44:7; 46:10; 48:3, 5; 58:5; 63:14; Jer 7:11; 8:5; 9:17; 11:11; 33:3; 37:7; 40:4; 42:14, 15, 17, 22; 43:7; Eze 6:11; 8:9; 10:16; 11:13; 16:37; 20:29; 21:20; 23:13; 24:16; 37:5; 40:40; 43:17; Da 2:29; 11:34; Am 4:3; 6:6; 8:12; Jnh 1:3; 4:3; Hag 1:5, 7; 2:15; Zec 2:2, 2; 3:8; 5:3; 6:5, 6, 6, 6; Mt 2:13; 4:13; 8:25; 9:9, 19; 17:22; 20:17; 24:39; 25:8, 14; 26:46, 58, 62; 28:7, 16; Mk 4:13, 38; 6:31; 9:31; 10:46; 14:42, 60; 15:4; 16:7; Lk 7:49; 8:24; 9:11, 44; 14:31; 15:26; 16:2; 18:5, 31, 36, 37; Jn 1:9, 51; 2:16; 3:8, 12, 26; 6:6, 67; 7:1, 35; 8:14, 21, 21, 22; 10:1, 24; 11:8, 31, 47; 12:33, 35; 13:6, 30, 36; 14:2, 4, 5, 12, 22, 28, 31; 16:4, 5, 5, 17, 20, 32; 18:4; 19:4; 21:3; Ac 1:6; 3:2; 7:28; 8:3; 16:16; 18:27; 20:22; 23:20; 26:17; 27:30; Ro 2:5; 15:26; 1Co 3:13; 5:1; 6:2, 2; 8:13; 2Co 2:2; 4:9; 8:2; 10:14; 12:5, 5; Gal 3:4; 4:19; Php 1:28, 28; 2:23; Col 1:6; 1Th 3:3, 3; Heb 6:1, 12; 11:1, 8, 20, 27; Jas 4:13; 1Pe 4:12; 5:9; 2Pe 3:11; 1Jn 2:11; 4:3; Jude 21; Rev 17:1

GONE (215)

Ge 7:13; 8:11; 12:19; 13:14; 21:15; 27:41; 28:7; 35:3; 37:13, 30; 42:36; 43:2, 10; 47:15, 16, 18; Ex 8:15; 12:32; 24:14; Lev 14:48; Nu 5:20; 11:6, 26; 16:3, 7; Dt 31:16; 32:36; Jdg 3:24; 4:12; 6:28; 20:3, 23; Ru 1:15; 1Sa 3:2, 3; 4:21; 9:7, 27; 14:17, 21; 20:41; 24:1, 7; 30:22; 2Sa 2:8; 6:13; 7:9; 24:8; 1Ki 2:41; 11:15; 14:10; 20:36; 2Ki 7:10; 9:16; 19:11; 25:3; 1Ch 17:8; 29:15; 2Ch 28:9; Ne 2:6; Job 4:20; 7:10, 21; 10:19; 11:16; 19:14; 24:24; 27:19, 21; 29:2; Ps 19:4; 32:5; 37:10, 36; 39:13; 58:3; 73:2, 20; 74:9; 77:8; 78:39; 90:10; 103:16; 105:38; 107:18; 115:17; Pr 12:7; 19:7; Ecc 6:12; 7:6; 9:6; 12:4; SS 2:11; 5:6; 6:1, 2; Isa 3:20, 24; 5:9; 14:11; 15:6; 16:6, 10, 10; 23:1, 13; 24:7, 9; 26:14; 27:4; 29:20; 30:2; 32:12, 13; 33:19; 34:12; 37:11; 40:2; 41:12; 50:1; 51:22; 59:15; Jer 4:25; 8:13, 20; 10:20; 14:16; 15:9, 18; 19:9; 22:20; 31:12; 37:9; 38:9; 48:33; 50:3; 51:30; 52:6; La 1:6; 3:18; Eze 5:16; 13:15; 19:5; 31:17; 32:24, 29; 34:4, 6; 37:11; Da 10:17; Hos 8:9; 10:11; 14:4; Joel 1:5, 10; Mic 4:9; Hab 1:11; 3:2; Zec 11:3; Mal 3:7; Mt 2:13; 6:30; 11:7; 25:10, 14; Mk 5:30; 7:30; 9:8; Lk 12:28; 19:7, 13; 23:45; 24:24, 28; Jn 4:8; 6:22; 12:19; 16:16, 19; 18:2; Ac 1:25; 2:40; 5:22; 8:27; 10:4, 7; 13:31; 27:20; Ro 2:28; 3:12; 10:18; 13:12; 2Co 5:17; 6:5; 11:27; Col 2:22; 1Ti 5:15; 6:17; 2Ti 1:15; 4:10, 10, 10; Heb 2:18; 4:14; 6:20; Jas 4:14; 1Pe 3:22; 2Pe 1:15; 2Jn 7; Rev 18:14, 14, 17, 19; 21:1, 4

HAD (2647)

Ge 1:31; 2:5, 8, 21; 3:1, 23; 4:22, 26; 5:4, 7, 10, 13, 16, 19, 22, 26, 30, 32; 6:4, 6, 10, 11, 22; 7:5, 9, 13, 16; 8:6, 20; 9:21, 24; 10:25; 11:11, 13, 15, 17, 19, 21, 23, 25, 27, 29; 12:4, 5; 13:3, 4, 10; 14:4, 14, 16, 20; 16:1, 13; 17:23; 18:15, 33; 19:27, 29; 20:2, 4, 8, 18; 21:1, 2, 4, 25, 31; 22:3, 9, 20, 24; 23:16; 24:1, 10, 16, 19, 19, 20, 22, 28, 29, 45, 48, 54, 59, 62; 25:10, 10, 34; 26:1, 15, 18, 18, 18, 20, 26, 32; 27:30, 30, 41; 28:6, 6, 7, 9, 18; 29:14, 16, 17, 28, 32, 33, 34, 35; 30:8, 19, 30; 31:10, 18, 24, 32, 34, 34; 34:5, 7, 7, 13, 27; 35:7, 13, 14, 15, 27; 36:4, 4, 5, 6, 12, 14; 37:1, 3, 5, 8, 9, 13; 38:3, 4, 5, 9, 13, 14, 14, 20, 21, 22, 27; 39:13, 13, 17, 23; 40:5, 5, 8, 10, 16, 22; 41:5, 11, 11, 15, 20, 22, 54; 42:5, 9, 9, 23, 24, 29; 43:2, 6, 7, 10, 21, 27; 44:6, 16, 19, 24, 27; 45:21, 27; 46:5, 6, 12, 27, 27; 47:11, 26; 48:2, 17; 49:33; 50:12, 13, 14; Ex 1:5, 7, 8; 2:11, 14, 16, 22; 3:4; 4:24, 27, 28, 30, 31, 31; 5:6; 6:9, 9, 28, 30; 7:6, 10, 13, 20, 22; 8:12, 13, 15, 17, 19, 24; 9:6, 11, 12, 21, 24, 32, 34, 35; 10:13, 15; 11:3, 9; 12:19, 28, 30, 35, 39, 39, 40, 42, 48; 13:19; 14:8, 19, 28, 29, 31; 15:19; 16:3, 3, 18, 18, 18, 18, 20, 21, 22, 34; 17:10, 11; 18:1, 1, 1, 2, 3, 4, 8, 8, 8, 9; 19:7, 9, 14, 18, 25; 21:4, 29; 24:3, 3; 32:14, 20, 20, 25, 35, 35; 33:5, 18; 34:4, 29, 32, 33, 34; 35:24, 29; 37:2, 18; 38:17, 22; 39:1, 5, 7, 21, 26, 29, 31, 32, 32, 43, 43; 40:16, 19, 21, 23, 25, 27, 29, 32, 35; Lev 8:9, 13, 17, 21, 29, 36; 9:5, 10, 15, 21; 10:1, 5, 16, 16, 19; 13:18; 15:33, 33; 16:1, 34; 19:20; 20:17; 21:3, 10; 23:43; 24:10, 23; Nu 1:19, 48, 54; 2:34, 34; 3:4, 4, 16, 17, 38, 42, 51; 4:37, 41, 45, 49, 49; 5:4; 7:2; 8:3, 4; 9:5, 6; 11:3, 5, 8, 18, 26, 28, 34; 12:1, 10, 14; 13:16, 24, 26, 26, 31; 14:2, 6, 36, 38; 15:36; 16:19, 31, 39, 42, 47, 49, 50; 17:8; 20:3, 29; 21:26, 26; 22:2, 15, 29; 24:11; 25:5, 9, 11; 26:1, 19, 19, 33, 46, 61, 64, 65; 27:4, 23; 29:40; 31:7, 10, 11, 14, 32, 41, 42, 47, 53; 32:13; 33:4, 4, 56; Dt 1:3, 4, 4, 4, 15, 25; 2:1, 10, 12, 12, 14, 14, 15, 15, 16, 22, 23, 36, 37; 3:6, 10; 4:3, 42, 46; 6:23; 7:8; 9:5, 9, 10, 10, 16, 16, 16, 18, 21, 28; 10:4, 5, 10; 19:6; 25:18; 29:1, 6, 26; 31:1, 24; 32:15, 17, 17, 18, 18, 30, 30, 45; 34:5, 9, 9; Jos 2:4, 6, 7, 22, 23; 3:17; 4:8, 10, 12, 14, 15, 23; 5:1, 4, 4, 5, 5, 6, 6, 6, 7, 7, 8; 6:15, 25; 7:1, 7, 22, 24; 8:20, 20, 21, 26, 27, 31, 33, 34, 35; 9:1, 3, 18; 10:1, 1, 1, 13, 17, 27, 28, 30, 33, 37, 39, 40; 11:1, 9, 10, 12, 15, 20, 23, 23; 12:1, 6; 13:8, 8, 12, 12, 14, 15, 21, 24, 29, 32, 33; 14:3, 4, 15, 15, 15; 15:13; 17:1, 3, 3, 4; 18:2; 19:9, 47, 50; 21:42, 43, 44, 45; 22:7, 11, 32; 23:1; 24:13, 30, 31, 31, 32, 32, 33; Jdg 1:7, 19, 20; 2:7, 7, 9, 10, 12, 17, 19; 3:1, 2, 4, 18; 4:3, 4, 11, 12; 6:11, 21, 27, 27, 28, 28, 28; 7:12, 13; 8:10, 18, 25, 30, 30, 31, 34, 35; 9:22, 46, 49, 56; 10:17; 11:2, 3, 11; 12:9, 14; 13:2; 14:8, 9, 19, 19, 20; 15:5; 16:9, 9, 18, 20, 30, 31; 17:6; 18:1, 1, 7, 14, 28, 29; 19:1, 6, 8, 21; 20:3, 3, 4, 17, 22, 23, 31, 32, 36, 39, 45; 21:1, 5, 8, 12, 15, 25; Ru 1:6, 7, 18; 2:19; 3:7, 16; 4:1; 1Sa 1:2, 2, 5, 6, 13; 2:12, 15, 15, 30; 3:2, 3, 7, 7, 15; 4:6, 7, 12, 13, 18, 18, 19, 21; 5:3, 4, 4, 11; 6:6, 7, 19; 7:2, 6, 7, 14, 14; 8:21; 9:15, 23, 25; 10:13, 16, 16, 21, 26; 13:4, 8, 13, 20, 22, 23; 14:3, 3, 4, 21, 24, 26, 27, 27, 30, 35, 47, 48, 49; 15:35; 16:13, 14; 17:12, 13, 39, 50, 57; 18:1, 6, 10, 12, 20, 25; 19:7, 7, 17, 18, 21; 20:9, 37, 41; 21:6; 22:15, 21; 23:13, 24; 24:1, 5, 7, 19; 25:2, 12, 21, 34, 36, 37, 37, 44; 26:12; 27:4, 8, 11; 28:3, 3, 3, 20, 24; 30:1, 1, 2, 3, 12, 14, 16, 18, 19, 21, 27, 31; 31:7, 11; 2Sa 1:2, 12, 13; 2:4, 8, 17, 24, 31; 3:1, 17, 23, 23, 30, 35, 35; 4:4, 6; 5:5, 12, 12, 13, 17, 21; 6:8, 13, 17, 18; 7:1, 17; 8:9, 10, 10, 11, 11; 9:1, 2, 10, 12; 10:5, 6, 19; 11:4, 8, 10, 27; 12:3, 8, 19; 13:1, 3, 15, 21, 22; 14:2, 6, 27, 30, 33; 15:18, 24, 32; 16:23, 23; 17:6, 14, 15, 15, 17, 17, 21, 24, 25, 25; 18:10, 13, 18, 18; 19:3, 5, 6, 6, 8, 24, 39, 41; 20:3, 5, 14; 21:2, 2, 7, 11, 12, 12, 13, 16; 22:1; 23:9, 14; 24:10, 19; 1Ki 1:4, 6, 6, 44, 51; 2:11, 27, 28, 28, 30, 40, 41, 41; 3:2, 10, 12, 15, 18, 28; 4:7, 25, 26; 5:1, 12; 7:3, 14, 20, 24, 30, 31, 32, 40, 46, 51; 8:9, 53, 54, 65, 66; 9:1, 2, 11, 12, 14, 16, 21, 24, 25; 10:2, 4, 7, 13, 19, 22, 24, 26; 11:2, 3, 4, 6, 9, 9, 10, 15, 15, 15, 16, 17, 23, 24; 12:1, 2, 6, 8, 12, 16, 24, 32, 32, 33; 13:5, 11, 11, 12, 13, 23, 28; 14:5, 18, 21, 24, 26; 15:3, 5, 5, 11, 12, 13, 15, 22, 26, 29, 30, 30, 30, 34; 16:7, 7, 7, 12, 16, 18, 19, 19, 26; 17:5, 16; 18:2, 4, 4, 4, 4, 16, 26, 30, 33; 19:1, 1, 4; 20:19, 36; 21:1, 11, 26, 26; 22:31, 38, 52, 53; 2Ki 1:17; 3:2, 3; 4:7, 17, 17, 40, 44; 5:1, 1, 2, 2, 4, 13, 14; 6:20, 29; 7:6, 10, 10, 13, 14, 15, 16, 17, 18, 19, 19; 8:1, 1, 4, 5, 6, 6, 7, 18, 19; 9:1, 12, 12, 14, 15, 15, 16, 21, 29, 30; 10:1, 6, 9, 15, 17, 24, 24, 25, 29, 31; 11:10, 20; 12:6, 10, 18, 18; 13:2, 5, 7, 11, 22, 25; 14:5, 24, 25, 26, 27, 28; 15:3, 9, 9, 18, 24, 28, 34; 16:2, 3, 14, 18; 17:7, 8, 8, 8, 9, 11, 11, 13, 15, 19, 23, 28, 29, 35; 18:3, 4, 4, 6, 12, 12, 12, 16, 36, 37; 19:8; 20:4, 8, 12, 12; 21:2, 3, 3, 4, 7, 7, 9, 20, 21, 24; 23:2, 4, 5, 5, 5, 8, 9, 11, 12, 12, 13, 15, 16, 16, 19, 19, 19, 22, 24, 25, 27, 32, 37; 24:2, 3, 4, 9, 13, 13, 19; 25:3, 5, 11, 16, 21, 23; 1Ch 1:19; 2:3, 4, 4, 7, 16, 17, 18, 19, 21, 26, 31, 31, 32, 33, 34, 34, 35, 49; 3:6, 9, 19; 4:5, 9, 27, 27, 40, 43; 5:9, 24, 25; 6:49; 7:4, 15, 23, 24, 30, 32; 8:8, 11, 38, 39, 40; 9:19, 20, 20, 21, 22, 44; 10:7, 11; 11:3, 6, 10, 16, 42; 12:22, 23, 27, 29, 39; 13:10, 11; 14:2, 2, 3, 8, 9, 12; 15:3, 15; 16:1, 2, 40; 17:15; 18:9, 10, 10, 11, 11; 19:5, 6, 7, 19; 20:1; 21:6, 19, 28; 22:4; 23:11, 17, 17, 24, 31; 24:2, 28; 25:3, 5; 26:5, 6, 27, 27; 27:1, 23; 28:12; 29:9; 2Ch 1:3, 4, 4, 12; 2:1, 17; 3:1, 1, 12; 4:3, 7, 11, 16, 17; 5:1, 10, 11; 6:13, 13; 7:6, 7, 9, 9, 10, 11; 8:1, 2, 8, 11, 12, 13; 9:2, 3, 6, 9, 11, 12, 18, 21, 23, 25; 10:1, 2, 6, 8, 12, 16; 11:15, 17, 19, 21; 12:5, 13; 13:13, 21; 14:8, 8; 15:8, 9, 9, 11, 15, 16, 18; 16:6, 14; 17:2; 18:30; 20:23, 24, 27, 29, 30; 21:3, 4, 6, 7, 10, 11, 11, 19; 22:1, 4, 7, 7; 23:9, 18, 21; 24:3, 7, 7, 9, 16, 24; 25:3, 5, 13, 24; 26:4, 8, 10, 11, 11, 16, 20, 21, 23; 27:2; 28:1, 3, 6, 17, 18, 18, 18, 19, 19, 23; 29:2, 15, 17, 24, 25, 34, 34, 36, 36; 30:3, 5, 17, 17, 18, 26; 31:6, 6, 10, 14, 18; 32:1, 27, 29, 31; 33:2, 3, 4, 7, 7, 9, 13, 15, 22, 22, 25; 34:4, 8, 9, 11, 14, 30; 35:3, 14, 16, 18, 18, 20, 22; 36:13, 15, 17, 21; Ezr 1:7, 7; 2:1, 61, 61, 62, 70; 3:1, 6, 6, 7, 8, 10, 11; 4:10, 24; 5:14, 14, 15; 6:14, 16, 20, 21, 21, 22; 7:6, 9, 10, 11; 8:15, 15, 22, 25, 35; 9:5; 10:5, 9, 17, 17, 18, 44, 44; Ne 1:2, 2; 2:1, 9, 10, 12, 12, 16, 16, 16, 18; 4:6, 15, 18; 5:8, 8, 12, 13, 15; 6:1, 1, 12, 12, 12, 15, 16, 18; 7:1, 5, 5, 6, 63, 63, 64, 73; 8:1, 4, 9, 12, 14, 15, 17, 17; 9:8, 15, 17, 23, 35; 10:28; 12:1, 8, 29, 43; 13:2, 4, 4, 5, 5, 5, 6, 7, 10, 10, 13, 23, 28; Est 1:7, 8; 2:1, 1, 1, 6, 7, 7, 10, 10, 14, 19, 19; 3:2, 4, 6; 4:1, 5, 7; 5:11, 11; 6:1, 2, 2, 4, 4, 13, 14; 7:4, 10; 8:1, 2, 17; 9:1, 4, 16, 24, 26, 31; 10:2; Job 1:2, 4, 21; 2:11; 3:13; 20:3; 22:18; 28:27; 29:12, 13, 22; 31:28, 35; 32:2, 3, 4, 5, 14; 41:32; 42:5, 7, 11, 12, 17; Ps 31:22; 44:20; 48:8; 51:T; 52:T; 55:6; 66:18; 73:15, 21, 21, 21; 78:11, 11, 30, 54, 57, 60; 94:17; 95:9; 103:16; 105:26, 28, 44; 106:13, 21, 30, 34; 116:3; 123:3, 4; 124:1, 2; 129:3; 139:16; Pr 5:12; 8:26; 23:5; Ecc 2:8, 8, 11; 6:4, 5; SS 3:4, 4; Isa 1:9; 7:2; 8:2, 3; 14:17; 34:6; 36:21, 22; 37:8; 38:15, 21, 22; 39:1, 1, 1; 40:15; 42:21; 48:18, 18; 52:15, 15; 53:9; 63:19; 66:3; Jer 2:7; 3:7, 8; 4:25, 26; 5:5; 11:19, 19; 13:5, 7; 15:10; 16:15; 18:4, 8, 10; 19:14; 20:2, 17, 17; 23:8, 22, 25; 26:8, 8, 19, 23; 28:11; 29:1, 2; 30:15; 31:20, 26; 32:3, 8, 8, 12, 16, 22; 34:9, 10, 11, 16; 35:8; 36:4, 16, 26, 27, 32, 32; 37:4, 12, 14, 15, 15; 38:1, 27, 27; 39:9, 11, 12, 15; 40:1, 1, 7, 11, 12, 15; 41:2, 4, 5, 5, 5, 8, 8, 10, 11, 13, 16, 18; 42:10; 43:1, 5, 5, 6; 44:15, 17, 17, 20; 45:1, 1, 3; 48:9; 51:60; 52:2, 6, 8, 15, 20, 27; La 1:10, 21; 3:18; 4:20; 5:21; Eze 1:6, 10, 11, 16, 23; 2:5; 3:23; 8:4, 5; 9:3; 10:8, 9, 10, 12, 14, 15, 20, 21, 22, 22; 11:25; 16:5, 17, 19, 20; 17:8, 10; 19:10; 20:6, 9, 12, 15, 16, 22, 26, 28; 23:10, 11; 24:18; 28:14; 31:8, 8, 17, 17, 17; 33:5, 21, 22; 35:5; 36:19, 21; 37:7, 8; 40:10, 25, 26, 28, 29, 31, 32, 34, 35, 36, 37; 41:23; 42:5, 11, 15; 43:3, 6; 47:6; Da 1:3, 9, 11, 15; 2:1, 2, 3, 15, 17, 24; 3:2, 3, 3, 7, 22, 27; 4:5, 12, 18, 21, 34; 5:2, 23; 6:10, 10, 23, 24, 24; 7:1, 5, 6, 6, 7, 8, 15, 20; 8:1, 3, 5, 6; 9:21; 10:1, 2, 3, 3, 3; 11:4; Hos 1:8; 13:6; Am 7:1, 4, 7; 8:10; Ob 16; Jnh 1:7, 17; 2:7; 3:10, 10, 10; Hag 1:12, 12; Zec 4:1, 1; 7:2, 12, 14; 8:10, 13; 10:6; 11:10, 10; Mt 2:12, 15, 16, 16; 3:3; 4:12, 23; 7:29; 9:20, 20; 11:1, 7, 20, 21, 23; 12:11; 13:6, 8, 23, 53; 14:3, 12, 14, 21, 24, 34; 15:31;

16:5, 21; 17:13, 20, 22, 25; 18:23, 25, 30, 31, 32, 33, 34; 19:1, 8, 22; 20:24; 22:5, 12, 26, 31, 34; 25:19, 20, 22; 26:1, 6, 24, 47, 48, 57, 57; 27:3, 3, 18, 19, 34, 35, 52, 54, 55, 60; 28:11, 11, 16; Mk 1:4, 22, 27, 28, 34, 45, 45; 3:8, 10, 22, 30; 4:6, 8, 20; 5:8, 15, 16, 18, 20, 25, 25, 26, 26, 26, 26, 27, 29, 30, 32, 33, 33, 43; 6:17, 17, 17, 29, 30, 30, 34, 44; 7:17, 25; 8:1, 9, 11, 14; 9:9, 9, 34; 10:22, 28, 41; 11:6, 18, 20, 21, 27; 12:22, 26, 28; 14:3, 11, 16, 21, 43, 44, 53; 15:10, 39, 41, 41, 41, 46; 16:4, 9, 11, 12, 14, 14, 19; Lk 1:7, 58, 65; 2:4, 15, 17, 17, 20, 20, 20, 26, 26, 36, 36, 38, 39; 3:3, 4, 19; 4:13, 37; 5:2, 4, 8, 14; 6:18; 7:1, 12, 17, 29, 30, 30, 39; 8:2, 2, 2, 4, 8, 8, 27, 29, 29, 35, 35, 36, 36, 38, 39, 40, 43, 43, 43, 43, 47, 47, 50, 53, 56; 9:10, 32, 36, 37, 53; 10:13; 11:1, 30; 12:16; 13:1, 11, 11, 14; 14:6, 7, 18, 19, 20, 21, 22, 24; 15:4, 11, 32; 16:8, 25, 25; 17:6, 16; 18:3, 9; 19:2, 15, 15, 32, 37; 20:31, 37; 22:13, 17, 19, 51, 61; 23:8, 8, 12, 25, 47, 48, 49, 51, 51, 53; 24:1, 2, 8, 9, 10, 12, 14, 21, 21, 23, 24, 35, 35; Jn 1:40, 50; 2:7, 9, 22; 4:1, 4, 8, 18, 27, 38, 39, 44, 45, 45, 46, 47, 52, 53; 5:5, 6, 13, 15, 18, 46; 6:22, 22, 23, 23, 41; 7:10, 11, 13, 30, 39, 39, 45, 50; 8:3, 20; 9:1, 14, 17, 18, 22, 24, 35; 11:13, 17, 19, 21, 30, 32, 46, 57; 12:1, 9, 11, 16, 17, 18, 20, 29, 37, 38; 13:1, 2, 3, 3, 5, 26, 27; 14:7; 15:20, 22; 17:1; 18:2, 3, 14, 18, 19, 26; 19:1, 23, 30, 38, 39; 20:1, 7, 12; 21:7, 14, 14, 20; Ac 2:30, 33, 44; 3:10, 11, 12, 18; 4:13, 13, 13, 14, 14, 22, 23, 32; 5:2, 7, 11, 13, 25, 34, 40, 41; 6:5; 7:5, 16, 21, 25, 35, 41; 8:4, 6, 7, 9, 14, 16, 16, 27, 32; 9:27, 27, 31, 33, 38, 39; 10:3, 8, 24, 41, 44, 45; 11:1, 4, 11, 12, 13, 13, 19, 22; 12:2, 11, 17, 17, 18, 25; 13:7, 12, 27, 29, 31, 34, 36; 14:8, 8, 9, 11, 23, 26, 26, 26, 27, 27; 15:4, 5, 12, 13, 24, 33, 38, 38; 16:6, 9, 13, 27; 17:9, 18, 23, 32; 18:2, 2, 17, 17, 18, 18, 24, 25, 27, 27; 19:12, 19, 20, 24; 20:13, 16, 21, 36, 38; 21:8, 9, 9, 10, 19, 29, 29, 33, 35; 22:11, 24, 29, 30; 23:12, 14, 28; 26:11; 27:7, 9, 21, 37; 28:6, 11, 15, 17, 19, 21, 25; Ro 2:12; 4:2, 2, 10, 11, 11, 12, 18, 19; 5:13; 7:7, 9; 9:7, 9, 11, 29; 10:19; 1Co 2:8; 3:1, 2; 4:15; 11:24; 12:19; 13:2, 2; 14:5; 15:3, 8; 2Co 3:18; 4:13; 7:7, 14; 8:15, 15; 9:4; 13:2; Gal 2:2, 6, 7, 7, 9, 11; 3:1; 4:1, 15, 22; Eph 2:12; 3:9; Php 2:5, 27; Col 2:18; 1Th 2:2, 7, 15; 3:5, 5; 2Th 2:2; 1Ti 1:13, 16; 2Ti 4:16; Heb 2:14; 4:8; 6:15; 7:2, 4, 6, 23; 8:7; 9:15, 19, 23, 23, 26, 26; 10:34; 11:7, 13, 15, 17, 18, 20, 23, 31, 33, 39, 40; Jas 5:6; 1Pe 1:10; 2:3; 4:1, 3; 2Pe 2:21; 1Jn 2:7; 3:12, 12; 2Jn 5; Jude 3; Rev 4:1, 4, 7, 7, 7, 8; 5:6, 6, 8; 6:9, 11; 7:2; 8:4; 9:1, 7, 7, 10, 15, 19; 10:2; 11:10; 12:6, 13, 13; 13:1, 2, 11, 12; 14:1, 3, 14, 17; 15:2, 2, 8; 16:2, 5; 17:1, 2, 3, 8; 19:20; 20:4, 4, 4, 5, 12; 21:1, 14

HADN'T (17)

Jdg 8:19; 14:18; 1Sa 30:12; 2Sa 2:27; Ps 119:92; Jer 40:7; Mt 11:20; 15:31; 16:7; Mk 8:16; Jn 6:17; 15:24; 20:9; 21:11; Ac 26:32; 2Co 1:17; 2:13

HAS (2109)

Ge 4:25; 5:29; 13:8; 14:20; 15:16; 16:2, 11; 19:13, 13; 21:6, 17, 31; 22:14; 24:27, 27, 35, 35, 35, 36, 50, 51, 56; 26:22, 29, 33; 27:27, 35, 36; 29:32, 33; 30:6, 6, 16, 18, 20, 23, 27, 30, 30; 31:1, 1, 5, 5, 7, 7, 9, 12, 15, 15, 16, 16, 32, 42; 32:30; 33:5, 11; 35:3, 8; 37:20, 33, 33; 38:8; 39:9, 9, 14; 41:28, 32, 39, 51, 52; 42:9, 12, 21, 21, 28, 32, 36; 45:7, 8, 9; 47:5; 48:9, 11, 15, 16; 49:9, 23; Ex 3:13, 14, 15, 15, 18; 4:5; 5:3, 10, 23; 6:7; 7:9, 16; 8:27; 10:6, 14; 11:6; 12:20, 25, 44, 44, 49; 13:3; 15:1, 1, 2, 4, 21, 21; 16:7, 8, 15, 23; 18:6, 10, 10; 20:20; 22:19, 31; 23:4, 18, 30; 24:3, 7, 8; 32:1, 1, 23, 33; 35:4, 10, 30, 31, 33, 34, 35; 36:1, 1, 5; Lev 1:6; 2:8; 6:2, 15, 30; 7:9, 35; 8:5, 34, 35; 9:7; 10:6, 11, 12, 13, 15, 19; 11:7, 9, 26, 35; 13:3, 4, 5, 6, 8, 10, 12, 13, 18, 18, 20, 20, 21, 24, 25, 26, 27, 28, 28, 29, 32, 32, 34, 36, 37, 37, 37, 38, 41, 49, 51, 52, 53, 55, 56; 14:3, 35, 39, 52; 15:2, 6, 7, 16, 19, 24, 32, 33, 33; 16:11, 20; 17:4; 18:25, 27; 19:20, 26; 20:11, 12, 14, 15, 17, 17, 18, 19, 19, 20, 20, 21, 24; 21:10, 10, 12, 18, 19, 20, 20, 20, 20, 21; 22:7, 8, 8, 13, 21, 22, 24; 23:4; 25:27, 29; 27:28; Nu 5:2, 2, 14, 18, 19, 27, 28, 30; 6:7, 19; 10:29; 11:18; 12:2; 14:24, 35, 40; 15:22, 23; 16:3, 9, 10, 28, 29, 46; 19:2, 2, 18, 18, 18, 20; 20:5, 24; 21:3, 29; 22:5, 10, 11, 11, 19; 23:8, 8, 19, 19, 20, 21, 22, 23, 23; 24:11, 16; 25:11; 27:8, 9, 10, 11, 18; 30:1; 31:21; 32:4, 7, 21, 31; 34:29; 35:6, 32; Dt 1:10, 21, 21, 31, 36, 41; 2:7, 7, 7, 29, 30; 3:18, 20, 20, 21; 4:7, 8, 23, 23, 32, 33, 34; 5:12, 15, 24, 33; 6:17, 20, 25; 7:6; 8:10, 20; 9:3, 4, 4; 10:21, 22; 11:4; 12:7, 20, 21; 13:14, 17; 14:2, 6, 8, 9, 21; 15:2, 6, 14, 21; 16:13; 17:2, 2, 4, 16; 18:8, 22; 19:3; 20:5, 6, 7, 14, 17; 21:3, 5, 15, 18, 22; 22:16, 17, 21, 23, 26; 24:4, 5, 12; 25:19; 26:3, 11, 16, 18; 27:20, 20, 21, 22, 23; 28:45, 52, 53, 55, 57, 63; 29:4, 12, 24; 30:1, 3; 31:2, 14; 32:6, 27; 33:17; 34:10; Jos 1:11, 13, 15; 2:9, 11; 5:9; 6:16; 7:8, 11, 12, 15, 15, 15, 15, 26; 8:8; 10:14, 19; 13:4; 14:10; 17:14; 18:3; 22:3, 4, 25; 23:3, 3, 9, 9, 10, 13, 14, 14, 15, 15, 16; 24:20, 27; Jdg 1:7; 3:28; 6:13, 13; 7:14, 15; 11:26, 36, 39; 16:17, 18, 23, 24; 18:10; 19:18, 30; 20:12; 21:3; Ru 1:13, 15, 20, 21, 21, 21; 2:7; 3:3, 18; 4:14, 15, 17; 1Sa 1:11, 27; 2:1, 5, 8; 4:17, 17, 22, 22; 6:4; 7:12; 9:12; 10:1, 24; 11:13; 12:7, 13, 24; 13:14, 14; 14:6, 29, 33, 45; 15:11, 11, 17, 23, 26, 28, 28, 33; 16:8, 9, 10, 18; 17:25, 33, 36; 18:7; 19:4; 20:3, 23, 32; 21:2, 11; 22:7, 7, 8; 23:7, 7, 22, 28; 24:6; 25:21, 26, 30, 30, 31, 32, 34, 39, 39, 40; 26:8, 11, 19, 20; 28:8, 9, 15, 16, 16, 17, 17, 18; 29:5; 30:23, 23; 2Sa 2:16; 3:9, 18, 29, 38; 4:8; 5:2, 20; 6:12, 12; 7:6; 10:3; 12:13; 13:20, 28, 30, 32; 14:2; 15:10, 13; 16:8, 10, 11, 21; 17:7, 8, 9, 13; 18:19, 25, 28, 31; 19:27; 20:21; 21:1; 22:33, 36; 23:5, 5; 24:17; 1Ki 1:11, 13, 18, 19, 19, 25, 25, 27, 29, 37, 43, 48; 2:22, 23, 24, 24; 3:12; 5:4; 8:15, 20, 46, 56, 56; 9:9; 10:9, 9, 12; 11:33, 33, 33; 12:24; 13:3, 26; 17:20; 18:10, 13, 22; 20:11; 21:5, 14, 20, 23, 29, 29; 22:8, 17, 23, 23, 28; 2Ki 1:9, 14; 2:2, 4, 6, 15, 16, 22; 3:7, 10; 4:1, 13, 27; 5:22; 6:11, 32, 33; 7:6, 12; 8:1, 4, 9, 10, 13, 22; 9:18, 20; 13:23; 17:26; 18:35; 19:3, 4, 21; 21:11, 11; 22:10, 13, 15; 23:25; 1Ch 11:2; 14:11; 15:2; 16:8, 12; 17:5, 27; 19:3; 21:11, 17, 24; 22:18, 18; 23:25; 28:4, 4, 5, 10; 29:1, 14; 2Ch 1:12; 2:4, 11, 12; 6:4, 10, 36, 41; 7:21; 8:11; 9:8, 8; 11:4; 14:7; 18:7, 16, 22, 22, 27; 19:2; 21:10; 23:3, 3; 24:20; 25:8, 16; 28:11; 29:8, 8, 11, 31; 30:8; 31:10; 32:11, 15; 34:17, 18, 21, 21, 23; 35:21; 36:23, 23; Ezr 1:2, 2; 4:15, 18, 19; 6:12; 7:25; 9:2, 6, 7, 8, 8, 8, 9; 10:14; Ne 1:3; 9:10, 32; 13:11; Est 1:16, 17; 4:11; 5:5, 12; 6:3, 13; 7:9; 8:7; 9:12; Job 1:11, 16, 21; 2:3, 4; 3:25, 25; 4:7, 18; 6:4, 4; 9:4, 8, 19; 12:6, 9; 14:13; 15:12, 12; 16:11, 11; 17:6; 19:6, 8, 9, 10, 10, 21, 26; 20:5, 5, 14, 26; 22:5; 23:10, 14, 16, 16; 26:2; 27:2, 2; 28:8, 8; 30:11, 11, 15, 19, 30; 31:2, 7, 9, 21; 32:12; 33:4; 34:5, 5, 7, 9, 13; 36:16, 25; 39:7, 17, 17; Ps 4:3; 6:8, 9; 13:6; 18:32, 35; 19:4; 22:15, 24, 24, 24, 31; 27:8; 28:5, 6; 31:10, 21; 32:2; 33:12; 40:3, 3, 7; 41:8, 9; 44:17; 45:2, 7; 47:5, 5; 50:1, 1; 53:5; 60:6; 62:11; 66:5; 68:16, 24; 71:11, 24; 74:3, 18; 75:9; 77:7, 9, 9; 79:2, 3; 83:8; 87:5, 6; 88:16; 89:18, 41; 93:2; 97:8; 98:1, 1, 2, 2, 3, 3; 102:23; 103:10, 12, 19, 22; 104:31; 105:1, 5; 106:31; 107:2, 2, 3; 108:7; 109:11; 110:4; 111:6, 9, 9, 9; 115:16; 116:7, 8, 12; 118:14, 15, 16, 17, 18, 18, 22, 24; 119:96; 126:2, 3; 129:4; 132:13, 13; 133:3; 135:4; 143:3, 3; 147:13, 19, 20; 148:14; Pr 2:17; 7:20, 26; 9:1, 2, 3; 10:2; 15:19; 16:4; 17:16; 23:24, 29, 29, 29, 29; 24:7; 30:4, 15; 31:21, 31; Ecc 1:9, 13; 3:10, 11, 11, 15; 5:20; 6:5, 10; 7:3, 13; 8:8, 17; 9:9, 13; 10:11; SS 1:6, 6; 2:12; 3:9; 6:1, 2; 8:11; Isa 1:21; 2:6, 7; 5:1, 9, 25; 6:7, 12; 7:17; 8:11, 17, 18, 18; 9:8, 17; 10:12, 22, 23; 12:2, 2, 4, 5; 13:4, 6; 14:4, 5, 11, 24, 27, 32; 16:9, 10, 13; 18:4; 19:12, 14, 17; 20:3; 21:10; 22:5, 14; 23:8, 9, 11; 24:3, 11, 11, 19, 19; 25:8; 26:18, 20; 27:7, 7, 8, 8, 9; 28:22, 26; 29:10, 10; 30:11, 33, 33; 31:4; 33:7, 9; 34:5, 16, 17; 36:20; 37:3, 4, 22; 38:12, 12, 20; 40:2, 5, 12, 12, 12, 14; 41:2, 4; 42:9, 21; 43:9, 10, 12; 44:13, 23, 23; 46:7; 48:14, 20; 49:2, 5, 5, 7, 13, 14, 14, 15, 21; 50:4, 5; 51:20, 20; 52:9, 9; 53:1, 11; 54:1, 6, 10; 59:2, 14; 61:1, 1, 2, 2, 3, 9, 10; 62:8, 11; 63:3, 4, 7, 7; 64:4, 4, 11; 66:8, 8, 8; Jer 2:10, 11, 14, 14, 15, 37; 3:6, 8, 9, 10, 10; 4:15, 18; 5:25, 25, 30; 7:28, 29, 29; 8:14, 14, 19; 9:12, 12, 13, 19, 20, 21, 21, 21; 10:12; 12:4, 13; 13:15; 14:7, 17; 15:9, 10, 18; 16:10; 17:11; 18:6, 13, 13; 19:4; 20:3, 18; 21:2, 2; 23:9, 18, 20, 33; 25:3, 4, 31, 33, 34, 38; 26:11, 13, 16; 27:8; 28:4, 11, 15; 29:4, 7, 15, 26, 31, 31, 32; 30:7, 15, 24; 31:11, 12; 32:24, 24, 31, 43; 33:10; 34:21; 36:7; 38:21; 40:2, 5, 14; 41:6; 42:19; 43:3; 44:7, 10; 45:3; 46:15; 47:4, 7; 48:8, 10, 11, 11, 11, 19, 20, 21, 25, 26, 32, 32, 36, 39, 42, 44; 49:24, 30; 50:14, 15, 15, 25, 27, 28, 29, 29, 31, 43; 51:5, 7, 8, 10, 10, 11, 13, 14, 14, 15, 29, 34, 34, 34, 42, 44, 44, 51; La 1:3, 3, 3, 5, 8, 8, 9, 10, 10, 13, 13, 13, 15, 15, 15, 16, 17; 2:1, 1, 2, 2, 2, 3, 5, 5, 5, 6, 6, 7, 7, 9, 11, 13, 17, 17, 22, 22; 3:1, 2, 3, 4, 4, 5, 6, 7, 7, 9, 9, 15, 15, 16, 16, 17; 4:1, 1, 4, 11, 16; 5:1, 2, 10, 15, 15, 16; Eze 5:6, 6, 6, 13; 7:6, 6, 7, 12, 13; 8:3, 12; 9:9; 11:15; 12:23; 16:57; 18:6, 10, 14; 19:14; 20:29; 21:24, 27, 29; 22:4; 24:13, 14, 22, 24, 26; 26:2, 2, 2; 28:5; 30:21, 21; 33:21, 33; 34:6, 10; 35:6; 43:22, 23; 45:20; Da 1:10; 2:10, 15, 20, 28, 29, 37, 38, 38, 39, 45; 4:2, 17, 24, 35; 5:11, 12, 24, 26, 26, 28; 6:27; 9:11, 12, 13, 14, 24, 27; 10:12; 11:36; 12:7; Hos 2:8; 4:1, 12; 5:6; 6:1, 1; 7:9, 9; 8:11, 14, 14; 9:7; 10:9; Joel 1:2, 6, 8, 12, 19, 20; 2:20, 21, 32, 32; Am 3:1, 5, 8, 8; 4:2; 5:2; 6:8; 8:7; Ob 8; Jnh 4:11; Mic 1:2, 9, 14; 2:4, 4; 4:4, 9; 6:2, 8; Na 2:6, 7; 3:19; Hab 1:4; 2:6, 13; Zep 1:7, 7, 7; 2:15; 3:17; Hag 1:2, 10; Zec 1:6, 10; 2:9; 3:2, 2; 4:9; 9:3, 3; 10:3; 12:10; 13:5; 14:3; Mal 2:8, 12, 14; 3:9; Mt 1:20; 4:16; 5:13, 23, 28, 32; 8:13; 9:18, 22, 33; 11:12, 27; 12:28; 13:28, 52; 15:22; 16:17; 17:12, 15; 18:12; 19:6, 9, 29; 20:23, 23; 21:42; 22:4; 24:21, 46; 26:12, 18, 45; 27:23; 28:6, 7; Mk 1:15, 27; 5:19, 19, 34; 6:16; 9:13, 21; 10:4, 9, 29, 40, 40, 52; 11:2, 21; 12:10, 43, 44, 44; 13:20; 14:8, 8, 41; 15:14; 16:6; Lk 1:2, 13, 25, 30, 36, 49, 52, 53, 54, 54, 68, 69, 72; 2:11, 15, 15; 4:18, 18, 19, 21; 7:16, 44, 45, 46, 47, 50; 8:39, 48; 10:22, 42; 11:6, 20, 30; 12:5, 43; 13:16, 25; 14:8; 15:8, 9, 24, 27, 27, 32; 16:17; 17:19, 23; 18:29, 42; 19:7, 9, 9, 25, 30; 20:17; 21:3, 4, 4, 8, 20; 22:18, 29, 31, 37; 23:2, 15, 22; 24:6, 34; Jn 1:18, 18; 2:4; 3:2, 31, 31, 32, 35; 4:10; 5:26, 26, 27, 36, 37; 6:27, 29, 37, 39, 46, 47; 7:8, 31; 8:29, 44; 9:32; 10:4, 13, 18, 20, 29; 11:11, 27, 39; 12:19, 23, 31, 38, 40; 13:10, 18, 31; 14:9, 9, 30; 15:9, 25; 16:5, 11, 13, 15, 21; 17:1; 18:11; 19:11; 20:21; Ac 1:8, 11, 21, 25; 2:11, 36, 40; 3:13, 16, 16; 4:11, 27; 5:3; 7:40; 9:13, 17; 10:28, 33; 11:18; 12:11; 13:11, 32; 15:14; 17:7, 18, 25, 31, 31; 19:26; 20:23, 28, 32; 22:14; 23:17, 18; 25:5, 11, 25; 26:24; 27:24; 28:20, 21; Ro 1:5, 5, 7, 17, 19; 2:4, 29; 3:2, 11, 21, 24, 24; 5:1, 2, 5, 11; 6:9, 15, 17; 8:2, 22, 23, 33, 33; 9:6, 22, 22, 23; 10:4, 16, 18; 11:1, 2, 7, 8, 8, 13, 17, 23, 28, 28, 31, 32; 12:1, 3, 4, 5, 6, 6, 8; 14:2, 3; 15:7, 17, 20, 20, 20, 22; 16:2, 6, 12, 13, 26; 1Co 1:4, 5, 20, 20, 21, 31; 2:9, 9, 9, 9, 10, 12, 12; 3:13; 4:9; 5:3, 7; 7:12, 13, 17, 19, 22, 25, 33, 34, 36, 37; 8:1, 4, 7, 10; 9:7, 17; 10:28; 11:15; 12:12, 14, 18, 24, 28; 13:5; 14:13, 13, 26; 15:13, 16, 17, 20, 20, 21, 27, 28, 31, 41, 48, 51; 2Co 1:4, 21, 22; 3:6, 11, 11; 4:1, 4, 5, 6, 12; 5:5, 5, 17, 18, 19; 6:7; 7:14; 8:1, 16, 22, 22; 10:15, 17; 13:7, 10; Gal 2:6, 17; 3:1, 11, 13, 14, 25; 4:6, 7, 9, 27; 5:1, 7, 10; Eph 1:3, 5, 6, 8, 9, 14, 18, 18, 22; 2:7, 10, 14, 14, 17, 18; 3:2, 5, 11; 4:7, 14, 14, 30, 32; 6:9; Php 1:12, 12, 26; 2:22, 22, 26; 3:3, 7; 4:6; Col 1:8, 12, 13, 13, 14, 14, 16, 22, 22, 22, 23, 25, 26, 27, 28; 2:7, 20; 3:25; 4:13; 1Th 1:10; 2:16; 3:6; 4:7, 9; 2Th 2:2; 1Ti 1:19; 4:8; 5:3, 4, 5, 10, 10, 10, 10, 10, 10, 16; 6:4, 12, 16, 18, 20; 2Ti 1:1, 7, 10, 14; 2:4, 10, 18; 4:5, 6, 10, 10, 10, 10, 14, 14; Tit 1:1, 3, 12; 2:11; Phm 1:7, 18; Heb 1:2, 9; 2:2, 13, 18; 3:4; 4:2, 2, 3, 14; 5:3, 4; 6:7, 18, 20, 20; 7:7, 15, 19, 21, 26, 26, 28; 8:6, 13; 9:11, 11, 15, 20, 24; 10:1, 20, 36; 11:16; 12:1; 13:5, 7; Jas 1:3, 9, 10, 12, 21; 2:10; 4:5, 12; 5:15, 16; 1Pe 1:2, 3, 4, 12, 16, 17; 2:7, 8, 14, 14, 21; 3:22; 4:10, 17; 2Pe 1:3, 4, 4, 9, 10, 14; 3:4, 7, 13; 1Jn 1:5, 10; 2:11, 18, 20, 23, 27; 3:8, 17; 4:2, 3, 6, 12, 12, 13, 18, 18, 21; 5:9, 10, 11, 11, 12, 12, 20, 20; 2Jn 6, 6; Jude 6; Rev 1:5, 6; 2:12, 17; 3:1, 7, 18; 5:5, 9; 6:17; 11:2, 15, 18; 12:10, 10, 12, 12; 13:18; 14:7, 15, 18; 17:17; 18:2, 6, 7, 20; 19:2, 2, 7, 7, 17; 21:23; 22:6

HASN'T (16)

Nu 12:2; 1Sa 3:13; 20:27; 2Sa 19:42; Pr 3:30; Jer 43:2; Eze 22:28; Lk 13:7; 23:41; 24: 18; Jn 7:15; Ac 22:25; 26:31; 1Co 4:7; Phm 1:11; Jas 2:5

HAVE (4502)

Ge 1:29, 30; 3:11, 14, 17, 22; 4:1, 10, 11, 14, 14, 23; 6:7, 13; 7:2, 4; 9:2, 3, 3, 4, 7, 13; 11:6, 30; 12:12, 18; 14:21, 22, 24; 15:2, 2, 3, 3, 4, 18; 16:2, 8, 13; 17:9, 11, 12, 17, 20; 18:5, 10, 12, 13, 14, 19, 19, 20, 27, 31; 19:5, 8, 12, 19, 19, 31; 20:9, 9, 10, 12, 13, 16, 17; 21:7, 7, 7, 10, 23, 26; 22:7, 12, 16, 16, 18; 23:4, 6, 9, 9; 24:14, 14, 19, 23, 25, 25, 31, 33, 33, 40, 44; 26:10, 10, 16, 27, 28, 29; 27:31, 33, 37, 37, 37, 45; 28:15, 15; 29:21, 27, 31, 34; 30:8, 16, 20, 26, 26, 27, 29, 33, 33, 34; 31:6, 8, 12, 26, 27, 28, 30, 36, 37, 37, 38, 41, 42, 43; 32:4, 5, 10, 28, 28, 30; 33:9, 9, 11, 13; 34:7, 11, 30; 35:3, 17; 37:16; 38:9, 22; 39:6; 40:14; 41:9, 15, 15, 28, 35, 40; 42:2, 7, 9, 10, 12, 16, 36; 43:6, 7, 10, 21, 22, 22, 23; 44:4, 5, 16, 18, 20, 28; 45:10, 13, 16; 46:30, 31, 32, 34, 34; 47:4, 6, 9, 18, 23, 25; 48:22; 50:20; Ex 1:18, 18, 19; 2:15, 22; 3:7, 7, 8, 9, 9, 9, 12, 12, 16; 4:2, 10, 10, 12, 17, 21, 23; 5:8, 17, 21, 22, 23; 6:5, 5, 29; 7:2, 16; 8:10, 22; 9:8, 15, 15, 15, 16; 10:1, 26; 12:13, 21, 31; 14:4, 5, 14; 15:4, 5, 13, 17, 17; 16:3, 3, 12, 12, 29; 17:16; 18:3, 11, 14; 19:4, 9, 10; 20:22; 21:16, 30; 23:20, 32; 24:12; 25:32, 40; 28:3; 29:19; 30:14; 31:2, 3, 6, 6, 6, 11; 32:7, 8, 8, 8, 9, 13, 29, 30, 31, 31; 33:1, 12, 12, 16, 17, 17, 22; 34:9, 10; 36:5, 6; Lev 2:14; 3:1, 6; 5:1, 3, 10, 15, 16, 18, 19; 6:2, 2, 4, 4, 5, 17; 7:18, 18, 34; 9:6; 10:13, 14, 18, 19; 11:3, 4, 4, 10, 12, 27; 13:17; 14:2, 32, 36, 43, 44, 48; 17:11, 14; 18:6, 7, 8, 9, 10, 11, 12, 13, 15, 16, 17, 23, 24; 20:3, 12, 13, 16, 24, 25, 26; 21:7, 15, 17; 22:4, 4, 6, 11; 23:14, 39; 24:3; 25:2, 5, 32, 32, 45, 54; 26:10, 13, 26, 26, 37, 41, 41; 27:22; Nu 1:52; 3:12; 4:15; 5:7, 19, 20, 28; 6:21, 21; 7:5; 8:7, 8, 13, 15, 16, 16, 19; 9:7, 8; 11:6, 12, 17, 18, 18, 20, 20; 12:11, 14; 13:19; 14:3, 9, 11, 14, 15, 17, 19, 20, 22, 23, 27, 27, 28, 31, 34, 35, 40, 43; 15:25, 31; 16:3, 3, 7, 15, 15, 28, 28, 30, 38, 38, 41; 18:6, 8, 8, 17, 24, 24; 19:20; 20:14, 17; 21:5, 7, 22, 30, 30, 34; 22:12, 20, 28, 29, 30, 32, 33, 34, 38, 38; 23:4, 4, 11, 11, 24; 24:10; 25:11; 27:7, 12, 13; 28:31; 31:15, 17, 19, 49; 32:5, 5, 11, 12, 17, 18, 19, 22, 23, 24, 27; 33:53; 34:14; 35:11, 28; Dt 1:6, 13, 20, 28, 28, 41; 2:3, 5, 7, 9, 19, 31; 3:2, 19, 20, 21, 24; 4:9, 25, 25, 30; 5:24, 24, 28, 28, 29; 6:3, 11; 7:13; 8:10, 12, 12, 13, 13; 9:7, 12, 12, 12, 13, 23, 24, 24; 10:9, 21; 11:2, 7, 8, 15; 12:7, 12, 21, 31, 31; 13:1, 6, 8, 10, 13, 17; 14:2, 7, 7, 10, 27, 29; 15:2, 18; 16:10, 13; 17:3, 11, 14; 18:2, 12, 16, 17; 19:9, 12; 20:9; 21:8, 14, 15; 22:8, 30; 23:13, 23, 23, 23; 24:8, 18; 26:1, 10, 10, 12, 13, 13, 13, 14, 14, 14, 14, 14, 15, 17, 17; 27:9; 28:13, 33, 41, 47, 47, 54, 57, 64; 29:2, 17; 30:1, 2, 3, 16, 19; 31:5, 13, 16, 17, 18, 21, 27, 29; 32:5, 21, 21, 46; 33:8; 34:4; Jos 1:3; 2:2, 3, 10, 11, 12, 16; 3:4; 5:9; 6:2, 5; 7:11, 11, 11, 19, 20, 25; 8:1, 6, 8, 31; 9:6, 9, 10, 19, 24; 10:4, 6; 13:6; 15:19; 17:14, 16, 18; 18:7, 10; 19:50; 22:2, 2, 2, 3, 3, 8, 22, 22, 23, 23, 24, 24, 25, 27, 27, 28, 31, 31; 23:3, 4, 4, 8; 24:22; Jdg 1:2, 15, 24; 2:2, 3, 20, 20; 3:19, 20; 4:9; 6:10, 14, 22; 7:2, 9; 8:1, 2, 3, 22, 24; 9:16, 16, 16, 18, 18, 19, 20, 31, 48; 10:10, 10, 10, 13, 14, 15; 11:26, 27, 27, 35, 36, 36, 38; 12:3; 13:3, 3, 22, 23, 23; 14:16, 18; 15:10, 10, 12, 18; 16:7, 9, 11, 12, 13, 14, 20; 17:3, 13; 18:9, 23, 24; 19:5, 8, 18, 19, 19, 22; 20:6, 10; 21:6, 7, 18, 22; Ru 2:9, 9, 11, 11, 12, 13; 4:5, 9, 10, 10; 1Sa 1:8, 8, 16, 17; 2:1, 3, 5, 23, 29, 34, 36; 3:13, 14; 4:7, 7, 9, 9, 16, 20; 6:4, 7, 7, 21; 8:5, 8; 9:7, 7, 8, 16, 16, 20, 27; 10:2, 2, 3, 14, 19, 19; 12:1, 2, 2, 3, 3, 3, 3, 3, 4, 4, 10, 13, 17, 19, 20; 13:11, 13, 13, 14; 14:1, 24, 29, 30, 43; 15:2, 13, 15, 23, 24, 24, 26, 30, 32; 16:1, 1, 1, 2, 5, 7, 11; 17:25, 25, 27, 29, 34, 36, 45; 18:21; 19:5, 17; 20:1, 1, 8, 26, 42, 42; 21:2, 3, 4, 4, 4, 8, 8, 9, 15; 22:8, 13, 13, 22; 23:10, 11, 23; 24:6, 11, 11, 11, 17, 18, 18, 19; 25:8, 8, 24, 27, 28, 28, 31; 26:18, 19, 21, 21, 24; 27:12; 28:8, 15, 15; 29:8, 9; 30:22; 2Sa 1:3, 4, 19, 25, 27; 2:6, 7, 14, 22, 27, 27; 3:8, 17, 18, 24, 33; 4:11; 6:22; 7:3, 6, 7, 7, 9, 9, 9, 10, 18, 21, 21, 22, 23, 25, 27, 27, 28; 9:9, 11; 10:9; 12:8, 9, 9, 10, 11, 13, 14, 21, 27; 13:16, 32; 14:7, 7, 13, 13, 13, 14, 15, 15, 22, 22, 32; 15:3; 16:11, 21; 17:10, 11, 13, 20; 18:3, 11, 18, 21, 26, 31, 33; 19:6, 7, 11, 20, 28, 30, 38, 42, 43; 20:1; 22:22, 22, 23, 24, 36, 37, 40, 40, 41; 24:10, 10, 17, 21, 21, 24; 1Ki 1:14, 24, 35, 42, 45, 45; 2:13, 14, 16, 20; 3:6, 7, 11, 11, 12, 16; 5:4, 8, 8; 8:12, 13, 16, 16, 20, 20, 21, 24, 24, 25, 27, 29, 33, 35, 35, 36, 43, 44, 44, 47, 48, 48, 50, 59; 9:3, 3, 3, 5, 7, 7; 11:11, 11, 22, 32, 36, 36; 12:16, 19; 13:7, 21, 21; 14:6, 8, 9, 9, 9, 9, 13, 15; 16:2, 2; 17:4, 9, 12, 12, 18, 18, 20; 18:9, 12, 18, 18, 18, 27, 36, 37; 19:2, 4, 10, 10, 14, 14, 18, 20; 20:4, 5, 18, 28, 31, 36, 40, 42; 21:15, 19, 20, 20, 22, 22; 22:28, 34; 2Ki 1:5, 6, 16, 17; 2:10, 19, 21; 3:17, 23, 27; 4:2, 10, 14, 28; 5:13, 20, 22, 25, 27; 6:19, 27; 7:4, 12, 12; 9:5, 15, 31; 10:2, 8, 30; 13:19, 19; 14:10; 17:26, 26; 18:14, 25, 33; 19:7, 11, 11, 11, 12, 17, 18, 20, 22, 23, 23, 23, 23, 23, 24, 25, 26, 27, 28, 30; 20:3, 5, 17, 19; 21:7, 15, 15; 22:4, 4, 6, 8, 9, 13, 13, 17, 17, 18, 19, 20; 23:17, 27; 1Ch 2:34; 4:43; 12:17, 17; 15:12; 16:22; 17:2, 5, 6, 8, 8, 8, 9, 16, 18, 19, 19, 20, 21, 22, 23, 25, 25, 26; 19:10; 21:8, 8, 17; 22:8, 8, 8, 9, 14, 14, 15; 23:5; 28:3, 6; 29:2, 3, 14, 14, 16, 17, 17, 19; 2Ch 1:8, 8, 9, 12; 6:1, 2, 5, 5, 6, 10, 10, 11, 15, 15, 16, 18, 20, 24, 26, 26, 27, 33, 34, 34, 37, 38, 38, 39; 7:12, 12, 16, 18, 19, 20, 20; 10:16, 19; 11:23; 12:5, 7; 13:9, 9, 10, 11; 14:11; 16:7, 9; 18:27, 33; 19:2, 3, 3, 11, 11; 20:11, 37; 21:12, 13, 13, 13; 24:20; 25:15, 16, 16, 16, 16; 26:18; 28:9, 11; 29:9, 18, 19; 30:6; 31:10, 11; 32:8, 8, 13; 33:7; 34:15, 21, 21, 24, 25, 25, 26, 27, 28; 35:21, 25; Ezr 4:2, 3, 3, 12, 14, 19, 19, 20, 20, 21; 5:16; 6:11, 12; 8:28; 9:1, 1, 2, 2, 7, 7, 8, 10, 13, 13; 10:2, 2, 10, 10; Ne 1:3, 6, 6, 7, 9; 2:3, 20; 4:5; 5:2, 3, 4, 5, 8, 10, 19; 6:7, 14, 14; 7:3; 8:10; 9:8, 10, 32, 33, 37, 37; 10:34; 13:14, 22, 29; Est 1:8; 4:14; 5:4; 6:9, 10, 10; 7:4, 4; 8:7; 9:12, 12, 13, 13; Job 1:5, 5, 7, 7, 8, 8, 10, 10, 17; 2:2, 2, 3, 3; 3:7, 26, 26; 4:3, 3, 4; 5:16, 21, 27; 6:5, 5, 8, 10, 11, 11, 12, 14, 15, 21, 21, 22, 22, 23, 23, 24; 7:3, 20, 20, 20; 9:15; 10:19, 19, 20, 20; 11:18, 18, 20; 12:12; 13:1, 12, 18, 23; 14:5, 6, 8; 15:4, 8, 18, 25, 30; 16:2, 3, 7, 8, 15; 17:4, 11; 18:3, 19; 19:3, 4, 13, 15, 19, 20, 20, 21, 21; 20:3; 21:3, 16, 17, 29, 31; 22:6, 7, 8, 9, 15, 18, 20, 20, 21; 23:11, 11, 12, 12; 24:21, 21, 22; 26:2, 2, 3, 3, 4; 27:3, 8, 12, 14, 16; 28:22; 30:11, 13, 19, 21, 27; 31:5, 7, 7, 8, 8, 9, 13, 13, 16, 17, 18, 18, 24, 26, 29, 30, 31, 32, 32, 33, 34, 37, 39; 32:11, 12; 33:1, 2, 8, 8, 9, 12, 24, 32; 34:2, 6, 10, 27, 31, 32, 33, 36, 37; 35:6, 16, 16; 36:2, 9, 16, 23; 38:3, 12, 13, 16, 16, 17, 22, 22, 23, 28; 39:1, 6, 19; 40:2, 5, 5, 7; 42:4, 5, 7, 8; Ps 1:5; 2:6, 7; 3:1; 4:1, 7, 7; 6:2; 7:3, 4; 8:2, 3; 9:1, 4, 4, 5, 5, 6, 10, 13, 14, 15, 15, 16; 11:3; 12:1, 5, 5, 5; 13:2, 4, 5; 14:3, 3; 16:1, 2, 6; 17:3, 3, 4, 4, 5, 5, 14, 15; 18:21, 21, 22, 23, 28, 35, 36, 39, 39, 40; 21:2, 2, 4, 5, 6, 6, 10; 22:1, 10, 12, 15, 16; 23:1; 24:5; 25:6, 16, 19; 26:1, 1, 3, 12; 27:9; 28:4, 5; 30:1, 10, 11, 11; 31:1, 7, 8, 8, 9, 12, 13, 19, 19, 22; 34:9; 35:21, 25, 27; 36:1, 12, 12; 37:16, 19, 25, 35, 38; 38:2, 18, 19; 40:4, 5, 6, 7, 9, 9, 10, 10, 10, 12; 41:4, 4, 10, 11, 12, 12; 42:3, 9; 43:2; 44:1, 1, 9, 11, 11, 13, 14, 17, 18, 18, 19, 19, 21; 47:9; 48:8; 50:8; 51:1, 4, 4, 8; 52:1, 9; 53:3, 3, 5; 55:12; 56:1, 8, 8, 13, 13; 57:1, 1, 6, 6, 6; 58:3; 59:1, 3, 3, 16; 60:1, 1, 2, 3, 4, 10; 61:5, 5; 62:11, 12; 63:2, 7; 64:6; 65:9; 66:10, 10, 18; 68:28; 69:19, 19, 20, 26, 26; 71:6, 6, 7, 15, 17, 17, 19, 20, 23; 72:12; 73:7, 15, 22, 25, 28; 74:1, 23; 75:2; 76:5; 77:8, 10, 11, 15; 78:3; 79:1, 1, 2, 7, 10, 12; 80:5, 6, 12, 15, 15; 81:9; 84:9, 9; 85:1, 1, 2, 2, 3, 3, 10, 10; 86:13, 16; 87:4; 88:1, 4, 5, 6, 8, 8, 15, 16, 17, 18; 89:3, 3, 19, 19, 20, 20, 35, 38, 39, 39, 40, 42, 43, 43, 44, 45, 51; 90:1; 92:4, 4, 10, 11, 11; 93:3; 94:15, 17; 99:4, 4; 101:3; 102:4, 10, 13; 104:24, 24; 105:15; 106:6, 6, 6; 108:11; 109:27; 112:9; 115:5, 5, 17; 116:2, 16; 119:4, 10, 11, 13, 13, 14, 22, 30, 30, 42, 45, 54, 65, 69, 74, 80, 81, 85, 92, 93, 94, 96, 99, 100, 101, 102, 107, 110, 118, 121, 126, 139, 140, 152, 153, 157, 165, 166, 167, 171, 173, 174, 176, 176; 123:3, 3, 3, 4; 124:3, 4, 4, 5; 125:5; 128:6; 129:1, 2, 2; 130:5; 131:2; 135:14, 16, 16; 137:8; 139:1; 140:5, 5, 5, 9; 141:9; 142:3; 143:5, 8; 144:15; 146:5; Pr 1:31; 2:21; 3:1; 4:10, 16, 16, 19; 5:9, 14; 6:2, 3, 3, 7, 34; 7:26; 8:6, 36; 9:5; 10:7, 9, 25; 11:20; 12:3, 9, 21; 13:3; 14:20, 29,

32; 15:16, 16, 21; 16:26, 32; 18:2; 19:19, 27; 20:4, 9; 21:20; 22:2, 20; 23:8, 18, 24, 35; 24:12, 14, 20; 27:10, 27; 28:14, 16, 19; 29:13, 14; 30:3, 27, 32; 31:21, 27; Ecc 1:16; 2:19; 3:10, 19; 4:1, 3; 5:6, 10, 11, 13, 16, 18; 6:1, 3, 3, 4, 4, 5, 5, 7, 8, 9, 9; 7:15, 22, 23, 29; 8:2, 9, 9, 10; 9:3, 5, 6, 11, 13; 10:5, 5, 7, 15, 20; SS 3:3; 4:8, 9; 5:2, 3, 3; 7:12, 12, 13; 8:8; Isa 1:2, 4, 4, 9, 19, 20, 22, 26; 2:6, 8; 3:6, 7, 8, 9, 14, 14; 4:3; 5:3, 4, 8, 19, 24, 24; 6:5; 7:11, 20, 21; 8:6, 18; 9:16; 10:10, 11, 13, 13, 14; 13:3, 3, 12, 18; 14:1, 12, 20, 22, 23, 24, 26; 16:4, 4, 6, 9, 10; 17:7, 8, 10; 19:9, 13, 25; 20:6; 21:8, 8, 10, 15, 17; 22:5, 8, 21, 25; 23:4, 13, 13; 24:5; 25:1; 26:12, 13, 15, 15, 18, 19, 21; 27:11; 28:12, 15, 15, 15, 17, 20, 20; 30:2, 2, 11, 15; 31:7; 33:1, 1, 2, 8, 8, 9, 13, 16; 34:5; 35:3, 3, 10; 36:10, 18; 37:7, 11, 11, 11, 12, 18, 19, 23, 24, 24, 24, 24, 24, 25, 26, 27, 28, 29, 31; 38:3, 5, 15, 16, 16, 17, 17; 39:6, 8; 40:21, 26, 28; 41:9, 9, 25, 26; 42:1, 3, 6, 6, 14, 14, 22, 22; 43:1, 1, 7, 8, 8, 10, 19, 21, 22, 23, 23, 23, 24, 24, 26, 28; 44:7, 8, 22, 22, 22; 45:4, 5, 13, 23; 46:3, 9, 11; 47:1, 6, 10, 12, 13, 15; 48:6, 6, 6, 8, 10, 10, 11, 11, 14, 15, 16, 16, 16, 18, 19, 19; 49:4, 13, 16; 50:2, 5, 7, 9; 51:11, 13, 16, 17, 17, 19, 20; 52:4; 53:5, 6, 6, 10; 54:8, 16, 16, 17; 55:1, 5, 7; 56:5, 6, 12; 57:7, 7, 8, 8, 9, 9, 11, 11, 16, 18, 19; 58:3, 3, 14; 59:2, 13, 13, 13, 20, 21, 21; 60:10, 10; 61:4; 62:6, 9; 63:2, 3, 3, 3, 17, 17, 18; 64:7; 65:1, 2, 8, 10, 11, 20, 22, 25; 66:2, 2, 2, 19, 21, 24; Jer 1:8, 9, 16, 18, 19; 2:3, 9, 11, 13, 13, 13, 15, 16, 17, 18, 19, 20, 22, 23, 25, 28, 28, 29, 30, 30, 31, 31, 31, 32, 35; 3:1, 2, 2, 3, 4, 6, 13, 20, 20, 21, 24, 25, 25; 4:10, 17, 18, 19, 22, 22, 28, 29, 30; 5:3, 7, 7, 12, 12, 21, 21, 22, 23, 23, 23; 6:19, 20, 24, 24, 27; 7:25, 26, 26, 30, 30, 31, 31; 8:2, 3, 5, 6, 8, 8, 9, 13, 19; 9:1, 10, 13, 13, 14, 16, 19, 24, 26; 10:14, 14, 20, 21, 25; 11:9, 10, 10, 10, 13, 15, 15, 16, 17, 17, 20; 12:2, 2, 4, 6, 6, 7, 7, 8, 8, 9, 10, 11, 13, 13, 15, 17; 13:22, 25, 25; 14:2, 7, 14, 15, 18, 19, 19, 20; 15:6, 20; 16:2, 5, 5, 10, 13, 18; 17:4, 4, 7, 13, 16, 16, 16; 18:15, 15, 18, 20, 22, 22; 19:4, 5, 5, 9, 15; 20:8, 10, 12, 15; 21:5, 7, 10, 12; 22:3, 21, 22, 22; 23:1, 2, 2, 3, 11, 12, 17, 21, 21, 22, 25, 32, 34, 38; 24:6, 10; 25:3, 3, 4, 6, 8, 9, 13, 18, 29, 29; 26:2, 4, 9, 11, 12, 15, 19; 27:5, 6, 11, 15; 28:4, 13, 13, 14, 14, 16; 29:6, 6, 9, 10, 11, 19, 19, 23, 23, 23, 27, 32; 30:2, 3, 5, 10, 11, 14, 14, 15, 21; 31:3, 3, 14, 18, 20, 25, 37; 32:7, 8, 17, 19, 20, 20, 23, 23, 24, 25, 30, 30, 33, 33, 34, 35, 35, 36, 42, 42, 42, 43, 44; 33:4, 5, 5, 10, 12, 13, 14, 17, 21, 24, 26; 34:5, 16, 17, 18, 19; 35:5, 8, 8, 8, 10, 10, 14, 15, 16, 16, 17, 18, 19, 19; 36:2, 3, 16, 30, 31; 37:17, 18, 18; 38:4, 9, 19, 22, 22; 39:16, 18; 40:3, 15; 42:10, 19, 21, 21; 43:10; 44:3, 8, 9, 10, 11, 17, 18, 18, 23, 23, 25, 25, 26, 29, 30; 45:3, 5; 46:12, 15, 21, 26, 27, 28; 48:2, 7, 25, 25, 29, 38, 46; 49:13, 14, 23, 24, 37; 50:6, 6, 6, 7, 15, 17, 21, 24, 24, 28, 33, 43; 51:9, 17, 17, 24, 30, 30, 58, 62, 63; La 1:2, 3, 5, 5, 8, 11, 16, 18, 20, 21, 22; 2:8, 9, 9, 11, 14, 16, 16, 21, 22; 3:17, 22, 42, 42, 43, 44, 45, 46, 52, 58, 59, 59, 60, 60, 61, 61, 64; 4:10, 12; 5:4, 7, 8, 16, 16, 20, 22; Eze 2:3, 5; 3:8, 9, 17, 19, 21; 4:8, 14, 14, 14; 5:7, 7, 9, 11, 13, 15, 17; 6:6, 11; 7:10, 27; 8:12, 15, 17; 9:5, 10, 10, 11; 11:6, 12, 12, 16; 12:9, 16, 28, 28; 13:3, 5, 5, 6, 7, 10, 16, 22, 22; 14:3, 3, 5, 9, 22; 15:6, 8; 16:22, 28, 30, 31, 31, 36, 36, 36, 37, 43, 43, 43, 45, 47, 50, 51, 54, 59, 61, 63; 17:21, 24, 24; 18:2, 6, 12, 22; 20:13, 21, 31, 32, 42, 43, 44, 48; 21:7, 10, 13, 17, 29, 32; 22:4, 10, 14, 14, 16, 22, 26, 30; 23:31, 34, 35, 37; 24:14, 23; 25:8, 12, 14, 15, 17, 17; 26:5, 14, 16, 17, 20, 21; 27:34, 36; 28:4, 5, 10, 19, 25; 29:3, 5, 13, 19, 20; 30:8, 11, 12, 21; 31:18, 18; 32:8, 9, 15, 16, 20, 21, 24, 25, 29, 30, 32, 32, 32; 33:5, 15, 16, 29, 30, 31; 34:4, 4, 4, 4, 4, 5, 6, 19, 19, 19, 24, 27; 35:12, 12, 12, 13; 36:2, 3, 4, 5, 6, 7, 7, 32, 35, 36; 37:11, 14, 14, 20, 21, 24, 28; 38:12; 39:5, 8, 19, 21, 21, 25; 40:4, 4; 42:6; 43:10, 11, 23, 25; 44:7, 7, 7, 8, 8, 9, 12, 13, 28; 47:22, 23; 48:33; Da 1:4, 10; 2:3, 9, 23, 23, 25, 47; 3:12, 12, 12, 14, 15, 18; 4:16, 18, 22, 26, 30; 5:11, 14, 14, 15, 22, 23, 23, 23, 23, 27, 27; 6:7, 22, 22; 8:17, 19; 9:5, 5, 6, 7, 8, 9, 10, 10, 11, 12, 13, 13, 15, 22, 26; 10:11, 11, 12, 16, 19, 20; 11:1, 12, 32, 37; 12:7, 9; Hos 1:2; 3:1, 3; 4:3, 6, 7, 10, 10, 11, 12; 5:1, 2, 2, 3, 7, 10; 6:5, 10, 10; 7:8, 11, 13, 13, 13; 8:1, 3, 4, 4, 5, 7, 8, 9, 9, 10, 14; 9:1, 13; 10:3, 6, 9, 13, 13; 12:14; 13:4, 8, 12, 13, 15; 14:1, 3; Joel 1:7, 12, 12, 20, 20; 2:2, 26, 28; 3:4, 4, 5, 5, 6, 7, 8, 21; Am 1:3, 5, 6, 8, 9, 11, 13, 15; 2:1, 3, 4, 4, 4, 6, 6, 16; 3:7, 10, 15; 4:3, 12; 5:11, 14, 15, 17, 18; 7:17; 8:3, 7; 9:7, 8, 9, 12, 12, 15; Ob 1, 4, 12, 12, 12, 12, 13, 13, 14, 14, 15, 18; Jnh 1:2, 6, 8, 14; 2:4, 6; 3:2, 9; Mic 1:11; 2:1, 5, 7, 8, 9, 10; 3:4; 4:6, 9, 9, 11; 6:3, 5, 12, 14; 7:2, 9, 9, 19; Na 1:12, 12, 14, 15; 3:16; Hab 1:12, 14, 16; 2:5, 7, 8, 8, 10, 18; 3:2, 2, 17; Zep 1:13, 13, 13, 17; 2:8, 10; 3:3, 6, 7, 19, 19, 20; Hag 1:6, 6, 6, 6, 10, 11, 11; 2:9, 19, 19, 23, 23; Zec 1:6, 11, 12, 16, 21; 2:4, 6; 3:4, 5, 9; 6:8, 15; 7:3; 8:9, 9, 19, 23; 10:8, 9, 12; 11:3, 5, 6; 12:5, 7, 10; 13:3; 14:17; Mal 1:2, 2, 4, 6, 6, 7, 7; 2:2, 2, 8, 8, 9, 9, 9, 11, 14, 17, 17, 17, 17; 3:7, 7, 8, 8, 10, 13, 13, 14, 14; Mt 1:21; 2:2, 2; 3:8; 4:16; 5:17, 21, 26, 27, 31, 33, 33, 38, 43; 6:2, 12, 12, 23, 25, 30; 7:3; 8:4, 4, 8, 9, 13, 20, 20, 20, 26, 29; 9:6, 13, 27; 10:8, 23, 25, 35; 11:4, 11, 21; 12:7, 18, 27; 13:11, 11, 12, 12, 15, 17, 17, 21; 14:5, 17, 31; 15:22, 32, 32, 34; 16:8; 17:9, 9, 15, 20, 25; 18:9, 15, 33; 19:12, 16, 21, 21, 28, 29; 20:23, 30, 31; 21:13, 16, 21; 22:4, 24; 23:8, 30, 37; 24:25; 25:9, 20, 21, 22, 23, 27, 27, 29, 29; 26:9, 11, 25, 32, 35, 50, 55, 62, 65; 27:4, 4, 46; 28:7, 18, 20; Mk 1:24, 44, 44; 2:10, 17; 3:9; 4:17, 25, 40; 5:34; 6:11, 31, 38, 38; 7:3, 4, 4, 11, 11, 29, 29; 8:2, 2, 3, 5, 18, 18; 9:22, 47, 50; 10:15, 21, 21, 30, 40, 47, 48; 11:17, 22, 24; 12:19, 27, 32, 38, 43; 13:23, 30; 14:5, 7, 31, 60, 64; 15:34, 45; Lk 1:1, 3, 14, 22, 31, 34, 38, 74; 2:30, 31, 48, 48, 49; 3:8, 11, 11; 4:34; 5:14, 14, 24, 26, 32; 6:9, 24, 30, 41; 7:8, 16, 22, 28, 40, 47; 8:10, 18; 9:5, 13, 53, 58, 58, 58; 10:13, 19, 23, 24, 24; 11:4, 6, 19, 35, 45, 48; 12:3, 3, 15, 18, 19, 21, 22, 28, 33, 33, 49, 51, 51, 59; 13:34; 14:9, 10, 15; 15:17, 18, 21, 23, 30, 31; 16:3, 4, 24, 28, 28, 29; 17:10, 13; 18:8, 17, 22, 22, 28, 38, 39; 19:8, 10, 17, 26, 44, 46; 20:28, 46; 21:4, 32; 22:15, 28, 31, 32, 32, 34, 35, 36, 38, 52, 71; 23:14, 16, 22, 29, 29; 24:4, 18, 26, 28, 39, 41; Jn 1:14, 16, 22, 25, 31, 41, 45; 2:3, 10, 18, 18; 3:11, 13, 15, 16, 18, 36; 4:9, 11, 15, 17, 17, 18, 32, 42; 5:7, 24, 24, 26, 29, 29, 34, 36, 36, 37, 38, 42, 43, 46; 6:14, 36, 38, 40, 46, 53, 54, 63, 68; 7:29, 46, 47; 8:7, 12, 16, 25, 26, 26, 28, 33, 42, 49, 50, 57; 9:37, 39, 39; 10:16, 17, 18, 25, 32, 33, 38, 41; 11:9, 21, 27, 32, 34; 12:5, 8, 28, 46, 47, 48; 13:14, 15, 15, 34; 14:7, 7, 9, 11, 12, 26, 29, 30; 15:3, 3, 9, 11, 15, 22, 27; 16:1, 3, 22, 24, 25, 33, 33, 33, 33; 17:2, 2, 3, 6, 6, 7, 8, 9, 10, 11, 12, 13, 14, 22, 26; 18:9, 20, 20, 20, 30, 35, 36, 39; 19:10, 11, 15, 22, 22; 20:2, 2, 13, 13, 15, 15, 18, 25, 29, 31; 21:5, 12; Ac 1:4, 24; 2:28, 29, 39; 3:6, 6; 4:7, 16, 20; 5:28; 6:14; 7:34, 34, 34; 8:19, 21; 9:12; 10:4, 14, 19, 20, 21, 31, 31, 36, 43, 47; 11:8; 13:2, 15, 28, 33, 46, 47; 14:15; 15:17, 21, 24, 26, 27; 16:17, 37; 17:6, 23; 19:26, 37, 37, 37, 38; 20:19, 19, 21, 25, 26, 33, 34, 34, 35; 21:20, 21, 22, 23, 23, 24, 37; 22:15, 16; 23:1, 11, 14, 14, 21, 30; 24:2, 2, 5, 10, 15, 19; 25:8, 11, 12, 26, 26; 26:5, 7, 7, 16, 20; 27:21, 21; 28:16, 21, 21, 27; Ro 1:6, 13, 14, 20, 20, 26; 2:1, 1, 6, 12, 14, 18, 20, 28; 3:9, 12, 12, 18, 22, 23, 27, 31; 4:2, 9, 11, 11, 12, 12, 15, 16, 17, 19; 5:1, 1, 9, 16; 6:2, 3, 5, 13, 17, 18, 22; 7:6, 7, 8; 8:9, 9, 10, 12, 23, 24, 25, 35; 9:4, 9, 17, 20, 21, 29, 30; 10:2, 12, 14, 18, 18; 11:3, 4, 4, 5, 7, 7, 14, 17, 25, 32, 33, 35; 12:4, 6, 8, 8, 20; 13:1; 14:5, 6, 9, 12, 22, 23; 15:15, 18, 19, 19, 21, 21, 21, 22, 23, 24, 26, 28; 16:3, 17; 1Co 1:2, 7, 11; 2:8, 8, 14, 15, 16; 3:10, 11, 18; 4:1, 3, 6, 7, 7, 7, 8, 8, 9, 11, 11, 12, 15, 18, 19; 5:1, 3, 10; 6:1, 4, 7, 9, 10, 11, 11, 11, 11; 7:2, 2, 10, 12, 14, 25, 27, 27; 8:6; 9:1, 4, 5, 6, 7, 7, 11, 12, 12, 15, 17, 19, 21; 11:6, 12, 14, 16, 22, 30; 12:11, 13, 13, 24, 28, 29, 30; 13:3; 14:12, 31, 35; 15:6, 10, 15, 18, 18, 19, 35, 38, 41, 52, 54; 16:2, 5, 17, 17, 18, 18, 20; 2Co 1:11, 12, 12, 12, 13, 20; 3:18; 4:13, 18; 5:1, 4, 10, 14, 16; 6:5, 6, 7, 7, 9, 10, 10, 11, 12; 7:1, 2, 2, 2, 4, 4, 4, 9, 9, 11, 13, 14, 16; 8:2, 2, 6, 7, 11, 12, 12, 14, 16; 9:2, 8; 10:2, 13; 11:6, 9, 9, 13, 16, 20, 23, 23, 26, 26, 26, 26, 26, 27, 27, 27, 27, 28; 12:6, 7, 11, 14, 15, 18, 21, 21; 13:2, 4, 5, 6, 7; Gal 2:2, 4, 10, 14, 16, 16, 19; 3:3, 4, 21, 21, 22, 27, 27; 4:2, 6, 9, 12, 15, 16; 5:4, 4, 13, 21, 24; 6:10, 15, 15; Eph 1:11, 13, 16; 2:5, 9, 13; 3:4, 6, 6, 7, 18; 4:1, 4, 4, 18, 19, 21, 21; 5:3; 6:9; Php 1:5, 7, 7, 14, 17, 20, 26, 29, 30; 2:20, 24, 27; 3:4, 4, 4, 8, 8, 12, 12, 16, 18; 4:10, 10, 11, 11, 12, 14, 18, 19; Col 1:4, 5, 9, 11, 23; 2:1, 1, 2, 2, 18, 18, 20, 23; 3:1, 5, 9, 10, 25; 4:1, 6, 8, 11, 16; 1Th 2:4, 6, 15; 3:7, 7, 9; 4:1, 6, 13, 13, 14, 16; 2Th 2:2; 3:9; 1Ti 1:6, 6, 19; 2:7, 12; 3:2, 8, 13; 4:6; 5:8, 14, 15, 20; 6:8, 10, 12, 21; 2Ti 1:5, 12, 13, 15; 2:2, 2, 9, 18, 18, 26; 3:3, 3, 10, 11, 14, 15, 15; 4:7, 7, 7; Tit 1:1, 3, 9, 11, 14; 2:2, 8, 15; 3:8, 10, 11, 12, 14, 14; Phm 1:7, 13, 15; Heb 1:5; 2:1, 8, 11, 15; 4:8, 13, 14; 5:2, 5, 12, 14; 6:4, 5, 10, 10, 18; 7:11; 8:5, 7; 9:7, 11, 26; 10:2, 2, 2, 2, 5, 7, 9, 18, 21, 22, 22, 23, 26, 29, 29, 29, 38, 39; 11:11, 12, 15, 39; 12:4, 5, 18, 22, 23, 23, 23, 23, 24; 13:2, 2, 5, 10, 10, 16, 22; Jas 2:1, 11, 13, 13, 14, 17, 18, 18, 18; 3:9; 4:2, 2, 2, 9, 12; 5:3, 3, 4, 4, 5, 6, 13, 14; 1Pe 1:2, 2, 8, 21, 22, 23; 2:3, 10, 24, 25; 4:1, 3, 5, 6, 13, 17, 18; 5:10, 12; 2Pe 1:1, 7, 9, 16, 19; 2:13, 15, 18; 3:1, 15, 16; 1Jn 1:1, 2, 3, 3, 6, 7, 8, 10; 2:7, 12, 13, 14, 14, 14, 14, 14, 15, 18, 18, 19, 22, 23, 24, 26, 27; 3:6, 9, 9, 11, 14, 15; 4:1, 2, 3, 4, 9, 14, 15, 16, 20; 5:7, 12, 12, 13, 18; 2Jn 4, 7, 8, 9, 9, 12; 3Jn 4, 6, 13; Jude 4, 4, 12, 15, 15, 19; Rev 1:19; 2:2, 2, 2, 3, 4, 5, 13, 14, 15, 20, 24, 24, 25, 28; 3:1, 4, 8, 8, 10, 11, 12, 12, 17; 5:10; 6:10; 7:3; 9:4; 11:6, 6, 17, 17, 18; 12:11; 13:10; 14:4, 11, 11, 11; 15:4; 16:6, 6; 17:2, 2, 10, 12; 18:3, 3, 3, 21; 22:10, 16

HAVEN'T (48)

Ge 27:36; Ex 5:14; 33:12; Nu 16:14; Jdg 8:6, 15; 14:16, 16; 16:15; 1Sa 13:12; 15:19; 26: 15; 2Sa 7:7; 1Ki 2:43; 22:3; 2Ki 5:25; 12:7; 1Ch 17:6; 2Ch 24:6; Ps 119:102; Ecc 2:21; Jer 2:23, 35; 35:9; 45:3; Mt 8:10; 12:3, 5; 19:4; 20:6, 13; 21:16; 22:31; Mk 2:25; 12:26; Lk 6:3; 7:9; 15:7; Jn 6:36; 14:5; 16:24; 20:17, 29; Ac 19:2; 27:33; Ro 9:19; 1Co 5:2; 9:1

HAVING (60)

Ge 2:2; 16:2; 18:11; 20:18; 29:35; 30:1; 31:35; 37:22; 38:9; 41:32; Ex 19:15; Lev 15:18; 18:7, 14, 19, 20, 23; Dt 4:42; 22:14; 1Sa 1:8; 11:11; 2Sa 11:4; 12:6; 21:5; 24:8; 1Ki 20:38; 1Ch 29:28; Ne 5:18; 12:46; Job 21:25; Pr 5:16; 22:1; 24:6; Ecc 7:4; 8:15; Isa 30:24; 56:5; Jer 2:19; Eze 1:12; 32:31; Zec 4:2; Mt 6:31; 16:8; Mk 8:17; Lk 1:3, 25; Jn 11:13; Ac 15:25; Ro 1:27; 3:19; 8:30; 1Co 15:24; 2Co 5:12, 12; 8:13; 10:8; Gal 6:4; Php 3:5; 1Ti 3:2; Tit 1:8

HE (8267)

Ge 1:4, 16, 27, 31, 31; 2:3, 8, 8, 9, 19, 19, 20, 21, 21; 3:1, 6, 10, 15, 16, 16, 17, 23, 23; 4:5, 9, 17, 20, 22, 26; 5:1, 2, 2, 4, 5, 7, 8, 10, 11, 13, 14, 16, 17, 19, 20, 22, 24, 24, 26, 27, 29, 29, 30, 31, 32; 6:5, 6, 9, 12; 7:6, 7, 7; 8:1, 6, 8, 12; 9:21, 21, 24, 25, 27, 29, 29; 10:9, 10, 11, 11; 11:6, 26, 28, 28; 12:4, 5, 8, 11, 18; 13:4, 8, 11, 18; 14:12, 14, 14, 14, 15, 20; 15:10, 10, 12; 16:12, 12; 17:17, 17; 18:1, 2, 2, 3, 8, 8, 15, 19, 33; 19:1, 1, 1, 2, 3, 7, 13, 14, 25, 27, 28, 30, 30, 33, 35, 37, 38; 20:4, 5, 7, 7, 8, 9, 14, 16, 16; 21:1, 10, 13, 14, 20, 20, 33; 22:1, 3, 3, 6, 9, 9, 11, 13; 23:3, 10, 11, 13, 13, 16, 17; 24:7, 7, 9, 10, 10, 12, 15, 19, 22, 23, 27, 27, 30, 30, 30, 34, 35, 36, 40, 48, 53, 53, 54, 56, 63, 63, 65, 67; 25:5, 6, 6, 8, 10, 20, 25, 25, 28, 34; 26:7, 7, 7, 12, 12, 13, 14, 16, 18, 22, 22, 24, 25, 34; 27:1, 7, 7, 10, 10, 11, 18, 23, 24, 25, 27, 27, 27, 31, 32, 34, 34, 35, 35, 36, 41, 41, 45; 28:4, 5, 6, 7, 9, 9, 11, 12, 12, 12, 13, 17, 18, 18, 18, 18, 19, 21, 22; 29:2, 6, 12, 12, 13, 18, 23, 30, 30; 30:2, 2, 6, 20, 35, 38, 40, 40, 42, 43; 31:4, 5, 5, 5, 7, 8, 8, 15, 15, 15, 18, 18, 23, 23, 23, 24, 25, 25, 33, 33, 33, 34, 36, 42, 46, 55, 55; 32:2, 2, 4, 7, 8, 11, 13, 16, 17, 17, 18, 20, 23, 25, 25, 27, 29, 30, 31, 31; 33:3, 3, 17, 19, 20; 34:2, 3, 4, 4, 5, 7, 8, 11, 19, 20, 31; 35:3, 4, 7, 9, 13, 14, 22, 29; 36:3, 6, 24, 35; 37:2, 3, 6, 8, 9, 10, 15, 15, 21, 22, 22, 27, 29, 29, 30, 33, 34, 35; 38:1, 2, 2, 9, 9, 11, 15, 16, 18, 20, 21, 22, 29, 29, 30; 39:1, 2, 3, 6, 6, 6, 8, 9, 10, 10, 11, 12, 12, 13, 14, 15, 15, 18, 20, 21; 40:3, 7, 9, 16, 16, 20, 20, 21, 22; 41:1, 5, 5, 8, 8, 9, 12, 13, 14, 14, 17, 25, 28, 32, 38, 42, 43, 46, 46, 46, 51, 52, 55, 55; 42:1, 7, 7, 9, 9, 9, 12, 17, 23, 23, 24, 24, 24, 24, 25, 25, 27, 28, 30, 38; 43:3, 7, 7, 7, 14, 16, 17, 18, 18, 23, 27, 27, 27, 28, 30, 30, 31, 31, 33, 34; 44:2, 5, 6, 20, 25, 31; 45:1, 1, 1, 1, 2, 3, 4, 4, 5, 8, 14, 21, 22, 22, 23, 24, 24, 26, 26, 27; 46:1, 1, 2, 29, 34; 47:10, 14, 22, 28, 28, 29, 30, 31; 48:1, 2, 4, 8, 12, 13, 14, 15, 16, 17, 17, 18, 19; 49:9, 11, 11, 15, 15, 17, 19, 23, 27, 27, 33; 50:5, 5, 6, 12, 16, 17, 20, 21, 22, 23, 24, 24, 25; Ex 1:8, 9, 18, 21; 2:2, 6, 10, 11, 11, 11, 13, 14, 14, 15, 15, 17, 18, 19, 20, 21, 22, 25; 3:1, 4, 6, 6, 6, 16, 20; 4:3, 6, 7, 14, 14, 14, 14, 14, 20, 21, 23, 27, 28; 5:6, 23; 6:1, 1, 1, 1, 13; 7:1, 2, 9, 13, 14, 15, 22; 8:12, 15, 15, 19, 20, 24, 25, 27; 9:5, 6, 6, 7, 7, 12, 27, 33, 34; 10:8, 16, 20, 24, 26, 27; 11:1, 1, 3, 10; 12:23, 23, 27, 27, 27, 31, 44; 13:5, 11, 19; 14:4, 7, 8, 24; 15:1, 1, 2, 2, 2, 4, 21, 21; 16:7, 8, 23, 32, 34; 17:6, 10, 11, 16; 18:1, 4, 5, 7, 8, 9, 9, 10, 10, 14, 25; 19:14, 15; 20:11, 19; 21:2, 2, 3, 3, 3, 3, 3, 4, 6, 8, 8, 8, 9, 9, 10, 10, 11; 22:16; 23:21, 21, 21; 24:4, 4, 5, 6, 7, 11, 18, 18; 28:3, 29, 30, 30, 35, 35, 35, 35, 38; 30:7, 8, 8; 31:4, 5, 5, 17, 18; 32:5, 11, 12, 14, 15, 17, 19, 20, 20, 20, 21, 21, 26, 27, 29; 33:8, 9, 18; 34:4, 6, 9, 14, 28, 28, 29, 29, 33, 34, 34, 34, 34, 35, 35; 35:32, 33, 33; 37:4, 5, 6, 7, 10, 13, 15, 16, 17, 23, 26, 29; 38:3, 4, 9, 23; 39:3; 40:19, 20, 20, 20, 21, 22, 23, 24, 25, 26, 27, 28, 29, 29, 30, 30, 33, 33; Lev 1:15, 17; 2:2; 4:3, 4, 10, 12, 18, 22, 22, 23, 23, 24, 26, 26; 5:9, 12, 16; 6:11, 12, 15; 7:38; 8:6, 7, 7, 9, 11, 12, 15, 15, 15, 16, 16, 20, 24, 24, 25, 26, 27, 27, 30, 30; 9:2, 9, 9, 10, 11, 12, 13, 14, 15, 15, 16, 17, 18, 19, 20, 22; 10:1, 3, 4, 16, 16, 17, 19, 20; 13:8, 13, 15, 31, 34, 36, 40, 41, 41, 41, 43, 55, 56; 14:4, 6, 13, 16, 27, 36, 37, 38, 44, 48, 50, 51, 51, 52, 53; 15:4, 4, 8, 12, 13, 13, 13, 14, 16, 16, 24, 24; 16:2, 3, 3, 4, 4, 7, 8, 11, 12, 12, 13, 13, 13, 14, 15, 15, 16, 16, 17, 19, 19, 20, 21, 21, 21, 23, 23, 23, 23, 24, 24, 25, 26, 32; 17:5; 20:15, 17, 18, 19, 20, 21; 21:4, 11, 12, 12, 14, 15, 18, 21, 21, 21, 22, 23; 27:8, 12; Nu 1:1; 3:4, 14; 5:10, 17, 18, 18, 21, 24, 26, 26; 6:11; 7:1, 7, 9, 14, 15, 20, 21, 26, 27, 32, 33, 38, 39, 44, 45, 50, 51, 56, 57, 62, 63, 68, 69, 74, 75, 80, 81, 89; 8:2, 2, 3, 21; 9:1, 18; 10:36; 11:2, 24, 25, 33; 12:1, 2, 5, 7, 8, 8, 9, 11; 13:3, 17, 30; 14:8, 8, 16, 16, 18, 18, 24, 24; 15:33; 16:3, 4, 5, 10, 26, 31, 38, 48; 17:8, 8, 9; 19:7, 7, 8, 10; 20:9, 9, 10, 10, 13, 14, 16, 20, 24; 21:1, 23, 26; 22:3, 5, 15, 15, 22, 30, 31, 36, 40, 41; 23:3, 7, 14, 16, 19, 19, 19, 19, 19, 20, 21, 22; 24:1, 1, 1, 2, 3, 8, 10, 21; 25:7, 7, 13, 13; 26:61; 27:3, 3, 4, 9, 10; 30:2, 2, 2, 5, 7, 8, 8, 12, 14, 14, 14, 15, 15; 31:15; 32:10, 15, 29, 42; 33:38, 39; Dt 1:4, 5, 11, 21, 30, 31, 32, 34, 34, 36, 36, 36, 37, 38, 45; 2:22, 22, 30, 30; 3:20, 21, 26, 26, 28, 28; 4:10, 13, 13, 15, 21, 30, 31, 31, 35, 36, 36, 36, 36, 37, 37, 38, 38, 46; 5:5, 5, 22, 22, 27; 6:10, 17, 23, 23, 23; 7:1, 4, 8, 8, 9, 10, 12, 13, 13, 13, 15, 15, 19, 19, 21, 23, 24; 8:3, 3, 10, 15, 15, 16, 16, 17, 18, 18; 9:3, 4, 5, 8, 10, 19, 20, 25, 28, 28, 28, 28, 28; 10:12, 15, 17, 18, 18, 21; 11:3, 4, 4, 6, 12, 14, 15, 17, 25; 12:5, 10, 18, 20; 13:17, 17; 14:2; 15:4, 6, 16, 16, 17, 20; 16:2, 11, 15, 16; 17:1, 16, 17, 18, 18, 19, 19, 19, 20, 20; 18:2, 6, 7, 8, 8, 18; 19:1, 8, 8, 9; 20:3, 4, 4; 21:15, 15, 16, 16, 17, 17, 20; 22:14, 16, 17, 17, 19, 19, 22, 23, 24, 25, 29, 29, 29, 29; 23:1, 5, 11, 11, 14, 14; 24:1, 5, 5; 25:7, 8, 8, 19; 26:3, 7, 9, 17, 18, 19, 19; 27:20; 28:8, 9, 11, 45, 55, 55, 55, 60; 29:1, 6, 6, 12, 13, 13, 13, 13, 24, 25; 30:3, 3, 5, 5, 9, 9, 20; 31:2, 3, 3, 4, 6, 7, 8, 8, 11, 25; 32:4, 4, 4, 4, 6, 6, 7, 8, 8, 10, 10, 10, 11, 13, 13, 13, 14, 14, 19, 20, 36, 36, 37, 39, 43, 43, 46; 33:2, 12, 17, 24, 24, 26, 27, 27, 29; 34:6, 7, 7; Jos 1:1, 12, 15, 17; 2:1; 3:10; 4:23, 23, 23, 24; 5:6, 6, 13, 14, 15; 6:7, 26, 26; 7:15, 15, 24; 8:14, 14, 18, 31; 9:9, 10, 27; 10:1, 1, 2, 4, 12, 18, 28, 28, 30, 40; 11:1, 15, 21, 23; 12:5; 13:32; 14:10, 14; 15:15; 17:1, 3; 19:50, 50, 50, 50; 21:43, 44; 22:2, 4, 7, 18, 20; 23:2, 10, 15, 15, 15, 15, 16; 24:9, 17, 17, 18, 19, 19, 20, 20, 26, 30, 33; Jdg 1:7, 25, 26, 26; 2:1, 9, 10, 14, 14, 15, 18, 20, 21; 3:2, 8, 10, 10, 16, 17, 19, 19, 20, 24, 27, 27, 28, 31; 4:13, 18, 19, 20, 21, 22; 5:17, 27, 27, 27; 6:8, 19, 19, 19, 20, 21, 22, 27, 27, 27, 30, 32, 34, 35, 38; 7:8, 15, 15, 16, 17; 8:8, 9, 14, 14, 17, 20, 20, 25, 30, 30, 31, 32, 32, 35; 9:1, 3, 4, 5, 7, 16, 17, 17, 18, 19, 21, 30, 31, 36, 38, 40, 43, 43, 45, 48, 48, 48, 48, 52, 54, 54, 55, 56; 10:1, 2, 2, 2, 5, 7, 16; 11:1, 3, 11, 11, 17, 20, 25, 25, 29, 30, 33, 35, 35, 35, 38; 12:6, 6, 7, 7, 8, 9, 9, 10, 10, 11, 12, 12, 14, 14, 15; 13:5, 5, 6, 6, 6, 7, 8, 11, 22, 23, 23, 24; 14:1, 2, 2, 6, 6, 6, 7, 8, 8, 8, 9, 9, 9, 9, 14, 16, 17, 19, 19; 15:1, 4, 4, 4, 5, 5, 5, 8, 8, 10, 14, 15, 17, 17, 18, 19, 19; 16:3, 3, 5, 13, 16, 17, 18, 18, 20, 20, 20, 21, 25, 25, 30, 30, 30, 30; 17:2, 3, 5, 5, 8, 8, 9, 12; 18:4, 4, 18, 20, 26; 19:1, 3, 4, 7, 8, 9, 10, 16, 16, 17, 17, 21, 27, 28, 28, 29, 29, 29; Ru 1:1; 2:4, 20, 22; 3:2, 3, 4, 4, 7, 8, 9, 13, 13, 15, 17, 18, 18; 4:1, 8, 13, 14, 15, 16, 17; 1Sa 1:1, 4, 5, 5, 11, 11, 13, 14, 27, 28; 2:3, 6, 7, 8, 8, 8, 9, 10, 10, 10, 11, 15, 18, 22, 22, 26, 28; 3:5, 5, 6, 7, 8, 9, 13, 15, 18, 18; 4:12, 16, 18, 18, 18; 5:7; 6:5; 7:3, 9, 12, 12, 16, 16, 17, 17; 8:1, 14, 15, 16, 17; 9:1, 3, 6, 6, 6, 12, 12, 13, 13, 16, 17, 26; 10:1, 10, 13, 15, 16, 18, 21, 21, 22, 22, 23, 25; 11:5, 5, 6, 7, 8, 11; 12:6, 8, 9, 22, 24; 13:1, 1, 2, 4, 4, 9, 15; 14:1, 6, 6, 10, 27, 27, 27, 35, 45, 45, 47, 47, 47, 48, 49, 52; 15:8, 11, 11, 11, 12, 13, 20, 23, 26, 29, 29, 29, 29, 32, 35, 35; 16:2, 4, 11, 12, 13, 18, 18; 17:4, 5, 6, 6, 12, 20, 23, 23, 25, 26, 26, 28, 28, 30, 33, 33, 34, 36, 37, 39, 39, 39, 40, 40, 43, 43, 49, 50, 51, 54, 55, 55; 18:1, 4, 8, 10, 10, 12, 14, 15, 16, 20, 21, 23, 25, 27, 29, 29; 19:2, 4, 4, 5, 7, 8, 11, 12, 14, 15, 15, 17, 18, 20, 21, 22, 23, 24; 20:1, 1, 2, 2, 3, 7, 7, 7, 12, 12, 13, 13, 17, 23, 25, 26, 28, 29, 29, 29, 29, 30, 32, 32, 34, 36, 39, 41; 21:1, 1, 2, 11, 13; 22:3, 7, 7, 9, 10, 14, 17, 17, 19, 21, 22; 23:7, 7, 9, 11, 13, 19, 22, 22, 23, 25, 25, 26; 24:1, 4, 5, 6, 9, 10, 14, 15, 15, 16, 17, 19; 25:2, 5, 5, 10, 13, 14, 21, 21, 25, 30, 36, 37, 37, 37, 38, 39; 26:4, 10, 11, 12, 13, 14, 20, 24; 27:4, 9, 9, 11, 11, 12; 28:3, 5, 6, 6, 8, 8, 14, 14, 14, 17, 17, 17, 20, 20, 21, 23; 29:3, 4, 4, 6; 30:7, 12, 13, 18, 23, 26, 26; 31:5; 2Sa 1:2, 2, 2, 7, 7, 8, 9, 10, 13, 18, 24; 2:5, 9, 10, 10, 11, 19, 19, 20, 20, 23, 30; 3:8, 11, 16, 17, 19, 24, 24, 25, 27, 28; 4:1, 4, 4, 5, 7, 10; 5:4, 4, 5, 5, 8, 9, 9, 13, 20, 25; 6:2, 8, 10, 12, 18, 19, 20, 21; 7:11, 13, 14, 14; 8:2, 2, 2, 4, 6, 6, 10, 11, 11, 13, 14, 14; 9:1, 1, 2, 3, 4, 6, 6, 6, 8, 11; 10:5, 7, 9, 9, 9, 10, 17; 11:2, 2, 3, 3, 4, 8, 8, 9, 10, 13, 13, 15, 16, 19, 20, 23; 12:3, 3, 3, 4, 5, 6, 6, 11, 16, 17, 18, 18, 19, 19, 20, 20, 23, 23, 31, 31; 13:2, 2, 3, 8, 8, 9, 10, 11, 13, 14, 14, 15, 15, 15, 17, 21, 22, 22, 24, 25, 27, 34, 38; 14:2, 2, 7, 11, 12, 14, 14, 20, 24, 25, 26, 26, 27, 32, 32, 32; 15:1, 2, 5, 8, 10, 10, 11, 12, 12, 14, 16, 25, 26, 30; 16:1, 3, 3, 6, 7, 13, 16, 16, 21; 17:2, 2, 5, 6, 8, 9, 9, 14, 15, 16, 16, 16, 18, 21, 23, 23, 27; 18:4, 9, 9, 14, 14, 18, 18, 23, 24, 24, 25, 25, 25, 26, 26, 27, 28, 29, 32, 33, 33, 33; 19:8, 15, 19, 21, 24, 32, 32, 34, 42; 20:3, 3, 3, 3, 5, 6, 8, 8, 12, 17, 17, 17, 22; 21:8, 8, 12, 14, 16, 16, 21; 22:2, 3, 4, 7, 10, 11, 12, 15, 17, 17, 18, 20, 20, 20, 21, 31, 33, 34, 35, 35, 42, 48, 48; 23:4, 5, 5, 8, 10, 16, 16, 17, 18, 18, 19, 20, 20, 20, 21, 23, 23; 24:1, 10, 10, 17, 20; 1Ki 1:1, 5, 9, 9, 10, 15, 16, 19, 19, 19, 24, 24, 25, 25, 25, 35, 35, 37, 37, 41, 42, 47, 48, 50, 51, 51, 52, 52, 52, 52, 53; 2:1, 4, 5, 8, 8, 11, 12, 13, 15, 17, 17, 19, 19, 19, 20, 22, 22, 24, 24, 28, 28, 29, 31, 32, 35, 40, 40, 40, 42; 3:1, 1, 6, 10, 15, 15, 15, 21, 25, 26; 4:11, 15, 31, 32, 33, 33; 5:1, 3, 3, 5, 7, 8, 10, 12, 14; 6:1, 15, 15, 16, 20, 21, 21, 22, 28, 33; 7:6, 8, 14, 14, 14, 16, 18, 21, 39, 40, 51; 8:15, 16, 20, 21, 23, 54, 54, 55, 56, 56, 57, 57, 58, 58, 64; 9:1, 1, 2, 11, 12, 13, 16, 17, 19, 19, 22, 23, 24, 24, 25, 25, 25; 10:4, 9, 9, 13, 15, 17, 26, 26; 11:1, 3, 6, 7, 10, 19, 21, 22, 24, 25, 26, 28, 28, 30, 31, 33, 33, 40, 43; 12:2, 2, 6, 9, 10, 13, 14, 18, 21, 25, 28, 29, 32, 32, 32, 32, 33, 33, 33; 13:1, 2, 2, 3, 4, 4, 10, 11, 12, 14, 14, 15, 16, 21, 22, 24, 26, 28, 30, 33; 14:4, 5, 6, 6, 13, 15, 15, 16, 19, 21, 21, 21, 26, 27, 31; 15:2, 3, 4, 8, 10, 12, 13, 13, 15, 15, 18, 19, 21, 23, 24, 25, 26, 27, 28, 29, 30, 30, 34; 16:6, 8, 11, 11, 15, 18, 19, 23, 24, 26, 26, 28, 29, 31, 31, 32, 33, 33, 34, 34; 17:6, 10, 10, 10, 10, 11, 17, 17, 19, 19, 21, 22, 23; 18:4, 7, 7, 10, 12, 17, 27, 27, 27, 27, 27, 27, 30, 31, 32, 32, 33, 33, 34, 34, 34, 43, 43, 43, 46; 19:1, 1, 3, 3, 4, 4, 4, 4, 5, 5, 6, 6, 8, 9, 9, 13, 14, 19, 21, 21; 20:7, 14, 15, 26, 32, 32, 36, 37, 39, 39; 21:6, 13, 18, 21, 22, 22, 26, 26, 27, 27, 29; 22:4, 8, 8, 18, 18, 20, 24, 28, 33, 35, 39, 40, 42, 42, 42, 43, 43, 45, 46, 50, 51, 52, 53; 2Ki 1:2, 2, 2, 5, 6, 7, 8, 8, 9, 13; 2:5, 14, 17, 17, 18, 21, 21, 23, 24; 3:1, 2, 2, 2, 3, 7, 11, 16, 18, 26, 26, 27; 4:1, 6, 7, 8, 8, 10, 10, 11, 12,

14, 18, 19, 20, 23, 25, 31, 33, 34, 35, 36, 38, 39, 41; **5:**1, 3, 7, 7, 8, 8, 11, 11, 13, 14, 21, 22, 23, 24, 25, 25, 27; **6:**2, 3, 5, 6, 8, 11, 15, 17, 17, 19, 21, 27, 30, 30, 32; **7:**17; **8:**1, 6, 8, 9, 9, 10, 14, 15, 17, 17, 18, 19, 21, 24, 26, 26, 27, 29; **9:**1, 4, 5, 5, 5, 5, 12, 16, 17, 18, 19, 20, 20, 24, 27, 27, 27, 34, 36, 36; **10:**9, 9, 12, 13, 13, 15, 17, 21, 25, 29, 31, 33, 35; **11:**4, 4, 10, 12, 17, 21; **12:**1, 3, 17, 18, 18; **13:**1, 2, 2, 3, 9, 10, 11, 11, 13, 14, 15, 17, 17, 17, 17, 19, 23, 23; **14:**2, 2, 3, 5, 6, 6, 7, 14, 14, 16, 19, 20, 24, 24, 27, 27, 28, 29; **15:**2, 2, 2, 3, 4, 5, 5, 7, 8, 9, 14, 16, 17, 18, 23, 24, 27, 28, 29, 29, 29, 30, 33, 33, 33, 35, 35, 38; **16:**2, 2, 2, 3, 3, 4, 6, 10, 10, 10, 11, 12, 15, 17, 18, 20; **17:**1, 2, 4, 5, 15, 18, 20, 26, 34, 34, 37, 39; **18:**2, 2, 2, 3, 4, 4, 6, 6, 7, 7, 8, 16, 16, 22, 23, 27, 28, 29, 32; **19:**1, 2, 7, 9, 14, 33, 33, 36, 37; **20:**1, 2, 3, 8, 9, 9, 11, 12, 13, 20; **21:**1, 1, 2, 3, 3, 3, 4, 5, 6, 6, 6, 7, 11, 11, 16, 17, 18, 19, 19, 20, 21, 22, 22, 26; **22:**1, 1, 2, 2, 3, 8, 11, 12; **23:**3, 3, 4, 5, 6, 6, 7, 8, 8, 11, 12, 14, 14, 15, 16, 16, 16, 19, 20, 20, 20, 24, 26, 31, 31, 32, 33, 34, 34, 36, 36, 37; **24:**3, 4, 8, 8, 12, 16, 17, 18, 18; **25:**9, 9, 19, 24, 27, 28, 29; **1Ch 1:**46; **2:**21, 34, 34; **3:**4, 4, 16, 19; **4:**10; **5:**1, 20; **6:**31; **8:**8; **9:**19; **10:**5, 13, 13, 13; **11:**6, 8, 11, 13, 18, 19, 20, 20, 21, 22, 22, 22, 23, 25, 25; **12:**1, 8, 18, 18, 19, 20, 22; **13:**2, 10, 10, 11, 13; **14:**8, 11, 16; **15:**1, 2, 3, 12; **16:**2, 3, 8, 12, 12, 14, 15, 15, 16, 16, 17, 19, 21, 21, 23, 24, 25, 25, 29, 33, 34, 40; **17:**1, 12, 13; **18:**4, 6, 6, 8, 10, 11, 11, 13, 13; **19:**5, 8, 10, 10, 10, 11, 17, 17; **20:**2, 3, 3, 7; **21:**4, 6, 7, 21, 22, 28, 30; **22:**2, 4, 10, 10, 18, 18, 18; **23:**1, 25; **24:**28; **26:**10, 24, 29, 30; **27:**3, 23; **28:**4, 4, 5, 6, 7, 7, 9, 12, 13, 15, 16, 18, 20, 20; **29:**1, 23, 25, 27, 28;
2Ch 1:2, 4, 13, 14; **2:**2, 3, 4, 11, 12, 13, 14, 14, 14, 14, 14, 17, 18; **3:**16, 16, 17, 17; **4:**2, 6, 8, 8, 9; **5:**1, 13; **6:**4, 4, 10, 13, 13, 13, 14; **7:**3, 7, 7, 11, 11, 22; **8:**2, 4, 5, 6, 6, 9, 11, 11, 12, 14, 14; **9:**3, 8, 8, 14, 16, 25, 26, 31, 31; **10:**2, 2, 3, 6, 9, 10, 13, 14, 18; **11:**1, 6, 11, 12, 15, 21, 22, 23; **12:**1, 3, 7, 12, 13, 13, 13, 14, 14, 16; **13:**2, 7, 12, 20, 21; **14:**1, 3, 3, 4, 6, 7, 8; **15:**2, 2, 2, 2, 8, 8, 8, 16, 18, 18; **16:**2, 3, 5, 8, 10, 12, 13, 14, 14, 14; **17:**1, 2, 2, 3, 4, 5, 6, 6, 8, 8, 13; **18:**1, 2, 7, 7, 17, 17, 19, 23, 27, 32, 34; **19:**2, 4, 5, 6, 6; **20:**3, 6, 15, 17, 31, 31, 31, 32, 33, 37; **21:**1, 3, 4, 5, 5, 6, 7, 9, 11, 19, 20, 20, 20, 20; **22:**2, 2, 4, 8, 9; **23:**1, 10, 18, 19; **24:**1, 1, 3, 5, 16, 16, 20, 20, 22, 25, 25; **25:**1, 1, 3, 4, 4, 5, 5, 6, 7, 8, 14, 14, 15, 24, 24, 27, 28; **26:**3, 3, 4, 6, 6, 8, 10, 10, 10, 10, 15, 15, 16, 16, 16, 19, 19, 21, 21, 21, 23, 23; **27:**1, 1, 2, 4, 5, 6, 8, 8, 8, 9, 9; **28:**1, 1, 1, 2, 3, 3, 4, 9, 19, 20, 22, 23, 23, 24, 25, 25, 27; **29:**1, 1, 2, 4, 5, 8, 19, 25; **30:**1, 1, 6, 8, 9; **31:**4, 21, 21; **32:**1, 3, 5, 6, 8, 12, 17, 19, 21, 24, 25, 27, 28, 28, 29, 30, 30, 30, 33; **33:**1, 1, 2, 3, 3, 3, 4, 5, 6, 6, 6, 7, 13, 14, 15, 15, 15, 16, 16, 19, 19, 20, 21, 21, 22, 22, 23; **34:**1, 1, 2, 2, 3, 3, 4, 4, 5, 5, 6, 7, 7, 7, 8, 10, 14, 19, 20, 31, 31, 32; **35:**3, 21, 22, 22, 22, 23, 24, 24; **36:**2, 2, 3, 4, 5, 5, 5, 6, 7, 8, 9, 9, 11, 11, 12, 12, 13, 13, 15, 18, 23; **Ezr 1:**2; **2:**69; **3:**11; **5:**5, 12; **6:**22; **7:**1, 6, 6, 9, 21, 21; **8:**18, 21, 23; **9:**8, 9, 9, 9; **10:**6, 6, 6, 11; **Ne 3:**12, 14, 15, 15, 15, 16, 31; **4:**1, 1; **6:**6, 6, 7, 10, 12; **7:**2; **8:**3, 15; **9:**5, 8; **13:**7, 26; **Est 1:**2, 3, 3, 8, 10, 11, 12, 13, 13, 21, 22; **2:**1, 1, 4, 5, 6, 9, 9, 9, 14, 15, 17, 17, 18; **3:**2, 4, 4, 4, 5, 6, 6, 6; **4:**1, 2, 4, 5, 8, 8; **5:**2, 2, 9, 9, 9, 10, 10, 11, 11, 13, 14; **6:**1, 2, 4, 7, 8; **7:**7, 7, 8, 8, 9, 10; **8:**2, 5, 7, 7, 10, 15; **9:**4, 12, 22, 25; **10:**3, 3; **Job 1:**1, 1, 2, 3, 3, 3, 5, 8, 8, 10, 10, 11, 11, 12, 16, 17, 18, 20, 21; **2:**3, 3, 3, 4, 4, 5, 7, 8, 11; **3:**1, 2; **4:**19; **5:**9, 9, 10, 10, 11, 11, 12, 13, 15, 15, 18, 18, 18, 19, 20; **6:**4, 9, 9; **8:**6, 20, 21; **9:**5, 6, 7, 8, 9, 10, 11, 11, 12, 16, 16, 17, 17, 18, 19, 22, 23, 24, 28; **11:**5, 5, 6, 10, 11, 11; **12:**14, 14, 15, 15, 17, 17, 18, 19, 19, 20, 20, 21, 22, 22, 23, 23, 23, 23, 24, 24, 25; **13:**9; **16:**9, 11, 12, 12, 12, 14; **19:**9, 10, 10, 11, 16, 25; **20:**7, 7, 8, 8, 10, 11, 12, 13, 14, 15, 15, 16, 17, 19, 19, 20, 20, 21, 22, 24, 26; **21:**17; **22:**4, 6, 13, 14, 14, 18, 25, 27; **23:**5, 6, 6, 8, 9, 10, 10, 10, 13, 13, 14, 14, 14; **24:**14, 15, 15; **25:**2; **26:**8, 9, 10, 10, 10, 12, 14; **28:**24, 25, 26, 27, 27, 27, 28; **29:**3; **30:**11, 18, 19; **31:**4, 6, 14, 15; **32:**1, 2, 2, 3, 4, 5, 5, 13; **33:**10, 11, 13, 15, 16, 17, 17, 18, 23, 26, 26, 27, 30; **34:**8, 8, 9, 11, 11, 17, 18, 19, 19, 19, 21, 24, 24, 25, 25, 26, 28, 29, 29, 30; **35:**14, 14, 15; **36:**5, 5, 6, 7, 9, 9, 10, 13, 15, 15, 27, 30, 31, 32, 32; **37:**4, 4, 6, 11, 12, 13, 16, 18, 22, 23, 23; **39:**17; **42:**7, 12, 13, 14, 17; **Ps 2:**5, 12; **3:**4; **7:**T, 11, 12, 13, 17; **9:**8, 12, 12; **10:**11; **11:**4, 5, 6, 7; **13:**6; **14:**2; **16:**8; **18:**T, 2, 3, 6, 9, 10, 11, 14, 16, 16, 17, 19, 19, 19, 20, 30, 32, 33, 34, 34, 41, 47, 47; **20:**2, 3, 4, 6; **21:**1, 2, 4; **22:**24, 24, 24, 28, 31; **23:**2, 2, 3, 3; **24:**2, 10; **25:**8, 9, 12, 14, 15; **27:**5, 5, 5; **28:**5, 6, 7; **29:**6; **31:**21, 21, 23; **33:**4, 5, 6, 7, 9, 12, 14, 15, 15, 19, 20; **34:**T, 4, 6, 6, 7, 16, 17, 18; **35:**9; **37:**4, 5, 6, 13, 23, 28, 28, 34, 39, 40; **40:**1, 2, 2, 3, 3; **41:**2, 5, 8, 8; **44:**21; **45:**11; **46:**8, 9, 9; **47:**2, 3, 4, 4, 9; **48:**3, 8, 14, 14; **49:**15; **50:**1, 4; **52:**5; **53:**2; **55:**18, 20, 20, 22, 22; **57:**T, 3; **59:**10; **60:**12; **61:**7; **62:**2, 6, 7; **64:**9; **66:**2, 5, 6, 6, 7, 7, 9, 16, 19; **68:**6, 19, 24; **69:**33; **72:**5, 8, 12, 12, 13, 13, 14; **73:**26; **75:**7, 8; **76:**2, 3, 12; **77:**2, 7, 9; **78:**4, 5, 5, 5, 11, 11, 12, 13, 14, 15, 16, 20, 20, 21, 23, 23, 24, 26, 27, 28, 29, 31, 31, 33, 38, 38, 39, 42, 44, 45, 46, 47, 48, 49, 49, 50, 50, 51, 52, 53, 54, 54, 55, 55, 55, 56, 59, 59, 60, 60, 61, 61, 62, 62, 66, 67, 67, 68, 68, 69, 70, 71, 72; **81:**5, 5; **82:**1; **84:**11; **85:**8; **87:**2, 6; **89:**7, 18, 24, 26; **91:**2, 2, 3, 4, 4, 11; **92:**15; **93:**1; **94:**10, 10, 10, 10, 14, 23; **95:**4, 5, 7, 7; **96:**2, 3, 4, 4, 8, 10, 13, 13; **97:**10; **98:**1, 1, 3, 9; **99:**1, 5, 6, 7, 7; **100:**3; **102:**16, 17, 17, 19, 23; **103:**2, 3, 4, 5, 7, 8, 9, 10, 10, 12, 14, 14, 19, 22; **104:**16, 31, 34; **105:**1, 5, 5, 7, 8, 8, 9, 9, 10, 12, 14, 14, 16, 17, 21, 22, 22, 25, 26, 29, 31, 32, 33, 34, 36, 37, 40, 40, 41, 42, 43, 44; **106:**1, 8, 9, 9, 10, 13, 15, 15, 23, 23, 23, 26, 26, 27, 31, 33, 40, 41, 43, 44, 45, 46; **107:**1, 2, 3, 6, 7, 9, 12, 13, 14, 14, 16, 16, 19, 20, 25, 28, 29, 30, 33, 34, 35, 36, 38, 41; **108:**13; **109:**11, 16, 16, 16, 17, 17, 18, 18, 31; **110:**5, 6, 6, 7, 7; **111:**3, 4, 5, 5, 6, 7, 9, 9, 9; **112:**1; **113:**6, 7, 8, 9; **114:**8; **115:**3, 3, 9, 9, 10, 10, 11, 11, 12, 12, 13, 16; **116:**1, 2, 5, 6, 8, 12; **117:**2; **118:**1, 7, 14, 18, 29; **120:**1, 3; **121:**3, 4; **127:**5, 5; **129:**4; **130:**8; **132:**1, 2, 2, 11, 13, 14, 18; **135:**7, 7, 8, 9, 10, 12, 21; **136:**1, 11, 12, 14, 15, 18, 23, 24, 25; **138:**6, 6; **140:**12; **143:**3, 3; **144:**1, 2, 2, 2; **145:**3, 9, 13, 13, 13, 17, 17, 19, 19, 20; **146:**6, 6, 9, 9; **147:**3, 4, 6, 8, 9, 13, 14, 15, 16, 16, 17, 18, 19, 20; **148:**5, 6, 14; **149:**4; **Pr 2:**7, 7, 8, 19; **3:**6, 10, 11, 12, 12, 19, 26, 32, 34; **5:**21, 23, 23; **6:**16, 28, 29, 30, 31, 31, 31, 32, 34; **7:**8, 8, 20, 20, 22, 23; **8:**22, 26, 27, 27, 28, 28, 29, 29, 31; **10:**3, 22; **11:**1, 8, 20; **12:**2, 22; **14:**26, 35; **15:**8, 9, 11, 25, 26, 29; **16:**7, 10, 11, 13; **19:**17; **20:**8, 23; **21:**1, 1, 12; **22:**12, 23; **23:**11; **24:**12, 12, 12, 12; **28:**16; **29:**3; **30:**5, 6, 31; **31:**23; **Ecc 3:**11, 18; **4:**8, 8, 14, 14, 16; **5:**2, 6; **6:**2, 3, 3, 4, 5, 5, 5, 6, 6; **7:**13; **12:**9, 9, 9, 10; **SS 1:**14; **2:**4, 4, 8, 9, 9, 16; **3:**1; **5:**2, 2, 6, 16; **6:**2, 3; **7:**10; **8:**7, 11; **Isa 2:**3, 13, 14, 15, 16, 21; **3:**2, 4, 7, 13; **4:**4; **5:**2, 2, 2, 7, 7, 7, 7, 12, 25, 26, 26; **6:**1, 6, 7, 9, 11; **7:**4, 12, 15, 16; **8:**13, 14, 14, 14, 17; **9:**4, 4, 7; **10:**7, 7, 8, 12, 12, 13, 17, 26, 27, 32, 33; **11:**3, 3, 4, 4, 5, 10, 12, 12, 15, 16, 16; **12:**1, 1, 2, 4, 4, 5; **14:**1; **18:**5; **19:**20, 22; **20:**2, 4; **21:**6, 7; **22:**11, 12, 17, 18, 21, 21, 22, 22, 23, 24, 24; **23:**11, 11, 12; **24:**1, 23; **25:**7, 8, 8, 9, 9, 11; **26:**5; **27:**7, 7, 8, 8, 9, 12; **28:**5, 6, 6, 9, 10, 21, 21, 21, 22, 24, 25, 27, 28, 28, 28, 29; **29:**10, 15, 16, 16, 16, 16; **30:**5, 11, 18, 19, 19, 20, 26, 28, 28, 30, 31; **31:**2, 2, 2, 4, 5, 5; **32:**2, 2; **33:**5, 6, 21, 22; **34:**2, 6, 16, 16, 17; **35:**4, 5, 5; **36:**7, 8, 12, 13, 14; **37:**1, 2, 7, 9, 14, 34, 34, 37, 38; **38:**1, 2, 3, 7, 7, 9, 15; **39:**1, 1, 2; **40:**10, 10, 10, 11, 11, 11, 14, 15, 19, 21, 22, 23, 24, 26, 26, 28, 29, 29; **41:**2, 2, 2, 3, 3, 4, 25, 25, 26; **42:**1, 1, 2, 2, 3, 3, 4, 5, 5, 5, 13, 13, 13, 14, 21, 21, 24, 25; **44:**13, 14, 14, 14, 15, 15, 15, 16, 17, 17, 17, 20, 20, 28, 28, 28; **45:**1, 13, 14, 18, 18, 18; **48:**14, 21, 21; **49:**1, 2, 2, 3, 5, 6, 7; **50:**4, 8; **51:**2; **52:**9, 13, 14, 15; **53:**3, 3, 3, 4, 5, 5, 5, 7, 7, 7, 7, 8, 8, 9, 9, 9, 9, 10, 10, 11, 11, 11, 11, 12, 12, 12; **54:**5; **55:**4, 6, 7, 7; **58:**9; **59:**1, 1, 2, 16, 16, 17, 17, 18, 19; **60:**9, 19; **61:**1, 2, 3, 10; **62:**7, 11, 11; **63:**7, 7, 8, 8, 9, 9, 9, 9, 10; **66:**15; **Jer 1:**3, 4; **2:**1, 17, 35; **3:**1; **5:**12, 24; **7:**1; **9:**20; **10:**10, 12, 12, 13, 13, 13, 16, 21; **11:**1; **13:**16, 20; **14:**1; **16:**1, 15; **18:**1, 3, 4, 4, 18; **19:**14, 14, 14; **20:**2, 4, 10, 13, 17; **21:**2, 2, 7, 10; **22:**10, 11, 12, 13, 14, 15, 16, 18, 18, 19, 28; **23:**5, 5, 8, 18, 33; **25:**30, 31, 38; **26:**7, 9, 11, 11, 12, 13, 13, 16, 18, 19, 20, 21; **27:**20; **28:**1, 6, 6, 9, 11; **29:**3, 4, 28, 28, 29, 31, 32; **30:**1, 21; **31:**35, 35; **32:**3, 6, 8, 8, 28; **33:**15, 21, 23; **34:**1, 1, 2, 9; **36:**12, 23, 25, 27, 30, 32, 32; **37:**1, 4, 4, 7, 12, 13, 14, 16, 21; **38:**1, 5, 9, 9, 10, 11, 11, 13; **39:**6, 7, 10, 12, 12, 12, 15; **40:**1, 3, 3, 5, 5, 7, 9; **41:**6, 6, 6, 9, 9, 10; **42:**4, 5, 8, 9, 12, 21; **43:**8, 10, 11, 11, 11, 11, 11, 12, 12, 12, 13, 13; **44:**22; **45:**1; **48:**32; **49:**22; **50:**34, 43; **51:**5, 6, 7, 15, 15, 15, 16, 16, 16, 19, 34, 34, 44, 55, 56, 59, 61; **52:**1, 1, 13, 13, 25, 29, 30, 31, 32, 33; **La 1:**13, 13, 13, 14; **2:**2, 2, 3, 4, 4, 5, 5, 6, 7, 7, 8, 8, 9, 17, 17, 17, 17; **3:**2, 3, 4, 4, 5, 6, 7, 7, 8, 9, 9, 10, 11, 12, 13, 15, 15, 16, 16, 32, 32, 33; **4:**11, 16; **Eze 1:**27, 27; **2:**2, 3, 10; **3:**2, 3, 4, 10, 16, 22, 24; **4:**16; **8:**2, 2, 3, 6, 7, 8, 9, 12, 13, 14, 15, 16, 17; **9:**4, 9; **10:**2, 7; **11:**5, 15; **12:**12, 12, 13, 13; **17:**3, 4, 4, 5, 13, 13, 16, 18, 19; **18:**6, 6, 7, 8, 13, 17, 18; **19:**3, 3, 4, 6, 6, 6, 7; **20:**49; **21:**21, 23; **24:**24, 27; **26:**8, 8, 9; **29:**19, 20, 20; **30:**11, 24, 25; **32:**31, 31; **33:**3, 6, 24; **34:**23; **36:**4, 20; **37:**2, 3, 4, 7, 9, 10, 11; **40:**2, 3, 3, 4, 6, 6, 8, 13, 14, 24, 28, 32, 32, 35, 35, 48, 48; **41:**1, 3, 3, 4, 5, 13; **42:**15, 16, 17; **43:**3, 18; **44:**3, 27, 27; **45:**17, 23; **46:**2, 2, 2, 5, 5, 5, 6, 7, 7, 7, 7, 7, 8, 8, 12, 12, 12, 12, 17, 18, 19, 20, 21; **47:**3, 3, 4, 5, 6, 6, 8; **Da 1:**2, 4, 8, 10, 10; **2:**1, 2, 2, 2, 3, 12, 12, 15, 16, 18, 20, 21, 21, 21, 22, 22, 28, 38, 46, 48; **3:**2, 2, 17, 18, 19, 20, 24, 26, 28; **4:**8, 17, 25, 29, 30, 30, 31, 32, 33, 33, 33, 35, 35, 37; **5:**2, 2, 7, 7, 11, 12, 12, 19, 19, 19, 19, 19, 19, 19, 20, 21, 21, 21, 21, 21, 21, 21, 29; **6:**1, 4, 10, 10, 10, 13, 14, 14, 18, 20, 20, 23, 24, 26, 26, 27, 27, 27; **7:**1, 1, 1, 9, 13, 14, 16, 23, 25, 25; **8:**11, 17, 18, 19, 24, 24, 24, 24, 25, 25, 25, 25; **9:**10, 13, 14, 14, 22, 27, 27, 27; **10:**11, 12, 15, 19, 19, 20; **11:**2, 3, 5, 7, 8, 8, 8, 13, 16, 17, 17, 18, 19, 19, 20, 21, 23, 23, 24, 24, 25, 28, 29, 30, 30, 32, 36, 36, 37, 37, 37, 38, 39, 39, 40, 41, 42, 43, 44, 44, 45, 45; **12:**8, 8, 9; **Hos 1:**2, 4; **5:**6, 13; **6:**1, 1, 1, 1, 2, 3; **7:**9, 10; **9:**8, 8, 9; **10:**12; **11:**2, 3; **12:**2, 3, 3, 3, 4, 4, 4; **Joel 2:**13, 13, 13, 14, 14, 17, 19, 23; **Am 1:**1, 2, 2; **3:**11, 11; **4:**12, 13; **5:**6, 8, 8, 9, 14, 19; **6:**8, 10, 10, 10; **7:**3, 7, 7, 10, 10, 11; **8:**2; **9:**1, 6; **Jnh 1:**3, 3, 3, 3, 6, 6, 10, 10; **2:**2, 2; **3:**4, 6, 6, 10, 10; **4:**1, 2, 5, 8, 8; **Mic 1:**3; **2:**4, 13; **3:**4; **4:**2, 9, 10, 12; **5:**4, 4, 5; **6:**2, 2, 8; **7:**9; **Na 1:**2, 3, 3, 7, 7, 8, 8, 9, 9, 15; **Hab 2:**1; **3:**3, 4, 6, 6, 6, 19; **Zep 1:**12, 18; **2:**11, 13; **3:**5, 17, 17, 17, 17; **Zec 1:**6, 6, 6, 19; **2:**2, 8, 12, 13; **3:**3, 4, 5; **4:**2, 6, 9, 13, 14; **5:**3, 6, 8, 11; **6:**5, 12, 12, 13, 13, 13; **9:**9, 9, 14; **10:**1, 3; **13:**5, 6; **14:**3, 18; **Mal 1:**8, 9; **2:**13, 13, 15, 17; **3:**1, 2, 2, 2, 3, 3, 4; **Mt 1:**20, 20, 21, 23, 24, 24; **2:**4, 4, 7, 8, 16, 16, 22, 22, 22, 23; **3:**3, 3, 4, 6, 7, 7, 7, 11, 12, 12, 14, 16; **4:**2, 6, 9, 12, 13, 18, 21, 21, 23, 24, 25; **5:**2, 45, 45; **6:**30, 33; **7:**29; **8:**1, 2, 3, 10, 10, 16, 16, 17, 18, 26; **9:**3, 4, 9, 12, 13, 15, 18, 23, 24, 28, 29, 32, 34, 34, 35, 35, 36, 37; **11:**1, 2, 9, 10, 11, 14, 18, 20; **12:**3, 4, 9, 10, 10, 11, 13, 15, 15, 16, 16, 18, 18, 19, 19, 20, 20, 22, 22, 24, 24, 26, 49; **13:**2, 2, 3, 4, 11, 29, 34, 37, 44, 44, 46, 46, 46, 52, 53, 54, 54, 54, 58; **14:**2, 2, 5, 7, 9, 9, 13, 13, 14, 14, 18, 19, 19, 19, 22, 23, 23, 26, 27, 30, 30, 30; **15:**7, 24, 26, 30, 36, 39; **16:**2, 7, 8, 12, 13, 15, 20, 20, 21, 21, 21, 21, 21, 22; **17:**5, 7, 12, 12, 12, 13, 15, 15, 23, 23, 25, 25, 25; **18:**3, 12, 12, 13, 13, 25, 25, 25, 27, 28, 28, 29, 30, 32, 34; **19:**1, 2, 5, 13, 15, 15, 22, 22; **20:**2, 3, 4, 4, 5, 6, 6, 8, 13, 17, 18, 19, 21, 23, 23; **21:**2, 3, 5, 7, 9, 10, 12, 13, 14, 17, 17, 18, 19, 19, 19, 25, 26, 29, 30, 30, 33, 34, 40, 41, 45; **22:**1, 3, 4, 5, 7, 8, 11, 12, 18, 20, 21, 32, 34, 42, 42, 45; **24:**2, 23, 26, 31, 47, 51; **25:**12, 14, 14, 15, 20, 31, 32, 33, 45; **26:**1, 18, 21, 23, 24, 26, 27, 27, 36, 37, 37, 38, 39, 40, 40, 42, 43, 44, 45, 47, 49, 53, 58, 66, 70, 72, 75; **27:**3, 3, 4, 9, 17, 18, 23, 24, 24, 26, 34, 34, 36, 42, 42, 42, 42, 43, 43, 47, 48, 50, 60, 60, 60, 63, 64; **28:**5, 6, 6, 6, 7, 7, 9; **Mk 1:**2, 3, 4, 5, 6, 7, 8, 9, 10, 13, 13, 15, 16, 20, 21, 22, 24, 26, 28, 31, 31, 34, 34, 34, 38, 39, 40, 41, 45, 45, 45; **2:**2, 2, 8, 14, 14, 16, 17, 20, 25, 26, 27; **3:**2, 2, 4, 5, 5, 5, 9, 12, 13, 14, 14, 15, 16, 16, 20, 20, 22, 26, 26, 30, 30, 31, 34; **4:**1, 2, 4, 8, 11, 27, 33, 34, 34, 34, 36, 39, 39, 40; **5:**4, 4, 4, 5, 6, 7, 15, 19, 20, 23, 30, 32, 34, 35, 39, 39, 40, 40, 41, 43; **6:**2, 2, 5, 6, 7, 8, 9, 10, 14, 15, 16, 20, 20, 20, 20, 21, 23, 26, 27, 34, 34, 34, 38, 41, 45, 46, 48, 48, 48, 49, 50, 51, 56; **7:**6, 9, 14, 17, 17, 18, 19, 20, 24, 24, 24, 29, 33, 33, 34, 36, 37, 37; **8:**5, 6, 9, 10, 11, 12, 12, 13, 13, 16, 17, 21, 23, 24, 25, 27, 31, 31, 31, 32, 32, 34, 34; **9:**6, 9, 9, 10, 13, 15, 16, 17, 17, 20, 21, 21, 25, 25, 26, 27, 31, 31, 31, 32, 32, 35, 35, 36, 36, 38; **10:**1, 4, 4, 5, 6, 10, 11, 13, 14, 14, 16, 17, 21, 21, 22, 22, 28, 28, 33, 34, 36, 40, 47, 48, 49, 52; **11:**2, 7, 9, 11, 11, 11, 13, 13, 13, 15, 16, 17, 20, 31; **12:**1, 2, 5, 6, 9, 12, 13, 16, 21, 27, 28, 28, 35, 37, 38, 43; **13:**20, 21, 27, 34, 34, 36; **14:**11, 11, 13, 14, 15, 20, 21, 22, 23, 23, 24, 33, 33, 34, 35, 35, 36, 37, 37, 40, 41, 41, 43, 45, 52, 54, 68, 68, 72; **15:**10, 14, 15, 23, 31, 31, 35, 36, 36, 39, 39, 41, 44, 45, 46, 46; **16:**6, 6, 7, 7, 9, 12, 12, 13, 14, 14, 14, 15, 19; **Lk 1:**9, 15, 15, 15, 16, 17, 17, 17, 17, 19, 21, 22, 22, 22, 23, 23, 25, 32, 33, 35, 38, 45, 48, 49, 49, 51, 52, 53, 54, 54, 55, 63, 63, 64, 68, 69, 70, 72, 73, 80, 80; **2:**4, 4, 5, 10, 21, 21, 23, 25, 25, 25, 26, 26, 28, 32, 32, 34, 34, 40, 44, 44, 46, 49, 50, 51, 52; **3:**4, 4, 13, 16, 17, 17, 18, 19, 21, 23; **4:**1, 2, 10, 13, 14, 15, 16, 16, 17, 18, 18, 20, 21, 23, 26, 30, 32, 32, 33, 35, 37, 38, 39, 41, 41, 43, 44; **5:**2, 3, 4, 4, 8, 9, 12, 12, 13, 14, 21, 22, 27, 35; **6:**3, 4, 8, 10, 12, 13, 14, 35; **7:**1, 3, 4, 5, 9, 9, 12, 13, 14, 14, 19, 21, 21, 22, 26, 27, 28, 33, 37, 39, 39, 40, 42, 43, 44, 49; **8:**1, 2, 2, 2, 5, 8, 8, 10, 23, 25, 27, 28, 28, 29, 29, 30, 39, 42, 48, 49, 50, 52; **9:**2, 3, 7, 9, 10, 11, 11, 16, 18, 20, 22, 23, 29, 31, 33, 34, 39, 42, 43, 45, 47, 48, 49, 52, 53, 59, 59; **10:**1, 16, 18, 23, 29, 30, 31, 31, 32, 33, 33, 34, 34, 35, 35, 39; **11:**1, 2, 5, 7, 8, 8, 15, 15, 16, 17, 17, 27, 28, 29, 37, 38; **12:**15, 16, 18, 28, 31, 36, 37, 38, 38, 44, 46, 47, 47; **13:**2, 6, 7, 11, 12, 13, 14, 17, 20, 22, 23, 25, 27; **14:**5, 7, 10, 12, 12, 17, 18, 18, 19, 20, 20, 22, 25, 32, 32; **15:**2, 13, 14, 15, 16, 17, 17, 20, 20, 20, 24, 24, 25, 25, 26, 27, 29, 32, 32; **16:**5, 5, 7, 15, 23, 25; **17:**3, 4, 7, 8, 9, 9, 11, 12, 14, 15, 15, 16, 16, 22, 22, 23; **18:**2, 4, 7, 7, 8, 13, 13, 15, 23, 23, 27, 32, 33, 34, 34, 36, 36, 38, 39, 40, 41, 43; **19:**2, 2, 3, 3, 4, 4, 5, 5, 7, 11, 11, 12, 13, 13, 13, 15, 15, 15, 29, 30, 40, 41, 46, 47, 48; **20:**3, 5, 6, 10, 11, 11, 12, 16, 19, 20, 23, 25, 30, 37, 37, 38, 41, 44, 45; **21:**1, 3, 8, 10, 29, 37; **22:**4, 5, 6, 10, 10, 12, 17, 17, 17, 19, 19, 19, 20, 36, 37, 38, 40, 41, 44, 44, 45, 46, 47, 51, 52, 57, 59, 60, 67, 70; **23:**2, 5, 5, 6, 7, 8, 9, 14, 20, 22, 22, 25, 25, 35, 35, 42, 46, 47, 50, 51, 51, 51, 52, 53; **24:**6, 6, 6, 7, 8, 12, 12, 16, 17, 19, 19, 21, 29, 30, 31, 32, 34, 35, 36, 38, 40, 40, 40, 41, 43, 44, 45, 46, 50, 51, 51; **Jn 1:**1, 1, 2, 3, 3, 8, 10, 11, 12, 14, 15, 15, 16, 18, 19, 20, 20, 21, 30, 30, 31, 33, 33, 33, 33, 34, 38, 39, 43, 51; **2:**5, 8, 9, 10, 10, 12, 14, 14, 15, 16, 22, 22, 23, 23, 24; **3:**2, 16, 30, 31, 31, 32, 32, 32, 34, 34, 35; **4:**3, 4, 5, 8, 12, 25, 25, 27, 32, 39, 40, 42, 44, 46, 46, 47, 47, 47, 51, 52; **5:**6, 6, 9, 11, 18, 19, 19, 20, 20, 21, 21, 26, 27, 27, 32, 33, 38, 46, 47; **6:**2, 2, 5, 6, 6, 6, 11, 14, 15, 20, 22, 29, 32, 39, 41, 42, 52, 59, 59, 61, 64, 65, 71; **7:**1, 15, 15, 26, 26, 27, 27, 27, 28, 28, 29, 35, 35, 36, 36, 39, 39, 41, 41, 51, 51; **8:**2, 2, 3, 7, 8, 20, 20, 22, 22, 23, 26, 27, 28, 29, 42, 44, 44, 44, 44, 54, 56, 56; **9:**1, 3, 6, 7, 9, 9, 11, 12, 12, 15, 15, 16, 17, 17, 18, 19, 19, 20, 21, 21, 23, 25, 26, 26, 30, 31, 33, 35, 36, 37, 38; **10:**3, 4, 4, 6, 7, 7, 12, 12, 12, 13, 19, 20, 23, 29, 39, 40; **11:**1, 4, 6, 6, 7, 11, 12, 12, 14, 17, 33, 34, 36, 37, 39, 51, 51, 54, 56; **12:**1, 6, 6, 6, 33, 33, 37, 41, 41; **13:**1, 3, 4, 5, 5, 6, 11, 11, 12, 21, 22, 25, 26, 26, 37; **14:**16, 17, 17, 26, 30; **15:**2, 2, 26; **16:**7, 8, 8, 13, 13, 13, 13, 13, 14, 14, 15, 17, 17, 17, 17, 18, 19, 23; **17:**1, 1, 2; **18:**4, 5, 6, 6, 7, 8, 9, 15, 17, 19, 22, 25, 28, 30, 32, 33, 38, 38; **19:**7, 7, 8, 9, 21, 26, 26, 26, 27, 28, 30, 30, 33, 38, 38; **20:**5, 5, 6, 8, 9, 15, 19, 20, 20, 20, 21, 22, 25, 26, 27; **21:**4, 5, 6, 7, 7, 12, 14, 17, 17, 19, 23; **Ac 1:**2, 3, 3, 3, 4, 4, 4, 7, 9, 9, 9, 11, 18, 18, 22, 22, 25, 25; **2:**25, 29, 29, 30, 30, 31, 33, 33, 34; **3:**2, 2, 3, 3, 7, 8, 8, 10, 11, 12, 16, 18, 20, 21, 22, 26; **4:**9, 10, 36, 37, 37; **5:**2, 2, 5, 15, 19, 31, 34, 34, 35, 36, 37, 37; **7:**2, 5, 8, 12, 15, 22, 23, 23, 24, 26, 26, 26, 27, 29, 31, 36, 38, 55, 56, 60, 60; **8:**3, 6, 6, 11, 11, 13, 13, 13, 18, 19, 22, 27, 27, 28, 28, 30, 31, 32, 32, 32, 33, 38, 40, 40; **9:**1, 1, 2, 2, 2, 3, 4, 8, 8, 9, 9, 10, 11, 12, 14, 16, 17, 18, 18, 19, 20, 20, 21, 26, 26, 27, 28, 29, 32, 33, 34, 39, 40, 40, 41, 41, 41; **10:**2, 2, 3, 3, 4, 6, 8, 10, 10, 11, 22, 23, 31, 32, 35, 39, 41, 42, 43, 48; **11:**5, 13, 14, 15, 16, 17, 23, 23, 23, 26, 26; **12:**2, 3, 6, 8, 9, 9, 11, 12, 13, 17, 17, 17, 19, 23, 23; **13:**7, 7, 8, 11, 12, 12, 16, 17, 18, 19, 22, 24, 25, 25, 27, 31, 36, 45, 47; **14:**8, 8, 9, 9, 12, 16, 17, 20, 20, 27; **15:**8, 8, 9, 9, 18; **16:**3, 9, 18, 18, 24, 27, 27, 30, 33, 34, 34; **17:**2, 2, 3, 3, 16, 16, 17, 17, 18, 18, 23, 24, 24, 24, 25, 25, 25, 26, 26, 26, 27, 30, 31, 31, 31; **18:**2, 3, 7, 16, 18, 19, 19, 20, 21, 21, 22, 25, 25, 27, 27, 28, 28; **19:**1, 1, 2, 3, 9, 16, 21, 22, 22, 24, 25, 33, 34, 35, 41; **20:**1, 2, 2, 2, 3, 3, 3, 3, 7, 7, 9, 10, 11, 13, 14, 16, 16, 17, 18, 32, 36, 36, 38; **21:**9, 11, 11, 11, 13, 26, 26, 28, 28, 32, 33, 33, 33, 34, 34, 37, 40; **22:**8, 12, 12, 13, 14, 22, 24, 29, 29, 30; **23:**5, 6, 17, 18, 22, 25, 27, 28, 34, 34; **24:**5, 6, 15, 23, 24, 25, 25, 26, 26, 27; **25:**1, 4, 5, 6, 8, 14, 20, 25, 25; **26:**32, 32; **27:**6, 10, 24, 25, 33, 35, 43, 43, 44; **28:**4, 6, 7, 8, 15, 16, 17, 17, 23, 23, 25, 30; **Ro 1:**7, 28; **2:**4, 7, 8, 12, 18; **3:**4, 4, 4, 5, 6, 24, 25, 26, 26, 29, 29, 29, 30; **4:**2, 9, 10, 10, 10, 10, 11, 12, 18, 19, 19, 20, 21, 21, 25, 25; **5:**5, 9; **6:**5, 9, 10, 10; **7:**2, 2; **8:**3, 4, 11, 11, 18, 23, 29, 30, 30, 30, 33, 34, 35; **9:**4, 5, 10, 10, 16, 18, 18, 19, 21, 22, 23, 23, 24, 26, 33; **11:**2, 4, 8, 9, 21, 21, 22, 23, 24, 26, 32, 35; **12:**1, 1; **14:**9; **15:**8, 9, 9, 12; **16:**5; **1Co 1:**2, 2, 4, 5, 8, 8, 9, 9, 9, 21, 27, 30, 30, 30; **2:**7; **3:**7; **4:**5, 17, 17; **5:**5; **6:**14, 16; **7:**7, 12, 13, 18, 18, 33, 36, 36, 37, 37, 37, 39; **9:**9, 10, 10; **10:**1, 5, 13, 13, 22; **11:**4, 23, 24, 24, 25, 26; **12:**8, 9, 10, 10, 11, 18, 18; **15:**4, 4, 5, 6, 7, 20, 24, 25, 28, 38; **16:**10, 11, 12, 12; **2Co 1:**3, 4, 10, 10, 11, 19, 19, 21, 22, 22; **2:**5, 6, 7, 7, 14; **3:**6, 17; **4:**13; **5:**5, 15, 16, 19; **7:**7, 7, 7, 15, 15; **8:**9, 9, 9, 16, 17, 17, 17, 18, 19, 22, 22, 23; **9:**10, 10; **10:**10; **12:**9; **13:**3, 4, 4; **Gal 1:**4, 6, 16, 23; **2:**3, 7, 11, 12, 12, 12; **3:**8, 13, 13, 14, 20; **4:**5, 7, 27; **5:**8, 22; **Eph 1:**4, 6, 7, 7, 8, 10, 11, 11, 13, 13, 14, 14, 14, 18, 18, 18, 21, 22; **2:**2, 4, 5, 5, 6, 7, 10, 10, 14, 15, 17; **3:**5, 16, 20, 21; **4:**7, 8, 8, 9, 11, 30; **5:**23, 25, 27, 28, 33; **6:**9, 22, 22; **Php 2:**6, 6, 7, 7, 8, 19, 19, 22, 25, 25, 26, 26, 26, 27, 27, 30, 30; **3:**21, 21; **4:**6; **Col 1:**7, 7, 8, 9, 13, 13, 15, 16, 17, 17, 18, 18, 20, 22, 22, 22; **2:**7, 10, 13, 14, 14, 15, 20; **3:**11, 12; **4:**7, 9, 10, 12, 13; **1Th 1:**4, 10; **2:**4, 12, 19; **3:**2, 6; **5:**10, 24; **2Th 1:**5, 6, 7, 10, 11; **2:**4, 4, 4, 6, 10, 14; **3:**3; **1Ti 1:**14, 17, 17; **2:**4, 5, 6, 13; **3:**1, 2, 2, 2, 3, 3, 4, 5, 6, 7, 12, 16, 16; **5:**1; **6:**16, 16; **2Ti 1:**1, 3, 9, 10, 12, 16, 16, 17, 17, 17, 18; **2:**8, 12, 13, 13, 26; **4:**1, 10, 11, 14, 15, 17; **Tit 1:**2, 3, 6, 7, 7, 7, 8, 8, 8, 9, 9, 9; **2:**14; **3:**5, 5, 6, 7; **Phm 1:**10, 11, 13, 16, 16, 16, 18; **Heb 1:**2, 2, 3, 3, 3, 5, 5, 6, 8, 13; **2:**4, 9, 11, 12, 13, 13, 14, 14, 15, 17, 17, 18, 18; **3:**2, 18, 18; **4:**3, 15, 15; **5:**1, 2, 2, 2, 3, 4, 4, 5, 7, 8, 8, 9; **6:**10, 15, 17, 20; **7:**2, 2, 3, 4, 8, 10, 16, 17, 20, 21, 25, 25, 26, 26, 26, 26, 27, 27; **8:**2, 4, 4, 6, 8, 13; **9:**7, 11, 12, 12, 12, 15, 19, 20, 21, 24, 25, 26, 26, 28, 28; **10:**5, 9, 9, 12, 13, 14, 14, 15, 17, 30, 36; **11:**4, 4, 5, 5, 5, 6, 7, 7, 8, 8, 9, 9, 9, 10, 16, 20, 21, 21, 22, 22, 22, 24, 25, 26, 26, 27, 27; **12:**2, 2, 2, 3, 5, 5, 6, 6, 6, 8, 16, 17, 17, 17, 21, 26; **13:**13, 20, 23; **Jas 1:**5, 5, 13, 17, 18; **2:**21, 21, 22, 22, 22, 23; **4:**6, 6, 7, 10, 12; **5:**9, 11, 17, 18; **1Pe 1:**11, 16, 17, 17, 18, 19, 20, 20; **2:**4, 4, 7, 8, 9, 12, 14, 22, 22, 23, 23, 23, 23, 23, 24; **3:**9, 18, 18, 18, 18, 18, 18, 19, 22; **4:**1, 19; **5:**1, 5, 6, 7, 8, 10, 10; **2Pe 1:**3, 4, 4, 17; **2:**4, 6, 6, 7, 8, 8, 10; **3:**4, 4, 5, 6, 9, 9, 9, 13, 16; **1Jn 1:**1, 2, 2, 2, 5, 9; **2:**1, 2, 2, 25, 27, 27, 27, 28; **3:**1, 2, 2, 6, 12, 20, 23, 24, 24; **4:**3, 3, 9, 10, 13; **5:**11, 14, 15, 15, 20, 20, 20; **2Jn** 6; **3Jn** 10, 10, 10, 10, 10; **Jude** 5, 14, 15, 15; **Rev 1:**2, 3, 6, 6, 7, 13, 16, 17; **2:**14; **3:**7, 7, 7; **5:**5, 6, 7, 8, 12; **6:**2; **7:**2, 14, 15, 17; **9:**1, 2; **10:**2, 2, 3, 3, 6, 6, 7, 9, 11; **11:**7, 15; **12:**4, 4, 12, 12, 13, 13, 17, 18; **13:**5, 5, 6, 7, 11, 11, 12, 12, 13, 14, 14, 14, 15, 16; **14:**4, 7, 7, 14, 17; **16:**19; **17:**1, 8, 11, 11, 14; **18:**2, 21; **19:**2, 2, 9, 10, 11, 12, 13, 15, 15, 15; **20:**2, 3, 3, 8, 8; **21:**3, 4, 5, 6, 10, 10, 16, 16, 17; **22:**9, 10, 20

HE'LL (3)

Ge 27:12, 12; **31:**31

HE'S (29)

Ge 29:6; **Jdg 9:**28, 28; **Ru 3:**2; **1Sa 16:**11; **19:**4; **20:**2, 2, 26; **25:**17; **29:**3; **2Sa 13:**20; **1Ki 21:**15; **Pr 7:**19; **Mt 11:**18, 19; **13:**55; **Mk 3:**21, 22; **6:**3; **9:**26; **10:**49; **Lk 7:**33, 34; **Jn 7:**12, 12; **10:**20; **Ac 17:**18; **20:**10

HER (1408)

Ge 2:22; 3:6, 6, 6, 15; 12:12, 14, 15, 15, 16, 19, 19; 16:1, 2, 2, 3, 4, 5, 6, 6, 8, 9, 13; 17:15, 15, 16, 16, 16, 16; 19:31, 33, 33, 34, 35; 20:2, 2, 4, 6, 7, 7, 7, 11, 12, 13; 21:9, 10, 14, 19; 23:2, 3, 6; 24:14, 15, 15, 16, 16, 17, 21, 22, 22, 22, 28, 30, 41, 44, 45, 45, 46, 47, 47, 51, 51, 53, 55, 57, 58, 59, 59, 60, 61, 65, 65, 67; 25:22, 23; 26:7, 9, 10; 27:6, 14; 29:9, 12, 12, 12, 12, 16, 18, 19, 20, 21, 23, 24, 29, 30, 31; 30:1, 4, 9, 14, 16, 17, 17, 21, 22, 22; 31:19, 19, 34; 33:2, 7; 34:2, 2, 2, 3, 4, 8, 8, 11, 14, 17; 35:18, 20; 38:2, 8, 9, 11, 11, 11, 13, 14, 14, 15, 15, 16, 18, 18, 19, 19, 20, 20, 20, 22, 23, 23, 24, 24, 25, 25, 25, 26; 39:7, 8, 10, 10, 16, 16, 17; 46:18, 25; 48:7; Ex 2:5, 5, 5, 6, 9, 9, 10; 4:25; 21:8, 8, 8, 8, 9, 9, 9, 10, 10, 10, 22; 22:16, 16, 17, 17, 17, 17; Lev 12:2, 4, 4, 5, 6, 7, 7, 8; 15:19, 19, 21, 23, 24, 24, 25, 26, 27, 30, 30, 33, 33; 18:7, 17, 17, 17, 17, 18, 18, 19, 19; 19:29; 20:14, 18; 21:9; 22:13, 13, 13, 28; Nu 5:12, 14, 15, 16, 16, 18, 18, 18, 18, 19, 27, 27, 27, 29, 30, 31; 12:12, 13, 14, 14, 14; 24:9; 30:3, 4, 4, 5, 5, 5, 5, 5, 5, 7, 7, 7, 8, 8, 8, 8, 9, 10, 11, 11, 11, 12, 12, 12, 13, 15; Dt 21:11, 11, 12, 12, 12, 13, 13, 13, 13, 14, 14, 14, 14, 14, 14; 22:13, 13, 14, 14, 15, 16, 16, 17, 17, 19, 20, 21, 21, 21, 23, 25, 27, 27, 29, 29, 29; 24:1, 1, 1, 1, 3, 4, 17; 25:5, 5, 8, 11, 12; 28:30, 56, 56; 32:11, 11; Jos 2:17; 6:17, 22, 22, 23, 23, 23, 25, 25; 15:18, 18, 18, 19; Jdg 1:14, 14, 14, 15; 4:5, 8, 18, 20, 22; 5:26, 26, 27, 29; 11:35, 38, 38, 39; 13:6, 9, 9, 10, 13, 24; 14:3, 7, 17, 17; 15:1, 1, 2, 2, 2, 2, 2, 6; 16:5, 9, 17, 18, 19; 17:3; 19:2, 3, 3, 3, 3, 4, 25, 25, 25, 25, 26, 27, 27, 27, 28, 28; 20:6; Ru 1:3, 5, 6, 6, 7, 8, 14, 15, 15, 15, 18, 18, 18, 22; 2:3, 14, 14, 15, 15, 16, 16, 16, 18, 18, 18, 19, 20, 23; 3:6, 15, 15, 15, 16, 16, 18; 4:5, 10, 13, 13, 13, 16; 1Sa 1:4, 5, 5, 6, 12, 13, 19, 22; 2:19; 4:19, 19, 19, 20, 21, 21; 25:14, 18, 19, 20, 20, 23, 35, 35, 36, 39, 42, 42; 28:7, 13; 2Sa 3:14, 15, 16; 6:16, 23; 11:4, 4, 4, 26, 27, 27; 12:24; 13:1, 1, 2, 8, 11, 14, 14, 15, 15, 15, 16, 17, 18, 19, 19, 19, 19, 20, 20; 14:2, 3, 4, 8; 17:3, 8, 20; 20:22; 1Ki 1:3, 4, 11, 16; 2:19, 19; 3:1, 19, 20, 20, 26; 9:24; 10:2, 3, 3, 13; 14:5, 5, 6, 6, 17; 15:13; 17:9, 10, 11, 13, 15, 15, 19, 20, 20; 21:6, 9; 2Ki 4:5, 5, 6, 6, 7, 9, 12, 13, 13, 13, 13, 14, 14, 15, 15, 18, 20, 22, 25, 26, 26, 27, 27, 27, 30, 37; 5:3; 6:28; 8:2, 3, 5, 5, 6, 6, 6; 9:10, 30, 30, 32, 33, 33, 33, 33, 35, 35, 35, 35, 37, 37; 11:1, 14, 15, 15, 15, 16, 16; 19:21; 22:20; 1Ch 4:19; 15:29; 2Ch 8:11; 9:2, 2, 2, 12; 15:16; 22:10; 23:13, 14, 14, 14, 15, 15, 15; 34:28; Ezr 2:61; Ne 6:14; 7:63; Est 1:11, 11; 2:7, 7, 7, 9, 9, 9, 9, 9, 9, 10, 10, 11, 13, 13, 13, 14, 14, 14, 15, 17, 17, 17, 17, 20; 4:4, 5, 8, 8, 8; 5:1, 2, 2, 3, 12; 7:2; Job 3:12; 24:3, 9; 31:10; 38:32; 39:13, 14, 16, 16, 17, 17; Ps 45:13, 14, 14; 48:3; 51:18; 84:3, 3; 102:13, 14, 14; 123:2; Pr 2:17, 18, 19; 3:14, 15, 16, 16, 17, 18, 18; 4:6, 8; 5:3, 5, 5, 8, 8, 19, 19; 6:25, 25, 29; 7:8, 13, 21, 21, 22, 25, 25, 26, 27, 27; 8:1; 9:1, 3, 14, 18; 12:4; 14:1, 1; 17:12; 27:16; 30:20, 20, 23; 31:11, 11, 12, 14, 15, 15, 16, 18, 19, 19, 20, 21, 22, 23, 26, 27, 28, 28, 28, 28, 31, 31, 31; Ecc 7:26, 26, 26, 26; SS 6:9, 9, 9; 8:5, 8, 9, 9; Isa 5:14, 14; 10:11; 16:8, 8; 23:16, 16, 17, 18, 18; 27:4, 6, 7, 7, 8, 8; 29:2, 7; 30:7; 32:2; 34:15, 15, 15, 15; 37:22; 40:2, 2, 2, 2, 2; 49:15; 50:1, 1; 51:3, 3; 54:6; 61:10; 62:1, 1, 1; 65:18; 66:10, 10, 10, 11, 12, 12, 12, 12; Jer 2:15, 32, 32; 3:1, 7, 8, 10, 20; 4:31; 6:5, 7, 7; 8:7, 19; 14:2, 5; 15:9; 20:17; 25:11; 30:18; 31:15, 15, 22; 33:6; 44:17, 18, 19, 19, 25; 46:22, 23; 48:2, 2, 2, 4, 5, 9, 11, 12, 12, 12, 13, 13, 15, 15, 17, 25, 25, 26, 26, 27, 29, 29, 29, 30, 30, 39, 41, 41; 49:2, 24, 24, 26, 26; 50:2, 2, 3, 3, 9, 14, 15, 15, 15, 19, 26, 26, 26, 26, 27, 29, 30, 30, 35, 36, 36, 37, 37, 37, 38, 46; 51:2, 2, 2, 2, 4, 6, 6, 8, 8, 9, 9, 9, 9, 9, 11, 28, 29, 30, 33, 36, 36, 41, 43, 47, 47, 47, 49, 52, 53, 53, 55, 55, 56, 57, 58, 64, 64; La 1:1, 2, 2, 2, 2, 2, 2, 3, 3, 4, 4, 5, 5, 5, 5, 5, 6, 7, 7, 7, 7, 7, 7, 8, 8, 8, 8, 9, 10, 10, 11, 17; 2:5, 7, 9, 9, 16, 17, 17; 4:13; Eze 4:7; 5:5, 6; 14:21; 16:2, 3, 32, 45, 45, 46, 46, 48, 49, 50, 57; 17:12, 14, 14, 15; 18:6; 19:2, 3, 5, 5; 20:5, 5, 6, 6; 21:2, 3; 22:2, 3; 23:4, 5, 5, 8, 8, 8, 8, 8, 9, 9, 10, 10, 10, 10, 11, 11, 11, 12, 13, 14, 16, 17, 17, 18, 19, 19, 31; 24:7, 8, 8, 9, 17; 25:3; 28:24; 29:7, 7, 7; 33:28, 28; 36:13, 38; 38:8, 8, 11; Da 11:6, 6, 6, 7; Hos 1:2; 2:2, 2, 2, 3, 3, 4, 6, 6, 6, 7, 8, 9, 9, 10, 10, 10, 11, 11, 11, 11, 12, 12, 12, 13, 13, 13, 13, 14, 14, 14, 15, 15, 15, 15; 3:1, 1, 2, 3; 4:16, 17; 5:3, 5, 5, 5; 9:13; 10:11, 11; Joel 1:8; 2:16; 3:17, 19; Am 5:2; Mic 1:6, 6, 6, 7, 7, 7; 5:3; 7:6, 6; Na 3:2, 4, 4, 9, 9, 10, 10; Zec 5:8; 12:4; Mal 2:14; Mt 1:19, 19, 20, 25; 2:18; 5:28, 31, 32; 8:15, 15; 9:18, 18, 22; 10:35, 35; 14:4, 7, 8, 11; 15:22, 22, 23, 23, 23, 28, 28; 19:7; 20:20; 23:37, 37; 26:10, 13; Mk 1:30, 31, 31, 31; 5:23, 23, 33, 34, 35, 41, 41, 42, 43; 6:17, 24, 24, 24, 28; 7:26, 27, 30; 10:4, 11, 12; 12:21, 22, 23; 14:5, 6, 6, 9; 16:11; Lk 1:28, 30, 36, 36, 41, 56, 58, 58, 58; 2:6, 7, 19, 36, 51; 4:38, 39, 39; 7:12, 13, 38, 38, 44, 44, 47; 8:47, 47, 48, 49, 54, 55, 55, 56; 10:38, 39, 40, 41, 42; 13:12, 12, 13, 14, 16, 34, 34; 15:9, 9, 9; 18:3, 4, 5; 20:31, 33; Jn 4:7, 16, 26, 28; 8:3, 5, 7, 10; 11:2, 2, 23, 25, 28, 31, 31, 33, 33; 12:3, 7; 16:21, 21; 19:26, 27; 20:13, 14, 14, 15; Ac 5:8, 10, 10, 10; 7:21; 9:37, 37, 37, 40, 41, 41; 16:14, 15, 15, 16, 18, 18, 18, 19; 19:27; Ro 7:2, 2, 2, 3, 3; 16:2, 2; 1Co 6:16; 7:2, 3, 3, 4, 4, 10, 11, 12, 13, 14, 34, 34, 39, 39, 40; 11:3, 5, 5, 5, 6, 6, 6, 10, 13, 15; Gal 4:25, 30; Eph 5:23, 25, 26, 27, 33; Col 4:15; 1Th 2:7; 5:3; 1Ti 5:3, 5, 9, 10; Heb 11:31; Jas 2:25; 1Pe 3:6, 6, 6, 7; 2Jn 1; Rev 2:21, 21, 22, 22, 23; 12:1, 1, 2, 4, 6, 14, 14, 16, 17; 14:8; 16:19; 17:2, 2, 4, 4, 5, 6, 16, 16, 16; 18:3, 3, 3, 4, 4, 4, 5, 5, 5, 6, 6, 6, 8, 8, 9, 9, 9, 9, 10, 10, 11, 15, 15, 19, 20, 20, 23, 23, 23, 24; 19:2; 21:2

HERS (3)

Pr 14:1; Isa 10:11; Jer 12:14

HERSELF (28)

Ge 18:12; 20:5; 21:16; 38:14, 14; Lev 18:23; 21:9; Nu 5:14, 27, 28, 29; 30:13; Dt 28:57; Jdg 5:29; Ru 2:3; Jer 3:8; La 1:9; Eze 23:7, 7, 11, 13, 16, 18, 18; Hos 2:15; Mk 5:28; Rev 2:20; 19:7

HIM (3969)

Ge 2:16, 18, 20; 3:2; 4:2, 6, 9, 15, 17, 25, 26; 5:24; 6:9, 22; 7:5, 23; 8:11; 9:23; 12:4, 4, 12, 18; 14:17, 18, 21; 15:1, 4, 5, 6, 7, 9; 16:11, 12, 15; 17:1, 3, 19, 19, 20, 20, 23; 18:9, 18, 19, 19, 23; 19:3, 6, 26, 29, 32, 32, 33, 34, 34, 35, 35, 37, 38; 20:2, 3, 7, 14, 15; 21:4, 17, 18, 18, 21; 22:2, 3, 3, 9, 11; 24:1, 10, 18, 21, 30, 32, 35, 36, 39, 54, 67; 25:2, 9, 25, 26; 26:2, 7, 7, 12, 14, 20, 22, 24, 32; 27:7, 12, 16, 17, 22, 25, 27, 31, 32, 33, 37, 39, 40, 42, 44; 28:1, 6; 29:13, 13, 13, 13, 15, 20, 21, 28, 32, 33, 34, 34, 35; 30:3, 4, 5, 6, 8, 10, 11, 13, 15, 16, 18, 20, 20, 24; 31:2, 7, 18, 21; 32:1, 19, 20, 24, 28, 29; 33:3, 4, 4, 4, 6; 34:8; 35:7, 9, 14, 15, 18, 18, 29; 37:3, 4, 5, 8, 10, 14, 15, 17, 18, 18, 18, 20, 20, 20, 21, 22, 22, 22, 24, 28, 28, 32, 32, 33, 35; 38:4, 5, 14, 16, 18, 22; 39:2, 3, 4, 4, 7, 7, 10, 12, 17, 20, 23; 40:1, 14, 18, 20, 23; 41:15, 17, 33, 42, 45, 45; 42:4, 6, 6, 8, 22, 24, 29, 30, 37, 38; 43:3, 4, 6, 7, 9, 10, 20, 23, 26, 26, 28, 34; 44:14, 20, 21, 21, 24, 28, 29, 32, 32, 34; 45:9, 13, 13, 15, 26, 27, 28; 46:2, 5, 8, 26, 32, 34, 34; 47:2, 7, 8, 20, 29; 48:1, 1, 2, 9, 10, 12; 49:9, 23, 23, 28; 50:1, 1, 14, 15, 18, 26; Ex 1:19; 2:2, 3, 4, 9, 9, 10, 10, 10, 10, 12, 19, 20, 20, 22; 3:2, 4, 5, 7, 12, 18; 4:2, 3, 4, 5, 11, 15, 15, 16, 16, 19, 21, 21, 22, 23, 24, 26, 27, 28; 5:1, 2, 15; 6:1, 11, 20, 23, 25; 7:2, 9, 15, 16, 16; 8:1, 20; 9:1, 13; 10:1, 7; 12:42; 13:19; 14:7, 31; 15:2, 2, 25, 25; 16:8; 17:12; 18:5, 6, 7, 7, 8, 12, 12, 13, 19; 19:3; 20:20; 21:2, 3, 4, 6, 6; 22:17; 23:21, 21, 22; 24:3; 28:39; 29:5, 18, 26, 29; 31:3, 3, 18; 32:1, 3, 29; 33:11; 34:4, 30, 31, 32, 34; 35:31, 34; 39:43; 40:13, 13, 16, 19; Lev 1:1; 7:30, 30; 8:7, 9, 12, 12, 13, 29; 9:9, 12, 13, 18; 10:1; 13:43, 44; 14:24; 15:10, 24; 16:5, 34; 19:22; 20:18; 21:15, 21; 23:13, 18; 24:14, 14, 23; 25:1; 27:26, 30, 32; Nu 5:9; 7:89, 89; 11:20; 12:8, 8; 13:3, 31; 14:24; 15:34, 34, 35, 36; 16:5, 9, 11, 37, 40, 47; 17:11; 20:29; 21:8, 27, 34, 34; 22:5, 7, 9, 16, 20, 31, 35, 36, 40, 41; 23:4, 4, 5, 13, 16, 16; 24:2, 8, 17, 17; 25:12, 12; 27:18, 18, 19, 19, 20, 20, 23, 23; 29:6, 40; 31:41, 54; 32:13, 15; 35:27, 27; Dt 1:3, 30, 36, 38; 2:24, 33, 33; 3:2, 2, 28; 4:7, 29, 29; 6:13, 24; 7:9, 10; 8:6; 9:7, 18, 20, 20, 23, 23; 10:12, 12, 20, 20; 11:13, 22; 13:3, 4, 4, 18, 18; 15:13, 14, 14; 16:10, 10; 17:17, 19, 20, 20; 18:18; 21:5, 15, 18, 21; 22:19; 23:21; 24:7, 7; 25:2, 6, 8, 8, 9; 26:3, 10; 30:6, 20, 20; 31:7, 14, 14; 32:5, 43, 43; 33:12; 34:1, 9, 9; Jos 4:14; 5:13, 13; 8:29, 29; 10:33; 13:1; 14:13; 15:18; 22:5, 5, 16, 29; 23:12, 15; 24:3, 3, 10, 14, 24, 30, 31; Jdg 1:5, 6, 7, 14, 24; 2:7, 9; 3:10, 10, 28; 4:6, 7, 10, 18, 18, 19, 19, 21, 22, 24; 5:25, 25; 6:12, 14, 16, 20, 31, 34; 7:5, 8, 19; 8:31; 9:4, 4, 29, 31, 33, 38, 54; 10:6; 11:3, 32, 34; 12:5, 6, 6, 6, 11; 13:12, 24, 24, 25; 14:6, 16, 17, 19; 15:1, 10, 12, 13, 13; 16:2, 5, 10, 12, 16, 19, 20, 21, 21, 24, 26, 27, 31, 31; 17:9; 18:3, 3, 15, 26; 19:2, 3, 3, 4, 7, 11, 21, 22, 25; Ru 2:10, 20; 3:13, 13; 4:1, 5, 13, 16, 17; 1Sa 1:11, 17, 20, 20, 22, 22, 24, 28; 2:19, 19, 27, 35; 3:13, 15, 16, 18, 19; 4:21; 8:5, 13; 9:6, 7, 7, 8, 13, 16, 25; 10:14, 14, 16, 21, 23, 23, 27, 27; 11:5, 15; 12:2, 13, 13, 15, 20, 24; 13:2, 8, 10, 14, 15; 14:8, 28, 39, 52; 15:12, 13, 13, 17, 22, 27, 27, 28, 31, 35; 16:1, 4, 7, 11, 12, 12, 13, 14, 17, 18, 21, 22; 17:7, 9, 24, 25, 25, 31, 41, 48, 56, 57; 18:2, 2, 4, 5, 8, 11, 12, 12, 13, 13, 14, 15, 17, 17, 21, 28, 29; 19:2, 2, 3, 4, 7, 9, 10, 11, 12, 15, 15, 17, 18, 18, 18, 20, 22; 20:3, 6, 8, 21, 22, 25, 25, 29, 30, 31, 31, 33, 35, 36, 40; 21:1, 6, 12; 22:1, 12, 13, 13, 13, 15; 23:2, 6, 7, 7, 11, 14, 14, 15, 16, 17, 19, 20, 20, 22, 23, 25, 25; 24:4, 5, 6, 8, 8, 10, 19; 25:1, 12, 17, 23, 25, 36, 37, 37, 38, 40; 26:1, 2, 7, 7, 8, 8, 9, 15, 19; 27:3, 4, 6, 12; 28:3, 6, 14, 23, 23; 29:3, 4, 4, 4; 30:6, 8, 11, 11, 12, 13; 31:3, 3; 2Sa 1:6, 7, 7, 10, 15, 15; 2:4, 5, 20, 21, 22, 32; 3:9, 10, 16, 19, 26, 26, 27, 27, 31, 35; 4:4, 4, 6, 10, 10, 10; 5:1, 3, 10, 11, 12, 17; 6:7, 11, 16, 20; 7:14, 15, 17; 8:2, 6; 9:3, 4, 5, 5, 10; 11:7, 10, 12, 13, 13, 21, 21, 26; 12:14, 17, 18, 18, 21, 23, 23, 24, 25; 13:4, 5, 5, 6, 6, 7, 8, 9, 10, 11, 25, 28; 14:3, 4, 7, 8, 14, 21, 22, 29, 29, 29, 32, 33; 15:1, 2, 5, 7, 8, 9, 11, 26, 26, 30, 32, 33; 16:1, 3, 10, 10, 11, 11, 11, 14, 17, 17, 20, 21, 21; 17:2, 6, 12, 16, 16, 21, 21, 22, 29; 18:9, 11, 11, 15, 19, 20, 30; 19:5, 8, 9, 15, 15, 17, 18, 25, 26, 30, 37, 37, 38, 39, 40, 41, 42, 43; 20:2, 5, 6, 6, 9, 9, 10, 10, 12, 12, 12, 21; 21:16; 22:1, 9, 13, 31; 23:10, 13, 21, 23; 24:1, 10, 13, 18, 19, 20, 24; 1Ki 1:1, 2, 4, 5, 6, 7, 13, 14, 15, 16, 23, 25, 31, 34, 35, 35, 42, 44, 44, 45, 47, 53, 53; 2:6, 6, 8, 9, 9, 12, 13, 17, 22, 25, 26, 29, 30, 31, 31, 32, 36, 46; 3:6, 6, 6, 26, 26, 26, 27, 27, 28; 4:21; 5:1, 3, 5, 11; 7:1, 40; 8:14, 18, 25, 59, 62; 9:3, 12; 10:1, 24, 24, 25, 26; 11:9, 11, 13, 19, 20, 22, 28, 29, 32; 12:1, 8, 18, 20, 27; 13:11, 11, 13, 14, 14, 18, 18, 18, 23, 24, 26, 29, 29, 32, 32; 14:3, 3, 8, 13, 13, 16, 18, 18; 15:3, 4, 27; 16:7, 9, 10, 10, 25, 30, 33; 17:5, 6, 19, 21, 23, 23; 18:1, 7, 7, 7, 16, 17, 21, 21, 30, 43, 44, 44; 19:5, 5, 7, 8, 9, 11, 15, 18, 19, 19, 20; 20:7, 13, 17, 23, 31, 33, 33, 34, 36, 36, 37, 39, 41, 42; 21:5, 10, 10, 10, 13, 19, 19, 22, 25; 22:7, 8, 13, 15, 17, 19, 24, 26, 27, 32, 33, 53; 2Ki 1:9, 9, 9, 11, 13, 15, 17; 2:3, 5, 15, 16, 17, 19, 20, 23; 3:7, 12, 27; 4:1, 8, 10, 15, 19, 20, 20, 21, 21, 27, 31, 33, 37, 38; 5:1, 3, 5, 6, 8, 10, 11, 13, 13, 14, 15, 16, 20, 20, 21, 21, 21, 21, 23, 25, 26; 6:1, 6, 7, 13, 16, 17, 22, 26, 29, 29, 29, 32, 32, 32; 7:20; 8:6, 8, 9, 10, 12, 14, 21, 21, 29; 9:1, 2, 3, 11, 15, 16, 21, 25, 25, 26, 26, 27, 27, 28, 28, 31, 32; 10:9, 15, 15, 15, 16, 18; 11:2, 2, 12, 12, 14; 12:2, 20, 20; 13:14, 14, 15, 19; 14:19, 19, 20; 15:10, 14, 19, 25, 30; 16:16; 17:2, 4, 4, 4, 26, 27, 36, 36, 36; 18:5, 7, 7, 30, 37; 19:3, 4, 7, 7, 7, 7, 9, 21, 37; 20:1, 4, 5, 14; 21:23, 23; 22:3, 4, 13, 18; 23:17, 25, 29, 29, 30, 30, 33; 24:1; 25:5, 6, 6, 7, 7, 18, 23, 25, 27, 28, 29, 30; 1Ch 2:3; 4:9, 10; 5:20; 7:22, 23; 9:20; 10:3, 3, 14; 11:1, 3, 9, 15, 23, 25, 42; 12:18; 13:10, 14; 14:1, 2, 8; 15:2, 29; 16:9, 27, 29, 30; 17:13, 14, 15; 18:2, 6; 19:3, 17; 21:6, 19, 20, 26; 22:6, 7, 9; 23:30; 25:5; 28:6, 9, 9, 9, 9; 29:1, 22, 23, 25, 30; 2Ch 1:1, 1, 14; 2:4, 6, 6, 6, 6, 14; 4:11; 6:3, 8, 16; 8:2, 18; 9:1, 2, 8, 12, 23, 23, 24, 25; 10:1, 8, 18; 12:1, 12; 13:5, 7, 10, 11, 20; 14:6, 6; 15:2, 2, 2, 2, 4, 4, 9, 15; 16:7, 9, 10; 17:11; 18:2, 2, 6, 7, 12, 14, 16, 23, 25, 26, 31, 31, 31, 32; 19:2; 20:21, 30; 21:9, 19; 22:3, 4, 6, 9, 9, 9, 11, 11; 23:11, 11, 13; 24:6, 19, 21, 25, 25, 27; 25:14, 16, 20, 23, 27, 27, 28; 26:5, 5, 7, 8, 15, 17, 20, 20; 27:2; 28:20, 21, 23; 29:4, 6, 11, 11, 18, 29; 30:9; 32:6, 15, 21, 24, 24, 25, 25, 29, 31, 33; 33:11, 11, 13, 18, 19, 24, 24; 34:21, 26; 35:20, 22, 23, 24, 24, 24; 36:1, 6, 8, 18, 23; Ezr 1:2; 4:2, 6, 11; 5:15; 7:6, 6, 7, 9, 22, 28; 8:17, 22, 22; 10:1; Ne 1:5; 2:6, 8; 3:4, 8, 10, 16, 20, 25, 29; 4:3; 6:12, 12, 18, 19; 8:5; 9:7, 7, 8, 8; 11:8; 13:26, 26, 26, 28; Est 1:10, 11; 2:21; 3:1, 2, 2, 4, 5; 4:4, 5, 5, 7, 7, 11, 17; 5:9, 11; 6:1, 5, 9, 11, 11, 13, 13; 8:3, 4; 10:3; Job 1:10, 10, 12, 12; 2:3, 4, 6, 9, 11, 12, 13; 5:8; 8:4; 9:3, 4, 11, 11, 12, 12, 13, 14, 16, 19, 22, 32, 32, 35; 11:8, 10, 13; 12:16; 13:8, 9, 10, 11, 15; 15:4, 26; 19:16, 27, 27; 20:7, 9, 14, 15, 16, 18, 22, 23, 23, 24, 25, 27, 28; 21:15; 22:2, 3, 4, 6, 14, 21, 27, 27, 29; 23:3, 7, 8, 9, 9, 13; 24:1, 15, 20, 20, 20; 25:5; 31:37, 37; 32:1, 2, 13; 33:13, 24, 24, 26, 26; 34:27, 29, 33; 35:6, 6, 7, 7, 15; 36:12, 13, 22, 23, 23, 30; 37:24, 24; 42:10, 11, 11, 11, 11, 11; Ps 2:12; 3:2; 4:3; 9:12; 13:4; 14:5; 18:T, 8, 30; 19:2; 20:6, 6; 21:2, 3, 5, 5, 6, 6, 7; 22:8, 8, 8, 23, 23, 23, 26, 27, 27, 30; 24:1; 25:14; 28:7; 31:23; 32:11; 33:1, 2, 3, 8, 18, 21; 34:T, 5, 7, 8, 9, 9, 17, 22, 22; 35:10, 21, 25; 37:5, 7, 22, 40; 40:15; 42:2, 5, 11; 43:5; 45:11; 47:7; 48:1; 50:3, 18; 51:T; 56:T; 59:T; 61:7; 62:1, 5, 8, 8; 63:11, 11; 64:10, 10; 66:17, 17; 67:7; 68:4; 69:30, 34, 36, 36; 70:3; 71:11, 11, 11; 72:2, 4, 9, 9, 10, 10, 11, 11, 12, 14, 15, 15, 15, 17, 17; 73:27; 74:14; 78:22, 34, 36, 36, 37, 40, 58, 70, 71; 81:15; 85:9, 13; 89:3, 19, 20, 21, 21, 22, 22, 23, 23, 24, 27, 28, 28, 28, 29, 33, 33, 38, 39, 40, 40, 41, 42, 43, 45, 45; 91:2; 92:15; 95:2, 2, 5; 96:6, 8, 9; 97:2, 3, 7; 100:2, 4; 102:24; 103:11, 13, 17, 21; 104:34; 105:2, 20, 20; 106:2, 7, 23, 43; 107:32; 109:6, 6, 7, 12, 17, 17, 18, 19, 19, 30; 111:2, 5, 10; 113:6; 116:15, 15; 117:1; 119:2; 120:1; 127:3; 128:4; 130:5; 132:7; 135:1, 6; 136:4, 5, 6, 7, 10, 13, 16, 17; 142:2, 2; 144:2; 145:18, 18, 19, 20; 147:9, 10, 11; 148:1, 2, 2, 3, 3, 4, 4, 8, 14; 150:1, 2, 3, 3, 4, 4, 5, 5; Pr 2:8; 5:22; 6:35; 7:10, 13, 13, 20, 21, 21, 23; 14:2, 31; 18:10; 21:3; 28:17, 17; 30:5; 31:1, 12, 12; Ecc 2:25, 26, 26; 3:14; 4:15, 16; 5:4; 8:3, 5; 9:15; 12:1, 2; SS 1:4; 2:8; 3:2, 3, 4, 4, 4, 4, 11; 4:16; 5:6, 6, 6, 8, 15; 6:1; Isa 2:3; 3:8; 5:9; 6:2; 7:4, 4, 14; 8:3, 13, 17; 10:7, 12; 11:2, 10; 12:2; 14:22, 27; 19:21; 21:7; 22:15, 22, 23; 25:9; 28:12, 26; 29:15; 30:18, 18; 32:1; 36:15, 22; 37:3, 4, 7, 7, 7, 9, 22, 38; 38:1, 5; 39:3; 40:10, 15, 16, 17, 18, 22; 41:2, 2, 25; 42:1, 1; 44:10, 12, 20; 45:1, 1, 24, 24, 25; 48:14, 15, 15; 49:5; 51:2, 2; 52:14; 53:2, 3, 4, 6, 8, 10, 10, 12; 55:6, 6; 56:6, 6; 61:11; 62:11; 63:10; 64:4; 66:5; Jer 2:19, 31; 3:13, 25; 5:19; 10:14; 11:19; 13:16; 18:18, 18; 20:2, 3, 10, 11, 16, 16; 21:1, 3; 22:1, 15, 16, 18; 26:8, 8, 8, 9, 19, 19, 21, 23, 23, 23, 24; 27:7, 8; 29:29, 31, 32; 30:21; 31:20, 20, 20, 20; 32:3, 5, 10; 33:1; 34:2; 35:8; 36:4, 8, 31; 37:13, 15, 17; 38:6, 8, 11, 13, 14, 16, 27, 27; 39:5, 5, 7, 7, 9, 12, 12, 14, 14; 40:1, 3, 5, 14, 15; 41:8, 10, 12, 12; 42:6, 12; 44:20, 23, 30; 45:1; 46:25; 50:43; 51:17, 31, 44; 52:8, 9, 9, 11, 11, 24, 31, 32, 33, 34; La 1:18; 2:8, 19; 3:24, 25, 25; Eze 1:28; 9:4, 5; 10:9; 12:12, 13, 13; 13:6; 17:7, 13, 16, 19, 20, 20, 20, 20; 19:4, 4, 5, 5, 7, 8, 8, 8, 8, 9, 9, 9; 21:27; 24:27; 28:12; 29:20; 32:2; 38:3, 14; 39:1; 40:46; 43:3; 46:12, 12, 16; Da 1:2, 2, 19; 2:1, 2, 15, 24, 24, 46, 46, 48; 3:13, 28; 4:8, 8, 9, 15, 15, 16, 19, 23, 23, 35, 35, 35; 5:6, 6, 7, 8, 11, 11, 13, 19, 19; 6:3, 11, 12, 16, 23; 7:10, 10, 14, 16; 8:11, 12; 9:3, 9, 14; 10:9, 13, 19; 11:6, 7, 8, 16, 17, 18, 22, 25, 30, 32, 38, 39, 40, 40, 44, 45; Hos 1:2, 9; 2:7; 5:6; 6:3; 7:5, 10, 10; 9:4, 8; 11:1, 2, 3, 3, 4; 12:4, 4; 13:10; 14:2; Joel 1:14; Am 2:4; 7:1, 4; Jnh 1:6, 11, 14, 15, 16, 16; 4:6; Mic 3:4; 4:2; 6:7, 7; 7:9, 17; Na 1:2, 7; Hab 2:20; 3:5; Zec 1:8; 2:3; 3:5; 4:7; 6:12; 12:10, 10; 13:3, 3; 14:5; Mal 2:17, 17, 17, 17; 3:2, 4, 16, 16; 4:4; Mt 1:20, 21, 25; 2:2, 7, 8, 8, 11, 11, 11, 16, 16, 19; 3:3, 5, 14, 15, 16, 17; 4:3, 4, 5, 8, 8, 10, 10, 20, 22, 24, 25; 5:3; 6:8, 26, 33; 7:11; 8:2, 3, 4, 4, 5, 7, 15, 19, 22, 25, 25, 27, 28, 29, 34; 9:2, 9, 9, 14, 18, 20, 24, 27, 28, 32, 38; 10:1, 4, 31; 11:4, 6, 7, 7, 27; 12:10, 15, 17, 18, 18, 29, 29, 42, 46; 13:10, 27, 56, 57; 14:6, 15, 26, 28, 31, 33, 36; 15:12, 16, 22, 23, 25, 30, 32; 16:1, 21, 22, 22; 17:5, 5, 16, 16, 18, 24, 25; 18:2, 21, 23, 24, 26, 27, 27, 28, 28, 29, 31; 19:2, 3, 10, 13, 21, 27; 20:17, 18, 19, 34; 21:7, 9, 14, 23, 25, 32, 32, 36, 38, 39, 39, 39, 41, 46; 22:13, 13, 15, 16, 19, 21, 33, 34, 35, 43, 45, 46, 46; 23:15; 24:1, 3, 51; 25:6, 10, 14, 31; 26:4, 15, 18, 22, 24, 25, 25, 48, 49, 50, 52, 56, 57, 59, 63, 67, 67, 69, 71, 73; 27:2, 2, 3, 11, 12, 19, 19, 22, 23, 26, 26, 28, 28, 29, 30, 30, 31, 31, 31, 32, 34, 35, 37, 38, 42, 42, 43, 44, 44, 48, 49, 49, 55, 58, 63; 28:4, 7, 9, 9, 17, 17; Mk 1:3, 10, 13, 18, 20, 25, 26, 36, 41, 43, 43, 44, 45, 45; 2:13, 14, 14, 16; 3:2, 2, 4, 8, 10, 10, 11, 11, 13, 13, 16, 19, 21, 27, 27, 31, 34; 4:10, 38, 41; 5:2, 4, 6, 6, 10, 20, 21, 22, 23, 24, 27, 30, 31, 33, 37, 40; 6:2, 3, 14, 20, 20, 25, 27, 30, 35, 49, 50, 54, 55, 56; 7:5, 17, 25, 26, 32, 32, 33; 8:11, 11, 22, 23, 23, 26, 30, 32, 32; 9:7, 11, 15, 17, 17, 18, 18, 18, 22, 22, 25, 26, 27, 27, 28, 32, 35, 38, 39; 10:2, 13, 21, 21, 32, 33, 33, 34, 34, 34, 34, 35, 48, 49, 49, 52; 11:9, 14, 18, 18, 27, 31; 12:3, 3, 4, 4, 6, 7, 8, 8, 12, 12, 12, 16, 17, 33, 34, 34, 37, 37, 43; 13:3, 3, 36; 14:1, 11, 12, 13, 19, 21, 29, 33, 35, 35, 44, 44, 45, 46, 50, 51, 55, 56, 57, 58, 61, 64, 65, 65, 65, 67, 69; 15:1, 3, 4, 8, 13, 14, 15, 15, 16, 17, 19, 19, 20, 20, 20, 21, 23, 24, 26, 27, 29, 32, 32, 36, 36, 36, 39, 41, 41, 44; 16:7, 9, 11, 12, 14; Lk 1:13, 31, 32, 50, 59, 62, 66; 2:5, 7, 7, 12, 21, 22, 22, 26, 27, 40, 43, 44, 45, 45, 46, 47, 48, 52; 3:4, 22; 4:2, 3, 4, 5, 5, 6, 8, 9, 13, 17, 20, 22, 29, 29, 29, 35, 35, 35, 36, 42, 42, 42; 5:1, 9, 14, 14, 15, 19, 27, 28; 6:7, 11, 16, 18, 19, 19; 7:3, 11, 11, 15, 19, 20, 22, 23, 24, 38, 39, 39, 41, 42, 42; 8:1, 4, 9, 19, 19, 24, 25, 27, 28, 29, 32, 39, 40, 41, 41, 42, 46, 47, 47, 51, 53; 9:9, 11, 12, 32, 35, 38, 39, 39, 39, 39, 41, 42, 42, 42, 45, 49, 50, 62; 10:2, 17, 22, 25, 28, 30, 30, 30, 31, 32, 34, 34, 34, 35, 37; 11:1, 5, 6, 13, 14, 22, 22, 30, 30, 31, 37, 39, 53, 54, 54; 12:7, 20, 24, 36, 46; 13:23, 31; 14:1, 4, 4, 5, 31; 15:15, 16, 16, 20, 20, 20, 21, 22, 28, 31; 16:2, 5, 6, 6, 25, 27, 28; 17:3, 4, 8, 16, 23; 18:3, 4, 7, 15, 19, 24, 31, 33, 33, 37, 40, 40; 19:5, 10, 13, 14, 14, 14, 35, 47; 20:1, 5, 10, 10, 13, 14, 15, 15, 19, 25, 26, 38, 44; 21:38; 22:2, 5, 6, 9, 10, 43, 47, 51, 54, 54, 56, 56, 58, 63, 64, 64, 65, 71; 23:3, 7, 8, 8, 11, 11, 14, 14, 15, 16, 16, 18, 21, 21, 22, 22, 22, 32, 35, 36, 36, 37, 38, 39, 49, 56; 24:16, 20, 20, 20, 29, 31, 35, 42, 52; Jn 1:4, 10, 10, 12, 12, 15, 18, 25, 29, 31, 32, 36, 39, 41, 43, 45, 50; 2:3, 3, 11, 25; 3:16, 18, 18, 23, 26, 28, 29, 33, 34, 35; 4:22, 23, 24, 27, 27, 30, 33, 40, 40, 42, 45, 47, 47, 50, 51, 53; 5:6, 6, 8, 14, 14, 15, 18, 20, 23, 27, 37; 6:2, 3, 5, 15, 15, 16, 21, 22, 24, 25, 40, 46, 64, 66, 71; 7:3, 5, 11, 11, 12, 13, 15, 26, 29, 29, 30, 30, 31, 39, 40, 43, 44, 44, 45, 45, 48; 8:6, 6, 29, 30, 30, 31, 44, 50, 55, 55, 55, 55, 59; 9:2, 3, 7, 8, 9, 21, 21, 23, 24, 28, 29, 30, 31, 34, 37, 39, 40; 10:3, 3, 4, 5, 19, 24, 31, 39, 41, 42; 11:3, 11, 15, 20, 27, 28, 29, 30, 34, 36, 36, 44, 44, 48, 48, 57, 57; 12:2, 4, 9, 11, 13, 18, 19, 29, 37, 42; 13:3, 5, 6, 11, 24, 27, 27, 29; 14:6, 7, 7, 9, 17, 17, 17, 22; 16:7, 19, 23; 17:2, 2; 18:3, 4, 12, 13, 24, 25, 30, 31, 31, 33, 33; 19:2, 3, 4, 4, 6, 6, 6, 9, 12, 12, 15, 15, 15, 16, 18, 18, 19, 37, 38; 20:2, 13, 14, 15, 15, 15, 16, 25, 29, 30, 31; 21:12, 15, 17, 19, 19, 21, 22, 23; Ac 1:6, 10, 11; 2:22, 23, 23, 24, 24, 24, 25, 33, 37; 3:4, 7, 9, 9, 13, 15, 26; 4:19; 5:6, 6, 6, 30, 30, 31, 32, 36, 37, 37; 6:9, 11, 12, 14; 7:3, 4, 5, 6, 7, 9, 9, 10, 10, 10, 10, 20, 21, 21, 24, 25, 27, 31, 33, 35, 38, 57, 58, 58, 59; 8:10, 26, 31, 35, 38, 39; 9:3, 4, 9, 10, 12, 12, 16, 17, 21, 23, 24, 25, 26, 27, 29, 30, 30, 34, 38, 39, 39; 10:3, 4, 6, 13, 19, 22, 24, 25, 26, 35, 38, 39, 39, 40, 40, 41, 43, 48; 11:2, 13, 13, 26, 26; 12:4, 4, 5, 7, 7, 8, 10, 17, 19, 20, 22; 13:7, 11, 11, 13, 22, 22, 22, 27, 28, 28, 29, 29, 30, 30, 31, 34, 39; 14:9, 10, 19, 20; 15:8, 39; 16:3, 9, 28, 32; 17:15, 15, 19, 23, 23, 27, 27, 28, 30, 31, 34; 18:6, 6, 9, 12, 17, 18, 20, 26, 26, 27, 27; 19:9, 30, 31, 31, 33; 20:4, 10, 10, 13, 17, 37, 38, 38; 21:12, 14, 27, 27, 29, 29, 30, 31, 33, 33, 35, 36, 36; 22:2, 13, 14, 20, 22, 24, 24, 25, 29; 23:2, 3, 4, 9, 9, 10, 10, 10, 10, 15, 17, 19, 19, 20, 21, 21, 22, 24, 27, 27, 28, 30, 30, 32, 35, 35; 24:5, 6, 8, 10, 23, 23, 26, 26, 26, 26; 25:2, 3, 9, 14, 15, 15, 18, 20, 21, 21, 25, 26, 26, 26, 27; 26:26, 28; 27:3; 28:4, 6, 6, 8, 8, 8, 30, 31; Ro 1:4, 5, 21, 21; 2:17; 3:7, 30; 4:2, 3, 10, 10, 11, 11, 17, 18, 22, 23; 6:3, 5, 9; 8:15, 30, 32; 9:4, 30, 33; 10:4, 6, 9, 11, 14, 14, 14, 14, 14; 11:35, 36, 36; 14:4, 6; 15:11, 12, 13, 16, 21, 21; 1Co 1:21; 2:9, 16; 6:17; 7:11, 12, 13, 14, 32; 8:6; 15:8, 27; 16:10, 11, 11, 11, 12; 2Co 1:20; 2:6, 7, 7, 8, 8, 10, 10, 13; 3:18; 5:9, 16, 18; 7:13, 14, 15, 15; 11:23; 12:18; 13:4; Gal 1:8, 18; 2:11; 3:6, 27, 29; 4:5; Eph 1:5, 19, 20, 22; 2:6, 13, 17, 22; 3:7, 12, 17; 4:18, 21; 5:2, 6; 6:20, 22; Php 1:29, 30; 2:9, 9, 13, 23, 26, 27, 28, 29, 29; 3:9,

10, 10, 20; **4:**6, 18; **Col 1:**9, 16, 16, 20, 21, 22; **2:**3, 6, 7, 7, 12; **3:**17; **4:**8; **1Th 3:**2, 13; **4:**15, 17; **5:**10; **2Th 1:**10, 10, 12; **2:**1, 6; **1Ti 1:**12, 16; **3:**4, 6, 7; **5:**1, 19; **6:**16, 16, 16; **2Ti 1:**12, 18; **2:**11, 11, 12, 12, 26; **4:**14, 15; **Tit 1:**3, 16; **Phm 1:**10, 12, 12, 13, 15, 17; **Heb 1:**3, 4, 6; **2:**3, 6, 6, 7, 7, 8, 10, 13; **3:**2, 8, 15, 18; **4:**7, 13, 14, 14; **5:**5, 6, 7, 9, 9, 10; **6:**6, 6, 10, 10, 18; **7:**1, 1, 4, 10, 25; **8:**5; **9:**28; **10:**22; **11:**5, 6, 6, 7, 8, 8, 9, 17, 18, 19, 23, 26; **12:**3, 28; **13:**13, 20, 20, 23; **Jas 1:**5, 6, 6, 12; **2:**5, 22, 23; **4:**10; **1Pe 1:**5, 8, 8, 8, 8, 9, 17, 20, 21; **2:**4, 5, 6, 7; **3:**6, 22; **4:**11; **5:**9; **2Pe 1:**17, 18; **2:**7, 16; **3:**15, 18; **1Jn 1:**1, 1, 2, 5, 9; **2:**3, 5, 5, 28; **3:**2, 2, 5, 6, 6, 12, 22, 22, 24; **4:**9, 13, 16, 17, 21; **5:**14; **2Jn** 10, 10, 11; **3Jn** 12; **Jude** 15, 25, 25; **Rev 1:**1, 5, 6, 7, 7, 7, 17; **4:**4; **7:**14, 15; **8:**3; **10:**9, 9; **11:**16; **12:**11; **13:**2, 4; **14:**1, 7, 7, 8; **16:**9; **17:**13, 16; **19:**1, 5, 7, 10, 12, 14, 20; **20:**2, 3, 6; **22:**3

HIMSELF (326)

Ge 1:27; **8:**21; **13:**11; **17:**17; **22:**6; **27:**22, 41; **33:**17; **39:**12; **43:**31, 32; **44:**18; **50:**1; **Ex 3:**3; **14:**14; **21:**10; **30:**12; **32:**16; **Lev 9:**8, 15; **15:**14; **16:**6, 11, 17, 24, 28; **18:**23; **21:**4, 11; **Nu 16:**4; **19:**7; **32:**42; **Dt 3:**14; **4:**34; **9:**10; **10:**9; **12:**5; **17:**16, 17, 17, 18; **18:**2; **23:**11; **28:**20; **31:**3; **Jos 7:**15; **8:**13; **22:**23; **Jdg 3:**16; **6:**31, 32; **Ru 1:**13; **1Sa 12:**22; **13:**9; **15:**12; **18:**17, 21; **19:**22; **20:**3, 17, 24, 26; **23:**7; **24:**3, 6; **27:**1, 12; **28:**8; **29:**4; **2Sa 3:**31; **6:**20; **12:**18, 20; **17:**15, 23; **18:**18, 18; **22:**12; **1Ki 1:**5, 5, 11, 50, 52; **3:**9; **7:**1; **12:**21, 26, 32, 33; **16:**18; **17:**21; **18:**6, 6, 27; **20:**38; **21:**25, 29; **22:**30; **2Ki 4:**35; **5:**14, 20; **12:**18; **15:**5; **18:**25; **24:**11; **1Ch 15:**1; **29:**1; **2Ch 2:**1, 12; **11:**1; **12:**12, 13; **16:**14; **18:**29, 34; **20:**29; **23:**16; **24:**21; **26:**20; **33:**23; **36:**12; **Ezr 1:**7; **10:**1; **Ne 9:**8; **Est 1:**8; **3:**1; **5:**10, 12; **6:**6; **10:**3; **Job 1:**5; **13:**3; **20:**21; **22:**25; **Ps 4:**3; **18:**11; **45:**2; **46:**5; **48:**3, 3; **50:**6; **64:**7; **68:**16; **78:**19; **110:**7; **121:**5; **130:**8; **135:**4; **Pr 23:**11; **Ecc 4:**8; **SS 3:**9; **Isa 7:**14; **19:**21; **28:**5; **36:**10; **38:**15; **44:**15, 15, 16, 20; **53:**12; **59:**16, 17; **Jer 20:**10; **25:**26; **41:**9; **43:**12; **La 4:**16; **Eze 44:**3, 25, 27; **45:**22; **Da 1:**8; **2:**22; **5:**5, 11; **6:**3, 14; **11:**28, 36; **Hos 7:**5; **Ob** 21; **Jnh 3:**6; **Mic 2:**13; **7:**8; **Zep 3:**15; **Mt 12:**26; **14:**13, 23; **24:**36; **27:**5, 42; **Mk 3:**26; **5:**5; **6:**46; **12:**36, 37; **13:**32; **14:**54, 67; **15:**31; **16:**S; **Lk 3:**21; **7:**39; **11:**18; **12:**37; **15:**17; **16:**3; **18:**4, 11; **19:**9; **20:**13, 42; **23:**35; **24:**15, 27, 36; **Jn 1:**8, 18; **4:**2; **5:**18, 19, 26, 26, 37; **6:**61; **8:**41, 59; **9:**21, 23; **11:**51; **16:**27; **18:**5, 18; **19:**7, 12, 17; **Ac 2:**29, 34; **7:**37; **8:**13, 34, 40; **9:**8; **12:**11; **13:**7; **14:**17; **15:**14; **16:**27; **17:**25; **19:**4; **20:**32; **25:**4; **Ro 1:**25; **3:**30; **8:**30, 33; **9:**5; **10:**3; **15:**3; **1Co 1:**30; **4:**4; **5:**5; **6:**16; **11:**23; **14:**37; **15:**27, 28; **2Co 4:**14; **5:**1, 5, 18, 19, 20; **8:**17; **10:**1; **11:**2, 14; **12:**12; **Gal 1:**1, 12; **2:**20; **3:**13; **4:**14; **Eph 1:**5; **2:**14, 15, 20; **3:**3; **5:**2, 27, 28, 33; **Php 1:**28; **2:**7, 8, 22; **3:**9; **Col 1:**20; **2:**2, 17; **1Th 3:**11; **4:**9, 16; **2Th 2:**4, 4, 4; **3:**16; **2Ti 2:**13; **Heb 2:**3, 18; **5:**5; **6:**17; **7:**27; **8:**8; **9:**14, 25; **10:**12; **12:**21, 23; **Jas 4:**6; **1Pe 1:**16; **4:**11; **5:**5; **1Jn 4:**21; **Rev 21:**3

HIS (5676)

Ge 1:27; **2:**2, 2, 3, 24, 24, 25; **3:**15, 20, 21, 23; **4:**1, 3, 4, 8, 8, 17, 21, 25, 26; **5:**3, 3, 6, 9, 12, 15, 18, 21, 24, 25, 28, 29; **6:**6, 9; **7:**7, 7, 13, 13; **8:**9, 18, 18; **9:**1, 8, 21, 22, 22, 24, 24, 26, 27; **10:**9, 10, 11, 25, 25; **11:**10, 12, 14, 16, 18, 20, 22, 24, 28, 28, 29, 31, 31, 31, 31; **12:**5, 5, 5, 5, 5, 12, 15, 20; **13:**1, 11, 11, 12, 18; **14:**5, 13, 14, 15, 16, 16, 17, 17; **15:**6; **16:**2, 12; **17:**11, 12, 19, 20, 23, 23, 25; **18:**1, 19, 29, 33, 33, 33; **19:**14, 16, 16, 30; **20:**2, 2, 2, 8, 14, 17; **21:**2, 3, 7, 11, 18, 21, 22, 32; **22:**3, 3, 3, 10, 13, 20, 24, 24; **23:**9; **24:**2, 2, 7, 10, 15, 30, 30, 38, 38, 38, 40, 47, 59, 67, 67, 67; **25:**1, 5, 6, 8, 9, 10, 17, 21, 26, 30, 33, 33, 34, 34; **26:**7, 11, 13, 15, 18, 19, 24, 25, 25, 26, 26; **27:**1, 14, 16, 18, 22, 23, 25, 27, 27, 30, 30, 31, 36, 37, 37, 39, 41; **28:**5, 5, 6, 7, 8, 9, 9; **29:**6, 10, 10, 10, 10, 11, 13, 20; **30:**4, 9, 14, 35, 40, 40; **31:**1, 7, 8, 17, 18, 18, 19, 21, 23, 25, 31, 35, 46, 53, 55; **32:**1, 3, 6, 7, 16, 18, 22, 23, 31; **33:**1, 2, 2, 3, 17, 17; **34:**4, 5, 5, 8, 8, 19, 20; **35:**2, 22, 27, 29, 29; **36:**3, 6, 6, 12, 18, 24, 25, 32; **37:**1, 2, 2, 2, 2, 2, 3, 3, 4, 5, 8, 8, 9, 10, 10, 10, 10, 11, 11, 14, 14, 17, 20, 22, 22, 23, 27, 27, 28, 29, 30, 34, 34, 35; **38:**6, 6, 7, 9, 9, 10, 11, 11, 11, 12, 12, 16, 20, 24, 26, 28, 29, 30; **39:**2, 4, 4, 5, 5, 8, 9, 11, 12, 12, 13, 15, 18, 19; **40:**9, 13, 14, 16, 20, 20, 21; **41:**2, 8, 37, 42, 42, 42, 43, 50, 51, 52; **42:**1, 6, 21, 21, 25, 25, 27, 27, 28, 37, 38, 38; **43:**2, 8, 9, 16, 29, 30, 30, 31, 32, 33; **44:**1, 1, 1, 2, 4, 9, 14, 16, 20, 20, 20, 20, 20, 22, 22, 29, 31, 33; **45:**1, 1, 2, 3, 3, 8, 15, 16, 23, 23, 24, 27; **46:**1, 1, 5, 6, 7, 22, 26, 29, 29, 29, 29, 31; **47:**2, 7, 11, 12, 26, 28, 29, 29, 31, 31; **48:**1, 1, 2, 10, 13, 14, 14, 14, 14, 17, 17, 18, 19, 19, 19; **49:**1, 10, 11, 11, 11, 11, 12, 12, 13, 15, 16, 22, 24, 24, 26, 27, 28, 31, 31, 33, 33; **50:**1, 2, 4, 5, 8, 13, 14, 14, 18, 22, 23, 23, 24, 26; **Ex 1:**1, 6, 9, 22; **2:**6, 11, 11, 13, 21, 21, 24; **3:**1, 6, 6, 13; **4:**6, 7, 14, 18, 20, 20, 24, 25; **5:**19, 21; **6:**1, 20; **7:**10, 10, 11, 19, 20, 20, 23, 23; **8:**5, 15, 16, 32; **9:**7, 23, 33, 34; **10:**1, 13, 22; **11:**5, 10; **12:**30, 42; **13:**3, 19; **14:**4, 5, 6, 6, 9, 10, 17, 18, 21, 27, 31; **15:**3, 26, 26; **16:**9; **17:**10, 11, 11, 12, 13; **18:**1, 2, 2, 2, 4, 4, 7, 8, 8, 11, 16, 17, 24, 24, 27, 27; **19:**19; **20:**7, 20; **21:**2, 3, 4, 4, 4, 6, 6, 6, 6, 7, 9, 9, 10; **22:**16; **23:**21; **24:**10, 13; **27:**21; **28:**1, 2, 2, 29, 29, 30, 38, 41, 43, 43; **29:**1, 4, 6, 7, 8, 9, 10, 15, 19, 20, 21, 22, 24, 27, 28, 29, 32, 35, 44; **30:**13, 19, 21, 30; **31:**6, 10; **32:**11, 14, 14, 15; **33:**11; **34:**4, 5, 5, 14, 29, 33, 35; **35:**19; **39:**27, 41; **40:**12, 14; **Lev 2:**3, 10; **4:**4, 6, 17, 22, 23, 23, 24, 24, 25, 30, 34; **6:**9, 10, 11, 16, 20, 25, 26; **7:**31, 35; **8:**2, 6, 7, 12, 14, 15, 18, 22, 23, 23, 27, 30, 30, 30, 31, 36; **9:**1, 9, 9, 12, 18, 22; **10:**6, 12, 19; **13:**2, 12, 40, 40, 41, 42; **14:**15, 16, 17, 26, 27, 28, 48; **15:**11, 13, 14, 15, 16; **16:**4, 4, 4, 4, 4, 4, 6, 11, 12, 14, 17, 19, 21, 24, 24, 24, 26, 28, 32; **17:**2; **18:**14; **20:**11, 12, 17, 17, 17, 17, 17, 19, 19, 19, 20, 20, 21, 21; **21:**4, 6, 6, 10, 10, 10, 11, 12, 12, 12, 14, 15, 15, 17, 20, 21, 21, 23, 24; **22:**2, 10, 11, 11, 11, 11, 18; **24:**9, 11, 14; **27:**12; **Nu 1:**20; **3:**6, 9, 10, 18, 19, 20, 38, 48, 51; **4:**5, 11, 15, 19, 27, 49; **5:**14, 15, 30, 30, 31; **6:**23, 26, 26, 27; **7:**11, 12, 18, 24, 30, 36, 42, 48, 54, 60, 66, 72, 78; **8:**13, 19, 22; **10:**10, 29; **11:**1, 28, 29; **14:**24; **15:**31, 39; **16:**4, 5, 5, 7, 17, 40; **17:**2, 9; **19:**3, 4, 7, 8, 10; **20:**11, 13, 20, 24, 25, 26, 26; **21:**23, 23, 26, 29, 29, 33, 34, 34, 35, 35; **22:**3, 5, 21, 22, 23, 27, 31, 36; **23:**2, 6, 19; **24:**10, 23; **25:**3, 4, 8, 13, 13; **26:**33; **27:**3, 8, 8, 9, 9, 10, 10, 11, 11, 11, 23, 23; **30:**16; **31:**28; **32:**21; **33:**40; **35:**28, 32; **36:**2; **Dt 1:**31, 36, 36; **2:**15, 24, 31, 31, 32, 33, 33, 34; **3:**1, 2, 2, 3, 4, 4, 11; **4:**12, 12, 13, 20, 25, 36, 36, 46, 47; **5:**5, 11, 22, 24, 24, 32; **6:**2, 13, 15, 22; **7:**6, 7, 9, 9, 12; **8:**2, 6, 11; **10:**6, 6, 8, 12, 15, 20; **11:**1, 2, 3, 22, 28; **12:**5, 11, 21; **13:**4, 4, 17; **14:**2, 23, 23, 24; **15:**17; **16:**2, 6, 11; **17:**16, 19, 20, 20; **18:**7, 7, 8, 22; **19:**9; **21:**16, 17, 17, 17, 18; **22:**13, 16, 30, 30; **23:**1; **25:**2, 5, 6, 7, 9, 9, 9, 9, 10; **26:**2, 5, 17, 17, 18, 18, 18; **27:**20, 20, 22, 22, 22, 23; **28:**9, 9, 12, 54, 54, 54, 55; **29:**2, 2, 13, 15, 20, 23, 24, 28; **30:**10, 16, 16; **31:**29; **32:**4, 5, 9, 10, 11, 11, 16, 16, 19, 36, 36, 36, 43, 43, 43, 43, 50; **33:**1, 2, 16, 17, 21, 24, 24, 27; **34:**7, 9, 11, 11, 12; **Jos 4:**14; **5:**14; **6:**19, 26, 26, 27; **7:**2, 24, 25; **8:**1, 1, 1, 10, 14, 26; **9:**24; **10:**2, 24, 25, 33, 33, 42; **11:**7, 15; **12:**2, 5; **19:**49; **22:**5, 5, 19, 27; **23:**16; **24:**3, 4, 28, 33; **Jdg 1:**6, 25; **2:**18; **3:**9, 15, 16, 16, 19, 20, 21, 21, 26; **4:**2, 7, 11, 11, 13, 13, 14, 15, 15, 21, 22; **5:**11, 17, 18, 26, 26, 26, 28, 28; **6:**21, 27, 27, 31, 31, 31; **7:**1, 5, 13, 14, 21; **8:**4, 20, 20, 27, 27, 32; **9:**1, 1, 3, 5, 5, 16, 17, 18, 18, 18, 19, 21, 26, 28, 31, 34, 35, 38, 41, 43, 43, 44, 48, 48, 48, 53, 54, 54, 56, 56; **10:**4; **11:**1, 3, 17, 19, 20, 20, 21, 32, 34, 34, 35, 39; **12:**4, 9, 9, 9, 9; **13:**2, 5, 6, 7, 7, 9, 9, 11, 19, 20, 21, 22, 23; **14:**2, 3, 3, 4, 5, 6, 6, 9, 9, 10, 11, 19, 19, 20; **15:**1, 6, 6, 14, 14; **16:**3, 9, 12, 13, 14, 17, 19, 19, 19, 19, 21, 22, 29, 29, 30, 31, 31, 31; **17:**2, 2, 4, 5, 12; **18:**4, 22, 27; **19:**1, 7, 9, 9, 10, 10, 12, 16, 25, 28, 29; **Ru 1:**1, 2, 6; **2:**5, 10, 14, 15, 20, 21, 22; **3:**2, 3, 4, 7, 7, 8; **4:**7, 8, 10; **1Sa 1:**3, 4, 9, 11, 11, 28; **2:**9, 10, 10, 19, 20, 22, 22, 28, 35, 35, 36; **3:**12, 13, 13, 14; **4:**12, 12, 12, 13, 18, 18; **5:**3, 4, 4; **7:**1, 15, 16, 17; **8:**1, 2, 11, 11, 12, 12, 12, 12, 14, 15, 16, 17; **9:**2, 4, 5, 11, 22, 27; **10:**1, 9, 10, 11, 12, 15, 16, 24, 26, 26; **11:**1, 11; **12:**3, 5, 14, 15, 22, 22; **13:**7, 8, 14, 14, 15; **14:**1, 1, 2, 6, 12, 13, 17, 20, 27, 36, 45, 47, 47, 50, 50, 52; **15:**4, 9, 22, 27, 29, 29, 34; **16:**1, 3, 5, 7, 8, 13; **17:**2, 6, 7, 15, 22, 22, 23, 25, 25, 26, 38, 40, 40, 41, 43, 47, 47, 49, 49, 51, 54, 55, 57, 58; **18:**4, 5, 7, 7, 10, 13, 13, 16, 22, 22, 27, 27, 29; **19:**1, 1, 1, 2, 4, 5, 8, 9, 10, 13, 15, 24; **20:**7, 17, 25, 29, 33, 33, 34, 35, 38, 40, 41; **21:**11, 11, 11, 13, 14; **22:**1, 4, 6, 6, 6, 7, 11, 17; **23:**5, 8, 8, 13, 16, 23, 24, 25, 26, 26; **24:**2, 3, 6, 7, 7, 14, 19, 19, 22; **25:**1, 1, 3, 3, 4, 5, 9, 13, 17, 20, 21, 22, 24, 25, 29, 37, 39, 39, 42, 43, 44; **26:**2, 4, 5, 7, 7, 11, 11, 16, 19, 23; **27:**2, 3, 8; **28:**3, 7, 7, 8, 8, 8, 18, 25; **29:**2, 4, 5, 5, 6; **30:**1, 3, 6, 6, 9, 10, 12, 16, 17, 18, 20, 20, 26, 27; **31:**2, 2, 4, 4, 4, 5, 5, 6, 6, 6, 7, 8, 9, 10, 10, 12; **2Sa 1:**1, 2, 2, 4, 6, 10, 10, 11, 12, 15, 15; **2:**2, 3, 6, 11, 16, 16, 19, 21, 23, 23, 28, 28, 29, 30, 30, 32, 32; **3:**7, 20, 21, 27, 27, 29, 29, 30, 32; **4:**1, 7, 7, 7, 8, 10, 11, 11, 12; **5:**6, 8, 9, 12, 12, 21; **6:**6, 11, 14, 20, 21; **7:**1, 12, 13, 14; **8:**3, 10, 10, 13; **9:**6, 9, 10, 11; **10:**1, 2, 2, 9, 9, 10, 11, 13, 19; **11:**11, 13, 19, 27; **12:**3, 3, 3, 4, 4, 8, 8, 9, 15, 20, 21, 24, 25, 29, 31; **13:**2, 3, 9, 17, 22, 24, 25, 27, 28, 31, 31, 32, 36, 37, 37, 39; **14:**7, 7, 24, 26, 27, 30, 30, 33; **15:**10, 11, 14, 15, 16, 16, 17, 20, 22, 23, 30, 30, 31, 32, 32; **16:**5, 8, 8, 9, 13, 15, 22; **17:**2, 8, 10, 12, 16, 18, 23, 23, 23, 23, 23, 24, 25, 25, 25; **18:**1, 2, 3, 5, 9, 9, 9, 13, 16, 18, 19, 20, 28, 33; **19:**2, 4, 4, 24, 24, 32, 39; **20:**3, 8, 8, 9, 10, 10, 10, 12, 14, 21, 22; **21:**1, 2, 3, 12, 15, 16, 17, 19, 22; **22:**1, 7, 7, 8, 9, 9, 10, 12, 15, 15, 15, 16, 23, 23, 25, 31, 51; **23:**2, 5, 8, 10, 10, 12, 15, 18, 23; **24:**2, 4, 14, 20, 20, 25; **1Ki 1:**2, 5, 6, 7, 9, 10, 27, 41, 47, 47; **2:**1, 3, 5, 12, 19, 19, 19, 19, 22, 23, 26, 27, 31, 33, 33, 33, 34, 40; **3:**1, 1, 3, 7, 15, 27; **4:**2, 21, 26, 27, 27, 30, 31; **5:**3, 3, 11; **6:**38; **7:**8, 14, 14, 51, 51; **8:**22, 54, 56, 56, 58, 59, 61, 61, 66, 66; **9:**8, 8, 9, 16, 18, 19, 19, 21, 22, 22, 24; **10:**5, 5; **11:**2, 3, 4, 4, 4, 6, 8, 9, 15, 17, 21, 23, 24, 26, 27, 27, 33, 34, 35, 36, 41, 43, 43; **12:**6, 8, 14, 16, 18, 25, 28; **13:**3, 5, 11, 23, 24, 26, 27, 30, 31, 31, 33, 34; **14:**2, 8, 19, 20, 21, 22, 29, 31, 31, 31; **15:**2, 3, 3, 3, 3, 4, 4, 5, 7, 8, 10, 11, 12, 13, 14, 15, 18, 20, 21, 23, 23, 23, 24, 24, 26, 31; **16:**5, 6, 7, 7, 13, 14, 20, 27, 27, 28, 34, 34, 34; **17:**19, 23; **18:**10, 43, 44, 46, 46; **19:**3, 3, 13, 13, 19, 19, 21, 21; **20:**1, 12, 15, 20, 33, 38, 41, 42, 42; **21:**4, 5, 6, 8, 25, 27, 29, 29, 29; **22:**3, 6, 8, 9, 19, 19, 19, 31, 32, 34, 34, 35, 35, 35, 36, 37, 38, 40, 40, 42, 43, 43, 45, 46, 50, 50, 52, 53; **2Ki 1:**2, 8, 13, 17; **2:**8, 12; **3:**2, 2, 4, 9, 26, 27; **4:**11, 12, 18, 19, 19, 20, 27, 34, 34, 34, 35, 37, 38, 42, 43; **5:**1, 3, 6, 7, 9, 11, 11, 13, 14, 15, 20, 21, 23, 25, 26, 27; **6:**5, 8, 11, 17, 17, 24, 30, 30, 32, 32; **7:**12, 13, 17, 17; **8:**6, 19, 21, 21, 23, 24, 24, 26, 28, 29; **9:**2, 3, 11, 15, 17, 24, 24, 24, 25, 25, 26, 27, 28, 28, 31, 33, 36; **10:**10, 11, 14, 15, 19, 24, 25, 31, 34, 35, 35; **11:**2, 3, 12, 14, 19; **12:**1, 2, 18, 19, 20, 21, 21; **13:**3, 4, 7, 8, 8, 9, 9, 12, 12, 12, 13, 13, 14, 16, 16, 21, 23, 23, 24; **14:**2, 3, 3, 5, 11, 13, 15, 15, 16, 16, 19, 20, 22, 28, 28, 28, 29, 29; **15:**2, 3, 5, 6, 7, 7, 9, 15, 18, 19, 19, 21, 22, 26, 29, 31, 33, 34, 36, 38, 38; **16:**2, 2, 3, 19, 20, 20; **17:**4, 13, 15, 15, 18, 23; **18:**2, 3, 5, 12, 12, 17, 17, 17, 22; **19:**1, 4, 7, 8, 19, 32, 33, 36, 36, 37, 37; **20:**2, 12, 13, 13, 13, 13, 20, 21; **21:**1, 3, 4, 6, 6, 7, 10, 17, 18, 19, 20, 21, 21, 22, 23, 24, 25, 26, 26; **22:**1, 2, 3, 11; **23:**3, 3, 3, 18, 18, 25, 26, 28, 29, 30, 30, 30, 31, 32, 34, 36, 37; **24:**2, 3, 5, 6, 8, 9, 12, 15, 18, 20, 20; **25:**1, 5, 7, 18, 29, 29, 30, 30; **1Ch 1:**19, 19, 33, 43, 50; **2:**4, 13, 13, 14, 14, 15, 15, 24, 29, 35; **3:**9, 16, 16, 20, 22; **4:**3, 9, 9, 9, 10, 27; **5:**1, 1, 1, 1; **6:**33, 49; **7:**14, 15, 16, 22, 23, 23, 35; **8:**8, 9, 29, 30; **9:**5, 6, 19, 35, 36; **10:**2, 2, 4, 4, 4, 5, 5, 6, 6, 7, 8, 9, 10, 10, 12, 14; **11:**6, 7, 11, 17, 20, 25, 45; **12:**3, 18, 19, 21, 27, 28, 30; **13:**1, 1, 9, 10, 14; **14:**2, 2, 8, 11; **15:**22; **16:**4, 5, 7, 8, 9, 9, 10, 11, 14, 15, 24, 27, 29, 32, 34, 37, 39, 41, 43; **17:**1, 11, 12, 13, 14; **18:**3, 10, 10; **19:**1, 2, 2, 7, 7, 8, 10, 10, 11, 12, 14, 17, 19; **20:**3, 8; **21:**2, 3, 13, 16, 20, 21, 28; **22:**5, 6, 9, 9, 9, 10, 10, 11, 18; **23:**1, 13, 13, 14, 22; **25:**9, 9, 10, 11, 12, 13, 14, 15, 16, 17, 18, 19, 20, 21, 22, 23, 24, 25, 26, 27, 28, 29, 30, 31; **26:**10, 11, 14, 14, 15, 22, 25, 26, 28, 29, 30; **27:**2, 4, 4, 5, 6, 6, 7, 7, 8, 9, 10, 11, 12, 13, 14, 15, 23; **28:**1, 5, 6, 7, 10; **29:**3, 23, 25, 28, 28, 30; **2Ch 1:**1, 8; **2:**3, 11, 14, 17; **5:**1, 13; **6:**12, 13; **7:**3, 6, 10, 21, 21, 22; **8:**1, 2, 6, 6, 8, 9, 9, 11, 14, 18; **9:**4, 4, 25, 31, 31; **10:**6, 8, 14, 16, 18; **11:**12, 14, 15, 18, 21, 23; **12:**8, 10, 13, 14, 16; **13:**2, 5, 6, 12, 13, 17, 19, 19, 20, 22; **14:**1, 2, 4, 4, 6, 10, 11, 13, 13; **15:**9, 16, 17, 18; **16:**4, 5, 10, 12, 12, 13, 14, 14; **17:**2, 3, 4, 4, 7, 7, 14, 16; **18:**1, 2, 5, 7, 8, 18, 18, 18, 30, 31, 33, 33, 34; **19:**9, 10; **20:**14, 18, 20, 21, 21, 25, 30, 31, 32, 33, 35; **21:**1, 1, 4, 7, 9, 9, 9, 10, 17, 17, 17, 19, 19, 19, 19; **22:**2, 3, 4, 4, 6, 9, 11; **23:**1, 11, 11, 13; **24:**1, 16, 22, 22, 25, 27, 27; **25:**1, 3, 11, 11, 14, 17, 21, 23, 27, 27, 28; **26:**2, 3, 4, 7, 7, 7, 8, 10, 11, 15, 16, 16, 19, 21, 23; **27:**1, 2, 6, 7, 9; **28:**1, 3, 5, 5, 5, 16, 19, 21, 23, 25, 26, 27; **29:**1, 2, 3, 6, 10, 11; **30:**2, 8, 8, 9, 12, 27; **31:**8, 8, 10, 12, 15, 20, 21, 21; **32:**1, 3, 5, 7, 14, 15, 16, 21, 21, 21, 26, 27, 27, 28, 28, 28, 31, 32, 33, 33; **33:**3, 4, 6, 6, 7, 10, 10, 11, 12, 12, 13, 13, 14, 18, 19, 20, 20, 22, 22, 23, 24, 25; **34:**2, 3, 3, 8, 8, 19, 31, 31, 31, 33; **35:**3, 4, 7, 9, 20, 20, 22, 22, 23, 24, 25, 26; **36:**5, 7, 8, 12, 15, 15, 15, 19, 20, 22; **Ezr 1:**1, 3, 7; **3:**2, 2, 8, 9, 9, 11; **4:**6; **5:**5, 13, 17; **6:**12; **7:**6, 9, 23, 23, 28, 28; **8:**17, 18, 19, 22, 25, 25, 36; **9:**4, 9; **10:**14, 18; **Ne 1:**5, 5, 11; **2:**1, 1, 20; **3:**10, 12, 17, 18, 28, 29, 30; **4:**2; **6:**5, 6, 10, 11, 13, 18, 18; **8:**4, 4; **9:**5, 8, 10, 10, 32; **10:**29; **11:**13, 14; **12:**8, 45; **13:**6, 26, 30; **Est 1:**2, 2, 3, 3, 4, 8, 13, 14, 15, 16, 21, 22; **2:**2, 7, 7, 16, 18, 20; **3:**10, 10, 10, 12; **4:**1, 11, 11; **5:**1, 5, 10, 10, 11, 11, 14; **6:**1, 3, 13, 13; **7:**7, 7, 8, 8, 9; **8:**2, 3, 8; **9:**4, 25; **10:**1, 2, 3; **Job 1:**5, 10, 10, 20, 20; **2:**3, 4, 5, 6, 8, 9, 13; **3:**1, 19; **4:**9, 18; **5:**18; **6:**4, 4, 9; **9:**5, 10, 13, 13, 34; **12:**6, 10, 13, 16; **13:**8, 10, 11, 16; **15:**11, 15; **16:**9, 9, 12, 13, 13; **19:**11, 12, 28; **20:**6, 7, 9, 9, 10, 10, 11, 12, 12, 13, 14, 18, 18, 21, 23, 25, 26, 26, 27, 28; **21:**17; **22:**22; **23:**3, 5, 6, 11, 12, 12, 13, 13, 15; **24:**15, 22; **25:**3, 3, 6; **26:**8, 9, 9, 11, 12, 12, 13, 13, 14, 14; **28:**8; **29:**25; **31:**7; **32:**1, 12; **33:**10, 16, 24, 25, 27; **34:**7, 8, 13, 14, 14, 22, 27, 29, 33, 35; **36:**7, 24, 26, 31, 32, 33, 33; **37:**2, 3, 4, 5, 7, 11, 12, 13, 15; **40:**9; **42:**8, 10, 10, 11, 11, 12, 14, 15, 16; **Ps 1:**2; **2:**2, 5, 12; **3:**T, 4; **7:**12, 12, 13, 13; **9:**7, 11, 16; **11:**4, 7; **14:**6, 7; **16:**9; **18:**T, 6, 6, 7, 8, 8, 9, 11, 12, 14, 14, 14, 22, 22, 24, 30, 50; **19:**1, 5; **20:**2, 6, 6, 6; **21:**2, 3, 4, 4, 4, 9; **22:**29, 31; **23:**3; **24:**3; **25:**9, 10, 10, 14; **27:**4, 5, 6; **28:**5, 8, 8; **29:**1, 2, 2, 9, 11; **30:**4, 5, 5; **31:**21; **33:**5, 9, 11, 12, 14, 18, 21; **34:**1, 3, 15, 16, 17; **35:**27; **37:**31, 34; **42:**8, 8; **47:**8; **48:**1; **50:**3, 4, 4, 6; **53:**6; **55:**20, 21, 21, 21; **57:**2, 3; **59:**10; **60:**6; **61:**6; **62:**9; **64:**7; **66:**2, 5, 6, 7, 8, 9, 20; **67:**1; **68:**4, 4, 4, 17, 19, 21, 33, 34, 34, 35, 35; **69:**33, 33, 35; **72:**6, 7, 9, 19, 19; **75:**8; **76:**1, 2, 3; **77:**3, 8, 8, 9; **78:**4, 5, 5, 7, 7, 10, 20, 21, 21, 26, 32, 37, 38, 38, 40, 42, 43, 43, 49, 49, 50, 52, 54, 56, 56, 60, 61, 61, 62, 62, 62, 66, 69, 70; **85:**8, 8, 9, 9, 12, 13; **89:**7, 22, 23, 25, 29, 30, 36, 36, 39, 41, 42, 43, 44, 44, 45; **90:**17; **91:**4, 4, 4, 11; **94:**14, 14; **95:**4, 5, 7, 7; **96:**2, 3, 6, 9, 11, 13; **97:**2, 3, 4, 6, 6, 10, 12; **98:**1, 2, 2, 3, 7; **99:**1, 5, 6, 6, 9; **100:**3, 3, 3, 4, 4, 4, 5, 5; **102:**15, 16, 19, 21; **103:**1, 7, 7, 11, 13, 17, 18, 18, 19, 20, 20, 20, 21, 22; **104:**32, 32; **105:**1, 2, 2, 3, 4, 7, 8, 18, 18, 19, 20, 26, 28, 28, 37, 42, 42, 43, 43, 44, 45, 45; **106:**1, 7, 8, 8, 12, 12, 12, 13, 23, 23, 24, 40, 40, 45, 45; **107:**1, 8, 8, 15, 15, 21, 21, 22, 24, 31, 31; **108:**7; **109:**7, 7, 8, 8, 9, 9, 10, 11, 12, 13, 13, 14, 14, 15, 18, 19; **110:**4, 5; **111:**1, 3, 3, 5, 6, 6, 7, 9, 9, 10; **113:**4, 8; **114:**2; **116:**13, 14, 18; **118:**1, 2, 3, 4, 29; **119:**2, 3; **123:**2; **125:**2; **126:**1; **127:**2, 5; **128:**1; **130:**5; **132:**13, 18; **133:**2, 2, 3; **135:**3, 4, 7, 9, 12, 14, 14; **136:**1, 2, 3, 4, 5, 6, 7, 8, 9, 10, 11, 12, 13, 14, 15, 15, 16, 16, 17, 18, 19, 20, 21, 22, 22, 23, 24, 25, 26; **138:**6, 8; **142:**T; **145:**3, 9, 21; **147:**5, 5, 10, 11, 15, 15, 17, 18, 18, 19, 19, 20; **148:**2, 5, 6, 13, 13, 14, 14; **149:**1, 3, 4, 9; **150:**1, 1, 2, 2; **Pr 2:**6; **3:**6, 20, 32, 33; **5:**22, 23; **6:**27, 28, 31, 32, 33, 33, 34, 34; **7:**23; **8:**30, 30, 30, 31; **12:**4; **14:**28; **15:**3; **16:**4, 12, 12, 15; **19:**12; **20:**2, 28; **23:**28; **24:**18; **25:**5; **26:**3, 11; **28:**16; **29:**3, 3, 4, 12; **30:**4, 4, 4, 4, 6, 10, 31; **31:**1, 11; **Ecc 5:**9; **6:**4; **9:**14; **12:**13; **SS 1:**4, 12; **2:**3, 3, 6, 6, 16; **3:**8, 11, 11, 11; **4:**16; **5:**6, 11, 11, 12, 13, 13, 13, 14, 14, 15, 16; **6:**2, 2; **8:**7; **Isa 1:**3, 4; **2:**3, 3, 10, 19, 19, 21; **3:**6, 8, 13, 13, 13; **5:**1, 7, 16, 16, 25, 25, 25, 25; **6:**1, 3; **7:**2, 17; **8:**7, 18; **9:**4, 6, 6, 7, 7, 12, 17, 21; **10:**4, 7, 12, 22, 26, 27, 32; **11:**4, 11, 15; **12:**4, 5, 6; **13:**5, 9; **14:**1, 3, 17, 22, 22, 22, 27, 27, 29, 29, 32; **18:**7; **19:**17; **22:**23, 24; **23:**9, 11; **24:**5, 5, 23, 23; **25:**8, 11; **26:**19; **27:**1, 12, 13; **28:**5, 13, 21, 25, 25, 27; **30:**2, 4, 18, 26, 27, 27, 28, 28, 30, 30, 30, 31, 32; **31:**2, 2, 3; **32:**3, 20; **33:**5, 17; **34:**2, 16; **35:**2; **36:**2, 7; **37:**1, 4, 7, 8, 20, 33, 34, 37, 37, 38, 38; **38:**2, 9, 20; **39:**1, 2, 2, 2, 2; **40:**10, 10, 11, 11, 11, 12, 12, 13, 17, 22, 28; **41:**2; **42:**2, 4, 10, 12, 13, 13, 21, 22, 24; **44:**10, 12, 12, 12, 15, 15, 16, 17; **45:**1, 13; **48:**14, 16, 20; **49:**2, 2, 5, 5, 10, 13, 24; **50:**4, 4, 7, 10; **51:**20; **52:**8, 9, 10, 15; **53:**1, 2, 4, 4, 7, 8, 10, 10, 11; **54:**5; **55:**13; **56:**6, 6, 10; **59:**16, 17, 17, 18, 18, 18; **61:**3, 10, 11, 11; **62:**3, 4, 5, 5, 6, 8, 11; **63:**1, 1, 7, 7, 9, 10, 11, 11, 11, 12, 12; **65:**11, 15; **66:**5, 6, 14, 14, 14, 15, 15, 15, 16; **Jer 3:**21; **4:**13, 13; **5:**8; **7:**29; **9:**23, 23, 23; **10:**10, 10, 12, 12, 12, 13, 16, 16, 23, 23; **11:**19, 19; **13:**18, 23; **14:**10; **18:**3, 6; **20:**9, 9; **21:**2, 2, 7; **22:**4, 10, 10, 11, 12, 13, 15, 18, 18, 18, 28, 30, 30; **23:**6, 20, 34; **24:**8; **25:**1, 3, 4, 12, 19, 19, 19, 30, 30, 31, 31, 31, 38; **26:**8, 12; **27:**6, 7, 7, 7, 8, 12; **28:**9, 14; **29:**31, 32, 32; **30:**24; **31:**10, 10, 32, 35; **33:**2, 11, 21; **34:**3, 21; **35:**3, 18; **36:**18, 21, 23, 24, 26, 30, 31, 31, 32; **37:**2, 12; **38:**6; **39:**1, 4, 6, 14, 14; **41:**2, 7, 13, 15, 16; **42:**7, 9, 11; **43:**5, 10, 10, 12; **44:**23, 30; **46:**2, 10, 17, 26; **48:**7; **49:**3, 22; **50:**18, 25, 25, 25, 28, 34; **51:**11, 11, 12, 14, 15, 15, 15, 16, 19, 19, 19, 34, 44; **52:**1, 3, 3, 4, 8, 10, 11, 24, 30, 30, 33, 33, 34, 34; **La 1:**12, 15, 15, 17; **2:**1, 1, 1, 2, 3, 3, 4, 4, 4, 4, 6, 6, 7, 7; **3:**3, 11, 12, 13, 22, 23, 23, 27, 32, 34; **4:**11, 20; **Eze 1:**27, 27; **2:**2; **3:**12; **9:**2, 2; **10:**7; **12:**12, 12, 12, 14, 27; **17:**17, 18; **18:**11, 14, 17, 18; **19:**9; **20:**1, 9; **21:**21; **24:**2; **26:**7, 10, 11; **29:**18, 19, 20; **30:**11, 21, 22, 22, 24, 25; **31:**2, 18; **32:**31, 32; **34:**12; **36:**20; **39:**11; **40:**3; **43:**2, 2; **44:**25, 26; **45:**1; **46:**2, 12, 16, 16, 17, 18, 18; **Da 1:**1, 2, 5, 5, 8, 15, 19, 20; **2:**1, 2, 10, 13, 17, 18, 24, 46, 48; **3:**19, 20, 22, 24, 28, 28; **4:**3, 3, 3, 3, 33, 33, 34, 34, 37; **5:**1, 2, 2, 2, 2, 3, 3, 3, 6, 6, 6, 7, 9, 9, 20, 20, 20, 22, 23, 29; **6:**3, 4, 5, 10, 10, 12, 13, 17, 17, 18, 18, 22, 22, 23, 26, 26, 27; **7:**1, 9, 9, 10, 13, 14, 14, 25, 26; **8:**10, 11, 16, 24; **9:**2, 10, 13, 20, 27; **10:**5, 6, 6, 6, 6, 6; **11:**1, 2, 4, 4, 4, 5, 9, 12, 12, 17, 17, 18, 18, 19, 20, 24, 24, 25, 26, 26, 26, 28, 30, 31, 32, 37, 38, 43, 45, 45; **12:**7; **Hos 1:**11, 11; **3:**5; **5:**7; **6:**2; **7:**10, 10; **11:**4; **12:**2, 3, 5; **13:**15; **Joel 2:**11, 11, 16, 18, 18, 23; **3:**16; **Am 1:**2, 2, 15; **2:**1; **3:**8; **4:**2, 13, 13, 13; **5:**8, 15, 19, 19; **6:**8; **7:**4; **8:**7; **9:**6; **Jnh 1:**14; **2:**1; **3:**6, 6, 7, 9; **4:**6, 8; **Mic 1:**2, 3, 4; **4:**2, 2, 12; **5:**3, 4, 4, 4; **6:**2, 9; **7:**6, 7, 9, 17, 18; **Na 1:**2, 3, 3, 3, 4, 5, 6, 6, 6, 6, 8, 8, 10; **2:**5; **Hab 2:**20; **3:**3, 3, 4, 4, 6; **Zep 1:**7, 18; **2:**3, 7, 13; **3:**5, 15, 17; **Hag 2:**12; **Zec 1:**17; **2:**1, 12, 13; **3:**4, 5, 5; **6:**5, 13, 13; **7:**12; **9:**10, 14, 14, 14, 15, 16, 16, 16; **10:**3; **11:**17, 17, 17, 17; **12:**4; **13:**3, 3; **14:**4, 5, 9; **Mal 1:**3, 6, 6, 13, 14; **2:**15; **3:**1, 14, 16; **4:**2, 6; **Mt 1:**2, 5, 5, 6, 11, 18, 21, 22, 24; **2:**2, 11, 13, 14, 20, 21; **3:**1, 4, 11, 12, 12, 16; **4:**6; **5:**1, 28, 28, 31, 32, 35, 41, 45; **6:**29; **7:**28; **8:**18, 21, 23; **9:**1, 9, 10, 10, 10, 11, 20, 21, 31, 37, 38; **10:**1, 11, 35; **11:**1, 2, 20; **12:**1, 3, 13, 19, 20, 21, 24, 26, 29, 46, 49; **13:**4, 10, 24, 25, 36, 44, 54, 54, 54, 55, 55, 56, 57, 57; **14:**2, 3, 9, 9, 11, 12, 22, 31, 36; **15:**23, 32; **16:**13, 21, 27; **17:**2, 2, 10; **18:**23, 24, 25, 25, 27, 29, 30; **19:**3, 5, 5, 9, 9, 13, 15, 23; **20:**1; **21:**29, 31, 31, 34, 34, 35, 36, 37, 38, 41, 45; **22:**2, 3, 5, 5, 6, 7, 8, 13, 22, 24, 33, 34, 45; **23:**1; **24:**1, 3, 31, 31, 33, 38, 45, 45; **25:**14, 15, 19, 19, 31, 31, 32, 33, 33, 41; **26:**1, 7, 28, 65, 65, 65; **27:**19, 24, 25, 29, 29, 31, 35, 38, 43, 50, 60, 64, 64; **28:**3, 3, 6, 7, 9, 13, 18; **Mk 1:**6, 6, 7, 16, 21, 22, 27, 29, 43, 45; **2:**1, 4, 4, 12, 14, 15, 15, 15, 16, 23, 25, 26; **3:**4, 5, 7, 8, 9, 14, 20, 21, 21, 27; **4:**4, 27, 34, 34, 35, 38; **5:**4, 23, 27, 28, 31, 33, 40; **6:**1, 1, 2, 3, 4, 4, 4, 5, 7, 17, 20, 21, 22, 26, 26, 28, 29, 31, 35, 45, 56; **7:**17, 24, 25, 32, 33, 33; **8:**1, 4, 6, 10, 23, 25, 25, 27, 32, 33, 34; **9:**3, 18, 27, 28, 31, 33, 36; **10:**2, 4, 7, 7, 10, 11, 14, 16, 16, 23, 46, 50; **11:**1; **12:**2, 2, 6, 8, 12, 19, 37, 43; **13:**1, 20, 27, 27, 29, 34, 34, 37; **14:**3, 24, 39, 50, 52, 63, 63, 64, 65; **15:**17, 20, 24, 27, 37, 43; **16:**6, 7, 12, S; **Lk 1:**2, 5, 8, 14, 15, 17, 22, 23, 24, 32, 33, 48, 50, 51, 54, 54, 55, 59, 60, 63, 67, 68, 69, 70, 72, 77, 80; **2:**5, 22, 28, 40, 40, 43, 47, 47, 48, 48, 51; **3:**1, 16, 17, 17, 19, 20, 23; **4:**10, 16, 22, 24, 36, 40, 41; **5:**8, 10, 15, 19, 25, 25, 27, 29; **6:**1, 3, 4, 9, 10, 13, 17, 20; **7:**3, 10, 11, 13, 15, 18, 36, 38, 38, 38, 40; **8:**1, 3, 5, 9, 22, 42, 44; **9:**1, 18, 29, 29, 42, 43, 47, 51, 52; **10:**2, 2, 29, 30, 34, 34, 35; **11:**1, 1, 7, 8, 15, 18, 18, 21, 22, 22, 37, 38, 49; **12:**1, 17, 22, 27, 37, 38, 42, 42, 47; **13:**6, 7, 17; **14:**12, 17, 21, 21, 23, 31, 31; **15:**12, 12, 12, 12, 13, 13, 14, 15, 17, 20, 20, 20, 21, 22, 22, 22, 27, 28, 31; **16:**1, 1, 2, 5, 18, 20, 21, 23, 24; **17:**1, 8, 8, 8, 22, 27; **18:**1, 7, 13, 13, 24; **19:**1, 6, 14, 28, 37; **20:**10, 10, 14, 16, 26, 28, 30, 44, 45; **21:**5; **22:**27, 44, 47, 50; **23:**11, 14, 26, 34, 46, 55, 55; **24:**9, 22, 22, 23, 26, 40, 40, 50; **Jn 1:**7, 11, 11, 14, 18, 27, 27, 35, 41, 45; **2:**2, 5, 8, 11, 11, 12, 12, 12, 17, 21; **3:**4, 16, 17, 22, 29, 35; **4:**2, 5, 8, 12, 12, 27, 34, 41, 44, 45, 46, 47, 51, 51, 51, 52, 53; **5:**18, 22, 26, 37, 38; **6:**2, 3, 12, 16, 22, 24, 40, 42, 52,

53, 60, 61, 66; **7:**1, 5, 10, 30, 39; **8:**6, 20, 27, 39, 44; **9:**2, 2, 2, 3, 3, 8, 18, 20, 27, 28, 31; **10:**3, 3, 4, 4, 5, 11, 12, 38, 41; **11:**1, 7, 8, 16, 17, 32, 44, 51, 54, 54; **12:**3, 4, 6, 16, 16, 23, 38, 47, 49, 50; **13:**1, 1, 1, 2, 4, 4, 12; **14:**10; **15:**10, 15; **16:**13, 29, 32; **18:**1, 2, 9, 19, 25, 28; **19:**2, 23, 23, 25, 26, 27, 29, 30, 30, 33, 34, 36; **20:**18, 20, 20, 25, 25; **21:**7, 14, 24; **Ac 1:**2, 3, 18, 18, 19, 20, 20; **2:**26, 29, 31, 40; **3:**8, 12, 13, 21, 26; **4:**26; **5:**1, 2, 7, 17, 21, 26, 28, 31, 35, 36, 37, 40; **6:**15; **7:**4, 5, 6, 10, 12, 13, 13, 14, 14, 15, 17, 20, 23, 24, 25, 27, 29, 35, 57, 60; **8:**28, 32, 33, 33, 39; **9:**9, 12, 17, 18, 22, 30, 32, 41; **10:**2, 7, 7, 22, 23, 24, 25, 41, 43; **11:**13; **12:**7, 11, 15, 21, 21; **13:**8, 11, 11, 16, 25, 25, 29, 31, 36, 36, 48; **14:**10, 17; **16:**3, 27, 32, 33, 34, 34; **17:**3, 7, 18, 25, 27, 28; **18:**2, 5, 6, 8, 14, 18; **19:**6, 9, 12, 22, 31; **20:**3, 9, 10, 28, 28, 32, 32; **21:**11, 19, 32; **22:**3, 12, 14, 15, 24, 30; **23:**10, 15, 23, 26, 30; **24:**23, 23, 24; **25:**1, 12, 13, 25; **26:**1, 1; **27:**3, 24; **28:**3, 8, 16, 30; **Ro 1:**1, 2, 3, 5, 7, 9, 17, 18, 20, 20; **2:**2, 8, 18, 26; **3:**3, 4, 7, 20, 21, 24, 25, 25, 26; **4:**1, 2, 9, 10, 13, 19, 20; **5:**5, 8, 10, 10, 10, 15; **6:**5, 8, 16; **8:**3, 3, 15, 16, 17, 17, 17, 17, 17, 19, 23, 28, 29, 29, 29, 30, 32, 33, 38; **9:**4, 4, 4, 5, 6, 11, 22, 22, 22, 23, 23, 28; **10:**12; **11:**1, 2, 11, 11, 17, 17, 22, 24, 28, 28, 28, 29, 30, 33, 33, 33, 34, 36, 36; **12:**2, 5; **15:**9, 10, 33; **16:**13, 13, 15, 23, 23, 23, 25; **1Co 1:**2, 3, 9, 21; **2:**2, 10, 10, 12; **5:**1, 5; **6:**14, 15; **7:**2, 3, 4, 4, 11, 14, 15, 25, 32, 33, 33, 34, 36, 36, 37; **9:**7, 7, 26; **10:**10; **11:**4, 7; **15:**6, 10, 10, 23, 25, 25, 27, 28; **16:**11, 15; **2Co 1:**2, 5, 22; **2:**11, 14; **3:**6, 7, 13, 18; **4:**1; **5:**5, 15; **7:**7, 9, 13; **8:**1, 9, 22; **9:**15; **10:**10, 10; **11:**15; **13:**3; **Gal 1:**6, 15, 16; **3:**6, 9, 10, 16, 16, 16, 17, 19, 20, 20, 29; **4:**1, 4, 5, 6, 6, 7, 22, 22, 23; **5:**24; **Eph 1:**4, 5, 5, 6, 7, 8, 9, 10, 13, 14, 18, 19, 23, 23; **2:**7, 8, 15, 15, 16, 20, 22; **3:**2, 3, 5, 10, 10, 11, 12, 16, 16, 18, 20; **4:**8, 10, 12, 15, 16, 30; **5:**1, 23, 23, 23, 25, 28, 29, 29, 30, 31, 31, 33; **Php 1:**6; **2:**1, 6, 22, 30; **3:**10, 21; **4:**7, 19; **Col 1:**11, 13, 14, 18, 19, 20, 21, 22, 22, 22, 24, 25, 25, 26, 27, 27; **2:**15, 19, 19; **3:**4, 16; **4:**3, 10, 11, 12, 14; **1Th 1:**1, 4; **2:**2, 11, 12, 12, 13; **4:**5, 6, 8; **5:**9, 10; **2Th 1:**5, 5, 6, 7, 9, 10, 11; **2:**6, 8, 8, 16; **3:**16; **1Ti 1:**13, 16; **2:**6; **3:**2, 2, 4, 5, 12, 12; **6:**1, 14; **2Ti 1:**9, 9, 12, 16; **2:**4, 5, 19, 21; **4:**1, 8, 8, 18; **Tit 1:**6, 6, 6, 8; **2:**14, 14; **3:**4, 5, 7; **Phm 1:**23; **Heb 1:**2, 3, 5, 6, 7, 8, 13; **2:**10, 11, 17; **3:**5, 7, 15, 16, 18, 19; **4:**1, 3, 3, 4, 7, 7, 13, 16; **5:**3, 7, 7; **6:**13, 17, 18, 18, 18; **7:**2, 3, 3, 3, 21, 23, 24, 28, 28; **9:**7, 12, 26; **10:**13, 13, 20, 23, 25, 27, 29, 30; **11:**2, 4, 7, 7, 8, 11, 17, 19, 20, 21, 22, 27; **12:**2, 5, 6, 7, 8, 8, 10, 16, 17, 18, 26; **13:**12, 12, 15, 20, 20; **Jas 1:**18, 18, 18, 18; **2:**13, 21, 22, 22; **5:**11; **1Pe 1:**2, 3, 4, 5, 11, 14, 15; **2:**5, 9, 9, 10, 21, 23, 24, 24; **3:**12, 12, 20; **4:**10, 13, 13, 16; **5:**1, 1, 4, 6, 10, 10, 11; **2Pe 1:**2, 3, 3, 4, 4, 16, 16, 19; **2:**2, 5, 16, 16; **3:**5, 9, 16, 16, 16; **1Jn 1:**3, 7, 10; **2:**3, 29; **3:**1, 1, 12, 12, 16, 23, 23; **4:**9, 10, 12, 13, 14, 18, 19; **5:**1, 2, 3, 6, 6, 9, 10, 11, 12, 14, 18, 20; **2Jn** 3, 11; **Jude** 3, 11, 14, 21, 24; **Rev 1:**4, 5, 6, 6, 6, 13, 14, 14, 14, 15, 15, 16, 16, 16, 17, 17; **2:**1; **3:**5, 21; **4:**3; **5:**10; **6:**2, 5; **7:**3, 15; **8:**7, 8, 10, 12; **9:**1, 11, 13; **10:**1, 1, 1, 2, 2, 2, 5, 7, 7; **11:**15, 15, 19; **12:**3, 4, 5, 7, 7, 9, 10; **13:**2, 6, 6, 17, 18; **14:**1, 1, 9, 9, 11, 11, 12, 14, 14, 16, 19; **15:**2, 2; **16:**2, 2, 3, 4, 8, 10, 10, 10, 12, 17, 19; **17:**10, 11, 12, 14, 16, 17; **18:**1; **19:**2, 2, 5, 7, 10, 12, 12, 13, 15, 16, 19, 20, 20; **20:**1, 4, 4, 7, 11; **21:**3, 3, 15; **22:**3, 4, 4, 6, 6, 16

I (9352)

Ge 1:29, 30; **2:**18; **3:**10, 10, 10, 10, 11, 12, 13, 17, 17; **4:**1, 9, 9, 15, 23; **6:**7, 7, 7, 7, 7, 13, 13, 17, 18; **7:**1, 2, 4, 4, 4; **8:**21; **9:**2, 3, 3, 9, 11, 12, 13, 14, 15, 16, 16; **12:**1, 2, 2, 2, 3, 7; **13:**15, 16, 17; **14:**22, 23, 23; **15:**1, 2, 2, 4, 7, 8, 14, 18; **16:**2, 5, 8, 10, 13; **17:**1, 2, 2, 4, 5, 6, 7, 7, 8, 8, 16, 16, 17, 19, 20, 20; **18:**10, 14, 14, 17, 19, 19, 19, 20, 21, 21, 26, 26, 27, 27, 28, 28, 29, 30, 31, 31, 32, 32; **19:**8, 19, 19, 21, 21, 22, 34; **20:**5, 6, 6, 6, 9, 11, 11, 12, 13, 16, 16; **21:**7, 7, 10, 13, 16, 18, 23, 24, 26, 30; **22:**1, 2, 5, 12, 16, 17, 17; **23:**4, 9, 9, 11, 11, 13, 13; **24:**5, 5, 13, 14, 14, 14, 33, 33, 33, 34, 37, 38, 38, 39, 39, 40, 42, 42, 43, 43, 45, 45, 45, 46, 46, 47, 47, 48, 48, 56, 58; **26:**3, 3, 3, 3, 4, 4, 5, 9, 24, 24, 24, 24; **27:**2, 2, 4, 4, 4, 6, 8, 13, 21, 25, 25, 31, 33, 33, 37, 37, 41, 45, 45; **28:**13, 13, 15, 15, 15, 15, 15, 15, 16, 21, 22; **29:**21, 25, 33, 34, 35; **30:**2, 8, 8, 11, 15, 16, 20, 25, 26, 26, 27, 28, 30, 30, 30, 33, 33; **31:**3, 6, 8, 10, 11, 12, 13, 27, 29, 30, 31, 31, 31, 32, 32, 36, 37, 38, 38, 38, 39, 39, 40, 43, 44, 50, 52, 53; **32:**4, 5, 5, 10, 10, 10, 11, 26, 30; **33:**8, 8, 9, 11, 12; **34:**4, 11, 12; **35:**3, 3, 3, 11, 12, 12, 12; **37:**10, 17, 30, 35; **38:**17, 18, 21, 26, 26; **39:**9, 9, 14, 18; **40:**9, 11, 11, 11, 12, 15, 15; **41:**9, 11, 13, 15, 15, 15, 17, 21, 22, 24, 28, 40, 40, 41, 44; **42:**2, 14, 15, 15, 18, 18, 20, 20, 22, 33, 34, 34, 37; **43:**9, 9, 14; **44:**15, 18, 21, 28, 30, 32, 32, 32, 32, 32, 34, 34; **45:**3, 4, 11, 12, 13, 28, 28; **46:**2, 3, 3, 4, 4, 30, 32; **47:**9, 9, 16, 23, 23, 30; **48:**4, 4, 5, 5, 7, 7, 9, 11, 11, 19, 21, 22, 22, 22; **49:**1, 6, 7, 18, 29, 31; **50:**5, 5, 5, 19, 20, 20, 20, 21, 24; **Ex 2:**7, 9, 10, 22; **3:**3, 4, 6, 7, 7, 7, 8, 9, 10, 11, 12, 12, 13, 13, 14, 14, 16, 17, 17, 19, 20, 21; **4:**1, 10, 11, 12, 12, 12, 15, 15, 17, 18, 18, 21, 21, 23, 23; **5:**2, 2, 2, 23; **6:**1, 2, 3, 3, 4, 4, 5, 5, 6, 6, 6, 7, 7, 7, 8, 8, 8, 12, 29, 29, 30; **7:**1, 2, 3, 3, 4, 4, 5, 5, 17, 17; **8:**2, 8, 9, 21, 22, 22, 23, 28, 29, 29, 29; **9:**14, 14, 15, 15, 16, 18, 27, 27, 28, 29, 29, 30; **10:**1, 1, 2, 2, 4, 10, 16, 29; **11:**1, 4, 8; **12:**12, 12, 12, 13, 13, 13, 17, 20; **13:**16; **14:**4, 4, 4, 4, 17, 17, 18, 18; **15:**1, 2, 2, 9, 9, 9, 21, 26, 26, 26; **16:**4, 12, 12, 29, 29; **17:**4, 6, 9, 14; **18:**3, 11, 16, 16; **19:**4, 4, 9, 9, 11, 22, 24; **20:**2, 5, 5, 5, 6, 22, 24, 24, 24; **21:**5, 5, 13; **22:**23, 24, 27, 27; **23:**7, 15, 20, 20, 22, 22, 23, 25, 25, 26, 27, 28, 29, 30, 31, 31; **24:**12, 12, 14; **25:**8, 8, 9, 16, 21, 22, 22, 40; **29:**42, 43, 44, 44, 45, 46, 46, 46, 46; **30:**6, 36; **31:**2, 3, 6, 6, 6, 11, 13, 15; **32:**8, 9, 10, 13, 13, 13, 24, 24, 30, 30, 33, 34, 34, 34; **33:**1, 1, 1, 2, 3, 3, 3, 5, 5, 5, 12, 13, 14, 14, 16, 17, 19, 19, 19, 19, 19, 19, 22, 22, 23; **34:**1, 6, 6, 6, 7, 7, 7, 9, 10, 10, 10, 11, 11, 18, 24; **Lev 6:**17; **7:**34; **8:**5, 31; **10:**3, 3, 13, 18, 19; **11:**12, 44, 44, 45, 45; **14:**34, 34; **16:**2; **17:**10, 10, 11, 12, 14; **18:**2, 3, 4, 5, 6, 21, 24, 25, 27, 30; **19:**2, 3, 4, 7, 10, 12, 14, 16, 18, 25, 28, 30, 31, 32, 34, 36, 37; **20:**3, 5, 6, 7, 8, 22, 23, 23, 24, 24, 25, 26, 26; **21:**8, 8, 12, 15, 23; **22:**2, 3, 8, 9, 16, 30, 31, 32, 32, 33, 33, 33; **23:**10, 22, 30, 43, 43; **24:**22; **25:**2, 17, 21, 38, 42, 55, 55; **26:**1, 2, 4, 6, 6, 9, 11, 11, 12, 12, 13, 13, 16, 17, 18, 19, 21, 22, 24, 24, 25, 25, 26, 28, 28, 30, 30, 30, 31, 31, 32, 33, 36, 41, 42, 42, 44, 44, 44, 45, 45, 45; **Nu 3:**12, 13, 13, 13, 41, 45; **5:**3; **6:**27; **8:**16, 16, 17, 17, 18, 19; **9:**8; **10:**10, 30, 30; **11:**11, 12, 13, 14, 17, 17, 17, 29; **12:**6, 7, 8, 13; **13:**2; **14:**11, 12, 12, 20, 21, 22, 23, 24, 27, 28, 28, 28, 28, 30, 31, 35, 35; **15:**2, 18, 41, 41, 41; **16:**15, 15, 21, 28, 28, 45; **17:**4, 5, 5; **18:**6, 7, 8, 8, 12, 19, 20, 21, 24, 24; **20:**12, 18, 24; **21:**16, 34; **22:**6, 6, 6, 8, 11, 12, 17, 18, 20, 28, 29, 29, 30, 30, 32, 33, 34, 34, 34, 35, 37, 37, 37, 38, 38, 38; **23:**3, 3, 4, 5, 8, 8, 9, 9, 9, 11, 12, 15, 20, 20, 26, 26, 27; **24:**10, 11, 12, 12, 13, 13, 13, 14, 17, 17; **25:**11, 11, 12; **27:**12; **32:**8, 11, 11; **33:**53, 56, 56; **34:**2; **35:**34, 34; **Dt 1:**8, 9, 12, 13, 15, 16, 17, 18, 20, 23, 29, 35, 36, 39, 42, 43; **2:**5, 5, 9, 9, 19, 19, 24, 24, 25, 26, 31; **3:**2, 12, 13, 15, 16, 18, 19, 20, 21, 23, 24; **4:**1, 2, 8, 10, 21, 22, 26, 40; **5:**1, 5, 5, 6, 9, 9, 9, 10, 28, 31, 31; **6:**3, 6; **7:**11; **8:**1, 19; **9:**6, 9, 9, 9, 12, 13, 14, 14, 15, 16, 17, 17, 18, 18, 19, 20, 21, 21, 21, 23, 24, 25, 26; **10:**2, 3, 3, 5, 5, 10, 10, 10, 11, 13; **11:**2, 8, 13, 22, 26, 27, 32; **12:**11, 14, 21, 30, 32; **13:**18; **15:**5, 11, 15, 16; **17:**3; **18:**17, 18, 18, 18, 19; **19:**7, 9; **22:**14, 14, 16; **24:**8, 18, 22; **26:**3, 10, 13, 13, 14, 14, 14, 14, 14; **27:**1, 3, 4, 10; **28:**1, 14, 15, 68; **29:**5, 19, 19; **30:**1, 2, 8, 11, 15, 16, 18, 19, 19; **31:**2, 2, 5, 14, 16, 17, 18, 20, 20, 21, 21, 23, 23, 27, 27, 28, 29, 29; **32:**1, 1, 3, 20, 20, 21, 21, 23, 24, 26, 27, 34, 35, 35, 39, 39, 39, 40, 40, 41, 41, 42, 46, 49, 52; **34:**4, 4, 4, 4; **Jos 1:**2, 3, 3, 3, 5, 5, 5, 6, 9; **2:**4, 5, 9, 12, 21; **3:**7, 7, 7; **5:**9, 14, 14; **6:**2, 10; **7:**8, 11, 12, 20, 21, 21, 21; **8:**1, 18; **10:**8; **13:**6, 6; **14:**7, 7, 8, 10, 11, 11, 11, 11, 12; **15:**16, 18; **17:**18; **18:**4, 6, 8; **20:**2; **22:**2; **23:**2, 4, 14; **24:**3, 3, 4, 4, 5, 5, 5, 7, 7, 7, 8, 8, 10, 10, 10, 11, 12, 13, 13, 13; **Jdg 1:**2, 7, 7, 12, 14; **2:**1, 1, 1, 1, 3, 20, 21, 22; **3:**19, 20; **4:**7, 7, 8, 9, 22; **5:**3, 3; **6:**8, 9, 10, 10, 14, 15, 15, 16, 18, 18, 22, 37, 37; **7:**2, 4, 7, 9, 13, 17, 17; **8:**2, 3, 5, 7, 9, 9, 19, 23, 24; **9:**2, 9, 11, 13, 29, 29, 29, 48; **10:**11, 12, 13; **11:**9, 27, 31, 31, 31, 35, 37; **12:**2, 3; **13:**6, 11, 13, 16, 16, 18; **14:**2, 2, 3, 12, 16, 16; **15:**2, 2, 3, 3, 7, 7, 11, 18; **16:**7, 7, 11, 11, 13, 17, 17, 20, 26, 28; **17:**2, 2, 3, 3, 9, 9, 10, 13, 13; **18:**24, 24; **19:**20, 24; **20:**4, 6, 28; **Ru 1:**11, 12, 12, 16, 17, 17, 21; **2:**9, 10, 11, 11, 11, 13, 13, 13, 19; **3:**1, 3, 5, 9, 11, 12, 12, 13, 13; **4:**1, 4, 4, 4, 6, 6, 9, 10; **1Sa 1:**11, 15, 15, 16, 16, 20, 22, 26, 27, 28; **2:**1, 1, 23, 24, 27, 28, 28, 30, 30, 30, 31, 32, 34, 34, 35, 35, 35; **3:**5, 5, 6, 6, 8, 11, 12, 13, 14, 16; **4:**16, 16; **7:**5; **8:**8; **9:**8, 16, 16, 17, 19, 19, 20, 24, 24, 27; **10:**1, 8, 8, 8, 18, 19; **11:**2; **12:**1, 2, 2, 2, 2, 3, 3, 3, 3, 3, 3, 3, 7, 17, 23, 23; **13:**11, 12, 12, 12; **14:**24, 29, 29, 38, 39, 40, 41, 43; **15:**1, 2, 11, 11, 13, 14, 20, 20, 20, 20, 24, 24, 24, 26, 30, 30, 32; **16:**1, 1, 2, 3, 5, 7, 22; **17:**8, 9, 10, 28, 29, 29, 34, 35, 35, 36, 39, 43, 45, 46, 46, 55; **18:**17, 18, 18, 21, 25, 25; **19:**3, 15, 17, 17; **20:**1, 1, 2, 3, 3, 3, 3, 3, 4, 6, 6, 8, 9, 9, 10, 12, 12, 12, 13, 14, 14, 20, 20, 21, 22, 29, 30, 31, 36; **21:**2, 2, 4, 5, 8, 9, 15; **22:**3, 9, 9, 15, 15, 22, 22, 22, 22, 23; **23:**2, 4, 10, 10, 11, 17, 22, 23; **24:**4, 6, 9, 10, 10, 10, 11, 11, 11, 11, 11, 12, 13, 17, 20; **25:**7, 11, 19, 24, 24, 25, 25, 27, 28, 34, 41; **26:**8, 11, 16, 18, 19, 19, 20, 21, 21, 21, 23, 24; **27:**1; **28:**2, 7, 8, 13, 15, 15, 21, 22; **29:**6, 6, 8, 8; **30:**8, 8, 13, 13, 15; **2Sa 1:**3, 6, 6, 7, 7, 8, 8, 9, 10, 10, 10, 10, 13, 26, 26; **2:**1, 1, 6, 7, 22, 22; **3:**8, 8, 9, 10, 10, 12, 13, 14, 18, 28, 28, 35, 39; **4:**9, 10, 10, 11, 11; **5:**8, 19, 19; **6:**9, 21, 21, 22, 22; **7:**2, 6, 6, 7, 7, 8, 9, 9, 9, 10, 11, 11, 12, 12, 13, 14, 14, 15, 15, 18, 20, 20, 27; **9:**2, 3, 3, 6, 7, 7, 9, 11; **10:**2, 11; **11:**11, 11, 11; **12:**7, 8, 8, 11, 11, 12, 13, 22, 22, 23, 23, 23, 27; **13:**4, 13, 34, 35; **14:**3, 5, 7, 7, 10, 11, 15, 15, 17, 18, 19, 22, 22, 32, 32; **15:**4, 4, 4, 7, 8, 8, 20, 20, 21, 21, 28, 28, 34, 34; **16:**3, 4, 4, 10, 10, 12, 18, 19, 19, 19, 20; **17:**2, 2, 3, 7, 11, 11; **18:**2, 10, 11, 12, 13, 18, 29, 31, 33; **19:**7, 11, 13, 19, 20, 20, 20, 22, 22, 26, 26, 26, 27, 27, 28, 28, 30, 33, 34, 35, 35, 35, 35, 36, 38, 38; **20:**16, 17, 19, 20, 21; **21:**3, 4, 4, 6; **22:**3, 4, 7, 7, 19, 22, 22, 23, 24, 24, 30, 30, 38, 38, 39, 39, 41, 43, 43, 44, 50, 50; **23:**15, 17; **24:**2, 10, 12, 12, 17, 21, 23, 24, 24; **1Ki 1:**14, 16, 21, 26, 30, 30, 35, 48; **2:**2, 7, 8, 8, 8, 13, 14, 16, 17, 18, 20, 20, 20, 26, 30, 38, 42, 42, 45; **3:**5, 7, 8, 9, 12, 12, 13, 14, 17, 17, 20, 21, 21, 21; **5:**4, 5, 5, 5, 6, 8, 8, 8; **6:**12, 12, 13; **8:**13, 16, 16, 16, 20, 20, 21, 27, 29, 43, 44, 48, 59; **9:**3, 3, 3, 5, 5, 7, 7, 7, 7, 7; **10:**6, 7, 7, 7, 7; **11:**11, 12, 12, 13, 22, 31, 31, 32, 32, 34, 34, 34, 35, 36, 37, 38, 38, 38, 38, 38, 38, 39; **12:**6, 9, 26; **13:**7, 8, 8, 14, 16, 16, 18, 31; **14:**2, 5, 6, 7, 8, 8, 10, 10, 11; **15:**19; **16:**2, 3, 3; **17:**1, 1, 4, 9, 12, 12, 12, 12, 12, 24; **18:**1, 8, 9, 10, 12, 12, 13, 14, 15, 15, 15, 18, 22, 23, 24, 36, 36, 41, 43, 44; **19:**2, 4, 4, 10, 10, 14, 14, 18, 20, 20; **20:**4, 5, 6, 7, 7, 9, 9, 13, 13, 28, 28, 34, 34, 39, 40, 42; **21:**2, 2, 2, 3, 6, 20, 29, 29, 29; **22:**4, 6, 7, 8, 14, 16, 17, 18, 19, 21, 22, 27, 28, 30, 34; **2Ki 1:**10, 12; **2:**2, 3, 4, 5, 6, 9, 9, 10, 18, 21; **3:**7, 13, 14, 14; **4:**2, 9, 12, 22, 24, 28, 28, 30; **5:**3, 5, 6, 6, 7, 7, 11, 11, 12, 15, 16, 16, 17, 17, 18, 20, 25, 26; **6:**3, 19, 21, 27, 27, 29, 31, 33; **7:**12; **8:**8, 12; **9:**3, 5, 6, 7, 9, 9, 17, 25, 26, 26, 26; **10:**9, 15, 15, 16, 18, 19, 30; **16:**7; **17:**13, 13, 38; **18:**14, 14, 31, 32; **19:**7, 7, 7, 20, 23, 23, 23, 24, 24, 25, 25, 25, 27, 27, 28, 28, 28, 34; **20:**3, 5, 5, 6, 6, 6, 8, 15, 15; **21:**7, 8, 8, 12, 13, 13, 13, 13, 14, 14; **22:**8, 16, 16, 17, 19, 19, 20, 20; **23:**27, 27, 27; **1Ch 4:**10; **11:**17, 19; **12:**17; **13:**12; **14:**10, 10; **15:**12; **16:**18, 22; **17:**1, 5, 5, 6, 6, 7, 8, 8, 8, 9, 10, 10, 10, 11, 11, 12, 13, 13, 13, 14, 16, 17, 18, 18, 25; **19:**2, 12; **21:**2, 8, 10, 10, 17, 17, 22, 23, 24, 24, 24; **22:**5, 7, 9, 9, 10, 10, 14, 14; **23:**5; **28:**2, 6, 6, 7, 8; **29:**2, 2, 3, 3, 4, 14, 17, 17, 17, 19; **2Ch 1:**7, 12, 12; **2:**4, 6, 8, 8, 9, 10, 13; **6:**2, 5, 5, 5, 6, 10, 10, 11, 18, 20, 33, 34, 38; **7:**12, 13, 13, 13, 14, 15, 16, 18, 18, 18, 19, 20, 20, 20, 20, 20; **9:**5, 6, 6, 6, 6; **10:**6, 9; **12:**5, 7, 7; **16:**3; **18:**3, 6, 7, 13, 15, 16, 17, 18, 20, 21, 26, 27, 29, 33; **25:**9, 9, 16, 16, 16; **28:**23; **29:**10; **32:**13, 15; **33:**7, 8, 8; **34:**15, 24, 25, 27, 27, 28, 28; **35:**21, 21, 21, 23; **Ezr 4:**19; **6:**8, 12; **7:**13, 14, 21, 24, 28, 28; **8:**15, 15, 15, 16, 16, 17, 21, 22, 24, 26, 26, 28; **9:**3, 3, 4, 5, 5, 5, 6, 6, 6; **Ne 1:**1, 2, 4, 4, 4, 5, 6, 6, 8, 9, 9, 11, 11; **2:**1, 1, 2, 3, 3, 4, 5, 6, 7, 8, 9, 9, 9, 12, 12, 12, 13, 14, 15, 15, 16, 16, 16, 16, 17, 18, 20; **4:**4, 13, 13, 14, 14, 19, 22, 23; **5:**6, 6, 7, 7, 7, 8, 9, 10, 12, 13, 14, 14, 14, 15, 16, 16, 17, 17, 18, 19; **6:**1, 2, 3, 3, 3, 4, 7, 9, 10, 11, 11, 12, 19; **7:**1, 2, 3, 5; **12:**31, 38, 40; **13:**6, 6, 6, 7, 8, 9, 9, 10, 11, 11, 13, 13, 14, 15, 15, 17, 19, 19, 21, 21, 22, 23, 25, 25, 25, 26, 28, 30, 31; **Est 3:**9; **4:**16, 16, 16, 16; **5:**3, 4, 6, 8, 8, 13; **6:**6; **7:**2, 4, 4; **8:**6, 7; **9:**12; **Job 1:**7, 15, 16, 17, 19, 21, 21, 21, 21; **2:**2; **3:**3, 11, 11, 13, 13, 14, 15, 16, 24, 25, 25, 26, 26; **4:**14, 16; **5:**3; **6:**3, 5, 7, 7, 8, 9, 9, 10, 10, 11, 11, 12, 13, 22, 22, 23, 23, 24, 24, 24, 28, 29, 30, 30; **7:**3, 4, 4, 4, 7, 8, 11, 11, 11, 12, 13, 13, 15, 16, 16, 20, 20, 20, 21, 21; **9:**2, 11, 11, 14, 14, 15, 15, 15, 16, 20, 20, 21, 21, 22, 27, 27, 28, 28, 29, 30, 31, 32, 34, 35, 35; **10:**1, 1, 2, 7, 9, 13, 14, 15, 15, 15, 16, 19, 19, 20, 20, 21; **11:**3, 4; **12:**3, 3, 4, 4; **13:**1, 1, 2, 2, 3, 3, 13, 14, 14, 15, 15, 16, 16, 16, 17, 18, 18, 19, 19, 20, 20, 22, 23, 28; **14:**13, 14, 15; **15:**6, 17; **16:**2, 3, 4, 4, 5, 5, 5, 6, 6, 12, 15, 15, 15, 17, 20, 22, 22; **17:**1, 2, 2, 7, 10, 13, 14; **19:**4, 6, 6, 7, 7, 10, 15, 16, 16, 17, 18, 19, 20, 25, 26, 27, 27, 27, 29; **20:**2, 2, 3; **21:**2, 3, 6, 6, 6, 16, 19, 27, 27, 29; **22:**13, 18; **23:**2, 3, 3, 4, 5, 7, 8, 8, 8, 9, 9, 9, 10, 11, 11, 12, 15, 15; **27:**2, 3, 3, 5, 5, 5, 6, 6, 11, 11, 12; **29:**2, 3, 7, 12, 13, 13, 14, 14, 15, 16, 17, 18, 18, 19, 22, 24, 25, 25; **30:**1, 1, 13, 14, 15, 19, 20, 20, 23, 25, 25, 26, 26, 28, 28, 29; **31:**1, 4, 4, 5, 7, 7, 8, 8, 9, 12, 13, 13, 14, 14, 16, 17, 18, 18, 19, 21, 21, 24, 25, 26, 28, 28, 29, 30, 32, 33, 34, 34, 35, 35, 35, 36, 36, 37, 37, 37, 39; **32:**6, 6, 6, 7, 11, 12, 14, 16, 16, 17, 17, 17, 18, 19, 20, 21, 22; **33:**1, 2, 3, 3, 6, 6, 7, 8, 9, 9, 9, 11, 12, 24, 27, 32, 32, 33; **34:**5, 6, 6, 31, 31, 32, 32, 32; **35:**2, 4; **36:**2, 2, 2, 3, 4, 4; **37:**1, 20; **38:**3, 4, 9, 10, 11, 23; **39:**6; **40:**4, 4, 4, 5, 5, 7, 14, 15, 15; **41:**12; **42:**2, 3, 3, 3, 4, 4, 5, 5, 6, 6, 6, 7, 8, 8; **Ps 2:**6, 7, 8; **3:**1, 4, 5, 5, 6; **4:**1, 3, 8; **5:**1, 2, 3, 7, 7; **6:**2, 3, 6; **7:**1, 3, 4, 8, 17, 17; **8:**3; **9:**1, 1, 2, 2, 13, 14, 14; **10:**1; **11:**1; **12:**5, 5, 5; **13:**2, 3, 5, 5, 6; **16:**1, 2, 2, 3, 4, 7, 8, 8; **17:**3, 3, 4, 5, 6, 6, 6, 15, 15, 15, 15, 15; **18:**1, 2, 3, 6, 6, 18, 21, 21, 22, 23, 23, 29, 29, 37, 37, 38, 40, 42, 42, 43, 49, 49; **19:**12, 13; **20:**6; **22:**2, 2, 6, 6, 9, 10, 10, 17, 22, 22, 25, 25; **23:**1, 1, 4, 4, 6; **25:**1, 2, 4, 5, 16, 19, 20, 21; **26:**1, 1, 3, 3, 4, 5, 5, 6, 6, 8, 11, 11, 12, 12; **27:**1, 1, 3, 4, 4, 6, 6, 8, 13, 13, 13; **28:**1, 2, 2, 7, 7; **30:**1, 2, 6, 6, 7, 8, 8, 9, 9, 12, 12; **31:**1, 4, 5, 6, 6, 7, 9, 10, 10, 11, 12, 12, 12, 13, 13, 14, 17, 22, 22; **32:**3, 3, 3, 5, 5, 5, 8, 8; **34:**1, 1, 2, 4, 6, 11; **35:**3, 7, 7, 9, 9, 10, 11, 12, 12, 13, 13, 14, 14, 15, 15, 15, 18, 18, 28, 28; **37:**25, 25, 25, 35, 36, 36, 36; **38:**6, 8, 9, 10, 13, 13, 14, 14, 15, 16, 17, 18, 18, 18, 19, 20; **39:**1, 1, 1, 1, 1, 2, 7, 8, 9, 9, 10, 12, 13, 13; **40:**1, 2, 5, 5, 6, 7, 7, 8, 9, 9, 10, 10, 10, 12, 12, 17; **41:**4, 4, 9, 10, 11, 12; **42:**1, 2, 2, 3, 4, 4, 5, 5, 5, 6, 6, 7, 8, 9, 9, 11, 11, 11; **43:**2, 4, 4, 5, 5, 5; **44:**6, 6; **45:**1, 10, 17; **46:**10, 10, 10; **49:**4; **50:**7, 7, 8, 9, 9, 10, 12, 12, 13, 13, 14, 14, 15, 21, 21, 21, 22, 23; **51:**3, 4, 4, 5, 7, 7, 13, 14, 15, 16, 16; **52:**8, 8, 9, 9; **54:**6, 6; **55:**2, 5, 6, 6, 6, 7, 8, 9, 12, 12, 16, 17, 23; **56:**3, 3, 4, 4, 4, 5, 9, 9, 10, 10, 11, 11, 12, 13; **57:**1, 1, 2, 4, 6, 7, 8, 9, 9; **59:**3, 9, 16, 16, 17; **60:**6, 6, 8; **61:**2, 8, 8; **62:**1, 2, 5, 6, 11; **63:**1, 2, 3, 4, 4, 5, 6, 7, 7, 8; **66:**13, 13, 14, 15, 15, 16, 17, 17, 18; **68:**22, 22; **69:**2, 2, 2, 3, 4, 4, 5, 7, 10, 11, 12, 13, 17, 19, 20, 29, 30, 30; **70:**5; **71:**3, 6, 8, 8, 14, 14, 15, 15, 15, 16, 16, 17, 18, 22, 22, 23, 24; **73:**2, 2, 3, 3, 13, 14, 15, 15, 16, 17, 17, 21, 21, 21, 21, 22, 22, 23, 25, 25, 28, 28; **75:**2, 2, 3, 4, 4, 9, 9, 10, 10; **77:**1, 2, 2, 2, 3, 3, 4, 5, 6, 10, 11, 11, 12; **78:**1, 2, 2; **81:**5, 6, 6, 7, 7, 7, 8, 10, 10, 12, 14, 16, 16; **82:**6; **84:**2, 2, 2, 10; **85:**8; **86:**1, 2, 2, 3, 7, 11, 11, 12, 12, 16; **87:**4; **88:**1, 4, 5, 5, 8, 9, 9, 13, 13, 15, 15; **89:**1, 3, 3, 4, 19, 19, 20, 20, 21, 21, 23, 25, 27, 28, 29, 32, 33, 34, 34, 34, 35, 35, 50; **91:**2, 2, 14, 14, 15, 15, 15, 16; **92:**4, 10, 11, 11; **94:**17, 18, 22; **95:**10, 10, 10, 11; **101:**1, 1, 2, 2, 3, 3, 3, 4, 5, 5, 6, 7; **102:**2, 4, 5, 6, 7, 9, 11, 24, 24; **103:**1, 1, 2, 22; **104:**1, 33, 33, 33, 34, 35; **105:**11, 15; **108:**1, 2, 3, 3, 7, 7, 9; **109:**1, 4, 4, 22, 23, 23, 24, 25, 28, 30; **110:**1; **111:**1, 1; **116:**1, 2, 2, 3, 4, 6, 7, 9, 9, 10, 10, 10, 11, 12, 13, 13, 14, 16, 16, 17, 18; **118:**5, 6, 7, 10, 11, 12, 17, 17, 19, 21, 28, 28; **119:**6, 6, 7, 7, 7, 8, 10, 11, 11, 13, 14, 15, 16, 17, 19, 19, 20, 22, 23, 25, 26, 27, 28, 30, 30, 31, 32, 34, 34, 39, 40, 42, 42, 44, 45, 45, 46, 46, 47, 47, 48, 48, 51, 52, 53, 55, 55, 57, 58, 59, 59, 60, 61, 62, 66, 67, 67, 69, 70, 74, 75, 75, 77, 78, 80, 80, 81, 81, 83, 83, 84, 87, 88, 92, 93, 94, 94, 95, 97, 97, 99, 99, 100, 100, 101, 101, 102, 104, 106, 107, 109, 110, 112, 113, 113, 115, 116, 117, 117, 119, 120, 120, 121, 124, 125, 127, 128, 129, 131, 133, 134, 139, 140, 141, 141, 143, 144, 145, 145, 146, 146, 147, 147, 148, 152, 153, 157, 158, 159, 162, 163, 163, 164, 166, 166, 167, 167, 168, 168, 173, 174, 175, 176, 176; **120:**1, 1, 5, 6, 7, 7; **121:**1; **122:**1, 8, 9; **123:**1; **130:**1, 5, 5, 5, 6; **131:**1, 2; **132:**3, 3, 4, 5, 11, 12, 14, 14, 14, 15, 16, 17, 18; **135:**5; **137:**5, 6, 6; **138:**1, 1, 2, 2, 2, 3, 3, 7; **139:**2, 3, 4, 4, 7, 7, 8, 8, 9, 9, 11, 12, 14, 15, 15, 16, 18, 18, 21, 21, 22; **140:**6, 12; **141:**1, 1, 3, 5, 8; **142:**1, 1, 2, 3, 3, 3, 4, 5, 5, 5, 6, 7; **143:**4, 4, 5, 5, 5, 6, 6, 7, 8, 8, 9, 12; **144:**2, 9, 9; **145:**1, 2, 2, 5, 6, 21; **146:**1, 2, 2, 2; **Pr 1:**24, 24, 25, 26, 26, 28, 30; **3:**1; **4:**2, 3, 10, 11, 20; **5:**7, 12, 12, 13, 13, 14, 14; **6:**9; **7:**6, 15, 15; **8:**4, 4, 6, 6, 7, 12, 12, 13, 17, 20, 21, 23, 24, 25, 27, 28, 29, 30, 30, 31; **9:**5; **20:**9, 9, 22; **22:**13, 13, 19, 20; **23:**15, 35, 35, 35, 35; **24:**29, 30, 31, 32, 32; **26:**13, 19; **27:**11, 11; **30:**1, 1, 2, 2, 3, 3, 7, 7, 9, 9, 9, 9, 18; **Ecc 1:**12, 12, 13, 13, 16, 16, 16, 17, 17; **2:**1, 1, 2, 3, 3, 3, 4, 5, 6, 7, 7, 8, 8, 8, 9, 9, 9, 10, 10, 10, 10, 11, 11, 12, 12, 14, 15, 15, 17, 18, 18, 19, 20, 21, 21, 21, 24, 24; **3:**10, 12, 14, 16, 17, 18, 22; **4:**1, 1, 2, 4, 7, 8, 8; **5:**13, 18; **6:**1, 3, 4; **7:**15, 23, 23, 23, 25, 25, 26, 27, 28, 29; **8:**9, 10, 12, 15, 16, 16; **9:**1, 11, 13, 16; **10:**5, 5, 7; **SS 1:**5, 7; **2:**1, 3, 5, 8, 16; **3:**1, 1, 2, 2, 3, 3, 4, 4, 4, 4; **4:**6, 9; **5:**1, 1, 1, 2, 2, 2, 3, 3, 3, 3, 3, 5, 5, 6, 6, 6, 6, 6, 8; **6:**3, 9, 11, 11, 12, 12; **7:**8, 8, 10, 12, 13; **8:**1, 2, 2, 4, 5, 10, 10, 12; **Isa 1:**2, 3, 11, 11, 11, 13, 14, 14, 15, 15, 18, 18, 18, 20, 24, 25, 25, 25, 26; **3:**7, 7; **5:**1, 1, 4, 4, 5, 5, 5, 6, 6, 6, 6, 9, 13; **6:**1, 5, 5, 5, 8, 8, 8, 9, 11, 11; **7:**9, 11, 11, 12; **8:**2, 2, 3, 16, 16, 17, 18; **10:**3, 4, 7, 13, 13, 14; **12:**2; **13:**3, 3, 3, 11, 11, 12, 13, 13, 17; **14:**13, 13, 14, 22, 22, 23, 23, 23, 24, 25, 25, 26, 30, 30, 30; **15:**9; **16:**9, 10, 11; **18:**3, 3, 4; **19:**2, 3, 4, 25; **20:**3; **21:**2, 2, 3, 3, 3, 4, 4, 8, 8, 10, 17; **22:**2, 4, 19, 19, 20, 22, 23, 25, 25; **23:**4, 4; **24:**16; **25:**1; **26:**9, 9; **27:**3, 3, 3, 4, 4; **28:**16, 17, 18, 18, 23; **29:**2, 3, 3, 6, 14, 14; **30:**7, 12; **31:**7; **32:**9; **33:**10, 13; **34:**5; **36:**16, 17; **37:**7, 7, 7, 24, 24, 24, 25, 25, 26, 26, 26, 28, 28, 29, 29, 29, 35; **38:**3, 5, 5, 6, 6, 8, 10, 10, 10, 11, 11, 11, 13, 13, 14, 14, 14, 15, 15, 15, 19, 20, 22; **39:**4, 4; **40:**3, 6, 6; **41:**4, 4, 9, 9, 10, 10, 10, 10, 10, 13, 13, 13, 13, 14, 14, 14, 17, 17, 18, 18, 19, 25, 25, 26, 27, 28; **42:**1, 1, 1, 6, 6, 6, 8, 8, 8, 9, 9, 9, 14, 14, 14, 14, 15, 15, 16, 16, 16, 16; **43:**1, 1, 2, 3, 3, 4, 4, 5, 5, 6, 7, 7, 10, 11, 12, 12, 12, 12, 12, 12, 13, 13, 14, 15, 16, 17, 17, 18, 19, 19, 19, 19, 20, 21, 23, 25, 25, 28; **44:**3, 3, 5, 5, 6, 7, 8, 19, 19, 21, 21, 22, 22, 22, 24, 24, 24, 25, 25, 26, 27, 28, 28; **45:**2, 2, 3, 3, 3, 4, 4, 5, 5, 6, 7, 7, 7, 8, 10, 11, 12, 12, 13, 13, 13, 18, 19, 19, 19, 19, 19, 19, 21, 22, 23, 23; **46:**3, 4, 4, 4, 4, 9, 9, 9, 9, 10, 10, 10, 10, 11, 11, 11, 11, 13, 13; **47:**3, 6, 7, 8, 10; **48:**3, 3, 4, 5, 5, 6, 6, 8, 8, 9, 10, 10, 11, 11, 12, 13, 15, 15, 15, 16, 17; **49:**2, 4, 4, 4, 4, 6, 8, 8, 8, 8, 9, 9, 11, 15, 16, 18, 21, 22, 23, 25, 25, 26, 26; **50:**1, 1, 2, 2, 2, 2, 2, 3, 4, 5, 5, 6, 6, 7, 7, 7, 7; **51:**2, 2, 5, 12, 12, 15, 16, 16, 16, 22, 23, 23; **52:**3, 3, 3, 6, 6; **53:**12; **54:**7, 7, 8, 8, 9, 9, 9, 9, 10, 11, 12, 13, 15, 15, 16, 16, 17; **55:**2, 3, 3, 3, 5, 11, 11, 11; **56:**1, 3, 4, 5, 5, 6, 7, 7, 8; **57:**6, 11, 12, 14, 15, 15, 16, 16, 16, 16, 17, 17, 18, 18, 18, 19; **58:**3, 6, 7, 9, 14, 14, 14; **59:**21, 21; **60:**7, 8, 10, 10, 15, 16, 17, 21, 22; **61:**8, 8, 8, 10, 10; **62:**1, 1, 1, 6, 8; **63:**1, 1, 3, 3, 3, 5, 5, 5, 5, 5, 6, 7, 7, 7; **65:**1, 1, 1, 2, 5, 6, 6, 6, 7, 8, 8, 8, 9, 9, 12, 12, 12, 12, 16, 17, 18, 19, 24, 24, 25; **66:**2, 2, 4, 4, 4, 4, 9, 9, 13, 18, 18, 18, 19, 19, 21, 21; **Jer 1:**5, 5, 5, 6, 6, 7, 7, 8, 8, 9, 10, 11, 11, 12, 12, 13, 13, 15, 16, 17, 17, 18, 19, 19, 19; **2:**2, 3, 7, 7, 9, 9, 19, 20, 21, 21, 22, 25, 25, 30, 31, 31, 35, 35; **3:**1, 7, 8, 12, 12, 13, 14, 14, 15, 18, 19, 19, 19, 19, 19, 22; **4:**6, 10, 12, 19, 19, 19, 21, 23, 23, 24, 25, 26, 27, 28, 31; **5:**1, 4, 5, 7, 7, 9, 9, 14, 15, 18, 22, 22, 29, 29; **6:**2, 8, 10, 10, 11, 11, 11, 12, 17, 19, 20, 21, 27, 30, 30; **7:**3, 5, 7, 7, 11, 12, 12, 13, 13, 14, 14, 14, 15, 15, 16, 18, 19, 20, 22, 22, 23, 23, 23, 25, 31, 34; **8:**3, 3, 5, 6, 6, 6, 10, 13, 13, 13, 17, 21, 21; **9:**1, 1, 2, 7, 7, 9, 9, 10, 11, 13, 15, 16, 16, 24, 24, 24, 25; **10:**18, 19, 20, 23, 24; **11:**4, 4, 4, 4, 5, 5, 5, 7, 7, 8, 9, 10, 11, 11, 14, 16, 16, 17, 19, 19, 20, 21, 22, 23; **12:**1, 7, 7, 8, 8, 11, 14, 14, 15, 15, 17; **13:**2, 5, 6, 7, 7, 8, 9, 11, 13, 14, 14, 17, 24, 25, 26, 27; **14:**10, 10, 12, 12, 12, 13, 14, 14, 15, 15, 16, 17, 18, 18, 18, 18; **15:**1, 3, 3, 4, 6, 6, 7, 7, 8, 8, 9, 10, 10, 10, 10, 10, 13, 14, 15, 15, 16, 17, 17, 17, 19, 20, 20, 20, 21, 21; **16:**5, 5, 9, 13, 13, 15, 15, 16, 16, 17, 17, 18, 21, 21; **17:**3, 4, 4, 10, 10, 10, 16, 16, 16, 22, 27; **18:**2, 3, 6, 7, 8, 8, 9, 9, 10, 10, 10, 11, 17, 17, 20; **19:**2, 3, 5, 7, 8, 9, 11, 12, 12, 15, 15; **20:**4, 4, 5, 7, 7, 7, 8, 8, 9, 9, 9, 10, 12, 13, 13, 14, 14, 15, 17, 18; **21:**4, 4, 5, 5, 6, 7, 10, 13, 14, 14; **22:**5, 6, 7, 14, 21, 24, 24, 24, 25, 26; **23:**1, 2, 3, 3, 3, 4, 5, 9, 9, 11, 12, 12, 13, 14, 15, 21, 21, 23, 23, 24, 25, 25, 30, 32, 34, 34, 38, 39, 39, 39, 40; **24:**1, 3, 5, 6, 6, 6, 6, 6, 7, 7, 8, 9, 9, 10, 10; **25:**3, 5, 6, 9,

9, 9, 9, 10, 12, 12, 13, 13, 14, 15, 16, 17, 18, 19, 21, 23, 24, 26, 27, 29, 29, 29, 29; 26:3, 3, 4, 5, 6, 6, 6, 12, 14; 27:5, 5, 5, 6, 6, 8, 8, 10, 11, 12, 12, 15, 15, 16, 22, 22; 28:2, 3, 4, 4, 4, 6, 6, 7, 14, 14; 29:9, 10, 10, 10, 11, 11, 12, 14, 14, 14, 14, 17, 18, 18, 18, 18, 19, 21, 23, 31, 32, 32, 32; 30:2, 3, 3, 3, 3, 5, 8, 9, 10, 11, 11, 11, 11, 11, 11, 14, 14, 15, 17, 18, 19, 20, 20, 21, 22; 31:1, 2, 2, 3, 3, 4, 8, 8, 9, 9, 13, 13, 14, 14, 14, 16, 18, 18, 18, 19, 19, 19, 19, 19, 20, 20, 20, 23, 25, 26, 27, 28, 28, 28, 31, 32, 32, 32, 33, 33, 33, 33, 34, 36, 36, 37, 37; 32:3, 5, 8, 8, 9, 10, 11, 12, 12, 13, 16, 16, 27, 28, 31, 33, 35, 36, 37, 37, 37, 38, 39, 40, 40, 41, 42, 42, 42, 42, 44, 44; 33:3, 5, 5, 6, 7, 8, 8, 9, 11, 13, 14, 14, 15, 22, 25, 25, 26, 26; 34:2, 5, 13, 13, 14, 17, 18, 19, 20, 21, 22, 22; 35:3, 4, 5, 14, 15, 15, 17, 17, 17, 19; 36:3, 3, 5, 18, 31, 31, 31; 37:14, 17, 18, 18, 18, 20, 20; 38:5, 14, 15, 15, 16, 19, 25; 39:16, 16, 16, 17, 18, 18; 40:4, 4, 10, 16; 42:4, 4, 4, 10, 10, 10, 10, 11, 12, 17, 19, 21; 43:10, 10, 10; 44:2, 4, 4, 10, 11, 12, 12, 13, 13, 26, 27, 29, 29, 29, 30, 30, 30; 45:3, 3, 3, 4, 4, 4, 4, 5, 5, 5; 46:18, 25, 25, 26, 26, 27, 28, 28, 28, 28, 28, 28; 48:12, 30, 31, 32, 32, 35, 38, 44, 47; 49:2, 5, 6, 8, 8, 10, 11, 13, 14, 15, 16, 19, 19, 19, 27, 32, 32, 35, 36, 36, 37, 37, 38, 38, 39; 50:9, 9, 18, 18, 19, 20, 20, 21, 21, 24, 31, 32, 40, 40, 44, 44, 44; 51:1, 20, 21, 22, 23, 24, 25, 25, 25, 36, 36, 36, 39, 39, 40, 44, 47, 53, 57, 64; La 1:11, 14, 16, 18, 19, 20; 2:11, 11, 13, 13, 22; 3:1, 7, 8, 17, 18, 18, 20, 20, 21, 21, 24, 24, 52, 54, 55; Eze 1:1, 1, 3, 4, 4, 8, 15, 15, 28, 28, 28; 2:1, 2, 3, 4, 8, 8, 9, 10; 3:1, 2, 3, 5, 6, 6, 7, 8, 9, 12, 14, 15, 15, 17, 18, 18, 20, 22, 23, 23, 23, 23, 26, 27, 27; 4:8, 13, 14, 14, 14, 14, 14, 14, 14, 16; 5:2, 5, 6, 8, 8, 9, 9, 10, 11, 11, 11, 12, 13, 13, 14, 15, 16, 17, 17; 6:3, 3, 4, 5, 6, 7, 8, 9, 10, 10, 10, 12, 13, 14, 14; 7:3, 3, 4, 4, 5, 8, 9, 9, 9, 20, 21, 22, 24, 24, 27, 27; 8:2, 3, 4, 5, 7, 8, 10, 10, 13, 15, 18, 18, 18; 9:5, 8, 8, 10, 10, 11; 10:1, 1, 2, 13, 15, 19, 20, 20, 20, 22; 11:1, 5, 5, 7, 8, 9, 10, 11, 12, 13, 13, 16, 16, 17, 17, 19, 19, 20, 21, 25; 12:7, 7, 7, 7, 7, 13, 13, 14, 15, 15, 16, 16, 20, 23, 25, 25, 25, 28, 28, 28; 13:7, 8, 9, 9, 9, 13, 14, 14, 15, 16, 20, 20, 21, 21, 22, 23, 23; 14:3, 4, 5, 7, 8, 8, 9, 9, 11, 13, 15, 17, 17, 19, 22; 15:6, 7, 7, 8; 16:6, 6, 7, 8, 8, 8, 9, 9, 10, 11, 14, 16, 17, 18, 19, 27, 27, 37, 37, 37, 38, 38, 39, 41, 42, 43, 48, 50, 53, 53, 59, 60, 60, 60, 61, 62, 62, 63; 17:9, 9, 9, 9, 12, 16, 19, 19, 20, 20, 21, 22, 22, 24, 24, 24, 24, 24; 18:3, 23, 23, 25, 29, 30, 32; 20:3, 3, 5, 5, 5, 6, 6, 6, 7, 7, 8, 9, 9, 10, 11, 12, 12, 13, 13, 14, 14, 14, 15, 15, 15, 16, 17, 18, 19, 19, 20, 21, 22, 23, 23, 23, 25, 26, 26, 26, 26, 26, 28, 28, 29, 31, 31, 31, 33, 33, 34, 35, 35, 36, 36, 37, 38, 38, 38, 40, 40, 41, 41, 42, 42, 42, 44, 44, 47, 48, 49; 21:3, 3, 4, 4, 5, 7, 7, 17, 17, 17, 27, 27, 30, 30, 30, 31, 31, 32; 22:4, 13, 14, 14, 14, 15, 16, 19, 20, 21, 22, 30, 30, 30, 30, 31, 31; 23:4, 4, 9, 13, 18, 18, 22, 24, 25, 27, 28, 31, 34, 43, 48, 49; 24:8, 9, 13, 14, 14, 14, 16, 18, 18, 18, 20, 21, 21, 24, 25, 25, 27; 25:4, 5, 5, 7, 7, 7, 7, 9, 10, 10, 11, 11, 13, 13, 13, 14, 14, 16, 16, 17, 17, 17; 26:2, 2, 3, 3, 4, 5, 6, 7, 13, 14, 14, 19, 20, 21, 21; 28:2, 2, 7, 9, 10, 14, 16, 16, 17, 18, 18, 22, 22, 22, 22, 23, 23, 24, 25, 25, 25, 25, 26, 26; 29:3, 3, 4, 5, 5, 6, 8, 9, 9, 10, 10, 12, 12, 13, 14, 16, 19, 20, 21, 21; 30:8, 8, 9, 10, 12, 12, 12, 13, 14, 15, 15, 16, 18, 19, 19, 21, 22, 22, 22, 23, 24, 24, 25, 25, 25, 26, 26; 31:9, 11, 11, 15, 15, 15, 16, 16, 18; 32:3, 4, 5, 6, 7, 7, 7, 8, 8, 9, 9, 10, 10, 10, 12, 13, 14, 15, 15, 16, 18, 32, 32; 33:2, 6, 7, 7, 8, 8, 11, 11, 11, 13, 13, 14, 18, 20, 22, 27, 28, 29, 29, 31; 34:8, 10, 10, 10, 10, 11, 12, 12, 13, 13, 14, 15, 16, 16, 16, 16, 16, 17, 20, 22, 22, 23, 24, 24, 25, 26, 26, 27, 27, 29, 30, 31; 35:3, 3, 4, 4, 5, 6, 6, 7, 8, 9, 9, 11, 11, 11, 11, 11, 12, 13, 14, 15, 15; 36:6, 7, 9, 9, 10, 11, 11, 11, 12, 15, 18, 19, 21, 22, 22, 23, 23, 23, 24, 25, 26, 26, 26, 27, 27, 28, 28, 29, 29, 29, 30, 32, 33, 33, 35, 36, 36, 36, 37, 37, 38, 38; 37:1, 3, 5, 6, 6, 6, 7, 7, 8, 10, 12, 12, 13, 14, 14, 14, 14, 14, 19, 19, 21, 21, 22, 23, 23, 23, 25, 26, 26, 26, 27, 27, 28; 38:3, 4, 4, 11, 12, 12, 16, 16, 17, 17, 17, 19, 21, 22, 22, 23, 23, 23; 39:1, 2, 3, 4, 5, 6, 6, 7, 7, 7, 8, 11, 13, 19, 21, 21, 21, 22, 23, 24, 25, 25, 25, 27, 28, 28, 29, 29; 40:2, 3, 4, 4, 5; 41:8; 43:3, 3, 6, 7, 7, 8, 9, 10, 27; 44:4, 4, 5, 8, 12, 28; 46:18, 21; 47:1, 2, 6, 14, 14, 23; Da 1:10; 2:3, 3, 3, 5, 6, 6, 8, 8, 8, 9, 23, 24, 25, 28, 30, 30, 36; 3:14, 15, 15, 25, 29; 4:2, 4, 5, 5, 5, 6, 7, 8, 9, 9, 10, 10, 10, 13, 13, 18, 19, 30, 34, 34, 36, 37; 5:14, 16, 17; 6:22, 22, 26; 7:2, 4, 5, 5, 7, 8, 9, 11, 11, 11, 13, 15, 15, 16, 19, 20, 21, 28, 28; 8:1, 2, 3, 3, 5, 6, 13, 15, 16, 17, 17, 17, 18, 19, 27, 27, 27; 9:2, 2, 3, 3, 4, 17, 20, 21, 21, 22, 23; 10:2, 3, 4, 5, 7, 8, 8, 9, 9, 11, 11, 11, 12, 13, 14, 15, 16, 16, 16, 16, 16, 17, 18, 19, 20, 20, 21, 21; 11:1, 2; 12:5, 8, 8, 8, 9; Hos 1:4, 5, 6, 7, 7, 9; 2:1, 2, 3, 3, 4, 4, 6, 6, 7, 7, 7, 8, 9, 9, 9, 9, 10, 11, 12, 12, 13, 14, 14, 15, 15, 17, 18, 18, 19, 20, 21, 23, 23, 23, 23, 23; 3:2, 3; 4:5, 6, 6, 9, 14; 5:2, 3, 10, 12, 12, 14, 14, 15; 6:4, 5, 5, 6, 6, 6, 10, 11; 7:1, 2, 2, 12, 12, 13, 15; 8:5, 10, 12, 13, 13, 14; 9:10, 10, 12, 12, 13, 14, 14, 15, 15, 15, 16; 10:10, 10, 11, 11, 12; 11:1, 1, 2, 3, 3, 4, 4, 4, 8, 8, 8, 9, 9, 9, 9, 9, 10, 11; 12:8, 8, 9, 9, 10; 13:4, 5, 7, 8, 8, 9, 11, 11, 14, 14, 14; 14:4, 5, 8, 8; Joel 2:19, 20, 20, 25, 25, 27, 27, 28, 28, 29, 30; 3:1, 2, 2, 4, 7, 7, 8, 8, 12, 17, 21, 21, 21; Am 1:3, 3, 4, 5, 5, 5, 6, 6, 7, 8, 8, 8, 9, 9, 10, 11, 11, 12, 13, 13, 14, 15; 2:1, 1, 2, 3, 3, 4, 4, 5, 6, 6, 9, 9, 9, 10, 11, 13, 16; 3:1, 2, 2, 7, 7, 8, 14, 14, 15, 15; 4:3, 6, 7, 7, 9, 10, 10, 10, 11, 11, 12, 12; 5:1, 12, 17, 17, 21, 22, 22, 23, 24, 27; 6:8, 8, 8, 14; 7:1, 2, 3, 4, 5, 6, 7, 8, 8, 8, 9, 14, 14; 8:1, 2, 2, 3, 7, 9, 10, 11; 9:1, 2, 2, 3, 3, 4, 4, 7, 7, 7, 8, 8, 8, 8, 9, 11, 11, 12, 12, 12, 14, 15, 15; Ob 2, 4, 4, 8, 15, 16, 18; Jnh 1:2, 9, 9, 12; 2:2, 2, 3, 3, 4, 4, 5, 6, 6, 7, 7, 9, 9; 3:2; 4:2, 2, 2, 2, 2, 3, 11; Mic 1:6, 6, 8, 8, 8, 15; 2:3, 3, 12, 12; 3:8, 8; 4:6, 7, 7, 13; 5:10, 11, 12, 13, 14, 15; 6:3, 4, 4, 5, 5, 11, 13, 13, 14, 16; 7:1, 7, 7, 8, 8, 8, 9, 9, 9, 10, 15, 15, 15; Na 1:12, 12, 13, 14, 14; 2:13; 3:5, 5, 6; Hab 1:2, 2, 3, 3, 3, 3, 5, 5, 6; 2:1, 3; 3:2, 2, 3, 7, 16, 16, 16, 16, 18, 18; Zep 1:2, 3, 3, 4, 4, 5, 6, 8, 9, 12, 17; 2:8, 9, 15; 3:6, 7, 7, 7, 8, 9, 11, 18, 19, 19, 19, 19, 20, 20, 20, 20; Hag 1:8, 9, 11, 13; 2:4, 5, 6, 6, 7, 7, 9, 9, 17, 19, 19, 21, 22, 22, 23, 23, 23, 23; Zec 1:2, 3, 6, 6, 8, 9, 9, 15, 15, 16, 18, 19, 21; 2:1, 1, 2, 2, 5, 5, 6, 9, 10, 11; 3:2, 4, 4, 5, 7, 8, 9, 9, 9; 4:1, 2, 2, 3, 4, 5, 11, 13; 5:1, 2, 2, 4, 6, 9, 10; 6:1, 4, 9; 7:13, 13, 14; 8:2, 3, 3, 7, 8, 8, 10, 11, 11, 12, 12, 13, 14, 14, 15, 17; 9:6, 8, 8, 10, 10, 11, 11, 12, 12, 13; 10:3, 6, 6, 6, 6, 6, 8, 8, 9, 10, 12, 12; 11:5, 6, 6, 6, 7, 7, 8, 8, 9, 9, 10, 10, 10, 12, 12, 13, 14, 16; 12:2, 3, 4, 4, 4, 6, 10; 13:2, 2, 6, 7, 9, 9, 9; 14:2; Mal 1:2, 2, 3, 3, 4, 6, 6, 10, 10, 10, 13, 14; 2:2, 2, 2, 3, 3, 4, 5, 8, 9, 16; 3:1, 5, 5, 5, 6, 6, 7, 10, 10, 11, 17, 17; 4:3, 4, 5, 6; Mt 2:8, 13, 15; 3:11, 11, 11, 14, 17; 4:9, 19; 5:17, 17, 17, 18, 20, 22, 26, 28, 32, 34, 37, 37, 39, 44; 6:2, 5, 16, 25; 7:23, 23; 8:3, 7, 8, 9, 9, 9, 9, 9, 10, 10, 11, 19, 20; 9:6, 6, 13, 13, 13, 21, 21, 28; 10:15, 16, 23, 23, 25, 27, 27, 32, 33, 34, 34, 35; 11:10, 11, 14, 16, 19, 21, 22, 23, 24, 28, 29, 30; 12:6, 7, 7, 8, 18, 18, 18, 27, 28, 36, 39, 40, 44, 44; 13:13, 13, 13, 14, 17, 18, 30, 35, 35, 37, 41; 14:8, 27; 15:10, 24, 32, 32; 16:4, 9, 10, 11, 11, 15, 18, 18, 19, 27, 28; 17:5, 9, 12, 16, 17, 17, 20; 18:3, 10, 18, 19, 20, 21, 26, 29, 32, 33; 19:9, 16, 20, 23, 24, 28, 28; 20:13, 14, 15, 15, 22, 23, 28; 21:21, 27, 29, 30, 31, 43; 22:8, 32, 44; 23:34, 36, 37, 39; 24:2, 5, 25, 34, 47; 25:12, 20, 21, 22, 23, 24, 25, 25, 25, 26, 26, 27, 35, 35, 35, 36, 36, 36, 40, 42, 42, 43, 43, 43, 45; 26:2, 11, 13, 18, 22, 24, 25, 29, 29, 32, 32, 33, 35, 35, 36, 39, 42, 45, 48, 53, 54, 55, 55, 61, 63, 70, 72, 74, 74; 27:4, 4, 19, 22, 22, 24, 43, 63; 28:5, 7, 18, 20, 20; Mk 1:2, 7, 7, 8, 11, 17, 24, 38, 38, 41; 2:10, 10, 17, 28; 3:28; 4:11, 12, 13, 14, 30, 30; 5:28, 28; 6:16, 22, 23, 24, 25, 50; 7:11, 11, 11, 27, 29; 8:2, 3, 12, 12, 19, 20, 24, 24, 27, 29, 38, 38; 9:1, 13, 17, 18, 19, 19, 23, 24, 25, 41; 10:15, 17, 20, 29, 38, 38, 40, 45, 51; 11:23, 33; 12:26, 33, 36, 43; 13:23, 30, 37, 37; 14:7, 9, 14, 19, 21, 25, 25, 25, 28, 28, 29, 31, 31, 32, 36, 41, 44, 48, 49, 58, 58, 62, 68, 71, 71; 15:9, 12, 12; Lk 1:3, 18, 19, 19, 20, 34, 34, 38, 38, 44, 46, 47, 66; 2:10, 29, 30, 48, 49; 3:16, 16, 16, 22; 4:6, 6, 7, 34, 43, 43; 5:13, 24, 24, 32; 6:5, 9, 27, 47; 7:6, 7, 8, 8, 8, 8, 8, 9, 9, 27, 28, 31, 31, 34, 40, 43, 44, 45, 47; 8:10, 10, 10, 28, 46; 9:9, 9, 18, 20, 22, 22, 22, 22, 26, 26, 27, 40, 41, 44, 57, 58, 61; 10:3, 13, 18, 19, 24, 25, 35, 40, 42; 11:6, 7, 8, 9, 18, 19, 20, 24, 24, 29, 49; 12:8, 8, 9, 18, 22, 37, 44, 49, 49, 50, 51, 51; 13:5, 18, 25, 27, 27, 32, 32, 33, 34; 14:24, 24; 15:12, 17, 18, 18, 19, 21, 21, 31, 31; 16:2, 3, 4, 4, 6, 9, 24, 28, 28; 17:3, 17; 18:4, 8, 8, 8, 11, 11, 11, 11, 11, 12, 12, 13, 14, 17, 18, 21, 29, 41; 19:5, 8, 8, 8, 10, 17, 20, 21, 22, 22, 23, 42; 20:8, 13, 13, 43; 21:3, 15, 32; 22:11, 15, 16, 16, 18, 20, 22, 27, 29, 32, 33, 35, 42, 52, 53, 57, 60, 67, 68, 69, 70; 23:4, 14, 16, 16, 22, 22, 43, 46; 24:38, 39, 39, 44, 44, 49; Jn 1:15, 15, 15, 15, 20, 23, 26, 27, 30, 30, 30, 30, 31, 31, 32, 33, 34, 34, 48, 50, 50; 2:19; 3:3, 11, 11, 12, 12, 13, 14, 28, 28, 28, 29, 29, 30, 31; 4:9, 10, 10, 14, 15, 17, 25, 26, 29, 32, 38, 39, 48; 5:7, 7, 7, 17, 19, 24, 25, 30, 30, 30, 31, 32, 34, 36, 40, 42, 43, 45, 47; 6:20, 26, 27, 32, 35, 37, 38, 38, 39, 39, 40, 41, 42, 43, 44, 46, 47, 48, 51, 53, 54, 56, 57, 58, 63, 65, 65, 70; 7:7, 8, 21, 23, 24, 28, 28, 29, 29, 33, 33, 34, 36; 8:11, 12, 14, 14, 14, 14, 15, 16, 16, 16, 18, 19, 21, 21, 22, 23, 23, 24, 24, 24, 24, 25, 25, 26, 26, 26, 26, 28, 28, 28, 29, 34, 37, 38, 38, 38, 40, 40, 42, 42, 43, 45, 46, 49, 49, 50, 51, 54, 55, 55, 55, 55, 58; 9:5, 5, 9, 11, 11, 12, 15, 17, 25, 25, 25, 25, 27, 36, 38, 39, 39; 10:1, 7, 7, 9, 11, 14, 14, 15, 15, 16, 16, 17, 17, 18, 18, 18, 25, 25, 27, 28, 30, 32, 34, 36, 37, 38, 38, 38; 11:4, 11, 15, 15, 22, 25, 27, 40, 42; 12:8, 26, 27, 27, 28, 28, 32, 32, 46, 47, 47, 48, 49, 49, 50, 50; 13:7, 8, 12, 14, 15, 15, 18, 18, 18, 19, 19, 26, 33, 33, 34, 34, 37, 37; 14:2, 2, 3, 3, 4, 6, 7, 9, 9, 10, 10, 11, 12, 12, 13, 14, 16, 18, 18, 19, 20, 20, 20, 21, 21, 23, 24, 25, 25, 26, 26, 27, 27, 28, 28, 28, 28, 28, 29, 30, 31, 31; 15:1, 3, 4, 5, 5, 9, 10, 11, 12, 12, 15, 15, 16, 16, 17, 19, 20, 22, 24, 24, 26; 16:1, 4, 4, 4, 5, 5, 7, 7, 7, 7, 10, 12, 15, 15, 16, 17, 19, 19, 19, 22, 25, 25, 26, 27, 28, 28, 32, 33, 33; 17:4, 6, 7, 8, 8, 11, 11, 12, 12, 13, 13, 13, 14, 14, 16, 18, 19, 20, 21, 21, 22, 23, 24, 25, 26, 26, 26; 18:5, 6, 8, 8, 8, 9, 11, 17, 20, 20, 20, 20, 20, 21, 23, 25, 26, 35, 36, 36, 36, 37, 37, 37, 37; 19:4, 4, 6, 10, 21, 22, 22, 28; 20:2, 13, 15, 17, 17, 18, 21, 25, 25; 21:15, 16, 17, 22, 22, 23, 23, 25; Ac 1:1, 4; 2:17, 18, 19, 25, 25, 29, 34; 3:6, 6, 17; 7:3, 7, 32, 34, 34, 34, 34, 43, 50, 56; 8:19, 23, 31, 36; 9:5, 12, 15, 16; 10:14, 20, 28, 29, 29, 30, 33, 34; 11:5, 5, 6, 6, 7, 8, 8, 11, 15, 15, 16, 17; 13:2, 22, 25, 25, 32, 33, 34, 34, 41, 47; 15:16, 16, 16, 16, 17; 16:15, 18, 30; 17:22, 23, 23, 23; 18:6, 6, 10, 14, 15, 21; 19:13, 15, 15, 21, 40; 20:18, 19, 19, 20, 21, 22, 24, 25, 25, 26, 27, 29, 29, 31, 32, 33, 34, 35; 21:13, 37, 39; 22:1, 3, 3, 3, 3, 3, 4, 5, 6, 7, 8, 8, 10, 10, 11, 13, 17, 17, 17, 18, 19, 19, 20, 20, 21, 27, 28, 28; 23:1, 5, 6, 6, 27, 27, 27, 28, 29, 30, 30, 30, 35; 24:4, 4, 10, 10, 11, 12, 12, 14, 14, 14, 14, 15, 16, 17, 18, 21, 21, 21, 21, 22; 25:8, 8, 10, 10, 11, 11, 11, 11, 15, 16, 17, 18, 20, 20, 21, 21, 25, 26, 26, 26; 26:2, 3, 4, 5, 6, 6, 7, 9, 9, 9, 10, 10, 11, 11, 11, 12, 14, 15, 15, 16, 16, 17, 17, 19, 20, 22, 22, 25, 25, 26, 26, 27, 29, 29; 27:10, 23, 23, 25; 28:17, 17, 19, 19, 20, 20, 20, 20, 26, 28; Ro 1:8, 9, 9, 9, 10, 11, 11, 12, 13, 13, 13, 13, 13, 14, 15, 16; 3:8; 4:17; 6:19; 7:7, 7, 9, 9, 9, 9, 9, 14, 15, 15, 15, 15, 15, 16, 16, 16, 17, 18, 18, 18, 18, 18, 18, 19, 19, 19, 19, 20, 20, 20, 21, 21, 22, 24, 25, 25; 8:38; 9:1, 1, 1, 3, 9, 13, 13, 15, 15, 15, 15, 17, 25, 25, 25, 33; 10:2, 19, 19, 20, 20, 21; 11:1, 1, 3, 4, 13, 13, 14, 14, 25, 27; 12:1, 3, 19, 19; 14:11, 14; 15:9, 9, 13, 14, 15, 15, 16, 18, 18, 18, 19, 19, 21, 22, 23, 23, 24, 24, 24, 24, 25, 25, 28, 28, 29, 29, 30, 31, 31, 32; 16:4, 7, 8, 17, 19, 22, 23; 1Co 1:4, 6, 10, 10, 12, 12, 12, 12, 13, 14, 14, 16, 16, 18, 19; 2:1, 1, 2, 3, 4, 5, 6, 6; 3:1, 1, 1, 1, 2, 4, 4, 10; 4:3, 3, 6, 8, 9, 14, 15, 15, 16, 16, 17, 17, 17, 18, 18, 19, 21, 21; 5:1, 1, 3, 3, 3, 4, 9, 9, 10, 11; 6:5, 12, 12, 12, 12; 7:7, 7, 8, 8, 10, 12, 12, 25, 25, 26, 28, 32, 35, 35, 40, 40, 40; 8:13, 13, 13, 13; 9:1, 1, 1, 2, 2, 2, 6, 15, 15, 15, 15, 16, 16, 16, 17, 17, 17, 18, 19, 19, 19, 20, 20, 20, 20, 20, 20, 21, 21, 21, 21, 21, 21, 22, 22, 22, 22, 22, 23, 23, 26, 26, 27, 27, 27; 10:1, 15, 19, 19, 20, 20, 23, 23, 30, 30, 33, 33, 33, 33, 33; 11:1, 2, 2, 3, 16, 17, 17, 18, 18, 21, 22, 22, 23, 23, 34; 12:1, 1, 3, 15, 15, 16, 16, 21, 21; 13:1, 1, 2, 2, 2, 2, 2, 2, 3, 3, 3, 3, 3, 11, 11, 11, 11, 12, 12; 14:5, 5, 6, 6, 11, 14, 14, 14, 15, 15, 15, 15, 15, 15, 15, 15, 18, 18, 19, 21, 26, 37; 15:1, 3, 8, 8, 9, 9, 9, 10, 10, 10, 11, 31, 31, 34, 50; 16:1, 2, 3, 3, 5, 5, 5, 6, 7, 7, 8, 10, 11, 12, 15, 17, 21; 2Co 1:8, 13, 15, 15, 16, 17, 17, 17, 18, 19, 23, 23, 23; 2:1, 1, 1, 2, 3, 3, 3, 3, 4, 4, 4, 4, 5, 5, 9, 9, 10, 10, 10, 12, 13, 13; 4:13, 13; 5:11, 16, 16; 6:2, 2, 13, 13, 16, 16, 17, 18; 7:3, 4, 7, 8, 8, 8, 8, 9, 9, 12, 14, 14, 14, 16, 16; 8:1, 3, 7, 8, 10, 13, 13, 16, 16; 9:1, 2, 2, 3, 3, 3, 3, 4, 4, 5, 5, 5; 10:1, 1, 1, 2, 2, 2, 8, 8, 12, 12; 11:1, 1, 2, 2, 3, 5, 5, 6, 6, 6, 6, 7, 7, 8, 8, 9, 9, 9, 9, 10, 11, 11, 12, 14, 16, 16, 17, 18, 21, 22, 22, 22, 23, 23, 23, 23, 25, 25, 25, 25, 26, 26, 26, 26, 26, 27, 27, 27, 28, 29, 30, 30, 30, 31, 32, 33, 33; 12:1, 2, 3, 4, 4, 5, 5, 6, 6, 6, 6, 7, 7, 8, 9, 10, 10, 10, 10, 11, 11, 12, 12, 12, 12, 13, 13, 14, 14, 14, 14, 15, 15, 15, 16, 16, 17, 18, 20, 20, 20, 20, 20, 20, 21, 21, 21; 13:1, 2, 2, 2, 2, 2, 3, 6, 10, 10, 10, 10, 10, 11; Gal 1:1, 6, 9, 10, 10, 10, 11, 11, 13, 13, 13, 13, 14, 14, 15, 16, 16, 17, 17, 17, 18, 19, 20, 20, 20, 21; 2:1, 2, 2, 2, 2, 2, 2, 2, 6, 10, 11, 14, 14, 15, 18, 18, 18, 19, 19, 19, 19, 19, 19, 20, 20, 21; 3:1, 5, 17; 4:9, 11, 11, 12, 12, 12, 12, 13, 13, 14, 15, 16, 16, 18, 19, 19, 20, 20, 20, 20; 5:2, 10, 10, 11, 11, 11, 11, 12, 16, 21; 6:11, 11, 14, 17, 17; Eph 1:15, 16, 16, 18, 18, 19; 3:1, 3, 4, 4, 7, 8, 8, 8, 9, 13, 14, 14, 16, 17; 4:1; 5:33; 6:19, 20, 20, 20, 21, 22; Php 1:3, 3, 4, 4, 6, 7, 7, 7, 7, 8, 9, 10, 12, 13, 18, 18, 19, 20, 20, 20, 20, 20, 20, 22, 22, 23, 23, 24, 25, 25, 26, 27, 27, 30; 2:12, 12, 16, 16, 17, 17, 17, 19, 20, 23, 23, 24, 24, 25, 25, 26, 27, 28, 28; 3:1, 1, 4, 4, 5, 5, 5, 5, 6, 6, 6, 7, 7, 8, 8, 9, 9, 10, 10, 11, 12, 12, 12, 12, 12, 13, 13, 13, 14, 15, 15, 18, 18; 4:1, 2, 3, 4, 8, 10, 10, 10, 11, 11, 11, 12, 12, 13, 13, 15, 16, 17, 17, 17, 18, 18, 18, 18; Col 1:23, 24, 24, 24, 29, 29; 2:1, 1, 2, 4, 5, 5; 4:3, 4, 4, 7, 8, 9, 13, 16; 1Th 2:18; 3:1, 5, 5, 5; 4:9, 13, 15; 5:1, 27; 2Th 2:5, 5; 3:1, 13, 17, 17; 1Ti 1:3, 3, 12, 13, 13, 13, 13, 15, 20; 2:1, 7, 8, 9, 12; 3:14, 14, 15; 4:13; 5:14, 15, 21; 6:13; 2Ti 1:3, 3, 3, 4, 4, 4, 5, 6, 6, 12, 12, 12, 12, 12, 12, 16; 2:7, 8, 9, 9, 10, 23; 3:10, 10, 10, 11, 11; 4:1, 7, 7, 7, 12, 13, 16, 16, 17, 20; Tit 1:1, 3, 5, 5; 3:8, 8, 12, 12; Phm 1:2, 4, 4, 5, 6, 7, 8, 8, 9, 10, 12, 13, 13, 14, 14, 17, 19, 19, 19, 21, 21, 21, 22; Heb 1:5, 5, 13; 2:12, 12, 13, 13; 3:10, 10, 10, 11; 4:3; 5:5; 6:14, 14; 7:14; 8:5, 8, 9, 9, 9, 10, 10, 10, 10, 12, 12; 10:5, 7, 7, 9, 16, 16, 16, 17, 30, 30, 38; 11:32; 12:21, 26; 13:5, 5, 6, 19, 19, 22, 22, 23, 23; Jas 2:18, 18, 18; 4:4; 1Pe 1:1, 16; 2:6, 11; 5:1, 1, 12, 12; 2Pe 1:1, 12, 13, 13, 13, 14, 15, 15, 15, 17; 3:1, 2, 3, 17, 17; 1Jn 2:1, 4, 7, 9, 12, 13, 13, 14, 14, 14, 21, 26; 4:20; 5:13, 16; 2Jn 1, 4, 5, 12, 12, 12; 3Jn 1, 2, 2, 4, 9, 10, 10, 13, 13, 14; Jude 1, 3, 3, 3, 4, 5, 6; Rev 1:8, 8, 9, 9, 10, 10, 12, 12, 17, 17, 17, 18, 18, 18; 2:2, 2, 2, 4, 5, 6, 9, 9, 10, 13, 14, 16, 17, 19, 19, 20, 21, 22, 23, 23, 23, 24, 24, 25, 26, 28, 28; 3:1, 3, 5, 5, 8, 8, 9, 9, 10, 11, 12, 15, 15, 16, 17, 17, 17, 17, 18, 19, 19, 20, 20, 21, 21; 4:1, 1, 1, 1, 2, 2; 5:1, 2, 4, 6, 6, 11, 11, 13; 6:1, 2, 3, 5, 5, 7, 8, 9, 12; 7:1, 2, 4, 9, 14; 8:2, 13, 13; 9:1, 13, 16, 17; 10:1, 4, 9, 10, 10; 11:1, 1, 3; 12:1, 1, 3, 3, 10; 13:1, 3, 11; 14:1, 2, 6, 13, 14; 15:1, 2, 5; 16:1, 5, 7, 13, 15; 17:1, 3, 6, 6, 7; 18:1, 4, 7, 7, 7, 21; 19:1, 6, 10, 10, 11, 17, 19; 20:1, 4, 4, 4, 9, 11, 11, 12; 21:1, 2, 3, 5, 5, 6, 6, 7, 9; 22:7, 8, 8, 8, 9, 12, 13, 16, 16, 16, 18, 20

I'D (5)

Ge 27:46; 29:19; Nu 11:15; Jnh 4:3; Ac 25:22

I'LL (80)

Ge 13:9, 9, 9; 14:24; 24:19, 44, 49; 27:9; 29:18; 30:1, 28, 31; 38:17; 40:18; 42:16, 16, 37; 46:31; Ru 4:4; 1Sa 2:16; 17:32, 36, 44; 18:17; 19:3, 3, 3; 20:5; 23:23, 23; 26:6, 8, 11; 2Sa 13:5; 14:8, 9; 18:4; 1Ki 12:10, 11, 11, 14, 14; 21:7; 2Ki 18:23; 2Ch 10:10, 11, 11, 14, 14; Ps 119:106; Pr 1:23; 3:28; 24:29; Isa 6:8; 36:8; Jer 20:9; Hos 2:5; Mic 2:11; Mal 2:14; Mt 17:4; 21:24; Mk 11:29; 12:9, 15; Lk 10:35; 12:5, 18, 18, 19; 13:8; 16:4; 20:13, 1[illegible]; Jn 4:15; 18:39; Ac 3:6; 24:25; 1Co 4:19; 11:34; Gal 5:3

I'M (75)

Ge 22:11; 25:30, 32; 27:12, 31, 46; 31:11, 35; 37:13, 13; 40:15; 48:19; Ex 4:10, 10, 10; 6:12, 30; 16:4; Jos 14:12; Jdg 4:19; 12:5; 15:7; 1Sa 1:15; 9:21; 14:7; 17:39; 20:2; 29:9; 2Sa 13:28; 16:18; 20:17; 1Ki 18:14; Job 10:15; 21:4; Ps 62:3; 94:18; Pr 26:13; Isa 44:20; 47:8; Jer 1:6; Am 7:14, 14; Zec 13:5, 5; Mt 25:26; 26:22, 25; Mk 14:19; Lk 1:18; 5:8; 12:42; 16:3, 3; 17:15; 18:5; 22:58; Jn 7:16; 16:4, 26; 17:15; 21:3; Ac 10:21, 26, 36; 17:3; 19:27, 27; 23:5; Ro 1:12; 2Co 7:3; 11:21, 21; Gal 1:10; Php 1:23; 2Ti 1:8

I'VE (28)

Ge 21:26; 27:19; 30:29; 41:19; Jdg 15:16, 16; 1Sa 9:6; 20:5; 25:11; 29:3, 6; 2Sa 9:7; Ps 27:12; 71:5; 119:106; Pr 7:14, 17; Hos 12:8; Mt 19:20; 24:33; Mk 10:20; 13:29; Lk 13:7; 15:29; 18:21; 21:31; Ac 9:13; 1Co 4:6

IF (1932)

Ge 2:17; 3:22; 4:7, 7, 24; 8:8; 11:6; 12:13; 13:9, 9; 15:5; 18:3, 26, 28, 29, 30; 20:7; 24:8, 14, 41, 42; 26:3; 27:12; 28:20, 21; 29:7, 18, 27; 30:33; 31:8, 32, 39, 50, 50; 32:8; 33:13; 34:15, 23; 38:23; 42:16, 18, 20, 33, 34, 37, 38; 43:4, 5, 7, 9, 10, 11, 14; 44:9, 19, 29, 32, 34; 47:6, 29; 50:23; Ex 1:10, 10; 3:13; 4:8, 9; 5:3, 8, 17; 8:2, 21, 26; 9:2, 14; 10:4, 10; 12:4, 19, 44, 48, 48; 13:13, 17; 15:26; 16:3; 18:23, 23; 19:5, 24; 20:7, 19, 25, 26; 21:2, 3, 3, 4, 6, 8, 9, 10, 11, 13, 14, 19, 20, 21, 22, 23, 23, 24, 24, 26, 27, 28, 29, 29, 31, 32, 35, 36; 22:2, 3, 3, 4, 5, 6, 7, 8, 12, 13, 14, 14, 15, 15, 16, 17, 23, 25, 26, 27; 23:4, 5, 22, 25, 33; 24:14; 28:35; 29:34; 32:17, 32; 33:3, 5, 13, 15, 16; 34:9, 12, 15, 20; 35:21; 40:37; Lev 1:3, 10, 14; 2:5, 7, 14; 3:1, 6, 7, 12; 4:3, 13, 22, 22, 27, 27, 32; 5:1, 2, 2, 3, 3, 4, 4, 7, 11, 15, 17, 17; 6:4, 27, 28, 28, 30; 7:12, 16, 18, 18, 21; 8:35; 10:6, 9, 19; 11:24, 25, 26, 27, 28, 31, 32, 33, 34, 35, 36, 37, 38, 39, 40; 12:5, 8; 13:2, 3, 4, 4, 5, 6, 7, 8, 10, 13, 13, 14, 16, 17, 18, 20, 20, 21, 21, 22, 23, 24, 25, 26, 27, 28, 29, 30, 31, 32, 32, 34, 35, 36, 37, 38, 39, 40, 41, 42, 43, 49, 51, 53, 55, 55, 56, 57, 58; 14:3, 37, 39, 43, 44, 48; 15:5, 6, 7, 8, 10, 11, 19, 21, 22, 24, 25, 25, 27; 16:13; 17:3, 8, 13, 15, 16; 18:5, 18; 19:7, 8, 20; 20:2, 4, 6, 10, 11, 12, 14, 15, 16, 17, 18, 19, 20, 21; 21:9, 11; 22:3, 4, 4, 10, 11, 11, 12, 13, 18, 19, 21, 23, 24; 25:18, 25, 26, 28, 30, 35, 39, 47, 47, 49, 51, 52, 54; 26:3, 14, 15, 18, 21, 23, 25, 26, 27; 27:2, 8, 9, 10, 11, 13, 14, 15, 16, 17, 18, 19, 20, 20, 22, 27, 27, 31, 33; Nu 5:6, 8, 14, 14, 15, 19, 20, 27, 28, 29, 30; 6:2, 7, 9, 21; 9:10, 10, 14, 19; 10:4; 11:18, 22, 22; 12:14; 14:8, 15; 15:6, 13, 14, 24, 27; 16:26, 29, 30, 40; 18:3, 5, 22, 32, 32; 19:12, 16, 16; 20:19; 21:2, 8; 22:18, 19, 29, 34; 23:3, 25; 24:13; 27:8, 9, 10, 11; 30:3, 5, 7, 8, 9, 11, 12, 14, 15; 32:5, 15, 20, 21, 23, 29, 30; 33:55; 35:11, 16, 17, 18, 20, 21, 24, 26, 30; 36:3; Dt 1:42; 4:6, 23, 26, 29, 32, 40; 5:11, 25, 29; 6:2; 7:12, 16, 22; 8:19; 9:28; 11:9, 13, 13, 13, 17, 27, 28; 12:21; 13:2, 3, 8, 14, 18; 14:7, 25; 15:5, 7, 9, 12, 21, 21; 17:4, 15, 20; 18:8, 22; 19:4, 6, 8, 9, 9, 16, 18; 20:5, 6, 8, 11, 12; 21:12, 14, 22; 22:1, 2, 3, 4, 6, 8, 9, 15, 22, 23, 25, 28; 23:1, 15, 21; 24:2, 7, 10, 12; 25:2, 5, 7, 8, 11; 26:19; 28:1, 2, 9, 13, 15, 45, 58, 58, 67, 67; 30:2, 10, 10, 16, 17, 17; Jos 2:5, 14, 18, 19, 20; 7:7, 7; 9:7, 20; 14:12; 17:15; 20:5; 22:18, 19, 22, 23, 28; 23:12, 15, 16; 24:15, 20, 27; Jdg 4:8, 20, 20; 6:13, 16, 17, 27, 31, 36, 37; 7:2, 10; 8:19; 9:7, 15, 15, 19, 20, 29; 11:8, 9, 9, 30; 12:5, 6; 13:18, 23; 14:6, 12, 13, 18; 15:14; 16:7, 9, 11, 12, 13, 17; Ru 1:12, 17; 2:7, 14; 3:13, 13; 4:4, 4, 4, 16; 1Sa 1:11; 2:25, 25; 3:9, 17; 4:3, 9; 6:3, 9, 9; 7:3; 9:9; 11:3; 12:10, 14, 14, 14, 15, 25; 14:9, 10, 30, 39, 44; 16:2; 17:9, 9, 35; 19:11, 17; 20:6, 7, 7, 8, 9, 12, 13, 13, 14, 21, 22, 28; 21:4, 9; 23:23, 23; 25:22, 28, 34, 40; 26:19, 19; 27:5; 28:16; 29:4; 30:15; 2Sa 2:22, 27, 27; 3:9, 27, 35; 7:14; 9:1, 3; 10:11, 11; 12:8; 13:5, 25, 26; 14:7, 9, 10, 32, 32; 15:8, 14, 25, 26, 33; 16:10; 17:6, 13; 18:3, 3, 3, 4, 13, 25, 33; 19:6, 7, 13; 20:11, 18, 21; 1Ki 1:12, 21, 52, 52; 2:4, 4, 23; 3:14; 6:12; 8:25, 31, 33, 33, 35, 37, 37, 38, 44, 44, 46, 48; 9:4, 6, 6; 11:38, 38; 12:7, 10; 13:8; 18:5, 14, 21, 21, 44; 19:2; 20:10, 39; 21:2; 22:28; 2Ki 1:10, 12; 2:10, 10; 3:11; 5:13; 6:27, 31; 7:2, 4, 4, 4, 4, 9, 13, 13, 19; 8:8, 9; 9:17; 10:6, 15, 24; 18:14, 21, 23, 27; 21:8; 1Ch 12:17, 17, 19; 13:2, 2; 19:12, 12; 22:13; 28:7, 9, 9; 2Ch 6:16, 22, 24, 24, 26, 28, 28, 29, 34, 34, 36, 38; 7:14, 17, 19, 19; 10:7, 10; 15:2; 18:27; 25:8; 28:23; 30:9, 9; 33:8; Ezr 4:13, 16; 5:17; 7:20, 25; 9:12; 10:8; Ne 1:8, 9, 9; 2:5, 5, 7; 4:2, 3; 5:13; 9:29; 10:29, 31; 13:21; Est 1:19; 3:4, 9; 4:14, 16; 5:3, 4, 6, 8; 6:7; 7:2, 3, 4; 8:5, 5;

9:12, 13; **Job 3:**13; **4:**18; **6:**2; **7:**13; **8:**5, 6; **9:**3, 7, 12, 15, 16, 24, 27, 27, 30, 33; **10:**14, 15, 15, 16; **11:**5, 5, 6, 10, 10, 13; **12:**15, 15; **13:**10, 16, 19; **14:**7, 14, 21; **15:**17; **16:**4, 6; **18:**2; **19:**4; **21:**15; **22:**3, 3, 21, 23, 29; **23:**3; **27:**14; **30:**5; **31:**7, 7, 7, 9, 9, 13, 13, 21, 23, 28, 35, 38, 39; **32:**14, 22; **33:**5, 23, 32, 33; **34:**14, 17; **35:**6, 6, 7, 12, 14; **36:**8, 11, 12; **38:**4, 18; **39:**16; **41:**8; **Ps 7:**2, 3, 4, 12; **14:**2; **22:**8; **27:**3, 10; **28:**1; **30:**9, 9; **31:**12, 12; **35:**14; **40:**5; **41:**6; **44:**20; **46:**2; **50:**12, 23; **51:**16; **53:**2; **62:**9, 10; **66:**18; **69:**20, 20; **73:**15; **81:**8; **89:**30, 31; **91:**9, 9; **104:**29; **109:**28; **119:**32, 92; **124:**1, 2; **129:**3; **130:**3; **132:**12; **137:**5, 6, 6; **139:**8, 8, 9, 9, 19; **141:**5; **Pr 1:**10; **3:**28; **4:**8, 12; **5:**9, 12; **6:**1, 2, 3, 31, 31; **9:**12, 12; **11:**27, 27, 31; **13:**18, 18, 24, 24; **14:**22, 22; **15:**31, 32, 32; **16:**21; **17:**13; **18:**14; **19:**7, 17, 18, 19, 25, 25, 27; **20:**4, 13, 16, 20; **21:**23; **22:**13, 27; **23:**2, 13, 15; **24:**10, 14; **25:**21, 21, 26; **26:**27, 27; **27:**11, 13, 14; **28:**13, 16; **29:**3, 9, 12, 24, 24, 24; **30:**4, 9, 9, 10, 32; **31:**5; **Ecc 2:**26; **4:**10; **5:**8; **6:**3; **8:**17; **9:**16; **10:**4, 6, 6; **11:**4; **SS 1:**8; **5:**8; **8:**1, 7, 8, 9, 9; **Isa 1:**9, 18, 19, 20; **6:**13; **7:**9; **8:**13, 20; **19:**12; **20:**6; **21:**12; **23:**12; **27:**4, 5; **28:**12; **29:**9; **30:**19; **36:**6, 8, 12; **41:**23; **43:**26; **44:**7; **45:**10; **47:**8; **49:**15; **50:**10; **54:**15; **55:**1; **57:**13, 16; **58:**8, 13; **63:**2, 3, 16; **66:**3; **Jer 2:**10, 28; **3:**1; **4:**1, 2; **5:**1, 14; **6:**8; **7:**3, 5, 6, 6, 6; **11:**4, 21; **12:**5, 5, 16, 16; **13:**17; **14:**18, 18; **15:**1, 2, 19, 19; **17:**24, 24, 27, 27; **18:**7, 9; **20:**9, 10; **22:**4, 5, 24; **23:**22, 26, 34; **25:**28; **26:**4, 5, 13, 15, 19; **27:**12, 18; **29:**7, 13; **32:**5; **33:**20; **35:**7; **36:**3; **37:**10; **38:**15, 15, 17, 18, 20, 21, 25, 26; **40:**4, 4, 5; **42:**5, 6, 10, 13, 14, 15; **49:**9, 12; **51:**9; **La 1:**12; **4:**19, 19; **Eze 1:**16; **3:**6, 18, 19, 20, 20, 21; **7:**13; **12:**2, 2, 18; **13:**7, 10; **14:**9, 14, 16, 18, 20; **15:**7; **18:**19, 21, 24, 27; **20:**39; **23:**43; **33:**4, 4, 5, 6, 8, 9, 12, 12, 15, 19; **43:**11; **44:**9; **46:**16, 17, 18; **Da 1:**10; **2:**5, 6, 9; **3:**15, 15, 17, 18, 29; **5:**16; **Hos 2:**3; **8:**7, 12; **9:**6, 12, 16; **Joel 3:**4; **Am 5:**6, 18; **6:**9; **7:**7; **8:**10; **9:**2, 2, 3, 3, 4; **Ob** 5; **Jnh 4:**5; **Mic 2:**7; **6:**9; **Na 3:**15; **Hab 1:**5; **2:**3; **Hag 2:**12, 13; **Zec 3:**7; **6:**15; **10:**7; **11:**9, 9, 12, 12; **13:**3, 6; **14:**18, 19; **Mal 3:**10; **4:**3; **Mt 4:**3, 6, 9, 24; **5:**13, 19, 21, 22, 22, 22, 23, 29, 29, 30, 30, 34, 35, 38, 38, 39, 40, 41, 46, 47; **6:**14, 15, 23, 30, 33; **7:**9, 10, 11; **8:**2, 9, 31; **9:**18, 21; **10:**13, 13, 14, 32, 33, 37, 37, 38, 39, 39, 41, 41, 42; **11:**14, 21, 23; **12:**7, 11, 26, 27, 28; **13:**29; **14:**28; **15:**5, 14; **16:**24, 25, 25, 26; **17:**4, 20; **18:**6, 8, 9, 12, 13, 15, 15, 16, 17, 17, 19, 35; **19:**17, 21; **21:**3, 19, 21, 22, 24, 25, 26; **22:**24; **24:**23, 24, 26, 46, 48; **26:**24, 33, 35, 39, 42, 54; **27:**22, 40, 64; **28:**14; **Mk 1:**40; **3:**2, 26; **4:**13; **5:**28; **6:**11; **8:**3, 11, 34, 35, 35, 36, 38; **9:**22, 23, 23, 41, 42, 43, 45, 47, 50; **10:**12; **11:**3, 13, 24, 29, 31; **12:**19; **13:**21, 22; **14:**21, 29, 31, 35; **15:**12; **16:**18; **Lk 2:**23; **3:**11, 11; **4:**3, 7, 9; **5:**5, 12; **6:**27, 29, 29, 33, 34, 37, 38; **7:**4, 8, 39; **9:**5, 23, 24, 24, 25, 26; **10:**6, 6, 8, 10, 13, 35; **11:**8, 11, 12, 13, 16, 18, 19, 20, 36; **12:**8, 9, 26, 28, 31, 43, 45, 58, 59; **13:**6, 9, 9, 31; **14:**5, 8, 8, 26, 27, 28, 32, 34; **15:**4; **16:**10, 11, 12, 30, 31, 31; **17:**3, 3, 4, 6; **19:**8, 22, 31, 40; **20:**5, 6, 19, 28; **21:**36; **22:**36, 42, 67, 67, 68; **23:**31, 35, 37; **Jn 1:**25; **2:**18; **3:**12, 12; **4:**10; **5:**23, 31, 46; **6:**30, 62; **7:**4, 4, 11, 23, 37, 38; **8:**12, 16, 17, 19, 31, 36, 39, 42, 54, 55; **9:**19, 33, 41; **10:**24, 35, 38, 38; **11:**12, 21, 32, 40, 48; **12:**26, 35, 44, 47; **13:**8; **14:**2, 7, 15, 28; **15:**4, 7, 14, 19, 20, 22, 24; **16:**7, 7; **18:**23, 30, 36, 39; **19:**12; **20:**15, 23, 23; **21:**12, 22, 23, 25; **Ac 5:**26, 38, 39; **10:**15, 18; **11:**9; **13:**15, 41; **15:**29; **16:**15; **17:**11; **18:**14; **19:**38, 39, 40; **20:**16; **24:**19; **25:**5, 11, 11; **26:**5, 32; **27:**10, 39; **Ro 2:**17, 21, 25, 25, 26; **3:**6, 7, 8, 31; **4:**2, 12, 14, 16, 24; **7:**2, 3, 3, 7, 8, 20; **8:**6, 6, 9, 13, 13, 17, 24, 25, 31, 35; **9:**3, 29; **10:**9, 14; **11:**6, 12, 16, 21, 22, 23, 24; **12:**6, 7, 7, 8, 8, 8, 8, 13, 14, 15, 20, 20; **13:**4, 8; **14:**14, 15, 15, 18, 20, 21, 23, 23; **15:**2; **1Co 2:**8; **3:**14, 15, 18; **4:**6, 7, 15, 19; **5:**6; **6:**4, 16; **7:**9, 11, 12, 13, 15, 21, 22, 22, 27, 27, 28, 28, 36, 37, 39, 40; **8:**8, 8, 13; **9:**2, 12, 16, 17; **10:**12, 15, 27, 27, 30; **11:**4, 5, 6, 16, 17, 27, 29, 31, 34; **12:**15, 16, 17, 19, 26, 26; **13:**1, 2, 2, 2, 3, 3; **14:**2, 6, 6, 8, 9, 14, 16, 23, 24, 28, 30, 35, 37, 38; **15:**2, 13, 14, 15, 16, 17, 19, 29, 32, 32; **16:**4, 7, 22; **2Co 1:**14; **2:**2; **3:**9, 11; **4:**3; **5:**13, 13; **6:**12; **8:**12, 23; **9:**4; **11:**4, 16, 30; **13:**5, 5, 7, 9; **Gal 1:**8, 9, 10; **2:**17, 18, 21; **3:**12, 16, 18, 20, 21; **4:**1, 15, 18, 19; **5:**2, 3, 4, 11, 15, 25; **6:**1, 3; **Eph 4:**28; **6:**3; **Php 1:**22; **2:**17, 17, 19; **3:**4, 4, 5, 15; **4:**7; **Col 3:**11, 21, 25; **4:**10; **2Th 2:**2; **1Ti 3:**1, 5, 10, 15; **4:**6; **5:**4, 16; **6:**2, 8; **2Ti 2:**10, 11, 12, 12, 13, 21; **3:**5; **Tit 3:**10; **Phm 1:**17, 17, 18; **Heb 2:**3; **3:**6, 14; **4:**8; **6:**8; **7:**11; **8:**4, 7; **9:**26; **10:**2, 26, 29; **11:**15, 19; **12:**8, 20, 25, 25; **13:**23; **Jas 1:**5, 5, 22, 23, 25, 25, 26; **2:**1, 3, 9, 11, 11, 13, 13, 14, 18; **3:**13, 13, 14; **4:**4, 11, 15; **5:**19; **1Pe 1:**7; **2:**12, 18, 18, 20, 20; **3:**7, 10, 13, 14, 15, 16, 17; **4:**1, 12, 14, 15, 17, 18, 19; **2Pe 2:**21; **1Jn 1:**6, 7, 8, 9, 10; **2:**1, 4, 17, 24; **3:**6, 13, 14, 17, 20, 21; **4:**1, 2, 2, 3, 6, 6, 12, 18, 20, 20; **5:**2, 15, 16; **2Jn** 9, 9, 10; **Rev 2:**5; **3:**20; **11:**5; **22:**18, 19

IN (9921)

Ge 1:1, 2, 14, 17, 26, 26, 26, 27, 31; **2:**1, 8, 8, 9, 15, 16; **3:**1, 8, 14; **4:**7, 16, 20, 25; **5:**1, 22, 23; **6:**3, 4, 4, 11, 12, 16, 18; **7:**3, 9, 11, 14, 16, 23; **8:**1, 6, 11, 17; **9:**2, 4, 6, 13, 14, 16, 21; **10:**5, 9, 9, 10, 30; **11:**2, 8, 28; **12:**5, 8, 10, 13, 14; **13:**2, 7, 9, 10, 12, 14, 17; **14:**1, 3, 4, 5, 5, 5, 6, 7, 8, 12, 14, 14, 17; **15:**1, 2, 10, 13, 14, 15; **16:**3; **17:**3, 12, 17, 23; **18:**4, 9, 26; **19:**2, 2, 10, 12, 15, 17, 27, 30, 30, 31, 33, 34, 35; **20:**3, 5, 16; **21:**2, 7, 15, 20, 22, 23, 23, 34; **22:**4, 12, 13, 13, 24; **23:**2, 4, 11, 17, 18, 19, 19; **24:**1, 2, 21, 35, 38, 40, 42, 62, 63; **25:**8, 9, 9, 11, 17, 18, 22, 23, 28; **26:**1, 3, 6, 18, 19, 27, 29, 30, 31; **27:**7, 15, 20, 43, 45; **28:**9, 16; **29:**1, 2, 2, 7, 17, 18, 22, 25; **30:**14, 15, 33, 35, 39, 40, 41; **31:**2, 9, 11, 18, 23, 23, 24, 25, 37, 38, 42, 46, 47, 47, 54; **32:**3, 16, 21, 24, 32; **33:**1, 4, 18; **34:**1, 5, 7, 8, 19, 28; **35:**2, 3, 5, 6, 8, 27, 29; **36:**5, 6, 8, 9, 16, 17, 21, 24, 30, 31, 31, 35, 40; **37:**1, 3, 7, 14, 18, 25, 29, 31, 32, 33, 35, 36; **38:**7, 12, 26, 27; **39:**1, 2, 3, 4, 5, 6, 8, 22, 22; **40:**3, 3, 4, 9, 9, 11, 11, 14, 15, 16, 17; **41:**2, 4, 10, 14, 14, 19, 19, 33, 33, 35, 39, 41, 42, 43, 44, 48, 48, 52, 54, 54, 54, 56; **42:**1, 2, 5, 6, 13, 16, 17, 19, 20, 27, 28, 29, 32, 38; **43:**12, 18, 19, 21, 33; **44:**1, 6, 8, 12, 13, 16, 18, 26, 29, 30, 31; **45:**3, 10, 13, 17, 18, 25; **46:**2, 4, 5, 6, 6, 12, 15, 15, 20, 27, 27, 34, 34; **47:**1, 4, 4, 4, 6, 12, 14, 14, 16, 17, 17, 19, 27, 27, 28, 29, 31; **48:**2, 3, 5, 6, 7, 9, 20; **49:**1, 3, 4, 6, 11, 16, 18, 27, 27, 29, 29, 30, 30, 33; **50:**5, 8, 13, 13, 22, 26, 26; **Ex 1:**5, 5, 6, 7, 14, 19, 19; **2:**3, 5, 12, 13, 15, 21, 22; **3:**2, 2, 6, 7, 16, 16, 22; **4:**2, 20, 21; **5:**1, 5, 12, 14, 19; **6:**1, 6, 7, 16, 26; **7:**3, 11, 15, 16, 18, 19, 19, 19, 21; **8:**3, 5, 9, 11, 13, 17, 20, 22, 22, 24, 24, 24, 25, 28, 31; **9:**13, 14, 18, 19, 20, 21, 24, 25, 25, 26, 31; **10:**5, 6, 7, 9, 14, 19; **11:**1, 3, 5, 5, 9, 10; **12:**1, 4, 4, 6, 11, 12, 16, 19, 20, 25, 27, 29, 29, 34, 40, 41, 46; **13:**4, 7, 7, 9, 13, 14; **14:**6, 9, 9, 10, 11, 11, 12, 12, 14, 24, 31; **15:**4, 6, 7, 8, 10, 11, 11, 13, 17, 20, 22, 26; **16:**3, 4, 6, 7, 8, 8, 12, 12, 14, 29, 31, 32, 33, 34, 35; **17:**9; **18:**3, 12, 12, 13, 23, 25; **19:**1, 9, 9, 18, 24; **20:**2, 4, 10, 11, 11, 12, 20, 21, 24; **21:**2, 3, 4, 11, 16, 22, 22, 26, 27, 28, 29, 32, 34, 36; **22:**2, 2, 3, 3, 5, 5, 11, 21, 21, 25; **23:**2, 3, 8, 9, 14, 15, 17, 18, 19, 24, 29, 31; **24:**3, 8, 11, 11; **25:**7, 29; **26:**4, 10, 11, 33; **27:**16, 17, 19, 21, 21; **28:**10, 11, 11, 20, 29, 29, 30, 32, 35, 43; **29:**3, 8, 9, 11, 21, 24, 26, 27, 28, 29, 30, 31, 31, 32, 33, 39, 39, 41, 41, 42; **30:**8, 20, 36, 36; **31:**3, 5, 5, 17; **32:**5, 6, 15, 17, 19, 20; **33:**8, 11, 22; **34:**2, 3, 4, 4, 5, 5, 6, 6, 9, 10, 10, 11, 12, 15, 18, 20, 24, 26, 28; **35:**3, 9, 12, 19, 25, 25, 29, 31, 33, 33, 33, 35, 35; **36:**11, 13, 17, 18, 18; **37:**14, 16; **38:**16, 20, 21, 22, 26, 26, 31; **39:**1, 6, 8, 10, 11, 12, 13, 13, 21, 23, 40, 41; **40:**4, 4, 6, 14, 22, 24, 25, 26, 26, 26, 31, 38; **Lev 1:**5, 5, 11, 12; **2:**4, 7, 11; **4:**4, 6, 7, 7, 12, 17, 18, 18, 20, 26, 31, 35; **5:**5, 10, 13, 15, 18; **6:**4, 6, 10, 14, 16, 20, 20, 25, 26, 27, 30; **7:**6, 7, 8, 9, 9, 26, 38; **8:**7, 10, 13, 14, 15, 26, 29, 30, 31, 34, 35; **9:**5, 16, 17; **10:**1, 1, 12, 13, 14, 17, 18; **11:**33, 34, 37; **13:**3, 4, 4, 5, 10, 11, 13, 19, 20, 20, 21, 21, 25, 25, 26, 26, 30, 31, 31, 33, 37, 46, 49, 53, 59, 59; **14:**8, 9, 13, 17, 17, 18, 18, 20, 23, 28, 29, 29, 31, 34, 36, 41, 42, 47, 52, 53, 53, 55, 55, 56, 56, 56; **15:**3, 5, 6, 10, 11, 13, 15, 17, 21, 27, 30, 31; **16:**2, 13, 16, 17, 19, 21, 22, 24, 24, 26, 28, 29, 30, 31, 32, 32; **17:**5, 7, 10, 11, 14, 14, 15; **18:**3, 9, 23, 24; **19:**4, 17, 24, 25, 25, 28, 32, 33, 34; **21:**17; **22:**10, 13; **23:**4, 5, 10, 24, 29, 37, 38, 38, 42, 43; **24:**3, 4, 6, 6, 6, 7, 9, 12, 12, 18, 20; **25:**8, 8, 12, 13, 18, 19, 21, 22, 22, 22, 28, 30, 31, 31, 31, 33, 33, 43, 45; **26:**1, 5, 6, 7, 16, 18, 31, 33, 34, 35, 35, 36, 36, 37, 37, 38, 39, 44, 44; **27:**10, 17, 18, 21, 24, 25, 28, 33; **Nu 1:**1, 1, 1, 19, 50; **2:**2, 16, 17, 17, 24, 32; **3:**4, 4, 7, 8, 13, 14, 31, 38, 38, 40, 45, 46, 50; **4:**3, 6, 12, 14, 16, 16, 19, 23, 24, 30, 35, 39, 43, 47; **5:**13, 17, 18, 24, 31; **6:**2, 11, 20; **7:**3, 85; **8:**2, 13, 14, 15, 16, 18, 19, 24, 26; **9:**1, 1, 3, 5, 10, 18, 22; **10:**9, 10, 11, 12, 12, 17, 28, 31; **11:**5, 7, 8, 8, 8, 10, 12, 18, 22, 25, 26, 26, 27, 31; **12:**5, 8, 14, 16; **13:**3, 19, 26, 27, 29, 29; **14:**2, 2, 2, 3, 13, 14, 14, 14, 16, 18, 22, 22, 25, 29, 29, 32, 33, 33, 33, 34, 35, 43, 45; **15:**2, 8, 18, 23, 26, 32, 34; **16:**3, 7, 9, 13, 38, 39, 49, 49, 49; **17:**4, 4, 7, 7; **18:**2, 6, 8, 21, 31; **19:**3, 7, 8, 9, 9, 13, 14, 15, 17, 18, 18; **20:**1, 1, 3, 24; **21:**1, 5, 11, 13, 14, 20, 23, 23, 25, 28, 32, 34; **22:**4, 5, 8, 22, 23, 23, 26, 27, 31, 31, 34; **23:**21, 21; **24:**7, 8, 14, 17, 17, 18, 19, 21; **25:**3, 4, 5, 11, 13; **26:**19, 51, 53, 59, 62, 64, 64, 64, 65; **27:**3, 11, 14, 14, 18; **28:**4, 4, 7, 8, 10, 15, 16, 23, 24, 31; **29:**1, 5, 6, 11, 16, 19, 22, 25, 28, 31, 34, 38, 39, 39; **30:**10; **31:**8, 21, 23, 26, 30, 30, 52; **32:**13, 15, 17, 26, 30, 41; **33:**3, 3, 11, 15, 36, 38, 40, 40, 47, 53, 54, 54, 55, 55, 55, 55; **34:**4; **35:**2, 4, 5, 6, 7, 8, 14, 20, 21, 24, 25; **36:**3, 8; **Dt 1:**1, 1, 3, 4, 4, 5, 8, 17, 21, 26, 27, 30, 31; **2:**3, 4, 8, 10, 12, 12, 12, 14, 14, 22, 23, 23, 29, 36, 37; **3:**2, 4, 6, 10, 11, 14, 19, 24, 27, 29; **4:**5, 11, 14, 16, 25, 25, 25, 28, 30, 34, 38, 39, 39, 40, 43, 43, 46; **5:**6, 8, 14, 15, 16, 31, 32, 33; **6:**1, 3, 11, 12, 18, 19, 20, 21; **7:**8, 13, 15, 24, 25; **8:**6, 7, 9, 11, 12, 14, 16, 20; **9:**1, 7, 15, 16, 21; **10:**1, 2, 5, 5, 6, 8, 10, 14, 19, 20, 22; **11:**3, 4, 5, 8, 9, 10, 14, 15, 17, 21, 22, 23, 24, 24, 24, 24, 25, 30, 30, 31; **12:**1, 4, 7, 7, 9, 10, 12, 12, 15, 18, 18, 18, 18, 19, 30, 31; **13:**5, 8, 9, 12, 14, 16; **14:**21, 23, 26, 27, 28, 29, 29; **15:**4, 7, 7, 10, 11, 12, 15, 17, 18, 20; **16:**1, 1, 3, 4, 5, 7, 10, 12, 16, 18; **17:**2, 2, 4, 7, 7, 8, 11, 14, 17, 18, 20, 20; **18:**1, 5, 6, 7, 9, 10, 22; **19:**1, 2, 3, 3, 5, 9, 10, 12, 14, 19; **20:**5, 6, 7, 11, 13, 16, 18; **21:**1, 1, 2, 5, 9, 13, 19, 21; **22:**6, 6, 6, 21, 21, 21, 22, 24, 25, 27, 28; **23:**1, 2, 3, 4, 6, 14, 16, 20, 20, 21, 24; **24:**13, 14, 17, 18, 19, 19, 21, 22; **25:**2, 2, 6, 7, 9, 9, 15, 19; **26:**1, 3, 5, 5, 5, 5, 11, 12, 13, 14, 15, 17; **27:**24; **28:**3, 3, 6, 6, 7, 8, 9, 10, 11, 12, 16, 16, 19, 19, 20, 21, 25, 29, 29, 30, 36, 48, 52, 52, 58, 61, 62, 63, 63, 66, 66, 67, 67, 68; **29:**1, 1, 2, 9, 15, 16, 19, 20, 21, 23, 27, 28; **30:**9, 9, 10, 10, 12, 14, 16, 18, 20; **31:**4, 12, 13, 15, 24, 29, 29; **32:**10, 10, 11, 24, 35, 47, 51; **33:**3, 3, 5, 12, 14, 16, 18, 18, 23, 24, 26, 28, 28, 28; **34:**5, 6, 6, 11, 12; **Jos 1:**4, 4, 7, 8, 11, 15; **2:**9, 11, 20, 24; **3:**6, 7, 13, 17; **4:**3, 5, 5, 6, 9, 10, 13, 14, 21; **5:**4, 5, 6, 8, 9, 13, 14; **6:**1, 6, 7, 8, 9, 11, 13, 13, 17, 17, 21, 23, 24, 25; **7:**6, 9, 12, 13, 14, 15, 21, 23; **8:**4, 9, 9, 12, 13, 16, 16, 17, 19, 20, 22, 25, 26, 29, 31, 34; **9:**1, 1, 9, 10, 17, 19, 22, 24; **10:**6, 10, 12, 13, 13, 16, 28, 28, 30, 35, 35, 39, 40, 42; **11:**2, 2, 3, 3, 3, 11, 17, 19, 21, 22, 22; **12:**2, 5, 5, 5, 7, 8, 22, 23, 23, 24; **13:**4, 4, 9, 10, 12, 16, 21, 21, 23, 27, 28, 30; **14:**1, 2, 4, 5, 10, 12; **15:**15, 16, 19, 21, 32, 33, 36, 48, 58, 61, 63; **16:**2, 9; **17:**5, 9, 15, 16; **18:**5, 5, 6, 8, 9, 9, 10; **19:**12, 15, 27, 34, 35, 50, 51; **20:**6, 6, 6, 7, 7, 7, 8, 8, 8, 8, 8, 9, 9, 9; **21:**2, 2, 6, 11, 27, 32, 38; **22:**5, 9, 10, 11, 14, 15, 16, 19, 22, 24, 29, 32; **23:**4, 6, 6, 7, 13, 13, 14; **24:**7, 13, 14, 15, 17, 18, 26, 30, 30, 32, 32, 33, 33; **Jdg 1:**3, 9, 10, 11, 12, 15, 16, 17, 18, 19, 21, 21, 25, 25, 27, 27, 29, 30, 32, 35; **2:**2, 3, 3, 9, 9, 11, 17; **3:**1, 1, 2, 3, 6, 7, 11, 12, 20, 22, 27; **4:**1, 2, 4, 5, 6, 6, 18; **5:**5, 6, 6, 7, 8, 11, 15, 16, 17, 20, 24, 25, 28, 31; **6:**1, 2, 4, 8, 10, 15, 15, 19, 19, 21, 24, 24, 28, 33, 37, 37, 40; **7:**1, 5, 5, 5, 5, 6, 8, 12, 13, 16, 20, 20, 21, 22, 23; **8:**9, 10, 14, 17, 25, 27, 31, 32, 32; **9:**3, 15, 16, 19, 19, 19, 20, 21, 24, 27, 29, 31, 31, 32, 33, 41, 43, 44, 44, 46, 47, 49, 51; **10:**1, 1, 2, 4, 5, 6, 8, 8, 9, 14, 17; **11:**3, 5, 7, 8, 11, 17, 21, 26, 29, 31, 35, 37, 39; **12:**1, 2, 7, 8, 9, 12, 15, 15; **13:**1, 1, 2, 2, 9, 20, 25; **14:**1, 2, 3, 4, 7, 8, 15, 16, 20; **15:**1, 2, 4, 5, 8, 8, 9, 11, 14, 19, 19; **16:**3, 4, 4, 9, 9, 12, 15, 19, 19, 21, 24; **17:**1, 3, 4, 6, 6, 7, 8, 9, 12; **18:**1, 1, 2, 2, 2, 6, 10, 12, 21, 28; **19:**1, 1, 1, 2, 7, 10, 11, 11, 12, 13, 14, 15, 15, 16, 16, 16, 17, 18, 18, 18, 18, 20, 22; **20:**1, 1, 2, 4, 10, 15, 21, 23, 26, 27, 27, 31, 32, 32, 33, 36, 36, 37, 37, 37, 39, 43, 44, 48; **21:**1, 2, 5, 5, 7, 12, 15, 18, 19, 20, 22, 22, 23, 23, 25, 25; **Ru 1:**1, 1, 1, 1, 2, 2, 6, 6, 22; **2:**1, 3, 7, 8, 14, 19, 22, 23; **3:**3, 7, 11, 13; **4:**4, 4, 5, 7, 7, 10, 11, 11, 14, 15; **1Sa 1:**1, 1, 10, 17, 20, 24; **2:**1, 1, 8, 8, 9, 17, 21, 27, 33; **3:**1, 3, 11, 15; **4:**6, 8, 20, 20; **5:**3, 4; **6:**1, 1, 2, 7, 10, 13, 18, 20; **7:**1, 2, 2, 6, 14; **8:**2, 12; **9:**2, 2, 6, 6, 9, 12, 16, 19, 21, 24; **10:**14, 24; **11:**5, 8, 15; **12:**4, 8, 11, 17, 20; **13:**2, 3, 6, 15, 16, 17, 19, 19; **14:**5, 5, 14, 15, 15, 15, 16, 16, 18, 19, 21, 22, 25, 33, 34, 45, 47; **15:**4, 5, 5, 9, 21, 21; **16:**4, 8, 10, 11; **17:**1, 8, 12, 12, 14, 15, 16, 24, 33, 39, 40, 42, 45, 45, 46, 49, 49, 54, 57, 58; **18:**5, 10, 10, 14, 18, 19, 20, 20, 25, 25; **19:**2, 4, 10, 10, 13, 15, 16, 19, 22, 22, 24; **20:**1, 5, 24, 29, 30, 34, 41, 42, 42; **21:**6, 9, 9; **22:**2, 2, 3, 4, 4, 6, 7, 15, 18; **23:**3, 7, 14, 14, 16, 16, 19, 19, 19, 23, 23, 24, 25, 26, 29; **24:**3, 10, 11, 18, 19; **25:**3, 16, 21, 24, 28, 29, 29, 35, 39; **26:**2, 6, 7, 10, 15, 23; **27:**5, 5, 9; **28:**1, 3, 10, 14, 15, 19; **29:**1, 2, 3, 4, 5, 9, 10; **30:**6, 6, 11, 14, 17; **31:**2, 7, 9, 10; **2Sa 1:**1, 2, 2, 6, 9, 11, 13, 18, 20, 20, 20, 23, 23, 24, 25; **2:**6, 19, 30; **3:**2, 5, 23, 27, 29, 32, 36, 37, 38; **4:**6, 11, 12, 12, 12; **5:**4, 6, 14, 24; **6:**4, 18, 19, 20, 21, 21, 22; **7:**1, 2, 2, 3, 5, 6, 8, 10, 18, 19, 23, 26; **8:**2, 2, 6, 13; **9:**1, 3, 4, 6, 13; **10:**2, 3, 4, 8, 9, 9, 17; **11:**1, 1, 11, 11, 12; **12:**1, 3, 11, 12, 31; **13:**1, 4, 12, 13, 13, 18, 19, 20, 31, 38; **14:**2, 2, 4, 6, 13, 20, 25, 28; **15:**6, 7, 8, 10, 12, 13, 13, 16, 19, 19, 28, 34; **16:**3, 4; **17:**5, 9, 18, 19, 23, 26; **18:**3, 6, 9, 10, 17, 18, 32; **19:**3, 13, 18, 20, 32, 33, 37, 41, 43, 43; **20:**3, 3, 8, 10, 10, 12, 12, 16, 19, 21, 24; **21:**2, 4, 5, 12, 14, 14, 14, 15, 19, 20; **22:**3, 6, 7, 12, 20, 25, 30; **23:**3, 4, 8, 9, 11, 11, 12, 13, 14, 15, 18, 39; **24:**2, 2, 2, 3, 5, 5, 6, 8, 9, 9; **1Ki 1:**2, 5, 5, 23, 28, 41, 42, 47, 47, 49; **2:**3, 3, 5, 6, 10, 11, 11, 13, 14, 26, 34, 35, 36, 38, 46; **3:**1, 5, 11, 13, 17, 17, 18, 20, 20, 21, 21, 25; **4:**6, 8, 9, 10, 11, 12, 13, 13, 13, 14, 15, 16, 16, 17, 18, 19, 25, 28, 30, 33; **5:**11, 14, 14, 14, 15; **6:**1, 1, 7, 9, 19, 25, 27, 30, 37, 38; **7:**3, 5, 5, 11, 14, 15, 20, 23, 32, 46, 46, 49, 51; **8:**1, 1, 1, 2, 5, 9, 12, 20, 22, 23, 31, 33, 37, 37, 40, 40, 47, 47, 54, 58, 59, 64, 64, 65, 65, 65, 65; **9:**11, 18, 19, 20, 21, 22, 26; **10:**2, 6, 9, 10, 17, 20, 21, 21, 23, 26, 26, 27, 27; **11:**4, 4, 6, 15, 15, 20, 21, 25, 26, 28, 29, 33, 36, 41, 41, 42, 43; **12:**16, 17, 18, 25, 28, 29, 29, 32, 32, 32, 33; **13:**4, 5, 5, 8, 11, 11, 16, 22, 25, 25, 28, 30, 30, 31, 32, 32, 34; **14:**6, 11, 11, 13, 15, 19, 20, 21, 21, 22, 25, 29, 29, 31; **15:**1, 1, 2, 4, 5, 5, 7, 7, 8, 9, 9, 10, 11, 13, 17, 17, 18, 18, 22, 23, 23, 23, 24, 25, 25, 25, 26, 28, 28, 31, 31, 33, 33, 33, 34; **16:**4, 4, 5, 5, 6, 7, 8, 8, 8, 9, 10, 10, 10, 14, 14, 15, 15, 15, 18, 19, 20, 23, 23, 23, 23, 24, 25, 27, 27, 28, 29, 29, 29, 30, 32; **17:**1, 7, 9, 12, 12, 12, 14, 16; **18:**1, 2, 3, 4, 4, 13, 15, 21, 27, 36, 38; **19:**3, 11, 11, 12, 13, 18; **20:**8, 12, 16, 21, 25, 27, 29, 30, 34, 34, 39, 42; **21:**1, 2, 5, 8, 9, 11, 18, 18, 20, 21, 24, 24, 25, 27, 27, 27; **22:**4, 10, 10, 17, 17, 23, 25, 27, 32, 35, 39, 39, 41, 41, 42, 43, 45, 45, 47, 50, 51, 51, 51, 52; **2Ki 1:**2, 3, 6, 16, 17, 18, 18; **2:**1, 12, 16, 19, 20, 24; **3:**1, 1, 1, 2, 3, 26; **4:**2, 9, 13, 15, 16, 25, 33, 35, 36, 38, 40; **5:**3, 7, 8, 10, 12, 12, 15, 15, 18, 19, 23, 25, 26; **6:**11, 12, 12, 20, 25, 30, 32; **7:**1, 10, 11, 12, 12, 15, 18; **8:**2, 4, 5, 9, 15, 16, 16, 17, 18, 23, 23, 24, 25, 25, 26, 27, 28, 28; **9:**5, 7, 8, 10, 15, 17, 18, 19, 21, 22, 24, 27, 28, 29, 29, 31, 36; **10:**1, 7, 8, 9, 11, 17, 23, 25, 26, 30, 34, 34, 35, 36; **11:**2, 3, 4, 4, 8, 10, 14, 14, 15, 15, 18; **12:**1, 1, 1, 2, 9, 18, 19, 19, 21; **13:**1, 1, 1, 2, 5, 5, 6, 8, 8, 9, 10, 10, 10, 11, 12, 12, 13, 14; **14:**1, 2, 3, 6, 7, 8, 9, 9, 11, 15, 15, 16, 18, 18, 19, 20, 23, 23, 23, 24, 26, 28, 28; **15:**1, 2, 3, 5, 5, 6, 6, 7, 8, 8, 8, 9, 10, 11, 11, 13, 13, 13, 15, 15, 17, 17, 17, 18, 19, 20, 20, 21, 21, 23, 23, 23, 24, 25, 26, 26, 27, 27, 27, 28, 30, 31, 31, 32, 32, 33, 34, 36, 36, 37, 38; **16:**1, 1, 2, 2, 3, 9, 10, 18, 19, 19, 20; **17:**1, 1, 1, 2, 4, 6, 6, 6, 6, 7, 9, 13, 14, 17, 18, 22, 24, 26, 29; **18:**1, 1, 2, 3, 5, 5, 6, 7, 9, 10, 11, 11, 11, 13, 15, 15, 17, 17, 19, 22, 22, 22, 23, 26, 26, 27, 28, 30, 37, 37; **19:**2, 9, 11, 12, 22, 24, 28, 28, 29, 30, 30, 37; **20:**1, 3, 13, 13, 15, 18, 20, 20; **21:**1, 2, 4, 5, 6, 6, 7, 7, 7, 11, 15, 16, 16, 17, 17, 18, 19, 20, 23, 25, 25, 26, 26; **22:**1, 2, 3, 8, 11, 11, 13, 13, 16, 19, 19, 20; **23:**2, 3, 3, 3, 5, 6, 8, 9, 10, 10, 12, 12, 16, 19, 21, 22, 23, 24, 24, 24, 24, 28, 28, 30, 30, 31, 32, 33, 33, 34, 35, 35, 36, 37; **24:**5, 5, 8, 9, 12, 13, 14, 18, 19, 20; **25:**3, 4, 7, 8, 9, 11, 12, 16, 19, 19, 21, 22, 24, 25, 26, 27, 27, 28; **1Ch 1:**43, 43, 46; **2:**4, 6, 22, 24; **3:**1, 4, 5, 16, 22, 23, 24; **4:**10, 23, 28, 32, 33, 39, 40; **5:**1, 7, 8, 9, 10, 11, 12, 16, 16, 17, 18, 18, 20, 22, 22; **6:**10, 32, 48, 55, 65, 67, 71, 76, 80; **7:**5, 7, 9, 28, 29, 40; **8:**1, 8, 13, 28, 28, 29, 32, 40; **9:**1, 1, 2, 3, 6, 9, 9, 13, 16, 19, 20, 20, 22, 22, 22, 25, 26, 28, 28, 29, 31, 32, 34, 34, 35, 38; **10:**2, 7, 7, 10, 10; **11:**5, 11, 12, 13, 13, 14, 15, 16, 17, 20; **12:**1, 8, 15, 17, 21, 30, 38, 38; **13:**2, 5, 10; **14:**3, 4, 9, 15; **15:**1, 13, 14, 24, 27; **16:**2, 3, 4, 10, 19, 19, 27, 29, 32, 40; **17:**1, 1, 1, 2, 4, 5, 7, 9, 16, 17, 21, 24; **18:**6, 12; **19:**2, 3, 4, 9, 10, 10, 17, 17; **20:**1, 1, 1, 6; **21:**2, 2, 2, 5, 5, 6, 25, 29; **22:**2, 3, 8, 9, 11, 17; **23:**13, 13, 24, 25, 28, 28, 29, 29, 31; **24:**5, 6, 19, 19, 30, 31; **25:**7, 7; **26:**6, 8, 11, 15, 20, 21, 22, 26, 27, 28, 30, 30, 31, 31, 31, 32; **27:**2, 3, 4, 5, 7, 8, 9, 10, 11, 12, 12, 13, 14, 14, 15, 23, 24, 25, 25, 26, 27, 28, 28, 29, 29, 30, 30, 31; **28:**1, 12, 13, 13, 19, 21; **29:**3, 3, 8, 10, 11, 12, 15, 22, 23, 25, 27, 28, 29; **2Ch 1:**3, 4, 5, 5, 6, 6, 7, 8, 14, 14, 15, 15; **2:**2, 14, 14, 14, 16, 17, 18; **3:**1, 2, 10, 12; **4:**2, 7, 8, 17, 17, 20; **5:**1, 1, 2, 2, 2, 3, 6, 10, 12, 13; **6:**1, 10, 11, 12, 14, 22, 24, 28, 28, 31, 31, 37, 37, 40, 41; **7:**7, 8, 8, 15; **8:**2, 4, 4, 6, 7, 8, 9, 11, 12, 14, 14, 14, 15, 17; **9:**5, 8, 11, 16, 19, 20, 20, 22, 25, 25, 27, 27, 29, 29, 29, 30, 31; **10:**5, 16, 17, 18; **11:**3, 5, 11, 11, 12, 21, 23; **12:**1, 2, 6, 12, 13, 13, 15, 15, 16; **13:**1, 1, 2, 4, 10, 16, 18, 22; **14:**1, 1, 2, 10, 11, 11, 12, 14; **15:**4, 8, 8, 8, 8, 10, 11, 16; **16:**1, 1, 1, 2, 4, 7, 7, 9, 11, 12, 13, 14, 14, 14; **17:**2, 7, 7, 13, 14, 15, 18, 19, 19; **18:**3, 3, 9, 9, 16, 16, 22, 24, 26, 31, 34; **19:**3, 4, 5, 6, 8, 8, 9, 10, 11, 11, 11; **20:**5, 6, 7, 9, 20, 20, 24, 26, 31, 32, 34, 34; **21:**1, 5, 6, 11, 13, 17, 19, 19, 20, 20, 20; **22:**2, 3, 4, 5, 9, 11, 11, 12; **23:**1, 2, 5, 7, 9, 13, 13, 13, 14, 14, 17, 18; **24:**1, 2, 6, 9, 13, 14, 16, 16, 21, 23, 25, 25, 25, 27; **25:**1, 2, 4, 5, 10, 14, 17, 18, 18, 21, 24, 26, 27, 28; **26:**3, 4, 5, 6, 6, 7, 7, 9, 9, 10, 10, 10, 17, 19, 21, 21, 23; **27:**1, 2, 2, 4, 4, 6, 7, 8, 9; **28:**1, 1, 3, 3, 6, 9, 14, 18, 18, 24, 25, 25, 26, 27, 27; **29:**1, 2, 3, 6, 9, 9, 11, 11, 15, 17, 17, 17, 19, 29, 30; **30:**2, 3, 5, 5, 5, 5, 12, 12, 13, 15, 16, 21, 25, 26, 27; **31:**3, 4, 4, 6, 6, 7, 11, 12, 13, 14, 15, 16, 17, 18, 18, 19, 19, 20, 20, 21, 21, 21; **32:**5, 6, 9, 10, 18, 20, 20, 21, 27, 30, 31, 31, 31, 32, 32, 33; **33:**1, 2, 4, 5, 6, 6, 6, 7, 7, 7, 11, 12, 14, 14, 15, 18, 18, 19, 21, 22, 24; **34:**1, 2, 3, 6, 8, 13, 15, 19, 19, 21, 24, 27, 27, 28, 30, 31, 31, 32; **35:**1, 1, 2, 3, 3, 5, 12, 13, 15, 17, 19, 24, 24, 25, 27; **36:**1, 5, 5, 6, 7, 7, 8, 9, 9, 10, 10, 11, 12, 12, 13, 14, 18, 22, 23; **Ezr 1:**1, 2, 3, 3, 4, 4, 6, 7, 7, 11; **2:**58, 65, 68, 70; **3:**1, 1, 1, 2, 4, 8, 8, 8, 9, 13, 13; **4:**3, 3, 7, 8, 10, 11, 14, 15, 15, 17, 19, 19, 24; **5:**1, 1, 2, 3, 8, 8, 14, 14, 15, 16, 17, 17, 17; **6:**1, 2, 3, 5, 7, 8, 9, 9, 11, 18, 18, 21; **7:**6, 7, 8, 8, 13, 14, 14, 15, 16, 17, 18, 19, 21, 24, 25, 27; **8:**25, 27, 29, 30, 32; **9:**1, 5, 8, 9, 9, 9, 12, 15, 15, 15; **10:**1, 2, 4, 6, 9, 9, 13, 13; **Ne 1:**1, 2, 3, 4, 11, 11; **2:**1, 3, 10, 12, 16, 17, 20; **3:**3, 11; **4:**2, 2, 4, 5, 7, 13; **5:**8, 9, 9; **6:**1, 2, 5, 7, 7, 8, 11, 11, 18; **7:**1, 3, 60, 67, 73, 73, 73; **8:**5, 13, 14, 15, 15, 15, 16, 16, 16, 17; **9:**1, 6, 9, 17, 19, 19, 21, 21, 22, 23, 24, 25, 25, 27, 27, 28, 30, 31, 36, 37, 37, 38, 38; **10:**28, 32, 34, 36, 37, 37, 38, 39; **11:**1, 2, 3, 3, 4, 6, 16, 18, 18, 20, 22, 24, 25, 26, 29, 30, 32, 36; **12:**7, 8, 22, 23, 25, 26, 26, 27, 27, 43, 44, 46, 46, 47, 47; **13:**6, 6, 7, 7, 13, 15, 16, 16, 17, 18, 19, 22, 24, 31; **Est 1:**1, 3, 5, 6, 7, 14, 22; **2:**3, 3, 8, 9, 13, 15, 16, 18, 20, 23; **3:**1, 7, 8, 12, 12, 12, 14, 15; **4:**3, 5, 6, 6, 8, 11, 11, 13, 16; **5:**2, 14; **6:**2, 4, 4, 5, 6, 9, 13; **7:**7, 8, 8, 9; **8:**2, 8, 8, 9, 10, 11, 13, 17; **9:**2, 4, 6, 11, 12, 12, 13, 14, 19, 19, 30, 32; **10:**2, 3; **Job 1:**1, 3, 3, 5, 5, 8, 10, 18, 19, 20, 22; **2:**3, 10; **3:**4, 9, 17, 18, 20, 23; **4:**3, 3, 9, 12, 12, 13, 20, 21; **5:**13, 14, 14, 20, 20; **6:**6, 10, 15, 17, 18; **7:**11, 21; **8:**16; **9:**2, 2, 3, 5, 24, 34, 35; **10:**1, 6, 10; **11:**4, 8, 10, 13, 15, 18; **12:**5, 6, 6, 6, 10, 14, 16, 24, 25; **13:**8, 10, 10, 10, 14, 27; **14:**4, 8, 11, 17, 20, 21, 22; **15:**15, 20, 24, 28, 31, 32; **16:**4, 5, 10, 15, 15, 19; **17:**6, 13, 16; **18:**4, 6, 8, 10, 19, 20, 20; **19:**24, 26, 29; **20:**8, 11, 13, 14, 22, 26, 28; **21:**5, 11, 13, 13, 17, 23, 25, 26, 30; **22:**11, 16, 20, 22, 26; **23:**6, 9, 10, 11, 12, 15; **24:**1, 5, 6, 7, 11, 13, 14, 16, 20, 22, 22, 23, 24; **25:**2, 4, 6; **26:**5, 6, 8; **27:**10, 14, 16, 20; **28:**10, 17, 18, 21; **29:**4, 4, 6, 6, 8, 9, 10, 12; **30:**6, 6, 10, 12, 15, 15, 22, 25, 28, 28; **31:**24, 26, 27, 33; **32:**2; **33:**8, 11, 12, 15, 15, 15, 16, 19, 30; **34:**13, 13, 20, 23, 24, 25; **35:**10, 15, 16; **36:**5, 12, 14, 16, 31; **37:**3, 5, 8, 8, 17, 21, 22; **38:**12, 14, 15, 26, 40, 40, 41; **39:**4, 6, 9, 14, 21; **40:**4, 13, 13, 24; **41:**6, 12, 22, 32; **42:**6, 7, 8, 10, 11, 12, 12, 15; **Ps 1:**1, 2, 3; **2:**4, 5, 6, 12, 12, 12; **3:**5, 7; **4:**5, 8; **5:**3, 4, 5, 8, 10, 11; **6:**1, 1, 2, 5, 10; **7:**5, 6; **8:**3, 6, 8, 8; **9:**3, 4, 9, 10, 11, 15, 16, 19, 20; **10:**2, 5, 8, 9, 14; **11:**1, 2, 4; **12:**6; **13:**2, 2, 5; **14:**1; **15:**1; **16:**3, 3, 4, 9, 10; **17:**3, 3, 7, 8, 12, 14; **18:**2, 5, 6, 11, 19, 24, 29; **19:**3, 4, 12; **20:**1, 7; **21:**1, 6, 7, 9, 9; **22:**4, 5, 12, 15, 16, 17, 25, 29; **23:**2, 5, 6; **24:**1, 3, 8; **25:**2, 2, 3, 5, 9, 13, 16, 20, 21; **26:**1, 5, 11; **27:**4, 4, 4, 5, 9, 13; **28:**3, 4, 7, 7, 9; **29:**2, 9; **31:**4, 6, 8, 9, 15, 16, 17, 20, 20, 22, 24; **32:**2, 4, 6, 11; **33:**7,

8, 8, 19, 21, 21, 22; **34:**T, 2, 6, 8, 10, 14, 18, 22; **35:**4, 5, 8, 8, 9, 15, 18, 24, 27; **36:**2, 7; **37:**3, 3, 4, 7, 9, 10, 11, 12, 19, 20, 23, 27, 39, 40; **38:**1, 1; **39:**1, 2, 6, 7; **40:**3, 4, 4, 6, 7, 8, 10, 10, 11, 14, 14; **41:**1; **42:**5, 9, 11; **43:**2, 5; **44:**1, 1, 5, 9, 19, 20, 25, 25; **45:**4, 6, 8, 11, 13, 14, 17; **46:**1, 5, 6, 9; **47:**9; **48:**1, 2, 3, 6, 9; **49:**1, 6, 14, 14, 18; **50:**2, 3, 12, 15; **51:**4, 4, 6, 10; **52:**7, 7, 8, 8, 9; **53:**1; **55:**3, 4, 9, 11, 17, 21; **56:**T, 1, 3, 4, 7, 8, 8, 11, 13, 13; **57:**6, 7, 9; **58:**7, 10; **59:**T, 10, 10, 13, 13, 16; **60:**T, 4, 8; **61:**4; **62:**4, 4, 5, 8, 9; **63:**T, 1, 2, 4, 7, 11, 11; **64:**8, 9, 10, 10; **65:**1, 4, 8; **66:**4, 6, 7, 9, 10, 11, 14, 18; **68:**2, 2, 3, 4, 6, 19, 23, 25, 28, 29, 30, 30, 31, 34, 35; **69:**2, 6, 11, 13, 17, 20, 29, 32, 34, 36; **70:**2, 2; **71:**9; **72:**2, 5, 9, 16, 16; **73:**8, 10, 19, 25; **74:**2, 5; **75:**3, 5, 8, 8; **76:**1, 1, 5; **77:**2, 12, 17; **78:**2, 6, 12, 14, 15, 17, 18, 19, 26, 30, 32, 32, 33, 39, 40, 40, 43, 51, 53; **81:**7, 13; **82:**5, 7; **83:**17; **84:**4, 5, 7, 10, 10, 10, 12; **85:**6; **87:**2, 7; **88:**8, 11, 11, 12; **89:**6, 7, 9, 11, 13, 15, 16, 16, 19, 25, 25, 30, 35, 37, 39, 40, 43, 50; **90:**5, 6, 12, 14, 15; **91:**1, 1, 6, 14, 15; **92:**2, 2, 8, 13, 14, 15; **93:**1, 1; **95:**8, 11; **96:**6, 9, 11; **97:**12; **98:**4, 7, 7, 8; **99:**2, 2, 9; **101:**2, 6; **102:**2, 6, 6, 14, 14, 16, 21, 21, 23, 25, 28, 28; **103:**22; **104:**2, 3, 17, 18, 24, 26, 31, 34; **105:**3, 12, 12, 18, 18, 21, 23, 23, 27, 28, 30, 35, 36; **106:**5, 5, 7, 14, 14, 16, 21, 22, 25, 26, 28, 30, 34, 39, 44; **107:**4, 6, 10, 10, 13, 17, 19, 23, 24, 26, 28, 39, 40, 43; **108:**1, 3, 9; **109:**13; **110:**1, 3, 3, 4, 5; **111:**2; **112:**1, 4, 9, 10; **115:**3, 8; **116:**9, 10, 11, 14, 18, 19, 19; **118:**5, 7, 8, 9, 10, 11, 12, 15, 16, 19, 24, 26; **119:**3, 11, 14, 14, 16, 18, 25, 39, 42, 43, 45, 47, 50, 51, 66, 69, 70, 72, 74, 74, 80, 81, 83, 88, 89, 92, 109, 120, 124, 143, 147, 149, 149, 156, 162; **122:**7; **123:**1; **125:**1, 4; **126:**5; **127:**4; **129:**5, 8; **130:**5, 7; **131:**3; **132:**4, 6, 6; **133:**1; **134:**1, 2; **135:**2, 2, 6, 8, 9, 18, 21; **137:**4; **138:**4; **139:**12, 13, 15, 15, 16, 18, 20, 24; **140:**2, 8, 11, 13; **141:**4, 4, 5; **142:**T, 5; **143:**3, 3, 8, 8, 11, 12; **144:**2, 12, 13, 14; **145:**13, 13, 17; **146:**3, 4, 5, 6, 10; **147:**8, 10, 11, 11; **149:**1, 2, 2, 4, 5, 6, 6; **150:**1, 1; **Pr 1:**3, 6, 12, 14, 20, 20, 21, 26, 33; **2:**14, 21, 21; **3:**1, 5, 6, 12, 16, 16, 26, 27; **4:**11; **5:**9, 11, 16, 18; **6:**21, 22, 31, 34, 34; **7:**9, 12, 20; **8:**8, 20, 20, 23, 30; **9:**10, 14, 17, 18; **10:**26, 28, 28; **11:**1, 20, 22, 26, 28, 28; **12:**22; **13:**13, 18; **14:**12, 33, 35; **15:**6, 8, 26, 32; **16:**2, 11, 25; **17:**1, 8, 12, 17; **18:**2, 15; **19:**10; **20:**4, 13, 17, 21, 21; **21:**9, 9, 12, 13, 16, 19, 22; **22:**1, 2, 13, 16, 19, 21, 22; **23:**26, 30, 32; **24:**14, 15; **25:**3, 8, 8, 11, 13, 19, 20, 20, 24, 24; **26:**5, 7, 9, 14, 17, 24, 27; **27:**10, 14, 18, 19, 25; **28:**8, 23, 26; **29:**2, 2, 13, 16, 23; **30:**4, 4, 27, 28, 32; **31:**6, 22, 23, 27, 29; **Ecc 1:**1, 11, 11, 12, 13, 16; **2:**1, 3, 3, 7, 9, 10, 16, 20, 20, 24; **3:**10, 11, 14, 15, 15, 15, 16, 17, 18, 22, 22; **4:**1, 3, 6, 7, 10, 14; **5:**2, 4, 4, 6, 7, 8, 13, 14, 19; **6:**1, 3, 3, 4, 5, 8, 12, 12; **7:**1, 6, 11, 14, 15, 20, 26; **8:**8, 9, 10, 14, 14, 15, 16, 17; **9:**1, 1, 6, 6, 9, 11, 12, 12, 14; **10:**8, 9, 16, 20; **11:**5, 8, 9; **12:**1, 10; **SS 1:**6, 14; **2:**3, 3, 9, 13, 15; **3:**1, 2, 2, 6, 10; **4:**1, 7; **5:**1, 2, 2, 15, 16; **6:**12; **7:**4, 5, 12; **8:**5, 13; **Isa 1:**7, 8, 13, 15, 29, 29; **2:**2, 2, 3, 5, 10, 12, 16, 17, 19, 19, 19, 21, 22; **3:**6, 8, 13, 16, 25; **4:**1, 2; **5:**2, 2, 8, 14, 15, 17; **6:**1, 3, 11; **7:**2, 17, 18, 19, 19, 19, 20, 22, 23; **8:**11, 17, 20; **9:**1, 2, 2, 5, 9, 10, 14, 17, 20; **10:**5, 10, 12, 17, 18, 20, 24, 25, 26, 27, 30, 32, 34; **11:**3, 6, 8, 9, 10, 11; **12:**1, 2, 4; **13:**6, 20, 22, 22; **14:**1, 2, 3, 6, 9, 11, 13, 18, 18, 19, 25, 30, 30, 31, 32; **15:**1, 2, 2, 4, 4; **16:**10, 10, 12, 12, 13; **17:**2, 3, 4, 5, 6, 14, 14; **18:**2, 6, 7; **19:**15, 16, 16, 17, 18, 19, 19, 20, 21, 22, 23; **20:**1, 5; **21:**1, 2, 13; **22:**2, 2, 9, 12, 16, 22, 23; **23:**1, 2, 18; **24:**9, 10, 11, 12, 14, 15, 18, 20, 21, 21, 22, 23, 23; **25:**2, 4, 6, 7, 9, 9, 9, 9; **26:**1, 1, 3, 3, 4, 16, 17, 17, 18, 19, 19; **27:**1, 2, 7, 8, 12, 12, 13, 13, 13; **28:**1, 4, 10, 12, 13, 14, 16, 18, 21, 25; **29:**6, 7, 8, 15, 18, 19, 23, 24; **30:**2, 3, 6, 12, 13, 15, 15, 19, 25; **31:**2, 4, 9; **32:**2, 2, 4, 5, 7, 9, 10, 10, 11, 12, 16, 16, 18, 20; **33:**2, 5, 6, 7, 9, 12, 14, 16, 17; **34:**1, 5, 6, 6, 13; **35:**1, 6, 8; **36:**1, 2, 4, 7, 7, 7, 8, 11, 11, 12, 13, 15, 22, 22; **37:**2, 9, 11, 12, 23, 25, 29, 29, 30, 31, 31, 38; **38:**1, 3, 10, 11, 11, 12, 14, 18, 18, 20; **39:**2, 2, 4, 7; **40:**2, 6, 10, 11, 12, 15, 15, 17, 19; **41:**1, 2, 5, 7, 12, 16, 16, 18, 18, 23; **42:**2, 5, 5, 7, 10, 11, 17, 17, 19, 25; **43:**9, 10, 14, 19, 20, 20, 20; **44:**7, 11, 11, 14, 17, 20, 23, 24, 26; **45:**3, 14, 14, 15, 18, 18, 19, 25, 25; **46:**3, 13; **47:**1, 5, 8, 9, 10, 14; **48:**1, 3, 10, 10; **49:**1, 2, 2, 4, 5, 9, 10, 13, 16, 20, 22; **50:**6, 10, 10, 11, 11; **51:**7, 9, 13, 13, 16, 16, 20, 20, 21; **52:**4, 5, 12, 15; **53:**2, 2, 9, 10; **54:**3, 4, 8, 9, 14, 17, 17; **55:**12; **56:**5, 7; **57:**2, 5, 6, 10, 13, 15; **58:**5, 5, 10, 13; **59:**5, 9, 9, 14, 16, 18, 20; **60:**7, 10, 11, 21; **61:**3, 6, 10, 10, 10, 11; **62:**3, 3, 4; **63:**1, 1, 3, 3, 6, 7, 9, 9; **64:**1; **65:**3, 5, 6, 6, 7, 14, 18, 19, 19, 21, 21, 23, 25; **66:**3, 5, 6, 8, 8, 11, 12, 17, 20, 20; **Jer 1:**1, 2, 3, 3, 5, 9, 17; **2:**3, 5, 8, 9, 12, 15, 15, 23, 23, 25, 26, 27, 28, 36, 37; **3:**2, 2, 10, 17, 18, 18, 19, 23, 25; **4:**7, 9, 9, 11, 19, 20, 20, 26, 28, 29, 30; **5:**1, 18, 19, 19, 22, 24, 26, 26, 30; **6:**1, 9, 11, 11, 16, 20, 21, 23, 26, 29; **7:**3, 7, 10, 17, 25, 29, 30, 31, 31, 32, 34, 34, 34; **8:**1, 16, 16, 22; **9:**2, 2, 7, 11, 16, 19, 21, 21, 21, 23, 23, 23, 24, 24, 25, 25, 26; **10:**2, 5, 7, 9, 13, 14, 24; **11:**4, 5, 6, 8, 13, 14, 15, 21, 22; **12:**2, 4, 4, 5; **13:**4, 4, 13, 18, 21, 24, 25, 27; **14:**2, 3, 8, 10, 12, 12, 14, 14, 15; **15:**4, 11, 17; **16:**2, 3, 6, 6, 9, 9, 16, 19; **17:**3, 5, 6, 6, 7, 13, 17, 19, 20, 25, 25; **18:**6, 6, 14, 16, 17, 21, 21, 23; **19:**11, 13, 14; **20:**1, 2, 3, 7, 8, 9, 9, 9, 9, 10, 17; **21:**2, 7, 9, 14; **22:**4, 4, 12, 15, 20, 20, 23, 23, 26, 30; **23:**3, 6, 6, 7, 8, 10, 11, 20, 23, 24, 25; **24:**1, 1, 8, 8; **25:**2, 5, 13, 14, 20, 23, 30, 33, 34, 36; **26:**1, 2, 6, 7, 9, 9, 12, 14, 15, 16, 23; **27:**1, 3, 11, 15, 18, 18, 18, 19, 19, 21, 21; **28:**1, 1, 5, 7; **29:**8, 9, 10, 12, 13, 15, 16, 18, 19, 20, 21, 23, 24, 25, 26, 26, 31; **30:**7, 7, 8, 10, 16, 24; **31:**1, 10, 13, 15, 19, 24, 27, 28, 28, 33, 40; **32:**1, 2, 2, 8, 8, 12, 15, 20, 20, 23, 29, 34, 35, 37, 37, 40, 41, 41, 43, 44, 44, 44, 44, 44, 44; **33:**1, 5, 10, 11, 13, 16, 16; **34:**4, 5, 9, 13, 15; **35:**7, 7, 8, 10, 11, 13, 15, 15, 18; **36:**1, 2, 3, 9, 12, 20, 22, 22, 29, 32; **37:**2, 15, 20, 21, 21, 21, 21; **38:**2, 6, 6, 7, 9, 9, 11, 22, 22, 28; **39:**1, 3, 3, 4, 5, 7, 7, 10, 14, 15; **40:**1, 1, 6, 6, 7, 7, 10, 11, 11; **41:**1, 1, 10; **42:**10, 12, 14, 17, 21, 22; **43:**4, 6, 9, 13, 13; **44:**1, 1, 2, 2, 7, 8, 9, 12, 13, 13, 15, 17, 17, 18, 21, 21, 24, 26, 26; **45:**1; **46:**2, 5, 10, 14, 14, 15, 22, 25; **47:**2, 2, 2, 5; **48:**1, 2, 6, 7, 8, 9, 11, 18, 20, 21, 26, 27, 28, 28, 32, 37, 38, 44, 47; **49:**1, 3, 4, 8, 16, 16, 16, 19, 23, 26, 30, 31, 32, 38, 39; **50:**3, 6, 11, 19, 20, 20, 20, 22, 23, 28, 30, 32, 34, 38, 42, 44; **51:**2, 4, 4, 6, 7, 10, 16, 17, 24, 29, 30, 32, 33, 35, 38, 43, 47, 50, 50, 56, 58, 64; **52:**1, 2, 3, 6, 7, 9, 11, 11, 12, 13, 15, 16, 20, 21, 25, 25, 27, 28, 29, 30, 30, 31, 31, 32; **La 1:**1, 4, 7, 9, 12, 13, 13, 14, 15, 19, 20; **2:**1, 1, 1, 2, 2, 7, 10, 10, 10, 10, 11, 12, 12, 13, 15, 19, 19, 21, 21, 22; **3:**6, 7, 7, 16, 24, 28, 29, 35, 36, 40, 41, 44, 63, 66; **4:**1, 2, 5, 5, 6, 10, 11, 12, 12, 17, 19, 20, 21, 22; **5:**9, 10, 11, 14; **Eze 1:**1, 3, 9, 10, 12, 12, 17, 20, 21, 28; **2:**3, 8; **3:**11, 12, 14, 15, 18, 19, 20, 23, 23, 24; **4:**1, 9, 13, 16, 17; **5:**3, 12, 13, 14, 15; **6:**4, 5, 11, 12, 14, 14; **7:**4, 18, 18, 19, 26, 27; **8:**1, 3, 4, 7, 9, 9, 10, 11, 12, 18; **9:**2, 2, 3, 8, 8, 11; **10:**2, 2, 3, 5, 6, 6, 7, 11, 11, 11, 17; **11:**2, 13, 13, 15, 15, 16, 16, 24; **12:**3, 4, 7, 7, 10, 12, 13, 19, 19, 22, 24, 25; **13:**4, 5, 5, 22; **14:**3, 4, 7, 11, 18, 22; **16:**4, 5, 5, 6, 7, 15, 22, 22, 22, 23, 24, 25, 31, 32, 36, 37, 38, 40, 41, 46, 46, 47, 52, 54, 56, 56, 63; **17:**5, 8, 10, 16, 16, 19, 20, 21, 21, 23; **18:**2, 3, 6, 7, 7, 12, 12, 14; **19:**4, 4, 7, 7, 7, 8, 9, 12, 13; **20:**1, 5, 8, 13, 13, 14, 15, 17, 18, 21, 22, 23, 32, 33, 36, 38, 41, 44, 49; **21:**5, 12, 30, 31, 32; **22:**2, 6, 9, 13, 14, 19, 20, 20, 22, 22, 24, 25, 30, 30, 31; **23:**3, 6, 8, 10, 11, 12, 14, 14, 17, 19, 21, 22, 27, 27, 29, 31, 32, 34, 34, 39, 39, 48, 48; **24:**6, 18, 21, 22, 26; **25:**3, 11; **26:**11, 15, 20, 20, 20; **27:**3, 10, 12, 15, 21, 22, 26, 26, 28, 30, 31, 31; **28:**2, 2, 8, 13, 13, 15, 15, 18, 23, 25, 26; **29:**3, 4, 5, 7, 14, 16, 16; **30:**5, 7, 9, 12, 13, 14, 16, 17, 21, 24, 24, 25; **31:**6, 6, 6, 8, 8, 8, 14, 14, 15, 16, 17; **32:**2, 3, 10, 18, 21, 23, 23, 24, 25, 25, 27, 30, 31; **33:**6, 8, 9, 11, 25, 27, 27, 27, 30; **34:**13, 14, 14, 15, 25, 25, 27, 28, 30; **35:**13, 15; **36:**17, 20, 26, 27, 28, 29, 33, 36; **37:**8, 14, 17, 19, 22, 25; **38:**8, 8, 11, 12, 14, 14, 15, 16, 17, 19, 19, 20, 21; **39:**5, 9, 11, 13, 15, 23, 24, 26, 26; **40:**2, 3, 11, 12, 16, 22, 24, 29, 29, 33, 36, 41, 46, 47, 47; **41:**6, 6, 10, 13, 22; **42:**5, 6, 12; **43:**3, 7, 8; **44:**1, 3, 4, 7, 7, 14, 15, 15, 17, 17, 19, 25, 25; **45:**4, 6, 15, 15, 16, 18, 20, 25; **46:**3, 9, 9, 21; **47:**6, 9, 10; **48:**1, 17, 18, 19, 21; **Da 1:**1, 2, 2, 3, 4, 4, 5, 17, 20, 20; **2:**2, 4, 9, 19, 22, 24, 28, 28, 31, 31, 45, 49, 49; **3:**1, 12, 13, 22, 22, 22, 24, 25, 28, 30; **4:**4, 4, 5, 6, 7, 8, 8, 9, 10, 10, 12, 12, 15, 18, 19, 21, 21, 23, 25, 26, 29, 32; **5:**2, 3, 7, 7, 8, 11, 13, 16, 16, 19, 29, 29; **6:**4, 5, 10, 15, 20, 22, 23, 27; **7:**1, 1, 2, 5, 7, 9, 18, 22, 23; **8:**2, 3, 8, 8, 12, 15, 17, 19, 24, 25; **9:**3, 7, 11, 12, 12, 13, 14, 15, 16, 18, 21, 24; **10:**1, 1, 2, 5, 12, 12, 14, 16, 21; **11:**5, 6, 11, 14, 15, 16, 17, 17, 18, 19, 20, 21, 21, 35, 44; **12:**1, 6, 7, 10; **Hos 1:**5, 5, 10, 11; **2:**1, 3, 4, 5, 6, 8, 10, 15, 16, 18, 21, 21; **3:**3, 5, 5; **4:**1, 5, 13, 15, 16, 19; **5:**8, 8, 8; **6:**1, 2, 2, 3, 4, 9, 10; **7:**6; **9:**3, 4, 5, 8, 8, 9, 10, 11; **10:**1, 4, 6, 9, 11, 13; **11:**6; **12:**6, 9, 9, 11, 14; **13:**1, 3, 4, 5, 5, 11, 11, 15; **14:**3, 3, 5, 9; **Joel 1:**2, 3, 13, 13, 16, 17, 18; **2:**1, 1, 3, 3, 3, 8, 13, 15, 17, 20, 23, 29, 30, 32; **3:**11, 14, 17, 18, 21; **Am 1:**1, 3, 5, 6, 11, 14; **2:**2, 2, 7, 8, 8, 9; **3:**4, 4, 5, 8, 12; **4:**2, 3, 10, 12; **5:**6, 11, 12, 16, 16, 17, 19, 19, 25, 26; **6:**1, 1, 1, 8, 9, 14, 14; **7:**2, 2, 13, 15, 17, 17, 17; **8:**1, 3, 3, 3, 5; **9:**1, 6, 9, 11, 11, 14, 15; **Ob** 3, 3, 8, 9, 10, 11, 14, 18, 19, 19, 20, 21; **Jnh 1:**3, 3, 5; **2:**2, 5, 6, 7; **3:**6; **4:**11; **Mic 1:**1, 3, 4, 5, 5, 8, 10, 10, 10, 13, 13, 16; **2:**3, 4, 5, 12, 12; **3:**4, 7; **4:**1, 1, 2, 4, 4, 6, 9, 9, 10, 10, 10; **5:**1, 2, 3, 4, 7; **6:**9, 10, 14; **7:**6, 8, 10, 11, 14, 14, 15, 16, 17, 18; **Na 1:**1, 3, 5, 6, 7, 8, 10, 14, 14; **2:**3, 5, 7, 10, 13, 13; **3:**3, 3, 7, 7, 10, 15, 17, 18; **Hab 1:**1, 4, 5, 12, 13, 13, 15, 16, 17; **2:**2, 4, 5, 7, 11, 11, 13, 17, 17, 18, 20; **3:**2, 2, 2, 4, 6, 7, 8, 12, 12, 16, 17, 18, 18; **Zep 1:**2, 3, 7, 7, 9, 11, 11, 12, 12, 13; **2:**4, 5, 7, 7, 7, 11, 11, 15, 15; **3:**2, 5, 6, 12, 13; **Hag 1:**4, 4, 6, 8, 9, 12; **2:**2, 3, 4, 6, 9, 12, 19; **Zec 1:**1, 8, 8; **2:**1, 7, 12; **3:**5, 7, 9; **4:**7, 7, 10; **5:**4, 5; **6:**10, 14; **7:**5, 5, 6, 11; **8:**3, 4, 8, 12, 16, 19, 21, 23; **9:**3, 7, 7, 9, 10, 11, 15, 16, 16; **10:**1, 3, 5, 5, 7, 9, 10, 12; **11:**3, 8, 10, 13; **12:**5, 6, 11, 11, 12, 12; **13:**3, 8, 8; **14:**1, 3, 5, 8, 8, 10, 12, 12, 13, 15, 16, 17, 20, 21, 21, 21, 21; **Mal 1:**4, 11; **2:**5, 9, 9, 11, 11, 11, 15; **3:**4, 10, 10, 16; **4:**2; **Mt 1:**20; **2:**1, 1, 1, 5, 6, 12, 13, 16, 18, 19, 19, 22, 23; **3:**1, 1, 3, 6, 12; **4:**13, 15, 15, 16, 16, 21, 23; **5:**6, 12, 14, 16, 19, 19, 22, 22, 23, 25, 28, 28, 45, 45, 48; **6:**1, 2, 2, 4, 5, 9, 10, 18, 19, 20, 26, 29; **7:**2, 3, 3, 4, 4, 5, 12, 21, 22, 22, 22, 25; **8:**4, 5, 6, 10, 11, 14, 20, 27, 28, 28, 30, 32; **9:**17, 25, 33, 35, 38; **10:**11, 17, 19, 23, 27, 27, 28, 32, 33, 36; **11:**1, 2, 7, 8, 8, 8, 11, 16, 21, 21, 21, 21, 23; **12:**3, 5, 5, 19, 32, 32, 34, 40, 40, 50; **13:**6, 21, 24, 30, 31, 32, 34, 35, 36, 43, 44, 44, 52, 54, 57, 57; **14:**9, 10, 13, 21, 24, 25, 26; **15:**22, 33, 38; **16:**3, 3, 17, 19, 19, 26, 27, 28; **17:**11, 18, 24, 27; **18:**1, 4, 6, 10, 10, 14, 18, 18, 19, 24, 24, 30, 32, 35; **19:**21, 25, 28, 29; **20:**3, 6, 7, 8, 12, 21, 21, 25, 32; **21:**9, 9, 9, 11, 14, 15, 18, 22, 28, 42, 45; **22:**10, 11, 28, 30, 31, 35, 36, 44; **23:**6, 6, 9, 13, 16, 21, 30, 31, 34, 35, 39; **24:**5, 7, 15, 16, 18, 19, 20, 22, 26, 30, 36, 37, 38, 40, 47, 51; **25:**10, 15, 18, 21, 23, 25, 31, 32, 36, 39, 43, 44; **26:**2, 6, 7, 13, 26, 29, 55, 56, 58, 61, 63, 64, 64, 67, 69, 70; **27:**1, 6, 16, 29, 29, 39, 40, 42, 51, 51, 59, 60; **28:**18, 19; **Mk 1:**2, 3, 4, 5, 9, 9, 19, 20, 23, 30, 39, 40, 44, 45; **2:**4, 25; **3:**3, 9, 11; **4:**6, 17, 26, 34, 34, 36, 40; **5:**1, 5, 23, 25, 26, 30, 34; **6:**2, 3, 4, 10, 19, 22, 26, 27, 29, 35, 39, 40, 47, 47, 48, 48, 49, 56, 56; **7:**4, 9, 13, 19, 26, 30; **8:**4, 9, 14, 17, 36, 38, 38; **9:**1, 12, 12, 15, 17, 28, 31, 33, 36, 39, 42, 50; **10:**10, 21, 26, 30, 30, 32, 37, 37, 42; **11:**4, 8, 8, 9, 9, 10, 11, 13, 13, 15, 16, 22, 23, 25, 27; **12:**10, 12, 23, 25, 26, 26, 33, 35, 36, 38, 38, 39, 40, 41, 41, 41, 42; **13:**1, 6, 8, 9, 11, 14, 16, 17, 18, 20, 32; **14:**3, 3, 9, 17, 22, 25, 49, 51, 55, 58, 62, 66; **15:**1, 8, 17, 19, 21, 25, 29, 29, 38, 38, 41, 44, 46, 46, 46; **16:**5, 17, 19; **Lk 1:**2, 6, 8, 9, 11, 15, 18, 19, 22, 26, 26, 26, 36, 36, 44, 47, 61, 66, 75, 79, 79, 80, 80; **2:**4, 4, 7, 7, 7, 8, 11, 12, 12, 14, 16, 19, 24, 25, 28, 29, 34, 36, 39, 43, 46, 49, 51, 52, 52; **3:**2, 4, 5, 5, 17, 20, 22; **4:**5, 15, 20, 23, 23, 24, 25, 25, 26, 27, 28, 31, 31, 33, 43, 44; **5:**1, 3, 7, 12, 12, 14, 17, 19, 29; **6:**1, 3, 6, 23, 38, 38, 41, 41, 42, 42, 42, 45; **7:**9, 24, 25, 25, 25, 25, 28, 30, 32, 45, 50; **8:**13, 16, 23, 26, 27, 37, 43, 48, 51, 54; **9:**4, 12, 12, 14, 25, 26, 26, 31, 38, 49, 58; **10:**1, 2, 7, 13, 13, 13, 13, 25; **11:**7, 27, 29, 37, 43, 44, 45, 45, 46, 49, 52; **12:**3, 3, 8, 11, 11, 17, 24, 27, 33, 33, 33, 36, 38, 44, 52, 54, 58; **13:**1, 4, 6, 10, 14, 16, 19, 24, 26, 29, 29, 33, 35; **14:**1, 3, 3, 10, 15; **15:**4, 7, 8, 9, 10, 10, 22, 23, 25, 25, 28, 29; **16:**2, 2, 9, 9, 10, 10, 15, 15, 16, 17, 19, 23, 23, 24, 24, 24, 25; **17:**2, 7, 10, 20, 22, 23, 26, 27, 28, 31, 34; **18:**2, 7, 13, 22, 26, 30, 30; **19:**2, 5, 6, 15, 23, 27, 27, 38, 38, 38, 43, 44, 47; **20:**1, 19, 26, 33, 35, 36, 42, 42, 46, 46, 46, 47; **21:**1, 2, 8, 11, 11, 21, 21, 23, 25, 25, 25, 34, 35; **22:**16, 19, 19, 24, 25, 28, 30, 32, 44, 53, 55, 56, 63, 69, 70; **23:**7, 14, 19, 19, 19, 25, 26, 43, 45, 48, 51, 53, 53; **24:**3, 4, 5, 6, 12, 17, 18, 25, 44, 47, 49, 53; **Jn 1:**1, 2, 4, 11, 23, 23, 26, 31, 39; **2:**1, 1, 11, 11, 14, 19, 20, 23; **3:**12, 14, 15, 16, 18, 20, 22, 27, 36; **4:**21, 23, 23, 24, 24, 39, 44, 45, 46, 46, 47, 48, 53, 54; **5:**7, 14, 18, 24, 25, 26, 26, 28, 29, 33, 38; **6:**21, 22, 29, 30, 35, 36, 40, 41, 45, 47, 49, 56, 56, 57, 59, 59; **7:**1, 5, 9, 13, 13, 19, 25, 26, 28, 31, 35, 38, 39, 42, 43, 45, 48; **8:**3, 3, 4, 6, 8, 9, 16, 20, 21, 24, 24, 30, 31, 37, 44, 49; **9:**3, 5, 7, 18, 24, 34, 35; **10:**9, 10, 16, 19, 22, 24, 25, 34, 38, 38, 38, 42; **11:**1, 4, 8, 15, 17, 25, 26, 44, 44, 45, 51, 55, 56; **12:**1, 2, 6, 7, 11, 13, 17, 21, 24, 25, 25, 35, 35, 36, 37, 42, 46, 46, 46; **13:**21, 26; **14:**1, 2, 10, 10, 10, 11, 11, 12, 13, 14, 17, 19, 20, 20, 20; **15:**4, 4, 5, 5, 7, 9, 10, 10, 12, 15; **16:**9, 16, 19, 25, 26, 29, 32, 33; **17:**2, 6, 20, 21, 21, 21, 23, 23, 26, 26; **18:**16, 20, 20, 20, 26, 28, 28; **19:**13, 17, 20, 23, 29, 36, 40; **20:**5, 5, 8, 11, 25, 25, 27, 30, 31; **21:**2, 3, 6, 6; **Ac 1:**1, 3, 4, 5, 8, 8, 17, 20, 20, 25, 26; **2:**1, 2, 4, 5, 11, 13, 15, 17, 18, 19, 24, 26, 27, 28, 31, 33, 34, 36, 38, 41, 42, 42, 45, 46; **3:**1, 2, 6, 11, 16, 17, 21, 25; **4:**5, 7, 7, 10, 11, 12, 12, 16, 17, 18, 24, 24, 27, 28, 29, 35, 37; **5:**6, 7, 10, 12, 16, 18, 25, 27, 28, 31, 40, 40, 42, 42; **6:**1, 3, 4, 7, 7, 15; **7:**2, 4, 6, 7, 7, 9, 10, 12, 14, 16, 16, 17, 20, 22, 27, 29, 30, 30, 34, 35, 38, 41, 42, 42, 43, 43, 44, 48, 50, 54, 55, 56; **8:**1, 8, 14, 16, 21, 25, 25, 28, 40; **9:**2, 2, 2, 10, 10, 12, 13, 14, 19, 20, 21, 21, 22, 25, 25, 26, 27, 27, 28, 28, 31, 31, 31, 32, 32, 36, 36, 37, 41, 42, 43; **10:**1, 3, 4, 12, 14, 24, 25, 30, 30, 30, 30, 32, 35, 37, 39, 43, 46, 48; **11:**1, 2, 5, 13, 17, 24, 28, 29, 29, 30; **12:**1, 5, 7, 13, 19, 22, 23, 25; **13:**5, 8, 9, 15, 17, 18, 19, 24, 27, 29, 32, 33, 34, 35, 38, 39, 41; **14:**1, 4, 10, 11, 11, 14, 15, 16, 21, 22, 23, 23, 25, 27, 28; **15:**3, 4, 21, 21, 22, 23, 23, 35, 38, 38; **16:**2, 3, 4, 5, 5, 9, 18, 20, 24, 32, 33, 34, 36; **17:**2, 11, 13, 13, 16, 16, 17, 21, 24, 24, 27, 28; **18:**2, 8, 9, 10, 12, 13, 17, 18, 23, 23, 24, 24, 26, 27, 27, 27, 28; **19:**1, 4, 5, 6, 7, 22, 23, 25, 26, 30, 32, 32, 33, 38, 39, 40; **20:**2, 6, 6, 16, 18, 20, 21, 23, 29, 30, 37; **21:**3, 11, 17, 18, 21, 24, 25, 27, 28, 29, 31, 34, 39, 40; **22:**2, 3, 3, 3, 5, 5, 12, 17, 19, 30; **23:**1, 6, 8, 11, 11, 33, 35; **24:**2, 2, 9, 11, 12, 12, 14, 15, 18, 20, 21, 23, 24, 27, 27; **25:**1, 5, 7, 15, 17, 20, 23, 24, 25; **26:**1, 4, 7, 10, 11, 11, 14, 18, 20, 20, 21, 26, 29; **27:**1, 5, 9, 11, 21, 24, 40; **28:**8, 15, 16, 17, 23, 30; **Ro 1:**2, 7, 8, 9, 11, 12, 12, 14, 14, 15, 17, 19, 26; **2:**2, 4, 5, 7, 13, 14, 19, 20, 27; **3:**1, 4, 4, 4, 20, 21, 21, 22, 22, 24, 25, 26, 26, 26, 31; **4:**14, 14, 17, 20, 20, 20, 24; **5:**1, 4, 9, 11, 11, 17, 18, 19, 21; **6:**2, 5, 6, 12, 20, 21, 22; **7:**4, 5, 6, 6, 25, 25; **8:**3, 9, 9, 11, 16, 21, 22, 26, 26, 27, 29, 35, 39, 39, 39; **9:**1, 13, 17, 25, 29, 32, 33, 33, 33; **10:**4, 8, 8, 9, 10, 11, 12, 14, 14, 19; **11:**5, 6, 14, 17, 17, 18, 21, 22, 31, 31, 32; **12:**3, 5, 10, 11, 12, 13, 16, 17, 18; **13:**1, 9, 12, 12, 13, 13, 13, 13; **14:**1, 5, 8, 8, 13, 13, 14, 15, 17, 19, 20, 23; **15:**2, 4, 5, 10, 13, 17, 19, 21, 22, 22, 23, 24, 24, 26, 26, 27, 30, 30, 31; **16:**1, 1, 2, 2, 2, 3, 4, 5, 5, 7, 9, 11, 16, 23; **1Co 1:**2, 10, 10, 13, 15, 21, 26, 27, 29, 30; **2:**3, 7; **3:**1, 6, 16, 19, 21; **4:**1, 2, 15, 17, 17; **5:**1, 1, 2, 3, 3, 4, 4, 9, 10, 11, 12; **6:**5, 6, 9, 9, 10, 19; **7:**1, 15, 15, 17, 24, 24, 25, 31, 32, 34, 34, 34, 40; **8:**5, 10; **9:**1, 4, 11, 12, 13, 14, 15, 21, 21, 23, 24, 24, 26; **10:**1, 2, 5, 7, 8, 8, 13, 16, 16, 25, 26, 33; **11:**2, 7, 11, 16, 18, 21, 25, 25, 31; **12:**2, 5, 6, 10, 22, 24, 28, 28, 30, 31; **13:**1, 1, 8, 12; **14:**2, 3, 4, 4, 5, 5, 6, 7, 9, 10, 13, 13, 14, 15, 15, 15, 15, 16, 16, 18, 19, 19, 20, 20, 21, 21, 22, 23, 26, 26, 27, 28, 28, 31, 32, 33, 35, 39, 40; **15:**2, 14, 18, 18, 19, 29, 31, 31, 32, 37, 40, 41, 52, 52, 54, 56; **16:**1, 2, 8, 15, 15, 19, 19, 19, 20, 24; **2Co 1:**1, 4, 6, 7, 8, 9, 12, 14, 20, 22, 24; **2:**3, 6, 9, 14; **3:**2, 4, 6, 6, 7, 10, 14; **4:**1, 6, 6, 7, 7, 10, 10, 11, 12, 12, 13; **5:**1, 1, 2, 6, 9, 10, 13, 19; **6:**3, 4, 5, 7, 16; **7:**3, 4, 4, 5, 9, 10, 10, 11, 12, 13, 16; **8:**1, 1, 2, 4, 4, 6, 6, 7, 7, 14, 17, 18, 22; **9:**1, 2, 2, 2, 3, 7, 10, 10, 11, 12; **10:**1, 1, 10, 11, 11, 16, 16; **11:**7, 10, 15, 20, 23, 26, 26, 32, 33, 33; **12:**6, 6, 7, 9, 13, 18; **13:**3, 4, 4, 4, 11, 12; **Gal 1:**2, 4, 4, 6, 15, 22, 22; **2:**4, 9, 13, 14, 16, 16, 16, 17, 20, 20, 20; **3:**3, 4, 6, 7, 9, 10, 13, 15, 22, 23, 23, 24, 25, 26, 27, 28; **4:**12, 14, 15, 19, 23, 25, 25; **5:**1, 3, 6, 6, 13, 13, 14, 16, 20, 20, 22, 25; **6:**2, 3, 11, 14, 14; **Eph 1:**1, 3, 4, 4, 7, 10, 12, 13, 15, 17, 20, 20, 21, 21; **2:**2, 4, 6, 7, 10, 12, 12, 15; **3:**3, 6, 8, 10, 10, 10, 12, 15, 17, 17, 21, 21; **4:**3, 6, 9, 13, 13, 15, 15, 21, 24, 28; **5:**1, 7, 11, 12, 16, 19, 20, 24, 28; **6:**9, 9, 12, 13, 16, 18, 18, 20, 21; **Php 1:**1, 5, 7, 7, 9, 11, 13, 13, 14, 20, 20, 27, 29, 30, 30, 30; **2:**1, 4, 7, 8, 10, 12, 13, 14, 15, 22, 25, 27; **3:**3, 3, 4, 4, 6, 10, 18; **4:**3, 3, 4, 5, 7, 11, 12, 14, 16, 19, 22; **Col 1:**2, 4, 7, 9, 12, 13, 16, 18, 19, 19, 20, 22, 23, 24, 25, 27, 27, 28; **2:**3, 5, 6, 7, 7, 9, 9, 10, 15, 19; **3:**1, 3, 4, 10, 11, 11, 14, 15, 15, 16, 16, 22; **4:**1, 3, 10, 13, 15, 18; **1Th 1:**1, 6, 6, 7, 8; **2:**12, 13, 14, 14, 14; **3:**1, 2, 2, 2, 7, 8, 9, 10; **4:**1, 1, 2, 4, 5, 5, 6, 10, 15, 17, 17; **5:**2, 4, 8, 12, 23, 26, 27; **2Th 1:**1, 3, 4, 6, 8; **2:**4, 13, 14, 15, 15, 16, 17; **3:**2, 4, 6, 11, 12, 14; **1Ti 1:**2, 3, 4, 4, 13, 13, 16, 18, 19; **2:**2, 2, 2, 9, 15; **3:**2, 8, 10, 11, 11, 13, 13, 15, 16, 16; **4:**1, 7, 8, 10, 10, 12, 12, 12; **5:**5, 5, 5, 8, 10, 18, 20, 21, 22, 22, 25; **6:**4, 16, 17, 17, 17, 18, 18; **2Ti 1:**1, 3, 8, 12, 12, 13, 13, 16; **2:**1, 4, 4, 7, 10, 14, 20, 23; **3:**1, 3, 10, 11, 12, 15, 16, 17; **4:**5, 17; **Tit 1:**4, 5, 8, 9, 10, 13; **2:**3, 6, 6, 10, 12; **3:**8, 9, 9; **Phm 1:**1, 2, 5, 6, 8, 9, 10, 11, 13, 16, 18, 19, 20, 23; **Heb 1:**1, 2, 2, 3, 8, 10, 13; **2:**6, 9, 13, 13, 14, 15, 17; **3:**5, 6, 6, 6, 8, 11, 14, 17; **4:**3, 5, 7, 13; **5:**1, 6, 6, 9, 10, 13; **6:**1, 4, 11, 13, 20, 20; **7:**2, 4, 5, 8, 9, 10, 14, 15, 17, 26; **8:**1, 1, 2, 5, 10; **9:**1, 2, 2, 4, 6, 6, 7, 8, 10, 11, 21, 22, 23, 23, 24; **10:**1, 7, 9, 16, 34, 35, 37, 38; **11:**2, 7, 9, 19, 20, 20, 21, 31, 34, 35, 36, 37, 37, 38, 38, 40; **12:**2, 2, 4, 10, 11, 14, 22, 23, 23; **13:**3, 3, 4, 10, 12, 14, 16, 18, 20, 22; **Jas 1:**4, 8, 10, 18, 20, 21, 21, 23, 27, 27; **2:**1, 2, 2, 2, 5, 5, 8, 19, 20; **3:**1, 2, 3, 9, 14; **5:**3, 5, 7, 7, 10, 10, 11, 14, 15; **1Pe 1:**1, 4, 5, 11, 12, 15, 17, 20, 21, 21, 23; **2:**6, 6, 21, 23, 24; **3:**1, 7, 7, 11, 16, 18, 19, 20, 22; **4:**3, 4, 6, 7, 11, 13; **5:**1, 4, 5, 6, 9, 10, 12, 13, 14, 14; **2Pe 1:**4, 8, 12, 19, 19, 19, 20; **2:**1, 3, 4, 11, 13, 13, 13; **3:**1, 3, 10, 10, 12, 16, 18; **1Jn 1:**5, 6, 6, 7, 10; **2:**4, 5, 6, 8, 9, 9, 10, 11, 14, 15, 16, 24, 25, 27, 27, 28, 28; **3:**5, 6, 9, 17, 17, 19, 23, 24, 24, 24; **4:**1, 4, 4, 12, 13, 13, 15, 15, 16, 16, 16, 16, 17, 17, 18; **5:**6, 10, 11, 13, 14, 16, 20, 20, 21; **2Jn 1:**2, 2, 3, 4, 7, 9, 10, 11, 12; **3Jn 1:**3, 4, 6, 13; **Jude** 1, 4, 6, 12, 12, 15, 16, 18, 18, 18, 19, 21, 21, 25; **Rev 1:**4, 9, 9, 9, 9, 10, 13, 15, 16, 16, 20; **2:**1, 1, 7, 8, 12, 13, 15, 17, 18, 19, 24; **3:**1, 2, 4, 4, 5, 7, 12, 12, 14, 20; **4:**1, 2, 2, 4, 5, 6, 6, 7; **5:**1, 3, 12, 13, 13; **6:**5, 9, 15; **7:**1, 9, 9, 9, 13, 14, 15, 15, 17; **8:**8, 9; **9:**6, 11, 11, 13, 17, 19, 19, 20; **10:**2, 6, 6, 6, 6, 10; **11:**3, 8, 12, 13, 13, 15, 19; **12:**1, 2, 3, 7, 12, 12, 14; **13:**1, 3, 6, 8; **14:**3, 10, 12, 13, 14, 15, 17, 20, 20; **15:**1, 5, 6; **16:**3, 5, 10, 16, 17, 18; **17:**3, 4, 5, 8, 18; **18:**4, 7, 8, 9, 10, 13, 16, 17, 18, 19, 23, 24; **19:**1, 10, 13, 14, 17, 17, 19; **20:**1, 2, 6, 12, 13, 13, 15; **21:**8, 10, 15, 16, 16, 22, 24, 27; **22:**7, 9, 11, 18, 19, 19, 19

INTO (1342)

Ge 1:9; **2:**7, 10, 21, 24; **4:**8; **6:**19; **7:**1, 9, 13, 15; **9:**23; **10:**25; **12:**15; **13:**1; **14:**10, 10, 14; **15:**5, 12; **17:**2; **21:**14, 16; **22:**17; **24:**20, 67; **27:**3; **30:**2; **31:**33, 33, 33, 34; **32:**7; **33:**2; **37:**20, 22, 24; **39:**20; **40:**11; **41:**35; **43:**22, 24, 30; **44:**1; **45:**4; **50:**20; **Ex 1:**22; **3:**1, 8, 18; **4:**7, 9, 27; **5:**1, 3, 8, 21; **6:**4, 8; **7:**15, 19, 22; **8:**3, 3, 14, 16, 17, 24, 25, 27; **9:**8, 10; **10:**19; **12:**22, 22; **13:**5, 11; **14:**17, 20, 21, 24, 27, 27, 28; **15:**1, 4, 19, 21, 22, 25; **16:**1, 3, 9, 33; **19:**18; **20:**21; **21:**33; **22:**2, 5, 6; **23:**23; **24:**6, 18; **25:**14; **26:**1, 3, 3, 9, 9, 19, 31, 32, 32, 36, 37, 37; **27:**5, 7, 10, 11, 12, 14, 15, 16; **28:**29, 30, 30; **30:**20, 25; **32:**4, 10, 12, 20, 24; **33:**4, 9; **34:**34; **35:**26; **36:**8, 35, 36, 36; **37:**5; **38:**4, 7, 14, 15, 19; **39:**3, 3, 3; **40:**18, 21; **Lev 1:**6; **2:**6; **4:**5, 6, 16, 17, 25, 30, 34; **5:**3; **6:**11, 21, 22, 30; **8:**20; **9:**9, 23; **10:**9, 18; **11:**32, 33, 36; **13:**2; **14:**6, 7, 15, 16, 26, 27, 40, 51; **16:**10, 14, 19, 21, 22, 26, 27; **24:**10; **25:**35; **Nu 4:**8; **5:**23; **6:**19; **7:**89; **8:**22; **11:**8, 31; **13:**17; **14:**8, 12, 16, 24, 31, 42; **16:**14, 30, 33, 38, 39; **17:**8; **19:**6, 18; **20:**4, 12; **22:**23; **24:**10; **25:**6, 8, 8, 18; **27:**17; **31:**2, 4, 6, 27; **32:**17, 32; **33:**8, 8, 51; **34:**2; **35:**10; **36:**3, 12; **Dt 1:**24, 28, 38, 41, 43; **2:**27, 29; **4:**11, 19, 21; **6:**10; **7:**1, 13, 23, 26; **8:**7; **9:**21, 21, 28; **10:**11, 22; **11:**29; **12:**30; **15:**17; **19:**3, 5; **20:**2; **23:**5; **24:**5; **26:**2, 3; **28:**24, 41; **29:**12, 23; **31:**7, 20, 23; **Jos 1:**2; **2:**3, 15, 19, 22; **3:**8; **4:**5; **6:**5, 19, 20; **8:**19, 33; **10:**5, 10, 27; **11:**8; **15:**3, 5; **16:**1; **18:**5, 9, 18; **22:**19; **24:**3, 4, 8; **Jdg 1:**16, 24, 34, 34; **2:**1; **3:**21; **4:**14, 15, 18, 18, 21, 22; **5:**15; **7:**5, 9, 13, 16; **9:**34, 39, 42, 43; **11:**18, 38; **14:**9; **15:**18; **16:**13, 13; **17:**4; **18:**13; **19:**29; **20:**6, 40, 45; **Ru 2:**2, 18; **3:**15; **4:**11; **1Sa 2:**14; **4:**3, 5, 7; **5:**2; **6:**14, 19; **7:**10; **8:**11, 20; **9:**10, 22; **10:**6; **11:**4, 7, 7, 11; **12:**8; **13:**7; **14:**27, 52; **17:**49; **18:**13, 16; **19:**10; **20:**35, 42; **23:**24, 25; **24:**1, 3, 4; **25:**20, 26; **26:**7, 12; **28:**25; **29:**4, 11; **30:**1; **2Sa 1:**15; **2:**16; **3:**31; **4:**6; **5:**8, 17; **6:**9, 10; **10:**14; **13:**10; **14:**24; **15:**25, 28; **16:**2, 13, 22; **17:**13,

13, 16; **18:**14, 17, 33; **19:**2, 3; **20:**6, 12; **22:**43; **23:**20; **24:**14, 14; **1Ki 1:**7, 15, 32; **2:**30; **5:**9; **6:**6; **8:**6; **11:**30; **12:**18; **13:**2; **15:**15; **16:**18, 21; **18:**23, 33, 44, 46; **19:**4; **20:**2, 27, 30, 33; **21:**22; **22:**20, 30, 30, 52; **2Ki 2:**11, 21; **3:**24; **4:**4, 4, 39, 39, 41; **5:**18; **6:**5, 6; **7:**4, 7, 8, 13; **9:**2, 6, 16, 25, 34; **10:**15, 23, 25, 27; **11:**19; **12:**7, 9, 10, 16; **13:**21; **18:**17, 30; **19:**1, 18, 25; **20:**18, 20; **21:**8, 11; **23:**15; **24:**20; **25:**21; **1Ch 1:**19; **5:**6, 10, 22; **6:**15, 15; **11:**22; **13:**12, 13; **16:**1; **18:**8; **19:**15; **21:**13, 13, 27; **22:**19; **23:**6; **24:**1, 3, 4, 4; **2Ch 5:**7; **10:**18; **13:**12; **15:**12, 15, 18; **16:**10; **18:**19, 29, 29; **20:**16, 20, 28; **23:**20; **24:**7; **25:**8; **26:**11; **28:**24; **29:**16; **30:**14; **31:**2; **33:**8; **34:**7, 11; **35:**22; **36:**17, 22; **Ezr 1:**1; **5:**14; **6:**5, 18; **7:**14; **Ne 1:**11; **4:**1, 22; **5:**5, 8; **9:**11, 23; **13:**2, 26, 26; **Est 2:**3, 4, 7, 9; **3:**9, 13, 15; **4:**1, 7; **7:**7; **9:**1, 22, 22; **Job 2:**12; **6:**27; **9:**31; **13:**11; **15:**22; **16:**11; **18:**8, 8, 18; **19:**8; **20:**22; **22:**24; **24:**5, 16; **28:**3, 4; **30:**19, 22; **35:**5; **36:**18, 21, 27; **39:**24; **42:**15; **Ps 7:**5, 15; **9:**15; **18:**42; **27:**12; **30:**3, 9, 11; **31:**5; **41:**12; **46:**2; **49:**17; **57:**T, 6; **58:**7, 8; **60:**9; **63:**9; **68:**15, 17, 24, 24; **69:**2; **73:**17; **78:**44, 55, 61; **80:**8; **88:**6; **92:**13; **100:**4; **102:**9; **104:**10, 22, 32; **105:**29; **107:**30, 33, 33, 34, 35, 35; **108:**10; **114:**8; **115:**17; **119:**34, 61, 85; **136:**15; **140:**10, 10; **141:**10; **147:**6; **148:**5; **Pr 1:**12; **6:**27; **7:**23; **11:**8; **13:**17; **17:**20; **18:**6, 7, 8; **22:**14; **24:**17; **26:**22; **27:**23; **28:**10, 10, 12, 17, 20; **29:**22; **31:**18; **Ecc 1:**7; **2:**7; **3:**21; **5:**14, 16; **7:**7, 13, 27; **SS 1:**4; **2:**9; **3:**4; **4:**16; **6:**11; **7:**8, 11; **Isa 2:**4, 4, 10, 19, 21; **3:**15; **5:**11, 13, 25, 29; **7:**3, 6, 6, 17; **8:**8, 22; **11:**15; **13:**21; **14:**17, 19, 23; **16:**8; **22:**17, 18, 18; **23:**13; **24:**18, 18; **25:**2; **28:**18; **30:**16; **33:**17; **36:**2, 15; **37:**1, 19, 26; **39:**7; **40:**26; **42:**15; **44:**23; **46:**2; **47:**6, 12; **48:**1, 13; **49:**11, 13, 21; **50:**2; **51:**23, 23; **52:**3, 9; **54:**1; **55:**12; **57:**8, 9; **58:**7; **60:**22; **63:**14; **Jer 2:**7, 21, 34, 37; **6:**28; **7:**15; **8:**6; **9:**11; **12:**10; **13:**17, 19; **14:**16, 18; **16:**13; **17:**4, 8; **18:**4; **19:**2, 4; **21:**4; **22:**13, 13; **23:**3, 13, 32; **24:**6; **25:**37; **28:**14; **29:**31; **30:**16; **31:**13, 35; **32:**14; **34:**3; **35:**2, 4; **36:**23; **37:**15, 16; **38:**6, 6, 9; **40:**12; **41:**7, 8, 15; **43:**3; **44:**6; **46:**3; **47:**6; **48:**44, 44; **50:**26; **51:**63; **52:**3, 27; **La 1:**3, 14; **2:**9; **3:**2, 13, 53; **4:**18; **Eze 1:**21; **2:**2; **3:**10, 22, 24; **5:**1, 4, 14; **7:**19; **8:**3, 8, 8, 16, 17; **9:**2; **10:**7, 16; **11:**5, 22; **12:**3, 6, 7, 7, 11; **14:**3, 4, 7, 19; **15:**5, 7; **16:**9; **17:**6, 8; **19:**9; **20:**10, 15, 28, 35; **21:**19; **23:**39; **24:**12; **25:**3, 5, 5; **26:**12; **27:**4, 26, 27; **31:**7, 15, 16; **32:**26; **37:**5, 6, 9, 22, 22; **38:**4, 8; **40:**7, 17, 18, 25, 27, 28, 30, 31, 34, 37, 38; **41:**1, 3, 6, 11, 17, 25; **43:**4, 5; **44:**7, 12; **46:**20; **47:**8; **Da 2:**5, 35, 44; **3:**6, 11, 13, 15, 17, 20, 21, 23, 24, 29; **4:**11, 20; **6:**1, 16, 24; **7:**13; **8:**22; **11:**4; **12:**1; **Hos 2:**12, 14, 15; **4:**13; **5:**1, 8; **14:**5; **Joel 1:**14; **2:**5, 20, 20, 20, 31; **3:**2, 10, 10; **Am 1:**6, 15; **4:**13; **5:**5, 8, 8, 15, 27; **6:**10, 12; **7:**11; **8:**10; **9:**2, 4; **Jnh 1:**12, 15; **2:**3; **Mic 1:**4, 6, 9, 11, 13; **4:**3, 3, 10; **7:**9, 19; **Na 1:**8; **2:**3; **3:**12, 14, 14; **Hab 2:**1; **Zep 1:**17; **Hag 1:**8; **Zec 2:**13; **3:**10; **5:**4, 4, 8, 9; **9:**4; **11:**6, 6, 6; **14:**2; **Mal 1:**3; **2:**8; **3:**10; **Mt 3:**9, 10; **4:**1, 3; **5:**25, 29, 30; **6:**22, 23; **7:**19; **8:**8, 12, 23, 24, 31, 32; **9:**1, 17, 28; **10:**12; **12:**4, 11, 43; **13:**2, 32, 36, 42, 47, 48, 50; **14:**19, 22, 23, 32; **15:**14, 36, 39; **17:**15, 15, 25; **18:**3, 6, 8, 9, 12; **19:**1, 5, 23; **21:**2, 13, 21, 31; **22:**13, 15; **23:**15; **24:**43; **25:**27, 30, 35, 41, 43, 46, 46; **26:**18, 45; **27:**7, 27, 53; **28:**4, 11; **Mk 1:**5, 12, 21, 26, 35; **2:**22, 26; **3:**1; **4:**1, 37; **5:**4, 12, 13, 18, 40; **6:**41, 45, 46, 51; **7:**17, 33; **8:**6, 10, 13, 26; **9:**20, 22, 22, 26, 42, 43, 45, 47; **10:**1, 8, 15, 16, 23, 24; **11:**2, 11, 17, 23; **12:**13; **13:**15; **14:**13, 13, 16, 41, 68; **15:**16; **16:**12, 15, 19; **Lk 1:**24; **3:**8, 9; **4:**1, 3, 42; **5:**3, 3, 19, 37, 38; **6:**4, 39, 49; **8:**14, 22, 29, 31, 32, 33; **9:**16, 39, 42; **10:**10, 38; **11:**24, 28, 34, 34, 54; **12:**5, 39; **14:**5, 21, 23; **17:**2, 6, 31; **18:**17, 24; **19:**30, 40, 46; **21:**1, 12; **22:**3; **23:**42, 46; **24:**7; **Jn 1:**9; **2:**16; **3:**4, 17, 19, 24; **4:**8, 43, 46; **5:**7, 13, 24; **6:**3, 15, 17, 24; **7:**39; **8:**6; **10:**36; **11:**27; **12:**16, 23; **13:**5, 27, 30, 31, 32; **14:**17; **15:**6; **16:**13, 21, 28; **17:**5, 18, 18, 23; **18:**11; **19:**9, 27; **20:**25, 25, 27; **21:**7; **Ac 1:**9, 9, 11, 22; **2:**20, 31, 34; **3:**2, 8; **5:**15; **7:**43, 45, 55; **8:**1, 3, 31, 38; **9:**6; **10:**10, 28; **11:**5; **14:**19, 20, 22; **16:**6, 23, 24, 34; **17:**7, 8; **20:**9, 10; **21:**29, 38; **22:**10, 11, 17, 23, 30; **27:**15; **28:**5, 23; **Ro 1:**3; **3:**19; **4:**17; **5:**2, 3; **7:**14; **8:**3, 15; **9:**6, 21; **11:**8, 23, 24, 24; **12:**2, 13; **15:**19; **1Co 1:**9, 13; **5:**5; **6:**16; **10:**12, 13; **12:**13; **14:**23, 24; **15:**21, 36, 36, 53, 54; **2Co 1:**24; **5:**4; **12:**2, 4; **Gal 1:**17, 21; **2:**17; **3:**20; **4:**6, 27; **6:**1, 15; **Eph 1:**5; **3:**12, 17; **5:**31; **Php 2:**12; **3:**5, 21; **4:**9; **Col 1:**13, 22; **2:**7; **1Th 2:**12; **2Th 3:**5; **1Ti 1:**15; **3:**7, 16; **4:**15; **5:**13; **6:**7, 9, 9; **2Ti 1:**6; **2:**8; **3:**6; **Heb 2:**10, 10; **4:**10, 12; **6:**14, 19; **9:**7, 12, 17, 24, 24; **10:**5, 22, 31, 34; **13:**11; **Jas 1:**25; **2:**2, 6; **3:**6, 9; **1Pe 1:**14; **2:**2, 5, 9; **4:**15; **2Pe 1:**11; **2:**4, 6, 14, 18; **1Jn 3:**9; **4:**3, 9; **2Jn** 7, 10; **Jude** 24; **Rev 2:**10; **5:**6; **8:**8; **9:**9; **11:**6; **12:**6; **14:**10, 19; **16:**10, 17, 19, 19; **17:**3, 17; **18:**21; **19:**20; **20:**3, 10, 14, 15; **21:**26

IS (6473)

Ge 2:4, 11, 11, 12, 13, 14, 14, 18, 23, 24; **4:**7, 9, 9, 13, 24; **5:**1; **6:**9, 13; **9:**5, 6, 13, 17, 18; **10:**1; **11:**9, 10, 27; **12:**12, 18, 19; **13:**18; **14:**3, 17, 24; **16:**5, 6; **17:**4, 9, 10, 17, 21; **18:**9, 12, 14, 15, 19, 20, 25; **19:**14, 20, 20; **20:**3, 5, 5, 6, 7, 9, 12; **21:**10, 12, 13, 22, 26, 26; **22:**7, 16; **23:**8, 9, 15, 15, 19; **24:**8, 14, 24, 47, 51, 65, 65; **25:**12, 13, 18, 19, 22, 32, 33; **26:**7, 9, 20, 27, 28; **27:**11, 11, 18, 19, 22, 27, 36, 37, 42, 43, 44; **28:**16, 17, 17; **29:**6, 25, 27, 27; **30:**2, 13, 28, 40; **31:**5, 36, 37, 42, 47; **32:**2, 11, 18, 20, 26, 27, 28, 29, 32; **33:**10, 10, 15, 17; **34:**8, 10, 15, 21; **35:**10, 16, 19, 27; **36:**1, 9, 24; **37:**2, 27, 30, 33; **38:**14, 25, 26; **40:**8, 8; **41:**15, 16, 25, 28, 33, 38, 38; **42:**2, 13, 13, 13, 15, 16, 28, 30, 32, 33, 36, 36, 38, 38; **43:**5, 21, 27, 27, 28, 29; **44:**16, 20, 20, 23, 26, 30, 31, 34; **45:**3, 9, 20, 26, 26, 28; **47:**3, 4, 4, 15, 16, 18, 26; **48:**7, 18; **49:**1, 7, 7, 9, 11, 14, 15, 17, 21, 22, 26, 27, 30, 32; **50:**5, 11, 13; **Ex 2:**20; **3:**8, 13, 14, 16; **4:**11, 14, 14, 22, 22; **5:**1, 2, 2, 16; **6:**17, 30; **7:**14; **8:**1, 10, 19, 20; **9:**1, 14, 27; **10:**3, 11; **11:**4; **12:**4, 10, 11, 22, 26, 27; **13:**3, 5, 8, 15, 16; **14:**25; **15:**2, 2, 2, 3, 3, 6, 11, 11, 23, 26; **16:**15, 15, 23, 25, 25, 26, 29; **17:**7, 15; **18:**11, 17, 18, 22; **20:**10, 11; **21:**2, 8, 8, 13, 19, 20, 21, 22, 23, 24, 26, 29, 30, 32; **22:**1, 1, 2, 2, 2, 3, 3, 3, 4, 5, 7, 7, 8, 9, 10, 10, 14, 15, 15, 15, 16; **23:**3, 8, 9, 15, 15, 21; **25:**3, 16; **26:**9, 33; **27:**16, 21; **28:**43; **29:**1, 16, 18, 18, 20, 22, 30, 34, 35, 38, 42; **30:**10, 12, 15, 21, 32, 33, 36, 37; **31:**4, 5, 5, 13, 14, 17; **32:**17, 18, 27; **33:**3, 13, 13; **34:**3, 9, 9, 10, 11, 14, 14, 20; **35:**2, 4, 5, 32, 33; **38:**21; **Lev 1:**3, 9, 10, 13, 17; **2:**2, 5, 6, 7, 15; **3:**4, 5, 10, 15, 17; **4:**10, 21, 21, 21, 24, 26, 31, 35; **5:**2, 2, 4, 11, 17, 19; **6:**11, 17, 18, 22, 25, 28, 28, 29; **7:**1, 4, 5, 6, 15, 16, 18, 20, 21, 21, 34, 35; **8:**31, 32, 33, 35; **10:**3, 7, 9, 10, 10, 10, 10, 12, 12, 12, 14, 17; **11:**5, 12, 26, 32, 32, 34, 35, 38, 39, 47, 47; **12:**2, 4, 4, 4, 5, 6; **13:**3, 4, 8, 11, 11, 11, 20, 21, 21, 22, 23, 25, 26, 26, 27, 28, 30, 30, 31, 31, 35, 39, 39, 39, 40, 41, 42, 44, 44, 49, 51, 51, 55, 55, 56, 57, 58, 59; **14:**5, 13, 29, 31, 44, 46, 48, 50, 57; **15:**2, 3, 3, 23, 31; **16:**2, 2, 8, 10, 17, 21, 29, 31, 34; **17:**7, 11, 11, 12, 13, 14, 14, 14; **18:**7, 9, 11, 12, 13, 14, 15, 18, 22, 23, 24, 25; **19:**7, 8, 10, 20; **20:**13, 14, 17, 21, 23; **21:**2, 11, 18, 20, 21; **22:**5, 5, 10, 13, 19, 22, 23, 24, 27, 30, 32; **23:**3, 14, 21, 27, 28, 31, 41; **24:**3; **25:**5, 16, 21, 26, 30, 34, 49; **26:**5, 17, 36, 37; **27:**3, 3, 4, 5, 5, 6, 6, 7, 7, 9, 10, 11, 17, 18, 20, 21, 22, 27, 33, 33; **Nu 1:**20, 51; **2:**9, 16, 24, 31; **3:**1, 15; **4:**7, 19; **5:**8, 12, 13, 15, 15, 21, 28, 29, 30; **6:**5, 7, 9, 13, 21, 21, 27; **8:**2, 24, 26; **10:**4, 8; **11:**12, 14, 17, 20, 23; **12:**7, 7, 8; **13:**18, 19, 20, 20, 23, 27, 27; **14:**3, 7, 8, 8, 9, 17, 18, 21, 24, 34, 42; **15:**3, 6, 11, 13, 15, 27; **16:**3, 5, 11, 11, 46; **18:**4, 9, 11, 13, 14, 15, 16, 19, 23, 24, 31; **19:**2, 6, 9, 9, 10, 14, 15, 18, 21; **20:**5, 14; **21:**5, 13, 16, 29; **22:**16; **23:**19, 19, 21, 21, 21, 22; **24:**3, 3, 9, 9, 15, 15, 20, 21; **26:**4, 57; **27:**21, 21; **28:**6, 8, 10, 15, 24; **29:**11, 12; **30:**1, 3, 9, 9, 10, 14; **31:**23, 49; **32:**4, 8, 11, 22, 29; **33:**1, 54; **34:**13; **35:**17, 18, 19, 20, 21, 30; **36:**6, 6; **Dt 1:**7, 8, 20, 30, 43; **2:**28; **3:**9, 14, 20, 24; **4:**1, 6, 7, 20, 21, 24, 25, 31, 34, 35, 35, 38, 39, 39, 40, 44; **5:**5, 14, 15; **6:**4, 10, 15, 18, 20, 24; **7:**8, 9, 9, 21, 21, 25; **8:**7, 8, 9, 9, 9, 9, 9, 9, 11, 14, 18; **9:**4, 4, 5, 6, 25; **10:**9, 9, 15, 17, 17, 21, 21; **11:**10, 11, 17, 31; **12:**1, 8, 9, 10, 16, 21, 23, 23; **13:**3, 12, 14, 18; **14:**11, 20, 23; **15:**2, 4, 7, 9, 11, 15, 16, 21; **16:**5, 11, 15, 18, 20; **17:**2, 4, 8, 8, 14, 20; **18:**1, 2, 6, 9, 12, 12, 16, 21; **19:**1, 2, 3, 7, 10, 14, 18; **20:**1, 4, 8, 16; **21:**1, 1, 2, 4, 9, 15, 17, 20, 20, 22, 23, 23; **22:**2, 17, 22, 23, 24, 26, 28, 28; **23:**1, 19, 22; **24:**1, 4, 6, 12, 18, 22; **25:**1, 1, 2, 9, 15, 19; **26:**1, 17, 19; **27:**2, 3, 15, 16, 17, 18, 19, 19, 20, 21, 22, 22, 23, 24, 25, 26; **28:**8, 40, 49, 55, 61; **29:**6, 12, 13, 14, 15, 27; **30:**11, 12, 13, 14, 14, 20; **31:**3, 8, 17, 29; **32:**3, 4, 4, 4, 4, 4, 6, 9, 28, 31, 33, 36, 36, 39, 49; **33:**1, 6, 17, 17, 20, 20, 22, 26, 27, 27, 29, 29; **34:**1, 4; **Jos 1:**2, 8, 9, 13, 15; **2:**9, 11, 13; **3:**10, 16; **4:**22; **5:**15; **6:**3, 19; **7:**12, 13, 26; **9:**12, 24, 25; **10:**13, 25; **12:**7; **13:**3; **14:**12; **15:**7, 8, 9, 13, 18, 25, 49, 54, 60; **16:**2, 8; **17:**7, 11, 15, 16; **18:**7, 13, 14, 17, 19, 28; **20:**6, 7; **21:**11; **22:**19, 19, 22, 22, 28, 28, 31, 34, 34; **24:**2, 17, 18, 19; **Jdg 1:**14, 26; **2:**23; **4:**6, 14, 20; **5:**24, 28; **6:**8, 12, 13, 15, 17, 23, 24, 25, 31, 37, 37, 39; **7:**1, 3; **8:**28, 35; **9:**18, 28, 28, 33, 37, 38, 38; **10:**8; **11:**10, 15, 27, 27, 35; **13:**8, 10, 17, 25; **14:**3, 18, 18; **15:**2, 2, 19; **16:**24; **18:**9, 12, 14; **19:**10, 22, 23; **20:**18; **21:**3, 6, 11, 11; **Ru 1:**19; **2:**5, 6, 19, 20, 20, 21, 22; **3:**2, 11, 12, 12, 12, 12, 13, 13; **4:**3, 11, 15, 18; **1Sa 1:**22, 23; **2:**2, 2, 2, 3, 8; **3:**4, 9, 10, 13, 18; **4:**4, 7, 14, 21, 21; **5:**5, 7; **6:**20; **8:**7, 11; **9:**6, 6, 7, 11, 12, 18, 21; **10:**2, 2, 5, 7, 11, 12, 12, 12, 22, 22, 24, 24; **11:**5, 7; **12:**5, 13, 16, 23; **13:**11; **14:**7, 28, 28, 33, 36, 39, 41, 41, 41; **15:**2, 14, 22, 22, 22, 23, 23, 28, 29, 29, 32; **16:**6, 8, 9, 11, 12, 15, 15, 16, 18, 18, 18, 18; **17:**9, 26, 26, 27, 27, 33, 46, 47, 55, 58; **18:**18, 18, 25, 25; **19:**5, 24; **20:**1, 1, 7, 7, 10, 13, 18, 21, 21, 22, 31, 37; **21:**1, 3, 4, 9, 9, 9; **22:**3, 8, 8, 12, 14, 14, 14; **23:**10, 17, 19, 19, 19, 21, 22, 22, 23; **24:**4, 6, 10, 11, 14, 14, 15, 15, 16; **25:**8, 10, 10, 17, 22, 25, 25, 26, 27; **26:**1, 14, 15, 17, 18, 19, 22; **27:**1, 1, 5; **28:**7, 7, 14; **29:**3, 4; **30:**25, 26; **2Sa 1:**18, 18; **2:**7, 20, 20, 26; **3:**8, 18; **4:**2, 8, 10; **5:**8, 24; **6:**2, 8; **7:**2, 3, 5, 8, 13, 18, 22, 22, 23, 26, 29; **9:**3, 3, 3, 4; **11:**3, 15; **12:**18, 19, 21, 23, 31; **13:**12, 16, 20, 30; **14:**7, 14; **15:**15, 26, 27, 36; **16:**2, 3, 8, 11, 17, 18; **17:**2, 3, 6, 8, 10, 12, 13, 14; **18:**3, 18, 20, 25, 27, 28, 29, 32, 32; **19:**10, 11, 20, 22, 27, 29, 36, 37, 42; **20:**6, 19, 21; **22:**2, 3, 3, 4, 31, 31, 32, 32, 33, 48; **23:**4, 5, 5, 17, 17; **24:**12, 14, 14, 16; **1Ki 1:**20, 23, 33, 41, 45, 45, 46; **2:**5, 14, 15, 16, 20, 22, 38, 42; **3:**9, 22, 22, 22, 23, 27; **5:**4, 6; **8:**18, 23, 28, 31, 32, 35, 36, 37, 37, 60, 60; **9:**8, 9, 13, 15; **10:**6, 9; **11:**22, 27, 31, 33; **12:**6, 9, 10, 10, 24, 24, 28; **13:**2, 21, 26, 31; **14:**5, 10, 13, 13; **17:**9, 14, 23; **18:**7, 8, 11, 14, 17, 21, 21, 22, 24, 27, 27, 27, 27, 27, 39, 39; **19:**7; **20:**2, 4, 5, 7, 13, 14, 23, 28, 28, 32, 32, 42; **21:**2, 5, 19, 20, 21, 22; **22:**8, 8, 11, 32; **2Ki 1:**3, 4, 6, 16, 16; **2:**3, 5, 14, 19, 19, 19, 21; **3:**11, 11, 11, 16, 18; **4:**1, 9, 14, 23, 25, 26, 26, 27, 27, 31; **5:**7, 8, 15, 21, 26; **6:**1, 11, 13, 13, 28, 33; **7:**1, 9, 9; **8:**5, 5, 6; **9:**3, 6, 11, 13, 18, 20, 32, 34; **10:**5, 27, 27; **11:**5; **12:**4; **13:**17; **14:**7; **17:**34, 39; **18:**17, 19, 21, 29, 31; **19:**3, 3, 3, 3, 6, 7, 10, 17, 20, 21, 26, 29, 32; **20:**1, 3, 5, 9, 17, 19; **21:**11, 12; **22:**13, 16, 17, 18; **23:**17, 17, 21; **1Ch 1:**24; **5:**1; **6:**54; **11:**7, 7, 11, 19, 19; **12:**18, 20; **13:**2, 3, 6, 11; **14:**15; **16:**14, 14, 16, 25, 25, 25, 28, 30, 31, 33, 34; **17:**1, 2, 4, 7, 12, 16, 20, 20, 21, 24, 27; **20:**3; **21:**10, 13, 13, 15, 24, 24; **22:**5, 10, 18; **24:**1; **25:**1; **27:**1; **28:**20, 20; **29:**1, 1, 1, 1, 2, 3, 5, 11, 11, 11, 11, 12; **2Ch 1:**10, 11; **2:**5, 7, 11, 13, 14, 14, 14, 14; **5:**13; **6:**8, 11, 14, 19, 22, 23, 26, 27, 28, 28; **7:**3, 18, 21, 22; **8:**11; **9:**5, 6, 8; **10:**6, 9, 10, 10; **11:**4, 4; **12:**5, 6, 8; **13:**8, 8, 10, 12, 12; **14:**7, 11; **18:**7, 7, 10, 31; **19:**3, 11, 11; **20:**2, 6, 9, 12, 15, 15, 17, 17, 21, 26, 34; **21:**12, 14, 14; **23:**4; **24:**20; **25:**7, 9, 19; **26:**18, 18; **28:**5, 9, 13, 13; **29:**8; **30:**9, 18; **32:**7, 10, 11, 12, 22, 32; **33:**13; **34:**24, 26; **35:**3, 21; **36:**23; **Ezr 1:**2; **2:**1, 2; **3:**11; **4:**9, 11, 13, 16; **5:**6, 8, 8, 8, 16; **6:**2, 9; **7:**14, 18, 18, 21; **8:**1, 28; **9:**7, 11; **10:**2, 4, 13, 24; **Ne 2:**3; **4:**14, 19, 20; **5:**9; **6:**6, 6, 7, 8; **7:**5, 6, 7, 73; **8:**9, 10, 10, 11; **9:**5, 18; **10:**37, 38; **11:**3; **12:**1; **Est 1:**18, 20; **3:**8, 8; **4:**11, 16; **5:**3, 3, 6, 6, 7, 8, 8, 13, 14; **6:**4, 5, 9, 11, 13; **7:**2, 2, 3, 3, 6; **8:**5, 5, 8; **9:**26, 26, 26; **Job 1:**8, 10; **2:**3; **3:**19, 22, 23; **4:**19; **5:**8, 24, 27; **6:**3, 6, 6, 12, 16, 18, 24; **7:**1, 1, 5, 7; **8:**3, 11, 11, 13, 18, 19; **9:**2, 4, 22, 22, 24, 32, 33; **10:**5, 5, 22, 22; **11:**2, 4, 6, 6, 7, 8, 8, 9, 10; **12:**10, 14; **13:**12, 16, 25; **14:**1, 1, 7, 7; **15:**11, 11, 16, 18, 23, 23; **16:**6, 13, 17, 19, 19; **17:**1, 1, 12, 12, 15; **18:**12; **19:**4, 6, 7, 17, 29; **20:**7, 21, 25, 29, 29; **21:**4, 7, 15, 16, 33; **22:**3, 4, 5, 10, 11, 12, 14, 29; **23:**2, 8, 9, 17, 17; **24:**14, 17, 18, 18, 23; **25:**2, 3, 4, 5; **26:**6, 6; **27:**6, 13, 13, 19; **28:**5, 13, 14, 14, 16, 17, 18, 19, 21, 28, 28, 28; **29:**20; **30:**16, 27; **31:**2, 3, 11, 12, 23; **32:**8, 13; **33:**10, 12, 23, 23, 28; **34:**4, 4, 6, 12, 22, 23, 29, 33; **35:**2, 7, 10, 11, 12, 13, 14, 14; **36:**5, 5, 20, 22, 22, 26; **37:**5, 17, 22, 23; **38:**2, 14, 15, 22, 24, 24, 29, 37; **39:**6, 11, 16, 16, 20, 22, 27; **40:**17, 19, 23; **41:**9, 11, 23, 24, 27, 27, 30, 33, 34, 34; **42:**3, 3; **Ps 1:**4; **5:**9, 9, 9; **6:**2, 6, 7; **7:**10, 11, 11, 11, 17; **8:**1; **9:**6, 9, 16, 17; **10:**4, 15, 16; **11:**4, 7, 7; **12:**8; **14:**1, 2, 5; **15:**2; **16:**5, 6, 8, 8, 9; **17:**14, 15; **18:**2, 2, 2, 3, 30, 30, 31, 31, 47; **19:**3, 7, 9, 9, 11; **22:**8, 11, 14, 14, 28; **23:**1; **24:**1, 8, 10, 10; **25:**8, 8, 9, 14; **26:**11; **27:**1, 4; **28:**7, 7; **29:**4, 4; **31:**1, 9, 15, 19; **32:**1, 1, 5, 6; **33:**1, 4, 5, 12, 16, 22; **34:**8, 12, 18; **35:**27; **36:**3, 3, 4, 5, 6, 7; **37:**16, 30, 39; **38:**3, 3, 4, 7; **39:**4, 5, 5, 5, 7, 9, 11; **40:**8, 11, 16, 17; **41:**8; **42:**3, 4, 10; **44:**7, 7, 15; **45:**1, 6, 7, 7, 11, 14; **46:**1, 7, 7, 11, 11; **47:**2, 2, 7, 9; **48:**1, 1, 2, 2, 3, 8, 10, 14, 14, 14; **49:**5, 11, 13; **50:**12, 14, 23; **51:**4, 4, 17; **53:**1, 2; **54:**T, 4, 4, 6; **55:**4, 10, 12, 12, 13, 19, 21, **56:**9; **57:**1, 7, 10; **58:**11, 11; **59:**12; **60:**7, 7, 11; **61:**2; **62:**2, 5, 6, 7, 8, 12; **63:**1, 3; **64:**10; **66:**2, 6, 15; **68:**4, 5, 5, 6, 13, 20, 34, 35; **69:**3, 7, 13, 16, 16; **70:**4; **71:**7, 8, 9, 11; **72:**3; **73:**1, 6, 11, 11, 11, 14, 16, 20, 20, 26, 28; **74:**1, 20; **75:**7, 8; **76:**1, 1, 2, 2, 12; **77:**8, 10, 13; **79:**3, 10; **81:**3, 3, 4, 4; **82:**5; **83:**8; **84:**1, 10, 11, 11; **85:**8, 9; **86:**8, 13; **87:**7; **88:**3, 4; **89:**2, 6, 7, 8, 8, 11, 11, 13, 13, 13, 14, 17, 36, 47, 49; **90:**6, 11; **91:**2, 2; **92:**1, 2, 7, 15, 15, 15; **93:**1, 1, 1, 1, 4, 5; **94:**9, 9, 13, 20, 22, 22; **95:**3, 7; **96:**4, 4, 4, 7, 10, 10, 13, 13; **97:**1; **98:**9; **99:**1, 3, 5, 9; **100:**3, 5; **102:**4, 13, 13; **103:**5, 8, 8, 11, 12, 13; **104:**24, 25, 30; **105:**7, 7, 9; **106:**1, 3, 40; **107:**1, 12; **108:**1, 4, 8, 8, 12; **109:**7, 18, 22, 23, 27; **111:**4, 7, 10; **113:**4, 4, 5; **115:**2, 3, 9, 9, 10, 10, 11, 11; **116:**5, 5; **118:**1, 6, 7, 8, 9, 14, 16, 23, 23, 24, 27, 29; **119:**35, 35, 38, 43, 49, 56, 63, 64, 72, 77, 105, 113, 114, 121, 126, 128, 128, 140, 142, 142, 147, 156, 174; **122:**3, 5, 9; **124:**7, 8; **127:**1, 2, 5, 5; **128:**4; **129:**3, 4; **130:**7; **131:**1, 2, 2; **132:**14, 14; **133:**1, 2, 3; **135:**3, 5, 13; **136:**1; **137:**8, 9; **138:**5, 6; **139:**6, 14; **141:**5; **143:**2; **144:**1, 2, 15; **145:**3, 3, 3, 8, 9, 13, 13, 13, 17, 17, 18; **146:**3, 5, 6, 6, 10; **147:**1, 2, 5, 5, 5, 10, 11; **148:**13; **149:**9; **Pr 1:**2, 3, 7, 19, 31; **2:**7, 9, 12, 15, 18, 19; **3:**13, 14, 15, 18, 26, 33, 33; **4:**7, 18, 19; **5:**3, 4, 19, 22; **6:**12, 23, 29, 30, 31, 32, 35; **7:**12, 16, 19, 27, 27; **8:**6, 8, 8, 11, 13; **9:**10, 13, 13, 17; **10:**15, 15, 18, 18, 20, 23, 23, 32; **11:**4, 12, 14, 15, 15, 17, 22, 22, 24; **12:**1, 4, 5, 8, 9, 10, 16; **13:**9, 9, 12, 14, 15, 19; **14:**3, 8, 12, 18, 18, 21, 24, 25, 27, 28, 28, 33, 33, 34, 35; **15:**3, 5, 6, 14, 15, 16, 17, 19, 23, 29; **16:**6, 8, 13, 14, 15, 17, 19, 21, 22, 22, 25, 26, 31, 31, 32, 32; **17:**1, 7, 12, 14, 16, 17, 17, 18, 21, 21, 22, 26, 27; **18:**1, 5, 9, 10, 11, 14; **19:**1, 2, 6, 8, 12, 12, 13, 18, 22; **20:**1, 2, 2, 3, 6, 11, 15, 21, 23, 24, 25, 28, 29, 29; **21:**1, 2, 3, 3, 6, 7, 9, 12, 15, 19, 27; **22:**1, 7, 11, 13, 14, 15, 18, 23; **23:**1, 11, 16, 22, 24, 27, 27, 29, 29, 30; **24:**3, 5, 5, 7, 10, 13, 13, 14, 16, 23, 26; **25:**2, 7, 11, 12, 14, 18, 19, 20, 20, 24, 25, 26, 27, 27, 28; **26:**6, 8, 9, 10, 12, 13, 17, 19; **27:**3, 3, 3, 4, 4, 5, 7, 8, 9, 10, 15, 16, 19, 20, 21, 25; **28:**1, 2, 2, 3, 4, 4, 6, 8, 11, 12, 15, 21, 24, 26; **29:**3, 5, 14, 15, 18, 19, 20, 21, 25; **30:**4, 9, 20; **31:**4, 6, 10, 14, 17, 23, 25, 26, 30; **Ecc 1:**2, 7, 8, 9, 10, 14, 15, 15; **2:**2, 13, 13, 14, 15, 15, 17, 17, 21, 23, 24, 24, 26; **3:**1, 12, 14, 14, 16, 22, 22; **4:**3, 4, 6, 6, 8, 8, 8, 12, 13, 15, 16; **5:**2, 5, 6, 7, 7, 8, 11, 13, 14, 14, 16, 16, 18, 18, 19, 19; **6:**1, 2, 9, 9; **7:**1, 1, 2, 2, 3, 5, 6, 6, 8, 8, 9, 11, 11, 14, 19, 20, 20, 24, 25, 25, 26, 26, 27; **8:**4, 5, 6, 7, 8, 11, 11, 14, 14, 14, 15, 16; **9:**3, 3, 4, 4, 6, 9, 11, 13, 16, 18; **10:**4, 5, 9, 12, 14, 16, 16, 17, 17; **11:**7, 8; **12:**2, 2, 6, 6, 6, 8, 12, 13, 13; **SS 1:**1, 2, 6, 10, 12, 13, 14; **2:**2, 3, 3, 6, 7, 9, 9, 9, 11, 11, 13, 14, 14, 16; **3:**5, 6, 6, 7, 10, 10; **4:**2, 4, 10, 10, 10, 11; **5:**2, 9, 10, 11, 11, 13, 14, 16, 16, 16; **6:**3, 5, 10; **7:**2, 2, 4, 4, 5, 5; **8:**4, 5, 6, 6, 9, 9, 10; **Isa 1:**2, 5, 5, 8, 8, 13, 21, 27; **2:**1, 8, 11; **3:**11, 11, 13, 14; **5:**5, 7, 8, 11, 12, 14, 16, 16, 18, 20, 20, 20, 20, 20, 20, 20, 21, 22, 25, 25, 25; **6:**3, 3, 5, 7, 11, 13; **7:**2, 3, 7, 8, 8, 9, 9, 14, 15, 15, 15, 22; **8:**4, 10, 13, 17, 20, 20; **9:**6, 6, 12, 17, 17, 18, 19, 21; **10:**1, 4, 5, 5, 7, 7, 12, 15, 15, 18, 24, 30; **12:**2, 4, 6; **13:**4, 7, 9, 15; **14:**4, 7, 7, 8, 9, 17, 17, 19, 22, 29, 29, 31; **15:**8; **16:**4, 5, 6, 10, 10; **17:**14; **18:**1; **19:**1, 11, 12; **20:**3; **21:**1, 3, 4, 5, 9, 12; **22:**1, 1, 2, 11, 14, 17, 17; **23:**1, 7, 10, 14; **24:**1, 1, 10, 12, 13, 13, 16, 16, 18, 19; **25:**9, 9; **26:**1, 4, 7, 8, 9, 12, 21; **27:**6, 11; **28:**1, 1, 4, 7, 8, 16, 16, 16, 17, 17, 20, 22, 24, 27, 27, 27, 27, 28, 29; **29:**1, 8, 8, 11, 14, 15, 15, 16, 16, 16, 22; **30:**1, 12, 14, 15, 16, 18, 21, 27; **31:**1; **32:**1, 15; **33:**1, 5, 6, 9, 9, 22; **34:**2, 2, 6, 6, 8; **35:**4, 4; **36:**2, 4, 6, 14, 16; **37:**3, 3, 3, 3, 6, 7, 10, 18, 21, 21, 22, 27, 30, 33; **38:**1, 3, 5, 7, 16; **39:**6, 8; **40:**7, 9, 10, 13, 14, 14, 20, 22, 22, 25, 28; **41:**1, 3, 4, 17, 20, 27; **42:**1, 5, 8, 19, 19, 19, 20, 21, 25; **43:**10, 11, 18, 28; **44:**6, 6, 7, 8, 8, 9, 13, 20, 20, 23, 28; **45:**1, 2, 4, 5, 6, 6, 9, 11, 14, 14, 14, 18, 18, 19, 21, 22, 24; **46:**4, 5, 7, 9, 10; **47:**4, 4, 14; **48:**2, 5, 10, 17, 22; **49:**7, 7, 8, 16, 22; **50:**1, 1, 2, 2, 2, 2, 8, 9, 11; **51:**5, 15, 18, 19, 19, 22, 22; **52:**3, 4, 5, 5, 6, 11; **53:**7, 10, 11, 12; **54:**5, 5, 14; **55:**1, 2, 3, 6, 11; **56:**1, 5; **57:**1, 8, 11, 11, 20, 21; **58:**4, 5; **59:**1, 1, 2, 3, 6, 6, 6, 8, 9, 9, 9, 11, 11, 14, 15, 15, 21; **60:**1, 4; **61:**1; **62:**11; **63:**1, 1, 1, 1, 1, 3, 10, 11, 11, 12, 13, 15; **64:**5, 10; **65:**6, 13; **66:**1, 1, 1, 3, 3, 3, 6, 6, 6, 13, 15; **Jer 2:**2, 5, 6, 8, 19, 34; **3:**1, 2, 3, 11, 12, 16; **4:**3, 7, 8, 10, 11, 11, 11, 12, 13, 16, 18, 20, 20, 27, 31; **5:**1, 6, 14, 15, 19, 19, 28; **6:**1, 4, 6, 6, 6, 8, 9, 14, 19, 20, 21, 22, 22, 23, 25, 29; **7:**4, 8, 11, 21, 23, 28, 28, 32; **8:**4, 6, 11, 16, 18, 18, 19, 20, 20, 22, 22, 22; **9:**10, 12, 17, 17, 23, 24, 24, 25; **10:**2, 6, 6, 7, 10, 10, 13, 15, 16, 16, 16, 17, 19, 19, 19, 20, 20, 23, 23; **11:**3, 3, 22; **12:**2, 11, 13, 14; **13:**1, 13, 16, 20, 22, 22, 22, 24, 25, 25, 27; **14:**4, 5, 6, 13; **15:**2, 3, 9, 10, 18, 18; **16:**3, 10, 11, 11, 14; **17:**5, 9, 9, 15, 16, 21; **18:**6, 7, 11, 11; **19:**3, 6, 9, 11, 11, 12, 15; **20:**4; **21:**4, 8, 12, 12; **22:**3, 3, 6, 11, 13, 15, 18, 18, 20, 28, 30; **23:**2, 5, 5, 6, 6, 9, 10, 10, 15, 15, 16, 18, 23, 28, 29, 31, 35, 35, 37, 37, 37, 38, 38; **24:**5; **25:**29, 32, 32, 36; **26:**4, 11, 15, 18; **27:**4, 6, 7, 15, 16, 16, 19, 21; **28:**9, 13; **29:**3, 10, 16, 17, 21, 25, 31; **30:**2, 3, 4, 5, 5, 12, 12, 13, 14, 15; **31:**7, 9, 15, 15, 17, 20, 23, 33, 35, 35, 35, 35, 38; **32:**3, 7, 8, 17, 20, 23, 27, 36; **33:**2, 3, 4, 10, 11, 12, 12, 15, 16, 17, 21, 24, 25; **34:**2, 4, 5, 13, 17; **35:**1, 11, 18; **36:**7, 29, 30; **37:**7, 7, 7; **38:**2, 4, 9, 21; **40:**3, 4; **42:**9, 15, 17; **44:**1, 2, 22, 23, 29; **45:**2, 4; **46:**7, 8, 10, 10, 12, 17, 18, 18, 18, 20, 20, 21; **47:**1, 2, 2, 4; **48:**1, 1, 2, 4, 11, 11, 12, 15, 16, 17, 17, 29, 31, 33, 39, 46, 47; **49:**1, 3, 7, 7, 12, 15, 19, 23, 28, 30, 35; **50:**2, 23, 34, 34, 38, 41, 42, 43, 44; **51:**1, 5, 6, 11, 13, 16, 18, 19, 19, 19, 30, 31, 32, 33, 41, 42, 43, 47, 52, 55, 56, 56, 57, 58, 64; **La 1:**1, 2, 8, 12, 12, 16, 18, 20, 20, 22; **2:**4, 4, 9, 11, 13, 15, 16, 17; **3:**3, 17, 18, 18, 19, 23, 24, 25, 26, 27, 29, 38, 51, 54; **4:**6, 8, 11, 22; **5:**4, 8, 18; **Eze 2:**3, 4; **3:**11, 27; **4:**13; **5:**5, 5, 7, 16; **6:**3, 7, 11; **7:**2, 2, 2, 5, 6, 7, 7, 9, 9, 10, 12, 12, 13, 14, 20, 23, 23; **8:**3, 17; **9:**5, 9, 9; **11:**3, 3, 5, 5, 5, 7, 7; **12:**10, 22; **13:**3, 3, 6, 7, 8, 8, 10, 10, 12, 13, 18, 18; **14:**9, 9, 21; **15:**2, 6; **16:**17, 23, 27, 36, 37, 57, 58, 59; **17:**10, 19, 24, 24; **18:**4, 5, 5, 7, 8, 9, 10, 16, 19, 20, 21, 25, 25, 27, 29, 29; **19:**2, 13, 13, 14, 14, 14; **20:**3, 29, 39; **21:**5, 5, 7, 9, 10, 11, 11, 15, 23, 24, 25, 28, 28; **22:**6, 18, 18, 26, 26, 26, 26, 26, 28; **23:**4, 4, 22, 25, 28, 32, 32, 44, 46; **24:**2, 6, 6, 6, 7, 9, 9, 13, 21, 24; **25:**8, 14; **26:**3, 14, 15; **27:**27; **28:**3, 6, 25; **29:**3, 9, 19; **30:**1, 3, 3, 6, 10, 13, 22; **31:**10, 15; **32:**3, 11, 16, 20, 29, 31; **33:**4, 5, 6, 14, 15, 16, 17, 17, 19, 20, 30; **34:**2, 10, 11, 17, 18, 18, 19, 19, 19, 20; **35:**10, 14; **36:**2, 5, 5, 13, 13, 23, 33, 35, 37; **37:**5, 9, 11, 19; **38:**1, 10, 11, 17; **39:**19; **40:**45, 46; **41:**4, 22; **42:**13; **43:**7, 12, 12, 12, 12, 13, 13, 14, 14, 16, 18, 18; **44:**5, 9, 23, 23, 23, 24, 25, 25; **45:**2, 9, 9, 13, 18; **46:**1, 5, 7, 11, 16, 20; **47:**13; **48:**1, 1, 1, 5, 8, 11, 12, 14, 20, 25, 27, 30, 35; **Da 2:**11, 22, 26, 28, 29, 30, 45, 45, 45, 47; **3:**14, 17, 29; **4:**8, 9, 9, 10, 17, 17, 18, 22, 24, 27, 31, 34, 34, 37; **5:**11, 12, 25, 26; **6:**12, 13, 26; **7:**1, 14, 23; **8:**23, 26; **9:**7, 9, 14, 18, 25, 27; **10:**17, 21, 21; **11:**12, 21, 35, 36, 36, 37, 45; **12:**1, 9, 11, 11; **Hos 1:**9; **2:**2, 5; **4:**1, 2, 3, 3, 3, 4, 6, 13, 15, 15, 16, 17, 18; **5:**9; **6:**8, 11; **7:**1, 4, 4, 9; **8:**3, 3, 6, 7; **9:**3, 4, 7, 7, 8; **10:**1, 11, 12; **11:**8, 12; **12:**2, 2, 5, 8, 11; **13:**4, 10; **14:**8; **Joel 1:**5, 6, 9, 13, 15, 18; **2:**1, 2, 3, 11, 11, 12, 12, 13, 13, 13, 13, 17; **3:**13, 13, 14; **Am 1:**2, 3, 3, 6, 9, 11, 13; **2:**1, 4, 6, 13; **3:**2, 11, 12; **4:**5, 13, 13; **5:**4, 8, 8, 8, 8, 13, 14, 14, 15, 16, 19, 23, 27; **6:**6, 8, 10, 10, 13; **7:**10, 10, 10, 11, 13, 17; **8:**9, 11; **9:**6, 6, 9, 11, 12; **Ob** 1, 15; **Jnh 1:**8, 8, 12; **3:**8; **4:**2, 3, 4, 8, 9, 10; **Mic 1:**3, 5, 5, 5, 9, 14; **2:**2, 3, 5, 7, 10; **3:**5, 9, 11; **4:**9, 12; **5:**1; **6:**1, 3, 8, 8, 8, 9, 9, 16; **7:**1, 2, 4, 4, 4, 4, 10, 10, 16, 18; **Na 1:**2, 3, 3, 7, 7, 11, 12, 14, 15, 15; **2:**6, 8, 10, 11; **3:**1, 18, 19, 19; **Hab 1:**1, 4, 4, 11, 12; **2:**5, 6, 20; **3:**3, 3, 6, 19, 19; **Zep 1:**14, 15, 15; **2:**2, 2, 3, 5, 5, 15, 15; **3:**5, 5, 8, 8, 12, 17; **Hag 1:**2, 5, 7, 10; **2:**3, 6, 8, 8, 11, 12, 14, 14, 14, 19; **Zec 1:**3, 4, 11, 14, 14, 16, 17; **2:**2, 13; **3:**2, 7; **4:**6, 6, 9; **5:**3, 4, 4, 5, 6, 6, 6, 8, 11; **6:**6, 6, 6, 12, 12; **7:**9, 12; **8:**2, 2, 4, 6, 6, 7, 9, 14, 16, 18, 19, 20, 23, 23; **9:**1, 2, 3, 9, 9, 9, 12, 13, 13, 13; **10:**1, 5; **11:**3, 4, 4, 17; **12:**1, 9; **13:**7, 9; **14:**1; **Mal 1:**1, 4, 4, 8, 11, 11, 14, 14; **2:**1, 5, 11, 13, 16, 17; **3:**1, 3, 6; **4:**1; **Mt 1:**1, 16, 18, 23; **2:**2, 5, 13, 18; **3:**2, 3, 10, 11, 11,

12, 15, 17; **4:**17; **5:**2, 3, 10, 13, 18, 25, 29, 29, 30, 30, 34, 34, 35, 35, 35, 37, 37, 38, 40, 46, 48; **6:**3, 5, 10, 16, 21, 22, 23, 34; **7:**6, 8, 12, 12, 13, 13, 14, 14, 19, 20, 20, 21, 24, 25, 26; **8:**27; **9:**3, 5, 34, 37, 38; **10:**7, 13, 24, 24, 26, 26, 40, 40; **11:**5, 7, 9, 10, 11, 11, 11, 14, 15, 19, 30; **12:**6, 6, 10, 12, 12, 18, 23, 25, 25, 26, 26, 30, 33, 34, 34, 39, 41, 42, 45, 48, 50; **13:**9, 13, 18, 22, 22, 24, 24, 27, 31, 31, 32, 33, 38, 39, 39, 43, 44, 45, 47, 47, 48, 49, 52, 57; **14:**2, 4, 15, 15; **15:**9, 22, 23, 28, 28; **16:**4, 13, 26; **17:**4, 5, 11, 22; **18:**1, 4, 5, 7, 8, 9, 12, 14, 18, 18; **19:**5, 10, 17, 17, 23, 24, 26, 26; **20:**1, 15, 16, 21; **21:**5, 5, 10, 42, 42, 43; **22:**4, 8, 12, 13, 17, 23, 29, 32, 36, 38, 39, 42, 42; **23:**5, 9, 10, 16, 17, 18, 19, 38; **24:**22, 23, 23, 26, 26, 28, 28, 32, 33, 39, 42, 45, 48; **25:**6, 25; **26:**13, 21, 23, 26, 28, 28, 34, 38, 39, 41, 41, 46, 56, 64, 66; **27:**8, 8, 11, 17, 22, 24, 37, 42, 42; **28:**7; **Mk 1:**3, 7, 7, 15, 27, 37, 38; **2:**7, 8, 9; **3:**4, 4, 4, 25, 26, 29, 33, 35; **4:**9, 14, 19, 19, 21, 22, 23, 26, 26, 29, 31, 31, 41; **5:**9, 23, 31, 35, 39; **6:**4, 11, 14, 18, 35, 35; **7:**4, 7, 11, 13, 19, 20, 37; **8:**37, 38; **9:**5, 7, 12, 12, 16, 17, 23, 31, 40, 40, 43, 45, 47, 50; **10:**7, 18, 23, 24, 25, 27, 27, 36; **11:**23; **12:**11, 11, 14, 18, 24, 27, 28, 29, 29, 31, 31, 32, 33, 33, 44; **13:**11, 21, 21, 28, 29; **14:**9, 14, 15, 15, 18, 18, 20, 20, 22, 24, 30, 34, 36, 38, 38, 42, 64, 69; **15:**2, 21; **16:**6, 7, 16; **Lk 1:**18, 20, 25, 28, 37, 42, 43, 49, 60, 61, 63, 66, 78; **2:**12, 23, 32, 32; **3:**4, 7, 9, 16, 16, 17; **4:**18, 24, 24, 43; **5:**4, 21, 21, 22, 23, 39; **6:**9, 9, 9, 20, 25, 33, 34, 35, 36, 38, 39, 40, 44, 45, 48, 48, 49; **7:**4, 22, 24, 26, 27, 28, 28, 28, 35, 39, 39, 47, 49; **8:**8, 11, 11, 14, 17, 25, 25, 30, 45, 49, 52; **9:**5, 7, 8, 9, 12, 26, 33, 35, 38, 39, 44, 48, 48, 50, 50, 60, 62; **10:**2, 2, 8, 9, 11, 12, 16, 16, 16, 29, 42; **11:**2, 7, 10, 17, 17, 18, 21, 21, 22, 23, 25, 26, 29, 31, 32, 33, 34, 35, 36, 49; **12:**2, 2, 6, 15, 21, 34, 41, 48, 48, 48, 48, 50, 50, 55, 57; **13:**2, 18, 19, 20, 21, 24, 35; **14:**3, 9, 22, 28, 31, 32, 32, 34, 35, 35, 35; **15:**10, 24, 27, 31, 32; **16:**8, 15, 16, 17, 25, 26, 26, 30; **17:**9, 9, 9, 21, 21, 22, 23, 37, 37; **18:**5, 5, 19, 22, 24, 25, 27, 27; **19:**42, 42; **20:**21, 22, 27, 34, 35, 38, 41, 41; **21:**4, 6, 28, 30, 31; **22:**11, 12, 12, 19, 20, 21, 22, 27, 53, 59, 69; **23:**2, 3, 5, 6, 31, 31, 35, 38; **24:**5, 23, 47; **Jn 1:**3, 9, 13, 15, 15, 15, 18, 18, 26, 29, 30, 30, 30, 33, 33, 34, 36, 45, 51; **2:**10; **3:**2, 5, 8, 12, 18, 19, 21, 26, 26, 28, 29, 31, 31, 33, 34, 34; **4:**1, 11, 20, 20, 20, 21, 23, 23, 23, 24, 25, 36, 42, 44; **5:**7, 20, 25, 25, 27, 28, 30, 30, 30, 32, 32, 34, 45; **6:**9, 12, 14, 26, 29, 33, 39, 40, 42, 45, 51, 55, 55, 60, 63, 65, 70; **7:**6, 17, 17, 22, 26, 26, 28, 35, 35, 40, 41, 48, 51, 51; **8:**17, 18, 19, 19, 22, 24, 26, 29, 34, 35, 35, 39, 41, 43, 44, 44, 44, 47, 54, 54, 55, 58; **9:**4, 8, 12, 16, 16, 17, 19, 20, 21, 23, 24, 25, 31, 36, 37; **10:**10, 10, 13, 25, 29, 34, 38; **11:**2, 3, 4, 9, 10, 10, 12, 12, 14, 28; **12:**15, 24, 27, 27, 34, 36, 38; **13:**11, 13, 16, 16, 17, 20, 20, 21, 25, 26; **14:**3, 7, 10, 11, 12, 17, 24, 28; **15:**1, 4, 6, 13, 13, 20, 24; **16:**2, 3, 7, 9, 10, 12, 15, 15, 20, 21, 23, 32, 32, 32; **17:**3, 7, 9, 21; **18:**20, 22, 29, 34, 36, 37, 38, 38; **19:**5, 12, 13, 14, 22, 25, 26, 27, 30, 35, 35, 40; **20:**31; **21:**1, 7, 18, 22, 23, 24, 24; **Ac 1:**13, 22; **2:**25, 25, 26, 29, 39; **3:**12, 13, 13, 24; **4:**2, 11, 12, 12, 27; **5:**32, 32, 38, 39, 42; **6:**13; **7:**42, 49, 49; **8:**21, 31, 32; **9:**11, 14, 15, 20, 36; **10:**4, 6, 15, 20, 22, 22, 28, 32, 35, 36, 36, 42, 43; **11:**9; **12:**14, 22; **13:**10, 22, 23, 23, 25, 26, 27, 33, 33, 34, 36, 38, 39, 47; **15:**15, 17, 19, 23, 23, 23; **16:**20; **17:**3, 23, 24, 24, 25, 27, 29, 31; **18:**5, 15, 28; **19:**2, 26, 28, 34, 34, 35, 36, 36, 40; **20:**24, 32, 35; **21:**25, 28, 39; **22:**5, 25, 26; **23:**4, 6, 8, 19; **24:**5, 5, 25; **25:**10, 14, 19, 24, 24, 26; **26:**7, 7, 14; **27:**10, 37; **28:**22, 28; **Ro 1:**1, 3, 8, 10, 16, 17, 17, 19, 25, 26; **2:**4, 5, 7, 13, 15, 15, 16, 17, 22, 25, 29, 29, 29; **3:**1, 4, 4, 5, 6, 6, 8, 8, 10, 11, 13, 13, 17, 19, 26, 27, 27, 29, 29, 29, 30, 30; **4:**6, 7, 8, 9, 9, 10, 11, 12, 13, 14, 14, 14, 15, 16, 16, 16, 17; **5:**7, 7, 16; **6:**13, 14, 19, 23, 23; **7:**1, 2, 3, 3, 4, 4, 7, 7, 7, 12, 13, 13, 14, 14, 15, 16, 16, 17, 18, 20, 21, 21, 23, 23, 23, 24, 25, 25; **8:**1, 6, 6, 7, 10, 17, 18, 19, 27, 31, 33, 34, 34, 37, 39; **9:**1, 2, 5, 5, 5, 6, 7, 8, 16; **10:**1, 2, 8, 8, 8, 8, 9, 10, 10, 15; **11:**5, 6, 6, 7, 9, 22, 22, 33, 34, 36; **12:**1, 2, 5, 6, 7, 8, 9, 12, 19; **13:**1, 7, 11, 11, 11, 11, 12; **14:**1, 2, 3, 5, 5, 14, 14, 14, 15, 16, 17, 20, 20, 22, 22, 23; **15:**8, 9, 10, 15, 17, 27; **16:**2, 4, 19, 22, 25, 25, 26, 27; **1Co 1:**1, 6, 9, 22, 22, 24, 25, 25, 30; **2:**7, 9, 11, 16; **3:**5, 5, 7, 7, 10, 13, 15, 17, 19; **4:**2, 4, 4, 5, 5, 7, 17, 17, 20, 20; **5:**1, 6, 11, 11, 12; **6:**1, 5, 7, 12, 13, 13, 13, 17, 18, 19; **7:**1, 2, 3, 6, 12, 12, 13, 13, 15, 17, 19, 26, 28, 28, 29, 34, 36, 36, 36, 37, 39, 39; **8:**1, 3, 4, 4, 6, 6, 10, 10, 12, 13; **9:**3, 6, 11, 16, 18, 18; **10:**10, 11, 13, 15, 20, 22, 23, 23, 24, 25, 26, 27, 29, 33, 33, 33; **11:**3, 3, 3, 3, 5, 6, 7, 7, 13, 15, 16, 17, 22, 23, 24, 24, 25, 27, 28, 30; **12:**3, 3, 3, 4, 4, 5, 6, 7, 10, 10, 10, 10, 10, 11, 12, 26, 27, 28, 29, 29, 31; **13:**4, 4, 5, 6, 7, 12, 13; **14:**2, 3, 4, 5, 6, 14, 21, 22, 22, 25, 26, 26, 28, 29, 30, 30, 33, 34, 35, 37, 40; **15:**1, 2, 10, 11, 13, 14, 14, 15, 16, 17, 20, 23, 26, 29, 31, 32, 37, 37, 40, 42, 45, 45, 50, 52, 54, 55, 55, 56, 58; **16:**9, 10, 12, 21, 22; **2Co 1:**1, 3, 6, 6, 12, 13, 18, 19, 19, 20, 21; **2:**2, 3, 7, 10, 15, 16, 17; **3:**2, 3, 3, 5, 6, 6, 8, 9, 14, 16, 17, 17; **4:**3, 3, 4, 4, 5, 6, 6, 7, 7, 7, 7, 16; **5:**1, 7, 9, 11, 13, 13, 14, 17, 17, 18, 19, 20; **6:**2, 2, 12, 12; **7:**4, 7, 10; **8:**8, 8, 18, 22, 22, 23, 24; **9:**5, 10; **10:**7, 8, 9, 10, 13, 16; **11:**10, 12, 15, 17, 29, 29, 31; **12:**1, 5, 9, 10, 19, 19; **13:**1, 3, 3, 5, 5, 8, 9; **Gal 1:**1, 1, 5, 7, 11; **3:**5, 9, 10, 11, 11, 12, 13, 13, 13, 15, 17, 19, 20, 21, 22, 28; **4:**15, 19, 25, 26, 27; **5:**6, 6, 8, 10, 17, 20, 23; **6:**1, 9, 14, 15; **Eph 1:**1, 1, 7, 9, 10, 14, 14, 19, 21, 23, 23; **2:**2, 4, 5, 8, 9, 20; **3:**6, 8, 13, 18, 19, 20; **4:**5, 6, 6, 8, 10, 11, 12, 15, 16, 16, 21, 22, 30; **5:**5, 9, 10, 12, 14, 14, 23, 23, 28, 29, 31, 32, 32; **6:**1, 2, 3, 17, 19; **Php 1:**1, 1, 6, 7, 18, 21, 21, 22, 24; **2:**1, 9, 11, 13, 17, 17, 19, 23, 25; **3:**5, 8, 14, 19, 19, 19; **4:**5, 7, 8, 12, 17, 18; **Col 1:**1, 2, 6, 6, 7, 7, 8, 15, 15, 16, 18, 18, 18, 18, 27, 27; **2:**2, 2, 5, 10; **3:**3, 4, 4, 5, 8, 10, 11, 14, 14, 18, 20, 24, 25; **4:**3, 3, 7, 10, 18; **1Th 1:**1, 1, 8, 10; **2:**4, 4, 5, 10, 19, 19; **3:**2, 5; **4:**8, 8, 10; **5:**3, 3, 3, 7, 12, 18, 21, 21, 24; **2Th 1:**1, 1, 3, 3, 12; **2:**3, 3, 4, 4, 6, 7, 7; **3:**3, 17; **1Ti 1:**1, 2, 5, 9, 9, 15, 16, 17, 17; **2:**3, 5, 5, 6, 7; **3:**1, 15, 15, 16; **4:**3, 4, 5, 6, 8, 9, 10, 10, 16; **5:**4, 4, 5, 5, 6, 9, 9; **6:**2, 2, 4, 5, 6, 10, 11; **2Ti 1:**1, 2, 3, 6, 9, 12, 12; **2:**5, 8, 11; **3:**3, 8, 10, 16, 16, 16, 16, 16, 17; **4:**2, 3, 6, 8, 11; **Tit 1:**1, 3, 4, 7, 8, 10, 13, 15, 15; **2:**3, 3, 14; **3:**1, 10; **Phm 1:**1, 1, 8, 8, 10, 11, 16, 16; **Heb 1:**4, 4, 8, 9, 9; **2:**6, 8, 9, 9, 11, 11, 18; **3:**4, 7, 13; **4:**4, 6, 7, 9, 12, 12, 13, 13, 14; **5:**1, 2, 2, 2, 3, 5, 11, 13, 13, 14, 14; **6:**4, 6, 8, 10, 11, 16, 18, 19; **7:**2, 3, 7, 7, 8, 12, 14, 15, 15, 19, 22, 23, 25, 26, 26; **8:**1, 3, 5, 6, 6, 10, 13; **9:**9, 15, 15, 16, 16, 17, 18, 22, 23, 27; **10:**4, 5, 7, 10, 14, 15, 16, 18, 20, 25, 26, 31, 36; **11:**1, 1, 1, 1, 4, 6, 6, 12, 16, 16, 18, 27; **12:**2, 7, 10, 11, 11, 11, 16, 23, 25, 29; **13:**6, 6, 8, 14, 14, 17, 18, 20, 20, 23; **Jas 1:**1, 1, 3, 4, 6, 6, 13, 13, 17, 21, 22, 23, 26; **2:**2, 8, 10, 17, 17, 19, 20, 25, 26, 26; **3:**5, 6, 6, 6, 8, 10, 14, 14, 16, 17, 17, 17, 17; **4:**1, 2, 3, 4, 11, 11, 14, 15, 16, 17; **5:**2, 8, 9, 9, 11, 11, 19; **1Pe 1:**1, 3, 4, 6, 6, 7, 7, 7, 7, 12, 15, 25; **2:**4, 4, 5, 7, 8, 9, 15, 16, 19, 20, 21, 21, 24; **3:**4, 5, 6, 7, 9, 14, 17, 17, 21, 21, 21, 22; **4:**6, 7, 13, 16, 19; **5:**1, 11, 12, 12; **2Pe 1:**1, 17; **2:**3, 10, 13, 14; **3:**1, 4, 8, 8, 9, 9, 11, 13, 15, 15, 16; **1Jn 1:**1, 1, 2, 2, 2, 3, 5, 5, 5, 7, 9; **2:**1, 1, 2, 4, 5, 7, 7, 8, 8, 8, 8, 8, 9, 10, 13, 14, 17, 18, 18, 22, 22, 27, 27, 27, 29, 29; **3:**2, 3, 5, 6, 7, 7, 7, 9, 11, 14, 15, 16, 19, 20, 21, 23; **4:**2, 3, 3, 3, 4, 6, 6, 7, 8, 10, 10, 15, 16, 18, 20; **5:**1, 1, 5, 6, 10, 11, 11, 15, 16, 17, 19, 20, 20; **2Jn** 1, 1, 5, 7; **3Jn** 1, 1, 2, 2, 2, 10, 10, 11; **Jude** 1, 14, 18, 21, 22, 24, 25; **Rev 1:**1, 3, 4, 4, 4, 5, 8, 8, 20; **2:**1, 6, 6, 7, 7, 7, 8, 8, 8, 9, 11, 11, 11, 12, 13, 17, 17, 17, 18, 20, 29, 29; **3:**1, 2, 2, 6, 6, 7, 7, 7, 13, 13, 14, 14, 21, 22, 22; **4:**8, 8, 8, 11; **5:**2, 5, 12, 12; **7:**15; **9:**11, 11, 12; **10:**8; **11:**5, 8, 14, 14, 17, 18; **13:**4, 4, 9, 10, 18, 18, 18; **14:**8, 8, 10, 15; **16:**5, 6, 17; **17:**1, 10, 11, 11, 14, 15; **18:**2, 2, 5, 8, 11, 17, 18, 19; **19:**1, 8, 10; **20:**5, 14; **21:**3, 5, 6, 8, 8, 23, 25; **22:**9, 10, 11, 11, 11, 11, 12, 18, 20

ISN'T (94)

Ge 19:31; **37:**32; **Ex 3:**3; **5:**16; **Nu 16:**13; **Dt 32:**6; **Jdg 14:**3; **18:**19; **1Sa 1:**8; **14:**17; **20:**2, 29; **21:**11, 11; **24:**10; **26:**16; **29:**5; **1Ki 18:**10; **21:**19; **22:**7; **2Ki 6:**19; **9:**20; **18:**22; **2Ch 18:**6; **Ezr 10:**13; **Job 8:**18; **15:**3; **35:**13; **Ps 10:**11; **94:**7; **Pr 19:**10; **Isa 36:**7; **Jer 2:**35; **22:**16; **39:**12; **Eze 18:**25; **Da 2:**10; **Am 3:**6; **Jnh 1:**14; **Zec 7:**7; **Mal 1:**8, 8; **Mt 9:**24; **12:**30, 30; **14:**16; **15:**26; **28:**6; **Mk 5:**39; **7:**27; **9:**38; **16:**6; **Lk 4:**22; **8:**52; **9:**49; **11:**23, 23; **17:**20; **19:**21; **24:**6; **Jn 7:**25; **10:**12; **13:**10; **14:**17, 27; **21:**23; **Ac 2:**15; **9:**21; **10:**15; **11:**9; **22:**22; **Ro 3:**5, 29; **1Co 4:**4; **5:**12; **6:**5; **7:**15; **9:**1, 7, 8; **10:**27; **11:**14, 15; **2Co 8:**12; **12:**19; **Gal 5:**8; **Eph 4:**20; **Heb 5:**13; **Jas 2:**6, 17; **4:**1; **2Pe 3:**9; **1Jn 5:**3; **Rev 17:**8

IT (4851)

Ge 1:4, 7, 9, 10, 11, 12, 15, 18, 21, 24, 25, 28, 30, 31; **2:**3, 3, 7, 15, 18, 21; **3:**2, 3, 3, 5, 6, 6, 12, 12, 13, 17, 18; **4:**7, 12, 17, 26; **6:**6, 11, 14, 15; **8:**8, 9, 12, 20; **9:**13, 23; **11:**9; **12:**10; **13:**8; **14:**10; **15:**8, 17; **16:**14; **17:**5, 7; **18:**3, 7, 8, 24, 24, 28, 29, 30, 31, 32; **19:**13, 14, 20; **21:**2, 2, 10, 22, 24, 26; **22:**9, 10, 13, 14; **23:**6, 11, 13, 17; **24:**7, 11, 65; **25:**22, 31, 33; **26:**20, 20, 21, 21, 22; **27:**4, 4, 4, 10, 14, 18, 19, 19, 20, 20, 25, 25, 31, 31, 33, 33, 39, 42; **28:**4, 8, 12, 13, 16, 17, 18, 18; **29:**3, 20, 23, 25; **30:**15, 28, 28, 33, 34; **31:**32, 37, 45, 47, 50, 50, 52; **32:**25, 26, 28; **33:**10, 10, 20; **34:**4, 12, 14; **35:**7, 12, 14, 20, 22; **36:**43; **37:**7, 9, 11, 11, 24, 25, 32, 32, 33, 33, 35; **38:**10, 17; **39:**9, 12; **40:**10, 11, 15, 18; **41:**7, 8, 13, 15, 16, 16, 28, 32, 35, 38; **42:**6, 16, 22, 35; **43:**11, 12, 14, 18, 21, 21, 23, 23; **44:**10, 15; **45:**1, 5, 8, 26, 28; **46:**3; **47:**24, 24, 25, 26, 26, 31; **48:**17, 17; **49:**7, 7, 10, 32; **50:**13; **Ex 2:**3, 3, 5, 6, 15, 16; **3:**2, 8, 15, 15, 21; **4:**3, 3, 3, 4, 4, 6, 7, 7, 9, 9, 11, 18; **5:**7, 11, 11, 16; **6:**8, 30; **7:**2, 9, 10, 18, 21; **8:**10, 10, 22, 25; **9:**6, 7, 7, 8, 9, 17, 25; **10:**14, 14; **11:**7; **12:**7, 9, 10, 14, 17, 20, 22, 22, 27, 39, 41, 42, 44, 45, 46; **13:**9, 9, 16, 16, 21; **14:**16; **15:**7, 23, 23, 25, 25; **16:**3, 6, 15, 15, 15, 16, 18, 19, 20, 20, 27, 31, 31, 32, 33, 33, 34; **17:**14, 15; **19:**18, 23; **20:**8, 11; **21:**13, 13, 24, 24, 29, 33, 33, 34, 36, 36; **22:**1, 3, 4, 5, 8, 10, 13, 14, 14, 14, 26, 27, 27, 30; **23:**4, 9, 12, 18, 19; **24:**6, 7, 15, 16; **25:**11, 11, 12, 14, 16, 17, 19, 20, 24, 24, 32; **26:**33, 36; **27:**5, 7, 8, 11, 16, 16, 16, 20, 21; **28:**7, 17, 21, 21, 32, 32, 35, 36, 38, 38; **29:**7, 11, 14, 16, 20, 20, 20, 21, 21, 25, 26, 26, 34, 34, 34, 36, 36, 36, 37, 41, 42; **30:**2, 16, 16, 18, 18, 32, 32, 32, 32, 33, 33, 35, 36, 36, 37, 37, 38; **31:**13, 14, 14, 15, 17; **32:**4, 4, 5, 8, 11, 13, 17, 18, 20, 20, 20, 20, 29; **33:**7; **34:**9, 15; **35:**24; **36:**35, 37; **37:**1, 2, 2, 5, 6, 8, 9, 11, 25; **38:**1, 9, 18, 19, 26; **39:**3, 3, 4, 9, 10, 23, 23, 30, 43; **40:**4, 7, 9, 18, 20, 21, 27, 29, 30, 30, 34, 35, 36, 37, 38; **Lev 1:**3, 4, 5, 9, 13, 17, 17; **2:**1, 1, 2, 3, 4, 4, 5, 5, 6, 6, 6, 7, 8, 8, 9, 9, 10, 15, 15, 15, 16; **3:**2, 5, 6, 6, 7, 8, 13; **4:**4, 6, 12, 14, 15, 17, 19, 21, 24, 25, 28, 29, 31, 32, 33, 34; **5:**3, 11, 11, 11, 15, 17, 18; **6:**3, 6, 12, 12, 13, 15, 16, 17, 17, 18, 21, 21, 21, 22, 22, 27, 28, 28, 29, 30; **7:**5, 6, 6, 9, 15, 15, 18, 18, 18, 18, 19, 19, 21, 24, 29, 30, 30, 30, 34, 35; **8:**8, 10, 11, 15, 15, 15, 15, 19, 19, 21, 23, 23, 28, 29, 31, 33; **9:**9, 9, 12, 15, 16, 18; **10:**1, 9, 12, 12, 12, 13, 13, 16, 17, 17; **11:**4, 4, 7, 7, 32, 32, 32, 35, 35, 35, 35, 38; **13:**3, 6, 8, 11, 11, 13, 20, 21, 22, 23, 25, 25, 27, 28, 30, 34, 37, 49, 50, 51, 52, 52, 53, 55, 55, 55, 58, 58; **14:**7, 13, 14, 16, 20, 21, 27, 35, 38, 45, 46, 53; **15:**2, 17, 23, 26; **16:**10, 10, 14, 19, 19, 19, 21, 21, 22, 29, 31; **17:**4, 4, 5, 6, 9, 9, 11, 13, 14; **18:**18, 22, 23, 28, 28; **19:**5, 5, 6, 6, 7, 7, 8, 10, 21, 23; **20:**16, 17, 18, 21, 23; **21:**2, 11, 12; **22:**14, 19, 19, 19, 20, 23, 23, 24, 27, 27, 29, 29, 30, 30, 32, 33; **23:**3, 3, 11, 11, 13, 13, 13, 14, 21, 22, 28, 31, 35, 41; **24:**2, 3, 3, 7, 18; **25:**10, 12, 12, 19, 23, 25, 26, 26, 27, 27, 27, 28, 28, 29, 29, 30, 30, 34, 50; **26:**5, 32, 34, 35, 35, 35, 43; **27:**16, 20, 21, 21, 24, 27, 27, 27, 27, 33; **Nu 1:**50, 50, 51, 51; **3:**1; **4:**5, 16, 27; **5:**7, 8, 15, 15, 17, 22, 24, 25, 25, 26; **6:**7, 18; **7:**1, 1, 10, 84, 88; **8:**4; **9:**15, 17, 22; **11:**8, 8, 8, 8, 8, 17, 18, 19, 20, 20, 25, 31; **13:**19, 20, 20, 23, 23, 27, 30; **14:**8, 8, 8, 13, 17, 23, 34, 41; **15:**3, 4, 9, 20, 24, 24, 24, 25, 25, 25; **16:**9, 13, 17, 42, 46, 46, 46; **18:**10, 10, 10, 23, 27, 30, 30, 31; **19:**3, 3, 4, 18; **20:**9, 13, 17, 19; **21:**8, 8, 9, 17, 27, 28, 28; **22:**23, 23, 25, 27, 27, 28; **23:**19, 20, 23, 27; **24:**17; **26:**62; **27:**13; **28:**2, 7, 8, 13, 27; **29:**2, 8, 12, 13, 36; **30:**2, 5, 7, 8, 11, 12, 12, 14, 14; **32:**4, 39; **33:**40, 53, 53; **34:**4, 4; **35:**16, 17, 18, 20, 21, 27; **36:**4, 6, 7; **Dt 1:**2, 7, 8, 8, 21, 21, 24, 25, 38, 39, 41, 41; **3:**9, 11, 14, 14, 26; **4:**14, 23, 34, 36, 38, 39; **5:**12; **6:**10; **7:**8, 19, 25, 25, 25; **8:**3, 8, 9, 9, 15, 17, 17, 18, 18; **9:**4, 4, 5, 6, 21, 21; **10:**11, 14; **11:**11, 12, 29; **12:**8, 16, 21; **13:**11, 14, 16, 16; **14:**7, 8, 8, 21, 21, 21, 23, 28, 29; **15:**2, 10, 17, 18, 21, 21, 22, 22, 23; **16:**2, 3, 6, 6, 7, 11, 15; **17:**4, 4, 11, 13, 14, 19, 20; **18:**12, 22; **19:**20; **20:**5, 6, 10, 13, 20; **21:**4, 4, 7, 21; **22:**1, 1, 2, 2, 2, 2, 3, 4, 6, 27; **23:**19, 22, 25; **24:**1, 6, 6, 11, 13, 13, 15, 15, 19, 19; **25:**4; **26:**1, 2, 4, 13, 14, 14, 14; **27:**7; **28:**24, 30, 40, 49, 49, 67, 67; **29:**8, 12, 22, 23, 27; **30:**12, 12, 12, 13, 13, 13, 14, 14; **31:**7, 9, 19, 19, 19, 21, 22, 26, 26; **32:**22, 27, 35; **33:**27; **34:**4, 4, 12; **Jos 1:**8, 8; **3:**11, 15; **4:**5, 20, 23, 23; **5:**12; **6:**6, 17, 20, 21, 24; **7:**3, 3, 9, 11, 19; **8:**7, 19, 19, 29; **9:**12, 24, 24, 24, 27; **10:**13, 28, 29, 31, 32, 34, 35, 37, 39; **11:**23; **13:**10, 11, 17, 26, 31; **14:**15; **15:**3, 3, 4, 4, 4, 7, 8, 9, 11, 11, 17, 18, 47; **16:**2, 3, 5, 7; **18:**11, 15, 16, 17, 18; **19:**7, 11, 13, 27, 47; **21:**42, 43; **22:**17, 23, 23, 27, 28, 28, 29, 34; **24:**12, 15, 18, 26, 27; **Jdg 1:**8, 13, 14, 26; **3:**16, 16, 21; **6:**17, 20, 22, 23, 24, 25, 27, 27, 28, 28, 28, 29, 37, 38, 39; **7:**5, 13, 13, 13, 16, 19; **8:**21, 27, 27, 27; **9:**9, 33, 38, 42, 50, 51, 54; **11:**23, 23, 23, 26, 31, 35, 39; **12:**1; **13:**16, 19, 21; **14:**6, 6, 6, 9, 9, 13, 14, 15, 17; **15:**15, 19; **16:**6, 13, 14, 16; **17:**2; **18:**9, 9, 19, 29; **19:**11, 26, 30; **21:**4, 6; **Ru 1:**12, 19; **2:**2, 3, 17, 18, 18; **3:**12, 14, 15, 15, 18; **4:**4, 4, 4, 4, 4, 4, 6, 6, 7, 7; **1Sa 1:**7; **2:**14, 15, 15, 16, 16, 19, 31; **3:**4, 8, 18; **4:**3, 3, 5, 6; **5:**1, 2, 3, 8, 8, 10, 11; **6:**2, 8, 9, 21; **7:**1, 1, 2, 6, 6, 9, 12, 12; **8:**7, 15; **9:**8, 10, 24, 24, 24, 24; **10:**1, 11, 12, 25; **12:**5, 6, 15, 17; **14:**27, 33, 33, 34, 39, 43, 45; **15:**16, 28; **16:**2, 13, 15; **17:**35, 35, 35, 36, 39, 39, 39, 47, 49, 51; **18:**5, 11, 17, 20; **19:**5, 5, 7, 13, 13, 16; **20:**2, 3, 22, 26; **21:**6, 9, 9, 9, 9; **22:**8, 12, 18, 22; **24:**3, 6, 6, 10, 11, 11, 18; **25:**2, 11, 21, 39; **26:**14, 22; **27:**5; **28:**14, 17, 24, 25; **29:**6, 10; **30:**7, 12, 25; **31:**4, 4; **2Sa 1:**18, 18, 18, 20; **2:**20; **3:**26, 28; **4:**12; **5:**9, 20; **6:**3, 4, 8, 10, 13, 17; **7:**10, 15, 25, 29, 29; **10:**3; **11:**14; **12:**3, 3, 3, 4, 4, 12, 29, 30, 30; **13:**2, 10, 10, 12, 13, 20, 20, 22, 28, 32, 33; **14:**6, 8, 8, 19, 20, 26, 26, 26; **15:**3, 14, 21, 24; **16:**5, 8, 11, 22, 23; **17:**3, 18, 19; **18:**3, 3, 3, 4, 12, 13, 17, 18, 20; **19:**6, 30; **20:**5, 10, 15, 22; **21:**1, 4, 4, 5, 6, 12; **23:**5, 10, 16, 16, 16, 17, 17, 18, 20, 21; **24:**12, 15, 22, 22, 23, 24; **1Ki 1:**11, 18, 36, 39, 48; **2:**5, 5, 14, 15, 16, 20; **3:**5, 15, 19, 21, 22; **6:**1, 3, 16, 38; **7:**1, 2, 3, 7, 23, 23, 26, 31, 31, 44; **8:**6, 8, 18, 19, 19, 24; **9:**3, 3, 8, 13, 16; **10:**7, 7, 7, 18, 20; **11:**11, 30; **12:**15, 25, 28, 32; **13:**4, 11, 24, 25, 25, 26, 28, 29; **14:**8, 10, 22; **15:**13, 18; **16:**7, 18, 24, 31, 34, 34; **17:**3, 11; **18:**7, 8, 17, 23, 23, 23, 23, 23, 25, 26, 34, 38, 39; **19:**11, 13; **20:**1, 14, 14; **21:**2, 2, 6, 7, 15, 16, 18, 29; **22:**3, 18, 21, 22; **2Ki 1:**8; **2:**3, 5, 8, 11, 12, 20, 20, 21, 21; **3:**13, 20, 22; **4:**10, 23, 27, 28, 40, 41, 41, 42, 43; **5:**7, 13, 17; **6:**5, 6, 6, 7, 7, 33; **7:**2, 2, 8, 9, 13, 15, 16, 19, 19, 20; **8:**6, 6, 15, 15; **9:**20; **10:**19, 24, 26, 27, 27; **11:**18; **12:**4, 7, 9, 10, 11, 14, 14, 16, 17; **13:**17; **14:**7, 7, 9, 10, 22; **16:**5, 8, 11, 11, 12, 13, 13, 14, 17; **18:**4, 4, 16, 21, 25, 26; **19:**3, 3, 14, 14, 17, 22, 25, 34; **20:**7, 10; **21:**7, 12, 13; **22:**5, 8, 10, 17; **23:**6, 6, 10, 16, 17, 18, 21; **24:**2, 10; **1Ch 4:**41; **5:**2; **9:**27, 27, 27, 30; **10:**4, 4; **11:**4, 7, 18, 18, 18, 19, 19, 20, 22, 23; **12:**19, 19; **13:**2, 3, 3, 4, 7, 11, 13; **14:**9, 11; **15:**1, 2, 3, 12, 13; **16:**1, 17, 32; **17:**9, 13, 23, 27, 27; **18:**8, 8; **19:**3; **20:**1, 2, 2; **21:**7, 10, 15, 23, 23, 23, 24, 24; **22:**5, 14; **23:**27; **24:**31; **26:**13; **27:**24; **28:**2, 2, 8, 20; **29:**1, 12, 16, 18; **2Ch 1:**4, 5, 6, 7; **2:**4, 11; **3:**8, 11, 14; **4:**2, 2, 5, 15; **5:**7, 9; **6:**8, 9, 9, 13, 15; **7:**2, 16, 20, 21; **8:**1, 3, 3, 11; **9:**6, 6, 6, 17, 18, 19; **10:**15; **11:**22; **12:**8; **14:**11; **15:**5, 15, 16, 16; **16:**2; **18:**14, 17, 20, 21; **20:**25, 25, 26; **21:**15, 18; **22:**7; **23:**17; **24:**10, 11, 13, 14; **25:**18; **26:**2, 18; **29:**16, 16, 22; **30:**5, 16; **32:**5, 12, 15, 18; **33:**7, 14, 14, 16, 19; **34:**4, 14, 18, 25; **35:**3; **36:**6, 22; **Ezr 1:**1; **3:**2; **4:**7, 13, 15, 15, 24; **5:**8, 15, 16, 16, 17; **6:**2, 2, 3, 7, 11, 12; **8:**26; **10:**4, 9; **Ne 1:**11; **2:**5, 7, 8, 17; **3:**1, 14, 15, 15; **4:**3, 10, 20; **5:**5, 19; **6:**6, 7, 11, 16; **8:**15; **9:**5, 38; **10:**31, 33, 35, 37; **13:**5, 13, 16, 18; **Est 1:**5, 5, 19, 19; **2:**15, 22; **3:**6, 8, 9, 9, 10, 15; **4:**4, 8, 8, 16; **5:**3, 3, 4, 6, 6, 14; **6:**4, 11, 13; **7:**2, 2, 9, 9; **8:**2, 5, 8; **9:**12, 12, 13, 26, 27, 32; **Job 1:**21; **3:**4, 4, 5, 5, 5, 7, 9, 9, 10, 21, 22; **4:**13, 16; **5:**21, 27; **6:**7, 7, 16; **7:**4; **8:**15, 15, 15, 17, 18, 18, 19; **9:**3, 7, 19, 20, 21, 22, 25, 26; **10:**22; **11:**8, 9, 16; **12:**8, 11; **14:**7, 9; **15:**3, 18, 23; **16:**6, 6, 18; **17:**15; **18:**4; **19:**6; **20:**12, 13, 13, 15, 29; **21:**15, 17; **22:**3, 3, 4, 5, 8; **23:**15; **24:**11; **27:**21, 22; **28:**13, 13, 14, 14, 15, 17, 18, 19, 21, 21, 23, 27, 27, 27; **31:**3, 12, 12, 14, 17, 21, 28, 36; **32:**8; **33:**8, 14, 27, 27, 32; **34:**3, 23; **35:**2, 3, 6, 12, 13, 14; **36:**21, 27, 28, 30; **37:**1, 2, 3, 21; **38:**8, 9, 10, 15, 18, 20, 21, 23, 34, 35, 35; **39:**6, 7, 7, 7, 8, 9, 10, 11, 11, 12, 20, 21, 21, 22, 22, 23, 24, 25, 25, 25, 27, 28, 29, 30; **40:**11, 15, 15, 19, 19, 20, 21, 22, 23, 23, 24, 24; **41:**2, 3, 4, 4, 5, 5, 6, 6, 8, 8, 9, 9, 9, 18, 18, 22, 25, 26, 28, 29, 30, 31, 34, 34; **42:**3; **Ps 4:**4; **7:**15, 16, 16; **10:**14; **15:**4; **17:**1; **19:**4, 5, 5; **24:**1, 2; **28:**4; **30:**9; **32:**9; **33:**1, 9, 17; **35:**21; **37:**8, 16, 35; **38:**4; **41:**6, 8; **42:**4, 4; **44:**1, 3, 3, 3, 7, 7, 21; **46:**5, 5; **48:**2, 2, 5, 8, 8, 8; **50:**12, 12; **51:**16; **52:**6; **54:**6; **55:**12, 12, 13; **57:**6; **60:**2, 2; **62:**10, 11; **64:**8; **65:**8, 9, 9, 9; **72:**17; **73:**13, 16, 28; **74:**7, 9; **75:**7, 8, 8, 8; **76:**10; **81:**4, 5, 10, 10; **84:**6; **87:**5; **89:**11, 49; **90:**6, 6; **91:**8; **92:**1, 2, 6; **93:**1; **95:**5; **96:**11; **98:**7; **104:**5, 7, 20, 27, 28, 28; **105:**10; **106:**15, 17; **109:**27; **116:**15; **118:**8, 9, 23, 24, 27; **119:**34, 49, 50, 71, 75, 97, 106, 126; **120:**5; **126:**1; **127:**1, 2; **132:**6, 13; **133:**1; **137:**7, 7; **139:**4, 14; **141:**5, 5, 5; **144:**15; **145:**15; **147:**1, 18; **Pr 1:**17, 19; **2:**5, 14, 18, 21; **3:**11, 27; **4:**19, 23; **5:**6, 17, 17; **6:**3, 4, 4, 29, 31, 31; **7:**23; **8:**8, 11, 33; **9:**13; **10:**17, 19, 22; **11:**11, 11, 12, 15, 24, 27; **12:**1, 9; **13:**13, 14, 16, 19, 23, 24; **14:**6, 9, 12, 21, 27, 30; **15:**16, 23; **16:**8, 14, 19, 22, 25, 26, 31, 32, 32; **17:**8, 12, 16, 18, 21, 26; **18:**5, 11, 14, 16; **19:**1, 10, 19, 22; **20:**5, 17, 24, 25; **21:**1, 9, 15, 19, 27; **22:**6, 14, 15, 18, 27; **23:**7, 7, 23, 24, 30, 32, 32, 35, 35; **24:**12, 13, 14, 23, 26, 31, 31, 32; **25:**2, 7, 12, 16, 16, 24, 26, 27, 27; **26:**26, 27, 27; **27:**2, 10, 14; **28:**6, 8, 8, 22; **29:**4, 11; **30:**10, 21, 32; **31:**4, 13, 16; **Ecc 1:**9, 10; **2:**2, 2, 9, 11, 11, 20, 21, 23, 26; **3:**14, 14; **4:**6, 8, 13, 16; **5:**5, 11, 11, 18, 19, 19; **6:**2, 2, 9, 10, 11; **7:**2, 2, 5, 11, 23; **8:**4, 8, 11, 17; **9:**3, 4, 11, 14, 14, 15; **10:**10, 11, 11, 12; **11:**3, 9, 9, 10; **12:**2, 7; **SS 1:**6; **3:**6, 7, 7; **4:**10; **5:**5, 9; **6:**5, 12; **8:**7, 13; **Isa 1:**8, 18, 31; **3:**9; **4:**6; **5:**2, 5, 5, 6, 6, 6, 22; **6:**7, 13; **7:**8, 11, 20; **8:**1, 2, 8, 16, 16, 20; **9:**9, 10, 18; **10:**6, 7, 15, 15, 18, 25, 27; **11:**8, 15; **13:**4, 9; **14:**7, 17, 24, 24; **16:**12; **17:**1; **19:**20; **22:**25, 25, 25; **23:**1, 9, 13; **24:**1, 20, 20; **25:**6; **26:**6; **27:**3; **28:**1, 2, 2, 2, 4, 4, 13, 16, 17, 17, 17, 17, 24, 27, 27, 28, 28, 28; **29:**3, 3, 9, 11, 11, 11, 12, 16, 17; **30:**5, 13, 13, 15, 26, 30, 33, 33; **31:**4, 4, 5, 5; **34:**1, 5, 6, 6, 8, 8, 11, 12, 16, 17, 17; **35:**8, 8, 8, 9; **36:**6, 10, 11; **37:**3, 3, 14, 14, 18, 23, 26, 35; **38:**12, 16, 17, 20, 21; **40:**5, 7, 20, 22; **41:**4, 7, 20, 20, 23; **42:**5, 5, 9, 20, 21, 21, 24, 24; **43:**7, 12, 18, 19; **44:**12, 13, 15, 15, 17, 17, 19, 19, 19, 24, 26; **45:**4, 9, 9, 10, 12, 14, 21; **46:**6, 6, 7, 7, 7, 7, 7, 7, 10, 11; **47:**11; **48:**5, 5, 6, 13, 15; **49:**4, 8; **50:**2, 2, 3; **51:**8, 8, 22, 23; **52:**6, 11, 11; **53:**4, 4, 10, 11; **54:**15; **55:**11, 11, 11, 11, 11, 11, 11, 13; **56:**5; **57:**11, 11, 20; **58:**3, 13; **59:**8, 9, 10, 11, 11; **60:**9, 22; **61:**2; **62:**9, 9; **63:**1, 1, 3, 18; **65:**9, 22; **66:**3, 3, 3, 6, 9; **Jer 1:**12; **2:**19, 30; **3:**5, 9; **4:**7, 11, 12, 13, 18, 20, 23, 27, 28, 30, 31; **5:**15, 31; **6:**11, 16, 19, 29; **7:**2, 13, 22, 28, 30, 31; **8:**8, 16, 16, 19; **9:**11, 12, 12, 21; **10:**4, 4, 4, 5, 5, 5, 12, 19, 20; **11:**5, 17; **12:**11, 13; **13:**1, 1, 2, 4, 5, 7, 7, 7, 16, 22, 25, 27; **14:**22, 22; **15:**9, 14, 18; **16:**11; **17:**9, 16, 22, 24; **18:**8, 9; **19:**3, 5, 8, 9; **20:**9, 10; **21:**10, 10; **22:**16, 23; **23:**10, 15, 20, 29, 36, 38; **25:**15, 16, 17, 28; **26:**15, 15; **27:**2, 8, 16; **28:**9, 10, 13; **29:**29, 29; **30:**3, 7, 18, 24; **31:**10, 18, 28, 28, 28, 28, 28, 35, 35; **32:**7, 7, 8, 8, 8, 9, 20, 23, 23, 24, 24, 25, 28, 31, 31, 34, 35, 36, 43; **33:**11, 12; **34:**2, 22, 22; **36:**7, 21, 21, 22, 23, 29, 29; **37:**5, 8; **38:**3, 6, 6, 18, 27; **39:**1; **40:**3, 9; **41:**9; **42:**6, 20; **44:**19, 22, 22, 25; **45:**5; **46:**8, 8, 10, 14, 14, 21; **47:**1, 2, 2, 7, 7; **48:**1, 16, 20, 29, 39, 44; **49:**2, 13, 18, 33, 37; **50:**27, 35, 36, 36, 37, 37, 38, 38, 39, 39, 40; **51:**6, 9, 14, 15, 37, 63, 63; **52:**20; **La 1:**12; **2:**6, 7, 8, 16, 17, 17; **3:**12, 26, 27, 36, 38; **4:**8, 13; **5:**7; **Eze 1:**4, 9, 11, 13, 16, 22, 28; **2:**9, 10; **3:**3, 3, 3, 13, 17, 23; **4:**1, 1, 2, 3, 3, 10, 11, 12, 16, 16; **5:**1, 2, 2, 2, 3; **7:**6, 7, 9, 13, 19, 19, 19, 20, 21, 21, 22, 25; **8:**4, 17; **9:**3, 9; **10:**10; **11:**3, 3, 5; **12:**3, 5, 13, 18, 23; **13:**5, 10, 10, 11, 11, 14, 14, 15, 15; **14:**9, 16, 16, 21; **15:**4, 4, 7; **16:**19, 20, 28, 41; **17:**4, 4, 5, 6, 6, 6, 8, 8, 9, 9, 9, 9, 10, 10, 10, 10, 10, 15, 22, 23, 23, 24, 24; **18:**25, 26, 28, 29; **19:**10, 11, 11, 14; **20:**9, 12, 46, 48; **21:**5, 7, 7, 10, 10, 11, 13, 14, 15, 15, 19, 23, 24, 27, 27, 27, 28, 29; **23:**34; **24:**4, 6, 7, 12, 13; **25:**14; **26:**4, 5; **27:**6; **28:**18, 18, 21; **29:**3, 9, 11, 12, 15; **30:**3, 12, 12, 18, 21, 21, 21, 25; **31:**4, 4, 5, 5, 7, 8, 8, 9, 10, 10, 11, 11, 11, 12, 12, 12, 14, 16, 16, 16; **33:**4, 17, 25, 32; **34:**18, 18; **35:**13; **36:**17, 22, 22, 32, 36; **37:**16, 16; **39:**7, 8, 12, 13, 23; **40:**6, 9, 20, 25, 26, 28, 28, 29, 31, 32, 32, 34, 35, 35, 37, 47, 49; **41:**5, 7, 7, 10, 12, 13; **42:**4, 5, 6, 7, 11, 13, 16, 20; **43:**11, 20, 21,

26; 44:1, 2, 2, 2, 5, 20, 20, 24, 25, 25; 45:1, 2, 3, 4, 4, 5, 5, 19; 46:1, 16, 17, 18, 20; 47:4, 8, 14, 16; 48:8, 12, 14, 14, 19, 23; Da 1:1, 11; 2:3, 4, 5, 6, 7, 9, 26, 30, 34, 36, 40, 42, 44, 44, 44; 3:1, 14; 4:7, 12, 12, 17, 18, 19, 21, 21, 23; 5:5, 7, 8, 26; 6:8, 12; 7:4, 4, 5, 5, 5, 5, 6, 6, 6, 7, 7, 7, 8, 14, 16, 16, 19, 19, 23, 23; 8:3, 4, 4, 4, 5, 7, 7, 7, 9, 10, 12, 14, 27; 9:1, 18, 23; 10:1; 11:4, 4, 15, 16, 27; 12:6, 7, 10; Hos 1:10; 2:8; 4:3, 6; 5:6; 7:6, 9, 13; 8:3, 6, 6, 7; 9:4, 10, 10, 12; 10:1, 5, 5, 9; 11:3, 3; 12:8, 8; 13:15; 14:5, 5; Joel 1:3, 6; 2:2, 11, 25; 3:13, 14; Am 1:3, 6, 9, 11, 13; 2:1, 4, 6, 10, 13; 3:6, 6, 10, 12, 13; 4:5, 7, 7; 5:7, 8, 8, 8, 8, 13, 18, 23, 25; 6:1, 4, 8, 14; 7:3, 5, 7, 7, 10; 8:1, 5, 9, 12; 9:5, 5, 6, 8, 11; Ob 7, 15, 17; Jnh 1:2, 10, 12, 13, 14; 2:10; 3:3, 3; 4:2, 4, 6, 7, 9, 10; Mic 1:9, 14, 14, 14; 2:1, 2, 2, 4, 10, 10; 3:6; 4:9; 6:14, 14; Na 1:12; 3:1, 14; Hab 1:5, 6; 2:2, 3, 3, 3, 9, 12, 15, 16, 19; 3:8; Zep 1:14, 15, 15; 2:5, 15, 15; 3:1, 2, 2, 2, 2, 8, 12; Hag 1:8, 9, 12; 2:3, 3, 3, 12, 13, 14; Zec 1:12; 2:2, 4; 3:9; 4:2, 6, 7, 7, 7, 9; 5:2, 4, 6, 6, 6, 7, 9; 6:14; 7:5, 14; 8:13; 9:3, 7, 8, 13; 10:1, 1, 6, 7; 11:10, 13; 12:3; 14:5, 7; Mal 1:8, 13; 2:2, 4, 16; 3:2, 10, 10, 10; Mt 2:2, 9, 12; 3:15; 4:9; 5:6, 12, 13, 13, 13, 15, 15, 25, 29, 29, 29, 29, 30, 30, 30, 30, 34, 35, 38, 38, 41; 6:2, 10, 16; 7:2, 14, 25, 25, 26, 27; 8:9; 9:5, 29; 10:12, 13, 13, 20, 20, 25, 29, 39, 39, 39; 11:12, 19, 23, 25, 26, 26; 12:2, 10, 11, 11, 12, 13, 23, 41, 42, 43, 44, 44; 13:4, 19, 20, 28, 32, 32, 40, 44, 46, 48, 49; 14:4, 11, 12, 15, 36; 15:22, 26, 26; 16:18, 25; 17:5, 18, 20, 25; 18:6, 7, 7, 8, 8, 8, 9, 9, 9, 13, 13, 14, 15, 17, 19, 26, 29; 19:8, 10, 23, 24, 24, 26, 27; 20:14, 15, 16, 23, 25, 26; 21:2, 7, 13, 19, 19, 21, 25, 25, 25, 26, 33, 42, 44, 44; 22:3, 12, 17, 20; 23:13, 15, 16, 16, 16, 20, 20, 21, 21, 23, 25, 27, 29; 24:14, 19, 22, 26, 27, 37, 37, 39; 25:15, 16, 25, 25, 28, 40, 40; 26:7, 9, 20, 24, 25, 26, 26, 26, 26, 26, 27, 27, 27, 28, 29, 39, 42, 61, 64, 70, 72; 27:6, 7, 11, 15, 29, 30, 34, 34, 37, 40, 48, 58, 59, 60, 65, 66; 28:2, 14, 15; Mk 1:27; 2:9; 3:2, 4, 4, 4, 5, 9, 29; 4:4, 4, 6, 7, 11, 15, 16, 21, 29, 30, 31, 32, 37; 5:16, 32; 6:11, 18, 21, 22, 27, 28, 28, 29, 35, 37, 56; 7:11, 20, 24, 27, 27; 8:17, 35; 9:3, 10, 12, 18, 18, 20, 42, 43, 43, 45, 45, 47, 47, 50, 50; 10:4, 23, 24, 25, 27, 36, 42, 43; 11:2, 2, 2, 3, 3, 5, 6, 7, 7, 11, 13, 13, 14, 17, 20, 24, 30, 31, 31, 32; 12:1, 11, 14, 16, 16, 33; 13:11, 14, 17, 19; 14:1, 5, 20, 21, 22, 22, 22, 22, 23, 23, 23, 25, 35, 68, 70; 15:2, 6, 17, 23, 25, 26, 29, 32, 36, 46, 46; 16:9, 18; Lk 1:5, 19, 57, 57, 66; 2:22, 34; 3:1, 11; 4:7, 17, 20, 35, 39; 5:3, 4, 17, 23, 36; 6:9, 9, 9, 10, 30, 37, 38, 39, 44, 48, 48, 48, 49; 7:4, 8, 14, 35; 8:5, 5, 5, 6, 10, 12, 15, 16, 16, 21, 34, 45; 9:5, 5, 8, 24, 34, 39, 39, 39, 40, 45, 45, 54; 10:5, 21, 21, 21, 26, 40, 42, 42; 11:8, 21, 24, 24, 24, 25, 28, 31, 32, 33, 33, 33, 42, 43, 44, 46, 47, 51, 52; 12:19, 20, 29, 32, 33, 33, 47, 50, 55, 58; 13:6, 7, 8, 8, 8, 9, 16, 18, 19, 19, 21, 25, 33; 14:3, 15, 17, 18, 30, 34, 34, 35; 15:4, 5, 8, 9, 22; 16:7, 8, 17; 17:1, 2, 5, 6, 21, 24, 24, 28, 30, 33, 33; 18:24, 25, 43; 19:20, 20, 23, 24, 30, 30, 30, 31, 33, 34, 35, 42, 46; 20:4, 5, 5, 6, 9, 18, 18, 22, 24, 31, 35, 41; 21:21, 23; 22:8, 16, 16, 17, 17, 19, 19, 19, 22, 22, 55, 57, 71; 23:3, 31, 39, 39, 44, 53, 53, 56; 24:4, 11, 25, 26, 29, 30, 30, 30, 36, 43, 46; Jn 1:5, 20, 39; 2:8, 9, 13, 18, 19, 20, 20; 3:8, 8, 17, 17; 4:14, 20, 20, 21, 27, 33, 53; 5:15, 25, 30, 30, 45; 6:4, 7, 40, 45, 50, 60, 63; 7:2, 4, 6, 7, 7, 22, 23, 26, 49, 51; 8:43, 44, 47, 54, 54, 55, 56; 9:2, 3, 11, 14, 15, 15, 27, 33; 10:7, 17, 18, 18, 22, 34, 36; 11:4, 4, 9, 38, 42, 51, 51, 52, 55; 12:3, 5, 7, 11, 14, 17, 22, 24, 24, 25, 25, 28, 28, 29, 35, 42, 47; 13:2, 7, 13, 16, 19, 25, 26, 26, 26, 27; 14:13, 14, 17; 15:4, 7, 13, 18, 18, 19, 19, 24; 16:7, 12, 21, 32; 18:18, 23, 27, 28; 19:2, 11, 14, 20, 21, 22, 22, 23, 24, 24, 29, 29, 29, 30, 30, 31, 35, 42; 20:1, 14, 25; 21:1, 6, 7, 7, 9, 12; Ac 1:9, 16, 20, 20, 21; 2:2, 6, 15, 36; 3:13; 4:3, 4, 11, 16; 5:2, 4, 5, 24, 38, 39; 6:9; 7:31, 31, 41, 42, 42, 44, 45, 47, 47, 53; 9:30, 31; 10:4, 9, 15, 28, 33, 46; 11:5, 9, 10, 26; 12:9, 9, 13, 15, 22; 13:15, 23, 33, 37, 41, 46, 46, 46; 14:6; 15:15, 16, 16, 23, 25, 28; 16:18, 28; 17:21, 23, 24; 18:15, 15; 19:15, 24, 34; 20:1, 24, 35; 21:3, 11, 14, 28; 22:25, 28; 23:19, 21, 29, 34; 24:10, 11, 25; 25:19, 27; 26:5, 7, 8, 14, 31; 27:2, 4, 9, 9, 13, 14, 14, 15, 25, 35, 44; 28:2, 4, 8, 11, 19, 28; Ro 1:3, 16, 17; 2:13, 22, 22, 23, 27; 3:5, 8, 19, 20, 20, 27; 4:2, 9, 10, 13, 15, 16, 24; 5:13; 6:2, 19, 21; 7:7, 11, 11, 13, 15, 17, 19, 20, 20, 21, 25; 8:7, 7, 13, 13, 21, 24, 35; 9:8, 16, 16, 16, 20; 10:2, 7, 8, 10, 10; 11:5, 6, 6, 11, 12, 15, 23, 33, 35; 12:5, 8, 8, 8, 16, 19, 19; 13:1, 7, 11; 14:2, 3, 14, 14, 15, 20, 20, 21, 22, 23; 15:10, 17, 21; 16:25; 1Co 1:21, 22, 22, 30; 2:7, 8, 14; 3:6, 6, 6, 10, 13; 4:3, 4, 20; 5:1, 12, 12; 6:1, 7, 15; 7:1, 18, 19, 21, 25, 26, 28, 28, 31, 36, 36, 40; 8:1, 4, 7, 8, 10, 10; 9:1, 6, 7, 9, 11, 14, 16, 16, 18, 25, 25, 27, 27; 10:13, 13, 25, 26, 27, 28, 29, 29, 30, 30; 11:6, 13, 14, 15, 15, 16, 17, 18, 23, 23, 24, 25; 12:4, 5, 6, 10, 11, 12, 15, 16, 18, 19, 26, 27; 13:2, 3, 5, 5, 6; 14:2, 5, 17, 20, 21, 34, 35; 15:1, 2, 2, 10, 10, 11, 27, 27, 29, 36, 36, 37, 38, 38, 42, 52; 16:2, 2, 4, 6; 2Co 1:6, 6, 8, 21; 2:1, 4, 4, 5, 7; 3:2, 3, 3, 5, 7; 4:3, 12; 5:11, 13, 13, 13, 14; 6:12; 7:8, 9, 9, 9; 8:3, 8, 8, 10, 11, 12, 14; 9:2, 3, 5; 10:2, 18; 11:6, 15, 15, 20, 21; 12:5, 6, 6, 8, 10, 15, 19; 13:5; Gal 1:9, 15, 18; 2:11; 3:4, 4, 4, 5, 9, 11, 11, 13, 15, 16, 16, 18, 18, 19, 21, 24; 4:1, 3, 15, 17; 5:3, 6, 8, 9, 10; 6:7, 12, 13, 15; Eph 1:1, 9, 23; 2:5, 8, 9, 11; 3:5, 5, 8, 11, 13, 19, 19; 4:9, 16; 5:8, 12, 13, 14, 14, 29, 32; Php 1:1, 5, 6, 7, 24; 3:8, 10, 15, 18; 4:4, 12; Col 1:2, 6, 6, 23, 23, 26, 27; 2:11, 14, 14, 14, 23; 3:11, 17; 4:16, 16; 1Th 1:1, 5, 6, 8; 2:6, 13, 19; 3:1, 5, 8, 11; 2Th 1:1; 2:7, 7; 3:1, 1, 8, 9; 1Ti 1:2, 13, 15; 2:14; 3:1; 4:3, 4, 4, 5, 8, 9; 5:18; 2Ti 1:2, 9, 9, 12; 2:10; 3:11, 16, 17; 4:16; Tit 1:3, 3, 9; 2:8; Phm 1:1, 8, 8, 14, 15, 18, 19; Heb 1:2; 2:1, 3, 6, 8, 8, 10, 17; 3:13, 17; 4:2, 2, 4, 8, 12, 12, 16; 6:4, 6, 7, 7, 8, 8, 9, 16, 18, 19; 7:2, 11, 12, 18, 22; 8:7, 13, 13; 9:8, 12, 16, 17, 23, 27; 10:4, 7, 29, 30, 31, 32, 34, 35; 11:1, 1, 4, 5, 6, 7, 8, 11, 13, 17, 20, 21, 22, 22, 23, 24, 26, 27, 28, 29, 30, 31, 32; 12:5, 8, 10, 11, 11, 15, 17, 20, 25; 13:2; Jas 1:1, 2, 4, 21, 22, 23, 25, 25; 2:6, 8, 14, 17, 17, 23; 3:4, 5, 6, 6, 6, 8, 9, 9, 17, 17, 17; 4:1, 2, 2, 2, 2, 3, 4, 11, 17, 17; 5:12, 13, 18; 1Pe 1:3, 4, 5, 6, 7, 7, 7, 10, 12, 22, 23; 2:6, 8, 15; 3:9, 14, 15, 17, 21; 4:11, 13, 15, 16, 17; 5:2, 2, 3; 2Pe 1:21; 2:21, 21; 3:5, 10, 12; 1Jn 2:7, 8, 15, 17, 19, 27; 3:7, 8, 14, 18, 19; 4:10, 18; 5:16; 2Jn 1, 12; 3Jn 1, 13; Jude 5, 11; Rev 1:3, 3, 10, 11, 11; 2:17; 3:3, 12; 4:2, 11; 5:1, 2, 3, 4, 9; 6:10; 8:5, 10, 11, 13; 9:2, 6; 10:4, 6, 6, 6, 7, 7, 9, 9, 9, 9, 9, 10, 10, 10; 11:2, 18; 12:4, 10; 13:1, 2, 15, 15, 18; 14:2, 10; 15:1, 2; 16:3, 6, 8, 12, 17; 18:7, 19, 21; 19:12, 15; 20:11, 13; 21:6, 11, 16, 16, 16, 16, 24

IT'S (81)

Ge 3:3; 16:5; 27:4, 19, 32, 32; 29:26; 37:32; 43:18; Ex 32:18; Jos 7:3; Jdg 9:36; 18:14; 19:9, 11; Ru 3:1; 1Sa 9:26; 15:15; 2Sa 15:3; 1Ki 18:17; 20:40; 22:36; 2Ki 3:23; 4:23, 41; 6:12; Job 19:28; Pr 3:27; 7:15; 16:21; 18:19; 20:14; Ecc 7:12; 11:7, 9; Isa 41:7; 44:15, 19; 49:20; 55:1; 58:3; Jer 20:9; 40:5; Eze 13:10; 21:7; 24:12; Mal 1:12, 13; Mt 12:2; 14:27, 28; 21:11; 27:6; Mk 2:24; 6:50; Lk 6:2, 47; 13:7; 17:21; 24:39; Jn 4:37; 5:10; Ac 2:15; 12:11; 17:20; 1Co 1:23; 7:6, 8, 9; 8:8; 11:14, 20; 13:11; 14:9; 2Co 5:4; 12:14; Gal 4:18; Heb 5:11; Jas 2:19; 4:14, 14

ITS (947)

Ge 1:2, 25; 2:17; 3:18; 6:14; 8:11; 10:5; 15:16; 22:13; 27:17; 31:44; 36:43; 37:31; 40:5; 41:2, 18; 49:9; Ex 4:4; 6:4; 7:19; 12:6, 46, 46; 13:13, 13; 14:27; 16:21; 19:12; 21:28, 36; 22:30, 31; 23:4, 19; 25:9, 12, 31, 39; 27:2, 18; 29:10, 12, 16, 19, 31; 30:10, 27, 27, 28, 28; 31:8, 8, 9, 9; 34:20, 20, 26; 35:11, 12, 13, 13, 14, 15, 16, 16, 21; 36:27; 37:3, 17, 24, 25; 38:8, 10, 30; 39:4, 33, 35, 36, 37, 39, 39; 40:9, 10, 11, 18; Lev 1:4, 8, 11, 15, 15, 17; 3:8, 13; 4:11, 16; 5:4, 8, 8; 7:2, 3; 8:7, 9, 11, 11, 14, 17, 18, 20, 22, 23; 11:28, 32, 39, 40, 40; 13:19; 14:25, 45; 16:15, 19; 17:11; 19:25, 26; 22:27; 23:5, 37; 25:29; 26:4, 34, 34, 43; 27:12, 14, 16, 23, 27, 27, 31; Nu 1:50, 50, 52; 2:2; 3:15, 25, 25; 4:9, 10, 25, 34, 38, 42, 47; 7:1, 1; 8:4, 4; 9:12; 10:21; 13:27; 19:4, 5; 20:8; 21:15, 25; 24:18, 20; 26:5, 5, 6, 6, 12, 12, 12, 13, 13, 15, 15, 15, 16, 16, 17, 17, 20, 20, 20, 23, 23, 24, 24, 26, 26, 26, 29, 29, 35, 35, 35, 38, 38, 38, 39, 39, 42, 44, 44, 44, 48, 48, 49, 49, 54, 57, 57, 57; 28:10, 15, 31; 29:11, 16, 19, 22, 25, 28, 31, 34, 38; 32:33, 42; 34:4; 35:8; 36:9; Dt 1:25; 3:12, 17; 13:15; 14:21; 20:6, 10; 22:1, 4, 8; 24:13; 28:30, 51; 29:14, 23; 32:22; 33:16; Jos 3:15; 4:18; 6:2, 2, 26, 26; 7:8, 14; 8:2; 10:1, 1, 30, 37, 39, 39; 11:10; 15:1, 47, 47; 19:18, 25, 33, 47; 21:11; Jdg 1:8; 7:15; 12:1; 16:3; 1Sa 5:5, 9, 11; 6:2; 17:35, 51; 19:13, 16; 2Sa 12:27; 20:8; 22:6; 1Ki 4:25; 6:20; 7:6, 12, 24, 26, 31; 8:1, 1, 4, 7; 13:3; 16:24; 20:27; 2Ki 1:1; 14:7, 12; 15:16; 16:9, 10; 18:8, 35; 19:23, 23, 23, 23, 32, 32; 22:16, 19; 25:1; 1Ch 2:23; 4:41; 5:16; 6:55, 57, 60, 66, 70, 71, 71, 75, 76, 77, 79, 81; 7:28, 28, 28, 28; 12:15; 15:15; 18:1; 21:22, 27; 23:26; 24:19; 28:6, 11; 2Ch 3:8; 4:3, 5, 18; 5:2, 2, 5, 8; 8:16, 16; 20:26; 21:17; 24:13; 25:22; 28:18, 18, 18; 29:18, 18; 32:21; 34:24, 27, 28; 36:21; Ezr 2:68; 3:3; 4:12, 13, 15, 16; 5:8; 6:3, 3, 7; 9:9; Ne 2:17; 3:1, 13, 15, 15; 4:6; 11:25, 25, 25, 27, 28, 30, 30, 31; 12:28; Est 1:22; 5:2; 6:8; Job 3:5, 9, 10; 4:15, 16; 5:23; 6:15; 8:16, 17, 19; 9:6, 6, 26; 14:8, 8; 15:33; 24:13, 13; 27:22; 28:16, 19; 31:22, 26, 34, 38, 39, 39; 36:32; 37:9; 38:5, 6, 6, 10, 20; 39:6, 8, 18, 19, 19, 20, 21, 26, 27, 28, 29, 30; 40:16, 16, 17, 17, 18, 18, 19, 24; 41:1, 2, 7, 7, 12, 13, 13, 14, 14, 15, 18, 19, 20, 21, 21, 22, 23, 24, 30, 31, 32; Ps 18:5; 19:6, 6; 24:1; 25:22; 33:7, 17; 55:10, 15; 65:10; 67:6; 68:13; 69:31; 75:3, 3; 77:16, 16; 78:7; 81:6; 83:4; 85:12; 104:5; 105:16; 116:3; 119:9, 96; 131:2; 132:15, 16, 16; 137:5; 145:4; Pr 1:12; 7:23; 14:10, 10; 24:4, 31; 26:2, 11, 14, 28; 27:8, 18; 28:2; Ecc 3:11, 15; 6:5; 8:1; SS 3:2, 10, 10, 10, 10; 4:16, 16; 7:7, 8; 8:6, 11, 12; Isa 4:2, 4; 5:2, 5, 5, 14; 6:4, 9; 7:6, 8, 8, 9, 9; 8:8; 9:2, 3, 18; 10:5, 6; 11:8; 13:11, 13, 22, 22, 22; 14:2, 15, 32; 15:5; 16:6, 14; 17:6, 14; 18:1; 19:19; 21:17; 23:11, 13, 13; 24:5, 6, 11, 12, 20; 26:5; 27:3, 11; 28:1, 3, 4, 25; 29:3; 30:24; 31:5; 34:5, 10, 12, 13, 13, 15; 35:9; 36:20; 37:24, 24, 24, 24, 33, 33; 40:26; 43:17; 45:9, 10; 49:8; 51:15, 17; 52:6; 54:9; 58:2; 66:11, 13; Jer 1:15; 2:7, 11, 11, 30; 4:7; 6:16; 7:20; 11:19; 12:10, 11, 15; 13:23; 18:8, 16; 19:12, 15; 22:13, 13; 23:10; 25:9, 38; 27:5; 31:23; 34:18; 39:16; 46:5, 20, 25; 48:45; 49:1, 10, 10, 10, 13, 19, 21, 38; 50:44; 51:41, 42; 52:4; La 2:2; 4:1, 11; Eze 1:11, 23; 3:1; 9:7; 15:3; 17:4, 5, 6, 6, 7, 9, 9, 23, 23; 19:11, 11, 11, 12, 12, 12, 14, 14; 21:5, 5, 7, 10, 20, 30; 25:2; 26:4, 4, 6; 29:12, 14, 15; 30:7, 18; 31:3, 5, 6, 6, 6, 7, 11, 12, 12, 13, 13, 14, 16, 17, 17; 32:7, 12, 16, 20, 21, 22, 24, 29; 34:29; 35:2; 36:30; 37:16; 38:6; 40:24, 29, 29, 31, 31, 33, 34, 34, 34, 37, 37, 48; 41:1, 12, 13, 15, 22; 43:10, 10, 11, 11, 13, 20; 46:21; 47:1, 9; 48:1, 4; Da 2:32, 32, 33, 33, 45; 4:12, 12, 14, 14, 14, 14, 14, 21, 21; 6:10; 7:4, 4, 5, 5, 6, 7, 7, 10, 11, 19, 19, 23, 24; 8:4, 4, 5, 7, 8, 8, 21, 23; 9:26; Hos 1:5, 10; 2:21; 5:14; 6:9; 7:1, 2, 16; 8:14; 10:5, 6, 7; 14:6; Joel 1:6; 2:3, 9; 3:13; Am 1:5, 7, 10, 14; 3:4, 4, 14; 9:5, 6, 8, 11, 11; Jnh 1:2; 4:6; Mic 1:5, 5; 2:12; Na 1:5; 2:2, 7, 9, 10; Hab 3:10; Zep 2:13, 14; 3:2, 3, 3, 4, 4; Hag 1:10; 2:9; Zec 1:8; 3:7; 5:4, 11; 8:12; 9:4, 5; 10:8; 14:10; Mt 4:16; 5:13, 18; 6:34; 7:13, 16; 12:33, 33, 33, 44; 13:14, 32; 21:2; 24:32, 32; Mk 4:12, 21, 28; 6:11, 11; 9:50; 13:28, 28; Lk 5:3; 7:17; 9:5, 5, 45; 10:10; 11:25; 13:19; 14:34; 16:17, 26; 18:34; 21:20; Jn 10:10; 11:38; 12:24; 16:8; 18:11; Ac 2:24; 10:11; 11:5; 16:26; 19:27; 28:11, 26; Ro 3:19; 6:6, 12; 7:4, 4, 6, 13; 8:13, 20; 10:5, 18; 1Co 1:17; 3:13; 9:23; 13:5; 15:56; Gal 3:12; Eph 3:10; 4:16; Col 1:25; 3:9, 10; 2Ti 4:17; Tit 3:1; Heb 7:19; 12:15; Jas 1:11; 3:3; 2Pe 2:20, 22; Rev 1:16; 2:5; 5:5, 9; 6:2, 4, 5, 8; 12:15, 16; 13:1; 16:8; 21:4, 12, 15, 15, 16, 22, 23, 24, 25

ITSELF (49)

Ge 32:16; Ex 29:5; 31:7; 37:25; Lev 8:7; 16:22; 25:2; Nu 4:25; 2Sa 22:6; 1Ki 6:34; 2Ki 11:5; 19:29; 2Ch 4:6; 29:17; Ps 18:5; 63:3; 78:69; Ecc 1:9; Isa 10:15; 37:30; Jer 14:22; 23:10; 49:10; Eze 27:8; 31:10; 41:2; 44:17; 47:20; Jnh 2:5; Zec 12:12; Mt 12:25, 25, 45; Mk 3:24, 25; Lk 11:17, 26; Jn 1:4; Ac 12:10; 28:3; Ro 7:12; 14:14; 1Co 1:30; Gal 5:6; Heb 3:3; 9:24; Jas 2:17; 3:6; 3Jn 12

LET (1048)

Ge 1:3, 6, 9, 11, 11, 14, 15, 20, 20, 22, 22, 24, 26; 9:27; 12:19; 18:5, 27, 30, 31; 19:9, 20; 20:6; 23:4, 9, 13; 24:3, 14, 37, 41, 44, 51; 27:13, 34; 29:31; 30:15, 26, 26, 32; 31:28, 32, 37; 32:26, 26; 33:15; 34:8, 9, 11; 38:18, 23, 26; 40:14; 41:34, 34; 42:4; 43:4, 5, 9, 10; 44:9, 18, 26, 33, 33; 46:30, 34; 47:25; 48:11; 49:21; Ex 3:18, 19, 20; 4:21, 23; 5:1, 2, 2, 3, 7, 17, 19; 6:1, 11, 13; 7:5, 14, 16, 8:1, 8, 20, 28, 29, 32; 9:1, 2, 7, 13, 16, 17, 28, 35; 10:3, 7, 7, 12, 20, 24, 27, 28; 11:1, 10; 12:4, 48; 13:9, 15, 17; 18:19; 19:24; 20:7, 19, 20; 22:17; 23:11, 11, 33; 32:25; 33:15, 18; 34:3; Lev 1:15; 21:10; 24:14; Nu 4:18; 5:22; 6:5, 11; 7:11; 10:35, 35; 11:31; 12:12; 20:17; 21:22, 23; 22:13, 16; 23:10, 10, 27; 24:14; 30:5, 5; 31:15; 32:5; 36:6; Dt 2:27, 29; 3:25; 4:9, 36, 36; 5:11; 7:3, 15; 11:16; 13:2, 6; 16:4, 4, 20; 18:10; 21:14; 22:7; 23:16; 29:19; 32:13, 38, 38, 43; 33:6, 10, 10; Jos 2:13, 15; 5:6; 7:7; 8:6; 9:20, 21; 10:12, 19; 22:22; Jdg 1:34; 5:23, 23; 6:31, 32, 39, 39; 7:2; 9:15, 54; 10:14; 11:17, 27, 37, 38; 13:8; 14:12; 15:1, 5; 16:30; 19:25; 21:22; Ru 2:2, 2, 15, 16; 3:3, 13; 4:4; 1Sa 3:18; 6:6, 8; 11:14; 12:9; 14:8, 24; 16:16, 22; 18:2, 17; 19:17; 20:12, 12; 21:15; 22:3; 23:14; 24:7, 19; 25:26, 31; 26:8, 19, 19, 22; 28:22; 2Sa 1:21; 3:21; 10:12; 12:22; 13:5, 6, 13, 27; 14:7, 11, 12, 32, 32; 15:5, 7, 18, 26, 28, 31; 16:9, 11; 17:1; 18:19, 22, 23; 19:37, 37; 21:6; 24:3, 13, 14, 14, 17; 1Ki 1:51; 2:6, 21; 5:6; 8:46; 11:13, 21, 34; 15:19; 17:21; 18:40; 19:20; 20:31, 32, 34; 21:21; 22:49; 2Ki 1:10, 12; 2:9; 3:10; 5:20; 6:17, 20; 7:4, 13; 9:15; 10:23, 24, 25; 12:5; 17:27; 18:29, 30; 19:10; 1Ch 12:18, 19; 13:2, 2; 16:8, 21, 23, 30, 31, 31, 32, 32, 33; 19:13; 21:12, 13, 13, 17, 22; 2Ch 6:36; 7:18; 13:9; 14:7, 11; 16:3; 20:10; 23:8; 25:8; 28:9; 32:15, 15; 33:13; Ezr 2:63; 4:2; 5:17; 6:7, 12; 9:12, 12; 10:3, 14; Ne 2:7, 17; 5:10; 6:10; 7:65; 9:28, 32; 10:30, 30; 13:25; Est 1:8; 2:2, 3; 3:8; 5:4; Job 3:4, 4, 4, 5, 5, 5, 6, 7, 7, 8, 9, 9, 12; 4:2; 9:18; 10:1, 18; 12:8; 13:13, 22; 14:6; 15:31; 16:18; 17:4, 5; 20:15; 21:3, 19, 20, 20; 31:6, 8, 8, 22, 22, 31, 35, 35, 40; 32:10, 20; 33:2, 31; 34:4, 4; 36:2, 6, 18; 40:11; Ps 2:3; 4:6; 5:10, 11, 11; 7:5, 5, 5; 9:19, 19, 20; 10:2, 16; 13:4, 4; 19:13; 22:8, 8, 29, 29; 24:7, 9; 25:2, 2, 20; 26:9; 27:12; 30:1; 31:1, 16, 17, 17, 17; 32:6; 33:1, 8, 8, 22; 34:2, 3, 3, 9; 35:3, 8, 8, 8, 19, 19, 24, 25, 27; 36:11, 11; 37:33, 33; 38:16; 40:15; 41:11; 43:3, 3; 46:3, 3; 48:11, 11; 50:6; 51:8; 55:15, 15; 56:7; 59:10, 12; 61:4; 64:1; 66:6, 7, 8; 68:1, 2, 3, 3, 3, 31, 31; 69:6, 6, 14, 15, 22, 22, 23, 23, 27, 28, 32; 70:3; 71:1, 18; 72:2, 19; 74:10, 14, 19, 21, 21; 76:11; 77:4; 79:8; 81:12; 83:4, 11, 11, 12, 17; 85:8; 89:33; 90:16, 16; 94:1; 95:1, 1, 2, 2, 6, 6; 96:1, 9, 11, 11, 11, 12, 12; 97:1, 1; 98:7, 7, 8, 8; 99:1, 1, 3; 102:18; 104:35, 35; 105:1, 14, 28; 106:5, 5, 5, 48; 107:8, 15, 21, 22, 31, 32; 109:7, 8, 8, 12, 12, 27, 28; 115:2; 118:2, 3, 4; 119:10, 22, 31, 76, 79, 116, 122, 171, 172, 175; 121:3; 122:1; 124:1, 6; 125:5; 129:1; 132:3, 4, 7, 7; 137:5; 140:8, 9, 10, 11; 141:4, 4, 4, 5, 5, 8, 10, 10; 143:8; 145:4; 148:5, 13; 149:5, 5, 6; 150:6; Pr 1:5, 5; 3:3; 4:21; 5:18, 19; 6:25; 7:5, 25; 8:5, 5; 10:3; 23:31; 24:11; 27:2; 31:7, 31; Ecc 5:2; 7:23; 11:8, 8; 12:1; SS 2:14, 14; 3:4; 4:16; 7:11, 12, 12; 8:13; Isa 1:16, 18, 19; 2:3, 5; 4:1, 1; 5:5, 5, 6, 23; 12:6; 14:21; 16:4; 18:3; 19:12; 22:4; 25:9; 26:11; 34:1; 36:14, 15, 18; 37:10; 41:21, 22; 42:11, 11, 12, 12; 43:26; 44:7, 7; 45:8, 22; 47:13; 48:11; 49:24; 50:8; 52:9; 54:9; 55:7, 7, 7; 56:3, 12; 60:1; 66:5; Jer 2:28, 36; 3:25; 5:24; 6:5; 7:3, 7; 9:18, 23, 24; 11:20; 12:1; 13:14; 15:15, 19; 18:21, 21, 21, 21, 21, 22, 23; 19:7; 20:5, 12, 16; 22:2, 30; 23:28, 28; 25:5, 29; 27:18, 18; 29:8; 30:6, 11; 31:6; 32:37; 40:4, 5, 15; 42:12; 46:28; 48:26; 50:14, 16, 22, 33; 51:3, 9, 10; La 1:17, 17; 2:18; 3:28, 29, 30, 30, 40, 40, 41, 65; 4:15; Eze 1:24; 3:10, 27; 6:8; 14:3; 17:9, 9; 18:12, 30; 20:26; 21:15; 23:43; 24:10, 16, 17; 28:18; 31:14; 32:14, 16; 34:3; 39:7, 23; 43:9; 44:20; Da 1:13; 4:15, 15, 16, 23, 23; 6:8; Hos 2:12; 5:4; 6:1, 3; 7:13; 11:8; 13:10; 14:9, 9; Joel 2:1, 17, 17, 17; 3:9, 12, 12, 13; Am 1:3, 6, 9, 11, 13; 2:1, 4, 6; Mic 1:2; 4:2; 6:1; 7:14; Hab 1:17; 2:20; Zec 3:7; 8:21, 23; 11:6; Mal 3:10; 4:2; Mt 5:15, 16; 6:13; 7:4; 8:4, 21, 22; 10:13; 11:29; 12:29; 13:15, 30; 14:36; 19:6, 12, 14; 20:21; 23:8, 10, 13, 37; 24:4; 26:39; 27:42, 43; Mk 1:44; 3:27; 5:37; 6:56; 7:12; 9:17; 10:9, 14; 13:5, 36; 15:32; Lk 5:4, 14; 6:42; 8:32, 51; 9:59, 60, 61; 11:4; 12:36; 13:34; 14:9; 18:16; 20:3; 21:8, 21, 34, 34; 22:34; 23:22, 35; Jn 6:21; 8:7, 50; 11:44, 50; 12:40; 18:8, 16; 21:19; Ac 1:20, 20; 2:36; 4:10, 21; 5:40; 8:19; 9:25; 10:11; 11:5; 13:40; 16:7, 35, 37; 17:7; 19:30, 38; 20:26; 21:39; 23:22; 27:3, 15, 32, 43; 28:27; Ro 1:8, 24, 28; 6:12, 13, 19; 7:2; 11:9, 9, 10, 10; 12:1, 2, 21; 13:14; 14:4, 15, 19; 1Co 1:10; 4:19; 5:6, 8; 6:7; 7:11, 15, 21, 29, 29, 36; 12:31; 14:1, 29, 29, 35; 15:1, 51; 16:7, 11; 2Co 4:6; 7:1, 1; 12:1, 1; Gal 1:8, 8, 9; 3:2, 24; 5:21, 25, 26; 6:17; Eph 4:17, 26, 29; 5:3, 4, 18; 6:22; Php 2:15; 4:5, 8; Col 2:7, 7, 8, 16, 18, 18; 3:2, 15, 16, 17; 4:6, 8; 1Th 3:10; 5:8; 2Th 2:1; 1Ti 1:4; 2:12, 12; 4:12; 6:8; 2Ti 2:4; Tit 2:7, 8, 15; Phm 1:22; Heb 1:6; 4:11, 14, 16; 6:1, 1; 10:22, 23, 25; 12:1, 1, 28; 13:13, 15; Jas 1:2, 4, 27; 4:9, 9, 9; 1Jn 3:7, 18, 18; 4:7; 3Jn 11; Rev 13:18; 14:12; 19:7; 20:7; 22:11, 17, 17, 17

LET'S (99)

Ge 4:8; 11:3, 4, 7; 12:12; 19:32, 34; 33:12; 34:21, 23; 37:20, 21, 22, 27, 27; Ex 14:25; Nu 13:30; 14:3, 4, 40; Dt 1:22; Jdg 14:13; 18:9; 19:11, 28; 1Sa 4:3; 9:5, 6, 9, 10; 14:1, 6, 19, 36, 36; 2Sa 2:14; 3:12; 17:5; 19:10; 20:1; 1Ki 3:23; 12:16; 20:31; 22:5, 8; 2Ki 3:23; 4:10; 6:2; 7:9; 2Ch 10:16; 18:4, 7; Ne 2:18; Ps 71:11; 74:8; Pr 1:11, 11, 12; 7:18, 18; Ecc 2:1, 1; SS 1:4; Isa 22:13; 56:12; 57:13; Jer 8:14; 11:19, 19; 18:18, 18; 46:16, 16; Eze 33:30, 30; Ob 1; Mt 21:38; 25:21, 23; 26:46; 27:49; Mk 4:35; 6:31; 12:7; 14:42; 15:36; Lk 2:15, 15; 8:22; 20:14; Jn 11:7, 15, 16; 14:31; 19:24; Ac 15:36; 1Co 8:1; 14:26; 15:32

LETS (9)

Ex 22:5; Job 9:24; Ps 23:2; Pr 11:8; Ecc 5:18; 10:18; Na 1:3; Mt 6:22; Lk 11:34

LETTING (15)

Ex 14:5; Lev 10:6; 25:36; Dt 8:3; Ru 3:2; 2Sa 3:24; 1Ki 1:27; Job 3:10; 20:12; 39:14; Ps 4:4; 36:8; Isa 47:6; Jer 41:8; Eph 4:26

LIKE (1422)

Ge 1:12, 26; 3:5; 10:9; 13:10, 16; 15:5; 18:12, 13; 19:2; 20:9, 15; 22:17; 27:4, 19, 23; 31:5, 26, 26; 33:10; 34:14, 15, 31; 38:11; 41:49; 42:34; 47:3, 6; 49:9, 9, 16; Ex 1:19; 2:13; 4:18; 5:15, 22; 7:1; 9:9, 14, 24; 10:6, 14; 12:36; 13:9, 16, 18; 14:29; 15:5, 8, 10, 11, 11, 16; 16:14, 31, 31; 19:18; 22:25; 23:9; 24:17; 25:33; 30:33; 32:8; 34:1, 4; 37:19; 38:18; 39:14; Lev 5:12; 6:17; 13:16; 14:35; 18:3, 3; 19:34; 25:31, 46; Nu 11:7, 8, 11, 12, 15; 12:12; 13:18, 33, 33; 14:33, 34; 16:13; 18:18; 22:4, 29, 30; 23:10, 10, 22, 24, 24; 24:6, 6, 6, 6, 8, 9, 9; 27:17; 32:15; 33:55; 36:6; Dt 1:23, 44; 5:29; 7:26; 9:3; 10:1, 3; 11:10; 12:16, 24; 15:23; 17:14; 18:1, 7, 15, 18; 21:14; 28:29, 49; 29:23; 31:21; 32:2, 2, 2, 2, 5, 11, 22, 31; 33:17, 20, 26, 29; 34:10; Jos 7:10; 10:14; 11:4; Jdg 5:31; 7:5, 12, 12; 8:18, 18; 9:36; 13:6; 17:11; 18:7, 23; 19:24; Ru 2:14; 4:11, 12; 1Sa 2:2, 2, 8, 18; 4:7; 6:4; 8:3, 5, 5, 20; 9:21; 14:29; 17:39; 18:10; 19:5; 20:2; 21:9, 15; 25:16, 29, 36; 26:20; 28:14; 30:24; 2Sa 2:7, 18; 3:8; 5:20, 24; 6:20, 21; 7:20, 22, 22, 23; 9:8; 11:11; 12:3; 14:2, 9, 14, 17; 17:12; 18:27; 19:5, 27; 20:3; 22:43; 23:4, 4, 4, 6; 1Ki 3:7; 5:6; 7:12, 19, 22, 26, 31; 8:23; 12:10; 14:8, 15; 16:7, 31; 19:2; 20:11, 25, 27; 21:2; 22:7, 8, 17; 2Ki 1:7; 4:16; 5:22; 8:13; 9:31, 37; 13:7; 14:3; 16:11; 17:11; 18:5, 32; 19:3, 26; 20:9; 23:22, 25, 25; 1Ch 12:22; 14:11, 15; 17:18, 20, 20, 21; 24:31; 26:12; 29:15; 2Ch 2:3, 17; 3:10; 4:5; 6:14; 10:10; 13:9; 18:6, 7, 16; 30:7, 26; 32:15; Ne 2:2, 19; 5:5, 14; 6:14; 9:11,

18; Est 3:11; 4:14; Job 2:10; 3:16, 16, 24; 7:1, 2, 2, 15; 8:2, 16; 9:26, 26, 32; 10:16; 11:16; 12:25; 13:28, 28; 14:2, 2, 6, 9; 15:24, 33, 33; 16:14; 19:6, 15; 20:7, 8, 8; 21:11, 18; 23:10; 24:5, 20, 24, 24; 27:7, 7; 29:14, 14, 19; 30:7; 31:36, 37; 32:19; 35:8, 16; 36:22; 37:18; 39:20; 40:9, 15; 41:5, 18, 20; Ps 1:3, 4; 2:9; 5:9; 7:2; 10:9, 9; 12:6; 14:4; 17:12, 12; 18:42; 19:5, 5; 22:12, 13, 14, 14, 15, 16; 26:11; 28:5, 9; 29:6, 6; 32:4, 9; 33:20; 35:5; 36:6, 6; 37:2, 2, 6, 20, 20, 35; 39:11; 42:10; 44:11, 22; 45:1, 16; 48:6, 7, 14; 49:10, 12, 14, 19, 20; 50:17; 52:2, 8; 53:4, 5; 55:6; 57:4, 4; 58:4, 4, 7, 8, 8; 59:6, 14; 66:10; 68:2, 2, 14; 69:8; 72:6, 16; 73:5, 5, 6, 22; 74:5; 77:20; 78:8, 13, 16, 39, 52, 65; 79:3, 5; 80:1; 83:11, 13, 13; 86:8, 8; 88:4, 17; 89:6, 46; 90:4, 5, 5; 92:7, 12, 12; 93:3; 97:5; 102:3, 3, 4, 6, 6, 11, 26, 26; 103:5, 13, 15, 15; 107:27, 41; 109:19, 19, 23, 23, 28; 110:3; 114:4, 4, 6, 6; 115:8; 118:12, 12; 119:83, 162, 176; 124:7; 126:1; 127:4; 128:3; 131:2; 135:18; 140:3; 143:3; 144:4, 4, 12, 12, 15; 147:16, 16, 17; Pr 1:27; 3:3; 4:18, 19; 6:5, 5, 11, 11; 7:4, 22, 22, 23; 10:20, 25, 26; 11:22, 28, 30; 12:6; 13:14; 16:15, 24; 17:8, 14; 18:19; 19:12, 12, 13; 20:2, 26; 21:1; 22:25; 23:28, 32, 32, 34; 24:15, 34, 34; 25:14, 16, 19, 25, 26; 26:2, 10; 27:4, 8, 16, 22; 28:3; 30:27; 31:14, 22; Ecc 1:14, 17; 2:11, 17, 26; 4:4, 16; 6:6, 9; 7:6; 8:13; 9:2, 12; 10:7, 7; 12:11; SS 1:7, 13, 14, 15; 2:2, 3, 9, 17; 3:6; 4:1, 1, 3, 3, 5, 11, 12, 12, 13; 5:12, 12, 13, 13, 13, 14, 14, 15; 6:5, 6, 7, 10; 7:1, 2, 3, 4, 7, 7, 8, 8; 8:6, 6, 6, 14; Isa 1:8, 10, 22, 22, 22, 26, 30, 31; 2:6; 3:9, 15, 26; 4:4; 5:24, 28, 29, 30; 6:13; 7:11, 12, 18, 18; 8:11; 9:3, 18; 10:6, 18, 18; 13:8, 14, 14, 19; 14:14, 19, 19; 16:2, 8; 17:5, 6, 9, 12, 13, 13, 13; 18:5; 19:14; 21:1, 3; 22:23; 23:10, 15; 24:13, 20, 20; 25:4, 5, 10; 26:17, 19; 27:11, 12; 28:2, 9, 17; 29:4, 5, 7, 7; 30:13, 14, 17, 22, 26, 27, 28, 29, 33; 33:12, 21; 34:4; 35:6; 36:17; 37:3, 27; 38:12, 14, 14; 40:6, 11, 22, 22, 24, 31; 41:24; 42:13, 13, 14; 43:17; 44:4, 4, 22, 22; 46:9; 48:18, 18; 49:2, 18; 50:7, 9; 51:6, 6, 6, 12; 53:2, 6, 9; 56:10; 57:20; 58:5, 8, 11, 11; 59:10, 10, 11, 11, 19; 60:8, 8, 18; 61:3, 10, 11; 62:1, 1; 63:13; 64:4, 5, 6, 6; 65:22, 25; 66:12, 15; Jer 1:18, 18; 2:23, 24, 26, 31; 3:2, 2, 6, 20; 4:4, 13, 13, 17, 31; 5:3, 14, 26, 27, 31; 6:7, 13, 23, 24; 8:2, 10, 17; 9:3, 7, 8, 22, 22, 26; 10:2, 5, 6, 7; 12:3, 8; 13:10, 21; 14:6, 8, 8; 15:7, 14, 18, 20; 16:4, 13; 17:6, 8, 11; 19:12, 13; 20:9, 9, 11, 16; 21:12; 22:19, 23, 28; 23:9, 9, 11, 19, 29, 29; 24:8; 25:30, 33, 34, 38; 26:9, 18; 29:17, 22; 30:6, 23; 31:12, 18, 32; 37:18; 38:5; 40:4, 5; 42:6; 44:6, 17; 46:7, 8, 21, 22, 23; 48:11, 26, 28, 36, 38; 49:18, 19, 19, 23; 50:11, 11, 17, 42, 43, 44, 44; 51:7, 14, 33, 34, 38, 40, 40; La 1:1, 6, 8, 12, 17; 2:3, 4, 5, 12, 18, 19; 3:6, 10, 52; 4:2, 3; Eze 1:4, 7, 7, 7, 13, 14, 22, 22, 24, 24, 24, 26, 26, 27, 27, 27, 28; 2:6, 6; 7:16, 19; 8:2, 2; 10:5, 8, 9, 21, 22; 11:3, 3; 12:3; 13:4, 20, 20; 15:3, 6; 16:7, 13, 30, 44, 44, 45; 17:15; 18:23, 24; 19:10; 20:32; 21:10, 15, 28; 22:22, 24, 27; 23:13, 15, 33, 43; 25:8; 26:3, 20; 27:5; 28:2, 10, 24; 29:6, 7; 31:3, 16; 32:27; 33:32; 34:12; 36:35, 38; 38:9, 9, 16; 40:3, 20, 25, 29; 42:10, 11; 43:2, 3; 47:22; Da 3:25, 29; 4:15, 25, 32, 33, 33; 5:21; 7:4, 4, 5, 6, 6, 8, 9, 13, 16; 8:15; 9:12; 10:6, 6, 6, 6, 6, 16, 17, 18; 11:10, 40; 12:3; Hos 1:10; 4:9, 9, 16; 5:3, 10; 6:4, 4, 7; 7:4, 6, 6, 9, 11, 12, 16; 8:1, 8, 9; 9:1, 10, 10, 11; 10:4, 7, 11; 11:8, 10, 11, 11; 12:7, 11; 13:3, 3, 3, 3, 7, 7, 8, 8, 13; 14:5, 5, 5, 6, 7, 7, 8; Joel 1:2; 2:2, 4, 5, 5, 5, 7, 7, 9, 26, 27; Am 1:14; 4:2, 10, 11; 5:6, 19; 8:8; 9:5, 11; Jnh 1:6; Mic 1:4, 4, 8, 8; 2:6, 11, 12, 12; 3:3, 12; 4:9, 12; 5:7, 7, 8; 7:1, 4, 10, 15, 17, 18; Na 1:6, 10, 10, 10; 2:4, 7, 8; 3:11, 12, 15, 15, 16, 17, 17; Hab 1:7, 8, 9, 9, 11; 3:14; Zep 2:2, 13; 3:3, 3; Hag 2:3, 23; Zec 1:4; 3:2; 5:9; 9:13, 14, 14, 15, 15, 16; 10:2, 3, 5, 7, 9; 11:12; 12:2, 6, 6, 8, 8, 11; 14:12; Mal 1:8; 3:2, 2, 3, 3; 4:1, 1, 1, 2; Mt 3:16; 5:14; 6:5, 8, 9, 32; 7:12, 24, 26; 8:10; 9:3, 33, 36; 10:41; 11:8, 16; 12:13, 34; 13:21, 24, 31, 33, 34, 43, 44, 45, 47, 52; 17:2; 18:5; 20:1; 21:21; 22:30; 23:27, 28; 24:37; 28:3; Mk 1:10; 2:12, 16; 4:17, 26, 31; 6:15, 22, 34; 8:24, 32; 9:37; 12:25; Lk 4:23, 37; 6:31, 40, 47, 48, 49; 7:9, 32; 8:13; 9:48; 11:44; 12:26; 13:18, 19, 20, 21; 16:15; 17:26; 18:11, 11; 19:10, 39; 20:36; 22:26, 31, 44; 24:11; Jn 1:32; 2:24; 5:6; 6:27; 7:4, 46; 8:40; 9:9, 36; 10:20, 21; 11:25; 14:27; 15:6, 7; 16:21; Ac 2:2, 3; 3:22; 5:4, 9; 7:37, 41; 9:18; 10:11, 26, 28; 11:5; 14:15; 20:29; 23:3; 25:22; Ro 1:21, 23; 3:13; 4:16; 8:3, 15, 15, 29, 36; 9:20; 13:12; 1Co 3:3, 4, 10, 15; 4:9, 10, 13, 13; 5:10; 6:11; 9:15, 26, 27; 10:33; 13:1, 11; 14:7; 15:48, 48, 49, 49; 16:16; 2Co 1:17; 2:14, 17; 3:13, 18; 5:2; 11:1, 12, 16, 17, 21, 23; 12:11, 11, 20, 20; Gal 1:13; 2:4, 14, 15; 3:27; 4:12, 25, 28; Eph 2:2, 3; 4:14, 14, 15; 5:2; Php 2:17, 20, 22, 29; 3:21; 1Th 4:13; 5:2, 4, 6; 2Ti 2:9, 17, 19; 3:5; Tit 3:11; Heb 1:11, 12, 12; 2:17; 5:11, 12; 6:9, 19; 7:15, 27; 8:9; 9:25; 10:39; 11:9, 12, 14; 12:16; Jas 1:7, 10, 23, 24; 4:14; 1Pe 1:24; 2:9, 25; 5:8; 2Pe 1:8, 19; 2:12; 3:8, 8; 1Jn 2:20; 3:2, 2, 12; 4:17; Jude 10, 11, 11, 12, 12, 12, 13, 16; Rev 1:10, 14, 14, 15; 2:14, 18, 18, 27; 3:16; 4:3, 6, 7; 6:1, 8, 13, 14; 8:10; 9:3, 5, 7, 8, 8, 9, 10, 17, 19; 10:1, 1, 3, 9; 12:14; 13:2, 11; 14:2, 2; 16:3, 13; 17:11; 18:16, 18; 19:6, 10, 12; 21:2, 11, 11; 22:9

MAY (827)

Ge 1:9; 2:16; 3:2; 9:25, 26, 26, 27, 27; 14:21; 16:6; 17:18; 19:2; 20:16; 23:9; 24:5, 60, 60; 27:28, 29, 29, 29; 28:3, 3, 4, 4; 30:24; 31:49; 33:13; 34:10; 42:19, 34, 37; 43:5, 14, 29; 44:10, 17, 23; 47:19, 25; 48:15, 16, 16, 16, 20; 49:6, 25, 25, 26; Ex 1:22; 5:21; 10:11; 12:15, 16, 18, 44, 45, 46, 48, 48; 13:13; 18:19; 19:12; 20:10, 26; 21:5, 8, 9, 10, 11, 26, 28, 30; 23:11, 18, 23; 25:2, 3; 28:3; 29:33, 33, 34, 44; 33:20, 20; 34:3, 20, 25; 40:15; Lev 2:4, 11, 12; 3:6, 6, 17; 6:17, 18, 23, 26, 29, 30; 7:6, 11, 15, 16, 16, 19, 19, 19, 24, 24; 10:6, 14; 11:2, 4, 4, 6, 7, 8, 9, 10, 21, 22, 32, 41, 47, 47; 14:8, 34; 16:17, 26; 19:25; 21:15, 18, 21, 22; 22:4, 7, 8, 10, 11, 11, 12, 13, 15, 19, 23, 23, 24; 23:3, 11, 36; 25:3, 6, 12, 25, 27, 31, 34, 44, 45, 45, 46, 48, 49; 27:26, 27, 27; Nu 5:10, 19, 21, 22, 24; 6:6, 20, 24, 25, 26; 8:15, 26, 26; 9:10; 12:14; 16:21; 18:4, 10, 11, 13, 17, 31; 19:7; 20:20; 21:27; 22:35; 28:17, 18, 25, 26; 29:1, 7, 12; 30:13; 31:18, 18, 24; 32:22, 23; 35:15, 28, 29, 30; 36:7, 9; Dt 1:11; 3:19, 20, 27; 4:1, 1; 5:14; 6:1; 9:14; 10:11; 11:8, 21; 12:14, 15, 15, 15, 20, 21, 21, 22, 27; 13:16; 14:4, 6, 7, 7, 8, 8, 9, 10, 11, 12, 19, 20, 21, 21, 25; 15:22, 22; 16:2, 8, 8, 20; 17:14; 18:3, 6, 7, 8, 21; 19:4, 13; 20:14, 14, 20; 21:12, 13, 14, 16; 22:7, 7, 19; 23:1, 2, 3, 8, 11, 17, 19, 20, 20, 24, 25, 25; 24:4; 25:3; 29:29; 30:6; 31:12, 19, 26; 32:52; 33:13, 16, 18, 18, 23, 24, 24, 24, 25, 25; Jos 1:8, 14, 15, 17; 6:26; 8:2; 9:23; 20:3; 22:23, 25, 29; Jdg 5:24, 31, 31; 7:3; 9:19, 19, 20, 20; 11:38; 13:16; 16:28; Ru 1:8, 9, 17; 2:12, 19, 20; 4:11, 11, 12, 14, 15; 1Sa 1:17, 23; 2:20; 3:17; 14:44; 15:13, 17; 17:37; 20:13, 13, 14, 16, 23; 24:15, 19; 25:22; 26:19, 24, 24; 2Sa 2:5, 6; 3:9, 29, 35, 39; 5:8; 7:26, 26, 29, 29; 9:7; 10:12; 11:12; 14:17, 24; 15:20; 18:32; 19:13; 22:47; 24:2, 3, 23; 1Ki 1:31, 36, 37, 37, 47, 47; 2:23, 33, 33, 44, 45, 45; 8:29, 29, 30, 46, 47, 52, 57, 57, 58, 59, 59, 60, 61, 61; 18:23; 19:2; 20:10, 34; 2Ki 5:18, 18; 6:31; 1Ch 12:17; 15:2; 17:23, 24, 24; 19:13; 21:2, 3, 12; 22:11, 12, 12, 14, 16; 28:8; 29:10; 2Ch 6:20, 20, 21, 36, 37, 41, 41; 13:10; 19:11; 23:6; 24:22; 25:19; 30:18; 32:8; 36:23, 23; Ezr 1:3, 3; 4:3; 6:12; 7:13, 16, 18, 20; 10:14; Ne 4:4, 4; 5:13; Job 1:12; 3:9; 5:1, 1, 3; 10:20; 14:9; 18:4; 20:23, 23; 21:3; 24:22, 23; 27:7, 16, 16; 31:10, 10; 33:30; 34:19; 36:18; Ps 3:8; 5:11; 6:10, 10; 12:3; 15:1, 1; 17:14, 14, 14; 18:46; 19:14; 20:1, 1, 2, 3, 4, 5, 5; 24:3, 3, 6; 25:21; 30:5; 31:18; 32:6; 35:26, 26; 40:14, 14, 16, 16; 48:13; 49:11; 51:15; 54:5; 57:5, 11; 58:7, 8; 61:6, 7; 67:1, 1, 2, 3, 3, 5, 5; 69:25; 70:2, 2, 4, 4; 71:13; 72:3, 3, 5, 6, 7, 7, 8, 15, 15, 16, 16, 17, 17, 17; 73:26, 26; 80:12, 16; 86:11, 11; 90:10, 12, 14, 17; 97:12; 101:6; 104:31, 34; 108:5; 109:9, 9, 10, 10, 11, 13, 13, 14, 14, 15, 15, 19, 19, 20; 115:14, 15; 119:17, 74, 77, 80, 101, 116, 144, 146, 175; 122:6, 7; 128:5, 5, 6, 6; 129:5, 6, 8; 132:9; 134:3; 137:6; 143:10; 144:12, 12, 13, 13, 14, 14; Pr 1:11; 5:19; 6:26; 13:23; 16:2, 33; 18:16; 19:2; 21:2; 22:21; 23:3, 14, 25, 26; 24:16; 25:10; 26:23, 24, 26; 29:19; 30:6, 9, 9; 31:5; Ecc 7:21; 10:8, 20; SS 6:8, 13; 7:8, 9; Isa 2:3; 10:30; 17:10, 11; 45:3; 54:10; 55:7; 57:19; Jer 4:14; 5:22; 6:27; 13:22; 20:14; 22:23; 28:6; 29:15, 22; 38:25, 25; 40:4; 42:5; 44:26; 51:35, 35; Eze 3:12; 4:15; 24:17; 30:21; 37:9; 40:46; 43:25; 44:3, 3, 5, 11, 11, 13, 13, 22, 22, 31; 45:21; 46:17, 18; 48:19; Da 4:17; 6:16; 10:19; Hos 4:15; 9:3, 4, 4; 10:12; 14:2; Am 5:14; Jnh 3:7; Mic 4:2; Hab 2:19; Zec 4:7, 7; 8:6; 11:1; Mal 1:4, 4; 2:4, 12; 3:3; Mt 6:9, 10, 10; 7:21; 12:5; 18:16; 21:19, 21; Mk 11:14, 23; Lk 1:38; 11:2, 2; 12:10, 38, 58; 17:6; 21:36; Jn 5:14; 6:51; 10:17; 15:7; 16:33; 17:22, 26; 20:31; Ac 4:30; 5:39; 8:20; 9:17; 21:37; 26:1, 18; Ro 1:7; 2:1; 6:4; 11:19; 14:22; 15:1, 5, 13, 33; 16:20; 1Co 1:3; 3:12; 6:12; 8:1; 10:12, 25, 33; 15:35; 16:23; 2Co 1:2, 17; 2:7; 4:10; 10:2, 8; 11:6; 12:9; 13:13; Gal 1:3; 6:16, 18; Eph 1:2; 2:18; 3:17, 18, 19, 21; 6:23, 24; Php 1:2, 10, 11; 3:1, 8; 4:23; Col 1:2, 11; 2:23; 4:18; 1Th 1:1; 3:10, 11, 12; 5:23, 23, 28; 2Th 1:2; 2:16; 3:5, 16, 18; 1Ti 1:2, 18; 3:10; 4:4; 6:3, 19, 21; 2Ti 1:2, 16, 18; 4:22; Tit 1:4; 3:15; Phm 1:3; Heb 2:1; 10:5; 13:20, 20, 25; Jas 2:18; 5:16; 1Pe 1:2; 3:7; 2Pe 1:2; 1Jn 1:3; 5:13; 2Jn 3; 3Jn 8, 15; Jude 2

ME (4054)

Ge 3:12, 12, 13; 4:10, 13, 14, 14, 14, 14, 23, 23, 24, 25; 12:13, 18, 18, 19; 15:3, 8, 9; 16:2, 5, 5, 13, 13; 17:1, 7; 18:5, 12, 13, 27, 30, 31; 19:19, 19, 19, 20; 20:5, 6, 9, 11, 13, 16; 21:6, 6, 23, 23, 23; 22:12, 16, 18; 23:4, 9, 11, 13, 13; 24:7, 12, 12, 17, 27, 37, 39, 40, 42, 43, 45, 47, 48, 49, 49, 54; 25:22, 30, 31, 32, 33; 26:5, 9, 9, 27; 27:3, 4, 9, 12, 12, 12, 13, 19, 19, 25, 26, 31, 32, 33, 34, 35, 36, 36, 38, 38; 28:20, 20, 20, 21, 22; 29:15, 18, 21, 27, 32, 33, 34; 30:1, 3, 6, 6, 13, 16, 18, 20, 20, 24, 26, 26, 27, 27, 30, 31, 32, 32; 31:5, 5, 5, 7, 7, 7, 9, 11, 13, 28, 29, 29, 31, 36, 37, 39, 42, 42, 52; 32:9, 9, 10, 11, 11, 12, 26, 26; 33:5, 11, 15, 15; 34:4, 11, 11, 12, 30; 35:1, 3; 37:9, 14; 38:16, 17; 39:8, 9, 12, 14, 15, 17; 40:8, 9, 14, 14, 14; 41:10, 15, 24, 51, 52; 42:20, 20, 33, 34, 36, 36; 43:5, 6, 7, 8, 9, 16, 29; 44:18, 18, 18, 23, 29, 33, 34; 45:5, 5, 7, 8, 8, 9, 9, 10, 13; 46:30, 31; 47:16, 29, 29, 30, 30; 48:3, 3, 4, 5, 9, 9, 11, 16; 49:1, 4, 29; 50:5, 5, 5, 19, 20; Ex 2:9, 14; 3:9, 11, 13, 13, 14, 15, 16; 4:1, 10, 23, 25; 5:22; 6:12, 30; 7:16, 16; 8:1, 8, 9, 9, 20, 28; 9:1, 13, 14; 10:3, 3, 8, 28; 11:8, 9; 12:32; 13:2; 14:15; 17:2, 4; 18:4, 15, 19; 19:5, 5, 6, 9, 23; 20:3, 5, 6, 24, 24; 22:23, 27, 29, 30, 30; 23:15, 16, 19; 24:1, 12; 25:2, 8, 30; 28:1, 3, 4; 30:30; 31:13; 32:2, 10, 23, 24, 24, 26, 32, 33; 33:12, 12, 12, 12, 12, 13, 13, 17, 18, 20, 21, 23; 34:2, 15, 16, 19, 20, 25; 40:13, 15; Lev 6:17; 10:3, 19; 21:18; 22:2; 23:2; 25:23, 23; 26:14, 18, 21, 23, 27, 40, 40; Nu 3:41; 8:14, 16; 11:11, 12, 15, 15, 15, 16, 21; 12:6; 14:11, 11, 22, 23, 24, 27, 29, 34, 35; 16:28, 29; 17:10; 18:8, 11; 20:12; 22:5, 6, 8, 10, 13, 17, 17, 18, 19, 28, 29, 29, 32, 33, 37, 38; 23:1, 3, 3, 7, 7, 7, 10, 11, 12, 13, 18, 26, 29, 29; 24:6, 13, 14; 28:2, 2; 32:11; Dt 1:9, 17, 23, 37, 37, 42; 2:1, 2, 17, 31; 3:2, 24, 25, 26, 26; 4:5, 5, 10, 10, 10, 14, 21, 26; 5:5, 7, 9, 10, 22, 23, 28, 29, 31; 6:1; 7:4; 9:10, 11, 12, 13, 14, 16, 19; 10:1, 1, 4, 5, 11; 18:15, 17, 20; 20:3; 25:7; 26:3, 10, 13, 14; 28:20; 31:2, 16, 20; 32:39, 41, 51; Jos 2:12, 12, 12, 13; 7:11, 19, 19; 8:31; 10:4, 22; 14:6, 7, 8, 9, 10, 11, 12, 12, 12; 15:19, 19, 19; 18:4, 8; 24:15; Jdg 1:7, 15, 15, 15; 3:28; 4:8, 19; 5:30; 6:10, 17, 17, 17, 36, 37, 37, 39, 39; 7:2, 17; 8:7, 15, 24; 9:7, 7, 15, 15, 54; 10:12, 13; 11:7, 7, 7, 9, 9, 27, 27, 30, 31, 35, 36, 37; 12:3, 3; 13:6, 6, 7, 10; 14:3, 12, 13, 16, 16, 16; 15:11, 12; 16:6, 10, 10, 10, 13, 13, 13, 15, 15, 15, 15, 17, 18, 28, 28, 30; 17:10, 10, 13; 19:20; 20:5; Ru 1:8, 8, 11, 13, 13, 16, 17, 20, 20, 20, 21, 21, 21; 2:2, 2, 7, 10, 13, 13, 21; 3:9, 17; 4:4; 1Sa 1:8, 11, 26, 27, 27; 2:1, 16, 28, 29, 30, 30, 35; 3:17, 17; 8:7, 7, 8; 9:18, 19, 21; 10:2, 8, 8, 19; 12:3, 3, 5, 12, 23; 13:9, 11; 14:12, 42, 43, 44; 15:1, 11, 11, 16, 20, 25, 30, 30, 32; 16:2, 3, 5, 17, 19; 17:9, 10, 10, 18, 35, 37, 37, 43, 45, 58; 18:8; 19:3, 15, 17, 17; 20:1, 2, 2, 4, 7, 8, 8, 8, 11, 13, 14, 21, 28; 21:2, 2, 2, 3, 9, 14; 22:3, 8, 8, 8, 8, 12, 13, 13, 13, 15, 17, 17, 23; 23:7, 11, 11, 12, 21; 24:10, 11, 11, 12, 15, 17, 18, 18, 18, 19, 21; 25:21, 22, 28, 31, 32, 33, 34, 34, 39; 26:6, 8, 18, 19, 19, 20, 24; 27:1, 1, 1, 12; 28:1, 8, 9, 9, 11, 12, 15, 15, 15, 15, 16, 19, 22; 29:3, 3; 30:7, 13, 15, 15, 15; 31:4, 4, 4; 2Sa 1:4, 7, 7, 8, 9, 9, 26; 2:7; 3:8, 9, 14, 21, 35, 39; 4:9, 10, 10; 5:19; 6:21, 21; 7:5, 7, 16, 18, 19, 21, 25, 27, 28, 29; 9:7, 8, 10; 10:2, 11, 11; 11:6; 12:10, 22, 23, 28; 13:6, 6, 10, 11, 12, 13, 16, 16, 24; 14:4, 8, 9, 10, 11, 12, 13, 15, 19, 19, 22, 32, 32, 32, 32, 32; 15:4, 7, 8, 25, 26, 28, 33, 35, 36, 36; 16:4, 9, 10, 11, 12; 17:1; 18:13, 19, 22, 23, 29; 19:12, 13, 19, 25, 26, 27, 28, 33, 37, 38; 20:16, 20, 21; 21:3, 4; 22:3, 4, 5, 5, 6, 6, 7, 17, 17, 18, 18, 18, 19, 19, 20, 20, 20, 21, 21, 23, 25, 34, 34, 35, 35, 36, 36, 40, 41, 44, 44, 44, 45, 45, 48, 48, 49, 49, 49; 23:2, 3, 5, 17; 24:10, 13, 14, 17, 24; 1Ki 1:13, 17, 29, 35, 51; 2:4, 4, 7, 8, 8, 15, 16, 17, 20, 22, 22, 23, 24, 24, 31; 3:7, 9, 14, 17, 20, 24; 5:4, 6, 9; 8:30; 9:4, 6; 11:21, 33; 12:5, 9, 27; 13:7, 8, 9, 15, 17, 18, 27, 31; 14:2, 8, 9, 9; 15:19; 17:10, 11, 13, 18, 19, 20; 18:9, 12, 37, 37; 19:2, 10, 11, 14, 20; 20:5, 10, 32, 35, 36, 37, 39; 21:6, 20, 23, 29; 22:4, 8, 14, 18, 24, 28, 30, 34; 2Ki 2:2, 4, 6, 9, 10, 20; 3:7, 7, 15; 4:2, 6, 13, 13, 16, 27, 30, 41; 5:7, 8, 11, 11, 17, 17, 18, 18, 22; 6:19, 26, 31, 32; 8:4, 9, 10, 13, 13, 14; 9:15, 18, 19; 10:6, 6, 15, 15, 16; 14:8; 16:7; 18:31; 19:6, 16, 27, 28; 20:8, 19; 21:15; 22:10, 13, 17, 19; 1Ch 4:10, 10, 10; 10:4, 4; 11:19; 12:17, 17; 14:10, 11; 17:4, 6, 12, 16, 17, 18, 23, 25, 26, 27; 19:2, 12, 12; 21:2, 8, 12, 13, 13, 17, 22, 24; 22:8, 8, 18; 28:3, 4, 4, 5, 5, 6, 19; 2Ch 1:8, 9, 10; 2:3, 7, 8; 6:21; 7:17, 19; 10:9; 12:5, 8; 13:4; 15:2; 16:3; 18:3, 7, 13, 17, 23, 27, 29, 33; 20:20; 25:17; 28:11, 23; 29:5; 32:13, 14, 15; 34:18, 21, 25, 27; 35:21, 21, 21, 23; 36:23, 23; Ezr 1:2, 2; 4:18; 6:10; 7:28, 28, 28, 28; 8:1; 9:1, 4; Ne 1:2, 3, 6, 9, 11, 11; 2:2, 5, 5, 7, 7, 8, 8, 9, 12, 18; 4:18, 23; 5:19; 6:2, 2, 2, 6, 7, 12, 13, 13, 13, 14, 19, 19; 7:5; 12:40; 13:22; Est 4:11, 16; 5:6, 8, 12, 12; 6:6, 6; 7:2, 3; 8:5; 9:12; Job 1:21; 2:3; 3:10, 12, 12, 25; 4:2, 12, 14; 6:4, 4, 9, 9, 11, 14, 23, 23, 24, 28; 7:8, 8, 12, 13, 14, 14, 16, 19, 20, 21; 9:16, 17, 18, 18, 20, 20, 21, 28, 31, 31, 32, 34; 10:1, 2, 2, 2, 3, 3, 7, 8, 8, 8, 9, 10, 11, 12, 12, 14, 15, 16, 16, 17, 17, 17, 18, 18, 20; 12:4, 4; 13:4, 13, 13, 15, 16, 17, 19, 19, 21, 21, 22, 22, 23, 23, 24, 24, 26; 14:3, 13, 13, 13, 14, 15; 16:7, 8, 9, 9, 9, 10, 10, 11, 11, 12, 12, 12, 12, 13, 13, 14, 14, 20, 21; 17:1, 2, 3, 6, 8, 16; 19:2, 2, 3, 3, 5, 6, 7, 9, 10, 11, 11, 12, 13, 15, 15, 18, 18, 19, 19, 21, 21, 22, 25, 28; 20:3; 21:2, 2, 3, 3, 3, 5, 27, 28, 34; 23:5, 6, 6, 10, 10, 13, 14, 15, 16, 17; 24:15, 25; 27:12; 29:2, 3, 5, 5, 8, 11, 11, 11, 11, 13, 14, 20, 21, 21, 23; 30:2, 9, 9, 10, 10, 11, 12, 12, 13, 14, 14, 15, 18, 19, 20, 21, 21, 22, 22, 23, 27; 31:6, 14, 15, 16, 20, 23, 35, 35, 35, 38; 32:10, 10, 13, 14, 18, 18, 20, 22; 33:2, 4, 4, 5, 7, 10, 10, 28, 31, 31, 33; 34:2, 6, 10, 32, 34, 34; 35:3; 36:2; 37:1; 38:4, 18; 40:8; 41:10, 11; 42:3, 7, 8; Ps 2:7; 3:1, 3, 4, 5, 6, 7; 4:1, 1, 1, 7, 8; 5:1, 8, 8, 8, 8; 6:1, 1, 2, 2, 3, 4, 4; 7:1, 1, 2, 2, 2, 5, 5, 8; 9:13, 13, 13, 14, 14; 11:1; 12:5; 13:1, 3, 5, 6; 16:1, 6, 7, 7, 8, 8, 11, 11; 17:2, 3, 4, 7, 8, 8, 9, 9, 9, 11, 11, 11, 12, 13, 14; 18:3, 4, 4, 5, 5, 6, 16, 16, 17, 17, 17, 18, 18, 19, 19, 19, 20, 20, 22, 24, 32, 33, 33, 34, 34, 35, 35, 35, 39, 40, 43, 43, 43, 44, 44, 47, 47, 48, 48, 48; 19:12, 13, 13; 22:1, 7, 7, 9, 9, 11, 11, 12, 12, 13, 14, 15, 15, 16, 16, 17, 20, 21; 23:2, 2, 3, 4, 4, 5, 5, 6; 25:2, 4, 4, 5, 5, 5, 15, 16, 16, 17, 19, 20, 20, 21; 26:1, 2, 2, 9, 9, 11; 27:1, 2, 2, 3, 3, 5, 5, 5, 6, 7, 8, 9, 9, 9, 10, 10, 11, 11, 11, 12, 12, 12; 28:1, 1, 3, 7; 30:1, 1, 3, 3, 6, 7, 7, 10, 10, 10, 11; 31:1, 1, 2, 2, 2, 2, 3, 4, 4, 5, 8, 8, 9, 11, 11, 13, 13, 15, 15, 16, 17, 21, 21; 32:4, 5, 7, 7; 34:4, 4, 6, 6, 11; 35:1, 1, 3, 4, 7, 7, 8, 8, 9, 11, 11, 12, 15, 15, 16, 16, 17, 19, 21, 22, 24, 24, 26, 27; 36:11, 11; 38:1, 1, 2, 4, 7, 12, 12, 15, 16, 19, 20, 20, 21, 22; 39:1, 2, 3, 4, 4, 8, 8, 10, 12, 13; 40:1, 1, 2, 2, 3, 6, 7, 11, 12, 13, 13, 14, 17, 17; 41:4, 4, 5, 6, 7, 7, 7, 9, 10, 10, 11, 11, 12; 42:3, 7, 8, 8, 9, 10; 43:1, 1, 2, 3, 3; 44:6; 45:10; 49:5, 15, 15; 50:5, 5, 11, 15, 15, 16, 22, 23; 51:1, 2, 2, 3, 4, 5, 6, 7, 7, 8, 8, 8, 10, 10, 11, 11, 12, 12, 14; 54:1, 1, 3, 3, 4, 7, 7; 55:2, 3, 3, 3, 4, 5, 12, 12, 16, 18, 18, 18, 18, 19, 20, 23; 56:1, 1, 1, 2, 2, 4, 5, 6, 6, 11, 13; 57:1, 2, 3, 3, 3, 6; 59:1, 1, 1, 2, 2, 3, 4, 4, 9, 10, 10, 16, 17; 60:9, 9; 61:2, 3, 4, 5; 62:3, 4, 4, 4, 7; 63:3, 5, 7, 8, 9; 64:1, 2; 66:14, 16, 20; 69:1, 2, 3, 4, 4, 4, 6, 6, 8, 8, 9, 9, 10, 11, 12, 13, 14, 14, 14, 14, 14, 15, 15, 15, 16, 17, 18, 18, 20, 21, 21, 29; 70:1, 1, 2; 71:1, 2, 2, 2, 3, 3, 4, 6, 6, 9, 9, 10, 10, 12, 13, 13, 14, 15, 17, 18, 18, 18, 20, 20, 20, 21, 21, 23, 24; 73:2, 14, 24, 24, 28; 75:9; 77:1, 2, 4, 7, 7; 81:7, 8, 11, 13, 13; 86:1, 2, 2, 4, 7, 11, 11, 13, 13, 14, 14, 16, 16, 17, 17, 17; 87:4; 88:5, 6, 7, 7, 8, 14, 14, 16, 16, 17, 17; 89:24, 26, 51; 91:14, 15; 92:4, 4, 10; 94:16, 16, 17, 18, 19; 95:10; 101:6, 6, 7; 102:2, 2, 8, 8, 10, 10, 23; 103:2, 4, 4, 22; 104:35; 106:4, 4, 5, 5, 5; 108:6, 10, 10; 109:2, 2, 3, 3, 4, 21, 21, 25, 26, 26, 28, 28, 28; 116:3, 4, 6, 7, 8, 12, 13, 16; 118:5, 5, 6, 6, 7, 7, 7, 10, 11, 12, 12, 13, 13, 18, 18, 19, 21; 119:8, 10, 12, 19, 22, 23, 24, 24, 25, 26, 27, 28, 29, 29, 31, 32, 33, 34, 35, 36, 36, 37, 38, 39, 41, 41, 42, 43, 49, 50, 50, 51, 52, 61, 64, 65, 66, 67, 68, 69, 71, 71, 72, 73, 73, 73, 74, 75, 76, 76, 77, 78, 79, 82, 84, 85, 86, 86, 87, 92, 94, 95, 98, 102, 104, 108, 110, 116, 117, 121, 122, 122, 124, 124, 125, 132, 134, 135, 135, 143, 144, 145, 146, 150, 153, 156, 157, 161, 169, 170, 171, 173, 175, 175, 176; 120:2, 5, 7; 122:1; 129:1, 2, 2, 4; 131:1, 2; 138:3, 3, 3, 7, 7, 8, 8; 139:1, 3, 3, 5, 6, 6, 10, 10, 11, 11, 13, 14, 15, 16, 17, 18, 23, 23, 24, 24; 140:1, 1, 4, 4, 4, 5, 7, 9; 141:4, 4, 4, 5, 5, 5, 8, 9, 9, 10; 142:3, 4, 4, 4, 4, 6, 6, 7, 7, 7; 143:1, 3, 3, 3, 7, 7, 8, 8, 8, 9, 9, 10, 10, 11, 11; 144:1, 2, 2, 7, 7, 11, 11; Pr 1:23, 28, 28, 32, 33; 2:1; 4:1, 4, 10; 5:7, 13; 7:24; 8:5, 5, 6, 14, 15, 17, 17, 17, 21, 22, 32, 34, 34, 34, 35, 36, 36; 9:4, 16; 23:26, 35, 35; 24:29; 30:4, 8, 8, 8, 18; Ecc 1:16; 2:7, 9; 8:17; 9:13; SS 1:2, 4, 4, 6, 6, 6, 6, 7; 2:4, 4, 5, 6, 7, 10, 14, 14, 17; 3:3, 5; 4:8; 5:2, 4, 7, 7, 8; 6:5, 8; 8:1, 2, 3, 6, 10, 13; Isa 1:2, 11, 13, 16, 19, 19; 3:7; 5:4, 13; 6:8, 10; 7:9, 9, 11; 8:1, 5, 11, 18; 10:14; 12:1, 1, 2; 14:28; 15:1; 17:1; 18:4; 19:1; 21:1, 3, 6, 11, 11, 13; 22:1, 4, 4, 4, 14, 15; 23:1; 28:22, 23; 29:13, 13, 16; 30:2, 15, 15; 31:4; 32:9; 36:16; 37:6, 17, 28, 29; 38:14, 16, 17, 17, 20; 39:8; 40:25; 41:1, 9; 42:6, 18; 43:4, 7, 10, 10, 20, 21, 22, 23, 23, 24, 24, 24, 24, 27; 44:1, 17, 22; 45:4, 5, 10, 11, 19, 21, 22, 23; 46:3, 5, 9, 12; 47:10, 10; 48:1, 11, 12, 16; 49:1, 1, 1, 2, 3, 3, 5, 5, 5, 5, 6, 16, 21, 21, 23; 50:4, 4, 5, 6, 6, 7, 8, 8, 9, 11; 51:1, 4, 4, 5, 7; 54:17; 55:3; 56:4, 4; 57:6, 7, 8, 8, 11, 11, 11, 11, 13, 20; 58:2, 2, 4; 61:1, 1, 1, 2, 10, 10; 63:3, 4; 65:1, 1, 1, 3, 5, 6, 7, 9, 10, 24, 24; 66:1, 1, 23, 24; Jer 1:4, 11, 13, 16; 2:1, 2, 2, 2, 5, 8, 8, 13, 20, 27, 27, 29, 32, 35; 3:1, 4, 6, 7, 8, 10, 11, 12, 13, 19, 19, 20, 22; 4:1, 12, 17, 19, 22; 5:7, 7, 11, 22, 23; 6:7, 19, 20, 20; 7:10, 16, 23, 24, 26; 8:19; 9:3, 6, 24; 10:20, 24, 24; 11:2, 4, 7, 9, 9, 10, 14, 18, 18, 19, 20, 21, 21; 12:1, 1, 3, 3, 5, 8, 9, 17; 13:1, 2, 3, 5, 6, 10, 11, 11, 14, 22, 25; 14:10, 11, 12; 15:1, 1, 6, 6, 7, 10, 13, 15, 15, 16, 16, 17, 19, 19; 16:1, 11, 11, 12, 17; 17:14, 15, 17, 18, 18, 19, 24, 27; 18:3, 5, 10, 15, 19, 19, 20, 22, 23; 19:1, 4, 15; 20:7, 7, 8, 10, 10, 10, 11, 11, 12, 13, 17; 21:5; 22:1, 4, 6, 16, 21; 23:21, 22, 24, 27; 24:1, 3, 4, 7, 7; 25:3, 6, 7, 7, 8, 15, 17, 27; 26:4, 12, 12, 14, 14, 15, 15; 27:2; 28:1, 8; 29:13, 13, 13, 19, 32; 30:6, 20, 21; 31:18, 18, 18, 34, 38; 32:6, 8, 25, 27, 30, 31, 33, 39, 40, 40; 33:3, 8, 9, 18, 21, 22; 34:15, 17; 35:13, 15, 16, 19; 36:18; 37:7, 20; 38:15, 15, 19, 19, 21, 24, 26; 39:18; 40:4, 10; 42:9, 20; 49:11, 19, 19; 50:44, 44; La 1:12, 13, 13, 14, 14, 16, 16, 19, 21, 21, 22; 3:2, 3, 3, 5, 5, 6, 7, 7, 9, 10, 11, 11, 11, 12, 14, 15, 15, 16, 16, 52, 53, 53, 56, 57, 59, 59, 60, 61, 62, 63; Eze 1:1, 3, 3, 4, 28, 28; 2:2, 2, 3, 3, 9; 3:1, 2, 7, 12, 12, 14, 14, 14, 16, 17, 22, 22, 24, 24, 24; 4:16; 6:1, 9; 7:1; 8:1, 3, 3, 3, 5, 6, 7, 8, 12, 14, 16, 17; 9:9, 11; 11:1, 1, 2, 5, 5, 12, 14, 24, 25; 12:1, 2, 8, 17, 21, 26; 13:1, 19; 14:1, 2, 3, 5, 7, 11, 12, 13; 15:1, 8; 16:1, 15, 17, 20, 43; 17:1, 11, 20; 18:1, 25; 20:1, 2, 8, 12, 13, 14, 21, 27, 31, 38, 39, 40, 40, 41, 45, 49; 21:1, 8, 18; 22:1, 12, 17, 23; 23:1, 4, 5, 35, 35, 36; 24:1, 15, 20, 25; 25:1, 14; 26:1; 27:1; 28:1, 11, 20; 29:1, 17, 20; 30:1, 20; 31:1; 32:1, 17; 33:1, 7, 21, 22, 23; 34:1; 35:1, 13; 36:5, 16, 17; 37:1, 2, 3, 4, 7, 9, 10, 11, 15; 38:1; 39:26; 40:1, 2, 2, 2, 3, 4, 17, 24, 28, 32, 35, 45, 48; 41:1, 4, 22; 42:1, 13, 15; 43:1, 5, 5, 6, 6, 7, 8, 18, 19; 44:1, 2, 4, 5, 7, 10, 10, 13, 15, 16, 19; 46:19, 19, 19, 21, 21, 24; 47:1, 2, 2, 3, 3, 4, 6, 6, 8; 48:11; Da 1:10; 2:3, 3, 5, 6, 6, 9, 9, 9, 9, 23, 23, 24, 26; 4:2, 5, 5, 6, 7, 8, 9, 18, 18, 18, 18, 27, 36, 36; 5:7, 16; 6:22; 7:15, 16, 23; 8:1, 3, 15, 18, 18; 9:18, 21, 22; 10:2, 7, 8, 10, 10, 11, 11, 13, 15, 16, 17, 18, 19, 21; Hos 1:2; 2:8, 13, 15, 16, 20; 3:1, 3; 4:6, 6, 7, 15; 5:3, 15, 15; 6:7; 7:7, 13, 13, 13, 14, 15, 16; 8:2, 13; 9:10; 11:5, 7, 7, 7, 8, 9, 12; 13:4, 6; Joel 2:12, 12; 3:4, 4; Am 4:1, 6, 8, 9, 10, 11; 5:4, 25; 7:1, 4, 7, 8, 15, 15; 8:1; 9:7; Jnh 1:12; 2:2, 2, 3, 4, 5, 6; 4:3; Mic 2:8; 3:8, 9;

4:13; 5:15; 6:1, 3, 3, 3; 7:7, 7, 7, 8, 9, 9, 9, 10; Hab 1:3; 2:1, 2; 3:16, 19, 19; Zep 1:6; 3:7, 11; Hag 2:17; Zec 1:3, 9, 13, 14, 19, 20; 2:1, 3, 8, 9, 11; 3:1, 8; 4:1, 1, 6, 8, 9, 14; 5:3, 5; 6:4, 8; 7:4, 5, 6, 13; 8:1, 6, 14, 18; 10:9; 11:8, 11, 12, 13, 13, 15; 12:10; Mal 2:2, 5, 6, 6, 9; 3:1, 5, 7, 8, 8, 8, 9, 10, 13; Mt 2:8; 3:14; 4:9; 7:4, 21, 22, 24; 8:2, 21, 22; 10:18, 22, 32, 33, 37, 37, 38, 39, 40, 40, 40; 11:6, 27, 28, 29; 12:29, 30, 30, 30, 30, 32; 13:15, 15; 14:28, 30, 31; 15:8, 22, 25, 32; 16:23, 23, 24, 25, 28; 17:4, 17; 18:5, 6, 21, 26, 32; 19:14, 17, 21; 20:15, 32; 21:24; 22:19; 23:37, 39; 24:9, 10; 25:20, 22, 35, 35, 35, 36, 36, 36, 40, 42, 42, 43, 43, 43, 45; 26:10, 12, 15, 21, 23, 23, 31, 34, 38, 39, 40, 55, 55, 64, 75; 27:17, 21, 46; 28:10; Mk 1:40; 3:27; 4:40; 5:7, 7, 31, 36; 6:22; 7:7; 8:2, 33, 34, 38; 9:19, 24, 37, 37, 37, 39, 42; 10:14, 18, 21, 47, 48, 51; 11:24, 29, 30; 12:15; 13:9, 13; 14:6, 18, 18, 20, 27, 30, 34, 36, 37, 48, 49, 49, 62, 72; 15:34; Lk 1:19, 43, 44, 48, 49; 2:29; 4:7, 18, 18, 18, 23; 5:8, 12; 6:22, 42, 46, 46, 47, 47; 7:23, 44, 45, 47; 8:28, 28, 45, 46, 46, 50; 9:23, 24, 26, 44, 48, 48, 48, 59, 61; 10:16, 16, 16, 16, 22, 40; 11:7, 18, 23, 23, 23, 23, 29, 30, 30; 12:8, 9, 13, 14, 50, 52; 13:16, 34, 35; 14:26, 27, 33; 15:19, 29, 29; 16:2, 4; 17:10; 18:5, 5, 13, 16, 19, 22, 38, 39, 41; 19:22, 27; 20:3, 24; 21:13, 17, 34; 22:19, 21, 28, 29, 32, 34, 34, 37, 37, 42, 48, 52, 53, 61, 67; 23:14, 28, 42, 43; 24:39, 39, 44, 47; Jn 1:33, 33, 48; 2:4, 17; 3:12, 15; 4:7, 9, 10, 15, 20, 21, 29, 34, 39, 48; 5:7, 7, 11, 11, 24, 30, 32, 32, 34, 36, 36, 37, 38, 39, 40, 41, 43, 46, 46; 6:26, 27, 35, 35, 36, 36, 37, 37, 38, 39, 44, 44, 44, 45, 47, 56, 57, 57, 57, 62, 64, 65, 65; 7:6, 7, 16, 19, 28, 29, 33, 34, 34, 36, 36, 37, 38; 8:12, 14, 15, 16, 16, 18, 19, 21, 26, 28, 28, 29, 29, 29, 37, 40, 42, 45, 46, 46, 49, 50, 54; 9:4, 11; 10:8, 9, 14, 15, 17, 18, 18, 25, 26, 27, 28, 29, 29, 32, 37, 38, 38; 11:15, 25, 26, 41, 42, 42; 12:26, 26, 27, 40, 40, 44, 44, 45, 45, 46, 47, 47, 48, 49, 49, 50, 50; 13:8, 13, 18, 20, 20, 20, 21, 31, 31, 32, 33, 33, 36, 36, 36, 38, 38; 14:1, 3, 6, 9, 10, 10, 10, 11, 11, 12, 15, 19, 20, 21, 21, 23, 24, 24, 28, 28, 30, 31; 15:4, 4, 5, 5, 6, 7, 9, 10, 14, 15, 16, 18, 20, 20, 21, 21, 23, 24, 25, 26, 27; 16:3, 5, 5, 9, 10, 14, 14, 15, 16, 16, 17, 17, 19, 19, 20, 20, 23, 27, 32, 32, 33; 17:4, 5, 6, 6, 8, 8, 9, 10, 11, 18, 20, 21, 21, 22, 23, 23, 23, 24, 24, 24, 24, 25, 26; 18:9, 11, 21, 21, 34, 39, 39; 19:10, 11, 11; 20:15, 17, 21, 29, 29; 21:15, 16, 17, 19, 22; Ac 1:8; 2:25, 25, 28, 28; 3:22; 4:10; 7:2, 7, 28, 37, 42, 49, 49; 8:19, 24, 24, 31; 9:4, 11, 16, 17; 10:28, 28, 29, 29, 30, 31; 11:5, 12, 12; 12:8, 11, 11; 13:16; 15:7, 13; 18:10; 20:19, 22, 23, 24, 25, 26, 26, 34; 21:39; 22:1, 5, 6, 7, 7, 9, 10, 13, 13, 14, 18, 18, 21, 27, 28; 23:3, 11, 18, 18, 19, 22; 24:4, 10, 13, 18, 18, 19, 20; 25:5, 9, 11, 11, 14, 15; 26:3, 7, 13, 14, 14, 18, 21, 21, 22, 28; 27:21, 23; 28:18, 18, 27, 27; Ro 1:8; 3:7, 8; 7:2, 7, 8, 10, 10, 11, 11, 14, 17, 17, 20, 23, 23, 23, 24; 9:20; 10:20, 20, 21, 21; 11:3, 13, 19; 14:11; 15:3, 15, 17, 17, 19, 24, 29, 30, 30, 30, 30; 16:2, 4, 7, 13, 19; 1Co 1:11, 17; 3:10; 4:1, 3, 4, 19; 7:10, 25, 29; 9:16, 17, 17, 19; 10:33; 11:2, 22, 24, 25; 12:31; 13:12; 14:11, 11, 21; 15:1, 3, 10, 10, 12, 51; 16:4, 6, 7, 9, 11, 17, 18, 20; 2Co 1:16; 2:2, 3, 5, 9, 12; 7:4, 4, 7, 7, 11, 14; 8:23; 9:4, 5; 11:1, 1, 9, 9, 10, 16, 24, 27, 32; 12:1, 1, 6, 7, 7, 7, 9, 11, 11, 13, 15, 21; 13:3, 10; Gal 1:2, 12, 15, 15, 16, 16, 22, 24; 2:2, 6, 7, 8, 9, 9, 20, 20, 20; 3:2, 24; 4:12, 14, 14, 14, 14, 15, 17, 21; 5:11, 21; 6:14, 14, 17; Eph 3:2, 3, 13; 4:17; 6:19, 19; Php 1:12, 16, 16, 17, 19, 19, 20, 21, 23, 26, 27, 30; 2:2, 18, 19, 19, 22, 23, 25, 27, 30; 3:9, 12, 12; 4:3, 8, 9, 9, 9, 10, 10, 10, 13, 14, 15, 18, 19, 21; Col 1:25, 29; 2:1; 4:7, 10, 11; 2Th 3:17; 1Ti 1:11, 12, 12, 13, 13, 14, 16, 16; 2Ti 1:8, 8, 11, 13, 15, 16, 16, 17, 18; 2:2, 3; 3:11; 4:6, 8, 8, 8, 10, 11, 11, 14, 16, 16, 17, 17, 17, 18, 18; Tit 3:12; Phm 1:13, 13, 16, 17, 17, 18, 19, 20, 20, 22, 22; Heb 2:13; 3:10; 8:11; 10:5, 7; 13:6, 23; Jas 1:13; 2:5; 2Pe 1:14; 3Jn 3, 3; Rev 1:10, 12, 17; 2:3, 4, 5, 13, 13, 26; 3:3, 4, 8, 18, 20, 21; 4:1; 5:5; 7:13, 14; 10:4, 8, 9, 11; 15:2; 16:15; 17:1, 1, 3, 15; 19:10; 21:5, 8, 9, 9, 10, 10, 15; 22:1, 6, 8, 9, 10, 12

MINE (81)

Ge 14:24; 16:5; 25:33; 30:13; 31:8, 43; Ex 13:2; Nu 3:12, 13, 13, 41, 45; 8:17; Dt 11:18; 2Sa 14:30; 1Ki 2:15; 3:20, 22, 22, 26; 20:3; 2Ch 7:20; Job 28:1, 4; 34:33; 41:11; Ps 16:5; 50:10, 12; 55:20; 60:7, 7; 73:26; 108:8, 8; 119:57; Pr 8:14, 18; SS 2:16; 6:3; Isa 8:20; 29:13; 43:1; 51:16; 56:3; 66:2; Jer 15:10; 27:5; 44:28; La 1:12; Eze 16:8; 18:4; 29:3, 9; 35:11; 43:8; Hos 2:20; Am 9:12; Mic 7:1; Hag 2:8, 8; Mt 10:37, 37, 38; 18:20; 20:23; 26:39; Mk 10:40; 14:36; Lk 4:6; 11:6; 15:24; 19:27; 22:42; Jn 12:30; 16:15; 17:10; Ac 15:17; 20:34; Php 3:17; Rev 3:5

MUST (1443)

Ge 3:1, 3; 4:7; 7:3; 9:4, 5, 5, 6, 7; 17:10, 10, 11, 12, 13; 24:40; 30:16; 31:30; 34:22; 38:8; 43:14, 23; 45:28; 50:25; Ex 1:10; 2:6; 3:3, 18; 5:1, 11, 18; 8:27; 10:9, 25, 26; 12:3, 5, 6, 8, 9, 10, 14, 15, 16, 19, 20, 24, 42, 46, 46, 47; 13:5, 7, 8, 12, 13, 13; 16:29; 19:13, 13, 13, 21, 22; 20:5, 23, 24; 21:1, 6, 6, 9, 12, 14, 15, 16, 17, 19, 19, 20, 22, 23, 23, 24, 28, 29, 29, 32, 34, 35, 36; 22:1, 3, 3, 4, 5, 6, 9, 9, 11, 11, 12, 13, 14, 16, 17, 18, 19, 20, 26, 29, 30; 23:14, 15, 16, 17, 18, 19, 19, 24, 25; 24:1, 2; 25:9, 15, 17, 30, 36, 36, 38; 26:2, 2, 7, 8, 16, 17, 35, 35; 27:8, 17, 19, 21; 28:5, 6, 38, 43; 29:15, 29, 34, 36; 30:2, 7, 8, 8, 10, 12, 14, 15, 15, 20, 32, 32, 32, 37; 31:11, 14, 15, 15, 16; 34:13, 14, 17, 20, 20, 21, 22, 23, 25, 26, 26; 35:1; Lev 1:2, 9, 12, 13, 15, 16; 2:1, 4, 5, 5, 7, 12; 3:1, 3, 6, 9, 14, 17; 4:3, 4, 7, 8, 10, 12, 14, 15, 18, 19, 21, 23, 26, 28, 31, 32, 35; 5:5, 7, 8, 11, 11, 12, 15, 15, 15, 16, 18, 18, 18; 6:4, 5, 6, 6, 9, 9, 10, 11, 12, 12, 12, 13, 13, 14, 16, 20, 21, 21, 21, 22, 23, 25, 27, 27, 28, 28, 30; 7:2, 6, 12, 13, 14, 15, 17, 19, 20, 21, 23, 25, 26, 27, 33; 8:32, 35; 10:9, 9, 11, 13, 15; 11:11, 13, 25, 28, 32, 33, 35, 40, 44, 45; 12:3, 4, 4, 4, 5, 6, 6, 8; 13:2, 3, 7, 8, 9, 11, 13, 15, 16, 19, 20, 22, 25, 25, 27, 28, 30, 31, 33, 33, 34, 36, 36, 39, 43, 44, 45, 45, 46, 49, 51, 52, 52, 55, 55, 57, 58; 14:2, 2, 8, 8, 9, 10, 19, 21, 22, 22, 23, 35, 36, 39, 40, 41, 44, 45, 45, 47, 57; 15:8, 12, 12, 13, 13, 14, 16, 17, 18, 21, 28, 29; 16:3, 3, 4, 4, 5, 7, 14, 15, 19, 20, 23, 23, 24, 25, 26, 28, 29; 17:4, 7, 12, 13, 14, 15; 18:3, 4, 6, 7, 21, 23, 23, 26, 26; 19:2, 3, 3, 6, 6, 8, 19, 20, 21, 34, 36, 36, 37; 20:2, 9, 10, 11, 12, 14, 15, 15, 16, 16, 17, 18, 22, 25, 25, 26, 27; 21:4, 5, 6, 6, 6, 7, 7, 8, 8, 9, 10, 11, 12, 13, 14, 14, 23; 22:3, 6, 14, 21, 22, 25, 27, 28, 29, 31, 32; 23:3, 3, 6, 7, 8, 8, 12, 13, 13, 14, 17, 19, 21, 21, 24, 25, 27, 31, 31, 32, 35, 36, 36, 38, 38, 41, 41, 42; 24:3, 3, 4, 5, 8, 9, 16, 17, 18, 19, 20, 21, 21; 25:2, 8, 12, 13, 14, 23, 24, 31, 33, 42, 46, 53, 53, 54; 26:2; 27:11, 13, 14, 15, 18, 19, 23, 25, 28, 29, 30, 31, 33; Nu 1:50, 50, 50; 3:10; 4:5, 6, 6, 7, 8, 9, 10, 10, 11, 12, 13, 13, 14, 14, 15, 15, 19, 19, 20, 25, 27, 32; 5:7, 8, 15, 16, 17, 18, 21, 30; 6:3, 3, 3, 3, 5, 5, 7, 9, 10, 11, 12, 12, 13, 17, 21; 8:10, 11, 24, 24, 25; 9:11, 11, 12, 12, 12, 14; 10:6, 9, 30; 14:25, 34; 15:3, 4, 5, 9, 12, 13, 14, 19, 24, 24, 27, 30, 31, 35, 35, 38, 40; 16:6, 22, 38; 17:3; 18:3, 4, 5, 7, 10, 10, 15, 23, 28, 28; 19:5, 6, 7, 8, 10, 12, 18, 18, 19, 19, 21; 20:8, 10; 23:26; 26:56; 27:7, 11; 28:3, 5, 7, 9, 13, 14, 15, 16, 18, 19, 22, 25, 26; 29:1, 2, 3, 5, 6, 7, 7, 8, 9, 11, 12, 13, 14, 16, 18, 19, 21, 22, 24, 25, 27, 28, 30, 31, 33, 34, 35, 36, 37, 38, 39; 30:2, 2, 9; 31:19, 19, 23, 23, 23, 24; 32:29, 30; 33:52, 52, 54; 35:6, 12, 16, 16, 17, 18, 18, 19, 21, 24, 25, 25, 30, 31, 31, 34; 36:7, 8, 9; Dt 1:16, 27; 3:18; 4:5, 14; 5:9, 14, 32; 6:5, 6, 13, 13, 14, 17, 21; 7:2, 5, 16, 25, 26; 10:19, 20, 20; 11:1, 29, 32; 12:1, 2, 5, 11, 12, 14, 16, 17, 18, 23, 27, 27, 31; 13:5, 5, 9, 9, 9, 14, 15, 16, 16; 14:3, 22; 15:1, 2, 2, 2, 12, 17, 19, 20, 21, 23; 16:2, 5, 6, 8, 10, 13, 16, 16, 16, 17, 19, 21; 17:5, 6, 7, 10, 11, 12, 12, 15, 16, 16, 16, 17, 17, 18, 19; 18:4, 13, 15, 20; 19:2, 9, 12, 15, 17, 18, 21; 20:12, 17; 21:2, 3, 4, 4, 5, 6, 7, 12, 13, 14, 17, 19, 20, 21, 23, 23; 22:5, 5, 8, 12, 15, 16, 17, 18, 21, 21, 22, 24, 24, 27, 29, 29, 30; 23:6, 10, 11, 13, 13, 14, 14; 24:4, 5, 5, 7, 7, 16, 16, 17, 17; 25:5, 5, 7, 9, 12, 13, 14; 26:5, 12, 13, 16, 18; 27:6, 8, 12, 13, 14; 28:14; 30:12, 13; 31:11, 23; 32:50; Jos 1:2, 14; 2:18; 4:5; 6:17, 19; 7:14, 14, 14; 9:20; 20:4, 5, 6, 6; Jdg 5:10; 6:10, 30; 11:36; 13:4, 5, 7, 14; 14:3, 13; 15:18; 20:7; 21:5, 17; Ru 3:14; 1Sa 1:14; 2:16, 24; 13:14; 14:38, 44; 18:17; 19:2; 20:22, 26, 26; 21:14; 26:20; 27:12; 2Sa 2:26; 12:6; 14:14, 24; 15:14; 17:16, 29; 18:3; 23:7; 1Ki 1:42; 2:2; 10:8; 11:22; 13:9, 17; 14:5; 18:5; 20:42, 42; 21:19; 22:16; 2Ki 1:11; 9:8, 20; 11:5, 6, 7, 8; 12:7; 14:6, 6; 17:36, 37, 39; 22:13; 23:21; 1Ch 15:12; 21:3; 22:5; 28:3; 2Ch 8:11; 9:7; 18:15; 19:9, 10; 23:4, 6, 7; 25:4, 4; 28:13; 32:12, 13; 34:21; Ezr 4:21, 22; 6:3, 8; 7:25; 10:12; Ne 5:5, 8, 11; 10:39; Est 1:15; 3:13; 4:16; Job 7:11, 11; 14:3; 16:22; 17:3; 19:22; 20:2, 10; 22:6, 7, 9; 24:1, 3, 4, 5, 10; 32:16, 20; 34:33; 36:10; 38:3, 11; 40:7; 42:4; Ps 13:2; 38:15; 42:9; 43:2; 49:10; 73:22; 75:8; 81:9, 9; 82:7; 97:7; 119:84; Pr 1:31, 31; 5:14; 12:1; 16:10; 19:19; Ecc 2:18, 21; 3:20; 6:6; 11:9; Isa 1:5; 6:11; 29:9; 38:10; 40:20, 22; 64:12; Jer 1:7; 4:21, 21; 5:19; 9:19; 10:19; 12:4; 23:33; 25:28; 27:8; 28:9, 16; 30:11; 34:14; 35:6; 36:16; 38:4; 46:28; 47:7; 49:12, 12, 12; 51:49; La 4:21; 5:9; Eze 2:7; 4:14; 16:21, 45; 18:13, 13; 20:39; 23:35, 36; 24:16, 23, 23; 34:18, 18; 42:14, 14, 14; 44:2, 2, 10, 12, 13, 17, 17, 18, 18, 19, 19, 20, 20, 21, 24, 24, 25, 27, 30; 45:1, 10, 13, 16, 21; 46:7, 7, 7, 8, 8, 9, 9, 9, 9, 13, 14, 15, 18; Da 2:3; 3:11; 8:17; 9:2; 10:20; Hos 3:3; 8:6; 10:2, 11; 13:16; Joel 2:17; Am 3:2; Jnh 3:8; Mic 4:10; Hab 1:2, 3, 15; Hag 2:3; Zec 8:16; 13:3; Mt 3:15, 15; 4:4, 10; 5:33; 9:17; 10:18; 12:36; 14:2; 15:4; 16:24; 17:10, 17, 17; 19:16, 20; 20:26, 27; 22:21, 37; 23:11; 24:6, 16, 17, 18, 44; 26:24, 54, 66, 73; 28:13; Mk 1:38; 6:14; 7:10; 8:34; 9:11, 12, 19, 19, 35, 50; 10:38, 43, 44; 12:17, 30; 13:7, 10, 14, 15, 16; 14:21, 70; Lk 1:15, 22; 2:23; 4:8, 43; 5:38; 6:36; 9:22, 23, 41; 10:25, 27; 12:40; 13:33; 14:26; 15:23; 17:8, 25, 31, 31; 18:1; 19:5; 20:25; 21:9, 21; 22:22, 58, 59; 24:7, 18, 44, 46; Jn 3:7, 14, 30, 30; 4:19, 24, 48; 6:30; 9:4, 17; 10:1, 16; 11:57; 12:24, 26, 26; 13:33; 15:27; 18:23; Ac 1:21, 21; 2:38; 3:18, 21; 5:29; 7:51; 9:16; 12:15; 14:22; 15:5, 29; 16:30; 19:21; 23:11; 26:20; Ro 6:19; 8:17, 25; 11:18; 13:5; 14:3, 3; 15:1, 25; 1Co 3:10; 4:2; 5:5, 13; 6:12, 20; 7:10, 11, 12, 13, 16, 16, 17, 34, 39; 8:9; 9:24; 10:8, 31; 11:19; 12:1; 14:26, 27, 27, 28, 30; 15:25, 53; 16:14, 18; 2Co 5:10; 8:8; 9:7; 10:7, 11; 11:30; 13:1; Gal 1:20; 3:12; 5:3, 11; Eph 4:23, 24; 5:24, 25, 33, 33; 6:9; Php 1:27; 2:12; 3:2, 16; Col 1:23; 2:6, 18; 3:12, 13, 13, 14, 18, 19, 20, 22; 4:1; 1Ti 3:2, 2, 2, 2, 2, 3, 3, 4, 6, 7, 8, 8, 8, 9, 9, 11, 11, 11, 12, 12, 15; 5:9, 10, 16; 2Ti 1:8; 2:19, 24, 24, 24; 3:5, 14; Tit 1:6, 6, 6, 7, 7, 7, 8, 8, 8, 8, 9, 11, 14; 2:2, 3, 3, 4, 7, 9, 9, 10, 15; 3:2, 2, 14; Heb 2:1; 3:7, 13, 15; 4:7, 13; 5:12; 7:12; 8:3; 11:6; 12:20; Jas 1:27; 5:7, 8; 1Pe 1:15, 16, 17; 2:2, 18; 3:1, 7, 15, 16; 4:1, 15, 17, 17; 2Pe 1:20; 3:8; 1Jn 2:24; 3:18, 23; 4:21, 21; Jude 3, 5, 17, 20; Rev 4:1; 10:11; 11:5; 13:15; 14:10

MY (4300)

Ge 2:23; 4:13, 14, 23; 6:3; 9:12, 13, 13, 15, 17, 26; 12:13, 13; 14:21, 24; 15:2, 2, 3, 3; 16:2, 8; 17:4, 13, 19, 21; 18:3, 4, 12, 12, 17, 27, 30; 19:2, 2, 2, 7, 8, 18, 19, 20; 20:5, 5, 9, 11, 12, 13, 13, 15; 21:10, 23, 23, 30; 22:7, 8, 16; 23:4, 9, 11, 13; 24:3, 4, 4, 4, 6, 7, 7, 7, 7, 8, 12, 12, 12, 14, 14, 24, 24, 27, 27, 35, 36, 36, 36, 37, 40, 40, 40, 41, 42, 42, 44, 47, 48, 48, 48, 49, 49, 54, 56, 56, 56, 65; 25:32; 26:5, 7, 24, 24; 27:1, 2, 4, 8, 11, 12, 18, 18, 20, 20, 24, 25, 25, 26, 27, 34, 36, 36, 38, 41; 28:21, 21; 29:14, 18, 21, 21, 32, 32, 34; 30:3, 6, 8, 15, 15, 16, 18, 18, 20, 23, 26, 26, 26, 30, 32, 33; 31:5, 11, 26, 28, 30, 35, 35, 36, 39, 41, 42, 42, 42, 42, 43, 43, 43, 50, 53; 32:4, 5, 9, 9, 9, 9, 10, 11, 11, 12, 30; 33:8, 11, 13, 15; 34:8, 11, 12; 35:3; 37:7, 16, 33, 35; 38:17, 25, 26, 26; 39:8, 14, 15, 18; 40:9, 11, 15, 16, 16; 41:9, 13, 16, 24, 33, 40, 40, 51, 51, 52; 42:10, 28, 28, 36, 37, 38, 38; 43:29; 44:2, 5, 16, 16, 17, 18, 19, 22, 27, 27, 29, 30, 30, 32, 32, 33, 34; 45:3, 9, 12, 13, 28; 46:30; 47:1, 6, 9, 29, 30; 48:5, 15, 15, 15, 16, 16, 16, 19, 22; 49:3, 3, 4, 4, 6, 29, 32; 50:5, 5, 5, 25; Ex 3:7, 10, 15, 15; 4:18, 18, 22; 5:1, 1; 6:1, 3, 5, 7, 12; 7:3, 5, 16; 8:1, 8, 20, 23; 9:1, 13, 16, 16, 17, 27, 27, 29; 10:1, 3, 16, 17; 15:2, 2, 2, 2, 2, 9, 9; 16:4, 28; 17:9, 15; 18:4, 4; 19:5, 5, 6, 10; 20:6, 6, 26; 21:5, 5, 5, 14; 22:24, 31; 23:13, 14, 20, 21, 21, 22, 23, 27; 24:12; 25:3, 22; 28:1, 41; 29:43, 44; 30:31; 31:13, 17; 32:10, 34; 33:17, 19, 19, 20, 22, 22, 23, 23; 34:27; Lev 10:19; 14:35; 15:31; 18:4, 4, 5, 26, 30; 19:3, 12, 19, 30, 30, 37; 20:3, 3, 8, 22, 26; 21:23; 22:2, 3, 31, 32; 25:18, 18, 21, 42, 55; 26:2, 2, 3, 3, 9, 12, 14, 15, 15, 28, 33, 40, 41, 42, 43, 43, 44, 45; Nu 6:27; 9:3; 10:30; 11:12, 12, 23, 23, 28, 29; 12:7, 7, 11; 14:22, 24; 15:40; 16:28; 20:12, 18, 24; 22:18, 34, 34; 23:10, 11; 24:10, 14; 25:11, 11, 11, 12; 27:14, 14; 28:2, 2; Dt 1:14; 4:5, 10; 5:10, 10, 29, 31; 9:15; 10:10; 12:28; 18:19; 22:16, 17; 25:7; 26:5, 13, 14; 29:19; 31:17, 17, 18, 20, 27, 29; 32:2, 2, 2, 21, 21, 22, 23, 34, 39, 40, 41, 41, 42, 42, 51; 33:17; Jos 1:2, 2, 6, 2:12, 13, 13; 7:11, 19, 21; 9:23; 14:7, 8, 8, 8, 9; 15:16; 23:3; 24:15; Jdg 1:7, 12; 2:1, 2, 20; 4:18; 5:3, 9, 21; 6:15, 15, 18; 7:13, 18; 8:2, 5, 19, 23; 9:11, 15, 16, 18; 11:7, 13, 31, 35, 35, 37; 12:3; 13:11, 18; 14:12, 16, 16, 18, 18; 15:7; 16:13, 17, 17, 17, 26, 28; 17:3, 13; 18:24, 24; 19:23, 23, 24; 20:4, 5; Ru 1:12, 13, 16, 16; 2:2, 8, 8; 3:1, 9, 10, 11, 18; 4:6, 10; 1Sa 1:11, 11, 15, 27; 2:1, 1, 24, 28, 28, 29, 29, 30, 31, 35; 3:6, 12, 16; 9:5, 16, 16, 17, 21; 10:2; 12:2, 5, 23; 13:11; 14:24, 29, 38, 39; 15:21, 25, 30; 16:1, 22; 17:34, 58; 18:17, 18, 18, 21, 25; 19:3, 17; 20:1, 8, 9, 12, 13, 15; 21:2, 5, 15; 22:3, 8, 8, 12, 15, 23; 23:12, 17, 17; 24:8, 10, 10, 11, 11, 15, 16, 21, 21; 25:11, 11, 24, 26, 33; 26:17, 17, 18, 19, 19, 19, 21, 21, 23, 24, 24, 25; 28:2, 21; 29:8, 9; 30:13, 15, 23; 2Sa 1:9, 10, 26; 2:7; 3:8, 13, 14, 18, 28; 4:9; 5:2, 20; 6:9, 21; 7:5, 6, 7, 8, 8, 10, 11, 13, 14, 15, 18, 25, 29; 9:7, 11; 11:11; 13:10, 11, 12, 13, 24, 25, 26, 28; 14:6, 7, 9, 11, 15, 15, 15, 18, 19, 24, 31; 15:27; 16:3, 9, 11; 18:5, 12, 18, 20, 22, 31, 33, 33, 33, 33, 33; 19:4, 4, 4, 12, 12, 12, 13, 19, 26, 26, 26, 28, 28, 29, 30, 35, 37, 37, 37; 20:6, 9; 22:2, 2, 2, 3, 3, 3, 3, 3, 3, 4, 7, 7, 7, 18, 21, 22, 25, 29, 29, 30, 33, 33, 37, 38, 39, 40, 44, 47, 47, 49, 49; 23:2, 5, 5; 24:17, 21, 22, 24; 1Ki 1:12, 13, 13, 17, 17, 20, 21, 24, 27, 30, 31, 33, 33, 35, 36, 48; 2:5, 15, 17, 17, 20, 22, 24, 24, 26, 31, 32, 38, 43, 44; 3:6, 7, 7, 11, 14, 17, 20, 20, 21, 21, 26; 5:3, 4, 5, 5, 5, 6, 9, 9; 6:12, 12, 13; 8:15, 16, 16, 16, 16, 17, 18, 20, 24, 25, 26, 28, 28, 28, 52, 59; 9:3, 4, 4, 6, 7, 13; 10:6, 7; 11:11, 11, 13, 13, 21, 32, 33, 33, 33, 34, 34, 36, 36, 38, 38, 38; 12:5, 9, 10, 10, 11, 11, 14, 14, 24; 13:6, 30, 31; 14:7, 8, 8; 15:19; 16:2, 2, 2; 17:9, 12, 18, 18, 20, 21; 18:5, 7, 9, 12, 13; 19:4, 4, 16, 20; 20:4, 6, 7, 9, 10, 32, 34, 34; 21:3, 20; 22:4, 4, 26, 49; 2Ki 1:13, 14; 2:12, 12, 19; 3:7, 7, 14; 4:1, 1, 13, 16, 19, 19, 24, 28, 28, 29; 5:3, 6, 15, 17, 18, 18, 20, 22; 6:5, 11, 12, 15, 21, 26, 28, 29; 8:5, 12; 9:7, 21, 32; 10:6, 9, 30; 13:14, 14; 14:9; 16:15; 17:13, 13; 18:23, 24, 27, 29, 34, 35; 19:23, 24, 28, 28, 31, 34, 34; 20:5, 6, 6, 15, 19; 21:7, 8, 8, 14, 15; 22:17, 17; 23:27, 27, 27; 1Ch 4:10; 11:2, 6; 12:17; 13:12; 14:11; 16:22; 17:4, 5, 6, 7, 7, 9, 10, 13, 13, 14, 14, 16, 19, 23, 25, 27; 21:3, 17, 17, 23; 22:5, 7, 8, 10, 10, 11; 28:2, 2, 2, 3, 4, 4, 4, 5, 6, 6, 7, 9, 20; 29:1, 2, 2, 3, 3, 3, 5, 14, 17, 19; 2Ch 1:8, 9, 11; 2:3, 4, 7, 8, 14; 6:4, 4, 5, 5, 5, 7, 8, 10, 15, 16, 16, 19, 19, 19, 40; 7:14, 14, 14, 16, 16, 16, 17, 20; 8:11; 9:5, 6; 10:5, 9, 10, 10, 11, 11, 14, 14; 11:4; 12:7; 16:3; 18:3, 13, 25; 25:16, 18, 19; 29:11; 32:10, 13, 15, 15, 17; 33:7, 8; 34:25; Ezr 4:21; 6:8, 10; 7:13, 14, 28; 9:3, 3, 5, 5, 5, 5, 6, 6; Ne 1:2, 6, 6, 9, 9, 11; 2:3, 5, 6, 7, 10, 11, 12, 14, 16, 18; 4:16, 23, 23; 5:10, 10, 13, 14, 15, 16, 17, 18, 19; 6:8, 11, 11, 14; 7:2, 5; 13:14, 14, 19, 22, 28, 29, 31, 31; Est 4:16; 5:7, 8; 6:10; 7:3, 3, 3, 3, 4, 8; 8:6, 6; Job 1:5, 8, 21; 2:3; 3:3, 10, 12, 24; 4:8, 12, 15, 15, 16; 5:3, 8, 27; 6:2, 2, 4, 7, 8, 8, 12, 15, 21, 22, 23, 26, 29; 7:5, 5, 6, 7, 11, 11, 13, 13, 16, 21, 21; 9:17, 18, 20, 21, 25, 27, 27, 30, 31, 35; 10:1, 1, 6, 6, 10, 11, 12, 14, 15, 16, 18; 11:4; 12:4; 13:3, 6, 6, 14, 14, 15, 18, 23, 23, 26, 27, 27, 27; 14:14, 16, 16, 17, 17; 15:17; 16:4, 4, 6, 7, 8, 9, 10, 13, 16, 16, 17, 18, 18, 19, 19, 20, 20; 17:1, 3, 6, 7, 7, 11, 11, 11, 13, 14, 14, 14, 15, 16; 19:4, 5, 5, 8, 8, 9, 9, 10, 12, 13, 13, 14, 14, 15, 16, 17, 17, 17, 19, 20, 21, 22, 23, 25, 26, 26, 27; 20:3; 21:4, 6; 23:2, 4, 4, 7, 12, 14, 16; 26:3; 27:2, 2, 4, 4, 5, 6, 6, 7, 7; 29:4, 4, 5, 6, 6, 7, 8, 18, 20, 21, 22, 23, 24; 30:1, 10, 11, 12, 12, 13, 13, 15, 16, 16, 17, 17, 18, 18, 23, 27, 30, 30, 31, 31; 31:1, 6, 7, 7, 9, 9, 10, 13, 15, 17, 18, 21, 22, 22, 24, 24, 25, 25, 27, 29, 31, 32, 33, 33, 34, 35, 35, 35, 35, 38; 32:10, 17, 17, 19, 20, 22; 33:8, 11, 28; 34:5, 6; 35:10; 36:3; 37:1; 38:2; 40:4, 4, 8; 42:3, 5, 6, 7, 8, 8, 8; Ps 2:6, 6, 7; 3:3, 3, 7, 7; 4:1, 1, 2; 5:1, 2, 2, 2, 3, 3, 8, 9; 6:2, 6, 6, 7, 7, 7, 8, 9, 9, 10; 7:1, 1, 3, 4, 5, 5, 6, 6, 10; 9:1, 3, 4, 6; 13:2, 2, 2, 3, 3, 4, 4; 14:4; 16:2, 3, 5, 5, 7, 9, 9, 9, 10; 17:1, 1, 1, 3, 3, 5; 18:1, 2, 2, 2, 2, 2, 2, 2, 2, 3, 6, 6, 6, 17, 20, 21, 24, 28, 28, 28, 29, 32, 36, 37, 38, 39, 39, 43, 46, 46, 48, 48; 19:12, 14, 14, 14, 14; 22:1, 1, 1, 2, 2, 9, 10, 10, 12, 14, 14, 14, 15, 15, 16, 16, 17, 17, 18, 18, 19, 19, 20, 22, 25; 23:1, 3, 5, 5, 5, 6; 25:1, 2, 2, 2, 5, 7, 11, 15, 15, 17, 18, 18, 20, 21; 26:2, 6, 6; 27:1, 2, 3, 4, 6, 6, 7, 8, 8, 9, 9, 10, 11; 28:1, 2, 2, 6, 7, 7, 7, 7; 30:1, 2, 2, 9, 11, 11, 12; 31:2, 3, 3, 4, 5, 7, 7, 8, 9, 9, 9, 10, 10, 11, 11, 11, 13, 13, 14, 15, 21, 22, 22; 32:3, 4, 5, 5, 5, 7; 34:4, 6, 6, 11; 35:2, 3, 10, 13, 14, 14, 17, 19, 19, 19, 23, 23, 23, 23, 24, 24, 24, 26, 27; 38:3, 3, 3, 4, 5, 5, 6, 7, 8, 9, 10, 10, 11, 11, 11, 12, 15, 16, 16, 18, 19, 21, 22; 39:1, 3, 4, 4, 4, 5, 5, 7, 7, 8, 9, 12, 12, 12, 12; 40:1, 2, 5, 8, 8, 10, 11, 12, 12, 12, 14, 17, 17, 17; 41:5, 6, 9, 9, 11, 12; 42:3, 4, 5, 5, 6, 9, 9, 11, 11, 11; 43:1, 2, 2, 4, 4, 4, 5, 5, 5; 44:4, 4, 6, 6; 45:1, 1; 49:3, 3, 15; 50:5, 7, 7, 8, 16, 17, 17, 21, 23; 51:1, 2, 2, 3, 5, 6, 7, 8, 9, 9, 15; 53:4; 54:2, 2, 4, 5, 7, 7; 55:1, 1, 2, 3, 4, 12, 13, 13, 15, 17, 17, 19; 56:1, 2, 3, 6, 8, 8, 9, 9, 12, 13; 57:3, 6, 6, 7, 8, 8; 59:1, 4, 4, 9, 9, 10, 10, 11, 14, 16, 17, 17; 60:7, 7, 8, 8; 61:1, 1, 2, 3, 3, 5, 8; 62:1, 2, 2, 2, 4, 4, 5, 6, 6, 6, 7, 7, 7, 8; 63:1, 1, 1, 4; 64:1, 1; 66:15, 18, 18, 19, 20; 68:22, 23, 24; 69:1, 3, 3, 3, 4, 5, 7, 8, 13, 16, 18, 19, 20, 21; 70:2, 5, 5, 5; 71:1, 2, 3, 3, 4, 5, 6, 7, 7, 9, 9, 10, 12, 17; 73:2, 13, 23, 26, 26, 26, 28; 74:12; 77:6, 6, 10, 12; 78:1, 1; 81:8, 11, 13, 13, 14; 83:13; 84:2, 3, 3, 8, 10; 86:1, 2, 4, 6, 6, 12, 12; 87:7; 88:1, 2, 2, 3, 8, 9, 9, 9, 15, 18; 89:3, 20, 20, 24, 26, 26, 26, 27, 28, 30, 30, 31, 31, 33, 34, 35, 35, 37, 47, 50; 91:2, 2, 2, 14, 16; 92:11, 11, 11, 11, 15; 94:19, 22, 22; 95:9, 9, 9, 11, 11; 101:2, 2, 7, 8; 102:1, 1, 2, 3, 3, 4, 4, 5, 8, 9, 9, 9, 11, 23, 24, 24; 103:1, 3, 3, 5, 5; 104:1, 33, 33; 105:15; 108:1, 1, 2, 8, 8, 9, 9; 109:5, 20, 20, 22, 24, 26, 29; 110:1, 1; 111:1; 116:1, 3, 8, 8, 11, 14, 16, 18; 118:5, 13, 14, 14, 14, 21, 28, 28; 119:5, 6, 10, 11, 18, 26, 34, 35, 37, 39, 40, 43, 49, 50, 54, 54, 56, 58, 59, 63, 69, 74, 77, 81, 82, 88, 92, 93, 95, 98, 98, 99, 100, 103, 105, 105, 107, 108, 109, 111, 113, 114, 114, 114, 115, 115, 116, 121, 123, 131, 133, 136, 139, 145, 147, 149, 149, 152, 153, 154, 154, 154, 156, 159, 161, 169, 170, 171, 172, 174; 120:1, 1; 121:1, 2; 122:8; 123:1; 129:1, 1, 2, 2, 3; 130:2, 2, 5; 131:1, 1, 2; 132:4, 4, 12, 14, 17, 17; 137:5, 6, 6, 6; 138:1, 7, 7, 8; 139:1, 2, 5, 13, 13, 16, 19, 22, 23, 23; 140:6, 6, 7, 9; 141:2, 2, 3, 6, 8; 142:2, 2, 3, 5, 6, 6; 143:1, 1, 3, 7, 9, 10, 12, 12; 144:1, 2, 2, 2, 2, 7, 11; 145:1; 146:2, 2; Pr 1:8, 10, 15, 25, 30; 2:1; 3:1, 1, 11, 21; 4:1, 2, 3, 3, 4, 4, 4, 5, 10, 13, 20, 21; 5:1, 1, 1, 7, 12, 13, 20; 6:1, 20; 7:1, 1, 1, 2, 6, 14, 14, 16, 17, 19, 24, 24; 8:4, 8, 9, 10, 16, 19, 19, 32, 33, 34, 34; 9:5; 19:27; 20:9; 22:17; 23:15, 16, 19, 26, 26; 24:13, 21; 27:11, 11; 30:8; 31:2, 2, 2; Ecc 1:18, 18; 2:6, 7, 10, 15, 18, 19, 19, 20, 21; 7:23, 23, 27; 8:16; 12:12, 13; SS 1:4, 6, 6, 6, 7, 8, 9, 12, 13, 13, 15, 16; 2:2, 3, 6, 8, 9, 10, 10, 10, 13, 13, 14, 16, 17; 3:1, 2, 4, 4; 4:1, 7, 8, 9, 9, 9, 10, 10, 11, 12, 12, 12, 16, 16; 5:1, 1, 1, 1, 1, 1, 1, 1, 2, 2, 2, 2, 2, 2, 2, 2, 3, 3, 4, 4, 5, 5, 6, 7, 8, 10, 16, 16; 6:3, 3, 4, 9, 9, 12; 7:6, 10, 11, 12, 13; 8:1, 1, 2, 2, 3, 10, 12, 12, 13, 14; Isa 1:3, 12, 13, 24, 24; 3:12, 12, 14, 15; 5:1, 4, 5, 9, 13, 29; 6:5, 7, 8, 9, 9; 7:13; 8:3, 6, 16, 17, 20, 21; 10:5, 5, 6, 7, 8, 13, 13, 14, 24, 25, 25; 11:9; 12:2, 2, 2; 13:3, 12, 13; 14:13, 24, 25, 25, 26, 30; 15:5; 16:9, 11; 18:3, 4; 19:25, 25; 20:3; 21:3, 4, 4, 8, 8, 10; 22:4, 20; 24:16; 25:1; 26:20; 27:4, 6; 29:22; 30:1, 1, 1; 31:6; 32:18; 33:10, 13, 14; 34:1, 5; 36:8, 9, 12, 19, 20; 37:21, 24, 25, 29, 29, 32, 35, 35; 38:10, 11, 12, 12, 13, 14, 15, 16, 17, 20; 39:4, 8; 40:1, 25; 41:8, 8, 8, 10, 25; 42:1, 1, 1, 6, 6, 6, 8, 8, 8, 14, 19, 19, 19, 19; 43:6, 7, 9, 10, 10, 13, 19, 20, 20, 22, 23, 25, 27; 44:1, 1, 2, 2, 3, 3, 8, 8, 17, 19, 19, 20, 21, 26, 28; 45:4, 4, 11, 12, 12, 13, 13, 13, 23, 23, 23, 24; 46:5, 11, 13; 47:6, 7, 8; 48:3, 5, 5, 6, 9, 9, 9, 11, 11, 11, 12, 13, 13, 18; 49:1, 2, 3, 4, 4, 4, 5, 5, 6, 9, 11, 12, 16, 21; 50:1, 4, 6, 6, 6, 7, 8, 9, 9; 51:4, 4, 4, 5, 5, 6, 7, 8, 8, 15, 16, 16, 22; 52:4, 5, 5, 6, 6, 13; 53:2, 11; 54:8, 9, 10; 55:4, 4, 8, 8, 9, 9, 11; 56:2, 3, 3, 4, 5, 5, 7, 7, 7, 8, 9, 10; 57:13, 14, 16, 21; 58:1, 2; 59:21, 21; 60:7, 7, 10, 10, 13, 13, 21; 61:8, 10; 62:1, 10; 63:3, 3, 3, 3, 3, 4, 5, 6, 8; 65:2, 2, 3, 5, 6, 9, 10, 12, 13, 14, 15, 16, 18, 19, 22,

25; 66:1, 1, 2, 2, 4, 5, 18, 19, 19, 19, 20, 21, 22, 22; Jer 1:5, 9, 9, 12, 16; 2:3, 3, 7, 9, 11, 13, 27, 27, 31, 31, 32; 3:4, 4, 12, 15, 19, 22; 4:2, 2, 4, 17, 19, 19, 19, 22, 28, 28, 28; 5:7, 22, 23, 26, 31; 6:2, 11, 13, 14, 15, 18, 19, 19, 21, 26, 27; 7:10, 11, 12, 12, 14, 20, 20, 23, 24, 25, 26, 30, 30, 31, 33; 8:2, 7, 10, 11, 18, 18, 19, 21, 22; 9:1, 1, 3, 13, 13; 10:18, 19, 19, 19, 20, 20, 21; 11:3, 4, 5, 15, 15, 17, 18, 20; 12:3, 3, 7, 7, 7, 8, 9, 10, 13, 14, 16, 16, 16, 16; 13:2, 11, 11, 11, 11, 14, 17; 14:10, 10, 12, 14, 15, 17, 17, 17; 15:1, 4, 6, 7, 10, 13, 14, 15, 16, 18, 18, 19; 16:5, 5, 5, 11, 18, 18, 19, 19, 21; 17:1, 4, 14, 16, 16, 17, 21; 18:6, 13, 15, 17, 17, 22; 19:5; 20:9, 9, 10, 12, 13, 13, 14, 15, 17, 17, 18; 21:12; 22:5, 24; 23:1, 1, 2, 3, 9, 11, 13, 16, 16, 17, 22, 22, 25, 27, 28, 28, 29, 32, 32, 39; 24:7; 25:9, 14, 14, 15, 15, 27, 29; 26:2, 5; 27:5, 6, 15, 16; 29:9, 19, 21, 23, 23, 32; 30:3, 7, 9, 10, 19, 22; 31:1, 3, 4, 9, 14, 14, 18, 19, 19, 20, 20, 21, 22, 26, 33, 33, 36; 32:7, 8, 12, 29, 32, 33, 34, 35, 37, 37, 38; 33:5, 9, 20, 21, 21, 21, 22, 25, 25, 26; 34:15, 15, 16; 36:2, 31; 37:20; 38:9, 10, 25; 42:18; 43:10; 44:3, 4, 5, 6, 8, 10, 11, 26, 26, 26; 45:3; 46:27, 28; 48:31, 36; 49:13, 19, 19, 37, 38; 50:6, 8, 11, 21, 44, 44; 51:20, 24, 25, 45; La 1:9, 13, 13, 14, 14, 14, 15, 15, 16, 16, 18, 18, 19, 19, 20, 20, 20, 21, 21, 21, 22, 22, 22; 2:11, 11, 11; 3:4, 4, 8, 9, 13, 14, 16, 18, 19, 20, 24, 48, 48, 49, 51, 52, 54, 56, 56, 57, 58, 58, 58, 59, 60, 62; 4:3, 6; Eze 1:1; 2:2, 7; 3:2, 4, 10, 20, 23, 24; 5:2, 6, 7, 11, 12, 13, 13, 13; 6:8, 12; 7:3, 4, 8, 12, 14, 22, 22, 23, 25; 8:1, 6, 17; 11:9, 20, 20, 24; 12:7, 7, 7, 7, 13, 13, 25; 13:6, 9, 10, 15, 18, 19, 19, 20, 20, 21, 23; 14:5, 7, 10, 11, 13, 19; 15:8; 16:8, 8, 18, 21, 26, 27, 38, 42, 42, 62; 17:19, 19, 20, 20; 18:4, 9, 17, 19, 21; 20:3, 8, 8, 9, 10, 11, 12, 12, 13, 13, 13, 13, 14, 14, 16, 16, 16, 19, 19, 20, 21, 21, 21, 21, 22, 22, 22, 24, 24, 24, 28, 39, 40, 41, 44; 21:3, 5, 5, 12, 17, 17, 28, 30, 31, 31; 22:8, 8, 12, 13, 14, 19, 20, 21, 22, 24, 26, 26, 26, 26, 26, 28, 31, 31; 23:25, 38, 38, 39, 39, 41, 41, 48; 24:8, 13, 14, 18, 21; 25:3, 6, 7, 11, 13, 14, 14, 16, 17; 28:22, 22, 25, 25, 25; 30:14, 15, 24, 25; 32:3, 10, 32; 33:15, 22; 34:5, 8, 8, 8, 10, 10, 10, 11, 12, 15, 16, 17, 17, 19, 21, 22, 23, 24, 24, 25, 26, 26, 27, 29, 30, 31, 31, 31; 35:3, 11; 36:5, 5, 7, 8, 12, 18, 20, 21, 21, 22, 23, 23, 27, 27, 28, 32; 37:12, 13, 14, 19, 23, 24, 24, 24, 25, 25, 26, 27, 27, 28; 38:14, 16, 16, 17, 18, 19, 20, 23; 39:7, 7, 13, 17, 20, 21, 23, 24, 25, 25, 27, 28, 28, 29, 29; 43:3, 7, 7, 7, 8, 8; 44:4, 7, 7, 7, 7, 8, 9, 12, 12, 13, 15, 15, 16, 16, 16, 23, 24, 24, 24; 45:4, 8, 8, 9; 46:18; 47:3, 4, 4, 7; Da 1:10, 10; 2:5, 23, 26; 3:14, 15; 4:4, 5, 6, 8, 9, 10, 18, 19, 30, 30, 30, 34, 36, 36, 36, 36; 5:13, 15; 6:22, 26; 7:2, 7, 13, 15, 28, 28; 8:18, 18, 27; 9:4, 18, 18, 19, 20, 20, 20; 10:8, 8, 9, 10, 13, 16, 16, 16, 17, 17, 18, 19; 12:8; Hos 1:2, 9, 9, 10; 2:1, 2, 4, 4, 7, 10, 16, 16, 19, 23, 23; 3:3; 4:4, 6, 6, 11; 5:10, 11, 15; 6:5, 5, 5, 7, 10, 11; 7:8, 12, 13; 8:1, 1, 4, 5, 12, 13; 9:8, 9, 15, 17; 10:12; 11:1, 4, 5, 7, 8, 8, 9, 10; 12:8, 10; 13:11, 11; 14:4, 4, 7, 8; Joel 1:6, 7, 13; 2:1, 21, 26, 27, 27, 28, 28, 29; 3:2, 2, 2, 3, 5, 5, 17, 21, 21, 21; Am 1:3, 6; 2:7, 9, 9, 11, 12; 3:7, 10; 5:23; 7:2, 8, 15, 15, 16; 8:2; 9:14; Ob 16, 16, 19; Jnh 1:2, 12; 2:2, 5, 6, 7, 7, 9, 9; Mic 1:9; 2:7, 8; 3:2, 3, 5; 4:6, 8; 5:15; 6:3, 5, 5; 7:1, 7, 8, 8, 9, 9, 9, 10, 10, 10; Na 1:12; Hab 1:12, 12; 2:1, 1, 2; 3:16, 16, 18, 19; Zep 1:4, 6; 2:8, 9, 12; 3:7, 8, 8, 8, 10, 11, 19; Hag 1:4, 8, 9; 2:5, 23, 23; Zec 1:6, 9, 14, 15, 15, 16; 2:8, 9, 11; 3:7, 7, 7, 7, 8; 4:4, 5, 6, 13; 5:4, 4; 6:4, 8, 15; 8:2, 7, 8, 11, 14, 15; 9:7, 8, 8, 13, 13, 13; 10:2, 3, 12, 12, 12; 11:4, 10, 11, 11, 12, 12, 14; 12:9; 13:5, 5, 7, 7, 9, 9; 14:5; Mal 1:2, 6, 7, 7, 11, 11, 11, 12, 14; 2:2, 2, 4, 5, 5; 3:1, 7, 10, 17, 17; 4:2, 4; Mt 2:6, 15; 3:17; 4:19; 5:11, 36; 7:21, 24, 26; 8:6, 8, 8, 9, 9, 9, 20, 20, 21; 9:9, 18; 10:18, 32, 33, 42; 11:10, 27, 29, 30; 12:18, 18, 18, 48, 48, 49, 50, 50; 13:12, 14, 41, 41; 15:13, 22; 16:17, 18, 24, 27, 28; 17:5, 15; 18:5, 10, 14, 19, 35; 19:28, 28, 29; 20:7, 15, 21, 23, 28; 21:13, 37; 22:44, 44; 24:5, 35, 48; 25:13, 21, 23, 27, 34, 40, 45; 26:12, 18, 18, 24, 26, 28, 29, 29, 38, 39, 42, 46, 50, 53; 27:46, 46; 28:10; Mk 1:2, 11, 17; 2:5, 14; 3:33, 33, 34, 35; 4:12, 25; 5:30; 6:23; 7:27; 8:34, 35, 38, 38; 9:7, 17, 37, 37, 39; 10:29, 39, 39, 45; 11:17; 12:6, 33, 33, 33, 33, 36, 36; 13:6, 9, 31; 14:8, 14, 21, 22, 24, 34, 42; 15:34, 34; 16:17; Lk 1:18, 20, 25, 43, 44, 47, 76; 2:49; 3:22; 5:27, 32; 6:47; 7:6, 7, 8, 8, 8, 27, 44, 45, 46, 46; 8:18, 21, 21, 54; 9:23, 26, 26, 35, 35, 38, 38, 48, 48, 58, 58, 59, 59, 61; 10:22, 29, 40, 41; 12:13, 18, 19, 45, 49; 13:32, 33; 14:26, 26, 27, 33; 15:12, 18, 29; 16:7, 24, 27; 18:12; 19:8, 27, 46; 20:13, 42, 42; 21:8, 12, 33; 22:11, 15, 19, 22, 28, 29, 30; 23:46; 24:39, 39, 47, 49; Jn 1:43; 2:4, 16; 3:7, 31; 4:34, 49; 5:17, 24, 25, 30, 30, 31, 31, 36, 36, 43; 6:32, 40, 51, 54, 54, 55, 55, 56, 56; 7:8, 16, 17, 17; 8:16, 18, 19, 19, 28, 31, 31, 37, 38, 42, 49, 51, 54, 56; 9:11, 15, 30; 10:10, 14, 15, 15, 16, 17, 18, 18, 18, 25, 26, 27, 27, 29, 32, 37; 11:21, 32; 12:7, 26, 26, 27, 35, 48, 49; 13:6, 8, 9, 9, 18, 20, 31, 32, 35; 14:2, 7, 10, 10, 13, 14, 15, 20, 21, 21, 23, 24, 24, 26; 15:1, 7, 8, 8, 9, 10, 10, 11, 14, 15, 16, 23, 24; 16:23, 24, 26; 17:9, 10, 12, 13, 21, 24; 18:36, 36; 19:24, 24; 20:13, 17, 17, 17, 25, 25, 27, 27, 28, 28; 21:15, 16, 17; Ac 1:1; 2:17, 18, 18, 26, 26, 26, 27, 34, 34; 5:38; 7:34, 49, 49, 59; 8:19; 9:15, 15; 10:14, 30; 13:22, 33; 15:19; 16:15; 20:24, 31, 31, 34; 21:13; 22:1, 11; 23:6, 6; 24:10, 17, 18; 25:25; 26:2, 4, 4, 10, 13, 14, 16, 16; 28:19, 26, 26; Ro 1:9; 2:16; 3:7; 7:7, 13, 13, 14, 16, 18, 22, 23, 25, 25; 9:1, 2, 3, 3, 17, 17, 25, 25, 26; 10:1, 1, 21; 11:27; 15:17, 18, 20, 22, 23, 24, 28, 30; 16:3, 5, 5, 6, 7, 7, 10, 10, 11, 14, 15, 17, 21, 21, 22; 1Co 1:15; 2:4, 4; 3:6; 4:3, 4, 14, 16, 17; 5:12; 7:6, 17, 40; 9:1, 1, 3, 3, 15, 17, 18, 18, 27; 10:14, 29; 11:1, 24, 25; 13:3; 14:14, 21, 26; 15:31, 58; 16:6, 21, 21, 24; 2Co 1:13, 16, 16, 16, 17, 17, 18, 23; 2:3, 3, 13; 6:13, 16, 18; 7:4, 7, 12, 14; 8:23; 9:3; 10:1, 8, 9; 11:16, 26, 29; 12:3, 3, 5, 6, 6, 7, 9, 9, 9, 10, 20; 13:2, 11; Gal 1:1, 12, 13, 14, 14; 2:2, 3, 20; 4:11, 14, 19; 6:11, 14, 17, 18; Eph 3:1, 14; Php 1:3, 4, 5, 7, 14, 17, 19, 20; 2:12, 16, 17, 17, 25, 28; 3:8, 9, 9, 13, 18; 4:1, 1, 1, 3, 3, 14, 21; Col 1:24; 2:2, 5; 4:11, 15, 18, 18, 18; 2Th 3:17, 17, 17; 1Ti 1:2, 5, 18, 18; 2Ti 1:2, 3, 3, 6; 2:1; 3:10, 10, 10, 10; 4:6, 6, 13, 13, 19; Tit 1:4; 3:15; Phm 1:7, 10, 10, 10, 12, 19, 23, 24; Heb 1:5, 5, 13; 2:12, 13; 3:9, 9, 11, 11; 4:3, 3, 5; 5:5; 8:9, 9, 10, 10; 10:16, 16; 12:5; 13:6, 24; Jas 1:16; 2:1, 18, 18; 3:10; 4:11; 5:9, 19; 1Pe 5:1, 12, 13; 2Pe 1:14, 17; 3:1; 1Jn 2:1, 12; 4:4; 3Jn 1, 4, 15; Jude 17; Rev 1:20; 2:13, 16, 20, 28; 3:5, 8, 10, 12, 12, 12, 12, 12, 16, 21, 21; 9:17; 10:10, 10; 11:3; 13:1; 18:4, 7; 21:7; 22:12, 16

MYSELF (135)

Ge 16:5; 31:31; 50:21; Ex 15:9; 19:4; Lev 10:3; 16:2; 20:3, 5; 26:24, 32; Nu 3:13; 6:27; 8:16, 17; 11:14; 18:6; 35:34; Dt 1:9, 12; 32:39; Jdg 16:20; 1Sa 2:27; 13:12; 18:17; 25:39; 2Sa 14:15; 22:24; 1Ki 1:26; 18:15; 22:30; 2Ki 19:7, 24, 28; 2Ch 18:29; Ne 2:8, 12; 5:10, 16; Job 9:30; 12:3; 16:6; 19:6, 27; Ps 18:23; 32:5; 37:35; 39:1; 73:13; 103:1, 2; 104:1; 119:29, 45, 94; 131:1, 2; 132:3; 146:1; Ecc 1:13, 16; 2:1, 3, 4, 10, 15; 3:17; 7:23, 25; SS 3:2; 6:12; Isa 14:22; 37:7, 25, 29; 42:14; 43:21; 44:24; 57:17; 60:21; Jer 3:19; 5:9, 29; 9:9; 13:26; 20:7; 21:5, 14; 31:3, 19; 49:37; La 3:24; Eze 5:8; 20:5; 24:9; 29:3; 31:11; 34:11, 15; 37:28; 38:23; Da 7:28; 9:3; Hos 2:5, 23; 11:4; 12:8; Zec 2:5; Mk 12:33; Lk 12:19; Jn 8:14, 50, 54; 12:32; 14:21, 26; 17:19; Ac 23:35; 25:22; Ro 7:15, 17, 18; 10:20; 11:1; 1Co 4:6; 9:27; 2Co 2:1; 11:7; 12:15; Gal 1:8; 2:18, 20; Php 2:24; 3:4; Phm 1:7

NO (1730)

Ge 2:5, 5, 20; 4:12, 12; 6:3; 8:9; 15:3, 4; 16:1; 17:5, 15; 19:2, 18; 21:26; 23:4, 11, 13; 24:6, 8, 16; 26:27; 27:36; 31:39; 32:28; 33:10, 15; 34:12, 19; 35:5, 10; 37:17, 35; 39:9, 11, 23; 40:8; 41:44; 42:10, 13; 43:1, 22; 44:17; 45:1; 47:4; 48:18; 49:4; 50:21; Ex 2:3, 12; 5:16, 18; 6:12, 30; 8:10, 22; 9:14, 21; 10:25; 12:5, 16, 19, 20, 22, 39, 43; 13:7; 16:25, 26; 17:1; 20:10; 21:9, 22; 22:10, 11, 13, 15, 15; 23:8, 18, 26, 32; 29:1, 2; 30:12; 32:18; 33:6, 20; 34:3, 3, 14, 17, 20, 24; 36:6; 40:35; Lev 1:3, 10; 2:5, 8, 11; 3:1, 6; 4:3, 23, 28, 32; 5:15, 18; 6:6; 7:18, 18; 9:2, 3; 10:12; 13:21, 23, 26, 26, 31, 32, 34; 14:10; 16:17, 17; 17:7; 21:3, 18; 22:10, 12, 13, 15, 19, 21; 23:12, 18, 25, 28, 31, 36; 25:26, 41; 26:13, 17, 20, 20, 31, 36, 37, 37; 27:33; Nu 3:4; 5:8, 13, 19; 6:12; 8:19; 10:30; 11:32; 14:9; 16:40, 40; 18:4, 20, 23, 24; 19:2; 20:2, 5, 5; 22:30, 38; 23:21, 21, 23, 23; 26:33; 27:4, 8, 9, 10, 11; 28:3, 9, 11, 17, 19, 31; 29:1, 2, 7, 8, 12, 13, 17, 20, 23, 26, 29, 32, 35, 36; 30:7, 9; 32:11; 33:14; 35:30, 33; 36:9; Dt 2:36; 3:26; 4:35, 39; 5:14; 7:2, 2, 16, 21, 24; 9:4, 9; 10:9, 17, 17; 11:25; 12:12; 13:8; 14:27, 29; 15:4; 16:4, 8; 18:2; 19:6; 22:26, 27; 23:3, 17; 25:3, 18; 28:26, 29, 31, 50, 50, 51, 54, 65, 66, 68; 29:6, 18, 18; 31:2, 17; 32:4, 36, 39, 39; 33:26; 34:6; Jos 1:5; 2:11, 11, 19; 5:12; 6:1; 7:3, 26; 10:21, 30, 39, 40; 11:19; 13:33; 14:4; 17:3; 22:25, 27, 33; 23:9, 13; 24:21; Jdg 2:3, 14, 21; 3:2; 4:9, 20; 5:19; 8:3; 9:37; 10:6; 11:25, 26, 28; 12:5; 13:2; 17:6; 18:1, 7, 28, 28; 19:1, 12, 12, 15, 18, 23, 28; 21:8, 9, 25; Ru 1:10, 12, 13; 3:14; 1Sa 1:5, 8, 13, 15, 18; 2:2, 2, 2, 4, 5, 9, 12, 16, 31, 32; 10:24; 11:11, 13; 12:4; 13:19; 14:3, 24, 37, 39; 17:33, 50; 19:5; 20:21; 21:1, 6; 25:17, 18, 39; 26:9, 19, 21; 27:11; 30:4, 23; 2Sa 1:21, 21; 3:34; 7:22, 22; 10:3, 15; 12:6; 13:12, 16, 16, 25, 32, 33; 14:6, 7, 8, 11, 25; 15:16, 21; 16:10; 17:19; 18:3, 18, 20, 22; 19:34, 35, 35; 20:1, 3; 22:42; 24:24; 1Ki 1:1, 4; 2:13, 30, 32; 3:12, 13, 22, 26; 5:4, 6; 8:5, 23, 35, 60; 10:20; 12:15, 16; 13:16; 14:2, 4; 17:1, 7, 16; 18:13, 18, 26, 29, 29, 29; 19:4; 21:25; 22:1, 30, 47; 2Ki 1:3, 6, 16; 2:16, 21; 3:9, 11, 13, 13; 4:13, 16, 31; 5:15; 7:5, 10; 9:10, 37; 12:15; 14:26; 19:3; 22:7; 23:10; 25:24; 1Ch 2:34; 15:2; 17:20, 20; 19:3, 16, 19; 21:24; 23:22, 26; 24:2, 5, 28; 2Ch 1:12; 5:6; 6:14, 26; 7:13; 9:19; 10:15, 16; 14:6, 11; 15:19; 18:29; 20:6; 21:20; 25:8; 28:24; 32:15; 35:21; 36:16, 16, 17; Ezr 4:3; 7:24; 9:14; Ne 2:12, 20; 6:1, 8, 11; 13:1, 19, 26; Est 1:8, 18; 4:2; 9:2, 15; Job 2:13; 3:7, 18, 23, 26, 26, 26; 4:6; 5:1, 1, 4, 14, 19, 21; 6:5, 5, 6, 13, 21; 8:11, 11; 9:15, 21, 34; 10:7; 11:20; 12:3, 14; 13:2, 10; 14:4, 12; 15:4, 4, 29, 31; 16:6; 17:3, 16; 18:3, 17; 19:7, 7; 20:18; 21:4, 14, 31, 31; 22:5; 23:6, 15; 24:15, 15, 18, 20, 21, 22; 26:2, 6; 27:4, 4, 15; 28:7, 7, 8, 8, 13; 29:12; 30:13, 24; 31:18, 30; 32:5, 15, 17; 34:10, 12, 22, 27, 31; 35:8; 36:23, 23; 37:24; 38:11, 26; 39:7, 13, 17; 40:24; 41:9, 10, 16, 26, 29; 42:2, 15; Ps 1:5; 5:4; 7:2; 10:18; 14:1, 1, 3, 3; 16:9; 18:41; 22:2, 11; 25:3; 27:3; 34:5; 35:7, 7; 36:1, 4; 37:38; 38:14; 39:5, 13; 40:4, 6; 44:9; 49:5, 8; 50:8, 9, 9, 16, 22; 53:1, 1, 3, 3; 57:7; 58:2, 5; 59:3, 5; 60:10; 62:7; 63:1; 66:7; 71:6, 11; 72:12; 74:9, 9; 75:6; 76:5, 7; 77:2, 19; 78:44; 79:3; 81:7, 11; 84:11; 86:8; 88:4, 8; 89:34, 48, 48; 91:10, 10; 105:37; 107:12; 108:1, 11; 109:3, 12, 12; 119:96, 104, 119, 129; 127:1; 142:4, 4, 4; 143:2; 144:14, 14, 14; 146:3; Pr 1:24, 30; 4:19; 6:7, 16, 34, 35; 10:2, 22; 12:9, 15, 21; 14:4, 10; 15:21; 17:16, 21; 18:2; 20:4; 21:10, 30; 24:20; 25:3; 28:1; 29:9; 30:15, 18, 21, 27, 29; 31:7, 21, 25; Ecc 1:8, 8, 11; 3:18, 19, 22; 4:1; 5:4; 6:3, 10; 8:4, 8, 17, 17; 9:1, 3, 5, 6, 10, 15; 10:11, 15; 12:1, 2, 12; SS 1:3; 4:12; 5:6; 8:1, 1; Isa 1:3, 16, 18, 31; 3:7; 5:6, 8, 29; 6:11; 7:8, 8, 9, 9, 12, 25; 8:20; 9:5, 17, 17, 19; 10:14, 20; 13:10, 17, 18, 18; 14:8, 17, 25; 16:10, 12, 12; 17:2, 8; 19:9; 22:11, 22, 22; 23:4, 12, 17; 24:7, 8; 26:10, 18, 21; 27:7, 11; 28:20, 22; 29:8, 21, 22; 30:16, 19; 31:4; 32:6; 33:8, 8, 21, 24; 34:10; 35:9; 37:3; 38:18; 40:15, 15, 28; 41:24, 26; 42:22; 43:10, 11, 12, 13, 13; 44:6, 8, 8, 9, 20; 45:5, 6, 6, 18, 19, 21, 21, 22; 46:7, 7, 9; 47:6, 10, 14; 48:16, 19, 22; 49:4, 15; 50:1, 2, 2; 51:22; 52:1, 3; 53:9; 54:1, 4, 4, 17; 55:1, 2; 56:10; 57:1, 1, 11, 21; 58:6; 59:4, 9, 9, 10, 10, 15, 16; 60:19; 62:6, 7, 12; 63:3, 5, 17; 64:4, 4, 7; 65:17, 19, 20, 20, 20, 25, 25; 66:3, 9; Jer 2:6, 13, 15, 19, 22, 30, 32; 3:8, 16, 16, 17; 4:1, 22, 22, 23, 30; 5:3, 12, 12, 13, 22, 28; 6:15, 16, 17, 20, 20, 23, 29; 7:16, 18, 28, 32, 33, 34; 8:6, 12, 15, 17, 19, 22, 22, 22; 9:5, 10, 11, 12, 21, 21, 22; 10:6, 7, 14, 14, 16, 20, 21, 23; 11:14, 19; 12:2, 6, 11, 12, 13; 13:13, 19; 14:5, 10, 12, 13, 15, 16, 19, 22; 16:4, 6, 7, 7, 9, 13, 14; 17:6, 6, 27; 19:6, 11; 21:13; 22:6; 23:7, 17, 21, 32; 25:10, 27, 29, 33, 35, 35; 26:19; 30:8, 10, 13, 15; 31:29; 33:21, 25; 34:9; 35:6; 36:30; 37:14; 38:6, 27; 44:2, 10, 10, 17, 22, 26; 45:3; 46:11; 48:2, 9, 33, 33, 42; 49:1, 4, 5, 7, 10, 10, 18, 33; 50:3, 14, 20, 32, 34, 40, 42; 51:3, 17, 17, 19, 30, 43, 44; La 1:2, 3, 4, 7, 9, 9, 16, 16, 17, 21; 2:1, 9, 9, 11, 18, 22; 4:4, 6, 8, 12, 14, 16, 16, 17; 5:5, 8, 14, 14; Eze 3:6; 5:11; 7:3, 4, 12, 14, 26, 26; 9:5, 5; 11:11; 12:25, 28; 13:10, 16, 21, 23; 14:14, 16; 15:4; 16:4, 5, 5, 34, 47; 17:9, 10, 16; 18:13, 19, 24; 21:30; 22:26, 30; 24:16, 17; 25:10; 26:13, 21; 27:36; 28:3, 9, 19, 24; 29:16, 18; 30:13; 31:8, 8, 8, 14; 32:19; 33:11, 15, 28, 31; 34:6, 10, 22, 28, 28, 28; 35:6; 36:15, 25; 37:8, 22; 39:26; 43:22, 23; 44:2, 7, 9, 17; 45:8, 18; 46:4, 6, 13; Da 2:10, 11, 27, 44; 3:29; 4:9, 18, 31, 35; 6:13, 15, 17; 8:4, 7; 10:3, 3, 3, 21; 11:19, 25, 27, 37, 45; Hos 1:6; 2:2, 2, 10, 17; 4:1, 1, 1, 10; 5:14; 7:7; 8:7, 8; 9:3, 14, 15, 16; 10:3, 9; 11:9; 12:7, 8; 13:4, 4; 14:3, 4; Joel 1:9, 9, 13, 16, 18, 20; 2:8, 10, 19; 3:15; Am 1:11; 3:5; 5:18, 23, 26; 6:2, 10; 7:8; 9:1; Ob 18; Jnh 3:7; Mic 1:14; 2:2, 5, 10; 3:11; 4:9, 9; 5:7, 8, 12; 6:8, 10, 12, 15; Na 1:14; 2:9; 3:5, 7, 15, 18, 19; Hab 1:4, 7, 14; 3:8, 17, 17; Zep 1:6, 6, 18; 2:15; 3:2, 3, 5, 5, 5, 6, 7, 11, 11, 11, 13, 13, 15, 18; Hag 2:12; Zec 4:5, 13; 7:14; 8:10, 10, 10, 13; 9:7, 8; 11:5, 6; 13:4, 4, 5; 14:6, 7, 17, 21; Mal 1:7; 2:13; Mt 4:4; 5:17, 37; 6:18, 24; 8:19, 20, 28, 29; 9:17; 10:34; 11:23, 27, 27; 12:24; 13:6, 22, 29; 15:23; 16:8; 18:22; 19:6, 6; 20:7, 23; 21:29; 22:12, 23, 46, 46; 24:36; 25:3, 43; 26:35, 60; Mk 2:22; 4:6, 7, 19; 5:4, 19, 26, 35; 6:8, 8, 8; 8:17; 9:2, 39; 10:8, 9, 40; 11:14; 12:18, 21, 22, 31, 32, 34; 13:32; 14:31, 61; 16:13; Lk 1:7, 25, 60, 61; 2:7; 3:13; 4:4, 24, 25, 40; 5:36, 37, 39; 7:25, 39; 8:16, 16, 39, 43, 46, 49; 9:57, 58; 10:15, 22, 22; 11:15, 33, 36; 12:33, 33, 33, 51; 13:5; 14:6, 33; 15:16, 19, 21; 16:13, 26, 30; 20:27, 28, 30, 31, 40; 22:35, 58; 23:22; Jn 1:18, 21, 21; 2:3, 25; 3:5, 18; 4:21, 32; 5:7, 44; 6:35; 7:6, 13, 27, 30, 44, 52; 8:11, 11, 39, 41, 44, 49, 49, 50; 9:9; 10:13, 18, 28, 29; 11:4, 10; 12:46; 13:8, 38; 14:5, 6, 18, 30; 15:15, 22, 24; 16:10, 22; 18:17, 40; 19:9, 11, 15; 21:5, 12; Ac 1:20; 2:14, 16, 26; 4:12, 12, 13, 34; 5:13, 23; 7:5, 5, 43; 8:21, 31, 33; 9:7; 10:38, 46; 13:8, 25, 28, 37; 15:9, 12, 24, 28; 16:24; 17:25; 18:10, 17; 19:2, 36, 40; 20:26; 21:39; 23:8; 24:11, 18, 18; 25:8, 10, 26; 27:21; 28:4, 6, 18, 19, 21, 31; Ro 1:20; 2:1, 5, 24, 25, 29; 3:9, 10, 11, 11, 12, 18, 20, 22, 27; 4:2, 8, 15; 5:7, 13; 6:6, 9, 14, 14; 7:2, 4, 6, 8, 18; 8:1, 4, 12, 33, 34, 35, 37; 9:6, 20; 11:2; 13:10; 14:14; 15:1; 1Co 1:15, 29; 2:7, 9, 9, 9, 11, 11; 3:11; 4:11; 6:9, 18; 7:19, 34, 37; 8:4; 9:17; 10:13, 20; 11:16; 12:3, 3, 29, 30; 13:2, 3, 5; 14:7, 17, 27, 28; 15:11, 12, 13, 15, 16, 32, 32; 2Co 1:17, 19; 2:1; 5:4, 12, 15, 19; 6:3, 3; 7:5, 8; 8:20; 10:16, 16; 11:8, 15; 12:6, 18; Gal 1:10, 12, 17; 2:6, 6, 16, 20, 21; 3:11, 15, 25, 28; 4:7, 14, 27; 5:6, 18, 23; Eph 2:19; 4:14, 17; 5:3, 3, 5, 11, 29; 6:9; Php 2:15, 20; 3:3, 9, 13; 4:15; Col 2:4, 23; 3:25; 1Th 3:1, 5; 4:13; 5:3, 15, 18; 2Th 3:12, 16; 1Ti 5:3; 6:2, 14, 16, 16; 2Ti 2:5; 3:3, 3; 4:3, 16; Phm 1:16; Heb 4:2; 5:4, 5; 6:13; 7:3, 3; 8:7; 9:16, 17, 22, 26; 10:6, 18, 26, 35, 38; 11:12, 13; 12:11, 15, 16, 22; 13:10; Jas 1:13; 2:13, 17; 3:8, 12, 17; 5:6, 12, 17; 1Pe 1:17; 2:20; 4:4, 16; 5:12; 2Pe 1:20; 3:9; 1Jn 1:5, 8, 10; 3:5; 4:12, 18; 3Jn 4; Rev 2:17; 3:7, 7, 8, 11; 5:3, 4; 10:6; 11:6, 9; 13:17; 14:3, 5, 11; 15:8; 18:7, 11, 22, 22, 22, 23; 19:10; 20:6, 11; 21:4, 22, 23, 25, 27; 22:3, 5, 5, 9

NOR (129)

Ge 45:6; 49:10; Ex 10:15; 32:18; 34:28; Lev 19:15; 27:10; Nu 14:44; Dt 4:28, 28, 28; 9:18; 12:17, 17, 17, 17; 13:6; 21:4, 7; 24:16; 28:64; 29:4, 4; 31:6, 8; Jos 22:23; Jdg 8:23, 35; 1Sa 5:5; 15:29; 2Sa 19:24; 1Ki 1:26; 3:26; 13:28; 2Ki 3:17; 4:23; 6:27; 14:6; 2Ch 6:5; 25:4; Ne 4:23, 23, 23; 5:14; 10:30; Est 9:28; Job 8:20; 14:12; 18:19, 19; 20:9; 28:14; 41:26, 26, 26; Ps 33:16; 37:25; 89:22, 33; 91:5, 6, 6; 103:9, 10; 121:6; 132:4; Pr 19:5; 30:3, 8; Ecc 9:5; Isa 42:24; 44:9; 49:10; Jer 10:5; 15:10; 31:34; 35:8; 36:24; 37:2, 2; 44:3, 3; 51:62; Eze 7:9, 19; 8:18; 13:23; 29:11; 33:12; 44:20; Da 5:23, 23; 11:4, 20, 37, 37; Hos 5:13; 14:3; Zec 4:6; 11:16, 16, 16; Lk 9:3, 3, 3; 14:35; 18:4; Jn 6:24; 13:16; Ac 15:10; 21:25, 25; 23:12, 14; 24:12; 25:11; Ro 8:26; 1Co 7:3; 10:9; 2Co 10:15; Gal 1:17; 1Ti 6:16; Heb 8:11; 9:25; 10:8; Rev 3:15; 9:20, 20; 20:4

NOT (3435)

Ge 2:5, 18; 3:1, 3, 3, 11, 17; 4:5, 15; 6:3; 7:8; 8:12; 11:30; 13:6; 14:23; 15:1, 4, 10; 17:4, 12; 18:15, 21, 24, 25, 28, 29, 30, 31, 32, 32; 19:17, 21; 20:4, 6, 9; 21:10, 12, 17; 22:12, 12, 16; 24:3, 21, 37; 26:2, 24, 29, 29; 27:23, 38; 28:1, 6; 29:26; 30:33, 33; 31:5, 7, 25, 35, 39, 52, 52; 32:10, 26; 36:7; 37:21, 27; 38:9, 9, 11, 14, 16; 41:8, 24, 49; 42:11, 15, 16, 20, 22, 31, 34, 38; 43:8; 44:23, 31, 34; 45:8; 46:3, 26; 47:9, 19, 26, 29; 48:1; 49:10; Ex 1:19; 3:5, 19, 21; 4:8, 9, 10, 10, 11, 11, 11, 11, 19, 21; 5:2, 7, 10, 19, 23; 6:3; 7:18; 8:31; 9:4, 30, 32, 32; 10:15, 19, 20, 23, 26, 27; 11:7, 9; 12:4, 10, 10, 13, 20, 23, 27, 30, 30, 38, 45, 46, 46; 13:3, 13, 17, 22; 14:5, 28; 15:26; 16:7, 8, 19, 21, 29, 29; 17:7; 18:17; 19:12, 12, 13, 21, 21, 23, 24; 20:3, 4, 5, 5, 7, 7, 13, 14, 15, 16, 17, 17, 23, 25, 26; 21:5, 7, 8, 8, 10, 18, 21, 28, 28, 29, 36; 22:2, 3, 8, 8, 14, 16, 18, 21, 22, 25, 27, 28, 29, 31; 23:1, 1, 2, 2, 3, 5, 6, 7, 9, 13, 19, 21, 21, 24, 29, 33; 24:2, 11; 28:32, 35, 43; 29:33, 34; 30:9, 15, 15, 33; 32:11, 32; 33:3, 20, 23; 34:3, 7, 15, 20, 25, 26; 35:3; 39:23; Lev 1:17; 2:11; 5:4, 11; 7:18, 19; 8:33; 10:6, 7, 18; 11:4, 4, 4, 4, 7, 7, 8, 10, 10, 12, 26, 44, 47; 12:4, 4; 13:4, 4, 5, 6, 11, 23, 28, 32, 32, 34, 53, 55, 55; 14:36, 48; 15:31; 16:2, 13, 29; 17:4, 9, 16; 18:3, 3, 7, 8, 9, 10, 11, 12, 13, 14, 15, 16, 17, 18, 19, 20, 21, 21, 22, 24, 26, 28, 30, 30; 19:4, 7, 9, 9, 10, 10, 11, 11, 11, 12, 13, 14, 16, 16, 17, 17, 19, 19, 19, 20, 20, 26, 26, 27, 29, 31, 33, 35; 20:23, 25; 21:4, 7, 12, 14, 15, 17, 21; 22:2, 4, 6, 20, 23, 25, 32; 23:14, 22, 22, 29; 25:4, 11, 11, 17, 20, 30, 30, 36, 37, 39, 53, 54; 26:1, 11, 14, 26, 44, 44; 27:11, 20, 22, 26, 27, 33; Nu 1:47, 49; 4:15, 19, 20; 5:3, 13, 14, 15, 18, 19, 28; 6:3, 3, 3, 4, 4, 6, 7; 8:26; 9:6, 12, 12, 13, 22; 10:30; 11:17, 23, 26; 12:7, 8, 8; 14:9, 16, 18, 22, 42, 42; 15:34; 16:14, 15, 15, 28, 29, 40; 18:3, 4, 17, 32, 32; 19:12, 13, 13, 15, 20, 20; 20:12, 12, 17, 20, 24; 21:22, 34, 35; 22:12, 12, 13, 26, 34, 37; 23:8, 8, 19, 19, 19; 24:1, 17; 25:9; 26:11, 62, 62, 64; 27:3, 17; 30:5; 31:23, 49; 32:11, 18, 19; 35:12, 23, 27, 33, 34; Dt 1:16, 35, 42, 42, 43; 2:5, 9, 9, 14, 19, 19, 34; 3:2, 22, 26, 27; 4:2, 9, 15, 16, 23, 25, 31; 5:3, 5, 7, 8, 9, 9, 11, 11, 17, 18, 19, 20, 21, 21; 6:10, 11, 11, 11, 12, 14, 16; 7:3, 7, 10, 15, 16, 21, 22, 25, 25, 26; 8:2, 11, 14, 15, 20; 9:5, 6, 6, 26; 11:2, 10, 16, 30; 12:4, 8, 13, 16, 17, 23, 25, 30, 30, 31, 32; 13:3, 8, 8; 14:3, 7, 7, 7, 8, 8, 8, 10, 10, 12, 19, 21, 21, 21, 27; 15:2, 3, 6, 7, 9, 13, 16, 18, 19, 19, 21, 23; 16:4, 5, 8; 17:11, 15, 16, 17, 17; 18:1, 9, 10, 19, 21, 22, 22, 22; 19:10, 13; 20:1, 3, 3, 5, 6, 15, 19, 19, 19, 20; 21:7, 8, 14, 14, 15, 15, 16, 17, 18, 23; 22:1, 2, 3, 4, 5, 5, 6, 8, 9, 10, 11, 14, 17, 20, 24, 28, 30; 23:1, 2, 4, 5, 7, 14, 15, 16, 18, 19, 20, 22, 24, 25; 24:4, 4, 5, 10, 12, 16, 21; 25:4, 5, 6; 26:13, 14, 14, 14; 27:6, 26; 28:13, 14, 15, 29, 39, 41, 44, 47, 49, 56, 58, 61, 62; 29:4, 5, 14, 20, 23, 26; 30:11, 12, 13, 18; 31:2, 6, 8, 13; 32:6, 17, 27, 31, 47, 52; 33:6; 34:4; Jos 1:5, 7, 9, 18; 2:19, 20; 5:6, 7; 6:10, 10, 10, 18; 7:11, 12; 8:1, 17, 17, 22, 27, 31; 9:14, 18, 26; 10:8, 8, 13, 13, 28, 37; 11:6, 8, 11, 13, 22; 13:4, 14; 15:63; 16:10; 17:12, 13, 15, 16; 18:2, 7; 20:5; 22:3, 17, 17, 19, 20, 22, 22, 23, 26, 27, 28, 31; 23:6, 7, 7, 14; 24:10, 12, 13, 13, 13, 19, 19; Jdg 1:32, 34; 2:2, 10, 17, 22, 23; 3:1, 29; 4:16; 5:8, 23; 6:10, 10, 23, 23; 7:4, 22; 8:20, 23, 26; 9:15, 20, 28; 10:6, 11, 13; 11:2, 15, 25, 27; 12:5; 13:4, 7, 9, 14, 16, 21; 16:7, 9; 18:1, 5, 9; 19:30; 20:8, 13, 17; 21:5, 7, 11, 14, 17, 22, 22; Ru 1:13; 2:9, 13; 3:10, 13; 1Sa 1:2, 7, 15, 22; 2:24; 3:3, 7; 4:20; 6:9; 8:3, 5, 7, 18; 12:14, 17, 22, 23; 13:14; 14:1, 9, 27, 34, 44, 45, 45; 15:11, 17, 19, 26, 29, 29; 16:8, 10, 11, 18; 17:39, 47, 47; 19:6; 20:2, 2, 10, 26; 21:2, 4; 22:8, 8, 15; 24:7, 11, 11, 21; 25:28, 34, 34, 35; 28:18; 30:15; 31:4; 2Sa 1:14, 22; 2:23, 29; 3:8, 13, 34, 34, 37, 38; 4:11; 5:8, 23; 6:10; 7:15; 11:25; 12:8; 13:30, 32; 14:11, 14, 24; 17:6, 12, 16, 17; 18:3, 20; 19:7, 13, 22, 24, 42; 20:10; 21:2, 2, 17; 22:22, 38, 39; 23:10, 17, 19, 23; 24:14; 1Ki 1:1, 10, 18, 19, 21, 26, 43, 51, 52, 52; 2:8, 9, 23, 26, 28, 42; 3:2, 11, 13, 26, 27; 5:3, 3; 6:6; 7:31, 47, 47; 8:8, 11, 19, 56; 9:12, 20, 21, 22; 10:7, 15, 21; 11:2, 10, 11, 12, 33, 33, 34, 39; 12:24, 31; 13:8, 8, 9, 9, 16, 17, 17, 22, 22, 28, 33; 14:8; 15:3, 14, 29; 16:11, 31; 18:23, 25; 19:11, 11, 12; 20:11, 25, 28, 36; 21:5, 7, 21, 29; 22:6, 15, 28, 33; 2Ki 1:17; 2:10, 17, 18; 3:2, 14; 4:27, 28, 40, 41; 5:16, 20; 6:9, 12, 22; 7:9, 10; 8:19; 9:18; 10:5, 10,

29, 31; **11:**2, 15; **12:**3, 6, 8, 8, 13, 16; **13:**23, 23; **14:**3, 4, 6, 6, 27; **15:**4, 20, 35; **16:**2, 5; **17:**2, 9, 14, 15, 22, 25, 26, 26, 35, 37, 38, 38, 40; **18:**27, 27, 36, 36; **19:**6, 10, 18, 25, 32, 32, 33; **20:**1, 13; **21:**8; **22:**2, 13, 13, 17, 20, 20; **23:**9, 18, 22, 26; **24:**4; **1Ch 3:**9; **5:**1; **10:**4; **11:**19, 21, 25; **13:**13; **14:**14; **15:**13; **16:**21, 22, 22; **17:**4, 13; **21:**3, 6, 13, 17, 24, 30; **22:**8, 13; **26:**10; **27:**23; **28:**3, 20; **29:**1; **2Ch 1:**11; **2:**6; **4:**6, 18; **5:**9, 11, 14; **6:**9, 42; **7:**2, 7, 18; **8:**7, 8, 9, 11, 15; **9:**6, 14, 20; **11:**4, 4, 14; **12:**7, 7, 12, 14; **13:**7, 10, 12, 12; **14:**11; **15:**5, 17; **16:**12; **17:**3; **18:**5, 14, 27, 32; **19:**6, 7, 10, 10, 10; **20:**7, 7, 10, 10, 12, 15, 15, 17, 17, 24; **21:**7, 12, 19, 20; **22:**11; **23:**8, 14; **24:**5, 5, 19, 25; **25:**2, 4, 4, 7, 7, 7, 15, 16, 20; **26:**7, 18, 18; **27:**2; **28:**1, 13, 21, 27; **29:**11; **30:**3, 3, 5, 7, 8, 9, 17, 18, 19, 26; **32:**25, 26; **33:**8, 23; **34:**2, 21, 21, 28, 28, 33; **35:**3, 15, 21, 22, 22; **Ezr 2:**59, 62, 63; **4:**14, 21, 22, 22; **5:**5, 16; **6:**7, 7, 8; **7:**25; **8:**15; **9:**1, 9, 12, 12, 12; **10:**6; **Ne 1:**3, 7; **2:**12, 16, 16, 16; **4:**5, 5, 23; **5:**9, 9, 15; **6:**1, 12; **7:**3, 61, 64, 65; **8:**17; **9:**17, 17, 19, 20, 21, 21, 29, 31, 32, 34, 35; **10:**30, 31, 39; **13:**2, 6, 10, 14, 19, 24, 25; **Est 1:**16; **2:**10, 10; **3:**5, 6, 8; **4:**11, 16; **5:**9, 12; **6:**10; **9:**10, 16; **Job 1:**9, 22; **3:**16; **5:**5, 6, 6, 12, 17, 22, 26; **6:**10, 11, 11; **7:**1, 8, 9, 16, 21; **8:**12, 15, 20; **9:**11, 13, 18, 24, 28, 32; **10:**7, 14; **11:**6; **13:**11, 16; **14:**5, 12, 12; **15:**11, 22, 29, 29, 30; **16:**5, 6, 18; **17:**4, 10; **18:**5; **19:**4; **20:**8, 18, 21; **21:**4, 9, 16, 18, 19, 21; **22:**5; **23:**2, 8, 9, 11, 12; **24:**6, 12, 13, 16; **25:**3; **26:**8; **27:**11, 15; **28:**13, 14; **30:**1, 25, 25; **31:**1, 20, 34; **32:**6, 9, 9, 12, 14; **33:**7, 9, 12, 13, 14, 20, 24, 27, 33; **34:**6, 12, 23, 33; **35:**12, 15; **36:**2, 5, 6, 20; **37:**4, 23; **39:**16, 22; **40:**23, 23; **41:**23; **42:**3, 7, 8, 8; **Ps 1:**1, 4; **3:**6; **5:**5; **6:**1; **7:**12; **9:**12, 18, 18, 19; **10:**5, 12; **14:**3; **15:**5; **16:**4, 8, 10; **17:**3, 5; **18:**21, 37, 38; **22:**2, 6, 11, 19, 24, 24; **23:**4; **24:**4; **25:**2, 20; **26:**4, 11; **27:**9, 9, 12; **30:**12; **31:**8; **32:**6, 9; **34:**20; **35:**22, 24; **37:**8, 24, 33, 36; **38:**21, 21; **39:**1, 2; **40:**9, 10, 17; **41:**11; **44:**3, 3, 6, 6, 17, 18, 18, 23; **46:**2; **49:**8, 12, 17; **50:**12; **51:**11, 16, 16, 17; **52:**7; **53:**3; **55:**1, 12, 12, 19, 22; **57:**T; **58:**T; **59:**T; **62:**6; **64:**1; **65:**9; **66:**18, 18, 20, 20; **69:**33; **70:**5; **71:**18; **75:**T; **78:**4, 6, 8, 10, 22, 37, 37, 38, 50, 53, 64, 67; **79:**6, 8; **81:**9, 11; **85:**8; **89:**22, 31, 34, 34; **91:**5, 7; **92:**6, 6; **94:**14, 14; **101:**5, 5, 7, 7; **102:**17; **103:**9, 10; **105:**14, 15, 15; **106:**7, 11, 23; **110:**4; **112:**6, 7; **115:**1; **118:**6, 17, 18; **119:**3, 6, 11, 16, 36, 43, 46, 51, 109, 110, 116, 133, 153, 155, 157, 165, 176; **121:**3, 3, 6; **124:**1, 2, 6; **125:**1, 3; **127:**5; **131:**1, 1; **132:**3, 3, 4, 10; **140:**8, 8; **147:**10, 20, 20; **Pr 1:**18, 28, 28, 29; **3:**5, 25, 27, 29, 31; **4:**14; **5:**6, 12; **6:**27, 28, 29; **7:**19; **8:**29; **10:**3; **12:**28; **13:**19; **14:**5, 33; **17:**7, 20; **19:**2, 5, 9; **20:**21, 23; **21:**17; **22:**22, 26, 28; **23:**18, 20; **24:**10, 14, 15, 17, 19, 28; **25:**27, 27; **26:**2; **27:**24; **28:**13; **29:**18, 19, 19; **30:**3, 6, 11, 18; **31:**3, 4, 4, 12, 27, 30; **Ecc 1:**8; **2:**10, 20, 21; **4:**12; **6:**3, 6; **7:**20, 28; **8:**5, 8, 11, 13, 14, 17; **9:**1, 3, 11, 16; **10:**17; **11:**2; **SS 2:**7; **3:**1, 5; **4:**2; **6:**6; **8:**4; **Isa 1:**3, 3, 9, 15; **3:**9; **5:**6, 10, 13, 25, 27, 27, 27; **6:**9, 9, 10, 12; **7:**1, 9, 10; **8:**11, 12, 13, 19, 19; **9:**1, 12, 13, 17, 18, 21; **10:**4, 4, 7, 24, 25; **11:**13; **12:**2; **13:**20; **14:**20, 20, 21, 29; **15:**9; **16:**3; **22:**4; **23:**18; **24:**20; **26:**7, 10, 11, 11; **28:**12, 25; **29:**9, 9, 9, 17; **30:**1, 5; **31:**2, 3, 3, 4, 8; **32:**5, 5; **34:**16, 16; **35:**4, 9; **36:**12, 12, 21, 21; **37:**6, 10, 19, 26, 33, 33, 34; **38:**1; **39:**2; **40:**9, 16, 16, 27, 31, 31; **41:**9, 10, 13, 28, 28; **42:**2, 3, 4, 8, 8, 16, 23, 24, 24; **43:**1, 2, 2, 2, 5, 19, 23, 23, 23, 24; **44:**2, 2, 8, 8, 8, 8, 21; **45:**4, 5, 13, 18, 19, 19, 19, 21, 21; **46:**8, 9, 13; **47:**3, 7, 8, 10, 14; **48:**6, 6, 7, 9, 10, 11, 11, 21; **49:**10, 15; **50:**1, 2, 5, 6, 7; **51:**7, 10, 14, 18, 21; **52:**12, 15, 15; **53:**3, 7; **54:**4, 14, 15; **55:**2; **56:**3, 6; **57:**6, 11, 16, 16; **58:**7; **59:**1, 1, 2, 8, 21; **60:**20; **62:**1; **63:**8; **64:**5; **65:**1, 6, 8, 8, 12, 12, 22, 23, 23; **66:**3, 4, 4, 9, 19; **Jer 1:**17; **2:**6, 8, 20, 23, 24, 35, 37; **3:**1, 2, 7, 12, 16; **4:**3, 6, 11, 22, 27, 28, 29; **5:**1, 7, 9, 9, 10, 15, 18, 19, 21, 21, 22, 24, 29, 29; **6:**8, 13, 15, 16, 28; **7:**4, 13, 16, 16, 17, 22, 24, 26, 27, 27, 28; **8:**2, 7, 7, 10, 12, 20; **9:**9, 9, 23, 25; **10:**2, 2, 5, 7, 11, 23, 24, 25; **11:**3, 8, 8, 11, 11, 12, 14, 14, 21, 23; **12:**6; **13:**1, 11, 14, 15; **14:**10, 11, 12, 14, 14, 18, 21, 21, 21; **15:**19, 20; **16:**2, 5, 6, 7, 8, 8, 11, 20; **17:**8, 11, 16, 16, 16, 17, 22, 23, 23, 24, 27; **18:**4, 6, 8, 10, 15; **20:**14, 17; **21:**10; **22:**3, 10, 13, 15, 18, 18, 20, 21; **23:**4, 16, 16, 20, 21, 24, 29, 29, 32, 38; **24:**2, 6, 6; **25:**3, 4, 6, 6, 7, 8, 29; **26:**4, 5, 5, 16, 24; **27:**9, 9, 14, 14, 15, 16, 17, 18; **28:**15; **29:**6, 8, 8, 9, 11, 16, 19, 31; **30:**10, 10, 11, 14, 21, 24; **31:**8, 9, 16, 20, 32, 34, 37; **32:**33, 40; **33:**20, 24; **34:**3, 4, 17; **35:**7, 14, 14, 15; **36:**25, 31; **37:**4, 9, 14, 19, 21; **38:**16, 17, 18, 23, 26; **39:**16; **42:**6, 10, 10, 11, 13, 19, 21; **44:**5, 7, 7, 7, 16, 19, 21, 27; **46:**27, 27, 28, 28; **48:**11, 27, 33, 44; **49:**9, 12; **50:**9, 15; **51:**5, 46, 50; **La 2:**14; **3:**31, 33, 38, 42, 49, 57; **4:**3, 12; **Eze 2:**5, 6, 6, 7, 8; **3:**5, 6, 11, 20; **7:**7, 13, 13, 25; **8:**18; **9:**5, 6, 10; **11:**3, 7, 11, 11; **13:**5, 7, 19, 19; **14:**11, 18, 20, 23; **16:**20, 22, 28, 31, 33, 42, 43, 47, 51, 61; **17:**14, 18; **18:**3, 6, 6, 7, 7, 15, 16, 16, 17, 17, 20, 20, 21, 23, 24, 28, 29; **20:**7, 8, 8, 15, 18, 24, 25, 31, 47, 48; **21:**4, 5, 24, 27; **22:**26, 26; **23:**8, 48; **24:**14, 16, 16, 17, 17, 22, 23, 23; **28:**2; **29:**11; **30:**21; **32:**7, 27, 31; **33:**9, 12, 15, 17, 17, 20; **34:**4, 4, 4, 18, 18; **36:**11, 15, 22, 32; **39:**7; **41:**6; **42:**6, 14; **43:**7; **44:**8, 9, 9, 13, 13, 18, 19, 22, 28; **46:**2, 18; **47:**11; **48:**11; **Da 1:**8, 13; **2:**11, 18, 30, 43, 43; **3:**16, 27, 27, 27; **4:**7, 19; **5:**22, 23; **6:**12, 22, 22, 23; **8:**24, 25, 26, 27; **9:**10, 10, 14, 18, 19; **11:**4, 14, 15, 21, 34, 42; **12:**8; **Hos 1:**6, 9, 9, 9, 10; **2:**4, 4, 7, 18, 23, 23; **3:**3, 3; **4:**3, 15; **5:**6; **7:**14; **8:**4, 6; **9:**1, 2, 4, 4, 9, 17; **10:**9; **11:**9, 9, 9, 9; **13:**14; **Joel 2:**2, 3, 13, 13; **3:**21; **Am 1:**3, 3, 6, 6, 9, 9, 11, 11, 13, 13; **2:**1, 1, 4, 4, 6, 6, 14; **3:**8; **5:**18, 22, 23; **7:**2, 3, 5, 13, 14; **8:**2, 11, 12; **9:**4, 7, 9; **Ob** 5, 8; **Jnh 3:**7; **4:**11; **Mic 1:**11, 14; **3:**7; **4:**12; **6:**15, 15; **7:**1, 2, 5, 8; **Na 1:**12; **3:**19; **Hab 1:**2, 2, 12; **2:**3, 13; **3:**6; **Zep 2:**5; **3:**2; **Hag 1:**2, 6, 6, 6; **2:**5; **Zec 1:**4, 4; **4:**6, 7, 10; **7:**10, 10, 11, 12, 13; **8:**11, 14, 17; **11:**6, 16; **12:**7; **13:**5; **Mal 1:**10, 10, 10; **2:**2, 6, 8, 9, 10, 10, 17; **3:**5, 6, 6, 11, 18; **Mt 1:**19, 20; **2:**6, 12; **3:**10, 11; **4:**7; **5:**17, 21, 27, 33; **6:**15, 27, 29; **7:**1, 10, 19, 21; **8:**8, 20; **9:**13; **10:**13, 24, 24, 29, 37, 37, 38; **11:**6, 8; **12:**7, 16, 19, 19, 20, 26; **13:**11, 12, 14, 14, 17; **15:**11, 13, 23, 24; **16:**17, 18, 20, 23, 28; **18:**14; **19:**8, 10, 11, 12, 13, 18, 18, 18, 18; **20:**28; **22:**17, 32; **23:**23; **24:**2, 17, 18, 20, 29, 34, 36, 43; **25:**13, 44; **26:**5, 11, 22, 25, 29, 35, 39; **Mk 1:**7; **2:**2, 17, 19, 27; **3:**12; **4:**12, 21, 25, 40; **5:**3, 10, 43; **6:**9, 52; **7:**3, 15, 36, 36; **8:**12, 30, 33; **9:**1, 9, 24, 40; **10:**13, 19, 19, 19, 19, 19, 27, 45; **11:**23; **12:**14, 15, 27, 34; **13:**2, 11, 14, 15, 16, 18, 24, 30, 32, 35; **14:**2, 7, 19, 25, 31, 36; **16:**6; **Lk 1:**54; **2:**26; **3:**9, 16; **4:**12, 26, 42; **5:**14, 32; **6:**35, 37, 40; **7:**6, 7, 23, 25; **8:**1, 18, 31, 56; **9:**3, 21, 27, 33, 45, 50, 58, 62; **10:**6, 24; **11:**12, 35, 42; **12:**6, 15, 21, 25, 27, 39, 48; **13:**3, 9, 14, 25; **14:**3, 14, 27, 32; **16:**12; **17:**9, 10, 31, 31; **18:**11, 13, 14, 15, 20, 20, 20, 20; **19:**14, 44; **20:**21, 22, 35, 38; **21:**6, 18, 21, 32; **22:**18, 27, 32, 34, 35, 40, 42, 58; **23:**2, 29, 51; **24:**39; **Jn 1:**8, 11, 13, 20, 26, 27; **2:**4, 9; **3:**16, 17, 18, 18, 28; **4:**35, 42; **5:**23, 30, 31, 34, 38, 38, 45; **6:**13, 26, 38, 39, 46, 58; **7:**6, 8, 8, 16, 23, 30, 34, 36, 39, 39; **8:**15, 16, 20, 20, 23, 29, 35, 37, 41, 42, 55; **9:**3, 16, 33; **10:**8, 16, 26, 33; **11:**4, 6, 21, 32, 52; **12:**6, 8, 30, 35, 37, 47, 47; **13:**9, 10, 11, 16, 18; **14:**2, 10, 18, 19, 22, 22, 24, 24; **15:**20, 22, 22, 24; **16:**13, 25, 26, 29, 32; **17:**9, 12, 14, 14, 15, 16, 20; **18:**9, 11, 17, 20, 25, 36, 36, 38, 40; **19:**4, 6, 12, 24, 36; **20:**24; **21:**25; **Ac 1:**4, 7, 9; **2:**24, 25, 27, 31, 31; **3:**23; **4:**4, 17, 32; **5:**4, 7, 39; **6:**2; **7:**5, 32; **8:**16, 21, 32; **10:**4, 41; **11:**6, 12; **12:**22; **13:**25, 35, 36, 37; **15:**38; **16:**6, 7, 37; **17:**6, 27; **19:**26, 27, 31, 37; **20:**22, 29; **21:**4, 12, 13, 21, 25; **23:**5, 21; **25:**8, 10, 16; **26:**19, 25, 26, 29; **27:**21, 34; **28:**4, 26, 26; **Ro 1:**16, 20, 25; **2:**3, 11, 13, 14, 21, 28, 29, 29; **3:**4, 6, 6, 9, 10, 12, 17, 21, 24, 25, 27, 28, 29, 31; **4:**4, 5, 11, 13, 16, 19; **5:**5, 13, 14; **6:**2, 12, 12, 13, 15, 21; **7:**3, 6, 7, 7, 7, 7, 8, 9, 13, 14, 19, 20; **8:**3, 9, 9, 9, 15, 32; **9:**1, 6, 8, 12, 14, 16, 19, 25, 25, 26, 29, 30, 32, 33; **10:**11, 16, 20, 20; **11:**1, 2, 4, 5, 6, 6, 7, 8, 8, 11, 18, 18, 21, 25; **13:**3; **14:**3, 3, 7, 13, 15, 16, 17, 22, 23, 23; **15:**18; **16:**4, 18; **1Co 1:**14, 17; **2:**4, 6, 6, 8, 12, 13; **3:**2, 4, 6, 9, 13; **4:**5, 5, 14, 20; **5:**3, 8, 9, 11; **6:**4, 7, 7, 12, 12, 13, 19; **7:**3, 5, 6, 7, 10, 10, 11, 12, 12, 13, 14, 15, 18, 18, 19, 25, 25, 27, 27, 27, 28, 28, 29, 30, 35, 36, 37, 37; **8:**4, 7, 9; **9:**1, 1, 2, 9, 15, 16, 19, 20, 21, 21, 26; **10:**5, 6, 8, 13, 20, 20, 23, 23, 25, 27, 29; **11:**7, 9, 11, 11, 20, 22, 29, 31, 32; **12:**14, 15, 15, 15, 16, 16, 23, 24, 29, 30; **13:**4, 5, 5; **14:**2, 11, 11, 21, 22, 22, 33, 34, 38, 38; **15:**9, 10, 10, 13, 14, 16, 17, 27, 29, 37, 50, 51; **16:**12, 22; **2Co 1:**9, 12, 18, 24; **2:**3, 5, 11, 17; **3:**3, 3, 5, 6, 7, 10, 13, 13, 15; **4:**2, 2, 7, 8, 18; **5:**1, 3, 4, 6, 7, 17; **6:**1, 12; **7:**2, 2, 2, 3, 9, 9, 12; **8:**3, 8, 12; **9:**5; **10:**4, 8, 8, 9, 13, 13, 14; **11:**6, 9, 14, 17, 21, 26, 29; **12:**5, 11, 14, 16, 18, 21; **13:**2, 3, 7, 7, 10; **Gal 1:**1, 7, 10, 10, 11, 16, 18, 20; **2:**2, 3, 14, 15, 16, 16, 17, 21; **3:**2, 4, 5, 10, 17, 18, 21; **4:**1, 8, 12, 14, 17, 18, 30, 31; **5:**6, 13, 21, 26; **6:**1, 15; **Eph 2:**9, 11, 12; **3:**5; **4:**30; **5:**4, 15; **6:**6, 12; **Php 1:**17, 17, 18, 29; **2:**6, 16, 16, 21, 27; **3:**13; **4:**11; **Col 2:**8, 11, 13, 16, 19; **3:**2, 22; **4:**5; **1Th 1:**5; **2:**1, 3, 4, 5, 8, 9; **4:**5, 7, 8, 12, 12, 13, 15; **5:**6, 9, 19, 20; **2Th 2:**3, 12; **3:**2, 8, 10, 10; **1Ti 1:**9, 20; **2:**9, 12, 14; **3:**3, 3, 6, 7, 8, 8, 11; **4:**4, 7, 14; **5:**7, 11, 14, 16, 18, 19, 22, 24; **6:**1, 17, 17; **2Ti 1:**7, 9, 12; **2:**4, 15, 24; **4:**2, 8, 16; **Tit 1:**6, 7, 7; **2:**3, 3, 5, 9; **3:**2, 5, 7, 9, 14; **Heb 2:**5, 8, 11, 16; **3:**12, 19; **4:**8, 8, 15; **5:**5; **6:**10, 10, 12; **7:**6, 13, 16, 21, 27; **8:**2, 4, 9, 9, 11; **9:**8, 9, 11, 11, 12, 24, 28; **10:**1, 4, 5, 6, 8, 25, 35, 37, 39; **11:**3, 16, 23, 27, 28, 31; **12:**4, 8, 9, 13, 14, 14, 18, 25, 26; **13:**6, 9, 9, 14, 17, 17; **Jas 1:**5, 7, 22; **2:**11, 11, 11, 13, 20, 24; **3:**1, 10, 15; **4:**11, 17; **5:**12; **1Pe 1:**8, 12, 18, 23; **2:**8, 9, 10, 16, 16, 18, 23, 23; **3:**7, 21; **4:**15; **5:**2, 2; **2Pe 1:**16; **2:**4, 5; **3:**8, 9, 17; **1Jn 1:**6, 10; **2:**1, 2, 4, 5, 7, 10, 15, 16, 19, 20, 21, 22, 27, 28; **3:**9, 10, 10, 10, 12; **4:**1, 3, 3, 6, 6, 8, 8, 10, 17, 18, 20, 21; **5:**6, 12, 12, 16, 16, 17, 18; **2Jn** 5, 7, 8, 9, 10; **3Jn** 7, 9, 10, 10, 11; **Jude** 5, 6, 9, 10, 12, 19; **Rev 2:**2, 11, 21, 24; **3:**4, 8, 9, 18; **7:**1; **9:**4, 4, 5, 6, 20, 21; **10:**4; **11:**2, 13; **12:**11; **13:**8, 10; **15:**4; **16:**9, 15; **17:**8, 12; **18:**4, 7; **20:**3, 4, 5, 15; **22:**10

NOW (1437)

Ge 2:25; **3:**1, 15; **4:**1, 12; **6:**5, 11; **8:**11; **9:**7, 19; **11:**30; **13:**5; **14:**2, 4, 7, 8, 8; **16:**5, 11; **17:**5, 15; **18:**10, 14; **19:**9, 15, 37, 38; **20:**1, 7; **21:**23; **22:**12, 14; **23:**2; **24:**1, 16, 29; **25:**1, 32, 33; **26:**1, 29; **27:**2, 8, 25, 36; **28:**4, 8; **29:**16, 21, 32, 34, 35; **30:**15, 20, 30, 37; **31:**13, 34, 37, 43, 44; **32:**3, 5, 10, 28; **33:**2; **35:**1, 3, 6, 10, 27; **37:**3, 30; **39:**1, 6; **40:**15, 19; **42:**22, 24, 36; **44:**30; **46:**30; **47:**1, 5; **48:**5, 10, 11; **50:**5, 15, 15; **Ex 2:**16; **3:**10, 16, 17; **4:**7, 10, 12, 14, 27; **5:**18; **6:**1, 5; **7:**16, 17; **8:**28; **9:**15; **10:**7; **11:**3, 9; **12:**1, 2, 42; **13:**11, 15; **16:**3, 12; **17:**16; **18:**5, 11, 19; **19:**5, 15; **20:**20; **21:**18, 22; **22:**10; **23:**31; **29:**19; **32:**10, 29, 32, 34; **33:**1; **35:**1; **36:**5; **40:**1, 36; **Lev 8:**2, 5; **13:**12, 47; **18:**28; **23:**39; **Nu 1:**17; **3:**40, 44; **4:**29; **5:**22; **8:**6; **9:**10; **10:**1; **11:**6, 18, 23, 31; **12:**3, 6; **13:**1, 23; **14:**15, 25, 28, 40, 41, 42; **16:**8, 10, 13; **18:**1, 22; **20:**16, 25; **21:**21; **22:**33; **23:**23; **24:**1, 11, 14; **26:**58; **30:**1, 6; **31:**17; **32:**1; **Dt 1:**20, 31, 40; **2:**24, 30, 31; **3:**8, 10, 28; **4:**1, 32; **5:**25; **6:**24; **9:**7; **10:**12, 22; **11:**2, 17; **12:**15, 22; **14:**24; **22:**16; **26:**10; **30:**15, 18; **31:**2, 19, 27, 28; **32:**21, 38, 39, 40; **33:**10; **34:**4, 9; **Jos 1:**2; **2:**12; **3:**7, 12, 15; **4:**2; **6:**1; **7:**8, 12, 25; **8:**20; **9:**1, 12, 13, 23, 25; **10:**1, 1, 6; **11:**17; **14:**10, 11; **18:**1; **20:**2; **22:**4, 4, 7; **23:**1, 2, 5, 8; **24:**13, 15; **Jdg 1:**7; **4:**11; **6:**10, 13; **7:**8; **9:**16, 18, 31, 38; **11:**1, 7, 13, 26, 26; **15:**18, 18; **16:**10, 15, 24, 25; **17:**3, 13; **18:**1; **19:**1; **20:**7; **21:**3; **Ru 2:**1; **3:**3, 10, 11, 13; **4:**11, 17; **1Sa 1:**23, 28; **2:**1, 4, 5, 5, 5, 12, 16, 18, 22; **3:**1, 2, 8; **6:**7; **8:**5, 8; **9:**5, 15; **10:**19; **11:**12; **12:**3, 7, 14, 16, 19, 20; **13:**4, 14; **14:**24, 29, 42, 47; **15:**1, 3, 25, 33; **16:**1, 14; **17:**1, 12, 29; **18:**12; **19:**1; **20:**1, 31; **21:**3, 7; **22:**22; **23:**7, 13, 14, 19, 26; **24:**20, 21; **25:**1, 26; **26:**1, 19, 24; **27:**12, 12; **28:**2, 22; **29:**1, 10; **30:**6; **31:**1; **2Sa 2:**7; **3:**17, 18, 35; **4:**2, 2, 11; **5:**7; **6:**9; **7:**6, 8, 9, 11, 19, 25, 29; **10:**6, 15; **12:**21, 28; **13:**3, 10, 16, 19, 24, 35, 39; **14:**7, 25; **15:**20, 31, 34; **16:**8, 19; **17:**1, 8, 24; **18:**1, 32; **19:**7, 10, 24, 31; **22:**44; **24:**3; **1Ki 1:**1, 6, 15, 20, 46; **2:**16, 26, 46; **3:**7; **5:**4, 6; **8:**16, 20, 25, 26; **9:**8, 10; **11:**1, 11; **12:**8; **13:**23; **14:**4, 14; **16:**3, 21, 24; **17:**1, 24; **18:**3, 8, 11, 14, 19, 23, 34, 46; **19:**10, 14; **20:**1, 19, 42; **21:**15; **22:**30, 31; **2Ki 1:**4, 6, 14, 16; **2:**19; **3:**15; **4:**1, 7, 13, 38, 41; **5:**2, 15, 17; **6:**15, 20; **7:**3; **8:**5, 7; **9:**14; **10:**1, 6, 16, 24; **12:**7; **13:**18, 19; **19:**19, 25; **20:**5, 8; **1Ch 10:**1; **11:**5; **13:**12; **14:**1; **15:**1; **17:**1, 5, 7, 8, 10, 17, 23, 27; **19:**6, 16; **22:**5, 11, 16, 18, 19; **23:**26; **28:**7, 8; **29:**2, 3, 5; **2Ch 1:**1, 8, 9; **2:**1; **6:**6, 10, 16, 17, 41; **7:**21; **8:**1, 2; **10:**8; **15:**7; **16:**9; **18:**1, 29, 30; **20:**10, 11; **21:**14; **23:**18; **24:**8, 20; **25:**16; **28:**10, 11; **29:**10, 19, 31; **30:**1; **31:**1; **35:**3; **Ezr 3:**1; **5:**17; **9:**8, 10, 13, 14; **10:**3, 10; **Ne 1:**11; **2:**17; **5:**10; **7:**73; **8:**7; **9:**32, 32, 36; **10:**29; **11:**1; **12:**12, 47; **13:**18; **Est 2:**5; **5:**6; **6:**4; **8:**3, 8; **9:**12; **Job 3:**13; **4:**5; **7:**8; **13:**13, 22; **16:**19; **19:**3; **20:**3; **22:**19; **24:**24; **30:**1, 6, 9, 15, 16; **32:**16; **33:**2, 28; **34:**16, 37; **42:**5, 8, 12; **Ps 2:**10; **12:**5; **18:**43; **20:**6; **27:**9; **30:**6; **35:**15, 22, 25; **37:**25; **40:**6, 15, 17; **42:**6; **44:**9; **48:**8; **50:**21; **51:**8; **56:**13; **60:**1; **66:**13; **68:**13, 18; **70:**3; **71:**9, 11, 18; **77:**6; **80:**12; **81:**6; **85:**4; **88:**2; **89:**4, 38; **102:**13, 13; **109:**17, 17, 19; **115:**18; **116:**7; **118:**22; **119:**26, 66, 67, 73, 76; **121:**8; **122:**2; **124:**1; **125:**2; **129:**1; **131:**3; **Pr 3:**28; **5:**7, 14; **6:**3, 4; **9:**18; **24:**29; **Ecc 1:**11, 17; **2:**1, 17; **4:**8; **7:**4; **12:**6; **SS 1:**6; **2:**9; **3:**2; **7:**8; **8:**10; **Isa 1:**15, 18, 21, 22; **2:**9; **5:**1, 3, 5; **6:**7; **7:**23; **9:**10; **10:**16, 28, 28; **12:**1; **14:**8, 10, 11; **16:**6, 9, 10, 14; **21:**4, 9; **23:**4, 4, 6, **24:**9, **25:**1; **26:**1; **28:**7; **30:**8; **33:**1, 7, 9; **37:**20, 26; **38:**10, 15, 22; **41:**1; **42:**9, 14; **43:**1; **44:**1, 13; **46:**13; **47:**5; **48:**6, 16, 20; **49:**5; **50:**8; **51:**21; **52:**3, 4, 5, 11; **54:**1, 9; **55:**6; **57:**12; **63:**15, 18; **65:**1; **Jer 1:**13; **2:**15, 25, 35; **3:**8, 9, 25; **4:**6, 10, 12; **5:**6, 19, 27; **6:**4, 11, 16, 20, 26; **7:**3, 6, 14, 25; **9:**15; **11:**13, 16; **12:**1, 14; **13:**7; **14:**9, 10, 17; **15:**9; **16:**16, 21; **17:**17; **20:**1, 3, 7, 13; **22:**6, 22; **23:**2, 14, 33; **25:**3, 7, 8, 27, 29, 30; **26:**18; **27:**6; **28:**7, 11; **30:**6, 17; **31:**7, 16; **32:**31, 36, 43; **33:**12; **34:**16; **36:**30; **37:**19; **38:**1; **40:**4; **42:**21; **44:**2, 6, 7, 26; **45:**3; **47:**6; **48:**11, 15, 34; **50:**8, 18, 33; **51:**8, 9, 9, 43; **La 1:**1, 1, 2, 7, 8, 9; **4:**2, 5, 5, 8, 11, 11; **5:**8; **Eze 4:**1, 4, 9, 14; **5:**8; **6:**11; **8:**8; **11:**15; **12:**3, 23, 28; **13:**17; **14:**21; **16:**57, 59; **17:**9; **19:**13, 14; **21:**10, 11, 13, 21, 24, 26, 28, 29; **22:**1, 13, 31; **23:**46; **24:**6, 11, 13; **26:**18; **27:**32, 34; **29:**8, 10; **32:**23, 24, 25, 26, 30; **33:**7, 25; **34:**10; **35:**15; **36:**2, 3, 13, 35, 35; **37:**12, 17; **38:**8, 12; **39:**17, 25; **43:**9; **47:**7, 14, 23; **Da 1:**9; **2:**28, 36; **4:**9, 15, 18, 37; **8:**7; **9:**7, 11, 23, 25; **10:**14, 19; **11:**2; **12:**6, 9; **Hos 2:**2, 7, 9, 23; **4:**6, 9; **5:**6, 7; **6:**1, 1; **7:**8, 15; **8:**2, 3, 10; **9:**2, 13; **10:**10, 11, 11, 12, 14; **12:**2, 6, 14; **13:**2, 7, 10, 10; **Joel 2:**12, 21; **3:**11, 13; **Am 3:**7, 9, 13; **5:**4; **7:**16; **8:**7; **9:**11; **Ob** 10; **Jnh 1:**17; **3:**4; **4:**3; **Mic 1:**7; **3:**6, 12; **4:**9; **6:**2; **7:**4; **Na 1:**13; **2:**11; **3:**5; **Hab 2:**1, 6, 8, 17, 17; **Zep 1:**5, 6; **2:**2, 9, 15; **3:**6, 7, 8; **Hag 1:**8; **2:**3, 4, 15, 19; **Zec 1:**5, 12; **3:**4, 9; **4:**2; **7:**6; **8:**3, 6, 11, 13, 19; **9:**4; **11:**5; **Mal 3:**7, 15; **Mt 1:**18; **3:**10; **6:**5; **8:**22; **9:**13; **10:**27; **11:**2, 12; **12:**37, 41, 42; **13:**18; **15:**1; **16:**18, 28; **19:**30; **20:**16, 16; **21:**33, 42; **22:**9, 17, 31; **23:**38; **24:**32; **25:**21, 23, 30; **26:**23, 54; **27:**11, 15; **28:**7; **Mk 4:**22; **5:**35; **6:**25; **7:**25; **8:**23; **9:**1, 11; **10:**30, 31, 32; **12:**10, 14, 26; **13:**28; **14:**1, 20; **15:**6, 10, 29; **16:**7; **Lk 1:**7, 18, 20, 48, 57, 71; **2:**25, 29, 37; **3:**1, 9; **5:**4, 10; **6:**21, 21, 24, 25; **7:**2; **8:**41, 49; **9:**27, 32; **10:**1, 3, 9, 36, 37; **11:**31, 32; **12:**19, 52; **13:**30, 30, 35; **15:**12, 24, 24, 32; **16:**3, 16, 25; **19:**27, 42; **20:**9, 17, 22, 37; **22:**7, 16, 29, 36, 63; **23:**11, 50; **24:**49; **Jn 2:**9, 10; **4:**18, 35, 35, 42, 49; **5:**14; **6:**12, 32; **7:**6; **8:**52; **9:**11, 12, 14, 25; **10:**22; **11:**11, 22, 30, 39, 55; **12:**27; **13:**1, 7, 17, 19, 21, 27, 34, 36, 37; **14:**1, 7, 17, 25, 28; **15:**15, 22; **16:**4, 5, 12, 22, 30; **17:**5, 7, 11, 13; **18:**3; **19:**4, 14, 28; **21:**12; **Ac 1:**6, 21; **2:**33; **3:**19; **4:**11, 29; **6:**3, 5; **7:**4, 34; **8:**12, 28; **9:**6, 10, 11; **10:**5, 29, 32, 33, 47; **12:**8, 20; **13:**11, 13, 32, 36; **14:**19, 26; **15:**10; **16:**19, 37; **17:**1, 6, 23, 30; **18:**6; **20:**18, 22, 25, 28, 32; **21:**22; **22:**16; **24:**10, 25; **26:**3, 6, 16; **27:**34; **Ro 1:**13; **3:**21, 24; **4:**9, 23; **5:**2, 7, 11, 21; **6:**4, 10, 17, 18, 19, 21, 22, 22; **7:**1, 4, 6, 6; **8:**1, 18, 24; **9:**25, 26; **11:**3, 12, 17, 28, 31; **13:**11; **15:**23, 33; **16:**17, 26; **1Co 1:**4, 7, 10, 15; **3:**10, 12; **4:**2; **6:**11; **7:**1, 8, 10, 12, 14, 18, 22, 22, 25, 29; **8:**1, 4; **9:**15; **10:**29; **11:**17; **12:**1, 4, 27; **13:**9, 12, 12, 12; **15:**1, 1, 6, 10, 21, 43, 43, 44, 49; **16:**1, 12, 12; **2Co 1:**14, 23; **2:**7, 8, 14; **3:**17; **4:**7, 18; **5:**16; **6:**2, 13; **7:**9, 14, 15, 16; **8:**1, 7, 11, 14, 22; **10:**1, 9; **11:**6; **12:**9, 14; **13:**2, 4; **Gal 1:**23; **3:**3, 4, 20, 24, 25, 29, 29; **4:**6, 7, 9, 9, 16, 18, 20, 24, 25, 27; **5:**1, 25; **6:**15, 17; **Eph 1:**9, 13, 21; **2:**13, 13, 18, 19; **3:**5, 11, 12, 20; **5:**8; **6:**4, 20; **Php 1:**5; **2:**12, 26; **3:**7; **4:**2, 8, 20; **Col 1:**22, 26; **2:**6; **3:**8; **1Th 1:**8; **2:**15; **3:**6; **4:**13; **5:**23; **2Th 2:**1, 14; **3:**6, 17; **1Ti 3:**14; **4:**1; **5:**15; **6:**14; **2Ti 1:**10; **4:**8; **Tit 1:**3; **3:**7; **Phm 1:**9, 11, 16; **Heb 1:**2; **2:**8, 9, 11; **5:**1, 12; **7:**5, 15, 19, 26; **8:**13; **9:**1, 5, 11, 16, 24; **10:**18, 25, 36; **11:**3; **12:**2, 23, 26; **13:**19, 20, 23; **Jas 2:**18; **5:**5; **1Pe 1:**3, 8, 12, 15, 20, 22; **2:**3, 5, 7, 10, 10, 25; **3:**13, 21, 22; **5:**1; **2Pe 3:**18; **1Jn 1:**2; **2:**28; **3:**10; **4:**14; **5:**20; **2Jn** 5; **Jude** 3, 14, 19, 24, 25; **Rev 1:**19; **3:**2; **5:**6; **11:**14, 15, 17, 18; **13:**1; **14:**13, 18; **16:**1; **17:**8, 9, 10; **18:**7, 19; **21:**3

O (754)

Ge 15:2, 8; **24:**12, 42; **27:**34, 38; **32:**9, 9, 11; **49:**2, 6, 18; **Ex 4:**10; **15:**6, 6, 11, 16, 17, 17; **32:**4, 8, 11; **34:**9; **Nu 10:**35, 36; **12:**13; **16:**22; **21:**17, 29, 29; **24:**5, 5, 9; **27:**16; **Dt 3:**24; **6:**4; **9:**1, 26; **21:**8; **26:**10; **27:**9; **32:**1, 1, 43; **33:**7, 8, 11, 23, 29; **Jos 7:**13; **Jdg 16:**28; **21:**3; **1Sa 1:**11; **14:**41; **23:**10, 11, 20; **26:**22; **2Sa 1:**19, 21, 24; **7:**18, 19, 22, 23, 24, 25, 27, 28, 29; **14:**4; **15:**31; **18:**33, 33; **19:**4, 4; **22:**29, 50; **1Ki 3:**7; **8:**12, 23, 25, 26, 28, 53; **12:**16, 28; **13:**2; **17:**18, 20, 21; **18:**26, 36, 37, 37; **2Ki 1:**13; **4:**16; **6:**17, 18, 20; **19:**15, 16, 16, 19, 19; **20:**3; **1Ch 16:**10, 13, 13, 28, 35; **17:**16, 17, 17, 19, 20, 21, 22, 23, 25, 26, 27; **21:**17; **29:**10, 11, 11, 13, 16, 18; **2Ch 6:**1, 14, 16, 17, 19, 40, 41, 41, 42; **10:**16; **13:**12; **14:**11, 11, 11; **20:**6, 7, 12, 17; **25:**7; **30:**6; **Ezr 9:**6, 10, 15; **Ne 1:**5, 11; **4:**4; **5:**19; **6:**14; **13:**14, 22, 29, 31; **Job 7:**7, 20; **9:**28; **13:**20; **16:**7, 18; **17:**3; **30:**20; **Ps 3:**1, 3, 7, 8; **4:**1, 8; **5:**1, 4, 8, 10, 12; **6:**1, 3, 4; **7:**1, 3, 6, 8, 8, 9; **8:**1, 9; **9:**2, 10, 19, 20; **10:**1, 12, 12; **12:**1; **13:**1, 3; **16:**1; **17:**1, 6, 13, 14; **18:**15, 49; **19:**14; **20:**9; **21:**1; **22:**19; **25:**1, 4, 6, 7, 11, 22; **26:**1, 6; **27:**7, 9, 11; **28:**1; **30:**2, 3, 7, 8, 10, 12; **31:**1, 14, 17; **35:**1, 17, 22, 22, 24; **36:**5, 6, 7; **38:**1, 15, 15, 22; **39:**12; **40:**5, 9, 17; **41:**4; **42:**1, 9; **43:**1, 4; **44:**1, 8, 23; **45:**3, 6, 10; **48:**9, 10; **50:**7, 7; **51:**1, 10, 14, 15, 17; **52:**9; **54:**1, 2, 6; **55:**1, 23; **56:**1, 4, 7, 10, 12, 13; **57:**1, 5, 7, 8, 11; **58:**6, 6; **59:**1, 3, 5, 9, 11, 17, 17; **60:**1, 10; **61:**1, 5; **62:**8, 11, 12; **63:**1; **64:**1; **65:**1, 5; **66:**10; **67:**3, 5; **68:**1, 7, 9, 10, 16, 24, 28, 28; **69:**1, 5, 6, 6, 13, 16, 29, 34; **70:**5, 5; **71:**1, 5, 5, 12, 16, 17, 18, 19, 19, 22, 22; **72:**1; **73:**17, 20; **74:**1, 10, 12, 22; **75:**1; **76:**6, 9; **77:**11, 13, 16; **78:**1; **79:**1, 5, 9, 12; **80:**1, 1, 3, 4, 7, 14, 19; **81:**8, 8; **82:**8; **83:**1, 13, 16; **84:**1, 3, 8, 8, 9, 12; **85:**4, 7; **86:**1, 3, 4, 5, 6, 8, 11, 12, 14, 15, 17; **87:**3; **88:**1, 9, 13, 14; **89:**8, 46, 51; **90:**13; **92:**5, 8; **93:**2, 3, 5; **94:**1, 1, 2, 3, 18; **96:**7; **97:**9; **99:**8; **100:**1; **102:**12; **104:**1, 24; **105:**3, 6, 6; **106:**47; **108:**1, 2, 5, 11; **109:**1, 21, 26; **113:**1; **114:**7; **115:**1, 9, 10; **116:**16; **118:**13; **119:**12, 33, 52, 55, 64, 75, 89, 107, 137, 149, 151, 169, 174; **120:**2, 3; **122:**2, 7, 9; **123:**1; **125:**4, 5; **130:**1, 2, 3, 7; **131:**3; **132:**8; **135:**13, 13, 19, 19, 20; **137:**5, 7, 8; **138:**1, 4, 8; **139:**1, 17, 19, 21, 23; **140:**1, 4, 6, 7, 8; **141:**1, 3, 8; **142:**5; **143:**1, 11; **144:**3, 9; **146:**10; **147:**12, 12; **149:**2, 2; **Pr 8:**5; **23:**26; **30:**1, 1, 7; **31:**2, 2, 2, 4; **SS 1:**4, 5, 7, 8; **2:**7; **3:**5, 11; **5:**8, 9, 16; **6:**1, 4, 13; **7:**1; **8:**4, 12, 13; **Isa 1:**2, 2; **3:**12; **13:**2; **14:**12; **21:**10, 13, 14; **23:**1, 12, 14; **25:**1, 4; **26:**11, 13; **30:**19; **34:**1; **37:**16, 17, 17, 20, 20; **38:**3; **40:**27; **41:**14; **43:**1, 10; **44:**2, 2, 21, 23, 23, 23; **45:**8, 15; **47:**1, 5; **48:**1, 12; **49:**13, 13, 13; **51:**17; **52:**1, 1, 2, 2; **54:**1, 1, 11; **62:**5, 6; **Jer 1:**6; **2:**31; **3:**12; **4:**1, 10, 14; **5:**15; **6:**2; **7:**2, 29; **10:**1, 7; **11:**20; **14:**8, 13; **15:**16; **17:**13, 14; **18:**6; **20:**7, 12; **22:**29; **31:**7, 23, 23; **32:**17, 25; **34:**4; **46:**11; **47:**6; **48:**43, 46; **49:**3, 3; **50:**31, 32; **51:**25; **La 1:**11; **2:**13, 13, 18, 20; **4:**21, 22; **5:**21; **Eze 4:**14; **7:**7; **9:**8; **11:**13; **13:**4; **18:**25, 29, 30, 31; **20:**31, 39, 44, 47, 49; **21:**3, 16, 25; **22:**3, 5; **26:**3, 17; **27:**3; **28:**16, 22; **29:**3, 8; **31:**18; **32:**19; **33:**11, 20; **35:**3; **36:**1, 4, 11, 32; **37:**3, 9, 12, 13; **39:**1; **44:**6; **Da 3:**16; **4:**9, 18, 27, 31; **5:**22; **9:**4, 8, 15, 17, 18, 19, 19, 19, 19; **10:**11; **Hos 2:**17; **4:**1, 14, 15; **5:**3, 8; **6:**4, 11; **8:**5; **9:**1, 10, 14; **10:**9; **13:**9, 14, 14; **14:**1, 8; **Joel 3:**11; **Am 3:**1; **6:**14; **7:**2, 5; **Jnh 1:**14, 14; **2:**4, 6; **Mic 2:**7, 12; **4:**8, 13; **5:**2; **6:**2, 3, 8; **7:**14; **Na 1:**12, 15; **2:**12; **3:**18; **Hab 1:**2, 12, 12; **Zep 3:**14, 14, 14; **Zec 1:**12; **2:**10; **3:**8; **9:**9, 9; **13:**7; **Mt 2:**6; **11:**25; **15:**22; **23:**37; **Mk 12:**29; **Lk 10:**21; **13:**34; **18:**13; **Jn 17:**25; **Ac 1:**24; **4:**24, 29; **26:**7, 19; **Ro 15:**10; **1Co 15:**55, 55; **Gal 4:**27; **Eph 5:**14; **Heb 1:**8; **10:**7; **Rev 4:**11; **6:**10; **12:**12; **15:**3, 4; **16:**5; **18:**20, 20

OF (23057)

Ge 1:2, 11, 11, 12, 20, 21, 21, 24, 25, 25; **2:**1, 3, 4, 4, 6, 7, 7, 9, 9, 9, 9, 9, 10, 11, 11, 12, 13, 14, 15, 17, 17, 17, 19, 21, 23, 23, 25; **3:**1, 1, 2, 3, 6, 14, 18, 20, 22, 22, 23, 24, 24; **4:**3, 4, 9, 16, 16, 18, 18, 18, 18, 20, 21, 22, 25; **5:**1, 1, 1, 3, 4, 5, 7, 8, 10, 11, 13, 14, 16, 17, 19, 20, 22, 26, 27, 29, 30, 31; **6:**2, 2, 4, 4, 5, 9, 13, 13, 19, 19, 20, 20, 20; **7:**1, 2, 2, 2, 3, 3, 3, 4, 8, 11, 14, 14, 14, 21; **8:**4, 16, 19; **9:**2, 12, 13, 17, 17, 18, 18, 19, 22, 25, 25, 25, 25, 27, 27; **10:**1, 1, 1, 2, 3, 4, 6, 7,

7, 8, 9, 10, 10, 12, 13, 15, 15, 19, 20, 21, 21, 21, 22, 23, 24, 24, 25, 26, 30, 30, 31, 32, 32; **11:**2, 3, 6, 6, 8, 10, 11, 13, 15, 17, 19, 21, 23, 25, 26, 27, 27, 28, 28, 29, 31, 31, 31; **12:**2, 3, 11, 13, 14, 16, 17, 20; **13:**7, 9, 9, 10, 10, 10, 10, 11, 12, 12, 13; **14:**1, 1, 1, 1, 2, 2, 2, 2, 2, 3, 3, 5, 6, 8, 8, 8, 9, 9, 10, 10, 13, 14, 15, 17, 17, 18, 18, 19, 20, 21, 22, 24, 24; **15:**2, 3, 4, 6, 7, 7, 12, 16, 17, 18, 19; **16:**3, 5, 5, 7, 9, 12, 12; **17:**4, 4, 5, 6, 7, 8, 9, 9, 11, 12, 13, 16, 17, 27; **18:**4, 6, 10, 11, 16, 18, 19, 20, 25, 28, 31, 32; **19:**1, 1, 4, 11, 12, 13, 14, 15, 15, 16, 25, 26, 28, 30, 33, 35, 36, 37, 38; **20:**8, 9, 9, 16, 17; **21:**9, 9, 10, 13, 13, 14, 14, 15, 17, 20, 26, 31, 32, 32; **22:**2, 2, 3, 4, 6, 11, 13, 14, 15, 17, 18, 21, 23; **23:**2, 4, 6, 8, 9, 9, 9, 10, 11, 12, 15, 16, 17, 18, 19; **24:**2, 3, 3, 7, 7, 10, 10, 12, 12, 13, 14, 15, 25, 27, 35, 35, 37, 42, 43, 44, 47, 48, 48, 51, 60, 67; **25:**4, 6, 9, 9, 9, 12, 12, 12, 13, 16, 16, 17, 18, 18, 19, 19, 19, 20, 20, 23, 23, 25, 27, 27, 28, 30, 32; **26:**1, 4, 8, 10, 14, 14, 14, 15, 15, 24, 24, 24, 31, 33, 34, 34, 34; **27:**3, 7, 10, 12, 16, 16, 16, 18, 24, 27, 27, 27, 28, 28, 29, 32, 37, 42, 45, 46, 46; **28:**1, 2, 2, 3, 5, 9, 9, 9, 12, 12, 13, 13, 13, 14, 14, 16, 17, 19, 19, 22; **29:**1, 2, 2, 3, 5, 10, 25, 26; **30:**1, 14, 35, 37, 39, 39, 41; **31:**3, 5, 11, 12, 13, 14, 15, 18, 18, 21, 22, 23, 23, 25, 26, 29, 32, 33, 36, 37, 38, 39, 40, 41, 42, 42, 42, 46, 48, 48, 49, 51, 52, 53, 53, 53, 53, 53; **32:**1, 3, 5, 6, 9, 10, 16, 19, 25, 30, 31, 32, 32; **33:**4, 10, 13, 14, 15, 19, 19; **34:**1, 2, 13, 19, 22, 25, 27, 29, 30; **35:**5, 8, 15, 16, 21, 22, 22, 23, 24, 25, 26; **36:**1, 1, 2, 2, 2, 3, 3, 5, 6, 7, 8, 9, 9, 10, 10, 11, 12, 13, 13, 14, 14, 15, 15, 15, 15, 16, 16, 17, 17, 17, 17, 17, 18, 18, 18, 18, 20, 20, 20, 21, 21, 22, 23, 24, 25, 26, 27, 28, 29, 30, 32, 32, 33, 34, 35, 35, 35, 36, 37, 38, 39, 39, 39, 40, 40, 43, 43, 43; **37:**1, 2, 2, 2, 3, 4, 7, 11, 14, 20, 25, 25, 28, 28, 29, 36, 36, 36; **38:**2, 5, 8, 8, 12, 12, 12, 14, 14, 22, 23, 24, 25, 27, 28, 28; **39:**1, 1, 1, 1, 2, 4, 10, 17, 22, 23; **40:**3, 3, 4, 9, 10, 13, 14, 15, 16, 17; **41:**1, 2, 5, 8, 8, 9, 10, 10, 12, 12, 12, 14, 15, 17, 18, 19, 20, 22, 23, 24, 26, 26, 27, 27, 29, 29, 30, 31, 33, 34, 35, 36, 38, 39, 41, 41, 42, 43, 43, 44, 45, 45, 45, 45, 46, 46, 46, 48, 49, 50, 50, 50, 50, 51, 52, 53, 54, 54, 55; **42:**6, 6, 6, 7, 13, 13, 13, 15, 16, 16, 19, 19, 21, 23, 25, 27, 29, 32, 32, 33, 33, 35, 35, 36, 38; **43:**8, 11, 14, 16, 18, 19, 23, 33, 33, 34; **44:**1, 1, 2, 4, 4, 7, 7, 9, 9, 10, 11, 17, 20, 20, 26, 28, 32, 33; **45:**1, 3, 5, 6, 8, 9, 10, 11, 11, 11, 15, 18, 18, 18, 20, 20, 21, 22, 22, 22, 23, 23, 25, 26; **46:**1, 3, 6, 8, 8, 9, 10, 11, 12, 12, 12, 13, 14, 15, 16, 17, 18, 19, 20, 20, 20, 22, 23, 24, 25, 26, 27, 27, 28, 31, 34, 34; **47:**1, 2, 4, 6, 6, 6, 6, 9, 11, 11, 12, 15, 15, 17, 20, 21, 24, 26, 26, 27, 27, 29, 30; **48:**3, 4, 4, 5, 5, 6, 7, 10, 14, 14, 16, 19, 20, 20, 21; **49:**2, 3, 4, 4, 5, 5, 7, 10, 11, 13, 14, 24, 24, 25, 25, 25, 25, 26, 26, 26, 26, 28, 30; **50:**3, 4, 5, 7, 7, 8, 8, 9, 10, 10, 11, 13, 13, 13, 17, 17, 19, 20, 21, 23, 23, 23, 24, 24, 24, 25, 26; **Ex 1:**1, 6, 8, 9, 11, 15, 21; **2:**1, 3, 3, 5, 5, 6, 7, 10, 11, 15, 16, 21, 23, 23; **3:**1, 1, 1, 2, 6, 6, 6, 6, 7, 7, 8, 9, 9, 10, 11, 12, 13, 13, 15, 15, 15, 15, 16, 16, 16, 17, 18, 18, 18, 18, 18, 19, 20, 20; **4:**4, 5, 5, 5, 5, 7, 15, 20, 20, 27, 29; **5:**1, 3, 6, 12, 13, 14, 16, 18; **6:**1, 4, 5, 5, 6, 9, 11, 13, 13, 14, 14, 14, 14, 15, 15, 16, 17, 17, 17, 18, 19, 19, 21, 22, 23, 23, 24, 24, 25, 25, 25, 25, 26, 26, 26, 27; **7:**2, 3, 4, 4, 4, 16, 17, 19, 20, 20, 21, 22, 23, 25; **8:**2, 3, 5, 5, 6, 9, 16, 16, 17, 19, 21, 22, 22, 24, 29; **9:**1, 4, 4, 4, 6, 7, 9, 13, 15, 18, 20, 21, 23, 24, 25, 26, 26, 33; **10:**3, 6, 6, 6, 9, 11, 12, 14, 15, 15, 19, 21, 23, 28; **11:**1, 1, 2, 3, 3, 5, 5, 5, 6, 8, 9; **12:**1, 2, 3, 4, 6, 6, 6, 7, 7, 7, 10, 12, 12, 12, 13, 13, 15, 15, 15, 16, 16, 16, 16, 17, 17, 17, 18, 18, 18, 18, 19, 19, 21, 21, 22, 22, 23, 27, 27, 28, 29, 29, 29, 29, 30, 30, 31, 33, 33, 35, 35, 37, 39, 40, 41, 42, 43, 46, 46, 47, 48, 50, 51, 51; **13:**2, 3, 4, 5, 7, 8, 14, 15, 16, 19, 19, 19, 20, 21, 21, 22, 22; **14:**4, 5, 7, 7, 7, 8, 9, 10, 16, 17, 17, 19, 19, 19, 20, 20, 22, 22, 23, 23, 24, 25, 28, 28, 29, 29, 30, 31; **15:**1, 4, 7, 8, 8, 10, 14, 15, 15, 15, 16, 19, 22, 26; **16:**2, 5, 6, 6, 6, 6, 7, 9, 10, 13, 17, 19, 20, 20, 20, 20, 22, 22, 23, 27, 29, 32, 32, 32, 33, 34, 35, 35; **17:**1, 3, 5, 5, 5, 5, 7, 7, 7, 7, 8, 8, 9, 9, 9, 10, 10, 13, 14; **18:**1, 1, 3, 4, 4, 4, 5, 9, 10, 12, 13, 16, 19, 21, 22, 25, 25; **19:**1, 2, 3, 3, 5, 6, 7, 8, 13, 16, 17, 18, 20, 20; **20:**4, 4, 5, 5, 7, 10, 10, 18, 20, 22, 23, 24, 26; **21:**7, 11, 16, 19, 21, 24, 24, 26, 27, 30, 30, 34, 35, 36; **22:**2, 3, 5, 6, 7, 9, 11, 11, 21, 26, 29, 29, 30; **23:**2, 3, 5, 7, 8, 9, 12, 15, 15, 16, 16, 16, 16, 19, 19, 21, 23, 24, 28, 31, 33; **24:**1, 1, 2, 4, 4, 4, 5, 7, 9, 9, 10, 10, 12, 13, 16, 17, 17; **25:**2, 3, 8, 10, 11, 12, 14, 16, 17, 17, 18, 19, 21, 21, 22, 22, 23, 24, 30, 31, 32, 33, 34, 35, 38, 39; **26:**1, 1, 3, 4, 4, 5, 5, 6, 6, 7, 7, 8, 9, 9, 9, 10, 12, 12, 14, 14, 14, 15, 15, 15, 18, 18, 20, 24, 25, 26, 26, 27, 28, 31, 31, 33, 34, 34, 34, 36; **27:**2, 2, 3, 7, 11, 11, 12, 18, 19, 19, 20, 21, 21; **28:**5, 6, 7, 8, 9, 9, 10, 12, 12, 13, 14, 14, 16, 16, 17, 21, 21, 21, 22, 23, 25, 25, 26, 28, 29, 29, 29, 29, 30, 31, 31, 32, 33, 33, 35, 36, 36, 37, 37, 38, 38, 39; **29:**1, 2, 3, 3, 4, 5, 10, 11, 12, 12, 12, 13, 15, 15, 16, 17, 20, 20, 20, 20, 20, 20, 21, 21, 22, 22, 22, 23, 23, 24, 26, 27, 28, 28, 34, 36, 40, 40, 40, 40, 41, 43, 45, 46; **30:**1, 2, 3, 4, 5, 6, 6, 10, 12, 12, 13, 13, 16, 23, 23, 23, 24, 24, 26, 28, 31, 32, 32, 33, 34, 35, 36, 36, 36, 36; **31:**2, 2, 2, 2, 3, 3, 6, 6, 6, 7, 7, 7, 9, 13, 13, 15, 16, 17, 18, 18; **32:**4, 4, 5, 8, 10, 11, 12, 13, 13, 15, 17, 18, 18, 18, 19, 23, 25, 25, 26, 27, 27, 29, 29, 31, 32; **33:**1, 7, 8, 9, 11, 11, 11, 22; **34:**2, 4, 5, 6, 7, 7, 10, 15, 18, 19, 21, 22, 22, 22, 22, 23, 23, 25, 25, 26, 26, 26, 27, 28, 29, 30, 30, 34; **35:**1, 2, 10, 12, 13, 13, 15, 16, 16, 17, 18, 21, 22, 22, 29, 30, 30, 30, 30, 31, 31, 34, 34, 34; **36:**3, 8, 10, 10, 11, 12, 12, 12, 13, 14, 16, 17, 18, 19, 19, 20, 20, 25, 27, 29, 30, 33, 34, 35, 36, 37; **37:**1, 2, 5, 6, 7, 7, 7, 8, 10, 12, 13, 15, 17, 18, 19, 20, 21, 23, 24, 25, 25, 26, 28, 29; **38:**1, 2, 2, 5, 6, 7, 8, 9, 9, 16, 17, 18, 18, 19, 19, 20, 21, 21, 21, 22, 22, 22, 22, 22, 23, 23, 23, 24, 24, 25, 26, 26, 26, 26, 27, 27, 28, 28, 29, 31, 31; **39:**1, 5, 6, 6, 6, 7, 10, 13, 14, 14, 14, 15, 16, 18, 18, 19, 21, 22, 22, 23, 23, 24, 24, 25, 25, 28, 29, 30, 30, 30, 34, 35, 35, 36, 38, 40, 40, 42, 42; **40:**2, 3, 5, 5, 6, 6, 8, 10, 12, 17, 20, 20, 20, 21, 22, 23, 24, 26, 28, 29, 33, 34, 35, 36, 38, 38; **Lev 1:**3, 5, 5, 7, 8, 11, 11, 12, 12, 15, 16, 17; **2:**1, 2, 2, 3, 3, 4, 4, 4, 5, 6, 7, 9, 10, 10, 11, 13, 14, 14, 16; **3:**2, 2, 3, 4, 5, 5, 8, 8, 8, 9, 9, 10, 13, 13, 13, 14, 15; **4:**4, 5, 6, 6, 7, 7, 7, 7, 7, 7, 9, 10, 11, 14, 14, 16, 17, 18, 18, 18, 18, 18, 18, 21, 21, 22, 23, 25, 25, 25, 25, 25, 27, 27, 28, 29, 30, 30, 30, 30, 32, 33, 34, 34, 34, 34, 35; **5:**1, 2, 2, 3, 3, 4, 4, 5, 5, 5, 7, 7, 8, 9, 9, 9, 9, 11, 11, 13, 15, 15, 16, 17, 17, 18, 19; **6:**2, 4, 5, 10, 12, 12, 14, 15, 16, 16, 17, 18, 18, 18, 20, 20, 22, 23, 23, 26, 29, 30, 30; **7:**2, 4, 7, 7, 8, 8, 11, 12, 13, 13, 14, 14, 15, 18, 24, 26, 29, 30, 32, 33, 34, 36, 38; **8:**2, 3, 3, 7, 12, 15, 15, 15, 15, 16, 17, 19, 20, 22, 23, 23, 23, 23, 24, 24, 24, 24, 24, 24, 25, 26, 26, 26, 26, 27, 28, 29, 29, 30, 30, 31, 31, 35; **9:**1, 5, 5, 6, 9, 9, 9, 10, 12, 17, 18, 19, 19, 20, 20, 23; **10:**1, 1, 4, 4, 5, 6, 6, 7, 7, 7, 12, 13, 14, 14, 15, 16, 17, 19, 19; **11:**5, 8, 14, 15, 16, 19, 22, 24, 25, 26, 27, 27, 29, 29, 31, 32, 34, 35, 36, 40, 44, 45; **12:**4, 4, 4, 4, 5, 6, 6, 7; **13:**2, 2, 3, 4, 6, 15, 16, 27, 30, 32, 42, 44, 48, 48, 52, 59; **14:**3, 4, 5, 6, 7, 9, 10, 10, 10, 10, 11, 12, 14, 14, 14, 14, 15, 15, 17, 17, 17, 17, 17, 19, 21, 21, 21, 22, 25, 25, 25, 25, 26, 26, 27, 28, 28, 28, 28, 28, 31, 32, 34, 35, 35, 37, 39, 41, 45, 50, 51, 54, 56, 56; **15:**2, 13, 14, 16, 23, 25, 28, 29, 31, 31, 32, 33;

16:1, 1, 2, 5, 7, 13, 13, 13, 14, 14, 14, 15, 16, 16, 18, 18, 21, 21, 21, 25, 31, 32; **17:**4, 4, 5, 6, 9, 11, 14, 14, 14, 15; **18:**3, 3, 8, 11, 11, 19, 21, 21, 24, 26, 26, 27, 29, 29, 30, 30; **19:**2, 3, 3, 4, 7, 8, 9, 10, 12, 14, 14, 16, 17, 19, 19, 19, 21, 22, 24, 26, 27, 30, 32, 32, 34, 36, 36, 37; **20:**2, 4, 4, 9, 11, 12, 13, 14, 16, 17, 17, 17, 18, 18, 19, 20, 21, 23, 27; **21:**5, 12, 12, 15, 21, 23; **22:**3, 4, 4, 4, 4, 6, 10, 11, 13, 14, 21, 30, 32; **23:**2, 3, 6, 7, 8, 10, 13, 13, 13, 15, 16, 17, 17, 17, 20, 22, 22, 24, 24, 27, 27, 28, 30, 32, 32, 32, 32, 34, 34, 36, 39, 39, 39, 39, 39, 42, 43, 43, 44; **24:**2, 3, 5, 5, 7, 8, 8, 9, 9, 10, 11, 11, 11, 11, 15, 15, 16; **25:**4, 5, 7, 9, 9, 10, 11, 13, 13, 14, 15, 15, 15, 16, 17, 17, 22, 24, 25, 27, 27, 27, 28, 30, 30, 31, 33, 34, 34, 35, 36, 38, 38, 39, 40, 42, 42, 42, 43, 45, 46, 47, 48, 50, 50, 50, 50, 51, 52, 53, 54, 55, 55, 55; **26:**2, 8, 8, 8, 10, 10, 13, 13, 18, 29, 31, 31, 34, 34, 36, 36, 36, 38, 39, 39, 40, 41, 43, 44, 45; **27:**2, 3, 3, 3, 4, 4, 5, 5, 5, 6, 6, 6, 6, 7, 7, 16, 16, 16, 16, 17, 18, 18, 21, 21, 22, 23, 23, 24, 25, 26, 26, 27, 27, 30, 30, 31, 33; **Nu 1:**1, 2, 2, 2, 5, 5, 6, 7, 8, 9, 10, 10, 10, 10, 11, 12, 13, 14, 15, 16, 18, 18, 19, 20, 32, 34, 44, 45, 49, 49, 50, 50, 52, 53, 53; **2:**2, 3, 3, 3, 3, 3, 5, 7, 9, 9, 10, 10, 10, 10, 10, 12, 14, 16, 16, 17, 18, 18, 18, 18, 18, 20, 22, 24, 24, 24, 25, 25, 25, 25, 25, 27, 29, 31, 31, 32, 34; **3:**1, 4, 4, 6, 8, 8, 10, 12, 12, 13, 13, 14, 15, 15, 18, 19, 20, 21, 21, 23, 24, 24, 25, 25, 26, 27, 27, 28, 29, 30, 30, 31, 32, 33, 33, 35, 35, 35, 36, 37, 38, 38, 38, 38, 38, 41, 41, 41, 42, 42, 43, 45, 45, 45, 45, 45, 45, 46, 46, 46, 47, 49, 49, 50, 50; **4:**2, 2, 2, 3, 4, 5, 6, 7, 8, 8, 9, 11, 12, 14, 15, 16, 16, 16, 22, 22, 22, 22, 23, 24, 24, 25, 25, 28, 29, 29, 29, 30, 31, 31, 33, 33, 34, 35, 37, 39, 41, 43, 45, 46, 47; **5:**2, 6, 6, 7, 12, 14, 15, 15, 15, 18, 18, 19, 23, 24, 31; **6:**1, 2, 2, 5, 6, 7, 10, 11, 12, 12, 13, 13, 13, 13, 15, 15, 17, 18, 19, 19, 20, 21, 23; **7:**2, 3, 5, 8, 8, 9, 9, 11, 12, 12, 12, 13, 13, 13, 17, 18, 18, 18, 19, 19, 19, 23, 24, 24, 24, 25, 25, 25, 29, 30, 30, 30, 31, 31, 31, 35, 36, 36, 36, 37, 37, 37, 41, 42, 42, 42, 43, 43, 43, 47, 48, 48, 48, 49, 49, 49, 53, 54, 54, 54, 55, 55, 55, 59, 60, 60, 60, 61, 61, 61, 65, 66, 66, 66, 67, 67, 67, 71, 72, 72, 72, 73, 73, 73, 77, 78, 78, 78, 79, 79, 79, 83, 84, 86, 86, 89, 89; **8:**4, 6, 6, 7, 8, 9, 9, 10, 11, 12, 13, 14, 14, 15, 16, 16, 16, 16, 17, 17, 18, 18, 19, 19, 20, 21, 24, 25; **9:**1, 1, 5, 6, 7, 10, 10, 12, 12, 13, 13, 15, 16, 17, 17, 22; **10:**2, 2, 3, 4, 4, 5, 10, 10, 10, 11, 12, 12, 14, 14, 15, 15, 16, 16, 17, 17, 18, 18, 19, 19, 20, 20, 21, 22, 22, 23, 23, 24, 24, 25, 25, 25, 25, 26, 26, 27, 27, 29, 33, 33, 33, 34, 36; **11:**1, 3, 4, 4, 10, 11, 16, 16, 17, 17, 20, 25, 28, 30, 33, 34; **12:**4, 4, 5, 5, 16; **13:**2, 2, 3, 3, 4, 4, 5, 6, 7, 8, 9, 10, 11, 11, 12, 13, 14, 15, 16, 19, 20, 21, 22, 22, 22, 23, 23, 23, 23, 24, 24, 26, 26, 27, 28, 29, 33; **14:**2, 3, 5, 6, 6, 6, 7, 9, 9, 9, 10, 14, 14, 14, 14, 14, 15, 18, 18, 19, 19, 22, 23, 24, 25, 29, 30, 30, 33, 34, 35, 38, 40, 44, 44; **15:**1, 3, 3, 3, 4, 4, 4, 5, 6, 6, 7, 8, 9, 9, 10, 12, 18, 20, 21, 22, 23, 24, 25, 26, 31, 32, 33, 38, 38, 39, 39, 39, 41, 41; **16:**1, 1, 1, 1, 1, 1, 2, 3, 3, 9, 9, 12, 13, 14, 15, 17, 18, 19, 22, 24, 25, 26, 27, 27, 34, 34, 37, 38, 38, 38, 38, 39, 40, 42, 43, 50; **17:**2, 3, 3, 3, 4, 4, 6, 6, 7, 8, 8, 10, 12, 13; **18:**1, 2, 2, 2, 2, 3, 4, 5, 7, 8, 8, 9, 10, 11, 11, 12, 13, 13, 15, 15, 16, 17, 18, 19, 20, 20, 20, 21, 21, 23, 24, 26, 26, 28, 29, 32, 32; **19:**2, 4, 4, 9, 9, 9, 10, 10, 12, 13, 13, 16, 17, 19, 20, 20, 21, 21; **20:**1, 1, 6, 6, 12, 13, 13, 14, 14, 16, 16, 18, 18, 19, 20, 22, 23, 23, 24, 24, 24, 27, 28; **21:**1, 1, 2, 4, 4, 5, 6, 8, 8, 9, 9, 11, 12, 13, 13, 14, 14, 14, 14, 14, 15, 15, 18, 21, 24, 25, 25, 26, 26, 27, 28, 28, 28, 29, 29, 29, 31, 31, 33, 34, 34; **22:**1, 1, 1, 2, 4, 4, 4, 5, 5, 5, 5, 7, 10, 10, 11, 15, 16, 17, 18, 22, 23, 24, 25, 26, 27, 31, 32, 34, 35, 36, 40, 41; **23:**2, 3, 6, 7, 10, 11, 13, 13, 14, 17, 18, 22, 23, 24, 28; **24:**2, 2, 3, 3, 3, 4, 6, 11, 13, 15, 15, 15, 16, 17, 17, 17, 19, 20, 20, 24; **25:**1, 2, 3, 3, 4, 5, 6, 6, 6, 7, 7, 11, 11, 12, 13, 14, 14, 14, 15, 15, 18, 18, 18, 18; **26:**1, 2, 2, 2, 2, 3, 3, 3, 4, 4, 4, 4, 7, 8, 9, 10, 10, 11, 12, 14, 15, 18, 19, 22, 23, 25, 26, 27, 34, 35, 37, 37, 37, 38, 41, 42, 43, 44, 47, 48, 50, 51, 54, 55, 55, 58, 58, 59, 59, 59, 61, 62, 62, 62, 63, 63, 63, 64, 65, 65, 65; **27:**1, 1, 1, 1, 1, 1, 2, 3, 4, 4, 7, 7, 8, 12, 12, 12, 14, 14, 14, 14, 16, 16, 17, 18, 19, 20, 21, 21, 21; **28:**1, 5, 5, 5, 7, 7, 9, 9, 11, 11, 12, 14, 14, 15, 18, 18, 18, 20, 21, 24, 24, 25, 25, 25, 26, 26, 26, 26, 26, 27, 28, 29; **29:**1, 1, 2, 3, 4, 7, 7, 8, 9, 9, 9, 10, 10, 11, 12, 12, 12, 13, 14, 14, 14, 14, 15, 17, 18, 18, 20, 21, 21, 23, 24, 24, 26, 27, 27, 29, 30, 30, 32, 33, 33, 35, 36, 37, 40, 40; **30:**1, 1, 4, 5, 7, 7, 8, 11, 12, 14, 15; **31:**3, 4, 5, 5, 6, 6, 8, 8, 12, 12, 13, 16, 19, 20, 21, 22, 23, 26, 26, 27, 28, 28, 29, 30, 30, 30, 30, 36, 37, 38, 39, 40, 42, 42, 47, 49, 50, 50, 51, 53, 54; **32:**1, 1, 1, 2, 4, 5, 7, 7, 9, 9, 11, 12, 12, 14, 18, 18, 19, 19, 22, 22, 22, 25, 26, 28, 29, 29, 30, 30, 30, 31, 32, 32, 33, 33, 33, 33, 33, 33, 33, 34, 34, 37, 37, 38, 38, 39, 39, 39, 40, 41, 41, 41, 41, 41, 41, 42; **33:**1, 1, 2, 2, 3, 3, 3, 4, 4, 6, 9, 15, 16, 36, 37, 38, 40, 40, 40, 44, 47, 48, 48, 49, 50, 51, 53, 54, 54, 54, 54; **34:**2, 3, 3, 3, 4, 5, 6, 11, 11, 11, 12, 14, 14, 14, 14, 15, 17, 19, 19, 20, 21, 22, 23, 23, 24, 24, 25, 26, 27, 28, 29, 29; **35:**1, 2, 6, 8, 8, 10, 10, 11, 12, 13, 14, 14, 15, 16, 25, 25, 26, 28, 28, 28, 30, 31, 31, 32, 32, 33, 34; **36:**1, 1, 1, 1, 1, 1, 2, 2, 3, 3, 3, 4, 4, 4, 5, 5, 6, 7, 7, 8, 9, 9, 10, 12, 12, 12, 13, 13; **Dt 1:**1, 1, 2, 4, 4, 5, 5, 5, 7, 7, 11, 17, 17, 19, 21, 21, 23, 24, 25, 26, 28, 28, 28, 33, 33, 35, 36, 36, 37, 38, 44; **2:**4, 5, 8, 9, 9, 10, 10, 10, 12, 15, 16, 18, 19, 19, 19, 19, 20, 22, 22, 23, 24, 25, 26, 26, 26, 28, 29, 35, 36; **3:**1, 2, 2, 4, 4, 6, 6, 8, 8, 10, 10, 11, 11, 11, 12, 12, 12, 12, 13, 13, 13, 13, 13, 14, 14, 14, 15, 16, 16, 17, 17, 18, 20, 21, 22, 26, 26; **4:**1, 3, 4, 8, 11, 16, 19, 19, 20, 21, 22, 23, 25, 25, 27, 32, 32, 33, 34, 37, 37, 41, 41, 43, 43, 43, 45, 46, 46, 47, 47, 47, 48, 49, 49; **5:**1, 3, 4, 5, 8, 8, 9, 9, 11, 14, 14, 22, 22, 24, 26, 26, 32; **6:**3, 9, 12, 14, 14, 15, 17, 20, 21, 23; **7:**1, 4, 6, 7, 12, 13, 13, 14, 14, 18, 18, 19, 21, 22, 24; **8:**3, 6, 7, 7, 8, 8, 14, 19; **9:**2, 3, 4, 4, 5, 5, 9, 11, 12, 14, 15, 23, 27; **10:**1, 2, 3, 4, 4, 5, 6, 6, 6, 7, 8, 8, 11, 12, 15, 17, 17, 19, 21, 22; **11:**2, 4, 6, 6, 10, 11, 11, 14, 18, 20, 25, 27, 28, 30, 30, 30, 30; **12:**1, 3, 6, 6, 7, 9, 12, 12, 14, 15, 17, 17, 18, 18, 21, 27, 27, 27, 27, 31; **13:**2, 5, 5, 7, 7, 10, 10, 12, 16, 17; **14:**1, 1, 2, 8, 13, 14, 15, 18, 22, 22, 23, 23, 23, 25, 26, 28, 28; **15:**1, 2, 5, 9, 9, 14, 15, 18, 19, 19, 20; **16:**1, 1, 3, 4, 4, 6, 9, 10, 13, 13, 14, 15, 16, 16, 16, 16, 18, 19, 19, 21; **17:**2, 2, 3, 3, 5, 6, 8, 8, 8, 12, 12, 16, 17, 18, 19, 19; **18:**1, 1, 1, 2, 4, 5, 5, 7, 8, 8, 9, 11, 12, 12, 16, 16; **19:**2, 3, 4, 5, 5, 5, 6, 7, 9, 10, 11, 11, 12, 12, 13, 15, 15, 15, 15, 16; **20:**1, 3, 5, 6, 9, 14, 15, 16, 18, 18; **21:**3, 6, 8, 8, 8, 9, 15, 16, 17, 17, 17, 19, 20, 21, 22, 23; **22:**8, 8, 9, 9, 11, 12, 14, 15, 15, 17, 17, 19, 19, 21, 21, 24, 24, 24, 26, 26, 28, 29; **23:**1, 2, 2, 3, 3, 4, 4, 8, 8, 10, 13, 13, 18, 18, 21, 24, 25; **24:**1, 6, 8, 14, 16, 16, 16, 17, 19, 20, 22; **25:**2, 5, 5, 6, 8, 9, 10, 11, 11, 18; **26:**2, 4, 5, 7, 8, 10, 11, 12, 13, 13, 14, 14; **27:**1, 3, 3, 8, 9, 12, 13, 14, 15, 22, 26; **28:**1, 9, 10, 10, 11, 13, 14, 17, 17, 21, 25, 25, 27, 31, 34, 36, 37, 42, 49, 53, 55, 55, 55, 58, 58, 60, 61, 62, 64, 64, 65, 67; **29:**1, 1, 3, 7, 7, 8, 8, 9, 10, 10, 15, 16, 16, 17, 18, 19, 19, 21, 21, 22, 23, 25, 25, 25, 25, 29; **30:**4, 6, 10; **31:**1, 3, 3, 4, 6, 6, 9, 9, 10, 10, 10, 11, 12, 15, 16, 18, 19, 19, 22, 23, 23, 24, 25, 26, 26, 26, 26, 28, 30; **32:**3, 7, 7, 8, 8, 9, 13, 14, 14, 15, 15, 22, 22, 24, 26, 27, 30, 31, 32, 32, 33, 33, 35, 38, 38, 42, 42, 43, 43, 44, 44, 46, 49, 49, 49,

51, 51, 51, 51, 52; **33:**1, 1, 4, 4, 5, 5, 6, 6, 7, 7, 8, 8, 11, 12, 12, 13, 13, 15, 16, 16, 16, 17, 17, 17, 17, 17, 18, 18, 18, 19, 19, 20, 21, 21, 22, 23, 23, 24, 25, 25, 25, 26, 28; **34:**1, 2, 2, 2, 3, 5, 5, 8, 8, 8, 9, 9, 9, 9, 11, 12; **Jos 1:**1, 1, 4, 8, 10, 11, 12, 12, 13, 14, 15, 15; **2:**1, 1, 2, 3, 6, 7, 9, 10, 11, 19, 24; **3:**1, 3, 3, 6, 7, 8, 8, 11, 11, 11, 13, 13, 13, 14, 14, 15, 16, 17, 17; **4:**3, 5, 5, 5, 5, 5, 7, 7, 8, 9, 9, 9, 10, 10, 11, 12, 12, 13, 14, 14, 16, 16, 18, 18, 19, 19, 24, 24; **5:**1, 1, 2, 3, 5, 9, 10, 10, 10, 12, 13, 14, 15; **6:**1, 1, 4, 5, 6, 6, 7, 7, 8, 8, 9, 10, 11, 12, 13, 13, 13, 13, 18, 20, 20, 23, 24, 26, 26, 26, 26; **7:**1, 1, 1, 1, 1, 1, 1, 1, 2, 2, 2, 3, 3, 4, 5, 6, 6, 9, 9, 13, 14, 15, 16, 16, 17, 17, 17, 17, 18, 19, 20, 21, 23, 24, 24, 26, 26; **8:**1, 3, 5, 7, 9, 10, 11, 12, 13, 13, 14, 20, 20, 21, 22, 22, 23, 25, 27, 28, 29, 29, 29, 30, 31, 32, 32, 33, 33, 33, 33, 33, 34; **9:**1, 1, 1, 3, 6, 6, 9, 9, 9, 10, 10, 10, 11, 15, 16, 17, 18, 18, 18, 19, 19, 23, 24, 26, 27, 27; **10:**1, 1, 3, 3, 3, 3, 3, 4, 6, 8, 8, 11, 12, 12, 12, 13, 13, 18, 19, 22, 23, 23, 24, 25, 26, 27, 27, 27, 28, 28, 28, 30, 30, 33, 37, 39, 40, 40, 42; **11:**1, 1, 1, 1, 2, 2, 2, 3, 3, 3, 3, 3, 3, 4, 6, 8, 10, 10, 12, 13, 14, 15, 16, 16, 17, 17, 17, 19, 20, 21, 21, 21, 22, 23, 23; **12:**1, 1, 2, 2, 2, 2, 2, 2, 3, 3, 3, 4, 4, 5, 5, 5, 5, 5, 5, 5, 6, 6, 6, 6, 7, 7, 7, 7, 9, 9, 10, 10, 11, 11, 12, 12, 13, 13, 14, 14, 15, 15, 16, 16, 17, 17, 18, 18, 19, 19, 20, 20, 21, 21, 22, 22, 23, 23, 23, 24; **13:**2, 3, 3, 3, 4, 4, 4, 4, 5, 5, 6, 6, 7, 8, 8, 8, 8, 9, 9, 10, 10, 10, 11, 11, 11, 11, 12, 12, 12, 13, 14, 14, 15, 15, 16, 16, 20, 21, 21, 21, 21, 22, 23, 23, 23, 24, 24, 25, 25, 25, 25, 25, 27, 27, 27, 27, 28, 28, 29, 29, 30, 30, 30, 31, 31, 31, 32, 32, 33, 33; **14:**1, 1, 2, 3, 3, 4, 5, 6, 6, 6, 7, 7, 9, 9, 12, 13, 14, 14, 14, 15; **15:**1, 1, 1, 1, 2, 3, 3, 3, 4, 5, 6, 6, 7, 7, 7, 8, 8, 8, 8, 8, 8, 8, 8, 9, 9, 10, 10, 10, 11, 11, 12, 12, 12, 13, 13, 13, 14, 15, 17, 20, 20, 21, 21, 32, 45, 45, 45, 47, 47, 52, 61, 62, 63, 63, 63; **16:**1, 1, 1, 1, 2, 3, 4, 5, 5, 5, 6, 8, 8, 9, 9, 10, 10, 10; **17:**1, 1, 1, 1, 1, 1, 2, 2, 3, 3, 4, 4, 5, 5, 6, 6, 6, 6, 7, 7, 7, 7, 7, 8, 8, 8, 9, 9, 9, 9, 10, 10, 10, 10, 10, 11, 12, 13, 14, 14, 15, 16, 17, 17, 18, 18; **18:**3, 3, 4, 4, 6, 7, 7, 7, 7, 7, 8, 10, 11, 11, 11, 11, 12, 12, 12, 13, 13, 14, 14, 14, 14, 15, 15, 16, 16, 16, 16, 16, 16, 16, 17, 17, 18, 19, 19, 19, 20, 20, 21, 21, 28, 28; **19:**1, 1, 1, 8, 8, 8, 8, 9, 9, 9, 10, 10, 10, 10, 11, 12, 14, 14, 16, 16, 16, 17, 17, 17, 23, 23, 23, 24, 24, 24, 27, 29, 31, 31, 31, 32, 32, 32, 34, 34, 39, 39, 39, 40, 40, 40, 47, 47, 47, 48, 48, 48, 49, 50, 51, 51, 51, 51, 51; **20:**2, 3, 3, 4, 5, 6, 6, 7, 7, 7, 7, 7, 8, 8, 8, 8, 8, 8, 8, 8, 9; **21:**1, 1, 1, 1, 1, 2, 3, 4, 4, 4, 4, 5, 5, 5, 6, 6, 6, 7, 7, 9, 10, 10, 10, 11, 11, 12, 13, 13, 17, 19, 20, 20, 20, 21, 23, 25, 26, 27, 27, 27, 27, 28, 30, 32, 32, 33, 34, 34, 36, 38, 38, 40, 41, 42, 44, 45; **22:**1, 1, 2, 3, 4, 4, 7, 7, 7, 7, 7, 8, 9, 9, 9, 9, 9, 10, 11, 11, 11, 13, 13, 13, 14, 14, 14, 15, 15, 15, 16, 16, 17, 17, 18, 19, 19, 20, 20, 20, 20, 21, 21, 24, 28, 28, 28, 29, 29, 30, 30, 31, 32, 32, 32, 33, 34; **23:**1, 2, 4, 4, 5, 6, 6, 7, 10, 10, 12, 14, 14, 16; **24:**1, 2, 2, 3, 4, 8, 8, 8, 9, 9, 9, 11, 12, 12, 15, 17, 23, 26, 26, 26, 26, 29, 29, 29, 30, 30, 31, 31, 32, 32, 32, 32, 32, 32, 33, 33, 33; **Jdg 1:**3, 3, 3, 4, 4, 8, 10, 11, 13, 16, 16, 16, 16, 18, 19, 19, 20, 20, 20, 21, 21, 22, 22, 24, 26, 27, 28, 29, 30, 31, 31, 32, 33, 33, 33, 33, 34, 35, 36; **2:**1, 1, 4, 6, 6, 7, 8, 8, 8, 9, 9, 11, 12, 12, 12, 13, 17; **3:**1, 2, 3, 7, 8, 9, 10, 10, 11, 12, 13, 14, 15, 15, 15, 15, 19, 27, 27, 28, 28, 29, 29, 31; **4:**2, 2, 4, 5, 5, 6, 6, 6, 6, 7, 9, 10, 11, 11, 11, 12, 13, 13, 14, 14, 16, 17, 17, 17, 20; **5:**1, 3, 4, 5, 5, 5, 6, 6, 6, 7, 11, 11, 11, 12, 13, 14, 15, 15, 16, 17, 19, 19, 22, 23, 23, 24, 28; **6:**3, 5, 7, 8, 8, 10, 11, 11, 11, 11, 11, 12, 13, 15, 19, 20, 21, 21, 22, 22, 24, 24, 26, 27, 27, 27, 27, 28, 28, 28, 29, 30, 33, 33, 33, 34, 34, 34, 34, 35, 38; **7:**1, 1, 1, 1, 2, 3, 6, 8, 11, 12, 12, 12, 12, 13, 14, 17, 18, 18, 19, 19, 22, 23, 23, 24, 24, 24, 25, 25, 25; **8:**1, 2, 2, 2, 3, 3, 5, 5, 6, 7, 9, 10, 10, 10, 11, 13, 14, 16, 17, 18, 21, 24, 24, 26, 26, 26, 28, 28, 29, 32, 32, 32, 33, 35; **9:**1, 2, 2, 3, 3, 4, 5, 6, 7, 7, 15, 16, 20, 20, 21, 23, 24, 25, 26, 26, 26, 27, 28, 28, 28, 29, 30, 31, 35, 36, 38, 39, 40, 41, 42, 43, 44, 46, 46, 46, 49, 49, 49, 50, 51, 57, 57, 57; **10:**1, 1, 1, 1, 1, 4, 4, 6, 6, 8, 8, 9, 10, 14, 17, 18, 18; **11:**1, 2, 2, 3, 3, 5, 5, 8, 11, 11, 11, 12, 13, 13, 16, 17, 17, 17, 18, 19, 21, 21, 21, 23, 25, 25, 25, 26, 27, 28, 29, 29, 31, 40; **12:**1, 2, 4, 4, 4, 5, 5, 5, 5, 6, 7, 7, 13, 15; **13:**2, 2, 3, 6, 6, 7, 7, 8, 9, 12, 13, 15, 16, 16, 17, 18, 20, 21, 25, 25, 25; **14:**5, 6, 6, 8, 8, 9, 9, 10, 12, 14, 17, 17, 18, 18, 19, 19, 19; **15:**4, 5, 8, 8, 9, 10, 11, 11, 12, 14, 14, 14, 16, 16, 18, 18, 18, 19, 19; **16:**1, 2, 2, 3, 3, 3, 4, 5, 5, 5, 9, 9, 9, 10, 13, 13, 13, 15, 24, 25, 27, 28, 29; **17:**1, 2, 3, 4, 5, 8, 10, 10, 11; **18:**1, 2, 2, 2, 6, 7, 9, 11, 12, 13, 13, 16, 18, 19, 19, 19, 21, 22, 22, 23, 25, 25, 26, 26, 27, 27, 28, 28, 28, 30, 30, 30, 31, 31; **19:**1, 1, 1, 6, 8, 8, 10, 14, 16, 16, 18, 18, 19, 22, 25, 26, 29; **20:**1, 1, 2, 2, 2, 2, 3, 4, 4, 5, 5, 6, 7, 8, 10, 10, 12, 13, 13, 15, 16, 16, 18, 20, 23, 24, 25, 25, 26, 27, 27, 28, 28, 31, 32, 32, 33, 33, 35, 35, 38, 40, 40, 43, 44, 45, 45, 46, 47; **21:**1, 2, 3, 3, 5, 5, 6, 12, 12, 13, 13, 14, 14, 14, 15, 16, 16, 17, 19, 19, 19, 20, 21, 21, 21, 22, 23, 23, 24; **Ru 1:**1, 1, 2, 8, 9, 13, 19, 22; **2:**1, 3, 9, 11, 12, 14, 16, 20, 20, 23; **3:**2, 6, 7, 9, 12, 15, 17; **4:**4, 5, 5, 7, 9, 10, 10, 11, 12, 12, 14, 15, 16, 17, 17, 18, 19, 19, 20, 20, 21, 21, 22, 22; **1Sa 1:**1, 1, 1, 1, 1, 3, 3, 4, 4, 6, 16, 17, 17, 24; **2:**8, 8, 10, 12, 13, 17, 18, 20, 21, 22, 22, 22, 27, 29, 30, 30, 30, 31, 32, 32, 36; **3:**3, 3, 14, 15, 20, 20, 20; **4:**1, 2, 3, 3, 3, 4, 4, 4, 4, 5, 5, 5, 6, 8, 11, 11, 12, 13, 13, 13, 17, 17, 19, 19, 19, 21, 22; **5:**1, 1, 2, 2, 2, 3, 3, 3, 4, 4, 5, 5, 6, 6, 7, 7, 8, 8, 8, 8, 8, 8, 9, 10, 10, 10, 10, 10, 11, 11; **6:**1, 2, 3, 3, 4, 5, 8, 9, 11, 12, 13, 14, 14, 15, 15, 15, 15, 17, 18, 18, 18, 19, 19, 20, 21; **7:**1, 1, 1, 1, 3, 3, 3, 4, 5, 10, 11, 12, 12, 14, 15, 16, 16; **8:**4, 12, 14, 15, 16, 17; **9:**1, 1, 1, 1, 1, 4, 4, 4, 4, 5, 6, 6, 10, 16, 16, 19, 19, 20, 21, 21, 22, 23, 23, 25, 27; **10:**1, 1, 2, 3, 3, 3, 4, 5, 5, 5, 6, 8, 10, 11, 12, 12, 17, 18, 18, 20, 21, 21, 21, 21, 25, 26; **11:**1, 1, 1, 2, 2, 3, 3, 6, 7, 7, 7, 8, 10, 11, 11; **12:**2, 3, 5, 6, 6, 7, 9, 9, 10, 12, 12, 17, 18, 18, 24; **13:**2, 2, 2, 2, 2, 3, 5, 5, 5, 6, 6, 7, 7, 13, 15, 15, 16, 17, 17, 18, 19, 21, 21, 21, 21, 22, 22, 23; **14:**2, 3, 3, 3, 3, 5, 5, 11, 16, 18, 21, 24, 27, 28, 29, 36, 39, 40, 41, 43, 43, 45, 47, 50, 50, 51; **15:**1, 2, 5, 6, 7, 9, 9, 14, 14, 15, 17, 17, 17, 17, 21, 22, 23, 23, 24, 26, 28, 29, 32, 33, 35; **16:**1, 1, 3, 4, 8, 10, 10, 13, 14, 15, 18, 18, 21; **17:**2, 4, 4, 4, 5, 7, 7, 10, 12, 12, 14, 16, 17, 17, 18, 19, 20, 22, 23, 25, 26, 26, 28, 34, 36, 37, 38, 41, 43, 45, 45, 45, 46, 52, 52, 52, 55; **18:**1, 1, 12, 15, 23, 29, 29, 30; **19:**1, 10, 13, 14, 16, 17, 20, 23, 24; **20:**5, 12, 14, 17, 20, 22, 27, 30, 31, 37, 39, 41; **21:**1, 3, 6, 9, 9, 10, 11, 12, 15; **22:**1, 2, 5, 5, 6, 7, 8, 8, 10, 12, 13, 14, 14, 15, 17, 19, 20, 20, 21, 22; **23:**5, 9, 10, 11, 11, 12, 13, 14, 14, 17, 18, 18, 19, 19, 19, 19, 22, 24, 24, 24, 24, 25, 26, 28, 29; **24:**1, 2, 4, 10, 11, 14, 15, 21; **25:**1, 2, 3, 5, 8, 10, 10, 11, 14, 16, 18, 18, 18, 21, 22, 29, 29, 30, 31, 32, 34, 34, 42, 43, 44; **26:**1, 2, 2, 3, 3, 5, 6, 10, 11, 11, 12, 16, 20, 20, 22; **27:**2, 3, 3, 5, 5, 6, 6, 10, 12; **28:**3, 4, 8, 8, 10, 13, 19, 19, 20, 21; **29:**2, 3, 5, 6, 6, 8, 9, 11; **30:**1, 5, 5, 5, 6, 10, 11, 12, 12, 13, 14, 14, 16, 16, 16, 17, 22, 25, 26, 26, 27, 29, 29; **31:**1, 2, 6, 7, 8, 9, 9, 10, 10, 10, 11, 12; **2Sa 1:**1, 9, 10, 12, 15, 18, 18, 18, 20, 21, 21, 21, 24, 26, 27; **2:**2, 3, 4, 4, 7, 8, 8, 9, 9, 10, 11, 12, 13, 13, 13, 14, 14, 16, 16, 17, 17, 17, 18, 21, 21, 23, 24, 24, 25, 25, 28, 31, 31; **3:**1, 2, 3, 3, 3, 7, 7, 10, 11, 12, 14, 15, 17, 19, 19, 19, 21, 22, 26, 28, 30, 34, 35, 39; **4:**2, 2, 2, 2, 3, 4, 4, 5, 8, 8;

5:1, 1, 2, 3, 3, 7, 7, 8, 8, 9, 11, 12, 14, 17, 18, 22, 24, 24; **6:**2, 2, 2, 3,
3, 4, 5, 5, 6, 6, 7, 9, 9, 10, 10, 10, 10, 11, 11, 12, 12, 12, 15, 15, 16,
16, 16, 17, 18, 19, 19, 19, 19, 20, 21, 21, 22, 23; **7:**2, 6, 7, 11, 12, 13,
19, 21, 22, 26, 27; **8:**2, 2, 3, 3, 3, 4, 5, 7, 8, 8, 9, 9, 10, 12, 12, 13, 14,
16, 16, 16, 17, 17, 18, 18; **9:**2, 3, 4, 4, 7, 11, 12; **10:**1, 2, 4, 6, 6, 6, 6,
8, 10, 10, 12, 16, 16, 16, 18; **11:**1, 1, 2, 2, 2, 3, 3, 9, 11, 11, 19, 24,
27, 27; **12:**4, 4, 7, 7, 7, 8, 9, 11, 12, 14, 17, 25, 26, 26, 28, 28, 29, 30,
30, 31, 31, 31; **13:**3, 4, 6, 9, 13, 15, 22, 25, 29, 32, 34, 34, 37, 37;
14:4, 6, 7, 7, 12, 13, 14, 14, 17, 17, 20, 25, 32; **15:**1, 2, 6, 6, 7, 10, 11,
12, 14, 14, 16, 17, 19, 24, 24, 25, 28, 29, 30, 30, 32, 32, 32; **16:**1, 1,
1, 1, 1, 1, 3, 5, 5, 5, 7, 8, 9, 10, 11, 12, 21, 23; **17:**4, 8, 9, 10, 10, 11,
12, 13, 13, 14, 14, 16, 19, 21, 24, 25, 25, 25, 26, 27, 27, 27, 27; **18:**2,
3, 3, 4, 4, 6, 8, 9, 9, 10, 11, 12, 14, 15, 16, 17, 17, 23, 23, 24, 27, 29,
32, 33; **19:**2, 2, 5, 6, 7, 9, 9, 11, 13, 13, 14, 15, 16, 16, 17, 17, 17, 21,
22, 22, 27, 30, 33, 40, 40, 41, 41, 41, 42, 42, 43, 43; **20:**1, 1, 1, 1, 2,
2, 3, 4, 11, 12, 13, 14, 14, 18, 21, 21, 23, 23, 23, 24, 24; **21:**1, 2, 2, 2,
6, 6, 7, 8, 8, 8, 8, 9, 9, 9, 10, 10, 12, 12, 12, 12, 12, 13, 13, 14, 14, 14,
14, 15, 16, 17, 17, 18, 19, 19, 19, 19, 20, 21, 22; **22:**3, 4, 5, 5, 8, 8,
11, 13, 16, 16, 16, 16, 17, 20, 21, 22, 25, 35, 36, 43, 45, 47, 49; **23:**1,
1, 1, 1, 2, 3, 3, 3, 4, 8, 8, 9, 9, 10, 11, 11, 12, 13, 13, 14, 15, 17, 17,
17, 18, 18, 18, 19, 19, 20, 20, 22, 23, 23, 23, 24, 24, 26, 29, 29, 29,
32, 33, 33, 34, 34, 36; **24:**1, 1, 2, 2, 4, 5, 5, 6, 7, 7, 9, 9, 11, 12, 13,
13, 13, 14, 16, 16, 18, 24; **1Ki 1:**4, 5, 5, 7, 8, 9, 9, 9, 9, 12, 15, 19, 25,
26, 27, 30, 32, 36, 36, 38, 39, 41, 42, 44, 48, 49, 50, 50, 50, 51; **2:**1,
3, 3, 3, 4, 4, 5, 5, 5, 5, 5, 5, 7, 7, 7, 8, 10, 11, 14, 16, 20, 22, 24, 25,
26, 27, 27, 28, 28, 28, 29, 29, 30, 31, 32, 32, 32, 32, 32, 32, 32, 32,
33, 34, 35, 35, 39, 39, 45, 46; **3:**1, 1, 1, 1, 2, 2, 3, 4, 7, 9, 11, 13, 15,
17, 18, 23, 25, 26, 28; **4:**2, 3, 3, 4, 4, 5, 5, 6, 6, 6, 7, 7, 8, 8, 10, 11,
12, 12, 13, 13, 13, 14, 15, 16, 17, 18, 19, 19, 19, 19, 19, 19, 20, 21,
21, 21, 22, 22, 24, 25, 25, 30, 30, 30, 31, 33, 33, 34; **5:**1, 1, 1, 3, 3, 5,
7, 7, 11, 11, 11, 12, 14, 17, 17, 18; **6:**1, 1, 1, 1, 1, 3, 3, 3, 5, 5, 5, 6, 7,
7, 8, 8, 9, 9, 10, 10, 10, 13, 16, 17, 18, 19, 19, 20, 21, 23, 24, 24, 27,
27, 29, 29, 31, 32, 33, 34, 35, 36, 36, 36, 37, 37, 37, 38, 38; **7:**2, 2, 2,
2, 3, 4, 4, 5, 6, 7, 7, 8, 9, 10, 11, 12, 12, 12, 12, 12, 14, 16, 16, 17, 18,
21, 24, 24, 25, 26, 26, 30, 30, 30, 31, 31, 31, 34, 34, 35, 36, 38, 39,
39, 40, 41, 41, 42, 42, 42, 45, 45, 47, 48, 48, 48, 49, 49, 50, 50, 51,
51; **8:**1, 1, 1, 1, 2, 3, 4, 5, 6, 6, 6, 8, 9, 9, 10, 10, 11, 14, 15, 16, 16,
17, 17, 19, 20, 20, 21, 22, 22, 22, 23, 23, 25, 26, 31, 31, 36, 37, 41,
42, 42, 43, 43, 47, 51, 51, 52, 53, 53, 54, 54, 55, 56, 59, 59, 63, 64,
64, 64, 65, 65, 65, 65, 65; **9:**1, 5, 5, 7, 7, 9, 10, 10, 11, 11, 11, 13, 14,
15, 15, 15, 16, 17, 17, 21, 22, 22, 23, 24, 25, 26, 26, 26, 27, 28; **10:**1,
1, 1, 2, 2, 2, 4, 5, 5, 7, 9, 10, 10, 10, 10, 11, 12, 12, 13, 14, 15, 15, 16,
16, 17, 17, 17, 17, 19, 19, 19, 20, 20, 21, 21, 21, 21, 21, 22, 25, 26,
26, 27, 29, 29, 29, 29, 29; **11:**4, 5, 5, 7, 7, 7, 7, 9, 11, 12, 13, 13, 13,
14, 17, 19, 19, 23, 23, 24, 24, 25, 26, 26, 26, 27, 27, 28, 28, 29, 31,
31, 31, 31, 32, 32, 32, 32, 33, 33, 33, 34, 34, 35, 36, 37, 39, 39, 40,
41, 41, 41, 43; **12:**2, 2, 3, 3, 8, 8, 13, 14, 15, 15, 15, 16, 17, 18, 19,
19, 20, 20, 20, 20, 21, 21, 22, 23, 23, 23, 24, 25, 25, 25, 26, 27, 27,
28, 28, 29, 31, 31, 32; **13:**1, 2, 3, 4, 5, 6, 6, 7, 8, 8, 11, 12, 14, 14, 15,
19, 21, 22, 22, 23, 24, 26, 29, 29, 31, 32, 33, 34, 34; **14:**3, 3, 3, 6, 7,
7, 8, 11, 13, 13, 13, 14, 15, 16, 17, 18, 19, 19, 19, 19, 19, 21, 21, 22,
22, 24, 24, 25, 25, 26, 27, 28, 29, 29, 29, 29, 31; **15:**1, 2, 3, 7, 7, 7, 7,
8, 9, 10, 15, 16, 16, 17, 18, 18, 18, 18, 18, 19, 19, 20, 20, 21, 21, 22,
22, 23, 23, 23, 23, 23, 23, 24, 25, 25, 26, 26, 27, 27, 27, 28, 28, 29,
29, 30, 30, 31, 31, 31, 31, 32, 33, 34, 34; **16:**1, 2, 2, 2, 3, 3, 4, 5, 5, 5,
5, 5, 7, 7, 7, 8, 8, 9, 9, 9, 10, 11, 12, 13, 13, 13, 13, 13, 14, 14, 14, 14,
15, 15, 15, 16, 17, 18, 19, 19, 20, 20, 20, 20, 20, 21, 21, 22, 22, 23,
23, 24, 24, 25, 26, 26, 26, 26, 27, 27, 27, 27, 27, 29, 29, 30, 31, 31,
33, 33, 33, 33, 34; **17:**1, 3, 9, 9, 10, 10, 11, 12, 12, 12, 13, 14, 14, 15,
18, 22, 24; **18:**1, 3, 3, 4, 5, 9, 10, 10, 12, 12, 13, 18, 18, 19, 19, 19,
21, 22, 23, 23, 24, 24, 25, 25, 25, 25, 26, 26, 26, 29, 30, 31, 31, 36,
38, 40, 42, 44, 46, 46; **19:**1, 6, 7, 7, 8, 10, 10, 12, 13, 14, 14, 15, 15,
16, 16, 16, 19, 19, 19, 19; **20:**1, 1, 2, 3, 6, 7, 9, 10, 11, 12, 14, 15, 15,
15, 17, 17, 22, 23, 25, 25, 27, 28, 28, 28, 28, 30, 31, 32, 32, 33, 33,
34, 35, 35, 36, 39, 39, 41, 41, 42, 43; **21:**4, 7, 8, 9, 10, 13, 18, 19, 21,
22, 22, 22, 22, 22, 23, 23, 24, 26; **22:**2, 2, 3, 4, 6, 7, 8, 8, 9, 9, 9, 10,
10, 10, 10, 10, 11, 11, 18, 19, 23, 24, 24, 26, 26, 28, 29, 29, 31, 31,
32, 33, 34, 34, 34, 34, 35, 38, 39, 39, 39, 39, 39, 41, 41, 42, 43, 44,
45, 45, 45, 45, 45, 46, 46, 48, 49, 50, 51, 51, 52, 52, 52, 52, 53, 53;
2Ki 1:1, 2, 2, 2, 3, 3, 3, 3, 6, 9, 9, 10, 11, 12, 12, 13, 13, 15, 16, 17,
17, 17, 17, 18, 18, 18, 18; **2:**3, 3, 5, 5, 7, 8, 11, 11, 12, 13, 14, 15, 16,
16, 19, 19, 23, 23, 24, 24, 24; **3:**1, 2, 3, 3, 3, 4, 4, 4, 4, 5, 5, 6, 7, 7, 7,
8, 9, 10, 10, 10, 11, 11, 11, 11, 12, 13, 13, 13, 13, 14, 15, 16, 18, 19,
20, 21, 24, 24, 24, 26, 26, 26; **4:**1, 1, 2, 6, 7, 8, 9, 13, 13, 16, 19, 21,
21, 22, 22, 25, 27, 27, 27, 31, 38, 39, 39, 40, 42, 42, 42, 42, 42, 43;
5:1, 1, 2, 2, 3, 5, 5, 5, 5, 5, 6, 6, 7, 8, 9, 10, 11, 12, 12, 14, 15, 17, 18,
22, 22, 22, 23, 23, 23; **6:**1, 2, 5, 6, 8, 9, 9, 10, 10, 11, 11, 11, 11, 12,
12, 12, 14, 15, 15, 17, 21, 22, 22, 23, 24, 25, 25, 25, 26, 26, 31, 32;
7:1, 1, 1, 1, 1, 2, 2, 2, 3, 5, 6, 6, 6, 6, 6, 8, 12, 12, 13, 13, 13, 15, 16,
16, 16, 16, 16, 17, 18, 18, 18, 18, 18, 18, 19, 19, 19; **8:**2, 2, 3, 4, 4, 5,
6, 6, 7, 7, 8, 9, 9, 11, 12, 13, 15, 16, 16, 16, 16, 18, 18, 18, 21, 21, 22,
23, 23, 23, 23, 24, 25, 25, 25, 26, 26, 27, 27, 28, 28, 29; **9:**1, 1, 1, 2,
2, 5, 6, 7, 7, 8, 9, 9, 9, 9, 9, 10, 11, 14, 14, 14, 14, 16, 17, 17, 20, 21,
21, 21, 22, 25, 25, 26, 27, 27, 28, 29, 31, 33, 34, 36, 37; **10:**1, 1, 1, 1,
3, 5, 6, 6, 6, 7, 8, 8, 10, 11, 12, 13, 13, 13, 13, 14, 14, 14, 15, 18, 18,
19, 19, 19, 19, 21, 22, 22, 22, 23, 23, 23, 24, 25, 25, 25, 26, 27, 27,
28, 29, 30, 30, 30, 31, 31, 31, 32, 32, 33, 33, 33, 34, 34, 34, 34; **11:**1,
1, 1, 2, 2, 3, 4, 4, 4, 5, 6, 9, 10, 11, 12, 14, 14, 15, 15, 15, 18, 18, 18,
18, 18, 19, 19, 19, 20; **12:**1, 4, 5, 6, 8, 9, 9, 9, 9, 9, 13, 13, 17, 18, 18,
19, 19, 19, 19, 21, 21, 21; **13:**1, 1, 2, 2, 2, 2, 3, 4, 5, 6, 7, 8, 8, 8, 8, 8,
10, 10, 11, 11, 12, 12, 12, 12, 12, 12, 14, 14, 16, 17, 19, 20, 21, 21,
22, 22, 23, 23, 24, 25, 25; **14:**1, 1, 1, 1, 3, 6, 6, 6, 6, 6, 6, 6, 7, 8, 8, 9,
9, 10, 11, 11, 12, 13, 13, 13, 14, 15, 15, 15, 15, 15, 15, 17, 17, 17, 18,
18, 18, 18, 20, 21, 22, 23, 23, 24, 24, 25, 25, 25, 26, 27, 27, 28, 28,
28, 28, 28, 28, 29; **15:**1, 1, 1, 1, 5, 5, 5, 6, 6, 6, 6, 7, 8, 8, 9, 9, 10, 11,
11, 11, 11, 12, 13, 13, 14, 15, 15, 15, 15, 16, 17, 17, 18, 18, 19, 19,
20, 20, 20, 20, 20, 21, 21, 21, 21, 23, 23, 24, 24, 25, 25, 25, 25, 26,
26, 26, 26, 27, 27, 28, 28, 29, 29, 29, 30, 30, 30, 31, 31, 31, 31, 32,
32, 33, 35, 35, 36, 36, 36, 36, 37, 37, 38; **16:**1, 1, 2, 3, 3, 3, 3, 5, 5, 6,
6, 6, 7, 7, 8, 9, 10, 10, 13, 14, 14, 15, 15, 17, 18, 18, 19, 19, 19, 19,
20; **17:**1, 1, 2, 3, 4, 4, 4, 4, 5, 6, 6, 6, 6, 7, 7, 8, 8, 9, 10, 11, 11, 15,
16, 16, 18, 19, 19, 20, 21, 21, 22, 22, 22, 23, 24, 24, 24, 24, 24, 25,
26, 26, 26, 27, 27, 27, 27, 28, 29, 29, 30, 33, 34, 34, 35, 36; **18:**1, 1,
2, 4, 5, 5, 7, 9, 9, 9, 9, 10, 10, 11, 11, 11, 13, 13, 13, 14, 14, 14, 14,
14, 15, 16, 17, 18, 18, 19, 20, 21, 23, 24, 24, 24, 26, 28, 31, 31, 32,
32, 32, 33, 33, 34, 34, 35, 37, 37; **19:**1, 2, 3, 4, 9, 10, 10, 11, 12, 12,
12, 13, 13, 13, 15, 15, 15, 16, 17, 18, 18, 18, 19, 20, 20, 20, 21, 21,
22, 23, 24, 25, 28, 30, 31, 31, 31, 32, 32, 34, 35, 36, 36, 37, 37, 37;
20:1, 5, 5, 5, 5, 6, 6, 8, 11, 12, 12, 14, 18, 18, 20, 20, 20, 20, 20; **21:**2,
2, 3, 3, 4, 5, 5, 7, 11, 11, 12, 12, 13, 13, 14, 15, 16, 17, 17, 17, 17, 18,
19, 21, 22, 24, 25, 25, 25, 25, 26; **22:**1, 2, 3, 3, 3, 3, 5, 7, 8, 9, 11, 12,
12, 14, 14, 14, 14, 14, 15, 18, 18; **23:**1, 2, 2, 2, 3, 3, 4, 4, 5, 5, 5, 7, 7,
8, 8, 8, 8, 8, 10, 10, 11, 11, 11, 11, 12, 12, 12, 13, 13, 13, 13, 13, 13,
13, 15, 16, 16, 16, 16, 17, 17, 17, 18, 19, 19, 20, 21, 22, 22, 23, 24,
24, 25, 26, 26, 27, 28, 28, 28, 28, 29, 29, 31, 33, 33, 33, 34, 34, 35,
36; **24:**1, 1, 2, 3, 3, 5, 5, 5, 5, 7, 7, 7, 8, 10, 10, 12, 13, 14, 16, 16, 17,
18, 20, 20; **25:**1, 1, 2, 3, 3, 4, 4, 5, 6, 7, 8, 8, 8, 8, 9, 9, 10, 10, 11, 11,
11, 12, 12, 15, 15, 16, 17, 17, 17, 18, 19, 19, 19, 19, 20, 21, 21, 21,
22, 22, 23, 23, 23, 23, 23, 24, 25, 25, 25, 25, 26, 26, 27, 27, 29, 30;
1Ch 1:1, 4, 5, 6, 7, 8, 9, 9, 10, 11, 13, 13, 17, 17, 18, 18, 19, 20, 23,
28, 29, 31, 32, 32, 33, 33, 34, 34, 35, 36, 37, 38, 39, 40, 40, 41, 41,
42, 42, 43, 43, 44, 45, 46, 46, 46, 47, 48, 49, 50, 50, 50, 51, 54; **2:**1,
5, 6, 7, 7, 8, 9, 10, 10, 10, 11, 11, 12, 12, 20, 20, 21, 22, 22, 23, 23,
23, 24, 24, 25, 25, 26, 27, 27, 28, 28, 29, 30, 31, 33, 35, 35, 36, 36,
37, 37, 38, 38, 39, 39, 40, 40, 41, 41, 42, 42, 42, 42, 43, 44, 44, 44,
45, 45, 46, 47, 48, 49, 49, 50, 50, 50, 50, 51, 51, 52, 52, 53, 53, 54,
54, 55, 55, 55; **3:**1, 2, 2, 5, 5, 9, 9, 10, 15, 17, 19, 19, 21, 23, 24; **4:**1,
1, 2, 2, 2, 3, 4, 4, 4, 4, 4, 5, 8, 8, 8, 9, 10, 11, 11, 11, 12, 12, 12, 13,
14, 14, 14, 14, 15, 15, 15, 16, 17, 17, 17, 18, 18, 18, 18, 18, 19, 19,
19, 19, 20, 20, 21, 21, 21, 21, 21, 22, 24, 25, 26, 27, 27, 31, 34, 34,
35, 35, 35, 37, 37, 37, 37, 37, 38, 38, 38, 39, 39, 40, 40, 41, 41, 41,
41, 41, 41, 42, 42, 42; **5:**1, 1, 1, 2, 3, 3, 4, 6, 6, 8, 8, 8, 9, 9, 10, 10,
11, 11, 12, 13, 14, 14, 14, 14, 14, 14, 14, 14, 15, 15, 15, 16, 17, 17,
17, 17, 18, 18, 22, 23, 24, 24, 25, 25, 26, 26, 26, 26; **6:**1, 2, 3, 3, 4, 4,
5, 5, 6, 6, 7, 7, 8, 8, 9, 9, 10, 11, 11, 12, 12, 13, 13, 14, 14, 15, 16, 17,
18, 19, 20, 22, 25, 28, 29, 31, 32, 33, 39, 44, 48, 49, 49, 49, 50, 54,
54, 54, 54, 56, 57, 57, 60, 60, 60, 61, 61, 61, 61, 62, 62, 62, 62, 63,
63, 64, 65, 65, 66, 66, 67, 67, 70, 70, 70, 71, 71, 71, 71, 72, 74, 76,
77, 77, 77, 78, 78, 80; **7:**1, 2, 2, 2, 2, 2, 3, 3, 3, 4, 4, 5, 5, 5, 5, 6, 7, 7,
7, 7, 8, 10, 10, 11, 11, 12, 12, 13, 13, 14, 14, 15, 16, 17, 17, 17, 19,
20, 23, 24, 25, 28, 29, 29, 29, 29, 30, 31, 31, 32, 33, 34, 35, 36, 38,
39, 40, 40, 40; **8:**1, 1, 3, 6, 6, 7, 8, 10, 12, 13, 13, 16, 18, 21, 25, 27,
28, 29, 32, 33, 33, 33, 34, 34, 35, 36, 36, 36, 37, 37, 37, 37, 38, 40,
40; **9:**1, 1, 1, 2, 3, 4, 4, 4, 4, 4, 4, 4, 6, 7, 7, 7, 7, 8, 8, 8, 8, 8, 8, 9, 9,
11, 11, 11, 11, 11, 11, 11, 12, 12, 12, 12, 12, 12, 12, 12, 13, 13, 14,
14, 14, 14, 15, 15, 15, 16, 16, 16, 16, 16, 16, 18, 19, 19, 19, 19, 20,
20, 21, 23, 26, 26, 27, 28, 31, 32, 32, 32, 34, 35, 38, 39, 39, 39, 40,
40, 41, 42, 42, 42, 43, 44; **10:**1, 2, 8, 9, 9, 10, 10, 11, 12, 14, 14;
11:1, 2, 3, 3, 4, 5, 5, 5, 6, 6, 6, 7, 8, 10, 11, 11, 12, 12, 13, 14, 15, 15,
16, 17, 19, 19, 19, 20, 20, 21, 21, 22, 22, 24, 25, 25, 25, 26, 28, 30,
31, 31, 34, 34, 35, 35, 37, 38, 38, 41, 42, 43, 44, 45, 46; **12:**1, 2, 2, 2,
3, 3, 7, 8, 15, 17, 18, 20, 20, 21, 22, 23, 23, 24, 25, 26, 27, 27, 28, 29,
29, 30, 31, 31, 31, 32, 32, 32, 33, 34, 35, 36, 37, 37, 37, 37, 38, 38,
40, 40; **13:**1, 2, 2, 3, 3, 5, 5, 5, 6, 6, 6, 7, 7, 8, 9, 10, 12, 12, 13, 13,
13, 14, 14; **14:**1, 2, 4, 9, 15, 15; **15:**1, 1, 2, 2, 3, 5, 6, 7, 8, 9, 10, 12,
12, 12, 13, 14, 14, 15, 16, 16, 17, 17, 17, 17, 22, 24, 24, 24, 25, 25,
25, 25, 26, 27, 28, 28, 28, 28, 29, 29, 29; **16:**1, 2, 3, 3, 3, 3, 4, 4, 5, 6,
7, 10, 12, 13, 13, 17, 18, 19, 25, 26, 28, 33, 35, 36, 37, 38, 39, 39, 40,
42, 42; **17:**1, 5, 6, 10, 11, 17, 20, 24; **18:**2, 3, 3, 4, 5, 7, 8, 8, 9, 9, 9,
10, 12, 12, 13, 15, 15, 15, 16, 16, 17, 17; **19:**1, 2, 6, 6, 7, 7, 9, 11, 11,
13, 16, 16, 16, 18, 19; **20:**1, 1, 1, 2, 2, 3, 3, 3, 4, 5, 5, 5, 5, 6, 7, 8, 8;
21:1, 2, 3, 5, 5, 6, 10, 12, 12, 12, 12, 12, 13, 15, 15, 16, 16, 18, 18,
25, 29, 29, 30, 30, 30; **22:**1, 1, 2, 2, 2, 3, 4, 4, 5, 5, 6, 7, 10, 11, 12,
14, 14, 14, 15, 16, 17, 19, 19, 19; **23:**2, 4, 4, 6, 7, 7, 8, 8, 9, 9, 9, 9,
10, 12, 13, 14, 14, 15, 16, 18, 19, 20, 21, 21, 22, 23, 24, 24, 24, 25,
28, 28, 28, 28, 28, 28, 29, 30, 31, 32, 32, 32; **24:**1, 3, 3, 3, 3, 4, 5, 5,
6, 6, 6, 6, 6, 19, 19, 19, 20, 20, 21, 22, 22, 23, 24, 24, 25, 25, 26, 26,
27, 28, 29, 30, 30, 31, 31, 31, 31; **25:**1, 1, 1, 2, 2, 3, 3, 5, 6, 6, 6, 6, 7,
8, 8, 9, 9, 9, 10, 11, 12, 13, 14, 15, 16, 17, 18, 19, 20, 21, 22, 23, 24,
25, 26, 27, 28, 29, 30, 31; **26:**1, 1, 1, 1, 2, 4, 6, 8, 8, 8, 10, 12, 12, 13,
14, 15, 17, 19, 19, 20, 20, 20, 21, 21, 22, 22, 22, 22, 24, 24, 24, 24,
26, 26, 27, 27, 28, 28, 28, 29, 30, 30, 30, 30, 30, 31, 31, 31, 31, 31,
32, 32, 32, 32, 32, 32, 32; **27:**1, 1, 2, 2, 3, 3, 4, 4, 5, 5, 7, 7, 8, 9, 9,
10, 10, 11, 11, 12, 12, 13, 13, 14, 15, 15, 16, 16, 16, 17, 18, 18, 19,
19, 20, 20, 21, 21, 22, 22, 22, 23, 24, 25, 25, 25, 25, 25, 26, 26, 27,
27, 28, 28, 28, 29, 29, 30, 30, 31, 31, 32, 34, 34; **28:**1, 1, 1, 2, 4, 4, 4,
5, 5, 8, 9, 11, 12, 12, 13, 13, 13, 15, 15, 16, 16, 16, 17, 17, 18, 18, 18,
19, 19, 20, 20, 21, 21, 21; **29:**1, 1, 2, 2, 2, 3, 3, 3, 3, 4, 4, 4, 6, 6, 6, 7,
7, 7, 7, 7, 7, 8, 8, 8, 8, 10, 10, 18, 20, 21, 23, 23, 24, 25, 25, 26, 29,
29, 29, 29, 30; **2Ch 1:**1, 1, 2, 4, 5, 5, 5, 5, 5, 6, 9, 10, 11, 13, 14, 15,
17, 17, 17, 17, 17; **2:**2, 4, 4, 7, 9, 10, 10, 10, 10, 11, 12, 14, 16, 17,
17, 18; **3:**1, 1, 2, 3, 4, 4, 4, 4, 5, 5, 6, 6, 7, 8, 8, 9, 11, 11, 11, 11, 12,
13, 13, 14, 14, 14, 15, 16, 16, 17, 17; **4:**3, 3, 4, 5, 5, 6, 10, 11, 12, 12,
13, 13, 13, 16, 16, 18, 19, 19, 20, 20, 21, 22, 22; **5:**1, 1, 1, 2, 2, 2, 2,
3, 4, 6, 7, 7, 7, 9, 10, 12, 13, 14, 14; **6:**3, 4, 5, 5, 7, 7, 9, 10, 10, 11,
12, 12, 12, 13, 14, 14, 16, 17, 22, 22, 27, 28, 32, 33, 33, 37, 41; **7:**1,
2, 2, 3, 3, 5, 5, 6, 7, 7, 8, 8, 8, 9, 9, 10, 11, 20, 20, 20, 22, 22; **8:**1, 3,
4, 5, 8, 9, 9, 10, 11, 11, 12, 12, 13, 13, 13, 14, 14, 14, 16, 16, 17, 17,
18, 18, 18; **9:**1, 1, 1, 1, 1, 3, 4, 4, 6, 9, 9, 9, 9, 10, 10, 11, 12, 12, 13,
14, 14, 15, 15, 16, 16, 16, 16, 18, 18, 18, 18, 19, 19, 20, 20, 20, 20,
20, 21, 24, 25, 26, 26, 27, 29, 29, 29, 29, 29, 29, 31; **10:**2, 2, 3, 8, 8,
13, 14, 15, 15, 15, 15, 17, 18, 19, 19; **11:**1, 1, 2, 3, 3, 4, 5, 10, 11, 11,
13, 16, 16, 17, 17, 17, 18, 18, 18, 18, 18, 20, 21, 23, 23; **12:**1, 2, 2, 3,
5, 6, 7, 9, 9, 9, 9, 9, 10, 10, 11, 12, 13, 15, 15, 15, 15, 15, 16; **13:**1, 2,
4, 4, 5, 5, 6, 6, 7, 8, 8, 9, 9, 9, 10, 11, 11, 12, 12, 13, 13, 15, 15, 15,
18, 19, 20, 21, 22, 22, 22; **14:**1, 2, 4, 4, 5, 5, 7, 8, 8, 8, 8, 8, 9, 9, 10,
12, 12, 13, 13, 14, 15; **15:**1, 1, 2, 4, 6, 7, 8, 8, 8, 8, 8, 9, 9, 10, 11, 12,
13, 14, 18, 19; **16:**1, 1, 2, 2, 3, 3, 4, 5, 5, 6, 6, 7, 7, 7, 7, 8, 9, 10, 11,
11, 11, 11, 12, 13, 14; **17:**2, 2, 2, 3, 3, 4, 4, 4, 5, 5, 6, 7, 7, 9, 9, 9, 9,
10, 10, 11, 13, 14, 14, 16, 17; **18:**1, 1, 2, 3, 5, 6, 7, 7, 8, 8, 8, 9, 9, 9,
9, 9, 10, 10, 17, 18, 19, 22, 23, 23, 25, 25, 27, 28, 28, 30, 30, 31, 32,
33, 33, 33, 33; **19:**1, 2, 4, 4, 7, 8, 8, 9, 10, 11, 11; **20:**1, 1, 4, 5, 5, 5,
6, 6, 6, 7, 10, 11, 13, 14, 14, 14, 14, 14, 14, 14, 15, 16, 16, 16, 17, 18,
19, 19, 20, 20, 20, 21, 21, 22, 23, 23, 23, 24, 24, 25, 26, 26, 27, 28,
28, 29, 29, 31, 31, 32, 33, 34, 34, 34, 34, 34, 34, 35, 35, 35, 36, 36,
37; **21:**1, 2, 3, 3, 3, 3, 4, 4, 6, 6, 6, 9, 10, 10, 11, 11, 12, 12, 12, 13,
13, 17, 19, 19, 20; **22:**1, 1, 1, 1, 2, 2, 3, 4, 4, 5, 5, 5, 6, 7, 7, 8, 8, 9, 9,
9, 9, 9, 10, 10, 10, 11, 11, 11, 12; **23:**1, 1, 1, 1, 1, 1, 3, 3, 4, 5, 6, 6, 8,
9, 10, 11, 12, 12, 13, 14, 14, 14, 17, 17, 17, 18, 18, 18, 19, 20, 21;
24:2, 4, 5, 5, 6, 6, 6, 6, 7, 7, 7, 7, 8, 9, 9, 11, 11, 12, 12, 13, 13, 14,
14, 14, 14, 16, 17, 18, 18, 18, 18, 20, 20, 21, 21, 23, 23, 24, 24, 24,
25, 25, 26, 26, 27, 27, 27, 27, 27; **25:**4, 4, 4, 4, 4, 4, 4, 5, 5, 6, 7, 7, 9,
9, 9, 11, 12, 13, 13, 13, 14, 14, 17, 17, 17, 18, 18, 19, 19, 19, 20, 21,
21, 22, 23, 23, 23, 24, 24, 24, 25, 25, 25, 26, 26, 26, 26, 28; **26:**1, 2,
5, 5, 6, 6, 7, 10, 10, 11, 11, 11, 11, 11, 12, 13, 14, 15, 15, 16, 17, 18,
18, 18, 21, 21, 21, 22, 22, 22; **27:**1, 2, 3, 4, 5, 5, 5, 5, 7, 7, 7, 7, 9;
28:1, 2, 2, 2, 3, 3, 3, 3, 5, 5, 5, 6, 6, 6, 8, 8, 9, 9, 9, 10, 12, 12, 12, 12,
12, 12, 14, 15, 16, 16, 17, 18, 19, 19, 20, 20, 21, 21, 23, 23, 23, 24,
24, 24, 25, 25, 25, 26, 26, 26, 26; **29:**1, 1, 3, 3, 3, 3, 4, 5, 5, 6, 7, 7, 8,
10, 12, 12, 12, 12, 12, 12, 12, 12, 12, 13, 13, 14, 14, 15, 16, 16, 17,
17, 18, 18, 18, 18, 19, 19, 20, 21, 21, 23, 24, 25, 26, 27, 27, 27, 30,
31, 35, 35, 35, 36; **30:**1, 1, 1, 1, 2, 5, 5, 6, 6, 6, 6, 7, 7, 10, 10, 10, 12,
12, 12, 13, 15, 16, 16, 17, 18, 19, 21, 21, 22, 25, 25, 26; **31:**1, 2, 3, 3,
4, 4, 5, 5, 5, 6, 6, 6, 7, 10, 11, 13, 14, 14, 14, 15, 16, 19, 20, 21, 21;
32:1, 3, 4, 4, 4, 5, 5, 7, 7, 9, 9, 10, 10, 11, 13, 13, 13, 13, 15, 17, 17,
17, 18, 19, 19, 20, 21, 21, 22, 22, 26, 26, 28, 30, 30, 30, 32, 32, 32,
32, 32, 32, 32, 33; **33:**2, 2, 3, 3, 4, 5, 5, 6, 6, 7, 9, 12, 14, 14, 14, 14,
14, 14, 16, 16, 16, 18, 18, 18, 18, 18, 18, 19, 19, 19, 19, 25; **34:**2, 3,
3, 4, 4, 5, 6, 7, 8, 8, 8, 8, 8, 9, 9, 9, 10, 11, 12, 12, 12, 12, 13, 13, 14,
14, 15, 17, 20, 20, 21, 21, 22, 22, 22, 22, 22, 23, 25, 26, 26, 29, 30,
30, 30, 31, 31, 32, 32, 32, 33, 33, 33; **35:**1, 1, 2, 4, 4, 4, 4, 8, 12, 15,
15, 16, 17, 18, 18, 18, 18, 19, 20, 21, 22, 24, 25, 25, 26, 26, 26, 26,
27, 27; **36:**1, 3, 3, 3, 3, 4, 4, 4, 5, 6, 7, 7, 8, 8, 8, 8, 10, 10, 12, 12, 13,
13, 14, 14, 14, 15, 16, 17, 18, 19, 19, 19, 20, 21, 22, 22, 22, 23, 23,
23, 23, 23; **Ezr 1:**1, 1, 1, 2, 2, 2, 2, 3, 3, 3, 4, 5, 5, 5, 5, 6, 7, 8, 8; **2:**1,
1, 1, 2, 2, 3, 4, 5, 6, 6, 7, 8, 9, 10, 11, 12, 13, 14, 15, 16, 16, 17, 18,
19, 20, 21, 22, 23, 24, 25, 26, 27, 28, 29, 30, 31, 32, 33, 34, 35, 36,
36, 37, 38, 39, 40, 40, 41, 41, 42, 42, 43, 55, 55, 58, 59, 59, 60, 60,
60, 61, 61, 61, 63, 63, 64, 68, 68, 68, 69, 69, 70, 70, 70; **3:**2, 2, 2, 2,
2, 2, 3, 4, 4, 4, 6, 6, 7, 7, 8, 8, 8, 8, 8, 8, 9, 9, 9, 9, 10, 10, 11, 12; **4:**1,
1, 2, 3, 3, 3, 4, 5, 5, 5, 6, 6, 6, 7, 7, 7, 9, 9, 10, 10, 10, 11, 11, 15, 15,
16, 17, 19, 19, 20, 22, 24, 24, 24, 24; **5:**1, 1, 1, 2, 2, 2, 2, 2, 3, 3, 4, 4,
5, 6, 6, 8, 8, 8, 11, 11, 11, 12, 12, 13, 13, 13, 14, 14, 14, 14, 15, 16,
16, 17; **6:**2, 3, 3, 4, 4, 5, 6, 6, 6, 7, 7, 7, 7, 8, 8, 9, 9, 10, 11, 12, 13,
13, 13, 14, 14, 14, 14, 15, 16, 16, 16, 17, 17, 18, 18, 21, 21, 22, 22,
22, 22, 22; **7:**1, 1, 1, 1, 1, 2, 2, 2, 3, 3, 3, 4, 4, 4, 5, 5, 5, 5, 6, 6, 6, 6,
7, 7, 7, 7, 8, 9, 10, 10, 11, 11, 12, 12, 12, 12, 13, 13, 14, 15, 16, 16,
16, 17, 17, 17, 17, 18, 19, 19, 19, 20, 21, 21, 21, 21, 21, 22, 22, 22,
22, 22, 23, 23, 24, 24, 25, 26, 26, 26, 27, 27, 28, 28, 28; **8:**1, 1, 1, 2,
2, 3, 3, 3, 4, 4, 5, 5, 6, 6, 7, 7, 8, 8, 9, 9, 10, 10, 11, 11, 12, 12, 13, 14,
15, 16, 17, 17, 18, 18, 18, 18, 18, 19, 19, 20, 21, 23, 24, 25, 25, 25,
26, 26, 26, 27, 28, 29, 29, 30, 30, 31, 33, 33, 33, 33, 33, 33, 35, 35,
36, 36, 36; **9:**1, 1, 1, 1, 2, 2, 4, 4, 4, 4, 4, 5, 7, 7, 7, 8, 8, 9, 9, 10, 11,
12, 13, 13, 15, 15; **10:**1, 1, 1, 2, 2, 2, 2, 3, 3, 5, 5, 6, 6, 6, 6, 6, 6, 8, 9,
9, 9, 9, 11, 11, 13, 14, 14, 14, 15, 15, 15, 16, 17, 18, 18, 20, 21, 22,
25, 25, 26, 27, 28, 29, 30, 31, 33, 34, 38, 43, 44; **Ne 1:**1, 1, 1, 1, 1, 2,
3, 3, 4, 5, 5, 9, 11, 11; **2:**1, 4, 7, 7, 8, 8, 8, 9, 9, 10, 17, 17, 17, 18, 19,
20; **3:**1, 1, 2, 2, 3, 4, 4, 4, 4, 4, 4, 6, 6, 7, 7, 7, 8, 8, 8, 9, 9, 9, 10, 10,
11, 11, 11, 11, 12, 12, 12, 12, 13, 14, 14, 15, 15, 15, 15, 15, 16, 16,
16, 16, 17, 17, 17, 17, 17, 17, 17, 18, 18, 18, 18, 19, 19, 19, 20, 20,
20, 21, 21, 21, 21, 21, 23, 23, 24, 24, 25, 25, 25, 26, 27, 27, 29, 29,
29, 30, 30, 30, 31; **4:**2, 2, 2, 3, 5, 10, 13, 14, 15, 16, 16, 20, 23; **5:**1,
1, 5, 8, 9, 10, 13, 14, 14, 14, 15, 15, 15, 15, 15, 18, 18, 18; **6:**1, 2, 2,
8, 10, 10, 10, 16, 17, 18, 18, 18; **7:**2, 2, 3, 3, 3, 5, 5, 6, 6, 6, 7, 7, 8, 9,
10, 11, 11, 12, 13, 14, 15, 16, 17, 18, 19, 20, 21, 21, 22, 23, 24, 25,
26, 27, 28, 29, 30, 31, 32, 33, 34, 35, 36, 37, 38, 39, 39, 40, 41, 42,
43, 43, 44, 44, 45, 45, 46, 57, 57, 60, 61, 61, 62, 62, 63, 63, 63, 65,
65, 66, 70, 71, 71, 72, 72, 73; **8:**1, 1, 2, 3, 5, 8, 8, 8, 9, 10, 10, 10, 12,
16, 16, 17, 17, 17, 18, 18, 18, 18, 18; **9:**2, 2, 3, 3, 4, 5, 6, 7, 8, 9, 11,
12, 12, 14, 15, 17, 17, 18, 19, 19, 22, 22, 22, 22, 22, 24, 25, 27, 30,
32, 32, 36, 37, 37, 37, 38, 38; **10:**1, 9, 9, 28, 28, 29, 29, 29, 30, 31,
32, 32, 32, 32, 33, 33, 33, 34, 34, 35, 36, 36, 37, 37, 37, 37, 37, 37,
38, 38, 38, 39, 39; **11:**1, 1, 1, 3, 3, 3, 3, 3, 4, 4, 4, 4, 4, 4, 4, 4, 4, 5, 5,
5, 5, 5, 5, 5, 5, 6, 7, 7, 7, 7, 7, 7, 7, 7, 8, 9, 9, 10, 11, 11, 11, 11, 11,
11, 11, 12, 12, 12, 12, 12, 12, 12, 13, 13, 13, 13, 13, 13, 14, 14, 15,
15, 15, 15, 16, 16, 17, 17, 17, 17, 17, 17, 19, 20, 20, 20, 21, 22, 22,
22, 22, 22, 22, 24, 24, 24, 24, 25, 25, 30, 30, 31, 31, 35, 36, 36; **12:**1,
1, 7, 7, 8, 8, 10, 10, 10, 11, 11, 12, 12, 12, 12, 12, 13, 13, 13, 13, 14,
14, 14, 14, 15, 15, 15, 15, 16, 16, 16, 16, 17, 17, 17, 17, 17, 17, 18,
18, 18, 18, 19, 19, 19, 19, 20, 20, 20, 20, 21, 21, 21, 21, 22, 22, 22,
22, 22, 23, 23, 23, 23, 24, 24, 24, 25, 26, 26, 26, 26, 26, 27, 27, 27,
27, 28, 29, 31, 31, 31, 31, 32, 35, 35, 35, 35, 35, 35, 36, 37, 37, 37,
38, 38, 38, 39, 39, 40, 40, 42, 43, 43, 44, 44, 44, 45, 45, 45, 46, 46,
46, 47, 47, 47, 47, 47; **13:**1, 1, 3, 4, 4, 4, 4, 5, 6, 6, 6, 7, 7, 7, 7, 8, 11,
12, 12, 13, 13, 13, 13, 14, 15, 15, 15, 16, 16, 17, 18, 18, 19, 19, 20,
22, 23, 23, 24, 24, 25, 25, 26, 27, 28, 28, 28, 28, 29, 31, 31; **Est 1:**1,
2, 3, 3, 4, 4, 5, 6, 7, 7, 9, 10, 14, 14, 18, 18, 19, 22, 22; **2:**4, 5, 5, 5, 5,
6, 8, 8, 10, 11, 12, 12, 13, 14, 14, 14, 15, 15, 16, 16, 17, 17, 21, 21,
23, 23; **3:**1, 6, 7, 7, 8, 8, 8, 8, 9, 10, 10, 12, 12, 12, 13, 13, 14, 15, 15;
4:2, 2, 3, 5, 6, 7, 8, 8, 16; **5:**1; **6:**1, 2, 2, 2, 4, 8, 9, 10; **7:**3, 9; **8:**1, 1,
2, 5, 7, 9, 9, 9, 10, 11, 11, 12, 12, 13, 14, 15, 15, 15, 15, 17, 17; **9:**1,
1, 2, 3, 3, 6, 10, 10, 10, 11, 11, 11, 12, 12, 13, 14, 16, 17, 18, 24, 24,
26, 26, 28, 28, 29, 29, 30, 30, 31, 31, 31, 32, 32; **10:**2, 2, 2, 2, 2, 3, 3,
3; **Job 1:**1, 1, 3, 5, 8, 16, 17, 21, 21, 22; **2:**3, 7, 8, 10, 11, 11; **3:**1, 3,
6; **4:**9, 11, 18, 19; **5:**5, 12, 15, 15, 16, 17, 17, 20, 20, 20, 21, 23; **6:**3,
6, 7, 10, 12, 13, 14, 21, 22, 26; **7:**1, 1, 3, 3, 5, 15, 17, 20; **8:**5, 8, 10,
13, 13, 17, 19, 20, 21, 22; **9:**2, 8, 9, 24, 24, 29, 34; **10:**1, 3, 4, 9, 17,
18, 20, 21, 22; **11:**2, 4, 6, 7, 11, 14, 15; **12:**7, 8, 10, 10, 17, 18, 19,
20, 24; **13:**7, 11, 20, 25, 26; **14:**1, 2, 5, 9, 13, 16; **15:**4, 18, 21, 30, 32;
16:3, 8, 11; **17:**6, 7, 10; **18:**5, 5, 7, 14, 14, 15, 15, 17, 21, 21; **19:**3, 5,
9, 15, 20, 21, 29; **20:**5, 5, 12, 16, 17, 17, 20, 22, 23, 25; **21:**11, 12,
14, 16, 16, 20, 20, 24, 28, 28, 30; **22:**2, 4, 5, 9, 11, 14, 16, 16, 18, 20,
28; **23:**15; **24:**2, 6, 8, 12, 17, 21, 24; **26:**6, 11, 14, 14, 14; **27:**14, 16,
18, 20; **28:**3, 7, 9, 16, 18, 21, 22, 26, 28; **29:**2, 4, 6, 10, 11, 11, 17,
24; **30:**2, 4, 8, 11, 18, 23, 27; **31:**6, 7, 16, 22, 23, 24, 28, 40, 40; **32:**2,
2, 2, 6, 8, 12, 14, 18; **33:**4, 4, 7, 15, 18, 22, 30; **34:**8, 27, 28; **35:**3, 9,
12; **36:**2, 3, 3, 4, 12, 13, 15, 20, 21, 24, 29, 30; **37:**1, 2, 4, 4, 5, 10,
13, 14, 19, 22, 23; **38:**4, 8, 13, 14, 15, 17, 17, 18, 21, 22, 23, 23, 24,
24, 25, 29, 30, 31, 32, 32, 33, 37, 38; **39:**2, 2, 7, 8, 13, 14, 17, 25, 25,
25, 30; **40:**10, 13, 16, 17, 18, 18, 19; **41:**13, 18, 20, 29, 34, 34; **42:**11,
11, 11, 12, 12, 15, 16; **Ps 1:**1, 1, 4, 5, 6, 6; **2:**2, 8, 10, 12; **3:**T, 6, 7;
4:T, 3, 6, 7; **5:**T, 7, 10, 12; **6:**T, 4, 7; **7:**T, T, T, 3, 6, 9, 17; **8:**T, 1, 3, 4,
6, 9; **9:**T, T, 1, 2, 6, 9, 13, 13, 17, 18; **10:**6, 7, 7, 10, 14, 14, 15, 17;
11:T, 3; **12:**T, 5; **13:**T; **14:**T, 4, 6; **15:**T, 3, 4; **16:**T, 4, 5, 11, 11, 11;
17:T, 8, 8, 14; **18:**T, T, 2, 3, 4, 4, 7, 7, 10, 12, 15, 15, 15, 16, 19, 20,
21, 24, 24, 34, 35, 44, 46, 48; **19:**T, 1, 1, 6, 7, 7, 8, 8, 9, 13, 13, 14,
14; **20:**T, 1, 1, 5, 7; **21:**T, 1, 3, 4, 6, 7, 10; **22:**T, T, 3, 12, 12, 14, 15,
16, 21, 22, 23, 23, 24, 25, 29, 30; **23:**T, 4, 5, 6, 6; **24:**T, 3, 6, 7, 8, 9,
10, 10; **25:**T, 7, 7, 11, 14, 15; **26:**T, 3, 5, 7, 7, 9; **27:**T, 4, 4, 4, 5, 6, 9,
11, 12, 13; **28:**T, 1, 4, 7; **29:**T, 2, 2, 3, 3, 4, 4, 4, 5, 5, 7, 8, 8, 9; **30:**T,
T, 3, 9, 11; **31:**T, 2, 3, 3, 7, 7, 9, 20; **32:**T, 1, 2, 4, 6, 7; **33:**3, 4, 4, 8,

10, 19; **34:**T, T, 3, 5, 7, 8, 12, 15, 20; **35:**T, 3, 5, 6, 10, 11, 16, 18, 20, 28; **36:**T, T, 1, 4, 7, 8, 8, 9; **37:**T, 6, 7, 13, 17, 17, 18, 23, 23, 28, 39; **38:**T, 3, 3, 5, 17; **39:**T, 2, 3, 5, 11; **40:**T, 2, 2, 2, 3, 4, 5, 10; **41:**T, 1, 1, 8, 13; **42:**T, T, 1, 3, 4, 4, 4, 6, 6, 7, 10; **43:**4, 4; **44:**T, T, 1, 13, 14, 16, 21, 26; **45:**T, T, 1, 2, 7, 8, 9, 12, 12; **46:**T, T, 1, 4, 4, 5, 7, 8, 11; **47:**T, T, 2, 4, 9, 9, 9; **48:**T, T, 1, 2, 4, 6, 7, 8, 8, 8, 10, 11, 12, 13; **49:**T, T, 5, 6, 13, 15, 19, 20; **50:**T, 2, 3, 10, 11, 11, 13, 15, 19, 22, 23; **51:**T, 1, 1, 1, 9, 12, 14, 18; **52:**T, 1, 5, 8, 9; **53:**T, 4, 5; **54:**T; **55:**T, 4, 7, 8, 14, 20, 22, 23; **56:**T, 8, 12; **57:**T, 1, 9; **58:**T, 1, 2, 5, 6, 10; **59:**T, 5, 9, 12, 12, 16, 16, 16; **60:**T, T, T, 4, 6; **61:**T, 2, 2, 4, 6; **62:**T, 3, 9, 10; **63:**T, T, 5, 5, 6, 7, 9, 10; **64:**T, 2, 2, 9; **65:**T, 5, 7, 8, 8, 8, 9, 9, 9, 13; **66:**2, 7, 11, 12, 15; **67:**4; **68:**T, 2, 5, 8, 8, 11, 12, 15, 17, 18, 21, 21, 22, 24, 26, 26, 27, 27, 27, 29, 30, 31, 32, 35; **69:**T, 6, 6, 11, 12, 14, 15, 16, 26, 28, 33, 35, 35, 36; **70:**T; **71:**3, 4, 4, 20, 22; **72:**T, 4, 7, 8, 10, 10, 15, 18, 20, 20; **73:**T, 2, 6, 11, 12, 17, 26; **74:**T, 1, 3, 14, 17, 20, 23; **75:**T, 1, 8, 9, 10, 10; **76:**T, 3, 3, 5, 5, 6, 9, 10, 12, 12; **77:**T, 3, 5, 10, 11, 14, 15, 15, 17, 20; **78:**T, 4, 4, 9, 9, 12, 14, 15, 21, 23, 25, 31, 31, 32, 33, 34, 39, 41, 43, 45, 45, 48, 49, 51, 51, 52, 54, 54, 55, 61, 67, 68, 71; **79:**T, 1, 2, 2, 2, 4, 9, 9, 9, 10, 11, 13; **80:**T, T, 1, 6, 16, 17; **81:**T, 1, 4, 4, 4, 6, 7, 10, 16; **82:**T, 3, 4, 6; **83:**T, 2, 4, 8, 12; **84:**T, T, 2, 6, 6, 6, 7, 8, 10, 10; **85:**T, T, 1, 2, 4; **86:**T, 5, 11, 13, 15, 17; **87:**T, T, 2, 3, 3, 4, 5, 6, 7; **88:**T, T, T, T, 1, 3, 8, 10, 11, 12, 12; **89:**T, 1, 1, 1, 5, 6, 7, 15, 18, 22, 24, 26, 29, 48, 50; **90:**T, T, 10, 11, 12, 14; **91:**1, 1, 2, 2, 5, 5, 5; **92:**3, 4, 7, 11, 11, 12, 13; **93:**4, 5; **94:**1, 2, 7, 23; **95:**1, 2, 4, 11; **96:**4, 5, 7, 12; **97:**2, 5, 8, 8, 10, 10; **98:**3, 6, 8; **99:**4, 7; **100:**T, 3; **101:**T, 1, 2, 8; **102:**T, 2, 5, 9, 10, 15, 17, 20, 25, 25, 28; **103:**T, 7, 8, 11, 17, 18, 18, 20, 20, 21; **104:**2, 2, 3, 3, 4, 6, 7, 7, 12, 13, 16, 16, 24, 24, 25, 27, 30, 31, 35; **105:**3, 5, 6, 6, 10, 11, 12, 16, 17, 20, 21, 23, 24, 27, 32, 32, 34, 36, 37, 38, 43, 44; **106:**2, 5, 5, 7, 8, 11, 16, 16, 17, 19, 20, 28, 38, 38, 39, 45, 48; **107:**11, 11, 16, 16, 20, 22, 23, 32, 33, 34, 34, 35, 38, 41, 43; **108:**T, 3, 7; **109:**T, 14, 18, 21, 22, 25, 26; **110:**T, 3, 4, 5; **111:**2, 6, 10, 10; **112:**2; **113:**1, 1, 2, 3, 8; **114:**1, 2, 3, 3, 5, 7, 7, 7, 8, 8; **115:**4, 10, 12, 12, 17; **116:**3, 4, 5, 6, 14, 16, 17, 17, 18, 19, 19; **117:**1, 2; **118:**2, 10, 11, 12, 15, 15, 15, 16, 16, 20, 26, 26; **119:**1, 1, 19, 27, 29, 33, 35, 38, 43, 54, 54, 55, 56, 59, 64, 99, 101, 104, 114, 115, 115, 119, 120, 121, 123, 128, 134, 136, 138, 159; **120:**5, 6; **122:**T, 1, 4, 4, 5, 5, 6, 8, 9, 9; **123:**3, 4, 4, 4; **124:**T, 3, 5; **126:**5; **127:**T, 1, 5; **128:**2; **130:**1, 3, 7, 8; **131:**T; **132:**2, 5, 6, 7, 8, 9, 10, 12, 16, 17; **133:**T, 2, 3; **134:**1, 1; **135:**1, 2, 2, 2, 5, 11, 11, 11, 15, 19; **136:**2, 3, 10, 11, 19, 20, 21, 26; **137:**1, 1, 2, 3, 3, 3, 4, 6, 7; **138:**T, 2, 4, 5, 7; **139:**T, 3, 5, 8, 9, 13, 15, 16, 18, 19, 24; **140:**T, 3, 4, 4, 7, 12; **141:**T, 3, 4, 4, 7, 9, 9, 9; **142:**T, 5, 7; **143:**T, 5, 8, 11, 11; **144:**T, 2, 4, 7, 8, 11, 11, 13, 13, 14; **145:**T, T, 3, 4, 7, 7, 8, 10, 11, 11, 12, 16, 19; **146:**5, 8, 8, 9; **147:**10, 10, 13, 14; **148:**2, 7, 11, 11, 13, 14; **149:**1, 2, 6, 9; **150:**3, 5; **Pr 1:**1, 1, 2, 6, 7, 7, 12, 12, 13, 19, 19, 21, 23, 31, 31, 33; **2:**5, 7, 8, 9, 16, 19, 20, 20; **3:**9, 14, 18, 20, 21, 25, 33, 33, 33; **4:**14, 18, 18, 18, 19, 21; **5:**3, 8, 10, 14, 16, 18, 18, 20, 23, 23; **6:**1, 3, 10, 12, 15, 23, 23, 24, 34; **7:**4, 5, 6, 8, 9, 10, 16, 18, 20, 26, 27; **8:**4, 7, 15, 20, 26, 28, 29; **9:**10, 10, 10; **10:**1, 3, 5, 7, 7, 11, 13, 14, 15, 15, 16, 20, 20, 21, 22, 24, 24, 27, 27, 28, 28; **11:**4, 5, 6, 6, 11, 18, 21, 26; **12:**2, 5, 5, 6, 6, 7, 10, 10, 12, 14, 18, 19, 21, 23, 27, 28; **13:**2, 9, 9, 14, 14, 25; **14:**3, 3, 3, 9, 11, 11, 19, 24, 26, 27, 27; **15:**6, 6, 8, 8, 9, 11, 17, 19, 22, 24, 25, 25, 26, 29, 33; **16:**6, 7, 14, 17, 23, 28, 28, 31; **17:**3, 5, 6, 6, 10, 10, 12, 17, 21, 21, 24; **18:**1, 4, 7, 10, 11, 11; **19:**6, 7, 14, 20, 23, 28, 28, 29; **20:**3, 10, 16, 16, 18, 20, 29, 29, 29; **21:**1, 9, 12, 13, 13, 16, 22, 23, 25, 27; **22:**4, 8, 8, 12, 13, 14, 17; **23:**5, 8, 10, 12, 18, 24, 26, 31; **24:**4, 5, 9, 15, 19, 23, 30, 30, 33; **25:**1, 1, 1, 3, 3, 7, 10, 13, 13, 16, 24; **26:**7, 13, 20, 25, 25; **27:**4, 9, 10, 13, 13, 21, 23, 26; **28:**8, 9, 19, 21; **29:**7, 13, 17, 22; **30:**1, 1, 5, 14, 17, 30, 33; **31:**1, 2, 2, 21, 21, 22, 25, 27; **Ecc 1:**1, 12, 16, 16; **2:**5, 7, 8, 8, 9, 13, 15, 15, 18, 23, 24; **3:**10, 11, 13, 16, 21; **4:**1, 3, 4, 7, 8, 16; **5:**1, 7, 7, 8, 11, 13, 15, 18; **6:**5, 8, 12; **7:**9, 13, 19, 28; **8:**8, 8, 8, 8; **9:**1, 7, 8, 9, 11, 13, 17, 17, 18; **10:**1, 1, 1, 2, 2, 6, 6, 9, 9, 10, 12, 20, 20; **11:**5, 6, 8, 9, 10; **12:**1, 2, 4, 5, 5, 6, 11, 12, 13; **SS 1:**1, 5, 5, 5, 7, 8, 10, 11, 11, 12, 13, 14, 14; **2:**1, 1, 7, 7, 12, 12, 15; **3:**5, 5, 6, 6, 7, 10, 10, 10, 11, 11; **4:**1, 1, 3, 4, 4, 5, 6, 6, 8, 9, 9, 10, 11, 11, 11, 12, 13, 15; **5:**1, 2, 2, 8, 9, 12, 13, 14, 15, 15, 15, 16; **6:**1, 4, 5, 5, 9, 11, 13, 13, 13; **7:**1, 2, 3, 4, 4, 5, 7, 8, 8; **8:**4, 6, 11, 11, 12, 12, 14; **Isa 1:**1, 1, 1, 4, 4, 9, 10, 10, 10, 10, 11, 11, 13, 14, 15, 17, 18, 21, 23, 23, 24, 26, 27, 29, 29, 29; **2:**1, 2, 3, 3, 3, 5, 5, 6, 7, 10, 10, 13, 13, 17, 19, 19, 21, 21, 21, 22; **3:**1, 5, 6, 6, 9, 14, 16, 17, 19, 24, 24, 24, 25, 26; **4:**1, 2, 2, 2, 3, 4, 4, 4, 5, 5; **5:**2, 3, 7, 7, 7, 7, 10, 10, 10, 10, 13, 14, 16, 18, 19, 24, 24, 24, 25, 25, 26, 28, 30, 30; **6:**1, 5, 6, 6, 10, 12; **7:**1, 1, 1, 1, 1, 1, 2, 3, 4, 4, 4, 5, 6, 9, 13, 13, 16, 17, 18, 18, 23, 23; **8:**2, 4, 4, 6, 7, 10, 10, 12, 14, 15, 16, 17; **9:**1, 1, 1, 4, 5, 6, 7, 7, 9, 15, 16, 16, 18, 19; **10:**2, 5, 7, 7, 8, 12, 12, 14, 14, 16, 16, 17, 20, 21, 22, 22, 24, 26, 27, 27, 28, 28, 29, 29, 29, 30, 31, 31, 32, 33; **11:**1, 1, 2, 2, 2, 2, 2, 4, 8, 10, 11, 11, 12, 12, 14; **12:**3, 6, 6; **13:**1, 1, 2, 4, 8, 8, 9, 9, 11, 11, 12, 17, 19, 19, 21, 22; **14:**1, 1, 1, 2, 4, 6, 8, 8, 9, 12, 12, 13, 15, 16, 18, 21, 21, 23, 23, 31, 32; **15:**1, 2, 3, 4, 4, 6, 7, 8, 8; **16:**1, 1, 2, 2, 7, 7, 7, 8, 8, 9, 10, 10, 12, 14, 14; **17:**1, 2, 3, 3, 3, 4, 5, 6, 6, 6, 6, 7, 7, 11, 14, 14; **18:**1, 1; **19:**1, 1, 5, 6, 6, 8, 11, 11, 11, 11, 13, 14, 14, 16, 17, 18, 18, 18, 19, 20; **20:**1, 1, 2, 3, 4, 4, 5, 5, 6; **21:**1, 2, 3, 3, 9, 10, 13, 14, 15, 16, 17, 17; **22:**5, 5, 5, 5, 5, 6, 9, 12, 14, 19, 20, 21, 22, 24; **23:**1, 2, 2, 3, 4, 7, 7, 8, 11, 12, 13, 13, 13, 14, 15; **24:**1, 5, 5, 7, 8, 8, 8, 9, 15, 15, 15, 16, 17, 21, 23, 23, 23; **25:**2, 4, 5, 5, 5, 5, 6, 7, 7, 12; **26:**1, 1, 7, 7, 10, 16, 18, 19, 19, 21; **27:**1, 2, 11, 12; **28:**1, 1, 1, 1, 3, 3, 3, 5, 5, 15, 17, 17, 17, 17, 20, 25, 28; **29:**1, 8, 8, 8, 10, 10, 13, 14, 17, 19, 22, 23, 23, 23, 23; **30:**1, 8, 10, 11, 11, 12, 12, 14, 15, 15, 16, 17, 17, 17, 17, 19, 19, 23, 25, 26, 29, 29, 29, 29, 29, 32, 33, 33; **31:**1, 1, 7, 8, 8; **32:**2, 4, 6, 7, 9, 11, 12, 14; **33:**2, 3, 4, 5, 6, 6, 9, 9, 14, 14, 16, 16, 18, 20, 21, 23, 24; **34:**1, 3, 6, 6, 8, 9, 10, 12, 14, 16, 16; **35:**2, 2, 2, 2, 5, 5, 7, 8, 10; **36:**1, 1, 1, 2, 3, 3, 4, 5, 6, 8, 9, 9, 9, 13, 16, 16, 17, 17, 18, 18, 19, 19, 20, 22, 22; **37:**1, 2, 3, 4, 9, 10, 10, 11, 12, 12, 12, 13, 13, 13, 16, 16, 16, 17, 18, 19, 19, 19, 20, 21, 21, 21, 22, 22, 23, 24, 25, 26, 29, 31, 32, 32, 32, 33, 33, 35, 36, 37, 37, 38, 38, 38; **38:**1, 5, 6, 8, 10, 10, 10, 11, 14, 15, 20, 20, 20, 22; **39:**1, 1, 3, 7, 7; **40:**3, 5, 6, 7, 8, 9, 9, 12, 13, 15, 16, 17, 21, 22, 23, 28, 28; **41:**4, 9, 14, 15, 16, 16, 17, 18, 18, 20, 21, 28; **42:**6, 7, 10, 11, 11, 13, 16, 19, 23; **43:**2, 2, 3, 6, 9, 9, 9, 14, 14, 17, 22, 25, 28; **44:**5, 5, 13, 13, 15, 15, 16, 17, 19, 19, 19, 19, 26, 26, 28; **45:**2, 2, 3, 4, 11, 11, 12, 14, 15, 17, 18, 19, 24, 25; **46:**1, 7, 11; **47:**1, 1, 4, 5, 5, 7, 7, 9, 12; **48:**1, 1, 1, 1, 1, 1, 2, 5, 8, 9, 10, 12, 13, 13, 14, 14, 14, 17, 20, 20; **49:**1, 2, 2, 5, 6, 6, 7, 7, 7, 8, 8, 9, 16, 19, 21, 24, 24, 25, 25, 26, 26; **50:**1, 1, 3, 4, 10; **51:**3, 3, 6, 6, 7, 9, 9, 10, 11, 12, 13, 13, 17, 17, 18, 22, 23; **52:**1, 2, 7, 7, 7, 9, 10, 10, 10, 11, 12, 12; **53:**3, 6, 6, 10, 11, 12, 12; **54:**4, 4, 5, 5, 8, 9, 10, 11, 11, 12, 12, 16, 17; **55:**1, 3, 5, 7, 12, 13; **56:**2, 6, 7, 7, 7, 8, 9, 9, 10, 11; **57:**3, 4, 8, 8, 9, 11, 11, 11, 12, 13, 19; **58:**1, 1, 2, 4, 5, 5, 6, 8, 12, 13, 14; **59:**2, 3, 3, 9, 17, 17, 19, 19, 21; **60:**1, 2, 2, 5, 6, 6, 6, 7, 7, 9, 9, 9, 11, 11, 13, 13, 14, 14, 14, 14, 16, 16, 18, 18, 20; **61:**1, 2, 2, 3, 3, 6, 6, 6, 7, 7, 10, 10, 11; **62:**3, 4, 4, 6, 7, 9, 11; **63:**1, 1, 7, 11, 11, 13, 14; **64:**11; **65:**3, 6, 7, 8, 9, 9, 9, 10, 10, 11, 11, 12, 16, 16, 18, 18, 19, 21; **66:**3, 3, 6, 8, 9, 11, 12, 14, 15, 15, 15, 19, 20, 21, 24; **Jer 1:**1, 1, 1, 1, 2, 3, 3, 3, 3, 8, 8, 12, 13, 14, 15, 15, 15, 15, 17, 17, 18, 18, 19; **2:**3, 4, 4, 4, 6, 6, 6, 8, 10, 10, 10, 13, 14, 16, 18, 19, 20, 21, 22, 23, 27, 27, 27, 29, 31, 31, 34; **3:**4, 6, 9, 9, 10, 14, 16, 17, 18, 20, 21, 23; **4:**2, 3, 3, 4, 7, 7, 8, 8, 11, 15, 16, 18, 19, 19, 20, 25, 28, 29, 31, 31; **5:**4, 4, 5, 10, 11, 11, 13, 13, 17, 17, 24, 24, 25, 25, 28; **6:**1, 6, 7, 10, 11, 11, 12, 14, 17, 18, 19, 23, 24, 26, 27, 27, 28, 28, 28; **7:**2, 2, 3, 4, 9, 11, 12, 12, 15, 17, 17, 18, 19, 20, 21, 22, 24, 24, 30, 31, 31, 31, 32, 32, 32, 33, 34, 34, 34; **8:**1, 1, 1, 3, 6, 7, 7, 8, 9, 11, 13, 14, 15, 16, 16, 16, 19, 21, 22; **9:**1, 4, 4, 4, 10, 10, 11, 11, 14, 15, 19, 20, 21, 22, 26, 26; **10:**1, 2, 5, 6, 7, 7, 7, 8, 8, 9, 16, 16, 21, 21, 22, 22; **11:**2, 2, 3, 3, 4, 6, 7, 9, 10, 12, 13, 13, 16, 16, 17, 20, 21, 23, 23; **12:**4, 6, 8, 12, 12, 13, 13, 15, 16, 16; **13:**7, 9, 12, 12, 12, 17, 19, 19, 22, 23, 27; **14:**4, 7, 8, 8, 14, 16, 16, 18, 18, 19, 19, 20, 21, 21, 22; **15:**1, 3, 4, 4, 4, 4, 4, 6, 7, 8, 8, 9, 11, 12, 12, 13; **16:**7, 7, 9, 9, 13, 14, 14, 15, 15, 18, 19; **17:**1, 4, 8, 11, 13, 13, 17, 19, 19, 20, 20, 25, 25, 26, 27, 27; **18:**4, 11, 11, 13, 14, 14, 15, 15; **19:**1, 1, 1, 2, 2, 3, 3, 3, 3, 4, 4, 4, 6, 6, 6, 7, 8, 11, 11, 13, 14, 14, 15; **20:**1, 1, 1, 2, 4, 4, 4, 5, 5, 9, 12, 14, 16; **21:**1, 1, 2, 4, 4, 4, 7, 8, 10, 11, 12, 12, 13; **22:**1, 2, 4, 4, 5, 6, 8, 17, 18, 19, 20, 22, 23, 23, 24, 24, 25, 25, 27, 30, 30; **23:**1, 1, 2, 2, 3, 4, 7, 7, 8, 8, 9, 9, 10, 12, 13, 13, 14, 14, 14, 15, 18, 18, 19, 20, 26, 27, 33, 33, 36, 40; **24:**1, 1, 1, 1, 1, 1, 5, 5, 8, 9, 10; **25:**1, 1, 1, 3, 3, 3, 9, 9, 9, 10, 11, 12, 12, 12, 15, 17, 18, 18, 20, 20, 20, 20, 20, 21, 22, 22, 24, 24, 24, 25, 26, 26, 26, 26, 27, 27, 29, 31, 31, 31, 32, 32, 34, 34, 36, 36, 38; **26:**1, 1, 1, 2, 2, 3, 6, 7, 9, 10, 10, 16, 17, 18, 18, 18, 18, 20, 22, 24; **27:**1, 1, 1, 3, 4, 5, 6, 9, 9, 11, 11, 12, 12, 14, 17, 18, 19, 20, 20, 20, 20, 21, 21; **28:**1, 1, 1, 1, 1, 2, 2, 2, 4, 4, 4, 5, 6, 7, 8, 9, 11, 11, 13, 14, 14, 14, 14; **29:**2, 3, 3, 4, 7, 8, 14, 18, 21, 21, 21, 22, 25, 25, 26, 26, 32; **30:**2, 3, 3, 7, 7, 13, 19, 19, 23, 24; **31:**1, 1, 2, 5, 6, 7, 7, 8, 9, 10, 12, 12, 12, 12, 14, 15, 16, 19, 23, 23, 27, 31, 32, 32, 33, 36, 37, 38, 39; **32:**1, 1, 1, 1, 1, 2, 3, 4, 7, 8, 9, 10, 11, 11, 12, 12, 12, 12, 14, 15, 19, 19, 20, 21, 22, 24, 27, 27, 28, 31, 32, 32, 32, 35, 35, 36, 36, 39, 44, 44, 44; **33:**1, 2, 4, 4, 4, 5, 5, 7, 8, 9, 9, 10, 11, 11, 11, 11, 13, 13, 13, 13, 13, 15, 17, 22, 25, 25, 26, 26; **34:**1, 1, 2, 2, 2, 3, 4, 6, 7, 13, 17, 18, 19, 21, 21, 21, 22; **35:**1, 1, 2, 2, 3, 3, 4, 4, 4, 4, 4, 5, 6, 8, 10, 11, 11, 13, 16, 17, 18, 19, 19, 19; **36:**1, 2, 3, 4, 6, 9, 9, 9, 9, 10, 10, 10, 11, 11, 12, 12, 12, 12, 14, 14, 14, 20, 22, 22, 23, 24, 26, 26, 29, 30, 30, 31, 31; **37:**1, 1, 1, 1, 3, 3, 5, 5, 5, 5, 7, 7, 10, 11, 12, 13, 13, 14, 15, 17, 19, 20, 21, 21; **38:**1, 1, 1, 1, 3, 3, 3, 4, 4, 4, 6, 6, 9, 10, 10, 13, 14, 17, 22, 23, 28; **39:**1, 3, 3, 4, 5, 5, 5, 5, 6, 8, 9, 9, 10, 13, 13, 14, 14, 14, 14, 16; **40:**1, 1, 2, 5, 5, 5, 5, 6, 7, 7, 7, 8, 8, 8, 8, 8, 8, 9, 11, 12, 13, 14, 14, 15; **41:**1, 1, 1, 2, 5, 7, 8, 9, 9, 9, 10, 10, 10, 11, 11, 15, 15, 16, 17, 18; **42:**1, 1, 8, 9, 11, 15, 15, 17, 17, 18, 18, 18, 19; **43:**2, 2, 3, 6, 7, 9, 9, 10, 10, 10, 11, 12, 12, 13, 13; **44:**1, 2, 2, 3, 3, 6, 6, 7, 7, 8, 8, 9, 9, 9, 11, 11, 12, 12, 14, 14, 15, 15, 17, 17, 17, 18, 18, 19, 19, 20, 21, 21, 22, 24, 25, 25, 26, 26, 26, 27, 30, 30, 30; **45:**1, 1, 1, 1, 2, 3; **46:**2, 2, 2, 2, 2, 2, 2, 2, 5, 9, 10, 10, 11, 12, 12, 14, 14, 16, 17, 19, 19, 21, 21, 25, 25, 25, 26, 26; **47:**1, 3, 3, 5, 5, 6, 7; **48:**1, 1, 1, 2, 3, 5, 5, 13, 13, 14, 17, 18, 19, 20, 21, 24, 25, 27, 27, 28, 28, 29, 29, 29, 31, 32, 33, 33, 34, 34, 37, 39, 39, 39, 40, 44, 46, 47, 47; **49:**1, 1, 2, 3, 3, 3, 4, 6, 7, 8, 10, 12, 13, 13, 17, 18, 19, 19, 20, 21, 21, 23, 23, 25, 27, 27, 28, 28, 29, 30, 30, 34, 34, 34, 35, 35, 36, 37, 39; **50:**1, 4, 7, 7, 8, 9, 11, 12, 13, 16, 17, 17, 18, 18, 18, 19, 19, 21, 21, 21, 22, 25, 26, 29, 31, 32, 32, 33, 34, 35, 35, 39, 39, 42, 43, 43, 44, 44, 45, 46, 46; **51:**1, 2, 4, 5, 11, 11, 13, 13, 14, 19, 19, 24, 25, 25, 27, 27, 28, 28, 28, 33, 34, 34, 35, 35, 37, 37, 38, 39, 44, 44, 46, 46, 48, 49, 52, 54, 54, 54, 55, 55, 58, 59, 59, 59, 59, 64, 64; **52:**1, 3, 3, 4, 4, 5, 6, 6, 7, 7, 8, 9, 9, 10, 10, 11, 12, 12, 12, 12, 13, 13, 14, 14, 15, 15, 15, 15, 15, 16, 19, 19, 20, 21, 22, 22, 23, 24, 25, 25, 25, 25, 26, 27, 27, 27, 28, 28, 30, 30, 31, 31, 33, 34; **La 1:**1, 3, 6, 7, 9, 12, 14, 21; **2:**1, 1, 1, 2, 3, 3, 6, 7, 8, 10, 10, 12, 13, 13, 15, 17, 17, 18, 21, 22, 22; **3:**1, 15, 19, 22, 27, 30, 32, 34, 35, 35, 48, 48, 48, 51, 51; **4:**2, 2, 3, 4, 4, 6, 6, 9, 9, 11, 12, 13, 13, 20, 21, 21, 21; **5:**7, 9, 10, 11, 13, 15; **Eze 1:**1, 1, 2, 3, 3, 3, 3, 5, 6, 8, 9, 9, 10, 10, 10, 11, 11, 11, 13, 14, 16, 17, 18, 20, 21, 23, 24, 24, 26, 26, 28; **2:**1, 3, 3, 6, 8, 10, 10; **3:**1, 1, 4, 4, 7, 7, 9, 10, 12, 13, 13, 13, 15, 16, 17, 18, 20, 22, 23, 26, 27; **4:**1, 1, 1, 1, 3, 4, 4, 5, 6, 7, 7, 8, 10, 11, 14, 14, 15, 16; **5:**1, 2, 2, 2, 3, 4, 4, 5, 5, 9, 10, 12, 12, 14, 15, 16, 16, 17, 17; **6:**2, 2, 3, 4, 5, 8, 8, 11, 11; **7:**2, 7, 7, 7, 7, 7, 10, 11, 12, 15, 19, 19, 20, 21, 24; **8:**1, 1, 1, 3, 3, 3, 4, 4, 5, 5, 6, 6, 7, 8, 10, 10, 11, 11, 11, 11, 12, 12, 14, 16, 17, 17; **9:**2, 3, 3, 3, 4, 4, 4, 7, 9, 9, 9; **10:**1, 1, 2, 3, 3, 4, 4, 4, 4, 5, 5, 6, 7, 7, 9, 11, 14, 14, 14, 14, 17, 18, 18, 19, 19, 19, 20, 22; **11:**1, 1, 1, 1, 2, 4, 5, 5, 7, 7, 9, 10, 11, 12, 13, 15, 16, 17, 18, 19, 19, 22, 22, 23, 24, 24; **12:**2, 6, 6, 9, 9, 10, 11, 13, 16, 18, 19, 19, 22, 22, 24, 25, 25, 27, 27; **13:**2, 2, 2, 4, 4, 5, 9, 13, 13, 13, 17, 18, 19, 19, 23; **14:**1, 1, 3, 4, 5, 6, 8, 9, 11, 13, 13, 15, 19, 21; **15:**2, 2, 6, 6; **16:**2, 10, 10, 13, 14, 16, 17, 22, 22, 25, 26, 29, 32, 34, 37, 37, 41, 43, 44, 53, 54, 61, 63; **17:**2, 2, 3, 3, 3, 5, 8, 12, 12, 12, 12, 13, 13, 15, 16, 16, 17, 17, 18, 21, 22, 22, 23; **18:**2, 14, 17, 22, 23, 24, 25, 26, 29, 29, 30, 30, 31; **19:**1, 3, 4, 5, 8, 9, 9, 10, 11, 11, 14; **20:**1, 1, 1, 1, 3, 3, 3, 4, 4, 6, 6, 7, 7, 8, 8, 9, 10, 12, 13, 14, 14, 14, 22, 22, 24, 27, 27, 30, 31, 32, 35, 36, 37, 38, 38, 38, 39, 39, 40, 41, 43, 44, 44, 46, 46, 47, 49; **21:**2, 6, 7, 9, 12, 14, 19, 19, 19, 21, 21, 23, 23, 23, 23, 24, 24, 25, 25, 28, 29, 30, 31; **22:**2, 2, 3, 3, 4, 4, 4, 4, 8, 12, 14, 15, 18, 18, 18, 20, 21, 24, 24, 24, 25, 29, 30, 31; **23:**2, 2, 4, 5, 7, 8, 8, 12, 14, 15, 17, 26, 29, 29, 32, 33, 34, 35, 36, 36, 39, 42, 44, 49; **24:**1, 2, 2, 3, 6, 8, 9, 13, 14, 16, 17, 21, 21, 23, 25; **25:**2, 2, 3, 5, 5, 6, 8, 12, 12, 13, 13, 14, 14, 15, 15, 16, 16; **26:**1, 2, 2, 3, 4, 5, 5, 7, 7, 8, 10, 13, 13, 14, 15, 15, 17, 19, 20, 20, 20; **27:**2, 3, 5, 6, 6, 6, 7, 7, 16, 18, 21, 22, 22, 25, 26, 26, 27, 27, 31, 32, 33, 33, 34, 36, 36; **28:**2, 2, 2, 7, 8, 10, 12, 12, 12, 13, 14, 14, 16, 16, 17, 17, 17, 18, 21, 21, 22, 25, 25; **29:**1, 2, 2, 3, 3, 6, 7, 9, 10, 10, 10, 13, 14, 14, 15, 16, 17, 18, 18, 18, 19, 19, 20, 21; **30:**2, 3, 3, 3, 4, 6, 6, 8, 9, 10, 10, 12, 13, 15, 15, 17, 18, 20, 21, 21, 21, 22, 22, 22, 24, 24, 24, 25, 25, 25, 25, 25; **31:**1, 2, 2, 3, 3, 5, 6, 8, 8, 8, 9, 9, 9, 9, 12, 12, 14, 15, 16, 16, 16, 18, 18, 18; **32:**1, 2, 2, 2, 3, 4, 4, 10, 10, 11, 11, 12, 12, 12, 14, 18, 18, 21, 22, 23, 23, 23, 24, 24, 25, 25, 26, 26, 26, 27, 28, 30, 30; **33:**2, 2, 7, 7, 10, 10, 11, 11, 12, 12, 12, 13, 16, 20, 20, 21, 22, 24, 24, 24, 27, 28, 29, 30, 31; **34:**2, 2, 2, 4, 6, 7, 8, 9, 13, 13, 14, 18, 25, 26, 27, 27, 29, 30, 31; **35:**2, 5, 6, 10, 10, 11, 12, 15, 15; **36:**1, 1, 1, 3, 3, 3, 4, 4, 6, 6, 8, 8, 10, 11, 17, 17, 20, 22, 26, 29, 32, 32, 38; **37:**1, 1, 3, 4, 7, 10, 11, 11, 12, 12, 16, 16, 21, 25, 26; **38:**2, 2, 2, 2, 6, 7, 8, 8, 12, 13, 13, 14, 18, 19, 23; **39:**1, 1, 1, 2, 7, 7, 8, 9, 11, 11, 11, 11, 11, 12, 14, 15, 17, 17, 18, 18, 18, 22, 24, 25, 27, 28; **40:**1, 1, 1, 2, 2, 4, 4, 6, 7, 7, 7, 8, 9, 10, 12, 12, 13, 13, 14, 15, 16, 16, 17, 17, 21, 21, 22, 25, 26, 30, 31, 33, 36, 38, 39, 40, 42, 42, 46, 46, 46, 47, 48, 49; **41:**1, 3, 3, 3, 5, 5, 7, 9, 10, 10, 14, 15, 16, 16, 18, 18, 19, 19, 19, 20, 20, 21, 22, 22, 25, 26; **42:**1, 1, 1, 1, 2, 3, 3, 3, 3, 4, 4, 5, 5, 5, 6, 8, 10, 10, 10, 11, 11, 11, 11, 12, 12, 12, 14; **43:**2, 2, 2, 2, 4, 5, 7, 7, 7, 7, 7, 10, 10, 10, 11, 11, 12, 12, 12, 13, 13, 15, 15, 16, 17, 18, 18, 18, 19, 19, 20, 20, 20, 25, 25, 27; **44:**2, 4, 4, 4, 5, 5, 6, 6, 6, 7, 8, 9, 10, 10, 10, 13, 13, 15, 15, 15, 22, 22, 25, 30, 30, 30; **45:**1, 1, 1, 2, 2, 3, 3, 5, 6, 7, 7, 7, 7, 8, 8, 9, 9, 11, 12, 13, 14, 16, 17, 18, 19, 19, 19, 19, 20, 21, 22, 22, 23, 23, 23, 24, 24, 25, 25; **46:**1, 1, 2, 3, 3, 4, 5, 5, 5, 5, 5, 7, 7, 7, 7, 7, 11, 11, 11, 11, 14, 14, 14, 16, 16, 17, 17, 17, 18, 19, 21, 22, 23, 23; **47:**1, 1, 2, 7, 8, 8, 9, 10, 10, 11, 12, 12, 12, 13, 13, 13, 16, 19, 19, 19, 21, 23; **48:**1, 1, 1, 1, 1, 2, 3, 4, 5, 7, 8, 10, 11, 11, 11, 12, 13, 14, 15, 15, 18, 21, 21, 21, 23, 23, 23, 24, 24, 25, 26, 27, 27, 28, 28, 28, 31, 35; **Da 1:**1, 1, 2, 2, 2, 2, 2, 3, 3, 3, 4, 4, 5, 5, 6, 6, 12, 13, 15, 16, 17, 17, 19, 19, 19, 20, 20, 21; **2:**1, 5, 10, 12, 13, 14, 18, 18, 19, 20, 21, 23, 23, 24, 24, 25, 25, 29, 30, 31, 31, 32, 32, 32, 32, 33, 33, 34, 35, 37, 38, 41, 42, 43, 44, 44, 45, 45, 47, 47, 48, 49, 49, 49; **3:**1, 1, 2, 4, 5, 7, 8, 10, 12, 12, 15, 20, 20, 26, 26, 26, 27, 28, 29, 29, 30; **4:**1, 6, 8, 9, 10, 15, 15, 15, 16, 16, 16, 17, 17, 17, 18, 18, 19, 22, 23, 23, 23, 23, 25, 25, 25, 29, 30, 30, 31, 32, 32, 33, 35, 35, 36, 37; **5:**1, 1, 3, 4, 5, 5, 7, 7, 8, 11, 11, 14, 16, 19, 20, 21, 21, 21, 23, 23, 23, 26, 31; **6:**3, 5, 5, 8, 12, 13, 14, 14, 15, 16, 17, 17, 20, 24, 25, 26, 27, 28, 28; **7:**1, 2, 3, 6, 7, 8, 9, 10, 10, 13, 14, 14, 16, 18, 19, 20, 22, 22, 24, 25, 27, 27, 28; **8:**1, 2, 2, 3, 3, 4, 8, 8, 9, 9, 10, 11, 12, 13, 13, 13, 15, 15, 16, 17, 17, 19, 19, 20, 21, 21, 22, 23, 23, 24, 25, 25, 26; **9:**1, 1, 1, 1, 2, 2, 2, 4, 6, 7, 7, 7, 11, 11, 11, 13, 15, 15, 16, 16, 16, 16, 20, 21, 23, 24, 24, 25, 25, 26, 26, 27, 27; **10:**1, 1, 1, 1, 5, 6, 6, 11, 13, 13, 13, 13, 13, 16, 20, 20, 20, 20, 21; **11:**1, 1, 2, 4, 5, 5, 6, 6, 6, 6, 6, 7, 7, 7, 7, 8, 9, 9, 9, 10, 10, 11, 11, 12, 12, 13, 14, 15, 15, 15, 16, 16, 17, 17, 23, 24, 24, 24, 24, 25, 25, 26, 28, 28, 30, 33, 35, 36, 36, 37, 37, 38, 38, 39, 40, 40, 40, 41, 41, 43; **12:**1, 1, 2, 4, 5, 6, 7, 9, 10, 12, 13; **Hos 1:**1, 1, 1, 1, 2, 3, 6, 7, 10, 10, 11, 11; **2:**3, 5, 13, 15, 15, 16, 17, 18, 21, 22, 23; **3:**2, 2, 2; **4:**1, 1, 1, 6, 7, 7, 11, 12, 13, 13, 18; **5:**1, 1, 1, 2, 5, 5, 7, 8, 9, 9, 10, 11; **6:**3, 3, 8, 8, 9, 9, 9, 11, 11; **7:**5, 5, 8, 9, 11, 16, 16; **8:**1, 3, 5, 7, 8, 9, 10, 13, 13; **9:**1, 3, 4, 5, 6, 7, 7, 8, 8, 10, 11, 15, 16, 17; **10:**1, 2, 5, 7, 8, 8, 9, 10, 11, 11, 12, 12, 12, 13, 13, 14, 15, 15, 15; **11:**1, 2, 3, 4, 11; **12:**1, 6, 9, 11, 11, 12, 13, 14; **13:**1, 1, 5, 10, 12, 15, 15, 16, 16; **14:**2, 4, 6, 6, 7, 7, 9; **Joel 1:**1, 2, 6, 6, 9, 9, 9, 10, 13, 13, 14, 14, 15, 16; **2:**1, 2, 2, 2, 3, 3, 3, 5, 5, 11, 14, 15, 17, 17, 17, 18, 19, 20, 22, 23, 23, 23, 27, 30, 31, 32; **3:**1, 2, 2, 3, 4, 6, 8, 8, 12, 13, 14, 14, 16, 18, 18; **Am 1:**1, 1, 1, 1, 2, 2, 3, 3, 4, 5, 5, 5, 6, 7, 8, 8, 9, 9, 10, 11, 12, 13, 14; **2:**1, 1, 2, 2, 4, 4, 5, 6, 6, 8, 8, 9, 10, 11, 11, 16; **3:**1, 7, 9, 9, 12, 14, 15; **4:**1, 2, 5, 5, 8, 10, 11, 11, 12, 13; **5:**1, 3, 4, 5, 5, 5, 12, 12, 15, 18, 20, 20, 21, 23, 24, 24, 27; **6:**2, 2, 3, 3, 4, 5, 8, 10, 12, 13, 14; **7:**1, 4, 9, 9, 9, 10, 11, 12, 12, 14, 14, 17; **8:**2, 2, 3, 3, 6, 6, 6, 7, 10, 10, 10, 11, 11, 11, 12, 14; **9:**1, 1, 2, 3, 3, 6, 7, 7, 8, 8, 11, 12, 13, 14; **Ob** 1, 6, 8, 8, 9, 9, 10, 11, 11, 13, 13, 14, 17, 18, 19, 19, 19, 19, 19, 20, 20, 21; **Jnh 1:**1, 2, 3, 7, 8, 9; **2:**2, 3, 6, 6, 6, 6, 9; **3:**2, 2, 5, 6, 6; **4:**1, 5, 6, 7; **Mic 1:**1, 1, 1, 2, 5, 5, 5, 6, 6, 6, 8, 9, 10, 11, 11, 11, 11, 12, 12, 13, 13, 14, 14, 14, 15, 15, 16; **2:**1, 2, 3, 4, 4, 7, 8, 9, 11, 11, 11, 12, 13, 13, 13; **3:**1, 4, 8, 9, 10, 11, 12; **4:**1, 2, 2, 2, 8, 10, 10, 12, 13; **5:**1, 2, 3, 4, 4, 5, 6, 6, 8, 9, 11, 13; **6:**2, 4, 5, 5, 6, 7, 7, 7, 7, 7, 9, 10, 10, 16, 16, 16; **7:**1, 4, 4, 4, 9, 10, 12, 13, 13, 14, 16, 18, 19; **Na 1:**4, 4, 8, 11, 14, 15, 15; **2:**2, 3, 10, 11, 11, 13, 13; **3:**1, 2, 3, 3, 4, 9, 9, 9, 10, 11, 12, 13, 15, 16, 17, 19; **Hab 1:**9, 9, 10, 12, 12, 16; **2:**9, 11, 13, 14, 14, 16, 17, 17; **3:**2, 4, 7, 8, 9, 11, 13, 18; **Zep 1:**1, 1, 1, 1, 1, 1, 3, 3, 3, 4, 4, 7, 7, 8, 8, 10, 10, 14, 15, 15, 15, 15, 18, 18, 18, 18; **2:**2, 2, 3, 5, 5, 6, 7, 7, 8, 8, 9, 9, 9, 10, 10, 13, 14, 14, 14, 15; **3:**1, 2, 3, 8, 8, 9, 10, 11, 12, 13, 14, 14, 15, 15, 15, 20, 20; **Hag 1:**1, 1, 1, 1, 1, 12, 12, 12, 14, 14, 14, 14, 14, 14, 15, 15; **2:**1, 2, 2, 2, 2, 4, 5, 7, 9, 10, 10, 12, 12, 13, 15, 17, 18, 18, 21, 22, 23; **Zec 1:**1, 1, 1, 1, 7, 7, 7, 7, 11, 12, 12, 16, 17; **2:**4, 5, 8, 12; **3:**1, 1, 5, 6, 7, 8, 9, 10; **4:**2, 2, 3, 7, 9, 10, 11, 14; **5:**4, 4, 6, 9, 11; **6:**5, 5, 8, 10, 10, 10, 11, 11, 12, 14, 14, 15, 15; **7:**1, 1, 2, 3, 3, 3, 3, 5, 6, 7, 7; **8:**3, 5, 6, 9, 11, 12, 12, 13, 13, 15, 17, 19, 19, 19, 21, 23; **9:**1, 1, 1, 1, 2, 5, 6, 6, 7, 9, 9, 10, 11, 12, 12, 15, 15, 17; **10:**1, 2, 3, 5, 7, 11, 11, 11, 11, 11; **11:**2, 2, 3, 6, 6, 8, 11, 12, 13, 14, 15, 16; **12:**1, 1, 3, 4, 4, 5, 5, 6, 6, 7, 7, 7, 7, 8, 8, 10, 10, 10, 11, 11, 12, 12, 13, 13, 14; **13:**1, 1, 2, 2, 2, 3, 4, 5, 6, 8; **14:**1, 1, 2, 4, 4, 5, 5, 6, 10, 10, 10, 10, 14, 14, 16, 16, 18, 20, 20, 21, 21; **Mal 1:**4, 7, 9, 11, 11, 13; **2:**3, 5, 5, 6, 7, 9, 9, 10, 10, 11, 12, 14, 15, 16, 17; **3:**1, 3, 4, 5, 5, 6, 7, 8, 10, 14, 15, 16, 16; **4:**1, 2, 4, 5, 6, 6; **Mt 1:**1, 1, 1, 1, 2, 2, 2, 3, 3, 3, 4, 4, 4, 5, 5, 5, 6, 6, 6, 7, 7, 7, 8, 8, 8, 9, 9, 9, 10, 10, 10, 11, 11, 12, 12, 13, 13, 13, 14, 14, 14, 15, 15, 15, 16, 16, 16, 20, 20, 22, 24; **2:**1, 1, 2, 3, 4, 4, 6, 9, 11, 13, 15, 17, 18, 19, 20; **3:**2, 3, 5, 7, 9, 9, 10, 16, 16; **4:**3, 3, 4, 5, 6, 8, 8, 10, 13, 13, 13, 15, 15, 17, 18, 23, 24, 25; **5:**3, 9, 10, 13, 14, 17, 17, 18, 19, 19, 20, 20, 21, 22, 22, 22, 27, 29, 30, 31, 31, 33, 35, 38, 38, 38, 43, 45; **6:**2, 7, 25, 27, 33; **7:**4, 4, 5, 9, 10, 12, 15, 20, 21, 29; **8:**4, 4, 4, 9, 10, 11, 12, 17, 18, 19, 19, 20, 20, 21, 28, 28, 29, 30, 31, 32; **9:**3, 3, 6, 13, 14, 18, 20, 26, 27, 29, 34, 35, 35, 35, 38; **10:**1, 2, 2, 3, 6, 7, 14, 15, 20, 22, 23, 23, 25, 25, 25, 26, 28, 31, 37, 37, 38, 41, 42, 42, 42; **11:**7, 11, 11, 12, 13, 16, 19, 19, 19, 20, 23, 23, 25, 28; **12:**1, 4, 5, 7, 8, 8, 10, 11, 17, 21, 23, 24, 27, 28, 28, 32, 34, 36, 38, 39, 40, 40, 40, 41, 41, 42, 42, 45, 50; **13:**11, 11, 12, 14, 15, 18, 22, 22, 23, 24, 27, 31, 32, 32, 33, 33, 33, 35, 36, 37, 38, 39, 40, 41, 42, 44, 45, 46, 47, 47, 49, 50, 52, 52, 52, 53, 58; **14:**3, 5, 8, 9, 9, 17, 19, 20, 22, 29, 33, 35, 36; **15:**1, 2, 3, 4, 6, 17, 21, 22, 24, 29, 31, 33, 34, 37, 39; **16:**3, 4, 5, 6, 6, 9, 10, 11, 11, 12, 13, 13, 14, 16, 17, 18, 19, 19, 21, 21, 23, 24, 27, 27, 28, 28; **17:**9, 10, 12, 13, 14, 22, 25, 27, 27; **18:**1, 1, 3, 4, 6, 8, 10, 10, 14, 19, 23, 24, 24, 31; **19:**1, 1, 7, 12, 12, 14, 23, 24, 24, 27, 28, 28; **20:**1, 1, 4, 7, 13, 18, 18, 20, 20, 21, 22, 28, 29, 30, 31; **21:**1, 1, 1, 5, 8, 8, 9, 9, 9, 10, 12, 12, 13, 13, 15, 15, 31, 31, 31, 34, 34, 36, 39, 40, 41, 43; **22:**2, 2, 6, 8, 13, 15, 16, 16, 16, 16, 23, 26, 26, 28, 28, 29, 31, 32, 32, 32, 32, 34, 35, 36, 40, 42, 43; **23:**2, 2, 8, 13, 13, 15, 15, 22, 23, 23, 23, 25, 25, 25, 26, 27, 27, 29, 29, 31, 31, 33, 33, 34, 35, 35, 36, 36, 39; **24:**2, 3, 3, 3, 3, 7, 8, 9, 12, 21, 22, 22, 27, 28, 29, 30, 30, 30, 30, 30, 30, 31, 31, 37, 39, 44, 45, 47, 51; **25:**1, 1, 2, 8, 9, 13, 14, 14, 15, 15, 15, 16, 17, 18, 19, 20, 20, 21, 22, 22, 24, 28, 30, 31, 34, 40, 40, 45; **26:**2, 3, 6, 7, 8, 14, 15, 17, 17, 21, 23, 24, 26, 27, 27, 28, 30, 31, 31, 32, 38, 39, 45, 45, 47, 47, 48, 51, 51, 53, 56, 57, 57, 58, 61, 63, 63, 64, 64, 64, 69, 70, 71, 73; **27:**3, 5, 8, 9, 9, 9, 11, 18, 21, 24, 24, 24, 27, 29, 29, 31, 37, 38, 40, 41, 42, 43, 47, 48, 52, 53, 54, 56, 56, 57, 60, 62; **28:**2, 7, 11, 12, 17, 19, 19, 20, 20; **Mk 1:**1, 2, 10, 13, 15, 16, 16, 21, 22, 24, 25, 27, 28, 28, 33, 34, 34, 34, 39, 40, 44, 44, 44; **2:**1, 4, 6, 6, 10, 14, 15, 16, 16, 19, 23, 26, 28, 28; **3:**3, 6, 8, 8, 11, 11, 11, 14, 16, 17, 17,

18, 21, 22, 22, 23; **4:**11, 19, 19, 21, 26, 26, 28, 30, 31, 31, 32, 32, 35,
37, 38; **5:**1, 1, 7, 8, 9, 11, 13, 13, 20, 21, 22, 27, 33, 38; **6:**1, 3, 3, 5,
15, 21, 23, 25, 26, 38, 40, 43, 47, 52, 52, 53, 56; **7:**1, 2, 2, 4, 4, 5, 10,
13, 14, 19, 21, 24, 24, 31, 31; **8:**1, 3, 5, 8, 10, 13, 14, 15, 15, 15, 19,
19, 20, 23, 27, 28, 31, 31, 33, 34, 35, 38, 38, 38, 38; **9:**1, 1, 2, 9, 11,
12, 14, 14, 17, 25, 25, 25, 31, 34, 35, 38, 39, 41, 42, 43, 47, 50; **10:**1,
1, 4, 6, 14, 15, 15, 23, 24, 25, 25, 32, 33, 33, 35, 37, 38, 38, 44, 45,
46, 47, 48, 48; **11:**1, 1, 1, 8, 9, 9, 10, 15, 15, 17, 17, 18, 18, 27; **12:**2,
2, 8, 9, 12, 13, 14, 18, 20, 22, 24, 26, 26, 26, 26, 26, 27, 28, 28, 28,
32, 33, 34, 35, 35, 36, 38, 38, 38, 39, 40, 40, 40, 44; **13:**1, 2, 3, 3, 4,
8, 8, 9, 13, 19, 20, 20, 25, 26, 27, 34, 34, 34, 34; **14:**1, 1, 3, 3, 4, 8,
10, 12, 12, 13, 13, 18, 18, 20, 21, 22, 23, 25, 26, 27, 28, 34, 36, 41,
41, 43, 43, 44, 47, 53, 54, 61, 62, 62, 62, 65, 66, 67, 69, 70; **15:**1, 2,
3, 7, 9, 10, 11, 11, 12, 17, 18, 20, 21, 26, 27, 31, 32, 35, 36, 39, 40,
40, 41, 42, 43, 43, 46, 46, 46, 47; **16:**1, 7, 19, S; **Lk 1:**2, 2, 3, 4, 4, 5,
5, 5, 5, 6, 9, 11, 11, 15, 17, 17, 17, 17, 19, 23, 25, 26, 27, 32, 32, 35,
35, 39, 41, 43, 48, 65, 66, 68, 69, 76, 77, 78, 79, 79; **2:**2, 4, 4, 7, 8, 9,
9, 10, 11, 12, 13, 13, 22, 22, 23, 24, 24, 32, 35, 36, 36, 36, 39, 39;
3:1, 1, 2, 3, 4, 7, 7, 8, 8, 9, 14, 19, 22, 23, 23, 24, 24, 24, 24, 24, 25,
25, 25, 25, 25, 26, 26, 26, 26, 26, 27, 27, 27, 27, 27, 28, 28, 28, 28,
28, 29, 29, 29, 29, 29, 30, 30, 30, 30, 30, 31, 31, 31, 31, 31, 32, 32,
32, 32, 32, 33, 33, 33, 33, 33, 33, 34, 34, 34, 34, 34, 35, 35, 35, 35,
35, 36, 36, 36, 36, 36, 37, 37, 37, 37, 37, 38, 38, 38, 38; **4:**1, 3, 3, 5,
5, 6, 9, 9, 16, 17, 18, 19, 22, 26, 26, 26, 27, 29, 34, 35, 37, 40, 41, 43,
43; **5:**1, 1, 1, 3, 7, 8, 9, 10, 12, 12, 14, 14, 14, 15, 15, 17, 19, 21, 24,
29, 29, 30, 33, 33, 36; **6:**1, 4, 5, 5, 7, 11, 13, 13, 15, 16, 17, 17, 17,
20, 22, 25, 28, 35, 42, 42, 42, 44, 49; **7:**2, 6, 8, 9, 11, 12, 16, 17, 18,
18, 21, 24, 28, 28, 32, 34, 34, 34, 35, 36, 39, 41, 42, 45, 46; **8:**1, 1, 3,
6, 10, 10, 11, 13, 14, 19, 21, 22, 26, 27, 28, 29, 29, 32, 33, 37, 37, 40,
41, 44; **9:**2, 2, 5, 6, 7, 10, 11, 13, 14, 17, 19, 22, 22, 23, 26, 26, 26,
26, 27, 27, 29, 31, 43, 44, 46, 53, 58, 58, 60, 60, 62; **10:**2, 4, 9, 11,
11, 11, 15, 15, 18, 19, 20, 21, 21, 26, 30, 31, 34, 35, 35, 36; **11:**1, 5,
6, 12, 14, 15, 18, 19, 20, 20, 22, 28, 29, 30, 30, 31, 31, 32, 32, 37, 39,
39, 42, 42, 43, 50, 50, 50, 51, 51, 53; **12:**1, 1, 1, 4, 6, 6, 6, 7, 8, 8, 8,
10, 23, 25, 26, 30, 31, 33, 38, 40, 42, 44, 50, 52, 56; **13:**4, 8, 12, 14,
14, 18, 20, 21, 21, 25, 28, 28, 29, 31, 32, 33, 35; **14:**1, 1, 5, 7, 9, 10,
10, 14, 15, 19, 21, 24, 24, 28, 29, 30, 31, 31, 32; **15:**2, 4, 8, 10, 12,
12, 17, 19, 21, 24, 26, 27, 30; **16:**4, 4, 6, 7, 8, 11, 12, 15, 16, 16, 16,
16, 23, 24, 28; **17:**2, 7, 10, 15, 20, 20, 21, 22, 22, 23, 24, 25, 26, 28,
30, 37; **18:**3, 8, 12, 16, 17, 17, 24, 25, 25, 29, 29, 31, 31, 36, 37, 38,
39, 39; **19:**2, 7, 9, 10, 11, 13, 17, 20, 27, 28, 29, 29, 36, 37, 37, 38,
39, 42, 46, 46, 47, 47, 48; **20:**1, 10, 10, 15, 15, 19, 21, 26, 27, 31, 35,
36, 37, 37, 37, 38, 39, 39, 41, 42, 46, 46, 46, 47, 47, 47; **21:**3, 4, 5, 5,
6, 7, 9, 12, 12, 15, 16, 17, 18, 20, 22, 22, 24, 24, 26, 26, 26, 27, 31,
34, 36, 37; **22:**1, 2, 3, 4, 7, 10, 16, 17, 18, 19, 19, 20, 20, 22, 22, 23,
25, 28, 30, 31, 39, 42, 44, 44, 47, 48, 50, 52, 53, 56, 58, 59, 63, 65,
66, 66, 69, 69, 70; **23:**3, 10, 14, 26, 28, 36, 37, 38, 39, 47, 50, 51, 51,
51, 53, 54; **24:**3, 7, 7, 10, 13, 13, 13, 18, 22, 24, 26, 27, 28, 30, 33,
35, 42, 47, 47, 48, 53; **Jn 1:**7, 12, 14, 14, 14, 19, 23, 28, 29, 29, 34,
35, 36, 39, 40, 42, 45, 47, 49, 49, 51, 51; **2:**1, 8, 9, 9, 11, 15, 16, 23;
3:3, 5, 5, 8, 13, 14, 18, 23, 26, 26, 31, 31, 36; **4:**5, 5, 15, 20, 27, 34,
35, 41, 42, 42, 43, 46, 46, 46, 51; **5:**1, 2, 3, 5, 7, 18, 25, 25, 27, 28,
30, 45; **6:**1, 1, 5, 10, 13, 27, 33, 34, 35, 38, 39, 39, 42, 48, 51, 53, 53,
57, 57, 57, 62, 64, 66, 69, 70, 71, 71, 71; **7:**1, 2, 7, 10, 12, 13, 16, 17,
19, 19, 22, 22, 22, 23, 25, 35, 37, 38, 39, 40, 42, 42, 48; **8:**1, 3, 3, 3,
4, 5, 9, 10, 12, 20, 23, 28, 33, 34, 35, 35, 37, 37, 38, 39, 41, 44, 44,
46, 46, 47; **9:**2, 2, 3, 3, 4, 5, 7, 11, 16, 16, 22, 28, 32, 34, 35; **10:**1, 4,
20, 21, 22, 25, 26, 32, 34, 36; **11:**4, 4, 9, 9, 10, 19, 27, 42, 45, 49, 51,
52, 52, 54, 55; **12:**1, 3, 3, 4, 6, 9, 11, 11, 12, 13, 13, 15, 16, 23, 24,
24, 31, 31, 34, 34, 36, 37, 41, 42, 42, 43, 48; **13:**1, 2, 10, 11, 17, 18,
18, 21, 21, 23, 26, 28, 31, 31; **14:**11, 13, 21, 26, 27, 30, 31; **15:**19,
21, 24, 26; **16:**5, 8, 8, 8, 11, 13, 21, 22, 25; **17:**10, 15, 16, 17, 20, 21;
18:1, 3, 5, 7, 9, 10, 13, 15, 17, 22, 25, 26, 26, 26, 28, 28, 33, 36, 38,
39, 39; **19:**2, 3, 5, 7, 12, 14, 14, 19, 19, 21, 21, 23, 25, 29, 32, 34, 36,
36, 38, 38, 39, 40, 41, 42; **20:**2, 12, 12, 19, 19, 24, 31; **21:**1, 2, 2, 6,
6, 10, 12, 15, 16, 16, 17, 19, 23, 24; **Ac 1:**3, 4, 8, 11, 12, 13, 13, 13,
13, 14, 14, 17, 19, 19, 19, 20, 22, 24; **2:**1, 2, 3, 3, 8, 9, 10, 14, 14, 15,
19, 20, 21, 22, 22, 23, 24, 28, 30, 32, 32, 33, 38, 38, 38, 38, 43, 47;
3:6, 6, 11, 12, 13, 13, 13, 13, 14, 15, 15, 16, 17, 19, 20, 20, 21, 25,
26, 26; **4:**1, 1, 2, 2, 4, 4, 5, 5, 6, 8, 10, 10, 12, 13, 13, 15, 22, 24, 26,
27, 30, 32, 33, 36, 36, 36; **5:**2, 3, 9, 9, 9, 14, 15, 15, 19, 19, 20, 21,
24, 30, 31, 31, 32, 35, 37, 37, 39, 40, 41; **6:**1, 1, 2, 2, 3, 3, 5, 5, 7, 7,
8, 9, 9, 10, 12, 13, 14; **7:**4, 5, 8, 8, 8, 8, 9, 9, 10, 10, 10, 10, 11, 16,
16, 17, 18, 22, 23, 24, 26, 29, 30, 31, 32, 32, 34, 36, 36, 37, 38, 38,
40, 40, 42, 43, 45, 45, 46, 46, 52, 53, 55, 55, 55, 56, 56, 58, 58; **8:**1,
1, 1, 5, 6, 10, 10, 11, 12, 12, 12, 14, 16, 16, 23, 25, 26, 27, 27, 27, 28,
32, 33, 39, 39, 40; **9:**2, 2, 7, 11, 11, 12, 15, 20, 25, 26, 27, 28, 30, 31,
31, 32, 35; **10:**1, 2, 3, 7, 7, 12, 22, 28, 30, 32, 33, 36, 36, 38, 39, 42,
42, 45, 48; **11:**1, 2, 3, 6, 12, 16, 18, 19, 20, 21, 21, 23, 24, 24, 26, 26,
28, 28, 28, 30; **12:**4, 4, 7, 12, 12, 14, 15, 17, 20, 22, 22, 23, 23; **13:**1,
1, 1, 4, 4, 5, 5, 7, 7, 10, 10, 10, 10, 10, 11, 13, 14, 15, 15, 15, 16, 16,
17, 17, 17, 18, 20, 21, 21, 21, 22, 23, 23, 26, 26, 26, 31, 31, 36, 44,
46, 47, 50, 50, 51, 51; **14:**1, 2, 3, 4, 5, 6, 6, 6, 13, 13, 13, 13, 19, 21,
22, 23, 26, 26, 27; **15:**1, 1, 5, 5, 11, 15, 16, 17, 20, 21, 22, 22, 26, 29,
30, 33, 35, 36; **16:**2, 3, 6, 6, 7, 7, 7, 8, 11, 12, 12, 14, 14, 14, 15, 16,
16, 17, 18, 18, 19, 20, 26, 32, 40; **17:**1, 3, 4, 4, 5, 6, 6, 7, 8, 11, 12,
13, 18, 19, 22, 23, 24, 27, 27, 28, 29, 32, 32, 34; **18:**2, 8, 11, 12, 13,
15, 15, 16, 17, 18, 19, 22, 25, 26, 27; **19:**3, 5, 8, 9, 10, 12, 13, 13, 14,
17, 17, 19, 19, 22, 24, 27, 27, 27, 27, 27, 28, 31, 31, 31, 32, 33, 34,
34, 35, 35, 35, 40; **20:**4, 4, 4, 7, 15, 15, 16, 16, 17, 18, 19, 21, 21, 24,
25, 30, 32, 34, 34, 35, 35, 38; **21:**1, 2, 3, 3, 5, 8, 8, 9, 10, 10, 11, 13,
14, 16, 16, 18, 19, 20, 20, 21, 25, 26, 27, 28, 30, 30, 31, 38; **22:**3, 4,
5, 8, 12, 12, 14, 16, 18, 23; **23:**3, 5, 6, 6, 8, 9, 9, 12, 13, 16, 17, 23,
29, 30; **24:**1, 3, 5, 8, 10, 12, 13, 14, 14, 16, 19, 21, 23; **25:**5, 11, 14,
16, 20, 23, 25, 26; **26:**1, 5, 5, 6, 7, 8, 9, 9, 10, 11, 12, 18, 31; **27:**1, 1,
2, 2, 4, 5, 5, 5, 7, 7, 7, 8, 9, 10, 11, 12, 12, 14, 17, 17, 22, 23, 27, 27,
34, 37, 38, 41, 41; **28:**1, 2, 3, 4, 7, 10, 17, 20, 23, 23, 23, 23, 27, 31;
Ro 1:4, 4, 8, 8, 10, 12, 14, 16, 16, 21, 23, 25, 27, 29, 29, 30, 30, 32;
2:5, 5, 5, 20, 23, 24, 24, 25, 26, 28, 28, 29, 29, 29; **3:**1, 1, 2, 2, 3, 4,
6, 8, 9, 13, 14, 18, 21, 23, 29, 29, 29, 30, 31; **4:**1, 1, 2, 2, 5, 5, 6, 6, 7,
9, 11, 12, 12, 16, 17, 18, 19, 22, 25; **5:**1, 2, 2, 4, 4, 9, 10, 11, 11, 14,
15, 16, 16, 16, 16, 17, 17, 18; **6:**2, 4, 7, 9, 10, 11, 13, 13, 13, 15, 17,
19, 19, 19, 20, 21, 22, 22, 23, 23; **7:**2, 6, 7, 7, 8, 8, 10, 11, 11, 13, 21,
25; **8:**2, 2, 3, 3, 4, 8, 9, 9, 10, 11, 13, 14, 14, 22, 23, 28, 34, 38, 39;
9:1, 4, 4, 5, 5, 7, 8, 8, 12, 12, 13, 14, 17, 21, 21, 22, 23, 23, 25, 26,
27, 29, 32, 33; **10:**1, 3, 3, 4, 5, 5, 6, 7, 13, 15, 17, 18, 19, 19; **11:**1, 1,
1, 1, 2, 5, 7, 7, 9, 11, 12, 13, 14, 15, 16, 17, 17, 17, 20, 25, 25, 28, 28,
28; **12:**1, 2, 3, 3, 5, 5, 5, 6, 7, 7, 9, 13, 16, 20, 21; **13:**2, 4, 8, 8, 10,
11, 12, 12, 12, 13, 14, 14; **14:**6, 9, 9, 10, 10, 12, 14, 14, 17, 17, 17,
17, 18, 20; **15:**1, 1, 5, 6, 6, 11, 13, 13, 14, 15, 18, 19, 19, 20, 21, 21,
23, 27, 28, 30, 30, 32; **16:**2, 5, 8, 10, 10, 11, 16, 19, 20, 20, 25;
1Co 1:1, 1, 2, 2, 2, 5, 5, 7, 10, 10, 11, 12, 12, 13, 13, 14, 16, 17, 18,
18, 24, 24, 25, 25, 25, 26, 29, 31; **2:**5, 6, 6, 6, 7, 7, 8, 13, 16; **3:**3, 4,
4, 5, 5, 10, 13, 13, 15, 16, 16, 16, 19, 20; **4:**1, 1, 6, 6, 9, 9, 10, 11, 17,
18, 20; **5:**2, 4, 4, 4, 5, 6, 8, 8; **6:**1, 6, 9, 10, 10, 11, 11, 11, 13, 15, 19;
7:3, 5, 5, 5, 5, 7, 7, 12, 16, 16, 22, 22, 26, 31, 31, 32; **8:**7, 7, 7, 9, 10,
11; **9:**1, 7, 7, 7, 7, 7, 9, 10, 10, 12, 13, 15, 15, 17, 19, 20, 21, 21;
10:1, 1, 1, 2, 3, 4, 5, 7, 8, 8, 9, 10, 10, 14, 16, 16, 16, 16, 16, 18, 19,
20, 21, 21, 21, 24, 24, 28, 28, 29, 31, 32; **11:**7, 10, 11, 11, 16, 18, 19,
19, 21, 22, 23, 24, 25, 25, 25, 27, 27, 27, 29, 30; **12:**1, 3, 4, 4, 5, 6, 7,
7, 8, 10, 12, 13, 15, 15, 16, 16, 22, 23, 27, 27, 27, 28, 28, 28, 28, 29,
30, 30, 30, 31; **13:**2, 2, 2, 3, 5, 9, 13; **14:**1, 2, 4, 5, 5, 7, 12, 13, 13,
18, 20, 20, 21, 22, 24, 24, 32, 33, 33, 36; **15:**1, 2, 6, 6, 8, 9, 9, 12, 12,
13, 15, 16, 20, 20, 22, 24, 27, 32, 34, 35, 37, 38, 38, 39, 39, 39, 40,
40, 41, 42, 43, 43, 47, 49, 50, 50, 51, 52; **16:**2, 2, 3, 8, 19, 23, 24;
2Co 1:1, 3, 3, 8, 14, 14, 15, 17, 18, 19, 20, 22, 24; **2:**6, 12, 12, 16,
17; **3:**1, 1, 2, 3, 4, 4, 5, 6, 6, 7, 7, 7, 10, 11, 13, 17, 18, 18, 18; **4:**2, 4,
4, 4, 4, 4, 5, 6, 6, 6, 10, 10, 10, 11, 11, 12, 13, 15; **5:**11, 12, 16, 18,
18; **6:**1, 2, 2, 4, 4, 6, 9, 12, 12, 16; **7:**2, 6, 7, 9, 10, 12, 14; **8:**3, 4, 5, 6,
7, 9, 13, 18, 22, 23, 23; **9:**2, 5, 10, 12, 13, 14, 14; **10:**1, 6, 7, 13, 13,
14, 17; **11:**2, 4, 10, 12, 13, 14, 15, 20, 22, 28, 31; **12:**6, 9, 16, 16, 17,
17, 18, 18, 20, 21, 21, 21; **13:**1, 1, 4, 11, 13, 13, 13; **Gal 1:**2, 5, 11,
13, 14, 14, 14, 17, 21, 24; **2:**2, 5, 6, 7, 7, 8, 8, 9, 12, 12, 14, 14, 16,
17, 20, 21, 21; **3:**1, 1, 2, 5, 5, 6, 7, 8, 9, 10, 12, 12, 12, 14, 16, 18, 19,
19, 22, 23, 26, 29; **4:**1, 3, 4, 6, 9, 13, 23, 23, 23, 23, 24, 28, 29, 29,
29, 30, 30, 31, 31, 31; **5:**3, 3, 9, 11, 15, 15, 19, 20, 21, 21, 21, 22, 24,
25, 26; **6:**2, 4, 6, 8, 9, 9, 12, 14, 14, 16, 18; **Eph 1:**1, 1, 3, 7, 10, 11,
15, 17, 17, 19, 20, 22, 22; **2:**1, 2, 2, 2, 2, 2, 3, 3, 5, 7, 7, 9, 11, 13, 13,
14, 15, 16, 17, 18, 18, 19, 19, 20, 22; **3:**1, 1, 2, 6, 6, 7, 8, 9, 12, 12,
13, 14, 14, 15, 17, 19, 19; **4:**1, 2, 7, 7, 8, 12, 13, 13, 15, 16, 18, 18,
19, 22, 22, 23, 30, 31, 31; **5:**2, 5, 5, 5, 6, 8, 8, 11, 16, 20, 21, 23, 23,
32; **6:**2, 3, 6, 6, 8, 11, 11, 12, 12, 12, 13, 13, 14, 14, 17, 17, 18;
Php 1:1, 1, 3, 4, 7, 7, 8, 11, 13, 14, 14, 15, 19, 25, 25, 27, 27, 29, 29,
30; **2:**3, 7, 9, 9, 10, 11, 15, 15, 15, 16, 17, 17, 30, 30; **3:**1, 5, 5, 5, 6,
7, 8, 9, 14, 15, 18, 18, 20, 21; **4:**3, 3, 4, 8, 9, 12, 13, 17, 19, 23;
Col 1:1, 2, 3, 4, 5, 5, 9, 13, 13, 15, 18, 18, 20, 22, 24, 25, 27; **2:**2, 2,
3, 5, 8, 9, 11, 12, 13, 15, 17, 19, 20, 20; **3:**1, 1, 5, 7, 8, 11, 14, 15, 16,
17, 22, 22; **4:**5, 9, 11, 12, 12, 12, 18; **1Th 1:**2, 3, 3, 3, 5, 5, 6, 8, 10,
10, 10; **2:**4, 7, 7, 10, 11, 13, 13, 13, 14, 15, 16, 17; **3:**2, 3, 5, 7, 9, 9;
4:1, 2, 3, 4, 5, 10, 13, 15, 16, 16; **5:**2, 4, 5, 5, 8, 8, 10, 13, 13, 14, 22,
23, 27, 28, 28; **2Th 1:**5, 8, 11, 12, 12, 12, 12; **2:**1, 2, 3, 4, 4, 7, 8, 8,
8, 9, 10, 14; **3:**5, 5, 6, 6, 8, 11, 12, 13, 13, 14, 15, 16, 17, 18; **1Ti 1:**1,
1, 4, 5, 7, 7, 13, 14, 15, 16, 20; **2:**1; **3:**5, 6, 7, 9, 10, 11, 15, 15, 15,
16; **4:**4, 5, 6, 6, 10, 10, 12, 14; **5:**4, 10, 12, 14, 15, 16, 20, 20, 21, 22,
23; **6:**1, 3, 4, 10, 10, 10, 15, 15, 19; **2Ti 1:**1, 5, 7, 7, 8, 8, 10, 10, 10,
11, 12, 12, 13, 14, 15, 16, 18; **2:**3, 4, 6, 9, 14, 15, 17, 17, 18, 18, 18,
20, 20, 22; **3:**6, 6, 11, 17; **4:**2, 5, 6, 8, 8, 10, 15, 19; **Tit 1:**1, 1, 2, 3, 5,
6, 10, 12, 12, 14; **2:**1, 2, 3, 5, 5, 7, 7, 11, 13, 14; **3:**2, 3, 5, 5, 6, 7, 9,
9, 12, 15; **Phm 1:**2, 5, 5, 6, 6, 7, 8, 8, 9, 9, 10, 10, 11, 11, 15, 25;
Heb 1:3, 3, 3, 3, 3, 6, 7, 9, 10, 10; **2:**2, 2, 4, 6, 6, 8, 10, 12, 14, 14,
14, 15, 16, 17; **3:**5, 6, 11, 13, 16, 18, 19; **4:**1, 1, 1, 2, 3, 3, 3, 5, 7, 8,
8, 8, 9, 11, 11, 12, 12, 14, 15, 15, 16; **5:**6, 7, 7, 9, 10; **6:**1, 1, 2, 2, 4,
5, 5, 5, 6, 7, 12, 12, 19, 20; **7:**1, 1, 1, 2, 2, 2, 3, 3, 3, 4, 4, 5, 5, 6, 8,
11, 11, 11, 11, 14, 16, 16, 16, 17, 17, 22, 22, 26, 26, 27, 28; **8:**1, 2, 4,
5, 5, 6, 8, 9, 9, 10, 13, 13; **9:**2, 4, 4, 5, 5, 6, 9, 11, 12, 13, 13, 14, 14,
15, 17, 17, 18, 19, 19, 19, 19, 22, 22, 22, 23, 23, 23, 24, 24, 25, 26,
26, 28; **10:**1, 1, 1, 2, 3, 4, 8, 10, 10, 12, 19, 19, 20, 22, 24, 24, 25, 26,
27, 28, 28, 29, 29, 31; **11:**1, 2, 2, 4, 7, 12, 13, 21, 22, 22, 22, 22, 23,
24, 25, 25, 25, 26, 26, 27, 27, 28, 28, 29, 30, 32, 32, 33, 34, 34, 37,
39, 39, 39, 40; **12:**1, 1, 2, 2, 7, 8, 9, 11, 15, 15, 15, 18, 22, 22, 23, 23,
23, 24, 24, 25; **13:**3, 5, 7, 7, 11, 11, 11, 15, 15, 20, 20, 20, 23;
Jas 1:1, 1, 6, 11, 12, 14, 18, 21, 27; **2:**9, 10, 10, 12, 14, 14, 21, 23,
25; **3:**1, 3, 6, 6, 6, 6, 7, 8, 9, 10, 11, 13, 14, 15, 16, 17, 17, 18, 18;
4:1, 4, 4, 9, 9; **5:**1, 1, 3, 4, 4, 4, 4, 8, 10, 10, 11, 11, 12, 14, 14, 16,
20; **1Pe 1:**1, 1, 1, 2, 3, 3, 4, 9, 11, 12, 13, 14, 17, 19, 19, 22, 23, 24,
25; **2:**1, 2, 3, 4, 5, 9, 9, 9, 10, 10, 12, 13, 18, 19, 20, 21, 23, 25; **3:**1,
4, 5, 5, 6, 7, 8, 8, 8, 12, 15, 21, 21, 21, 22; **4:**2, 2, 3, 3, 4, 7, 8, 8, 10,
10, 13, 14, 16; **5:**1, 2, 2, 5, 5, 6, 9, 10, 12, 12, 14; **2Pe 1:**1, 1, 4, 5, 5,
5, 8, 9, 11, 11, 12, 13, 16, 19; **2:**2, 3, 5, 5, 5, 6, 6, 6, 6, 7, 7, 9, 12, 14,
15, 15, 17, 20; **3:**1, 5, 7, 10, 16, 16, 16, 16, 17, 17, 18; **1Jn 1:**1, 7, 7;
2:2, 12, 15, 17, 18, 20, 26, 28; **3:**4, 4, 8, 8, 9, 10, 10, 17, 23; **4:**2, 2, 3,
6, 6, 7, 14, 15, 17, 18, 19; **5:**1, 4, 5, 10, 13, 18, 18, 19, 19, 20; **2Jn** 4,
9, 9, 13; **3Jn** 3, 5, 6, 10, 10, 12, 15; **Jude** 1, 1, 1, 1, 2, 3, 4, 5, 5, 6, 6,
6, 6, 7, 7, 7, 8, 9, 9, 9, 11, 11, 12, 13, 13, 14, 15, 15, 15, 17, 20, 23,
24; **Rev 1:**2, 2, 4, 5, 5, 7, 7, 7, 9, 9, 13, 13, 14, 18, 20, 20; **2:**1, 2, 6, 7,
7, 8, 9, 9, 10, 10, 10, 12, 13, 14, 16, 17, 18, 18, 18, 23, 23, 24, 24, 24;
3:1, 1, 2, 2, 5, 7, 7, 10, 12, 12, 14, 14, 16; **4:**1, 3, 5, 5, 5, 5, 6, 6, 7, 7,
7, 8; **5:**1, 1, 5, 5, 5, 6, 6, 7, 8, 11, 11; **6:**1, 1, 5, 6, 6, 8, 8, 9, 9, 11, 11,
11, 13, 14, 14, 15, 15, 16, 16, 17; **7:**1, 2, 3, 3, 4, 4, 9, 13, 14, 14, 15,
15, 17, 17; **8:**3, 3, 4, 4, 7, 7, 8, 8, 9, 9, 10, 10, 10, 11, 11, 12, 12, 12,
12, 12, 13; **9:**1, 4, 5, 8, 8, 9, 9, 13, 13, 15, 16, 16, 17, 18, 18, 20, 21;
10:1, 3, 6, 10; **11:**1, 1, 4, 5, 6, 7, 8, 10, 11, 13, 13, 15, 15, 18, 19, 19;
12:1, 1, 2, 4, 8, 10, 10, 11, 11, 11, 14, 15, 16, 17, 18; **13:**1, 3, 3, 6, 8,
11, 11, 11, 12, 14, 14, 14, 17, 18, 18; **14:**2, 2, 2, 3, 3, 7, 8, 8, 10, 10,
10, 11, 11, 14, 18, 18, 19; **15:**3, 3, 3, 3, 6, 7, 7, 7; **16:**1, 2, 3, 9, 9, 9,
10, 11, 11, 13, 14, 14, 17, 19, 19, 19, 19, 21; **17:**1, 2, 2, 4, 4, 4, 5, 6,
7, 7, 8, 8, 8, 9, 9, 15, 15, 17, 18; **18:**2, 3, 3, 3, 6, 8, 9, 11, 12, 12, 12,
17, 17, 20, 22, 22, 22, 23, 24; **19:**1, 2, 6, 6, 6, 7, 8, 9, 10, 10, 10, 12,
13, 14, 15, 15, 16, 16, 18, 18, 18, 19, 20, 20, 20, 21, 21, 21; **20:**4, 4,
4, 5, 6, 6, 7, 8, 9, 10, 12, 14, 14, 15, 15; **21:**2, 3, 4, 6, 6, 9, 9, 10, 11,
12, 12, 14, 14, 14, 16, 18, 19, 21, 23, 23, 24, 24, 25, 27; **22:**1, 1, 1, 2,
2, 2, 2, 3, 3, 9, 14, 14, 16, 17, 18, 19, 19, 19, 21

OH (98)

Ge 19:2, 18; **27:**36; **44:**16; **Ex 16:**3; **Nu 11:**4; **12:**11; **Dt 5:**29; **30:**19;
32:29, 29; **1Sa 1:**15, 18; **2:**1; **10:**15; **15:**25; **2Sa 1:**26; **14:**9; **23:**15;
1Ki 3:26; **13:**30; **18:**9; **2Ki 19:**4; **1Ch 4:**10; **11:**17; **Job 3:**20; **6:**8;
7:16; **13:**3; **16:**21; **19:**23, 23; **Ps 1:**1; **14:**7; **25:**17; **32:**1; **34:**8; **40:**4;
41:1; **51:**8; **53:**6; **55:**6; **60:**11; **77:**1; **78:**40; **79:**8, 9; **81:**13, 13; **95:**7;
108:12; **119:**5, 97; **134:**1; **Pr 5:**13; **SS 2:**5; **4:**3; **5:**1; **7:**6; **8:**1;
Isa 1:4; **12:**4; **22:**5; **37:**4; **42:**18; **44:**22; **48:**18; **64:**1, 3, 9; **Jer 8:**19;
9:1, 2; **15:**10; **20:**17; **41:**6; **48:**9; **La 1:**21; **Da 4:**19; **Hos 6:**3; **11:**8;
Jnh 1:10; **Mt 18:**26; **20:**22; **Mk 10:**39; **Lk 1:**46; **5:**8; **23:**6;
Jn 16:12; **Ro 4:**7; **7:**24; **11:**33; **1Co 1:**16; **2Co 6:**11; **10:**12; **Gal 3:**1;
4:19; **1Ti 1:**14

ON (3855)

Ge 1:8, 13, 19, 23, 31; **2:**2, 5; **3:**14, 15, 17; **4:**12, 12, 15; **6:**1, 4, 9,
17; **7:**11, 11, 18, 19, 21, 22, 23; **8:**4, 20; **9:**16, 21, 25; **12:**8, 8; **13:**9;
17:12, 15, 23; **18:**5, 8, 16, 22, 27, 33; **19:**2, 22, 24, 29; **22:**1, 2, 4, 6,
6, 8, 9, 9, 13, 14, 17; **24:**15, 30, 45; **25:**11, 34; **26:**24; **27:**13, 23;
28:4, 12, 13, 20; **29:**1, 9, 12; **30:**26, 37; **31:**17, 18, 34, 53; **32:**1, 6,
16, 21, 23; **33:**3, 14, 17, 19; **34:**17, 19, 22, 28; **35:**1, 2, 12, 16, 19, 21;
36:37; **37:**14, 20, 34; **38:**9, 14, 19, 30; **39:**10; **40:**6, 14, 16, 19, 22;
41:1, 5, 6, 13, 17, 22, 42, 49; **42:**18, 19, 33; **43:**8, 31; **44:**3, 12;
45:23; **46:**28, 29; **47:**26, 31; **48:**7, 14, 14, 14, 17, 17, 18; **49:**3, 13,
26; **50:**1, 4; **Ex 2:**25; **3:**5, 18; **4:**3, 9, 14, 20, 24; **5:**19; **7:**15; **8:**7; **9:**9,
10, 11, 22; **10:**7, 12, 15, 21; **11:**1, 3, 5; **12:**2, 3, 4, 7, 12, 13, 15, 16,
16, 16, 17, 23, 29, 34, 36, 37, 41; **13:**6, 9, 9, 16, 17, 20; **14:**16, 22,
22, 24, 26, 29, 29, 30; **15:**17, 19, 19, 26; **16:**5, 22, 22, 23, 25, 26, 26,
29, 29, 29, 30; **17:**5, 6, 12, 12; **19:**4, 11, 12, 16, 18, 20, 23; **20:**6, 10,
11, 20, 24; **21:**29; **22:**30; **23:**1, 2, 12; **24:**2, 12, 16, 17, 18; **25:**3, 12,
20, 21, 30, 40; **26:**13, 14, 17, 20, 22, 25, 30, 32, 34, 35, 37; **27:**5, 8,
9, 11, 12, 14, 14, 15; **28:**9, 10, 12, 14, 21, 24, 25, 28, 29, 38; **29:**5, 6,
10, 12, 13, 15, 16, 18, 19, 20, 20, 20, 21, 21, 25, 35, 38; **30:**4, 6, 7, 9,
10, 32, 33; **31:**14, 15, 17, 18; **32:**15, 16, 26, 27, 30; **33:**16, 21; **34:**1,
1, 2, 3, 21, 28, 28, 32, 35; **35:**2, 3, 35; **36:**5, 13, 20, 22, 31; **37:**9, 16,
27; **38:**4, 14, 14, 15, 23; **39:**6, 17, 18, 21, 30, 41; **40:**2, 4, 9, 9, 10, 17,
19, 20, 23, 24, 27, 29, 36, 38; **Lev 1:**4, 7, 8, 9, 11, 12, 12, 13, 15, 17,
17; **2:**1, 2, 5, 6, 9, 12, 14, 15; **3:**2, 5, 5, 5, 8, 11, 13, 16; **4:**4, 5, 7, 10,
12, 15, 18, 19, 24, 25, 26, 29, 30, 31, 33, 34, 35, 35; **5:**11, 12; **6:**9,
10, 12, 12, 12, 13, 15, 15, 20, 21, 22; **7:**3, 5, 9, 15, 16, 16, 18, 31, 38;
8:8, 9, 12, 14, 15, 16, 18, 20, 21, 22, 23, 24, 26, 28, 28, 30, 30, 30;
9:1, 9, 10, 13, 14, 17, 20, 20, 24, 24; **10:**19; **11:**27, 29, 32, 35, 37, 38,
42; **12:**3; **13:**2, 5, 5, 6, 18, 22, 24, 27, 28, 29, 33, 34, 38, 41, 42, 51,
55; **14:**9, 10, 14, 14, 14, 17, 17, 17, 20, 23, 25, 25, 25, 28, 28, 28, 37,
39, 39; **15:**4, 4, 8, 9, 14, 20, 22, 24, 26, 27, 29; **16:**4, 4, 13, 13, 14,
15, 18, 21, 21, 24, 25, 29, 30, 32; **17:**6; **19:**5, 6, 6, 7, 8, 27, 31; **21:**10,
20; **22:**20, 22, 25, 27, 28, 29, 30; **23:**3, 5, 7, 8, 8, 11, 11, 14, 24, 24,
25, 27, 27, 30, 32, 34, 35, 36, 36, 37, 39, 40; **24:**4, 6, 8, 14; **25:**1, 5,
9, 11, 15, 23, 27, 36, 37, 46, 50, 53; **26:**46; **27:**23, 33, 34; **Nu 1:**18;
2:3, 9, 10, 16, 18, 24, 25, 31; **3:**1, 8, 38, 50; **4:**7, 8, 10, 12, 14; **5:**15,
23, 24, 26; **6:**7, 10, 18, 25; **7:**1, 9, 11, 12, 18, 24, 30, 36, 42, 48, 54,
60, 66, 72, 78, 89; **8:**10, 12, 17, 19, 22; **9:**3, 5, 10, 11, 13, 15, 21, 22,
22; **10:**5, 5, 6, 6, 12, 29, 34; **11:**9; **12:**3; **13:**23; **14:**5, 25; **15:**32; **16:**1,
17, 18, 22, 28, 45, 46, 46; **17:**2, 3, 5; **18:**17, 22; **19:**4, 12, 12, 13, 18,
18, 18, 19, 19, 19, 20; **20:**6, 16, 17, 19, 23, 26, 28, 28; **21:**1, 11, 11,
15, 18, 22; **22:**6, 13, 30, 31, 35, 36, 36; **23:**2, 4, 14, 14, 24, 30; **24:**18;
25:11, 18; **26:**3, 63; **27:**11, 18, 23; **28:**2, 9, 11, 14, 15, 16, 17, 18, 18,
24, 25, 25, 26, 26; **29:**1, 1, 2, 7, 12, 17, 20, 23, 26, 29, 32, 35, 35;
30:5, 7, 8, 12, 14; **31:**2, 12, 19, 24; **32:**19, 19, 22, 32; **33:**3, 6, 38, 39,
44, 48, 49, 50; **34:**3, 4, 8, 11, 15; **35:**1, 14, 14, 23, 30; **36:**9, 11, 13;
Dt 1:1, 1, 3, 7, 22, 28, 40, 41; **2:**27, 27, 32, 36; **3:**10, 16, 17, 21, 24,
25; **4:**5, 7, 9, 13, 15, 22, 32, 36, 39, 43; **5:**4, 5, 10, 14, 22, 33; **6:**7, 8,
9, 9; **7:**6, 7, 15; **8:**3; **9:**9, 10, 10, 11; **10:**1, 2, 2, 4, 4, 10; **11:**18, 19,
20, 20; **12:**2, 2, 16, 24, 27; **13:**17; **15:**23; **16:**6, 8, 8, 16; **17:**6, 9, 18,
18; **18:**19, 22; **19:**15, 17; **20:**19; **21:**22, 23, 23; **22:**4, 6, 8, 12; **23:**19;
24:15; **25:**5; **27:**3, 6, 7, 8, 12, 13, 18; **28:**49, 55, 57; **29:**20, 21, 27;
30:1, 3, 7, 14, 19; **31:**17, 18, 21, 29; **32:**2, 2, 2, 11, 13, 41, 43, 46, 50,
50; **33:**10, 16, 29; **34:**4, 8, 9; **Jos 1:**3, 4, 4, 8, 14, 15; **2:**1, 8, 16, 19,
21; **3:**16, 17, 17; **4:**5, 11, 19, 22; **5:**7, 10, 10, 12; **6:**4, 5, 14, 15, 16,
18, 26; **7:**6, 7, 10, 23, 25, 25; **8:**8, 11, 12, 19, 20, 29, 30, 31; **9:**5, 23;
10:12, 13, 24, 26, 32, 33; **11:**2, 3, 4, 13; **12:**2, 7; **13:**3, 4, 8, 9, 14, 16,
17, 19, 32; **14:**3, 9, 11; **15:**7, 7, 8, 9, 10, 10; **16:**3, 6; **17:**1, 2, 8, 13;
18:7, 8, 17; **19:**26, 34, 34; **20:**8; **21:**44; **22:**4, 19; **23:**15; **24:**5, 7, 8,
27; **Jdg 1:**8, 24; **2:**18; **3:**25, 26; **4:**15, 17, 23, 24; **5:**1, 6, 10, 10, 18,
21; **6:**5, 20, 26, 26, 28, 32, 37; **7:**6, 12, 17, 18; **9:**3, 5, 18, 25, 38, 45,
48, 49, 53, 53; **10:**4; **11:**16, 18, 34; **12:**14; **13:**19; **14:**15, 17; **15:**1, 7,
14, 15, 16; **16:**3, 13, 27, 29, 30; **18:**6, 7, 21, 26; **19:**5, 8, 9, 12, 14, 18,
27, 28; **20:**10, 30; **21:**4; **Ru 1:**8, 11, 14, 19; **2:**16; **3:**3, 15, 18; **4:**5,
10; **1Sa 1:**4, 21; **2:**15, 28, 32, 34; **3:**5, 6; **4:**6, 12, 17; **5:**5; **6:**8, 11, 15;
8:10; **9:**12, 12, 16, 19, 19, 26, 27; **10:**1, 2, 3, 5, 25; **11:**2; **12:**20;
13:15; **14:**1, 2, 5, 5, 10, 12, 12, 24, 24, 25, 43, 45, 47; **15:**12, 18;
16:13, 13; **17:**3, 35, 39; **18:**2, 9, 9, 25; **19:**23, 24; **20:**5, 21; **21:**2, 5, 5,
5, 13; **22:**6, 8, 18; **23:**15, 19, 26, 26; **24:**7; **25:**8, 13, 18, 19, 31, 31,
37; **26:**1, 20, 20, 25; **28:**20, 23; **29:**4, 11; **30:**14, 17, 20, 25; **31:**1, 2,
4, 5, 7, 8; **2Sa 1:**2, 2, 4, 6, 6, 6, 19; **2:**14, 21, 21; **3:**6, 21, 25, 29, 31;
4:7, 8, 11; **5:**23; **6:**3, 4; **7:**23; **8:**2, 10; **9:**11, 12; **10:**9; **11:**2, 8, 15, 21,
24; **12:**10, 16, 18, 20, 30; **13:**19, 25, 27, 29, 30, 31, 34; **14:**11, 14, 30,
31; **15:**17, 19, 20, 32, 36; **16:**2, 13, 13, 22; **17:**11, 12, 19, 21, 22;
18:9, 18; **19:**4, 9, 40; **20:**1, 13; **21:**6, 9, 10, 20, 20; **22:**4, 11, 11, 28;
24:5, 18, 22, 24; **1Ki 1:**2, 4, 17, 24, 30, 33, 35, 38, 39, 41, 44, 46, 48,
53; **2:**2, 4, 12, 17, 19, 19, 22, 24, 37, 37, 45; **3:**19; **4:**20; **5:**4, 5; **6:**6,
8, 10; **7:**2, 3, 4, 9, 19, 20, 21, 21, 22, 22, 25, 30, 31, 39, 39, 41, 42,
42, 49, 49, 51; **8:**27, 33, 36, 65; **9:**5, 25; **10:**2, 5, 9, 19, 19, 20; **11:**2,
7, 29, 37; **12:**4, 10, 11, 11, 14, 14, 28, 32, 33, 33; **13:**2, 2, 3, 24, 29;
14:9, 10, 12, 23; **16:**24; **17:**19, 20; **18:**10, 23, 23, 23, 24, 24, 25, 26,
26, 27, 33, 33, 39; **19:**4, 6, 11, 20; **20:**10, 20, 23, 29, 30, 31, 32;
22:10, 17, 19, 19, 19; **2Ki 1:**4, 6, 9, 16; **2:**2, 4, 6, 8, 16; **3:**7, 27; **4:**8,
10, 20, 24, 29, 31, 31, 32, 34, 34, 34, 34, 35, 38; **5:**11, 17, 18; **6:**10,
16, 16, 33; **7:**9; **8:**1; **9:**11, 13, 17, 26, 26, 27, 32, 33, 37; **10:**6; **11:**5,
5, 7, 12, 19; **12:**7, 7, 9, 11, 18, 20; **13:**16, 16, 25; **14:**9, 10, 13, 17, 20;
15:19; **16:**4, 5, 12, 13, 14, 17, 18; **17:**34; **18:**9, 21, 23, 26, 28; **19:**1,
26, 28, 33; **20:**9, 11; **21:**12; **22:**20; **23:**4, 12, 16, 20, 20; **25:**1, 5, 8,
17, 27; **1Ch 1:**48; **2:**7; **6:**32, 49; **9:**18, 24, 32, 33; **10:**1, 2, 4, 5, 8;
12:8, 14, 14, 15, 18, 40; **13:**7, 10; **14:**14; **15:**15, 28; **16:**11, 21, 39,
40; **17:**21; **18:**10; **19:**10; **20:**2, 6, 6; **21:**16, 23, 24, 26; **23:**29, 31;
24:2; **27:**1, 2, 4, 5, 7, 8, 9, 10, 11, 12, 13, 14, 15, 29; **28:**5, 15, 16;
29:11, 15, 21; **2Ch 1:**6; **2:**4; **3:**1, 1, 7, 14, 17, 17; **4:**4, 12, 13, 13;
5:11; **6:**13, 18, 24, 27; **7:**3, 6, 9; **8:**12, 13, 13; **9:**2, 4, 8, 18, 18, 19;
10:4, 10, 11, 11, 14, 14; **12:**7; **13:**4, 11, 17; **15:**5, 11, 15; **16:**8, 9, 14;
17:10; **18:**9, 16, 18, 18, 18; **20:**1, 20, 23, 24, 26, 30; **23:**4, 4, 6, 11,
20; **24:**6, 11, 27; **25:**12, 18, 19, 25, 28; **26:**6, 10, 10, 15, 16, 19; **27:**3;
28:4, 5, 15; **29:**6, 17, 21, 22, 22, 23, 24, 27; **30:**12, 15, 16; **32:**7, 12,
18, 23; **33:**15, 16; **34:**5, 28; **35:**1, 3, 11, 16, 20, 22; **36:**15, 17;
Ezr 2:68; **3:**2, 3, 10; **4:**5, 24; **5:**4, 16; **6:**3, 7, 15, 19; **7:**6, 9, 9, 9, 14,
17, 28; **8:**18, 31, 33; **10:**9, 14, 16; **Ne 2:**7, 8, 18; **3:**8, 9, 17, 25, 26;
4:4, 11, 15, 16, 17, 21, 22; **5:**4, 11, 14, 15, 16, 16; **6:**15; **7:**3, 3; **8:**2,
4, 5, 9, 13, 16, 18, 18; **9:**1, 1, 4, 11, 13, 29, 35, 38; **10:**31, 31, 33, 34;

11:21; 12:37, 37, 39, 39, 43, 44; 13:1, 15, 15, 15, 16, 19, 19, 21, 22, 25; Est 1:6, 8, 10, 11, 11; 2:17, 21, 22, 23; 3:6, 12, 13, 13, 14; 4:1; 5:1, 1, 10, 14, 14; 6:8, 9, 11, 11; 7:8, 9, 10; 8:1, 7, 9, 13, 13, 14, 14, 15; 9:1, 1, 5, 15, 17, 17, 18, 18, 21, 24, 25, 27; Job 1:4, 7, 19; 2:2, 13; 3:4; 6:2, 11, 22; 7:4, 8, 12, 15, 15, 16; 8:2, 9, 14, 14; 9:8, 11, 26; 11:3; 12:4, 14; 14:3; 15:5, 8, 10, 21, 32; 16:18, 19; 18:10; 19:10, 18, 21, 23, 28; 20:4, 19, 28; 22:14, 15, 28; 25:3; 26:7; 27:22; 28:4; 29:20; 31:2, 6, 25, 40; 32:1, 18; 33:15; 35:6, 14; 36:2, 17, 21; 37:6, 13; 38:26; 39:12, 14, 28, 28, 30; 40:10, 12; 41:8, 15, 20, 33; 42:8; Ps 2:6; 3:6, 8; 4:1, 6; 6:2; 7:7, 8, 16, 16; 9:13; 10:5, 7, 9; 11:4, 6; 14:2; 15:1, 5; 17:5; 18:T, 3, 10, 10; 20:3; 21:3, 4; 22:8, 16; 24:2, 2; 25:16; 26:2; 27:5; 30:5, 10; 31:9, 11, 16; 32:4; 33:2, 2, 3, 14, 17, 18, 20; 35:1, 2, 17; 36:10; 37:32; 38:17; 39:4; 40:2, 8, 12; 41:4, 10; 44:3, 6; 45:3, 7, 7; 47:8; 48:1, 9, 11; 50:10; 51:1, 18, 19; 53:2; 55:3, 16; 56:T, 1, 1, 6, 9, 9; 57:1; 58:9, 11; 59:4, 10, 12; 60:3; 62:9; 63:6; 65:5, 5; 66:4, 6, 11; 68:14, 34; 69:2, 4, 13, 24; 71:13, 14, 22; 72:16; 73:11, 18, 24, 25; 74:2, 7; 75:6; 77:9; 78:7, 12, 17, 32, 43, 49; 79:6, 6, 12; 80:13, 18; 82:1, 2; 84:5, 9; 85:1; 86:3, 4, 16; 87:1; 88:7, 13; 89:4, 14, 17, 27, 36, 46; 90:13; 91:12, 15; 92:T; 93:4; 94:8, 20; 97:11, 11; 99:1, 6; 101:6; 102:7, 13; 103:15; 104:5, 13, 21, 27; 105:4, 14, 16, 31; 107:24, 40; 109:6, 28; 113:5; 116:4, 9, 17; 118:27; 119:8, 15, 19, 23, 27, 44, 48, 52, 55, 78, 95, 101, 117, 135, 143; 123:2, 3; 124:1, 2; 129:6; 130:5, 5; 132:11; 133:3; 135:6, 14; 136:6; 137:2, 7; 139:5; 140:7, 10, 11; 143:10; 145:5, 6, 9, 18, 18, 21; 149:5, 7, 7; Pr 1:10, 14, 22; 2:2, 20; 3:5, 7, 21, 23, 33, 33; 4:6, 9, 25; 6:11, 28; 7:3, 19; 8:2, 27; 9:14; 10:8, 16, 17, 26; 11:4, 7, 29, 31; 15:3, 14, 21; 16:12, 22, 26; 17:10, 24; 18:20; 19:12, 27; 20:3; 21:12; 22:3, 16, 18; 23:9, 19, 21; 24:6, 25, 34; 25:3, 19, 22; 26:2, 13, 14, 27; 27:12, 15; 30:19, 24, 29; 31:3, 3, 27; Ecc 4:11; 5:2, 5, 14, 15, 20; 7:3, 15, 15, 17, 21; 8:9, 16; 9:6; 10:13; 12:12; SS 1:6, 12, 16; 2:8, 14, 17; 3:8, 11; 4:16; 5:7; 6:11; 8:5, 6, 14; Isa 1:15, 24, 31; 2:2; 3:9, 11, 16, 26; 5:1, 6, 8, 29; 6:1; 7:17, 22; 8:1; 9:1, 2, 6, 17, 21, 21; 10:20, 22; 11:2, 14; 13:2, 4, 8, 18; 14:1, 13, 17, 22, 25; 16:12; 17:6, 6, 8, 11, 13; 18:3, 4, 4; 19:1, 3, 14; 20:5, 6; 21:1, 5, 6, 7, 8, 9; 22:13; 23:4, 8; 24:13, 13, 18, 21, 23; 25:10; 26:3, 19; 27:10, 13; 28:16, 20, 27, 27, 28; 29:10, 15; 30:6, 17, 28, 30; 31:4, 4; 32:14; 33:16, 23; 34:10; 35:8; 36:6, 8, 11, 13; 37:1, 27, 29, 34; 38:8, 8; 40:15, 20, 24, 31, 31; 41:3, 18, 19, 25, 25, 27; 42:15, 20, 25, 25; 44:3, 4, 5, 20; 45:12, 23; 46:1, 7; 48:1, 1, 2, 15; 49:8, 9, 13, 16, 22; 50:9, 10; 51:5, 6, 23; 52:1, 7; 53:3, 6; 54:8, 9, 10, 11, 15; 55:2, 6, 7, 10; 56:11, 12, 12; 57:7, 10, 17, 19; 58:2, 3, 4, 13; 59:4, 13, 17, 17, 18, 21, 21; 60:6, 10, 18; 62:6; 63:15; 64:5, 7; 65:3, 7, 7, 25; 66:3, 14, 17, 20, 20; Jer 1:14, 16; 2:8, 9, 17, 20, 27, 28, 32, 37; 3:5, 6, 21, 23, 24; 4:8, 13, 21; 5:6, 13; 6:11, 11, 11; 7:11, 20, 24, 28, 29; 8:2, 2; 9:17; 10:25, 25; 11:19; 12:2, 5, 6, 9, 15; 13:13, 13, 16, 27; 14:2, 6, 16, 17; 15:6, 11, 17; 16:4; 17:1, 1, 2, 6, 8, 18, 21, 21, 22, 24, 24, 25, 25, 27, 27; 18:15, 17, 18; 19:3, 13; 20:3, 10; 21:2, 13; 22:2, 4, 4, 7, 18, 24, 30; 23:2, 5, 19, 26; 24:9; 25:3, 7, 30, 33; 26:3, 6, 15, 15, 15, 18, 19; 27:2, 13; 28:4, 14; 29:16, 25; 30:18, 23; 31:5, 12, 20, 33, 33, 40; 32:29, 33; 33:17, 20, 21, 22, 26; 36:6, 6, 6, 9, 9, 18, 28, 30, 31, 31, 32; 37:12; 38:11; 39:2, 5; 40:2; 42:14, 15, 17, 18, 18, 22; 43:10; 44:5, 6, 12; 46:2, 3, 4, 10, 20; 47:7; 48:8, 21, 21, 22, 23, 24, 37, 38, 40, 45; 49:3, 8, 11, 19; 50:19, 44; 51:3, 33, 60, 61; 52:4, 8, 12, 22, 23, 23, 31; La 1:4, 12; 2:4, 10, 10, 20; 3:16, 53, 55; 4:20; Eze 1:1, 10, 10, 11, 15; 2:2; 3:14, 17, 19, 24; 4:1, 4, 4, 4, 6, 9; 6:12, 13; 7:11; 8:1, 9; 9:1, 4, 10; 12:3, 3, 3, 7, 7, 19; 13:5, 18, 18; 16:5, 14, 14, 25, 31; 17:22; 18:11, 15; 19:9; 20:1, 8, 13, 15, 21, 28, 40, 47; 21:7, 19, 19, 29, 31, 31; 22:6, 22, 31, 31; 23:6, 12, 14, 24, 27, 30, 35, 37, 39, 40, 41, 41, 42, 42; 24:1, 2, 3, 5, 7, 8, 10, 11, 14, 25, 26; 25:4, 11; 26:1, 16; 27:10, 11, 11, 27, 27, 29, 30, 35; 28:2, 8, 13, 18; 29:1, 4, 5, 7, 7, 17; 30:8, 9, 15, 20; 31:1, 12, 13; 32:1, 4, 4, 4, 10, 17; 33:21, 30, 32; 34:12, 13, 14; 36:5, 11, 12, 18, 25; 37:6, 10, 16, 16; 38:8, 9, 19; 39:4, 6, 6, 6, 13, 20, 21, 22, 23, 25, 29; 40:1, 2, 7, 10, 20, 20, 21, 23, 23, 31, 34, 37, 38, 39, 40, 42, 43, 49; 41:2, 3, 6, 6, 8, 12, 19, 19, 25, 26; 42:10, 10, 11, 12, 14, 20; 43:17, 20, 22, 24, 27, 27, 27; 44:17, 19, 24; 45:7, 18, 19, 19, 20, 21, 22, 23; 46:1, 3, 10, 12; 47:1, 7, 12, 15, 16, 16, 17, 20; 48:1, 1, 16, 20, 30, 32, 34; Da 1:12; 2:21, 28, 35; 3:1, 8, 27; 4:29, 35; 5:5, 15, 27; 6:23, 24, 27; 7:4, 5, 6, 9, 20; 8:13, 25; 9:17, 20, 27; 10:4; 11:16, 28, 34, 38; 12:5, 7; Hos 2:3, 10, 13, 21; 4:13; 5:8, 10; 6:3; 7:5, 14; 8:1, 14; 9:1, 3, 5, 5; 10:1, 7, 8, 11; 12:1, 6, 6; 13:2, 10; Joel 1:15; 2:1, 29, 30, 32, 32; 3:4, 12; Am 1:2, 2, 4, 7, 10, 12, 14; 2:2, 5, 15, 16; 3:2, 3, 9, 14; 4:2, 4, 7, 7; 5:2, 8, 15; 6:2, 4; 7:10, 12; 8:5, 11; 9:1, 6, 6, 13; Ob 8, 9, 15, 16, 16; Jnh 1:3, 6, 8; 2:8, 10; 3:4, 6, 9, 10; 4:8, 8; Mic 1:3; 3:5, 10, 11, 12; 4:1, 12; 5:7, 15; 7:2, 10, 19; Na 1:2, 14; 2:8; 3:8, 13; Hab 1:6, 8, 9, 9, 15; 2:2, 7, 15; 3:17; Zep 1:8, 10, 17, 18, 18; 2:3; 3:8, 9, 11, 16, 20; Hag 1:1, 11, 14, 15; 2:1, 10, 15, 18, 20, 23; Zec 1:7, 8; 2:11; 3:5, 5, 9, 10; 4:2, 3, 11; 5:9, 11; 6:7, 11; 7:1, 3; 8:10, 10, 13; 9:1, 4, 7, 9, 9, 17; 11:6; 12:3, 4, 6, 8, 10, 10, 10, 11; 13:1, 2, 6, 9; 14:2, 4, 4, 4, 6, 8, 9, 12, 13, 18, 20, 21; Mal 1:7; 2:6, 14, 16; 3:5, 15, 17; 4:1, 3, 4; Mt 3:16; 4:4, 6, 17; 5:14, 15, 39, 45, 45; 6:5, 7, 7, 10, 19; 7:7, 7, 7, 22, 24, 25, 26; 8:13, 28; 9:2, 6, 6, 27; 10:15, 30, 32, 33; 11:21, 22, 24; 12:1, 2, 5, 5, 10, 11, 12, 36, 41, 42; 13:2, 4, 5, 8, 19, 45; 14:8, 11, 14, 19, 19, 25, 28, 29; 15:22, 35; 16:19, 19, 21, 21; 17:6, 15, 24; 18:5, 18, 18, 19, 33, 33; 19:13, 15, 28; 20:7, 17, 19, 23, 30, 31; 21:1, 1, 5, 5, 7, 8, 8, 19, 38, 44; 22:20, 26, 40; 23:5, 5, 7, 8, 9, 18, 19, 20, 22, 27, 27; 24:2, 3, 20, 30; 25:14, 15, 34, 41; 26:12, 16, 17, 26, 36, 39, 39, 64; 27:19, 28, 29, 30, 30, 31, 32, 38, 48, 62; 28:1, 2, 11, 18; Mk 1:10, 14, 38, 43, 45; 2:3, 4, 10, 11, 24; 3:2, 4, 13; 4:4, 5, 8, 15, 21, 27, 28, 38; 5:11, 21, 23, 32; 6:5, 25, 28, 34, 39, 41, 47, 48, 49, 53, 55, 56; 7:9, 32; 8:6, 23, 23, 26; 9:1, 22, 33, 37; 10:16, 17, 32, 34, 40, 47, 48, 49; 11:1, 1, 7, 8, 13, 21; 12:16; 13:2, 3, 26, 34; 14:12, 16, 22, 35, 35, 62; 15:17, 19, 19, 20, 27, 36, 42; 16:1, 2, 3, 5, 9, 18; Lk 1:8, 50, 66; 2:14, 15; 3:3, 22; 4:11, 16, 29; 5:1, 1, 7, 10, 18, 19, 24, 24; 6:2, 6, 7, 9, 17, 29, 37, 44, 44, 48; 7:38, 38; 8:5, 5, 6, 8, 12, 23, 32, 40, 43; 9:14, 16, 48, 56; 10:1, 4, 12, 13, 14, 30, 32, 34, 38; 11:9, 9, 9, 29, 31, 32, 33, 36, 44, 53; 12:7, 8, 9, 37, 52, 58; 13:4, 6, 14, 14, 14, 15, 15, 16, 22, 32, 33; 14:3, 5, 12; 15:5, 13, 19, 22, 26, 30; 17:11, 13, 16, 31; 18:33, 38, 39; 19:8, 23, 28, 29, 35, 36, 43, 48; 20:18, 24, 34; 21:5, 6, 25, 27, 35, 37; 22:30; 23:11, 14, 30, 33, 33, 54; 24:1, 28, 30, 32, 33, 46; Jn 1:14; 3:12, 12, 14, 14, 19, 26; 4:4, 43, 51; 5:3, 9, 10, 31, 45; 6:10, 19, 22; 7:8, 21, 22, 23, 23, 30, 37, 49; 8:28, 28, 33, 42; 9:6, 14, 16; 11:2, 19, 24, 53; 12:12, 14, 15, 32, 49; 13:12; 14:7; 16:26, 33; 17:4, 8, 26; 18:22; 19:2, 2, 13, 13, 18, 27, 29, 37; 20:19, 22; 21:4, 6, 7; Ac 1:3, 15; 2:1, 3, 19, 21, 30, 33; 3:8, 25; 4:2, 12; 5:15, 34, 38; 6:6; 7:33, 38, 38; 8:19, 39; 9:3, 12, 17, 17, 27, 30; 11:15, 15, 25; 12:6, 7, 8, 8, 21, 21; 13:3, 3, 14; 14:13, 25; 15:4, 21, 22, 25, 28; 16:1, 3, 8, 13, 18, 31; 17:11, 14, 23; 18:6; 19:6, 6, 10, 12, 15, 16, 17, 21, 22; 20:7, 9, 9, 9, 13, 26; 21:3, 4, 8, 12, 21, 40; 22:6, 16, 19; 23:2, 6, 15, 30, 32; 24:12, 21; 25:6, 7, 20; 26:3, 6, 12, 13; 27:2, 4, 6, 10, 19, 26, 27, 44; 28:1, 1, 2, 3, 8, 9, 10, 11, 15, 23, 23; Ro 2:8, 9, 17; 3:27, 27; 4:13, 13, 15; 6:1, 15; 7:4; 8:13, 20; 9:27, 32; 10:8, 13, 14; 11:13, 32; 12:9; 13:6; 14:3, 10, 14; 15:12, 24, 28; 1Co 1:8, 18; 2:2, 2; 3:10, 10, 12; 4:3, 7, 8, 9; 5:1, 6, 6, 13; 6:3; 7:15, 17, 20, 35; 8:5, 8; 10:1; 11:2, 5, 7, 10, 23, 23; 13:1; 14:25; 15:1, 3, 3, 4, 10, 40; 16:2, 6, 7, 11, 13; 2Co 1:9, 9, 12, 12, 14, 16, 16, 16; 2:3, 13; 3:3, 3; 4:8; 5:2, 3, 12; 6:2, 12; 8:22; 10:7; 11:1, 9, 20, 26; 12:1; 13:2, 4; Gal 1:8, 11; 2:4; 3:1, 1, 8, 10, 13, 13, 20; 4:10; 5:2; 6:17, 17; Eph 1:6, 8, 9, 10; 2:20; 3:15; 4:30; 5:13; 6:11, 14, 15, 17, 18, 20; Php 1:6, 9; 2:3, 8, 10, 27, 27; 3:9, 9, 13, 15, 15, 19; 4:8, 12, 15; Col 1:20, 20, 22, 29; 2:15, 18, 20; 3:1, 2; 4:8, 16; 1Th 3:13; 4:12, 17; 5:6, 9, 17, 21; 2Th 1:8, 8, 10, 11; 2:10, 15; 1Ti 1:13, 16, 18; 3:16; 4:13, 14, 16, 16; 5:9, 11, 16; 2Ti 1:6, 13, 18; 2:2, 22; 3:13; 4:8; Tit 1:5, 10, 14; 2:5; 3:8; Phm 1:13; Heb 1:9, 9; 2:3; 4:4; 5:7, 13; 6:1, 2, 7, 11, 16, 18; 7:8, 11, 25, 27; 8:4, 5, 6, 9, 10, 10; 9:1, 2, 4, 4, 21, 21; 10:6, 8, 16, 16, 28, 29, 39; 11:12, 13, 21, 27, 27, 28, 29; 12:2, 2, 2, 12, 15, 27; 13:10; Jas 2:3, 21; 3:5, 6; 4:10; 5:3, 3, 5, 13; 1Pe 1:5, 7, 17; 2:24; 3:3; 4:19; 5:10; 2Pe 1:12, 13, 14, 18; 2:3, 10; 3:7, 10, 12; 1Jn 1:6; 3:6, 8, 9; 4:17; 5:6, 18; 3Jn 6; Jude 20; Rev 1:17; 2:17; 3:11, 12, 21, 21; 4:2, 3, 4, 4, 8, 9; 5:1, 1, 2, 3, 7, 10, 13, 13; 6:1, 2, 16, 16; 7:3, 10, 15; 8:3, 7, 9, 10; 9:3, 4, 7, 15, 17, 18; 10:2, 2, 5, 5, 8, 8; 11:16, 16, 18; 12:1, 3, 12, 18; 13:1, 1, 14, 16, 16; 14:1, 1, 4, 9, 13, 14, 14, 15, 15, 16, 19; 15:2; 16:1, 2, 3, 4, 6, 8, 10, 12, 14; 17:1, 1, 3, 5; 18:7, 10, 19, 20; 19:4, 11, 12, 12, 14, 16, 19, 20, 21; 20:4, 4, 9, 9, 11; 21:5, 12, 13, 14, 19; 22:2, 4, 5

OR (1707)

Ge 2:5; 3:3, 3; 13:10; 14:23; 17:27; 18:21; 19:12, 15, 17, 33, 35; 21:23; 24:21, 49, 49; 26:11; 27:18; 30:1, 32, 33, 33; 31:39, 50; 34:12; 41:44; 42:16, 20; 44:8, 19; Ex 1:8; 4:11, 11, 11; 5:3, 14; 9:19; 12:3, 4, 5, 9, 49; 13:7, 9, 16, 21, 22; 16:23, 24; 17:7; 18:22; 19:12, 13, 13, 22, 24; 20:4, 4, 5, 17, 17, 17, 23, 23, 25; 21:4, 10, 10, 15, 16, 17, 18, 20, 26, 27, 28, 31, 32, 33, 33; 22:1, 1, 4, 4, 5, 5, 6, 7, 8, 9, 10, 10, 10, 12, 14, 22, 28; 23:4, 7, 13, 24, 26; 28:43; 29:28, 34; 30:9, 9, 20, 33; 34:3, 10; 35:23, 23; 38:26; Lev 1:10, 14; 2:4, 11; 3:1, 6, 6, 17; 4:10; 5:2, 2, 3, 4, 4, 6, 7, 11, 11; 6:2, 2, 2, 2, 3, 3, 3, 4, 4, 4, 5, 6, 18, 27; 7:9, 10, 16, 21, 23, 23, 24, 26; 8:32; 10:6, 9; 11:4, 8, 9, 11, 23, 26, 29, 32, 35, 36, 40, 46; 12:6, 6, 7, 8; 13:2, 2, 2, 5, 19, 24, 28, 29, 29, 30, 38, 42, 47, 48, 48, 49, 49, 52, 52, 53, 55, 56, 59, 59, 59, 59; 14:22, 30, 37, 47, 56, 57, 57; 15:3, 10, 14, 17, 20, 23, 25, 26, 27, 29, 32, 33; 17:3, 3, 3, 8, 10, 10, 12, 13, 14, 14, 14, 15; 18:3, 9, 9, 9, 10, 17, 17; 19:4, 6, 13, 18, 26, 27, 28, 29, 35, 36; 20:6, 9, 17, 19, 25, 25, 27; 21:2, 2, 3, 5, 7, 10, 11, 14, 18, 18, 19, 19, 20, 20, 20, 20, 20, 20, 23; 22:4, 4, 5, 5, 8, 10, 13, 18, 19, 21, 21, 22, 22, 23, 23, 24, 25, 27, 27, 28; 23:14, 14; 24:16; 25:4, 5, 11, 14, 20, 36, 37, 40, 44, 49; 26:1, 1, 14, 44; 27:10, 20, 26, 28, 28, 30, 31, 33; Nu 1:3, 18, 20, 45; 3:15, 22, 28, 34, 38, 39, 40, 43; 4:15, 19, 20, 27; 5:2, 2, 6, 15, 18, 30; 6:2, 3, 3, 4, 4, 7, 10; 7:9; 9:10, 10, 21, 22, 23; 11:8, 19, 19, 19, 19, 23; 13:18, 18, 19, 19, 20; 14:2, 29; 15:3, 3, 3, 8, 8, 11, 30; 16:14; 18:3, 15, 17, 20, 27, 30; 19:16, 16, 16, 18, 18, 18, 18; 20:5, 18; 21:22, 22; 26:2, 62; 29:39, 39; 30:2, 3, 4, 5, 6, 7, 8, 9, 10, 11, 12, 13, 13, 15; 31:19, 20, 22; 32:11; 35:17, 20, 21, 22, 23; Dt 2:6, 9, 19; 3:24; 4:2, 16, 17, 18, 23, 31, 31; 5:8, 8, 9, 21, 21, 21, 21; 7:7, 14, 25, 25; 8:2, 4; 9:23, 28; 10:9; 11:2; 12:15, 21, 22, 32; 13:1, 1, 2, 5, 6, 7, 8, 8; 14:1, 7, 8, 21, 26; 15:2, 7, 12, 21, 21, 22, 22; 16:2, 19; 17:1, 1, 2, 3, 3, 5, 6, 8, 8, 8, 12; 18:10, 10, 10, 10, 11, 11, 11, 11, 16, 20, 21; 19:15; 20:3; 21:3, 14, 18; 22:1, 2, 3, 4, 6, 6, 9; 23:1, 3, 3, 6, 7, 14, 17, 18, 19; 24:3, 5, 6, 7, 14; 26:13; 27:15, 16, 22; 28:39, 51, 56; 29:6, 6, 18; 30:11; 31:8; 32:36; 33:20; Jos 1:5, 9; 5:13; 6:1, 18, 19, 24; 7:3; 8:1, 17, 22; 10:14, 25; 22:19, 23, 23, 28, 29, 29; 23:7; 24:12, 15; Jdg 2:10, 22, 23; 5:8, 30; 7:3; 8:26; 9:2; 11:15, 27; 13:4, 4, 7, 7, 14, 14, 14; 14:3, 6, 15, 16; 18:5; 19:13; 20:28; Ru 1:5; 3:10; 1Sa 2:13, 16; 3:14; 4:20; 5:11; 12:3, 4, 19, 21; 13:20, 21, 21, 22; 14:6, 9, 41; 15:6, 9, 22; 16:7; 17:34, 39; 20:8, 10, 12, 27; 21:3, 8; 22:2, 2; 24:14; 25:21; 26:10, 10, 12; 28:6, 6, 15; 30:12, 15, 19, 19, 19; 2Sa 1:20, 20, 21, 21; 3:29, 29, 29, 29; 14:2; 15:14, 21; 17:9; 19:24, 42; 21:6; 24:13; 1Ki 1:10, 10, 10; 2:42; 3:11, 11, 12; 4:23; 6:7; 8:23, 37, 37, 37, 37, 37, 38, 46; 9:6; 10:12; 13:8, 9, 16, 17, 22; 14:10; 15:17; 17:1; 18:27, 27, 27; 19:18; 20:18, 39; 21:2, 6, 7, 21; 22:6, 15; 2Ki 2:16, 21; 3:9; 4:13, 40; 5:17; 9:32; 12:4, 13, 13; 13:19, 23; 17:35, 35, 35; 18:5; 20:9, 13; 23:10, 18; 25:15; 1Ch 11:4; 12:2; 21:12; 22:13; 23:3, 24, 27; 24:31; 25:8, 8; 26:13; 28:20, 20; 2Ch 1:11, 11, 12; 5:11; 6:28, 28, 28, 28, 28, 29, 36; 7:13, 13; 15:13, 13; 16:1; 18:5, 14; 19:7, 10, 10; 20:9, 17; 21:12; 25:8; 31:16, 17; 32:7, 15; 35:21; Ezr 2:59; 3:8; 6:12; 7:20, 24, 26; 10:6, 13; Ne 2:16, 16, 20; 7:61; 8:16; 9:5, 20, 31, 34; 10:31, 31, 35; 13:1, 20, 24; Est 2:13; 3:2, 5; 4:16, 16; 5:9; 6:3; 8:11, 11; Job 6:27; 9:14, 22, 32; 11:10; 13:9, 22; 14:21; 20:17; 24:7; 27:14; 28:15, 16; 31:5, 7, 7, 9, 13, 16, 24, 26, 29, 30, 39, 39; 32:12, 21; 33:19; 34:32; 36:18; 37:8, 13; 38:31, 32, 40; 39:15, 19; 40:24; 41:1, 2, 3, 5, 7; Ps 1:1, 1; 2:12; 5:8; 6:1; 7:3, 4; 13:3; 15:3, 3; 16:4, 10; 19:3; 25:2; 26:4; 28:5; 32:9; 35:14; 36:3; 37:7, 33; 38:16; 40:4, 6, 6; 44:20; 48:7; 50:8, 22; 51:16; 62:3, 10; 69:15, 15, 31; 73:5; 75:5, 6, 6; 78:22; 83:9; 90:2, 5; 105:37; 109:18, 18; 115:5, 6, 7, 7, 7; 131:1; 135:16, 17; 139:2; 140:10, 10; 143:7; Pr 2:4; 3:25; 4:5, 12, 14; 5:20; 6:1, 7, 35; 7:22; 8:8; 10:26; 17:26; 18:5, 21; 19:10, 26; 20:20; 21:30; 22:1, 16, 22, 25, 26; 25:3, 6, 10, 16, 17, 18, 19, 20, 26; 26:1, 2, 4, 5, 6, 10, 21; 27:10, 16; 28:15; 30:6, 14, 32; Ecc 2:19, 25; 3:14; 4:8; 5:12, 14; 6:5; 7:12, 16; 8:4; 9:1, 2, 2, 2, 2, 10, 10, 10, 12; 11:3; 12:14; SS 2:9, 17; 6:11; 8:6, 14; Isa 1:6, 8, 11, 30; 3:7; 5:6, 9, 12, 27, 27; 8:4, 20; 10:4, 14, 26; 11:3, 9; 13:10, 10, 17; 14:21; 17:6, 6, 8, 8, 13; 18:4; 19:9, 15, 15; 23:4; 24:13; 25:5; 27:9, 11; 28:22; 29:22; 30:14; 38:11, 14; 39:2; 40:12, 13, 14, 20, 21, 26, 28, 28; 41:22, 23, 23; 42:2, 3; 43:24; 47:7, 8; 49:18; 50:5; 51:7, 18; 53:2; 55:1; 57:1, 11, 12; 58:13; 59:8; 60:19; 61:10; 62:4; 64:7; 65:5, 16, 25; 66:3, 3, 8, 19; Jer 1:17, 18, 18; 2:6, 22; 3:16; 4:4; 5:12; 7:16, 26, 32; 8:2; 9:22, 23, 23; 10:14, 21; 11:14; 13:14, 14; 14:13, 14, 14, 15; 15:12; 16:2, 4, 6, 6, 7; 17:1, 8, 11, 23, 24; 18:7, 9; 19:4, 6; 20:4, 9; 21:7, 8, 9, 12; 22:10; 23:4, 32, 33, 33, 34, 35, 37; 25:4, 33; 30:13; 31:40; 32:23, 33; 33:26, 26; 34:19, 19; 35:7, 7, 8, 9, 9, 9, 14, 15, 17; 36:23, 24; 37:18; 38:2, 16, 24; 42:6; 43:3; 44:5, 7, 10, 26, 28; 46:18; 49:31; 50:20; 51:3, 17, 43; 52:19; La 2:18, 22; 3:10, 33; 5:22; Eze 1:13, 24, 24; 2:5, 7; 3:9, 11; 4:14; 5:9; 7:2, 12; 9:10; 12:16; 13:19; 14:15, 17, 19; 16:5; 17:9; 18:6, 6, 10, 25; 20:8, 31; 21:21; 22:11, 24; 23:27; 24:17, 17, 22, 23; 32:13; 33:32; 34:4, 29; 36:14, 15; 39:10, 26; 43:7; 44:13, 17, 22, 22, 25, 31, 31; 45:13, 20; 46:12; 48:14, 14; Da 1:13; 2:10, 27; 3:7, 7, 12, 14, 18, 28, 29, 29; 4:35; 5:8, 17; 6:7, 12, 13; 8:4; 10:3; 11:33; Hos 1:6, 7; 2:3; 3:4, 4; 6:3; 7:10; 9:11, 11, 17; 11:3; 13:7; Joel 1:9, 13; 2:5; Am 5:5, 20; 8:6, 11; Jnh 3:7; Mic 2:2; 4:12; 5:7; 7:1, 5; Zep 1:6; 2:15; 3:2, 13; Hag 2:12, 12, 12; Zec 7:12; 8:10, 13; 9:7; 12:6; Mal 2:2, 6; 3:2, 3, 5, 14; Mt 4:24, 24, 24; 5:17, 36, 37; 6:20, 24, 26, 26, 28, 31, 31; 7:10, 16, 20; 8:9, 9; 9:5; 10:5, 10, 11, 14, 37, 37, 37; 11:3, 8; 12:19, 20, 25, 31, 32, 37; 13:21, 23; 15:4, 32; 16:12, 14; 17:15, 25; 18:8, 8, 16, 16, 17, 20; 19:29, 29, 29, 29, 29, 29; 21:25; 22:17; 23:17, 19; 24:20, 21, 23, 26, 36, 36; 25:13, 37, 38, 38, 39, 44, 44, 44, 44, 44; 26:5; 27:17; Mk 2:9; 3:4, 4; 4:17, 20, 21, 22; 6:11, 40; 7:10; 8:17; 9:22; 10:29, 29, 29, 29, 29, 29; 11:30; 12:5, 14, 15; 13:21, 32, 32, 35; 14:2; Lk 1:15; 2:24; 4:27; 5:23; 6:9, 9, 37, 38, 44; 7:8, 8, 19, 20, 25; 8:16, 17; 9:8, 13, 25; 10:4, 4; 11:12, 33; 12:22, 24, 24, 27, 38, 41, 52, 58; 13:15; 14:3, 5, 12, 31; 15:8; 16:13; 17:7, 21, 23, 23; 18:29, 29, 29, 29; 20:4, 22; 21:24, 29; 22:35; Jn 1:13, 25, 25; 3:8, 34; 4:11, 21, 27; 5:3, 14, 37, 41; 6:19; 7:17, 35, 48; 9:2, 3, 21; 10:20; 13:29; 14:11, 27; 16:3; 18:34; 19:10; Ac 2:3, 27; 4:7, 18, 34; 5:4; 8:7, 34; 13:27; 15:20, 29; 17:29, 29; 18:14; 19:12; 20:20, 33; 21:21; 23:8, 8, 9, 21, 29; 24:12; 25:6, 8, 8; 26:29, 31; 28:6, 17, 21; Ro 1:21, 23; 2:4, 15, 28; 3:9, 22, 30; 4:9, 10, 16; 6:3, 16; 8:35, 35, 35, 35, 35, 35, 39; 9:11, 12, 16; 12:13; 13:13, 13; 14:1, 4, 7, 17, 21, 21; 1Co 1:12, 12, 26, 26; 3:1, 7, 12, 13; 4:3, 5, 19, 21; 5:10, 10, 10, 11, 11, 11, 11, 11; 6:19; 7:11, 15, 15, 19, 30, 30, 34; 8:9; 9:6; 10:7, 25, 31, 31, 32, 32, 33; 11:4, 5, 6, 22, 27, 29; 12:10, 17; 13:1, 1, 4, 4, 5; 14:6, 6, 6, 7, 23, 24, 27, 29, 37; 15:11, 37, 39; 2Co 1:17; 3:1; 5:9, 10; 6:8, 8; 7:1, 3, 12; 9:7; 11:4, 4; 12:3; 13:1; Gal 1:1, 11; 2:2; 3:15, 28, 28, 28; 4:9, 10, 10, 10, 10, 14; 5:6, 26, 26; 6:15; Eph 1:21, 21, 21, 21, 21; 3:20; 4:14, 29; 5:3, 5, 27, 27; 6:8; Php 1:18, 20, 27; 3:9, 12; 4:11, 12, 12, 12; Col 2:16, 16, 16, 16; 3:11, 11, 11, 17; 1Th 2:3, 3, 6; 5:10; 2Th 2:2; 1Ti 1:9, 9; 2:9, 9, 9, 12; 3:3; 5:4, 19, 21; 2Ti 2:5; 4:2; Tit 1:6, 7, 7; 2:10, 15; 3:9, 12; Phm 1:18; Heb 2:1; 7:3, 3, 3; 10:6, 8, 8, 8, 28; 12:16; Jas 1:17; 2:3, 12, 15, 15, 16; 3:12; 4:11, 12, 13, 15; 5:9, 12, 12, 12; 1Pe 1:17, 18; 2:8; 3:3; 4:9, 15; 2Pe 1:9, 10, 21; 2:17; 1Jn 2:5; 3:6, 17; 4:6; 2Jn 10; Rev 2:4, 16; 3:15; 5:3, 3; 6:6; 7:3, 3, 16; 9:4, 4, 21, 21, 21; 12:9; 13:16, 17, 17; 14:2, 9, 9, 11; 18:4, 22; 19:6, 6; 20:4, 4; 21:4, 4, 4, 23; 22:5

OTHER (1038)

Ge 1:20, 30; 4:22; 5:4, 7, 10, 13, 16, 19, 22, 26, 30; 7:8; 8:5; 9:23; 11:7, 11, 13, 15, 17, 19, 21, 23, 25; 14:16; 17:23, 27; 18:22; 19:9, 12, 25; 20:17; 22:24; 25:22, 23, 26, 30; 28:17; 30:13; 31:50, 53; 32:8, 23; 37:3; 38:29; 39:22; 41:3, 19; 42:28; 45:23; 48:20; 49:16; Ex 2:17; 8:2; 9:14; 14:26; 18:11, 13; 20:3, 5; 21:1, 18, 29; 22:9, 10, 20; 23:13, 24; 24:2, 6, 14; 25:7, 20; 26:3, 5, 9, 28, 35; 29:17, 19, 39, 41; 32:27; 33:16; 34:14, 16, 16; 35:9, 27; 36:1, 10, 18, 33; 37:9; Lev 5:7, 12; 6:3; 7:10, 24; 10:9; 11:23; 12:8; 14:22, 31, 42; 15:15, 30; 19:19; 20:24, 26; 22:13; 23:40; 25:14, 17; 26:37; Nu 3:38; 4:27, 34; 5:19; 6:3, 3, 11; 8:12; 12:3; 13:31; 15:3; 16:2; 18:7, 11, 22; 23:9; 28:4; 32:2, 19; 35:3, 6; Dt 1:1; 3:25; 4:6, 32, 34, 35, 39; 5:7, 9, 14; 7:4, 7; 8:19, 20; 9:4; 10:9, 15; 11:16; 12:27; 13:6; 15:11; 17:3, 14; 18:1, 12; 19:5; 20:14; 21:15; 22:4, 9, 9, 22; 24:5; 25:1, 11; 26:19; 28:14, 64; 29:6, 18, 26; 30:17; 31:18, 20; 32:21, 39; 33:24; Jos 1:14; 2:1; 4:11; 6:23; 7:7, 9; 8:21, 33, 33; 10:3; 11:12; 12:5; 13:17; 19:12; 21:1, 5; 22:3, 4, 7; 23:7, 16; 24:2, 16, 18, 20; Jdg 2:12, 17, 19; 4:11; 6:27, 29; 7:5, 8, 18, 22; 9:44; 10:13, 18; 11:18; 13:4, 7, 10, 11, 14; 16:31; 20:3; Ru 1:4, 11; 2:8, 22; 3:14; 4:7, 8; 1Sa 2:20; 3:20; 8:5, 8; 13:2; 14:20; 17:3, 21; 19:20, 21; 20:23, 41, 42; 21:6; 22:1; 29:6; 30:31; 31:7; 2Sa 2:13, 15, 17, 26; 3:18; 7:14, 22, 23, 23; 8:11; 10:16; 11:9, 17; 13:29; 16:11; 17:4, 22; 18:20; 23:23, 24; 1Ki 1:9; 3:13, 22, 23, 26; 6:7; 7:4, 5, 51; 8:60; 9:6, 9; 10:13, 20, 20, 23; 11:10; 14:9; 16:21, 33; 18:23; 19:21; 20:12, 21, 29; 21:8, 11; 22:12; 2Ki 2:9; 3:17, 23; 5:17; 7:3, 9; 8:1; 9:5; 10:5, 15, 21; 11:7; 12:7, 12, 13; 13:18; 17:7, 24, 35, 37, 38; 18:33; 19:12; 20:13; 21:7, 16; 23:8, 9, 24; 25:14, 15, 19, 28; 1Ch 2:54; 3:6, 20; 4:34; 5:13; 6:48, 49; 8:30, 32; 9:12, 33, 36, 38; 11:25; 12:3; 13:5; 16:26, 38, 42; 17:20, 21, 21; 18:11; 19:9, 16; 23:10, 28, 29; 24:20; 26:11, 12, 20, 26, 28; 28:1, 1, 16; 29:2, 5, 21; 2Ch 1:12; 2:4, 5; 3:11, 12, 17; 5:13; 7:6, 19, 22; 8:6; 9:19, 19, 22, 28; 11:21, 23; 12:15; 18:11; 19:10; 20:23, 25; 21:2, 4; 24:14; 26:6, 17, 20; 27:7; 28:25; 29:27; 31:3; 32:13, 17, 27; 33:7; 34:12, 22; Ezr 1:10; 2:1, 70; 3:5, 12; 4:2, 3; 5:6; 6:6, 20; 7:24; 8:3, 4, 5, 6, 7, 8, 9, 10, 11, 12, 13, 14, 24, 25, 33; 9:1, 11; 10:25; Ne 1:2; 3:1, 12, 18, 32; 4:16, 19; 5:17; 7:6, 71; 10:31, 31, 33, 37; 11:1, 20; 12:24, 24, 38, 38; 13:24; Est 1:6; 2:8, 17; 3:8; 4:13, 14; 5:11; 9:16, 19, 22; Job 31:7, 10; 34:37; 35:8; 42:15; Ps 10:16; 12:2; 13:1; 16:4; 19:6; 31:11; 44:1, 24; 64:5; 73:5; 78:58; 86:8; 87:2; 96:5; 106:17; 111:6; 126:2; 135:5; 147:20; Pr 18:24; 30:15; 31:23; Ecc 4:10, 11; 7:17; 8:9; SS 1:1; 2:2, 3; 3:6; 4:14; Isa 1:11; 3:5; 8:8; 11:13; 15:8; 19:2; 32:12; 35:9; 36:18; 37:12; 39:2; 43:10, 11; 44:6, 8, 8; 45:5, 6, 6, 18, 21, 22; 53:3; 54:1, 3; 65:4, 5; 66:17; Jer 1:15, 16; 2:25; 3:6; 5:26; 7:9, 18; 9:5; 10:2, 2, 11; 12:12; 13:14; 16:11; 17:19, 27; 22:9; 23:30, 35; 24:2; 25:9, 18, 26, 33; 26:22; 27:19, 20; 28:4; 29:25; 32:29; 33:10; 35:15; 36:2; 39:13; 40:11, 12, 13; 41:8, 10; 43:2; 44:3; 46:12, 16, 25; 50:37; 51:46; 52:10, 18, 19, 25, 32; La 3:30; Eze 1:11; 2:10; 3:13; 6:6, 9; 9:5; 16:23, 34; 18:24; 19:6; 21:20; 23:5, 23, 30; 25:8; 29:12, 12; 30:5, 7; 31:5, 8, 9, 14, 16, 18; 32:18, 19, 30; 34:28; 36:13; 37:23; 38:21; 40:15, 28, 32, 35, 42, 44; 41:6, 11, 19, 19; 42:3, 11, 14; 43:7; 44:7, 12, 19, 22; 45:17; 48:12; Da 1:3, 8, 10, 13; 2:18, 43; 3:5, 29; 6:3, 4, 7; 7:7, 12, 20, 24; 8:3, 13, 14; 11:27, 27, 37; Hos 1:2, 2; 2:5; 3:1; 4:10, 12, 13; 6:10; 9:1; 13:1, 4; Joel 2:8; Am 9:7, 9; Mic 5:8; Zep 3:13; Hag 1:11; 2:12, 22; Zec 1:11, 15; 2:4; 3:8; 5:3; 7:10; 8:10, 16, 17; 9:7; 11:7, 9, 14; 14:13, 15, 18, 19; Mal 1:11; 2:10, 14; 3:16; Mt 4:21; 5:39; 6:7, 24, 24; 8:18, 28; 9:10; 12:13, 45; 13:5, 7; 14:22; 15:19; 16:5, 14; 18:15, 17, 31; 20:21, 24; 21:23, 30; 22:1, 4, 40; 24:7, 10, 40, 41, 49; 25:4, 11; 26:3, 35, 47, 57, 65, 73; 27:1, 3, 12, 20, 41, 54, 61; 28:1; Mk 1:38; 2:15; 4:5, 7, 8, 27, 35, 36; 5:1, 21; 6:15, 53; 8:13, 28; 9:10, 14, 50; 10:28, 37, 41; 11:27; 12:31, 32, 38; 13:8; 14:43, 53, 56, 63, 70; 15:1, 41; Lk 1:2, 42; 2:15, 44; 3:19; 4:43; 5:7, 21, 29; 6:29, 39; 7:41; 8:6, 7, 8, 22, 37, 40; 9:8, 19; 10:1, 31, 32; 11:26; 12:1, 45, 52; 13:2; 14:10; 15:1; 16:12, 13, 13; 17:17, 34, 35; 18:10; 19:47; 20:1, 14, 31; 21:10, 29; 22:23, 49, 52, 71; 23:13, 40, 51; 24:20, 32, 33; Jn 3:26; 4:33; 5:44; 6:52; 7:35; 8:18; 9:8; 10:16; 11:33, 47, 56; 12:19; 13:22, 34, 34; 14:22; 15:12, 17; 16:17; 18:14, 15, 16; 20:2, 3, 4, 8, 30; 21:2, 25; Ac 1:14, 26; 2:4, 12,

14, 37, 42; 4:6, 12, 16, 23; 7:26; 9:25, 39; 10:23; 11:1; 12:17; 16:15, 25; 17:6, 9; 19:6, 39; 21:21; 23:14; 24:9; 25:2, 15; 26:16; 27:1; 28:4, 9; Ro 1:12, 13, 14, 26, 27, 27; 5:15, 19; 9:7; 10:19; 11:16; 12:5, 10, 10, 16; 13:9; 14:13, 18, 19; 15:5, 5, 7, 32; 16:14, 15, 16; 1Co 3:3, 11; 6:1, 18; 7:5; 8:4, 12; 9:5; 10:24, 29; 11:16, 33, 34; 12:24, 25; 14:17, 31, 33; 15:10, 22, 41; 16:11, 12, 15, 20, 20; 2Co 8:8, 14; 10:12, 12, 16; 11:8; 12:13, 14, 18; 13:11, 12; Gal 1:8, 8, 9, 19; 2:13; 4:27; 5:17, 21; Eph 2:16; 4:2, 16, 25, 32; 5:27; Php 1:9; 2:2, 9; 4:15, 22; Col 2:1; 3:9, 16; 1Th 3:12; 4:18; 5:11, 11, 13, 15, 26; 2Th 1:3, 4; 3:11; 1Ti 1:9; 3:10; 5:10, 13; Heb 3:13; 4:5; 5:1; 6:10; 7:20, 27; 10:6, 8, 25, 26; 12:15; 13:1, 24; Jas 3:2; 4:11, 11, 11; 5:9, 16, 16; 1Pe 1:22, 22; 3:8; 4:8, 15; 5:5, 14; 2Pe 1:7; 3:16; 1Jn 1:7; 2:10, 11; 3:10, 14, 18; 4:11, 12, 19; Rev 1:1; 2:4; 3:15; 11:10; 17:11; 19:10

OTHER'S (14)

Ge 31:49; Ex 18:7; 1Sa 20:42; 2Sa 2:16; Pr 7:18; 12:12; Da 11:27; Zec 11:6; Jn 13:14; Ro 1:24; 2Co 12:18; Gal 6:2; Eph 4:2; Col 3:13

OTHERS (372)

Ge 7:2; 12:2; 23:10, 10; 37:26; 42:5; 43:34; Ex 24:2; 35:23, 24, 34; Nu 14:24; Jos 6:17; 11:19; 24:11; Jdg 7:6, 7; 18:14; 1Sa 2:6; 8:12, 12; 9:24; 14:41; 17:26, 30; 22:2; 2Sa 15:12; 19:43; 1Ki 11:18; 19:18; 20:20; 2Ki 9:6; 13:7; 1Ch 9:5, 29; 12:16; 16:41; 28:21; 2Ch 32:22; 34:13; Ezr 3:12; 6:21; 10:3; Ne 2:12; 5:3, 4, 5; Est 2:6; Job 4:13; 5:5; 8:19; 24:24; 31:31; 32:4; 34:24; Ps 5:9; 7:15, 16; 9:15; 10:2; 15:3; 25:3; 28:4; 34:14; 37:8, 26; 49:11, 19; 52:4; 71:17; 73:8; 105:44; 106:3; 107:2; 109:16, 17, 17; Pr 10:17; 11:25; 12:15; 13:7; 17:5; 20:18; 21:10; 25:10, 18; 26:27, 27; 27:2; Ecc 2:7, 18; 6:2, 8; 7:21, 22; SS 5:10; Isa 5:8; 26:13; 32:8; 33:1; 43:4; 44:5; 56:8; Jer 1:10; 6:13, 28; 7:5; 8:10, 10; 9:12; 36:12; 39:3; 49:16; 50:15, 29; 51:49; La 1:21; Eze 7:27; 10:22; 13:18; 18:8; 19:11; 22:9; 23:48; 31:10, 16; 38:6; 40:24, 25, 25, 29, 29, 33, 36; 43:3; 48:14; Da 2:21, 42; 6:2; 7:3, 19, 20, 23; 11:2, 4; 12:5; Hos 9:1; Am 2:11; Mic 2:5; Zec 3:4, 7; Mt 5:19; 6:15; 7:1, 2, 2, 12; 13:11; 15:30; 16:14; 18:7, 12, 16; 19:12; 20:7, 28; 21:8, 41; 22:6; 23:13, 34; 25:8, 9; 26:50; 27:42; Mk 1:36; 4:10, 13, 14; 6:15, 15; 7:13; 8:28; 10:45; 11:8; 12:5, 9, 43; 14:31, 46, 60, 69; 15:7, 31; 16:13; Lk 2:13, 34; 3:20; 5:9; 6:31, 37, 37, 37; 8:3, 36; 9:8, 19, 32; 11:16, 49, 52; 15:4, 7; 16:9; 19:24; 20:16, 21; 23:32, 35; 24:10; Jn 4:38; 5:43; 7:12, 41, 41; 9:8, 9, 16; 10:8, 21; 12:17, 29; 13:28; 15:27; 18:8, 34; 19:18; 20:24; 21:8, 18; Ac 2:13; 4:35; 5:11, 36; 8:35; 9:36; 10:27; 11:18; 12:6; 15:35; 17:18, 32, 34; 18:8, 19, 25; 19:25; 20:24; 26:30; 27:44; 28:15; Ro 1:9, 32; 2:3, 21, 21; 3:9; 11:4; 12:5, 7, 8, 8, 9, 15; 13:8; 14:5; 15:2, 14; 1Co 1:12; 2:15; 3:10; 4:15; 7:7; 9:2, 12, 27; 10:13; 11:21, 21; 12:23, 28, 28; 13:1, 2, 3; 14:3, 19, 29; 15:8; 16:16, 19; 2Co 1:4, 4; 2:14; 5:11, 16, 19; 6:10; 9:8; 11:18; 13:2; Gal 2:14; 5:9; Eph 4:28; 5:2; Php 1:7, 14, 15, 17; 2:3, 3, 4, 21; 3:4; 4:3; Col 1:8, 10; 3:13; 1Th 4:12; 5:6; 1Ti 1:16; 2:2; 3:11, 13; 4:6; 5:20, 22, 24, 25; 6:18; 2Ti 1:1, 8; 2:2; 3:3, 13; 4:5; Tit 1:9; 2:3, 3; 3:3, 3, 14; Heb 5:12; 6:11; 10:33; 11:31, 35, 36, 37; Jas 2:1, 13, 18; 3:17; 4:2; 1Pe 2:9; 3:11; 4:11; 3Jn 10; Jude 16, 23, 23; Rev 18:6

OTHERS' (1)

Eze 1:23

OUR (1316)

Ge 1:26; 11:4; 13:8; 19:31, 32, 32, 34, 34; 23:6; 24:60; 26:20; 29:26; 31:1, 1, 14, 15, 16, 16, 37, 48, 52, 53; 33:14; 34:9, 9, 17, 21, 31; 37:8, 20, 22, 26, 27; 38:8, 23; 41:12; 42:9, 13, 13, 13, 13, 32; 43:7, 7, 8, 8, 18, 18, 20, 21, 21, 22; 44:8, 16, 16, 16, 24, 26, 26, 30, 31; 46:34, 34; 47:3, 4, 15, 18, 18, 18, 19, 19, 25; 50:5; Ex 1:10; 2:14, 19; 3:18; 5:3, 16; 8:10, 26, 27; 10:9, 9, 25, 25, 26, 26, 26; 12:27; 13:14; 14:12; 15:12; 16:23; 17:3, 3; 34:9, 9; Nu 10:29, 32; 11:6, 22; 14:3; 20:3, 4, 15, 19, 20; 27:3, 4, 4; 31:49, 50, 50; 32:4, 5, 16, 16, 17, 17, 18, 19, 26, 32; 36:2, 3, 4; Dt 1:6, 19, 20, 25, 28, 41; 2:8, 29, 33, 36, 37; 3:3; 4:7; 5:2, 3, 24, 25, 27; 6:4, 20, 22, 23, 24, 24, 25; 21:7; 26:3, 7, 7, 15; 29:18, 29, 29; 32:3, 27, 31, 31; Jos 2:11, 14, 14, 19; 6:17; 8:5; 9:11, 11, 11, 13, 13, 20, 24; 17:4; 18:6; 21:2; 22:17, 19, 19, 19, 22, 23, 25, 25, 27, 27, 28, 28, 29, 29, 34; 24:17, 17, 17, 17, 18, 24; Jdg 6:13; 8:22, 22; 9:8, 10, 12, 14; 10:10, 15; 11:2, 6, 10, 24; 12:2; 13:23; 14:3; 16:23, 23, 24, 24, 24; 18:5; 19:18, 19; 20:23, 28; 21:3, 5, 6, 7, 18; Ru 2:14, 20, 20; 4:3, 12; 1Sa 2:2; 4:3; 5:7; 6:9; 7:8; 8:20; 9:7; 11:3; 12:10, 19; 14:30; 17:9; 20:3, 23; 25:14, 17; 30:14; 2Sa 1:4; 2:14, 26; 5:2; 7:29; 10:12, 12; 11:24; 14:14; 19:9, 10, 42, 43; 22:32; 1Ki 1:11, 43; 8:21, 40, 53, 57, 57, 58, 59, 59, 61; 20:31; 22:3; 2Ki 2:16; 6:8, 16; 18:22; 19:19; 22:13; 1Ch 11:2; 12:17, 19; 13:2, 3; 15:13; 16:14, 35; 17:27; 19:13, 13; 28:8; 29:10, 13, 15, 15, 16, 17, 18; 2Ch 2:4, 5; 6:31; 13:10, 11, 12; 14:7, 7, 11, 11; 19:7; 20:6, 7, 10, 12; 23:3; 28:13, 13; 29:6, 6, 9, 9; 32:7, 8, 8, 11; 34:21; Ezr 5:12; 7:27; 8:18, 21, 21, 21, 22, 23, 23, 28, 30, 31, 33, 33; 9:6, 6, 6, 7, 7, 7, 8, 8, 8, 8, 9, 9, 9, 10, 12, 12, 12, 13, 13, 13, 15; 10:2, 3, 3, 3, 14, 14; Ne 2:17, 19; 4:4, 9, 11, 15, 15, 20, 23, 23; 5:3, 4, 4, 5, 5, 5, 5, 8, 9, 14; 6:1, 9, 16, 16; 8:10; 9:9, 12, 16, 22, 25, 32, 32, 34, 36, 37, 37, 38; 10:30, 30, 32, 33, 34, 35, 36, 36, 36, 37, 37, 37, 37, 37, 37, 38, 39; 13:2, 4, 18, 18; Est 7:6; Job 8:8, 9; 14:5; 15:10; 22:20; 31:2; 37:19; Ps 8:1, 9; 12:4, 4, 4; 18:31; 20:5, 7, 9, 9; 22:4, 30; 33:4, 21, 22; 35:21; 39:6; 40:3; 44:1, 1, 2, 2, 5, 5, 7, 9, 10, 10, 13, 15, 16, 16, 17, 18, 20, 20, 24; 46:1, 4, 7, 11; 47:3, 3, 4, 6; 48:1, 8, 14, 14; 50:3; 51:19; 59:11; 60:1, 2, 10, 11, 12; 62:8; 65:1, 2, 3, 5, 5; 66:5, 8, 9, 9, 11, 12; 67:6; 68:19, 20; 74:10; 76:5; 78:2, 3, 4, 5; 79:4, 8, 8, 9, 9, 12; 80:4, 6, 10, 10, 11, 11, 12, 12, 14, 16; 81:1; 83:12; 84:9, 11; 85:4, 9, 12; 89:17, 18, 18; 90:1, 8, 8, 9, 9, 12, 14, 15, 16, 17, 17, 17; 92:13; 94:23; 95:1, 6, 7; 98:3; 99:5, 8, 9, 9; 103:10, 12, 15; 105:7; 106:6, 7, 28, 47; 107:43; 108:11, 12, 13; 111:4; 113:5; 115:3; 119:138; 122:9; 123:2, 3, 4; 124:1, 2, 5, 8; 126:4; 130:3; 135:2, 5; 136:23, 24; 137:2, 3, 3; 140:11; 144:4, 12, 12, 13, 13, 14, 14; 147:1, 5, 7; Pr 1:13, 14; 7:18; 16:1, 9, 9; 20:24; Ecc 4:1, 3, 7; 6:1, 12, 12; 8:8, 8, 14, 17; 9:13; SS 7:13; Isa 1:10; 3:6; 4:1; 7:6; 9:10; 16:3, 4, 4; 25:9; 26:1, 8, 13, 15, 15, 18; 30:16; 33:2, 2, 21, 22, 22, 22; 35:2; 36:7; 37:20; 40:3, 8, 16; 45:15; 47:4; 52:10; 53:1, 3, 4, 4, 5, 6; 55:7; 59:12, 13, 13, 14; 61:6; 63:15, 16, 16, 16, 18; 64:3, 6, 6, 7, 8, 9, 11; Jer 3:22, 23, 23, 23, 24, 25, 25; 4:13, 13; 5:19, 24; 8:14, 14; 9:19, 19, 21, 21, 21; 11:8; 14:7, 8, 20, 20, 22; 16:10, 10, 19; 18:12, 18; 20:10; 21:13; 23:6, 36; 26:16; 28:6; 29:28; 31:6; 32:23; 33:16; 34:5, 18; 35:6, 8, 8, 8, 10; 37:3; 38:16; 42:6, 6, 20; 43:2; 44:17, 17, 19; 46:16; 50:28; 51:10, 34, 34, 34; La 3:39, 40, 41, 44, 46; 4:7, 17, 18, 18, 18, 19, 20, 20, 20; 5:2, 2, 3, 5, 7, 8, 9, 10, 11, 12, 15, 15, 16, 17, 17; Eze 4:14; 8:12; 11:3; 16:61; 33:10, 21; 40:1; Da 1:13; 6:5; 9:6, 7, 7, 8, 9, 10, 11, 12, 13, 13, 14, 15, 16, 16, 17, 18; Hos 2:23; 6:1; 8:2; 14:2, 3, 3; Joel 1:16, 16, 16; Am 5:18; 6:13; Ob 1; Jnh 1:6, 14; Mic 1:10; 2:4, 4, 6; 4:5; 5:5, 5, 5, 6; 6:7, 7; 7:17, 19, 20; Hab 1:12, 12; 3:2; Zec 9:7; 13:9; Mal 1:5; 2:10; 3:14; Mt 6:9, 11, 12; 8:17, 17; 15:2, 2; 25:8; 27:25; Mk 7:5; 9:38; 11:10; 12:29; 14:15; Lk 1:55, 71, 72, 73, 74; 9:49; 10:11; 11:3, 4; 12:13; 13:26; 17:10; 18:28; 19:33; 22:12; 23:2, 41; 24:20, 22, 24, 32; Jn 4:12, 20; 6:31, 34; 7:26; 8:39, 41, 53, 54; 9:20; 11:11, 48, 48; 12:38; 19:7; Ac 1:6; 2:11, 39; 3:12, 13; 4:8, 25; 5:30; 6:2, 4; 7:2, 2, 11, 17, 19, 39, 44; 10:14; 11:8; 13:17, 32, 32; 15:10, 25, 25, 26; 17:6; 19:25, 27, 37; 20:21; 21:3, 6, 10, 15, 21, 23, 28; 22:3, 5, 14; 24:4, 8, 14; 26:5, 6; 27:10; 28:12, 17, 17, 25; Ro 1:4, 7, 14; 3:5, 22, 24, 25, 27, 27, 27; 4:1, 24, 25; 5:1, 2, 4, 5, 11, 11, 15, 21; 6:6, 6, 23; 7:5, 25; 8:3, 3, 4, 16, 23, 26, 38, 38, 39; 9:10, 12; 10:16; 12:4; 13:11, 13; 14:7; 15:6, 30; 16:1, 9, 18, 20; 1Co 1:1, 2, 3, 7, 8, 9, 21, 30, 30; 2:7, 8; 4:5, 5, 10, 11, 12, 12; 5:7; 6:11, 13, 13, 14, 14; 9:1; 10:1; 12:6, 18; 15:3, 14, 30, 42, 43, 48, 53, 54, 57; 16:12, 22; 2Co 1:1, 2, 3, 4, 11, 12, 12, 14, 22; 2:15; 3:2, 2, 4, 5; 4:7, 7, 7, 10, 11, 14, 16, 16, 17; 5:2, 2, 4, 4, 9, 10, 13, 21; 6:3, 6, 6, 6, 6, 6, 7, 9, 10, 11, 12; 7:1, 3, 4, 10, 13; 8:5, 9, 17, 19, 24; 9:2; 10:11, 13, 13, 15; 11:31; 12:18; 13:7, 8, 13; Gal 1:3, 4, 4, 19; 2:4, 16; 3:13, 23, 24, 25; 4:26, 31; 5:6, 22, 25; 6:5, 10, 14, 18; Eph 1:2, 2, 3, 7, 7, 12, 14, 17; 2:3, 5, 16; 3:11, 12; 4:13, 14; 5:20; 6:24; Php 1:2; 3:17, 20; 4:20; Col 1:1, 2, 3, 7, 14, 14; 2:13, 19; 4:15; 1Th 1:3, 3, 5; 2:1, 2, 4, 4, 5, 8, 9, 10, 13, 17, 17, 19, 19, 20; 3:2, 2, 5, 6, 7, 11, 11, 12, 13, 13; 5:8, 8, 9, 23, 28; 2Th 1:1, 2, 8, 11, 12, 12; 2:1, 14, 16, 16; 3:6, 7, 18; 1Ti 1:1, 1, 2, 2, 11, 12; 2:3; 3:16; 4:10; 6:14, 17; 2Ti 1:2, 2, 8, 10; 3:16; Tit 1:3, 4, 5; 2:10, 13; 3:3, 4, 5, 6, 14; Phm 1:1, 1, 2, 3, 9; Heb 1:1; 2:17; 3:6, 6; 4:11, 12, 15, 16; 6:1, 1, 11, 19, 20; 7:14; 8:1, 3, 6; 9:12, 14, 14, 24, 28; 10:12, 22, 22, 25, 39; 12:1, 2, 2, 9, 9, 10, 25, 29; 13:14, 14, 15, 18, 20, 23; Jas 1:14, 27; 2:1, 8, 21; 3:9; 1Pe 1:3; 2:24; 3:18; 2Pe 1:1, 2, 8, 11, 16, 16; 2:20; 3:2, 15, 18; 1Jn 1:1, 1, 3, 4, 9, 10; 2:2, 2, 16, 19; 3:1, 5, 16, 16, 18, 19, 20, 20, 21; 4:10, 14, 16, 17, 21; 5:15; 2Jn 2, 3, 12; 3Jn 9, 15; Jude 4, 17, 21, 25, 25; Rev 1:5; 4:11; 6:10; 7:10, 12; 11:15; 12:10, 10, 10; 19:1, 5, 6

OURS (23)

Ge 31:16, 32; 34:23; Dt 21:20; Jos 22:24, 27; Ru 3:2; 1Sa 4:9; 17:47; 2Ch 14:7; Ps 116:5; Ecc 9:11; Eze 35:10; Ro 8:3, 3, 17, 37; 1Co 3:9; 15:50; 2Co 4:10; 11:12; Php 3:21; Heb 4:15

OURSELVES (42)

Ge 1:26; Nu 32:17; Dt 2:35; 3:7; Jos 22:23; Jdg 19:19; 21:8; 1Ki 20:31; Ezr 8:21; Ne 2:17; 4:9, 10; Job 34:4; Ps 2:3; 48:8; Da 3:16; Zec 8:21; Mt 21:38; Mk 12:7; Lk 20:14; 22:71; Jn 4:42; Ac 23:14; Ro 15:1; 1Co 9:6; 11:31; 15:30; 2Co 1:9; 3:5; 4:5, 5; 5:12; 6:6, 7; 7:1; 12:19; 13:7; 2Pe 1:18; 1Jn 1:3, 8; 3Jn 8, 12

OUT (1977)

Ge 2:6, 23; 3:14, 23; 4:7, 8, 10; 6:7, 14; 7:23; 8:8, 9, 19; 12:10, 20; 13:7; 14:1, 17; 15:7; 18:7, 19; 19:2, 5, 10, 12, 14, 14, 15, 27, 28; 21:14; 22:2, 3; 24:10, 11, 13, 30, 53, 63; 25:11; 26:8; 27:3, 9, 13, 34; 29:13; 30:16, 32, 35; 31:4, 18, 20, 23, 37, 49; 32:25; 34:5, 6; 35:5; 37:7, 28, 29; 38:14, 24, 25, 28, 28, 29; 39:10, 18; 40:13, 14; 41:2, 18, 20, 23, 30; 42:16, 16, 33, 35; 43:23, 31; 44:3, 4; 45:1, 1; 46:1; 47:15, 30; 48:14; 50:24; Ex 1:10; 2:10, 11, 13, 23; 3:8, 10, 11, 12, 20; 4:4, 6, 7, 9, 27; 5:1; 6:26; 7:4, 17, 23; 8:3, 25; 9:9, 10, 11, 21, 33; 10:4, 6, 11, 19, 28; 12:17, 33, 39, 42, 51; 13:3, 14, 16, 19; 14:6, 10, 11, 12, 15, 16, 25; 15:22, 25; 16:4, 6, 10, 17, 27, 32; 17:3, 6, 6, 10, 14; 18:1, 7, 9, 12, 18; 19:3, 17; 21:24, 24, 27; 22:6, 23, 27, 31; 23:28, 30, 31; 25:17, 20, 29, 32; 28:33, 35, 39; 29:12, 46; 30:1, 34; 32:4, 8, 23, 24, 25, 32, 33; 33:1, 2, 8, 19; 34:5, 11, 24, 34; 37:1, 2, 7, 9, 10, 16, 18; 40:36; Lev 1:15; 4:7, 18, 25, 30, 34; 5:9, 12; 6:10, 12, 13; 8:15; 9:9, 23; 10:5; 13:12, 20, 25, 45; 14:45; 16:17, 18, 21, 24, 26; 17:7, 13; 18:25, 28, 28; 19:36; 20:14, 22; 24:8; 25:38, 42, 55; 26:25, 44, 45; Nu 2:17; 3:10; 5:15; 8:15, 22; 10:12, 18, 22, 25, 35; 11:24, 26, 32, 32, 33; 12:4, 4, 11, 13; 13:3, 17, 18; 14:3, 25, 40; 15:22, 41; 16:13, 27, 39, 40, 47; 17:9; 20:8, 11, 16, 16, 18, 20, 20; 21:4, 5, 7, 9, 18, 30, 32; 22:7, 11, 36, 41; 23:22; 24:1, 7, 11; 26:2, 4; 27:12; 28:7; 31:6, 28, 49; 32:21, 23, 39; 33:1, 3, 52, 55; Dt 1:22, 44; 2:1, 12; 4:9, 37, 38; 5:15; 6:19, 21, 23; 7:19, 20, 22; 8:2, 4; 9:3, 5, 7, 12, 23; 10:6; 11:10, 23; 12:2, 16, 24, 27, 29; 13:5; 15:9, 23; 16:1; 18:5, 12; 20:1, 1, 3; 22:25, 27; 23:4; 24:11, 15; 25:4, 13; 26:7, 8; 29:5, 7, 21, 25; 32:41, 49; 33:6, 21, 22, 27; Jos 2:1, 1, 1, 2, 3, 19; 3:6, 10, 14; 4:5, 10, 16, 18; 6:1, 22, 23; 7:2, 7, 14, 14, 14, 16, 17, 17, 18; 8:3, 3, 5, 14, 16, 22, 25, 26; 9:13, 16, 17; 10:6, 7, 20, 23; 13:6, 12, 13; 14:12; 15:14, 63; 16:10; 17:12, 13, 15, 18; 18:4, 8; 23:5, 9, 13, 13, 15, 16; 24:5, 7, 12, 18; Jdg 1:19, 20, 21, 24, 27, 28, 29, 30, 31, 32, 33; 2:1, 3, 12, 15, 21, 23; 3:9, 15, 19, 21, 25; 4:3, 18, 22; 5:4, 9, 28; 6:6, 7, 8, 9, 13, 19, 22, 27, 30, 38; 7:4; 8:1, 24, 25; 9:15, 20, 20, 29, 32, 33, 35, 38, 41, 42, 43; 10:10, 12, 14; 11:13, 31, 34, 35, 35; 12:4; 14:14, 14; 15:4, 18, 19, 19; 16:3, 5, 9, 12, 14, 20, 21, 25; 18:1, 2, 11, 14, 18; 19:22, 24, 25; 20:21, 23, 24, 30, 31; 21:3, 6, 21, 21; Ru 1:7; 2:2, 3, 16, 17; 3:15, 15; 4:1; 1Sa 1:15, 16; 2:32, 32; 3:3, 4, 6, 12, 16; 4:1; 5:7, 10; 6:10, 20; 7:6; 9:11, 14; 10:23; 11:2, 7, 10; 12:6, 8, 19; 13:10, 14; 14:11, 15, 17, 20, 23, 24, 34, 38; 15:11, 13, 20; 16:11; 17:4, 20, 22, 23, 25, 41, 48, 49, 55, 56; 18:6, 17, 27; 19:2, 3, 3, 8, 10, 11, 12, 14, 16; 20:11, 11, 20, 35, 41; 22:10; 24:8; 25:33, 34; 26:4, 11, 17, 20; 28:13, 24, 25; 29:2; 30:9, 16; 31:8; 2Sa 1:7, 9; 2:20, 23, 24, 24; 5:6, 18, 19, 22; 6:6, 7, 8, 20; 7:2, 6, 8, 23; 8:3; 10:3, 5, 9; 11:2, 2, 3, 23; 13:9, 15, 17, 18; 14:4, 6, 14, 26; 15:2, 14, 16, 17, 23; 16:5, 7; 17:1, 9, 21; 18:2, 13, 28; 19:7, 8, 9, 11; 20:5, 7, 10, 13, 16, 22; 21:2, 17, 17; 22:7, 17; 23:16; 24:4; 1Ki 2:30; 3:26; 6:6; 7:26; 8:10, 16, 21, 25, 44, 51, 52, 53; 9:9; 11:32; 12:16, 28; 13:3, 5, 6, 21, 24, 28, 30; 14:6; 16:2; 17:20, 21, 21; 18:16, 28, 39, 43; 19:11, 13; 20:15, 17, 19, 26, 39; 21:10; 22:5, 22, 25, 32, 34; 2Ki 2:12, 14, 21, 24; 3:10, 24; 4:1, 18, 26, 35, 39, 40; 5:5, 10, 11; 6:7, 13, 15, 19, 32; 7:4, 5, 6, 8, 10, 12, 13, 16, 17; 9:8, 13, 17, 17, 18, 18, 19, 21, 26, 32, 33, 35; 10:9, 12, 15, 26; 11:1, 12, 15, 16; 12:14; 14:9, 27; 16:6; 17:7, 36; 18:31; 19:14, 31, 35; 20:5; 21:15; 23:16, 29; 25:7; 1Ch 5:20; 8:6, 13; 9:28; 10:8, 12; 11:18; 12:15, 17, 19; 13:9, 10, 11; 14:8, 10; 15:13; 16:35; 17:1, 5, 7, 21; 18:3; 19:3, 5, 10; 20:4; 21:16; 23:29, 32; 24:19; 27:24; 28:18; 2Ch 3:13; 4:5, 16; 5:8; 6:5, 12, 16, 34; 7:22; 8:16; 10:16; 12:7; 13:2, 14; 14:11; 15:2, 4, 14; 16:6, 14; 17:7, 8; 18:4, 21, 24, 31, 33; 19:2, 4; 20:7, 9, 11, 16, 17, 20, 25, 37; 21:15, 19; 22:5, 7, 7, 10; 23:11, 14, 15; 24:6; 25:18; 26:18, 19, 20, 20; 28:9, 11; 29:7, 16, 16; 32:1, 20; 33:12; 34:21, 25; 35:13, 20, 23, 24; Ezr 1:7; 4:22; 6:3; 10:13; Ne 2:12, 13, 16; 3:8; 4:2, 5, 19; 5:7, 13; 6:1; 8:1, 16; 9:4, 5, 18, 21; 13:21, 25, 30; Est 1:18; 2:11; 3:15; 4:1, 5, 6, 11; 5:2; 6:5, 8, 10; 7:7; 8:4, 5, 14; 9:28; Job 3:24; 4:2; 6:9; 9:8; 10:17, 18; 13:9, 17; 15:22; 16:18, 20; 18:4, 5; 19:7; 23:4; 24:11; 29:6; 31:12, 22, 35; 32:5, 19; 34:28; 35:9, 12, 15; 36:13, 18; 37:3; 38:25, 41; Ps 3:4; 6:6, 7; 9:5; 18:6, 16; 19:4; 22:14, 14; 25:4; 27:5, 12; 28:2, 4, 7; 30:2, 8; 31:3, 17, 22; 32:1; 34:6; 36:10; 40:2, 2, 9, 12; 41:8; 43:3; 44:2; 45:4, 7; 51:1; 57:2, 3; 58:2; 59:3, 13, 14; 60:6; 62:8; 66:17; 69:14, 24; 75:8; 77:1; 78:20, 55; 79:6; 81:7; 83:4; 85:1; 88:1, 13; 90:8; 94:18; 97:4; 98:4, 8; 101:8; 102:T, 10, 26; 103:20; 104:2, 3; 105:37, 39, 41, 43; 106:29; 107:2; 108:7; 109:13; 114:3, 5; 116:11; 119:115, 146, 147; 120:1; 136:11; 138:8; 139:16, 19, 24; 140:4, 5; 141:9, 9; 142:1, 2, 7; 143:6, 11; 147:7; Pr 1:20, 21, 23, 24; 2:3; 4:13, 26; 6:3, 19; 7:6, 15; 8:1; 9:3, 15; 13:9; 14:3; 17:14; 20:5, 20, 26; 21:23; 22:10; 23:30; 24:20; 25:17; 26:13, 20; 27:11; 28:7; 29:10; 30:1, 15, 17; 31:16; Ecc 4:10; 5:6; 7:13, 28; SS 1:6; 3:11; 5:2; 6:11; 7:11, 12; Isa 1:9, 18, 24, 31; 2:3; 3:8, 24; 5:30; 7:3; 8:19, 19, 22; 9:8; 10:30; 11:1, 8; 14:8, 10, 30, 31; 15:4; 16:8, 8, 10; 17:6; 19:17; 21:6, 8; 22:19, 25, 25; 23:11, 11; 24:10, 11; 26:7, 17, 21; 28:7, 13; 29:10; 30:5, 22, 28, 28; 32:4; 36:3, 16; 37:14, 32, 36; 40:4, 12, 22, 26, 29; 42:5, 13, 16, 25; 43:8, 17, 25; 44:3, 13, 24, 26; 45:8, 12; 46:6, 7; 47:11, 12; 48:9, 13, 21; 49:9; 50:3, 6, 11; 51:6, 17, 20; 54:2, 9; 55:11; 57:4; 58:10; 62:10, 10, 10; 63:2, 11, 11; 65:4, 6; 66:5, 24, 24; Jer 1:12, 14, 17; 2:6, 27, 27; 5:6, 18; 6:11, 25; 7:13, 20, 22, 25, 27; 8:2, 2; 9:5; 10:12, 25; 11:4, 7, 14; 12:14; 13:7, 25, 27; 14:16, 16, 18; 15:1; 16:13; 17:4, 19, 27; 18:4, 21, 23; 19:2, 13; 20:8, 13; 21:9; 22:7, 7, 19; 23:2, 19; 26:2, 3; 29:14; 30:23; 31:7, 32, 39, 40; 32:10, 21, 29; 36:30, 31; 38:10, 13, 22, 23, 27; 39:4, 7, 14; 40:12; 41:3, 12; 42:6, 18, 18; 44:19, 25, 28; 46:14; 48:4, 12, 21; 49:3, 28; 50:25, 29; 51:15, 26, 27, 34, 34, 48; 52:11; La 1:9; 2:4, 6, 11, 14, 19, 19; 3:2, 8, 18, 46, 54; 4:11; Eze 1:11, 22, 23; 2:9; 3:22, 25; 4:10, 11, 16, 16; 5:2, 4; 6:11; 7:8, 19; 8:3; 9:8, 8, 8; 10:7, 7; 11:9, 9, 13; 12:5, 7, 13; 13:12, 17; 14:19; 16:16, 50; 17:7, 9, 9; 19:8, 11; 20:6, 8, 10, 13, 14, 21, 22, 28, 34, 36, 38, 46, 48; 21:12, 19, 24, 31, 32; 22:22, 31; 24:6; 25:9, 13, 14, 15, 16; 27:28; 29:4, 7; 30:15, 15; 32:3, 7, 15; 35:15; 36:18, 26; 37:20; 38:4; 39:9, 29; 40:18; 42:1, 3, 15; 45:3, 9; 46:2; 47:2; Da 2:12; 3:4, 22, 26, 26; 4:30, 36; 6:2, 14, 19, 20; 7:3, 8; 8:4, 16; 9:11, 27; 11:3, 40, 44, 45; Hos 2:13, 14; 4:16; 7:7, 14; 9:1, 4, 13; 10:10, 11; 11:1; 12:13; 14:6; Joel 1:14, 20; 2:28, 28, 29; 3:4, 9, 11; Am 2:9; 7:12; 8:3, 5, 5; 9:3, 7, 7; Ob 5, 16; Jnh 1:14; 2:2, 6, 7; 3:10; 4:5; Mic 2:1, 13, 13; 3:8; 4:2; 5:7, 8, 9, 15; 6:4, 9, 10; 7:9, 17; Hab 1:12, 15; 2:11; 3:10, 13, 14; Zep 1:15, 17; 2:4; 3:3, 6, 8; Hag 2:5; Zec 1:10; 3:7; 4:7, 12; 5:3; 6:5, 12; 9:14; 11:12; 12:1, 10; 14:3, 8; Mal 2:14; 3:10; 4:2; Mt 2:15; 3:5, 16; 4:1, 10, 19; 5:13, 16, 29, 33, 38, 38; 6:23; 7:22; 8:31, 32, 34; 9:33, 34, 38; 10:1, 5, 8, 13, 16; 11:7, 8; 12:11, 13, 13, 23, 24, 26, 27, 28; 13:3, 7, 22, 28, 30, 40, 52; 14:31; 15:17, 33; 16:6; 17:4, 19; 18:9, 12, 15; 19:27; 20:1, 2, 7; 21:12, 23, 28, 33, 39; 22:7, 9, 13; 24:1, 6, 26; 25:6, 8; 26:28, 30, 47, 51, 71; 27:5, 18, 27, 33, 46, 50, 60; 28:1; Mk 1:5, 10, 13, 17, 25, 34, 35, 36, 45; 2:13; 3:5, 5, 7, 14, 15, 21, 22, 23, 31; 4:3, 7, 19, 21, 36; 5:2, 8, 13, 14, 30; 6:6, 7, 7, 12, 13, 24, 38, 45, 47, 54, 56; 7:19, 21; 8:1, 7, 23; 9:18, 25, 28, 29, 33, 38, 47, 48; 10:17, 47; 11:11, 15, 28; 12:1, 8, 40; 13:7, 9, 23; 14:24, 26, 43, 47, 68; 15:10, 16, 34, 46; 16:1, 9, 17, S; Lk 1:21, 22, 66, 80; 3:2, 5; 4:1, 35, 41, 42; 5:3, 4, 13; 6:10, 10, 18, 19; 7:12, 17, 21, 24; 8:2, 2, 5, 7, 8, 14, 22, 27, 27, 29, 29, 33, 46; 9:1, 2, 11, 33, 38, 40, 49, 51; 10:2, 3, 10; 11:1, 7, 14, 15, 18, 19, 20, 27, 34; 13:15, 28, 31, 32; 14:5, 16, 19, 23, 29, 30; 15:14, 28; 16:3; 17:13, 23; 18:4, 5; 19:15, 36, 45; 20:2, 9, 15, 47; 21:30, 34; 22:20, 35; 23:32, 37, 53; 24:13, 24, 40; Jn 1:15, 31; 2:3, 8, 10, 15, 15, 16; 4:40; 6:11, 17, 19, 20, 51; 7:1, 10, 28, 38; 8:41; 9:4, 34; 10:3, 37; 11:42, 43, 44; 12:18, 31, 35; 13:2, 30; 15:19; 17:15; 18:26, 29, 38; 19:4, 5, 13, 34; 20:2, 20; 21:3, 5, 6, 8, 18; Ac 1:18; 2:17, 18, 33; 3:11; 4:15; 5:6, 9, 10, 15, 19, 25; 7:7, 11, 31, 36, 40, 45, 57, 58; 8:3, 7, 39; 10:45; 12:4, 15, 16, 17; 13:4, 17, 44, 46, 50; 14:14, 19; 16:18, 30, 39; 17:5, 6; 18:9, 16; 19:12, 13, 13; 20:31; 21:30, 32, 34, 38; 22:24, 30; 23:28; 24:8, 21; 25:16; 27:4, 14, 19, 20, 29, 30, 43; 28:3; Ro 1:1; 2:8; 4:7; 9:21, 23, 27, 28, 29; 10:18; 12:6, 13; 13:11; 16:13, 17; 1Co 2:10; 4:19; 5:5; 8:8; 9:9; 10:13, 28; 13:6; 14:5; 15:10; 2Co 2:9; 6:17; 9:3, 11; 11:12; Gal 1:16; 2:17; 4:15; 5:15; Eph 1:6; 3:11; 5:10, 21; Php 1:7, 15, 19; 2:17, 23; 3:2; Col 1:6; 4:17; 1Th 1:8; 2:15; 3:5; 5:9; 2Th 2:7; 1Ti 5:18; 2Ti 1:1; 3:16; 4:6; Tit 3:6; Heb 1:9, 11; 2:8; 3:16; 5:7; 7:17; 8:9, 13; 9:5, 6; 11:22; 12:13, 15, 15, 24; 13:13, 23; Jas 1:18; 2:13; 3:9, 10, 11; 5:4; 1Pe 2:2, 9; 5:2, 8; 2Pe 2:7, 11; 3:17; 1Jn 4:2; 2Jn 7, 8; 3Jn 10; Jude 12; Rev 2:23; 3:16; 4:7, 8; 5:6; 6:1, 2; 7:2, 14; 8:4, 10; 9:2; 11:7; 12:2, 8, 16; 13:1, 11; 14:10, 15; 15:8; 16:1, 2, 2, 3, 4, 6, 8, 10, 12, 17; 17:1, 8, 17; 18:6, 10, 16; 19:4, 21; 20:7, 8; 21:2, 10

OVER (1008)

Ge 1:2, 26, 28, 31; 9:14, 23; 11:4, 8; 13:8, 9; 14:17; 19:4; 20:15; 21:12; 22:9; 24:17; 26:20, 21; 27:21, 22, 25, 27; 28:18; 29:3, 4, 10, 27; 31:5; 32:23; 35:5, 14, 20; 37:13; 38:12; 39:6, 22; 41:3, 34; 42:30; 43:19; 45:4, 8, 9, 15, 26; 47:26; 48:8, 9, 18; 49:22; 50:1, 4; Ex 1:11; 3:3, 16; 4:18; 5:6; 9:9, 17; 10:12, 14, 22; 12:13, 23, 27; 14:16, 21, 26, 26, 27; 16:18; 18:21, 25, 25; 22:28; 24:8; 25:22; 26:9, 12, 14; 28:29, 30; 29:2, 7; 32:26; 34:25, 31, 33; 39:9; 40:19, 35; Lev 7:16, 17; 8:32; 10:1; 11:46; 12:4; 13:12; 14:5, 7, 18, 29, 50; 16:2, 13, 19, 21; 25:43; 26:17, 18, 24, 28, 37; Nu 3:32; 4:7, 8, 11, 14; 8:21; 9:15, 17, 18, 19, 20; 10:10, 34; 11:32; 14:14; 16:25, 33; 19:17; 20:8; 21:3, 34; 22:11; 24:18, 20, 21; 27:9, 12; 32:27, 30; Dt 1:15, 36; 2:31, 33; 3:2, 3; 7:2, 16, 23; 9:3; 11:12; 15:6; 19:12; 20:13; 21:6, 10; 24:20; 25:9; 27:12; 31:3, 5; 32:10, 11, 13; 34:8; Jos 3:16; 4:11, 13, 23; 7:26; 8:29; 10:8, 12, 12, 12, 19; 11:8; 16:2, 3; 24:8, 11; Jdg 1:2, 4; 2:14, 18; 3:8, 10, 12, 20, 28; 4:2, 7, 9, 14; 6:1, 13, 20; 7:7, 9, 13, 14, 15; 8:3, 7, 23, 23; 9:9, 11, 13, 22, 45; 10:7, 18; 11:8, 9, 9, 21, 30, 36; 12:1, 3; 13:1; 14:4; 15:11, 12, 13; 16:23;

18:15; 20:28; Ru 2:5, 7, 8, 14, 18; 3:8, 9; 4:1; 1Sa 1:9; 2:13; 4:3, 14; 8:1; 10:1; 11:12; 12:12, 13; 13:13, 14; 14:1, 8, 14, 21, 33, 40, 40; 15:32; 17:4, 6, 30, 39, 44, 50, 51; 18:13; 23:7, 20; 26:5, 8, 22; 28:19; 2Sa 1:1, 9; 2:4, 9; 3:10, 12, 21; 5:5, 5, 12, 19; 7:26; 8:15; 10:11, 14; 11:2, 27; 16:9; 17:19; 18:17, 28, 33; 19:10; 20:12, 16, 21, 21; 21:6; 22:5, 44, 44; 24:13; 1Ki 1:34, 35; 2:11; 3:19; 4:1, 5, 7, 12, 19, 24; 5:3; 7:18; 8:7, 7, 16, 25, 29, 55, 60, 66; 9:3, 5; 10:16; 11:37, 42; 12:5, 17, 20; 13:29; 14:7, 14; 15:1, 9, 25, 33; 16:8, 15, 18, 23, 29; 17:21; 18:30, 33; 19:19; 20:13, 38; 22:36, 41, 51; 2Ki 3:1, 18; 4:7, 43, 44; 5:11; 6:11; 8:15, 16, 25; 9:3, 3, 6, 6, 12, 29; 10:36; 11:3, 14, 18; 12:1; 13:1, 10, 14, 17; 14:1, 23; 15:1, 8, 13, 17, 23, 27, 30, 32; 16:1, 13, 15; 17:1, 20, 24; 18:1, 30; 20:7; 21:14; 23:14, 17; 25:22, 28; 1Ch 4:22; 10:14; 12:18; 14:2, 8, 10; 17:14, 24; 18:14; 19:12; 21:3, 12, 16; 22:10, 12, 18; 23:1, 32; 28:4, 4, 18; 29:4, 9, 11, 12, 26; 2Ch 1:9, 13; 5:8, 8; 6:16, 20; 7:18; 9:15, 26, 30; 10:17; 11:16; 13:1, 16; 16:8; 17:5, 10; 20:27, 29, 31; 22:12; 23:5, 13, 17; 24:7; 28:14; 32:6; 34:4; 35:18; 36:17; Ezr 1:11; 4:20; 5:5; 7:18; 8:15; Ne 2:13; 3:27; 4:14; 6:7; 8:13; 9:22, 25, 27, 32, 37, 37; 11:9; 13:26; Est 1:1, 5; 5:11; Job 2:12; 13:19; 14:17; 16:11; 17:11; 21:5; 26:7; 29:9, 25; 33:18; 40:4; Ps 1:6; 3:5; 4:4; 8:6; 12:6; 18:4, 43, 43; 29:3, 10; 30:1; 31:8; 32:8; 33:18; 34:15; 35:19, 19, 26; 38:6, 16; 41:11; 42:7; 44:7; 45:16; 47:7; 49:14; 54:7; 57:5, 11; 60:8, 9; 61:7; 67:7; 69:7; 73:18; 78:50, 62; 80:14; 82:1; 83:18; 95:7; 97:9; 103:19; 105:21; 106:41, 41; 108:5, 9, 10; 110:2, 6; 118:18; 121:3, 4, 5, 8; 133:2; 135:7; 148:13; Pr 2:11; 4:19; 5:9; 8:10; 17:2; 19:10; 20:14, 26; 22:1; 24:12; 26:14; 28:13; Ecc 3:19; 6:6, 8; SS 2:8, 11; 7:9; 8:6; Isa 1:8; 2:2; 3:4, 12; 4:1; 5:30, 30; 6:6; 8:6; 10:26; 11:15; 14:2, 9; 19:4; 21:11; 23:3, 10, 11, 13; 24:1; 25:7; 27:3; 28:10, 10, 13, 13, 13; 29:8; 31:5, 5; 34:17; 36:15; 38:12, 13, 21; 41:2, 3, 7, 25; 54:3; 60:2; 62:5, 5, 8; 64:7; Jer 4:20; 6:11, 12, 17, 21; 10:4, 13; 11:7, 7; 13:21; 15:9, 13; 20:4; 21:7; 22:1, 25; 25:1, 12; 26:2, 10, 24; 27:7; 29:21; 31:10, 39; 32:3, 24, 28; 34:2, 21; 36:6, 9; 38:3, 16, 18, 19, 20; 40:7; 43:10; 44:6, 27, 30, 30; 46:16, 24, 26; 51:14, 16, 42; 52:32; La 2:1, 17; 3:20, 51; 5:2; Eze 1:26; 4:6, 12; 6:2; 7:12, 12; 10:1, 2, 4, 12; 11:1, 9; 16:27; 17:20; 18:28; 20:25; 21:27, 31; 22:13, 18; 23:9, 12, 24, 28, 46; 25:10, 10; 26:2; 30:12; 31:11; 34:23; 37:8; 38:2; 40:6; 41:25; Da 1:2, 11; 2:37, 38, 47, 48, 48; 4:17, 25, 32; 5:11, 21, 31; 6:1, 3, 17; 7:14, 22; 11:6, 21, 31, 32, 43; 12:1; Hos 7:12; 9:6, 8; 10:5; Joel 2:9, 20; Am 6:2, 12; 7:1; 8:5; Ob 12, 13, 14, 19, 21; Jnh 1:4; 4:6; Mic 4:1, 11; 5:5, 6; 7:8; Na 1:15; 3:3; Hab 2:15; 3:19; Zep 3:15, 17, 17; Zec 3:7; 5:3; 12:4; 14:9, 10; Mt 2:9; 3:5; 4:25; 5:25; 8:4, 9, 11; 9:31; 10:17; 11:27; 12:9; 14:29; 15:37, 39; 16:9, 10; 17:5, 7; 18:2, 13, 13; 20:19, 25; 21:2, 7, 12, 19, 25, 44; 24:9; 26:7, 48, 69, 73; 27:26; Mk 1:5, 29, 33, 44; 3:7, 23; 7:3; 8:8, 10, 25, 34; 9:7, 35; 10:30, 33, 35, 42; 11:2, 7, 13, 15, 31; 12:4, 41; 13:9, 27; 14:3, 44; 15:15; Lk 1:23, 33; 2:43; 3:1, 1, 1, 1; 4:6, 29; 5:26, 26; 6:17, 38; 7:8, 14, 17; 8:22, 37; 9:18, 34, 43; 10:19, 22, 32, 40, 41; 11:41, 44; 12:14, 26, 58; 13:12, 29; 15:7, 7, 14; 16:24, 26, 26; 17:21; 18:11, 30, 32; 19:3, 19, 30, 35; 20:5, 18; 22:4, 47; 23:1, 5, 25; 24:20; Jn 2:9, 15, 15, 16; 3:25, 26, 35; 4:47; 6:1, 22; 9:6, 11, 15; 10:1; 13:3, 10; 14:30; 16:20; 17:2; 18:30; 19:11, 19; 20:14; 21:9, 20; Ac 2:43; 3:13; 4:1; 7:10, 27, 35, 57; 8:1, 29, 30; 9:11; 10:19; 13:31; 14:23; 15:39; 16:9; 19:21; 20:1, 10, 28, 31; 21:11; 22:27; 23:5, 18; 25:1, 11; 26:31; 28:17; Ro 4:25; 5:17, 17, 21; 6:9; 8:3; 9:5, 32; 14:20; 15:12, 19, 19; 1Co 7:4, 4; 15:24, 27, 27, 28, 28, 57; 2Co 2:4; 3:13; 4:18; 8:15; 9:8; 10:14; 11:10; Eph 4:6, 19, 26; Col 1:6, 15, 23; 2:10, 15; 1Ti 1:4, 20; 2:12; 4:7; 6:4; 2Ti 2:14; Heb 2:8; 6:1, 1; 9:5, 11; 10:21; 11:38; 13:17; Jas 2:3, 13; 5:14; 1Pe 3:1, 12; 5:2, 3, 9; Jude 12; Rev 2:26; 6:8; 10:1; 11:2; 13:7; 14:16; 15:2; 16:2, 5; 17:1, 3, 14, 14, 18; 18:20, 24

SAID (2363)

Ge 1:3, 6, 9, 11, 14, 20, 24, 26, 29; 2:18; 3:14, 16, 17, 22; 4:1, 10, 23, 25; 5:29; 6:3, 7, 13; 7:1; 8:15, 21; 9:12, 17, 26; 11:3, 6; 12:7, 11; 13:8, 14; 15:1, 4, 18; 16:2, 5, 8, 9, 11, 13; 17:1, 3, 18; 18:3, 5, 5, 6, 10, 13, 15, 23, 28, 31, 31, 32, 32; 19:2, 2, 15, 21, 31, 34; 20:4, 5, 11, 16; 21:2, 16, 22, 26; 22:7, 7, 12; 23:3, 7, 11; 24:2, 18, 19, 27, 30, 33, 33, 45, 46, 54, 55, 56, 57, 59; 25:30, 32; 26:2, 7, 16, 20, 22, 24, 32; 27:1, 2, 6, 13, 18, 21, 22, 25, 25, 27, 31, 33, 35, 36, 37, 39, 41, 46; 28:1, 13, 16, 17; 29:4, 15, 21, 32, 33, 34, 35; 30:6, 8, 11, 13, 15, 16, 18, 20, 23, 24, 25, 34; 31:1, 3, 8, 8, 11, 12, 14, 31, 48, 49; 32:26, 30; 33:10, 12, 15; 34:14, 21, 30; 35:1, 10, 11; 37:8, 9, 13, 14, 21, 26, 33; 38:8, 26; 39:17; 40:9, 12, 16; 41:9, 13, 17, 38, 39, 41, 44, 51, 52; 42:1, 9, 13, 14, 18, 21, 28, 31, 37; 43:2, 3, 5, 8, 11, 16, 18, 20, 27; 44:4, 16, 17, 18, 20, 21, 22, 24, 25, 27; 45:3, 4, 4, 12, 17, 28; 46:3, 30, 31; 47:1, 5, 15, 18, 23, 29; 48:3, 4, 9, 11, 15, 18, 19, 21; 49:1; 50:5, 6, 11, 15, 18, 25; Ex 2:6, 10, 13, 22; 3:3, 6, 15, 16; 4:6, 7, 8, 14, 18, 19, 25, 27; 5:21; 6:9, 10, 26, 28; 7:1, 8, 14, 19; 8:1, 5, 10, 10, 16, 24, 25, 29; 9:6, 8, 13, 20, 22; 10:1, 3, 8, 12, 16, 21, 24, 25; 11:1; 12:21, 43; 13:1, 3, 17; 14:15, 26; 15:9; 16:4, 9, 11, 25, 33; 17:5, 16; 18:3, 4, 10, 14, 27; 19:3, 7, 9, 9, 24, 25; 20:19, 20, 22; 24:8, 12; 25:1; 30:11, 17, 22; 31:1; 32:1, 2, 9, 23, 30, 31; 33:1, 12, 15, 18; 34:6, 9, 27; 35:4; 40:1; Lev 1:1; 4:1; 5:14; 6:1, 8, 19, 24; 7:22, 28; 8:1, 31, 35; 9:2, 7; 10:3, 3, 4, 6, 8, 12, 19; 11:1; 12:1; 13:1; 14:1, 33; 15:1; 16:2; 17:1, 12; 18:1; 19:1; 20:1; 21:1, 16; 22:1, 17, 26; 23:1, 26, 33; 24:1, 13; 25:1; 27:1; Nu 1:1, 48; 3:5, 11, 14, 40, 44; 4:1, 17, 21; 5:5, 11; 6:1, 22; 7:4, 11; 8:1, 5; 9:7; 10:1, 29; 11:11, 16, 21, 23; 12:2, 4, 6, 14; 13:1, 30; 14:7, 11, 17, 20, 26, 31, 40, 41; 15:17, 35, 37; 16:3, 5, 15, 16, 20, 23, 28, 36, 44, 46; 17:1, 10, 12; 18:1, 20, 24; 19:1; 20:3, 7, 12, 18, 23; 21:16, 34; 22:4, 8, 10, 37; 23:1, 3, 4, 5, 7, 15, 16, 23, 25, 27; 24:12; 25:10, 16; 26:1, 52, 65; 27:3, 12, 15; 28:1; 30:2; 31:1, 3, 21, 25, 49; 32:2, 20, 24, 27, 29, 31; 33:50; 34:1, 16; 35:1, 9; 36:2; Dt 1:6, 20, 27, 29, 37, 42; 2:2, 17, 24, 31; 3:21, 23; 5:1, 5, 22, 24, 28, 28; 6:19; 9:12, 13, 26; 10:1, 10, 11; 18:17; 23:23; 29:2; 31:2, 7, 14, 16; 32:20, 48; 33:6, 7, 8, 12, 13, 18, 20, 22, 23, 24; 34:4, 5; Jos 1:1; 2:24; 3:6; 4:1, 15, 21; 5:9, 14; 6:2, 6, 22; 7:10, 19, 22, 25; 8:1, 18; 9:22; 10:8, 12, 22; 11:6; 13:1; 14:6, 6, 12; 15:16, 19; 17:4, 16, 17; 19:50; 20:1; 22:8, 15, 34; 23:2; 24:2, 19, 22, 23, 24, 27, 27; Jdg 1:3, 7, 12, 15, 24; 2:1, 20; 3:19, 20, 28; 4:6, 14, 18, 19, 22; 5:23; 6:8, 12, 14, 16, 20, 25, 29, 36, 39; 7:2, 9, 13, 14, 17; 8:7, 9, 15, 20, 21, 22; 9:1, 8, 10, 12, 14, 36, 37, 38, 54, 54; 10:15, 18; 11:2, 5, 7, 9, 11, 30, 36, 38; 12:2, 5; 13:3, 8, 15, 22, 23; 14:12, 14, 15, 16; 15:3, 11, 12, 16; 16:5, 6, 10, 13, 18, 23, 26; 17:2, 3, 10, 13; 18:5, 14, 18, 19, 23, 25; 19:5, 6, 8, 9, 11, 12, 20, 28, 30; 20:4, 23, 28; 21:5, 6, 11; Ru 1:8, 10, 15; 2:2, 2, 4, 8, 19, 21, 22; 3:1, 14, 15, 17, 18; 4:3, 8, 9, 14, 17; 1Sa 1:17, 20; 2:23, 34; 3:6, 6, 8, 9, 11, 15, 19; 4:3, 16, 20, 22; 7:3, 12; 8:11, 19, 21; 9:5, 6, 8, 17, 24, 27; 10:1, 16, 19, 24; 11:2, 12, 14; 12:12; 13:11, 11, 12; 14:1, 6, 12, 19, 28, 33, 36, 36, 38, 40, 42, 44, 45; 15:1, 10, 13, 16, 19, 28, 32, 33; 16:1, 7, 8, 9, 10, 11, 12, 15, 17, 18; 17:17, 34, 37, 55, 58; 18:8, 17, 21, 21, 23; 20:3, 3, 18, 26, 41, 42; 21:2, 14; 22:9, 18; 23:3, 11, 19, 21; 24:4, 6, 10, 17; 25:12, 18, 24, 39; 26:9, 25; 27:5; 28:7, 8, 11, 13, 17, 21; 30:7, 20, 22, 23, 26; 2Sa 1:8, 13, 15, 16; 2:27; 3:18, 21, 31, 38; 4:9; 6:20; 7:2, 4, 17; 9:6, 7, 9; 10:2, 3; 11:23, 25; 12:7, 18, 22; 13:4, 5, 10, 24, 26, 32, 35; 14:2, 10, 11, 12, 15, 22, 30, 33; 15:7, 21, 25; 16:3, 10, 11; 17:5, 6, 14, 15, 29; 18:14, 18, 19, 21, 23, 27, 28, 31; 19:5, 21, 30, 33; 20:3, 6, 9, 17, 17; 21:1, 6; 23:3; 24:2, 10, 16, 17, 18, 22; 1Ki 1:14, 28, 33, 42; 2:13, 20, 26, 30, 30, 31, 44; 3:5, 22, 23, 25, 26, 27; 5:7; 8:12, 17, 25, 29; 9:3; 11:11, 21, 31; 12:4, 22, 28; 13:3, 7, 8, 11, 13, 15, 26, 27, 31; 14:12; 17:2, 8, 12, 13, 15, 18, 23; 18:1, 5, 15, 21, 22, 25, 33, 34, 34, 34, 41, 43, 43; 19:4, 7, 9, 13, 20; 20:5, 7, 22, 23, 28, 28, 31, 34, 37, 39, 42; 21:2, 15, 17; 22:3, 8, 9, 12, 13, 17, 18, 20, 21, 22, 28, 30; 2Ki 1:6, 9, 11, 15, 16; 2:2, 4, 6, 9, 16, 16, 17, 20, 21, 22; 3:12, 13, 13, 16; 4:3, 6, 7, 9, 12, 13, 15, 17, 19, 23, 24, 25, 27, 28, 28, 29, 30, 36, 36, 38, 41, 41, 42; 5:3, 4, 6, 7, 11, 13, 15, 17, 19, 20, 22; 6:3, 7, 29, 32, 33; 7:2, 9, 18, 19; 8:4, 8, 9; 9:5, 6, 12, 12, 18, 25, 26, 34; 10:1, 4, 8, 15, 15, 16, 18, 23, 30; 12:4; 13:17; 14:27; 16:15; 18:26, 37; 19:23, 29; 20:7, 8, 16, 19; 21:4, 10; 22:8, 10, 15, 19; 23:27; 24:13; 1Ch 11:5, 6; 12:17, 18, 19; 15:12; 16:19; 17:1, 3, 15; 19:2, 3; 21:8, 11, 15, 17, 22, 23; 22:1, 5, 8; 23:4, 25; 28:3, 6; 29:1, 20; 2Ch 1:7, 11; 6:1, 7, 16, 20; 7:12, 18; 8:11; 10:4; 11:2; 12:6; 18:7, 8, 11, 12, 16, 17, 19, 20, 21, 27, 29; 20:9, 15, 20, 37; 22:9; 23:3; 24:20; 25:7, 16; 26:18; 28:9, 23; 29:5; 30:6, 18; 32:4, 11; 33:4; 34:15, 18, 23, 27; 36:21; Ezr 4:2; 6:2; 8:28; 9:1; 10:2, 5, 10; Ne 1:3, 5; 2:7, 16, 17; 4:14; 5:3, 4, 8, 13; 6:6, 10, 19; 7:3; 8:9, 15; 9:18; 13:1, 21; Est 3:8; 5:5, 6; 6:6, 10, 10, 13; 7:9; 8:5, 7; 9:12, 13; Job 1:5, 12, 21; 2:6, 9, 10, 13; 3:2; 4:16; 16:3; 22:17; 26:3; 32:6; 33:8, 9, 12; 34:1, 5, 9; 35:1; 38:11; 40:1, 5; 42:4, 6, 7, 7, 8; Ps 2:7; 16:2; 30:6; 32:5; 39:1; 40:7, 15; 54:T; 69:19; 70:3; 74:23; 77:10; 81:5; 83:12; 87:3, 5; 89:3, 19, 34; 95:10; 105:12; 110:1; 122:1; 126:2; 132:14; 140:6; Pr 6:2; 7:13; Ecc 1:16; 2:1, 2, 15; 3:17; 7:23, 28; 10:20; SS 2:10; 3:2, 3; 5:2, 3; 7:8; Isa 6:5, 7, 8, 9, 11; 7:3, 12, 13; 8:1, 3, 5, 11; 14:13; 16:13; 20:3; 21:6, 9, 10; 30:16; 36:11, 22; 37:24, 30; 38:10, 11, 21; 39:5, 8; 40:6; 41:26; 45:10; 46:11; 47:10; 48:15; 49:3; 53:7; 63:8; 65:1; Jer 1:4, 6, 9, 11, 12, 14; 2:1; 3:6, 11; 4:10, 10; 5:4, 12; 6:17; 7:1; 11:1, 4, 5, 6, 9, 19, 21; 13:1, 6; 14:11, 13, 14; 15:1, 10, 15; 16:1; 17:19; 18:1, 10, 13, 18; 19:1, 14; 20:3; 22:1; 24:3, 8; 25:2, 15, 27; 26:2, 11, 12, 16, 18; 27:2, 12, 16; 28:1, 6, 11, 15; 29:3, 25, 28, 28; 30:1, 2; 31:3; 32:6, 8, 8, 13, 24; 33:23; 35:6, 18; 36:5, 15, 16, 27, 29; 37:2, 13, 17; 38:4, 5, 9, 14, 15, 17, 19, 24; 39:12; 40:2, 3, 9, 14, 16; 41:6; 42:2, 5, 9, 21; 43:2, 8; 44:20, 24, 25; 45:1, 3; 50:7; 51:61, 62; La 1:17; 2:14; Eze 2:1, 3; 3:1, 3, 4, 16, 22, 24; 4:14, 15; 7:13; 8:5, 6, 8, 9, 12; 9:4, 9, 11; 10:2, 6; 11:2; 13:6; 16:6; 17:24; 20:7, 29, 49; 21:8; 22:14; 23:36, 43; 24:20, 25; 25:8; 29:3, 9; 33:21; 35:10, 12; 36:20; 37:4, 9, 11; 40:4, 45; 43:7, 18; 44:2, 5; 46:24; 47:8; Da 1:4, 10, 12; 2:3, 5, 7, 8, 24, 25, 26, 47; 3:9, 14, 24, 28; 4:9, 19, 30; 5:7, 10; 6:6, 15, 16; 7:23; 8:13, 17, 19; 10:11, 11, 12, 16, 19, 19; 12:8, 9, 9; Hos 1:2, 4, 6, 9, 10; 2:5; 3:1, 3; 10:12; Joel 2:32; Am 2:12; 7:2, 3, 5, 6, 8; 8:2; 9:1; Jnh 1:12; 2:2, 4; 4:9, 10; Hab 2:2; Hag 2:14; Zec 1:4, 6, 6, 6, 6, 7, 14; 2:4, 8; 3:2, 4, 4, 5, 6; 4:6, 14; 5:3, 5, 8; 6:7, 8; 11:12, 13, 15; Mal 3:13, 14, 16; Mt 1:20; 2:5, 13; 3:3, 14, 15, 17; 4:3, 6, 9; 8:2, 3, 4, 7, 8, 10, 13, 17, 19, 20, 21; 9:2, 3, 6, 9, 18, 22, 24, 29, 34, 37; 11:14, 28; 12:3, 13, 24, 27, 38, 49; 13:35, 36, 37, 51, 54; 14:2, 15, 18, 27, 29, 31; 15:7, 10, 12, 15, 23, 24, 26, 28, 32; 16:8, 22, 23, 24; 17:5, 5, 7, 14, 26; 18:3, 32; 19:5, 10, 11, 14, 23, 26, 27; 20:18, 25, 33; 21:2, 6, 13, 19, 30, 38; 22:1, 8, 13, 18, 21, 24, 31, 43, 44; 23:1; 25:20, 23, 24; 26:1, 8, 21, 25, 27, 36, 40, 45, 47, 50, 55, 61, 62, 63, 69, 70, 71, 72, 73, 74; 27:6, 14, 43, 49, 54, 63; 28:5, 6, 9, 10, 15; Mk 1:2, 37, 40, 41; 2:5, 6, 8, 10, 14, 16, 24, 27; 3:3, 5, 21, 22, 23, 32, 34; 4:8, 26, 35, 39, 41; 5:8, 19, 23, 31, 34, 36, 41; 6:10, 16, 22, 31, 35, 37, 50; 7:6, 9, 14, 29, 37; 8:12, 17, 19, 20, 24, 33; 9:7, 17, 19, 25, 31, 35, 36, 38, 39; 10:4, 14, 23, 24, 27, 28, 35, 37, 39, 39, 42, 49, 49, 51, 52; 11:6, 14, 21, 22; 12:7, 14, 15, 17, 26, 32, 34, 36, 36, 43; 13:1; 14:16, 18, 24, 29, 32, 36, 37, 41, 43, 62, 63, 67, 68, 71; 15:5, 36; 16:6, 20; Lk 1:13, 18, 19, 20, 28, 38, 45, 60; 2:10, 15, 17, 20, 33, 34, 48; 3:4, 22; 4:3, 9, 21, 23, 32; 5:4, 8, 12, 13, 14, 20, 21, 24, 27; 6:2, 8, 9, 10, 20; 7:4, 9, 13, 14, 20, 39, 40, 43, 44, 48, 49, 50; 8:8, 22, 25, 38, 45, 48, 50, 52, 54; 9:9, 12, 13, 22, 23, 35, 41, 43, 48, 49, 50, 54, 57, 59, 59, 61; 10:16, 21, 23, 35, 37, 40, 41; 11:1, 2, 15, 17, 19, 29, 39, 45, 45, 46, 49; 12:3, 12, 15, 18, 20, 22, 54; 13:7, 12, 14, 18, 31; 14:12, 18, 19, 20, 21, 21, 23, 25; 15:17, 21, 22, 31; 16:2, 7, 15, 19, 25, 27, 29, 31; 17:1, 5, 14, 19, 22; 18:2, 4, 6, 16, 22, 24, 26, 28, 34, 42; 19:5, 8, 11, 12, 19, 20, 25, 32, 39, 48; 20:14, 17, 21, 23, 25, 39, 41, 42, 45; 21:3, 5; 22:8, 13, 15, 17, 20, 33, 34, 36, 38, 47, 48, 51, 56, 57, 58, 60, 60, 61, 67; 23:4, 28, 34, 35, 42, 47; 24:8, 17, 19, 23, 24, 25, 27, 32, 36, 44, 46; Jn 1:15, 20, 29, 30, 32, 39, 40, 42, 43, 46, 47, 51; 2:8, 10, 22; 3:2, 26, 26; 4:7, 9, 11, 15, 17, 19, 25, 32, 39, 42, 44; 5:7, 10, 11, 12; 6:32, 34, 41, 42, 43, 53, 59, 60, 61, 65, 65, 70; 7:12, 12, 25, 31, 39, 41, 41; 8:4, 7, 10, 11, 11, 12, 21, 23, 24, 28, 31, 33, 49, 52, 55, 57; 9:9, 9, 16, 16, 22, 23, 28, 35, 37, 38; 10:7, 19, 20, 21, 32, 34; 11:4, 7, 8, 11, 12, 16, 21, 24, 32, 36, 37, 39, 41, 42, 49; 12:4, 14, 19, 21, 33, 39; 13:6, 11, 26, 31, 36; 14:5, 8, 22; 15:25; 16:19, 19, 29; 17:1; 18:5, 6, 8, 11, 17, 20, 21, 23, 25, 37; 19:4, 5, 6, 11, 13, 14, 21, 21, 24, 26, 27, 28, 30; 20:2, 9, 15, 16, 17, 19, 21, 22, 26, 27; 21:3, 3, 6, 7, 10, 12, 15, 16, 16, 17, 17, 19, 23, 23; Ac 1:9, 11, 24; 2:13, 17, 25, 34, 34, 37, 41; 3:4, 6, 12, 17, 22, 23, 25; 4:8, 23; 5:3, 9; 6:2, 13; 7:26, 33; 8:26, 29, 36; 9:11, 15, 17, 27, 34, 40; 10:3, 13, 19, 21, 22, 26; 11:3, 5, 16, 18; 12:7, 11, 15, 17; 13:2, 8, 9, 16, 22, 40, 45, 47; 15:13, 36; 16:15, 18; 17:3, 18, 18, 19, 32; 18:6, 14, 18; 19:4, 4, 21, 35, 36; 20:1, 10, 38; 21:6, 11, 13, 14, 20, 37; 22:1, 10, 13, 21, 25; 23:3, 4, 11, 17; 24:9, 10, 21, 22; 25:5, 8, 22, 24; 26:1, 22, 32; 27:10, 21, 24, 25, 31, 33; 28:4, 17, 25; Ro 4:18; 7:7; 9:15, 29, 33; 10:16, 19, 21; 11:2, 4, 9, 26; 15:12; 1Co 4:13; 9:9; 11:23, 24; 12:10; 14:13, 26, 29; 15:3, 4, 15; 2Co 2:1, 13; 4:6, 13; 6:16; 7:3; 12:9; Gal 2:14; 3:8; Eph 5:14; 1Th 1:5; 2:13; 5:21; 2Ti 4:15; Tit 1:12; Heb 1:5, 5, 5, 6, 13; 2:12, 13, 13; 3:10; 4:3, 5; 5:5, 6; 7:17; 8:8; 9:20; 10:5, 7, 8, 30, 30; 12:5, 21; 13:5, 22; Jas 2:11, 11; 1Pe 1:16; 2Pe 3:2; Jude 9, 14; Rev 1:11, 17; 4:1; 5:5, 14; 6:6, 10; 7:12, 14, 14; 10:4, 6, 9, 11; 11:17; 17:1, 15; 19:5, 9, 10; 21:5, 5, 6, 9; 22:6, 9

SAY (823)

Ge 3:1; 12:12, 13; 14:23; 18:13; 20:13; 21:26; 24:43, 50; 26:3, 9; 31:24, 29; 32:19, 20; 37:4, 17, 35; 42:18, 34; 43:7; 44:16, 18; 48:20; 50:17; Ex 4:1, 12, 15, 16, 28; 6:6; 7:2, 9, 16, 16; 8:20; 13:8, 16; 16:9; 20:22; 30:31; 32:12; Lev 14:35; 18:2; 19:2; 24:15; Nu 5:12, 19, 22; 9:10; 10:36; 14:15, 28; 15:38; 18:26, 30; 22:8, 19, 35, 35, 38; 23:12, 17; 24:13; 28:3; 35:10; Dt 1:3, 28; 6:3; 9:4, 6, 28, 28; 12:30; 13:2; 17:10; 18:18; 20:3, 5, 8; 21:7; 22:14; 25:7, 9; 26:3, 5; 28:67, 67, 67; 31:17; 32:1, 27; Jos 7:8; 8:6; 9:22; 22:24, 27, 28; Jdg 4:20; 6:13; 9:29; 11:10; 12:6, 6; 16:15; 18:25; Ru 3:5; 1Sa 2:20, 36; 3:9, 17; 8:7, 22; 9:9; 10:15; 11:9; 14:9, 10; 16:2, 19; 18:22; 20:26; 24:9; 25:24; 28:22; 2Sa 3:11; 7:8, 20, 26; 14:3, 19; 15:3; 18:12; 19:11; 24:12; 1Ki 1:13; 2:42; 12:23; 18:11, 14; 20:9, 35; 22:8, 14, 14; 2Ki 2:16; 6:8; 9:3; 18:22; 19:6; 1Ch 17:7, 18, 24; 21:10; 2Ch 11:3; 18:7, 13, 13; 19:11, 11; 32:15; Ezr 9:10; 10:12; Ne 5:8, 12; 7:73; 9:5; Est 4:14; Job 4:2; 9:22; 10:2; 13:14, 17; 15:5, 13; 16:4, 8; 17:12; 18:21; 21:14, 19, 19; 22:20, 29; 28:22; 31:14; 32:17; 33:1, 13, 24, 31, 32; 34:31, 34; 35:13, 13, 14; 36:23; 37:19; 40:5, 8; Ps 4:6; 10:6, 11; 11:1; 12:4; 14:1; 17:3; 27:8; 35:3, 21, 25, 27; 36:3; 39:1, 9; 41:5, 8; 45:10; 51:4; 52:4, 6; 53:1; 56:5; 58:11; 59:12; 64:6; 66:3; 71:11; 82:6; 83:4; 87:6; 89:26; 94:7; 106:48; 115:2; 122:8; 124:1; 129:1; 139:4, 4; 141:3; 142:5; Pr 1:11; 3:28; 4:10, 20; 5:7, 12; 8:6; 12:14; 15:23; 20:6, 9, 22; 23:7, 33, 35; 24:7, 29; 30:9, 20; Ecc 5:5; 6:3; 8:17; 9:4, 16; Isa 2:3; 3:6, 11; 4:1; 5:9, 19, 20; 7:9; 8:4; 9:9; 10:8; 14:4; 19:25; 20:6; 22:13; 28:9, 15; 29:11, 12, 13, 15, 16, 16; 30:10, 11, 21, 22; 33:24; 35:4; 36:7; 37:6; 38:15; 40:27, 27; 41:7, 13; 42:14; 44:5, 26, 27, 28, 28; 45:14; 47:8; 48:5, 7; 49:20; 50:4; 56:4, 12; 57:14; 58:3; 65:5, 8; Jer 1:7, 7, 17; 2:23, 23, 25, 27, 27, 31, 35; 3:4, 12; 4:11; 5:24; 7:23, 28; 8:4, 6, 8, 14; 9:20; 10:11; 11:3, 6; 12:4; 13:18; 14:7, 15, 17; 15:2; 16:14, 15, 19; 17:15, 20; 18:11; 19:3, 11; 20:9, 10, 10, 10; 21:11; 22:1, 8; 23:7, 8, 16, 17, 25, 26, 31, 37, 38; 25:30; 26:4, 8; 27:9; 28:6; 29:22; 31:23; 32:7, 36, 43; 33:10; 34:5; 35:13; 36:29; 38:25; 39:16; 42:13; 43:3, 10; 46:16, 17; 48:2; 49:14; 51:35, 51, 62, 64; La 2:16; 3:24, 41; Eze 2:4, 8; 3:11, 27; 9:5; 11:3, 5; 12:10; 13:8, 15; 16:44; 17:12; 18:3, 25; 20:32; 22:28; 32:19; 33:7, 18, 32; 36:35; 37:4, 9, 19; 38:11; 39:17; Da 10:11, 15; Hos 2:23; 10:3; 12:8; 14:2; Joel 2:17; 3:9; Am 5:18; 6:10; 7:16; 9:10; Ob 1; Jnh 4:2; Mic 2:5, 6, 6, 11; 3:11; 4:2; Na 3:7; Hab 2:1; Hag 2:2; Zec 1:3, 17; 2:4; 7:5; 8:21, 23; 11:5; 12:5; 13:5, 6, 9, 9; Mal 1:4, 5, 13; 3:13, 15; Mt 2:4; 3:9; 4:4, 6, 7, 10; 5:22, 22, 28, 32, 34, 34, 35, 37, 39, 44; 8:8, 9, 9; 9:5; 10:19; 11:10, 14, 18, 19; 12:10, 16, 34, 37; 13:13; 15:5, 10, 11; 16:11, 13, 14, 14, 14, 15, 18; 17:20; 18:16; 19:7, 24; 20:23; 21:3, 16, 21, 25, 26; 22:23; 23:3, 16, 16, 18, 30, 39; 25:34, 41; 26:31, 62, 64; 27:11; 28:13, 15; Mk 2:9; 3:12; 7:11, 11, 15; 8:27, 28, 28, 28, 29, 32; 9:1, 6; 10:3, 40; 11:3, 6, 14, 23, 31, 32; 12:18; 13:11, 11, 37, 37; 14:14, 27, 40, 49, 58, 60; 15:2, 4; Lk 1:36; 3:8; 4:4, 8, 10, 12; 5:5, 23, 39; 6:27, 45; 7:6, 7, 8, 8, 27, 33, 34, 40; 8:10; 9:18, 19, 19, 19, 20, 44, 61; 10:9, 10, 26, 36; 11:5, 18; 12:11, 19, 54, 55; 13:26, 35; 14:9, 10, 30; 15:18; 17:6, 10, 21; 19:14, 31; 20:5, 6, 20, 27; 22:11, 71; 23:3, 29; Jn 1:22; 5:47; 6:31, 42; 7:26, 40; 8:5, 24, 26, 26, 30, 48, 52, 54, 57; 9:17; 10:34; 11:51; 12:49, 50, 50; 14:10, 23, 24; 16:15; 18:37, 37; 19:36; Ac 4:14; 6:14; 8:6; 9:15; 10:15; 11:7, 9; 19:40; 20:26; 21:21; 23:5, 8; 26:7; 28:26; Ro 1:8, 17; 2:1, 22, 24; 3:4, 5, 8, 8, 10; 8:31, 36; 9:7, 14, 17, 19, 20, 20, 26, 30; 10:8, 15; 11:2, 8, 19; 12:20; 13:3; 14:11; 15:3; 16:8, 12; 1Co 1:15, 19, 23, 31; 2:9; 3:19; 5:13; 6:12, 13, 16; 7:8, 29, 40; 9:8; 10:7, 15, 19, 23, 23; 11:16, 22; 12:3, 21, 21; 14:24; 15:27, 33, 34; 2Co 1:12, 17, 20; 2:5; 4:5; 8:15, 23; 9:9; 10:1, 10, 11, 12, 17; 11:21, 22, 22, 23; 13:1; Gal 1:9; 2:12; 3:10, 11, 16, 17; 4:9, 22, 30; 5:3, 11; Eph 4:8, 17, 29; 5:31, 33; Php 3:2, 12, 18; 4:4, 8, 17; Col 2:18, 18; 3:17; 4:17; 2Th 2:2, 3, 17; 3:13, 14; 1Ti 4:3; 5:14; 2Ti 2:23; Tit 2:8, 15; Heb 5:11; 7:9, 21; 9:22; 10:23; 11:32; 13:6, 17; Jas 1:13; 2:3, 16, 18, 23; 4:4, 5, 6, 13, 15; 5:12; 1Pe 2:8; 3:9, 10; 4:4; 1Jn 1:6, 8; 2:6; 2Jn 12, 12; 3Jn 12; Jude 4; Rev 2:2, 9; 3:9, 17; 4:10; 6:3, 5, 7; 18:18, 19; 22:17, 17

SAYING (263)

Ge 1:22; 12:19; 38:28; Ex 5:17; 6:30; 17:7; 32:8; Nu 11:13; 14:27; 16:4, 41; 24:23; Dt 9:2; 20:9; 31:1; Jos 21:2; 24:21; Jdg 5:28; 7:11, 24; 8:15; 9:9, 11, 30; 10:10; 16:2, 24; 20:12; 1Sa 10:12; 14:24; 19:4; 20:16; 25:21; 2Sa 3:12, 35; 5:8; 19:9, 27; 20:18; 1Ki 1:47, 53; 2Ki 6:33; 18:30, 32; 2Ch 7:3; 16:10; Ne 4:2, 11; 5:2; 6:7; Job 12:3; 13:1; 15:23; 19:28; 21:2, 6; 27:12; 36:2; Ps 3:2; 13:4; 22:7; 30:8; 31:14; 42:3; 78:1, 19; 85:8; 90:3; Pr 20:14; 22:13; 24:12; 26:13; 28:24; Isa 7:5; 36:15, 18; 45:9; 49:9; Jer 5:2; 12:16; 20:1; 23:17, 18, 35, 37; 26:8, 9, 19, 21; 31:18, 34; 32:36; 33:24, 24; 38:1, 22; 42:20; La 2:15; Eze 3:18; 8:12; 9:9; 11:5, 15; 12:27; 13:10; 18:29; 20:49; 26:2; 32:21; 33:10, 17, 20, 24, 30, 30; 35:13; 36:2, 13; 37:11; Da 2:20; 4:23, 35; 7:5; Hos 4:1; Am 7:10, 10, 11; Jnh 3:6; Mic 6:1; 7:10; Hab 2:6; Hag 1:2; Zec 8:9; Mal 1:7, 12; Mt 7:4; 9:18; 16:2, 7; 19:1; 21:16; 22:15; 23:31; 24:5; 26:1, 26, 44, 68; 27:24; Mk 1:11; 3:30; 6:14; 7:19; 8:16, 26; 9:32; 12:13, 32; 14:22, 70; 16:8; Lk 2:28; 3:16; 5:26; 6:42; 7:1, 16; 9:7, 8, 33, 34; 11:54; 18:13; 19:39; 21:8; 22:19, 70; Jn 4:37; 8:6, 43; 9:9, 22, 40; 12:28, 34, 36; 13:18; 16:26; 17:1; 18:1; Ac 2:15, 31; 4:25; 6:1, 11; 9:4, 20; 10:43, 44; 13:35; 14:2; 16:14; 17:20; 18:21; 21:1; 22:7, 18; 26:14; Ro 2:1; 3:8; 4:9, 14; 8:27; 9:1; 11:13; 1Co 1:12, 12; 4:6; 6:5; 7:35; 10:19, 20; 11:25; 14:5, 14, 16, 26, 27, 37; 15:12, 50; 2Co 7:3; 8:8; 12:19; Gal 1:20, 23; 1Th 5:3; 1Ti 1:15; 3:1; 5:13; 2Ti 2:7, 11; Heb 4:4; 6:13; 8:11; Jas 2:14; 1Jn 3:18; 5:16; 3Jn 10; Jude 4; Rev 2:7, 11, 17, 29; 3:6, 13, 22; 4:8; 14:13; 16:5, 7, 17; 21:3

SAYS (842)

Ge 3:3; 21:12; 22:16; 24:14; 45:9; Ex 4:22; 5:1; 7:17; 8:1, 20; 9:1, 13; 10:3; 11:4; 16:16; 20:19; 32:27; Nu 22:16; 24:13; 30:4, 14; Dt 5:27; 13:6; 15:16; Jos 3:9; 7:13; 24:2; Jdg 6:8; 11:15; 1Sa 2:30; 9:6; 15:2; 20:7; 24:13; 2Sa 7:5, 8; 12:7; 24:12; 1Ki 3:23; 11:31; 12:24; 13:2, 21; 17:14; 20:2, 5, 13, 14, 28, 32, 42; 21:19; 22:5, 11, 19; 2Ki 1:4, 11, 16; 2:21; 3:16, 17; 4:43; 5:13; 7:1; 9:3, 6, 26; 18:19, 29; 19:3, 6, 17, 20, 32, 33; 20:1, 5, 17; 21:12; 22:13, 16, 18, 19; 1Ch 17:4, 7; 21:10; 2Ch 11:4; 12:5; 18:4, 10, 18; 20:15; 21:12; 24:20; 32:10; 34:21, 24, 26, 27; 36:23; Ezr 1:2; Job 23:5; 24:15; 28:14, 14, 28; 34:18; 36:10; Ps 32:8; 50:16; 68:22; 75:2, 10; 91:14; 95:8; 145:13; Pr 9:4, 16; 24:24; 26:19; Ecc 1:2; 7:27; 12:8; Isa 1:2,

11, 18, 24; 7:7; 8:20; 10:24; 14:22; 16:14; 17:3, 6; 19:4; 21:16; 22:19, 25; 23:4, 12; 28:16; 29:13, 22; 30:1, 15; 31:9; 33:10; 36:4, 14; 37:3, 6, 18, 21, 33, 34; 38:1, 5; 39:6; 40:1; 41:21; 42:5; 43:1, 10, 12, 14; 44:2, 6, 17, 24; 45:1, 2, 11, 14, 18; 48:17, 22; 49:6, 7, 8, 14, 18, 22, 25; 51:16, 22; 52:3, 4; 54:1, 6, 8, 10; 55:8; 56:1, 8; 57:15, 19, 21; 59:20, 21; 65:1, 7, 8, 13; 66:1, 9, 12, 17, 20, 22; Jer 2:2, 5, 12, 29; 3:1, 10, 12, 14, 16, 20, 22; 4:1, 3, 9, 17, 22, 27; 5:1, 11, 14, 15, 18; 6:6, 9, 12, 15, 16, 21, 22; 7:3, 11, 13, 20, 21, 30, 32; 8:1, 4, 12, 17; 9:3, 6, 7, 11, 15, 17, 22, 23, 25; 10:2, 18; 11:3, 11, 22; 12:14; 13:9, 11, 12, 14, 25; 14:15; 15:2, 3, 6, 9; 16:3, 5, 9, 14, 16, 21; 17:1, 5, 21, 24; 18:11, 18; 19:3, 6, 11, 12, 15; 20:4; 21:4, 7, 8, 10, 12, 14; 22:3, 5, 6, 11, 13, 14, 24, 30; 23:1, 2, 4, 5, 7, 11, 15, 16, 17, 30, 32, 33, 34, 38; 24:5; 25:7, 8, 12, 27, 28, 32; 26:4, 18; 27:4, 8, 15, 16, 19, 21, 22; 28:2, 13, 14, 16; 29:8, 9, 11, 14, 16, 17, 19, 21, 23, 25, 31; 30:2, 5, 8, 10, 11, 12, 17, 18, 21; 31:1, 7, 15, 16, 17, 23, 27, 28, 31, 32, 33, 34, 35, 38; 32:3, 14, 15, 30, 36; 33:2, 4, 10, 11, 12, 14, 17; 34:2, 4, 5, 13, 17; 35:13, 17, 18; 36:29, 30; 37:7, 9; 38:2, 3, 17; 39:16; 42:4, 11, 15, 15, 18, 20; 43:10; 44:2, 11, 25, 26, 29; 45:2, 4; 46:5, 18, 23, 25, 28; 47:2; 48:1, 12, 15, 25, 30, 35, 40, 43, 44, 47; 49:1, 2, 2, 5, 6, 7, 12, 13, 15, 16, 18, 23, 26, 28, 30, 31, 32, 35, 37, 38, 39; 50:2, 4, 10, 18, 20, 21, 30, 31, 33, 35, 40; 51:1, 20, 24, 25, 26, 33, 35, 36, 39, 48, 52, 53, 57, 58; Eze 2:4; 3:11, 27; 4:13; 5:5, 7, 11; 6:3, 11; 7:2, 5; 11:5, 7, 8, 21; 12:10, 25; 13:3, 8, 8, 13, 18, 20; 14:11, 21, 23; 15:6, 8; 16:8, 14, 19, 23, 30, 36, 43, 48, 58, 59, 63; 17:12, 16, 19, 22; 18:3, 9, 30, 32; 20:31, 33, 36, 39, 40, 44; 21:7, 24, 26; 22:12, 31; 23:22, 28, 32, 35, 46; 24:6, 9, 14, 21; 25:6, 8, 12, 13, 15, 16; 26:3, 5, 7, 15, 19; 28:6, 25; 29:8, 13, 19, 20; 30:6, 6, 10, 13, 22; 31:10, 15; 32:3, 11, 14, 31; 33:11; 34:8, 10, 11, 15, 17, 20, 30, 31; 35:6, 11, 14; 36:2, 5, 7, 13, 14, 15, 23, 32, 33, 37; 37:5, 9, 19; 38:10, 17, 18, 21; 39:5, 8, 10, 13, 17, 20, 25, 29; 43:18, 19, 27; 44:9, 12, 15, 27; 45:9, 15, 18; 46:1, 16; 47:13; 48:29; Hos 2:13, 16, 21; 9:10, 15; 10:9; 11:11; 14:4; Joel 2:12, 25; 3:1; Am 1:3, 6, 9, 11, 13; 2:1, 4, 6; 3:10, 11, 12, 13; 4:5, 6, 8, 9, 10, 11; 5:3, 4, 16, 27; 6:8, 14; 7:17; 8:9, 11; 9:8, 13, 15; Ob 2, 8; Mic 2:3; 3:5; 4:6, 13; 5:10; 7:15; Na 1:12, 14; 2:13; Zep 1:2, 3, 8, 10; 2:9, 12; 3:8; Hag 1:2, 5, 7, 8, 9, 13; 2:4, 4, 4, 6, 7, 8, 9, 11, 14, 17, 23, 23; Zec 1:3, 3, 4, 14, 16, 16, 17; 2:5, 6, 10; 3:7, 9, 10; 4:6, 6; 5:3, 3, 4; 6:12; 7:9, 13; 8:2, 3, 4, 6, 7, 9, 11, 14, 14, 17, 19, 20, 23; 11:4, 6; 12:4; 13:2, 7, 8; Mal 1:2, 4, 6, 8, 10, 11, 13, 14; 2:2, 4, 8, 16, 16; 3:1, 5, 7, 10, 11, 12, 13, 17; 4:1, 3; Mt 5:21, 27, 31, 33, 38, 43; 12:44; 13:14; 15:4, 18; 26:18; 27:9; Lk 2:23; 4:17; 11:24; Jn 5:32; 7:36; 8:5, 17, 54; 10:36; 16:17, 17; 19:24; Ac 1:20; 4:11; 7:48; 10:15; 11:9; 13:33, 34; 15:17; 17:28; Ro 2:14; 3:4; 9:25; 10:6, 7; 12:19; 14:11; 15:21; 16:23, 25; 1Co 1:9; 3:4, 4; 9:9; 12:15, 16; 14:21, 34; 15:27; 2Co 6:2, 17, 18; Gal 3:12; 4:21; Eph 4:9; 1Ti 5:18; Heb 1:8; 2:6, 8; 3:7; 8:8, 9, 10; 10:15, 16; Jas 1:25; 1Pe 1:24; 1Jn 2:4, 9, 22; 4:20; Rev 1:3, 8; 14:13; 22:20

SHE (994)

Ge 2:23, 23, 23; 3:6, 6, 13, 20; 4:1, 1, 1, 2, 25, 25, 25; 12:15, 18, 19; 16:2, 4, 4, 4, 5, 6, 8, 13; 17:16, 17; 18:12, 12, 13, 15, 15; 19:26, 26, 37, 38; 20:5, 5, 12; 21:2, 10, 14, 15, 16, 16, 16, 19, 19; 23:2; 24:8, 14, 16, 16, 18, 18, 19, 20, 20, 21, 24, 36, 44, 45, 46, 46, 46, 47, 47, 55, 57, 58, 60, 64, 65, 67, 67; 25:2, 21, 22, 22; 26:7, 7, 7, 9, 9; 27:6, 14, 15, 16, 16, 17, 42; 28:9; 29:9, 10, 32, 32, 33, 33, 33, 34, 34, 34, 35, 35, 35, 35; 30:1, 1, 1, 3, 6, 8, 9, 9, 11, 13, 16, 17, 18, 18, 19, 20, 20, 21, 23, 23, 24, 24; 31:34; 35:8, 18; 38:3, 4, 5, 5, 11, 14, 14, 15, 16, 17, 18, 18, 18, 19, 25, 26, 27, 28; 39:10, 12, 12, 13, 13, 14, 14, 16, 17, 17; Ex 2:2, 3, 3, 3, 5, 6, 6, 7, 10; 4:25, 26, 26; 6:20, 23, 25; 21:7, 8, 11; Lev 12:2, 2, 4, 4, 5, 5, 5, 6, 7, 8, 8; 15:19, 20, 22, 25, 26, 27, 28, 28, 29; 18:7, 9, 9, 11, 12, 13, 14, 15; 19:20; 20:16, 18; 21:3, 9, 14; 22:12, 13, 13, 13; 24:11; Nu 5:13, 13, 14, 15, 27, 27, 28, 28; 12:14, 14, 15; 25:15; 26:59; 30:3, 9, 10, 13; Dt 21:12, 13; 22:14, 17, 21, 24, 26, 27; 24:2, 4; 25:6, 7, 9; 27:22; 28:56, 56, 57, 57, 57, 57; Jos 2:6, 9, 15, 16, 21, 21; 6:17, 25, 25; 15:18, 18, 19; Jdg 1:14, 14, 15; 4:5, 6, 6, 9, 18, 19, 21, 22; 5:24, 25, 26, 26, 26, 26, 28, 29; 11:36, 38, 38, 39, 39; 13:9, 10, 14; 14:3, 17, 17, 17; 15:2; 16:8, 9, 9, 14, 16, 18, 18, 19, 20; 17:3; 19:2, 3, 26, 27; 20:5; Ru 1:7, 7, 9, 18, 20; 2:3, 4, 6, 7, 7, 7, 10, 13, 14, 14, 17, 18, 19, 19, 23, 23; 3:6, 9, 14, 17; 4:3, 5, 10, 13; 1Sa 1:10, 11, 12, 13, 15, 18, 18, 18, 20, 20, 22, 23; 2:19, 20; 4:19, 20, 20, 20, 21, 21, 22; 19:12, 13, 14; 25:18, 18, 19, 19, 20, 20, 23, 24, 36, 36, 37, 41, 42, 42; 28:12, 13, 14, 21, 24, 24, 25; 2Sa 4:4, 4; 6:16, 16; 11:3, 3, 4, 4, 4, 5, 5, 26, 27, 27; 12:24; 13:2, 5, 8, 8, 9, 11, 12, 14, 18, 19; 14:4, 5, 9, 11, 12, 13, 18, 27; 17:20; 20:3, 17, 18; 21:10; 1Ki 1:2, 4, 17, 22, 28; 2:13, 14, 16, 19, 20, 21; 3:17, 18, 19, 20, 20, 27; 9:16; 10:1, 2, 2, 2, 4, 5, 5, 6, 10, 13, 13; 11:20; 14:5, 17; 15:13; 17:11, 12, 15, 15, 18; 21:8, 9, 15; 2Ki 4:2, 5, 5, 5, 6, 7, 8, 9, 12, 13, 13, 13, 14, 15, 16, 17, 21, 22, 23, 24, 25, 27, 27, 28, 36, 37, 37; 6:28, 29; 8:2, 3, 3, 4, 6, 6; 9:30, 31, 34; 11:1, 13, 14, 14, 16; 22:14, 15; 1Ch 2:26, 49; 4:18; 7:16, 23, 24; 15:29, 29; 2Ch 9:1, 1, 2, 2, 3, 4, 4, 5, 9, 12, 12, 12; 15:16; 22:10, 11; 23:12, 13, 13; 34:22, 23; Est 1:11, 12, 19; 2:1, 12, 13, 13, 14, 14, 14, 14, 15, 15, 15, 20, 20, 20, 22; 4:4, 4, 5; 5:12, 12; 8:4; Job 3:12; 39:14, 15, 16, 16, 18, 18; Ps 45:14; 113:9; Pr 1:20, 21, 22; 2:17, 17; 3:16, 17; 4:6, 6, 8, 8, 9, 9; 5:6, 6, 19; 7:11, 12, 13, 13, 21, 21, 26; 8:2, 3; 9:2, 3, 3, 4, 4, 13, 14, 15, 16, 16; 23:22, 25, 28; 31:10, 11, 12, 13, 14, 14, 15, 16, 16, 17, 18, 20, 21, 22, 22, 24, 25, 25, 26, 26, 27, 31; SS 6:13; 8:5, 9, 9; Isa 1:21; 7:14; 8:3; 21:2; 23:16, 16, 17, 17, 17; 34:15; 49:15, 15; Jer 2:14, 26; 3:1, 7, 7, 7, 8, 8, 9, 10; 6:6, 7; 15:9; 17:11; 46:24; 48:9, 11, 11, 11, 26, 27, 39, 42; 50:9, 14, 15, 15, 29, 29; 51:8, 35, 42, 43, 53, 56, 62; La 1:1, 1, 2, 3, 3, 7, 7, 8, 8, 9, 9, 9, 10, 10, 11, 18; Eze 5:6, 6; 16:50; 19:2, 3, 5; 23:5, 7, 8, 8, 8, 9, 10, 11, 11, 12, 13, 14, 14, 16, 16, 16, 17, 18, 19, 19, 20; 24:6, 7, 7, 16; 25:3; 26:2, 2; 29:7, 16; Da 5:10, 10; 11:6, 6; Hos 1:3, 8; 2:2, 3, 3, 3, 5, 7, 7, 7, 7, 8, 8, 8, 12, 13, 13, 15, 15, 15; 3:1; 4:16, 17; 5:5; 10:11; Am 5:2; Na 3:1, 4; Mal 2:14; Mt 1:18, 18, 21, 23, 25; 5:32; 8:15; 9:20, 21, 25; 12:42; 13:33; 14:7; 15:23, 25, 27; 20:20, 21; 22:26, 27, 28, 28; 26:9, 12; Mk 1:31; 5:23, 23, 26, 26, 26, 26, 27, 27, 28, 29, 29, 33, 39; 6:17, 19, 24; 7:25, 25, 26, 26, 28, 30; 10:12; 12:23, 44, 44, 44; 14:3, 5, 8, 8, 67; 16:10, 11, 11; Lk 1:25, 27, 36, 40; 2:7, 7, 36, 36, 37, 37, 38, 38, 38; 4:39; 7:38, 38, 38, 44, 45, 46, 47; 8:43, 43, 44, 47, 47, 47, 50, 52, 52, 53, 55; 10:40, 40; 11:31; 13:11, 13, 13, 21; 15:8, 8, 9, 9, 9; 18:4, 5, 5; 20:33; 21:4, 4, 4; 22:56; Jn 2:3; 4:9, 11; 8:11; 11:20, 27, 28, 28, 31, 32; 12:3, 7; 16:21; 18:16; 19:27; 20:2, 2, 11, 11, 12, 13, 14, 14, 15, 15, 16, 18; Ac 5:8, 10, 10; 9:36, 37, 40, 40, 40, 41; 12:14, 14, 14, 15; 16:14, 14, 14, 15, 15, 16, 17; Ro 7:3, 3, 3, 3; 9:11, 12; 16:2; 1Co 7:11, 12, 13, 39, 39, 40; 11:5, 6, 6, 6; Gal 4:25, 26; Eph 5:27; 1Ti 5:4, 5, 10, 10, 10, 10, 10, 10, 10, 10, 16; Heb 11:31; Jas 2:25, 25; 1Pe 3:6, 7, 7; Rev 2:20, 21, 22; 12:2, 2, 2, 4, 5, 14, 14; 14:8; 17:4, 6; 18:2, 6, 6, 6, 7, 7, 8, 12, 13, 13, 16, 19, 21, 24; 19:8

SHE'S (3)

Mt 9:24; Lk 1:36; 7:39

SHOULD (526)

Ge 18:17, 25; 20:9; 24:49; 26:28; 27:43, 45; 30:30; 32:18; 34:7, 31; 37:22; 41:38; 42:38; 47:15, 19, 26; Ex 2:7; 3:13; 5:2; 6:30; 9:30; 16:16; 17:4; 18:19, 20; 21:21, 27; Lev 10:18; 19:34; 24:12; 25:15; 27:10; Nu 9:7; 10:31; 12:8; 16:40; 17:10; 23:19, 19; 27:4, 21; 35:24, 28; Dt 1:22; 5:25; 8:5; 15:4; 19:21; 22:25; 23:15; Jos 18:10; Jdg 1:1; 9:9, 11, 13, 28, 28, 38; 11:23; 13:12; 14:16; 18:9; 20:7, 18, 23, 28, 28; Ru 1:11, 15, 21; 4:4; 1Sa 5:8; 6:2, 4; 14:37, 45; 15:29; 18:18; 19:5; 20:3, 32; 21:15; 22:10; 23:2, 9; 24:14; 25:11; 26:11, 19; 28:6; 29:6; 30:8; 2Sa 2:1, 1; 3:10, 10, 33; 4:11, 11; 5:19; 9:8; 12:23, 25; 13:4; 14:14; 15:20, 27; 16:9, 20; 17:6, 11; 18:22; 19:21, 42; 20:3; 21:17; 23:17; 1Ki 1:27; 2:4; 5:5; 8:16; 12:6, 9, 10; 20:11, 14; 21:3; 22:6, 15; 2Ki 3:10; 5:13, 20; 6:21, 33; 7:3; 13:19; 16:15; 19:11, 25; 21:4; 1Ch 11:19; 12:38; 14:10; 28:14; 2Ch 6:5; 10:6, 9, 10; 18:5, 14; 19:2; 20:3; 23:5; 25:9; 29:24; 32:4; 33:4; Ezr 1:4; 5:13; 7:23; 10:7; Ne 2:9; 5:9; 6:11, 11; 8:14, 15; 10:31, 34; 13:1, 19; Est 1:8, 19, 22; 6:6, 8; Job 2:10; 3:20; 6:14; 7:17; 9:14; 11:3; 13:8; 15:6; 19:3; 21:15, 19; 28:25; 29:25; 31:11, 28; 32:7, 16; 37:20; Ps 8:4, 4; 25:4, 12; 27:1, 1; 48:1; 56:4, 11; 79:10; 111:2; 119:7; 142:3; 144:3, 3; Pr 5:17; 31:4; Ecc 3:13, 14; 7:2, 17; SS 1:7; 5:3, 3; Isa 6:8; 14:32; 29:16; 37:11, 26; 40:6; 44:19; 48:17; Jer 5:9, 9, 29, 29; 8:14; 9:9, 9; 18:20; 23:35, 37, 38; 25:29; 26:11; 27:13, 17; 29:28, 28; 31:34; 36:19; 37:18; 40:15, 15; 48:27; La 2:20, 20; 3:39; Eze 7:13; 13:19, 19; 14:3; 16:20, 52; 17:9; 18:13, 24, 31; 20:31; 21:30; 33:11, 24, 25, 26; 36:32; Da 6:7, 26; Hos 4:14; 6:4; 9:14; 13:14, 14; Jnh 1:11; Mic 2:7; 6:6, 7, 7; Hab 1:13; Zec 7:3; Mal 1:9, 13; 2:7, 7; 3:8; Mt 9:15; 11:3, 15; 13:9, 43; 18:14, 21; 19:3; 20:15, 26; 22:24; 23:23, 23; 25:27; 27:22; Mk 1:4; 4:9, 23, 30; 6:24; 7:27; 10:2, 17, 43; 12:15, 15, 19; 13:14; 15:9, 12; Lk 1:63; 2:1, 49; 3:3, 10, 12, 14; 7:19, 20; 8:8; 9:54; 11:2, 42, 42; 14:35; 16:12; 17:10; 18:18; 20:16, 28; 21:21; 22:26, 26, 32, 49; Jn 5:17; 6:39, 39, 40, 40; 7:23; 11:50, 51; 12:5, 27, 49; 13:34; 18:14, 23; Ac 2:37; 4:16; 6:2; 10:28; 14:15; 15:19, 20; 17:21, 26, 27; 20:35; 21:4, 25, 25; 23:15; 27:21; Ro 1:28; 2:1; 6:1, 11; 8:15, 15, 26, 26; 9:20; 13:4, 13; 14:4, 5, 23; 15:2; 1Co 1:31; 3:5; 4:21, 21; 5:6; 6:3, 15; 7:2, 2, 3, 3, 5, 9, 18, 18, 20, 29, 30, 31; 8:1, 4; 9:10, 14, 27; 10:9, 25, 27, 29, 30; 11:1, 6, 6, 7, 10, 28; 12:11, 23, 31; 14:6, 13, 27, 34, 34, 37; 15:30; 16:1, 2; 2Co 8:11, 13, 13, 20; 9:5, 7; 10:17; Gal 2:2; 4:9; 6:1, 4, 6, 10, 14; Eph 1:12; 3:13, 18; 5:8; 6:20; Php 1:7; 2:5, 18, 25; 3:13; Col 2:5; 4:4, 16; 1Th 3:1; 4:3, 9, 11; 2Th 3:10; 1Ti 1:15; 2:9, 10, 11; 3:10; 4:4, 9; 5:3, 11, 17, 20; 6:1, 2, 17, 18, 18; 2Ti 2:25; 3:1; 4:5; Tit 2:3; 3:1, 2, 14; Heb 2:6, 6, 10; 8:11; 12:9; Jas 1:7, 9, 10, 13; 3:1; 5:13, 13, 14; 1Pe 2:15; 3:4, 7, 8; 2Pe 1:13; 3:11, 12; 1Jn 2:6; 3:11; 5:16, 16; 2Jn 5; 3Jn 8; Rev 2:7, 11, 17, 29; 3:6, 13, 22; 13:9

SHOULDN'T (40)

Ge 29:15; Jdg 19:30; 1Sa 11:12; 24:6; 2Sa 16:11, 19; 24:10; 1Ki 22:8; 2Ki 5:12; 1Ch 21:8; 2Ch 18:7; Ne 2:3; Job 4:6; 11:2, 3; Ps 139:21, 21; Eze 34:2; Am 3:4; Ob 12, 12, 12, 12, 13, 13, 14, 14; Jnh 4:11; Mt 12:2; 18:33; Mk 2:24; 8:32; Lk 6:2; Jn 6:27; Ac 17:29; 19:36; Ro 14:23; 1Co 9:12; 2Co 3:8; 1Ti 5:13

SO (3565)

Ge 1:7, 9, 9, 11, 15, 21, 24, 27, 30; 2:1, 19, 21; 3:6, 6, 6, 7, 8, 10, 14, 23; 4:6, 6, 16; 6:6, 13, 22; 7:5; 8:3, 9, 17, 18; 9:23; 12:4, 10, 18; 13:1, 6, 7, 12, 16; 14:23; 15:3, 18; 16:1, 2, 3, 4, 6, 15; 18:6, 12, 15, 19, 20; 19:3, 5, 11, 14, 19, 33, 35, 36; 20:2, 4, 17; 21:10, 14, 23, 31; 22:2, 13; 23:6, 8, 9, 13, 16, 19; 24:5, 9, 20, 27, 32, 42, 45, 46, 47, 49, 50, 58, 59, 65; 25:21, 22, 25, 25, 26, 33, 33; 26:1, 6, 17, 20, 21, 22, 28, 30, 33; 27:4, 5, 14, 19, 20, 22, 23, 25, 27, 31; 28:1, 5, 9; 29:7, 7, 12, 20, 20, 21, 22, 28, 30, 32; 30:4, 9, 16, 16, 38, 39, 42; 31:5, 16, 17, 25, 34, 35, 38, 45, 53; 32:2, 21; 33:11, 14, 15, 16; 34:5, 23, 24, 30; 35:2, 4, 19, 27; 36:8, 29; 37:1, 3, 8, 14, 17, 23, 28; 38:7, 9, 10, 11, 14, 16, 17, 18, 21, 22; 39:4, 6; 40:7, 11; 41:8, 17, 30, 31, 35, 43, 45, 49, 56; 42:3, 5, 17, 26, 29; 43:7, 11, 14, 15, 17, 25, 34; 44:2, 6, 21, 24; 45:4, 7, 10, 12, 16, 21, 24; 46:1, 5, 26, 27, 33; 47:1, 11, 17, 19, 19, 20, 20, 23, 27, 28, 30, 31; 48:1, 7, 10, 13, 14, 17, 20; 49:11, 17; 50:7, 9, 12, 16, 17, 20, 22, 26; Ex 1:7, 9, 11, 19, 20; 2:8, 9, 18; 3:8, 20, 21; 4:3, 3, 4, 6, 11, 17, 20, 21, 23, 27, 29; 5:2, 3, 10, 12, 15, 17, 22; 6:1, 9; 7:3, 4, 6, 10, 15, 16, 20, 21, 22; 8:1, 5, 6, 8, 12, 16, 17, 20, 30; 9:1, 10, 13, 18, 23, 33; 10:1, 3, 3, 5, 8, 13, 18, 22, 27; 11:1, 4, 7, 10; 12:28, 36, 42, 50; 13:3, 10, 15, 18; 14:4, 4, 6, 8, 22, 27; 15:11, 25; 16:17, 23, 29, 30, 35; 17:2, 10, 12, 16; 18:7, 23; 19:8, 9, 14, 20, 25; 21:22; 23:23; 24:13; 25:37; 26:17, 25; 27:2, 18, 20; 28:3, 32, 38, 41; 29:49, 46; 30:30; 31:6; 32:2, 6, 10, 11, 12, 14, 24, 31; 33:6, 13, 13; 34:4, 7; 35:20, 21, 29; 36:2, 6, 6, 18, 22, 30; 37:8; 39:4, 23, 32, 42; 40:15, 17, 30, 33, 38; Lev 1:3, 4; 8:4, 36; 9:5, 8; 10:2, 5, 7; 11:6, 44, 47; 13:6; 14:7, 36; 15:5, 31; 16:13; 17:5, 11, 14; 18:3, 30; 19:5, 12, 17; 20:7, 23; 21:24; 22:2, 29; 23:11, 44; 24:2, 11; 25:21, 42; 26:13, 13, 22, 26; Nu 1:19, 54; 2:9, 16, 24, 31, 34; 3:16, 39, 42, 49; 4:15, 19, 28, 33, 34, 37, 41, 45, 46, 49; 5:3, 4, 22, 24; 7:6, 84; 8:2, 3, 3, 19, 20, 22; 9:4, 6, 6, 20, 23; 10:9, 12; 11:11, 17, 24, 26, 32, 34; 12:4, 11, 13, 15; 13:3, 21, 23, 32; 14:16, 18, 40; 15:36; 16:15, 17, 18, 21, 25, 27, 33, 39, 45; 17:6, 11; 20:2, 9, 11, 27; 21:1, 6, 7, 9, 25, 31; 22:4, 6, 8, 10, 14, 21, 22, 25, 26, 35; 23:3, 14, 16, 17, 28, 30; 24:1; 25:4, 5, 8, 11, 12; 26:3, 51, 63; 27:5, 17, 20, 22; 29:40; 30:13; 31:3, 5, 31, 36, 50, 51, 54; 32:1, 17, 28, 33, 40; 35:20; 36:5, 8; Dt 1:5, 15, 23, 34, 41, 46; 2:4, 7, 8, 14, 21, 22, 29, 30; 3:3, 29; 4:1, 1, 16, 23, 35, 36, 36, 38, 39, 48; 5:31, 31, 32; 6:1, 2, 18, 23; 7:17; 8:5, 6, 15, 17; 9:3, 4, 14, 15, 17, 20; 10:3, 11; 11:8, 14, 18, 21; 12:14, 21, 28; 14:7, 25, 29; 16:3, 12, 20; 17:13; 18:6; 19:3, 13; 20:5, 6; 22:7; 23:20; 24:1, 13; 25:6, 15; 26:8, 12; 27:10; 28:33, 53, 56, 56, 57, 60; 29:6, 9, 18, 18, 24, 29; 30:6, 6, 12, 12, 13, 13, 14; 31:9, 12, 13, 14, 17, 19, 22, 26, 28, 30; 32:11, 26, 44, 46, 52; 33:11, 28; 34:5, 9; Jos 1:8, 18; 2:1, 3, 7; 3:6, 9; 4:4, 8, 17, 24; 5:1, 3, 7, 9, 12; 6:6, 11, 25, 27; 7:1, 4, 21, 22, 26; 8:3, 9, 13, 22, 25, 28; 9:11, 14, 21, 24; 10:3, 5, 7, 13, 20, 23, 40; 11:7, 15, 16, 20, 23, 23; 13:6, 13; 14:5, 9, 12, 13; 15:13, 17, 19, 63; 16:10; 17:4, 14, 17; 19:9, 47, 51; 21:3, 8, 19, 26, 33, 40, 43; 22:4, 6, 9, 22, 26; 23:6, 11; 24:1, 10, 14, 18, 20, 25; Jdg 1:3, 13, 15, 17, 21, 25, 29; 2:5, 14, 20; 3:5, 11, 12, 16, 19, 22, 22, 25, 28, 30; 4:2, 9, 14, 18, 19, 21, 22, 23; 5:28; 6:1, 2, 6, 27, 40; 7:1, 8, 11; 8:7, 9, 21; 9:3, 34, 48, 49, 49, 54, 57; 10:7, 13; 11:3, 11, 17, 21, 23, 32, 39; 12:3, 3, 4, 6; 13:1, 10, 12; 14:14, 16, 17, 18, 20; 15:2, 6, 8, 11, 13, 19; 16:2, 5, 6, 6, 8, 9, 12, 13, 15, 16, 18, 18, 21, 24, 25, 25, 28, 30; 17:4, 6, 12; 18:2, 7, 11, 15, 20, 26, 31; 19:4, 6, 7, 8, 10, 14, 15, 21, 22, 28; 20:6, 11, 13, 19, 24, 29, 32, 34, 35, 42, 46; 21:8, 10, 16, 17, 23, 24, 25; Ru 1:6, 18, 19, 22; 2:3, 10, 13, 14, 17, 19, 19, 23; 3:1, 6, 14; 4:1, 1, 4, 8, 13, 15; 1Sa 1:8, 23; 2:3, 15, 17, 29, 31, 36; 3:5, 8, 9, 9, 14, 18; 4:4, 5, 10; 5:3, 8, 8, 10, 11; 6:3, 10, 14, 21; 7:1, 4, 6, 6, 9, 13; 8:10, 19, 21; 9:4, 10, 11, 14, 24, 24, 26; 10:12, 14, 19, 20, 22, 23; 11:5, 9, 11, 15; 12:9, 18; 13:3, 4, 9, 12, 12, 20, 22; 14:13, 19, 23, 24, 34, 37, 45, 52; 15:4, 6, 11, 23, 31; 16:4, 12, 13, 19, 21; 17:3, 20, 39, 50; 18:5, 9, 16, 19, 22, 26, 27, 30; 19:6, 12, 15, 18; 20:1, 2, 3, 13, 16, 24, 29, 31, 33, 36, 36, 38; 21:6, 8, 10, 13; 22:1, 5, 18; 23:4, 5, 8, 13, 13, 18, 24, 28; 24:2, 7, 13, 22; 25:8, 12, 17, 36, 42; 26:2, 4, 7, 12, 15, 19; 27:2, 4, 6; 28:7, 8, 15, 22, 23, 24; 29:6, 11; 30:7, 9, 10, 16, 22; 31:4, 6, 7, 9; 2Sa 1:10, 10, 12, 15; 2:2, 5, 15, 16, 23, 28; 3:15, 16, 21, 30, 37, 39; 4:6, 12; 5:3, 9, 19, 20, 20, 21, 25; 6:10, 12, 13, 15, 21, 23; 7:17, 26, 29; 8:6, 13; 9:3, 5, 7; 10:2, 3, 4, 6, 15; 11:6, 10, 12, 14, 15, 16, 20, 22; 12:1, 14, 18, 28, 29; 13:2, 4, 4, 6, 7, 8, 9, 10, 18, 20, 20, 29; 14:2, 21, 24, 30, 30, 33; 15:6, 9, 16, 22, 29, 37; 16:11, 13, 14, 22; 17:12, 14, 17, 19, 22, 23; 18:4, 6, 30; 19:8, 15, 26, 27, 28, 39, 43; 20:2, 3, 5, 7, 10, 12, 16, 17, 22; 21:1, 2, 3, 6, 9, 13; 22:39; 23:12, 16, 17; 24:2, 2, 4, 13, 15, 19, 21, 24; 1Ki 1:2, 3, 5, 15, 28, 36, 38, 40, 50, 53; 2:3, 16, 19, 24, 25, 27, 30, 34, 38, 42, 46; 3:4, 8, 9, 11, 22, 24; 4:1; 5:1, 5, 10, 12, 14; 6:6, 7, 14, 22, 36, 38; 7:12, 14, 22, 40, 47, 48, 51; 8:8, 59, 63, 64; 9:1, 3, 13, 17, 21, 25; 10:9, 10, 13, 23; 11:11, 13, 22, 36; 12:5, 15, 16, 20, 24, 28, 33; 13:4, 6, 10, 12, 19, 27, 29; 14:2, 2, 4, 6, 17; 15:19, 29; 16:3, 12, 17, 22; 17:5, 10, 15; 18:2, 3, 6, 16, 17, 20, 26, 28, 34, 37, 40, 42; 19:2, 6, 8, 19; 20:3, 9, 9, 12, 15, 25, 28, 31, 32, 34, 37, 43; 21:2, 4, 5, 8, 11, 13, 16, 20, 25; 22:6, 9, 17, 20, 23, 29, 30, 30, 32, 37; 2Ki 1:2, 4, 5, 11, 15, 17; 2:2, 4, 6, 17, 20; 3:6, 12, 27, 27; 4:5, 20, 22, 24, 30, 40, 42, 43; 5:4, 5, 8, 9, 12, 13, 14, 19, 21; 6:10, 14, 23, 29, 29; 7:4, 4, 5, 7, 10, 12, 14, 16, 17, 20; 8:2, 6, 9, 18, 21; 9:4, 6, 12, 14, 15, 17, 18, 19, 20, 26, 27, 33, 37; 10:1, 5, 8, 11, 15, 16, 20, 22, 24, 25; 11:2, 9, 16, 20; 12:3, 7, 8, 18; 13:3, 5, 17, 18, 21, 25; 14:11; 15:12, 20; 16:9, 10; 17:3, 4, 11, 20, 23, 24, 26, 28, 41; 18:7, 19, 27, 35; 19:24, 26; 20:11; 21:12; 22:10, 14, 19, 20; 23:10, 18, 26; 24:14, 20; 25:1, 21; 1Ch 1:24; 2:3, 4; 4:9, 14, 27; 5:9, 20, 22, 26; 6:57, 60, 64; 10:4, 6, 7, 9, 13, 14; 11:3, 6, 14, 18, 19; 12:18; 13:5, 10, 13; 14:8, 10, 11, 11, 12, 16, 17; 15:12, 14, 17, 28; 16:1, 35; 17:15, 24, 27; 18:6; 19:2, 3, 4, 6, 16; 20:4; 21:2, 4, 6, 11, 14, 16, 19, 22, 25; 22:2, 5, 5, 8, 14, 19; 23:32; 24:2, 5; 28:8, 8, 10; 29:15, 23, 25, 26; 2Ch 1:8; 2:6, 7; 3:1, 13; 4:11, 19; 5:9, 13; 7:3, 5, 6, 7, 10, 11, 13; 8:8, 16; 9:8, 8, 22; 10:5, 15, 16; 11:4, 12; 12:5, 8, 9; 13:12, 18, 20; 14:5, 7, 10, 12, 13; 15:19; 16:3, 10, 13; 17:5, 5, 10, 12; 18:5, 8, 16, 19, 22, 28, 29, 29, 31; 19:4, 10; 20:4, 10, 24, 25, 30, 31, 37; 21:6, 9, 14; 22:1, 8, 11; 23:8, 15, 21; 24:5, 6, 8, 13, 16, 20, 24; 25:10, 16, 21; 26:21, 23; 28:14, 20, 23, 24; 29:8, 10, 17, 22, 30, 31, 34, 35, 36; 30:5, 6, 8, 13, 15, 21, 22, 23; 31:4; 32:17, 18, 21, 22, 25, 26, 30; 33:11, 13; 34:5, 18, 22, 27, 28, 33; 35:12, 13, 22, 24; 36:17, 21; Ezr 2:62, 64, 70; 3:2, 11; 4:2; 5:10, 16, 17; 6:1, 6, 8, 14, 20, 22; 8:16, 23, 30, 32; 9:2, 9; 10:5, 8, 13, 14, 16; Ne 2:2, 2, 6, 15, 18; 4:10, 13; 5:2; 6:3, 7, 9, 15; 7:5, 64, 66, 73; 8:2, 12, 16, 17; 9:11, 12, 25, 27, 30, 36; 10:32, 39; 11:30; 12:40, 45, 47; 13:10, 15, 17, 18, 19, 19, 25, 28, 30; Est 1:19, 21; 2:2, 4, 17; 3:2, 4, 6, 7, 8, 9, 14; 4:6, 9, 12, 17; 5:2, 5, 14; 6:1, 1, 5, 6, 7, 11; 7:1, 3, 10; 8:4, 9, 14; 9:1, 14, 19, 23, 26, 32; Job 1:12; 2:7, 10; 5:12, 13, 16, 19; 6:3, 18, 29; 7:17; 8:4, 9, 16; 9:4, 4, 29, 31, 32; 10:5, 9, 15, 20; 12:11; 14:6, 19; 15:3, 33; 16:3; 17:5; 19:3; 21:4, 16; 22:12, 18; 23:7, 14, 15; 24:15, 18; 25:5; 30:6, 11, 26; 31:28, 34; 32:6, 10, 20; 33:7, 13, 30; 34:4, 28, 30; 37:7, 19, 23; 38:4, 21; 39:11; 40:8; 41:16, 17, 33; 42:9, 12; Ps 3:1, 1, 2; 5:11; 9:14, 14; 10:1, 18; 11:1; 13:6; 18:38; 22:1, 8, 11; 26:11; 27:1, 1; 28:4, 5; 31:19, 19, 24; 32:11; 33:15; 35:8; 37:31; 39:7, 13; 40:12; 41:10; 42:1, 5, 11; 43:5; 45:3, 3; 46:2; 49:8, 13, 16; 51:6; 55:12; 56:4, 11, 13; 62:3; 65:9; 69:4, 9, 16, 23; 73:2, 4, 10, 16, 22; 74:1, 8; 78:6, 7, 20, 33, 44, 53, 62; 80:12, 18; 81:12; 82:5; 85:6; 86:5, 5, 5; 89:38, 50; 90:12, 14; 95:11; 101:6; 102:18, 21, 24; 104:5, 9, 10; 105:43, 45; 106:8, 10, 15, 23, 29, 31, 44, 47; 109:21; 113:9; 116:5, 7, 9, 10; 118:6; 119:77, 133, 140, 166, 175; 125:2; 127:2; 136:5; 139:14; 141:7; 142:7; 144:5; Pr 1:24, 26; 5:7; 6:29; 7:21; 8:29, 32; 9:8; 10:24; 15:7, 12; 17:14; 19:24; 20:19; 22:7, 19; 23:25, 35; 24:6; 25:9, 23; 26:11, 14, 15; 27:19, 20; 30:33; Ecc 1:8, 17; 2:9, 9, 11, 11, 12, 15, 15, 15, 17, 17, 20, 22, 24; 3:11, 12, 18, 19, 22; 4:2, 6, 8, 8, 16; 5:2, 4, 11, 16, 18; 6:10, 11; 7:16, 18; 8:14, 15; 9:3, 7, 15, 17; 10:15; 11:10; 12:10; SS 1:6; 2:4; 3:2, 3; 4:7, 7; 6:13, 13; Isa 1:21, 22; 2:3, 9; 4:1; 5:8, 8, 13; 7:2, 16; 8:19; 10:11, 19, 24; 11:9; 14:22; 16:6, 9; 17:9, 11; 19:12, 14; 22:25; 23:16; 25:5; 28:13, 22, 28; 29:13; 30:14, 18, 26; 33:4; 36:4, 12, 20; 37:25, 27; 38:8; 40:7, 20, 21; 41:7, 9; 43:14, 20; 44:9; 45:3, 6, 8, 19; 47:11, 11; 48:7, 8, 16; 49:4; 50:4; 51:12; 52:14; 54:9; 55:9; 57:7, 12, 13, 14; 58:2; 59:16; 60:15; 63:2, 5, 17; 64:5, 9; 65:8, 16, 17; 66:18, 22; Jer 2:5; 3:5, 9, 9; 4:8; 5:6, 17; 6:5, 11, 12, 16; 7:14, 18, 20, 32, 32; 8:8, 9; 9:12, 15; 10:4, 24; 11:5, 5, 15, 19, 22; 12:1, 1, 8; 13:2, 5, 7, 11, 12, 13; 14:7, 10, 22; 15:18, 19; 16:13, 21; 17:3, 11; 18:3, 4, 6, 11, 21; 19:6, 11; 20:2, 8; 22:15, 25; 25:17, 20; 27:8, 15; 28:9; 29:7, 22, 27; 30:10; 31:37; 32:8, 9, 31, 35, 42; 33:20, 22; 34:6, 12; 35:3, 8, 11, 15; 36:4, 6, 14, 18; 37:4, 21, 21; 38:4, 5, 6, 8, 10, 11, 13, 16; 39:4, 13, 14, 17; 40:6, 8; 42:8, 12, 18, 22; 43:3, 4; 44:4, 6; 48:9; 50:2, 15, 29; 51:9, 49, 62; 52:3, 4, 27; La 1:8; 2:14; 3:26, 44; 4:14, 15; 5:20; Eze 1:20; 3:2, 9, 23, 25, 26; 4:8, 17; 5:7, 14; 6:12; 7:27; 8:5, 5, 8, 10, 11; 9:6, 7, 10; 10:6; 11:8, 15, 20, 24; 12:3, 3, 4, 7, 16; 13:20; 14:4, 7; 16:8, 13, 13, 15, 31, 34, 37, 45, 50, 52; 17:7, 8, 9, 10, 14, 19; 19:9; 20:10, 11, 13, 21, 26; 21:13, 24; 22:19, 26, 30, 31; 23:7, 9, 9, 16, 17, 18, 21, 24; 24:6, 8, 12, 18, 20, 27; 28:16, 17, 18; 29:8, 18; 30:19, 21; 31:4, 10; 32:19; 33:5, 11, 22, 28, 31; 34:5, 22, 29; 36:18, 27; 37:7, 9, 10, 20; 39:14, 15, 16, 25; 40:4, 41; 42:12, 19, 20; 43:8, 10, 11; 44:9, 12, 19, 30; 46:11; 47:17; 48:22; Da 1:14, 16, 19; 2:1, 15, 16, 18; 3:7, 19, 21, 23, 26; 4:6, 6, 36; 5:2, 3, 9, 10, 13, 19, 24; 6:5, 6, 8, 9, 12, 16, 17, 22, 28; 7:14, 16, 19, 19; 8:5, 17, 26; 9:3, 11, 18, 23; 10:8; 11:6; 12:8; Hos 1:2, 3; 2:18, 18; 3:2; 4:5, 8, 9, 16, 19; 5:10; 6:2, 11; 9:2, 7;

10:4, 6; **12:**6, 14; **13:**7; **14:**2; **Joel 2:**14, 17; **Am 1:**4, 7, 10, 12, 14; **2:**2, 5, 10, 13; **3:**12; **4:**5; **5:**13, 27; **7:**3; **8:**5; **9:**1, 1; **Ob** 15, 16; **Jnh 1:**6; **3:**3; **4:**2, 7; **Mic 1:**6, 13; **3:**12; **4:**2, 13; **5:**13; **6:**12; **7:**16; **Na 3:**5; **Hab 2:**2, 13, 15; **Zep 1:**4, 5; **2:**14, 15; **3:**7, 8, 9; **Hag 1:**3, 11, 14; **2:**5, 15, 17; **Zec 1:**10; **2:**4; **3:**4, 5; **6:**7; **7:**3, 12, 12, 14, 14; **8:**13, 15, 19; **9:**2, 3, 5; **10:**1, 2; **11:**1, 7, 9, 12, 13; **12:**7; **13:**2; **Mal 1:**10; **2:**4, 9, 15, 16; **3:**1, 3, 10, 10; **Mt 1:**19; **2:**8, 21, 23; **3:**11, 14, 15; **4:**15, 24; **5:**16, 19, 23, 29; **6:**16, 25, 30, 30, 31, 32, 34; **7:**19; **8:**4, 26, 28, 31, 32; **9:**4, 9, 33, 36, 37, 37, 38; **10:**31; **11:**2, 17, 25; **12:**1, 10, 22, 27, 40, 44, 45; **13:**15, 22, 40, 56, 58; **14:**7, 10, 15, 29; **15:**6, 14, 35; **16:**8, 8, 11; **17:**2, 16, 27; **18:**8, 16, 25; **19:**13; **20:**4, 16; **21:**20, 27, 36, 39; **22:**4, 10, 25, 26, 28, 32; **23:**3, 24, 25; **24:**2, 14, 24, 26, 27, 28, 33, 42; **25:**13, 21, 23, 25, 27; **26:**19, 44, 49, 59; **27:**3, 21, 24, 26, 40, 42, 48, 64, 66; **28:**15; **Mk 1:**7, 34, 39, 44; **2:**2, 4, 8, 14; **4:**7, 12, 12, 19, 36, 40; **5:**1, 13, 20, 23, 27, 30; **6:**12, 20, 20, 25, 27, 31, 34, 36, 40; **7:**5, 29; **8:**6, 7, 13, 14, 17, 17; **9:**10, 18, 20; **10:**13, 42, 46, 49; **11:**11, 13, 18, 25, 33; **12:**8, 12, 21, 23, 27, 28; **13:**2, 22, 29, 35; **14:**11, 13, 16, 55; **15:**15, 32, 36, 44; **16:**5, 6; **Lk 1:**21, 35, 62, 74; **2:**22, 24, 27, 52; **3:**16, 20; **4:**44; **5:**3, 5, 6, 14, 19, 22, 28, 33; **6:**8, 33, 46; **7:**4, 6, 18, 32, 36, 42, 47; **8:**10, 14, 18, 22, 24, 26, 33, 37, 39; **9:**6, 9, 12, 15, 39, 45, 47, 56; **10:**2, 2, 21, 29, 41; **11:**8, 9, 17, 19, 25, 26, 37, 39, 41; **12:**7, 18, 22, 28, 28, 32; **14:**18, 20, 23, 23, 33; **15:**3, 12, 16, 20, 24; **16:**2, 5, 6, 8, 25, 28; **17:**37; **18:**7, 15, 38; **19:**4, 4, 17, 22, 23, 32, 35; **20:**11, 15, 20, 26, 31, 33, 38; **21:**6, 14, 28, 31; **22:**6, 6, 8, 32, 54; **23:**3, 16, 24, 39, 56; **24:**3, 9, 11, 17, 25, 29; **Jn 1:**7, 14, 22, 34; **2:**3, 8; **3:**7, 8, 14, 15, 16, 16, 21; **4:**3, 20, 22, 24, 30, 40; **5:**10, 14, 16, 17, 18, 23, 28, 34, 40; **6:**10, 12, 15, 27, 51, 53, 61; **7:**9, 15, 16, 23, 23, 43; **8:**7, 28, 36, 43, 45; **9:**3, 7, 15, 16, 18, 19, 24; **10:**7, 12, 29, 35; **11:**3, 29, 31, 31, 41, 42, 49, 53, 55, 57; **12:**18, 35, 40, 46, 50; **13:**4, 18, 19, 30, 34; **14:**2, 3, 5, 9, 27, 29, 31; **15:**2, 11, 16, 19; **16:**1, 4, 12, 19, 33; **17:**1, 10, 11, 12, 13, 19, 21, 22, 24, 26; **18:**12, 15, 29, 39; **19:**11, 16, 20, 24, 25, 29, 31, 32, 33, 35, 42; **20:**21, 31; **21:**3, 6, 6, 11, 23; **Ac 1:**12, 21, 23; **2:**36; **3:**2, 10, 12, 19; **4:**4, 15, 18; **5:**15, 21, 22, 31, 32, 38; **6:**2, 11, 12; **7:**4, 8, 10, 12, 15, 19, 24, 34, 35, 41, 43, 51; **8:**8, 19, 27, 30, 35; **9:**1, 9, 12, 17, 17, 24, 25, 38, 39; **10:**21, 22, 23, 27, 29, 33, 48; **11:**29; **12:**9, 10, 14, 20, 23; **13:**3, 16, 45, 49; **14:**8, 10, 18; **15:**6, 7, 17, 19, 25, 27, 39, 41; **16:**3, 5, 8, 10, 18, 19, 24, 27, 36, 37; **17:**5, 5, 22; **18:**11, 21; **19:**9, 10, 12, 20; **20:**3; **21:**11, 26, 34, 35, 40; **22:**5, 24, 27; **23:**6, 9, 18, 31; **24:**26; **25:**5, 10, 21, 23, 26, 26; **26:**1, 11, 18, 19, 22, 28; **27:**3, 4, 7, 9, 13, 15, 17, 25, 29, 32, 40, 43, 44; **28:**2, 13, 14, 20, 20, 23, 27, 28; **Ro 1:**5, 11, 15, 20, 24, 25, 27; **2:**5, 23, 27; **3:**28; **4:**2, 3, 11, 14, 16; **5:**11, 12, 20, 21; **6:**1, 6, 11, 15, 19; **7:**3, 4, 10, 13, 18, 25; **8:**1, 4, 12, 15, 29; **9:**16, 17, 18, 31; **11:**7, 7, 8, 8, 10, 17, 25, 26, 32, 35; **12:**1, 5, 6; **13:**2, 3, 5, 6, 10, 12, 13; **14:**4, 6, 8, 9, 10, 13, 19; **15:**7, 9, 13, 14, 15, 16, 17, 22; **16:**4, 6, 12, 23, 26; **1Co 1:**10, 20, 23, 29; **2:**5, 12; **3:**18, 21; **4:**1, 5, 10, 10, 16; **5:**1, 2, 5, 7, 8; **6:**3, 18, 20; **7:**2, 5, 5, 5, 24, 29, 33, 38; **8:**4, 7, 11; **9:**19, 20, 20, 22, 22, 23, 26; **10:**6, 13, 13, 14, 33; **11:**2, 10, 19, 27, 33, 34; **12:**3, 12, 23, 24, 25; **13:**2; **14:**5, 10, 12, 13, 22, 23, 31, 39; **15:**11, 21, 28, 39, 44, 49, 52, 58; **16:**17, 18; **2Co 1:**4, 6, 6, 11, 15, 24; **2:**1, 3, 7, 10, 11, 13; **3:**11, 13, 14, 18; **4:**1, 4, 7, 10, 11, 12, 13, 18; **5:**4, 6, 9, 11, 12, 15, 16, 21; **6:**3; **7:**7, 9, 12; **8:**6, 7, 7, 9, 13, 24; **9:**4, 5, 11, 12; **11:**8, 15, 19, 22, 22, 22; **12:**1, 4, 9, 9; **Gal 1:**6, 16; **2:**16, 19, 19, 20; **3:**4, 6, 9, 15, 22, 23, 24, 26; **4:**5, 17, 17, 20, 31; **5:**1, 7, 16; **6:**9, 13; **Eph 1:**6, 7, 17, 18; **2:**4, 4, 7, 9, 10, 19; **3:**13, 13, 19; **4:**10, 16, 25, 29; **5:**15, 24, 33; **6:**11, 13, 15; **Php 1:**10, 18, 25, 25; **2:**10, 12, 15, 16, 27, 28; **3:**5, 6, 7, 8, 11; **4:**1, 14; **Col 1:**9, 11, 18, 21, 28; **2:**4, 7, 16, 18, 20; **3:**5, 13; **4:**6, 10, 14, 16; **1Th 1:**6; **2:**3, 5, 8, 9, 10; **3:**7; **4:**1, 3, 10, 13, 18; **5:**6, 10, 11; **2Th 1:**11; **2:**2, 11; **3:**8, 14; **1Ti 1:**7, 16, 20; **2:**2, 8; **3:**6, 7, 15; **4:**15; **5:**7, 14, 20, 23; **6:**1, 8, 11, 12, 16, 19; **2Ti 1:**8; **2:**15; **4:**1, 21, 21; **Tit 1:**5, 13; **2:**8, 15; **3:**8; **Phm 1:**6, 7, 9, 15, 17, 24; **Heb 2:**1, 4, 11, 17; **3:**1, 10, 11, 13, 19; **4:**1, 6, 7, 9, 16; **5:**8, 11, 11; **6:**1, 3, 17, 18; **8:**9, 10, 10; **9:**11, 14, 15, 28; **10:**5, 15, 16, 16, 19, 36; **11:**6, 9, 12, 12, 22, 28; **12:**1, 3, 12, 15, 19, 21, 27; **13:**6, 9, 12, 13, 19; **Jas 1:**4, 11, 16, 21; **2:**11, 12, 17, 22, 23, 23, 24, 26; **3:**5, 10, 13; **4:**2, 2, 7, 12; **5:**12, 16; **1Pe 1:**6, 7, 12, 13, 17, 22; **2:**1, 2, 8, 9, 11, 24; **3:**4, 14, 19; **4:**1, 6, 10, 19; **5:**6, 13; **2Pe 1:**5, 10, 15; **2:**9, 10, 12; **3:**9, 14, 15, 17; **1Jn 1:**3, 4, 6; **2:**1, 21, 24, 27, 27, 28; **3:**1, 6, 9, 10, 13, 16, 19; **4:**5, 9, 17; **5:**7, 12, 13, 20; **2Jn** 8, 8, 8; **3Jn** 8, 8; **Rev 1:**1; **3:**11, 18, 18; **8:**11; **10:**9, 10; **11:**6; **13:**15; **14:**16, 19; **16:**2, 6, 12, 15, 19; **17:**3, 7, 17; **18:**6, 7, 14, 14, 16; **20:**3; **21:**10; **22:**14

THAT (5637)

Ge 1:4, 10, 11, 12, 18, 21, 25, 31; **2:**9, 12; **3:**3, 5, 7, 11; **4:**26; **5:**29; **6:**5, 7, 17; **7:**2, 3, 8, 13, 22; **8:**7, 11, 20, 20; **9:**4, 5, 15, 15, 22; **10:**32; **11:**4, 8, 8, 9, 9; **12:**1, 6, 8, 10; **13:**1, 7, 9, 11, 16; **14:**3, 14, 16, 17, 23; **15:**5, 8, 12, 13, 14, 18; **16:**14, 16; **17:**10, 11, 22, 23, 24; **18:**15, 15, 19, 19, 20, 20, 25; **19:**1, 21, 22, 22, 29, 32, 33, 34, 35; **20:**2, 3, 6, 7, 9, 13; **21:**7, 10, 22, 23, 23, 25, 29, 30, 31, 31, 33; **22:**11, 12, 16, 20; **23:**15, 17; **24:**3, 7, 9, 14, 28, 37, 49, 65; **25:**16, 25, 30, 33, 34; **26:**7, 12, 15, 22, 25, 28, 29, 32, 33, 33; **27:**4, 11, 12, 25, 27, 33, 37; **28:**6, 6, 7, 8, 12; **29:**12, 20, 23, 27, 33; **30:**1, 9, 15, 16, 27, 32, 33, 33, 35, 35, 35, 38; **31:**1, 10, 12, 12, 26, 32, 32, 37, 38, 42, 43, 49; **32:**5, 6, 11, 21, 25, 32, 32; **33:**13, 16, 17; **34:**5, 7, 7, 30; **35:**5, 16, 19; **36:**20; **37:**19, 20, 22, 26, 29; **38:**11, 13, 14, 16, 22, 22, 24, 26; **39:**3, 13, 13, 16, 17, 22, 23; **40:**10, 16; **41:**1, 15, 15, 20, 30, 31, 32, 32, 33, 36, 49; **42:**1, 6, 15, 16, 23, 29, 34; **43:**3, 5, 12, 14, 16, 18; **44:**7, 9, 10, 15, 27, 28, 31, 32; **45:**3, 5, 7, 10, 12; **46:**3, 31; **47:**5, 17, 19, 22, 26, 29, 30, 31; **48:**1, 2, 7, 17, 20, 22; **49:**9, 17, 27, 28, 32; **50:**5, 13, 15; **Ex 1:**6, 7, 19; **2:**13, 14, 14, 16; **3:**3, 4, 12, 16, 19, 21; **4:**5, 26, 31, 31; **5:**2, 2, 6, 9, 16, 19; **6:**1, 5, 7, 13, 28; **7:**2, 5, 9, 9, 15, 17, 21; **8:**9, 10, 15, 22, 22, 26, 26; **9:**4, 5, 7, 14, 14, 15, 16, 16, 24, 26, 29, 30; **10:**2, 5, 5, 6, 7, 11, 13, 15, 19, 23; **11:**1, 1, 7, 7; **12:**3, 8, 10, 12, 17, 20, 37, 41, 51; **13:**15, 15, 16, 17, 17, 19, 21; **14:**4, 5, 13, 18, 21, 30, 31; **15:**17, 23, 25; **16:**3, 4, 6, 12, 13, 16, 26, 29, 29, 29, 32; **18:**9, 11, 14, 22; **19:**12, 13; **20:**10, 11, 22, 25; **21:**6, 29; **22:**3, 31; **23:**2, 3, 4, 8, 11, 15, 15, 18, 33; **24:**12; **25:**2, 22, 40; **26:**25; **27:**10, 10, 16, 16; **28:**2, 3, 15, 21; **29:**13, 22, 23, 25, 27, 27, 37, 44, 46, 46; **30:**6; **31:**13, 14; **32:**13, 21, 25, 28; **33:**1, 1, 13, 16; **34:**1, 9, 10, 18, 24, 28, 28, 29; **35:**2, 2, 3, 10; **38:**4, 18, 25, 31; **39:**34; **40:**23; **Lev 1:**5; **2:**14; **4:**7, 18; **5:**2, 2, 2, 10; **6:**2, 4, 11, 15, 18, 30; **7:**9, 11, 16, 19, 19, 20, 21, 21, 36; **8:**26, 30, 31, 32, 33; **9:**22; **10:**11, 14, 14, 15, 16; **11:**3, 10, 12, 20, 21, 21, 23, 26, 26, 27, 27, 29, 32, 32, 34, 34, 35, 39, 41, 42, 44, 46; **12:**4; **13:**2, 8, 10, 11, 11, 12, 18, 19, 20, 20, 21, 22, 23, 25, 26, 27, 27, 31, 32, 34, 34, 37, 55, 56; **14:**3, 5, 7, 11, 19, 29, 40, 42, 44, 48, 50; **15:**10, 13, 17, 19, 20, 26, 28, 31, 31; **16:**12, 13, 13, 18, 34; **17:**4, 6, 11, 12, 13, 14, 15, 15; **18:**10, 25; **19:**6, 10, 26, 34; **20:**23, 24, 25; **21:**15, 17; **22:**2, 3, 4, 5, 8, 21, 22, 22, 33; **23:**6, 12, 14, 17, 21, 24, 25, 27, 27, 28, 29, 30, 32, 32, 36, 38, 39, 40, 43; **24:**18; **25:**4, 5, 5, 6, 10, 11, 11, 11, 12, 12, 13, 20, 24, 27, 29, 33, 41, 50, 54; **26:**10, 22, 36, 46; **27:**2, 4, 5, 6, 9, 11, 16, 22, 34; **Nu 1:**18; **2:**17; **3:**26; **4:**8, 15, 26; **5:**9, 10, 18, 19, 21, 22, 27, 30; **6:**4, 5, 11, 12, 20; **7:**86, 89; **8:**2, 22; **9:**6, 6, 11, 15; **10:**3, 14, 18, 22, 25, 32; **11:**3, 5, 12, 17, 22, 22, 25, 25, 29, 29, 31, 32, 34; **12:**7, 14; **13:**23, 24; **14:**8, 14, 14, 14, 14, 15, 17, 22, 24, 40, 44; **15:**13, 19, 22, 28, 39, 40, 41; **16:**9, 11, 13, 13, 17, 21, 26, 28, 28, 30, 34, 39, 40, 42, 45, 49; **17:**8; **18:**8, 9, 9, 13, 15, 18, 19, 24; **19:**2, 14, 14, 15, 16, 18, 19, 22; **20:**2, 15, 20, 29; **21:**1, 7; **22:**5, 6, 6, 9, 20, 22, 26, 28, 36, 38; **23:**13, 19, 19, 26; **24:**1, 8, 13; **25:**12; **26:**3, 10, 11, 64; **27:**7; **28:**2, 18, 25, 26, 27, 31; **29:**1, 2, 7, 12, 13, 35; **31:**2, 23, 23, 23, 28, 30, 32, 52, 54; **32:**1, 13, 23, 41, 42; **33:**4, 40, 40; **34:**13; **35:**22, 33; **36:**4, 8, 13; **Dt 1:**1, 9, 14, 17, 18, 20, 25, 28, 28; **2:**7, 8, 12, 14, 20; **3:**18, 18, 21, 21, 23; **4:**1, 1, 8, 10, 14, 14, 20, 20, 21, 28, 34, 35, 35, 40, 44, 45, 47; **5:**14, 15, 15, 15, 22, 29, 29, 33; **6:**1, 10, 18, 20; **7:**8, 9, 17; **8:**3, 5, 7, 11, 11, 14, 14, 15, 17, 17, 18; **9:**1, 3, 4, 5, 9, 9, 9, 20, 21, 25; **10:**1, 2, 8, 9, 13, 21; **11:**6, 12, 17, 21, 27, 31; **12:**2, 8, 15, 16, 21, 22, 28, 31; **13:**6, 7, 13, 14, 15, 16, 17; **14:**3, 6, 10, 11, 20, 21; **15:**5, 11, 12, 15, 15, 17, 17, 18; **16:**1, 3, 5, 8, 12, 20; **17:**2, 4, 5, 8, 15, 19, 20; **18:**1, 1, 3, 12, 15, 16, 18, 22; **19:**3, 7, 10, 11, 12, 13; **20:**14, 19, 20; **21:**3, 3, 4, 13, 23; **22:**8, 17, 26, 27; **23:**19, 21; **24:**1, 4, 18, 18, 18, 22, 22; **25:**1, 6, 8, 15; **26:**3, 3, 12, 17, 18, 18, 19; **27:**1, 10, 11; **28:**10, 50, 53, 55, 57, 57, 58, 60, 64, 66; **29:**4, 4, 4, 6, 9, 13, 18, 18, 26, 26, 27, 29, 29; **30:**2, 5, 5, 6, 12, 13, 14, 18, 19, 19; **31:**2, 7, 13, 17, 18, 22, 28, 29; **32:**1, 5, 11, 24, 27, 28, 29, 29, 48; **33:**1, 14; **34:**12; **Jos 1:**2, 8, 15; **2:**1, 8, 12, 12, 19, 23; **3:**7, 10, 16; **4:**7, 14, 19, 20, 24, 24; **5:**2, 9, 10, 12, 12; **6:**11, 26; **7:**8, 11, 12, 12, 14, 14, 21, 26; **8:**9, 9, 12, 13, 21, 21, 25, 29, 31, 31; **9:**22, 24, 24, 27, 27; **10:**1, 1, 11, 14, 14, 17, 20, 21, 28; **13:**3; **14:**9, 9, 11, 12, 12; **15:**7, 9, 13, 25, 49, 54, 60; **16:**2; **17:**11; **18:**1, 13, 14, 28; **19:**51; **20:**6, 6, 6, 7; **21:**4, 11, 45; **22:**5, 9, 17, 20, 23, 24, 27, 28, 29, 29, 34; **23:**13, 14; **24:**12, 25, 31; **Jdg 1:**26, 27; **2:**1, 10, 18, 21, 23; **3:**16, 22, 30; **4:**12, 23, 24; **5:**1, 14, 21; **6:**2, 17, 22, 25, 25, 28, 28, 29, 37, 38, 40; **7:**1, 2; **8:**3, 10, 14, 28, 35; **9:**9, 13, 16, 24, 25, 26, 36, 38, 38, 47, 53, 54, 55; **10:**8, 8, 17; **11:**21, 29, 35; **12:**6; **14:**4, 6, 8; **15:**5, 12, 15, 19; **16:**2, 7, 9, 11, 28; **17:**8; **18:**4, 26; **19:**9, 10, 16; **20:**3, 5, 21, 32, 34, 35, 36, 39, 44, 46; **21:**5, 5, 8, 17, 18, 19; **Ru 1:**6, 7, 18; **2:**3, 5, 17, 18, 20; **3:**1, 1, 6, 12, 14; **4:**3, 4, 4, 5, 5, 9; **1Sa 1:**3, 8, 11, 17; **2:**14, 15, 18, 22, 30, 34; **3:**13, 14, 20; **4:**1, 5, 10, 12, 19, 19; **5:**5; **6:**3, 4, 7, 9, 15, 16, 17; **7:**2, 2, 6, 6, 7, 7, 10, 14, 14; **8:**18; **9:**20, 20, 21, 23; **10:**2, 2, 6, 9, 12, 16, 18; **11:**8, 9, 11; **12:**5, 12, 17, 20, 20, 21, 22; **13:**3, 4, 4, 8; **14:**3, 4, 10, 10, 17, 18, 23, 24, 28, 28, 29, 29, 32, 33, 33, 34, 37, 39, 43; **15:**9, 11, 11, 15, 29; **16:**2, 2, 13, 14, 15, 18; **17:**5, 7, 12, 26, 27, 43, 46, 47, 51; **18:**2, 5, 9, 18, 25, 25; **19:**8, 8, 16, 18, 19; **20:**1, 3, 9, 12, 21, 22, 26, 26, 29, 30, 31, 33, 34; **21:**6, 6, 7, 8, 9; **22:**8, 8, 21, 22; **23:**1, 7, 10, 13, 15, 22, 25, 27, 28; **24:**1, 3, 11, 11, 13, 16, 20, 21, 21; **25:**4, 7, 17, 34, 36, 39; **26:**8, 11, 12, 16, 16, 17; **27:**4; **28:**1, 9, 14; **30:**1, 8, 15, 17, 19; **31:**5, 6, 7, 7; **2Sa 1:**2, 5, 12, 16, 18; **2:**4, 7, 16, 18, 20, 23, 29, 30; **3:**1, 8, 9, 19, 23, 25, 28, 37, 38; **5:**8, 12, 17, 20, 24, 24; **6:**8, 8, 17; **7:**4, 11, 18, 23, 25, 26, 27, 29; **8:**9; **9:**1, 7, 7, 9, 11, 11; **10:**3, 9, 15, 19; **11:**5, 9, 11, 11, 12, 15, 26; **12:**3, 7, 8, 20, 21, 25, 31; **13:**2, 2, 20; **14:**7, 8, 10, 11, 14, 17, 20, 22; **15:**10, 21, 30, 31, 35; **16:**4, 12, 21; **17:**3, 8, 9, 11, 11, 11, 12, 12, 14, 21; **18:**3, 7, 19, 20, 32; **19:**1, 2, 6, 7, 8, 11, 20, 26, 27, 27, 29, 34, 41; **20:**3, 4, 6, 10, 12; **21:**1, 2, 3, 14, 17; **23:**4, 6, 10, 15, 17, 18, 22; **24:**2, 4, 15, 16, 16, 18, 21, 24; **1Ki 1:**5, 11, 11, 13, 17, 24, 24, 30, 40, 51, 51, 51; **2:**3, 5, 5, 8, 9, 15, 19, 22, 22, 41; **3:**2, 3, 5, 9, 10, 21, 23; **4:**30, 33; **5:**1, 3, 5, 6, 14; **6:**1, 2, 22, 36; **7:**3, 6, 12, 18, 32, 32, 41, 42, 42, 45; **8:**5, 8, 9, 12, 21, 24, 28, 36, 43, 44, 44, 47, 53, 58, 59, 59, 60, 60, 64; **9:**3, 7, 9, 13, 15, 21; **10:**22, 27, 29; **11:**21, 22, 36, 37; **12:**4, 16, 32, 33; **13:**3, 4, 4, 11; **14:**1, 2, 5, 11, 13, 15, 22; **15:**15, 18, 19, 19, 22, 22, 26, 29, 34; **16:**16, 18, 19, 26, 34; **17:**12, 13, 24, 24; **18:**1, 9, 10, 10, 11, 14, 14, 15, 16, 30, 36, 36, 36, 37, 37; **19:**1, 4, 11; **20:**4, 5, 7, 10, 13, 23, 25, 27, 28, 28, 31; **21:**3, 3, 5, 23; **22:**3, 8, 13, 16, 20, 35, 47, 49; **2Ki 1:**11; **2:**3, 5, 21; **3:**2, 3, 25, 26; **4:**8, 13, 16, 17, 22; **5:**7, 8, 15, 22, 26; **6:**9, 17, 20, 23, 28, 30; **7:**2, 5, 10, 15, 16, 16, 19; **8:**1, 5, 6, 6, 6, 7, 10, 13, 14, 19, 22; **9:**11, 12, 21, 26, 26, 30, 37; **10:**9, 10, 10, 10, 19, 22, 23, 27, 29, 31, 32; **11:**1, 9, 10, 17; **12:**5, 10, 16, 18; **13:**2, 11, 17, 25; **14:**10, 24; **15:**9, 16, 18, 20, 24, 28; **16:**6, 18; **17:**9, 13, 19, 29, 37; **18:**4, 11, 17, 19, 20, 21, 27, 27, 35; **19:**7, 9, 10, 17, 19, 21, 24, 25, 26, 29, 29, 35; **20:**1, 8, 8, 9, 12, 13; **21:**6, 8, 8, 12, 16, 21; **22:**13, 19; **23:**2, 3, 4, 7, 11, 12, 12, 15, 16, 17, 17, 22, 24, 33; **24:**7, 13; **25:**8, 13, 23, 24, 25, 27; **1Ch 2:**7; **4:**10, 10; **5:**2, 8, 9, 25; **6:**49; **7:**28; **9:**4, 4, 23; **10:**5, 7, 7; **11:**7, 17, 19, 20, 24; **12:**38; **13:**11, 11; **14:**2, 8, 11, 15, 15; **16:**7, 23, 28, 31, 40; **17:**3, 10, 16, 21, 23, 24, 25, 27; **18:**9; **19:**3, 7, 10, 16, 19; **20:**3; **21:**4, 15, 15, 22, 24, 28, 29, 29; **22:**3, 12, 13, 14, 19; **23:**27, 29, 31; **24:**5; **26:**23, 26, 30; **27:**1; **28:**8, 20; **29:**12, 14, 16, 17, 18, 22, 30; **2Ch 1:**3, 7, 15, 17; **2:**1, 3, 8, 11, 15; **3:**1, 9, 12, 15; **4:**3, 7, 12, 13, 13, 18; **5:**6, 9, 10, 11, 13; **6:**1, 6, 6, 11, 15, 19, 27, 33, 34, 34, 37; **7:**13, 20, 20, 22; **8:**2, 3, 8, 16; **9:**27; **10:**4, 16; **11:**22; **12:**8; **13:**5, 8, 8, 14, 17; **14:**11, 13, 14; **15:**9, 11, 13, 18; **16:**3, 3, 6, 7, 8, 10, 10; **17:**2, 10; **18:**7, 12, 15, 19, 34; **19:**6, 6, 10, 11; **20:**3, 12, 16, 25, 26, 27, 29; **21:**7, 10, 14, 18; **22:**7, 10, 11; **23:**3, 8, 9, 16; **24:**5, 6, 9, 20, 22; **25:**5, 13, 16, 19, 24; **26:**18; **28:**5, 16, 24; **29:**8, 10, 24, 25, 27; **30:**3, 6, 8; **31:**6, 14, 21; **32:**2, 4, 10, 12, 22, 24, 31; **33:**6, 8, 13, 14, 15; **34:**4, 4, 9, 17, 21, 30, 31; **35:**1, 1, 6, 16; **36:**10; **Ezr 2:**59; **3:**13; **4:**1, 9, 12, 13, 15, 16, 19, 21; **5:**1, 6, 8, 10, 11, 13, 14, 14, 17; **6:**1, 2, 8, 8, 9, 12, 22; **7:**8, 13, 16, 18, 24; **8:**15, 21, 23, 25; **9:**7, 9, 11, 12, 12; **10:**2, 5, 5, 7, 13, 14, 16; **Ne 1:**6, 7; **2:**10, 12; **3:**15, 25, 32; **4:**1, 3, 7, 7, 10, 10, 15, 15, 22; **5:**14, 14, 15, 19; **6:**1, 1, 6, 6, 6, 7, 7, 7, 9, 12, 12, 14, 16; **7:**4, 61, 73; **8:**4, 14, 14, 14, 15; **9:**10, 12, 13, 13, 21, 36; **10:**31, 32, 38; **12:**40, 43, 44; **13:**1, 1, 5, 6, 7, 9, 10, 14, 15, 16, 18, 18, 19, 19, 21, 23, 25, 30, 31, 31; **Est 1:**2, 8, 17, 19, 19, 19, 19, 22; **2:**3, 4, 14, 17; **3:**5, 6, 9, 13, 14; **4:**8, 11, 13, 14; **5:**14; **6:**1, 4; **7:**2, 3, 4, 7, 9; **8:**1, 8, 13, 13; **9:**1, 11, 12, 18, 26; **10:**3; **Job 1:**3; **2:**13; **3:**4, 6, 7, 8; **4:**6, 8; **5:**3, 13, 19, 24, 27; **6:**3, 8, 8, 11, 15; **7:**1, 7, 12, 17; **8:**19; **9:**14, 22, 26, 35; **10:**6, 9, 15, 20; **12:**9; **13:**9, 16, 25; **14:**7; **15:**9, 9, 13, 24, 28, 33; **16:**3, 5, 21, 22; **17:**12; **18:**4, 5; **19:**4, 23, 23, 25, 25, 29; **20:**4, 29; **21:**7, 16, 19; **22:**4, 8, 10, 11, 18, 18; **24:**18; **25:**5; **27:**5, 11, 17, 17, 19; **28:**7; **29:**16; **30:**13, 23; **31:**8, 11, 12, 23, 25, 34, 35, 40; **32:**2, 2, 5, 8, 14, 16; **33:**2, 23; **34:**10; **35:**9; **36:**20, 21, 29; **37:**18, 20, 23; **38:**2, 15, 27; **39:**15, 15, 27; **41:**8; **42:**2, 3, 16; **Ps 8:**4, 4, 8; **9:**14; **10:**4; **14:**7; **16:**5; **20:**6; **21:**2; **26:**11; **27:**13; **30:**12; **31:**18; **32:**6, 9; **34:**8, 12; **35:**15, 21; **37:**18; **39:**4, 4; **40:**6; **41:**8, 11; **44:**3, 3; **46:**5, 10; **48:**13, 14; **49:**20; **50:**16, 23; **51:**15; **52:**T, 4; **53:**6; **55:**12; **58:**4, 8; **59:**7, 7, 12, 13; **60:**3; **66:**15; **68:**30; **69:**4, 34; **71:**8, 16, 18; **72:**6; **73:**13, 20; **74:**2, 7, 9, 15; **77:**1, 10, 20; **78:**6, 35, 35, 39; **79:**6, 6; **80:**12, 15; **81:**5, 7, 13, 13; **83:**18, 18; **86:**11, 11; **90:**5, 5, 12; **91:**6, 6; **94:**11, 20; **95:**7; **96:**2, 7, 10; **100:**3; **102:**18; **104:**6, 16, 19; **105:**44; **106:**9, 14, 22, 26, 27, 31, 40; **107:**12, 30; **109:**23, 27, 27; **110:**3; **113:**9; **114:**1, 5, 5; **119:**5, 11, 17, 35, 41, 75, 101, 116, 128, 140, 144, 146, 152; **128:**4; **130:**4; **132:**1, 6, 12; **133:**2, 2, 3; **135:**5; **139:**24; **144:**3, 3; **148:**8; **150:**6; **Pr 1:**31; **3:**25; **5:**22; **6:**17, 18, 18, 35; **7:**23; **8:**13; **9:**18; **10:**26, 31, 32; **11:**21, 30, 31; **12:**20, 20; **14:**12; **16:**5, 17, 25; **19:**24; **24:**31; **25:**3, 14; **26:**15; **27:**8; **28:**3, 24; **30:**15, 15, 17, 18, 20, 21, 24; **31:**1, 9, 27; **Ecc 1:**10, 13, 17; **2:**1, 9, 14, 18, 24; **3:**12, 14, 14, 16, 18, 18, 18, 21, 22, 22; **4:**1, 2, 3, 4; **5:**1, 5, 6, 6, 10, 14, 18, 19; **6:**4; **7:**12, 14, 14, 14, 15, 25, 25, 26, 29; **8:**8, 8, 9, 10, 12, 14, 15, 16, 16, 17; **9:**3, 3, 9, 13, 16, 18; **10:**15; **11:**8, 9, 10; **SS 3:**6; **4:**11, 12; **5:**8, 9; **6:**13; **8:**13; **Isa 1:**31; **2:**1, 3, 12; **3:**15; **4:**1, 4; **5:**2, 11, 15, 20, 20, 20, 25, 25; **6:**10, 13, 13; **7:**3, 11, 12, 18, 20, 22, 23; **8:**2, 4, 12, 14, 14, 14, 18; **9:**1, 1, 2, 4, 4, 5, 8, 17; **10:**7, 17, 19, 19, 22, 27, 32, 33; **11:**6, 10, 11, 15; **12:**1, 4; **14:**3, 29, 29, 29, 32, 32; **16:**5, 9; **17:**4, 11; **19:**16, 18, 19, 21, 22, 23; **22:**14, 14, 25, 25; **23:**7, 13, 16; **24:**21, 23; **25:**7, 7, 9; **26:**1; **27:**1, 2, 13; **28:**1, 15, 16, 19, 22; **29:**14, 16, 18, 22; **30:**1, 1, 13, 14, 14, 24, 25; **31:**7; **32:**5, 12; **33:**6, 13, 17, 21; **34:**11; **35:**8; **36:**2, 4, 5, 6, 12, 12, 20; **37:**7, 7, 9, 10, 18, 20, 22, 25, 26, 27, 30, 30, 36; **38:**1, 7, 22; **39:**1, 1, 2; **40:**2, 2, 6, 6, 20, 26, 28; **41:**20, 23, 26; **42:**8, 21, 23, 25; **43:**4, 9, 10, 12, 18, 20, 28; **44:**9, 10, 13, 20, 20, 25, 28, 28; **45:**3, 20, 21; **47:**11; **48:**5, 5, 7, 8, 11, 11, 13, 18, 20; **49:**8, 9, 15, 23, 24, 26; **50:**1, 2, 2, 4, 7, 9; **51:**23; **52:**6, 7; **53:**4, 5, 8, 8, 11; **54:**9, 9, 14, 16, 17; **55:**2, 2, 2, 3, 7; **56:**3, 10; **57:**1, 11, 11, 12, 13, 15; **58:**2, 13; **59:**5, 9, 9, 13, 15, 16; **60:**7, 12, 16; **61:**1, 2, 9; **62:**9; **63:**3, 10; **64:**1, 9; **65:**5, 17, 20; **66:**1, 6, 19, 22, 24, 24; **Jer 1:**3, 7, 12, 16, 18; **2:**5, 13, 22, 23; **3:**1, 3, 7, 8, 13, 13, 17; **4:**9, 14, 31; **5:**7, 14, 19, 22, 31; **6:**1, 9, 13, 24, 27; **7:**7, 8, 14, 14, 14, 29, 32, 32; **8:**1, 10; **9:**1, 2, 12, 24, 24, 24; **10:**7, 16, 23, 25, 25; **11:**19; **13:**6, 13, 20, 22, 25; **14:**15, 20; **15:**10, 18, 19; **16:**11, 15, 21; **17:**4, 8, 11; **18:**7, 8, 9, 10, 10; **19:**2, 3, 9; **20:**6, 16, 17, 17; **21:**13, 14; **22:**5, 15, 16, 16, 18, 21, 23, 30; **23:**6, 7, 13, 14, 15, 19, 29, 32, 34, 39; **24:**2, 6, 7; **25:**5, 18, 19, 20, 33; **26:**9, 9, 12, 13, 15, 15; **27:**8, 8, 11, 13, 16, 18, 18; **28:**1, 3, 4, 4, 9, 11, 11, 11; **29:**7, 10, 15, 22, 28; **30:**3, 8, 15, 16, 23; **31:**1, 18, 32, 33; **32:**6, 8, 22, 23; **33:**15, 16, 20, 24, 26; **34:**1, 14, 22; **35:**11, 15; **36:**1, 4, 6, 6, 9, 23, 32; **37:**7, 9, 17, 18, 21, 21; **38:**4, 4, 7, 7, 25; **39:**1, 12; **40:**3, 4, 7, 7, 9, 11, 11, 14; **41:**8, 18; **42:**17, 22; **43:**10; **44:**3, 4, 12, 15, 19, 20, 21, 22, 25, 26, 29, 29; **45:**4; **46:**8; **48:**9, 11, 27, 28, 44; **49:**13, 14, 16, 25, 27; **50:**2, 3, 5, 17, 21, 25, 32, 43; **51:**19, 60, 62, 62; **52:**12, 17, 31; **La 1:**9, 10, 13; **3:**1; **4:**6, 11, 14, 17, 20; **5:**1; **Eze 1:**4, 5, 6, 26; **2:**3, 10; **4:**6, 14, 14, 14, 17; **5:**13; **6:**7, 9, 10, 10, 10, 11, 13, 14; **7:**4, 9, 19, 20, 27; **8:**2, 3, 5, 17; **9:**2; **11:**5, 5, 10, 12; **12:**11, 15, 16, 20, 22; **13:**9, 11, 14, 21, 23, 23; **14:**3, 8, 9, 16, 18, 20, 23; **15:**7, 7; **16:**20, 27, 29, 31, 41, 47, 55, 62, 63; **17:**15, 21, 24; **18:**10, 11, 14, 14, 19, 23; **19:**5; **20:**5, 6, 9, 12, 14, 15, 20, 25, 26, 38, 38, 40, 42, 44, 48; **21:**5, 12, 19; **22:**16, 18, 18, 22, 26, 30; **23:**14, 19, 25, 31, 32, 34, 39, 41, 44, 49; **24:**24, 24, 26, 27; **25:**5, 7, 8, 11, 17; **26:**6; **27:**3, 27; **28:**2, 22, 23, 24, 26, 26; **29:**6, 9, 11, 16, 18, 21; **30:**1, 5, 8, 9, 9, 19, 21, 25, 26; **31:**3, 4, 11, 17; **32:**9, 13, 15, 31; **33:**2, 8, 13, 14, 28, 29; **34:**12, 19, 19, 27, 30, 30; **35:**4, 9, 10, 12, 13, 15; **36:**4, 7, 11, 13, 23, 34, 36, 38, 38; **37:**2, 3, 6, 9, 13, 14, 14, 28; **38:**1, 10, 12, 16, 17, 19, 23; **39:**6, 7, 8, 13, 22, 22, 28; **40:**5, 6, 16, 27, 28, 32, 35; **41:**1, 1, 5, 8, 19, 19, 22; **42:**7, 13, 13; **43:**14, 19, 20, 20, 22, 23; **44:**4, 12, 18, 24, 31, 31; **45:**15, 17, 20, 21; **46:**7, 17; **47:**3, 9, 14; **48:**13, 18, 20, 21, 24, 29, 35; **Da 1:**10, 16, 20; **2:**1, 1, 2, 3, 9, 9, 15, 19, 30, 35, 35, 36, 39, 40, 40, 41, 41, 43, 44, 45; **3:**7, 11, 11, 14, 18, 19, 19, 27; **4:**5, 5, 9, 9, 17, 17, 18, 18, 22, 25, 26, 26, 32, 33; **5:**2, 2, 5, 6, 14, 14, 16, 19, 21, 23, 25, 30; **6:**7, 7, 7, 10, 12, 12, 13, 15, 15, 17, 18, 22, 23, 26; **7:**2, 7, 8, 13, 14, 17, 20, 20, 20, 23, 24, 24, 28; **8:**1, 5, 6, 13, 17, 17, 22, 22; **9:**2, 12, 18, 26, 27, 27; **10:**3, 21; **11:**10, 14, 24, 31, 37; **12:**1, 1, 11; **Hos 1:**10, 11; **2:**1, 8, 16, 18, 18, 18, 21, 23; **3:**4; **4:**3, 13; **5:**7; **6:**3; **7:**4, 16; **8:**8; **9:**3, 10, 14, 14; **10:**9, 9, 11, 12, 13, 15; **11:**3; **13:**5, 7; **14:**2, 8; **Joel 1:**15; **2:**12, 14, 27, 27, 31; **3:**1, 14, 17, 18; **Am 2:**4, 16; **3:**1, 2, 5; **5:**14, 18, 19, 24; **6:**6; **7:**2, 6, 7; **8:**3, 9, 10; **9:**1, 8, 9, 11; **Ob** 1, 1, 8, 14, 18; **Jnh 1:**3, 4, 10, 12; **3:**3, 10; **4:**2, 2, 2, 7; **Mic 2:**4, 6, 7; **3:**7, 9; **4:**2, 6, 12; **5:**10, 15; **6:**7, 7, 12, 16; **7:**9, 10, 10, 10, 11, 16; **Na 2:**11; **3:**12, 17; **Hab 1:**1, 14; **2:**2, 13, 15; **3:**8; **Zep 1:**4, 8, 10, 14, 18; **2:**3, 14, 15, 15; **3:**9, 9, 16, 20; **Hag 1:**10; **2:**1, 14, 21; **Zec 1:**8, 15, 19, 21; **2:**4, 4, 9, 11, 11; **3:**2, 10; **4:**9, 10, 12; **5:**3, 3, 3, 4; **6:**12; **7:**5, 12, 12, 14, 14; **8:**7, 16, 16, 17, 18, 23; **9:**3, 12, 16; **10:**1, 1, 8; **11:**1, 4, 7, 10, 11, 11, 14, 16; **12:**2, 3, 4, 6, 6, 7, 8, 9, 11; **13:**1, 2, 2, 2, 9; **14:**2, 4, 6, 8, 9, 12, 13, 17, 18, 20, 21; **Mal 1:**1, 8, 8, 8, 9, 10, 10, 13; **2:**4, 17; **3:**2, 2, 3, 5, 6, 14; **4:**1, 4; **Mt 2:**1, 8, 14, 16, 22; **3:**8, 9, 10, 11, 15; **4:**12, 24; **5:**16, 21, 23, 24, 26, 27, 31, 32, 33, 37, 38, 41, 43, 45, 46, 46, 47; **6:**5, 16, 23, 30; **7:**4, 12, 15, 19, 20, 25, 27; **8:**9, 11, 13, 16, 28, 28, 31; **9:**6, 10, 17, 22, 35, 36; **10:**7, 14, 15, 23, 26, 32, 33, 34; **11:**7, 8; **12:**1, 2, 4, 5, 15, 22, 23, 36, 38, 45, 45; **13:**1, 7, 8, 13, 19, 25, 27, 35, 41, 44, 47, 49, 53; **14:**2, 6, 15, 16; **15:**27, 38; **16:**9, 12, 13, 18, 20, 21, 28; **17:**2, 10, 18, 19; **18:**1, 6, 10, 10, 13, 14, 15, 16, 17, 17, 25, 32; **19:**4, 12, 28; **20:**6, 8, 16, 25, 30, 30; **21:**43, 43, 44, 45; **22:**3, 12, 21, 23, 29, 34, 46; **23:**16, 16, 16, 17, 18, 19, 31, 37; **24:**2, 14, 15, 20, 21, 22, 28, 32, 39, 46, 47, 51; **26:**3, 16, 47, 53, 54, 55, 56, 63, 68; **27:**3, 8, 9, 17, 18, 19, 24, 24, 51, 54, 63, 64, 64; **Mk 1:**4, 4, 7, 26, 28, 32, 38, 45; **2:**2, 10, 13, 15, 15, 16, 24, 26; **3:**10, 28; **4:**1, 7, 7, 8, 12, 15, 22, 38, 41; **5:**20, 29, 30; **6:**1, 11, 11, 14, 20, 22, 31, 48; **7:**2, 18, 19, 20, 24; **8:**9, 11, 31, 32, 38; **9:**1, 11, 12, 17, 25, 28, 30, 41, 42; **10:**28, 29, 32, 42, 47; **11:**2, 2, 5, 13, 19, 23, 23, 25, 32, 32; **12:**17, 19, 24, 28, 32, 34, 35; **13:**1, 2, 14, 18, 20, 24, 28, 29, 34; **14:**15, 15, 25, 25, 35, 43, 48, 65, 69; **15:**7, 10, 34, 44, 46; **16:**4, 11, S; **Lk 1:**1, 8, 22, 43, 45, 58, 61; **2:**1, 1, 8, 15, 26, 27, 44, 49; **3:**3, 3, 7, 8, 8, 9, 16; **4:**2, 18, 18, 18, 19, 22, 23, 38, 40, 43; **5:**17, 24, 33; **6:**2, 4, 23, 23, 32, 33, 33, 34, 35, 42, 49; **7:**8, 17, 21, 24, 29, 39, 42; **8:**4, 7, 10, 12, 17, 23, 25, 37, 47, 47, 55, 56; **9:**5, 5, 26, 27, 39; **10:**3, 35, 40; **11:**25, 26, 27, 30, 30, 35, 38, 48, 53; **12:**2, 8, 9, 14, 16, 26, 28, 43, 44, 48, 49, 59; **13:**1, 2, 5, 14, 32, 32, 34; **14:**7, 17, 23, 30; **15:**2, 16, 29; **16:**1, 6, 8, 17, 17, 25; **17:**15, 23, 23, 23, 24, 31, 34, 37; **18:**1, 3, 5, 11, 11, 37, 40; **19:**11, 25, 30, 30, 39, 42, 47; **20:**16, 18, 19, 20, 21, 25, 28, 35, 40, 41; **21:**6, 15, 20, 30, 31, 34, 35, 36; **22:**5, 12, 12, 16, 30, 32, 34, 40, 44, 52, 61, 61, 64, 70; **23:**7, 12, 29, 29, 48, 48, 53, 56; **24:**2, 7, 7, 8, 13, 14, 18, 19, 21, 25, 26, 31, 39, 39, 39, 44, 46; **Jn 1:**3, 7, 34; **2:**4, 9, 22, 23; **3:**2, 2, 7, 12, 15, 16, 16, 21, 25, 28, 28, 33; **4:**1, 5, 15, 20, 20, 23, 47, 51, 53; **5:**10, 12, 23, 25, 32, 36, 40, 44; **6:**9, 12, 15, 16, 22, 22, 24, 27, 27, 34, 39, 39, 40, 40, 46, 51, 61, 65, 65, 68; **7:**24, 26, 26, 32, 38, 42; **8:**12, 17, 24, 24, 24, 27, 28, 28, 29, 34, 37, 40, 41, 48, 52, 59; **9:**8, 20, 22, 39; **10:**16, 17,

20, 34, 35, 38; **11:**12, 17, 20, 22, 40, 49, 51, 52, 53, 57; **12:**5, 6, 11, 12, 14, 16, 16, 18, 27, 34, 42, 46; **13:**1, 3, 3, 10, 11, 16, 17, 19, 31, 35, 38; **14:**3, 10, 11, 20, 22, 29, 31, 31; **15:**2, 2, 11, 12, 16, 16, 24, 24; **16:**1, 4, 7, 15, 15, 16, 19, 22, 23, 27, 30, 30, 33; **17:**7, 8, 11, 12, 21, 21, 22, 23, 23, 26; **18:**4, 8, 13, 14, 15, 20, 22, 37, 37, 37; **19:**4, 10, 13, 19, 20, 24, 25, 28, 31, 31, 33, 35, 36; **20:**1, 7, 9, 17, 19, 31, 31, 31; **21:**7, 9, 17, 22, 23, 23, 23, 23, 24, 24, 25; **Ac 1:**3, 9, 21; **2:**5, 15, 20, 30, 31, 31, 36, 40; **3:**11, 17, 18, 23; **4:**2, 2, 4, 10, 11, 13, 27, 32; **5:**8, 9, 10, 15, 25, 34, 36, 41; **6:**1, 14; **7:**3, 5, 6, 7, 8, 10, 12, 20, 25, 28, 29, 34, 45, 49, 60; **8:**1, 8, 14, 18, 19, 23, 24, 26; **9:**8, 9, 12, 14, 17, 21, 22, 24, 28, 38, 41; **10:**28, 34, 36, 38, 42, 43, 45, 47; **11:**1, 6, 26, 28; **12:**1, 14; **13:**10, 20, 27, 33, 34, 42, 46, 49; **14:**1, 8, 12, 12, 15, 22, 27; **15:**3, 5, 7, 7, 8, 10, 11, 17, 19, 20, 24, 31, 39; **16:**3, 4, 6, 9, 10, 13, 15, 18, 21, 33, 38; **17:**10, 13, 21, 22, 27, 33; **18:**7, 13, 18; **19:**2, 10, 12, 12, 16, 21, 23, 25, 26, 27, 27, 35; **20:**18, 19, 23, 23, 25, 26, 27, 28, 29, 32, 34, 38; **21:**4, 14, 21, 21, 22, 24, 24, 29, 31; **22:**5, 10, 13, 19, 22; **23:**3, 4, 6, 9, 10, 11, 27, 31; **24:**9, 10, 11, 11, 14, 15, 26; **25:**4, 16, 23, 26; **26:**2, 5, 7, 8, 9, 11, 19, 20, 22, 23, 29; **27:**4, 6, 16, 37; **28:**1, 11, 11, 20, 20, 22, 23, 28; **Ro 1:**5, 8, 11, 13, 17, 20, 21, 26, 28; **2:**2, 3, 7, 13, 14, 15, 17, 19, 20, 29; **3:**3, 5, 8, 8, 9, 20, 25, 27, 31; **4:**2, 10, 11, 11, 13, 13, 14, 14, 14, 17, 18, 19, 19, 21, 23, 24; **5:**3, 16, 20; **6:**1, 3, 6, 16, 19, 21, 22; **7:**1, 3, 4, 5, 7, 7, 7, 8, 13, 16, 16, 16, 17, 21, 23, 23, 24; **8:**2, 3, 4, 5, 9, 16, 19, 22, 23, 24, 26, 28, 29, 38, 39; **9:**1, 3, 7, 8, 11, 17, 17, 20, 20, 33, 33; **10:**1, 5, 8, 9, 9, 10, 10, 15; **11:**1, 6, 9, 14, 15, 18, 25, 35; **12:**6, 7, 9, 14, 17, 19; **13:**4, 8, 11, 13; **14:**9, 13, 14, 14, 22; **15:**1, 8, 8, 9, 13, 14, 14, 15, 16, 29, 31, 31; **16:**5, 17, 19, 26; **1Co 1:**4, 6, 14, 17, 21, 23, 26, 29; **2:**5, 6, 6, 9, 11; **3:**3, 5, 12, 14, 16, 16, 17, 20; **4:**4, 7, 17, 18; **5:**1, 1, 5, 6, 6, 7, 10, 11; **6:**2, 3, 7, 9, 11, 15, 16, 19; **7:**5, 10, 16, 16, 21, 25, 28, 29, 33; **8:**1, 1, 1, 4, 4, 4, 6, 7, 8, 10; **9:**1, 2, 13, 14, 15, 17, 20, 20, 22, 22, 24, 24, 25, 27; **10:**1, 4, 4, 6, 10, 13, 13, 13, 13, 17, 18, 19, 19, 20, 25, 28, 33; **11:**2, 14, 15, 16, 18, 19, 21, 27, 28, 30; **12:**2, 10, 15, 16, 22, 23, 24, 24, 25, 28, 31; **13:**2, 12, 13; **14:**5, 6, 6, 12, 18, 19, 22, 26, 31, 32, 36, 37, 40; **15:**2, 2, 3, 6, 11, 12, 15, 15, 18, 20, 24, 28, 34, 37, 45, 50, 52, 53, 54, 56, 58; **16:**6, 15, 17, 22; **2Co 1:**4, 5, 6, 7, 10, 12, 12, 18, 20, 23, 24; **2:**3, 3, 3, 4, 5, 7, 8, 11, 17; **3:**5, 7, 7, 10, 15, 18, 18, 18; **4:**2, 3, 4, 5, 6, 6, 7, 7, 7, 10, 11, 14, 16, 17; **5:**1, 4, 4, 6, 7, 11, 13, 14, 14, 15, 16, 17, 21; **6:**3, 4; **7:**1, 3, 8, 8, 8, 10, 10, 11, 12; **8:**3, 9, 10, 13, 13, 16, 16, 17, 19, 20, 23, 24; **9:**2, 2, 3, 3, 4, 11, 13; **10:**1, 5, 7, 7, 7, 11, 12, 15, 15, 16; **11:**3, 12, 16, 21, 21, 29, 30; **12:**4, 4, 5, 9, 12, 15, 19, 19, 20, 20, 21; **13:**2, 3, 5, 6, 7, 7, 10; **Gal 1:**5, 6, 7, 9, 11, 16, 18, 19, 20, 23; **2:**2, 3, 4, 7, 10, 10, 14, 16, 16, 17, 19; **3:**10, 11, 11, 16, 16, 22, 25, 29; **4:**5, 8, 9, 9, 11, 13, 15, 17, 20, 22, 27, 30; **5:**1, 10, 11, 11, 11, 12, 17, 20, 21, 21; **6:**1, 7, 12, 14, 14, 17; **Eph 1:**7, 12, 13, 14, 14, 17, 18, 18, 19, 20; **2:**3, 5, 5, 10, 11, 14, 15; **3:**9, 13, 16, 17, 19, 15; **4:**8, 9, 9, 10, 13, 16, 20, 21, 29, 30; **5:**2, 5, 12, 18; **6:**2, 8, 11, 13, 15, 15, 19, 20; **Php 1:**6, 6, 7, 9, 9, 10, 11, 12, 12, 13, 18, 19, 20, 20, 20, 20, 22, 23, 24, 25, 27, 28, 28, 30; **2:**5, 9, 10, 11, 12, 15, 16, 16, 17, 24, 26, 27, 28; **3:**5, 6, 8, 10, 11, 12, 12, 12, 18, 21; **4:**5, 8, 8, 10, 11, 18; **Col 1:**4, 4, 6, 6, 8, 11, 11, 12, 27, 27, 29; **2:**4, 8, 14, 22; **3:**5, 10, 11, 15, 24; **4:**1, 3, 3, 3, 4, 6, 13; **1Th 1:**4, 4, 5, 5; **2:**1, 3, 5, 8, 9, 10, 11, 12, 13; **3:**1, 3, 4, 5, 5, 5, 6, 6, 6, 10, 13; **4:**1, 9, 14, 14; **5:**2, 10, 12, 15, 21, 23; **2Th 1:**3, 10, 11, 11; **2:**2, 3, 4, 5, 10, 13, 13; **3:**1, 2, 4, 4, 5, 7, 8, 9, 11, 17; **1Ti 1:**5, 10, 11, 16, 16, 16; **2:**2, 6; **3:**1, 6, 7, 15; **4:**1, 1, 10, 11, 15; **5:**4, 7, 15, 20, 24; **6:**1, 2, 9, 12, 14, 16, 19; **2Ti 1:**5, 9, 12, 12, 13; **2:**2, 8, 8, 16, 18, 22, 22, 23; **3:**1, 5, 5, 15; **4:**8, 8, 17; **Tit 1:**1, 3, 4, 8; **2:**1, 3, 8, 13; **3:**7, 8, 10, 10, 11, 13; **Phm 1:**2, 6, 8, 10, 19, 21, 22; **Heb 1:**4; **2:**3, 3, 6, 6, 10, 11, 16, 17, 17; **3:**7, 12, 13, 14, 18, 19; **4:**1, 2, 7, 11, 13, 14; **5:**3, 5; **6:**7, 8, 9, 9, 9, 11, 11, 16, 17, 17; **7:**8, 9, 11, 15, 16, 19, 20, 23; **8:**2, 5, 5, 6, 10; **9:**1, 4, 4, 8, 9, 10, 10, 11, 11, 12, 14, 14, 15, 15, 15, 16, 18, 22, 23, 24, 26, 27, 27; **10:**5, 5, 11, 14, 15, 16, 20, 25, 26, 27, 36, 39; **11:**1, 3, 3, 3, 4, 4, 5, 6, 6, 7, 7, 8, 8, 11, 11, 12, 13, 14, 16, 17, 19, 20, 21, 22, 22, 23, 23, 24, 26, 27, 28, 28, 29, 30, 31, 39, 40; **12:**1, 1, 1, 3, 7, 8, 15, 15, 16, 19, 21, 25, 27, 27, 28; **13:**6, 7, 17, 19, 20, 23; **Jas 1:**6, 6, 7, 12, 25, 27; **2:**1, 4, 9, 12, 12, 14, 16, 16, 17, 19, 20, 20, 21, 22; **3:**6, 13, 14, 17; **4:**2, 4, 4, 5, 15; **5:**12, 16, 17, 20, 20, 20; **1Pe 1:**3, 7, 12, 12, 13, 17, 18, 22, 24, 25, 25; **2:**2, 3, 5, 7, 8, 8, 8, 9, 15; **3:**3, 4, 5, 9, 17, 18, 20; **4:**3, 5, 6, 6, 10, 11; **5:**9, 12; **2Pe 1:**4, 4, 4, 9, 10, 14, 19, 20; **2:**21; **3:**3, 5, 7, 8, 12, 15, 17; **1Jn 1:**2, 3, 4, 10; **2:**1, 3, 4, 5, 15, 15, 18, 19, 20, 22, 28, 29, 29; **3:**1, 2, 5, 14, 15, 17, 19, 22; **4:**2, 2, 3, 6, 6, 9, 10, 10, 11, 13, 14, 15, 18, 20, 21; **5:**1, 3, 5, 6, 9, 10, 13, 14, 15, 16, 16, 16, 18, 19, 19, 20, 20, 21; **2Jn** 2, 5, 7, 8, 8; **3Jn** 2, 3, 4, 6, 8, 11, 11, 11; **Jude** 3, 4, 5, 7, 12, 15, 18, 21, 21, 23; **Rev 1:**1, 1, 10, 19, 19; **2:**6, 13, 13, 17, 17, 20, 20, 23, 25; **3:**1, 5, 8, 9, 10, 11, 12, 15, 17, 18; **4:**11; **5:**6, 6; **6:**1; **7:**15; **9:**1, 10, 13, 17, 18, 20; **11:**4, 6, 7, 13; **12:**12, 13, 15, 16, 17; **13:**1, 3, 15, 15, 17; **14:**8, 17; **15:**2, 5; **16:**12, 13, 14, 19; **17:**1, 3, 6, 11, 17, 18; **18:**2, 10, 14, 16; **19:**3, 5, 9, 20, 20, 21; **20:**2, 10; **21:**8; **22:**18, 19, 19

THAT'S (42)

Ge 3:13; **31:**14; **42:**21; **Nu 13:**33; **Dt 3:**26; **1Sa 9:**17; **20:**2, 29; **2Sa 4:**10; **18:**4; **1Ki 1:**45; **Est 5:**12; **Job 1:**7; **2:**2; **13:**5; **16:**5; **18:**8; **22:**13; **Ecc 10:**10; **Isa 41:**23; **Jer 1:**12; **2:**23; **6:**16; **37:**14; **Hos 6:**6; **Am 6:**12; **Mic 2:**11; **Mt 18:**35; **27:**4; **Mk 3:**22; **7:**28; **11:**23; **Lk 7:**43; **22:**38; **Jn 9:**23, 30; **Ac 2:**13; **Ro 4:**16; **8:**8; **2Co 10:**18; **11:**33; **Gal 4:**3

THE (52785)

Ge 1:1, 1, 1, 2, 2, 4, 4, 5, 5, 6, 7, 7, 8, 8, 9, 9, 10, 10, 11, 11, 11, 12, 13, 14, 14, 14, 14, 14, 15, 16, 16, 16, 16, 16, 16, 16, 16, 16, 17, 17, 18, 18, 18, 19, 20, 20, 22, 22, 22, 23, 24, 26, 26, 26, 26, 26, 28, 28, 28, 29, 29, 30, 30, 31; **2:**1, 1, 1, 2, 3, 3, 4, 4, 4, 4, 4, 4, 4, 5, 5, 5, 6, 6, 7, 7, 7, 7, 7, 8, 8, 8, 9, 9, 9, 9, 9, 9, 10, 10, 11, 11, 12, 13, 13, 13, 14, 14, 14, 14, 15, 15, 15, 16, 16, 17, 17, 18, 18, 19, 19, 20, 21, 21, 22, 22, 24; **3:**1, 1, 1, 1, 1, 1, 1, 2, 3, 3, 3, 3, 4, 6, 6, 6, 8, 8, 8, 9, 11, 11, 12, 12, 13, 13, 13, 14, 14, 14, 14, 14, 15, 16, 17, 17, 19, 19, 20, 21, 22, 22, 22, 22, 23, 23, 24, 24, 24, 24, 24; **4:**1, 1, 3, 4, 4, 6, 7, 8, 9, 10, 10, 11, 12, 13, 15, 15, 16, 16, 18, 18, 18, 18, 20, 20, 21, 21, 21, 22, 25, 26; **5:**1, 1, 1, 3, 4, 5, 7, 8, 10, 11, 13, 14, 16, 17, 19, 20, 22, 26, 27, 29, 29, 30, 31, 32; **6:**1, 1, 2, 2, 2, 3, 3, 4, 4, 4, 5, 5, 5, 6, 7, 7, 8, 9, 9, 9, 11, 12, 13, 13, 16, 16, 16, 16, 16, 17, 18, 19, 19, 21; **7:**1, 1, 1, 1, 1, 2, 3, 4, 4, 5, 6, 7, 8, 8, 9, 10, 10, 11, 11, 11, 11, 11, 11, 12, 13, 14, 15, 16, 17, 17, 17, 18, 18, 18, 18, 19, 19, 19, 20, 21, 21, 23, 24, 24; **8:**1, 1, 1, 1, 2, 2, 3, 4, 4, 4, 4, 5, 6, 6, 7, 9, 9, 9, 9, 10, 11, 11, 12, 13, 13, 13, 14, 16, 17, 18, 19, 20, 20, 21, 21, 21, 22; **9:**1, 2, 2, 7, 7, 10, 11, 13, 13, 13, 14, 14, 14, 16, 16, 16, 17, 17, 17, 18, 18, 18, 19, 19, 20, 22, 23, 23, 25, 25, 25, 25, 25, 26, 27, 27, 28; **10:**1, 1, 1, 1, 2, 3, 4, 5, 6, 7, 7, 9, 9, 10, 10, 10, 12, 12, 13, 13, 14, 14, 15, 15, 15, 15, 19, 20, 21, 21, 21, 22, 23, 24, 24, 25, 25, 25, 26, 30, 30, 30, 31, 32, 32, 32, 32; **11:**1, 1, 2, 2, 4, 4, 5, 5, 5, 5, 8, 8, 8, 8, 9, 9, 9, 9, 10, 10, 11, 13, 15, 17, 19, 21, 23, 25, 26, 27, 27, 28, 28, 29, 31, 31, 31; **12:**1, 1, 2, 3, 3, 4, 5, 6, 6, 7, 7, 8, 8, 8, 8, 9, 10, 11, 12, 13, 15, 15, 17, 20; **13:**1, 3, 4, 4, 4, 6, 6, 7, 7, 9, 10, 10, 10, 10, 10, 10, 10, 10, 11, 11, 12, 12, 13, 13, 14, 17, 18, 18; **14:**1, 2, 3, 3, 3, 4, 5, 5, 5, 5, 6, 6, 6, 7, 7, 8, 8, 8, 8, 9, 10, 10, 10, 10, 10, 10, 11, 11, 13, 13, 13, 13, 14, 15, 16, 16, 17, 17, 18, 20, 21, 21, 22, 23, 24; **15:**1, 4, 5, 5, 5, 5, 6, 6, 7, 7, 7, 9, 10, 10, 10, 11, 12, 13, 14, 14, 16, 16, 17, 17, 18, 18, 18, 18, 19, 19; **16:**2, 3, 3, 5, 5, 7, 7, 7, 8, 9, 9, 10, 11, 11, 12, 13, 13, 13; **17:**1, 3, 4, 5, 7, 9, 9, 9, 10, 11, 12, 12, 12, 13, 14, 14, 16, 17, 17, 22, 26, 27, 27; **18:**1, 1, 1, 2, 4, 6, 7, 8, 8, 8, 8, 9, 10, 11, 13, 14, 16, 16, 17, 17, 18, 18, 19, 19, 20, 20, 22, 22, 24, 25, 25, 25, 25, 25, 25, 26, 26, 28, 28, 29, 30, 31, 31, 31, 32, 32, 32, 33; **19:**1, 1, 1, 1, 2, 2, 2, 2, 3, 4, 4, 4, 4, 5, 5, 6, 9, 10, 10, 11, 11, 12, 12, 13, 13, 13, 13, 14, 14, 14, 15, 15, 15, 15, 16, 16, 16, 16, 17, 17, 17, 19, 21, 23, 23, 24, 24, 25, 25, 27, 27, 28, 28, 29, 29, 29, 30, 30, 31, 33, 34, 34, 35, 37, 37, 37, 38, 38, 38, 38; **20:**1, 8, 8, 12, 13, 17, 17, 18, 18; **21:**1, 2, 5, 8, 9, 10, 12, 12, 13, 14, 14, 14, 15, 15, 16, 16, 17, 17, 17, 17, 17, 19, 20, 20, 26, 31, 32, 32, 33, 33; **22:**2, 2, 3, 3, 4, 4, 4, 4, 5, 5, 5, 6, 6, 6, 6, 7, 7, 7, 7, 7, 9, 9, 9, 9, 10, 10, 11, 11, 12, 12, 12, 13, 13, 14, 14, 14, 14, 15, 15, 16, 17, 17, 17, 17, 18, 18, 21, 21, 21, 23; **23:**2, 3, 5, 6, 9, 9, 9, 10, 10, 10, 10, 11, 11, 11, 12, 12, 13, 15, 16, 17, 17, 17, 17, 18, 18, 18, 18, 19, 20, 20, 20; **24:**1, 2, 3, 3, 5, 7, 7, 9, 10, 10, 11, 11, 11, 11, 12, 13, 13, 14, 15, 16, 17, 18, 20, 20, 20, 20, 21, 21, 21, 22, 23, 25, 26, 26, 26, 27, 27, 27, 28, 30, 30, 30, 31, 31, 31, 32, 32, 35, 35, 37, 40, 42, 42, 44, 44, 45, 45, 46, 47, 47, 47, 48, 48, 48, 48, 48, 50, 51, 51, 52, 52, 54, 54, 54, 56, 59, 60, 61, 62, 63, 63, 65, 65, 66, 66, 67; **25:**3, 6, 6, 9, 9, 9, 10, 10, 11, 12, 12, 12, 13, 16, 16, 17, 18, 18, 18, 19, 19, 19, 20, 20, 20, 21, 22, 22, 23, 23, 23, 23, 24, 24, 25, 26, 26, 27, 27, 27, 28, 33, 34; **26:**1, 1, 2, 4, 4, 4, 7, 8, 12, 14, 15, 16, 16, 17, 18, 18, 18, 19, 20, 20, 22, 22, 24, 24, 25, 28, 29, 30, 31, 33, 33, 33, 34, 34, 34, 34, 34; **27:**3, 4, 4, 5, 5, 7, 9, 10, 13, 13, 14, 14, 15, 16, 16, 16, 17, 18, 19, 19, 20, 22, 22, 25, 25, 27, 27, 27, 27, 27, 29, 31, 39; **28:**2, 4, 5, 5, 8, 9, 9, 9, 11, 12, 13, 13, 13, 13, 13, 13, 13, 14, 14, 14, 14, 16, 17, 17, 18, 18, 19, 19, 19, 21; **29:**1, 1, 2, 2, 2, 3, 3, 3, 3, 3, 3, 4, 5, 6, 7, 7, 8, 8, 8, 8, 9, 10, 10, 10, 16, 19, 20, 21, 22, 25, 26, 27, 30, 31, 32, 33, 35; **30:**2, 13, 14, 14, 15, 16, 24, 27, 30, 32, 32, 35, 35, 35, 35, 37, 38, 39, 39, 40, 40, 40, 41, 41, 42, 42, 42; **31:**3, 3, 4, 4, 5, 8, 8, 8, 8, 10, 10, 10, 11, 12, 12, 13, 13, 13, 13, 16, 18, 18, 18, 19, 21, 21, 23, 24, 25, 26, 29, 32, 33, 33, 34, 34, 37, 39, 39, 39, 39, 40, 40, 41, 42, 42, 42, 46, 49, 53, 53, 53, 53, 53, 54, 54, 55; **32:**2, 3, 6, 6, 7, 7, 8, 10, 12, 12, 13, 17, 17, 19, 19, 19, 20, 21, 21, 22, 22, 23, 24, 25, 25, 25, 26, 27, 28, 29, 30, 31, 32, 32; **33:**1, 2, 5, 5, 6, 8, 10, 12, 13, 13, 17, 18, 19, 19; **34:**1, 1, 2, 2, 5, 6, 7, 10, 12, 20, 21, 24, 25, 27, 28, 28, 29, 29, 30, 30; **35:**1, 3, 4, 5, 5, 8, 8, 8, 8, 11, 12, 13, 14, 14, 15, 17, 18, 19, 21, 22, 22, 23, 24, 25, 26, 26; **36:**1, 1, 2, 2, 2, 2, 3, 3, 5, 6, 6, 8, 9, 9, 10, 10, 11, 13, 14, 15, 15, 15, 15, 16, 16, 17, 17, 17, 17, 17, 18, 18, 18, 18, 19, 20, 20, 20, 20, 21, 21, 21, 22, 23, 24, 24, 24, 25, 26, 27, 28, 29, 29, 30, 30, 31, 34, 34, 35, 35, 35, 35, 36, 37, 37, 39, 39, 40, 40, 40, 43, 43, 43, 43, 43; **37:**1, 2, 2, 2, 5, 7, 8, 9, 13, 14, 14, 15, 17, 18, 24, 24, 25, 26, 28, 28, 28, 29, 30, 31, 32, 32, 36, 36, 36; **38:**2, 3, 5, 7, 7, 8, 9, 9, 10, 10, 12, 12, 12, 12, 13, 14, 14, 14, 14, 18, 20, 20, 20, 21, 21, 21, 21, 21, 22, 22, 23, 23, 23, 23, 25, 25, 26, 27, 28, 28, 28, 29, 29, 29, 30, 30; **39:**1, 1, 1, 1, 1, 2, 2, 3, 5, 5, 6, 11, 12, 14, 14, 16, 20, 20, 21, 21, 22, 22, 22, 23, 23; **40:**3, 3, 3, 3, 5, 5, 6, 6, 9, 11, 11, 11, 12, 12, 15, 15, 16, 16, 17, 17, 18, 20, 21, 22; **41:**1, 1, 2, 3, 3, 4, 4, 4, 6, 6, 7, 8, 8, 8, 9, 10, 10, 10, 10, 11, 12, 12, 12, 13, 14, 17, 17, 18, 19, 19, 20, 20, 23, 23, 24, 24, 25, 26, 26, 27, 27, 29, 29, 30, 30, 31, 31, 32, 32, 33, 34, 34, 34, 35, 35, 35, 36, 36, 36, 38, 38, 39, 39, 39, 39, 41, 42, 43, 43, 44, 44, 45, 45, 46, 46, 46, 47, 48, 48, 49, 49, 49, 49, 50, 50, 50, 51, 53, 54, 54, 54, 55, 55, 56, 56, 56, 57, 57; **42:**5, 6, 6, 6, 7, 9, 12, 13, 15, 16, 18, 19, 19, 20, 24, 25, 25, 26, 27, 27, 27, 29, 30, 30, 32, 32, 33, 33, 33, 33, 35, 35, 35, 35, 38; **43:**1, 1, 2, 3, 5, 7, 8, 9, 11, 11, 11, 12, 13, 14, 14, 15, 15, 16, 17, 18, 19, 19, 19, 19, 21, 21, 22, 23, 23, 24, 24, 27, 29, 31, 32, 33, 34, 34; **44:**1, 2, 2, 2, 3, 4, 5, 6, 6, 7, 8, 9, 10, 10, 11, 12, 12, 12, 13, 13, 14, 16, 17, 17, 17, 22, 26, 26, 29, 30, 30, 31, 31, 32, 32, 33, 33, 34; **45:**2, 2, 9, 10, 16, 18, 18, 18, 18, 20, 20, 21, 21, 23, 24, 25, 26, 26, 27, 27; **46:**1, 2, 3, 3, 5, 6, 6, 8, 8, 8, 9, 10, 11, 12, 12, 12, 13, 14, 16, 17, 18, 19, 20, 22, 23, 24, 25, 25, 26, 27, 28, 31, 34, 34; **47:**1, 4, 4, 6, 6, 11, 11, 12, 13, 13, 14, 14, 15, 17, 18, 19, 20, 20, 20, 21, 22, 22, 23, 23, 24, 26, 26, 26, 26, 27, 27, 29; **48:**3, 5, 6, 6, 6, 6, 7, 7, 7, 8, 9, 10, 12, 13, 14, 14, 14, 14, 14, 15, 15, 16, 16, 20, 20, 21, 22, 22; **49:**1, 3, 3, 4, 4, 7, 10, 10, 10, 10, 10, 11, 13, 13, 14, 15, 15, 15, 17, 17, 17, 17, 22, 24, 24, 24, 25, 25, 25, 25, 25, 26, 26, 26, 26, 26, 26, 27, 27, 27, 28, 28, 29, 30, 30, 30, 32, 32, 33; **50:**2, 3, 4, 5, 7, 8, 8, 10, 10, 11, 11, 11, 13, 13, 13, 13, 13, 15, 17, 17, 17, 17, 20, 20, 23, 24, 24, 25, 26; **Ex 1:**1, 7, 8, 10, 11, 11, 11, 11, 12, 12, 12, 12, 14, 14, 15, 15, 16, 16, 16, 17, 17, 17, 18, 18, 18, 19, 20, 20, 21, 22, 22, 22; **2:**1, 2, 3, 3, 3, 3, 3, 4, 5, 5, 5, 5, 5, 6, 6, 6, 7, 7, 7, 7, 8, 8, 8, 9, 9, 10, 10, 10, 10, 11, 11, 12, 12, 13, 13, 13, 14, 15, 16, 16, 17, 17, 17, 18, 18, 19, 21, 23, 23, 25; **3:**1, 1, 1, 1, 2, 2, 2, 4, 4, 6, 6, 6, 6, 7, 7, 8, 8, 8, 9, 9, 9, 10, 11, 12, 13, 13, 14, 15, 15, 15, 15, 15, 16, 16, 16, 16, 17, 17, 17, 17, 18, 18, 18, 18, 18, 18, 18, 18, 19, 20, 21, 22, 22; **4:**1, 2, 3, 3, 4, 5, 5, 5, 5, 5, 6, 7, 7, 8, 8, 8, 9, 9, 10, 11, 11, 14, 14, 15, 16, 17, 19, 20, 20, 21, 21, 21, 22, 24, 24, 25, 25, 26, 26, 27, 27, 27, 28, 28, 29, 30, 30, 31, 31, 31; **5:**1, 1, 1, 2, 2, 3, 3, 3, 3, 3, 4, 6, 6, 7, 8, 10, 10, 12, 12, 13, 14, 14, 15, 16, 17, 18, 19, 21, 21, 22; **6:**1, 1, 2, 3, 4, 5, 5, 5, 6, 6, 7, 8, 8, 9, 9, 9, 10, 11, 13, 13, 14, 14, 14, 15, 15, 16, 16, 17, 17, 18, 19, 19, 19, 21, 22, 23, 24, 24, 25, 25, 26, 26, 26, 26, 26, 27, 27, 27, 28, 29, 29, 30, 30; **7:**1, 2, 3, 4, 5, 5, 5, 6, 7, 8, 10, 10, 11, 13, 14, 14, 15, 15, 15, 15, 16, 16, 16, 16, 17, 17, 17, 17, 17, 18, 18, 18, 18, 19, 19, 19, 19, 19, 20, 20, 20, 20, 21, 21, 21, 21, 21, 22, 22, 23, 24, 24, 25, 25, 25, 25; **8:**1, 1, 2, 3, 3, 5, 5, 5, 6, 7, 7, 7, 8, 8, 8, 8, 9, 9, 9, 9, 10, 11, 11, 12, 12, 13, 13, 13, 13, 13, 14, 15, 15, 16, 16, 16, 16, 17, 17, 17, 17, 17, 18, 18, 18, 19, 19, 19, 20, 20, 20, 21, 22, 22, 22, 22, 24, 24, 24, 25, 26, 26, 26, 27, 27, 28, 29, 29, 29, 29, 30, 30, 31, 31, 31, 32; **9:**1, 1, 1, 1, 3, 4, 4, 4, 4, 5, 5, 5, 6, 6, 6, 6, 7, 7, 8, 8, 9, 10, 10, 10, 11, 11, 12, 12, 13, 13, 13, 13, 13, 14, 14, 15, 15, 16, 19, 19, 20, 20, 21, 21, 21, 22, 22, 22, 22, 23, 23, 23, 23, 23, 24, 25, 25, 26, 26, 26, 27, 28, 29, 29, 29, 29, 29, 30, 31, 31, 31, 32, 32, 32, 33, 33, 33, 33, 35, 35; **10:**1, 2, 2, 2, 3, 3, 3, 4, 5, 5, 5, 5, 6, 6, 6, 7, 7, 7, 8, 9, 10, 11, 11, 11, 12, 12, 12, 12, 12, 12, 13, 13, 13, 13, 14, 14, 14, 15, 15, 15, 15, 15, 15, 15, 15, 15, 16, 17, 18, 19, 19, 19, 19, 20, 20, 21, 21, 22, 23, 23, 24, 25, 26, 27, 28; **11:**1, 1, 1, 2, 3, 3, 3, 3, 3, 4, 5, 5, 5, 5, 5, 5, 6, 7, 7, 7, 8, 9, 9, 9, 10, 10, 10; **12:**1, 1, 1, 2, 2, 3, 3, 4, 4, 4, 6, 6, 6, 7, 7, 7, 7, 7, 9, 9, 10, 11, 11, 12, 12, 12, 12, 12, 13, 13, 13, 14, 15, 15, 15, 15, 16, 16, 16, 16, 16, 17, 18, 18, 18, 18, 18, 18, 19, 19, 21, 21, 21, 22, 22, 22, 22, 22, 23, 23, 23, 23, 23, 23, 23, 23, 25, 25, 27, 27, 27, 27, 27, 27, 28, 28, 29, 29, 29, 29, 29, 29, 29, 29, 29, 30, 30, 30, 31, 31, 33, 33, 33, 34, 35, 35, 36, 36, 36, 36, 36, 37, 37, 38, 39, 39, 40, 41, 41, 41, 41, 42, 42, 42, 43, 43, 43, 43, 46, 47, 47, 48, 48, 48, 48, 50, 50, 51, 51; **13:**1, 2, 3, 3, 3, 3, 4, 5, 5, 5, 5, 6, 6, 7, 8, 9, 9, 10, 11, 11, 11, 11, 12, 13, 13, 13, 14, 14, 15, 15, 15, 15, 15, 15, 16, 17, 17, 17, 17, 18, 18, 18, 19, 19, 20, 20, 21, 21, 22, 22; **14:**1, 2, 2, 2, 3, 3, 4, 4, 4, 4, 4, 5, 5, 6, 7, 7, 8, 8, 9, 9, 9, 9, 9, 10, 10, 10, 10, 11, 12, 13, 13, 13, 14, 15, 15, 16, 16, 16, 17, 17, 17, 17, 17, 18, 19, 19, 19, 20, 20, 20, 20, 20, 20, 21, 21, 21, 21, 21, 22, 22, 23, 23, 23, 24, 24, 24, 24, 25, 25, 26, 26, 26, 26, 26, 27, 27, 27, 27, 27, 27, 28, 28, 28, 28, 28, 28, 29, 29, 29, 29, 30, 30, 30, 30, 30, 30, 31, 31, 31, 31, 31; **15:**1, 1, 1, 1, 2, 3, 3, 4, 4, 4, 5, 5, 6, 7, 8, 8, 8, 8, 8, 8, 9, 9, 10, 10, 11, 12, 13, 14, 14, 15, 15, 15, 16, 17, 17, 18, 19, 19, 19, 19, 20, 20, 21, 21, 22, 22, 22, 23, 23, 24, 25, 25, 25, 25, 25, 25, 25, 26, 26, 26, 26, 26, 27; **16:**1, 2, 3, 4, 4, 5, 6, 6, 6, 6, 7, 7, 7, 7, 8, 8, 8, 8, 9, 9, 10, 10, 10, 10, 11, 11, 12, 12, 12, 12, 13, 13, 13, 13, 14, 14, 14, 15, 15, 15, 16, 17, 21, 21, 21, 21, 22, 22, 22, 22, 23, 23, 24, 24, 25, 25, 26, 26, 26, 27, 28, 28, 29, 29, 29, 29, 30, 30, 31, 32, 32, 32, 32, 32, 34, 34, 34, 35, 35, 36, 36; **17:**1, 1, 1, 2, 2, 4, 5, 5, 5, 5, 5, 5, 6, 6, 6, 6, 7, 7, 7, 7, 7, 7, 8, 8, 9, 9, 9, 9, 9, 10, 10, 11, 11, 11, 11, 11, 12, 13, 14, 15, 16, 16; **18:**1, 1, 1, 3, 3, 4, 4, 4, 4, 5, 5, 8, 8, 8, 8, 8, 9, 10, 10, 10, 11, 11, 12, 13, 13, 14, 14, 15, 16, 16, 16, 18, 19, 22, 22, 22, 22, 22, 23, 25, 26, 26; **19:**1, 1, 2, 3, 3, 3, 3, 3, 4, 5, 5, 5, 6, 7, 7, 7, 7, 8, 8, 8, 9, 9, 9, 9, 10, 10, 11, 11, 12, 12, 13, 13, 13, 13, 13, 13, 14, 16, 16, 16, 16, 17, 17, 17, 18, 18, 18, 18, 18, 19, 20, 20, 20, 20, 20, 21, 21, 21, 21, 22, 22, 23, 23, 23, 24, 24, 24, 24, 24, 25, 25; **20:**1, 2, 4, 5, 5, 5, 5, 7, 7, 8, 10, 10, 11, 11, 11, 11, 11, 11, 11, 11, 12, 12, 18, 18, 18, 18, 18, 18, 18, 21, 21, 21, 22, 22, 24, 24, 25, 26; **21:**2, 3, 4, 4, 5, 6, 6, 7, 7, 8, 8, 8, 9, 13, 14, 18, 19, 19, 19, 19, 20, 21, 21, 21, 21, 22, 22, 22, 22, 22, 22, 23, 23, 23, 24, 24, 24, 24, 24, 26, 26, 26, 26, 27, 27, 27, 28, 28, 29, 29, 29, 29, 29, 29, 29, 30, 30, 30, 30, 30, 31, 31, 32, 32, 32, 34, 34, 34, 35, 35, 35, 35, 35, 36, 36, 36, 36, 36; **22:**1, 1, 2, 2, 2, 2, 3, 3, 3, 3, 4, 4, 5, 5, 6, 6, 6, 6, 6, 7, 7, 7, 7, 8, 8, 8, 9, 9, 11, 11, 11, 11, 11, 12, 12, 13, 14, 14, 14, 15, 15, 15, 16, 17, 17, 20, 21, 24, 27, 29, 29, 30, 30, 30, 31; **23:**1, 2, 2, 2, 5, 8, 8, 8, 9, 9, 11, 11, 11, 11, 11, 11, 12, 12, 15, 15, 15, 15, 16, 16, 16, 16, 16, 16, 17, 18, 19, 19, 20, 23, 23, 24, 25, 27, 28, 29, 29, 30, 31, 31, 31, 31, 31, 31; **24:**1, 2, 2, 2, 2, 3, 3, 3, 3, 4, 4, 4, 4, 4, 4, 5, 5, 6, 6, 6, 7, 7, 7, 7, 8, 8, 8, 8, 9, 9, 10, 10, 12, 12, 12, 12, 12, 13, 14, 15, 15, 16, 16, 16, 16, 16, 16, 17, 17, 17, 17, 17, 17, 18, 18, 18; **25:**1, 2, 6, 6, 6, 7, 7, 8, 9, 14, 14, 14, 14, 15, 16, 16, 16, 16, 17, 17, 18, 18, 19, 19, 20, 20, 21, 21, 21, 21, 21, 22, 22, 22, 22, 22, 23, 26, 26, 26, 27, 27, 27, 27, 30, 30, 30, 31, 31, 32, 33, 34, 34, 35, 36, 36, 37, 37, 38, 39, 40, 40; **26:**1, 2, 3, 4, 4, 5, 5, 5, 5, 5, 6, 6, 6, 7, 8, 9, 9, 9, 9, 9, 10, 10, 11, 12, 12, 13, 14, 15, 15, 17, 17, 18, 20, 22, 24, 24, 24, 25, 26, 26, 26, 27, 27, 27, 28, 28, 28, 28, 29, 29, 29, 30, 30, 31, 31, 31, 32, 33, 33, 33, 33, 33, 34, 34, 34, 34, 34, 35, 35, 35, 35, 35, 35, 35, 36, 36, 37; **27:**2, 2, 2, 3, 5, 5, 5, 6, 7, 7, 7, 8, 8, 9, 9, 9, 10, 10, 10, 11, 11, 11, 12, 12, 13, 14, 14, 14, 15, 15, 16, 16, 17, 17, 17, 18, 18, 19, 19, 19, 19, 19, 20, 20, 21, 21, 21, 21, 21, 21, 21; **28:**1, 3, 6, 7, 8, 8, 9, 9, 10, 10, 11, 11, 12, 12, 12, 12, 13, 14, 14, 14, 15, 15, 15, 17, 18, 19, 20, 21, 21, 22, 22, 23, 23, 24, 24, 25, 25, 25, 25, 25, 26, 26, 26, 27, 27, 28, 28, 28, 28, 28, 28, 29, 29, 29, 29, 29, 29, 29, 30, 30, 30, 30, 30, 30, 30, 31, 31, 32, 32, 33, 33, 34, 34, 34, 35, 35, 35, 35, 36, 36, 37, 38, 38, 38, 38, 39, 43, 43, 43; **29:**1, 1, 3, 3, 3, 3, 4, 4, 5, 5, 5, 5, 5, 6, 6, 7, 10, 10, 10, 11, 11, 11, 12, 12, 12, 12, 13, 13, 13, 13, 13, 13, 14, 14, 14, 14, 15, 15, 16, 16, 17, 17, 17, 17, 17, 17, 18, 18, 19, 20, 20, 20, 20, 20, 20, 20, 21, 21, 21, 21, 22, 22, 22, 22, 22, 22, 22, 22, 22, 22, 23, 23, 24, 24, 25, 25, 25, 26, 26, 27, 27, 27, 27, 27, 27, 28, 28, 28, 28, 30, 30, 30, 31, 31, 32, 32, 32, 33, 33, 33, 34, 36, 36, 36, 37, 37, 38, 39, 39, 39, 41, 41, 41, 41, 41, 42, 42, 43, 43, 44, 44, 45, 46, 46, 46; **30:**2, 2, 2, 3, 3, 3, 4, 4, 4, 5, 5, 6, 6, 6, 6, 6, 6, 7, 7, 8, 8, 10, 10, 10, 10, 10, 11, 12, 12, 12, 13, 14, 15, 15, 16, 16, 16, 17, 18, 18, 20, 20, 20, 20, 22, 26, 26, 26, 27, 27, 27, 28, 28, 31, 32, 33, 34, 34, 34, 35, 35, 36, 36, 36, 37, 38; **31:**1, 2, 3, 6, 6, 6, 7, 7, 7, 7, 7, 7, 7, 8, 8, 8, 9, 9, 10, 10, 10, 11, 11, 11, 11, 12, 13, 13, 13, 14, 14, 15, 15, 16, 16, 17, 17, 18, 18, 18, 18; **32:**1, 1, 3, 4, 4, 4, 4, 5, 5, 5, 5, 6, 6, 7, 7, 7, 8, 9, 11, 11, 12, 12, 12, 12, 13, 14, 14, 15, 15, 15, 15, 16, 17, 17, 17, 18, 19, 19, 19, 19, 19, 19, 20, 20, 20, 21, 24, 25, 25, 26, 26, 26, 26, 27, 27, 27, 28, 29, 29, 29, 30, 30, 30, 30, 31, 32, 33, 34, 34, 34, 34, 35, 35, 35; **33:**1, 2, 3, 4, 5, 6, 6, 7, 7, 7, 7, 8, 8, 9, 9, 9, 9, 10, 11, 11, 11, 11, 11, 12, 14, 16, 17, 19, 19, 21, 22, 22; **34:**1, 1, 1, 1, 2, 2, 2, 3, 3, 3, 4, 4, 4, 4, 5, 5, 6, 6, 6, 7, 7, 7, 8, 10, 10, 10, 10, 10, 10, 10, 11, 11, 12, 12, 13, 14, 15, 15, 18, 18, 20, 20, 20, 21, 21, 22, 22, 22, 22, 22, 22, 23, 23, 24, 24, 25, 25, 25, 26, 26, 26, 26, 27, 27, 28, 28, 28, 28, 29, 29, 29, 29, 29, 30, 30, 31, 32, 32, 32, 34, 34, 34, 34, 34, 35, 35, 35; **35:**1, 1, 2, 2, 4, 4, 5, 8, 8, 8, 9, 9, 10, 11, 11, 11, 12, 12, 12, 12, 12, 13, 13, 13, 14, 14, 14, 14, 15, 15, 15, 15, 16, 16, 16, 16, 17, 17, 17, 17, 17, 17, 18, 18, 19, 19, 19, 19, 20, 21, 21, 22, 22, 24, 25, 26, 26, 27, 27, 27, 27, 28, 28, 28, 29, 29, 29, 30, 30, 31, 34, 34, 35, 35, 35; **36:**1, 1, 1, 1, 2, 2, 3, 3, 3, 3, 4, 5, 5, 6, 6, 6, 7, 8, 8, 9, 10, 11, 11, 12, 12, 12, 12, 12, 13, 13, 13, 14, 15, 16, 16, 17, 17, 18, 18, 18, 19, 19, 19, 20, 20, 22, 22, 23, 25, 25, 27, 27, 29, 29, 30, 31, 31, 32, 32, 33, 33, 33, 33, 34, 34, 34, 35, 36, 37, 37, 38, 38; **37:**1, 2, 5, 5, 5, 5, 6, 6, 7, 7, 8, 9, 9, 9, 11, 12, 12, 12, 13, 14, 14, 15, 16, 16, 17, 18, 18, 19, 20, 20, 21, 22, 22, 23, 23, 23, 24, 25, 25, 26, 26, 26, 27, 27, 28, 29, 29, 29, 29, 29; **38:**1, 2, 2, 3, 3, 3, 4, 5, 5, 6, 7, 7, 7, 7, 8, 8, 8, 8, 9, 9, 10, 11, 12, 12, 13, 14, 14, 14, 14, 15, 15, 16, 16, 17, 17, 17, 17, 17, 18, 18, 18, 18, 19, 19, 19, 20, 21, 21, 21, 21, 21, 21, 21, 22, 22, 22, 23, 24, 24, 25, 26, 26, 27, 27, 27, 27, 27, 28, 28, 28, 28, 28, 29, 30, 30, 30, 30, 30, 31, 31, 31, 31, 31, 31, 31, 31, 31, 31, 31; **39:**1, 1, 1, 1, 2, 3, 3, 4, 5, 5, 6, 6, 6, 6, 6, 7, 7, 8, 8, 8, 10, 11, 12, 13, 14, 14, 14, 15, 15, 16, 16, 17, 17, 17, 18, 18, 18, 18, 18, 19, 19, 19, 20, 20, 21, 21, 21, 21, 21, 21, 21, 21, 22, 22, 23, 23, 24, 24, 25, 25, 25, 26, 26, 26, 28, 28, 28, 29, 29, 29, 30, 30, 30, 30, 30, 31, 31, 32, 32, 32, 33, 33, 33, 34, 34, 34, 35, 35, 35, 35, 36, 36, 36, 37, 37, 37, 38,

38, 38, 38, 38, 38, 39, 39, 39, 40, 40, 40, 40, 40, 40, 40, 40, 40, 40, 41, 41, 41, 41, 42, 42, 43; **40:**1, 2, 2, 2, 3, 3, 3, 3, 3, 4, 4, 4, 4, 5, 5, 5, 5, 5, 5, 5, 6, 6, 7, 7, 7, 8, 8, 8, 8, 8, 9, 9, 10, 10, 10, 11, 12, 12, 13, 15, 16, 17, 17, 17, 18, 18, 19, 19, 19, 19, 20, 20, 20, 20, 20, 20, 20, 21, 21, 21, 21, 21, 22, 22, 22, 22, 22, 23, 23, 23, 23, 23, 24, 24, 24, 24, 24, 25, 25, 25, 26, 26, 26, 26, 27, 27, 28, 28, 28, 29, 29, 29, 30, 30, 30, 30, 31, 32, 32, 32, 33, 33, 33, 33, 33, 33, 33, 33, 34, 34, 34, 34, 35, 35, 35, 35, 35, 36, 36, 36, 37, 38, 38, 38, 38, 38, 38; **Lev 1:**1, 1, 2, 2, 2, 3, 3, 3, 3, 4, 5, 5, 5, 5, 5, 5, 5, 6, 7, 7, 7, 8, 8, 8, 9, 9, 9, 9, 9, 10, 11, 11, 11, 11, 11, 11, 11, 12, 12, 12, 12, 12, 12, 12, 13, 13, 13, 13, 13, 14, 15, 15, 15, 15, 15, 15, 15, 16, 16, 16, 16, 16, 16, 17, 17, 17, 17, 17, 17; **2:**1, 1, 2, 2, 2, 2, 3, 3, 3, 3, 4, 8, 8, 8, 9, 9, 9, 9, 10, 10, 10, 10, 11, 11, 11, 12, 12, 12, 14, 14, 16, 16, 16, 16; **3:**1, 1, 1, 2, 2, 2, 2, 2, 2, 2, 3, 3, 3, 4, 4, 4, 4, 4, 4, 5, 5, 5, 5, 5, 6, 6, 7, 8, 8, 8, 8, 8, 8, 9, 9, 9, 9, 9, 9, 10, 10, 10, 10, 10, 10, 11, 11, 11, 12, 13, 13, 13, 13, 13, 13, 14, 14, 14, 15, 15, 15, 15, 15, 15, 16, 16, 16, 16, 16; **4:**1, 2, 2, 2, 3, 3, 3, 4, 4, 4, 4, 4, 4, 5, 5, 5, 6, 6, 6, 6, 7, 7, 7, 7, 7, 7, 7, 7, 7, 7, 7, 7, 8, 8, 8, 9, 9, 9, 9, 9, 10, 10, 11, 11, 12, 12, 12, 12, 13, 13, 13, 13, 13, 14, 14, 14, 14, 15, 15, 15, 16, 16, 17, 17, 17, 18, 18, 18, 18, 18, 18, 18, 18, 18, 18, 18, 19, 19, 19, 20, 20, 20, 20, 20, 21, 21, 21, 21, 21, 21, 22, 24, 24, 24, 25, 25, 25, 25, 25, 25, 25, 25, 25, 26, 26, 26, 26, 26, 27, 27, 29, 29, 29, 30, 30, 30, 30, 30, 30, 30, 30, 30, 31, 31, 31, 31, 31, 31, 31, 32, 33, 33, 33, 33, 34, 34, 34, 34, 34, 34, 34, 34, 35, 35, 35, 35, 35, 35, 35; **5:**1, 2, 2, 4, 5, 6, 6, 6, 7, 7, 7, 7, 8, 8, 8, 8, 8, 9, 9, 9, 9, 9, 9, 9, 10, 10, 10, 10, 11, 12, 12, 12, 12, 13, 13, 13, 13, 13, 14, 15, 15, 15, 15, 15, 15, 15, 16, 16, 16, 17, 18, 18, 18, 18, 18, 19; **6:**1, 2, 2, 5, 5, 6, 6, 6, 7, 7, 8, 9, 9, 9, 9, 9, 9, 10, 10, 10, 10, 10, 11, 11, 12, 12, 12, 12, 12, 12, 12, 13, 13, 14, 14, 14, 14, 15, 15, 15, 15, 16, 16, 16, 16, 17, 17, 17, 17, 18, 18, 18, 19, 20, 20, 20, 20, 21, 22, 22, 22, 22, 23, 23, 24, 25, 25, 25, 25, 25, 26, 26, 26, 26, 27, 27, 28, 30, 30, 30, 30; **7:**1, 1, 2, 2, 2, 2, 3, 3, 3, 3, 3, 3, 4, 4, 4, 4, 4, 4, 5, 5, 5, 6, 7, 7, 7, 7, 7, 7, 8, 8, 8, 8, 8, 9, 10, 11, 11, 11, 12, 14, 14, 14, 14, 15, 15, 15, 16, 16, 17, 18, 18, 18, 18, 20, 20, 21, 21, 22, 23, 24, 25, 25, 26, 27, 28, 29, 29, 29, 30, 30, 30, 30, 30, 31, 31, 31, 31, 32, 32, 33, 33, 33, 33, 33, 34, 34, 34, 34, 34, 35, 35, 35, 35, 36, 36, 36, 36, 36, 36, 37, 37, 37, 37, 37, 37, 37, 38, 38, 38, 38; **8:**1, 2, 2, 2, 2, 2, 3, 3, 3, 4, 4, 4, 5, 7, 7, 7, 7, 7, 7, 8, 8, 8, 9, 9, 9, 10, 10, 11, 11, 12, 13, 14, 14, 15, 15, 15, 15, 15, 15, 15, 15, 16, 16, 16, 16, 16, 16, 17, 17, 17, 17, 18, 18, 18, 19, 19, 19, 20, 20, 20, 20, 21, 21, 21, 21, 21, 21, 21, 22, 22, 23, 23, 23, 24, 24, 24, 24, 24, 24, 24, 24, 25, 25, 25, 25, 25, 25, 25, 25, 25, 26, 26, 27, 27, 28, 28, 28, 28, 28, 29, 29, 29, 29, 30, 30, 30, 31, 31, 31, 31, 31, 33, 33, 33, 34, 35, 35, 35, 35, 36; **9:**1, 1, 1, 2, 3, 4, 4, 5, 5, 5, 5, 5, 6, 6, 6, 7, 7, 7, 7, 8, 8, 9, 9, 9, 9, 9, 9, 9, 10, 10, 10, 10, 10, 10, 10, 11, 11, 11, 12, 12, 12, 12, 12, 13, 13, 13, 14, 14, 14, 15, 15, 15, 16, 16, 17, 17, 17, 17, 18, 18, 18, 18, 18, 18, 19, 19, 19, 19, 19, 19, 19, 19, 19, 20, 20, 21, 21, 22, 22, 22, 22, 22, 23, 23, 23, 23, 23, 24, 24, 24, 24, 24, 24; **10:**1, 2, 2, 3, 3, 4, 4, 4, 4, 5, 6, 6, 6, 6, 6, 7, 7, 7, 7, 8, 9, 11, 11, 11, 12, 12, 12, 12, 13, 13, 13, 14, 14, 14, 15, 15, 15, 15, 15, 16, 16, 17, 17, 17, 17, 17, 17, 18, 18, 18, 18, 19, 19, 19; **11:**1, 2, 2, 2, 3, 4, 4, 4, 4, 5, 5, 6, 7, 7, 8, 13, 13, 13, 13, 14, 16, 16, 16, 17, 17, 17, 18, 18, 18, 19, 19, 19, 20, 24, 25, 26, 26, 27, 27, 29, 29, 29, 29, 29, 30, 30, 30, 30, 30, 31, 32, 33, 33, 34, 35, 36, 36, 36, 37, 37, 37, 38, 38, 38, 41, 44, 44, 45, 45, 45, 46, 46, 46, 46, 46, 46; **12:**1, 1, 3, 3, 4, 4, 4, 4, 5, 6, 6, 6, 6, 6, 7, 7, 7, 7, 8, 8, 8, 8; **13:**1, 2, 2, 3, 3, 3, 3, 3, 3, 4, 4, 4, 4, 4, 4, 5, 5, 5, 5, 5, 5, 6, 6, 6, 6, 6, 6, 6, 6, 7, 7, 7, 8, 8, 9, 10, 10, 11, 11, 11, 11, 12, 12, 13, 13, 13, 13, 13, 13, 14, 15, 15, 16, 16, 16, 16, 16, 17, 17, 17, 18, 19, 20, 20, 20, 20, 20, 20, 21, 21, 21, 21, 22, 22, 22, 22, 23, 23, 23, 23, 24, 24, 25, 25, 25, 25, 25, 25, 26, 26, 26, 26, 26, 27, 27, 27, 27, 28, 28, 28, 28, 28, 29, 30, 30, 30, 30, 30, 30, 30, 31, 31, 31, 31, 32, 32, 32, 33, 33, 33, 33, 33, 34, 34, 34, 35, 35, 36, 36, 36, 37, 37, 37, 37, 37, 38, 39, 39, 39, 39, 42, 42, 43, 43, 44, 44, 44, 46, 46, 48, 49, 49, 49, 49, 49, 49, 50, 50, 51, 51, 51, 51, 52, 52, 52, 53, 53, 53, 53, 53, 54, 54, 55, 55, 55, 55, 55, 56, 56, 56, 56, 56, 56, 57, 57, 57, 58, 58, 59, 59; **14:**1, 2, 2, 3, 3, 3, 5, 5, 6, 6, 6, 6, 6, 6, 7, 7, 7, 7, 7, 7, 7, 7, 7, 8, 8, 8, 9, 9, 9, 10, 10, 10, 11, 11, 11, 11, 11, 12, 12, 12, 12, 13, 13, 13, 13, 13, 13, 14, 14, 14, 14, 14, 14, 14, 14, 14, 15, 15, 15, 16, 16, 17, 17, 17, 17, 17, 17, 17, 17, 17, 17, 18, 18, 18, 18, 18, 18, 19, 19, 19, 19, 19, 19, 19, 20, 20, 20, 20, 20, 21, 21, 22, 22, 22, 22, 23, 23, 23, 23, 23, 23, 23, 24, 24, 24, 24, 24, 25, 25, 25, 25, 25, 25, 25, 25, 25, 26, 26, 26, 27, 27, 28, 28, 28, 28, 28, 28, 28, 28, 28, 28, 29, 29, 29, 29, 29, 30, 30, 30, 30, 31, 31, 31, 31, 31, 32, 32, 32, 33, 34, 35, 35, 36, 36, 36, 36, 36, 37, 37, 37, 37, 38, 39, 39, 39, 39, 39, 40, 40, 40, 40, 41, 41, 41, 41, 41, 42, 42, 43, 44, 44, 44, 44, 44, 45, 46, 47, 48, 48, 48, 48, 48, 49, 49, 50, 51, 51, 51, 51, 51, 51, 51, 52, 53, 53, 53, 53, 53, 54, 54; **15:**1, 2, 3, 3, 5, 6, 6, 7, 7, 7, 8, 9, 11, 12, 12, 13, 14, 14, 14, 14, 14, 15, 15, 15, 15, 15, 15, 17, 18, 18, 22, 25, 25, 25, 25, 28, 29, 29, 29, 29, 30, 30, 30, 30, 31, 32; **16:**1, 1, 1, 2, 2, 2, 2, 2, 2, 2, 2, 3, 4, 4, 4, 5, 6, 7, 7, 7, 7, 8, 8, 9, 9, 10, 10, 10, 10, 10, 11, 11, 12, 12, 12, 12, 13, 13, 13, 13, 13, 13, 13, 14, 14, 14, 14, 14, 14, 15, 15, 15, 15, 15, 15, 15, 15, 16, 16, 16, 16, 16, 17, 17, 17, 18, 18, 18, 18, 18, 18, 19, 19, 20, 20, 20, 20, 21, 21, 21, 21, 21, 21, 21, 22, 22, 22, 22, 23, 23, 23, 23, 24, 24, 24, 25, 25, 25, 26, 26, 26, 26, 27, 27, 27, 27, 27, 27, 28, 28, 28, 29, 29, 29, 30, 31, 32, 32, 32, 33, 33, 33, 33, 33, 34, 34; **17:**1, 2, 2, 3, 4, 4, 4, 4, 5, 5, 5, 5, 5, 5, 6, 6, 6, 6, 6, 6, 7, 7, 7, 8, 9, 9, 9, 9, 10, 11, 11, 11, 12, 12, 13, 13, 14, 14, 14, 14, 14, 15, 15; **18:**1, 2, 2, 3, 3, 4, 5, 6, 9, 11, 21, 21, 24, 24, 25, 25, 25, 26, 27, 27, 27, 28, 28, 29, 30; **19:**1, 2, 2, 3, 4, 5, 6, 6, 6, 6, 7, 7, 8, 8, 8, 8, 9, 9, 9, 10, 10, 10, 10, 10, 10, 10, 12, 12, 14, 14, 14, 15, 15, 16, 16, 18, 20, 20, 21, 21, 21, 21, 22, 22, 22, 22, 22, 23, 23, 23, 24, 24, 24, 25, 25, 25, 27, 27, 28, 28, 29, 30, 31, 32, 32, 32, 33, 34, 34, 36, 36, 37; **20:**1, 2, 2, 2, 3, 4, 4, 4, 5, 6, 6, 7, 8, 10, 10, 11, 11, 13, 15, 16, 17, 17, 17, 17, 18, 18, 20, 21, 22, 23, 23, 24, 26; **21:**1, 1, 5, 5, 6, 6, 6, 7, 7, 8, 10, 10, 10, 12, 12, 12, 13, 15, 15, 16, 21, 22, 22, 22, 23, 23, 23, 24; **22:**1, 2, 2, 2, 3, 3, 3, 4, 4, 4, 6, 7, 7, 8, 8, 9, 9, 10, 10, 11, 12, 12, 13, 13, 14, 14, 14, 15, 15, 15, 16, 16, 16, 17, 18, 18, 18, 21, 21, 22, 22, 23, 24, 26, 27, 27, 28, 28, 28, 29, 30, 30, 30, 30, 31, 32, 32, 33; **23:**1, 2, 2, 2, 3, 3, 4, 4, 4, 4, 5, 6, 6, 6, 6, 6, 7, 7, 7, 8, 8, 8, 8, 8, 9, 10, 10, 10, 10, 11, 11, 11, 11, 12, 13, 15, 15, 15, 15, 16, 16, 16, 17, 17, 17, 18, 18, 18, 20, 20, 20, 20, 20, 20, 22, 22, 22, 22, 22, 22, 22, 23, 24, 24, 24, 24, 25, 26, 27, 27, 27, 27, 28, 28, 29, 32, 32, 33, 34, 34, 34, 34, 34, 35, 36, 36, 36, 36, 37, 37, 37, 38, 38, 38, 39, 39, 39, 39, 39, 39, 39, 40, 40, 40, 41, 42, 43, 43, 44, 44, 44; **24:**1, 2, 2, 3, 3, 3, 3, 3, 4, 4, 4, 6, 6, 6, 6, 7, 7, 8, 8, 8, 9, 9, 9, 10, 11, 11, 11, 11, 11, 12, 12, 12, 13, 14, 14, 14, 15, 15, 16, 16, 16, 18, 19, 22, 23, 23, 23, 23; **25:**1, 2, 2, 2, 2, 4, 4, 4, 5, 5, 5, 6, 6, 7, 7, 9, 9, 9, 9, 10, 11, 11, 11, 12, 12, 13, 13, 15, 15, 15, 15, 15, 15, 15, 16, 16, 16, 16, 16, 16, 16, 16, 16, 17, 18, 19,

20, 21, 21, 21, 22, 22, 22, 22, 22, 22, 22, 23, 24, 26, 26, 27, 27, 27, 27, 27, 27, 27, 27, 28, 28, 28, 28, 28, 28, 29, 29, 29, 30, 30, 30, 30, 30, 30, 31, 31, 31, 32, 32, 32, 33, 33, 33, 33, 33, 33, 34, 34, 36, 38, 38, 40, 42, 42, 44, 45, 46, 48, 49, 50, 50, 50, 52, 53, 54, 54, 55, 55, 55; **26:**1, 2, 4, 4, 4, 5, 6, 6, 8, 10, 10, 13, 13, 13, 19, 19, 26, 29, 32, 33, 34, 34, 34, 35, 35, 36, 36, 36, 38, 38, 39, 40, 41, 42, 43, 43, 43, 44, 44, 45, 45, 46, 46, 46; **27:**1, 2, 2, 2, 2, 3, 3, 6, 8, 8, 8, 8, 9, 9, 10, 10, 10, 11, 11, 11, 13, 13, 13, 14, 14, 14, 15, 15, 15, 15, 16, 16, 17, 17, 17, 17, 18, 18, 18, 18, 18, 18, 19, 19, 19, 19, 20, 20, 20, 21, 21, 21, 21, 21, 22, 23, 23, 23, 23, 23, 23, 24, 24, 24, 25, 25, 26, 26, 26, 27, 27, 27, 28, 28, 29, 30, 30, 30, 31, 31, 32, 33, 33, 33, 33, 34, 34, 34; **Nu 1:**1, 1, 1, 1, 2, 2, 2, 3, 5, 5, 5, 5, 16, 17, 18, 18, 18, 19, 19, 19, 20, 44, 44, 45, 46, 47, 48, 49, 49, 49, 49, 50, 50, 50, 50, 51, 51, 51, 53, 53, 53, 53, 53, 53, 53, 54, 54; **2:**1, 2, 2, 2, 2, 3, 3, 3, 3, 3, 3, 3, 9, 9, 9, 9, 9, 10, 10, 10, 10, 10, 10, 16, 16, 16, 16, 17, 17, 17, 17, 17, 17, 17, 18, 18, 18, 18, 18, 18, 24, 24, 24, 24, 24, 25, 25, 25, 25, 25, 25, 31, 31, 31, 31, 31, 32, 33, 33, 34, 34, 34; **3:**1, 1, 2, 4, 4, 4, 5, 6, 6, 7, 7, 8, 8, 8, 8, 9, 10, 10, 10, 11, 12, 12, 12, 12, 12, 13, 13, 13, 13, 13, 13, 14, 14, 15, 16, 18, 19, 20, 20, 21, 21, 23, 23, 23, 24, 24, 25, 25, 26, 26, 26, 26, 26, 26, 26, 27, 27, 28, 28, 29, 29, 30, 30, 31, 31, 31, 31, 31, 31, 31, 31, 31, 32, 32, 32, 32, 32, 33, 33, 35, 35, 35, 35, 36, 36, 36, 36, 36, 36, 36, 37, 37, 38, 38, 38, 38, 38, 38, 38, 38, 38, 39, 39, 40, 40, 41, 41, 41, 41, 41, 41, 42, 42, 42, 43, 44, 45, 45, 45, 45, 45, 45, 45, 45, 45, 46, 46, 47, 47, 48, 48, 48, 49, 49, 50, 51, 51; **4:**1, 2, 2, 2, 3, 3, 3, 4, 4, 4, 4, 5, 5, 5, 5, 5, 6, 6, 6, 6, 7, 7, 7, 7, 7, 7, 8, 8, 8, 9, 10, 10, 11, 11, 11, 12, 12, 12, 13, 13, 13, 14, 14, 14, 14, 14, 15, 15, 15, 15, 15, 15, 15, 15, 16, 16, 16, 16, 16, 16, 16, 16, 17, 18, 18, 19, 20, 20, 21, 22, 22, 22, 23, 23, 23, 24, 24, 24, 25, 25, 25, 25, 25, 25, 26, 26, 26, 26, 26, 26, 26, 27, 27, 27, 28, 28, 28, 28, 29, 29, 29, 30, 30, 30, 31, 31, 31, 31, 31, 32, 32, 32, 33, 33, 33, 33, 34, 34, 34, 35, 35, 35, 36, 37, 37, 37, 37, 38, 39, 39, 39, 40, 41, 41, 41, 41, 42, 43, 43, 43, 44, 45, 45, 45, 46, 46, 47, 47, 49, 49, 49; **5:**1, 2, 2, 3, 4, 4, 4, 5, 6, 6, 6, 7, 8, 8, 8, 9, 9, 10, 11, 12, 13, 15, 15, 16, 16, 17, 18, 18, 18, 18, 18, 19, 19, 19, 19, 21, 21, 21, 21, 22, 22, 23, 23, 24, 24, 24, 25, 25, 25, 25, 25, 26, 26, 26, 27, 27, 29, 30, 30, 30, 31; **6:**1, 1, 2, 2, 2, 4, 5, 5, 6, 6, 7, 7, 8, 10, 10, 10, 10, 11, 11, 11, 11, 11, 12, 12, 12, 13, 13, 13, 13, 13, 14, 16, 16, 16, 16, 17, 17, 17, 17, 18, 18, 18, 18, 18, 19, 19, 19, 19, 20, 20, 20, 20, 20, 20, 20, 21, 21, 21, 22, 23, 24, 25, 26, 27; **7:**1, 1, 1, 2, 2, 2, 3, 3, 4, 5, 5, 5, 5, 6, 6, 7, 8, 8, 8, 9, 9, 9, 9, 10, 10, 10, 10, 11, 11, 11, 12, 12, 13, 17, 18, 18, 19, 23, 24, 24, 25, 29, 30, 30, 31, 35, 36, 36, 37, 41, 42, 42, 43, 47, 48, 48, 49, 53, 54, 54, 55, 59, 60, 60, 61, 65, 66, 66, 67, 71, 72, 72, 73, 77, 78, 78, 79, 83, 84, 84, 84, 84, 85, 86, 86, 86, 87, 87, 88, 88, 88, 89, 89, 89, 89, 89, 89, 89, 89, 89; **8:**1, 2, 2, 3, 3, 4, 4, 4, 5, 6, 6, 6, 7, 9, 9, 9, 9, 10, 10, 10, 11, 11, 11, 11, 12, 12, 12, 12, 12, 12, 13, 13, 14, 14, 14, 14, 15, 16, 16, 16, 16, 16, 17, 17, 17, 17, 17, 18, 18, 19, 19, 19, 19, 19, 20, 20, 20, 21, 21, 21, 22, 22, 22, 22, 22, 23, 24, 24, 24, 24, 25, 26, 26, 26; **9:**1, 1, 1, 1, 1, 2, 2, 2, 3, 4, 4, 5, 5, 5, 5, 6, 7, 7, 7, 7, 8, 9, 10, 10, 10, 10, 11, 11, 11, 12, 12, 12, 12, 13, 13, 13, 13, 13, 13, 14, 14, 14, 14, 15, 15, 15, 15, 16, 16, 16, 17, 17, 17, 17, 17, 18, 18, 18, 19, 19, 19, 19, 20, 20, 20, 20, 21, 21, 21, 21, 22, 22, 22, 23, 23; **10:**1, 2, 2, 3, 3, 3, 4, 4, 5, 5, 5, 5, 6, 6, 6, 7, 7, 8, 8, 9, 9, 10, 10, 10, 10, 10, 11, 11, 11, 11, 12, 12, 12, 12, 13, 13, 13, 14, 14, 14, 15, 16, 17, 17, 17, 17, 17, 18, 18, 19, 20, 21, 21, 21, 21, 21, 21, 22, 22, 23, 24, 25, 25, 25, 25, 25, 26, 27, 28, 28, 29, 29, 29, 31, 31, 32, 32, 33, 33, 33, 33, 34, 34, 35, 36, 36; **11:**1, 1, 1, 1, 1, 1, 2, 2, 2, 3, 3, 3, 4, 4, 4, 4, 5, 5, 7, 8, 8, 9, 9, 9, 9, 10, 10, 11, 11, 12, 14, 16, 16, 16, 17, 17, 17, 17, 18, 18, 18, 20, 22, 22, 23, 24, 24, 24, 24, 25, 25, 25, 25, 25, 25, 26, 26, 26, 26, 26, 27, 29, 29, 30, 30, 31, 31, 31, 31, 31, 32, 32, 32, 32, 32, 33, 33, 33, 33, 34, 34, 35; **12:**2, 2, 4, 4, 4, 5, 5, 5, 5, 6, 6, 8, 9, 10, 10, 13, 14, 14, 15, 15, 16; **13:**1, 2, 2, 2, 3, 3, 4, 4, 4, 16, 16, 16, 17, 17, 17, 17, 18, 18, 20, 20, 20, 20, 20, 21, 21, 22, 22, 22, 23, 23, 24, 24, 24, 25, 25, 26, 26, 26, 26, 26, 27, 28, 28, 29, 29, 29, 29, 29, 29, 29, 29, 30, 30, 31, 31, 32, 32, 32, 32, 33; **14:**1, 2, 3, 5, 5, 6, 6, 7, 7, 8, 9, 9, 9, 9, 10, 10, 10, 10, 10, 11, 11, 13, 13, 13, 14, 14, 14, 14, 15, 16, 16, 16, 18, 18, 18, 18, 19, 20, 21, 21, 22, 22, 23, 24, 24, 25, 25, 25, 25, 25, 26, 27, 28, 28, 29, 30, 30, 31, 33, 33, 33, 34, 34, 34, 34, 35, 35, 36, 36, 36, 36, 37, 38, 38, 39, 39, 39, 40, 40, 40, 40, 41, 41, 42, 42, 43, 43, 43, 44, 44, 44, 44, 44, 44, 45, 45; **15:**1, 1, 2, 3, 3, 3, 4, 6, 7, 8, 9, 10, 10, 11, 13, 14, 14, 15, 15, 15, 16, 16, 17, 18, 18, 18, 19, 19, 20, 20, 20, 20, 21, 21, 21, 22, 23, 23, 24, 24, 24, 24, 24, 25, 25, 25, 26, 26, 26, 26, 27, 27, 28, 28, 28, 29, 30, 30, 30, 31, 31, 32, 32, 32, 33, 33, 35, 35, 35, 35, 36, 36, 36, 36, 37, 38, 38, 38, 38, 39, 39, 39, 40, 41, 41, 41; **16:**1, 1, 2, 3, 3, 4, 5, 5, 7, 7, 7, 9, 9, 9, 9, 10, 11, 11, 12, 14, 15, 16, 17, 18, 18, 19, 19, 19, 19, 19, 20, 22, 22, 22, 23, 24, 24, 25, 25, 26, 26, 27, 27, 27, 28, 29, 30, 30, 30, 30, 31, 31, 32, 32, 32, 33, 33, 34, 34, 35, 35, 36, 37, 37, 37, 37, 38, 38, 38, 38, 38, 38, 38, 38, 39, 39, 39, 39, 39, 40, 40, 40, 40, 41, 41, 41, 42, 42, 42, 42, 42, 43, 43, 44, 45, 46, 46, 46, 46, 47, 47, 47, 48, 48, 48, 49, 50, 50, 50; **17:**1, 3, 3, 3, 4, 4, 4, 5, 5, 6, 6, 6, 7, 7, 7, 7, 8, 8, 8, 8, 9, 9, 9, 10, 10, 10, 11, 12, 13, 13; **18:**1, 1, 1, 1, 2, 2, 2, 2, 3, 3, 3, 4, 4, 4, 5, 5, 5, 5, 5, 6, 6, 6, 7, 7, 7, 7, 7, 7, 8, 8, 8, 8, 9, 9, 9, 9, 9, 10, 11, 11, 11, 12, 12, 12, 12, 12, 13, 13, 13, 13, 14, 15, 15, 15, 16, 16, 16, 17, 17, 17, 17, 18, 18, 18, 19, 19, 19, 20, 20, 21, 21, 21, 21, 22, 22, 23, 23, 23, 23, 24, 24, 24, 24, 25, 26, 26, 26, 26, 26, 26, 27, 27, 28, 28, 28, 28, 28, 29, 29, 29, 30, 30, 31, 32, 32, 32, 32, 32; **19:**1, 2, 2, 3, 3, 4, 4, 5, 6, 6, 6, 7, 7, 8, 8, 9, 9, 9, 9, 9, 9, 9, 10, 10, 10, 10, 12, 12, 12, 12, 13, 13, 13, 13, 14, 14, 15, 16, 17, 17, 17, 18, 18, 18, 18, 18, 18, 19, 19, 19, 19, 19, 20, 20, 20, 20, 21, 21; **20:**1, 1, 2, 3, 3, 4, 6, 6, 6, 6, 6, 6, 7, 8, 8, 8, 8, 8, 8, 9, 9, 9, 10, 10, 11, 11, 11, 12, 12, 12, 13, 13, 13, 14, 14, 14, 15, 16, 16, 17, 17, 18, 19, 19, 20, 22, 23, 23, 23, 24, 24, 24, 24, 24, 27, 27, 27, 28, 28, 28, 29; **21:**1, 1, 1, 1, 1, 2, 2, 3, 3, 3, 3, 4, 4, 4, 4, 4, 4, 5, 6, 7, 7, 7, 7, 7, 8, 8, 9, 9, 10, 11, 11, 12, 13, 13, 13, 13, 13, 13, 13, 13, 13, 14, 14, 14, 14, 14, 14, 14, 15, 15, 16, 16, 16, 16, 17, 18, 18, 20, 20, 21, 21, 22, 23, 24, 24, 24, 24, 24, 24, 25, 25, 25, 26, 26, 26, 27, 28, 28, 28, 28, 29, 30, 31, 31, 31, 32, 32, 32, 32, 34, 34, 34; **22:**1, 1, 1, 2, 2, 2, 4, 4, 5, 5, 5, 6, 6, 6, 8, 8, 8, 11, 11, 13, 13, 14, 15, 18, 18, 19, 21, 21, 22, 22, 22, 23, 23, 23, 23, 23, 23, 24, 24, 24, 25, 25, 25, 25, 25, 26, 26, 26, 26, 27, 27, 28, 28, 30, 30, 31, 31, 31, 31, 31, 32, 32, 33, 33, 34, 34, 34, 35, 35, 36, 36, 36, 38, 40, 40, 40, 41, 41; **23:**2, 3, 3, 5, 6, 6, 7, 7, 7, 8, 9, 9, 10, 12, 13, 14, 15, 15, 16, 17, 17, 17, 17, 18, 21, 24, 24, 26, 28, 28; **24:**1, 1, 2, 2, 3, 3, 3, 3, 4, 4, 6, 6, 6, 8, 11, 13, 13, 13, 14, 14, 15, 15, 15, 15, 16, 16, 16, 17, 17, 17, 17, 17, 19, 20, 20, 21, 21, 22, 24; **25:**1, 1, 1, 2, 2, 3, 3, 4, 4, 4, 4, 4, 6, 6, 6, 6, 6, 6, 7, 7, 8, 8, 8, 8, 8, 8, 8, 10, 11, 11, 13, 14, 14, 14, 14, 15, 15, 15, 16, 17, 18, 18, 18; **26:**1, 1, 1, 2, 3, 3, 3, 3, 3, 4, 4, 4, 4, 5, 5, 5, 6, 6, 7, 7, 8, 9, 9, 9, 10, 10, 10, 11, 12, 12, 12, 12, 13, 13,

14, 14, 15, 15, 15, 15, 15, 16, 16, 17, 17, 18, 18, 19, 20, 20, 20, 20, 21, 21, 21, 21, 22, 22, 23, 23, 23, 23, 24, 24, 25, 25, 26, 26, 26, 26, 26, 27, 27, 29, 29, 29, 30, 30, 30, 30, 31, 31, 32, 32, 34, 34, 35, 35, 35, 35, 35, 36, 36, 36, 37, 37, 38, 38, 38, 38, 38, 39, 39, 40, 40, 40, 40, 41, 41, 42, 42, 42, 43, 43, 44, 44, 44, 44, 44, 45, 45, 45, 45, 47, 47, 48, 48, 48, 48, 49, 49, 50, 50, 51, 51, 52, 53, 53, 53, 54, 54, 54, 55, 55, 55, 56, 57, 57, 57, 57, 57, 58, 58, 58, 58, 58, 58, 58, 59, 59, 59, 61, 62, 62, 62, 62, 62, 62, 63, 63, 63, 63, 63, 64, 64, 65, 65, 65; **27:**1, 1, 2, 2, 2, 2, 2, 3, 3, 4, 4, 5, 6, 7, 7, 8, 11, 11, 11, 12, 12, 12, 12, 12, 12, 14, 14, 14, 14, 14, 15, 16, 16, 16, 17, 17, 18, 18, 19, 19, 19, 19, 20, 21, 21, 21, 21, 21, 22, 22, 22, 23; **28:**1, 1, 2, 2, 2, 3, 4, 4, 4, 6, 6, 7, 7, 7, 8, 8, 8, 8, 9, 10, 10, 11, 11, 12, 13, 14, 14, 14, 15, 15, 15, 16, 16, 17, 18, 18, 18, 19, 20, 21, 24, 24, 24, 24, 24, 25, 25, 25, 26, 26, 26, 26, 26, 27, 28, 29, 31, 31; **29:**1, 1, 1, 2, 3, 3, 4, 6, 7, 7, 7, 8, 9, 9, 9, 10, 11, 11, 12, 12, 12, 12, 13, 14, 14, 15, 16, 17, 18, 19, 20, 20, 21, 22, 23, 23, 24, 25, 26, 26, 27, 28, 29, 29, 30, 31, 32, 32, 33, 34, 35, 35, 35, 36, 37, 38, 39, 39, 40, 40; **30:**1, 1, 1, 2, 3, 4, 5, 5, 5, 7, 8, 8, 12, 12, 14, 15, 16, 16; **31:**1, 2, 2, 3, 3, 6, 6, 6, 6, 6, 7, 7, 8, 8, 8, 9, 9, 10, 10, 11, 12, 12, 12, 12, 13, 13, 13, 13, 14, 14, 15, 16, 16, 16, 16, 16, 16, 17, 17, 18, 19, 19, 21, 21, 21, 21, 21, 23, 23, 24, 24, 25, 26, 26, 26, 26, 26, 27, 27, 27, 27, 27, 28, 28, 28, 28, 29, 29, 30, 30, 30, 30, 30, 31, 31, 32, 32, 32, 36, 36, 36, 37, 38, 39, 40, 41, 41, 41, 42, 42, 42, 42, 42, 47, 47, 47, 47, 47, 48, 49, 50, 50, 50, 50, 51, 51, 51, 52, 52, 52, 53, 53, 54, 54, 54, 54, 54, 54, 54; **32:**1, 1, 2, 2, 2, 4, 4, 5, 6, 6, 7, 7, 7, 7, 8, 9, 9, 9, 9, 9, 10, 11, 12, 12, 12, 13, 13, 13, 14, 14, 15, 17, 17, 18, 19, 19, 19, 19, 20, 21, 21, 22, 22, 22, 22, 22, 22, 22, 22, 22, 23, 25, 26, 27, 28, 29, 29, 29, 29, 29, 30, 30, 31, 31, 32, 32, 32, 33, 33, 33, 33, 33, 33, 34, 34, 37, 37, 38, 38, 39, 39, 39, 40, 41, 41, 41, 41, 41, 42; **33:**1, 1, 1, 2, 2, 2, 2, 3, 3, 3, 3, 3, 4, 4, 4, 4, 4, 5, 6, 6, 8, 8, 8, 10, 11, 11, 12, 14, 15, 16, 36, 37, 38, 38, 38, 38, 38, 40, 40, 40, 40, 41, 44, 47, 47, 48, 48, 48, 48, 49, 49, 50, 50, 50, 51, 51, 51, 52, 53, 54, 54, 54, 54, 54, 54, 54, 55, 55, 55; **34:**1, 2, 2, 2, 3, 3, 3, 3, 3, 3, 4, 5, 5, 5, 6, 6, 7, 10, 11, 11, 11, 11, 12, 12, 12, 13, 13, 13, 13, 13, 14, 14, 14, 15, 15, 16, 17, 17, 17, 17, 18, 19, 19, 19, 29, 29, 29, 29, 29; **35:**1, 1, 1, 2, 2, 2, 3, 4, 4, 4, 5, 5, 5, 5, 5, 6, 7, 7, 8, 8, 8, 8, 8, 9, 10, 10, 10, 12, 12, 12, 14, 14, 14, 14, 15, 16, 17, 18, 18, 19, 19, 19, 19, 20, 21, 21, 21, 23, 24, 24, 24, 24, 25, 25, 25, 25, 25, 26, 26, 27, 27, 28, 28, 28, 28, 28, 28, 28, 30, 31, 32, 32, 32, 33, 33, 33, 33, 34, 34, 34; **36:**1, 1, 1, 2, 2, 2, 2, 2, 3, 3, 4, 4, 5, 5, 5, 5, 6, 6, 7, 7, 8, 8, 8, 10, 10, 12, 13, 13, 13, 13, 13; **Dt 1:**1, 1, 1, 1, 1, 1, 3, 3, 3, 4, 5, 5, 5, 5, 6, 7, 7, 7, 7, 7, 7, 7, 7, 7, 7, 7, 8, 8, 10, 10, 11, 11, 15, 16, 16, 17, 19, 19, 19, 19, 20, 20, 21, 21, 22, 22, 24, 24, 25, 25, 26, 26, 27, 28, 28, 28, 28, 28, 30, 31, 31, 32, 33, 34, 35, 36, 36, 37, 37, 38, 38, 39, 39, 40, 40, 41, 41, 41, 41, 42, 43, 43, 44, 44, 45; **2:**1, 1, 1, 2, 4, 4, 4, 4, 4, 5, 7, 7, 8, 8, 8, 8, 9, 9, 9, 10, 10, 10, 11, 11, 11, 11, 12, 12, 12, 12, 12, 13, 14, 14, 14, 14, 15, 16, 17, 18, 19, 19, 19, 19, 20, 20, 20, 21, 21, 21, 22, 22, 22, 23, 23, 23, 24, 24, 24, 24, 25, 26, 27, 27, 28, 29, 29, 29, 29, 29, 30, 31, 33, 35, 35, 36, 36, 36, 36, 36, 36, 37, 37, 37, 37, 37, 37; **3:**1, 2, 2, 3, 4, 5, 6, 6, 7, 7, 8, 8, 8, 8, 9, 9, 10, 10, 10, 11, 11, 11, 12, 12, 12, 12, 13, 13, 13, 13, 13, 14, 14, 14, 14, 14, 14, 15, 16, 16, 16, 16, 16, 16, 16, 17, 17, 17, 17, 17, 17, 17, 18, 18, 18, 18, 19, 20, 20, 20, 20, 20, 20, 20, 21, 21, 21, 21, 21, 22, 22, 23, 25, 25, 25, 25, 25, 25, 26, 27, 27, 28, 28, 28, 29; **4:**1, 1, 1, 2, 3, 3, 3, 4, 5, 5, 6, 7, 9, 10, 10, 10, 11, 11, 11, 11, 12, 12, 13, 14, 14, 14, 15, 15, 15, 19, 19, 19, 19, 19, 19, 20, 20, 21, 21, 21, 21, 22, 22, 22, 23, 23, 23, 24, 25, 25, 25, 25, 26, 26, 27, 27, 29, 30, 30, 31, 31, 32, 32, 32, 32, 33, 34, 35, 39, 40, 40, 40, 41, 43, 43, 43, 43, 43, 44, 44, 45, 45, 46, 46, 46, 46, 47, 47, 48, 48, 48, 49, 49, 49, 49; **5:**1, 1, 2, 3, 4, 4, 4, 4, 5, 5, 5, 6, 8, 9, 9, 9, 9, 9, 11, 11, 11, 12, 12, 14, 14, 15, 15, 15, 16, 16, 16, 22, 22, 22, 23, 23, 23, 24, 24, 24, 25, 26, 26, 26, 26, 27, 28, 28, 31, 31, 32, 32, 32, 33, 33, 33; **6:**1, 1, 1, 2, 3, 3, 3, 4, 4, 5, 9, 10, 10, 11, 12, 12, 13, 14, 15, 15, 15, 16, 17, 17, 17, 18, 18, 18, 19, 19, 20, 20, 20, 21, 22, 24, 24, 25, 25; **7:**1, 1, 1, 2, 4, 4, 6, 6, 6, 7, 7, 8, 8, 8, 9, 9, 12, 13, 14, 14, 15, 15, 16, 16, 18, 18, 19, 19, 19, 19, 19, 19, 20, 20, 21, 22, 22, 23, 24, 24, 25, 25; **8:**1, 1, 1, 2, 2, 3, 5, 6, 6, 7, 7, 9, 10, 10, 11, 11, 14, 14, 14, 15, 15, 16, 18, 18, 19, 20, 20; **9:**1, 1, 1, 2, 2, 2, 3, 3, 4, 4, 4, 4, 5, 5, 6, 7, 7, 7, 8, 9, 9, 9, 9, 10, 10, 10, 10, 10, 10, 11, 11, 11, 11, 11, 12, 12, 12, 13, 15, 15, 15, 16, 16, 16, 16, 17, 17, 18, 18, 19, 20, 20, 21, 21, 21, 21, 21, 22, 23, 23, 23, 23, 24, 25, 26, 27, 28, 28, 28, 28; **10:**1, 1, 1, 2, 2, 2, 2, 2, 2, 2, 3, 3, 3, 4, 4, 4, 4, 4, 4, 4, 4, 4, 5, 5, 5, 5, 5, 5, 6, 6, 6, 6, 8, 8, 8, 8, 8, 9, 9, 9, 9, 10, 10, 10, 10, 11, 11, 11, 12, 13, 14, 14, 14, 15, 15, 17, 17, 17, 18, 19, 20, 21, 21, 22, 22, 22; **11:**1, 2, 2, 3, 4, 4, 4, 5, 5, 6, 6, 7, 8, 9, 9, 10, 10, 12, 12, 13, 13, 14, 16, 17, 17, 17, 17, 20, 21, 21, 21, 21, 22, 22, 23, 23, 24, 24, 24, 24, 24, 24, 24, 24, 25, 25, 26, 27, 27, 28, 28, 29, 29, 30, 30, 30, 30, 30, 30, 30, 31, 31, 31, 32; **12:**1, 1, 1, 1, 2, 2, 2, 2, 3, 4, 4, 5, 5, 5, 6, 6, 7, 7, 7, 9, 9, 10, 10, 10, 11, 11, 12, 12, 12, 14, 14, 15, 16, 16, 16, 17, 17, 18, 18, 18, 18, 18, 18, 19, 20, 21, 21, 21, 21, 21, 23, 23, 23, 23, 23, 23, 24, 24, 25, 25, 26, 26, 27, 27, 27, 27, 27, 27, 27, 28, 29, 29, 31, 31, 31, 32; **13:**1, 2, 2, 2, 3, 4, 5, 5, 5, 5, 5, 7, 7, 7, 9, 9, 9, 10, 10, 10, 10, 12, 12, 14, 15, 16, 16, 16, 16, 16, 16, 17, 17, 18, 18; **14:**1, 1, 1, 1, 1, 2, 2, 2, 4, 4, 4, 4, 5, 5, 5, 5, 5, 5, 6, 7, 7, 7, 7, 7, 8, 8, 8, 12, 12, 12, 12, 13, 15, 15, 15, 16, 16, 16, 17, 17, 17, 18, 18, 18, 21, 22, 23, 23, 23, 23, 23, 24, 24, 25, 25, 25, 25, 26, 26, 26, 27, 28, 28, 28, 29, 29, 29, 29, 29; **15:**1, 2, 2, 3, 4, 4, 5, 5, 6, 7, 7, 9, 9, 9, 9, 10, 11, 12, 14, 14, 15, 15, 17, 17, 18, 18, 18, 19, 19, 19, 19, 20, 20, 20, 21, 23, 23; **16:**1, 1, 1, 1, 2, 2, 2, 2, 3, 3, 4, 4, 4, 5, 5, 5, 6, 6, 6, 6, 7, 7, 7, 7, 8, 8, 8, 8, 9, 10, 10, 10, 11, 11, 11, 11, 13, 13, 13, 13, 13, 14, 15, 15, 15, 16, 16, 16, 16, 16, 16, 17, 17, 18, 18, 18, 18, 19, 19, 19, 19, 20, 20, 21, 21, 22; **17:**1, 2, 2, 2, 2, 3, 3, 3, 4, 5, 5, 6, 7, 7, 7, 8, 8, 9, 9, 9, 10, 10, 10, 11, 11, 12, 12, 12, 12, 14, 14, 14, 15, 15, 16, 16, 17, 17, 18, 18, 18, 19, 19, 19, 20; **18:**1, 1, 1, 1, 1, 1, 1, 2, 2, 3, 3, 3, 3, 3, 3, 3, 4, 4, 4, 4, 4, 4, 5, 5, 5, 6, 6, 7, 7, 7, 8, 9, 9, 9, 9, 11, 11, 12, 12, 12, 13, 14, 14, 15, 16, 16, 16, 17, 18, 19, 19, 21, 21, 22, 22, 22, 22; **19:**1, 1, 2, 2, 3, 3, 3, 4, 5, 5, 5, 5, 5, 5, 6, 6, 6, 6, 6, 8, 8, 9, 9, 10, 10, 10, 11, 12, 12, 12, 12, 12, 13, 14, 14, 14, 15, 15, 15, 15, 17, 17, 17, 18, 19, 19, 19; **20:**1, 2, 2, 4, 5, 5, 5, 5, 7, 8, 9, 9, 9, 11, 11, 12, 13, 13, 14, 14, 14, 15, 16, 16, 16, 17, 17, 18, 18, 18, 18, 19, 19, 19, 19, 20, 20; **21:**1, 1, 1, 2, 3, 4, 5, 5, 5, 6, 6, 6, 6, 8, 8, 9, 9, 10, 11, 15, 15, 15, 15, 16, 16, 16, 16, 16, 17, 17, 17, 17, 17, 17, 19, 19, 19, 19, 21, 21, 23, 23, 23, 23, 23; **22:**2, 2, 3, 4, 4, 5, 6, 6, 6, 6, 6, 7, 7, 8, 8, 8, 9, 9, 9, 9, 9, 12, 15, 15, 15, 15, 15, 17, 17, 17, 18, 18, 19, 19, 19, 19, 20, 21, 21, 21, 21, 21, 22, 22, 24, 24, 24, 24, 24, 25, 25, 25, 25, 26, 27, 27, 28, 29; **23:**1, 1, 2, 2, 3, 3, 5, 5, 5, 6, 6, 7, 7, 7, 7, 8, 8, 8, 10, 11, 12, 13, 13, 14, 14, 18, 18, 18, 18, 19, 20, 20, 21, 21, 23; **24:**3, 4, 4, 4, 4, 5, 5, 6, 6, 7, 7, 8, 8, 8, 9, 10, 11, 12, 13, 13, 15, 16, 16, 18, 19, 19, 20, 20, 20, 20, 21, 21, 21, 22; **25:**1, 1, 2, 2, 2, 2, 2, 4, 5, 5, 5, 6, 6, 6, 7, 7, 7,

7, 8, 8, 9, 9, 9, 10, 10, 11, 11, 11, 15, 15, 16, 17, 19, 19, 19; **26:**1, 1, 2, 2, 2, 3, 3, 3, 4, 4, 4, 4, 5, 5, 6, 7, 7, 8, 10, 10, 10, 10, 11, 11, 11, 11, 11, 12, 13, 13, 13, 13, 14, 14, 15, 16, 17, 18, 19; **27:**1, 1, 2, 2, 2, 3, 3, 3, 3, 3, 3, 4, 5, 6, 6, 6, 7, 8, 8, 9, 9, 9, 10, 11, 12, 12, 12, 13, 14, 14, 15, 15, 15, 16, 17, 18, 18, 19, 20, 21, 22, 22, 23, 24, 25, 26, 26; **28:**1, 1, 1, 1, 1, 2, 3, 7, 8, 8, 8, 9, 9, 9, 10, 10, 10, 11, 11, 12, 12, 12, 12, 13, 13, 13, 13, 13, 14, 15, 15, 16, 20, 21, 21, 22, 23, 23, 24, 24, 25, 25, 25, 26, 27, 27, 27, 28, 29, 31, 33, 34, 35, 36, 36, 37, 37, 39, 39, 39, 40, 40, 40, 43, 44, 44, 45, 45, 47, 47, 48, 49, 49, 49, 50, 50, 52, 52, 52, 52, 52, 53, 53, 53, 54, 55, 55, 55, 56, 56, 56, 57, 57, 57, 58, 58, 58, 59, 60, 61, 61, 62, 62, 62, 63, 63, 63, 64, 64, 64, 64, 65, 66, 67, 67, 67, 68; **29:**1, 1, 1, 1, 1, 1, 2, 2, 3, 3, 3, 4, 5, 6, 8, 8, 9, 10, 10, 11, 12, 12, 14, 14, 15, 16, 16, 18, 18, 19, 20, 20, 20, 21, 21, 21, 21, 22, 22, 22, 22, 22, 22, 23, 24, 24, 25, 25, 25, 25, 25, 25, 26, 27, 27, 28, 29, 29, 29; **30:**1, 1, 1, 1, 2, 2, 3, 3, 4, 4, 4, 5, 6, 6, 7, 8, 8, 9, 9, 10, 10, 10, 10, 13, 13, 14, 16, 16, 16, 18, 18, 19, 19, 20, 20, 20; **31:**1, 2, 2, 3, 3, 3, 4, 4, 4, 4, 4, 5, 5, 6, 7, 7, 7, 8, 8, 9, 9, 9, 9, 10, 10, 10, 11, 11, 11, 12, 12, 12, 13, 13, 13, 14, 14, 14, 14, 15, 15, 15, 16, 16, 16, 16, 18, 19, 19, 20, 20, 21, 22, 22, 22, 23, 23, 23, 25, 25, 25, 26, 26, 26, 26, 26, 27, 28, 29, 29, 29, 30; **32:**1, 3, 3, 4, 6, 6, 7, 7, 8, 8, 8, 8, 8, 8, 9, 9, 12, 13, 13, 13, 13, 13, 14, 14, 14, 14, 14, 14, 15, 15, 15, 18, 18, 19, 21, 22, 22, 22, 22, 22, 24, 24, 25, 25, 26, 27, 27, 27, 28, 30, 31, 32, 32, 33, 33, 36, 37, 38, 38, 39, 39, 42, 42, 42, 42, 42, 43, 43, 44, 44, 46, 47, 47, 48, 49, 49, 49, 49, 49, 50, 51, 51, 51, 51, 52, 52, 52; **33:**1, 1, 1, 2, 3, 4, 4, 4, 5, 5, 5, 5, 6, 6, 7, 7, 8, 8, 8, 8, 8, 9, 10, 11, 11, 12, 12, 12, 13, 13, 13, 13, 13, 14, 14, 14, 15, 15, 15, 15, 16, 16, 16, 16, 16, 16, 16, 17, 17, 17, 17, 17, 17, 18, 18, 18, 19, 19, 19, 19, 19, 19, 20, 20, 21, 21, 21, 21, 21, 22, 23, 23, 23, 23, 24, 25, 25, 26, 26, 26, 27, 27, 28, 29; **34:**1, 1, 1, 2, 2, 2, 2, 3, 3, 3, 4, 4, 4, 5, 5, 5, 5, 6, 8, 8, 8, 9, 9, 9, 10, 11, 11, 11, 12, 12; **Jos 1:**1, 1, 1, 2, 2, 4, 4, 4, 4, 4, 4, 4, 4, 4, 4, 6, 7, 8, 9, 10, 11, 11, 11, 11, 11, 12, 12, 13, 13, 13, 14, 14, 14, 14, 15, 15, 15, 15, 15, 15, 15, 15, 17; **2:**1, 1, 1, 1, 1, 1, 2, 2, 3, 3, 3, 4, 4, 5, 5, 6, 7, 7, 7, 7, 7, 7, 7, 8, 8, 9, 10, 10, 10, 10, 11, 11, 11, 11, 11, 12, 14, 14, 14, 15, 15, 16, 16, 17, 18, 18, 19, 21, 21, 22, 22, 22, 22, 22, 23, 23, 23, 24, 24, 24, 24; **3:**1, 1, 1, 1, 2, 2, 3, 3, 3, 3, 3, 4, 5, 5, 6, 6, 6, 6, 6, 6, 7, 7, 7, 8, 8, 8, 8, 8, 8, 9, 9, 10, 10, 11, 11, 11, 11, 11, 13, 13, 13, 13, 13, 13, 13, 13, 14, 14, 14, 14, 14, 15, 15, 15, 15, 15, 15, 15, 16, 16, 16, 16, 16, 16, 17, 17, 17, 17, 17, 17, 17; **4:**1, 1, 1, 3, 3, 3, 3, 3, 4, 5, 5, 5, 5, 5, 6, 7, 7, 7, 7, 8, 8, 8, 8, 8, 8, 8, 9, 9, 9, 9, 9, 9, 10, 10, 10, 10, 10, 10, 10, 11, 11, 11, 11, 12, 12, 12, 12, 12, 13, 13, 14, 14, 14, 14, 15, 16, 16, 16, 16, 17, 18, 18, 18, 18, 18, 19, 19, 19, 19, 19, 20, 20, 21, 21, 22, 22, 23, 23, 23, 24, 24, 24, 24, 24; **5:**1, 1, 1, 1, 1, 1, 1, 2, 2, 3, 4, 4, 5, 5, 5, 6, 6, 6, 6, 6, 6, 7, 7, 8, 8, 9, 9, 10, 10, 10, 10, 10, 10, 11, 11, 12, 12, 13, 14, 14, 15, 15; **6:**1, 1, 1, 2, 3, 4, 4, 4, 4, 4, 5, 5, 5, 5, 5, 5, 5, 6, 6, 6, 7, 7, 7, 7, 7, 7, 8, 8, 8, 8, 8, 8, 8, 8, 8, 9, 9, 9, 9, 11, 11, 11, 11, 11, 12, 12, 12, 12, 13, 13, 13, 13, 13, 13, 13, 13, 13, 14, 14, 14, 15, 15, 15, 15, 16, 16, 16, 16, 16, 16, 17, 17, 17, 17, 18, 19, 20, 20, 20, 20, 20, 20, 22, 22, 23, 23, 23, 24, 24, 24, 24, 24, 25, 25, 25, 25, 26, 26, 26, 26, 26, 27, 27; **7:**1, 1, 1, 1, 1, 1, 1, 1, 2, 4, 5, 5, 5, 5, 5, 6, 6, 6, 7, 7, 7, 9, 9, 9, 9, 9, 9, 10, 11, 11, 12, 12, 13, 13, 13, 13, 14, 14, 14, 14, 14, 14, 14, 14, 14, 15, 15, 15, 16, 16, 16, 16, 17, 17, 17, 17, 17, 19, 19, 19, 20, 20, 21, 21, 21, 22, 22, 22, 22, 23, 23, 23, 23, 23, 23, 24, 24, 24, 24, 24, 25, 25, 26, 26, 26; **8:**1, 1, 1, 2, 2, 2, 3, 4, 5, 6, 6, 7, 7, 8, 8, 9, 9, 9, 10, 10, 11, 11, 12, 12, 13, 13, 13, 13, 13, 14, 14, 14, 14, 14, 14, 14, 15, 15, 16, 16, 16, 17, 17, 18, 18, 19, 19, 19, 20, 20, 20, 20, 20, 20, 21, 21, 21, 21, 22, 22, 22, 22, 22, 23, 24, 24, 24, 25, 27, 27, 27, 27, 27, 29, 29, 29, 29, 30, 30, 31, 31, 31, 31, 31, 31, 32, 32, 32, 32, 33, 33, 33, 33, 33, 33, 33, 33, 33, 33, 33, 33, 33, 34, 34, 34, 35, 35, 35, 35; **9:**1, 1, 1, 1, 1, 1, 1, 1, 1, 2, 3, 6, 6, 7, 9, 9, 10, 10, 11, 12, 14, 14, 15, 16, 17, 17, 18, 18, 18, 18, 18, 18, 19, 19, 19, 19, 21, 21, 21, 21, 21, 22, 23, 24, 24, 26, 27, 27, 27, 27, 27, 27; **10:**1, 1, 2, 2, 4, 6, 6, 6, 7, 8, 9, 10, 10, 10, 10, 10, 10, 11, 11, 11, 11, 11, 11, 11, 12, 12, 12, 12, 12, 12, 12, 12, 12, 13, 13, 13, 13, 13, 13, 14, 14, 15, 16, 16, 18, 18, 18, 18, 19, 19, 19, 19, 20, 20, 20, 21, 22, 22, 22, 22, 23, 23, 23, 24, 24, 25, 26, 27, 27, 27, 27, 27, 27, 27, 28, 28, 28, 28, 28, 29, 30, 30, 30, 30, 30, 31, 32, 32, 32, 33, 33, 34, 35, 37, 39, 40, 40, 40, 40, 40, 40, 40, 40, 40, 42, 42, 43; **11:**1, 1, 1, 2, 2, 2, 2, 2, 2, 2, 2, 3, 3, 3, 3, 3, 3, 3, 3, 3, 3, 3, 3, 4, 4, 4, 5, 6, 7, 8, 8, 8, 9, 9, 9, 10, 10, 11, 11, 11, 12, 12, 12, 13, 14, 14, 14, 14, 15, 15, 16, 16, 16, 16, 16, 16, 16, 17, 17, 17, 17, 17, 19, 19, 19, 20, 20, 20, 21, 21, 21, 22, 23, 23, 23, 23, 23, 23; **12:**1, 1, 1, 1, 1, 2, 2, 2, 2, 2, 2, 2, 2, 2, 3, 3, 3, 3, 3, 4, 4, 5, 5, 5, 5, 5, 5, 5, 6, 6, 6, 6, 6, 6, 7, 7, 7, 7, 7, 7, 7, 8, 8, 8, 8, 8, 8, 8, 8, 8, 8, 8, 8, 8, 9, 9, 10, 10, 11, 11, 12, 12, 13, 13, 14, 14, 15, 15, 16, 16, 17, 17, 18, 18, 19, 19, 20, 20, 21, 21, 22, 22, 23, 23, 23, 24; **13:**1, 2, 2, 2, 2, 3, 3, 3, 3, 4, 4, 4, 4, 4, 4, 4, 4, 4, 4, 5, 5, 5, 5, 6, 6, 6, 6, 6, 7, 7, 7, 8, 8, 8, 8, 8, 8, 9, 9, 9, 9, 9, 9, 10, 10, 10, 11, 11, 12, 12, 12, 13, 13, 13, 14, 14, 14, 14, 14, 14, 15, 15, 15, 16, 16, 16, 16, 16, 16, 17, 17, 19, 19, 20, 21, 21, 21, 21, 21, 21, 21, 22, 22, 22, 23, 23, 23, 23, 23, 23, 24, 24, 24, 25, 25, 25, 27, 27, 27, 27, 27, 27, 28, 28, 28, 29, 29, 29, 30, 30, 31, 32, 32, 32, 33, 33, 33; **14:**1, 1, 1, 2, 3, 3, 3, 4, 4, 4, 5, 5, 5, 6, 6, 6, 6, 7, 7, 7, 8, 8, 8, 9, 9, 10, 10, 12, 12, 12, 12, 12, 12, 14, 14, 14, 14, 15, 15; **15:**1, 1, 1, 1, 1, 2, 2, 2, 3, 4, 4, 5, 5, 5, 5, 5, 5, 5, 5, 6, 7, 7, 7, 7, 7, 7, 8, 8, 8, 8, 8, 8, 8, 8, 8, 8, 8, 9, 9, 9, 9, 9, 9, 10, 10, 10, 11, 11, 11, 11, 12, 12, 12, 12, 12, 12, 13, 13, 14, 15, 15, 16, 17, 17, 19, 19, 20, 20, 20, 21, 21, 21, 33, 33, 45, 45, 45, 46, 46, 47, 47, 47, 48, 48, 52, 61, 61, 62, 63, 63, 63, 63, 63; **16:**1, 1, 1, 1, 1, 1, 2, 2, 3, 3, 3, 4, 5, 5, 5, 5, 6, 6, 6, 6, 7, 8, 8, 8, 8, 8, 8, 9, 9, 10, 10, 10; **17:**1, 1, 1, 1, 1, 1, 1, 2, 2, 2, 2, 4, 4, 4, 4, 4, 5, 5, 6, 6, 6, 6, 6, 7, 7, 7, 7, 7, 7, 8, 8, 8, 8, 9, 9, 9, 9, 9, 9, 10, 10, 10, 10, 10, 10, 10, 10, 11, 11, 12, 12, 13, 13, 13, 14, 14, 15, 15, 15, 16, 16, 16, 16, 17, 17, 18, 18, 18, 18, 18; **18:**1, 1, 1, 3, 3, 3, 4, 4, 5, 5, 5, 5, 6, 6, 7, 7, 7, 7, 7, 7, 7, 7, 8, 8, 8, 8, 8, 8, 8, 9, 9, 9, 9, 10, 10, 11, 11, 11, 11, 11, 12, 12, 12, 12, 12, 13, 13, 13, 14, 14, 14, 14, 14, 14, 14, 15, 15, 15, 15, 16, 16, 16, 16, 16, 16, 16, 16, 16, 17, 17, 17, 18, 18, 18, 18, 18, 19, 19, 19, 19, 19, 20, 20, 20, 20, 20, 21, 21, 21, 28, 28, 28; **19:**1, 1, 1, 8, 8, 8, 8, 8, 9, 9, 10, 10, 10, 10, 11, 12, 12, 12, 14, 14, 15, 16, 16, 16, 17, 17, 17, 18, 22, 22, 23, 23, 23, 24, 24, 24, 26, 26, 27, 29, 29, 29, 29, 31, 31, 31, 32, 32, 32, 33, 33, 34, 34, 34, 34, 34, 34, 34, 35, 39, 39, 39, 40, 40, 40, 41, 46, 47, 47, 47, 48, 48, 48, 49, 49, 49, 50, 50, 50, 51, 51, 51, 51, 51, 51, 51, 51, 51, 51; **20:**1, 2, 2, 3, 3, 3, 3, 4, 4, 4, 4, 4, 4, 5, 5, 5, 5, 5, 5, 6, 6, 6, 6, 6, 6, 6, 6, 6, 7, 7, 7, 7, 8, 8, 8, 8, 8, 8, 8, 8, 8, 9, 9; **21:**1, 1, 1, 1, 1, 2, 2, 3, 3, 3, 3, 4, 4, 4, 4, 5, 5, 5, 5, 6, 6, 6, 7, 7, 8, 8, 8, 9, 9, 9, 10, 10, 10, 10, 11, 12, 12, 12, 13, 13, 13, 17, 17, 17, 19, 19, 20, 20, 20, 20, 23, 23, 23, 25, 25, 25, 26, 26, 27, 27, 27, 28, 30, 32, 33, 34, 34, 34, 34, 34, 36, 38, 40, 41, 41, 43, 43, 44, 44, 45, 45; **22:**1, 1, 2, 2, 3, 3, 3, 3, 3, 4, 4, 4, 4, 4, 4, 4, 5, 5, 5, 7, 7, 7, 7, 7, 7, 8, 9, 9, 9, 9, 9, 9, 9, 10, 10, 10, 11, 11, 11, 11, 12, 13, 13, 13, 13, 14, 14, 15, 15, 15, 16, 16, 16, 16, 17, 17, 17, 18, 18, 19, 19, 19, 19, 19, 20, 20, 20, 20, 20, 21, 21, 22, 22, 22, 22, 23, 23, 24, 24, 24, 25, 25, 25, 25, 26, 27, 27, 27, 28, 28, 28, 29, 29, 29, 29, 30, 30, 30, 30, 31, 31, 31, 31, 32, 32, 32, 32, 32, 33, 34, 34, 34; **23:**1, 1, 1, 2, 3, 3, 4, 4, 4, 4, 4, 4, 5, 5, 5, 6, 6, 6, 7, 7, 7, 8, 9, 10, 10, 11, 12, 13, 13, 14, 14, 14, 15, 15, 16, 16, 16; **24:**1, 2, 2, 2, 2, 2, 3, 3, 3, 4, 6, 6, 7, 7, 7, 7, 7, 8, 8, 8, 8, 11, 11, 11, 11, 11, 11, 11, 11, 11, 12, 12, 13, 14, 14, 14, 14, 15, 15, 15, 15, 15, 15, 16, 16, 17, 17, 17, 17, 18, 18, 18, 18, 18, 19, 19, 20, 21, 21, 22, 23, 23, 23, 24, 24, 25, 25, 26, 26, 26, 26, 26, 27, 27, 28, 29, 29, 29, 30, 30, 31, 31, 31, 31, 32, 32, 32, 32, 32, 32, 32, 33, 33; **Jdg 1:**1, 1, 1, 2, 2, 3, 3, 3, 3, 3, 4, 4, 4, 4, 5, 6, 8, 8, 9, 9, 9, 9, 10, 10, 11, 11, 12, 13, 13, 15, 15, 16, 16, 16, 16, 16, 16, 17, 17, 17, 18, 19, 19, 19, 19, 19, 19, 20, 20, 20, 21, 21, 21, 21, 22, 22, 22, 24, 24, 25, 26, 26, 26, 26, 27, 27, 27, 28, 28, 28, 29, 29, 29, 30, 30, 31, 31, 32, 32, 32, 33, 33, 33, 33, 33, 33, 34, 34, 34, 34, 35, 35, 35, 36, 36; **2:**1, 1, 1, 2, 3, 4, 4, 4, 5, 5, 6, 6, 6, 7, 7, 7, 7, 7, 7, 8, 8, 8, 9, 9, 10, 10, 11, 11, 11, 12, 12, 12, 12, 12, 13, 13, 14, 15, 15, 16, 16, 17, 17, 17, 18, 18, 18, 18, 19, 19, 20, 20, 21, 22, 23, 23; **3:**1, 1, 1, 3, 3, 3, 3, 3, 3, 3, 4, 4, 4, 5, 6, 7, 7, 7, 7, 7, 8, 8, 9, 9, 9, 10, 10, 10, 11, 12, 12, 12, 13, 14, 15, 15, 15, 15, 17, 18, 18, 19, 19, 19, 21, 21, 22, 22, 22, 22, 22, 23, 23, 23, 24, 24, 24, 24, 25, 25, 25, 26, 26, 27, 27, 28, 28, 28, 28, 29, 30; **4:**1, 1, 2, 2, 3, 3, 3, 4, 5, 5, 5, 6, 6, 6, 6, 7, 9, 9, 10, 11, 11, 11, 13, 14, 14, 14, 15, 16, 16, 17, 17, 17, 20, 20, 21, 21, 22, 22, 22, 23; **5:**2, 2, 3, 3, 3, 4, 4, 4, 5, 5, 5, 5, 5, 5, 6, 6, 6, 7, 8, 9, 10, 11, 11, 11, 11, 11, 11, 11, 11, 13, 13, 13, 13, 14, 14, 14, 15, 15, 15, 16, 16, 16, 17, 17, 18, 19, 20, 20, 21, 21, 22, 22, 22, 23, 23, 23, 23, 23, 23, 24, 24, 26, 26, 28, 28, 28, 30, 31, 31; **6:**1, 1, 1, 1, 2, 2, 2, 3, 3, 3, 4, 4, 4, 5, 6, 6, 6, 7, 8, 8, 8, 8, 9, 10, 10, 10, 11, 11, 11, 11, 11, 11, 11, 12, 12, 12, 13, 13, 13, 13, 13, 14, 14, 14, 15, 15, 15, 16, 16, 17, 18, 19, 19, 19, 19, 20, 20, 20, 20, 21, 21, 21, 21, 21, 21, 21, 22, 22, 22, 22, 23, 24, 24, 24, 24, 24, 25, 25, 25, 25, 26, 26, 26, 26, 26, 26, 27, 27, 27, 27, 28, 28, 28, 28, 28, 28, 29, 29, 30, 30, 31, 31, 33, 33, 33, 33, 33, 34, 34, 34, 34, 37, 37, 37, 37, 38, 38, 39, 39, 40, 40, 40; **7:**1, 1, 1, 1, 2, 2, 2, 3, 4, 4, 5, 5, 5, 5, 5, 6, 6, 6, 7, 7, 7, 8, 8, 8, 8, 8, 9, 9, 9, 10, 11, 11, 11, 12, 12, 12, 12, 12, 13, 13, 14, 14, 15, 15, 15, 15, 16, 17, 17, 18, 18, 18, 18, 19, 19, 19, 19, 19, 19, 20, 20, 20, 21, 21, 22, 22, 22, 22, 22, 23, 23, 23, 24, 24, 24, 24, 24, 25, 25, 25, 25, 25, 25, 25; **8:**1, 1, 2, 2, 3, 3, 3, 4, 4, 5, 5, 5, 6, 7, 7, 7, 8, 9, 10, 10, 11, 11, 12, 14, 14, 14, 15, 16, 16, 16, 17, 17, 17, 18, 18, 19, 21, 21, 22, 23, 24, 24, 26, 26, 26, 26, 26, 26, 26, 27, 27, 28, 28, 28, 32, 32, 32, 33, 33, 34, 35, 35; **9:**1, 2, 3, 4, 5, 5, 6, 6, 6, 7, 8, 8, 9, 9, 10, 11, 11, 12, 13, 13, 13, 14, 14, 15, 15, 16, 17, 20, 20, 23, 24, 24, 25, 25, 26, 26, 27, 27, 27, 27, 28, 28, 30, 30, 31, 32, 33, 33, 35, 36, 36, 36, 37, 37, 37, 38, 38, 39, 40, 40, 40, 42, 42, 42, 43, 43, 43, 44, 44, 44, 45, 45, 45, 45, 45, 46, 46, 46, 46, 47, 47, 49, 49, 49, 49, 49, 50, 51, 51, 51, 51, 52, 52, 53, 54, 56, 57, 57; **10:**1, 1, 1, 1, 4, 4, 6, 6, 6, 6, 7, 7, 7, 8, 8, 8, 8, 9, 9, 9, 9, 10, 10, 11, 11, 11, 11, 11, 12, 12, 12, 14, 15, 15, 16, 16, 17, 18, 18, 18; **11:**1, 2, 2, 3, 4, 5, 5, 5, 6, 7, 8, 8, 9, 9, 9, 10, 10, 11, 11, 11, 11, 11, 12, 13, 13, 13, 13, 13, 13, 13, 14, 16, 16, 17, 17, 17, 18, 18, 18, 18, 19, 21, 21, 21, 21, 22, 22, 22, 22, 23, 23, 23, 23, 24, 26, 26, 26, 27, 28, 29, 29, 29, 29, 30, 30, 31, 31, 32, 32, 33, 33, 35, 36, 36, 36, 37, 38, 40; **12:**1, 2, 2, 3, 3, 4, 4, 4, 5, 5, 5, 5, 5, 6, 6, 6, 7, 15, 15; **13:**1, 1, 1, 1, 2, 2, 3, 3, 5, 6, 7, 7, 8, 8, 9, 9, 10, 10, 11, 11, 12, 13, 13, 13, 15, 15, 16, 16, 16, 16, 16, 17, 17, 18, 18, 19, 19, 20, 20, 20, 20, 20, 20, 20, 21, 21, 21, 23, 24, 25, 25, 25; **14:**3, 3, 3, 4, 4, 5, 6, 6, 6, 7, 8, 8, 8, 8, 8, 9, 9, 9, 9, 9, 10, 10, 10, 11, 12, 14, 14, 15, 15, 15, 16, 16, 17, 17, 17, 17, 17, 17, 18, 18, 18, 18, 19, 19, 19, 19, 20, 20; **15:**1, 5, 5, 5, 5, 5, 5, 6, 6, 6, 6, 8, 8, 9, 9, 10, 10, 10, 11, 11, 11, 12, 12, 13, 13, 14, 14, 14, 14, 15, 16, 16, 17, 17, 18, 18, 18, 19, 19, 19, 20, 20; **16:**1, 1, 2, 2, 2, 2, 3, 3, 3, 3, 3, 4, 5, 5, 8, 9, 9, 9, 9, 12, 12, 12, 12, 13, 13, 13, 13, 13, 14, 14, 14, 14, 14, 18, 18, 18, 18, 20, 20, 21, 21, 23, 24, 24, 25, 25, 25, 25, 25, 25, 26, 26, 26, 27, 27, 27, 28, 28, 28, 29, 29, 30, 30, 30, 30; **17:**1, 2, 2, 2, 3, 3, 4, 5, 6, 11, 12, 13; **18:**1, 1, 1, 2, 2, 2, 2, 3, 6, 6, 7, 7, 7, 7, 7, 8, 9, 9, 10, 11, 13, 13, 14, 14, 14, 15, 15, 16, 16, 16, 17, 17, 17, 17, 17, 17, 18, 18, 18, 19, 20, 20, 20, 20, 22, 22, 23, 25, 26, 27, 27, 27, 27, 27, 28, 28, 28, 28, 28, 28, 29, 30, 30, 30, 31, 31; **19:**1, 1, 5, 5, 5, 6, 6, 6, 7, 7, 8, 8, 8, 9, 10, 10, 11, 11, 13, 14, 14, 15, 15, 15, 16, 16, 16, 17, 17, 18, 18, 18, 18, 18, 20, 20, 20, 22, 22, 22, 22, 22, 22, 23, 25, 25, 25, 25, 26, 26, 26, 26, 27, 27; **20:**1, 1, 1, 1, 2, 2, 2, 2, 2, 3, 3, 3, 4, 4, 4, 4, 4, 5, 5, 6, 6, 7, 8, 10, 10, 10, 11, 11, 12, 12, 13, 14, 15, 18, 18, 18, 18, 18, 19, 19, 20, 21, 21, 22, 22, 22, 23, 23, 23, 23, 24, 25, 26, 26, 26, 26, 27, 27, 27, 27, 28, 28, 28, 28, 29, 30, 30, 31, 31, 31, 31, 31, 32, 32, 32, 32, 32, 32, 33, 33, 34, 34, 35, 35, 36, 36, 37, 38, 39, 39, 39, 40, 40, 40, 40, 41, 42, 42, 43, 43, 45, 45, 45, 45, 45, 46, 47, 48, 48, 48, 48; **21:**1, 1, 2, 2, 4, 4, 5, 5, 5, 6, 6, 7, 7, 8, 9, 11, 12, 12, 12, 13, 13, 13, 14, 14, 15, 15, 15, 16, 16, 16, 16, 17, 19, 19, 19, 19, 20, 20, 21, 21, 22, 23, 23, 23, 23, 24, 25; **Ru 1:**1, 1, 1, 1, 2, 2, 4, 4, 6, 7, 7, 8, 8, 9, 9, 13, 15, 17, 19, 19, 19, 20, 21, 21, 21, 22, 22, 22; **2:**2, 3, 3, 4, 4, 4, 4, 6, 6, 7, 7, 8, 9, 9, 9, 9, 11, 11, 12, 12, 14, 15, 16, 17, 18, 19, 19, 19, 19, 20, 21, 22, 23, 23, 23, 23, 23; **3:**2, 3, 6, 6, 7, 9, 10, 13, 13, 14, 14, 15, 15, 18; **4:**1, 1, 2, 3, 3, 4, 4, 4, 5, 5, 5, 5, 6, 6, 7, 7, 7, 8, 8, 9, 9, 9, 10, 10, 10, 10, 11, 11, 11, 11, 11, 12, 12, 13, 14, 14, 14, 15, 16, 17, 17, 17, 18, 19, 19, 20, 20, 21, 21, 22, 22; **1Sa 1:**1, 1, 1, 1, 3, 3, 3, 3, 3, 4, 4, 5, 6, 7, 7, 8, 9, 9, 9, 9, 10, 11, 12, 15, 17, 17, 19, 19, 19, 19, 20, 21, 21, 22, 22, 22, 23, 23, 24, 24, 24, 25, 25, 26, 26, 27, 28, 28, 28; **2:**1, 1, 2, 3, 5, 5, 6, 6, 7, 8, 8, 8, 8, 8, 9, 10, 10, 10, 10, 11, 11, 11, 12, 12, 13, 13, 14, 14, 14, 14, 15, 15, 15, 16, 16, 16, 16, 17, 17, 17, 18, 19, 20, 20, 20, 21, 21, 21, 22, 22, 22, 22, 23, 23, 24, 24, 25, 25, 25, 26, 26, 27, 27, 28, 28, 29, 30, 30, 30, 30, 31, 32, 34, 36; **3:**1, 1, 1, 3, 3, 3, 4, 6, 7, 7, 8, 8, 8, 10, 11, 14, 15, 15, 15, 17, 18, 19, 20, 20, 20, 20, 21, 21; **4:**1, 1, 1, 1, 2, 2, 3, 3, 3, 3, 3, 3, 3, 4, 4, 4, 4, 4, 4, 4, 5, 5, 5, 5, 5, 5, 6, 6, 6, 6, 6, 7, 8, 8, 8, 9, 10, 10, 10, 11, 11, 12, 12, 13, 13, 13, 13, 13, 13, 13, 14, 14, 16, 17, 17, 17, 18, 18, 18, 19, 19, 20, 21, 21, 21, 22, 22; **5:**1, 1, 1, 1, 2, 2, 2, 3, 3, 3, 3, 3, 3, 4, 4, 4, 4, 4, 4, 4, 5, 5, 6, 6, 6, 7, 7, 7, 8, 8, 8, 8, 8, 8, 8, 8, 9, 9, 10, 10, 10, 10, 10, 11, 11, 11, 11, 11, 11; **6:**1, 1, 2, 2, 2, 3, 3, 3, 3, 3, 4, 5, 6, 7, 7, 7, 8, 8, 8, 8, 8, 9, 9, 9, 9, 10, 11, 11, 11, 11, 11, 12, 12, 12, 12, 13, 13, 13, 14, 14, 14, 14, 14, 14, 14, 15, 15, 15, 15, 15, 15, 15, 15, 15, 16, 17, 17, 17, 17, 18, 18, 18, 18, 18, 18, 18, 19, 19, 19, 19, 19, 20, 20, 20, 21, 21, 21, 21; **7:**1, 1, 1, 1, 2, 2, 3, 3, 3, 3, 4, 4, 5, 6, 6, 7, 7, 7, 8, 8, 9, 9, 9, 10, 10, 10, 10, 10, 11, 11, 12, 12, 12, 13, 13, 13, 14, 14, 14, 14, 14, 14, 15, 16, 17; **8:**4, 4, 5, 6, 7, 8, 10, 10, 11, 13, 14, 16, 18, 19, 20, 21, 21, 22, 22; **9:**1, 1, 1, 1, 2, 2, 4, 4, 4, 4, 4, 5, 5, 6, 6, 8, 9, 10, 10, 11, 11, 12, 12, 13, 13, 13, 14, 14, 14, 15, 15, 16, 16, 16, 17, 17, 18, 18, 19, 19, 19, 19, 20, 21, 21, 21, 22, 22, 22, 22, 23, 23, 23, 23, 24, 25, 25, 25, 25, 26, 26, 27, 27; **10:**1, 1, 1, 2, 2, 3, 3, 4, 5, 5, 5, 5, 6, 6, 10, 10, 11, 12, 12, 12, 13, 13, 14, 14, 14, 16, 17, 17, 18, 18, 18, 18, 19, 20, 20, 20, 21, 21, 21, 21, 22, 22, 22, 24, 24, 24, 24, 24, 25, 25, 25, 25; **11:**1, 1, 2, 3, 4, 4, 5, 5, 5, 6, 7, 7, 7, 7, 9, 9, 10, 11, 11, 11, 11, 12, 13, 14, 15, 15, 15; **12:**1, 3, 5, 6, 6, 7, 7, 7, 8, 8, 9, 9, 9, 9, 9, 10, 10, 10, 11, 12, 12, 13, 13, 14, 14, 14, 15, 16, 16, 17, 17, 17, 17, 18, 18, 18, 18, 19, 20, 22, 23, 24, 24; **13:**2, 2, 2, 2, 2, 2, 2, 3, 3, 3, 3, 4, 4, 4, 4, 4, 5, 5, 5, 6, 6, 7, 7, 9, 9, 9, 10, 11, 12, 12, 12, 13, 13, 13, 14, 14, 14, 15, 15, 15, 15, 15, 16, 16, 16, 17, 17, 17, 18, 18, 18, 18, 19, 19, 19, 20, 21, 22, 23, 23; **14:**1, 1, 2, 2, 3, 3, 3, 3, 3, 3, 3, 3, 4, 5, 5, 5, 5, 6, 6, 7, 10, 11, 11, 12, 13, 15, 15, 15, 15, 16, 18, 18, 18, 19, 19, 19, 20, 20, 21, 21, 21, 21, 22, 22, 22, 22, 23, 23, 24, 25, 25, 26, 26, 27, 28, 28, 30, 30, 31, 32, 32, 32, 33, 33, 34, 34, 34, 34, 34, 34, 35, 35, 36, 36, 37, 38, 39, 39, 39, 39, 40, 41, 41, 41, 41, 42, 43, 45, 45, 45, 46, 46, 46, 47, 47, 48, 50, 50, 52, 52; **15:**1, 1, 2, 2, 3, 5, 5, 6, 6, 6, 6, 7, 7, 8, 9, 9, 9, 10, 11, 12, 13, 13, 14, 15, 15, 15, 15, 16, 17, 17, 17, 18, 18, 18, 19, 19, 19, 20, 20, 21, 21, 21, 22, 22, 23, 23, 23, 24, 24, 25, 26, 26, 28, 28, 29, 30, 30, 31, 32, 33, 33, 35; **16:**1, 2, 2, 3, 4, 4, 4, 5, 5, 5, 6, 7, 7, 7, 7, 8, 8, 9, 9, 10, 10, 11, 11, 11, 11, 12, 12, 13, 13, 13, 14, 14, 14, 16, 16, 16, 18, 18, 18, 19, 23, 23, 23; **17:**1, 2, 3, 3, 4, 4, 7, 8, 8, 10, 11, 12, 12, 13, 14, 14, 14, 15, 16, 16, 19, 19, 19, 20, 20, 20, 20, 20, 20, 20, 21, 22, 22, 23, 23, 23, 24, 25, 25, 25, 25, 25, 26, 26, 26, 27, 27, 27, 28, 28, 30, 30, 31, 33, 34, 35, 35, 35, 36, 36, 37, 37, 37, 37, 37, 37, 39, 43, 44, 45, 45, 45, 45, 46, 46, 46, 46, 47, 47, 49, 49, 49, 49, 50, 51, 51, 52, 52, 52, 52, 52, 52, 53, 53, 54, 55, 56, 57; **18:**1, 1, 2, 4, 5, 6, 6, 6, 10, 10, 11, 12, 14, 17, 17, 18, 19, 19, 20, 21, 22, 22, 23, 23, 24, 25, 25, 26, 26, 27, 28, 28, 29, 30, 30, 30; **19:**2, 4, 5, 5, 5, 6, 8, 9, 9, 9, 10, 10, 10, 10, 11, 14, 16, 19, 20, 20, 21, 22, 23, 23, 24, 24, 24; **20:**2, 3, 5, 5, 5, 5, 8, 9, 11, 12, 12, 12, 12, 13, 13, 14, 14, 15, 16, 18, 18, 19, 19, 19, 20, 20, 21, 21, 22, 22, 23, 24, 24, 24, 25, 27, 27, 34, 35, 35, 36, 36, 36, 37, 37, 37, 38, 38, 40, 40, 41, 41, 41, 42, 42, 42; **21:**1, 1, 2, 4, 4, 6, 6, 6, 6, 6, 6, 7, 8, 9, 9, 9, 9, 9, 11, 11, 11, 11; **22:**1, 2, 3, 4, 5, 5, 5, 5, 6, 6, 6, 6, 7, 9, 9, 10, 10, 10, 14, 15, 16, 17, 17, 18, 19, 19, 19, 19, 20, 21, 21, 22, 23; **23:**1, 1, 2, 2, 3, 4, 4, 4, 5, 5, 6, 6, 6, 9, 9, 9, 11, 11, 12, 13, 14, 14, 14, 15, 15, 17, 18, 18, 19, 19, 19, 19, 21, 23, 24, 24, 24, 25, 25, 25, 27, 28, 28, 28, 28, 29; **24:**1, 1, 2, 2, 3, 3, 4, 4, 6, 6, 6, 7, 8, 9, 10, 10, 10, 12, 12, 14, 15, 15, 18, 19, 19, 21; **25:**1, 2, 11, 14, 15, 16, 21, 25, 26, 26, 28, 28, 29, 29, 29, 30, 31, 31, 32, 32, 33, 34, 34, 36, 37, 38, 39, 39, 40, 41; **26:**1, 2, 3, 3, 5, 6, 7, 7, 8, 9, 10, 11, 11, 12, 12, 13, 13, 15, 16, 16, 16, 16, 17, 19, 19, 19, 19, 20, 20, 20, 20, 23, 23, 23, 24; **27:**1, 1, 2, 5, 5, 6, 6, 7, 8, 8, 8, 8, 9, 9, 10, 10, 10, 11, 12; **28:**1, 3, 4, 4, 5, 6, 6, 6, 8, 9, 9, 9, 10, 10, 10, 11, 12, 13, 13, 14, 15, 16, 17, 17, 18, 18, 19, 19, 19, 19, 19, 20, 21, 21, 22, 23, 23, 23, 24, 25, 25; **29:**1, 1, 1, 2, 2, 3, 3, 4, 4, 5, 5, 6, 6, 6, 8, 8, 9, 10, 11, 11, 11; **30:**1, 1, 1, 2, 3, 5, 6, 7, 7, 8, 8, 10, 10, 10, 13, 14, 14, 14, 14, 15, 16, 16, 16, 16, 16, 16, 16, 17, 17, 18, 20, 21, 22, 23, 23, 24, 26, 26, 26, 27, 27, 27, 29, 29, 29, 29, 31; **31:**1, 1, 1, 2, 3, 3, 5, 7, 7, 7, 7, 7, 8, 8, 8, 8, 9, 9, 9, 10, 10, 10, 10, 11, 11, 12, 12, 12, 13; **2Sa 1:**1, 1, 2, 2, 2, 3, 3, 4, 4, 4, 6, 6, 10, 11, 12, 12, 13, 13, 14, 15, 15, 16, 18, 18, 18, 18, 19, 19, 20, 20, 20, 20, 21, 21, 21, 25, 25, 26, 27; **2:**1, 1, 1, 2, 3, 4, 4, 5, 6, 7, 8, 9, 9, 9, 10, 13, 13, 13, 13, 16, 16, 16, 16, 17, 17, 17, 17, 17, 18, 21, 23, 23, 23, 24, 24, 24, 24, 25, 25, 25, 26, 28, 29, 29, 29, 31; **3:**1, 2, 2, 3, 3, 3, 3, 4, 4, 5, 6, 9, 10, 12, 14, 17, 18, 18, 18, 19, 19, 19, 21, 23, 24, 26, 27, 28, 29, 29, 30, 31, 31, 32, 32, 33, 34, 34, 35, 35, 36, 36, 38, 39, 39; **4:**2, 3, 4, 4, 4, 4, 5, 6, 6, 6, 7, 7, 8, 8, 8, 9, 9, 9, 10, 11, 12; **5:**1, 2, 2, 2, 3, 3, 6, 6, 6, 6, 7, 7, 8, 8, 8, 8, 8, 8, 8, 8, 8, 9, 9, 9, 9, 10, 12, 12, 14, 17, 17, 18, 18, 19, 19, 19, 19, 20, 20, 20, 21, 22, 22, 23, 23, 23, 24, 24, 24, 24, 24, 25, 25, 25; **6:**2, 2, 2, 2, 3, 3, 3, 4, 5, 5, 6, 6, 6, 7, 7, 8, 9, 9, 9, 10, 10, 10, 10, 11, 11, 11, 11, 12, 12, 12, 12, 13, 14, 15, 15, 16, 16, 16, 16, 16, 17, 17, 17, 17, 18, 18, 18, 20, 20, 21, 21, 21, 21, 21, 22, 23; **7:**1, 1, 1, 2, 2, 3, 4, 5, 5, 6, 6, 7, 8, 8, 9, 10, 11, 11, 13, 13, 17, 18, 21, 23, 26, 26, 26; **8:**1, 2, 2, 2, 2, 3, 3, 4, 6, 6, 6, 7, 9, 11, 11, 11, 13, 14, 14, 16, 16, 17, 17, 18; **9:**2, 3, 4, 4, 7, 7, 8, 8, 8, 9, 10, 10, 12, 13; **10:**1, 2, 3, 4, 5, 6, 6, 6, 6, 7, 8, 8, 8, 8, 8, 8, 9, 9, 9, 10, 10, 10, 10, 11, 11, 12, 12, 13, 14, 14, 14, 14, 15, 16, 16, 16, 16, 17, 17, 17, 18, 18, 18, 19, 19; **11:**1, 1, 1, 1, 1, 1, 2, 2, 2, 3, 3, 3, 4, 4, 6, 7, 7, 8, 9, 9, 10, 11, 11, 11, 12, 12, 13, 14, 15, 15, 15, 16, 16, 19, 19, 19, 20, 20, 20, 21, 22, 23, 23, 24, 24, 24, 25, 25, 27, 27, 27; **12:**1, 1, 2, 3, 3, 4, 4, 4, 5, 6, 6, 7, 7, 7, 8, 9, 9, 10, 11, 12, 13, 13, 14, 14, 15, 16, 16, 17, 17, 18, 18, 18, 18, 19, 20, 20, 20, 20, 21, 21, 22, 22, 22, 24, 24, 25, 25, 25, 26, 26, 28, 28, 28, 28, 29, 30, 30, 30, 30, 31, 31, 31, 31; **13:**3, 4, 4, 6, 8, 9, 10, 13, 13, 17, 18, 18, 18, 23, 24, 24, 24, 25, 25, 26, 27, 28, 28, 29, 29, 30, 31, 31, 32, 34, 34, 34, 34, 34, 34, 34, 34, 35, 36, 37; **14:**1, 3, 3, 4, 4, 4, 5, 5, 6, 7, 7, 7, 7, 8, 9, 10, 11, 11, 13, 14, 14, 15, 17, 17, 18, 19, 19, 20, 21, 21, 22, 22, 24, 24, 25, 28, 30, 32, 32, 33, 33; **15:**2, 2, 2, 3, 4, 5, 6, 6, 7, 7, 9, 10, 10, 12, 12, 14, 14, 16, 16, 17, 17, 17, 18, 18, 19, 19, 19, 20, 21, 21, 23, 23, 23, 23, 24, 24, 24, 24, 25, 25, 25, 25, 25, 27, 27, 27, 28, 28, 28, 29, 29, 30, 30, 30, 30, 32, 32, 32, 32, 34, 35, 35; **16:**1, 1, 1, 2, 2, 2, 2, 2, 2, 3, 3, 4, 5, 6, 6, 6, 8, 8, 9, 10, 10, 11, 11, 12, 13, 14, 14, 14, 16, 16, 16, 17, 18, 18, 21, 22, 22, 23; **17:**2, 3, 3, 4, 5, 8, 8, 10, 10, 11, 11, 11, 11, 12, 12, 13, 13, 13, 13, 14, 14, 14, 14, 15, 16, 16, 16, 17, 17, 19, 19, 19, 19, 20, 21, 21, 21, 22, 22, 22, 22, 24, 24, 25, 26, 26, 27, 29; **18:**2, 2, 3, 4, 4, 4, 4, 4, 5, 5, 5, 6, 6, 7, 8, 8, 8, 8, 9, 9, 9, 12, 12, 13, 13, 13, 14, 16, 16, 17, 17, 18, 18, 19, 19, 19, 20, 21, 21, 23, 23, 23, 24, 24, 24, 24, 24, 25, 25, 25, 26, 26, 27, 27, 27, 28, 28, 28, 28, 29, 30, 31, 31, 31, 32, 32, 32, 33, 33; **19:**1, 2, 2, 2, 3, 4, 5, 5, 7, 7, 8, 8, 8, 8, 8, 9, 9, 9, 9, 9, 11, 11, 11, 11, 12, 14, 14, 15, 15, 15, 15, 16, 16, 16, 17, 17, 17, 17, 18, 18, 18, 18, 18, 19, 19, 20, 21, 22, 24, 24, 24, 25, 26, 26, 31, 31, 31, 32, 32, 33, 35, 35, 36, 36, 38, 39, 39, 39, 40, 40, 40, 40, 41, 41, 41, 41, 41, 42, 42, 43, 43, 43, 43, 43; **20:**2, 2, 2, 3, 3, 4, 4, 5, 5, 7, 8, 8, 8, 9, 10, 10, 10, 12, 12, 12, 13, 14, 15, 16, 17, 18, 19, 21, 21, 21, 21, 22, 22, 22, 22, 22, 23, 23, 24, 24, 25, 25, 26; **21:**1, 1, 1, 1, 2, 2, 2, 3, 4, 4, 6, 6, 6, 6, 7, 7, 8, 8, 9, 9, 9, 9, 9, 10, 10, 10, 10, 12, 12, 12, 12, 12, 12, 13, 13, 13, 13, 14, 14, 14, 14, 14, 15, 15, 16, 17, 17, 18, 18, 19, 19, 20, 20, 21, 22; **22:**1, 1, 2, 2, 3, 3, 4, 5, 5, 6, 6, 7, 8, 8, 8, 10, 11, 11, 14, 14, 16, 16, 16, 16, 16, 16, 16, 19, 21, 22, 22, 25, 26, 27, 27, 28, 31, 32, 34, 36, 40, 42, 43, 43, 43, 44, 47, 47, 48, 48, 49, 50; **23:**1, 1, 1, 1, 1, 1, 2, 2, 3, 3, 3, 3, 4, 4, 4, 4, 4, 6, 6, 8, 8, 8, 8, 8, 9, 9, 9, 10, 10, 10, 10, 11, 11, 11, 12, 12, 12, 12, 13, 13, 13, 13, 13, 14, 14, 14, 15, 15, 15, 16, 16, 16, 16, 17, 17, 17, 17, 18, 18, 18, 18, 19, 19, 19, 20, 20, 21, 21, 22, 22, 23, 23, 23, 24, 29, 31, 32, 39; **24:**1, 1, 1, 1, 2, 2, 2, 2, 2, 2, 3, 3, 4, 4, 4, 5, 5, 5, 5, 6, 7, 7, 7, 8, 9, 9, 10, 10, 10, 11, 11, 11, 11, 11, 12, 13, 13, 14, 14, 15, 15, 16, 16, 16, 16, 16, 16, 16, 17, 17, 17, 18, 18, 18, 19, 20, 20, 20, 21, 21, 21, 22, 22, 22, 23, 24, 24, 24, 24, 25, 25, 25; **1Ki 1:**3, 3, 4, 4, 4, 7, 8, 8, 9, 9, 9, 9, 10, 10, 11, 12, 13, 15, 17, 17, 18, 19, 19, 19, 20, 22, 22, 23, 23, 23, 24, 25, 25, 25,

25, 26, 27, 28, 29, 29, 30, 30, 30, 32, 32, 32, 33, 34, 34, 34, 36, 36,
36, 37, 38, 38, 38, 39, 39, 39, 39, 40, 40, 40, 40, 41, 41, 41, 42, 44,
44, 44, 44, 44, 45, 45, 45, 46, 47, 47, 48, 48, 49, 50, 50, 50, 51, 51,
53, 53; **2:**1, 3, 3, 3, 3, 4, 4, 4, 5, 7, 7, 8, 8, 8, 10, 12, 15, 15, 15, 15,
15, 17, 18, 19, 21, 22, 22, 23, 24, 24, 24, 26, 26, 26, 26, 27, 27, 27,
27, 28, 28, 28, 28, 30, 30, 30, 30, 31, 31, 31, 32, 32, 32, 32, 32, 33,
34, 34, 35, 35, 35, 35, 36, 36, 37, 37, 38, 42, 42, 43, 44, 44, 44, 45,
46, 46; **3:**1, 1, 1, 1, 1, 1, 2, 2, 2, 3, 3, 3, 4, 4, 5, 9, 10, 11, 13, 13, 15,
15, 16, 17, 17, 18, 19, 20, 21, 21, 22, 22, 22, 22, 22, 22, 23, 23, 23,
23, 23, 24, 25, 26, 26, 26, 26, 26, 27, 27, 27, 28, 28, 28; **4:**2, 3, 3, 4,
4, 5, 5, 6, 7, 7, 7, 8, 8, 8, 10, 12, 13, 13, 19, 19, 19, 19, 20, 20, 20, 21,
21, 21, 21, 21, 21, 22, 23, 24, 24, 24, 25, 27, 28, 28, 28, 30, 30, 30,
31, 31, 31, 33, 33, 34; **5:**1, 3, 3, 3, 3, 4, 5, 5, 5, 5, 7, 7, 8, 9, 9, 9, 9, 9,
9, 12, 15, 16, 17, 17, 17, 17, 18, 18, 18; **6:**1, 1, 1, 1, 1, 1, 2, 2, 3, 3, 3,
3, 3, 3, 3, 4, 5, 5, 5, 5, 5, 6, 6, 6, 6, 6, 6, 6, 6, 6, 7, 7, 7, 7, 7, 7, 7, 8,
8, 8, 8, 8, 8, 9, 10, 10, 10, 11, 12, 13, 14, 15, 15, 15, 16, 16, 16, 17,
17, 17, 18, 18, 18, 19, 19, 19, 19, 19, 20, 21, 21, 21, 21, 22, 22, 22,
23, 24, 24, 25, 27, 27, 27, 27, 28, 29, 29, 29, 30, 31, 31, 32, 33, 33,
35, 36, 36, 37, 37, 37, 38, 38, 38; **7:**1, 2, 2, 2, 4, 5, 6, 7, 7, 7, 8, 10,
11, 11, 12, 12, 12, 12, 12, 14, 16, 16, 18, 18, 18, 19, 19, 19, 20, 20,
20, 21, 21, 21, 21, 21, 21, 21, 21, 21, 22, 22, 22, 22, 23, 24, 24, 24,
25, 26, 26, 29, 29, 29, 30, 30, 31, 31, 31, 31, 31, 31, 32, 32, 32, 33,
34, 34, 34, 35, 35, 35, 36, 37, 37, 39, 39, 39, 39, 39, 39, 40, 40, 40,
41, 41, 42, 42, 42, 42, 42, 43, 43, 44, 44, 45, 45, 45, 45, 45, 46, 46,
47, 47, 47, 48, 48, 48, 48, 48, 48, 48, 49, 49, 49, 49, 49, 50, 50, 50,
50, 50, 50, 51, 51, 51, 51, 51, 51, 51, 51; **8:**1, 1, 1, 1, 1, 1, 2, 2, 3, 3,
3, 4, 4, 4, 4, 4, 5, 5, 6, 6, 6, 6, 6, 6, 6, 6, 7, 7, 7, 8, 8, 8, 9, 9, 9, 9, 9,
10, 10, 10, 10, 11, 11, 11, 11, 14, 14, 15, 15, 15, 16, 16, 16, 17, 17,
17, 18, 18, 19, 20, 20, 20, 20, 21, 21, 21, 22, 22, 22, 27, 28, 28, 29,
30, 31, 32, 32, 32, 32, 35, 36, 37, 37, 37, 39, 40, 43, 43, 44, 48, 51,
52, 53, 53, 54, 54, 54, 55, 56, 56, 57, 58, 58, 59, 59, 59, 59, 60, 60,
61, 62, 62, 63, 63, 63, 63, 64, 64, 64, 64, 64, 64, 64, 65, 65, 65, 65,
65, 65, 65, 65, 65, 65, 66, 66, 66, 66; **9:**1, 1, 1, 2, 3, 5, 5, 7, 7, 8, 9, 9,
9, 10, 10, 10, 10, 10, 11, 11, 11, 11, 12, 15, 15, 15, 15, 15, 15, 15, 16,
16, 16, 17, 17, 18, 19, 20, 21, 21, 22, 23, 24, 24, 24, 25, 25, 25, 25,
25, 26, 26, 26, 27; **10:**1, 1, 1, 3, 4, 4, 5, 5, 5, 5, 5, 5, 6, 7, 9, 9, 9, 10,
10, 12, 12, 12, 12, 12, 12, 13, 13, 15, 15, 15, 15, 17, 17, 17, 18, 19,
19, 19, 19, 20, 20, 21, 21, 21, 22, 22, 23, 24, 26, 27, 27, 27, 28, 28,
29, 29, 29; **11:**1, 2, 2, 3, 4, 5, 5, 5, 5, 6, 6, 7, 7, 7, 7, 9, 9, 9, 10, 11,
11, 12, 12, 13, 13, 14, 14, 15, 16, 17, 19, 21, 24, 25, 26, 27, 27, 27,
27, 28, 28, 29, 29, 29, 30, 31, 31, 31, 31, 31, 32, 32, 32, 33, 33, 33,
33, 33, 34, 34, 34, 34, 35, 35, 36, 36, 36, 37, 39, 41, 41, 41, 41, 43,
43; **12:**3, 3, 4, 5, 6, 6, 7, 7, 8, 8, 8, 8, 9, 10, 12, 12, 13, 13, 14, 14, 15,
15, 15, 15, 15, 15, 16, 16, 17, 17, 18, 19, 20, 20, 20, 21, 21, 21, 22,
23, 24, 24, 24, 24, 24, 25, 25, 25, 26, 26, 27, 27, 28, 28, 28, 28, 29,
30, 31, 31, 31, 31, 32, 32, 32, 33, 33, 33; **13:**1, 1, 2, 2, 2, 2, 2, 3, 3, 3,
4, 4, 4, 4, 5, 5, 5, 5, 5, 6, 6, 6, 6, 6, 6, 7, 7, 7, 8, 8, 9, 9, 11, 11, 12, 12,
13, 13, 13, 14, 14, 14, 15, 17, 17, 18, 18, 18, 19, 19, 20, 20, 20, 21,
21, 21, 21, 21, 22, 23, 23, 24, 24, 24, 24, 25, 25, 25, 25, 26, 26, 26,
26, 26, 26, 27, 28, 28, 28, 28, 28, 28, 29, 29, 29, 29, 29, 30, 31, 31,
31, 32, 32, 32, 32, 32, 33, 33, 33, 34, 34; **14:**2, 2, 2, 3, 5, 5, 6, 7, 7, 7,
7, 8, 8, 11, 11, 11, 11, 12, 12, 13, 13, 13, 13, 13, 14, 14, 15, 15, 15,
15, 17, 17, 18, 18, 18, 19, 19, 19, 19, 19, 20, 21, 21, 21, 21, 22, 22,
24, 24, 24, 24, 24, 24, 24, 25, 26, 26, 26, 26, 27, 27, 28, 28, 28, 28,
28, 29, 29, 29, 29, 29, 31, 31; **15:**1, 2, 3, 3, 3, 4, 5, 5, 5, 5, 7, 7, 7, 7,
7, 8, 8, 9, 10, 11, 12, 12, 12, 13, 13, 14, 14, 15, 15, 15, 15, 18, 18, 18,
18, 18, 19, 20, 20, 22, 22, 22, 23, 23, 23, 23, 23, 23, 23, 23, 24, 24,
25, 26, 26, 26, 27, 27, 27, 28, 28, 29, 29, 29, 29, 30, 30, 30, 30, 30,
31, 31, 31, 31, 31, 33, 34, 34, 34; **16:**1, 1, 2, 2, 3, 4, 4, 4, 5, 5, 5, 5, 5,
5, 6, 7, 7, 7, 7, 7, 8, 9, 9, 9, 9, 10, 10, 11, 12, 12, 12, 13, 13, 13, 13,
13, 14, 14, 14, 14, 14, 15, 15, 15, 16, 16, 17, 18, 18, 18, 18, 19, 19,
19, 20, 20, 20, 20, 20, 21, 21, 21, 22, 22, 23, 24, 24, 25, 25, 26, 26,
26, 26, 26, 27, 27, 27, 27, 27, 27, 28, 29, 30, 30, 31, 31, 33, 33, 33,
33, 34, 34, 34, 34; **17:**1, 1, 1, 1, 1, 2, 3, 3, 4, 4, 5, 6, 6, 7, 7, 8, 9, 9,
10, 10, 12, 12, 12, 12, 12, 14, 14, 14, 14, 14, 16, 16, 17, 19, 19, 19,
20, 21, 21, 22, 22, 22, 23, 24, 24; **18:**1, 1, 1, 2, 3, 3, 4, 6, 7, 9, 10, 10,
10, 10, 12, 12, 12, 13, 13, 15, 18, 18, 18, 18, 19, 19, 20, 20, 21, 21,
22, 22, 23, 23, 23, 23, 23, 24, 24, 24, 24, 24, 24, 24, 25, 25, 25, 25,
26, 26, 26, 26, 28, 29, 29, 30, 30, 30, 31, 32, 32, 32, 33, 33, 33, 33,
33, 33, 33, 34, 35, 35, 35, 36, 36, 36, 36, 38, 38, 38, 38, 38, 38, 38,
38, 39, 39, 39, 40, 40, 40, 42, 42, 43, 43, 44, 44, 44, 44, 45, 46, 46,
46; **19:**1, 2, 4, 5, 7, 7, 8, 8, 9, 9, 10, 10, 11, 11, 11, 11, 11, 11, 11, 11,
11, 11, 12, 12, 12, 12, 12, 13, 13, 14, 14, 15, 15, 15, 19, 20, 21, 21,
21, 21; **20:**1, 1, 2, 3, 6, 7, 7, 7, 8, 9, 9, 9, 9, 9, 10, 11, 12, 12, 13, 13,
14, 14, 14, 14, 14, 15, 15, 15, 16, 17, 17, 17, 19, 20, 20, 21, 21, 22,
22, 23, 23, 23, 24, 25, 25, 25, 26, 26, 27, 27, 27, 27, 28, 28, 28, 28,
28, 28, 28, 28, 29, 29, 29, 29, 30, 30, 30, 30, 31, 32, 32, 33, 33, 34,
35, 35, 35, 35, 36, 36, 36, 37, 37, 38, 38, 38, 39, 39, 39, 40, 40, 41,
41, 41, 41, 42, 42, 42, 43; **21:**1, 2, 3, 3, 4, 4, 5, 5, 7, 8, 8, 9, 10, 11,
11, 11, 12, 13, 13, 13, 14, 15, 15, 16, 17, 19, 19, 19, 20, 21, 22, 22,
23, 23, 23, 23, 24, 24, 24, 25, 26, 26, 26, 26, 26, 28; **22:**2, 3, 3, 5, 6,
7, 7, 8, 9, 10, 10, 11, 11, 12, 12, 13, 13, 13, 14, 14, 15, 15, 15, 16, 16,
16, 17, 17, 18, 19, 19, 19, 20, 21, 22, 22, 22, 23, 23, 23, 24, 24, 24,
26, 26, 27, 27, 28, 29, 31, 31, 32, 32, 33, 33, 34, 34, 34, 34, 34, 35,
35, 35, 35, 36, 36, 37, 38, 38, 38, 38, 39, 39, 39, 39, 39, 39, 39, 39,
40, 41, 42, 43, 43, 43, 43, 44, 45, 45, 45, 45, 45, 45, 45, 46, 46, 46,
46, 48, 49, 50, 50, 51, 52, 52, 52, 52, 53, 53, 53; **2Ki 1:**1, 2, 2, 2, 3, 3,
3, 3, 3, 3, 4, 4, 4, 5, 5, 6, 6, 6, 6, 6, 7, 8, 9, 9, 10, 11, 11, 11, 12, 13,
13, 13, 14, 14, 15, 15, 15, 16, 16, 16, 16, 17, 17, 17, 17, 18, 18, 18,
18, 18; **2:**1, 2, 2, 3, 3, 4, 4, 5, 5, 6, 6, 6, 7, 7, 8, 8, 8, 9, 12, 13, 13, 14,
14, 14, 14, 14, 15, 16, 16, 16, 16, 19, 19, 19, 19, 21, 21, 21, 21, 22,
23, 23, 24, 24, 24; **3:**1, 2, 2, 3, 3, 4, 4, 5, 5, 6, 7, 7, 8, 9, 9, 9, 10, 10,
10, 10, 11, 11, 12, 12, 13, 13, 13, 13, 14, 15, 15, 15, 15, 16, 17, 18,
18, 19, 19, 20, 20, 20, 20, 21, 21, 22, 22, 22, 23, 23, 23, 24, 24, 24,
24, 24, 25, 25, 25, 26, 26, 26, 26, 27, 27, 27; **4:**1, 1, 2, 4, 4, 4, 6, 6, 7,
7, 8, 10, 12, 13, 13, 13, 13, 15, 15, 17, 17, 18, 19, 20, 21, 21, 21, 22,
22, 24, 24, 25, 25, 25, 26, 27, 27, 27, 27, 27, 29, 29, 29, 30, 30, 31,
31, 31, 32, 32, 33, 33, 34, 34, 34, 34, 34, 35, 35, 35, 36, 38, 38, 39,
39, 39, 40, 41, 42, 42, 42, 43, 43, 44; **5:**1, 1, 1, 2, 3, 3, 4, 4, 5, 5, 5, 6,
6, 7, 8, 8, 9, 10, 11, 11, 11, 12, 12, 13, 14, 14, 15, 15, 16, 16, 17, 18,
18, 18, 18, 18, 20, 22, 23, 23, 24, 24, 24, 24, 24, 24, 26, 27; **6:**1, 2, 4,
5, 6, 6, 6, 6, 6, 7, 8, 9, 9, 9, 10, 10, 10, 10, 11, 11, 11, 12, 12, 12, 12,
12, 13, 13, 14, 14, 15, 15, 15, 17, 17, 18, 18, 19, 19, 19, 20, 21, 23,
23, 23, 25, 26, 26, 26, 26, 27, 28, 28, 28, 29, 30, 30, 30, 30, 31, 32,
32, 32, 32, 32, 33, 33, 33, 33; **7:**1, 1, 1, 2, 2, 2, 2, 2, 3, 3, 4, 4, 4, 5, 5,
6, 6, 6, 6, 6, 6, 6, 7, 8, 8, 8, 9, 9, 10, 10, 10, 10, 10, 11, 11, 11, 11, 12,
12, 12, 12, 12, 12, 12, 13, 13, 14, 14, 15, 15, 15, 15, 15, 16, 16, 16,
17, 17, 17, 17, 17, 17, 18, 18, 18, 19, 19, 19, 19, 20, 20; **8:**1, 1, 2, 2,
2, 2, 3, 3, 3, 4, 4, 4, 4, 4, 5, 5, 5, 5, 5, 5, 6, 6, 7, 7, 7, 8, 8, 8, 8, 9, 9,
10, 11, 12, 12, 12, 12, 13, 13, 14, 15, 15, 15, 16, 16, 18, 18, 18, 19,
20, 21, 21, 22, 23, 23, 23, 23, 23, 24, 24, 25, 25, 27, 27, 27, 28; **9:**1,
1, 3, 3, 3, 3, 4, 5, 6, 6, 6, 6, 6, 6, 7, 7, 7, 8, 9, 9, 10, 10, 10, 11, 12,
12, 13, 14, 14, 15, 15, 17, 17, 18, 18, 18, 18, 19, 19, 20, 20, 21, 22,
23, 24, 24, 25, 25, 26, 26, 26, 27, 27, 28, 29, 30, 31, 31, 32, 33, 33,
33, 34, 34, 36, 36, 36, 37; **10:**1, 1, 1, 1, 1, 1, 1, 2, 3, 5, 5, 5, 5, 6, 6, 6,
6, 6, 7, 7, 7, 8, 8, 8, 8, 9, 9, 9, 10, 10, 10, 12, 12, 13, 13, 14, 15, 16,
17, 18, 18, 18, 19, 19, 21, 21, 22, 22, 23, 23, 23, 24, 24, 25, 25, 25,
25, 26, 26, 27, 27, 29, 29, 30, 30, 30, 30, 31, 31, 31, 31, 32, 32, 32,
33, 33, 33, 33, 34, 34, 34, 34, 34, 35; **11:**1, 1, 1, 2, 2, 2, 2, 3, 3, 3, 4,
4, 4, 4, 4, 4, 4, 4, 4, 5, 5, 6, 6, 6, 6, 7, 7, 7, 7, 8, 8, 9, 9, 9, 9, 9, 10, 10,
10, 11, 11, 11, 11, 11, 11, 12, 12, 12, 12, 13, 13, 13, 13, 14, 14, 14,
14, 14, 15, 15, 15, 15, 15, 15, 16, 16, 17, 17, 17, 17, 17, 17, 18, 18,
18, 18, 18, 18, 18, 18, 18, 18, 19, 19, 19, 19, 19, 19, 19, 19, 19, 19,
19, 19, 19, 20, 20, 20, 20; **12:**1, 2, 2, 3, 3, 4, 4, 4, 5, 5, 6, 6, 6, 7, 7, 7,
8, 8, 8, 8, 9, 9, 9, 9, 9, 9, 9, 9, 9, 9, 9, 10, 10, 10, 10, 10, 11, 11, 11,
11, 11, 11, 12, 12, 12, 12, 12, 13, 13, 13, 13, 14, 14, 15, 16, 16, 16,
18, 18, 18, 18, 18, 18, 19, 19, 19, 19, 19, 20, 21, 21, 21; **13:**1, 2, 2, 2,
3, 4, 4, 4, 4, 5, 5, 5, 5, 6, 7, 7, 8, 8, 8, 8, 8, 8, 9, 10, 11, 11, 12, 12, 12,
12, 12, 12, 13, 14, 15, 16, 16, 16, 17, 17, 18, 18, 18, 18, 19, 19, 20,
21, 21, 21, 21, 22, 23, 23, 24, 25, 25; **14:**1, 1, 3, 3, 4, 4, 5, 6, 6, 6, 6,
6, 6, 6, 6, 6, 7, 8, 9, 9, 10, 11, 12, 13, 13, 14, 14, 14, 14, 14, 15, 15,
15, 15, 15, 15, 16, 17, 18, 18, 18, 18, 18, 20, 21, 22, 23, 23, 24, 24,
25, 25, 25, 25, 25, 26, 26, 27, 27, 27, 28, 28, 28, 28, 28, 28, 28, 29,
29; **15:**1, 1, 3, 4, 4, 5, 5, 5, 5, 5, 5, 5, 6, 6, 6, 6, 6, 7, 7, 8, 9, 9, 10, 11,
11, 11, 11, 11, 12, 12, 13, 14, 15, 15, 15, 15, 15, 16, 16, 16, 16, 16,
17, 18, 18, 19, 20, 20, 20, 20, 20, 21, 21, 21, 21, 21, 22, 23, 24, 24,
25, 25, 25, 25, 25, 26, 26, 26, 26, 26, 27, 28, 28, 29, 29, 29, 30, 31,
31, 31, 31, 31, 32, 33, 34, 35, 35, 35, 35, 35, 35, 36, 36, 36, 36, 36,
37, 38, 38; **16:**1, 2, 2, 3, 3, 3, 3, 3, 3, 3, 3, 4, 4, 6, 6, 6, 7, 8, 8, 8, 8, 8,
9, 9, 10, 10, 11, 11, 12, 12, 13, 13, 14, 14, 14, 14, 14, 14, 14, 15, 15,
15, 15, 15, 15, 15, 15, 15, 15, 15, 16, 17, 17, 17, 17, 17, 17, 17, 18,
18, 18, 18, 18, 18, 18, 19, 19, 19, 19, 19, 20, 20; **17:**1, 2, 2, 4, 4, 4, 5,
5, 6, 6, 6, 6, 6, 6, 7, 7, 7, 8, 8, 8, 8, 8, 8, 9, 9, 9, 9, 10, 11, 11, 11, 11,
11, 11, 12, 13, 13, 13, 14, 14, 15, 15, 15, 15, 16, 16, 16, 17, 17, 18,
18, 18, 19, 19, 19, 19, 20, 20, 21, 21, 21, 22, 22, 23, 23, 24, 24, 24,
24, 24, 25, 25, 26, 26, 26, 26, 26, 27, 27, 27, 27, 27, 27, 28, 28, 28,
29, 29, 31, 31, 32, 32, 33, 33, 33, 34, 34, 34, 35, 35, 36, 37, 38, 39,
39, 40, 41, 41; **18:**1, 2, 3, 4, 4, 4, 4, 4, 4, 5, 5, 5, 6, 6, 6, 7, 7, 8, 9, 9,
9, 10, 10, 11, 11, 11, 11, 11, 11, 12, 12, 12, 13, 13, 14, 14, 15, 15, 15,
15, 16, 16, 16, 16, 16, 17, 17, 17, 17, 17, 17, 18, 18, 18, 18, 19, 19,
21, 22, 22, 22, 23, 24, 24, 25, 25, 26, 26, 26, 27, 28, 28, 28, 29, 30,
30, 30, 31, 31, 31, 32, 33, 33, 34, 34, 35, 36, 37, 37, 37, 37, 37; **19:**1,
1, 2, 2, 2, 2, 3, 4, 4, 4, 5, 6, 6, 6, 7, 8, 9, 10, 11, 12, 12, 12, 13, 13, 13,
14, 14, 14, 15, 15, 15, 15, 15, 15, 16, 17, 17, 18, 18, 18, 19, 19, 20,
20, 21, 21, 21, 21, 22, 23, 23, 23, 24, 25, 26, 26, 27, 28, 29, 29, 29,
30, 30, 31, 31, 32, 32, 33, 33, 33, 34, 35, 35, 35, 35, 35, 37, 37, 37;
20:1, 1, 1, 2, 2, 4, 4, 5, 5, 5, 5, 5, 6, 6, 7, 8, 8, 8, 9, 9, 9, 9, 10, 11, 11,
11, 13, 13, 13, 13, 13, 14, 14, 16, 17, 17, 17, 18, 19, 19, 20, 20, 20,
20, 20, 20, 20, 21; **21:**2, 2, 2, 2, 2, 2, 3, 3, 4, 4, 4, 4, 5, 5, 6, 6, 7, 7, 7,
7, 7, 8, 8, 9, 9, 9, 9, 9, 10, 10, 11, 11, 12, 12, 12, 13, 13, 13, 13, 16,
16, 16, 16, 17, 17, 17, 17, 17, 17, 18, 18, 18, 19, 20, 21, 21, 22, 22,
22, 24, 24, 24, 25, 25, 25, 25, 25, 26, 26; **22:**1, 2, 2, 3, 3, 3, 3, 4, 4, 4,
4, 4, 5, 5, 5, 5, 6, 6, 6, 7, 7, 8, 8, 8, 8, 8, 8, 9, 9, 9, 9, 9, 9, 10, 10, 10,
11, 11, 11, 12, 12, 12, 13, 13, 13, 13, 13, 13, 14, 14, 14, 14, 14, 14,
15, 15, 15, 16, 16, 18, 18, 18, 18, 18, 19, 19, 20, 20, 20; **23:**1, 1, 2, 2,
2, 2, 2, 2, 2, 2, 2, 2, 2, 3, 3, 3, 3, 3, 3, 3, 3, 3, 3, 4, 4, 4, 4, 4, 4, 4,
4, 4, 4, 4, 5, 5, 5, 5, 5, 5, 5, 5, 6, 6, 6, 6, 6, 6, 7, 7, 7, 7, 7, 7, 8, 8, 8,
8, 8, 8, 8, 8, 8, 8, 9, 9, 9, 9, 10, 10, 10, 10, 11, 11, 11, 11, 11, 11, 11,
11, 11, 11, 11, 12, 12, 12, 12, 12, 12, 12, 12, 12, 12, 13, 13, 13, 13,
13, 13, 13, 13, 13, 14, 14, 15, 15, 15, 15, 15, 16, 16, 16, 16, 16, 16,
16, 16, 16, 16, 17, 17, 17, 17, 17, 17, 18, 19, 19, 19, 19, 19, 20, 20,
20, 21, 21, 21, 21, 21, 22, 22, 22, 22, 23, 23, 24, 24, 24, 24, 24, 24,
24, 25, 25, 26, 26, 27, 27, 27, 28, 28, 28, 28, 28, 29, 29, 30, 30, 31,
32, 33, 35, 35, 36, 37; **24:**1, 2, 2, 3, 3, 4, 5, 5, 5, 5, 5, 6, 7, 7, 7, 7, 7,
8, 9, 10, 11, 11, 12, 12, 12, 13, 13, 13, 13, 13, 13, 14, 14, 14, 14, 14,
15, 16, 17, 17, 18, 19, 20, 20, 20; **25:**1, 1, 2, 3, 3, 3, 3, 4, 4, 4, 4, 4, 4,
4, 4, 4, 4, 4, 5, 5, 5, 6, 7, 8, 8, 8, 9, 9, 9, 9, 9, 9, 10, 10, 10, 10, 11, 11,
11, 11, 11, 11, 12, 12, 12, 12, 13, 13, 13, 13, 13, 13, 14, 14, 14, 15,
15, 15, 16, 16, 16, 16, 16, 16, 17, 17, 17, 18, 18, 18, 18, 19, 19, 19,
19, 19, 20, 20, 21, 21, 21, 22, 23, 23, 23, 23, 24, 24, 24, 25, 26, 26,
26, 26, 26, 27, 27, 28, 29, 29, 30, 30; **1Ch 1:**1, 4, 5, 6, 7, 8, 9, 9, 10,
10, 11, 11, 12, 12, 13, 13, 13, 13, 17, 17, 18, 18, 19, 19, 19, 20, 24,
28, 29, 29, 31, 32, 32, 33, 34, 34, 35, 36, 37, 38, 39, 40, 40, 41, 41,
42, 42, 43, 45, 45, 46, 46, 46, 46, 47, 48, 48, 50, 50, 51, 54; **2:**1, 3, 3,
5, 6, 7, 8, 9, 10, 10, 11, 11, 12, 12, 20, 20, 21, 22, 22, 23, 23, 24, 24,
25, 25, 25, 26, 27, 27, 28, 28, 29, 30, 31, 35, 36, 36, 37, 37, 38, 38,
39, 39, 40, 40, 41, 41, 42, 42, 42, 42, 43, 44, 44, 44, 45, 45, 46, 47,
49, 49, 50, 50, 50, 51, 51, 52, 52, 52, 53, 53, 53, 54, 54, 54, 54, 54,
55, 55, 55, 55; **3:**1, 1, 1, 2, 2, 2, 3, 3, 4, 5, 5, 5, 9, 9, 10, 15, 15, 15,
15, 15, 17, 17, 19, 19, 21, 23, 24; **4:**1, 2, 2, 2, 2, 3, 4, 4, 4, 4, 4, 5, 8,
8, 10, 10, 11, 11, 11, 12, 12, 12, 13, 14, 14, 14, 14, 15, 15, 16, 17, 17,
17, 18, 18, 18, 18, 19, 19, 19, 19, 19, 20, 20, 21, 21, 21, 21, 22, 23,
23, 24, 25, 26, 27, 31, 38, 38, 39, 39, 39, 40, 40, 41, 41, 41, 41, 41,
41, 42, 43; **5:**1, 1, 1, 1, 2, 2, 2, 2, 3, 3, 4, 6, 6, 7, 8, 9, 9, 9, 9, 10, 10,
10, 10, 10, 11, 11, 11, 12, 12, 13, 15, 16, 16, 16, 17, 17, 18, 18, 19,
19, 19, 19, 20, 20, 21, 21, 22, 22, 23, 23, 24, 25, 25, 25, 26, 26, 26,
26, 26, 26; **6:**1, 2, 3, 3, 4, 4, 5, 5, 6, 6, 7, 7, 8, 8, 9, 9, 10, 10, 10, 11,
11, 12, 12, 13, 13, 14, 14, 15, 15, 16, 17, 18, 19, 19, 19, 20, 22, 25,
28, 28, 28, 29, 31, 31, 31, 31, 31, 32, 32, 32, 32, 33, 33, 33, 39, 44,
48, 48, 49, 49, 49, 49, 49, 49, 49, 50, 54, 54, 54, 56, 57, 57, 60, 60,
61, 61, 61, 62, 62, 62, 62, 63, 63, 64, 64, 65, 65, 66, 66, 67, 70, 70,
70, 71, 71, 71, 71, 72, 74, 76, 77, 77, 77, 78, 78, 80; **7:**1, 2, 2, 2, 2, 3,
3, 3, 4, 5, 5, 5, 7, 7, 7, 8, 10, 10, 11, 11, 12, 12, 13, 14, 14, 16, 17, 19,
20, 21, 23, 24, 28, 28, 28, 28, 28, 28, 29, 29, 29, 30, 31, 31, 32, 33,
34, 35, 36, 38, 39, 40, 40; **8:**1, 1, 3, 6, 6, 7, 8, 10, 12, 13, 13, 13, 16,
18, 21, 25, 27, 28, 28, 29, 32, 33, 33, 33, 34, 34, 35, 36, 36, 36, 37,
37, 37, 37, 38, 39, 39, 39, 40; **9:**1, 1, 1, 1, 1, 2, 2, 3, 5, 5, 6, 6, 7, 9,
10, 11, 11, 13, 14, 16, 17, 17, 18, 18, 18, 18, 19, 19, 19, 19, 19, 19,
19, 19, 20, 20, 21, 21, 22, 23, 23, 23, 23, 24, 25, 26, 26, 26, 27, 27,
27, 28, 28, 29, 29, 29, 29, 30, 30, 31, 31, 31, 31, 32, 32, 32, 33, 33,
34, 35, 38, 39, 39, 39, 40, 40, 41, 42, 42, 42, 43, 44; **10:**1, 1, 1, 2, 3,
3, 7, 7, 7, 8, 8, 8, 8, 9, 9, 9, 10, 10, 10, 11, 11, 12, 12, 13, 13, 14, 14;
11:2, 2, 2, 3, 3, 3, 4, 4, 5, 5, 5, 6, 6, 6, 6, 6, 6, 7, 7, 8, 8, 8, 8, 9, 10,
10, 11, 11, 11, 11, 11, 12, 13, 13, 13, 13, 14, 14, 14, 14, 15, 15, 15,
15, 15, 15, 16, 16, 16, 17, 17, 17, 18, 18, 18, 18, 19, 19, 19, 20, 20,
20, 20, 21, 21, 21, 22, 22, 23, 23, 24, 24, 25, 25, 25, 31, 32, 34, 38,
41, 42, 44, 46; **12:**1, 1, 2, 3, 4, 8, 8, 8, 8, 14, 14, 15, 15, 15, 15, 15,
15, 16, 17, 18, 18, 18, 19, 19, 19, 20, 20, 22, 23, 23, 24, 25, 26, 27,
29, 29, 30, 31, 31, 31, 32, 32, 32, 32, 32, 33, 34, 35, 36, 37, 37, 37,
37, 38, 38, 40, 40; **13:**1, 2, 2, 2, 2, 2, 2, 3, 3, 4, 4, 4, 5, 5, 5, 5, 6, 6, 6,
6, 7, 7, 9, 9, 9, 10, 10, 10, 11, 12, 13, 13, 13, 14, 14, 14; **14:**2, 2, 4, 8,
9, 9, 10, 10, 10, 11, 11, 12, 13, 13, 14, 15, 15, 15, 15, 16, 16, 17, 17;
15:1, 1, 2, 2, 2, 2, 2, 3, 3, 3, 3, 4, 5, 6, 7, 11, 12, 12, 12, 12, 12, 12,
13, 13, 13, 13, 13, 14, 14, 14, 14, 14, 15, 15, 15, 16, 16, 17, 17, 17,
18, 18, 19, 20, 21, 22, 22, 23, 24, 24, 24, 25, 25, 25, 25, 25, 25, 26,
26, 26, 27, 27, 27, 27, 28, 28, 28, 28, 29, 29, 29, 29; **16:**1, 1, 2, 2, 2,
4, 4, 4, 4, 4, 4, 5, 5, 5, 5, 6, 6, 6, 7, 8, 8, 10, 11, 12, 12, 12, 14, 14, 15,
16, 16, 17, 18, 23, 23, 23, 24, 24, 25, 26, 26, 26, 28, 28, 28, 29, 29,
29, 30, 30, 31, 31, 31, 31, 32, 32, 33, 33, 33, 33, 34, 35, 36, 36, 36,
36, 37, 37, 39, 39, 39, 39, 39, 40, 40, 40, 40, 40, 41, 41, 42, 42, 43;
17:1, 1, 1, 4, 4, 5, 5, 6, 7, 7, 8, 9, 10, 10, 12, 15, 16, 18, 21, 24, 24,
24; **18:**1, 2, 2, 3, 3, 4, 6, 6, 6, 7, 8, 8, 8, 8, 8, 8, 9, 11, 11, 11, 12, 13,
13, 15, 15, 16, 16, 17, 17; **19:**1, 2, 3, 4, 5, 6, 6, 7, 7, 7, 9, 9, 9, 9, 9,
10, 10, 10, 11, 11, 11, 11, 12, 12, 13, 13, 14, 15, 15, 15, 16, 16, 16,
16, 16, 17, 17, 18, 18, 18, 19, 19, 19; **20:**1, 1, 1, 1, 1, 1, 1, 2, 2, 2, 2,
3, 3, 3, 4, 4, 4, 5, 5, 5, 6, 6, 7, 8; **21:**1, 2, 2, 2, 2, 2, 3, 3, 4, 4, 4, 5, 6,
6, 6, 7, 8, 9, 9, 10, 11, 11, 12, 12, 12, 12, 13, 13, 14, 15, 15, 15, 15,
15, 15, 15, 16, 16, 16, 16, 17, 17, 17, 18, 18, 18, 18, 18, 19, 19, 20,
20, 21, 21, 22, 22, 23, 23, 23, 23, 23, 24, 24, 25, 26, 26, 26, 26, 27,
27, 27, 28, 29, 29, 29, 29, 29, 30, 30, 30; **22:**1, 1, 1, 1, 1, 2, 2, 2, 3, 3,
3, 3, 4, 5, 5, 5, 6, 6, 7, 7, 8, 8, 8, 9, 10, 10, 11, 11, 11, 12, 12, 12, 13,
13, 14, 14, 14, 16, 16, 17, 18, 18, 18, 19, 19, 19, 19, 19, 19, 19, 19;
23:2, 2, 2, 3, 3, 4, 4, 4, 5, 5, 6, 6, 6, 7, 7, 8, 8, 9, 9, 9, 11, 12, 13, 13,
13, 13, 14, 14, 15, 16, 16, 17, 18, 18, 19, 19, 19, 19, 19, 20, 20, 20,
21, 21, 22, 23, 24, 24, 24, 24, 25, 25, 26, 26, 27, 28, 28, 28, 28, 28,
28, 28, 28, 28, 29, 29, 29, 29, 29, 29, 29, 29, 30, 31, 31, 31, 31, 31,
31, 32, 32, 32, 32, 32, 32, 32; **24:**1, 1, 3, 4, 5, 5, 5, 6, 6, 6, 6, 6, 6, 6,
7, 7, 8, 8, 9, 9, 10, 10, 11, 11, 12, 12, 13, 13, 14, 14, 15, 15, 16, 16,
17, 17, 18, 18, 19, 19, 19, 19, 19, 19, 20, 20, 20, 20, 20, 21, 21, 22,
22, 22, 22, 23, 23, 24, 24, 24, 24, 25, 25, 25, 26, 26, 26, 26, 27, 27,
28, 28, 29, 29, 30, 30, 30, 31, 31, 31, 31, 31; **25:**1, 1, 1, 2, 2, 2, 3, 3,
3, 3, 5, 5, 6, 6, 6, 6, 6, 6, 7, 8, 9, 9, 9, 10, 11, 12, 13, 14, 15, 16, 17,
18, 19, 20, 21, 22, 23, 24, 25, 26, 27, 28, 29, 30, 31; **26:**1, 1, 1, 1, 2,
2, 2, 2, 2, 3, 3, 3, 4, 4, 4, 4, 4, 4, 5, 5, 5, 6, 10, 10, 10, 11, 11, 11, 12,
12, 12, 12, 13, 14, 14, 14, 15, 15, 16, 16, 16, 17, 17, 17, 17, 18, 18,
18, 18, 19, 19, 19, 20, 20, 20, 21, 21, 21, 22, 22, 22, 22, 23, 24, 24,
24, 26, 26, 26, 26, 26, 26, 27, 27, 27, 28, 28, 28, 28, 29, 30, 30, 30,
30, 30, 30, 30, 31, 31, 31, 31, 31, 31, 31, 31, 32, 32, 32, 32, 32, 32,
32, 32; **27:**1, 1, 1, 1, 2, 2, 3, 3, 4, 4, 5, 5, 5, 6, 6, 7, 7, 7, 8, 8, 8, 9, 9,
10, 10, 11, 11, 12, 12, 12, 13, 13, 14, 14, 15, 15, 16, 16, 17, 22, 22,
23, 23, 23, 24, 24, 24, 25, 25, 25, 26, 26, 27, 27, 27, 28, 28, 28, 29,
29, 29, 29, 30, 30, 30, 31, 31, 32, 32, 32, 33, 33, 33, 34; **28:**1, 1, 1, 1,
1, 1, 1, 1, 1, 1, 1, 2, 2, 2, 4, 4, 4, 4, 4, 5, 5, 8, 8, 8, 9, 9, 10, 10, 11, 11,
11, 11, 11, 11, 11, 11, 12, 12, 12, 12, 12, 12, 12, 13, 13, 13, 13, 13,
13, 13, 13, 14, 15, 15, 15, 15, 16, 16, 16, 16, 16, 17, 17, 17, 17, 17,
18, 18, 18, 18, 18, 19, 19, 20, 20, 20, 20, 20, 20, 20, 21, 21, 21, 21;
29:1, 1, 1, 1, 1, 2, 3, 3, 3, 4, 4, 5, 5, 5, 6, 6, 6, 6, 6, 6, 7, 7, 8, 8, 8, 8,
9, 9, 9, 10, 10, 10, 10, 11, 11, 11, 11, 11, 11, 11, 15, 18, 19, 20, 20,
20, 20, 20, 20, 20, 21, 21, 22, 22, 23, 23, 24, 24, 24, 25, 25, 29, 29,
29, 29, 29, 29, 29, 30, 30; **2Ch 1:**1, 1, 1, 2, 2, 2, 2, 3, 3, 3, 3, 3, 4, 4,
5, 5, 5, 5, 5, 6, 6, 6, 9, 9, 11, 12, 13, 13, 14, 15, 15, 16, 16, 17, 17, 17;
2:1, 1, 2, 3, 4, 4, 4, 4, 4, 4, 6, 7, 9, 11, 12, 12, 12, 12, 12, 14, 15, 16,
16, 16, 16, 16, 17, 17, 18; **3:**1, 1, 1, 1, 1, 1, 1, 2, 2, 3, 3, 4, 4, 4, 4, 4,
4, 4, 4, 4, 4, 5, 5, 6, 6, 6, 7, 7, 7, 8, 8, 8, 9, 9, 10, 11, 11, 11, 11, 11,
11, 11, 12, 12, 12, 12, 12, 12, 13, 13, 13, 14, 14, 15, 15, 16, 16, 16,
17, 17, 17, 17, 17, 17, 17, 17, 17, 17, 17; **4:**2, 3, 3, 3, 4, 5, 5, 6, 6, 6,
6, 6, 6, 6, 7, 7, 7, 7, 8, 8, 8, 9, 9, 9, 10, 10, 10, 11, 11, 12, 12, 13, 13,
13, 13, 13, 14, 14, 15, 15, 16, 16, 16, 16, 16, 16, 17, 17, 19, 19, 19,
19, 19, 19, 20, 20, 21, 22, 22, 22, 22, 22, 22; **5:**1, 1, 1, 1, 1, 1, 1, 1, 2,
2, 2, 2, 2, 2, 3, 3, 4, 4, 4, 5, 5, 5, 6, 6, 7, 7, 7, 7, 7, 7, 7, 7, 8, 8, 8, 9, 9,
9, 10, 10, 10, 10, 11, 11, 11, 12, 12, 12, 13, 13, 13, 13, 13, 14, 14, 14,
14; **6:**3, 3, 4, 4, 4, 5, 5, 5, 7, 7, 7, 8, 8, 9, 10, 10, 10, 10, 11, 11, 11,
11, 11, 12, 12, 12, 13, 13, 13, 13, 18, 19, 19, 20, 21, 22, 23, 23, 23,
23, 26, 27, 28, 28, 28, 30, 31, 33, 33, 38, 40; **7:**1, 1, 1, 1, 2, 2, 2, 2, 2,
3, 3, 3, 3, 3, 3, 3, 4, 4, 4, 5, 5, 5, 6, 6, 6, 6, 6, 6, 6, 6, 7, 7, 7, 7, 7, 7,
8, 8, 8, 8, 8, 8, 9, 9, 9, 9, 10, 10, 10, 10, 11, 11, 11, 12, 12, 13, 18, 19,
20, 20, 21, 22, 22, 22; **8:**1, 1, 2, 3, 4, 4, 5, 6, 7, 8, 8, 9, 10, 11, 11, 11,
11, 12, 12, 12, 12, 13, 13, 13, 13, 13, 13, 13, 14, 14, 14, 14, 14, 14,
14, 14, 15, 15, 16, 16, 16, 16, 16, 17, 17, 17, 18; **9:**1, 3, 3, 4, 4, 4, 4,
4, 4, 5, 6, 8, 8, 9, 9, 10, 11, 11, 11, 11, 11, 11, 12, 12, 14, 14, 14, 14,
16, 16, 16, 17, 18, 18, 18, 18, 19, 19, 20, 20, 20, 21, 21, 21, 22, 23,
25, 26, 26, 26, 26, 26, 27, 27, 27, 29, 29, 29, 29, 29, 29, 29, 31, 31;
10:3, 4, 5, 6, 6, 7, 7, 8, 8, 8, 8, 9, 10, 12, 12, 13, 13, 14, 14, 15, 15,
15, 15, 15, 15, 16, 17, 17, 18, 18, 19; **11:**1, 1, 1, 2, 2, 3, 4, 4, 4, 5, 10,
13, 13, 14, 14, 15, 15, 16, 16, 16, 16, 16, 17, 17, 17, 18, 18, 20, 22,
22, 23, 23; **12:**1, 1, 2, 2, 5, 5, 6, 6, 6, 7, 7, 9, 9, 9, 9, 10, 10, 11, 11,
11, 11, 11, 12, 12, 13, 13, 13, 13, 14, 15, 15, 15, 15, 15, 15, 15, 16,
16; **13:**1, 4, 4, 4, 5, 5, 5, 8, 8, 8, 9, 9, 9, 9, 10, 10, 10, 10, 11, 11, 11,
11, 11, 11, 11, 12, 12, 13, 14, 14, 14, 14, 14, 15, 15, 15, 15, 16, 18,
18, 20, 22, 22, 22, 22; **14:**1, 1, 1, 2, 2, 3, 3, 3, 3, 4, 4, 4, 5, 5, 6, 6, 7,
7, 7, 8, 8, 9, 10, 11, 11, 11, 12, 12, 12, 12, 12, 13, 13, 14, 14, 14, 15;
15:1, 2, 2, 3, 4, 4, 5, 8, 8, 8, 8, 8, 8, 8, 8, 9, 9, 9, 10, 10, 11, 11, 11,
12, 12, 13, 13, 14, 15, 16, 16, 17, 17, 18, 18, 18, 19; **16:**1, 2, 2, 2, 2,
3, 4, 4, 6, 6, 6, 7, 7, 7, 7, 7, 8, 8, 9, 9, 9, 11, 11, 11, 11, 12, 12, 12, 13,
14, 14, 14; **17:**1, 2, 2, 2, 3, 3, 3, 4, 4, 5, 5, 5, 6, 6, 6, 6, 7, 7, 8, 9, 9, 9,
9, 9, 10, 10, 10, 11, 11, 14, 16, 17, 19, 19, 19; **18:**1, 2, 4, 6, 6, 7, 8, 9,
9, 10, 10, 11, 11, 12, 12, 12, 13, 14, 15, 15, 15, 16, 16, 17, 18, 18, 18,
19, 20, 20, 21, 21, 22, 22, 22, 23, 23, 23, 25, 25, 26, 26, 27, 28, 30,
30, 31, 31, 31, 31, 32, 32, 33, 33, 33, 33, 33, 34, 34, 34; **19:**2, 2, 2, 2,
2, 3, 3, 4, 4, 4, 4, 4, 5, 5, 6, 6, 7, 7, 7, 8, 8, 8, 9, 9, 10, 11, 11, 11, 11,
11; **20:**1, 1, 1, 2, 3, 4, 4, 5, 5, 5, 5, 6, 6, 6, 7, 10, 13, 13, 14, 14, 14,
15, 15, 16, 16, 16, 16, 17, 17, 18, 18, 18, 18, 19, 19, 19, 19, 20, 20,
20, 20, 20, 21, 21, 21, 21, 21, 21, 22, 22, 22, 23, 23, 24, 24, 24, 24,
24, 25, 26, 26, 26, 26, 26, 27, 28, 28, 28, 29, 29, 29, 29, 31, 31, 32,
32, 33, 33, 33, 34, 34, 34, 34, 34, 35, 36, 37, 37; **21:**1, 1, 2, 3, 3, 4, 6,
6, 6, 7, 8, 9, 10, 10, 10, 11, 11, 12, 12, 12, 12, 13, 13, 14, 16, 16, 16,
16, 17, 18, 18, 19, 19, 19, 20, 20; **22:**1, 1, 1, 3, 4, 4, 5, 5, 5, 7, 7, 8, 9,
9, 9, 9, 9, 9, 10, 10, 11, 11, 11, 11, 11, 11, 12, 12; **23:**1, 1, 2, 3, 3, 3,
3, 3, 4, 4, 5, 5, 5, 5, 5, 6, 6, 6, 6, 6, 6, 7, 7, 7, 8, 8, 8, 8, 8, 8, 9, 9, 9,
10, 10, 10, 10, 10, 10, 11, 11, 11, 12, 12, 12, 12, 12, 13, 13, 13, 13,
13, 13, 14, 14, 14, 14, 14, 14, 15, 15, 16, 16, 16, 17, 17, 17, 17, 17,

17, 18, 18, 18, 18, 18, 18, 19, 19, 20, 20, 20, 20, 20, 20, 20, 20, 20, 21, 21, 21; **24:**2, 2, 2, 4, 4, 5, 5, 5, 5, 5, 6, 6, 6, 6, 6, 6, 6, 6, 6, 6, 7, 7, 7, 7, 7, 7, 7, 8, 8, 8, 9, 9, 9, 9, 9, 9, 10, 10, 10, 11, 11, 11, 11, 11, 11, 11, 11, 12, 12, 12, 12, 12, 12, 13, 13, 13, 14, 14, 14, 14, 14, 14, 14, 14, 14, 14, 16, 16, 17, 17, 18, 18, 18, 18, 19, 19, 20, 20, 20, 20, 20, 21, 21, 21, 22, 23, 23, 23, 23, 23, 23, 24, 24, 24, 24, 24, 24, 25, 25, 25, 25, 25, 26, 26, 26, 27, 27, 27, 27, 27, 27, 27, 27, 27; **25:**2, 3, 4, 4, 4, 4, 4, 4, 4, 4, 4, 5, 5, 7, 7, 8, 9, 9, 9, 9, 9, 10, 11, 12, 12, 13, 13, 14, 14, 15, 16, 16, 17, 18, 18, 19, 20, 21, 22, 23, 23, 24, 24, 24, 24, 24, 24, 25, 26, 26, 26, 26, 27, 28; **26:**1, 2, 4, 5, 5, 5, 5, 6, 6, 6, 7, 7, 7, 8, 9, 9, 9, 9, 10, 10, 10, 10, 10, 10, 11, 11, 11, 11, 13, 13, 14, 15, 15, 15, 15, 15, 16, 16, 16, 16, 17, 17, 18, 18, 18, 18, 18, 18, 19, 19, 19, 19, 20, 20, 20, 20, 21, 21, 21, 21, 21, 21, 22, 22, 22, 23, 23; **27:**1, 2, 2, 2, 2, 3, 3, 3, 3, 4, 4, 5, 5, 6, 7, 7, 7, 7, 9, 9; **28:**1, 1, 2, 2, 2, 3, 3, 3, 3, 3, 3, 3, 3, 4, 4, 5, 5, 5, 6, 6, 7, 7, 7, 8, 9, 9, 9, 9, 10, 11, 12, 12, 13, 13, 14, 14, 14, 14, 14, 15, 15, 15, 15, 15, 16, 17, 18, 18, 18, 18, 19, 19, 21, 21, 21, 21, 22, 23, 23, 23, 24, 24, 24, 24, 24, 25, 25, 25, 25, 26, 26, 26, 26, 27, 27; **29:**1, 1, 2, 3, 3, 3, 3, 3, 4, 4, 4, 5, 5, 5, 5, 5, 6, 6, 6, 7, 7, 7, 7, 7, 8, 10, 10, 11, 11, 12, 12, 12, 13, 13, 14, 14, 15, 15, 15, 15, 16, 16, 16, 16, 16, 16, 16, 16, 17, 17, 17, 17, 17, 17, 18, 18, 18, 18, 18, 18, 18, 19, 19, 19, 19, 20, 20, 20, 20, 21, 21, 21, 21, 21, 21, 21, 22, 22, 22, 22, 22, 22, 22, 22, 23, 23, 23, 23, 24, 24, 24, 24, 24, 25, 25, 25, 25, 25, 25, 25, 26, 26, 26, 26, 26, 27, 27, 27, 27, 27, 28, 28, 28, 28, 28, 29, 30, 30, 30, 30, 30, 31, 31, 31, 31, 32, 32, 34, 34, 34, 34, 34, 35, 35, 35, 35, 36, 36; **30:**1, 1, 1, 1, 1, 2, 2, 3, 4, 4, 4, 5, 5, 5, 5, 5, 5, 5, 6, 6, 6, 6, 6, 6, 7, 7, 8, 8, 9, 9, 10, 10, 10, 10, 12, 12, 12, 12, 12, 12, 12, 13, 14, 14, 14, 15, 15, 15, 15, 15, 16, 16, 16, 16, 16, 16, 16, 16, 17, 17, 17, 18, 18, 19, 19, 19, 20, 20, 21, 21, 21, 21, 22, 22, 22, 22, 22, 22, 22, 23, 23, 24, 24, 25, 25, 25, 25, 25, 25, 26, 26, 27, 27; **31:**1, 1, 1, 1, 1, 1, 1, 2, 2, 2, 2, 2, 3, 3, 3, 3, 3, 3, 4, 4, 4, 4, 4, 5, 5, 5, 6, 6, 6, 6, 6, 7, 7, 8, 9, 10, 10, 10, 10, 10, 11, 11, 12, 12, 12, 13, 13, 13, 14, 14, 14, 14, 14, 14, 14, 15, 15, 15, 16, 16, 16, 17, 17, 17, 18, 18, 18, 18, 18, 19, 19, 19, 19, 19, 19, 19, 20, 20, 20, 21, 21, 21, 21; **32:**1, 3, 3, 3, 4, 4, 4, 4, 4, 5, 5, 5, 5, 5, 6, 6, 6, 7, 8, 8, 9, 9, 9, 11, 11, 12, 12, 12, 12, 13, 13, 13, 13, 16, 17, 17, 17, 17, 17, 17, 18, 18, 18, 18, 18, 18, 18, 18, 19, 19, 20, 21, 21, 21, 22, 22, 22, 22, 23, 23, 24, 25, 25, 26, 26, 30, 30, 30, 30, 31, 31, 32, 32, 32, 32, 32, 32, 33, 33, 33; **33:**2, 2, 2, 2, 2, 2, 3, 3, 3, 4, 4, 4, 4, 5, 5, 6, 6, 6, 6, 7, 7, 7, 8, 8, 9, 9, 9, 9, 9, 10, 11, 11, 12, 12, 13, 13, 13, 14, 14, 14, 14, 14, 14, 14, 15, 15, 15, 15, 15, 15, 15, 15, 15, 16, 16, 16, 16, 16, 17, 17, 17, 18, 18, 18, 18, 18, 18, 18, 18, 18, 19, 19, 19, 19, 19, 20, 22, 22, 23, 25, 25, 25; **34:**2, 2, 3, 3, 3, 3, 3, 3, 4, 4, 4, 4, 4, 4, 5, 5, 6, 6, 7, 7, 7, 7, 7, 8, 8, 8, 8, 8, 8, 8, 9, 9, 9, 9, 9, 9, 9, 10, 10, 10, 10, 10, 10, 11, 11, 12, 12, 12, 12, 13, 13, 14, 14, 14, 14, 14, 14, 15, 15, 15, 15, 15, 16, 16, 17, 17, 17, 17, 18, 18, 18, 19, 19, 20, 20, 21, 21, 21, 21, 21, 21, 21, 22, 22, 22, 22, 22, 22, 23, 23, 23, 24, 24, 24, 25, 26, 26, 26, 26, 26, 27, 28, 28, 28, 29, 29, 30, 30, 30, 30, 30, 30, 30, 30, 30, 30, 30, 30, 31, 31, 31, 31, 31, 31, 31, 31, 32, 32, 32, 33, 33, 33, 33, 33; **35:**1, 1, 1, 1, 2, 2, 2, 3, 3, 3, 3, 4, 4, 4, 5, 5, 6, 6, 6, 7, 8, 8, 8, 8, 9, 9, 10, 10, 10, 10, 11, 11, 11, 11, 11, 11, 11, 11, 12, 12, 12, 12, 12, 12, 12, 13, 13, 13, 14, 14, 14, 14, 14, 14, 15, 15, 15, 15, 15, 16, 16, 16, 16, 16, 17, 17, 18, 18, 18, 18, 18, 19, 20, 20, 21, 22, 22, 23, 23, 24, 25, 25, 26, 26, 26, 26, 27, 27; **36:**1, 1, 1, 3, 4, 4, 4, 5, 5, 7, 7, 7, 8, 8, 8, 8, 8, 8, 9, 10, 10, 10, 10, 10, 12, 12, 12, 12, 12, 13, 13, 14, 14, 14, 14, 14, 14, 14, 15, 15, 16, 16, 16, 17, 17, 17, 17, 17, 18, 18, 18, 18, 18, 18, 18, 19, 19, 19, 20, 20, 20, 21, 21, 21, 21, 22, 22, 22, 23, 23, 23, 23, 23, 23, 23; **Ezr 1:**1, 1, 1, 2, 2, 2, 2, 2, 3, 3, 4, 4, 5, 5, 5, 5, 5, 5, 6, 6, 7, 7, 7, 8, 8, 8, 9, 11; **2:**1, 1, 1, 1, 2, 2, 3, 4, 5, 6, 7, 8, 9, 10, 11, 12, 13, 14, 15, 16, 17, 18, 19, 20, 21, 22, 23, 24, 25, 26, 27, 28, 29, 30, 31, 32, 33, 34, 35, 36, 36, 36, 37, 38, 39, 40, 40, 41, 41, 42, 42, 43, 43, 55, 58, 58, 59, 60, 61, 63, 63, 63, 63, 63, 68, 68, 68, 68, 69, 69, 70, 70, 70, 70, 70, 70, 70, 70, 70; **3:**1, 1, 2, 2, 2, 2, 3, 3, 3, 3, 3, 4, 4, 4, 4, 5, 5, 5, 5, 5, 5, 5, 6, 6, 6, 6, 6, 7, 7, 7, 7, 7, 8, 8, 8, 8, 8, 8, 8, 9, 9, 9, 9, 10, 10, 10, 10, 10, 10, 11, 11, 11, 11, 11, 12, 12, 12, 12, 13, 13; **4:**1, 1, 1, 1, 2, 3, 3, 3, 3, 4, 4, 5, 5, 6, 6, 7, 7, 7, 7, 8, 8, 8, 8, 9, 9, 9, 9, 9, 9, 10, 10, 10, 10, 10, 10, 11, 11, 11, 12, 12, 13, 15, 15, 16, 16, 17, 17, 17, 17, 18, 19, 20, 20, 22, 23, 24, 24, 24, 24; **5:**1, 1, 1, 1, 2, 2, 2, 3, 3, 4, 4, 4, 5, 5, 6, 6, 6, 6, 6, 8, 8, 8, 8, 8, 9, 10, 11, 11, 11, 12, 12, 13, 13, 14, 14, 14, 14, 15, 15, 15, 16, 16, 16, 17, 17, 17; **6:**1, 2, 2, 3, 3, 3, 3, 4, 5, 5, 6, 6, 6, 7, 7, 7, 7, 7, 8, 8, 8, 9, 9, 9, 9, 9, 10, 12, 12, 12, 13, 13, 13, 14, 14, 14, 14, 14, 14, 15, 15, 16, 16, 16, 16, 16, 16, 17, 17, 17, 18, 18, 18, 18, 19, 20, 20, 20, 20, 21, 21, 21, 21, 21, 21, 22, 22, 22, 22, 22, 22, 22, 22; **7:**1, 1, 5, 6, 6, 6, 6, 6, 6, 6, 7, 7, 7, 9, 10, 10, 10, 11, 11, 11, 12, 12, 12, 12, 12, 13, 13, 14, 15, 16, 16, 16, 16, 16, 17, 17, 17, 17, 18, 19, 19, 19, 19, 20, 21, 21, 21, 21, 21, 21, 23, 23, 23, 25, 25, 25, 25, 25, 26, 26, 26, 27, 27, 27, 27, 27, 28, 28, 28, 28; **8:**1, 1, 1, 2, 2, 3, 3, 4, 5, 6, 7, 8, 9, 10, 11, 12, 13, 14, 15, 15, 15, 15, 15, 16, 17, 17, 17, 17, 18, 19, 20, 20, 21, 22, 22, 22, 24, 25, 25, 25, 25, 25, 25, 25, 26, 26, 28, 28, 28, 29, 29, 29, 29, 29, 30, 30, 30, 30, 31, 31, 31, 33, 33, 33, 33, 34, 35, 35, 35, 35, 36, 36, 36, 36, 36, 36; **9:**1, 1, 1, 1, 1, 1, 1, 2, 2, 2, 2, 4, 4, 4, 4, 5, 5, 5, 6, 7, 7, 7, 8, 9, 9, 11, 11, 11, 11, 11, 11, 12, 12; **10:**1, 1, 2, 3, 3, 3, 3, 5, 5, 5, 5, 6, 6, 6, 6, 6, 6, 7, 8, 8, 8, 9, 9, 9, 9, 9, 9, 10, 11, 11, 11, 11, 12, 13, 14, 14, 14, 15, 16, 16, 16, 16, 17, 17, 18, 18, 20, 21, 22, 23, 24, 24, 25, 25, 26, 27, 28, 29, 30, 31, 33, 34, 38, 43; **Ne 1:**1, 1, 1, 2, 2, 3, 3, 3, 4, 5, 7, 8, 9, 9, 9, 10, 11, 11, 11; **2:**1, 1, 1, 2, 3, 3, 3, 4, 4, 5, 6, 6, 6, 7, 7, 7, 7, 8, 8, 8, 8, 8, 8, 8, 9, 9, 9, 9, 9, 10, 10, 12, 12, 12, 13, 13, 13, 13, 14, 14, 14, 15, 15, 15, 16, 16, 16, 16, 17, 17, 18, 18, 18, 18, 19, 19, 20; **3:**1, 1, 1, 1, 1, 1, 1, 2, 3, 3, 3, 3, 3, 3, 4, 5, 6, 6, 6, 6, 7, 7, 7, 7, 8, 8, 9, 9, 9, 10, 11, 11, 11, 12, 12, 12, 12, 13, 13, 13, 13, 13, 14, 14, 14, 14, 14, 15, 15, 15, 15, 15, 15, 15, 15, 15, 16, 16, 16, 16, 16, 16, 16, 17, 17, 17, 17, 17, 18, 18, 18, 18, 19, 19, 19, 20, 20, 20, 20, 21, 21, 21, 21, 22, 22, 23, 24, 24, 24, 25, 25, 25, 25, 25, 25, 25, 26, 26, 26, 26, 26, 26, 27, 27, 27, 28, 28, 28, 28, 28, 29, 29, 29, 30, 30, 31, 31, 31, 31, 31, 31, 31, 32, 32, 32; **4:**1, 1, 2, 2, 2, 3, 3, 5, 5, 6, 6, 6, 7, 7, 7, 7, 9, 10, 10, 12, 12, 13, 13, 13, 13, 14, 14, 14, 14, 14, 15, 16, 16, 16, 17, 17, 18, 18, 18, 19, 19, 19, 19, 20, 20, 21, 22, 22, 23; **5:**1, 2, 3, 4, 5, 7, 7, 8, 8, 9, 10, 11, 12, 12, 12, 13, 13, 13, 13, 14, 14, 14, 14, 15, 15, 15, 16, 16, 17, 18, 18, 18; **6:**1, 1, 1, 1, 1, 2, 2, 4, 4, 5, 6, 6, 7, 9, 9, 10, 10, 11, 14, 14, 14, 15, 16, 16, 17, 18; **7:**1, 1, 1, 1, 2, 2, 2, 3, 3, 3, 3, 3, 3, 4, 4, 4, 5, 5, 5, 5, 5, 6, 6, 6, 6, 7, 8, 9, 10, 11, 12, 13, 14, 15, 16, 17, 18, 19, 20, 21, 22, 23, 24, 25, 26, 27, 28, 29, 30, 31, 32, 33, 34, 35, 36, 37, 38, 39, 39, 39, 40, 41, 42, 43, 43, 44, 44, 45, 45, 46, 46, 57, 60, 60, 61, 62, 63, 65, 65, 65, 65, 65, 70, 70, 70, 70, 70, 71, 71, 71, 72, 72, 72, 73, 73, 73, 73, 73, 73, 73; **8:**1, 1, 1, 1, 1, 1, 1, 2, 2, 2, 2, 2, 2, 3, 3, 3, 3, 3, 4, 4, 5, 5, 5, 6, 6, 6, 6, 6, 7, 7, 8, 8, 8, 8, 9, 9, 9, 9, 9, 9, 9, 9, 10, 10, 11, 11, 12, 13, 13, 13, 14, 14, 14, 14, 15, 15, 15, 15, 16,

16, 16, 16, 16, 16, 17, 17, 17, 17, 18, 18, 18, 18, 18; **9:**1, 2, 3, 3, 3, 3, 4, 4, 4, 5, 5, 5, 5, 6, 6, 6, 6, 6, 6, 7, 7, 8, 8, 9, 9, 10, 11, 11, 11, 11, 12, 14, 15, 15, 17, 19, 19, 19, 19, 19, 21, 22, 22, 22, 23, 23, 23, 24, 24, 24, 24, 26, 30, 30, 30, 32, 32, 32, 32, 36, 37, 37, 37, 38; **10:**1, 1, 1, 1, 1, 8, 9, 9, 14, 28, 28, 28, 28, 28, 29, 29, 29, 29, 30, 30, 31, 31, 31, 31, 32, 32, 32, 33, 33, 33, 33, 33, 33, 33, 33, 33, 33, 33, 33, 34, 34, 34, 34, 34, 34, 35, 35, 35, 36, 36, 36, 36, 37, 37, 37, 37, 37, 37, 37, 37, 37, 38, 38, 38, 38, 39, 39, 39, 39, 39, 39, 39, 39; **11:**1, 1, 1, 1, 1, 1, 2, 3, 3, 3, 3, 4, 4, 4, 5, 7, 9, 10, 11, 11, 12, 15, 16, 16, 17, 18, 19, 19, 20, 20, 20, 20, 21, 21, 22, 22, 24, 25, 30, 30, 30, 31, 35, 36, 36; **12:**1, 1, 1, 7, 7, 7, 8, 8, 9, 10, 10, 10, 10, 11, 11, 12, 12, 12, 12, 13, 13, 14, 14, 15, 15, 16, 16, 17, 17, 17, 18, 18, 19, 19, 20, 20, 21, 21, 22, 22, 22, 22, 22, 22, 23, 23, 23, 23, 23, 24, 24, 24, 24, 24, 25, 25, 25, 26, 26, 26, 26, 27, 27, 27, 27, 27, 27, 27, 28, 28, 28, 29, 29, 30, 30, 30, 30, 31, 31, 31, 31, 31, 31, 31, 32, 36, 36, 36, 37, 37, 37, 37, 37, 37, 37, 37, 38, 38, 38, 38, 38, 38, 38, 38, 38, 39, 39, 39, 39, 39, 39, 39, 39, 40, 40, 40, 41, 42, 42, 42, 43, 43, 43, 43, 43, 44, 44, 44, 44, 44, 44, 44, 44, 44, 44, 45, 45, 45, 45, 45, 46, 46, 46, 47, 47, 47, 47, 47, 47, 47, 47; **13:**1, 1, 1, 2, 2, 3, 4, 4, 4, 5, 5, 5, 5, 5, 5, 6, 6, 6, 7, 7, 7, 8, 9, 9, 9, 9, 10, 10, 10, 11, 11, 11, 12, 12, 13, 13, 13, 13, 14, 15, 16, 16, 17, 17, 18, 18, 18, 19, 19, 19, 19, 19, 20, 21, 21, 21, 22, 22, 22, 22, 23, 23, 24, 24, 25, 25, 28, 28, 28, 29, 29, 29, 30, 31, 31, 31, 31, 31, 31; **Est 1:**1, 2, 3, 3, 3, 4, 4, 5, 5, 5, 5, 5, 6, 7, 8, 8, 8, 9, 9, 9, 10, 10, 10, 11, 11, 12, 12, 13, 14, 14, 14, 15, 15, 15, 16, 16, 17, 18, 18, 18, 18, 18, 19, 19, 21, 22, 22; **2:**1, 2, 2, 3, 3, 3, 4, 4, 4, 5, 5, 8, 8, 8, 9, 9, 9, 11, 11, 12, 12, 13, 13, 14, 14, 14, 14, 14, 14, 14, 14, 15, 15, 15, 15, 16, 16, 17, 17, 17, 18, 18, 19, 19, 21, 21, 21, 21, 22, 22, 22, 22, 23, 23, 23; **3:**1, 1, 1, 1, 2, 2, 3, 3, 3, 4, 6, 6, 7, 7, 7, 7, 7, 8, 8, 8, 8, 9, 9, 10, 10, 10, 10, 11, 11, 12, 12, 12, 12, 12, 12, 13, 13, 13, 13, 13, 14, 14, 15, 15, 15, 15, 15, 15; **4:**1, 2, 2, 3, 3, 3, 4, 5, 6, 6, 7, 7, 7, 7, 8, 8, 8, 11, 11, 11, 11, 13, 14, 14, 16, 16, 16, 16; **5:**1, 1, 1, 1, 1, 2, 2, 3, 3, 4, 4, 5, 5, 6, 6, 8, 9, 9, 11, 11, 11, 12, 12, 12, 13, 13, 14, 14, 14, 14, 14; **6:**1, 1, 2, 2, 2, 2, 2, 3, 4, 4, 4, 4, 4, 4, 5, 5, 5, 6, 6, 7, 8, 8, 9, 9, 9, 9, 9, 9, 9, 10, 10, 10, 10, 10, 11, 11, 11, 11, 12, 14, 14; **7:**1, 2, 2, 3, 4, 6, 7, 7, 8, 8, 8, 8, 8, 8, 8, 9, 9, 9, 9, 10, 10; **8:**1, 1, 1, 1, 1, 2, 3, 3, 4, 4, 5, 5, 5, 7, 7, 7, 7, 8, 8, 8, 8, 9, 9, 9, 9, 9, 9, 9, 9, 10, 10, 10, 10, 10, 11, 11, 11, 12, 12, 12, 13, 13, 14, 14, 14, 14, 14, 15, 15, 15, 15, 16, 17, 17, 17, 17, 17; **9:**1, 1, 1, 1, 1, 2, 2, 3, 3, 3, 3, 3, 3, 4, 4, 5, 5, 5, 6, 10, 10, 10, 11, 11, 11, 12, 12, 12, 12, 13, 13, 13, 14, 14, 14, 14, 15, 16, 16, 17, 17, 18, 18, 18, 20, 20, 22, 22, 23, 24, 24, 24, 24, 24, 25, 25, 26, 27, 27, 27, 28, 28, 28, 28, 29, 29, 29, 29, 30, 30, 30, 31, 31, 31, 31, 31, 32, 32, 32; **10:**1, 2, 2, 2, 2, 2, 2, 3, 3, 3, 3, 3; **Job 1:**1, 3, 5, 6, 6, 6, 7, 7, 7, 8, 8, 8, 9, 12, 12, 13, 14, 15, 15, 15, 15, 16, 16, 16, 17, 19, 19, 19, 19, 20, 21, 21, 21, 21; **2:**1, 1, 1, 2, 2, 2, 3, 3, 3, 4, 6, 7, 8, 10, 11, 11, 11, 11, 12, 13; **3:**1, 3, 3, 5, 5, 6, 6, 6, 6, 8, 9, 11, 14, 16, 17, 17, 19, 20, 22; **4:**1, 3, 4, 7, 7, 8, 11, 11, 11, 17, 20; **5:**1, 2, 2, 3, 5, 6, 6, 10, 10, 11, 12, 12, 14, 14, 15, 15, 15, 15, 15, 16, 16, 16, 17, 17, 17, 20, 20, 23, 23, 26; **6:**2, 3, 3, 4, 6, 7, 10, 10, 10, 11, 14, 14, 15, 17, 17, 17, 17, 18, 18, 19, 30; **7:**1, 2, 4, 21; **8:**1, 3, 5, 5, 8, 8, 10, 13, 13, 13, 16, 16, 16, 19, 19, 22, 22; **9:**2, 5, 6, 7, 7, 8, 8, 8, 9, 9, 9, 9, 9, 13, 22, 22, 22, 23, 24, 24, 24, 24, 24, 28, 29, 34; **10:**1, 2, 3, 3, 10, 19, 19, 21, 22; **11:**1, 4, 6, 7, 7, 8, 8, 9, 9, 10, 16, 17, 20; **12:**7, 7, 7, 8, 8, 8, 9, 10, 10, 11, 11, 11, 12, 15, 15, 15, 15, 18, 19, 20, 20, 20, 21, 22, 22, 24, 25; **13:**3, 5, 13, 25, 26; **14:**2, 5, 6, 8, 9, 12, 13, 19, 19, 20; **15:**1, 7, 7, 15, 15, 18, 18, 19, 21, 21, 22, 25, 29, 30, 30, 30, 32, 33, 34; **16:**4, 11, 11, 12, 13, 15; **17:**1, 6, 8, 8, 8, 9, 12, 13, 14, 14, 16, 16; **18:**1, 4, 5, 5, 5, 5, 6, 6, 7, 7, 8, 8, 9, 10, 11, 14, 14, 15, 15, 17, 18, 20, 20, 21, 21; **19:**9, 15, 15, 20, 21, 24, 25, 27; **20:**1, 4, 5, 5, 5, 5, 6, 6, 6, 8, 10, 11, 12, 14, 15, 16, 16, 19, 20, 22, 25, 25, 25, 27, 27, 29, 29, 29; **21:**7, 7, 12, 12, 13, 15, 17, 18, 18, 19, 20, 20, 22, 24, 25, 26, 26, 27, 29, 32, 33, 33, 33; **22:**1, 3, 6, 6, 7, 7, 8, 8, 9, 11, 12, 12, 13, 14, 15, 16, 16, 17, 19, 19, 19, 20, 20, 23, 24, 25, 26, 28, 29; **23:**9, 9, 16; **24:**1, 1, 1, 2, 3, 4, 4, 5, 5, 5, 5, 6, 6, 7, 8, 9, 9, 10, 11, 12, 12, 12, 12, 13, 14, 14, 14, 15, 15, 16, 16, 17, 17, 17, 18, 20, 20, 21, 21, 22; **25:**1, 2, 3, 4, 5; **26:**2, 5, 5, 6, 6, 7, 7, 8, 8, 8, 10, 10, 10, 11, 12, 12, 13, 13, 14, 14; **27:**2, 2, 7, 8, 10, 11, 13, 13, 15, 16, 16, 17, 17, 18, 18, 19, 20, 20, 21; **28:**2, 3, 3, 4, 5, 5, 5, 8, 9, 10, 11, 11, 13, 14, 14, 16, 18, 19, 21, 21, 21, 24, 24, 25, 26, 26, 26, 28, 28; **29:**2, 3, 3, 4, 5, 7, 7, 7, 8, 8, 9, 10, 10, 12, 12, 13, 15, 15, 16, 17, 19, 19, 23; **30:**3, 3, 4, 6, 7, 7, 11, 18, 19, 22, 22, 23, 24, 25, 26, 28; **31:**2, 3, 6, 8, 16, 16, 23, 23, 26, 26, 26, 28, 28, 34, 35, 35, 36; **32:**2, 2, 4, 6, 8, 8, 9, 9, 18; **33:**3, 4, 4, 4, 6, 11, 15, 18, 18, 20, 22, 28, 30, 30, 30; **34:**3, 3, 3, 8, 10, 12, 13, 13, 17, 19, 19, 20, 21, 22, 24, 25, 28, 28, 28, 30, 30, 33, 36, 36; **35:**3, 5, 5, 9, 9, 9, 9, 10, 10, 11, 11, 13; **36:**2, 3, 4, 6, 6, 7, 9, 9, 13, 17, 20, 27, 28, 28, 29, 29, 29, 30, 30, 30, 31, 33, 33; **37:**2, 3, 4, 4, 4, 4, 5, 5, 6, 6, 6, 8, 8, 9, 9, 9, 10, 11, 12, 12, 14, 15, 15, 16, 17, 18, 18, 19, 21, 21, 21, 21, 22, 23, 23; **38:**1, 1, 4, 4, 5, 7, 7, 8, 8, 8, 12, 12, 12, 13, 13, 13, 13, 14, 14, 14, 14, 15, 15, 15, 15, 16, 16, 17, 17, 18, 18, 19, 19, 22, 22, 22, 23, 23, 24, 24, 24, 24, 25, 25, 25, 26, 27, 27, 27, 28, 29, 29, 29, 29, 30, 30, 30, 31, 31, 31, 32, 32, 32, 32, 32, 33, 33, 33, 34, 37, 37, 38, 39, 40, 41; **39:**1, 1, 2, 4, 5, 6, 6, 7, 7, 8, 9, 11, 12, 13, 13, 13, 14, 14, 18, 19, 20, 21, 22, 23, 23, 24, 24, 25, 25, 25, 25, 25, 25, 26, 26, 26, 27, 27, 28, 30, 30; **40:**1, 2, 2, 3, 4, 6, 6, 11, 12, 12, 13, 13, 13, 15, 16, 17, 20, 20, 21, 21, 22, 22, 22, 23; **41:**2, 8, 9, 10, 12, 12, 15, 18, 22, 25, 27, 29, 29, 30, 30, 31, 31, 31, 32, 32, 34, 34, 34; **42:**1, 7, 7, 9, 9, 9, 9, 9, 10, 10, 11, 11, 12, 12, 12, 14, 14, 15, 15; **Ps 1:**1, 1, 1, 2, 3, 4, 4, 5, 5, 6, 6, 6, 6, 6; **2:**1, 1, 2, 2, 2, 2, 4, 4, 6, 6, 7, 7, 7, 8, 8, 8, 10, 11, 12; **3:**T, 3, 4, 5, 7, 7, 7; **4:**T, 3, 3, 3, 5, 6; **5:**T, T, 3, 4, 5, 6, 8, 9, 12; **6:**T, 5, 8, 9, 9; **7:**T, T, 5, 5, 6, 7, 8, 8, 9, 9, 9, 11, 14, 17, 17, 17; **8:**T, 1, 1, 1, 3, 3, 3, 3, 7, 7, 7, 8, 8, 8, 8, 8, 9, 9; **9:**T, T, T, 1, 5, 5, 6, 7, 8, 8, 9, 9, 11, 11, 12, 13, 13, 15, 15, 16, 16, 17, 17, 17, 17, 18, 18, 18, 19; **10:**1, 2, 2, 3, 3, 7, 8, 9, 10, 10, 10, 11, 12, 12, 13, 14, 14, 14, 15, 15, 16, 16, 17, 17, 18, 18; **11:**T, 1, 1, 2, 2, 2, 3, 3, 4, 4, 5, 5, 5, 6, 7; **12:**T, 1, 1, 1, 3, 5, 5, 5, 5, 6, 7, 8, 8; **13:**T, 1, 2, 3, 6; **14:**T, 2, 2, 4, 6, 6, 6, 6, 7; **15:**2, 4, 4, 5, 5; **16:**2, 2, 3, 3, 4, 6, 7, 8, 10, 10, 11, 11, 11; **17:**3, 8, 8, 11, 13, 14, 14; **18:**T, T, T, T, T, T, 2, 2, 3, 4, 4, 5, 5, 6, 7, 7, 7, 9, 10, 10, 12, 12, 13, 13, 15, 15, 15, 15, 15, 18, 20, 21, 21, 24, 24, 25, 26, 26, 27, 30, 31, 33, 35, 39, 41, 42, 42, 43, 46, 46, 47, 47, 48, 49; **19:**T, 1, 1, 1, 3, 4, 4, 4, 4, 5, 6, 6, 6, 7, 7, 7, 7, 7, 7, 8, 8, 8, 8, 8, 9, 9, 9, 10, 10, 12, 14, 14; **20:**T, 1, 1, 5, 6, 7; **21:**T, 1, 4, 6, 7, 7, 7, 7, 9, 10, 10; **22:**T, T, T, 3, 8, 8, 8, 8, 8, 10, 15, 15, 21, 21, 22, 23, 24, 24, 25, 25, 26, 26, 27, 27, 28, 28, 29, 29, 30, 30; **23:**1, 4, 5, 6, 6, 6; **24:**1, 1, 1, 2, 2, 2, 3, 3, 5, 6, 7, 8, 8, 8, 9, 10, 10, 10; **25:**4, 4, 5, 7, 7, 8, 8, 9, 10, 11, 12, 12, 13, 14, 14, 15, 15; **26:**1, 5, 5, 8, 9, 12; **27:**1, 1, 4, 4, 4, 4, 4, 4, 4, 6, 10, 11, 13, 13, 13, 14, 14; **28:**3, 4, 5, 6, 7, 8; **29:**1, 1, 2, 2, 2, 2, 3, 3, 3, 3, 3, 3, 4, 4, 4, 4, 5, 5, 5, 5, 5, 7, 7, 8, 8, 8, 8, 8, 9, 9, 9, 10, 10, 10, 11, 11; **30:**T, T, 3, 3, 4, 5, 8, 9, 9,

9; **31:**T, 3, 4, 6, 7, 11, 11, 13, 17, 17, 18, 19, 20, 21, 22, 23, 23, 24; **32:**2, 4, 5, 6, 6, 8, 8, 10, 10, 11; **33:**1, 1, 2, 2, 2, 3, 4, 4, 5, 6, 6, 6, 6, 7, 7, 8, 8, 9, 10, 10, 10, 11, 12, 12, 13, 13, 14, 16, 18, 20; **34:**T, 1, 2, 3, 4, 6, 7, 7, 8, 8, 9, 10, 11, 15, 15, 16, 16, 17, 18, 18, 19, 19, 20, 21, 21, 22; **35:**3, 5, 5, 5, 6, 6, 8, 8, 9, 10, 10, 10, 10, 12, 16, 18, 18, 27; **36:**T, T, T, 1, 5, 5, 6, 6, 7, 8, 9, 9, 11, 11; **37:**1, 3, 3, 4, 5, 6, 6, 6, 7, 7, 9, 9, 9, 10, 11, 12, 12, 13, 14, 14, 14, 15, 17, 17, 17, 17, 18, 18, 20, 20, 21, 21, 22, 22, 23, 23, 23, 24, 24, 25, 26, 27, 28, 28, 28, 28, 29, 29, 30, 32, 33, 33, 33, 33, 34, 34, 34, 38, 39, 39, 40, 40; **38:**T, 17, 20; **39:**T, 1, 2, 2, 5, 10, 11; **40:**T, 1, 2, 2, 2, 3, 4, 4, 4, 5, 10, 12, 16, 17; **41:**T, 1, 1, 1, 2, 3, 6, 7, 9, 9, 13, 13; **42:**T, T, 1, 2, 4, 4, 4, 6, 6, 6, 7, 7, 8; **43:**3, 4, 4; **44:**T, T, 2, 2, 3, 11, 13, 14, 14, 15, 16, 19, 21, 24, 25, 25; **45:**T, T, T, 1, 1, 2, 5, 7, 8, 9, 12, 13, 14, 15, 17; **46:**T, T, 2, 2, 3, 3, 3, 4, 4, 4, 5, 6, 6, 7, 7, 8, 8, 8, 9, 9, 9, 9, 10, 11, 11; **47:**T, T, 2, 2, 2, 3, 4, 4, 5, 7, 7, 8, 9, 9, 9, 9, 9; **48:**T, 1, 1, 2, 2, 2, 2, 4, 4, 4, 6, 7, 8, 8, 8, 8, 10, 10, 11, 11, 12, 12, 13, 13; **49:**T, T, 1, 9, 10, 11, 12, 13, 14, 14, 14, 14, 15, 16, 17, 18, 19, 20; **50:**1, 1, 2, 3, 6, 6, 8, 10, 10, 10, 11, 11, 11, 12, 13, 13, 14, 16, 23; **51:**T, T, T, 1, 5, 6, 9, 12, 17, 18; **52:**T, T, T, 5, 5, 6, 8, 9; **53:**T, 2, 5; **54:**T, T, T, 4, 4; **55:**T, 4, 7, 7, 9, 10, 10, 11, 14, 15, 16, 17, 18, 22, 22, 23, 23; **56:**T, T, T, T, 1, 7, 9; **57:**T, T, T, T, 1, 5, 5, 8, 9, 9, 10, 10, 11, 11; **58:**T, T, 1, 1, 1, 5, 5, 6, 8, 10, 10, 10; **59:**T, T, T, 5, 6, 7, 7, 8, 12, 12, 13, 14, 16, 17; **60:**T, T, T, T, T, 2, 4, 6, 8, 9; **61:**T, 2, 2, 2, 4, 6, 6, 6; **62:**T, 9, 9, 9, 10; **63:**T, 5, 6, 7, 9, 9, 10, 10, 11; **64:**T, 2, 2, 2, 3, 3, 4, 6, 6, 9, 9, 10, 10; **65:**T, 5, 6, 7, 7, 7, 8, 8, 8, 9, 9, 10, 10, 10, 10, 11, 11, 12, 12, 13, 13; **66:**T, 1, 2, 2, 6, 7, 8, 11, 13, 14, 15, 18; **67:**T, 2, 3, 3, 4, 4, 4, 5, 5, 6, 7; **68:**T, 2, 2, 2, 3, 4, 4, 5, 6, 6, 7, 8, 8, 8, 8, 9, 11, 11, 12, 12, 13, 14, 14, 15, 15, 16, 17, 18, 18, 18, 19, 20, 21, 21, 22, 22, 22, 24, 24, 26, 26, 27, 27, 27, 28, 29, 29, 30, 30, 30, 32, 32, 33, 33, 33, 34, 35; **69:**T, T, 1, 2, 2, 4, 10, 12, 12, 13, 14, 15, 15, 15, 19, 19, 22, 26, 28, 28, 31, 32, 33, 33, 34, 35, 35, 36, 36; **70:**T, T; **71:**3, 4, 4, 4, 17, 19, 20, 20, 22; **72:**1, 1, 2, 2, 3, 3, 3, 4, 4, 4, 5, 5, 5, 6, 6, 6, 7, 7, 8, 8, 8, 9, 10, 10, 10, 12, 12, 13, 13, 15, 15, 15, 16, 16, 16, 17, 17, 18, 18, 19, 20; **73:**2, 2, 3, 9, 9, 10, 11, 16, 17, 17, 18, 26, 28, 28; **74:**1, 2, 2, 3, 3, 3, 5, 6, 7, 7, 7, 8, 9, 12, 13, 13, 14, 14, 15, 16, 16, 17, 17, 20, 21; **75:**T, T, 2, 2, 3, 3, 4, 4, 5, 6, 8, 8, 8, 8, 9, 10, 10, 10, 10; **76:**T, 3, 3, 3, 4, 5, 5, 8, 9, 9, 11, 11, 12, 12, 12; **77:**T, 2, 5, 6, 7, 9, 10, 10, 14, 14, 15, 16, 16, 17, 17, 17, 18, 18, 18, 18, 19, 19; **78:**4, 4, 4, 4, 6, 6, 9, 9, 11, 12, 12, 13, 13, 14, 15, 15, 16, 16, 17, 17, 18, 19, 21, 21, 23, 23, 25, 26, 26, 26, 27, 27, 28, 29, 30, 31, 31, 32, 34, 35, 40, 40, 41, 43, 44, 48, 50, 50, 51, 51, 51, 52, 53, 54, 55, 55, 56, 60, 60, 61, 62, 65, 67, 68, 69, 70, 71, 71; **79:**2, 2, 2, 2, 3, 6, 7, 8, 9, 9, 10, 10, 11, 11, 12, 13; **80:**T, T, T, 1, 5, 6, 8, 9, 9, 10, 10, 11, 11, 13, 13, 13, 16, 17, 17; **81:**T, 1, 2, 2, 2, 3, 3, 3, 4, 4, 7, 10, 10, 15, 16, 16; **82:**1, 2, 3, 3, 3, 3, 3, 4, 4, 5, 5, 6, 8, 8; **83:**2, 4, 8, 9, 9, 10, 13, 18, 18, 18; **84:**T, T, 2, 2, 2, 3, 3, 5, 6, 6, 9, 9, 10, 10, 10, 10, 11, 11; **85:**T, T, 1, 2, 8, 11, 12, 13; **86:**8, 9, 13; **87:**T, 1, 1, 1, 2, 5, 6, 6, 7, 7, 7; **88:**T, T, T, T, T, 6, 6, 10, 10, 11, 11, 12, 12; **89:**T, 1, 1, 2, 3, 6, 6, 7, 9, 9, 10, 10, 11, 11, 11, 15, 15, 18, 18, 19, 22, 22, 25, 25, 25, 25, 26, 27, 29, 32, 36, 37, 37, 38, 39, 40, 48, 48, 50, 51, 52; **90:**T, 1, 2, 2, 2, 5, 6, 10, 11, 11, 12, 14, 14, 15, 17; **91:**1, 1, 1, 1, 2, 3, 5, 5, 5, 5, 6, 6, 8, 9, 9, 14; **92:**T, 1, 1, 2, 2, 3, 3, 3, 7, 8, 11, 11, 12, 12, 13, 13, 15; **93:**1, 1, 1, 2, 3, 3, 3, 3, 4, 4, 4, 4, 4, 5; **94:**1, 2, 2, 2, 3, 7, 7, 9, 9, 10, 11, 13, 14, 15, 16, 17, 21, 21, 22, 23, 23; **95:**1, 1, 3, 3, 4, 4, 4, 5, 5, 6, 7, 7, 8, 8; **96:**1, 1, 1, 2, 2, 3, 3, 4, 4, 5, 5, 5, 7, 7, 7, 8, 8, 9, 9, 10, 10, 10, 11, 11, 11, 12, 12, 12, 13, 13, 13, 13, 13; **97:**1, 1, 1, 2, 4, 4, 5, 5, 5, 5, 6, 8, 9, 10, 10, 10, 10, 11, 12; **98:**1, 2, 3, 3, 4, 4, 5, 5, 5, 6, 6, 6, 6, 7, 7, 8, 8, 9, 9, 9, 9, 9; **99:**1, 1, 1, 1, 2, 2, 5, 6, 7, 7, 9, 9; **100:**1, 2, 3, 3, 5; **101:**6, 8, 8; **102:**T, 6, 7, 11, 13, 13, 14, 15, 15, 15, 15, 16, 17, 17, 18, 19, 19, 20, 20, 21, 22, 25, 25, 25, 25, 27, 28; **103:**1, 2, 2, 5, 6, 7, 8, 11, 11, 11, 12, 12, 13, 16, 17, 17, 17, 19, 19, 20, 21, 22, 22; **104:**1, 2, 2, 3, 3, 3, 3, 3, 4, 5, 6, 6, 7, 7, 7, 8, 9, 9, 10, 10, 11, 11, 12, 12, 12, 12, 13, 13, 13, 14, 14, 16, 16, 16, 17, 17, 17, 18, 18, 18, 19, 19, 19, 20, 20, 21, 23, 24, 25, 26, 26, 30, 30, 31, 31, 31, 32, 32, 33, 34, 35, 35, 35, 35, 35; **105:**1, 1, 3, 4, 5, 5, 5, 7, 7, 8, 9, 9, 10, 11, 16, 19, 19, 20, 20, 21, 21, 22, 22, 23, 24, 24, 25, 25, 25, 26, 27, 27, 28, 29, 29, 30, 30, 31, 32, 33, 35, 35, 36, 36, 38, 39, 39, 41, 44, 45; **106:**1, 1, 2, 2, 5, 5, 7, 7, 8, 9, 9, 11, 14, 16, 16, 16, 17, 17, 18, 19, 22, 23, 23, 24, 24, 25, 26, 27, 28, 28, 29, 30, 30, 32, 34, 34, 34, 35, 37, 38, 38, 38, 39, 40, 47, 48, 48, 48, 48; **107:**1, 2, 3, 4, 8, 9, 9, 11, 11, 11, 14, 15, 20, 21, 23, 23, 24, 24, 25, 25, 26, 26, 26, 29, 29, 31, 32, 32, 32, 34, 34, 35, 36, 40, 41, 42, 42, 43, 43; **108:**2, 3, 3, 4, 4, 5, 5, 7, 9, 10; **109:**T, 2, 14, 14, 14, 15, 16, 16, 18, 18, 20, 21, 30, 31; **110:**1, 2, 3, 4, 4, 5, 5, 6, 6, 7; **111:**1, 1, 2, 2, 4, 6, 10, 10, 10; **112:**1, 1, 4, 7, 10; **113:**1, 1, 1, 1, 2, 2, 3, 3, 4, 4, 4, 5, 6, 6, 7, 7, 7, 7, 8, 9, 9; **114:**1, 1, 2, 3, 3, 3, 4, 4, 7, 7, 7, 7, 8; **115:**1, 2, 3, 9, 10, 11, 11, 12, 12, 12, 12, 13, 14, 15, 16, 16, 16, 17, 17, 17, 17, 18, 18; **116:**1, 3, 3, 4, 4, 5, 6, 7, 9, 12, 13, 14, 14, 15, 16, 17, 17, 18, 18, 19, 19, 19, 19; **117:**1, 1, 2, 2, 2; **118:**1, 2, 3, 4, 5, 5, 6, 7, 8, 9, 10, 10, 11, 11, 12, 12, 13, 14, 15, 15, 15, 15, 16, 16, 16, 16, 17, 18, 19, 19, 19, 20, 20, 20, 22, 22, 22, 23, 24, 24, 26, 26, 26, 26, 26, 27, 27, 27, 29; **119:**1, 1, 13, 18, 19, 25, 27, 29, 35, 41, 51, 53, 54, 54, 59, 64, 71, 73, 78, 83, 90, 95, 95, 109, 110, 112, 115, 119, 119, 119, 121, 123, 127, 130, 134, 147, 148, 155, 169; **120:**T, 1; **121:**T, 1, 2, 2, 2, 3, 5, 5, 6, 6, 7, 8; **122:**T, 1, 1, 4, 4, 4, 4, 4, 5, 5, 5, 6, 8, 9, 9, 9; **123:**T, 2, 2, 4, 4, 4, 4; **124:**T, 1, 2, 4, 5, 6, 7, 8, 8, 8; **125:**T, 1, 2, 2, 3, 3, 3; **126:**T, 1, 2, 2, 3, 4, 6; **127:**T, 1, 1, 1, 1, 3, 5, 5; **128:**T, 1, 2, 4, 5; **129:**T, 4, 4, 4, 7, 7, 8, 8; **130:**T, 1, 5, 6, 6, 6, 7, 7; **131:**T, 3; **132:**T, 2, 2, 5, 5, 6, 6, 7, 7, 8, 8, 10, 10, 11, 12, 12, 13, 14, 16, 17; **133:**T, 2, 2, 3, 3, 3; **134:**T, 1, 1, 1, 1, 2, 3; **135:**1, 1, 1, 1, 2, 2, 2, 2, 3, 3, 4, 5, 5, 6, 6, 7, 7, 7, 7, 7, 8, 11, 11, 14, 19, 19, 20, 20, 20, 21, 21; **136:**1, 2, 3, 5, 6, 6, 7, 8, 8, 9, 9, 10, 13, 15, 16, 19, 21, 26; **137:**1, 2, 2, 4, 4, 5, 6, 7, 7, 7, 7, 8, 9, 9; **138:**1, 2, 3, 4, 5, 5, 5, 6, 6, 6, 7, 8; **139:**T, 3, 8, 8, 9, 9, 9, 11, 11, 12, 13, 15, 15, 18, 18, 19, 24; **140:**T, 3, 4, 4, 5, 5, 6, 7, 9, 10, 11, 12, 12, 12, 13; **141:**4, 5, 5, 7, 7, 7, 9, 9, 10; **142:**T, 1, 1, 3, 7; **143:**3, 3, 5, 8, 11; **144:**1, 2, 5, 5, 7, 8, 10, 11, 11, 11, 13, 13, 15; **145:**3, 7, 8, 9, 11, 12, 13, 14, 14, 16, 17, 18, 19, 20, 20, 21; **146:**1, 1, 2, 4, 5, 5, 6, 6, 6, 7, 7, 7, 7, 8, 8, 8, 8, 8, 8, 8, 9, 9, 9, 9, 9, 10, 10; **147:**1, 2, 2, 3, 4, 6, 6, 6, 6, 7, 8, 8, 8, 9, 9, 10, 10, 11, 12, 13, 14, 15, 16, 16, 17, 18, 20; **148:**1, 1, 1, 1, 2, 4, 5, 7, 7, 7, 11, 11, 13, 13, 13, 14, 14; **149:**1, 1, 1, 1, 4, 4, 5, 6, 7, 7, 9, 9, 9; **150:**1, 3, 3, 4, 6, 6; **Pr 1:**1, 2, 4, 6, 7, 7, 11, 12, 12, 12, 13, 19, 20, 20, 21, 21, 22, 23, 25, 29, 31, 31, 31; **2:**5, 6, 7, 8, 9, 16, 16, 16, 17, 18, 19, 19, 20, 20, 20, 21, 21, 22, 22, 22; **3:**1, 5, 7, 9, 9, 10, 11, 12, 13, 14, 19, 19, 19, 20, 20, 20, 25, 25, 26, 32, 32, 33, 33, 33, 33, 33, 33, 34, 34, 35; **4:**7, 14, 14, 16, 18, 18, 18, 18, 19, 19, 26; **5:**3, 4, 5, 6, 8, 10, 14, 16, 18, 20, 21; **6:**1, 6, 8, 10, 16, 17, 22, 23, 23, 23, 24, 24, 29, 32, 34; **7:**5, 6, 8, 8, 8, 9, 9, 10, 11, 12, 20, 22, 23, 26, 27, 27, 27; **8:**2, 2, 3, 3, 3, 7, 13, 19, 22, 22, 23, 23, 24, 24, 25, 25, 26, 26, 27, 27, 27,

28, 28, 28, 29, 29, 29, 30, 31, 35; **9:**2, 2, 3, 3, 4, 5, 7, 8, 8, 9, 9, 10,
10, 10, 12, 12, 13, 14, 14, 16, 17, 18, 18; **10:**1, 3, 3, 3, 3, 5, 6, 7, 7, 8,
11, 11, 13, 14, 15, 15, 15, 15, 16, 16, 17, 19, 20, 20, 20, 21, 22, 22,
23, 24, 24, 24, 24, 25, 25, 26, 26, 27, 27, 27, 28, 28, 28, 28, 29, 29,
29, 30, 30, 30, 31, 31, 32, 32; **11:**1, 4, 5, 5, 6, 6, 7, 8, 8, 9, 10, 10, 10,
11, 11, 18, 18, 18, 20, 21, 21, 23, 23, 25, 26, 28, 29, 29, 29, 30, 31,
31, 31; **12:**2, 3, 5, 5, 5, 5, 6, 6, 6, 6, 7, 7, 7, 10, 10, 10, 10, 12, 13, 13,
14, 14, 15, 17, 18, 18, 19, 21, 21, 22, 26, 26, 27, 27, 28, 28; **13:**2, 5,
6, 8, 8, 9, 9, 9, 12, 14, 14, 14, 20, 21, 22, 22, 25, 25, 25; **14:**2, 2, 2, 3,
3, 3, 8, 9, 11, 11, 11, 11, 13, 13, 15, 16, 18, 18, 19, 19, 19, 20, 20, 21,
24, 24, 26, 27, 27, 31, 31, 32, 32; **15:**2, 3, 3, 3, 4, 6, 6, 6, 6, 7, 8, 8, 8,
8, 8, 9, 9, 9, 10, 11, 11, 11, 12, 13, 14, 15, 15, 16, 19, 19, 21, 23, 23,
24, 24, 24, 25, 25, 25, 25, 26, 26, 26, 27, 28, 28, 29, 29, 29, 29, 30,
31, 33; **16:**1, 1, 2, 3, 4, 4, 5, 5, 6, 7, 7, 9, 10, 11, 11, 13, 14, 14, 14,
15, 17, 17, 19, 19, 20, 21, 23, 23, 24, 24, 28, 33, 33; **17:**2, 3, 3, 3, 5,
5, 6, 6, 6, 10, 14, 15, 15, 15, 20, 20, 21, 21, 23, 24, 24, 26; **18:**3, 5, 5,
7, 10, 10, 10, 11, 13, 14, 14, 17, 20, 20, 20, 21, 21, 22, 22, 23, 23;
19:2, 3, 6, 7, 7, 7, 12, 12, 14, 16, 17, 17, 20, 20, 21, 23, 25, 25, 25,
28, 28, 29; **20:**2, 4, 4, 5, 7, 8, 8, 8, 10, 11, 12, 14, 14, 16, 16, 17, 18,
20, 21, 22, 22, 23, 24, 24, 25, 26, 26, 27, 27, 28, 29, 29, 29, 29, 29,
30; **21:**1, 1, 2, 2, 3, 7, 8, 8, 9, 12, 12, 12, 12, 13, 13, 15, 16, 16, 16,
17, 18, 18, 18, 18, 19, 20, 22, 22, 22, 22, 25, 26, 27, 29, 29, 30, 31,
31, 31; **22:**2, 2, 2, 3, 3, 3, 4, 5, 6, 7, 7, 7, 7, 9, 10, 11, 12, 12, 12, 13,
13, 14, 14, 16, 16, 17, 17, 19, 21, 22, 22, 23, 28; **23:**3, 5, 8, 9, 10, 10,
17, 19, 23, 24, 30, 30, 31, 32; **24:**7, 7, 9, 13, 13, 14, 15, 15, 15, 15,
16, 18, 19, 20, 21, 21, 22, 22, 22, 23, 24, 24, 25, 30, 30, 33; **25:**1, 2,
3, 3, 3, 3, 4, 4, 4, 5, 5, 6, 6, 7, 7, 9, 12, 13, 13, 22, 23, 24, 25, 26, 26,
27; **26:**7, 13, 13, 14; **27:**1, 3, 4, 7, 9, 12, 12, 12, 13, 13, 14, 15, 16,
18, 19, 19, 21, 23, 24, 24, 25, 25, 25, 26; **28:**1, 1, 3, 3, 4, 4, 4, 5, 7, 8,
8, 9, 9, 10, 10, 11, 12, 12, 14, 15, 17, 18, 20, 20, 23, 25, 27, 28, 28,
28; **29:**2, 2, 2, 3, 6, 7, 7, 7, 7, 10, 10, 10, 10, 13, 13, 13, 13, 14, 16,
16, 16, 18, 19, 24, 25, 26, 26, 27, 27, 27, 27; **30:**1, 3, 4, 4, 4, 9, 10,
14, 14, 14, 14, 15, 16, 16, 16, 16, 17, 17, 19, 19, 21, 25, 26, 29, 30,
31, 31, 33, 33; **31:**1, 6, 9, 15, 18, 20, 20, 23, 23, 24, 25, 26, 27, 29,
30; **Ecc 1:**1, 1, 2, 5, 6, 7, 7, 7, 7, 7, 7, 9, 12, 13, 13, 14, 14, 16, 17, 18,
18; **2:**1, 2, 3, 6, 7, 8, 9, 11, 12, 14, 14, 14, 15, 16, 16, 16, 17, 17, 18,
20, 24, 26, 26; **3:**10, 11, 11, 13, 15, 15, 16, 16, 16, 19, 19, 20, 20, 21,
21, 21, 22; **4:**1, 1, 1, 1, 1, 2, 2, 3, 4, 6, 8, 10, 11, 15, 16, 16, 16; **5:**1,
4, 6, 6, 7, 8, 8, 9, 9, 11, 11, 11, 12, 13, 13, 13, 14, 15, 15, 16, 18, 19,
20; **6:**2, 3, 5, 6, 9, 11, 11, 12, 12; **7:**1, 1, 1, 1, 4, 7, 9, 10, 13, 13, 15,
17, 19, 20, 25, 27, 27; **8:**2, 3, 4, 8, 8, 8, 9, 9, 10, 10, 10, 13, 13, 15,
16, 17; **9:**1, 2, 2, 4, 5, 5, 9, 9, 9, 10, 11, 11, 11, 11, 11, 11, 11, 11, 13,
15, 17, 17; **10:**2, 2, 2, 2, 3, 3, 5, 9, 10, 10, 12, 14, 14, 15, 16, 16, 17,
18, 18, 20; **11:**3, 3, 5, 5, 7, 8, 10; **12:**1, 2, 2, 2, 4, 5, 5, 6, 6, 6, 6, 6, 6,
7, 7, 7, 8, 9, 9, 10, 10, 11, 11, 13; **SS 1:**3, 5, 5, 6, 6, 6, 7, 8, 8, 12, 12,
14, 16; **2:**1, 1, 1, 3, 3, 4, 7, 7, 7, 7, 8, 8, 9, 9, 9, 11, 11, 12, 12, 12, 13,
13, 14, 15, 15, 15, 16, 17, 17, 17; **3:**2, 3, 5, 5, 5, 5, 6, 6, 8, 8, 10, 11,
11; **4:**1, 4, 4, 5, 6, 6, 6, 6, 8, 10, 11, 11, 11, 13, 15, 15; **5:**2, 2, 2, 2, 4,
5, 7, 7, 7, 11, 15, 15; **6:**2, 3, 4, 5, 9, 9, 10, 10, 10, 11, 11, 11, 11, 11;
7:1, 4, 4, 4, 5, 8, 8, 9, 10, 11, 11, 11, 12, 12, 12, 12, 13, 13, 13; **8:**4,
5, 5, 6, 6, 13, 14; **Isa 1:**1, 2, 2, 3, 3, 3, 4, 4, 8, 9, 10, 10, 10, 11, 11,
11, 13, 13, 13, 14, 15, 17, 17, 17, 18, 18, 20, 21, 23, 23, 23, 24, 24,
24, 26, 26, 26, 27, 27, 28, 29, 29, 31, 31, 31; **2:**2, 2, 2, 2, 2, 3, 3, 3, 3,
3, 4, 4, 5, 5, 6, 6, 6, 6, 8, 8, 9, 10, 10, 10, 10, 11, 11, 12, 12, 12, 13,
13, 14, 16, 16, 16, 17, 17, 17, 19, 19, 19, 19, 19, 19, 19, 20, 21, 21,
21, 21, 21, 21; **3:**1, 1, 1, 2, 2, 8, 9, 9, 11, 11, 13, 13, 14, 14, 14, 14,
14, 15, 15, 15, 16, 16, 16, 16, 16, 17, 17, 18, 25, 25, 26, 26, 26; **4:**2,
2, 2, 2, 2, 2, 3, 4, 4, 4, 5, 5, 5; **5:**1, 2, 2, 2, 2, 3, 3, 5, 6, 6, 6, 7, 7, 7, 7,
8, 9, 9, 11, 12, 12, 13, 13, 14, 15, 15, 15, 16, 16, 17, 19, 22, 23, 23,
24, 24, 24, 24, 25, 25, 25, 25, 25, 25, 26, 26, 26, 28, 28, 30, 30, 30,
30, 30; **6:**1, 1, 1, 1, 2, 3, 3, 4, 4, 4, 5, 5, 6, 6, 8, 10, 11, 12, 12, 13;
7:1, 1, 1, 1, 2, 2, 2, 2, 3, 3, 3, 3, 3, 3, 3, 4, 5, 6, 7, 10, 12, 12, 13, 14,
14, 14, 15, 16, 16, 17, 17, 17, 18, 18, 18, 19, 19, 19, 20, 22, 22, 22,
23, 24, 25, 25; **8:**1, 2, 2, 3, 4, 5, 6, 7, 7, 7, 8, 9, 11, 11, 12, 13, 13, 14,
16, 17, 17, 18, 18, 18, 18, 19, 19, 19, 19, 20, 22; **9:**1, 1, 1, 1, 1, 1, 2,
2, 3, 4, 4, 4, 6, 7, 7, 7, 8, 9, 10, 10, 11, 11, 12, 12, 12, 13, 13, 14, 14,
14, 14, 14, 15, 15, 15, 15, 16, 16, 16, 17, 17, 17, 17, 18, 19, 19, 19,
19, 19, 20, 21; **10:**1, 2, 2, 2, 4, 4, 5, 7, 7, 12, 12, 12, 15, 15, 15, 15,
16, 16, 17, 17, 17, 17, 18, 20, 20, 20, 21, 22, 22, 22, 22, 23, 23, 24,
24, 24, 24, 26, 26, 26, 26, 26, 26, 27, 27, 27, 28, 29, 29, 29, 29, 30,
31, 31, 32, 32, 33, 33, 33, 34, 34, 34; **11:**1, 1, 2, 2, 2, 2, 2, 2, 2, 3, 4,
4, 4, 4, 6, 6, 6, 6, 7, 7, 9, 9, 9, 9, 10, 10, 10, 10, 11, 11, 11, 11, 12, 12,
12, 12, 13, 14, 14, 14, 14, 15, 15, 15, 16; **12:**1, 2, 3, 4, 4, 5, 5, 6, 6;
13:1, 2, 2, 2, 2, 3, 4, 4, 4, 4, 4, 4, 5, 5, 6, 6, 6, 7, 8, 8, 9, 9, 9, 9, 9, 10,
11, 11, 11, 11, 11, 11, 11, 12, 13, 13, 13, 16, 17, 18, 18, 18, 19, 19,
20, 21, 21, 21, 21; **14:**1, 1, 1, 2, 2, 2, 3, 4, 4, 5, 6, 6, 7, 8, 8, 8, 8, 9, 9,
11, 12, 12, 12, 12, 13, 13, 13, 14, 14, 15, 15, 16, 16, 16, 16, 17, 17,
17, 17, 18, 18, 19, 19, 21, 21, 21, 21, 22, 23, 23, 23, 24, 25, 26, 26,
27, 28, 29, 30, 30, 30, 31, 32, 32, 32; **15:**2, 3, 3, 4, 4, 4, 5, 5, 6, 6, 6,
7, 7, 7, 8, 8, 9, 9; **16:**1, 2, 2, 2, 4, 6, 7, 7, 8, 8, 8, 8, 8, 8, 8, 9, 9, 10,
10, 10, 10, 10, 10, 12, 12, 12, 13, 13, 14, 14; **17:**2, 2, 3, 3, 3, 3, 3, 4,
4, 5, 5, 5, 6, 6, 6, 6, 6, 6, 6, 6, 7, 7, 8, 9, 9, 9, 10, 10, 10, 11, 12, 12,
13, 14, 14, 14; **18:**1, 1, 1, 1, 2, 3, 3, 3, 4, 4, 4, 4, 5, 6, 6, 6, 6, 7, 7, 7,
7, 7; **19:**1, 1, 1, 1, 2, 3, 4, 4, 5, 5, 5, 5, 6, 6, 6, 7, 7, 7, 8, 9, 9, 10, 10,
11, 11, 12, 13, 13, 13, 14, 14, 16, 16, 16, 17, 17, 18, 18, 18, 18, 19,
19, 19, 20, 20, 20, 20, 21, 21, 21, 21, 22, 22, 22, 23, 23, 24, 25, 25;
20:1, 1, 2, 3, 3, 3, 4, 4, 4, 5, 5, 6; **21:**1, 1, 1, 2, 2, 2, 3, 4, 6, 6, 7, 8, 8,
9, 9, 9, 9, 10, 10, 11, 12, 13, 15, 16, 16, 17, 17; **22:**1, 2, 3, 5, 5, 5, 5,
5, 6, 6, 6, 6, 8, 9, 9, 10, 10, 11, 11, 11, 12, 12, 13, 14, 14, 14, 14, 14,
15, 15, 15, 16, 17, 19, 21, 22, 22, 22, 22, 24, 25, 25, 25, 25; **23:**1, 2,
2, 3, 3, 3, 4, 4, 5, 6, 7, 8, 9, 10, 10, 11, 11, 11, 11, 13, 13, 13, 13, 15,
15, 16, 17, 17, 18, 18, 18; **24:**1, 1, 1, 1, 1, 3, 3, 4, 4, 4, 5, 5, 5, 6, 7, 7,
7, 8, 8, 8, 8, 9, 9, 10, 11, 11, 12, 13, 13, 13, 13, 13, 13, 13, 14, 14, 15,
15, 15, 15, 15, 15, 16, 16, 16, 16, 17, 18, 18, 18, 19, 20, 21, 21, 21,
21, 21, 23, 23, 23, 23, 23; **25:**4, 4, 4, 4, 4, 4, 5, 5, 5, 5, 5, 5, 6, 6, 7, 7,
7, 8, 8, 9, 9, 9, 10, 12; **26:**1, 1, 2, 2, 4, 4, 4, 5, 5, 5, 6, 7, 7, 9, 10, 10,
16, 18, 18, 19, 19, 19, 20, 21, 21, 21, 21; **27:**1, 1, 1, 1, 1, 2, 3, 6, 6, 7,
7, 8, 9, 9, 10, 10, 11, 11, 11, 11, 12, 12, 12, 12, 12, 12, 13, 13; **28:**1,
1, 1, 1, 2, 2, 2, 3, 3, 3, 5, 5, 5, 6, 7, 9, 13, 14, 15, 15, 16, 17, 17, 17,
17, 18, 18, 18, 18, 20, 20, 21, 21, 21, 22, 22, 24, 26, 27, 28, 29, 29;
29:1, 4, 5, 6, 7, 7, 8, 10, 10, 13, 14, 15, 15, 15, 16, 16, 16, 16, 16, 17,
17, 18, 19, 19, 19, 21, 21, 22, 22, 23, 23, 23, 24; **30:**1, 6, 6, 6, 7, 8, 9,
10, 10, 12, 12, 14, 15, 15, 16, 16, 18, 18, 19, 20, 21, 23, 24, 24, 24,
26, 26, 26, 26, 26, 26, 27, 28, 29, 29, 29, 29, 29, 29, 30, 31, 31, 32,
32, 33, 33, 33, 33; **31:**1, 1, 2, 3, 4, 4, 4, 4, 5, 5, 6, 7, 7, 8, 8, 8, 8, 9, 9;
32:2, 2, 2, 2, 4, 6, 6, 6, 7, 7, 7, 7, 10, 14, 14, 14, 14, 15, 15, 15, 16,
16, 17, 19, 19; **33:**3, 3, 3, 4, 4, 5, 6, 6, 6, 8, 8, 9, 9, 10, 14, 14, 15, 16,
16, 16, 17, 17, 18, 21, 22, 23, 23, 23, 24, 24; **34:**1, 1, 2, 2, 3, 3, 3, 4,
4, 4, 5, 5, 6, 6, 6, 6, 7, 7, 7, 8, 8, 8, 9, 9, 10, 10, 11, 11, 11, 11, 12, 13,
14, 14, 14, 15, 15, 16, 16, 16, 17; **35:**1, 1, 2, 2, 2, 2, 2, 5, 5, 5, 5, 6, 6,
6, 7, 7, 8, 9, 10; **36:**1, 1, 2, 2, 2, 2, 2, 2, 3, 3, 3, 3, 4, 4, 6, 7, 7, 7, 8, 9,
9, 10, 10, 11, 11, 11, 12, 13, 13, 13, 14, 15, 15, 15, 16, 16, 16, 18, 18,
18, 19, 19, 20, 21, 22, 22, 22, 22, 22; **37:**1, 1, 2, 2, 2, 2, 3, 4, 4, 4, 5,
6, 6, 6, 7, 8, 9, 10, 11, 12, 12, 12, 13, 13, 13, 14, 14, 14, 15, 16, 16,
16, 16, 16, 17, 18, 18, 19, 19, 19, 20, 20, 21, 21, 22, 22, 22, 22, 23,
24, 24, 24, 25, 26, 27, 27, 28, 29, 30, 30, 30, 31, 31, 32, 32, 33, 33,
34, 34, 34, 35, 36, 36, 36, 36, 36, 38, 38, 38; **38:**1, 1, 1, 2, 2, 4, 5, 5,
6, 7, 7, 8, 8, 8, 8, 10, 10, 10, 11, 11, 11, 18, 19, 19, 20, 20, 20, 21, 22,
22; **39:**2, 2, 2, 2, 2, 3, 3, 5, 6, 6, 6, 7, 8, 8; **40:**2, 3, 3, 3, 3, 4, 4, 4, 4,
5, 5, 5, 6, 6, 7, 7, 7, 7, 8, 8, 8, 9, 9, 10, 11, 11, 12, 12, 12, 12, 12, 12,
13, 13, 14, 15, 15, 15, 15, 15, 17, 17, 21, 21, 21, 22, 22, 22, 22, 22,
23, 23, 24, 25, 26, 26, 27, 28, 28, 28, 28, 28, 29, 31; **41:**1, 1, 2, 2, 2,
2, 4, 4, 4, 4, 4, 5, 5, 6, 7, 7, 7, 7, 7, 7, 7, 9, 9, 13, 14, 14, 16, 16, 16,
16, 16, 17, 17, 17, 18, 18, 18, 20, 20, 21, 21, 22, 23, 25, 25, 27, 27,
29; **42:**1, 3, 4, 4, 5, 5, 5, 5, 6, 6, 7, 7, 7, 8, 9, 10, 10, 10, 10, 11, 11,
11, 11, 12, 12, 13, 15, 15, 15, 16, 16, 19, 19, 19, 21, 21, 23, 23, 24,
24, 24; **43:**1, 2, 2, 3, 3, 6, 6, 8, 9, 9, 9, 10, 11, 12, 12, 14, 14, 14, 15,
16, 16, 16, 17, 17, 19, 19, 20, 20, 20, 20, 20, 21, 24, 25, 26, 27; **44:**2,
5, 5, 5, 6, 6, 6, 6, 7, 11, 12, 13, 13, 13, 14, 14, 14, 14, 14, 15, 15, 16,
19, 19, 19, 20, 21, 22, 22, 22, 23, 23, 24, 24, 24, 24, 25, 25, 26, 26,
27, 28; **45:**1, 2, 2, 3, 3, 3, 3, 4, 5, 6, 6, 7, 7, 7, 7, 7, 7, 8, 8, 9, 9, 9, 11,
11, 11, 12, 12, 12, 12, 13, 14, 14, 14, 17, 17, 18, 18, 18, 18, 19, 19,
21, 22, 24, 24, 24, 25, 25; **46:**1, 1, 1, 2, 2, 2, 2, 2, 2, 9, 11, 13; **47:**1,
1, 2, 4, 4, 5, 6, 7, 7, 8, 8, 9, 12, 12, 13; **48:**1, 1, 1, 1, 1, 2, 2, 2, 3, 7, 7,
9, 10, 10, 11, 12, 12, 13, 13, 13, 13, 14, 14, 14, 16, 17, 17, 17, 17, 19,
19, 20, 20, 20, 20, 20, 21, 21, 22, 22; **49:**1, 1, 2, 4, 5, 5, 6, 6, 6, 6, 7,
7, 7, 7, 7, 7, 7, 7, 8, 8, 8, 8, 9, 10, 10, 11, 11, 12, 13, 14, 14, 18, 19,
20, 21, 22, 22, 23, 23, 23, 24, 24, 25, 25, 25, 26, 26, 26; **50:**1, 2, 2, 2,
3, 3, 4, 5, 7, 9, 10, 10, 11; **51:**1, 1, 1, 3, 3, 3, 3, 4, 5, 5, 6, 6, 6, 6, 6, 6,
8, 8, 9, 9, 9, 10, 10, 10, 11, 12, 12, 13, 13, 13, 13, 13, 13, 15, 15, 15,
16, 16, 16, 17, 17, 17, 20, 20, 22, 22, 23, 23; **52:**2, 2, 3, 4, 5, 7, 7, 7,
7, 8, 8, 9, 9, 10, 10, 10, 10, 10, 10, 11, 11, 11, 12, 12; **53:**1, 2, 3, 6, 6,
7, 7, 8, 10, 10, 12, 12; **54:**1, 1, 1, 3, 4, 4, 5, 5, 5, 5, 6, 8, 9, 9, 10, 10,
10, 11, 16, 16, 16, 16, 16, 17, 17, 17; **55:**2, 3, 3, 4, 5, 5, 5, 6, 7, 7, 7,
8, 9, 9, 10, 10, 10, 10, 10, 10, 10, 11, 12, 12, 12, 13; **56:**1, 3, 3, 4, 5,
5, 6, 6, 6, 8, 8, 9, 9, 10, 10; **57:**1, 1, 1, 2, 5, 6, 6, 7, 9, 9, 13, 14, 14,
15, 15, 15, 16, 19, 20, 21; **58:**1, 2, 5, 5, 5, 6, 7, 8, 8, 8, 9, 9, 10, 10,
10, 11, 12, 12, 13, 13, 13, 13, 14, 14, 14; **59:**1, 3, 9, 13, 14, 15, 16,
17, 17, 19, 19, 19, 19, 19, 20, 20, 21, 21, 21; **60:**1, 1, 1, 2, 2, 2, 2, 5,
5, 6, 6, 6, 7, 7, 9, 9, 9, 9, 11, 11, 11, 11, 12, 13, 13, 14, 14, 14, 14, 16,
16, 16, 18, 18, 19, 19, 20, 20, 20, 22, 22, 22, 22; **61:**1, 1, 1, 1, 1, 2, 2,
2, 3, 4, 6, 6, 6, 8, 9, 9, 10, 10, 11, 11, 11; **62:**1, 2, 2, 3, 3, 4, 4, 4, 4, 4,
6, 6, 7, 7, 7, 8, 9, 9, 9, 9, 10, 10, 10, 10, 11, 11, 12, 12, 12, 12, 12;
63:1, 1, 1, 1, 3, 4, 6, 6, 7, 7, 9, 11, 11, 11, 12, 12, 13, 13, 13, 13, 14,
14, 15, 15, 18; **64:**1, 1, 2, 2, 3, 4, 6, 8, 8, 11, 11; **65:**1, 3, 4, 7, 7, 7, 8,
9, 10, 10, 11, 11, 11, 12, 12, 13, 15, 16, 16, 17, 19, 21, 21, 22, 22, 22,
23, 25, 25, 25, 25; **66:**1, 1, 2, 3, 3, 4, 5, 5, 6, 6, 6, 6, 6, 7, 8, 8, 8, 9, 9,
12, 12, 12, 14, 14, 15, 15, 15, 16, 16, 16, 17, 19, 19, 19, 19, 19, 20,
20, 20, 21, 22, 24, 24, 24; **Jer 1:**1, 1, 1, 2, 2, 3, 3, 3, 4, 5, 7, 8, 8, 9,
11, 12, 13, 13, 14, 14, 14, 15, 15, 15, 15, 15, 15, 18, 19; **2:**1, 2, 2, 3,
3, 3, 4, 4, 5, 6, 6, 7, 8, 8, 8, 8, 8, 8, 9, 9, 10, 10, 12, 12, 13, 15, 15, 17,
17, 18, 18, 18, 19, 19, 19, 20, 21, 21, 22, 23, 23, 23, 24, 29, 29, 31,
31, 33, 34, 34, 34, 37, 37; **3:**1, 1, 2, 2, 2, 2, 3, 4, 5, 6, 6, 9, 10, 11, 12,
13, 13, 14, 14, 16, 16, 16, 16, 16, 17, 17, 17, 18, 18, 18, 19, 19, 20,
21, 21, 21, 22, 22, 22, 23, 23, 25; **4:**1, 2, 2, 3, 3, 3, 4, 5, 5, 5, 6, 8, 8,
9, 9, 9, 9, 9, 10, 10, 11, 11, 11, 11, 15, 16, 16, 16, 17, 18, 19, 19, 20,
22, 23, 23, 24, 25, 25, 25, 26, 26, 26, 27, 27, 28, 28, 29, 29, 29, 29,
29, 29, 31; **5:**1, 1, 1, 2, 4, 4, 4, 5, 5, 6, 6, 7, 9, 10, 10, 10, 10, 10, 11,
11, 12, 14, 14, 15, 18, 19, 22, 22, 22, 22, 22, 22, 24, 24, 27, 28, 28,
29, 31, 31, 31; **6:**1, 1, 3, 4, 4, 6, 6, 6, 6, 7, 8, 9, 9, 9, 10, 10, 11, 11,
12, 12, 13, 13, 15, 15, 16, 16, 16, 17, 17, 19, 19, 21, 22, 22, 23, 24,
25, 25, 25, 26, 26, 26, 27, 28, 29, 29, 30; **7:**1, 2, 2, 2, 2, 3, 3, 4, 4, 8,
11, 11, 12, 12, 12, 12, 13, 15, 17, 17, 18, 18, 18, 18, 19, 19, 20, 20,
21, 21, 24, 25, 28, 28, 29, 29, 30, 30, 31, 31, 31, 31, 32, 32, 32, 32,
32, 32, 33, 33, 34, 34, 34, 34, 34; **8:**1, 1, 1, 1, 1, 1, 2, 2, 2, 2, 3, 3, 4,
4, 4, 6, 7, 7, 7, 7, 7, 7, 7, 8, 8, 9, 9, 10, 10, 12, 12, 13, 13, 14, 14, 14,
14, 16, 16, 16, 16, 16, 16, 16, 16, 16, 17, 19, 19, 19, 19, 19, 20, 20,
20, 21, 22; **9:**2, 3, 3, 5, 6, 7, 9, 10, 10, 10, 10, 11, 11, 12, 12, 13, 13,
14, 15, 15, 16, 16, 17, 17, 18, 19, 20, 20, 21, 21, 21, 22, 22, 22, 23,
23, 23, 23, 24, 24, 25, 26, 26, 26, 26; **10:**1, 1, 2, 2, 7, 7, 7, 7, 8, 8, 10,
10, 10, 10, 10, 10, 11, 11, 12, 12, 13, 13, 13, 13, 13, 13, 14, 15, 16,
16, 16, 17, 18, 21, 21, 22, 22, 22, 25, 25; **11:**1, 2, 2, 3, 3, 3, 5, 6, 6, 6,
6, 8, 9, 9, 10, 10, 11, 12, 12, 16, 16, 17, 17, 18, 18, 19, 20, 21, 21, 22;
12:1, 4, 4, 4, 4, 4, 4, 4, 5, 5, 5, 8, 9, 10, 11, 12, 12, 12, 12, 12, 13, 13,
14, 14, 14, 16, 16, 16, 17; **13:**1, 2, 2, 3, 4, 4, 4, 5, 5, 6, 6, 6, 7, 7, 7, 8,
9, 9, 11, 12, 12, 13, 13, 13, 13, 13, 14, 14, 15, 16, 16, 17, 18, 18, 19,
19, 19, 20, 20, 21, 23, 24, 24, 25, 27, 27; **14:**1, 1, 2, 2, 3, 3, 3, 4, 4, 5,
6, 6, 7, 7, 8, 8, 10, 11, 13, 14, 15, 16, 16, 17, 18, 18, 18, 18, 18, 21,
21, 22, 22, 22; **15:**1, 2, 3, 3, 3, 3, 3, 4, 4, 4, 6, 7, 8, 8, 8, 9, 9, 9, 11,
12, 13, 17, 19, 20; **16:**1, 3, 3, 4, 4, 5, 6, 6, 7, 7, 9, 9, 9, 9, 10, 10, 10,
11, 14, 14, 14, 14, 14, 15, 15, 15, 15, 15, 16, 16, 19, 19, 20, 21, 21;
17:1, 1, 4, 5, 5, 6, 6, 6, 6, 7, 7, 8, 8, 9, 10, 11, 13, 13, 13, 15, 17, 19,
19, 19, 19, 19, 20, 20, 21, 21, 22, 24, 24, 25, 25, 26, 26, 26, 26, 26,
26, 27, 27, 27, 27, 27, 27; **18:**1, 2, 3, 4, 4, 4, 5, 6, 6, 11, 13, 13, 14,
14, 14, 14, 15, 15, 17, 18, 18, 21; **19:**1, 1, 1, 1, 2, 2, 2, 2, 2, 3, 3, 3, 3,
4, 4, 4, 6, 6, 6, 6, 6, 7, 7, 7, 7, 8, 8, 8, 9, 9, 10, 11, 11, 11, 12, 13, 13,
13, 13, 14, 14, 14, 15, 15; **20:**1, 1, 1, 2, 2, 2, 3, 3, 3, 4, 4, 4, 4, 4, 4, 5,
5, 5, 7, 8, 8, 9, 10, 10, 11, 12, 13, 13, 14, 14, 15, 16, 16; **21:**1, 1, 2, 2,
2, 4, 4, 4, 4, 4, 7, 7, 8, 8, 9, 10, 10, 11, 11, 12, 12, 12, 14; **22:**1, 1, 2,
3, 3, 4, 4, 4, 5, 6, 6, 6, 7, 8, 8, 9, 9, 10, 10, 11, 13, 16, 16, 17, 17, 18,
18, 19, 20, 20, 23, 24, 24, 25, 27, 29, 30, 30, 30; **23:**1, 1, 1, 1, 2, 2, 2,
3, 4, 5, 5, 5, 6, 7, 7, 7, 7, 8, 8, 8, 8, 8, 9, 9, 9, 10, 10, 10, 11, 11, 11,
12, 13, 14, 14, 15, 15, 16, 16, 17, 18, 19, 19, 19, 20, 20, 20, 23, 24,
24, 25, 27, 29, 30, 31, 32, 33, 33, 33, 33, 33, 34, 35, 35, 36, 36, 36,
36, 37, 37, 37, 38, 38, 38, 40; **24:**1, 1, 1, 1, 2, 3, 4, 5, 5, 5, 5, 5, 5, 7,
8, 8, 8, 10; **25:**1, 1, 1, 1, 2, 2, 3, 3, 3, 4, 5, 5, 5, 5, 6, 7, 7, 8, 9, 9, 9,
10, 11, 12, 12, 12, 12, 12, 13, 13, 13, 14, 14, 15, 15, 15, 15, 16, 17,
17, 17, 17, 18, 18, 20, 20, 20, 20, 20, 21, 22, 22, 22, 22, 23, 24, 24,
24, 24, 25, 26, 26, 26, 26, 26, 26, 26, 26, 27, 27, 27, 28, 28, 29, 29,
29, 29, 30, 30, 30, 30, 31, 31, 31, 31, 31, 31, 31, 31, 32, 32, 32, 33,
33, 33, 33, 34, 34, 34, 36, 36, 36, 36, 36, 37, 38, 38, 38; **26:**1, 1, 2, 2,
2, 2, 3, 4, 4, 5, 6, 6, 7, 7, 7, 7, 8, 8, 8, 8, 9, 9, 9, 10, 10, 10, 10, 11, 11,
11, 12, 12, 13, 15, 15, 16, 16, 16, 16, 16, 16, 17, 17, 18, 18, 18, 18,
18, 18, 19, 19, 19, 19, 20, 20, 20, 21, 21, 21, 23, 24, 24; **27:**1, 1, 2, 3,
4, 4, 5, 6, 7, 8, 9, 11, 11, 11, 11, 12, 13, 14, 14, 15, 16, 16, 16, 16, 17,
18, 18, 18, 18, 18, 18, 19, 19, 19, 19, 19, 19, 19, 20, 21, 21, 21, 21,
21, 22; **28:**1, 1, 1, 1, 2, 2, 2, 2, 3, 4, 4, 4, 4, 5, 5, 6, 6, 7, 7, 8, 9, 9, 10,
10, 11, 11, 11, 11, 11, 12, 13, 14, 14, 14, 14, 15, 15, 15, 16, 16; **29:**1,
1, 2, 2, 2, 2, 3, 4, 4, 4, 5, 7, 7, 8, 8, 8, 9, 10, 10, 11, 11, 14, 14, 15, 16,
16, 17, 18, 19, 20, 21, 21, 22, 22, 22, 23, 24, 24, 25, 25, 25, 25, 26,
26, 26, 26, 26, 28, 29, 30, 31, 31, 31, 32, 32; **30:**1, 2, 2, 2, 3, 3, 3, 4,
4, 5, 5, 7, 8, 8, 9, 10, 11, 11, 12, 13, 17, 18, 18, 21, 23, 23, 23, 24, 24,
24; **31:**1, 1, 1, 2, 2, 2, 3, 5, 6, 6, 6, 7, 7, 7, 8, 8, 8, 8, 8, 10, 10, 10, 11,
12, 12, 12, 12, 12, 13, 13, 13, 14, 14, 15, 16, 16, 16, 17, 18, 18, 20,
21, 22, 23, 23, 23, 23, 25, 25, 27, 27, 27, 27, 28, 28, 28, 29, 29, 29,
30, 30, 31, 31, 31, 32, 32, 32, 32, 33, 33, 33, 34, 34, 34, 34, 35, 35,
35, 35, 35, 35, 35, 36, 37, 37, 37, 37, 38, 38, 38, 38, 39, 40, 40, 40,
40, 40, 40, 40, 40, 40; **32:**1, 1, 1, 1, 1, 2, 2, 2, 2, 3, 3, 4, 4, 5, 6, 7,
8, 8, 8, 8, 8, 8, 9, 10, 10, 11, 11, 11, 11, 12, 12, 12, 12, 14, 14, 14, 15,
15, 16, 16, 17, 18, 18, 19, 20, 20, 22, 24, 24, 24, 24, 25, 25, 25, 26,
27, 27, 27, 27, 28, 29, 29, 29, 29, 29, 30, 31, 32, 32, 32, 32, 32, 32,
32, 35, 35, 36, 36, 36, 37, 39, 42, 42, 43, 44, 44, 44, 44, 44, 44; **33:**1,
1, 1, 2, 2, 2, 2, 4, 4, 4, 4, 4, 4, 4, 5, 5, 6, 7, 9, 9, 9, 9, 9, 10, 10, 10, 11,
11, 11, 11, 11, 11, 11, 11, 11, 12, 12, 13, 13, 13, 13, 13, 13, 13, 13,
14, 14, 14, 15, 15, 16, 17, 17, 19, 20, 20, 21, 21, 22, 22, 22, 22, 22,
23, 24, 25, 26, 26, 26; **34:**1, 1, 1, 1, 2, 2, 2, 3, 4, 4, 5, 6, 6, 7, 7, 8, 8,
8, 9, 10, 10, 10, 11, 12, 13, 13, 16, 17, 17, 17, 18, 18, 20, 21, 21, 22,
22; **35:**1, 1, 2, 2, 2, 2, 2, 3, 4, 4, 4, 4, 4, 4, 4, 7, 10, 11, 12, 13, 13, 13,
14, 15, 16, 17, 17, 17, 18, 18, 18, 19, 19; **36:**1, 1, 2, 2, 2, 2, 3, 3, 4, 4,
5, 6, 6, 6, 6, 7, 7, 8, 8, 8, 9, 9, 9, 9, 9, 10, 10, 10, 10, 10, 11, 11, 12,
12, 12, 12, 12, 13, 13, 14, 14, 14, 15, 15, 16, 16, 19, 20, 20, 20, 20,
20, 21, 21, 21, 22, 22, 23, 23, 23, 23, 24, 25, 25, 26, 26, 27, 27, 28,
29, 29, 29, 29, 30, 30, 31, 31, 32, 32; **37:**1, 2, 2, 2, 3, 3, 5, 5, 5, 6, 7,
7, 7, 8, 8, 9, 9, 10, 10, 11, 12, 12, 12, 13, 13, 13, 13, 14, 15, 15, 17,
17, 17, 17, 18, 18, 19, 20, 20, 20, 20, 21, 21, 21, 21, 21, 21, 21; **38:**1,
2, 2, 3, 3, 3, 3, 4, 4, 4, 4, 6, 6, 6, 6, 6, 7, 7, 7, 7, 8, 9, 9, 9, 9, 9, 10, 10,
11, 11, 11, 11, 12, 13, 13, 13, 14, 14, 14, 14, 15, 16, 16, 17, 17, 17,
18, 18, 19, 19, 19, 20, 21, 22, 22, 22, 22, 22, 23, 23, 25, 27, 27, 27,
27, 27, 27, 28, 28, 28; **39:**1, 2, 2, 2, 3, 3, 3, 3, 4, 4, 4, 4, 4, 4, 5, 5, 5,
5, 5, 6, 8, 8, 8, 8, 9, 9, 9, 9, 10, 13, 13, 13, 13, 14, 14, 15, 15, 16, 16,
16, 18; **40:**1, 1, 1, 2, 2, 2, 3, 4, 5, 5, 6, 6, 7, 7, 7, 7, 7, 8, 8, 8, 8, 8, 9,
9, 10, 10, 10, 11, 11, 11, 11, 12, 12, 13, 15, 15; **41:**1, 2, 3, 4, 5, 5, 7,
8, 9, 9, 9, 9, 10, 10, 10, 10, 11, 11, 12, 13, 14, 15, 16, 17, 18, 18, 18;
42:1, 1, 1, 1, 2, 2, 3, 4, 5, 6, 7, 8, 8, 8, 8, 9, 9, 10, 11, 11, 13, 15, 15,
15, 15, 16, 17, 17, 18, 18, 18, 19, 20, 20, 21, 21; **43:**1, 1, 2, 2, 3, 4, 4,
4, 5, 5, 6, 6, 6, 6, 6, 7, 7, 7, 8, 9, 9, 9, 10, 10, 10, 11, 11, 11, 12, 12,
12, 13, 13, 13, 13; **44:**1, 1, 1, 2, 2, 2, 4, 6, 6, 7, 7, 7, 8, 8, 8, 9, 9, 9, 9,
10, 11, 11, 12, 12, 15, 15, 15, 15, 16, 17, 17, 17, 18, 18, 19, 19, 21,
21, 21, 21, 22, 22, 23, 23, 24, 24, 25, 25, 25, 26, 26, 26, 26, 26, 29,
29, 30; **45:**1, 1, 1, 2, 3, 4, 5; **46:**1, 1, 1, 2, 2, 2, 2, 2, 2, 4, 5, 5, 5, 6, 6,
6, 6, 7, 7, 8, 8, 9, 10, 10, 10, 10, 10, 10, 10, 10, 12, 12, 13, 13, 14, 14,
15, 16, 16, 17, 18, 18, 18, 19, 20, 22, 23, 24, 25, 25, 25, 25, 26, 26,
26, 28, 28; **47:**1, 1, 1, 1, 2, 2, 2, 2, 2, 3, 3, 3, 4, 4, 4, 4, 5, 5, 6, 7, 7, 7,
7; **48:**1, 1, 1, 1, 1, 2, 2, 3, 5, 6, 8, 8, 8, 8, 10, 10, 12, 12, 12, 15, 15,
17, 17, 18, 19, 19, 20, 20, 20, 21, 21, 24, 25, 25, 26, 27, 27, 28, 28,
28, 29, 30, 31, 32, 32, 33, 33, 34, 34, 35, 35, 39, 39, 40, 40, 41, 42,
43, 44, 44, 44, 45, 45, 46, 46, 47, 47, 47, 47; **49:**1, 1, 1, 2, 2, 2, 2, 3,
3, 5, 5, 6, 6, 6, 7, 7, 9, 10, 11, 12, 12, 13, 14, 14, 15, 15, 16, 16, 16,
16, 17, 18, 18, 19, 19, 19, 19, 19, 20, 20, 20, 21, 21, 21, 21, 22, 22,
23, 23, 23, 26, 26, 27, 27, 28, 28, 28, 28, 30, 31, 31, 32, 32, 34, 34,
34, 34, 35, 35, 35, 36, 36, 36, 37, 37, 37, 38, 39, 39, 39; **50:**1, 1, 1, 1,
2, 2, 3, 4, 4, 4, 5, 5, 6, 6, 7, 7, 8, 8, 9, 9, 9, 10, 10, 12, 13, 13, 14, 15,
16, 16, 16, 16, 17, 17, 18, 18, 18, 18, 19, 19, 20, 20, 21, 21, 21, 21,
22, 22, 23, 23, 23, 24, 25, 25, 25, 25, 25, 27, 28, 28, 29, 29, 29, 30,
30, 31, 31, 32, 33, 33, 34, 34, 34, 35, 35, 35, 35, 38, 38, 39, 39, 40,
41, 42, 43, 43, 44, 44, 44, 44, 44, 45, 45, 45, 46, 46, 46; **51:**1, 1, 3, 4,
4, 5, 5, 6, 7, 7, 10, 10, 11, 11, 11, 11, 11, 11, 12, 12, 12, 12, 13, 14,
15, 15, 16, 16, 16, 16, 16, 16, 17, 18, 19, 19, 19, 20, 21, 21, 24, 24,
24, 25, 25, 25, 26, 27, 27, 28, 28, 28, 28, 28, 29, 30, 30, 30, 31, 32,
32, 32, 33, 33, 35, 35, 35, 35, 36, 38, 39, 40, 41, 41, 42, 44, 44, 44,
45, 46, 46, 47, 47, 48, 48, 48, 49, 49, 50, 50, 51, 51, 52, 52, 52, 52,
53, 53, 54, 54, 54, 54, 55, 55, 55, 56, 57, 57, 58, 58, 58, 58, 59, 59,
60, 63, 63, 64, 64; **52:**1, 2, 3, 3, 3, 4, 4, 5, 6, 6, 6, 6, 7, 7, 7, 7, 7, 7, 7,
7, 7, 7, 7, 8, 8, 9, 9, 10, 10, 11, 12, 12, 12, 13, 13, 13, 13, 13, 13, 14,
14, 14, 14, 15, 15, 15, 15, 15, 15, 15, 15, 16, 16, 17, 17, 17, 17, 17,
17, 18, 18, 18, 19, 19, 19, 20, 20, 20, 20, 20, 20, 21, 22, 22, 23,
23, 23, 24, 24, 24, 24, 25, 25, 25, 25, 25, 26, 26, 27, 27, 27, 28, 28,
30, 31, 31, 32, 33, 33, 34, 34; **La 1:**1, 2, 4, 4, 4, 5, 6, 6, 7, 9, 9, 9, 10,
10, 10, 12, 12, 14, 15, 15, 16, 17, 18, 19, 20, 20, 21; **2:**1, 1, 1, 1, 1, 2,
2, 2, 3, 3, 3, 3, 5, 6, 6, 7, 7, 8, 8, 8, 9, 9, 9, 10, 10, 10, 11, 11, 12, 13,
13, 14, 15, 15, 15, 17, 17, 18, 19, 19, 19, 20, 21, 21, 21, 22, 22, 22,
22; **3:**1, 1, 1, 1, 9, 11, 16, 18, 19, 22, 22, 24, 25, 26, 27, 27, 28, 29,
30, 30, 31, 32, 34, 35, 36, 36, 37, 38, 40, 45, 48, 50, 51, 51, 54, 54,
55, 59, 60, 61, 61, 62, 64, 66; **4:**1, 1, 1, 1, 2, 3, 3, 3, 4, 4, 4, 5, 5, 5, 5,
6, 9, 10, 11, 11, 11, 12, 12, 12, 13, 13, 14, 15, 16, 16, 18, 19, 19, 19,
20, 20, 21, 21, 21; **5:**1, 7, 7, 9, 9, 10, 11, 11, 12, 13, 13, 14, 14, 14,
15, 16, 19, 21; **Eze 1:**1, 1, 1, 2, 3, 3, 3, 3, 3, 3, 4, 4, 4, 5, 5, 9, 9, 9, 9,
10, 10, 10, 10, 10, 10, 10, 11, 11, 11, 12, 13, 14, 15, 16, 16, 17, 17,
18, 18, 18, 19, 19, 19, 20, 20, 20, 20, 20, 20, 21, 21, 21, 21, 21, 21,
21, 21, 21, 21, 22, 23, 23, 24, 24, 24, 24, 25, 26, 28, 28, 28, 28, 28;
2:1, 2, 3, 3, 4; **3:**1, 1, 2, 4, 7, 7, 11, 12, 12, 12, 13, 13, 13, 13, 14, 14,
15, 15, 16, 16, 16, 17, 18, 18, 18, 20, 22, 22, 23, 23, 23, 23, 24, 25,
26, 27; **4:**1, 2, 3, 3, 3, 4, 4, 7, 8, 9, 12, 12, 13, 13, 14, 14, 15, 16, 16,
17; **5:**1, 2, 2, 2, 2, 2, 3, 4, 5, 5, 5, 6, 6, 7, 8, 8, 10, 10, 10, 11, 12, 12,
12, 12, 13, 14, 14, 15, 15, 15, 16, 16, 17, 17, 17, 17; **6:**1, 2, 3, 3, 3, 3,
3, 6, 7, 7, 8, 8, 9, 10, 11, 11, 11, 13, 14, 14, 14, 14; **7:**1, 2, 2, 4, 5, 6,
7, 7, 7, 9, 9, 10, 10, 12, 12, 12, 14, 15, 16, 16, 19, 21, 23, 24, 26, 26,
26, 27, 27, 27, 27, 27, 27; **8:**1, 1, 1, 2, 2, 3, 3, 3, 3, 3, 3, 3, 4, 4, 4, 5,
5, 5, 5, 5, 5, 5, 5, 6, 6, 7, 7, 7, 8, 8, 9, 10, 10, 10, 11, 12, 12, 12, 14,
14, 14, 16, 16, 16, 16, 16, 16, 16, 17, 17; **9:**1, 1, 1, 2, 2, 2, 3, 3, 3, 3,
3, 3, 3, 3, 4, 4, 4, 5, 5, 5, 6, 6, 6, 7, 7, 7, 7, 8, 9, 9, 9, 9, 9, 9, 9, 11, 11,
11; **10:**1, 1, 1, 2, 2, 2, 2, 2, 3, 3, 3, 3, 3, 3, 4, 4, 4, 4, 4, 4, 4, 4, 4, 5, 5,
5, 5, 6, 6, 6, 6, 6, 6, 7, 7, 7, 7, 7, 7, 8, 9, 9, 10, 11, 11, 11, 12, 12, 12,
13, 13, 14, 14, 14, 14, 14, 14, 14, 14, 15, 15, 15, 16, 16, 16, 16, 17,
17, 17, 17, 17, 18, 18, 18, 18, 18, 19, 19, 19, 19, 19, 20, 20, 20, 22,
22, 22, 22; **11:**1, 1, 1, 1, 1, 2, 2, 2, 3, 5, 5, 5, 5, 6, 7, 7, 7, 7, 8, 8, 10,
10, 10, 11, 11, 12, 12, 12, 13, 14, 15, 15, 16, 16, 16, 16, 17, 17, 17,
18, 21, 22, 22, 22, 22, 23, 23, 23, 23, 23, 24, 24, 24, 25, 25; **12:**1, 2,
3, 4, 4, 5, 6, 6, 7, 7, 7, 7, 7, 8, 8, 9, 10, 10, 12, 13, 13, 14, 14, 15, 15,
16, 17, 19, 19, 20, 20, 20, 21, 23, 23, 23, 23, 24, 25, 25, 26, 27, 28,
28; **13:**1, 2, 2, 2, 3, 3, 4, 5, 5, 5, 5, 5, 6, 6, 7, 8, 8, 9, 9, 9, 10, 12, 12,

12, 13, 14, 14, 15, 15, 16, 17, 18, 18, 20, 21, 21, 22, 22, 23; **14:**1, 2, 4, 4, 4, 5, 6, 6, 7, 8, 9, 9, 11, 11, 12, 13, 14, 15, 15, 16, 16, 16, 17, 18, 18, 18, 19, 19, 20, 20, 21, 23; **15:**1, 2, 5, 6, 6, 6, 6, 7, 8, 8; **16:**1, 3, 5, 5, 7, 8, 13, 14, 14, 14, 15, 16, 17, 18, 19, 19, 20, 22, 23, 26, 27, 28, 30, 34, 35, 36, 39, 43, 46, 46, 48, 49, 53, 57, 57, 58, 59, 60, 61, 62, 63; **17:**1, 2, 3, 3, 6, 7, 8, 9, 10, 10, 10, 11, 12, 12, 12, 12, 13, 16, 16, 16, 16, 17, 17, 18, 19, 19, 21, 21, 21, 21, 22, 22, 22, 24, 24, 24, 24, 24, 24, 24; **18:**1, 2, 2, 2, 3, 4, 4, 6, 7, 7, 7, 9, 11, 11, 12, 15, 16, 16, 16, 17, 18, 18, 19, 19, 19, 20, 20, 20, 20, 20, 20, 22, 23, 25, 25, 27, 29, 29, 30, 32; **19:**1, 2, 4, 4, 5, 6, 7, 8, 8, 9, 9, 10, 10, 11, 12, 12, 12, 13, 13, 13, 14, 14; **20:**1, 1, 1, 2, 3, 3, 3, 3, 4, 5, 5, 6, 7, 7, 8, 9, 9, 10, 12, 13, 13, 13, 14, 14, 15, 15, 15, 17, 19, 20, 21, 22, 22, 23, 23, 24, 26, 26, 27, 27, 28, 30, 30, 31, 32, 33, 34, 35, 35, 36, 36, 37, 37, 38, 38, 38, 39, 40, 40, 41, 42, 42, 43, 44, 44, 45, 46, 46, 46, 47, 47, 47, 47, 47, 48, 48; **21:**1, 3, 3, 3, 4, 4, 5, 5, 6, 7, 7, 7, 8, 9, 9, 11, 11, 13, 13, 14, 14, 15, 16, 16, 17, 18, 19, 19, 19, 20, 21, 21, 21, 21, 22, 22, 22, 22, 23, 23, 23, 23, 24, 24, 26, 26, 26, 26, 27, 27, 27, 28, 28, 29, 29, 29, 30, 31, 32, 32; **22:**1, 3, 4, 4, 12, 14, 15, 16, 16, 17, 18, 18, 18, 19, 20, 21, 22, 23, 24, 24, 25, 25, 26, 28, 28, 29, 29, 30, 30, 30, 30, 30, 31, 31, 31; **23:**1, 2, 4, 5, 7, 8, 10, 13, 15, 17, 22, 23, 23, 23, 24, 25, 27, 28, 29, 29, 31, 32, 32, 32, 33, 34, 34, 35, 35, 36, 39, 42, 42, 44, 45, 46, 48, 49, 49; **24:**1, 1, 2, 3, 3, 4, 4, 4, 5, 5, 5, 5, 5, 5, 5, 6, 6, 6, 7, 9, 9, 9, 10, 10, 10, 10, 10, 10, 11, 11, 11, 12, 12, 13, 14, 14, 14, 14, 15, 17, 18, 18, 18, 18, 19, 20, 21, 21, 21, 21, 22, 23, 24, 25, 25, 27; **25:**1, 2, 3, 3, 3, 3, 4, 5, 5, 5, 5, 6, 6, 7, 8, 8, 8, 10, 10, 10, 11, 11, 11, 12, 12, 12, 13, 13, 14, 14, 15, 15, 16, 16, 16, 16, 16, 16, 17; **26:**1, 1, 2, 2, 2, 2, 3, 3, 3, 4, 5, 5, 5, 6, 6, 7, 7, 7, 10, 10, 10, 11, 12, 13, 13, 14, 14, 14, 15, 15, 15, 15, 15, 15, 16, 16, 17, 17, 18, 18, 19, 19, 20, 20, 20, 20, 20, 20, 20, 21; **27:**1, 3, 3, 3, 3, 4, 5, 6, 6, 7, 9, 21, 21, 22, 25, 25, 26, 26, 26, 27, 27, 28, 29, 29, 29, 32, 32, 33, 33, 33, 33, 34, 34, 35, 36, 36, 36; **28:**1, 2, 2, 2, 2, 6, 7, 7, 8, 8, 8, 10, 10, 11, 12, 12, 12, 13, 13, 13, 14, 14, 14, 15, 15, 16, 16, 17, 17, 17, 18, 18, 20, 21, 22, 22, 22, 23, 23, 24, 25, 25, 25, 25, 25, 25, 26, 26; **29:**1, 1, 2, 2, 3, 3, 3, 3, 4, 5, 5, 5, 6, 6, 7, 8, 9, 9, 9, 9, 10, 10, 10, 12, 13, 13, 13, 13, 13, 14, 14, 15, 15, 16, 17, 17, 18, 18, 19, 19, 20, 20, 21, 21, 21; **30:**1, 2, 3, 3, 3, 3, 4, 4, 6, 6, 6, 6, 8, 8, 9, 10, 10, 11, 11, 11, 12, 12, 12, 12, 13, 13, 13, 13, 15, 15, 17, 17, 18, 19, 20, 20, 21, 21, 22, 22, 22, 22, 22, 22, 23, 23, 24, 24, 25, 25, 25, 25, 25, 25, 26, 26, 26; **31:**1, 1, 3, 4, 4, 5, 5, 6, 6, 6, 6, 8, 8, 8, 9, 9, 9, 9, 10, 10, 10, 12, 12, 12, 12, 12, 13, 13, 14, 14, 14, 14, 15, 15, 15, 15, 15, 15, 16, 16, 16, 16, 16, 16, 16, 16, 16, 16, 17, 18, 18, 18, 18, 18, 18; **32:**1, 1, 2, 3, 3, 4, 4, 4, 4, 4, 5, 5, 6, 6, 6, 6, 6, 7, 7, 7, 7, 8, 8, 10, 11, 11, 11, 12, 12, 12, 12, 13, 14, 14, 15, 16, 16, 16, 17, 17, 18, 18, 18, 18, 19, 19, 19, 20, 20, 20, 20, 21, 21, 21, 22, 22, 23, 23, 23, 23, 24, 24, 24, 24, 24, 24, 25, 25, 25, 25, 25, 26, 26, 26, 27, 27, 27, 28, 28, 29, 29, 29, 30, 30, 30, 30, 30, 30, 31, 32, 32, 32, 32; **33:**1, 2, 3, 3, 3, 3, 4, 5, 5, 5, 6, 6, 6, 6, 6, 7, 10, 11, 11, 12, 12, 17, 20, 21, 21, 22, 22, 22, 23, 24, 24, 24, 24, 25, 25, 25, 26, 27, 27, 27, 27, 27, 28, 28, 29, 29, 30, 30, 30; **34:**1, 2, 2, 2, 3, 3, 3, 4, 4, 4, 6, 6, 6, 7, 7, 8, 8, 9, 9, 10, 10, 10, 11, 12, 13, 13, 13, 13, 14, 15, 16, 16, 17, 17, 17, 18, 18, 18, 18, 18, 20, 20, 20, 24, 24, 25, 25, 25, 25, 27, 27, 29, 30, 30, 30, 31, 31; **35:**1, 3, 4, 5, 6, 8, 8, 9, 10, 10, 11, 12, 12, 14, 14, 15, 15; **36:**1, 1, 2, 2, 3, 3, 3, 4, 4, 4, 5, 6, 6, 6, 6, 7, 8, 10, 10, 11, 11, 13, 13, 14, 15, 16, 17, 18, 19, 20, 20, 20, 20, 21, 22, 22, 22, 23, 23, 23, 23, 23, 24, 28, 29, 30, 31, 32, 33, 33, 34, 35, 36, 36, 36, 36, 36, 37, 38, 38, 38, 38; **37:**1, 1, 1, 2, 2, 2, 3, 4, 4, 5, 6, 7, 7, 8, 9, 9, 9, 10, 10, 11, 12, 12, 13, 14, 14, 15, 16, 19, 19, 20, 20, 21, 21, 21, 21, 22, 25, 25, 28, 28; **38:**1, 2, 2, 2, 3, 6, 6, 7, 8, 8, 8, 9, 10, 12, 12, 13, 14, 15, 16, 16, 16, 16, 17, 17, 18, 18, 19, 20, 20, 21, 21, 23, 23, 23; **39:**1, 1, 2, 2, 4, 4, 5, 5, 6, 6, 7, 7, 7, 8, 9, 9, 10, 10, 11, 11, 11, 11, 11, 11, 11, 12, 12, 12, 13, 14, 14, 14, 14, 15, 15, 16, 17, 17, 17, 17, 17, 18, 18, 19, 20, 21, 21, 21, 22, 22, 23, 24, 25, 25, 27, 27, 28, 29; **40:**1, 1, 1, 2, 2, 4, 5, 5, 5, 5, 6, 6, 6, 6, 6, 7, 7, 7, 7, 7, 7, 8, 8, 9, 9, 9, 10, 10, 10, 11, 11, 11, 11, 12, 12, 13, 13, 13, 13, 14, 14, 14, 14, 15, 15, 15, 16, 16, 16, 16, 16, 17, 17, 17, 17, 17, 17, 17, 17, 18, 18, 18, 18, 18, 18, 19, 19, 19, 19, 20, 20, 20, 20, 21, 21, 21, 21, 22, 22, 22, 22, 22, 22, 22, 22, 23, 23, 23, 23, 23, 24, 24, 24, 24, 25, 25, 25, 25, 25, 25, 25, 26, 27, 27, 27, 27, 28, 28, 28, 28, 28, 29, 29, 29, 29, 29, 30, 30, 30, 31, 31, 31, 32, 32, 32, 32, 33, 33, 33, 33, 33, 34, 35, 35, 35, 35, 36, 36, 36, 36, 36, 37, 37, 38, 38, 38, 38, 38, 39, 39, 40, 40, 40, 41, 42, 42, 42, 43, 43, 43, 44, 44, 44, 44, 44, 45, 45, 45, 45, 45, 46, 46, 46, 46, 46, 46, 46, 47, 47, 47, 47, 47, 48, 48, 48, 49, 49, 49; **41:**1, 1, 1, 1, 1, 2, 2, 2, 3, 3, 3, 3, 3, 3, 3, 3, 3, 4, 4, 5, 5, 5, 6, 6, 6, 6, 6, 7, 7, 7, 7, 7, 7, 8, 8, 9, 9, 10, 10, 10, 10, 10, 11, 11, 11, 12, 12, 13, 13, 13, 13, 14, 14, 14, 15, 15, 15, 15, 15, 15, 16, 16, 16, 16, 16, 17, 17, 17, 18, 18, 19, 19, 19, 19, 19, 19, 19, 20, 20, 20, 20, 20, 21, 21, 21, 21, 21, 22, 22, 22, 23, 23, 25, 25, 25, 25, 25, 26; **42:**1, 1, 1, 1, 1, 1, 2, 3, 3, 3, 3, 3, 4, 4, 4, 4, 4, 5, 5, 5, 6, 6, 6, 7, 7, 8, 8, 8, 8, 9, 9, 10, 10, 10, 10, 10, 10, 10, 11, 11, 11, 11, 11, 11, 11, 11, 12, 12, 12, 12, 12, 12, 13, 13, 13, 13, 13, 13, 13, 14, 14, 14, 14, 14, 14, 14, 15, 15, 15, 16, 17, 17, 18, 18, 19, 20, 20, 20; **43:**1, 1, 2, 2, 2, 2, 2, 2, 3, 3, 3, 4, 4, 4, 4, 5, 5, 5, 5, 5, 6, 6, 7, 7, 7, 7, 9, 10, 10, 11, 12, 12, 12, 12, 12, 12, 12, 13, 13, 13, 13, 13, 14, 14, 14, 14, 14, 14, 15, 15, 15, 15, 16, 16, 17, 17, 17, 17, 18, 18, 18, 18, 18, 19, 19, 19, 20, 20, 20, 20, 20, 20, 21, 21, 21, 21, 22, 22, 22, 23, 23, 24, 24, 24, 25, 26, 27, 27, 27, 27, 27, 27; **44:**1, 1, 1, 2, 2, 2, 3, 3, 3, 4, 4, 4, 4, 4, 4, 4, 4, 4, 4, 5, 5, 5, 5, 6, 6, 7, 8, 9, 9, 9, 10, 10, 10, 11, 11, 12, 12, 13, 13, 13, 14, 14, 15, 15, 15, 15, 15, 15, 16, 16, 17, 17, 17, 17, 19, 19, 19, 19, 19, 21, 21, 22, 22, 22, 23, 24, 24, 24, 25, 27, 27, 27, 27, 28, 29, 29, 29, 29, 29, 29, 29, 29, 30, 30, 30, 30, 30, 30, 30, 30, 31; **45:**1, 1, 1, 1, 2, 3, 3, 3, 4, 4, 4, 5, 5, 5, 6, 7, 7, 7, 7, 7, 7, 7, 7, 7, 8, 8, 8, 8, 9, 11, 11, 11, 12, 12, 13, 13, 15, 15, 15, 16, 16, 17, 17, 17, 17, 17, 17, 18, 18, 18, 19, 19, 19, 19, 19, 19, 19, 19, 19, 19, 20, 20, 20, 21, 21, 21, 22, 22, 22, 23, 23, 23, 24, 25, 25, 25, 25, 25, 25, 25; **46:**1, 1, 1, 1, 1, 2, 2, 2, 2, 2, 2, 2, 2, 2, 3, 3, 3, 4, 4, 5, 6, 7, 7, 8, 8, 8, 8, 9, 9, 9, 9, 9, 9, 9, 9, 9, 10, 10, 11, 11, 11, 12, 12, 12, 12, 12, 12, 13, 14, 14, 14, 15, 15, 15, 16, 16, 17, 17, 17, 17, 17, 17, 17, 18, 19, 19, 19, 19, 19, 19, 19, 20, 20, 20, 20, 20, 20, 20, 20, 21, 23, 23, 23, 24, 24, 24, 24, 24; **47:**1, 1, 1, 1, 1, 1, 2, 2, 2, 2, 2, 2, 2, 3, 3, 4, 5, 6, 7, 8, 8, 8, 8, 8, 8, 9, 9, 10, 10, 10, 10, 10, 10, 10, 11, 12, 12, 12, 12, 12, 12, 13, 13, 13, 13, 15, 15, 16, 16, 17, 17, 17, 17, 17, 18, 18, 18, 18, 19, 19, 19, 19, 19, 19, 20, 20, 20, 20, 20, 21, 21, 22, 22, 22, 23, 23, 23; **48:**1, 1, 1, 1, 1, 1, 1, 1, 1, 1, 8, 8, 8, 8, 9, 9, 10, 10, 10, 11, 11, 11, 11, 11, 12, 12, 12, 12, 12, 13, 13, 13, 13, 14, 15, 15, 16, 17, 18, 18, 18, 18, 18, 18, 18, 19, 19, 20, 20, 21, 21, 21, 21, 21, 21, 21, 22, 22, 22, 22, 22, 23, 23, 23, 23, 23, 24, 25, 25, 26, 26, 27, 27, 27, 28, 28, 28, 28, 29, 29, 30, 30, 30, 31, 31, 31, 32, 32, 33, 34, 34, 35, 35, 35, 35, 35; **Da 1:**1, 2, 2, 2, 2, 2, 3, 3, 3, 3, 4, 4, 4, 4, 5, 5, 5, 6, 6, 7, 8, 8, 8, 9, 10, 10, 10, 11, 11, 13, 13, 13, 13, 14, 15, 15, 15, 15, 15, 16, 16, 17, 17, 17, 18, 18, 18, 18, 19, 20, 20, 20, 21; **2:**1, 2, 4, 4, 4, 4, 5, 5, 6, 6, 7, 8, 9, 9, 10, 10, 11, 11, 12, 12, 13, 14, 14, 14, 15, 16, 16, 16, 18, 18, 18, 19, 19, 20, 21, 21, 21, 21, 23, 24, 24, 24, 24, 25, 25, 25, 26, 27, 28, 28, 29, 30, 32, 32, 34, 35, 35, 35, 35, 35, 35, 36, 37, 38, 38, 38, 38, 39, 39, 41, 44, 44, 45, 45, 45, 45, 45, 45, 45, 46, 47, 47, 47, 48, 48, 49, 49, 49, 49; **3:**1, 1, 2, 2, 2, 2, 3, 4, 5, 5, 5, 7, 7, 7, 7, 7, 8, 8, 8, 9, 10, 10, 10, 10, 12, 12, 14, 15, 15, 15, 15, 17, 17, 18, 19, 20, 20, 21, 22, 22, 22, 22, 22, 23, 24, 25, 25, 25, 26, 26, 26, 26, 27, 27, 28, 28, 29, 30, 30; **4:**1, 1, 2, 2, 6, 7, 7, 8, 8, 8, 9, 9, 10, 10, 11, 11, 11, 12, 14, 14, 14, 14, 15, 15, 15, 15, 15, 15, 16, 17, 17, 17, 17, 17, 17, 17, 17, 18, 18, 18, 18, 19, 19, 19, 19, 19, 20, 20, 22, 22, 23, 23, 23, 23, 23, 23, 23, 24, 24, 25, 25, 25, 25, 25, 25, 26, 26, 26, 27, 29, 29, 30, 32, 32, 32, 32, 32, 33, 33, 34, 34, 35, 35, 35, 35, 37; **5:**2, 2, 3, 3, 5, 5, 5, 5, 5, 5, 7, 7, 7, 7, 8, 8, 9, 10, 10, 10, 11, 11, 11, 12, 12, 13, 13, 14, 14, 15, 16, 16, 17, 17, 18, 21, 21, 21, 21, 21, 21, 23, 23, 23, 25, 26, 27, 27, 28, 29, 29, 30, 31, 31, 31; **6:**1, 1, 2, 2, 2, 3, 3, 3, 4, 4, 5, 6, 6, 7, 7, 8, 9, 10, 11, 12, 12, 12, 12, 12, 13, 13, 14, 14, 14, 14, 15, 15, 15, 15, 15, 15, 15, 16, 16, 16, 17, 17, 17, 17, 17, 17, 18, 18, 19, 19, 19, 20, 20, 21, 22, 23, 23, 24, 24, 24, 24, 24, 24, 25, 25, 26, 26, 27, 27, 27, 28, 28, 28; **7:**1, 1, 2, 3, 3, 4, 4, 6, 7, 8, 8, 9, 10, 10, 11, 11, 12, 13, 13, 14, 14, 16, 17, 18, 18, 18, 18, 19, 19, 19, 19, 20, 20, 20, 20, 20, 20, 21, 22, 22, 22, 22, 22, 22, 23, 23, 23, 23, 24, 25, 25, 25, 26, 27, 27, 27, 27, 28, 28; **8:**1, 1, 2, 2, 2, 3, 3, 3, 3, 4, 4, 4, 4, 5, 5, 5, 6, 6, 7, 7, 7, 7, 7, 7, 8, 8, 8, 8, 8, 9, 9, 9, 9, 10, 10, 10, 10, 11, 11, 12, 12, 12, 13, 13, 13, 13, 13, 14, 14, 15, 16, 16, 17, 17, 17, 17, 17, 18, 19, 19, 20, 20, 21, 21, 21, 21, 21, 22, 22, 22, 22, 23, 24, 25, 26, 27, 27; **9:**1, 1, 1, 1, 1, 2, 2, 2, 2, 2, 2, 3, 4, 6, 6, 6, 7, 7, 9, 10, 10, 10, 11, 11, 11, 12, 13, 13, 13, 14, 14, 14, 16, 16, 20, 20, 21, 21, 21, 23, 23, 24, 24, 25, 25, 25, 25, 26, 26, 26, 26, 26, 27, 27, 27; **10:**1, 1, 1, 1, 4, 6, 7, 7, 9, 11, 12, 13, 13, 13, 13, 13, 14, 15, 16, 16, 16, 18, 20, 20, 20, 20, 21; **11:**1, 1, 1, 2, 2, 2, 4, 4, 4, 4, 5, 5, 6, 6, 6, 6, 6, 6, 6, 6, 6, 7, 7, 7, 7, 8, 8, 9, 9, 9, 9, 9, 10, 10, 10, 10, 10, 11, 11, 11, 11, 11, 12, 12, 12, 13, 13, 13, 14, 14, 14, 15, 15, 15, 15, 15, 15, 16, 16, 16, 17, 17, 17, 17, 18, 20, 20, 21, 21, 24, 24, 24, 24, 24, 25, 25, 25, 25, 27, 27, 28, 28, 28, 28, 28, 29, 29, 29, 30, 30, 30, 31, 31, 31, 31, 32, 32, 35, 35, 35, 36, 36, 36, 37, 37, 38, 39, 39, 40, 40, 40, 40, 40, 40, 41, 41, 43, 43, 44, 44, 45, 45; **12:**1, 1, 3, 4, 4, 4, 5, 6, 6, 7, 7, 7, 7, 7, 9, 9, 10, 11, 11, 11, 12, 12, 13, 13, 13, 13; **Hos 1:**1, 1, 2, 2, 2, 3, 4, 4, 4, 5, 6, 6, 7, 7, 9, 10, 10, 10, 10, 10, 11, 11; **2:**1, 2, 3, 6, 8, 8, 8, 8, 8, 9, 9, 12, 13, 13, 14, 15, 16, 18, 18, 18, 18, 18, 21, 21, 21, 21, 22, 22, 22, 22, 22, 22; **3:**1, 1, 1, 5, 5, 5, 5; **4:**1, 1, 1, 3, 4, 6, 7, 7, 7, 7, 8, 8, 8, 8, 9, 9, 10, 12, 12, 13, 13, 13, 14, 15, 16, 18; **5:**1, 1, 1, 4, 5, 6, 7, 7, 8, 8, 8, 10, 11, 13; **6:**1, 3, 3, 3, 4, 4, 4, 9, 11; **7:**3, 3, 3, 3, 4, 4, 5, 5, 6, 6, 10, 11, 12, 16, 16; **8:**1, 1, 1, 1, 3, 4, 7, 7, 7, 8, 8, 9, 10, 10, 13; **9:**2, 3, 4, 4, 4, 5, 7, 7, 7, 7, 7, 7, 8, 8, 9, 10, 10, 10, 10, 10, 11, 11, 15, 16, 17, 17; **10:**1, 1, 1, 1, 1, 1, 1, 1, 2, 2, 2, 3, 3, 5, 5, 5, 6, 8, 8, 8, 8, 9, 9, 10, 10, 11, 11, 11, 12, 12, 12, 12, 13, 14, 15, 15; **11:**2, 2, 2, 3, 4, 7, 9, 10, 10, 10, 11, 12; **12:**1, 1, 1, 1, 2, 4, 5, 5, 6, 7, 9, 9, 11, 11, 12, 13, 13, 14, 14; **13:**1, 1, 1, 1, 1, 2, 3, 3, 3, 4, 5, 7, 10, 10, 12, 13, 14, 15, 15, 15, 15, 15, 16, 16, 16; **14:**1, 2, 2, 3, 3, 4, 5, 5, 5, 6, 7, 7, 8, 8, 9, 9, 9; **Joel 1:**1, 2, 3, 3, 4, 4, 4, 4, 4, 5, 6, 7, 9, 9, 9, 9, 9, 10, 10, 10, 10, 11, 11, 12, 12, 12, 12, 13, 13, 13, 14, 14, 14, 14, 14, 15, 15, 15, 15, 15, 16, 17, 17, 17, 17, 18, 18, 18, 19, 19, 19, 20, 20, 20; **2:**1, 1, 1, 1, 2, 2, 3, 3, 5, 5, 5, 5, 6, 7, 8, 8, 9, 9, 9, 10, 10, 10, 10, 11, 11, 11, 12, 13, 14, 15, 15, 16, 16, 16, 16, 16, 17, 17, 17, 17, 17, 18, 18, 19, 20, 20, 20, 20, 20, 20, 20, 20, 21, 22, 22, 22, 23, 23, 23, 23, 24, 24, 25, 25, 25, 25, 25, 26, 26, 27, 30, 30, 31, 31, 31, 32, 32, 32, 32, 32; **3:**1, 1, 2, 2, 2, 2, 6, 6, 8, 8, 8, 9, 9, 11, 12, 12, 12, 13, 13, 13, 13, 13, 14, 14, 14, 15, 15, 16, 16, 16, 17, 18, 18, 18, 18, 18, 21; **Am 1:**1, 1, 1, 2, 2, 2, 2, 3, 3, 4, 5, 5, 5, 5, 5, 6, 6, 7, 8, 8, 8, 8, 9, 9, 10, 11, 11, 11, 12, 13, 13, 14, 14, 15; **2:**1, 1, 1, 2, 2, 2, 2, 2, 2, 3, 4, 4, 4, 4, 4, 5, 6, 6, 7, 7, 8, 9, 9, 9, 10, 10, 10, 11, 12, 14, 14, 15, 15, 15, 16, 16; **3:**1, 1, 2, 2, 3, 6, 6, 6, 7, 7, 8, 8, 9, 9, 9, 10, 11, 12, 12, 13, 13, 14, 14, 14, 14, 14, 15, 15, 15; **4:**1, 1, 2, 2, 3, 3, 3, 4, 5, 5, 6, 7, 7, 8, 9, 10, 10, 10, 10, 11, 13, 13, 13, 13, 13, 13, 13; **5:**2, 2, 3, 4, 4, 5, 5, 5, 6, 6, 7, 8, 8, 8, 8, 8, 8, 9, 10, 11, 11, 11, 12, 12, 12, 14, 15, 16, 16, 16, 16, 17, 18, 18, 18, 19, 20, 20, 21, 25, 25, 26, 27; **6:**1, 2, 2, 3, 4, 5, 5, 6, 7, 8, 8, 8, 10, 10, 10, 10, 10, 10, 11, 11, 12, 14, 14, 14, 14; **7:**1, 1, 1, 1, 1, 2, 3, 3, 4, 4, 4, 4, 4, 6, 6, 7, 8, 8, 9, 9, 9, 10, 10, 11, 12, 13, 15, 16, 17, 17; **8:**1, 2, 3, 3, 3, 3, 4, 4, 5, 5, 5, 6, 6, 7, 7, 7, 8, 8, 8, 9, 9, 9, 11, 11, 11, 11, 11, 12, 12, 13, 14; **9:**1, 1, 1, 1, 1, 1, 1, 1, 2, 2, 2, 3, 3, 3, 3, 4, 5, 5, 5, 5, 5, 6, 6, 6, 6, 6, 6, 6, 7, 7, 7, 7, 8, 8, 8, 8, 9, 10, 10, 11, 12, 12, 13, 13, 13, 13, 13, 15, 15; **Ob** 1, 1, 1, 1, 1, 2, 2, 3, 4, 4, 5, 8, 8, 8, 9, 9, 9, 10, 13, 13, 14, 14, 15, 15, 15, 16, 16, 17, 18, 18, 18, 19, 19, 19, 19, 19, 19, 19, 20, 20, 20, 20, 20, 20, 21, 21; **Jnh 1:**1, 2, 3, 3, 3, 3, 3, 3, 4, 4, 4, 4, 5, 5, 5, 5, 6, 7, 7, 7, 7, 9, 9, 9, 9, 10, 10, 11, 11, 12, 13, 13, 13, 14, 15, 15, 15, 16, 16, 17, 17; **2:**1, 1, 2, 2, 2, 3, 3, 3, 5, 5, 6, 6, 6, 6, 6, 7, 9, 10, 10, 10; **3:**1, 2, 2, 3, 4, 4, 4, 5, 5, 5, 6, 7, 7, 7, 10; **4:**2, 4, 5, 5, 5, 6, 6, 6, 7, 7, 7, 7, 8, 8, 9, 10, 10, 11; **Mic 1:**1, 1, 1, 1, 2, 2, 2, 2, 3, 3, 4, 5, 5, 6, 6, 6, 6, 7, 9, 10, 10, 11, 11, 11, 12, 12, 12, 13, 13, 14, 14, 15, 16; **2:**1, 3, 3, 5, 5, 6, 7, 8, 8, 11, 11, 12, 13, 13; **3:**2, 2, 3, 4, 4, 5, 6, 6, 6, 8, 8, 11, 11, 11, 12, 12; **4:**1, 1, 1, 1, 1, 2, 2, 2, 2, 2, 3, 3, 4, 5, 5, 6, 7, 8, 8, 10, 10, 10, 12, 13, 13, 13, 13, 13; **5:**1, 1, 1, 2, 3, 3, 3, 4, 4, 4, 4, 4, 5, 5, 6, 6, 6, 6, 7, 7, 7, 7, 8, 8, 8, 9, 10, 11, 13, 14, 15; **6:**1, 1, 2, 2, 2, 5, 6, 7, 7, 8, 9, 9, 9, 10, 10, 12, 12, 14, 15, 16, 16; **7:**1, 1, 2, 2, 3, 4, 4, 6, 6, 6, 7, 8, 9, 9, 9, 9, 10, 10, 10, 12, 12, 12, 12, 13, 13, 14, 15, 16, 16, 16, 17, 18, 18, 19, 19; **Na 1:**2, 3, 3, 3, 3, 3, 3, 4, 4, 4, 5, 5, 5, 6, 7, 8, 9, 11, 12, 12, 14, 14, 14, 14, 15; **2:**1, 1, 1, 2, 2, 3, 3, 4, 4, 4, 5, 5, 6, 6, 6, 7, 8, 8, 9, 9, 10, 10, 11, 11, 11, 13, 13, 13; **3:**1, 2, 2, 2, 2, 3, 3, 3, 3, 3, 4, 4, 5, 5, 6, 9, 9, 9, 10, 10, 10, 11, 12, 12, 12, 13, 13, 14, 14, 14, 14, 15, 15, 15, 15, 16, 16, 17, 17, 17, 17, 18, 18; **Hab 1:**1, 1, 1, 4, 4, 4, 4, 5, 5, 6, 6, 6, 9, 11, 12, 13, 16; **2:**1, 2, 3, 3, 4, 4, 5, 6, 8, 8, 9, 10, 11, 11, 11, 11, 11, 13, 13, 14, 14, 14, 14, 14, 14, 16, 16, 17, 17, 20, 20; **3:**1, 2, 3, 3, 3, 3, 6, 6, 6, 6, 6, 7, 8, 8, 9, 10, 10, 10, 10, 11, 11, 12, 12, 13, 13, 15, 15, 16, 16, 17, 17, 17, 17, 17, 17, 17, 18, 18, 19, 19, 19; **Zep 1:**1, 1, 2, 3, 3, 3, 3, 3, 3, 3, 4, 4, 5, 5, 6, 7, 7, 7, 7, 7, 8, 8, 10, 10, 10, 10, 10, 11, 12, 13, 13, 13, 13, 14, 15, 16, 17, 17, 17, 18, 18, 18, 18; **2:**2, 2, 2, 2, 3, 3, 5, 5, 5, 6, 7, 7, 7, 7, 8, 8, 9, 9, 10, 10, 10, 11, 11, 11, 11, 11, 12, 13, 13, 13, 14, 14, 14, 14, 14, 14, 15, 15; **3:**1, 2, 2, 2, 4, 5, 5, 5, 8, 8, 8, 8, 8, 8, 9, 9, 10, 11, 12, 12, 12, 12, 13, 15, 15, 15, 15, 16, 17, 18, 19, 20, 20, 20; **Hag 1:**1, 1, 1, 1, 2, 2, 2, 2, 2, 3, 3, 5, 7, 8, 8, 9, 10, 10, 10, 11, 12, 12, 12, 12, 12, 12, 12, 12, 13, 13, 13, 13, 14, 14, 14, 14, 14, 14, 15; **2:**1, 1, 2, 2, 2, 3, 4, 4, 4, 4, 4, 6, 6, 6, 6, 6, 7, 7, 7, 7, 8, 8, 8, 9, 9, 9, 10, 10, 10, 11, 11, 11, 12, 13, 13, 14, 15, 15, 16, 17, 17, 18, 18, 18, 19, 19, 19, 19, 19, 19, 20, 21, 21, 21, 22, 22, 23, 23, 23; **Zec 1:**1, 1, 1, 2, 3, 3, 3, 4, 4, 6, 6, 6, 7, 7, 7, 8, 9, 9, 10, 10, 10, 10, 10, 11, 11, 11, 11, 11, 11, 12, 12, 12, 13, 13, 14, 14, 15, 15, 16, 16, 16, 17, 17, 17, 19, 19, 20, 21, 21, 21; **2:**3, 4, 4, 5, 5, 5, 6, 6, 6, 8, 8, 9, 10, 11, 11, 12, 12, 12, 13; **3:**1, 1, 1, 1, 1, 2, 2, 2, 3, 4, 4, 5, 5, 6, 6, 7, 8, 8, 8, 9, 9, 9, 10; **4:**1, 2, 3, 4, 5, 6, 6, 7, 7, 7, 8, 9, 9, 9, 10, 10, 10, 10, 10, 10, 11, 11, 12, 14, 14, 14; **5:**1, 2, 3, 3, 3, 3, 3, 4, 4, 4, 5, 5, 6, 6, 7, 7, 8, 8, 8, 8, 9, 9, 9, 10, 10, 11, 11, 11, 11; **6:**2, 2, 3, 3, 4, 5, 5, 5, 6, 6, 6, 7, 7, 7, 7, 8, 8, 9, 10, 10, 11, 11, 11, 11, 12, 12, 12, 12, 12, 13, 13, 14, 14, 14, 15, 15, 15, 15, 15; **7:**1, 1, 2, 2, 3, 3, 3, 3, 3, 3, 4, 5, 5, 7, 7, 7, 7, 7, 7, 8, 9, 12, 12, 12, 12, 12, 13, 14, 14; **8:**1, 2, 3, 3, 3, 3, 3, 4, 4, 5, 5, 6, 6, 7, 7, 7, 9, 9, 9, 9, 9, 9, 10, 10, 10, 11, 11, 12, 12, 12, 12, 12, 12, 13, 13, 14, 14, 15, 16, 17, 18, 19, 19, 19, 20, 20, 21, 21, 21, 21, 22, 22, 23, 23, 23; **9:**1, 1, 1, 1, 1, 1, 2, 3, 4, 4, 4, 5, 6, 6, 6, 7, 7, 7, 10, 10, 10, 10, 10, 10, 10, 11, 12, 13, 14, 14, 14, 14, 15, 15, 15, 15, 16, 17, 17; **10:**1, 1, 1, 3, 4, 4, 4, 4, 5, 5, 5, 5, 6, 7, 7, 8, 9, 11, 11, 11, 11, 11, 11, 11, 12; **11:**2, 2, 2, 3, 3, 3, 3, 4, 5, 5, 5, 5, 6, 6, 6, 6, 6, 7, 7, 7, 10, 10, 11, 11, 13, 13, 13, 13, 13, 13, 14, 15, 15, 16, 16, 16, 16, 16, 16, 17, 17; **12:**1, 1, 1, 1, 1, 1, 1, 2, 3, 3, 4, 4, 4, 5, 5, 5, 6, 6, 6, 7, 7, 7, 7, 7, 8, 8, 8, 8, 8, 8, 9, 10, 10, 11, 11, 11, 12, 12, 12, 13, 13, 14; **13:**1, 1, 2, 2, 2, 2, 2, 2, 3, 3, 4, 5, 6, 7, 7, 7, 7, 7, 8, 8, 8, 8, 9, 9; **14:**1, 1, 2, 2, 2, 2, 2, 2, 2, 3, 4, 4, 4, 4, 4, 4, 5, 5, 5, 6, 7, 8, 8, 9, 9, 10, 10, 10, 10, 10, 10, 10, 10, 12, 12, 13, 14, 14, 15, 15, 15, 16, 16, 16, 16, 16, 16, 17, 17, 17, 18, 18, 18, 18, 18, 19, 19, 20, 20, 20, 20, 20, 20, 20, 20, 21, 21, 21; **Mal 1:**1, 1, 1, 2, 2, 4, 4, 4, 4, 4, 5, 5, 6, 6, 6, 7, 7, 7, 8, 9, 10, 10, 11, 11, 11, 12, 13, 13, 13, 14, 14, 14, 14; **2:**2, 2, 3, 3, 4, 4, 5, 5, 6, 6, 7, 7, 7, 7, 8, 8, 8, 9, 9, 9, 10, 10, 10, 11, 11, 12, 12, 12, 13, 14, 14, 14, 14, 15, 15, 16, 16, 16, 17, 17, 17; **3:**1, 1, 1, 1, 1, 3, 3, 3, 4, 4, 4, 5, 5, 6, 7, 7, 8, 10, 10, 10, 10, 11, 12, 13, 14, 14, 15, 16, 16, 16, 17, 17, 18, 18, 18; **4:**1, 1, 1, 1, 2, 3, 3, 3, 4, 4, 5, 5, 5, 6, 6, 6; **Mt 1:**1, 1, 2, 2, 2, 3, 3, 3, 4, 4, 4, 5, 5, 5, 6, 6, 6, 7, 7, 7, 8, 8, 8, 9, 9, 9, 10, 10, 10, 11, 11, 11, 12, 12, 12, 13, 13, 13, 14, 14, 14, 15, 15, 15, 16, 16, 16, 16, 17, 17, 17, 18, 18, 19, 20, 20, 20, 20, 22, 23, 24, 24; **2:**1, 1, 2, 2, 4, 4, 4, 5, 6, 7, 7, 7, 8, 9, 9, 9, 9, 10, 11, 11, 13, 13, 13, 13, 13, 14, 15, 15, 16, 16, 16, 16, 17, 19, 20, 20, 20, 22, 23, 23; **3:**1, 1, 2, 3, 3, 5, 5, 6, 8, 9, 10, 10, 11, 12, 12, 12, 12, 12, 13, 14, 16, 16, 16; **4:**1, 1, 1, 3, 3, 4, 5, 5, 5, 6, 6, 7, 7, 8, 8, 8, 8, 10, 10, 11, 13, 13, 15, 15, 15, 16, 16, 17, 18, 18, 21, 22, 23, 23, 23, 24, 24, 25, 25; **5:**1, 1, 3, 5, 9, 10, 12, 13, 13, 14, 14, 14, 16, 17, 17, 17, 18, 19, 19, 19, 19, 19, 20, 20, 20, 21, 22, 22, 23, 23, 24, 26, 27, 31, 33, 33, 33, 35, 35, 35, 35, 38, 38, 38, 38, 38, 39, 39, 43, 45, 45, 45, 45; **6:**1, 2, 2, 2, 5, 5, 5, 6, 13, 16, 16, 23, 23, 24, 24, 26, 28, 32, 33; **7:**4, 5, 5, 6, 7, 8, 12, 12, 13, 13, 13, 13, 14, 14, 16, 19, 20, 20, 21, 21, 23, 25, 25, 25, 27, 27, 28, 29; **8:**1, 2, 3, 4, 4, 4, 4, 8, 8, 9, 10, 10, 10, 11, 11, 11, 12, 13, 13, 15, 16, 16, 17, 17, 18, 18, 18, 19, 20, 23, 23, 24, 25, 26, 27, 27, 28, 28, 28, 28, 30, 31, 32, 32, 32, 32, 32, 32, 32, 33, 33, 33, 34; **9:**1, 2, 3, 6, 6, 6, 7, 8, 9, 11, 13, 14, 14, 14, 15, 15, 16, 16, 17, 17, 17, 17, 17, 17, 18, 19, 19, 20, 22, 23, 23, 23, 24, 24, 25, 25, 25, 26, 26, 27, 28, 31, 33, 33, 33, 34, 34, 35, 35, 35, 35, 36, 37, 37, 38, 38; **10:**2, 2, 3, 4, 5, 5, 5, 6, 7, 8, 8, 11, 13, 14, 15, 15, 17, 17, 18, 19, 19, 20, 20, 22, 23, 23, 23, 24, 24, 25, 25, 25, 25, 25, 25, 25, 25, 25, 26, 27, 27, 29, 30, 34, 40, 41, 42; **11:**1, 2, 2, 2, 3, 5, 5, 5, 5, 5, 5, 5, 7, 7, 8, 10, 10, 11, 11, 11, 12, 12, 12, 13, 13, 14, 14, 16, 18, 19, 19, 20, 21, 22, 23, 23, 23, 24, 25, 25, 27, 27, 27, 27, 27, 30; **12:**1, 1, 2, 2, 3, 4, 4, 4, 4, 5, 5, 5, 5, 6, 7, 8, 8, 9, 10, 10, 11, 12, 13, 13, 13, 14, 15, 17, 18, 20, 21, 21, 22, 23, 23, 23, 24, 24, 24, 27, 28, 28, 31, 32, 32, 32, 37, 39, 39, 39, 40, 40, 40, 40, 40, 41, 41, 42, 42, 43, 44, 45, 45, 45, 46, 50; **13:**1, 1, 2, 2, 4, 5, 6, 6, 6, 7, 10, 11, 11, 14, 15, 18, 18, 18, 19, 19, 19, 19, 19, 19, 20, 20, 21, 22, 22, 22, 22, 22, 23, 23, 24, 25, 26, 26, 27, 27, 28, 28, 29, 30, 30, 30, 30, 30, 31, 32, 32, 33, 33, 33, 34, 35, 35, 35, 36, 36, 36, 36, 36, 37, 37, 37, 38, 38, 38, 38, 38, 38, 38, 38, 39, 39, 39, 39, 39, 39, 39, 39, 39, 40, 40, 40, 41, 42, 43, 43, 44, 44, 44, 45, 45, 47, 47, 48, 48, 48, 48, 49, 49, 49, 49, 49, 49, 50, 50, 52, 52, 52, 52, 53, 54; **14:**2, 3, 5, 8, 8, 8, 9, 9, 10, 11, 13, 13, 14, 15, 15, 15, 19, 19, 19, 19, 19, 19, 19, 19, 21, 22, 22, 22, 22, 23, 24, 25, 25, 26, 29, 29, 29, 30, 32, 32, 33, 33, 34, 35, 35, 36, 36; **15:**3, 5, 6, 10, 12, 12, 14, 17, 17, 18, 19, 21, 24, 24, 24, 26, 26, 29, 30, 31, 31, 31, 31, 32, 33, 33, 35, 35, 36, 36, 36, 36, 36, 37, 38, 39, 39; **16:**1, 2, 3, 3, 3, 3, 3, 4, 4, 4, 5, 5, 5, 6, 6, 9, 9, 10, 11, 11, 12, 12, 13, 13, 14, 14, 16, 16, 16, 18, 19, 19, 20, 21, 21, 21, 21, 21, 24, 26, 26, 27, 27, 28; **17:**1, 2, 2, 5, 6, 6, 9, 9, 9, 10, 10, 12, 13, 13, 14, 14, 15, 15, 17, 18, 18, 18, 19, 22, 23, 23, 24, 24, 24, 25, 25, 26, 26, 27, 27, 27, 27, 27; **18:**1, 1, 2, 3, 4, 4, 6, 6, 7, 7, 8, 10, 12, 12, 12, 13, 14, 15, 15, 17, 17, 17, 23, 24, 25, 25, 26, 26, 27, 28, 28, 28, 30, 30, 31, 31, 32, 32, 34, 34; **19:**1, 1, 1, 4, 4, 5, 12, 12, 13, 14, 14, 17, 18, 20, 21, 21, 22, 23, 23, 24, 24, 25, 25, 28, 28, 28, 30, 30; **20:**1, 1, 2, 3, 3, 4, 4, 5, 7, 7, 7, 8, 8, 8, 12, 13, 14, 15, 17, 17, 18, 18, 18, 19, 19, 19, 20, 20, 21, 22, 23, 23, 24, 25, 28, 29, 29, 30, 31, 32; **21:**1, 1, 1, 2, 3, 4, 5, 6, 7, 7, 8, 8, 8, 8, 9, 9, 9, 9, 9, 9, 9, 10, 11, 11, 12, 12, 12, 12, 12, 13, 14, 14, 14, 15, 15, 15, 15, 15, 16, 18, 19, 19, 20, 20, 21, 23, 23, 23, 23, 24, 26, 28, 28, 29, 30, 30, 31, 31, 31, 32, 32, 33, 33, 34, 34, 34, 35, 36, 36, 36, 37, 38, 38, 38, 39, 40, 40, 41, 41, 41, 41, 42, 42, 42, 42, 42, 43, 43, 45, 45, 46; **22:**1, 2, 2, 3, 4, 5, 7, 7, 8, 8, 8, 9, 10, 10, 11, 11, 11, 12, 13, 13, 15, 16, 16, 16, 17, 19, 19, 19, 24, 24, 25, 25, 25, 26, 26, 26, 28, 28, 29, 29, 30, 30, 31, 31, 32, 32, 32, 32, 32, 32, 33, 34, 34, 36, 36, 37, 38, 40, 40, 40, 41, 42, 42, 43, 43, 44, 45; **23:**1, 2, 2, 2, 2, 4, 6, 6, 6, 7, 7, 8, 10, 11, 13, 15, 16, 16, 17, 17, 17, 18, 18, 18, 19, 19, 19, 19, 20, 21, 22, 22, 23, 23, 23, 23, 25, 25, 25, 26, 26, 26, 27, 27, 29, 29, 29, 30, 31, 31, 33, 35, 35, 35, 35, 36, 36, 36, 37, 37, 39, 39, 39; **24:**1, 1, 3, 3, 3, 3, 5, 6, 7, 7, 8, 8, 9, 12, 13, 14, 14, 14, 14, 15, 15, 15, 15, 16, 17, 18, 20, 21, 22, 22, 23, 26, 26, 27, 27, 27, 28, 28, 29, 29, 29, 29, 29, 30, 30, 30, 30, 30, 30, 30, 30, 31, 31, 31, 32, 33, 33, 34, 36, 36, 36, 36, 36, 37, 38, 38, 38, 39, 39, 39, 40, 40, 41, 41, 43, 44, 44, 45, 45, 46, 46, 47, 48, 49, 50, 51, 51; **25:**1, 1, 1, 3, 4, 5, 6, 6, 7, 8, 8, 9, 10, 10, 10, 11, 11, 13, 14, 14, 15, 16, 16, 16, 17, 17, 18, 18, 18, 18, 20, 20, 20, 21, 22, 22, 22, 22, 23, 24, 24, 25, 26, 27, 28, 28, 28, 31, 31, 32, 32, 32, 33, 33, 34, 34, 34, 34, 34, 40, 40, 41, 41, 41, 41, 45, 46; **26:**2, 2, 3, 3, 3, 5, 6, 8, 9, 9, 11, 13, 13, 14, 14, 16, 17, 17, 17, 17, 18, 18, 18, 19, 19, 20, 20, 21, 22, 24, 24, 25, 25, 26, 28, 28, 29, 30, 31, 31, 31, 31, 32, 34, 34, 35, 35, 38, 39, 40, 41, 41, 44, 45, 45, 45, 45, 47, 47, 47, 48, 49, 50, 51, 51, 52, 52, 54, 55, 55, 56, 56, 56, 56, 57, 57, 57, 57, 58, 58, 58, 59, 59, 61, 62, 63, 63, 63, 63, 63, 64, 64, 64, 64, 65, 69, 69, 71, 72, 74, 74, 75; **27:**1, 1, 1, 2, 3, 3, 5, 5, 5, 6, 6, 6, 6, 7, 8, 8, 9, 9, 9, 9, 10, 10, 11, 11, 11, 11, 12, 14, 15, 15, 15, 17, 17, 18, 19, 20, 20, 21, 21, 22, 23, 23, 24, 24, 24, 25, 26, 27, 27, 29, 30, 30, 31, 32, 34, 35, 35, 37, 37, 37, 37, 39, 40, 40, 40, 41, 41, 41, 42, 42, 43, 44, 44, 45, 47, 47, 49, 51, 51, 51, 52, 52, 53, 53, 54, 54, 54, 54, 54, 56, 56, 59, 60, 60, 61, 62, 62, 62, 62, 63, 64, 64, 65, 66; **28:**1, 1, 1, 2, 2, 4, 5, 5, 6, 7, 8, 8, 8, 8, 11, 11, 11, 11, 11, 12, 12, 13, 13, 14, 15, 15,

15, 16, 16, 19, 19, 19, 19, 19, 20, 20, 20; **Mk 1:**1, 1, 1, 2, 2, 3, 3, 4, 4, 5, 5, 8, 9, 10, 10, 10, 12, 12, 13, 15, 15, 16, 16, 19, 20, 20, 21, 21, 21, 22, 23, 24, 25, 26, 26, 27, 28, 29, 31, 31, 33, 34, 35, 35, 36, 39, 39, 42, 42, 44, 44, 44, 44, 45, 45, 45; **2:**1, 1, 2, 2, 2, 4, 4, 4, 5, 6, 9, 10, 10, 10, 12, 12, 12, 13, 13, 15, 16, 18, 18, 19, 19, 21, 21, 22, 22, 22, 22, 24, 24, 24, 25, 26, 26, 26, 26, 26, 27, 27, 28, 28; **3:**1, 2, 2, 2, 3, 4, 5, 5, 6, 6, 7, 8, 8, 9, 11, 13, 16, 16, 17, 18, 20, 20, 22, 22, 22, 29, 31; **4:**1, 1, 2, 4, 5, 6, 6, 6, 7, 10, 10, 11, 11, 12, 13, 14, 14, 15, 15, 15, 16, 16, 17, 18, 18, 19, 19, 19, 19, 20, 21, 24, 24, 26, 27, 27, 27, 28, 28, 28, 29, 29, 30, 31, 32, 33, 34, 35, 35, 36, 36, 37, 38, 38, 39, 39, 39, 41; **5:**1, 1, 1, 1, 2, 3, 4, 4, 5, 5, 5, 6, 7, 8, 8, 9, 10, 11, 12, 13, 13, 13, 13, 13, 13, 14, 14, 14, 14, 15, 16, 16, 17, 18, 18, 19, 20, 20, 20, 21, 21, 21, 22, 24, 25, 26, 27, 27, 29, 30, 33, 33, 35, 35, 37, 38, 38, 38, 38, 39, 39, 40, 40, 40, 40, 42; **6:**1, 2, 2, 2, 3, 3, 12, 14, 14, 15, 15, 15, 16, 16, 21, 22, 22, 24, 25, 25, 25, 25, 26, 27, 27, 27, 28, 30, 31, 33, 34, 35, 36, 36, 39, 39, 41, 41, 41, 41, 41, 41, 45, 45, 45, 46, 47, 47, 47, 47, 48, 48, 48, 49, 51, 51, 52, 52, 52, 53, 53, 53, 54, 55, 56, 56, 56, 56, 56; **7:**2, 3, 3, 4, 5, 5, 13, 14, 17, 17, 19, 20, 24, 24, 26, 27, 27, 27, 28, 28, 28, 30, 31, 31, 31, 32, 32, 33, 33, 33, 33, 35, 36, 36, 36, 36; **8:**1, 3, 4, 6, 6, 6, 6, 6, 7, 8, 9, 10, 11, 13, 13, 13, 14, 14, 15, 15, 15, 19, 20, 22, 23, 23, 23, 23, 24, 25, 25, 26, 27, 28, 28, 29, 31, 31, 31, 31, 34, 35, 35, 36, 36, 38, 38, 38; **9:**1, 2, 2, 7, 9, 9, 9, 10, 11, 11, 12, 12, 13, 14, 14, 14, 15, 17, 17, 18, 18, 18, 19, 20, 20, 20, 20, 20, 21, 22, 22, 24, 25, 25, 26, 26, 26, 26, 27, 28, 31, 31, 33, 33, 34, 35, 35, 35, 36, 41, 42, 42, 43, 47, 48, 48, 50; **10:**1, 1, 1, 1, 6, 8, 10, 10, 13, 14, 14, 15, 16, 19, 20, 21, 21, 22, 23, 24, 25, 25, 26, 26, 28, 29, 30, 31, 31, 32, 32, 32, 32, 33, 33, 33, 33, 35, 37, 38, 38, 40, 40, 41, 42, 44, 45, 46, 48, 49, 51, 52, 52; **11:**1, 1, 3, 4, 4, 4, 7, 8, 8, 8, 8, 9, 9, 9, 9, 9, 9, 10, 11, 11, 11, 12, 13, 14, 14, 15, 15, 15, 15, 15, 17, 18, 18, 19, 19, 20, 20, 20, 20, 21, 21, 21, 22, 23, 27, 27, 27, 27, 28, 28, 32; **12:**1, 1, 2, 3, 3, 4, 4, 5, 6, 7, 7, 7, 8, 9, 9, 9, 10, 10, 10, 10, 11, 12, 12, 12, 13, 14, 14, 18, 19, 19, 20, 21, 21, 21, 22, 22, 23, 24, 24, 25, 25, 26, 26, 26, 26, 26, 26, 26, 27, 27, 27, 28, 28, 28, 28, 29, 29, 29, 30, 31, 32, 32, 33, 33, 34, 35, 35, 35, 35, 35, 36, 36, 36, 37, 37, 38, 38, 39, 39, 40, 40, 41, 41, 41, 43; **13:**1, 1, 1, 3, 3, 3, 3, 6, 7, 8, 8, 8, 9, 9, 10, 11, 13, 14, 14, 14, 15, 15, 16, 19, 20, 20, 20, 21, 24, 24, 25, 25, 25, 26, 26, 27, 27, 27, 28, 29, 29, 30, 32, 32, 32, 32, 34, 34, 34, 34, 35; **14:**1, 1, 1, 1, 2, 3, 3, 3, 4, 5, 5, 7, 9, 9, 10, 10, 11, 11, 12, 12, 12, 12, 12, 13, 13, 14, 14, 14, 14, 14, 15, 16, 16, 16, 17, 17, 18, 18, 19, 21, 21, 22, 24, 25, 26, 27, 27, 27, 28, 30, 30, 31, 31, 34, 35, 35, 37, 38, 38, 41, 41, 41, 41, 43, 43, 43, 43, 44, 45, 46, 47, 49, 49, 51, 53, 53, 54, 54, 54, 54, 55, 55, 60, 60, 61, 61, 61, 61, 62, 62, 62, 63, 65, 66, 66, 66, 67, 67, 68, 69, 69, 72, 72, 72; **15:**1, 1, 1, 1, 2, 2, 3, 6, 6, 7, 8, 9, 9, 10, 11, 11, 11, 12, 12, 14, 14, 15, 15, 16, 16, 18, 19, 20, 21, 21, 24, 25, 25, 26, 26, 26, 26, 29, 29, 30, 31, 32, 32, 33, 35, 35, 38, 38, 39, 39, 40, 40, 42, 42, 42, 43, 43, 44, 45, 45, 45, 46, 46, 46, 46, 47; **16:**1, 1, 1, 2, 3, 3, 3, 3, 4, 5, 5, 5, 6, 6, 6, 8, 8, 9, 9, 9, 10, 12, 13, 14, 15, 15, 18, 19, 19, 20, 20, 99; **Lk 1:**1, 2, 2, 3, 4, 5, 5, 6, 8, 9, 9, 9, 9, 10, 11, 11, 11, 11, 13, 15, 15, 15, 16, 17, 17, 17, 17, 17, 17, 17, 18, 19, 19, 20, 20, 21, 22, 23, 25, 26, 26, 28, 29, 30, 32, 32, 32, 32, 34, 35, 35, 35, 35, 35, 35, 38, 38, 39, 39, 40, 41, 41, 43, 44, 45, 46, 49, 51, 52, 53, 53, 58, 58, 59, 59, 59, 62, 65, 65, 65, 66, 66, 67, 68, 68, 69, 73, 76, 76, 76, 76, 78, 79, 79, 80; **2:**1, 1, 2, 4, 6, 7, 8, 8, 9, 9, 9, 10, 11, 11, 11, 11, 13, 13, 14, 15, 15, 15, 16, 16, 16, 17, 17, 18, 20, 20, 20, 20, 21, 21, 21, 22, 22, 22, 22, 23, 23, 23, 24, 24, 25, 25, 26, 26, 27, 27, 27, 27, 27, 28, 30, 32, 32, 34, 35, 36, 36, 36, 37, 38, 39, 39, 39, 40, 41, 42, 43, 44, 46, 46; **3:**1, 1, 1, 2, 2, 3, 4, 4, 5, 5, 5, 5, 6, 7, 8, 8, 9, 9, 10, 11, 13, 15, 15, 16, 17, 17, 17, 17, 17, 18, 18, 21, 21, 22, 22, 23, 23, 24, 24, 24, 24, 24, 25, 25, 25, 25, 25, 26, 26, 26, 26, 26, 27, 27, 27, 27, 27, 28, 28, 28, 28, 28, 29, 29, 29, 29, 29, 30, 30, 30, 30, 30, 31, 31, 31, 31, 31, 32, 32, 32, 32, 32, 33, 33, 33, 33, 33, 33, 34, 34, 34, 34, 34, 35, 35, 35, 35, 35, 36, 36, 36, 36, 36, 37, 37, 37, 37, 37, 38, 38, 38, 38; **4:**1, 1, 1, 1, 2, 3, 3, 4, 5, 5, 5, 6, 6, 8, 8, 9, 9, 9, 9, 10, 12, 12, 13, 13, 14, 14, 16, 16, 16, 16, 17, 17, 17, 17, 17, 18, 18, 18, 18, 18, 19, 19, 20, 20, 20, 22, 24, 25, 26, 27, 27, 28, 28, 29, 29, 29, 29, 30, 31, 32, 32, 33, 34, 35, 35, 35, 35, 35, 35, 36, 37, 37, 38, 39, 40, 40, 40, 41, 41, 41, 42, 42, 42, 43, 43; **5:**1, 1, 1, 2, 2, 3, 3, 3, 3, 7, 7, 9, 9, 10, 12, 12, 12, 12, 13, 13, 14, 14, 14, 15, 16, 17, 18, 19, 19, 19, 20, 21, 24, 24, 24, 25, 27, 29, 30, 33, 33, 33, 33, 34, 36, 36, 36, 37, 37, 37, 37, 39, 39, 39, 39; **6:**1, 1, 2, 2, 3, 4, 4, 4, 4, 5, 5, 6, 7, 7, 7, 7, 8, 8, 8, 9, 10, 10, 11, 15, 17, 17, 17, 17, 17, 20, 21, 22, 23, 26, 28, 29, 32, 35, 35, 39, 39, 39, 40, 40, 40, 42, 42, 42, 44, 48, 48, 48, 49; **7:**2, 3, 4, 5, 6, 6, 7, 8, 9, 9, 10, 10, 11, 12, 12, 12, 12, 13, 14, 14, 15, 16, 16, 17, 18, 18, 19, 19, 20, 20, 21, 22, 22, 22, 22, 22, 22, 22, 24, 24, 25, 27, 27, 28, 28, 29, 29, 30, 32, 33, 34, 34, 35, 36, 36, 39, 39, 39, 40, 41, 43, 43, 44, 44, 45, 46, 48, 49, 49, 50; **8:**1, 1, 1, 3, 5, 7, 9, 10, 10, 10, 11, 11, 11, 12, 12, 12, 12, 13, 13, 13, 14, 14, 14, 14, 15, 16, 16, 19, 21, 22, 22, 23, 23, 24, 24, 24, 24, 25, 26, 26, 26, 27, 28, 28, 29, 29, 29, 29, 30, 31, 31, 32, 32, 32, 33, 33, 33, 33, 33, 33, 34, 34, 34, 34, 35, 35, 36, 36, 37, 37, 37, 37, 38, 39, 39, 39, 40, 40, 40, 41, 42, 43, 44, 44, 47, 47, 49, 49, 51, 51, 52, 52, 53, 54; **9:**2, 2, 2, 5, 5, 6, 6, 6, 7, 8, 10, 10, 11, 11, 12, 12, 12, 12, 12, 14, 15, 16, 16, 16, 16, 16, 16, 19, 19, 19, 20, 22, 22, 22, 22, 22, 23, 25, 25, 26, 26, 26, 26, 27, 29, 32, 32, 35, 36, 37, 37, 38, 39, 40, 42, 42, 42, 42, 42, 43, 43, 44, 46, 48, 48, 51, 53, 53, 58, 59, 60, 60, 62, 62; **10:**1, 1, 2, 2, 2, 2, 4, 6, 6, 9, 9, 11, 11, 12, 12, 13, 14, 15, 15, 16, 17, 17, 19, 19, 21, 21, 21, 21, 22, 22, 22, 22, 22, 23, 26, 27, 27, 29, 30, 31, 31, 31, 32, 33, 34, 34, 35, 35, 35, 35, 35, 36, 37, 37, 37, 38, 39, 40, 40, 41; **11:**7, 7, 9, 10, 13, 14, 14, 15, 18, 19, 20, 20, 24, 24, 26, 26, 27, 27, 27, 28, 29, 29, 29, 29, 30, 30, 31, 31, 32, 32, 33, 34, 35, 37, 37, 38, 39, 39, 39, 39, 40, 40, 41, 42, 42, 42, 43, 43, 43, 43, 44, 46, 47, 48, 49, 50, 50, 50, 51, 51, 51, 51, 52, 52, 52, 53; **12:**1, 1, 1, 2, 3, 3, 3, 4, 5, 6, 7, 8, 8, 10, 10, 11, 12, 13, 24, 26, 27, 30, 31, 32, 33, 36, 36, 36, 38, 38, 39, 40, 40, 42, 42, 42, 43, 43, 44, 45, 45, 46, 46, 46, 47, 49, 51, 52, 54, 54, 55, 56, 56, 56, 58, 58, 58, 59; **13:**1, 4, 4, 4, 8, 14, 14, 14, 14, 14, 14, 15, 15, 15, 16, 16, 17, 17, 18, 19, 20, 21, 21, 22, 24, 25, 25, 25, 25, 28, 28, 29, 29, 32, 33, 34, 34, 35, 35, 35; **14:**1, 1, 1, 3, 3, 3, 4, 5, 7, 7, 7, 8, 9, 9, 9, 10, 10, 10, 11, 11, 13, 13, 13, 13, 14, 14, 15, 15, 17, 21, 21, 21, 21, 21, 21, 21, 22, 23, 23, 23, 24, 28, 28, 29, 30, 31, 32, 35; **15:**2, 4, 4, 4, 7, 8, 10, 10, 11, 12, 14, 14, 16, 16, 16, 17, 22, 22, 22, 23, 23, 24, 25, 25, 25, 26, 27, 28, 30; **16:**1, 3, 3, 4, 5, 5, 6, 6, 7, 7, 7, 8, 8, 8, 8, 11, 13, 13, 14, 15, 16, 16, 16, 16, 16, 16, 17, 17, 21, 21, 22, 22, 22, 23, 23, 23, 24, 24, 27, 29, 30, 30, 31, 31; **17:**1, 1, 2, 2, 2, 5, 5, 6, 6, 9, 10, 11, 14, 16, 17, 19, 20, 20, 20, 21, 22, 22, 22, 23, 24, 24, 24, 25, 26, 26, 26, 27, 27, 27, 27, 28, 28, 29, 30, 30, 31, 31, 31, 34, 35, 35, 37, 37, 37; **18:**4, 6, 7, 8, 10, 10, 11, 13, 14, 14, 14, 15, 16, 16, 16, 16, 17, 20, 21, 22, 22, 23, 24, 25, 25, 26, 29, 29, 30, 31, 31, 31, 31, 32, 33, 35, 36, 39, 39, 40, 41, 43; **19:**1, 2, 2, 3, 4, 7, 7, 8, 8, 10, 11, 11, 11, 15, 15, 15, 15, 16, 16, 17, 17, 18, 18, 19, 20, 20, 22, 23, 23, 24, 24, 24, 24, 24, 26, 29, 29, 31, 32, 33, 34, 34, 35, 36, 36, 37, 37, 37, 37, 38, 38, 38, 39, 39, 40, 40, 41, 42, 44, 44, 45, 45, 46, 47, 47, 47, 47, 47, 48; **20:**1, 1, 1, 2, 2, 6, 9, 10, 10, 10, 11, 11, 12, 13, 14, 14, 14, 15, 15, 15, 16, 17, 17, 17, 17, 19, 19, 19, 19, 20, 20, 21, 22, 26, 26, 28, 28, 29, 30, 31, 31, 32, 33, 35, 35, 35, 37, 37, 37, 37, 37, 37, 38, 38, 38, 39, 41, 41, 42, 42, 44, 45, 46, 46, 46, 47, 47; **21:**1, 1, 1, 3, 5, 5, 5, 5, 6, 8, 8, 9, 11, 14, 15, 20, 21, 21, 22, 22, 23, 24, 24, 24, 24, 24, 24, 25, 25, 25, 25, 26, 26, 26, 26, 26, 27, 27, 29, 30, 31, 31, 32, 34, 35, 36, 37, 37, 37, 38; **22:**1, 1, 2, 3, 4, 4, 4, 6, 7, 7, 8, 10, 11, 11, 11, 11, 12, 13, 13, 14, 14, 14, 16, 18, 19, 20, 20, 21, 22, 23, 24, 24, 25, 25, 26, 26, 26, 27, 27, 29, 30, 34, 35, 37, 37, 39, 39, 39, 44, 45, 48, 49, 49, 50, 51, 51, 52, 52, 52, 52, 53, 53, 53, 54, 55, 55, 56, 57, 60, 61, 61, 61, 62, 63, 66, 66, 66, 66, 67, 69, 69, 69, 70; **23:**1, 1, 2, 2, 3, 3, 4, 4, 7, 8, 10, 10, 13, 13, 15, 15, 18, 19, 22, 23, 25, 26, 29, 29, 29, 29, 30, 30, 31, 33, 33, 33, 34, 35, 35, 35, 36, 37, 37, 38, 38, 38, 39, 39, 40, 44, 45, 45, 45, 45, 47, 47, 47, 48, 48, 49, 50, 51, 51, 51, 51, 53, 53, 54, 54, 55, 55, 56, 56, 56; **24:**1, 1, 1, 2, 2, 3, 3, 5, 5, 6, 7, 7, 7, 10, 10, 10, 10, 11, 12, 12, 13, 18, 18, 18, 19, 19, 19, 21, 24, 25, 25, 26, 26, 27, 27, 27, 28, 29, 32, 32, 33, 33, 33, 33, 34, 35, 35, 35, 37, 44, 44, 46, 46, 46, 47, 49, 49, 49, 53; **Jn 1:**1, 1, 2, 5, 5, 5, 6, 7, 8, 8, 9, 9, 9, 10, 10, 12, 14, 14, 14, 14, 15, 15, 15, 16, 17, 18, 19, 19, 19, 20, 21, 23, 23, 23, 24, 25, 25, 26, 28, 29, 29, 29, 29, 30, 31, 32, 33, 33, 33, 33, 33, 34, 35, 36, 39, 39, 39, 39, 41, 41, 41, 42, 43, 45, 45, 45, 48, 49, 49, 50, 51, 51, 51; **2:**1, 1, 2, 3, 3, 3, 5, 7, 7, 7, 7, 8, 9, 9, 9, 9, 10, 10, 10, 12, 13, 14, 15, 15, 15, 15, 16, 17, 18, 22, 22, 22, 23, 23, 23; **3:**3, 5, 5, 5, 6, 8, 8, 13, 14, 14, 14, 16, 17, 18, 19, 19, 19, 19, 20, 20, 20, 21, 23, 26, 26, 26, 26, 26, 28, 28, 29, 29, 29, 31, 31, 35, 36, 36; **4:**1, 4, 5, 5, 6, 6, 8, 8, 9, 10, 14, 15, 17, 18, 19, 20, 21, 21, 22, 22, 23, 23, 23, 25, 25, 25, 26, 28, 28, 28, 29, 30, 30, 31, 33, 34, 35, 35, 35, 36, 36, 36, 36, 37, 38, 38, 39, 39, 42, 42, 42, 43, 43, 45, 45, 46, 46, 46, 46, 49, 50, 51, 52, 53, 53, 53; **5:**1, 2, 2, 2, 3, 5, 7, 7, 7, 9, 9, 9, 10, 10, 10, 11, 13, 13, 14, 15, 15, 16, 16, 18, 18, 18, 19, 19, 19, 19, 20, 20, 20, 21, 21, 22, 23, 23, 23, 23, 25, 25, 25, 25, 26, 27, 28, 28, 28, 30, 30, 33, 33, 34, 36, 36, 37, 38, 39, 39, 44, 45; **6:**1, 1, 2, 3, 4, 5, 10, 10, 11, 11, 11, 11, 12, 13, 13, 14, 14, 15, 16, 17, 17, 18, 19, 19, 21, 22, 22, 22, 22, 23, 23, 23, 23, 24, 24, 26, 26, 27, 27, 27, 29, 31, 31, 32, 33, 33, 33, 35, 37, 38, 39, 39, 40, 41, 41, 42, 44, 44, 44, 45, 45, 46, 48, 49, 50, 51, 51, 52, 53, 53, 54, 55, 55, 57, 57, 57, 58, 58, 59, 62, 63, 63, 64, 65, 67, 68, 69, 70, 71; **7:**1, 2, 3, 4, 6, 7, 10, 11, 11, 12, 12, 13, 13, 14, 14, 15, 17, 18, 19, 20, 21, 22, 22, 23, 23, 23, 23, 25, 25, 26, 27, 28, 30, 31, 31, 31, 32, 32, 32, 33, 35, 35, 35, 35, 37, 37, 37, 37, 38, 39, 39, 40, 40, 41, 41, 42, 42, 42, 42, 43, 45, 45, 46, 47, 50, 52, 53; **8:**1, 2, 2, 3, 3, 3, 4, 5, 6, 7, 8, 9, 9, 9, 9, 9, 12, 12, 12, 12, 12, 13, 16, 18, 20, 20, 20, 22, 25, 26, 28, 28, 28, 29, 31, 32, 32, 35, 35, 36, 38, 40, 44, 44, 44, 44, 44, 44, 45, 46, 47, 48, 50, 52, 52, 53, 57, 58, 59; **9:**3, 4, 4, 4, 5, 5, 5, 6, 6, 6, 6, 7, 7, 8, 9, 9, 11, 11, 11, 13, 13, 14, 15, 15, 15, 16, 16, 17, 17, 17, 18, 22, 22, 22, 24, 24, 24, 25, 27, 30, 32, 32, 34, 35, 35, 36, 38, 39, 39, 40; **10:**1, 1, 2, 3, 3, 3, 7, 7, 8, 9, 10, 11, 11, 11, 12, 12, 12, 13, 13, 14, 15, 15, 17, 18, 18, 19, 21, 21, 22, 23, 23, 24, 24, 25, 25, 30, 31, 32, 34, 35, 36, 36, 36, 36, 38, 38, 40, 40; **11:**2, 2, 2, 3, 3, 4, 4, 6, 8, 9, 12, 16, 18, 19, 25, 25, 27, 27, 27, 27, 28, 28, 30, 30, 31, 31, 33, 36, 38, 39, 39, 39, 41, 42, 45, 46, 47, 47, 47, 48, 48, 50, 50, 51, 52, 52, 52, 53, 54, 54, 54, 55, 55, 55, 55, 56, 56, 57; **12:**1, 1, 1, 1, 2, 3, 4, 5, 5, 6, 6, 8, 9, 9, 9, 10, 11, 12, 12, 12, 12, 13, 13, 13, 13, 13, 14, 16, 17, 18, 19, 19, 20, 23, 23, 24, 24, 26, 27, 29, 29, 30, 31, 31, 31, 32, 34, 34, 34, 35, 35, 36, 36, 37, 37, 38, 38, 39, 40, 41, 42, 42, 42, 43, 44, 45, 46, 47, 48, 48, 49, 50; **13:**1, 1, 1, 2, 3, 4, 5, 5, 10, 14, 16, 16, 17, 18, 18, 19, 20, 21, 22, 23, 23, 26, 26, 26, 27, 28, 28, 29, 29, 30, 31, 31, 31, 33, 35, 38; **14:**5, 6, 6, 6, 6, 8, 9, 9, 10, 10, 10, 11, 11, 12, 12, 12, 13, 13, 13, 16, 17, 17, 19, 21, 22, 22, 24, 26, 26, 26, 26, 27, 27, 27, 28, 30, 31, 31, 31; **15:**1, 1, 2, 3, 4, 5, 5, 9, 12, 13, 15, 16, 18, 19, 19, 20, 21, 21, 25, 26, 26, 26, 27; **16:**2, 2, 3, 5, 7, 8, 8, 9, 10, 11, 13, 13, 15, 15, 17, 17, 20, 21, 21, 23, 23, 25, 25, 26, 27, 28, 28, 28, 28, 32, 32, 33; **17:**1, 2, 3, 3, 3, 5, 5, 6, 8, 9, 11, 12, 12, 14, 14, 15, 15, 18, 18, 21, 22, 23, 24, 24, 25; **18:**1, 2, 3, 3, 6, 8, 10, 10, 11, 11, 12, 12, 13, 13, 14, 14, 15, 15, 15, 16, 16, 16, 16, 17, 18, 18, 19, 20, 20, 22, 22, 22, 22, 23, 24, 25, 26, 26, 26, 26, 28, 28, 28, 28, 28, 29, 31, 31, 32, 33, 33, 36, 37, 37, 38, 39, 39; **19:**2, 3, 4, 5, 5, 5, 6, 7, 7, 9, 10, 11, 11, 12, 13, 13, 13, 14, 14, 14, 15, 17, 17, 19, 19, 20, 20, 20, 21, 21, 21, 21, 23, 23, 23, 24, 25, 25, 26, 28, 31, 31, 31, 31, 31, 32, 32, 32, 34, 36, 38, 38, 39, 40, 40, 41, 42, 42, 42; **20:**1, 1, 1, 2, 2, 2, 2, 3, 3, 4, 5, 6, 7, 7, 8, 9, 9, 11, 12, 12, 12, 13, 15, 17, 18, 18, 19, 19, 19, 19, 21, 22, 24, 24, 24, 25, 25, 25, 26, 26, 27, 30, 31, 31; **21:**1, 1, 2, 2, 2, 3, 4, 4, 6, 6, 6, 7, 7, 7, 7, 8, 8, 8, 8, 10, 11, 11, 11, 12, 13, 13, 14, 14, 16, 17, 18, 20, 20, 23, 23, 25, 25, 25; **Ac 1:**2, 2, 3, 3, 3, 4, 5, 6, 7, 8, 8, 8, 9, 11, 12, 12, 12, 13, 13, 13, 13, 14, 14, 16, 16, 16, 17, 18, 19, 19, 19, 19, 20, 21, 21, 22, 22, 24, 25, 26; **2:**1, 1, 2, 2, 2, 4, 4, 6, 8, 8, 9, 10, 11, 13, 14, 14, 15, 16, 17, 19, 19, 20, 20, 20, 21, 21, 23, 23, 24, 25, 27, 27, 28, 30, 31, 31, 31, 31, 31, 32, 33, 33, 33, 34, 37, 38, 38, 38, 38, 39, 39, 41, 42, 42, 42, 43, 44, 45, 46, 46, 47, 47, 47, 47; **3:**1, 1, 2, 2, 2, 2, 2, 2, 5, 6, 7, 7, 7, 8, 9, 10, 10, 11, 12, 13, 13, 13, 13, 13, 14, 15, 16, 17, 18, 18, 20, 20, 21, 21, 22, 25, 25, 25; **4:**1, 1, 1, 1, 1, 2, 2, 4, 4, 5, 5, 5, 6, 6, 7, 8, 10, 10, 10, 10, 11, 11, 11, 11, 13, 13, 13, 14, 14, 15, 18, 20, 21, 22, 23, 23, 24, 24, 25, 25, 25, 26, 26, 26, 26, 27, 27, 27, 30, 31, 31, 32, 33, 33, 33, 35, 35, 36, 36, 36, 36, 37, 37; **5:**2, 2, 2, 3, 3, 4, 4, 5, 8, 8, 9, 9, 9, 9, 10, 10, 11, 12, 12, 12, 12, 12, 14, 15, 15, 16, 17, 18, 18, 19, 19, 19, 20, 20, 21, 21, 21, 21, 21, 21, 22, 22, 22, 22, 23, 23, 23, 24, 24, 24, 25, 25, 25, 25, 26, 26, 26, 27, 27, 28, 29, 30, 30, 31, 31, 32, 33, 34, 34, 34, 36, 37, 37, 40, 40, 40, 41, 41, 41, 42, 42; **6:**1, 1, 2, 2, 2, 3, 4, 5, 5, 5, 5, 6, 7, 7, 8, 9, 9, 10, 12, 12, 12, 12, 13, 13, 13, 14, 14, 15; **7:**1, 3, 4, 4, 4, 5, 7, 7, 8, 8, 8, 8, 8, 10, 10, 13, 16, 16, 17, 17, 18, 22, 22, 23, 24, 26, 27, 27, 29, 29, 30, 30, 31, 31, 32, 32, 33, 34, 35, 35, 35, 36, 36, 37, 38, 38, 38, 38, 38, 42, 42, 42, 42, 43, 43, 43, 44, 44, 44, 45, 45, 45, 45, 46, 46, 48, 48, 49, 49, 51, 51, 52, 52, 52, 52, 53, 54, 55, 55, 55, 56, 56, 56, 58, 58, 58; **8:**1, 1, 1, 1, 1, 3, 4, 4, 5, 5, 5, 6, 10, 10, 10, 10, 10, 11, 12, 12, 12, 13, 14, 14, 15, 16, 16, 16, 17, 18, 18, 19, 22, 24, 25, 25, 25, 25, 26, 26, 27, 27, 27, 28, 28, 29, 29, 30, 30, 31, 31, 32, 32, 32, 33, 34, 35, 36, 38, 38, 39, 39, 39, 39, 40, 40, 40; **9:**1, 1, 2, 2, 2, 4, 5, 5, 6, 7, 7, 8, 9, 10, 11, 11, 13, 13, 14, 15, 15, 15, 17, 17, 17, 19, 20, 20, 21, 21, 22, 22, 23, 24, 25, 25, 25, 26, 27, 27, 27, 27, 27, 28, 28, 28, 30, 31, 31, 31, 31, 31, 31, 32, 32, 32, 35, 35, 36, 39, 39, 39, 40, 40, 41, 41, 42, 42, 42; **10:**1, 2, 3, 4, 4, 4, 6, 7, 9, 9, 9, 11, 12, 15, 16, 16, 17, 17, 17, 17, 18, 19, 19, 21, 22, 22, 23, 23, 23, 24, 25, 27, 28, 30, 31, 32, 32, 33, 33, 36, 36, 37, 38, 38, 41, 41, 42, 42, 42, 43, 43, 44, 44, 45, 45, 45, 45, 47, 47, 48; **11:**1, 1, 1, 1, 2, 3, 5, 6, 9, 10, 11, 12, 12, 12, 15, 15, 15, 16, 16, 17, 17, 18, 18, 18, 19, 19, 19, 20, 20, 21, 21, 21, 22, 23, 23, 24, 24, 26, 26, 28, 28, 28, 28, 29, 29, 30, 30; **12:**1, 2, 3, 3, 4, 4, 5, 6, 6, 7, 7, 7, 7, 7, 8, 8, 9, 9, 9, 10, 10, 10, 10, 10, 11, 11, 12, 12, 13, 13, 14, 14, 16, 17, 17, 18, 19, 20, 21, 22, 22, 23, 23, 23; **13:**1, 1, 1, 1, 2, 2, 2, 3, 4, 4, 4, 5, 5, 5, 6, 7, 7, 7, 8, 8, 8, 8, 9, 9, 9, 10, 10, 10, 11, 12, 12, 13, 14, 14, 14, 15, 15, 15, 15, 16, 17, 18, 20, 20, 21, 21, 22, 24, 24, 25, 26, 27, 27, 27, 27, 29, 29, 30, 31, 33, 34, 34, 34, 35, 36, 39, 40, 42, 42, 42, 43, 43, 44, 44, 44, 44, 45, 45, 47, 47, 47, 47, 48, 48, 49, 50, 50, 50, 50, 51, 51, 52, 52; **14:**1, 2, 2, 3, 3, 3, 3, 4, 4, 4, 4, 6, 6, 6, 6, 7, 10, 11, 12, 12, 13, 13, 13, 13, 13, 13, 13, 13, 14, 15, 15, 15, 16, 18, 19, 19, 20, 20, 20, 21, 22, 22, 22, 23, 23, 26, 26, 27, 27, 27, 28; **15:**1, 1, 2, 3, 3, 3, 3, 3, 4, 4, 5, 5, 6, 7, 7, 7, 8, 10, 11, 11, 11, 12, 12, 14, 14, 15, 16, 16, 17, 17, 17, 17, 19, 20, 22, 22, 22, 22, 23, 23, 23, 26, 28, 29, 30, 30, 30, 31, 32, 33, 33, 35, 35, 36, 36, 36, 40, 40, 41; **16:**2, 3, 3, 4, 4, 4, 5, 6, 6, 6, 7, 7, 7, 8, 10, 11, 11, 12, 13, 13, 14, 15, 16, 17, 18, 18, 19, 19, 20, 21, 22, 23, 24, 24, 25, 26, 26, 26, 27, 27, 27, 29, 29, 31, 32, 32, 33, 35, 35, 35, 35, 36, 38, 38, 39, 39, 40, 40; **17:**1, 2, 2, 2, 3, 3, 3, 3, 3, 4, 5, 5, 5, 5, 6, 6, 6, 6, 8, 8, 8, 9, 9, 10, 10, 11, 11, 11, 12, 13, 14, 14, 16, 16, 17, 17, 17, 17, 18, 19, 21, 21, 21, 22, 24, 24, 26, 26, 27, 31, 31, 31, 32, 34; **18:**4, 4, 5, 5, 6, 6, 6, 7, 8, 8, 8, 9, 11, 11, 12, 13, 16, 17, 17, 17, 17, 18, 18, 19, 19, 19, 19, 22, 22, 22, 23, 23, 24, 25, 25, 26, 26, 27, 27, 28, 28, 28; **19:**1, 2, 3, 4, 4, 5, 5, 6, 8, 8, 8, 9, 9, 9, 9, 10, 10, 10, 11, 13, 13, 13, 15, 16, 17, 17, 17, 17, 19, 19, 20, 20, 21, 22, 23, 24, 25, 26, 27, 27, 27, 27, 27, 28, 29, 29, 30, 31, 31, 31, 32, 33, 33, 34, 34, 34, 35, 35, 35, 35, 37, 38, 38, 38, 38, 40; **20:**1, 2, 2, 2, 4, 4, 6, 7, 7, 7, 7, 8, 9, 11, 12, 15, 15, 15, 15, 16, 16, 17, 17, 18, 18, 19, 19, 19, 19, 20, 21, 22, 23, 24, 24, 24, 24, 25, 28, 29, 30, 31, 32, 34, 35, 35, 35, 38; **21:**1, 1, 1, 2, 3, 3, 3, 4, 4, 5, 5, 5, 5, 5, 7, 7, 8, 8, 8, 9, 10, 11, 11, 11, 11, 12, 13, 13, 14, 14, 16, 16, 17, 18, 18, 18, 19, 19, 20, 21, 21, 21, 24, 24, 24, 24, 25, 26, 26, 26, 26, 26, 27, 27, 27, 28, 28, 28, 29, 29, 30, 30, 30, 30, 31, 31, 32, 32, 32, 32, 33, 33, 34, 34, 34, 35, 35, 35, 36, 37, 37, 38, 38, 38, 40, 40, 40, 40; **22:**2, 4, 4, 5, 5, 5, 6, 7, 8, 9, 9, 9, 10, 11, 12, 12, 14, 14, 15, 16, 16, 17, 18, 20, 21, 21, 22, 23, 24, 24, 25, 26, 26, 27, 28, 29, 29, 30, 30, 30, 30, 30; **23:**1, 2, 2, 3, 4, 5, 5, 6, 6, 6, 7, 7, 7, 8, 8, 9, 10, 10, 10, 10, 11, 11, 11, 12, 14, 15, 15, 15, 15, 16, 17, 17, 18, 18, 19, 19, 20, 21, 22, 22, 23, 25, 27, 31, 32, 32, 32, 33, 35, 35, 35; **24:**1, 1, 1, 2, 2, 5, 5, 5, 5, 5, 6, 8, 9, 10, 11, 12, 12, 12, 13, 14, 14, 14, 14, 15, 15, 18, 19, 20, 21, 21, 22, 22, 22, 22, 25, 27; **25:**2, 6, 7, 8, 8, 8, 8, 9, 10, 14, 15, 17, 17, 17, 18, 21, 22, 23, 23, 23, 24, 24, 25, 26, 27, 27; **26:**2, 2, 4, 5, 5, 6, 7, 7, 8, 9, 10, 10, 11, 12, 12, 13, 15, 15, 16, 17, 17, 18, 20, 20, 21, 22, 22, 22, 23, 23, 23, 25, 27, 29, 30, 30, 30; **27:**1, 1, 1, 2, 2, 3, 4, 4, 4, 5, 5, 5, 6, 7, 7, 7, 8, 8, 9, 9, 9, 11, 11, 11, 11, 12, 12, 12, 12, 13, 13, 14, 14, 15, 15, 15, 16, 17, 17, 17, 17, 17, 17, 17, 18, 18, 18, 18, 19, 19, 20, 20, 20, 21, 21, 22, 23, 27, 27, 27, 27, 28, 29, 29, 29, 30, 30, 30, 30, 31, 31, 31, 32, 32, 32, 33, 33, 37, 38, 38, 38, 39, 39, 39, 40, 40, 40, 40, 41, 41, 41, 41, 41, 41, 42, 42, 43, 44, 44; **28:**1, 2, 2, 2, 3, 3, 4, 4, 4, 5, 5, 6, 7, 7, 7, 9, 9, 10, 10, 11, 11, 11, 13, 13, 15, 15, 15, 15, 17, 17, 17, 18, 18, 19, 19, 20, 20, 22, 23, 23, 23, 23, 23, 23, 23, 25, 25, 27, 28, 30, 31, 31; **Ro 1:**2, 3, 4, 4, 4, 5, 7, 8, 9, 10, 10, 11, 12, 14, 16, 17, 18, 19, 20, 20, 20, 21, 23, 25, 25, 25, 26, 26, 27, 27; **2:**5, 5, 7, 8, 9, 9, 10, 10, 12, 12, 12, 13, 13, 14, 16, 19, 20, 20, 23, 24, 24, 24, 25, 26, 26, 28, 29; **3:**1, 1, 2, 2, 4, 4, 5, 6, 8, 8, 9, 10, 13, 13, 19, 19, 20, 20, 21, 21, 21, 25, 28, 29, 29, 29, 29, 31, 31; **4:**1, 3, 6, 8, 9, 10, 11, 11, 12, 12, 13, 13, 14, 15, 15, 15, 16, 16, 17, 17, 17, 17, 18, 18, 19, 24, 25; **5:**5, 6, 9, 10, 12, 13, 16, 16, 16, 17; **6:**4, 4, 4, 7, 9, 10, 11, 12, 13, 14, 15, 17, 19, 21, 21, 22, 23, 23; **7:**1, 1, 2, 2, 4, 4, 4, 4, 4, 5, 6, 6, 6, 6, 6, 6, 7, 7, 7, 7, 9, 9, 9, 10, 10, 10, 11, 11, 12, 13, 14, 14, 14, 15, 16, 20, 20, 23, 23, 25; **8:**2, 2, 2, 3, 4, 4, 4, 5, 5, 5, 6, 7, 8, 9, 9, 9, 11, 11, 11, 13, 13, 14, 18, 21, 22, 22, 23, 23, 26, 26, 27, 27, 27, 28, 29, 33, 34, 34, 36, 38, 38, 38, 39, 39, 39; **9:**1, 1, 4, 4, 6, 7, 7, 7, 8, 8, 12, 12, 13, 13, 17, 17, 17, 20, 20, 21, 22, 22, 23, 23, 23, 24, 24, 25, 25, 26, 27, 27, 27, 27, 28, 28, 29, 30, 31, 31, 32, 32, 33; **10:**1, 1, 3, 4, 4, 5, 6, 7, 7, 8, 8, 8, 9, 11, 12, 12, 13, 13, 15, 15, 16, 16, 17, 18, 18, 18, 18, 19, 19, 19; **11:**1, 1, 2, 2, 2, 2, 4, 5, 5, 7, 7, 7, 7, 7, 8, 11, 11, 12, 12, 12, 12, 13, 13, 14, 15, 15, 15, 16, 16, 16, 16, 17, 17, 18, 18, 20, 21, 21, 23, 23, 23, 24, 24, 25, 25, 26, 28, 28, 28, 30, 31, 31, 31, 34; **12:**1, 2, 2, 5, 6, 6, 8, 9, 9, 11, 13, 13, 13, 16, 19, 20, 21; **13:**1, 1, 2, 2, 3, 4, 4, 5, 6, 8, 8, 9, 11, 12, 12, 12, 12, 14; **14:**4, 4, 5, 6, 6, 6, 8, 8, 8, 10, 11, 11, 14, 14, 17, 17, 19, 20, 22; **15:**1, 2, 3, 4, 5, 5, 6, 8, 8, 9, 9, 9, 10, 11, 11, 12, 12, 12, 13, 13, 16, 16, 18, 18, 19, 19, 19, 19, 20, 20, 21, 21, 25, 26, 26, 27, 27, 27, 27, 27, 30, 30, 31, 31, 32; **16:**1, 2, 4, 4, 5, 5, 5, 7, 8, 10, 10, 11, 11, 12, 12, 13, 14, 15, 16, 19, 20, 20, 22, 23, 23, 25, 25, 25, 26, 26, 27; **1Co 1:**1, 2, 2, 3, 4, 5, 7, 8, 8, 9, 10, 10, 10, 13, 16, 17, 17, 18, 18, 18, 18, 19, 20, 20, 20, 21, 22, 22, 23, 23, 24, 24, 25, 25, 26, 27, 28, 28, 29, 30, 31, 31, 31; **2:**2, 4, 5, 6, 6, 6, 7, 7, 7, 8, 9, 12, 12, 13, 13, 14, 14, 15, 16, 16; **3:**1, 3, 5, 5, 5, 6, 7, 7, 7, 7, 8, 8, 8, 10, 11, 13, 13, 14, 14, 15, 15, 15, 16, 16, 19, 19, 20, 20, 20, 22, 22, 22; **4:**4, 5, 5, 6, 6, 9, 9, 13, 13, 15, 17, 17, 17, 19, 20; **5:**1, 1, 1, 3, 3, 4, 4, 4, 4, 4, 5, 5, 8, 8, 8, 12, 13, 13, 13; **6:**1, 2, 2, 4, 5, 7, 8, 9, 10, 11, 11, 13, 13, 13, 13, 14, 14, 16, 16, 17, 17, 18, 19, 19; **7:**1, 3, 3, 4, 4, 5, 5, 7, 7, 7, 10, 11, 12, 12, 14, 14, 15, 15, 17, 17, 18, 19, 22, 22, 22, 22, 23, 25, 25, 25, 26, 27, 28, 29, 31, 31, 32, 32, 34, 34, 34, 35, 38, 38, 39; **8:**1, 2, 3, 3, 6, 7, 10, 10; **9:**1, 2, 4, 5, 5, 5, 7, 7, 8, 9, 9, 10, 10, 12, 12, 13, 13, 13, 13, 13, 14, 14, 14, 16, 18, 18, 20, 20, 20, 20, 21, 21, 21, 21, 23, 24, 26; **10:**1, 1, 1, 2, 2, 3, 4, 4, 5, 7, 7, 9, 11, 12, 13, 13, 14, 16, 16, 16, 16, 16, 16, 16, 18, 18, 19, 19, 21, 21, 21, 21, 21, 22, 25, 26, 26, 27, 28, 28, 29, 30, 31, 32, 33; **11:**2, 5, 7, 8, 8, 10, 11, 12, 16, 16, 20, 22, 22, 23, 23, 23, 25, 25, 25, 25, 26, 27, 27, 27, 27, 28, 28, 29, 29, 29, 32, 32, 33, 34; **12:**1, 1, 3, 3, 4, 4, 5, 5, 6, 6, 7, 8, 8, 8, 9, 9, 9, 10, 10, 10, 10, 10, 10, 11, 12, 12, 12, 13, 14, 15, 15, 15, 16, 16, 16, 17, 21, 21, 21, 21, 22, 22, 23, 23, 23, 24, 25, 25, 26, 26, 28, 28, 28, 29, 30, 30, 31; **13:**2, 2, 2, 2, 3, 6, 9, 10, 13; **14:**1, 1, 1, 2, 2, 2, 3, 4, 4, 5, 5, 7, 7, 7, 7, 7, 8, 8, 9, 10, 12, 13, 13, 15, 15, 16, 17, 21, 21, 21, 22, 26, 29, 30, 30, 31, 33, 34, 34, 36, 37; **15:**1, 2, 3, 4, 4, 4, 5, 7, 8, 8, 9, 9, 9, 9, 10, 11, 12, 12, 13, 15, 15, 16, 19, 19, 20, 20, 20, 21, 21, 21, 22, 22, 24, 24, 24, 26, 27, 28, 29, 29, 31, 32, 35, 36, 37, 37, 38, 40, 40, 40, 40, 40, 41, 41, 41, 42, 42, 42, 45, 45, 45, 46, 46, 47, 47, 47, 47, 49, 49, 49, 50, 52, 52, 52, 52, 54, 56, 56, 58, 58; **16:**1, 1, 1, 1, 3, 6, 7, 8, 8, 10, 11, 12, 12, 15, 17, 19, 19, 19, 19, 20, 22, 23, 23; **2Co 1:**1, 2, 3, 3, 3, 4, 5, 5, 6, 8, 8, 9, 13, 14, 14, 17, 19, 19, 19, 21, 22, 22, 23, 23; **2:**3, 3, 5, 5, 12, 12, 12, 14, 14, 17; **3:**2, 3, 3, 6, 6, 6, 6, 6, 7, 7, 7, 8, 9, 9, 10, 10, 11, 11, 13, 13, 14, 14, 14, 16, 16, 17, 17, 17, 17, 18, 18, 18, 18; **4:**2, 2, 3, 4, 4, 4, 4, 4, 4, 4, 5, 6, 6, 6, 6, 10, 10, 11, 12, 13, 13, 14, 18, 18, 18; **5:**2, 6, 8, 10, 11,

12, 14, 16, 17, 17, 18, 19, 19, 21; **6:**2, 2, 2, 3, 3, 6, 6, 7, 15, 16, 16, 17, 18; **7:**4, 6, 7, 7, 9, 9, 10, 11, 12, 12, 13, 14, 15; **8:**1, 4, 4, 4, 5, 6, 8, 10, 10, 15, 16, 18, 18, 19, 19, 19, 20, 21, 23, 24; **9:**1, 5, 6, 7, 9, 9, 10, 10, 10, 12, 12, 13, 14; **10:**1, 4, 6, 7, 7, 8, 8, 11, 13, 14, 14, 14, 15, 16, 17, 17, 17, 18; **11:**2, 3, 4, 4, 4, 9, 10, 12, 12, 15, 17, 20, 24, 26, 26, 26, 26, 26, 28, 28, 30, 31, 31, 32, 32, 33; **12:**1, 1, 2, 6, 8, 9, 13, 13, 14, 14, 15, 15, 17, 18, 18; **13:**1, 1, 1, 1, 3, 4, 4, 4, 5, 6, 8, 8, 10, 10, 11, 12, 13, 13, 13, 13; **Gal 1:**1, 1, 2, 2, 3, 5, 6, 7, 7, 7, 8, 9, 11, 13, 13, 14, 14, 16, 16, 17, 19, 21, 22, 22, 23, 23; **2:**2, 2, 2, 5, 5, 6, 6, 6, 7, 7, 7, 7, 7, 8, 8, 8, 8, 8, 9, 9, 9, 9, 10, 10, 12, 12, 13, 14, 14, 14, 14, 14, 15, 16, 16, 16, 18, 19, 19, 20, 21, 21; **3:**1, 1, 2, 2, 2, 2, 3, 4, 5, 5, 5, 6, 7, 8, 8, 8, 9, 10, 10, 10, 11, 11, 12, 12, 13, 13, 13, 13, 13, 14, 14, 14, 14, 16, 16, 16, 17, 17, 18, 18, 18, 19, 19, 19, 19, 19, 21, 22, 22, 23, 23, 23, 24, 25, 29, 29; **4:**3, 3, 4, 4, 5, 6, 9, 12, 13, 16, 21, 21, 22, 23, 23, 23, 23, 23, 24, 24, 26, 26, 27, 27, 28, 29, 29, 29, 29, 29, 30, 30, 30, 30, 30, 30, 31, 31, 31; **5:**1, 3, 3, 4, 5, 7, 8, 9, 9, 10, 11, 11, 11, 14, 16, 17, 17, 17, 17, 18, 18, 19, 20, 21, 22, 23, 24, 25, 25; **6:**1, 1, 2, 4, 6, 8, 8, 8, 9, 10, 12, 13, 14, 14, 16, 17, 18; **Eph 1:**3, 3, 4, 6, 7, 10, 10, 11, 12, 13, 13, 13, 14, 15, 17, 18, 19, 19, 20, 20, 20, 21, 22, 22, 22, 23; **2:**2, 2, 2, 2, 2, 2, 2, 3, 5, 6, 6, 7, 9, 10, 11, 11, 12, 13, 14, 15, 15, 15, 18, 18, 20, 20, 20, 20, 21; **3:**5, 6, 6, 6, 6, 6, 6, 6, 7, 8, 8, 8, 9, 9, 10, 10, 14, 14, 15, 17, 18, 19, 19, 21; **4:**1, 3, 4, 4, 7, 8, 8, 9, 10, 10, 10, 10, 11, 11, 11, 11, 11, 11, 12, 12, 13, 13, 14, 14, 15, 15, 15, 16, 16, 16, 17, 17, 18, 21, 25, 26, 27, 30, 30, 30; **5:**2, 5, 5, 6, 7, 8, 10, 11, 12, 13, 14, 16, 17, 18, 19, 20, 20, 22, 23, 23, 23, 24, 25, 25, 28, 29, 31, 31, 32, 32, 33; **6:**1, 1, 2, 2, 3, 4, 4, 4, 6, 7, 8, 8, 9, 9, 10, 11, 12, 12, 12, 13, 13, 13, 14, 14, 15, 15, 16, 17, 17, 17, 18, 18, 19, 19, 19, 21, 23, 23; **Php 1:**1, 2, 5, 5, 6, 7, 7, 7, 8, 11, 12, 13, 13, 14, 16, 16, 18, 18, 19, 20, 25, 27, 27, 29, 29, 30, 30; **2:**1, 5, 7, 9, 10, 10, 11, 11, 13, 13, 16, 16, 17, 19, 21, 22, 24, 28, 30, 30, 30; **3:**1, 3, 3, 5, 5, 5, 5, 6, 6, 8, 10, 10, 11, 11, 13, 14, 14, 14, 16, 18, 20, 21; **4:**1, 1, 2, 3, 3, 3, 4, 5, 7, 9, 10, 10, 12, 13, 13, 15, 15, 18, 18, 21, 21, 22, 23, 23; **Col 1:**2, 3, 5, 5, 5, 6, 6, 7, 7, 8, 8, 8, 10, 10, 10, 11, 12, 12, 12, 13, 13, 13, 15, 15, 16, 16, 16, 18, 18, 18, 18, 20, 22, 22, 23, 23, 23, 23, 24, 25, 27, 27, 28; **2:**1, 3, 7, 8, 9, 10, 10, 11, 12, 12, 14, 14, 15, 15, 17, 19, 19, 20, 20; **3:**1, 1, 4, 5, 5, 8, 12, 13, 13, 14, 15, 16, 17, 17, 17, 18, 20, 22, 22, 23, 24, 24, 25; **4:**5, 6, 7, 9, 11, 11, 11, 12, 13, 16, 16, 17, 17, 18; **1Th 1:**1, 1, 1, 3, 5, 5, 5, 5, 6, 6, 6, 6, 7, 8, 8, 9, 9, 10, 10, 10, 10, 10; **2:**2, 4, 4, 4, 13, 13, 14, 14, 15, 15, 16, 16, 16; **3:**2, 3, 5, 5, 6, 8, 9, 12; **4:**1, 1, 2, 2, 5, 6, 9, 10, 12, 13, 14, 15, 15, 16, 16, 16, 16, 16, 17, 17, 17, 17; **5:**2, 2, 2, 4, 4, 4, 5, 5, 6, 7, 7, 8, 8, 8, 10, 12, 19, 23, 27, 27, 27, 28; **2Th 1:**1, 1, 2, 4, 7, 8, 9, 11, 12, 12; **2:**1, 2, 2, 3, 3, 4, 7, 7, 8, 8, 8, 8, 9, 10, 12, 12, 13, 13, 13, 13, 14, 14; **3:**1, 2, 3, 3, 4, 4, 5, 5, 5, 6, 6, 9, 12, 12, 13, 16, 16, 17, 18; **1Ti 1:**1, 2, 5, 5, 7, 10, 11, 13, 14, 14, 15, 15, 16, 17, 17, 18, 18, 18; **2:**4, 5, 6, 6, 6, 7, 7, 9, 10, 14, 14; **3:**6, 7, 7, 8, 9, 9, 10, 11, 15, 15, 15, 15, 15, 16, 16, 16, 16, 16; **4:**1, 1, 3, 5, 6, 6, 6, 8, 10, 10, 10, 12, 13, 13, 13, 14, 14, 14, 14; **5:**1, 2, 2, 3, 6, 7, 7, 8, 9, 10, 11, 11, 14, 16, 16, 16, 18, 18, 20, 21, 21, 22, 23, 25; **6:**1, 2, 3, 3, 3, 4, 5, 7, 10, 10, 10, 12, 12, 15, 15, 15, 17, 19, 21; **2Ti 1:**1, 3, 5, 5, 6, 8, 8, 8, 9, 10, 10, 10, 10, 12, 12, 13, 13, 14, 14, 15, 15, 16, 18, 18; **2:**1, 4, 4, 5, 5, 6, 6, 7, 8, 8, 9, 15, 18, 18, 18, 18, 18, 19, 19, 20, 20, 21, 22, 22, 24, 25, 25, 26; **3:**1, 5, 6, 6, 6, 7, 8, 11, 14, 15, 15, 15; **4:**1, 1, 2, 2, 4, 5, 5, 6, 7, 8, 8, 8, 8, 8, 10, 13, 14, 14, 16, 16, 17, 17, 17, 18, 18, 19, 21, 22; **Tit 1:**1, 2, 2, 3, 3, 4, 4, 5, 9, 11, 12, 13, 14, 14, 16; **2:**1, 2, 3, 3, 4, 5, 6, 6, 7, 10, 11, 13, 15; **3:**1, 5, 5, 6, 8, 11, 12, 13, 15; **Phm 1:**1, 2, 2, 3, 5, 6, 7, 8, 8, 9, 11, 13, 16, 17, 20, 25, 25; **Heb 1:**1, 2, 2, 2, 3, 3, 3, 3, 3, 3, 3, 4, 4, 6, 6, 7, 9, 10, 10, 10, 10, 10, 12; **2:**1, 2, 2, 2, 3, 4, 4, 5, 6, 6, 7, 9, 9, 10, 11, 11, 12, 13, 13, 14, 14, 14, 15, 16, 16, 17, 17; **3:**3, 4, 5, 6, 6, 7, 8, 12, 14, 15, 16, 17, 17; **4:**3, 4, 4, 4, 5, 6, 7, 8, 9, 10, 11, 12, 12, 13, 14, 15, 16; **5:**2, 2, 6, 7, 8, 9, 10, 12, 12, 13, 14; **6:**1, 1, 2, 2, 2, 4, 4, 5, 5, 5, 5, 6, 6, 7, 7, 7, 7, 8, 12, 17, 19, 20; **7:**1, 2, 3, 4, 5, 5, 5, 6, 6, 7, 7, 7, 8, 9, 9, 10, 10, 11, 11, 11, 11, 12, 12, 13, 13, 14, 14, 15, 15, 16, 16, 16, 17, 17, 18, 18, 19, 21, 22, 23, 26, 26, 27, 27, 27, 27, 28, 28; **8:**1, 1, 2, 2, 2, 4, 4, 5, 5, 5, 5, 6, 6, 6, 7, 8, 8, 8, 8, 9, 9, 9, 9, 10, 10, 10, 11, 11, 11, 13; **9:**2, 2, 2, 3, 3, 3, 4, 4, 4, 4, 4, 4, 5, 5, 5, 5, 6, 6, 7, 7, 7, 7, 8, 8, 8, 8, 8, 9, 9, 9, 9, 9, 11, 11, 12, 13, 13, 13, 14, 14, 14, 14, 15, 15, 15, 15, 15, 16, 16, 17, 17, 17, 17, 17, 17, 18, 19, 19, 19, 19, 20, 21, 21, 22, 22, 23, 23, 23, 23, 24, 24, 25, 25, 25, 26, 26, 26, 26, 28; **10:**1, 1, 1, 1, 1, 1, 1, 2, 2, 3, 4, 5, 6, 7, 8, 8, 9, 9, 10, 10, 11, 11, 11, 12, 15, 16, 16, 19, 20, 20, 22, 23, 25, 26, 27, 27, 28, 28, 29, 29, 29, 29, 29, 30, 30, 31, 31, 33, 35, 35, 37; **11:**1, 1, 3, 7, 7, 7, 9, 9, 12, 12, 12, 12, 13, 15, 18, 19, 20, 22, 23, 24, 25, 25, 26, 26, 26, 26, 27, 27, 27, 28, 28, 28, 28, 29, 29, 29, 30, 30, 31, 31, 31, 32, 32, 32, 33, 34, 34, 34, 35, 37, 38, 40, 40, 40, 40; **12:**1, 1, 1, 2, 2, 2, 5, 5, 6, 9, 9, 10, 14, 15, 16, 18, 20, 21, 22, 22, 22, 23, 23, 23, 23, 24, 24, 24, 24, 25, 25, 25, 25, 26, 26, 26, 27; **13:**3, 5, 6, 7, 7, 7, 8, 10, 10, 11, 11, 11, 11, 11, 11, 11, 12, 13, 13, 15, 20, 20, 20, 20, 20, 24, 24; **Jas 1:**1, 1, 6, 6, 7, 10, 11, 11, 11, 12, 12, 14, 21, 21, 25, 27, 27; **2:**3, 3, 3, 5, 5, 5, 6, 6, 7, 8, 9, 10, 10, 10, 11, 11, 12, 12, 14, 19, 21, 23, 23, 25, 26; **3:**1, 4, 4, 5, 6, 6, 8, 9, 10, 13, 14, 15, 17; **4:**1, 1, 2, 5, 5, 6, 6, 6, 7, 9, 10, 11, 12, 12, 14, 15; **5:**1, 3, 3, 4, 4, 4, 4, 4, 4, 4, 5, 7, 7, 7, 7, 7, 7, 8, 8, 9, 9, 10, 10, 10, 11, 13, 14, 14, 14, 14, 15, 15, 16, 17, 18, 18, 19, 20, 20; **1Pe 1:**1, 1, 2, 2, 3, 3, 3, 4, 5, 7, 7, 9, 10, 11, 12, 12, 12, 13, 13, 17, 18, 18, 19, 19, 20, 20, 21, 22, 22, 23, 23, 24, 24, 24, 24, 25, 25, 25; **2:**2, 3, 4, 4, 5, 6, 7, 7, 7, 8, 8, 8, 8, 9, 9, 10, 12, 13, 13, 14, 14, 17, 18, 19, 20, 23, 24, 25; **3:**1, 1, 1, 3, 4, 4, 5, 5, 5, 7, 10, 12, 12, 12, 18, 19, 21, 22, 22; **4:**1, 2, 2, 3, 3, 4, 5, 5, 6, 6, 7, 7, 11, 12, 13, 13, 14, 16, 17, 18, 18, 19; **5:**1, 1, 2, 3, 4, 5, 5, 5, 5, 6, 8, 9, 9, 12, 12; **2Pe 1:**1, 4, 5, 8, 8, 11, 11, 12, 14, 16, 17, 18, 18, 19, 19, 19, 20, 21, 21; **2:**3, 4, 4, 5, 5, 5, 6, 6, 6, 7, 7, 8, 9, 9, 9, 10, 11, 11, 12, 13, 15, 15, 17, 20, 20, 21, 21, 22; **3:**2, 3, 3, 4, 4, 5, 5, 5, 5, 6, 6, 7, 7, 7, 8, 9, 10, 10, 10, 10, 12, 12, 12, 12, 13, 15, 15, 16, 16, 17, 18; **1Jn 1:**1, 1, 1, 1, 2, 2, 3, 5, 6, 7, 7, 8; **2:**1, 1, 2, 2, 2, 4, 5, 7, 7, 8, 8, 9, 10, 11, 13, 13, 14, 14, 14, 15, 15, 15, 16, 16, 16, 16, 17, 18, 18, 18, 18, 20, 20, 21, 21, 22, 22, 22, 22, 22, 23, 23, 23, 23, 24, 24, 24, 25, 27, 27; **3:**1, 4, 4, 8, 8, 8, 8, 10, 11, 11, 12, 13, 19, 19, 22, 23, 24; **4:**1, 1, 1, 2, 2, 2, 3, 3, 3, 4, 4, 4, 5, 5, 6, 6, 9, 14, 14, 14, 15, 17; **5:**1, 1, 4, 5, 5, 5, 5, 6, 6, 6, 8, 8, 8, 9, 10, 13, 18, 19, 19, 19, 20, 20, 20; **2Jn** 1, 1, 1, 2, 4, 4, 5, 6, 7, 8, 9, 9, 9, 9, 10, 13; **3Jn** 1, 1, 3, 3, 4, 5, 6, 7, 8, 9, 9, 10, 10, 10, 10, 12, 12; **Jude** 1, 1, 1, 3, 3, 3, 4, 5, 5, 6, 6, 6, 6, 7, 7, 8, 8, 9, 9, 9, 10, 11, 12, 12, 12, 12, 13, 13, 14, 15, 15, 15, 15, 15, 17, 18, 19, 20, 20, 21, 23, 25; **Rev 1:**1, 1, 2, 2, 3, 3, 3, 4, 4, 4, 4, 5, 5, 5, 5, 5, 5, 7, 7, 7, 8, 8, 8, 8, 8, 8, 8, 9, 9, 9, 10, 10, 11, 13, 13, 13, 16, 17, 17, 18, 18, 18, 19, 19, 20, 20, 20, 20, 20, 20, 20, 20; **2:**1, 1, 1, 1, 1, 1, 1, 2, 2, 5, 6, 6, 7, 7, 7, 7, 7, 8, 8, 8, 8, 8, 8, 9, 10, 10, 10, 11, 11, 11, 11, 12, 12, 12, 12, 13, 14, 15, 15, 15, 16, 17, 17, 17, 17, 17, 17, 18, 18, 18, 18, 19, 23, 23, 23, 24, 26, 26, 27, 28, 28, 29, 29, 29; **3:**1, 1, 1, 1, 1, 1, 1, 2, 2, 5, 6, 6, 6, 7, 7, 7, 7, 7, 7, 8, 9, 10, 10, 12, 12, 12, 13, 13, 13, 14, 14, 14, 14, 14, 14, 14, 15, 15, 19, 20, 20, 22, 22, 22; **4:**1, 1, 1, 2, 3, 3, 3, 5, 5, 5, 5, 6, 6, 6, 7, 7, 7, 7, 7, 7, 8, 8, 9, 9, 9, 9, 10, 10, 10; **5:**1, 1, 1, 1, 1, 1, 2, 3, 3, 4, 5, 5, 5, 5, 5, 6, 6, 6, 6, 7, 7, 7, 7, 8, 8, 8, 8, 9, 10, 11, 11, 11, 11, 12, 12, 13, 13, 13, 13, 13, 13, 14, 14, 14; **6:**1, 1, 1, 1, 1, 2, 3, 3, 3, 4, 4, 5, 5, 5, 6, 6, 7, 7, 8, 8, 8, 9, 9, 9, 9, 9, 10, 10, 11, 11, 12, 12, 12, 12, 13, 13, 13, 14, 14, 14, 15, 15, 15, 15, 15, 15, 15, 15, 15, 16, 16, 16, 16, 16, 16, 16, 17; **7:**1, 1, 1, 1, 1, 1, 2, 2, 2, 3, 3, 3, 3, 3, 4, 4, 9, 9, 10, 10, 11, 11, 11, 11, 11, 13, 14, 14, 14, 14, 14, 15, 15, 16, 17, 17, 17; **8:**1, 1, 2, 3, 3, 3, 3, 4, 4, 4, 4, 4, 4, 5, 5, 5, 5, 6, 6, 7, 7, 7, 7, 7, 8, 8, 8, 8, 9, 9, 9, 10, 10, 10, 10, 11, 11, 11, 11, 12, 12, 12, 12, 12, 12, 13, 13; **9:**1, 1, 1, 1, 1, 2, 2, 3, 3, 4, 4, 4, 5, 7, 8, 8, 11, 11, 11, 12, 13, 13, 13, 13, 14, 14, 14, 14, 14, 15, 15, 17, 17, 17, 17, 17, 18, 18, 18, 18, 18, 19, 20; **10:**1, 2, 2, 3, 3, 4, 4, 5, 5, 5, 6, 6, 6, 6, 7, 7, 8, 8, 8, 8, 8, 9, 10, 10, 10; **11:**1, 1, 1, 2, 2, 2, 4, 4, 4, 4, 5, 5, 6, 6, 6, 6, 7, 7, 8, 8, 8, 10, 10, 10, 11, 13, 13, 13, 14, 14, 15, 15, 15, 16, 17, 18, 18, 18, 18, 18, 18, 19, 19, 19, 19; **12:**1, 1, 2, 4, 4, 4, 4, 5, 5, 6, 6, 7, 7, 8, 8, 9, 9, 9, 9, 9, 10, 10, 10, 10, 10, 11, 11, 12, 12, 12, 12, 13, 13, 13, 13, 14, 14, 15, 15, 16, 16, 16, 16, 17, 17, 17, 18, 18; **13:**1, 2, 3, 3, 3, 3, 3, 4, 4, 4, 4, 5, 7, 8, 8, 8, 8, 8, 8, 10, 11, 11, 12, 12, 12, 12, 14, 14, 14, 14, 14, 14, 15, 16, 16, 17, 17, 17, 18, 18, 18, 18; **14:**1, 2, 2, 2, 3, 3, 3, 3, 4, 4, 4, 4, 6, 6, 6, 7, 7, 7, 8, 8, 8, 8, 9, 9, 9, 10, 10, 10, 10, 11, 11, 11, 12, 13, 13, 14, 15, 15, 15, 15, 15, 15, 15, 16, 16, 16, 16, 17, 18, 18, 18, 18, 18, 18, 19, 19, 19, 19, 20, 20, 20, 20; **15:**1, 2, 2, 2, 3, 3, 3, 3, 3, 5, 6, 6, 6, 6, 7, 7, 7, 8, 8, 8, 8; **16:**1, 1, 1, 1, 2, 2, 2, 2, 2, 3, 3, 3, 3, 4, 4, 5, 6, 7, 8, 8, 9, 10, 10, 10, 11, 12, 12, 12, 12, 13, 13, 13, 13, 14, 14, 14, 16, 17, 17, 17, 17, 18, 19, 19, 19, 19, 20, 21, 21, 21; **17:**1, 1, 1, 1, 2, 2, 2, 2, 3, 3, 4, 4, 5, 5, 6, 7, 7, 7, 8, 8, 8, 8, 8, 8, 9, 9, 9, 9, 10, 10, 11, 11, 11, 12, 14, 14, 14, 15, 15, 15, 16, 16, 17, 17, 18, 18, 18; **18:**1, 2, 3, 3, 3, 3, 3, 8, 8, 9, 9, 9, 11, 11, 14, 14, 15, 17, 17, 17, 17, 18, 18, 19, 21, 21, 22, 23, 23, 23, 24, 24, 24, 24; **19:**1, 2, 2, 2, 3, 4, 4, 4, 5, 5, 5, 6, 6, 6, 6, 6, 7, 7, 7, 8, 8, 8, 9, 9, 9, 10, 11, 11, 13, 14, 15, 15, 15, 17, 17, 17, 17, 18, 19, 19, 19, 19, 19, 20, 20, 20, 20, 20, 20, 20, 21, 21, 21, 21, 21, 21, 21; **20:**1, 1, 2, 2, 3, 3, 3, 3, 4, 4, 4, 4, 4, 4, 5, 5, 5, 5, 6, 6, 7, 8, 8, 8, 9, 9, 9, 9, 10, 10, 10, 10, 11, 11, 12, 12, 12, 12, 12, 12, 13, 13, 13, 13, 14, 14, 14, 14, 15, 15; **21:**1, 1, 1, 2, 2, 3, 3, 4, 5, 5, 6, 6, 6, 6, 6, 6, 8, 8, 8, 8, 9, 9, 9, 9, 9, 9, 10, 11, 12, 12, 12, 14, 14, 14, 14, 14, 15, 15, 16, 17, 17, 18, 18, 19, 19, 19, 19, 19, 19, 20, 20, 20, 20, 20, 20, 20, 20, 21, 21, 22, 22, 22, 23, 23, 23, 23, 24, 24, 24, 24, 25, 26, 26, 27; **22:**1, 1, 1, 1, 2, 2, 2, 2, 2, 3, 3, 5, 6, 6, 6, 7, 8, 8, 9, 10, 10, 11, 11, 11, 11, 13, 13, 13, 13, 13, 13, 14, 14, 14, 14, 15, 15, 15, 15, 15, 15, 16, 16, 16, 16, 17, 17, 17, 17, 18, 18, 19, 19, 19, 20, 21, 21

THEIR (4131)

Ge 1:12, 15, 30; **3:**7, 7, 7; **6:**2, 5, 18; **7:**7, 13; **8:**2, 18; **9:**4, 18, 23, 23; **10:**5, 20, 31, 32; **11:**6, 29; **12:**13, 15, 20; **13:**6; **14:**3, 11; **17:**8, 23; **18:**16, 19, 24, 26; **19:**36; **21:**14, 32; **22:**17, 24; **24:**32, 60; **25:**13, 16; **30:**39; **31:**22; **32:**1, 15; **33:**2, 6, 7, 13; **34:**7, 13, 21, 23, 25, 25, 26, 27, 28; **35:**4, 4; **36:**7, 14, 30; **37:**4, 12, 16, 32, 33; **40:**6; **42:**6, 24, 25, 26, 29, 35; **43:**11, 14, 24, 24, 25, 26, 32, 33, 33, 34; **44:**1, 3, 3, 11, 11, 13; **45:**17, 17, 18, 19, 25; **46:**5, 6, 15, 17, 20, 31, 32; **47:**1, 12, 17, 20, 20, 22, 27; **48:**12; **49:**6, 6, 7, 7, 7; **50:**8, 15, 22; **Ex 1:**1, 7, 11, 13, 19, 21; **2:**16, 17, 17, 17, 18, 20, 23, 23, 24, 25; **3:**7, 7, 7, 8, 22, 22; **4:**5, 31, 31; **5:**4, 5, 8, 8; **6:**9, 14, 15, 16, 16, 19, 24, 25; **7:**7, 11, 12, 12, 22; **8:**7, 17, 18; **9:**6, 20; **10:**7; **11:**2; **12:**27, 29, 34, 34, 34, 34; **13:**17, 22; **14:**5, 25, 25, 31; **15:**25; **17:**16; **18:**8, 19, 20; **19:**10, 14; **20:**5; **21:**16; **23:**13, 24, 24, 32, 33; **25:**20, 37; **26:**21; **28:**10, 42, 43; **29:**8, 9, 9, 10, 13, 15, 19, 20, 20, 21, 21, 22, 25, 33, 35, 45, 46, 46; **30:**14, 19, 38; **32:**2, 3, 25, 32, 34; **33:**1, 4, 8, 10; **34:**7, 12, 13, 13, 15, 15, 16; **35:**17, 18, 20, 20, 21, 21, 22, 22, 24, 26, 29, 34; **36:**4, 6, 7, 38; **37:**9; **39:**43; **40:**14, 15, 18, 31, 36, 38; **Lev 2:**10; **4:**14, 15, 28, 28, 28, 32; **5:**2, 5, 5, 6, 6, 7, 11, 12, 15, 16, 17; **6:**2, 2, 4, 5, 16, 17, 18, 22; **7:**10, 34, 35, 36, 38; **8:**2, 13, 13, 13, 14, 16, 18, 22, 24, 24, 24, 25, 30, 30; **9:**15; **10:**1, 5, 19, 19; **11:**8, 11, 11, 21, 24, 42; **13:**2, 45, 45, 45; **14:**8, 8, 8, 9, 9, 47; **17:**5; **18:**3; **19:**17; **20:**2, 3, 9, 24; **21:**5, 5, 5, 17; **22:**3, 6; **23:**7, 8, 43; **24:**14, 15; **25:**34, 41, 41, 50, 52, 54; **26:**4, 39, 39, 40, 40, 41, 41, 41, 43, 44, 44, 45, 45; **Nu 1:**2, 16, 18, 18, 44; **2:**2, 3, 3, 3, 10, 10, 10, 18, 18, 18, 25, 25, 25, 32, 34; **3:**4, 7, 9, 20, 23, 26, 29, 31, 35, 36, 37; **4:**27, 31, 31, 32, 32, 46; **5:**7; **6:**4, 5, 5, 5, 6, 7, 7, 7, 9, 9, 9, 11, 11, 12, 12, 12, 13, 15, 18, 21, 21; **7:**2, 5, 7, 8, 8, 9, 10, 87; **8:**2, 3, 7, 7, 10, 12, 15, 16, 21, 22, 26; **9:**6, 13; **10:**14, 18, 22, 25; **11:**1, 10, 12, 12; **13:**3, 19, 27, 28; **14:**2, 6, 18, 23, 24; **15:**25, 25, 31; **16:**15, 18, 26, 27, 27, 30, 32, 33, 34, 38; **17:**10; **18:**3, 4, 17, 17, 21; **19:**13, 19, 19, 21; **20:**8, 11, 11, 21; **21:**2, 3, 3, 18, 24, 35; **23:**21, 21; **24:**7, 7, 7, 8, 25; **25:**2; **26:**10, 21, 21, 30, 30, 31, 31, 32, 32, 36, 40, 40, 45, 45, 53, 57, 59; **27:**1, 5, 7, 7; **28:**31; **29:**6, 11; **31:**9, 9, 29; **32:**1, 17, 18, 29, 36; **33:**2, 2, 4, 52, 52, 54; **34:**14; **35:**2, 3, 3; **36:**3, 4, 6, 8, 8, 11, 12, 12; **Dt 1:**8, 28, 28, 41, 42; **2:**5, 5, 9, 9, 19, 19, 21, 22, 29; **4:**10, 37, 38; **5:**9, 29, 30, 31; **7:**3, 5, 5, 5, 5, 16, 24, 24, 25; **8:**3; **9:**5, 5, 14; **10:**8, 9, 11, 15; **11:**4, 6, 9, 14; **12:**2, 3, 3, 3, 3, 3, 4, 12, 29, 30, 30, 30, 30, 31, 31, 31; **13:**13; **15:**2, 2; **18:**1, 2, 2, 3, 18; **19:**1, 14; **20:**9, 18, 18; **21:**6; **23:**2, 3, 15; **24:**15, 16, 16, 16; **25:**19; **26:**6; **29:**8, 8, 17, 20, 25, 28; **31:**3, 7, 7, 20, 21; **32:**15, 17, 20, 21, 21, 27, 29, 30, 32, 32, 32, 33, 35, 35, 35, 36, 37, 38, 38, 49; **33:**6, 7, 7, 7, 9, 11, 11, 11, 13, 18, 18, 29; **34:**4; **Jos 1:**5, 6, 11, 14; **2:**13, 21; **3:**13; **4:**19; **5:**7, 7, 10; **6:**13, 13, 16; **7:**5, 6, 6, 11, 12, 25; **8:**20; **9:**2, 4, 11, 14, 15, 17, 18, 18, 21; **10:**1, 5, 5, 6, 13, 15, 19, 20, 21, 42, 43; **11:**4, 4, 5, 6, 6, 8, 12, 20, 21, 23; **12:**1, 6, 7, 24; **13:**8, 9, 14, 16, 25, 30, 33; **14:**2, 4; **15:**4, 32, 36, 41, 44, 46, 51, 54, 57, 59, 60, 62; **16:**4, 5, 5; **17:**3, 4, 11; **18:**2, 4, 7, 7, 7, 8, 24, 28; **19:**1, 6, 7, 9, 15, 22, 30, 38, 47, 47, 48; **21:**3, 3, 13, 17, 25, 26, 27, 29, 31, 32, 33, 35, 37, 39, 43, 44, 44, 44; **22:**9, 12; **23:**1, 7; **24:**1, 8, 26; **Jdg 1:**3, 18, 27; **2:**2, 3, 12, 14, 14, 16, 17, 18, 19, 19, 20, 22; **3:**4, 6, 6, 6, 7, 15, 25, 29; **4:**5, 16; **5:**16, 20; **6:**3, 5, 9, 28, 35; **7:**2, 5, 5, 5, 6, 6, 6, 12, 19, 20, 20, 20, 20, 22, 22; **8:**12, 21, 26, 33, 34, 34; **9:**3, 3, 6, 25, 43, 55, 57; **10:**16, 16; **11:**4, 11, 16, 17, 19; **13:**20; **14:**18, 19, 19; **15:**4, 5, 5; **16:**23, 24; **17:**6; **18:**2, 7, 8, 21, 21, 26, 29, 30; **19:**21, 21; **20:**2, 14, 15; **21:**1, 2, 4, 14, 21, 22, 23, 23, 24, 25; **Ru 1:**2, 2, 19, 19; **4:**18, 18; **1Sa 1:**21, 21; **2:**13, 25, 31, 32, 33; **4:**3, 3, 5, 7, 10; **6:**2, 7, 10, 18; **7:**4, 7; **8:**3, 6, 7; **9:**16; **10:**3; **11:**4, 10, 11; **12:**9; **13:**6, 16, 20; **14:**1, 11, 14, 34; **17:**1, 18, 51; **18:**7, 8, 27; **22:**18; **23:**5, 18; **24:**22; **25:**10, 13; **27:**2, 8; **28:**1, 4; **29:**2, 5; **30:**1, 3, 6, 22; **31:**7, 7, 7, 9, 12, 13; **2Sa 1:**11, 22, 27; **2:**3, 7, 26; **3:**18, 21, 30, 39; **4:**12, 12; **5:**2, 17, 21; **6:**5; **7:**10, 23, 24; **8:**1; **10:**3, 4, 5, 5, 8, 18, 19; **12:**26; **13:**29, 31; **15:**2, 4, 22, 30, 36; **16:**21; **18:**7, 17; **19:**8, 43; **20:**2, 3, 22; **21:**10, 12; **22:**46, 46; **23:**17, 19; **24:**8; **1Ki 1:**41, 49; **2:**4; **3:**2; **4:**34; **6:**1, 27, 27; **7:**50; **8:**7, 8, 11, 25, 33, 34, 34, 35, 36, 37, 38, 38, 44, 45, 45, 46, 48, 48, 49, 49, 50, 65; **9:**9, 9; **10:**5, 5, 13; **11:**2, 4, 8; **12:**16, 27, 27; **13:**12; **14:**15, 22, 22; **16:**13, 16, 21; **18:**23, 28, 39; **19:**10, 14, 21; **20:**12, 16, 23; **22:**10, 17, 29, 46; **2Ki 3:**9, 19, 19, 19, 19, 21, 25, 27; **5:**2; **6:**9, 10, 20, 22, 23; **7:**7, 7, 12, 15; **8:**12, 12, 12, 12, 20; **9:**13, 21; **10:**7, 25, 25; **11:**11, 12; **12:**16; **14:**6, 6, 6, 11, 21; **16:**15; **17:**7, 7, 9, 9, 14, 14, 15, 16, 17, 19, 20, 21, 29, 29, 30, 30, 31, 31, 34, 40, 41, 41; **18:**8, 8, 12, 27, 27, 33, 37; **19:**1, 11, 24, 26, 29, 32, 32, 37; **21:**8, 14, 15; **23:**20, 35; **25:**11, 21, 23, 23; **1Ch 2:**3, 4, 16; **4:**31, 32, 33, 33, 33, 39, 41; **5:**7, 7, 13, 15, 20, 20, 22, 24, 25, 25; **6:**19, 32, 33, 48, 73; **7:**4, 5, 7, 7, 9, 9, 9, 11, 22, 29, 40; **8:**12, 28; **9:**2, 2, 9, 17, 19, 22, 22, 23, 23, 25, 25, 27, 27, 34, 44; **10:**7, 7, 7, 9, 10, 12, 12; **11:**2, 10, 14, 19, 21; **12:**2, 2, 3, 9, 32, 38, 39, 39; **13:**2, 8; **14:**8, 12; **15:**5, 6, 7, 8, 9, 10, 15, 18; **16:**21, 32, 42, 43; **17:**9, 21, 22; **19:**4, 4, 5, 5, 9, 18; **21:**16, 16; **23:**7, 22, 24, 32; **24:**2, 3, 19, 30, 31; **25:**1, 1, 2, 3, 6, 6, 7, 8; **26:**7, 7, 8, 8, 12, 28; **27:**1, 16; **29:**17, 18, 20, 22, 22, 22, 24; **2Ch 2:**11; **4:**6, 20; **5:**8, 9, 12, 13, 14; **6:**16, 24, 25, 25, 26, 27, 28, 29, 29, 34, 35, 35, 36, 38, 38, 39, 39; **7:**6, 14, 14, 14, 22; **8:**5, 14, 14, 14, 14; **9:**4, 4, 12; **10:**16; **11:**11, 14, 16; **12:**7; **13:**10, 12, 15, 18, 19; **14:**4; **15:**12, 12, 14, 15, 15; **16:**8, 8; **18:**9, 16, 28; **19:**4; **20:**13, 23, 27, 33; **21:**3, 8; **22:**1, 5; **23:**8, 10; **24:**10, 17, 18, 18, 23, 24; **25:**4, 4, 4, 15, 21; **26:**1; **27:**2; **28:**6, 15, 15; **29:**6, 15, 15, 22, 23, 24, 26, 26, 31, 34; **30:**7, 9, 15, 16, 17, 19, 22, 22; **31:**1, 4, 5, 5, 6, 6, 10, 15, 15, 16, 16, 16, 17, 17; **32:**1, 13, 17; **33:**8, 17; **34:**4, 5, 32, 32, 33, 33; **35:**2, 2, 5, 9, 10, 10, 12, 15, 15, 15, 15, 23; **36:**15, 16; **Ezr 1:**4, 6; **2:**1, 2, 59, 62, 69; **3:**1, 10, 10, 10, 10; **4:**4, 5, 9, 13, 17, 21, 23; **5:**3, 5, 10, 11, 15; **6:**3, 7, 11, 11, 13, 14, 18, 21; **7:**16; **9:**2, 12, 12; **10:**3, 8, 12, 16, 19, 19; **Ne 2:**7; **3:**5, 23; **4:**4, 4, 5, 5, 11, 15, 17, 17, 18, 22; **5:**1, 1, 6, 8, 11, 11, 15; **6:**6; **7:**3, 3, 6, 7, 61, 64, 73, 73; **8:**5, 6, 6, 15, 16, 16; **9:**1, 2, 2, 3, 3, 3, 4, 4, 9, 11, 12, 17, 20, 21, 21, 23, 23, 27, 27, 27, 28, 29, 30, 35, 35, 37; **10:**10, 29, 30; **11:**3, 9, 12, 13, 14, 19, 20, 23, 30; **12:**7, 9, 27, 29, 40, 44, 45; **13:**10, 11, 12, 13, 13, 13, 15, 15, 15, 15, 24, 25, 25; **Est 1:**13, 17, 18, 20, 20; **3:**8, 12, 14; **8:**11, 11, 11, 13; **9:**2, 5, 5, 16, 16, 17, 18, 18, 22, 22, 22, 27, 28, 31; **Job 1:**4, 5, 18; **2:**11, 12, 12, 12; **3:**14; **4:**19, 21; **5:**4, 5, 5, 12, 13, 13; **6:**6, 20; **7:**10; **8:**4, 15; **11:**11, 20; **12:**18; **14:**10, 12, 21, 22; **15:**18, 20, 23, 25, 26, 28, 29, 29, 31, 34, 35; **17:**4, 5, 5, 5; **18:**5, 6, 7, 7, 10, 12, 13, 13, 14, 16, 16, 17, 19, 20; **19:**18; **20:**19; **21:**8, 8, 9, 10, 10, 11, 13, 16, 16, 19, 19, 19, 20, 20, 21, 28, 32, 33; **22:**16, 18; **24:**5, 5, 12, 17, 18; **26:**5; **27:**8, 9, 13, 14, 15, 19; **29:**9, 9, 10, 12, 17, 25; **30:**9, 9; **31:**13, 29; **32:**3; **33:**16, 17, 19, 20; **34:**11, 11, 24, 26; **35:**12; **36:**9, 10, 11, 11, 14, 15, 15; **37:**8; **38:**16, 40, 41; **39:**2, 2, 3, 3, 4, 4; **40:**20; **41:**6; **42:**15, 15; **Ps 1:**3; **2:**1, 3; **5:**9, 9, 9, 10, 10; **7:**16; **9:**5, 6, 6, 6, 15, 16; **10:**3, 5, 7, 7, 9, 14, 17; **11:**2, 2; **12:**3, 3; **14:**1, 1; **15:**3, 3, 4; **16:**4, 4; **17:**7, 10, 12, 13, 14, 14, 14; **18:**45, 45; **19:**3, 4, 4; **20:**7; **21:**10, 11; **22:**5, 5, 7, 13, 24, 26; **24:**5; **25:**13; **26:**10; **27:**12; **28:**3, 3, 4, 4; **31:**18; **32:**6; **33:**10, 15; **34:**5, 15, 16, 17, 20; **35:**6, 17, 20; **36:**1, 2, 4; **37:**7, 13, 14, 14, 15, 15, 23, 25, 26, 31, 39; **38:**13; **39:**11, 11; **40:**3, 15; **41:**2, 3; **42:**10; **44:**2, 3, 3, 14; **45:**16; **49:**6, 10, 11, 11, 11, 12, 14, 14, 14, 16, 17, 18, 20; **52:**7, 7; **53:**1, 1; **55:**3, 9, 19; **56:**5, 7; **58:**3, 6, 7, 7, 10; **59:**7, 7, 11, 12, 12, 12, 12; **62:**4; **64:**5, 6, 8, 8; **65:**7; **68:**1, 12, 21, 23, 23; **69:**20, 22, 23, 23, 25, 25, 27, 28, 32; **70:**3; **72:**4, 14; **73:**3, 4, 6, 7, 8, 9, 10, 12, 20; **74:**4, 4, 23; **76:**6; **77:**17, 20; **78:**5, 6, 8, 8, 9, 12, 17, 18, 28, 28, 29, 30, 31, 33, 35, 35, 36, 36, 37, 38, 42, 44, 46, 46, 47, 47, 48, 48, 53, 55, 55, 57, 58, 63, 63, 63, 64, 64, 64; **79:**10; **81:**6, 12, 12, 14, 14, 15; **83:**5, 10, 11, 11; **84:**5; **85:**2, 8; **89:**9, 17, 32, 32; **91:**12; **94:**4, 20, 20, 23; **96:**12; **97:**7; **98:**8, 8; **101:**5, 8; **102:**17, 28; **104:**11, 15, 17, 17, 21, 22, 23, 27, 29; **105:**14, 24, 33; **106:**10, 10, 11, 14, 18, 20, 21, 25, 27, 35, 36, 36, 37, 37, 38, 39, 39, 42, 42, 43, 44, 44, 46; **107:**6, 6, 13, 13, 14, 16, 16, 17, 17, 18, 19, 19, 26, 27, 28, 28, 36, 37, 37, 37, 38, 40, 41, 41; **109:**3, 10, 25, 29; **110:**6; **112:**2, 3, 5, 8, 9, 10, 10; **114:**3, 5; **115:**2, 4, 6, 6, 7, 7, 7; **119:**2, 70, 110; **122:**4; **123:**2, 2; **124:**3, 5, 6; **126:**6; **135:**6, 12, 15, 17, 17; **140:**2, 3, 3, 8, 8, 10; **141:**5, 6, 10; **144:**8, 11, 12; **145:**14, 15, 19; **146:**4, 4, 5, 5, 8; **147:**3, 11; **149:**5, 6, 6, 8, 8; **Pr 1:**15, 18, 31, 32; **2:**7, 15; **3:**31; **4:**15, 16, 22; **6:**6, 13, 13, 13, 14, 21, 22; **8:**21, 24, 29; **9:**15; **10:**6, 8, 11, 15, 15, 16, 16, 21, 26; **11:**3, 3, 5, 5, 7, 7, 26, 26, 29; **12:**10, 11, 12, 13, 14, 21, 22, 23, 23, 26, 28; **13:**2, 3, 6, 22, 25; **14:**3, 14, 15, 20, 26, 29, 31, 32; **15:**20, 20; **16:**2, 2, 7, 21, 27, 29, 30; **17:**2, 5, 6, 24, 28; **18:**2, 7, 7, 11; **19:**3, 3, 7, 11, 14, 18, 19, 26, 26; **20:**7, 11, 29; **21:**7, 10, 13, 13, 25, 25; **22:**8, 23; **23:**6, 8, 11, 11, 21; **24:**1, 2, 2, 20, 29; **25:**13, 22; **26:**4, 5, 5, 24, 25, 26; **27:**18, 22; **28:**7, 10, 11, 13, 27; **29:**5; **30:**11, 11, 26; **31:**5, 7, 7; **Ecc 1:**3; **2:**3, 22, 23; **3:**9, 13, 17, 18, 22; **4:**4, 4, 9; **5:**15, 16, 17, 18; **6:**7; **7:**29; **8:**10, 13; **9:**3, 6; **10:**6, 13, 13, 17; **12:**3; **SS 3:**3; **4:**8; **5:**7; **7:**13; **Isa 1:**3; **2:**4, 4, 9, 17, 20; **3:**9, 9, 9, 16, 16, 16, 17, 18, 18, 19, 20, 21, 23, 24, 24; **5:**18, 24, 24, 28, 28, 28, 28, 29, 30; **6:**2, 2, 10, 10, 10, 10, 10, 11, 11; **8:**4, 19, 20, 20, 21, 21, 21; **9:**9, 11, 20, 20; **10:**13, 13, 14, 27, 28, 29; **13:**8, 11, 14, 16, 16, 16, 16, 20, 22; **14:**1, 2, 18, 25; **15:**2, 2, 2, 5; **16:**3, 9, 10, 12, 12; **17:**7, 8, 8, 8, 9; **18:**2, 7; **19:**3, 3, 11, 11, 11, 13, 14, 17, 21, 22, 23, 24; **20:**4, 5; **23:**18; **25:**11, 11; **26:**19, 21; **28:**6, 6, 7, 8, 12; **29:**13, 13, 13, 15, 21, 23; **30:**28, 30; **31:**1, 2, 3, 9; **32:**20; **33:**1, 7, 8, 15, 16, 23, 23, 24; **34:**2, 2, 3, 3, 14; **36:**12, 12, 18, 22; **37:**1, 11, 25, 27, 30, 33, 33, 38; **38:**18; **40:**6, 11, 24; **41:**2, 17; **42:**15, 17; **43:**4, 7, 9, 17; **44:**5, 5, 7, 9, 9, 18, 18, 25; **45:**1, 9, 14, 14, 20; **46:**6, 7; **47:**6, 14; **48:**11; **49:**13, 22, 22, 26, 26; **51:**7; **52:**8; **53:**8, 8, 11; **54:**3, 13, 17; **55:**7, 7, 12; **56:**4, 7, 11; **57:**1, 19; **58:**1, 2, 12; **59:**4, 4, 5, 6, 6, 7, 18, 20; **60:**8, 9, 16, 21; **61:**2, 6, 8, 9; **63:**3, 4, 8, 9, 10, 11; **65:**2, 3, 3, 7, 7, 21, 22, 23, 23, 24, 24; **66:**3, 3, 3; **Jer 1:**15, 16, 18; **2:**8, 11, 16, 27, 37; **3:**17, 18, 21, 24, 24; **4:**19, 31; **5:**5, 5, 6, 6, 6, 13, 16, 16, 27, 28; **6:**3, 10, 12, 12, 12, 12, 19, 23; **7:**18, 19, 24, 26, 28, 28, 30, 31; **8:**2, 2, 4, 5, 6, 9, 10, 10, 13, 13, 19; **9:**3, 4, 5, 8, 8, 14, 14, 16; **10:**2, 2, 3, 5, 9, 14, 21, 21; **11:**2, 8, 10, 10, 11, 12, 15, 15, 16, 22, 22, 23; **12:**2, 2, 7, 9, 14, 15; **13:**10, 19; **14:**3, 4, 6, 12, 13, 14, 16, 16, 18; **15:**7, 11, 13, 14, 17, 17, 21; **16:**3, 4, 5, 6, 6, 8, 15, 15, 18, 18, 18, 20; **17:**1, 1, 1, 2, 2, 5, 5, 7, 8, 10, 10, 11, 11, 11, 25, 26, 26; **18:**16, 16, 16, 17, 17, 17, 21, 21, 21, 21, 21, 22, 23, 23, 23; **19:**4, 5, 8, 9; **20:**11; **21:**12; **22:**3, 7, 9, 9; **23:**3, 8, 8, 10, 11, 12, 12, 14, 17, 22, 27, 28, 30, 32, 36; **24:**6, 7, 10; **25:**12, 18, 33, 36, 38; **26:**3, 3, 11, 19; **27:**3, 4, 11; **29:**8, 22, 23; **30:**3, 6, 8, 8, 8, 9, 9, 10, 10, 20, 21; **31:**9, 12, 12, 13, 13, 17, 29, 30, 32, 33, 33, 33, 34, 34, 34, 34, 37; **32:**18, 19, 22, 30, 30, 33, 34, 35, 38, 39, 39, 40; **33:**5, 7, 8, 8, 13, 16, 20, 26; **34:**7, 9, 11, 13; **35:**14, 16; **36:**3, 7, 31; **37:**5, 10; **40:**8, 12; **41:**2, 5, 5, 7, 8, 12; **43:**1, 12; **44:**3, 5, 15; **46:**27; **47:**3, 4; **48:**10, 34, 35, 36, 37, 37; **49:**18, 20, 23, 23, 29, 29, 32, 35, 37; **50:**4, 6, 6, 7, 7, 7, 16, 17, 33, 40, 42, 45; **51:**3, 3, 5, 5, 14, 17, 28, 30, 30, 38, 39, 56, 56, 58; **52:**15, 27; **La 1:**4, 11, 14, 17, 17, 19, 22; **2:**4, 4, 8, 9, 10, 10, 12, 12, 16, 17, 20, 20; **3:**14, 30, 35, 63,

63; 4:2, 3, 3, 4, 4, 8, 8, 8, 10, 20; 5:12; Eze 1:7, 7, 8, 24, 24, 25, 26; 2:3, 6, 6; 3:9, 13, 18, 19, 20, 20; 4:4, 5, 17; 5:10, 10; 6:9, 9, 13, 13, 13, 14; 7:11, 11, 11, 12, 13, 16, 17, 18, 19, 19, 19, 20, 20, 24, 24, 24; 8:11, 12, 16, 17; 9:1, 8; 10:8, 11, 12, 12, 12, 12, 19, 21, 22; 11:15, 15, 18, 18, 19, 20, 21, 22, 22; 12:11, 16, 19, 19, 19, 19; 13:2, 3, 6, 9, 9, 11, 17, 18, 22; 14:3, 4, 5, 7, 10, 11, 13, 14, 20, 23; 16:33, 45, 45, 55; 18:2, 20, 20, 21, 22, 23, 24, 24, 26, 27, 27, 28; 19:4, 7, 7, 7, 8, 8; 20:4, 8, 16, 16, 18, 18, 18, 21, 24, 26, 26, 28, 28, 28; 21:12, 15, 21, 23, 23, 28; 22:9, 10, 11, 11, 11, 25, 27, 31; 23:6, 7, 8, 10, 15, 15, 17, 18, 23, 30, 36, 37, 37, 39, 39, 47, 47, 47, 48; 24:25, 25, 25, 25, 25; 25:4, 4, 9, 9, 13; 26:5, 14, 16, 16, 17; 27:10, 11, 20, 23, 29, 30, 31, 35, 36; 28:7, 25, 26, 26, 26; 29:18, 18, 19; 30:4, 4, 5, 6, 8; 31:6; 32:10, 10, 13, 23, 23, 23, 25, 26, 27, 27, 27, 27, 27; 33:4, 5, 6, 6, 8, 8, 8, 9, 11, 12, 13, 13, 13, 14, 16, 19, 29, 30, 31, 31; 34:2, 10, 10, 10, 10, 13, 24, 26, 27, 30; 35:5; 36:7, 12, 12, 17, 17, 17, 23, 37; 37:8, 10, 21, 23, 23, 23, 24, 25, 25, 25, 25, 26, 27; 38:5, 13, 13, 14; 39:10, 22, 23, 23, 24, 26, 26, 27, 28; 40:16; 43:7, 7, 7, 8, 9, 9, 10; 44:10, 12, 20, 22, 24, 28, 29; 45:4, 5, 5, 9, 9, 16; 46:18; 47:12, 22; 48:12; Da 3:7, 27, 27, 28, 29, 29; 5:4, 16; 6:24; 7:12, 25; 8:23, 23; 11:8, 32, 39; 12:10; Hos 1:7, 7, 9; 2:5, 17; 3:5, 5; 4:8, 9, 11, 12, 15, 18, 18, 18; 5:6, 7, 7, 15; 6:9; 7:2, 3, 6, 6, 7, 8, 9, 12, 14, 16, 16, 16; 8:3, 4, 4, 13, 13, 13, 14, 14, 14; 9:9, 15, 15, 15, 16, 16; 10:1, 2, 2, 5, 11; 11:6, 6, 6, 6; 12:11, 14, 14; 13:1, 15, 15, 16, 16, 16, 16; 14:7; Joel 1:7; 2:17, 20; 3:3, 6; Am 1:9, 11, 11, 13, 13, 15; 2:3, 3, 4, 8, 8, 8, 9, 9, 15, 16, 16; 3:10, 11, 11, 15, 15, 15; 5:9; 6:8, 8; 7:8, 17; 8:2; 9:14, 14, 14; Ob 11, 11, 13, 13, 14, 17, 20, 20; Jnh 1:5, 5; 2:8; 3:5, 8, 8, 10; Mic 1:11, 11; 2:9, 9, 9; 3:2, 3, 3; 4:3, 3, 4, 7; 5:3, 3, 9, 9, 14; 6:12; 7:2, 3, 16, 17; Na 2:3, 3, 5, 5, 7, 10; 3:3, 10, 19; Hab 1:7, 8, 8, 8, 9, 10, 10, 11, 11, 14, 15, 15, 16, 17; 2:4, 4, 5, 5, 6, 15; 3:13, 14; Zep 1:4, 5, 7, 9, 12; 2:7, 7, 8, 9, 9, 10, 11; 3:3, 3, 4, 6, 6, 6, 7, 10, 20; Hag 1:12, 12, 14, 14; 2:19, 22, 22; Zec 1:5; 2:4, 9; 5:9; 6:7, 11; 7:2, 11, 11, 12, 14; 8:8; 9:5, 8, 15, 15, 16; 10:5, 5, 6, 6, 7, 7, 7, 8, 9; 11:3, 3, 5, 6, 8, 16; 12:2, 5; 13:1; 14:12, 12, 12, 12, 12, 12, 21; Mal 1:4, 4; 3:5; 4:6, 6; Mt 1:3, 21; 2:3, 9, 11; 3:6, 11; 4:4, 6, 8, 20, 21, 21, 22, 24; 5:3; 6:2, 7, 7, 16, 28; 8:22; 9:2, 8, 29, 36; 10:21, 21, 41; 11:16, 20, 21, 21, 21; 12:25; 13:15, 15, 15, 15, 15, 19, 21, 43, 58; 14:14, 35, 35; 15:5, 8, 8, 9, 9, 27; 16:27; 17:12, 24, 25; 18:10; 19:2, 15; 20:10, 11, 34; 21:7, 8, 12; 22:5, 7, 16, 18, 34; 23:3, 5, 5; 24:19; 25:1, 3, 7, 15, 19; 26:43, 67; 27:12, 13, 21, 27, 38, 39; 28:11, 15; Mk 1:4, 5, 18, 19, 20, 34; 2:5; 3:5; 4:12, 17; 5:36; 6:5, 6, 12, 30, 47, 52; 7:3, 3, 4, 4, 7, 7, 7, 7, 11, 12; 10:13, 15, 16, 34; 11:7, 8, 15; 12:15, 40, 40, 41, 44; 13:12, 12, 17; 14:40, 55, 59, 65; 15:1, 16, 19, 27, 29; 16:14, 14, 18; Lk 1:2, 16, 17, 52, 77; 2:3, 8, 20, 34, 44; 3:3, 16; 4:4, 11, 15, 18, 40; 5:2, 6, 7, 9, 15, 20, 30, 32; 6:1, 8, 13, 26, 34; 7:21, 32, 42; 8:3, 13; 9:6, 47, 60; 10:7, 13, 13, 13, 38; 11:17; 12:1, 27; 13:15, 29; 16:14, 16, 29, 30; 17:14, 28; 18:1, 15, 17; 19:8, 14, 15, 27, 35, 36, 45; 20:20, 23, 40, 47, 47; 21:1, 4, 23; 22:25; 23:2, 2, 10, 23; 24:17, 28, 31, 33, 35, 45, 53; Jn 2:14, 15; 3:19, 19, 20; 4:40; 5:24, 28; 6:21, 22; 7:18, 43; 8:17; 10:12, 19; 11:19, 19; 12:16, 25, 25, 40, 40, 40, 40, 42, 46; 13:12, 29; 15:13, 13, 22; 17:20; 18:12, 35; 19:3, 31, 31, 31; 20:20; Ac 1:10; 2:6, 45, 46, 47; 4:4, 17, 24, 25, 29, 29, 32; 5:16, 31, 31, 36, 38, 42; 6:1, 6; 7:9, 19, 34, 35, 42, 45, 54, 57, 57, 57, 58; 8:7, 17, 18; 9:2, 24; 10:43, 47; 11:12, 18, 30; 12:20, 20, 25; 13:3, 3, 5, 17, 19, 27, 51; 14:3, 4, 5, 6, 11, 14, 16, 26, 27; 15:4, 5, 9, 24, 26, 32, 38, 39; 16:3, 5, 24, 33, 38; 17:21, 26, 27; 19:12, 18, 19, 28; 21:21, 21, 23, 24, 26, 26, 35, 40; 22:2, 23; 23:16, 21, 28, 29, 30; 25:2, 3, 13, 14, 16, 19; 26:18, 18, 20; 27:19, 43; 28:6, 27, 27, 27, 27, 27; Ro 1:19, 21, 24, 26, 28, 29, 30, 31; 2:14, 15; 3:3, 13, 13, 13, 14; 4:4, 5, 5; 8:8; 9:5, 32; 10:3; 11:6, 8, 8, 9, 9, 10, 10, 15, 16, 23, 27, 32; 12:15; 15:8, 12; 16:2, 4, 5, 16, 18, 21; 1Co 1:19, 20, 22; 3:8, 19; 7:5, 29; 8:7, 10; 9:13, 21, 22; 14:25, 25, 32, 32, 35; 15:41; 16:15, 19; 2Co 3:14, 15; 6:16, 17; 8:2, 3, 5; 9:9, 12; 10:5; 11:8, 12, 15, 18, 20; 12:14, 14; 13:12; Gal 2:4, 6, 9, 9, 13; 3:7, 8, 9; 4:1, 2, 2; 5:24; 6:6, 8, 13; Eph 2:11, 11, 11; 4:12, 18, 18, 18, 19; 5:14, 28, 28; Php 1:18; 3:2, 4, 19, 19, 19; 4:21, 22; Col 1:28; 2:18; 3:16; 1Th 2:14, 14, 15, 16; 4:5, 15, 16; 5:13; 2Th 2:10; 1Ti 1:6, 9, 19, 19; 2:9, 9; 3:10, 11, 13; 4:2, 14; 5:4, 4, 8, 11, 11, 12, 13, 14, 17, 18; 6:1, 5, 17, 17, 18, 19, 20; 2Ti 2:6, 26; 3:2, 2, 4, 6, 8, 8; 4:3; Tit 1:11, 12, 14, 15; 2:4, 4, 5, 5, 9, 9; 3:13; Heb 1:4; 2:10, 15; 3:10, 19; 4:10; 5:1, 1, 1, 3; 6:12; 7:5, 9, 25, 27; 8:9, 10, 10, 10, 11, 11, 12, 12; 9:5, 6, 10; 10:2, 3, 16, 16, 17, 39, 39; 11:2, 14, 16, 28, 34, 35, 35, 36, 39; 13:3, 7, 17, 24; Jas 1:8, 11, 27; 3:2; 5:4, 15; 1Pe 1:12, 24; 3:5, 12; 4:3, 3, 3, 6; 2Pe 1:9, 19; 2:1, 1, 2, 3, 3, 9, 10, 13, 13, 14, 14, 18; 3:4; 1Jn 2:6; 3Jn 6, 15; Jude 4, 7, 8, 10, 10, 11, 13, 23; Rev 2:22; 3:4, 5; 4:4, 8, 10; 6:9, 17; 7:9, 14, 17, 17; 8:6, 13; 9:4, 7, 8, 8, 9, 11, 17, 19, 19, 19, 19, 20, 21, 21, 21, 21; 11:5, 7, 8, 8, 9, 12, 16, 16; 12:11; 14:1, 11, 13, 13; 15:6; 16:6, 6, 6, 10, 11, 11, 12, 15, 16; 17:12, 13, 17, 17; 18:11, 17, 19, 19; 19:3, 10, 18, 19, 21; 20:4, 4, 4, 13; 21:4, 7, 8, 24, 26; 22:4, 12, 14

THEIRS (15)

Ex 33:3; Nu 23:10; 2Ki 6:16; Ne 5:5; Jer 44:28; Eze 3:18, 20; 16:15; 33:5; Mt 5:10; 10:41; Ro 15:28; 1Co 1:2; 2Pe 2:1; Rev 2:9

THEM (5038)

Ge 1:22, 27, 27, 28, 28; 2:1, 19, 19, 25; 3:24; 5:1, 2, 2, 2; 6:6, 7, 13, 13, 19; 7:8, 14, 16; 9:1, 2, 3, 4; 10:1; 11:6, 7, 8, 9, 9; 12:20; 13:11; 14:11, 14, 14, 15; 15:10, 11, 14; 17:6, 23; 18:2, 2, 8, 10, 16; 19:1, 1, 1, 3, 5, 5, 6, 8, 12, 16, 25; 20:8, 14; 21:28; 22:6; 23:7; 24:14, 32, 32; 25:6; 26:4, 18, 18, 27, 30, 31; 27:9, 14, 15, 46; 29:3, 4; 30:14, 26, 26, 32, 33, 35, 36, 37, 38, 40, 41; 31:5, 5, 19, 23, 26, 28, 32, 32, 34, 34, 34, 35, 37, 39, 41, 46, 55; 32:2, 4, 16, 19; 33:4, 10, 11; 34:14, 21, 21, 21; 35:4, 5; 36:7, 40; 37:5, 13, 16, 17, 25; 38:25, 28; 40:3, 4, 17; 41:8, 8, 24, 34, 35, 48, 55; 42:4, 7, 8, 9, 17, 18, 23, 23, 24, 24, 25, 27, 35; 43:11, 11, 16, 16, 17, 23, 23, 27, 32, 33, 34; 44:4, 4, 4, 6, 6, 11, 28; 45:1, 3, 15, 18, 18, 21, 21, 22, 24; 46:5, 32; 47:2, 3, 6, 6, 6, 6; 48:9, 9, 10; 49:6, 19, 29; 50:4, 5, 12, 19, 21, 21; Ex 1:9, 11, 11, 11, 12, 14, 21; 2:17, 21; 3:8, 8, 9, 13, 13, 14, 15, 16; 4:1, 20, 28, 30, 31; 5:5, 7, 9, 9, 9, 20, 21, 21, 23; 6:1, 1, 3, 4, 4, 5, 28; 7:5, 6, 10, 20; 8:3, 3, 17, 19, 21, 21, 26; 9:2, 2, 11, 17, 21; 10:1, 11, 12, 16, 27; 12:4, 34, 34, 38; 13:8, 14, 17, 18, 19, 19, 21; 14:10, 10, 19, 19, 23, 24; 15:5, 7, 9, 9, 9, 9, 9, 10, 13, 16, 17, 17, 19, 25; 16:4, 5, 6, 12, 15, 19, 20, 20, 29, 32; 17:8; 18:1, 9, 16, 20, 20, 20, 21, 25; 19:7, 10, 10, 12, 14, 14, 15, 17, 22, 23, 24, 25; 20:5, 11, 25; 21:16, 35; 22:23; 23:23, 24, 24, 30, 31, 32, 33; 24:1, 11, 12; 25:8, 12, 13, 18, 28, 37; 26:1, 11, 14; 27:6; 28:9, 23, 26, 27, 33, 33, 40, 41, 41, 42; 29:2, 3, 4, 8, 13, 17, 18, 29, 33, 40, 46, 46; 30:12, 29, 29, 29, 30; 31:17; 32:2, 8, 10, 10, 10, 12, 12, 12, 13, 16, 17, 19, 21, 24, 24, 24, 27, 34; 33:1, 1, 5; 34:1, 15, 15, 31, 32, 33; 35:1, 25, 29, 30, 35; 36:3, 8; 37:4, 7, 13, 15; 39:16, 40, 43; 40:9, 10, 11, 12, 14, 15; Lev 1:16; 3:4, 10, 11, 15, 16; 4:9, 10, 31, 35; 5:6, 7, 8, 16, 17; 6:4, 7, 10; 7:4; 8:5, 6, 10, 11, 13, 16, 27, 28, 30; 9:2, 4, 4, 4, 6, 14, 20, 22; 10:2, 4, 5; 11:10; 12:7, 8; 14:3, 12, 12, 24, 31; 15:29, 31, 31; 16:7; 17:5, 5, 7, 8; 18:5, 25, 30; 19:10, 31, 34; 20:2, 3, 3, 5, 5, 6, 6, 8, 14, 17, 18, 23; 21:8, 8, 23; 22:3, 4, 7, 8, 9, 9, 16, 16, 16, 31; 23:37, 43; 24:9; 25:25, 32, 35, 35, 36, 36, 37, 39, 40, 43, 43, 45, 46, 53; 26:7, 16, 41, 44, 44, 44; Nu 1:49; 2:34; 3:6, 16; 4:14, 19, 37, 41, 45; 5:3, 23; 6:1, 9, 19, 19, 27; 7:5; 8:2, 6, 7, 7, 8, 10, 11, 12, 13, 15, 15, 16, 17, 19, 19, 21, 21, 21; 9:18, 23; 10:10, 17, 33, 33, 34, 35; 11:1, 1, 1, 3, 12, 16, 17, 18, 21, 22, 24, 25, 26, 28, 29, 31, 33; 12:2, 4, 6, 9; 13:17, 23, 23, 26, 31, 33, 33; 14:9, 11, 12, 12, 14, 14, 16, 16, 16, 19, 20, 28, 31, 45, 45; 16:7, 9, 15, 15, 17, 18, 21, 26, 28, 30, 31, 32, 33, 34, 45, 46, 46, 47; 17:9; 18:11, 16, 18, 21, 24; 19:6, 9, 10, 13, 17, 20; 20:6, 12, 12, 13, 20, 26, 27, 28; 21:1, 3, 3, 6, 6, 16, 23, 23, 24, 25, 30, 30, 33; 22:6, 6, 6, 7, 11, 11, 11, 12, 12, 18, 20; 23:2, 9, 9, 11, 21, 22, 22, 25, 25, 27; 24:8, 8, 8, 10; 25:2, 2, 4, 11, 17; 26:10, 65; 27:7, 7, 14, 17, 17; 28:3; 30:1, 5; 31:6, 6, 12, 13, 18, 47; 32:7, 8, 9, 10, 13, 15, 17, 29; 33:51, 56; 34:18; 35:6; 36:3, 3, 6; Dt 1:3, 13, 15, 17, 42, 42; 2:5, 5, 6, 9, 9, 11, 15, 15, 19, 19, 20, 21, 30; 3:3, 20, 28; 4:1, 2, 5, 5, 6, 7, 9, 10, 10, 13, 19, 19; 5:1, 1, 9, 22, 30, 31, 31, 31; 6:1, 7, 7, 8, 8, 9, 21; 7:2, 2, 2, 2, 3, 12, 15, 16, 18, 19, 22, 23, 23, 24, 26; 8:19; 9:3, 3, 3, 3, 11, 12, 14, 17, 17, 28, 28, 28, 28, 28, 28, 28; 10:1, 4, 4, 9, 9, 18, 22; 11:4, 4, 6, 6, 18, 18, 19, 19, 20; 12:18, 29, 32, 32; 13:3, 5, 8, 9, 13; 15:7, 8; 16:17, 22; 18:2, 10, 12; 19:1, 5, 8; 20:16, 20; 21:5, 10; 22:16, 24, 24; 23:15, 16, 16; 24:8, 15; 25:5; 26:16; 27:2, 3, 4, 15, 26; 28:12, 13, 14, 25, 26, 32, 39, 41, 44, 55, 57, 57; 29:1, 2, 7, 20, 20, 21, 21, 25, 26, 26, 28; 30:1; 31:5, 6, 7, 10, 12, 13, 15, 16, 17, 17, 17, 17, 18, 19, 19, 20, 21, 21, 21, 23, 28, 28; 32:10, 10, 10, 10, 11, 11, 12, 13, 13, 13, 14, 14, 15, 20, 23, 23, 24, 26, 26, 30, 30, 30, 34, 35, 38, 46, 47; 33:7, 7, 7, 8, 8, 10, 10, 12, 12, 17, 21, 27; 34:4; Jos 1:2, 7, 12, 14, 14, 15, 15; 2:1, 5, 6, 6, 8, 9, 15, 16, 19, 21, 22, 23; 3:3, 4, 14, 17; 4:3, 5, 7, 8, 8, 22; 5:4, 6; 6:8; 7:11, 21, 21, 23, 23, 24; 8:2, 3, 5, 6, 11, 16, 20, 22, 33, 34; 9:13, 15, 19, 20, 21, 21, 26; 10:4, 8, 8, 8, 10, 10, 10, 10, 11, 19, 19, 19, 26, 30, 32, 41; 11:6, 8, 8, 12, 20, 21; 13:8, 12, 12, 14; 14:8, 12; 17:4, 13; 18:3, 4, 7, 8; 19:9; 20:4, 5, 9; 21:2, 10, 44, 44, 44; 22:2, 4, 6, 6, 7, 7, 8, 9, 31, 34; 23:2, 5, 6, 7, 7, 13; 24:7, 8, 11, 13, 25, 32; Jdg 1:2, 4, 7, 16, 22, 25, 28, 29, 30, 30, 32, 34, 34; 2:1, 6, 12, 12, 14, 14, 14, 15, 15, 17, 19, 19, 23; 3:6, 8, 9, 15, 19, 29; 4:2, 10; 5:21, 23; 6:1, 19, 19, 35; 7:1, 3, 4, 8, 9, 17, 24; 8:6, 12, 15, 16, 16, 19, 20, 21, 34, 34; 9:1, 33, 36, 38, 43, 44, 48, 49, 49, 52; 10:7, 8, 14; 11:7, 17, 20; 12:4; 13:1, 1; 14:9, 12; 15:6, 8, 11; 16:3, 3, 3, 8, 12, 18, 26, 29; 17:2, 4; 18:1, 2, 4, 8, 20, 21, 22, 23, 26; 19:6, 15, 17, 21, 23, 24, 24; 20:13, 23, 28, 32, 32, 39, 40, 42, 42, 43, 43, 45; 21:7, 12, 14, 14, 18, 21, 22, 22, 22, 22, 23, 23; Ru 1:6, 7, 9, 13, 19, 20; 2:9, 16, 16, 23, 23; 4:2; 1Sa 2:8, 8, 10, 23, 25; 3:13; 5:11; 6:2, 6, 7, 12, 14, 15, 21; 7:2, 5, 10, 11, 11; 8:8, 9, 9, 11, 13, 14, 22; 9:3, 14, 16, 22, 22; 10:6, 10, 14, 18, 21, 25, 27; 11:7, 7, 7, 8, 11, 11, 12, 12; 12:8, 8, 9, 20; 13:7, 16, 19, 20; 14:8, 9, 10, 11, 12, 13, 24, 32, 34, 34, 34, 36, 37, 48; 15:6, 9, 15; 16:5; 17:3, 18, 23, 26, 30, 39, 39, 40, 52; 18:1, 17, 25, 30; 19:8, 14, 15; 20:23, 36, 40, 41; 21:15; 22:18, 18; 23:2, 13, 18; 24:7; 25:5, 7, 7, 14, 15, 18, 43; 26:12; 29:3, 6, 7, 9; 30:8, 8, 8, 15, 15, 16, 17, 17, 20, 21, 21, 22, 22; 31:12, 13; 2Sa 1:10; 2:5, 16; 3:17, 20, 22, 26, 36; 4:7, 12; 5:8, 19, 21, 23, 23, 23; 6:2; 7:7, 10, 21; 8:2, 5, 10; 9:1, 3; 10:3, 4, 7, 9, 9, 19; 11:23; 12:11, 17, 19, 31; 13:36; 14:6, 10; 15:4, 5, 5, 5, 35; 16:5, 6, 13, 21; 17:10, 11, 16, 17, 18, 18, 20; 18:14, 24, 26; 19:7, 13, 18; 20:3, 3, 8; 21:2, 2, 3, 6, 8, 8, 9, 9, 10, 14; 22:28, 37, 38, 39, 39, 41, 42, 42, 43, 43; 23:6, 7; 24:1; 1Ki 1:33; 2:4, 7, 11, 40, 40, 40, 44; 3:17; 4:7; 5:9, 9, 14; 6:27; 7:20, 46, 51; 8:4, 21, 34, 35, 36, 46, 46, 46, 50, 52; 9:7, 9, 12, 21, 22, 23; 10:26, 28; 11:2, 2, 16, 18, 18, 29; 12:7, 9, 13, 30; 13:12; 14:15, 27, 28, 28; 16:23; 17:4; 18:4, 4, 6, 13, 13, 21, 22, 27, 37, 40, 40, 40; 19:21; 20:7, 13, 18, 20, 23, 25, 25, 30, 33; 21:8, 8; 22:6, 6, 10, 11, 13, 17, 27; 2Ki 1:3, 5, 10, 12; 2:8, 11, 11, 16, 17, 24, 24, 24; 3:9, 21, 24; 4:39, 39, 41; 5:12, 22; 6:2, 5, 18, 18, 19, 19, 20, 21, 21, 22, 22, 23, 23; 7:13, 13; 9:11, 12, 18, 19, 20; 10:7, 8, 8, 9, 9, 13, 14, 14, 14, 14, 18, 19, 22, 24, 25, 25; 11:4, 4, 4, 5, 9, 10; 12:7, 18; 13:3, 18, 18, 23, 23, 23; 14:26, 27; 15:20; 16:9; 17:7, 8, 11, 15, 15, 18, 20, 20, 21, 23, 24, 25, 25, 26, 26, 34, 35, 35, 35, 35; 18:11, 13, 18, 23, 27, 36; 19:12, 12, 18, 18, 29; 20:13, 13, 13, 13, 15; 21:3, 8, 9, 14, 16; 22:6, 15, 17; 23:2, 12, 14, 16, 20, 26, 35; 24:20; 25:5, 20, 21, 24, 24, 26; 1Ch 5:22, 26; 6:32, 49; 7:2, 4, 5, 7, 22; 8:7; 9:2, 28; 11:14, 14; 12:2, 14, 17, 18, 18, 19, 19; 13:2; 14:8, 10, 12, 14, 14, 14; 15:2, 12; 16:21; 17:6, 9, 19; 18:5, 10; 19:3, 4, 8, 10, 10; 20:3; 22:2, 18; 23:4; 25:7; 26:8, 32, 32; 28:2, 2; 2Ch 1:10, 14, 16; 2:8, 18; 3:10, 16, 16; 4:7, 8, 9, 17; 5:5; 6:25, 26, 27, 36, 36, 36; 7:20, 22, 22; 8:2, 8, 9, 10; 9:25; 10:7, 7, 9, 13; 11:11, 11, 14, 23, 23, 23; 12:5, 7, 7, 10, 10, 11, 11; 13:7, 10, 13, 15, 16, 17; 14:7, 7, 13; 15:3, 9, 15; 16:8; 17:8, 10; 18:5, 5, 9, 10, 12, 16, 26; 19:6, 9, 10, 10; 20:10, 10, 12, 16, 16, 23, 25, 27, 27, 29; 21:3; 22:8; 23:3, 4, 18; 24:5, 19, 22, 24; 25:8, 10, 10, 12, 12, 12, 14, 14, 14; 27:5, 5; 28:9, 9, 9, 15, 21, 23, 24; 29:3, 5, 23, 34; 30:10, 12, 14, 17, 17, 18, 27; 31:6, 13; 32:6, 6, 18, 22, 26; 33:3, 8, 15; 34:4, 23, 25, 30; 35:2, 12, 13, 13, 15; 36:7, 15, 17, 17, 17; Ezr 1:4, 6, 6, 8; 2:63, 66; 3:7; 4:4, 5, 12; 5:2, 2, 5, 12; 6:9, 22, 22; 7:19, 25; 8:17, 26, 29; 9:2; 10:3, 10, 15; Ne 1:2; 2:7, 9, 17, 18; 3:2, 2, 7, 9, 19, 23; 4:11, 11, 14, 15; 5:7, 7, 8, 8, 8, 11; 6:2, 3; 7:3, 3, 65, 68; 8:9, 11, 12, 16; 9:3, 6, 10, 13, 13, 14, 14, 15, 15, 15, 17, 17, 17, 19, 19, 19, 20, 20, 21, 23, 24, 24, 26, 27, 27, 27, 27, 28, 28, 29, 30, 30, 30, 31, 31, 35, 35, 37; 10:36, 39; 12:8, 9, 24, 32, 38, 38; 13:2, 10, 11, 15, 15, 21, 25, 25, 25, 25, 29; Est 3:4, 8, 13; 5:11; 8:8, 11, 17; 9:1, 2, 2, 2, 5, 16, 21, 22, 24; 10:3; Job 1:4, 5, 6, 14; 2:1; 3:18; 4:18; 5:4, 15; 9:5, 24, 30; 10:4; 12:6, 23, 23, 24, 25; 14:20, 20, 20; 15:24, 30, 31; 17:4; 18:6, 9, 9, 11, 12, 17; 19:15; 20:19; 21:9, 17, 19, 20, 31, 31; 22:9, 19, 20, 22; 24:23; 27:8, 9, 15, 20, 21, 21, 22, 23, 23; 29:12, 17, 22, 24, 24, 25, 25; 30:5; 31:20, 27; 32:8, 8; 33:16, 17, 17, 18, 22, 30; 34:19, 25, 25, 26; 35:9; 36:7, 8, 9, 9, 13, 31; 38:3; 39:14, 15, 15; 40:7, 13, 13; 41:16, 17; 42:4, 9, 11, 15; Ps 2:4, 5, 5, 9, 9; 5:10, 10, 10, 11, 11, 12; 7:5, 7, 16; 9:20, 20; 10:2, 5, 9, 14, 15, 17, 18; 11:6; 12:5, 7; 13:4; 14:5; 16:3; 17:13, 13; 18:36, 37, 38, 40, 41, 41, 42, 42; 19:11, 11, 13; 21:9, 9, 9, 12; 22:4, 5; 25:9, 12, 14, 17, 20; 28:4, 4, 4, 5, 9, 9; 29:11; 31:17, 19, 20, 20, 20; 32:5; 33:19, 19; 34:7, 17, 19, 20; 35:4, 5, 6, 7, 7, 8, 8, 8, 10, 13, 13, 25, 27; 36:1, 8, 8; 37:10, 12, 24, 28, 32, 36, 36, 40, 40, 40; 38:13, 19; 40:5, 15; 41:1, 2, 2, 2, 2, 3, 10; 43:3, 3; 44:3, 3, 3, 10; 45:16; 48:13; 49:14, 17, 17, 19; 51:16; 53:5, 5, 5; 54:5, 5; 55:9, 12, 15, 15, 19; 56:7, 7; 58:9; 59:3, 8, 11, 11, 11, 12, 13, 13; 62:3, 3, 9; 64:7, 7, 8, 8; 65:3; 67:4; 68:2, 2, 3, 3, 6, 22, 25; 69:6, 22, 24, 24, 27, 28, 34; 70:3; 72:12, 13, 14; 73:3, 18, 18, 20; 74:10; 76:6, 11; 77:12; 78:5, 6, 11, 13, 13, 13, 14, 15, 21, 22, 24, 24, 25, 29, 31, 33, 34, 38, 42, 45, 45, 49, 49, 50, 50, 52, 53, 54, 54, 55, 55, 56, 59, 66, 72, 72; 81:12; 82:4; 83:8, 9, 13, 15, 15, 16, 17, 17; 84:7; 85:8; 86:14; 88:8; 89:9, 42; 90:8; 91:15, 15, 15, 16, 16; 92:7; 94:13, 23, 23, 23; 95:10, 10; 97:10; 99:3, 6, 7, 7, 8, 8; 101:3; 102:19, 26; 104:14, 15, 15, 24, 27, 28, 29; 105:14, 17, 37, 38, 39, 39, 40, 40; 106:7, 8, 10, 10, 11, 15, 23, 23, 24, 26, 27, 29, 34, 38, 41, 41, 41, 42, 42, 43, 44, 45, 46; 107:6, 7, 8, 8, 12, 12, 13, 14, 15, 15, 19, 21, 21, 22, 28, 30, 31, 31, 32, 38, 40; 109:4, 4, 27, 28, 31, 31; 110:1, 6; 111:2, 6, 9; 112:7; 113:8; 114:3; 115:8, 8, 8; 118:10, 11, 12; 119:19, 22, 47, 83, 93, 129, 130, 140, 144, 167; 125:5; 126:2; 127:5; 129:8; 132:12; 135:18, 18, 18; 137:2, 9; 138:4; 139:18, 22; 140:10; 141:6, 8; 144:6; 145:15, 19; 146:6; 147:4; 148:6, 13; 149:5, 9; Pr 1:2, 9, 10, 12, 15, 19, 30, 32; 2:4; 3:3, 3, 21, 27; 4:13, 13, 21; 6:7, 21; 7:2, 3, 3, 5; 11:6, 6, 26; 12:14, 26; 13:19, 24, 24; 14:3; 15:12, 18; 16:7, 26, 29; 17:9; 18:7, 15; 19:4, 7, 7, 7, 16, 19; 20:7, 26, 26; 21:7, 10; 22:2, 23, 25; 23:13, 14; 24:11, 18, 22, 28, 29; 25:2, 9, 18, 18, 18, 21, 21; 26:24; 27:22; 28:1, 4, 13, 15; 31:7, 21, 29; Ecc 1:16; 2:5, 15; 3:18, 22; 4:1; 5:18, 20; 6:2, 2; 8:6, 15; 9:1; 10:2, 2, 12, 20; 11:8, 8; 12:9, 12; SS 1:10; 3:3; 5:3; 7:13; 8:11; Isa 1:3, 13, 14, 23; 2:12; 3:4, 8, 9, 9, 10, 12, 17, 24; 4:1; 5:7, 13, 18, 25, 29, 29; 6:11; 7:25; 8:7, 14, 14, 15, 20; 9:4, 11, 16; 10:6, 6, 17, 19, 20, 21, 22, 23, 25, 26; 11:4, 6, 11; 13:2, 2, 3, 4, 5, 8, 10, 17, 19; 14:1, 1, 2, 21, 25, 32; 16:4, 12, 12; 17:2, 11, 11, 13; 19:3, 12, 14, 17, 20, 20, 20, 21, 22, 24; 20:4; 22:4, 22, 22; 24:16, 16; 25:1, 1; 26:7, 10, 11, 14, 14; 27:3, 4, 11, 11, 12, 12; 28:11, 13; 29:6, 11; 30:17, 17, 18, 22, 22, 26, 28, 28, 28, 31, 32; 31:3, 8; 32:4; 33:1, 8, 16; 34:2, 15; 36:1, 3, 8, 12, 21; 37:12, 12, 19, 19, 30; 39:2, 2, 2, 2, 4; 40:11, 22, 23, 24, 24, 26, 26; 41:2, 3, 12, 16, 16, 16, 17, 17, 18, 18, 21, 22, 25; 42:5, 6, 12, 16, 16, 16, 16, 17, 22, 24, 25, 25; 43:7, 7, 9, 17, 19, 20, 25; 44:7, 7, 9, 25; 45:8; 46:2; 47:6, 6, 12, 13, 14; 48:6, 11, 21, 21; 49:10, 10, 11, 13, 21; 50:8; 51:8, 8, 20; 52:5, 6; 54:15; 55:7, 7, 7; 56:3, 3, 5, 5, 7, 7, 11; 57:1, 6, 8, 11, 12, 13, 13, 17, 18, 18, 19; 58:6, 6, 7; 59:4, 7, 8, 16, 21, 21; 60:9, 21; 61:3, 4, 8; 63:4, 6, 9, 9, 9, 9, 10, 12, 13, 14; 65:1, 6, 6, 7, 8, 8, 24; 66:4, 19, 20, 24, 24, 24; Jer 1:10, 10, 10, 17, 17, 17; 2:3, 5, 15, 24, 25, 27, 28, 30, 31, 34; 4:5, 10; 5:3, 4, 5, 6, 6, 9, 10, 14, 29; 6:13, 21, 28, 29, 29, 30, 30; 7:16, 16, 21, 22, 23, 27, 27, 27, 28, 28, 33; 8:2, 3, 5, 7, 10, 13; 9:2, 7, 7, 7, 8, 9, 11, 13, 14, 15, 15, 16, 16, 16, 22, 24; 10:2, 14, 20, 21; 11:3, 4, 7, 8, 11, 12, 12, 14, 14, 16, 16, 16, 20, 22, 22, 23; 12:2, 3, 6, 8, 8, 13, 13, 14, 15, 15; 13:12, 13, 14, 14, 19; 14:12, 12, 13, 14, 14, 14, 15, 16, 16, 17; 15:1, 1, 1, 2, 3, 8, 14, 14, 15, 15, 19, 19; 16:4, 4, 5, 5, 6, 6, 7, 8, 11, 11, 15, 15, 16, 16, 17, 18, 21; 17:16, 18; 18:11, 17, 20, 20, 22, 23, 23; 19:2, 3, 7, 11; 20:4, 4, 12; 21:7, 7, 12; 22:3, 7, 20, 20, 20; 23:2, 2, 2, 3, 3, 4, 4, 8, 9, 12, 14, 15, 15, 18, 21, 32; 24:6, 6, 6, 6, 6, 6, 7, 8, 9, 9, 10; 25:3, 9, 13, 14, 16, 27, 28, 30, 33, 33; 26:2, 3, 4, 5, 5, 19, 19; 27:4, 17, 18, 18, 20, 22, 22; 28:14; 29:6, 9, 17, 17, 18, 18, 18, 18, 19, 21, 31; 30:3, 9, 10, 19, 20, 20; 31:8, 9, 10, 10, 11, 12, 13, 23, 32, 32, 32, 33, 37; 32:12, 14, 14, 19, 23, 23, 33, 37, 37, 37, 39, 40, 40, 41, 41, 42, 42, 44; 33:5, 5, 14, 24, 26, 26; 34:11, 12, 13, 14, 16; 35:2, 2, 2, 4, 5, 5, 14; 36:3, 7, 13, 14, 14, 18, 26, 31; 38:11, 19, 20, 26; 39:10; 40:9, 9, 10, 14; 41:1, 6, 6, 7, 8, 10, 17; 42:9; 43:5, 10; 44:2, 3, 4, 12, 13, 13, 20, 24; 46:4, 15, 26, 26, 27; 48:9, 10, 21; 49:32, 37, 37; 50:6, 6, 7, 7, 7, 9, 17, 21, 27, 27, 32, 33, 33, 34, 34, 34, 34, 36, 38; 51:17, 39, 39, 40; 52:3, 8, 26, 27; La 1:10, 17, 21, 22; 2:4, 9, 21, 21, 21, 22; 3:28, 29, 29, 30, 30, 30, 33, 63, 64, 65, 65, 66, 66; 4:4, 6, 8, 10, 14, 15, 15, 16, 16; Eze 1:13, 15, 19, 22, 25; 2:4, 5, 6, 7, 8; 3:7, 9, 10, 11, 13, 15, 19, 20, 20, 21, 26, 27, 27; 4:9, 13; 5:4, 4, 12, 12, 13, 13; 6:2, 10, 12, 14; 7:11, 12, 14, 18, 19, 19, 20, 27; 8:11, 17, 18, 18; 9:1, 1, 2, 4, 6, 10, 10, 10; 10:2, 7, 7, 16, 16, 16, 19; 11:1, 4, 19, 19, 19, 21, 22, 22; 12:3, 10, 11, 14, 15, 16, 23, 28; 13:2, 6, 18, 20, 22, 22; 14:3, 3, 4, 8, 8, 9, 13, 23; 15:6; 16:17, 18, 19, 20, 21, 33, 34, 37, 47, 54; 17:3, 12; 18:6, 12, 16, 23, 30; 19:6; 20:4, 4, 4, 5, 6, 7, 8, 10, 11, 11, 11, 12, 12, 12, 12, 12, 13, 13, 13, 14, 14, 15, 15, 15, 16, 16, 17, 17, 18, 19, 21, 21, 21, 22, 22, 23, 23, 25, 26, 26, 26, 26, 26, 28, 28, 28, 29, 31, 36, 38, 40; 21:6, 7, 13, 14, 23, 28; 22:9, 19, 26, 26, 28, 31, 31, 31; 23:4, 12, 16, 16, 17, 18, 23, 24, 40, 41, 43, 45, 46, 46, 47, 47; 24:3, 20; 25:17, 17; 26:10; 28:9, 25, 25, 26; 29:3, 18; 30:9; 31:16; 32:10, 18, 19, 20, 25; 33:7, 8, 9, 11, 12, 12, 13, 13, 27, 28, 31, 32, 33, 33; 34:2, 4, 6, 8, 10, 12, 13, 13, 14, 15, 16, 16, 16, 23, 23, 23, 25, 27, 27, 28, 28, 29, 30; 35:3, 5, 5, 10; 36:1, 6, 15, 18, 19, 19, 20, 37, 38; 37:8, 10, 12, 17, 19, 19, 19, 20, 21, 21, 22, 22, 23, 23, 25, 26, 26, 26, 26, 27, 28; 38:7, 9, 12, 13, 13; 39:9, 9, 10, 10, 14, 15, 15, 15, 17, 21, 23, 23, 24, 26, 26, 27, 28, 28, 29, 29; 40:4, 7, 10, 48; 41:3; 42:5; 43:8, 8, 9, 9, 10, 11, 11, 24, 24, 24; 44:18, 19, 19; 45:9, 15; 46:20; 47:8; Da 1:2, 5, 5, 7, 8, 14, 16, 19, 19; 2:14, 18, 18, 18, 34, 35; 3:14, 20, 21, 21, 24, 27, 27; 4:7, 17, 25, 32; 5:1, 2, 3, 4, 8, 17, 21, 23; 6:24, 24, 24; 7:8, 12, 21, 24, 27; 8:10, 13, 22, 25, 25, 26; 11:11, 14, 32, 34, 37, 39, 39, 40; 12:6, 10; Hos 1:6, 7; 2:5, 7, 7, 7, 12, 23; 3:1; 4:8, 12, 12, 12, 14, 19; 5:2, 6, 7, 10, 13, 14, 14; 7:2, 2, 2, 12, 12, 12, 13, 13, 15, 15, 16; 8:3, 10, 12, 12, 13; 9:9, 12, 15, 15, 15; 10:4, 6, 8, 8, 8; 11:6, 6, 11; 12:13, 14; 13:1, 10, 10, 11, 14, 14; 14:9; Joel 1:4, 12, 18; 2:2, 3, 3, 3, 3, 5, 8, 11, 17, 17, 20, 20; 3:2, 5, 6, 7, 7, 8, 12, 12; Am 1:3, 6, 6, 9, 11, 11, 13; 2:1, 4, 6, 12; 3:11; 5:17; 9:2, 2, 3, 3, 3, 3, 4, 4, 4, 14, 15, 15; Ob 12, 14; Jnh 1:4, 7, 10, 13; 3:10; Mic 1:12, 16; 2:8; 3:3; 4:7, 12; 5:8; 6:2, 9, 15; 7:3, 3, 4, 10, 14, 14, 16, 19; Na 2:3, 7, 7; 3:3, 4, 17, 18; Hab 1:7, 9, 9, 10, 14, 16, 17; 2:6, 15; 3:8; Zep 1:4, 5, 12; 2:9, 11; 3:7, 8, 13; Hag 1:6; Zec 1:4, 12, 15, 21, 21; 2:9, 9; 6:10; 7:12, 12, 13, 14; 8:8, 8, 11, 14, 22; 10:2, 3, 5, 6, 6, 6, 8, 8, 9, 10, 10, 10; 11:2, 5, 6, 6, 9, 11, 11, 12, 13; 12:8, 8; 13:1, 2, 9, 9; 14:18; Mal 1:4, 7; 2:2, 5, 5, 7, 13, 17; 3:3, 7, 11, 15, 17; Mt 2:4, 7, 8, 9, 9, 9, 12, 16; 3:6, 7; 4:19, 21, 24; 5:1, 2, 3, 5, 17, 19; 6:5, 8, 16, 26; 7:2, 9, 10, 12, 16; 8:16, 32, 34; 9:4, 15, 28, 30; 10:1, 7, 18, 21; 11:4; 12:2, 3, 15, 16, 37, 39; 13:4, 11, 12, 15, 30, 34, 42, 42, 57; 14:14, 16, 18, 19, 25, 27, 36; 15:14, 18, 30, 30, 32, 33, 36, 36, 36; 16:1, 4, 4, 6, 15, 20, 21; 17:1, 5, 7, 8, 9, 14, 20, 22, 27; 18:2, 20; 19:4, 6, 6, 13, 13, 13, 14, 15, 26; 20:2, 4, 4, 4, 6, 7, 8, 12, 13, 17, 22, 23, 25, 25, 31, 34; 21:1, 2, 2, 3, 3, 8, 14, 21, 42, 45; 22:1, 4, 5, 6, 6, 22, 26, 28, 35, 41; 23:30, 34; 24:2, 4, 39; 25:2, 14, 19, 32, 40; 26:18, 19, 27, 31, 36, 38, 40, 42, 43, 43, 48, 53, 73; 27:17, 22, 26, 48, 56; 28:8, 9, 10, 11, 16, 17, 19; Mk 1:5, 17, 20, 29, 31, 38; 2:2, 8, 17, 20, 27; 3:5, 12, 14, 14, 14, 15, 17, 21, 23, 23, 30, 31; 4:15, 21, 25, 34, 40; 5:10, 13, 17, 19, 20, 26, 40, 43, 43; 6:4, 5, 5, 7, 8, 8, 9, 13, 22, 33, 33, 34, 34, 37, 48, 48, 50,

56; 7:12, 36; 8:1, 3, 3, 3, 4, 6, 6, 6, 7, 9, 13, 14, 15, 21, 24, 27, 30, 31, 34; 9:7, 8, 9, 14, 15, 19, 31, 31, 33, 34, 36, 36; 10:1, 3, 6, 9, 9, 11, 13, 13, 13, 14, 14, 16, 24, 27, 32, 33, 42, 42; 11:1, 2, 6, 8, 17; 12:1, 9, 12, 15, 17, 20, 38, 38; 13:9, 12; 14:7, 10, 13, 13, 23, 24, 27, 34, 39, 40, 40, 41, 44, 48, 65, 69, 70; 15:12, 15, 24, 36; 16:11, 13, 14, 15, 18, 18, 19, 20, S; Lk 1:22, 55, 68, 72; 2:7, 9, 9, 10, 17, 19, 20, 34, 46, 51, 51; 4:6, 26, 30, 39, 41, 41, 42; 5:2, 22, 31, 35, 36; 6:10, 13, 30, 31, 35, 35; 7:4, 6, 19, 30, 31, 38, 38, 42, 42, 44, 44; 8:2, 12, 18, 23, 25, 29, 31, 32, 32, 37, 37, 39, 55; 9:1, 2, 3, 10, 11, 11, 13, 14, 18, 20, 21, 34, 34, 34, 45, 46, 46, 48, 54, 55; 10:1, 2, 9, 18, 19, 34, 38; 11:5, 11, 12, 29, 29, 44, 49; 12:1, 5, 6, 24, 33, 37, 37; 13:4, 15; 14:5, 7, 17, 19, 24, 25; 15:2, 4, 11; 16:15, 28, 29, 30; 17:14, 15, 27, 29; 18:1, 7, 8, 15, 15, 15, 16, 31, 34; 19:8, 13, 27, 27, 30, 33, 46; 20:9, 16, 17, 19, 41, 43, 46; 21:3, 8, 13, 29; 22:4, 5, 23, 25, 35, 40, 45, 50, 55, 58; 23:2, 20, 25, 28, 30, 30; 24:4, 5, 15, 15, 16, 18, 23, 25, 29, 29, 30, 35, 36, 40, 40, 41, 50, 50, 51, 51; Jn 1:26, 38, 38; 2:15, 16, 24; 3:32, 36; 4:2, 14, 14, 14, 27, 41, 52; 5:15; 6:7, 10, 11, 18, 20, 29, 31, 32, 37, 39, 40, 44, 44, 54, 56, 61, 65, 69; 7:16, 18, 33, 40, 49; 8:2, 10, 14, 14, 21, 23, 27, 42, 59; 9:11, 15, 16, 19; 10:3, 4, 7, 8, 12, 16, 20, 27, 28, 28, 29, 29, 39; 11:2, 6, 14, 34, 39, 44, 46, 49; 12:11, 26, 30, 36, 40, 42; 13:5, 16, 17; 14:21, 21, 21, 23, 23, 23; 15:5, 22, 24; 17:6, 6, 8, 8, 10, 10, 11, 11, 11, 12, 12, 13, 13, 14, 14, 15, 15, 17, 17, 18, 21, 22, 23, 23, 26, 26, 26; 18:4, 5, 7, 18, 19, 28, 29, 31, 38; 19:13, 16, 18, 23; 20:17, 18, 18, 19, 20, 20, 21, 22, 22, 23, 25, 26, 26; 21:13, 20, 24; Ac 1:3, 3, 4, 4, 10, 15; 2:2, 3, 4, 8, 35, 37, 43; 3:3, 5, 8; 4:1, 3, 3, 8, 12, 13, 14, 17, 17, 18, 21, 21, 21, 23, 24, 33, 34, 34; 5:13, 13, 15, 18, 19, 19, 26, 26, 33, 39, 40, 40, 40, 41; 6:3, 6, 6, 10; 7:7, 16, 25, 26, 34, 36, 42, 42, 43, 44, 45, 56, 58, 60; 8:3, 16, 25; 9:2, 21, 21, 27, 27, 28, 39, 39, 40, 41; 10:8, 8, 13, 20, 20, 23, 28, 46, 48, 48; 11:3, 4, 7, 12, 15, 15, 21, 26, 28; 12:10, 17, 17, 19, 21, 25; 13:2, 3, 3, 5, 13, 15, 16, 17, 17, 18, 21, 42, 43, 44, 50, 51; 14:2, 3, 4, 5, 15, 18, 22, 22, 23, 23; 15:2, 3, 7, 8, 9, 12, 14, 20, 20, 22, 23, 33, 38, 40, 40; 16:3, 6, 7, 14, 19, 22, 24, 30, 34, 34, 37, 39, 39, 39, 40; 17:5, 6, 6, 7, 16, 18, 22, 23, 33, 34; 18:3, 5, 16, 23, 23, 27, 28; 19:2, 6, 6, 12, 16, 16, 19, 19, 25, 32, 35, 38, 38, 41; 20:1, 11, 17, 36; 21:4, 24, 24, 24, 25, 25, 26, 40; 22:5, 18, 30; 23:10, 13, 14; 24:24, 25; 25:16; 26:10, 11, 11, 11, 11; 27:35, 40, 43; 28:3, 14, 15, 17, 23, 23, 27; Ro 1:5, 19, 24, 26, 28, 28, 32, 32; 2:3, 3, 15, 15, 15, 26; 3:3, 16, 18; 4:8; 5:18, 21; 8:9, 28, 29, 30, 30, 30, 30; 9:3, 4, 4, 4, 7, 19, 33, 33; 10:12, 14, 14, 15, 21; 11:5, 8, 9, 9, 14, 23, 27; 12:1, 7, 9, 13, 14, 14, 15, 20, 20; 13:6, 7, 12; 14:1, 3, 4, 4; 15:1, 2, 2, 9, 14, 18, 19, 27, 27, 31; 16:4, 7, 14, 15, 17; 1Co 1:20, 28; 2:10, 14; 6:13; 7:5, 15, 15, 25, 31, 31, 36; 8:12; 9:19, 20, 20, 20, 21, 21, 22, 22; 10:1, 1, 1, 3, 4, 4, 5, 5, 7, 8, 8, 9, 10, 10, 11, 24, 33; 12:1, 4, 31; 14:3, 10, 26, 34, 35; 16:16, 16, 20; 2Co 1:4; 2:1, 17; 3:1, 1; 4:4; 5:15, 16, 19; 6:16, 16, 17, 17; 8:5, 14, 22, 24; 9:2, 3, 4, 11, 13; 10:5; 13:2, 2; Gal 1:13; 2:2, 5, 13; 3:10; 4:15, 17; 5:24; 6:6; Eph 2:12; 3:8; 4:29; 5:11, 13; 6:4, 4, 5, 9; Php 1:28; 2:15; 3:7, 21; Col 1:28, 28, 28; 2:2, 15, 15, 18, 22; 3:7, 19, 22, 22; 4:16; 1Th 1:8; 2:16; 4:10, 17; 5:3, 13, 13; 2Th 2:2, 10, 11; 3:12, 14, 15, 15; 1Ti 1:13, 15, 20; 2:1, 12, 12; 4:11, 13; 5:4, 14, 15, 16; 6:2, 5, 9, 18, 18; 2Ti 2:2, 14, 14; 3:5; 4:3, 16; Tit 1:1, 1, 2, 2, 12, 13, 13; 2:7, 9, 15, 15; 3:8, 12; Heb 1:12, 13; 2:10, 11; 3:10, 10; 4:2, 2, 2, 8; 6:16; 8:9, 9, 9, 10, 10, 10; 9:4, 9, 15, 15, 17; 10:3, 8, 16, 16, 16; 11:12, 13, 16, 22, 22, 23, 33, 39, 40; 12:18; 13:3, 9, 17; Jas 1:9, 10, 17; 2:25; 4:2; 5:14, 14, 14, 15; 1Pe 1:11, 11; 2:8, 8, 14; 3:1, 9; 4:4, 10; 5:3; 2Pe 1:9, 12, 15; 2:1, 2, 3, 4, 6, 6, 12, 21; 3:1, 10, 16; 1Jn 2:11; 3:9, 14, 15, 24; 4:1, 5, 15, 16; 5:18, 18; 2Jn 4; 3Jn 6, 8, 8, 10, 10; Jude 6, 6, 10, 11, 19, 23; Rev 2:14, 16, 20, 24, 27, 28; 3:7, 7, 12, 12; 4:4; 5:10; 6:11; 7:14, 15, 15, 17; 8:4; 9:5, 5, 10, 17; 11:5, 5, 7, 7, 7, 9, 10, 11, 11; 13:7; 14:5, 8, 9, 13; 15:2; 17:14; 19:15; 20:4, 6, 8, 9, 9, 10, 13; 21:3, 3, 14, 17; 22:5, 8, 17, 17

THEMSELVES (257)

Ge 3:7, 8; 21:28; 42:21; 43:15; Ex 5:7; 18:22, 26; 19:9, 22; 32:6, 7, 31; 38:6; 40:30; Lev 9:3; 14:8, 9; 18:24; 21:1; 25:35, 39, 47, 49, 51; Nu 6:2, 12; 8:21; 11:18; 14:4; 19:12, 13, 19, 20; 23:9; 25:1; 31:53; Dt 9:12; 29:19; 31:14; 33:21; Jos 7:13; 8:27; 9:4; 11:14; 24:1, 25; Jdg 2:17; 6:2; 7:2; 8:27, 33; 9:34, 51; 16:2; 19:22; 2Sa 10:8, 17; 1Ki 6:6; 18:28; 2Ki 3:21; 11:11; 12:8; 17:9, 15, 17, 32; 23:3; 1Ch 4:41; 15:14; 19:9; 2Ch 5:11; 7:14; 12:6, 7; 20:22, 33; 21:11; 29:15, 34; 30:11, 15, 17, 18, 24; 31:4, 6, 18; 32:26; 35:14; Ezr 6:20, 20; 9:1; Ne 4:4, 16; 5:8; 9:2, 25; 10:28, 29; 12:30; 13:22; Est 8:17; 9:2, 31; Job 1:6; 2:1; 5:5; 15:31; 24:10, 17; Ps 7:15; 9:16; 10:6, 11; 22:18; 49:7, 11, 18; 57:6; 106:39; 112:3; 119:118; Pr 1:18; 8:36; 11:25; 13:13; 14:8; 19:24; 26:15, 16; 28:11; 31:8; Ecc 3:12, 18; Isa 1:4; 5:21; 44:9; 47:14; 56:2, 3, 6; 66:17; Jer 1:16; 2:5, 13; 5:13; 7:19; 9:5; 14:15; 16:6; 41:5; 46:16; 50:5; Eze 6:9; 7:18; 14:11, 14; 20:18, 26; 23:3; 25:12; 27:31; 32:4; 34:10; 36:5; 37:7, 23; 40:12; 44:24; Da 2:43; Hos 6:10; 7:14; 8:4, 9, 10; 9:4, 10; Am 2:14; Hab 2:4; Zec 2:11; 12:5; Mt 8:27; 9:3; 11:25; 14:15; 21:25; 23:12, 12; Mk 2:6, 8; 3:8; 4:41; 5:14; 6:36; 9:10; 11:31; Lk 7:49; 8:35; 10:21; 20:5; 22:24; Jn 5:43; 7:18, 25; 18:28; 19:24; Ac 2:7, 42; 4:15; 16:37; 23:12; 25:16; 28:25; Ro 1:18, 27; 2:8; 11:11; 14:20, 22; 1Co 3:15; 7:5, 9; 10:7; 2Co 5:15; 8:5; 10:12, 12, 12, 18; 11:13; Gal 5:12; Eph 4:19; Php 2:21; 1Th 1:9; 1Ti 2:9, 10; 3:15; 6:10; 2Ti 3:2, 13; Tit 2:10; 3:11; Heb 5:14; 6:16; Jas 3:2; 5:6; 1Pe 3:5; 2Pe 1:20; 2:14, 18, 19; 1Jn 3:3; Jude 12, 18; Rev 6:15; 19:21

THEN (3757)

Ge 1:3, 4, 11, 11, 22, 26, 31; 2:8, 10, 22; 3:6, 13, 16, 19, 20, 22, 22; 4:7, 15, 17, 5:24, 6:3, 14, 16; 7:3, 16; 8:8, 15, 20; 9:8, 17, 25, 26; 11:7; 12:1, 7, 9, 12, 13, 16, 20; 13:3, 8, 9, 9, 18; 14:7, 11, 18, 20; 15:4, 5, 7, 9, 13; 16:5, 9; 17:3, 15, 17; 18:7, 10, 13, 16, 19, 21, 27, 29, 31, 31, 32; 19:1, 2, 11, 20, 24, 32; 20:7, 9, 14, 16, 17; 21:1, 16, 17, 19, 25, 27, 33; 22:3, 5, 9, 13, 15, 19; 23:3, 7; 24:5, 8, 22, 33, 48, 49, 50, 53, 54, 55, 61, 66; 25:26, 33, 34; 26:11, 20, 21, 25, 31; 27:4, 10, 12, 15, 17, 21, 25, 25, 25, 31, 33, 38, 40, 41, 46; 28:16, 18, 20, 21; 29:11, 13, 30, 35; 30:3, 7, 12, 19, 22, 38, 40; 31:3, 8, 11, 33, 33, 36, 43, 46, 54, 55; 32:9, 26, 29; 33:1, 3, 4, 5, 6, 18; 34:11, 27; 35:11, 13, 14, 21, 29; 36:6; 37:7, 9, 14, 20, 22, 25, 30, 31, 34, 35; 38:4, 8, 11, 14, 18, 23, 29, 30; 40:11, 19, 21; 41:3, 4, 6, 7, 9, 19, 21, 23, 42, 54; 42:16, 16, 24, 25, 33, 34, 34, 37; 43:9, 11, 13, 14, 18, 23, 24, 27, 28, 30, 31; 44:2, 18, 27; 45:2, 12, 15, 15, 28; 46:30; 47:7, 10, 16, 19, 20, 23, 24, 26; 48:8, 11, 13, 15, 21; 49:1, 29, 33; 50:2, 14, 18, 25; Ex 1:8, 10, 15, 18, 22; 2:4, 7, 17, 19, 20; 3:6, 7, 12, 13, 18, 20; 4:2, 4, 5, 6, 9, 14, 18, 21, 22, 28; 5:14; 6:10; 7:1, 4, 8, 11, 12, 14, 19, 24; 8:1, 2, 5, 8, 9, 10, 22; 9:8, 13, 22, 27, 29; 10:1, 12, 21, 24; 11:1, 6, 7, 8, 8; 12:6, 21, 22, 26, 27, 43, 48; 13:1, 6, 14; 14:1, 3, 11, 15, 16, 17, 19, 21, 23, 26; 15:1, 20, 22, 24, 26; 16:1, 4, 6, 9, 12, 19, 20, 32, 33; 17:4, 5, 6, 12, 14; 18:7, 12, 23; 19:3, 9, 9, 10, 13, 15, 21; 20:1, 11, 12; 21:3, 3, 4, 6, 10, 14, 21, 22, 23, 26, 33, 34, 35, 36; 22:1, 4, 5, 6, 11, 23, 27, 30; 23:11, 22; 24:1, 4, 5, 7, 8, 9, 12, 15, 18; 25:17, 18, 21, 23, 37; 26:3, 6, 34; 27:9; 28:15, 23, 26, 28, 40, 41; 29:2, 5, 7, 9, 10, 11, 14, 21, 23, 26; 30:1, 12, 22; 31:12, 18; 32:2, 4, 7, 9, 10, 15, 20, 29, 32; 33:10, 15, 18, 23; 34:5, 9, 11, 16, 32, 34; 35:4; 36:8, 13, 17, 19, 31, 36, 37; 37:4, 6, 10, 13, 17, 29; 38:3, 9; 39:3, 20, 27; 40:4, 8, 10, 14, 19, 20, 21, 25, 33, 34; Lev 1:5, 8, 9, 12, 13, 15, 17, 17; 3:2, 8, 13; 4:1, 5, 10, 15, 18, 18, 21, 25, 30, 31, 34, 35; 5:9, 14, 16; 6:6, 7, 8, 11, 12, 24; 7:3, 14, 18, 21, 22, 28, 31; 8:3, 6, 8, 10, 12, 14, 18, 19, 23, 24, 28, 29, 31, 32; 9:3, 6, 7, 7, 10, 14, 16, 18, 19, 20, 21, 22; 10:3, 4, 6, 8, 12, 15, 19; 11:1, 40; 12:4, 5, 7, 7; 13:3, 3, 5, 8, 17, 20, 21, 25, 25, 26, 28, 31, 33, 37, 37, 45, 54, 55, 58; 14:6, 8, 9, 11, 13, 14, 15, 17, 18, 19, 25, 28, 29, 30, 33, 35, 36, 40, 48, 51; 15:6, 11, 13; 16:4, 5, 7, 11, 12, 14, 14, 15, 18, 19, 21, 24, 26; 17:1, 15; 18:1, 18; 19:22; 20:5; 21:16; 23:6, 9, 19, 26, 40; 24:13, 14; 25:9, 19, 25, 27, 27, 28, 30, 52, 54; 26:4, 21, 24, 28, 34, 34, 41, 42; 27:8, 9, 10, 11, 15, 17, 19, 23, 33; Nu 2:1, 17; 3:5, 40; 4:1, 6, 8, 10, 11, 13, 17; 5:5, 16, 21, 23, 24, 25, 26; 6:1, 9, 9, 11, 17, 18, 20, 22; 7:2, 4; 8:5, 7, 9, 13, 21, 22; 9:15, 18, 20; 10:4, 17, 18, 22; 11:4, 8, 16, 23, 24, 30; 12:5, 16; 14:1, 4, 5, 10, 12, 20, 26, 36, 45; 15:9, 35; 16:5, 7, 8, 12, 15, 19, 24, 27, 29, 30, 35, 38, 38, 50; 17:1, 5, 12; 19:6, 7, 9, 12, 18, 19; 20:6, 10, 11, 23, 28; 21:2, 4, 7, 8, 11, 13, 18, 20, 33, 35; 22:1, 6, 11, 15, 24, 26, 28, 31, 34, 39; 23:3, 3, 5, 11, 13, 15, 16, 25, 27; 24:2, 20, 21, 25; 25:6, 7, 10, 16; 26:52; 27:8, 15; 30:4, 5, 14, 15; 31:1, 6, 9, 21, 23, 24, 27, 48; 32:10, 17, 20, 22, 23, 25, 29, 30, 39; 33:6, 8, 40, 42; 34:1, 4, 8, 11, 12, 13; 36:1, 4; Dt 1:19, 41, 45; 2:1, 2, 8, 13, 24, 26, 31, 32; 3:13, 20; 4:26, 32, 40, 41; 5:16, 27, 33; 6:3, 18, 21; 7:4, 20, 26; 8:1, 3; 9:12, 14, 18; 10:2, 5, 7; 11:14, 17, 23; 12:25; 13:2, 9, 11, 16, 17; 14:26, 29; 16:7, 10; 17:5, 7, 13, 14; 18:17; 19:2, 11, 17; 20:5, 8, 11; 21:3, 7, 8, 13, 14, 21, 22; 22:2, 17, 18, 19, 25, 29; 24:2, 19; 25:8, 9; 26:4, 5, 10, 13, 19; 27:1, 3, 5, 9, 14; 28:10, 36, 59, 68; 29:22; 30:3, 8, 18, 20; 31:7, 10, 14, 17, 20, 21, 23; 32:15, 37, 50; 34:1, 4; Jos 1:8, 10, 12, 15; 2:1, 15, 16, 23; 3:5, 16; 4:7, 21, 22; 5:9; 6:5, 7, 10, 11, 22, 24; 7:7, 9, 14, 17, 17, 19, 23, 24, 25; 8:1, 7, 18, 22, 30, 31, 33, 34; 9:15; 10:10, 15, 21, 22, 26, 27, 29, 30, 34, 38, 43; 11:6, 9, 10, 11; 14:11; 15:3, 6, 8, 8, 9, 11, 15; 16:3, 3, 6, 6; 17:7, 17; 18:3, 6, 8, 9, 12, 14, 17, 18; 19:13, 27, 29, 34; 20:6; 21:1; 22:1, 19, 21, 27, 32; 23:13; 24:1, 5, 7, 9, 15, 19, 23, 28; Jdg 1:3, 9, 12, 17; 2:2, 8, 11, 16; 3:8, 11, 23, 27; 4:3, 14, 15, 21; 5:11, 22, 26, 31; 6:6, 11, 14, 19, 21, 26, 32, 34, 36, 37, 39; 7:11, 15, 17, 20, 23; 8:1, 4, 6, 15, 15, 16, 18, 21, 22, 29; 9:6, 10, 12, 14, 19, 20, 21, 38, 39, 50; 10:16; 11:12, 13, 17, 19, 23; 12:1, 6, 15; 13:8, 15, 17, 19; 14:13, 17, 19; 15:4, 5, 8, 15, 19; 16:3, 5, 13, 15, 20, 28, 29; 17:5; 18:5, 13, 27, 28, 30; 19:6, 8, 25, 29; 20:1, 3, 7, 20, 23, 26, 32, 33, 36, 37, 48; 21:5, 14, 19, 23; Ru 1:6, 9, 12; 2:5, 9, 21, 23; 3:3, 4, 7, 13, 13, 15, 18; 4:2, 4, 5, 6, 9, 11; 1Sa 1:11, 18, 19, 22; 2:1, 11, 16, 35, 36; 3:6, 8, 11, 15; 4:3, 22; 5:6; 6:2, 3, 5, 8, 11, 16; 7:3, 3, 5, 12, 16, 16, 17; 8:22; 9:18, 22, 23; 10:1, 8, 10, 21, 24, 25, 25; 11:6, 10, 12, 14, 15; 12:1, 10, 11, 14, 15, 17; 13:15; 14:8, 9, 10, 12, 15, 18, 20, 34, 36, 38, 40, 41, 42, 46; 15:5, 7, 10, 12, 14, 16, 21, 24, 30, 32, 34; 16:5, 8, 11, 13, 22, 23; 17:4, 9, 31, 38, 40, 46, 52, 53; 18:22; 19:3, 5, 7, 11, 13, 15, 18; 20:3, 7, 7, 10, 12, 18, 21, 21, 22, 33, 40, 41, 42; 22:2, 9, 10, 18, 19; 23:18, 23, 29; 24:4, 5, 9, 16; 25:1, 31, 35, 39; 26:11, 12, 14, 19, 19, 21, 25; 27:1; 28:2, 7, 8, 25; 30:7, 8, 15, 25; 31:9, 13; 2Sa 1:9, 10, 13, 15, 17; 2:1, 4, 14, 17, 27, 32; 3:12, 14, 16, 19, 21, 21, 26, 27, 31, 33, 38; 4:6, 12; 5:1, 6, 11; 6:1, 7, 12, 19, 19; 7:18; 8:4, 6; 9:3, 9, 12; 10:11, 17; 11:4, 4, 8, 13, 13, 15, 18, 21, 27; 12:7, 9, 13, 18, 20, 20, 24, 31; 13:8, 10, 15, 19, 26, 28, 29, 32, 34; 14:3, 3, 11, 23, 26, 29, 31, 32, 33; 15:3, 4, 14, 19, 23, 24, 26, 27, 34; 16:11, 20, 21; 17:2, 3, 5, 6, 10, 13, 14, 15, 21; 18:14, 15, 16, 19, 21, 23, 28, 31; 19:5, 7, 11, 14, 16, 21, 23, 37, 40; 20:1, 4, 6, 18, 22; 21:4, 5, 10; 22:8, 16; 23:20; 24:5, 6, 7, 8; 1Ki 1:11, 13, 31, 32, 34, 39, 47, 49; 2:4, 10, 21, 23, 26, 32, 35, 36, 43, 46; 3:15, 15, 20, 22, 23, 25, 26, 27; 5:2, 8, 9, 13; 6:11, 21, 33; 7:13, 23, 51; 8:1, 4, 6, 12, 14, 17, 22, 32, 34, 35, 36, 39, 40, 43, 43, 45, 48, 49, 62, 65; 9:2, 5, 7; 10:10, 13, 18, 29; 11:14, 18, 31, 38, 43; 12:4, 5, 6, 25; 13:2, 7, 15, 20, 27; 14:2, 6, 12, 15, 28, 31; 15:8, 22, 24, 27; 16:6, 9, 10, 15, 24, 28, 33; 17:2, 8, 12, 18, 20, 23, 24; 18:21, 21, 22, 24, 25, 26, 26, 30, 32, 33, 40, 41, 43, 44; 19:4, 5, 7, 15, 16, 20, 21, 21; 20:7, 10, 13, 13, 15, 27, 28, 28, 31, 34, 36, 37, 41; 21:10, 13, 14, 28; 22:2, 4, 5, 19, 24, 26, 28, 38, 40, 50; 2Ki 1:9, 10, 15; 2:4, 5, 6, 8, 10, 10, 13, 14, 21, 24; 3:8, 12; 4:4, 6, 8, 10, 21, 28, 29, 34, 35, 36, 37, 41, 41; 5:10, 15, 17, 24; 6:6, 17, 19, 23, 28, 29; 7:11, 12, 16; 8:8, 11, 13, 15, 24; 9:3, 6, 10, 16, 21, 23, 24, 34; 10:11, 12, 15, 16, 18, 20, 23, 25, 35; 11:4, 12, 15, 17, 19; 12:9, 11, 17, 21; 13:4, 5, 9, 13, 16, 17, 17, 17, 19, 20, 25; 14:9, 13, 16, 21, 29; 15:7, 10, 14, 19, 25, 25, 30, 38; 16:5, 8, 10, 14, 17, 20; 17:4, 5, 21, 27; 18:14, 19, 26, 28, 31, 32, 37; 19:7, 19, 20, 29, 36, 37; 20:3, 7, 14, 16, 19; 21:10, 14, 18, 23, 26; 22:5, 8, 12; 23:1, 4, 6, 10, 14, 16, 16, 19, 21, 30, 34; 24:1, 2, 12, 17, 20; 25:4, 5, 7, 10, 11, 22, 26; 1Ch 1:51; 3:4; 5:10; 6:32; 10:9, 12; 11:1, 4, 22; 12:17, 18; 13:2, 6, 10; 14:3; 15:2, 3, 11, 15, 25; 16:3, 5, 43; 17:16; 18:3, 4, 6; 19:12, 15, 17; 20:3; 21:4, 8, 9, 18, 22, 27; 22:1, 6, 17; 23:4, 6; 25:1; 28:11, 20; 29:1, 5, 6, 10, 20, 28; 2Ch 1:3, 13, 17; 3:17; 4:2, 7, 8; 5:2, 7, 11; 6:1, 3, 7, 12, 13, 23, 25, 26, 27, 30, 31, 33, 33, 35, 38, 39; 7:4, 7, 10, 12, 14, 18, 20; 8:12; 9:9, 12, 17, 31; 10:4, 6; 12:4, 5, 11, 16; 13:2, 7, 14; 14:1, 11; 15:1, 9, 12; 16:6; 17:1, 10; 18:2, 4, 18, 23, 25, 27, 34; 20:17, 18, 19, 27, 37; 21:1, 12, 16; 22:1, 9; 23:9, 11, 11, 14, 16, 20; 24:9, 11, 18, 20, 21, 23, 25; 25:5, 11, 18, 23, 24; 26:1, 6, 23; 28:7, 12, 15, 15, 24, 27; 29:12, 15, 17, 18, 23, 24, 25, 26, 27, 29, 31; 30:15, 16, 23, 27; 31:2, 12; 32:5, 6, 9, 20, 23, 26, 33; 33:16, 20; 34:3, 5, 7, 10, 15, 20, 29; 35:1, 5, 7, 11, 13, 24; 36:1, 3, 4, 6, 8, 19; Ezr 1:5; 3:2, 3, 7, 11; 4:4, 13, 17; 5:17; 6:10, 11, 16, 18; 8:35, 36; 9:1, 4; 10:2, 6, 7, 10, 12, 13; Ne 1:5; 2:2, 14, 18; 3:1, 4, 11, 15, 17, 22, 27, 31; 4:4, 10, 14, 16, 19, 20; 5:7, 9, 12, 12; 6:13, 19; 8:6, 6, 9, 18; 9:3, 5, 5, 11, 22; 12:30, 35, 37, 39, 39, 40; 13:9, 11, 19, 22; Est 2:22; 3:3, 8, 15; 4:5, 10, 15, 16; 5:3, 8, 10, 12, 13; 7:7, 9, 9; 8:1, 7, 15; 9:15, 17, 18, 29; Job 1:8, 20; 2:3, 8, 13; 4:1; 5:3; 6:1, 24; 8:1; 9:1, 24, 35; 10:18, 19; 11:1, 15; 12:1; 14:2, 10, 16, 20; 15:1; 16:1, 12; 17:15; 18:1; 19:1, 29; 20:1; 21:1, 13; 22:1, 6, 25, 26, 30; 23:1, 5; 24:15; 25:1; 26:1; 28:27; 31:8, 10, 22, 40; 32:2; 33:25, 33; 34:1; 35:1; 36:11, 27; 37:4; 38:1; 39:4; 40:1, 3, 6, 10, 14; 42:1, 11, 17; Ps 2:5, 10; 7:5, 15; 18:7, 15; 19:13; 22:8, 22; 27:6; 30:7; 34:13; 35:9, 18, 28; 37:3; 40:7; 50:6; 51:13, 14, 19; 53:5; 55:6; 58:11; 59:13; 61:8; 64:9; 67:6; 68:27; 69:30; 71:22; 73:17, 21; 74:8; 78:8, 35, 60, 65; 79:13; 80:3, 7, 18, 19; 81:14; 86:17; 89:32; 104:9, 21, 23; 105:17, 20, 23, 25, 30, 36; 106:11, 12, 12, 28; 107:2; 109:28; 116:4, 6; 119:6, 42, 80, 88, 117, 125, 134; 125:3; 132:6, 12; 142:5; 147:18; Pr 2:5, 9; 3:4, 8, 10, 28; 4:26; 5:2; 16:3; 19:3; 20:14, 26; 24:32; 25:10; 26:19; 27:10, 11; 28:24; 30:20; Ecc 1:7; 2:15, 24; 3:18; 4:4, 8, 16; 6:2; 7:13; 9:16; 12:2, 7; SS 8:1; Isa 1:19, 26; 3:4; 4:5; 5:2, 25; 6:5, 6, 8, 11; 7:3, 6, 13, 14; 8:3, 5, 10; 9:12, 17, 21; 10:4, 20, 25; 11:13; 16:5; 17:7; 20:3; 21:8, 9, 12; 22:20; 23:15; 24:23; 26:11; 28:5; 29:9, 24; 30:8, 22, 23; 32:3, 15; 34:5; 36:2, 4, 11, 13, 16, 17, 22; 37:7, 20, 21, 30, 37, 38; 38:3, 4, 14; 39:3, 5, 8; 40:5, 18; 41:7, 17; 43:12; 44:13, 15, 17; 46:6; 48:3, 18, 19; 49:21, 23; 52:6; 54:10; 57:19; 58:9, 10, 12; 59:4, 19; 62:5; 63:11; 64:2; 66:9; Jer 1:9, 11, 13; 2:31, 36; 3:11; 4:2, 10; 5:4; 7:7, 10; 8:5, 14; 10:4, 9; 11:4, 5, 6, 12, 18; 12:5, 16; 13:3, 8, 13, 16; 14:11, 13, 14; 15:1, 10, 15, 18; 17:19, 19, 25, 27; 18:5, 8, 10, 13, 18; 19:1, 9, 11, 14; 20:10; 21:7; 22:1; 23:4, 8, 25, 38; 24:3, 4; 25:5, 6, 12, 15, 21, 27; 26:3, 6, 12, 16, 17, 19, 22, 23; 27:3, 7, 12, 16; 28:10, 15; 29:6, 10, 30; 30:6; 31:19; 32:8, 8, 11, 13, 16, 26; 33:9, 19, 21, 21, 24; 34:3; 35:8, 12, 18; 36:3, 5, 20, 23, 26, 29, 32; 37:6, 8, 18; 38:12, 17, 22, 24, 25; 39:7, 9; 40:5, 5, 12, 15; 41:3, 16; 42:1, 5, 15; 43:8, 10; 44:15, 20, 24, 25, 28; 46:9, 13; 48:3, 12; 49:2; 50:4, 17; 51:46, 62, 63, 64; 52:3, 7, 8, 11, 14, 15, 29; La 1:7; 2:8, 12; 3:29, 39, 65; Eze 2:9; 3:1, 4, 10, 11, 12, 15, 20, 22, 24, 27; 4:1, 3, 11, 12, 14, 16; 5:4, 4, 13; 6:7, 9, 9, 13, 14; 7:1, 4, 9, 27; 8:1, 3, 5, 7, 12, 13, 16; 9:1, 3, 5, 9, 11; 10:2, 4, 7, 15, 18; 11:1, 2, 5, 10, 13, 14, 20, 22, 23; 12:4, 7, 11, 13, 16, 17, 20, 24, 26; 13:1, 9, 14, 15, 21, 23; 14:1, 4, 7, 8, 12, 22; 15:1; 16:1, 9, 18, 20, 26, 39, 42, 54, 61; 17:1, 4, 5, 7, 10, 11, 21; 18:1; 19:4, 8; 20:2, 7, 8, 18, 39, 42, 45, 49; 21:1, 8, 14, 18, 22, 23, 27; 22:17, 22; 23:5, 14, 25, 34, 38, 40, 43, 49; 24:3, 10, 15, 19, 22, 25, 27; 25:1, 5, 7, 11, 17; 26:6, 8, 17; 27:1, 6; 28:1, 9, 11, 20, 23, 24; 29:16, 16, 21, 21; 30:26; 32:14, 15; 33:4, 8, 13, 13, 14, 15, 23, 29, 33; 34:1, 25, 27; 35:4, 9, 12, 15; 36:11, 16, 21, 23, 25, 31, 36; 37:3, 4, 6, 8, 8, 9, 11, 12, 14, 16, 20, 23; 38:14, 16, 23; 39:6, 9, 23, 26, 28; 40:4, 6, 13, 17, 19, 24, 28, 32, 35, 47, 48; 41:3, 5, 13; 42:1, 13; 43:3, 5, 18, 21, 22, 27; 44:1, 4, 26; 45:7; 46:2, 2, 12, 19, 21; 47:1, 1, 5, 6, 8, 15, 16, 19; 48:1, 4, 6, 7, 26, 28; Da 1:3, 5, 13; 2:4, 9, 17, 19, 24, 25, 46, 48; 3:2, 13, 15, 20, 26, 27, 28, 30; 4:13, 23, 27; 5:29; 6:4, 13, 18, 24, 25; 7:3, 5, 6, 7, 10, 19, 22, 23, 24, 26, 27; 8:13, 14, 19, 27; 9:27; 10:10, 12, 13, 16, 18, 20; 11:2, 3, 11, 15, 25, 28, 29, 40, 44; 12:1, 5, 13; Hos 1:10, 11; 2:7, 14, 22, 23; 3:1, 3; 5:6, 15; 6:3; 7:11, 16; 8:10; 9:5, 10; 10:3; 12:13; 13:6; 14:4; Joel 1:4; 2:18, 27, 28; 3:4, 17; Am 1:8; 3:11; 4:5; 5:14, 18; 6:2, 10; 7:2, 4, 5, 6, 7, 12, 16; 8:1, 2, 6; 9:1, 1, 5, 13, 15; Ob 19; Jnh 1:7, 10, 14, 15; 2:1, 4, 10; 3:1, 7; 4:5, 9, 10; Mic 2:5; 3:4, 7; 4:7, 13; 5:3, 4, 7; 7:10; Na 3:16; Hab 1:16; 2:2; Zep 1:5; 2:11; 3:11; Hag 1:8, 12, 13; 2:1, 13, 13, 14; Zec 1:7, 11, 14, 18, 20; 2:3, 9; 3:1, 5, 6, 7; 4:1, 4, 6, 7, 8, 9, 11, 14; 5:3, 5, 9; 6:1, 8, 9, 11; 7:8; 8:1, 3; 11:7, 10, 14, 15; 12:10; 13:3, 4, 6; 14:3, 5, 10; Mal 1:7, 14; 2:4, 10; 3:1, 4, 12, 16, 18; Mt 2:7, 8, 11, 22; 3:12, 13, 15; 4:1, 3, 5, 11, 17; 5:24; 6:1, 6, 18; 7:5, 6; 8:4, 8, 13, 15, 19, 23, 26; 9:6, 13, 15, 29; 10:2; 11:20, 25, 28; 12:9, 13, 14, 22, 28, 29, 37, 44, 45, 49; 13:11, 19, 30, 36, 43, 52, 57; 14:12, 19, 28, 33; 15:10, 12, 15, 17, 21, 23, 24, 32, 36, 39; 16:4, 12, 15, 20, 21, 24; 17:13, 18, 25, 26; 18:3, 21, 27, 32, 34; 19:7, 10, 10, 21, 23, 25, 27, 30, 30; 20:7, 16, 16, 19, 20, 34; 21:17, 19, 21, 27, 30, 31, 33, 42; 22:7, 13, 15, 21, 25, 27, 41, 43; 23:1, 15, 16, 24, 26, 30; 24:9, 14, 16, 23, 30; 25:8, 15, 24, 31, 34, 37, 41, 44; 26:14, 26, 30, 36, 40, 45, 50, 55, 57, 62, 63, 65, 67; 27:2, 5, 19, 26, 29, 31, 33, 36, 40, 50, 60, 64; 28:5, 10, 16; Mk 1:26, 43; 2:4, 10, 12, 13, 20, 26, 27; 3:4, 5, 14, 27, 34; 4:8, 15, 21, 21, 27, 28; 5:9, 10, 33, 37, 40; 6:4, 6, 22, 23, 26, 31, 39, 51; 7:9, 14, 17, 19, 20, 24, 31, 33; 8:6, 23, 25, 29, 31, 33, 34; 9:4, 7, 12, 15, 26, 35, 36; 10:1, 16, 21, 26, 28, 31, 31, 35, 52; 11:7, 11, 11, 14, 22, 33; 12:1, 1, 4, 17, 18, 20, 21, 40, 42; 13:11, 14, 21, 26; 14:10, 22, 26, 37, 39, 44, 46, 54, 59, 60, 61, 63, 65, 67, 68; 15:3, 15, 18, 20, 21, 24, 30, 34, 37, 41, 46; 16:15, S; Lk 1:19, 22, 23, 38, 56, 67, 80; 2:17, 22, 34, 51; 3:3, 6, 17; 4:1, 3, 5, 9, 14, 21, 23, 31, 35; 5:14, 24, 35, 36, 36; 6:4, 9, 10, 20, 35, 39, 42, 47; 7:14, 15, 22, 38, 38, 40, 41, 44, 48; 8:12, 16, 25, 36, 54, 55; 9:2, 10, 20, 23, 30, 35, 42, 46, 48, 62; 10:16, 21, 23, 33, 34, 37; 11:5, 20, 26, 33, 36, 39; 12:5, 13, 15, 18, 20, 22, 36, 54; 13:6, 13, 18, 25, 29, 30, 30; 14:5, 9, 10, 10, 12, 14, 28, 29, 32; 15:5; 16:4, 15, 27, 30; 17:3, 29; 18:6, 9, 16, 22, 24, 26, 41; 19:12, 24, 36, 45; 20:8, 17, 25, 27, 29, 35, 41, 45, 47; 21:2, 10, 20, 21, 27, 29; 22:3, 14, 17, 19, 23, 35, 39, 43, 52, 61, 64, 70; 23:1, 5, 11, 13, 16, 18, 26, 42, 46, 53, 56; 24:5, 8, 12, 18, 22, 25, 27, 30, 35, 41, 44, 45, 50, 52; Jn 1:21, 22, 24, 32, 36, 37, 40, 42, 51; 2:10, 16, 17; 4:15, 26, 27, 34, 42, 50, 53; 5:15, 23; 6:3, 8, 11, 21, 41, 52, 62, 65, 67, 70; 7:14, 30, 33, 50, 53; 8:8, 10, 19, 23, 28, 30; 9:6, 13, 17, 28, 39; 10:38; 11:11, 14, 28, 35, 38, 41, 43, 47, 48; 12:3, 10, 19, 28, 30, 36; 13:5, 9, 27, 33; 14:7; 16:16, 17, 19, 22, 26, 29; 17:6, 23; 18:10, 16, 24, 28, 31, 33, 36, 37, 38; 19:1, 5, 11, 12, 13, 16, 21, 27, 30, 31; 20:6, 8, 9, 10, 18, 22, 27, 29; 21:6, 7, 13, 15, 16, 17, 19; Ac 1:13, 24, 26; 2:3, 14, 38, 40; 3:7, 8, 20, 23; 4:8, 21, 24; 5:3, 6, 19, 21, 25, 27, 31, 35, 40; 6:4; 7:1, 4, 14, 18, 42, 57; 8:13, 17, 35; 9:18, 27, 28, 31, 35, 40, 41; 10:13, 16, 17, 34, 38, 40, 46; 11:4, 11, 16, 25; 12:8, 10, 17; 13:4, 9, 17, 19, 21, 46, 50; 14:24, 25; 15:5, 22, 32, 33; 16:1, 4, 7, 23, 32, 34, 39, 40; 17:15, 19; 18:1, 18, 21, 22; 19:3, 6, 8, 9, 41; 20:1, 2, 11, 11, 38; 21:1, 6, 8, 11, 20, 24, 26, 33; 22:14, 22; 23:23, 25, 28, 34, 35; 24:9, 22, 27; 25:9, 12, 24; 26:1, 18, 20, 30; 27:9, 17, 30, 35, 36, 40, 43; 28:9; Ro 2:21; 3:1, 5, 9, 27, 31; 4:9, 10, 13, 14; 6:1; 7:4, 7, 14; 8:34; 9:6, 19, 30; 11:1, 6, 11, 27; 12:2; 14:14, 16, 19; 15:6, 7, 32; 16:7; 1Co 4:5, 8, 19; 5:5; 9:17, 18; 10:9, 25; 11:6; 12:17, 28; 13:12, 12; 14:15, 21; 15:1, 5, 7, 13, 14, 16, 17, 23, 28, 29, 38, 46, 52, 54; 16:2, 4, 6, 7; 2Co 1:6, 14, 16; 3:11, 16; 5:8; 8:14; 9:8, 10; 10:16, 16; 11:28; 12:10, 20; 13:11; Gal 1:15, 16, 21; 2:1, 13, 17, 21; 3:7, 18, 19, 21; 4:15; 5:2, 16; 6:4; Eph 3:19; 4:14, 28; 5:19; Php 1:26, 27; 2:2, 19; 4:15; Col 1:10; 2:13; 1Th 2:14; 4:4, 17; 5:3; 2Th 1:12; 2:8, 12; 1Ti 1:16; 3:10; 5:12, 14, 16; 6:14; 2Ti 2:4, 26; Tit 1:9; 2:5, 8, 10; 3:4; Heb 1:6; 2:17; 3:12; 5:14; 6:6, 12, 15; 7:2, 4, 27; 9:3, 20; 10:7, 9, 12, 17, 36; 12:13; Jas 1:25; 2:13, 16; 3:13; 4:11, 14, 17; 5:18; 1Pe 1:14; 3:16; 4:1, 11, 11, 14; 2Pe 1:5; 2:5, 20, 21; 3:4, 6, 10; 1Jn 1:2, 7; 2Jn 12; 3Jn 14; Rev 3:18; 4:1; 5:4, 11, 13; 6:1, 11, 13, 15; 7:1, 13, 14; 8:3, 5, 6, 8, 10, 12, 13; 9:1, 3, 13; 10:1, 5, 8, 11; 11:1, 12, 15, 19; 12:1, 7, 10, 15, 17, 18; 13:5, 11, 14, 15; 14:1, 8, 9, 14, 15, 18; 15:1, 5; 16:1, 3, 4, 8, 10, 12, 17, 18; 17:11; 18:4, 21; 19:4, 6, 10, 11, 11, 17, 19; 20:1, 3, 4, 10; 21:1, 5, 9, 17; 22:6, 10

THERE (2016)

Ge 1:3, 3, 6, 11; 2:5, 5, 8, 12, 20; 4:8; 7:3; 8:22; 9:15; 10:11; 11:2, 9, 31; 12:7, 8, 10; 13:4, 6, 9, 11, 18; 14:15; 17:27; 18:8, 24, 28, 29, 29, 30, 31, 32; 19:1, 19, 20, 20, 22, 28, 30, 31; 20:2; 22:2, 5; 23:2, 6, 10, 13, 19; 24:4, 5, 6, 7, 8, 11, 54; 26:2, 7, 17, 21, 23, 25, 33; 27:15, 37, 44; 28:11; 29:3, 5, 14; 31:3, 33, 54; 32:29; 33:15, 17, 20; 34:25, 27; 35:1, 1, 7, 7, 15, 20, 22; 36:7, 31; 37:15, 17; 38:2, 21, 22; 39:6, 21; 40:8, 10, 16; 41:22, 30, 35, 36, 47, 49, 54, 54; 42:1, 2, 13, 13, 23, 35; 43:1, 21, 23, 25, 30; 45:3, 6, 11, 11; 46:3, 27, 28; 47:4, 4, 27; 48:7; 49:31, 31, 31; 50:3, 13; Ex 1:9, 19; 2:20; 4:2; 5:5; 7:15, 21; 8:5, 22, 24; 9:14, 24; 10:5, 6, 14, 22, 23, 26; 11:6, 6; 12:19, 30, 37, 48; 13:7; 14:2, 4, 11; 15:25, 27, 27; 16:1, 2, 3, 3, 22, 25, 26, 27, 29, 35; 17:1, 1, 15; 19:2, 16, 16; 20:24; 22:9, 10, 14, 15; 23:23, 26; 24:10, 10, 12, 14; 25:15, 22, 22; 26:7, 17, 20, 22, 25; 27:5; 29:43; 30:6, 12, 19; 32:5, 17; 33:5, 7; 34:2, 5; 36:22; 38:2, 10, 10; 40:38; Lev 4:4, 15, 21; 8:3; 9:5; 10:2, 12; 11:21; 13:21, 26, 31; 14:13; 15:15, 31; 16:2, 13, 15, 23; 18:25, 28; 25:10, 24, 26; 26:25, 36; Nu 1:19; 3:14, 22, 28, 34, 39; 5:8, 13; 7:3, 89; 9:5; 11:3, 16, 17, 21, 23, 26, 31, 34, 35; 13:18, 20, 24, 28, 28, 32, 33; 14:34, 39; 15:19; 17:3; 19:9; 20:1, 2, 5, 8, 15, 26, 26, 28; 21:5, 10, 12, 16, 17, 32; 22:3, 8, 25, 41; 23:4, 13, 14, 27; 32:39, 40; 33:9, 14, 38, 39, 52; 34:11; 35:15, 30, 34; Dt 1:28, 44, 46; 2:22, 22; 3:22, 24; 4:12, 26, 28, 29, 35, 39; 9:9, 16; 10:5, 7, 22; 11:3, 6; 12:2, 6, 7, 12, 14, 18; 13:1; 14:23, 26; 15:4, 7, 11; 16:6; 17:6, 14, 16; 18:7, 7, 9; 19:3, 6; 21:4, 5; 22:6, 27; 25:7; 26:1; 27:5, 7; 28:26, 31, 61, 64, 65, 68; 29:29; 31:3, 5, 14, 20; 32:39, 50, 51; 33:19, 20, 26; 34:5, 10; Jos 2:1, 16, 22; 3:13, 17; 4:8, 9, 20; 7:3, 22; 8:14, 17, 29; 10:14, 30; 14:12; 15:4, 7, 9, 9, 32, 36, 42, 55, 58, 60, 61, 63; 16:5; 17:12, 18; 18:2, 10, 13, 15, 16, 18; 19:11, 12, 47, 50; 20:4; 21:43; 22:19; 23:5, 5; 24:11; Jdg 1:7, 11, 16, 19, 20, 29, 36; 3:11; 4:7, 20, 22; 5:7, 15, 16, 30, 31; 6:24; 7:4; 8:8, 14; 9:5, 36, 51; 14:3; 16:2, 27, 27; 18:2, 10, 14, 26, 28, 28; 19:1, 4, 12, 15, 26, 27, 28; 20:15; 21:10, 14, 17; Ru 1:17; 2:1, 4, 5, 7, 17, 22; 3:4, 12, 12; 4:1, 11; 1Sa 1:1, 22, 28; 2:2, 2; 3:21; 4:16; 5:9, 12; 6:18; 7:6, 14, 17; 9:6, 19, 25; 10:8, 8, 27; 11:8, 9; 13:8, 19; 14:20, 34, 40; 15:4; 16:1, 11, 13; 17:26, 33, 46; 18:1; 19:3, 5, 15; 20:5, 11, 19, 21, 29; 21:3, 4, 6, 7, 9, 9, 11; 22:1, 9, 14, 22; 23:22, 25; 24:10; 25:2, 10, 17; 26:6, 15; 27:7; 28:7; 29:4; 2Sa 1:6, 21, 21; 2:9, 13, 23, 23, 25, 32; 3:23; 4:2, 7; 5:3, 20, 21; 6:11, 12; 7:22, 22; 8:10; 10:17; 11:20; 12:1; 13:35, 38; 14:6, 32; 15:10, 18, 23, 24, 28, 29, 35, 37; 17:9, 13, 19, 23; 18:7, 11, 22, 29; 19:7, 8, 9, 33, 43; 20:10, 18; 21:1, 10, 18; 23:13, 20, 39; 24:2, 3, 3, 9, 21, 25; 1Ki 1:34, 39; 2:5, 31, 36; 3:4, 18; 4:19, 24; 5:6; 6:8, 10, 34, 36; 7:4, 6, 7, 12, 24, 34, 35, 36, 36, 47; 8:8, 9, 21, 23, 35, 37, 55, 60, 64; 9:3, 20; 10:12; 11:15, 16, 40; 12:32; 13:1, 9, 11, 17, 24, 28; 14:24, 30; 15:6, 7, 16, 32; 17:1, 7, 9, 9, 13, 14, 16; 18:25, 26, 29, 40; 19:3, 7, 9, 11, 11, 12, 12, 15, 19, 20; 20:10; 22:1, 7, 8, 10, 20, 20, 32, 37, 43, 47; 2Ki 1:3, 6, 16; 2:25; 3:9, 11, 11, 20; 4:6, 7, 8, 8, 21, 31, 32, 38, 43, 43, 44; 5:8, 15, 18, 26; 6:2, 2, 9, 10, 15, 16, 25; 7:3, 5, 10, 10; 8:29; 9:5, 16, 16, 22, 27; 10:8, 15, 17; 11:4, 16; 12:3; 14:19, 19; 16:6, 10; 18:5; 19:36; 20:13, 19; 22:7; 23:2, 17, 22, 25, 25; 25:21; 1Ch 1:43; 4:9, 14, 40, 41, 43; 5:18; 6:31, 32, 32; 7:9, 40; 9:22, 33; 10:6; 11:3, 15, 22; 12:24, 25, 26, 29, 30, 32, 33, 34, 35, 36, 37, 40; 13:10, 14; 14:11, 12; 15:1, 5, 6, 7, 8, 9, 10; 17:20, 20; 18:10; 21:2, 5, 20, 22, 26, 28, 30; 24:4, 5; 25:2; 26:1, 32; 27:2, 4, 5, 7, 8, 9, 10, 11, 12, 13, 14, 15; 29:2, 17; 2Ch 1:6; 2:16; 4:3; 5:9, 10; 6:11, 14, 26, 28; 7:7; 8:7, 11; 9:9, 11, 18; 12:12; 13:17; 14:1, 14; 15:19; 17:14, 17; 18:6, 7, 9, 19, 19, 31; 19:3; 20:14, 17, 24, 25, 26; 23:15; 25:27, 27; 26:19; 28:9, 24; 29:16, 34, 35; 30:17, 26; 32:7, 21, 22; 34:30; 35:18, 24; 36:16; Ezr 1:11; 2:63; 4:19; 5:15; 6:6, 22; 7:1; 8:15, 21; 9:4, 11; 10:2, 6; Ne 2:16; 4:8, 10; 6:7, 8; 7:5, 65; 8:7; 10:32; 11:1, 6, 8, 12, 13, 18; 12:17; 13:16, 26; Est 1:7, 18; 2:5, 14, 14; 3:8; 4:3, 13; 5:2, 13; 6:5; Job 1:1; 3:19; 4:16; 6:6, 18, 18; 8:11, 11; 9:33, 33; 11:7; 12:14; 13:20; 14:7, 13; 16:19; 19:7, 29; 22:14; 23:3, 8; 26:6; 28:8; 31:23; 32:15; 33:23; 34:7, 12; 38:20; 39:29; 41:33; 42:15; Ps 14:1, 2; 19:11; 27:5; 32:6; 37:29; 39:2; 43:4; 49:5; 53:1, 2; 55:11; 58:11, 11; 59:3; 63:1; 68:6, 10; 69:35, 36; 71:11; 72:7, 16; 74:4, 4; 76:3; 77:2, 13, 19; 78:69; 81:7; 84:3; 86:8, 8; 89:8; 92:7, 15; 95:9; 103:19; 104:17; 105:18, 37; 107:34, 36, 38; 118:20; 121:1; 122:7; 128:3; 130:7; 137:3; 139:8, 8, 10; 144:14; 146:3, 3; Pr 6:16, 35; 8:8, 27, 28, 29; 11:14; 13:12; 14:7, 12; 15:6; 16:15, 25; 17:21; 18:24; 19:18; 20:13; 26:12, 13, 13; 28:2, 2; 29:9, 20; 30:15, 18, 21, 24, 29; 31:29; Ecc 1:6; 2:11, 24; 3:1, 12, 16, 22; 5:7, 13, 14; 6:1; 7:2, 20; 8:6, 8, 15, 16; 9:3, 4, 10, 14, 15, 15; 10:5, 9; 11:3; 12:2, 12; SS 1:8; 2:9; 5:6; 6:8; 7:12, 13; 8:2, 11; Isa 2:2, 3; 4:5, 5; 5:17, 29; 7:25; 8:20, 22; 9:1; 10:31; 11:16; 13:20, 21; 14:1, 9, 9, 16; 17:2; 19:19, 19; 22:18, 18; 23:5; 24:7, 23; 27:9, 10; 29:2; 30:14, 23, 25; 34:10, 14, 14, 15; 35:2, 2, 8, 9; 37:37; 39:2, 8; 41:11, 17; 43:10, 10, 11; 44:6, 8, 8; 45:5, 6, 6, 18, 21, 22; 46:7, 7, 9; 48:19, 22; 51:3; 53:2; 55:13; 57:7, 21; 59:2, 15; 60:18, 21; 63:3; 65:8, 8, 8, 9; 66:13, 19; Jer 2:10, 28, 36; 3:2, 14, 16, 17; 4:23; 5:12, 28; 6:20, 29; 7:11, 12, 32; 8:14, 19, 22, 22, 22, 22; 10:5, 6, 7, 13; 11:13; 13:4, 6; 14:5, 6, 16, 18; 15:8; 16:13; 17:25; 18:2; 19:5, 8, 11, 14; 20:6; 22:4; 23:28; 25:35; 26:2, 17; 27:22; 29:8, 20; 30:5, 6, 7, 13, 19; 31:5, 17; 32:3, 5, 12, 35; 33:10, 18; 36:6, 12; 37:20, 21; 38:6, 6, 26; 39:5; 40:5; 42:16, 17; 46:17, 19; 48:2, 2, 19, 33; 49:1, 7, 10, 17, 18, 33; 50:13, 34, 39, 40; 51:16, 37, 46; 52:10, 11, 23, 27; La 1:2, 7, 12, 20; 2:13; 3:29; 4:15, 19; 5:8; Eze 1:3, 22; 3:15, 22, 23, 25; 4:4, 7; 5:2; 6:6; 7:12; 8:3, 4, 5, 9, 11, 11, 14; 11:24; 12:13, 25; 13:10, 16; 14:1, 14, 16, 20, 22; 16:6, 6, 28; 17:6, 20; 20:11, 13, 35, 36, 40; 22:12, 26; 23:2; 24:16, 17; 26:20, 20; 27:32; 28:8; 30:13, 24; 31:4, 12, 16, 18; 32:19, 22, 24, 26, 29, 30, 30, 30, 32; 34:14; 35:10; 37:7, 25; 39:9, 11, 16, 16, 17; 40:2, 7, 10, 16, 16, 20, 21, 22, 23, 25, 26, 31, 33, 34, 37, 40, 41, 42, 43, 44, 47, 49; 41:5, 18, 21, 22, 25, 26; 42:6, 7, 9, 10, 11, 12, 13; 43:13, 17; 47:1, 2, 12, 12; 48:10, 18, 31, 35; Da 1:21; 2:10, 27, 28, 40; 3:12, 29; 4:13; 5:11; 6:20; 8:7, 18; 9:12; 10:8, 9, 13, 21; 11:14, 36, 45, 45, 45; 12:1, 4, 11; Hos 2:14, 15; 4:1, 2, 7; 5:13, 14; 8:7; 9:4, 4, 15; 10:6, 9, 14; 12:4; 13:4; Joel 1:9, 9, 13, 14, 16, 18; 2:12, 32; 3:2, 12, 14; Am 1:14; 3:5; 4:8; 5:16, 17; 6:2, 9, 10; 7:12; 8:12; 9:4, 15; Jnh 4:6, 10; Mic 1:14; 4:1, 2, 4, 10; 5:4, 12; 6:10; 7:13; Na 2:9; 3:15, 18, 19; Hab 1:4; 3:17; Zep 1:11, 17; 2:2, 7, 14, 15; 3:5, 6, 11, 13; Hag 2:2, 3; Zec 3:1, 3, 4; 5:7, 11; 6:8, 13; 8:10, 10; 9:12; 10:10; 14:7, 7, 9, 21; Mal 2:11; 3:10; Mt 2:13, 15; 4:1; 5:24; 6:21; 8:12, 27; 12:6, 45; 13:42, 50, 54, 58; 14:14, 23; 15:22, 37, 38; 16:21; 17:20; 18:20; 19:2; 21:2, 2, 14, 19, 19; 22:13, 23, 25, 31; 23:10; 24:3, 7, 23, 28, 30, 46, 51; 25:30; 26:5, 19, 32, 55, 60; 27:16, 36; 28:2, 7, 10; Mk 1:13, 45; 2:2, 6, 15; 3:10, 32; 4:1, 1, 39; 5:9, 11, 15, 25; 6:31, 34, 54; 7:13, 24; 8:8, 9, 14; 9:2, 26; 10:1; 11:2, 2, 13; 12:6, 18, 20, 22, 28, 32; 13:4, 8, 21; 14:2, 15, 16, 28, 49, 51, 69; 15:40; 16:5, 7; Lk 1:61; 2:4, 6, 7, 16, 25, 28, 36, 37, 40, 45; 4:22, 25, 25, 31, 32; 5:3, 29; 6:17; 7:37; 8:43; 9:12, 14, 14, 36, 46; 10:6, 31, 32, 42; 11:26; 12:12, 34, 37, 38, 43, 50, 53; 13:6, 7, 14, 28; 14:2, 2, 22, 28; 15:10, 13; 16:19, 21, 23, 26, 26; 17:1, 12, 21, 37; 18:2, 11, 22, 31; 19:2, 2, 4, 8, 30, 30; 20:19, 27, 29, 39; 21:7, 11, 11, 11, 12, 23, 25; 22:12, 13, 40, 53, 55; 23:10, 33, 50; 24:18, 36, 41, 47; Jn 1:3, 29, 36, 39, 46; 2:6; 3:18, 22, 23, 23, 26; 4:6, 46; 5:5, 7; 6:13, 24; 7:12, 25, 48; 8:44; 9:4, 16, 40; 10:16, 42; 11:8, 9, 10, 10, 15, 31, 54; 12:36; 14:2, 4; 16:12; 18:2, 5, 18, 22, 26; 19:18, 18, 26, 29, 31, 41, 42; 20:4, 5, 6, 19; 21:2, 6, 9, 9, 11; Ac 1:10, 18; 2:2, 12; 3:11; 4:2, 6, 12, 12, 14, 34, 36; 5:1, 23, 36, 37; 6:1; 7:11, 12, 15, 45; 8:5, 8, 9, 14, 31, 40; 9:2, 9, 10, 33, 36; 10:1, 36, 46; 11:26, 26; 12:7, 18, 24; 13:5, 13, 38; 14:3, 7, 17, 28; 15:12, 31, 35, 41; 16:1, 10, 12, 12, 26; 17:1, 6, 10, 13, 17, 25; 18:2, 11, 17, 19, 22, 27; 19:2, 7, 32, 39, 40; 20:14, 22; 21:2, 5; 22:5, 10, 12, 20, 25; 23:8, 13, 21; 24:18, 19; 25:4, 9, 14, 26; 27:4, 6, 10, 12; 28:4, 13, 14; Ro 2:5, 9, 10; 3:1, 30, 30; 5:13; 7:8, 23; 8:1, 6, 6; 11:20, 21; 13:1; 14:20, 22; 15:25, 31; 16:7; 1Co 1:10, 10; 3:13; 5:3, 4; 6:5, 11; 7:2, 24, 37; 8:4, 5, 6, 6; 11:3, 18, 19; 12:4, 5, 6, 20; 13:13; 14:10; 15:12, 13, 15, 16, 23, 29, 32, 32, 32, 39, 39, 40, 40, 44, 44; 16:2, 9, 9; 2Co 1:13; 2:17; 4:6, 15; 6:12, 15, 16; 7:5, 5, 5; 8:13; 10:13, 16; 12:3; 13:2; Gal 1:18; 2:2, 2, 4, 6, 21; 3:19, 21, 28; 4:20; 5:23, 24; Eph 3:8; 4:5, 6, 23; 5:3, 4; Php 2:1; 3:5, 18; 4:21; 1Th 2:2, 9; 5:3; 2Th 2:3, 4; 1Ti 1:3, 5; 2:5; 4:13; 5:19, 24, 25; 2Ti 3:1; Tit 1:5, 10; 3:12; Heb 3:9; 4:1, 6, 9, 16; 5:11; 6:13, 13, 20; 7:3, 23; 8:2, 4, 7; 9:1, 2, 3, 22; 10:13, 18, 26, 27; 11:6, 9, 12; 12:11; 13:3, 24; Jas 2:3, 13, 19; 3:14, 16, 16; 4:9, 9, 9, 13, 13; 1Pe 1:6; 2Pe 1:18; 2:1, 1; 3:3; 1Jn 1:5; 2:1; 3:5; 4:1; 5:16; 3Jn 15; Jude 18, 23; Rev 2:6; 3:4; 5:1; 6:4, 12; 7:4; 8:1, 5; 9:16; 11:13, 15, 19; 12:7; 13:4; 16:18, 21; 17:3; 18:11, 18, 22, 22, 23; 19:11; 20:10; 21:4, 13, 25; 22:3, 5, 5

THERE'S (13)

Ge 31:14; Jos 7:3; 1Ki 20:25; 2Ki 4:40; Pr 26:13; Ecc 6:10; Am 3:5; Mk 5:35; Lk 8:49; 14:30; Jn 6:9; Ac 8:36; 1Co 8:10

THESE (1546)

Ge 1:5, 17; 2:11; 9:10, 19; 10:20, 31, 32, 32; 14:24; 15:10; 18:21; 19:8; 24:3, 45; 25:4, 16; 26:4, 15; 27:46; 28:1; 30:29, 38; 31:32, 43, 43, 43; 32:5, 17, 17, 18; 33:5, 5; 35:22, 26; 36:5, 12, 13, 16, 17, 18, 19, 20, 21, 31, 40, 43; 38:18; 40:2; 41:3, 3, 6, 7, 15, 20, 24, 32, 35; 43:16; 44:1; 45:6; 46:8, 15, 18, 22, 25, 32; 48:5, 8, 9, 16; 49:26, 28, 28; 50:11; Ex 1:1, 9; 4:9; 5:9; 6:14, 16, 19, 25; 10:7, 26; 11:10; 12:6, 16, 19, 24, 43; 13:8, 11; 14:1, 5; 16:28; 17:4; 18:22, 23, 26; 19:3; 21:11; 23:17, 24; 24:6, 8; 25:15, 27, 28; 26:1, 3, 7, 8, 9, 14, 18, 20, 24, 24; 28:5, 11, 12, 20, 36, 41, 43; 29:3, 24, 28, 30, 33; 30:20, 25, 34; 31:12; 32:4, 8, 9, 16, 22, 31; 33:1, 4, 12; 34:27; 35:1, 5; 36:10, 16, 29, 29; 37:14, 16; 38:7; 39:7, 13, 24, 30; Lev 2:12; 3:5, 16; 5:5; 6:4, 14, 25; 7:1, 5, 11, 23, 29, 36, 37, 38; 8:26, 26, 27; 9:4, 5, 6, 20, 20; 10:13, 14; 11:8, 13, 21, 22, 29, 31, 44, 46; 12:1, 7; 13:59, 59; 14:32, 43, 54, 57; 15:2, 32; 16:3, 4, 13, 34; 17:2; 18:24, 26, 27, 29, 30; 20:2, 23; 21:24; 22:9, 13, 18; 23:10, 17, 18, 20, 20, 24, 37, 38, 38, 44; 24:22, 23; 25:2; 26:25, 46; 27:26, 34; Nu 1:5, 16, 44; 2:1, 2, 3, 9, 10, 16, 18, 25; 3:20, 22, 25, 28, 31, 34, 36, 50; 4:15, 15, 26, 28, 33; 5:1, 6, 23; 6:1, 14, 16, 20; 7:3, 5, 13, 19, 25, 31, 37, 43, 49, 55, 61, 67, 73, 79; 9:1, 14; 10:9; 11:8, 13, 14; 13:4, 16, 17; 14:11, 13, 15, 22, 35; 15:1, 11, 13, 22; 16:3, 18, 21, 26, 28, 29, 30, 38, 38, 45; 17:4; 18:5, 8, 8, 11, 18, 19; 21:2; 22:9, 12, 17, 20, 28, 35; 23:24; 25:2; 26:3, 5, 12, 15, 21, 23, 26, 29, 30, 35, 37, 38, 40, 42, 43, 44, 45, 48, 63; 27:2, 14; 28:1, 12, 20, 23, 24, 28, 31; 29:3, 6, 6, 9, 14, 18, 21, 24, 27, 30, 33, 37, 39, 39, 40; 30:16; 31:16, 23; 32:36; 33:2; 34:2, 2, 12, 17, 19, 29; 35:3, 4, 8, 12, 15, 24, 29; 36:13; Dt 1:3, 27; 2:4, 7; 3:5, 21; 4:1, 2, 5, 6, 9, 19, 35, 43, 45; 5:22; 6:1, 6, 20, 24; 7:1, 2, 11, 12, 17; 8:4; 9:5, 27, 28; 10:8; 11:18, 30; 12:1, 4, 18, 30, 31; 14:4, 8, 12; 15:20; 16:12, 16, 16; 17:18, 20; 18:3, 12, 12; 19:3, 3, 4; 20:15; 21:9; 23:4; 26:12, 16; 27:1, 4, 10, 15; 28:2, 13, 15, 22, 45, 46, 59; 29:1, 18, 29; 30:1, 7; 31:1, 7, 13, 16, 17, 21, 23, 25; 32:34, 45, 47; 33:16; Jos 3:3, 8; 4:6, 6, 7, 13, 21; 7:1, 13; 8:4, 27; 9:1, 2, 7, 13, 16, 17; 10:5, 42; 11:4, 10; 12:1, 8; 13:6, 32; 14:2, 10; 15:12, 32, 42, 55; 17:4, 12; 18:21; 19:15, 25, 48, 51; 20:3, 4, 9, 9; 21:8, 16, 20, 42; 22:21; 23:12; 24:26; Jdg 2:20; 3:3, 4; 5:29; 6:5; 7:7; 11:2; 13:23; 14:12; 15:18; 17:3, 4; 18:2, 23; 20:6, 13; Ru 3:17; 4:4; 1Sa 2:17; 4:8; 6:5, 10; 7:16; 9:24; 10:7; 16:10, 11; 17:17, 18, 39; 18:23; 21:12; 22:17; 23:12; 25:10, 31; 29:3; 30:20; 31:4; 2Sa 3:2, 5, 39, 39; 5:14; 7:21, 28; 8:11; 10:3, 16; 16:2, 12; 21:22; 22:2; 23:1, 8, 17, 22; 24:12, 17; 1Ki 1:48; 2:33; 3:4, 25; 4:2, 8; 6:32, 35; 7:9, 30, 30, 34, 45; 8:8, 54, 59; 9:9, 13, 13, 21; 10:8, 17, 29; 11:31; 12:6, 9, 28, 29; 15:22; 18:37; 20:13, 34; 22:11, 31; 2Ki 1:13; 4:38; 10:9, 22; 11:6; 13:21; 17:22, 25, 29, 32, 41; 18:18, 31; 19:17, 18; 21:5; 22:12; 23:4, 14, 16; 24:3; 25:16, 23; 1Ch 1:23, 31, 33, 43, 54; 2:23, 33, 50, 55; 3:1, 4, 5, 9; 4:2, 4, 12, 22, 31, 33, 38, 42; 5:8, 14, 17, 24, 24; 6:33, 64, 66, 70; 7:2, 3, 7, 17, 29, 40; 8:10, 28, 32, 38, 40; 9:9, 18, 23, 34, 38, 44; 10:4; 11:10, 19, 24, 26; 12:3, 14, 23, 32, 38; 14:4; 15:2, 4, 11; 16:22; 17:19, 26; 18:11; 19:3, 7, 16; 20:8; 21:2, 10, 11, 17; 23:9, 24; 24:20, 30; 25:5, 6; 26:1, 8, 12, 19, 23, 27; 27:22, 31; 29:16, 19, 30; 2Ch 1:17; 2:4; 3:10; 4:16; 5:1, 9, 13; 7:22; 8:8, 18; 9:7, 16; 10:6, 9; 11:10, 12; 13:9, 9; 14:7, 14; 16:6; 17:7, 19; 18:10, 30; 19:6, 9; 23:2; 24:5; 26:12; 28:10, 11, 18, 23; 29:12, 15; 31:7, 8, 13; 32:8, 19; 33:5; 34:20; 35:14, 25, 25; 36:16; Ezr 1:8, 9; 2:36, 40, 55; 4:21; 5:14; 6:8; 7:17; 8:28, 28, 29, 30; 9:2, 2, 12, 14; 10:2, 11, 18, 23, 24, 25, 44, 44; Ne 1:1; 2:8; 5:7, 19; 7:39, 43, 57; 8:15, 17; 10:8, 38, 39; 12:7, 24, 26, 44; 13:5, 13; Est 1:14; 2:3; 3:11, 12; 9:20, 21, 22, 27, 28, 28, 31, 31; Job 1:4, 5; 7:16; 12:3; 15:13, 27; 26:4, 14; 27:12; 30:12; 33:29; 36:25; Ps 4:2; 10:4, 15; 19:12; 22:20, 21; 35:17; 43:1, 1; 58:3, 6; 59:2, 2; 68:30, 30; 69:4, 14; 73:7, 12; 74:18, 19, 21, 22, 23; 78:4; 82:5; 83:6, 12; 90:10; 91:7; 93:4; 94:4; 104:27, 34; 105:15; 106:29; 107:42; 109:15; 116:11; 119:85, 126, 158; 120:5, 5; 136:21; Pr 1:1, 2, 3, 4, 5, 6, 18; 2:13; 6:23, 24; 22:18; 25:1; 31:1; Ecc 1:1; 2:9; 3:13; Isa 1:1; 2:8; 6:10; 7:20; 8:16; 9:6; 10:13; 13:3; 19:18; 21:14; 27:5; 29:11, 13, 14; 30:8, 9; 31:3; 33:16, 19; 34:16; 36:3, 16; 37:18, 19; 41:21; 42:16, 23; 44:9, 11; 45:7, 21; 47:9, 12; 49:21, 21; 50:4; 51:19; 54:17; 57:8, 8, 17; 58:8; 59:21; 66:14; Jer 1:1; 2:25, 28; 3:12; 5:25, 25; 6:15; 7:13, 16; 8:5, 9, 12, 17; 9:24, 26; 10:9, 9; 11:14, 23; 12:3, 16; 13:10; 14:11, 14, 15; 15:1, 21; 16:10; 17:27; 18:15; 19:10; 20:8; 23:2, 14, 16, 17, 18, 21, 25, 27, 28, 30, 31; 25:30; 27:5, 15, 15, 18; 28:7, 14; 29:23; 32:25, 29, 42; 35:7, 8; 36:8, 17; 38:4, 9, 11, 12; 40:3, 8; 43:10; 44:4, 5, 23; 45:5; 49:32; 52:20; La 1:16; Eze 1:15; 5:4; 7:11, 22; 8:6, 13, 15, 17; 10:15, 20; 11:2; 12:6, 9, 10; 13:4, 10, 10, 11; 14:3, 16, 18, 21, 23; 16:30, 37, 39, 43, 43; 17:12, 21; 18:9; 23:16, 38, 43, 44, 45; 24:3, 27; 27:14; 31:18; 32:23; 33:25, 33; 34:10; 36:5, 20, 37; 37:3, 4, 7, 9, 11, 16, 16; 38:11; 39:10; 40:7, 42; 41:6, 6, 9; 42:9, 10, 13, 13, 13, 14, 15; 43:11, 13, 18, 25; 44:6, 8, 15; 45:8, 15, 25; 46:10, 19, 22, 23, 24; 47:12, 13, 21, 23; 48:13, 21, 23, 29, 30; Da 1:4, 7, 17, 20; 2:43, 44; 3:3; 4:28, 31, 35; 5:3, 7, 16, 23, 26; 7:6, 17, 28; 8:26; 10:19, 21; 11:27, 33, 34, 38; 12:6, 7, 10; Hos 1:1; 5:1; 8:11; 13:2; 14:9; Joel 1:9; 2:20, 26, 32; 3:7, 13; Am 4:12; 9:12; Ob 12; Jnh 4:2; Mic 1:1, 7; 4:12; Hab 1:12, 16; 2:3; Zep 1:1; 2:4; 3:8; Zec 1:19, 19, 21; 3:4, 7; 4:4, 10, 10, 11; 6:4, 5; 8:12, 17; 10:3; 11:8; 13:9; 14:20, 21; Mal 1:10, 13; 3:5; Mt 3:9; 4:3; 6:32; 10:5; 11:1, 16; 12:49; 13:13, 15, 34, 53; 15:8, 20, 32; 18:6, 10, 14; 19:1, 14, 20; 21:15, 16, 24; 22:40; 24:2, 6, 28, 34, 36; 25:37, 40, 45; 26:1, 62; 27:21; 28:20; Mk 3:16, 34; 4:11; 7:7, 23; 8:2, 7, 38; 9:42; 10:14, 20; 11:29; 12:14, 31, 38; 13:1, 2, 7, 9, 30, 32; 14:49, 60; 15:4; 16:17, S; Lk 1:3, 66; 2:19, 51; 3:8; 4:6; 5:17; 8:10; 10:2, 36, 41; 11:29, 30; 12:30, 56; 15:29; 16:24; 17:2, 37; 18:16, 21; 19:27; 20:36, 46; 21:6, 9, 28, 32, 36; 22:60; 23:31, 34, 38; 24:26, 45, 48; Jn 1:40; 2:16, 18; 3:10; 6:5, 59; 7:49; 8:14, 20, 30, 54; 10:19, 32; 11:42; 12:16, 36; 13:17, 18, 33; 14:25, 29; 16:1, 4, 25; 17:1, 6, 20, 24, 25; 18:1, 8; 19:36; 20:31; 21:15, 24, 24; Ac 1:3, 4, 24; 2:7, 11, 15, 29; 3:18; 4:16; 5:5, 32, 35, 38, 38; 6:6; 7:1, 9; 8:15, 17, 24; 10:44; 11:12, 17, 21; 13:2, 31, 42; 14:11, 15; 15:18, 21, 25, 28; 16:17, 20; 17:8, 30; 19:37; 20:34; 21:4, 30, 39; 23:8; 24:13, 15, 20; 25:11, 20; 26:2, 22, 26, 26, 29; 28:22, 27; Ro 1:32; 2:1; 7:5, 17; 8:31, 37; 9:30; 11:17; 13:6; 14:20; 15:1, 1, 14, 15, 22, 23, 23; 1Co 2:10, 14, 15, 16; 4:14, 19; 5:12; 6:2, 5, 10; 9:15; 10:6, 11, 19, 20; 11:22; 12:11; 13:10, 13; 14:20, 23, 24; 15:50; 2Co 4:10, 15; 5:1, 4, 6, 8; 7:1; 8:23; 9:3, 5; 10:5, 5, 12; 11:5, 13; 12:11; 13:11; Gal 2:12, 14; 3:10; 4:12, 24; 5:10, 17, 19; 6:11, 17; Eph 4:11; 5:4, 6, 7, 13, 16; Php 3:7, 12, 15, 21; 4:3; Col 2:17, 18, 23; 4:11; 1Th 4:8, 18; 5:4; 2Th 2:11, 15; 1Ti 1:4, 6, 8, 10; 3:14; 4:2, 11, 15; 5:7, 14, 21; 6:2, 3, 3, 5, 11; 2Ti 2:2, 7, 14; 3:8; Tit 2:4, 15; 3:8, 8, 9; Phm 1:13; Heb 1:2; 6:18; 9:5, 6, 8; 10:26; 11:13, 33, 39; Jas 1:15; 1Pe 1:7, 12, 12, 20; 4:13; 2Pe 1:5, 9, 12, 13, 15; 2:10, 11, 12, 17, 22; 3:14, 16, 17; 1Jn 1:4; 2:16, 19, 26; 3:8; 4:4, 5; 5:7; Jude 8, 10, 12, 14, 16; Rev 1:3, 5; 2:19; 4:1, 7, 8; 5:9; 6:10; 7:13, 14; 9:18, 20; 11:4; 16:9, 14; 18:15; 19:9; 21:7; 22:6, 8, 8, 20

THEY (7440)

Ge 1:11, 14, 26; 3:7, 7, 8, 8, 22, 22; 4:2, 8, 15, 17; 6:2, 3, 3, 4; 7:9, 15, 23; 8:17; 9:23, 23, 23, 25; 11:2, 3, 3, 6, 6, 6, 7, 31; 12:6, 12, 13, 14, 15; 13:1, 1, 3, 3, 16; 14:4, 4, 5, 7, 12; 15:13, 14; 17:11, 27; 18:5, 8, 9, 20; 19:1, 2, 3, 4, 5, 8, 9, 9, 11, 11, 15, 33, 35; 20:11, 17; 21:27, 30, 31, 32; 22:8, 9, 17, 19; 23:18; 24:19, 20, 41, 54, 57, 58, 58, 59, 60; 25:16, 25, 26; 26:7, 15, 20, 20, 20, 24, 28, 30, 31, 32, 32; 28:14; 29:4, 5, 7, 8; 30:36, 38, 38; 31:1, 19, 20, 20, 38, 47, 54; 32:12, 18, 23; 33:7, 8, 13, 13, 18, 18; 34:5, 7, 14, 21, 22, 22, 23, 26, 28, 28, 29, 30, 31; 35:4, 5, 6, 16, 16; 37:4, 8, 13, 17, 17, 18, 19, 23, 25, 25, 32, 32; 38:5, 14, 21, 22, 25, 26, 28; 40:4, 8, 8, 20; 41:8, 19, 21, 24, 38, 55; 42:6, 7, 10, 13, 20, 21, 23, 26, 27, 28, 29, 30, 35; 43:2, 7, 15, 15, 18, 18, 18, 18, 19, 20, 25, 25, 25, 26, 27, 28, 28, 34; 44:1, 4, 11, 13, 14; 45:3, 4, 15, 21, 24, 25, 26, 27; 46:5, 6, 6, 28, 32, 32; 47:1, 1, 3, 15, 15, 17, 17, 18, 22, 25, 26, 27; 48:5, 6, 16, 16, 20; 49:6, 6; 50:8, 10, 10, 11, 13, 15, 16, 17, 18, 23, 26; Ex 1:7, 7, 10, 10, 11, 14, 16, 17, 19, 19, 19; 2:11, 19, 22, 23; 3:13, 13, 21; 4:1, 1, 5, 5, 8, 8, 9, 11, 18, 28, 30, 31, 31; 5:1, 1, 3, 8, 8, 8, 13, 14, 14, 15, 19, 20, 20; 6:4, 9, 9, 27; 7:5, 7, 10, 11, 16, 22, 24; 8:1, 3, 3, 7, 8, 14, 18, 20, 26, 26; 9:1, 10, 13, 20, 32, 34; 10:3, 5, 6, 15, 23; 11:8; 12:1, 4, 4, 7, 19, 21, 33, 34, 36, 36, 36, 37, 39, 39, 39, 48, 48, 48; 13:2, 17, 19, 20, 21; 14:3, 4, 5, 9, 10, 11, 17, 20, 31; 15:5, 10, 16, 22, 22, 23, 23, 24, 27, 27; 16:1, 1, 3, 4, 4, 10, 10, 15, 15, 21, 29, 35; 17:1, 2, 3, 4, 12, 16; 18:5, 7, 8, 12, 13, 22, 22, 25, 26, 26; 19:1, 2, 8, 9, 11, 13, 13, 13, 17, 21, 24; 20:18, 18, 19; 21:4, 16, 22; 22:7, 23; 23:6, 27, 33; 24:3, 7, 10, 11; 25:15, 35, 36, 37; 26:17, 19; 27:10; 28:1, 4, 4, 4, 41, 43; 29:9, 21, 29, 33, 44, 46; 30:20, 20, 20, 20, 30; 31:6, 10, 11; 32:1, 6, 8, 8, 8, 8, 13, 15, 19, 20, 21, 22, 23, 24, 31, 35; 33:4, 6, 8, 16; 34:13, 15, 15, 16, 27, 30; 35:21, 21, 22, 25, 28, 35; 36:5, 17, 18, 19, 20, 22, 23, 25, 29, 30, 31, 32, 37; 37:8, 8, 9, 21, 22; 39:4, 5, 15, 16, 30, 30, 33; 40:15, 32, 32, 37; Lev 3:17; 4:14, 20, 27, 27, 28, 28, 29, 31, 33, 35; 5:1, 1, 1, 2, 2, 2, 3, 3, 3, 3, 3, 4, 4, 4, 4, 5, 7, 8, 10, 11, 11, 12, 13, 15, 16, 16, 16, 16, 17, 17, 18, 18, 19; 6:2, 2, 3, 3, 3, 4, 4, 4, 4, 5, 5, 5, 6, 7, 20, 22, 22; 7:35; 9:13, 23, 23, 24; 10:1, 2, 5, 7, 15; 11:4, 6, 8, 11, 13; 13:2, 45, 45, 46; 14:8, 8, 9, 9; 15:18, 31; 16:1; 18:17, 18; 19:34; 20:2, 3, 9, 11, 12, 13, 16, 23, 27; 21:6, 6, 6, 8; 22:2, 3, 3, 4, 4, 6, 6, 6, 7, 9, 11, 11, 25; 23:17; 24:9, 12, 23; 25:32, 33, 40, 41, 41, 42, 48, 48, 49, 49, 51, 51, 51, 52, 54; 26:17, 26, 32, 41, 43, 44; 27:32; Nu 1:45, 50, 50; 2:17, 24, 31; 3:3, 4, 4, 7, 8, 13, 23, 28, 29, 35, 37; 4:6, 6, 7, 8, 8, 9, 11, 15, 15, 19, 19, 20, 20, 25, 26, 27, 27, 28, 31, 33; 5:3, 6, 7, 7; 6:3, 3, 3, 3, 4, 4, 5, 5, 5, 6, 7, 8, 9, 9, 10, 11, 11, 12, 13, 21, 21; 7:3, 3, 5, 9, 10; 8:3, 7, 15, 19, 19, 22, 24, 25, 26, 26; 9:5, 6, 6, 10, 10, 11, 11, 12, 12, 12, 13, 14, 18, 18, 18, 20, 22, 23, 23; 10:3, 21, 25, 33, 34; 11:4, 8, 8, 12, 13, 17, 18, 25, 26, 26, 32, 33, 34, 35; 12:1, 2, 5, 15, 16; 13:19, 19, 21, 22, 23, 23, 23, 24, 26, 26, 26, 30, 31, 32; 14:1, 2, 4, 7, 9, 9, 11, 12, 13, 13, 14, 14, 14, 19, 22, 22, 23, 31, 33, 35, 40, 40; 15:14, 25, 25, 30, 31, 31, 32, 34, 34; 16:2, 3, 4, 12, 19, 22, 30, 32, 33, 33, 34, 37, 38, 39, 42; 18:3, 3, 3, 6, 16, 17, 19, 22, 22, 23, 24, 32; 19:9, 12, 12, 12, 12, 19, 20, 20; 20:1, 2, 6; 21:5, 5, 8, 9, 11, 12, 13, 20, 24, 32, 33; 22:3, 5, 6, 7, 16; 23:24, 24, 24; 24:6, 6, 7, 24, 24; 25:6, 18; 26:61, 62, 65; 27:3, 21; 28:2, 2, 9; 29:6; 31:5, 6, 7, 7, 8, 10, 11, 12, 16; 32:1, 2, 2, 9, 9, 11, 12, 16, 17, 30, 30, 38, 38, 39, 40; 33:1, 2, 3, 6, 7, 8, 8, 9, 10, 11, 12, 13, 14, 15, 16, 17, 18, 19, 20, 21, 22, 23, 24, 25, 26, 27, 28, 29, 30, 31, 32, 33, 34, 35, 36, 37, 38, 42, 43, 44, 45, 46, 47, 48, 49, 50, 55; 35:11, 19, 21, 23, 25, 25; 36:2, 3, 6, 12, 13; Dt 1:1, 1, 5, 17, 22, 24, 25, 25, 28, 28, 39, 39, 42, 42, 44; 2:10, 12, 21, 22, 25, 25; 3:17, 20; 4:6, 6, 10, 10, 10, 45, 46, 46, 49; 5:24, 28, 29, 29, 29, 29, 31; 7:4, 16, 23, 25, 26; 9:1, 2, 12, 13, 14, 26, 28, 29; 10:4, 7, 11; 11:3, 4, 4, 5, 6, 23, 30; 12:2, 12, 31; 13:1, 5, 5, 7, 8, 10; 14:7, 10, 27, 29; 15:2, 2, 6, 8, 18; 16:16, 16, 17, 18; 17:10, 10, 11, 11, 17; 18:2, 17; 19:18; 20:9, 11, 12, 19; 21:4, 4, 5, 7, 8, 18, 20; 22:17, 19; 23:4, 16; 24:15, 15, 21; 25:18, 18, 18; 26:5, 12; 28:7, 7, 7, 10, 41, 44, 44, 48, 51, 52, 52, 60; 29:1, 23, 25, 25, 26, 28; 31:11, 12,

16, 16, 17, 17, 18, 20, 20, 20, 20, 20, 21; 32:5, 5, 5, 5, 7, 12, 15, 15, 16, 16, 17, 17, 20, 21, 21, 24, 29, 29, 31, 37, 46, 47; 33:3, 9, 10, 11, 19, 19, 21; Jos 1:15, 16; 2:3, 4, 5, 5, 17, 19, 19, 22, 24; 3:1, 4, 6, 7, 17; 4:7, 8, 8, 8, 13, 14, 14, 19; 5:1, 4, 6, 6, 8, 8, 10, 11; 6:8, 14, 14, 15, 15, 20, 20, 21, 23; 7:3, 3, 4, 5, 9, 11, 11, 11, 21, 22, 23, 24, 26; 8:5, 6, 6, 6, 9, 11, 13, 15, 16, 19, 20, 21, 24, 29, 31; 9:4, 4, 5, 5, 6, 6, 8, 9, 13, 14, 24; 10:2, 4, 5, 6, 11, 17, 23, 24, 24, 27, 27, 30, 35, 35, 36, 37, 37, 38, 39, 39, 39, 39; 11:5, 6, 14, 20; 13:13; 16:10; 17:12, 13, 13, 16, 16, 18; 18:4, 7, 9, 9; 19:47, 47, 47; 20:4, 9; 21:2, 28, 30, 32, 36, 38, 43; 22:9, 10, 10, 11, 13, 13, 15, 15, 28, 30, 34; 23:13; 24:1, 2, 8, 14, 22, 30, 32; Jdg 1:4, 5, 7, 9, 11, 16, 17, 19, 19, 23, 24, 25, 28, 28, 30, 32, 33, 35; 2:3, 5, 5, 9, 12, 12, 13, 14, 17, 19, 19, 22; 3:4, 6, 7, 7, 24, 25, 25, 25, 25, 28, 29; 4:13, 24; 5:11, 14, 15, 19, 23, 30, 30; 6:2, 4, 5, 7, 13, 27, 29, 30; 7:2, 19, 20, 21, 24, 25, 25; 8:1, 3, 4, 4, 5, 5, 18, 18, 18, 19, 25, 25, 34, 35; 9:2, 3, 4, 5, 8, 10, 12, 23, 31, 46, 49, 51, 55; 10:4, 6, 6, 8, 10, 12; 11:2, 2, 5, 8, 13, 17, 17, 18, 18, 18; 12:1, 5, 6, 6; 13:2, 20, 24; 14:9, 13, 14, 15; 15:11, 11, 13, 13, 14, 14; 16:2, 9, 12, 21, 23, 24, 31; 17:2; 18:1, 2, 3, 5, 7, 7, 7, 12, 13, 19, 21, 23, 23, 25, 27, 28, 29, 30, 30; 19:8, 11, 14, 14, 15, 15, 17, 17, 21, 21, 22, 22, 23, 25; 20:5, 10, 11, 14, 20, 22, 23, 23, 24, 26, 30, 31, 31, 31, 33, 33, 36, 38, 39, 42, 45, 45, 47, 48, 48; 21:3, 5, 5, 8, 8, 9, 10, 11, 12, 12, 19, 20, 23, 23, 23, 24; Ru 1:2, 7, 9, 10, 14, 19, 22; 2:9, 9; 4:1, 17; 1Sa 1:7, 9, 19, 24, 25, 28; 2:17, 20, 29, 36; 4:3, 4, 6, 7, 7, 8, 9, 20; 5:1, 2, 3, 7, 8, 8, 10, 10, 10; 6:3, 4, 4, 6, 8, 9, 9, 12, 13, 13, 18, 19, 20, 21; 7:1, 6, 6, 6, 7, 7, 8; 8:3, 3, 3, 5, 7, 7, 7, 8, 8, 9, 19, 22; 9:4, 5, 9, 10, 11, 11, 12, 14, 14, 20, 25, 27; 10:2, 4, 5, 5, 10, 11, 14, 21, 22, 23, 27; 11:1, 5, 15, 15, 15; 12:4, 5, 10, 19, 21; 13:5, 6, 15, 19, 20; 14:9, 10, 11, 12, 13, 14, 17, 17, 22, 25, 26, 26, 26, 30, 31, 31, 32, 32; 15:2, 6, 9, 15, 18, 24; 16:4, 6, 15; 17:11, 14, 24, 51; 18:1, 6, 8; 19:8, 11, 16, 16, 20, 20, 21, 22; 20:11, 41; 21:5, 5, 11; 22:12, 17, 17, 17; 23:5, 12, 19; 25:1, 8, 15, 16, 40; 27:7; 28:25, 25; 29:4; 30:1, 2, 4, 4, 6, 9, 11, 12, 16, 20, 21, 22, 22, 31; 31:2, 7, 8, 9, 9, 10, 10, 12, 12, 13, 13; 2Sa 1:11, 12, 22, 23, 23, 23, 27; 2:3, 13, 23, 24, 24, 29, 29, 29, 32; 3:21, 26, 32; 4:2, 3, 6, 7, 7, 8, 8, 12, 12, 12; 5:3, 6, 17, 17; 6:3, 6, 13; 7:10, 10; 10:3, 5, 6, 6, 14, 15, 15, 16, 19, 19; 11:1, 20; 12:18, 19, 21, 24; 13:9, 29, 30, 35, 36; 14:10, 30; 15:2, 2, 11, 17, 23, 24, 30, 32, 36; 16:14, 14, 21, 22; 17:8, 8, 10, 17, 18, 19, 20, 20, 20, 21, 21, 22, 28, 29; 18:3, 3, 17; 19:3, 3, 14, 14, 17, 18, 18, 35; 20:8, 15, 22, 22; 21:2, 5, 18, 22; 22:8, 15, 19, 38, 39, 39, 42, 42, 45, 45, 46; 23:6, 7; 24:4, 5, 5, 7, 7, 8, 17; 1Ki 1:3, 3, 7, 25, 32, 41, 44, 45, 53; 2:4, 7, 39; 3:8, 22, 28; 4:7, 20, 28; 7:5, 8, 19, 24, 28; 8:1, 2, 8, 9, 25, 33, 33, 35, 39, 40, 40, 42, 42, 43, 43, 44, 46, 47, 48, 51, 52, 66, 66, 66; 9:8, 9, 21, 28; 10:2, 11, 21; 11:2, 3, 4, 18, 18; 12:4, 7, 16, 20, 24, 27, 27, 27; 13:11, 12, 13, 19, 20, 25, 27; 14:15, 18, 23; 15:20; 16:13, 16; 17:16; 18:6, 23, 26, 26, 26, 26, 28, 28, 29, 30, 33, 34, 34, 39; 19:10, 14, 21; 20:1, 6, 12, 12, 17, 18, 23, 25, 32, 33, 34; 21:12, 19; 22:6, 12, 30, 32, 32, 33, 48; 2Ki 1:6, 8, 9; 2:2, 4, 6, 9, 11, 12, 15, 15, 16, 17, 18, 19, 20, 23; 3:4, 21, 22, 24, 24, 25, 26, 27; 4:4, 39, 40, 40, 42, 43; 5:15, 24; 6:4, 4, 20, 20, 20; 7:3, 4, 4, 5, 6, 7, 7, 8, 9, 10, 10, 12, 12, 12, 13, 15; 9:12, 13, 17, 21, 27, 28, 33, 35, 35, 36; 10:4, 6, 7, 8, 13, 14, 15, 20, 21, 24, 25, 26, 27; 11:9, 11, 12, 16, 17, 18, 18, 19; 12:8, 11, 12, 12, 15; 13:5, 6, 6, 7, 19, 21, 21, 21, 23; 14:19, 20, 26; 16:5, 6, 9; 17:6, 8, 9, 10, 11, 12, 14, 15, 15, 15, 15, 16, 16, 17, 17, 19, 20, 21, 22, 23, 25, 26, 29, 29, 32, 33, 33, 33, 34, 41; 18:12, 12, 18, 27, 34, 37, 37; 19:3, 11, 11, 18, 18, 26, 26, 32, 35, 37; 20:7, 14, 14, 15, 15, 18; 21:15, 24; 22:5, 6, 7, 7, 17, 20; 23:5, 5, 8, 9, 11, 18, 19, 29; 24:13; 25:1, 4, 4, 6, 7, 10, 13, 14, 23, 26; 1Ch 2:17, 19, 21, 35; 4:23, 23, 28, 40, 41, 41, 43, 43; 5:6, 9, 9, 10, 18, 19, 20, 20, 22, 22, 23, 25, 25, 26; 6:32, 32, 49, 49, 49, 60, 72, 74, 76, 78, 80; 7:11, 13, 30, 32, 40; 8:7, 13, 13, 28, 28, 40; 9:1, 9, 13, 13, 18, 22, 22, 26, 27, 28, 33, 33, 34; 10:2, 7, 8, 9, 9, 10, 10, 12, 12; 11:3, 10; 12:1, 2, 2, 8, 15, 19, 19, 21, 21, 23, 33, 39; 13:7, 9; 14:3, 8, 8; 15:24, 26, 26; 16:1, 1, 5, 19, 20, 39, 40, 42; 17:9, 9; 19:3, 5, 6, 7, 7, 15, 16, 16, 17, 19, 19; 20:1, 4, 8; 21:3, 17; 22:3, 16, 18; 23:28, 28, 29, 29, 30, 31, 31; 24:2, 31; 25:2, 3, 6, 7, 8; 26:12, 13, 27, 30, 32; 29:7, 8, 9, 20, 21, 21, 22, 22, 22, 22; 2Ch 3:9, 13; 4:3; 5:2, 3, 9, 10, 11, 12, 13; 6:16, 24, 24, 26, 30, 31, 31, 32, 33, 33, 34, 36, 37, 38; 7:3, 6, 7, 8, 8, 9, 9, 10, 21, 22; 8:8; 9:2, 10, 20; 10:4, 7, 16; 11:4, 15, 16, 17, 17, 21; 12:2, 8, 8; 13:11, 11, 11, 14, 14, 18; 14:7, 9, 13, 13, 14, 14, 15; 15:9, 11, 11, 12, 13, 14, 15, 15, 15; 16:4; 17:9, 17; 18:2, 5, 11, 29, 31, 31, 32; 20:2, 9, 10, 11, 11, 21, 22, 23, 23, 24, 25, 25, 26, 27, 28, 36; 21:17, 19; 22:4, 5, 9, 9; 23:3, 3, 6, 10, 11, 11, 15, 15, 16, 17, 17, 20, 20; 24:7, 10, 12, 13, 13, 14, 18, 18, 21, 22, 23, 23, 25; 25:10, 11, 12, 27, 28; 26:11, 13, 18, 20; 28:6, 8, 11, 13, 15, 15, 15, 18, 23, 23; 29:6, 6, 7, 7, 7, 15, 15, 15, 16, 16, 17, 17, 19, 21, 22, 22, 30, 33; 30:5, 6, 8, 9, 14, 14, 15, 16, 18, 19, 22, 22, 23; 31:1, 4, 5, 5, 6, 8, 15, 16, 17, 18; 32:3, 4, 4, 8; 33:10, 11, 11, 25; 34:9, 10, 11, 11, 16, 25, 28, 32, 33; 35:5, 12, 12, 12, 13, 13, 24, 24; 36:14, 16, 17, 20; Ezr 1:6; 2:1, 59, 59, 62, 62, 66, 68, 70; 3:2, 3, 3, 3, 4, 5, 6, 7, 8, 9, 11, 12, 12; 4:2, 5, 9, 10, 11, 12, 23; 5:4; 6:5, 8, 9, 10, 11, 14, 20, 22; 8:18, 19, 20, 35, 35; 9:1; 10:5, 5, 9, 13, 16, 17, 19, 19; Ne 1:3, 3; 2:10, 18, 18, 19, 19; 3:1, 1, 3, 6, 8, 13; 4:2, 2, 2, 2, 4, 5, 7, 8, 11, 12, 22; 5:2, 7, 8, 12, 12, 13, 13; 6:2, 4, 9, 9, 13, 13, 16, 16, 19, 19; 7:6, 61, 61, 64, 64, 68; 8:1, 5, 5, 6, 6, 8, 9, 12, 14, 14, 15, 15, 18; 9:1, 2, 3, 5, 11, 11, 12, 15, 15, 16, 17, 17, 18, 18, 21, 22, 24, 24, 25, 25, 26, 26, 26, 26, 26, 27, 29, 29, 29, 29, 30, 35, 35, 35, 37; 10:29, 29, 29, 38; 11:1, 23, 26, 29, 30, 32; 12:27, 29, 36, 37, 37, 40, 42, 44, 45, 47; 13:2, 2, 2, 10, 15, 15, 16, 21, 25, 29; Est 1:8, 12, 14, 17; 2:3; 3:4, 4, 8, 9, 9, 14; 4:3; 5:6; 6:1, 2, 9, 13, 14; 7:2, 10; 8:1, 9, 11, 17; 9:5, 5, 6, 7, 10, 12, 13, 14, 15, 16, 16, 17, 19, 26, 27, 27, 31; Job 1:4, 4, 5, 15; 2:11, 11, 12, 12, 12, 13, 13; 3:21, 21, 22, 22; 4:9, 9, 10, 10, 19, 20, 20, 21; 5:1, 13, 14, 14, 14; 6:3, 5, 5, 18; 7:6, 10; 8:10, 12, 12, 14, 14, 15, 15; 11:20; 12:4, 5, 7, 7, 9, 15, 18, 25; 14:10, 10, 10, 12, 14, 20, 21, 22; 15:21, 21, 22, 22, 23, 23, 24, 25, 26, 28, 29, 30, 30, 31, 32, 32, 33, 33, 35; 16:8, 10; 17:2, 5, 6, 8, 12, 12; 18:8, 14, 14, 18, 19, 21; 19:12, 12, 18, 23; 21:7, 8, 8, 12, 12, 13, 13, 14, 17, 18, 18, 21, 21, 29, 31, 32; 22:16, 17, 18, 20; 24:2, 3, 5, 6, 6, 6, 7, 8, 8, 9, 10, 10, 11, 11, 11, 13, 13, 16, 16, 17, 18, 18, 21, 21, 22, 22, 23, 24, 24; 27:10, 10, 14, 16, 20, 21, 22; 28:2, 3, 3, 4, 4, 8, 10, 11, 12, 20; 29:8, 13, 21, 21, 22, 23, 23, 23, 24, 25; 30:2, 3, 4, 4, 5, 5, 6, 7, 7, 7, 8, 9, 10, 11, 12, 12, 13, 13, 14, 14, 15, 24; 31:20; 32:3, 4, 5; 33:15, 20, 21, 22, 30; 34:6, 20, 20, 21, 25, 27, 27, 28, 30; 35:9, 10, 12; 36:8, 9, 10, 11, 11, 12, 12, 13, 14; 37:7, 11, 12; 38:40, 41; 39:2, 3, 13, 16, 16; 40:12; 41:6, 16, 17, 30; 42:11; Ps 1:2, 2, 3, 3, 3, 4, 5; 2:3; 5:10; 6:10; 7:2, 14, 15, 16, 16; 8:2; 9:3, 15, 15, 20; 10:2, 3, 3, 4, 5, 5, 5, 5, 6, 8, 8, 9, 9, 10, 13, 14; 11:2; 12:4, 5; 14:1, 4, 4; 15:5; 17:10, 11, 12, 14; 18:7, 14, 18, 37, 38, 38, 41, 41, 44, 44, 45; 19:2, 2, 3, 10, 10, 11; 21:10, 11, 12, 12; 22:5, 7, 13, 16, 18, 31; 24:5, 6; 25:12, 13, 19; 26:10; 27:2, 3, 12; 28:4, 4, 5, 5; 31:11, 11; 32:6; 33:15; 34:9, 17; 35:7, 7, 8, 8, 11, 12, 13, 14, 15, 15, 15, 16, 16, 20, 20, 21, 21, 21; 36:1, 2, 2, 3, 3, 4, 4, 12, 12; 37:2, 2, 10, 11, 12, 15, 18, 19, 19, 20, 24, 24, 30, 31, 31, 33, 36, 38, 40; 38:12, 12, 19, 20; 40:3, 12, 12, 15; 41:3, 5, 6, 6, 6, 6, 6, 8; 42:10; 44:3, 3; 45:15; 47:9; 48:5, 5, 5, 6; 49:6, 7, 11, 11, 11, 12, 12, 13, 14, 17, 17, 18, 19, 20; 51:3, 13; 52:6, 7; 53:1, 4, 4, 5; 54:3; 55:3, 19; 56:5, 5, 6; 57:6, 6; 58:3, 4, 4, 5, 7, 8, 10, 10; 59:3, 4, 6, 6, 7, 12, 14, 15; 62:4, 4, 4, 4, 9, 12; 63:9, 10; 64:3, 3, 4, 5, 5, 6, 6; 65:9, 13; 66:4; 68:13, 13; 69:4, 8, 8, 10, 11, 19, 21, 21, 23, 26, 26; 70:3; 71:10, 11; 72:12, 16; 73:4, 5, 6, 8, 8, 9, 11, 19, 20; 74:4, 5, 6, 7, 7, 8, 8; 76:5; 77:12; 78:6, 8, 10, 10, 11, 17, 18, 18, 19, 22, 25, 25, 29, 30, 30, 32, 34, 35, 36, 36, 37, 39, 40, 41, 42, 43, 53, 56, 56, 57, 57, 58, 58; 79:1, 2, 7, 10, 12; 80:16; 82:5, 5; 83:3, 4, 5, 10, 12, 16, 17, 18; 84:6, 7; 86:9; 87:4; 88:5, 11, 17, 17; 89:4, 15, 16, 16, 31, 51; 90:4, 10; 91:12, 15; 92:13, 13, 14, 14, 15; 93:3; 94:2, 5, 6, 7, 11, 21; 95:8, 9, 9, 10, 10, 11; 99:6, 7, 8; 101:6; 102:8, 26, 26, 26; 104:9, 11, 21, 22, 23, 27, 28, 28, 29, 29; 105:12, 13, 18, 24, 25, 27, 28, 30, 35, 38, 40, 44, 45; 106:7, 7, 12, 13, 13, 15, 19, 20, 21, 24, 25, 28, 29, 32, 33, 35, 36, 37, 38, 38, 39, 43, 43; 107:5, 6, 7, 11, 12, 13, 17, 19, 20, 24, 27, 28, 37, 38, 39, 43; 109:3, 3, 4, 5, 10, 19, 25, 28, 28, 28; 111:8; 112:3, 4, 7, 7, 8, 9, 9, 10, 10, 10; 115:5, 5, 5, 6, 17; 116:15; 118:11, 12, 12; 119:3, 3, 24, 52, 87, 103, 111, 118, 130, 138, 150, 155, 158; 120:7; 122:1, 4; 124:3; 125:1; 126:6, 6, 6, 6; 127:3; 128:3; 129:2, 6; 135:16, 16, 16, 17; 137:7; 138:5; 139:17, 18, 20; 140:4, 5, 5, 9, 10, 12, 13; 141:5, 6, 9; 142:6; 144:5, 8, 8, 11, 11; 145:7, 11, 11, 12, 15; 146:4; 147:20; 148:5; 149:5; Pr 1:4, 11, 12, 12, 16, 16, 18, 18, 28, 28, 28, 29, 30, 31, 31, 31, 32, 32; 2:14, 14, 15; 3:2, 22, 23, 29; 4:13, 16, 16, 16, 17, 19, 22; 5:22; 6:7, 8, 12, 14, 15, 22, 22; 8:29; 9:8, 9, 9; 10:26; 11:7, 10, 26, 31; 12:14, 15, 27, 27; 13:16; 14:14, 15, 32, 35; 15:12, 24; 16:14, 30, 30, 33; 17:8, 8, 11, 28, 28, 28; 18:2, 6, 8, 11, 15; 19:7, 11, 24, 25; 20:6, 11; 21:2, 20, 22, 24, 26; 22:6, 6, 9, 22, 29; 23:5, 7, 7, 7, 8, 9, 13, 21, 35, 35; 24:2, 12, 16, 16, 17; 25:13, 21, 27; 26:4, 5, 12, 15, 22, 25; 28:13, 13; 29:2, 17, 18, 19; 30:12, 12, 13, 14, 14, 25, 25, 26, 26, 27, 27, 28, 28; 31:5, 5, 9; Ecc 2:19, 23; 3:12, 18, 18, 20, 20, 22; 4:3, 6, 9, 10; 5:12, 14, 15, 16, 16, 17, 18; 6:2, 2, 7, 11; 7:10, 29; 8:7, 10, 10, 13, 14, 14, 15, 17, 17, 17; 9:2, 3, 3, 4, 5, 5, 5, 6, 6, 16, 16; 10:3, 6, 6, 15; 11:6; SS 2:13, 15; 3:3, 8; 4:2; 5:7, 7, 12; 6:9, 10; Isa 1:3, 4, 4, 4, 7, 28; 2:6, 8, 19, 20, 21, 21, 22, 22; 3:8, 8, 9, 9, 9, 12, 24, 24, 24; 5:7, 13, 19, 21, 22, 23, 23, 24, 24, 24, 26, 27, 27, 29, 29; 6:2, 2, 2, 3, 10; 7:5, 18, 18, 19, 19, 21; 8:21, 21, 22, 22; 9:3, 9, 12, 17, 20, 20, 20; 10:2, 2, 18, 20, 24, 28, 28, 29; 11:13, 14, 14, 14, 16; 13:2, 3, 5, 5, 5, 8, 18; 14:10, 11, 22, 25; 15:2, 3, 3, 5, 7; 16:3, 12; 17:8, 8, 8, 9, 11, 11, 13, 13; 18:7; 19:3, 3, 11, 11, 12, 14, 16, 18, 21, 21, 23; 20:6; 21:5, 5, 15; 22:3, 3, 7; 23:3, 13; 24:5, 6, 16, 22, 22; 26:10, 11, 11, 11, 14, 14, 21; 27:5; 28:2, 7, 7, 9, 11, 12, 12, 13, 13; 29:11, 12, 13, 13, 15, 23, 23, 23; 30:6, 8, 10, 10, 16; 31:3, 3, 8, 9; 32:6, 6, 6, 7, 8, 18, 20; 33:8, 8, 14, 16, 18, 19; 34:17; 35:10; 36:12, 19, 22, 22; 37:3, 11, 11, 19, 19, 27, 27, 33, 36, 38; 38:18; 39:3, 3, 4, 4, 7; 40:15, 15, 17, 24, 31, 31, 31; 41:6, 7, 7, 12, 18, 21, 29; 42:17, 22, 22, 24, 25, 25; 43:9, 14, 17, 21; 44:4, 7, 9, 11, 11, 18, 18, 26, 27; 45:14, 14, 14, 17, 20, 21, 25; 46:2, 6, 7, 7; 47:14, 14; 48:7, 13, 21; 49:9, 10, 18, 22, 22, 23, 23, 26; 50:6; 51:5, 11; 52:4, 6, 6, 8, 14, 15, 15, 15, 15; 53:8; 55:5, 10; 56:3, 3, 5, 10, 10, 11, 11, 12; 57:6, 13, 17, 18, 19; 58:2, 2, 2, 3, 6; 59:4, 5, 6, 6, 7, 7, 7, 8, 8, 19, 21; 60:5, 6, 9, 9, 14, 21; 61:4, 4, 4, 5, 9; 62:6, 12; 63:3, 8, 8, 10, 11, 11, 13; 64:6; 65:2, 2, 3, 3, 4, 4, 5, 5, 7, 13, 13, 20, 21, 23, 23, 24, 24; 66:2, 3, 3, 3, 4, 4, 4, 4, 5, 5, 18, 18, 19, 20, 20, 20, 24, 24; Jer 1:15, 15, 16, 16, 19, 19; 2:5, 6, 13, 13, 27, 27, 27, 27, 28, 30, 34; 3:17, 18, 21; 4:17, 22, 22, 22, 24, 29; 5:2, 2, 3, 3, 3, 3, 4, 4, 5, 7, 7, 7, 8, 10, 12, 14, 17, 17, 17, 22, 23, 24, 26, 27, 28, 28; 6:3, 4, 10, 10, 10, 13, 14, 14, 15, 15, 15, 15, 19, 19, 23, 23, 23, 23, 25, 28, 28; 7:17, 18, 19, 19, 24, 24, 26, 30, 31, 31, 32; 8:2, 4, 4, 4, 7, 7, 9, 9, 10, 11, 11, 11, 12, 12, 12, 12, 12, 12, 17, 19; 9:2, 3, 3, 3, 4, 5, 5, 5, 6, 8, 10, 13, 14, 16, 24; 10:3, 4, 5, 8, 9, 9, 9, 14, 14, 14, 15, 15, 21, 21, 22, 25; 11:6, 8, 8, 8, 10, 10, 11, 11, 14, 15, 15, 19, 19, 21, 21; 12:2, 2, 6, 6, 9, 11, 13, 13, 16, 16, 16; 13:10, 10, 11, 11, 12, 13, 19; 14:4, 6, 12, 12, 14, 14, 14, 15, 15, 15, 16, 18, 18; 15:2, 7, 10, 15, 16, 20, 20; 16:4, 4, 4, 10, 11, 11, 11, 15, 17, 19, 20, 21; 17:6, 6, 8, 8, 11, 13, 13, 23, 23, 26; 18:12, 15, 15, 15, 19, 20, 20, 22, 22; 19:4, 5, 5, 8, 9, 11; 20:4, 10, 10, 10, 11, 11, 11, 11; 21:1; 22:7, 9, 20; 23:1, 1, 3, 4, 7, 8, 8, 12, 12, 13, 14, 14, 14, 16, 16, 16, 17, 17, 21, 21, 22, 22, 23, 25, 26, 26, 26, 27, 32, 38; 24:6, 7, 7, 9, 10; 25:14, 14, 16, 16, 18, 19, 28, 30, 33; 26:3, 8, 10, 11, 18, 19, 19, 23; 27:10, 14, 15, 18, 22; 28:5; 29:3, 9, 11, 19, 22, 23; 30:3, 6, 7, 20, 21; 31:1, 2, 9, 12, 12, 32, 33, 34, 34; 32:13, 23, 23, 29, 30, 33, 34, 35, 35, 38, 40; 33:11, 20, 24; 34:5, 5, 5, 11, 11, 11, 20, 22; 35:6, 6; 36:3, 7, 15, 16, 16, 17, 24, 31; 37:5, 9, 10, 15; 38:13, 18, 19, 22, 22, 25, 27; 39:4, 4, 5, 6, 14; 40:8, 12, 12, 12, 14; 41:1, 3, 5, 5, 7, 8, 12, 12, 13, 16, 17, 17, 18, 18; 42:2, 5, 18; 43:5; 44:2, 3, 3, 5, 6, 12, 12; 46:5, 6, 15, 16, 17, 21, 22, 23, 23; 48:2, 12, 18, 19, 30, 35, 37, 42; 49:4, 5, 9, 17, 23, 24, 31, 36; 50:5, 5, 6, 7, 9, 13, 28, 36, 37, 42, 42, 42; 51:2, 4, 14, 17, 17, 17, 18, 18, 24, 28, 30, 30, 35, 39, 39, 57; 52:4, 7, 7, 9, 10, 11, 14, 17, 18, 21; La 1:2, 8, 11, 11, 19, 19, 21; 2:7, 10, 12, 14, 14, 15, 16, 19, 20; 3:14, 35, 36, 36, 49, 53, 59, 61, 61, 63, 64; 4:3, 5, 7, 14, 15, 19, 19; 5:7, 7; Eze 1:12, 12, 17, 17, 18, 19, 24, 24, 24, 25; 2:3, 4, 5, 5, 5, 5, 6, 6, 7, 7, 7; 3:6, 7, 7, 8, 9, 11, 13, 18, 19, 19, 20, 20, 21, 21, 26, 27; 4:17; 5:15; 6:8, 9, 9, 9, 9, 10, 11, 13, 13, 14; 7:12, 13, 18, 18, 19, 20, 21, 25, 26, 26, 27, 27, 27, 27; 8:6, 12, 16, 17, 18; 9:2, 4, 6, 7, 7, 8, 9, 10; 10:11, 11, 11, 16, 16, 20, 22; 11:3, 15, 18, 20, 20; 12:2, 2, 2, 2, 2, 3, 3, 4, 4, 4, 5, 6, 11, 15, 16, 16, 16, 19, 22; 13:5, 5, 6, 6, 9, 9, 16, 21, 22; 14:1, 3, 4, 7, 11, 18, 18, 20, 20, 22, 22; 15:6, 7, 7; 16:27, 37, 39, 39, 39, 40, 41, 45, 47, 51, 61; 18:12, 21, 22, 22, 24, 24, 26, 26, 27, 28, 28; 19:4, 7, 8, 9, 9; 20:1, 8, 8, 8, 11, 13, 13, 13, 16, 20, 21, 21, 23, 24, 24, 28, 28, 28, 28, 28, 38, 38, 47, 49; 21:7, 13, 14, 21, 21, 22, 22, 22; 22:12, 18, 25, 25, 26, 26, 27, 28, 28; 23:3, 3, 4, 6, 10, 15, 17, 24, 24, 24, 25, 25, 26, 29, 37, 38, 39, 39, 40, 42, 43, 44, 44, 45, 45, 45, 47; 24:27; 25:4, 4, 11, 14, 17, 17; 26:4, 6, 11, 12, 12, 16, 16, 17; 27:5, 6, 6, 6, 7, 10, 15, 16, 24, 30, 30, 31, 31, 32, 32; 28:7, 8, 13, 24, 26, 26; 29:13, 14, 19, 21; 30:6, 11, 14, 19, 26; 31:14, 17; 32:10, 12, 14, 16, 21, 21, 23, 24, 24, 24, 25, 25, 25, 25, 26, 26, 27, 27, 27, 27, 29, 29, 30, 30; 33:4, 5, 5, 5, 6, 8, 9, 9, 11, 12, 12, 13, 13, 14, 14, 14, 15, 15, 15, 15, 16, 16, 17, 18, 19, 29, 30, 31, 31, 31, 32, 32, 33, 33; 34:5, 6, 8, 12, 14, 19, 21, 22, 26, 27, 27, 28, 28, 30, 30, 30; 35:5, 12, 12; 36:5, 8, 17, 18, 19, 20, 20, 35; 37:2, 7, 8, 9, 10, 10, 11, 21, 22, 23, 23, 24, 24, 25, 25, 27; 38:12, 23; 39:6, 9, 10, 10, 10, 10, 11, 18, 23, 26, 26; 40:24, 46; 41:1; 42:6, 13, 14, 14, 14, 14; 43:7, 8, 8, 10, 11, 11, 11, 11; 44:9, 11, 11, 12, 12, 13, 13, 13, 13, 14, 15, 16, 16, 17, 17, 17, 18, 18, 19, 19, 19, 19, 19, 20, 20, 22, 22, 23, 24, 24; 45:4, 8; 46:9, 9, 9, 9, 20; 47:10, 11, 12, 22, 22, 23; Da 1:4, 5, 19; 2:2, 2, 7, 11, 18; 3:9, 10, 12, 13, 21, 22, 24, 25, 27, 28, 29; 4:6, 7; 5:3, 4, 5, 15; 6:4, 5, 12, 13, 22, 24; 7:12, 18, 25, 27; 10:7; 11:14, 33, 35; Hos 1:10, 11; 2:4, 4, 18, 23; 3:5, 5; 4:6, 7, 7, 10, 10, 10, 10, 12, 12, 12, 13, 13, 15, 18, 19, 19; 5:6, 6, 6, 7, 11, 13, 15, 15; 7:4, 4, 7, 8, 9, 12, 13, 13, 14, 14, 14, 15, 16, 16; 8:1, 4, 7, 8, 9, 10, 10, 12, 13, 14; 9:4, 4, 7, 9, 10, 10, 10, 16, 16, 17, 17; 10:1, 1, 1, 2, 3, 4, 4, 6, 6, 8, 14; 11:5, 7, 7, 11, 11; 12:1, 1, 1, 7, 11; 13:2, 2, 3, 13, 13, 15, 16, 16; 14:7, 7; Joel 1:7, 20; 2:2, 4, 4, 5, 5, 7, 8, 8, 9, 9, 10, 11, 17, 20; 3:3, 3, 8, 19; Am 1:3, 6, 9, 11, 11, 13, 13; 2:1, 4, 4, 6, 7, 8, 8; 5:11, 23; 6:2, 2, 9; 8:3, 12; 9:2, 2, 3, 3, 4, 13, 14, 14, 14, 15; Ob 5, 7, 7, 12, 12, 12, 13; Jnh 1:7, 8, 10, 10, 11, 13, 14, 14, 16; 3:5, 10; Mic 1:1, 4, 7; 4:7, 12, 13; 5:1, 6, 6, 6, 7; 7:2, 3, 3, 3, 9, 10, 10, 14, 16, 16, 17, 17, 17, 17; Na 1:12, 15; 2:5; 3:2, 12, 15, 16; Hab 1:6, 7, 7, 7, 8, 8, 9, 10, 10, 11, 11, 13, 13, 15, 16, 16, 17; 2:4, 5, 5, 5, 7, 8, 13, 19, 19; Zep 1:5, 5, 5, 6, 13, 13, 13, 13, 13; 2:7, 10, 10; 3:3, 7, 7, 7, 12, 13, 20; Hag 1:9, 14; 2:14, 14; Zec 1:6, 6, 10, 21; 2:4, 11; 3:5; 4:4, 14; 5:9, 10, 11, 11; 6:5, 7, 10; 7:3, 11, 12, 12, 13, 13, 14; 8:8, 19, 23; 9:2, 7, 15, 15, 15, 16, 17; 10:5, 5, 5, 8, 9, 9, 11, 12, 12; 11:6, 8, 11, 12, 13; 12:6, 10, 10, 10; 13:9, 9; 14:13, 13, 19; Mal 1:4, 11; 2:5, 6, 6, 6, 6, 6; 3:3, 11, 16, 17, 17; 4:1, 3; Mt 2:5, 7, 10, 10, 11, 11, 11, 12, 15, 18, 23; 3:6; 4:4, 6, 18, 20, 22, 24; 5:4, 6, 7, 8, 9, 10; 6:2, 2, 5, 7, 16, 19, 20, 20, 26, 26, 28, 28, 29; 7:6, 10, 16, 21, 21, 21; 8:9, 9, 9, 27, 28, 29, 34; 9:4, 8, 8, 11, 13, 15, 28, 28, 30, 31, 32, 33, 36, 36; 10:28, 28; 11:10, 16, 20; 12:1, 4, 10, 10, 15, 23, 24, 27, 27, 41, 45, 47; 13:6, 12, 12, 13, 13, 13, 13, 15, 15, 16, 16, 17, 21, 21, 21, 21, 28, 41, 42, 48, 51, 57; 14:12, 15, 17, 20, 20, 20, 24, 26, 32, 33, 34, 34; 15:2, 2, 2, 9, 14, 14, 15, 23, 30, 31, 32, 32, 32, 34, 37, 37; 16:5, 5, 7, 7, 8, 12, 14; 17:8, 8, 9, 14, 16, 22, 25, 26; 18:20, 31, 31; 19:4, 6, 7, 25; 20:7, 10, 10, 10, 11, 11, 18, 19, 22, 24, 30, 30, 31, 33, 34, 34; 21:1, 7, 10, 15, 16, 20, 23, 25, 27, 31, 37, 38, 39, 45, 45, 46, 46; 22:3, 10, 15, 16, 19, 21, 22, 23, 30, 30, 33, 34, 42; 23:3, 3, 3, 4, 5, 5, 5, 6, 7, 7, 7, 32; 24:2, 5, 30, 31; 25:5, 6, 10, 11, 19, 29, 29, 29, 44, 46; 26:5, 8, 8, 15, 21, 22, 26, 30, 43, 47, 59, 60, 66, 67; 27:2, 4, 6, 7, 7, 9, 15, 22, 28, 29, 29, 29, 30, 31, 31, 31, 32, 32, 32, 33, 35, 36, 42, 53, 54, 63, 66; 28:4, 4, 8, 8, 9, 9, 10, 12, 13, 13, 15, 15, 17, 17; Mk 1:4, 5, 16, 18, 20, 22, 27, 27, 29, 30, 34, 37; 2:4, 4, 4, 8, 12, 12, 16, 17, 19, 19, 20, 24; 3:2, 4, 11, 13, 21, 21, 30, 31; 4:10, 12, 12, 12, 12, 17, 17, 17, 17, 25, 33, 36, 38, 41; 5:1, 13, 14, 15, 15, 38; 6:2, 3, 12, 13, 29, 30, 30, 32, 33, 34, 36, 37, 38, 40, 42, 42, 43, 48, 49, 49, 50, 50, 51, 51, 52, 52, 53, 53, 55, 56; 7:2, 3, 4, 4, 4, 5, 7, 23, 36, 37, 37; 8:2, 2, 3, 5, 8, 8, 9, 11, 11, 14, 15, 16, 16, 17, 19, 20, 22, 22, 24, 27, 28; 9:6, 8, 9, 9, 10, 10, 11, 14, 15, 18, 20, 28, 30, 32, 32, 33, 33, 34, 34; 10:4, 8, 10, 26, 30, 32, 33, 34, 35, 37, 39, 41, 46, 49, 49; 11:1, 5, 6, 6, 7, 12, 15, 18, 18, 20, 27, 27, 31, 32, 33; 12:4, 6, 8, 12, 12, 12, 16, 18, 25, 25, 38, 38, 39, 40, 40, 40, 44; 13:6, 33, 34; 14:2, 4, 5, 11, 11, 16, 18, 19, 22, 23, 26, 32, 40, 40, 43, 45, 52, 55, 56, 59, 64, 65, 65, 65; 15:1, 13, 17, 18, 19, 20, 20, 21, 22, 23, 24, 24, 29, 31, 41, 41; 16:2, 3, 4, 4, 5, 6, 8, 11, 12, 13, 13, 14, 17, 17, 18, 18, 18, 20, S; Lk 1:2, 7, 7, 22, 59, 61, 62; 2:6, 9, 16, 20, 24, 36, 39, 42, 43, 44, 44, 45, 45, 46, 50; 3:3, 14, 15; 4:6, 11, 22, 28, 29, 29, 41, 42, 42; 5:6, 11, 17, 18, 19, 19, 22, 26, 32, 33, 35, 39; 6:7, 17, 18, 19, 35; 7:4, 4, 6, 8, 8, 8, 10, 16, 24, 27, 29, 29, 30, 32, 32, 47; 8:10, 10, 10, 10, 13, 13, 14, 16, 18, 18, 19, 20, 22, 23, 25, 25, 26, 33, 34, 34, 35, 35, 40, 51, 53, 55, 56; 9:6, 10, 10, 11, 12, 13, 17, 17, 19, 31, 31, 32, 36, 36, 37, 40, 43, 45, 45, 45, 53, 54, 56, 57; 10:6, 7, 17, 23, 24, 30, 38; 11:12, 19, 19, 26, 32, 44, 48, 49, 53, 54; 12:4, 4, 24, 27, 27, 27, 37, 48; 13:1, 2, 4; 14:4, 6, 12, 18, 21, 30; 16:28, 28, 29, 30, 31, 31; 17:14; 18:1, 33, 34, 34, 35, 37; 19:7, 14, 15, 25, 26, 26, 29, 32, 33, 35, 37, 37, 37, 40, 41, 44, 48; 20:2, 5, 6, 7, 13, 14, 15, 19, 19, 19, 19, 20, 21, 24, 26, 26, 26, 28, 36, 36, 36, 38, 46, 46, 46, 47, 47, 47; 21:4, 7, 24, 26; 22:2, 2, 5, 5, 6, 9, 13, 13, 24, 25, 35, 38, 49, 54, 64, 64, 65, 67, 70, 71; 23:2, 5, 7, 11, 18, 21, 24, 25, 25, 26, 29, 33, 34, 34, 35, 37, 48, 55, 56, 56, 56; 24:1, 2, 3, 3, 4, 8, 9, 10, 11, 14, 14, 16, 17, 19, 20, 22, 23, 23, 28, 29, 30, 31, 32, 33, 33, 33, 35, 35, 36, 37, 41, 42, 43, 52, 53; Jn 1:13, 21, 38, 39, 39, 47; 2:3, 6, 8, 20, 22; 3:19, 20, 20, 20, 20, 21, 22; 4:27, 27, 36, 40, 40, 42, 45, 52; 5:10, 12, 23, 24, 24, 29, 36, 36, 39; 6:2, 11, 11, 14, 15, 17, 18, 19, 19, 19, 21, 22, 24, 24, 25, 25, 28, 30, 31, 34, 42, 45, 49, 52, 58; 7:3, 13, 15, 15, 25, 26, 31, 32, 35, 45, 49, 52; 8:3, 3, 4, 6, 6, 7, 9, 19, 25, 27, 33, 39, 41, 59; 9:10, 11, 12, 13, 18, 19, 22, 22, 23, 24, 26, 28, 34, 34, 39, 39; 10:4, 4, 5, 5, 5, 9, 9, 12, 14, 16, 27, 28, 33, 39, 41; 11:8, 9, 9, 13, 25, 26, 31, 31, 34, 38, 41, 42, 45, 47, 55, 56, 56, 56, 57; 12:9, 13, 16, 18, 21, 22, 26, 40, 42, 43; 14:21, 29, 29; 15:2, 20, 20, 20, 20, 21, 22, 22, 24, 24, 25; 16:2, 3, 4, 19; 17:6, 6, 6, 7, 8, 8, 9, 10, 10, 11, 13, 14, 16, 19, 21, 21, 22, 24; 18:3, 5, 6, 7, 13, 18, 21, 25, 28, 30, 40; 19:2, 3, 3, 6, 13, 15, 16, 18, 23, 23, 24, 24, 25, 29, 31, 33, 33, 33, 37, 37, 40, 42; 20:2, 2, 9, 10, 13, 13, 19, 20, 20, 23, 23, 25; 21:3, 3, 3, 4, 5, 6, 6, 8, 9, 9, 12; Ac 1:6, 7, 9, 10, 11, 12, 13, 13, 14, 19, 23, 24, 24, 26; 2:2, 6, 6, 6, 7, 7, 12, 12, 13, 18, 37, 42, 44, 45, 46; 3:2, 10, 10, 10, 11; 4:2, 3, 7, 13, 13, 13, 13, 15, 16, 16, 18, 21, 21, 23, 24, 28, 31, 31, 31, 32, 32, 32, 32; 5:9, 10, 16, 18, 21, 21, 22, 24, 25, 26, 26, 27, 38, 40, 40, 40, 42; 6:2, 5, 6, 9, 11, 12; 7:6, 7, 9, 11, 13, 13, 19, 21, 25, 40, 41, 41, 41, 52, 54, 57, 57, 58, 59; 8:7, 14, 15, 15, 16, 17, 19, 25, 36, 36, 38, 39; 9:7, 7, 21, 24, 24, 26, 26, 29, 30, 35, 38, 38, 39; 10:18, 22, 24, 27, 39, 46, 47; 11:3, 18, 18, 19, 22, 29, 30; 12:10, 10, 15, 15, 16, 16, 20, 20, 25; 13:5, 6, 6, 6, 14, 27, 27, 28, 28, 29, 29, 40, 45, 45, 48, 50, 51; 14:6, 6, 7, 8, 11, 12, 13, 14, 19, 22, 22, 22, 23, 24, 25, 26, 26, 26, 27, 28; 15:3, 3, 4, 4, 7, 13, 22, 23, 24, 30, 31, 33, 39, 41; 16:1, 3, 4, 7, 8, 17, 19, 20, 21, 23, 23, 23, 31, 32, 34, 37, 37, 39, 39, 40; 17:5, 5, 5, 6, 6, 6, 7, 7, 9, 10, 10, 11, 11, 11, 13, 13, 15, 18, 19, 19, 32; 18:2, 3, 13, 19, 20, 26, 27; 19:2, 3, 5, 5, 6, 12, 13, 15, 16, 28, 32, 34, 37, 39, 41; 20:4, 5, 11, 18, 37, 37, 38, 38; 21:6, 16, 20, 20, 20, 21, 22, 25, 25, 27, 29, 29, 31, 32, 35; 22:2, 19, 20, 20, 22, 23, 25, 29; 23:9, 10, 12, 14, 14, 15, 20, 21, 21, 21, 27, 32, 33, 33; 24:13, 14, 19, 19, 24; 25:3, 7, 16, 17; 26:5, 5, 7, 7, 10, 18, 18, 20, 20, 21, 26, 31, 31; 27:3, 13, 13, 14, 15, 15, 17, 19, 19, 28, 28, 29, 29, 30, 30, 39, 39, 40, 40, 42; 28:2, 6, 6, 15, 18, 21, 22, 25, 25, 27, 27, 28; Ro 1:5, 20, 20, 21, 21, 21, 22, 23, 24, 25, 25, 25, 27, 28, 30, 30, 31, 32, 32, 32; 2:1, 6, 12, 12, 12, 14, 14, 15, 15; 3:3, 15, 16, 17, 18, 26, 30; 4:4, 11, 12, 14; 5:3, 3, 14, 14, 20; 9:4, 4, 7, 11, 11, 19, 26, 30, 32, 32; 10:2, 3, 3, 3, 12, 14, 14, 14, 14, 15, 15, 18, 18, 19, 21; 11:3, 3, 6, 7, 8, 8, 10, 20, 24, 31; 12:13, 15, 20, 20, 20; 13:3, 3, 6; 14:1, 4, 4, 4, 6, 22, 23, 23, 23; 15:4, 12, 27, 27, 27, 27, 27; 16:3, 4, 7, 18, 18, 26; 1Co 1:15, 22, 22, 27; 2:8, 8, 9, 16; 3:8, 19, 20; 4:19; 6:13; 7:5, 5, 9, 9, 14; 8:7, 7, 10, 12; 9:10, 19, 25; 10:2, 4, 6, 7, 11,

33; **14:**2, 7, 8, 9, 9, 11, 11, 16, 16, 21, 23, 24, 24, 25, 25, 27, 27, 28, 34, 35; **15:**11, 35, 42, 42, 43, 43, 43, 43, 43, 44, 44, 44; **16:**15, 17, 18, 18; **2Co 1:**17; **3:**14, 15, 15; **4:**3, 4, 4, 17; **5:**15, 17; **6:**8, 8, 16; **8:**2, 3, 3, 3, 4, 5, 14, 23; **9:**11, 12, 14; **10:**7, 12, 12; **11:**4, 13, 15, 20, 21, 22, 22, 22, 22, 22, 22, 23, 23; **12:**4, 6, 16; **Gal 1:**23, 24; **2:**2, 3, 3, 4, 7, 9, 9, 9, 10, 14; **3:**19; **4:**1, 1, 2, 2, 17, 19; **6:**12, 13, 13, 16; **Eph 3:**10, 13; **4:**17, 18, 18, 19, 19; **5:**28; **6:**6; **Php 1:**16, 16, 16, 17, 17, 28; **2:**4; **3:**18, 19, 19; **4:**3, 3, 18; **Col 2:**2, 2, 18, 18, 19, 23, 23; **3:**21, 22; **4:**11, 11, 16; **1Th 1:**9, 10; **2:**15, 15, 16; **3:**4; **5:**12; **2Th 1:**9; **2:**2, 3, 10, 11, 12, 12; **3:**14, 17; **1Ti 1:**4, 6, 7, 7, 7, 7, 8, 9, 9, 16, 18, 20; **2:**9, 9, 10; **3:**8, 9, 10, 10, 10, 10, 11, 11; **4:**1, 2, 3; **5:**11, 12, 13, 13, 24; **6:**3, 5, 18, 19, 19; **2Ti 2:**14, 18, 18, 19, 24, 25, 25, 26, 26; **3:**2, 2, 3, 3, 3, 4, 5, 5, 5, 6, 7, 9, 9, 13, 13, 14, 15; **4:**3, 3, 4; **Tit 1:**9, 10, 11, 11, 12, 14, 16, 16, 16, 16; **2:**2, 3, 3, 5, 6, 8, 9, 10, 10; **3:**1, 2, 2, 2, 3, 11, 11, 13, 13, 14; **Heb 1:**11, 11, 12, 14; **3:**8, 8, 9, 10, 11, 15, 16, 16, 18, 19; **4:**2, 3, 5, 6; **5:**2, 2; **6:**6, 16; **7:**5, 8, 27; **8:**5, 9, 10, 10, 10, 11, 11; **9:**6, 15; **10:**1, 2, 8, 16, 16; **11:**11, 13, 13, 13, 14, 15, 15, 15, 16, 22, 23, 23, 29, 29, 33, 34, 35, 38, 38, 40; **12:**10, 13, 19, 19, 20, 25; **13:**7, 17, 17, 17; **Jas 1:**8, 8, 8, 10, 12; **2:**5, 7, 19; **4:**5; **5:**7, 13, 14; **1Pe 1:**10, 10, 11, 11, 12, 23; **2:**8, 8, 8, 11, 12, 12, 12, 18, 18, 18; **3:**1, 5, 16, 16; **4:**4, 4, 5, 6; **2Pe 1:**9, 19, 21; **2:**1, 3, 4, 11, 12, 12, 12, 13, 13, 13, 13, 13, 14, 14, 14, 14, 15, 17, 18, 18, 19, 19, 20, 21, 22; **3:**3, 5, 16; **1Jn 2:**6, 11, 16, 19, 19, 19, 19, 22; **3:**1, 7, 8, 9, 9; **4:**1, 2, 5, 6, 6, 15; **5:**10; **2Jn** 7; **3Jn** 5, 6, 7, 10, 11, 11; **Jude** 4, 6, 10, 10, 10, 11, 11, 11, 12, 12, 12, 12, 12, 12, 12, 13, 13, 15, 16, 16, 16, 19, 19, 19, 19; **Rev 2:**2, 2, 9, 9, 9, 22, 24, 27, 28; **3:**4, 4, 5, 9, 9, 12, 12, 12; **4:**4, 5, 8, 10, 11; **5:**8, 9, 10, 12, 13; **6:**8, 10, 10, 11, 16; **7:**9, 10, 11, 12, 13, 14, 15, 16, 16; **8:**2, 12; **9:**3, 4, 5, 6, 7, 7, 9, 10, 16, 20, 21; **11:**2, 3, 6, 6, 6, 6, 7, 11, 12, 17; **12:**11, 11, 17; **13:**4, 4, 4, 8; **14:**4, 4, 5, 10, 11, 11, 13, 13, 18; **15:**2, 3; **16:**4, 9, 9, 11, 11, 15, 16, 21; **17:**9, 12, 13, 14, 16, 17; **18:**9, 10, 10, 14, 14, 15, 18, 18, 18, 19, 19; **19:**4; **20:**4, 4, 6, 9, 10, 11, 12, 13; **21:**3, 7; **22:**4, 5, 14

THEY'LL (3)

Ge 29:7; **Ex 4:**1; **1Sa 18:**8

THEY'RE (2)

1Sa 20:21; **Ac 2:**13

THIS (4240)

Ge 1:7, 8, 13, 19, 23, 31; **2:**4, 16, 24; **3:**14; **4:**5; **5:**1, 29; **6:**7, 9, 12; **8:**11, 12; **9:**17, 23; **10:**1; **11:**4, 6, 10, 10, 27; **12:**7, 12, 18; **13:**4, 8, 9, 10, 13, 15; **14:**1, 19; **15:**7, 16, 18; **16:**3, 5, 5, 12; **17:**3, 4, 7, 8, 9, 10, 11, 11, 12, 21; **18:**4, 10, 10; **19:**12, 31; **20:**9, 9, 9, 9, 10, 11, 16, 16; **21:**6, 11, 22, 23, 26, 26, 30; **22:**14, 16, 20; **23:**8, 17; **24:**7, 8, 13, 14, 14, 38, 42, 42, 43, 49, 52, 58, 60; **25:**10, 12, 19, 22, 30; **26:**3, 3, 5, 10, 11, 20, 24, 27, 33; **27:**43; **28:**4, 15, 16, 17, 20, 20, 22; **29:**9, 25, 25; **30:**33, 40, 42; **31:**9, 13, 26, 26, 48, 49, 49, 51, 51, 52; **32:**2, 4, 24; **34:**4, 14, 19, 20, 23, 23, 30; **35:**8, 20; **36:**1, 9, 24; **37:**2, 6, 9, 10, 12, 22, 24, 32; **38:**1, 11, 25, 25, 28; **39:**3, 7, 14; **41:**4, 5, 16, 22, 28, 31, 40, 50, 52; **42:**15, 20, 20, 21, 21, 33; **43:**10, 11, 16, 29; **44:**13, 18, 34; **45:**5, 9, 16; **46:**34; **47:**26, 29; **48:**1, 4, 18, 20, 20; **49:**30, 33; **50:**11, 13, 16, 24; **Ex 1:**10, 15, 18, 22; **2:**1, 5, 9, 16, 17; **3:**3, 6, 12, 12, 15, 22, 22; **4:**5, 7, 22; **5:**1, 1, 6, 15, 21, 22; **6:**26, 30; **7:**1, 9, 17; **8:**1, 2, 18, 19, 20, 23, 25; **9:**1, 16, 18, 28, 29, 34; **10:**3, 6, 17, 17; **11:**4, 9; **12:**2, 3, 4, 5, 6, 11, 11, 13, 14, 17, 17, 17, 19, 25, 26, 26, 42, 42, 47, 49; **13:**3, 4, 5, 5, 7, 8, 9, 10, 14, 16; **14:**4, 4, 30; **15:**1, 13, 21, 22, 25; **16:**3, 4, 9, 17, 22, 23, 25, 32, 32, 34; **17:**14; **18:**2, 12, 14, 17, 18, 23, 27; **19:**6; **20:**10, 20, 22; **21:**6, 29; **22:**15; **23:**7, 12, 15, 29; **24:**8; **25:**9; **26:**11, 12, 14, 17, 30, 32, 33, 37; **27:**21; **28:**16, 28, 29, 35, 37, 39, 43; **29:**1, 9, 18, 21, 22, 27, 32, 35, 38, 42; **30:**8, 9, 10, 10, 14, 15, 16, 21, 26, 29, 30, 31, 36, 37; **32:**1, 6, 12, 13, 23, 24, 27, 29; **33:**1, 13, 13, 15, 21; **34:**7, 9, 10; **35:**4; **36:**6, 18, 22, 36, 38; **38:**2, 26; **39:**1, 7, 21, 21, 23, 26, 28, 31; **40:**15, 38; **Lev 2:**2, 2; **3:**3, 3, 9, 9, 14, 14, 17; **4:**20, 21, 24, 26, 31, 35; **5:**6, 10, 12, 12, 13, 18, 19; **6:**6, 12, 14, 15, 16, 17, 18, 21, 22, 29; **7:**13, 14, 18, 35, 36; **8:**15, 21, 29, 30, 35, 35; **9:**24; **10:**1, 3, 9, 19, 20; **11:**32, 42; **12:**4; **13:**7, 8, 15, 39, 42, 59; **14:**18, 20, 29, 31, 52, 53; **15:**3, 15, 24, 30, 31; **16:**11, 16, 19, 21, 21, 24, 27, 29, 30, 31, 34; **17:**5, 7, 8, 13, 15; **18:**2, 8, 16, 17, 23, 24, 26; **19:**2, 25; **20:**4; **21:**23; **22:**7, 8; **23:**6, 13, 14, 14, 18, 21, 31, 32, 32, 34, 36, 39, 41, 41, 43; **24:**3, 8, 11; **25:**10, 46, 46; **26:**18, 23, 27, 44; **27:**28; **Nu 1:**20, 47; **2:**33; **3:**1, 4; **4:**11, 19, 37, 41, 45; **5:**3, 19, 21, 21, 22, 29, 30, 31; **6:**8, 11, 13, 20, 21, 23, 27; **7:**17, 23, 29, 35, 41, 47, 53, 59, 65, 71, 77, 83, 84, 88; **8:**3, 7, 14, 15, 24, 26; **9:**3, 9, 16, 18; **10:**8, 25, 28; **11:**6, 11, 15, 15, 25; **12:**11; **13:**16, 27; **14:**3, 14, 14, 14, 19, 27, 28, 29, 32, 33, 35; **15:**7, 10, 12, 15, 17, 21, 29; **16:**6, 10, 13, 28, 40; **17:**5, 10; **18:**13, 19, 23, 24, 26, 27, 28, 31; **19:**9, 10, 12, 14, 21; **20:**4, 5, 5, 10, 13, 14, 14; **21:**2, 5, 14, 17, 18, 21, 27, 27; **22:**4, 5, 10, 15, 16, 16, 27, 30; **23:**7, 16, 18; **24:**3, 3, 15, 15, 20, 23; **25:**7, 13; **26:**4, 9, 10, 36, 57, 64; **27:**8, 11, 21; **28:**6, 10, 13, 14, 15, 24; **29:**11, 17; **30:**1; **31:**21, 29, 30, 47, 50; **32:**4, 5, 8, 15, 15, 32; **33:**1, 38, 54; **34:**9, 13; **35:**5, 10, 24, 33; **36:**3, 5, 6; **Dt 1:**1, 4, 6, 8, 23, 31, 35, 36, 43; **2:**3, 7, 14, 22, 26; **3:**12, 14, 18, 18; **4:**6, 8, 22, 23, 25, 32, 39, 44, 46; **5:**3, 5, 14, 22, 25, 29; **6:**11, 23; **7:**19; **8:**16, 19; **9:**4, 4, 6, 13, 18, 23; **11:**4; **12:**31; **13:**8; **14:**23, 23; **15:**2, 3, 5, 15, 21; **16:**3, 14, 15, 15; **17:**4, 7, 15, 19, 19, 20, 20; **18:**16, 16; **19:**9, 19; **20:**9, 18; **21:**7, 8, 12, 20, 21, 21; **22:**5, 15, 16, 22, 23, 24, 26, 30; **24:**18, 21, 22; **25:**9, 19; **26:**3, 9, 9; **27:**3, 8, 11, 26; **28:**58, 58, 61, 67; **29:**4, 9, 12, 14, 15, 18, 19, 19, 20, 21, 24, 25, 27, 27; **30:**10, 11, 16; **31:**9, 10, 11, 12, 13, 13, 19, 21, 24, 26, 30; **32:**6, 19, 27, 29, 44, 46; **33:**1, 6, 7, 8, 12, 13, 17, 18, 20, 22, 23, 24; **34:**4, 6; **Jos 1:**8, 13; **2:**9, 18, 19, 20; **3:**4; **4:**9, 22, 24; **5:**9, 14, 15; **6:**13, 14, 15, 25, 26; **7:**5, 10, 13, 26; **8:**2, 16, 28, 33; **9:**12, 24, 27; **10:**2, 13, 18, 25, 27; **11:**6, 18, 19, 21; **12:**2, 7, 8; **13:**3, 4, 6, 7, 8, 13, 23, 28, 31; **14:**10; **15:**4, 20, 63; **16:**8, 10; **18:**14, 20, 28; **19:**8, 16, 23, 31, 35, 39, 48; **20:**9; **22:**14, 22, 23, 24, 28, 28, 30; **23:**5, 13, 15; **24:**2, 22, 27, 29, 32; **Jdg 1:**21, 25, 26; **2:**1, 2, 3, 14, 22; **3:**2; **4:**6, 9; **5:**1; **6:**8, 13, 20, 24, 26, 29, 37, 39; **7:**13; **8:**1, 9, 10, 13; **9:**7; **10:**6; **11:**4, 14, 15, 26, 26; **12:**1; **13:**8, 17, 20, 23; **14:**4, 15; **15:**3, 6, 7, 18, 19; **17:**11; **18:**12, 23, 28, 30; **19:**8, 10, 11, 12, 23, 24, 24, 30; **20:**3, 6, 7, 10, 13, 41; **21:**3, 11, 15, 18; **Ru 1:**5; **2:**7, 19, 22; **3:**18; **4:**6, 7, 10, 12, 15, 18; **1Sa 1:**11, 27; **2:**14, 20, 27; **4:**7, 7, 16, 21; **5:**4, 5; **6:**9, 16, 20; **7:**12; **8:**11, 18; **9:**6, 12, 16, 21; **10:**1, 18, 24, 27; **11:**7, 7; **12:**8, 17; **13:**3, 11; **14:**29, 44; **15:**1, 2, 6, 11; **16:**6, 8, 9, 12; **17:**8, 8, 11, 17, 26, 26, 32, 33, 36, 36, 37, 42; **18:**7, 8, 8, 10, 11, 15, 24; **20:**2, 5, 8, 12, 15, 21; **21:**5, 11, 15; **22:**15, 15; **24:**10, 11; **25:**3, 5, 8, 9, 10, 10, 21, 24, 31; **26:**8, 16, 19; **27:**6, 11; **28:**10, 18; **29:**3, 5, 8; **30:**24, 25; **2Sa 2:**1, 5; **3:**8, 8, 8, 14, 28, 33, 36; **6:**7, 22; **7:**2, 5, 8, 18, 19, 27; **8:**1, 14; **10:**1, 7, 18; **12:**1, 9, 10, 12, 13; **13:**12, 17, 30, 32; **14:**9, 13, 22, 24; **15:**1, 6; **16:**9, 11, 17; **17:**3, 4, 5, 7; **18:**5, 5, 14, 18; **19:**5, 22, 42; **20:**1; **21:**18; **22:**1, 50; **23:**17, 17, 17; **24:**3, 10, 11, 12, 13, 14; **1Ki 1:**27; **2:**1, 4, 23, 24, 29, 31, 45; **3:**6, 9, 17; **5:**2, 8, 14; **6:**1, 11, 12, 20; **7:**8; **8:**8, 14, 17, 20, 26, 27, 29, 29, 29, 30, 31, 33, 34, 35, 38, 42, 43, 44, 44, 48, 48, 55; **9:**3, 5, 7, 7, 8, 15, 21; **10:**15; **11:**12, 27, 31, 34; **12:**5, 10, 15, 18, 19, 24, 30; **13:**2, 3, 3, 8, 9, 16, 17, 18, 21, 22, 22, 33, 34; **14:**7, 13, 14, 15; **15:**18, 30; **16:**1, 7, 10, 13, 34; **17:**12, 14, 20, 21; **18:**33, 36; **19:**2, 2; **20:**2, 2, 5, 6, 7, 9, 9, 10, 11, 12, 13, 14, 24, 26, 28, 28, 33, 39, 42; **21:**19, 19, 19, 27, 29; **22:**11, 22, 27, 27; **2Ki 1:**4, 6, 7, 13, 16, 16, 17; **2:**19, 21, 21; **3:**7, 16, 16, 17, 18; **4:**9, 16, 35, 40, 43; **5:**6, 7, 8, 10, 17, 18, 20, 26, 27; **6:**1, 10, 11, 19, 28, 30, 31, 33, 33; **7:**1, 1, 1, 9, 9, 13, 18; **8:**5, 6, 22; **9:**1, 3, 6, 7, 25, 34, 36; **10:**2, 4, 5, 6, 10, 27, 30; **11:**5, 14; **12:**17; **13:**17, 23; **14:**7, 8, 9; **16:**6, 7; **17:**4, 7, 23, 34, 41; **18:**14, 15, 19, 19, 27, 27, 28, 29, 30, 32; **19:**3, 3, 6, 6, 9, 10, 10, 15, 20, 20, 21, 25, 29, 29, 31, 32, 33; **20:**1, 1, 1, 2, 4, 5, 6, 6, 7, 9, 11, 12, 16, 19; **21:**7, 8, 11, 12, 16; **22:**5, 13, 13, 13, 16, 16, 17, 18, 19, 19, 20, 20; **23:**3, 8, 16, 21, 23, 24; **24:**4; **1Ch 1:**24; **4:**33; **5:**1, 26; **6:**54, 55; **9:**18; **11:**19, 19, 19; **12:**27, 28, 29; **13:**4; **15:**2; **16:**5, 7, 16, 19, 38; **17:**1, 4, 7, 16, 25; **18:**1, 13; **19:**1, 8, 18; **20:**4; **21:**3, 8, 9, 10, 12, 13, 22; **22:**1, 17; **24:**1; **27:**1, 6; **28:**8, 8, 10, 19; **29:**3, 11, 17, 19; **2Ch 1:**3, 10; **2:**3, 5, 11; **5:**9; **6:**3, 7, 10, 17, 18, 20, 20, 20, 21, 22, 24, 25, 26, 29, 32, 33, 34, 34, 38, 38, 40, 41; **7:**7, 12, 15, 16, 18, 20, 20, 21; **8:**3, 6, 8; **9:**8, 14; **10:**10, 15, 18, 19; **11:**4, 17; **12:**1, 5, 6, 7; **14:**6, 11; **15:**8, 15; **16:**2, 10; **18:**10, 20, 26, 26; **19:**10; **20:**1, 2, 3, 7, 7, 8, 9, 12, 15, 15, 21; **21:**10, 12, 12, 18; **22:**7, 7, 11; **23:**4, 13; **24:**6, 10, 11, 20; **25:**9, 10, 15, 16, 16, 17, 18; **26:**11, 18, 18; **28:**12, 21, 25; **29:**18, 24; **30:**4, 9, 18, 26; **31:**1, 9, 11, 20; **32:**1, 6, 9, 10, 15, 18; **33:**7, 8, 14; **34:**21, 21, 24, 24, 25, 26, 27, 28, 28, 32; **35:**3, 19, 21, 25; **36:**22, 23, 23; **Ezr 1:**1, 2, 3; **2:**2, 59, 60, 61; **3:**3, 6, 7, 9, 11; **4:**3, 5, 11, 12, 13, 14, 14, 15, 16, 17, 23; **5:**3, 3, 6, 9, 9, 11, 12, 16, 17; **6:**2, 6, 8, 11, 12, 12, 12; **7:**6, 10, 11, 21, 24; **8:**28, 35; **9:**3, 4, 8, 10, 12, 14; **10:**1, 2, 9, 13, 13, 13, 14, 15, 16, 24; **Ne 1:**4; **2:**1, 17, 19, 20; **4:**2, 23; **5:**1, 10, 11, 15; **6:**3, 6, 7, 12, 16; **7:**5, 7, 61, 62, 63; **8:**9, 10, 11, 17; **9:**1, 18, 26, 36, 37, 38, 38; **10:**33; **11:**1; **12:**25, 36; **13:**3, 4, 7, 14, 17, 18, 18, 21, 22, 26, 27, 31; **Est 1:**1, 8, 12, 18, 20, 21; **2:**4, 7, 23; **3:**4, 13, 14; **4:**10, 13, 14, 14, 15; **5:**7, 8, 13, 14, 14; **6:**3, 9, 11, 13; **7:**6; **8:**12, 13; **9:**17, 19, 22, 23, 26, 27, 31; **Job 1:**5, 14, 16, 17, 18, 22; **2:**10; **3:**10; **4:**12; **5:**8, 27; **6:**10; **7:**1, 15; **8:**2; **9:**2; **10:**13, 19; **11:**2; **12:**9; **13:**16, 19; **14:**14; **15:**2; **16:**2; **18:**21; **20:**29; **21:**14; **27:**2, 12, 13, 13; **28:**27, 28; **32:**11; **33:**12, 31; **34:**12; **35:**7; **36:**21; **37:**1; **38:**2, 21; **42:**3; **Ps 1:**4; **2:**3; **4:**3; **9:**17; **12:**7; **18:**T, 49; **22:**8; **31:**3; **35:**22; **40:**7, 10; **42:**3, 10; **44:**17; **49:**1, 13, 18; **50:**21; **52:**1; **55:**8, 20; **56:**9; **57:**1; **60:**6; **63:**1; **68:**5, 30; **69:**13, 31; **71:**18; **72:**20; **73:**15, 20; **77:**10; **78:**30, 32, 54, 56; **80:**14, 15; **81:**4; **83:**5; **87:**5, 6; **89:**3, 46, 47; **91:**2; **92:**6; **102:**18; **105:**9, 12, 45; **106:**17, 36; **107:**43; **108:**7; **109:**27; **112:**10; **116:**5; **118:**23, 24; **119:**55, 56; **122:**6; **129:**8; **132:**14, 14, 15; **143:**11; **144:**15; **147:**20; **149:**5, 9; **Pr 6:**9, 23, 24; **20:**22; **22:**2, 21; **24:**32; **29:**13; **Ecc 1:**17; **2:**1, 3, 3, 15, 20, 21, 24, 26; **3:**10, 14; **4:**4, 8; **5:**16, 16, 20; **6:**2, 8; **7:**6, 14, 15, 27, 27; **8:**2, 14, 14, 14, 15, 17; **9:**1, 1, 7, 9, 11; **12:**13; **SS 1:**1; **3:**3, 6; **5:**1, 8, 9; **6:**10, 13; **8:**5; **Isa 1:**2, 18; **2:**1, 21; **3:**6; **5:**5, 7, 14; **6:**7, 9, 11; **7:**7, 7, 10, 10, 15, 20; **8:**1, 4, 4, 8; **9:**7, 13, 18; **10:**24; **13:**1, 3; **14:**8, 16, 17, 17, 21, 22, 24, 28; **15:**1; **16:**6, 13; **17:**1, 14; **18:**4, 7, 7; **19:**1; **20:**3, 6; **21:**1, 11, 13; **22:**1, 2, 11, 14, 15; **23:**1, 7, 8; **25:**9, 9; **26:**1, 19; **27:**9; **28:**9, 13, 14, 16, 19; **29:**14; **30:**6, 11, 12, 21; **31:**4; **32:**17; **33:**6, 14, 18; **34:**10, 16; **35:**3; **36:**4, 4, 12, 12, 13, 14, 15, 17; **37:**3, 3, 6, 6, 9, 10, 10, 15, 21, 21, 21, 22, 26, 30, 30, 32, 33, 34; **38:**1, 1, 1, 2, 4, 5, 6, 6, 7, 9, 11, 15, 15, 17; **39:**1, 5, 8; **41:**2, 20, 26, 26, 28; **43:**12; **44:**6, 9, 20, 20, 23; **45:**1, 2, 3, 4, 10, 11, 14; **46:**8; **48:**14, 15, 16; **49:**8, 8, 22; **50:**11; **51:**21, 22; **52:**3, 4, 5; **55:**13; **56:**2, 4, 12; **57:**6, 8, 15; **58:**2, 4, 5, 5, 13; **59:**9, 21; **62:**11; **63:**1, 1; **64:**12; **65:**13; **66:**1, 5, 8, 9, 9; **Jer 1:**14; **2:**2, 5, 10, 17, 21, 21, 25, 26; **3:**7, 7, 10, 12, 19; **4:**3, 18, 18, 21, 27; **5:**9, 9, 14, 14, 19, 20, 29, 29, 30; **6:**1, 6, 6, 8, 9, 12, 18, 21, 22; **7:**2, 2, 7, 11, 14, 14, 14, 20, 21, 23, 27, 28, 29; **8:**3, 4; **9:**9, 9, 12, 13, 17, 23, 24; **10:**2, 11, 18; **11:**3, 5, 6, 7, 17, 19, 22; **12:**1, 4, 14; **13:**1, 8, 9, 10, 13, 13, 22, 25; **14:**1, 17; **15:**2; **16:**2, 3, 3, 6, 9, 11, 13, 15; **17:**5, 15, 20, 21, 22, 25, 25; **18:**5, 6, 11; **19:**3, 3, 3, 4, 4, 4, 6, 11, 11, 12, 12, 12, 14, 15, 15; **20:**4; **21:**4, 4, 6, 8, 10, 11, 12, 13; **22:**2, 3, 5, 5, 6, 8, 11, 18, 26, 28, 29, 30, 30; **23:**2, 6, 15, 15, 16, 20, 26, 31, 36, 37, 38, 38, 38, 39; **24:**1, 4, 5; **25:**1, 1, 5, 5, 9, 11, 13, 15, 18, 27, 32; **26:**1, 4, 6, 9, 11, 11, 12, 12, 13, 15, 16, 18, 19, 20; **27:**1, 4, 4, 12, 15, 15, 16, 17, 19, 21; **28:**6, 12, 13, 16; **29:**2, 3, 4, 16, 17, 20, 21, 23, 24, 25, 30, 31; **30:**2, 3, 4, 5, 12, 15, 18, 24; **31:**7, 10, 15, 23, 26, 28, 29, 32, 33, 35; **32:**1, 3, 3, 3, 12, 14, 15, 20, 22, 23, 26, 28, 31, 36, 36, 37, 41, 43; **33:**1, 2, 4, 4, 5, 9, 10, 10, 11, 12, 12, 17, 19, 25; **34:**1, 2, 2, 4, 4, 5, 7, 8, 12, 13, 14, 17, 21, 22; **35:**1, 4, 6, 11, 12, 18, 19; **36:**1, 6, 9, 10, 18, 29, 29, 30, 32; **37:**5, 6, 7, 8, 10, 18; **38:**2, 4, 4, 18, 21, 23, 24, 26; **39:**16; **40:**2, 2, 13; **42:**9, 10, 15, 19; **43:**1, 3; **44:**1, 2, 10, 12, 24, 26, 26, 29; **45:**2, 4, 4; **46:**2, 7, 10, 13; **47:**1, 2; **48:**1, 1, 47; **49:**1, 1, 2, 7, 7, 12, 12, 15, 23, 23, 28, 28, 34, 35; **50:**1, 2, 33, 39; **51:**1, 11, 14, 47, 58, 59, 59, 61, 64, 64; **La 2:**15, 16, 20, 20; **3:**20, 21, 54; **Eze 1:**2, 23, 26, 28; **2:**3, 4; **3:**1, 11, 11, 27; **4:**3, 9, 10, 13; **5:**4, 5, 5, 7; **6:**3, 3, 10, 11; **7:**1, 2, 5; **8:**15, 17; **10:**2, 4; **11:**2, 5, 7, 7, 11, 14, 16; **12:**3, 8, 9, 10, 17, 19, 23, 23, 23, 26, 28; **13:**1, 3, 7, 8, 13, 18; **14:**2, 4, 5, 6, 11, 12, 21; **15:**1, 6, 7; **16:**3, 35, 36, 37, 58, 59; **17:**1, 2, 3, 8, 9, 11, 12, 15, 19, 20; **18:**2, 3, 4, 15, 16; **19:**1, 14; **20:**2, 3, 3, 5, 16, 27, 29, 29, 30, 31, 39, 45, 47, 48; **21:**1, 3, 9, 18, 24, 28; **22:**1, 2, 3, 17, 19, 24; **23:**1, 22, 27, 28, 30, 32, 46, 48; **24:**1, 2, 6, 9, 15, 18, 19, 21, 21; **25:**1, 3, 14; **26:**1, 3, 14, 15, 17; **27:**1, 3, 32; **28:**1, 2, 6, 11, 12, 22, 25; **29:**1, 3, 17, 19; **30:**1, 2, 6, 10, 13, 20, 22; **31:**1, 2, 5, 8, 9, 10, 15, 18; **32:**1, 2, 3, 11, 16; **33:**2, 10, 12, 15, 22, 23, 25, 27; **34:**1, 2, 10, 11, 17, 20, 30; **35:**3, 14; **36:**1, 2, 3, 5, 6, 13, 16, 22, 32, 33, 35, 36, 37; **37:**5, 9, 12, 13, 16, 16, 19, 21; **38:**1, 3, 10, 14, 16, 17; **39:**1, 11, 19; **40:**9, 13, 14, 18, 18, 23, 26, 36, 39; **41:**4, 8, 9, 10, 22; **42:**2, 8, 11; **43:**1, 3, 7, 12, 12, 13, 14, 14, 18, 20, 26; **44:**2, 3, 6, 7, 9, 19; **45:**1, 2, 4, 6, 9, 13, 18, 19, 20, 21, 23; **46:**1, 3, 14, 16, 20; **47:**1, 4, 8, 8, 9, 9, 13, 14, 18, 19; **48:**11, 14, 18, 20; **Da 1:**10; **2:**5, 11, 12, 26, 41, 43, 43, 47; **3:**29, 29; **4:**1, 10, 12, 17, 17, 19, 19, 24, 25, 26, 30, 30, 31, 31, 32, 33, 34; **5:**7, 10, 11, 12, 15, 22, 24, 25, 26; **6:**8, 14, 14, 25; **7:**1, 6, 8, 16, 20, 21, 23; **8:**2, 5, 12, 13, 15, 16, 26; **9:**7, 26, 27, 27; **10:**2, 7, 8, 11, 14; **11:**5, 18, 24, 29, 35, 39; **12:**4, 7, 8; **Hos 1:**2; **3:**3, 4; **5:**1; **8:**5, 5, 6; **9:**3, 4, 7; **10:**6, 6; **Joel 1:**1, 2, 2; **2:**11, 14, 25, 26, 27; **Am 1:**1, 1, 2, 3, 6, 9, 11, 13; **2:**1, 4, 6, 11; **3:**1, 7, 9, 12, 13; **4:**2, 5; **5:**1, 4, 16; **6:**8, 8, 13; **7:**1, 6, 8, 16, 17, 17; **8:**2, 4, 7; **9:**8; **Ob** 1, 12; **Jnh 1:**1, 5, 6, 7, 8, 10, 11, 12, 14, 14; **3:**3, 7; **4:**1, 2, 4, 6, 8; **Mic 1:**5, 8; **2:**3, 4, 8, 10; **3:**5; **4:**4, 10; **6:**8; **Na 1:**1, 11, 12, 14; **3:**4; **Hab 1:**1, 3, 12, 13, 17; **3:**1, 2, 16, 19; **Zep 2:**5, 15; **Hag 1:**2, 3, 5, 7, 13, 15; **2:**2, 3, 6, 7, 7, 9, 9, 10, 11, 11, 14, 14, 15, 18, 18, 19, 20, 23; **Zec 1:**1, 3, 4, 12, 12, 14, 14, 16, 17, 17; **3:**2, 7, 9; **4:**6, 9; **5:**3, 4, 4; **6:**15, 15; **7:**3, 4, 7, 8, 9, 11; **8:**2, 4, 6, 6, 6, 7, 9, 14, 16, 17, 19, 20, 23; **9:**1, 12; **11:**4, 8, 13, 16, 16, 16, 17; **12:**1, 1; **14:**5, 7, 15; **Mal 1:**1, 4; **2:**1, 4, 5, 5, 12; **Mt 1:**1, 18, 20, 22; **2:**5, 7, 9, 15, 23; **3:**17; **4:**14; **5:**2; **6:**9; **7:**12; **8:**9, 10, 10, 11, 17, 27; **9:**3, 8, 12, 13, 18, 26, 30, 33; **10:**18; **11:**7, 13, 16, 25, 26; **12:**7, 17, 29, 32, 36, 41, 42, 45; **13:**3, 14, 22, 33, 35; **14:**2, 15, 22; **16:**7, 17, 17, 18, 22; **17:**4, 5, 20; **18:**4, 5, 18, 19, 23, 31; **19:**3, 5, 9, 11, 12, 16, 22; **20:**14, 25; **21:**4, 10, 20, 21, 21, 28, 32, 33, 38, 42, 42; **22:**16, 17, 23, 26, 31, 35, 38; **23:**36, 39; **24:**3, 8, 34, 43; **25:**21, 23, 28, 30; **26:**8, 12, 13, 26, 28, 34, 39, 42, 47, 56, 61, 71, 72; **27:**9, 16, 19, 24, 37, 54, 64; **28:**20; **Mk 1:**4, 15, 27; **2:**7, 8, 12, 15, 17; **3:**4, 27, 30; **4:**2, 13, 19, 24, 31, 41; **5:**3, 9, 31, 39; **6:**14, 35, 37, 45; **7:**4, 10, 13, 19; **8:**1, 10, 12, 12, 16, 32; **9:**5, 7, 16, 18, 21, 25, 29, 37; **10:**2, 7, 21, 22, 24, 42; **11:**23, 27; **12:**7, 10, 11, 12, 17, 18, 22, 26, 29, 33, 34, 38, 40, 43; **13:**4, 4, 8, 9, 30; **14:**4, 9, 22, 24, 30, 36, 43, 57, 58, 71; **15:**11, 12, 32, 32, 39, 42; **16:**6, 7; **Lk 1:**18, 19, 43, 66, 67; **2:**2, 3, 5, 12, 15, 17, 34, 48; **3:**2, 20; **4:**3, 21, 22, 22, 28, 36; **5:**6, 21, 21, 22, 36; **6:**9, 11; **7:**1, 8, 9, 9, 24, 29, 31, 39, 41, 44, 49; **8:**4, 6, 8, 8, 11, 14, 25, 29, 45; **9:**7, 9, 12, 13, 21, 33, 34, 35, 36, 43, 48; **10:**21, 25, 28; **11:**2, 5, 7, 8, 29, 31, 32, 49, 50; **12:**8, 20, 33, 39, 41; **13:**1, 6, 16, 17, 30; **14:**7, 9, 10, 10, 15, 16, 22; **15:**2, 3, 11, 13, 24, 30, 32; **16:**1, 2, 8, 9, 14, 15, 28; **17:**6, 16, 18, 22, 23, 25, 33, 33, 37; **18:**5, 6, 9, 11, 14, 18, 23, 26, 30; **19:**9, 9, 24, 28; **20:**9, 14, 19, 28, 37, 47; **21:**3, 7, 12, 13, 23, 29, 32, 34; **22:**15, 15, 17, 19, 19, 20, 21, 25, 37, 42, 47, 53, 56, 59, 66; **23:**2, 4, 14, 14, 15, 38, 41, 44, 47, 54; **24:**8, 22, 28, 47; **Jn 1:**4, 13, 13, 15, 19, 28, 34, 50, 50; **2:**11, 17, 18, 19, 20, 21, 22; **3:**19, 23, 24; **4:**11, 11, 12, 13, 29, 54; **5:**9, 20, 40, 45; **6:**1, 9, 14, 29, 39, 42, 51, 51, 52, 58, 60, 61, 66; **7:**1, 4, 8, 22, 24, 25, 27, 31, 35, 40, 40, 46; **8:**4, 9, 14, 23; **9:**2, 8, 16, 17, 19, 20, 22, 25, 29, 33; **10:**6, 16, 18, 21, 41; **11:**2, 4, 9, 15, 26, 37, 45, 47, 50, 51; **12:**16, 18, 25, 25, 31, 33, 34, 38, 41, 46; **13:**1, 18, 19, 24; **14:**2, 24, 30; **15:**8, 11, 25; **16:**3, 11, 15, 24, 25, 30, 33; **17:**3, 16, 26; **18:**2, 9, 21, 29, 32, 34, 36, 40; **19:**8, 12, 13, 24, 27, 27, 35; **20:**26, 30; **21:**1, 14, 19, 24; **Ac 1:**4, 9, 12, 15, 16, 20, 25, 26; **2:**4, 6, 7, 12, 14, 16, 25, 29, 32, 32, 36, 39, 40; **3:**12, 12, 13, 13, 14, 15, 16, 16; **4:**7, 22, 27, 31; **5:**2, 4, 8, 9, 20, 24, 28, 31, 33, 42; **6:**3, 5, 12, 13, 14, 15; **7:**2, 7, 19, 24, 40, 41, 45, 60; **8:**18, 19, 21, 32, 35; **9:**3, 13, 21, 37; **10:**18, 28; **11:**10, 18, 23, 27, 28, 30; **12:**3, 10; **13:**15, 17, 20, 26, 32, 33, 34, 36, 38, 46, 47, 48; **14:**15; **15:**2, 6, 15, 17, 22, 23, 23, 29, 31, 39; **16:**18; **17:**3, 18, 19, 23, 27, 29, 31, 32; **18:**10, 14, 27; **19:**5, 10, 13, 14, 25, 26, 26, 27, 28, 36, 40; **20:**16; **21:**11, 12, 13, 20, 28; **22:**5, 26; **23:**7, 10, 17, 18, 22, 25, 27; **24:**3, 4, 10, 16, 27; **25:**10, 20, 24; **26:**7, 16, 21, 29, 31; **27:**21, 29; **28:**20, 25, 28; **Ro 1:**1, 2, 12, 16, 17, 17, 19; **2:**16; **3:**8, 22, 24, 26, 31; **4:**1, 6, 9, 17, 20, 23; **5:**2, 5, 15, 15, 17, 17; **6:**9, 15, 19; **7:**4, 8, 23, 24; **8:**4, 11, 24; **9:**8, 10, 11, 20, 30, 33; **10:**12, 17; **11:**2, 7, 8, 9, 13, 13, 25, 25, 26, 28; **12:**1, 2, 3; **13:**9; **14:**5, 9, 18; **15:**5, 15, 19, 27, 28, 28, 30; **16:**19, 22, 26; **1Co 1:**1, 6, 9, 9, 18, 20, 25; **2:**5, 6, 6, 8, 13; **3:**1, 10, 17, 18, 19; **4:**3, 11, 17; **5:**2, 3, 5, 6, 7, 10; **6:**5, 13, 18; **7:**5, 6, 17, 29, 31, 32, 35, 39, 40; **8:**7, 9, 10, 10; **9:**3, 8, 9, 12, 15, 17, 17, 19, 21, 23; **10:**5, 11, 27, 28; **11:**5, 13, 16, 16, 17, 22, 23, 24, 24, 25, 25, 26, 26, 27, 27, 31; **12:**24, 25; **13:**11; **14:**20, 31, 38; **15:**1, 2, 12, 19, 23, 31, 54; **16:**2, 7; **2Co 1:**1; **2:**10, 15, 16; **3:**4, 6, 12, 14, 14; **4:**1, 4, 6, 7, 7; **5:**1, 5, 9, 9, 11, 11, 17, 18, 19; **6:**1; **7:**3, 11, 13; **8:**6, 7, 8, 10, 11, 14, 15, 20; **9:**1, 6; **10:**8, 9, 11, 13; **11:**6, 10, 12, 16, 28; **12:**1, 11, 13, 19, 19; **13:**1, 2, 7, 10; **Gal 1:**1, 4, 16, 21; **2:**1, 20; **3:**2, 8, 8, 12, 15, 17, 19, 19; **4:**1, 3, 9, 20; **5:**2, 14, 17, 22; **6:**2, 14, 16; **Eph 1:**1, 5, 10, 14, 19, 21, 22; **2:**8, 12, 17, 22; **3:**2, 3, 4, 6, 7, 8, 9, 10, 11; **4:**9, 17; **5:**5, 9, 14, 27, 32; **6:**1, 2, 3, 12, 20, 22; **Php 1:**1, 11, 19, 25, 28, 30, 30; **2:**9, 18; **3:**1, 1, 13, 19; **4:**7, 8, 15, 17, 19; **Col 1:**1, 5, 6, 21, 22, 23, 26, 27, 27, 29; **2:**4, 8, 15, 18, 20; **3:**5, 7, 10, 11, 20; **4:**4, 8, 16; **1Th 1:**1, 6; **2:**13, 14, 16; **4:**1, 6, 11, 15; **5:**1, 18, 24, 27; **2Th 1:**1, 5, 12; **2:**5, 7, 9; **3:**6, 10, 14, 17; **1Ti 1:**1, 6, 15, 20; **2:**2, 3, 6, 7; **3:**15, 16; **4:**6, 8, 9; **5:**4, 5; **6:**4, 17, 19; **2Ti 1:**1, 6, 9, 10, 11; **2:**4, 8, 9, 11, 17, 17, 19; **3:**1, 9; **4:**10; **Tit 1:**1, 2, 3, 3, 4, 10, 13; **2:**12, 15; **Phm 1:**1, 9, 15, 19, 20, 20, 21; **Heb 1:**4; **2:**3, 8, 15; **3:**1; **4:**2, 7, 8, 13, 15; **5:**4, 9, 11; **6:**9, 19; **7:**1, 4, 17, 20, 22, 27, 27; **8:**5, 9, 10; **9:**2, 2, 9, 11, 20, 28; **10:**15, 16, 20, 35; **11:**10, 12, 38; **12:**2, 7, 11, 27; **13:**2, 14, 17, 22; **Jas 1:**1; **2:**4, 5, 19, 25; **3:**10; **4:**4, 4, 15; **5:**3; **1Pe 1:**1, 5, 10, 10, 11, 12, 20, 20, 23; **2:**2, 9, 21; **3:**16, 21; **5:**1, 12; **2Pe 1:**1, 8, 10, 17; **3:**1, 4, 15; **1Jn 1:**2, 5; **2:**1, 7, 8, 15, 16, 17, 18, 25; **3:**1, 3, 7, 11, 23; **4:**2, 5, 10, 17, 18; **5:**4, 5, 6, 10, 10, 11, 11, 13; **2Jn** 1, 5; **3Jn** 1, 9, 11; **Jude** 1, 3, 4, 9; **Rev 1:**1, 3, 4, 20; **2:**1, 1, 4, 6, 8, 8, 12, 12, 18, 18, 20, 24; **3:**1, 1, 7, 7, 10, 14, 14; **5:**2; **6:**10; **7:**9; **8:**13; **9:**10, 15; **11:**5, 10; **12:**9, 14; **13:**2, 3, 8, 12, 14, 15, 18; **14:**3, 3, 6, 12, 13; **16:**5, 9; **17:**2, 7, 8, 8, 9, 9, 18; **18:**1, 18, 21, 23; **19:**1, 9, 16; **20:**5, 14; **21:**5, 8; **22:**7, 9, 16, 18, 18, 19, 19

THOSE (1460)

Ge 6:4; **7:**8, 8, 23; **12:**3, 3; **19:**9; **31:**15, 38; **34:**21; **37:**27; **41:**48; **Ex 4:**19; **8:**11; **9:**21; **12:**19, 20; **13:**7; **14:**3; **15:**7; **16:**18, 18; **19:**12, 21; **20:**5, 6; **23:**22; **28:**3; **30:**38; **34:**11, 24; **35:**24; **36:**2; **38:**26; **Lev 4:**2, 31, 35; **5:**10, 13, 18; **10:**3; **11:**3, 27, 42, 42; **13:**45; **14:**2, 2, 32, 40; **16:**29; **20:**2, 5; **22:**18; **24:**14, 15; **25:**45; **26:**36, 39; **Nu 4:**37, 41, 45; **5:**18; **9:**13; **14:**23, 45; **15:**30; **16:**5, 49; **19:**11, 13, 14, 14, 19, 20, 21; **21:**8, 9; **22:**15, 32; **23:**8, 8; **26:**64; **32:**11; **33:**55; **Dt 1:**17; **4:**30; **5:**9, 10; **7:**9, 10, 21, 22; **12:**3; **13:**1; **19:**20; **23:**2; **24:**16; **25:**16, 18; **28:**61, 65; **29:**19; **32:**35, 38, 38, 41; **Jos 5:**5, 5, 7; **11:**17; **21:**13, 21; **23:**4; **24:**31; **Jdg 2:**7, 19; **3:**1, 3, 18; **5:**9, 14, 31; **7:**5, 5, 18, 22; **9:**33; **13:**2; **17:**6; **18:**1; **19:**1; **20:**27, 36, 37; **21:**25; **Ru 4:**7, 12; **1Sa 2:**4, 4, 5, 5, 10, 30, 30, 33; **3:**1; **5:**12; **6:**4; **7:**14; **9:**9, 20; **11:**12; **13:**19; **14:**6, 48; **17:**28; **25:**29; **26:**19; **30:**5, 24, 24; **2Sa 3:**1, 1, 6, 31; **5:**8; **13:**18; **14:**14, 16; **16:**2; **17:**29; **18:**31; **19:**6, 6, 14, 28; **22:**18, 26, 28, 48; **1Ki 1:**8; **4:**21; **10:**10; **11:**2; **12:**10, 31; **14:**11; **16:**4, 4; **19:**2, 17; **21:**24; **22:**28; **2Ki 10:**21, 23; **11:**9; **14:**6; **15:**37; **17:**30, 30, 30; **19:**4; **20:**14; **21:**12, 14, 24; **23:**18; **25:**11; **1Ch 9:**22; **27:**23; **2Ch 2:**14; **9:**9; **10:**10; **11:**16; **13:**8; **14:**6; **15:**5; **16:**9; **17:**19; **18:**27; **19:**2, 11; **20:**7, 10; **23:**8, 19; **25:**4, 7; **28:**15; **29:**31; **30:**18, 18, 25; **32:**13; **33:**25; **34:**4; **35:**6; **Ezr 1:**4; **6:**11; **7:**10, 25; **8:**1, 22, 22; **9:**12; **10:**8; **Ne 1:**3, 5, 11, 11; **4:**2; **6:**17; **7:**5; **9:**2; **13:**3; **Est 1:**8; **3:**8, 13; **6:**2, 9, 11; **7:**4; **9:**5, 16; **Job 3:**8, 8, 20, 23, 23; **4:**3, 4, 6, 8, 19; **5:**13, 17; **7:**9; **8:**10, 22; **10:**4; **11:**11; **12:**5, 6, 12; **15:**19; **17:**9; **19:**19; **20:**7; **21:**29; **22:**8; **27:**15; **28:**8; **29:**6, 7, 13, 25; **30:**1, 2, 25, 31; **31:**3; **32:**7;

36:15; **Ps 1:**1; **4:**7; **5:**6; **7:**9, 10; **9:**10, 12, 13; **10:**16; **11:**2, 7; **14:**4, 5; **15:**2, 3, 4, 5; **16:**4; **17:**2, 7, 14; **18:**17, 25, 27, 47; **19:**11, 11; **20:**8; **21:**8; **22:**25, 29, 31; **24:**4; **25:**3, 8, 10, 12, 14; **26:**5; **28:**3, 3; **31:**6, 15, 18, 19, 19, 20, 23; **32:**1, 2, 10; **33:**18, 18; **34:**5, 8, 9, 10, 15, 16, 18, 21, 22; **35:**1, 1, 4, 10, 19, 26, 26, 27; **36:**10, 10; **37:**1, 9, 11, 14, 22, 22, 32, 37, 37; **40:**4, 4, 14, 14, 16; **41:**1; **44:**7; **49:**10; **50:**5; **53:**4; **57:**3; **58:**11; **59:**1; **60:**4; **61:**5; **63:**9; **64:**2, 10; **65:**4, 4, 5, 8; **68:**1, 18, 21, 30; **69:**4, 6, 9, 14, 26, 26, 36, 36; **70:**2, 2, 4; **71:**13, 13; **73:**1, 27, 27; **76:**9; **79:**4, 11; **81:**15; **84:**4, 5, 11, 12; **85:**9; **86:**17; **87:**4; **88:**11; **89:**7, 15, 23; **91:**1, 14, 14; **94:**5, 12, 12, 15; **97:**7, 11; **101:**6; **102:**20; **103:**11, 13, 17, 18, 18; **106:**3, 5, 41; **107:**34, 43; **109:**20, 31; **111:**5; **112:**1, 1, 5, 6, 9; **115:**8, 13; **116:**6; **118:**7, 20; **119:**2, 21, 38, 42, 53, 84, 86, 113, 122, 150, 165; **125:**1, 4, 5, 5; **126:**5; **128:**1, 3, 4; **129:**8; **135:**18; **137:**3; **139:**21, 21; **140:**1, 2, 4, 12; **141:**4, 9; **143:**3; **144:**15, 15; **145:**14, 19, 20; **146:**5, 8; **147:**11, 11; **Pr 1:**5, 5, 21; **2:**7, 8, 12, 21; **3:**12, 18, 18, 27; **4:**19; **5:**13; **8:**9, 17, 21, 34, 36; **9:**4, 16; **10:**9, 17; **11:**13, 20, 24, 25, 26, 29, 30; **12:**2, 2, 22, 22; **13:**2, 3, 4, 5, 10, 13, 14; **14:**2, 2, 6, 17, 21, 26, 29, 29, 31, 31, 35; **15:**9, 12, 21, 27; **16:**13, 20, 20, 22; **17:**5, 5, 8, 15; **18:**21; **21:**13, 17; **22:**8, 9, 14, 21; **24:**11, 25; **28:**5, 7, 10, 14, 18, 26, 27; **29:**8; **31:**3, 5, 6, 8, 8; **Ecc 1:**11; **2:**26, 26; **4:**3; **5:**10; **7:**18, 26; **8:**3, 3, 5, 5, 8, 12; **9:**11, 16; **SS 8:**12; **Isa 2:**3; **3:**6, 10; **4:**3; **5:**17, 18, 20, 21, 22, 26; **7:**4; **10:**1, 10, 17, 20; **13:**8; **14:**2, 2, 19; **15:**9, 9; **16:**8; **17:**14; **19:**8, 8, 13, 20; **24:**14, 18, 18; **26:**7, 14, 19, 19, 21; **29:**7, 11, 12, 15, 19, 20, 20, 21, 21, 24, 24; **30:**18; **31:**1, 2, 3; **32:**3, 4, 12; **33:**15, 15; **34:**17; **35:**1, 3, 3, 4, 6, 8, 10; **37:**4; **38:**11, 18; **39:**3; **40:**29, 31; **42:**3, 7, 17; **43:**14; **44:**9, 9; **45:**9; **47:**9, 15; **49:**23, 25; **50:**6, 6; **51:**11, 23, 23; **52:**5, 7; **53:**12; **56:**2, 2, 2; **57:**15, 15, 18, 20; **58:**6, 6, 7, 10; **59:**8, 9, 20; **60:**14; **61:**2; **63:**11; **64:**4, 5; **65:**7, 9, 21, 25; **66:**2, 3, 17, 19, 21, 24; **Jer 2:**3, 24; **3:**16, 18; **5:**18; **7:**4, 9, 10; **9:**25; **10:**11; **15:**2, 2, 2, 2, 9; **16:**7; **17:**5, 7, 11; **19:**3, 9; **20:**12; **21:**9, 12; **22:**3, 25; **23:**14, 17; **24:**8; **25:**33; **29:**12, 16; **30:**16, 16; **31:**11, 30; **38:**2; **39:**9, 17; **43:**6, 11, 11, 11; **44:**14, 17, 28; **46:**26; **47:**4; **48:**10, 18, 19, 44, 44; **49:**9, 31; **50:**16, 20, 28; **51:**11; **52:**15; **La 2:**20; **3:**25, 30; **4:**5, 9, 9; **5:**5; **Eze 6:**12, 12; **7:**15; **9:**4, 7; **11:**21; **12:**19; **13:**15, 15, 19, 19; **14:**7, 16; **16:**37, 37; **17:**21; **20:**11, 38; **21:**10; **23:**12, 12, 22, 27, 28; **26:**20, 20; **28:**9; **30:**4; **31:**12, 17; **32:**13, 18, 22, 24, 29; **33:**4, 27, 27, 27; **34:**4, 16, 27; **36:**7, 15, 36; **38:**12; **39:**10, 11; **40:**21, 22, 29, 33; **44:**9; **46:**9; **48:**19; **Da 2:**44; **3:**11; **4:**35, 37; **5:**19, 19, 19, 19; **7:**16; **9:**4; **11:**26, 30, 32, 33, 39; **12:**2, 3, 3, 10, 12; **Hos 2:**23, 23; **4:**15; **7:**5; **8:**12; **9:**7; **14:**6, 9, 9; **Joel 2:**20, 20, 29; **Am 2:**7; **4:**11; **5:**13; **8:**14; **9:**1, 10; **Ob** 5, 14, 17, 19; **Jnh 2:**8; **Mic 2:**4, 8; **3:**5; **4:**2; **6:**14, 16; **7:**13, 15; **Na 3:**12; **Hab 3:**14; **Zep 1:**6, 8, 9, 9, 12; **2:**9; **3:**12, 19; **Zec 1:**9; **5:**3, 3, 9; **6:**8, 14; **7:**5; **8:**23; **11:**9, 11; **13:**6; **14:**3; **Mal 3:**5, 15, 15, 16, 16, 18, 18; **Mt 1:**17; **2:**20; **3:**1, 11; **4:**16; **5:**3, 4, 5, 6, 7, 8, 9, 10, 42, 42, 44, 46; **6:**12, 14; **7:**11; **8:**4, 12, 22; **9:**13; **10:**8, 10, 22, 26, 28; **11:**6, 8, 25, 27; **12:**7, 20; **13:**12, 12, 19, 20, 22, 23; **14:**21; **15:**31, 31; **19:**11, 30; **20:**9, 10, 12, 16, 23; **21:**12, 40; **23:**12, 12, 31; **24:**13, 16, 19, 29, 38; **25:**10, 29, 29, 34, 41; **26:**52, 69, 71; **Mk 1:**44; **2:**17; **3:**11, 34; **4:**15, 16, 18, 20, 25, 25; **5:**12, 16; **6:**44; **7:**37; **10:**5, 31, 40; **11:**15; **13:**13, 14, 17, 19, 20, 24; **14:**4, 67; **16:**14, 17; **Lk 1:**79; **3:**11; **4:**23; **5:**14, 32; **6:**27, 28, 28, 32, 33, 34, 35; **7:**15, 23, 35; **8:**12, 13, 14, 16, 18, 18, 21, 36; **9:**11, 60; **10:**6, 7, 21, 22; **11:**4, 13; **12:**4, 10, 33, 37, 48, 48; **13:**2, 14; **14:**14, 24; **17:**27; **18:**26; **19:**10, 26, 26; **20:**15, 35; **21:**16, 21, 21, 21, 22; **22:**26, 37; **23:**46; **Jn 1:**22, 24; **3:**18, 18, 21, 33, 36; **4:**24; **5:**24, 25, 29, 29; **6:**35, 37, 39, 54, 57; **7:**16, 18, 18; **8:**7, 29, 52; **9:**2, 31, 39; **10:**6, 9, 35; **11:**25; **12:**17, 25, 25, 26; **14:**21, 23; **15:**5; **16:**2; **17:**9, 11; **18:**9, 21; **20:**29; **Ac 1:**7, 13; **2:**18, 41, 45, 47; **3:**25; **4:**37; **5:**16, 32; **6:**1, 1; **7:**42; **10:**35, 41; **13:**13, 15, 31; **15:**17, 33; **16:**35; **17:**11, 15; **18:**27; **20:**32, 34; **22:**19; **23:**2, 4; **25:**5, 24; **26:**20; **Ro 1:**6, 32; **2:**7, 8, 13; **3:**8, 19, 25; **4:**7, 8, 11, 12, 14, 15; **6:**20, 22; **8:**1, 5, 5, 8, 9, 28; **9:**22, 23, 25, 25; **10:**15, 20; **11:**15, 19, 20, 22; **12:**19; **13:**2, 3, 4, 12; **14:**3, 3, 3, 3, 6, 6, 6, 9, 9, 22; **15:**1, 3, 21, 21, 31; **1Co 1:**18, 24, 27, 27, 27; **2:**9, 14; **3:**4, 19; **4:**12, 12; **5:**12, 13; **6:**9, 9; **7:**8, 10, 31; **9:**3, 10, 13, 13, 14, 14, 20, 22; **11:**19; **12:**23, 23, 24, 28, 28, 28, 28, 28; **14:**10, 11, 12, 16; **15:**20, 29, 32, 33; **2Co 2:**15, 15, 16, 16, 17; **4:**4; **5:**12, 15, 17; **6:**14; **7:**6; **8:**15, 15, 23; **9:**11; **10:**2, 6, 7; **11:**12; **13:**2; **Gal 1:**7, 17; **2:**21; **3:**7, 10; **4:**1, 15, 17, 29; **5:**12, 20, 24; **6:**6, 8, 8, 12, 13, 16; **Eph 1:**18; **2:**2, 12; **4:**29; **5:**6, 6, 15; **6:**12; **Php 1:**11, 17; **3:**2, 2, 2, 17; **4:**2, 22; **Col 3:**6, 18; **4:**5, 15; **1Th 3:**13; **4:**15; **5:**12, 14, 14, 14; **2Th 1:**6, 8, 8, 10; **2:**2, 10; **3:**14; **1Ti 1:**3, 10; **3:**13; **4:**3, 10, 16; **5:**8, 8, 10, 17, 18; **6:**17, 18, 20; **2Ti 2:**10, 14, 19, 19, 22, 25, 25; **3:**14; **4:**19; **Tit 1:**1, 9, 10, 15, 15; **2:**8; **Heb 1:**14; **2:**3, 15; **3:**16, 18; **4:**3, 6; **5:**9, 14; **6:**4, 4, 12, 17; **7:**28; **8:**6; **9:**28; **10:**1, 3, 14, 29, 30, 32, 34, 39; **11:**6; **12:**6, 6, 11, 13, 14; **13:**3, 3, 4, 9, 16; **Jas 1:**10, 12; **2:**5, 25; **3:**2, 9, 18; **5:**11, 13; **1Pe 1:**12; **2:**7, 14, 15; **3:**1, 12, 12, 20; **4:**6, 9, 17; **2Pe 1:**9, 10; **2:**10, 18; **3:**16; **1Jn 2:**5, 6, 11, 26; **3:**4, 6, 9, 24; **4:**6; **5:**10, 16, 18; **3Jn** 7, 11, 11; **Jude** 5, 7, 22; **Rev 1:**7; **2:**2, 9; **3:**9, 9, 10; **7:**2; **9:**6; **11:**3; **12:**14; **13:**10, 11, 12; **14:**3, 13; **19:**9; **20:**4, 4, 6; **21:**8, 27; **22:**7, 14

TO (20812)

Ge 1:6, 7, 14, 14, 16, 17, 18, 18, 25, 26, 30; **2:**5, 14, 15, 18, 19, 19, 20, 21, 22, 24; **3:**3, 6, 7, 9, 11, 14, 14, 16, 17, 17, 17, 17, 19, 19, 19, 23, 24, 24; **4:**1, 2, 3, 7, 7, 8, 9, 10, 12, 13, 13, 14, 15, 15, 15, 17, 20, 22, 22, 23, 23, 24, 25, 26; **6:**1, 4, 13, 13, 17, 18, 19, 20, 20; **7:**1, 1, 3, 7, 12; **8:**1, 1, 3, 4, 5, 5, 8, 9, 9, 11, 13, 15, 20, 21; **9:**3, 6, 6, 11, 11, 13, 13, 17, 25; **10:**1, 11, 19, 19, 20, 21, 31, 32; **11:**3, 3, 4, 4, 5, 6, 7, 30, 31, 31; **12:**1, 2, 2, 6, 7, 7, 7, 7, 10, 10, 11, 15, 18, 19; **13:**3, 8, 9, 9, 11, 12, 14, 15, 15, 16, 18, 18; **14:**4, 7, 13, 15, 17, 24; **15:**1, 1, 3, 4, 4, 5, 7, 8, 11, 16, 18, 18; **16:**2, 2, 3, 4, 5, 5, 7, 8, 9, 9, 11, 11, 13, 13; **17:**1, 2, 3, 8, 8, 9, 12, 12, 14, 17, 17, 18, 20, 21; **18:**1, 1, 1, 2, 2, 4, 5, 6, 6, 7, 7, 8, 10, 12, 13, 19, 21, 27, 31, 31, 33; **19:**1, 1, 1, 2, 2, 4, 5, 5, 6, 6, 9, 9, 13, 14, 14, 15, 16, 17, 19, 19, 19, 27, 28, 29, 30, 31, 31, 31, 34, 37, 38; **20:**1, 2, 3, 7, 7, 9, 9, 10, 11, 11, 13, 13, 14, 14, 15, 16, 16, 17, 18; **21:**2, 8, 10, 10, 14, 16, 17, 18, 22, 23, 23, 23, 23, 24, 25, 27, 30, 32; **22:**2, 2, 3, 3, 9, 10, 10, 11, 15, 19, 19, 24; **23:**3, 4, 5, 6, 8, 9, 9, 11, 11, 11, 12, 13, 13, 17, 20; **24:**2, 4, 4, 5, 6, 7, 7, 7, 7, 8, 8, 10, 10, 11, 12, 12, 13, 14, 16, 17, 18, 20, 20, 21, 23, 26, 27, 27, 27, 28, 30, 30, 32, 32, 33, 36, 38, 38, 38, 38, 38, 39, 41, 41, 42, 42, 43, 43, 44, 45, 45, 48, 49, 49, 52, 53, 54, 55, 56, 56, 58, 59, 65, 67; **25:**5, 6, 6, 16, 18, 18, 21, 22, 22, 27, 30, 32, 33, 33, 34; **26:**1, 2, 2, 3, 4, 5, 7, 7, 9, 13, 16, 17, 22, 23, 24, 24, 33; **27:**2, 4, 4, 5, 6, 7, 7, 9, 10, 12, 18, 20, 21, 21, 21, 22, 22, 25, 31, 33, 37, 37, 39, 41, 42, 42, 43, 46; **28:**2, 2, 4, 4, 4, 5, 5, 6, 6, 6, 7, 8, 9, 11, 11, 12, 13, 13, 14, 14, 15, 17, 21; **29:**2, 3, 3, 4, 7, 10, 11, 13, 15, 19, 19, 20, 20, 21, 21, 22, 23, 24, 26, 27, 28, 29; **30:**1, 2, 4, 9, 9, 14, 14, 14, 16, 17, 18, 21, 23, 25, 25, 25, 26, 31, 32, 33, 37, 38, 40, 41, 42; **31:**1, 2, 3, 3, 3, 4, 5, 7, 8, 11, 12, 13, 13, 14, 15, 16, 18, 24, 24, 29, 29, 31, 32, 33, 37, 37, 39, 39, 41, 42, 42, 43, 43, 46, 46, 48, 49, 50, 52, 52, 53, 53, 54, 54; **32:**1, 3, 4, 5, 5, 6, 9, 9, 9, 9, 10, 11, 12, 12, 12, 16, 17, 18, 19, 19, 19, 20, 20, 20, 20, 30; **33:**4, 5, 8, 10, 11, 11, 15, 15, 15, 16, 17; **34:**1, 3, 4, 4, 6, 8, 9, 10, 10, 11, 13, 14, 14, 16, 20, 21, 21, 23, 26, 30; **35:**1, 1, 1, 1, 3, 3, 7, 9, 12, 12, 12, 13, 14, 14, 14, 15, 18, 19, 20, 26, 27; **36:**5, 7, 12, 20, 43; **37:**2, 3, 4, 5, 5, 6, 8, 9, 12, 13, 13, 13, 13, 14, 17, 17, 18, 21, 22, 22, 22, 24, 25, 25, 26, 27, 28, 29, 30, 32, 32, 35, 35, 36; **38:**1, 6, 8, 9, 9, 9, 10, 10, 11, 11, 11, 11, 11, 11, 11, 12, 12, 14, 14, 14, 14, 16, 18, 20, 20, 20, 21, 22, 23, 25, 25, 26, 29; **39:**5, 5, 6, 6, 7, 7, 10, 14, 14, 17; **40:**4, 8, 10, 13, 14, 14, 15, 16, 20, 21, 22; **41:**8, 12, 13, 16, 24, 25, 28, 36, 39, 39, 40, 41, 44, 49, 50, 53, 55, 55, 56, 57, 57; **42:**1, 2, 3, 3, 4, 5, 6, 6, 7, 7, 9, 9, 10, 12, 18, 20, 20, 21, 22, 22, 23, 25, 25, 27, 27, 28, 28, 28, 29, 30, 34, 34, 34, 36, 37, 37, 38, 38; **43:**2, 5, 6, 7, 8, 9, 11, 11, 13, 15, 15, 16, 17, 18, 18, 19, 19, 20, 20, 20, 21, 22, 23, 24, 29, 30, 32, 33, 33, 33, 34, 34, 34; **44:**1, 1, 4, 5, 6, 12, 13, 14, 15, 16, 16, 17, 18, 21, 22, 24, 26, 27, 28, 29, 29, 30, 31, 32, 32, 34, 34, 34; **45:**1, 1, 2, 3, 3, 5, 5, 6, 7, 8, 9, 9, 11, 13, 14, 16, 17, 17, 17, 18, 18, 18, 18, 18, 19, 19, 19, 22, 23, 25; **46:**1, 1, 2, 3, 3, 3, 4, 5, 8, 15, 18, 25, 26, 28, 28, 29, 29, 30, 31, 31, 31; **47:**1, 2, 4, 4, 5, 6, 7, 11, 12, 12, 13, 14, 15, 17, 17, 19, 20, 21, 22, 22, 23, 24, 24, 24, 25, 27, 29; **48:**1, 1, 2, 3, 3, 4, 4, 6, 7, 9, 10, 11, 12, 14, 17, 20, 21, 21, 21; **49:**1, 1, 1, 2, 6, 9, 10, 11, 11, 13, 15, 15, 26, 28, 33; **50:**2, 4, 4, 5, 5, 5, 5, 6, 13, 14, 14, 15, 16, 17, 17, 17, 17, 19, 20, 21, 22, 23, 24, 24, 24, 24, 25, 25; **Ex 1:**1, 8, 9, 10, 10, 11, 11, 13, 14, 14, 15, 16, 17, 17, 18, 20, 22; **2:**2, 4, 4, 5, 5, 7, 10, 11, 11, 12, 13, 14, 14, 15, 15, 16, 16, 17, 18, 21, 21, 21, 23, 24; **3:**2, 3, 3, 4, 6, 8, 10, 11, 11, 12, 13, 13, 14, 15, 16, 16, 17, 17, 18, 18, 18, 21; **4:**1, 5, 6, 10, 12, 14, 15, 15, 15, 15, 16, 16, 16, 17, 18, 18, 18, 19, 19, 19, 19, 20, 21, 21, 23, 24, 25, 26, 27, 27, 27, 28, 28, 29, 29; **5:**1, 1, 1, 2, 3, 4, 6, 8, 8, 8, 9, 9, 10, 15, 16, 17, 17, 18, 18, 21, 21, 22, 23, 23; **6:**1, 1, 1, 3, 3, 3, 3, 4, 5, 6, 8, 8, 10, 11, 11, 12, 12, 13, 13, 13, 16, 16, 18, 19, 20, 25, 26, 27, 27, 27, 28, 30; **7:**1, 1, 1, 2, 2, 2, 3, 4, 4, 5, 7, 8, 9, 9, 10, 13, 14, 14, 14, 15, 15, 15, 16, 16, 16, 16, 17, 17, 18, 19, 19, 20, 22, 22, 23, 24, 25; **8:**1, 1, 2, 2, 5, 5, 7, 7, 8, 8, 9, 15, 15, 16, 16, 18, 19, 19, 20, 20, 25, 26, 26, 27, 27, 28, 28, 29, 29, 29, 29, 29, 30, 31, 32; **9:**1, 2, 2, 3, 6, 7, 7, 7, 8, 9, 10, 11, 12, 13, 13, 14, 14, 17, 19, 22, 22, 28, 29, 29, 29, 33, 34, 35; **10:**1, 1, 1, 2, 2, 2, 3, 3, 3, 5, 7, 7, 7, 8, 8, 9, 10, 10, 12, 12, 13, 14, 16, 17, 21, 25, 26; **11:**1, 1, 1, 2, 3, 4, 5, 8, 9, 9; **12:**1, 3, 4, 7, 14, 17, 17, 19, 21, 22, 23, 25, 25, 29, 33, 36, 39, 39, 39, 42, 42, 42, 42, 43, 43, 48, 49, 50, 51; **13:**1, 2, 3, 3, 3, 5, 6, 8, 8, 9, 9, 11, 12, 13, 15, 15, 17, 17; **14:**1, 2, 5, 5, 8, 10, 10, 11, 12, 14, 15, 15, 15, 19, 20, 25, 25, 26, 27; **15:**1, 1, 5, 6, 13, 21, 23, 24, 25, 25, 25, 25, 26, 27; **16:**3, 3, 3, 4, 4, 4, 5, 8, 9, 9, 9, 10, 11, 12, 21, 23, 25, 27, 27, 28, 32, 33, 35, 36; **17:**1, 1, 1, 2, 2, 3, 4, 5, 6, 7, 8, 9, 10, 10, 12, 12, 13, 14, 16; **18:**2, 5, 6, 7, 7, 7, 7, 8, 10, 12, 12, 13, 14, 14, 15, 15, 18, 18, 19, 19, 20, 22, 23, 23, 24, 26, 26, 27, 27; **19:**2, 3, 3, 3, 4, 4, 5, 6, 6, 8, 9, 9, 9, 9, 13, 14, 17, 19, 20, 21, 21, 22, 23, 23, 23, 24, 25; **20:**5, 5, 8, 10, 19, 19, 20, 22, 22, 22, 24; **21:**1, 2, 4, 6, 6, 8, 8, 8, 9, 10, 12, 12, 13, 14, 15, 17, 19, 23, 28, 30, 30, 32, 33, 34, 36, 36, 36; **22:**3, 5, 7, 9, 9, 10, 10, 12, 16, 17, 18, 20, 23, 25, 27, 27, 30, 31; **23:**2, 4, 5, 7, 7, 9, 11, 11, 12, 12, 13, 13, 15, 16, 19, 20, 20, 21, 22, 22, 28, 29, 30, 31, 31, 32; **24:**1, 2, 2, 2, 3, 3, 5, 5, 7, 10, 12, 12, 16; **25:**1, 2, 7, 8, 9, 12, 14, 15, 16, 18, 19, 21, 22, 27, 27, 29, 40; **26:**1, 5, 6, 7, 9, 12, 17, 26, 28, 29, 30; **27:**7, 8, 10, 10, 16, 16, 17, 19, 20; **28:**1, 2, 2, 2, 3, 4, 4, 13, 14, 15, 17, 22, 22, 23, 25, 26, 26, 27, 28, 28, 30, 30, 33, 34, 35, 35, 36, 37, 40, 42, 42, 42, 43; **29:**10, 18, 18, 21, 24, 24, 25, 26, 27, 28, 30, 32, 35, 36, 38, 41, 42, 42; **30:**4, 5, 8, 8, 10, 11, 12, 13, 14, 15, 15, 16, 17, 20, 20, 20, 21, 21, 22, 26, 29, 30, 31, 34, 35; **31:**1, 4, 6, 6, 6, 10, 12, 13, 13, 15; **32:**1, 1, 1, 2, 2, 5, 6, 8, 8, 11, 12, 13, 17, 19, 21, 21, 23, 23, 23, 24, 25, 26, 27, 30, 30, 30, 31, 33, 34, 34; **33:**1, 1, 1, 2, 3, 4, 5, 5, 7, 7, 8, 11, 11, 11, 11, 12, 12, 13, 17, 19, 19, 19; **34:**2, 2, 6, 7, 7, 8, 10, 11, 12, 15, 15, 15, 15, 16, 18, 19, 20, 20, 22, 24, 25, 26, 27, 29, 29, 30, 31, 31, 34, 35; **35:**2, 4, 5, 5, 9, 12, 17, 19, 19, 20, 20, 21, 21, 22, 22, 24, 26, 27, 29, 29, 32, 34, 34; **36:**2, 4, 5, 5, 7, 10, 13, 16, 16, 18, 18, 22, 23, 29, 31, 33, 34, 36, 37, 38; **37:**3, 5, 9, 13, 14, 14, 16, 16, 27; **38:**3, 5, 10, 17, 18, 21, 28, 28, 30, 31, 31; **39:**1, 4, 6, 7, 9, 15, 15, 16, 18, 19, 19, 20, 21, 21, 21, 24, 26, 26, 30, 30, 31, 33, 41, 41, 42; **40:**1, 3, 9, 11, 12, 13, 15, 16, 21, 30, 32, 32, 35; **Lev 1:**1, 1, 2, 2, 3, 9, 13, 14, 15, 16, 17; **2:**1, 1, 2, 2, 3, 3, 8, 8, 9, 10, 10, 11, 11, 12, 12, 13, 13, 13, 14, 16; **3:**1, 1, 3, 4, 5, 6, 7, 9, 10, 11, 12, 14, 15, 16, 16; **4:**1, 3, 4, 12, 24, 29, 31, 33, 35; **5:**1, 1, 1, 6, 6, 7, 7, 8, 11, 12, 12, 13, 14, 15, 16, 18; **6:**1, 2, 2, 4, 5, 6, 8, 11, 12, 14, 15, 16, 17, 17, 18, 18, 19, 20, 20, 20, 21, 24, 28, 30; **7:**4, 5, 7, 8, 9, 10, 11, 14, 14, 16, 18, 20, 22, 25, 28, 29, 29, 29, 30, 30, 30, 31, 32, 32, 33, 35, 35, 36, 36, 36, 38, 38, 38; **8:**1, 3, 3, 5, 5, 15, 18, 21, 21, 27, 28, 28, 31, 33, 34; **9:**2, 2, 3, 4, 4, 4, 4, 5, 6, 7, 7, 7, 8, 13, 17, 21, 23; **10:**3, 4, 4, 6, 7, 8, 10, 12, 12, 13, 13, 14, 14, 15, 15, 16, 16, 17, 19, 19; **11:**1, 2, 10, 11, 12, 20, 23, 34, 35, 37, 42, 45; **12:**1, 1, 2, 4, 5, 5, 6, 7, 7, 8; **13:**1, 2, 2, 3, 4, 7, 7, 9, 12, 13, 16, 18, 19, 19, 20, 21, 21, 25, 26, 26, 30, 32, 34, 35, 45, 45, 49, 49, 54, 56; **14:**1, 2, 5, 7, 8, 13, 17, 23, 23, 24, 28, 30, 31, 32, 33, 35, 37, 42, 45, 49, 57; **15:**1, 2, 5, 6, 10, 11, 14, 14, 24, 25, 27, 29; **16:**1, 2, 2, 4, 6, 7, 8, 8, 8, 9, 9, 10, 10, 17, 18, 19, 21, 24, 26, 26, 27, 27, 28, 29, 29, 34, 34; **17:**1, 4, 4, 4, 5, 5, 5, 6, 6, 7, 7, 7, 8, 8, 9, 9, 9, 12, 13, 13, 14, 15; **18:**1, 2, 3, 4, 17, 18, 21, 23, 23, 26, 26, 28, 30; **19:**1, 2, 5, 8, 10, 12, 15, 16, 20, 20, 21, 24, 37; **20:**1, 2, 2, 2, 2, 3, 4, 4, 7, 9, 10, 12, 12, 13, 14, 14, 15, 16, 16, 18, 22, 26, 27; **21:**1, 1, 6, 6, 7, 8, 9, 10, 12, 16, 17, 17, 18, 21, 21, 22, 24, 24; **22:**1, 2, 9, 9, 13, 13, 13, 15, 16, 16, 17, 18, 18, 18, 18, 21, 21, 22, 23, 24, 25, 25, 26, 27, 29; **23:**1, 2, 3, 3, 4, 4, 6, 8, 8, 10, 10, 12, 13, 13, 14, 16, 17, 17, 18, 18, 18, 20, 20, 24, 24, 24, 24, 25, 25, 26, 27, 27, 33, 34, 34, 36, 36, 37, 37, 38, 38, 38, 38, 39, 39, 41, 43, 44; **24:**1, 2, 3, 7, 7, 9, 9, 11, 13, 14, 14, 15, 16, 17, 19, 20, 21, 22, 23, 23; **25:**1, 2, 2, 4, 5, 7, 8, 10, 10, 10, 13, 13, 14, 18, 20, 21, 23, 25, 26, 26, 26, 27, 27, 28, 28, 28, 29, 29, 30, 31, 32, 32, 35, 38, 38, 39, 41, 41, 46, 47, 50, 53; **26:**1, 3, 5, 6, 10, 10, 14, 16, 16, 21, 23, 25, 25, 25, 26, 26, 26, 27, 28, 32, 35, 37, 41, 41, 46; **27:**1, 2, 2, 2, 3, 8, 8, 8, 8, 9, 9, 11, 11, 13, 14, 14, 15, 15, 16, 16, 17, 18, 19, 19, 20, 20, 22, 23, 24, 26, 26, 27, 29, 30, 30, 31, 32, 34; **Nu 1:**1, 3, 3, 3, 18, 20, 20, 20, 44, 45, 45, 48, 53, 53; **2:**1, 3, 9, 9, 10, 17, 18, 25, 31, 31, 33; **3:**1, 3, 4, 5, 6, 9, 10, 11, 14, 20, 23, 25, 26, 31, 36, 38, 40, 44, 46, 48, 50, 51; **4:**1, 3, 4, 5, 11, 11, 14, 15, 17, 19, 21, 23, 26, 27, 28, 28, 30, 31, 32, 32, 33, 36, 37, 40, 41, 44, 49; **5:**1, 2, 3, 5, 6, 6, 7, 8, 8, 8, 9, 9, 11, 12, 12, 15, 15, 15, 18, 18, 19, 22, 25, 26, 27, 28, 29, 30; **6:**1, 1, 2, 4, 5, 6, 7, 8, 10, 11, 12, 13, 14, 21, 22, 23, 25; **7:**3, 4, 5, 5, 6, 7, 8, 9, 9, 11, 86, 89, 89, 89; **8:**1, 2, 4, 4, 5, 11, 11, 12, 12, 13, 14, 15, 19, 20, 21, 21, 22, 26; **9:**1, 2, 3, 4, 6, 10, 13, 13, 14, 14, 14, 14, 15, 16, 18; **10:**1, 2, 2, 3, 4, 5, 6, 7, 8, 8, 8, 9, 10, 13, 29, 29, 29, 30, 33, 33, 36; **11:**1, 1, 2, 2, 4, 4, 5, 6, 11, 11, 12, 12, 12, 13, 16, 16, 16, 17, 17, 18, 18, 18, 18, 20, 23, 23, 24, 25, 26, 27, 30, 33, 35; **12:**4, 4, 6, 6, 8, 8, 8, 11, 13, 14; **13:**1, 2, 2, 16, 16, 17, 20, 23, 23, 26, 26, 27, 27, 30, 30, 32, 33, 33; **14:**3, 3, 3, 4, 7, 8, 8, 9, 10, 10, 11, 14, 16, 16, 17, 18, 18, 22, 23, 24, 26, 28, 30, 34, 35, 39, 40, 41, 41; **15:**1, 1, 2, 3, 3, 4, 7, 8, 10, 11, 13, 13, 14, 14, 15, 16, 16, 17, 19, 21, 21, 21, 22, 23, 24, 25, 29, 34, 35, 35, 36, 37, 38, 38, 39, 39, 40; **16:**3, 3, 4, 5, 5, 5, 8, 9, 9, 9, 9, 9, 10, 12, 13, 14, 15, 16, 19, 20, 23, 24, 25, 26, 28, 36, 37, 37, 38, 39, 40, 40, 40, 40, 42, 42, 44, 46, 46, 49, 50; **17:**1, 5, 5, 6, 9, 10, 10, 10, 12, 13; **18:**1, 1, 2, 3, 4, 6, 6, 7, 8, 8, 8, 9, 11, 11, 12, 13, 13, 14, 15, 17, 19, 19, 20, 22, 24, 26, 26, 27, 28, 28, 29, 29, 29, 30, 32, 32; **19:**1, 2, 2, 3, 7, 9, 12, 17; **20:**2, 4, 5, 5, 6, 6, 7, 8, 8, 10, 12, 12, 12, 14, 15, 15, 16, 17, 19, 20, 21, 21, 21, 23, 24; **21:**1, 2, 4, 4, 5, 5, 5, 5, 7, 8, 9, 10, 11, 12, 13, 13, 16, 16, 20, 21, 23, 24, 27, 30, 32, 34, 34, 34; **22:**1, 2, 4, 5, 5, 5, 6, 7, 7, 7, 7, 8, 9, 10, 11, 11, 12, 14, 14, 16, 18, 18, 19, 19, 19, 20, 20, 20, 22, 22, 25, 28, 28, 32, 34, 34, 35, 36, 38, 39, 40, 41; **23:**1, 3, 3, 3, 3, 3, 4, 5, 7, 11, 11, 13, 14, 15, 15, 16, 17, 19, 20, 24, 25, 25, 27, 27, 27, 28; **24:**1, 1, 9, 10, 11, 13, 13, 14, 14, 25; **25:**2, 2, 3, 4, 5, 10, 11, 16; **26:**1, 1, 2, 3, 10, 52, 53, 57, 60; **27:**6, 7, 8, 8, 9, 10, 11, 12, 12, 14, 14, 15, 19, 20, 22, 23; **28:**1, 1, 2, 2, 2, 2, 3, 3, 6, 7, 8, 10, 10, 11, 13, 15, 15, 19, 22, 23, 24, 24, 24, 26, 27, 30, 31; **29:**2, 5, 6, 6, 6, 8, 11, 12, 13, 16, 19, 22, 25, 28, 31, 34, 35, 36, 38, 39, 39, 40; **30:**2, 3, 5, 8, 11, 12, 13, 14, 15; **31:**1, 3, 3, 12, 12, 13, 16, 16, 21, 23, 24, 25, 26, 27, 27, 28, 29, 29, 30, 30, 36, 41, 42, 42, 43, 47, 47, 48, 49, 50, 52, 54, 54, 54; **32:**2, 6, 7, 7, 8, 9, 11, 16, 16, 17, 18, 22, 22, 23, 27, 27, 28, 29, 30, 32, 33, 39, 40, 41; **33:**14, 38, 50, 51, 53, 53, 54, 54, 54, 55, 56, 56, 56; **34:**1, 2, 4, 4, 7, 8, 9, 10, 11, 12, 13, 16, 17, 18, 29; **35:**1, 2, 2, 2, 4, 7, 8, 8, 9, 10, 11, 11, 12, 16, 18, 19, 25, 28, 29, 29, 30, 31, 31, 32, 32, 32, 34; **36:**1, 2, 2, 2, 3, 4, 4, 4, 7, 8, 9, 9, 13; **Dt 1:**1, 2, 2, 3, 3, 5, 6, 7, 7, 7, 7, 7, 7, 8, 8, 8, 8, 9, 15, 16, 16, 17, 18, 20, 22, 22, 23, 24, 25, 26, 27, 29, 31, 32, 33, 35, 35, 36, 37, 38, 39, 41, 42, 42, 43, 44, 45; **2:**2, 4, 4, 11, 12, 13, 14, 17, 19, 20, 22, 24, 26, 28, 29, 30, 30, 31, 31, 31, 31, 33, 37; **3:**3, 8, 12, 13, 13, 14, 15, 16, 16, 16, 17, 18, 18, 20, 20, 20, 21, 21, 21, 24, 25, 26, 27; **4:**1, 1, 2, 3, 4, 5, 5, 5, 5, 6, 7, 7, 9, 9, 9, 10, 10, 10, 12, 13, 14, 14, 15, 20, 22, 23, 26, 30, 30, 32, 36, 37, 44, 45, 48; **5:**1, 1, 4, 4, 5, 5, 9, 9, 14, 15, 22, 22, 23, 24, 25, 27, 28, 28, 30, 30, 31, 31, 33, 33; **6:**1, 1, 3, 3, 6, 7, 8, 10, 12, 18, 23, 24, 24; **7:**1, 2, 4, 6, 6, 8, 10, 12, 13, 13, 16, 17, 18, 18, 20, 23, 24, 25, 25; **8:**1, 1, 2, 2, 3, 3, 5, 11, 12, 14, 16, 16, 18, 18, 19; **9:**1, 1, 1, 1, 2, 3, 4, 5, 5, 5, 8, 10, 12, 12, 13, 16, 17, 19, 19, 20, 23, 25, 26, 28, 28, 28, 28; **10:**1, 1, 1, 4, 4, 6, 7, 7, 8, 8, 8, 10, 11, 11, 12, 12, 12, 12, 13, 14, 18, 18, 19, 20; **11:**2, 3, 4, 4, 4, 6, 6, 6, 8, 8, 8, 9, 9, 9, 10, 15, 15, 16, 18, 18, 19, 21, 22, 22, 22, 24, 24, 25, 29, 31, 31, 32; **12:**5, 6, 6, 11, 11, 11, 13, 16, 17, 19, 21, 23, 26, 26, 26, 28, 30, 31, 31, 32; **13:**3, 3, 4, 4, 5, 5, 5, 5, 6, 9, 9, 10, 10, 13, 16, 16, 17, 18; **14:**2, 2, 21, 21, 21, 23, 23, 23, 23, 23, 24, 25, 26, 29, 29; **15:**2, 3, 3, 6, 6, 9, 9, 11, 19, 21; **16:**2, 2, 6, 7, 10, 10, 11, 11, 12, 15, 16, 17, 17; **17:**1, 5, 5, 6, 8, 8, 9, 12, 12, 13, 14, 14, 16, 16, 16, 19; **18:**1, 4, 5, 6, 9, 10, 12, 14, 14, 15, 16, 16, 17, 18, 19, 20, 20; **19:**2, 3, 4, 5, 5, 6, 6, 7, 11, 12, 12, 14, 18, 20; **20:**1, 2, 3, 3, 9, 10, 11, 12, 12, 13, 15, 15, 18, 19, 20, 20; **21:**3, 4, 5, 5, 5, 10, 10, 11, 11, 12, 16, 17, 20, 21; **22:**1, 1, 2, 4, 9, 15, 16, 16, 19, 21, 21, 23, 24, 24, 26, 26, 27, 29, 29; **23:**4, 4, 5, 6, 9, 11, 14, 14, 15, 18, 18, 19, 20, 20, 20, 21, 22, 23, 23; **24:**1, 4, 5, 5, 6, 6, 9, 10, 10, 11, 12, 13, 15, 16, 17, 17, 19, 19, 21; **25:**1, 2, 2, 2, 6, 7, 7, 7, 7, 7, 8, 8, 9, 9, 9, 10, 11, 16, 17, 19; **26:**2, 2, 3, 3, 3, 5, 7, 9, 11, 11, 12, 12, 13, 14, 16, 16, 17, 19; **27:**3, 5, 6, 11, 12, 13, 14, 15, 19, 25; **28:**9, 11, 12, 12, 12, 13, 14, 15, 15, 21, 25, 25, 26, 29, 30, 31, 31, 31, 33, 35, 36, 36, 37, 44, 44, 45, 45, 45, 51, 52, 52, 55, 55, 56, 56, 56, 57, 58, 62, 63, 63, 64, 65, 65, 65, 66, 68, 68, 68, 68; **29:**1, 1, 2, 2, 4, 7, 8, 8, 12, 13, 13, 13, 18, 19, 21, 22, 24, 26, 26, 28, 29, 29; **30:**1, 1, 2, 2, 5, 5, 9, 9, 10, 11, 12, 13, 13, 16, 16, 16, 17, 17, 18, 19, 20, 20, 20, 20; **31:**1, 2, 5, 7, 7, 7, 9, 9, 11, 12, 13, 13, 14, 14, 14, 15, 15, 16, 16, 19, 19, 20, 20, 21, 22, 23, 25, 28, 28, 29, 29, 30; **32:**8, 8, 9, 11, 17, 17, 17, 17, 19, 20, 22, 26, 30, 37, 40, 41, 44, 45, 46, 46, 47, 48, 49, 49, 49, 51, 51, 52; **33:**1, 7, 7, 8, 8, 9, 9, 10, 10, 17, 19, 19, 20, 21, 26; **34:**1, 2, 4, 4, 4, 4, 6, 10, 11; **Jos 1:**1, 4, 4, 5, 6, 6, 8, 11, 14, 15, 15, 18; **2:**1, 2, 3, 3, 3, 5, 6, 7, 8, 8, 10, 11, 12, 12, 16, 19, 22, 23, 23; **3:**3, 6, 7, 8, 9, 11, 14, 16; **4:**1, 3, 6, 6, 8, 9, 10, 13, 15, 16, 21; **5:**2, 4, 4, 6, 6, 7, 7, 9, 9, 11, 13, 14, 14; **6:**1, 2, 3, 4, 6, 7, 8, 10, 11, 14, 17, 19, 22, 22, 23, 25, 25, 26; **7:**2, 3, 3, 7, 7, 8, 9, 10, 11, 13, 14, 19, 19, 22, 22, 23, 24, 25, 26; **8:**1, 1, 3, 5, 7, 12, 16, 18, 20, 23, 28, 30, 31, 33, 34, 35; **9:**2, 3, 4, 4, 4, 6, 6, 7, 10, 11, 17, 18, 21, 22, 24, 26, 27, 27; **10:**3, 6, 7, 8, 8, 8, 10, 12, 15, 18, 19, 20, 21, 21, 22, 25, 25, 27, 27, 29, 31, 32, 33, 34, 41, 41, 43; **11:**1, 4, 5, 6, 7, 15, 17, 17, 18, 20, 23; **12:**1, 2, 3, 5, 5, 5, 6, 7, 7, 7; **13:**1, 1, 2, 3, 3, 4, 4, 4, 5, 5, 6, 6, 6, 8, 9, 13, 13, 13, 14, 14, 15, 16, 23, 24, 26, 26, 28, 29, 31, 33, 33; **14:**3, 4, 5, 6, 6, 6, 7, 12, 13, 14; **15:**1, 1, 3, 3, 4, 4, 5, 6, 6, 7, 7, 7, 8, 8, 9, 9, 10, 10, 10, 10, 11, 13, 13, 16, 18, 19, 20, 33, 63; **16:**1, 2, 3, 3, 3, 5, 5, 6, 6, 7, 8, 8, 10; **17:**1, 1, 2, 4, 4, 5, 5, 6, 7, 7, 8, 8, 9, 9, 10, 10, 10, 11, 12, 12, 13, 14, 17; **18:**3, 3, 4, 4, 6, 6, 8, 8, 9, 10, 11, 11, 13, 13, 13, 14, 15, 16, 16, 17, 17, 17, 21, 28; **19:**1, 9, 10, 11, 12, 12, 12, 13, 17, 24, 26, 27, 27, 29, 32, 33, 34, 40, 49, 51; **20:**1, 2, 3, 3, 4, 5, 5, 6, 6, 9; **21:**1, 2, 2, 2, 4, 8, 8, 10, 10, 12, 13, 19, 23, 25, 26, 33, 40, 41, 41, 43, 43; **22:**3, 3, 4, 5, 5, 5, 7, 9, 9, 9, 12, 12, 13, 15, 16, 23, 24, 24, 25, 26, 27, 27, 27, 27, 29, 31, 32, 32; **23:**2, 4, 4, 6, 8, 9, 10, 11, 13; **24:**1, 1, 2, 4, 4, 7, 9, 10, 11, 12, 15, 19, 19, 20, 21, 22, 23, 24, 25, 27, 27, 27, 27, 28, 32, 33; **Jdg 1:**3, 3, 3, 7, 7, 9, 12, 14, 15, 17, 19, 20, 21, 21, 23, 24, 26, 26, 27, 27, 28, 29, 29, 30, 30, 30, 31, 33, 33, 35, 35, 36; **2:**1, 1, 2, 2, 3, 5, 6, 6, 13, 14, 14, 14, 15, 16, 17, 17, 17, 17, 19, 19, 19, 22, 22, 23; **3:**1, 2, 2, 3, 4, 4, 4, 6, 8, 8, 9, 9, 10, 14, 15, 15, 15, 15, 16, 17, 19, 19, 20, 21, 24, 26, 27; **4:**2, 3, 5, 5, 6, 7, 9, 12, 13, 14, 16, 17, 18, 18, 19, 21, 22; **5:**3, 3, 9, 9, 11, 11, 14, 16, 23, 23, 29; **6:**1, 2, 4, 5, 6, 6, 7, 8, 10, 11, 11, 12, 13, 13, 14, 16, 17, 17, 17, 18, 19, 20, 22, 24, 24, 25, 25, 26, 28, 29, 30, 31, 31, 34, 34, 36, 36, 36, 37, 37, 39; **7:**2, 2, 3, 4, 5, 10, 10, 11, 11, 11, 12, 15, 17, 17, 22, 22, 22, 24, 25, 25; **8:**1, 2, 3, 4, 8, 9, 15, 15, 20, 21, 21, 22, 35; **9:**1, 1, 1, 1, 2, 3, 3, 4, 4, 5, 7, 7, 7, 7, 7, 8, 8, 9, 10, 11, 12, 13, 14, 15, 18, 26, 29, 31, 31, 31, 36, 40, 42, 44, 47, 48, 51, 51, 52, 52, 52, 54, 55; **10:**1, 7, 8, 9, 10, 12, 14, 17, 18; **11:**7, 7, 10, 11, 12, 12, 13, 13, 14, 17, 17, 19, 19, 19, 19, 20, 22, 22, 23, 23, 25, 25, 26, 26, 28, 30, 31, 31, 33, 34, 34, 35, 35, 36, 36, 40, 40; **12:**1, 1, 1, 1, 2, 2, 3, 3, 5, 6, 9, 9; **13:**1, 2, 3, 3, 3, 5, 5, 6, 6, 7, 7, 8, 8, 8, 9, 10, 11, 15, 15, 16, 17, 19, 20, 21, 22, 23, 23, 25; **14:**2, 3, 3, 4, 5, 8, 8, 9, 11, 12, 14, 14, 15, 15, 15, 15, 16, 16, 17, 18, 18, 19, 19, 19, 20; **15:**1, 2, 3, 3, 4, 5, 6, 6, 6, 8, 10, 10, 11, 11, 11, 11, 12, 13, 18, 19, 19; **16:**1, 2, 3, 5,

6, 6, 9, 10, 12, 14, 17, 19, 19, 20, 21, 21, 22, 24, 25, 26, 26, 28, 31; **17:**2, 3, 3, 4, 8, 8, 9, 10, 11; **18:**1, 1, 1, 2, 2, 2, 7, 8, 9, 12, 13, 14, 14, 15, 19, 19, 20, 26, 27, 27, 28; **19:**1, 2, 2, 3, 3, 3, 4, 5, 5, 6, 7, 7, 8, 8, 9, 10, 11, 11, 12, 13, 14, 15, 18, 18, 20, 22, 23, 23, 24, 24, 24, 25, 26, 27, 29; **20:**1, 3, 4, 4, 5, 9, 10, 11, 12, 14, 15, 18, 18, 20, 23, 24, 26, 26, 31, 31, 31, 32, 33, 36, 36, 39, 47, 48; **21:**1, 1, 2, 5, 7, 8, 10, 10, 11, 12, 13, 14, 14, 19, 21, 22, 22, 23, 24; **Ru 1:**1, 6, 6, 6, 7, 8, 8, 8, 8, 10, 10, 11, 11, 12, 12, 12, 13, 13, 13, 15, 15, 15, 16, 17, 18, 19, 21; **2:**2, 2, 3, 3, 8, 8, 9, 9, 10, 11, 12, 13, 13, 14, 14, 15, 17, 18, 20, 20, 21; **3:**1, 3, 4, 4, 6, 7, 8, 12, 13, 13, 14, 15, 15, 16, 17, 18; **4:**1, 1, 1, 1, 2, 3, 3, 4, 4, 7, 7, 8, 9, 9, 10, 10, 10, 13, 13, 13, 14, 15; **1Sa 1:**3, 3, 3, 4, 7, 7, 9, 9, 9, 10, 11, 11, 12, 15, 18, 19, 19, 20, 21, 21, 22, 24, 25, 26, 27, 28, 28; **2:**6, 10, 11, 14, 14, 16, 19, 20, 20, 22, 23, 25, 25, 25, 26, 27, 27, 28, 28, 28, 28, 28, 31, 31, 34, 34, 35, 35, 36; **3:**2, 5, 5, 6, 6, 8, 9, 9, 11, 11, 12, 15, 15, 16, 17, 20, 21, 21; **4:**1, 3, 3, 4, 4, 4, 7, 10, 12, 13, 14, 16, 18, 20; **5:**1, 3, 3, 5, 6, 8, 8, 10, 10, 11; **6:**2, 2, 5, 5, 7, 7, 9, 10, 14, 15, 16, 17, 20, 21; **7:**1, 1, 1, 3, 3, 3, 3, 5, 5, 8, 9, 9, 11, 12, 14, 17, 17; **8:**1, 4, 6, 7, 10, 12, 13, 14, 19, 19, 20; **9:**5, 6, 7, 7, 8, 9, 11, 12, 13, 13, 14, 16, 19, 19, 20, 21, 23, 25, 25, 26, 27; **10:**1, 3, 3, 4, 8, 8, 9, 10, 13, 14, 14, 14, 16, 17, 24, 26, 27; **11:**2, 3, 3, 3, 4, 5, 7, 7, 7, 8, 9, 9, 10, 10, 12, 14, 14, 14, 15, 15; **12:**8, 8, 8, 10, 11, 12, 12, 14, 15, 15, 16, 17, 18, 19, 19, 19, 21, 23, 24, 25; **13:**2, 2, 3, 6, 10, 12, 12, 14, 15, 15, 18, 20, 20, 20; **14:**1, 1, 4, 4, 6, 6, 9, 9, 12, 12, 16, 18, 19, 19, 20, 21, 23, 30, 31, 33, 34, 35, 38, 38, 42, 45, 45, 45; **15:**1, 1, 1, 2, 4, 5, 6, 6, 7, 9, 10, 11, 11, 11, 12, 12, 12, 12, 12, 15, 15, 16, 16, 19, 21, 21, 22, 22, 22, 25, 27, 27, 27, 28, 28, 30, 32, 33, 34, 34, 35; **16:**1, 1, 1, 2, 2, 3, 3, 5, 5, 5, 7, 8, 10, 10, 11, 13, 16, 18, 19, 19, 20, 21, 22; **17:**4, 8, 8, 8, 9, 13, 17, 17, 18, 22, 22, 23, 24, 25, 25, 26, 26, 26, 26, 28, 28, 28, 30, 31, 34, 35, 36, 36, 39, 39, 40, 44, 45, 45, 46, 47, 47, 48, 48, 49, 51, 54, 55, 57; **18:**3, 5, 6, 6, 10, 10, 11, 11, 14, 17, 17, 17, 17, 19, 21, 21, 21, 21, 22, 22, 23, 24, 26, 27, 27, 27; **19:**1, 3, 3, 4, 5, 5, 6, 7, 10, 11, 11, 14, 15, 15, 16, 17, 17, 18, 18, 18, 18, 20, 20, 22, 23, 23; **20:**1, 2, 3, 3, 6, 6, 7, 8, 9, 11, 12, 13, 19, 20, 21, 23, 24, 26, 28, 29, 30, 32, 33, 33, 34, 35, 38, 40, 40, 40, 41, 41, 42, 42; **21:**1, 1, 2, 2, 3, 5, 8, 9, 10, 12, 13, 14; **22:**1, 3, 3, 5, 5, 7, 8, 9, 10, 12, 13, 13, 17, 18, 19, 20, 23; **23:**1, 3, 3, 3, 4, 5, 6, 6, 7, 8, 8, 9, 10, 11, 12, 13, 15, 15, 16, 16, 17, 17, 19, 19, 20, 22, 23, 25, 26, 28, 29; **24:**2, 3, 4, 4, 6, 6, 9, 9, 9, 10, 11, 11, 12, 12, 14, 16, 17, 18, 20, 21, 22; **25:**1, 5, 5, 6, 8, 9, 11, 13, 14, 14, 14, 15, 16, 17, 17, 18, 21, 24, 24, 25, 27, 31, 32, 32, 34, 39, 39, 39, 40, 41, 41, 41, 44; **26:**1, 1, 2, 4, 5, 5, 6, 8, 8, 8, 8, 14, 15, 16, 16, 19, 20, 21, 23, 25; **27:**1, 1, 1, 1, 2, 4, 5, 6, 6, 8, 9, 11, 11, 12, 12; **28:**1, 6, 7, 7, 8, 8, 8, 9, 10, 11, 14, 15, 15, 17, 19, 22, 23, 25; **29:**3, 4, 8, 9, 11; **30:**1, 3, 6, 7, 9, 10, 11, 11, 11, 12, 13, 15, 15, 15, 16, 20, 21, 22, 24, 24, 26, 27; **31:**1, 4, 8, 9, 10, 11, 12, 12; **2Sa 1:**2, 2, 6, 7, 7, 8, 9, 10, 13, 14, 15, 18; **2:**1, 1, 3, 4, 5, 6, 7, 8, 10, 12, 14, 15, 17, 22, 22, 22, 23, 24, 25, 26, 30, 32; **3:**1, 1, 2, 5, 6, 8, 8, 10, 12, 12, 14, 17, 18, 19, 19, 20, 21, 21, 21, 21, 24, 25, 25, 26, 27, 31, 31, 35, 35, 38, 39; **4:**3, 5, 8, 8, 9, 12; **5:**1, 4, 6, 6, 11, 11, 13, 17, 19, 19, 20, 23, 24, 25; **6:**2, 2, 6, 10, 10, 12, 17, 19, 20, 20, 20, 21, 21, 21, 22; **7:**1, 4, 5, 5, 6, 7, 8, 8, 11, 14, 17, 19, 21, 21, 23, 27, 28, 29, 29; **8:**2, 2, 3, 5, 7, 10, 11, 15; **9:**1, 3, 3, 6, 7, 7, 7, 7, 8, 8, 9, 10, 10, 13, 13; **10:**2, 2, 2, 2, 2, 3, 3, 3, 4, 5, 5, 7, 8, 9, 9, 10, 12, 13, 14, 17, 19, 19; **11:**1, 1, 1, 3, 4, 5, 6, 8, 11, 12, 13, 13, 13, 14, 14, 14, 16, 16, 18, 19, 20, 22, 22, 23, 25, 27, 27; **12:**1, 3, 4, 5, 6, 7, 10, 10, 11, 11, 11, 12, 13, 14, 15, 16, 17, 18, 18, 20, 20, 21, 22, 23, 23, 24, 27, 29, 31, 31, 31; **13:**4, 5, 5, 5, 5, 6, 6, 6, 6, 7, 7, 8, 9, 10, 10, 10, 11, 12, 12, 13, 14, 15, 16, 16, 16, 22, 22, 23, 23, 24, 24, 27, 30, 34, 37, 39, 39; **14:**1, 2, 3, 3, 3, 4, 6, 7, 8, 8, 10, 11, 13, 13, 14, 15, 15, 15, 18, 19, 20, 22, 23, 23, 24, 25, 26, 26, 28, 29, 29, 29, 29, 30, 30, 30, 31, 32, 32; **15:**1, 2, 2, 3, 4, 5, 7, 7, 7, 7, 7, 8, 8, 8, 9, 10, 10, 13, 16, 18, 18, 19, 19, 20, 21, 25, 25, 26, 27, 29, 30, 34, 35, 36, 37; **16:**2, 2, 2, 4, 8, 10, 10, 10, 11, 11, 11, 11, 16, 20, 21, 22; **17:**1, 2, 3, 3, 4, 4, 12, 14, 15, 16, 17, 17, 17, 17, 18, 18, 18, 19, 20, 21, 23; **18:**1, 3, 3, 5, 5, 9, 12, 13, 17, 18, 18, 18, 19, 20, 21, 22, 23, 24, 25, 28, 28, 28, 29, 33; **19:**5, 5, 6, 6, 8, 8, 10, 10, 11, 11, 11, 12, 13, 14, 14, 15, 15, 15, 16, 17, 17, 18, 20, 22, 23, 24, 27, 30, 31, 33, 35, 36, 37, 37, 39, 40, 41, 41, 43, 43, 43; **20:**1, 2, 3, 3, 4, 4, 5, 6, 6, 8, 8, 9, 10, 11, 12, 13, 14, 16, 16, 16, 17, 18, 18, 19, 19, 20, 21, 21, 22, 22, 22, 22; **21:**2, 2, 3, 4, 5, 5, 6, 12, 16, 17, 17; **22:**1, 7, 7, 20, 22, 26, 26, 27, 27, 28, 31, 35, 37, 42, 42, 42, 50, 51, 51, 51; **23:**1, 3, 6, 7, 8, 10, 10, 13, 15, 16, 16, 17, 17, 18; **24:**1, 2, 2, 3, 3, 4, 5, 6, 6, 6, 7, 7, 8, 9, 10, 10, 11, 12, 13, 13, 14, 16, 16, 17, 18, 18, 18, 19, 20, 21, 21, 21, 22, 22, 23, 24, 24, 25; **1Ki 1:**3, 5, 5, 7, 8, 8, 9, 11, 12, 13, 13, 17, 20, 23, 25, 30, 33, 33, 33, 34, 35, 36, 38, 40, 42, 44, 47, 48, 48, 50, 52; **2:**1, 4, 7, 8, 8, 9, 13, 13, 14, 15, 15, 16, 17, 17, 18, 19, 19, 19, 20, 22, 22, 22, 25, 25, 26, 26, 26, 28, 29, 30, 30, 30, 32, 33, 33, 34, 35, 35, 36, 39, 40, 40, 40, 41, 42, 43, 44, 44; **3:**1, 5, 5, 6, 6, 6, 6, 8, 9, 13, 15, 15, 16, 16, 17, 20, 21, 23, 24, 25, 27, 27, 28; **4:**5, 11, 12, 12, 15, 20, 21, 21, 21, 24, 25, 29, 33, 34, 34; **5:**1, 2, 3, 3, 5, 5, 5, 7, 8, 9, 9, 9, 12, 14, 16; **6:**6, 8, 8, 10, 11, 12, 15, 16, 21, 21, 22, 27, 31, 33, 34, 38; **7:**1, 7, 7, 9, 11, 13, 14, 18, 20, 23, 32, 33, 40, 50; **8:**1, 1, 1, 4, 8, 14, 15, 16, 16, 17, 17, 18, 18, 18, 19, 20, 23, 23, 24, 25, 25, 26, 28, 28, 31, 33, 33, 34, 36, 36, 40, 41, 43, 44, 44, 46, 47, 48, 48, 48, 50, 52, 52, 52, 53, 54, 56, 58, 58, 61, 62, 63, 64, 65, 66, 66; **9:**1, 2, 3, 5, 5, 7, 8, 8, 11, 12, 15, 16, 19, 21, 22, 23, 24, 25, 25, 27, 28, 28; **10:**1, 1, 3, 3, 6, 8, 8, 10, 12, 12, 13, 24, 24, 25, 29, 29; **11:**2, 2, 4, 6, 8, 8, 9, 10, 11, 11, 14, 15, 15, 18, 18, 18, 21, 21, 22, 23, 24, 25, 31, 31, 31, 35, 36, 36, 38, 38, 38, 40, 40; **12:**1, 1, 2, 2, 3, 5, 6, 7, 9, 12, 13, 15, 15, 17, 18, 18, 18, 19, 19, 20, 21, 21, 21, 22, 23, 23, 26, 26, 27, 27, 27, 28, 28, 32, 32, 33, 33; **13:**1, 1, 2, 3, 3, 6, 6, 6, 7, 7, 7, 8, 9, 11, 15, 16, 17, 18, 18, 18, 20, 21, 22, 22, 26, 27, 29, 29, 31, 32, 33, 33; **14:**2, 3, 4, 5, 6, 8, 8, 12, 17, 21, 27, 28, 28; **15:**1, 4, 4, 9, 14, 17, 18, 20, 20, 21, 22, 22, 22, 25, 26, 27, 30, 33, 34; **16:**1, 2, 2, 7, 8, 9, 13, 15, 17, 19, 21, 23, 26, 29, 31, 31, 33, 34; **17:**2, 3, 4, 8, 10, 11, 11, 12, 13, 15, 18, 18, 18, 19, 20, 20, 20, 21, 21, 22, 23; **18:**1, 1, 2, 4, 5, 5, 5, 7, 9, 9, 10, 10, 10, 10, 12, 13, 15, 16, 16, 18, 19, 20, 21, 22, 23, 23, 24, 25, 25, 27, 27, 30, 31, 32, 32, 36, 37, 40, 41, 42, 42, 43, 43, 43, 44, 46, 46; **19:**2, 2, 3, 8, 8, 9, 9, 10, 14, 15, 15, 16, 16, 18, 19, 20, 20, 21, 21, 21, 21; **20:**1, 2, 2, 6, 7, 8, 9, 9, 10, 10, 12, 12, 13, 13, 17, 19, 22, 23, 27, 28, 31, 32, 33, 35, 35, 35, 37, 38, 39, 43; **21:**2, 2, 2, 2, 4, 4, 4, 6, 6, 8, 10, 13, 14, 14, 15, 16, 16, 17, 18, 20, 20, 21, 21, 22, 25, 28, 29; **22:**2, 3, 4, 4, 4, 6, 7, 8, 11, 12, 13, 13, 14, 15, 18, 19, 20, 22, 24, 24, 24, 26, 26, 28, 30, 31, 34, 35, 37, 41, 43, 48, 48, 49, 51; **2Ki 1:**2, 2, 3, 3, 4, 5, 6, 6, 6, 6, 6, 9, 9, 9, 10, 11, 13, 15, 15, 16, 16, 16, 17; **2:**1, 1, 2, 2, 2, 2, 3, 3, 4, 4, 4, 4, 5, 5, 6, 6, 6, 9, 9, 13, 15, 18, 20, 21, 23, 25, 25; **3:**1, 3, 4, 7, 7, 10, 11, 11, 12, 13, 13, 13, 26, 26, 27; **4:**1, 1, 1, 2, 5, 6, 6, 7, 7, 8, 8, 8, 9, 9, 10, 11, 11, 11, 12, 12, 12, 13, 13, 13, 13, 15, 16, 18, 19, 19, 21,

22, 22, 24, 24, 25, 26, 27, 27, 27, 28, 29, 29, 29, 31, 33, 34, 38, 38, 39, 42, 43; **5:**2, 3, 3, 5, 5, 6, 6, 7, 7, 7, 8, 8, 10, 11, 11, 13, 13, 13, 14, 15, 16, 17, 17, 18, 20, 21, 22, 22, 22, 23, 25, 26, 26; **6:**1, 2, 2, 6, 7, 9, 10, 10, 13, 14, 15, 19, 19, 21, 22, 23, 26, 27, 30, 32, 32, 32; **7:**2, 2, 3, 4, 5, 6, 6, 9, 10, 10, 11, 12, 13, 13, 14, 14, 15, 15, 17, 17, 17, 18, 19, 20; **8:**1, 1, 3, 3, 5, 5, 5, 5, 6, 6, 6, 7, 8, 8, 8, 9, 9, 12, 12, 13, 16, 19, 19, 21, 22, 25, 27, 29, 29, 29; **9:**1, 1, 3, 3, 4, 7, 11, 15, 15, 15, 15, 15, 16, 16, 16, 17, 17, 18, 18, 18, 19, 19, 21, 21, 23, 25, 27, 27, 28, 30, 35, 37; **10:**1, 1, 1, 1, 3, 3, 5, 6, 6, 7, 8, 9, 9, 13, 14, 15, 15, 15, 15, 16, 18, 18, 19, 19, 19, 19, 19, 19, 20, 21, 22, 23, 24, 27, 29, 30, 30, 30, 30, 31, 31, 32, 33; **11:**1, 2, 2, 4, 4, 5, 6, 9, 10, 11, 13, 13, 15, 16, 18, 18; **12:**1, 4, 4, 5, 8, 8, 10, 11, 11, 12, 12, 13, 14, 16, 17, 17, 18, 20; **13:**1, 2, 3, 5, 6, 7, 10, 11, 11, 16, 20, 21, 23, 23; **14:**1, 6, 7, 7, 8, 9, 9, 9, 11, 13, 13, 13, 14, 19, 20, 22, 23, 24, 24, 26, 27, 28; **15:**1, 8, 9, 9, 12, 12, 13, 14, 16, 17, 18, 18, 19, 23, 24, 24, 27, 28, 28, 29, 30, 32, 37, 37; **16:**1, 6, 6, 7, 8, 10, 10, 10, 15, 18, 18; **17:**1, 3, 3, 4, 4, 4, 6, 9, 9, 13, 14, 15, 17, 19, 20, 23, 23, 25, 26, 26, 26, 27, 28, 28, 29, 31, 32, 33, 34, 35, 36, 37, 40, 41; **18:**1, 4, 4, 6, 7, 8, 11, 12, 12, 13, 14, 15, 16, 17, 17, 18, 19, 21, 23, 26, 26, 27, 27, 28, 28, 29, 30, 31, 31, 32, 32, 32, 32, 34, 35, 36, 37, 37; **19:**1, 2, 3, 3, 5, 6, 7, 7, 8, 9, 9, 9, 13, 13, 14, 16, 16, 20, 25, 29, 32, 33, 35, 36, 36, 37; **20:**1, 1, 2, 2, 3, 3, 4, 5, 5, 6, 6, 7, 8, 8, 8, 9, 9, 11, 11, 13, 14, 16, 16, 17, 19, 20; **21:**9, 9, 16, 16, 16, 16, 22; **22:**3, 4, 5, 5, 5, 5, 6, 6, 7, 8, 8, 9, 9, 10, 10, 12, 13, 13, 14, 14, 15, 18, 18, 20, 20; **23:**2, 2, 2, 3, 3, 4, 4, 4, 5, 5, 5, 6, 6, 8, 8, 8, 8, 9, 9, 10, 10, 11, 11, 12, 15, 16, 17, 20, 20, 21, 21, 23, 24, 25, 27, 29, 29, 29, 30, 33, 34, 34, 34, 35, 35, 35; **24:**2, 3, 3, 3, 7, 12, 15, 17; **25:**4, 6, 7, 11, 12, 12, 13, 16, 20, 21, 24, 25, 26, 26, 26, 27, 27, 28, 29, 29, 30; **1Ch 1:**36; **2:**24, 35, 46, 48, 49; **3:**1, 4, 4, 5; **4:**6, 7, 10, 39, 42; **5:**1, 2, 8, 9, 20, 23, 26, 26, 26; **6:**19, 31, 32, 48, 49, 54, 56, 60, 64; **7:**9, 9, 14, 16, 18, 21, 22, 23, 28, 28, 28, 28; **8:**6, 9, 11; **9:**1, 1, 2, 2, 18, 19, 21, 23, 25, 25, 27, 27, 28, 28, 32; **10:**1, 4, 6, 8, 9, 10, 11, 12, 13, 13, 14; **11:**1, 4, 4, 5, 6, 8, 10, 11, 15, 17, 18, 18, 19, 19, 20; **12:**8, 16, 17, 17, 17, 17, 18, 19, 19, 19, 20, 20, 23, 29, 32, 33, 38, 40; **13:**2, 2, 3, 4, 4, 5, 5, 6, 6, 9, 13, 13; **14:**1, 1, 8, 8, 10, 10, 11, 11, 12, 14, 15, 16, 17; **15:**1, 2, 2, 3, 3, 3, 12, 12, 13, 13, 14, 14, 16, 16, 16, 17, 19, 20, 21, 23, 24, 24, 25, 25, 25, 28; **16:**3, 4, 4, 7, 7, 8, 9, 15, 16, 17, 17, 20, 23, 25, 29, 29, 33, 34, 36, 37, 37, 39, 40, 40, 41, 41, 42, 42, 43, 43; **17:**1, 3, 4, 4, 5, 6, 7, 7, 10, 15, 17, 19, 21, 22, 25, 26, 27; **18:**3, 5, 7, 10, 11, 14; **19:**2, 2, 2, 2, 2, 3, 3, 3, 4, 5, 5, 6, 8, 9, 10, 10, 11, 13, 14, 15, 19, 19; **20:**1, 1, 3, 3; **21:**1, 2, 2, 3, 3, 4, 4, 5, 8, 9, 10, 11, 12, 13, 15, 15, 15, 16, 16, 17, 18, 18, 18, 21, 22, 22, 23, 23, 23, 24, 24, 26, 26, 27, 30, 30; **22:**2, 4, 6, 7, 7, 8, 8, 8, 9, 10, 13, 14, 14, 15, 17, 18, 18, 19; **23:**1, 3, 4, 13, 13, 13, 13, 24, 24, 26, 26, 27, 28, 29, 30, 30, 31; **24:**2, 3, 5, 7, 7, 8, 8, 9, 9, 10, 10, 11, 11, 12, 12, 13, 13, 14, 14, 15, 15, 16, 16, 17, 17, 18, 18, 19, 19, 31, 31; **25:**1, 1, 3, 3, 6, 8, 8, 9, 9, 10, 11, 12, 13, 14, 15, 16, 17, 18, 19, 20, 21, 22, 23, 24, 25, 26, 27, 28, 29, 30, 31; **26:**13, 14, 14, 15, 16, 17, 17, 17, 17, 18, 18, 18, 18, 26, 27, 28, 29, 30, 31, 32, 32; **27:**23, 32, 32; **28:**1, 2, 3, 3, 4, 4, 4, 5, 6, 7, 8, 8, 9, 10, 13, 14, 17, 19, 20, 20; **29:**1, 1, 3, 3, 3, 4, 5, 5, 5, 9, 14, 16, 16, 16, 18, 18, 19, 19, 20, 20, 21, 24, 29, 30, 30, 30; **2Ch 1:**3, 4, 5, 6, 7, 7, 8, 8, 9, 10, 10, 11, 11, 11, 13, 17, 17; **2:**1, 3, 3, 4, 4, 4, 4, 4, 4, 6, 6, 6, 8, 9, 11, 14, 16, 16; **3:**1, 1, 8, 16, 16, 17, 17; **4:**2, 6, 6, 6, 7, 11, 20, 22; **5:**1, 2, 2, 2, 5, 9, 13, 13; **6:**3, 4, 5, 5, 7, 7, 8, 8, 8, 9, 10, 14, 14, 15, 16, 16, 17, 19, 19, 22, 24, 24, 25, 27, 27, 31, 32, 32, 33, 34, 34, 36, 37, 38, 38, 38, 40, 40; **7:**4, 8, 10, 10, 11, 12, 13, 15, 16, 18, 20, 21, 21, 21; **8:**2, 6, 8, 9, 10, 11, 12, 13, 13, 14, 14, 14, 14, 16, 16, 17, 18, 18; **9:**1, 1, 2, 2, 5, 7, 7, 8, 8, 9, 11, 11, 12, 14, 18, 23, 23, 24, 26, 29; **10:**1, 1, 2, 2, 3, 6, 7, 7, 9, 12, 13, 15, 15, 17, 18, 18, 18, 19, 19; **11:**1, 1, 1, 2, 3, 3, 14, 14, 15, 16, 16, 16, 17, 20, 21, 23, 23; **12:**2, 4, 5, 5, 6, 7, 7, 8, 8, 9, 10, 11, 11, 13, 13, 15; **13:**1, 4, 4, 6, 7, 9, 11, 13, 14, 15, 16; **14:**4, 4, 6, 6, 7, 9, 11, 13, 15; **15:**2, 2, 3, 4, 5, 9, 11, 12, 13, 13, 14, 17; **16:**1, 2, 4, 4, 6, 6, 6, 7, 7, 8, 8, 9, 9, 10, 11; **17:**1, 2, 2, 5, 6, 7, 14, 19; **18:**1, 2, 2, 2, 2, 3, 5, 6, 7, 10, 11, 12, 12, 13, 14, 17, 18, 19, 21, 23, 23, 23, 25, 25, 27, 29, 30, 31, 31, 33; **19:**1, 2, 3, 4, 4, 4, 6, 6, 8, 9, 10, 10; **20:**4, 4, 7, 9, 9, 9, 11, 12, 12, 12, 17, 18, 19, 20, 20, 21, 21, 21, 22, 22, 25, 25, 27, 28, 28, 33, 33, 34, 37; **21:**7, 7, 9, 10, 11, 11, 13, 14, 15, 16, 19, 19; **22:**4, 5, 6, 6, 6, 6, 7, 7, 7, 7, 8, 9, 10, 11; **23:**1, 2, 2, 3, 3, 5, 9, 10, 12, 12, 12, 14, 15, 17, 18, 18, 18, 19; **24:**4, 5, 6, 7, 8, 8, 9, 9, 11, 11, 12, 12, 13, 14, 14, 15, 17, 17, 18, 19, 19, 21, 21, 23, 25; **25:**4, 5, 5, 6, 7, 8, 8, 9, 9, 10, 11, 12, 12, 14, 15, 16, 17, 18, 18, 18, 19, 20, 23, 23, 23, 24, 26, 27, 28; **26:**2, 8, 8, 11, 13, 15, 16, 18, 18, 19, 20, 22, 23; **27:**3, 6, 6; **28:**5, 5, 5, 8, 9, 10, 11, 13, 13, 15, 15, 15, 15, 15, 19, 19, 21, 22, 22, 23, 23, 23, 24, 25, 26; **29:**4, 5, 5, 7, 11, 11, 11, 11, 11, 12, 15, 15, 16, 16, 16, 18, 20, 21, 24, 25, 27, 30, 31, 31, 32, 34, 35; **30:**1, 1, 1, 1, 1, 2, 4, 5, 5, 5, 5, 6, 6, 8, 8, 9, 9, 9, 9, 9, 10, 11, 12, 13, 14, 15, 16, 16, 17, 17, 18, 18, 19, 20, 21, 22, 23, 25; **31:**1, 1, 2, 2, 2, 4, 4, 4, 6, 6, 7, 10, 10, 10, 11, 12, 14, 16, 16, 16, 17, 17, 17, 18, 19, 19, 19, 21; **32:**1, 1, 2, 3, 4, 5, 6, 8, 8, 9, 11, 12, 12, 13, 13, 14, 15, 17, 18, 18, 18, 20, 21, 24, 25, 27, 30, 31, 31, 31; **33:**9, 10, 11, 12, 13, 13, 13, 14, 16, 17, 18, 18, 22; **34:**3, 3, 4, 4, 7, 8, 10, 10, 11, 15, 15, 16, 16, 17, 18, 18, 20, 21, 21, 22, 22, 23, 25, 26, 26, 28, 28, 30, 30, 30, 31, 31, 32, 33; **35:**2, 3, 3, 3, 4, 5, 5, 6, 8, 9, 10, 11, 12, 12, 15, 15, 20, 20, 21, 21, 21, 22, 22, 22, 23, 24, 25, 26, 27; **36:**4, 4, 6, 6, 10, 10, 10, 12, 13, 13, 15, 17, 18, 19, 20, 20, 20, 22, 22, 23, 23; **Ezr 1:**1, 1, 2, 3, 3, 5, 5, 5, 6, 8, 8, 8, 11, 11, 11; **2:**1, 1, 1, 59, 61, 62, 64, 65, 69, 70; **3:**2, 3, 3, 5, 5, 6, 6, 6, 7, 10, 10, 11; **4:**1, 2, 4, 4, 5, 5, 7, 11, 12, 13, 13, 13, 13, 14, 14, 15, 16, 17, 18, 19, 21, 22, 23, 23, 23; **5:**1, 3, 5, 6, 7, 8, 8, 9, 12, 12, 15, 15, 15, 17, 17; **6:**3, 5, 5, 6, 6, 6, 8, 9, 10, 10, 11, 11, 12, 18, 21, 22; **7:**6, 6, 7, 9, 10, 10, 10, 11, 11, 12, 13, 13, 14, 15, 15, 16, 17, 19, 19, 21, 21, 22, 22, 23, 24, 25, 25, 25, 26, 27, 28, 28, 28; **8:**15, 17, 17, 17, 20, 21, 22, 22, 25, 26, 26, 27, 28, 28, 28, 29, 30, 31, 33, 33, 35, 35, 36; **9:**1, 2, 5, 5, 6, 6, 6, 8, 9, 9, 11, 12, 12, 12, 12, 13; **10:**1, 2, 2, 3, 3, 4, 4, 6, 7, 8, 10, 11, 16, 16, 19; **Ne 1:**2, 3, 3, 4, 6, 9, 9, 9, 9, 11, 11, 11, 11; **2:**4, 5, 5, 7, 7, 7, 7, 8, 8, 8, 9, 9, 9, 13, 13, 14, 14, 16, 16, 17; **3:**1, 2, 5, 7, 9, 10, 11, 13, 16, 16, 19, 20, 20, 21, 23, 24, 25, 25, 27, 29, 30, 32; **4:**5, 6, 8, 8, 9, 9, 10, 10, 13, 14, 15, 18, 18, 19, 20, 21, 22; **5:**2, 3, 4, 4, 5, 5, 5, 5, 5, 7, 8, 8, 8, 8, 8, 9, 11, 12, 13, 14, 15, 16, 16, 16, 18; **6:**2, 2, 3, 3, 6, 6, 6, 7, 7, 9, 9, 10, 10, 10, 11, 12, 13, 13, 14, 18, 18, 19; **7:**2, 3, 3, 5, 5, 6, 6, 6, 61, 63, 64, 66, 67, 70, 71, 73; **8:**1, 1, 2, 3, 3, 4, 4, 5, 6, 9, 9, 12, 12, 12, 13, 14, 15, 15, 15, 15, 15, 16; **9:**3, 4, 5, 5, 6, 8, 8, 13, 14, 15, 15, 16, 17, 17, 17, 17, 19, 20, 23, 26, 26, 27, 27, 28, 28, 29, 29, 29, 30, 32, 34, 35, 36; **10:**28, 28, 29, 29, 29, 30, 30, 31, 31, 31, 31, 31, 32, 32, 32, 33, 34, 34, 34, 35, 35, 36, 36, 36, 37, 37, 38, 39, 39; **11:**1, 2, 3, 3, 30, 36; **12:**23, 24, 27, 27, 27, 27, 31, 31, 31, 37, 38, 38, 39, 39, 39, 40, 44, 44, 46, 46, 47; **13:**1, 2, 2, 5, 6, 6, 10, 10, 11, 12, 13, 13, 15, 15, 16, 18, 19, 19, 21, 22, 22, 22, 22, 26,

30; **Est 1:**1, 5, 6, 8, 8, 11, 11, 11, 12, 12, 15, 15, 17, 17, 18, 18, 22, 22; **2:**2, 3, 4, 6, 8, 10, 11, 11, 11, 12, 13, 13, 13, 14, 14, 14, 15, 15, 16, 18, 18, 19, 20, 21, 22, 23; **3:**1, 1, 2, 2, 4, 4, 4, 4, 6, 6, 7, 7, 8, 8, 9, 10, 12, 13, 13, 14, 14, 14, 15; **4:**2, 4, 4, 5, 5, 6, 7, 8, 8, 8, 8, 8, 8, 8, 8, 9, 10, 10, 11, 11, 11, 12, 13, 14, 15, 16, 16; **5:**2, 3, 4, 5, 5, 5, 5, 6, 6, 8, 8, 11, 12, 12, 14, 14; **6:**1, 1, 2, 2, 4, 4, 5, 6, 6, 6, 7, 9, 9, 9, 9, 10, 10, 11, 11, 12, 13, 13, 14, 14; **7:**1, 2, 3, 4, 4, 7, 7, 9, 9; **8:**1, 2, 2, 3, 4, 5, 6, 7, 7, 8, 9, 9, 9, 11, 11, 11, 11, 13, 13, 13, 17; **9:**1, 2, 2, 12, 13, 16, 19, 19, 20, 21, 22, 22, 22, 24, 25, 27, 27, 27, 27, 27, 28, 28, 29, 30, 31, 31; **10:**1, 3; **Job 1:**4, 4, 5, 6, 8, 9, 11, 12, 15, 16, 17, 19, 20; **2:**1, 3, 3, 4, 4, 5, 6, 7, 9, 9, 11, 12; **3:**4, 4, 6, 6, 8, 10, 10, 16, 18, 20, 20, 23, 23, 25, 25; **4:**1, 3; **5:**1, 4, 8, 8, 8, 9, 11, 11, 26, 27, 27; **6:**5, 11, 11, 14, 18, 18, 21, 22, 23, 23, 25, 28; **7:**2, 2, 4, 10, 13, 16, 20, 20; **8:**1, 5, 8, 12, 12, 13, 15, 15, 17, 19; **9:**3, 3, 3, 10, 12, 12, 14, 16, 21, 22, 27, 27, 30, 30, 32, 35; **10:**2, 3, 6, 6, 9, 14, 19, 21; **11:**1, 7, 8, 10, 10, 13, 19; **12:**5, 8, 8, 12, 12, 17, 22; **13:**3, 3, 3, 6, 6, 15, 17, 17, 20, 22; **14:**13, 21; **15:**2, 3, 5, 19, 28, 29, 35; **16:**5, 6, 8, 11, 12, 20; **17:**1, 4, 13, 16; **18:**2, 4, 12, 14; **19:**2, 3, 5, 12, 15, 17, 17, 18, 20; **20:**3, 3, 6, 24; **21:**2, 2, 7, 8, 8, 10, 12, 13, 14, 16, 21, 22, 28, 29, 30, 32, 33, 33; **22:**2, 2, 3, 3, 6, 6, 8, 8, 17, 18, 19, 19, 22, 23, 26, 27, 27, 28; **23:**2, 3, 3, 5, 5, 9, 13; **24:**5, 5, 10, 11, 12, 13, 14, 20, 21, 23; **25:**3, 4, 5; **27:**9, 10, 12, 12, 14, 15, 15, 19, 19, 22; **28:**1, 2, 3, 6, 9, 11, 12, 13, 18, 20, 28, 28; **29:**7, 12, 13, 16, 21, 21, 22, 23, 24; **30:**1, 2, 3, 10, 12, 13, 13, 20, 20, 23, 29, 29; **31:**1, 5, 10, 12, 13, 13, 16, 16, 17, 20, 27, 29, 32, 33, 34, 35, 35, 35; **32:**1, 1, 2, 3, 4, 6, 10, 11, 11, 16, 19, 20, 21; **33:**1, 1, 2, 7, 7, 10, 13, 17, 21, 23, 23, 26, 26, 27, 31, 32, 32, 32, 33; **34:**2, 9, 10, 11, 11, 14, 15, 16, 17, 18, 19, 19, 22, 23, 23, 23, 24, 28, 30, 31, 33, 37; **35:**2, 7, 9, 13, 13, 14; **36:**6, 9, 12, 12, 13, 13, 21, 23, 23; **37:**2, 6, 6, 13, 15, 19, 19, 19, 20; **38:**12, 12, 13, 13, 13, 13, 20, 20, 24, 29, 30, 31, 34, 35, 37, 38, 41; **39:**3, 3, 7, 9, 10, 11, 12, 12, 18, 20, 20, 21, 26, 27, 27; **40:**1, 2, 3, 5, 8, 11; **41:**4, 5, 5, 6, 9, 9, 10, 10, 10, 12, 27; **42:**1, 6, 7, 7, 8, 16; **Ps 1:**6; **2:**7, 12; **3:**4; **4:**T, 3; **5:**T, 1, 2, 2, 3, 3, 5, 8, 8, 9; **6:**T; **7:**T, 1, 2, 2, 14, 15, 17; **8:**T, 2; **9:**T, T, 2, 11, 12, 17; **10:**4, 4, 6, 6, 9, 11, 13, 17, 18; **11:**1, 1; **12:**T, 2, 3, 4, 5, 5, 5; **13:**3, 6, 6; **14:**2, 4, 7; **15:**3, 5, 5; **16:**1, 2, 10; **17:**1, 1, 3, 6, 10, 11, 12, 13, 14, 15; **18:**T, 6, 6, 19, 21, 25, 25, 26, 26, 28, 30, 34, 36, 41, 41, 41, 49, 50, 50, 50; **19:**2, 4, 4, 5, 6, 8, 8, 11, 14; **20:**1, 5, 9, 9; **21:**4; **22:**T, T, 2, 9, 15, 19, 22, 24, 27, 29, 31; **23:**3; **24:**1; **25:**1, 3, 3, 4, 8, 15, 16, 17; **26:**3, 5, 6, 6; **27:**2, 4, 7, 11, 11; **28:**1, 2, 2, 3, 4, 4, 8; **29:**1, 1, 2, 6; **30:**1, 2, 4, 8, 12; **31:**1, 1, 2, 8, 11, 13, 17, 19, 23; **32:**3, 5, 5, 5, 5, 6, 9, 10; **33:**1, 1, 3, 16, 17, 20; **34:**T, 4, 5, 6, 11, 11, 12, 15, 17, 18; **35:**2, 4, 8, 10, 23, 27; **36:**1, 1, 3, 4, 10, 12; **37:**5, 7, 8, 14, 14, 16, 16, 26, 32, 34; **38:**T, T, 4, 12, 13, 14, 22; **39:**1, 2, 3, 5, 6, 12; **40:**1, 1, 3, 3, 5, 5, 5, 9, 12, 14, 14; **41:**1; **42:**4, 4, 8; **43:**3, 3, 4, 4; **44:**2, 6, 8, 9, 10, 11, 13, 13, 17, 20; **45:**T, T, 1, 4, 4, 10, 10, 14, 17; **46:**T, 1, 4, 9; **47:**1, 6, 6, 9; **48:**2, 10, 13; **49:**1, 4, 5, 7, 9, 11, 14; **50:**1, 5, 8, 11, 12, 14, 14, 14, 16, 23, 23; **51:**T, 6, 12, 12, 13, 13; **52:**T, 4, 7; **53:**2, 4, 5, 6; **54:**T, T, 2, 2, 3, 5, 6, 7; **55:**T, 1, 7, 14, 19, 22, 22, 23, 23; **56:**T, T, 4, 5, 6, 6, 7, 9, 11, 12; **57:**T, T, 1, 2, 2, 3, 3, 10; **58:**T, T, 4; **59:**T, T, T, T, 1, 4, 5, 5, 7, 9, 11, 15, 17; **60:**T, T, 1, 5; **61:**T, 1, 2, 2, 6, 7, 8; **62:**3, 3, 4, 4, 8, 9, 10, 11, 12; **63:**3, 4, 9, 9; **64:**1, 5, 5; **65:**1, 1, 2, 4, 8; **66:**1, 3, 12, 12, 13, 13, 13, 15, 17, 19; **67:**T; **68:**4, 4, 4, 5, 9, 16, 18, 29, 31, 32, 32, 33, 35, 35; **69:**T, T, 1, 2, 3, 4, 6, 11, 13, 21, 26, 26; **70:**T, T, 2, 2, 5; **71:**2, 3, 3, 7, 10, 11, 12, 13, 14, 18, 18, 19, 20, 20, 21, 22, 24; **72:**1, 1, 4, 4, 4, 8, 8, 12, 12, 14, 15; **73:**1, 1, 2, 4, 8, 15, 16, 18, 22, 23, 24, 28; **74:**7, 10, 12, 15, 16, 21; **75:**T, T, 8, 9; **76:**T, 9, 9, 11, 11; **77:**1, 1, 4, 9, 10, 16; **78:**1, 1, 2, 3, 5, 5, 5, 5, 8, 8, 10, 15, 22, 23, 24, 28, 32, 34, 36, 37, 39, 45, 45, 46, 48, 48, 50, 54, 54, 56, 56, 58, 61, 62, 66; **79:**3, 4, 6, 8, 10, 11, 11, 13; **80:**T, T, 2, 2, 3, 7, 11, 11, 19; **81:**T, 1, 1, 5, 7, 8, 12, 13; **82:**3, 5, 8; **83:**9, 9, 9, 16; **84:**T, 2, 2, 5, 7; **85:**4, 5, 8, 8, 8, 9; **86:**2, 5, 6, 7, 11, 12, 14, 14, 15, 16, 17; **88:**T, T, 1, 2, 5, 6, 8, 9, 10, 13, 15; **89:**3, 15, 19, 19, 19, 24, 25, 26, 28, 30, 31, 33, 35, 43, 49; **90:**3, 3, 10, 12, 13, 14, 15; **91:**11, 12; **92:**T, 1, 1, 1, 1, 2; **94:**1, 2, 3, 21; **95:**1, 1, 5, 7, 10; **96:**1, 1, 2, 4, 8, 8, 13; **97:**7; **98:**1, 2, 3, 3, 4, 5, 9; **99:**6, 7; **100:**1, 4, 5; **101:**2, 2, 3, 3, 6, 7, 7, 8; **102:**1, 2, 5, 12, 13, 13, 14, 17, 18, 19, 20, 20, 20, 22, 24; **103:**6, 7, 7, 8, 13, 13, 17, 18; **104:**8, 14, 14, 14, 14, 15, 15, 19, 19, 22, 23, 26, 27, 28, 29, 30, 33, 33; **105:**1, 2, 8, 9, 10, 10, 13, 17, 19, 28, 39, 41, 42; **106:**1, 4, 4, 7, 8, 8, 9, 23, 24, 24, 25, 27, 28, 30, 34, 34, 36, 37, 38, 41, 43, 44, 46, 48; **107:**1, 7, 7, 8, 15, 21, 26, 26, 29, 31, 36, 40, 43; **108:**4, 6; **109:**4, 6, 6, 6, 8, 12, 16, 16, 17, 19, 25, 29, 30, 30, 31; **110:**1, 5; **111:**5, 6, 8, 10; **112:**7, 9; **113:**3, 6; **115:**1, 1, 16, 16, 17; **116:**7, 11, 14, 15, 18; **118:**1, 5, 6, 8, 8, 9, 9, 13, 17, 18, 20, 23, 29; **119:**4, 10, 17, 18, 29, 30, 30, 31, 31, 32, 33, 40, 41, 45, 46, 49, 57, 59, 60, 61, 61, 62, 67, 71, 71, 72, 73, 80, 82, 83, 85, 87, 88, 90, 93, 94, 95, 101, 101, 103, 112, 112, 115, 119, 121, 123, 123, 125, 126, 144, 146, 150, 169, 170, 173, 173; **120:**T, 1, 1, 3, 5; **121:**T, 1; **122:**T, 1, 1, 4, 4; **123:**T, 1, 2; **124:**T; **125:**T, 3, 4, 5; **126:**T, 1, 6; **127:**T, 2, 2, 2, 4, 5; **128:**T, 6; **129:**T, 2, 4, 8; **130:**T, 2, 4; **131:**T; **132:**T, 2, 5, 7, 11; **133:**T; **134:**T; **135:**7, 12, 13; **136:**1, 2, 3, 4, 5, 6, 7, 8, 9, 10, 13, 16, 17, 22, 25, 26; **137:**6, 6, 7, 8; **138:**2; **139:**3, 4, 6, 8, 8, 11, 11, 12, 12; **140:**5, 6, 6, 8, 11; **141:**1, 1, 2, 6, 8; **142:**1, 4, 4, 5; **143:**1, 2, 2, 3, 3, 8, 8, 8, 9, 9, 10; **144:**8, 9, 10, 11, 12; **145:**8, 9, 15, 18, 18; **146:**2, 4, 4, 7, 7; **147:**1, 1, 2, 7, 7, 9, 15, 19, 19; **148:**5, 14; **149:**1, 7, 8, 9; **150:**6; **Pr 1:**2, 2, 4, 5, 8, 16, 16, 21, 21, 23, 24, 29, 32, 33; **2:**1, 2, 5, 7, 8, 9, 13, 18, 18; **3:**18, 21, 27, 32, 32, 34, 35; **4:**1, 1, 4, 5, 10, 13, 16, 20, 22, 26; **5:**1, 1, 2, 5, 5, 6, 7, 7, 9, 13, 13, 14; **6:**3, 7, 9, 10, 13, 18, 23, 23, 26, 31; **7:**5, 15, 22, 24, 24, 27; **8:**3, 4, 4, 4, 6, 6, 9, 9, 9, 12, 14, 18, 32, 33, 34; **9:**3, 3, 4, 6, 6, 11, 12, 12, 15, 16; **10:**1, 1, 3, 3, 8, 11, 17, 18, 18, 18, 18, 23, 26; **11:**2, 12, 15, 15, 23, 24, 26, 29; **12:**1, 1, 9, 9, 15, 26, 28, 28; **13:**1, 5, 7, 7, 10, 19, 19, 22, 22, 24, 24, 25; **14:**6, 8, 21, 23, 34; **15:**16, 16, 18, 20, 21, 23, 24, 27, 30, 31, 32, 33; **16:**3, 8, 14, 16, 19, 19, 20, 22, 24, 26, 32, 32, 32; **17:**4, 4, 8, 12, 12, 16, 16, 17, 18, 18, 19, 21, 23, 24, 25, 25, 26, 26, 28; **18:**2, 3, 5, 10, 13, 13, 15, 19, 19, 21; **19:**1, 1, 8, 8, 10, 10, 13, 16, 17, 19, 22, 24, 27; **20:**1, 2, 2, 4, 12, 12, 13, 16, 17, 18, 22, 25, 25; **21:**5, 5, 7, 9, 10, 12, 13, 15, 17, 18, 19, 25, 26, 28, 31; **22:**4, 6, 7, 17, 17, 18, 21, 25; **23:**1, 2, 4, 8, 12, 12, 13, 17, 21, 22, 24, 28, 34; **24:**6, 7, 11, 12, 12, 13, 14, 16, 22, 23, 24, 26, 29, 33; **25:**2, 2, 7, 7, 7, 8, 8, 20, 21, 21, 24, 25, 27, 27; **26:**3, 5, 6, 8, 11, 15, 19, 25, 26, 26; **27:**7, 7, 10, 10, 10, 10, 11, 11, 13, 14, 16, 16, 18; **28:**4, 4, 4, 4, 6, 7, 8, 11, 15, 20, 22, 22, 25, 27, 27; **29:**1, 3, 4, 5, 5, 7, 9, 11, 13, 14, 15, 16, 25; **30:**2, 4, 5, 6, 8, 8, 10, 28, 33; **31:**4, 5, 5, 7, 15, 16, 20, 20, 24, 24, 27; **Ecc 1:**5, 7, 7, 10, 13, 13, 13, 16, 17, 18; **2:**1, 2, 2, 3, 3, 4, 6, 6, 11, 12, 12, 15, 16, 18, 20, 21, 21, 24, 24, 26, 26; **3:**2, 2, 2, 2, 3, 3, 3, 3, 4, 4, 4, 4, 5, 5, 5, 5, 6, 6, 6, 6, 7, 7, 7, 7, 8, 8, 10, 11, 12, 12, 14, 17, 18, 20, 20, 22, 22; **4:**1, 4, 5, 6, 6, 8, 13, 13, 15, 15; **5:**1, 2, 4, 4, 5, 5, 10, 11, 11, 13, 14, 14, 15, 18, 19, 19, 19; **6:**2, 2, 3, 5, 7, 8; **7:**2, 2, 5, 5, 12, 18, 23, 23,

23, 24, 25, 25, 25, 25, 27, 28, 29, 29; **8:**1, 1, 1, 2, 3, 5, 7, 8, 9, 11, 15, 15, 16; **9:**3, 3, 4, 10, 15; **10:**1, 2, 2, 6, 11, 12, 12, 12, 14, 14, 17, 17, 18; **11:**1, 5, 6, 7, 8, 8, 9, 9, 9; **12:**1, 2, 2, 3, 7, 7, 11, 12; **SS 1:**6, 6, 8; **2:**2, 3, 3, 4, 7, 10, 17; **3:**2, 3, 4, 5, 8, 11; **4:**6, 6, 16; **5:**2, 4, 5, 6, 6, 8, 9; **6:**2, 2, 2, 2, 8, 11, 11, 11, 13; **7:**12; **8:**2, 2, 4, 4, 7, 8, 11, 12, 13; **Isa 1:**1, 5, 6, 10, 10, 11, 13, 15, 17, 19, 20, 23, 26, 28, 28, 29, 31; **2:**2, 3, 3, 4, 12, 19, 20, 21, 21, 22; **3:**4, 6, 7, 8, 11, 12, 14, 17, 17, 24; **5:**4, 5, 5, 6, 7, 7, 8, 11, 15, 19, 21, 22, 23, 25, 25, 26, 26, 29; **6:**4, 6, 8, 10, 12; **7:**2, 3, 3, 3, 4, 4, 9, 9, 10, 11, 13, 14, 15, 15, 20, 20, 21, 25; **8:**1, 2, 4, 5, 6, 8, 9, 11, 14, 14, 15, 16, 16, 17, 19, 19; **9:**6, 6, 11, 12, 13, 17, 20, 21; **10:**3, 4, 7, 12, 21, 22, 23, 25, 26, 30, 31; **11:**10, 10, 10, 11, 12, 14, 14, 14, 15; **12:**2, 5; **13:**2, 2, 3, 3, 4, 6, 8, 14, 16, 20, 20, 21; **14:**1, 2, 2, 8, 9, 12, 13, 13, 14, 15, 15, 19, 24, 28, 29, 31; **15:**1, 5, 5, 5, 8, 8, 9; **16:**1, 8, 12, 12, 12; **17:**1, 2, 8; **18:**2, 2, 6, 7; **19:**1, 3, 3, 4, 4, 5, 11, 12, 12, 12, 14, 17, 18, 19, 19, 20, 20, 21, 21, 21, 22, 22, 24; **20:**4, 6, 6; **21:**1, 5, 6, 6, 7, 11, 11, 12, 13, 14, 16; **22:**1, 1, 3, 4, 4, 8, 9, 9, 10, 10, 11, 12, 12, 12, 12, 14, 15, 15, 17, 17, 18, 20, 21, 22, 22, 22, 23, 24, 25; **23:**1, 4, 6, 7, 9, 12, 13, 15, 17, 18, 18; **24:**1, 4, 10, 15, 16, 16, 16, 23; **25:**2, 4, 4, 10, 12; **26:**2, 2, 5, 8, 8, 9, 10, 11, 17, 18, 18, 19, 21, 21; **27:**3, 9, 9, 12, 12, 13, 13; **28:**2, 6, 6, 9, 9, 11, 11, 14, 15, 15, 16, 17, 17, 18, 18, 19, 20, 20, 21, 22, 23, 26; **29:**8, 11, 11, 12, 12, 13, 15, 15, 15, 16, 21, 21, 22; **30:**1, 2, 2, 4, 5, 6, 6, 8, 9, 9, 11, 11, 14, 15, 16, 18, 18, 18, 19, 20, 22, 26, 28, 29, 29; **31:**1, 1, 3, 4, 6; **32:**3, 6, 7, 8, 9, 10; **33:**1, 1, 1, 2, 6, 11, 13, 15, 15, 15, 15, 16, 18; **34:**8, 10, 11, 14, 17, 17; **35:**4, 4, 4, 10; **36:**1, 2, 2, 3, 4, 6, 8, 11, 11, 12, 12, 13, 13, 14, 15, 16, 16, 17, 17, 19, 20, 21, 22, 22; **37:**1, 2, 3, 3, 5, 6, 7, 7, 8, 9, 9, 9, 13, 13, 14, 17, 17, 21, 21, 26, 30, 33, 34, 36, 37, 37, 38; **38:**1, 1, 2, 2, 3, 3, 4, 5, 5, 7, 8, 10, 14, 16, 16, 17, 18, 19, 21, 22; **39:**2, 3, 5, 5, 6, 8; **40:**2, 9, 9, 11, 13, 13, 16, 16, 17, 18, 18, 19, 20, 21, 22, 23, 25, 26, 27, 29, 29; **41:**2, 2, 7, 13, 13, 16, 22, 27; **42:**1, 3, 5, 6, 6, 6, 6, 8, 10, 14, 18, 20, 21, 22, 24, 25; **43:**4, 6, 10, 13, 14, 18, 18, 19, 19, 22; **44:**1, 3, 3, 5, 7, 9, 9, 12, 14, 15, 15, 15, 16, 16, 17, 19, 19, 19, 20, 21, 22, 22, 25, 25, 25, 25, 27; **45:**1, 1, 6, 10, 12, 13, 14, 14, 14, 18, 18, 19, 19, 20, 22, 23, 23, 24; **46:**3, 5, 6, 7, 7, 10, 10, 12, 13, 13, 13; **47:**2, 6, 8, 10, 10, 11, 11, 12, 14, 15; **48:**1, 3, 5, 5, 6, 11, 12, 14, 14, 18, 19, 20, 21; **49:**1, 3, 4, 5, 5, 5, 6, 6, 6, 7, 7, 8, 8, 8, 9, 12, 17, 18, 18, 21, 22, 22, 23, 23; **50:**1, 2, 2, 2, 3, 4, 4, 4, 5, 6, 6, 7, 8; **51:**1, 4, 4, 6, 7, 8, 11, 13, 15, 16, 18, 18, 19, 19, 21, 23; **52:**4, 6, 6, 6, 8, 11; **53:**1, 2, 2, 6, 7, 8, 10, 11, 12; **54:**1, 10, 15, 15, 17; **55:**2, 3, 3, 3, 5, 7, 7, 10, 10, 11, 13; **56:**1, 1, 2, 2, 3, 4, 4, 4, 6, 7, 10, 10; **57:**1, 1, 1, 7, 9, 9, 9, 13, 15; **58:**2, 2, 2, 2, 2, 6, 6, 7, 7, 7, 14; **59:**1, 7, 7, 8, 10, 11, 11, 14, 15, 15, 16, 16, 16, 20, 20; **60:**1, 3, 3, 5, 7, 8, 8, 9, 9, 10, 11, 12, 13, 15, 16, 19, 20, 21, 22; **61:**1, 1, 1, 1, 2, 3, 11; **62:**3, 6, 8, 8, 10, 10, 11; **63:**1, 3, 4, 4, 5, 6, 7, 7, 11, 15, 17, 19; **64:**2, 2, 7, 12, 12; **65:**1, 2, 3, 4, 5, 9, 10, 12, 12, 22, 23, 24, 24; **66:**4, 5, 5, 7, 9, 12, 17, 19, 19, 19, 19, 19, 19, 19, 20, 20, 21, 23, 23, 23; **Jer 1:**2, 3, 5, 10, 10, 10, 10, 11, 13, 15, 15, 17, 18, 18; **2:**2, 3, 4, 5, 5, 7, 9, 10, 10, 17, 18, 19, 20, 24, 24, 25, 27, 27, 27, 30, 31, 31, 31, 31, 33, 36; **3:**1, 1, 1, 4, 6, 7, 8, 10, 10, 11, 12, 12, 13, 14, 16, 17, 18, 19, 19, 19, 19, 22; **4:**1, 2, 2, 3, 5, 5, 5, 5, 10, 11, 16, 18, 31; **5:**3, 3, 5, 6, 10, 19, 19, 20, 20, 23, 28, 28; **6:**1, 6, 9, 10, 10, 12, 13, 13, 13, 18, 19, 19, 23, 24, 25, 25, 29; **7:**1, 2, 2, 2, 2, 5, 6, 7, 7, 10, 10, 12, 12, 13, 13, 13, 14, 14, 16, 16, 18, 18, 18, 19, 24, 25, 26, 26, 27, 27, 28, 28, 31, 33, 34; **8:**3, 4, 5, 6, 10, 10, 10, 10, 14, 14, 14, 14, 16, 19; **9:**3, 3, 3, 6, 6, 8, 8, 12, 12, 12, 13, 15, 15, 17, 20, 20, 20, 20, 20, 22; **10:**2, 5, 7, 9, 11, 13, 14, 17, 17, 20, 23, 25; **11:**1, 3, 4, 5, 5, 6, 7, 8, 9, 10, 10, 10, 11, 11, 12, 13, 14, 14, 15, 15, 16, 16, 17, 19, 19, 20; **12:**3, 3, 5, 7, 9, 9, 12, 15, 15, 16, 16, 17; **13:**1, 4, 6, 6, 6, 7, 10, 10, 11, 11, 11, 11, 11, 11, 12, 13, 16, 16, 17, 18, 19, 20, 22, 26; **14:**1, 2, 3, 6, 6, 8, 9, 10, 10, 11, 12, 14, 16, 16, 17, 22; **15:**1, 2, 2, 2, 2, 2, 3, 3, 3, 3, 4, 5, 6, 7, 7, 8, 9, 9, 10, 10, 11, 13, 14, 14, 15, 19, 19, 19; **16:**5, 5, 7, 7, 8, 9, 10, 11, 12, 12, 15, 15, 15, 17, 19; **17:**1, 2, 3, 4, 10, 16, 19, 20, 20, 21, 22, 23, 23, 26, 27, 27, 27, 27, 27; **18:**1, 2, 2, 6, 6, 7, 10, 10, 11, 12, 12, 13, 15, 16, 17, 18, 18, 19, 19, 19, 20, 20; **19:**1, 1, 2, 2, 3, 3, 4, 5, 5, 5, 8, 9, 9, 9, 9, 11, 12, 12, 13, 13, 14, 15, 15; **20:**3, 4, 4, 5, 6, 6, 7, 12, 13; **21:**1, 2, 2, 3, 7, 9, 10, 10, 11, 11, 12, 12; **22:**1, 1, 1, 2, 5, 5, 6, 7, 8, 10, 16, 16, 20, 23, 23, 25, 25, 25, 27, 28, 28, 29, 30, 30; **23:**1, 2, 2, 2, 2, 4, 8, 8, 15, 16, 16, 16, 17, 17, 18, 18, 20, 21, 22, 25, 25, 27, 27, 29, 36, 36, 37, 38, 39; **24:**1, 3, 5, 7, 8, 9, 10; **25:**1, 2, 3, 4, 5, 7, 8, 14, 15, 15, 15, 17, 18, 19, 19, 21, 23, 23, 24, 25, 26, 27, 27, 28, 29, 30, 33, 33, 35, 35, 36, 36; **26:**1, 2, 2, 3, 3, 4, 4, 5, 5, 5, 7, 8, 9, 10, 11, 12, 13, 15, 16, 16, 17, 18, 18, 19, 19, 21, 21, 22, 22, 23, 24, 24, 24; **27:**1, 2, 3, 3, 5, 6, 8, 8, 9, 10, 11, 11, 11, 12, 12, 12, 13, 13, 14, 16, 16, 17, 17, 18, 18, 20, 22, 22; **28:**3, 4, 5, 7, 7, 11, 11, 12, 15; **29:**1, 1, 3, 3, 4, 4, 5, 7, 8, 11, 14, 16, 17, 19, 19, 19, 20, 21, 22, 23, 24, 25, 25, 25, 26, 26, 26, 27, 27, 28, 28, 28, 28, 29, 29, 30, 31, 31, 32; **30:**1, 2, 3, 3, 6, 6, 13, 15, 21, 21, 24; **31:**2, 2, 3, 3, 6, 6, 8, 10, 15, 16, 17, 18, 18, 20, 21, 22, 25, 25, 34, 34, 34, 35, 35, 36, 36, 38, 39, 40, 40; **32:**1, 3, 3, 3, 4, 4, 5, 7, 7, 7, 8, 8, 12, 13, 14, 16, 16, 18, 19, 20, 20, 23, 23, 24, 25, 25, 26, 28, 28, 29, 29, 29, 29, 31, 33, 35, 35, 35, 35, 36, 36, 37, 39, 40, 40, 41, 44; **33:**3, 4, 4, 5, 11, 11, 11, 15, 18, 18, 19, 21, 23, 24, 26; **34:**1, 2, 2, 2, 3, 3, 4, 6, 8, 9, 9, 17, 18, 20, 21, 22; **35:**2, 2, 3, 4, 4, 4, 5, 11, 11, 12, 13, 13, 14, 14, 14, 15, 15, 15, 15, 15, 16, 16, 17, 18; **36:**1, 2, 3, 5, 5, 5, 6, 8, 9, 10, 12, 13, 14, 14, 14, 14, 15, 18, 20, 21, 21, 22, 25, 26, 29, 30, 30, 30, 31, 32; **37:**2, 3, 3, 6, 7, 7, 7, 7, 7, 8, 10, 10, 12, 12, 12, 13, 17, 20, 21; **38:**2, 3, 4, 5, 6, 8, 11, 11, 11, 12, 12, 13, 14, 14, 14, 15, 16, 17, 17, 18, 18, 18, 19, 19, 19, 19, 20, 20, 21, 21, 22, 22, 23, 24, 25, 25, 26, 26, 27; **39:**1, 5, 7, 9, 9, 10, 11, 14, 14, 14, 15, 16, 16; **40:**1, 1, 4, 4, 4, 4, 5, 5, 5, 6, 7, 8, 9, 9, 10, 10, 12, 12, 12, 12, 12, 13, 14, 14, 14, 15, 15, 16, 16; **41:**1, 5, 6, 6, 8, 9, 12, 14, 17, 17; **42:**1, 2, 2, 3, 3, 3, 4, 5, 5, 5, 6, 7, 8, 9, 9, 10, 12, 13, 14, 15, 15, 17, 19, 20, 20; **43:**1, 2, 2, 2, 3, 4, 4, 5, 7, 7, 8, 10, 10, 11, 11, 12; **44:**2, 2, 4, 5, 8, 10, 10, 10, 11, 12, 12, 14, 14, 15, 16, 17, 17, 17, 18, 19, 20, 21, 23, 23, 23, 24, 24, 25, 25, 26, 27, 28, 28, 29, 30, 30, 30; **45:**1, 1, 2; **46:**1, 4, 6, 11, 11, 13, 16, 19, 24, 26, 26, 28; **47:**1, 2, 4; **48:**2, 7, 10, 11, 11, 12, 14, 15, 16, 19, 19, 34, 34, 35, 35, 39, 41, 44, 45, 45; **49:**1, 7, 10, 11, 14, 14, 15, 20, 21, 22, 24, 30, 32, 34, 36, 36, 37; **50:**5, 5, 6, 6, 7, 9, 9, 14, 15, 15, 16, 19, 19, 19, 25, 27, 28, 29, 29, 29, 29, 33, 38, 42, 43, 45; **51:**2, 4, 9, 11, 14, 16, 17, 24, 25, 27, 31, 31, 33, 35, 36, 36, 39, 40, 40, 53, 58, 59, 59, 61, 61, 63, 64; **52:**7, 9, 11, 15, 16, 16, 17, 20, 26, 27, 28, 31, 31, 32, 33, 33, 34; **La 1:**2, 3, 4, 4, 5, 6, 7, 7, 9, 10, 11, 12, 14, 14, 14, 15, 16, 18, 19, 19, 21, 21; **2:**1, 2, 4, 5, 7, 8, 9, 11, 13, 14, 14, 17, 19, 19, 20, 22; **3:**10, 15, 21, 24, 25, 26, 27, 27, 30, 32, 40, 41, 56, 59; **4:**4, 4, 6, 8, 10, 11, 14, 15, 17, 17, 18, 19; **5:**1, 2, 2, 4, 4, 6, 6, 6, 8, 13, 15, 19, 20, 21; **Eze 1:**1, 3, 9, 11, 12, 14, 15, 23, 28, 28; **2:**1, 2, 3, 3, 4, 4, 8, 8, 9; **3:**1, 1, 4, 5, 6, 7, 7, 7, 10, 11, 11, 11, 15, 17, 18, 19, 19, 20, 22, 22, 24, 26, 26, 27; **4:**3, 4, 8, 8, 9, 10, 16; **5:**1, 1, 2, 5, 6, 6, 7, 10, 12, 13, 14, 15, 16; **6:**1, 3, 3, 3, 10, 11, 13, 14; **7:**1, 2, 3, 8, 12, 12, 13, 13, 14, 16, 20, 20, 21, 24, 27; **8:**2, 3, 3, 3, 5, 5, 5, 6, 7, 8, 8, 12, 14, 16, 17; **9:**1, 1, 2, 3, 3, 4, 5, 9, 11; **10:**1, 2, 4, 6, 13, 19; **11:**1, 2, 3, 3, 5, 5, 8, 9, 10, 11, 12, 13, 14, 15, 16, 18, 23, 24, 24, 24; **12:**1, 2, 2, 3, 3, 3, 4, 6, 8, 10, 11, 13, 14, 16, 17, 21, 23, 23, 23, 26; **13:**1, 2, 2, 5, 5, 6, 7, 10, 14, 15, 16, 19, 19, 19, 19, 20, 22; **14:**2, 4, 5, 5, 7, 10, 11, 12, 13, 13, 13, 15, 15, 17, 17, 19, 22, 22, 23; **15:**1, 2, 3, 6, 7, 8; **16:**1, 5, 7, 8, 8, 15, 16, 18, 18, 20, 20, 21, 23, 24, 25, 26, 27, 29, 30, 31, 33, 33, 33, 35, 36, 36, 37, 39, 39, 40, 41, 41, 43, 47, 51, 57, 61; **17:**1, 2, 3, 4, 9, 11, 12, 12, 12, 15, 15, 17, 17, 18, 20, 21, 24, 24; **18:**1, 4, 7, 10, 10, 12, 15, 16, 21, 23, 23, 24, 24, 25, 28, 30, 32; **19:**3, 3, 4, 5, 6, 11, 12, 14; **20:**1, 1, 2, 3, 5, 6, 7, 8, 8, 9, 9, 9, 12, 12, 13, 13, 13, 14, 14, 15, 16, 18, 19, 20, 21, 21, 22, 25, 25, 26, 26, 27, 28, 28, 29, 30, 30, 31, 31, 31, 31, 31, 31, 32, 35, 37, 39, 41, 42, 45, 47; **21:**1, 3, 3, 4, 5, 8, 13, 14, 14, 16, 16, 18, 19, 20, 20, 21, 21, 22, 22, 24, 27, 27, 28, 30, 31, 32; **22:**1, 2, 2, 7, 9, 17, 19, 23, 26, 28, 30, 30; **23:**1, 3, 5, 9, 10, 11, 11, 16, 16, 16, 16, 16, 16, 18, 19, 21, 24, 27, 28, 28, 29, 30, 34, 34, 36, 39, 40, 40, 43, 45, 46, 48, 48, 48; **24:**1, 3, 5, 7, 7, 7, 10, 11, 13, 15, 16, 17, 18, 18, 19, 20, 20, 21, 21, 22, 24, 25, 26, 27; **25:**1, 4, 7, 10, 13, 17; **26:**1, 2, 5, 14, 15, 20, 20, 21; **27:**1, 3, 3, 5, 9, 15, 16, 19, 24, 25, 29, 36; **28:**1, 8, 9, 9, 11, 13, 14, 17, 17, 18, 19, 20, 22, 25; **29:**1, 4, 5, 5, 6, 10, 12, 13, 14, 15, 16, 16, 17, 18, 19, 19, 21; **30:**1, 6, 9, 11, 12, 12, 16, 18, 20, 21, 21, 22, 23, 25; **31:**1, 2, 2, 4, 6, 8, 8, 8, 10, 11, 15, 16, 16, 17, 18, 18; **32:**1, 3, 4, 6, 6, 9, 10, 10, 17, 18, 18, 19, 19, 20, 24, 24, 27, 27, 29, 30, 31, 32; **33:**1, 3, 4, 5, 6, 7, 8, 8, 9, 11, 12, 13, 18, 20, 21, 22, 23, 24, 26, 28, 31, 32, 33; **34:**1, 6, 8, 8, 10, 10, 10, 12, 13, 15, 18, 18, 19, 19, 21, 23, 25, 26; **35:**1, 3, 5, 7, 11, 11, 12, 12; **36:**1, 2, 4, 4, 6, 8, 9, 11, 12, 15, 15, 16, 17, 19, 19, 20, 22, 24, 30, 33, 34, 34, 37, 37; **37:**1, 3, 4, 4, 4, 5, 6, 8, 9, 9, 10, 10, 11, 12, 12, 14, 15, 19, 19, 21, 28; **38:**1, 4, 4, 10, 12, 13, 13, 16, 20, 23; **39:**4, 9, 10, 10, 11, 12, 14, 14, 15, 17, 17, 23, 24, 26, 27, 28; **40:**2, 2, 4, 4, 4, 6, 7, 9, 14, 15, 22, 22, 23, 24, 26, 28, 31, 32, 32, 34, 35, 35, 37, 38, 40, 43, 43, 45, 46, 46, 47, 48, 48, 49; **41:**3, 3, 7, 7, 13, 14, 15, 20, 21; **42:**1, 5, 8, 9, 13, 13, 14, 14, 15, 20; **43:**1, 3, 6, 7, 8, 9, 10, 11, 11, 14, 14, 18, 19, 24, 24, 24, 24, 26; **44:**1, 2, 3, 4, 4, 5, 5, 5, 5, 7, 8, 10, 11, 12, 12, 13, 14, 14, 15, 16, 17, 18, 19, 19, 19, 24, 24, 26, 27, 28, 29, 29, 30, 30, 30; **45:**2, 4, 5, 6, 6, 8, 8, 12, 13, 17, 17, 18, 19, 23; **46:**4, 5, 5, 5, 7, 7, 9, 11, 11, 12, 12, 12, 13, 14, 14, 16, 16, 17, 17, 17, 18, 19, 19, 20, 20, 21, 21, 24, 24, 24; **47:**1, 1, 2, 3, 3, 4, 4, 4, 5, 6, 7, 8, 10, 14, 14, 15, 16, 16, 17, 17, 17, 19, 19, 20, 22, 23; **48:**1, 1, 1, 1, 1, 2, 3, 4, 7, 12, 13, 13, 14, 18, 18, 19, 21, 21, 21, 21, 22, 23, 23, 24, 26, 27, 28, 28, 30; **Da 1:**1, 2, 3, 3, 3, 4, 5, 8, 8, 8, 10, 11, 13, 13, 14, 18, 19, 20; **2:**5, 8, 9, 10, 12, 13, 14, 16, 18, 18, 19, 21, 21, 23, 24, 24, 24, 24, 25, 26, 29, 30, 34, 39, 39, 39, 39, 43, 45, 46, 46, 47, 47, 48, 49; **3:**2, 2, 2, 4, 5, 5, 6, 7, 8, 9, 10, 11, 12, 12, 13, 14, 14, 14, 15, 16, 17, 20, 24, 26, 28, 28, 28, 30; **4:**1, 1, 2, 9, 9, 11, 12, 17, 17, 19, 19, 19, 20, 21, 22, 22, 24, 25, 27, 27, 27, 28, 32, 34, 35, 35, 36, 37; **5:**2, 4, 7, 7, 10, 10, 11, 15, 17, 18, 19, 19, 19, 19, 21, 24, 26, 28; **6:**1, 1, 2, 2, 3, 4, 6, 7, 7, 7, 10, 11, 12, 12, 12, 12, 13, 13, 14, 14, 14, 15, 15, 16, 16, 18, 19, 20, 22, 24, 25, 25; **7:**4, 5, 6, 8, 9, 10, 10, 11, 12, 16, 19, 22, 23, 25, 27, 28; **8:**1, 3, 4, 4, 4, 10, 10, 11, 13, 15, 17, 17, 18, 18, 19, 19, 23; **9:**3, 4, 4, 6, 6, 6, 6, 7, 11, 11, 13, 15, 18, 21, 22, 22, 23, 24, 24, 24, 24, 24, 24, 24, 25, 26, 26, 27, 27; **10:**1, 2, 7, 8, 9, 10, 11, 11, 11, 11, 11, 11, 12, 12, 12, 13, 14, 14, 14, 15, 15, 16, 16, 17, 19, 20, 21; **11:**2, 2, 2, 3, 3, 4, 6, 6, 8, 9, 14, 15, 15, 16, 17, 17, 18, 18, 18, 20, 21, 21, 25, 25, 27, 31, 32, 33, 35, 35, 36, 39, 39, 44, 45; **12:**2, 2, 3, 7, 11, 13; **Hos 1:**1, 2, 2, 2, 2, 4, 4, 5, 6, 6, 6, 7, 8, 10; **2:**2, 2, 2, 3, 5, 6, 7, 7, 9, 10, 11, 13, 14, 15, 15, 17, 20, 21, 23, 23; **3:**1, 1, 1, 3, 5, 5, 5; **4:**3, 4, 6, 6, 6, 8, 10, 12, 12, 13, 13, 13, 14, 16, 17, 18, 19; **5:**2, 4, 6, 6, 11, 13, 13, 14, 15, 15; **6:**1, 3, 3, 5, 5, 6, 6, 9, 11; **7:**1, 7, 10, 10, 11, 11, 13, 14, 16, 16; **8:**6, 9, 9, 10, 11, 12, 13, 13, 13; **9:**1, 1, 2, 3, 4, 4, 4, 4, 10, 12, 13, 15; **10:**4, 6, 6, 8, 8, 10, 11, 12, 14; **11:**2, 2, 2, 3, 4, 5, 5, 5, 5, 7, 9, 9, 12; **12:**2, 4, 4, 6, 7, 10, 12, 14; **13:**1, 2, 2, 8, 9, 16; **14:**1, 2, 2, 5, 7, 8; **Joel 1:**1, 3, 3, 6, 9, 9, 13, 14, 20, 20; **2:**5, 12, 13, 13, 14, 14, 17, 19, 25; **3:**3, 3, 4, 5, 6, 7, 8, 8, 9, 10, 12, 12, 12, 16, 16; **Am 1:**1, 5, 5, 8, 9, 13; **2:**1, 4, 7, 11, 11, 12, 12, 14, 15, 15, 15; **3:**1, 5, 6, 8, 9, 10, 12, 13, 14; **4:**1, 4, 5, 6, 6, 6, 8, 8, 9, 10, 11, 12; **5:**1, 2, 2, 3, 4, 4, 5, 5, 6, 6, 7, 16, 16, 19, 23, 23, 24, 25, 27; **6:**1, 2, 2, 2, 5, 5, 6, 7, 8, 10, 11, 12, 12, 14, 14; **7:**1, 4, 7, 8, 9, 10, 10, 12, 12, 14, 15, 16, 17; **8:**3, 4, 5, 5, 5, 10, 12, 14; **9:**2, 3, 4, 4, 4, 7, 10, 12; **Ob** 1, 1, 1, 2, 7, 10, 11, 11, 11, 12, 14, 14, 15, 15, 17, 20, 20, 21, 21; **Jnh 1:**1, 2, 3, 3, 3, 3, 4, 4, 5, 5, 6, 7, 8, 11, 11, 13, 14, 16, 17; **2:**1, 2, 2, 3, 6, 7, 7, 9, 10; **3:**1, 2, 3, 3, 4, 5, 5, 5, 8, 8, 10; **4:**2, 2, 2, 3, 4, 5, 5, 5, 5, 6, 8, 8, 9, 9, 9, 10, 11; **Mic 1:**1, 1, 3, 5, 7, 7, 9, 9, 10, 12, 13, 14, 15, 15, 16; **2:**1, 1, 2, 3, 4, 7, 8, 11, 11, 11, 13; **3:**1, 4, 5, 5, 6, 6, 9, 11, 12; **4:**1, 2, 2, 3, 4, 8, 8, 9, 9, 10, 11, 12, 13, 13; **5:**1, 3, 3, 3, 4, 5, 5, 6, 8, 9, 12, 12, 15; **6:**1, 1, 2, 2, 3, 4, 5, 5, 5, 6, 6, 7, 8, 8, 8, 9, 12, 13, 14, 14, 14, 15, 15, 16; **7:**1, 1, 3, 7, 7, 9, 12, 12, 14, 16, 17, 17, 20; **Na 1:**1, 3, 6, 9, 11, 14, 14; **2:**1, 5, 5, 5, 6, 7, 9, 11, 12; **3:**1, 3, 4, 10, 10, 13, 14, 14, 17, 17, 18; **Hab 1:**2, 3, 6, 8, 12, 12, 14, 14; **2:**1, 1, 2, 13, 16, 18, 18, 19, 19, 19; **3:**2, 2, 10, 11, 13, 13, 13, 19; **Zep 1:**1, 3, 4, 5, 5, 5, 6, 9, 12, 12, 12, 13, 18; **2:**3, 7, 14; **3:**2, 2, 2, 6, 7, 7, 8, 9, 10, 11, 13, 13, 13, 16, 17, 19; **Hag 1:**1, 1, 2, 6, 6, 6, 6, 6, 6, 11, 11, 11, 11; **2:**2, 2, 2, 3, 7, 10, 12, 15, 16, 17, 17, 17, 20, 21; **Zec 1:**1, 3, 3, 3, 4, 6, 7, 10, 11, 12, 13, 14, 14, 16, 16, 21, 21; **2:**2, 2, 3, 4, 6, 7, 9, 10, 11, 11, 12; **3:**2, 4, 4, 6, 8, 8, 8, 10; **4:**6, 6, 8, 10, 10, 14; **5:**2, 3, 11; **6:**5, 7, 7, 14, 15; **7:**1, 2, 3, 3, 5, 8, 9, 10, 11, 11, 13, 13, 13; **8:**1, 3, 6, 8, 13, 14, 15, 16, 16, 17, 17, 18, 20, 21, 21, 21, 21, 21, 21, 22, 22, 22, 22; **9:**4, 9, 10, 10, 10, 12; **10:**2, 3, 8, 8, 9; **11:**3, 11, 12, 12, 13, 13, 13, 14, 15; **12:**2, 2, 3, 4, 4, 5, 7, 9; **13:**1, 4, 4; **14:**2, 3, 4, 5, 10, 10, 10, 10, 11, 16, 16, 16, 17, 17, 17, 18, 18, 19, 20, 21, 21, 21, 21; **Mal 1:**1, 4, 6, 8, 8, 9, 9, 12, 13, 14, 14; **2:**2, 2, 3, 5, 6, 7, 8, 10, 12, 13, 14, 14, 15, 16; **3:**1, 2, 2, 3, 4, 7, 7, 7, 8, 10, 10, 14, 15, 16, 16, 16; **4:**2, 4, 6, 6; **Mt 1:**11, 17, 17, 17, 18, 18, 19, 19, 20, 20, 20, 21, 22, 23, 24; **2:**2, 7, 7, 8, 9, 9, 12, 12, 12, 13, 13, 13, 13, 13, 16, 16, 18, 19, 20, 20, 21, 22, 22; **3:**2, 5, 5, 7, 7, 8, 10, 11, 11, 12, 13, 13, 14, 14, 14; **4:**1, 3, 5, 5, 6, 6, 8, 9, 12, 13, 13, 17, 17, 19, 19, 21, 24; **5:**1, 3, 5, 14, 16, 17, 17, 19, 21, 22, 22, 23, 24, 24, 25, 25, 29, 29, 29, 30, 30, 30, 32, 33, 37, 40, 42, 42, 45, 47, 48; **6:**1, 2, 2, 2, 3, 5, 6, 13, 15, 16, 24, 26, 26, 27, 33; **7:**2, 5, 6, 6, 8, 11, 11, 11, 12, 13, 14, 20, 21, 24; **8:**2, 3, 4, 4, 4, 8, 9, 9, 10, 13, 16, 16, 18, 18, 19, 20, 20, 25, 25, 29, 33, 33, 34, 34; **9:**1, 2, 2, 5, 6, 6, 9, 10, 13, 13, 14, 18, 19, 22, 32, 36, 37, 38, 38; **10:**1, 1, 1, 5, 6, 7, 10, 10, 13, 14, 17, 18, 18, 18, 19, 21, 21, 22, 22, 23, 25, 27, 28, 29, 31, 34, 34, 34, 35, 38, 39, 42; **11:**1, 2, 4, 5, 5, 7, 7, 8, 10, 13, 14, 15, 16, 19, 20, 20, 21, 23, 23, 25, 26, 27, 27, 28; **12:**2, 3, 7, 9, 10, 11, 12, 13, 16, 18, 22, 22, 32, 38, 38, 38, 41, 42, 42, 42, 44, 46, 46, 47, 47, 49; **13:**1, 3, 9, 10, 11, 11, 12, 12, 12, 15, 17, 26, 30, 30, 34, 34, 35, 38, 43, 44, 44, 44, 54, 57; **14:**2, 2, 3, 4, 7, 9, 11, 11, 13, 13, 15, 15, 19, 19, 19, 21, 22, 23, 25, 27, 28, 28, 28, 30, 35, 36; **15:**1, 4, 5, 5, 10, 10, 10, 12, 20, 21, 22, 23, 23, 24, 24, 26, 26, 27, 28, 29, 31, 32, 32, 32, 33, 35, 36, 36, 38, 39; **16:**1, 1, 5, 5, 13, 17, 18, 20, 21, 21, 21, 21, 22, 23, 23, 24, 24, 25, 27; **17:**4, 5, 11, 16, 17, 20, 20, 22, 22, 24, 25, 25, 25, 27, 27; **18:**1, 2, 6, 6, 7, 7, 8, 8, 8, 9, 9, 9, 12, 17, 17, 21, 23, 23, 23, 25, 28, 31, 34, 35, 35; **19:**1, 3, 3, 5, 8, 10, 10, 12, 13, 13, 14, 14, 16, 16, 17, 21, 21, 23, 23, 24, 24, 27, 27, 30; **20:**1, 2, 2, 8, 10, 13, 14, 15, 17, 17, 17, 18, 18, 18, 19, 19, 20, 20, 21, 22, 22, 23, 23, 26, 27, 28, 28, 28, 31, 32, 33; **21:**1, 4, 5, 7, 12, 14, 16, 17, 18, 19, 19, 21, 23, 23, 24, 32, 32, 33, 33, 33, 34, 36, 38, 38, 40, 41, 41, 42, 43, 44, 46, 46, 46; **22:**1, 3, 3, 4, 5, 5, 7, 8, 9, 11, 13, 15, 15, 16, 16, 17, 17, 18, 21, 21, 21, 21, 26, 31, 34, 35, 44, 46; **23:**1, 1, 3, 4, 6, 15, 16, 16, 18, 18, 23, 25, 28, 34, 35, 37, 38; **24:**1, 3, 3, 8, 9, 13, 16, 17, 18, 24, 26, 32, 33, 38, 39, 43, 45; **25:**1, 4, 9, 10, 10, 14, 15, 15, 15, 15, 16, 17, 19, 20, 20, 22, 28, 29, 34, 37, 40, 40, 41, 42, 45, 45; **26:**1, 4, 4, 4, 9, 10, 12, 14, 15, 15, 16, 17, 17, 22, 26, 27, 27, 28, 30, 32, 35, 36, 36, 37, 38, 40, 40, 43, 44, 45, 48, 49, 53, 55, 55, 56, 57, 58, 58, 58, 58, 59, 59, 60, 61, 62, 62, 62, 63, 65, 68, 69, 71, 73; **27:**1, 1, 1, 1, 2, 3, 3, 6, 7, 14, 15, 15, 17, 17, 20, 20, 20, 20, 21, 21, 26, 26, 26, 31, 32, 33, 34, 35, 37, 48, 51, 53, 55, 58, 58, 58, 62, 64, 66; **28:**1, 5, 7, 8, 8, 9, 10, 10, 11, 12, 15, 16, 16, 20, 20; **Mk 1:**4, 4, 4, 5, 7, 12, 14, 14, 17, 17, 21, 24, 27, 29, 31, 31, 32, 33, 34, 34, 34, 35, 36, 38, 38, 40, 40, 41, 44, 44, 45, 45, 45; **2:**1, 2, 4, 5, 6, 8, 9, 9, 10, 10, 13, 14, 15, 16, 17, 18, 24, 24, 26, 27, 27, 27; **3:**2, 3, 4, 4, 4, 4, 5, 6, 7, 8, 9, 9, 10, 12, 13, 13, 14, 14, 15, 20, 20, 20, 21, 22, 23, 31; **4:**2, 3, 9, 11, 11, 13, 14, 21, 22, 23, 24, 24, 25, 25, 25, 30, 32, 33, 33, 34, 35, 35, 37, 38, 39; **5:**2, 4, 6, 8, 10, 10, 11, 14, 14, 16, 16, 17, 18, 19, 20, 20, 21, 23, 23, 26, 28, 31, 32, 33, 34, 35, 36, 38, 39, 40, 41, 43, 43, 43; **6:**1, 2, 3, 5, 6, 7, 8, 9, 9, 11, 11, 12, 14, 17, 17, 18, 20, 20, 22, 22, 23, 25, 26, 27, 27, 27, 28, 28, 30, 31, 35, 36, 37, 39, 41, 41, 41, 45, 46, 48, 48, 50, 55, 56; **7:**1, 2, 4, 9, 9, 10, 11, 11, 11, 11, 11, 13, 14, 14, 14, 17, 23, 24, 24, 25, 26, 27, 27, 31, 31, 32, 32, 32, 33, 34, 36, 36; **8:**2, 4, 6, 6, 6, 7, 10, 11, 11, 11, 13, 14, 17, 22, 22, 27, 30, 31, 33, 34, 34, 35; **9:**1, 2, 6, 7, 9, 10, 12, 15, 17, 18, 18, 19, 19, 20, 22, 24, 25, 26, 27, 30, 31, 31, 31, 32, 35, 35, 36, 38, 38, 38, 39, 41, 42, 42, 43, 43, 43, 45, 45, 45, 47, 47, 47; **10:**1, 2, 2, 4, 5, 7, 13, 13, 14, 14, 14, 17, 17, 21, 23, 23, 24, 25, 25, 28, 28, 30, 31, 32, 32, 32, 32, 33, 33, 33, 33, 35, 35, 37, 37, 38, 38, 38, 40, 40, 43, 44, 45, 45, 45, 47, 49, 50, 51, 51, 52; **11:**1, 6, 6, 7, 11, 11, 13, 14, 15, 18, 21, 22, 23, 24, 27, 29; **12:**1, 1, 2, 7, 7, 9, 11, 12, 12, 13, 13, 14, 14, 15, 16, 17, 17, 17, 17, 23, 26, 26, 28, 33, 33, 33, 34, 34, 36, 37, 38, 38, 38, 40, 41, 43; **13:**3, 4, 6, 8, 9, 9, 9, 10, 11, 11, 12, 12, 13, 13, 14, 15, 16, 22, 27, 28, 29, 34, 34, 34, 37, 37; **14:**1, 1, 5, 6, 7, 10, 10, 10, 10, 11, 12, 12, 13, 14, 15, 19, 22, 23, 23, 24, 26, 28, 29, 31, 32, 33, 34, 37, 40, 40, 41, 44, 45, 48, 49, 51, 53, 55, 55, 57, 60, 60, 63, 64, 65, 70; **15:**1, 1, 4, 5, 6, 8, 8, 11, 15, 15, 15, 15, 19, 20, 21, 22, 24, 24, 26, 36, 38, 41, 43, 43, 43; **16:**1, 2, 3, 7, 7, 8, 8, 12, 13, 14, 14, 15, 16, 18, 18, S, S; **Lk 1:**3, 4, 6, 9, 11, 13, 16, 16, 17, 17, 18, 19, 20, 21, 22, 26, 27, 27, 27, 28, 29, 30, 31, 35, 36, 38, 39, 39, 42, 50, 50, 54, 55, 55, 56, 57, 58, 58, 59, 62, 63, 66, 72, 73, 77, 78, 79, 79, 79, 79, 80; **2:**3, 3, 4, 4, 6, 7, 14, 14, 15, 15, 15, 16, 17, 20, 22, 22, 22, 23, 24, 25, 26, 27, 27, 27, 31, 32, 32, 34, 34, 38, 38, 39, 41, 43, 44, 45, 45, 48, 48, 48, 49, 51, 51; **3:**2, 3, 3, 3, 3, 7, 7, 8, 9, 11, 12, 13, 15, 15, 16, 17, 18, 20; **4:**1, 3, 5, 6, 6, 7, 9, 9, 10, 11, 14, 16, 16, 16, 17, 17, 18, 18, 18, 20, 26, 26, 29, 29, 31, 34, 35, 38, 39, 39, 40, 41, 42, 44; **5:**1, 1, 3, 4, 6, 8, 8, 10, 12, 12, 12, 13, 14, 14, 15, 15, 16, 18, 18, 19, 20, 21, 23, 24, 24, 25, 27, 30, 32, 32, 32, 36, 39; **6:**2, 4, 7, 7, 7, 8, 9, 9, 9, 9, 10, 11, 11, 12, 12, 12, 13, 18, 18, 19, 20, 20, 25, 27, 27, 30, 30, 31, 33, 33, 34, 34, 35, 35, 35, 35, 38, 38, 38, 38, 39, 42, 47, 47; **7:**1, 3, 3, 4, 6, 6, 7, 8, 8, 9, 10, 11, 14, 15, 15, 15, 19, 19, 20, 20, 21, 22, 22, 22, 24, 24, 25, 27, 32, 35, 36, 36, 36, 39, 40, 40, 40, 41, 41, 41, 44, 44, 44, 46, 48, 50; **8:**1, 3, 4, 4, 5, 6, 8, 10, 10, 15, 17, 17, 18, 18, 18, 18, 18, 19, 19, 20, 22, 22, 23, 23, 24, 25, 27, 28, 29, 31, 32, 34, 35, 37, 37, 37, 38, 39, 41, 47, 47, 48, 49, 50, 55, 55; **9:**1, 1, 2, 2, 5, 7, 9, 12, 12, 12, 13, 14, 16, 16, 16, 18, 21, 23, 23, 24, 28, 28, 31, 31, 33, 35, 38, 40, 42, 42, 43, 44, 44, 45, 46, 47, 48, 49, 49, 49, 51, 52, 52, 53, 53, 53, 53, 54, 54, 56, 57, 58, 58, 59, 60, 61, 62; **10:**1, 1, 2, 2, 2, 4, 6, 7, 7, 10, 13, 15, 15, 16, 17, 21, 21, 22, 22, 23, 23, 24, 25, 25, 29, 30, 31, 34, 35, 36, 38, 38, 39, 40, 40, 40, 41; **11:**1, 1, 4, 5, 5, 5, 6, 10, 13, 13, 13, 14, 16, 16, 18, 24, 29, 30, 30, 30, 30, 31, 31, 31, 32, 33, 33, 38, 38, 39, 39, 41, 42, 46, 49, 51, 52, 54; **12:**1, 3, 4, 4, 5, 5, 7, 11, 11, 12, 13, 14, 17, 18, 19, 19, 20, 21, 22, 22, 22, 24, 24, 25, 29, 31, 32, 33, 36, 36, 39, 42, 42, 47, 48, 48, 49, 49, 51, 51, 51, 54, 54, 56, 58, 58, 58; **13:**3, 6, 7, 11, 14, 14, 16, 24, 24, 24, 29, 31, 31, 31, 33, 34, 35; **14:**3, 4, 5, 5, 7, 7, 8, 9, 12, 15, 17, 17, 18, 18, 19, 23, 25, 26, 28, 28, 31, 31, 32, 35; **15:**1, 1, 4, 6, 7, 9, 11, 12, 13, 14, 15, 15, 16, 17, 17, 17, 18, 20, 20, 21, 22, 24, 29, 29, 31, 32, 32; **16:**1, 1, 2, 3, 3, 3, 4, 5, 5, 8, 9, 13, 15, 15, 16, 22, 23, 24, 25, 26, 26, 26, 27, 28, 28, 29, 30, 31; **17:**1, 1, 2, 2, 5, 5, 6, 9, 14, 15, 18, 18, 19, 21, 22, 22, 23, 27, 27, 30, 31, 31, 32, 33; **18:**1, 1, 3, 4, 5, 7, 8, 9, 10, 10, 13, 13, 15, 15, 16, 16, 16, 18, 22, 24, 24, 25, 25, 30, 31, 32, 32, 34, 39, 40, 41, 41; **19:**3, 3, 6, 7, 8, 8, 9, 9, 10, 11, 11, 12, 12, 13, 14, 14, 15, 15, 17, 21, 24, 24, 26, 27, 29, 35, 35, 37, 41, 41, 44, 45, 47; **20:**1, 9, 9, 9, 9, 10, 14, 14, 15, 16, 18, 19, 20, 20, 20, 20, 22, 22, 25, 25, 25, 25, 26, 33, 35, 36, 37, 37, 38, 40, 41, 42, 45, 46, 46, 46, 47; **21:**8, 13, 14, 15, 16, 17, 21, 24, 24, 28, 37, 37, 37, 38; **22:**2, 4, 4, 4, 4, 5, 6, 9, 11, 12, 13, 15, 15, 16, 19, 20, 23, 24, 24, 28, 30, 31, 31, 32, 33, 33, 33, 35, 37, 39, 44, 45, 45, 47, 49, 52, 52, 54; **23:**1, 2, 2, 2, 2, 4, 4, 5, 7, 7, 8, 8, 9, 11, 14, 15, 15, 18, 20, 22, 22, 24, 25, 25, 26, 28, 30, 30, 32, 33, 37, 38, 41, 48, 51, 52, 56; **24:**1, 4, 4, 4, 9, 10, 12, 12, 13, 17, 19, 20, 20, 21, 24, 25, 25, 26, 29, 30, 30, 32, 32, 33, 34, 35, 40, 41, 45, 47, 47, 50, 50, 51, 52; **Jn 1:**4, 7, 8, 9, 9, 12, 12, 15, 15, 16, 18, 19, 19, 22, 22, 25, 27, 31, 31, 33, 34, 39, 41, 42, 43, 43, 43, 45; **2:**2, 3, 6, 7, 8, 12, 13, 16, 18, 18, 20, 25; **3:**2, 2, 13, 13, 17, 17, 20, 21, 23, 26, 26, 28, 31; **4:**3, 3, 4, 5, 5, 7, 7, 8, 9, 9, 9, 15, 15, 18, 25, 27, 27, 28, 30, 31, 33, 36, 38, 40, 40, 41, 42, 47, 47, 47, 47, 47, 52; **5:**1, 6, 7, 7, 10, 10, 11, 14, 15, 18, 18, 21, 22, 23, 24, 26, 27, 29, 29, 30, 31, 33, 33, 36, 37, 38, 39, 40, 40, 41, 43, 43; **6:**5, 5, 6, 7, 10, 11, 11, 13, 15, 16, 16, 20, 21, 22, 24, 24, 26, 28, 29, 30, 31, 33, 35, 37, 38, 38, 39, 41, 44, 44, 45, 50, 52, 60, 61, 62, 63, 65, 65, 67, 67, 68; **7:**1, 1, 3, 3, 4, 6, 8, 8, 11, 13, 14, 14, 17, 18, 19, 20, 22, 23, 25, 26, 29, 30, 31, 32, 33, 34, 35, 35, 35, 36, 37, 37, 39, 45, 45, 51; **8:**1, 4, 5, 6, 10, 12, 12, 21, 22, 23, 25, 26, 26, 27, 29, 31, 33, 37, 40, 42, 43, 44, 47, 50, 50, 56, 59; **9:**4, 11, 13, 21, 23, 24, 27, 27, 29, 31, 31, 32, 34, 36, 37, 39, 39, 39, 39; **10:**3, 7, 8, 10, 10, 16, 18, 18, 18, 20, 24, 29, 31, 32, 34, 39, 40, 41; **11:**3, 6, 7, 7, 8, 15, 16, 19, 20, 21, 28, 28, 29, 31, 31, 31, 38, 41, 46, 47, 47, 51, 53,

54, 54, 56; 12:5, 9, 9, 10, 12, 13, 13, 17, 18, 19, 20, 20, 21, 21, 22, 23, 26, 28, 29, 32, 33, 33, 38, 40, 41, 42, 44, 46, 47, 47, 49, 50, 50; 13:1, 1, 2, 2, 3, 5, 5, 6, 6, 6, 8, 10, 10, 14, 15, 15, 18, 23, 24, 24, 26, 26, 29, 29, 29, 31, 31, 33, 35, 37; 14:2, 4, 6, 9, 12, 13, 18, 20, 21, 22, 22, 22, 22, 23, 28, 28, 30, 30; 15:6, 7, 8, 12, 13, 16, 17, 19, 19, 20, 20, 21, 22, 26; 16:4, 5, 7, 10, 12, 14, 15, 17, 19, 20, 20, 20, 21, 23, 23, 28, 30; 17:1, 1, 2, 3, 3, 3, 4, 4, 6, 6, 8, 9, 10, 10, 11, 13, 14, 15, 15, 19, 24, 26; 18:3, 4, 4, 4, 6, 9, 11, 13, 15, 16, 22, 24, 28, 28, 29, 30, 31, 33, 33, 37, 37, 38, 39, 39; 19:4, 4, 4, 7, 10, 10, 10, 11, 11, 12, 13, 14, 16, 16, 17, 21, 21, 24, 26, 27, 28, 29, 31, 33, 38, 39; 20:1, 3, 3, 7, 17, 17, 17, 20, 21, 22, 23, 27; 21:1, 7, 8, 11, 14, 15, 18, 18, 19, 19, 20, 22, 22, 23, 23; Ac 1:1, 2, 3, 3, 3, 3, 6, 7, 8, 10, 12, 13, 16, 16, 17, 20, 21, 24, 25; 2:6, 6, 10, 14, 23, 24, 27, 29, 33, 34, 36, 37, 37, 38, 39, 39, 41, 42, 47; 3:1, 1, 3, 8, 11, 11, 13, 13, 15, 17, 19, 20, 22, 23, 25, 25, 26, 26; 4:1, 1, 8, 9, 10, 10, 11, 12, 12, 14, 17, 17, 18, 19, 21, 28, 33, 35, 35, 35, 37; 5:2, 2, 3, 4, 4, 4, 4, 5, 9, 10, 13, 14, 20, 21, 22, 22, 28, 31, 31, 31, 32, 33, 35, 35, 36, 36, 37, 39, 40, 41, 42; 6:5, 6, 9, 10, 11, 14; 7:2, 2, 2, 3, 4, 5, 9, 12, 13, 13, 14, 14, 15, 16, 17, 18, 19, 21, 23, 24, 25, 26, 27, 28, 30, 31, 31, 33, 34, 34, 35, 35, 38, 38, 39, 39, 41, 42, 42, 43, 44, 51, 58, 60; 8:3, 3, 3, 5, 6, 6, 9, 10, 15, 18, 22, 24, 24, 25, 25, 25, 26, 26, 26, 27, 27, 29, 31, 31, 32, 35, 36, 38, 40; 9:1, 1, 2, 2, 2, 4, 4, 6, 9, 10, 11, 11, 11, 13, 14, 15, 15, 15, 15, 17, 21, 21, 21, 23, 26, 26, 27, 27, 29, 30, 30, 32, 32, 32, 34, 35, 38, 39, 40, 40; 10:2, 2, 4, 5, 5, 6, 8, 9, 9, 13, 16, 19, 22, 22, 23, 24, 25, 28, 31, 32, 33, 33, 39, 40, 40, 41, 41, 41, 42, 42, 42, 47, 48, 48; 11:5, 6, 10, 12, 12, 13, 13, 13, 17, 19, 20, 20, 21, 22, 23, 23, 24, 25, 25, 26, 27, 28, 29, 29, 30, 30, 30; 12:1, 4, 6, 7, 10, 10, 10, 11, 11, 11, 12, 13, 17, 17, 18, 19, 19, 20, 21, 23, 25; 13:4, 5, 6, 7, 7, 7, 8, 8, 8, 11, 13, 14, 14, 16, 16, 19, 22, 24, 24, 25, 27, 28, 28, 31, 31, 31, 32, 32, 34, 34, 34, 35, 36, 36, 37, 40, 42, 43, 44, 46, 46, 47, 47, 47, 48, 51; 14:1, 3, 5, 6, 6, 9, 10, 10, 13, 13, 15, 15, 16, 18, 21, 22, 23, 23, 24, 25, 26, 26, 27; 15:1, 2, 2, 2, 3, 3, 3, 5, 6, 7, 7, 8, 10, 13, 14, 17, 19, 20, 20, 20, 22, 22, 23, 25, 25, 27, 28, 28, 29, 30, 32, 33, 33, 35, 36, 36, 36, 37, 40, 41; 16:1, 1, 3, 3, 3, 4, 4, 6, 7, 8, 10, 10, 11, 13, 13, 14, 15, 15, 16, 17, 17, 18, 18, 21, 23, 25, 26, 27, 27, 28, 29, 30, 35, 36, 37, 37, 38, 39, 39, 39, 40; 17:1, 2, 2, 5, 5, 7, 10, 10, 11, 11, 11, 14, 15, 15, 15, 17, 17, 17, 17, 19, 20, 21, 23, 23, 25, 30, 30, 31, 32; 18:1, 2, 4, 5, 6, 7, 9, 10, 13, 13, 14, 14, 14, 14, 15, 18, 18, 19, 19, 20, 22, 23, 23, 25, 27, 27, 27, 27, 27, 28; 19:1, 4, 4, 4, 4, 8, 11, 13, 13, 13, 17, 21, 21, 21, 21, 22, 29, 29, 30, 31, 31, 33, 33, 35, 35, 35, 40; 20:2, 3, 3, 3, 7, 9, 11, 13, 13, 14, 15, 16, 16, 16, 17, 17, 17, 19, 21, 22, 25, 30, 32, 32, 34, 35, 35, 38; 21:1, 1, 1, 3, 4, 5, 5, 8, 8, 11, 12, 12, 13, 13, 16, 18, 21, 21, 23, 24, 24, 25, 26, 26, 28, 31, 34, 34, 35, 35, 35, 37, 37, 39, 40, 40; 22:1, 3, 3, 4, 4, 5, 5, 5, 5, 7, 7, 10, 11, 12, 13, 14, 14, 15, 17, 18, 21, 21, 22, 22, 24, 24, 25, 25, 25, 26, 29, 30, 30; 23:2, 2, 3, 3, 4, 4, 4, 9, 9, 10, 10, 11, 12, 14, 14, 15, 15, 15, 16, 17, 17, 18, 18, 18, 19, 20, 20, 20, 21, 21, 21, 21, 23, 24, 24, 25, 26, 27, 27, 28, 28, 28, 30, 30, 30, 32, 32, 33; 24:1, 2, 2, 3, 5, 5, 6, 10, 11, 16, 17, 17, 17, 17, 19, 19, 23, 23, 23, 25, 27; 25:1, 3, 3, 3, 6, 9, 9, 9, 10, 11, 11, 11, 11, 11, 12, 12, 13, 13, 15, 16, 16, 20, 20, 20, 21, 21, 21, 21, 22, 25, 25, 26, 27, 27; 26:1, 3, 6, 6, 7, 8, 9, 9, 9, 10, 10, 10, 11, 11, 11, 11, 12, 14, 14, 16, 16, 16, 16, 17, 17, 18, 18, 18, 19, 20, 20, 20, 21, 22, 22, 22, 23, 23, 26, 29, 32, 32; 27:2, 3, 3, 4, 4, 7, 9, 10, 11, 11, 12, 12, 12, 13, 14, 17, 17, 18, 21, 23, 24, 30, 30, 31, 33, 33, 35, 39, 41, 42, 42, 43, 43, 44; 28:2, 2, 4, 4, 6, 6, 7, 10, 13, 13, 14, 14, 15, 16, 17, 17, 18, 19, 19, 20, 22, 23, 25, 26, 27, 28, 28, 31; Ro 1:1, 1, 4, 5, 5, 6, 6, 7, 9, 10, 10, 11, 12, 12, 12, 13, 13, 13, 14, 14, 15, 15, 15, 17, 19, 21, 22, 23, 25, 25, 26, 26, 28, 28, 30, 31, 32; 2:4, 5, 5, 6, 7, 8, 21, 22; 3:5, 5, 6, 8, 15, 18, 19, 19, 19, 22, 25, 25, 26, 27; 4:2, 3, 6, 11, 13, 13, 13, 15, 15, 15, 16, 16, 17, 19, 19, 20, 21, 22, 23, 24, 25, 25; 5:2, 3, 5, 7, 7, 8, 10, 12, 13, 14, 15, 15, 16, 17, 21; 6:2, 2, 3, 6, 10, 11, 11, 12, 13, 13, 13, 14, 14, 16, 16, 16, 18, 19, 19, 21, 22; 7:1, 2, 2, 4, 6, 9, 10, 11, 13, 15, 18, 19, 19, 20, 21, 21, 23, 25, 25; 8:1, 2, 3, 7, 11, 12, 12, 16, 17, 17, 18, 20, 22, 23, 24, 24, 25, 28, 28, 29, 30, 30, 34, 34, 39; 9:3, 4, 4, 4, 6, 6, 8, 10, 11, 12, 15, 15, 15, 16, 16, 18, 18, 18, 20, 20, 21, 21, 21, 22, 22, 23, 23, 31, 32, 33; 10:1, 3, 3, 5, 6, 6, 6, 6, 7, 7, 7, 7, 12, 14, 17, 18, 18, 20, 21; 11:2, 3, 4, 8, 9, 11, 11, 13, 14, 14, 15, 18, 18, 19, 22, 22, 22, 23, 24, 24, 24, 25, 25, 28, 28, 28, 30, 31, 33, 34, 35, 36; 12:1, 1, 1, 2, 5, 5, 6, 6, 8, 8, 13, 16, 17, 18, 19, 20, 20; 13:2, 2, 4, 4, 5, 5, 6, 6, 7, 7, 7, 10, 14; 14:2, 3, 4, 4, 6, 6, 6, 6, 6, 8, 8, 8, 11, 11, 12, 12, 13, 14, 19, 20, 21, 22; 15:1, 4, 6, 8, 8, 8, 8, 9, 9, 9, 12, 14, 15, 16, 16, 16, 17, 17, 18, 20, 22, 23, 24, 24, 25, 25, 25, 27, 27, 28, 28, 30, 30, 30, 31, 31, 32, 32, 32; 16:1, 4, 5, 5, 6, 8, 10, 10, 12, 12, 13, 13, 14, 15, 15, 17, 19, 19, 19, 23, 25, 26, 27; 1Co 1:1, 2, 2, 4, 8, 10, 10, 10, 17, 17, 18, 18, 20, 21, 21, 22, 22, 22, 24, 24, 27, 27, 28, 28, 30, 30, 30, 30, 31; 2:1, 1, 2, 3, 6, 6, 6, 10, 13, 13, 14; 3:1, 1, 1, 1, 2, 3, 5, 6, 8, 9, 10, 13, 13, 13, 18, 19, 21, 22, 22, 23, 23; 4:5, 5, 5, 5, 5, 6, 6, 9, 9, 9, 10, 11, 11, 12, 13, 14, 14, 15, 15, 16, 17; 5:4, 6, 9, 9, 10, 10, 11, 11, 12, 12; 6:1, 1, 1, 2, 2, 3, 4, 5, 5, 7, 12, 12, 12, 15, 15, 16, 17, 19, 19; 7:1, 4, 4, 5, 5, 5, 6, 7, 7, 8, 8, 9, 9, 11, 12, 12, 13, 14, 14, 15, 15, 18, 19, 21, 26, 28, 31, 32, 32, 33, 33, 34, 34, 35, 35, 36, 37, 37, 39, 39, 39; 8:1, 2, 4, 5, 7, 7, 9, 10, 10, 10, 12, 13, 13; 9:2, 3, 4, 5, 6, 6, 7, 7, 7, 10, 11, 12, 12, 13, 15, 15, 16, 18, 19, 19, 20, 20, 20, 21, 22, 22, 22, 23, 25, 26, 27, 27; 10:1, 1, 6, 8, 9, 10, 11, 11, 11, 13, 15, 19, 19, 20, 20, 20, 22, 23, 23, 25, 27, 27, 28, 28, 32, 33; 11:2, 3, 3, 3, 3, 6, 6, 13, 13, 14, 15, 16, 18, 21, 22, 22, 22, 23; 12:1, 3, 3, 3, 7, 8, 8, 8, 9, 9, 9, 10, 10, 10, 10, 10, 21, 21, 24, 28, 29, 30; 13:2, 2, 3; 14:2, 2, 2, 2, 5, 6, 8, 9, 9, 11, 12, 12, 13, 20, 21, 21, 26, 27, 28, 31, 34, 35, 35, 37, 39; 15:1, 3, 3, 9, 11, 20, 22, 22, 23, 24, 26, 28, 34, 34, 38, 50, 51; 16:1, 2, 2, 3, 3, 4, 5, 5, 5, 6, 7, 7, 11, 11, 12, 12, 13, 15, 15, 16, 17, 18, 18, 18, 20, 24; 2Co 1:1, 1, 1, 3, 4, 6, 8, 9, 9, 10, 11, 15, 16, 16, 16, 19, 20, 21, 23, 23, 24, 24, 24; 2:1, 2, 3, 4, 4, 4, 7, 7, 9, 9, 10, 12, 12, 13, 13, 14, 14, 14, 15, 16, 16, 17; 3:1, 1, 1, 6, 7, 7, 14, 16; 4:2, 4, 13, 14, 15, 18, 18; 5:4, 4, 9, 10, 11, 12, 12, 13, 13, 14, 14, 15, 15, 18, 18, 19, 19, 20, 20, 20, 21; 6:1, 2, 3, 4, 5, 7, 7, 9, 10, 11, 13, 13; 7:2, 2, 3, 7, 8, 8, 9, 9, 10, 11, 11, 11, 11, 11, 12, 12, 13, 13, 14, 15; 8:1, 5, 5, 5, 6, 6, 6, 7, 7, 8, 8, 10, 10, 11, 11, 12, 12, 12, 16, 17, 19, 19, 19, 21, 21, 23, 23, 24; 9:1, 1, 2, 2, 2, 2, 3, 3, 4, 5, 5, 7, 7, 8, 9, 10, 10, 10, 11, 11, 12, 13, 13, 13; 10:2, 4, 5, 7, 7, 8, 8, 8, 8, 8, 9, 13, 14, 14, 16, 17; 11:2, 3, 4, 5, 7, 9, 9, 12, 15, 16, 16, 16, 19, 21, 21, 21, 26, 27, 31, 32; 12:5, 5, 6, 6, 7, 7, 8, 9, 11, 11, 12, 13, 13, 14, 14, 16, 17, 18, 19, 20, 21; 13:1, 5, 7, 7, 7, 7, 7, 8, 8, 9, 9, 10, 10, 10, 10, 10; Gal 1:2, 4, 5, 6, 7, 10, 10, 10, 13, 14, 15, 16, 16, 16, 16, 17, 17, 17, 18, 23, 23, 24; 2:1, 2, 2, 2, 2, 4, 4, 4, 5, 5, 5, 6, 6, 6, 7, 7, 9, 9, 10, 10, 11, 11, 13, 14, 14, 17, 19, 19, 21; 3:1, 3, 4, 8, 8, 10, 11, 12, 14, 16, 16, 16, 17, 17, 18, 19, 19, 19, 19, 19, 19, 20, 22, 22, 23, 23, 24, 29, 29, 29; 4:2, 3, 4, 5, 5, 7, 8, 9, 9, 10, 12, 12, 14, 15, 17, 17, 17, 18, 20, 21, 21, 23, 24, 27, 29, 31, 31; 5:1, 2, 3, 4, 5, 5, 6, 7, 8, 9, 10, 10, 12, 13, 13, 13, 16, 16, 17, 18, 24, 24; 6:1, 3, 4, 4, 4, 8, 8, 10, 10, 12, 12, 12, 13, 17; Eph 1:1, 1, 2, 3, 4, 5, 5, 6, 9, 9, 12, 14, 14, 17, 18, 18, 18, 19, 21; 2:2, 2, 3, 7, 11, 12, 13, 13, 14, 15, 16, 16, 17, 17, 18; 3:1, 2, 3, 5, 5, 8, 8, 9, 9, 10, 10, 13, 14, 14, 18, 20, 20, 20; 4:1, 4, 7, 8, 8, 9, 11, 12, 12, 13, 13, 14, 15, 19, 25, 27, 28, 29, 30, 32; 5:2, 2, 4, 6, 10, 10, 12, 17, 17, 19, 20, 21, 22, 22, 23, 24, 24, 26, 27, 27, 28, 31; 6:1, 1, 4, 6, 11, 13, 16, 19, 22; Php 1:1, 1, 3, 10, 11, 12, 12, 12, 16, 17, 17, 18, 21, 23, 23, 26, 26, 27, 28, 28, 28; 2:1, 3, 6, 9, 11, 12, 12, 13, 13, 15, 16, 17, 17, 17, 17, 19, 19, 21, 23, 23, 23, 24, 25, 25, 26, 28, 28, 28, 29, 30; 3:2, 5, 9, 9, 10, 12, 12, 13, 14, 14, 15, 16, 20, 21; 4:1, 1, 2, 2, 3, 10, 11, 12, 14, 17, 18, 19, 20, 21; Col 1:1, 2, 3, 5, 6, 6, 9, 9, 9, 10, 12, 12, 19, 20, 23, 23, 25, 26, 27, 28, 28, 28; 2:1, 2, 4, 6, 6, 11, 12, 14, 18, 19, 23; 3:1, 4, 5, 5, 7, 8, 9, 12, 15, 16, 16, 17, 18, 18, 22; 4:1, 2, 3, 3, 8, 8, 12, 15, 15, 16, 16, 17, 17; 1Th 1:1, 1, 3, 4, 7, 8, 8, 9, 10; 2:1, 2, 2, 2, 4, 4, 5, 5, 7, 9, 9, 12, 12, 13, 13, 16, 16, 16, 17, 17, 18; 3:2, 2, 2, 3, 3, 3, 5, 6, 6, 10, 10, 11, 11, 12, 12, 13; 4:1, 1, 3, 7, 7, 8, 8, 9, 9, 9, 10, 11, 12, 12, 13, 13, 14, 15, 17; 5:1, 1, 3, 5, 9, 9, 13, 14, 15, 15, 15, 18, 21, 27, 27; 2Th 1:1, 1, 5, 8, 10, 11, 12; 2:1, 2, 9, 10, 10, 10, 13, 13, 14; 3:1, 1, 7, 8, 9, 9, 9, 9, 11, 12, 12, 13, 14, 15, 15, 15, 17; 1Ti 1:2, 3, 7, 11, 12, 12, 13, 15, 17, 18, 19, 20, 20; 2:1, 4, 4, 6, 6, 7, 8, 8, 9, 9, 10, 10, 15; 3:1, 2, 2, 6, 9, 12, 14, 14, 16, 16; 4:2, 3, 3, 3, 6, 12, 13, 14, 15, 16; 5:1, 1, 1, 1, 3, 4, 7, 9, 10, 10, 11, 11, 13, 13, 14, 14, 19, 19, 21, 21, 23; 6:2, 4, 5, 5, 9, 11, 12, 13, 16, 17, 17, 18, 18, 18, 18, 20; 2Ti 1:2, 4, 6, 8, 8, 9, 9, 9, 10, 10, 11, 12, 12, 13, 13, 14, 16, 17; 2:2, 2, 2, 6, 10, 10, 14, 15, 16, 19, 21, 22, 24, 24, 26, 26; 3:2, 12, 14, 15, 16, 16, 16, 17; 4:1, 3, 3, 5, 6, 8, 10, 10, 10, 11, 12, 13, 17, 18, 18, 19; Tit 1:1, 1, 1, 1, 3, 3, 4, 6, 9, 13, 14, 15, 15; 2:2, 2, 2, 3, 4, 5, 5, 5, 5, 5, 6, 7, 8, 8, 9, 10, 11, 12, 12, 13, 14, 14, 14, 14, 15, 15; 3:1, 1, 1, 2, 3, 8, 8, 9, 10, 12, 12, 12, 12, 13, 14, 15; Phm 1:1, 2, 2, 2, 6, 6, 8, 9, 10, 11, 11, 12, 13, 14, 14, 14, 14, 16, 16, 22; Heb 1:1, 2, 2, 3, 5, 5, 6, 8, 13, 13, 14; 2:1, 3, 3, 4, 10, 11, 12, 12, 15, 16, 16, 17, 18; 3:1, 1, 2, 7, 10, 14, 14, 15, 18, 18, 19; 4:1, 1, 2, 2, 6, 6, 7, 11, 13, 14, 14, 16, 16; 5:1, 1, 2, 2, 3, 4, 5, 5, 6, 7, 10, 11, 11, 11, 12, 12, 14; 6:1, 3, 4, 4, 5, 6, 6, 6, 6, 9, 10, 11, 12, 13, 13, 16, 16, 18, 18, 18; 7:2, 3, 5, 6, 7, 8, 9, 11, 12, 13, 16, 19, 21, 23, 25, 25, 25, 27; 8:3, 5, 5, 6, 7, 9, 11, 11, 11, 13; 9:7, 7, 8, 9, 9, 14, 14, 15, 17, 17, 22, 23, 23, 24, 25, 25, 26, 26, 28, 28, 28; 10:1, 1, 1, 4, 7, 9, 9, 10, 12, 18, 22, 23, 23, 24, 24, 27, 27, 28, 28, 29, 31, 33, 36; 11:1, 2, 4, 4, 4, 5, 5, 6, 6, 6, 7, 8, 8, 9, 10, 11, 12, 12, 14, 15, 16, 17, 19, 19, 20, 22, 22, 24, 25, 26, 26, 26, 28, 28, 31, 31, 32, 32, 34, 34, 35, 35; 12:1, 2, 2, 3, 5, 9, 14, 14, 18, 18, 19, 20, 22, 22, 22, 23, 23, 23, 24, 24, 25, 25, 25, 25, 25; 13:1, 2, 2, 4, 4, 6, 10, 12, 13, 14, 14, 15, 16, 16, 16, 17, 17, 17, 18, 19, 20, 20, 22, 23, 23, 24, 24; Jas 1:1, 3, 5, 5, 6, 7, 12, 13, 13, 15, 15, 17, 18, 19, 19, 19, 21, 22, 22, 23, 26, 27; 2:3, 5, 5, 5, 9, 13, 17, 19, 22, 22, 23; 3:4, 17, 17; 4:2, 2, 4, 5, 6, 6, 8, 8, 11, 12, 12, 13, 15, 15, 17, 17; 5:6, 7, 11, 13, 13, 16, 18; 1Pe 1:1, 3, 5, 6, 7, 7, 7, 7, 10, 10, 11, 12, 13, 13, 15, 17, 17, 18, 20, 20, 21, 22, 25; 2:1, 4, 4, 7, 8, 11, 12, 12, 14, 14, 16, 16, 21, 23, 24, 25; 3:1, 1, 4, 7, 9, 12, 13, 13, 15, 16, 17, 17, 18, 18, 19, 21, 22, 22; 4:1, 1, 1, 2, 5, 6, 8, 9, 10, 10, 11, 11, 12, 13, 16, 19, 19; 5:1, 1, 1, 2, 2, 3, 5, 7, 7, 8, 10, 12, 12, 14; 2Pe 1:1, 1, 2, 3, 5, 5, 5, 6, 6, 6, 7, 7, 9, 10, 11, 12, 14, 15, 15, 15, 19, 21, 21; 2:3, 6, 9, 10, 12, 13, 14, 15, 17, 19, 19, 21, 21, 21, 22, 22; 3:1, 1, 2, 3, 4, 6, 8, 9, 9, 9, 10, 11, 12, 13, 14, 14, 15, 15, 16, 16, 17, 18; 1Jn 1:2, 2, 2, 5, 5, 8, 9, 9, 9; 2:1, 1, 3, 4, 5, 7, 10, 12, 13, 13, 14, 14, 14, 21, 24, 24, 26, 26, 26, 27, 27, 28; 3:1, 1, 4, 5, 6, 8, 8, 10, 12, 14, 16, 17, 17, 21; 4:1, 1, 2, 3, 4, 5, 5, 6, 6, 6, 7, 10, 11, 12, 14; 5:4, 13, 14, 16, 16, 17; 2Jn 1, 1, 4, 5, 6, 7, 10, 12, 12, 12, 12, 12, 12; 3Jn 1, 4, 5, 6, 9, 9, 10, 10, 13, 13, 14, 14, 15; Jude 1, 1, 3, 3, 3, 3, 4, 15, 16, 18, 20, 20, 21, 22, 22, 23, 23, 24, 24, 25, 25; Rev 1:1, 3, 3, 4, 4, 5, 5, 5, 6, 8, 9, 11, 12, 12; 2:1, 5, 7, 7, 7, 8, 10, 10, 11, 11, 11, 12, 13, 13, 14, 14, 14, 16, 17, 17, 17, 18, 20, 20, 20, 21, 23, 25, 26, 26, 29, 29, 29; 3:1, 3, 3, 6, 6, 6, 7, 9, 9, 10, 10, 10, 11, 12, 13, 13, 14, 18, 18, 21, 22, 22, 22; 4:1, 8, 9, 11; 5:2, 3, 4, 5, 5, 5, 9, 10, 12, 13, 13, 13; 6:2, 4, 8, 10, 10, 10, 11, 11, 13, 16, 17; 7:2, 2, 9, 12, 14, 14, 17; 8:3, 3, 4, 6, 13, 13; 9:1, 1, 3, 4, 4, 5, 5, 6, 10, 14, 15, 19, 20, 20; 10:4, 4, 5, 7, 8, 9, 11; 11:2, 3, 5, 5, 6, 6, 6, 9, 9, 10, 10, 10, 12, 13, 17, 17, 18, 18; 12:4, 4, 4, 4, 5, 5, 5, 6, 9, 10, 11, 12, 13, 13, 14, 14, 15, 17; 13:4, 5, 5, 7, 7, 7, 8, 8, 9, 10, 12, 12, 13, 14, 14, 14, 15, 15, 15, 16, 18; 14:4, 4, 6, 6, 6, 6, 7, 12, 12, 15, 15, 18, 18, 18; 15:1, 2; 16:1, 6, 8, 11, 14, 15, 16; 17:1, 1, 2, 8, 8, 10, 11, 12, 12, 12, 13, 13, 15, 17, 17; 18:5, 6, 6, 11, 19; 19:1, 5, 8, 9, 10, 10, 11, 17, 19; 20:1, 4, 4, 5, 8, 11, 12, 12, 13; 21:5, 6, 9, 10, 15, 15, 17, 24, 27; 22:2, 6, 6, 8, 8, 11, 11, 11, 12, 12, 15, 16, 16, 17, 18, 18, 20

TOO (439)

Ge 3:6; 4:13; 6:7; 8:9; 13:6; 15:5; 18:14; 19:31; 24:14, 19, 44, 46; 26:16; 27:34, 38; 29:27, 28, 30; 30:15; 32:12; 33:13, 13; 38:10; 39:21; 40:16; 41:54; 42:36; 44:29; 46:6; 47:6; 48:11, 19; Ex 1:17; 6:9; 7:12, 22; 8:7, 28; 9:11; 12:4; 16:2; 17:12; 18:18, 18, 22, 22; 23:29; 24:2; Nu 1:51; 3:10, 38; 10:10; 11:14, 32; 12:2; 16:3, 7, 34; 18:7, 22; 19:8; 24:24; 28:8; Dt 1:9, 17; 2:20, 36; 7:22; 10:19; 17:8; 19:6; 30:11; Jos 1:15; 10:30, 32; 17:16, 18; 19:9; 22:22, 27, 34; 24:18; Jdg 6:5; 7:2, 4, 12; 18:26; 19:11; Ru 1:12; 2:23; 1Sa 4:17; 5:10; 7:17; 10:10; 16:5; 17:36; 18:11; 19:21, 23, 24; 30:10, 21; 2Sa 2:6; 3:39; 10:11, 11; 11:21; 13:25; 14:26; 15:3, 14; 18:22; 19:34; 22:18; 23:10; 1Ki 3:3, 8; 4:29; 7:34; 8:43, 64; 10:3; 12:28; 13:18; 16:19; 17:11; 19:10, 14; 21:19; 22:7; 2Ki 5:18; 6:1; 9:16, 27; 25:16; 1Ch 19:12, 12; 26:28; 2Ch 6:33; 8:3; 9:2; 14:14; 18:6; 28:9, 23; 29:31, 34; 32:23; Ne 8:11; 11:1; Est 7:4; Job 2:13; 5:9; 6:21; 7:3; 9:10; 10:15; 15:11; 32:13; 33:6; 35:4; 36:17; 37:19; 40:5; 42:3; Ps 10:4; 18:17; 38:4; 40:5, 12; 77:4; 83:8; 95:5; 103:22; 105:24; 106:4, 32; 107:24; 131:1; 139:6, 6; 142:6; Pr 4:3; 10:19; 19:2; 20:4, 19; 23:21; 24:7; 25:16, 17, 27; 27:14; 30:2, 9; Ecc 2:1; 4:4; 5:3, 16; 7:16, 16, 17; 9:1; 12:2, 3, 3; SS 8:8, 13; Isa 3:11; 9:18; 22:3; 26:18; 28:20, 20; 31:2; 33:1; 34:7; 43:20; 48:19; 50:1, 2; 56:3, 8; 58:11; 59:1; 65:5, 23; Jer 1:6; 3:8; 5:5; 13:16; 14:4, 20; 18:13; 22:2; 24:8; 25:19; 27:15; 29:17; 31:11; 32:17, 27, 44; 36:7, 14; 38:4; 46:25; 48:2, 18, 21; 49:8, 11; 50:27, 35; 51:8; 52:20; La 1:6; 4:21, 21; Eze 1:19, 20; 3:21; 10:22; 15:4; 16:28, 53; 19:6; 20:21; 21:17; 27:23; 30:18; 31:3, 17, 18; 32:28; 38:5; 39:7; 40:21; 44:20; 47:5; Da 4:9; 5:9; Hos 1:10; 4:9; 5:5, 6; 7:1; 8:3; 9:2, 7; 10:10; 12:11; Joel 1:4, 6; Am 3:15; 7:6; 9:7; Jnh 1:13; Mic 1:9; Na 2:6; Hab 2:8; Zep 1:5; 2:4, 5; Hag 2:6; Zec 2:11; 9:2; 10:7; 11:8; 14:14; Mal 1:13; Mt 2:8; 4:21; 5:12, 25, 39, 40, 45; 12:4, 27; 13:22, 44; 20:10; 23:26; Mk 1:20, 38; 2:26; 4:19; 5:18; 8:7, 17; 11:13, 25; 12:21, 22; 16:8; Lk 4:43; 5:8; 6:4; 8:14, 38; 11:19, 32, 45; 13:25; 16:3; 18:43; 19:3, 42; 20:12, 32; 22:59; 23:36, 39; Jn 6:67; 7:22, 47, 52; 8:19; 9:27; 10:16; 11:16; 12:10; 14:19; 15:23; 21:3; Ac 2:15; 5:9, 37; 6:7; 8:19, 25; 10:45; 14:27; 15:3; 22:28; 26:24; Ro 1:15, 32; 2:3; 4:9, 19, 24; 5:3; 8:17, 23; 9:7; 11:3, 16, 31; 12:1; 13:6; 14:18; 16:22; 1Co 9:11; 10:12, 21, 21, 33; 15:8; 16:18; 2Co 2:10; 5:11; 8:13; 9:15; 10:8, 14; 11:18, 21; 13:4; Gal 2:1; 3:8; 6:3; Eph 6:19, 21; Php 2:4; 4:22; Col 1:27; 4:3, 16; 1Th 2:8; 2Th 3:2; 1Ti 1:16; Tit 3:3; Heb 8:3; 11:11, 12, 32, 38; 12:17; Jas 5:8; 1Pe 4:1; 5:1, 1; 1Jn 4:21; 5:1; Rev 7:9; 17:11

UP (1388)

Ge 1:5; 2:6, 21; 4:2, 26; 6:3; 8:13; 9:24; 12:6, 8; 14:14; 15:5; 18:2, 16; 19:1, 2, 19, 27, 33, 35; 20:8; 21:14, 20; 22:3, 9, 10, 13; 24:16, 23, 63, 64; 25:27, 34; 26:15, 25, 33; 27:19, 31; 28:11, 12, 16, 18; 29:25; 30:38, 41; 31:23, 25, 25, 35, 45, 46, 55; 32:22; 33:18; 35:13, 14, 20; 37:7, 7; 38:6, 14, 20; 41:2, 3, 4, 7, 7, 9, 18, 19, 20, 21, 24, 56; 42:24, 26; 44:3, 6, 30; 48:2; Ex 2:11, 23; 3:2, 3; 5:19; 7:12; 8:3, 7, 20; 9:13; 12:30; 14:9, 16, 21, 29, 30; 15:8, 9, 12; 16:4, 5, 16, 21, 29; 17:11, 12, 12; 18:13; 19:2, 12, 21, 23, 24; 20:26; 23:11; 24:1, 4, 9, 12, 13, 15, 18; 26:28, 30; 27:10, 10, 11; 29:17, 24, 26, 27, 28; 32:6; 33:7, 8, 12; 34:2, 28; 36:33; 38:10, 17; 39:40; 40:2, 4, 5, 8, 17, 21, 25, 33; Lev 6:22, 23, 30; 7:17, 19, 30; 8:27, 29, 32; 9:21; 10:2, 14, 15, 15, 16; 11:28, 45; 13:55, 57; 14:12, 21, 24, 38; 15:3; 18:9; 19:9, 10, 32; 21:8; 23:11, 15, 17, 20, 22; 24:3; 25:8; 26:1, 30, 34; Nu 1:51; 2:31, 34; 5:25; 6:3, 20, 20; 7:1; 8:2, 3; 9:15; 10:21; 13:21, 31, 32; 14:40; 16:19, 25, 30, 32, 35; 18:11, 18; 19:9, 10; 20:25, 27; 21:12, 17; 22:13, 20, 41; 23:18, 24; 24:8; 25:7; 26:10; 32:9; 33:5, 38; 34:13; Dt 2:8; 4:19, 46; 6:7, 15; 9:2, 23; 10:3, 11; 11:6, 17, 19; 12:2; 16:21, 22; 17:16; 18:15, 18; 19:14; 25:9; 27:2, 4, 15; 30:12; 32:8, 16, 30, 34; Jos 2:5, 6, 8, 22; 3:6, 13, 16; 4:3, 5, 16, 18, 20, 23, 23; 5:1, 7, 13, 13; 6:6, 12, 15, 26; 7:10, 13; 8:7, 19; 10:8; 11:17; 12:7; 15:3, 8; 18:1; 19:12; 22:3; Jdg 2:1, 10, 16, 19; 3:9, 15; 4:10, 12, 21; 5:3, 12, 12, 12, 12; 6:8, 13, 21, 38; 7:1, 5, 9, 13, 15; 8:8; 9:23, 43, 51; 11:2, 37; 13:20, 24; 14:17; 15:9, 12, 13, 13, 15; 16:3, 5, 6, 7, 8, 10, 11, 12, 13, 14, 20; 17:5; 18:13, 23, 30; 19:5, 7, 8, 9, 28, 30; 20:3, 8, 13, 23, 26, 27, 33, 38; Ru 1:11, 13, 18; 2:16; 3:8, 14; 1Sa 1:17, 19; 2:6, 7, 14, 21, 35; 3:5, 6, 8, 15, 19; 5:3; 6:10, 14; 7:12, 16; 9:12, 13, 19, 25, 26, 26; 13:15, 16; 14:9, 10, 10, 12, 13; 15:6, 6, 12; 17:40; 20:38; 22:9; 26:12, 14, 19; 28:4, 8, 11, 11, 13, 23; 29:10; 30:20; 31:3; 2Sa 2:23; 3:10, 26; 5:8; 6:15; 7:12; 10:8; 12:3, 17, 18, 20; 13:31; 14:14; 15:2, 10, 30; 16:1, 22; 17:2, 6, 26; 18:33; 22:29, 39; 1Ki 1:49; 3:15, 20; 6:8; 8:3, 4, 35, 54; 9:17; 10:26; 11:14, 20, 23; 12:8, 25, 25, 33; 14:10, 10, 14, 23, 25; 16:33, 34; 17:7, 19; 18:36, 38, 38; 19:5, 7, 8; 20:7, 26, 27, 33; 21:7; 22:12, 24, 35; 2Ki 1:6, 15; 2:1, 13, 23; 3:2, 19, 22, 25; 4:11, 21, 35, 37; 5:23; 6:15, 17; 9:19, 32; 13:5, 6, 18, 18; 14:10, 11; 16:7; 17:10, 16; 18:4; 19:14, 24, 29, 29, 35; 20:17; 21:3, 7; 22:4; 23:2, 16; 24:10; 25:13; 1Ch 10:3; 14:12; 15:1, 25, 28; 17:11; 19:9; 21:1, 16, 26; 26:16, 18; 2Ch 1:6, 14; 2:16; 3:17; 5:5; 6:26; 7:1, 13; 10:8; 11:6; 13:7; 14:6; 15:16; 18:11, 23, 34; 20:16; 21:16; 23:1; 25:14, 19, 21; 28:24; 31:6; 32:30; 33:3, 7, 19; 34:30; 35:20; Ezr 3:8; 7:6, 7, 22; 9:1, 5, 6; 10:5; Ne 2:15; 3:1, 6, 28; 9:5, 37; 12:37; Est 5:9, 14, 14; 7:9, 10; Job 1:5, 16, 20; 2:4; 4:15; 8:6, 19; 11:13; 12:23; 13:26; 14:12, 21; 15:30; 16:12; 17:3; 18:16; 19:12; 22:14, 23, 24, 26, 29; 27:19; 28:11; 32:18; 34:23, 24; 35:5; 36:27, 30; 38:27; 39:4, 18; 41:10, 30; Ps 2:12; 3:5; 7:6, 6; 12:5; 14:4; 18:28, 38; 20:8; 22:15; 24:7, 7, 9, 9; 25:1; 28:1; 30:3; 31:19; 35:2, 3, 23, 23; 38:12; 39:6; 40:12; 43:1; 44:23, 23, 26; 53:4; 57:8, 8; 59:4, 5; 60:6; 63:4; 68:22; 69:1, 27; 71:20; 72:16; 74:4, 15; 75:6; 76:9; 77:18; 78:13, 65; 80:16; 82:8; 85:11; 86:14; 88:10; 90:5; 94:16; 97:3; 102:10; 105:35, 41; 106:17; 107:25; 108:1, 2, 7; 116:13; 119:8, 69, 147; 121:1; 124:2; 139:2, 8, 18; 140:2; 141:7, 7; 145:14; 147:3; Pr 1:19; 5:2; 6:9, 14, 22; 10:6, 11, 12; 12:25; 15:1; 21:16, 29; 22:26, 28; 23:8, 35, 35; 24:2; 28:8; 30:4, 4, 25; 31:8, 9, 15; Ecc 3:7; 4:8, 16; 5:8; 6:5; 8:1; 12:4; SS 2:10, 12; 3:2; 5:5; 7:8, 12, 13; 8:5; Isa 1:15, 16; 2:3; 5:8, 11, 14, 19; 6:6; 9:18; 10:14, 25; 13:17; 15:6; 19:6, 7; 22:6, 9, 18; 24:4, 22; 25:8; 26:19; 27:4; 28:4; 30:1, 10; 32:20; 33:3, 10, 12; 37:14, 25, 30, 30, 36; 39:6; 40:15, 26, 30; 41:2, 18, 25; 42:15; 43:2; 45:8, 8, 13; 47:13; 51:6, 9, 10, 15, 17, 17; 52:1, 1; 53:2; 55:13; 57:8, 10, 20; 59:5, 12; 61:11; 63:9, 12; Jer 1:10, 10, 17; 4:3, 28, 30; 5:1, 7, 14; 6:1, 3; 7:30; 8:2, 4; 9:3; 14:7, 14; 15:3; 18:9, 14; 21:14; 23:10, 16; 24:6; 25:33; 27:7; 29:15; 30:9, 13; 31:6, 21, 21, 26, 28; 32:32, 34; 36:2, 23; 40:5; 41:12; 42:10; 44:11, 25; 46:11, 19; 48:34; 49:27, 31; 50:9, 17, 21, 32, 38; 51:1, 11, 11, 36, 57; 52:17; La 2:19; Eze 1:19, 21, 27; 2:1; 3:12, 14, 23, 24; 4:8; 5:3, 4; 8:2, 3; 9:3; 10:4; 11:23; 14:3, 4, 7; 15:3; 16:7, 44; 17:6; 18:10; 19:12; 20:28; 21:22; 23:24; 24:9; 25:4, 7, 9; 30:12, 14, 21; 32:2; 33:16; 34:4, 16; 36:24; 37:10; 39:9, 15; 40:14, 22, 26, 40, 41, 49; 41:7; 43:5, 15, 17; 45:7; 47:3, 4, 4; Da 1:8; 2:44; 3:1, 2, 3, 7, 12, 14, 18, 21, 24, 24; 4:22, 34; 7:3, 5, 5, 20; 8:3, 27; 9:27; 10:5, 11, 11; 11:2, 6, 25, 31; 12:2, 4, 11; Hos 2:7; 4:13, 18; 7:8; 8:8, 9; 9:12, 16; 10:4, 8, 11, 12; 11:8; 12:11; 13:1, 15; Joel 1:5, 6; 2:8, 12, 19, 20; 3:2; Am 1:2; 2:12; 4:4, 13; 5:2, 8; 7:1, 4, 17; 8:8; 9:2, 2, 6; Ob 3, 11, 16, 21; Jnh 1:2, 3, 6, 15; 2:10; 3:2; Mic 1:6, 7; 2:1, 10; 3:3; 4:2, 13; 5:9; 6:1, 6; 7:9; Na 1:4, 10; 2:5, 13; 3:14, 17; Hab 1:6, 13, 15; 2:1, 5, 6, 7; Zep 1:5; 3:8, 16; Hag 1:6, 8; Zec 1:18; 5:1, 5, 9, 9; 6:1; 9:3; 12:6; 14:10, 16; Mal 1:13; 4:1; Mt 1:24; 2:13, 20; 3:12, 16; 4:21; 5:1; 6:19; 8:15, 24, 25, 26; 9:5, 6, 7, 9, 20, 25; 10:38, 39; 12:29, 41, 42; 13:5, 7, 48; 14:19, 20, 23; 15:13, 37; 16:25; 17:1, 7, 17; 18:23; 19:27, 29; 21:19, 21, 23; 22:34; 24:24, 27, 38; 25:7; 26:46, 62; 27:6, 48, 50; 28:14; Mk 1:10, 19, 31, 31; 2:9, 9, 11, 12; 3:13, 27; 4:5, 7, 38, 39; 5:27, 41, 42; 6:23, 41, 43, 46; 7:34; 8:8, 19, 20, 27, 35; 9:17, 19, 27; 10:10, 17, 28, 29, 49, 50; 11:23, 27; 12:3, 40; 13:22; 14:15, 42, 45, 57, 60; 15:11, 36; 16:4, 19; Lk 1:80; 2:40, 44; 3:17; 4:5, 16, 20, 29, 39; 5:17, 19, 23, 24, 25, 28; 7:14, 15, 40; 8:7, 16, 24, 44, 45, 54, 55; 9:16, 17, 24, 32, 41, 54; 10:25, 30; 11:8, 31, 32; 12:21, 33; 13:7, 11; 14:33; 16:6, 9; 17:19, 27, 30; 18:1, 29; 19:5; 20:1, 10, 11, 36, 47; 21:26, 28; 22:12, 32, 45, 46; 24:51; Jn 1:51; 2:19; 3:14, 14; 5:7, 8, 8, 9, 11; 6:3, 8; 7:14, 50, 53; 8:7, 10, 28, 59; 10:31; 11:11, 41; 12:32; 13:4; 17:1; 18:12; 19:29, 30; 20:7; Ac 1:9, 15; 3:6, 7, 8, 22, 26; 5:34; 7:37, 42; 8:31, 39; 9:6, 8, 18, 34, 40, 40, 41; 10:9, 13, 16, 26, 26, 27; 11:7, 10, 28; 12:7; 13:18, 50; 14:2, 10, 20; 15:5; 16:27; 17:11, 13, 18; 18:22; 19:34; 20:32; 21:14; 22:3, 10, 16; 23:9; 26:16; 27:12, 13, 15; 28:6, 13; Ro 1:21; 2:5; 8:22, 32; 9:10, 16; 13:9, 11; 14:19; 15:2, 16, 26; 1Co 1:8; 3:15;

4:13; 8:1; 9:12; 10:13; 12:12; 13:7, 11; 14:26; 15:54; 16:17; 2Co 1:17; 4:1, 8, 9, 16; 5:4; 6:14; 9:2, 7; 10:8; 11:20; 12:2, 4, 7; 13:10; Gal 1:17; 2:4; 4:1; 5:1, 14; 6:9; Eph 4:12, 13; 5:14, 25; 6:4; Php 2:9, 19; 3:14; Col 2:7; 1Th 2:16, 16; 3:10; 4:17; 5:11; 1Ti 2:8; 3:16; 5:10; 6:4, 19; 2Ti 2:4; 3:4; 4:1; Heb 1:12; 3:6; 6:6, 7; 10:20; 11:5, 5, 24; 12:3, 15, 15; Jas 1:8, 11; 4:10; 2Pe 1:16; 2:3, 9, 20; 3:5; 1Jn 3:16, 16; Jude 13; Rev 2:14; 3:2; 4:1; 6:2, 5, 8, 14; 8:4, 13; 11:7, 11, 12; 12:5; 13:1, 11; 16:12; 17:8; 18:21; 20:9, 13, 13; 22:10

UPON (269)

Ge 1:15, 16; 12:17; 23:9; 42:21; Ex 6:1; 19:11, 16; 23:4, 27; 24:16; 32:21, 35; Lev 4:3; 10:7; 16:22; 22:16; 26:9; Nu 5:21; 11:17, 17, 25, 25, 25, 26, 29; 24:2; Dt 4:30; 24:4; 32:23; 33:2; Jos 20:4; Jdg 3:10; 9:8; 11:29; 1Sa 1:11; 6:9; 10:6, 10; 11:6; 12:15, 15; 14:32; 16:13; 19:9, 20, 23; 2Sa 1:21, 25; 17:14; 18:9; 23:2; 24:15; 1Ki 1:13; 6:34; 9:9; 2Ki 3:15; 7:9; 17:7; 1Ch 12:18; 21:14; 2Ch 7:22; 14:14; 15:1; 20:14; 24:20; 29:8; 32:16; Ne 9:32, 32; 13:18, 18; Job 10:17; 12:21; 19:25; 20:23, 25; 27:9; 28:8; 30:14, 27; 31:1; 36:8; 40:23; Ps 22:10; 42:8; 46:8; 63:2; 67:1; 78:53; 79:6; 80:3, 7, 19; 81:14; 84:9; 94:23; 104:3; 106:18; 118:27; 119:78, 153; 129:8; 137:5; 147:16; Pr 1:23; 3:25; 22:6; 28:27; Ecc 8:6; SS 3:11; Isa 10:3; 20:3; 21:3; 22:5; 28:2; 29:2; 30:13; 32:15; 34:5; 42:1; 47:9, 9, 11; 60:1; 61:1; Jer 2:3; 4:6, 8, 18; 5:12; 6:9, 19, 26; 9:6, 19; 10:18, 25; 11:8, 11, 23; 12:13; 13:16; 15:8; 17:18; 18:22; 19:15; 20:4; 21:6, 10; 23:1, 12; 25:13, 32; 27:8; 29:17; 31:28; 32:23, 42; 35:17; 39:5; 42:10, 17; 45:5; 49:5, 32, 37; 50:25; 51:60, 64; La 1:18; 3:3, 65; 5:16; Eze 6:3; 11:5; 14:21; 22:21; 30:9; 32:32; 33:10; 39:29; Da 4:19; Hos 10:12; Joel 2:1, 28; 3:14; Am 4:12; 9:4; Jnh 1:14; Zec 1:12; Mal 4:3; Mt 9:18; 11:29; 12:18; 16:18; 19:28; 23:36; 25:31; Lk 1:35, 65, 66, 78; 2:40; 4:18; 6:48; 18:32; 21:23, 26, 35; Jn 1:32, 33, 51; 3:34, 36; 6:18; Ac 1:8; 2:17, 18, 33; 4:33; 7:11; 8:16, 17, 18; 9:3; 10:44, 45; 11:21, 28; 12:20; 13:11, 11; 14:8, 27; 18:6; Ro 5:18; 9:23, 24, 28; 1Co 1:2; 3:17; 11:29, 34; 2Co 1:23; 4:4; Gal 1:9; 3:2, 13; 6:16; Eph 5:6; 6:24; Col 3:6; 1Th 5:3; 2Th 2:11; 1Ti 2:1; Tit 3:6; Heb 7:6; 1Pe 4:14; 1Jn 2:20; Rev 2:22; 3:3, 10, 12; 7:1; 8:5, 7, 10; 11:6

US (1594)

Ge 1:26; 5:29; 11:4, 4; 17:7; 19:9, 9, 13, 31; 20:9, 10; 23:6; 24:23, 31, 33, 65; 26:10, 10, 16, 22, 28, 29, 29; 31:14, 14, 14, 15, 15, 37, 48, 49, 52, 53; 32:5, 18, 20, 20; 33:14; 34:10, 10, 10, 21, 22, 23, 30; 37:26; 39:14; 40:8; 41:10, 12; 42:2, 12, 13, 13, 21, 28, 30, 30, 33; 43:2, 4, 7, 7, 18, 18; 44:7, 9, 9, 16, 19, 21, 23, 25, 26, 26, 27, 31; 45:11; 47:15, 19, 19, 25; 50:15, 16, 17, 25; Ex 1:9, 10; 2:19, 19; 3:18, 18; 5:3, 3, 10, 15, 17, 21, 21; 8:26, 26, 27; 10:9, 26; 12:27, 31; 13:8, 14, 15; 14:11, 11, 11, 12, 25; 16:3, 3, 3, 7, 8; 17:2, 3, 3, 7; 19:8; 20:19, 19; 24:3, 14; 32:1, 1, 1, 23, 23, 23; 33:15, 15, 16; 34:9, 9; 36:5; Nu 10:29, 31, 32; 11:13; 12:2, 11; 13:27; 14:3, 3, 8, 8, 8, 8, 9, 9, 40; 16:3, 5, 13, 13, 13, 14, 14, 14; 20:5, 5, 16, 16, 17; 21:2, 5, 22; 22:14; 27:4; 31:49; 32:5, 5; Dt 1:6, 19, 20, 22, 22, 25, 25, 27, 27, 28, 41; 2:9, 13, 27, 29, 29, 29, 32, 33, 36, 36, 37; 3:1, 3; 4:7; 5:2, 3, 24, 25, 27; 6:20, 21, 23, 23, 24, 25; 9:4; 13:2, 6; 17:14; 26:6, 6, 7, 8, 9, 9, 15; 29:7, 29; 30:13; 31:17; 33:2, 4; Jos 1:16, 16; 2:3, 14, 14, 20, 24, 24; 4:7; 5:6; 7:3, 3, 7, 7, 9, 9, 25; 8:6, 6; 9:6, 11, 20, 22, 22; 10:6, 6; 17:4, 14, 14, 16, 16; 21:2; 22:18, 19, 19, 19, 23, 28, 29, 31, 34; 24:17, 17, 27; Jdg 1:3, 3, 24; 6:13, 13, 13, 13, 13, 13; 8:1, 1, 22; 10:15, 15; 11:6, 8, 24, 27; 12:1, 2; 13:8, 8, 23, 23, 23; 14:15, 15; 15:10, 10, 11, 11; 16:5, 23, 24, 24, 25; 18:10, 19, 19, 23, 25; 19:18; 20:8, 10; 21:22; Ru 1:17; 2:8, 20; 1Sa 2:36; 4:3, 3, 3, 8; 5:7, 10, 11; 6:2, 9; 7:8, 12; 8:5, 20, 20, 20; 9:5, 6; 10:27; 11:1, 3, 3, 10, 12, 14; 12:4, 10, 19; 13:12; 14:6, 8, 9, 10, 12, 29, 29, 37, 41; 16:16; 17:47; 20:23; 22:23; 24:12, 15; 25:7, 8, 8, 15, 15, 15, 16, 40; 28:15; 29:4, 4, 4, 6; 30:22, 23, 23, 23; 2Sa 10:12; 11:23, 24; 14:7, 14, 14, 16, 16, 17, 20; 15:19, 20, 22; 18:3, 3, 3; 19:5, 6, 9, 10, 14, 42, 42, 43; 20:6; 21:5, 5, 6; 24:14; 1Ki 3:18, 26; 5:6; 8:30, 57, 57, 58; 12:4; 15:19; 18:26; 20:25; 2Ki 1:6, 6, 9; 3:10, 10, 11, 13; 4:13; 5:7; 6:2, 3, 12, 33; 7:4, 4, 6, 9, 12, 12, 13; 9:5, 12, 22; 10:5; 18:25, 26, 30, 32; 19:4, 19; 22:13; 1Ch 12:19, 19; 13:2, 2, 2; 15:13; 16:35, 35; 19:13; 23:25; 29:14, 15; 2Ch 6:21; 10:4; 12:6; 13:10, 12, 12; 14:7, 7, 11; 16:3; 20:9, 9, 9, 11, 11, 11, 12; 29:8, 10; 30:6; 32:8, 8, 11; 34:21; Ezr 4:2, 2, 3; 5:17; 8:17, 18, 18, 21, 21, 21, 22, 22, 23, 31, 31; 9:8, 8, 8, 9, 9, 9, 9, 11, 12, 13, 14, 15; 10:3, 4, 13, 14, 14; Ne 1:7, 11; 2:12, 17, 20; 4:4, 12, 12, 20, 23, 23; 5:8, 10; 6:9, 10; 9:32, 32, 33, 33, 37, 37; 10:31; 13:18; Est 1:18; 2:2; 5:12; 7:4; Job 1:15; 7:17, 18, 18; 8:10; 9:33; 14:6, 6, 6; 15:2; 18:2; 21:15; 22:14, 17, 17; 31:2, 15; 32:13; 34:4, 4, 33; 35:11; 37:19, 23; Ps 2:3; 4:6, 6; 8:4, 4, 5, 5, 6, 6; 10:6, 13; 12:4; 33:20, 20, 20, 22; 34:3, 3; 38:T; 40:5, 5; 44:1, 7, 7, 9, 10, 11, 11, 12, 12, 13, 13, 14, 19, 19, 23, 26, 26; 46:7, 11; 47:3, 9; 59:7; 60:1, 1, 1, 3, 3, 3, 5, 10, 11; 65:4; 66:6, 10, 10, 11, 12; 67:1, 1, 6, 7; 68:18, 19, 20, 30; 70:T; 74:1, 9, 9; 76:5, 5; 78:3, 19; 79:4, 5, 8, 9, 9, 9, 10; 80:2, 2, 3, 3, 5, 5, 6, 6, 7, 7, 8, 8, 9, 13, 13, 18, 19, 19; 81:5; 83:4, 12; 84:11; 85:4, 4, 5, 6, 7, 7; 89:18; 90:10, 12, 13, 14, 15, 16, 17; 95:1, 1, 2, 2, 6, 6; 100:3; 103:9, 10, 10, 12; 106:47, 47; 108:11, 12; 115:1, 12, 12; 117:2; 118:25, 25, 27; 119:4, 13; 122:1; 123:3; 124:2, 3, 3, 4, 4, 6; 126:3; 132:7, 7; 136:24; 137:3, 3, 8; 144:3, 3; 146:9; Pr 1:11, 14; Ecc 7:3; 8:8, 8; 12:14; SS 5:9; 6:13; 7:11, 12, 12; Isa 1:9, 18; 2:3, 3, 5; 4:1, 1; 5:19; 6:8; 7:2, 14; 8:10, 17; 9:6, 6; 10:9; 14:8; 16:3, 3, 3, 3; 20:6; 25:9, 9; 26:12, 13; 28:9, 10, 15; 29:15, 16; 30:10, 10, 10, 16; 32:15; 33:2, 14, 22, 22; 36:10, 11, 15, 18; 37:4, 20; 41:22, 23; 43:26; 49:14, 14; 53:2, 6, 6; 59:9, 9, 11, 12; 63:15, 16, 17, 17, 17, 19; 64:5, 5, 6, 7, 7, 9, 9, 12, 12; Jer 2:6, 6; 3:25; 4:8, 13; 5:12, 12, 19, 24, 24, 24; 6:5, 24; 8:14; 9:19; 13:12; 14:7, 7, 8, 9, 9, 9, 19, 21, 21, 21, 22, 22; 16:10; 18:18; 21:2, 13; 26:16, 19; 31:6; 35:6; 36:15, 17; 37:3; 38:25, 25; 40:10, 15; 42:2, 3, 5, 5, 6, 20; 43:2; 44:17, 19; 51:10, 10, 34, 34, 34, 35; La 1:16; 3:40, 40, 41, 42, 43, 43, 43, 45, 46; 4:15, 17, 19, 19; 5:1, 5, 8, 16, 20, 20, 21, 21, 21, 22, 22; Eze 8:12; 11:15; 20:32; 24:19; 33:10, 24, 30; 35:12; 36:2; Da 1:12, 13; 2:4, 7, 23; 3:17, 17; 9:7, 7, 7, 10, 11, 12, 13, 14; Hos 6:1, 1, 1, 1, 2, 3, 3; 8:2; 10:3; 14:2, 3; Joel 1:19; 2:1; Am 5:18; 7:13; 9:10; Ob 3; Jnh 1:6, 8, 14, 14; 3:9, 9; Mic 2:4, 4; 3:11, 11; 4:2, 2, 5; 5:5, 5, 6; 7:19, 20; Hab 1:12, 12, 13, 16; 3:2, 2, 2, 16; Zec 5:9; 8:21, 21, 23; Mal 1:2; 2:14; Mt 1:23; 6:11, 12, 12, 13, 13; 8:25, 29, 29, 31, 31; 9:27; 12:38; 13:56; 15:23; 17:27; 18:1; 20:7, 12, 30, 31; 22:17, 28; 25:8, 9, 11; 26:17, 53, 63, 68; Mk 1:24, 24; 5:9, 12; 6:3; 8:11; 9:22, 22, 40, 40; 10:35; 12:14, 19, 23; 13:4; 14:12; Lk 1:1, 2, 69, 71, 78, 79; 2:15, 48; 4:34, 34; 7:5, 16, 20; 9:13; 10:17; 11:1, 3, 4, 4, 4, 45; 12:41; 13:25; 16:26, 26; 17:5, 13; 20:6, 22, 28, 33; 22:9, 21, 38, 67; 23:15, 18, 39; 24:32, 32; Jn 1:14, 16, 18, 22, 22; 2:18; 3:2, 11, 26; 4:12, 25, 35, 42; 6:28, 30, 30, 30, 34, 52; 7:48; 8:25; 9:4, 4, 34; 10:24, 24; 14:8, 22; 15:24; 17:21; 21:20; Ac 1:17, 17, 21, 22, 22, 24, 25; 2:29, 33; 3:4, 12; 4:19; 5:4, 28; 6:14; 7:27, 35, 38, 40, 40, 40; 10:41, 42; 11:12, 13, 15, 17; 13:15, 26, 47; 15:8, 9, 24, 25, 28; 16:9, 10, 14, 15, 15, 17, 37, 37, 37, 37; 17:19, 27; 19:35; 20:5, 13, 14; 21:5, 11, 16, 16, 17, 18; 24:2, 2; 27:2, 6, 7, 16, 37; 28:2, 2, 2, 7, 7, 14, 15, 15; Ro 1:5, 12, 17, 17; 3:5, 5, 21, 24, 24, 25, 25; 4:3, 16, 24, 24, 24, 25; 5:1, 2, 3, 3, 4, 5, 5, 5, 6, 8, 8, 9, 11, 11, 17, 21; 6:1, 15; 7:5; 8:3, 3, 3, 4, 16, 16, 18, 23, 23, 23, 26, 26, 27, 31, 31, 32, 32, 32, 33, 33, 34, 34, 34, 34, 35, 35, 37, 38, 39; 9:16, 24, 29; 10:11; 11:33; 12:5, 5, 6; 14:10, 12, 19; 15:4, 4, 33; 1Co 1:30, 30; 2:10, 10, 12, 12, 13, 15; 3:5, 5, 5; 4:8, 9, 10, 11, 12, 12, 13; 5:7, 8; 8:1; 9:5, 10; 10:6, 11, 11; 12:1, 6, 7, 13, 30; 15:22, 43, 45, 51, 51, 57; 2Co 1:3, 4, 4, 5, 6, 10, 10, 11, 11, 13, 14, 14, 21, 21, 22, 22; 2:11, 14, 14, 14, 17, 17; 3:3, 6, 9, 12, 18, 18; 4:1, 5, 6, 7, 9, 14, 14, 17; 5:1, 4, 5, 5, 12, 14, 18, 18, 19, 20; 6:7, 8, 8, 8, 8, 8, 12, 12, 13; 7:1, 1, 2, 5, 6, 9, 10, 12; 8:4, 5, 7, 19; 10:8, 13; Gal 1:4, 23; 2:4, 4, 9, 17; 3:13, 21, 23, 24; 4:3, 5, 5, 29; 5:1, 5, 17, 22, 25, 26; Eph 1:3, 4, 4, 5, 5, 6, 8, 9, 11, 14, 14, 14, 19; 2:3, 4, 5, 6, 7, 7, 7, 9, 10, 10, 14, 14, 14, 17, 18, 18; 3:20; 4:6, 6, 6, 7, 14, 14; 6:8; Php 3:3, 9, 14; 4:19; Col 1:7, 8, 13, 13, 28; 2:14; 3:11, 14; 4:3, 3; 1Th 1:6, 8, 9, 10; 2:2, 2, 5, 15, 15, 16, 18, 19, 19; 3:3, 6, 8, 10, 11; 4:7; 5:8, 9, 9, 10, 25; 2Th 1:7; 2:1, 2, 13, 16, 16; 3:1, 9; 1Ti 4:1; 6:7, 7, 8, 17; 2Ti 1:7, 9, 9, 9, 10, 10, 14; 2:12; 3:16, 16, 16, 16, 17, 17; Tit 2:8, 14, 14, 14; 3:3, 4, 5, 5, 6, 7, 15; Phm 1:11; Heb 1:2, 3; 2:3, 3, 9, 17, 18; 4:2, 11, 12, 14, 16, 16; 6:1, 1, 18, 19, 20; 8:6; 9:26; 10:1, 10, 20, 20, 22, 22, 23, 25; 11:4, 40; 12:1, 1, 1, 1, 9, 10, 10, 25, 28; 13:13, 15, 18; Jas 1:17, 18, 18, 27; 4:5, 5, 6, 12, 15; 1Pe 1:3; 3:18; 2Pe 1:1, 1, 3, 3, 4; 3:11; 1Jn 1:2, 2, 3, 5, 7, 9, 9; 2:19, 19, 19, 19, 25; 3:1, 1, 16, 18, 18, 20, 23, 24, 24; 4:6, 6, 7, 9, 10, 11, 12, 12, 13, 13, 16, 18, 19; 5:6, 11, 14, 15, 19, 20; 2Jn 2, 3, 6, 6; 3Jn 10; Jude 4; Rev 1:5, 5, 5, 6; 6:10, 16, 16; 18:19; 19:7

WAS (4748)

Ge 1:2, 2, 3, 4, 7, 9, 10, 11, 12, 12, 15, 18, 21, 24, 25, 30, 31; 2:1, 3, 5, 20, 23; 3:1, 6, 6, 10, 10, 12; 4:2, 18, 18, 18, 18, 21, 22, 22, 26; 5:3, 3, 3, 6, 6, 9, 9, 12, 12, 15, 15, 18, 18, 21, 21, 25, 25, 28, 28, 32; 6:6, 9, 11; 7:6, 11, 23, 23; 8:7, 9, 11, 13, 13, 14, 21; 9:22, 29; 10:8, 9, 13, 15, 15, 21, 24, 24, 25, 25, 26, 32; 11:9, 9, 10, 10, 12, 12, 14, 14, 16, 16, 18, 18, 20, 20, 22, 22, 24, 24, 26, 27, 28, 28, 30; 12:4, 6, 10, 11, 15, 18, 19; 13:2, 4, 5, 5, 10, 10, 14; 14:10, 13; 15:12; 16:4, 14, 16; 17:1, 24, 25; 18:1, 1, 8, 10, 11, 15; 19:1, 14, 16, 22, 23, 26, 27, 30, 33, 35; 20:2; 21:4, 5, 8, 11, 15, 20, 31; 22:21, 21; 23:1, 10, 16, 17; 24:1, 2, 11, 15, 15, 15, 16, 16, 21, 30, 33, 36, 38, 38, 47, 62, 63, 67; 25:1, 10, 13, 20, 21, 25, 25, 25, 26, 26, 27, 29, 30; 26:7, 7, 7, 9, 9, 21; 27:1, 27, 33, 35, 42; 28:8, 9, 9, 17, 19; 29:3, 9, 9, 10, 12, 16, 17, 18, 20, 23, 25, 31, 31, 33; 30:16, 25, 36, 38; 31:4, 19, 24, 25, 31, 34, 39, 49; 32:6, 7, 13, 20, 31; 33:17; 34:3, 19; 35:3, 7, 8, 18, 19, 22; 36:3, 7, 22, 24, 25, 25, 35, 39; 37:2, 22, 24, 24, 25, 29, 35, 36; 38:7, 9, 11, 11, 11, 12, 14, 15, 15, 16, 21, 24, 29, 29, 30, 30; 39:1, 1, 2, 3, 5, 6, 11, 11, 12, 18, 19, 21, 23; 40:3, 11, 15; 41:1, 7, 12, 13, 13, 14, 17, 25, 43, 43, 46, 49, 54, 57; 42:1, 6, 6, 23, 35; 43:1, 2, 7, 12, 16, 17, 21, 30, 34; 44:2, 12, 14; 45:1, 2, 3, 8, 16, 26; 46:8, 10, 17, 20, 23, 26; 47:20, 22, 28; 48:1, 7, 10, 13, 13, 14, 14, 17; 49:28; 50:3, 4, 15, 22, 26; Ex 1:5; 2:2, 10, 12, 13, 14, 21; 3:1, 2, 2, 6; 4:3, 6, 7, 24, 26, 31; 6:15; 7:7, 7, 21; 8:24; 9:7, 25, 26, 31, 31; 10:14, 22, 23; 11:3, 3; 12:30, 30, 39, 41; 13:9, 16, 17, 19, 21; 14:12, 30; 15:23, 23, 25; 16:6, 13, 20, 20, 22, 24, 27, 27, 31, 36; 17:1, 6; 18:3, 3, 4, 4, 6, 9, 12, 14; 19:16, 16, 18; 20:21; 21:3, 3, 4, 29, 36; 22:3, 7, 8, 12, 13, 14, 15, 15; 29:23; 31:17; 33:7; 34:18, 28; 36:6, 9, 10, 13, 14, 15, 18, 19, 19, 21, 27, 27, 33, 35, 36, 37, 38; 37:1, 2, 6, 8, 11, 12, 20, 21, 24, 25, 25; 38:1, 1, 2, 7, 7, 9, 11, 12, 13, 14, 14, 14, 15, 15, 18, 18, 19, 22, 23, 24, 25, 25, 28, 30, 31; 39:1, 2, 7, 8, 9, 13, 21, 21, 22, 23, 26, 31, 32; 40:17, 35, 35, 38; Lev 7:20; 8:17, 21, 21, 22, 26, 28, 29, 30, 34; 10:3, 17, 18; 13:6; 14:30; 15:10; 17:15; 18:9; 21:3; 22:33; 23:15; 24:11, 11, 11, 18; 25:1; Nu 1:46; 3:1, 24, 30, 32, 35, 38, 38, 43; 4:37, 38, 41, 42, 45, 49, 49; 5:7, 8, 13; 7:3, 8, 10, 14, 17, 20, 23, 26, 29, 32, 35, 38, 41, 44, 47, 50, 53, 56, 59, 62, 65, 68, 71, 74, 77, 80, 83, 84, 84, 88, 88; 8:4, 4; 9:9, 15, 16; 10:15, 16, 17, 19, 20, 23, 24, 26, 27, 28, 36; 11:3, 10, 25, 25, 34; 12:3, 9, 15, 15; 13:22, 27; 14:16, 39; 15:24, 24, 25, 26, 33; 16:40, 48; 19:13, 15, 16, 18, 18; 20:1, 2, 9, 9, 13, 13, 14, 21; 21:24, 35; 22:5, 22, 22, 36; 23:6, 7, 18; 24:20; 25:3, 8, 13, 14, 15, 15, 18; 26:3, 8, 9, 36, 58, 59, 59, 62; 27:1, 1, 3; 31:12, 14, 47; 32:9, 10, 13; 33:14, 38, 39, 40; 35:1; 36:7; Dt 1:4, 14, 25, 37; 2:20, 34; 3:11, 11, 26; 4:11, 12, 14, 21, 46; 5:22, 23; 7:8, 8; 8:15, 17; 9:8, 9, 9, 9, 19, 20, 25; 10:6; 16:1; 19:6, 6; 21:6; 22:14, 17, 27; 25:10; 26:5, 5, 14; 29:24; 30:9; 32:19, 19, 27; 33:21; 34:6, 7, 7, 7, 8, 9, 12; Jos 1:5, 17; 2:7, 15; 3:7, 15, 15, 16; 4:11, 20; 5:12, 15; 6:1, 11, 27; 7:1, 1, 1, 15, 16, 17, 17, 18, 18, 26; 8:14, 17, 17, 18, 20, 21, 23, 25, 26, 33, 35; 9:12; 10:2, 27, 28, 32, 37, 42; 11:8, 11, 15, 22; 12:1, 2, 5; 13:1, 12, 21, 21, 27, 31, 31, 32; 14:5, 7, 11; 15:4, 6, 12, 13, 17, 20; 16:5, 9; 17:1, 1, 1, 1, 2, 3, 6, 10, 10; 18:1, 14, 17, 20, 20, 28; 19:1, 8, 9, 16, 23, 31, 39, 48, 49, 51; 20:3, 5, 6, 6; 21:11, 20; 22:7, 17, 20; 23:1; 24:12, 18, 32, 33; Jdg 1:13, 17, 19, 20, 22; 2:11, 18; 3:7, 9, 11, 12, 15, 15, 16, 17, 20, 24, 30, 30; 4:1, 2, 4, 12, 16, 17; 5:15, 16, 31; 6:1, 5, 6, 19, 20, 22, 27, 28, 29, 32, 40, 40; 7:8, 13, 19, 25; 8:20, 20, 26, 28, 32, 32, 33; 9:3, 21, 30, 30, 35, 40, 40, 51, 55; 10:1, 2, 2, 5, 16; 11:1, 1, 1, 12, 17, 23; 12:6, 7, 7, 10, 12, 14, 15; 13:1, 2, 6, 6, 9, 9, 16, 21, 24; 14:1, 4, 7, 10, 10, 17, 19, 20; 15:6, 15, 17, 18, 19, 20; 16:2, 9, 17, 21, 25, 26, 27, 31; 17:2, 8; 18:1, 4, 7, 20, 28, 31; 19:1, 2, 5, 8, 10, 11, 14, 16, 16, 26, 26, 27, 28; 20:5, 27, 28, 34, 39, 41; 21:5, 8, 9; Ru 1:2, 2, 3, 19; 2:1, 1, 4, 18; 3:7, 8, 14, 14; 4:7, 18, 19, 19, 20, 20, 21, 21, 22, 22; 1Sa 1:1, 1, 7, 9, 10, 12, 15, 18, 24; 2:13, 17, 18, 22, 22, 25; 3:1, 2, 3, 8, 8, 15, 19, 19, 20; 4:1, 1, 3, 4, 5, 6, 8, 10, 10, 11, 13, 15, 16, 18, 19; 5:4, 7, 9, 11, 12; 6:9, 9, 9; 7:6, 10, 13, 14; 8:6; 9:1, 1, 2, 10, 14, 24, 27; 10:20, 21, 21; 11:5, 9, 11; 12:2, 6, 12, 15; 13:1, 3, 10, 21; 14:1, 3, 3, 3, 3, 5, 5, 15, 18, 19, 20, 38, 39, 42, 43, 45, 47, 49, 50, 50, 52; 15:9, 11, 16, 24, 35; 16:12; 17:4, 7, 12, 12, 14, 20, 23, 28, 29, 31, 33, 39, 51; 18:1, 5, 6, 7, 12, 12, 12, 14, 16, 20, 25, 26, 28, 30; 19:2, 7, 9, 14, 16, 19; 20:7, 9, 25, 27, 33, 34, 41; 21:6, 6, 7, 8, 12; 22:2, 4, 6, 9, 9, 15, 17; 23:7, 15, 28; 24:1, 4; 25:2, 2, 3, 3, 3, 4, 7, 13, 15, 19, 20, 21, 36, 36, 37, 39; 26:3, 13; 27:11, 11; 28:3, 14, 20, 21; 30:6, 8, 13, 19; 31:4, 5; 2Sa 1:2, 21, 26; 2:10, 19, 24; 3:1, 2, 2, 3, 3, 3, 3, 4, 4, 4, 4, 5, 5, 11, 23, 37; 4:2, 4, 4, 4, 5, 10; 5:2, 4, 10, 17; 6:8, 9, 12, 16, 17, 21; 7:1; 8:14, 15, 16, 16, 17, 18; 9:1, 6, 6, 13; 10:2, 10, 14, 17; 11:3, 3, 5, 7, 17, 21, 26, 27, 27; 12:1, 1, 5, 18, 21, 22, 30, 30; 13:2, 3, 8, 11, 14, 14, 18, 18, 21, 32, 33; 14:6, 6, 25, 25, 26, 27, 27; 15:8, 10, 12, 23, 30, 31, 34; 16:1, 1, 5; 17:14, 23, 23, 24, 25, 25, 25, 27; 18:7, 24, 29, 29, 33; 19:1, 2, 8, 9, 18, 32, 32; 20:8, 12, 23, 24, 24, 25, 26; 21:1, 2, 5, 7, 8, 12, 16, 16, 16, 18, 19, 21; 22:19; 23:8, 8, 9, 10, 10, 11, 13, 13, 14, 18, 18, 19, 19, 19, 20, 21, 23, 23; 24:11, 11, 16, 16, 25; 1Ki 1:1, 4, 5, 6, 15, 15, 22, 26, 40, 42, 50, 51; 2:5, 5, 8, 10, 12, 13, 15, 25, 32, 34, 46; 3:4, 6, 10, 10, 17, 20, 21, 22, 24, 26; 4:1, 2, 3, 4, 5, 6, 6, 11, 15, 19, 24, 31; 5:1, 3, 7, 14; 6:1, 1, 2, 3, 5, 6, 7, 8, 10, 10, 15, 16, 16, 17, 18, 20, 24, 26, 30, 34, 36, 37, 38; 7:2, 2, 6, 6, 6, 7, 7, 12, 14, 14, 14, 17, 22, 23, 23, 24, 31, 31, 35, 36, 37, 38, 39; 8:9, 57, 64, 66; 9:12; 10:3, 4, 5, 5, 7, 21, 27; 11:6, 9, 17, 20, 25, 26, 26, 27, 28, 28, 29, 30, 43; 12:4, 10, 11, 14, 15, 18, 32; 13:1, 4, 11, 18, 24; 14:4, 21, 21, 21, 22, 22, 30, 31, 31; 15:2, 3, 5, 6, 7, 8, 10, 11, 16, 18, 18, 21, 24, 26, 29, 30, 32, 34; 16:1, 6, 7, 7, 9, 15, 19, 22, 25, 28, 30, 34; 17:1, 7, 11, 12, 16; 18:3, 3, 7, 10, 13, 26, 29, 45; 19:3, 5, 11, 11, 11, 11, 12, 12, 12, 19; 20:34, 39, 40; 21:1, 3, 13, 17, 25, 26, 28; 22:1, 33, 35, 36, 37, 38, 40, 42, 42, 43, 43, 47, 50, 52; 2Ki 1:2, 3, 7, 8, 8; 2:1, 11, 17, 18, 23; 3:2, 2, 9, 13, 15, 20, 20, 20, 22, 25, 26, 27; 4:5, 6, 18, 18, 28, 31, 32, 38, 38, 44; 5:1, 2, 14, 26, 27, 27; 6:5, 5, 8, 17, 25, 26, 30, 32, 33; 7:5, 10, 10, 16, 17, 20; 8:4, 5, 6, 6, 16, 17, 18, 18, 19, 24, 25, 26, 26, 27, 27, 28, 29; 9:4, 16, 16, 27, 27; 10:10, 11, 12, 15, 17, 19, 35; 11:1, 2, 13, 14, 16, 20, 21; 12:1, 2, 13, 14, 15, 16, 16, 16, 21; 13:2, 3, 4, 7, 9, 11, 13, 14, 15, 19, 20, 23; 14:2, 2, 3, 5, 7, 12, 16, 19, 20, 24, 29; 15:2, 2, 3, 5, 7, 9, 18, 24, 28, 33, 33, 34, 35, 38; 16:2, 2, 10, 11, 20; 17:2, 3, 18, 23, 26; 18:2, 2, 3, 4, 5, 7, 7, 9, 22; 19:8, 9, 22, 25, 37; 20:13, 19; 21:1, 1, 2, 6, 8, 16, 16, 18, 19, 19, 20, 26; 22:1, 1, 2, 2, 11, 14; 23:8, 16, 23, 27, 29, 31, 31, 32, 34, 36, 36, 37; 24:8, 8, 9, 18, 18, 19; 25:2, 4, 4, 6, 8, 16, 17, 17, 17, 19, 25, 27; 1Ch 1:10, 10, 11, 13, 13, 18, 18, 19, 19, 20, 34, 36, 39, 41, 46, 50; 2:3, 8, 10, 10, 11, 11, 12, 12, 13, 13, 13, 14, 14, 15, 15, 20, 20, 21, 22, 26, 31, 36, 36, 37, 37, 38, 38, 39, 39, 40, 40, 41, 41, 42, 42, 44, 44, 44, 45, 45, 46; 3:1, 1, 1, 1, 2, 2, 2, 2, 3, 3, 3, 3, 5, 16, 16, 17, 21, 21, 21, 21; 4:2, 2, 9, 9, 10, 11, 11, 12, 12, 14, 14, 15, 18, 18, 19, 19, 19, 21, 33, 40; 5:1, 1, 2, 6, 12, 12, 15, 22; 6:4, 4, 5, 5, 6, 6, 7, 7, 8, 8, 9, 9, 10, 11, 11, 12, 12, 13, 13, 14, 14, 33, 33, 39, 39, 44, 44, 60; 7:2, 2, 3, 4, 5, 7, 10, 12, 14, 15, 15, 16, 17, 25, 40; 8:29, 30, 32, 33, 33, 33, 34, 34, 35, 36, 36, 36, 37, 37, 37, 37; 9:1, 4, 11, 17, 19, 23, 27, 27, 30, 31, 35, 36, 38, 39, 39, 39, 40, 40, 42, 42, 42, 43, 43, 43, 43; 10:4, 5, 13; 11:2, 9, 11, 11, 12, 13, 15, 15, 16, 20, 20, 21, 21, 21, 22, 23, 23, 25, 25; 12:1, 3, 3, 8, 9, 9, 9, 10, 10, 11, 11, 12, 12, 13, 13, 20, 40; 13:4, 11, 12; 14:8, 11; 15:22, 26, 27, 27, 29; 17:1; 18:13, 14, 15, 15, 16, 17; 19:2, 11, 17; 20:2, 2, 5, 7; 21:6, 7, 9, 15, 15, 20, 30, 30; 23:1, 11, 11, 27, 28, 29; 24:3, 3, 20, 20, 21, 22, 22, 23, 23, 23, 23, 24, 24, 25, 26, 28, 29, 31; 25:7; 26:1, 10, 13, 14, 21, 24, 24, 31, 31; 27:2, 2, 3, 3, 4, 4, 4, 5, 5, 6, 6, 7, 7, 7, 8, 8, 9, 9, 10, 10, 11, 11, 12, 12, 13, 13, 14, 14, 15, 15, 24, 25, 25, 26, 27, 27, 28, 28, 29, 29, 30, 30, 31, 32, 32, 33, 33, 34, 34; 28:2, 4, 19; 29:9; 2Ch 1:1, 3, 3, 5, 15; 2:3; 3:1, 3, 4, 4, 5, 8, 8, 8, 11, 11, 13; 4:2, 2, 3, 10; 5:10; 8:1, 3, 16, 16; 9:2, 3, 4, 4, 6, 18, 20, 27, 31; 10:4, 10, 11, 14, 15, 18; 11:18; 12:1, 12, 12, 13, 13, 14, 16; 13:2, 6, 7; 14:1, 1, 2, 6, 6; 15:2, 3, 5, 6, 9, 19; 16:2, 5, 14, 14; 17:3, 6, 14, 15, 16, 18; 18:32, 34; 20:2, 3, 14, 14, 25, 30, 31, 31, 32, 32, 35; 21:1, 3, 5, 6, 6, 7, 17, 18, 20, 20, 20; 22:2, 2, 4, 7, 8, 9, 9, 9, 10; 23:12, 21; 24:1, 1, 2, 9, 11, 14, 16, 22, 24, 25; 25:1, 1, 2, 3, 5, 20, 22, 27, 28; 26:3, 3, 4, 10, 19, 19, 19, 20, 21, 23; 27:1, 1, 2, 6, 8, 9; 28:1, 1, 9, 9, 19, 27; 29:1, 1, 2, 6, 17, 19, 27, 34, 35, 35; 30:3, 12, 18, 26; 31:7, 11, 12, 14, 14, 20, 21; 32:5, 14, 22, 27, 31, 33; 33:1, 2, 6, 13, 14, 14, 20, 21, 22; 34:1, 2, 2, 3, 14, 17, 19, 22; 35:10, 16, 24; 36:2, 3, 5, 5, 9, 9, 10, 11, 12, 13, 16, 21; Ezr 2:63; 3:6, 8; 4:7, 15, 23; 5:5, 5, 11, 11; 6:2, 2, 3, 14, 15, 16, 21, 22; 7:1, 1, 6, 6, 9, 10, 28; 8:18, 18, 18, 22, 34, 34, 35; 9:11; 10:6, 7, 9, 16, 24; Ne 1:1, 11; 2:1, 2, 8, 10, 12, 16; 3:2, 3, 6, 8, 8, 9, 10, 12, 14, 16, 17, 20, 24, 29; 4:1, 3, 6, 7, 10; 5:6, 14, 15; 6:8, 10, 15, 18, 18, 19; 7:1, 2, 4, 4, 5, 65; 8:8, 15, 17; 9:3, 28; 10:1; 11:9, 9, 12, 14, 17, 20, 22, 24; 12:8, 10, 10, 10, 11, 11, 12, 12, 12, 13, 13, 14, 14, 15, 15, 16, 16, 17, 17, 17, 18, 18, 19, 19, 20, 20, 21, 21, 22; 13:1, 3, 4, 6, 10, 13, 21, 26, 26, 31, 31; Est 1:5, 5, 6, 7, 8, 10, 11; 2:4, 5, 5, 5, 7, 8, 9, 11, 12, 12, 13, 14, 14, 15, 15, 16, 17, 20, 20, 21, 23, 23, 23; 3:4, 5, 6, 6, 7, 13, 14, 15; 4:2, 3, 4, 5, 5; 5:1, 9, 9; 7:7, 8, 10; 8:1, 9, 12, 13, 14; 9:2, 11, 14, 17, 22, 32; 10:3, 3; Job 1:1, 1, 3, 5, 16, 17, 18; 2:13; 3:3, 16; 4:12, 16; 8:4; 10:12, 13, 14; 15:19; 16:12; 18:21; 20:11, 20; 29:4, 5, 14, 16, 24; 30:25; 31:19; 32:2, 2, 3; 33:6, 27; 36:21; 38:21; 42:3, 7, 8; Ps 3:5; 18:18; 22:9, 10, 10; 30:6, 7; 31:21; 32:3, 4; 35:14; 37:25; 42:4; 44:3, 3, 3; 51:5; 63:T; 66:14; 73:2, 13, 22; 74:8; 77:2, 19; 78:21, 30, 35, 35, 38, 46, 59, 62; 81:7, 10; 83:5; 95:10; 105:17, 21, 38, 38; 106:9, 30, 39; 107:18, 30; 116:6; 119:71; 122:1; 126:1; 132:6; 133:2; 139:15, 15, 16, 16, 16; Pr 4:3; 7:6, 8, 8, 9, 11, 15, 23; 8:23, 24, 25, 27, 28, 29, 30, 30, 31; 24:31, 31; 26:19; Ecc 1:12, 17; 2:1, 11, 11, 11, 20; 4:14; 5:6; 6:10; 7:25; 9:14, 15, 15; 12:9; SS 3:2, 10; 5:2, 2, 6, 6; 8:1; Isa 6:1, 4; 7:1, 1, 17; 8:2; 10:26; 12:1; 14:6, 29; 16:8; 20:2; 23:7, 17; 29:16; 36:7; 37:8, 9, 23, 26, 38; 38:9, 12, 13, 13, 17; 39:2, 8; 41:26, 27; 42:24, 24; 43:7; 45:10, 21; 47:6; 48:3, 5, 13; 49:21; 50:1, 2; 51:2; 52:14; 53:2, 3, 3, 4, 4, 5, 5, 5, 7, 7, 8, 8, 9, 9, 10, 12; 57:17; 58:2; 59:15, 15, 16; 63:3, 5; Jer 2:3; 3:24; 4:23, 23; 7:14, 22; 13:7, 7; 14:1; 15:17; 18:4; 20:1, 13, 14, 18; 22:11, 15, 30; 24:2, 2; 25:1, 5; 26:6, 10, 20, 21; 29:2; 30:18; 31:18, 19, 19; 32:1, 2, 2, 8, 31; 33:1, 11; 34:7, 9, 14, 15; 35:1, 4; 36:1, 10, 12, 13, 22, 22, 23; 37:1, 13, 13, 16, 21, 21, 21; 38:1, 6, 6, 7, 7, 12, 13, 28; 39:1, 5, 14, 15; 40:11; 41:1, 9; 44:22; 46:2; 47:1; 48:1, 13, 27; 49:1, 7, 14, 23, 28; 51:5, 59; 52:1, 1, 2, 5, 7, 7, 9, 12, 20, 21, 22, 22, 25, 28, 31; La 1:7; 2:8; 4:18, 20; 5:7; Eze 1:1, 13, 20, 21, 22, 26, 26, 26, 28, 28; 3:13, 14; 4:14; 6:10; 8:3, 4, 11; 9:2, 3, 8; 10:4, 14, 14, 14, 14, 17, 20; 11:13; 12:7; 13:16; 16:3, 4, 15, 20, 46, 46, 47, 50; 17:8; 18:18; 19:4, 10, 12, 12; 20:12; 23:4, 4, 8, 10, 11, 13, 18, 19, 41; 24:21; 25:3; 27:12, 25, 32; 28:13, 15, 17; 29:7, 16, 20; 31:3, 3, 4, 4, 7, 9; 33:24; 36:17, 21; 37:1, 7; 38:17; 39:23, 23; 40:3, 5, 5, 6, 7, 7, 9, 11, 12, 13, 14, 15, 18, 19, 20, 21, 22, 23, 23, 25, 25, 27, 27, 29, 38, 43, 48, 49, 49; 41:2, 2, 3, 4, 5, 5, 5, 7, 8, 8, 9, 11, 12, 13, 14, 15, 17, 18, 22, 25; 42:2, 5, 6, 7, 7, 9, 11, 11, 12, 16, 18, 19, 20; 43:2, 3, 6; 44:1; 46:22, 23; 47:3, 4, 4, 5; Da 1:3, 7, 7, 7, 7, 10, 18; 2:5, 12, 19, 26, 29, 32, 34, 36; 3:19, 24, 27, 27; 4:4, 8, 10, 12, 12, 18, 19, 21, 29, 31, 33, 33, 33, 33, 36; 5:2, 10, 11, 13, 13, 20, 21, 21, 21, 25, 29, 29, 29, 30; 6:4, 4, 14, 17, 20, 23, 23; 7:4, 4, 4, 5, 6, 7, 7, 8, 8, 9, 11, 11, 12, 13, 14, 15, 19, 20, 20, 21, 21, 28, 28, 28; 8:2, 3, 5, 7, 7, 8, 12, 12, 12, 15, 17, 18, 27, 27; 9:1, 2, 21, 23, 23; 10:4, 6, 8, 15; 12:6, 7; Hos 1:1; 2:3, 3, 7, 8, 15; 8:6; 9:10, 10; 10:9; 11:1, 3, 3;

12:3; 13:15; Joel 1:4; 2:25; Am 1:1, 1, 1; 2:10; 4:8; 5:25, 26; 6:5; 7:1, 1, 2, 4, 7, 7, 10; Ob 1; Jnh 1:4, 5, 10, 11, 13, 17; 2:3, 5, 6; 3:6; 4:6; Hab 3:1, 8; Zep 1:1, 1; 2:14; Hag 1:15; 2:3, 18; Zec 1:2, 8, 9, 11, 15, 19; 2:3, 3; 3:1, 3; 5:5, 7, 7; 6:2, 4; 7:5, 12; 8:9, 10; 11:7, 11, 11, 14; 13:6; Mal 1:2; 2:4, 5; 3:16; Mt 1:2, 2, 2, 3, 3, 3, 3, 4, 4, 4, 5, 5, 5, 5, 5, 6, 6, 6, 7, 7, 7, 8, 8, 8, 9, 9, 9, 10, 10, 10, 11, 12, 12, 13, 13, 13, 14, 14, 14, 15, 15, 15, 16, 16, 18, 18, 18, 25; 2:1, 3, 3, 9, 12, 16, 22, 22, 22, 23; 3:1, 4; 4:1, 18; 6:29; 8:10, 12, 13, 14, 18, 24, 26, 30; 9:9, 18, 22, 25, 28, 32; 11:2, 2; 12:1, 4, 16, 22, 22, 23, 40, 46; 13:8, 54; 14:5, 5, 9, 10, 11, 13, 14, 23, 26, 30; 15:7, 24, 28, 31; 16:7, 11, 20; 17:12, 14, 18; 18:24, 27; 19:8; 20:3, 4, 6, 17, 17, 30; 21:4, 9, 10, 18, 18, 25, 25, 26, 26, 31, 45; 22:3, 3, 10, 26, 28; 24:1, 37, 39, 43; 25:5, 10, 14, 21, 25, 35, 35, 35, 36, 36, 36, 42, 42, 43, 43, 43; 26:6, 20, 47, 55, 58, 58, 60, 69, 71; 27:3, 9, 11, 15, 16, 19, 24, 32, 37, 47, 51, 54, 57, 63; 28:1, 2, 3, 5, 6, 12; Mk 1:4, 4, 6, 9, 13, 13, 14, 16, 23, 30, 34, 42; 2:2, 2, 23, 26, 26, 27; 3:2, 5, 9, 12, 20, 21, 31, 32; 4:1, 8, 10, 34, 36, 37, 38, 39; 5:2, 4, 4, 4, 6, 15, 20, 22, 25, 26, 35, 40, 42; 6:6, 15, 15, 19, 19, 20, 20, 21, 26, 26, 34, 47, 49; 7:6, 24, 25, 26, 30, 30, 32; 8:11, 14, 16, 25; 9:2, 8, 13, 21, 25, 28, 32, 34; 10:6, 10, 14, 14, 17, 20, 32, 32, 46, 46, 46, 47; 11:9, 11, 13, 13, 20, 27, 30, 31, 32, 32; 12:5, 6, 12, 28, 35; 13:1; 14:1, 3, 4, 43, 49, 51, 53, 66; 15:6, 7, 21, 21, 25, 26, 35, 38, 39, 41, 43, 44, 47; 16:6, 9, 9, 11, 13, 19; Lk 1:5, 5, 5, 7, 8, 8, 9, 9, 10, 11, 12, 19, 21, 23, 27, 36, 41, 57, 57, 59, 67; 2:2, 2, 4, 5, 7, 13, 16, 21, 21, 21, 22, 24, 25, 25, 25, 28, 33, 36, 36, 36, 36, 37, 38, 40, 42, 43, 44, 46, 51, 52; 3:1, 1, 1, 1, 1, 2, 15, 21, 21, 23, 23, 23, 24, 24, 24, 24, 24, 25, 25, 25, 25, 25, 26, 26, 26, 26, 26, 27, 27, 27, 27, 27, 28, 28, 28, 28, 28, 29, 29, 29, 29, 29, 30, 30, 30, 30, 30, 31, 31, 31, 31, 31, 32, 32, 32, 32, 32, 33, 33, 33, 33, 33, 33, 34, 34, 34, 34, 34, 35, 35, 35, 35, 35, 36, 36, 36, 36, 36, 37, 37, 37, 37, 37, 38, 38, 38, 38; 4:1, 2, 15, 17, 25, 26, 26, 29, 33, 41, 43; 5:1, 9, 17, 17, 26; 6:1, 4, 6, 6, 19; 7:2, 9, 12, 12, 18, 29, 37, 39, 39, 39; 8:5, 23, 24, 27, 27, 29, 30, 32, 35, 42, 42, 43, 49, 52; 9:7, 11, 18, 29, 31, 33, 34, 36, 43, 43, 45, 46; 10:21, 30, 30, 36, 36, 40, 40; 11:14, 16, 27, 30, 37, 38, 48, 51; 12:27, 39; 13:1, 6, 6, 10, 11, 14; 14:1, 2, 17, 17, 21, 30; 15:2, 4, 6, 16, 20, 24, 24, 25, 26, 27, 28, 32, 32; 16:1, 7, 19, 19, 22, 22; 17:15, 16, 28; 18:2, 2, 10, 10, 21, 23, 34, 34, 35, 36, 37; 19:2, 2, 3, 11, 11, 12, 13, 21; 20:1, 4, 5, 6, 6, 11, 12, 12, 19; 21:1; 22:1, 3, 5, 37, 44, 49, 53, 54, 56, 66; 23:7, 7, 8, 19, 26, 26, 38, 44, 45, 45, 47, 50, 50, 51, 54, 55, 56; 24:16, 19, 19, 21, 23, 24, 29, 35, 36, 37, 44, 46, 51, 51; Jn 1:1, 1, 2, 4, 8, 8, 9, 10, 11, 14, 15, 17, 19, 28, 30, 31, 33, 35, 39, 40, 41, 44; 2:1, 9, 11, 13, 22, 23; 3:23, 23, 24, 24, 26; 4:6, 8, 9, 27, 46, 46, 47, 47, 51, 51, 53, 54; 5:2, 9, 10, 15; 6:4, 6, 6, 46, 59, 71; 7:2, 12, 28, 39, 42, 43; 8:2, 3, 4, 9, 20, 20, 27, 38, 44, 56, 58; 9:1, 2, 2, 3, 3, 9, 15, 16, 19, 20, 22, 25; 10:22, 22, 23, 36, 40; 11:1, 2, 6, 13, 17, 18, 20, 31, 33, 33, 38, 38, 49, 51, 52, 55; 12:2, 3, 5, 6, 6, 11, 12, 16, 18, 21, 29, 30, 33, 36, 41, 41; 13:2, 12, 21, 23, 29, 29; 16:4; 17:12, 13; 18:4, 5, 14, 15, 15, 18, 25, 28, 36, 37, 40; 19:8, 14, 20, 20, 20, 23, 28, 29, 31, 31, 33, 41, 41, 42, 42; 20:1, 7, 11, 14, 15, 19, 24, 26, 26; 21:4, 7, 9, 9, 12, 14, 17; Ac 1:3, 4, 9, 9, 16, 16, 17, 20, 22, 22, 26; 2:2, 4, 6, 16, 29, 30, 31, 31, 32; 3:2, 2, 10, 11, 16, 17, 18; 4:3, 6, 9, 10, 14, 21, 32, 33, 34, 36, 36; 5:1, 2, 4, 4, 5, 8, 8, 10, 23, 23, 33, 34, 34, 34, 36, 36, 37, 37; 6:7, 9, 10; 7:2, 8, 8, 8, 9, 11, 12, 20, 22, 23, 31, 35, 38, 38, 42, 43, 44, 45, 45, 47; 8:1, 3, 8, 11, 13, 13, 18, 28, 28, 32, 32, 33, 33, 34; 9:1, 1, 3, 8, 10, 18, 19, 22, 24, 26, 28, 34, 36, 36, 38, 39, 41; 10:1, 2, 2, 7, 9, 10, 10, 11, 16, 16, 17, 18, 18, 19, 24, 29, 30, 30, 33, 38, 44; 11:5, 5, 10, 11, 15, 17, 21, 23, 24, 26, 28, 28; 12:4, 5, 6, 6, 7, 9, 9, 14, 18, 20, 21, 23, 24; 13:8, 12, 25, 36, 37, 46; 14:3, 9, 12, 12, 12, 13, 14; 15:12, 31, 39; 16:1, 1, 2, 3, 10, 14, 14, 14, 15, 16, 23, 26, 26; 17:1, 2, 3, 13, 16, 16, 23, 27; 18:3, 19, 22; 19:1, 4, 13, 17, 19, 29, 32, 33, 34, 35; 20:1, 3, 7, 7, 8, 12, 12, 16, 31; 21:3, 7, 14, 30, 30, 31, 33, 37; 22:2, 3, 6, 11, 12, 12, 17, 20, 20, 29, 29, 30; 23:5, 9, 27, 27, 29, 30, 34; 24:2, 6, 9, 10, 11, 18, 18, 22, 24, 25, 27; 25:3, 4, 14, 15, 19, 20; 26:4, 11, 12, 19; 27:2, 2, 2, 3, 6, 7, 9, 9, 12, 12, 16, 20, 27, 28, 36, 41; 28:2, 3, 5, 6, 7, 8, 11, 12, 16, 16, 17, 23, 25; Ro 1:2, 4, 13, 20, 21, 21, 25; 3:19, 25; 4:1, 2, 9, 10, 10, 10, 10, 11, 11, 12, 13, 19, 21, 21, 24, 25, 25; 5:13, 13, 14, 20; 6:4, 5, 20, 21, 21; 7:4, 7, 9, 10, 13; 8:20, 34; 9:5, 10, 12, 14, 20; 10:20; 11:11, 24, 30; 16:5; 1Co 1:13, 23; 2:4, 7; 3:1, 6, 6; 5:11; 6:11, 19; 7:18, 18; 9:9, 10; 10:4, 5, 25; 11:9, 9, 23; 13:11; 15:2, 3, 4, 4, 5, 6, 7, 10, 10, 14, 23, 32, 46, 47; 16:12; 2Co 1:15, 23; 2:4, 6; 3:7, 9, 10, 11; 5:15, 19; 7:5, 5, 5, 7, 7, 7, 8, 8, 9, 12, 12, 13, 14; 8:5, 9, 9, 17, 19; 9:2, 3; 11:3, 9, 25, 25, 25, 32, 33; 12:2, 3, 4, 7, 12, 13, 16, 16; 13:2; Gal 1:1, 13, 14, 15, 17, 18, 19, 23; 2:2, 3, 6, 10, 11, 11, 12, 13, 21; 3:4, 4, 13, 16, 16, 19, 19, 19, 19, 19, 23, 24; 4:3, 11, 13, 14, 23, 23, 29; Eph 1:12; 2:15, 16; 3:8, 9, 10, 11; 5:2, 2; Php 1:7, 7; 2:6, 12, 16, 25, 26, 26, 27, 30; 3:5, 5, 5, 5, 6; 4:11, 16; Col 1:7, 19, 26; 2:11, 13; 3:7; 1Th 1:5, 5, 5; 2:1, 13; 3:5, 5; 4:14; 2Th 2:5; 1Ti 1:14, 15; 2:14, 14, 14; 3:16, 16, 16, 16, 16; 5:9; 2Ti 1:9, 16, 16; 2:8, 8; 3:11; 4:16, 16; Tit 1:9; Heb 2:3, 3, 9, 10, 10, 17; 3:2, 2, 5, 5, 6, 10, 18, 18; 4:2, 8; 5:4, 5, 7, 8; 6:13, 13; 7:1, 1, 4, 4, 6, 10, 11, 11, 18, 18, 28; 8:2, 5; 9:2, 3, 3, 4, 8, 18, 22, 24; 10:1, 28, 34; 11:3, 4, 4, 5, 5, 5, 5, 7, 7, 8, 8, 9, 10, 11, 11, 11, 12, 17, 17, 17, 19, 20, 20, 21, 21, 22, 22, 22, 23, 24, 26, 26, 27, 27, 28, 29, 30, 31, 34; 12:2, 7, 17, 17, 21; Jas 2:21, 22, 22, 22, 23, 25; 5:17; 1Pe 1:10, 11, 18, 20, 25; 2:4, 7, 23; 3:18, 20; 4:6; 2Pe 1:21; 2:7, 7, 8, 8, 16; 3:4; 1Jn 1:2, 2, 2; 3:12, 12; 5:6; 2Jn 4; Jude 4, 9; Rev 1:1, 4, 8, 9, 10, 10, 12, 13, 13, 16; 2:13; 3:21; 4:2, 3, 6, 8; 5:1, 1, 1, 3, 4, 6, 12; 6:2, 4, 4, 5, 8, 8, 8, 11, 12, 14; 8:1, 3, 5, 7, 7, 8, 11, 11, 12, 12; 9:1, 8, 10, 17, 19; 10:2, 4, 10; 11:1, 1, 8, 13, 13, 17, 19, 19, 19; 12:2, 4, 4, 5, 5, 5, 7, 8, 9, 14; 13:3, 5, 5, 7, 7, 8, 8, 13, 14, 14, 15, 17; 14:2, 16; 15:1, 5, 8; 16:5, 6, 9, 10, 18, 19, 21, 21; 17:5, 6, 8, 11; 18:16, 24, 24; 19:4, 11, 11, 12, 13, 13, 16, 20, 21; 20:10, 11, 15, 15; 21:1, 11, 16, 16, 16, 18, 18, 19, 19, 21

WASN'T (30)

Ge 28:16; 30:1, 9, 15; 43:3; Ex 34:29; Dt 9:28; Jdg 9:38; 1Sa 30:12; 2Sa 11:21; 1Ki 3:21; Ne 13:18, 26; Jer 38:27; Mt 16:12; 17:12; 22:11; 27:24; Mk 2:2; Lk 13:16; 24:26; Jn 6:24; 11:15; Ac 2:29; Ro 4:23; 1Co 5:10; 9:10; 2Th 3:9; Heb 3:17; 7:10

WE (2351)

Ge 3:2, 3, 3, 3, 22; 12:12; 13:8, 9; 19:5, 9, 13, 32, 32; 20:12, 13; 22:5, 5, 7; 24:25, 25, 31, 50, 55; 26:22, 28, 28, 28, 29, 29, 29; 28:4; 29:5, 8, 15, 21; 31:44, 44, 49, 49; 33:14; 34:9, 9, 14, 15, 16, 17, 21, 23, 30, 30; 35:3; 37:7, 20, 22, 26, 32; 38:23, 23; 40:8; 41:12; 42:2, 7, 10, 11, 11, 21, 21, 21, 22, 22, 31, 31, 32; 43:3, 4, 5, 7, 7, 7, 8, 8, 8, 10, 18, 21, 21, 21, 21, 22, 22, 23; 44:7, 8, 8, 8, 16, 16, 16, 16, 16, 19, 20, 20, 22, 24, 26, 26, 26, 31; 46:34; 47:3, 4, 4, 15, 18, 19, 19; 48:7; 50:15, 17, 18; Ex 1:10, 10, 19; 5:3, 3, 3, 16, 16, 16, 17; 8:26, 26, 27; 10:9, 9, 25, 26, 26, 26; 12:33; 13:8, 15; 14:5, 12, 12; 15:24; 16:3, 3, 23; 17:3; 19:8; 20:19, 19; 24:3, 7, 7, 14; 32:1; 33:16; 36:5; Lev 25:20, 20; Nu 9:7, 7; 10:29, 29, 31, 32; 11:5, 5, 5, 5, 6, 18, 18, 20, 22, 22; 12:11; 13:27, 28, 30, 31, 31, 32, 32, 33, 33, 33; 14:2, 2, 7, 40, 40, 40; 16:7, 12, 14; 17:12, 12, 13; 20:3, 3, 10, 14, 15, 16, 16, 17, 17, 17, 17, 19, 19, 19; 21:2, 5, 7, 22, 22, 22, 30, 30; 31:49, 50, 50; 32:5, 16, 17, 17, 17, 18, 19, 19, 19, 25, 31, 32; Dt 1:6, 19, 19, 22, 28, 28, 41, 41; 2:1, 1, 8, 8, 13, 14, 14, 27, 28, 28, 28, 28, 29, 33, 34, 35, 35, 37; 3:1, 3, 4, 5, 6, 6, 6, 6, 7, 8, 10, 12, 29; 4:7; 5:2, 24, 24, 24, 25, 25, 27; 6:21, 25, 25; 7:17, 17; 9:4; 17:14; 18:21; 21:7; 26:7; 29:7, 7, 8, 16, 16, 16, 29; 30:12, 13; Jos 1:16, 16, 17, 17; 2:9, 10, 10, 14, 14, 17, 19, 19, 20; 4:6, 23; 7:7; 8:5, 6; 9:6, 7, 7, 8, 9, 9, 10, 12, 13, 19, 19, 20, 20, 21, 24, 24, 24, 24, 25; 14:6, 12; 22:17, 19, 22, 22, 23, 23, 23, 24, 24, 26, 27, 31, 31; 23:4; 24:15, 16, 17, 18, 21, 22, 24, 24; Jdg 1:3, 24; 5:28; 8:6, 15, 15; 9:28, 28, 38; 10:10, 10, 15; 11:8, 8, 10, 23, 24; 12:1; 13:15, 17, 22, 22; 14:15; 15:10, 12, 13, 13; 16:2; 18:9, 14; 19:12, 12, 13, 18, 18, 19, 19, 19, 22, 30; 20:9, 13, 23, 28, 28, 32, 39; 21:5, 6, 7, 7, 8, 16, 18, 18, 22, 22, 22; Ru 1:10; 3:18; 4:11; 1Sa 2:36; 4:3, 7, 9; 5:7, 7, 8; 6:2, 4, 9, 9, 20; 8:19, 20; 9:7, 7, 8; 10:14, 14, 14, 19; 11:1, 3, 9, 10, 12; 12:10, 10, 19, 19; 14:8, 9, 10, 30, 37, 38; 15:15; 16:11; 17:8, 9, 58; 18:22; 20:5, 8, 18, 42, 42; 21:4, 15; 23:3, 19, 20; 25:7, 8, 15, 21, 35; 27:5; 28:2; 30:14, 14, 24; 2Sa 2:26, 26, 27; 5:1; 7:22; 11:23; 12:18, 21; 13:25, 25; 14:7, 14; 15:14, 14, 14, 15, 20; 17:6, 12, 12, 13; 18:3, 3, 12; 19:5, 5, 6, 10, 42, 43, 43; 20:1, 1, 6, 21, 21; 21:4, 6, 17; 1Ki 1:2; 3:18; 5:9, 9; 8:30, 47; 11:22; 12:4, 16; 18:5, 5; 20:14, 23, 25, 25, 31; 22:3, 15, 30; 2Ki 2:19; 3:8, 8, 10, 11; 4:13, 13, 14; 6:1, 2, 8, 13, 15, 22, 28, 29, 29; 7:3, 4, 4, 4, 4, 4, 4, 9, 9, 12, 13; 9:15; 10:4, 5, 5, 13, 13; 18:22, 25, 26; 22:13, 13; 1Ch 11:1; 12:17, 18, 18; 13:3; 15:2, 13; 16:35; 17:20; 29:11, 13, 14, 14, 14, 15, 16; 2Ch 2:16; 6:21, 37; 10:4, 16; 13:10, 11; 14:7, 11, 11; 18:3, 5, 14, 29; 20:9, 9, 9, 12, 12, 12; 24:5; 28:13; 29:18, 19; 31:10; 32:8; 34:21, 21; Ezr 4:2, 2, 3, 3, 13, 14, 14, 14, 15, 16, 22; 5:8, 8, 9, 10, 10, 11, 11, 17; 7:15, 15, 19, 23; 8:15, 21, 21, 22, 23, 31, 32, 32; 9:7, 7, 7, 8, 9, 9, 10, 10, 11, 12, 12, 12, 13, 13, 13, 14, 15; 10:2, 2, 2, 3, 3, 4, 10, 10, 12, 13; Ne 1:6, 7, 10; 2:12, 20; 4:1, 4, 9, 10, 11, 15, 15, 19, 21, 23, 23; 5:2, 2, 2, 2, 3, 4, 5, 5, 5, 5, 8, 8, 12, 12, 18; 6:1, 15; 9:5, 32, 33, 33, 36, 36, 37, 37, 38; 10:30, 31, 31, 31, 32, 34, 35, 36, 36, 37, 37, 37, 39; 12:39, 41; Est 1:19; 6:3; 7:4; Job 2:10; 5:27; 8:9; 14:2, 2, 5, 5, 6; 15:9, 9; 17:16; 18:3, 3; 21:14, 15, 15; 28:22; 36:26; 37:5, 19, 20, 20, 21, 23; Ps 10:6; 12:4, 7; 13:4; 20:5, 5, 7, 8; 21:13, 13; 33:20, 21; 35:21, 25, 25, 25; 36:9; 39:6, 6; 44:1, 5, 5, 8, 13, 14, 15, 16, 16, 17, 18, 20, 22, 22, 25; 46:2; 48:1, 8, 8, 9, 9, 14; 54:T; 55:14, 14; 60:12; 64:6; 65:1; 66:12; 74:2, 9; 75:1, 1; 78:3, 4, 4; 79:4, 8, 13; 80:3, 7, 8, 9, 11, 14, 16, 18, 18, 19; 83:4; 90:7, 7, 9, 9, 10, 12, 14; 95:7; 100:3, 3; 103:10, 14, 14, 15, 16, 16; 106:6, 6, 6, 47; 108:13; 115:18; 118:24, 26; 122:2; 123:2, 3, 4; 124:7, 7; 126:2, 2; 129:8; 130:4; 132:6, 6; 137:1, 1, 2, 4; 144:4; Pr 10:7; 16:1, 9, 33; 20:24, 24; 21:3, 3; Ecc 1:8, 8, 8, 8, 11, 11; 6:12; 12:14; SS 1:4, 4, 11, 16; 6:1, 13; 8:8, 8, 9, 9; Isa 1:9; 2:3; 4:1, 1; 5:19; 7:6, 6; 9:10, 10; 10:9, 9, 9, 9, 10, 11, 11; 14:10, 32; 16:6; 20:6, 6; 22:13; 25:9, 9; 26:1, 8, 12, 13, 14, 15, 16, 16, 17, 17, 18, 18, 19; 27:2; 28:9, 9, 15; 29:11, 12; 30:10, 11, 11, 16; 33:2, 24; 36:7, 10, 11; 40:18, 18; 42:24; 48:7; 49:20; 53:3, 3, 4, 5, 5, 6; 56:12; 58:3, 3; 59:9, 9, 9, 10, 10, 10, 11, 11, 11, 11, 12, 12, 13, 13, 13, 13, 13; 63:17, 17, 19, 19; 64:5, 5, 6, 6, 6, 6, 8, 8, 9, 9; Jer 2:23, 31, 31; 3:22, 24, 25, 25; 5:4; 6:16, 17, 24, 24, 25; 7:10; 8:8, 8, 14, 14, 15, 15, 20; 9:19, 19; 13:12; 14:7, 9, 19, 19, 20, 20, 22; 15:2; 16:10; 17:12; 18:12, 12, 18, 18; 20:10, 10; 21:13; 26:19; 29:28, 28, 28; 35:4, 6, 8, 8, 9, 10, 11, 11, 11; 36:16, 16; 38:4, 25; 40:15; 42:2, 2, 5, 6, 6, 6, 6, 13, 20; 43:3; 44:16, 17, 17, 17, 17, 17, 17, 17, 18, 18, 19; 46:16; 48:2, 14, 29, 29; 49:29; 50:7; 51:9, 9, 51, 51; La 2:12, 16, 16; 3:22, 39, 39, 42, 47, 47; 4:17, 17, 18, 18, 19, 19, 20, 20; 5:1, 3, 4, 5, 6, 7, 9, 16, 21; Eze 11:3; 20:32; 33:10, 10, 24; 35:10, 10; 37:11; 42:1; Da 1:13; 2:4, 7, 23; 3:16, 17, 17, 18, 24, 24; 6:7; 9:5, 5, 6, 8, 8, 9, 10, 10, 13, 14, 15, 18, 18; Hos 6:2, 3; 10:3, 3; 14:2, 3, 3; Joel 1:16; Am 6:13; 7:2, 5; Ob 1; Jnh 1:11; Mic 2:4; 4:2, 5; 5:5; 6:6, 6, 7, 7; Hab 1:14, 14, 15; Zec 1:6, 6, 11; 7:3, 3; 8:21, 23; Mal 1:4, 4, 6, 7; 2:10, 10, 10, 17; 3:7, 7, 8, 13, 14, 14, 15; Mt 2:2, 2; 3:15; 6:12; 7:22; 9:14, 28; 11:3, 17, 17; 12:38; 13:28, 51, 55; 14:17; 15:33; 17:19, 27; 19:27; 20:18, 22, 33; 21:25, 25, 26, 27; 22:16; 23:30; 25:9, 37, 39, 44; 26:65, 73; 27:4, 6, 25, 25, 42, 63, 64, 64; 28:13; Mk 1:38; 4:38; 6:38; 8:4; 9:5, 28, 38, 38; 10:33, 35, 37, 39; 11:31, 31, 32, 33; 12:14, 15, 15; 14:58, 63; 15:32; Lk 1:71, 74, 74; 3:10, 12, 14; 5:5, 26; 7:16, 19, 20, 32, 32; 9:13, 33, 49, 49, 54; 10:11, 17; 11:4, 7; 12:15; 13:7, 9, 26; 14:10; 15:23, 23, 27, 27, 30, 32; 17:5, 10, 10; 18:28, 31, 31; 20:5, 5, 6, 7, 21; 22:8, 38, 49, 49, 71, 71; 23:41; 24:21; Jn 1:14, 16, 22, 41, 45; 3:2, 11; 4:20, 22, 42, 42; 6:5, 14, 42, 68, 69, 69; 7:27, 46; 8:33, 33, 41, 48, 52; 9:20, 21, 24, 28, 29, 29, 40; 11:47, 48; 12:21, 34; 14:5, 5, 5, 8, 23; 16:18, 30, 30; 17:5, 11, 22; 18:30; 19:15; 20:25; 21:24; Ac 1:21, 21; 2:8, 8, 9, 11, 32, 37; 3:12, 15; 4:9, 16, 16, 17, 20, 20; 5:23, 28, 29, 32; 6:2, 3, 4, 11, 14; 7:40; 9:14, 21; 10:22, 33, 39, 41, 47; 11:6, 12, 17; 13:46; 14:15, 15; 15:10, 11, 11, 19, 20, 24, 27, 27, 36; 16:10, 10, 11, 11, 12, 12, 13, 13, 13, 15, 16, 16, 28, 37; 17:20, 28, 28, 29, 32; 19:2, 2, 40, 40; 20:6, 6, 7, 8, 13, 14, 15, 15, 15, 17; 21:1, 1, 2, 3, 4, 5, 5, 6, 7, 8, 12, 12, 14, 14, 15, 23, 25, 25; 23:9, 14, 14, 15; 24:3, 5, 6; 25:26; 26:14; 27:1, 2, 3, 4, 4, 5, 7, 7, 7, 8, 9, 10, 16, 16, 17, 26, 27, 29, 37; 28:1, 1, 1, 7, 10, 10, 11, 12, 13, 13, 14, 14, 15, 16, 20, 21, 21, 22, 22; Ro 2:2; 3:8, 9, 9, 20, 20, 22, 22, 22, 22, 22, 25, 25, 27, 27, 28, 31, 31, 31, 31; 4:9, 16, 16, 16, 24; 5:1, 1, 2, 2, 3, 3, 3, 5, 6, 8, 9, 10, 10, 10, 11, 16, 16; 6:1, 2, 2, 3, 3, 4, 4, 5, 5, 6, 7, 7, 8, 8, 8, 9, 15; 7:5, 6, 6, 6, 6, 13; 8:16, 17, 17, 17, 17, 18, 22, 23, 23, 23, 24, 24, 25, 25, 25, 26, 26, 26, 28, 31, 35, 36, 36, 39; 9:14, 16, 29, 30; 10:8; 11:33; 12:5, 5, 5; 13:11, 13, 13; 14:7, 7, 7, 8, 8, 8, 8, 8, 17; 15:1, 1, 1, 2, 2, 2, 4, 32; 1Co 1:2, 18, 23; 2:7, 10, 12, 13, 13, 13, 15, 16, 16; 3:5, 6, 9, 11; 4:8, 9, 10, 10, 11, 11, 11, 12, 12, 12, 13, 13; 6:2, 3; 7:7; 8:4, 4, 6, 6, 6, 8, 8, 8, 8, 8, 8; 9:4, 5, 11, 12, 12, 12, 25; 10:6, 8, 9, 16, 16, 16, 16, 17, 17, 22; 11:16, 31, 31, 32, 32; 12:5, 13, 13, 23, 23, 23; 13:9, 12, 12; 15:11, 12, 15, 15, 19, 19, 30, 32, 49, 49, 51, 52, 52, 57; 16:4; 2Co 1:1, 4, 4, 5, 6, 6, 6, 7, 8, 8, 8, 8, 9, 9, 10, 12, 12, 12, 12, 14, 20, 20, 24, 24; 2:11, 14, 16, 16, 17, 17, 17; 3:1, 1, 2, 4, 5, 5, 8, 12, 13, 18, 18; 4:1, 2, 2, 2, 2, 3, 4, 5, 5, 5, 5, 8, 8, 8, 8, 9, 9, 9, 11, 11, 12, 13, 13, 14, 16, 18, 18, 18, 18, 18; 5:1, 1, 1, 1, 2, 2, 2, 3, 3, 4, 4, 6, 6, 6, 6, 7, 8, 8, 8, 9, 10, 10, 10, 10, 11, 11, 11, 12, 12, 13, 13, 14, 14, 14, 14, 14, 16, 20, 20, 21; 6:1, 3, 3, 4, 4, 4, 4, 5, 6, 7, 7, 8, 8, 9, 9, 9, 9, 9, 10, 10, 10, 10, 10, 11, 16; 7:1, 1, 2, 2, 2, 3, 5, 10, 13, 13; 8:6, 18, 19, 20, 20, 20, 21, 21, 21, 22; 9:11; 10:2, 3, 3, 4, 5, 5, 5, 6, 7, 11, 11, 13, 13, 14, 14, 14, 15, 15, 16; 11:4, 6, 21; 12:18, 19, 19, 19, 19; 13:4, 4, 4, 6, 7, 7, 7, 7, 9, 9; Gal 1:4, 8; 2:5, 5, 10, 16, 16, 16, 16, 16, 17, 17, 21; 3:14, 21, 22, 23, 23, 23, 24, 25; 4:3, 15, 29, 31, 31; 5:5, 6, 6, 25; 6:5, 9, 10, 10, 15, 15; Eph 1:3, 3, 6, 6, 11, 12; 2:3, 3, 5, 6, 6, 9, 10, 10, 20, 21; 3:12, 20; 4:4, 4, 4, 9, 13, 13, 14, 14, 15, 25; 5:30; 6:8, 8, 12, 22; Php 1:7, 30; 3:3, 3, 3, 16, 16, 20, 20; Col 1:3, 3, 4, 9, 9, 9, 9, 11, 16, 16, 28, 28, 28, 28; 2:19, 19, 19, 22; 4:8, 11; 1Th 1:2, 3, 3, 4, 5, 5, 5, 8, 8, 8; 2:2, 2, 2, 2, 3, 4, 5, 5, 6, 7, 7, 8, 8, 9, 9, 9, 10, 11, 12, 13, 13, 13, 13, 17, 17, 18, 19; 3:1, 1, 2, 2, 4, 4, 6, 7, 9, 9, 10; 4:1, 1, 1, 2, 6, 10, 11, 14, 14, 15, 17; 5:5, 10, 10, 14; 2Th 1:3, 3, 4, 10, 11, 11; 2:1, 13, 13, 14, 15; 3:2, 4, 4, 6, 6, 7, 7, 8, 8, 8, 9, 9, 10, 10, 11, 12, 12, 14; 1Ti 1:8; 2:2; 4:1, 4, 4, 5, 10; 5:8; 6:7, 7, 7, 7, 8, 12, 17; 2Ti 1:4, 4, 9; 2:11, 11, 12, 12, 12, 13; 4:15; Tit 1:3, 4; 2:12, 12, 13; 3:3, 3, 3, 5, 7, 7; Phm 1:6; Heb 2:1, 1, 1, 3, 3, 5, 8, 9, 16, 18; 3:1, 6, 6, 14, 14, 14, 19; 4:1, 3, 4, 12, 13, 13, 14, 15, 16, 16, 16; 5:11; 6:1, 3, 9, 9, 9, 18, 18; 7:8, 9, 13, 19, 26; 9:5, 14, 22; 10:19, 21, 23, 23, 26, 26, 30, 39, 39; 11:1, 1, 3, 3, 39, 40; 12:1, 2, 9, 9, 10, 25, 28; 13:6, 10, 14, 18, 18; Jas 1:18, 27; 2:24, 24; 3:1, 2, 3, 3; 4:13, 13, 15; 5:11, 11, 17; 1Pe 1:3; 2:24; 4:17; 2Pe 1:1, 3, 3, 16, 16, 16, 18, 18, 19; 3:13; 1Jn 1:1, 1, 2, 2, 3, 3, 4, 6, 6, 6, 6, 7, 7, 8, 8, 8, 9, 10, 10, 10; 2:3, 3, 5, 16, 18, 25, 29, 29; 3:1, 1, 2, 2, 2, 2, 2, 2, 6, 6, 10, 11, 11, 12, 14, 14, 16, 16, 18, 19, 19, 19, 19, 21, 22, 22, 22, 23, 24; 4:6, 6, 9, 10, 11, 12, 13, 14, 16, 16, 17, 17, 17, 17, 18, 19, 20, 20, 20, 20, 21; 5:2, 2, 2, 7, 9, 9, 14, 14, 15, 15, 15, 15, 18, 19, 19, 20, 20, 20, 20; 2Jn 4, 5, 5, 8; 3Jn 8, 8, 12, 12, 14; Jude 3; Rev 1:9; 3:20; 7:3; 11:17

WE'D (1)

Ge 38:23

WE'LL (21)

Ge 13:9; 19:2, 9; 24:57; 37:20; 42:16, 19; 1Sa 9:19; 14:9, 12, 36; 26:11; Pr 1:13, 13, 14; Mt 21:26; 27:64; 28:14; Lk 5:5; Jn 21:3; Ac 4:17

WE'RE (11)

Jdg 19:18; 20:32, 39; 1Sa 23:3; Mt 3:9, 9; 8:25; Lk 3:8, 8; 8:24; 1Co 3:5

WE'VE (16)

Ge 26:32; 38:21; Jdg 15:10; 1Sa 23:7; Ps 40:15; 70:3; Mic 6:6; Mt 11:3; 19:27; Mk 2:12; 10:28; Lk 7:19, 20; Jn 7:15; 12:19; Ac 4:9

WENT (895)

Ge 7:7; 8:14; 9:22; 12:4, 10; 13:11; 15:17; 18:16, 22, 33; 19:3, 30, 33, 35; 21:8, 16; 22:6, 8; 23:3; 24:10, 16, 32, 45, 59; 25:22, 34; 27:22, 27; 28:5; 29:4, 10; 30:16, 35; 31:33, 33; 33:3; 34:1; 35:13; 37:12, 30; 38:11, 12, 15, 19, 23; 41:3, 14, 43; 42:3; 43:19; 44:28; 46:8, 26; 47:1; 48:1; 50:7; Ex 1:1; 2:11; 3:1; 4:18; 5:1, 15, 22; 6:27; 7:10; 9:10, 33; 10:3; 12:38; 16:17, 27; 17:10; 18:7, 7; 19:14, 25; 24:9, 15; 32:1, 15; 33:4, 8, 9; 34:34; 35:20; Lev 9:8, 23; Nu 7:89; 8:22; 11:24, 32; 12:4; 13:21; 16:3, 33; 17:8; 20:6, 15, 27, 28; 21:11, 20, 24; 22:7, 16, 35, 36; 23:3; 27:2; 31:13, 49; 32:9, 39; Dt 1:43; 2:8; 10:22; 26:5; 31:14; 34:1; Jos 2:5, 7, 8, 8, 22; 3:2, 14; 4:7; 5:13; 6:15, 23; 8:14, 24; 9:15; 10:29, 31, 34; 14:8; 15:3, 3, 7, 8, 10; 17:7; 18:11, 12, 13, 16, 17, 18; 19:1, 10, 11, 12, 17, 24, 26, 32, 40; 24:4; Jdg 1:3; 2:1, 15; 3:10, 22; 4:9, 18, 18, 22; 7:1, 3, 11; 8:1, 8; 9:1, 34, 42, 45; 11:11, 18, 29, 38; 12:3; 14:19, 19; 15:4, 6, 8, 11; 16:1, 5, 31; 18:7, 13, 15, 26, 26; 19:14; 20:18, 24, 26, 27, 30; 21:2; Ru 1:1, 21; 2:3, 8, 15; 3:6, 7, 16; 4:1; 1Sa 1:7, 9, 18, 19, 21; 3:9; 4:1; 5:3; 6:12, 12; 7:6; 8:6; 10:14, 14; 11:15; 13:2, 10, 15, 15, 15, 17, 18; 15:5, 12, 12, 12, 31, 34, 35; 16:21; 17:15; 18:27; 19:18, 22; 20:11, 35; 21:1, 10; 22:3, 5, 19; 23:5, 6, 16, 19, 25, 29; 24:2, 3, 22, 22; 25:14, 42; 26:2, 7, 25; 27:2; 28:8, 25; 29:11; 31:8; 2Sa 1:4; 3:6, 16, 19; 4:5, 6; 5:1, 17, 20; 6:12, 19; 7:17, 18; 8:6, 14; 11:2, 22; 12:16, 20; 13:8, 19, 24; 14:23; 15:2, 9, 22, 23, 30; 16:13, 16, 22; 17:22, 23; 18:33, 33; 19:5, 8, 8, 40; 20:5, 13, 22; 21:12; 23:13; 24:4, 5, 7, 19; 1Ki 1:9, 11, 15, 23, 47, 49; 2:15, 19, 30, 40; 3:4; 8:65, 66; 11:18, 18; 12:1, 3, 5, 6, 24, 25, 33; 13:1, 10, 19, 25, 28; 14:4, 28; 16:18; 17:10; 18:2, 6, 6, 16, 16, 43, 43; 19:3, 4, 13, 19, 19, 21; 20:1, 28, 32, 43; 21:4, 4, 16, 27; 22:2, 13, 30, 32; 2Ki 1:4, 15; 2:2, 4, 6, 7, 8, 14, 15, 21, 23, 25; 3:12, 24; 4:8, 11, 18, 33, 39; 5:9, 12, 14, 15, 21, 25; 6:15, 19; 7:5, 8, 10, 15; 8:3, 7, 9, 14, 21, 29; 9:4, 6, 11, 18, 34, 35; 10:8, 9, 23, 25; 11:18, 19; 12:17; 15:14; 16:10; 18:37, 37; 19:1, 8, 14, 35, 36; 20:1, 14; 22:14; 23:2, 29; 25:25; 1Ch 4:42; 6:15; 10:8, 12; 11:1, 4, 15; 12:17, 19; 13:6; 14:11; 15:25; 17:15, 16; 18:6, 13; 26:14, 15; 2Ch 1:6; 8:17; 10:1, 3, 5, 6; 12:11; 14:7; 15:2; 18:2, 12, 29, 31; 19:2, 4; 20:10, 20, 25; 21:9; 22:5, 6, 7; 23:17, 20; 24:11; 26:17; 28:9; 29:16, 18, 20; 30:10, 11; 31:1; 34:22, 30; Ezr 4:5; 5:8; 8:15; 10:6; Ne 2:13, 14, 15; 4:23; 6:10, 17; 8:12, 16; 9:24; 12:37, 38, 39, 41; Est 3:15; 4:1, 6, 17; 5:5, 10; 7:1, 7; 9:5; Job 29:7; Ps 57:T; 66:6, 12; 73:17; 99:8; 107:23; SS 6:11; Isa 36:3, 22, 22; 37:1, 8, 14, 36, 37; 38:1; 39:3; 50:1; 52:4; 53:3; 57:10, 17; Jer 7:24; 13:5, 7; 22:16; 25:18, 19, 21, 23, 24, 26; 29:3; 35:3, 4; 36:12, 14, 20; 38:4, 11; 39:4; 40:12; 41:3, 6; 43:7; 51:59; La 2:8; Eze 1:12, 19, 20, 20; 3:14, 23; 8:10; 9:2, 7; 10:3, 4, 6, 7, 11; 11:23; 12:7; 25:3; 31:7, 12, 15, 16; 32:27; 40:6; 41:3, 10; 47:3; Da 2:16, 17, 24; 3:8; 6:6, 10, 11, 12, 15; 9:20; Hos 2:13; Jnh 1:3, 3, 3, 6; 2:7; 3:3; 4:5; Hab 3:13; Zec 2:3; 6:8; Mt 2:9, 9, 12, 23; 3:5, 13; 4:11, 13, 20, 25; 5:1; 8:25; 9:1, 7, 25, 28, 35; 11:1, 7; 12:4, 9; 13:1, 3, 36; 14:13, 23, 29; 15:21; 16:4; 17:25; 18:28, 31; 19:1, 22; 20:1; 21:19, 29; 22:5, 22; 25:1, 10, 17; 26:14, 30, 39, 44, 58, 75; 27:5, 33, 53, 58, 62; 28:1, 9, 11; Mk 1:14, 18, 20, 21, 21, 29, 31, 35, 36, 45; 2:13, 26; 3:1, 6, 7, 13; 4:3, 27, 27; 5:21, 24, 39; 6:6, 12, 24, 46, 56; 7:17, 24, 31; 8:27; 9:1; 10:1, 22; 11:11, 11, 13; 12:12, 41; 14:10, 16, 26, 35, 68; 15:43; 16:1, 10, 20; Lk 1:24, 56; 2:20, 41, 45; 3:3; 4:16, 31, 38, 40, 42; 5:19, 25; 6:4, 12, 19; 7:1, 6, 11, 24; 8:5, 39, 42; 9:56; 11:5, 37; 13:22, 22; 16:1, 23; 17:14, 28; 18:10; 19:28, 32; 20:11, 31; 21:37; 22:4, 13, 39; 23:48,

52, 56; **24:**3, 10, 12, 29; **Jn 1:**39, 45; **2:**12, 13; **4:**28, 43, 47; **5:**15; **6:**2, 3, 15, 16, 24; **7:**10, 14, 53; **9:**7, 11; **10:**40; **11:**20, 29, 46, 54; **12:**13, 18, 22, 36; **18:**29, 33, 38; **19:**4, 17; **20:**6, 8, 10; **21:**3, 11; **Ac 1:**13; **3:**1, 8; **5:**15, 22, 26, 36; **7:**13, 15, 31; **8:**3, 4, 5, 13, 38, 39; **9:**1, 9, 17; **10:**9, 21, 23, 27, 38; **11:**5, 20, 25; **12:**12, 16, 17; **13:**4, 5, 5, 14, 51; **14:**1, 6, 20, 25; **15:**30; **16:**1, 4, 8, 13, 18; **17:**2, 10, 13, 15, 17; **18:**1, 19, 22, 22, 23; **19:**8, 10; **20:**5, 10, 11, 13, 13; **21:**1, 4, 6, 8, 18, 26, 26; **22:**26, 27; **23:**14, 16; **24:**27; **28:**8, 23; **2Co 1:**8; **2:**13; **8:**5; **Gal 1:**17, 18, 21; **2:**1, 2; **Heb 9:**6; **11:**8, 29, 37; **1Pe 3:**19; **Rev 20:**9

WERE (2828)

Ge 2:5, 25; **3:**7, 11, 19; **4:**8; **6:**5; **7:**8, 8, 14, 23, 23; **10:**1, 2, 3, 4, 6, 7, 7, 20, 21, 22, 23, 25, 31; **11:**5; **12:**19; **13:**6, 7, 13; **14:**13, 21; **17:**26, 27; **18:**11; **19:**4; **22:**24; **23:**20; **24:**11; **25:**3, 3, 4, 4, 18, 24, 26; **26:**12, 15; **27:**15, 20; **29:**10; **30:**35, 35, 39, 41, 42; **31:**1, 8, 8, 10, 20, 36, 39; **32:**21, 23; **33:**4, 8; **34:**5, 7, 7, 24, 25; **35:**16, 23, 24, 25, 26, 26; **36:**5, 10, 11, 12, 13, 13, 14, 16, 17, 21, 22, 23, 24, 26, 27, 28, 29, 31; **37:**2, 7, 11, 17, 25; **38:**5, 25, 26, 28; **39:**20; **40:**10, 16, 17, 20; **41:**3, 6, 10, 19, 21, 22, 22, 37, 47, 49, 50, 54; **42:**28; **43:**18, 18, 21, 24, 25, 32; **44:**1, 3, 4, 15, 18; **45:**3, 3, 16, 21; **46:**9, 10, 11, 12, 12, 13, 14, 15, 16, 17, 17, 18, 19, 20, 21, 22, 24, 25, 27; **47:**17, 17, 22, 26; **48:**5, 7; **49:**24; **50:**23, 23; **Ex 1:**14; **2:**11; **4:**28, 31; **5:**13, 19, 20; **6:**4, 16; **8:**7, 14, 15, 24; **9:**7, 11, 25, 31, 32; **10:**8; **12:**1, 29, 37, 37, 38, 39; **14:**4, 5, 9, 9, 12, 26; **15:**27; **16:**3, 15, 35; **17:**8, 13; **18:**5, 13, 25, 26; **22:**21; **26:**30; **27:**8; **28:**21; **29:**27; **30:**34; **32:**5, 15, 16, 16; **33:**5; **34:**1, 30; **35:**21, 22, 25, 26; **36:**2, 3, 7, 10, 11, 13, 16, 18, 22, 22, 29, 34, 34, 35, 36, 38, 38; **37:**3, 8, 8, 9, 14, 16, 17, 22, 22, 27, 28, 28; **38:**2, 5, 6, 6, 7, 8, 10, 10, 12, 16, 17, 17, 17, 19, 19, 20, 26; **39:**4, 6, 6, 10, 10, 11, 12, 13, 14, 17, 18, 19, 20, 21, 24, 24, 25, 27, 28, 29; **40:**32; **Lev 5:**4, 4; **7:**35, 36; **8:**26; **10:**14; **14:**42; **19:**34; **Nu 1:**16, 18, 18, 20, 44, 45, 45; **2:**33; **3:**2, 3, 17, 18, 19, 20, 20, 21, 22, 23, 25, 27, 28, 28, 29, 31, 33, 34, 35, 36, 37, 39, 43; **4:**35, 37, 39, 41, 43, 45, 47; **6:**12, 20; **7:**9, 13, 19, 25, 31, 37, 43, 49, 55, 61, 67, 73, 79, 86, 87, 87, 88; **9:**1, 18; **10:**17; **11:**4, 18, 26, 26, 29, 31, 33; **12:**1; **13:**4, 32; **14:**29, 34, 37; **15:**32; **16:**4, 32, 35, 38, 39, 40; **18:**27, 32; **19:**14; **20:**1; **21:**1, 6, 9; **22:**3, 3, 18, 22, 34, 40; **23:**17; **24:**13; **25:**1, 2, 6; **26:**5, 10, 12, 15, 21, 23, 26, 28, 29, 30, 33, 35, 37, 38, 40, 42, 43, 44, 45, 48, 57, 58, 60, 62, 62, 62, 65; **31:**21, 37, 38, 39, 40; **32:**1, 36, 39; **33:**4, 38, 40, 50; **35:**23; **36:**2, 13; **Dt 1:**1, 1, 5, 6, 15, 18, 39; **2:**10, 12, 12, 21; **3:**5, 10; **4:**4, 43; **5:**2, 5, 15; **6:**21; **7:**7, 7; **10:**2, 4, 4, 19, 22; **11:**4; **15:**15; **16:**12; **18:**16; **24:**9, 18, 22; **25:**18, 18; **28:**67, 67; **29:**1, 26; **32:**29; **33:**9, 21; **Jos 2:**4, 4, 5, 22; **3:**14, 15, 17; **4:**1, 9, 10, 10, 13, 23; **5:**1, 4, 6, 8, 10; **6:**1, 1, 13, 23, 24, 25; **7:**4, 4, 5, 5, 12; **8:**15, 16, 16, 22, 22, 27, 33; **9:**1, 13, 17, 24; **10:**1, 2, 24; **11:**19, 20; **12:**8, 24; **13:**21, 23, 27, 28; **14:**4, 6, 9; **15:**32, 33, 36, 37, 42, 52, 55, 58, 60, 61; **17:**3, 11, 12; **18:**8, 9, 21; **19:**35; **20:**7, 8, 9; **21:**3, 4, 4, 4, 5, 10, 12, 13, 17, 19, 23, 26, 33, 34, 40; **22:**10, 14, 30, 33; **24:**11, 32; **Jdg 1:**5, 16, 20, 21, 27, 33, 35; **2:**2, 2, 14, 15, 18; **3:**3, 4, 6, 8, 14, 26; **5:**7, 15; **6:**2, 16; **7:**1, 3, 12, 22, 24; **8:**3, 4, 10, 15, 18, 19; **9:**29, 40, 47; **10:**9, 17; **12:**6; **13:**23; **14:**5, 6, 11, 14; **15:**14; **16:**9, 12, 12, 17, 27, 27, 27; **17:**4; **18:**7, 7, 22, 23, 26, 27; **19:**9, 17, 17, 22; **20:**11, 16, 21, 25, 31, 33, 35, 36, 37, 43; **21:**13, 14, 14, 14, 23; **Ru 1:**2, 2, 12, 12; **4:**16; **1Sa 1:**3, 9; **2:**4, 4, 5, 5, 12, 14, 22, 22, 27; **3:**1, 1; **4:**1, 6, 11, 17, 19, 21; **5:**4, 12; **6:**3, 4, 6, 10, 10, 10, 11, 13, 13, 15, 17, 17, 18; **7:**7, 7, 10, 13, 14; **8:**3, 3; **9:**11, 20, 26; **10:**9, 14, 18, 25, 27; **11:**8, 11, 15; **12:**8, 12, 18; **13:**7, 8, 15, 16, 19; **14:**2, 4, 14, 17, 22, 24, 31, 41, 41, 51, 51; **15:**4, 6; **16:**10; **17:**11, 14, 19, 25, 52; **19:**5, 11, 24; **20:**20, 41; **22:**2, 2; **23:**1, 25, 26, 27; **24:**3; **25:**15, 15, 16; **26:**5, 7, 12, 16; **28:**23; **29:**2, 4; **30:**5, 6, 10, 14, 16, 26, 27; **31:**1, 7; **2Sa 1:**14, 23, 23, 23, 23; **2:**2, 15, 18, 30; **3:**1, 2, 2, 5, 6, 31, 34, 34, 34; **4:**1, 2, 2, 2, 4; **5:**2, 6, 14, 17; **6:**3, 5, 13; **7:**8; **8:**2, 17; **9:**11, 12; **10:**5, 15, 16, 19; **11:**7, 16, 24; **12:**1, 18, 21, 26; **13:**23, 30; **15:**2, 4, 18, 30, 30; **16:**14; **17:**17, 19, 20, 22, 29; **18:**2, 7, 8; **19:**3, 9, 17, 43, 43; **20:**3, 25; **21:**2, 2, 15, 15, 22, 22; **22:**10, 15, 16, 18, 38; **23:**13, 39; **24:**9; **1Ki 1:**8, 26, 39, 41; **2:**15, 32, 39; **3:**6, 18, 18, 28; **4:**2, 3, 4, 7, 7, 20, 20, 22; **6:**1, 6, 6, 7, 8, 25, 29, 32, 32, 34, 35, 35, 36; **7:**4, 5, 5, 8, 9, 10, 10, 11, 11, 12, 19, 19, 22, 24, 26, 28, 29, 29, 30, 30, 31, 32, 32, 32, 33, 33, 34, 34, 35, 36, 37, 37, 42, 45, 47; **8:**1, 8, 9, 66; **9:**20, 20, 21; **10:**10, 19, 21, 21, 21, 28, 29; **11:**21, 29; **12:**8, 31; **13:**20, 28; **14:**24; **15:**14, 27; **16:**21, 31; **18:**21, 34; **19:**11, 19; **20:**12, 16, 21, 21, 33; **22:**10, 10, 20, 48; **2Ki 2:**1, 11; **3:**4; **4:**39; **6:**15, 20; **7:**3, 10, 10, 14, 16, 16; **9:**7, 25; **10:**4, 6, 22, 24; **11:**2, 9, 10, 14, 14, 15; **12:**15, 21; **13:**7, 19, 21, 21, 23; **17:**6, 6, 9, 14, 20; **18:**36; **19:**12, 18; **20:**14; **22:**19; **23:**3, 4, 7, 8, 9, 9, 11; **24:**14, 16; **25:**7, 13, 21, 26; **1Ch 1:**1, 4, 5, 6, 7, 8, 9, 9, 17, 17, 19, 23, 28, 29, 31, 32, 32, 33, 33, 34, 35, 36, 37, 38, 39, 40, 40, 41, 42, 42, 43, 51, 54; **2:**1, 3, 4, 5, 6, 9, 16, 18, 23, 25, 27, 28, 28, 29, 30, 33, 43, 47, 50, 50, 52, 54, 55; **3:**1, 1, 4, 9, 10, 15, 17, 19, 19, 20, 21, 22, 23, 24; **4:**1, 2, 3, 4, 12, 13, 13, 15, 16, 17, 20, 20, 21, 23, 24, 25, 26, 31, 38; **5:**3, 4, 6, 11, 13, 14, 17, 18, 18, 20, 22, 22, 23, 24, 25; **6:**1, 2, 3, 3, 16, 19, 20, 22, 25, 28, 29, 48, 50, 54, 56, 57, 60, 65, 70, 72, 76; **7:**1, 2, 3, 5, 6, 7, 7, 7, 8, 9, 10, 11, 12, 13, 13, 14, 16, 17, 19, 20, 21, 29, 30, 31, 32, 33, 34, 35, 36, 38, 39, 40, 40; **8:**3, 6, 7, 12, 13, 16, 18, 21, 25, 27, 28, 28, 30, 38, 40, 40; **9:**1, 1, 2, 9, 9, 10, 12, 13, 13, 14, 17, 18, 19, 22, 22, 22, 23, 24, 26, 26, 28, 29, 32, 33, 33, 34, 34, 36, 41, 44, 44; **10:**1, 7; **11:**2, 15, 26; **12:**1, 2, 2, 3, 6, 8, 14, 21, 23, 24, 25, 26, 28, 29, 30, 31, 32, 33, 33, 34, 35, 36, 37, 40; **13:**8; **14:**4, 8; **15:**4, 5, 6, 7, 8, 9, 10, 16, 18, 19, 20, 21, 23, 24, 24, 24, 27; **16:**5, 19, 42; **17:**7, 17; **18:**16; **19:**5, 7, 16, 19; **20:**4, 8, 8; **21:**5, 20, 29; **23:**3, 3, 7, 8, 9, 9, 10, 11, 13, 13, 14, 15, 21, 23, 24, 27, 29, 29, 31; **24:**1, 1, 2, 4, 4, 5, 5, 20, 26, 27, 30, 30, 31; **25:**2, 4, 5, 6, 7, 8, 8; **26:**2, 4, 7, 7, 8, 9, 12, 13, 15, 16, 16, 17, 18, 19, 20, 22, 25, 26, 28, 29, 30, 30, 31, 32, 32; **27:**1, 2, 4, 5, 7, 8, 9, 10, 11, 12, 13, 14, 15, 16, 22, 23, 31; **28:**13, 18; **29:**8, 15; **2Ch 1:**15, 16, 17; **2:**3, 7; **3:**4, 6, 7, 7, 9, 10, 15; **4:**3, 5, 7, 7, 13, 18; **5:**1, 2, 9, 11, 11, 12, 12, 12, 12; **7:**6, 10; **8:**1, 7, 7, 8, 13; **9:**18, 20, 20, 20, 28; **10:**8; **12:**2, 15; **13:**14, 17; **14:**8, 13, 13, 14, 14; **15:**4, 15, 17; **17:**14, 17, 17, 19; **18:**9, 9, 19; **19:**9; **20:**24; **21:**2, 13; **22:**8, 11; **23:**8, 9, 13, 13, 13, 14, 19; **24:**14, 14, 22, 26; **26:**11, 13; **28:**15, 15; **29:**6, 15, 21, 23, 27, 28, 31, 34; **30:**6, 8, 12, 18, 21, 22; **31:**12, 13, 13, 15, 17, 17, 18, 19, 19; **32:**13, 19; **33:**15; **34:**4, 4, 9, 12, 13, 16, 27, 31; **35:**1, 3, 15, 15, 16; **36:**10, 20; **Ezr 1:**9, 11; **2:**2, 59, 62; **3:**3, 5, 7, 8, 8, 9, 9, 12; **4:**1; **5:**2, 4, 5, 10, 14; **6:**1, 5, 5, 14, 17, 17, 18, 20; **8:**16, 16, 20, 20, 33, 33, 36; **9:**9, 9; **10:**9, 9, 10, 23, 24, 25; **Ne 1:**2; **2:**10; **3:**4, 5, 7, 18, 25; **4:**1, 7, 10, 11, 17, 21, 23; **5:**2, 18, 18; **6:**2, 9, 13, 16; **7:**1, 4, 7, 61, 64; **8:**7, 9, 15; **9:**4, 4, 10, 13, 13, 15, 15, 16, 24, 25, 26, 30, 33; **10:**1, 8, 9, 14, 28; **11:**1, 1, 1, 6, 8, 13, 13, 16, 18, 21, 23, 29, 30, 30, 32, 36; **12:**7, 8, 12, 23, 24, 25, 27, 27, 28, 40, 40, 43, 44, 44; **13:**3, 10, 15, 15, 16, 16; **Est 1:**7, 14, 14; **2:**21, 23; **3:**7, 7, 12; **5:**6; **6:**14; **7:**2; **8:**1, 9, 11, 16, 16; **9:**1, 24, 25, 30; **Job 1:**13, 14, 18; **2:**11; **3:**15; **4:**3; **5:**14; **8:**9; **9:**15, 30, 33; **13:**16; **15:**7, 7, 7, 8; **16:**4; **20:**4; **22:**3, 16, 16; **29:**5, 7, 21, 23, 24; **30:**5, 17; **32:**4; **34:**14; **38:**4, 5, 21; **39:**16; **42:**15; **Ps 8:**2; **18:**9, 14, 15, 17, 37; **22:**5; **31:**12, 12; **33:**6, 6; **35:**13, 14, 14; **37:**36; **39:**12; **48:**5, 5, 6; **50:**12; **73:**2; **77:**6; **78:**37, 39, 53, 57, 57, 63, 64; **80:**8, 10, 10; **83:**10; **90:**2; **99:**6, 8; **105:**12, 30, 37, 38; **106:**7, 16, 43; **107:**17, 18, 20, 26, 27; **126:**2; **Pr 8:**24, 25; **24:**31; **Ecc 2:**7; **4:**3; **5:**15; **7:**10; **8:**10, 14, 14; **SS 1:**6; **5:**7; **6:**11, 11; **8:**1; **Isa 5:**2; **6:**2; **10:**10; **14:**11; **23:**3, 12; **26:**16, 17; **27:**13; **36:**21; **37:**12, 19; **39:**3; **42:**25; **45:**24; **46:**3; **47:**8; **48:**21; **49:**9, 15, 21, 21; **51:**1, 1; **52:**14; **53:**4, 5, 12; **54:**6; **55:**13; **57:**11; **59:**10; **60:**15; **63:**3, 13; **65:**1; **Jer 1:**3, 5; **2:**2, 3; **4:**25; **5:**7, 14; **6:**9; **7:**13; **9:**1; **11:**18, 19; **13:**11; **16:**11, 19; **19:**13; **22:**16, 21, 24; **23:**1, 13, 14; **24:**2; **28:**4; **29:**16; **30:**14; **32:**12; **35:**11; **36:**12, 16; **37:**2, 10, 15; **38:**25; **40:**1, 6, 7; **41:**1, 3, 7, 18; **42:**2, 18, 20; **43:**6, 6; **44:**17, 19, 21, 22; **46:**1, 2, 16; **49:**28; **52:**10, 17, 21, 23, 27; **La 1:**21; **2:**4, 6, 7, 22; **4:**7, 7, 17, 18, 18, 19, 19; **Eze 1:**1, 7, 7, 9, 18, 18; **2:**10; **3:**19; **7:**20; **8:**1, 11, 14, 16, 16; **9:**7, 8; **10:**3, 11, 12, 15, 20, 20, 22; **11:**1, 1; **12:**18; **13:**16; **14:**1, 13, 14, 15, 16, 17, 18, 19, 20; **16:**4, 4, 5, 5, 7, 8, 13, 13, 13, 13, 27, 28, 48, 49, 60; **19:**5, 7, 7; **20:**4, 8, 16, 23; **23:**2, 2, 6, 14, 15, 20, 42; **27:**5, 7, 8, 11, 14, 15, 19, 25, 33; **28:**12, 13, 13, 13, 15, 15, 18; **29:**18, 18; **31:**12, 16, 17; **32:**22, 27, 29; **34:**8, 8, 12; **35:**5; **36:**11, 17, 20, 22; **37:**2; **39:**18; **40:**7, 10, 10, 12, 16, 16, 16, 17, 21, 22, 22, 24, 26, 29, 30, 31, 33, 33, 34, 37, 39, 39, 40, 41, 41, 42, 42, 43, 44, 49; **41:**1, 2, 6, 12, 15, 16, 16, 18, 19, 21, 21, 22, 25, 26; **42:**3, 6, 10, 10, 11; **47:**7; **Da 1:**5, 6, 19; **2:**13, 30, 32, 32, 33, 33, 35, 41; **3:**3, 13, 28; **4:**26, 33; **5:**9, 11, 20; **7:**4, 8, 9, 10, 12; **10:**6, 7; **Hos 1:**1, 10; **2:**4, 8; **5:**13; **7:**1; **10:**9, 14; **13:**6; **Am 1:**11; **2:**9; **4:**11; **5:**18, 25; **6:**2, 2; **Ob** 11, 12, 13; **Jnh 1:**10, 16; **4:**2; **Mic 1:**1, 7, 13; **2:**11; **3:**7; **Na 2:**12; **3:**9, 10, 10, 10; **Hab 3:**8, 8, 9; **Zep 3:**19; **Hag 1:**6, 9; **2:**15; **Zec 1:**8; **5:**9; **6:**7; **7:**3, 5, 7, 7; **8:**10, 10; **11:**11; **Mal 2:**14; **4:**3; **Mt 2:**10, 11, 13, 16, 20; **3:**4, 16; **4:**18, 24, 24, 24, 24; **5:**1, 12; **7:**23, 28; **8:**16, 28, 28; **9:**4, 11, 19, 36, 36; **11:**8, 9; **12:**1, 3, 10, 15, 46; **13:**57; **14:**24, 24, 35, 36; **15:**31, 31, 31, 37, 37, 37, 38, 38; **16:**8, 9; **17:**6, 23; **18:**31; **19:**13, 25; **20:**9, 10, 24, 30; **21:**9, 15, 19, 19, 20, 36, 45, 46; **22:**3, 25, 33; **24:**38; **25:**2, 2, 3, 4, 6, 10, 10, 40, 45; **26:**3, 8, 21, 26, 59, 60, 69; **27:**31, 32, 38, 44, 52, 54, 55, 56, 61, 64; **28:**8, 11, 13, 15; **Mk 1:**6, 16, 22, 29, 32; **2:**6, 8, 15, 16, 25; **3:**10, 30; **4:**10, 33, 41; **5:**15, 42; **6:**2, 3, 14, 14, 31, 34, 47, 48, 50, 51, 52, 56; **7:**37; **8:**7, 8, 8, 8, 9, 15, 17, 27; **9:**6, 8, 14, 32, 33; **10:**1, 26, 32, 32, 32, 41; **11:**5, 6, 9, 12, 13, 18, 18, 32; **12:**5, 5, 12, 12, 20, 22, 23; **13:**34; **14:**1, 4, 11, 12, 18, 22, 35, 55, 55, 65, 67; **15:**20, 27, 32, 40; **16:**3, 5, 8, 10, 12, 14; **Lk 1:**4, 6, 7, 21; **2:**6, 8, 9, 18, 33, 47; **3:**2, 15, 21; **4:**22, 22, 25, 28, 32, 40, 41; **5:**2, 6, 7, 9, 10, 17, 22, 29, 33; **6:**3, 7, 11, 17, 19, 23; **7:**12, 25, 26; **8:**2, 3, 23, 25, 56; **9:**7, 8, 11, 14, 31, 31, 32, 33, 45, 53, 57; **10:**2, 23; **11:**53; **12:**1, 17, 36, 49; **13:**1, 2, 4; **14:**1, 2, 7, 25; **15:**27; **16:**16; **17:**26; **19:**7, 15, 33; **20:**19, 19, 26, 26, 29, 33, 39; **22:**2, 5, 7, 37; **23:**32, 33, 56; **24:**4, 5, 10, 13, 14, 22, 28, 31, 33, 33, 33, 35, 36, 37; **Jn 1:**24; **2:**2, 6, 6, 23, 24; **3:**19; **4:**27, 31; **5:**31; **6:**11, 13, 13, 15, 19, 19, 21, 61; **7:**1, 13, 15, 21, 32, 35; **8:**6, 39, 41, 42, 48; **9:**22, 33, 34, 40, 41; **10:**8, 19, 35; **11:**8, 31, 36, 45; **12:**17; **14:**2; **17:**6, 6; **18:**18, 36; **19:**11, 18, 25; **20:**19, 19, 20, 26, 26; **21:**2, 6, 8, 9, 11, 12, 18, 18, 25; **Ac 1:**6, 9, 10, 12, 13, 13, 15, 21; **2:**1, 2, 5, 6, 7, 8, 13, 41, 47; **3:**7, 10; **4:**1, 2, 2, 13, 13, 23, 24, 27, 31, 31, 32; **5:**12, 12, 14, 15, 16, 17, 22, 24, 25, 26, 37; **6:**1, 1, 6, 7, 9; **7:**9, 13, 16, 29, 42, 54; **8:**7, 7, 12; **9:**21, 24, 26, 31, 39; **10:**9, 12, 22, 27, 38, 41, 45; **11:**18, 24, 26; **12:**11, 12, 16, 20, 24; **13:**1, 2, 45, 48, 48, 52; **14:**4, 8, 17; **15:**1, 2, 3, 4, 10, 22, 33, 35; **16:**4, 5, 16, 19, 23, 23, 25, 25, 33, 38, 38; **17:**4, 5, 8, 11, 11, 34; **18:**3, 8, 14; **19:**5, 7, 12, 12, 13, 14, 29, 32, 32; **20:**4, 4, 4, 34; **21:**12, 18, 19, 27, 30, 31; **22:**29; **23:**6, 6, 6, 9, 10, 13, 27; **24:**19; **26:**10, 26; **27:**1, 17, 17, 27, 29, 30; **28:**1, 1, 2, 9, 10, 15; **Ro 2:**28; **3:**2, 3; **4:**1; **5:**6, 8, 10, 10, 20; **6:**3, 4, 6, 7, 17, 20; **7:**5, 5, 8; **9:**5, 11, 25, 26, 30, 32; **10:**20, 20; **11:**7, 12, 15, 16, 17, 17, 18, 19, 20, 24, 30; **15:**4, 27; **16:**7; **1Co 1:**13, 15, 26; **2:**4; **3:**1; **4:**8; **6:**11, 13, 13; **7:**17, 20, 22, 22, 24; **9:**17; **10:**2, 11; **12:**2, 2, 17, 17; **14:**5; **16:**15; **2Co 1:**8; **2:**6; **3:**14; **5:**16, 20; **7:**7, 7, 9, 13; **8:**10, 10; **9:**2; **10:**14; **11:**21; **Gal 1:**10, 17, 23; **2:**6, 9, 14; **3:**23, 23; **4:**3, 5, 8, 12, 14, 20; **5:**7, 11; **Eph 1:**12; **2:**1, 3, 3, 5, 11, 11, 12, 12, 13, 17, 17; **4:**20; **5:**8; **6:**7; **Php 2:**12, 30; **3:**7; **4:**15; **Col 1:**21, 21; **2:**7, 11, 12, 12, 12, 13, 17; **3:**23; **4:**10; **1Th 2:**2, 3, 5, 7, 10, 17; **3:**3, 4; **2Th 3:**7, 7, 10; **1Ti 1:**9; **5:**1; **Tit 3:**3, 3, 3; **Phm 1:**14, 17; **Heb 2:**2; **3:**16, 19; **6:**4; **7:**23, 28, 28; **8:**4; **9:**1, 2, 2, 4, 4, 5, 5, 6, 8, 23; **10:**1, 1, 6, 8, 29, 33, 33, 33, 34; **11:**11, 13, 16, 23, 29, 29, 35, 36, 36, 36, 37, 37, 38; **13:**3, 11; **Jas 5:**3; **1Pe 1:**12, 22; **2:**10, 25; **3:**20; **4:**6, 11, 12; **2Pe 1:**16, 18; **2:**1, 21; **Jude** 7, 7; **Rev 1:**14, 14, 15; **3:**15; **4:**4, 5, 6, 8, 11; **5:**9; **6:**8, 11; **7:**4, 4, 4, 9, 10, 11; **8:**2, 7, 7, 9; **9:**2, 3, 4, 5, 8, 15, 16, 17, 18; **10:**1; **11:**11, 15, 18; **12:**11; **13:**1, 8; **14:**1, 20; **15:**1, 2, 3, 6; **16:**20; **17:**6, 8; **18:**23; **19:**12, 12, 20; **20:**3, 12, 12, 13, 14; **21:**12, 12, 13, 14, 16, 21; **22:**2

WEREN'T (17)

Ex 14:11; **Dt 11:**3, 6; **1Sa 21:**11; **Eze 16:**29; **Mt 11:**17, 17; **Lk 7:**32, 32; **22:**6; **Jn 18:**30; **Ac 5:**4; **25:**18; **Ro 6:**20; **1Co 16:**17; **2Co 9:**4; **Heb 3:**16

WHAT (2460)

Ge 2:19; **3:**22; **4:**10; **9:**24; **11:**6; **12:**18; **13:**9; **14:**24; **15:**2; **18:**19, 25; **19:**9; **20:**8, 9, 9; **21:**1; **22:**16; **23:**15; **24:**49, 50, 57; **25:**32; **27:**12, 13, 37, 39, 42, 43, 45; **28:**17; **29:**25, 25; **30:**13, 30, 31; **31:**15, 24, 26, 29, 36, 36, 37, 43; **32:**27, 29, 32; **33:**8, 9, 10; **34:**12, 13; **37:**8, 10, 11, 15, 20, 26, 30; **38:**17, 18, 29; **39:**6; **40:**8, 8, 12, 18; **41:**8, 8, 12, 15, 16, 24, 25, 28; **42:**21, 28, 34; **44:**5, 5, 7, 7, 15, 16, 24, 34; **45:**9; **47:**3; **48:**19, 22; **49:**1; **50:**20; **Ex 1:**8; **2:**2, 4, 13, 14; **3:**13, 13, 16; **4:**1, 2, 12, 14, 15, 16, 22, 25; **5:**1; **6:**1, 9; **8:**1, 20; **9:**1, 20; **10:**3, 11; **11:**4; **12:**26, 26; **13:**8, 14; **14:**5; **15:**24, 26; **16:**15, 18, 23; **17:**4, 10; **19:**4, 7, 9, 25; **20:**19; **22:**7, 10; **23:**9; **29:**38; **32:**1, 21, 22, 27; **33:**5, 13, 17; **35:**4; **Lev 4:**21; **5:**4; **8:**5, 34, 35; **10:**3, 10, 10, 10, 10, 12, 16; **11:**47, 47; **19:**8, 9; **23:**22; **25:**20, 51; **Nu 4:**19, 49; **5:**7; **6:**21; **11:**11; **12:**10; **13:**18, 19, 23, 26, 33; **14:**13, 31, 34; **15:**11, 34; **16:**3, 4; **22:**2, 7, 16, 20, 28, 35; **23:**5, 11, 12, 17, 23; **24:**12, 13, 14; **27:**21; **30:**1, 2, 9; **32:**8; **33:**56; **36:**6; **Dt 1:**43; **4:**3, 6, 7, 8, 9, 20, 30, 34; **5:**5, 27, 28; **6:**18, 20; **7:**18; **9:**18; **10:**12; **11:**4, 6; **12:**25, 28; **13:**18; **17:**9, 10; **18:**16, 18; **21:**9; **24:**9; **25:**9, 17; **31:**21, 29; **Jos 1:**3, 13; **2:**10; **3:**9; **4:**6, 21; **5:**14; **7:**8, 9, 13, 15, 19; **9:**1, 3, 10; **11:**1; **14:**6; **15:**18, 18; **19:**9; **20:**4; **22:**24, 32; **24:**2, 7; **Jdg 1:**7, 14, 14; **2:**11; **3:**7, 12; **4:**1, 6; **6:**1, 8, 27; **7:**11; **8:**2, 3, 18; **9:**30, 46; **11:**11, 15, 35, 36; **13:**1, 12, 17; **14:**18, 18, 19; **15:**10, 11, 11; **16:**5, 6, 6, 15; **18:**3, 8, 14, 18, 23, 24, 24, 25; **20:**7, 12; **21:**11; **Ru 1:**12; **3:**4, 11, 16, 18; **1Sa 2:**3, 22, 34, 35; **3:**4, 5, 6, 8, 15, 17, 18; **4:**13, 14, 16, 18; **5:**7, 8; **6:**2, 4, 18, 19; **8:**21; **9:**8, 19; **10:**11, 15, 25; **11:**7, 9; **12:**23; **13:**11; **14:**1, 7, 38, 39, 43; **15:**2, 9, 14, 16, 16, 19, 22, 24; **17:**26, 27, 28, 28, 29, 39; **18:**18, 25; **19:**2, 7, 21, 24; **20:**1, 1, 4, 32, 39; **21:**3, 12; **22:**3, 10, 12; **23:**9; **24:**11, 12; **25:**12, 19, 24, 37; **26:**11, 18, 18; **28:**2, 6, 7, 13, 14, 15, 22; **29:**3, 4, 8; **30:**3, 23; **31:**11; **2Sa 1:**4; **2:**6, 24, 27; **3:**11, 24, 24; **4:**11; **5:**23, 25; **7:**3, 5, 8, 18, 20, 20, 23, 23; **10:**5, 17; **11:**10, 27; **12:**11, 18, 19; **13:**5, 12, 16, 21, 22; **14:**3, 19, 33; **15:**15, 21, 26, 28, 36; **16:**2, 10, 20; **17:**5, 6, 6, 10, 15, 15; **18:**10, 11, 21, 29, 29, 32; **19:**22, 27; **20:**19; **21:**3, 4, 11; **24:**12, 13, 17, 19; **1Ki 1:**6, 16, 45; **2:**6, 14, 16, 20, 30; **3:**5, 12, 13; **8:**20, 36, 43; **9:**13; **10:**7, 8; **11:**6, 22, 31, 33, 38; **12:**6, 9, 10, 10, 24, 24; **13:**2, 11, 11, 21; **14:**3, 22; **15:**5, 11, 21, 26, 34; **16:**7, 19, 25, 30; **17:**4, 14, 18; **18:**9; **19:**1, 9, 13, 20; **20:**2, 5, 13, 14, 28, 42; **21:**5, 5, 19, 20, 25, 29; **22:**5, 8, 11, 14, 19, 28, 43, 52; **2Ki 1:**4, 7, 16; **2:**9, 15, 21; **3:**2, 8, 10, 11, 16; **4:**2, 2, 7, 13, 14, 27, 43; **5:**4; **6:**15, 27, 28; **7:**1, 10, 12, 14; **8:**14, 18, 27; **9:**3, 6, 11, 12, 15, 18, 19, 27; **10:**4, 27; **11:**5, 13; **12:**2, 18; **13:**2, 11; **14:**3, 24; **15:**3, 9, 18, 24, 28, 34; **16:**2; **17:**2; **18:**3, 19, 19, 23, 29, 34, 34, 35, 35, 37; **19:**3, 6, 11, 13, 13, 20, 25, 29, 29, 32; **20:**1, 3, 5, 8, 14, 15; **21:**2, 12, 20; **22:**2, 2, 11, 13, 16, 18, 19; **23:**17, 32, 37; **24:**9, 19; **25:**26; **1Ch 10:**11; **14:**14, 16; **16:**8; **17:**2, 4, 7, 16, 18, 18, 21, 21; **19:**5, 17; **21:**6, 10, 12, 17, 24, 24; **29:**14; **2Ch 1:**7; **6:**10, 27, 33; **9:**6, 7; **10:**6, 9, 10, 10; **11:**4, 4; **12:**5; **14:**2; **16:**5, 8, 9; **18:**4, 7, 10, 13, 18, 27; **19:**2, 11; **20:**10, 12, 15, 21, 32; **21:**6, 12; **22:**4; **23:**4, 12; **24:**2, 20, 22; **25:**2, 9; **26:**4; **27:**2; **28:**1, 10; **29:**2, 6, 36; **31:**20; **32:**10, 10, 13, 14, 31; **33:**2, 22; **34:**2, 2, 11, 19, 21, 24, 26, 27; **35:**21; **36:**5, 9, 12, 23; **Ezr 1:**2; **4:**15; **6:**2; **9:**10; **10:**11; **Ne 1:**8; **2:**16, 19; **4:**2; **5:**9, 12; **6:**6, 19; **7:**5; **8:**8; **9:**8, 31, 33; **12:**47; **13:**10, 21, 26; **Est 1:**15, 15, 18; **2:**1, 11, 15; **4:**1, 5; **5:**3, 3, 6, 6, 8, 9; **6:**3, 6, 9, 11, 13; **7:**2, 2; **8:**17; **9:**12, 12, 26, 28; **Job 3:**25, 25; **6:**24, 25; **7:**17, 20; **8:**3; **9:**12; **10:**3; **11:**5, 8; **12:**14; **13:**1, 9, 14, 16, 17, 23; **15:**3, 5, 9, 9, 12, 12; **16:**2, 3, 5; **21:**2, 6, 15, 21, 31; **22:**13, 17; **23:**5; **26:**3; **27:**8, 13; **28:**28; **29:**25; **31:**2, 2, 7, 14, 23, 37; **32:**6; **33:**1; **34:**4, 4, 25, 32; **35:**6, 6, 7, 14; **36:**2, 23, 26; **37:**19; **38:**6; **42:**7, 8; **Ps 2:**12; **5:**8; **8:**4; **11:**3, 7; **15:**2; **16:**6; **17:**3, 15; **25:**8, 9; **26:**11; **28:**4, 5, 5; **30:**9; **31:**1; **32:**1, 2; **33:**12; **35:**25; **36:**3; **37:**30; **38:**9, 18; **39:**1, 1; **40:**3; **45:**7, 7, 10, 15; **48:**14; **50:**14; **51:**4, 4; **52:**7, 9; **55:**14; **56:**4, 5, 11; **62:**12; **64:**10; **65:**1, 4, 4; **66:**5, 5, 16; **69:**4, 19; **72:**3; **73:**11, 11, 16; **75:**9; **78:**1, 11, 29; **83:**2; **84:**11; **85:**8; **87:**3; **88:**10; **89:**6; **92:**4, 5; **94:**10; **95:**10; **104:**24; **105:**1; **106:**3, 13, 15; **107:**30; **111:**9; **112:**1; **114:**5; **116:**12; **118:**6, 17; **119:**121; **120:**3; **122:**9; **126:**2, 3; **137:**7, 8; **139:**4; **141:**3; **142:**4; **143:**5; **144:**3; **Pr 1:**3, 8, 9; **2:**5, 9, 15; **4:**19, 20, 25; **5:**7, 21; **6:**2; **8:**31; **10:**32; **11:**31; **14:**8, 14, 35; **16:**14; **18:**8, 13, 13; **21:**2, 3, 7, 12; **23:**1, 16, 24; **24:**12; **26:**22; **27:**1; **30:**4; **Ecc 1:**3, 10, 11, 11, 15, 15; **2:**2, 15, 22; **3:**9; **5:**11; **6:**9, 9, 10, 12; **7:**13; **8:**5, 7; **9:**16; **10:**14, 20; **11:**2; **SS 1:**6, 9, 16; **5:**9; **8:**8; **Isa 1:**2, 3, 4; **3:**11, 12; **5:**4, 5, 12, 19, 19; **6:**9; **7:**7, 9, 15, 15; **8:**6, 16; **10:**3, 24, 30; **12:**4; **14:**22, 32; **16:**5; **17:**8; **19:**11, 12, 12; **20:**6; **21:**3, 6; **22:**1, 2, 5, 5, 9; **23:**7; **26:**9; **28:**16, 26; **29:**15, 15; **30:**11, 12; **32:**6; **33:**13; **34:**16; **36:**4, 4, 8, 14, 19, 19, 20, 20, 22; **37:**3, 6, 11, 13, 13, 21, 26, 30, 30, 33; **38:**1, 3, 5, 15, 22; **39:**3, 4; **40:**6, 14, 14, 18; **41:**21, 22, 22, 23; **42:**20, 22; **43:**12, 13, 18; **44:**6, 7, 8; **45:**1, 2, 11, 11, 14, 19, 19, 20, 21; **46:**10; **47:**11, 13; **48:**3, 5, 8, 16, 17; **49:**8, 22; **50:**4; **51:**18, 22; **52:**3, 4, 5, 15, 15; **53:**11; **56:**1, 4; **57:**18; **58:**4, 5, 6; **59:**8, 8, 12; **60:**8; **63:**5; **65:**12, 13; **66:**1, 4, 6, 6, 18, 18; **Jer 1:**11, 13; **2:**2, 5, 5, 10, 18, 18, 19; **3:**6, 12; **4:**3, 10, 27, 30; **5:**4, 4, 5, 14, 31; **6:**6, 9, 13, 21, 22; **7:**12, 17, 21, 23; **8:**4, 6, 6, 7, 10, 17; **9:**7, 15, 17, 17, 20, 23; **10:**2, 21; **11:**3, 15, 22; **12:**5, 14; **13:**1, 13; **14:**18; **15:**2, 3, 10, 15, 16; **16:**3, 10, 10; **17:**5, 10, 15, 21; **18:**11, 11, 18, 19; **19:**3, 11, 12, 15; **20:**1, 4; **21:**4, 8, 12, 12; **22:**3, 3, 6, 11, 16, 30; **23:**2, 5, 15, 18, 23, 33, 35, 35, 37, 37, 37, 38; **24:**3, 5; **25:**20, 32; **26:**4, 9, 9, 10, 11, 18, 19, 21; **27:**4, 15, 16, 19, 21; **28:**13; **29:**3, 16, 17, 21, 25, 31; **30:**2, 5, 12; **31:**7, 15, 23, 35; **32:**3, 35, 36; **33:**3, 4, 10, 11, 12, 15, 17, 24; **34:**2, 4, 13, 15, 17; **35:**18; **36:**16, 24, 29, 30; **37:**2, 7, 7, 18, 18; **38:**1, 2, 19, 21, 22, 25; **40:**15; **41:**6, 11, 18; **42:**2, 3, 15, 20, 21; **44:**2, 2; **45:**2, 4, 4; **47:**2; **48:**1, 19; **49:**1, 1, 7, 12, 15, 19, 23, 28, 35; **50:**2, 44; **51:**1, 44, 58; **52:**2; **La 1:**21; **2:**11, 13; **3:**17; **Eze 1:**26; **2:**4, 8, 8; **3:**1, 11, 19, 27; **4:**13; **5:**5, 5, 7, 15; **6:**3, 11; **7:**2, 5, 13; **8:**3, 6, 12; **10:**1, 8, 21; **11:**5, 5, 7; **12:**3, 3, 9, 10, 11, 12, 22, 24, 25; **13:**3, 8, 8, 13, 18; **14:**21, 22; **15:**6; **16:**30, 36, 37, 59, 59; **17:**19, 24; **18:**5, 10, 12, 18, 19, 19, 21, 27; **19:**2; **20:**29, 32, 39; **21:**13, 24; **22:**14, 26, 26, 26; **23:**10, 11, 22, 28, 32, 44, 45, 46; **24:**6, 9, 19, 19, 21, 26; **25:**17; **26:**3, 15, 16; **28:**6, 22, 25; **29:**19; **30:**6, 10, 13, 22; **31:**10, 15; **32:**3, 11; **33:**7, 14, 15, 15, 16, 19, 30, 31, 32; **34:**10, 10, 11, 17, 19, 20; **35:**10, 11, 14; **36:**2, 5, 13, 33, 37; **37:**5, 9, 18, 19; **38:**10, 16, 17; **40:**2; **43:**11, 18; **44:**9, 23, 23, 23; **45:**9, 9, 18; **46:**1, 16; **47:**6, 13; **Da 2:**2, 3, 3, 4, 5, 5, 6, 6, 6, 7, 8, 9, 16, 17, 22, 23, 23, 26, 26, 28, 29, 30, 36, 45; **3:**15; **4:**6, 7, 9, 10, 18, 19, 24, 24, 27, 35; **5:**7, 8, 10, 12, 17, 26; **7:**1, 7, 16, 19; **8:**19, 19; **9:**12, 23; **10:**1, 11, 14, 21; **11:**36; **12:**8, 8, 9, 10; **Hos 1:**11; **4:**12; **5:**2, 3; **6:**4; **8:**3; **9:**5, 5, 9, 14; **10:**3; **Joel 1:**4; **2:**25; **3:**4; **Am 1:**2, 3, 6, 9, 11, 13; **2:**1, 4, 6; **3:**10, 12; **5:**4, 11, 14, 15, 16, 18; **6:**2, 8; **7:**8, 10, 10, 17; **8:**2; **9:**12; **Jnh 1:**8, 8, 8, 8, 11; **3:**6; **Mic 2:**3, 7; **3:**5; **6:**1, 3, 6, 6, 8, 8, 8; **7:**1, 16, 17; **Na 1:**12, 14; **Hab 1:**5; **2:**1, 6, 18, 18, 19; **3:**3; **Zep 2:**3; **3:**6; **Hag 1:**2, 5, 7; **2:**6, 11; **Zec 1:**3, 4, 6, 6, 9, 14, 16, 17, 19, 21; **3:**7; **4:**2, 4, 4, 6, 11, 12; **5:**2, 4, 6; **6:**4; **7:**9; **8:**2, 4, 6, 7, 9, 9, 13, 14, 16, 19, 20, 23; **11:**4; **13:**6; **Mal 1:**4; **2:**5, 15; **3:**8, 13, 14, 16; **Mt 1:**24; **2:**5, 15, 23; **5:**2, 13, 46; **6:**3, 8, 18; **7:**6, 7, 12; **8:**13, 33; **9:**4; **10:**19, 27, 27; **11:**4, 14, 19, 21; **12:**3, 15, 27, 27, 34, 34; **13:**12, 13, 13, 14, 17, 56; **14:**12; **15:**10, 11, 11, 12, 15, 15, 20; **16:**8, 21; **17:**9, 25; **18:**12, 31, 35; **19:**8, 16, 17, 20, 27; **20:**15, 17, 21, 22, 24, 32; **21:**3, 16, 28, 40, 43; **22:**17, 21, 42; **23:**3, 32; **24:**15, 39, 42; **25:**29, 29; **26:**8, 50, 54, 58, 62, 66, 70; **27:**4, 22, 23, 63; **28:**11, 15; **Mk 1:**27, 27, 28, 45; **2:**7, 8, 25; **3:**21; **4:**10, 12, 24, 25, 26, 30; **5:**9, 16, 19, 20, 33, 33, 43; **6:**24, 29, 30, 37, 51; **7:**11, 15, 15, 17, 18, 23; **8:**17, 19; **9:**6, 9, 10, 16, 23, 32, 32, 33; **10:**3, 14, 17, 36, 38, 41, 51; **11:**3, 5, 6, 18, 21; **12:**9, 17; **13:**11, 11, 37; **14:**8, 40, 49, 60, 64, 68; **15:**4, 12, 14; **16:**20; **Lk 1:**2, 20, 29, 43, 45, 61, 65, 66; **2:**17, 17, 20, 24, 33, 48, 50; **3:**10, 12, 14; **4:**36, 37, 40; **5:**8, 14, 22; **6:**3, 11, 24, 25, 25, 26, 30, 34, 38, 39, 45, 47; **7:**17, 22, 31, 39, 39; **8:**9, 10, 10, 18, 18, 30, 35, 36, 50, 56; **9:**33, 36, 44, 45; **10:**7, 13, 23, 24, 25, 26, 39; **11:**8, 9, 19, 19, 30, 30, 41, 45, 48, 49; **12:**3, 6, 11, 12, 15, 29, 33, 57; **13:**4, 18, 20; **14:**8, 15, 21, 24, 31; **15:**26; **16:**3, 15; **17:**9, 16, 32; **18:**18, 27, 34, 36, 41; **19:**15, 15, 21, 26, 26, 31; **20:**13, 15, 17, 21, 21, 25; **22:**49, 60, 71; **23:**22, 31, 34, 47; **24:**4, 6, 9, 10, 12, 17, 19, 27; **Jn 1:**22, 25, 38, 40; **2:**18, 20, 24; **3:**4, 9, 11, 12, 21, 21, 32, 32; **4:**27, 36, 42; **5:**19, 20, 47,

47; 6:6, 9, 28, 29, 30, 38, 43, 52, 62, 65; 7:36, 49; 8:5, 22, 26, 28, 33, 38, 43; 9:10, 26, 35; 10:6, 25, 38; 11:46, 47, 56; 12:27, 38, 49; 13:11, 12, 28; 14:11, 23, 24, 28, 31; 15:20, 25; 16:13, 15, 17, 17, 18, 19, 20; 18:19, 20, 21, 29, 35, 37, 38; 19:15, 22, 25; 21:19, 21, 22, 23, 23; Ac 1:4; 2:3, 6, 12, 16, 37, 41; 3:6, 12, 17, 18, 24; 4:7, 16, 23, 27, 32; 5:7, 11, 35; 7:31, 40; 8:6, 30; 9:6, 15, 27; 10:4, 8, 17, 35, 37; 11:4, 22; 12:11, 11, 17, 17, 18; 13:8, 12, 12, 33; 14:11, 14; 15:4, 15, 17, 27; 16:14, 30; 17:20; 19:2, 3, 17, 36, 40; 20:22; 21:22, 25, 33; 22:10, 15, 26, 30; 23:3, 14, 19, 28, 34; 24:20; 25:18, 26; 26:22; 28:22, 26; Ro 1:5, 21, 25; 2:1, 6, 7, 14, 15, 18; 3:4, 8, 17, 20, 22; 4:1, 4, 7, 8, 9, 17, 17; 5:1, 11, 14, 15; 6:13, 20, 21; 7:9, 13, 15, 16, 20, 21, 21, 24; 8:12, 18, 26, 27, 31; 9:1, 14, 19, 30; 10:2, 15, 18; 11:2, 6, 14, 20, 26, 33, 34; 12:1, 2, 9, 20, 20; 13:3, 7; 14:1, 15, 17, 20, 22; 15:2, 9; 16:17, 19; 1Co 1:6, 9, 22, 28, 31; 2:9, 9, 11, 14, 16; 3:13; 4:3, 3, 4, 6, 7, 7, 17; 5:11; 6:11; 8:4, 8, 10, 13; 9:7, 7, 18, 27; 10:1, 13, 15, 19, 20, 22, 24, 25, 29, 33, 33, 33; 11:13, 22, 22, 23; 12:3, 10, 19; 13:2; 14:5, 6, 9, 13, 14, 15, 16, 24, 26, 26, 27, 29, 37; 15:3, 3, 11, 29, 31, 32, 35, 36, 37, 46, 50; 16:2, 13; 2Co 4:5, 18; 5:16, 17, 18; 6:15, 16; 7:7, 11; 8:1, 3, 10, 11, 12, 12, 15; 10:12, 17; 11:6; 12:6, 14, 20; 13:9; Gal 1:13, 15, 20; 2:2, 6, 11, 12, 16, 17; 3:1, 17; 4:10, 20, 21, 27, 30; 5:6, 16, 17, 17; 6:4, 7, 9, 11, 15; Eph 1:18; 2:18; 3:4, 4, 13; 4:14, 20; 5:9, 10, 17; Php 1:10, 26; 2:4, 13, 21, 23; 3:3, 7, 10, 13; 4:6, 8, 17; Col 1:9, 24; 2:16; 3:14, 20, 25; 4:11; 1Th 1:5; 2:13, 19, 19; 4:2, 13; 5:18, 21; 2Th 1:10; 2:3, 6; 3:14, 16; 1Ti 1:7, 9, 9; 4:1, 12, 16; 5:8; 6:11, 12, 20; 2Ti 1:12, 14; 2:7; 3:3, 9, 10, 10, 16, 16, 16; 4:14; Tit 2:3, 14, 15; 3:1, 6; Phm 1:21; Heb 1:5, 9, 9; 2:3, 6, 9; 3:10; 4:2, 12; 5:13, 14; 6:11, 15; 7:4, 14; 10:10, 35, 36; 11:1, 1, 3, 13, 20, 23, 33; 13:5, 6, 16, 17, 22; Jas 1:5, 24, 25, 25; 2:16, 21, 22, 24; 3:5; 4:1, 2, 2, 2, 3, 5, 12, 14, 15, 17; 1Pe 1:10, 11, 17; 2:21, 24; 3:6, 6, 9, 14, 16, 17; 4:17, 18, 19; 5:2, 7, 12; 2Pe 1:19; 2:6; 3:2, 2, 11, 16; 1Jn 1:3; 2:24, 27, 27, 27, 29; 3:2, 7, 12, 12, 16; 5:10, 11, 15; 2Jn 6; 3Jn 11; Jude 17; Rev 1:3, 11, 19; 2:7, 10, 11, 17, 25, 29; 3:2, 2, 3, 6, 11, 13, 22; 4:1; 6:10; 8:13; 10:4; 13:5; 15:2; 19:6, 12; 20:12; 21:5; 22:6, 6, 9, 18

WHAT'S (40)

Ge 17:5; 21:17; 28:15; Nu 16:14; Ru 2:21; 1Sa 1:8; 4:6, 6; 11:5; 16:4; 18:8; 28:19; 2Sa 11:10; 13:4; 14:5; 1Ki 1:41; 2Ki 8:12; 18:25; Ne 4:11; Est 4:14; Job 9:29; 35:3; Ps 114:5; Pr 28:24; 30:20; Ecc 6:6; Isa 22:13; 36:10; 44:17; Hos 10:3; Mal 3:14; Lk 1:36; 12:26; 16:2; Ac 27:24; Ro 3:1; Gal 3:8; Php 3:5; Jas 2:14; 1Pe 2:5

WHEN (2835)

Ge 2:3, 4; 3:5; 4:1, 2, 17, 26; 5:1, 3, 6, 9, 12, 15, 18, 21, 25, 28; 6:1; 7:1, 6, 11; 8:13; 9:14, 16, 24, 29; 11:6, 10, 12, 14, 16, 18, 20, 22, 24, 26; 12:4, 12, 14, 15; 14:14; 15:2, 16; 16:4; 17:1; 18:8, 12, 33; 19:1, 16, 37, 38; 20:8, 13; 21:15, 28; 22:9; 23:1; 24:19, 22, 30, 30, 31, 36, 42, 47, 49, 64; 25:20, 24, 26, 29; 26:7; 27:1, 5, 27, 34, 45; 29:23, 25; 30:1, 30, 38, 39; 31:8, 23, 25, 49; 32:2, 10, 17, 19, 25; 34:2, 25; 35:1, 3, 5, 7, 9; 36:33, 34, 35, 36, 37, 38, 39; 37:2, 13, 15, 18, 23, 28, 29; 38:5, 6; 39:1, 11, 13, 15, 16; 40:14, 16; 41:36, 46, 46; 42:1, 27; 43:2, 3, 16, 18, 26; 44:1, 4, 14, 25, 31; 45:1, 27, 27; 46:1, 28, 33, 34; 47:15, 24, 28, 30; 48:2, 17; 49:15, 33; 50:4, 10, 17, 22, 25; Ex 1:16; 2:3, 5, 10, 11, 15, 15, 18; 3:4, 6, 12; 4:6, 7, 9, 14, 21, 24, 26, 31; 6:1; 7:5, 9; 8:9, 15; 9:34; 10:13; 12:13, 13, 23, 25; 13:5, 8, 11, 17, 19; 14:5, 18, 26, 31; 15:19, 23; 16:14, 15, 32; 17:5; 18:3, 9, 14, 16; 20:18, 18; 21:3, 7; 22:29; 23:2, 16; 24:3; 25:16; 26:33; 28:4, 29, 30; 30:7, 8, 15; 32:1, 5, 17, 19, 20, 24, 25, 34; 33:4; 34:18, 24, 29, 30, 33; 39:26; Lev 1:6; 2:1, 4; 4:14, 23, 28; 5:5, 16, 17; 6:5; 7:29, 38; 9:6, 23, 24; 10:3, 16, 20; 11:38; 12:2, 6; 14:34, 57, 57; 15:13, 28; 16:1, 3, 10, 20, 23; 19:5, 9, 23, 35; 22:3, 7, 27, 29; 23:2, 10, 22, 28, 43; 25:2, 10, 14, 15, 51; 26:17, 36, 41; 27:21; Nu 1:49; 3:1, 4; 4:5, 15, 19; 5:18, 21; 8:2, 10, 19; 9:17, 21; 10:3, 5, 6, 7, 9, 13, 21, 36; 11:1, 2, 26; 12:10; 13:23; 14:13, 39, 43; 15:2, 3, 8, 18; 16:4, 22, 31; 17:8, 9; 18:16, 26, 30; 19:14, 14; 20:16, 29; 22:3, 25, 27, 36, 37; 23:6; 24:22, 23; 25:7; 26:61, 62; 27:14, 21; 28:3, 26; 30:10; 32:1, 8, 22, 29; 33:39, 51; 34:2; 35:10, 19, 21; 36:4; Dt 1:6, 17, 19, 34; 2:16, 23, 25; 3:12, 20, 20; 4:5, 6, 10, 19, 25, 30, 45; 5:23; 6:7, 7, 7, 7, 11, 13, 16, 25; 7:1, 2, 13, 19; 8:10, 12, 13; 9:9, 25; 10:22; 11:6, 19, 19, 19, 19, 29, 31; 12:2, 9, 10, 20, 29; 14:26; 15:7, 13, 18; 16:1, 3; 17:4, 18; 18:9, 16; 19:14; 20:1, 9, 13, 19; 21:16; 22:14, 17; 23:4, 9, 21; 24:19, 20; 25:13, 18, 19; 26:1, 6; 27:2, 4, 12; 28:7; 29:7, 25; 31:1, 11, 24; 32:5, 8, 8, 36, 41, 45; 33:5, 5, 21; 34:7; Jos 2:10, 13, 14; 3:3, 8, 13, 14; 4:1, 7, 11, 23; 5:1, 4, 6; 6:5, 20; 7:3, 9; 8:5, 14, 20, 21, 24; 9:3, 6, 12, 13, 22; 10:2, 14, 17; 11:1; 13:1, 7; 14:6, 7, 11; 15:18; 17:13, 14; 22:11, 15, 20, 30; 24:6, 7, 11, 14, 32; Jdg 1:4, 14, 16, 28, 35; 2:4, 19, 21; 3:9, 15, 19, 25, 25, 27; 4:12, 15, 21, 22; 5:2, 4, 8; 6:7, 22, 38; 7:5, 15, 17, 19, 22; 8:1, 3, 5, 15, 32; 9:7, 17, 30, 33, 35, 36, 42, 43, 46, 55; 10:2, 5, 12; 11:2, 5, 7, 13, 16, 31, 34, 35, 39; 12:7, 10, 12; 13:12, 17, 20, 24; 14:1, 2, 7, 8; 15:17; 16:2, 15, 20, 24, 30; 18:2, 8, 10, 18, 22, 26; 19:3, 11, 17, 27, 29; 20:31, 33, 40; 21:5, 8, 21, 22, 22; Ru 1:1, 18, 19, 21; 2:8, 9, 15, 17; 3:16; 4:1, 13; 1Sa 1:9, 19, 24; 2:19, 27; 4:5, 6, 8, 13, 18, 19; 5:3, 7, 9, 10; 6:13; 7:7, 7; 8:18; 9:17, 25, 27; 10:2, 3, 5, 8, 10, 11, 13, 21, 26; 11:4, 5, 8, 9; 12:8, 12; 13:1, 6, 11, 15; 14:11, 17, 22, 47; 15:2, 6, 11, 13; 16:4, 6; 17:11, 28, 34, 51; 18:6, 15, 19, 20, 23, 24, 28; 19:11, 14, 16, 19, 20, 21; 20:15, 18, 24, 27, 37; 21:1, 5; 22:7, 9, 12, 21, 22; 23:25; 24:4, 8, 18, 19, 21; 25:4, 23, 29, 30, 31, 36, 37, 39, 40; 26:15, 23; 28:5, 12, 21; 30:1, 3, 16, 21, 24, 26; 31:5, 7, 8, 11; 2Sa 1:7, 11; 2:4, 10, 20, 23, 24, 26, 30; 3:13, 20, 23, 27, 28; 4:1, 4, 4; 5:4, 8, 17, 24; 6:6, 16, 18, 20; 7:1, 8, 12, 23, 29; 8:3, 5, 9; 9:6; 10:2, 5, 7, 9, 13, 14, 15, 17, 19; 11:1, 4, 5, 7, 10, 26, 27; 12:18, 19, 23; 13:5, 6, 8, 9, 21, 23; 14:4, 14, 26; 15:2, 5, 31; 16:1, 14, 16; 17:6, 9, 12, 20, 23, 27; 18:29; 19:15, 19; 20:3, 15; 21:11, 12, 15; 22:19; 23:9, 13; 24:17, 20; 1Ki 1:32, 35, 41; 2:7, 8, 19, 28, 29, 39, 40; 3:19, 21, 21; 5:1, 7; 8:3, 21, 30, 30, 41, 42, 53, 54; 9:16; 10:1, 2, 4, 4, 11; 11:21, 28, 43; 12:2, 16, 18, 20, 21, 27; 13:13, 26, 31; 14:6, 12, 18, 20, 21, 31; 15:8, 24; 16:6, 15, 18, 28, 34, 34; 17:14; 18:4, 10, 12, 13, 17, 34, 39; 19:1, 13, 15; 20:7, 33, 36; 21:15, 27; 22:15, 16, 24, 25, 32, 32, 40, 42, 50; 2Ki 1:5; 2:1, 9, 10, 15, 18; 3:20, 21, 22, 24, 26; 4:7, 12, 15, 18, 27, 32, 36; 5:7, 8, 13, 18, 18, 21, 24, 25, 26, 27; 6:4, 6, 8, 15, 17, 21, 30, 32, 32; 7:8, 17; 8:8, 14, 17, 24, 26, 28; 9:5, 25, 27, 30, 31, 35, 36; 10:7, 15, 17, 35; 11:1, 13, 14, 21; 13:9, 13, 14, 21; 14:2, 5, 16, 29; 15:2, 7, 22, 33, 38; 16:2, 11, 12, 20; 17:4, 21, 25; 18:2, 32; 19:1, 3, 35; 20:2, 17, 21; 21:1, 9, 18, 19; 22:1, 11, 19; 23:15, 22, 29, 31, 36; 24:6, 8, 18; 25:23; 1Ch 1:44, 45, 46, 47, 48, 49, 50; 2:21; 5:6; 6:15; 8:7; 10:5, 7, 8, 11; 11:15; 12:17, 19; 13:9; 14:8, 15; 15:2, 29; 16:2, 19; 17:1, 7, 11, 21, 27; 18:3, 5, 9; 19:2, 5, 8, 10, 14, 15, 17, 19; 20:1, 2; 21:21, 26, 28; 23:1; 27:23; 29:17; 2Ch 2:3; 5:1, 4, 10; 6:21, 21, 32; 7:1, 3, 18; 9:1, 2, 3, 3, 10, 31; 10:2, 16, 18; 11:1; 12:1, 7, 13, 16; 13:4, 7, 14; 14:1; 15:8, 9; 16:12; 18:14, 15, 23, 24, 31; 19:1, 6; 20:7, 10, 24, 29, 31; 21:1, 4, 5, 20, 20; 22:2, 10; 23:4, 12, 13; 24:1, 14, 27; 25:1, 3, 14, 16; 26:3, 16, 20; 27:1, 8, 9; 28:1, 9, 20, 22, 27; 29:1, 19; 31:1, 8; 32:2, 14, 21, 31, 33; 33:1, 9, 13, 20, 21; 34:1, 19, 27; 35:10; 36:2, 5, 9, 11; Ezr 1:11; 2:68; 3:1, 10, 12; 4:6, 23; 9:3; Ne 1:4; 2:6, 9, 10, 19; 4:1, 7, 15, 20, 23; 5:6, 7; 6:1, 16; 7:73; 8:5; 9:8, 15, 15, 28, 32; 10:34; 12:12; 13:2, 3, 7; Est 1:5, 10, 12, 17, 20; 2:7, 13, 15, 16, 20, 23; 3:5; 4:1, 4, 13; 5:2, 9, 14; 6:13; 9:11, 19, 22, 22, 25; Job 1:4, 5, 13, 15, 21; 2:11, 12; 3:3, 22, 22; 4:5, 7; 5:17, 21, 24; 6:5, 5, 6, 7, 16, 17, 26; 7:4, 4, 21; 8:18; 9:11, 11, 23; 11:3; 12:2, 14; 14:10; 17:8; 19:18; 21:6, 17, 21, 32; 23:10, 15; 26:10; 27:8, 9; 28:27; 29:2, 3, 7, 8, 24; 30:14, 24; 31:14, 29, 29; 32:5; 33:15, 26; 34:23, 29, 29; 36:13, 20; 37:4, 17, 20, 21; 38:4, 41; 39:1, 21, 24; 40:23; 41:18, 25; 42:10; Ps 4:1, 3; 8:3; 10:1; 14:7; 15:4; 17:15; 18:18; 20:5; 21:9, 12; 22:9; 23:4; 27:2, 2, 5; 30:6; 31:11, 21; 32:3; 33:9; 34:17; 35:13; 37:33, 36; 39:1, 8, 11; 41:3, 6; 42:2; 48:5; 49:5, 5, 16, 17; 50:18; 53:6; 56:3; 58:10; 63:T; 66:14; 68:7, 7, 18; 69:10, 11; 71:9; 72:12; 73:3, 20, 20; 74:9; 75:3; 76:6, 7; 77:2, 6, 16; 78:9, 21, 34, 59; 81:3, 3, 5, 7; 84:6; 87:6; 89:9; 91:15; 94:8, 19; 99:8; 101:2; 102:2, 22; 104:19, 20, 28, 29, 30; 105:12, 31, 38; 106:4; 107:39; 109:7, 25, 28; 112:4, 10; 114:1, 1; 116:15; 119:6, 7, 82, 84; 120:7; 122:1; 124:2; 126:1; 127:5; 129:6; 133:1; 138:3; 139:2, 2, 18; 141:1, 6; 145:16; 146:4; Pr 1:17, 26, 26, 27, 27, 27, 28, 30; 3:11, 11, 27; 5:11; 6:9, 22, 22; 8:27, 27, 28, 28, 29, 29; 9:8; 11:7, 10, 10, 17, 17; 12:16; 13:12; 14:13, 32; 16:7, 15; 17:28, 28; 18:3; 20:8; 21:3, 3, 27; 22:6; 23:1, 16, 22, 35, 35; 24:7, 17, 17, 23; 26:4, 5, 20; 28:1, 2, 12, 12, 28, 28; 29:2, 2, 16, 18; 31:26, 26; Ecc 4:6, 10; 5:4; 7:14; 8:11; 9:10, 12; 10:8, 8, 9, 9; 11:3, 3, 8; 12:2, 4, 4; SS 6:9; Isa 1:15, 29, 29; 2:11, 19; 5:4, 22; 7:21; 9:1, 4; 10:3, 11, 24, 26, 26; 11:16; 13:3, 12, 19; 14:3, 25, 27; 16:4; 17:9; 18:3, 3, 7; 19:20; 20:1; 21:3, 7, 11; 22:25; 23:5; 26:9, 11, 17; 27:6, 9, 12; 28:18; 29:8, 11, 12, 23; 30:25, 26, 29; 31:3, 4, 7, 9; 33:3, 18; 34:5, 8; 35:5; 37:1, 3, 36; 38:2, 9, 12; 39:6; 40:24; 41:17, 28; 43:2, 2, 2; 44:26, 27, 28; 45:4; 46:7, 7; 48:21; 49:7; 50:2; 51:2, 2, 9, 10; 52:3, 14; 53:3, 10, 11; 56:3, 10; 57:13; 58:4, 9, 11; 59:1, 9, 10; 63:11, 12; 64:3, 6; 65:12, 12, 20, 22; 66:3, 3, 3, 4, 4, 14; Jer 2:7, 17, 21, 26, 28; 3:16, 16; 4:11; 5:2, 19, 31; 6:9, 10, 14, 15; 7:22, 32; 8:4, 4, 8, 11, 12, 12; 9:25; 10:13, 15; 11:4, 7, 12, 14, 23; 12:1; 13:16, 21; 14:12, 12; 16:10, 14; 19:6; 20:3; 21:1; 22:18, 21; 23:5, 7, 12, 16; 25:1, 16; 26:8, 10, 18, 21; 27:20; 28:9; 29:3, 12, 13, 29, 31; 30:3, 18; 31:6, 23, 27, 31, 32, 38; 33:6, 14; 34:13, 18; 35:1, 11, 17; 36:11, 13, 25; 37:5, 11; 38:12, 22; 39:4; 40:11; 41:6, 9, 11, 13, 18; 42:18, 20; 43:1, 11; 46:2; 47:6, 7; 48:12; 49:8; 50:36, 36, 37, 37; 51:16, 18, 25, 46, 47, 52, 59, 61, 63; 52:1; La 1:21, 21; 3:21, 39; Eze 1:19, 19, 21, 21, 21, 24, 28; 3:3; 5:13, 15; 6:7, 9, 10, 13; 10:3, 16, 16, 17, 20; 11:18; 12:4, 15; 13:7, 10, 12, 14, 16, 22; 14:21, 23; 15:7; 16:4, 8, 22, 60, 63; 17:10, 10, 17; 18:8, 26; 19:5, 7; 20:5, 28, 31, 38, 41, 42, 44; 21:7, 7; 22:16, 28; 23:8, 8, 16, 19, 21, 40; 24:24, 27; 25:3, 17; 28:22, 26; 29:6, 7, 20, 21; 30:8, 18, 25; 31:15; 32:7, 9, 15, 31; 33:2, 3, 13, 18, 22, 29, 33; 34:8, 26, 27; 35:5, 5, 14; 36:17, 20, 23, 33, 35; 37:13, 18; 38:14, 17, 18; 39:13, 27; 42:14, 15; 43:3, 18, 23; 44:10, 15, 17, 19; 45:1; 46:9; 48:11, 12; Da 1:2, 18; 2:12, 14; 3:3, 5, 10, 13, 15; 4:7, 26, 36; 5:8, 10, 20; 6:10, 20; 8:23; 10:2, 9, 11; 11:7, 8, 21; 12:7; Hos 1:1, 2, 10, 11; 2:7, 13, 15, 15; 4:8, 8; 5:9, 13; 9:10, 10, 12; 10:6, 14, 15; 11:1; 12:3, 9; 13:1, 6; Joel 1:8, 15; 3:1; Am 1:1, 13; 2:13; 3:5, 6, 6, 12; 4:2, 7; 5:3, 3; 6:10, 11, 12; 7:10; 8:11; 9:13; Ob 11, 12, 13, 15; Jnh 1:7, 10; 2:7; 3:6, 10; Mic 1:1; 2:2, 2; 5:3, 5, 6; 6:5; 7:15; Na 1:7; 3:17; Hab 2:3, 6, 14; 3:6, 6, 16, 16; Zep 1:1, 14, 15; 3:8; Hag 1:9; 2:5, 16, 16, 18, 23; Zec 1:4; 2:1; 5:7, 11; 6:15; 7:5, 7, 13, 13; 8:14; 9:16; 10:8; 14:1; Mal 1:5, 8, 9; 2:14; 3:2, 2, 7, 8, 17; 4:3; Mt 1:24; 2:7, 8, 10, 12, 16, 19, 22; 3:3, 6, 7; 4:12; 5:11; 6:2, 3, 5, 6, 7, 16, 17; 7:3, 4, 27; 8:5, 10, 14, 15, 16, 18, 28; 9:12, 23, 25, 32; 10:12, 19, 23, 26, 27; 11:1, 7, 10; 12:3, 24, 43; 13:10, 26, 34, 46, 48, 53, 54; 14:1, 26, 30, 32; 15:7, 15, 37; 16:13; 17:8, 14; 18:28, 31; 19:22, 28; 20:9, 10, 11, 18, 24, 30; 21:20, 23, 32, 38, 40, 45; 22:3, 11, 19, 30, 33, 34; 23:20, 21, 22; 24:3, 15, 27, 32, 33, 36, 37, 39, 43, 44; 25:5, 11, 31, 37, 39, 40, 44, 45; 26:1, 8, 20, 48; 27:3, 12, 21, 31, 34; 28:4, 17; Mk 1:5, 10; 2:16, 17, 25, 26; 3:20, 21; 4:10, 34, 39; 5:6, 15, 18, 21, 38; 6:10, 16, 29, 49, 50, 53; 7:6, 30; 8:8, 11, 12, 20, 22, 38; 9:20, 25, 28; 10:10, 14, 33, 41, 47, 49; 11:15, 18, 25; 12:16, 25; 13:4, 4, 9, 11, 14, 28, 29, 32, 33, 35, 36; 14:11, 25, 41, 44, 51; 15:20, 25, 39; 16:1, 4, 9, 11, 13, 19; Lk 1:5, 11, 22, 44, 59; 2:2, 15, 21, 27, 36, 39, 42, 44, 45; 3:4, 21, 23; 4:13, 16, 25, 28, 33, 42; 5:4, 8, 12; 6:3, 17, 21, 23, 30, 41, 42, 46, 47, 48, 49; 7:1, 3, 9, 10, 13, 27, 29, 39, 44; 8:8, 13, 19, 29, 34, 47, 50, 51; 9:4, 5, 7, 10, 26, 36, 54; 10:7, 17, 17, 23, 31, 33; 11:1, 21, 24, 24; 12:2, 11, 39, 40, 54, 55; 13:4, 12, 25; 14:4, 7, 10, 12, 17; 15:6, 9, 10, 17, 25, 30; 16:4, 28; 17:7, 10, 15, 20, 22, 24, 26, 30; 18:8, 23, 31, 36, 40; 19:5, 15; 20:14, 19, 37; 21:6, 7, 9, 20, 28, 30, 31; 22:6, 7, 17, 19, 32, 35, 49, 53, 69; 23:7, 29, 31, 31, 40, 42, 47, 48; 24:33, 44; Jn 1:10, 15, 19, 30, 33, 33, 39; 2:7, 9, 10; 3:12; 4:21, 23, 25, 40, 47, 52; 5:6, 7, 25, 28; 6:14, 19, 24, 25, 65; 7:15, 15, 22, 27, 32, 36, 39, 40; 8:9, 28, 38, 41, 44, 45; 9:15, 35; 10:12, 18, 19, 36; 11:4, 17, 20, 24, 31, 32, 33, 45; 12:9, 29, 31, 32, 35, 41, 45; 13:6, 11, 19, 26; 14:3, 20, 26, 29; 15:10, 13, 18; 16:2, 4, 8, 13, 15, 17, 17, 20, 21, 25, 32; 17:1; 18:5, 36; 19:6, 8, 13, 23, 26, 30, 33, 38; 20:20, 24; 21:7, 9, 18, 18; Ac 1:6, 8, 12, 15; 2:6, 29; 3:3, 10, 26; 4:13; 5:10, 21, 22, 23, 24; 7:8, 17, 21, 23, 29, 45; 8:14, 18, 18, 19, 31, 39; 9:11, 26, 30, 35, 40; 11:2, 6, 16, 17, 18, 22, 23, 26; 12:3, 14, 15, 16, 19, 21, 25; 13:12, 29, 33, 45, 47, 48; 14:6, 11, 14; 15:4, 13; 16:38; 17:10, 13, 18, 32; 18:6, 12, 19, 26, 27; 19:2, 6, 12, 15, 34; 20:1, 3, 17, 18, 36; 21:5, 11, 12, 14, 26, 27, 32; 22:2, 18, 20, 29; 23:27, 27, 30, 33, 35; 24:2, 6, 21, 25; 25:15, 17; 26:10; 27:1, 3, 13, 39; 28:6, 10, 15, 16, 19, 25; Ro 1:4, 28; 2:1, 3, 5, 12, 12, 14, 16; 3:5, 22, 25, 25, 26, 31; 4:4, 17, 18; 5:3, 6, 12; 6:3, 7, 20; 7:2, 3, 4, 5, 9, 9, 19, 19, 21; 8:19, 21, 23; 9:10, 21, 33; 10:15; 11:9, 12, 30; 12:1, 6, 13, 15; 13:11; 14:7, 7, 8; 15:9, 24, 29; 1Co 1:8, 23, 26; 2:1, 6, 9, 13; 3:1, 4; 4:5, 13, 15; 5:5, 9; 6:1, 11; 7:17, 18, 20, 22, 22, 24, 40; 8:7, 12; 9:9, 20, 20, 21, 22; 10:11, 13, 16, 16; 11:7, 17, 17, 18, 20, 23, 24, 32, 33, 34; 12:2; 13:5, 10, 11, 11; 14:16, 20, 26; 15:23, 24, 27, 28, 36, 42, 43, 43, 44, 52, 52, 54, 54; 16:3, 10, 11, 12; 2Co 1:4, 6, 6, 14, 17, 20; 2:3, 5, 6, 10, 10, 12; 3:8, 15; 4:13; 5:1, 1, 2; 7:5, 7, 15; 8:14; 9:11; 10:2, 14, 18, 18; 11:7, 9, 20, 32; 12:10, 12, 18, 20, 21; 13:2, 10; Gal 1:13, 16; 2:11, 12, 12, 14, 19; 3:8, 8, 13, 17, 20; 4:4, 12, 13, 18, 27; 5:6, 18, 19, 22; Eph 1:13; 2:5, 8; 3:10, 14; 4:8, 20; 5:13, 28; 6:6; Php 1:6, 7, 7, 26; 2:12, 16, 19; 3:5, 8, 12; 4:15, 16; Col 1:23, 24; 2:11, 12, 23; 3:3, 4, 7, 22; 1Th 1:5; 2:13, 19; 3:1, 5, 13, 13; 4:14, 15; 5:1, 3, 3, 4, 7, 23; 2Th 1:7, 10; 2:5, 6, 14; 3:1, 7; 1Ti 1:3, 8; 4:14; 6:7, 7; 2Ti 1:4, 6, 17; 4:1, 3, 11, 13; Tit 2:13, 15; Phm 1:4; Heb 1:6; 2:8, 18; 3:8, 8, 14, 15, 18; 4:16; 6:7, 16; 7:1, 10, 12, 17, 23, 27; 8:5, 8, 8, 9, 13; 9:6, 16; 10:5, 18, 32, 34; 11:8, 9, 17, 21, 22, 22, 24, 29; 12:3, 5, 5, 17, 18, 25, 26; Jas 1:3, 4, 6; 2:8, 20, 21, 25; 4:3, 5, 10; 5:17; 1Pe 1:7, 11, 11, 17, 22; 2:12, 19, 23, 23; 3:6, 6, 9, 16, 18, 20; 4:4, 13; 5:1, 4; 2Pe 1:16, 17, 18; 2:4, 16, 20; 3:7, 12; 1Jn 2:15, 19, 28; 3:2, 2, 7, 8, 19; 5:15; 3Jn 5, 10, 10; Jude 9, 12; Rev 1:3, 12, 17; 2:10, 13; 6:3, 5, 7, 9, 10; 8:1, 13; 9:2; 10:3, 4, 7, 9; 11:7; 12:13; 14:7; 20:7; 21:16; 22:8

WHICH (433)

Ge 1:11; 2:11, 13, 14, 21; 3:19, 23; 13:18; 17:2; 21:23; 22:2; 23:19; 25:18; 26:18; 27:15; 31:47; 35:27; 38:14; 44:5; 45:6; 49:28, 30; Ex 3:13; 7:4; 10:26; 15:23; 16:7, 36; 25:16, 21; 26:27; 29:18; 36:27; 38:24, 30; 39:4; Lev 3:4, 10, 15; 7:1, 4; 8:22; 11:35; 15:4, 4, 9, 20, 22, 24, 26, 27; 16:8, 8; 17:8; 20:2, 22; 22:18; 23:5; 27:22; Nu 7:14, 20, 26, 32, 38, 44, 50, 56, 62, 68, 74, 80; 10:28; 18:24; 21:15, 16, 18, 18; 31:12, 37, 38, 39, 42; 34:2, 4; 36:3; Dt 1:19, 22; 3:10; 4:13; 7:25; 9:10; 10:5; 11:10; 15:14; 17:3; 20:18; 21:2; 28:27, 37; 29:23; 30:1; 32:49; 34:1; Jos 3:11, 16; 4:10; 7:14, 26; 10:27; 11:17; 12:2, 2, 5, 7; 13:3, 4; 14:9; 15:4, 7, 13; 17:7; 18:6, 7, 10, 17, 19; 24:13, 32, 33; Jdg 1:1; 4:5; 6:11, 32; 8:28; 9:4; 10:4; 11:27; 13:25; 18:12; 20:18, 39; Ru 2:9; 1Sa 6:18; 9:6; 10:4; 16:3; 21:4; 23:19; 24:15; 26:1; 27:6; 2Sa 2:1; 5:20; 6:2, 8; 14:14; 17:14; 23:20; 1Ki 7:6; 8:21; 9:10; 10:1; 11:32; 13:12, 12; 16:15; 2Ki 1:4, 6, 16; 6:11; 9:5, 36; 14:28; 15:5; 16:14; 17:13, 13, 33; 18:9, 20; 19:28, 28, 33; 25:8; 1Ch 11:22; 13:6, 11; 14:11; 16:40; 27:2, 4, 5, 7, 8, 9, 10, 11, 12, 13, 14, 15; 28:13, 16; 29:8, 19; 2Ch 1:14; 12:15; 15:8; 20:11, 26, 34; 26:16; 28:8; 29:17; 30:6, 8; 32:32; 35:21; Ezr 1:7; 2:70; 6:5; 7:6, 14, 15, 16, 17; Ne 3:1; 8:1, 2, 15; 9:29; 11:23; 13:1; Est 8:2; Job 16:22; 38:16; Ps 5:8; 7:T; 17:4; 25:6; 36:9; 48:1; 78:68; 104:26; 119:38; 140:10; Pr 4:18; 21:22; Ecc 3:20, 20; 11:6; SS 3:11; 8:11; Isa 3:14; 9:1; 18:1; 19:3; 33:14; 36:5; 37:29, 29, 34; 43:9; 51:1, 1; 63:7; Jer 5:17; 7:11; 13:25; 16:15; 23:8; 24:10; 27:13; 31:21; 32:11, 43; 40:12; 43:5; 46:28; 49:28; 51:7; 52:12; La 1:12; Eze 10:11; 13:20; 16:17; 23:22; 29:13, 14; 31:18; 34:12, 26; 36:21, 22; 38:8; 39:16; 40:7, 11; 41:8, 11; 42:8; 45:25; 46:17, 19; 47:16; 48:26, 30; Da 6:8, 12; 8:5; Hos 2:21; Joel 3:3, 7, 21; Jnh 1:7; Mic 5:7; Na 3:9; Zec 11:13; 14:4; Mt 12:31; 13:14; 18:1; 19:18; 21:31; 22:15, 36; 23:17, 19; 26:28, 48; 27:9, 17, 21, 33, 46, 60; Mk 9:34; 12:13, 28; 14:44; 15:22, 34; Lk 2:15; 4:29; 9:46; 10:36; 11:27; 13:16; 14:5; 22:1, 23; Jn 1:38, 41, 42; 8:46; 10:32; 19:31; Ac 1:19, 24; 4:36; 6:10; 9:36; 10:3; 17:26; 21:39; 24:14; Ro 6:14, 16; 7:10, 13, 18; 10:8; 1Co 2:7; 4:21; 6:15; 7:3; 11:24; 12:11; 15:42; 16:21; 2Co 3:9, 9, 11, 11; 12:13; Gal 1:4, 11; 3:12; 5:17; Eph 4:9, 22; 5:29; 6:17; Php 1:22; 3:14; 4:7, 19; Col 1:18; 2:2; 1Th 2:13; 2Th 1:5, 11; 3:17; 1Ti 3:15; 6:12, 17; Tit 1:2; Heb 7:10, 11; 9:4, 7, 23; 12:24; 13:9, 10, 14; 1Pe 3:4, 21; 2Jn 3, 8; Jude 7; Rev 1:1; 5:6; 10:2; 11:8; 12:4; 13:8, 17; 15:1; 16:21; 17:16; 20:3, 8

WHO (4628)

Ge 2:18; 3:6, 11, 12; 4:14, 15, 15, 20, 23, 24, 24; 6:4; 7:23; 9:5, 6; 10:8; 12:3, 3, 5; 13:5; 14:12, 13, 13, 20, 21, 23; 15:7; 16:13, 13, 13; 17:6, 14, 21; 19:5, 9, 15; 21:6, 7, 26; 24:2, 5, 7, 15, 31, 43, 59, 65; 25:11, 27; 26:11; 27:18, 29, 29, 32, 33; 29:16; 31:32, 37, 53; 33:5; 34:1; 35:1, 3; 36:3, 9, 21, 24, 30, 31, 32, 35, 40; 38:8, 9, 9, 21, 21, 25, 28; 41:12, 38, 38, 38; 42:30; 44:10, 15, 16, 17; 45:1, 8; 46:8, 15, 26, 27; 48:5, 15, 16; 49:9, 23, 26; 50:14, 23; Ex 1:1, 8; 2:10, 14, 14, 16; 3:11, 14; 4:11, 11, 19; 5:2, 4, 20; 6:5, 7, 27, 30; 9:21; 11:5; 12:15, 19, 29, 38, 44, 46, 48, 49; 13:9, 16; 14:8, 19, 28; 15:7, 11, 11, 26; 16:6, 18, 18; 18:16, 21, 27; 19:12, 21, 22; 20:2, 5, 5, 6, 24; 21:8, 8, 12, 15, 17, 24, 24; 22:1, 2, 3, 3, 6, 8, 9, 14, 16, 19, 20, 28; 23:5, 8, 22; 24:14; 25:2; 28:3; 29:29, 46; 30:12, 14, 33, 33, 38; 31:13, 14, 14, 15; 32:1, 1, 4, 8, 23, 26; 33:7, 11; 34:11, 14, 16; 35:2, 10, 24, 25, 26, 29; 36:2; 38:8, 26; Lev 2:8; 4:2, 31, 35; 5:8, 10, 12, 13, 18; 6:6, 26, 27; 7:9, 14, 19, 20, 25, 27, 33; 10:3; 11:36, 45; 13:9, 45; 14:2, 3, 21, 32, 32, 46, 47; 15:2, 7, 32, 33, 33; 16:1, 28, 29, 32; 17:10, 12; 18:25, 26, 28; 19:10, 20, 33, 36; 20:2, 5, 8, 9, 24, 27; 21:3, 6, 7, 10, 17, 18, 23; 22:5, 9, 14, 16, 18, 32, 33; 23:29, 30, 42; 24:9, 10, 14, 15, 16, 16, 17, 18, 19, 22; 25:6, 10, 26, 27, 29, 38, 40, 44, 45, 49; 26:13, 32, 36; Nu 1:3, 20, 45, 51; 3:10, 15, 17, 38, 38, 40, 43, 46, 49; 4:3, 23, 30, 35, 37, 39, 41, 43, 45, 47; 5:2, 2, 7, 8, 18; 7:2; 9:13; 11:4, 20, 28, 34; 13:28, 31, 32; 14:6, 14, 23, 29, 34, 35, 36, 38, 45; 15:30, 41; 16:5, 5, 5, 7, 11, 32, 35, 38, 39, 40, 49; 17:13; 18:4, 7, 11, 13; 19:8, 9, 10, 10, 11, 13, 14, 14, 16, 16, 18, 18, 18, 18, 18, 19, 20, 21, 21; 20:16; 21:1, 8, 9, 32, 34; 22:5, 9, 40; 23:9, 10, 10; 24:4, 4, 4, 9, 9, 9, 16, 16, 16, 16, 19, 23; 25:5, 18; 26:2, 4, 9, 19, 57, 62; 27:3, 17, 18, 21; 30:2, 16; 31:14, 16, 16, 17, 18, 19, 21, 27, 47, 49; 32:11, 27, 29, 39; 33:40, 55, 55; 34:17; 35:6, 12, 15, 32, 34; 36:8; Dt 1:4, 4, 13, 17, 33, 39, 44; 2:4, 8, 23, 29; 3:2, 24; 4:3, 4, 42; 5:3, 6, 9, 9, 10; 6:12, 15; 7:6, 9, 9, 10; 8:14, 18; 9:2; 10:17, 21, 21; 11:2, 30; 12:12, 18; 13:1, 5, 5, 7, 7, 10; 14:29; 15:11; 16:11, 15; 17:12; 18:6, 7, 12, 19, 20, 20; 19:3, 6, 17, 20; 20:1; 21:1, 17, 17, 18; 22:2, 5, 23, 26, 28; 23:8, 10; 25:9, 16, 18; 26:5; 27:15, 16, 17, 18, 19, 20, 21, 22, 23, 24, 25, 26; 29:11, 15, 19, 22; 30:12, 13; 31:5, 7, 8, 9, 13, 25; 32:4, 6, 15, 18, 18, 27, 35, 38, 39, 39, 41; 33:16, 20, 27, 29; Jos 1:18; 2:3, 4, 16, 22; 3:8, 14, 15, 17; 4:9, 10; 5:1, 4, 5, 6, 7, 7; 6:23, 25, 26; 7:5, 15; 8:17, 20, 22, 26, 35; 9:1, 8, 10; 10:6; 11:21; 12:1, 2, 8; 13:10, 12, 21, 21, 31; 14:8; 15:16, 17, 63; 17:3, 12; 18:2, 8; 20:3, 3, 4, 6, 6, 9; 21:4, 10, 13, 21; 22:20; 23:1; 24:11, 17, 18, 31, 31; Jdg 1:12, 13, 16, 20, 21, 24, 30; 2:7, 7, 10, 12, 14, 17, 18, 19; 3:1, 2, 15, 17, 18; 4:2, 3, 4, 6; 5:9, 10, 10, 14, 24, 31; 6:9, 19, 27, 29, 31; 7:3, 4, 4, 5, 5, 22, 23, 25; 8:31, 34; 9:4, 25, 28, 28, 33, 38, 46, 49; 10:8; 11:7, 19, 21, 23, 27; 12:14; 13:1, 8, 10, 11; 14:4, 14, 19, 20; 15:6, 19; 16:4, 24, 26, 27; 17:2, 2, 4; 18:1, 2, 3, 14; 19:22, 30; 20:4, 9, 15, 21, 37, 47; 21:5, 7, 11, 12, 13, 14, 16, 18, 20, 23; Ru 1:11; 2:1, 2, 5, 6, 19; 3:9, 12; 4:3, 5, 11, 12, 14, 15, 15; 1Sa 1:1, 26; 2:3, 4, 4, 5, 5, 10, 12, 14, 22, 25, 30, 30, 33, 35; 3:2, 8; 4:4, 8, 8, 15; 5:5, 12; 6:9, 20; 9:6; 10:3, 12, 27; 11:7, 12; 12:6; 13:15; 14:1, 3, 3, 17, 21, 22, 24, 28, 39, 41, 41, 45, 48, 49, 52; 15:28, 29; 16:1, 17; 17:10, 25, 26, 37; 18:10, 18; 19:24; 22:2, 2, 9, 11, 14;

23:22; 24:9, 14, 14, 19; 25:2, 10, 10, 10, 11, 11, 29, 32, 34, 39; 26:9, 14; 27:8; 28:7, 8, 23; 29:3; 30:17, 21, 24, 24, 26; 2Sa 1:8, 13, 13; 2:7, 23; 3:1, 1, 2, 6, 29, 29, 29, 29, 31; 4:2, 2, 4, 6, 8, 9, 11; 5:2, 14, 20; 6:2, 13, 21; 7:13, 18; 8:2; 9:2, 10, 13; 10:10; 11:3, 21; 12:5; 13:28; 14:2, 2, 16; 15:12, 18, 30; 16:2, 6, 10, 14, 18; 17:8, 25, 29; 18:13, 28, 28, 31; 19:6, 6, 8, 14, 28, 32; 20:19, 21; 21:5, 7, 12; 22:3, 4, 18, 28, 31, 32, 32, 41, 48, 48; 23:3, 3, 8, 13, 17, 21; 24:11, 17; 1Ki 1:2, 8, 20, 27, 29, 48; 2:32; 3:7, 9, 26, 26, 27; 4:7; 5:6; 8:15, 23, 32, 46, 50, 56; 9:8, 9, 20; 10:25; 11:9, 15, 18, 20, 34; 12:6, 8, 8, 9, 17, 18, 28, 31; 13:2, 14, 26, 33; 14:2, 8, 9, 11, 11, 13, 14; 15:18; 16:4, 4, 9; 17:1, 9, 20; 18:3, 12, 19, 22, 24; 19:17, 17, 18; 20:11; 21:10, 17, 18, 24, 24, 28; 22:13, 20, 46, 52; 2Ki 1:3, 7; 3:13, 15, 21, 24, 27; 4:1, 9, 18, 28; 5:2; 6:11, 33; 9:7, 16, 31, 32; 10:9, 9, 13, 15, 17, 19, 21, 23, 23; 11:2, 5, 7, 8, 9, 15, 15; 12:11, 14; 14:5, 7; 15:35; 17:2, 7, 28, 36, 39; 18:22; 19:4, 8, 11, 12, 25, 30, 30; 20:18; 21:11, 12, 14, 24; 22:15, 18; 23:5, 8, 9, 16, 17, 25; 25:11, 11, 19, 25; 1Ch 1:10, 36, 43, 43, 46; 2:22, 55; 3:1, 17; 4:8, 9, 10, 17, 18, 22, 23, 39, 41, 43; 5:11; 6:15, 33, 54; 7:15; 8:12, 32; 9:10, 14, 16, 17, 30; 11:2, 11, 15, 19, 23, 42; 12:1, 6, 18, 18, 18, 20, 21, 23, 27, 28; 13:6; 14:4, 11; 15:4, 16, 27; 17:12, 13, 16; 19:11; 21:17, 17, 20, 20, 27; 22:9, 10; 23:3; 24:3, 3; 25:2, 3; 26:6, 11, 31; 27:1, 6, 23, 26; 29:5, 5, 11, 14, 14; 2Ch 1:10; 2:6, 6, 7, 7, 7, 7, 12, 12; 5:11, 12, 12; 6:4, 14, 23, 36, 39; 7:6, 14, 18, 21, 22; 8:7; 9:24; 10:6, 8, 8, 9, 17, 18; 11:16; 12:5; 13:6; 15:9, 13; 16:2; 17:15, 16, 18; 18:2, 12, 19; 19:2, 11; 20:6, 7, 14, 35; 21:13, 16; 22:8, 9, 9, 11; 23:7, 8, 14, 14, 19; 24:12, 12; 25:3, 15; 26:5, 10, 10, 18; 28:15, 15, 23; 29:21, 23; 30:6, 7, 12, 16, 18, 18, 19, 21, 25, 25, 25; 31:1, 6, 14, 16, 17, 17, 19; 32:12, 18, 21, 22, 24; 33:25; 34:4, 9, 10, 23, 26; 35:3, 6, 11, 21; 36:3, 12, 20, 23; Ezr 1:3, 3, 4; 2:1, 2, 36, 40, 63; 3:8, 8; 4:12, 15; 5:3, 4, 9, 10, 12; 6:11, 12, 16, 21, 21; 7:11, 15, 25, 26, 27; 8:1, 13, 15, 16, 16, 18, 22, 22, 35, 36; 9:4, 14; 10:3, 8, 14, 17, 18, 23, 24, 24, 25; Ne 1:2, 2, 3, 5, 5, 11; 2:10; 3:8, 11, 17, 20, 24, 26, 27; 4:3, 12, 14, 17, 23; 5:8, 15; 6:10, 14; 7:2, 5, 6, 7, 39, 43, 65; 8:3, 7, 9, 10, 17; 9:7, 18, 24, 26, 27, 30, 32; 10:1, 9, 14, 28, 28, 36, 37; 11:2, 3, 6, 9, 12, 13, 16, 17, 17, 19, 36; 12:1, 8, 8, 24, 35, 40; 13:4, 4, 10, 26; Est 1:1, 8, 10, 13, 15; 2:4, 7, 15, 21; 3:13; 4:5, 11, 14; 6:2, 4, 6, 10, 13; 7:4, 5, 9; 8:10, 11; 9:2, 5, 16, 27; 10:3; Job 1:1, 15, 16, 17, 19; 3:8, 8, 16; 4:2, 3, 4, 6, 8; 5:3, 13; 7:2, 9; 8:10, 13, 22; 9:4, 12, 12, 14, 19, 24, 33; 11:8, 10, 11; 12:3, 4, 5, 5, 6, 12; 13:19; 14:4; 15:18; 18:21; 19:6; 20:7; 21:15, 19, 22, 28, 29; 22:8; 23:13; 24:21, 25; 25:3, 4, 6; 26:2, 14; 27:2, 2, 15; 29:11, 11, 12, 13, 25, 25; 30:1, 23, 31; 31:3, 16, 19, 35; 32:7; 34:2, 10, 13, 13, 29, 29; 35:10, 11; 36:15, 22; 37:24; 38:2, 5, 6, 8, 25, 25, 26, 27, 29, 29, 36, 37, 37, 41; 39:5, 26; 41:9, 10, 11, 13, 13, 14; 42:3, 17; Ps 1:1; 2:4, 12; 3:3, 6; 4:1, 6, 7; 5:5, 6, 11, 11; 6:5, 5, 8; 7:9, 11; 8:2; 9:10, 10, 11, 12, 12, 13, 17; 10:8, 16; 11:2, 5, 7; 12:4; 14:2, 4, 5; 15:1, 1, 2, 3, 4, 5, 5; 16:4, 7; 17:2, 7, 9, 9; 18:3, 17, 27, 30, 31, 31, 40, 47, 47; 19:11, 11; 21:8; 22:7, 8, 23, 25, 26; 24:3, 3, 4, 8, 10; 25:3, 3, 5, 8, 10, 12, 12, 14; 26:5; 27:6; 28:3, 3; 31:6, 15, 19, 19, 20, 23, 23, 24; 32:10, 11; 33:14, 18, 18; 34:T, 2, 5, 7, 8, 9, 10, 15, 16, 18, 21, 22, 22; 35:1, 1, 10, 10, 10, 10, 19, 20, 26, 26, 27, 27; 36:10; 37:1, 7, 9, 11, 14, 32, 37, 37; 38:13; 40:4, 4, 4, 14, 14, 16, 16; 41:1, 7, 9, 13; 42:8; 44:7, 7, 7; 49:10, 20; 50:5, 22; 51:14; 52:1, 7; 53:2, 4; 54:4; 55:12, 12, 19; 57:2, 3, 4; 58:8, 11, 11; 59:1, 7, 17; 60:4, 9, 9; 61:5; 63:11; 64:2, 5, 8, 10; 65:4, 5, 8; 66:6, 16, 20; 68:1, 4, 18, 20, 21, 30, 33; 69:4, 4, 6, 9, 14, 32, 33, 36, 36; 70:2, 2, 4, 4; 71:13, 13, 18, 19, 24; 72:12, 18; 73:27, 27; 75:3, 7, 7, 7; 76:7, 9; 80:1, 12; 81:10, 15; 84:4, 5, 5, 11, 12; 85:9; 86:5, 17; 87:4; 88:4; 89:6, 7, 9, 10, 15, 23, 41; 90:11; 91:1, 14, 14; 94:9, 9, 15, 16, 16, 20; 97:7, 7, 10, 11, 12; 101:5, 6; 102:24; 103:6, 11, 13, 17, 18, 18, 20, 21; 105:17; 106:2, 2, 3, 5, 21, 41; 107:34, 43; 108:10, 10; 109:20, 31; 111:2, 4, 5, 10; 112:1, 1, 5, 5, 6; 113:5, 5; 115:8, 8, 11, 13, 15; 118:4, 7, 26; 119:1, 2, 21, 38, 42, 53, 55, 63, 63, 74, 78, 79, 84, 85, 86, 113, 118, 122, 132, 162, 165; 120:6; 121:2, 3, 4; 122:6; 124:6, 8; 125:1, 4, 5, 5; 126:5; 128:1, 1, 4; 129:5, 8; 130:3; 134:1, 3; 135:1, 2, 18, 18, 20; 136:4, 5, 6, 7, 10, 13, 16, 17; 137:8, 9; 139:21, 21; 140:1, 2, 4; 141:4, 9; 144:1, 10, 15; 145:18, 18, 19, 20; 146:5, 6, 6, 7; 147:11, 11, 17; 148:14; Pr 1:5, 5, 19, 32, 33; 2:7, 8, 19, 21; 3:13, 18, 18, 27, 30; 4:19, 22; 5:13; 6:19, 19, 29, 29, 30, 32; 7:7, 11; 8:9, 13, 17, 17, 21, 32, 34, 36, 36; 9:7, 7, 15; 10:5, 9, 10, 17, 17; 11:13, 20, 22, 24, 25, 26, 26, 29, 30; 12:2, 2, 22, 22; 13:2, 3, 4, 5, 7, 7, 10, 13, 13, 14; 14:2, 2, 17, 21, 26, 29, 31, 31, 35, 35; 15:9, 12, 21, 27; 16:13, 20, 20, 22; 17:5, 5, 8, 15, 16, 19, 19; 18:9, 14, 21, 22, 24; 19:2, 6, 8, 26; 20:6, 6, 9, 16, 19, 24; 21:13, 16, 17; 22:8, 9, 11, 16, 21, 23; 23:6, 22, 25, 28, 29, 29, 29, 29, 29, 29, 30; 24:8, 11, 22, 24, 25; 25:12, 14; 26:10, 10, 12, 19; 27:4, 7, 8, 10, 13, 18, 18; 28:3, 5, 7, 7, 8, 8, 9, 10, 13, 14, 18, 20, 26, 27; 29:3, 4, 8, 14, 20, 21; 30:4, 4, 4, 4, 5, 9, 22, 22, 23, 23, 30; 31:3, 5, 8, 8, 10, 30; Ecc 1:1, 16; 2:7, 9, 19, 21, 25, 26, 26; 3:21; 4:3, 8, 8, 8, 10, 13; 5:1, 10, 12, 15, 20; 6:12, 12; 7:13, 18, 20, 26; 8:3, 3, 5, 5, 8, 10, 12; 9:2, 2, 11, 15, 16; 10:14; 12:7; SS 3:6, 6; 6:10; 8:1, 1, 5, 12; Isa 1:4; 2:6; 3:10, 16; 4:3, 5; 5:8, 11, 18, 20, 21, 22, 22; 6:8; 8:16; 9:2, 2; 10:1, 6, 7, 15, 15, 20; 11:9; 12:6; 13:15; 14:2, 2, 12, 16, 17, 17, 27, 27, 29, 30; 15:9, 9; 16:5; 17:10, 10, 14; 18:2, 7; 19:8, 8, 20, 20; 20:5; 22:11, 16; 23:6, 8; 24:14, 18, 18; 26:2, 3, 7, 19, 19, 21; 27:11, 13; 28:6, 9, 11; 29:7, 11, 12, 15, 15, 16, 16, 19, 20, 20, 21, 21, 22, 24; 30:9, 18, 19; 31:1, 2; 32:3, 3, 4, 9; 33:1, 15, 15, 15, 15, 15, 15, 15, 16; 35:3, 3, 4, 6, 8, 10; 36:3, 7; 37:4, 8, 11, 12, 26, 31, 31; 38:11, 18; 39:7; 40:12, 12, 12, 13, 13, 22, 22, 25, 26, 29, 31; 41:2, 2, 2, 4, 11, 20, 24, 26, 26; 42:3, 3, 5, 7, 10, 10, 17, 19, 19, 19, 24; 43:1, 7, 7, 8, 8, 9, 16, 25; 44:2, 7, 9, 9, 10, 11, 11, 19, 24, 25; 45:3, 7, 7, 7, 9, 9, 12, 16, 20, 21, 24; 46:3, 5, 11; 48:1, 1, 17; 49:5, 5, 7, 7, 17, 19, 21, 21, 21, 23, 24, 24, 25; 50:3, 6, 6, 8, 8, 9, 10, 11; 51:1, 7, 10, 11, 12, 12, 13, 15, 16, 19, 19, 21, 23, 23; 52:5, 6, 7, 11; 53:1, 8, 12, 12; 54:1, 10, 16, 17; 56:2, 2, 2, 4, 4, 6, 6, 8; 57:2, 15, 18, 20; 58:6, 6, 7, 7, 12; 59:8, 9, 14, 15, 20; 60:14, 18; 61:2, 3; 62:6; 63:1, 1, 1, 1, 11, 11, 13; 64:4, 4, 5, 5; 65:1, 1, 10, 16; 66:2, 2, 3, 8, 10, 17, 19, 19, 21, 24, 24; Jer 2:3, 6, 24, 24, 29; 3:6, 15, 20; 4:22, 30; 5:1, 6, 21, 21, 22, 26; 6:9, 10, 17; 7:2, 4, 28; 8:3; 9:1, 12, 12, 24, 25, 26; 10:2, 7, 8, 9, 11, 11; 11:3, 17; 12:17; 14:18; 15:2, 2, 2, 2, 5, 5, 5, 9, 10, 10; 16:7, 14, 14, 15, 16, 16; 17:5, 7, 9, 11, 13, 18; 18:16; 19:3, 8; 20:3, 10, 12, 15; 21:4, 9, 9, 12; 22:3, 7, 11, 13, 18, 25; 23:5, 7, 8, 14, 17, 17, 18, 23, 30, 31; 24:8; 25:23; 26:2, 19; 27:6, 9, 14, 16; 28:8, 9; 29:1, 8, 16, 16, 19, 21, 26, 27; 30:16, 16, 16, 20, 21; 31:10, 30, 35, 35; 32:12, 12, 24; 33:21, 22; 35:19; 37:2, 7, 19; 38:2, 2, 3, 16, 19, 19; 39:5, 9, 14; 40:1, 6, 7, 8, 10, 15, 15; 41:1, 3, 10; 42:17; 43:5; 44:7, 14, 15, 20, 24, 28, 30; 46:7, 9, 17, 18, 25, 26; 48:10, 10, 18, 19, 44, 44; 49:1, 9, 11, 17, 19, 19, 32; 50:7, 13, 16, 28, 28, 34, 44, 44; 51:11, 50, 56; 52:15, 15, 25, 30; La 1:8, 12, 16; 2:13, 15, 17; 3:1, 25, 30, 38; 4:5, 5, 9, 13; 5:5, 7; Eze 5:10, 14; 6:12, 12, 12; 7:9, 15, 15, 16; 9:3, 4, 11; 11:1, 2, 9, 21; 12:2; 13:2, 3, 15, 15, 16, 17, 18, 19, 19, 19; 14:4, 5, 7, 7, 10; 16:15, 32, 44, 46, 46, 57; 17:16, 24, 24; 18:4, 4, 9, 10, 14, 20, 20, 25, 29; 20:9, 11, 14, 22, 32, 38; 21:27, 31; 22:6, 9, 10, 11, 11, 27, 30; 23:2, 10, 42; 25:16; 26:2, 20, 20; 27:35; 28:9, 18, 19; 30:4; 31:12, 18; 32:18, 20, 22, 23, 24, 24, 27, 29, 30, 32; 33:4, 17, 21, 32; 34:2, 4, 16, 16, 27; 35:7, 7, 15; 36:34; 38:2, 11, 12, 13, 13; 39:6, 10, 11; 40:45; 42:13; 43:6, 19; 44:5, 5, 7, 9, 10, 16, 16; 45:4, 5, 15, 20; 46:9; 47:22; 48:11, 19; Da 1:3, 3, 11, 13, 15; 2:10, 24, 25, 27, 28; 3:6, 11, 28, 29; 4:34, 35, 37; 5:11, 13, 23; 6:7, 12, 24; 7:13, 24; 8:7, 15; 9:1, 4, 6; 10:7, 16, 18; 11:3, 20, 21, 30, 32, 32, 33, 34, 35, 39; 12:1, 3, 3, 6, 7, 7, 10, 12; Hos 2:8; 4:15; 7:5, 13; 9:4, 7; 11:3, 3; 12:9, 11, 13; 13:4, 13; 14:8, 9, 9; Joel 1:13; 2:11, 14, 17, 17, 25, 26, 32, 32; 3:6; Am 2:7, 10; 3:12; 4:1, 1, 11, 13; 5:8, 8, 8, 10, 13, 15, 18, 19; 6:1, 4, 10; 8:4, 14; 9:1, 10; Ob 3, 5, 8, 14, 17; Jnh 1:8, 9; 2:8; 3:9; Mic 1:5; 2:1, 4, 8, 8, 12; 3:2, 5, 5; 4:6, 6; 6:11, 14, 16; 7:1, 13, 18; Na 1:1, 2, 6, 6, 7, 11, 11; 3:7, 10, 12, 19, 19; Hab 1:3, 6, 12, 13, 13, 16; 2:9, 12, 15, 19; 3:14, 16; Zep 1:6, 9, 9, 11, 11, 12; 2:3, 3, 5, 9; 3:3, 10, 12, 12, 13, 18, 19, 19, 19; Hag 2:3; Zec 1:4, 9, 11, 13, 19; 2:3, 3, 7, 8, 8; 3:2; 4:1, 9, 14; 5:3, 3, 4, 5; 6:4, 5, 8, 14; 10:1, 6; 11:9, 11, 16, 17; 12:1, 3, 8, 10; 13:7; 14:16, 18, 21; Mal 1:14; 2:4, 11, 12; 3:2, 2, 5, 5, 5, 15, 15, 16, 16, 18, 18; 4:2; Mt 1:16; 2:6, 16, 20; 3:7, 11, 11, 14; 4:16, 16, 23; 5:3, 4, 5, 6, 7, 9, 10, 19, 28, 32, 32, 38, 42, 42, 44, 46; 6:4, 5, 6, 12, 14, 16, 18, 18, 32; 7:8, 8, 8, 11, 13, 15, 21, 24, 24, 26, 26, 29; 8:4, 17, 22, 27, 28; 9:13, 16, 20, 32, 38; 10:4, 10, 22, 26, 28, 28, 40, 40, 40, 41; 11:2, 6, 7, 8, 11, 15, 25, 28; 12:6, 7, 16, 20, 22, 30, 30, 32, 48, 48, 50; 13:9, 12, 12, 19, 20, 22, 23, 24, 37, 38, 39, 41, 43, 52, 52; 14:11, 36; 15:4, 18, 22, 31, 31, 36, 38; 16:13, 15; 18:4, 5, 6, 7, 7, 21, 23, 23, 24, 28; 19:9, 12, 25, 28, 29, 30, 30; 20:1, 12, 16, 16, 23; 21:9, 10, 23, 24, 41, 44; 22:2, 11, 23, 24; 23:12, 12, 21, 22, 31, 39; 24:13, 43, 45; 25:1, 3, 10, 16, 18, 22, 29, 29, 34; 26:6, 23, 25, 52, 57, 59, 60, 61, 68; 27:3, 17, 22, 32, 44, 52, 55, 57; 28:5, 11; Mk 1:7, 22, 24, 34, 34, 44; 2:6, 7, 16, 17, 21; 3:12, 19, 22, 29, 33, 33, 35; 4:9, 10, 14, 15, 16, 18, 20, 23, 25, 25, 41; 5:15, 16, 18, 25, 30, 31, 32, 42; 6:2, 28, 56; 7:10, 37; 8:6, 27, 29; 9:35, 37, 37, 37, 39, 40, 42; 10:15, 26, 29, 31, 31, 40; 11:9, 28, 29; 12:5, 15, 18, 19; 13:11, 13, 34; 14:3, 18, 20, 55, 65, 66; 15:21, 24, 32, 39, 43; 16:3, 6, 9, 10, 12, 13, 14, 16, 16, 17; Lk 1:5, 19, 50, 66, 71, 79; 2:5, 18, 25, 38, 47, 52; 3:2, 7, 11, 16; 4:22, 25, 27, 27, 34; 5:14, 21, 21, 32, 39; 6:16, 20, 21, 21, 22, 24, 25, 25, 26, 27, 28, 28, 30, 32, 33, 34, 35, 40, 48, 49, 49; 7:12, 23, 24, 25, 28, 35, 39, 39, 42, 47, 49; 8:3, 8, 12, 13, 14, 15, 18, 18, 21, 25, 27, 35, 36, 38, 43, 45; 9:9, 11, 18, 20, 38, 48, 48, 48, 50, 60, 62; 10:2, 6, 7, 16, 16, 16, 21, 29, 36, 37; 11:4, 10, 10, 10, 13, 14, 21, 22, 23, 23, 28, 33, 51; 12:4, 5, 10, 10, 14, 20, 37, 38, 39, 48; 13:4, 11, 27, 30, 30, 35; 14:7, 14, 28, 30, 31, 35; 15:7, 7; 16:5, 11, 14, 18, 18, 19, 19, 26; 17:1, 10; 18:2, 3, 7, 8, 9, 17, 26, 26, 29, 43; 19:10, 24, 26, 26, 27, 38; 20:2, 18, 27, 28, 39; 22:3, 21, 24, 26, 37, 52, 64; 23:12, 26, 29, 49; 24:5, 10, 16, 18, 19, 21, 23, 38, 47; Jn 1:9, 9, 12, 15, 18, 21, 22, 22, 24, 27, 29, 30, 33, 40; 2:16; 3:15, 16, 18, 18, 21, 33, 36, 36; 4:10, 12, 23, 24, 25, 29, 33, 34, 47; 5:10, 11, 12, 15, 23, 24, 24, 25, 29, 29, 30, 43, 45; 6:33, 35, 35, 38, 40, 44, 45, 46, 47, 50, 51, 54, 56, 57, 57, 58, 63, 64, 64, 71; 7:16, 17, 18, 18, 25, 33, 39, 45, 48, 50; 8:7, 16, 18, 19, 19, 24, 25, 26, 29, 30, 31, 34, 51, 52, 53, 53, 53, 54; 9:1, 4, 8, 10, 17, 17, 17, 21, 22, 24, 31, 36, 39, 40; 10:1, 6, 8, 9, 35, 36; 11:2, 25, 27, 31, 36, 45, 49; 12:4, 6, 13, 17, 20, 21, 25, 25, 26, 34, 38, 44, 45, 46, 48, 49; 13:10, 11, 16, 18, 20, 20, 20, 24, 25; 14:7, 7, 9, 9, 10, 12, 16, 17, 21, 21, 23, 24, 24, 28; 15:5, 6, 21, 23; 16:2, 5; 17:20; 18:14, 21, 37; 19:11, 12, 24, 38, 39; 20:15, 29; 21:4, 20, 20, 24; Ac 1:13, 16, 21; 2:21, 39, 41, 47; 3:13, 23; 4:4, 13, 13, 14, 22, 34; 5:1, 5, 9, 11, 17, 32, 32, 34, 36; 6:1, 1, 3, 5, 6; 7:18, 27, 35, 35, 38, 40, 40, 47, 52; 8:4, 7, 33; 9:5, 17, 21, 21, 33, 39; 10:1, 2, 2, 6, 22, 32, 35, 36, 38, 41, 43, 44, 45; 11:11, 12, 17, 19, 20; 13:16, 21, 23, 26, 31, 39, 43, 48; 14:2, 15; 15:5, 8, 18, 19, 26, 33, 35; 16:13, 16, 32; 17:4, 17, 23, 24, 31, 32; 18:2, 7, 24, 27; 19:13, 15, 18, 19, 24, 29; 20:34, 34; 21:8, 9, 10, 12, 23, 28, 33, 38; 22:8, 19, 25, 29; 23:5, 9; 24:5, 22, 24; 25:19; 26:15, 18; 27:43; 28:14, 21, 30; Ro 1:3, 6, 16, 18, 25, 32; 2:2, 7, 8, 8, 9, 10, 13, 14, 19, 27, 27; 3:8, 22, 24, 25; 4:6, 11, 12, 14, 15, 16, 17, 17, 24; 5:7, 14, 17; 7:1, 1, 4, 24; 8:1, 4, 5, 5, 8, 9, 11, 14, 19, 27, 28, 31, 32, 33, 33, 34, 34, 37; 9:5, 8, 10, 20, 20, 22, 25, 31, 33; 10:4, 11, 12, 12, 13, 15, 16, 20, 20; 11:4, 15, 17, 22, 24, 34, 34, 35; 12:19; 13:1, 2, 3, 3, 4, 12; 14:1, 2, 3, 3, 3, 3, 4, 6, 6, 6, 9, 9, 22; 15:1, 3, 5, 13, 21, 21, 26, 31, 33; 16:2, 4, 6, 7, 12, 13, 14, 15, 17, 22, 27; 1Co 1:2, 9, 18, 18, 21, 27, 27, 27, 30, 31; 2:6, 9, 14, 14, 15, 16, 16; 3:3, 4, 5, 5, 6, 7, 7, 8, 8, 9, 12, 17, 19; 4:1, 2, 4, 12, 12; 5:1, 3, 9, 10, 10, 11, 12; 6:1, 4, 5, 8, 9, 9, 9, 17, 19; 7:8, 10, 12, 13, 15, 18, 18, 25, 34, 38, 38; 8:2, 3, 6, 10; 9:3, 6, 7, 10, 12, 13, 13, 14, 14, 20, 21, 22, 26; 10:11, 18, 27, 28; 11:19; 12:4, 6, 11, 28, 28, 28, 28, 28; 14:3, 4, 4, 10, 11, 13, 16, 23, 24, 28, 30, 31, 32; 15:10, 18, 20, 22, 27, 28, 29, 33, 52, 52, 57; 16:9, 16, 18, 19; 2Co 1:3, 9, 17, 21; 2:2, 3, 5, 14, 16, 16, 16, 17, 17; 3:6, 13; 4:2, 4, 4, 6, 14; 5:12, 15, 15, 17, 18, 21; 6:14; 7:6, 6, 12, 12; 8:6, 15, 15, 22, 23, 23; 9:6, 6, 7, 10, 11; 10:2, 6, 7, 11, 12, 17; 11:9, 12, 19, 26, 29, 29, 31; 12:21; 13:2; Gal 1:1, 6, 7, 8, 17, 23; 2:4, 6, 8, 9, 12, 20, 21; 3:7, 9, 10, 10, 13, 19, 27; 4:5, 17, 21, 27, 29, 29; 5:5, 5, 7, 8, 10, 12, 24; 6:1, 6, 8, 8, 12, 13, 16; Eph 1:1, 3, 12, 19, 23; 2:2, 11, 17, 17, 21; 4:6, 10, 10, 11, 15, 29, 30; 5:2, 5, 6, 6, 15; 6:12, 24; Php 1:1, 6; 2:20; 3:2, 3, 3, 5, 15, 17; 4:13, 15, 19, 21, 22; Col 1:2, 7, 8, 12, 12, 13, 18, 21; 2:1, 12; 3:4, 6, 10, 13, 18, 25; 4:5, 7, 10, 15; 1Th 1:1, 10; 2:2, 4, 4, 4, 13, 14; 3:13; 4:8, 8, 12, 13, 13, 14, 15, 15, 16, 17; 5:8, 12, 14, 14, 14, 18, 24; 2Th 1:1, 6, 7, 8, 8; 2:2, 3, 7, 10, 13, 16; 3:6, 14, 15; 1Ti 1:3, 9, 9, 9, 9, 9, 10, 10, 17; 2:2, 5, 10, 14; 3:3, 4, 8, 13; 4:3, 6, 10, 10, 16; 5:3, 5, 5, 6, 8, 9, 9, 10, 14, 16, 17, 17, 18, 20; 6:1, 4, 9, 13, 13, 17, 17, 20; 2Ti 1:9, 10, 14, 15; 2:2, 4, 14, 15, 15, 19, 19, 22, 25; 3:6, 6, 12, 14; 4:1, 3, 8; Tit 1:6, 9, 10, 10, 14, 15; 2:8; 3:8, 14, 15; Heb 1:14; 2:3, 9, 10, 14, 15; 3:1, 2, 3, 4, 16, 16, 17, 17, 18; 4:3, 3, 6, 10, 11, 14; 5:5, 7, 9, 12, 13, 14; 6:4, 4, 5, 6, 12, 17, 18; 7:5, 6, 6, 7, 7, 8, 9, 15, 22, 25, 28; 8:4, 6, 6; 9:9, 15, 15, 16, 17, 25, 28; 10:1, 21, 28, 29, 29, 30, 30, 33, 34, 38, 39; 11:6, 6, 7, 12, 14, 14, 17, 27, 31; 12:7, 9, 11, 13, 14, 23, 23, 24, 25, 25; 13:2, 4, 4, 7, 9, 20; Jas 1:9, 10, 12, 12, 13, 17; 2:2, 5, 5, 6, 7, 10, 10, 11, 15; 3:1, 2, 9, 18; 4:11, 12, 13; 5:6, 7, 10, 11, 11, 13, 15, 20; 1Pe 1:1, 12, 15; 2:4, 4, 5, 6, 7, 7, 14, 14, 15, 18, 21, 23; 3:1, 12, 12, 13, 20; 4:5, 6, 9, 17, 19; 5:1, 14; 2Pe 1:1, 1, 9, 21; 2:1, 7, 8, 10, 10, 12, 15, 18; 3:3, 16; 1Jn 1:1, 2, 2; 2:1, 5, 6, 9, 10, 11, 13, 13, 13, 14, 14, 14, 22, 22, 23, 23, 26, 29; 3:1, 3, 4, 6, 6, 8, 9, 10, 10, 10, 12, 14, 15, 24; 4:1, 4, 4, 6, 7, 8, 15, 16; 5:1, 1, 5, 5, 10, 10, 13, 16, 18; 2Jn 1, 3, 11; 3Jn 5, 7, 9, 11, 11; Jude 1, 5, 6, 7, 8, 11, 14, 19, 24, 24, 25; Rev 1:3, 3, 4, 4, 4, 5, 5, 6, 7, 8, 8, 8, 12, 18; 2:1, 1, 2, 7, 7, 8, 8, 11, 12, 14, 14, 15, 17, 17, 17, 20, 22, 23, 24, 26, 26, 26, 29; 3:1, 4, 5, 6, 7, 7, 9, 9, 10, 12, 13, 14, 19, 21, 22; 4:8, 8, 8, 9, 10; 5:1, 2, 2, 4, 12; 6:8, 9, 10, 16, 17; 7:2, 4, 13, 13, 14, 15, 17; 8:2, 13; 9:4, 14, 14, 15, 20; 10:6, 6, 8; 11:5, 10, 10, 11, 13, 17, 17, 18, 18; 12:5, 10, 12, 13, 17; 13:4, 6, 6, 8, 8, 9, 10, 10, 12, 14, 14, 18; 14:1, 3, 6, 7, 9, 9, 13, 18; 15:2, 4, 6, 7; 16:2, 2, 5, 5, 5, 9, 15, 15; 17:1, 1, 2, 6, 8, 8, 12, 16; 18:8, 9, 15, 23, 24; 19:2, 4, 5, 9, 10, 20, 20, 20; 20:4, 4, 6, 10, 11; 21:6, 7, 8, 8, 9, 15, 27; 22:6, 7, 8, 8, 9, 11, 11, 11, 11, 14, 15, 17, 17, 18, 20

WHO'S (1)

Jn 7:20

WHOM (231)

Ge 10:14; 17:12; 21:12; 22:2; 45:4; 48:15; 49:10, 10; Ex 6:17, 26; 10:8; 15:13, 16; 22:9; 32:11; 33:12; 36:1; Lev 10:6; 20:23; 25:42, 55; 26:45; 27:24; Nu 5:8; 16:7; 23:8, 8; 31:40; 33:4; Dt 9:29; 21:8; 28:48, 53; 29:14; 34:10; Jos 24:15; Jdg 20:16, 25, 35; Ru 4:11; 1Sa 17:45; 21:9; 29:5; 30:13; 2Sa 6:22; 7:15; 19:10; 22:3; 23:1; 1Ki 5:5; 8:51; 11:34; 17:1; 19:2; 21:26; 2Ki 3:14; 5:16; 17:26; 19:22, 22, 22; 21:2, 9; 24:16; 1Ch 1:12; 2:53; 7:16; 15:24; 29:1; 2Ch 22:7; 28:3; 33:2, 9; 34:12; 35:22; Ezr 4:10; 5:14; 8:33; Ne 9:37; Est 6:6; 7:5; 10:2; Job 15:19; Ps 18:2; 47:4; 73:25; 94:1, 12, 12; 105:26; 109:1; Pr 3:12; Isa 6:8; 10:3; 25:9; 37:23, 23, 23; 40:18, 25; 42:1, 24; 46:5; 47:15; 51:2; 53:1; 57:4; Jer 6:10; 14:16; 20:6; 22:25; 25:9, 15; 29:22; 30:9, 17; 41:2; 42:6; 43:6; La 3:52; Eze 16:37; 21:29; 23:9; 31:2; 47:23; Da 3:12, 17; 5:12; 6:16, 20; 9:21; Joel 2:32; Am 6:1; Hag 1:12; Zec 12:10; Mal 1:4; 3:1; Mt 8:12; 11:10, 27; 12:18; 19:11; 21:44; 22:18; 23:35; 24:45; 25:20; Mk 12:6; 16:9; Lk 2:14; 7:27, 43; 8:2, 2; 9:9; 10:22; 12:5, 42, 48, 48; 19:15; 20:18; Jn 5:45; 6:68; 12:38; 13:22, 26; 17:24; 18:4, 7; 19:37; 20:2; 21:7; Ac 2:32, 36; 3:13; 4:10, 27; 7:52; 10:41; 13:22, 37; 14:23; 19:13; 20:25, 28; 25:19; 27:23, 23; Ro 1:9; 3:19; 8:33; 9:7, 24, 25; 11:2; 13:7; 14:15; 16:8, 10, 13; 1Co 8:6, 6, 11; 10:19; 15:6; 2Co 1:19; Gal 3:19; Eph 1:13; Col 1:16; 3:12; 1Th 1:10; 2Th 2:8; 2Ti 1:12; Heb 2:10; 3:1, 18; 4:13; 10:14; 11:9, 18; 12:2; Jas 4:5; 5:4; 1Pe 1:11, 17; 5:12; 1Jn 4:20; 2Jn 1; 3Jn 1; Jude 23

WHOSE (168)

Ge 24:23, 40, 47, 62; 32:17, 17; Ex 6:15; 23:27; 35:22; Lev 16:27; Nu 24:3, 15; Dt 19:1; 21:6; 25:10; 28:49; Jos 2:10; 12:1; 24:15; Jdg 6:10; 18:27; Ru 2:12, 19; 1Sa 10:26; 12:3; 17:55; 28:11; 2Sa 3:2, 3, 3, 4, 4, 5; 21:8; 1Ki 1:5; 2:13; 18:15; 2Ki 8:1; 17:34; 1Ch 3:1, 1, 2, 2, 3, 3; 11:23; 28:18; 2Ch 16:9; 29:31; Ne 11:21, 22; Job 3:15; 15:33; 26:4; 29:19, 19; 30:1; Ps 7:10; 17:14; 24:4; 32:1, 1, 2, 2, 11; 33:12, 12; 57:4, 4; 68:5; 73:1; 95:10; 125:4; 127:5; 144:15; 146:5; Pr 2:12; 25:20; Ecc 10:16, 16, 17, 17; Isa 4:3; 10:10; 26:3; 31:9; 45:1; 47:4; 48:2; 57:15; 63:12; Jer 5:15, 15; 7:28; 9:24; 31:30; 44:28; 46:18; 48:15; 51:57; Eze 1:26; 3:5; 7:13; 9:5; 17:16; 23:20; 31:16; 40:3; 42:2; 48:7; Da 8:9; 9:26; 12:1, 2; Hos 13:8; Am 5:27; Mic 5:2; Zep 1:13, 13; Mt 5:8; 21:23; 22:20, 28, 42; Mk 5:22; 7:25; 11:28; 12:16, 23; Lk 14:2; 20:2, 24, 33; Jn 4:46; 8:47; 18:26; Ac 4:7; 13:37; 16:1, 1; 19:35; 25:14, 24; 27:2; Ro 2:29; 4:7, 7, 8; Php 3:18; 4:3; 1Ti 3:2; 5:24, 25; Tit 1:15; Heb 3:17; 7:13; 12:23; Jas 2:7; Jude 18, 22; Rev 2:18, 18; 6:8; 13:8, 12; 17:8; 20:15; 21:27

WILL (11210)

Ge 1:11, 14, 26; 2:17, 18, 18, 23; 3:3, 5, 5, 14, 14, 15, 15, 15, 15, 16, 16, 16, 17, 18, 18, 19, 19, 22; 4:7, 12, 12, 14, 15, 15, 24; 5:29; 6:3, 3, 7, 7, 9, 13, 17, 17, 20; 7:3, 4, 4; 8:21, 22; 9:2, 14, 15, 15, 15, 16; 11:4, 6, 6; 12:1, 2, 2, 2, 3, 3, 12, 13, 13; 13:9; 14:23; 15:1, 1, 2, 3, 4, 4, 5, 8, 13, 13, 14, 14, 15, 16; 16:5, 10, 11, 12, 12, 12, 12; 17:2, 2, 4, 5, 5, 5, 6, 6, 6, 7, 7, 7, 8, 8, 11, 13, 14, 15, 15, 16, 16, 16, 19, 19, 19, 20, 20, 20, 21; 18:10, 10, 14, 14, 18, 18, 19, 19, 21, 23, 24, 26, 28, 28, 29, 30, 31, 32, 32; 19:13, 15, 17, 20, 21, 21, 31, 32, 32, 34; 20:4, 7, 7, 11, 11, 16; 21:6, 12, 13, 18, 23; 22:2, 5, 5, 5, 8, 14, 14, 17, 17, 17, 18; 23:6, 11, 13; 24:3, 5, 7, 7, 14, 14, 14, 40, 40, 40, 41, 43, 44, 46, 49, 58; 25:23, 23, 23; 26:3, 3, 4, 4, 4, 5, 11, 22, 24, 24, 24, 24, 29; 27:4, 25, 25, 37, 39, 40, 40, 40, 41, 41, 45; 28:13, 14, 14, 14, 15, 15, 15, 15, 20, 21, 21, 22, 22; 29:32, 34, 35; 30:3, 13, 15, 15, 20, 33, 33, 34; 31:3, 12, 14, 32, 44, 44, 48, 50, 52, 52; 32:5, 17, 20, 26, 28; 33:12, 14; 34:9, 11, 12, 15, 16, 17, 22, 23, 23, 30, 30; 35:3, 10, 11, 12, 12; 37:10, 22, 35; 38:8, 16, 17, 17; 40:13, 19, 19; 41:16, 16, 28, 29, 30, 30, 30, 31, 31, 32, 35, 36, 36, 36, 40, 40, 44; 42:15, 15, 18, 19, 20, 20, 33, 34, 34, 38; 43:4, 8, 8, 16, 18; 44:9, 10, 17, 31, 31, 32; 45:6, 6, 7, 10, 11, 11, 18, 18, 28; 46:3, 3, 4, 4, 4, 32, 34; 47:6, 16, 19, 19, 23, 24, 29, 31; 48:4, 4, 5, 5, 6, 6, 9, 19, 19, 19, 20, 20, 21, 21; 49:1, 4, 7, 8, 8, 8, 9, 10, 10, 13, 13, 13, 15, 16, 17, 19, 19, 20, 26, 29; 50:5, 15, 21, 24, 24, 24; Ex 1:10, 10; 2:9; 3:10, 12, 12, 12, 13, 15, 15, 17, 18, 19, 20, 20, 21, 21, 21, 22, 22, 22; 4:5, 5, 8, 9, 12, 12, 14, 15, 15, 16, 16, 21, 21, 22, 23; 5:2, 3, 9, 18; 6:1, 1, 1, 1, 6, 6, 7, 7, 7, 8, 8; 7:1, 1, 1, 2, 3, 4, 4, 4, 5, 9, 9, 17, 17, 18, 18, 18, 19; 8:2, 3, 3, 3, 4, 5, 8, 9, 9, 9, 10, 10, 11, 16, 21, 21, 21, 22, 22, 22, 23, 23, 26, 28, 29; 9:3, 4, 4, 9, 14, 14, 18, 19, 28, 29, 29, 29; 10:2, 3, 4, 5, 5, 6, 7, 9, 9, 10, 21, 26, 26, 28, 29; 11:1, 1, 1, 1, 4, 5, 5, 6, 6, 7, 7, 7, 8, 8, 8, 9, 9; 12:2, 7, 12, 12, 13, 13, 13, 14, 15, 17, 17, 19, 23, 23, 23, 25, 26, 27, 33, 48; 13:4, 6, 6, 9, 14, 14, 16; 14:3, 4, 4, 4, 4, 13, 14, 16, 16, 17, 17, 17, 18, 26; 15:1, 2, 2, 9, 9, 9, 9, 13, 13, 14, 14, 15, 15, 15, 16, 16, 17, 18, 21, 26, 26; 16:4, 4, 6, 7, 8, 12, 12, 12, 23, 25, 26, 28, 29, 32; 17:3, 6, 6, 6, 9, 14, 16; 18:22, 23, 23; 19:5, 5, 6, 8, 9, 11, 12, 21, 22, 24; 20:5, 7, 12, 12, 19, 19, 24; 21:2, 3, 3, 4, 4, 6, 7, 13, 19, 28, 30, 35, 36; 22:8, 11, 13, 23, 24, 24, 24, 24, 27, 27; 23:7, 12, 12, 15, 21, 22, 22, 23, 23, 25, 25, 26, 26, 27, 27, 28, 29, 30, 31, 31, 31, 33; 24:3, 7, 7, 12; 25:9, 16, 20, 21, 22, 22, 27, 31, 32, 33, 34, 35, 39; 26:11, 12, 13, 14, 15, 17, 18, 19, 20, 22, 24, 24, 25, 27, 28, 32, 33, 37; 27:3, 9, 10, 10, 11, 12, 13, 14, 14, 15, 16, 18, 18, 21, 21; 28:1, 1, 2, 3, 4, 7, 8, 10, 12, 14, 15, 15, 16, 17, 17, 18, 19, 20, 20, 21, 21, 24, 25, 28, 29, 29, 30, 30, 32, 32, 35, 35, 35, 37, 38, 38, 43; 29:9, 9, 10, 11, 16, 21, 25, 28, 29, 30, 35, 35, 37, 37, 41, 42, 43, 43, 44, 44, 45, 46; 30:6, 10, 12, 13, 16, 16, 19, 20, 29, 31, 33,

36, 38; **31:**14; **32:**5, 10, 12, 13, 13, 13, 29, 30, 30, 33, 34, 34; **33:**2, 3, 12, 13, 14, 14, 14, 16, 16, 17, 19, 19, 19, 19, 22, 23, 23, 23; **34:**1, 10, 10, 10, 11, 12, 15, 16, 16, 24, 24, 24; **35:**2; **36:**1; **40:**10; **Lev 1:**3, 4, 5, 7, 8, 9, 11, 12, 13, 15, 17, 17; **2:**2, 3, 3, 8, 9, 9, 10, 10, 16; **3:**2, 5, 8, 11, 13, 16, 16; **4:**5, 7, 12, 13, 16, 18, 20, 20, 22, 24, 25, 26, 26, 27, 28, 30, 31, 31, 31, 31, 34, 35, 35, 35; **5:**1, 2, 3, 4, 6, 6, 7, 7, 8, 8, 9, 9, 10, 10, 10, 12, 12, 12, 13, 13, 13, 16, 16, 17, 18, 18; **6:**6, 7, 7, 12, 15, 15, 15, 16, 18, 21, 22, 27; **7:**3, 5, 14, 18, 18, 18, 18, 18, 31, 31; **8:**33, 35; **9:**4, 6; **10:**3, 3, 6, 6, 9, 15; **11:**11, 24, 25, 26, 27, 28, 31, 32, 32, 32, 33, 34, 34, 35, 35, 36, 36, 37, 38, 39, 40; **12:**2, 5, 7, 7, 8, 8, 8; **13:**3, 4, 5, 5, 6, 6, 6, 13, 14, 17, 23, 34, 34, 37, 46, 50, 54, 58, 59; **14:**3, 4, 5, 6, 7, 7, 7, 8, 9, 11, 12, 13, 13, 14, 15, 16, 17, 18, 18, 19, 20, 20, 21, 24, 25, 26, 27, 28, 29, 29, 30, 31, 36, 36, 38, 40, 42, 42, 46, 48, 49, 50, 51, 51, 53, 53, 53; **15:**4, 5, 5, 6, 6, 9, 10, 10, 11, 11, 13, 15, 15, 16, 17, 18, 19, 19, 20, 21, 24, 24, 24, 25, 26, 27, 27, 27, 28, 30, 30, 31, 31, 31; **16:**6, 8, 8, 9, 10, 10, 11, 12, 12, 13, 13, 13, 15, 16, 16, 18, 19, 21, 21, 22, 24, 27, 30, 30, 31, 31, 32, 32; **17:**4, 5, 5, 6, 6, 9, 10, 10, 15, 15, 16; **18:**5, 18, 25, 28, 29; **19:**5, 7, 7, 8, 17, 20, 22, 22, 24, 25, 29, 31; **20:**3, 5, 6, 17, 20, 21, 22, 23, 24; **21:**17; **22:**6, 7, 9, 19, 25, 27, 29; **23:**2, 11, 13, 13, 17, 18, 18, 20, 20, 24, 28, 28, 29, 30, 32, 32, 34, 35, 36, 39, 39, 43; **24:**3, 7, 12, 15, 16; **25:**4, 7, 10, 10, 11, 12, 15, 19, 19, 20, 21, 21, 22, 22, 27, 28, 28, 30, 30, 31, 40, 41, 41, 50, 51, 52; **26:**4, 4, 4, 5, 5, 5, 6, 6, 6, 7, 8, 8, 8, 9, 10, 10, 11, 11, 12, 12, 12, 16, 16, 16, 16, 17, 17, 17, 17, 18, 19, 20, 20, 20, 21, 22, 22, 22, 22, 24, 24, 25, 25, 25, 26, 26, 26, 26, 28, 28, 29, 30, 30, 30, 31, 31, 32, 32, 33, 33, 33, 34, 34, 35, 36, 36, 36, 36, 36, 37, 37, 38, 39, 40, 41, 41, 42, 42, 43, 43, 44, 44, 45; **27:**8, 8, 9, 10, 12, 12, 14, 15, 16, 17, 19, 21, 21, 24, 33, 33; **Nu 1:**51, 51, 52, 53; **2:**2, 2, 2, 16, 17, 24; **3:**7, 8, 41, 45; **4:**4, 15, 15, 16, 16, 19, 20, 24, 27, 28, 31, 31; **5:**3, 9, 18, 19, 22, 23, 24, 25, 26, 26, 27, 27, 27, 28, 28, 30, 31, 31; **6:**9, 11, 11, 16, 18, 19, 20, 27, 27; **8:**7, 12, 12, 14, 14, 19, 19, 26; **9:**13, 13; **10:**3, 4, 5, 6, 9, 10, 29, 30, 32; **11:**17, 17, 17, 17, 17, 18, 18, 18, 20, 23; **13:**32; **14:**3, 8, 8, 11, 11, 12, 12, 13, 14, 15, 20, 22, 23, 23, 24, 24, 27, 28, 29, 30, 30, 31, 31, 32, 33, 33, 34, 35, 35, 42, 43, 43; **15:**7, 10, 16, 19, 24, 25, 25, 26, 28, 28, 30, 39, 40; **16:**5, 5, 7, 14, 16, 17, 26, 28, 30, 38; **17:**5, 5; **18:**1, 1, 3, 5, 7, 15, 18, 20, 21, 22, 23, 23, 24, 27, 30, 32, 32; **19:**3, 4, 7, 8, 9, 9, 10, 11, 12, 12, 13, 14, 16, 19, 20, 21, 22; **20:**8, 12, 17, 17, 18, 19, 19, 24, 26, 26; **21:**2, 2, 7, 8, 16, 22, 22, 34; **22:**4, 6, 8, 11, 13, 17, 18, 34, 38; **23:**3, 3, 3, 13, 23, 27, 27; **24:**7, 7, 7, 13, 14, 17, 17, 17, 18, 18, 19, 19, 22, 24, 24, 24; **25:**4, 13; **26:**65; **27:**13, 17, 17, 20, 21, 21, 21, 21; **28:**4, 12, 13, 17, 20, 23, 24, 24, 27, 27, 28; **29:**1, 2, 8, 13, 36; **30:**4, 5, 5, 7, 8, 11, 12, 12, 15; **31:**2, 50; **32:**11, 15, 17, 17, 17, 18, 22, 22, 23, 23, 25, 26, 27, 31, 32, 32; **33:**54, 54, 54, 55, 55, 56; **34:**2, 3, 3, 4, 4, 4, 5, 6, 7, 9, 10, 11; **35:**3, 3, 4, 5, 7, 8, 8, 8, 8, 12, 27, 33, 33; **36:**3, 3, 4, 8; **Dt 1:**13, 17, 17, 22, 30, 35, 36, 36, 37, 38, 39, 39, 41, 42, 42; **2:**4, 4, 5, 9, 18, 19, 24, 24, 25, 25, 27, 28; **3:**18, 21, 22, 28, 28; **4:**6, 6, 10, 10, 10, 22, 22, 23, 25, 26, 26, 26, 27, 27, 28, 29, 29, 30, 31, 40, 40, 40; **5:**9, 11, 16, 16, 25, 27, 31, 33; **6:**2, 3, 3, 10, 11, 11, 11, 15, 18, 18, 19, 20; **7:**1, 4, 4, 4, 12, 13, 13, 13, 14, 14, 14, 15, 15, 15, 16, 17, 19, 20, 22, 22, 23, 23, 24, 24, 24, 24, 25, 26; **8:**1, 1, 19, 20; **9:**3, 3, 3, 5, 6, 14, 28; **10:**2, 12; **11:**9, 14, 15, 15, 17, 17, 17, 17, 23, 24, 24, 25, 25, 27, 28; **12:**5, 6, 7, 7, 8, 10, 11, 12, 14, 18, 25, 25, 28, 28; **13:**11, 11, 17, 17, 18; **14:**29; **15:**4, 5, 6, 6, 6, 6, 6, 9, 10, 11, 16, 17, 18; **16:**3, 6, 14, 15, 18; **17:**7, 7, 8, 9, 10, 13, 14, 14, 17, 19, 20, 20, 20, 20; **18:**1, 1, 2, 12, 15, 17, 18, 18, 18, 19, 19, 21; **19:**1, 1, 9, 10, 10, 19, 19, 20; **20:**2, 3, 4, 4, 5, 8, 9, 11, 18; **21:**8, 9, 18, 21, 21; **22:**8, 19, 19, 19, 21, 22, 24, 29; **23:**21; **24:**11, 13, 19; **25:**2, 6, 6, 8, 9, 10, 15; **26:**4, 12, 19, 19, 19; **27:**3, 15, 16, 17, 18, 19, 20, 21, 22, 23, 24, 25, 26; **28:**1, 2, 3, 4, 4, 5, 6, 7, 7, 7, 8, 8, 8, 9, 10, 10, 11, 12, 12, 12, 13, 13, 15, 16, 17, 18, 18, 19, 20, 21, 22, 22, 23, 23, 24, 24, 25, 25, 25, 25, 26, 26, 27, 28, 29, 29, 29, 29, 30, 30, 30, 30, 30, 30, 31, 31, 31, 31, 32, 32, 32, 33, 33, 34, 35, 36, 36, 37, 38, 38, 39, 39, 39, 40, 40, 40, 41, 41, 41, 42, 43, 44, 44, 44, 45, 46, 48, 48, 48, 48, 49, 49, 51, 51, 51, 52, 52, 53, 53, 54, 55, 55, 56, 57, 57, 57, 59, 59, 60, 60, 61, 62, 63, 64, 64, 65, 65, 66, 66, 66, 67, 67, 67, 68, 68, 68; **29:**9, 20, 20, 20, 20, 21, 22, 22, 23, 23, 24, 25; **30:**3, 3, 4, 5, 5, 5, 6, 6, 7, 8, 9, 9, 9, 9, 10, 12, 13, 16, 16, 18, 18, 20; **31:**2, 3, 3, 3, 3, 4, 5, 5, 6, 6, 7, 7, 8, 8, 13, 13, 14, 16, 16, 17, 17, 17, 17, 17, 18, 20, 20, 20, 20, 20, 21, 21, 21, 23, 27, 29, 29, 29, 29; **32:**1, 2, 2, 2, 3, 7, 7, 20, 20, 21, 21, 23, 24, 24, 25, 25, 35, 35, 35, 35, 35, 36, 36, 37, 41, 42, 42, 43, 43, 46, 47, 52; **33:**10, 17, 28, 29, 29; **34:**4; **Jos 1:**3, 5, 5, 5, 6, 7, 8, 11, 16, 16, 17, 18; **2:**12, 13, 14, 19, 19, 19, 24; **3:**4, 5, 7, 7, 10, 10, 11, 13, 13, 13; **4:**6, 6, 7, 21; **6:**4, 5, 7, 17, 18, 18, 26, 26; **7:**9, 9, 12, 13, 14, 14, 14, 14, 15, 25; **8:**2, 5, 5, 6, 6, 7, 7, 18; **9:**8, 21, 23; **10:**8, 8; **11:**6; **13:**6; **14:**9, 12, 12; **15:**16; **17:**17, 18; **18:**4, 4, 5, 6, 6, 7, 8; **20:**4; **22:**18, 19, 23, 24, 27, 27; **23:**5, 5, 5, 10, 13, 13, 13, 14, 15, 15, 16, 16; **24:**15, 15, 15, 18, 19, 20, 24, 24, 27; **Jdg 1:**3, 12, 24; **2:**3, 3, 3, 21; **4:**7, 7, 8, 9, 9, 9, 14, 22; **5:**3, 3; **6:**16, 16, 18, 23, 31, 31, 37, 37; **7:**2, 4, 4, 4, 7, 11, 11; **8:**5, 6, 7, 9, 15, 22, 23, 23, 23; **10:**13, 18; **11:**2, 8, 8, 9, 24, 31, 31, 37; **13:**3, 5, 5, 5, 7, 7, 16, 16, 22; **14:**12, 15; **15:**7, 13; **16:**2, 5, 7, 11, 13, 20; **17:**3, 10, 13; **18:**5, 6, 10; **19:**12, 13, 20, 24; **20:**8, 9, 9, 10, 10, 28; **21:**17, 18, 22; **Ru 1:**16, 16, 16, 17, 17; **2:**2, 22; **3:**1, 2, 4, 5, 11, 13, 13, 18; **4:**5, 12; **1Sa 1:**11, 11, 11, 11, 22, 28; **2:**3, 5, 9, 9, 9, 10, 30, 30, 31, 31, 31, 31, 32, 32, 33, 33, 34, 34, 35, 35, 35, 35, 36, 36, 36; **3:**14, 18; **4:**3, 9; **5:**5, 7, 11; **6:**3, 3, 5, 9, 9; **7:**3, 5; **8:**9, 11, 11, 12, 12, 12, 12, 13, 14, 15, 16, 17, 17, 18, 18, 20; **9:**5, 16, 16, 17, 19; **10:**2, 2, 3, 3, 3, 3, 4, 5, 5, 5, 6, 6, 6, 7, 8, 8; **11:**1, 2, 3, 3, 7, 9, 10, 12, 13; **12:**3, 10, 10, 14, 14, 15, 17, 17, 19, 22, 23, 23, 25; **14:**6, 8, 9, 10, 10, 10, 12, 28, 37, 39, 40, 45; **15:**6, 26, 29, 29, 33; **16:**2, 3, 11, 16, 16; **17:**8, 8, 9, 9, 10, 25, 25, 26, 37, 46, 46, 46, 46, 47, 47; **19:**6, 11; **20:**7, 7, 10, 12, 12, 18, 20, 21, 21, 22; **22:**16, 23; **23:**4, 11, 11, 11, 12, 12, 17, 17, 20; **24:**4, 10, 12, 12, 12, 13, 15, 20, 21; **25:**8, 19, 28, 29, 35, 40; **26:**6, 10, 10, 21, 25; **27:**1, 1, 12; **28:**1, 2, 2, 8, 10, 19, 19, 19; **30:**8, 8, 15, 15, 15, 24; **2Sa 1:**20, 20, 21; **2:**6, 22, 26, 26; **3:**12, 13, 21, 21; **4:**9; **5:**2, 2, 19, 19, 24; **6:**22; **7:**9, 10, 10, 11, 11, 12, 12, 13, 13, 14, 14, 14, 15, 16, 16, 21, 25, 26, 27; **9:**7, 10, 11; **10:**11, 12; **11:**11, 15; **12:**10, 11, 11, 11, 12, 14, 18, 22, 23, 28; **13:**13; **14:**7, 7, 7, 10, 11, 15, 17; **15:**10, 14, 14, 20, 21, 25, 28, 33, 34, 36; **16:**3, 4, 8, 12, 12, 19, 21, 21; **17:**2, 2, 2, 2, 3, 3, 9, 9, 10, 11, 13, 16; **18:**3, 3, 22, 26; **19:**7, 7, 23, 29, 33, 38, 38; **20:**21, 21; **21:**3, 4, 6, 6; **22:**4, 50, 50; **23:**5, 7; **24:**12, 12, 13, 21, 23; **1Ki 1:**2, 2, 2, 14, 20, 21, 24, 24, 30, 30, 35, 35, 51, 52, 52; **2:**3, 4, 4, 9, 17, 18, 24, 26, 30, 31, 32, 37, 37, 38, 42; **3:**5, 12, 12, 12, 13, 13, 14, 26; **5:**5, 5, 6, 8, 9, 9, 9; **6:**12, 13; **8:**19, 19, 23, 25, 27, 40, 42, 43, 43, 58; **9:**3, 3, 4, 5, 5, 7, 7, 7, 8, 8, 9; **11:**11, 12, 12, 13, 31, 32, 34, 34, 35, 36, 36, 37, 37, 38, 38, 38, 39; **12:**4, 7, 15, 26, 27, 27; **13:**2, 2, 2, 3, 3, 7, 22, 32; **14:**2, 3, 5, 5, 10, 10, 11, 11, 12, 13, 13, 14, 14, 14, 15, 15, 15, 16; **15:**19; **16:**3, 4, 4; **17:**1, 9, 12, 13, 14; **18:**1, 12, 12, 15, 23, 24, 37, 44; **19:**17, 17, 18, 20; **20:**6, 6, 9, 13, 13, 14, 14, 25, 25, 28, 28, 31, 34, 34, 36, 39, 42; **21:**2, 2, 10, 18, 19, 21, 23, 24, 24, 29, 29, 29; **22:**4, 6, 11, 12, 14, 15, 22, 22, 22, 25, 30, 30; **2Ki 1:**3, 4, 4, 6, 6, 6, 16, 16, 16; **2:**2, 4, 6, 10, 16, 21; **3:**7, 8, 8, 12, 16, 17, 17, 17, 18, 19, 19; **4:**7, 10, 16, 43, 43; **5:**5, 8, 10, 10, 16, 17, 17, 20, 27; **6:**3, 8, 13, 15, 19, 32; **7:**1, 1, 2, 4, 4, 9, 12, 18, 18, 19; **8:**1, 8, 9, 10, 10, 12, 12, 14; **9:**7, 9, 10, 10, 26, 36, 37, 37; **10:**5, 5, 10, 18, 19, 24, 30; **11:**6; **13:**17, 19; **14:**10; **15:**12; **16:**15; **17:**39; **18:**14, 14, 20, 21, 21, 22, 23, 23, 26, 27, 27, 27, 29, 30, 30, 31, 32, 32; **19:**4, 7, 7, 7, 7, 10, 19, 28, 28, 29, 29, 29, 29, 29, 30, 30, 31, 31, 32, 32, 33, 33, 34; **20:**1, 5, 5, 6, 6, 6, 8, 8, 8, 9, 9, 17, 17, 18, 18, 18, 19; **21:**7, 8, 8, 12, 12, 13, 13, 14, 14; **22:**6, 7, 16, 17, 20, 20; **23:**27, 27; **25:**24; **1Ch 11:**2, 2, 5, 6; **12:**19; **13:**2; **14:**10, 10, 15; **16:**18; **17:**8, 9, 9, 10, 10, 11, 11, 12, 12, 13, 13, 13, 14, 14, 19, 23, 24, 25, 27; **19:**12, 13; **21:**10, 10, 22, 22, 23, 24; **22:**1, 5, 8, 9, 9, 9, 9, 9, 10, 10, 10, 10, 13; **23:**4, 5, 5, 25, 26; **28:**6, 6, 7, 9, 9, 20, 20, 21, 21; **29:**1, 5; **2Ch 1:**7, 12, 12, 12; **2:**4, 5, 8, 9, 9, 10, 12, 14, 16, 16; **6:**9, 9, 14, 16, 18, 31, 33, 33; **7:**14, 14, 14, 15, 16, 18, 18, 20, 20, 20, 21, 21, 22; **10:**4, 7, 15; **12:**7, 7, 7, 8; **13:**12; **15:**2, 2, 2, 7; **16:**3, 9; **18:**3, 3, 5, 10, 11, 13, 14, 20, 21, 21, 24, 29, 29; **19:**6, 10, 10, 11, 11, 11; **20:**9, 16, 17, 20, 20, 37; **21:**15; **23:**3, 4, 5, 5; **25:**7, 8, 8, 19; **26:**18; **28:**23; **29:**10, 10; **30:**6, 8, 9, 9, 9; **32:**11, 15, 17; **33:**7, 8, 8; **34:**24, 24, 25, 25, 28, 28; **35:**21; **Ezr 4:**3, 12, 13, 13, 15, 16; **6:**3, 3, 4, 4, 5, 8, 10, 11, 11, 11; **7:**17, 18, 24, 26; **9:**14; **10:**3, 3, 4, 14; **Ne 1:**8, 9; **2:**6, 6, 8, 20, 20; **4:**11, 12, 20; **5:**12, 12; **6:**7; **7:**3; **9:**29; **10:**31, 32, 33, 33, 36, 37, 37, 38, 38; **13:**21; **Est 1:**17, 18, 18, 18, 20; **2:**3, 4; **3:**9; **4:**13, 14, 14, 16, 16; **5:**3, 6, 8, 8; **6:**13, 13; **7:**2, 3, 8; **9:**12, 12; **Job 1:**8, 11, 21; **2:**3, 4, 5; **4:**2, 6, 8, 10, 11, 11, 19; **5:**12, 19, 20, 21, 21, 22, 22, 23, 23, 24, 24, 25, 25, 26, 26; **6:**24; **7:**4, 7, 8, 8, 9, 13, 13, 21, 21; **8:**2, 6, 7, 10, 10, 14, 15, 20, 20, 21, 22, 22; **9:**18, 28, 29; **10:**1, 2, 9; **11:**15, 15, 16, 16, 17, 17, 18, 18, 18, 18, 19, 19, 20; **12:**2, 7, 7, 8; **13:**8, 8, 10, 13, 14, 16, 18, 20, 22; **14:**5, 7, 12; **15:**17, 17, 22, 28, 28, 29, 29, 29, 30, 30, 30, 31, 32, 32, 33, 34; **16:**22; **17:**3, 9, 9, 10, 16, 16; **18:**4, 4, 5, 5, 6, 6, 7, 7, 15, 16, 16, 17, 17, 18, 19, 21; **19:**2, 2, 25, 26, 27, 27, 29; **20:**7, 7, 8, 8, 9, 10, 11, 15, 16, 16, 17, 18, 18, 21, 22, 22, 24, 24, 26, 26, 27, 27, 28, 28; **21:**15, 16, 19, 21, 28; **22:**15, 18, 19, 19, 20, 21, 21, 23, 25, 25, 26, 27, 27, 27, 28, 28, 29, 30; **23:**10, 14; **24:**13, 15, 15, 20, 20, 20, 24; **27:**4, 4, 5, 5, 6, 9, 11, 11, 13, 14, 15, 17, 17; **29:**18; **31:**35; **32:**17, 17, 17; **33:**12, 24, 25, 26, 26, 27, 33; **34:**12, 31, 32, 34, 34; **35:**3, 4, 6, 14, 14; **36:**2, 3, 11, 11, 12, 17, 20; **38:**11; **39:**9, 9, 10; **40:**4; **41:**3, 4, 6, 6, 7, 8, 8, 9, 11; **42:**4, 8, 8, 8, 15; **Ps 1:**5, 5; **2:**8, 9, 12, 12; **3:**2; **4:**2, 2, 2, 3, 6, 8, 8; **5:**2, 5, 6, 7, 8; **6:**9; **7:**2, 12, 12, 13, 17, 17; **9:**1, 1, 2, 2, 8, 17, 18, 18; **10:**6, 6, 11, 13, 17, 18; **11:**7; **12:**4, 5, 7; **13:**1, 1, 2, 3, 5, 6; **14:**4, 5, 6, 7, 7; **15:**5; **16:**4, 4, 7, 8, 10, 11; **17:**6, 15, 15, 15; **18:**3, 49, 49; **19:**13; **20:**6, 8, 8; **21:**7, 8, 8, 9, 9, 9, 10, 10, 11, 12; **22:**22, 22, 25, 25, 26, 26, 26, 27, 27, 30, 30, 31, 31; **23:**4, 6, 6; **24:**5; **25:**3, 12, 13, 13; **26:**12; **27:**2, 3, 5, 5, 5, 6, 6, 10, 13; **28:**5, 5; **30:**1, 9, 12; **32:**5, 8, 8; **34:**1, 1, 2, 5, 5, 9, 10, 11, 16, 20, 21, 21, 22, 22; **35:**9, 9, 10, 17, 18, 18, 25, 28, 28; **37:**3, 4, 5, 6, 6, 9, 9, 10, 10, 11, 11, 15, 15, 17, 18, 19, 19, 20, 20, 22, 22, 24, 27, 28, 28, 28, 29, 29, 31, 33, 34, 34, 38; **39:**1, 1, 4; **40:**3, 3, 8; **41:**5, 8; **42:**5, 5, 6, 11, 11; **43:**4, 4, 5, 5; **45:**1, 12, 12, 16, 16, 17, 17; **46:**2, 5, 10, 10; **48:**8, 10, 14; **49:**11, 12, 12, 13, 14, 14, 14, 15, 15, 17, 19, 20; **50:**4, 6, 15, 15, 21, 22, 22, 23; **51:**4, 7, 7, 13, 13, 14, 17, 19, 19; **52:**5, 5, 6, 6, 9, 9; **53:**4, 5, 5, 5, 6, 6; **54:**6, 6, 7; **55:**16, 16, 19, 19, 22, 22, 23, 23; **56:**9, 12; **57:**1, 2, 3, 3, 8, 9, 9; **58:**8, 9, 10, 10, 11; **59:**10, 10, 13, 16, 16; **60:**6, 6, 7, 7, 8, 8, 8, 9, 9, 10, 12, 12; **61:**2, 8; **62:**2, 6; **63:**4, 5, 9, 9, 10, 11, 11, 11; **64:**5, 7, 7, 8, 8, 9, 10, 10; **65:**1, 2, 9; **66:**4, 4, 15, 16; **67:**4, 6, 6, 7, 7; **68:**16, 18, 21, 22, 22, 23, 23; **69:**13, 30, 30, 31, 32, 35, 35, 36, 36; **71:**14, 14, 15, 15, 16, 16, 20, 21, 22, 22, 23, 24; **72:**9, 9, 10, 10, 11, 11, 12, 12, 13, 14; **73:**20, 24, 27, 28; **74:**9, 9, 10, 10; **75:**2, 7, 7, 9, 9, 10, 10; **77:**7; **78:**2, 2, 4, 4, 4, 8; **79:**5, 5, 13; **80:**3, 4, 7, 18, 19; **81:**6, 6, 10; **82:**2, 2, 7; **83:**4; **84:**2, 6, 7, 7, 11; **85:**5, 5, 9, 12; **86:**7, 7, 9, 9, 12, 12, 17; **87:**4, 5, 5, 6, 7; **88:**13; **89:**1, 1, 2, 4, 4, 5, 5, 15, 21, 21, 22, 22, 23, 24, 24, 25, 26, 27, 28, 28, 29, 29, 32, 33, 34, 34, 36, 46, 46, 46, 48; **90:**13; **91:**1, 3, 4, 4, 7, 8, 8, 10, 10, 12, 13, 13, 14, 14, 15, 15, 15, 16; **92:**9, 9, 12, 14, 14, 15; **94:**3, 8, 14, 14, 15, 15, 16, 16, 23, 23, 23; **95:**11; **96:**10, 13; **98:**9; **101:**1, 1, 2, 2, 2, 3, 3, 4, 5, 5, 6, 6, 7, 7, 8; **102:**12, 12, 13, 15, 15, 16, 16, 17, 17, 18, 21, 26, 26, 26, 26, 28, 28; **103:**1, 9, 21, 22; **104:**33, 33, 35; **105:**11; **107:**42, 43, 43; **108:**2, 3, 3, 7, 7, 8, 8, 9, 9, 9, 10, 10, 11, 13, 13; **109:**28, 28, 28, 30; **110:**2, 2, 3, 3, 4, 5, 6, 6, 7, 7; **111:**1; **112:**2, 2, 3, 3, 4, 6, 6, 9, 9, 10, 10, 10; **115:**12, 12, 13; **116:**2, 13, 13, 14, 17, 18; **118:**6, 7, 7, 17, 17, 19, 24, 28, 28; **119:**6, 7, 8, 15, 16, 23, 27, 32, 32, 34, 34, 42, 44, 45, 46, 46, 60, 78, 80, 82, 84, 93, 95, 106, 109, 110, 117, 117, 125, 133, 145, 160, 164; **120:**3, 3, 4; **121:**3, 3, 6; **122:**8, 9; **125:**1, 1, 3; **126:**5; **127:**1, 5; **128:**2, 2, 3; **130:**8; **132:**3, 3, 4, 9, 11, 11, 12, 14, 14, 15, 16, 16, 17, 17, 18, 18; **135:**14; **137:**8; **138:**1, 2, 4, 4, 5, 7, 7, 7, 8; **139:**10, 10; **140:**12, 12, 13; **141:**5, 6, 7; **142:**4, 7; **143:**7, 10; **144:**9, 9; **145:**1, 2, 2, 5, 6, 6, 7, 7, 10, 10, 11, 11, 12, 21, 21; **146:**2, 2, 10; **148:**6; **Pr 1:**3, 4, 4, 9, 12, 22, 22, 22, 26, 26, 28, 28, 32, 33; **2:**5, 5, 9, 9, 10, 10, 11, 11, 12, 16, 19, 21, 21, 22, 22; **3:**2, 4, 4, 6, 6, 8, 10, 10, 17, 26; **4:**4, 6, 6, 8, 8, 9, 9, 10, 11, 13; **5:**2, 2, 9, 10, 10, 11, 12, 23, 23; **6:**9, 9, 11, 11, 15, 22, 22, 24, 26, 29, 31, 33, 34, 34, 35; **8:**13, 17; **9:**7, 7, 8, 8, 9, 9, 11, 12, 12; **10:**3, 9, 13, 17, 24, 24, 30, 30, 31; **11:**18, 21, 21, 24, 25, 27, 27, 29, 31; **13:**3, 4, 13, 13, 18, 18, 19, 20, 20, 24; **14:**11, 11, 19, 19, 22, 22, 26, 29; **15:**10, 10, 27, 31; **16:**3, 5, 20, 20; **17:**2, 2, 5, 11, 13, 20; **18:**21; **19:**5, 5, 7, 8, 9, 9, 17, 18, 19, 21, 25, 25, 29, 29; **20:**4, 5, 6, 13, 13, 20, 22; **21:**12, 13, 16, 21, 23, 25, 28, 28; **22:**5, 6, 8, 8, 10, 14, 15, 16, 19, 23, 25, 27, 29; **23:**8, 8, 9, 11, 15, 16, 18, 28, 33, 33, 34, 35, 35; **24:**8, 12, 14, 14, 16, 18, 18, 20, 22, 22, 24, 34, 34; **25:**4, 5, 10, 16, 17, 22, 22; **26:**2, 4, 5, 26, 27, 27; **27:**1, 11, 11, 14, 18, 26, 26, 27; **28:**8, 8, 10, 10, 13, 13, 16, 16, 17, 18, 18, 20, 20, 21, 27, 27; **29:**1, 8, 9, 12, 14, 16, 17, 21, 24, 24; **30:**6, 10, 10, 17; **31:**11, 12, 30; **Ecc 1:**11; **2:**15, 15, 16, 19, 19; **3:**15, 17, 22; **5:**10, 16; **6:**12; **7:**14, 18, 26, 26, 26; **8:**3, 5, 5, 8, 12, 13, 13, 15; **9:**1, 5, 10, 16, 16; **10:**1, 13; **11:**1, 4, 6, 6, 8; **12:**2, 3, 3, 3, 3, 4, 4, 5, 5, 5, 7, 7, 14; **SS 1:**7, 11; **3:**2; **4:**6; **6:**1; **7:**8, 12; **8:**8, 9, 9, 12; **Isa 1:**15, 15, 19, 19, 20, 24, 25, 25, 25, 26, 26, 27, 28, 29, 29, 30, 31, 31, 31; **2:**2, 2, 3, 3, 3, 4, 4, 4, 4, 9, 11, 11, 12, 13, 14, 15, 16, 17, 17, 17, 18, 19, 19, 20, 21, 21; **3:**1, 2, 4, 4, 5, 5, 5, 6, 7, 8, 9, 10, 10, 11, 14, 16, 17, 17, 18, 20, 24, 24, 24, 24, 24, 24, 25, 26, 26; **4:**1, 1, 1, 2, 2, 3, 4, 4, 5, 5, 6; **5:**1, 5, 5, 6, 6, 6, 6, 9, 10, 10, 13, 13, 13, 14, 15, 15, 17, 17, 24, 24, 25, 26, 26, 26, 27, 27, 27, 28, 28, 29, 29, 29, 30, 30, 30; **6:**8, 9, 9, 9, 9, 10, 13, 13, 13, 13; **7:**3, 6, 6, 7, 8, 11, 14, 14, 14, 14, 15, 16, 17, 17, 17, 18, 18, 18, 19, 19, 20, 21, 22, 22, 23, 24, 25, 25, 25; **8:**4, 6, 7, 8, 8, 9, 9, 12, 14, 14, 14, 15, 15, 16, 16, 16, 16, 17, 21, 21, 22, 22; **9:**1, 1, 1, 1, 2, 2, 3, 3, 3, 4, 5, 5, 5, 6, 6, 7, 7, 7, 9, 10, 10, 11, 12, 12, 13, 14, 17, 20, 20, 21, 21, 21, 21; **10:**3, 3, 3, 4, 4, 4, 6, 6, 7, 7, 8, 8, 9, 9, 9, 11, 12, 16, 16, 17, 17, 17, 18, 18, 18, 19, 20, 20, 21, 22, 25, 25, 25, 26, 27, 27, 33, 33, 34; **11:**1, 2, 3, 3, 4, 4, 5, 6, 6, 6, 6, 7, 7, 7, 8, 8, 9, 9, 10, 10, 10, 11, 12, 12, 13, 13, 14, 14, 14, 15, 15, 16; **12:**1, 2, 3, 4; **13:**3, 5, 9, 10, 10, 11, 11, 12, 12, 13, 13, 13, 14, 15, 16, 16, 17, 17, 18, 18, 18, 19, 20, 20, 20, 20, 20, 21, 21, 21, 21, 22, 22, 22; **14:**1, 1, 1, 1, 2, 2, 2, 2, 4, 4, 8, 13, 13, 14, 15, 16, 19, 19, 20, 20, 22, 22, 23, 23, 24, 24, 25, 25, 25, 29, 29, 30, 30, 30, 30, 31, 32; **15:**1, 2, 2, 3, 3, 4, 4, 9; **16:**5, 5, 9, 10, 11, 11, 12, 12, 12, 12, 14, 14; **17:**1, 1, 2, 2, 2, 3, 3, 3, 4, 4, 5, 6, 6, 7, 8, 8, 9, 9, 11, 11, 13, 13; **18:**4, 5, 5, 6, 6, 6, 7, 7, 7; **19:**2, 3, 3, 3, 3, 4, 5, 5, 6, 6, 7, 7, 7, 8, 8, 9, 9, 10, 11, 11, 16, 16, 17, 18, 18, 18, 19, 19, 20, 20, 20, 21, 21, 21, 21, 22, 22, 22, 22, 23, 23, 23, 24, 24, 24, 25; **20:**3, 4, 4, 5, 6; **21:**2, 2, 11, 12, 16, 17; **22:**14, 18, 18, 18, 19, 19, 20, 21, 21, 22, 22, 22, 22, 22, 23, 23, 24, 24, 25, 25, 25; **23:**5, 12, 12, 12, 15, 15, 16, 16, 17, 17, 17, 18, 18, 18; **24:**2, 3, 6, 7, 7, 7, 7, 8, 8, 8, 14, 14, 17, 18, 18, 20, 21, 22, 23, 23, 23, 23; **25:**1, 2, 3, 3, 6, 6, 7, 8, 8, 8, 9, 10, 10, 11, 11, 12; **26:**1, 3, 9, 11, 12, 14, 19, 19, 19, 19, 21, 21; **27:**1, 2, 3, 3, 3, 4, 4, 5, 6, 6, 9, 10, 10, 11, 12, 12, 12, 13, 13; **28:**1, 2, 2, 3, 4, 4, 5, 5, 6, 6, 11, 12, 13, 13, 13, 17, 17, 17, 18, 18, 18, 19, 19, 21, 21, 21, 22; **29:**2, 2, 2, 3, 3, 3, 4, 4, 5, 6, 7, 7, 8, 11, 12, 14, 14, 17, 17, 17, 18, 18, 19, 19, 20, 20, 21, 21, 22, 23, 23, 24, 24; **30:**1, 3, 5, 5, 6, 8, 13, 13, 13, 14, 15, 16, 16, 17, 17, 17, 19, 19, 19, 20, 20, 21, 22, 22, 22, 23, 23, 24, 25, 26, 26, 26, 28, 28, 29, 29, 30, 30, 30, 31, 31, 32, 33; **31:**2, 2, 2, 2, 3, 3, 4, 4, 5, 5, 5, 7, 7, 8, 8, 8, 8, 9; **32:**1, 2, 2, 3, 3, 4, 4, 5, 5, 6, 7, 8, 8, 9, 10, 10, 10, 12, 13, 13, 14, 14, 14, 15, 15, 16, 17, 17, 18, 18, 19, 20, 20, 20; **33:**1, 4, 5, 6, 10, 11, 11, 12, 16, 16, 16, 16, 17, 17, 18, 19, 19, 20, 20, 21, 21, 22, 23, 23, 24, 24; **34:**2, 3, 3, 3, 4, 4, 5, 6, 6, 7, 7, 8, 9, 9, 10, 10, 10, 10, 11, 11, 12, 12, 13, 13, 13, 14, 14, 14, 15, 15, 15, 16, 16, 16, 16, 16, 17; **35:**1, 1, 2, 2, 2, 5, 6, 6, 6, 6, 7, 7, 7, 8, 8, 8, 8, 8, 9, 9, 9, 10, 10, 10; **36:**5, 6, 6, 7, 8, 8, 11, 12, 12, 12, 14, 15, 15, 16, 17, 18; **37:**4, 7, 7, 7, 7, 10, 20, 29, 29, 30, 30, 30, 30, 30, 31, 31, 32, 32, 33, 33, 34, 34, 35; **38:**1, 5, 6, 6, 7, 7, 8, 11, 11, 15, 20, 21, 22, 22; **39:**6, 6, 7, 7, 7, 8; **40:**5, 5, 10, 11, 11, 11, 25, 30, 30, 31, 31, 31, 31; **41:**9, 10, 10, 10, 11, 12, 12, 14, 15, 15, 16, 16, 16, 16, 16, 17, 17, 18, 18, 18, 18, 19, 20, 23, 23, 25, 25, 25; **42:**1, 2, 2, 3, 3, 4, 4, 6, 6, 7, 7, 8, 8, 9, 9, 13, 13, 13, 13, 14, 14, 14, 15, 15, 15, 16, 16, 16, 16, 17, 23; **43:**2, 2, 2, 2, 5, 6, 7, 10, 14, 14, 19, 19, 20, 20, 21, 25; **44:**3, 3, 4, 5, 5, 5, 5, 11, 11, 21, 26, 26, 26, 27, 28, 28; **45:**1, 1, 1, 2, 2, 3, 3, 6, 13, 13, 13, 14, 14, 14, 14, 14, 16, 17, 17, 23, 23, 23, 24, 24, 25, 25; **46:**4, 4, 4, 5, 10, 11, 11, 11; **47:**1, 3, 3, 3, 5, 7, 8, 9, 9, 11, 11, 11, 14, 15; **48:**6, 8, 9, 11, 11, 11, 14, 15, 15; **49:**3, 4, 6, 6, 6, 7, 7, 8, 8, 8, 8, 8, 9, 10, 10, 10, 11, 11, 12, 13, 17, 17, 18, 18, 19, 19, 20, 21, 22, 22, 22, 23, 23, 23, 23, 23, 25, 25, 25, 25, 26, 26, 26; **50:**4, 7, 7, 7, 8, 9, 9, 11, 11; **51:**3, 3, 3, 3, 4, 4, 5, 5, 6, 6, 6, 6, 8, 8, 8, 8, 11, 11, 11, 13, 13, 14, 14, 22, 23, 23; **52:**1, 6, 6, 6, 10, 10, 12, 12, 12, 13, 13, 15, 15, 15, 15; **53:**1, 10, 10, 10, 11, 11, 11, 12; **54:**3, 3, 4, 4, 5, 7, 8, 9, 10, 10, 11, 12, 13, 13, 14, 14, 14, 14, 15, 15, 17, 17, 17; **55:**2, 3, 5, 5, 7, 11, 11, 12, 12, 12, 13, 13, 13, 13; **56:**5, 5, 6, 7, 7, 7, 7, 8, 12, 12; **57:**2, 12, 12, 13, 14, 16, 16, 18, 18, 19, 19; **58:**3, 4, 5, 8, 8, 8, 8, 9, 9, 10, 10, 11, 11, 12, 12, 14, 14; **59:**2, 18, 18, 19, 19, 20, 21, 21, 21; **60:**2, 2, 3, 3, 4, 5, 5, 5, 5, 6, 6, 7, 7, 7, 9, 9, 9, 10, 10, 10, 11, 11, 12, 13, 13, 14, 14, 14, 15, 15, 15, 16, 16, 17, 17, 18, 18, 18, 18, 19, 19, 19, 20, 20, 20, 20, 21, 21, 21, 22, 22, 22; **61:**1, 1, 3, 4, 4, 5, 5, 6, 6, 6, 7, 8, 9, 9, 11, 11, 11; **62:**1, 2, 2, 2, 3, 4, 4, 4, 5, 5, 6, 8, 8, 9, 9, 12, 12; **63:**7, 7, 7, 8; **64:**12; **65:**5, 6, 6, 6, 7, 8, 8, 8, 9, 9, 10, 10, 12, 12, 13, 13, 13, 13, 13, 13, 14, 15, 15, 16, 16, 17, 18, 18, 19, 19, 20, 20, 20, 20, 21, 22, 22, 22, 23, 23, 23, 24, 24, 25, 25, 25, 25; **66:**2, 3, 4, 5, 8, 8, 12, 12, 12, 13, 14, 14, 14, 15, 16, 16, 17, 18, 18, 19, 19, 19, 20, 20, 20, 21, 22, 22, 22, 23, 24, 24, 24, 24; **Jer 1:**8, 12, 14, 15, 15, 16, 17, 18, 19, 19, 19; **2:**9, 9, 19, 19, 35, 36, 37, 37; **3:**12, 14, 15, 15, 16, 16, 16, 17, 17, 17, 18, 18, 22, 22, 23; **4:**1, 2, 2, 2, 4, 7, 9, 9, 11, 12, 13, 14, 27, 27, 28, 28, 28, 30, 30; **5:**1, 5, 5, 6, 6, 6, 12, 12, 13, 14, 14, 15, 17, 17, 17, 18, 19, 31; **6:**2, 3, 3, 8, 9, 9, 10, 11, 12, 12, 12, 15, 15, 16, 19, 21, 21, 21, 26, 29, 30; **7:**3, 5, 7, 8, 14, 15, 16, 20, 20, 23, 23, 23, 28, 32, 32, 33, 33, 34, 34, 34; **8:**1, 2, 2, 2, 3, 3, 9, 10, 12, 12, 13, 13, 13, 14, 17, 17, 17; **9:**7, 10, 11, 11, 11, 15, 16, 16, 16, 22, 22, 25; **10:**11, 14, 15, 18, 18, 20, 22, 22; **11:**4, 4, 11, 11, 12, 12, 14, 19, 22, 22, 22, 23, 23; **12:**5, 5, 12, 13, 14, 14, 15, 15, 16, 17; **13:**9, 10, 12, 12, 12, 13, 13, 14, 14, 16, 17, 17, 17, 18, 19, 19, 19, 19, 21, 21, 24, 26, 27; **14:**10, 10, 10, 12, 12, 12, 13, 13, 15, 15, 15, 16, 16, 16, 16, 22; **15:**3, 3, 4, 5, 5, 5, 6, 7, 7, 8, 8, 8, 9, 11, 11, 13, 14, 14, 19, 19, 20, 20, 20, 20, 21, 21; **16:**4, 4, 4, 4, 4, 6, 6, 6, 7, 7, 9, 9, 10, 13, 13, 14, 15, 15, 16, 16, 18, 19, 21, 21; **17:**3, 4, 4, 4, 6, 11, 11, 13, 13, 25, 25, 25, 25, 26, 26, 27, 27, 27; **18:**2, 8, 9, 10, 12, 16, 16, 17, 17; **19:**3, 3, 6, 7, 7, 8, 8, 8, 9, 9, 9, 11, 11, 12, 12, 13, 15; **20:**4, 4, 4, 4, 5, 5, 6, 6, 10, 10, 10, 11, 11, 11, 13; **21:**2, 2, 4, 4, 5, 6, 6, 7, 7, 9, 9, 10, 10, 12, 13, 14, 14, 14; **22:**4, 4, 5, 6, 7, 7, 7, 8, 9, 10, 11, 12, 14, 18, 18, 19, 21, 22, 23, 24, 25, 26, 26, 27, 30, 30; **23:**1, 2, 3, 3, 3, 4, 4, 4, 5, 5, 5, 6, 6, 7, 8, 8, 12, 12, 12, 12, 15, 17, 17, 20, 20, 26, 33, 34, 39, 39, 40, 40; **24:**6, 6, 6, 6, 7, 7, 7, 7, 7, 8, 9, 9, 10; **25:**5, 6, 9, 9, 9, 10, 10, 10, 10, 11, 11, 12, 12, 13, 14, 14, 16, 16, 27, 29, 29, 30, 30, 31, 31, 31, 32, 33, 33, 33, 34, 35, 35, 37, 38; **26:**3, 3, 4, 5, 6, 6, 9, 9, 13, 15, 15, 18, 18, 18, 19; **27:**6, 7, 7, 8, 8, 9, 10, 11, 13, 14, 15, 15, 16, 17, 18, 22, 22, 22; **28:**2, 3, 4, 4, 11, 16; **29:**7, 10, 10, 10, 12, 13, 14, 14, 14, 17, 18, 18, 18, 21, 22, 22, 28, 28, 32, 32, 32; **30:**3, 3, 3, 7, 7, 8, 8, 9, 9, 10, 10, 10, 10, 10, 11, 11, 11, 16, 16, 16, 16, 17, 18, 18, 19, 19, 20, 20, 20, 21, 21, 21, 22, 22, 24, 24; **31:**1, 1, 2, 2, 4, 4, 5, 6, 6, 8, 8, 8, 9, 9, 9, 10, 12, 12, 12, 12, 13, 13, 13, 13, 14, 14, 16, 16, 17, 20, 22, 22, 22, 23, 24, 27, 27, 28, 29, 30, 30, 30, 31, 31, 32, 33, 33, 33, 33, 33, 34, 34, 34, 34, 34, 37, 38, 39, 40, 40; **32:**4, 5, 5, 5, 7, 15, 15, 24, 25, 28, 28, 29, 29, 36, 37, 37, 37, 38, 38, 39, 40, 40, 40, 41, 41, 42, 43, 44, 44; **33:**3, 5, 6, 6, 7, 8, 8, 9, 9, 9, 10, 11, 11, 11, 12, 13, 14, 14, 15, 15, 16, 16, 16, 17, 18, 21, 21, 22, 26, 26, 26; **34:**2, 3, 3, 3, 3, 4, 5, 5, 5, 17, 17, 18, 19, 20, 20, 20, 21, 22, 22, 22, 22; **35:**7, 17, 19; **36:**3, 3, 6, 7, 30, 30, 31, 31; **37:**8, 17, 20; **38:**2, 2, 3, 3, 4, 5, 9, 15, 16, 17, 17, 18, 18, 18, 19, 19, 20, 20, 22, 22, 23, 23, 23, 23, 24, 25; **39:**16, 16, 16, 17, 18; **40:**4, 9, 10, 15; **42:**4, 4, 4, 6, 6, 10, 10, 11, 12, 12, 13, 14, 16, 16, 17, 17, 17, 18, 18, 18, 20, 21, 22; **43:**3, 10, 10, 10, 11, 11, 11, 11, 12, 12, 12, 13, 13; **44:**7, 8, 12, 12, 12, 12, 12, 13, 14, 16, 17, 17, 25, 26, 27, 27, 28, 28, 29, 29, 30; **45:**4, 4, 5, 5; **46:**8, 10, 10, 11, 12, 14, 17, 19, 23, 24, 24, 25, 25, 26, 26, 27, 27, 27, 27, 27, 28, 28; **47:**2, 2, 2, 5, 5, 5, 6; **48:**1, 1, 1, 2, 2, 2, 2, 3, 4, 5, 7, 7, 8, 9, 12, 12, 13, 15, 18, 18, 26, 32, 35, 38, 41, 41, 41, 42, 43, 44, 44, 44, 47; **49:**2, 2, 2, 2, 3, 4, 5, 5, 5, 6, 8, 10, 10, 10, 10, 11, 11, 12, 13, 13, 13, 15, 15, 16, 17, 17, 17, 18, 18, 19, 19, 19, 19, 20, 20, 21, 21, 22, 22, 22, 25, 26, 26,

27, 27, 29, 29, 29, 32, 32, 32, 33, 33, 33, 35, 36, 36, 36, 37, 37, 37, 38, 38, 39; **50:**2, 2, 2, 2, 3, 3, 3, 3, 4, 5, 5, 5, 5, 9, 9, 9, 9, 10, 12, 12, 13, 13, 13, 18, 19, 20, 20, 21, 25, 27, 30, 30, 32, 32, 32, 32, 34, 34, 35, 35, 36, 36, 37, 37, 38, 39, 39, 39, 39, 40, 40, 44, 44, 44, 44, 45, 45, 46, 46; **51:**1, 2, 2, 3, 3, 4, 6, 9, 12, 14, 14, 17, 18, 20, 21, 22, 23, 24, 25, 25, 26, 26, 26, 29, 33, 36, 36, 36, 37, 37, 39, 39, 40, 44, 44, 46, 46, 47, 47, 47, 48, 48, 52, 52, 53, 55, 57, 57, 58, 58, 58, 62, 62, 62, 64, 64; **La 1:**21; **3:**20, 24, 49; **4:**21, 22, 22, 22; **Eze 2:**5; **3:**18, 18, 19, 19, 20, 20, 20, 21, 21, 22, 25, 26, 27, 27, 27, 27; **4:**3, 3, 5, 8, 9, 13, 13, 16, 16, 16, 16, 17, 17, 17; **5:**2, 4, 5, 8, 9, 9, 10, 10, 10, 11, 11, 12, 12, 12, 13, 13, 13, 14, 15, 15, 15, 16, 16, 17, 17, 17; **6:**3, 4, 4, 4, 5, 6, 6, 7, 8, 8, 9, 9, 9, 10, 12, 12, 12, 12, 13, 14, 14; **7:**3, 3, 4, 4, 5, 7, 8, 9, 9, 9, 11, 11, 11, 12, 13, 13, 13, 15, 15, 16, 17, 17, 18, 18, 18, 19, 19, 20, 21, 21, 22, 24, 24, 25, 25, 25, 26, 26, 26, 26, 27, 27, 27, 27, 27; **8:**6, 13, 15, 18, 18, 18; **9:**8, 10, 10; **11:**3, 7, 8, 9, 9, 10, 10, 11, 11, 11, 12, 16, 17, 17, 18, 19, 19, 20, 20, 20, 21; **12:**3, 3, 6, 11, 11, 12, 12, 12, 13, 13, 13, 13, 14, 15, 16, 16, 19, 19, 20, 20, 23, 23, 24, 25, 25, 28; **13:**8, 9, 9, 9, 9, 9, 11, 11, 11, 12, 13, 14, 14, 14, 15, 15, 20, 21, 21, 21, 23, 23, 23, 23; **14:**4, 5, 7, 8, 8, 9, 10, 11, 11, 11, 21, 22, 22, 22, 22, 23; **15:**7, 7, 7, 8; **16:**37, 37, 38, 38, 39, 39, 39, 39, 40, 41, 41, 42, 42, 42, 42, 43, 44, 53, 53, 54, 55, 55, 59, 60, 60, 61, 61, 62, 62, 63; **17:**9, 9, 9, 10, 10, 10, 12, 16, 17, 18, 19, 20, 20, 21, 21, 21, 22, 22, 23, 23, 24, 24; **18:**3, 4, 9, 17, 17, 18, 19, 20, 20, 20, 20, 21, 22, 22, 24, 24, 26, 26, 27, 28, 28, 30; **20:**3, 11, 16, 31, 32, 33, 34, 35, 35, 36, 37, 38, 38, 38, 38, 40, 40, 40, 41, 41, 42, 43, 44, 47, 47, 47, 47, 48, 48; **21:**4, 4, 5, 5, 7, 7, 7, 7, 10, 10, 12, 12, 13, 14, 16, 17, 17, 21, 21, 21, 22, 22, 22, 23, 23, 23, 27, 27, 27, 29, 30, 31, 31, 32, 32; **22:**4, 5, 14, 14, 15, 16, 19, 20, 21, 22, 22, 24, 31, 31; **23:**22, 23, 23, 24, 24, 24, 25, 25, 25, 25, 25, 25, 26, 27, 27, 28, 29, 29, 31, 32, 32, 33, 34, 34, 45, 45, 47, 47, 48, 48, 49, 49, 49; **24:**8, 9, 13, 14, 14, 16, 21, 21, 22, 22, 23, 23, 23, 24, 24, 25, 26, 27, 27, 27; **25:**4, 4, 4, 5, 5, 7, 7, 7, 7, 9, 10, 10, 11, 11, 13, 13, 13, 14, 14, 14, 16, 16, 17, 17; **26:**2, 3, 4, 4, 5, 5, 5, 6, 6, 7, 8, 8, 9, 10, 10, 11, 11, 11, 12, 12, 13, 13, 14, 14, 15, 16, 16, 17, 19, 19, 19, 20, 20, 20, 21, 21, 21, 21; **27:**36; **28:**7, 7, 8, 8, 9, 9, 10, 22, 22, 23, 23, 23, 23, 23, 24, 24, 25, 25, 25, 26, 26; **29:**4, 5, 5, 6, 8, 9, 9, 10, 11, 11, 12, 12, 12, 12, 13, 14, 14, 15, 16, 16, 16, 19, 19, 21, 21, 21, 21; **30:**4, 4, 4, 4, 5, 6, 6, 6, 7, 7, 8, 9, 9, 10, 11, 12, 12, 13, 13, 13, 14, 14, 15, 15, 16, 16, 16, 16, 17, 17, 18, 18, 18, 19, 19, 22, 22, 23, 24, 24, 24, 25, 25, 26, 26; **31:**14, 18, 18, 18, 18; **32:**3, 4, 4, 4, 5, 6, 7, 7, 7, 8, 8, 9, 10, 10, 10, 11, 12, 12, 12, 13, 13, 14, 14, 15, 16, 18, 20, 20, 21, 28, 31, 32; **33:**6, 6, 8, 8, 9, 9, 12, 12, 13, 13, 13, 14, 15, 16, 16, 18, 19, 20, 27, 27, 27, 28, 28, 28, 28, 29, 33, 33; **34:**10, 10, 10, 10, 11, 12, 12, 13, 13, 14, 14, 15, 16, 16, 16, 16, 16, 17, 20, 22, 22, 22, 23, 23, 24, 24, 25, 25, 26, 26, 26, 27, 27, 27, 28, 28, 28, 28, 29, 29, 30, 30; **35:**3, 4, 4, 6, 7, 8, 8, 9, 9, 9, 10, 10, 11, 11, 11, 12, 14, 15, 15, 15; **36:**7, 8, 8, 9, 9, 10, 10, 11, 11, 11, 11, 12, 12, 12, 14, 15, 15, 23, 23, 24, 25, 25, 25, 25, 26, 26, 26, 27, 27, 28, 28, 28, 29, 29, 29, 30, 30, 31, 33, 33, 34, 35, 36, 36, 38, 38, 38; **37:**6, 6, 6, 6, 12, 12, 13, 14, 14, 14, 14, 19, 19, 21, 21, 22, 22, 22, 23, 23, 23, 23, 23, 24, 24, 24, 25, 25, 25, 26, 26, 26, 27, 27, 27, 28, 28; **38:**4, 4, 5, 6, 8, 8, 8, 9, 10, 10, 11, 11, 12, 12, 13, 14, 15, 16, 16, 16, 16, 16, 18, 20, 20, 20, 20, 21, 21, 22, 22, 23, 23, 23; **39:**2, 3, 4, 4, 5, 6, 6, 7, 7, 7, 8, 8, 9, 9, 9, 10, 10, 10, 11, 11, 11, 12, 13, 13, 14, 14, 15, 15, 16, 16, 21, 21, 22, 23, 25, 25, 26, 26, 27, 28, 28, 29, 29; **40:**4; **42:**13, 13; **43:**7, 7, 7, 9, 10, 11, 18, 20, 20, 25, 27, 27; **44:**2, 2, 9, 15, 15, 16, 16, 23, 24, 24, 28, 29, 29, 30, 30; **45:**1, 1, 2, 3, 4, 4, 4, 5, 5, 6, 6, 7, 7, 7, 7, 8, 8, 8, 11, 11, 12, 15, 15, 17, 17, 19, 20, 21, 22, 23, 23, 23, 24, 25; **46:**1, 1, 2, 2, 2, 2, 3, 4, 5, 6, 10, 11, 12, 12, 12, 12, 14, 16, 17, 17, 17, 20, 20; **47:**8, 9, 9, 9, 9, 10, 10, 10, 11, 11, 12, 12, 12, 12, 12, 13, 14, 14, 15, 16, 17, 18, 19, 19, 20, 22, 22; **48:**8, 8, 9, 10, 12, 12, 12, 13, 13, 14, 15, 16, 17, 18, 18, 21, 21, 22, 29, 30, 31, 31, 32, 33, 34, 35, 35; **Da 1:**10; **2:**4, 5, 5, 6, 7, 9, 9, 9, 24, 25, 28, 28, 36, 39, 39, 40, 40, 41, 42, 43, 43, 44, 44, 44, 44, 44, 45; **3:**6, 15, 15, 15, 15, 17, 18, 29, 29; **4:**3, 24, 25, 25, 25, 25, 25, 26, 27, 32, 32, 32, 32; **5:**7, 7, 7, 12, 16, 16, 16, 17; **6:**5, 7, 7, 12, 26, 26, 26; **7:**14, 14, 17, 18, 18, 23, 23, 23, 24, 24, 24, 25, 25, 25, 26, 26, 27, 27, 27; **8:**13, 13, 13, 14, 14, 19, 22, 23, 24, 24, 24, 25, 25, 25, 25, 26; **9:**25, 25, 26, 26, 26, 26, 27, 27, 27; **10:**14, 21; **11:**2, 2, 2, 3, 3, 4, 4, 4, 4, 5, 5, 5, 6, 6, 6, 6, 6, 7, 8, 8, 9, 9, 10, 10, 11, 11, 12, 12, 12, 13, 14, 14, 14, 15, 15, 16, 16, 16, 17, 17, 17, 17, 18, 18, 18, 19, 19, 19, 20, 20, 21, 21, 22, 23, 23, 24, 24, 24, 25, 25, 25, 26, 26, 26, 27, 27, 27, 28, 28, 29, 29, 30, 30, 30, 31, 32, 32, 32, 33, 33, 33, 34, 34, 35, 35, 36, 36, 36, 37, 37, 38, 39, 39, 40, 40, 40, 41, 41, 41, 42, 42, 43, 43, 44, 44, 45, 45, 45, 45; **12:**1, 1, 1, 2, 3, 3, 4, 4, 6, 7, 7, 8, 10, 10, 10, 10, 11, 13, 13; **Hos 1:**2, 2, 5, 6, 7, 7, 10, 10, 10, 10, 11, 11, 11, 11; **2:**1, 1, 3, 3, 4, 6, 6, 7, 7, 9, 9, 10, 10, 11, 12, 12, 12, 13, 14, 14, 15, 15, 16, 17, 17, 18, 18, 18, 19, 20, 20, 21, 21, 22, 22, 23, 23, 23, 23; **3:**3, 4, 5, 5, 5; **4:**5, 5, 5, 6, 9, 10, 10, 14, 16, 16, 19, 19; **5:**2, 5, 5, 6, 6, 6, 7, 9, 10, 11, 12, 12, 14, 14, 14, 15, 15; **6:**1, 1, 2, 3, 5; **7:**12, 12, 13, 16, 16; **8:**3, 5, 7, 7, 10, 10, 13, 13, 13, 14; **9:**2, 2, 3, 3, 4, 4, 4, 4, 5, 5, 6, 6, 6, 6, 7, 9, 9, 11, 11, 12, 12, 13, 14, 15, 15, 16, 16, 17, 17, 17; **10:**2, 3, 5, 6, 6, 7, 7, 8, 8, 8, 10, 10, 11, 11, 12, 14, 14, 15, 15; **11:**5, 5, 6, 6, 9, 9, 9, 10, 10, 10, 11, 11, 11; **12:**9, 14; **13:**3, 7, 8, 8, 14, 15, 15, 15, 15, 16; **14:**3, 4, 4, 4, 5, 5, 5, 6, 7, 7, 7; **Joel 1:**15; **2:**2, 14, 14, 14, 17, 18, 19, 19, 20, 20, 20, 20, 20, 20, 22, 22, 22, 23, 24, 24, 25, 26, 26, 26, 27, 27, 28, 28, 28, 28, 29, 30, 31, 31, 32, 32, 32; **3:**2, 2, 4, 7, 7, 8, 8, 12, 14, 15, 15, 16, 16, 16, 17, 17, 17, 18, 18, 18, 18, 19, 20, 20, 21, 21; **Am 1:**3, 3, 4, 4, 5, 5, 5, 6, 6, 7, 7, 8, 8, 8, 9, 9, 10, 10, 11, 11, 12, 12, 13, 13, 14, 14, 14, 15; **2:**1, 1, 2, 2, 2, 3, 4, 4, 5, 5, 6, 6, 13, 14, 14, 14, 15, 16; **3:**11, 11, 12, 12, 14, 14, 15; **4:**2, 2, 2, 3, 3, 12; **5:**3, 3, 5, 5, 6, 11, 11, 13, 14, 15, 16, 17, 17, 18, 18, 19, 20, 22, 23, 24, 27; **6:**1, 4, 7, 7, 8, 9, 10, 10, 10, 11, 14; **7:**2, 5, 8, 8, 9, 9, 10, 11, 11, 17, 17, 17, 17, 17; **8:**2, 3, 3, 3, 7, 8, 8, 8, 9, 10, 10, 10, 10, 11, 12, 12, 13, 14; **9:**1, 1, 1, 1, 2, 2, 3, 3, 4, 8, 8, 9, 10, 10, 11, 11, 12, 12, 13, 13, 13, 14, 14, 14, 14, 15, 15; **Ob** 2, 2, 4, 5, 6, 6, 7, 7, 7, 7, 8, 8, 9, 9, 10, 15, 15, 15, 16, 16, 17, 17, 17, 18, 18, 19, 19, 19, 20, 20, 21, 21; **Jnh 1:**6, 12; **2:**4, 9, 9; **3:**4, 9; **Mic 1:**6, 6, 6, 7, 7, 7, 8, 8, 8, 15, 15, 16, 16, 16; **2:**1, 3, 3, 4, 5, 5, 6, 7, 12, 12, 12, 13, 13, 13, 13; **3:**6, 6, 6, 6, 7, 7, 7, 12, 12, 12; **4:**1, 1, 2, 2, 2, 3, 3, 3, 3, 4, 4, 5, 6, 7, 7, 8, 8, 10, 10, 10, 13, 13; **5:**1, 2, 3, 3, 4, 4, 4, 5, 5, 6, 6, 7, 7, 8, 8, 9, 9, 10, 11, 12, 12, 13, 13, 14, 15; **6:**2, 10, 13, 13, 14, 14, 14, 14, 14, 15, 15, 15, 16, 16; **7:**6, 7, 8, 8, 9, 9, 9, 9, 10, 10, 10, 11, 11, 12, 13, 15, 16, 16, 16, 16, 17, 17, 17, 19, 19, 20; **Na 1:**9, 10, 12, 12, 13, 14, 14, 15; **2:**2, 13, 13, 13, 13; **3:**1, 5, 5, 6, 7, 7, 11, 11, 12, 12, 13, 13, 15, 15, 15, 15, 17, 19; **Hab 1:**5, 6, 13, 16, 16, 17, 17; **2:**1, 1, 1, 3, 3, 3, 4, 6, 6, 7, 7, 8, 9, 9, 12, 13, 14, 14, 15, 16, 16, 17, 17, 19; **3:**16, 16, 18, 18, 19; **Zep 1:**2, 3, 3, 3, 4, 4, 4, 5, 6, 8, 9, 10, 10, 11, 12, 12, 13, 13, 13, 13, 14, 15, 17, 17, 17, 18, 18, 18; **2:**3, 4, 5, 5, 6, 7, 7, 7, 9, 9, 9, 10, 11, 11, 12, 13, 13, 14, 14, 14, 14, 14, 15; **3:**1, 7, 7, 8, 8, 9, 9, 10, 11, 11, 11, 11, 12, 13, 13, 13, 15, 15, 15, 15, 15, 16, 17, 17, 17, 18, 18, 19, 19, 19, 19, 20, 20, 20; **Hag 1:**8; **2:**6, 6, 7, 7, 7, 9, 9, 12, 13, 19, 22, 22, 22, 22, 23, 23; **Zec 1:**3, 9, 12, 16, 16, 17, 17, 21; **2:**4, 4, 4, 5, 5, 9, 9, 9, 11, 11, 11, 11, 12, 12; **3:**7, 7, 9, 9, 10; **4:**7, 7, 7, 7, 9, 9; **5:**3, 3, 4, 11, 11; **6:**10, 12, 13, 13, 13, 13, 13, 14, 15, 15, 15; **8:**3, 3, 3, 4, 5, 7, 8, 8, 8, 11, 12, 12, 12, 12, 13, 15, 19, 20, 21, 22, 23, 23; **9:**4, 4, 5, 5, 5, 5, 5, 5, 5, 6, 6, 7, 7, 7, 8, 8, 10, 10, 10, 10, 11, 12, 13, 14, 14, 14, 14, 15, 15, 15, 15, 16, 16, 17, 17; **10:**1, 3, 3, 4, 5, 5, 6, 6, 6, 6, 7, 7, 7, 7, 8, 8, 9, 9, 10, 11, 11, 11, 11, 11, 12, 12; **11:**5, 5, 6, 6, 6, 6, 9, 16, 16, 16, 16, 17, 17; **12:**2, 3, 3, 4, 4, 4, 5, 6, 6, 7, 7, 8, 8, 8, 10, 10, 10, 11, 12, 12, 14; **13:**1, 2, 2, 2, 3, 3, 4, 4, 5, 6, 7, 7, 8, 8, 9, 9, 9, 9, 9; **14:**1, 2, 2, 2, 2, 3, 4, 4, 4, 5, 5, 5, 5, 6, 7, 7, 7, 8, 9, 9, 9, 10, 10, 10, 11, 12, 12, 12, 12, 13, 13, 14, 14, 15, 16, 17, 18, 19, 20, 20, 21, 21, 21; **Mal 1:**4, 4, 4, 4, 5, 10; **2:**2, 2, 3, 3, 4; **3:**1, 1, 2, 2, 2, 3, 3, 4, 5, 5, 5, 7, 10, 10, 10, 11, 11, 11, 12, 12, 15, 17, 17, 17, 18; **4:**1, 1, 2, 2, 3, 6, 6; **Mt 1:**21, 21, 23, 23, 23; **2:**6, 6, 23; **3:**10, 11, 12; **4:**6, 9, 9, 19; **5:**4, 5, 6, 7, 8, 9, 13, 16, 18, 19, 19, 37, 45; **6:**1, 2, 4, 5, 6, 10, 14, 15, 16, 16, 18, 18, 20, 20, 21, 23, 24, 33, 34; **7:**1, 2, 2, 5, 6, 7, 7, 7, 11, 15, 22, 23, 27; **8:**4, 7, 8, 11, 12, 12, 19; **9:**6, 15, 15, 21, 29; **10:**15, 15, 17, 18, 19, 20, 21, 21, 21, 22, 22, 23, 25, 26, 26, 32, 33, 36, 39, 39, 41, 41, 42; **11:**10, 22, 23, 23, 24, 28, 29; **12:**18, 18, 19, 19, 20, 21, 26, 27, 32, 33, 33, 37, 37, 39, 40, 41, 42, 44, 45, 50; **13:**12, 12, 12, 14, 14, 14, 14, 30, 35, 35, 40, 41, 41, 42, 42, 43, 49, 49, 50; **15:**13, 14, 32; **16:**4, 18, 18, 19, 19, 19, 22, 25, 25, 27, 27, 28; **17:**12, 23, 23, 27; **18:**3, 7, 7, 12, 13, 14, 19, 26, 29, 35; **19:**21, 27, 28, 29, 29, 30, 30; **20:**16, 16, 18, 18, 19, 19, 21, 23, 23; **21:**2, 3, 13, 21, 22, 25, 30, 31, 37, 40, 41, 41, 43, 43, 44, 44; **22:**24, 28, 30, 31; **23:**12, 12, 13, 15, 16, 23, 25, 26, 27, 29, 33, 34, 34, 35, 36, 39; **24:**2, 2, 3, 3, 5, 5, 6, 7, 7, 8, 9, 9, 10, 11, 11, 12, 12, 13, 14, 14, 14, 15, 15, 19, 20, 21, 21, 22, 22, 24, 27, 29, 29, 29, 29, 30, 30, 30, 31, 31, 34, 35, 35, 36, 37, 39, 40, 40, 41, 41, 44, 46, 47, 50, 51, 51; **25:**21, 23, 29, 29, 29, 30, 31, 32, 32, 33, 34, 37, 40, 41, 44, 45, 46, 46; **26:**2, 5, 11, 11, 13, 15, 18, 18, 21, 23, 24, 29, 31, 31, 31, 32, 33, 34, 35, 39, 41, 42, 48, 52, 64, 75; **27:**25, 42, 49, 63, 64; **28:**7, 10, 14; **Mk 1:**2, 8, 17, 38, 44; **2:**10, 20, 20; **3:**24, 29, 35; **4:**12, 13, 21, 22, 24, 25, 25; **5:**28; **6:**22, 23; **8:**3, 12, 35, 35, 38; **9:**1, 5, 31, 31, 39, 41, 49; **10:**15, 21, 30, 30, 31, 31, 33, 33, 34, 34, 39, 40; **11:**2, 3, 17, 23, 24, 25, 31; **12:**6, 9, 9, 19, 23, 25, 26, 35, 40; **13:**2, 2, 4, 4, 4, 6, 6, 7, 8, 8, 8, 9, 9, 9, 11, 12, 12, 12, 13, 13, 14, 14, 17, 18, 19, 19, 20, 22, 24, 24, 25, 25, 26, 27, 30, 31, 31, 32, 33, 35; **14:**2, 7, 7, 9, 13, 15, 18, 21, 25, 27, 27, 27, 28, 29, 30, 31, 36, 38, 44, 58, 58, 62, 72; **15:**36; **16:**7, 16, 16, 17, 17, 17, 18, 18; **Lk 1:**13, 14, 14, 15, 15, 16, 17, 17, 17, 17, 18, 20, 31, 32, 32, 32, 33, 33, 35, 35, 35, 35, 48, 66, 71, 76, 76, 77; **2:**12, 12, 34, 34, 34, 35, 35; **3:**6, 9, 16, 17; **4:**6, 7, 7, 11, 18, 18, 18, 23; **5:**4, 14, 24, 35, 35; **6:**21, 21, 21, 25, 34, 35, 35, 37, 37, 37, 38, 38, 38, 39, 40, 42, 47, 49; **7:**7, 27, 31; **8:**17, 18, 18, 50; **9:**22, 22, 22, 24, 24, 26, 27, 33, 57, 61; **10:**6, 6, 12, 14, 15, 15, 19, 28; **11:**8, 9, 9, 9, 13, 19, 24, 29, 30, 31, 32, 36, 41, 42, 43, 44, 46, 47, 49, 49, 50, 51, 52; **12:**2, 2, 3, 3, 8, 9, 10, 12, 20, 20, 29, 31, 33, 33, 34, 36, 37, 37, 38, 40, 43, 44, 46, 46, 47, 48, 52, 53, 55; **13:**3, 5, 23, 24, 25, 25, 25, 26, 27, 28, 28, 28, 29, 30, 30, 32, 32, 35; **14:**9, 9, 9, 10, 10, 11, 11, 12, 14, 23, 24, 32; **15:**7, 9, 18; **16:**11, 13, 30; **17:**1, 1, 20, 22, 23, 24, 24, 26, 28, 30, 33, 33, 34, 34, 34, 35, 35, 37; **18:**7, 7, 8, 8, 14, 14, 17, 22, 30, 31, 32, 33, 33; **19:**8, 8, 17, 26, 26, 30, 43, 44, 44, 46; **20:**5, 6, 13, 13, 15, 16, 18, 18, 28, 33, 35, 36, 37, 47; **21:**6, 6, 7, 7, 8, 10, 11, 11, 11, 12, 12, 12, 13, 15, 15, 16, 16, 17, 18, 19, 20, 22, 22, 23, 23, 24, 24, 25, 25, 26, 26, 27, 32, 33, 33, 35; **22:**10, 12, 18, 20, 21, 22, 30, 34, 37, 40, 42, 46, 61, 69; **23:**16, 16, 22, 29, 30, 31, 43; **24:**49; **Jn 1:**27, 42, 50, 51; **2:**19; **3:**13, 15, 16, 20, 20, 29, 36; **4:**21, 23, 23, 25, 25, 34, 35, 38, 48, 50, 53; **5:**20, 20, 21, 23, 24, 25, 25, 28, 29, 29, 29, 30, 45, 45, 47; **6:**30, 35, 35, 37, 37, 38, 39, 40, 44, 45, 51, 54, 57, 58, 62; **7:**6, 17, 17, 24, 27, 27, 33, 33, 34, 36, 38, 41, 42; **8:**12, 21, 24, 24, 28, 32, 32, 36, 51, 52; **9:**31; **10:**5, 9, 9, 12, 12, 16, 16, 28, 28, 38; **11:**4, 4, 11, 15, 22, 23, 25, 26, 39, 40, 42, 48, 48, 56; **12:**8, 8, 24, 24, 25, 25, 26, 28, 31, 32, 34, 35, 35, 36, 38, 46, 48; **13:**7, 8, 18, 19, 21, 31, 32, 35, 36, 38; **14:**3, 3, 8, 12, 13, 14, 16, 16, 16, 17, 18, 18, 19, 19, 19, 19, 20, 21, 21, 21, 23, 23, 23, 24, 26, 26, 28, 28, 29, 31, 31; **15:**2, 4, 5, 7, 11, 11, 16, 16, 20, 21, 26, 26, 26; **16:**2, 2, 4, 7, 7, 8, 10, 11, 13, 13, 13, 13, 14, 15, 16, 16, 17, 19, 19, 20, 20, 20, 20, 21, 22, 22, 23, 24, 24, 25, 25, 25, 26, 26, 28, 32, 33; **17:**11, 20, 21, 21, 21, 23, 23, 26, 26; **19:**36, 37; **20:**15, 31; **21:**18, 18, 20; **Ac 1:**5, 8, 8, 11, 22; **2:**17, 17, 17, 17, 18, 18, 19, 20, 20, 21, 25, 27, 28, 38; **3:**20, 20, 22, 23, 23, 25; **4:**28; **5:**9, 38, 39; **6:**3, 14; **7:**3, 7, 7, 34, 37, 43; **8:**19, 22; **9:**6, 16; **10:**43; **11:**14, 14, 16; **13:**10, 11, 22, 34, 35, 36, 46; **15:**16, 16, 16, 16, 29; **16:**31; **18:**6, 10, 21; **19:**27, 27; **20:**25, 29, 30; **21:**14, 22, 24; **22:**10, 14, 21; **23:**3, 15, 35; **24:**15, 22; **26:**14, 16, 17, 18; **27:**22, 22, 24, 25, 26, 31, 34; **28:**4, 26, 26, 26, 26, 28; **Ro 1:**5, 11, 12; **2:**2, 3, 6, 7, 8, 9, 10, 12, 12, 13, 16, 16, 27; **3:**3, 4, 4, 5; **4:**18, 24; **5:**5, 9, 10, 17, 19; **6:**5, 8, 9, 19; **7:**24; **8:**7, 10, 11, 13, 13, 17, 18, 19, 20, 21, 23, 27, 33, 34, 34, 39; **9:**7, 9, 9, 12, 15, 15, 16, 25, 25, 26, 27, 28, 33; **10:**9, 11, 13, 15, 19, 19; **11:**12, 15, 15, 16, 16, 22, 23, 24, 25, 25, 26, 26, 26, 27, 31; **12:**1, 2, 2, 2, 14, 19, 19, 20; **13:**2, 3, 4, 8, 12; **14:**2, 4, 10, 11, 11, 12, 13, 16, 18, 18; **15:**2, 7, 9, 9, 12, 12, 12, 13, 21, 21, 24, 28, 29, 31, 31, 32, 32, 32; **16:**1, 20; **1Co 1:**1, 8, 8, 9, 19; **3:**8, 13, 14, 15, 15, 17, 18; **4:**4, 5, 5, 5, 17, 18, 19, 19; **5:**4, 4, 5, 5, 6, 13; **6:**3, 9, 10, 13, 14; **7:**12, 25, 31, 35, 40; **8:**10, 10, 11, 13; **9:**17, 24, 25; **10:**13, 13, 13; **11:**19, 31, 32; **12:**1; **13:**8, 8, 10, 12, 12, 13; **14:**2, 2, 2, 6, 7, 8, 9, 11, 11, 12, 15, 15, 15, 15, 15, 17, 19, 21, 21, 23, 24, 24, 25, 25, 26, 26, 26, 26, 26, 31, 31, 38; **15:**12, 20, 22, 23, 24, 24, 28, 28, 29, 29, 32, 35, 35, 37, 42, 42, 43, 43, 44, 48, 49, 51, 51, 52, 52, 52, 52, 53, 54, 54; **16:**3, 6, 7, 8, 12; **2Co 1:**4, 5, 7, 10, 11, 11, 13, 14, 22, 24; **2:**3, 11; **4:**11, 14, 15, 15, 17, 18, 18; **5:**1, 2, 3, 3, 4, 8, 10, 15, 15; **6:**3, 16, 16, 16, 17, 18, 18; **7:**10, **8:**3, 14, 20; **9:**6, 6, 8, 8, 9, 10, 10, 11, 11, 12, 12, 12, 13, 13, 14; **10:**6, 8, 11, 13, 15, 15, 16, 16; **11:**1, 3, 9, 10, 12, 15, 18; **12:**14, 15, 20, 21, 21; **13:**2, 3, 7, 11; **Gal 1:**9; **2:**16; **3:**8; **4:**17, 19, 30; **5:**10, 19, 21, 22; **6:**4, 7, 8, 8, 9; **Eph 1:**10, 14, 18, 19; **3:**4, 10, 16, 17, 19, 19; **4:**13, 14, 15, 29, 30; **5:**5, 14, 14, 18, 19, 20, 21, 22, 27; **6:**3, 6, 8, 11, 13, 15, 16, 20, 21, 22, 22; **Php 1:**6, 9, 9, 11, 18, 19, 20, 20, 20, 25, 25, 26, 27, 28; **2:**10, 11, 16, 17, 24, 28, 28; **3:**12, 15, 15, 21, 21; **4:**7, 7, 9, 19; **Col 1:**10, 10, 10, 11, 11, 18, 27; **2:**2, 4, 7; **3:**4, 6, 21, 24, 25; **4:**3, 4, 6, 7, 9, 12; **1Th 2:**13, 19; **3:**13; **4:**4, 12, 12, 13, 13, 14, 15, 16, 16, 17; **5:**1, 2, 3, 3, 18, 24; **2Th 1:**5, 5, 6, 7, 7, 9, 10, 11, 11, 12, 12; **2:**1, 3, 4, 4, 7, 8, 8, 9, 10, 11, 11, 12; **3:**1, 2, 3, 4, 14; **1Ti 1:**16; **2:**15; **3:**6, 7, 13, 13, 15; **4:**1, 1, 3, 6, 10, 15, 16; **5:**7, 11, 11, 14, 20, 24, 24; **6:**1, 15, 16, 17, 19; **2Ti 1:**1, 4; **2:**7, 10, 11, 12, 12, 21, 21, 21, 25, 25, 26; **3:**1, 2, 2, 2, 3, 3, 3, 4, 5, 5, 9, 12, 13, 13, 13; **4:**1, 3, 3, 3, 3, 4, 8, 11, 14, 16, 18, 18; **Tit 1:**9; **2:**5, 8, 10, 13; **3:**7, 8; **Phm 1:**6, 6, 16, 19, 21, 22; **Heb 1:**5, 5, 11, 11, 12, 12, 12, 14; **2:**5, 12, 12, 13; **3:**11, 13, 14; **4:**3, 5, 10, 11, 16, 16; **6:**3, 8, 10, 11, 11, 12, 12, 14, 14; **7:**8, 21, 24; **8:**8, 8, 9, 10, 10, 10, 10, 10, 10, 10, 11, 11, 11, 12, 12; **9:**14, 16, 16, 17, 17, 28, 28; **10:**7, 9, 16, 16, 16, 16, 16, 17, 26, 27, 27, 29, 30, 30, 30, 36, 36, 36, 37, 38, 38; **11:**18; **12:**10, 11, 13, 13, 14, 15, 26, 27, 27; **13:**4, 5, 5, 6, 20, 23; **Jas 1:**4, 5, 5, 10, 11, 12, 25; **2:**5, 12, 13, 13, 18, 20; **3:**1, 13, 13, 16, 18; **4:**3, 7, 8, 10, 13, 13, 14, 15, 16; **5:**3, 3, 9, 12, 15, 15, 15, 20; **1Pe 1:**5, 5, 7, 9, 13, 17, 23, 23, 25; **2:**6, 8, 12, 12, 15; **3:**1, 1, 7, 9, 13, 14, 16; **4:**2, 2, 5, 5, 11, 13, 13, 14, 18, 19, 19; **5:**1, 2, 4, 6, 10, 10; **2Pe 1:**4, 4, 5, 7, 8, 10, 11, 15; **2:**1, 1, 1, 2, 2, 3, 6, 12; **3:**3, 3, 4, 7, 7, 10, 10, 10, 10, 12, 12; **1Jn 1:**4; **2:**1, 17, 17, 24, 28; **3:**2, 2, 2, 3, 19, 22; **4:**17; **5:**14, 14, 15, 16; **2Jn** 2, 8, 9, 9, 12; **3Jn** 10, 14; **Jude** 7, 11, 11, 11, 15, 15, 24; **Rev 1:**1, 3, 7, 7, 19; **2:**5, 7, 10, 10, 10, 11, 16, 17, 17, 17, 22, 22, 23, 23, 23, 24, 26, 27, 28, 28; **3:**3, 4, 5, 5, 5, 9, 9, 10, 10, 11, 12, 12, 12, 12, 12, 16, 18, 18, 18, 20, 20, 21; **4:**1; **5:**10; **6:**10, 10, 17; **7:**15, 16, 16, 17, 17, 17; **8:**13; **9:**6, 6, 6, 6; **10:**6, 7, 7, 9, 9; **11:**2, 3, 3, 3, 6, 7, 7, 8, 9, 9, 10, 15, 18, 18; **12:**12; **13:**10, 10; **14:**7, 10, 11, 13; **15:**4, 4; **16:**15, 15; **17:**1, 7, 8, 8, 10, 11, 12, 13, 14, 14, 16, 16, 17, 17, 17; **18:**4, 7, 8, 8, 9, 10, 10, 11, 14, 15, 15, 17, 18, 18, 19, 19, 21, 21, 22, 22, 23, 23, 23; **20:**6, 6, 7, 8, 8, 10; **21:**3, 3, 3, 4, 4, 6, 7, 7, 7, 9, 24, 24, 26, 27; **22:**3, 3, 3, 4, 4, 5, 5, 5, 6, 18, 19

WITH (5639)

Ge 1:11, 12, 20, 20; **3:**6, 16; **4:**1, 1, 11, 22, 25; **5:**22, 24; **6:**3, 4, 8, 9, 11, 13, 14, 17, 18, 19; **7:**1, 8, 8, 13, 14, 14, 23, 23; **8:**11, 21; **9:**9, 10, 10, 12, 15, 15, 17, 18; **10:**5, 10, 32; **11:**4; **12:**4, 20; **13:**1, 5, 5, 6, 8, 11, 11; **14:**10, 11, 14, 16, 19; **15:**14, 18; **16:**2, 4, 4, 5, 6, 12; **17:**2, 4, 19, 21, 27; **18:**16, 22, 25, 33; **19:**3, 3, 5, 5, 8, 25, 30, 32, 32, 33, 34, 34, 34, 35; **20:**4, 18; **21:**6, 10, 14, 20, 21, 22, 32; **22:**3, 3, 5; **23:**4; **24:**8, 10, 10, 15, 16, 31, 32, 39, 40, 45, 54, 58, 59, 59, 60, 61, 65; **25:**21, 21, 22, 25, 26; **26:**3, 10, 15, 20, 20, 24, 26, 28; **27:**15, 17, 33, 44; **28:**5, 15, 15, 20; **29:**6, 9, 17, 18, 22, 23, 30; **30:**3, 4, 5, 8, 10, 15, 16, 16, 16, 26, 32, 35, 42, 43; **31:**3, 5, 5, 7, 10, 12, 14, 16, 19, 21, 23, 25, 27, 38; **32:**4, 6, 6, 7, 11, 15, 20, 24, 28; **33:**1, 2, 5, 6, 7, 12; **34:**6, 8, 10, 16, 16, 20, 21; **35:**3, 14, 18, 22; **37:**2, 13; **38:**9, 14, 16, 18, 26, 30; **39:**1, 2, 3, 4, 4, 6, 7, 8, 10, 12, 15, 16, 21, 21, 23; **40:**2; **41:**5, 10, 38, 55, 56; **42:**4, 5, 6, 13, 13, 19, 24, 25, 26, 28, 32, 33, 38; **43:**4, 5, 6, 8, 11, 16, 16, 30, 32, 34; **44:**1, 2, 3, 4, 6, 9, 18, 23, 26, 26, 31, 33, 34; **45:**1, 5, 10, 14, 15, 21, 23, 23, 27; **46:**1, 4, 4, 8, 15, 26, 30, 32; **47:**1, 2, 23, 29; **48:**1, 7, 20, 21, 22; **49:**4, 25, 28, 29; **50:**7, 10, 14, 25; **Ex 1:**1, 1, 14; **2:**3, 21; **3:**8, 9, 12, 17, 18, 20, 21, 22; **4:**6, 10, 10, 14, 18, 18, 18; **5:**3, 7, 9, 15, 21; **6:**4, 5, 6, 30; **7:**4, 4, 11, 17; **8:**3, 3, 7, 8, 12, 16, 18, 21, 21; **9:**15, 24; **10:**4, 6, 10, 17, 18, 24, 26; **11:**8, 8; **12:**4, 5, 8, 15, 19, 19, 20, 22, 34, 38, 38, 48; **13:**5, 9, 14, 16, 17, 19, 19; **14:**7, 7, 7, 9, 18, 21, 22; **15:**9, 10, 13, 15; **16:**12, 13, 20; **17:**2, 4, 4, 7, 9, 11, 16; **18:**2, 5, 6, 19; **19:**13, 17, 18, 18, 24; **20:**5, 18, 25; **21:**3, 6, 8, 10, 18, 19; **22:**16, 19, 24, 30; **23:**1, 7, 18, 25, 32, 32, 33; **24:**8, 12, 14, 14; **25:**11, 13, 16, 20, 21, 22, 24, 28, 33, 34, 34, 36; **26:**1, 1, 11, 21, 23, 24, 29, 29, 31, 32, 37; **27:**2, 4, 6, 9, 10, 11, 16, 18; **28:**5, 6, 7, 8, 15, 15, 28, 32, 33, 36, 38, 41; **29:**1, 2, 2, 3, 4, 5, 6, 9, 12, 13, 21, 22, 23, 32, 36, 40, 40, 41, 42; **30:**2, 3, 5, 6, 18, 18, 28, 28, 36; **31:**3, 8, 9, 17, 18, 18; **32:**6, 11, 11, 11, 13, 15, 20; **33:**3, 3, 5, 7, 9, 12, 12, 14, 15, 16, 16, 17, 22; **34:**3, 9, 10, 12, 14, 15, 15, 15, 22, 25, 27, 27, 28, 29, 31, 33, 34, 35; **35:**16, 31; **36:**1, 2, 4, 24, 26, 29, 30, 34, 35, 36, 37, 38, 38; **37:**2, 4, 11, 11, 15, 19, 20, 22, 24, 25, 26, 28; **38:**2, 2, 3, 6, 10, 11, 11, 12, 17, 18, 19, 30; **39:**2, 3, 6, 8, 14, 23, 23, 26, 29, 30, 31, 33; **40:**7, 12, 13, 15, 20, 30, 35; **Lev 1:**3, 9, 10, 13; **2:**1, 2, 2, 4, 4, 4, 13, 15, 16, 16; **3:**4, 4, 10, 10, 15, 15; **4:**2, 3, 9, 10, 20, 21, 23, 26, 28, 31, 32, 35; **5:**3, 11, 13, 16; **6:**2, 6, 15, 15, 17, 21, 28; **7:**4, 4, 10, 12, 14, 30, 30; **8:**2, 6, 7, 7, 7, 9, 15, 21, 25, 25, 26, 26, 31; **9:**2, 3, 4, 19, 24; **10:**6, 15, 16; **11:**21, 42, 42; **13:**44, 49, 59; **14:**4, 5, 6, 10, 10, 10, 11, 13, 20, 21, 21, 24, 31, 34, 44, 50, 54, 57; **15:**6, 12, 12, 17, 24, 32, 33, 33, 33, 33; **16:**12, 12, 15, 24; **17:**13; **18:**6, 7, 7, 8, 9, 10, 11, 12, 13, 14, 15, 16, 17, 19, 20, 23, 23; **19:**10, 14, 19, 19, 20, 22, 28, 29; **20:**5, 10, 11, 12, 14, 15, 16, 17, 17, 18, 19, 20, 24; **21:**6; **22:**2, 6, 11, 19, 20, 27; **23:**12, 13, 13, 18, 18, 18, 20, 24, 35; **24:**2, 6, 10, 19; **25:**6, 14, 23, 24, 35, 36, 40; **26:**7, 9, 13, 15, 16, 16, 21, 33, 36, 42, 42, 42, 44, 45; **Nu 1:**50, 52; **2:**17; **3:**4, 25, 32; **4:**5, 6, 6, 9, 9, 10, 10, 11, 12, 13, 19, 25, 31, 32; **5:**8, 13, 15, 15, 17, 19, 20, 29, 30; **6:**15, 15, 15, 17, 20, 23; **7:**1, 1, 13, 13, 14, 19, 19, 20, 25, 25, 26, 31, 31, 32, 37, 37, 38, 43, 43, 44, 49, 49, 50, 55, 55, 56, 61, 61, 62, 67, 67, 68, 73, 73, 74, 79, 79, 80, 86, 87, 89; **8:**7, 8, 8; **9:**7, 11; **10:**9, 10, 14, 14, 17, 18, 18, 22, 22, 25, 29, 32, 33; **11:**4, 8, 9, 16, 17, 21, 30; **12:**6, 7, 7, 9, 10; **13:**27, 31; **14:**8, 8, 9, 12, 13, 14, 21, 23, 37, 42; **15:**3, 4, 6, 9, 12, 20, 24, 24, 25, 25, 31, 34, 38; **16:**1, 3, 4, 13, 14, 16, 17, 18, 18, 22, 27, 32, 32, 33; **17:**4; **18:**1, 4, 4, 7, 21; **19:**12, 15, 16; **20:**3, 4, 11, 13, 14, 18, 20, 20; **21:**18, 21; **22:**7, 8, 9, 12, 13, 14, 18, 20, 21, 23, 27, 29, 31, 35, 35, 40; **23:**6, 13, 21; **24:**4, 7, 8, 13, 16; **25:**1, 2, 12, 14, 18; **26:**9, 10; **27:**4, 7, 19; **28:**3, 5, 5, 7, 7, 8, 9, 9, 11, 12, 12, 12, 13, 14, 14, 17, 19, 20, 20, 20, 21, 28, 28, 28, 29, 31; **29:**2, 3, 3, 3, 4, 6, 8, 9, 9, 9, 10, 11, 13, 14, 16, 17, 19, 20, 22, 23, 25, 26, 28, 29, 31, 32, 34, 36, 38, 39; **31:**8, 14, 17, 23; **32:**5, 10, 13, 14, 29, 30, 33, 36; **33:**4; **34:**18; **35:**2, 5, 7, 16, 17, 18, 21; **36:**1, 3; **Dt 1:**28, 37, 42; **2:**7, 9, 19, 25, 26, 35; **3:**5, 12, 17, 23, 26; **4:**11, 21, 23, 29, 31, 37, 40; **5:**2, 3, 3, 9, 15, 22, 23, 31; **6:**3, 3, 5, 10, 11, 18, 21; **7:**2, 3, 8, 12, 19, 25; **8:**3, 7, 13, 15, 16, 18; **9:**1, 9, 9, 11, 20, 23; **10:**7, 12; **11:**6, 7, 9, 10, 11, 13; **12:**12, 15, 18, 22, 23, 25, 28; **13:**3; **14:**26; **15:**11, 11, 14, 14, 16, 21; **16:**3, 8, 11, 14, 14; **17:**19; **18:**14, 19; **19:**3, 5, 13; **20:**1, 2, 4; **21:**4, 8; **22:**6, 6, 10, 13, 14, 23, 30; **23:**4, 8, 13, 15, 19, 25; **25:**2, 8, 16; **26:**3, 8, 9, 15; **27:**2, 3, 4, 6, 7, 8, 20, 21, 22, 23; **28:**4, 4, 5, 5, 5, 5, 8, 17, 17, 18, 18, 22, 22, 22, 27, 27, 28, 35, 47, 59, 66; **29:**1, 1, 2, 11, 12, 12, 12, 14, 14, 15, 15, 18, 23, 25; **30:**6, 10; **31:**3, 5, 8, 14, 16, 20, 23, 23, 27; **32:**13, 13, 14, 14, 16, 19, 21, 23, 38, 42, 43, 44, 51; **33:**2, 4, 8, 13, 14, 15, 16; **34:**3; **Jos 1:**5, 5, 9, 14, 17, 17; **2:**5, 8, 13; **3:**7, 7; **4:**11; **5:**1, 6, 13, 14; **6:**4, 8, 9, 13, 13, 22, 23, 25, 27; **7:**1, 5, 12, 14, 15, 15, 21, 22; **8:**4, 11, 31, 33; **9:**4, 6, 7, 11, 15, 15, 20; **10:**1, 4, 6, 11, 11, 18, 27, 33; **11:**4, 19; **13:**21, 21; **14:**2, 5, 8, 12; **15:**1, 32, 36, 41, 44, 46, 47, 47, 51, 54, 57, 59, 60, 62; **16:**9; **17:**4, 4, 6, 10, 11; **18:**4, 8, 24, 28; **19:**6, 7, 15, 22, 30, 38, 46, 48; **21:**1, 3, 11, 13, 17, 25, 26, 27, 29, 32, 35, 37, 39; **22:**5, 8, 8, 13, 18, 19, 27, 28; **23:**7, 12; **24:**1, 6, 7, 25, 32; **Jdg 1:**3, 3, 7, 16, 17, 18, 19, 22; **2:**1, 1, 2, 14, 18, 20, 20; **3:**6, 8, 13, 21, 31; **4:**7, 8, 9, 9, 10, 10, 17, 18, 21, 22; **5:**15, 21, 26, 26; **6:**4, 5, 12, 13, 14, 16, 19, 21, 37, 39, 39, 40; **7:**2, 4, 5, 5, 6, 7, 8, 10, 14, 16, 19, 22; **8:**1, 4, 7, 10, 16; **9:**16, 26, 32, 33,

33, 40, 54; **10:**7, 15; **11:**9, 11, 37; **12:**1; **13:**9, 11, 20; **14:**6, 7, 7, 15, 17, 18, 18, 19; **15:**1, 8, 13, 15, 16, 16; **16:**1, 3, 4, 7, 8, 11, 12, 13, 14, 18, 19, 21, 27, 29, 30; **17:**10; **18:**4, 14, 19, 20, 23, 27; **19:**20, 21, 22, 22, 27; **20:**2, 10, 15, 17, 25, 35; **21:**10, 12, 18; **Ru 1:**3, 7, 8, 9, 10, 11, 14, 18; **2:**4, 6, 8, 14, 19, 21, 22, 23, 23, 23; **3:**2; **4:**10, 13, 13, 18; **1Sa 1:**19, 22; **2:**3, 5, 13, 17, 19, 26, 26, 32; **3:**19; **4:**1, 3, 8; **5:**3, 6, 7, 8, 9, 12; **6:**3, 6, 10; **7:**8, 9, 10, 14; **8:**4, 6; **9:**3, 24; **10:**6, 6, 7; **11:**1, 7; **12:**20; **13:**2, 2, 7, 10, 15, 15, 16; **14:**7, 21, 34, 52; **15:**2, 6, 25, 26, 30, 31, 35; **16:**1, 2, 5, 12, 14, 18, 20, 20, 22; **17:**3, 7, 10, 14, 15, 19, 20, 20, 20, 22, 23, 35, 37, 40, 41, 43, 45, 50, 57; **18:**1, 2, 6, 8, 8, 12, 14, 20, 28; **19:**1, 3, 4, 8, 13, 16, 18; **20:**5, 11, 13, 13, 14, 15, 16, 25, 30, 35, 41; **21:**1, 4, 5, 6, 11; **22:**9, 16, 17, 23, 23; **23:**6, 6, 23, 23; **24:**4, 10; **25:**13, 15, 22, 28, 33, 36, 42; **26:**6, 6, 7; **27:**3, 5; **28:**1, 5, 15, 19, 20, 20, 23; **29:**2, 3, 4, 4, 6, 9, 10; **30:**10, 16, 21, 22, 23; **31:**3; **2Sa 1:**6, 21; **2:**6, 8, 26; **3:**7, 8, 9, 13, 14, 17, 19, 20, 20, 21, 22, 26, 26, 27, 29, 31; **4:**1, 7; **5:**3, 10, 11; **6:**4, 4, 5, 11, 12, 14, 15, 16; **7:**3, 9, 19; **8:**2, 8, 10, 11; **9:**7, 10, 11; **11:**4, 9, 10, 11, 17, 27; **12:**3, 11, 17, 17, 24, 30, 31, 31; **13:**1, 2, 4, 11, 19, 20, 24, 36, 39; **14:**4, 15, 17; **15:**11, 15, 18, 18, 19, 19, 20, 20, 22, 26, 27, 30, 33; **16:**1, 1, 2, 10, 13, 14, 17, 21, 22; **17:**10, 16, 19, 22, 29; **18:**2, 5, 11, 19, 22, 27, 28, 33; **19:**4, 14, 16, 17, 22, 25, 26, 33, 36, 37, 38, 39, 40, 43; **20:**1, 2, 3, 7, 8, 9, 10, 13, 13, 22; **21:**12, 15, 16, 20, 20; **22:**12, 26, 30, 40; **23:**5, 7, 21, 21, 21; **24:**20; **1Ki 1:**4, 5, 14, 22, 25, 37, 37, 40, 40, 44; **2:**4, 5, 6, 8, 23, 26; **3:**1, 10, 17, 28; **4:**13, 13, 20, 33; **5:**3, 8, 9; **6:**15, 15, 16, 18, 20, 21, 22, 28, 29, 30, 31, 32, 32, 35, 35; **7:**7, 12, 17, 28, 28, 29, 30, 31, 32, 34, 35, 50, 50; **8:**4, 9, 21, 22, 24, 24, 46, 48, 54, 57, 57, 62; **9:**4, 12, 27; **10:**1, 2, 2, 2, 7, 9, 9, 18, 19, 20, 22, 22; **11:**2, 9, 15, 38; **12:**3, 6, 8, 16; **13:**4, 7, 8, 15, 18, 24; **14:**8, 9, 16, 22; **15:**3, 18, 18, 19, 20, 24; **16:**13; **18:**4, 13, 19, 28, 33, 45; **19:**10, 14, 19, 19, 20, 21; **20:**9, 24; **21:**4, 8; **22:**11, 13, 19, 44, 49, 50; **2Ki 1:**6, 9, 9, 11, 13, 13, 15; **2:**8, 14, 20, 21; **3:**11, 12, 14, 16, 17, 19, 25; **4:**4, 10, 18, 26, 26, 26, 30, 30, 37, 39, 43; **5:**6, 9, 10, 13, 17, 17; **6:**1, 3, 8, 8, 14, 17, 32; **7:**3, 9, 13, 14; **8:**4, 9, 11, 19, 21, 24; **9:**1, 5, 14, 15, 28; **10:**2, 4, 5, 6, 16, 16, 23, 24, 24, 25, 31, 35; **11:**4, 10, 11, 12; **12:**18, 18, 21; **13:**3, 9, 12, 13, 19, 23; **14:**9, 10, 15, 16, 20, 29; **15:**5, 25, 25, 38; **16:**7, 10, 10, 20; **17:**15, 35, 36, 38; **18:**7, 16, 17, 18, 23, 24, 24, 31, 32; **19:**7, 10, 23, 24, 32, 37; **21:**6, 12, 16; **22:**14, 17; **23:**2, 3, 5, 9, 25, 29; **24:**4, 12, 15; **25:**3, 11, 17, 18, 25, 25, 29; **1Ch 4:**10; **5:**1, 12, 18, 25; **6:**32, 33, 57, 60, 66, 70, 71, 71, 73, 75, 76, 77, 79, 81; **7:**23; **9:**2, 6, 20, 31; **10:**3; **11:**3, 9, 10, 13, 23, 23, 42; **12:**2, 8, 18, 19, 19, 24, 28, 32, 34, 37, 38, 39; **13:**1, 7, 8, 14; **14:**1; **15:**5, 6, 7, 8, 9, 10, 15, 25, 28, 29; **16:**16, 32, 33; **17:**2, 2, 8; **18:**8, 10, 11; **20:**2, 3, 3, 4, 5, 6, 6; **21:**7, 16, 16, 20; **22:**9, 11, 16, 18, 18, 19; **23:**2, 5, 14, 22, 31; **24:**3, 25; **25:**5; **26:**6; **28:**8, 9, 9, 20, 21; **29:**9, 17, 22; **2Ch 1:**1; **2:**7, 7, 12, 14, 14; **3:**4, 5, 5, 5, 6, 6, 7, 8, 9, 10, 14; **4:**9, 22; **5:**5, 10, 13; **6:**11, 12, 15, 15, 36, 38, 41; **7:**6, 8; **8:**18; **9:**1, 1, 1, 2, 6, 8, 17, 18, 19, 21; **10:**3, 6, 8, 16; **11:**13, 23; **12:**3, 5, 10, 14, 15; **13:**5, 8, 9, 12, 19; **14:**7, 7, 8, 8, 9; **15:**2, 2, 6, 9, 9, 12, 14, 15; **16:**2, 3, 8, 10, 14; **17:**3, 8, 16, 17; **18:**2, 10, 12, 18; **19:**6, 7, 9, 9, 11; **20:**9, 13, 17, 17, 18, 19, 27, 35, 37, 37; **21:**1, 7, 9, 14, 15, 18; **22:**5, 7, 9; **23:**1, 3, 9, 10, 11, 13; **24:**10, 24; **25:**7, 8, 10, 14, 16, 17, 18, 24, 28; **26:**7, 7, 7, 14, 17, 19; **28:**9, 12, 15, 18, 18, 18; **29:**10, 18, 18, 22, 25, 26, 26, 29, 30, 35; **30:**21; **31:**5; **32:**3, 6, 9, 21, 21, 23; **33:**6; **34:**22, 25, 30, 31, 32; **35:**12, 21, 21, 21, 21, 21, 21, 23; **36:**18, 23; **Ezr 1:**3, 4; **2:**66; **3:**2, 2, 7, 9, 11; **4:**2; **5:**2, 8, 8; **6:**9, 12, 13, 16; **7:**7, 13, 15, 25, 28; **8:**1, 18, 19, 33; **9:**4, 5, 11, 14; **10:**1, 3, 3, 14, 17; **Ne 1:**2, 5; **2:**2, 4, 5, 6, 12, 12, 18; **4:**13, 16, 17, 18, 23, 23; **5:**7; **6:**3, 5, 7, 16; **7:**2, 5, 68, 73; **8:**6, 10, 10, 12, 13, 17; **9:**8, 24, 25, 30; **10:**1, 29, 38; **11:**12, 17, 25, 25, 25, 27, 28, 30, 30, 31, 36; **12:**1, 8, 8, 27, 27, 33, 38, 40, 40, 41; **13:**7, 20, 25; **Est 1:**6, 10, 11, 12, 13; **2:**6, 8, 9, 9, 12, 12, 17; **3:**4, 5, 11, 12; **4:**1, 9; **5:**8, 8, 12, 14; **6:**8; **7:**3, 6, 7; **8:**3, 5, 8, 8, 10, 16; **9:**5, 5, 17, 22, 29; **10:**3; **Job 1:**6, 8, 12, 14, 14, 16, 17, 18; **2:**1, 3, 6, 7, 8, 13; **3:**14, 15, 15, 18, 23; **4:**14, 18; **5:**4, 23, 23; **6:**4, 16, 19; **7:**5, 13, 14, 14; **8:**6, 7, 7, 21, 21, 22; **9:**14, 18, 25, 30, 30, 32; **10:**1, 8, 11, 15; **12:**2, 13, 16, 18, 22; **13:**3, 4, 10, 15, 19, 21; **14:**13; **15:**16; **16:**9, 13, 16; **17:**5, 7, 9, 16; **19:**2, 3, 16, 22, 24, 24, 27; **20:**25; **21:**3, 4, 4, 12, 16, 17; **22:**18, 18, 21, 21; **23:**3, 6, 7; **24:**16, 17; **26:**8, 9; **27:**15; **28:**17; **29:**5, 19; **30:**1, 3, 9, 17, 18, 21, 30; **31:**1, 1, 10, 17, 17, 21; **32:**3, 7, 14, 14, 15, 22; **33:**3, 10, 16, 19, 19, 26, 28; **34:**7, 8, 33; **36:**7, 11, 17, 18, 32; **37:**11, 11, 16; **38:**2, 9, 32; **39:**18, 19, 29; **40:**2, 9, 12; **41:**1, 2, 2, 5, 30, 31; **42:**3, 5, 7, 7, 11, 15; **Ps 1:**1, 1; **2:**1, 5, 9, 11, 11; **5:**7, 9, 11, 12; **7:**2, 11, 14; **8:**5; **9:**1, 2, 4, 8, 8; **10:**13; **11:**6; **12:**2; **13:**2, 2; **14:**2, 5, 7; **16:**4, 8, 9, 11; **17:**4, 7, 13; **18:**11, 25, 29, 32, 39; **21:**1, 3, 5, 6, 13; **22:**13, 26; **23:**5, 5; **24:**5; **25:**10, 14, 14; **26:**1, 4, 4, 5, 9, 10; **27:**6, 6, 8; **28:**3, 3, 7, 7; **29:**7, 11; **30:**5, 11; **31:**7; **32:**7; **33:**1, 2, 3; **34:**5, 14; **35:**6, 10, 12, 12, 16, 21, 26, 27; **36:**10; **37:**15, 31; **38:**6, 6; **40:**16; **41:**11; **43:**4; **44:**1, 3, 19; **45:**1, 8, 8, 12, 13; **46:**9; **47:**1, 5, 5, 7; **48:**6, 10; **49:**3, 4, 17; **50:**3, 5, 18, 19; **51:**T, 16, 18, 19, 19; **53:**2, 6; **54:**1, 1; **56:**7; **57:**8; **59:**11, 16; **60:**1, 6, 10, 12; **63:**5; **65:**3, 5, 6, 7, 10, 10, 11, 11, 12, 13, 13; **66:**13; **67:**1, 4; **68:**3, 10, 13, 16, 25, 31; **69:**3, 4, 13, 24, 30, 30, 31; **70:**4; **71:**6, 19, 22, 22; **72:**19; **73:**5, 24; **74:**6; **75:**5, 8; **77:**2, 3, 6, 20; **78:**17, 36, 36, 47, 47, 58, 62, 72, 72; **79:**5; **80:**5, 10, 10; **81:**10, 16, 16; **83:**8, 15, 15; **84:**2, 2, 9; **85:**5, 9; **86:**12; **88:**4, 8; **89:**3, 6, 10, 20, 24, 28, 32, 32, 38, 39, 49; **90:**9, 10, 14, 15; **91:**4, 4, 8, 12, 15, 16; **92:**4, 7, 11, 11; **93:**1; **95:**2, 10; **96:**12, 12, 13, 13; **98:**5, 5, 6, 9, 9; **99:**4; **100:**1, 2, 2, 4, 4; **101:**1, 3, 6; **102:**T; **103:**1, 4, 5, 10, 17; **104:**1, 1, 6, 13, 25; **105:**9, 18, 26, 37, 43, 43; **106:**3, 4, 5, 15, 29, 38, 45, 46; **107:**9, 12; **108:**2, 7, 11, 13; **109:**3, 21, 29; **110:**6; **111:**1, 1, 8, 9; **113:**5; **115:**6, 6, 7, 7, 7; **117:**2; **119:**2, 3, 6, 20, 28, 34, 36, 40, 53, 58, 69, 77, 79, 81, 83, 92, 124, 135, 139, 145, 155, 171; **120:**4, 4, 5; **122:**8; **125:**4, 5; **126:**2, 5, 6; **127:**1; **129:**3; **130:**7; **131:**1, 2; **132:**8, 15, 18; **135:**3, 7, 17, 17; **136:**12; **138:**1; **139:**18, 22; **140:**11; **143:**4; **144:**9, 13, 14; **145:**7, 17; **146:**2; **147:**8, 14, 20; **149:**3, 4, 8, 8; **150:**3, 3, 4, 4, 5, 5; **Pr 1:**9, 9, 13, 14, 14, 15; **2:**7, 10; **3:**4, 5, 7, 9, 9, 10, 10, 15, 22; **4:**9; **5:**15, 16, 17, 20; **6:**13, 26, 29, 29; **7:**5, 13, 16, 17, 20, 21, 21; **8:**9, 11, 12, 16, 31; **9:**1, 4, 16; **10:**6, 9, 13, 13, 22; **11:**2, 12, 14, 20; **12:**8, 9; **13:**15, 20, 20; **14:**1, 6, 16, 18, 18, 29, 35; **15:**16, 16, 17, 17; **16:**7, 10, 13, 19, 19, 30; **17:**1, 27; **18:**19, 19, 23; **19:**11, 14; **20:**7, 19; **21:**9, 19, 24, 27, 29; **22:**15, 20; **23:**1, 6, 20, 21; **24:**4, 18, 21, 22, 31, 31; **25:**6, 9, 18, 18, 18, 19, 24, 26, 28; **26:**1, 1, 1, 3, 3, 3, 4, 5, 24; **27:**16, 22; **28:**2, 24; **29:**3; **30:**14, 20, 32; **31:**16, 23, 25, 25; **Ecc 2:**3, 5, 9, 21, 23; **3:**10; **4:**1; **5:**20; **6:**10; **8:**3, 10, 15; **9:**7, 8, 9, 14, 14; **10:**4, 9; **11:**10; **12:**3, 4; **SS 1:**4, 6, 10, 10; **2:**5; **3:**7, 11; **4:**4, 8, 13; **5:**1, 1, 1, 2, 2, 5, 5, 8, 14, 14; **6:**4, 10, 12; **7:**2, 2; **8:**7, 10; **Isa 1:**4, 6, 12, 13, 15, 21; **2:**6, 8, 19; **3:**14, 16, 16, 16; **5:**2, 6, 9, 14, 18; **6:**2, 2, 2, 2, 3, 4, 6, 7, 10, 10, 10, 11; **7:**2, 2, 14, 17; **8:**3, 7, 10; **9:**1, 3, 4, 7, 10, 10, 12, 12, 17; **10:**11, 26; **11:**4, 5, 9; **12:**1, 3, 6; **13:**5, 7, 8, 9, 15, 18; **14:**6, 10, 11, 19, 23, 23, 30; **15:**9, 9; **16:**1; **18:**5; **19:**1, 3, 6, 8, 13; **21:**3, 3; **22:**24, 25; **24:**12, 16; **25:**2, 5, 6, 11; **27:**6, 10; **28:**8, 27, 27; **29:**2, 6, 6, 13, 19, 22; **30:**6, 20, 20, 23, 27, 27, 29, 30, 30, 30, 31, 32, 33; **31:**9; **32:**13; **33:**14, 19, 23; **34:**3, 6, 6, 7, 7, 9, 9, 14, 15, 15; **35:**1, 3, 10; **36:**2, 3, 8, 9, 9, 16, 17; **37:**7, 10, 24, 25, 33, 38; **38:**11, 20; **40:**7, 10, 10, 11, 12, 15, 19, 19; **41:**2, 6, 10, 10, 15, 23; **42:**1, 6, 8; **43:**2, 5, 17, 23, 23, 24, 24, 24; **44:**11, 12; **45:**1, 9, 9, 9, 12, 14, 14, 17, 24; **46:**4; **47:**3, 6, 15; **48:**16; **49:**19, 26, 26; **50:**2; **51:**9, 11; **52:**1, 8, 11; **53:**3, 10; **54:**7, 8; **55:**3, 3, 11; **56:**7; **57:**5, 6, 8, 15, 15; **58:**1, 4, 5, 7, 13; **59:**3, 3, 6, 16, 17, 21; **60:**5, 9, 9, 21; **61:**2, 6, 8, 10, 10, 10, 11; **62:**5, 11; **63:**1, 11, 14; **64:**6, 7, 9; **65:**10; **66:**10, 10, 12, 15, 15, 22, 24; **Jer 1:**8, 19; **2:**18, 22, 25, 31, 34, 35, 37; **3:**1, 2, 12, 15, 16; **4:**8, 9, 30; **5:**3, 13, 27, 27, 31; **6:**7, 11, 24; **7:**21; **8:**19, 21; **9:**5, 5, 7, 11, 15, 16; **10:**4, 4, 13; **11:**2, 5, 10, 16; **13:**17; **14:**3, 7, 17, 17, 18, 21; **15:**1, 11, 17; **16:**8, 18, 18; **17:**1, 1, 3, 6, 8, 26; **18:**23; **19:**4, 10; **20:**4, 16, 18; **21:**1, 5; **22:**4, 6, 9, 13, 14, 14, 22, 23; **23:**5, 15, 16, 33, 34, 39; **24:**1, 2, 2; **25:**15, 20, 31; **26:**11, 14, 22, 23, 24; **27:**2, 18, 20; **28:**13; **29:**3, 18, 23; **30:**11; **31:**3, 3, 4, 7, 7, 9, 14, 14, 31, 32, 33, 36; **32:**5, 21, 21, 22, 30, 40; **33:**9, 11, 20, 21, 21; **34:**1, 7, 8, 13, 15; **36:**2, 12, 12, 18; **37:**15; **38:**8, 11; **40:**4, 5, 6, 10, 12, 15; **41:**3, 9, 10, 12; **42:**6, 9, 11; **43:**5, 6; **44:**4, 14, 19; **45:**3; **46:**9, 10, 12, 22, 28; **47:**4; **48:**7, 9, 33, 45; **49:**3, 16, 21, 23, 37, 37; **50:**5, 10, 12, 38, 38, 43, 46; **51:**5, 13, 14, 14, 16, 20, 21, 22, 23, 34, 39, 59; **52:**6, 15, 20, 21, 22, 24, 33; **La 1:**1, 1, 4, 9, 9, 9, 13, 15; **2:**14, 19; **3:**5, 9, 9, 11, 15, 43, 47, 63; **4:**4, 6, 7; **5:**12, 17, 22; **Eze 1:**1, 4, 4, 18, 19, 25, 27; **2:**1, 10; **3:**4, 6, 25; **4:**2, 7, 8, 15, 16, 16; **5:**2, 2, 11, 12, 16, 17; **6:**7; **7:**5, 7, 23, 27; **8:**10, 11, 12, 16, 18; **9:**1, 6, 7, 9; **10:**4, 4, 12, 16, 16, 19; **11:**6, 22; **12:**7, 7, 7, 12, 18, 19; **13:**10, 13, 13, 13, 15, 18, 22; **14:**11, 22; **16:**2, 4, 8, 13, 26, 27, 28, 37, 38, 40, 42, 46, 46, 60, 60, 61, 62; **17:**3, 4, 7, 13, 14, 15, 20; **18:**6; **19:**9; **20:**6, 7, 15, 18, 26, 33, 33, 34; **21:**6, 7, 15, 22, 23, 24, 29, 30, 31; **22:**5, 9, 10, 10, 11, 28; **23:**7, 8, 14, 17, 17, 18, 18, 23, 23, 24, 24, 24, 25, 29, 30, 31, 41, 43, 44, 44, 47; **24:**4, 5, 6, 10; **25:**6, 13; **26:**7, 9, 9, 10, 16, 17, 20; **27:**6, 7, 9, 20, 22, 23, 24, 31, 34, 35, 35; **28:**4, 8, 13, 16, 17, 18, 26; **29:**4; **30:**5, 16, 21, 22; **31:**3, 14, 16, 16, 16, 18; **32:**2, 5, 5, 6, 7, 12, 13, 18, 20, 24, 27, 29, 29, 30; **33:**25, 31, 32; **34:**4, 10, 18, 25, 30; **35:**8, 8, 11; **36:**10, 18, 26, 35, 38; **37:**1, 6, 23, 26; **38:**5, 6, 11, 12, 12, 15, 22; **39:**19; **40:**7, 9, 16, 21, 48, 49; **41:**6, 15, 16, 18, 18, 24, 25, 26; **42:**20; **43:**2, 3, 8, 13, 15, 17, 22; **44:**4; **45:**7, 7, 18, 24, 25; **46:**4, 5, 5, 6, 7, 7, 7, 7, 10, 11, 11, 11, 11, 13, 14, 14, 23; **47:**10, 23; **48:**1, 8, 10, 15, 25, 27; **Da 1:**1, 2, 4, 7, 11, 19; **2:**14, 18, 43; **3:**19, 19; **4:**12, 15, 15, 21, 23, 23, 23, 25, 25, 32, 33, 35, 36; **5:**1, 6, 12, 14, 20, 21; **6:**5, 10, 14, 17, 24, 26; **7:**2, 4, 4, 7, 9, 13, 19, 28; **8:**3, 18, 18, 22; **9:**3, 3, 7, 8, 20, 25, 26, 27; **10:**5, 7, 9, 11, 13; **11:**5, 6, 8, 8, 12, 13, 17, 17, 23, 25, 28, 40; **Hos 2:**6, 7, 7, 18; **3:**3, 3; **4:**2, 3, 4, 14, 15; **5:**2, 5, 6, 7; **6:**4, 5, 5, 8; **7:**1, 3, 4, 5, 6, 8, 9, 14; **8:**2, 4; **9:**7; **10:**1, 6; **11:**4, 12, 12; **12:**1, 1, 3, 3, 4, 10, 11; **13:**1, 2; **Joel 1:**8, 12, 18; **2:**6, 11, 12, 13, 22, 24, 24; **3:**13, 18, 18, 21; **Am 1:**3, 9, 11, 13; **2:**7, 8, 13; **3:**10, 12, 15; **4:**2, 5, 9; **5:**2, 9, 16, 23; **6:**4, 6, 10; **7:**4, 7, 8, 13; **8:**1, 6; **9:**13; **Ob** 10; **Jnh 2:**9; **4:**2; **Mic 1:**7; **2:**2, 3, 3, 7, 10, 12; **3:**8, 8; **4:**6; **5:**1, 4, 6, 8, 14; **6:**6, 8, 10, 16; **7:**3, 3, 10, 18, 20; **Na 1:**2, 9, 15; **2:**3, 11, 12; **3:**1, 4, 6, 16; **Hab 1:**4, 17; **2:**5, 6, 8, 12, 14, 19; **3:**2, 3, 8, 9, 14, 15, 16; **Zep 1:**3, 4, 9, 12; **2:**13; **3:**14, 17, 17, 19; **Hag 1:**6, 13; **2:**4, 7, 14; **Zec 1:**2, 8, 9, 12, 13, 15, 15, 17, 19; **2:**1, 3, 4; **3:**7, 9; **4:**1, 2, 2; **5:**5, 6, 9, 9; **6:**4, 6, 6, 6; **7:**2, 7, 12, 14; **8:**2, 4, 5, 12, 13, 23, 23; **9:**5, 5, 7, 11, 11, 15, 15, 15, 15; **10:**5, 9; **11:**8, 10, 11; **12:**12, 12; **14:**5, 13, 18, 20; **Mal 1:**4, 10, 12; **2:**3, 4, 5, 6, 8, 13, 13, 15, 17; **3:**16; **4:**2, 2, 6; **Mt 1:**20, 23; **2:**10, 13, 14, 21; **3:**11, 11, 11, 12, 12, 17; **4:**6, 18, 20, 21; **5:**1, 22, 25, 28, 28, 37; **7:**5, 27; **8:**2, 5, 6, 11, 14, 23, 24; **9:**8, 10, 11, 15, 16; **10:**5, 8, 9, 10; **12:**10, 18, 20, 25, 30, 46; **13:**5, 20; **14:**7; **15:**8, 9, 20, 23, 30, 32; **16:**9, 10, 10, 27; **17:**3, 5, 8, 17, 17, 23; **18:**6, 8, 16, 23, 26, 27, 32; **19:**3, 16, 26; **20:**8, 15, 20; **21:**2, 28; **22:**10, 16, 18, 33, 34, 35, 37; **23:**4, 5, 27, 28; **24:**30, 31, 51; **25:**10, 17, 22, 24, 28, 31, 41; **26:**7, 11, 18, 20, 23, 29, 35, 37, 38, 38, 40, 47, 47, 51, 55, 58, 67, 69, 71, 72; **27:**3, 22, 26, 30, 34, 38, 44, 46, 48, 55; **28:**4, 8, 20; **Mk 1:**8, 8, 11, 16, 18, 20, 20, 29, 30, 40, 41; **2:**2, 15, 16, 16, 19, 19, 21; **3:**1, 6, 13, 21, 24, 31; **4:**5, 10, 10, 16, 27, 29, 32, 34, 34, 38, 41; **5:**3, 5, 17, 23, 24, 35, 37; **6:**1, 7, 8, 13, 20, 37; **7:**7, 7, 19, 32, 33; **8:**2, 10, 11, 14, 19, 20, 32, 38; **9:**4, 8, 12, 14, 19, 19, 28, 31, 42, 43, 43, 45, 45, 49, 50; **10:**2, 10, 14, 27, 27, 30, 32, 32, 34, 38, 38, 39; **11:**11; **12:**15, 30, 33, 37; **13:**26, 34; **14:**3, 7, 14, 17, 18, 20, 31, 33, 33, 34, 34, 37, 43, 43, 48, 54, 57, 58, 65, 67; **15:**7, 12, 15, 19, 23, 27, 32, 34, 36, 41; **16:**18, 19, 20, S; **Lk 1:**5, 12, 14, 15, 17, 28, 37, 41, 53, 53, 56, 58, 67, 72; **2:**5, 25, 37, 38, 40, 44, 46, 51; **3:**11, 14, 16, 16, 16, 17, 17, 22; **4:**11, 14, 32, 38; **5:**7, 9, 12, 17, 26, 29, 30, 32, 34; **6:**6, 8, 11, 11, 17, 21, 22, 42; **7:**4, 6, 11, 11, 12, 13, 31, 37, 38, 44, 44, 46; **8:**1, 2, 6, 13, 25, 29, 30, 32, 40, 41, 42, 49, 51, 52; **9:**10, 30, 32, 41, 41, 53; **10:**21, 27, 30, 34; **11:**17, 23, 36, 36, 48, 53; **12:**13, 21, 46; **13:**26; **14:**15, 16, 31; **15:**2, 2, 6, 9, 20, 23, 29; **16:**7, 10, 11, 12, 12, 22, 23; **17:**2, 20, 22; **18:**2, 5, 7, 27; **19:**15, 17, 21, 44; **20:**41, 45; **21:**27, 34; **22:**1, 11, 15, 15, 20, 33, 33, 47, 48, 52; **23:**4, 13, 18, 20, 32, 38, 43, 46, 51; **24:**22, 29, 29, 32, 33, 36, 41, 44, 47, 49, 52; **Jn 1:**1, 2, 26, 31, 33, 33, 35, 39; **2:**7, 12; **3:**2, 2, 25, 29, 29; **4:**9, 18, 47, 51; **5:**2, 18; **6:**3, 9, 9, 11, 13, 13, 26, 52; **7:**13, 50; **8:**6, 9, 9, 15, 16, 29, 38, 44; **9:**6; **10:**16; **11:**1, 2, 16, 33, 33, 38, 45, 54; **12:**2, 3, 3, 3, 8; **13:**5, 36; **14:**3, 9, 12, 17, 22, 23, 25, 27; **15:**11, 27; **16:**4, 32; **17:**13, 13, 24; **18:**1, 2, 3, 5, 15, 15, 18, 26; **19:**1, 3, 15, 15, 18, 18, 32, 34, 40; **20:**19, 20, 21, 24, 26, 26; **21:**8; **Ac 1:**4, 5, 5, 6, 14, 17, 18, 20, 21, 21, 26; **2:**4, 7, 14, 23, 25, 26, 30, 42, 45, 46; **3:**8, 24; **4:**6, 8, 13, 16, 25, 31, 31; **5:**1, 17, 21, 23, 25, 26, 28, 34; **6:**9; **7:**9, 32, 38, 44, 44, 45, 46, 57, 60, 60; **8:**2, 20, 31, 35; **9:**1, 7, 7, 17, 19, 21, 26, 28, 29, 39, 39, 43; **10:**6, 20, 23, 36, 38, 38, 38, 41, 45, 48; **11:**3, 12, 16, 16, 23, 26; **12:**2, 6, 20, 20, 20, 21, 23, 23, 25; **13:**5, 9, 11, 13, 18, 22, 31, 39, 52, 52; **14:**1, 4, 4, 5, 8, 20, 23, 28; **15:**2, 10, 15, 22, 23, 24, 25, 33, 39; **16:**9, 13, 15, 22, 29, 31, 32, 40; **17:**15, 15, 17, 18, 31, 33; **18:**2, 2, 3, 7, 10, 18, 19, 25, 28; **19:**9, 16, 24, 25, 29, 40; **20:**4, 8, 19, 28, 31, 32, 34, 36; **21:**4, 5, 11, 12, 18, 18, 24, 26, 29, 33, 37; **22:**9, 22, 22, 24, 30; **23:**9, 12, 27; **24:**1, 12, 17, 22, 24, 25, 26, 27; **25:**2, 5, 12, 13, 14, 16, 23; **26:**1, 12; **27:**2, 3, 8, 12, 16, 17, 24, 39; **28:**8, 10, 11, 14, 20, 25, 31; **Ro 1:**9, 11, 24, 26, 27, 27, 27; **2:**4, 17, 29; **3:**2, 13, 25, 28, 30; **4:**11, 13, 25; **5:**1, 5, 10, 11, 21; **6:**3, 3, 4, 5, 6, 7, 8, 17, 20; **7:**1, 4, 4, 6, 14, 14, 14, 22, 23; **8:**10, 26, 27, 29, 30, 33, 35; **9:**1, 2, 4, 22, 28, 30, 31, 32; **10:**3, 3, 3, 4, 5, 6, 9, 10, 10, 21; **11:**27; **12:**1, 5, 10, 15, 16, 18; **13:**12; **14:**1, 8, 18, 20, 22; **15:**5, 5, 6, 10, 13, 32, 33; **16:**7, 14, 15, 20; **1Co 1:**5, 9, 10, 17, 22; **2:**6; **3:**1, 2, 2, 3, 8; **4:**8, 12, 12, 21, 21; **5:**1, 3, 3, 4, 9, 11, 11; **6:**11, 13, 16, 17, 20, 20; **7:**9, 12, 13, 15, 24, 25, 28, 31, 35; **8:**1, 9, 9, 10; **9:**1, 5, 12, 20, 20, 21, 21, 22, 22, 26; **10:**4, 5, 7, 20; **11:**21, 32; **12:**12, 18, 23, 26; **13:**12; **14:**16, 36; **15:**52; **16:**6, 10, 11, 11, 12, 14, 16, 19, 21, 23; **2Co 1:**5, 6, 12, 21, 24; **2:**1, 10, 11, 13, 17, 17; **3:**1, 3, 3, 7, 7, 9, 10, 15; **4:**14, 14; **5:**6, 8, 20, 21; **6:**3, 11, 14, 14, 14, 15; **7:**3, 7, 15; **8:**14, 18, 20, 22, 23; **9:**3, 4, 8, 14; **10:**1, 1, 2, 3, 5, 5, 7, 12, 13, 14; **11:**1, 1, 2, 9, 20, 25, 27, 27, 29; **12:**10, 10, 12, 18; **13:**3, 4, 10, 11, 11, 13; **Gal 1:**16, 17, 18, 18; **2:**1, 2, 9, 12, 12, 12, 16, 17, 19; **3:**1, 10, 11, 14, 17, 21, 23, 24, 27; **4:**3, 10, 12, 18, 20, 20, 30; **5:**2, 3, 4, 5, 7, 23; **6:**7, 17, 18; **Eph 1:**3, 8, 18, 23; **2:**3, 6, 6, 6, 19; **3:**6, 19; **4:**2, 3, 17, 19; **5:**2, 18, 25; **6:**2, 4, 5, 6, 7, 10, 23, 24; **Php 1:**4, 8, 11, 15, 17, 23, 25; **2:**2, 2, 12, 12, 17, 18, 22, 29, 29; **3:**8, 9, 9, 10, 18; **4:**2, 3, 3, 9, 12, 12, 12, 13, 14, 18, 18, 21, 23; **Col 1:**9, 11, 11, 14, 20, 28; **2:**4, 5, 7, 8, 10, 12, 12, 13, 20; **3:**1, 3, 5, 10, 12, 16, 25; **4:**2, 7, 10, 11, 18; **1Th 1:**5, 5, 6; **2:**3, 4, 5, 12, 16; **3:**4, 6, 13; **4:**11, 14, 16, 16, 16, 17, 17, 18; **5:**10, 13, 14, 28; **2Th 1:**7, 9, 12; **2:**5, 8, 9, 15; **3:**6, 7, 10, 16, 17, 18; **1Ti 1:**5, 14, 16; **2:**8; **3:**4, 9, 13, 14; **4:**3, 4; **5:**2; **6:**6, 7, 7, 10, 11, 14, 14, 18, 20, 20, 21; **2Ti 1:**3, 4, 8, 8, 14; **2:**1, 3, 11, 11, 12, 19, 22, 24; **3:**4, 6, 9, 9; **4:**2, 11, 11, 13, 16, 17, 22, 22; **Tit 1:**9; **2:**2, 12; **3:**10, 13, 15; **Phm 1:**12, 13, 25; **Heb 2:**7, 9, 13; **3:**2, 10; **4:**1; **5:**1, 2, 7; **6:**1, 9, 17, 18; **7:**14, 25, 28; **8:**6, 8, 8, 9, 10; **9:**4, 4, 7, 10, 12, 19, 20, 22, 23, 28; **10:**6, 6, 8, 16, 22, 22, 22, 34, 34; **11:**10, 11, 12, 22, 31, 33, 36, 37; **12:**1, 12, 14, 19, 28; **13:**1, 3, 5, 6, 15, 16, 17, 20, 20, 23, 25; **Jas 1:**11; **2:**21, 24, 25; **3:**1, 11; **4:**4; **5:**1, 14; **1Pe 1:**3, 8, 19, 22; **2:**1, 19, 20; **3:**7, 8, 9, 11; **4:**1, 6, 9, 11, 13; **5:**12, 12; **2Pe 1:**1, 2, 16, 17, 18; **2:**5, 12, 13, 14, 16, 18, 18, 20; **3:**5, 6, 10, 13, 14, 15; **1Jn 1:**1, 1, 2, 3, 3, 3, 6, 7; **2:**13, 14, 14, 17, 19, 19, 19, 24, 24, 28; **3:**21, 24, 24; **4:**4, 14, 17; **5:**14; **2Jn** 3, 9, 9, 12; **3Jn** 2, 8, 15; **Jude** 7, 9, 14, 24; **Rev 1:**1, 7, 13; **2:**16, 22, 22, 27; **3:**4, 4, 21, 21; **4:**1, 5, 6, 7, 8; **5:**1, 2, 8, 9; **6:**1, 8, 15; **7:**4, 10; **8:**3, 3, 4, 5, 6, 7; **9:**5, 10, 19; **10:**1, 2; **11:**18; **12:**1, 1, 3, 3, 5, 9, 15; **13:**1, 11, 14; **14:**1, 10, 18, 18; **15:**2, 6, 7, 8; **16:**8, 19; **17:**1, 2, 3, 6, 7, 12, 16, 16; **18:**1, 1, 3, 4, 7, 16, 23; **19:**2, 13, 15, 15, 20, 20; **20:**1, 4, 6, 10; **21:**3, 3, 8, 9, 11, 12, 19; **22:**1, 2, 12, 21

WON'T (223)

Ge 3:4; **11:**7; **21:**10, 23; **24:**49; **27:**11; **31:**50; **43:**5; **44:**26; **Ex 3:**13; **4:**1, 1; **6:**12; **8:**26; **10:**5, 26; **14:**14; **Lev 22:**20; **Nu 11:**19; **14:**41; **20:**17; **Dt 2:**27; **28:**31; **Jos 7:**3; **18:**7; **Jdg 15:**7, 12, 13; **16:**13; **Ru 3:**18; **1Sa 9: 13; 20:**3; **25:**31; **26:**8; **28:**15; **29:**6; **2Sa 7:**10; **12:**13; **14:**11; **17:**8; **21:**4; **1Ki 2:**20, 20; **2Ki 2:**10; **4:**30; **7:**2, 13, 19; **1Ch 17:**9; **2Ch 20:**12; **Ne 6:**11; **Job 3:**21; **7:**19; **8:**15; **9:**7, 7; **11:**12; **14:**6; **16:**3; **20:**15; **30:**10; **32:**21; **Ps 39:**9; **85:**6; **94:**10; **Pr 4:**12; **7: 20; 11:**4; **13:**8; **14:**7; **19:**24; **23:**13; **26:**15; **27:**10; **30:**30; **Isa 4:**1; **27:**9; **30:**14; **40:**20; **41:**7; **42:**18; **47:**11, 11, 11; **Jer 2:**31; **3:**5; **5:**12; **6:**17; **7:**32; **10:**4; **12:**4; **38:**15, 20; **Eze 2:**7; **3:**7, 20, 26; **4:**8; **7:**19; **12:**2, 27; **17:**9; **24:**14; **39:**10; **Hos 2:**7; **5:**4; **Am 2:**15, 15; **5:**6, 22; **7:**3, 6; **Ob 1:**7; **Mic 2:**3; **3:**4, 11; **Na 1:**9; **Hab 2:**3; **Zep 3:**7; **Zec 2:**4; **10:**10; **11:**9; **Mal 3:**10; **Mt 5: 26, 37; 6:**30; **7:**21, 25; **10:**20; **16:**9; **18:**12, 17; **21:**27, 29; **22:**30; **23:**13, 13, 24; **24:**6, 48; **Mk 6:**11; **7:**18; **8:**17; **9:**17; **11:**33; **12:**25; **13:**7; **16:**18; **Lk 1:**20; **6:**46; **9:**5; **10:**42; **11:**8, 8; **12:**28, 45, 59; **15:**8; **16:**10, 10, 28, 31, 31; **17:**21, 22; **20:**8, 35; **21:**9; **22:**16, 67, 68; **Jn 3:**11; **4:**15; **7:**34, 36; **8:**12, 26; **10:**5; **13:**8; **16:**1, 7, 16, 17, 19, **23; 19:**10; **20:**25; **Ac 8:**24; **19:**40; **22:**18; **Ro 2:**5, 26; **8:**32; **10:**3; **11:**21; **14:**3, 3, 6; **1Co 1:**10; **4:**6; **7:**5; **10:**25; **11:**34; **14:**2; **2Co 2:**1, 1, 7; **4:**17; **10:**2; **12:**6, 20, 20; **13:**10; **Gal 5:**16; **6:**4; **1Th 5:**4; **1Ti 5:**8, 25; **2Ti 3:**9; **Tit 2:**8; **Phm 1:**19; **1Pe 4:**2; **1Jn 3:**6

WOULD (859)

Ge 2:19; **3:**6, 20; **10:**9; **18:**25; **19:**19, 19; **20:**15; **21:**2, 7, 7; **24:**9, 23, 37; **25:**25; **26:**7, 9, 10; **29:**3; **30:**38; **31:**27, 42; **34:**14; **37:**22, 26, 35; **38:**9, 9, 11; **39:**9; **41:**13; **42:**38; **43:**7, 25; **44:**8, 15, 22, 29, 32, 34; **47:**30; **48:**11; **Ex 2:**4, 17; **4:**18; **5:**19; **8:**26; **9:**5, 15; **10:**27; **13:**19, 19; **16:**3; **20:**25; **21:**5; **23:**29, 29, 33; **33:**1, 3, 5, 7, 8, 8, 9, 10, 11, 11; **34:**34, 35, 35; **39:**23; **40:**36, 37; **Lev 10:**19; **15:**26; **18:**8, 10, 16, 17; **21:**23; **22:**8, 16; **25:**35, 50; **26:**13; **Nu 9:**20, 20, 20; **10:**21, 35, 36; **11:**22, 22, 29; **14:**31; **16:**34, 40, 40; **18:**24; **22:**18, 29, 33, 37; **27:**7; **30:**2, 5; **32:**19; **Dt 1:**39, 41, 43; **3:**26; **4:**21, 35; **5:**29, 29; **6:**19; **7:**22; **8:**2, 17; **18:**16; **19:**6; **20:**5, 6, 7, 18; **22:**30; **23:**5; **24:**4, 15; **25:**3; **28:**56, 62, 68; **29:**6, 18, 18, 19; **30:**19; **32:**26; **34:**4; **Jos 5:**6; **9:**20, 27; **24:**10, 15, 16; **Jdg 1:**34; **2:**1, 22; **3:**4; **4:**5; **6:**3, 27; **9:**29, 29; **11:**38; **12:**5, 5, 6, 6, 6; **16:**6, 17, 17; **19:**23; **20:**13, 32; **Ru 1:**7, 13; **1Sa 1:**3, 4, 7, 7, 7, 8; **2:**13, 14, 15, 15, 16, 20, 30; **7:**17, 17; **9:**9; **12:**22; **13:**11, 13, 19; **14:**39; **16:**23, 23, 23; **18:**25; **20:**9; **22:**3, 22; **24:**19; **25:**8, 34; **27:**5, 10, 10; **28:**17; **31:**4; **2Sa 2:**23, 27, 27; **9:**1; **10:**9; **11:**20; **12:**5, 8; **13:**13, 24, 25; **14:**16; **15:**2, 2, 3, 4, 8; **18:**11, 13, 13; **19:**6, 35, 38; **20:**3; **23:**15; **1Ki 1:**13, 13, 17, 17; **2:**8, 42; **5:**14; **6:**19; **8:**12, 29; **11:**2; **13:**8, 8; **14:**2, 28; **17:**10; **21:**2; **22:**7; **2Ki 1:**2; **3:**14, 27; **4:**8, 28, 40; **5:**3, 3, 11, 22; **6:**8, 9, 10; **7:**4; **8:**19; **10:**10; **11:**17; **13:**19; **14:**27; **17:**14, 23, 40; **20:**9; **22:**19; **24:**4; **25:**26; **1Ch 4:**10; **9:**27; **10:**4; **11:**17; **19:**10; **22:**3; **24:**5; **28:**11, 15, 16; **2Ch 6:**1, 20; **11:**14, 22; **12:**11; **15:**13; **18:**6; **20:**10; **21:**7; **23:**16; **24:**19; **25:**20; **32:**18; **35:**1, 22, 22; **Ezr 2:**63; **8:**21, 23; **9:**11, 12, 12; **10:**5, 8; **Ne 4:**3; **5:**14; **6:**13; **7:**65; **8:**15; **13:**25; **Est 2:**11, 14, 14; **3:**2, 4, 5, 13, 14; **6:**6; **7:**4, 4, 5; **8:**13; **9:**22, 27, 28, 28, 28; **Job 1:**4, 5, 5; **3:**13, 14, 15; **6:**3, 8, 9, 9, 27, 28; **7:**15; **9:**3, 15, 16, 20, 20, 28, 28, 31, 31, 31, 34; **10:**14, 19, 19; **11:**5, 5, 6, 13; **13:**16, 19, 25, 25; **14:**13, 14, 14, 15, 15, 15, 16, 17, 17; **16:**5, 5, 5, 21; **22:**3; **23:**3, 4, 5, 6, 6, 7; **30:**24; **31:**12, 23, 28, 34, 35, 36, 36, 37, 37; **32:**14, 22; **34:**15, 15; **40:**14, 14; **41:**10, 21, 32; **Ps 14:**7; **40:**5; **44:**21; **50:**12; **51:**16, 16, 16; **53:**6; **55:**6, 7, 8; **66:**18; **69:**20, 20; **73:**15; **77:**1; **81:**8, 13, 13, 14, 14, 15, 15, 16, 16; **84:**10; **92:**6, 6; **94:**17; **95:**7; **104:**5, 9; **105:**45; **106:**23, 26, 27; **119:**5, 92; **124:**3, 4, 4, 5; **139:**19; **Pr 2:**4; **7:**23, 23; **8:**29; **Ecc 2:**12; **5:**6; **6:**3, 4, 5, 5, 10; **SS 6:**9; **8:**1, 2, 2, 2, 3, 3, 7; **Isa 1:**9; **10:**20; **28:**12; **30:**15; **33:**18; **40:**16; **41:**26; **42:**24, 24; **43:**12; **44:**10; **45:**10, 21; **46:**11; **48:**16, 16, 18, 19, 19; **49:**15; **52:**14; **54:**9; **56:**5; **57:**16; **58:**2, 2; **63:**16, 16; **64:**1, 1, 2, 2; **66:**9, 9; **Jer 2:**20; **3:**1, 7, 19, 19; **7:**13, 24; **9:**1, 1; **10:**7, 24; **11:**8, 21; **13:**11; **17:**23; **18:**10; **20:**6; **22:**24; **23:**22; **25:**7; **26:**5; **30:**21; **32:**8, 24, 33; **33:**25, 25; **35:**15; **36:**29, 31; **37:**10, 19; **38:**26; **40:**3, 9; **41:**18; **44:**5; **49:**9; **51:**9, 60; **La 1:**9; **4:**12, 15; **Eze 3:**6; **4:**12; **6:**10; **12:**2; **13:**16; **14:**14, 16, 16, 16, 18, 20; **17:**5, 14; **18:**11; **20:**5, 6, 8, 13, 15, 21, 23, 25; **31:**2; **33:**22; **38:**17; **44:**18; **47:**14; **Da 1:**5; **2:**18; **4:**19; **6:**22; **7:**14; **9:**12; **Hos 2:**4; **Joel 3:**3; **Am 5:**18; **Ob** 5; **Jnh 4:**2, 5; **Mic 2:**7, 7, 11; **6:**7, 7; **Na 3:**10; **Hab 3:**14; **Zec 1:**4, 6, 6; **7:**11, 13; **Mal 1:**10; **Mt 2:**4; **7:**12; **9:**16, 17; **11:**14, 21, 23; **12:**7, 10, 11, 39; **14:**5; **15:**33; **16:**4, 21, 21, 21, 21; **17:**20, 20; **18:**6; **20:**4, 10; **23:**30; **24:**43; **25:**25; **26:**25, 53, 54, 59;

28:6; Mk 2:21, 22; 3:2, 11, 26; 4:21; 5:5; 6:37; 8:31, 31, 31; 9:33, 42; 11:32; 14:55; 15:24; 16:3; Lk 1:45; 2:26, 49; 5:36, 37; 6:7, 31; 7:39; 8:16; 9:46; 10:13, 36; 11:5, 7, 48; 12:39; 14:15, 28, 29, 30, 31; 15:5, 6; 16:21; 17:2, 6; 19:11, 40, 42; 20:19, 20; 22:23, 24; 24:7, 26, 28; Jn 4:10, 10, 11; 5:6, 31, 46; 6:7, 64, 68, 71; 7:31, 39; 8:16, 19, 39, 42, 55; 9:22, 36; 11:21, 32, 52; 12:4, 34, 42; 13:3, 11, 24; 14:2, 7; 15:19, 20, 22, 24; 17:13; 18:28, 32, 36; 19:11; 20:9; 21:19; Ac 2:30, 31, 31; 5:24, 26, 31; 7:5, 6, 6, 17, 19, 25; 18:14; 19:4; 20:38; 21:26, 26; 23:10; 24:26; 25:4, 20; 26:5, 22, 23; 27:21, 29; 28:10; Ro 4:2, 18; 7:3, 7, 8; 8:4, 29; 9:3, 3, 29; 11:6, 11, 35; 14:23; 1Co 1:17, 21; 2:8; 3:1; 4:8; 5:10; 7:5, 14; 9:12, 15, 15, 17; 10:6; 12:16, 17, 19; 13:1, 2, 2, 3; 14:6, 19; 15:15; 2Co 1:8; 2:9; 3:13; 5:8; 6:13; 9:3, 4, 4; 10:1; 11:16, 30; 12:6, 6; Gal 1:10; 2:2, 12; 3:8, 17, 18; 4:15; 5:11, 12; Eph 3:20; 6:5; Php 1:23; 2:27; 1Th 2:5, 9, 12; 3:4; 2Th 2:10; 3:8, 15; 1Ti 1:5, 20; 5:1, 2, 12; Phm 1:13, 17; Heb 2:17; 3:5, 18; 4:8; 5:11; 6:17; 7:20; 8:4, 7; 9:26; 10:2, 2, 2; 11:8, 11, 15, 26, 28, 32, 40; 12:2; 13:17; Jas 5:17; 1Pe 1:11, 12; 2Pe 2:21; 1Jn 2:19; Jude 18; Rev 2:21; 12:14; 15:1; 20:3

WOULDN'T (81)

Ge 9:23; 18:25, 25; 42:4, 21, 22; Ex 5:8, 17; 6:9; 8:19; 11:10; Nu 12:14; Jdg 8:19; 11:17; 13:18, 23, 23; 14:18; 15:1; 19:25; 1Sa 2:25; 6:6; 13:19; 18:2; 20:2; 2Sa 11:9; 13:14, 16, 25; 15:5; 18:12, 20; 1Ki 21:15; 2Ki 5:13; Ne 9:30; Ps 14:4; 53:4; 81:11; 106:13, 24; Ecc 6:4; Isa 7:12; Jer 15:1; 36:25; 37:14; Eze 14:16; 20:9, 13, 14; 22:30; 33:5; Am 4:6, 8, 9, 10, 11; Hab 1:5; Mt 12:11; 18:30; 23:37; Mk 3:4; 5:37; Lk 5:36; 8:51; 13:33, 34; 15:4, 28; Jn 8:40; 9:18, 41; 12:42; 18:28, 30; 21:23; Ac 13:41; 19:30; Ro 1:21; 2Co 10:12; Gal 2:4, 12

YOU (14828)

Ge 1:29; 2:16, 17, 17; 3:1, 4, 5, 5, 9, 10, 11, 11, 11, 11, 12, 13, 14, 14, 14, 14, 14, 15, 15, 16, 17, 17, 17, 18, 18, 19, 19, 19, 19, 19; 4:6, 6, 7, 7, 7, 7, 7, 10, 11, 11, 12, 12, 12, 14, 14, 15; 6:18, 19, 20; 7:1; 8:16; 9:2, 3, 3, 4, 6, 7, 9, 10, 10, 12, 12, 13, 15; 12:1, 2, 2, 2, 2, 3, 3, 3, 11, 12, 13, 13, 13, 18, 18, 19; 13:9, 9, 9, 9, 14, 15, 16, 17; 14:20, 21, 21, 23, 23; 15:1, 3, 4, 4, 5, 7, 7, 8, 13, 15; 16:5, 5, 6, 6, 8, 8, 10, 10, 11, 11; 17:2, 2, 4, 4, 5, 5, 6, 7, 8, 9, 10, 10, 11, 12, 15, 16, 19, 19, 20, 21; 18:3, 5, 5, 14, 15, 23, 24, 24, 25, 25, 25, 28; 19:2, 2, 5, 8, 9, 9, 9, 9, 9, 12, 15, 17, 19, 19, 20, 22, 34; 20:3, 3, 4, 6, 6, 6, 7, 7, 7, 7, 7, 9, 9, 10, 13, 15, 16; 21:17, 22, 22, 23, 23, 23, 23, 26, 29, 30; 22:2, 2, 12, 12, 16, 17, 18; 23:6, 6, 6, 8, 11, 11, 13; 24:3, 7, 7, 8, 8, 8, 14, 14, 23, 31, 31, 31, 33, 40, 40, 40, 41, 41, 42, 44, 49, 49, 49, 50, 58, 60; 26:3, 3, 3, 3, 9, 10, 10, 16, 24, 24, 24, 27, 27, 28, 29, 29, 29, 29, 29; 27:4, 8, 10, 13, 19, 19, 19, 20, 21, 21, 24, 25, 28, 29, 29, 29, 29, 31, 32, 33, 36, 39, 40, 40, 40, 42, 43, 45, 45, 45; 28:3, 3, 4, 4, 13, 13, 13, 14, 15, 15, 15, 15, 15, 15; 29:4, 5, 7, 7, 15, 15, 18, 19, 25, 27, 27; 30:2, 15, 15, 15, 16, 16, 26, 26, 26, 27, 28, 29, 29, 30, 30, 31, 31, 33, 33, 33, 33, 34; 31:3, 6, 12, 12, 13, 13, 13, 16, 16, 24, 26, 26, 27, 27, 28, 28, 29, 29, 30, 30, 30, 30, 32, 32, 36, 36, 37, 37, 37, 38, 39, 39, 39, 40, 41, 42, 42, 43, 44, 50, 50, 52, 52; 32:5, 5, 9, 9, 10, 12, 17, 17, 17, 18, 19, 19, 26, 26, 28, 29; 33:5, 9, 12, 13, 14, 15, 15; 34:9, 10, 10, 10, 11, 12, 14, 14, 15, 16, 16, 30; 35:1, 1, 10, 12, 12, 17; 37:8, 8, 10, 10, 13, 15, 16; 38:8, 8, 16, 17, 17, 17, 18, 18, 25, 29; 39:9, 9; 40:7, 8, 13, 13, 14, 18; 41:10, 10, 15, 15, 16, 16, 25, 28, 33, 39, 39, 40, 40, 41, 55; 42:1, 7, 9, 9, 12, 12, 14, 15, 16, 16, 16, 16, 18, 18, 19, 19, 19, 20, 20, 20, 22, 22, 33, 34, 34, 34, 34, 34, 34, 36, 36, 37, 37, 38, 38; 43:4, 5, 5, 5, 6, 6, 6, 8, 9, 10, 12, 14, 14, 27, 29, 29; 44:4, 5, 5, 7, 7, 7, 9, 10, 15, 15, 16, 17, 18, 18, 18, 19, 21, 22, 23, 23, 23, 24, 26, 27, 29, 29, 32; 45:1, 4, 5, 5, 7, 7, 8, 10, 10, 10, 11, 11, 12, 13, 18, 18; 46:3, 4, 4, 30, 30, 31, 33, 33, 34, 34; 47:5, 6, 8, 16, 23, 23, 23, 24, 25, 25, 29, 29, 31; 48:4, 4, 6, 11, 20, 21, 21, 22; 49:1, 1, 3, 3, 4, 4, 4, 4, 8, 8, 8, 18, 25, 25; 50:6, 17, 17, 17, 19, 20, 21, 24, 24, 24, 25, 25; Ex 1:16, 18, 18, 22; 2:7, 9, 13, 14, 14, 14, 14, 14, 18, 20; 3:5, 7, 10, 10, 11, 12, 12, 12, 12, 13, 13, 14, 15, 16, 16, 16, 17, 17, 18, 19, 20, 21, 21, 21, 22, 22; 4:1, 2, 5, 5, 9, 9, 10, 12, 12, 12, 14, 14, 15, 15, 15, 16, 17, 17, 19, 21, 21, 22, 23, 23, 25; 5:4, 4, 5, 10, 11, 11, 13, 14, 17, 17, 17, 18, 18, 21, 21, 22, 22, 23; 6:1, 5, 6, 6, 7, 7, 7, 8, 29; 7:1, 1, 2, 4, 9, 9, 16, 17; 8:2, 4, 9, 9, 9, 9, 10, 10, 21, 22, 28, 29, 29; 9:2, 14, 14, 14, 15, 15, 15, 16, 16, 17, 17, 28, 29, 30, 30, 30; 10:2, 3, 4, 5, 7, 7, 8, 10, 10, 11, 16, 24, 24, 28, 28, 28, 29; 11:1, 1, 1, 7, 8, 9; 12:2, 11, 13, 13, 13, 14, 14, 15, 15, 17, 17, 19, 19, 20, 20, 24, 25, 25, 25, 27, 31, 31, 32, 46, 46, 48, 48, 48, 49; 13:3, 3, 3, 5, 5, 6, 6, 8, 8, 9, 9, 9, 11, 13, 13, 14, 14, 16; 14:4, 11, 11, 12, 13, 13, 13, 14, 14, 15, 16; 15:7, 7, 11, 11, 12, 13, 13, 13, 16, 17, 17, 26, 26, 26; 16:3, 4, 6, 6, 7, 8, 12, 12, 12, 15, 23, 26, 29, 29, 32; 17:2, 2, 3, 3, 5, 5, 6; 18:6, 10, 14, 18, 19, 19, 19, 20, 22, 22, 22, 23, 23, 23; 19:4, 4, 4, 4, 5, 5, 6, 9, 9, 9, 23, 23, 24; 20:2, 5, 7, 7, 10, 10, 12, 12, 19, 20, 20, 22, 22, 23, 24, 24, 24, 25, 26, 26; 21:1, 2, 2; 22:21, 23, 24, 24, 25, 26, 26, 27, 28, 29, 29, 30, 31; 23:2, 4, 5, 5, 8, 8, 9, 9, 11, 14, 15, 15, 16, 16, 16, 19, 19, 20, 20, 20, 22, 22, 23, 23, 23, 24, 25, 25, 25, 25, 26, 27, 27, 28, 31, 31, 31, 33, 33, 33, 33; 24:2, 8, 8, 12, 12, 14; 25:3, 9, 9, 16, 21, 22, 22, 22, 30, 39, 40, 40; 26:30; 27:8, 20; 28:15; 29:9, 11, 35, 36, 38, 42, 42; 30:6, 12, 12, 16, 32, 32, 36, 37; 31:6, 11, 13, 13, 13; 32:4, 7, 8, 10, 11, 11, 12, 13, 21, 21, 22, 26, 29, 29, 29, 30, 30, 32, 34, 34; 33:1, 2, 3, 3, 3, 5, 5, 5, 5, 12, 12, 12, 12, 12, 13, 13, 14, 14, 14, 15, 16, 16, 17, 17, 17, 19, 19, 20, 22, 22, 23; 34:1, 3, 10, 10, 10, 11, 12, 12, 12, 13, 14, 14, 15, 15, 15, 16, 17, 18, 18, 20, 20, 20, 21, 22, 24, 25, 26, 26, 27; 35:1, 10; 36:6; 40:15; Lev 1:2, 2, 4, 12, 14; 2:1, 1, 4, 11, 12, 13, 14; 3:1, 1, 6, 6, 7, 12, 17, 17; 6:21; 7:12, 16, 18, 18, 18, 23, 26, 29, 32; 8:3, 31, 34, 35, 35, 35; 9:6, 6; 10:6, 6, 7, 7, 9, 9, 9, 9, 10, 11, 13, 14, 15, 17, 17, 18, 18; 11:2, 4, 8, 8, 9, 10, 10, 11, 11, 12, 13, 13, 20, 21, 23, 24, 24, 24, 25, 25, 25, 26, 26, 26, 27, 27, 27, 28, 28, 28, 29, 31, 31, 31, 39, 39, 40, 40, 40, 44, 45, 45, 47; 14:34, 34; 15:5, 5, 5, 6, 6, 6, 7, 8, 8, 10, 10, 10, 11, 11, 11, 19, 19, 21, 21, 21, 22, 27, 27, 27, 27, 31; 16:29, 29, 29, 30, 30, 31, 31, 34; 17:8, 8, 9, 10, 11, 11, 11, 12, 12, 13, 13, 13, 15, 15, 15, 15, 15, 16, 16; 18:3, 3, 3, 4, 5, 5, 6, 7, 10, 21, 26, 26, 26, 26, 27, 28; 19:2, 3, 3, 5, 6, 6, 8, 8, 9, 10, 17, 19, 23, 25, 31, 34, 34, 34, 36, 37; 20:2, 8, 14, 22, 22, 22, 23, 24, 24, 25, 25, 26, 26, 27; 21:8, 8, 8; 22:18, 18, 21, 21, 25, 28, 29, 31, 32, 33; 23:2, 3, 3, 6, 10, 10, 10, 12, 13, 14, 14, 14, 17, 19, 21, 21, 21, 22, 22, 24, 24, 25, 25, 27, 28, 30, 31, 31, 31, 32, 32, 36, 36, 38, 38, 39, 39, 41, 41, 42; 24:2, 3, 5, 16, 22; 25:2, 2, 3, 6, 6, 8, 10, 10, 11, 12, 12, 12, 13, 14, 14, 15, 15, 16, 18, 19, 20, 21, 21, 22, 22, 22, 23, 35, 35, 36, 36, 37, 38, 38, 39, 40, 40, 41, 44, 44, 45, 45, 46, 53; 26:2, 3, 5, 6, 6, 6, 7, 8, 8, 9, 9, 10, 10, 11, 11, 12, 12, 13, 13, 13, 14, 15, 16, 16, 16, 17, 17, 17, 17, 17, 18, 18, 21, 21, 23, 24, 24, 25, 25, 25, 25, 26, 26, 27, 28, 29, 30, 33, 33, 35, 35, 36, 36, 36, 36, 36, 36, 36, 37, 37, 37, 38; 27:2, 8, 8, 11, 13, 13, 14, 15, 15, 15, 16, 19, 19, 19, 20, 22, 22, 23, 24, 26, 27, 27, 31, 31; Nu 1:3, 49, 50, 50; 4:19, 32; 5:3, 19, 19, 19, 20, 21, 21, 22; 6:24, 24, 25, 25, 26, 26; 8:10, 14, 15, 26; 9:8, 14, 14, 14; 10:3, 4, 5, 6, 6, 7, 9, 9, 9, 9, 10, 29, 31, 32, 35; 11:11, 12, 12, 15, 16, 17, 17, 17, 17, 18, 18, 20, 20, 20, 20, 20, 21, 23, 29; 12:4, 8, 13; 13:20, 27; 14:12, 13, 14, 14, 14, 15, 17, 17, 19, 20, 25, 28, 28, 29, 29, 29, 30, 31, 31, 32, 33, 34, 34, 41, 42, 42, 43, 43, 43, 43; 15:2, 2, 3, 5, 8, 12, 12, 13, 13, 14, 15, 16, 16, 18, 18, 19, 19, 20, 20, 21, 22, 22, 26, 29, 38, 39, 39, 39, 40, 40, 41; 16:3, 3, 3, 6, 7, 8, 9, 9, 9, 10, 10, 11, 11, 13, 13, 14, 14, 17, 22, 26, 26, 28, 30, 41; 17:4, 5; 18:1, 1, 2, 2, 3, 4, 4, 5, 5, 7, 7, 8, 9, 9, 10, 10, 11, 12, 13, 14, 15, 17, 19, 19, 19, 20, 23, 26, 26, 28, 28, 29, 30, 31, 31, 32, 32, 32, 32; 19:2; 20:4, 5, 8, 8, 10, 10, 12, 12, 14, 18, 20, 24, 26; 21:2, 5, 7, 29, 34, 34, 34, 34; 22:6, 6, 8, 9, 12, 13, 16, 17, 17, 20, 20, 28, 29, 29, 30, 32, 32, 33, 34, 34, 35, 35, 37, 37, 37, 37; 23:3, 5, 11, 11, 11, 13, 25, 26, 27, 27; 24:9, 9, 10, 10, 11, 11, 12, 13, 14, 21, 22; 25:18, 18; 26:55; 27:7, 13, 13, 14, 14; 28:2, 3, 3, 5, 7, 14, 15, 16, 18, 19, 22, 23, 24, 25, 26, 26, 31; 29:1, 2, 5, 7, 8, 11, 12, 13, 16, 19, 22, 25, 28, 31, 34, 35, 36, 38, 39, 39; 31:2, 15, 18, 19, 19, 24, 24, 26; 32:5, 6, 6, 7, 14, 14, 15, 15, 20, 22, 22, 23, 23, 23, 23, 24, 27, 29, 29, 30, 30; 33:51, 52, 52, 53, 54, 55, 55, 55, 56; 34:2, 2, 13; 35:6, 10, 29, 29, 31, 33, 34, 34; 36:2, 2; Dt 1:6, 8, 9, 9, 10, 11, 11, 14, 15, 15, 16, 16, 17, 17, 17, 18, 18, 19, 20, 20, 21, 21, 22, 26, 27, 29, 30, 30, 30, 31, 31, 31, 32, 33, 33, 35, 37, 37, 39, 40, 41, 43, 43, 43, 44, 44, 45, 46; 2:3, 4, 5, 6, 7, 7, 7, 9, 18, 19, 24, 24, 25, 25, 30, 30, 31; 3:2, 2, 2, 18, 19, 20, 20, 20, 21, 22, 24, 26, 27, 27, 28, 28; 4:1, 1, 1, 1, 2, 3, 3, 4, 5, 5, 5, 5, 6, 6, 8, 9, 9, 9, 10, 11, 12, 12, 13, 14, 14, 15, 15, 19, 20, 20, 21, 21, 22, 23, 23, 23, 25, 26, 26, 26, 26, 26, 26, 27, 27, 28, 29, 29, 29, 30, 30, 30, 31, 31, 33, 34, 35, 35, 36, 36, 36, 36, 37, 38, 38, 38, 40, 40, 40, 40, 40; 5:1, 4, 5, 5, 5, 6, 9, 11, 11, 12, 14, 14, 14, 15, 15, 15, 16, 16, 16, 22, 23, 27, 27, 28, 31, 31, 31, 32, 33, 33, 33; 6:1, 1, 1, 2, 2, 2, 2, 3, 3, 3, 5, 6, 6, 7, 7, 7, 7, 10, 10, 11, 11, 11, 11, 11, 11, 12, 13, 13, 13, 14, 15, 15, 15, 16, 16, 17, 17, 18, 18, 19, 19, 20, 21; 7:1, 1, 1, 1, 2, 2, 2, 4, 4, 5, 6, 6, 7, 7, 7, 7, 8, 8, 11, 12, 12, 13, 13, 13, 13, 13, 13, 14, 15, 15, 15, 16, 16, 16, 16, 17, 19, 19, 19, 20, 21, 22, 22, 22, 22, 23, 24, 24, 24, 25, 25, 26, 26; 8:1, 1, 1, 2, 2, 2, 2, 3, 3, 3, 3, 3, 5, 5, 5, 7, 10, 10, 11, 12, 14, 15, 15, 16, 16, 16, 17, 17, 18, 19, 19, 19, 20; 9:1, 1, 3, 3, 4, 5, 5, 5, 6, 6, 6, 6, 7, 7, 7, 8, 8, 9, 10, 12, 16, 16, 16, 18, 19, 19, 21, 22, 23, 23, 23, 24, 24, 25, 28, 29; 10:2, 4, 4, 10, 12, 12, 13, 15, 18, 19, 19, 20, 21, 22; 11:1, 4, 5, 5, 7, 8, 8, 8, 9, 9, 9, 10, 10, 10, 13, 13, 13, 13, 14, 15, 15, 17, 17, 17, 17, 19, 19, 19, 19, 21, 22, 23, 24, 25, 25, 25, 25, 26, 27, 27, 27, 28, 28, 29, 29, 31, 31, 31, 32, 32; 12:1, 1, 1, 2, 2, 5, 6, 7, 7, 7, 7, 8, 8, 9, 9, 10, 10, 10, 11, 11, 12, 14, 14, 14, 15, 15, 15, 15, 15, 15, 16, 16, 18, 18, 19, 20, 20, 21, 21, 21, 21, 22, 23, 25, 25, 27, 27, 28, 28, 29, 31, 32; 13:1, 1, 3, 3, 5, 5, 5, 5, 5, 6, 6, 7, 9, 9, 10, 10, 11, 12, 12, 13, 14, 14, 14, 15, 16, 17, 17, 17, 18, 18; 14:1, 2, 2, 3, 4, 7, 8, 8, 9, 10, 10, 11, 12, 19, 20, 21, 21, 21, 21, 22, 22, 23, 25, 26, 26, 27, 29, 29, 29; 15:1, 3, 4, 4, 4, 5, 5, 5, 6, 6, 6, 6, 7, 7, 9, 9, 10, 10, 11, 11, 12, 12, 13, 14, 15, 15, 15, 16, 16, 16, 17, 18, 18, 18, 18, 19, 20, 21, 23; 16:1, 3, 3, 3, 3, 3, 5, 8, 10, 10, 11, 12, 15, 18, 19, 20, 20, 21; 17:2, 2, 4, 7, 7, 8, 10, 14, 14, 14, 14, 15, 15, 16, 16; 18:4, 9, 9, 12, 13, 14, 14, 15, 15, 16, 16, 16, 16, 16, 18, 21; 19:1, 1, 2, 2, 3, 7, 8, 9, 9, 9, 9, 9, 10, 10, 10, 13, 14, 14, 19, 19, 21; 20:1, 1, 1, 1, 2, 3, 3, 4, 4, 4, 5, 6, 7, 8, 8, 10, 11, 11, 12, 13, 14, 14, 14, 16, 17, 17, 18, 18, 19, 20, 20, 20; 21:1, 1, 8, 9, 10, 10, 10, 11, 11, 12, 13, 14, 14, 14, 14, 14, 21, 21, 23, 23; 22:1, 2, 3, 3, 4, 6, 7, 7, 8, 8, 9, 9, 12, 21, 24, 24; 23:4, 4, 4, 5, 6, 6, 7, 8, 9, 13, 13, 13, 14, 14, 14, 15, 16, 19, 20, 20, 20, 20, 21, 21, 21, 21, 21, 23, 23, 23, 24, 25, 25; 24:4, 4, 7, 7, 9, 10, 11, 13, 15, 15, 17, 17, 18, 18, 18, 19, 19, 19, 20, 22, 22; 25:13, 13, 14, 15, 15, 17, 17, 18, 18, 19, 19, 19; 26:1, 1, 1, 5, 10, 10, 11, 11, 12, 12, 13, 13, 14, 15, 15, 16, 16, 17, 17, 17, 18, 18, 19, 19, 19, 19; 27:1, 2, 2, 3, 3, 3, 4, 4, 6, 8, 9, 10, 12; 28:1, 1, 1, 2, 2, 3, 4, 4, 5, 6, 6, 7, 7, 7, 8, 8, 8, 9, 9, 10, 10, 11, 12, 12, 12, 13, 13, 13, 14, 14, 15, 15, 15, 16, 17, 18, 18, 19, 19, 20, 20, 20, 21, 21, 21, 22, 22, 22, 24, 25, 25, 25, 25, 27, 27, 28, 29, 29, 29, 29, 29, 30, 30, 30, 30, 31, 31, 32, 32, 32, 33, 33, 33, 34, 34, 35, 36, 36, 36, 36, 37, 37, 38, 39, 39, 40, 40, 41, 41, 43, 43, 44, 44, 44, 45, 45, 45, 45, 46, 47, 47, 48, 48, 48, 48, 48, 49, 49, 49, 51, 51, 52, 52, 52, 53, 53, 54, 56, 58, 58, 59, 59, 60, 60, 60, 61, 61, 62, 62, 62, 63, 63, 63, 63, 64, 64, 64, 65, 66, 66, 67, 67, 67, 67, 67, 68, 68, 68, 68; 29:2, 4, 5, 6, 6, 6, 9, 9, 10, 11, 11, 12, 12, 13, 13, 14, 15, 16, 17, 18, 18, 18; 30:1, 1, 1, 1, 2, 2, 2, 3, 3, 3, 4, 4, 4, 5, 5, 5, 6, 6, 8, 8, 9, 9, 9, 9, 10, 10, 10, 11, 11, 12, 13, 14, 15, 16, 16, 16, 16, 16, 17, 17, 18, 18, 18, 18, 19, 19, 19, 19, 20; 31:2, 3, 3, 3, 5, 5, 5, 6, 6, 6, 7, 7, 8, 8, 8, 8, 11, 13, 13, 14, 14, 16, 16, 23, 23, 27, 27, 27, 27, 29, 29, 29, 29; 32:2, 6, 6, 6, 6, 6, 7, 7, 14, 18, 18, 18, 18, 38, 38, 46, 47, 47, 50, 51, 51, 52, 52; 33:3, 8, 8, 9, 10, 23, 23, 26, 27, 27, 29, 29, 29, 29; 34:4, 4; Jos 1:2, 3, 3, 3, 3, 5, 5, 5, 5, 5, 6, 7, 7, 7, 8, 8, 9, 9, 9, 11, 11, 13, 13, 13, 15, 15, 15, 16, 16, 17, 17; 2:5, 5, 9, 9, 10, 10, 10, 10, 12, 12, 13, 14, 16, 18, 20; 3:3, 4, 4, 4, 4, 5, 7, 7, 8, 10, 10, 11; 4:3, 5, 6, 7, 22, 23, 24; 5:13, 14; 6:2, 4, 5, 10, 10, 16, 18, 18; 7:7, 7, 10, 12, 12, 12, 13, 13, 13, 14, 19, 25, 25; 8:1, 2, 2, 2, 7, 7, 8, 18; 9:6, 7, 7, 7, 8, 8, 12, 22, 22, 22, 22, 23, 23, 24, 25; 10:8, 8, 19, 19; 13:1, 6, 7; 14:6, 9, 9, 10, 12, 12; 15:18, 19; 17:14, 15, 17, 17, 18, 18; 18:3, 3; 22:2, 2, 2, 2, 3, 3, 4, 5, 8, 16, 16, 18, 18, 19, 19, 24, 25, 27, 31, 31; 23:3, 3, 3, 4, 5, 5, 7, 8, 9, 9, 10, 10, 12, 12, 13, 13, 13, 14, 15, 15, 15, 15, 15, 16, 16, 16, 16; 24:5, 6, 7, 7, 7, 7, 8, 8, 8, 8, 9, 10, 10, 11, 11, 11, 11, 12, 12, 13, 13, 13, 13, 13, 13, 13, 15, 15, 15, 15, 19, 20, 20, 20, 20, 22, 22, 23, 27, 27; Jdg 1:3, 14, 15, 24; 2:1, 1, 2, 2, 2, 3, 3; 3:19, 20, 28; 4:6, 7, 8, 9, 9, 9, 14, 14, 20, 22, 22; 5:3, 3, 4, 10, 10, 14, 16, 31; 6:8, 9, 9, 9, 10, 10, 10, 10, 12, 14, 14, 16, 16, 16, 17, 18, 18, 23, 26, 31, 31, 36, 36, 37, 37; 7:2, 2, 2, 4, 7, 7, 9, 10, 11, 11, 15, 18; 8:1, 1, 1, 2, 3, 5, 6, 15, 15, 18, 18, 19, 19, 22, 22, 23, 23, 24, 24; 9:7, 7, 10, 12, 14, 15, 16, 16, 16, 17, 17, 18, 18, 19, 19, 19, 20, 31, 33, 33, 33, 38, 38; 10:10, 10, 11, 12, 12, 12, 13, 13, 14, 14, 15; 11:2, 2, 7, 7, 8, 8, 8, 9, 9, 10, 23, 23, 24, 24, 25, 26, 26, 27, 27, 30, 35, 36, 36, 36, 36, 38; 12:1, 1, 1, 2, 2, 2, 3, 3, 5; 13:3, 3, 4, 5, 7, 7, 11, 15, 16, 17, 18, 18, 18; 14:3, 3, 12, 12, 12, 13, 13, 15, 15, 16, 16, 16, 16, 16, 18, 18; 15:2, 3, 7, 7, 10, 11, 11, 12, 12, 12, 13, 13, 13, 18; 16:5, 6, 6, 9, 10, 10, 12, 13, 13, 13, 13, 14, 15, 15, 15, 15, 15, 20; 17:2, 2, 2, 9, 10, 10; 18:3, 3, 3, 6, 8, 9, 10, 10, 18, 23, 23, 24, 25, 25; 19:5, 8, 9, 20, 20, 20, 20, 22, 24, 24, 24; 20:12, 28; 21:11, 21, 22, 22; Ru 1:8, 9, 10, 11, 13, 13, 15, 16, 16, 16, 17, 21; 2:4, 4, 8, 9, 9, 10, 11, 11, 12, 12, 13, 13, 14, 14, 19, 19, 19, 22; 3:1, 1, 2, 3, 3, 4, 5, 9, 9, 10, 10, 11, 12, 13, 13, 13; 4:1, 3, 4, 4, 4, 4, 4, 4, 5, 6, 8, 9, 10, 11, 12, 14, 15, 15, 15; 1Sa 1:8, 8, 8, 11, 11, 14, 17, 18, 23, 23, 26; 2:2, 3, 3, 16, 20, 23, 23, 24, 28, 29, 29, 29, 30, 32; 3:5, 5, 6, 6, 8, 17, 17, 17; 4:9, 9, 20; 6:3, 4, 5; 7:3, 3, 5, 5; 8:5, 5, 7, 8, 11, 13, 17, 18, 18, 18; 9:3, 16, 17, 18, 19, 19, 19, 20, 20, 21, 24, 26, 27; 10:1, 2, 2, 2, 2, 2, 3, 3, 3, 4, 4, 4, 5, 5, 6, 6, 6, 7, 7, 8, 8, 14, 18, 18, 18, 19, 19; 11:2, 9, 10, 10, 10; 12:1, 1, 3, 3, 4, 4, 5, 5, 7, 7, 10, 10, 10, 11, 11, 12, 12, 12, 12, 13, 13, 14, 14, 14, 15, 15, 17, 17, 17, 20, 20, 20, 21, 22, 23, 23, 24, 25, 25; 13:11, 11, 11, 11, 12, 13, 13, 14; 14:7, 7, 7, 9, 9, 12, 36, 37, 40, 43, 44, 44; 15:1, 6, 6, 13, 17, 17, 17, 18, 18, 19, 19, 23, 23, 26, 26, 26, 28, 28; 16:1, 2, 2, 3, 4, 7, 11, 15, 16, 16, 16, 16; 17:8, 8, 9, 25, 25, 27, 28, 28, 33, 33, 37, 43, 45, 45, 45, 46, 46, 47; 18:17, 17, 21, 22, 22; 19:2, 3, 3, 4, 4, 5, 5, 5, 11, 11, 17; 20:3, 7, 7, 9, 9, 9, 12, 12, 12, 12, 13, 13, 13, 13, 14, 18, 19, 21, 21, 22, 22, 22, 30, 30, 30, 36, 37; 21:1, 1, 3, 4, 8, 9, 9, 14; 22:3, 7, 7, 7, 8, 8, 12, 13, 13, 13, 13, 15, 16, 18, 23; 23:4, 12, 17, 17, 17, 20, 21, 23; 24:4, 9, 9, 10, 10, 10, 10, 11, 11, 11, 11, 12, 12, 12, 13, 13, 16, 17, 17, 18, 18, 18, 19, 19, 20, 21; 25:6, 6, 7, 8, 8, 8, 19, 25, 26, 26, 27, 28, 28, 28, 29, 29, 30, 31, 31, 32, 33, 34, 34, 40; 26:6, 8, 11, 15, 15, 16, 16, 17, 18, 19, 19, 21, 21, 23, 23, 23, 25, 25; 27:5, 10; 28:1, 2, 2, 8, 9, 9, 9, 10, 11, 12, 13, 15, 15, 16, 17, 18, 19, 19, 22, 22; 29:6, 6, 9; 30:8, 8, 13, 13, 15, 15, 15, 15, 24, 24, 24, 26; 2Sa 1:3, 5, 8, 10, 13, 14, 16, 16, 16, 21, 24, 26, 26; 2:5, 6, 6, 6, 6, 7, 20, 22, 26, 26, 27, 27; 3:8, 8, 8, 12, 13, 13, 13, 17, 21, 21, 21, 24, 24, 25, 25, 25, 34, 38; 4:8, 8, 9; 5:2, 2, 2, 2, 6, 19, 19, 24, 24; 6:22; 7:3, 3, 5, 7, 8, 8, 9, 9, 11, 11, 12, 15, 18, 19, 19, 20, 21, 22, 22, 22, 23, 23, 23, 23, 24, 24, 25, 27, 27, 28, 28, 29, 29, 29; 9:2, 7, 7, 7, 7, 10, 11; 10:3, 11, 11; 11:10, 10, 12; 12:7, 7, 7, 8, 8, 9, 9, 10, 11, 11, 12, 12, 13, 13, 14, 21, 21, 21, 28; 13:5, 5, 5, 5, 5, 12, 13, 13, 16, 20, 25, 26; 14:2, 3, 9, 9, 10, 11, 12, 13, 13, 13, 13, 14, 15, 17, 17, 19, 19, 20, 20, 20, 22, 32; 15:10, 10, 13, 15, 15, 19, 19, 20, 20, 20, 20, 21, 27, 28, 33, 33, 34; 16:2, 4, 4, 4, 7, 7, 8, 8, 8, 8, 10, 17, 17, 19, 19, 21, 21; 17:3, 3, 8, 11, 11, 11, 13, 20, 29; 18:2, 3, 3, 3, 3, 4, 11, 11, 12, 13, 20, 21, 22, 22, 28, 31, 31, 33; 19:5, 6, 6, 6, 6, 6, 6, 7, 7, 7, 11, 11, 12, 12, 13, 13, 14, 19, 20, 22, 25, 26, 27, 27, 28, 28, 29, 29, 30, 33, 36, 37, 37, 38, 42, 43, 43; 20:1, 9, 11, 16, 17, 18, 19, 19, 21, 21; 21:3, 4, 17; 22:26, 26, 27, 27, 28, 29, 29, 36, 37, 40, 40, 41, 44, 44, 49, 49, 50, 51, 51; 24:3, 3, 12, 13, 21, 22, 22, 23; 1Ki 1:2, 2, 6, 11, 12, 13, 14, 14, 16, 17, 18, 20, 21, 21, 23, 24, 30, 35, 37, 42, 42; 2:3, 3, 3, 4, 5, 6, 9, 9, 13, 14, 15, 16, 17, 18, 20, 20, 20, 20, 22, 22, 22, 26, 26, 26, 26, 30, 37, 37, 42, 42, 42, 42, 42, 43, 44, 44, 44; 3:5, 5, 6, 6, 6, 7, 11, 12, 12, 12, 13, 13, 13, 14, 14, 23; 5:3, 6, 6, 6, 8, 8, 9, 9, 9; 6:12, 12, 12; 8:12, 12, 13, 13, 18, 19, 23, 23, 23, 24, 24, 24, 25, 25, 27, 28, 29, 29, 29, 29, 30, 30, 30, 33, 33, 33, 34, 35, 35, 36, 39, 39, 40, 40, 41, 42, 43, 43, 43, 44, 46, 46, 47, 48, 48, 48, 49, 50, 51, 52, 53, 53, 53, 61, 61, 61; 9:3, 4, 4, 5, 6, 6; 10:9, 9, 9, 9; 11:11, 11, 12, 22, 22, 22, 31, 35, 37, 37, 38, 38, 38, 38, 38, 38; 12:7, 10, 10, 10, 11, 11, 14, 14, 28, 28; 13:2, 2, 7, 8, 8, 8, 9, 9, 9, 14, 17, 17, 17, 18, 18, 21, 21, 22, 22; 14:2, 5, 5, 5, 6, 6, 7, 7, 8, 8, 9, 9, 9, 9, 12; 15:19; 16:2, 2, 2, 2, 3; 17:4, 4, 9, 10, 13, 18, 18, 20, 24, 24; 18:7, 9, 9, 10, 11, 12, 12, 12, 13, 14, 17, 18, 18, 21, 25, 25, 36, 37, 37, 44, 44; 19:2, 7, 9, 10, 13, 14, 15, 15, 16, 20, 20; 20:5, 6, 9, 9, 13, 13, 13, 25, 28, 28, 31, 34, 34, 36, 36, 36, 39, 40, 42, 42; 21:2, 2, 2, 3, 5, 5, 7, 7, 15, 15, 15, 19, 19, 20, 21, 21, 22, 29; 22:3, 4, 4, 6, 8, 11, 12, 13, 16, 16, 18, 22, 22, 23, 23, 24, 25, 25, 28, 30; 2Ki 1:3, 4, 4, 4, 5, 6, 6, 6, 6, 6, 9, 10, 11, 12, 16, 16, 16, 16, 16, 16; 2:2, 2, 3, 3, 4, 4, 5, 5, 6, 6, 9, 10, 10, 10, 10, 10, 18, 19, 23, 23; 3:7, 7, 13, 14, 17, 17, 18, 19, 19; 4:1, 1, 2, 2, 3, 4, 7, 14, 16, 24, 26, 28, 28, 30, 30; 5:5, 6, 8, 10, 13, 13, 13, 22, 25, 26, 26, 27, 27; 6:1, 1, 11, 12, 19, 19, 19, 27, 27; 7:2, 2, 19, 19; 8:9, 10, 12, 12, 13, 14, 14; 9:1, 3, 5, 5, 6, 7, 11, 15, 18, 18, 19, 19, 22, 25, 25, 31, 31, 31; 10:2, 2, 2, 5, 5, 6, 9, 10, 13, 15, 15, 15, 24, 24, 30; 11:5, 5, 6, 8; 12:7; 13:17, 19, 19, 19; 14:10, 10; 17:13, 26, 36, 36, 37, 37, 38, 39, 39; 18:14, 14, 19, 19, 20, 20, 21, 21, 22, 23, 23, 23, 23, 24, 25, 27, 27, 29, 29, 30, 31, 32, 32, 35; 19:10, 10, 11, 11, 15, 15, 15, 19, 21, 21, 21, 22, 22, 22, 22, 23, 23, 25, 25, 26, 27, 27, 27, 28, 28, 29, 29, 29, 29, 30, 30; 20:1, 1, 3, 5, 5, 6, 9, 9, 17, 19; 22:15, 16, 18, 18, 19, 19, 19, 19, 20, 20; 23:17, 21; 25:24; 1Ch 4:10; 11:2, 2, 2, 2, 5; 12:17, 17, 17, 18, 18, 18; 13:2; 14:10, 10, 15, 15; 15:12, 12, 12, 13; 16:18, 35; 17:2, 2, 4, 6, 7, 7, 8, 8, 10, 11, 13, 16, 17, 17, 18, 18, 19, 20, 20, 21, 21, 21, 21, 22, 22, 23, 25, 25, 26, 26, 27, 27, 27; 19:3, 12, 12; 21:3, 3, 10, 11, 12, 22, 23, 23, 23; 22:8, 8, 8, 8, 9, 11, 11, 11, 12, 12, 12, 13, 13, 14, 15, 15, 16, 18, 18, 19; 28:3, 3, 8, 8, 9, 9, 9, 9, 10, 20, 20, 20; 29:10, 11, 12, 12, 13, 14, 14, 14, 14, 16, 16, 17, 17, 17, 18, 18; 2Ch 1:7, 7, 8, 8, 9, 11, 11, 12, 12, 12, 12; 2:11, 13, 15, 16, 16; 6:1, 1, 2, 2, 8, 9, 14, 14, 14, 15, 15, 15, 16, 16, 18, 19, 20, 20, 20, 20, 21, 21, 21, 24, 24, 24, 25, 26, 26, 27, 30, 30, 31, 31, 32, 33, 33, 33, 34, 34, 36, 36, 37, 38, 38, 38, 39, 39, 40; 7:13, 17, 17, 18, 19, 19, 19; 9:8, 8, 8, 8; 10:7, 10, 10, 10, 11, 11, 14, 14; 12:5, 5; 13:5, 8, 8, 8, 9, 9, 11, 12, 12, 12; 14:11, 11, 11, 11; 15:2, 2, 2, 2, 2, 2, 2, 4, 4, 6, 7; 16:3, 7, 7, 8, 8, 8, 9, 9; 18:3, 3, 3, 5, 7, 10, 11, 12, 15, 15, 17, 20, 21, 22, 22, 23, 24, 24, 27, 29; 19:2, 2, 2, 3, 3, 3, 6, 6, 6, 6, 9, 10, 10, 10, 10, 11, 11; 20:2, 6, 6, 6, 6, 7, 7, 8, 9, 9, 10, 11, 12, 12, 15, 16, 17, 17, 17, 20, 20, 20, 37; 21:12, 13, 13, 13, 13, 14, 15; 23:4, 7; 24:6, 20, 20, 20, 20; 25:8, 8, 8, 8, 9, 15, 15, 16, 16, 16, 19, 19; 26:18, 18, 18; 28:9, 9, 10, 11, 11, 13; 29:5, 8, 11; 30:7, 8, 9, 9, 9; 32:10, 10, 10, 11, 11, 12, 13, 14, 15, 15, 15; 34:23, 24, 26, 26, 27, 27, 27, 27, 28, 28; 35:3, 5, 21, 21, 21; 36:23, 23; Ezr 1:3, 3; 4:2, 2, 3, 13, 13, 14, 14, 14, 15, 15, 16, 18; 5:3, 8, 9, 10, 17; 6:8, 8; 7:13, 14, 15, 15, 16, 16, 18, 19, 20, 20, 21, 21, 22, 25, 25, 25; 8:28, 29; 9:6, 12, 12, 12, 13, 15, 15; 10:3, 10, 10, 12, 12; Ne 1:6, 7, 8, 8, 8, 9, 9, 9, 10, 11; 2:2, 2, 2, 2, 4, 5, 6, 6, 17, 19, 20; 4:5, 20; 5:7, 8, 9, 9, 11, 11, 12, 13, 13; 6:3, 6, 6, 6, 7, 7, 7, 7, 8, 8, 10; 9:6, 6, 6, 6, 6, 7, 8, 8, 8, 8, 9, 9, 10, 10, 10, 11, 11, 12, 13, 13, 14, 14, 15, 15, 15, 17, 17, 17, 18, 19, 20, 20, 21, 22, 22, 23, 23, 24, 26, 26, 27, 27, 27, 27, 28, 28, 28, 28, 29, 29, 30, 30, 30, 31, 31, 32, 33, 33, 33, 35, 35, 35, 36, 37; 13:17, 18, 21, 21, 21, 27; Est 1:19, 19; 2:4; 3:3, 11; 4:13, 14, 14, 14; 5:3, 3, 6, 6, 8, 14; 6:10, 10, 13, 13; 7:2, 2, 5, 5; 8:8; 9:12, 12; Job 1:7, 8, 10, 10, 11, 12, 12, 15, 16, 17, 19; 2:2, 3, 3, 4, 4, 5, 6, 9, 10; 4:2, 3, 3, 4, 5, 6, 6; 5:1, 1, 1, 8, 17, 19, 19, 20, 21, 22, 22, 23, 23, 24, 24, 26, 26; 6:14, 15, 21, 21, 21, 22, 22, 23, 23, 26, 26, 27, 30; 7:8, 12, 14, 14, 17, 18, 19, 20, 20, 20, 21; 8:2, 5, 6, 7, 7, 10, 10, 22; 9:12, 28, 31; 10:2, 3, 3, 4, 6, 7, 8, 8, 8, 9, 10, 11, 11, 12, 14, 16, 17, 17, 18, 18; 11:3, 3, 3, 4, 5, 6, 6, 6, 7, 7, 8, 8, 13, 14, 15, 16, 18, 18, 18, 19, 19; 12:2, 2, 2, 2, 7, 7, 8, 8; 13:1, 1, 2, 2, 4, 4, 5, 7, 8, 8, 8, 9, 9, 9, 9, 10, 10, 11, 19, 20, 20, 22, 22, 24, 24, 25, 25, 26, 27, 27, 27; 14:3, 5, 5,

6, 6, 13, 15, 15, 16, 17, 19, 20, 20; **15:**2, 2, 2, 4, 6, 7, 7, 8, 8, 9, 9, 11, 13, 17, 17; **16:**2, 3, 3, 4, 4, 4, 5, 7, 8; **17:**3, 4, 10, 10; **18:**2, 2, 3, 3, 4; **19:**2, 2, 3, 3, 5, 22, 22, 28, 29, 29, 29; **20:**4; **21:**2, 3, 14, 19, 27, 28, 29, 29, 34; **22:**3, 3, 4, 6, 6, 6, 7, 8, 9, 10, 11, 11, 13, 15, 21, 21, 21, 23, 23, 26, 27, 27, 27, 28, 28, 29; **26:**2, 2, 3, 3, 4, 4; **27:**5, 11, 12, 12; **30:**20, 20, 20, 20, 21, 21, 22, 23; **32:**6, 6, 11, 12, 15, 16; **33:**5, 6, 7, 7, 8, 9, 12, 12, 12, 13, 13, 32, 32, 33; **34:**2, 2, 10, 17, 18, 33, 36, 36, 37; **35:**2, 2, 3, 4, 5, 6, 6, 6, 7, 7, 14, 15, 16, 16; **36:**2, 3, 4, 16, 16, 16, 17, 18, 19, 21, 23; **37:**15, 16, 17, 18, 19, 19; **38:**3, 3, 4, 4, 5, 11, 12, 13, 16, 16, 17, 17, 18, 18, 20, 20, 21, 21, 21, 22, 22, 31, 31, 32, 33, 34, 35, 35, 39; **39:**1, 1, 2, 2, 10, 10, 11, 11, 12, 19, 20, 26; **40:**2, 2, 2, 7, 7, 8, 8, 8, 9, 9, 14, 14, 15; **41:**1, 2, 3, 3, 4, 4, 5, 8, 8, 8; **42:**2, 2, 3, 4, 4, 4, 5, 5, 7, 7, 7, 8, 8, 8, 8, 8; **Ps 2:**7, 8, 9, 10, 10, 12; **3:**3, 8; **4:**2, 2, 2, 3, 4, 7, 8; **5:**2, 3, 4, 4, 5, 6, 10, 11, 12; **6:**3, 5, 5, 8; **7:**1, 2, 7, 9, 9; **8:**2, 2, 3, 4, 4, 5, 5, 6, 6; **9:**1, 1, 2, 3, 4, 4, 5, 5, 10, 10, 10, 14, 14, 19; **10:**1, 1, 1, 14, 14, 14, 14, 17, 17, 18; **11:**1; **12:**7; **13:**1, 1, 5; **16:**1, 2, 2, 5, 5, 6, 10, 11, 11; **17:**2, 3, 3, 5, 6, 6, 7, 15, 15; **18:**1, 1, 25, 25, 26, 26, 27, 27, 28, 28, 35, 36, 39, 39, 40, 43, 43, 48, 48, 49, 50, 50; **19:**14; **20:**1, 2, 2; **21:**2, 2, 3, 3, 4, 4, 5, 6, 6, 8, 8, 9, 9, 10, 11, 13; **22:**1, 1, 1, 2, 2, 2, 3, 4, 4, 5, 5, 9, 9, 10, 10, 15, 19, 22, 23, 23, 23, 25, 25; **23:**4, 5, 5; **25:**1, 2, 3, 5, 5, 6, 7, 20, 21; **27:**8, 9; **28:**1, 1, 2; **29:**1; **30:**1, 1, 1, 2, 2, 3, 3, 4, 7, 8, 9, 9, 11, 11, 12, 12; **31:**1, 1, 3, 4, 5, 7, 7, 8, 14, 14, 17, 19, 19, 19, 19, 20, 20, 22, 23, 24; **32:**5, 5, 6, 7, 7, 7, 8, 8, 8, 11, 11; **33:**17, 17, 22; **34:**11, 12; **35:**3, 10, 17, 18, 18, 22, 24, 28; **36:**6, 8, 9, 10; **37:**3, 4, 5, 5, 10, 27, 34, 34, 34; **38:**9, 9, 15, 15; **39:**5, 7, 9, 9, 11; **40:**5, 6, 6, 6, 9, 16, 17; **41:**4, 11, 11, 12, 12; **42:**1, 9; **43:**2, 2, 3, 4; **44:**1, 2, 2, 3, 4, 4, 7, 7, 8, 9, 9, 10, 11, 11, 12, 12, 13, 14, 17, 18, 19, 19, 23, 24, 24; **45:**2, 2, 3, 5, 7, 7, 7, 8, 12, 16, 17; **48:**10, 13; **49:**1; **50:**7, 8, 12, 13, 14, 15, 15, 16, 17, 18, 18, 18, 20, 21, 21, 21, 21, 22, 22, 22, 23, 23; **51:**4, 4, 4, 4, 6, 6, 8, 12, 13, 15, 16, 16, 16, 17, 17, 19; **52:**1, 1, 1, 2, 3, 4, 4, 5, 5, 5, 9, 9; **53:**5; **54:**5, 6, 7; **55:**13, 22, 23, 23; **56:**3, 8, 8, 8, 9, 12, 13, 13; **57:**1, 7, 9; **58:**1, 1, 2; **59:**8, 8, 9, 9, 9, 16, 17, 17; **60:**1, 1, 2, 3, 4, 4, 10, 10; **61:**2, 3, 5, 5; **62:**9, 11, 12; **63:**1, 1, 1, 1, 2, 3, 4, 4, 5, 5, 6, 6, 7, 8; **65:**1, 1, 2, 2, 3, 4, 5, 5, 6, 7, 8, 9, 9, 10, 10, 11; **66:**4, 10, 10, 11, 12, 12, 13, 14, 15, 16, 16; **67:**3, 3, 4, 5, 5; **68:**7, 7, 8, 9, 10, 16, 18, 18, 18, 18, 23, 26, 28, 32; **69:**5, 5, 6, 9, 13, 13, 19, 19, 26, 26; **70:**4, 5; **71:**1, 2, 3, 5, 5, 6, 6, 6, 7, 8, 14, 14, 15, 16, 17, 17, 19, 19, 20, 20, 21, 22, 22, 22, 23; **73:**18, 20, 20, 22, 23, 23, 24, 25, 25, 27, 27, 28; **74:**1, 2, 2, 9, 10, 10, 10, 11, 12, 13, 14, 15, 15, 16, 16, 17, 17, 18, 22; **75:**1, 1; **76:**4, 6, 7, 7, 8, 8, 9, 10; **77:**4, 11, 13, 14, 14, 15, 16, 20; **78:**2, 2; **79:**5, 6, 12, 13; **80:**1, 4, 5, 6, 8, 8, 9, 12, 14, 15, 15, 17, 18; **81:**7, 7, 7, 8, 8, 9, 9, 10, 16, 16; **82:**2, 2, 6, 7, 7, 8; **83:**2, 2, 5, 9, 9, 18, 18; **84:**9, 12; **85:**1, 1, 2, 2, 3, 3, 5, 5, 6, 6; **86:**2, 2, 2, 2, 3, 4, 5, 7, 7, 8, 9, 9, 10, 10, 11, 12, 13, 14, 15, 17; **87:**3; **88:**1, 6, 8, 8, 9, 10, 13, 14, 14, 18; **89:**5, 8, 9, 9, 10, 10, 11, 12, 14, 17, 19, 26, 38, 38, 38, 39, 39, 40, 42, 43, 44, 45, 46, 49, 51; **90:**1, 2, 2, 3, 4, 5, 8, 8, 8, 11, 13; **91:**3, 3, 4, 4, 7, 7, 8, 8, 9, 9, 10, 11, 11, 12, 12, 13, 13; **92:**4, 4, 4, 5, 8, 8, 10; **93:**2; **94:**5, 8, 8, 10, 10, 12, 12, 13; **95:**7; **97:**9, 9, 10; **99:**4, 4, 8, 8, 8; **101:**1, 2; **102:**2, 10, 12, 13, 13, 25, 26, 26, 27; **103:**20, 20, 21; **104:**1, 1, 2, 2, 3, 3, 3, 5, 6, 8, 9, 10, 13, 13, 14, 14, 14, 19, 20, 24, 24, 26, 27, 28, 28, 29, 29, 30; **105:**11; **106:**4, 5, 47; **107:**2, 2; **108:**1, 3, 11, 11; **109:**17, 17, 21, 27, 28; **110:**2, 3, 4, 5; **114:**5, 5, 6; **115:**1, 11, 14, 15; **116:**10, 11, 16, 17; **117:**1, 1; **118:**13, 21, 26, 28, 28, 28, 28; **119:**4, 7, 10, 11, 12, 13, 21, 26, 26, 32, 38, 41, 55, 57, 58, 62, 63, 65, 65, 67, 68, 71, 73, 73, 74, 75, 76, 79, 82, 84, 90, 93, 102, 107, 113, 114, 115, 116, 118, 119, 120, 126, 132, 137, 146, 151, 154, 164, 168, 169, 170, 171, 175; **120:**3, 4; **121:**3, 3, 5, 5, 6, 7, 8, 8; **122:**8, 9; **123:**1; **125:**4; **127:**2; **128:**2, 2, 5, 5, 5, 6; **129:**8, 8; **130:**3, 4, 4; **132:**10; **134:**1, 1, 3; **135:**1, 2, 20; **137:**5, 6, 8, 8, 8; **138:**1, 3, 3, 4, 7, 7, 8; **139:**1, 2, 2, 3, 3, 4, 5, 5, 8, 8, 12, 12, 12, 13, 14, 15, 16, 18, 19, 19, 20, 21, 21, 24; **140:**6, 7; **141:**1, 1, 2, 8, 8; **142:**3, 5, 5, 5, 7, 7; **143:**1, 2, 5, 6, 6, 8, 8, 9, 10; **144:**3, 3, 9, 10, 10; **145:**1, 2, 2, 10, 10, 13, 15, 15, 16, 16; **146:**3; **147:**13, 14; **148:**3, 7; **Pr 1:**8, 9, 9, 9, 10, 14, 22, 22, 22, 22, 23, 23, 24, 24, 24, 24, 25, 26, 26, 26, 27, 27, 27; **2:**4, 5, 5, 9, 9, 10, 11, 11, 12, 16; **3:**1, 2, 3, 4, 4, 6, 8, 11, 11, 15, 16, 17, 22, 22, 23, 24, 25, 28, 28, 29, 30; **4:**2, 4, 6, 6, 7, 7, 8, 8, 8, 9, 10, 11, 11, 12, 12, 12, 13, 23, 25; **5:**2, 9, 9, 9, 11, 12, 17, 18, 19, 19; **6:**1, 1, 2, 2, 3, 3, 4, 6, 9, 9, 9, 9, 11, 11, 22, 22, 22, 22, 22, 22, 23, 24, 25, 26, 26; **7:**5, 15, 15, 15; **8:**4, 4, 5, 5, 5, 6, 11; **9:**8, 8, 12, 12, 12, 12; **11:**17, 17, 17, 21, 27, 27, 27, 27, 28; **12:**1; **13:**18, 18, 18, 18, 24, 24, 24, 24; **14:**7, 22, 22, 22, 22; **15:**17, 17, 31, 31, 32, 32, 32, 32; **17:**13; **18:**16; **19:**17, 17, 17, 18, 18, 19, 19, 20, 21, 25, 25, 27, 27; **20:**4, 4, 13, 13, 20; **21:**23, 23; **22:**19, 19, 19, 20, 21, 21, 25, 27, 27, 29; **23:**1, 2, 8, 8, 11, 13, 15, 16, 18, 18, 22, 25, 31, 33, 33, 34, 35; **24:**10, 12, 12, 12, 14, 14, 18, 22, 24, 34, 34; **25:**7, 8, 10, 10, 16, 16, 17, 22, 22; **26:**4, 27, 27, 27, 27; **27:**1, 10, 11, 14, 22, 22, 27, 27; **29:**17, 24, 24, 24, 24, 24, 24; **30:**4, 6, 6, 7, 9, 10, 10, 10, 32; **31:**29; **Ecc 1:**10, 10; **5:**1, 2, 3, 3, 4, 4, 5, 6, 6, 6, 8, 11, 11; **6:**9, 9, 11; **7:**1, 1, 2, 2, 10, 12, 14, 14, 17, 21, 21, 22, 22, 26; **8:**2; **9:**9, 9, 9, 10, 10; **10:**3, 4, 8, 8, 8, 8, 9, 9, 9, 10, 11, 20; **11:**1, 2, 4, 4, 6, 9, 9, 9; **12:**1, 1, 3, 4, 4, 4, 5, 5, 5, 6; **SS 1:**3, 4, 6, 7, 7, 8, 9, 11, 15, 16; **2:**14, 14; **3:**3; **4:**1, 7, 9, 12, 12, 13, 15; **5:**8, 9; **6:**1, 4, 4, 13, 13; **7:**6, 7, 12, 13; **8:**1, 1, 2, 2, 2, 4, 5, 5, 5, 12; **Isa 1:**5, 5, 6, 7, 10, 10, 12, 13, 15, 15, 18, 18, 18, 19, 19, 19, 20, 20, 22, 22, 24, 25, 25, 26, 26, 29, 29, 29, 29, 29, 29, 30, 31; **3:**6, 6, 10, 11, 11, 12, 12, 14, 14, 15; **4:**1; **5:**3, 3, 3, 8, 8, 11, 12, 12, 19, 19; **6:**9, 9, 9, 9; **7:**3, 3, 5, 9, 9, 9, 11, 11, 13, 13, 13, 16, 17, 17, 18, 20, 20; **8:**9, 9, 12, 13, 13, 14, 19; **10:**3, 3, 3, 4, 4, 24, 25, 30, 30; **12:**1, 3, 4, 6; **14:**4, 4, 6, 9, 10, 11, 12, 12, 12, 13, 15, 16, 19, 19, 20, 20, 20, 29, 29, 29, 30, 30, 31, 31; **16:**4, 7; **17:**10, 10, 10, 10, 11, 11; **18:**5, 5; **19:**12; **21:**1, 2, 2, 5, 10, 12; **22:**8, 9, 9, 10, 11, 11, 12, 12, 13, 13, 13, 14, 14, 16, 16, 17, 17, 17, 17, 18, 18, 18, 18, 19, 19, 20; **23:**1, 2, 2, 3, 3, 4, 6, 7, 12, 12, 12, 12, 12; **24:**17, 18, 18; **25:**1, 1, 1, 1, 2, 3, 4, 4, 5, 5; **26:**3, 3, 3, 7, 7, 9, 9, 11, 12, 12, 13, 14, 15, 15, 15, 16; **28:**14, 15, 15, 15, 17, 18, 18, 19, 20, 20, 20, 22; **29:**1, 2, 4, 9, 9, 9, 9, 9, 10, 11, 12, 15, 16, 16, 16; **30:**1, 1, 2, 2, 3, 5, 6, 12, 12, 13, 14, 15, 15, 16, 16, 16, 17, 17, 17, 18, 18, 19, 19, 20, 20, 20, 20, 21, 22, 22, 22, 23, 29; **31:**6, 7; **32:**9, 9, 10, 11; **33:**1, 1, 1, 1, 1, 1, 2, 3, 11, 11, 13, 13, 17, 18, 20, 20; **35:**4; **36:**4, 4, 5, 5, 6, 6, 7, 8, 8, 8, 8, 9, 10, 12, 12, 14, 14, 15, 16, 17, 18, 20; **37:**10, 10, 11, 11, 16, 16, 16, 20, 22, 22, 22, 23, 23, 23, 23, 24, 24, 26, 26, 27, 28, 28, 28, 29, 29, 30, 30, 30, 30, 31, 31; **38:**1, 1, 3, 6, 7, 16, 17, 18, 19; **39:**6, 8; **40:**21, 21, 21, 25, 27, 27, 28, 28; **41:**1, 8, 9, 9, 9, 9, 10, 10, 10, 10, 11, 12, 13, 13, 13, 14, 14, 15, 15, 16, 16, 16, 23, 24, 24, 24, 26, 26, 28; **42:**6, 6, 6, 6, 7, 7, 9, 10, 10, 11, 18, 18, 18, 20, 20, 20, 23, 23; **43:**1, 1, 1, 1, 2, 2, 2, 2, 2, 2, 2, 4, 4, 4, 4, 5, 5, 10, 10, 10, 12, 12, 19, 22, 22, 23, 23, 23, 24, 24, 26, 26; **44:**2, 2, 3, 7, 7, 8, 8, 17, 21, 21, 21, 22; **45:**2, 3, 3, 3, 4, 4, 4, 5, 5, 9, 9, 10, 11, 11, 14, 14, 14, 14, 14, 15, 20, 21; **46:**3, 3, 3, 3, 4, 4, 4, 4, 5, 8, 10, 12; **47:**1, 3, 3, 5, 6, 6, 7, 7, 8, 8, 8, 9, 9, 10, 10, 10, 11, 11, 11, 11, 11, 11, 12, 12, 13, 13, 14, 15; **48:**1, 1, 2, 3, 4, 4, 5, 5, 6, 6, 6, 6, 7, 8, 8, 8, 9, 10, 10, 11, 14, 14, 16, 16, 17, 17, 17, 18, 18, 19, 20; **49:**1, 3, 3, 6, 6, 6, 7, 7, 7, 8, 8, 8, 9, 9, 15, 17, 18, 18, 19, 21, 22, 23, 23, 23, 25; **50:**1, 1, 1, 2, 10, 10, 11, 11, 11; **51:**1, 1, 2, 7, 9, 10, 10, 12, 12, 13, 13, 13, 14, 16, 16, 17, 17, 18, 18, 19, 21, 22, 23, 23; **52:**3, 3, 3, 11, 11, 11, 11, 12, 12, 12; **54:**1, 3, 4, 6, 6, 7, 7, 8, 9, 10, 10, 11, 14, 14, 15, 15, 17; **55:**1, 2, 2, 2, 3, 3, 5, 5, 6, 8, 12; **56:**1; **57:**3, 3, 3, 4, 4, 5, 5, 6, 7, 7, 8, 8, 8, 9, 9, 10, 10, 10, 11, 11, 11, 11, 12, 12, 13, 13, 16; **58:**2, 3, 3, 3, 3, 3, 3, 3, 4, 4, 5, 5, 5, 5, 6, 6, 7, 8, 8, 8, 9, 10, 11, 11, 11, 11, 12, 13, 13, 14, 14; **59:**1, 1, 1, 2, 21; **60:**1, 2, 5, 5, 6, 7, 9, 10, 10, 10, 14, 14, 14, 15, 15, 15, 15, 16, 18, 19, 19; **61:**6, 6, 7; **62:**2, 3, 4, 4, 4, 5, 5, 6, 8, 9, 9, 9, 9; **63:**2, 14, 15, 16, 16, 16, 17, 17, 17, 19, 19, 19; **64:**1, 3, 3, 4, 5, 7, 7, 8, 8, 11, 12, 12; **65:**5, 5, 11, 12, 12, 12, 12, 12, 12, 13, 13, 13, 14, 15; **66:**1, 1, 5, 5, 10, 13, 14, 22; **Jer 1:**5, 5, 5, 5, 5, 6, 7, 7, 7, 8, 8, 10, 10, 10, 11, 13, 17, 17, 18, 18, 18, 19, 19; **2:**2, 2, 4, 7, 7, 7, 9, 9, 10, 17, 17, 17, 18, 18, 19, 19, 20, 20, 21, 21, 22, 22, 23, 23, 23, 23, 24, 24, 24, 25, 25, 27, 27, 28, 28, 28, 28, 29, 29, 30, 33, 33, 34, 35, 35, 35, 35, 36, 36, 37, 37, 37; **3:**1, 1, 2, 2, 2, 2, 2, 3, 4, 4, 5, 5, 5, 5, 6, 12, 13, 13, 14, 14, 14, 15, 15, 16, 16, 19, 19, 19, 20, 20, 20, 22; **4:**1, 2, 2, 6, 10, 10, 14, 14, 18, 18, 30, 30, 30, 30, 30, 30, 30; **5:**1, 3, 3, 3, 7, 14, 15, 15, 15, 17, 18, 19, 19, 19, 21, 22, 22, 25, 25, 31; **6:**1, 2, 2, 3, 8, 9, 16, 16, 16, 17, 17, 18, 22, 23, 26, 27, 27; **7:**2, 3, 3, 5, 6, 6, 6, 6, 7, 8, 8, 9, 9, 11, 13, 13, 13, 13, 13, 14, 14, 15, 16, 17, 23; **8:**8, 17, 17, 17, 17, 17; **9:**20; **10:**5, 5, 6, 6, 7, 7, 7, 18, 18, 18, 25; **11:**4, 4, 4, 5, 5, 13, 20, 20, 20; **12:**1, 1, 1, 2, 2, 3, 3, 5, 5, 5, 5, 6, 6; **13:**4, 6, 12, 16, 16, 16, 16, 17, 20, 21, 21, 21, 22, 22, 23, 23, 24, 25, 25, 25, 26, 27; **14:**7, 8, 8, 9, 9, 9, 10, 10, 10, 13, 19, 19, 19, 20, 22, 22, 22; **15:**2, 5, 5, 5, 6, 6, 6, 7, 7, 11, 11, 15, 19, 19, 19, 19, 19, 19, 19, 20, 20, 20, 20, 21, 21; **16:**10, 12, 12, 13, 13, 13, 13, 13, 13, 19, 19; **17:**4, 4, 4, 13, 14, 14, 14, 15, 16, 17, 20, 20, 24, 24, 27, 27; **18:**2, 2, 6, 6, 11, 11, 23, 23; **19:**1, 2, 3, 10, 10, 13, 15; **20:**3, 4, 4, 6, 6, 6, 6, 6, 7, 7, 7, 10, 12, 12, 12, 15; **21:**4, 5, 5, 12, 14, 14; **22:**2, 4, 5, 6, 6, 6, 7, 17, 17, 17, 20, 21, 21, 21, 21, 21, 22, 23, 24, 24, 24, 25, 25, 25, 26, 26, 27; **23:**2, 2, 2, 16, 16, 17, 18, 20, 33, 33, 33, 33, 33, 35, 37, 38, 38, 38, 39, 39, 39, 40; **24:**3; **25:**3, 3, 4, 4, 5, 5, 5, 5, 6, 6, 7, 7, 7, 8, 9, 9, 9, 15, 27, 27, 28, 28, 29, 29, 34, 34, 34, 35; **26:**4, 4, 5, 5, 5, 9, 9, 11, 13, 13, 14, 15, 15, 15, 15; **27:**8, 9, 10, 10, 12, 13, 13, 13, 14, 14, 15, 15, 15, 15, 17, 18; **28:**6, 7, 8, 13, 13, 15, 16, 16; **29:**5, 7, 7, 8, 10, 10, 10, 11, 11, 12, 13, 13, 13, 14, 14, 14, 14, 15, 15, 19, 20, 21, 22, 25, 25, 25, 26, 26, 27, 27, 31, 31, 32; **30:**2, 6, 10, 11, 11, 11, 11, 11, 11, 13, 13, 14, 14, 14, 15, 15, 16, 16, 16, 17, 17, 18, 22, 24; **31:**3, 3, 4, 4, 5, 10, 16, 16, 18, 18, 18, 21, 22, 23, 34; **32:**5, 5, 7, 7, 8, 17, 17, 18, 18, 19, 19, 19, 20, 20, 20, 21, 22, 22, 23, 23, 23, 24, 25, 36, 43; **33:**3, 4, 10, 20, 24; **34:**3, 3, 3, 4, 5, 15, 15, 16, 16, 17, 17, 17, 18, 18, 18, 18, 19, 19, 19, 20, 20; **35:**6, 7, 7, 14, 14, 15, 15, 15, 15, 15, 16, 17, 18; **36:**2, 6, 17, 19, 19, 28, 29; **37:**7, 7, 10, 13, 17, 17, 18, 19, 19, 20; **38:**5, 5, 12, 14, 15, 15, 15, 15, 16, 16, 16, 17, 17, 18, 18, 20, 20, 20, 21, 22, 22, 22, 22, 23, 23, 24, 24, 25, 25, 25, 25, 25, 26, 26, 26; **39:**16, 17, 17, 18, 18; **40:**4, 4, 4, 4, 4, 4, 4, 4, 5, 5, 5, 9, 10, 10, 14, 14, 15, 16, 16; **42:**2, 4, 4, 6, 9, 10, 10, 10, 10, 10, 10, 11, 11, 11, 12, 12, 13, 14, 14, 14, 15, 16, 16, 16, 17, 17, 17, 17, 18, 18, 18, 18, 19, 19, 19, 20, 20, 20, 21, 21, 21, 22, 22, 22; **43:**2, 3; **44:**2, 3, 7, 7, 7, 7, 8, 8, 9, 9, 10, 10, 10, 11, 19, 21, 21, 22, 23, 23, 24, 25, 25, 25, 26, 26, 27, 27, 27, 27, 29, 29, 29; **45:**2, 3, 5, 5, 5; **46:**9, 9, 11, 14, 19, 27, 28, 28, 28, 28, 28; **47:**5, 5, 6; **48:**2, 7, 7, 14, 17, 18, 27, 27, 27, 28, 32, 32, 32, 44; **49:**1, 1, 2, 2, 4, 4, 4, 4, 5, 5, 8, 8, 11, 12, 12, 12, 15, 15, 16, 16, 16, 16, 16, 16, 30, 30, 30; **50:**11, 11, 11, 12, 14, 21, 24, 24, 24, 32, 32, 41, 42; **51:**13, 14, 20, 20, 21, 22, 23, 24, 25, 25, 25, 26, 26, 36, 46, 50, 50, 50, 61, 62, 62, 63; **La 1:**12, 12, 20, 21, 21, 21, 21, 22; **2:**13, 13, 14, 14, 15, 16, 20, 21, 22, 22; **3:**42, 43, 44, 44, 45, 56, 56, 56, 57, 58, 58, 59, 60, 61, 61; **4:**15, 21, 21, 21, 22; **5:**19, 20, 20, 21, 22, 22; **Eze 2:**1, 3, 4, 7, 8, 8; **3:**1, 5, 5, 6, 7, 7, 8, 9, 11, 17, 17, 18, 18, 18, 19, 19, 19, 19, 20, 20, 21, 21, 22, 25, 25, 26, 27, 27, 27, 27; **4:**1, 3, 4, 4, 5, 8, 8, 9, 12, 15; **5:**7, 8, 9, 10, 11, 11, 11, 14, 15, 15, 15, 16, 16, 17, 17, 17; **6:**3, 6, 6, 7; **7:**2, 3, 3, 4, 4, 9, 9, 9; **8:**6, 6, 6, 12, 13, 15, 15, 17; **9:**7, 11; **11:**5, 6, 7, 7, 8, 8, 9, 9, 9, 10, 10, 11, 11, 11, 12, 12, 12, 12, 13, 16, 16, 17, 17, 17; **12:**2, 3, 3, 4, 9, 18, 20, 23, 24, 25; **13:**7, 7, 8, 8, 9, 12, 14, 14, 15, 18, 18, 18, 18, 19, 19, 19, 20, 21, 22, 22, 23, 23, 23, 23; **14:**8, 22, 22, 22, 23, 23; **15:**7; **16:**3, 4, 4, 4, 5, 5, 5, 5, 5, 6, 6, 7, 7, 7, 8, 8, 8, 8, 8, 9, 10, 11, 13, 13, 13, 13, 14, 15, 15, 15, 15, 16, 16, 16, 17, 17, 18, 18, 18, 19, 19, 20, 20, 20, 21, 22, 22, 24, 25, 26, 27, 27, 28, 28, 28, 29, 29, 30, 31, 31, 31, 32, 33, 33, 33, 34, 34, 34, 35, 36, 36, 36, 37, 37, 37, 37, 37, 38, 38, 39, 39, 39, 39, 40, 40, 41, 41, 42, 42, 43, 43, 43, 44, 45, 45, 47, 47, 47, 48, 50, 51, 51, 52, 52, 53, 54, 54, 55, 56, 57, 59, 59, 59, 60, 60, 60, 61, 61, 62, 62, 63, 63, 63; **17:**12, 12, 21; **18:**2, 3, 19, 23, 25, 25, 29, 30, 30, 31, 31, 32; **20:**3, 3, 7, 20, 29, 30, 30, 31, 31, 31, 31, 31, 31, 32, 32, 33, 34, 34, 35, 35, 36, 37, 37, 38, 38, 39, 39, 40, 41, 41, 41, 42, 42, 43, 43, 44, 44, 47; **21:**7, 10, 10, 16, 16, 24, 24, 24, 24, 24, 25, 30, 30, 31, 31, 31, 32, 32; **22:**2, 2, 4, 4, 4, 5, 8, 9, 14, 15, 15, 16, 16, 19, 19, 20, 21, 21, 22, 22, 22, 24; **23:**21, 21, 22, 22, 24, 24, 24, 24, 25, 25, 26, 27, 27, 28, 28, 29, 29, 29, 29, 30, 31, 31, 32, 32, 33, 34, 34, 35, 35, 36, 40, 40, 41, 41, 49, 49, 49; **24:**13, 13, 13, 13, 14, 16, 17, 17, 19, 22, 22, 22, 23, 23, 23, 23, 24, 24, 24, 26, 26, 27, 27; **25:**3, 4, 5, 6, 7, 7, 7, 7, 7; **26:**3, 8, 8, 14, 17, 17, 18, 19, 19, 20, 20, 21, 21, 21, 21; **27:**3, 4, 4, 5, 5, 6, 7, 7, 10, 15, 20, 26, 31, 31, 33, 34, 34, 36, 36; **28:**2, 2, 2, 2, 3, 3, 4, 5, 5, 6, 6, 7, 8, 8, 9, 9, 9, 10, 12, 13, 13, 13, 13, 14, 14, 15, 15, 15, 15, 16, 16, 16, 16, 17, 17, 17, 18, 18, 18, 18, 19, 19, 19, 22, 22, 22, 23; **29:**3, 3, 4, 5, 5, 5, 6, 6, 7, 7, 7, 7, 8, 9, 10; **31:**2, 3, 18, 18, 18; **32:**2, 2, 3, 3, 4, 4, 4, 7, 7, 8, 9, 10, 11, 12, 15, 15, 19, 28; **33:**7, 8, 8, 9, 9, 10, 11, 20, 20, 25, 25, 25, 25, 26, 30, 30, 31, 32, 32; **34:**2, 3, 3, 4, 4, 4, 4, 7, 8, 8, 8, 8, 9, 17, 18, 18, 18, 18, 19, 19, 21, 31, 31; **35:**3, 3, 4, 4, 5, 6, 6, 9, 9, 10, 11, 11, 12, 12, 12, 13, 14, 15, 15, 15, 15; **36:**2, 3, 3, 3, 6, 9, 9, 11, 11, 11, 11, 12, 12, 12, 13, 14, 15, 15, 22, 22, 22, 22, 23, 23, 24, 24, 25, 25, 25, 26, 26, 26, 27, 27, 28, 28, 29, 29, 30, 31, 31, 32, 32, 32, 33, 35; **37:**3, 5, 5, 6, 6, 6, 6, 6, 12, 12, 13, 14, 14, 14, 14, 18, 20; **38:**4, 4, 4, 5, 6, 7, 8, 8, 9, 10, 11, 13, 13, 14, 15, 16, 16, 16, 17, 17, 21, 22; **39:**2, 2, 2, 3, 4, 4, 5, 19, 19, 19; **40:**4, 4, 4, 4, 4; **43:**10, 20, 22, 23, 24, 27; **44:**5, 7, 7, 7, 7, 8, 8, 8; **45:**1, 1, 9, 10, 13, 13, 20, 21; **46:**14; **47:**14, 22, 22, 22; **Da 1:**10, 10, 13; **2:**4, 5, 5, 6, 6, 7, 8, 8, 9, 9, 9, 9, 11, 23, 23, 23, 23, 26, 28, 28, 28, 29, 29, 30, 30, 31, 31, 34, 37, 37, 38, 38, 41, 47; **3:**5, 10, 12, 12, 14, 15, 15, 15, 15, 15, 15, 16, 18; **4:**1, 2, 9, 9, 18, 18, 19, 20, 22, 22, 23, 24, 25, 25, 25, 25, 25, 25, 26, 26, 27, 31, 31, 32, 32, 32, 32, 32, 35; **5:**12, 13, 14, 14, 14, 16, 16, 16, 16, 16, 17, 22, 22, 22, 23, 23, 23, 23, 23, 27; **6:**12, 13, 16, 16, 20, 20, 22, 25; **8:**17, 17, 19, 19; **9:**4, 4, 4, 5, 7, 7, 7, 7, 8, 12, 12, 12, 15, 18, 22, 23, 23, 23, 23; **10:**11, 11, 12, 17, 19, 19, 19, 20, 21; **11:**2; **12:**4, 13, 13, 13, 13; **Hos 1:**2, 10, 10; **2:**1, 1, 16, 17, 18, 18, 19, 19, 20, 20, 20, 23, 23; **3:**1, 3, 3; **4:**1, 2, 4, 4, 5, 5, 6, 6, 6, 6, 14, 14, 14; **5:**1, 1, 1, 1, 1, 2, 2, 2, 3, 3, 3, 4, 4, 4, 9; **6:**4, 5, 5, 5, 5, 6, 6, 7, 11; **8:**2, 5, 5, 5, 6; **9:**1, 2, 2, 3, 3, 3, 4, 4, 5, 5, 6, 6, 6, 10, 12, 12; **10:**9, 10, 10, 12, 12, 13, 13, 15; **11:**8, 8, 8, 9, 9; **12:**9, 9, 9, 9, 10; **13:**4, 4, 5, 6, 6, 7, 8, 8, 8, 9, 10, 10, 10, 11; **14:**1, 2, 3, 4, 8, 8, 8; **Joel 1:**2, 5, 11, 11, 13, 13, 13, 20; **2:**13, 14, 14, 14, 14, 17, 19, 19, 22, 23, 25, 25, 25, 26, 26, 26, 26, 27; **3:**4, 4, 4, 4, 4, 4, 5, 5, 6, 7, 7, 7, 11, 17; **Am 2:**10, 10, 10, 11, 12, 12, 13, 14; **3:**1, 2, 2, 7; **4:**1, 1, 2, 2, 3, 3, 5, 5, 6, 7, 8, 9, 10, 10, 11, 11, 12, 12; **5:**1, 6, 6, 7, 7, 7, 10, 10, 11, 11, 11, 11, 11, 12, 14, 14, 16, 18, 18, 18, 19, 25, 26, 27; **6:**1, 1, 1, 1, 2, 3, 4, 5, 5, 6, 6, 7, 10, 10, 12, 12, 13, 14, 14; **7:**2, 5, 8, 10, 12, 16, 17, 17; **8:**2, 4, 5, 5, 5, 6, 6, 6, 7, 10; **9:**7, 7, 7; **Ob** 2, 2, 3, 3, 3, 4, 4, 5, 5, 7, 7, 7, 7, 7, 10, 10, 11, 11, 11, 11, 12, 12, 12, 12, 13, 13, 14, 14, 15, 15, 16, 16, 16, 16, 16; **Jnh 1:**6, 8, 8, 8, 10, 11, 14; **2:**2, 2, 3, 4, 6, 7, 9; **3:**2; **4:**2, 2, 2, 4, 9, 10, 10; **Mic 1:**2, 10, 11, 13, 13, 13, 15, 16, 16, 16; **2:**1, 1, 1, 2, 2, 2, 2, 2, 3, 3, 3, 4, 7, 7, 7, 8, 8, 9, 10, 11, 11, 11, 12, 12, 13, 13, 13, 13; **3:**1, 1, 2, 2, 3, 3, 4, 4, 4, 4, 5, 5, 5, 5, 5, 5, 6, 6, 6, 6, 7, 7, 7, 9, 9, 10, 11, 11, 11, 11, 11, 11, 11, 11, 12; **4:**8, 8, 9, 9, 9, 9, 9, 9, 10, 10, 10, 10, 10, 11, 13, 13, 13; **5:**2, 2, 13; **6:**3, 4, 4, 4, 5, 5, 5, 5, 8, 9, 12, 13, 13, 14, 14, 14, 14, 15, 15, 15, 16, 16, 16, 16, 16, 16; **7:**12, 15, 15, 16, 18, 18, 18, 19, 19, 20, 20; **Na 1:**9, 9, 12, 13, 14, 14, 14; **2:**1, 12, 12, 12, 13; **3:**6, 6, 7, 8, 11, 11, 15, 15, 15, 15; **Hab 1:**2, 2, 5, 5, 12, 12, 13, 13, 13, 17; **2:**6, 6, 6, 6, 7, 7, 7, 8, 8, 8, 8, 9, 9, 10, 10, 11, 12, 15, 15, 15, 17, 17, 17, 17, 17, 18, 18, 19, 19, 19, 19; **3:**2, 2, 2, 8, 8, 8, 9, 9, 12, 13, 13, 14, 15; **Zep 1:**11, 17, 17, 18; **2:**1, 3, 3, 3, 3, 5, 5, 5, 5, 12; **3:**11, 11, 11, 15, 15, 17, 17, 17, 18, 18, 19, 20, 20, 20, 20; **Hag 1:**4, 5, 6, 6, 6, 6, 6, 6, 6, 7, 9, 9, 9, 11, 11, 13; **2:**3, 4, 4, 5, 5, 12, 15, 15, 16, 16, 16, 16, 17, 19, 19, 19, 23, 23, 23; **Zec 1:**3, 9, 12, 12; **2:**2, 6, 7, 8, 8, 9, 10, 11, 11, 11; **3:**2, 4, 7, 7, 7, 8, 8, 10; **4:**2, 5, 9, 13; **5:**2; **6:**15, 15; **7:**5, 5, 6; **8:**6, 6, 7, 9, 12, 13, 13, 16, 19, 23, 23; **9:**9, 11, 12, 12; **11:**2, 2, 2, 9, 9, 9, 9, 12, 12; **13:**3, 3; **14:**1, 5, 5, 5; **Mal 1:**2, 2, 2, 2, 5, 5, 6, 6, 7, 7, 7, 8, 9, 9, 9, 10, 10, 12, 12, 13, 13, 13; **2:**1, 1, 2, 2, 2, 3, 4, 4, 8, 8, 8, 9, 9, 13, 13, 14, 14, 14, 14, 14, 15, 15, 17, 17, 17, 17; **3:**1, 1, 5, 5, 6, 7, 7, 7, 8, 8, 8, 8, 8, 9, 10, 10, 10, 10, 12, 13, 13, 13, 13, 14, 18; **4:**2, 2, 3, 5; **Mt 1:**21; **2:**6, 6, 8, 13; **3:**7, 7, 8, 8, 11, 14, 14; **4:**3, 6, 6, 6, 6, 9, 9, 10, 19; **5:**11, 11, 11, 12, 13, 13, 14, 18, 19, 19, 20, 20, 20, 21, 21, 21, 22, 22, 22, 22, 22, 22, 22, 23, 23, 23, 25, 26, 26, 26, 27, 29, 29, 30, 30, 31, 33, 33, 33, 34, 35, 36, 38, 39, 40, 40, 41, 43, 44, 45, 46, 46, 47, 47, 48; **6:**1, 2, 2, 3, 4, 5, 5, 6, 6, 6, 7, 8, 8, 14, 14, 14, 15, 16, 16, 17, 18, 18, 18, 23, 23, 23, 24, 24, 25, 25, 26, 30, 30, 33, 33, 33; **7:**1, 2, 2, 2, 2, 3, 4, 4, 4, 5, 6, 7, 7, 7, 9, 9, 10, 11, 12, 12, 13, 15, 16, 16, 16, 23, 23; **8:**2, 2, 4, 8, 8, 10, 11, 13, 19, 19, 26, 26, 29, 29, 31; **9:**4, 6, 13, 18, 18, 22, 28, 28; **10:**8, 9, 11, 11, 12, 14, 14, 14, 15, 16, 17, 18, 18, 19, 19, 20, 20, 22, 23, 23, 23, 25, 26, 27, 28, 31, 37, 37, 37, 37, 37, 38, 38, 39, 39, 39, 39, 40, 41, 41, 41, 41, 42, 42; **11:**3, 4, 7, 7, 8, 9, 10, 10, 11, 14, 17, 17, 18, 19, 21, 21, 22, 22, 23, 23, 23, 23, 24, 24, 25, 26, 28, 28, 29, 29, 29, 30; **12:**3, 5, 6, 7, 7, 7, 11, 11, 11, 27, 27, 28, 29, 34, 34, 34, 36, 36, 36, 37, 37, 37, 38, 38, 41, 42, 47; **13:**10, 10, 11, 14, 14, 14, 14, 17, 17, 27, 29, 35, 51; **14:**4, 16, 28, 28, 31, 31, 33; **15:**3, 5, 5, 5, 6, 7, 7, 11, 11, 11, 11, 12, 12, 12, 15, 15, 16, 17, 20, 20, 20, 34; **16:**2, 3, 3, 8, 8, 9, 9, 10, 11, 15, 16, 17, 17, 17, 18, 18, 19, 19, 19, 22, 23, 23, 24, 24, 25, 25, 25, 25, 26, 26, 28, 28, 28; **17:**4, 4, 9, 12, 17, 17, 17, 17, 20, 20, 20, 20, 25, 27, 27; **18:**3, 3, 3, 8, 9, 10, 10, 15, 15, 16, 16, 16, 17, 18, 18, 18, 19, 19, 19, 19, 32, 32, 32, 33, 33, 35, 35; **19:**4, 9, 17, 17, 21, 21, 21, 23, 27, 28, 28; **20:**6, 12, 13, 14, 15, 21, 21, 22, 22, 22, 23, 25, 26, 26, 32, 32; **21:**2, 3, 5, 13, 16, 16, 16, 16, 19, 21, 21, 21, 21, 21, 21, 22, 22, 22, 23, 23, 24, 24, 28, 30, 31, 31, 32, 32, 32, 32, 40, 42, 43; **22:**9, 12, 16, 16, 16, 17, 18, 18, 29, 29, 31, 37, 42; **23:**3, 4, 8, 8, 8, 10, 11, 13, 13, 13, 13, 15, 15, 15, 15, 15, 16, 16, 16, 16, 18, 20, 20, 21, 21, 22, 22, 23, 23, 23, 23, 23, 23, 24, 24, 24, 25, 25, 25, 25, 27, 27, 27, 28, 29, 29, 29, 30, 31, 33, 34, 34, 35, 35, 36, 37, 38, 39, 39, 39; **24:**2, 2, 4, 9, 9, 15, 23, 25, 26, 32, 33, 33, 34, 42, 44, 47; **25:**12, 13, 20, 21, 21, 22, 23, 23, 24, 24, 24, 26, 26, 26, 27, 34, 34, 35, 35, 35, 36, 36, 36, 37, 37, 37, 38, 38, 39, 39, 40, 40, 40, 41, 41, 42, 42, 43, 43, 43, 44, 44, 45, 45, 45; **26:**2, 11, 11, 11, 13, 15, 15, 17, 18, 18, 21, 23, 25, 27, 29, 31, 32, 32, 33, 34, 35, 35, 40, 41, 48, 50, 53, 55, 55, 62, 62, 63, 63, 64, 64, 65, 68, 68, 69, 70, 73, 75; **27:**11, 11, 13, 13, 17, 17, 21, 21, 40, 40, 40, 46, 64, 65; **28:**5, 7, 7, 7, 13, 14, 20, 20; **Mk 1:**2, 8, 8, 11, 11, 17, 24, 24, 24, 37, 40, 40, 44; **2:**8, 11, 25; **3:**11, 27, 28, 32; **4:**11, 13, 13, 24, 24, 24, 38, 40, 40; **5:**7, 8, 19, 31, 31, 34, 34; **6:**10, 11, 11, 11, 11, 18, 22, 22, 23, 23, 37, 38; **7:**6, 6, 8, 9, 10, 11, 11, 11, 12, 13, 14, 15, 15, 15, 15, 18, 18, 18, 18, 20, 23, 23, 29; **8:**5, 12, 12, 17, 17, 18, 18, 18, 18, 18, 19, 20, 21, 23, 28, 29, 29, 33, 34, 34, 35, 35, 35, 35, 36, 36; **9:**1, 1, 1, 5, 13, 17, 19, 19, 19, 19, 22, 23, 25, 33, 41, 41, 41, 43, 45, 47, 50, 50; **10:**15, 18, 19, 21, 21, 21, 28, 29, 35, 37, 38, 38, 38, 38, 39, 42, 43, 43, 49, 51, 51, 52; **11:**2, 2, 3, 5, 17, 21, 23, 23, 23, 23, 23, 24, 24, 24, 25, 25, 28, 28, 29; **12:**9, 9, 10, 14, 14, 14, 15, 15, 24, 24, 26, 27, 30, 32, 34, 43; **13:**5, 9, 9, 11, 11, 11, 13, 14, 21, 23, 28, 29, 29, 30, 33, 35, 36, 37; **14:**7, 7, 7, 7, 7, 9, 12, 13, 13, 15, 18, 18, 20, 27, 28, 28, 29, 30, 31, 31, 36, 37, 37, 38, 44, 44, 48, 49, 60, 60, 61, 62, 64, 65, 65, 67, 70, 70, 72; **15:**2, 2, 4, 4, 9, 12, 29, 29, 29, 34; **16:**6, 7, 7, 7; **Lk 1:**3, 4, 4, 13, 13, 14, 14, 19, 20, 20, 28, 30, 31, 31, 35, 35, 35, 38, 42, 44, 45, 45, 76, 76, 77; **2:**10, 12, 12, 29, 31, 48, 48, 49, 49; **3:**7, 7, 8, 8, 11, 11, 13, 13, 14, 16, 22, 22; **4:**3, 6, 7, 7, 8, 9, 10, 11, 11, 23, 23, 23, 34, 34, 34, 41; **5:**4, 5, 8, 12, 12, 14, 22, 24, 30; **6:**2, 3, 9, 20, 20, 21, 21, 21, 21, 22, 22, 23, 24, 24, 25, 25, 25, 26, 27, 27, 28, 28, 29, 30, 30, 30, 31, 31, 32, 32, 32, 33, 33, 34, 34, 35, 36, 37, 37, 37, 37, 38, 38, 38, 38, 38, 41, 42, 42, 42, 42, 45, 46, 46, 47; **7:**7, 7, 9, 19, 20, 22, 24, 24, 25, 26, 27, 27, 28, 32, 32, 33, 34, 40, 42, 44, 45, 46, 47, 50; **8:**10, 18, 20, 28, 28, 39, 45, 48; **9:**4, 5, 5, 5, 13, 13, 19, 20, 20, 23, 23, 24, 24, 24, 24, 25, 25, 27, 27, 27, 33, 41, 41, 41, 48, 50, 50, 57, 57, 61; **10:**3, 5, 6, 7, 7, 8, 8, 9, 9, 10, 13, 13, 14, 15, 15, 15, 16, 19, 19, 19, 20, 21, 21, 23, 23, 24, 24, 26, 27, 28, 36, 40, 41; **11:**2, 5, 5, 7, 8, 8, 8, 8, 9, 9, 9, 9, 11, 11, 12, 13, 18, 19, 19, 20, 27, 27, 31, 32, 34, 35, 35, 36, 36, 39, 39, 41, 41, 42, 42, 42, 42, 42, 43, 43, 43, 44, 44, 45, 45, 46, 46, 46, 47, 47, 48, 48, 49, 50, 51, 52, 52, 52, 52; **12:**3, 3, 4, 4, 5, 7, 8, 11, 12, 12, 14, 15, 19, 20, 20, 22, 22, 24, 28, 28, 29, 31, 31, 31, 32, 33, 33, 36, 36, 37, 40, 44, 51, 54, 54, 54, 55, 56, 56, 56, 57, 58, 58, 58, 59, 59; **13:**2, 3, 3,

5, 5, 5, 9, 12, 15, 15, 15, 25, 25, 26, 26, 26, 27, 27, 27, 28, 28, 31, 31, 34, 35, 35, 35; **14:**5, 5, 8, 9, 10, 10, 10, 12, 12, 12, 14, 14, 23, 26, 26, 26, 27, 27, 28, 29, 29, 34; **15:**4, 4, 4, 5, 6, 6, 6, 12, 18, 21, 29, 29, 29, 30, 31; **16:**2, 5, 7, 9, 9, 10, 10, 10, 10, 11, 11, 12, 12, 13, 13, 15, 25, 25, 25, 26; **17:**3, 4, 6, 6, 6, 6, 6, 10, 10, 19, 21, 21, 22, 22, 23, 24; **18:**7, 8, 11, 12, 14, 17, 19, 20, 22, 22, 22, 28, 29, 31, 41, 41, 42, 42; **19:**17, 17, 17, 17, 19, 21, 21, 22, 22, 23, 30, 30, 31, 33, 42, 42, 43, 43, 44, 44, 44, 44, 46; **20:**2, 2, 3, 15, 16, 21, 21; **21:**3, 8, 9, 12, 12, 14, 15, 16, 16, 16, 17, 19, 20, 20, 30, 31, 31, 32, 34, 34, 36; **22:**9, 10, 10, 12, 15, 16, 19, 20, 20, 26, 28, 29, 30, 31, 31, 32, 32, 33, 33, 34, 34, 34, 34, 35, 35, 35, 36, 40, 42, 46, 46, 48, 52, 53, 58, 60, 61, 64, 64, 67, 67, 67, 68, 68, 70, 70, 70; **23:**3, 3, 14, 37, 39, 40, 40, 42, 43, 43; **24:**5, 6, 6, 17, 17, 18, 25, 25, 36, 38, 38, 39, 39, 41, 44, 44, 48, 49; **Jn 1:**21, 21, 21, 22, 22, 25, 25, 26, 33, 33, 38, 38, 42, 42, 48, 48, 48, 49, 50, 50, 50, 50, 51; **2:**4, 5, 10, 18, 18, 20; **3:**2, 2, 3, 3, 3, 4, 7, 8, 8, 9, 10, 10, 11, 11, 11, 12, 12, 12, 12, 26, 26, 28, 28; **4:**9, 9, 10, 10, 10, 10, 11, 11, 12, 12, 17, 18, 18, 19, 20, 21, 22, 22, 32, 35, 35, 37, 38, 38, 38, 42, 48; **5:**6, 10, 14, 14, 19, 20, 23, 23, 24, 25, 32, 33, 34, 34, 35, 37, 38, 38, 38, 39, 39, 40, 40, 42, 42, 43, 43, 43, 44, 44, 44, 45, 45, 45, 46, 46, 47, 47; **6:**25, 26, 26, 26, 27, 27, 29, 30, 30, 30, 30, 32, 32, 36, 36, 47, 53, 53, 53, 61, 62, 62, 63, 64, 67, 68, 69, 70; **7:**4, 4, 4, 6, 7, 8, 19, 19, 20, 21, 22, 22, 23, 24, 28, 28, 28, 29, 31, 34, 34, 36, 36, 37, 38, 45, 47, 52; **8:**5, 10, 12, 12, 12, 13, 14, 15, 19, 19, 19, 19, 21, 21, 22, 23, 23, 24, 24, 24, 25, 26, 28, 28, 31, 31, 32, 32, 33, 34, 36, 36, 37, 37, 38, 38, 39, 39, 40, 40, 41, 41, 42, 42, 43, 43, 44, 44, 45, 46, 46, 46, 47, 48, 48, 49, 51, 52, 52, 53, 53, 53, 53, 54, 55, 55, 57, 57, 57; **9:**10, 17, 26, 27, 27, 27, 27, 28, 30, 34, 34, 35, 37, 37, 40, 41, 41, 41, 41, 41; **10:**1, 7, 24, 24, 25, 25, 26, 26, 32, 33, 34, 35, 36, 38, 38; **11:**3, 8, 8, 15, 21, 22, 22, 26, 27, 28, 32, 34, 40, 40, 41, 42, 42, 49, 56; **12:**8, 8, 8, 34, 34, 35, 35, 35, 35, 35, 35, 36, 44, 44, 45, 45; **13:**6, 7, 7, 8, 8, 8, 10, 11, 12, 13, 13, 13, 14, 15, 15, 17, 18, 18, 19, 19, 21, 33, 33, 33, 34, 34, 34, 35, 36, 36, 36, 37, 37, 38, 38; **14:**1, 2, 2, 3, 3, 4, 5, 7, 7, 7, 9, 9, 9, 10, 11, 13, 15, 16, 16, 17, 17, 17, 18, 18, 19, 19, 20, 20, 20, 22, 25, 25, 26, 26, 26, 27, 28, 28, 28, 28, 29, 29, 30; **15:**3, 3, 4, 4, 5, 5, 7, 7, 7, 7, 9, 10, 10, 11, 11, 12, 12, 14, 14, 15, 15, 15, 16, 16, 16, 16, 16, 17, 18, 18, 19, 19, 19, 19, 19, 20, 20, 20, 20, 21, 21, 26, 26, 26, 27, 27; **16:**1, 1, 2, 2, 4, 4, 4, 4, 4, 5, 6, 7, 7, 10, 12, 12, 13, 13, 13, 14, 15, 16, 16, 17, 17, 19, 19, 19, 20, 20, 20, 22, 22, 22, 22, 23, 23, 23, 24, 24, 24, 25, 26, 27, 27, 29, 30, 30, 30, 31, 32, 33, 33, 33; **17:**1, 2, 2, 3, 3, 4, 4, 6, 6, 6, 7, 8, 8, 8, 9, 9, 10, 10, 11, 11, 13, 15, 18, 19, 21, 21, 21, 21, 22, 23, 23, 23, 23, 24, 24, 25, 25, 26, 26; **18:**4, 7, 8, 8, 9, 17, 21, 23, 23, 25, 26, 30, 33, 34, 35, 35, 37, 37, 37, 39, 39; **19:**4, 6, 9, 10, 10, 10, 10, 11, 11, 11, 11, 12, 12, 35; **20:**13, 15, 15, 15, 15, 19, 21, 21, 23, 23, 26, 29, 29, 31, 31; **21:**5, 15, 15, 15, 16, 16, 16, 17, 17, 17, 17, 18, 18, 18, 18, 18, 18, 18, 18, 20, 22, 22, 23; **Ac 1:**1, 4, 4, 5, 6, 7, 8, 8, 11, 11, 11, 24, 24; **2:**14, 15, 16, 22, 23, 23, 27, 28, 28, 33, 36, 38, 38, 39; **3:**6, 6, 13, 14, 15, 16, 17, 19, 20, 22, 25, 25, 26, 26, 26; **4:**7, 9, 10, 10, 11, 19, 19, 25, 27; **5:**3, 3, 4, 4, 4, 8, 9, 9, 28, 28, 28, 30, 35, 39, 39, 42; **7:**3, 4, 26, 26, 27, 28, 28, 33, 34, 34, 35, 42, 43, 43, 49, 49, 51, 51, 51, 52, 53, 53; **8:**20, 21, 23, 30, 30; **9:**4, 5, 5, 6, 6, 11, 17, 17, 34; **10:**6, 19, 21, 21, 22, 22, 26, 28, 29, 33, 33, 33, 36, 37, 38; **11:**3, 14, 14, 16; **13:**10, 10, 11, 11, 15, 16, 25, 26, 26, 32, 33, 34, 35, 40, 41, 41, 41, 46, 46, 47; **14:**15, 15, 15, 17, 17; **15:**1, 1, 7, 7, 10, 14, 24, 24, 25, 27, 28, 29, 29, 29; **16:**15, 17, 18, 31, 36; **17:**3, 20, 22, 23, 23; **18:**5, 10, 10, 14, 14, 15, 28; **19:**2, 2, 2, 3, 13, 15, 25, 26, 36, 37; **20:**18, 20, 25, 27, 28, 28, 29, 30, 31, 31, 32, 32, 32, 34, 35, 35; **21:**13, 20, 21, 21, 22, 24, 37, 37, 38; **22:**3, 7, 8, 8, 10, 10, 14, 15, 15, 18, 18, 19, 21, 25, 26, 27; **23:**3, 3, 3, 5, 11, 11, 15, 15, 18, 18, 19, 20, 21, 22, 30, 30; **24:**2, 3, 4, 8, 10, 11, 21, 25; **25:**5, 5, 9, 10, 11, 12, 12, 22, 26, 26; **26:**1, 2, 3, 8, 14, 14, 15, 15, 16, 16, 16, 16, 17, 24, 24, 27, 27, 28, 28, 29; **27:**21, 21, 22, 24, 24, 31, 33; **28:**20, 20, 21, 22, 26, 26, 26, 26, 28; **Ro 1:**6, 7, 7, 8, 9, 9, 10, 11, 11, 11, 11, 12, 13, 13, 13, 15; **2:**1, 1, 1, 1, 1, 1, 1, 3, 3, 3, 4, 4, 4, 4, 4, 5, 5, 17, 17, 17, 18, 18, 18, 19, 19, 20, 20, 20, 20, 21, 21, 21, 21, 22, 22, 22, 23, 23, 24, 25, 25, 25, 27, 27, 28, 28, 28; **3:**8, 8; **4:**14, 14, 17; **6:**3, 11, 12, 13, 14, 14, 14, 16, 16, 16, 16, 17, 17, 17, 18, 18, 19, 19, 19, 20, 20, 21, 21, 22, 22; **7:**1, 1, 4, 4, 4, 4, 25; **8:**2, 9, 9, 9, 9, 10, 10, 11, 11, 12, 12, 13, 13, 13, 13, 15, 15, 24, 24; **9:**17, 17, 18, 19, 20, 20, 26, 26; **10:**6, 7, 9, 9, 10, 10, 19; **11:**2, 4, 4, 13, 14, 17, 17, 18, 18, 19, 20, 20, 21, 22, 22, 22, 22, 24, 24, 25, 25, 26, 28, 30, 30, 31; **12:**1, 1, 1, 2, 2, 2, 2, 3, 3, 6, 6, 6, 7, 8, 8, 8, 9, 12, 14, 14, 16, 17, 20, 21; **13:**3, 4, 4, 4, 4, 5, 7, 8, 8, 8, 11, 14; **14:**4, 10, 10, 13, 15, 15, 15, 16, 16, 18, 18, 18, 20, 22, 22, 23, 23, 23; **15:**3, 5, 6, 7, 9, 10, 11, 11, 11, 13, 13, 13, 13, 14, 14, 14, 15, 16, 16, 16, 22, 23, 24, 26, 28, 29, 30, 30, 32, 33; **16:**1, 2, 16, 17, 19, 19, 20, 21, 23, 23, 25, 25; **1Co 1:**2, 2, 3, 4, 4, 6, 7, 7, 7, 8, 8, 9, 9, 10, 10, 12, 13, 13, 14, 26, 26, 30; **2:**1, 1, 3, 4, 5, 13; **3:**1, 1, 1, 1, 2, 2, 2, 3, 3, 3, 3, 4, 4, 5, 9, 16, 16, 16, 17, 18, 18, 18, 18, 21, 22, 23; **4:**3, 6, 6, 7, 7, 7, 7, 7, 8, 8, 8, 8, 8, 8, 10, 10, 10, 14, 14, 15, 15, 15, 15, 16, 17, 17, 18, 18, 21; **5:**1, 1, 2, 2, 2, 3, 3, 4, 4, 4, 5, 6, 6, 6, 7, 7, 9, 9, 10, 11, 13, 13; **6:**1, 1, 2, 2, 2, 3, 3, 4, 4, 5, 7, 8, 9, 11, 11, 11, 11, 12, 12, 13, 15, 16, 19, 19, 19, 19, 20, 20; **7:**1, 12, 16, 16, 16, 16, 17, 17, 17, 20, 20, 20, 21, 21, 21, 22, 22, 22, 22, 22, 23, 24, 24, 25, 26, 27, 27, 28, 28, 32, 32, 35, 35, 35, 40; **8:**1, 9, 10, 10, 10, 12, 12; **9:**1, 2, 2, 7, 9, 11, 12, 12, 13, 24, 24; **10:**1, 12, 12, 12, 13, 13, 13, 13, 15, 20, 21, 21, 22, 22, 23, 25, 25, 27, 27, 27, 28, 28, 29, 31, 31, 31; **11:**1, 2, 2, 2, 3, 13, 17, 17, 18, 18, 19, 19, 20, 20, 21, 22, 22, 22, 22, 23, 24, 25, 25, 26, 26, 28, 29, 29, 30, 33, 34, 34, 34, 34; **12:**2, 2, 2, 3, 17, 17, 21, 21, 27, 27, 31, 31; **14:**2, 2, 2, 5, 5, 5, 6, 6, 6, 6, 9, 9, 9, 9, 12, 16, 16, 16, 16, 16, 17, 18, 22, 23, 24, 24, 25, 26, 36, 36, 36, 37, 37, 37, 38, 38; **15:**1, 1, 1, 2, 2, 2, 3, 11, 11, 12, 17, 21, 31, 34, 36, 37, 37, 51, 58, 58; **16:**1, 2, 2, 3, 5, 6, 6, 12, 12, 13, 14, 15, 15, 17, 18, 19, 20, 23, 24; **2Co 1:**2, 5, 6, 6, 7, 7, 8, 11, 12, 13, 13, 14, 14, 14, 15, 16, 16, 17, 19, 21, 23, 24, 24, 24, 24; **2:**2, 2, 3, 4, 4, 4, 6, 8, 9, 9, 10, 13, 17; **3:**1, 1, 2, 2, 3; **4:**12, 14; **5:**11, 12, 12, 20, 20, 20; **6:**1, 2, 2, 2, 11, 11, 12, 17, 18; **7:**3, 3, 3, 4, 4, 4, 4, 7, 7, 7, 8, 8, 9, 9, 9, 11, 11, 11, 11, 12, 12, 12, 13, 14, 14, 14, 15, 15, 16; **8:**1, 6, 6, 7, 7, 7, 8, 9, 9, 10, 10, 10, 10, 11, 11, 11, 11, 12, 12, 12, 12, 12, 13, 13, 14, 14, 14, 15, 16, 17, 17, 22, 23, 24; **9:**1, 2, 2, 3, 3, 3, 4, 4, 5, 7, 7, 8, 8, 8, 10, 10, 11, 11, 11, 13, 13, 14, 14; **10:**1, 1, 6, 7, 7, 7, 8, 8, 9, 12, 13, 14, 14, 15, 16; **11:**1, 2, 2, 3, 3, 4, 4, 4, 4, 6, 7, 7, 8, 9, 9, 9, 11, 13, 16, 16, 19, 19, 20, 20, 20, 20, 20; **12:**9, 11, 11, 12, 12, 12, 12, 13, 14, 14, 14, 14, 15, 15, 16, 16, 16, 17, 17, 18, 18, 19, 19, 20, 20, 21, 21; **13:**1, 3, 3, 3, 3, 4, 5, 5, 5, 6, 7, 7, 7, 9, 10, 10, 10, 10, 11, 12, 13; **Gal 1:**6, 6, 7, 8, 9, 11, 13, 20; **2:**5, 14, 14, 14, 15; **3:**1, 1, 1, 2, 2, 2, 2, 3, 3, 4, 4, 5, 5, 5, 5, 5, 5, 8, 12, 12, 26, 28, 28, 29, 29, 29, 29; **4:**6, 6, 7, 7, 7, 8, 8, 9, 9, 9, 10, 10, 11, 11, 12, 12, 12, 12, 13, 13, 14, 14, 14, 15, 16, 17, 17, 18, 18, 19, 20, 20, 21, 21, 27, 28; **5:**1, 2, 2, 2, 2, 3, 3, 4, 4, 4, 7, 7, 7, 8, 9, 10, 10, 11, 12, 13, 15, 16, 16, 18, 18, 19, 21; **6:**1, 3, 3, 3, 3, 4, 4, 4, 7, 7, 7, 12, 13, 13, 18; **Eph 1:**2, 13, 13, 13, 13, 13, 16, 16, 17, 17, 18, 18, 19; **2:**1, 2, 5, 8, 8, 8, 11, 11, 12, 12, 12, 12, 13, 13, 13, 14, 17, 19, 19, 19, 22; **3:**1, 2, 2, 4, 4, 13, 13, 16, 17, 18, 19, 19, 19; **4:**1, 1, 20, 20, 21, 24, 24, 26, 26, 28, 29, 30, 30, 30, 32; **5:**1, 2, 3, 4, 5, 8, 9, 14, 15, 17, 18, 19, 20, 21, 22, 22, 24, 25; **6:**1, 3, 3, 4, 4, 5, 7, 9, 9, 11, 13, 15, 16, 21, 22, 22, 22, 23; **Php 1:**2, 3, 4, 5, 5, 6, 7, 7, 8, 8, 9, 10, 10, 11, 12, 19, 24, 25, 25, 26, 26, 27, 27, 27, 27, 28, 29, 30, 30; **2:**12, 12, 12, 13, 13, 14, 15, 15, 17, 17, 18, 19, 19, 22, 23, 24, 25, 26, 26, 28, 28, 30, 30; **3:**1, 1, 2, 15, 15, 15, 18; **4:**1, 1, 1, 2, 3, 5, 5, 6, 7, 7, 7, 9, 9, 10, 10, 10, 14, 15, 15, 15, 16, 17, 17, 18, 21; **Col 1:**2, 3, 4, 4, 5, 5, 5, 5, 6, 6, 7, 8, 9, 9, 9, 9, 10, 10, 10, 11, 11, 11, 11, 12, 21, 21, 22, 22, 22, 22, 23, 23, 23, 24, 25, 27, 27, 27; **2:**1, 1, 4, 4, 5, 5, 5, 5, 6, 6, 7, 7, 8, 10, 11, 11, 11, 12, 12, 12, 13, 13, 16, 16, 18, 20, 20, 20; **3:**1, 3, 4, 5, 7, 9, 10, 10, 10, 11, 12, 12, 13, 13, 13, 13, 14, 15, 16, 17, 18, 19, 20, 21, 22, 22, 22, 23, 23, 24, 24, 25, 25, 25; **4:**1, 1, 3, 6, 7, 8, 8, 9, 10, 10, 12, 12, 13, 13, 16, 16, 17, 18; **1Th 1:**1, 2, 2, 3, 4, 4, 5, 5, 5, 5, 6, 6, 6, 7, 8, 9, 9, 10; **2:**1, 1, 2, 2, 2, 3, 5, 5, 5, 6, 7, 7, 8, 8, 9, 9, 9, 10, 10, 11, 11, 11, 12, 12, 12, 12, 13, 13, 13, 13, 14, 14, 17, 17, 17, 19, 19, 20; **3:**2, 2, 2, 3, 3, 3, 4, 4, 4, 5, 5, 6, 6, 6, 7, 8, 9, 9, 10, 10, 11, 12, 13; **4:**1, 1, 1, 1, 2, 2, 3, 3, 4, 6, 8, 9, 9, 10, 11, 12, 12, 13, 13, 15; **5:**1, 2, 4, 4, 5, 11, 12, 12, 14, 18, 23, 24, 27, 28; **2Th 1:**1, 2, 3, 3, 4, 5, 5, 6, 7, 10, 10, 11, 11, 11, 11, 12, 12; **2:**1, 5, 5, 5, 6, 13, 13, 13, 14, 14, 14, 15, 17, 17; **3:**1, 1, 3, 3, 4, 4, 4, 5, 6, 6, 7, 7, 7, 8, 9, 9, 10, 10, 11, 13, 15, 16, 16, 18; **1Ti 1:**2, 3, 18, 18, 18; **2:**1, 1, 8; **3:**14, 14, 15; **4:**6, 6, 6, 12, 12, 12, 12, 14, 14, 14, 16, 16; **5:**1, 2, 7, 21, 23, 23, 23; **6:**2, 2, 11, 12, 12, 13, 14, 14, 20, 20, 21; **2Ti 1:**2, 3, 3, 4, 5, 5, 6, 6, 6, 8, 8, 13, 13, 14, 15, 18; **2:**1, 2, 4, 4, 7, 15, 21, 21, 21, 21, 22; **3:**1, 5, 10, 10, 10, 11, 11, 14, 14, 14, 14, 14, 14, 15, 15; **4:**1, 5, 5, 9, 11, 11, 13, 21, 21, 22; **Tit 1:**4, 5, 5, 5; **2:**1, 7, 7, 15, 15, 15, 15; **3:**8, 8, 10, 12, 12, 13, 15; **Phm 1:**3, 4, 6, 6, 6, 8, 8, 9, 10, 11, 12, 14, 14, 14, 15, 15, 16, 17, 17, 18, 18, 19, 21, 22, 23; **Heb 1:**5, 9, 9, 9, 10, 11, 12, 12, 12; **2:**6, 6, 7, 7, 8, 12; **3:**7, 12, 13, 13, 15; **4:**1, 7; **5:**5, 6, 11, 11, 12, 12, 12, 12, 12; **6:**2, 9, 9, 10, 10, 10, 11, 11, 12, 12, 14; **7:**17, 21; **8:**5, 5, 11; **9:**20; **10:**5, 5, 5, 6, 8, 8, 32, 32, 33, 33, 34, 34, 34, 34, 34, 34, 35, 36, 36, 36; **11:**6; **12:**3, 4, 5, 5, 5, 5, 7, 7, 8, 8, 13, 15, 15, 18, 22, 23, 23, 23, 24, 25, 25; **13:**3, 3, 5, 5, 5, 7, 16, 19, 20, 20, 20, 22, 23, 23, 24, 25; **Jas 1:**4, 5, 5, 5, 6, 6, 22, 22, 23, 24, 24, 25, 25, 25, 25, 25, 26, 26; **2:**1, 1, 3, 3, 3, 4, 6, 6, 6, 7, 8, 9, 9, 9, 11, 11, 11, 12, 12, 12, 12, 13, 13, 13, 13, 13, 14, 14, 15, 16, 16, 16, 17, 18, 18, 19, 20, 21, 22, 24; **3:**1, 12, 13, 13, 13, 13, 14, 14, 16; **4:**1, 1, 2, 2, 2, 2, 2, 2, 2, 2, 3, 3, 3, 3, 4, 4, 4, 4, 5, 7, 8, 8, 8, 8, 9, 10, 10, 10, 11, 11, 11, 11, 12, 13, 14, 15, 16, 17; **5:**1, 1, 3, 3, 3, 4, 4, 4, 5, 5, 6, 6, 7, 7, 8, 9, 12, 13, 14, 16, 19, 20; **1Pe 1:**2, 2, 2, 2, 4, 5, 5, 5, 6, 7, 8, 8, 8, 8, 8, 10, 12, 13, 14, 14, 15, 15, 16, 17, 17, 17, 18, 18, 19, 20, 21, 22, 22, 22, 22, 23, 23, 25; **2:**2, 2, 3, 5, 5, 7, 9, 9, 9, 9, 9, 10, 10, 10, 10, 11, 11, 12, 12, 15, 16, 16, 18, 19, 19, 20, 20, 20, 21, 21, 24, 25, 25; **3:**1, 4, 6, 6, 7, 7, 7, 7, 7, 8, 9, 9, 9, 10, 13, 13, 14, 14, 15, 15, 16, 16, 16, 21; **4:**1, 1, 1, 2, 2, 3, 4, 4, 10, 10, 11, 11, 11, 12, 12, 13, 13, 14, 14, 15, 19, 19, 19; **5:**1, 1, 2, 2, 2, 5, 5, 6, 7, 7, 9, 10, 10, 10, 10, 10, 12, 12, 12, 13, 14; **2Pe 1:**1, 2, 2, 4, 4, 4, 7, 8, 8, 10, 10, 11, 12, 12, 13, 15, 15, 16, 20; **2:**1, 9, 13, 13, 19, 19; **3:**1, 2, 3, 8, 11, 12, 14, 15, 17, 17, 17; **1Jn 1:**2, 3, 3, 5; **2:**1, 1, 1, 1, 7, 7, 8, 12, 13, 13, 13, 14, 14, 14, 14, 14, 14, 15, 15, 15, 15, 16, 17, 17, 18, 20, 20, 21, 21, 21, 24, 24, 24, 24, 26, 26, 26, 27, 27, 27, 27, 27, 27, 28; **3:**5, 7, 13, 15, 17; **4:**1, 3, 4, 4, 4; **5:**13, 13, 16, 16, 16; **2Jn** 5, 6, 8, 8, 9, 9, 9, 9, 12, 12, 12; **3Jn** 2, 3, 5, 5, 5, 6, 11, 12, 13, 14, 15, 15; **Jude** 2, 3, 3, 4, 5, 5, 6, 9, 12, 12, 17, 17, 19, 20, 20, 21, 21, 21, 23, 23, 24, 24; **Rev 1:**11, 19, 20; **2:**2, 2, 2, 2, 3, 4, 4, 4, 5, 5, 5, 6, 6, 9, 9, 10, 10, 10, 10, 13, 13, 13, 13, 14, 14, 14, 15, 15, 16, 19, 20, 20, 23, 23, 24, 24, 25, 25; **3:**1, 1, 1, 3, 3, 3, 8, 8, 8, 8, 9, 10, 10, 11, 15, 15, 15, 16, 16, 17, 17, 17, 18, 18, 18, 18, 20; **4:**1, 11, 11; **5:**9, 9, 10; **6:**10, 10; **7:**14; **10:**9, 11; **11:**17, 17, 18, 18, 18; **12:**12, 12; **14:**15; **15:**4, 4; **16:**5, 6; **17:**1, 7, 7, 8, 18; **18:**4, 14, 14, 20, 20; **19:**10; **21:**5, 9; **22:**6, 9, 10, 16, 21

YOU'D (1)

1Sa 25:17

YOU'LL (8)

Ge 29:18; **1Sa 20:**31; **2Sa 5:**6; **13:**5; **1Ki 18:**27; **Mt 13:**29; **Lk 5:**10; **Jn 21:**6

YOU'RE (19)

Ex 5:17; **18:**18; **Jdg 11:**7; **1Sa 17:**28; **22:**8; **23:**20; **26:**15; **29:**9; **2Ki 9:**12; **Job 12:**3; **Ps 52:**2; **Mk 14:**68, 71; **Lk 23:**39, 39; **Jn 4:**17, 18; **7:**20; **Ac 12:**15

YOU'VE (11)

Ge 25:30; **39:**17; **Dt 9:**2; **Jdg 16:**15; **18:**24; **1Sa 28:**12; **2Sa 15:**3; **Job 12:**3; **Mt 20:**12; **Jn 17:**24; **21:**10

YOUR (6301)

Ge 1:29; **3:**5, 14, 15, 15, 16, 16, 16, 17, 17, 19, 19; **4:**9, 10, 11, 14, 15; **6:**18, 18, 21; **7:**1; **9:**2, 9; **12:**1, 1, 1, 7, 18, 19, 19; **13:**9, 15; **14:**20; **15:**1, 2, 4, 4, 4, 5, 13, 16, 18; **16:**5, 6, 9, 11; **17:**5, 7, 7, 7, 8, 9, 9, 10, 12, 12, 13, 15, 18, 19; **18:**4, 5, 6, 9, 10; **19:**2, 2, 15, 15, 17, 21; **20:**7, 16; **21:**12, 12, 13; **22:**2, 2, 12, 16, 17, 18; **23:**11, 15; **24:**5, 14, 19, 23, 33, 40, 41, 44, 46, 51, 60; **25:**23, 23, 23, 31; **26:**3, 3, 4, 4, 9, 9, 10, 24, 27; **27:**3, 6, 9, 10, 19, 19, 20, 29, 29, 29, 31, 32, 35, 35, 37, 40, 40, 43, 44; **28:**2, 2, 3, 4, 13, 13, 13, 14, 14, 14; **29:**18; **30:**29, 30, 32; **31:**3, 3, 5, 6, 9, 12, 29, 30, 32, 38, 39, 41, 42, 53; **32:**4, 10, 18, 20, 27, 28, 29; **33:**8, 10; **34:**8, 9, 9; **35:**1, 2, 10, 11, 12; **37:**7, 10, 10, 13, 14, 17; **38:**8, 18, 18; **40:**13, 19, 19, 19; **41:**44; **42:**15, 15, 16, 16, 19, 20, 33, 33, 34, 34; **43:**5, 7, 11, 12, 13, 23, 23, 23, 27, 29; **44:**8, 9, 16, 16, 17, 23; **45:**4, 5, 7, 9, 10, 10, 11, 17, 18, 19, 19, 20; **46:**3, 4, 4, 33; **47:**3, 5, 16, 16, 19, 23, 24, 24, 24; **48:**4, 6, 8, 11, 18, 20, 21, 22; **49:**2, 8, 8, 8, 25, 26; **50:**6, 16, 17, 17, 18, 21; **Ex 2:**9, 13; **3:**5, 6, 13, 15, 16, 18, 22; **4:**2, 6, 6, 7, 7, 14, 16, 17, 18, 23; **5:**13, 14, 16, 22, 23, 23; **6:**6, 7, 7, 7, 8; **7:**1, 1, 9; **8:**2, 3, 3, 3, 3, 3, 4, 9, 9, 9, 21, 22, 23, 25, 28, 29, 29; **9:**3, 14, 19, 22, 30; **10:**1, 2, 6, 6, 8, 10, 10, 12, 16, 17, 21, 24, 24; **11:**8; **12:**11, 11, 11, 11, 13, 15, 17, 19, 21, 23, 23, 24, 26, 32; **13:**3, 4, 5, 7, 7, 8, 9, 9, 9, 9, 11, 14, 16, 16; **14:**14, 16, 26; **15:**6, 6, 7, 7, 8, 10, 12, 13, 13, 16, 16, 17, 17, 17, 26; **16:**7, 8, 8, 9, 12, 25, 29; **17:**5; **18:**6, 6, 14; **20:**2, 5, 5, 7, 9, 10, 10, 10, 10, 10, 12, 12, 16, 17, 17, 17, 20, 24, 24, 24, 24, 26, 26; **21:**3; **22:**24, 24, 26, 27, 27, 29, 29, 29, 30; **23:**2, 3, 4, 9, 10, 11, 12, 12, 12, 12, 15, 16, 19, 19, 21, 22, 25, 26, 30, 31; **28:**1; **29:**12; **30:**16; **32:**2, 8, 11, 12, 12, 12, 13, 13, 13, 13, 13, 24, 27, 27, 29; **33:**5, 13, 13, 16, 18; **34:**9, 9, 11, 11, 16, 16, 24, 24, 24, 24, 26; **35:**3; **Lev 1:**2, 3, 4, 4, 10; **2:**5, 7, 13, 13, 14; **3:**2, 7, 8, 12, 13, 17; **7:**12, 18, 26, 30, 32; **9:**7, 7; **10:**4, 6, 6, 6, 9, 13, 13, 14, 14, 15; **11:**25, 28, 40, 44, 45; **14:**34; **15:**5, 6, 10, 11, 21, 27; **16:**2, 30; **17:**11, 15, 16; **18:**2, 2, 4, 7, 7, 7, 8, 8, 9, 9, 9, 10, 10, 10, 11, 11, 12, 12, 12, 13, 13, 13, 14, 14, 14, 15, 15, 16, 16, 18, 20, 21, 21, 30; **19:**2, 3, 3, 4, 4, 5, 9, 9, 10, 10, 12, 13, 14, 15, 16, 16, 17, 17, 17, 18, 19, 19, 25, 27, 27, 28, 29, 31, 32, 33, 34, 36, 36, 36; **20:**7, 24; **21:**8; **22:**20, 25, 25, 29, 33; **23:**10, 10, 11, 14, 17, 20, 21, 22, 22, 22, 24, 28, 28, 35, 38, 38, 40, 43; **24:**22; **25:**3, 3, 3, 4, 4, 5, 6, 6, 7, 10, 10, 11, 13, 15, 17, 17, 19, 25, 35, 36, 36, 37, 38, 38, 39, 43, 43, 45, 45, 46, 46, 46, 47, 53, 55; **26:**1, 1, 5, 5, 5, 5, 6, 6, 7, 7, 8, 8, 9, 12, 13, 13, 13, 16, 16, 16, 16, 17, 18, 19, 20, 20, 20, 21, 22, 22, 22, 22, 23, 24, 25, 25, 26, 26, 29, 30, 30, 30, 30, 31, 31, 31, 32, 32, 33, 33, 34, 34, 36, 37, 38; **27:**8, 9, 9, 11, 16, 22, 26, 32; **Nu 5:**20, 22; **10:**9, 9, 9, 9, 10, 10, 10, 10, 35; **11:**11, 18; **14:**14, 15, 17, 19, 31, 32, 33, 33, 34, 42; **15:**3, 3, 21, 23, 38, 39, 39, 40, 41, 41, 41; **16:**6, 10, 13, 16, 17; **18:**1, 1, 1, 2, 2, 3, 6, 6, 7, 7, 8, 8, 9, 11, 11, 13, 15, 19, 19, 19, 20, 20, 21, 27, 27, 27, 29, 30, 31, 31; **20:**14, 16, 17, 17, 17, 19, 19; **21:**22, 22, 22, 22, 22, 29; **22:**28, 32, 32; **23:**3, 15; **24:**5, 5, 11, 12, 14, 21; **27:**13, 18, 20; **28:**3, 18, 23, 25, 26, 26; **29:**6, 39; **31:**2, 19, 20, 24; **32:**6, 8, 20, 21, 22, 22, 23, 23, 24, 24, 25, 25; **33:**54, 55, 55; **34:**2, 3, 6, 7, 9, 12; **Dt 1:**8, 10, 11, 12, 13, 15, 21, 23, 26, 27, 30, 31, 32, 34, 35, 38, 39, 41; **2:**4, 7, 7, 7, 7, 27, 28, 30; **3:**18, 18, 18, 18, 19, 20, 21, 22, 24, 24; **4:**1, 2, 3, 4, 6, 9, 9, 10, 19, 21, 21, 23, 23, 24, 25, 29, 29, 30, 31, 31, 34, 34, 37, 40, 40; **5:**6, 9, 9, 11, 12, 13, 14, 14, 14, 14, 14, 14, 15, 15, 16, 16, 16, 20, 21, 21, 21, 23, 28, 32, 33; **6:**1, 2, 2, 3, 5, 5, 5, 5, 7, 8, 8, 9, 9, 10, 10, 11, 13, 15, 16, 17, 18, 19, 20; **7:**1, 2, 3, 4, 6, 6, 8, 8, 9, 12, 12, 13, 13, 13, 14, 14, 15, 16, 18, 19, 19, 19, 20, 21, 22, 23, 24, 25, 26; **8:**1, 2, 2, 3, 4, 4, 5, 6, 7, 10, 10, 11, 11, 13, 13, 14, 16, 16, 17, 18, 18, 19, 20, 20; **9:**3, 4, 5, 5, 6, 7, 14, 16, 16, 17, 21, 23, 26, 26, 26, 27, 29, 29, 29; **10:**9, 12, 12, 13, 14, 15, 16, 17, 20, 20, 21, 21, 22, 22; **11:**1, 2, 2, 7, 9, 10, 10, 12, 13, 13, 15, 16, 17, 18, 18, 19, 20, 20, 21, 21, 22, 23, 24, 24, 25, 27, 28, 29, 31; **12:**1, 4, 5, 6, 6, 6, 6, 6, 6, 6, 7, 7, 9, 10, 10, 11, 11, 11, 11, 11, 11, 12, 12, 12, 12, 13, 14, 14, 15, 17, 17, 17, 17, 17, 18, 18, 18, 18, 18, 19, 20, 20, 21, 21, 21, 25, 26, 26, 27, 27, 27, 27, 28, 28, 29, 31; **13:**3, 3, 4, 5, 5, 6, 6, 10, 12, 16, 17, 18; **14:**1, 1, 2, 21, 22, 23, 23, 23, 24, 24, 25, 25, 26, 26, 27, 28, 29, 29, 29; **15:**1, 3, 4, 5, 6, 7, 7, 10, 11, 12, 14, 14, 14, 14, 15, 16, 16, 17, 17, 18, 18, 19, 19, 19, 19, 19, 20, 20, 21, 22; **16:**1, 2, 2, 2, 4, 5, 6, 6, 7, 7, 8, 9, 10, 11, 11, 11, 11, 14, 14, 14, 15, 15, 15, 16, 17, 18, 20, 21, 22; **17:**1, 2, 2, 2, 8, 12, 14, 15; **18:**5, 5, 9, 10, 10, 12, 13, 14, 15, 15, 16, 16; **19:**1, 2, 3, 8, 8, 9, 10, 14, 14, 21; **20:**1, 1, 1, 4, 4, 5, 7, 13, 14, 14, 16, 17, 18; **21:**1, 2, 5, 8, 8, 9, 10, 10, 12, 13, 23; **22:**1, 3, 3, 4, 4, 5, 8, 9, 12; **23:**5, 5, 7, 9, 13, 14, 14, 14, 18, 18, 20, 21, 21, 21, 23, 24, 24, 25; **24:**4, 9, 10, 10, 12, 13, 13, 14, 18, 19, 19, 19, 20, 21; **25:**3, 15, 16, 19, 19; **26:**1, 2, 3, 4, 4, 5, 10, 11, 11, 12, 12, 13, 13, 15, 15, 16, 17, 19; **27:**2, 3, 3, 5, 6, 7, 9, 10; **28:**1, 1, 2, 3, 7, 8, 8, 9, 11, 13, 15, 16, 24, 25, 26, 31, 31, 31, 31, 32, 32, 36, 38, 40, 42, 45, 46, 47, 48, 51, 51, 52, 52, 53, 53, 55, 55, 57, 57, 58, 59, 62, 64, 65, 65, 65, 66, 67, 68; **29:**2, 5, 6, 10, 10, 10, 10, 11, 11, 11, 11, 12, 13, 13, 15, 22; **30:**1, 2, 2, 3, 3, 3, 4, 5, 5, 6, 6, 6, 7, 7, 9, 9, 9, 10, 10, 10, 14, 14, 16, 16, 17, 19, 20, 20, 20; **31:**3, 3, 6, 11, 12, 12, 13, 13, 16, 26, 28; **32:**6, 7, 7, 46, 47, 50, 50; **33:**3, 3, 3, 3, 8, 9, 9, 10, 10, 25, 25, 27, 29, 29, 29; **Jos 1:**9, 11, 13, 14, 14, 15, 17, 18, 18; **2:**3, 11, 14, 16, 17, 18, 18, 18, 21; **3:**3, 9; **4:**5, 5, 6, 21, 23, 23, 24; **5:**9, 14, 14, 15; **6:**3, 22; **7:**9, 10, 13, 19; **8:**7, 7, 8, 18; **9:**8, 9, 24, 25; **10:**6, 19, 24, 25; **14:**9, 9; **18:**3, 8; **22:**3, 4, 5, 5, 5, 8, 8, 8, 8, 8, 19, 24, 25, 25, 27, 27; **23:**3, 3, 3, 5, 5, 8, 10, 11, 13, 13, 13, 13, 13, 14, 14, 15, 16; **24:**2, 3, 6, 7, 12, 14, 15, 19, 23, 27; **Jdg 1:**3; **2:**1, 2, 3, 3; **3:**28; **5:**12, 31; **6:**9, 10, 25, 25, 26, 30; **7:**10, 14, 17, 18; **8:**6, 7, 15, 22, 22, 24; **9:**2, 15, 16, 18, 18, 54; **10:**14; **11:**24, 36; **12:**1; **13:**7, 12, 13, 17; **14:**13, 15, 15; **15:**2, 18; **16:**13; **17:**10; **18:**6, 25; **19:**9; **21:**21, 22, 22; **Ru 1:**8, 8, 8, 10, 11, 12, 15, 16, 16; **2:**11, 11, 11, 11, 13, 14, 20; **3:**3, 9, 9, 12, 15, 17; **4:**5, 11, 15, 15, 15; **1Sa 1:**14, 23; **2:**1, 3, 27, 28, 29, 30, 31, 31, 32, 34, 36; **3:**9, 10; **4:**17; **6:**4, 4, 5, 5; **7:**3, 3; **8:**5, 11, 13, 14, 15, 16, 16, 17; **9:**19, 20, 26; **10:**2, 24; **11:**1, 3; **12:**2, 6, 7, 12, 12, 13, 14, 14, 15, 19, 20, 20, 25; **13:**13, 13, 14; **14:**28; **15:**15, 21, 22, 22, 24, 30, 33, 33; **16:**1, 19; **17:**9, 9, 17, 18, 28, 44, 46, 46, 58; **18:**17; **20:**1, 3, 3, 5, 6, 8, 10, 15, 16, 18, 30, 30; **21:**4; **22:**14, 14, 14, 16, 22; **24:**4, 4, 10, 11, 15, 20; **25:**6, 7, 7, 8, 13, 26, 26, 27, 28, 29, 29, 29, 31, 31, 33, 35; **26:**8, 15, 16, 16, 22, 22; **27:**10; **28:**1, 16, 17, 19, 21, 22; **29:**10; **31:**4; **2Sa 1:**13, 19, 21, 26; **2:**5, 22, 26; **3:**8, 17, 21, 21, 31, 34, 34; **4:**8, 11; **5:**1; **6:**21; **7:**8, 9, 9, 11, 12, 16, 16, 16, 21, 21, 23, 23, 24, 26, 26, 26, 28, 28, 29; **9:**6, 7, 7, 9, 10; **10:**3; **12:**10, 10, 11, 11, 14, 21; **13:**5, 20, 30, 32, 33, 35; **14:**7, 11, 11, 13, 17, 22, 31; **15:**9, 19, 20, 21, 27, 34, 34; **16:**2, 5, 8, 17, 19, 21; **17:**6, 8, 8, 9, 9, 9, 10, 13, 29; **18:**28, 32; **19:**5, 5, 5, 5, 23, 28, 29; **20:**17, 20; **22:**28, 30, 36, 36, 50, 51, 51; **24:**3, 3, 13, 13, 17, 21, 23, 23; **1Ki 1:**2, 2, 12, 12, 13, 17, 17, 19, 19, 20, 24, 25, 26, 30, 47, 47; **2:**3, 4, 7, 21, 26, 37, 37, 38, 43; **3:**8, 9, 11, 13, 14, 22; **5:**5, 5, 6, 8; **6:**12; **8:**19, 23, 23, 24, 24, 24, 25, 25, 25, 26, 28, 29, 30, 32, 33, 33, 35, 36, 36, 36, 36, 37, 38, 39, 40, 41, 42, 42, 43, 43, 44, 44, 44, 48, 50, 51, 51, 52, 52, 53, 53; **9:**3, 3, 4, 5, 5, 6; **10:**6, 7, 8, 8, 9; **11:**11, 12, 12, 37; **12:**4, 4, 4, 6, 7, 9, 16, 24; **13:**6, 21, 22, 22; **14:**7, 9, 9, 10, 10, 10, 11, 13; **15:**19, 19; **16:**3, 4; **17:**12, 13, 14, 19, 23; **18:**8, 10, 11, 14, 18, 24, 25, 36, 36, 44; **19:**2, 10, 10, 14, 14; **20:**3, 3, 5, 6, 6, 32, 33, 34, 40, 40, 42; **21:**2, 19, 21, 22, 23, 24; **22:**4, 23, 30, 49; **2Ki 1:**10, 12, 13; **2:**3, 5, 9, 10, 16; **3:**7, 13, 17, 17; **4:**3, 4, 4, 4, 7, 7, 16, 26, 26, 36; **5:**10, 27, 27; **6:**12, 29; **8:**1, 9; **9:**3, 7, 22; **10:**2, 3, 5, 15, 24, 30; **11:**8; **12:**7; **14:**9, 10; **15:**12; **16:**7, 7; **17:**13, 13, 39, 39; **18:**20, 21, 21, 23, 24, 25, 31, 31; **19:**4, 6, 16, 20, 22, 23, 27, 28, 28, 28, 30; **20:**1, 3, 5, 5, 5, 6, 15, 17, 18; **22:**9, 19; **23:**21; **1Ch 10:**4; **11:**1, 2; **12:**18, 18; **15:**12; **16:**18, 29, 35; **17:**7, 8, 8, 10, 11, 19, 21, 21, 22, 24, 24, 24, 26; **19:**3; **21:**3, 12, 17, 17; **22:**11, 12, 18, 19, 19; **28:**6, 8, 8, 9, 9, 21; **29:**11, 12, 12, 13, 16, 17, 18, 19, 20; **2Ch 1:**9, 11, 11, 11; **2:**8, 10, 14, 14; **6:**9, 14, 14, 15, 15, 15, 15, 16,

16, 16, 17, 19, 20, 21, 23, 24, 24, 26, 26, 27, 27, 27, 27, 28, 29, 30, 31, 32, 32, 33, 33, 34, 34, 34, 38, 39, 41, 41, 41, 41, 42, 42, 42; **7:**12, 13, 17, 18, 18; **9:**5, 6, 7, 7, 8; **10:**4, 4, 4, 6, 7, 7, 9, 16; **11:**4; **13:**8, 8, 9, 12; **14:**11; **15:**7; **16:**3, 3, 7, 7, 7; **18:**22, 29; **19:**11; **20:**7, 7, 8, 9, 9, 11, 17, 20, 37; **21:**12, 12, 12, 13, 14, 14, 14, 15; **23:**7; **24:**5; **25:**8, 16, 18, 19; **28:**9, 10, 10, 11; **29:**5, 11, 31; **30:**7, 8, 9, 9, 9; **32:**14, 15; **34:**16, 27; **35:**3, 3, 3, 4, 5; **36:**23; **Ezr 1:**3; **4:**2, 11, 13, 14, 15; **6:**6, 8; **7:**14, 14, 17, 18, 18, 19, 20, 25, 26; **9:**10, 11, 14, 14, 15; **10:**4, 11, 11; **Ne 1:**6, 7, 8, 10, 10; **2:**5, 5, 7; **4:**14, 14, 14; **5:**7, 13, 13, 13; **6:**8, 10; **8:**9, 10; **9:**5, 8, 11, 14, 14, 14, 16, 18, 19, 20, 22, 24, 25, 26, 28, 28, 28, 29, 29, 29, 30, 30, 31, 34, 34, 35; **13:**18, 22; **Est 1:**16, 18, 18, 19, 20; **3:**8, 9; **4:**14; **5:**3, 4, 6, 8, 14; **6:**13; **7:**2, 3; **8:**5; **9:**13; **Job 1:**11, 14, 16, 17, 17, 18, 19; **2:**5, 9; **4:**4, 6; **5:**8, 24, 24, 25, 25; **6:**22, 25, 26, 28; **7:**8, 20; **8:**2, 4, 6, 21, 21; **10:**3, 4, 5, 5, 7, 8, 12, 12, 13, 13, 16; **11:**13, 13, 14, 15, 16, 17; **13:**8, 10, 10, 11, 11, 12, 12, 21, 21, 24; **14:**6, 13, 13, 15; **15:**5, 5, 5, 6, 10, 12, 12; **16:**3, 5; **18:**4; **19:**2, 29; **20:**3; **21:**5, 5, 14, 27, 34; **22:**4, 5, 5, 6, 22, 23, 24, 24, 25, 25, 27, 30; **30:**21; **32:**11; **33:**5, 5, 8; **34:**33, 33, 37; **35:**4, 8, 8; **36:**19; **37:**17; **38:**11; **39:**9, 11, 12, 27; **40:**10, 10, 11, 14; **41:**4, 5; **42:**7, 8; **Ps 2:**7, 8, 8, 12; **3:**8, 8; **4:**6; **5:**5, 7, 7, 7, 11, 12; **6:**1, 1, 4; **7:**7; **8:**1, 1, 2, 3, 9; **9:**2, 4, 10, 19; **10:**5; **13:**5; **15:**1, 1, 1; **16:**10, 11; **17:**4, 5, 7, 7, 8, 8, 13, 14; **18:**15, 15, 29, 35, 35, 35, 49, 50, 50; **20:**1, 3, 3, 4, 4, 5, 5; **21:**1, 1, 5, 6, 8, 8, 12, 13, 13; **22:**3, 22, 22; **23:**4, 4, 6; **25:**5, 6, 7, 11; **26:**3, 3, 6, 7, 8, 8, 11; **27:**9; **28:**2, 9, 9, 9; **30:**7, 9; **31:**3, 5, 7, 15, 16, 16, 16, 19, 20, 20, 24; **32:**4, 8; **33:**17, 22; **34:**13, 13; **35:**2, 2, 3, 3, 28; **36:**5, 5, 6, 6, 7, 7, 8, 8, 10; **37:**4, 6, 6, 8, 8; **38:**1, 1, 2, 2, 3; **39:**10, 12; **40:**5, 5, 7, 8, 8, 9, 9, 10, 10, 11, 11, 16; **41:**12; **42:**6, 7; **43:**3, 3, 3; **44:**3, 4, 5, 5, 8, 12, 17, 18, 22, 26; **45:**2, 3, 4, 5, 5, 5, 6, 6, 7, 8, 9, 9, 10, 10, 11, 11, 11, 12, 16, 17; **47:**1; **48:**9, 9, 10, 10, 11; **50:**7, 8, 9, 9, 14, 14, 15, 18, 19, 19, 20; **51:**1, 1, 4, 4, 11, 11, 12, 13, 14, 19; **52:**2, 5, 9, 9; **53:**5; **54:**1, 6; **55:**22; **56:**4, 7, 8, 8, 10, 10, 12, 13, 13; **57:**1, 5, 7, 9, 10, 10, 11; **58:**2; **59:**11, 13, 16, 16; **60:**1, 5, 5; **61:**4, 4, 5, 7, 8; **62:**8, 10, 10; **63:**2, 2, 3, 7, 8; **65:**4, 4, 6, 8; **66:**3, 3, 3, 4, 4, 11, 13; **67:**2, 2; **68:**1, 7, 10, 10, 23, 23, 24, 28, 28, 29; **69:**7, 9, 13, 13, 16, 16, 17, 24, 24, 29; **70:**4; **71:**2, 8, 15, 15, 16, 18, 18, 19, 22, 23, 24; **72:**2; **73:**15, 17, 24; **74:**1, 1, 2, 2, 3, 4, 7, 10, 11, 11, 13, 18, 19, 19, 20, 21, 22, 23; **75:**1, 4, 4, 5; **76:**7, 8, 10, 11; **77:**11, 13, 14, 15, 15, 15, 17, 18, 19, 19, 20; **78:**1; **79:**1, 1, 1, 2, 2, 5, 6, 6, 7, 8, 9, 9, 10, 10, 11, 13, 13, 13; **80:**1, 2, 3, 7, 8, 16, 17, 18, 19; **81:**6, 6, 7, 10, 10; **83:**2, 2, 3, 3, 15, 15, 16; **84:**1, 3, 4, 4, 10; **85:**1, 2, 3, 3, 4, 5, 6, 7, 7; **86:**1, 5, 9, 11, 11, 12, 13, 16, 16, 17; **88:**5, 7, 9, 10, 11, 11, 12, 12, 14, 15, 16, 16; **89:**1, 2, 2, 4, 4, 5, 5, 8, 10, 10, 12, 13, 13, 13, 14, 15, 16, 16, 17, 19, 39, 46, 49, 50, 51; **90:**7, 7, 9, 11, 11, 13, 14, 16, 16; **91:**4, 7, 8, 9, 9, 10, 12, 13; **92:**2, 2, 5, 9, 10; **93:**2, 5, 5; **94:**1, 5, 9, 9, 12, 18, 19; **95:**8, 9; **96:**8; **97:**8; **98:**5; **99:**3, 3; **101:**1; **102:**2, 10, 12, 14, 25, 27, 28, 28; **104:**3, 3, 4, 4, 7, 7, 13, 13, 24, 28, 30; **105:**11; **106:**4, 4, 5, 5, 5, 47; **107:**2; **108:**1, 3, 4, 4, 5, 6, 6; **109:**21, 26, 27, 28; **110:**1, 1, 2, 2, 3, 3, 5; **115:**1, 9, 9, 10, 10, 11, 11, 14; **116:**16, 16, 16; **118:**13; **119:**4, 5, 6, 7, 8, 9, 10, 11, 12, 14, 15, 15, 16, 16, 17, 17, 18, 19, 20, 21, 22, 23, 24, 25, 26, 27, 27, 28, 29, 30, 31, 32, 33, 34, 35, 36, 37, 38, 39, 40, 40, 41, 42, 43, 43, 44, 45, 46, 47, 48, 48, 49, 50, 51, 52, 53, 54, 55, 56, 57, 58, 59, 60, 61, 62, 63, 64, 64, 66, 67, 68, 69, 70, 71, 72, 73, 74, 75, 76, 76, 77, 77, 78, 79, 80, 81, 81, 82, 83, 85, 86, 87, 88, 88, 89, 90, 91, 91, 92, 93, 94, 95, 96, 97, 98, 98, 99, 100, 101, 102, 103, 104, 105, 106, 108, 109, 110, 110, 111, 112, 113, 114, 117, 118, 119, 120, 123, 123, 124, 124, 125, 125, 126, 127, 128, 129, 130, 131, 132, 132, 133, 134, 135, 136, 137, 138, 139, 140, 141, 142, 142, 143, 144, 145, 146, 147, 148, 149, 149, 150, 151, 152, 153, 155, 156, 156, 157, 158, 159, 159, 160, 160, 161, 162, 163, 164, 165, 166, 166, 167, 168, 171, 172, 172, 173, 174, 174, 175, 176; **120:**3; **121:**5, 7; **122:**2, 7, 7; **128:**2, 2, 3, 3, 3, 6; **130:**1; **131:**3; **132:**8, 8, 9, 9, 10, 10, 11, 11, 12, 12; **134:**2; **135:**13, 13; **137:**9; **138:**1, 2, 2, 2, 2, 2, 4, 7, 7, 8; **139:**5, 7, 7, 10, 10, 14, 16, 17, 20, 20, 22; **140:**13, 13; **143:**2, 5, 8, 10, 10, 11, 11, 12, 12; **144:**6, 6, 6, 9, 10; **145:**1, 4, 5, 5, 6, 6, 7, 7, 10, 10, 11, 11, 12, 12, 13, 16; **146:**3, 10; **147:**7, 12, 13, 13, 14; **149:**2, 2; **Pr 1:**8, 8, 10, 14, 22; **2:**2, 10; **3:**1, 3, 5, 5, 6, 7, 7, 9, 9, 10, 10, 23, 23, 26, 26, 27, 28, 29; **4:**1, 6, 9, 21, 23, 25, 26, 27; **5:**9, 10, 10, 11, 15, 15, 15, 16, 18, 18; **6:**2, 3, 3, 3, 20, 20, 21, 21, 26; **7:**2, 3, 3, 4, 25; **9:**6, 11, 11; **10:**2; **11:**17, 28; **13:**24, 24; **16:**3, 3; **17:**13; **19:**16, 18, 20, 27; **20:**2, 13, 20, 20; **21:**23; **22:**6, 17, 18, 25, 27, 28, 28; **23:**2, 4, 8, 9, 12, 13, 18, 19, 22, 22, 25, 26, 26; **24:**10, 12, 14, 14, 17, 27, 27; **25:**8, 10, 17, 17, 21; **27:**10, 10, 10, 14, 23, 23, 23, 26, 26, 27, 27; **28:**24; **29:**17; **30:**32, 32; **31:**3; **Ecc 5:**1, 1, 2, 6, 11, 19, 19; **6:**10; **7:**2, 12, 17, 21; **8:**3; **9:**7, 7, 9, 9; **10:**4, 9, 20; **11:**1, 2; **12:**1, 1, 2, 3, 3, 3, 4, 4, 5, 6; **SS 1:**2, 3, 3, 4, 7, 7, 7, 8, 10, 10, 10, 15; **2:**5, 5, 5, 14, 14, 15; **4:**1, 1, 1, 2, 3, 3, 3, 3, 4, 5, 9, 9, 10, 10, 11, 11, 11; **5:**9; **6:**1, 5, 5, 5, 6, 7, 7; **7:**1, 1, 2, 2, 3, 4, 4, 4, 5, 5, 5, 7, 8, 8, 9; **8:**3, 3, 5, 6, 6, 13, 13; **Isa 1:**5, 5, 7, 7, 7, 11, 11, 11, 12, 13, 13, 13, 14, 15, 15, 15, 16, 16, 18, 20, 23, 25, 25, 29, 29, 31; **2:**11, 22; **3:**11, 11, 12, 14; **4:**1; **5:**8, 9, 12; **6:**7, 7, 7; **7:**3, 11, 17, 17, 20, 20, 20; **8:**9, 10, 10, 10, 19; **10:**3, 16, 16, 16; **14:**4, 5, 5, 6, 6, 8, 9, 11, 11, 11, 11, 19, 20, 20, 20; **15:**1, 2; **17:**11; **18:**2, 2, 5, 5, 5, 6; **19:**12; **20:**2, 2; **21:**5; **22:**3, 7, 7, 8, 11, 12, 12, 12, 18, 18, 19, 21, 21, 21; **23:**1, 2, 7, 9, 10, 14; **24:**17; **25:**1, 3; **26:**8, 8, 10, 11, 11, 11, 11, 11, 16, 17, 20, 20; **28:**17, 18, 19, 22; **29:**1, 3, 4, 5, 8, 10; **30:**1, 2, 5, 10, 11, 15, 16, 19, 20, 20, 22, 23, 25; **31:**7; **32:**9, 10, 11, 11, 11, 12, 12, 13, 13; **33:**1, 3, 6, 7, 8, 11, 11, 12, 17, 18, 18, 18; **35:**4, 4; **36:**5, 6, 6, 8, 9, 10, 16, 16; **37:**4, 6, 17, 21, 23, 24, 28, 29, 29, 29, 31; **38:**1, 3, 5, 5, 5, 5, 16, 18, 19; **39:**4, 6, 7; **40:**1, 9, 27, 27; **41:**1, 1, 10, 11, 13, 13, 14, 15, 21, 28, 29; **43:**3, 3, 3, 5, 12, 14, 14, 15, 24, 24, 25, 26, 27, 27, 28; **44:**3, 3, 3, 22, 22, 24; **45:**8, 21, 21; **46:**4, 4, 4; **47:**1, 2, 2, 6, 7, 9, 9, 10, 10, 11, 15; **48:**1, 4, 8, 14, 17, 17, 19, 20; **49:**9, 16, 17, 18, 19, 19, 19, 22, 22, 23, 23, 25, 26, 26; **50:**1, 1, 1, 1, 10, 11, 11; **51:**2, 5, 7, 10, 13, 13, 14, 15, 16, 18, 19, 20, 22, 22, 23; **52:**1, 1, 2, 11, 12; **54:**2, 2, 3, 4, 5, 5, 5, 6, 6, 8, 11, 12, 12, 13, 14, 15, 15; **55:**1, 2, 3, 3, 5, 9, 9; **57:**4, 5, 5, 6, 6, 8, 9, 10, 12, 13; **58:**3, 5, 7, 7, 7, 8, 8, 8, 10, 11, 12, 12, 13, 13, 14, 14, 14; **59:**2, 2, 3, 3, 3, 3, 21, 21, 21; **60:**1, 3, 3, 4, 4, 5, 5, 9, 10, 11, 12, 14, 14, 16, 16, 17, 17, 17, 17, 17, 18, 19, 19, 19, 20, 20, 21; **61:**5, 5, 5, 5; **62:**2, 2, 4, 5, 6, 8, 8, 11; **63:**1, 2, 14, 15, 15, 17, 17, 17, 18, 19; **64:**1, 2, 2, 2, 5, 7, 8, 9, 10; **65:**15; **66:**5, 9, 14, 20; **Jer 1:**5, 9; **2:**5, 9, 17, 18, 19, 19, 20, 20, 24, 25, 30, 30, 33, 34, 34, 36, 37, 37; **3:**2, 2, 13, 13, 14, 16, 19, 22; **4:**1, 3, 3, 4, 4, 5, 7, 7, 12, 14, 14, 15, 18, 18, 30, 30, 30; **5:**3, 7, 17, 17, 17, 17, 17, 17, 19, 19, 19, 25, 25; **6:**1, 3, 8, 16, 20, 20, 20; **7:**3, 3, 4, 5, 6, 6, 7, 14, 15, 21, 22, 23, 25, 27, 29; **8:**8; **9:**4, 4, 18, 18, 20, 20; **10:**6, 11, 17, 25, 25, 25; **11:**4, 4, 5, 6, 7, 8, 13, 13, 20; **12:**2, 6, 6; **13:**1, 12, 16, 17, 18, 18, 18, 20, 20, 21, 22, 25, 25, 27, 27, 27; **14:**7, 9, 10, 10, 21, 21, 21; **15:**6, 7, 11, 15, 16, 16, 17, 18; **16:**9, 9, 11, 12, 12, 13; **17:**3, 3, 3, 3, 4, 12, 15, 16, 16, 21, 22, 22, 24; **18:**11, 12, 20, 23; **19:**9, 13, 13; **20:**3, 4, 5, 5, 6, 6, 12; **21:**4, 4, 8, 12, 14, 14; **22:**2, 2, 3, 6, 7, 15, 20, 22, 22, 22, 26, 27; **23:**17, 39, 40; **25:**5, 7, 10, 10, 10, 34; **26:**11, 13, 13, 14; **27:**2, 6, 8, 9, 10, 13, 16; **28:**2, 4, 6, 15, 16; **29:**14, 14, 14, 16, 21, 25; **30:**10, 13, 14, 14, 14, 14, 15, 15, 15, 16, 17, 17, 18, 18, 22; **31:**5, 5, 7, 16, 17, 17, 21; **32:**7, 17, 20, 23; **34:**5, 5, 5, 13, 15, 16, 17, 18, 19, 20, 20; **35:**6, 15, 15, 18; **37:**18, 19; **38:**12, 17, 20, 22, 22, 22, 23; **39:**18; **40:**2, 4; **42:**2, 3, 4, 5, 9, 12, 13, 18, 20, 21; **44:**3, 7, 9, 9, 10, 16, 21, 21, 22, 25, 25, 25, 25; **46:**3, 4, 4, 4, 10, 11, 12, 12, 12, 15, 27; **47:**6; **48:**6, 7, 7, 18, 18, 27, 28, 32, 32, 43, 44, 46, 46; **49:**2, 3, 3, 4, 4, 5, 5, 5, 11, 30; **50:**12, 14, 31, 31; **51:**9, 13, 13, 14, 25, 26, 36, 36, 50; **La 2:**13, 13, 14, 14, 16, 18, 19, 19, 19, 20, 21; **3:**43, 55, 65, 66; **4:**21, 22, 22, 22; **5:**19; **Eze 2:**8; **3:**10, 11, 18, 19, 20, 21, 24, 26, 26, 27; **4:**4, 4, 6, 7, 7, 8, 9, 12, 15; **5:**1, 2, 2, 3, 7, 8, 9, 12, 17, 17; **6:**3, 4, 4, 4, 4, 5, 5, 5, 5, 6, 6, 6, 6, 11, 11; **7:**2, 3, 4, 6, 7, 8, 8, 9, 10; **9:**6, 8; **11:**5, 6, 7, 16; **12:**3, 3, 3, 4, 4, 5, 6, 6, 6, 11, 18, 18, 18, 25; **13:**7, 8, 13, 14, 20, 20, 21, 21, 22, 23, 23; **14:**6, 6, 22; **16:**3, 3, 4, 6, 7, 7, 8, 9, 9, 12, 12, 12, 13, 14, 14, 14, 15, 15, 16, 18, 20, 20, 22, 22, 23, 23, 25, 25, 26, 26, 27, 27, 27, 28, 29, 31, 31, 31, 33, 36, 36, 36, 37, 38, 39, 39, 39, 39, 41, 41, 41, 41, 43, 43, 43, 45, 45, 45, 45, 46, 46, 48, 51, 51, 52, 52, 54, 55, 56, 57, 58, 58, 59, 59, 61, 61, 63, 63; **18:**30, 30, 31; **19:**2, 10; **20:**7, 7, 19, 20, 27, 30, 31, 36, 39, 40, 42, 43, 44; **21:**3, 3, 12, 14, 24, 24, 24, 24, 25, 26, 28, 29, 30, 30, 32, 32, 32; **22:**4, 4, 6, 8, 11, 13, 15, 25, 26, 27, 28; **23:**21, 22, 25, 25, 26, 27, 28, 29, 31, 32, 32, 33, 34, 35, 35, 40, 40, 42, 42, 42, 49, 49; **24:**13, 14, 16, 17, 17, 21, 21, 23, 23, 23, 27; **25:**4, 4, 4, 4; **26:**3, 3, 8, 9, 9, 10, 10, 11, 11, 12, 12, 12, 12, 12, 13, 13, 14, 15, 17, 18, 20; **27:**4, 4, 6, 7, 8, 8, 9, 10, 10, 11, 11, 11, 11, 12, 12, 14, 15, 16, 17, 18, 19, 19, 21, 22, 25, 25, 26, 26, 26, 27, 27, 27, 28, 28, 33, 34, 34, 35; **28:**2, 4, 4, 5, 5, 7, 7, 8, 13, 16, 16, 17, 17, 17, 17, 18, 18, 18, 19, 22, 23, 23, 23; **29:**3, 4, 4, 5, 10, 21; **31:**2, 18; **32:**2, 2, 5, 5, 6, 8, 9, 10, 13, 15; **33:**2, 11, 12, 17, 20, 30, 30; **34:**2, 3, 18, 31; **35:**3, 4, 5, 6, 6, 8, 8, 8, 8, 9, 11, 11; **36:**2, 3, 9, 9, 11, 14, 14, 15, 24, 25, 26, 28, 28, 29, 30, 30, 31, 33, 33; **37:**12, 14, 17, 18, 18; **38:**3, 4, 4, 4, 9, 10, 15, 15, 15, 21, 22; **39:**1, 3, 3, 4, 6, 9; **44:**5, 6, 7, 30, 30; **45:**9, 11, 14, 15; **47:**14, 14, 20; **Da 1:**10; **2:**5, 7, 8, 10, 11, 25, 25, 28, 28, 29, 30, 31, 31, 36, 37, 38, 39, 39, 45, 47; **3:**12, 12, 17, 17, 18, 18, 24; **4:**19, 22, 22, 22, 24, 26, 27; **5:**11, 11, 16, 17, 18, 18, 23, 23, 23, 26, 28; **6:**7, 7, 8, 12, 13, 15, 16, 20, 22; **8:**17; **9:**4, 4, 5, 6, 6, 11, 11, 15, 15, 16, 16, 16, 16, 16, 17, 17, 17, 18, 18, 19, 19, 19, 19, 23, 24, 24; **10:**12, 12, 12, 14, 17, 21; **11:**14; **12:**1, 1, 13; **Hos 1:**6; **2:**1, 1, 17; **3:**1, 3; **4:**1, 3, 4, 5, 5, 5, 6, 6, 6, 13, 13; **5:**4, 4, 9; **6:**4, 6; **8:**6; **9:**1, 2, 2, 6, 6, 10, 11, 12, 14; **10:**10, 10, 12, 13, 13, 14, 14, 15; **12:**6, 6, 9, 9; **13:**4, 4, 9, 10, 14, 14; **14:**1, 1, 2, 4; **Joel 1:**2, 3, 5, 13, 14; **2:**12, 13, 13, 13, 13, 14, 17, 19, 23, 26, 27, 28, 28, 28; **3:**5, 8, 9, 9, 10, 10, 10, 11, 17; **Am 2:**11, 12, 14, 16; **3:**2, 9; **4:**1, 2, 3, 4, 4, 4, 5, 5, 7, 9, 9, 10, 10, 11, 12; **5:**3, 6, 12, 14, 15, 21, 21, 22, 22, 23, 23, 26, 26, 26, 26; **6:**3, 6, 7, 13, 14; **7:**2, 9, 10, 12, 13, 14, 17, 17, 17; **8:**5, 8, 10, 10, 10, 10; **9:**15; **Ob** 3, 4, 5, 7, 7, 7, 7, 10, 11, 12, 13, 15, 15; **Jnh 1:**6, 8, 8, 14; **2:**3, 4, 4, 7; **4:**2; **Mic 1:**10, 13, 15, 16, 16; **2:**3, 4, 4, 5, 10, 12, 13, 13, 13, 13; **3:**6, 6, 7, 7; **4:**8, 10, 11, 11; **5:**1, 10, 10, 11, 11, 13, 13, 14, 14; **6:**1, 1, 3, 4, 5, 8, 10, 11, 12, 13, 14, 14, 15, 15; **7:**4, 4, 5, 5, 6, 6, 11, 11, 14, 14, 18, 19, 20; **Na 1:**13, 14, 14, 15, 15, 15, 15; **2:**1, 2, 12, 12, 12, 12, 12, 13, 13, 13, 13; **3:**5, 5, 5, 7, 12, 13, 13, 15, 16, 17, 18, 18, 19, 19, 19, 19; **Hab 1:**5, 12; **2:**6, 7, 9, 9, 10, 10, 11, 15, 15, 16, 16, 17, 17, 18, 18; **3:**2, 2, 2, 8, 9, 11, 11, 12, 13, 13, 15; **Zep 1:**2, 17, 17, 18; **2:**2; **3:**14, 15, 15, 17, 17, 20; **Hag 1:**6, 6, 9, 9, 11, 11, 11; **2:**17, 19; **Zec 1:**2, 4, 4, 4, 5, 6; **3:**2, 4, 10, 10, 10; **6:**15; **7:**5, 5, 6, 11; **8:**14, 16; **9:**9, 10, 11, 12; **10:**3; **11:**1, 1, 9; **13:**6; **14:**1; **Mal 1:**2, 6, 6, 8, 10, 12, 13; **2:**3, 3, 3, 8, 9, 13, 14, 14, 14, 14, 15, 15, 15, 16, 17; **3:**7, 9, 11, 11, 12; **4:**3; **Mt 1:**20; **3:**2, 8, 10; **4:**6, 7, 10, 17; **5:**15, 16, 16, 22, 24, 24, 25, 29, 29, 29, 29, 30, 30, 30, 30, 33, 37, 37, 40, 40, 43, 43, 44, 45, 47, 48; **6:**1, 1, 3, 3, 4, 4, 6, 6, 8, 9, 10, 10, 14, 15, 15, 17, 17, 18, 18, 20, 21, 21, 22, 22, 22, 26, 27, 27, 28, 32, 32, 33; **7:**3, 3, 4, 4, 5, 5, 9, 11, 11, 22, 22, 22; **8:**4; **9:**2, 5, 6, 11, 13, 14, 18, 22, 29; **10:**12, 13, 14, 18, 19, 20, 22, 27, 28, 28, 29, 30, 36, 36, 37, 37, 38, 39; **11:**10, 29; **12:**2, 7, 13, 27, 34, 37, 47, 47; **13:**16, 16; **15:**2, 3, 4, 5, 6, 28, 28; **16:**24, 24, 25, 25, 26, 26; **17:**16, 24; **18:**3, 8, 8, 9, 17, 33, 35, 35; **19:**8, 17, 19, 19; **20:**21, 21, 21, 21, 26, 27; **21:**5, 27, 32; **22:**18, 29, 37, 37, 37, 37, 39, 44, 44; **23:**9, 23, 24, 28, 29, 29, 34, 37, 38; **24:**3, 9, 20, 42; **25:**8, 25, 35, 43; **26:**18, 39, 42, 52, 66, 73; **27:**4; **Mk 1:**2, 15, 44; **2:**5, 9, 9, 11, 18; **3:**5, 32, 32; **4:**10; **5:**9, 19, 23, 34, 35; **6:**11, 18; **7:**5, 8, 9, 10, 13, 19, 29; **8:**17, 26, 34, 34, 35, 35, 36, 37; **9:**18, 38, 43, 45, 47; **10:**5, 19, 19, 37, 37, 37, 43, 52, 52; **11:**14, 23, 23, 25, 25, 33; **12:**15, 24, 30, 30, 30, 30, 30, 31, 36, 36; **13:**9, 11, 13, 18; **14:**36, 64; **Lk 1:**13, 13, 36, 42, 44, 61; **2:**32, 35, 48; **3:**8, 9, 13, 14; **4:**8, 11, 12, 21, 23; **5:**4, 14, 20, 23, 24; **6:**10, 23, 24, 25, 27, 29, 29, 35, 35, 36, 38, 41, 41, 42, 42, 42, 42, 45; **7:**4, 27, 44, 48, 50; **8:**20, 20, 25, 30, 39, 48, 49; **9:**5, 5, 23, 23, 24, 24, 25, 40, 49, 60; **10:**5, 11, 11, 16, 17, 20, 27, 27, 27, 27, 27, 27; **11:**2, 2, 11, 13, 13, 19, 27, 34, 34, 34, 36, 42, 47, 48; **12:**7, 11, 25, 25, 30, 30, 31, 32, 33, 34, 34, 36, 58; **13:**3, 12, 15, 15, 34, 35; **14:**5, 5, 10, 12, 26, 26, 27; **15:**5, 6, 6, 12, 19, 21, 27, 27, 30, 32; **16:**2, 2, 7, 9, 9, 12, 15, 16, 25, 29; **17:**19; **18:**20, 20, 42; **19:**5, 17, 39, 43, 43, 44, 44; **20:**8, 43, 43; **21:**13, 15, 16, 17, 18, 19, 28; **22:**27, 32, 32, 36, 36, 42, 53; **23:**14, 28, 42, 46; **Jn 3:**2; **4:**16, 50, 53; **5:**8, 11, 38, 41, 45; **6:**27, 49, 58; **7:**3, 3, 23; **8:**10, 15, 17, 19, 21, 24, 24, 37, 38, 41, 42, 44, 52, 56; **9:**17, 19; **10:**34; **11:**15, 23; **12:**15, 28, 30; **13:**14, 35; **15:**11; **16:**20, 23, 26; **17:**1, 6, 14, 17, 26; **18:**11, 29, 31, 34, 35; **19:**14, 15, 26, 27; **20:**17, 17, 27, 27; **21:**6, 18; **Ac 2:**17, 17, 17, 27, 28, 34, 35, 38, 38, 39; **3:**16, 17, 19, 19, 20, 22, 22, 25, 25, 26; **4:**25, 27, 28, 29, 30, 30; **5:**3, 8, 8, 9, 28; **7:**3, 3, 32, 33, 37, 43, 43, 51, 52; **8:**20, 21, 22, 22; **9:**17, 34; **10:**4, 31, 31; **11:**14; **12:**8, 8, 15; **13:**33, 35, 38, 41; **15:**23, 27; **16:**31; **17:**23, 28; **18:**6, 6, 15; **20:**20; **22:**13, 16, 18, 20; **23:**35, 35; **24:**2, 4; **25:**5; **26:**1, 13, 17; **27:**22, 34, 34; **Ro 1:**8, 9, 12; **2:**4, 5, 5, 17; **4:**18; **6:**13, 13, 14, 16, 17, 18, 18; **8:**6, 6, 6, 9, 10, 10, 11, 12, 36; **9:**7, 12, 12; **10:**8, 8, 9, 9, 10, 10, 19; **11:**3, 3, 28; **12:**1, 3, 3, 7, 8, 11, 18, 20; **13:**6, 7, 8, 8, 9, 12, 14; **14:**15; **15:**9, 24, 30; **16:**6, 20; **1Co 1:**5, 11; **3:**3, 3, 6; **4:**6, 7, 8, 15; **5:**1, 2, 6, 12; **6:**8, 11, 15, 18, 19, 20; **7:**1, 14, 16, 16, 24, 35; **8:**1, 11; **9:**4, 4; **10:**13, 24, 25, 27; **11:**2, 21, 22; **12:**1, 17; **14:**1, 2, 20, 23, 24, 28; **15:**1, 14, 17, 17, 34, 34, 55, 55; **16:**3, 11; **2Co 1:**6, 15, 24, 24; **2:**3, 5, 6, 10; **3:**2; **4:**5, 15; **5:**13; **6:**12, 13, 18; **7:**2, 7, 9; **8:**6, 6, 8, 9, 24; **9:**2, 3, 7, 11, 13, 13; **10:**7, 15; **11:**3; **12:**9, 15, 19, 21; **13:**5, 9, 11; **Gal 3:**3, 3, 3; **4:**6, 6, 15, 16, 17, 17, 19; **5:**13, 14, 16, 16, 17, 19, 19, 20; **6:**4; **Eph 1:**15, 15, 17, 18; **2:**1; **3:**17, 17; **4:**1, 2, 22, 22, 23, 25, 28, 29; **5:**2, 8, 8, 14, 18, 19, 22, 24, 25; **6:**1, 2, 3, 4, 5, 6, 6, 9, 14, 16, 17, 18; **Php 1:**9, 9, 11, 11, 25, 28; **2:**1, 4, 5, 12, 15, 17, 20, 25; **3:**1, 17; **4:**2, 7, 8, 17, 19, 23; **Col 1:**7, 9, 21, 27; **2:**5, 6, 7, 7, 10, 11, 13, 13; **3:**1, 2, 3, 4, 7, 9, 15, 16, 18, 19, 20, 21, 22, 22, 24; **4:**1, 6, 9, 10, 12; **1Th 1:**3, 3, 3, 8; **2:**5, 12, 14; **3:**2, 5, 6, 7, 10, 12, 13; **4:**4, 10, 11, 11, 11, 12; **5:**6, 12, 13, 23; **2Th 1:**3, 4, 11; **2:**13, 17; **3:**12; **1Ti 1:**19, 19; **2:**1; **4:**6, 7, 12, 12, 12, 15, 15, 15, 16; **5:**1, 1, 2, 2, 23; **6:**2, 2; **2Ti 1:**4, 5, 5; **2:**21; **4:**2, 22; **Tit 1:**11; **2:**7, 8, 15; **3:**1, 12; **Phm 1:**2, 5, 5, 6, 6, 7, 7, 9, 13, 14, 17, 19, 22, 25; **Heb 1:**5, 8, 8, 9, 10, 13, 13; **2:**12, 12; **3:**8, 9, 12, 15; **4:**7; **5:**5; **6:**10, 14; **10:**7, 9; **11:**18; **12:**4, 4, 12, 12, 13; **13:**3, 7, 9, 17, 17, 17, 19, 24; **Jas 1:**2, 3, 3, 4, 5, 20, 21, 21, 21, 23, 23, 26, 26; **2:**2, 8, 14, 18; **3:**6, 6, 14; **4:**3, 4, 8, 8, 10, 11, 12, 14, 16; **5:**2, 2, 3, 3, 5, 5, 5, 16; **1Pe 1:**7, 7, 7, 9, 9, 14, 17, 18, 21, 22, 22, 23, 23; **2:**2, 11, 12, 12, 15, 16, 17, 18, 19, 21, 25, 25; **3:**1, 1, 2, 6, 7, 7, 7, 10, 10, 15, 15, 16, 21; **4:**2, 4, 7, 9; **5:**3, 3, 4, 7, 8, 9, 13; **2Pe 1:**5, 5, 8, 19; **2:**3; **3:**1, 1, 2, 9, 17; **1Jn 2:**12, 13, 14, 14; **4:**4; **5:**21; **2Jn** 4, 8, 10, 10, 13; **3Jn** 2, 2, 3, 6, 6, 15; **Jude** 20, 20; **Rev 1:**9; **2:**2, 2, 5, 5, 9, 9, 19, 19, 19, 19, 19; **3:**2, 9, 11, 18, 18, 19; **4:**11; **5:**9; **10:**9; **11:**17, 18, 18, 18, 18, 18; **13:**10; **14:**18; **15:**3, 3, 4, 4; **16:**1, 6, 6, 7; **17:**18; **18:**6, 20; **22:**9

YOURS (84)

Ge 16:12; **31:**38; **41:**40; **45:**20; **47:**18; **48:**5; **Nu 18:**15, 18; **Dt 3:**24; **11:**24; **Jos 17:**18; **23:**5; **Jdg 9:**38; **1Sa 1:**11; **26:**24; **1Ki 1:**37, 47; **3:**9, 22, 23, 26; **5:**6; **20:**4, 9; **22:**4; **2Ki 3:**7; **1Ch 12:**18; **21:**24; **29:**11, 11; **2Ch 1:**10; **6:**41; **13:**9; **18:**3; **20:**15; **21:**14; **Job 19:**4; **34:**33; **Ps 42:**3, 10; **52:**1; **62:**12; **86:**8; **89:**11, 11, 11; **119:**94; **Pr 27:**10; **Isa 10:**30; **23:**7; **43:**4; **45:**14; **55:**8; **60:**13; **66:**14; **Jer 7:**9; **30:**12; **49:**32; **Eze 13:**4; **16:**37; **33:**25; **35:**15; **Da 2:**39; **9:**18; **Mic 7:**10; **Na 1:**11; **Mt 27:**24; **Lk 5:**33; **15:**30, 31; **19:**21; **Jn 17:**6, 19; **Ac 5:**4, 4; **Ro 1:**7, 12; **1Co 8:**9; **Gal 1:**3; **Eph 1:**2; **Col 1:**6; **1Th 1:**1; **1Pe 1:**12; **Rev 18:**14

YOURSELF (178)

Ge 14:21; **Ex 18:**18, 18; **29:**26; **32:**22; **34:**2; **Lev 9:**7; **18:**20; **19:**18, 34; **Nu 5:**19, 20; **16:**16; **Dt 23:**13; **26:**16; **30:**20; **Jdg 8:**21; **19:**6, 9; **Ru 2:**9, 14; **1Sa 15:**17; **18:**17; **20:**8, 30; **25:**26; **28:**2; **2Sa 1:**16; **7:**23; **14:**13; **18:**13; **22:**26, 27, 27; **1Ki 3:**11; **14:**2; **18:**1, 37; **21:**20; **22:**25; **2Ki 2:**2, 4, 6; **4:**30; **5:**10; **22:**19; **1Ch 17:**21; **2Ch 18:**24; **19:**3; **20:**37; **21:**15; **34:**27, 27; **Job 5:**27; **22:**26; **33:**12; **35:**8; **36:**18; **38:**3; **40:**7; **Ps 18:**25, 26, 26; **27:**9; **52:**1; **65:**6; **80:**3, 7, 15, 15, 19; **89:**46; **93:**2; **109:**27; **Pr 6:**2, 3, 5; **11:**17; **15:**32; **22:**18; **23:**4, 12; **26:**27; **27:**2; **29:**24; **Ecc 5:**6; **7:**16, 22; **12:**4; **Isa 14:**13; **22:**16; **47:**2; **48:**2; **49:**21; **51:**9, 9; **57:**10; **Jer 3:**1; **13:**22; **14:**21; **32:**8; **45:**5; **La 3:**44; **Eze 3:**10, 24; **4:**4, 9, 10; **16:**15, 36; **23:**21, 30, 30, 30; **28:**3; **32:**2; **38:**14; **Da 5:**22; **10:**12; **Am 7:**17; **Mal 2:**15, 16; **Mt 6:**6; **16:**25; **19:**19; **22:**39; **26:**25, 62; **27:**40; **Mk 8:**11, 35; **12:**31; **14:**60; **15:**30; **Lk 4:**23; **7:**6; **9:**24; **10:**27; **23:**37, 39; **Jn 1:**22, 46; **7:**52; **8:**13; **10:**33; **14:**22; **Ac 5:**3; **21:**24; **23:**3; **24:**8; **Ro 2:**1, 5, 17, 21; **11:**20; **13:**9; **14:**22; **1Co 6:**19; **11:**28, 29; **Gal 5:**14; **6:**1, 3, 4; **Php 2:**3; **1Ti 4:**7, 15, 16; **5:**22; **2Ti 2:**4, 21; **Tit 2:**7; **Heb 13:**3; **Jas 1:**22, 24, 26; **2:**8; **1Pe 4:**19

YOURSELVES (175)

Ge 35:2; **45:**5, 12; **47:**24, 24; **Ex 5:**11; **22:**21; **30:**15, 32, 37; **34:**17; **Lev 11:**43, 44; **17:**15; **18:**24, 30; **19:**4; **20:**7, 25; **23:**27, 32; **Nu 18:**5; **28:**22, 30; **29:**5; **31:**18, 19; **32:**20; **34:**13; **35:**13; **Dt 1:**19; **4:**16, 25; **6:**6; **7:**17; **9:**4; **10:**19, 21; **11:**15, 18; **14:**1, 21; **18:**16; **20:**14; **28:**68; **Jos 3:**5; **6:**18; **7:**14; **8:**2; **17:**15; **22:**19; **Jdg 15:**12; **1Sa 10:**19; **16:**5; **2Ki 3:**17; **1Ch 15:**12; **2Ch 29:**5; **30:**7, 8; **35:**6; **Ezr 10:**11; **Job 19:**29; **27:**12; **42:**8; **Pr 5:**17; **Isa 1:**16; **8:**9; **29:**15; **33:**1; **50:**11; **52:**1, 11; **58:**3, 5, 5; **62:**9; **Jer 2:**17, 20, 30; **5:**19; **6:**26; **7:**8, 21; **25:**7; **37:**9; **44:**7, 8, 8; **49:**16, 30; **51:**6, 45; **La 2:**18; **Eze 13:**18; **16:**28; **18:**31; **20:**7, 30, 30, 31, 43; **23:**40; **24:**22; **34:**2, 8, 18, 18; **36:**31; **39:**19; **47:**22; **Hos 4:**6; **9:**1; **Joel 1:**13; **Am 5:**26; **6:**5, 6; **Ob** 3, 13; **Mic 1:**16; **6:**15; **Zep 3:**11; **Zec 7:**6; **Mal 1:**5; **Mt 23:**13, 15, 31; **25:**9; **Mk 9:**50; **Lk 11:**48, 52; **12:**57; **17:**14; **22:**17; **23:**28; **Jn 3:**28; **16:**19; **Ac 2:**40; **5:**39; **6:**3; **13:**46; **14:**15; **Ro 6:**11, 13, 19; **12:**3, 19; **13:**12; **1Co 1:**10; **3:**18; **5:**2; **6:**2, 7, 8, 9; **10:**15; **11:**34; **2Co 3:**2; **6:**17; **7:**11; **13:**5, 5; **Gal 5:**4, 15; **Eph 4:**3, 3; **5:**19; **Col 3:**10, 12; **4:**2; **1Th 1:**7; **2:**1, 10; **Jas 4:**7; **1Pe 4:**1; **5:**6

SELECTED INDEX TO THE FOOTNOTES OF THE NEW LIVING TRANSLATION

FEATURES OF THE SELECTED INDEX TO NLT FOOTNOTES

NLT WORD HEADING
The indexed word as spelled in NLT footnotes (see the introduction, page ix).

FREQUENCY COUNT
Total number of occurrences in this index (see the introduction, page ix).

ADAR (10)

NLT CONTEXT
Locates the footnote within the NLT text (see the introduction, page ix).

BRACES { }
Enclose the text of the NLT context (see the introduction, page ix).

ELLIPSES (...)
Used to abridge the footnote text (see the introduction, page ix).

Ezr 6:15 {on March 12,} Aramaic *on the third day of the month* ***A****,* of the Hebrew calendar....

BIBLICAL REFERENCE
See the abbreviations in the first table below.

INDEXED WORD
Abbreviated by its first letter, ***bold italic*** or **bold** depending on whether the indexed word is *italic* or roman in the footnote (see the introduction, page ix).

Est 9:17 {the following day} Hebrew *on the fourteenth day,* of the Hebrew month of **A**.

ABBREVIATIONS USED FOR CONTEXTS

BOOKS OF THE BIBLE

1Ch	1 Chronicles
1Co	1 Corinthians
1Jn	1 John
1Ki	1 Kings
1Pe	1 Peter
1Sa	1 Samuel
1Th	1 Thessalonians
1Ti	1 Timothy
2Ch	2 Chronicles
2Co	2 Corinthians
2Jn	2 John
2Ki	2 Kings
2Pe	2 Peter
2Sa	2 Samuel
2Th	2 Thessalonians
2Ti	2 Timothy
3Jn	3 John
Ac	Acts
Am	Amos
Col	Colossians
Da	Daniel
Dt	Deuteronomy
Ecc	Ecclesiastes
Eph	Ephesians
Est	Esther
Ex	Exodus
Eze	Ezekiel
Ezr	Ezra
Gal	Galatians
Ge	Genesis
Hab	Habakkuk
Hag	Haggai
Heb	Hebrews
Hos	Hosea
Isa	Isaiah
Jas	James
Jdg	Judges
Jer	Jeremiah
Jn	John
Jnh	Jonah
Job	Job
Joel	Joel
Jos	Joshua
Jude	Jude
La	Lamentations
Lev	Leviticus
Lk	Luke
Mal	Malachi
Mic	Micah
Mk	Mark
Mt	Matthew
Na	Nahum
Ne	Nehemiah
Nu	Numbers
Ob	Obadiah
Phm	Philemon
Php	Philippians
Pr	Proverbs
Ps	Psalms
Rev	Revelation
Ro	Romans
Ru	Ruth
SS	Song of Songs
Tit	Titus
Zec	Zechariah
Zep	Zephaniah

OTHER

S	Shorter Endingof Mark
T	Psalm Titles

ABBREVIATIONS USED WITHIN FOOTNOTES

1 Kgs	1 Kings
1 Sam	1 Samuel
2 Chr	2 Chronicles
2 Kgs	2 Kings
2 Sam	2 Samuel
Dan	Daniel
Deut	Deuteronomy
Exod	Exodus
Ezek	Ezekiel
Ezra	Ezra
Gen	Genesis
Hab	Habakkuk
Hag	Haggai
Hos	Hosea
Isa	Isaiah
Jer	Jeremiah
Judg	Judges
Josh	Joshua
Lev	Leviticus
Mal	Malachi
Matt	Matthew
Mic	Micah
Neh	Nehemiah
Num	Numbers
Prov	Proverbs
Ps	Psalm
Pss	Psalms
Zech	Zechariah
Zeph	Zephaniah

A

AARON (2)
1Ch 15: 4 {are the priests} Hebrew *descendants of* ***A***.
Heb 7:11 {and Aaron?} Greek *according to the order of* ***A***.

ABADDON (2)
Pr 15:11 {Death and Destruction} Hebrew *Sheol and* ***A***.
27:20 {Death and Destruction} Hebrew *Sheol and* ***A***.

ABARIM (4)
Nu 27:12 {of the river,} Hebrew *the mountains of* ***A***.
33:47 {of the river,} Hebrew *the mountains of* ***A***;...
Dt 32:49 {of the river,} Hebrew *the mountains of* ***A***.
Jer 22:20 {of the river.} Hebrew *in* ***A***.

ABBA (5)
Mk 14:36 {"Abba,} ***A*** is an Aramaic term for "father."
Ro 8:15 {"Father, dear Father."} Greek *"**A**, Father."* ***A*** is an Aramaic term for "father."
Gal 4: 6 {your dear Father.} Greek *into your hearts, crying, "**A**, Father."* **A** is an Aramaic term for "Father."

ABDOMEN (2)
Nu 5:21 {makes you infertile.} Hebrew *when he causes your thigh to waste away and your* ***a*** *to swell.*
5:22 {make you infertile.} Hebrew *enter your body so that your* ***a*** *swells and your thigh wastes away.*

ABDON (1)
2Ch 34:20 {son of Micaiah,} As in parallel text at 2 Kgs 22:12; Hebrew reads ***A*** *son of Micah.*

ABEL-BETH-MAACAH (1)
2Ch 16: 4 {Ijon, Dan, Abel-beth-maacah,} As in parallel text at 1 Kgs 15:20; Hebrew reads *Abel-maim,* another name for **A**.

ABEL-MAIM (1)
2Ch 16: 4 {Ijon, Dan, Abel-beth-maacah,} As in parallel text at 1 Kgs 15:20; Hebrew reads ***A***, another name for Abel-beth-maacah.

ABEL-MIZRAIM (1)
Ge 50:11 {the place Abel-mizraim,} ***A*** means "mourning of the Egyptians."

ABI (1)
2Ki 18: 2 {mother was Abijah,} As in parallel text at 2 Chr 29:1; Hebrew reads ***A***, a variant name for Abijah.

ABIASAPH (2)
1Ch 6:23 {Elkanah, Abiasaph,} Hebrew *Ebiasaph,* a variant name for **A** (also in 6:37); compare parallel text at Exod 6:24.
9:19 {descendant of Abiasaph,} Hebrew *Ebiasaph,* a variant name for **A**; compare Exod 6:24.

ABIATHAR (1)
2Sa 15:27 {You and Abiathar} Hebrew lacks *and* ***A***; compare 15:29.

ABIB (4)
Ex 13: 4 {in early spring} Hebrew *in the month of* ***A***....
23:15 {in early spring,} Hebrew *in the month of* ***A***....
34:18 {in early spring,} Hebrew *in the month of* ***A***....
Dt 16: 1 {in early spring,} Hebrew *in the month of* ***A***....

ABIEL (1)
1Ch 11:32 {Abi-albon} As in parallel text at 2 Sam 23:31; Hebrew reads ***A***.

ABIHAIL (1)
Est 2:15 {was Esther's turn} Hebrew *the turn of Esther, the daughter of* ***A***, *who was Mordecai's uncle, who had adopted her.*

ABIJAH (3)
1Ki 14:31 {his son Abijam} Also known as ***A***.
15: 1 {Abijam} Also known as ***A***.
2Ki 18: 2 {mother was Abijah,} As in parallel text at 2 Chr 29:1; Hebrew reads *Abi,* a variant name for **A**.

ABIMELECH (2)
2Sa 11:21 {son Abimelech killed} Hebrew *Was not* ***A*** *son of Jerubbesheth killed.*
1Ch 18:16 {Ahitub and Ahimelech} As in some Hebrew manuscripts, Syriac version, and Latin Vulgate (see also 2 Sam 8:17); most Hebrew manuscripts read ***A***.

ABISHALOM (1)
1Ki 15: 2 {daughter of Absalom.} Hebrew ***A*** (also in 15:10), a variant name for Absalom; compare 2 Chr 11:20.

ABOMINATION (5)
Da 9:27 {that causes desecration,} Hebrew *an* ***a*** *of desolation.*
11:31 {that causes desecration.} Hebrew *the* ***a*** *of desolation.*
12:11 {that causes desecration} Hebrew *the* ***a*** *of desolation.*
Mt 24:15 {that causes desecration} Greek *the* ***a*** *of desolation.* See Dan 9:27; 11:31; 12:11.
Mk 13:14 {that causes desecration} Greek *the* ***a*** *of desolation.* See Dan 9:27; 11:31; 12:11.

ABOMINATIONS (1)
Da 9:27 {his terrible deeds,} Hebrew *on the wing of* ***a***; the meaning of the Hebrew is uncertain.

ABOVE (2)
Jn 3: 3 {are born again,} Or *born from* ***a***; also in 3:7.
Jas 1:17 {all heaven's lights.} Greek *from* ***a***, *from the Father of lights.*

ABRAHAM (7)
Ge 17: 5 {known as Abraham,} *Abram* means "exalted father"; ***A*** means "father of many."
24: 9 {solemn oath} Hebrew *put his hand under the thigh of* ***A*** *his master and swore an oath.*
Lk 13:16 {this dear woman} Greek *this woman, a daughter of* ***A***.
Jn 8:39 {his good example.} Some manuscripts read *if you are children of* ***A***, *follow his example.*
8:57 {have seen Abraham?} Some manuscripts read *How can you say* ***A*** *has seen you?*
8:58 {was even born!"} Or *"Truly, truly, before* ***A*** *was, I am."*
Heb 7: 5 {their own relatives.} Greek *their brothers, who are descendants of* ***A***.

ABRAHAM'S (1)
Lk 16:22 {be with Abraham.} Greek *into* ***A*** *bosom.*

ABRAM (1)
Ge 17: 5 {known as Abraham,} ***A*** means "exalted father"; *Abraham* means "father of many."

ABSALOM (2)
2Sa 13:39 {his son Absalom.} Or *no longer felt a need to go out after* ***A***.
1Ki 15: 2 {daughter of Absalom.} Hebrew *Abishalom* (also in 15:10), a variant name for **A**; compare 2 Chr 11:20.

ACCEPTABLE (2)
Isa 61: 2 {favor has come,} Or *to proclaim the* ***a*** *year of the LORD.*
Lk 4:18[-19] {favor has come.} Or *and to proclaim the* ***a*** *year of the Lord.* Isa 61:1-2.

ACCEPTING (1)
1Ti 2:15 {saved through childbearing} Or *will be saved by* ***a*** *their role as mothers,* or *will be saved by the birth of the Child.*

ACCO (1)
Mic 1:10 {weep at all.} Greek version reads *weep not in* ***A***.

ACCOMPANIED (1)
Ac 16:10 {So we} Luke, the writer of this book, here joined Paul and **a** him on his journey.

ACCOMPLISHED (1)
Ro 8: 4 {accomplished for us} Or ***a*** *by us.*

ACCORDING (23)
Ex 30:13 {of an ounce} Hebrew *half a shekel* [6 grams], ***a*** *to the sanctuary shekel, 20 gerahs to each shekel.*
30:24 {and one gallon} Hebrew *500 shekels* [5.7 kilograms] *of cassia,* ***a*** *to the sanctuary shekel, and 1 hin* [3.8 liters].
38:24 {about 2,200 pounds,} Hebrew *29 talents* [2,175 pounds or 986 kilograms] *and 730 shekels* [18.3 pounds or 8.3 kilograms], ***a*** *to the sanctuary shekel.*
38:25 {about 7,545 pounds.} Hebrew *100 talents* [7,500 pounds or 3,400 kilograms] *and 1,775 shekels* [44.4 pounds or 20.2 kilograms], ***a*** *to the sanctuary shekel.*
38:26 {ounce of silver} Hebrew *1 beka* [6 grams] *per person, that is, half a shekel,* ***a*** *to the sanctuary shekel.*
Lev 27: 3 {pieces of silver} Hebrew *50 shekels of silver,* ***a*** *to the standard sanctuary shekel,* each about 0.4 ounces or 11 grams in weight. The term *shekels* also appears in 27:4, 5, 6, 7, 16.
27:25 {standard sanctuary shekel.} Hebrew *measured* ***a*** *to the sanctuary shekel, 20 gerahs to each shekel.* Each sanctuary shekel was about 0.4 ounces or 11 grams in weight.
Nu 3:47 {standard sanctuary shekel.} Hebrew *5 shekels* [2 ounces or 57 grams] *apiece,* ***a*** *to the sanctuary shekel, 20 gerahs to each shekel.*
3:50 {pounds in weight.} Hebrew *1,365 shekels* [15.5 kilograms], ***a*** *to the sanctuary shekel.*
7:13 {about 1 3/4 pounds.} Hebrew *silver platter weighing 130 shekels* [1.5 kilograms] *and a silver basin weighing 70 shekels* [0.8 kilograms], ***a*** *to the sanctuary shekel;* also in 7:19, 25, 31, 37, 43, 49, 55, 61, 67, 73, 79, 85.
18:16 {standard sanctuary shekel.} Hebrew *5 shekels* [about 2 ounces or 57 grams] *of silver,* ***a*** *to the sanctuary shekel, 20 gerahs to each shekel.*
1Ch 15:20 {play the lyres.} Hebrew adds *a to Alamoth,* which is probably a musical term. The meaning of the Hebrew is uncertain.
15:21 {play the harps.} Hebrew adds ***a*** *to the Sheminith,* which is probably a musical term. The meaning of the Hebrew is uncertain.
Ps 6: T {an eight-stringed instrument.} Hebrew *with stringed instruments;* ***a*** *to the sheminith.*
8: T {a stringed instrument.} Hebrew ***a*** *to the gittith.*
12: T {an eight-stringed instrument.} Hebrew ***a*** *to the sheminith.*
46: T {by soprano voices.} Hebrew ***a*** *to alamoth.*
81: T {a stringed instrument.} Hebrew ***a*** *to the gittith.*
84: T {a stringed instrument.} Hebrew ***a*** *to the gittith.*
Da 1: 1 {reign in Judah,} The third year of Jehoiakim's reign, **a** to the Babylonian system of reckoning, was 605 B.C.
Hab 3: 1 {the prophet Habakkuk:} Hebrew adds ***a*** *to shigionoth,* probably indicating the musical setting for the prayer.
Mt 2:16 {two years earlier.} Or ***a*** *to the time he calculated from the wise men.*
Heb 7:11 {Levi and Aaron?} Greek ***a*** *to the order of Aaron.*

ACCOUNT (2)
Ecc 3:15 {in its turn.} Hebrew *For God calls the past to* ***a***.
Jn 1:51 {Son of Man."} See Gen 28:10-17, the **a** of Jacob's ladder.

ACCUSER (1)
Zec 3: 1 {Satan} Or *The* ***A***; Hebrew reads *The Adversary;* also in 3:2.

ACCUSERS (1)
Ac 24: 6 {we arrested him.} Some manuscripts add *We would have judged him by our law, [7]but Lysias, the commander of the garrison, came and took him violently away from us, [8]commanding his* ***a*** *to come before you.*

ACHAIA (7)
Ac 18: 1 {went to Corinth.} *Athens* and *Corinth* were major cities in **A**, the region on the southern end of the Greek peninsula.
Ro 15:26 {believers in Greece} Greek *Macedonia and* ***A***, the northern and southern regions of Greece.
1Co 16:15 {Christians in Greece,} Greek *were the firstfruits in* ***A***, the southern region of the Greek peninsula.
2Co 1: 1 {Christians throughout Greece.} Greek ***A***, the southern region of the Greek peninsula.
9: 2 {Christians in Greece} Greek ***A***, the southern region of the Greek peninsula.
11:10 {all over Greece.} Greek ***A***.
1Th 1: 7 {Christians in Greece.} Greek *Macedonia and* ***A***, the northern and southern regions of Greece; also in 1:8.

ACHAR (2)
1Ch 2: 7 {Achan} Hebrew ***A***; compare Josh 7:1. ***A*** means "disaster."

ACHOR (2)
Jos 7:26 {Valley of Trouble} Hebrew *valley of* ***A***.
Hos 2:15 {Valley of Trouble} Hebrew *valley of* ***A***.

ACQUIRE (1)
Ge 4: 1 {birth to Cain,} *Cain* sounds like a Hebrew term that can mean "bring forth" or "**a**."

ACQUIRED (1)
Ge 4: 1 {have brought forth} Or *I have* ***a***.

ACQUIRING (1)
Eph 1:18 {to his people.} Or *realize how much God has been honored by* ***a*** *his people.*

ACT (1)
Lev 19:16 {among your people.} Hebrew *Do not* ***a*** *as a merchant toward your own people.*

ACTS (1)
1Sa 13: 1 {for forty-two years.} Hebrew *reigned...and two;* the number is incomplete in the Hebrew. Compare **A** 13:21.

ACZIB (1)
Mic 1:14 {town of Aczib} ***A*** means "deception."

ADAM'S (1)
Ge 2:21 {of Adam's ribs} Or *took a part of A side.*

ADAR (10)
Ezr 6:15 {on March 12,} Aramaic *on the third day of the month A,* of the Hebrew calendar....
Est 3:7 {a year later.} As in Greek version, which reads *the thirteenth day of the twelfth month, the month of A* (see also 3:13). Hebrew reads *in the twelfth month,* of the Hebrew calendar....
3:13 {on March 7.} Hebrew *on the thirteenth day of the twelfth month, the month of A,* of the Hebrew calendar....
8:12 {the next year.} Hebrew *the thirteenth day of the twelfth month, the month of A,* of the Hebrew calendar....
9:1 {on March 7} Hebrew *on the thirteenth day of the twelfth month, the month of A,* of the Hebrew calendar....
9:15 {on March 8} Hebrew *the fourteenth day of the month of A,* of the Hebrew calendar....
9:17 {on March 7.} Hebrew *on the thirteenth day of the month of A,* of the Hebrew calendar....
9:17 {the following day} Hebrew *on the fourteenth day,* of the Hebrew month of A.
9:18 {the third day,} Hebrew *killing their enemies on the thirteenth day and the fourteenth day, and then rested on the fifteenth day,* of the Hebrew month of A.
9:19 {in late winter,} Hebrew *on the fourteenth day of the month of A....*

ADD (42)
Ge 30:24 {named him Joseph,} *Joseph* means "may he **a**."
1Sa 1:11 {never be cut."} Some manuscripts **a** *He will drink neither wine nor intoxicants.*
1:22 {the LORD permanently."} Some manuscripts **a** *I will offer him as a Nazirite for all time.*
Eze 40:8 {of the gateway} Many Hebrew manuscripts **a** *which faced inward toward the Temple; it was one rod* [10.5 feet or 3.2 meters] *deep.* [9]*Then he measured the foyer of the gateway,...*
Mt 5:22 {angry with someone,} Some manuscripts **a** *without cause.*
5:44 {love your enemies!} Some manuscripts **a** *Bless those who curse you, do good to those who hate you.*
6:13 {the evil one.} Or *from evil.* Some manuscripts **a** *For yours is the kingdom and the power and the glory forever. Amen.*
17:20 {would be impossible."} Some manuscripts **a** verse 21, *But this kind of demon won't leave unless you have prayed and fasted.*
18:10 {heavenly Father.} Some manuscripts **a** verse 11, *And I, the Son of Man, have come to save the lost.*
19:9 {has been unfaithful.} Some manuscripts **a** *And the man who marries a divorced woman commits adultery.*
23:13 {go in yourselves.} Some manuscripts **a** verse 14, *How terrible it will be for you teachers of religious law and you Pharisees. Hypocrites! You shamelessly cheat widows out of their property, and then, to cover up the kind of people you really are, you make long prayers in public. Because of this, your punishment will be the greater.*
27:35 {by throwing dice.} Greek *by casting lots.* A few late manuscripts **a** *This fulfilled the word of the prophet: "They divided my clothes among themselves and cast lots for my robe."* See Ps 22:18.
27:49 {and save him."} Some manuscripts **a** *And another took a spear and pierced his side, and out came water and blood.*
Mk 7:4 {pitchers, and kettles.} Some Greek manuscripts **a** *and dining couches.*
7:15 {say and do!} Some manuscripts **a** verse 16, *Anyone who is willing to hear should listen and understand.*
7:24 {region of Tyre.} Some Greek manuscripts **a** *and Sidon.*
9:29 {only by prayer.} Some manuscripts **a** *and fasting.*
9:43 {with two hands.} Some manuscripts **a** verse 44 (which is identical with 9:48).
9:45 {with two feet.} Some manuscripts **a** verse 46 (which is identical with 9:48).
9:49 {purified with fire.} Greek *salted with fire.* Some manuscripts **a** *and every sacrifice will be salted with salt.*
10:24 {is very hard} Some manuscripts **a** *for those who trust in riches.*
11:25 {your sins, too.} Some manuscripts **a** verse 26, *But if you do not forgive, neither will your Father who is in heaven forgive your sins.*
13:33 {and keep watch.} Some manuscripts **a** *and pray.*
15:27 {side of his.} Some manuscripts **a** verse 28, *And the Scripture was fulfilled that said, "He was counted among those who were rebels."* See Isa 53:12.
Lk 1:28 {is with you!} Some manuscripts **a** *Blessed are you among women.*
9:54 {burn them up} Some manuscripts **a** *as Elijah did.*
9:55 {and rebuked them.} Some manuscripts **a** *And he said, "You don't realize what your hearts are like.* [56]*For the Son of Man has not come to destroy men's lives, but to save them."*
11:2[-4] {yield to temptation.} Some manuscripts **a** additional portions of the Lord's Prayer as it reads in Matt 6:9-13.
11:11 {your children ask} Some manuscripts **a** *for bread, do you give them a stone? Or if they ask.*
15:21 {called your son.} Some manuscripts **a** *Please take me on as a hired man.*
17:35 {the other left.} Some manuscripts **a** verse 36, *Two men will be working in the field; one will be taken, the other left.*
23:16 {will release him."} Some manuscripts **a** verse 17, *For it was necessary for him to release one [prisoner] for them during the feast.*
Jn 3:13 {Son of Man,} Some manuscripts **a** *who lives in heaven.*
5:3 {on the porches.} Some manuscripts **a** *waiting for a certain movement of the water,* [4]*for an angel of the Lord came from time to time and stirred up the water. And the first person to step down into it afterward was healed.*
Ac 8:36 {I be baptized?"} Some manuscripts **a** verse 37, *"You can," Philip answered, "if you believe with all your heart." And the eunuch replied, "I believe that Jesus Christ is the Son of God."*
15:33 {had sent them.} Some manuscripts **a** verse 34, *But Silas decided to stay there.*
24:6 {we arrested him.} Some manuscripts **a** *We would have judged him by our law,* [7]*but Lysias, the commander of the garrison, came and took him violently away from us,* [8]*commanding his accusers to come before you.*
28:28 {will accept it."} Some manuscripts **a** verse 29, *And when he had said these words, the Jews departed, greatly disagreeing with each other.*
Ro 16:23 {a Christian brother.} Some manuscripts **a** verse 24, *May the grace of our Lord Jesus Christ be with you all. Amen.*
1Co 16:24 {in Christ Jesus.} Some manuscripts **a** *Amen.*
Heb 2:7 {glory and honor.} Some manuscripts **a** *You put him in charge of everything you made.*
1Jn 5:7 {these three witnesses} Some very late manuscripts **a** *in heaven—the Father, the Word, and the Holy Spirit, and these three are one. And we have three witnesses on earth.*

ADDITIONAL (1)
Lk 11:2[-4] {yield to temptation.} Some manuscripts add **a** portions of the Lord's Prayer as it reads in Matt 6:9-13.

ADDON (1)
Ne 7:61 {Tel-harsha, Kerub, Addan,} As in parallel text at Ezra 2:59; Hebrew reads *A.*

ADDS (7)
Jdg 19:28 {was no answer.} Greek version **a** *for she was dead.*
1Sa 14:41 {among the others?"} Greek version **a** *If the fault is with me or my son Jonathan, respond with Urim; but if the men of Israel are at fault, respond with Thummim.*
1Ch 15:20 {play the lyres.} Hebrew **a** *according to Alamoth,* which is probably a musical term. The meaning of the Hebrew is uncertain.
15:21 {play the harps.} Hebrew **a** *according to the Sheminith,* which is probably a musical term. The meaning of the Hebrew is uncertain.
Ps 18:13 {a mighty shout.} As in Greek version (see also 2 Sam 22:14); Hebrew **a** *raining down hail and burning coals.*
Hab 3:1 {the prophet Habakkuk:} Hebrew **a** *according to shigionoth,* probably indicating the musical setting for the prayer.
3:3 {and Mount Paran.} Hebrew **a** *selah;* also in 3:9, 13. The meaning of this Hebrew term is uncertain; it is probably a musical or literary term.

ADINO (1)
2Sa 23:8 {a single battle.} As in some Greek manuscripts (see also 1 Chr 11:11); the Hebrew is uncertain, though it might be rendered *the Three. It was A the Eznite who killed eight hundred men at one time.*

ADJOINING (1)
Mic 1:11 {people of Beth-ezel} *Beth-ezel* means "**a** house."

ADONIRAM (1)
2Ch 10:18 {Adoniram,} Hebrew *Hadoram,* a variant name for A; compare 1 Kgs 4:6; 5:14; 12:18.

ADOPTED (1)
Est 2:15 {was Esther's turn} Hebrew *the turn of Esther, the daughter of Abihail, who was Mordecai's uncle, who had **a** her.*

ADORAM (2)
2Sa 20:24 {Adoniram} As in Greek version (see also 1 Kgs 4:6; 5:14); Hebrew reads *A.*
1Ki 12:18 {Rehoboam sent Adoniram,} As in some Greek manuscripts and Syriac version (see also 4:6; 5:14); Hebrew reads *A.*

ADRIA (1)
Ac 27:27 {Sea of Adria,} The *Sea of A* is in the central Mediterranean; it is not to be confused with the Adriatic Sea.

ADRIATIC (1)
Ac 27:27 {Sea of Adria,} The *Sea of Adria* is in the central Mediterranean; it is not to be confused with the **A** Sea.

ADULT (1)
Ac 4:4 {women and children.} Greek *5,000 **a** males.*

ADULTEROUS (1)
Pr 20:16 {of a foreigner.} An alternate reading in the Hebrew text is *the debt of an **a** woman;* compare 27:13.

ADULTERY (1)
Mt 19:9 {has been unfaithful.} Some manuscripts add *And the man who marries a divorced woman commits **a**.*

ADVERSARY (1)
Zec 3:1 {Satan} Or *The Accuser;* Hebrew reads *The A;* also in 3:2.

ADVISERS (1)
Da 3:3 {all these officials} Aramaic *the princes, prefects, governors, **a**, counselors, judges, magistrates, and all the provincial officials.*

ADVOCATE (3)
Jn 14:16 {you another Counselor,} Or *Comforter,* or *Encourager,* or *A.* Greek *Paraclete;* also in 14:26.
15:26 {you the Counselor} Or *Comforter,* or *Encourager,* or *A.* Greek *Paraclete.*
16:7 {don't, the Counselor} Or *Comforter,* or *Encourager,* or *A.* Greek *Paraclete.*

AFFAIRS (1)
Lk 2:49 {my Father's house."} Or *"Didn't you realize that I should be involved with my Father's **a**?"*

AFFECTION (1)
Ge 29:34 {Levi,} *Levi* sounds like a Hebrew term that means "being attached" or "feeling **a** for."

AFRICA (3)
Mt 27:32 {from Cyrene,} *Cyrene* was a city in northern **A**.
Mk 15:21 {from Cyrene,} *Cyrene* was a city in northern **A**.
Lk 23:26 {of Cyrene,} *Cyrene* was a city in northern **A**.

AFTER (13 of 16)
Ge 5:3 {of his father.} Hebrew *was in his own likeness, **a** his image.*
5:4 {birth of Seth,} Or *A the birth of this ancestor of Seth;* similarly in 5:7, 10, 13, 16, 19, 22, 26.
11:12[-13] {sons and daughters.} Greek version reads [12]*When Arphaxad was 135 years old, his son Cainan was born.* [13]*A the birth of Cainan, Arphaxad lived another 430 years and had other sons and daughters, and then he died. When Cainan was 130 years old, his son Shelah was born. A the birth of Shelah, Cainan lived another 330 years and had other sons and daughters, and then he died.*
Nu 26:23 {its ancestor Puah.} As in Samaritan Pentateuch, Greek and Syriac versions, and Latin Vulgate (see also 1 Chr 7:1); Hebrew reads *The Punite clan, named **a** its ancestor Puvah.*
26:40 {their ancestor Ard.} As in Samaritan Pentateuch, some Greek manuscripts, and Latin Vulgate; Hebrew lacks *named **a** their ancestor Ard.*
2Sa 13:39 {his son Absalom.} Or *no longer felt a need to go out **a** Absalom.*
Da 9:26 {sets of seven,} Hebrew *A 62 sevens.*
Zec 6:6 {is going west,} Hebrew *is going **a** them.*
Mt 16:2[-3] {of the times!} Several manuscripts do not include any of the words in 16:2-3 **a** *He replied.*
27:51[-53] {to many people.} Or *The earth shook, rocks split apart, tombs opened, and many bodies of godly men and women who had died were raised from the dead. A Jesus' resurrection, they left the cemetery, went into the holy city of Jerusalem, and appeared to many people.*
27:62 {the Passover ceremonies} Or *On the next day, which is **a** the Preparation.*
28:1 {on Sunday morning,} Greek *A the Sabbath, on the first day of the week.*
1Co 14:35 {in church meetings.} Some manuscripts place verses 34-35 **a** 14:40.

AFTERWARD (1)
Jn 5:3 {on the porches.} Some manuscripts add *waiting for a certain movement of the water,* [4]*for an angel of the Lord came from time to time and stirred up the water. And the first person to step down into it **a** was healed.*

AGAG (1)

1Sa 15:32 {have been spared!"} Dead Sea Scrolls and Greek version read *A arrived hesitantly, for he thought, "Surely this is the bitterness of death."*

AGE (4)

Mt 24: 3 {of the world} Or *the **a**.*
24:34 {you, this generation} Or *this **a**,* or *this nation.*
Mk 13:30 {you, this generation} Or *this **a**,* or *this nation.*
Lk 21:32 {you, this generation} Or *this **a**,* or *this nation.*

AGES (1)

Rev 15: 3 {of the nations.} Some manuscripts read *King of the **a**;* other manuscripts read *King of the saints.*

AGRIPPA (1)

Ac 25:13 {his sister, Bernice,} Greek *A the king and Bernice arrived.*

AHASUERUS (2)

Ezr 4: 6 {Xerxes} Hebrew *A*, another name for Xerxes.
Est 1: 1 {King Xerxes,} Hebrew *A*, another name for Xerxes; also throughout the book of Esther.

AHAZ (1)

1Ch 9:41 {Tahrea, and Ahaz.} As in Syriac version and Latin Vulgate (see also 8:35); Hebrew lacks *and A.*

AHAZIAH (2)

2Ch 21:17 {youngest son, Ahaziah,} Hebrew *Jehoahaz*, a variant name for A; compare 22:1.
22: 8 {and Ahaziah's relatives} As in Greek version (see also 2 Kgs 10:13); Hebrew reads *and sons of the brothers of A.*

AI (1)

Jos 8:28 {So Ai} *A* means "ruin."

AKRABBIM (3)

Nu 34: 4 {past Scorpion Pass} Hebrew *the ascent of A.*
Jos 15: 3 {of Scorpion Pass} Hebrew *A.*
Jdg 1:36 {from Scorpion Pass} Hebrew *A.*

ALABASTER (3)

Mt 26: 7 {beautiful jar} Greek *an **a** jar.*
Mk 14: 3 {of expensive perfume.} Greek *an **a** jar of expensive ointment, pure nard.*
Lk 7:37 {a beautiful jar} Greek *an **a** jar.*

ALAMOTH (2)

1Ch 15:20 {play the lyres.} Hebrew adds *according to A*, which is probably a musical term. The meaning of the Hebrew is uncertain.
Ps 46: T {by soprano voices.} Hebrew *according to **a**.*

ALGUM (2)

2Ch 2: 8 {cypress, and almug} Hebrew ***a**;* compare 9:10-11 and parallel text at 1 Kgs 10:11-12.
9:10 {of almug wood} Hebrew ***a** wood* (also in 9:11); compare parallel text at 1 Kgs 10:11-12.

ALIAH (1)

1Ch 1:51 {were Timna, Alvah,} As in parallel text at Gen 36:40; Hebrew reads *A.*

ALIAN (1)

1Ch 1:40 {Shobal were Alvan,} As in many Hebrew manuscripts and a few Greek manuscripts (see also Gen 36:23); most Hebrew manuscripts read *A.*

ALLON-BACUTH (1)

Ge 35: 8 {"Oak of Weeping."} Hebrew *A.*

ALLOW (1)

1Sa 10:27 {Saul ignored them.} Dead Sea Scroll 4QSam[a] continues: *Nahash, king of the Ammonites, had been grievously oppressing the Gadites and Reubenites who lived east of the Jordan River. He gouged out the right eye of each of the Israelites living there, and he didn't **a** anyone to come and rescue them. In fact, of all the Israelites east of the Jordan, there wasn't a single one whose right eye Nahash had not gouged out. But there were seven thousand men who had escaped from the Ammonites, and they had settled in Jabesh-gilead.*

ALMOND (1)

Jer 1:12 {I am watching,} The Hebrew word for "watching" sounds like the word for "**a** tree."

ALONG (1)

Jos 5: 1 {the Mediterranean coast} Hebrew ***a** the sea.*

ALREADY (2)

Ac 27: 9 {in the fall,} Greek *because the fast was now **a** gone by.* This fast happened on the Day of Atonement (*Yom Kippur*), which occurred in late September or early October.
1Co 5: 6[-7] {can stay pure.} Greek *Don't you realize that even a little leaven spreads quickly through the whole batch of dough? [7]Purge out the old leaven so that you can be a new batch of dough, just as you are **a** unleavened.*

ALTAR (4)

1Ki 6:20 {made of cedar.} Or *overlaid the **a** with cedar.* The meaning of the Hebrew is uncertain.
2Ki 23:16 {man of God} As in Greek version; Hebrew lacks *as Jeroboam stood beside the **a** at the festival. Then Josiah turned and looked up at the tomb of the man of God.*
Isa 29: 1 {certain for Ariel,} *Ariel* sounds like a Hebrew term that means "hearth" or "**a**."
Eze 43:13 {of the altar} Hebrew *measurements of the **a** in long cubits, each being a cubit* [18 inches or 45 centimeters] *and a handbreadth* [3 inches or 8 centimeters] *in length.* In this chapter, the distance measures are calculated using the Hebrew long cubit, which equals 21 inches or 53 centimeters.

ALTERNATE (1)

Pr 20:16 {of a foreigner.} An **a** reading in the Hebrew text is *the debt of an adulterous woman;* compare 27:13.

AMALEK (1)

1Ch 1:36 {born to Timna.} As in some Greek manuscripts (see also Gen 36:12); Hebrew reads *Kenaz, Timna, and A.*

AMAVITES (1)

Nu 22: 5 {land of Pethor} Or *who was at Pethor in the land of the A.*

AMEN (5)

Jer 11: 5 {"So be it,} Hebrew *A.*
Mt 6:13 {the evil one.} Or *from evil.* Some manuscripts add *For yours is the kingdom and the power and the glory forever. A.*
Ro 9: 5 {eternal praise! Amen.} Or *May God, who rules over everything, be praised forever. A.*
16:23 {a Christian brother.} Some manuscripts add verse 24, *May the grace of our Lord Jesus Christ be with you all. A.*
1Co 16:24 {in Christ Jesus.} Some manuscripts add *A.*

AMMINADAB (1)

SS 6:12 {my beloved one.} Or *among the royal chariots of my people,* or *among the chariots of A.* The meaning of the Hebrew is uncertain.

AMMONITE (1)

Nu 21:24 {Ammonites was fortified.} Or *because the terrain of the A frontier was rugged;* Hebrew *because the boundary of the Ammonites was strong.*

AMMONITES (7)

Nu 21:24 {Ammonites was fortified.} Or *because the terrain of the Ammonite frontier was rugged;* Hebrew *because the boundary of the A was strong.*
1Sa 10:27 {Saul ignored them.} Dead Sea Scroll 4QSam[a] continues: *Nahash, king of the A, had been grievously oppressing the Gadites and Reubenites who lived east of the Jordan River. He gouged out the right eye of each of the Israelites living there, and he didn't allow anyone to come and rescue them. In fact, of all the Israelites east of the Jordan, there wasn't a single one whose right eye Nahash had not gouged out. But there were seven thousand men who had escaped from the A, and they had settled in Jabesh-gilead.*
2Sa 12:30 {the king's head,} Greek version reads *removed the crown of Milcom;* compare 1 Kgs 11:5. Milcom, also called Molech, was the god of the **A**.
1Ch 20: 2 {the king's head,} Greek version and Latin Vulgate read *removed the crown of Milcom;* compare 1 Kgs 11:5. Milcom, also called Molech, was the god of the **A**.
2Ch 20: 1 {of the Meunites} As in some Greek manuscripts (see also 26:7); Hebrew reads *A.*
26: 8 {The Meunites} As in Greek version; Hebrew reads *A.* Compare 26:7.

AMON (2)

Ne 7:59 {Pokereth-hazzebaim, and Ami.} As in parallel text at Ezra 2:57; Hebrew reads *A.*
Mt 1:10 {father of Amos.} *Amos* is the same person as **A**. See 1 Chr 3:14.

AMONG (10)

SS 1: 9 {my beloved one!} Hebrew *I compare you, my beloved, to a mare **a** Pharaoh's chariots.*
6:12 {my beloved one.} Or ***a** the royal chariots of my people,* or *among the chariots of Amminadab.* The meaning of the Hebrew is uncertain.
6:12 {my beloved one.} Or *among the royal chariots of my people,* or ***a** the chariots of Amminadab.* The meaning of the Hebrew is uncertain.
Mt 27:35 {by throwing dice.} Greek *by casting lots.* A few late manuscripts add *This fulfilled the word of the prophet: "They divided my clothes **a** themselves and cast lots for my robe."* See Ps 22:18.
Mk 15:27 {side of his.} Some manuscripts add verse 28, *And the Scripture was fulfilled that said, "He was counted **a** those who were rebels."* See Isa 53:12.
Lk 1:28 {is with you!} Some manuscripts add *Blessed are you **a** women.*
2:14 {whom God favors.} Or *and peace on earth for all those pleasing God;* some manuscripts read *and peace on earth, goodwill **a** people.*
1Co 3:16 {God lives in} Or ***a**.*
1Th 2: 7 {as a mother} Some manuscripts read *we were as infants **a** you; we were as a mother.*
Jude 1:12 {can shipwreck you.} Or *they are contaminants **a** you,* or *they are stains.*

AMOS (5)

Ge 10:14 {the Philistines came.} Hebrew *Casluhites, from whom the Philistines came, Caphtorites.* Compare Jer 47:4; **A** 9:7.
1Ch 1:12 {the Philistines came.} Hebrew *Casluhites, from whom the Philistines came, Caphtorites.* See Jer 47:4; **A** 9:7.
Mt 1:10 {father of Amos.} *A* is the same person as Amon. See 1 Chr 3:14.
Ac 7:42[-43] {away in Babylon.'} **A** 5:25-27.
15:16[-18] {known long ago.'} **A** 9:11-12; Isa 45:21.

ANCESTOR (7)

Ge 4:18 {the father of} Or *the **a** of,* and so throughout the verse.
5: 3 {Seth was born,} Or *his son, the **a** of Seth, was born;* similarly in 5:6, 9, 12, 15, 18, 21, 25.
5: 4 {birth of Seth,} Or *After the birth of this **a** of Seth;* similarly in 5:7, 10, 13, 16, 19, 22, 26.
11:12 {Shelah was born.} Or *his son, the **a** of Shelah, was born;* similarly in 11:14, 16, 18, 20, 22, 24.
Nu 26:23 {its ancestor Puah.} As in Samaritan Pentateuch, Greek and Syriac versions, and Latin Vulgate (see also 1 Chr 7:1); Hebrew reads *The Punite clan, named after its **a** Puvah.*
26:40 {their ancestor Ard.} As in Samaritan Pentateuch, some Greek manuscripts, and Latin Vulgate; Hebrew lacks *named after their **a** Ard.*
Mt 1: 8 {was the father} Or ***a**;* also in 1:11.

ANGEL (1)

Jn 5: 3 {on the porches.} Some manuscripts add *waiting for a certain movement of the water, [4]for an **a** of the Lord came from time to time and stirred up the water. And the first person to step down into it afterward was healed.*

ANGELS (6)

Dt 32: 8 {of angelic beings.} As in Dead Sea Scrolls, which read *of the sons of God,* and Greek version, which reads *of the **a** of god;* Masoretic Text reads *of the sons of Israel.*
Ps 8: 5 {lower than God,} Or *a little lower than the **a**;* Hebrew reads *Elohim.*
Ac 7:53 {hands of angels.} Greek *received the Law as it was ordained by **a**.*
1Co 13: 1 {or on earth} Greek *in tongues of people and **a**.*
2Pe 2:10 {the glorious ones} *The glorious ones* are probably evil **a**; also in 2:11.
Jude 1: 8 {the glorious ones.} *The glorious ones* are probably evil **a**.

ANGER (1)

Mk 1:41 {Moved with pity,} Some manuscripts read *Moved with **a**.*

ANIMAL (1)

Lev 6: 6 {value in silver.} Or *and the **a** must be of the proper value;* Hebrew lacks *in silver;* compare 5:15.

ANIMALS (2)

Lev 11: 4 {animals named here} The identification of some of the **a**, birds, and insects in this chapter is uncertain.
Dt 14: 4 {are the animals} The identification of some of the **a** and birds listed in this chapter is uncertain.

ANOINTED (1)

Da 9:25 {the Anointed One} Or *an **a** one.*

ANOINTING (2)

1Jn 2:20 {come upon you,} Greek *But you have an **a** from the Holy One.*
2:27 {the Holy Spirit,} Greek *the **a**.*

ANSWERED (1)

Ac 8:36 {I be baptized?"} Some manuscripts add verse 37, *"You can," Philip **a**, "if you believe with all your heart." And the eunuch replied, "I believe that Jesus Christ is the Son of God."*

ANSWERING (1)

2Sa 22:36 {your help} As in Dead Sea Scrolls; most Hebrew manuscripts read *your **a***.

ANTIPAS (2)

Lk 3: 1 {Antipas was ruler} Greek *Herod was tetrarch.* Herod **A** was a son of King Herod.
Ac 12: 1 {King Herod Agrippa} Greek *Herod the king.* He was the nephew of Herod **A** and a grandson of Herod the Great.

ANY (1)

Mt 16: 2[-3] {of the times!} Several manuscripts do not include **a** of the words in 16:2-3 after *He replied.*

ANYONE (6)

1Sa 10:27 {Saul ignored them.} Dead Sea Scroll 4QSama continues: *...He gouged out the right eye of each of the Israelites living there, and he didn't allow **a** to come and rescue them....*
Isa 28:16 {run away again.} Greek version reads ***A** who believes in him will not be disappointed.*
Hab 2: 4 {lives are crooked;} Greek version reads *I will have no pleasure in **a** who turns away.*
Mk 7:15 {say and do!} Some manuscripts add verse 16, ***A** who is willing to hear should listen and understand.*
Jn 7:37[-38] {out from within."} Or *"Let **a** who is thirsty come to me and drink. [38]For the Scriptures declare that rivers of living water will flow from the heart of those who believe in me."*
16:30 {tell you anything.} Or *don't need that **a** should ask you anything.*

ANYTHING (4)

Mt 5:37 {something is wrong.} Or ***A** beyond this is from the evil one.*
Jn 16:30 {tell you anything.} Or *don't need that anyone should ask you **a**.*
Ac 10:14 {our Jewish laws.} Greek ***a** common and unclean.*
11: 8 {our Jewish laws.} Greek ***a** common or unclean.*

APART (2)

Mt 27:51[-53] {to many people.} Or *The earth shook, rocks split **a**, tombs opened, and many bodies of godly men and women who had died were raised from the dead. After Jesus' resurrection, they left the cemetery, went into the holy city of Jerusalem, and appeared to many people.*
Heb 11:40 {finish the race.} Greek *for us, for they **a** from us can't finish.*

APIECE (1)

Nu 3:47 {standard sanctuary shekel.} Hebrew *5 shekels* [2 ounces or 57 grams] ***a**, according to the sanctuary shekel, 20 gerahs to each shekel.*

APOSTLES (2)

Mk 3:14 {calling them apostles.} Some manuscripts do not include *calling them **a**.*
2Co 8:23 {brothers are representatives} Greek ***a**.*

APPEARANCE (2)

Zec 5: 6 {with the sins} As in Greek version; Hebrew reads *the **a**.*
Php 2: 7 {in human form.} Greek *he was born in the likeness of men and was found in **a** as a man.*

APPEARED (2)

1Sa 5: 6 {plague of tumors.} Greek version and Latin Vulgate read *tumors. And rats **a** in their land, and death and destruction were throughout the city.*
Mt 27:51[-53] {to many people.} Or *The earth shook, rocks split apart, tombs opened, and many bodies of godly men and women who had died were raised from the dead. After Jesus' resurrection, they left the cemetery, went into the holy city of Jerusalem, and **a** to many people.*

APPEARING (1)

2Sa 22:11 {soaring} As in some Hebrew manuscripts (see also Ps 18:10); other Hebrew manuscripts read ***a***.

APPEARS (1)

Lev 27: 3 {pieces of silver} Hebrew *50 shekels of silver, according to the standard sanctuary shekel,* each about 0.4 ounces or 11 grams in weight. The term *shekels* also **a** in 27:4, 5, 6, 7, 16.

APPLE (3)

Dt 32:10 {most precious possession.} Hebrew *as the **a** of his eye.*
Pr 7: 2 {most precious possession.} Hebrew *as the **a** of your eye.*
Zec 2: 8 {most precious possession.} Hebrew *harms the **a** of my eye.*

APPOINTED (5)

Ge 4:25 {named him Seth,} *Seth* probably means "granted"; the name may also mean "**a**."
1Sa 10: 1 {his people Israel.} Greek version reads *Israel. And you will rule over the LORD's people and save them from their enemies around them. This will be the sign to you that the LORD has **a** you to be leader over his inheritance.*
Job 15:23 {'Where is it?'} Greek version reads *He is **a** to be food for a vulture.*
Hos 12: 9 {Festival of Shelters.} Hebrew *as in the days of your **a** feast.*
Mic 6: 9 {is sending them.} Hebrew *"Listen to the rod. Who **a** it?"*

APPROACHED (1)

Lev 16: 1 {LORD had commanded.} Hebrew *when they **a** the LORD's presence;* compare 10:1.

ARABAH (18)

Dt 1: 1 {the Jordan Valley} Hebrew *the **A**;* also in 1:7.
3:17 {the Dead Sea,} Hebrew *from Kinnereth to the sea of the **A**, the Salt Sea.*
4:49 {the Dead Sea,} Hebrew *took the **A** on the east side of the Jordan as far as the sea of the **A**.*
11:30 {the Jordan Valley,} Hebrew *the **A**.*
Jos 3:16 {the Dead Sea} Hebrew *the sea of the **A**, the Salt Sea.*
8:14 {the Jordan Valley.} Hebrew *the **A**.*
11: 2 {the Jordan Valley} Hebrew *the **A**;* also in 11:16.
12: 1 {the Jordan Valley.} Hebrew *the **A**;* also in 12:3, 8.
12: 3 {the Dead Sea,} Hebrew *the sea of the **A**, the Salt Sea.*
18:18 {the Jordan Valley.} Hebrew *the **A**.*
2Sa 2:29 {the Jordan Valley.} Hebrew *the **A**.*
4: 7 {the Jordan Valley} Hebrew *the **A**.*
2Ki 14:25 {the Dead Sea,} Hebrew *the sea of the **A**.*
25: 4 {the Jordan Valley.} Hebrew *the **A**.*
Jer 39: 4 {the Jordan Valley.} Hebrew *the **A**.*
52: 7 {the Jordan Valley.} Hebrew *the **A**.*
Eze 47: 8 {the Jordan Valley,} Hebrew *the **A**.*

ARAM (10)

Ge 24:10 {traveled to Aram-naharaim} *Aram-naharaim* means "**A** of the two rivers," thought to have been located between the Euphrates and Balih Rivers in northwestern Mesopotamia.
Dt 23: 4 {Pethor in Aram-naharaim} *Aram-naharaim* means "**A** of the two rivers," thought to have been located between the Euphrates and Balih Rivers in northwestern Mesopotamia.
Jdg 3: 8 {Cushan-rishathaim of Aram-naharaim.} *Aram-naharaim* means "**A** of the two rivers," thought to have been located between the Euphrates and Balih Rivers in northwestern Mesopotamia.
2Sa 8:12 {Edom,} As in a few Hebrew manuscripts and Greek and Syriac versions (see also 8:14; 1 Chr 18:11); most Hebrew manuscripts read ***A***.
2Ki 16: 6 {king of Edom} As in Latin Vulgate; Hebrew reads *Rezin king of **A**.*
16: 6 {Elath for Edom.} As in Latin Vulgate; Hebrew reads ***A***.
1Ch 1:17 {of Aram were} As in one Hebrew manuscript and some Greek manuscripts (see also Gen 10:23); most Hebrew manuscripts lack *The descendants of **A** were.*
2Ch 20: 2 {army from Edom} As in one Hebrew manuscript; most Hebrew manuscripts and ancient versions read ***A***.
Eze 16:57 {is scorned—by Edom} Many ancient manuscripts read ***A***.
Mt 1: 3 {father of Ram.} Greek ***A**;* also in 1:4. See 1 Chr 2:9-10.

ARAM-NAHARAIM (3)

Ge 24:10 {traveled to Aram-naharaim} ***A*** means "Aram of the two rivers," thought to have been located between the Euphrates and Balih Rivers in northwestern Mesopotamia.
Dt 23: 4 {Pethor in Aram-naharaim} ***A*** means "Aram of the two rivers," thought to have been located between the Euphrates and Balih Rivers in northwestern Mesopotamia.
Jdg 3: 8 {Cushan-rishathaim of Aram-naharaim.} ***A*** means "Aram of the two rivers," thought to have been located between the Euphrates and Balih Rivers in northwestern Mesopotamia.

ARAMAIC (39)

Ge 31:47 {language and Galeed} *Jegar-sahadutha* means "witness pile" in **A**; *Galeed* means "witness pile" in Hebrew.
Ezr 4: 8 {Rehum} The original text of 4:8—6:18 is in **A**.
4:10 {and noble Ashurbanipal} **A** *Osnappar,* another name for Ashurbanipal.
5: 2 {son of Jehozadak} **A** *Jozadak,* a variant name for Jehozadak.
5:12 {Nebuchadnezzar of Babylon,} **A** *Nebuchadnezzar the Chaldean.*
6: 3 {be ninety feet.} **A** *Its height will be 60 cubits* [27 meters], *and its width will be 60 cubits.* It is commonly held that this verse should be emended to read: "Its height will be 45 feet, its length will be 90 feet, and its width will be 30 feet"; compare 1 Kgs 6:2. The emendation regarding the width is supported by the Syriac version.
6:11 {pile of rubble.} **A** *a dunghill.*
6:15 {completed on March 12,} **A** *on the third day of the month Adar,* of the Hebrew calendar. This event occurred on March 12, 515 B.C.; also see note on 3:1.
7:12 {"Greetings} The original text of 7:12-26 is in **A**.
7:22 {to 7,500 pounds} **A** *100 talents* [3.4 metric tons].
7:22 {500 bushels} **A** *100 cors* [18.2 kiloliters].
7:22 {of olive oil,} **A** *100 baths* [2.1 kiloliters] *of wine, 100 baths of olive oil.*
Jer 10:11 {from the earth."} The original text of this verse is in **A**.
Da 2: 4 {king in Aramaic,} The original text from this point through chapter 7 is in **A**.
2:34 {by supernatural means.} **A** *not by human hands;* also in 2:45.
3: 1 {nine feet wide} **A** *60 cubits* [27 meters] *tall and 6 cubits* [2.7 meters] *wide.*
3: 3 {all these officials} **A** *the princes, prefects, governors, advisers, counselors, judges, magistrates, and all the provincial officials.*
3: 7 {the musical instruments,} **A** *the horn, flute, zither, lyre, harp, and other instruments of the musical ensemble.*
3: 8 {of the astrologers} **A** *Chaldeans.*
3:10 {the musical instruments.} **A** *the horn, flute, zither, lyre, harp, pipes, and other instruments of the musical ensemble;* also in 3:15.
3:25 {a divine being} **A** *like a son of the gods.*
4:13 {saw a messenger,} **A** *a watcher;* also in 4:23.
4:17 {by the messengers} **A** *the watchers.*
5: 2 {that his predecessor,} **A** *father;* also in 5:11, 13, 18.
5:22 {are his successor,} **A** *son.*
5:28 {*Parsin*} **A** *Peres,* the singular of *Parsin.*
7: 9 {the Ancient One} **A** *an Ancient of Days;* also in 7:13, 22.
7:12 {a while longer.} **A** *for a season and a time.*
7:13 {like a man} Or *a Son of Man;* **A** reads *a son of man.*
Mt 5:22 {friend, 'You idiot,'} Literally *'Raca,'* an **A** term of contempt.
23: 7 {being called 'Rabbi.'} *Rabbi,* from **A**, means "master" or "teacher."
Mk 5:41 {up, little girl!"} Greek text uses **A** *"Talitha cumi"* and then translates it as "Get up, little girl."
7:34 {commanded, "Be opened!"} Greek text uses **A** *"Ephphatha"* and then translates it as "Be opened."
14:36 {"Abba,} *Abba* is an **A** term for "father."
Ac 9:36 {Greek is Dorcas} The names *Tabitha* in **A** and *Dorcas* in Greek both mean "gazelle."
22: 2 {their own language,} Greek *in **A**.*
Ro 8:15 {"Father, dear Father."} Greek *"Abba, Father." Abba* is an **A** term for "father."
1Co 16:22 {Our Lord, come!} From **A**, *Marana tha.*
Gal 4: 6 {your dear Father.} Greek *into your hearts, crying, "Abba, Father."* Abba is an **A** term for "Father."

ARAMEANS (2)

2Sa 8:13 {eighteen thousand Edomites} As in a few Hebrew manuscripts and Greek and Syriac versions (see also 8:14; 1 Chr 18:12); most Hebrew manuscripts read ***A***.
2Ki 16: 6 {and sent Edomites} As in marginal *Qere* reading of the Masoretic Text, Greek version, and Latin Vulgate; Hebrew reads ***A***.

ARAUNAH (2)

1Ch 21:15 {floor of Araunah} As in parallel text at 2 Sam 24:16; Hebrew reads *Ornan,* another name for **A**; also in 21:18-28.
2Ch 3: 1 {floor of Araunah} Hebrew reads *Ornan,* another name for **A**; compare 2 Sam 24:16.

ARD (1)

Nu 26:40 {their ancestor Ard.} As in Samaritan Pentateuch, some Greek manuscripts, and Latin Vulgate; Hebrew lacks *named after their ancestor **A**.*

AREOPAGITE (1)

Ac 17:34 {of the Council,} Greek *an **A**.*

AREOPAGUS (2)

Ac 17:19 {Council of Philosophers.} Greek *the **A**.*
17:22 {before the Council,} Or *in the middle of Mars Hill;* Greek reads *in the middle of the **A**.*

ARGUING (1)

Nu 20:13 {waters of Meribah,} *Meribah* means "**a**."

ARGUMENTS (1)

Ac 26:28 {Christian so quickly?"} Or *"A little more, and your **a** would make me a Christian."*

ARIEL (2)

Isa 29: 1 {certain for Ariel,} ***A*** sounds like a Hebrew term that means "hearth" or "altar."
29: 7 {fighting against Jerusalem} Hebrew ***A***.

ARK (2 of 13)

Ge 6:14 {"Make a boat} Traditionally rendered *an **a**.*

1Sa 14:18 {of the Israelites.} As in some Greek manuscripts; Hebrew reads *"Bring the **A** of God." For at that time the **A** of God was with the Israelites.*

ARMIES (1)
SS 6:13 {lines of dancers?} Or *as you would at the movements of two **a**?* or *as you would at the dance of Mahanaim?* The meaning of the Hebrew is uncertain.

ARMS (1)
Isa 9:20 {their own children.} Or *eat their own **a**.*

ARNI (1)
Lk 3:33 {son of Arni.} ***A*** is the same person as Ram; see 1 Chr 2:9-10.

AROD (1)
Nu 26:17 {its ancestor Arodi.} As in Samaritan Pentateuch and Syriac version (see also Gen 46:16); Hebrew reads ***A***.

AROER (1)
Jer 48: 6 {in the wilderness!} Or *Be like* [the town of] ***A*** *in the wilderness.*

AROUND (1 of 2)
1Sa 10: 1 {his people Israel.} Greek version reads *Israel. And you will rule over the LORD's people and save them from their enemies **a** them. This will be the sign to you that the LORD has appointed you to be leader over his inheritance.*

ARPHAXAD (4)
Ge 10:24 {father of Shelah,} Greek version reads ***A*** *was the father of Cainan, Cainan was the father of Shelah.*
11:12[-13] {sons and daughters.} Greek version reads [12]*When **A** was 135 years old, his son Cainan was born.* [13]*After the birth of Cainan, **A** lived another 430 years and had other sons and daughters, and then he died....*
1Ch 1:24 {Shem: Arphaxad, Shelah,} Some Greek manuscripts read ***A**, Cainan, Shelah.* See notes on Gen 10:24 and 11:12-13.

ARRIVED (4)
Ge 8:14 {months went by,} Hebrew *The twenty-seventh day of the second month **a**;* see note on 8:13.
1Sa 15:32 {have been spared!"} Dead Sea Scrolls and Greek version read *Agag **a** hesitantly, for he thought, "Surely this is the bitterness of death."*
Ac 2: 1 {after Jesus' resurrection,} Greek *When the day of Pentecost **a**.* This annual celebration came 50 days after the Passover ceremonies. See Lev 23:16.
25:13 {his sister, Bernice,} Greek *Agrippa the king and Bernice **a**.*

ARROWS (1)
2Ch 26:15 {and hurl stones} Or *designed by brilliant men to protect those who shot **a** and stones.*

ARTEMIS (1)
Ac 19:24 {Greek goddess Artemis.} ***A*** is otherwise known as Diana.

ASA (1)
Mt 1: 7 {father of Asaph.} *Asaph* is the same person as **A**; also in 1:8. See 1 Chr 3:10.

ASAPH (1)
Mt 1: 7 {father of Asaph.} ***A*** is the same person as Asa; also in 1:8. See 1 Chr 3:10.

ASARELAH (1)
1Ch 25:14 {fell to Asarelah} Hebrew *Jesharelah,* a variant name for **A**; compare 25:2.

ASCENT (1)
Nu 34: 4 {past Scorpion Pass} Hebrew *the **a** of Akrabbim.*

ASHAMED (1)
Jer 48:13 {calf at Bethel.} Hebrew ***a*** *when they trusted in Bethel.*

ASHAN (1)
1Ch 6:59 {Ain,} As in parallel text at Josh 21:16; Hebrew reads ***A***.

ASHDOD (1)
Am 3: 9 {leaders of Philistia} Hebrew ***A***.

ASHER (1)
Ge 30:13 {named him Asher,} ***A*** means "happy."

ASHURBANIPAL (1)
Ezr 4:10 {and noble Ashurbanipal} Aramaic *Osnappar,* another name for **A**.

ASIA (2)
Ac 16: 6[-7] {province of Bithynia,} *Phrygia, Galatia, **A**, Mysia,* and *Bithynia* were all districts in the land now called Turkey.
1Co 16:19 {province of Asia} ***A*** was a Roman province in what is now western Turkey.

ASIDE (1)
Php 2: 7 {made himself nothing;} Or *He laid **a** his mighty power and glory.*

ASK (2)
Lk 11:11 {your children ask} Some manuscripts add *for bread, do you give them a stone? Or if they **a**.*
Jn 16:30 {tell you anything.} Or *don't need that anyone should **a** you anything.*

ASKED (1)
1Sa 1:20 {named him Samuel,} *Samuel* sounds like the Hebrew term for "**a** of God" or "heard by God."

ASSEMBLY (1)
Hos 7:12 {their evil ways.} Hebrew *I will punish them because of what was reported against them in the **a**.*

ASSHUR (1)
Nu 24:22 {when Assyria} Hebrew ***A**;* also in 24:24.

ASSOCIATED (1)
Eze 30: 5 {Ethiopia, Libya,} Hebrew *Put...Kub.* Both *Put* and *Kub* are **a** with Libya.

ASSYRIA (2)
Ezr 6:22 {king of Assyria} King Cyrus of Persia is here identified as the king of **A** because Persia had conquered the Babylonian Empire, which included the earlier Assyrian Empire.
Isa 33: 1 {for you Assyrians,} Hebrew *for you, O destroyer...O betrayer.* The Hebrew text does not specifically name **A** as the object of this prophecy.

ASSYRIAN (1)
Ezr 6:22 {king of Assyria} King Cyrus of Persia is here identified as the king of Assyria because Persia had conquered the Babylonian Empire, which included the earlier **A** Empire.

ASTROLOGERS (1)
Mt 2: 1 {some wise men} Or *royal **a**,* Greek *magi;* also in 2:7, 16.

ASWAN (1)
Isa 49:12 {south as Egypt.} As in Dead Sea Scrolls, which read *from the region of **A**,* which is in southern Egypt. Masoretic Text reads *from the region of Sinim.*

ATHENS (1)
Ac 18: 1 {went to Corinth.} ***A*** and *Corinth* were major cities in Achaia, the region on the southern end of the Greek peninsula.

ATONEMENT (2 of 4)
Lev 8:15 {atonement for it.} Or *that **a** may be made on it.*
25: 9 {the fiftieth year,} Hebrew *on the tenth day of the seventh month, on the Day of **A**;* see 23:27 and the note there.

ATTACHED (1)
Ge 29:34 {named him Levi,} *Levi* sounds like a Hebrew term that means "being **a**" or "feeling affection for."

ATTACKED (1)
2Ki 3:25 {came under attack.} Hebrew *until only Kir-hareseth was left, with its stones, but the slingers surrounded and **a** it.*

AUTHORITY (4)
Mt 21:23 {from the Temple?} Or *By whose **a** do you do these things?*
Mk 11:28 {from the Temple?} Or *By whose **a** do you do these things?*
Lk 20: 2 {from the Temple?} Or *By whose **a** do you do these things?*
1Co 15:24 {of every kind.} Greek *every ruler and every **a** and power.*

AVEN (2)
Hos 10: 8 {shrines of Aven,} ***A*** is a reference to Beth-aven; see 10:5 and the note there.
Am 1: 5 {valley of Aven.} ***A*** means "wickedness."

AVOID (1)
Lk 11: 8 {won't be damaged.} Greek *in order to **a** shame,* or *because of [your] persistence.*

AWAKEN (3)
SS 2: 7 {time is right.} Or *not to **a** love until it is ready.*
3: 5 {time is right.} Or *not to **a** love until it is ready.*
8: 4 {time is right.} Or *not to **a** love until it is ready.*

AWAY (10)
Nu 5:21 {makes you infertile.} Hebrew *when he causes your thigh to waste **a** and your abdomen to swell.*
5:22 {make you infertile.} Hebrew *enter your body so that your abdomen swells and your thigh wastes **a**.*
5:27 {will become infertile,} Hebrew *Her body will swell and her thigh will waste **a**.*
Ezr 10:44 {by these wives.} Or *and they sent them **a** with their children.* The meaning of the Hebrew is uncertain.
Jer 48: 4 {will cry out.} Greek version reads *Her cries are heard as far **a** as Zoar.*
Hab 2: 4 {lives are crooked;} Greek version reads *I will have no pleasure in anyone who turns **a**.*
Mt 11: 6 {offended by me.} Or *who don't fall **a** because of me.*
Lk 7:23 {offended by me.} Or *who don't fall **a** because of me.*
Ac 2:39 {to the Gentiles} Greek *to those far **a**.*
24: 6 {we arrested him.} Some manuscripts add *We would have judged him by our law,* [7]*but Lysias, the commander of the garrison, came and took him violently **a** from us,* [8]*commanding his accusers to come before you.*

AWEN (1)
Eze 30:17 {Heliopolis and Bubastis} Hebrew *of **A** and Pi-beseth.*

AZAREL (1)
1Ch 25:18 {fell to Uzziel} Hebrew ***A**,* a variant name for Uzziel; compare 25:4.

AZARIAH (6)
2Ki 14:21 {sixteen-year-old son, Uzziah,} Hebrew ***A**,* a variant name for Uzziah.
15: 1 {Uzziah} Hebrew ***A**,* a variant name for Uzziah; also in 15:6, 7, 8, 17, 23, 27.
1Ch 3:12 {Amaziah, Uzziah,} Hebrew ***A**,* a variant name for Uzziah.
2Ch 22: 6 {and King Ahaziah} Some Hebrew manuscripts, Greek and Syriac versions, and Latin Vulgate (see also 2 Kgs 8:29); most Hebrew manuscripts read ***A***.
Ne 7: 7 {Jeshua, Nehemiah, Seraiah,} As in parallel text at Ezra 2:2; Hebrew reads ***A***.
Jer 42: 1 {Kareah and Jezaniah} Greek version reads ***A**;* compare 43:2.

AZAZEL (1)
Lev 16: 8 {the scapegoat.} Hebrew ***a**,* which in this context means "the goat of removal"; also in 16:10, 26.

AZMAVETH (1)
Ezr 2:24 {people of Beth-azmaveth} As in parallel text at Neh 7:28; Hebrew reads ***A***.

AZUBAH (1)
Isa 62: 4 {the Godforsaken City} Hebrew ***A**,* which means "forsaken."

B

BAAL (2)
1Ch 4:33 {away as Baalath.} As in some Greek manuscripts (see also Josh 19:8); Hebrew reads ***B***.
Hos 2:16 {'my master.'} Hebrew *'my **b**.'*

BAAL-BERITH (1)
Jdg 9:46 {temple of Baal-berith.} Hebrew *El-berith,* another name for **B**; compare 9:4.

BAALAH (1)
2Sa 6: 2 {Baalah of Judah} ***B*** *of Judah* is another name for Kiriath-jearim; compare 1 Chr 13:6.

BABBLING (1)
Pr 10:10 {reproof promotes peace.} As in Greek version; Hebrew reads *but **b** fools fall flat on their faces.*

BABEL (1)
Ge 11: 9 {was called Babel,} ***B*** sounds like a Hebrew term that means "confusion."

BABOONS (2)
1Ki 10:22 {apes, and peacocks.} Or *and **b**.*
2Ch 9:21 {apes, and peacocks.} Or *and **b**.*

BABYLON (5 of 7)

Jer 25:26 {king of Babylon} Hebrew *of Sheshach,* a code name for **B**.
51:20 {"You} Possibly Cyrus, who was used of God to conquer **B**. Compare Isa 44:28; 45:1.
51:41 {"How Babylon} Hebrew *Sheshach,* a code name for **B**.
1Pe 5:13 {here in Rome} Greek *The elect one in* **B**. **B** was probably a code name for Rome.

BABYLONIA (1)

Jer 51: 1 {people of Babylonia.} Hebrew *of Leb-kamai,* a code name for **B**.

BACA (1)

Ps 84: 6 {Valley of Weeping,} Hebrew *valley of* **B**.

BAD (1)

Ecc 9: 2 {good or bad,} As in Greek and Syriac versions, and Latin Vulgate; Hebrew lacks *or* ***b***.

BAHARUM (1)

1Ch 11:33 {Azmaveth from Bahurim} As in parallel text at 2 Sam 23:31; Hebrew reads ***B***.

BANI (1)

Ezr 8:10 {family of Bani} As in some Greek manuscripts (see also 1 Esdras 8:36); Hebrew lacks ***B***.

BARABBAS (1)

Mt 27:16 {man named Barabbas.} Some manuscripts read *Jesus* ***B****;* also in 27:17.

BARBARIAN (1)

Col 3:11 {uncircumcised, barbaric, uncivilized,} Greek ***B****, Scythian.*

BARLEY (8)

2Ki 7: 1 {ounce of silver.} Hebrew *2 seahs* [12 liters] *of* ***b*** *grain will cost 1 shekel* [11 grams]; also in 7:16, 18.
2Ch 2:10 {bushels of barley,} Hebrew *20,000 cors* [3,640 kiloliters] *of crushed wheat, 20,000 cors of* ***b***.
27: 5 {bushels of barley.} Hebrew *10,000 cors* [1,820 kiloliters] *of wheat, and 10,000 cors of* ***b***.
Eze 45:13 {for every sixty} Hebrew *1/6 of an ephah from each homer of wheat…and of* ***b***.
Hos 3: 2 {measure of wine.} As in Greek version, which reads *a homer* [182 liters] *of* ***b*** *and a measure of wine;* Hebrew reads *a homer of* ***b*** *and a lethech* [2.5 bushels or 91 liters] *of* ***b***.
Rev 6: 6 {day's pay.} Greek *A choinix of wheat for a denarius, and 3 choinix of* ***b*** *for a denarius.*

BARREN (1)

Heb 11:11 {keep his promise.} Some manuscripts read *It was by faith that Sarah was able to have a child, even though she was too old and* ***b***. *Sarah believed that God would keep his promise.*

BASE (1)

Ex 38:27 {for each base.} Hebrew *100 talents* [3,400 kilograms] *of silver, 1 talent* [34 kilograms] *for each* ***b***.

BASIC (1)

Col 2: 8 {of this world,} Or *from the* ***b*** *principles of this world;* also in 2:20.

BASICS (1)

Heb 6: 1 {basics of Christianity} Or *the* ***b*** *about Christ.*

BATCH (2)

1Co 5: 6[-7] {can stay pure.} Greek *Don't you realize that even a little leaven spreads quickly through the whole* ***b*** *of dough? [7]Purge out the old leaven so that you can be a new* ***b*** *of dough, just as you are already unleavened.*

BATH (5)

Isa 5:10 {even six gallons} Hebrew *a* ***b*** [21 liters].
Eze 45:10 {liquid volume measures.} Hebrew *use honest scales, an honest ephah, and an honest* ***b***.
45:11 {and the bath} The *ephah* is a dry measure; the ***b*** is a liquid measure.
45:14 {your olive oil,} Hebrew *the portion of oil, measured by the* ***b****, is 1/10 of a* ***b*** *from each cor, which consists of 10 baths or 1 homer, for 10 baths are equivalent to a homer.*

BATHS (12)

1Ki 5:11 {and 110,000 gallons} As in Greek version, which reads *20,000* ***b*** [420 kiloliters] (see also 2 Chr 2:10); Hebrew reads *20 cors,* about 800 gallons or 3.6 kiloliters in volume.
7:26 {about 11,000 gallons} Hebrew *2,000* ***b*** [42 kiloliters].
7:38 {hold 220 gallons} Hebrew *40* ***b*** [840 liters].
2Ch 2:10 {of olive oil.} Hebrew *20,000* ***b*** [420 kiloliters] *of wine, and 20,000* ***b*** *of olive oil.*
4: 5 {about 16,500 gallons} Hebrew *3,000* ***b*** [63 kiloliters].
Ezr 7:22 {of olive oil,} Aramaic *100* ***b*** [2.1 kiloliters] *of wine, 100* ***b*** *of olive oil.*
Eze 45:14 {your olive oil,} Hebrew *the portion of oil, measured by the bath, is 1/10 of a bath from each cor, which consists of 10* ***b*** *or 1 homer, for 10* ***b*** *are equivalent to a homer.*
Lk 16: 6 {four hundred gallons.} Greek *100* ***b****…50 [****b****].*

BATHSHEBA (1)

1Ch 3: 5 {and Solomon. Bathsheba,} Hebrew *Bathshua,* a variant name for **B**.

BATHSHUA (1)

1Ch 3: 5 {and Solomon. Bathsheba,} Hebrew ***B****,* a variant name for Bathsheba.

BATTLE (1)

Isa 22: 2 {famine and disease.} Hebrew *killed, but not by sword and not in* ***b***.

BATTLEMENTS (1)

SS 8: 9 {off from men.} Hebrew *If she is a wall, we will build* ***b*** *of silver on her; but if she is a door, we will surround her with panels of cedar.*

BAVVAI (1)

Ne 3:18 {led by Binnui} As in a few Hebrew manuscripts, some Greek manuscripts, and Syriac version (see also 3:24; 10:9); most Hebrew manuscripts read ***B***.

BAZLITH (1)

Ne 7:54 {Bazluth,} As in parallel text at Ezra 2:52; Hebrew reads ***B***.

BEAR (1)

Job 11:12 {bear human offspring} Or ***b*** *a tame colt.*

BEARD (1)

Isa 7:20 {and your people.} Hebrew *shave off the head, the hair of the legs, and the* ***b***.

BEASTS (2)

Ps 76: 4 {the everlasting mountains.} As in Greek version; Hebrew reads *than mountains filled with* ***b*** *of prey.*
1Co 15:32 {men of Ephesus} Greek *fighting wild* ***b*** *in Ephesus.*

BEATING (1)

Lk 23:48 {in deep sorrow.} Greek ***b*** *their breasts.*

BED (1)

Ge 47:31 {on his staff.} As in Greek version; Hebrew reads *bowed in worship at the head of his* ***b***.

BEDAN (1)

1Sa 12:11 {Barak,} As in Greek and Syriac versions; Hebrew reads ***B***.

BEDROOM (1)

SS 1: 4 {bedroom, O my king.} Or *The king has brought me into his* ***b***.

BEELIADA (1)

1Ch 14: 7 {Elishama, Eliada,} Hebrew ***B****,* a variant name for Eliada; compare 3:8 and parallel text at 2 Sam 5:16.

BEELZEBOUL (6)

Mt 10:25 {prince of demons,} Greek ***B***.
12:24 {Satan,} Greek ***B***.
12:27 {prince of demons,} Greek *by* ***B***.
Mk 3:22 {Satan,} Greek ***B***.
Lk 11:15 {Satan,} Greek ***B***.
11:18 {prince of demons.} Greek *by* ***B****;* also in 11:19.

BEER (1)

Nu 21:16 {traveled to Beer,} ***B*** means "well."

BEER-LAHAIROI (1)

Ge 16:14 {was named Beer-lahairoi,} ***B*** means "well of the Living One who sees me."

BEEROTH (1)

Dt 10: 6 {people of Jaakan} Or *set out from* ***B*** *of Bene-jaakan.*

BEGAN (2 of 5)

Ge 1: 1 {beginning God created} Or *In the beginning when God created,* or *When God* ***b*** *to create.*
Mk 8:32 {things like that.} Or *and* ***b*** *to correct him.*

BEGINNING (5 of 7)

Eze 40: 1 {On April 28,} Hebrew *At the* ***b*** *of the year, on the tenth day of the month,* of the Hebrew calendar.…
1Co 14:33 {the other churches.} The phrase *as in all the other churches* could be joined to the **b** of 14:34.
Col 1:18 {from the dead,} Greek *He is the* ***b****, the firstborn from the dead.*
2Th 2:13 {among the first} Some manuscripts read *God chose you from the very* ***b***.
1Jn 1: 1 {from the beginning} Greek *What was from the* ***b***.

BEGINS (1 of 2)

Eze 45:25 {in early autumn,} Hebrew *the festival which* ***b*** *on the fifteenth day of the seventh month* (see Lev 23:33). This day of the Hebrew lunar calendar occurs in late September or October.

BEHALF (4)

2Co 5:14 {used to live.} Greek *Since one died on* ***b*** *of all, then all died.*
Col 1: 7 {in your place.} Greek *he is ministering on your* ***b****;* other manuscripts read *he is ministering on our* ***b***.
Heb 9:24 {as our Advocate.} Greek *on our* ***b***.

BEHEMOTH (1)

Job 40:15 {the mighty hippopotamus.} Hebrew *at* ***b***.

BEHIND (2)

2Sa 13:34 {the Horonaim road} As in Greek version; Hebrew reads *from the road* ***b*** *him.*
Eze 3:12 {in his place!)} A likely reading for this verse is *Then the Spirit lifted me up, and as the glory of the* LORD *rose from its place, I heard* ***b*** *me a loud rumbling sound.*

BEING (1 of 8)

2Co 4:16 {our spirits are} Greek *our inner* ***b*** *is.*

BEKA (1)

Ex 38:26 {ounce of silver} Hebrew *1* ***b*** [6 grams] *per person, that is, half a shekel, according to the sanctuary shekel.*

BELIAL (1)

1Ki 21:10 {Find two scoundrels} Hebrew *two sons of* ***B****;* also in 21:13.

BELIAR (1)

2Co 6:15 {and the Devil} Greek *and* ***B***.

BELIEVE (4)

Jn 7:37[-38] {out from within."} Or *"Let anyone who is thirsty come to me and drink. [38]For the Scriptures declare that rivers of living water will flow from the heart of those who* ***b*** *in me."*
20:31 {you may believe} Some manuscripts read *may continue to* ***b***.
Ac 8:36 {I be baptized?"} Some manuscripts add verse 37, *"You can," Philip answered, "if you* ***b*** *with all your heart." And the eunuch replied, "I* ***b*** *that Jesus Christ is the Son of God."*

BELIEVED (1)

Heb 11:11 {keep his promise.} Some manuscripts read *It was by faith that Sarah was able to have a child, even though she was too old and barren. Sarah* ***b*** *that God would keep his promise.*

BELIEVES (1)

Isa 28:16 {run away again.} Greek version reads *Anyone who* ***b*** *in him will not be disappointed.*

BELOVED (3)

SS 1: 9 {my beloved one!} Hebrew *I compare you, my* ***b****, to a mare among Pharaoh's chariots.*
Lk 9:35 {my Chosen One.} Some manuscripts read *This is my* ***b*** *Son.*
Jas 1:19 {Dear friends,} Greek *Know this, my* ***b*** *brothers.*

BEN (1)

Ne 12:24 {Binnui,} Hebrew *son of* (i.e., ***b***), which should probably be read here as the proper name Binnui; compare Ezra 3:9 and the note there.

BEN-AMMI (1)

Ge 19:38 {Ben-ammi.} ***B*** means "son of my people."

BEN-ONI (1)

Ge 35:18 {Benjamin.} ***B*** means "son of my sorrow"; *Benjamin* means "son of my right hand."

BENE (2)

Ezr 3: 9 {descendants of Hodaviah.} Hebrew *sons of Judah* (i.e., ***b*** *Yehudah*). ***B*** might also be read here as the proper name Binnui; *Yehudah* is probably another name for Hodaviah. Compare 2:40; Neh 7:43; 1 Esdras 5:58.

BENE-JAAKAN (1)
Dt 10: 6 {people of Jaakan} Or *set out from Beeroth of* ***B***.

BENJAMIN (2)
Ge 35:18 {called him Benjamin.} *Ben-oni* means "son of my sorrow"; ***B*** means "son of my right hand."
1Sa 13:15 {land of Benjamin.} As in Greek version; Hebrew reads *Samuel left Gilgal and went to Gibeah in the land of* ***B***.

BENJAMINITE (1)
2Sa 16:11 {relative of Saul} Hebrew *this* ***B***.

BERACAH (1)
2Ch 20:26 {Valley of Blessing,} Hebrew *valley of* ***B***.

BERIAH (1)
1Ch 7:23 {named him Beriah} ***B*** sounds like a Hebrew term meaning "tragedy" or "misfortune."

BERNICE (1)
Ac 25:13 {his sister, Bernice,} Greek *Agrippa the king and* ***B*** *arrived.*

BESIDE (1)
2Ki 23:16 {man of God} As in Greek version; Hebrew lacks *as Jeroboam stood* ***b*** *the altar at the festival. Then Josiah turned and looked up at the tomb of the man of God.*

BETAH (1)
2Sa 8: 8 {cities of Tebah} As in some Greek manuscripts (see also 1 Chr 18:8); Hebrew reads ***B***.

BETH-AVEN (4)
Hos 4:15 {and at Beth-aven.} ***B*** means "house of wickedness"; it is being used as another name for Bethel, which means "house of God."
5: 8 {cry in Beth-aven} ***B*** means "house of wickedness"; it is being used as another name for Bethel, which means "house of God."
10: 5 {idol at Beth-aven.} ***B*** means "house of wickedness"; it is being used as another name for Bethel, which means "house of God."
10: 8 {shrines of Aven,} *Aven* is a reference to **B**; see 10:5 and the note there.

BETH-EZEL (1)
Mic 1:11 {people of Beth-ezel} ***B*** means "adjoining house."

BETH-LEAPHRAH (1)
Mic 1:10 {Beth-leaphrah,} ***B*** means "house of dust."

BETH-SHAN (4)
Jos 17:11 {to Manasseh: Beth-shan,} Hebrew *Beth-shean,* a variant name for **B**; also in 17:16.
Jdg 1:27 {living in Beth-shan,} Hebrew *Beth-shean,* a variant name for **B**.
1Ki 4:12 {all of Beth-shan} Hebrew *Beth-shean,* a variant name for **B**; also in 4:12b.
1Ch 7:29 {towns of Beth-shan,} Hebrew *Beth-shean,* a variant name for **B**.

BETH-SHEAN (4)
Jos 17:11 {to Manasseh: Beth-shan,} Hebrew ***B***, a variant name for Beth-shan; also in 17:16.
Jdg 1:27 {living in Beth-shan,} Hebrew ***B***, a variant name for Beth-shan.
1Ki 4:12 {all of Beth-shan} Hebrew ***B***, a variant name for Beth-shan; also in 4:12b.
1Ch 7:29 {towns of Beth-shan,} Hebrew ***B***, a variant name for Beth-shan.

BETH-ZATHA (1)
Jn 5: 2 {pool of Bethesda,} Some manuscripts read ***B***; other manuscripts read *Bethsaida.*

BETHEL (7)
Ge 35: 7 {named it El-bethel,} *El-bethel* means "the God of **B**."
Jos 8:17 {Ai or Bethel} Some manuscripts lack *or* ***B***.
16: 2 {(that is, Luz)} As in Greek version (also see 18:13); Hebrew reads *From* ***B*** *to Luz.*
Jer 48:13 {calf at Bethel.} Hebrew *ashamed when they trusted in* ***B***.
Hos 4:15 {and at Beth-aven.} *Beth-aven* means "house of wickedness"; it is being used as another name for **B**, which means "house of God."
5: 8 {cry in Beth-aven} *Beth-aven* means "house of wickedness"; it is being used as another name for **B**, which means "house of God."
10: 5 {idol at Beth-aven.} *Beth-aven* means "house of wickedness"; it is being used as another name for **B**, which means "house of God."

BETHEL-SHAREZER (1)
Zec 7: 2 {Sharezer and Regemmelech,} Or ***B*** *had sent Regemmelech.*

BETHER (1)
SS 2:17 {the rugged mountains.} Or *on the hills of* ***B***.

BETHSAIDA (1)
Jn 5: 2 {pool of Bethesda,} Some manuscripts read *Beth-zatha;* other manuscripts read ***B***.

BETRAYER (1)
Isa 33: 1 {for you Assyrians,} Hebrew *for you, O destroyer. . . O* ***b***. The Hebrew text does not specifically name Assyria as the object of this prophecy.

BETWEEN (2 of 6)
Ge 16: 5 {this to me!} Hebrew *Let the* L*ORD* *judge* ***b*** *you and me.*
Zec 13: 6 {on your chest} Or *scars* ***b*** *your hands.*

BEULAH (1)
Isa 62: 4 {Bride of God,} Hebrew ***B***, which means "married."

BEYOND (2)
Mt 5:37 {something is wrong.} Or *Anything* ***b*** *this is from the evil one.*
1Co 4: 6 {to the Scriptures,} Or *You must learn not to go* ***b*** *"what is written," so that.*

BIGTHAN (1)
Est 2:21 {king's eunuchs, Bigthana} Hebrew ***B***; compare 6:2.

BINNUI (4)
Ezr 3: 9 {descendants of Hodaviah.} Hebrew *sons of Judah* (i.e., *bene Yehudah*). *Bene* might also be read here as the proper name **B**; *Yehudah* is probably another name for Hodaviah. Compare 2:40; Neh 7:43; 1 Esdras 5:58.
10:37[-38] {family of Binnui} As in Greek version; Hebrew reads *Jaasu,* [38]*Bani,* ***B***.
Ne 7:15 {family of Bani} As in parallel text at Ezra 2:10; Hebrew reads ***B***.
12:24 {Sherebiah, Jeshua, Binnui,} Hebrew *son of* (i.e., *ben*), which should probably be read here as the proper name **B**; compare Ezra 3:9 and the note there.

BIRTH (3 of 5)
Ge 11:12[-13] {sons and daughters.} Greek version reads [12]*When Arphaxad was 135 years old, his son Cainan was born.* [13]*After the* ***b*** *of Cainan, Arphaxad lived another 430 years and had other sons and daughters, and then he died. When Cainan was 130 years old, his son Shelah was born. After the* ***b*** *of Shelah, Cainan lived another 330 years and had other sons and daughters, and then he died.*
1Ti 2:15 {saved through childbearing} Or *will be saved by accepting their role as mothers,* or *will be saved by the* ***b*** *of the Child.*

BITHRON (1)
2Sa 2:29 {through the morning,} Or *continued on through the* ***B***. The meaning of the Hebrew is uncertain.

BITTER (2)
Ru 1:20 {call me Mara,} *Naomi* means "pleasant"; *Mara* means "**b**."
Mic 1:12 {people of Maroth} *Maroth* sounds like the Hebrew term for "**b**."

BITTERNESS (1)
1Sa 15:32 {have been spared!"} Dead Sea Scrolls and Greek version read *Agag arrived hesitantly, for he thought, "Surely this is the* ***b*** *of death."*

BLASPHEMOUS (1)
2Pe 2:11 {out disrespectfully against} Greek *never bring* ***b*** *judgment from the Lord against.*

BLESS (1)
Mt 5:44 {love your enemies!} Some manuscripts add ***B*** *those who curse you, do good to those who hate you.*

BLESSED (1)
Lk 1:28 {is with you!} Some manuscripts add ***B*** *are you among women.*

BLIND (1)
Isa 61: 1 {will be freed.} Greek version reads *and the* ***b*** *will see.*

BLOOD (6)
Lev 17: 4 {a capital offense.} Hebrew ***b*** *guilt.*
Mt 27:25 {and our children!"} Greek *"His* ***b*** *be on us and on our children."*
27:49 {and save him."} Some manuscripts add *And another took a spear and pierced his side, and out came water and* ***b***.
Ac 20:26 {blamed on me,} Greek *I am innocent of the* ***b*** *of all.*
Col 1:14 {with his blood} Some manuscripts do not include *with his* ***b***.
1Jn 5: 6 {on the cross} Greek *This is he who came by water and* ***b***.

BOANERGES (1)
Mk 3:17 {"Sons of Thunder"} Greek *whom he named* ***B***, *which means Sons of Thunder.*

BOAZ (2)
1Ki 7:21 {Boaz.} Jakin probably means "he establishes"; **B** probably means "in him is strength."
2Ch 3:17 {Boaz.} Jakin probably means "he establishes"; **B** probably means "in him is strength."

BODIES (1)
Mt 27:51[-53] {to many people.} Or *The earth shook, rocks split apart, tombs opened, and many* ***b*** *of godly men and women who had died were raised from the dead. After Jesus' resurrection, they left the cemetery, went into the holy city of Jerusalem, and appeared to many people.*

BODILY (1)
Col 2: 9 {human body,} Greek *in him dwells all the fullness of the Godhead* ***b***.

BODY (8)
Nu 5:22 {make you infertile.} Hebrew *enter your* ***b*** *so that your abdomen swells and your thigh wastes away.*
5:27 {will become infertile,} Hebrew *Her* ***b*** *will swell and her thigh will waste away.*
Job 19:26 {will see God} Or *without my* ***b*** *I will see God.*
Ro 6:12 {way you live;} Or *Do not let sin reign in your* ***b***, *which is subject to death.*
7:24 {dominated by sin?} Greek *from this* ***b*** *of death?*
1Co 11:29 {body of Christ,} Greek *the* ***b***; some manuscripts read *the Lord's* ***b***.
13: 3 {boast about it;} Some manuscripts read *and even gave my* ***b*** *to be burned.*

BOKIM (1)
Jdg 2: 5 {the place "Weeping,"} Hebrew ***B***.

BONES (1)
Hab 3:16 {way beneath me,} Hebrew *Decay entered my* ***b***.

BORN (3 of 6)
Ge 11:12[-13] {sons and daughters.} Greek version reads [12]*When Arphaxad was 135 years old, his son Cainan was* ***b***. [13]*After the birth of Cainan, Arphaxad lived another 430 years and had other sons and daughters, and then he died. When Cainan was 130 years old, his son Shelah was* ***b***. *After the birth of Shelah, Cainan lived another 330 years and had other sons and daughters, and then he died.*
Php 2: 7 {in human form.} Greek *he was* ***b*** *in the likeness of men and was found in appearance as a man.*

BOSOM (2)
Lk 16:22 {be with Abraham.} Greek *into Abraham's* ***b***.
Jn 13:23 {at the table.} Greek *was reclining on Jesus'* ***b***. The "disciple whom Jesus loved" was probably John.

BOSOR (1)
2Pe 2:15 {son of Beor,} Other manuscripts read ***B***.

BOUNDARY (2)
Nu 21:24 {Ammonites was fortified.} Or *because the terrain of the Ammonite frontier was rugged;* Hebrew *because the* ***b*** *of the Ammonites was strong.*
Hos 5:10 {bad as thieves.} Hebrew *have become as those who move a* ***b*** *marker.*

BOWED (1)
Ge 47:31 {on his staff.} As in Greek version; Hebrew reads ***b*** *in worship at the head of his bed.*

BOWL (2)
Mt 26:23 {with me now} Or *The one who has dipped his hand in the* ***b*** *with me.*
Mk 14:20 {with me now.} Or *one who is dipping bread into the* ***b*** *with me.*

BOWSHOT (1)
Ge 21:16 {a hundred yards} Hebrew *a* ***b***.

BRACELETS (1)
Ge 24:22 {large gold bracelets} Hebrew *a gold nose-ring weighing a half shekel* [0.2 ounces or 6 grams] *and two gold* ***b*** *weighing 10 shekels* [4 ounces or 114 grams].

BRANCH (6)
Ge 15:18 {border of Egypt} Hebrew *the river of Egypt,* referring either to an eastern **b** of the Nile River or to the brook of Egypt in the Sinai (see Num 34:5).
Ps 51: 7 {from my sins,} Hebrew *Purify me with the hyssop **b**.*
Isa 23: 3 {grain from Egypt} Hebrew *from Shihor,* a **b** of the Nile River.
Jer 2:18 {of the Nile} Hebrew *of Shihor,* a **b** of the Nile River.
33:15 {a righteous descendant,} Hebrew *a righteous **B**.*
Da 11: 7 {of her relatives} Hebrew *a **b** from her roots.*

BREAD (7)
Mk 14:20 {with me now.} Or *one who is dipping **b** into the bowl with me.*
Lk 11:11 {your children ask} Some manuscripts add *for **b**, do you give them a stone? Or if they ask.*
Ac 12: 3 {the Passover celebration} Greek *the days of unleavened [**b**].*
20: 6 {the Passover season} Greek *the days of unleavened **b**.*
20: 7 {the Lord's Supper.} Greek *to break **b**.*
20:11 {Lord's Supper together.} Greek *broke the **b**.*
1Co 5: 8 {the new bread} Greek *but with unleavened **b**.*

BREAK (1)
Ac 20: 7 {the Lord's Supper.} Greek *to **b** bread.*

BREAKING (1)
Ge 38:29 {was called Perez.} *Perez* means "**b** out."

BREASTS (1)
Lk 23:48 {in deep sorrow.} Greek *beating their **b**.*

BREATH (1)
Mal 2:15 {you are his.} Or *Did not one God make us and preserve our life and **b**? or Did not one God make her, both flesh and spirit?* The meaning of the Hebrew is uncertain.

BRIDLE (2)
2Sa 8: 1 {their largest city.} Hebrew *by conquering Metheg-ammah,* a name which means "the **b**," possibly referring to the size of the city or the tribute money taken from it. Compare 1 Chr 18:1.
Job 41:13 {layer of armor} As in Greek version; Hebrew reads *its **b**.*

BRIGHT (1)
Rev 15: 6 {spotless white linen} Some manuscripts read *in **b** and sparkling stone.*

BRIGHTNESS (1)
Ge 38:30 {was named Zerah.} *Zerah* means "scarlet" or "**b**."

BRILLIANT (1)
2Ch 26:15 {and hurl stones} Or *designed by **b** men to protect those who shot arrows and stones.*

BRING (5)
Ge 4: 1 {birth to Cain,} *Cain* sounds like a Hebrew term that can mean "**b** forth" or "acquire."
1Sa 14:18 {of the Israelites.} As in some Greek manuscripts; Hebrew reads *"**B** the Ark of God." For at that time the Ark of God was with the Israelites.*
Jn 13:32 {God will bring} Some manuscripts read *And if God is glorified in him [the Son of Man], God will **b**.*
Ro 8:10 {spirit is alive} Or *the Spirit will **b** you eternal life.*
2Pe 2:11 {out disrespectfully against} Greek *never **b** blasphemous judgment from the Lord against.*

BRINGING (1)
Ps 68:30 {tribute from us.} Or *Humble them until they submit, **b** pieces of silver as tribute.*

BROKE (1)
Ac 20:11 {Lord's Supper together.} Greek ***b** the bread.*

BROKEN (2)
Isa 10:27 {from their shoulders.} As in Greek version; Hebrew reads *The yoke will be **b**, for you have grown so fat.*
1Co 11:24 {which is given} Some manuscripts read ***b**.*

BRONZE (1 of 2)
2Ki 18: 4 {was called Nehushtan.} *Nehushtan* sounds like the Hebrew terms that mean "snake," "**b**," and "unclean thing."

BROTHER (17)
Ge 10:21 {brother of Japheth.} Or *Shem, whose older **b** was Japheth.*
2Ch 36:10 {appointed Jehoiachin's uncle,} As in parallel text at 2 Kgs 24:17; Hebrew reads ***b**,* or *relative.*
Jer 22:13 {certain for Jehoiakim,} The **b** and successor of the exiled Jehoahaz.
Ob 1:10 {relatives in Israel.} Hebrew *your **b** Jacob.*
Ro 14:10 {condemn another Christian} Greek *your **b**;* also in 14:10b, 13, 15, 21.
1Co 5:11 {be a Christian} Greek *a **b**.*
6: 6 {instead, one Christian} Greek *one **b**.*
7:12 {a Christian man} Greek *a **b**.*
8:11 {a weak Christian,} Greek ***b**;* also in 8:13.
1Th 4: 6 {cheat another Christian} Greek *a **b**.*
2Th 3: 6 {from any Christian} Greek ***b**;* also in 3:15.
1Ti 6: 2 {helping another believer} Greek *a **b**.*
Jas 1: 9 {Christians who are} Greek *The **b** who is.*
1Jn 2: 9 {rejects another Christian} Greek *hates his **b**;* also in 2:11.
3:10 {love other Christians} Greek *his **b**;* also in 3:15.
4:20 {hates another Christian,} Greek ***b**.*
5:16 {see any Christian} Greek *your **b**.*

BROTHERLY (1)
Heb 13: 1 {true Christian love.} Greek *with **b** love.*

BROTHERS (63)
2Ch 22: 8 {and Ahaziah's relatives} As in Greek version (see also 2 Kgs 10:13); Hebrew reads *and sons of the **b** of Ahaziah.*
Jn 21:23 {community of believers} Greek *the **b**.*
Ac 3:17 {"Friends,} Greek ***B**.*
6: 3 {among yourselves, friends,} Greek ***b**.*
9:30 {When the believers} Greek ***b**.*
10:23 {some other believers} Greek ***b**.*
11: 1 {and other believers} Greek ***b**;* also in 11:29b.
15: 1 {teach the Christians} Greek ***b**;* also in 15:32, 33.
15: 3 {visit the believers.} Greek ***b**;* also in 15:23, 36, 40.
16: 2 {by the believers} Greek ***b**;* also in 16:40.
17: 6 {the other believers} Greek ***b**;* also in 17:10, 14.
18:18 {to the Christians} Greek ***b**;* also in 18:27.
21: 7 {greeted the believers} Greek ***b**;* also in 21:17.
28:14 {found some believers,} Greek ***b**;* also in 28:15.
Ro 1:13 {know, dear friends,} Greek ***b**.*
7: 1 {Now, dear friends} Greek ***b**;* also in 7:4.
8:12 {dear Christian friends,} Greek ***b**.*
10: 1 {Dear friends,} Greek ***B**.*
11:25 {mystery, dear friends,} Greek ***b**.*
12: 1 {dear Christian friends,} Greek ***b**.*
15:14 {convinced, dear friends,} Greek ***b**;* also in 15:30.
16:14 {the other Christians} Greek ***b**.*
1Co 1:11 {arguments, dear friends.} Greek *my **b**.*
8:12 {against other Christians} Greek ***b**.*
15: 6 {of his followers} Greek *the **b**.*
15:31 {swear, dear friends,} Greek ***b**.*
16:11 {other believers.} Greek *the **b**;* also in 16:12, 20.
2Co 1: 8 {know, dear friends,} Greek ***b**.*
8: 1 {you, dear friends,} Greek ***b**.*
11:26 {but are not.} Greek *from false **b**.*
13:11 {Dear friends,} Greek ***B**.*
Gal 1: 2 {All the Christians} Greek ***b**.*
1:11 {Dear friends,} Greek ***B**.*
2: 4 {there—false ones, really} Greek *some false **b**.*
3:15 {Dear friends,} Greek ***B**.*
4:12 {Dear friends,} Greek ***b**;* also in 4:31.
5:11 {Dear friends,} Greek ***b**;* also in 5:13.
6: 1 {if a Christian} Greek ***B**, if a man.*
6:18 {dear Christian friends,} Greek ***B**.*
Eph 6:23 {peace, dear friends,} Greek ***b**.*
Php 1:12 {know, dear friends,} Greek ***b**.*
1:14 {of the Christians} Greek ***b** in the Lord.*
3: 1 {happens, dear friends,} Greek ***b**;* also in 3:13, 17.
4: 8 {now, dear friends,} Greek ***b**.*
1Th 2:17 {Dear friends,} Greek ***B**.*
3: 7 {comforted, dear friends,} Greek ***b**.*
4:10 {all the Christians} Greek *the **b**.*
4:10 {so, dear friends,} Greek ***b**.*
5:26 {in Christian love.} Greek *Greet all the **b** with a holy kiss.*
5:27 {all the Christians.} Greek *the **b**.*
Heb 2:11 {brothers and sisters.} Greek *his **b**;* also in 2:17.
2:12 {brothers and sisters.} Greek *my **b**.* Ps 22:22.
3: 1 {belong to God} Greek *holy **b**.*
3:12 {then, dear friends.} Greek ***b**.*
7: 5 {their own relatives.} Greek *their **b**, who are descendants of Abraham.*
10:19 {so, dear friends,} Greek ***b**.*
13:22 {you, dear friends,} Greek ***b**.*
Jas 1:19 {Dear friends,} Greek *Know this, my beloved **b**.*
1Pe 5: 9 {Remember that Christians} Greek *your **b**.*
2Pe 1:10 {So, dear friends,} Greek ***b**.*
1Jn 3:14 {love other Christians,} Greek *the **b**.*
3:16 {our Christian friends.} Greek *the **b**.*
Rev 19:10 {and other believers} Greek ***b**.*

BROUGHT (2)
Ge 49:10 {whom it belongs,} Or *until tribute is **b** to him and the peoples obey;* traditionally rendered *until Shiloh comes.*
SS 1: 4 {bedroom, O my king.} Or *The king has **b** me into his bedroom.*

BUILD (1)
SS 8: 9 {off from men.} Hebrew *If she is a wall, we will **b** battlements of silver on her; but if she is a door, we will surround her with panels of cedar.*

BUILDS (1)
Pr 17:19 {who speaks boastfully} Or *who **b** up defenses;* Hebrew reads *who makes a high gate.*

BUL (1)
1Ki 6:38 {detail by midautumn} Hebrew *in the month of **B**, which is the eighth month....*

BULLS (1)
1Sa 1:24 {a three-year-old bull} As in Dead Sea Scrolls, Greek and Syriac versions; Hebrew reads *3 **b**.*

BURIED (3)
Dt 34: 6 {He was buried} Hebrew *He **b** him,* that is, "The LORD **b** him." Samaritan Pentateuch and some Greek manuscripts read *They **b** him.*

BURNED (2)
1Co 13: 3 {boast about it;} Some manuscripts read *and even gave my body to be **b**.*
2Pe 3:10 {exposed to judgment.} Some manuscripts read *will be **b** up.*

BURNING (5)
Dt 9:22 {angry at Taberah,} *Taberah* means "place of **b**." See Num 11:1-3.
Ps 18:13 {a mighty shout.} As in Greek version (see also 2 Sam 22:14); Hebrew adds *raining down hail and **b** coals.*
Pr 26:23 {Smooth} As in Greek version; Hebrew reads ***B**.*
Lk 20:37 {to the Lord} Greek *when he wrote about the **b** bush, he referred to the Lord.*
Ro 12:20 {done to you."} Greek *and you will heap **b** coals on their heads.* Prov 25:21-22.

BURY (2)
Mt 8:22 {their own dead."} Greek *Let the dead **b** their own dead.*
Lk 9:60 {their own dead.} Greek *Let the dead **b** their own dead.*

BUSH (2)
Mk 12:26 {said to Moses,} Greek *in the story of the **b**? God said to him.*
Lk 20:37 {to the Lord} Greek *when he wrote about the burning **b**, he referred to the Lord.*

C

CAB (1)
2Ki 6:25 {about two ounces} Hebrew *sold for 80 shekels* [0.9 kilograms] *of silver, and 1/4 of a **c*** [0.3 liters] *of dove's dung cost 5 shekels* [57 grams]. *Dove's dung* may be a variety of wild vegetable.

CAIN (1)
Ge 4: 1 {birth to Cain,} ***C*** sounds like a Hebrew term that can mean "bring forth" or "acquire."

CAINAN (7)
Ge 10:24 {father of Shelah,} Greek version reads *Arphaxad was the father of **C**, **C** was the father of Shelah.*
11:12[-13] {sons and daughters.} Greek version reads *[12]When Arphaxad was 135 years old, his son **C** was born. [13]After the birth of **C**, Arphaxad lived another 430 years and had other sons and daughters, and then he died. When **C** was 130 years old, his son Shelah was born. After the birth of Shelah, **C** lived another 330 years and had other sons and daughters, and then he died.*
1Ch 1:24 {Shem: Arphaxad, Shelah,} Some Greek manuscripts read *Arphaxad, **C**, Shelah.* See notes on Gen 10:24 and 11:12-13.

CAKES (1)
Hos 3: 1 {them choice gifts.} Hebrew *raisin **c**.*

CALEB (1)
1Ch 2: 9 {Ram, and Caleb.} Hebrew *Kelubai,* a variant name for **C**; compare 2:18.

CALL (3 of 4)
Ac 10:15 {say it isn't."} Greek *"What God calls clean you must not **c** unclean."*
11: 9 {say it isn't.'} Greek *'What God calls clean you must not **c** unclean.'*
1Co 5: 4 {of the church,} Or *In the name of the Lord Jesus, you are to **c** a meeting of the church.*

CALLED (4 of 16)
Jn 11:16 {nicknamed the Twin,} Greek *the one who was **c** Didymus.*
20:24 {(nicknamed the Twin} Greek *the one who was **c** Didymus.*
21: 2 {(nicknamed the Twin} Greek *the one who was **c** Didymus.*
Ac 13: 1 {"the black man"} Greek *who was **c** Niger.*

CALLING (1)
Mk 3:14 {calling them apostles.} Some manuscripts do not include *c them apostles.*

CALLS (3)
Ecc 3:15 {in its turn.} Hebrew *For God c the past to account.*
Ac 10:15 {say it isn't."} Greek *"What God c clean you must not call unclean."*
11:9 {say it isn't.'} Greek *'What God c clean you must not call unclean.'*

CALVARY (1)
Lk 23:33 {called The Skull.} Sometimes rendered *C*, which comes from the Latin word for "skull."

CAMP (1)
Jdg 18:12 {is called Mahaneh-dan} *Mahaneh-dan* means "the **c** of Dan."

CAMPS (1)
Ge 32:2 {the place Mahanaim.} *Mahanaim* means "two **c**."

CANAAN (2)
Isa 19:18 {the Hebrew language.} Hebrew *the language of C.*
23:11 {out against Phoenicia} Hebrew *C.*

CANAANITE (1)
Mt 15:22 {A Gentile} Greek *C.*

CANAANITES (1)
Zec 14:21 {longer be traders} Hebrew *C.*

CANANEAN (2)
Mt 10:4 {Simon (the Zealot} Greek *the C.*
Mk 3:18 {Simon (the Zealot} Greek *the C.*

CANDACE (1)
Ac 8:27 {queen of Ethiopia.} Greek *under the C, the queen of Ethiopia.*

CAPHTOR (3)
Dt 2:23 {Caphtorites from Crete} Hebrew *from C.*
Jer 47:4 {colonists from Crete.} Hebrew *from C.*
Am 9:7 {Philistines from Crete} Hebrew *C.*

CAPHTORITES (2)
Ge 10:14 {the Philistines came.} Hebrew *Casluhites, from whom the Philistines came, C.* Compare Jer 47:4; Amos 9:7.
1Ch 1:12 {the Philistines came.} Hebrew *Casluhites, from whom the Philistines came, C.* See Jer 47:4; Amos 9:7.

CAPTAINS (1)
1Ch 11:11 {among David's men.} As in some Greek manuscripts (see also 2 Sam 23:8); Hebrew *commander of the Thirty*, or *commander of the c.*

CAPTIVE (2)
Mic 2:4 {who betrayed us.} Or *to those who took us c.*
2Ti 3:6 {the confidence of} Greek *and take c.*

CAPTURED (2)
2Sa 12:27 {its water supply.} Or *c the city of water.*
1Ch 2:23 {Towns of Jair} Or *c Havvoth-jair.*

CARCASS (2)
Mt 24:28 {end is near.} Greek *Wherever the c is, the vultures gather.*
Lk 17:37 {end is near."} Greek *Wherever the c is, the vultures gather.*

CARE (2)
Ps 8:4 {care for us?} Hebrew *What is man that you should think of him, the son of man that you should c for him?*
Isa 33:8 {made before witnesses.} As in Dead Sea Scrolls; Masoretic Text reads *c nothing for the cities.*

CARED (1)
Ac 13:18 {up with them} Other manuscripts read *He c for them;* compare Deut 1:31.

CARMEL (1)
1Sa 30:29 {Racal,} Greek version reads *C.*

CARRIED (1)
Isa 53:4 {was our sorrows} Or *Yet it was our sicknesses he c; it was our diseases.*

CARRY (1)
Mt 3:11 {be his slave.} Greek *to c his sandals.*

CASLUHITES (2)
Ge 10:14 {the Philistines came.} Hebrew *C, from whom the Philistines came, Caphtorites.* Compare Jer 47:4; Amos 9:7.
1Ch 1:12 {the Philistines came.} Hebrew *C, from whom the Philistines came, Caphtorites.* See Jer 47:4; Amos 9:7.

CASSIA (1)
Ex 30:24 {and one gallon} Hebrew *500 shekels* [5.7 kilograms] *of c, according to the sanctuary shekel, and 1 hin* [3.8 liters].

CAST (5)
Ps 22:18 {and throw dice} Hebrew *c lots.*
Mt 12:29 {house be robbed!} Or *One cannot rob Satan's kingdom without first tying him up. Only then can his demons be c out.*
27:35 {by throwing dice.} Greek *by casting lots.* A few late manuscripts add *This fulfilled the word of the prophet: "They divided my clothes among themselves and c lots for my robe."* See Ps 22:18.
Mk 3:27 {house be robbed!} Or *One cannot rob Satan's kingdom without first tying him up. Only then can his demons be c out.*
Jn 19:24 {but throw dice} Greek *c lots.*

CASTING (3)
Mt 27:35 {by throwing dice.} Greek *by c lots.* A few late manuscripts add *This fulfilled the word of the prophet: "They divided my clothes among themselves and cast lots for my robe."* See Ps 22:18.
Mk 15:24 {clothes, throwing dice} Greek *c lots.* See Ps 22:18.
Lk 23:34 {by throwing dice.} Greek *by c lots.* See Ps 22:18.

CASTOR (1)
Ac 28:11 {the twin gods} The *twin gods* were the Roman gods **C** and Pollux.

CASTRATE (1)
Gal 5:12 {would mutilate themselves.} Or *c themselves;* Greek reads *cut themselves off.*

CATTLE (1)
Job 36:33 {his indignant anger.} Or *even the c know when a storm is coming.* The meaning of the Hebrew is uncertain.

CAUSE (2)
Mt 5:22 {angry with someone,} Some manuscripts add *without c.*
1Ti 1:4 {and spiritual pedigrees.} Greek *in myths and endless genealogies, which c speculation.*

CAUSED (1)
1Ki 2:5 {time of peace,} Or *He murdered them during a time of peace as revenge for deaths they had c in time of war.*

CAUSES (2)
Nu 5:21 {makes you infertile.} Hebrew *when he c your thigh to waste away and your abdomen to swell.*
Ps 29:9 {twists mighty oaks} Or *c the deer to writhe in labor.*

CAUSING (1)
Ge 41:51 {older son Manasseh,} *Manasseh* sounds like a Hebrew term that means "**c** to forget."

CAUTIOUS (1)
Pr 12:26 {to their friends;} Or *The godly are c in friendship,* or *the godly are freed from evil.* The meaning of the Hebrew is uncertain.

CEDAR (2)
1Ki 6:20 {made of cedar.} Or *overlaid the altar with c.* The meaning of the Hebrew is uncertain.
SS 8:9 {off from men.} Hebrew *If she is a wall, we will build battlements of silver on her; but if she is a door, we will surround her with panels of c.*

CELEBRATION (1 of 2)
Jn 10:22 {time of Hanukkah.} Or *the Dedication C.*

CEMETERY (1)
Mt 27:51[-53] {to many people.} Or *The earth shook, rocks split apart, tombs opened, and many bodies of godly men and women who had died were raised from the dead. After Jesus' resurrection, they left the c, went into the holy city of Jerusalem, and appeared to many people.*

CENTER (1)
Jdg 9:37 {from the hills.} Or *the c of the land.*

CENTRAL (1)
Ac 27:27 {Sea of Adria,} The *Sea of Adria* is in the **c** Mediterranean; it is not to be confused with the Adriatic Sea.

CEPHAS (7)
Jn 1:42 {(which means Peter} The names *C* and *Peter* both mean "rock."
1Co 1:12 {"I follow Peter,} Greek *C.*
3:22 {Apollos and Peter} Greek *C.*
9:5 {brothers and Peter} Greek *C.*
15:5 {seen by Peter} Greek *C.*
Gal 1:18 {visit with Peter} Greek *C.*
2:9 {fact, James, Peter,} Greek *C;* also in 2:11, 14.

CERTAIN (1)
Jn 5:3 {on the porches.} Some manuscripts add *waiting for a c movement of the water,* [4]*for an angel of the Lord came from time to time and stirred up the water. And the first person to step down into it afterward was healed.*

CHAINS (1)
2Pe 2:4 {in gloomy caves} Some manuscripts read *c of gloom.*

CHALDEA (7)
Isa 23:13 {land of Babylonia} Or *C.*
47:1 {O daughter of Babylonia,} Or *C;* also in 47:5.
Jer 50:10 {Babylonia} Or *C.*
51:24 {people of Babylonia} Or *C;* also in 51:35.
Eze 11:24 {again to Babylonia,} Or *C.*
16:29 {land of Babylonia} Or *C.*
23:15 {land of Babylonia.} Or *C;* also in 23:16.

CHALDEAN (11)
2Ki 24:2 {bands of Babylonian,} Or *C.*
25:10 {the entire Babylonian} Or *C;* also in 25:24.
Ezr 5:12 {Nebuchadnezzar of Babylon,} Aramaic *Nebuchadnezzar the C.*
Isa 48:14 {destroying the Babylonian} Or *C.*
Jer 22:25 {the mighty Babylonian} Or *C.*
35:11 {of the Babylonian} Or *C.*
37:5 {When the Babylonian} Or *C;* also in 37:10, 11.
41:3 {officials and Babylonian} Or *C.*
52:14 {the entire Babylonian} Or *C.*
Eze 23:14 {wall—pictures of Babylonian} Or *C.*
Da 5:30 {Belshazzar, the Babylonian} Or *C.*

CHALDEANS (27)
2Ki 25:4 {by the Babylonians,} Or *the C;* also in 25:5, 13, 25, 26.
2Ch 36:17 {them. The Babylonians} Or *C.*
Isa 43:14 {And the Babylonians} Or *C.*
48:20 {and the Babylonians,} Or *the C.*
Jer 21:4 {and the Babylonians} Or *C;* also in 21:9.
24:5 {of the Babylonians.} Or *C.*
25:12 {of the Babylonians} Or *C.*
32:4 {by the Babylonians} Or *C;* also in 32:5, 24, 25, 28, 29, 43.
33:5 {the Babylonians} Or *C.*
37:8 {Then the Babylonians} Or *C;* also in 37:9, 13.
38:2 {to the Babylonians} Or *C;* also in 38:18, 19, 23.
39:5 {But the Babylonians} Or *C;* also in 39:8.
40:9 {to the Babylonians.} Or *C;* also in 40:10.
41:18 {what the Babylonians} Or *C.*
43:3 {by the Babylonians} Or *C.*
50:1 {the Babylonians.} Or *C;* also in 50:8, 25, 35, 45.
51:4 {of the Babylonians,} Or *C;* also in 51:54.
52:7 {by the Babylonians,} Or *C;* also in 50:8, 17.
Eze 1:3 {of the Babylonians,} Or *C.*
12:13 {of the Babylonians,} Or *C.*
Da 1:4 {of the Babylonians.} Or *of the C.*
2:2 {and astrologers,} Or *C;* also in 2:4, 5, 10.
3:8 {of the astrologers} Aramaic *C.*
4:7 {magicians, enchanters, astrologers,} Or *C.*
5:7 {the enchanters, astrologers,} Or *C;* also in 5:11.
9:1 {of the Babylonians.} Or *the C.*
Hab 1:6 {up the Babylonians} Or *C.*

CHARGE (1)
Heb 2:7 {glory and honor.} Some manuscripts add *You put him in c of everything you made.*

CHARIOTEERS (11)
2Sa 8:4 {seventeen hundred charioteers} Greek version reads *1,000 chariots and 7,000 c;* compare 1 Chr 18:4.
1Ki 1:5 {chariots and horses} Or *and c.*
4:26 {twelve thousand horses.} Or *12,000 c.*
9:19 {chariots and horses} Or *and c.*
10:26 {twelve thousand horses.} Or *12,000 c.*
2Ki 18:24 {chariots and horsemen} Or *and c.*
2Ch 1:14 {twelve thousand horses.} Or *12,000 c.*
8:6 {chariots and horses} Or *and c.*
9:25 {twelve thousand horses.} Or *12,000 c.*
16:8 {chariots and horsemen} Or *and c.*
Isa 36:9 {chariots and horsemen} Or *and c.*

CHARIOTS (5)

2Sa 8: 4 {seventeen hundred charioteers} Greek version reads *1,000 **c** and 7,000 charioteers;* compare 1 Chr 18:4.
Ps 20: 7 {armies and weapons,} Hebrew *c and horses.*
SS 1: 9 {my beloved one!} Hebrew *I compare you, my beloved, to a mare among Pharaoh's **c**.*
6:12 {my beloved one.} Or *among the royal **c** of my people,* or *among the **c** of Amminadab.* The meaning of the Hebrew is uncertain.

CHEAT (1)

Mt 23:13 {go in yourselves.} Some manuscripts add verse 14, *How terrible it will be for you teachers of religious law and you Pharisees. Hypocrites! You shamelessly **c** widows out of their property, and then, to cover up the kind of people you really are, you make long prayers in public. Because of this, your punishment will be the greater.*

CHEESE (1)

Job 10:10 {in the womb.} Hebrew *You poured me out like milk and curdled me like **c**.*

CHERUB (4)

2Sa 22:11 {a mighty angel,} Hebrew *c.*
Ps 18:10 {a mighty angel,} Hebrew *a **c**.*
Eze 10:14 {of an ox,} Hebrew *the face of a **c**;* compare 1:10.
28:14 {mighty angelic guardian.} Hebrew *guardian **c**;* also in 28:16.

CHERUBIM (1)

Ge 3:24 {mighty angelic beings} Hebrew *c.*

CHIEF (1)

Da 10:13 {of the archangels,} Hebrew *the **c** princes.*

CHILD (2)

1Ti 2:15 {saved through childbearing} Or *will be saved by accepting their role as mothers,* or *will be saved by the birth of the **C**.*
Heb 11:11 {keep his promise.} Some manuscripts read *It was by faith that Sarah was able to have a **c**, even though she was too old and barren. Sarah believed that God would keep his promise.*

CHILDREN (7)

Ezr 10:44 {by these wives.} Or *and they sent them away with their **c**.* The meaning of the Hebrew is uncertain.
Eze 20:31 {burned as sacrifices,} Or *and make your little **c** pass through the fire.*
Mt 27:25 {and our children!"} Greek *"His blood be on us and on our **c**."*
Mk 7:27 {family, the Jews.} Greek *Let the **c** eat first.*
Lk 7:35 {who follow it.} Or *But wisdom is justified by all her **c**.*
Jn 8:39 {his good example.} Some manuscripts read *if you are **c** of Abraham, follow his example.*
2Jn 1: 1 {to her children,} Or *the church God has chosen and her members,* or *the chosen Kyria and her **c**.*

CHOICE (1)

1Ki 4:22 {bushels of meal,} Hebrew *30 cors* [5.5 kiloliters] *of **c** flour and 60 cors* [11 kiloliters] *of meal.*

CHOINIX (2)

Rev 6: 6 {day's pay.} Greek *A **c** of wheat for a denarius, and 3 **c** of barley for a denarius.*

CHOSEN (6)

1Sa 10:20 {Benjamin was chosen.} Hebrew *c by lot;* also in 10:21.
14:41 {Saul were chosen} Hebrew *c by lot.*
2Sa 21: 6 {the LORD.} As in Greek version (see also 21:9); Hebrew reads *at Gibeah of Saul, the **c** of the LORD.*
Jn 1:34 {Son of God.} Some manuscripts read *the **c** One of God.*
2Jn 1: 1 {to her children,} Or *the church God has **c** and her members,* or *the **c** Kyria and her children.*

CHR (54)

Ge 10: 4 {Kittim, and Rodanim.} As in some Hebrew manuscripts and Greek version (see also 1 **C** 1:7); most Hebrew manuscripts read *Dodanim.*
36:39 {Baal-hanan died, Hadad} As in some Hebrew manuscripts, Samaritan Pentateuch, and Syriac version (see also 1 **C** 1:50); most Hebrew manuscripts read *Hadar.*
46:13 {were Tola, Puah,} As in Syriac version and Samaritan Pentateuch (see also 1 **C** 7:1); Hebrew reads *Puvah.*
46:13 {Jashub,} As in some Greek manuscripts and Samaritan Pentateuch (see also Num 26:24; 1 **C** 7:1); Hebrew reads *Iob.*
46:27 {had two sons} Greek version reads *nine sons,* probably including Joseph's grandsons through Ephraim and Manasseh (see 1 **C** 7:14-20).
Nu 26:23 {its ancestor Puah.} As in Samaritan Pentateuch, Greek and Syriac versions, and Latin Vulgate (see also 1 **C** 7:1); Hebrew reads *The Punite clan, named after its ancestor Puvah.*
Jos 7: 1 {family of Zimri,} As in Greek version (see also 1 **C** 2:6); Hebrew reads *Zabdi.* Also in 7:17, 18.
2Sa 5:14 {in Jerusalem: Shimea,} As in parallel text at 1 **C** 3:5; Hebrew reads *Shammua,* a variant name for Shimea.
5:25 {way from Gibeon} As in Greek version (see also 1 **C** 14:16); Hebrew reads *Geba.*
6: 2 {Baalah of Judah} *Baalah of Judah* is another name for Kiriath-jearim; compare 1 **C** 13:6.
6: 5 {might, singing songs} As in Greek version (see also 1 **C** 13:8); Hebrew reads *cypress trees.*
8: 1 {their largest city.} Hebrew *by conquering Metheg-ammah,* a name which means "the bridle," possibly referring to the size of the city or the tribute money taken from it. Compare 1 **C** 18:1.
8: 4 {seventeen hundred charioteers} Greek version reads *1,000 chariots and 7,000 charioteers;* compare 1 **C** 18:4.
8: 8 {cities of Tebah} As in some Greek manuscripts (see also 1 **C** 18:8); Hebrew reads *Betah.*
8:12 {Edom,} As in a few Hebrew manuscripts and Greek and Syriac versions (see also 8:14; 1 **C** 18:11); most Hebrew manuscripts read *Aram.*
8:13 {eighteen thousand Edomites} As in a few Hebrew manuscripts and Greek and Syriac versions (see also 8:14; 1 **C** 18:12); most Hebrew manuscripts read *Arameans.*
8:18 {as priestly leaders.} Hebrew *David's sons were priests;* compare parallel text at 1 **C** 18:17.
10:18 {forty thousand horsemen,} Some Greek manuscripts read *foot soldiers;* compare parallel text at 1 **C** 19:18.
13: 3 {David's brother Shimea.} Hebrew *Shimeah* (also in 13:32), a variant name for Shimea; compare 1 **C** 2:13.
17:25 {an Ishmaelite.} As in some Greek manuscripts (see also 1 **C** 2:17); Hebrew reads *an Israelite.*
21:19 {son of Jair} As in parallel text at 1 **C** 20:5; Hebrew reads *son of Jaare-oregim.*
21:19 {Goliath of Gath.} As in parallel text at 1 **C** 20:5; Hebrew reads *killed Goliath of Gath.*
21:21 {Shimea.} As in parallel text at 1 **C** 20:7; Hebrew reads *Shimei,* a variant name for Shimea.
23: 8 {Jashobeam the Hacmonite,} As in parallel text at 1 **C** 11:11; Hebrew reads *Josheb-basshebeth the Tahkemonite.*
23: 8 {a single battle.} As in some Greek manuscripts (see also 1 **C** 11:11); the Hebrew is uncertain, though it might be rendered *the Three. It was Adino the Eznite who killed eight hundred men at one time.*
23:26 {Helez from Pelon} As in parallel text at 1 **C** 11:27 (see also 1 **C** 27:10); Hebrew reads *from Palti.*
23:27 {Sibbecai} As in some Greek manuscripts (see also 1 **C** 11:29); Hebrew reads *Mebunnai.*
23:29 {Heled} As in some Hebrew manuscripts (see also 1 **C** 11:30); most Hebrew manuscripts read *Heleb.*
23:29 {Ithai} As in parallel text at 1 **C** 11:31; Hebrew reads *Ittai.*
23:30 {Hurai} As in some Greek manuscripts (see also 1 **C** 11:32); Hebrew reads *Hiddai.*
23:33 {son of Shagee} As in parallel text at 1 **C** 11:34; Hebrew reads *Jonathan, Shammah;* some Greek manuscripts read *Jonathan son of Shammah.*
24:13 {you choose three} As in Greek version (see also 1 **C** 21:12); Hebrew reads *seven.*
1Ki 4:26 {four thousand} As in some Greek manuscripts (see also 2 **C** 9:25); Hebrew reads *40,000.*
5:11 {and 110,000 gallons} As in Greek version, which reads *20,000 baths* [420 kiloliters] (see also 2 **C** 2:10); Hebrew reads *20 cors,* about 800 gallons or 3.6 kiloliters in volume.
5:16 {and thirty-six hundred} As in some Greek manuscripts (see also 2 **C** 2:2, 18); Hebrew reads *3,300.*
7:13 {man named Huram} Hebrew *Hiram* (also in 7:40, 45); compare 2 **C** 2:13. This is not the same person mentioned in 5:1.
8:65 {Festival of Shelters.} Hebrew *seven days and seven days, fourteen days;* compare parallel text at 2 **C** 7:8-10.
8:66 {festival was over,} Hebrew *On the eighth day,* probably referring to the day following the seven-day Festival of Shelters; compare parallel text at 2 **C** 7:9-10.
12: 2 {returned from Egypt,} As in Greek version and Latin Vulgate (see also 2 **C** 10:2); Hebrew reads *he lived in Egypt.*
15: 2 {daughter of Absalom.} Hebrew *Abishalom* (also in 15:10), a variant name for Absalom; compare 2 **C** 11:20.
2Ki 12:21 {assassins were Jozacar} As in Greek and Syriac versions; Hebrew reads *Jozabad;* compare parallel text at 2 **C** 24:26.
18: 2 {mother was Abijah,} As in parallel text at 2 **C** 29:1; Hebrew reads *Abi,* a variant name for Abijah.
25:17 {was 7 1/2 feet} As in parallel texts at 1 Kgs 7:16, 2 **C** 3:15, and Jer 52:22, all of which read *5 cubits* [2.3 meters]; Hebrew reads *3 cubits,* which is 4.5 feet or 1.4 meters.
1Ch 11:12 {son of Dodai,} As in parallel text at 2 Sam 23:9 (see also 1 **C** 27:4); Hebrew reads *Dodo,* a variant name for Dodai.
2Ch 13: 2 {mother was Maacah,} As in most Greek manuscripts and Syriac version (see also 2 **C** 11:20-21; 1 Kgs 15:2); Hebrew reads *Micaiah.*
Ezr 7: 1 {was the son} Or *descendant;* see 1 **C** 6:14.
7: 3 {of Azariah, son} Or *descendant;* see 1 **C** 6:6-10.
Mt 1: 3 {father of Ram.} Greek *Aram;* also in 1:4. See 1 **C** 2:9-10.
1: 7 {father of Asaph.} *Asaph* is the same person as Asa; also in 1:8. See 1 **C** 3:10.
1: 8 {father of Jehoram.} Greek *Joram.* See 1 Kgs 22:50 and note at 1 **C** 3:11.
1:10 {father of Amos.} *Amos* is the same person as Amon. See 1 **C** 3:14.
1:11 {father of Jehoiachin} Greek *Jeconiah;* also in 1:12. See 2 Kgs 24:6 and note at 1 **C** 3:16.
Lk 3:33 {son of Arni.} *Arni* is the same person as Ram; see 1 **C** 2:9-10.

CHRIST (8)

Ac 8:36 {I be baptized?"} Some manuscripts add verse 37, *"You can," Philip answered, "if you believe with all your heart." And the eunuch replied, "I believe that Jesus **C** is the Son of God."*
Ro 16:23 {a Christian brother.} Some manuscripts add verse 24, *May the grace of our Lord Jesus **C** be with you all. Amen.*
1Co 3: 1 {the Christian life.} Greek *in **C**.*
2Co 12: 2 {I} Greek *I know a man in **C** who.*
Eph 3:14 {to the Father,} Some manuscripts read *the Father of our Lord Jesus **C**.*
2Th 1:12 {Lord, Jesus Christ.} Or *of our God and the Lord Jesus **C**.*
Heb 6: 1 {basics of Christianity} Or *the basics about **C**.*
1Jn 2: 1 {pleases God completely.} Greek *Jesus **C**, the righteous.*

CHRISTIAN (2)

Ac 26:28 {Christian so quickly?"} Or *"A little more, and your arguments would make me a **C**."*
1Co 7:39 {to the Lord.} Or *but only to a **C**;* Greek reads *but only in the Lord.*

CHRISTIANS (1)

2Co 1:21 {firm for Christ.} Or *who has identified us and you as genuine **C**.*

CHURCH (6)

Ac 18:22 {church at Jerusalem} Greek *the **c**.*
1Co 5: 4 {of the church,} Or *In the name of the Lord Jesus, you are to call a meeting of the **c**.*
Gal 1:13 {persecuted the Christians.} Greek *the **c** of God.*
1Ti 5: 7 {widows you support} Or *so the **c**;* Greek reads *so they.*
2Jn 1: 1 {to her children,} Or *the **c** God has chosen and her members,* or *the chosen Kyria and her children.*
1:13 {of your sister,} Or *from the members of your sister **c**.*

CHURCHES (1)

1Co 14:33 {the other churches.} The phrase *as in all the other **c*** could be joined to the beginning of 14:34.

CILICIA (6)

1Ki 10:28 {imported from Egypt} Possibly *Muzur,* a district near **C**; also in 10:29.
10:28 {and from Cilicia} Hebrew *Kue,* probably another name for **C**.
2Ki 7: 6 {Hittites and Egyptians} Possibly *and the people of Muzur,* a district near **C**.
2Ch 1:16 {imported from Egypt} Possibly *Muzur,* a district near **C**; also in 1:17.
1:16 {and from Cilicia} Hebrew *Kue,* probably another name for **C**.
9:28 {imported from Egypt} Possibly *Muzur,* a district near **C**.

CIRCUMCISION (1)

Ac 11: 2 {the Jewish believers} Greek *those of the **c**.*

CISTERN (1)

Pr 5:15 {with your wife.} Hebrew *Drink water from your own **c**, flowing water from your own well.*

CITIES (2 of 4)

Isa 33: 8 {made before witnesses.} As in Dead Sea Scrolls; Masoretic Text reads *care nothing for the **c**.*
Eze 30:17 {and the women} Or *her **c**.*

CITY (16)

Jdg 1:16 {Judah left Jericho,} Hebrew *the **c** of palms.*
3:13 {possession of Jericho.} Hebrew *the **c** of palms.*
1Sa 5: 6 {plague of tumors.} Greek version and Latin Vulgate read *tumors. And rats appeared in their land, and death and destruction were throughout the **c**.*
2Sa 8: 1 {their largest city.} Hebrew *by conquering Metheg-ammah,* a name which means "the bridle," possibly referring to the size of the **c** or the tribute money taken from it. Compare 1 Chr 18:1.
12:27 {its water supply.} Or *captured the **c** of water.*
2Ki 10:25 {into the fortress} Hebrew *c.*
2Ch 25:28 {City of David.} As in some Hebrew manuscripts and other ancient versions (see also 2 Kgs 14:20); most Hebrew manuscripts read *the **c** of Judah.*
Isa 22: 9 {walls of Jerusalem} Hebrew *the **c** of David.*

Eze 11: 3 {from all harm.} Hebrew *This **c** is the pot, and we are the meat.*
Mt 27:32 {was from Cyrene,} *Cyrene* was a **c** in northern Africa.
27:51[-53] {to many people.} Or *The earth shook, rocks split apart, tombs opened, and many bodies of godly men and women who had died were raised from the dead. After Jesus' resurrection, they left the cemetery, went into the holy **c** of Jerusalem, and appeared to many people.*
Mk 15:21 {was from Cyrene,} *Cyrene* was a **c** in northern Africa.
Lk 23:26 {Simon of Cyrene,} *Cyrene* was a **c** in northern Africa.
Ac 7: 2 {moved to Haran.} *Mesopotamia* was the region now called Iraq. *Haran* was a **c** in what is now called Syria.
17: 5 {to the crowd.} Or *the **c** council.*
Rev 11: 8 {street of Jerusalem,} Greek *the great **c**.*

CLAN (2)

Nu 26:23 {its ancestor Puah.} As in Samaritan Pentateuch, Greek and Syriac versions, and Latin Vulgate (see also 1 Chr 7:1); Hebrew reads *The Punite **c**, named after its ancestor Puvah.*
1Ch 6:39 {clan of Gershon.} Hebrew lacks *from the **c** of Gershon;* see 6:43.

CLAUDA (1)

Ac 27:16 {island named Cauda,} Some manuscripts read ***C**.*

CLEAN (2)

Ac 10:15 {say it isn't."} Greek *"What God calls **c** you must not call unclean."*
11: 9 {say it isn't.'} Greek *'What God calls **c** you must not call unclean.'*

CLEANSE (1)

Isa 52:15 {will again startle} Or ***c**.*

CLEANSED (2)

1Co 6:11 {been washed away,} Or *you have been **c**.*
Eph 5:26 {and God's word.} Greek *having **c** her by the washing of water with the word.*

CLIP (3)

Jer 9:26 {in distant places,} Or *the people who **c** the corners of their hair.*
25:23 {in distant places.} Or *who **c** the corners of their hair.*
49:32 {in distant places.} Or *who **c** the corners of their hair.*

CLOSED (1)

Ne 7: 3 {of the day.} Or *Keep the gates of Jerusalem **c** until the sun is hot.*

CLOTHES (1)

Mt 27:35 {by throwing dice.} Greek *by casting lots.* A few late manuscripts add *This fulfilled the word of the prophet: "They divided my **c** among themselves and cast lots for my robe."* See Ps 22:18.

CLOTHING (2)

2Ki 1: 8 {hairy man,} Or *He was wearing **c** made of hair.*
Jude 1:23 {by their sins.} Greek *mercy, hating even the **c** stained by the flesh.*

COALS (2)

Ps 18:13 {a mighty shout.} As in Greek version (see also 2 Sam 22:14); Hebrew adds *raining down hail and burning **c**.*
Ro 12:20 {done to you."} Greek *and you will heap burning **c** on their heads.* Prov 25:21-22.

COAT (1)

Ge 37: 3 {a beautiful robe.} Traditionally rendered *a **c** of many colors.* The exact meaning of the Hebrew is uncertain.

COLD (1)

Zec 14: 6 {no longer shine,} Hebrew *there will be no light, no **c** or frost.* The meaning of the Hebrew is uncertain.

COLLECTORS (3)

Mt 9:11 {with such scum} Greek *with tax **c** and sinners.*
Mk 2:16 {with such scum} Greek *with tax **c** and sinners.*
Lk 5:30 {with such scum} Greek *with tax **c** and sinners.*

COLONNADE (1)

1Ch 26:18 {to the courtyard.} Or *the **c**.* The meaning of the Hebrew is uncertain.

COLORS (1)

Ge 37: 3 {a beautiful robe.} Traditionally rendered *a coat of many **c**.* The exact meaning of the Hebrew is uncertain.

COLT (1)

Job 11:12 {bear human offspring} Or *bear a tame **c**.*

COMFORT (1)

Ge 5:29 {his son Noah,} *Noah* sounds like a Hebrew term that can mean "relief" or "**c**."

COMFORTER (3)

Jn 14:16 {you another Counselor,} Or ***C***, or *Encourager,* or *Advocate.* Greek *Paraclete;* also in 14:26.
15:26 {you the Counselor} Or ***C***, or *Encourager,* or *Advocate.* Greek *Paraclete.*
16: 7 {don't, the Counselor} Or ***C***, or *Encourager,* or *Advocate.* Greek *Paraclete.*

COMMANDER (3)

1Ch 11:11 {among David's men.} As in some Greek manuscripts (see also 2 Sam 23:8); Hebrew ***c** of the Thirty,* or ***c** of the captains.*
Ac 24: 6 {we arrested him.} Some manuscripts add *We would have judged him by our law, [7]but Lysias, the **c** of the garrison, came and took him violently away from us, [8]commanding his accusers to come before you.*

COMMANDERS (3)

Nu 31:14 {the military commanders} Hebrew *the **c** of thousands, and the **c** of hundreds;* also in 31:48, 52, 54.
1Ki 1:25 {of the army,} As in Greek version; Hebrew reads *invited the **c** of the army.*

COMMANDS (1)

Isa 29:13 {learned by rote.} Greek version reads *Their worship is a farce, for they merely teach human **c** and teachings.*

COMMITS (1)

Mt 19: 9 {has been unfaithful.} Some manuscripts add *And the man who marries a divorced woman **c** adultery.*

COMMON (2)

Ac 10:14 {our Jewish laws.} Greek *anything **c** and unclean.*
11: 8 {our Jewish laws.} Greek *anything **c** or unclean.*

COMPARE (86)

Ge 10:14 {the Philistines came.} Hebrew *Casluhites, from whom the Philistines came, Caphtorites.* **C** Jer 47:4; Amos 9:7.
11:32 {for 205 years} Some ancient versions read *145 years;* **c** 11:26; 12:4.
36:26 {sons of Dishon} Hebrew *Dishan,* a variant name for Dishon; **c** 36:21, 28.
Ex 19: 1 {they left Egypt.} Hebrew *in the third month...on the very day,* i.e., two lunar months to the day after leaving Egypt. This day of the Hebrew lunar calendar occurs in late May or early June; **c** note on 13:4.
Lev 6: 6 {value in silver.} Or *and the animal must be of the proper value;* Hebrew lacks *in silver;* **c** 5:15.
16: 1 {LORD had commanded.} Hebrew *when they approached the LORD's presence;* **c** 10:1.
Jdg 9:46 {temple of Baal-berith.} Hebrew *El-berith,* another name for Baal-berith; **c** 9:4.
1Sa 1: 1 {lived in Ramah} Hebrew *Ramathaim-zophim;* **c** 1:19.
13: 1 {for forty-two years.} Hebrew *reigned...and two;* the number is incomplete in the Hebrew. **C** Acts 13:21.
2Sa 6: 2 {Baalah of Judah} *Baalah of Judah* is another name for Kiriath-jearim; **c** 1 Chr 13:6.
8: 1 {their largest city.} Hebrew *by conquering Metheg-ammah,* a name which means "the bridle," possibly referring to the size of the city or the tribute money taken from it. **C** 1 Chr 18:1.
8: 4 {seventeen hundred charioteers} Greek version reads *1,000 chariots and 7,000 charioteers;* **c** 1 Chr 18:4.
8:18 {as priestly leaders.} Hebrew *David's sons were priests;* **c** parallel text at 1 Chr 18:17.
10:18 {forty thousand horsemen,} Some Greek manuscripts read *foot soldiers;* **c** parallel text at 1 Chr 19:18.
12:30 {the king's head,} Greek version reads *removed the crown of Milcom;* **c** 1 Kgs 11:5. Milcom, also called Molech, was the god of the Ammonites.
13: 3 {David's brother Shimea.} Hebrew *Shimeah* (also in 13:32), a variant name for Shimea; **c** 1 Chr 2:13.
15:27 {You and Abiathar} Hebrew lacks *and Abiathar;* **c** 15:29.
1Ki 4:19 {land of Gilead,} Greek version reads *of Gad;* **c** 4:13.
7:13 {man named Huram} Hebrew *Hiram* (also in 7:40, 45); **c** 2 Chr 2:13. This is not the same person mentioned in 5:1.
8:65 {Festival of Shelters.} Hebrew *seven days and seven days, fourteen days;* **c** parallel text at 2 Chr 7:8-10.
8:66 {festival was over,} Hebrew *On the eighth day,* probably referring to the day following the seven-day Festival of Shelters; **c** parallel text at 2 Chr 7:9-10.
15: 2 {Absalom.} Hebrew *Abishalom* (also in 15:10), a variant name for Absalom; **c** 2 Chr 11:20.
15:10 {His grandmother} Hebrew *his mother* (also in 15:13); **c** 15:2.
2Ki 12:21 {assassins were Jozacar} As in Greek and Syriac versions; Hebrew reads *Jozabad;* **c** parallel text at 2 Chr 24:26.
25: 3 {Zedekiah's eleventh year,} Hebrew *By the ninth day,* that is, "of the fourth month of Zedekiah's eleventh year" (**c** Jer 52:6 and the note there)....
1Ch 1:42 {sons of Dishan} Hebrew *Dishon;* **c** 1:38 and parallel text at Gen 36:28.
2: 7 {Achan} Hebrew *Achar;* **c** Josh 7:1. *Achar* means "disaster."
2: 9 {Ram, and Caleb.} Hebrew *Kelubai,* a variant name for Caleb; **c** 2:18.
2:19 {Caleb married Ephrathah,} Hebrew *Ephrath,* a variant name for Ephrathah; **c** 2:50 and 4:4.
3: 6 {Elpelet,} Hebrew *Eliphelet;* **c** parallel text at 14:5-7.
6:23 {Elkanah, Abiasaph,} Hebrew *Ebiasaph,* a variant name for Abiasaph (also in 6:37); **c** parallel text at Exod 6:24.
7:35 {his brother Helem} Possibly another name for *Hotham;* **c** 7:32.
7:37 {Shamma, Shilshah, Ithran,} Possibly another name for *Jether;* **c** 7:38.
8: 3 {Addar, Gera, Abihud,} Possibly *Gera the father of Ehud;* **c** 8:6.
9:19 {descendant of Abiasaph,} Hebrew *Ebiasaph,* a variant name for Abiasaph; **c** Exod 6:24.
14: 4 {in Jerusalem: Shimea,} Hebrew *Shammua,* a variant name for Shimea; **c** 3:5.
14: 7 {Eliada,} Hebrew *Beeliada,* a variant name for Eliada; **c** 3:8 and parallel text at 2 Sam 5:16.
14:12 {abandoned their idols} Hebrew *their gods;* **c** parallel text at 2 Sam 5:21.
18: 8 {cities of Tebah} Hebrew reads *Tibhath,* a variant name for Tebah; **c** parallel text at 2 Sam 8:8.
19: 1 {his son Hanun} Hebrew lacks *Hanun;* **c** parallel text at 2 Sam 10:1.
20: 2 {the king's head,} Greek version and Latin Vulgate read *removed the crown of Milcom;* **c** 1 Kgs 11:5. Milcom, also called Molech, was the god of the Ammonites.
23: 7 {descent from Libni} Hebrew *Ladan* (also in 23:8-9), another name for Libni; **c** 6:17.
24:20 {leader was Shebuel.} Hebrew *Shubael* (also in 24:20b), a variant name for Shebuel; **c** 23:16 and 26:24.
24:22 {leader was Shelomith.} Hebrew *Shelomoth* (also in 24:22b), a variant name for Shelomith; **c** 23:18.
24:23 {was the leader,} Hebrew *From the descendants of Jeriah;* **c** 23:19.
25: 4 {Mattaniah, Uzziel, Shubael,} Hebrew *Shebuel,* a variant name for Shubael; **c** 25:20.
25:11 {fell to Zeri} Hebrew *Izri,* a variant name for Zeri; **c** 25:3.
25:14 {fell to Asarelah} Hebrew *Jesharelah,* a variant name for Asarelah; **c** 25:2.
25:18 {fell to Uzziel} Hebrew *Azarel,* a variant name for Uzziel; **c** 25:4.
25:22 {fell to Jerimoth} Hebrew *Jeremoth,* a variant name for Jerimoth; **c** 25:4.
25:24 {fell to Joshbekashah} Hebrew *Joshbekasha,* a variant name for Joshbekashah; **c** 25:4.
25:29 {fell to Geddalti} Hebrew *Giddalti,* a variant name for Geddalti; **c** 25:4.
26:14 {went to Meshelemiah} Hebrew *Shelemiah,* a variant name for Meshelemiah; **c** 26:2.
26:21 {family of Libni} Hebrew *Ladan,* another name for Libni; **c** 6:17.
26:21 {of Gershon, Jehiel} Hebrew *Jehieli* (also in 26:22), a variant name for Jehiel; **c** 23:8.
26:31 {Hebron came Jeriah,} Hebrew *Jerijah,* a variant name for Jeriah; **c** 23:19.
27: 8 {Shammah} Hebrew *Shamhuth,* another name for Shammah; **c** 11:27 and 2 Sam 23:25.
27:15 {Heled,} Hebrew *Heldai,* a variant name for Heled; **c** 11:30 and 2 Sam 23:29.
2Ch 2: 8 {cypress, and almug} Hebrew *algum;* **c** 9:10-11 and parallel text at 1 Kgs 10:11-12.
3: 1 {floor of Araunah} Hebrew reads *Ornan,* another name for Araunah; **c** 2 Sam 24:16.
9:10 {of almug wood} Hebrew *algum wood* (also in 9:11); **c** parallel text at 1 Kgs 10:11-12.
10:18 {Rehoboam sent Adoniram,} Hebrew *Hadoram,* a variant name for Adoniram; **c** 1 Kgs 4:6; 5:14; 12:18.
21:17 {youngest son, Ahaziah,} Hebrew *Jehoahaz,* a variant name for Ahaziah; **c** 22:1.
24:26 {assassins were Jozacar,} Hebrew *Zabad;* **c** parallel text at 2 Kgs 12:21, and see note there.
26: 8 {The Meunites} As in Greek version; Hebrew reads *Ammonites.* **C** 26:7.
Ezr 3: 9 {descendants of Hodaviah.} Hebrew *sons of Judah* (i.e., *bene Yehudah*). *Bene* might also be read here as the proper name Binnui; *Yehudah* is probably another name for Hodaviah. **C** 2:40; Neh 7:43; 1 Esdras 5:58.
6: 3 {be ninety feet.} Aramaic *Its height will be 60 cubits* [27 meters], *and its width will be 60 cubits.* It is commonly held that this verse should be emended to read: "Its height will be 45 feet, its length will be 90 feet, and its width will be 30 feet"; **c** 1 Kgs 6:2. The emendation regarding the width is supported by the Syriac version.

Ne 1: 1 {King Artaxerxes' reign,} Hebrew *In the month of Kislev of the twentieth year....* The *twentieth year* probably refers to the reign of King Artaxerxes I; **c** 2:1; 5:14.
12: 3 {Shecaniah, Harim,} Hebrew *Rehum;* **c** 7:42; 12:15; Ezra 2:39.
12: 5 {Miniamin, Moadiah,} Hebrew *Mijamin, Maadiah;* **c** 12:17.
12: 11 {father of Johanan.} Hebrew *Jonathan;* **c** 12:22.
12: 20 {family of Sallu.} Hebrew *Sallai;* **c** 12:7.
12: 23 {Johanan, the grandson} Hebrew *son;* **c** 12:10-11.
12: 24 {Sherebiah, Jeshua, Binnui,} Hebrew *son of* (i.e., *ben*), which should probably be read here as the proper name Binnui; **c** Ezra 3:9 and the note there.
Est 2: 21 {king's eunuchs, Bigthana} Hebrew *Bigthan;* **c** 6:2.
Pr 20: 16 {of a foreigner.} An alternate reading in the Hebrew text is *the debt of an adulterous woman;* **c** 27:13.
SS 1: 9 {my beloved one!} Hebrew *I* **c** *you, my beloved, to a mare among Pharaoh's chariots.*
Jer 42: 1 {Kareah and Jezaniah} Greek version reads *Azariah;* **c** 43:2.
51: 20 {"You} Possibly Cyrus, who was used of God to conquer Babylon. **C** Isa 44:28; 45:1.
Eze 10: 14 {of an ox,} Hebrew *the face of a cherub;* **c** 1:10.
45: 1 {6 2/3 miles wide.} Reflecting the Greek reading *25,000 cubits* [13.3 kilometers] *long and 20,000 cubits* [10.6 kilometers] *wide;* Hebrew reads *25,000 cubits long and 10,000 cubits wide.* **C** 45:3, 5; 48:9. In this chapter, the distance measures are calculated using the Hebrew long cubit, which equals 21 inches or 53 centimeters.
48: 9 {6 2/3 miles wide.} Reflecting the Greek reading in 45:1: *25,000 cubits* [13.3 kilometers] *long and 20,000 cubits* [10.6 kilometers] *wide;* Hebrew reads *25,000 cubits long and 10,000 cubits wide.* **C** 45:1-5; 48:10-13. In this chapter, the distance measures are calculated using the Hebrew long cubit, which equals 21 inches or 53 centimeters.
Da 8: 26 {evenings and mornings} Hebrew *about the evenings and mornings;* **c** 8:14.
Zec 6: 14 {who gave it—Heldai,} As in Syriac version (**c** 6:10); Hebrew reads *Helem.*
6: 14 {Jedaiah, and Josiah} As in Syriac version (**c** 6:10); Hebrew reads *Hen.*
Ac 13: 18 {up with them} Other manuscripts read *He cared for them;* **c** Deut 1:31.

COMPATRIOT (1)

Ro 16: 11 {Herodion, my relative.} Or **c**.

COMPATRIOTS (1)

Ro 16: 7 {my relatives,} Or **c**; also in 16:21.

COMPLAINT (1)

Hos 4: 4 {is with you!} Hebrew *Your people are like those with a* **c** *against the priests.*

COMPLETELY (1)

Heb 7: 25 {forever, to save} Or *able to save* **c**.

COMPULSION (1)

Ac 20: 22 {the Holy Spirit,} Or *by my spirit,* or *by an inner* **c**; Greek reads *by the spirit.*

CONCERN (1)

Jn 2: 17 {burns within me."} Or "**C** *for God's house will be my undoing."* Ps 69:9.

CONCERNING (1)

Isa 22: 1 {me concerning Jerusalem} Hebrew **c** *the Valley of Vision.*

CONEY (2)

Lev 11: 5 {the rock badger} Or **c**, or *hyrax.*
Dt 14: 7 {the rock badger.} Or **c**, or *hyrax.*

CONEYS (2)

Ps 104: 18 {for rock badgers.} Or **c**, or *hyraxes.*
Pr 30: 26 {Rock badgers} Or **c**, or *hyraxes.*

CONFIRMED (2)

Heb 2: 3 {was passed on} Or *and* **c**.
Rev 19: 10 {witness for Jesus.} Or *is the message* **c** *by Jesus.*

CONFRONT (1)

Job 41: 11 {and remain safe} As in Greek version; Hebrew reads **c** *me that I must pay.*

CONFRONTED (2)

Ex 4: 24 {LORD confronted Moses} Or **c** *Moses' son;* Hebrew reads **c** *him.*

CONFUSION (1)

Ge 11: 9 {was called Babel,} *Babel* sounds like a Hebrew term that means "**c**."

CONIAH (2)

Jer 22: 24 {abandon you, Jehoiachin} Hebrew **C**, a variant name for Jehoiachin; also in 22:28, 30.
37: 1 {Josiah succeeded Jehoiachin} Hebrew **C**, a variant name for Jehoiachin.

CONQUERING (1)

2Sa 8: 1 {their largest city.} Hebrew *by* **c** *Metheg-ammah,* a name which means "the bridle," possibly referring to the size of the city or the tribute money taken from it. Compare 1 Chr 18:1.

CONQUEROR (1)

Mic 1: 15 {people of Mareshah,} *Mareshah* sounds like the Hebrew term for "**c**."

CONSECRATION (28)

Lev 27: 21 {specially set apart} The Hebrew term used here refers to the complete **c** of things or people to the LORD, either by destroying them or by giving them as an offering; also in 27:28, 29.
Nu 18: 14 {for the LORD} The Hebrew term used here refers to the complete **c** of things or people to the LORD, either by destroying them or by giving them as an offering.
21: 2 {will completely destroy} The Hebrew term used here refers to the complete **c** of things or people to the LORD, either by destroying them or by giving them as an offering; also in 21:3.
Dt 2: 34 {and completely destroyed} The Hebrew term used here refers to the complete **c** of things or people to the LORD, either by destroying them or by giving them as an offering.
3: 6 {We completely destroyed} The Hebrew term used here refers to the complete **c** of things or people to the LORD, either by destroying them or by giving them as an offering.
7: 2 {must completely destroy} The Hebrew term used here refers to the complete **c** of things or people to the LORD, either by destroying them or by giving them as an offering; also in 7:26.
13: 15 {and completely destroy} The Hebrew term used here refers to the complete **c** of things or people to the LORD, either by destroying them or by giving them as an offering; also in 13:17.
20: 17 {must completely destroy} The Hebrew term used here refers to the complete **c** of things or people to the LORD, either by destroying them or by giving them as an offering.
Jos 2: 10 {you completely destroyed.} The Hebrew term used here refers to the complete **c** of things or people to the LORD, either by destroying them or by giving them as an offering.
6: 17 {be completely destroyed} The Hebrew term used here refers to the complete **c** of things or people to the LORD, either by destroying them or by giving them as an offering; also in 6:18, 21.
7: 1 {for the LORD.} The Hebrew term used here refers to the complete **c** of things or people to the LORD, either by destroying them or by giving them as an offering; also in 7:11, 12, 13, 15.
8: 26 {was completely destroyed.} The Hebrew term used here refers to the complete **c** of things or people to the LORD, either by destroying them or by giving them as an offering.
10: 1 {and completely destroyed} The Hebrew term used here refers to the complete **c** of things or people to the LORD, either by destroying them or by giving them as an offering; also in 10:28, 35, 37, 39, 40.
11: 11 {Israelites completely destroyed} The Hebrew term used here refers to the complete **c** of things or people to the LORD, either by destroying them or by giving them as an offering; also in 11:12, 20, 21.
22: 20 {for the LORD} The Hebrew term used here refers to the complete **c** of things or people to the LORD, either by destroying them or by giving them as an offering.
Jdg 1: 17 {they completely destroyed} The Hebrew term used here refers to the complete **c** of things or people to the LORD, either by destroying them or by giving them as an offering.
21: 11 {said. "Completely destroy} The Hebrew term used here refers to the complete **c** of things or people to the LORD, either by destroying them or by giving them as an offering.
1Sa 15: 3 {and completely destroy} The Hebrew term used here refers to the complete **c** of things or people to the LORD, either by destroying them or by giving them as an offering; also in 15:8, 9, 15, 18, 20, 21.
1Ki 9: 21 {not completely destroyed.} The Hebrew term used here refers to the complete **c** of things or people to the LORD, either by destroying them or by giving them as an offering.
20: 42 {must be destroyed,} The Hebrew term used here refers to the complete **c** of things or people to the LORD, either by destroying them or by giving them as an offering.
1Ch 2: 7 {for the LORD.} The Hebrew term used here refers to the complete **c** of things or people to the LORD, either by destroying them or by giving them as an offering.
4: 41 {and completely destroyed} The Hebrew term used here refers to the complete **c** of things or people to the LORD, either by destroying them or by giving them as an offering.
Isa 34: 2 {will completely destroy} The Hebrew term used here refers to the complete **c** of things or people to the LORD, either by destroying them or by giving them as an offering; also in 34:5.
43: 28 {of complete destruction} The Hebrew term used here refers to the complete **c** of things or people to the LORD, either by destroying them or by giving them as an offering.
Jer 25: 9 {will completely destroy} The Hebrew term used here refers to the complete **c** of things or people to the LORD, either by destroying them or by giving them as an offering.
50: 21 {and completely destroy} The Hebrew term used here refers to the complete **c** of things or people to the LORD, either by destroying them or by giving them as an offering.
51: 3 {be completely destroyed.} The Hebrew term used here refers to the complete **c** of things or people to the LORD, either by destroying them or by giving them as an offering.
Eze 44: 29 {anyone sets apart} The Hebrew term used here refers to the complete **c** of things or people to the LORD, either by destroying them or by giving them as an offering.

CONSISTS (1)

Eze 45: 14 {your olive oil,} Hebrew *the portion of oil, measured by the bath, is 1/10 of a bath from each cor, which* **c** *of 10 baths or 1 homer, for 10 baths are equivalent to a homer.*

CONSORTED (1)

Eze 19: 7 {in nearby nations} As in Greek version; Hebrew reads *He* **c** *with widows.*

CONSULT (2)

Ezr 2: 63 {of sacred lots.} Hebrew **c** *the Urim and Thummim about the matter.*
Ne 7: 65 {of sacred lots.} Hebrew **c** *the Urim and Thummim about the matter.*

CONTAGIOUS (7)

Ex 4: 6 {leprosy.} Or *with a* **c** *skin disease.* The Hebrew word used here can describe various skin diseases.
Nu 12: 10 {leprosy.} Or *with a* **c** *skin disease.* The Hebrew word used here can describe various skin diseases.
2Sa 3: 29 {leprosy} Or *or a* **c** *skin disease.* The Hebrew word used here can describe various skin diseases.
2Ki 5: 1 {suffered from leprosy.} Or *from a* **c** *skin disease.* The Hebrew word used here and throughout this passage can describe various skin diseases.
7: 3 {men with leprosy} Or *with a* **c** *skin disease.* The Hebrew word used here and throughout this passage can describe various skin diseases.
15: 5 {king with leprosy,} Or *with a* **c** *skin disease.* The Hebrew word used here and throughout this passage can describe various skin diseases.
2Ch 26: 19 {LORD's Temple, leprosy} Or *a* **c** *skin disease.* The Hebrew word used here and throughout this passage can describe various skin diseases.

CONTAMINANTS (1)

Jude 1: 12 {can shipwreck you.} Or *they are* **c** *among you,* or *they are stains.*

CONTEMPT (1)

Mt 5: 22 {friend, 'You idiot,'} Literally *'Raca,'* an Aramaic term of **c**.

CONTEMPTIBLE (1)

1Sa 3: 13 {are blaspheming God} As in Greek version; Hebrew reads *his sons have made themselves* **c**.

CONTEND (1)

Jude 1: 3 {the Good News.} Greek *to* **c** *for the faith.*

CONTENTS (1)

Lev 1: 16 {and the feathers} Or *the crop and its* **c**. The meaning of the Hebrew is uncertain.

CONTINUE (2)

1Ki 11: 36 {continue to reign} Hebrew *will* **c** *to have a lamp.*
Jn 20: 31 {you may believe} Some manuscripts read *may* **c** *to believe.*

CONTINUED (1)

2Sa 2: 29 {through the morning,} Or **c** *on through the Bithron.* The meaning of the Hebrew is uncertain.

CONTROL (1)

Ge 3: 16 {for your husband,} Or *And though you may desire to* **c** *your husband.*

COR (2)

Eze 45: 14 {your olive oil,} Hebrew *the portion of oil, measured by the bath, is 1/10 of a bath from each* **c**, *which consists of 10 baths or 1 homer, for 10 baths are equivalent to a homer.*
2Co 8: 19 {offering to Jerusalem} See 1 **C** 16:3-4.

CORBAN (1)
Mk 7:11 {given to you.'} Greek *'What I could have given to you is **C**' (that is, a gift).*

CORINTH (1)
Ac 18:1 {went to Corinth.} *Athens* and ***C*** were major cities in Achaia, the region on the southern end of the Greek peninsula.

CORNERS (3)
Jer 9:26 {in distant places,} Or *the people who clip the **c** of their hair.*
25:23 {in distant places.} Or *who clip the **c** of their hair.*
49:32 {in distant places.} Or *who clip the **c** of their hair.*

CORPSES (1)
2Ch 20:25 {of equipment, clothing,} As in some Hebrew manuscripts and Latin Vulgate; most Hebrew manuscripts read ***c***.

CORRECT (1)
Mk 8:32 {things like that.} Or *and began to **c** him.*

CORS (9)
1Ki 4:22 {bushels of meal,} Hebrew *30 **c*** [5.5 kiloliters] *of choice flour and 60 **c*** [11 kiloliters] *of meal.*
5:11 {of 100,000 bushels} Hebrew *20,000 **c*** [3,640 kiloliters].
5:11 {and 110,000 gallons} As in Greek version, which reads *20,000 baths* [420 kiloliters] (see also 2 Chr 2:10); Hebrew reads *20 **c***, about 800 gallons or 3.6 kiloliters in volume.
2Ch 2:10 {bushels of barley,} Hebrew *20,000 **c*** [3,640 kiloliters] *of crushed wheat, 20,000 **c** of barley.*
27:5 {bushels of barley.} Hebrew *10,000 **c*** [1,820 kiloliters] *of wheat, and 10,000 **c** of barley.*
Ezr 7:22 {silver, 500 bushels} Aramaic *100 **c*** [18.2 kiloliters].

COST (3)
2Ki 6:25 {about two ounces} Hebrew *sold for 80 shekels* [0.9 kilograms] *of silver, and 1/4 of a cab* [0.3 liters] *of dove's dung **c** 5 shekels* [57 grams]. *Dove's dung* may be a variety of wild vegetable.
7:1 {ounce of silver,} Hebrew *1 seah* [6 liters] *of fine flour will **c** 1 shekel* [11 grams]; also in 7:16, 18.
7:1 {ounce of silver.} Hebrew *2 seahs* [12 liters] *of barley grain will **c** 1 shekel* [11 grams]; also in 7:16, 18.

COUCHES (1)
Mk 7:4 {pitchers, and kettles.} Some Greek manuscripts add *and dining **c**.*

COUNCIL (1)
Ac 17:5 {to the crowd.} Or *the city **c**.*

COUNSELOR (1)
Isa 9:6 {titles: Wonderful Counselor,} Or *Wonderful, **C**.*

COUNSELORS (1)
Da 3:3 {all these officials} Aramaic *the princes, prefects, governors, advisers, **c**, judges, magistrates, and all the provincial officials.*

COUNTED (1)
Mk 15:27 {side of his.} Some manuscripts add verse 28, *And the Scripture was fulfilled that said, "He was **c** among those who were rebels."* See Isa 53:12.

COURT (2)
Job 9:3 {God to court,} Or *If God wanted to take a person to **c**.*
Jer 31:22 {embrace her God.} Hebrew *a woman will **c** a suitor.*

COURTYARD (1)
Mk 15:16 {into their headquarters} Greek *the **c**, which is the praetorium.*

COVENANT (8)
Lev 16:13 {of the Covenant.} Hebrew *on the Testimony,* referring to the terms of God's **c** with Israel, which were kept in the Ark.
Nu 18:19 {an unbreakable covenant} Hebrew *a **c** of salt.*
1Ch 16:15 {by his covenant} As in some Greek manuscripts (see also Ps 105:8); Hebrew reads *Remember his **c** forever.*
2Ch 13:5 {an unbreakable covenant} Hebrew *a **c** of salt.*
Mt 26:28 {seals the covenant} Some manuscripts read *the new **c**.*
Mk 14:24 {sealing the covenant} Some manuscripts read *the new **c**.*
Heb 9:16 {wrote the will} Or **c**.
9:16 {is dead.} Or *Now when someone makes a **c**, it is necessary to ratify it with the death of a sacrifice.*

COVER (1)
Mt 23:13 {go in yourselves.} Some manuscripts add verse 14, *How terrible it will be for you teachers of religious law and you Pharisees. Hypocrites! You shamelessly cheat widows out of their property, and then, to **c** up the kind of people you really are, you make long prayers in public. Because of this, your punishment will be the greater.*

COW (3)
Lev 9:4 {take a bull} Or ***c***; also in 9:18, 19.
17:3 {sacrifices a bull} Or ***c***.
22:23 {If the bull} Or ***c***; also in 22:27.

CRAVING (1)
Dt 9:22 {and Kibroth-hattaavah.} *Kibroth-hattaavah* means "graves of **c**." See Num 11:31-34.

CREATE (1)
Ge 1:1 {beginning God created} Or *In the beginning when God created,* or *When God began to **c**.*

CREATED (1)
Ge 1:1 {beginning God created} Or *In the beginning when God **c**,* or *When God began to create.*

CREATION (1)
Col 1:15 {all creation.} Greek *He is the firstborn of all **c**.*

CRIED (1)
La 2:18 {Cry aloud} Hebrew *Their heart **c**.*

CRIES (1)
Jer 48:4 {will cry out.} Greek version reads *Her **c** are heard as far away as Zoar.*

CROP (1)
Lev 1:16 {and the feathers} Or *the **c** and its contents.* The meaning of the Hebrew is uncertain.

CROSSING (2)
2Sa 15:28 {the Jordan River} Hebrew *at the **c** points of the wilderness.*
17:16 {the Jordan River} Hebrew *at the **c** points of the wilderness.*

CROWED (1)
Mk 14:68 {a rooster crowed.} Some manuscripts do not include *Just then, a rooster **c**.*

CROWN (3)
2Sa 12:30 {the king's head,} Greek version reads *removed the **c** of Milcom;* compare 1 Kgs 11:5. Milcom, also called Molech, was the god of the Ammonites.
1Ch 20:2 {the king's head,} Greek version and Latin Vulgate read *removed the **c** of Milcom;* compare 1 Kgs 11:5. Milcom, also called Molech, was the god of the Ammonites.
La 5:16 {The garlands have} Or *The **c** has.*

CROWNS (1)
Zec 6:11 {make a crown} As in Greek and Syriac versions; Hebrew reads ***c***.

CRUSHED (1)
2Ch 2:10 {bushels of barley,} Hebrew *20,000 cors* [3,640 kiloliters] *of **c** wheat, 20,000 cors of barley.*

CRY (1)
Pr 30:15 {out, "More, more!"} Hebrew *two daughters who **c** out, "Give, give!"*

CRYING (1)
Gal 4:6 {dear Father.} Greek *into your hearts, **c**, "Abba, Father."* Abba is an Aramaic term for "Father."

CUBIT (36)
Ge 6:16 {boat, 18 inches} Hebrew *1 **c*** [45 centimeters].
Ex 25:10 {2 1/4 feet high.} Hebrew *2 1/2 cubits* [1.1 meters] *long, 1 1/2 cubits* [0.7 meters] *wide, and 1 1/2 cubits high.* In this chapter, the distance measures are calculated from the Hebrew **c** at a ratio of 18 inches or 45 centimeters per **c**.
26:2 {six feet wide.} Hebrew *28 cubits* [12.6 meters] *long and 4 cubits* [1.8 meters] *wide.* In this chapter, the distance measures are calculated from the Hebrew **c** at a ratio of 18 inches or 45 centimeters per **c**.
27:1 {4 1/2 feet high.} Hebrew *5 cubits* [2.3 meters] *wide, 5 cubits long, and 3 cubits* [1.4 meters] *high.* In this chapter, the distance measures are calculated from the Hebrew **c** at a ratio of 18 inches or 45 centimeters per **c**.
30:2 {three feet high,} Hebrew *1 **c*** [45 centimeters] *square and 2 cubits* [90 centimeters] *high.*
36:9 {six feet wide.} Hebrew *28 cubits* [12.6 meters] *long and 4 cubits* [1.8 meters] *wide.* In this chapter, the distance measures are calculated from the Hebrew **c** at a ratio of 18 inches or 45 centimeters per **c**.
37:1 {2 1/4 feet high.} Hebrew *2 1/2 cubits* [1.1 meters] *long, 1 1/2 cubits* [0.7 meters] *wide, and 1 1/2 cubits high.* In this chapter, the distance measures are calculated from the Hebrew **c** at a ratio of 18 inches or 45 centimeters per **c**.
38:1 {4 1/2 feet high.} Hebrew *5 cubits* [2.3 meters] *square at the top, and 3 cubits* [1.4 meters] *high.* In this chapter, the distance measures are calculated from the Hebrew **c** at a ratio of 18 inches or 45 centimeters per **c**.
Jdg 3:16 {was eighteen inches} Hebrew *1 **c*** [45 centimeters].
1Ki 6:2 {and 45 feet high.} Hebrew *60 cubits* [27 meters] *long, 20 cubits* [9 meters] *wide, and 30 cubits* [13.5 meters] *high.* In this chapter, the distance measures are calculated from the Hebrew **c** at a ratio of 18 inches or 45 centimeters per **c**.
7:2 {and 45 feet high.} Hebrew *100 cubits* [45 meters] *long, 50 cubits* [22.5 meters] *wide, and 30 cubits* [13.5 meters] *high.* In this chapter, the distance measures are calculated from the Hebrew **c** at a ratio of 18 inches or 45 centimeters per **c**.
7:24 {gourds per foot} Or *20 gourds per meter;* Hebrew reads *10 per **c**.*
7:35 {rim 9 inches wide.} Hebrew *half a **c** wide* [22.5 centimeters].
2Ch 3:3 {thirty feet wide.} Hebrew *60 cubits* [27 meters] *long and 20 cubits* [9 meters] *wide.* In this chapter, the distance measures are calculated from the Hebrew **c** at a ratio of 18 inches or 45 centimeters per **c**.
4:1 {and 15 feet high.} Hebrew *20 cubits* [9 meters] *long, 20 cubits wide, and 10 cubits* [4.5 meters] *high.* In this chapter, the distance measures are calculated from the Hebrew **c** at a ratio of 18 inches or 45 centimeters per **c**.
4:3 {oxen per foot} Or *20 oxen per meter;* Hebrew reads *10 per **c**.*
Eze 40:5 {was 10 1/2 feet} Hebrew *6 long cubits* [3.2 meters], *each being a **c*** [18 inches or 45 centimeters] *and a handbreadth* [3 inches or 8 centimeters] *in length.* In this chapter, the distance measures are calculated using the Hebrew long **c**, which equals 21 inches or 53 centimeters.
41:1 {were 10 1/2 feet} Hebrew *6 cubits* [3.2 meters]. In this chapter, the distance measures are calculated using the Hebrew long **c**, which equals 21 inches or 53 centimeters.
42:2 {87 1/2 feet wide.} Hebrew *100 cubits* [53 meters] *long and 50 cubits* [26.5 meters] *wide.* In this chapter, the distance measures are calculated using the Hebrew long **c**, which equals 21 inches or 53 centimeters.
43:13 {of the altar} Hebrew *measurements of the altar in long cubits, each being a **c*** [18 inches or 45 centimeters] *and a handbreadth* [3 inches or 8 centimeters] *in length.* In this chapter, the distance measures are calculated using the Hebrew long **c**, which equals 21 inches or 53 centimeters.
45:1 {6 2/3 miles wide.} Reflecting the Greek reading *25,000 cubits* [13.3 kilometers] *long and 20,000 cubits* [10.6 kilometers] *wide;* Hebrew reads *25,000 cubits long and 10,000 cubits wide.* Compare 45:3, 5; 48:9. In this chapter, the distance measures are calculated using the Hebrew long **c**, which equals 21 inches or 53 centimeters.
46:22 {52 1/2 feet wide,} Hebrew *40 cubits* [21.2 meters] *long and 30 cubits* [15.9 meters] *wide.* The distances are calculated using the Hebrew long **c**, which equals 21 inches or 53 centimeters.
47:3 {for 1,750 feet} Hebrew *1,000 cubits* [530 meters]; also in 47:4, 5. The distances are calculated using the Hebrew long **c**, which equals 21 inches or 53 centimeters.
48:9 {6 2/3 miles wide.} Reflecting the Greek reading in 45:1: *25,000 cubits* [13.3 kilometers] *long and 20,000 cubits* [10.6 kilometers] *wide;* Hebrew reads *25,000 cubits long and 10,000 cubits wide.* Compare 45:1-5; 48:10-13. In this chapter, the distance measures are calculated using the Hebrew long **c**, which equals 21 inches or 53 centimeters.

CUBITS (85)
Ge 6:15 {45 feet high.} Hebrew *300 **c*** [135 meters] *long, 50 **c*** [22.5 meters] *wide, and 30 **c*** [13.5 meters] *high.*
7:20 {than twenty-two feet} Hebrew *15 **c*** [6.8 meters].
Ex 25:10 {2 1/4 feet high.} Hebrew *2 1/2 **c*** [1.1 meters] *long, 1 1/2 **c*** [0.7 meters] *wide, and 1 1/2 **c** high.* In this chapter, the distance measures are calculated from the Hebrew cubit at a ratio of 18 inches or 45 centimeters per cubit.
26:2 {six feet wide.} Hebrew *28 **c*** [12.6 meters] *long and 4 **c*** [1.8 meters] *wide.* In this chapter, the distance measures are calculated from the Hebrew cubit at a ratio of 18 inches or 45 centimeters per cubit.
27:1 {4 1/2 feet high.} Hebrew *5 **c*** [2.3 meters] *wide, 5 **c** long, and 3 **c*** [1.4 meters] *high.* In this chapter, the distance measures are calculated from the Hebrew cubit at a ratio of 18 inches or 45 centimeters per cubit.
30:2 {three feet high,} Hebrew *1 cubit* [45 centimeters] *square and 2 **c*** [90 centimeters] *high.*

36: 9 {six feet wide.} Hebrew *28 c* [12.6 meters] *long and 4 c* [1.8 meters] *wide.* In this chapter, the distance measures are calculated from the Hebrew cubit at a ratio of 18 inches or 45 centimeters per cubit.
37: 1 {2 1/4 feet high.} Hebrew *2 1/2 c* [1.1 meters] *long, 1 1/2 c* [0.7 meters] *wide, and 1 1/2 c high.* In this chapter, the distance measures are calculated from the Hebrew cubit at a ratio of 18 inches or 45 centimeters per cubit.
38: 1 {4 1/2 feet high.} Hebrew *5 c* [2.3 meters] *square at the top, and 3 c* [1.4 meters] *high.* In this chapter, the distance measures are calculated from the Hebrew cubit at a ratio of 18 inches or 45 centimeters per cubit.
Nu 11:31 {above the ground.} Or *there were quail 3 feet* [2 c or 90 centimeters] *deep on the ground.*
35: 4 {extend 1,500 feet} Hebrew *1,000 c* [450 meters].
35: 5 {off 3,000 feet} Hebrew *2,000 c* [900 meters].
Dt 3:11 {six feet wide.} Hebrew *9 c* [4.1 meters] *long and 4 c* [1.8 meters] *wide.*
Jos 3: 4 {half mile} Hebrew *about 2,000 c* [900 meters].
1Sa 17: 4 {over nine feet} Hebrew *6 c* [9 feet or 2.7 meters] *and 1 span* [9 inches or 23 centimeters]; Greek version reads *4 c* [6 feet or 1.8 meters] *and 1 span,* about 6.75 feet or 2 meters in length.
1Ki 6: 2 {and 45 feet high.} Hebrew *60 c* [27 meters] *long, 20 c* [9 meters] *wide, and 30 c* [13.5 meters] *high.* In this chapter, the distance measures are calculated from the Hebrew cubit at a ratio of 18 inches or 45 centimeters per cubit.
7: 2 {and 45 feet high.} Hebrew *100 c* [45 meters] *long, 50 c* [22.5 meters] *wide, and 30 c* [13.5 meters] *high.* In this chapter, the distance measures are calculated from the Hebrew cubit at a ratio of 18 inches or 45 centimeters per cubit.
2Ki 14:13 {six hundred feet} Hebrew *400 c* [180 meters].
25:17 {27 feet} Hebrew *18 c* [8.1 meters].
25:17 {7 1/2 feet} As in parallel texts at 1 Kgs 7:16, 2 Chr 3:15, and Jer 52:22, all of which read *5 c* [2.3 meters]; Hebrew reads *3 c,* which is 4.5 feet or 1.4 meters.
1Ch 11:23 {a half feet} Hebrew *5 c* [2.3 meters].
2Ch 3: 3 {thirty feet wide.} Hebrew *60 c* [27 meters] *long and 20 c* [9 meters] *wide.* In this chapter, the distance measures are calculated from the Hebrew cubit at a ratio of 18 inches or 45 centimeters per cubit.
3: 4 {was thirty feet} As in some Greek and Syriac manuscripts, which read *20 c* [9 meters]; Hebrew reads *120 c,* which is 180 feet or 54 meters.
3:15 {that were 27 feet} As in Syriac version (see also 1 Kgs 7:15; 2 Kgs 25:17; Jer 52:21), which reads *18 c* [8.1 meters]; Hebrew reads *35 c,* which is 52.5 feet or 15.8 meters.
4: 1 {and 15 feet high.} Hebrew *20 c* [9 meters] *long, 20 c wide, and 10 c* [4.5 meters] *high.* In this chapter, the distance measures are calculated from the Hebrew cubit at a ratio of 18 inches or 45 centimeters per cubit.
6:13 {4 1/2 feet high} Hebrew *5 c* [2.3 meters] *long, 5 c wide, and 3 c* [1.4 meters] *high.*
25:23 {six hundred feet} Hebrew *400 c* [180 meters].
Ezr 6: 3 {ninety feet.} Aramaic *Its height will be 60 c* [27 meters], *and its width will be 60 c.* It is commonly held that this verse should be emended to read: "Its height will be 45 feet, its length will be 90 feet, and its width will be 30 feet"; compare 1 Kgs 6:2. The emendation regarding the width is supported by the Syriac version.
Ne 3:13 {fifteen hundred feet} Hebrew *1,000 c* [450 meters].
Est 5:14 {stands seventy-five feet} Hebrew *50 c* [22.5 meters].
7: 9 {stands seventy-five feet} Hebrew *50 c* [22.5 meters].
Jer 52:21 {18 feet in circumference.} Hebrew *18 c* [8.1 meters] *tall and 12 c* [5.4 meters] *in circumference.*
52:22 {was 7 1/2 feet} Hebrew *5 c* [2.3 meters].
Eze 40: 5 {was 10 1/2 feet} Hebrew *6 long c* [3.2 meters], *each being a cubit* [18 inches or 45 centimeters] *and a handbreadth* [3 inches or 8 centimeters] *in length.* In this chapter, the distance measures are calculated using the Hebrew long cubit, which equals 21 inches or 53 centimeters.
41: 1 {were 10 1/2 feet} Hebrew *6 c* [3.2 meters]. In this chapter, the distance measures are calculated using the Hebrew long cubit, which equals 21 inches or 53 centimeters.
42: 2 {87 1/2 feet wide.} Hebrew *100 c* [53 meters] *long and 50 c* [26.5 meters] *wide.* In this chapter, the distance measures are calculated using the Hebrew long cubit, which equals 21 inches or 53 centimeters.
43:13 {of the altar} Hebrew *measurements of the altar in long c, each being a cubit* [18 inches or 45 centimeters] *and a handbreadth* [3 inches or 8 centimeters] *in length.* In this chapter, the distance measures are calculated using the Hebrew long cubit, which equals 21 inches or 53 centimeters.
45: 1 {6 2/3 miles wide.} Reflecting the Greek reading *25,000 c* [13.3 kilometers] *long and 20,000 c* [10.6 kilometers] *wide;* Hebrew reads *25,000 c long and 10,000 c wide.* Compare 45:3, 5; 48:9. In this chapter, the distance measures are calculated using the Hebrew long cubit, which equals 21 inches or 53 centimeters.
46:22 {52 1/2 feet wide,} Hebrew *40 c* [21.2 meters] *long and 30 c* [15.9 meters] *wide.* The distances are calculated using the Hebrew long cubit, which equals 21 inches or 53 centimeters.
47: 3 {for 1,750 feet} Hebrew *1,000 c* [530 meters]; also in 47:4, 5. The distances are calculated using the Hebrew long cubit, which equals 21 inches or 53 centimeters.
48: 9 {6 2/3 miles wide.} Reflecting the Greek reading in 45:1: *25,000 c* [13.3 kilometers] *long and 20,000 c* [10.6 kilometers] *wide;* Hebrew reads *25,000 c long and 10,000 c wide.* Compare 45:1-5; 48:10-13. In this chapter, the distance measures are calculated using the Hebrew long cubit, which equals 21 inches or 53 centimeters.
48:16 {measure 1 1/2 miles} Hebrew *4,500 c* [2.4 kilometers]; also in 48:30, 32, 33, 34.
48:17 {for 150 yards} Hebrew *250 c* [133 meters].
48:35 {be six miles.} Hebrew *18,000 c* [9.6 kilometers].
Da 3: 1 {nine feet wide} Aramaic *60 c* [27 meters] *tall and 6 c* [2.7 meters] *wide.*
Zec 5: 2 {fifteen feet wide.} Hebrew *20 c* [9 meters] *long and 10 c* [4.5 meters] *wide.*
Jn 21: 8 {three hundred feet.} Greek *200 c* [90 meters].
Rev 21:17 {216 feet thick} Greek *144 c* [65 meters].

CUMI (1)
Mk 5:41 {up, little girl!"} Greek text uses Aramaic *"Talitha c"* and then translates it as "Get up, little girl."

CUMIN (1)
Mt 23:23 {of your income,} Greek *to tithe the mint, the dill, and the c.*

CURDLED (1)
Job 10:10 {in the womb.} Hebrew *You poured me out like milk and c me like cheese.*

CURSE (1)
Mt 5:44 {love your enemies!} Some manuscripts add *Bless those who c you, do good to those who hate you.*

CURTAIN (2)
Ex 27:21 {in the Tabernacle.} Hebrew *in the Tent of Meeting, outside of the inner c, in front of the Testimony.*
Lev 24: 3 {in the Tabernacle} Hebrew *the c of the Testimony in the Tent of Meeting.*

CUSH (17)
2Ki 19: 9 {Tirhakah of Ethiopia} Hebrew *of C.*
Est 1: 1 {India to Ethiopia.} Hebrew *to C.*
8: 9 {India to Ethiopia.} Hebrew *to C.*
Job 28:19 {Topaz from Ethiopia} Hebrew *from C.*
Ps 68:31 {let Ethiopia} Hebrew *C.*
87: 4 {even distant Ethiopia.} Hebrew *C.*
Isa 11:11 {Upper Egypt, Ethiopia,} Hebrew *Pathros, C.*
18: 1 {land of Ethiopia,} Hebrew *C.*
20: 3 {Egypt and Ethiopia.} Hebrew *C;* also in 20:5.
37: 9 {Tirhakah of Ethiopia} Hebrew *of C.*
43: 3 {gave Egypt, Ethiopia,} Hebrew *C.*
Jer 46: 9 {Libya, and Lydia} Hebrew *C, Put, and Lud.*
Eze 29:10 {border of Ethiopia.} Hebrew *C.*
30: 4 {land of Ethiopia} Hebrew *C;* also in 30:5, 9.
38: 5 {Ethiopia, and Libya} Hebrew *Paras, C, and Put.*
Na 3: 9 {Ethiopia} Hebrew *C.*
Zep 3:10 {rivers of Ethiopia} Hebrew *C.*

CUSHITE (4)
2Ch 14: 9 {Once an Ethiopian} Hebrew *a C.*
Jer 13:23 {Can an Ethiopian} Hebrew *a C.*
38: 7 {Ebed-melech the Ethiopian,} Hebrew *the C.*
39:16 {Ebed-melech the Ethiopian,} Hebrew *the C.*

CUSHITES (9)
2Ch 12: 3 {Sukkites, and Ethiopians.} Hebrew *and C.*
14:12 {defeated the Ethiopians} Hebrew *C;* also in 14:13.
16: 8 {to the Ethiopians} Hebrew *C.*
21:16 {near the Ethiopians,} Hebrew *the C.*
Isa 20: 4 {Egyptians and Ethiopians} Hebrew *C.*
45:14 {"The Egyptians, Ethiopians,} Hebrew *C.*
Da 11:43 {Libyans and Ethiopians} Hebrew *C.*
Am 9: 7 {than the Ethiopians} Hebrew *the C.*
Zep 2:12 {"You Ethiopians} Hebrew *C.*

CUT (1)
Gal 5:12 {would mutilate themselves.} Or *castrate themselves;* Greek reads *c themselves off.*

CYPRESS (1)
2Sa 6: 5 {might, singing songs} As in Greek version (see also 1 Chr 13:8); Hebrew reads *c trees.*

CYRENE (3)
Mt 27:32 {from Cyrene,} *C* was a city in northern Africa.
Mk 15:21 {from Cyrene,} *C* was a city in northern Africa.
Lk 23:26 {of Cyrene,} *C* was a city in northern Africa.

CYRUS (4)
Ezr 5:13 {Cyrus of Babylon,} King *C* of Persia is here identified as the king of Babylon because Persia had conquered the Babylonian Empire.
6:22 {king of Assyria} King *C* of Persia is here identified as the king of Assyria because Persia had conquered the Babylonian Empire, which included the earlier Assyrian Empire.
Jer 51:20 {"You} Possibly *C,* who was used of God to conquer Babylon. Compare Isa 44:28; 45:1.
Da 6:28 {Cyrus the Persian.} Or *of Darius, that is, the reign of C the Persian.*

D

DAN (9)
Ge 30: 6 {named him Dan,} ***D*** is a play on the Hebrew term meaning "to vindicate" or "to judge."
Jdg 18:12 {is called Mahaneh-dan} *Mahaneh-dan* means "the camp of **D**."
Mt 24:15 {that causes desecration} Greek *the abomination of desolation.* See **D** 9:27; 11:31; 12:11.
24:30 {and great glory.} See **D** 7:13.
26:64 {clouds of heaven."} See Ps 110:1; **D** 7:13.
Mk 13:14 {that causes desecration} Greek *the abomination of desolation.* See **D** 9:27; 11:31; 12:11.
13:26 {power and glory.} See **D** 7:13.
14:62 {clouds of heaven."} See Ps 110:1; **D** 7:13.
Lk 21:27 {and great glory.} See **D** 7:13.

DANCE (1)
SS 6:13 {lines of dancers?} Or *as you would at the movements of two armies?* or *as you would at the **d** of Mahanaim?* The meaning of the Hebrew is uncertain.

DANIEL (1 of 2)
1Ch 3: 1 {second was Kileab,} As in parallel text at 2 Sam 3:3; Hebrew reads ***D.***

DARA (1)
1Ch 2: 6 {Calcol, and Darda} As in many Hebrew manuscripts, some Greek manuscripts, and Syriac version (see also 1 Kgs 4:31); Hebrew reads ***D.***

DARICS (5)
1Ch 29: 7 {10,000 gold coins,} Hebrew *10,000 **d*** [a Persian coin] *of gold,* about 185 pounds or 84 kilograms in weight.
Ezr 2:69 {61,000 gold coins,} Hebrew *61,000 **d** of gold,* about 1,100 pounds or 500 kilograms in weight.
8:27 {1,000 gold coins,} Hebrew *1,000 **d**,* about 19 pounds or 8.6 kilograms in weight.
Ne 7:70 {1,000 gold coins,} Hebrew *1,000 **d** of gold,* about 19 pounds or 8.6 kilograms in weight.
7:71 {20,000 gold coins} Hebrew *20,000 **d** of gold,* about 375 pounds or 170 kilograms in weight; also in 7:72.

DARIUS (2)
Ne 12:22 {Darius II of Persia,} Hebrew ***D** the Persian.*
Da 6:28 {Cyrus the Persian.} Or *of **D**, that is, the reign of Cyrus the Persian.*

DARKEST (1)
Ps 23: 4 {valley of death,} Or *the **d** valley.*

DAUGHTER (25)
Dt 18:10 {a burnt offering.} Or *never make your son or **d** pass through the fire.*
2Ki 23:10 {in the fire} Or *to make a son or **d** pass through the fire.*
Est 2:15 {was Esther's turn} Hebrew *the turn of Esther, the **d** of Abihail, who was Mordecai's uncle, who had adopted her.*
Ps 45:12 {princes of Tyre} Hebrew *The **d** of Tyre.*
Isa 1: 8 {Jerusalem} Hebrew *The **d** of Zion.*
16: 1 {lambs to Jerusalem} Hebrew *to the **d** of Zion.*
62:11 {people of Israel,} Hebrew *Tell the **d** of Zion.*
Jer 4:31 {of Jerusalem's people} Hebrew *the **d** of Zion.*
6:23 {destroy you, Jerusalem.} Hebrew ***d** of Zion.*
La 1: 6 {majesty of Jerusalem} Hebrew *the **d** of Zion.*
1:15 {his beloved city} Hebrew *the virgin **d** of Judah.*
2: 1 {shadow over Jerusalem.} Hebrew *the **d** of Zion;* also in 2:8, 10, 18.
2: 2 {walls of Jerusalem.} Hebrew *the **d** of Judah;* also in 2:5.
2: 4 {on beautiful Jerusalem.} Hebrew *on the tent of the **d** of Zion.*
2:15 {and insult Jerusalem,} Hebrew *the **d** of Jerusalem.*
4:22 {O Jerusalem,} Hebrew ***d** of Zion.*
Mic 1:13 {you led Jerusalem} Hebrew *the **d** of Zion.*
4:10 {people of Jerusalem,} Hebrew *O **d** of Zion.*
4:13 {the nations, O Jerusalem!"} Hebrew *"Rise up and thresh, O **d** of Zion."*
Zec 2:10 {and rejoice, O Jerusalem,} Hebrew *O **d** of Zion.*
9: 9 {Rejoice greatly, O people} Hebrew ***d.***

Mt 21: 5 {people of Israel,} Greek *Tell the **d** of Zion.* Isa 62:11.
Mk 6:22 {also named Herodias,} Some manuscripts read *the **d** of Herodias herself.*
Lk 13:16 {this dear woman} Greek *this woman, a **d** of Abraham.*
Jn 12:15 {people of Israel.} Greek ***d** of Zion.*

DAUGHTERS (6)

Ge 11:12[-13] {sons and daughters.} Greek version reads [12]*When Arphaxad was 135 years old, his son Cainan was born.* [13]*After the birth of Cainan, Arphaxad lived another 430 years and had other sons and **d**, and then he died. When Cainan was 130 years old, his son Shelah was born. After the birth of Shelah, Cainan lived another 330 years and had other sons and **d**, and then he died.*
2Ki 17:17 {in the fire.} Or *They even made their sons and **d** pass through the fire.*
Pr 30:15 {out, "More, more!"} Hebrew *two **d** who cry out, "Give, give!"*
Isa 3:16 {women of Jerusalem,} Hebrew *the **d** of Zion.*
4: 4 {women of Jerusalem.} Hebrew *from the **d** of Zion.*

DAVID (9)

1Sa 20:16 {covenant with David,} Hebrew *with the house of **D**.*
2Ki 8:19 {to rule forever.} Hebrew *promised to give a lamp to **D** and his descendants forever.*
2Ch 6:42 {your servant David.} Or *Remember the faithfulness of your servant **D**.*
17: 3 {father's early years} Some Hebrew manuscripts read *the example of his father, **D**.*
21: 7 {to rule forever.} Hebrew *promised to give a lamp to **D** and his descendants forever.*
Isa 22: 9 {walls of Jerusalem} Hebrew *the city of **D**.*
Hos 3: 5 {descendant, their king.} Hebrew *to **D** their king.*
Rev 5: 5 {to David's throne,} Greek *the root of **D**.*
22:16 {to his throne.} Greek *I am the root and offspring of **D**.*

DAVID'S (2)

2Sa 8:18 {as priestly leaders.} Hebrew ***D** sons were priests;* compare parallel text at 1 Chr 18:17.
Isa 11: 1 {of David's family} Hebrew *the line of Jesse.* Jesse was King **D** father.

DAWNS (1)

2Pe 1:19 {in your hearts.} Or *until the day **d** and the morning star rises in your hearts.*

DAY (151 of 157)

Ge 8: 4 {the flood began,} Hebrew *on the seventeenth **d** of the seventh month;* see 7:11.
8: 5 {half months later,} Hebrew *On the first **d** of the tenth month;* see 7:11 and note on 8:4.
8:13 {the flood began,} Hebrew *on the first **d** of the first month;* see 7:11.
8:14 {months went by,} Hebrew *The twenty-seventh **d** of the second month arrived;* see note on 8:13.
Ex 16: 1 {after leaving Egypt.} Hebrew *on the fifteenth **d** of the second month.* The Exodus had occurred on the fourteenth **d** of the first month (see 12:6).
19: 1 {they left Egypt.} Hebrew *in the third month…on the very **d**,* i.e., two lunar months to the **d** after leaving Egypt. This **d** of the Hebrew lunar calendar occurs in late May or early June; compare note on 13:4.
40: 2 {the new year.} Hebrew *the first **d** of the first month.* This **d** of the Hebrew lunar calendar occurs in March or early April.
40:17 {the new year.} Hebrew *the first **d** of the first month, in the second year.* See note on 40:2b.
Lev 16:29 {in early autumn,} Hebrew *On the tenth **d** of the seventh month.* This **d** of the Hebrew lunar calendar occurs in September or early October.
23: 5 {in early spring.} Hebrew *on the fourteenth **d** of the first month.* This **d** of the Hebrew lunar calendar occurs in late March or early April.
23: 6 {the Passover celebration,} Hebrew *On the fifteenth **d** of the same month.*
23:24 {in early autumn,} Hebrew *On the first **d** of the seventh month.* This **d** of the Hebrew lunar calendar occurs in September or early October.
23:27 {Festival of Trumpets.} Hebrew *on the tenth **d** of the seventh month;* see 23:24 and the note there.
23:32 {Day of Atonement} Hebrew *the evening of the ninth **d** of the month;* see 23:24, 27 and the notes there.
23:34 {Day of Atonement.} Hebrew *on the fifteenth **d** of the seventh month;* see 23:24, 27 and the notes there.
23:39 {Festival of Shelters,} Hebrew *on the fifteenth **d** of the seventh month;* see 23:24 and the note there.
25: 9 {the fiftieth year,} Hebrew *on the tenth **d** of the seventh month, on the **D** of Atonement;* see 23:27 and the note there.
Nu 1: 1 {day in midspring,} Hebrew *On the first **d** of the second month.* This **d** of the Hebrew lunar calendar occurs in April or early May.
1:18 {that very day.} Hebrew *on the first **d** of the second month;* see 1:1.
9: 3 {in early spring.} Hebrew *on the fourteenth **d** of the first month.* This **d** of the Hebrew lunar calendar occurs in late March or early April.
9: 5 {the appointed day.} Hebrew *on the fourteenth **d** of the first month;* see note on 9:3.
9:11 {one month later,} Hebrew *on the fourteenth **d** of the second month.* This **d** of the Hebrew lunar calendar occurs in late April or early May.
10:11 {day in midspring,} Hebrew *On the twentieth **d** of the second month.* This **d** of the Hebrew lunar calendar occurs in late April or early May.
28:16 {in early spring,} Hebrew *On the fourteenth **d** of the first month.* This **d** of the Hebrew lunar calendar occurs in late March or early April.
29: 1 {in early autumn} Hebrew *on the first **d** of the seventh month.* This **d** of the Hebrew lunar calendar occurs in September or early October.
29: 7 {"Ten days later,} Hebrew *On the tenth **d** of the seventh month;* see 29:1 and the note there.
29:12 {"Five days later,} Hebrew *On the fifteenth **d** of the seventh month;* see 29:1, 7 and the notes there.
33: 3 {in early spring.} Hebrew *on the fifteenth **d** of the first month.* This **d** of the Hebrew lunar calendar occurs in late March or early April.
33:38 {day in midsummer,} Hebrew *on the first **d** of the fifth month.* This **d** of the Hebrew lunar calendar occurs in July or early August.
Dt 1: 3 {day in midwinter,} Hebrew *on the first **d** of the eleventh month.* This **d** of the Hebrew lunar calendar occurs in January or early February.
Jos 4:19 {exodus from Egypt.} Hebrew *the tenth **d** of the first month.* This **d** of the Hebrew lunar calendar occurs in late March or early April.
5:10 {exodus from Egypt.} Hebrew *the fourteenth **d** of the first month.* This **d** of the Hebrew lunar calendar occurs in late March or early April.
1Sa 14:14 {half an acre.} Hebrew *half a yoke;* a "yoke" was the amount of land plowed by a pair of yoked oxen in one **d**.
1Ki 8:66 {festival was over,} Hebrew *On the eighth **d**,* probably referring to the **d** following the seven-day Festival of Shelters; compare parallel text at 2 Chr 7:9-10.
12:32 {day in midautumn,} Hebrew *on the fifteenth **d** of the eighth month* (also in 12:33). This **d** of the Hebrew lunar calendar occurs in late October or early November, exactly one month after the annual Festival of Shelters in Judah (see Lev 23:34).
2Ki 25: 1 {So on January 15,} Hebrew *on the tenth **d** of the tenth month,* of the Hebrew calendar. A number of events in 2 Kings can be cross-checked with dates in surviving Babylonian records and related accurately to our modern calendar. This event occurred on January 15, 588 B.C.
25: 3 {Zedekiah's eleventh year,} Hebrew *By the ninth **d**,* that is, "of the fourth month of Zedekiah's eleventh year" (compare Jer 52:6 and the note there). …
25:27 {of that year.} Hebrew *on the twenty-seventh **d** of the twelfth month,* of the Hebrew calendar. This **d** was April 2, 560 B.C.; also see note on 25:1.
2Ch 3: 2 {began in midspring,} Hebrew *on the second **d** of the second month.* This **d** of the Hebrew lunar calendar occurs in April or early May.
5: 3 {in early autumn.} Hebrew *at the festival that is in the seventh month.* The Festival of Shelters began on the fifteenth **d** of the seventh month of the Hebrew lunar calendar. This occurs on our calendar in late September or early October.
7:10 {of the celebration,} Hebrew *Then on the twenty-seventh **d** of the seventh month.* This **d** of the Hebrew lunar calendar occurs in late September or early October.
29:17 {in early spring,} Hebrew *on the first **d** of the first month.* This **d** of the Hebrew lunar calendar occurs in March or early April.
30:15 {day in midspring,} Hebrew *On the fourteenth **d** of the second month.* This **d** of the Hebrew lunar calendar occurs in late April or early May.
35: 1 {in early spring.} Hebrew *on the fourteenth **d** of the first month.* This **d** of the Hebrew lunar calendar occurs in late March or early April.
Ezr 3: 6 {of Shelters began,} Hebrew *On the first **d** of the seventh month.* This day of the Hebrew lunar calendar occurs in September or early October. The Festival of Shelters began on the fifteenth **d** of the seventh month.
6:15 {completed on March 12,} Aramaic *on the third **d** of the month Adar,* of the Hebrew calendar. This event occurred on March 12, 515 B.C.;…
6:19 {On April 21} Hebrew *On the fourteenth **d** of the first month,* of the Hebrew calendar.…
7: 9 {Babylon on April 8} Hebrew *on the first **d** of the first month,* of the Hebrew calendar. This event occurred on April 8, 458 B.C.; also see note on 3:1.
7: 9 {August 4,} Hebrew *on the first **d** of the fifth month,* of the Hebrew calendar. This event occurred on August 4, 458 B.C.; also see note on 3:1.
8:31 {Canal on April 19} Hebrew *on the twelfth **d** of the first month,* of the Hebrew calendar. This event occurred on April 19, 458 B.C.; see note on 7:9a.
10: 9 {place on December 19,} Hebrew *on the twentieth **d** of the ninth month,* of the Hebrew calendar. This event occurred on December 19, 458 B.C.; also see note on 7:9a.
10:16 {name. On December 29,} Hebrew *On the first **d** of the tenth month,* of the Hebrew lunar calendar. This event occurred on December 29, 458 B.C.; also see note on 7:9a.
10:17 {the next year} Hebrew *By the first **d** of the first month,* of the Hebrew calendar. This event occurred on March 27, 457 B.C.; also see note on 7:9a.
Ne 6:15 {So on October 2} Hebrew *on the twenty-fifth **d** of the month Elul,* of the Hebrew calendar. This event occurred on October 2, 445 B.C.; also see note on 1:1.
8: 2 {So on October 8} Hebrew *on the first **d** of the seventh month,* of the Hebrew calendar. This event occurred on October 8, 445 B.C.; also see note on 1:1.
8:13 {On October 9} Hebrew *On the second **d**,* of the seventh month of the Hebrew calendar. This event occurred on October 9, 445 B.C.; also see notes on 1:1 and 8:2.
8:18 {Then on October 15} Hebrew *on the eighth **d**,* of the seventh month of the Hebrew calendar. This event occurred on October 15, 445 B.C.; also see notes on 1:1 and 8:2.
9: 1 {On October 31} Hebrew *On the twenty-fourth **d** of that same month,* the seventh month of the Hebrew calendar. This event occurred on October 31, 445 B.C.; also see note on 1:1.
9: 3 {about three hours.} Hebrew *for a quarter of a **d**.*
13:19 {every Friday evening,} Hebrew *on the **d** before the Sabbath.*
Est 3: 7 {a year later.} As in Greek version, which reads *the thirteenth **d** of the twelfth month, the month of Adar* (see also 3:13). Hebrew reads *in the twelfth month,* of the Hebrew calendar. The date selected was March 7, 473 B.C.; also see note on 2:16.
3:12 {On April 17} Hebrew *On the thirteenth **d** of the first month,* of the Hebrew calendar. This event occurred on April 17, 474 B.C.; also see note on 2:16.
3:13 {later on March 7.} Hebrew *on the thirteenth **d** of the twelfth month, the month of Adar,* of the Hebrew calendar. The date selected was March 7, 473 B.C.; also see note on 2:16.
8: 9 {So on June 25} Hebrew *on the twenty-third **d** of the third month, the month of Sivan,* of the Hebrew calendar.…
8:12 {the next year.} Hebrew *the thirteenth **d** of the twelfth month, the month of Adar,* of the Hebrew calendar. The date selected was March 7, 473 B.C.; also see note on 2:16.
9: 1 {So on March 7} Hebrew *on the thirteenth **d** of the twelfth month, the month of Adar,* of the Hebrew calendar. This event occurred on March 7, 473 B.C.; also see note on 2:16.
9:15 {March 8} Hebrew *the fourteenth **d** of the month of Adar,* of the Hebrew calendar.…
9:17 {March 7.} Hebrew *on the thirteenth **d** of the month of Adar,* of the Hebrew calendar. This event occurred on March 7, 473 B.C.;…
9:17 {the following day} Hebrew *on the fourteenth **d**,* of the Hebrew month of Adar.
9:18 {the third day,} Hebrew *killing their enemies on the thirteenth **d** and the fourteenth **d**, and then rested on the fifteenth **d**,* of the Hebrew month of Adar.
9:19 {in late winter,} Hebrew *on the fourteenth **d** of the month of Adar.* This **d** of the Hebrew lunar calendar occurs in late February or early March.
Jer 39: 2 {on July 18,} Hebrew *On the ninth **d** of the fourth month of the eleventh year of Zedekiah.* This event occurred on July 18, 586 B.C.;…
52: 4 {So on January 15,} Hebrew *on the tenth **d** of the tenth month,* of the Hebrew calendar.…
52: 6 {Zedekiah's eleventh year,} Hebrew *By the ninth **d** of the fourth month* [of Zedekiah's eleventh year].…
52:12 {of that year,} Hebrew *On the tenth **d** of the fifth month,* of the Hebrew calendar. This **d** was August 17, 586 B.C.; also see note on 52:4a.
52:31 {of that year.} Hebrew *on the twenty-fifth **d** of the twelfth month,* of the Hebrew calendar. This **d** was March 31, 560 B.C.; also see note on 52:4a.
Eze 1: 1 {July 31} Hebrew *On the fifth **d** of the fourth month,* of the Hebrew calendar (also in 1:2).…
8: 1 {September 17,} Hebrew *on the fifth **d** of the sixth month,* of the Hebrew calendar.…
20: 1 {August 14,} Hebrew *In the fifth month, on the tenth **d**,* of the Hebrew calendar. This event occurred on August 14, 591 B.C.;…
24: 1 {January 15,} Hebrew *On the tenth **d** of the tenth month,* of the Hebrew calendar. This event occurred on January 15, 588 B.C.;…
26: 1 {King Jehoiachin's captivity,} Hebrew *In the eleventh year, on the first **d** of the month,* of the Hebrew calendar year. Since an element is missing in the date formula here, scholars have reconstructed this probable reading: *On the first **d** of the eleventh month, during the twelfth year.…*
29: 1 {January 7,} Hebrew *On the twelfth **d** of the tenth month,* of the Hebrew calendar.…
29:17 {April 26,} Hebrew *On the first **d** of the first month,* of the Hebrew calendar.…
30:20 {April 29,} Hebrew *On the seventh **d** of the first month,* of the Hebrew calendar. This event occurred on April 29, 587 B.C.; also see note on 29:1.

31: 1 {On June 21,} Hebrew *On the first **d** of the third month,* of the Hebrew calendar. This event occurred on June 21, 587 B.C.; also see note on 29:1.
32: 1 {March 3,} Hebrew *On the first **d** of the twelfth month,* of the Hebrew calendar. This event occurred on March 3, 585 B.C.; also see note on 29:1.
32:17 {March 17,} Hebrew *On the fifteenth **d** of the month,* presumably in the twelfth month of the Hebrew calendar (see 32:1). This would put this message at the end of King Jehoiachin's twelfth year of captivity, on March 17, 585 B.C.; also see note on 29:1. Greek version reads *On the fifteenth **d** of the first month,* which would put this message on April 27, 586 B.C., at the beginning of Jehoiachin's twelfth year.
33:21 {January 8,} Hebrew *On the fifth **d** of the tenth month,* of the Hebrew calendar. This event occurred on January 8, 585 B.C.; also see note on 29:1.
40: 1 {April 28,} Hebrew *At the beginning of the year, on the tenth **d** of the month,* of the Hebrew calendar. A number of events in Ezekiel can be cross-checked with dates in surviving Babylonian records and related accurately to our modern calendar. This event occurred on April 28, 573 B.C.
45:18 {each new year,} Hebrew *On the first **d** of the first month,* of the Hebrew calendar. This **d** of the Hebrew lunar calendar occurs in late March or early April.
45:25 {in early autumn,} Hebrew *the festival which begins on the fifteenth **d** of the seventh month* (see Lev 23:33). This **d** of the Hebrew lunar calendar occurs in late September or October.

Hag 1: 1 {On August 29} Hebrew *On the first **d** of the sixth month,* of the Hebrew calendar. A number of events in Haggai can be cross-checked with dates in surviving Persian records and related accurately to our modern calendar. This event occurred on August 29, 520 B.C.
1:15 {was on September 21} Hebrew *on the twenty-fourth **d** of the sixth month,* of the Hebrew calendar. This event occurred on September 21, 520 B.C.; also see note on 1:1a.
2: 1 {Then on October 17} Hebrew *on the twenty-first **d** of the seventh month,* of the Hebrew calendar. This event occurred on October 17, 520 B.C.; also see note on 1:1a.
2:10 {On December 18} Hebrew *On the twenty-fourth **d** of the ninth month,* of the Hebrew calendar (also in 2:18). This event occurred on December 18, 520 B.C.; also see note on 1:1a.
2:20 {on December 18} Hebrew *on the twenty-fourth **d** of the month;* see note on 2:10.

Zec 1: 7 {Then on February 15} Hebrew *on the twenty-fourth **d** of the eleventh month, the month of Shebat,* of the Hebrew calendar. This event occurred on February 15, 519 B.C.; also see note on 1:1.
7: 1 {On December 7} Hebrew *On the fourth **d** of the ninth month, the month of Kislev,* of the Hebrew calendar. This event occurred on December 7, 518 B.C.; also see note on 1:1.

Mt 27:62 {the Passover ceremonies} Or *On the next **d**, which is after the Preparation.*
28: 1 {on Sunday morning,} Greek *After the Sabbath, on the first **d** of the week.*

Mk 15:42 {day of preparation,} Greek *on the **d** of preparation.*
16: 2 {on Sunday morning,} Greek *on the first **d** of the week;* also in 16:9.

Lk 17:30 {of Man returns.} Or *on the **d** the Son of Man is revealed.*
23:54 {day of preparation} Greek *on the **d** of preparation.*
24: 1 {on Sunday morning} Greek *But on the first **d** of the week, very early in the morning.*

Jn 2: 1 {The next day} Greek *On the third **d**;* see 1:35, 43.
20: 1 {Early Sunday morning,} Greek *On the first **d** of the week.*

Ac 2: 1 {after Jesus' resurrection,} Greek *When the **d** of Pentecost arrived.* This annual celebration came 50 days after the Passover ceremonies. See Lev 23:16.

1Co 16: 2 {every Lord's Day,} Greek *every first **d** of the week.*

1Pe 2:12 {judge the world.} Or *on the **d** of visitation.*

2Pe 1:19 {in your hearts.} Or *until the **d** dawns and the morning star rises in your hearts.*

DAYS (9)

1Ki 8:65 {Festival of Shelters.} Hebrew *seven **d** and seven **d**, fourteen **d**;* compare parallel text at 2 Chr 7:8-10.

Est 1: 4 {lasted six months} Hebrew *180 **d**.*

Da 7: 9 {the Ancient One} Aramaic *an Ancient of **D**;* also in 7:13, 22.

Hos 12: 9 {Festival of Shelters.} Hebrew *as in the **d** of your appointed feast.*

Ac 2: 1 {after Jesus' resurrection,} Greek *When the day of Pentecost arrived.* This annual celebration came 50 **d** after the Passover ceremonies. See Lev 23:16.
12: 3 {the Passover celebration} Greek *the **d** of unleavened bread.*
20: 6 {the Passover season} Greek *the **d** of unleavened bread.*

DEACONS (1)

1Ti 3:11 {way, their wives} Or *the women **d**.* The Greek word can be translated *women* or *wives.*

DEAD (27)

Ex 1: 5 {Jacob had seventy} **D** Sea Scrolls and Greek version read *seventy-five;* see notes on Gen 46:27.

Dt 31: 1 {had finished saying} As in **D** Sea Scrolls and Greek version; Masoretic Text reads *Moses went and spoke.*
32: 8 {of angelic beings.} As in **D** Sea Scrolls, which read *of the sons of God,* and Greek version, which reads *of the angels of god;* Masoretic Text reads *of the sons of Israel.*
32:43 {God worship him,} As in **D** Sea Scrolls and Greek version; Masoretic Text reads *Rejoice with his people, O nations.*

Jdg 19:28 {was no answer.} Greek version adds *for she was **d**.*

Ru 2:20 {your dead husband.} Hebrew *to the living and to the **d**.*

1Sa 1:24 {a three-year-old bull} As in **D** Sea Scrolls, Greek and Syriac versions; Hebrew reads *3 bulls.*
2:33 {a violent death.} As in **D** Sea Scrolls, which read *die by the sword;* Masoretic Text reads *die like mortals.*
10:27 {Saul ignored them.} **D** Sea Scroll 4QSam[a] continues: *Nahash, king of the Ammonites, had been grievously oppressing the Gadites…*
11: 8 {addition to 30,000} **D** Sea Scrolls and Greek version read *70,000.*
15:32 {have been spared!"} **D** Sea Scrolls and Greek version read *Agag arrived hesitantly, for he thought, "Surely this is the bitterness of death."*

2Sa 22:36 {your help} As in **D** Sea Scrolls; most Hebrew manuscripts read *your answering.*

Pr 2:18 {road to hell.} Hebrew *to the spirits of the **d**.*

Isa 15: 9 {stream near Dibon} As in **D** Sea Scrolls, some Greek manuscripts, and Latin Vulgate; Hebrew reads *Dimon;* also in 15:9b.
21: 8 {Then the watchman} As in **D** Sea Scrolls and Syriac version; Hebrew reads *a lion.*
33: 8 {made before witnesses.} As in **D** Sea Scrolls; Masoretic Text reads *care nothing for the cities.*
45: 2 {level the mountains.} As in **D** Sea Scrolls and Greek version; Masoretic Text reads *the swellings.*
49:12 {south as Egypt.} As in **D** Sea Scrolls, which read *from the region of Aswan,* which is in southern Egypt. Masoretic Text reads *from the region of Sinim.*
49:24 {that a tyrant} As in **D** Sea Scrolls, Syriac version, and Latin Vulgate (also see 49:25); Masoretic Text reads *a righteous person.*

Hab 2: 5 {Wealth} As in **D** Sea Scroll 1QpHab; other Hebrew manuscripts read *Wine.*

Mt 8:22 {their own dead."} Greek *Let the **d** bury their own **d**.*
27:51[-53] {to many people.} Or *The earth shook, rocks split apart, tombs opened, and many bodies of godly men and women who had died were raised from the **d**. After Jesus' resurrection, they left the cemetery, went into the holy city of Jerusalem, and appeared to many people.*

Lk 9:60 {their own dead.} Greek *Let the **d** bury their own **d**.*

1Co 15:52 {who have died} Greek *the **d**.*

Col 1:18 {from the dead,} Greek *He is the beginning, the firstborn from the **d**.*

DEATH (8)

1Sa 5: 6 {plague of tumors.} Greek version and Latin Vulgate read *tumors. And rats appeared in their land, and **d** and destruction were throughout the city.*
15:32 {have been spared!"} Dead Sea Scrolls and Greek version read *Agag arrived hesitantly, for he thought, "Surely this is the bitterness of **d**."*

Pr 21: 6 {deadly trap.} As in Greek version; Hebrew reads *mist for those who seek **d**.*

Ro 6:12 {way you live;} Or *Do not let sin reign in your body, which is subject to **d**.*
7:24 {dominated by sin?} Greek *from this body of **d**?*
8:13 {turn from it} Greek *put it to **d**.*

Heb 9:16 {is dead.} Or *Now when someone makes a covenant, it is necessary to ratify it with the **d** of a sacrifice.*

Rev 6: 8 {famine and disease} Greek ***d**.*

DEATHS (1)

1Ki 2: 5 {time of peace,} Or *He murdered them during a time of peace as revenge for **d** they had caused in time of war.*

DEBIR (1)

Jos 13:26 {Mahanaim to Lo-debar.} Or *to the territory of **D**.*

DEBT (1)

Pr 20:16 {of a foreigner.} An alternate reading in the Hebrew text is *the **d** of an adulterous woman;* compare 27:13.

DECAPOLIS (3)

Mt 4:25 {the Ten Towns,} Greek ***D**.*

Mk 5:20 {the Ten Towns} Greek ***D**.*
7:31 {the Ten Towns.} Greek ***D**.*

DECAY (1)

Hab 3:16 {way beneath me,} Hebrew ***D** entered my bones.*

DECEIVES (4)

Ge 25:26 {called him Jacob.} *Jacob* means "he grasps the heel"; this can also figuratively mean "he **d**."
27:36 {name is Jacob,} *Jacob* means "he grasps the heel"; this can also figuratively mean "he **d**."
35:10 {be called Israel."} *Jacob* means "he grasps the heel"; this can also figuratively mean "he **d**"; *Israel* means "God struggles" or "one who struggles with God."

Hos 12: 2 {to punish Jacob} *Jacob* means "he grasps at the heel"; this can also figuratively mean "he **d**."

DECEPTION (1)

Mic 1:14 {town of Aczib} *Aczib* means "**d**."

DECIDED (1)

Ac 15:33 {had sent them.} Some manuscripts add verse 34, *But Silas **d** to stay there.*

DECLARE (2)

Ex 22: 9 {whom God declares} Or *whom the judges **d**.*

Jn 7:37[-38] {out from within."} Or *"Let anyone who is thirsty come to me and drink. [38]For the Scriptures **d** that rivers of living water will flow from the heart of those who believe in me."*

DECLARES (1)

Pr 30: 1 {worn out, O God.} The Hebrew can also be translated *The man **d** this to Ithiel, to Ithiel and to Ucal.*

DEDICATION (1)

Jn 10:22 {time of Hanukkah.} Or *the **D** Celebration.*

DEEP (4)

Nu 11:31 {above the ground.} Or *there were quail 3 feet* [2 cubits or 90 centimeters] ***d** on the ground.*

Eze 40: 6 {10 1/2 feet deep.} Greek version; Hebrew reads *1 rod* [10.5 feet or 3.2 meters] ***d**, and one threshold, one rod **d**.*
40: 8 {of the gateway} Many Hebrew manuscripts add *which faced inward toward the Temple; it was one rod* [10.5 feet or 3.2 meters] ***d**. [9]Then he measured the foyer of the gateway,…*

DEER (2)

Ps 29: 9 {twists mighty oaks} Or *causes the **d** to writhe in labor.*

Hab 3:19 {as a deer} Or *will give me the speed of a **d**.*

DEFENSES (1)

Pr 17:19 {who speaks boastfully} Or *who builds up **d**;* Hebrew reads *who makes a high gate.*

DEFILED (2)

Mal 1: 7 {defiled the sacrifices} As in Greek version; Hebrew reads ***d** you.*

Rev 14: 4 {pure as virgins,} Greek *they are virgins who have not **d** themselves with women.*

DEFILES (1)

Mt 15:11 {say and do.} Or *what comes out of the mouth **d** a person.*

DELIGHT (1)

Isa 62: 4 {of God's Delight} Hebrew *Hephzibah,* which means "my **d** is in her."

DEMON (1)

Mt 17:20 {would be impossible."} Some manuscripts add verse 21, *But this kind of **d** won't leave unless you have prayed and fasted.*

DEMONS (2)

Mt 12:29 {house be robbed!} Or *One cannot rob Satan's kingdom without first tying him up. Only then can his **d** be cast out.*

Mk 3:27 {house be robbed!} Or *One cannot rob Satan's kingdom without first tying him up. Only then can his **d** be cast out.*

DENARII (7)

Mt 18:28 {few thousand dollars.} Greek *100 **d**.* A denarius was the equivalent of a full day's wage.

Mk 6:37 {a small fortune} Greek *200 **d**.* A denarius was the equivalent of a full day's wage.
14: 5 {small fortune} Greek *300 **d**.* A denarius was the equivalent of a full day's wage.

Lk 7:41 {pieces of silver} Greek *500 **d**.* A denarius was the equivalent of a full day's wage.

10:35 {pieces of silver} Greek *2 **d**.* A denarius was the equivalent of a full day's wage.
Jn 6: 7 {small fortune} Greek *200 **d**.* A denarius was the equivalent of a full day's wage.
12: 5 {small fortune.} Greek *300 **d**.* A denarius was equivalent to a full day's wage.

DENARIUS (13)

Mt 18:28 {few thousand dollars.} Greek *100 denarii.* A **d** was the equivalent of a full day's wage.
20: 2 {normal daily wage} Greek *a **d**,* the payment for a full day's labor; also in 20:9, 10, 13.
22:19 {him the coin,} Greek *a **d**.*
Mk 6:37 {a small fortune} Greek *200 denarii.* A **d** was the equivalent of a full day's wage.
12:15 {a Roman coin,} Greek *a **d**.*
14: 5 {small fortune} Greek *300 denarii.* A **d** was the equivalent of a full day's wage.
Lk 7:41 {pieces of silver} Greek *500 denarii.* A **d** was the equivalent of a full day's wage.
10:35 {pieces of silver} Greek *2 denarii.* A **d** was the equivalent of a full day's wage.
20:24 {a Roman coin.} Greek *a **d**.*
Jn 6: 7 {small fortune} Greek *200 denarii.* A **d** was the equivalent of a full day's wage.
12: 5 {small fortune.} Greek *300 denarii.* A **d** was equivalent to a full day's wage.
Rev 6: 6 {day's pay.} Greek *A choinix of wheat for a **d**, and 3 choinix of barley for a **d**.*

DEPARTED (1)

Ac 28:28 {will accept it."} Some manuscripts add verse 29, *And when he had said these words, the Jews **d**, greatly disagreeing with each other.*

DERBE (1)

Ac 14: 1 {In Iconium,} *Iconium,* as well as *Lystra* and ***D*** (14:6), were cities in the land now called Turkey.

DESCENDANT (4)

2Sa 21:16 {of the giants} As in Greek version; Hebrew reads *a **d** of the Rephaites;* also in 21:18, 20, 22.
1Ch 20: 4 {of the giants,} Hebrew ***d** of the Rephaites;* also in 20:6, 8.
Ezr 7: 1 {was the son} Or ***d**;* see 1 Chr 6:14.
7: 3 {of Azariah, son} Or ***d**;* see 1 Chr 6:6-10.

DESCENDANTS (7)

2Ki 8:19 {to rule forever.} Hebrew *promised to give a lamp to David and his **d** forever.*
1Ch 1:17 {of Aram were} As in one Hebrew manuscript and some Greek manuscripts (see also Gen 10:23); most Hebrew manuscripts lack *The **d** of Aram were.*
3:16 {his uncle Zedekiah.} Hebrew *The **d** of Jehoiakim were his son Jeconiah* [a variant name for Jehoiachin] *and his son Zedekiah.*
15: 4 {are the priests} Hebrew ***d** of Aaron.*
24:23 {was the leader,} Hebrew *From the **d** of Jeriah;* compare 23:19.
2Ch 21: 7 {to rule forever.} Hebrew *promised to give a lamp to David and his **d** forever.*
Heb 7: 5 {their own relatives.} Greek *their brothers, who are **d** of Abraham.*

DESERT (1)

Isa 21: 1 {land of Babylonia} Hebrew *the **d** of the sea.*

DESIGNED (1)

2Ch 26:15 {and hurl stones} Or ***d** by brilliant men to protect those who shot arrows and stones.*

DESIRE (1)

Ge 3:16 {for your husband,} Or *And though you may **d** to control your husband.*

DESOLATE (1)

Isa 62: 4 {the Desolate Land.} Hebrew *Shemamah,* which means "**d**."

DESOLATION (5)

Da 9:27 {that causes desecration,} Hebrew *an abomination of **d**.*
11:31 {that causes desecration.} Hebrew *the abomination of **d**.*
12:11 {that causes desecration} Hebrew *the abomination of **d**.*
Mt 24:15 {that causes desecration} Greek *the abomination of **d**.* See Dan 9:27; 11:31; 12:11.
Mk 13:14 {that causes desecration} Greek *the abomination of **d**.* See Dan 9:27; 11:31; 12:11.

DESTINATION (1)

2Sa 16:14 {the Jordan River.} As in Greek version (see also 17:16); Hebrew reads *when they reached their **d**.*

DESTROY (1)

Lk 9:55 {and rebuked them.} Some manuscripts add *And he said, "You don't realize what your hearts are like.* [56]*For the Son of Man has not come to **d** men's lives, but to save them."*

DESTROYED (2)

2Ch 36:19 {everything of value.} Or ***d** all the valuable Temple utensils.*
Am 4:11 {as I destroyed} Hebrew *as when God **d**.*

DESTROYER (1)

Isa 33: 1 {for you Assyrians,} Hebrew *for you, O **d**...O betrayer.* The Hebrew text does not specifically name Assyria as the object of this prophecy.

DESTRUCTION (6)

Nu 21: 3 {been called Hormah} *Hormah* means "**d**."
Jdg 1:17 {was named Hormah.} *Hormah* means "**d**."
1Sa 5: 6 {plague of tumors.} Greek version and Latin Vulgate read *tumors. And rats appeared in their land, and death and **d** were throughout the city.*
Mt 7:13 {highway to hell} Greek *The way that leads to **d**.*
1Co 5: 5 {will be destroyed} Or *so that he will die;* Greek reads *for the **d** of the flesh.*
2Th 2: 3 {who brings destruction.} Greek *the son of **d**.*

DETAINED (1)

1Sa 21: 7 {for ceremonial purification.} Hebrew *was **d** before the LORD.*

DEUT (51)

2Ki 14: 6 {their own crimes."} **D** 24:16.
2Ch 25: 4 {their own crimes."} **D** 24:16.
Mt 4: 4 {word of God.'} **D** 8:3.
4: 7 {Lord your God.'} **D** 6:16.
4:10 {serve only him.'} **D** 6:13.
5:21 {subject to judgment.'} Exod 20:13; **D** 5:17.
5:27 {not commit adultery.'} Exod 20:14; **D** 5:18.
5:31 {letter of divorce.'} **D** 24:1.
5:38 {who did it.'} Greek *'An eye for an eye and a tooth for a tooth.'* Exod 21:24; Lev 24:20; **D** 19:21.
15: 4 {put to death.'} Exod 20:12; 21:17; Lev 20:9; **D** 5:16.
19: 7 {send her away?"} **D** 24:1.
19:18[-19] {neighbor as yourself.'} Exod 20:12-16; Lev 19:18; **D** 5:16-20.
22:24 {the brother's heir.'} **D** 25:5-6.
22:37 {all your mind.'} **D** 6:5.
Mk 7:10 {put to death.'} Exod 20:12; 21:17; Lev 20:9; **D** 5:16.
10: 4 {send her away."} **D** 24:1.
10:19 {father and mother.'} Exod 20:12-16; **D** 5:16-20.
12:19 {the brother's heir.} **D** 25:5-6.
12:29[-30] {all your strength.'} **D** 6:4-5.
Lk 4: 4 {for their life.'} **D** 8:3.
4: 8 {serve only him.'} **D** 6:13.
4:12 {Lord your God.'} **D** 6:16.
10:27 {neighbor as yourself.' "} **D** 6:5; Lev 19:18.
18:20 {father and mother.'} Exod 20:12-16; **D** 5:16-20.
20:28 {the brother's heir.} **D** 25:5-6.
Jn 1:21 {you the Prophet?"} See **D** 18:15, 18; Mal 4:5-6.
6:14 {is the Prophet} See **D** 18:15, 18.
7:40 {is the Prophet."} See **D** 18:15, 18.
8:17 {accepted as fact.} See **D** 19:15.
Ac 3:22 {he tells you.'} **D** 18:15.
3:23 {and utterly destroyed.'} **D** 18:19; Lev 23:29.
7:37 {your own people.'} **D** 18:15.
13:18 {up with them} Other manuscripts read *He cared for them;* compare **D** 1:31.
Ro 7: 7 {"Do not covet."} Exod 20:17; **D** 5:21.
10: 6[-8] {in your heart."} **D** 30:12-14.
10:19 {the foolish Gentiles."} **D** 32:21.
11: 8 {do not hear."} **D** 29:4; Isa 29:10.
12:19 {who deserve it,"} **D** 32:35.
15:10 {people, the Jews."} **D** 32:43.
1Co 5:13 {from among you."} **D** 17:7.
9: 9 {out the grain."} **D** 25:4.
2Co 13: 1 {or three witnesses."} **D** 19:15.
Gal 3:10 {of the Law."} **D** 27:26.
3:13 {on a tree."} **D** 21:23.
Eph 6: 2[-3] {full of blessing."} Exod 20:12; **D** 5:16.
1Ti 5:18 {deserve their pay!"} **D** 25:4; Luke 10:7.
Heb 1: 6 {God worship him."} **D** 32:43.
10:30 {his own people."} **D** 32:35-36.
12:21 {terrified and trembling."} **D** 9:19.
13: 5 {never forsake you."} **D** 31:6, 8.
Jas 2:11 {"Do not murder."} Exod 20:13-14; **D** 5:17-18.

DEVIL (1)

1Ti 3: 6 {make him fall.} Or *he might fall into the same judgment as the **D**.*

DEVOURER (1)

Mal 3:11 {insects and disease.} Hebrew *from the **d**.*

DIANA (1)

Ac 19:24 {Greek goddess Artemis.} *Artemis* is otherwise known as **D**.

DIBLAH (1)

Eze 6:14 {south to Riblah} As in some Hebrew manuscripts; most Hebrew manuscripts read ***D**.*

DIDYMUS (3)

Jn 11:16 {nicknamed the Twin,} Greek *the one who was called **D**.*
20:24 {(nicknamed the Twin} Greek *the one who was called **D**.*
21: 2 {(nicknamed the Twin} Greek *the one who was called **D**.*

DIE (3)

1Sa 2:33 {a violent death.} As in Dead Sea Scrolls, which read ***d** by the sword;* Masoretic Text reads ***d** like mortals.*
1Co 5: 5 {will be destroyed} Or *so that he will **d**;* Greek reads *for the destruction of the flesh.*

DIED (5)

Ge 11:12[-13] {sons and daughters.} Greek version reads [12]*When Arphaxad was 135 years old, his son Cainan was born.* [13]*After the birth of Cainan, Arphaxad lived another 430 years and had other sons and daughters, and then he **d**. When Cainan was 130 years old, his son Shelah was born. After the birth of Shelah, Cainan lived another 330 years and had other sons and daughters, and then he **d**.*
Mt 27:51[-53] {to many people.} Or *The earth shook, rocks split apart, tombs opened, and many bodies of godly men and women who had **d** were raised from the dead. After Jesus' resurrection, they left the cemetery, went into the holy city of Jerusalem, and appeared to many people.*
2Co 5:14 {used to live.} Greek *Since one **d** on behalf of all, then all **d**.*

DILL (1)

Mt 23:23 {of your income,} Greek *to tithe the mint, the **d**, and the cumin.*

DIMON (1)

Isa 15: 9 {stream near Dibon} As in Dead Sea Scrolls, some Greek manuscripts, and Latin Vulgate; Hebrew reads ***D**;* also in 15:9b.

DINING (1)

Mk 7: 4 {pitchers, and kettles.} Some Greek manuscripts add *and **d** couches.*

DIPHATH (1)

1Ch 1: 6 {were Ashkenaz, Riphath,} As in some Hebrew manuscripts and Greek version (see also Gen 10:3); most Hebrew manuscripts read ***D**.*

DIPPED (1)

Mt 26:23 {with me now} Or *The one who has **d** his hand in the bowl with me.*

DIPPING (1)

Mk 14:20 {with me now.} Or *one who is **d** bread into the bowl with me.*

DIRECTION (1)

1Ch 28:19 {of the LORD.} Or *was written under the **d** of the LORD.*

DISAGREEING (1)

Ac 28:28 {will accept it."} Some manuscripts add verse 29, *And when he had said these words, the Jews departed, greatly **d** with each other.*

DISAPPOINTED (1)

Isa 28:16 {run away again.} Greek version reads *Anyone who believes in him will not be **d**.*

DISASTER (1)

1Ch 2: 7 {Achan} Hebrew *Achar;* compare Josh 7:1. *Achar* means "**d**."

DISCHARGE (1)

Lev 15: 2 {genital discharge} Hebrew *a **d** from his flesh;* also in 15:32.

DISCIPLE (2)

Jn 13:23 {at the table.} Greek *was reclining on Jesus' bosom.* The "**d** whom Jesus loved" was probably John.
Ac 9:10 {was a believer} Greek ***d**;* also in 9:36.

DISCIPLES (13)

Jn 13: 1 {of his love.} Or *He loved his **d** to the very end.*
Ac 6: 1 {as the believers} Greek ***d**;* also in 6:2, 7.
9: 1 {the Lord's followers,} Greek ***d**.*
9:19 {with the believers} Greek ***d**;* also in 9:26.
9:25 {the other believers} Greek *his **d**.*
11:26 {that the believers} Greek ***d**;* also in 11:29a.
13:52 {And the believers} Greek *the **d**.*
14:20 {as the believers} Greek ***d**;* also in 14:22, 28.
15:10 {the Gentile believers} Greek ***d**.*
18:23 {all the believers,} Greek ***d**;* also in 18:27.
19: 1 {found several believers.} Greek ***d**;* also in 19:9, 30.
20: 1 {for the believers} Greek ***d**.*
21: 4 {the local believers,} Greek ***d**;* also in 21:16.

DISCUSSIONS (1)
Tit 3: 9 {about spiritual pedigrees} Greek *d and genealogies.*

DISEASE (7)
Ex 4: 6 {snow with leprosy.} Or *with a contagious skin d.* The Hebrew word used here can describe various skin diseases.
Nu 12:10 {snow with leprosy.} Or *with a contagious skin d.* The Hebrew word used here can describe various skin diseases.
2Sa 3:29 {sores or leprosy} Or *or a contagious skin d.* The Hebrew word used here can describe various skin diseases.
2Ki 5: 1 {suffered from leprosy.} Or *from a contagious skin d.* The Hebrew word used here and throughout this passage can describe various skin diseases.
7: 3 {men with leprosy} Or *with a contagious skin d.* The Hebrew word used here and throughout this passage can describe various skin diseases.
15: 5 {king with leprosy,} Or *with a contagious skin d.* The Hebrew word used here and throughout this passage can describe various skin diseases.
2Ch 26:19 {LORD's Temple, leprosy} Or *a contagious skin d.* The Hebrew word used here and throughout this passage can describe various skin diseases.

DISEASES (12)
Ex 4: 6 {snow with leprosy.} Or *with a contagious skin disease.* The Hebrew word used here can describe various skin **d.**
Lev 13: 2 {contagious skin disease,} Traditionally rendered *leprosy.* The Hebrew word used throughout this passage is used to describe various skin **d.**
13:47 {an infectious mildew} Traditionally rendered *leprosy.* The Hebrew term used throughout this passage is the same term used for the various skin **d** described in 13:1-46.
Nu 5: 2 {contagious skin disease} Traditionally rendered *leprosy.* The Hebrew word used here describes various skin **d.**
12:10 {snow with leprosy.} Or *with a contagious skin disease.* The Hebrew word used here can describe various skin **d.**
Dt 24: 8 {contagious skin diseases} Traditonally rendered *leprosy.* The Hebrew word used here can describe various skin **d.**
2Sa 3:29 {or leprosy} Or *or a contagious skin disease.* The Hebrew word used here can describe various skin **d.**
2Ki 5: 1 {leprosy.} Or *from a contagious skin disease.* The Hebrew word used here and throughout this passage can describe various skin **d.**
7: 3 {leprosy} Or *with a contagious skin disease.* The Hebrew word used here and throughout this passage can describe various skin **d.**
15: 5 {leprosy,} Or *with a contagious skin disease.* The Hebrew word used here and throughout this passage can describe various skin **d.**
2Ch 26:19 {leprosy} Or *a contagious skin disease.* The Hebrew word used here and throughout this passage can describe various skin **d.**
Isa 53: 4 {our sorrows} Or *Yet it was our sicknesses he carried; it was our d.*

DISHAN (1)
Ge 36:26 {sons of Dishon} Hebrew *D*, a variant name for Dishon; compare 36:21, 28.

DISHON (2)
Ge 36:26 {sons of Dishon} Hebrew *Dishan*, a variant name for **D**; compare 36:21, 28.
1Ch 1:42 {sons of Dishan} Hebrew *D;* compare 1:38 and parallel text at Gen 36:28.

DISPERSION (1)
Jas 1: 1 {among the nations.} Greek *To the twelve tribes in the d.*

DISTRESS (1)
1Ch 4: 9 {named him Jabez} *Jabez* sounds like a Hebrew term meaning "**d**" or "pain."

DISTURBING (1)
Jdg 9:23 {stirred up trouble} Hebrew *sent a d spirit.*

DIVIDED (1)
Mt 27:35 {by throwing dice.} Greek *by casting lots.* A few late manuscripts add *This fulfilled the word of the prophet: "They d my clothes among themselves and cast lots for my robe."* See Ps 22:18.

DIVINE (1)
Ps 45: 6 {Your throne, O God,} Or *Your d throne.*

DIVORCED (1)
Mt 19: 9 {has been unfaithful.} Some manuscripts add *And the man who marries a d woman commits adultery.*

DOCTORS (1)
Lk 8:43 {had on doctors} Some manuscripts omit *She had spent everything she had on d.*

DODAI (1)
1Ch 11:12 {son of Dodai,} As in parallel text at 2 Sam 23:9 (see also 1 Chr 27:4); Hebrew reads *Dodo*, a variant name for **D.**

DODANIM (1)
Ge 10: 4 {Kittim, and Rodanim.} As in some Hebrew manuscripts and Greek version (see also 1 Chr 1:7); most Hebrew manuscripts read *D.*

DODO (1)
1Ch 11:12 {son of Dodai,} As in parallel text at 2 Sam 23:9 (see also 1 Chr 27:4); Hebrew reads *D*, a variant name for Dodai.

DOG (1)
2Ki 8:13 {nobody like me} Hebrew *a d.*

DOGS (1)
Mt 7: 6 {to unholy people.} Greek *Don't give the sacred to d.*

DONKEY (1)
Lk 14: 5 {If your son} Some manuscripts read *d.*

DOOR (1)
SS 8: 9 {off from men.} Hebrew *If she is a wall, we will build battlements of silver on her; but if she is a d, we will surround her with panels of cedar.*

DORCAS (1)
Ac 9:36 {Greek is Dorcas} The names *Tabitha* in Aramaic and *D* in Greek both mean "gazelle."

DOUBLE (3)
1Sa 1: 5 {special portion} Or *a d portion.* The meaning of the Hebrew is uncertain.
2Ki 2: 9 {your rightful successor."} Hebrew *Let me inherit a d share of your spirit.*
1Ti 5:17 {be paid well,} Greek *should be worthy of d honor.*

DOUGH (3)
Ro 11:16 {also be holy.} Greek *If the d offered as firstfruits is holy, so is the whole lump.*
1Co 5: 6[-7] {can stay pure.} Greek *Don't you realize that even a little leaven spreads quickly through the whole batch of d?* [7]*Purge out the old leaven so that you can be a new batch of d, just as you are already unleavened.*

DOVE'S (2)
2Ki 6:25 {about two ounces} Hebrew *sold for 80 shekels* [0.9 kilograms] *of silver, and 1/4 of a cab* [0.3 liters] *of d dung cost 5 shekels* [57 grams]. *D dung* may be a variety of wild vegetable.

DRACHMA (1)
Lk 15: 8 {valuable silver coins} Greek *10 drachmas.* A **d** was the equivalent of a full day's wage.

DRACHMAS (1)
Lk 15: 8 {valuable silver coins} Greek *10 d.* A drachma was the equivalent of a full day's wage.

DRAGON (1)
Isa 51: 9 {of the Nile.} Hebrew *slew Rahab the d.* Rahab is the name of a mythical sea monster that represents chaos in ancient literature. The name is used here as a poetic name for Egypt.

DRAW (2)
Ex 2:10 {named him Moses,} *Moses* sounds like a Hebrew term that means "to **d** out."
1Sa 14:42 {said, "Now choose} Hebrew *d lots.*

DRINK (4)
1Sa 1:11 {never be cut."} Some manuscripts add *He will d neither wine nor intoxicants.*
Pr 5:15 {with your wife.} Hebrew *D water from your own cistern, flowing water from your own well.*
Jn 7:37[-38] {out from within."} Or *"Let anyone who is thirsty come to me and d.* [38]*For the Scriptures declare that rivers of living water will flow from the heart of those who believe in me."*
1Co 12:13 {the same Spirit.} Greek *we were all given one Spirit to d.*

DROPSY (1)
Lk 14: 2 {legs were swollen.} Traditionally translated *who had d.*

DULL (1)
Ge 29:17 {had pretty eyes,} Or *d eyes.* The meaning of the Hebrew is uncertain.

DUMAH (1)
Isa 21:11 {me concerning Edom} Hebrew *D*, which means "silence" or "stillness." It is a wordplay on the word *Edom.*

DUNG (2)
2Ki 6:25 {about two ounces} Hebrew *sold for 80 shekels* [0.9 kilograms] *of silver, and 1/4 of a cab* [0.3 liters] *of dove's d cost 5 shekels* [57 grams]. *Dove's d* may be a variety of wild vegetable.

DUNGHILL (1)
Ezr 6:11 {pile of rubble.} Aramaic *a d.*

DURING (3 of 5)
1Ki 2: 5 {time of peace,} Or *He murdered them d a time of peace as revenge for deaths they had caused in time of war.*
Eze 26: 1 {King Jehoiachin's captivity,} Hebrew *In the eleventh year, on the first day of the month,* of the Hebrew calendar year. Since an element is missing in the date formula here, scholars have reconstructed this probable reading: *On the first day of the eleventh month, d the twelfth year.* This reading would put this message on February 3, 585 B.C.; also see note on 1:1.
Lk 23:16 {will release him."} Some manuscripts add verse 17, *For it was necessary for him to release one [prisoner] for them d the feast.*

DUST (1)
Mic 1:10 {people in Beth-leaphrah,} *Beth-leaphrah* means "house of **d.**"

DWELLINGS (1)
Ps 87: 2 {city in Israel.} Hebrew *He loves the gates of Zion more than all the d of Jacob.*

DWELLS (1)
Col 2: 9 {human body,} Greek *in him d all the fullness of the Godhead bodily.*

E

EAGER (1)
Mt 11:12 {people attack it.} Or *until now, e multitudes have been pressing into the Kingdom of Heaven.*

EARTH (7)
Ge 1:26 {livestock, wild animals,} As in Syriac version; Hebrew reads *all the e.*
Mic 7:13 {But the land} Or *e.*
Mt 27:51[-53] {to many people.} Or *The e shook, rocks split apart, tombs opened, and many bodies of godly men and women who had died were raised from the dead. After Jesus' resurrection, they left the cemetery, went into the holy city of Jerusalem, and appeared to many people.*
Lk 2:14 {whom God favors.} Or *and peace on e for all those pleasing God;* some manuscripts read *and peace on e, goodwill among people.*
Eph 4: 9 {which we live.} Or *to the lowest parts of the e.*
1Jn 5: 7 {these three witnesses} Some very late manuscripts add *in heaven—the Father, the Word, and the Holy Spirit, and these three are one. And we have three witnesses on e.*

EARTHEN (1)
2Co 4: 7 {our weak bodies.} Greek *But we have this treasure in e vessels.*

EARTHLY (1)
2Pe 1:14 {soon to die.} Greek *I must soon put off this e tent.*

EAST (7)
Dt 4:49 {the Dead Sea,} Hebrew *took the Arabah on the e side of the Jordan as far as the sea of the Arabah.*
1Sa 10:27 {Saul ignored them.} Dead Sea Scroll 4QSam[a] continues: *Nahash, king of the Ammonites, had been grievously oppressing the Gadites and Reubenites who lived e of the Jordan River.…In fact, of all the Israelites e of the Jordan, there wasn't a single one whose right eye Nahash had not gouged out.…*
Ps 80:11 {the Euphrates River.} Hebrew *west to the sea,…e to the river.*
Eze 40:44 {beside the south} As in Greek version; Hebrew reads *e.*
42:10 {On the south} As in Greek version; Hebrew reads *e.*
Mt 2: 2 {as it arose,} Or *in the e.*

EASTERN (3 of 4)
Eze 47:18 {the Dead Sea} Hebrew *the e sea.*

Joel 2:20 {into the Mediterranean.} Hebrew *the **e** sea;...the western sea.*
Zec 14: 8 {toward the Mediterranean,} Hebrew *half toward the **e** sea and half toward the western sea.*

EAT (3)
Isa 9:20 {their own children.} Or ***e** their own arms.*
Mk 7:27 {family, the Jews.} Greek *Let the children **e** first.*
Jas 5: 3 {flesh in hell.} Or *will **e** your flesh like fire.*

EBAL (1)
1Ch 1:22 {Obal,} As in some Hebrew manuscripts and Syriac version (see also Gen 10:28); most Hebrew manuscripts read ***E***.

EBIASAPH (2)
1Ch 6:23 {Elkanah, Abiasaph,} Hebrew ***E***, a variant name for Abiasaph (also in 6:37); compare parallel text at Exod 6:24.
9:19 {descendant of Abiasaph,} Hebrew ***E***, a variant name for Abiasaph; compare Exod 6:24.

EBRON (1)
Jos 19:28 {Abdon,} As in some Hebrew manuscripts (see also 21:30); most Hebrew manuscripts read ***E***.

EDGE (1)
1Sa 20:41 {the stone pile.} As in Greek version; Hebrew reads *near the south **e***.

EDH (1)
Jos 22:34 {the altar "Witness,"} Hebrew ***e***. Some manuscripts lack this word.

EDOM (3)
Isa 21:11 {concerning Edom} Hebrew *Dumah,* which means "silence" or "stillness." It is a wordplay on the word **E**.
21:11 {Someone from Edom} Hebrew *Seir,* another name for **E**.
Eze 27:16 {"Aram} Some manuscripts read ***E***.

EFFEMINATE (1)
2Sa 3:29 {walks on crutches} Or *who is **e**;* Hebrew reads *who handles a spindle.*

EGYPT (10 of 16)
Ge 10: 6 {were Cush, Mizraim,} Or ***E**;* also in 10:13.
15:18 {border of Egypt} Hebrew *the river of **E**,* referring either to an eastern branch of the Nile River or to the brook of **E** in the Sinai (see Num 34:5).
47:21 {servants to Pharaoh.} As in Greek version and Samaritan Pentateuch; Hebrew reads *He moved the people into the towns throughout the land of **E**.*
1Ki 12: 2 {returned from Egypt,} As in Greek version and Latin Vulgate (see also 2 Chr 10:2); Hebrew reads *he lived in **E**.*
2Ki 17: 4 {So of Egypt} Or *by asking the king of **E** at Sais.*
1Ch 1: 8 {were Cush, Mizraim,} Or ***E**;* also in 1:11.
13: 5 {to the other,} Hebrew *from the Shihor of **E** to Lebo-hamath.*
Isa 11:15 {the Red Sea.} Hebrew *sea of **E**.*
Zec 10:11 {sea of distress,} Or *the sea of **E**,* referring to the Red Sea.

EGYPTIANS (1)
Ge 50:11 {the place Abel-mizraim,} *Abel-mizraim* means "mourning of the **E**."

EHUD (1)
1Ch 8: 3 {Addar, Gera, Abihud,} Possibly *Gera the father of **E**;* compare 8:6.

EIGHT (2)
2Sa 23: 8 {a single battle.} As in some Greek manuscripts (see also 1 Chr 11:11); the Hebrew is uncertain, though it might be rendered *the Three. It was Adino the Eznite who killed **e** hundred men at one time.*
2Ch 36: 9 {Jehoiachin was eighteen} As in one Hebrew manuscript, some Greek manuscripts, and Syriac version (see also 2 Kgs 24:8); most Hebrew manuscripts read **e**.

EIGHTH (5)
1Ki 6:38 {detail by midautumn} Hebrew *in the month of Bul, which is the **e** month....*
8:66 {festival was over,} Hebrew *On the **e** day,* probably referring to the day following the seven-day Festival of Shelters; compare parallel text at 2 Chr 7:9-10.
12:32 {day in midautumn,} Hebrew *on the fifteenth day of the **e** month* (also in 12:33). This day of the Hebrew lunar calendar occurs in late October or early November, exactly one month after the annual Festival of Shelters in Judah (see Lev 23:34).
Ne 8:18 {Then on October 15} Hebrew *on the **e** day,* of the seventh month of the Hebrew calendar. This event occurred on October 15, 445 B.C.; also see notes on 1:1 and 8:2.

Zec 1: 1 {In midautumn} Hebrew *In the **e** month.* A number of events in Zechariah can be cross-checked with dates in surviving Persian records and related accurately to our modern calendar. This month of the Hebrew lunar calendar occurred in October and November 520 B.C.

EL (1)
Ex 6: 3 {as God Almighty,} Hebrew ***E** Shaddai.*

EL-BERITH (1)
Jdg 9:46 {temple of Baal-berith.} Hebrew ***E***, another name for Baal-berith; compare 9:4.

EL-BETHEL (1)
Ge 35: 7 {named it El-bethel,} ***E*** means "the God of Bethel."

EL-ELOHE-ISRAEL (1)
Ge 33:20 {called it El-Elohe-Israel.} ***E*** means "God, the God of Israel."

EL-ROI (1)
Ge 16:13 {who sees me,"} Hebrew ***E***.

ELDER (3)
1Ti 5: 1 {an older man,} Or *an **e**.*
2Jn 1: 1 {John, the Elder.} Greek *From the **e**.*
3Jn 1: 1 {John, the Elder.} Greek *From the **e**.*

ELDERS (1)
Ac 24: 1 {and the lawyer} Greek *some **e** and an orator.*

ELECT (1)
1Pe 5:13 {here in Rome} Greek *The **e** one in Babylon.* Babylon was probably a code name for Rome.

ELEVENTH (5 of 8)
Dt 1: 3 {day in midwinter,} Hebrew *on the first day of the **e** month.* This day of the Hebrew lunar calendar occurs in January or early February.
Jer 39: 2 {later, on July 18,} Hebrew *On the ninth day of the fourth month of the **e** year of Zedekiah.* This event occurred on July 18, 586 B.C.; also see note on 39:1.
Eze 26: 1 {King Jehoiachin's captivity,} Hebrew *In the **e** year, on the first day of the month,* of the Hebrew calendar year. Since an element is missing in the date formula here, scholars have reconstructed this probable reading: *On the first day of the **e** month, during the twelfth year.* This reading would put this message on February 3, 585 B.C.; also see note on 1:1.
Zec 1: 7 {Then on February 15} Hebrew *on the twenty-fourth day of the **e** month, the month of Shebat,* of the Hebrew calendar. This event occurred on February 15, 519 B.C.; also see note on 1:1.

ELIADA (1)
1Ch 14: 7 {Elishama, Eliada,} Hebrew *Beeliada,* a variant name for **E**; compare 3:8 and parallel text at 2 Sam 5:16.

ELIEZER (1)
Ex 18: 4 {son was Eliezer,} ***E*** means "God is my helper."

ELIJAH (4)
2Ki 2:15 {become Elijah's successor!"} Hebrew *The spirit of **E** rests upon Elisha.*
3:11 {Elijah's personal assistant.} Hebrew *He used to pour water on the hands of **E**.*
Mt 17:10 {the Messiah comes} Greek *that **E** must come first.*
Lk 9:54 {burn them up} Some manuscripts add *as **E** did.*

ELIPHELET (1)
1Ch 3: 6 {Elpelet,} Hebrew ***E**;* compare parallel text at 14:5-7.

ELISHA (1)
2Ki 2:15 {become Elijah's successor!"} Hebrew *The spirit of Elijah rests upon **E**.*

ELISHAMA (1)
1Ch 3: 6 {sons: Ibhar, Elishua,} As in some Hebrew and Greek manuscripts (see also 14:5-7 and 2 Sam 5:15); most Hebrew manuscripts read ***E***.

ELOHIM (1)
Ps 8: 5 {lower than God,} Or *a little lower than the angels;* Hebrew reads ***E***.

ELON-MEONENIM (1)
Jdg 9:37 {the Diviners' Oak.} Hebrew ***E***.

ELOTH (3)
1Ki 9:26 {port near Elath} As in Greek version (see also 2 Kgs 14:22; 16:6); Hebrew reads ***E***.

2Ch 8:17 {Ezion-geber and Elath,} As in Greek version (see also 2 Kgs 14:22; 16:6); Hebrew reads ***E***.
26: 2 {town of Elath} As in Greek version (see also 2 Kgs 14:22; 16:6); Hebrew reads ***E***.

ELUL (1)
Ne 6:15 {So on October 2} Hebrew *on the twenty-fifth day of the month **E**,* of the Hebrew calendar. This event occurred on October 2, 445 B.C.; also see note on 1:1.

EMBITTERED (1)
Ps 106:33 {made Moses angry,} Hebrew *They **e** his spirit.*

EN-HAKKORE (1)
Jdg 15:19 {Who Cried Out,"} Hebrew ***E***.

ENCOURAGER (3)
Jn 14:16 {another Counselor,} Or *Comforter,* or ***E***, or *Advocate.* Greek *Paraclete;* also in 14:26.
15:26 {the Counselor} Or *Comforter,* or ***E***, or *Advocate.* Greek *Paraclete.*
16: 7 {the Counselor} Or *Comforter,* or ***E***, or *Advocate.* Greek *Paraclete.*

END (4 of 6)
Zec 9:10 {of the earth.} Or *the **e** of the land.*
Lk 16: 9 {you in heaven.} Or *Then when you run out at the **e** of this life, your friends will welcome you into eternal homes.*
Jn 13: 1 {of his love.} Or *He loved his disciples to the very **e**.*
Ro 10: 4 {the whole purpose} Or *the **e**.*

ENDEARMENT (4)
Dt 32:15 {But Israel} Hebrew *Jeshurun,* a term of **e** for Israel.
33: 5 {king in Israel} Hebrew *in Jeshurun,* a term of **e** for Israel.
33:26 {God of Israel.} Hebrew *of Jeshurun,* a term of **e** for Israel.
Isa 44: 2 {be afraid. O Israel,} Hebrew *Jeshurun,* a term of **e** for Israel.

ENDLESS (1)
1Ti 1: 4 {and spiritual pedigrees.} Greek *in myths and **e** genealogies, which cause speculation.*

ENEMIES (3)
Dt 32:31 {even they recognize.} The meaning of the Hebrew is uncertain. Greek version reads *our **e** are fools.*
1Sa 10: 1 {his people Israel.} Greek version reads *Israel. And you will rule over the LORD's people and save them from their **e** around them. This will be the sign to you that the LORD has appointed you to be leader over his inheritance.*
Est 9:18 {the third day,} Hebrew *killing their **e** on the thirteenth day and the fourteenth day, and then rested on the fifteenth day,* of the Hebrew month of Adar.

ENGLISH (4)
Ex 16: 1 {the Sin} Not to be confused with the **E** word *sin.*
17: 1 {the Sin} Not to be confused with the **E** word *sin.*
Nu 33:11 {the Sin} Not to be confused with the **E** word *sin.*
Jer 48: 2 {city of Madmen,} *Madmen* sounds like the Hebrew word for "silence"; it should not be confused with the **E** word *madmen.*

ENLARGE (1)
Mt 23: 5 {Scripture verses inside,} Greek *They **e** their phylacteries.*

ENOCH (1)
Jude 1:14[-15] {spoken against him."} The quotation comes from the Apocrypha: **E** 1:9.

ENOS (1)
Lk 3:38 {son of Enosh.} Greek ***E**;* see Gen 5:6.

ENOUGH (2)
Job 7:19 {for a moment} Hebrew *long **e** to swallow my spittle.*
Ps 59:15 {to sleep unsatisfied.} Or *and growl if they don't get **e**.*

ENSEMBLE (2)
Da 3: 7 {the musical instruments,} Aramaic *the horn, flute, zither, lyre, harp, and other instruments of the musical **e**.*
3:10 {the musical instruments.} Aramaic *the horn, flute, zither, lyre, harp, pipes, and other instruments of the musical **e**;* also in 3:15.

ENTERED (1)
Hab 3:16 {way beneath me,} Hebrew *Decay **e** my bones.*

ENVY (2)

Jas 4: 5 {to be faithful} Or *the spirit that God placed within us tends to* **e**, or *the Holy Spirit, whom God has placed within us, opposes our* **e**.

EPHAH (33)

Ex 16:36 {about two quarts.)} Hebrew *An omer is one tenth of an* **e**.
29:40 {quart of wine} Hebrew *1/10 of an* **e** [2 liters] *of fine flour…1/4 of a hin* [1 liter] *of olive oil…1/4 of a hin of wine.*
Lev 5:11 {bring two quarts} Hebrew *1/10 of an* **e** [2 liters].
6:20 {of two quarts} Hebrew *1/10 of an* **e** [2 liters].
14:10 {with five quarts} Hebrew *3/10 of an* **e** [5.4 liters].
14:21 {with two quarts} Hebrew *1/10 of an* **e** [2 liters].
19:36 {must be accurate.} Hebrew *Use an honest* **e** [a measure for dry goods] *and an honest hin* [a measure for liquids].
23:13 {of three quarts} Hebrew *2/10 of an* **e** [3.6 liters]; also in 23:17.
24: 5 {using three quarts} Hebrew *2/10 of an* **e** [3.6 liters].
Nu 5:15 {of two quarts} Hebrew *1/10 of an* **e** [2 liters].
15: 4 {of two quarts} Hebrew *1/10 of an* **e** [2 liters].
15: 6 {give three quarts} Hebrew *2/10 of an* **e** [3.6 liters].
15: 9 {include five quarts} Hebrew *3/10 of an* **e** [5.4 liters].
28: 5 {of two quarts} Hebrew *1/10 of an* **e** [2 liters]; also in 28:13, 21, 29.
28: 9 {of three quarts} Hebrew *2/10 of an* **e** [3.6 liters]; also in 28:12, 20, 28.
28:12 {olive oil—five quarts} Hebrew *3/10 of an* **e** [5.4 liters]; also in 28:20, 28.
29: 3 {olive oil—five quarts} Hebrew *3/10 of an* **e** [5.4 liters]; also in 29:9, 14.
29: 3 {bull, three quarts} Hebrew *2/10 of an* **e** [3.6 liters]; also in 29:9, 14.
29: 4 {and two quarts} Hebrew *1/10 of an* **e** [2 liters]; also in 29:10, 15.
Jdg 6:19 {half a bushel} Hebrew *1* **e** [18 liters].
Ru 2:17 {half a bushel.} Hebrew *about an* **e** [18 liters].
1Sa 1:24 {half a bushel} Hebrew *and an* **e** [18 liters].
17:17 {"Take this half-bushel} Hebrew **e** [18 liters].
Isa 5:10 {only one measure} Hebrew *A homer* [5 bushels or 182 liters] *of seed will yield only an* **e** [0.5 bushels or 18.2 liters].
Eze 45:10 {liquid volume measures.} Hebrew *use honest scales, an honest* **e**, *and an honest bath.*
45:11 {and the bath} The **e** is a dry measure; the *bath* is a liquid measure.
45:13 {for every sixty} Hebrew *1/6 of an* **e** *from each homer of wheat…and of barley.*
45:24 {of olive oil} Hebrew *an* **e** [18 liters] *of flour…a hin* [3.8 liters] *of olive oil.*
46: 5 {of olive oil} Hebrew *an* **e** [18 liters] *of flour…a hin* [3.8 liters] *of olive oil;* also in 46:7, 11.
46:14 {of olive oil} Hebrew *1/6 of an* **e** [2.9 liters] *of flour with 1/3 of a hin* [1.3 liters] *of olive oil.*
Mic 6:10 {in short measures.} Hebrew *by using the short* **e**; the **e** was a unit for measuring grain.
Zec 5: 6 {for measuring grain,} Hebrew *an* **e**, about half a bushel or 18 liters; also in 5:7, 8, 9, 10, 11.

EPHESIAN (1)

Ac 21:29 {Gentile from Ephesus,} Greek *Trophimus, the* **E**.

EPHESUS (2)

1Co 15:32 {men of Ephesus} Greek *fighting wild beasts in* **E**.
Eph 1: 1 {people in Ephesus,} Some manuscripts do not include *in* **E**.

EPHOD (4)

1Sa 2:18 {of a priest.} Hebrew *He wore a linen* **e**.
2:28 {the priestly garments} Hebrew *an* **e**.
2Sa 6:14 {a priestly tunic.} Hebrew *a linen* **e**.
1Ch 15:27 {a priestly tunic.} Hebrew *a linen* **e**.

EPHPHATHA (1)

Mk 7:34 {commanded, "Be opened!"} Greek text uses Aramaic *"E"* and then translates it as "Be opened."

EPHRAIM (22)

Ge 41:52 {second son Ephraim,} *E* sounds like a Hebrew term that means "fruitful."
46:27 {two sons} Greek version reads *nine sons*, probably including Joseph's grandsons through **E** and Manasseh (see 1 Chr 7:14-20).
2Ch 28:12 {Israel} Hebrew *E*, referring to the northern kingdom of Israel.
Isa 7: 2 {Israel} Hebrew *E*, referring to the northern kingdom of Israel; also in 7:5, 8, 9, 17.
9: 9 {Israel} Hebrew *of E*, referring to the northern kingdom of Israel.
11:13 {Israel} Hebrew *E*, referring to the northern kingdom of Israel.
17: 3 {of Israel} Hebrew *of E*, referring to the northern kingdom of Israel.
28: 1 {of Israel} Hebrew *of E*, referring to the northern kingdom of Israel; also in 28:3.
Jer 7:15 {of Israel.} Hebrew *of E*, referring to the northern kingdom of Israel.
31:18 {Israel} Hebrew *E*, referring to the northern kingdom of Israel; also in 31:20.
Eze 47:13 {shares of land.} A share of land for each of Joseph's two oldest sons, **E** and Manasseh.
Hos 5: 9 {Israel} Hebrew *E*, referring to the northern kingdom of Israel; also in 5:11, 12, 13, 14.
6: 4 {"O Israel} Hebrew *E*, referring to the northern kingdom of Israel.
7: 8 {Israel} Hebrew *E*, referring to the northern kingdom of Israel; also in 7:11.
8: 9 {Israel} Hebrew *E*, referring to the northern kingdom of Israel; also in 8:11.
9: 8 {Israel,} Hebrew *E*, referring to the northern kingdom of Israel; also in 9:11, 13, 16.
10:11 {"Israel} Hebrew *E*, referring to the northern kingdom of Israel.
11: 3 {Israel} Hebrew *E*, referring to the northern kingdom of Israel; also in 11:8, 9, 12.
12: 1 {Israel} Hebrew *E*, referring to the northern kingdom of Israel; also in 12:8, 14.
14: 8 {"O Israel,} Hebrew *E*, referring to the northern kingdom of Israel.
Zec 9:10 {from Israel} Hebrew *from E;* also in 9:13.
10: 7 {of Israel} Hebrew *of E.*

EPHRATH (1)

1Ch 2:19 {Caleb married Ephrathah,} Hebrew *E*, a variant name for Ephrathah; compare 2:50 and 4:4.

EPHRATHAH (1)

1Ch 2:19 {Caleb married Ephrathah,} Hebrew *Ephrath*, a variant name for **E**; compare 2:50 and 4:4.

EPHRON (1)

Jos 18:15 {it ran westward} Or *it went to E, and.* The meaning of the Hebrew is uncertain.

ESAU (3)

Ge 25:25 {called him Esau.} *E* sounds like a Hebrew term that means "hair."
Jer 49: 8 {disaster on Edom,} Hebrew *E;* also in 49:10.
Ob 1: 6 {cranny of Edom} Hebrew *E;* also in 8b, 9, 18, 19, 21.

ESCAPED (1)

1Sa 10:27 {Saul ignored them.} Dead Sea Scroll 4QSam[a] continues: *…But there were seven thousand men who had* **e** *from the Ammonites, and they had settled in Jabesh-gilead.*

ESDRAS (5)

Ezr 3: 9 {descendants of Hodaviah.} Hebrew *sons of Judah* (i.e., *bene Yehudah*). *Bene* might also be read here as the proper name Binnui; *Yehudah* is probably another name for Hodaviah. Compare 2:40; Neh 7:43; 1 **E** 5:58.
8: 5 {family of Zattu} As in some Greek manuscripts (see also 1 **E** 8:32); Hebrew lacks *Zattu.*
8:10 {family of Bani} As in some Greek manuscripts (see also 1 **E** 8:36); Hebrew lacks *Bani.*
10: 6 {spent the night} As in parallel text at 1 **E** 9:2; Hebrew reads *He went.*
10:25 {Mijamin, Eleazar, Hashabiah,} As in parallel text at 1 **E** 9:26; Hebrew reads *Malkijah.*

ESEK (1)

Ge 26:20 {the well "Argument,"} Hebrew *E.*

ESHBAAL (4)

1Sa 14:49 {included Jonathan, Ishbosheth,} Hebrew *Ishvi*, a variant name for Ishbosheth; also known as **E**.
2Sa 2: 8 {Saul's son Ishbosheth.} Also known as *E.*
3: 7 {One day Ishbosheth,} Also known as *E.*
4: 1 {When Ishbosheth} Also known as *E.*

ESTABLISHES (2)

1Ki 7:21 {the north Boaz.} Jakin probably means "he**e**"; Boaz probably means "in him is strength."
2Ch 3:17 {the north Boaz.} Jakin probably means "he**e**"; Boaz probably means "in him is strength."

ESTHER (1 of 3)

Est 2:15 {was Esther's turn} Hebrew *the turn of E, the daughter of Abihail, who was Mordecai's uncle, who had adopted her.*

ETERNAL (2)

Lk 16: 9 {you in heaven.} Or *Then when you run out at the end of this life, your friends will welcome you into* **e** *homes.*
Ro 8:10 {spirit is alive} Or *the Spirit will bring you* **e** *life.*

ETHANIM (1)

1Ki 8: 2 {in early autumn.} Hebrew *at the festival in the month E, which is the seventh month.* The Festival of Shelters began on the fifteenth day of the seventh month on the Hebrew lunar calendar. This occurs on our calendar in late September or early October.

ETHIOPIA (1)

Ac 8:27 {queen of Ethiopia.} Greek *under the Candace, the queen of E.*

EUNUCH (1)

Ac 8:36 {I be baptized?"} Some manuscripts add verse 37, *"You can," Philip answered, "if you believe with all your heart." And the* **e** *replied, "I believe that Jesus Christ is the Son of God."*

EUNUCHS (1)

Jer 41:16 {and palace officials.} Or **e**.

EVE (1)

Ge 3:20 {his wife Eve,} *E* sounds like a Hebrew term that means "to give life."

EVENING (1)

Lev 23:32 {Day of Atonement} Hebrew *the* **e** *of the ninth day of the month;* see 23:24, 27 and the notes there.

EVERY (6)

Isa 2:16 {great trading ships} Hebrew **e** *ship of Tarshish.*
Mk 9:49 {purified with fire.} Greek *salted with fire.* Some manuscripts add *and* **e** *sacrifice will be salted with salt.*
Lk 11:42 {of your income,} Greek *to tithe the mint and the rue and* **e** *herb.*
1Co 15:24 {of every kind.} Greek **e** *ruler and* **e** *authority and power.*
16: 2 {every Lord's Day,} Greek **e** *first day of the week.*

EVERYTHING (4)

Lk 8:43 {had on doctors} Some manuscripts omit *She had spent* **e** *she had on doctors.*
Ro 8:28 {to work together} Some manuscripts read *And we know that* **e** *works together.*
9: 5 {eternal praise! Amen.} Or *May God, who rules over* **e**, *be praised forever. Amen.*
Heb 2: 7 {glory and honor.} Some manuscripts add *You put him in charge of* **e** *you made.*

EVIL (7)

Pr 12:26 {to their friends;} Or *The godly are cautious in friendship,* or *the godly are freed from* **e**. The meaning of the Hebrew is uncertain.
Mt 5:37 {something is wrong.} Or *Anything beyond this is from the* **e** *one.*
6:13 {the evil one.} Or *from* **e**. Some manuscripts add *For yours is the kingdom and the power and the glory forever. Amen.*
Eph 6:16 {you by Satan.} Greek *by the* **e** *one.*
2Th 3: 3 {the evil one.} Or *from* **e**.
2Pe 2:10 {the glorious ones} *The glorious ones* are probably **e** angels; also in 2:11.
Jude 1: 8 {the glorious ones.} *The glorious ones* are probably **e** angels.

EXALTED (1)

Ge 17: 5 {known as Abraham,} *Abram* means "**e** father"; *Abraham* means "father of many."

EXAMINE (1)

1Co 9: 3 {as an apostle.} Greek *those who* **e** *me.*

EXAMPLE (2)

2Ch 17: 3 {father's early years} Some Hebrew manuscripts read *the* **e** *of his father, David.*
Jn 8:39 {his good example.} Some manuscripts read *if you are children of Abraham, follow his* **e**.

EXCEPT (2)

Da 10:21 {your spirit prince.} Hebrew *against these* **e** *Michael, your prince.*
Jn 13:10 {for the feet,} Some manuscripts do not include **e** *for the feet.*

EXCHANGE (1)

Hos 4: 7 {They have exchanged} As in Syriac version and an ancient Hebrew tradition; Masoretic Text reads *I will* **e**.

EXOD (32)

Ge 46:27 {there were seventy} Greek version reads *seventy-five;* see note on **E** 1:5.
Dt 9:22 {Massah,} *Massah* means "place of testing." See **E** 17:1-7.
33: 8 {the sacred lots} Hebrew *given your Thummim and Urim.* See **E** 28:30.
1Ch 6:23 {Elkanah, Abiasaph,} Hebrew *Ebiasaph*, a variant name for Abiasaph (also in 6:37); compare parallel text at **E** 6:24.
9:19 {descendant of Abiasaph,} Hebrew *Ebiasaph*, a variant name for Abiasaph; compare **E** 6:24.
Mt 5:21 {subject to judgment.'} **E** 20:13; Deut 5:17.
5:27 {not commit adultery.'} **E** 20:14; Deut 5:18.
5:38 {who did it.'} Greek *'An eye for an eye and a tooth for a tooth.'* **E** 21:24; Lev 24:20; Deut 19:21.
15: 4 {put to death.'} **E** 20:12; 21:17; Lev 20:9; Deut 5:16.
19:18[-19] {neighbor as yourself.'} **E** 20:12-16; Lev 19:18; Deut 5:16-20.
22:32 {God of Jacob.'} **E** 3:6.

Mk 7:10 {put to death.'} **E** 20:12; 21:17; Lev 20:9; Deut 5:16.
10:19 {father and mother.'} **E** 20:12-16; Deut 5:16-20.
12:26 {God of Jacob.'} **E** 3:6.
Lk 2:23 {to the Lord."} **E** 13:2.
18:20 {father and mother.'} **E** 20:12-16; Deut 5:16-20.
20:37 {God of Jacob.'} **E** 3:6.
Jn 6:31 {heaven to eat.'} **E** 16:4; Ps 78:24.
19:36 {will be broken,"} **E** 12:46; Num 9:12; Ps 34:20.
Ac 7: 5[-7] {in this place.'} Gen 12:7; 15:13-14; **E** 3:12.
7:31[-34] {you to Egypt.'} **E** 3:5-10.
23: 5 {rules over you.'} **E** 22:28.
Ro 7: 7 {"Do not covet."} **E** 20:17; Deut 5:21.
9:15 {anyone I choose."} **E** 33:19.
9:17 {throughout the earth."} **E** 9:16.
1Co 10: 7 {in pagan revelry."} **E** 32:6.
2Co 8:15 {little had enough."} **E** 16:18.
Eph 6: 2[-3] {full of blessing."} **E** 20:12; Deut 5:16.
Heb 8: 5 {on the mountain."} **E** 25:40; 26:30.
9:20 {made with you."} **E** 24:8.
12:20 {stoned to death."} **E** 19:13.
Jas 2:11 {"Do not murder."} **E** 20:13-14; Deut 5:17-18.

EXPENSE (1)

Ac 28:30 {own rented house.} Or *at his own **e**.*

EXPENSIVE (1)

Mk 14: 3 {of expensive perfume.} Greek *an alabaster jar of **e** ointment, pure nard.*

EXPLAIN (1)

Eph 6:19 {the Gentiles, too.} Greek ***e** the mystery of the gospel.*

EXPLAINING (2)

1Co 2:13 {explain spiritual truths.} Or ***e** spiritual truths in spiritual language,* or ***e** spiritual truths to spiritual people.*

EYE (7 of 8)

Dt 32:10 {most precious possession.} Hebrew *as the apple of his **e**.*
1Sa 10:27 {Saul ignored them.} Dead Sea Scroll 4QSam[a] continues: *...He gouged out the right **e** of each of the Israelites living there, and he didn't allow anyone to come and rescue them. In fact, of all the Israelites east of the Jordan, there wasn't a single one whose right **e** Nahash had not gouged out....*
Pr 7: 2 {most precious possession.} Hebrew *as the apple of your **e**.*
Zec 2: 8 {most precious possession.} Hebrew *harms the apple of my **e**.*
Mt 5:38 {who did it.'} Greek *'An **e** for an **e** and a tooth for a tooth.'* Exod 21:24; Lev 24:20; Deut 19:21.

EYES (2)

Ge 29:17 {had pretty eyes,} Or *dull **e**.* The meaning of the Hebrew is uncertain.
Zec 3: 9 {with seven facets.} Hebrew *7 **e**.*

EZEK (2)

2Co 6:16 {be my people.} Lev 26:12; **E** 37:27.
6:17 {will welcome you.} Isa 52:11; **E** 20:34.

EZEL (1)

1Sa 20:19 {the stone pile.} Hebrew *the stone **E**.* The meaning of the Hebrew is uncertain.

EZNITE (1)

2Sa 23: 8 {a single battle.} As in some Greek manuscripts (see also 1 Chr 11:11); the Hebrew is uncertain, though it might be rendered *the Three. It was Adino the **E** who killed eight hundred men at one time.*

EZRA (18 of 19)

Ne 7: 7 {Seraiah,} As in parallel text at **E** 2:2; Hebrew reads *Azariah.*
7: 7 {Reelaiah,} As in parallel text at **E** 2:2; Hebrew reads *Raamiah.*
7: 7 {Mispar,} As in parallel text at **E** 2:2; Hebrew reads *Mispereth.*
7: 7 {Rehum,} As in parallel text at **E** 2:2; Hebrew reads *Nehum.*
7:15 {family of Bani} As in parallel text at **E** 2:10; Hebrew reads *Binnui.*
7:24 {family of Jorah} As in parallel text at **E** 2:18; Hebrew reads *Hariph.*
7:25 {family of Gibbar} As in parallel text at **E** 2:20; Hebrew reads *Gibeon.*
7:43 {(descendants of Hodaviah} As in parallel text at **E** 2:40; Hebrew reads *Hodevah.*
7:47 {Keros, Siaha,} As in parallel text at **E** 2:44; Hebrew reads *Sia.*
7:52 {Besai, Meunim, Nephusim,} As in parallel text at **E** 2:50; Hebrew reads *Nephushesim.*
7:54 {Bazluth,} As in parallel text at **E** 2:52; Hebrew reads *Bazlith.*
7:57 {Sotai, Sophereth, Peruda,} As in parallel text at **E** 2:55; Hebrew reads *Perida.*
7:58 {Jaalah,} As in parallel text at **E** 2:56; Hebrew reads *Jaala.*
7:59 {Pokereth-hazzebaim, and Ami.} As in parallel text at **E** 2:57; Hebrew reads *Amon.*
7:61 {Tel-harsha, Kerub, Addan,} As in parallel text at **E** 2:59; Hebrew reads *Addon.*
7:68 {horses, 245 mules,} As in some Hebrew manuscripts (see also **E** 2:66); most Hebrew manuscripts lack this verse.
12: 3 {Shecaniah, Harim,} Hebrew *Rehum;* compare 7:42; 12:15; **E** 2:39.
12:24 {Sherebiah, Jeshua, Binnui,} Hebrew *son of* (i.e., *ben*), which should probably be read here as the proper name Binnui; compare **E** 3:9 and the note there.

F

FACE (4)

Ne 4: 5 {the presence of} Or *for they have thrown insults in the **f** of.*
Eze 10:14 {of an ox,} Hebrew *the **f** of a cherub;* compare 1:10.
1Co 13:12 {with perfect clarity.} Greek *see **f** to **f**.*

FACED (1)

Eze 40: 8 {of the gateway} Many Hebrew manuscripts add *which **f** inward toward the Temple; it was one rod* [10.5 feet or 3.2 meters] *deep. [9]Then he measured the foyer of the gateway,...*

FACES (1)

Pr 10:10 {reproof promotes peace.} As in Greek version; Hebrew reads *but babbling fools fall flat on their **f**.*

FACT (1)

1Sa 10:27 {Saul ignored them.} Dead Sea Scroll 4QSam[a] continues: *...In **f**, of all the Israelites east of the Jordan, there wasn't a single one whose right eye Nahash had not gouged out....*

FACTS (1)

2Co 10: 7 {basis of appearance.} Or *Look at the obvious **f**.*

FAILED (1)

1Sa 25:37 {had a stroke,} Hebrew *his heart **f** him.*

FAITH (6)

2Co 1:24 {faith into practice.} Greek *want to lord it over your **f**.*
1Ti 1: 4 {faith in God.} Greek *a stewardship of God in **f**.*
Heb 4: 2 {God told them.} Some manuscripts read *they didn't share the **f** of those who listened [to God].*
11:11 {keep his promise.} Some manuscripts read *It was by **f** that Sarah was able to have a child, even though she was too old and barren. Sarah believed that God would keep his promise.*
12: 2 {start to finish.} Or *Jesus, the Originator and Perfecter of our **f**.*
Jude 1: 3 {the Good News.} Greek *to contend for the **f**.*

FAITHFUL (1)

Hos 11:12 {the Holy One.} Or *and Judah is unruly against God, the **f** Holy One.*

FAITHFULNESS (3)

2Sa 15:20 {love and faithfulness.} As in Greek version; Hebrew reads *and may unfailing love and **f** go with you.*
2Ch 6:42 {your servant David.} Or *Remember the **f** of your servant David.*
Hab 2: 4 {by their faith.} Or *the just will live by their **f**.*

FALL (4)

Pr 10:10 {reproof promotes peace.} As in Greek version; Hebrew reads *but babbling fools **f** flat on their faces.*
Mt 11: 6 {offended by me.} Or *who don't **f** away because of me.*
Lk 7:23 {offended by me.} Or *who don't **f** away because of me.*
1Ti 3: 6 {make him fall.} Or *he might **f** into the same judgment as the Devil.*

FALSE (2)

2Co 11:26 {but are not.} Greek *from **f** brothers.*
Gal 2: 4 {there—false ones, really} Greek *some **f** brothers.*

FAMILY (2)

Nu 1:20[-21] {clan and family} In the Hebrew text, *number of men...**f*** is repeated in 1:22, 24, 26, 28, 30, 32, 34, 36, 38, 40, 42.
Ne 12:17 {was also a} Hebrew lacks the name of this **f** leader.

FAR (5)

Dt 4:49 {the Dead Sea,} Hebrew *took the Arabah on the east side of the Jordan as **f** as the sea of the Arabah.*
Jos 7: 5 {as the quarries,} Or *as **f** as Shebarim.*
Ps 48: 2 {the holy mountain,} Or *Mount Zion, in the **f** north;* Hebrew reads *Mount Zion, the heights of Zaphon.*
Jer 48: 4 {will cry out.} Greek version reads *Her cries are heard as **f** away as Zoar.*
Ac 2:39 {to the Gentiles} Greek *to those **f** away.*

FARCE (1)

Isa 29:13 {learned by rote.} Greek version reads *Their worship is a **f**, for they merely teach human commands and teachings.*

FAST (3)

Zec 7: 3 {the Temple's destruction,} Hebrew *mourn and **f** in the fifth month.* This month of the Hebrew lunar calendar usually occurs in July and August.
Ac 27: 9 {in the fall,} Greek *because the **f** was now already gone by.* This **f** happened on the Day of Atonement (*Yom Kippur*), which occurred in late September or early October.

FASTED (2)

Zec 7: 5 {in early autumn,} Hebrew ***f** and mourned in the fifth and seventh months.* The fifth month of the Hebrew lunar calendar occurs during our months of July and August. The seventh month occurs during September and October; both the Day of Atonement and the Festival of Shelters were celebrated in the seventh month.
Mt 17:20 {would be impossible."} Some manuscripts add verse 21, *But this kind of demon won't leave unless you have prayed and **f**.*

FASTING (1)

Mk 9:29 {only by prayer.} Some manuscripts add *and **f**.*

FAT (1)

Isa 10:27 {from their shoulders.} As in Greek version; Hebrew reads *The yoke will be broken, for you have grown so **f**.*

FATHER (27)

Ge 10:24 {father of Shelah,} Greek version reads *Arphaxad was the **f** of Cainan, Cainan was the **f** of Shelah.*
17: 5 {known as Abraham,} *Abram* means "exalted **f**"; *Abraham* means "**f** of many."
19:37 {named him Moab.} *Moab* sounds like a Hebrew term that means "from **f**."
1Sa 2:28 {your ancestor Aaron} Hebrew *your **f**.*
10:12 {become a prophet."} Hebrew *responded, "Who is their **f**?"*
1Ch 2:24 {(the father of} Or *the founder of;* also in 2:42, 45, 49-52 and perhaps other instances where the text reads *the **f** of.*
4: 3 {The descendants of} As in Greek version; Hebrew reads ***f** of.* The meaning of the Hebrew is uncertain.
4: 4 {(the father of} Or *the founder of;* also in 4:12, 14, 17-18, and perhaps other instances where the text reads *the **f** of.*
4:14 {Valley of Craftsmen,} Or *Joab, the **f** of Ge-harashim.*
8: 3 {Addar, Gera, Abihud,} Possibly *Gera the **f** of Ehud;* compare 8:6.
2Ch 17: 3 {father's early years} Some Hebrew manuscripts read *the example of his **f**, David.*
Isa 11: 1 {of David's family} Hebrew *the line of Jesse.* Jesse was King David's **f**.
Da 5: 2 {that his predecessor,} Aramaic ***f**;* also in 5:11, 13, 18.
Mk 11:25 {your sins, too.} Some manuscripts add verse 26, *But if you do not forgive, neither will your **F** who is in heaven forgive your sins.*
14:36 {"Abba,} *Abba* is an Aramaic term for "**f**."
Lk 3:22 {pleased with you.} Some manuscripts read *and today I have become your **F**.*
Jn 14: 7 {my Father is.} Some manuscripts read *If you really have known me, you will know who my **F** is.*
Ro 8:15 {"Father, dear Father."} Greek *"Abba, **F**."* *Abba* is an Aramaic term for "**f**."
2Co 1: 3 {is the source} Greek *the **F**.*
Gal 4: 6 {your dear Father.} Greek *into your hearts, crying, "Abba, **F**."* Abba is an Aramaic term for "**F**."
Eph 3:14 {to the Father,} Some manuscripts read *the **F** of our Lord Jesus Christ.*
Jas 1:17 {all heaven's lights.} Greek *from above, from the **F** of lights.*
1Jn 5: 7 {these three witnesses} Some very late manuscripts add *in heaven—the **F**, the Word, and the Holy Spirit, and these three are one. And we have three witnesses on earth.*

FATHER'S (2)

1Sa 2:30 {tribe of Levi} Hebrew *that your house and your **f** house.*
Lk 2:49 {my Father's house."} Or *"Didn't you realize that I should be involved with my **F** affairs?"*

FATHER-IN-LAW (2)

Ex 3: 1 {his father-in-law, Jethro,} Moses' **f** went by two names, Jethro and Reuel.
Jdg 4:11 {of Moses' brother-in-law} Or *f.*

FATHERS (2)

Mal 4: 6 {hearts of parents} Hebrew *f;* also in 4:6b.
Ac 7:12 {sent his sons} Greek *our f;* also in 7:15.

FATHOMS (2)

Ac 27:28 {found only 90 feet.} Greek *20 f...15 f* [37 meters...27 meters].

FAULT (2)

1Sa 14:41 {among the others?"} Greek version adds *If the f is with me or my son Jonathan, respond with Urim; but if the men of Israel are at f, respond with Thummim.*

FEAR (3)

Ps 72: 5 {May he live} As in Greek version; Hebrew reads *May they f you.*
Pr 14:16 {wise are cautious} Hebrew *The wise f.*
28:14 {a tender conscience,} Hebrew *those who f.*

FEAST (2)

Hos 12: 9 {Festival of Shelters.} Hebrew *as in the days of your appointed f.*
Lk 23:16 {will release him."} Some manuscripts add verse 17, *For it was necessary for him to release one [prisoner] for them during the f.*

FEELING (1)

Ge 29:34 {named him Levi,} *Levi* sounds like a Hebrew term that means "being attached" or "**f** affection for."

FEET (2 of 15)

Jn 13:10 {for the feet,} Some manuscripts do not include *except for the f.*
1Ti 5:10 {other Christians humbly?} Greek *Has she washed the f of saints?*

FELT (1)

2Sa 13:39 {his son Absalom.} Or *no longer f a need to go out after Absalom.*

FESTIVAL (2 of 19)

2Ki 23:16 {man of God} As in Greek version; Hebrew lacks *as Jeroboam stood beside the altar at the f. Then Josiah turned and looked up at the tomb of the man of God.*
Ac 18:21 {come back later,} Some manuscripts read *"I must by all means be at Jerusalem for the upcoming f, but I will come back later."*

FIELD (1)

Lk 17:35 {the other left.} Some manuscripts add verse 36, *Two men will be working in the f; one will be taken, the other left.*

FIFTEENTH (11 of 14)

Ex 16: 1 {after leaving Egypt.} Hebrew *on the f day of the second month.* The Exodus had occurred on the fourteenth day of the first month (see 12:6).
Lev 23: 6 {the Passover celebration,} Hebrew *On the f day of the same month.*
23:34 {Day of Atonement.} Hebrew *on the f day of the seventh month;* see 23:24, 27 and the notes there.
23:39 {Festival of Shelters,} Hebrew *on the f day of the seventh month;* see 23:24 and the note there.
Nu 29:12 {"Five days later,} Hebrew *On the f day of the seventh month;* see 29:1, 7 and the notes there.
33: 3 {in early spring.} Hebrew *on the f day of the first month.* This day of the Hebrew lunar calendar occurs in late March or early April.
1Ki 12:32 {day in midautumn,} Hebrew *on the f day of the eighth month* (also in 12:33). This day of the Hebrew lunar calendar occurs in late October or early November, exactly one month after the annual Festival of Shelters in Judah (see Lev 23:34).
Est 9:18 {the third day,} Hebrew *killing their enemies on the thirteenth day and the fourteenth day, and then rested on the f day,* of the Hebrew month of Adar.
Eze 32:17 {On March 17,} Hebrew *On the f day of the month,* presumably in the twelfth month of the Hebrew calendar (see 32:1). This would put this message at the end of King Jehoiachin's twelfth year of captivity, on March 17, 585 B.C.; also see note on 29:1. Greek version reads *On the f day of the first month,* which would put this message on April 27, 586 B.C., at the beginning of Jehoiachin's twelfth year.
45:25 {in early autumn,} Hebrew *the festival which begins on the f day of the seventh month* (see Lev 23:33). This day of the Hebrew lunar calendar occurs in late September or October.

FIFTH (14 of 17)

Nu 33:38 {day in midsummer,} Hebrew *on the first day of the f month....*
2Ki 25: 8 {of that year,} Hebrew *On the seventh day of the f month,* of the Hebrew calendar....
Ezr 7: 8 {Jerusalem in August} Hebrew *in the f month....*
7: 9 {Jerusalem on August 4,} Hebrew *on the first day of the f month,* of the Hebrew calendar....
Jer 1: 3 {of that year,} Hebrew *In the f month,* of the Hebrew calendar....
28: 1 {in late summer} Hebrew *In the f month,* of the Hebrew calendar....
52:12 {of that year,} Hebrew *On the tenth day of the f month,* of the Hebrew calendar....
Eze 1: 1 {On July 31} Hebrew *On the f day of the fourth month,* of the Hebrew calendar (also in 1:2)....
8: 1 {Then on September 17,} Hebrew *on the f day of the sixth month,* of the Hebrew calendar....
20: 1 {On August 14,} Hebrew *In the f month, on the tenth day,* of the Hebrew calendar....
33:21 {On January 8,} Hebrew *On the f day of the tenth month,* of the Hebrew calendar....
Zec 7: 3 {the Temple's destruction,} Hebrew *mourn and fast in the f month....*
7: 5 {in early autumn,} Hebrew *fasted and mourned in the f and seventh months....*
8:19 {autumn, and winter} Hebrew *in the fourth, f, seventh, and tenth months....*

FIGHTING (1)

1Co 15:32 {men of Ephesus} Greek *f wild beasts in Ephesus.*

FIGURATIVELY (4)

Ge 25:26 {called him Jacob.} *Jacob* means "he grasps the heel"; this can also **f** mean "he deceives."
27:36 {name is Jacob,} *Jacob* means "he grasps the heel"; this can also **f** mean "he deceives."
35:10 {be called Israel."} *Jacob* means "he grasps the heel"; this can also **f** mean "he deceives"; *Israel* means "God struggles" or "one who struggles with God."
Hos 12: 2 {to punish Jacob} *Jacob* means "he grasps at the heel"; this can also **f** mean "he deceives."

FILLED (1)

Ps 76: 4 {the everlasting mountains.} As in Greek version; Hebrew reads *than mountains f with beasts of prey.*

FINGERS (1)

Jer 52:21 {walls 3 inches thick.} Hebrew *4 f thick* [8 centimeters].

FIRE (13)

Nu 21:30 {Nophah and Medeba.} Or *until f spread to Medeba.* The meaning of the Hebrew is uncertain.
Dt 18:10 {a burnt offering.} Or *never make your son or daughter pass through the f.*
2Ki 16: 3 {in the fire.} Or *even making his son pass through the f.*
17:17 {in the fire.} Or *They even made their sons and daughters pass through the f.*
21: 6 {in the fire.} Or *even made his son pass through the f.*
23:10 {in the fire} Or *to make a son or daughter pass through the f.*
2Ch 28: 3 {in the fire.} Or *even making his sons pass through the f.*
33: 6 {in the fire} Or *even made his sons pass through the f.*
Eze 20:31 {burned as sacrifices,} Or *and make your little children pass through the f.*
Mt 3:11 {and with fire.} Or *in the Holy Spirit and in f.*
Mk 9:49 {purified with fire.} Greek *salted with f.* Some manuscripts add *and every sacrifice will be salted with salt.*
Lk 3:16 {and with fire.} Or *in the Holy Spirit and in f.*
Jas 5: 3 {flesh in hell.} Or *will eat your flesh like f.*

FIRST (67 of 76)

Ge 8: 5 {half months later,} Hebrew *On the f day of the tenth month;* see 7:11 and note on 8:4.
8:13 {the flood began,} Hebrew *on the f day of the f month;* see 7:11.
Ex 40: 2 {the new year.} Hebrew *the f day of the f month....*
40:17 {the new year.} Hebrew *the f day of the f month, in the second year.* See note on 40:2b.
Lev 23: 5 {in early spring.} Hebrew *on the fourteenth day of the f month....*
23:24 {in early autumn,} Hebrew *On the f day of the seventh month....*
Nu 1: 1 {day in midspring,} Hebrew *On the f day of the second month....*
1:18 {that very day.} Hebrew *on the f day of the second month;* see 1:1.
9: 1 {in early spring,} Hebrew *in the f month....*
9: 3 {in early spring.} Hebrew *on the fourteenth day of the f month....*
9: 5 {the appointed day.} Hebrew *on the fourteenth day of the f month;* see note on 9:3.
20: 1 {In early spring} Hebrew *In the f month....*
28:16 {in early spring,} Hebrew *On the fourteenth day of the f month....*
29: 1 {in early autumn} Hebrew *on the f day of the seventh month....*
33: 3 {in early spring.} Hebrew *on the fifteenth day of the f month....*
33:38 {day in midsummer,} Hebrew *on the f day of the fifth month....*
Dt 1: 3 {day in midwinter,} Hebrew *on the f day of the eleventh month....*
Jos 4:19 {exodus from Egypt.} Hebrew *the tenth day of the f month....*
5:10 {exodus from Egypt.} Hebrew *the fourteenth day of the f month....*
2Ch 29:17 {in early spring,} Hebrew *on the f day of the f month....*
30: 3 {in early spring,} Hebrew *in the f month....*
35: 1 {in early spring.} Hebrew *on the fourteenth day of the f month....*
Ezr 3: 6 {of Shelters began,} Hebrew *On the f day of the seventh month....*
6:19 {On April 21} Hebrew *On the fourteenth day of the f month,* of the Hebrew calendar....
7: 9 {Babylon on April 8} Hebrew *on the f day of the f month,* of the Hebrew calendar....
7: 9 {Jerusalem on August 4,} Hebrew *on the f day of the fifth month,* of the Hebrew calendar....
8:31 {Canal on April 19} Hebrew *on the twelfth day of the f month,* of the Hebrew calendar....
10:16 {name. On December 29,} Hebrew *On the f day of the tenth month,* of the Hebrew calendar....
10:17 {the next year} Hebrew *By the f day of the f month,* of the Hebrew calendar....
Ne 8: 2 {So on October 8} Hebrew *on the f day of the seventh month,* of the Hebrew calendar....
Est 3: 7 {month of April,} Hebrew *in the f month, the month of Nisan....*
3:12 {On April 17} Hebrew *On the thirteenth day of the f month,* of the Hebrew calendar....
Eze 26: 1 {King Jehoiachin's captivity,} Hebrew *In the eleventh year, on the f day of the month,* of the Hebrew calendar year. Since an element is missing in the date formula here, scholars have reconstructed this probable reading: *On the f day of the eleventh month, during the twelfth year.* This reading would put this message on February 3, 585 B.C.; also see note on 1:1.
29:17 {On April 26,} Hebrew *On the f day of the f month,* of the Hebrew calendar....
30:20 {On April 29,} Hebrew *On the seventh day of the f month,* of the Hebrew calendar...
31: 1 {On June 21,} Hebrew *On the f day of the third month,* of the Hebrew calendar....
32: 1 {On March 3,} Hebrew *On the f day of the twelfth month,* of the Hebrew calendar....
32:17 {On March 17,} Hebrew *On the fifteenth day of the month,* presumably in the twelfth month of the Hebrew calendar (see 32:1). This would put this message at the end of King Jehoiachin's twelfth year of captivity, on March 17, 585 B.C.; also see note on 29:1. Greek version reads *On the fifteenth day of the f month,* which would put this message on April 27, 586 B.C., at the beginning of Jehoiachin's twelfth year.
45:18 {each new year,} Hebrew *On the f day of the f month,* of the Hebrew calendar....
Da 10: 4 {On April 23,} Hebrew *On the twenty-fourth day of the f month....*
Hag 1: 1 {On August 29} Hebrew *On the f day of the sixth month,* of the Hebrew calendar....
Mt 12:29 {house be robbed!} Or *One cannot rob Satan's kingdom without f tying him up. Only then can his demons be cast out.*
17:10 {the Messiah comes} Greek *that Elijah must come f.*
19:30 {the greatest then.} Greek *But many who are f will be last; and the last, f.*
28: 1 {on Sunday morning,} Greek *After the Sabbath, on the f day of the week.*
Mk 3:27 {house be robbed!} Or *One cannot rob Satan's kingdom without f tying him up. Only then can his demons be cast out.*
7:27 {family, the Jews.} Greek *Let the children eat f.*
10:31 {the greatest then.} Greek *But many who are f will be last; and the last, f.*
16: 2 {on Sunday morning,} Greek *on the f day of the week;* also in 16:9.
Lk 13:30 {be despised then.} Greek *Some are last who will be f, and some are f who will be last.*
24: 1 {on Sunday morning} Greek *But on the f day of the week, very early in the morning.*
Jn 5: 3 {on the porches.} Some manuscripts add *waiting for a certain movement of the water, [4]for an angel of the Lord came from time to time and stirred up the water. And the f person to step down into it afterward was healed.*
20: 1 {Early Sunday morning,} Greek *On the f day of the week.*
1Co 16: 2 {every Lord's Day,} Greek *every f day of the week.*
Heb 9: 6 {the first room} Greek *f tent;* also in 9:8.

FIRSTBORN (3)

Col 1:15 {over all creation.} Greek *He is the f of all creation.*
1:18 {from the dead,} Greek *He is the beginning, the f from the dead.*
Heb 1: 6 {presented his honored} Greek *f.*

FIRSTFRUITS (4)
Jer 2: 3 {of my children.} Hebrew the f of his harvest.
Ro 11:16 {also be holy.} Greek If the dough offered as f is holy, so is the whole lump.
1Co 16:15 {Christians in Greece,} Greek were the f in Achaia, the southern region of the Greek peninsula.
Rev 14: 4 {a special offering} Greek as f.

FIST (1)
Mk 7: 3 {their cupped hands,} Greek washed with the f.

FLAT (1)
Pr 10:10 {reproof promotes peace.} As in Greek version; Hebrew reads but babbling fools fall f on their faces.

FLESH (8)
Lev 15: 2 {genital discharge} Hebrew a discharge from his f; also in 15:32.
Eze 11:19 {them tender hearts} Hebrew hearts of f.
36:26 {new, obedient heart.} Hebrew a heart of f.
Mal 2:15 {you are his.} Or Did not one God make us and preserve our life and breath? or Did not one God make her, both f and spirit? The meaning of the Hebrew is uncertain.
1Co 5: 5 {will be destroyed} Or so that he will die; Greek reads for the destruction of the f.
Heb 10:20 {death for us.} Greek his f.
Jas 5: 3 {flesh in hell.} Or will eat your f like fire.
Jude 1:23 {by their sins.} Greek mercy, hating even the clothing stained by the f.

FLOOR (2 of 3)
1Ki 7: 7 {floor to ceiling.} As in Syriac version and Latin Vulgate; Hebrew reads from f to f.

FLOW (2)
Pr 4:23 {everything you do.} Hebrew for from it f the springs of life.
Jn 7:37[-38] {out from within."} Or "Let anyone who is thirsty come to me and drink. [38]For the Scriptures declare that rivers of living water will f from the heart of those who believe in me."

FLOWING (2)
Pr 5:15 {with your wife.} Hebrew Drink water from your own cistern, f water from your own well.
Isa 8: 6 {my gentle care} Hebrew rejected the gently f waters of Shiloah.

FLUTE (2)
Da 3: 7 {the musical instruments,} Aramaic the horn, f, zither, lyre, harp, and other instruments of the musical ensemble.
3:10 {the musical instruments.} Aramaic the horn, f, zither, lyre, harp, pipes, and other instruments of the musical ensemble; also in 3:15.

FOLLOW (1)
Jn 8:39 {his good example.} Some manuscripts read if you are children of Abraham, f his example.

FOOD (1)
Job 15:23 {'Where is it?'} Greek version reads He is appointed to be f for a vulture.

FOOL (2)
1Sa 25:25 {his name suggests.} The name Nabal means "f."
Mt 5:22 {you curse someone,} Greek if you say, 'You f.'

FOOLS (2)
Dt 32:31 {even they recognize.} The meaning of the Hebrew is uncertain. Greek version reads our enemies are f.
Pr 10:10 {reproof promotes peace.} As in Greek version; Hebrew reads but babbling f fall flat on their faces.

FOOT (1)
2Sa 10:18 {forty thousand horsemen,} Some Greek manuscripts read f soldiers; compare parallel text at 1 Chr 19:18.

FOOTSTOOL (1)
La 2: 1 {to his Temple.} Hebrew f.

FORESKINS (1)
Jos 5: 3 {Israel at Gibeath-haaraloth.} Gibeath-haaraloth means "hill of f."

FOREVER (5)
2Ki 8:19 {to rule forever.} Hebrew promised to give a lamp to David and his descendants f.
1Ch 16:15 {by his covenant} As in some Greek manuscripts (see also Ps 105:8); Hebrew reads Remember his covenant f.
2Ch 21: 7 {to rule forever.} Hebrew promised to give a lamp to David and his descendants f.
Mt 6:13 {the evil one.} Or from evil. Some manuscripts add For yours is the kingdom and the power and the glory f. Amen.
Ro 9: 5 {eternal praise! Amen.} Or May God, who rules over everything, be praised f. Amen.

FORGET (1)
Ge 41:51 {older son Manasseh,} Manasseh sounds like a Hebrew term that means "causing to f."

FORGIVE (2)
Mk 11:25 {your sins, too.} Some manuscripts add verse 26, But if you do not f, neither will your Father who is in heaven f your sins.

FORGIVENESS (2)
Mk 1: 4 {to be forgiven.} Greek preaching a baptism of repentance for the f of sins.
Lk 3: 3 {to be forgiven.} Greek preaching a baptism of repentance for the f of sins.

FORGOTTEN (1)
Ecc 8:10 {and are praised} As in some Hebrew manuscripts and Greek version; many Hebrew manuscripts read and are f.

FORSAKEN (1)
Isa 62: 4 {the Godforsaken City} Hebrew Azubah, which means "f."

FORTH (1)
Ge 4: 1 {birth to Cain,} Cain sounds like a Hebrew term that can mean "bring f" or "acquire."

FORTUNE (1)
Ge 30:11 {named him Gad,} Gad means "good f."

FORTY-TWO (1)
2Ch 22: 2 {Ahaziah was twenty-two} As in some Greek manuscripts and Syriac version (see also 2 Kgs 8:26); Hebrew reads f.

FOUND (2)
Ps 145:13 {all he does.} The last two lines of 145:13 are not f in many of the ancient manuscripts.
Php 2: 7 {in human form.} Greek he was born in the likeness of men and was f in appearance as a man.

FOUNDER (5)
1Ch 2:24 {(the father of} Or the f of; also in 2:42, 45, 49-52 and perhaps other instances where the text reads the father of.
2:55 {family of Recab.} Or the f of Beth-recab.
4: 4 {(the father of} Or the f of; also in 4:12, 14, 17-18, and perhaps other instances where the text reads the father of.
8:29 {(the father of} Or the f of.
9:35 {(the father of} Or the f of.

FOURTEEN (1)
1Ki 8:65 {Festival of Shelters.} Hebrew seven days and seven days, f days; compare parallel text at 2 Chr 7:8-10.

FOURTEENTH (13 of 14)
Lev 23: 5 {in early spring.} Hebrew on the f day of the first month....
Nu 9: 3 {in early spring.} Hebrew on the f day of the first month....
9: 5 {the appointed day.} Hebrew on the f day of the first month; see note on 9:3.
9:11 {one month later,} Hebrew on the f day of the second month....
28:16 {in early spring,} Hebrew On the f day of the first month....
Jos 5:10 {exodus from Egypt.} Hebrew the f day of the first month....
2Ch 30:15 {day in midspring,} Hebrew On the f day of the second month....
35: 1 {in early spring.} Hebrew on the f day of the first month....
Ezr 6:19 {On April 21} Hebrew On the f day of the first month, of the Hebrew calendar....
Est 9:15 {together on March 8} Hebrew the f day of the month of Adar, of the Hebrew calendar....
9:17 {the following day} Hebrew on the f day, of the Hebrew month of Adar.
9:18 {the third day,} Hebrew killing their enemies on the thirteenth day and the f day, and then rested on the fifteenth day, of the Hebrew month of Adar.
9:19 {in late winter,} Hebrew on the f day of the month of Adar....

FOURTH (7 of 15)
Jer 39: 2 {later, on July 18,} Hebrew On the ninth day of the f month of the eleventh year of Zedekiah....
52: 6 {Zedekiah's eleventh year,} Hebrew By the ninth day of the f month [of Zedekiah's eleventh year]....
Eze 1: 1 {On July 31} Hebrew On the fifth day of the f month, of the Hebrew calendar (also in 1:2)....
Zec 7: 1 {On December 7} Hebrew On the f day of the ninth month, the month of Kislev, of the Hebrew calendar....
8:19 {autumn, and winter} Hebrew in the f, fifth, seventh, and tenth months....
Mt 14:25 {in the morning} Greek In the f watch of the night.
Mk 6:48 {in the morning} Greek About the f watch of the night.

FOYER (1)
Eze 40: 8 {of the gateway} Many Hebrew manuscripts add which faced inward toward the Temple; it was one rod [10.5 feet or 3.2 meters] deep. [9]Then he measured the f of the gateway,...

FREE (1)
1Co 9: 1 {as anyone else?} Greek Am I not f?

FREED (1)
Pr 12:26 {to their friends;} Or The godly are cautious in friendship, or the godly are f from evil. The meaning of the Hebrew is uncertain.

FRIENDS (1)
Lk 16: 9 {you in heaven.} Or Then when you run out at the end of this life, your f will welcome you into eternal homes.

FRIENDSHIP (1)
Pr 12:26 {to their friends;} Or The godly are cautious in f, or the godly are freed from evil. The meaning of the Hebrew is uncertain.

FRONTIER (1)
Nu 21:24 {Ammonites was fortified.} Or because the terrain of the Ammonite f was rugged; Hebrew because the boundary of the Ammonites was strong.

FROST (1)
Zec 14: 6 {no longer shine,} Hebrew there will be no light, no cold or f. The meaning of the Hebrew is uncertain.

FRUITFUL (1)
Ge 41:52 {second son Ephraim,} Ephraim sounds like a Hebrew term that means "f."

FULFILL (1)
Mt 3:15 {that is right.} Or we must f all righteousness.

FULFILLED (3)
Mt 27:35 {by throwing dice.} Greek by casting lots. A few late manuscripts add This f the word of the prophet: "They divided my clothes among themselves and cast lots for my robe." See Ps 22:18.
Mk 15:27 {side of his.} Some manuscripts add verse 28, And the Scripture was f that said, "He was counted among those who were rebels." See Isa 53:12.
Lk 1: 1 {that took place} Or have been f.

FULLNESS (1)
Col 2: 9 {human body,} Greek in him dwells all the f of the Godhead bodily.

G

GAASH (2)
2Sa 23:30 {from Nahale-gaash} Or from the ravines of G.
1Ch 11:32 {near Nahale-gaash} Or from the ravines of G.

GAD (2)
Ge 30:11 {named him Gad,} G means "good fortune."
1Ki 4:19 {land of Gilead,} Greek version reads of G; compare 4:13.

GADARENES (2)
Mk 5: 1 {of the Gerasenes.} Some manuscripts read G; others read Gergesenes. See Matt 8:28; Luke 8:26.
Lk 8:26 {of the Gerasenes,} Some manuscripts read G; other manuscripts read Gergesenes. See Matt 8:28; Mark 5:1.

GADITES (1)
1Sa 10:27 {Saul ignored them.} Dead Sea Scroll 4QSam[a] continues: Nahash, king of the Ammonites, had been grievously oppressing the G and Reubenites who lived east of the Jordan River....

GALAL (1)
Jos 5: 9 {been called Gilgal} Gilgal sounds like the Hebrew word g, meaning "to roll."

GALATIA (1)

Ac 16: 6[-7] {province of Bithynia,} *Phrygia, **G**, Asia, Mysia,* and *Bithynia* were all districts in the land now called Turkey.

GALEED (1)

Ge 31:47 {language and Galeed} *Jegar-sahadutha* means "witness pile" in Aramaic; ***G*** means "witness pile" in Hebrew.

GALILEE (4)

Jos 12:23 {Goyim in Gilgal} Greek version reads *Goyim in **G**.*
Lk 4:44 {synagogues throughout Judea.} Some manuscripts read ***G***.
5: 1 {Sea of Galilee,} Greek *Lake Gennesaret,* another name for the Sea of **G**.
Jn 21: 1 {Sea of Galilee.} Greek *Sea of Tiberias,* another name for the Sea of **G**.

GALL (3)

Job 16:13 {with my blood.} Hebrew *my **g**.*
20:25 {glistens with blood.} Hebrew *with **g**.*
La 3:19 {bitter beyond words.} Hebrew *is wormwood and **g**.*

GAMBLE (1)

Job 6:27 {orphan into slavery} Hebrew *even **g** over an orphan.*

GARRISON (1)

Ac 24: 6 {we arrested him.} Some manuscripts add *We would have judged him by our law, [7]but Lysias, the commander of the **g**, came and took him violently away from us, [8]commanding his accusers to come before you.*

GASHMU (1)

Ne 6: 6 {"Geshem} Hebrew ***G***, another name for Geshem.

GATE (6 of 8)

1Ch 26:16 {to the Temple.} Or *the **g** of Shalleketh on the upper road* (also in 26:18). The meaning of the Hebrew is uncertain.
Pr 17:19 {who speaks boastfully} Or *who builds up defenses;* Hebrew reads *who makes a high **g**.*
Da 8: 2 {the Ulai River.} Or *the Ulai **G**;* also in 8:16.
8: 3 {beside the river.} Or *the **g**;* also in 8:6.

GATES (3)

Ne 7: 3 {of the day.} Or *Keep the **g** of Jerusalem closed until the sun is hot.*
Ps 87: 2 {city in Israel.} Hebrew *He loves the **g** of Zion more than all the dwellings of Jacob.*
Mt 16:18 {powers of hell} Greek *and the **g** of Hades.*

GATEWAY (1)

Eze 40: 8 {of the gateway} Many Hebrew manuscripts add *which faced inward toward the Temple; it was one rod* [10.5 feet or 3.2 meters] *deep. [9]Then he measured the foyer of the **g**,...*

GATEWAYS (1)

2Ch 9:11 {to make steps} Or ***g***. The meaning of the Hebrew is uncertain.

GATH (2)

2Sa 21:19 {Goliath of Gath.} As in parallel text at 1 Chr 20:5; Hebrew reads *killed Goliath of **G**.*
Mic 1:10 {city of Gath} ***G*** sounds like the Hebrew term for "tell."

GATHER (3)

Mt 18:20 {they are mine,} Greek ***g** together in my name.*
24:28 {end is near.} Greek *Wherever the carcass is, the vultures **g**.*
Lk 17:37 {end is near."} Greek *Wherever the carcass is, the vultures **g**.*

GAZELLE (1)

Ac 9:36 {Greek is Dorcas} The names *Tabitha* in Aramaic and *Dorcas* in Greek both mean "**g**."

GE-HARASHIM (2)

1Ch 4:14 {Valley of Craftsmen,} Or *Joab, the father of **G**.*
Ne 11:35 {Valley of Craftsmen.} Or *and **G**.*

GEBA (2)

Jdg 20:10 {revenge on Gibeah} Hebrew ***G***, in this case, a variant for Gibeah; also in 20:33.
2Sa 5:25 {way from Gibeon} As in Greek version (see also 1 Chr 14:16); Hebrew reads ***G***.

GEDDALTI (1)

1Ch 25:29 {fell to Geddalti} Hebrew *Giddalti,* a variant name for **G**; compare 25:4.

GEN (48)

Ex 1: 5 {Jacob had seventy} Dead Sea Scrolls and Greek version read *seventy-five;* see notes on **G** 46:27.
Nu 26:17 {its ancestor Arodi.} As in Samaritan Pentateuch and Syriac version (see also **G** 46:16); Hebrew reads *Arod.*
1Ch 1: 4 {of Noah were} As in Greek version (see also **G** 5:3-32); Hebrew lacks *The sons of Noah were.*
1: 6 {were Ashkenaz, Riphath,} As in some Hebrew manuscripts and Greek version (see also **G** 10:3); most Hebrew manuscripts read *Diphath.*
1:17 {of Aram were} As in one Hebrew manuscript and some Greek manuscripts (see also **G** 10:23); most Hebrew manuscripts lack *The descendants of Aram were.*
1:17 {Gether, and Mash.} As in parallel text at **G** 10:23; Hebrew reads *and Meshech.*
1:22 {Obal,} As in some Hebrew manuscripts and Syriac version (see also **G** 10:28); most Hebrew manuscripts read *Ebal.*
1:24 {Shem: Arphaxad, Shelah,} Some Greek manuscripts read *Arphaxad, Cainan, Shelah.* See notes on **G** 10:24 and 11:12-13.
1:36 {Zepho,} As in many Hebrew manuscripts and a few Greek manuscripts (see also **G** 36:11); most Hebrew manuscripts read *Zephi.*
1:36 {born to Timna.} As in some Greek manuscripts (see also **G** 36:12); Hebrew reads *Kenaz, Timna, and Amalek.*
1:39 {and Heman.} As in parallel text at **G** 36:22; Hebrew reads *and Homam.*
1:40 {Alvan,} As in many Hebrew manuscripts and a few Greek manuscripts (see also **G** 36:23); most Hebrew manuscripts read *Alian.*
1:40 {Manahath, Ebal, Shepho,} As in some Hebrew manuscripts (see also **G** 36:23); most Hebrew manuscripts read *Shephi.*
1:41 {Dishon were Hemdan,} As in many Hebrew manuscripts and some Greek manuscripts (see also **G** 36:26); most Hebrew manuscripts read *Hamran.*
1:42 {Akan.} As in many Hebrew and Greek manuscripts (see also **G** 36:27); most Hebrew manuscripts read *Jaakan.*
1:42 {sons of Dishan} Hebrew *Dishon;* compare 1:38 and parallel text at **G** 36:28.
1:50 {city of Pau.} As in many Hebrew manuscripts, some Greek manuscripts, Syriac version, and Latin Vulgate (see also **G** 36:39); most Hebrew manuscripts read *Pai.*
1:51 {Alvah,} As in parallel text at **G** 36:40; Hebrew reads *Aliah.*
7:13 {Jahzeel,} As in parallel text at **G** 46:24; Hebrew reads *Jahziel,* a variant name for Jahzeel.
7:13 {Shillem.} As in some Hebrew and Greek manuscripts (see also **G** 46:24; Num 26:49); most Hebrew manuscripts read *Shallum.*
Mt 19: 4 {male and female.'} **G** 1:27; 5:2.
19: 5 {united into one.'} **G** 2:24.
Mk 10: 6 {male and female.'} **G** 1:27; 5:2.
10: 7[-8] {united into one.'} **G** 2:24.
Lk 3:38 {son of Enosh.} Greek *Enos;* see **G** 5:6.
Jn 1:51 {Son of Man."} See **G** 28:10-17, the account of Jacob's ladder.
Ac 3:25 {will be blessed.'} **G** 22:18.
7: 3 {will show you.'} **G** 12:1.
7: 5[-7] {in this place.'} **G** 12:7; 15:13-14; Exod 3:12.
Ro 4: 3 {to be righteous."} **G** 15:6.
4:17 {of many nations."} **G** 17:5.
4:18 {as the stars,"} **G** 15:5.
9: 7 {will be counted,"} **G** 21:12.
9: 9 {have a son."} **G** 18:10, 14.
9:12 {your younger son."} **G** 25:23.
1Co 6:16 {united into one."} **G** 2:24.
15:45 {a living person."} **G** 2:7.
Gal 3: 6 {of his faith."} **G** 15:6.
3: 8 {blessed through you."} **G** 12:3; 18:18; 22:18.
3:16 {and his child.} Greek *seed;* also in 3:16c, 19. See **G** 12:7.
4:22 {his freeborn wife.} See **G** 16:15; 21:2-3.
4:30 {free woman's son."} **G** 21:10.
Eph 5:31 {united into one."} **G** 2:24.
Heb 4: 4 {all his work."} **G** 2:2.
6:14 {into countless millions."} **G** 22:17.
11: 5 {God took him."} **G** 5:24.
11:18 {will be counted."} **G** 21:12.
Jas 2:23 {to be righteous."} **G** 15:6.

GENDER (1)

SS 1: 1 {*Young Woman:*} The headings identifying the speakers are not in the original text, though the Hebrew usually gives clues by means of the **g** of the person speaking.

GENEALOGIES (2)

1Ti 1: 4 {and spiritual pedigrees.} Greek *in myths and endless **g**, which cause speculation.*
Tit 3: 9 {about spiritual pedigrees} Greek *discussions and **g**.*

GENNESARET (1)

Lk 5: 1 {Sea of Galilee,} Greek *Lake **G**,* another name for the Sea of Galilee.

GENTILES (2)

Eph 4:17 {as the ungodly} Greek ***G***.
3Jn 1: 7 {are not Christians.} Greek *from **G**.*

GENTLY (1)

Isa 8: 6 {my gentle care} Hebrew *rejected the **g** flowing waters of Shiloah.*

GENUINE (1)

2Co 1:21 {firm for Christ.} Or *who has identified us and you as **g** Christians.*

GERA (1)

1Ch 8: 3 {Addar, Gera, Abihud,} Possibly ***G** the father of Ehud;* compare 8:6.

GERAHS (4)

Ex 30:13 {of an ounce} Hebrew *half a shekel* [6 grams], *according to the sanctuary shekel, 20 **g** to each shekel.*
Lev 27:25 {standard sanctuary shekel.} Hebrew *measured according to the sanctuary shekel, 20 **g** to each shekel.* Each sanctuary shekel was about 0.4 ounces or 11 grams in weight.
Nu 3:47 {standard sanctuary shekel.} Hebrew *5 shekels* [2 ounces or 57 grams] *apiece, according to the sanctuary shekel, 20 **g** to each shekel.*
18:16 {standard sanctuary shekel.} Hebrew *5 shekels* [about 2 ounces or 57 grams] *of silver, according to the sanctuary shekel, 20 **g** to each shekel.*

GERASENES (1)

Mt 8:28 {of the Gadarenes,} Some manuscripts read ***G**;* other manuscripts read *Gergesenes.* See Mark 5:1; Luke 8:26.

GERGESENES (3)

Mt 8:28 {of the Gadarenes,} Some manuscripts read *Gerasenes;* other manuscripts read ***G***. See Mark 5:1; Luke 8:26.
Mk 5: 1 {of the Gerasenes,} Some manuscripts read *Gadarenes;* others read ***G***. See Matt 8:28; Luke 8:26.
Lk 8:26 {of the Gerasenes,} Some manuscripts read *Gadarenes;* other manuscripts read ***G***. See Matt 8:28; Mark 5:1.

GERSHOM (4)

Ex 2:22 {named him Gershom,} ***G*** sounds like a Hebrew term that means "a stranger here."
18: 3 {son was Gershom,} ***G*** sounds like a Hebrew term that means "a stranger here."
1Ch 6:16 {Levi were Gershon,} Hebrew ***G***, a variant name for Gershon (see 6:1); also in 6:17, 20, 43, 62, 71.
15: 7 {clan of Gershon,} Hebrew ***G***, a variant name for Gershon.

GERSHON (3)

1Ch 6:16 {Levi were Gershon,} Hebrew *Gershom,* a variant name for **G** (see 6:1); also in 6:17, 20, 43, 62, 71.
6:39 {clan of Gershon.} Hebrew lacks *from the clan of **G**;* see 6:43.
15: 7 {clan of Gershon,} Hebrew *Gershom,* a variant name for **G**.

GESHEM (1)

Ne 6: 6 {"Geshem} Hebrew *Gashmu,* another name for **G**.

GIBEAH (3)

Jdg 20:10 {revenge on Gibeah} Hebrew *Geba,* in this case, a variant for **G**; also in 20:33.
1Sa 13:15 {land of Benjamin.} As in Greek version; Hebrew reads *Samuel left Gilgal and went to **G** in the land of Benjamin.*
2Sa 21: 6 {of the LORD.} As in Greek version (see also 21:9); Hebrew reads *at **G** of Saul, the chosen of the LORD.*

GIBEATH-ELOHIM (1)

1Sa 10: 5 {Gibeah of God,} Hebrew ***G***.

GIBEATH-HAARALOTH (1)

Jos 5: 3 {Israel at Gibeath-haaraloth.} ***G*** means "hill of foreskins."

GIBEON (2)

1Ch 6:60 {were given Gibeon,} As in parallel text at Josh 21:17; Hebrew lacks ***G***.
Ne 7:25 {family of Gibbar} As in parallel text at Ezra 2:20; Hebrew reads ***G***.

GIDDALTI (1)

1Ch 25:29 {fell to Geddalti} Hebrew ***G***, a variant name for Geddalti; compare 25:4.

GIDEON (1)

1Sa 12:11 {LORD sent Gideon,} Hebrew *Jerubbaal,* another name for **G**; see Judg 7:1.

GIFT (2)

Mk 7:11 {given to you.'} Greek *'What I could have given to you is Corban' (that is, a* ***g****).*
2Co 9:15 {wonderful for words!} Greek *Thank God for his indescribable* ***g****.*

GILBOA (1)

Jdg 7: 3 {afraid may leave} Hebrew *leave Mount Gilead.* The identity of Mount Gilead is uncertain in this context. It is perhaps used here as another name for Mount **G**.

GILEAD (4)

Jdg 7: 3 {afraid may leave} Hebrew *leave Mount* ***G****.* The identity of Mount **G** is uncertain in this context. It is perhaps used here as another name for Mount Gilboa.
2Sa 24: 6 {land of Tahtim-hodshi} Greek version reads *to* ***G*** *and to Kadesh in the land of the Hittites.*
1Ch 27:21 {Manasseh (east)} Hebrew *in* ***G****.*

GILGAL (2)

Jos 5: 9 {been called Gilgal} ***G*** sounds like the Hebrew word *galal,* meaning "to roll."
1Sa 13:15 {land of Benjamin.} As in Greek version; Hebrew reads *Samuel left* ***G*** *and went to Gibeah in the land of Benjamin.*

GINNETHOI (1)

Ne 12: 4 {Iddo, Ginnethon,} As in some Hebrew manuscripts and Latin Vulgate (see also 12:16); most Hebrew manuscripts read ***G****.*

GITTITH (3)

Ps 8: T {stringed instrument.} Hebrew *according to the* ***g****.*
81: T {stringed instrument.} Hebrew *according to the* ***g****.*
84: T {stringed instrument.} Hebrew *according to the* ***g****.*

GLAD (1)

1Pe 1: 6 {be truly glad!} Or *So you are truly* ***g****.*

GLOOM (1)

2Pe 2: 4 {in gloomy caves} Some manuscripts read *chains of* ***g****.*

GLORIFIED (1)

Jn 13:32 {God will bring} Some manuscripts read *And if God is* ***g*** *in him [the Son of Man], God will bring.*

GLORY (9)

Ps 16: 9 {and my mouth} As in Greek version; Hebrew reads ***g****.*
Jer 2:11 {their glorious God} Hebrew *their* ***G****.*
Eze 3:12 {in his place!)} A likely reading for this verse is *Then the Spirit lifted me up, and as the* ***g*** *of the* LORD *rose from its place, I heard behind me a loud rumbling sound.*
Mic 1:15 {And the leaders} Hebrew *the* ***g****.*
Mt 6:13 {the evil one.} Or *from evil.* Some manuscripts add *For yours is the kingdom and the power and the* ***g*** *forever. Amen.*
Jn 9:24 {telling the truth,} Or *Give* ***g*** *to God, not to Jesus;* Greek reads *Give* ***g*** *to God.*
Php 2: 7 {made himself nothing;} Or *He laid aside his mighty power and* ***g****.*
1Ti 3:16 {up into heaven.} Greek *in* ***g****.*

GOAT (2)

Lev 16: 8 {be the scapegoat.} Hebrew *azazel,* which in this context means "the **g** of removal"; also in 16:10, 26.
17: 7 {to evil spirits} Or ***g*** *idols.*

GOATS (1)

Zec 10: 3 {punish these leaders.} Or *these male* ***g****.*

GOD (80 of 91)

Ge 1: 1 {beginning God created} Or *In the beginning when* ***G*** *created,* or *When* ***G*** *began to create.*
16:11 {name him Ishmael,} *Ishmael* means "**G** hears."
32:28 {is now Israel,} *Israel* means "**G** struggles" or "one who struggles with **G**."
33:20 {called it El-Elohe-Israel.} *El-Elohe-Israel* means "**G**, the **G** of Israel."
35: 7 {El-bethel,} *El-bethel* means "the **G** of Bethel."
35:10 {be called Israel."} *Jacob* means "he grasps the heel"; this can also figuratively mean "he deceives"; *Israel* means "**G** struggles" or "one who struggles with **G**."
41:45 {renamed him Zaphenath-paneah} *Zaphenath-paneah* probably means "**G** speaks and lives."
Ex 18: 4 {son was Eliezer,} *Eliezer* means "**G** is my helper."
Dt 4:33 {voice of God} Or *voice of a* ***g****.*
6: 4 {the LORD alone.} Or *The* LORD *our* ***G*** *is one* LORD, or *The* LORD *our* ***G****, the* LORD *is one,* or *The* LORD *is our* ***G****, the* LORD *is one.*
32: 8 {of angelic beings.} As in Dead Sea Scrolls, which read *of the sons of* ***G****,* and Greek version, which reads *of the angels of* ***g****;* Masoretic Text reads *of the sons of Israel.*
1Sa 1:20 {named him Samuel,} *Samuel* sounds like the Hebrew term for "asked of **G**" or "heard by **G**."
4: 7 {"The gods have} Or *A* ***g*** *has.*
14:18 {of the Israelites.} As in some Greek manuscripts; Hebrew reads *"Bring the Ark of* ***G****." For at that time the Ark of* ***G*** *was with the Israelites.*
2Sa 12:30 {the king's head,} Greek version reads *removed the crown of Milcom;* compare 1 Kgs 11:5. Milcom, also called Molech, was the **g** of the Ammonites.
2Ki 23:16 {man of God} As in Greek version; Hebrew lacks *as Jeroboam stood beside the altar at the festival. Then Josiah turned and looked up at the tomb of the man of* ***G****.*
Job 1: 6 {the angels} Hebrew *the sons of* ***G****.*
2: 1 {the angels} Hebrew *the sons of* ***G****.*
9: 3 {God to court,} Or *If* ***G*** *wanted to take a person to court.*
19:26 {will see God} Or *without my body I will see* ***G****.*
32: 3 {had condemned God} As in ancient Hebrew scribal tradition; the Masoretic Text makes no reference to **G**.
38: 7 {all the angels} Hebrew *sons of* ***G****.*
Ps 56: 9 {on my side.} Or *By this I will know that* ***G*** *is on my side.*
Ecc 3:15 {in its turn.} Hebrew *For* ***G*** *calls the past to account.*
Jer 50:40 {just as I} Hebrew *just as* ***G****.*
Hos 1:11 {day of Jezreel} *Jezreel* means "**G** plants."
4:15 {and at Beth-aven.} *Beth-aven* means "house of wickedness"; it is being used as another name for Bethel, which means "house of **G**."
5: 8 {cry in Beth-aven} *Beth-aven* means "house of wickedness"; it is being used as another name for Bethel, which means "house of **G**."
10: 5 {idol at Beth-aven.} *Beth-aven* means "house of wickedness"; it is being used as another name for Bethel, which means "house of **G**."
11:12 {the Holy One.} Or *and Judah is unruly against* ***G****, the faithful Holy One.*
Am 4:11 {as I destroyed} Hebrew *as when* ***G*** *destroyed.*
5:26 {you yourselves made.} Greek version reads *You took up the shrine of Molech, and the star of your* ***g*** *Rephan, and the images you made for yourselves.*
Mal 2:15 {you are his.} Or *Did not one* ***G*** *make us and preserve our life and breath?* or *Did not one* ***G*** *make her, both flesh and spirit?* The meaning of the Hebrew is uncertain.
Mt 7: 2 {you treat them.} Or *For* ***G*** *will treat you as you treat others;* Greek reads *For with the judgment you judge you will be judged.*
22:31 {died, God said,} Greek *in the Scriptures?* ***G*** *said.*
Mk 1: 1 {Son of God.} Some manuscripts do not include *the Son of* ***G****.*
12:26 {said to Moses,} Greek *in the story of the bush?* ***G*** *said to him.*
Lk 2:14 {whom God favors.} Or *and peace on earth for all those pleasing* ***G****;* some manuscripts read *and peace on earth, goodwill among people.*
7:29 {plan was right,} Or *praised* ***G****.*
11:49 {said about you:} Greek *Therefore, the wisdom of* ***G*** *said.*
Jn 1:34 {Son of God.} Some manuscripts read *the chosen One of* ***G****.*
9:24 {telling the truth,} Or *Give glory to* ***G****, not to Jesus;* Greek reads *Give glory to* ***G****.*
9:35 {Son of Man} Some manuscripts read *the Son of* ***G****.*
13:32 {God will bring} Some manuscripts read *And if* ***G*** *is glorified in him [the Son of Man],* ***G*** *will bring.*
Ac 8:36 {I be baptized?"} Some manuscripts add verse 37, *"You can," Philip answered, "if you believe with all your heart." And the eunuch replied, "I believe that Jesus Christ is the Son of* ***G****."*
10:15 {say it isn't."} Greek *"What* ***G*** *calls clean you must not call unclean."*
11: 9 {say it isn't.'} Greek *'What* ***G*** *calls clean you must not call unclean.'*
Ro 3: 2 {revelation of God.} Greek *the oracles of* ***G****.*
9: 5 {eternal praise! Amen.} Or *May* ***G****, who rules over everything, be praised forever. Amen.*
2Co 9:15 {wonderful for words!} Greek *Thank* ***G*** *for his indescribable gift.*
Gal 1:13 {persecuted the Christians.} Greek *the church of* ***G****.*
6:16 {people of God.} Greek *the Israel of* ***G****.*
Eph 1:18 {to his people.} Or *realize how much* ***G*** *has been honored by acquiring his people.*
6:15 {prepared.} Or *For shoes, put on the readiness to preach the Good News of peace with* ***G****.*
Php 3: 3 {in the Spirit} Or *in spirit;* some manuscripts read *worship by the Spirit of* ***G****.*
2Th 1:12 {Lord, Jesus Christ.} Or *of our* ***G*** *and the Lord Jesus Christ.*
2:13 {among the first} Some manuscripts read ***G*** *chose you from the very beginning.*
1Ti 1: 4 {faith in God.} Greek *a stewardship of* ***G*** *in faith.*
3:16 {Christ} Greek *Who;* some manuscripts read **G**.
Heb 4: 2 {God told them.} Some manuscripts read *they didn't share the faith of those who listened [to* ***G****].*
5:12 {about the Scriptures.} Or *about the oracles of* ***G****.*
11:11 {keep his promise.} Some manuscripts read *It was by faith that Sarah was able to have a child, even though she was too old and barren. Sarah believed that* ***G*** *would keep his promise.*
Jas 4: 5 {to be faithful} Or *the spirit that* ***G*** *placed within us tends to envy,* or *the Holy Spirit, whom* ***G*** *has placed within us, opposes our envy.*
2Pe 1: 2 {God and Lord,} Or ***G*** *and Jesus our Lord.*
2Jn 1: 1 {to her children,} Or *the church* ***G*** *has chosen and her members,* or *the chosen Kyria and her children.*
Rev 21: 3 {be with them.} Some manuscripts read ***G*** *himself will be with them, their* ***G****.*

GOD'S (3 of 4)

Jn 2:17 {burns within me."} Or *"Concern for* ***G*** *house will be my undoing."* Ps 69:9.
1Co 2: 7 {wisdom of God,} Greek *we speak* ***G*** *wisdom in a mystery.*
Eph 1:11 {inheritance from God,} Or *we have become* ***G*** *inheritance.*

GODHEAD (1)

Col 2: 9 {human body,} Greek *in him dwells all the fullness of the* ***G*** *bodily.*

GODLY (3)

Pr 12:26 {to their friends;} Or *The* ***g*** *are cautious in friendship,* or *the* ***g*** *are freed from evil.* The meaning of the Hebrew is uncertain.
Mt 27:51[-53] {to many people.} Or *The earth shook, rocks split apart, tombs opened, and many bodies of* ***g*** *men and women who had died were raised from the dead. After Jesus' resurrection, they left the cemetery, went into the holy city of Jerusalem, and appeared to many people.*

GODS (5)

1Sa 28:13 {see a god} Or ***g****.*
1Ch 14:12 {abandoned their idols} Hebrew *their* ***g****;* compare parallel text at 2 Sam 5:21.
Da 3:25 {a divine being} Aramaic *like a son of the* ***g****.*
Ac 28:11 {the twin gods} The *twin* ***g*** were the Roman **g** Castor and Pollux.

GOOD (4)

Ge 30:11 {named him Gad,} *Gad* means "**g** fortune."
Mt 5:44 {love your enemies!} Some manuscripts add *Bless those who curse you, do* ***g*** *to those who hate you.*
19:16 {this question: "Teacher,} Some manuscripts read ***G*** *Teacher.*
Eph 6:15 {be fully prepared.} Or *For shoes, put on the readiness to preach the* ***G*** *News of peace with God.*

GOODWILL (1)

Lk 2:14 {whom God favors.} Or *and peace on earth for all those pleasing God;* some manuscripts read *and peace on earth,* ***g*** *among people.*

GOSPEL (1 of 3)

Eph 6:19 {the Gentiles, too.} Greek *explain the mystery of the* ***g****.*

GOUGED (2)

1Sa 10:27 {Saul ignored them.} Dead Sea Scroll 4QSam[a] continues: *...He* ***g*** *out the right eye of each of the Israelites living there, and he didn't allow anyone to come and rescue them. In fact, of all the Israelites east of the Jordan, there wasn't a single one whose right eye Nahash had not* ***g*** *out....*

GOVERNORS (1)

Da 3: 3 {all these officials} Aramaic *the princes, prefects,* ***g****, advisers, counselors, judges, magistrates, and all the provincial officials.*

GOYIM (1)

Jos 12:23 {Goyim in Gilgal} Greek version reads ***G*** *in Galilee.*

GRACE (4)

Jn 1:14 {love and faithfulness.} Greek ***g*** *and truth;* also in 1:17.
1:16 {blessing after another} Greek ***g*** *upon* ***g****.*
Ro 16:23 {a Christian brother.} Some manuscripts add verse 24, *May the* ***g*** *of our Lord Jesus Christ be with you all. Amen.*

GRANTED (1)

Ge 4:25 {named him Seth,} *Seth* probably means "**g**"; the name may also mean "appointed."

GRASPS (4)

Ge 25:26 {called him Jacob.} *Jacob* means "he **g** the heel"; this can also figuratively mean "he deceives."
27:36 {name is Jacob,} *Jacob* means "he **g** the heel"; this can also figuratively mean "he deceives."
35:10 {be called Israel."} *Jacob* means "he **g** the heel"; this can also figuratively mean "he deceives"; *Israel* means "God struggles" or "one who struggles with God."
Hos 12: 2 {to punish Jacob} *Jacob* means "he **g** at the heel"; this can also figuratively mean "he deceives."

GRASS (1)

Ps 58: 7 {in their hands.} Or *Let them be trodden down and wither like* ***g****.* The meaning of the Hebrew is uncertain.

GRAVES (1)

Dt 9:22 {and Kibroth-hattaavah.} *Kibroth-hattaavah* means "**g** of craving." See Num 11:31-34.

GREAT (8 of 9)

Jos 1: 4 {the Mediterranean Sea} Hebrew *the **G** Sea.*
9: 1 {the Mediterranean Sea} Hebrew *the **G** Sea.*
15:12 {the Mediterranean Sea.} Hebrew *the **G** Sea;* also in 15:47.
23: 4 {the Mediterranean Sea} Hebrew *the **G** Sea.*
Eze 47:10 {fill the Mediterranean} Hebrew *the **g** sea;* also in 47:15, 17, 19, 20.
48:28 {to the Mediterranean.} Hebrew *the **g** sea.*
Da 12: 1 {Michael, the archangel} Hebrew *the **g** prince.*
ARevl 1: 8 {street of Jerusalem,} Greek *the **g** city.*

GREATER (1)

Mt 23:13 {go in yourselves.} Some manuscripts add verse 14, *How terrible it will be for you teachers of religious law and you Pharisees. Hypocrites! You shamelessly cheat widows out of their property, and then, to cover up the kind of people you really are, you make long prayers in public. Because of this, your punishment will be the **g**.*

GREATLY (1)

Ac 28:28 {will accept it."} Some manuscripts add verse 29, *And when he had said these words, the Jews departed, **g** disagreeing with each other.*

GREEK (717)

Ge 10: 4 {Kittim, and Rodanim.} As in some Hebrew manuscripts and **G** version (see also 1 Chr 1:7); most Hebrew manuscripts read *Dodanim.*
10:24 {father of Shelah,} **G** version reads *Arphaxad was the father of Cainan, Cainan was the father of Shelah.*
11:12[-13] {sons and daughters.} **G** version reads *[12]When Arphaxad was 135 years old, his son Cainan was born. [13]After the birth of Cainan, Arphaxad lived another 430 years and had other sons and daughters, and then he died. When Cainan was 130 years old, his son Shelah was born. After the birth of Shelah, Cainan lived another 330 years and had other sons and daughters, and then he died.*
46:13 {Jashub,} As in some **G** manuscripts and Samaritan Pentateuch (see also Num 26:24; 1 Chr 7:1); Hebrew reads *Iob.*
46:16 {Gad were Zephon,} As in **G** version and Samaritan Pentateuch (see also Num 26:15); Hebrew reads *Ziphion.*
46:27 {had two sons} **G** version reads *nine sons,* probably including Joseph's grandsons through Ephraim and Manasseh (see 1 Chr 7:14-20).
46:27 {there were seventy} **G** version reads *seventy-five;* see note on Exod 1:5.
47:21 {servants to Pharaoh.} As in **G** version and Samaritan Pentateuch; Hebrew reads *He moved the people into the towns throughout the land of Egypt.*
47:31 {on his staff.} As in **G** version; Hebrew reads *bowed in worship at the head of his bed.*
Ex 1: 5 {Jacob had seventy} Dead Sea Scrolls and **G** version read *seventy-five;* see notes on Gen 46:27.
Nu 3:28 {There were 8,600} Some **G** manuscripts read *8,300;* see total in 3:39.
26:23 {its ancestor Puah.} As in Samaritan Pentateuch, **G** and Syriac versions, and Latin Vulgate (see also 1 Chr 7:1); Hebrew reads *The Punite clan, named after its ancestor Puvah.*
26:39 {its ancestor Shupham.} As in some Hebrew manuscripts, Samaritan Pentateuch, **G** and Syriac versions, and Latin Vulgate; most Hebrew manuscripts read *Shephupham.*
26:40 {their ancestor Ard.} As in Samaritan Pentateuch, some **G** manuscripts, and Latin Vulgate; Hebrew lacks *named after their ancestor Ard.*
Dt 31: 1 {had finished saying} As in Dead Sea Scrolls and **G** version; Masoretic Text reads *Moses went and spoke.*
32: 8 {of angelic beings.} As in Dead Sea Scrolls, which read *of the sons of God,* and **G** version, which reads *of the angels of god;* Masoretic Text reads *of the sons of Israel.*
32:26 {to scatter them,} As in **G** version; the meaning of the Hebrew is uncertain.
32:31 {even they recognize.} The meaning of the Hebrew is uncertain. **G** version reads *our enemies are fools.*
32:43 {God worship him,} As in Dead Sea Scrolls and **G** version; Masoretic Text reads *Rejoice with his people, O nations.*
33: 2 {dawned upon us} As in **G** and Syriac versions; Hebrew reads *upon them.*
34: 6 {He was buried} Hebrew *He buried him,* that is, "The LORD buried him." Samaritan Pentateuch and some **G** manuscripts read *They buried him.*
Jos 7: 1 {family of Zimri,} As in **G** version (see also 1 Chr 2:6); Hebrew reads *Zabdi.* Also in 7:17, 18.
12:23 {Goyim in Gilgal} **G** version reads *Goyim in Galilee.*
15:18 {she urged him} Some **G** manuscripts read *Othniel urged her.*
16: 2 {(that is, Luz)} As in **G** version (also see 18:13); Hebrew reads *From Bethel to Luz.*
18:28 {Gibeah, and Kiriath-jearim} As in **G** version; Hebrew reads *Kiriath.*
Jdg 1:14 {she urged him} **G** version and Latin Vulgate read *he urged her.*
9:29 {I would say} As in **G** version; Hebrew reads *And he said.*
14:15 {On the fourth} As in **G** version; Hebrew reads *seventh.*
16:13 {the loom shuttle,} As in **G** version; Hebrew lacks *on your loom and tighten it with the loom shuttle.*
18:30 {descendant of Moses,} As in an ancient Hebrew tradition, some **G** manuscripts, and Latin Vulgate; Masoretic Text reads *of Manasseh.*
19:28 {was no answer.} **G** version adds *for she was dead.*
1Sa 1:24 {a three-year-old bull} As in Dead Sea Scrolls, **G** and Syriac versions; Hebrew reads *3 bulls.*
2:20 {to the LORD.} As in **G** version; Hebrew reads *this one she requested of the LORD in prayer.*
3:13 {are blaspheming God} As in **G** version; Hebrew reads *his sons have made themselves contemptible.*
5: 6 {plague of tumors.} **G** version and Latin Vulgate read *tumors. And rats appeared in their land, and death and destruction were throughout the city.*
6:19 {killed seventy men} As in a few Hebrew manuscripts; most Hebrew manuscripts and **G** version read *50,070 men.* Perhaps the text should be understood to read *the LORD killed 70 men and 50 oxen.*
7:12 {Mizpah and Jeshanah.} As in **G** version; Hebrew reads *Shen.*
8:16 {of your cattle} As in **G** version; Hebrew reads *young men.*
9:25 {for him there.} As in **G** version; Hebrew reads *and talked with him there.*
10: 1 {his people Israel.} **G** version reads *Israel. And you will rule over the LORD's people and save them from their enemies around them. This will be the sign to you that the LORD has appointed you to be leader over his inheritance.*
11: 1 {month later,} As in **G** version; Hebrew lacks *About a month later.*
11: 8 {addition to 30,000} Dead Sea Scrolls and **G** version read *70,000.*
12:11 {Barak,} As in **G** and Syriac versions; Hebrew reads *Bedan.*
12:11 {Samuel} **G** and Syriac versions read *Samson.*
13: 1 {Saul was thirty} As in a few **G** manuscripts; the number is missing in the Hebrew.
13: 5 {of three thousand} As in **G** and Syriac versions; Hebrew reads *30,000.*
13:15 {land of Benjamin.} As in **G** version; Hebrew reads *Samuel left Gilgal and went to Gibeah in the land of Benjamin.*
13:20 {axes, or sickles,} As in **G** version; Hebrew reads *or plowshares.*
14:18 {of the Israelites.} As in some **G** manuscripts; Hebrew reads *"Bring the Ark of God." For at that time the Ark of God was with the Israelites.*
14:41 {others?"} **G** version adds *If the fault is with me or my son Jonathan, respond with Urim; but if the men of Israel are at fault, respond with Thummim.*
15:32 {have been spared!"} Dead Sea Scrolls and **G** version read *Agag arrived hesitantly, for he thought, "Surely this is the bitterness of death."*
17: 4 {over nine feet} Hebrew *6 cubits* [9 feet or 2.7 meters] *and 1 span* [9 inches or 23 centimeters]; **G** version reads *4 cubits* [6 feet or 1.8 meters] *and 1 span,* about 6.75 feet or 2 meters in length.
17:52 {far as Gath} As in some **G** manuscripts; Hebrew reads *a valley.*
20:25 {sitting opposite him} As in **G** version; Hebrew reads *with Jonathan standing.*
20:41 {the stone pile.} As in **G** version; Hebrew reads *near the south edge.*
25: 1 {wilderness of Maon.} As in **G** version; Hebrew reads *Paran.*
30:29 {Racal,} **G** version reads *Carmel.*
2Sa 5:25 {way from Gibeon} As in **G** version (see also 1 Chr 14:16); Hebrew reads *Geba.*
6: 5 {might, singing songs} As in **G** version (see also 1 Chr 13:8); Hebrew reads *cypress trees.*
8: 4 {seventeen hundred charioteers} **G** version reads *1,000 chariots and 7,000 charioteers;* compare 1 Chr 18:4.
8: 8 {cities of Tebah} As in some **G** manuscripts (see also 1 Chr 18:8); Hebrew reads *Betah.*
8:12 {Edom,} As in a few Hebrew manuscripts and **G** and Syriac versions (see also 8:14; 1 Chr 18:11); most Hebrew manuscripts read *Aram.*
8:13 {eighteen thousand Edomites} As in a few Hebrew manuscripts and **G** and Syriac versions (see also 8:14; 1 Chr 18:12); most Hebrew manuscripts read *Arameans.*
10:18 {horsemen,} Some **G** manuscripts read *foot soldiers;* compare parallel text at 1 Chr 19:18.
12:30 {the king's head,} **G** version reads *removed the crown of Milcom;* compare 1 Kgs 11:5. Milcom, also called Molech, was the god of the Ammonites.
13:34 {the Horonaim road} As in **G** version; Hebrew reads *from the road behind him.*
15: 7 {After four years,} As in **G** and Syriac versions; Hebrew reads *40 years.*
15:20 {love and faithfulness.} As in **G** version; Hebrew reads *and may unfailing love and faithfulness go with you.*
15:27 {the priest, "Look,} As in **G** version; Hebrew reads *Are you a seer?* or *Do you see?*
16:14 {Jordan River.} As in **G** version (see also 17:16); Hebrew reads *when they reached their destination.*
17: 3 {that you seek.} As in **G** version; Hebrew reads *like the return of all is the man whom you seek.*
17:25 {an Ishmaelite.} As in some **G** manuscripts (see also 1 Chr 2:17); Hebrew reads *an Israelite.*
20:24 {Adoniram} As in **G** version (see also 1 Kgs 4:6; 5:14); Hebrew reads *Adoram.*
21: 6 {of the LORD.} As in **G** version (see also 21:9); Hebrew reads *at Gibeah of Saul, the chosen of the LORD.*
21: 8 {Saul's daughter Merab,} As in a few Hebrew and **G** manuscripts and Syriac version (see also 1 Sam 18:19); most Hebrew manuscripts read *Michal.*
21:16 {of the giants} As in **G** version; Hebrew reads *a descendant of the Rephaites;* also in 21:18, 20, 22.
23: 8 {a single battle.} As in some **G** manuscripts (see also 1 Chr 11:11); the Hebrew is uncertain, though it might be rendered *the Three. It was Adino the Eznite who killed eight hundred men at one time.*
23:27 {Sibbecai} As in some **G** manuscripts (see also 1 Chr 11:29); Hebrew reads *Mebunnai.*
23:30 {Hurai} As in some **G** manuscripts (see also 1 Chr 11:32); Hebrew reads *Hiddai.*
23:33 {son of Shagee} As in parallel text at 1 Chr 11:34; Hebrew reads *Jonathan, Shammah;* some **G** manuscripts read *Jonathan son of Shammah.*
24: 6 {land of Tahtim-hodshi} **G** version reads *to Gilead and to Kadesh in the land of the Hittites.*
24:13 {you choose three} As in **G** version (see also 1 Chr 21:12); Hebrew reads *seven.*
1Ki 1: 9 {stone of Zoheleth} Or *to the Serpent's Stone;* **G** version supports reading *Zoheleth* as a proper name.
1:25 {of the army,} As in **G** version; Hebrew reads *invited the commanders of the army.*
4:19 {land of Gilead,} **G** version reads *of Gad;* compare 4:13.
4:19 {land of Judah.} As in some **G** manuscripts; Hebrew lacks *of Judah.* The meaning of the Hebrew is uncertain.
4:26 {had four thousand} As in some **G** manuscripts (see also 2 Chr 9:25); Hebrew reads *40,000.*
5:11 {and 110,000 gallons} As in **G** version, which reads *20,000 baths* [420 kiloliters] (see also 2 Chr 2:10); Hebrew reads *20 cors,* about 800 gallons or 3.6 kiloliters in volume.
5:16 {thirty-six hundred} As in some **G** manuscripts (see also 2 Chr 2:2, 18); Hebrew reads *3,300.*
6: 8 {the bottom floor} As in **G** version; Hebrew reads *middle floor.*
9:26 {port near Elath} As in **G** version (see also 2 Kgs 14:22; 16:6); Hebrew reads *Eloth.*
12: 2 {returned from Egypt,} As in **G** version and Latin Vulgate (see also 2 Chr 10:2); Hebrew reads *he lived in Egypt.*
12:18 {Rehoboam sent Adoniram,} As in some **G** manuscripts and Syriac version (see also 4:6; 5:14); Hebrew reads *Adoram.*
2Ki 8:21 {town of Zair.} **G** version reads *Seir.*
10: 1 {of the city,} As in some **G** manuscripts and Latin Vulgate (see also 10:6); Hebrew reads *of Jezreel.*
12:21 {assassins were Jozacar} As in **G** and Syriac versions; Hebrew reads *Jozabad;* compare parallel text at 2 Chr 24:26.
15:16 {town of Tappuah} As in some **G** manuscripts; Hebrew reads *Tiphsah.*
16: 6 {and sent Edomites} As in marginal *Qere* reading of the Masoretic Text, **G** version, and Latin Vulgate; Hebrew reads *Arameans.*
23:16 {man of God} As in **G** version; Hebrew lacks *as Jeroboam stood beside the altar at the festival. Then Josiah turned and looked up at the tomb of the man of God.*
1Ch 1: 4 {of Noah were} As in **G** version (see also Gen 5:3-32); Hebrew lacks *The sons of Noah were.*
1: 6 {were Ashkenaz, Riphath,} As in some Hebrew manuscripts and **G** version (see also Gen 10:3); most Hebrew manuscripts read *Diphath.*
1:17 {of Aram were} As in one Hebrew manuscript and some **G** manuscripts (see also Gen 10:23); most Hebrew manuscripts lack *The descendants of Aram were.*
1:24 {Shem: Arphaxad, Shelah,} Some **G** manuscripts read *Arphaxad, Cainan, Shelah.* See notes on Gen 10:24 and 11:12-13.
1:36 {Zepho,} As in many Hebrew manuscripts and a few **G** manuscripts (see also Gen 36:11); most Hebrew manuscripts read *Zephi.*
1:36 {Timna.} As in some **G** manuscripts (see also Gen 36:12); Hebrew reads *Kenaz, Timna, and Amalek.*
1:40 {Shobal were Alvan,} As in many Hebrew manuscripts and a few **G** manuscripts (see also Gen 36:23); most Hebrew manuscripts read *Alian.*
1:41 {Dishon were Hemdan,} As in many Hebrew manuscripts and some **G** manuscripts (see also Gen 36:26); most Hebrew manuscripts read *Hamran.*
1:42 {Zaavan, and Akan.} As in many Hebrew and **G** manuscripts (see also Gen 36:27); most Hebrew manuscripts read *Jaakan.*
1:50 {city of Pau.} As in many Hebrew manuscripts, some **G** manuscripts, Syriac version, and Latin Vulgate (see also Gen 36:39); most Hebrew manuscripts read *Pai.*

2: 6 {Calcol, and Darda} As in many Hebrew manuscripts, some **G** manuscripts, and Syriac version (see also 1 Kgs 4:31); Hebrew reads *Dara.*
2: 11 {father of Salmon.} As in **G** version (see also Ruth 4:21); Hebrew reads *Salma.*
3: 6 {sons: Ibhar, Elishua,} As in some Hebrew and **G** manuscripts (see also 14:5-7 and 2 Sam 5:15); most Hebrew manuscripts read *Elishama.*
4: 3 {The descendants of} As in **G** version; Hebrew reads *father of.* The meaning of the Hebrew is uncertain.
4: 13 {Hathath and Meonothai.} As in some **G** manuscripts and Latin Vulgate; Hebrew lacks *and Meonothai.*
4: 33 {away as Baalath.} As in some **G** manuscripts (see also Josh 19:8); Hebrew reads *Baal.*
6: 27 {Elkanah, and Samuel.} As in some **G** manuscripts (see also 6:33-34); Hebrew lacks *and Samuel.*
6: 28 {Samuel were Joel} As in some **G** manuscripts and the Syriac version (see also 6:33 and 1 Sam 8:2); Hebrew lacks *Joel.*
6: 77 {of Jokneam, Kartah,} As in **G** version (see also Josh 21:34); Hebrew lacks *Jokneam, Kartah.*
7: 13 {Jezer, and Shillem.} As in some Hebrew and **G** manuscripts (see also Gen 46:24; Num 26:49); most Hebrew manuscripts read *Shallum.*
8: 29 {Jeiel} As in some **G** manuscripts (see also 9:35); Hebrew lacks *Jeiel.*
8: 30 {Kish, Baal, Ner,} As in some **G** manuscripts (see also 9:36); Hebrew lacks *Ner.*
9: 42 {father of Jadah.} As in some Hebrew manuscripts and **G** version (see also 8:36); Hebrew reads *Jarah.*
11: 11 {among David's men.} As in some **G** manuscripts (see also 2 Sam 23:8); Hebrew *commander of the Thirty,* or *commander of the captains.*
16: 15 {by his covenant} As in some **G** manuscripts (see also Ps 105:8); Hebrew reads *Remember his covenant forever.*
17: 6 {to Israel's leaders,} As in **G** version (see also 2 Sam 7:7); Hebrew reads *judges.*
20: 2 {the king's head,} **G** version and Latin Vulgate read *removed the crown of Milcom;* compare 1 Kgs 11:5. Milcom, also called Molech, was the god of the Ammonites.
23: 10 {were Jahath, Ziza,} As in **G** version and Latin Vulgate (see also 23:11); Hebrew reads *Zina.*
25: 3 {Zeri, Jeshaiah, Shimei,} As in one Hebrew manuscript and some **G** manuscripts (see also 25:17); most Hebrew manuscripts lack *Shimei.*
25: 9 {sons and relatives.} As in **G** version; Hebrew lacks *and twelve of his sons and relatives.*
2Ch 3: 4 {was thirty feet} As in some **G** and Syriac manuscripts, which read *20 cubits* [9 meters]; Hebrew reads *120 cubits,* which is 180 feet or 54 meters.
8: 17 {Ezion-geber and Elath,} As in **G** version (see also 2 Kgs 14:22; 16:6); Hebrew reads *Eloth.*
13: 2 {mother was Maacah,} As in most **G** manuscripts and Syriac version (see also 2 Chr 11:20-21; 1 Kgs 15:2); Hebrew reads *Micaiah.*
20: 1 {of the Meunites} As in some **G** manuscripts (see also 26:7); Hebrew reads *Ammonites.*
22: 2 {Ahaziah was twenty-two} As in some **G** manuscripts and Syriac version (see also 2 Kgs 8:26); Hebrew reads *forty-two.*
22: 6 {and King Ahaziah} Some Hebrew manuscripts, **G** and Syriac versions, and Latin Vulgate (see also 2 Kgs 8:29); most Hebrew manuscripts read *Azariah.*
22: 8 {and Ahaziah's relatives} As in **G** version (see also 2 Kgs 10:13); Hebrew reads *and sons of the brothers of Ahaziah.*
26: 2 {town of Elath} As in **G** version (see also 2 Kgs 14:22; 16:6); Hebrew reads *Eloth.*
26: 7 {Arabs of Gur} As in **G** version; Hebrew reads *Gur-baal.*
26: 8 {The Meunites} As in **G** version; Hebrew reads *Ammonites.* Compare 26:7.
36: 9 {Jehoiachin was eighteen} As in one Hebrew manuscript, some **G** manuscripts, and Syriac version (see also 2 Kgs 24:8); most Hebrew manuscripts read *eight.*
Ezr 2: 25 {peoples of Kiriath-jearim,} As in some Hebrew manuscripts and **G** version (see also Neh 7:29); Hebrew reads *Kiriath-arim.*
8: 5 {family of Zattu} As in some **G** manuscripts (see also 1 Esdras 8:32); Hebrew lacks *Zattu.*
8: 10 {family of Bani} As in some **G** manuscripts (see also 1 Esdras 8:36); Hebrew lacks *Bani.*
10: 37[-38] {family of Binnui} As in **G** version; Hebrew reads *Jaasu, [38]Bani, Binnui.*
Ne 3: 18 {led by Binnui} As in a few Hebrew manuscripts, some **G** manuscripts, and Syriac version (see also 3:24; 10:9); most Hebrew manuscripts read *Bavvai.*
6: 2 {of the villages} As in **G** version; Hebrew reads *at Kephirim.*
12: 14 {family of Malluch.} As in **G** version (see also 10:4; 12:2); Hebrew reads *Malluchi.*
12: 14 {family of Shecaniah.} As in many Hebrew manuscripts, some **G** manuscripts, and Syriac version (see also 12:3); most Hebrew manuscripts read *Shebaniah.*
12: 15 {family of Meremoth.} As in some **G** manuscripts (see also 12:3); Hebrew reads *Meraioth.*
Est 3: 7 {a year later.} As in **G** version, which reads *the thirteenth day of the twelfth month, the month of Adar* (see also 3:13). Hebrew reads *in the twelfth month,* of the Hebrew calendar. The date selected was March 7, 473 B.C.; also see note on 2:16.
Job 15: 23 {'Where is it?'} **G** version reads *He is appointed to be food for a vulture.*
41: 11 {and remain safe} As in **G** version; Hebrew reads *confront me that I must pay.*
41: 13 {layer of armor} As in **G** version; Hebrew reads *its bridle.*
Ps 8: 2 {give you praise.} As in **G** version; Hebrew reads *to show strength.*
16: 9 {and my mouth} As in **G** version; Hebrew reads *glory.*
18: 13 {a mighty shout.} As in **G** version (see also 2 Sam 22:14); Hebrew adds *raining down hail and burning coals.*
72: 5 {May he live} As in **G** version; Hebrew reads *May they fear you.*
76: 4 {the everlasting mountains.} As in **G** version; Hebrew reads *than mountains filled with beasts of prey.*
112: 4 {They are} **G** version reads *The LORD is.*
Pr 10: 10 {reproof promotes peace.} As in **G** version; Hebrew reads *but babbling fools fall flat on their faces.*
14: 33 {wisdom is not} As in **G** version; Hebrew lacks *not.*
21: 6 {deadly trap.} As in **G** version; Hebrew reads *mist for those who seek death.*
24: 5 {strong man,} As in **G** version; Hebrew reads *A wise man is strength.*
26: 23 {Smooth} As in **G** version; Hebrew reads *Burning.*
31: 21 {them have warm} As in **G** version; Hebrew *scarlet.*
Ecc 8: 10 {and are praised} As in some Hebrew manuscripts and **G** version; many Hebrew manuscripts read *and are forgotten.*
9: 2 {good or bad,} As in **G** and Syriac versions, and Latin Vulgate; Hebrew lacks *or bad.*
SS 7: 9 {lips and teeth.} As in **G** and Syriac versions and Latin Vulgate; Hebrew reads *over lips of sleepers.*
Isa 5: 17 {lambs and kids} As in **G** version; Hebrew reads *strangers.*
10: 27 {their shoulders.} As in **G** version; Hebrew reads *The yoke will be broken, for you have grown so fat.*
15: 9 {stream near Dibon} As in Dead Sea Scrolls, some **G** manuscripts, and Latin Vulgate; Hebrew reads *Dimon;* also in 15:9b.
28: 16 {run away again.} **G** version reads *Anyone who believes in him will not be disappointed.*
29: 13 {learned by rote.} **G** version reads *Their worship is a farce, for they merely teach human commands and teachings.*
45: 2 {level the mountains.} As in Dead Sea Scrolls and **G** version; Masoretic Text reads *the swellings.*
61: 1 {be freed.} **G** version reads *and the blind will see.*
66: 19 {to the Libyans} As in some **G** manuscripts, which read *Put* [Libya]; Hebrew reads *Pul.*
Jer 23: 33 {are the burden!} As in **G** version and Latin Vulgate; Hebrew reads *What burden?*
42: 1 {Kareah and Jezaniah} **G** version reads *Azariah;* compare 43:2.
48: 4 {will cry out.} **G** version reads *Her cries are heard as far away as Zoar.*
Eze 19: 7 {in nearby nations} As in **G** version; Hebrew reads *He consorted with widows.*
22: 25 {Your princes} As in **G** version; Hebrew reads *prophets.*
27: 15 {you from Dedan.} **G** version reads *Rhodes.*
32: 17 {On March 17,} Hebrew *On the fifteenth day of the month,* presumably in the twelfth month of the Hebrew calendar (see 32:1). This would put this message at the end of King Jehoiachin's twelfth year of captivity, on March 17, 585 B.C.; also see note on 29:1. **G** version reads *On the fifteenth day of the first month,* which would put this message on April 27, 586 B.C., at the beginning of Jehoiachin's twelfth year.
38: 14 {will rouse yourself.} As in **G** version; Hebrew reads *then you will know.*
40: 6 {10 1/2 feet deep.} **G** version; Hebrew reads *1 rod* [10.5 feet or 3.2 meters] *deep, and one threshold, one rod deep.*
40: 44 {the south} As in **G** version; Hebrew reads *east.*
42: 10 {On the south} As in **G** version; Hebrew reads *east.*
45: 1 {6 2/3 miles wide.} Reflecting the **G** reading *25,000 cubits* [13.3 kilometers] *long and 20,000 cubits* [10.6 kilometers] *wide;* Hebrew reads *25,000 cubits long and 10,000 cubits wide.* Compare 45:3, 5; 48:9....
45: 5 {for their towns.} As in **G** version; Hebrew reads *They will have as their possession 20 rooms.*
47: 18 {south as Tamar.} As in **G** version; Hebrew reads *you will measure.*
48: 9 {6 2/3 miles wide.} Reflecting the **G** reading in 45:1: *25,000 cubits* [13.3 kilometers] *long and 20,000 cubits* [10.6 kilometers] *wide;* Hebrew reads *25,000 cubits long and 10,000 cubits wide.* Compare 45:1-5; 48:10-13....
Da 10: 13 {kingdom of Persia.} As in one **G** version; Hebrew reads *and I was left there with the kings of Persia.* The meaning of the Hebrew is uncertain.
10: 16 {like a man} As in most manuscripts of the Masoretic Text; one manuscript of the Masoretic Text and one **G** version read *Then something that looked like a human hand.*
Hos 3: 2 {measure of wine.} As in **G** version, which reads *a homer* [182 liters] *of barley and a measure of wine;* Hebrew reads *a homer of barley and a lethech* [2.5 bushels or 91 liters] *of barley.*
4: 18 {love for honor.} As in **G** version; the meaning of the Hebrew is uncertain.
11: 2 {the more I} As in **G** version; Hebrew reads *they.*
12: 4 {spoke to him} As in **G** and Syriac versions; Hebrew reads *to us.*
13: 10 {Where now is} As in **G** and Syriac versions and Latin Vulgate; Hebrew reads *I will be.*
Am 5: 26 {you yourselves made.} **G** version reads *You took up the shrine of Molech, and the star of your god Rephan, and the images you made for yourselves.*
Mic 1: 10 {weep at all.} **G** version reads *weep not in Acco.*
Hab 2: 4 {lives are crooked;} **G** version reads *I will have no pleasure in anyone who turns away.*
Zec 5: 6 {with the sins} As in **G** version; Hebrew reads *the appearance.*
6: 11 {make a crown} As in **G** and Syriac versions; Hebrew reads *crowns.*
14: 5 {ones with him.} As in **G** version; Hebrew reads *with you.*
Mal 1: 7 {defiled the sacrifices} As in **G** version; Hebrew reads *defiled you.*
Mt 1: 3 {father of Ram.} **G** *Aram;* also in 1:4. See 1 Chr 2:9-10.
1: 8 {father of Jehoram.} **G** *Joram.* See 1 Kgs 22:50 and note at 1 Chr 3:11.
1: 11 {father of Jehoiachin} **G** *Jeconiah;* also in 1:12. See 2 Kgs 24:6 and note at 1 Chr 3:16.
2: 1 {some wise men} Or *royal astrologers,* **G** *magi;* also in 2:7, 16.
3: 11 {be his slave.} **G** *to carry his sandals.*
4: 3 {Then the Devil} **G** *the tempter.*
4: 25 {the Ten Towns,} **G** *Decapolis.*
5: 3 {need for him,} **G** *the poor in spirit.*
5: 22 {you curse someone,} **G** *if you say, 'You fool.'*
5: 29 {your good eye} **G** *your right eye.*
5: 30 {your stronger hand} **G** *your right hand.*
5: 38 {who did it.'} **G** *'An eye for an eye and a tooth for a tooth.'* Exod 21:24; Lev 24:20; Deut 19:21.
5: 41 {for a mile,} **G** *milion* [4,854 feet or 1,478 meters].
7: 2 {you treat them.} Or *For God will treat you as you treat others;* **G** reads *For with the judgment you judge you will be judged.*
7: 6 {to unholy people.} **G** *Don't give the sacred to dogs.*
7: 13 {highway to hell} **G** *The way that leads to destruction.*
8: 22 {their own dead."} **G** *Let the dead bury their own dead.*
9: 11 {with such scum} **G** *with tax collectors and sinners.*
10: 4 {Simon (the Zealot} **G** *the Cananean.*
10: 25 {prince of demons,} **G** *Beelzeboul.*
10: 41 {speaks for God,} **G** *welcome a prophet in the name of a prophet.*
11: 23 {of the dead.} **G** *to Hades.*
12: 24 {power from Satan,} **G** *Beelzeboul.*
12: 27 {prince of demons,} **G** *by Beelzeboul.*
12: 42 {queen of Sheba} **G** *The queen of the south.*
13: 33 {a large amount} **G** *3 measures.*
14: 1 {When Herod Antipas} **G** *Herod the tetrarch.* He was a son of King Herod and was one of four rulers in Palestine.
14: 25 {in the morning} **G** *In the fourth watch of the night.*
15: 22 {A Gentile} **G** *Canaanite.*
16: 17 {son of John,} **G** *Simon son of Jonah;* see John 1:42; 21:15-17.
16: 18 {powers of hell} **G** *and the gates of Hades.*
17: 4 {make three shrines,} Or *shelters;* **G** reads *tabernacles.*
17: 10 {the Messiah comes} **G** *that Elijah must come first.*
17: 25 {you think, Peter} **G** *Simon.*
18: 8 {to enter heaven} **G** *enter life;* also in 18:9.
18: 20 {they are mine,} **G** *gather together in my name.*
18: 24 {millions of dollars.} **G** *10,000 talents.*
18: 28 {few thousand dollars.} **G** *100 denarii.* A denarius was the equivalent of a full day's wage.
19: 28 {in the Kingdom,} **G** *in the regeneration.*
19: 30 {the greatest then.} **G** *But many who are first will be last; and the last, first.*
20: 2 {normal daily wage} **G** *a denarius,* the payment for a full day's labor; also in 20:9, 10, 13.
21: 5 {people of Israel,} **G** *Tell the daughter of Zion.* Isa 62:11.
21: 7 {sat on it.} **G** *over them, and he sat on them.*
21: 9 {"Praise God} **G** *Hosanna,* an exclamation of praise that literally means "save now"; also in 21:9b, 15.
22: 19 {him the coin,} **G** *a denarius.*
22: 31 {died, God said,} **G** *in the Scriptures? God said.*
23: 5 {Scripture verses inside,} **G** *They enlarge their phylacteries.*
23: 23 {of your income,} **G** *to tithe the mint, the dill, and the cumin.*
24: 15 {that causes desecration} **G** *the abomination of desolation.* See Dan 9:27; 11:31; 12:11.
24: 17 {outside the house} **G** *on the roof.*
24: 28 {end is near.} **G** *Wherever the carcass is, the vultures gather.*
25: 15 {bags of gold} **G** *talents;* also throughout the story. A talent is equal to 75 pounds or 34 kilograms.
26: 7 {beautiful jar} **G** *an alabaster jar.*

26:31 {'God'} G *I.*
26:53 {Father for thousands} G *12 legions.*
26:59 {entire high council} G *the Sanhedrin.*
27:9[-10] {the Lord directed.} G *as the Lord directed me.* Zech 11:12-13; Jer 32:6-9.
27:25 {and our children!"} G *"His blood be on us and on our children."*
27:35 {by throwing dice.} G *by casting lots.* A few late manuscripts add *This fulfilled the word of the prophet: "They divided my clothes among themselves and cast lots for my robe."* See Ps 22:18.
28:1 {on Sunday morning,} G *After the Sabbath, on the first day of the week.*
Mk 1:4 {to be forgiven.} G *preaching a baptism of repentance for the forgiveness of sins.*
1:7 {be his slave.} G *to stoop down and untie his sandals.*
2:16 {who were Pharisees} G *the scribes of the Pharisees.*
2:16 {with such scum} G *with tax collectors and sinners.*
3:17 {"Sons of Thunder"} G *whom he named Boanerges, which means Sons of Thunder.*
3:18 {Simon (the Zealot)} G *the Cananean.*
3:22 {possessed by Satan,} G *Beelzeboul.*
5:20 {the Ten Towns} G *Decapolis.*
5:41 {up, little girl!"} G text uses Aramaic *"Talitha cumi"* and then translates it as "Get up, little girl."
6:3 {of James, Joseph,} G *Joses;* see Matt 13:55.
6:37 {a small fortune} G *200 denarii.* A denarius was the equivalent of a full day's wage.
6:48 {in the morning} G *About the fourth watch of the night.*
7:3 {their cupped hands,} G *washed with the fist.*
7:4 {pitchers, and kettles.} Some G manuscripts add *and dining couches.*
7:11 {given to you.'} G *'What I could have given to you is Corban' (that is, a gift).*
7:24 {region of Tyre.} Some G manuscripts add *and Sidon.*
7:27 {family, the Jews.} G *Let the children eat first.*
7:31 {the Ten Towns.} G *Decapolis.*
7:34 {commanded, "Be opened!"} G text uses Aramaic *"Ephphatha"* and then translates it as "Be opened."
9:5 {make three shrines} Or *shelters;* G reads *tabernacles.*
9:43 {to enter heaven} G *enter life;* also in 9:45.
9:49 {purified with fire.} G *salted with fire.* Some manuscripts add *and every sacrifice will be salted with salt.*
10:31 {the greatest then.} G *But many who are first will be last; and the last, first.*
11:9 {"Praise God!} G *Hosanna,* an exclamation of praise that literally means "save now"; also in 11:10.
11:19 {and the disciples} G *they;* some manuscripts read *he.*
12:15 {a Roman coin,} G *a denarius.*
12:26 {said to Moses,} G *in the story of the bush? God said to him.*
12:42 {in two pennies.} G *2 lepta, which is a kodrantes.*
13:6 {be the Messiah.} G *name, saying, 'I am.'*
13:14 {that causes desecration} G *the abomination of desolation.* See Dan 9:27; 11:31; 12:11.
13:15 {outside the house} G *on the roof.*
14:3 {of expensive perfume.} G *an alabaster jar of expensive ointment, pure nard.*
14:5 {small fortune} G *300 denarii.* A denarius was the equivalent of a full day's wage.
14:27 {'God} G *I.*
14:55 {entire high council} G *the Sanhedrin.*
15:1 {entire high council} G *the Sanhedrin;* also in 15:43.
15:16 {into their headquarters} G *the courtyard, which is the praetorium.*
15:24 {clothes, throwing dice} G *casting lots.* See Ps 22:18.
15:40 {and of Joseph} G *Joses;* also in 15:47. See Matt 27:56.
15:42 {day of preparation,} G *on the day of preparation.*
16:2 {on Sunday morning,} G *on the first day of the week;* also in 16:9.
Lk 1:33 {reign over Israel} G *over the house of Jacob.*
3:1 {Antipas was ruler} G *Herod was tetrarch.* Herod Antipas was a son of King Herod.
3:1 {Philip was ruler} G *tetrarch;* also in 3:1c, 19.
3:3 {to be forgiven.} G *preaching a baptism of repentance for the forgiveness of sins.*
3:16 {be his slave.} G *to untie his sandals.*
3:32 {son of Salmon.} G *Sala;* see Ruth 4:22.
3:38 {son of Enosh.} G *Enos;* see Gen 5:6.
5:1 {Sea of Galilee,} G *Lake Gennesaret,* another name for the Sea of Galilee.
5:30 {with such scum} G *with tax collectors and sinners.*
7:37 {a beautiful jar} G *an alabaster jar.*
7:41 {pieces of silver} G *500 denarii.* A denarius was the equivalent of a full day's wage.
9:7 {reached Herod Antipas,} G *Herod the tetrarch.* He was a son of King Herod and was one of four rulers in Palestine.
9:33 {make three shrines} Or *shelters;* G reads *tabernacles.*
9:60 {their own dead.} G *Let the dead bury their own dead.*
10:15 {of the dead.} G *to Hades.*
10:32 {A Temple assistant} G *A Levite.*
10:35 {pieces of silver} G *2 denarii.* A denarius was the equivalent of a full day's wage.
11:8 {won't be damaged.} G *in order to avoid shame, or because of [your] persistence.*
11:15 {power from Satan,} G *Beelzeboul.*
11:18 {prince of demons.} G *by Beelzeboul;* also in 11:19.
11:21 {For when Satan,} G *the strong one.*
11:31 {queen of Sheba} G *the queen of the south.*
11:42 {of your income,} G *to tithe the mint and the rue and every herb.*
11:49 {said about you:} G *Therefore, the wisdom of God said.*
12:38 {just before dawn.} G *in the second or third watch.*
13:16 {this dear woman} G *this woman, a daughter of Abraham.*
13:21 {a large amount} G *3 measures.*
13:30 {be despised then.} G *Some are last who will be first, and some are first who will be last.*
14:26 {me more than} G *you must hate.*
15:8 {valuable silver coins} G *10 drachmas.* A drachma was the equivalent of a full day's wage.
16:6 {four hundred gallons.} G *100 baths...50 [baths].*
16:7 {eight hundred bushels.} G *100 korous...80 [korous].*
16:22 {be with Abraham.} G *into Abraham's bosom.*
16:23 {of the dead.} G *to Hades.*
17:31 {outside the house} G *on the roof.*
17:37 {end is near."} G *Wherever the carcass is, the vultures gather.*
19:13 {pounds of silver} G *10 minas;* 1 mina was worth about 3 months' wages.
20:24 {a Roman coin.} G *a denarius.*
20:37 {to the Lord} G *when he wrote about the burning bush, he referred to the Lord.*
21:2 {in two pennies.} G *2 lepta.*
21:8 {be the Messiah} G *name, saying, 'I am.'*
22:66 {this high council,} G *before their Sanhedrin.*
23:34 {by throwing dice.} G *by casting lots.* See Ps 22:18.
23:48 {in deep sorrow.} G *beating their breasts.*
23:54 {day of preparation} G *on the day of preparation.*
24:1 {on Sunday morning} G *But on the first day of the week, very early in the morning.*
24:13 {Emmaus, seven miles} G *60 stadia* [11.1 kilometers].
24:34 {appeared to Peter} G *Simon.*
Jn 1:14 {love and faithfulness.} G *grace and truth;* also in 1:17.
1:16 {blessing after another} G *grace upon grace.*
1:19 {and Temple assistants} G *and Levites.*
1:27 {be his slave.} G *to untie his sandals.*
2:1 {The next day} G *On the third day;* see 1:35, 43.
2:6 {to thirty gallons} G *2 or 3 measures* [75 to 113 liters].
3:5 {and the Spirit.} Or *spirit.* The G word for *Spirit* can also be translated *wind;* see 3:8.
3:7 {statement that you} The G word for *you* is plural; also in 3:12.
3:14 {on a pole,} G *must be lifted up.*
4:20 {at Mount Gerizim,} G *on this mountain.*
4:26 {am the Messiah!"} G *"I am, the one speaking to you."*
6:7 {small fortune} G *200 denarii.* A denarius was the equivalent of a full day's wage.
6:19 {or four miles} G *25 or 30 stadia* [4.6 or 5.5 kilometers].
6:41 {Then the people} G *Jewish people;* also in 6:52.
8:31 {the people} G *Jewish people;* also in 8:48, 52, 57.
9:24 {telling the truth,} Or *Give glory to God, not to Jesus;* G reads *Give glory to God.*
10:19 {things, the people} G *Jewish people.*
11:16 {nicknamed the Twin,} G *the one who was called Didymus.*
11:18 {a few miles} G *was about 15 stadia* [about 2.8 kilometers].
11:19 {of the people} G *Jewish people;* also in 11:31, 33, 36, 45, 54.
11:47 {the high council} G *the Sanhedrin.*
12:3 {twelve-ounce jar} G *took 1 litra* [327 grams].
12:5 {small fortune.} G *300 denarii.* A denarius was equivalent to a full day's wage.
12:9 {all the people} G *Jewish people;* also in 12:11.
12:13 {"Praise God!} G *Hosanna,* an exclamation of praise that literally means "save now."
12:15 {people of Israel.} G *daughter of Zion.*
13:23 {at the table.} G *was reclining on Jesus' bosom.* The "disciple whom Jesus loved" was probably John.
14:16 {you another Counselor,} Or *Comforter,* or *Encourager,* or *Advocate.* G *Paraclete;* also in 14:26.
15:26 {you the Counselor} Or *Comforter,* or *Encourager,* or *Advocate.* G *Paraclete.*
16:7 {don't, the Counselor} Or *Comforter,* or *Encourager,* or *Advocate.* G *Paraclete.*
17:12 {kept them safe.} G *I have kept in your name those whom you have given me.*
18:5 {"I am he,"} G *I am;* also in 18:6, 8.
18:20 {heard by people} G *Jewish people;* also in 18:38.
19:14 {to the people,} G *Jewish people;* also in 19:20.
19:24 {but throw dice} G *cast lots.*
19:39 {about seventy-five pounds} G *100 litras* [32.7 kilograms].
20:1 {Early Sunday morning,} G *On the first day of the week.*
20:16 {and exclaimed, "Teacher!"} G *and said in Hebrew, "Rabboni," which means "Teacher."*
20:24 {(nicknamed the Twin} G *the one who was called Didymus.*
21:1 {Sea of Galilee.} G *Sea of Tiberias,* another name for the Sea of Galilee.
21:2 {(nicknamed the Twin} G *the one who was called Didymus.*
21:8 {three hundred feet.} G *200 cubits* [90 meters].
21:23 {community of believers} G *the brothers.*
Ac 1:12 {the half mile} G *a Sabbath day's journey.*
2:1 {after Jesus' resurrection,} G *When the day of Pentecost arrived.* This annual celebration came 50 days after the Passover ceremonies. See Lev 23:16.
2:27 {among the dead} G *in Hades;* also in 2:31.
2:39 {to the Gentiles} G *to those far away.*
3:17 {"Friends,} G *Brothers.*
4:4 {women and children.} G *5,000 adult males.*
4:15 {the council chamber} G *the Sanhedrin.*
5:21 {the high council,} G *Sanhedrin;* also in 5:27, 41.
5:42 {in their homes,} G *from house to house.*
6:1 {as the believers} G *disciples;* also in 6:2, 7.
6:3 {among yourselves, friends,} G *brothers.*
6:12 {the high council.} G *Sanhedrin;* also in 6:15.
7:12 {sent his sons} G *our fathers;* also in 7:15.
7:44 {carried the Tabernacle} G *the tent of witness.*
7:53 {hands of angels.} G *received the Law as it was ordained by angels.*
7:54 {fists in rage.} G *they were grinding their teeth against him.*
8:27 {queen of Ethiopia.} G *under the Candace, the queen of Ethiopia.*
9:1 {the Lord's followers,} G *disciples.*
9:10 {was a believer} G *disciple;* also in 9:36.
9:19 {with the believers} G *disciples;* also in 9:26.
9:25 {the other believers} G *his disciples.*
9:30 {When the believers} G *brothers.*
9:36 {Greek is Dorcas} The names *Tabitha* in Aramaic and *Dorcas* in G both mean "gazelle."
10:14 {our Jewish laws.} G *anything common and unclean.*
10:15 {say it isn't."} G *"What God calls clean you must not call unclean."*
10:23 {some other believers} G *brothers.*
10:41 {the general public,} G *the people.*
11:1 {and other believers} G *brothers;* also in 11:29b.
11:2 {the Jewish believers} G *those of the circumcision.*
11:3 {home of Gentiles} G *of uncircumcised men.*
11:8 {our Jewish laws.} G *anything common or unclean.*
11:9 {say it isn't.'} G *'What God calls clean you must not call unclean.'*
11:20 {preaching to Gentiles} G *the Greeks;* other manuscripts read *the Hellenists.*
11:26 {that the believers} G *disciples;* also in 11:29a.
12:1 {King Herod Agrippa} G *Herod the king.* He was the nephew of Herod Antipas and a grandson of Herod the Great.
12:3 {the Passover celebration} G *the days of unleavened bread.*
13:1 {"the black man"} G *who was called Niger.*
13:1 {King Herod Antipas} G *Herod the tetrarch.*
13:25 {be his slave.} G *to untie his sandals.*
13:52 {And the believers} G *the disciples.*
14:15 {"Friends,} G *Men.*
14:20 {as the believers} G *disciples;* also in 14:22, 28.
15:1 {teach the Christians} G *brothers;* also in 15:32, 33.
15:3 {visit the believers.} G *brothers;* also in 15:23, 36, 40.
15:10 {the Gentile believers} G *disciples.*
15:14 {Peter} G *Simon.*
16:2 {by the believers} G *brothers;* also in 16:40.
17:6 {the other believers} G *brothers;* also in 17:10, 14.
17:19 {Council of Philosophers.} G *the Areopagus.*
17:22 {before the Council,} Or *in the middle of Mars Hill;* G reads *in the middle of the Areopagus.*
17:30 {turn to him.} G *everywhere to repent.*
17:34 {of the Council,} G *an Areopagite.*
18:1 {went to Corinth.} *Athens* and *Corinth* were major cities in Achaia, the region on the southern end of the G peninsula.
18:18 {to the Christians} G *brothers;* also in 18:27.
18:22 {church at Jerusalem} G *the church.*
18:23 {all the believers,} G *disciples;* also in 18:27.
19:1 {found several believers.} G *disciples;* also in 19:9, 30.
19:19 {several million dollars.} G *50,000 pieces of silver,* each of which was the equivalent of a day's wage.
20:1 {for the believers} G *disciples.*
20:6 {the Passover season} G *the days of unleavened bread.*
20:7 {the Lord's Supper.} G *to break bread.*
20:11 {Lord's Supper together.} G *broke the bread.*
20:22 {the Holy Spirit,} Or *by my spirit,* or *by an inner compulsion;* G reads *by the spirit.*
20:26 {blamed on me,} G *I am innocent of the blood of all.*
20:28 {you as elders.} G *overseers.*
21:4 {the local believers,} G *disciples;* also in 21:16.
21:7 {greeted the believers} G *brothers;* also in 21:17.
21:29 {Gentile from Ephesus,} G *Trophimus, the Ephesian.*
22:2 {their own language,} G *in Aramaic.*
22:30 {Jewish high council.} G *Sanhedrin.*

23: 1 {the high council,} **G** *Sanhedrin;* also in 23:6, 15, 20, 28.
24: 1 {and the lawyer} **G** *some elders and an orator.*
24:20 {Jewish high council} **G** *Sanhedrin.*
25:13 {his sister, Bernice,} **G** *Agrippa the king and Bernice arrived.*
26: 9 {Jesus of Nazareth.} **G** *oppose the name of Jesus the Nazarene.*
26:14 {against my will.} **G** *It is hard for you to kick against the oxgoads.*
27: 9 {in the fall,} **G** *because the fast was now already gone by.* This fast happened on the Day of Atonement (*Yom Kippur*), which occurred in late September or early October.
27:28 {found only 90 feet.} **G** *20 fathoms...15 fathoms* [37 meters...27 meters].
28:14 {found some believers,} **G** *brothers;* also in 28:15.
28:22 {about these Christians} **G** *this sect.*
Ro 1:13 {know, dear friends,} **G** *brothers.*
1:19 {to them instinctively.} **G** *is manifest in them.*
3: 2 {revelation of God.} **G** *the oracles of God.*
3: 9 {better than others?} **G** *Are we better?*
7: 1 {Now, dear friends} **G** *brothers;* also in 7:4.
7:24 {dominated by sin?} **G** *from this body of death?*
8: 2 {For the power} **G** *the law;* also in 8:2b.
8:12 {dear Christian friends,} **G** *brothers.*
8:13 {turn from it} **G** *put it to death.*
8:15 {"Father, dear Father."} **G** *"Abba, Father." Abba* is an Aramaic term for "father."
9:33 {stone in Jerusalem} **G** *in Zion.*
10: 1 {Dear friends,} **G** *Brothers.*
11: 5 {God. A few} **G** *A remnant.*
11:16 {also be holy.} **G** *If the dough offered as firstfruits is holy, so is the whole lump.*
11:25 {dear friends,} **G** *brothers.*
11:26 {come from Jerusalem,} **G** *from Zion.*
11:26 {will turn Israel} **G** *Jacob.*
12: 1 {dear Christian friends,} **G** *brothers.*
12:20 {done to you."} **G** *and you will heap burning coals on their heads.* Prov 25:21-22.
14:10 {condemn another Christian} **G** *your brother;* also in 14:10b, 13, 15, 21.
15:12 {to David's throne} **G** *The root of Jesse.*
15:14 {convinced, dear friends,} **G** *brothers;* also in 15:30.
15:26 {believers in Greece} **G** *Macedonia and Achaia,* the northern and southern regions of Greece.
16:14 {the other Christians} **G** *brothers.*
16:16 {in Christian love.} **G** *with a sacred kiss.*
16:26 {as the prophets} **G** *the prophetic writings.*
1Co 1:11 {arguments, dear friends.} **G** *my brothers.*
1:12 {"I follow Peter,} **G** *Cephas.*
1:24 {Jews and Gentiles,} **G** *Greeks.*
2: 1 {you God's message.} **G** *mystery;* other manuscripts read *testimony.*
2: 7 {wisdom of God,} **G** *we speak God's wisdom in a mystery.*
3: 1 {the Christian life.} **G** *in Christ.*
3: 4 {are not Christians?} **G** *aren't you merely human?*
3:22 {Apollos and Peter} **G** *Cephas.*
5: 5 {will be destroyed} Or *so that he will die;* **G** reads *for the destruction of the flesh.*
5: 5 {and he himself} **G** *and the spirit.*
5: 6[-7] {can stay pure.} **G** *Don't you realize that even a little leaven spreads quickly through the whole batch of dough? [7]Purge out the old leaven so that you can be a new batch of dough, just as you are already unleavened.*
5: 8 {the old bread} **G** *not with old leaven.*
5: 8 {the new bread} **G** *but with unleavened [bread].*
5:11 {be a Christian} **G** *a brother.*
6: 6 {instead, one Christian} **G** *one brother.*
7:12 {a Christian man} **G** *a brother.*
7:23 {by the world.} **G** *don't become slaves of people.*
7:39 {to the Lord.} Or *but only to a Christian;* **G** reads *but only in the Lord.*
8:11 {a weak Christian,} **G** *brother;* also in 8:13.
8:12 {against other Christians} **G** *brothers.*
9: 1 {as anyone else?} **G** *Am I not free?*
9: 3 {as an apostle.} **G** *those who examine me.*
9: 5 {Christian wife} **G** *a sister, a wife.*
9: 5 {brothers and Peter} **G** *Cephas.*
9:21 {the Jewish law,} **G** *those without the law.*
10: 3 {the same miraculous} **G** *spiritual;* also in 10:4.
11: 4 {man dishonors Christ} **G** *his head.*
11: 5 {dishonors her husband} **G** *her head.*
11:29 {body of Christ,} **G** *the body;* some manuscripts read *the Lord's body.*
12:13 {the same Spirit.} **G** *we were all given one Spirit to drink.*
13: 1 {or on earth} **G** *in tongues of people and angels.*
13:12 {with perfect clarity.} **G** *see face to face.*
14:21 {in the Scriptures,} **G** *in the law.*
15: 5 {seen by Peter} **G** *Cephas.*
15: 6 {of his followers} **G** *the brothers.*
15:24 {of every kind.} **G** *every ruler and every authority and power.*
15:31 {swear, dear friends,} **G** *brothers.*
15:32 {men of Ephesus} **G** *fighting wild beasts in Ephesus.*
15:52 {who have died} **G** *the dead.*
16: 2 {every Lord's Day,} **G** *every first day of the week.*
16:11 {the other believers.} **G** *the brothers;* also in 16:12, 20.
16:15 {Christians in Greece,} **G** *were the firstfruits in Achaia,* the southern region of the **G** peninsula.
16:20 {in Christian love.} **G** *with a sacred kiss.*
2Co 1: 1 {Christians throughout Greece.} **G** *Achaia,* the southern region of the **G** peninsula.
1: 3 {is the source} **G** *the Father.*
1: 8 {know, dear friends,} **G** *brothers.*
1:19 {Silas,} **G** *Silvanus.*
1:24 {faith into practice.} **G** *want to lord it over your faith.*
4: 7 {our weak bodies.} **G** *But we have this treasure in earthen vessels.*
4:16 {our spirits are} **G** *our inner being is.*
5:14 {used to live.} **G** *Since one died on behalf of all, then all died.*
6:15 {and the Devil} **G** *and Beliar.*
8: 1 {you, dear friends,} **G** *brothers.*
8:23 {brothers are representatives} **G** *apostles.*
9: 1 {Christians in Jerusalem.} **G** *about the offering for the saints.*
9: 2 {Christians in Greece} **G** *Achaia,* the southern region of the **G** peninsula.
9:10 {harvest of generosity} **G** *righteousness.*
9:15 {wonderful for words!} **G** *Thank God for his indescribable gift.*
11: 2 {pure bride} **G** *a virgin.*
11:10 {all over Greece.} **G** *Achaia.*
11:26 {but are not.} **G** *from false brothers.*
12: 2 {I} **G** *I know a man in Christ who.*
12: 4 {know that I} **G** *he.*
13:11 {Dear friends,} **G** *Brothers.*
13:12 {in Christian love.} **G** *with a sacred kiss.*
Gal 1: 2 {All the Christians} **G** *brothers.*
1:11 {Dear friends,} **G** *Brothers.*
1:13 {persecuted the Christians.} **G** *the church of God.*
1:18 {visit with Peter} **G** *Cephas.*
2: 3 {was a Gentile.} **G** *a G.*
2: 4 {there—false ones, really} **G** *some false brothers.*
2: 9 {fact, James, Peter,} **G** *Cephas;* also in 2:11, 14.
3:15 {Dear friends,} **G** *Brothers.*
3:16 {and his child.} **G** *seed;* also in 3:16c, 19. See Gen 12:7.
3:16 {to his children,} **G** *seeds.*
3:28 {Jew or Gentile,} **G** *Jew or G.*
4: 6 {dear Father.} **G** *into your hearts, crying, "Abba, Father."* Abba is an Aramaic term for "Father."
4:12 {Dear friends,} **G** *brothers;* also in 4:31.
5:11 {Dear friends,} **G** *brothers;* also in 5:13.
5:12 {would mutilate themselves.} Or *castrate themselves;* **G** reads *cut themselves off.*
6: 1 {if a Christian} **G** *Brothers, if a man.*
6:16 {people of God.} **G** *the Israel of God.*
6:18 {dear Christian friends,} **G** *Brothers.*
Eph 4:17 {as the ungodly} **G** *Gentiles.*
5:26 {and God's word.} **G** *having cleansed her by the washing of water with the word.*
6:16 {you by Satan.} **G** *by the evil one.*
6:19 {the Gentiles, too.} **G** *explain the mystery of the gospel.*
6:23 {peace, dear friends,} **G** *brothers.*
Php 1: 1 {to the elders} **G** *overseers.*
1:11 {of your salvation} **G** *the fruit of righteousness.*
1:12 {know, dear friends,} **G** *brothers.*
1:14 {of the Christians} **G** *brothers in the Lord.*
2: 7 {in human form.} **G** *he was born in the likeness of men and was found in appearance as a man.*
2:29 {with Christian love} **G** *in the Lord.*
3: 1 {happens, dear friends,} **G** *brothers;* also in 3:13, 17.
4: 3 {my true teammate,} **G** *true yokefellow,* or *loyal Syzygus.*
4: 8 {now, dear friends,} **G** *brothers.*
Col 1: 7 {in your place.} **G** *he is ministering on your behalf;* other manuscripts read *he is ministering on our behalf.*
1:15 {over all creation.} **G** *He is the firstborn of all creation.*
1:18 {from the dead,} **G** *He is the beginning, the firstborn from the dead.*
2: 9 {human body,} **G** *in him dwells all the fullness of the Godhead bodily.*
3:11 {or a Gentile,} **G** *G.*
3:11 {uncircumcised, barbaric, uncivilized,} **G** *Barbarian, Scythian.*
1Th 1: 1 {from Paul, Silas,} **G** *Silvanus.*
1: 7 {Christians in Greece.} **G** *Macedonia and Achaia,* the northern and southern regions of Greece; also in 1:8.
2:17 {Dear friends,} **G** *Brothers.*
3: 7 {comforted, dear friends,} **G** *brothers.*
4: 4 {control your body} Or *will know how to take a wife for himself;* **G** reads *will know how to possess his own vessel.*
4: 6 {cheat another Christian} **G** *a brother.*
4:10 {all the Christians} **G** *the brothers.*
4:10 {dear friends,} **G** *brothers.*
5:26 {in Christian love.} **G** *Greet all the brothers with a holy kiss.*
5:27 {all the Christians.} **G** *the brothers.*
2Th 1: 1 {from Paul, Silas,} **G** *Silvanus.*
2: 3 {who brings destruction.} **G** *the son of destruction.*
3: 6 {from any Christian} **G** *brother;* also in 3:15.
1Ti 1: 4 {and spiritual pedigrees.} **G** *in myths and endless genealogies, which cause speculation.*
1: 4 {faith in God.} **G** *a stewardship of God in faith.*
3: 1 {be an elder,} **G** *overseer;* also in 3:2.
3: 2 {to his wife.} **G** *be the husband of one wife;* also in 3:12.
3:11 {their wives} Or *the women deacons.* The **G** word can be translated *women* or *wives.*
3:16 {Christ} **G** *Who;* some manuscripts read *God.*
3:16 {up into heaven.} **G** *in glory.*
4: 2 {consciences are dead.} **G** *are seared.*
5: 7 {widows you support} Or *so the church;* **G** reads *so they.*
5: 9 {to her husband.} **G** *was the wife of one man.*
5:10 {other Christians humbly?} **G** *Has she washed the feet of saints?*
5:17 {be paid well,} **G** *should be worthy of double honor.*
6: 2 {helping another believer} **G** *a brother.*
2Ti 3: 6 {the confidence of} **G** *and take captive.*
4:13 {especially my papers.} **G** *especially the parchments.*
4:17 {from certain death.} **G** *from the mouth of a lion.*
Tit 1: 6 {to his wife,} Or *have only one wife,* or *be married only once;* **G** reads *be the husband of one wife.*
1: 7 {An elder} **G** *overseer.*
3: 5 {the Holy Spirit.} **G** *He saved us through the washing of regeneration and renewing of the Holy Spirit.*
3: 9 {about spiritual pedigrees} **G** *discussions and genealogies.*
Heb 1: 6 {presented his honored} **G** *firstborn.*
2:11 {brothers and sisters.} **G** *his brothers;* also in 2:17.
2:12 {brothers and sisters.} **G** *my brothers.* Ps 22:22.
3: 1 {belong to God} **G** *holy brothers.*
3:12 {then, dear friends.} **G** *brothers.*
7: 5 {their own relatives.} **G** *their brothers, who are descendants of Abraham.*
7:11 {Levi and Aaron?} **G** *according to the order of Aaron.*
9: 6 {the first room} **G** *first tent;* also in 9:8.
9:24 {as our Advocate.} **G** *on our behalf.*
10:19 {so, dear friends,} **G** *brothers.*
10:20 {death for us.} **G** *his flesh.*
11:40 {finish the race.} **G** *for us, for they apart from us can't finish.*
13: 1 {true Christian love.} **G** *with brotherly love.*
13:22 {you, dear friends,} **G** *brothers.*
Jas 1: 1 {among the nations.} **G** *To the twelve tribes in the dispersion.*
1: 9 {Christians who are} **G** *The brother who is.*
1:17 {all heaven's lights.} **G** *from above, from the Father of lights.*
1:19 {Dear friends,} **G** *Know this, my beloved brothers.*
2: 2 {into your meeting} **G** *synagogue.*
1Pe 2: 6 {stone in Jerusalem,} **G** *in Zion.*
3:20 {that terrible flood.} **G** *saved through water.*
5: 9 {Remember that Christians} **G** *your brothers.*
5:12 {help of Silas,} **G** *Silvanus.*
5:13 {here in Rome} **G** *The elect one in Babylon.* Babylon was probably a code name for Rome.
5:14 {in Christian love.} **G** *with a kiss of love.*
2Pe 1: 1 {is from Simon} **G** *Simeon.*
1:10 {So, dear friends,} **G** *brothers.*
1:14 {soon to die.} **G** *I must soon put off this earthly tent.*
2: 4 {them into hell,} **G** *Tartaros.*
2:11 {out disrespectfully against} **G** *never bring blasphemous judgment from the Lord against.*
1Jn 1: 1 {from the beginning} **G** *What was from the beginning.*
2: 1 {pleases God completely.} **G** *Jesus Christ, the righteous.*
2: 9 {rejects another Christian} **G** *hates his brother;* also in 2:11.
2:20 {come upon you,} **G** *But you have an anointing from the Holy One.*
2:27 {the Holy Spirit,} **G** *the anointing.*
3:10 {love other Christians} **G** *his brother;* also in 3:15.
3:14 {love other Christians,} **G** *the brothers.*
3:16 {our Christian friends.} **G** *the brothers.*
4:19 {love each other} Or *We love him;* **G** reads *We love.*
4:20 {hates another Christian,} **G** *brother.*
5: 6 {on the cross} **G** *This is he who came by water and blood.*
5:16 {see any Christian} **G** *your brother.*
5:21 {in your hearts.} **G** *keep yourselves from idols.*
2Jn 1: 1 {John, the Elder.} **G** *From the elder.*
3Jn 1: 1 {John, the Elder.} **G** *From the elder.*
1: 7 {for the Lord} **G** *the Name.*
1: 7 {are not Christians.} **G** *from Gentiles.*
Jude 1: 3 {the Good News.} **G** *to contend for the faith.*
1:20 {the Holy Spirit.} **G** *Pray in the Holy Spirit.*
1:23 {by their sins.} **G** *mercy, hating even the clothing stained by the flesh.*
Rev 1: 4 {the sevenfold Spirit} **G** *the seven spirits.*
1:13 {Son of Man.} Or *one who looked like a man;* **G** reads *one like a son of man.*
1:18 {and the grave.} **G** *and Hades.*
3: 1 {the sevenfold Spirit} **G** *the seven spirits.*
5: 5 {to David's throne,} **G** *the root of David.*
6: 6 {day's pay.} **G** *A choinix of wheat for a denarius, and 3 choinix of barley for a denarius.*
6: 8 {by the Grave.} **G** *by Hades.*
6: 8 {famine and disease} **G** *death.*
8:11 {star was Bitterness.} **G** *Wormwood.*
11: 8 {street of Jerusalem,} **G** *the great city.*
12:14 {from the dragon} **G** *the serpent;* also in 12:15. See 12:9.
14: 4 {pure as virgins,} **G** *they are virgins who have not defiled themselves with women.*
14: 4 {a special offering} **G** *as firstfruits.*
14:14 {Son of Man} Or *one who looked like a man;* **G** reads *one like a son of man.*

14:20 {about 180 miles} **G** *1,600 stadia* [296 kilometers].
16:21 {weighing seventy-five pounds} **G** *1 talent* [34 kilograms].
19:10 {and other believers} **G** *brothers.*
20:13 {and the grave} **G** *and Hades;* also in 20:14.
21:16 {each 1,400 miles.} **G** *12,000 stadia* [2,220 kilometers].
21:17 {216 feet thick} **G** *144 cubits* [65 meters].
22:16 {to his throne.} **G** *I am the root and offspring of David.*

GREEKS (2)
Ac 11:20 {preaching to Gentiles} Greek *the **G**;* other manuscripts read *the Hellenists.*
1Co 1:24 {Jews and Gentiles,} Greek **G**.

GRIEVOUSLY (1)
1Sa 10:27 {Saul ignored them.} Dead Sea Scroll 4QSam[a] continues: *Nahash, king of the Ammonites, had been **g** oppressing the Gadites and Reubenites…*

GRINDING (1)
Ac 7:54 {fists in rage.} Greek *they were **g** their teeth against him.*

GROUND (1)
Nu 11:31 {above the ground.} Or *there were quail 3 feet* [2 cubits or 90 centimeters] *deep on the **g**.*

GROWL (1)
Ps 59:15 {to sleep unsatisfied.} Or *and **g** if they don't get enough.*

GROWN (1)
Isa 10:27 {from their shoulders.} As in Greek version; Hebrew reads *The yoke will be broken, for you have **g** so fat.*

GUESTS (1)
Zep 1:7 {chosen their executioners.} Hebrew *has prepared a sacrifice and sanctified his **g**.*

GUILT (1)
Lev 17:4 {a capital offense.} Hebrew *blood **g**.*

GUM (1)
Nu 11:7 {yellow in color.} Hebrew *the color of **g** resin.*

GUR-BAAL (1)
2Ch 26:7 {Arabs of Gur} As in Greek version; Hebrew reads **G**.

H

HAB (4)
Ac 13:41 {you about it.'} **H** 1:5.
Ro 1:17 {person has life."} **H** 2:4.
Gal 3:11 {person has life."} **H** 2:4.
Heb 10:37[-38] {who turns away."} **H** 2:3-4.

HADAR (1)
Ge 36:39 {Baal-hanan died, Hadad} As in some Hebrew manuscripts, Samaritan Pentateuch, and Syriac version (see also 1 Chr 1:50); most Hebrew manuscripts read **H**.

HADES (8)
Mt 11:23 {of the dead.} Greek *to **H**.*
16:18 {powers of hell} Greek *and the gates of **H**.*
Lk 10:15 {of the dead.} Greek *to **H**.*
16:23 {of the dead.} Greek *to **H**.*
Ac 2:27 {among the dead} Greek *in **H**;* also in 2:31.
Rev 1:18 {and the grave.} Greek *and **H**.*
6:8 {by the Grave.} Greek *by **H**.*
20:13 {and the grave} Greek *and **H**;* also in 20:14.

HADORAM (2)
1Ch 18:10 {his son Joram} As in parallel text at 2 Sam 8:10; Hebrew reads ***H***, a variant name for Joram.
2Ch 10:18 {Rehoboam sent Adoniram,} Hebrew ***H***, a variant name for Adoniram; compare 1 Kgs 4:6; 5:14; 12:18.

HADRACH (1)
Zec 9:1 {land of Aram} Hebrew *land of **H**.*

HAG (1)
Heb 12:26 {the heavens also."} **H** 2:6.

HAIL (1)
Ps 18:13 {a mighty shout.} As in Greek version (see also 2 Sam 22:14); Hebrew adds *raining down **h** and burning coals.*

HAIR (8)
Ge 25:25 {called him Esau.} *Esau* sounds like a Hebrew term that means "**h**."
1Ki 1:52 {not be harmed.} Hebrew *not a **h** on his head will be touched.*
2Ki 1:8 {hairy man,} Or *He was wearing clothing made of **h**.*
Isa 7:20 {and your people.} Hebrew *shave off the head, the **h** of the legs, and the beard.*
Jer 9:26 {in distant places,} Or *the people who clip the corners of their **h**.*
25:23 {in distant places.} Or *who clip the corners of their **h**.*
49:32 {in distant places.} Or *who clip the corners of their **h**.*
1Co 11:6 {wear a covering.} Or *then she should have long **h**.*

HALF (8)
Ge 24:22 {large gold bracelets} Hebrew *a gold nose-ring weighing a **h** shekel* [0.2 ounces or 6 grams] *and two gold bracelets weighing 10 shekels* [4 ounces or 114 grams].
Ex 30:13 {of an ounce} Hebrew ***h** a shekel* [6 grams], *according to the sanctuary shekel, 20 gerahs to each shekel.*
38:26 {ounce of silver} Hebrew *1 beka* [6 grams] *per person, that is, **h** a shekel, according to the sanctuary shekel.*
1Sa 14:14 {half an acre.} Hebrew ***h** a yoke;* a "yoke" was the amount of land plowed by a pair of yoked oxen in one day.
1Ki 7:35 {rim 9 inches wide.} Hebrew ***h** a cubit wide* [22.5 centimeters].
Zec 5:6 {for measuring grain,} Hebrew *an ephah,* about **h** a bushel or 18 liters; also in 5:7, 8, 9, 10, 11.
14:8 {toward the Mediterranean,} Hebrew ***h** toward the eastern sea and **h** toward the western sea.*

HAM (1)
Ps 78:51 {land of Egypt.} Hebrew *in the tents of **H**.*

HAMRAN (1)
1Ch 1:41 {Dishon were Hemdan,} As in many Hebrew manuscripts and some Greek manuscripts (see also Gen 36:26); most Hebrew manuscripts read **H**.

HAND (10)
Ge 24:3 {"Swear} Hebrew *Put your **h** under my thigh, and I will make you swear.*
24:9 {solemn oath} Hebrew *put his **h** under the thigh of Abraham his master and swore an oath.*
35:18 {called him Benjamin.} *Ben-oni* means "son of my sorrow"; *Benjamin* means "son of my right **h**."
1Sa 14:19 {let's get going!"} Hebrew *Withdraw your **h**.*
Ps 89:25 {in the east.} Hebrew *I will set his **h** on the sea, his right **h** on the rivers.*
Isa 21:16 {within a year,"} Hebrew *Within a year, like the years of a hired **h**.* Some ancient manuscripts read *Within three years,* as in 16:14.
Da 10:16 {like a man} As in most manuscripts of the Masoretic Text; one manuscript of the Masoretic Text and one Greek version read *Then something that looked like a human **h**.*
Mt 5:30 {your stronger hand} Greek *your right **h**.*
26:23 {with me now} Or *The one who has dipped his **h** in the bowl with me.*

HANDBREADTH (7)
Ex 25:25 {about three inches} Hebrew *a **h*** [8 centimeters].
37:12 {rim about 3 inches} Hebrew *a **h*** [8 centimeters].
1Ki 7:26 {about three inches} Hebrew *a **h*** [8 centimeters].
2Ch 4:5 {about three inches} Hebrew *a **h*** [8 centimeters].
Eze 40:5 {was 10 1/2 feet} Hebrew *6 long cubits* [3.2 meters], *each being a cubit* [18 inches or 45 centimeters] *and a **h*** [3 inches or 8 centimeters] *in length.* In this chapter, the distance measures are calculated using the Hebrew long cubit, which equals 21 inches or 53 centimeters.
40:43 {each three inches} Hebrew *a **h*** [8 centimeters].
43:13 {of the altar} Hebrew *measurements of the altar in long cubits, each being a cubit* [18 inches or 45 centimeters] *and a **h*** [3 inches or 8 centimeters] *in length.* In this chapter, the distance measures are calculated using the Hebrew long cubit, which equals 21 inches or 53 centimeters.

HANDLES (1)
2Sa 3:29 {walks on crutches} Or *who is effeminate;* Hebrew reads *who **h** a spindle.*

HANDS (5)
Ex 17:16 {throne, so now} Or ***H** have been lifted up to the LORD's throne, and now.*
2Ki 3:11 {Elijah's personal assistant.} Hebrew *He used to pour water on the **h** of Elijah.*
Da 2:34 {by supernatural means.} Aramaic *not by human **h**;* also in 2:45.
Jnh 4:11 {in spiritual darkness,} Hebrew *people who don't know their right **h** from their left.*
Zec 13:6 {on your chest} Or *scars between your **h**.*

HANUN (1)
1Ch 19:1 {his son Hanun} Hebrew lacks ***H**;* compare parallel text at 2 Sam 10:1.

HAPPEN (1)
Lk 23:31 {it is dry?} Or *If these things are done to me, the living tree, what will **h** to you, the dry tree?*

HAPPY (1)
Ge 30:13 {named him Asher,} *Asher* means "**h**."

HARAN (1)
Ac 7:2 {moved to Haran.} *Mesopotamia* was the region now called Iraq. ***H*** was a city in what is now called Syria.

HARD (1)
Ac 26:14 {against my will.} Greek *It is **h** for you to kick against the oxgoads.*

HAREM (1)
Est 2:14 {the second harem,} Or *to another part of the **h**.*

HARIPH (1)
Ne 7:24 {family of Jorah} As in parallel text at Ezra 2:18; Hebrew reads ***H***.

HARMON (1)
Am 4:3 {from your fortresses.} Hebrew *thrown out toward **H**,* possibly a reference to Mount Hermon.

HARMS (1)
Zec 2:8 {most precious possession.} Hebrew ***h** the apple of my eye.*

HAROR (1)
1Ch 11:27 {Shammah from Harod;} As in parallel text at 2 Sam 23:25; Hebrew reads *Shammoth from **H**.*

HARP (2)
Da 3:7 {the musical instruments,} Aramaic *the horn, flute, zither, lyre, **h**, and other instruments of the musical ensemble.*
3:10 {the musical instruments.} Aramaic *the horn, flute, zither, lyre, **h**, pipes, and other instruments of the musical ensemble;* also in 3:15.

HARVEST (1)
Jer 2:3 {of my children.} Hebrew *the firstfruits of his **h**.*

HASHEM (1)
1Ch 11:34 {sons of Jashen} As in parallel text at 2 Sam 23:32; Hebrew reads *sons of **H**.*

HASRAH (1)
2Ch 34:22 {grandson of Harhas,} As in parallel text at 2 Kgs 22:14; Hebrew reads *son of Tokhath, son of **H**.*

HASSOPHERETH (1)
Ezr 2:55 {Sotai, Sophereth,} As in parallel text at Neh 7:57; Hebrew reads ***H***.

HATE (2)
Mt 5:44 {love your enemies!} Some manuscripts add *Bless those who curse you, do good to those who **h** you.*
Lk 14:26 {me more than} Greek *you must **h**.*

HATES (1)
1Jn 2:9 {rejects another Christian} Greek ***h** his brother;* also in 2:11.

HATING (1)
Jude 1:23 {by their sins.} Greek *mercy, **h** even the clothing stained by the flesh.*

HAVVOTH-JAIR (4)
Nu 32:41 {Towns of Jair.} Hebrew ***H***.
Dt 3:14 {Towns of Jair,} Hebrew ***H***.
Jdg 10:4 {Towns of Jair.} Hebrew ***H***.
1Ch 2:23 {Towns of Jair} Or *captured **H**.*

HEAD (6)
Ge 47:31 {on his staff.} As in Greek version; Hebrew reads *bowed in worship at the **h** of his bed.*
Lev 21:10 {hair hang loose} Or *uncover his **h**.*
1Ki 1:52 {not be harmed.} Hebrew *not a hair on his **h** will be touched.*
Isa 7:20 {and your people.} Hebrew *shave off the **h**, the hair of the legs, and the beard.*
1Co 11:4 {man dishonors Christ} Greek *his **h**.*
11:5 {dishonors her husband} Greek *her **h**.*

HEADS (3)
Lev 10:6 {hair hang loose} Or *by uncovering your **h**.*
13:45 {to hang loose.} Or *and uncover their **h**.*
Ro 12:20 {done to you."} Greek *and you will heap burning coals on their **h**.* Prov 25:21-22.

HEALED (1)

Jn 5: 3 {on the porches.} Some manuscripts add *waiting for a certain movement of the water, [4]for an angel of the Lord came from time to time and stirred up the water. And the first person to step down into it afterward was **h**.*

HEALING (1)

Mal 4: 2 {in his wings.} Or *the sun of righteousness will rise with **h** in its wings.*

HEAP (1)

Ro 12:20 {done to you."} Greek *and you will **h** burning coals on their heads.* Prov 25:21-22.

HEAR (1)

Mk 7:15 {say and do!} Some manuscripts add verse 16, *Anyone who is willing to **h** should listen and understand.*

HEARD (4)

1Sa 1:20 {named him Samuel,} *Samuel* sounds like the Hebrew term for "asked of God" or "**h** by God."
Ps 19: 3 {in the skies;} Or *There is no speech or language where their voice is not **h**.*
Jer 48: 4 {will cry out.} Greek version reads *Her cries are **h** as far away as Zoar.*
Eze 3:12 {in his place!)} A likely reading for this verse is *Then the Spirit lifted me up, and as the glory of the LORD rose from its place, I **h** behind me a loud rumbling sound.*

HEARS (2)

Ge 16:11 {name him Ishmael,} *Ishmael* means "God **h**."
29:33 {named him Simeon,} *Simeon* probably means "one who **h**."

HEART (6)

1Sa 25:37 {had a stroke,} Hebrew *his **h** failed him.*
La 2:18 {Cry aloud} Hebrew *Their **h** cried.*
Eze 36:26 {new, obedient heart.} Hebrew *a **h** of flesh.*
Jn 7:37[-38] {out from within."} Or *"Let anyone who is thirsty come to me and drink. [38]For the Scriptures declare that rivers of living water will flow from the **h** of those who believe in me."*
Ac 8:36 {I be baptized?"} Some manuscripts add verse 37, *"You can," Philip answered, "if you believe with all your **h**." And the eunuch replied, "I believe that Jesus Christ is the Son of God."*
1Pe 1:22 {all your hearts.} Some manuscripts read *with a pure **h**.*

HEARTH (1)

Isa 29: 1 {certain for Ariel,} *Ariel* sounds like a Hebrew term that means "**h**" or "altar."

HEARTHS (1)

Ge 49:14 {among the sheepfolds.} Or *saddlebags,* or ***h**.*

HEARTS (2 of 4)

Lk 9:55 {and rebuked them.} Some manuscripts add *And he said, "You don't realize what your **h** are like. [56]For the Son of Man has not come to destroy men's lives, but to save them."*
Gal 4: 6 {your dear Father.} Greek *into your **h**, crying, "Abba, Father."* Abba is an Aramaic term for "Father."

HEAVEN (7)

Mt 11:12 {people attack it.} Or *until now, eager multitudes have been pressing into the Kingdom of **H**.*
Mk 11:25 {your sins, too.} Some manuscripts add verse 26, *But if you do not forgive, neither will your Father who is in **h** forgive your sins.*
Lk 24:51 {up to heaven.} Some manuscripts do not include *and was taken up to **h**.*
Jn 3:13 {Son of Man,} Some manuscripts add *who lives in **h**.*
3:31 {come from heaven.} Some manuscripts omit *but he has come from **h**.*
Php 3:14 {up to heaven.} Or *from **h**.*
1Jn 5: 7 {these three witnesses} Some very late manuscripts add *in **h**—the Father, the Word, and the Holy Spirit, and these three are one. And we have three witnesses on earth.*

HEBREW (1979)

Ge 1:26 {make people} **H** *man;* also in 1:27.
1:26 {livestock, wild animals,} As in Syriac version; **H** reads *all the earth.*
2:19 {them to Adam} **H** *the man,* and so throughout this chapter.
3: 9 {called to Adam,} **H** *the man,* and so throughout this chapter.
3:20 {his wife Eve,} *Eve* sounds like a **H** term that means "to give life."
3:24 {mighty angelic beings} **H** *cherubim.*
4: 1 {Now Adam} **H** *the man.*
4: 1 {birth to Cain,} *Cain* sounds like a **H** term that can mean "bring forth" or "acquire."
5: 1 {God created people,} **H** *man.*
5: 2 {called them "human."} **H** *man.*
5: 3 {of his father.} **H** *was in his own likeness, after his image.*
5:29 {his son Noah,} *Noah* sounds like a **H** term that can mean "relief" or "comfort."
6: 4 {even afterward, giants} **H** *Nephilim.*
6:15 {45 feet high.} **H** *300 cubits* [135 meters] *long, 50 cubits* [22.5 meters] *wide, and 30 cubits* [13.5 meters] *high.*
6:16 {boat, 18 inches} **H** *1 cubit* [45 centimeters].
7:20 {than twenty-two feet} **H** *15 cubits* [6.8 meters].
8: 4 {the flood began,} **H** *on the seventeenth day of the seventh month;* see 7:11.
8: 5 {half months later,} **H** *On the first day of the tenth month;* see 7:11 and note on 8:4.
8:13 {the flood began,} **H** *on the first day of the first month;* see 7:11.
8:14 {months went by,} **H** *The twenty-seventh day of the second month arrived;* see note on 8:13.
9:27 {prosperity of Shem;} **H** *may he live in the tents of Shem.*
10: 4 {and Rodanim.} As in some **H** manuscripts and Greek version (see also 1 Chr 1:7); most **H** manuscripts read *Dodanim.*
10: 9 {the LORD's sight.} **H** *a mighty hunter before the LORD;* also in 10:9b.
10:10 {land of Babylonia,} **H** *Shinar.*
10:14 {the Philistines came.} **H** *Casluhites, from whom the Philistines came, Caphtorites.* Compare Jer 47:4; Amos 9:7.
11: 2 {land of Babylonia} **H** *Shinar.*
11: 9 {was called Babel,} *Babel* sounds like a **H** term that means "confusion."
12: 7 {to your offspring.} **H** *seed.*
13:15 {and your offspring} **H** *seed.*
14: 1 {Amraphel of Babylonia,} **H** *Shinar;* also in 14:9.
14: 3 {the Dead Sea} **H** *Salt Sea.*
14: 8 {the Dead Sea} **H** *in Siddim Valley;* see 14:3.
15:18 {border of Egypt} **H** *the river of Egypt,* referring either to an eastern branch of the Nile River or to the brook of Egypt in the Sinai (see Num 34:5).
16: 5 {this to me!} **H** *Let the LORD judge between you and me.*
16:13 {who sees me,"} **H** *El-roi.*
17: 7 {and your offspring} **H** *seed;* also in 17:8.
18: 6 {Get three measures} **H** *3 seahs,* about 15 quarts or 18 liters.
19:37 {named him Moab.} *Moab* sounds like a **H** term that means "from father."
20:16 {pieces of silver} **H** *1,000 shekels of silver,* about 25 pounds or 11.4 kilograms in weight.
21:16 {a hundred yards} **H** *a bowshot.*
22:14 {LORD Will Provide."} **H** *Yahweh Yir'eh.*
22:18 {through your descendants,} **H** *seed.*
23:15 {four hundred pieces} **H** *400 shekels,* about 10 pounds or 4.6 kilograms in weight; also in 23:16.
24: 3 {"Swear} **H** *Put your hand under my thigh, and I will make you swear.*
24: 7 {to my offspring.} **H** *seed.*
24: 9 {solemn oath} **H** *put his hand under the thigh of Abraham his master and swore an oath.*
24:22 {large gold bracelets} **H** *a gold nose-ring weighing a half shekel* [0.2 ounces or 6 grams] *and two gold bracelets weighing 10 shekels* [4 ounces or 114 grams].
25:18 {to one another.} The meaning of the **H** is uncertain.
25:25 {called him Esau.} *Esau* sounds like a **H** term that means "hair."
26: 4 {through your descendants} **H** *seed.*
26:20 {the well "Argument,"} **H** *Esek.*
26:21 {named it "Opposition."} **H** *Sitnah.*
26:22 {it "Room Enough,"} **H** *Rehoboth.*
26:33 {the well "Oath,"} **H** *Shibah,* which can mean "oath" or "seven."
28:14 {and your descendants.} **H** *seed.*
29:17 {had pretty eyes,} Or *dull eyes.* The meaning of the **H** is uncertain.
29:32 {named him Reuben,} *Reuben* means "Look, a son!" It also sounds like the **H** for "He has seen my misery."
29:34 {named him Levi,} *Levi* sounds like a **H** term that means "being attached" or "feeling affection for."
29:35 {named him Judah,} *Judah* sounds like the **H** term for "praise."
30: 6 {named him Dan,} *Dan* is a play on the **H** term meaning "to vindicate" or "to judge."
30:18 {named him Issachar,} *Issachar* sounds like a **H** term that means "reward."
31:47 {language and Galeed} *Jegar-sahadutha* means "witness pile" in Aramaic; *Galeed* means "witness pile" in **H**.
32:31 {he left Peniel,} **H** *Penuel,* a variant name for Peniel.
33:19 {pieces of silver.} **H** *100 kesitahs;* the value or weight of the kesitah is no longer known.
34: 7 {against Jacob's family,} **H** *in Israel.*
35: 8 {"Oak of Weeping."} **H** *Allon-bacuth.*
35:21 {Jacob} **H** *Israel;* also in 35:22a.
36:26 {sons of Dishon} **H** *Dishan,* a variant name for Dishon; compare 36:21, 28.
36:37 {the Euphrates River} **H** *the river.*
36:39 {Baal-hanan died, Hadad} As in some **H** manuscripts, Samaritan Pentateuch, and Syriac version (see also 1 Chr 1:50); most **H** manuscripts read *Hadar.*
37: 3 {Now Jacob} **H** *Israel;* also in 37:13.
37: 3 {gift—a beautiful robe.} Traditionally rendered *a coat of many colors.* The exact meaning of the **H** is uncertain.
37:28 {when the traders} **H** *Midianites;* also in 37:36.
37:28 {for twenty pieces} **H** *20 shekels,* about 8 ounces or 228 grams in weight.
38:21 {find the prostitute} **H** *shrine prostitute;* also in 38:21b, 22.
41:45 {priest of Heliopolis.} **H** *of On;* also in 41:50.
41:51 {older son Manasseh,} *Manasseh* sounds like a **H** term that means "causing to forget."
41:52 {second son Ephraim,} *Ephraim* sounds like a **H** term that means "fruitful."
42: 5 {So Jacob's} **H** *Israel's.*
43: 6 {another brother?" Jacob} **H** *Israel;* also in 43:11.
45:21 {sons of Jacob} **H** *Israel;* also in 45:28.
45:22 {three hundred pieces} **H** *300 shekels,* about 7.5 pounds or 3.4 kilograms in weight.
46: 1 {So Jacob} **H** *Israel;* also in 46:30.
46:13 {Puah,} As in Syriac version and Samaritan Pentateuch (see also 1 Chr 7:1); **H** reads *Puvah.*
46:13 {Jashub,} As in some Greek manuscripts and Samaritan Pentateuch (see also Num 26:24; 1 Chr 7:1); **H** reads *Iob.*
46:16 {Gad were Zephon,} As in Greek version and Samaritan Pentateuch (see also Num 26:15); **H** reads *Ziphion.*
46:20 {priest of Heliopolis.} **H** *of On.*
47:21 {servants to Pharaoh.} As in Greek version and Samaritan Pentateuch; **H** reads *He moved the people into the towns throughout the land of Egypt.*
47:31 {and Jacob} **H** *Israel.*
47:31 {on his staff.} As in Greek version; **H** reads *bowed in worship at the head of his bed.*
48: 8 {Then Jacob} **H** *Israel;* also in 48:10, 11, 13, 14, 21.
48:22 {an extra portion} Or *give you the ridge of land.* The meaning of the **H** is uncertain.
49:28 {with which Jacob} **H** *Israel.*
Ex 1: 1 {sons of Jacob} **H** *Israel.*
2:10 {named him Moses,} *Moses* sounds like a **H** term that means "to draw out."
2:22 {named him Gershom,} *Gershom* sounds like a **H** term that means "a stranger here."
3: 1 {wilderness near Sinai,} **H** *Horeb,* another name for Sinai.
3:15 {'The LORD,} **H** *Yahweh;* traditionally rendered *Jehovah.*
4: 6 {snow with leprosy.} Or *with a contagious skin disease.* The **H** word used here can describe various skin diseases.
4:24 {LORD confronted Moses} Or *confronted Moses' son;* **H** reads *confronted him.*
5:21 {situation with Pharaoh} **H** *for making us a stench in the nostrils of Pharaoh.*
6: 3 {God Almighty,} **H** *El Shaddai.*
6: 3 {the LORD,} **H** *Yahweh;* traditionally rendered *Jehovah.*
10:19 {the Red Sea.} **H** *sea of reeds.*
13: 4 {in early spring} **H** *in the month of Abib.* This month of the **H** lunar calendar usually occurs in March and April.
13:18 {the Red Sea,} **H** *sea of reeds.*
15: 4 {the Red Sea.} **H** *sea of reeds;* also in 15:22.
16: 1 {after leaving Egypt.} **H** *on the fifteenth day of the second month.* The Exodus had occurred on the fourteenth day of the first month (see 12:6).
16:16 {up two quarts} **H** *1 omer* [2 liters]; also in 16:18, 32, 33.
16:22 {the ground—four quarts} **H** *2 omers* [4 liters].
16:33 {a sacred place} **H** *before the LORD.*
16:34 {of the Covenant.} **H** *in front of the Testimony.*
16:36 {about two quarts.)} **H** *An omer is one tenth of an ephah.*
17: 6 {at Mount Sinai.} **H** *Horeb,* another name for Sinai.
17:15 {Is My Banner."} **H** *Yahweh Nissi.*
18: 3 {son was Gershom,} *Gershom* sounds like a **H** term that means "a stranger here."
19: 1 {they left Egypt.} **H** *in the third month…on the very day,* i.e., two lunar months to the day after leaving Egypt. This day of the **H** lunar calendar occurs in late May or early June; compare note on 13:4.
21:32 {thirty silver coins} **H** *30 shekels of silver,* about 12 ounces or 342 grams in weight.
23:15 {in early spring,} **H** *in the month of Abib.* This month of the **H** lunar calendar usually occurs in March and April.
23:31 {the Mediterranean Sea,} **H** *from the sea of reeds to the sea of the Philistines.*
23:31 {the Euphrates River.} **H** *the river.*
25:10 {2 1/4 feet high.} **H** *2 1/2 cubits* [1.1 meters] *long, 1 1/2 cubits* [0.7 meters] *wide, and 1 1/2 cubits high.* In this chapter, the distance measures are calculated from the **H** cubit at a ratio of 18 inches or 45 centimeters per cubit.
25:16 {of the covenant,} **H** *place inside it the Testimony;* also in 25:21.
25:25 {about three inches} **H** *a handbreadth* [8 centimeters].
25:39 {need seventy-five pounds} **H** *1 talent* [34 kilograms].
26: 2 {six feet wide.} **H** *28 cubits* [12.6 meters] *long and 4 cubits* [1.8 meters] *wide.* In this chapter, the distance measures are calculated from the **H** cubit at a ratio of 18 inches or 45 centimeters per cubit.

27: 1 {4 1/2 feet high.} **H** *5 cubits* [2.3 meters] *wide, 5 cubits long, and 3 cubits* [1.4 meters] *high.* In this chapter, the distance measures are calculated from the **H** cubit at a ratio of 18 inches or 45 centimeters per cubit.
27:21 {in the Tabernacle.} **H** *in the Tent of Meeting, outside of the inner curtain, in front of the Testimony.*
28:16 {pouch nine inches} **H** *1 span* [23 centimeters].
28:32 {a woven collar} The meaning of the **H** is uncertain.
28:43 {enter the Tabernacle} **H** *Tent of Meeting.*
29: 4 {of the Tabernacle,} **H** *Tent of Meeting;* also in 29:10, 11, 30, 32, 42, 44.
29:40 {quart of wine} **H** *1/10 of an ephah* [2 liters] *of fine flour…1/4 of a hin* [1 liter] *of olive oil…1/4 of a hin of wine.*
30: 2 {three feet high,} **H** *1 cubit* [45 centimeters] *square and 2 cubits* [90 centimeters] *high.*
30:13 {of an ounce} **H** *half a shekel* [6 grams], *according to the sanctuary shekel, 20 gerahs to each shekel.*
30:16 {of the Tabernacle.} **H** *Tent of Meeting;* also in 30:18, 20, 26, 36.
30:23 {myrrh, 6 1/4 pounds} **H** *500 shekels* [5.7 kilograms] *of pure myrrh, 250 shekels* [2.9 kilograms].
30:24 {and one gallon} **H** *500 shekels* [5.7 kilograms] *of cassia, according to the sanctuary shekel, and 1 hin* [3.8 liters].
31: 7 {of the Covenant;} **H** *the Tent of Meeting; the Ark of the Testimony.*
31:18 {of the covenant,} **H** *the Testimony.*
32:13 {Isaac, and Jacob.} **H** *Israel.*
32:15 {of the covenant.} **H** *the Testimony.*
33: 6 {left Mount Sinai,} **H** *Horeb,* another name for Sinai.
34:18 {in early spring,} **H** *in the month of Abib.* This month of the **H** lunar calendar usually occurs in March and April.
34:29 {of the covenant,} **H** *the Testimony.*
35:21 {for the Tabernacle} **H** *Tent of Meeting.*
36: 9 {six feet wide.} **H** *28 cubits* [12.6 meters] *long and 4 cubits* [1.8 meters] *wide.* In this chapter, the distance measures are calculated from the **H** cubit at a ratio of 18 inches or 45 centimeters per cubit.
37: 1 {2 1/4 feet high.} **H** *2 1/2 cubits* [1.1 meters] *long, 1 1/2 cubits* [0.7 meters] *wide, and 1 1/2 cubits high.* In this chapter, the distance measures are calculated from the **H** cubit at a ratio of 18 inches or 45 centimeters per cubit.
37:12 {rim about 3 inches} **H** *a handbreadth* [8 centimeters].
37:24 {from seventy-five pounds} **H** *1 talent* [34 kilograms].
38: 1 {4 1/2 feet high.} **H** *5 cubits* [2.3 meters] *square at the top, and 3 cubits* [1.4 meters] *high.* In this chapter, the distance measures are calculated from the **H** cubit at a ratio of 18 inches or 45 centimeters per cubit.
38: 8 {of the Tabernacle.} **H** *Tent of Meeting;* also in 38:30.
38:21 {of the Covenant.} **H** *the Tabernacle, the Tabernacle of the Testimony.*
38:24 {about 2,200 pounds,} **H** *29 talents* [2,175 pounds or 986 kilograms] *and 730 shekels* [18.3 pounds or 8.3 kilograms], *according to the sanctuary shekel.*
38:25 {about 7,545 pounds.} **H** *100 talents* [7,500 pounds or 3,400 kilograms] *and 1,775 shekels* [44.4 pounds or 20.2 kilograms], *according to the sanctuary shekel.*
38:26 {ounce of silver} **H** *1 beka* [6 grams] *per person, that is, half a shekel, according to the sanctuary shekel.*
38:27 {for each base.} **H** *100 talents* [3,400 kilograms] *of silver, 1 talent* [34 kilograms] *for each base.*
38:28 {about 45 pounds,} **H** *1,775 shekels* [20.2 kilograms].
38:29 {brought 5,310 pounds} **H** *70 talents* [5,250 pounds or 2,380 kilograms] *and 2,400 shekels* [60 pounds or 27.4 kilograms].
39: 9 {pouch, nine inches} **H** *1 span* [23 centimeters].
39:23 {a woven collar,} The meaning of the **H** is uncertain.
39:32 {the Tabernacle} **H** *the Tabernacle, the Tent of Meeting;* also in 39:40.
40: 2 {the Tabernacle} **H** *the Tabernacle, the Tent of Meeting;* also in 40:6, 29.
40: 2 {the new year.} **H** *the first day of the first month.* This day of the **H** lunar calendar occurs in March or early April.
40: 7 {between the Tabernacle} **H** *Tent of Meeting;* also in 40:12, 22, 24, 26, 30, 32, 34, 35.
40:17 {the new year.} **H** *the first day of the first month, in the second year.* See note on 40:2b.
40:20 {of the covenant,} **H** *the Testimony.*
Lev 1: 1 {the Tabernacle} **H** *Tent of Meeting;* also in 1:3, 5.
1:16 {and the feathers} Or *the crop and its contents.* The meaning of the **H** is uncertain.
3: 2 {of the Tabernacle.} **H** *Tent of Meeting;* also in 3:8, 13.
4: 4 {of the Tabernacle,} **H** *Tent of Meeting;* also in 4:5, 7, 14, 16, 18.
4:27 {citizens of Israel} **H** *people of the land.*
5:11 {bring two quarts} **H** *1/10 of an ephah* [2 liters].
6: 6 {value in silver.} Or *and the animal must be of the proper value;* **H** lacks *in silver;* compare 5:15.
6:16 {of the Tabernacle.} **H** *Tent of Meeting;* also in 6:26, 30.
6:20 {of two quarts} **H** *1/10 of an ephah* [2 liters].
6:21 {mixed and broken} The meaning of this **H** term is uncertain.
8: 3 {of the Tabernacle.} **H** *Tent of Meeting;* also in 8:4, 31, 33, 35.
9: 5 {of the Tabernacle,} **H** *Tent of Meeting;* also in 9:23.
10: 7 {of the Tabernacle,} **H** *Tent of Meeting;* also in 10:9.
12: 6 {of the Tabernacle.} **H** *Tent of Meeting.*
13: 2 {contagious skin disease,} Traditionally rendered *leprosy.* The **H** word used throughout this passage is used to describe various skin diseases.
13:47 {an infectious mildew} Traditionally rendered *leprosy.* The **H** term used throughout this passage is the same term used for the various skin diseases described in 13:1-46.
14:10 {with five quarts} **H** *3/10 of an ephah* [5.4 liters].
14:10 {of a pint} **H** *1 log* [0.3 liters]; also in 14:21.
14:11 {of the Tabernacle.} **H** *Tent of Meeting;* also in 14:23.
14:21 {with two quarts} **H** *1/10 of an ephah* [2 liters].
15: 2 {genital discharge} **H** *a discharge from his flesh;* also in 15:32.
15:14 {of the Tabernacle} **H** *Tent of Meeting;* also in 15:29.
16: 1 {LORD had commanded.} **H** *when they approached the LORD's presence;* compare 10:1.
16: 7 {of the Tabernacle.} **H** *Tent of Meeting;* also in 16:16, 17, 20, 23, 33.
16: 8 {be the scapegoat.} **H** *azazel,* which in this context means "the goat of removal"; also in 16:10, 26.
16:13 {of the Covenant.} **H** *on the Testimony,* referring to the terms of God's covenant with Israel, which were kept in the Ark.
16:29 {in early autumn,} **H** *On the tenth day of the seventh month.* This day of the **H** lunar calendar occurs in September or early October.
17: 4 {the Tabernacle} **H** *Tent of Meeting;* also in 17:5, 6, 9.
17: 4 {a capital offense.} **H** *blood guilt.*
19:16 {among your people.} **H** *Do not act as a merchant toward your own people.*
19:21 {of the Tabernacle.} **H** *Tent of Meeting.*
19:23 {consider it forbidden.} **H** *consider it uncircumcised.*
19:36 {must be accurate.} **H** *Use an honest ephah* [a measure for dry goods] *and an honest hin* [a measure for liquids].
21: 4 {among his relatives,} The meaning of the **H** is uncertain.
23: 5 {in early spring.} **H** *on the fourteenth day of the first month.* This day of the **H** lunar calendar occurs in late March or early April.
23: 6 {the Passover celebration,} **H** *On the fifteenth day of the same month.*
23:13 {three quarts} **H** *2/10 of an ephah* [3.6 liters]; also in 23:17.
23:13 {one quart} **H** *1/4 of a hin* [1 liter].
23:24 {in early autumn,} **H** *On the first day of the seventh month.* This day of the **H** lunar calendar occurs in September or early October.
23:27 {Festival of Trumpets.} **H** *on the tenth day of the seventh month;* see 23:24 and the note there.
23:32 {Day of Atonement} **H** *the evening of the ninth day of the month;* see 23:24, 27 and the notes there.
23:34 {Day of Atonement.} **H** *on the fifteenth day of the seventh month;* see 23:24, 27 and the notes there.
23:39 {Festival of Shelters,} **H** *on the fifteenth day of the seventh month;* see 23:24 and the note there.
24: 3 {in the Tabernacle} **H** *the curtain of the Testimony in the Tent of Meeting.*
24: 5 {using three quarts} **H** *2/10 of an ephah* [3.6 liters].
25: 9 {the fiftieth year,} **H** *on the tenth day of the seventh month, on the Day of Atonement;* see 23:27 and the note there.
27: 3 {pieces of silver} **H** *50 shekels of silver, according to the standard sanctuary shekel,* each about 0.4 ounces or 11 grams in weight. The term *shekels* also appears in 27:4, 5, 6, 7, 16.
27:16 {five bushels} **H** *1 homer* [182 liters].
27:21 {specially set apart} The **H** term used here refers to the complete consecration of things or people to the LORD, either by destroying them or by giving them as an offering; also in 27:28, 29.
27:25 {standard sanctuary shekel.} **H** *measured according to the sanctuary shekel, 20 gerahs to each shekel.* Each sanctuary shekel was about 0.4 ounces or 11 grams in weight.
Nu 1: 1 {day in midspring,} **H** *On the first day of the second month.* This day of the **H** lunar calendar occurs in April or early May.
1: 1 {the Tabernacle} **H** *Tent of Meeting.*
1:18 {that very day.} **H** *on the first day of the second month;* see 1:1.
1:20[-21] {clan and family} In the **H** text, *number of men…family* is repeated in 1:22, 24, 26, 28, 30, 32, 34, 36, 38, 40, 42.
1:20[-21] {Reuben (Jacob's} **H** *Israel's.*
2: 2 {banners. The Tabernacle} **H** *Tent of Meeting;* also in 2:17.
2:14[-15] {son of Deuel} As in many **H** manuscripts, Samaritan Pentateuch, and Latin Vulgate (see also 1:14); most **H** manuscripts read *son of Reuel.*
3: 7 {around the Tabernacle.} **H** *around the Tent of Meeting, doing service at the Tabernacle.*
3: 8 {the sacred tent,} **H** *Tent of Meeting.*
3:38 {toward the sunrise} **H** *toward the sunrise, in front of the Tent of Meeting.*
3:47 {standard sanctuary shekel.} **H** *5 shekels* [2 ounces or 57 grams] *apiece, according to the sanctuary shekel, 20 gerahs to each shekel.*
3:50 {pounds in weight.} **H** *1,365 shekels* [15.5 kilograms], *according to the sanctuary shekel.*
4: 3 {the Tabernacle.} **H** *Tent of Meeting;* also in 4:4, 15, 23, 25, 28, 30, 31, 33, 35, 37, 39, 41, 43, 47.
5: 2 {contagious skin disease} Traditionally rendered *leprosy.* The **H** word used here describes various skin diseases.
5:15 {of two quarts} **H** *1/10 of an ephah* [2 liters].
5:21 {makes you infertile.} **H** *when he causes your thigh to waste away and your abdomen to swell.*
5:22 {make you infertile.} **H** *enter your body so that your abdomen swells and your thigh wastes away.*
5:27 {will become infertile,} **H** *Her body will swell and her thigh will waste away.*
6:10 {of the Tabernacle.} **H** *Tent of Meeting;* also in 6:13, 18.
6:27 {as my people,} **H** *will put my name on the people of Israel.*
7: 5 {of the Tabernacle.} **H** *Tent of Meeting;* also in 7:89.
7:13 {about 1 3/4 pounds.} **H** *silver platter weighing 130 shekels* [1.5 kilograms] *and a silver basin weighing 70 shekels* [0.8 kilograms], *according to the sanctuary shekel;* also in 7:19, 25, 31, 37, 43, 49, 55, 61, 67, 73, 79, 85.
7:14 {about four ounces,} **H** *10 shekels* [114 grams]; also in 7:20, 26, 32, 38, 44, 50, 56, 62, 68, 74, 80, 86.
7:85 {weighed about 60 pounds,} **H** *2,400 shekels* [27.4 kilograms].
7:86 {about three pounds,} **H** *120 shekels* [1.4 kilograms].
8: 9 {of the Tabernacle.} **H** *Tent of Meeting;* also in 8:15, 19, 22, 24, 26.
9: 1 {in early spring,} **H** *in the first month.* This month of the **H** lunar calendar usually occurs in March and April.
9: 3 {in early spring.} **H** *on the fourteenth day of the first month.* This day of the **H** lunar calendar occurs in late March or early April.
9: 5 {the appointed day.} **H** *on the fourteenth day of the first month;* see note on 9:3.
9:11 {one month later,} **H** *on the fourteenth day of the second month.* This day of the **H** lunar calendar occurs in late April or early May.
9:15 {cloud covered it.} **H** *covered the Tabernacle, the Tent of the Testimony.*
10: 3 {of the Tabernacle.} **H** *Tent of Meeting.*
10:11 {day in midspring,} **H** *On the twentieth day of the second month.* This day of the **H** lunar calendar occurs in late April or early May.
11: 7 {yellow in color.} **H** *the color of gum resin.*
11:16 {to the Tabernacle} **H** *Tent of Meeting.*
11:24 {around the Tabernacle.} **H** *the tent;* also in 11:26.
11:32 {than fifty bushels} **H** *10 homers* [1.8 kiloliters].
12: 4 {to the Tabernacle,} **H** *Tent of Meeting.*
12: 5 {of the Tabernacle.} **H** *the tent;* also in 12:10.
12:10 {snow with leprosy.} Or *with a contagious skin disease.* The **H** word used here can describe various skin diseases.
13:29 {the Mediterranean Sea} **H** *the sea.*
13:33 {even saw giants} **H** *nephilim.*
14:10 {above the Tabernacle.} **H** *Tent of Meeting.*
14:25 {the Red Sea.} **H** *sea of reeds.*
15: 4 {two quarts} **H** *1/10 of an ephah* [2 liters].
15: 4 {one quart} **H** *1/4 of a hin* [1 liter]; also in 15:5.
15: 6 {three quarts} **H** *2/10 of an ephah* [3.6 liters].
15: 6 {pints} **H** *1/3 of a hin* [1.3 liters]; also in 15:7.
15: 9 {five quarts} **H** *3/10 of an ephah* [5.4 liters].
15: 9 {two quarts} **H** *1/2 of a hin* [2 liters]; also in 15:10.
16:18 {the Tabernacle} **H** *Tent of Meeting;* also in 16:19, 42, 43, 50.
17: 4 {of the Covenant,} **H** *in the Tent of Meeting before the Testimony.*
17:10 {of the Covenant} **H** *before the Testimony.*
18: 4 {of the Tabernacle,} **H** *Tent of Meeting;* also in 18:6, 21, 22, 23, 31.
18:14 {for the LORD} The **H** term used here refers to the complete consecration of things or people to the LORD, either by destroying them or by giving them as an offering.
18:16 {standard sanctuary shekel.} **H** *5 shekels* [about 2 ounces or 57 grams] *of silver, according to the sanctuary shekel, 20 gerahs to each shekel.*
18:19 {an unbreakable covenant} **H** *a covenant of salt.*
19: 4 {of the Tabernacle.} **H** *Tent of Meeting.*
20: 1 {In early spring} **H** *In the first month.* This month of the **H** lunar calendar usually occurs in March and April.
20: 6 {of the Tabernacle,} **H** *Tent of Meeting.*
21: 2 {will completely destroy} The **H** term used here refers to the complete consecration of things or people to the LORD, either by destroying them or by giving them as an offering; also in 21:3.
21: 4 {the Red Sea} **H** *sea of reeds.*
21:24 {Ammonites was fortified.} Or *because the terrain of the Ammonite frontier was rugged;* **H** *because the boundary of the Ammonites was strong.*

21:30 {Nophah and Medeba.} Or *until fire spread to Medeba.* The meaning of the **H** is uncertain.
22: 5 {the Euphrates River.} **H** *the river.*
24:22 {when Assyria} **H** *Asshur;* also in 24:24.
24:24 {coasts of Cyprus} **H** *Kittim.*
25: 1 {camped at Acacia,} **H** *Shittim.*
25: 6 {of the Tabernacle.} **H** *Tent of Meeting.*
26: 5 {from Reuben, Jacob's} **H** *Israel's.*
26:17 {its ancestor Arodi.} As in Samaritan Pentateuch and Syriac version (see also Gen 46:16); **H** reads *Arod.*
26:23 {its ancestor Puah.} As in Samaritan Pentateuch, Greek and Syriac versions, and Latin Vulgate (see also 1 Chr 7:1); **H** reads *The Punite clan, named after its ancestor Puvah.*
26:39 {its ancestor Shupham.} As in some **H** manuscripts, Samaritan Pentateuch, Greek and Syriac versions, and Latin Vulgate; most **H** manuscripts read *Shephupham.*
26:40 {their ancestor Ard.} As in Samaritan Pentateuch, some Greek manuscripts, and Latin Vulgate; **H** lacks *named after their ancestor Ard.*
27: 2 {of the Tabernacle.} **H** *Tent of Meeting.*
27:12 {of the river,} **H** *the mountains of Abarim.*
27:14 {Meribah at Kadesh} **H** *waters of Meribath-kadesh.*
27:21 {of sacred lots.} **H** *of the Urim.*
28: 5 {two quarts} **H** *1/10 of an ephah* [2 liters]; also in 28:13, 21, 29.
28: 5 {one quart} **H** *1/4 of a hin* [1 liter]; also in 28:7.
28: 9 {three quarts} **H** *2/10 of an ephah* [3.6 liters]; also in 28:12, 20, 28.
28:12 {five quarts} **H** *3/10 of an ephah* [5.4 liters]; also in 28:20, 28.
28:14 {two quarts} **H** *1/2 of a hin* [2 liters].
28:14 {a half pints} **H** *1/3 of a hin* [1.3 liters].
28:14 {and one quart} **H** *1/4 of a hin* [1 liter].
28:16 {in early spring,} **H** *On the fourteenth day of the first month.* This day of the **H** lunar calendar occurs in late March or early April.
29: 1 {in early autumn} **H** *on the first day of the seventh month.* This day of the **H** lunar calendar occurs in September or early October.
29: 3 {five quarts} **H** *3/10 of an ephah* [5.4 liters]; also in 29:9, 14.
29: 3 {three quarts} **H** *2/10 of an ephah* [3.6 liters]; also in 29:9, 14.
29: 4 {two quarts} **H** *1/10 of an ephah* [2 liters]; also in 29:10, 15.
29: 7 {"Ten days later,} **H** *On the tenth day of the seventh month;* see 29:1 and the note there.
29:12 {"Five days later,} **H** *On the fifteenth day of the seventh month;* see 29:1, 7 and the notes there.
31:14 {the military commanders} **H** *the commanders of thousands, and the commanders of hundreds;* also in 31:48, 52, 54.
31:52 {about 420 pounds.} **H** *16,750 shekels* [191 kilograms].
31:54 {to the Tabernacle} **H** *Tent of Meeting.*
32:41 {Towns of Jair.} **H** *Havvoth-jair.*
33: 3 {in early spring.} **H** *on the fifteenth day of the first month.* This day of the **H** lunar calendar occurs in late March or early April.
33: 8 {the Red Sea} **H** *the sea.*
33:10 {the Red Sea.} **H** *sea of reeds;* also in 33:11.
33:38 {day in midsummer,} **H** *on the first day of the fifth month.* This day of the **H** lunar calendar occurs in July or early August.
33:45 {They left Iye-abarim} As in 33:44; **H** reads *Iyim,* another name for Iye-abarim.
33:47 {of the river,} **H** *the mountains of Abarim;* also in 33:48.
34: 3 {the Dead Sea.} **H** *Salt Sea;* also in 34:12.
34: 4 {past Scorpion Pass} **H** *the ascent of Akrabbim.*
34: 5 {Mediterranean Sea.} **H** *the sea;* also in 34:6, 7.
34:11 {Sea of Galilee,} **H** *sea of Kinnereth.*
35: 4 {extend 1,500 feet} **H** *1,000 cubits* [450 meters].
35: 5 {off 3,000 feet} **H** *2,000 cubits* [900 meters].
Dt 1: 1 {the Jordan Valley} **H** *the Arabah;* also in 1:7.
1: 2 {from Mount Sinai} **H** *Horeb,* another name for Sinai; also in 1:6, 19.
1: 3 {day in midwinter,} **H** *on the first day of the eleventh month.* This day of the **H** lunar calendar occurs in January or early February.
1: 7 {the western foothills,} **H** *the Shephelah.*
1:40 {the Red Sea.} **H** *sea of reeds.*
2: 1 {the Red Sea,} **H** *sea of reeds.*
2:23 {Caphtorites from Crete} **H** *from Caphtor.*
2:34 {and completely destroyed} The **H** term used here refers to the complete consecration of things or people to the LORD, either by destroying them or by giving them as an offering.
3: 6 {We completely destroyed} The **H** term used here refers to the complete consecration of things or people to the LORD, either by destroying them or by giving them as an offering.
3:11 {six feet wide.} **H** *9 cubits* [4.1 meters] *long and 4 cubits* [1.8 meters] *wide.*
3:14 {Towns of Jair,} **H** *Havvoth-jair.*
3:17 {the Dead Sea,} **H** *from Kinnereth to the sea of the Arabah, the Salt Sea.*
4:10 {at Mount Sinai,} **H** *Horeb,* another name for Sinai; also in 4:15.
4:48 {to Mount Sirion,} As in Syriac version (see also 3:9); **H** reads *Mount Sion.*
4:49 {the Dead Sea,} **H** *took the Arabah on the east side of the Jordan as far as the sea of the Arabah.*
5: 2 {at Mount Sinai,} **H** *Horeb,* another name for Sinai.
7: 2 {must completely destroy} The **H** term used here refers to the complete consecration of things or people to the LORD, either by destroying them or by giving them as an offering; also in 7:26.
7:20 {will send hornets} Or *will spread panic,* or *will send a plague.* The meaning of the **H** is uncertain.
9: 8 {at Mount Sinai,} **H** *Horeb,* another name for Sinai.
11: 4 {the Red Sea} **H** *sea of reeds.*
11:24 {in the west.} **H** *to the western sea.*
11:30 {the Jordan Valley,} **H** *the Arabah.*
13:15 {and completely destroy} The **H** term used here refers to the complete consecration of things or people to the LORD, either by destroying them or by giving them as an offering; also in 13:17.
16: 1 {in early spring,} **H** *in the month of Abib.* This month of the **H** lunar calendar usually occurs in March and April.
18:16 {at Mount Sinai.} **H** *Horeb,* another name for Sinai.
20:17 {must completely destroy} The **H** term used here refers to the complete consecration of things or people to the LORD, either by destroying them or by giving them as an offering.
22:19 {pieces of silver,} **H** *100 shekels of silver,* about 2.5 pounds or 1.1 kilograms in weight.
22:29 {pieces of silver} **H** *50 shekels of silver,* about 1.25 pounds or 570 grams in weight.
24: 8 {contagious skin diseases} Traditonally rendered *leprosy.* The **H** word used here can describe various skin diseases.
29: 1 {at Mount Sinai.} **H** *Horeb,* another name for Sinai.
31:14 {to the Tabernacle,} **H** *Tent of Meeting;* also in 31:14b.
32: 5 {really his children?} The meaning of the **H** is uncertain.
32:10 {most precious possession.} **H** *as the apple of his eye.*
32:15 {But Israel} **H** *Jeshurun,* a term of endearment for Israel.
32:22 {of the grave.} **H** *of Sheol.*
32:26 {to scatter them,} As in Greek version; the meaning of the **H** is uncertain.
32:31 {even they recognize.} The meaning of the **H** is uncertain. Greek version reads *our enemies are fools.*
32:44 {came with Joshua} **H** *Hoshea,* a variant name for Joshua.
32:49 {of the river,} **H** *the mountains of Abarim.*
32:51 {Meribah at Kadesh} **H** *waters of Meribath-kadesh.*
33: 2 {dawned upon us} As in Greek and Syriac versions; **H** reads *upon them.*
33: 2 {his right hand.} Or *came from myriads of holy ones, from the south, from his mountain slopes.* The meaning of the **H** is uncertain.
33: 4 {assembly of Israel.} **H** *of Jacob.*
33: 5 {king in Israel} **H** *in Jeshurun,* a term of endearment for Israel.
33: 6 {tribe of Reuben:} **H** lacks *Moses said this about the tribe of Reuben.*
33: 8 {the sacred lots} **H** *given your Thummim and Urim.* See Exod 28:30.
33:18 {Zebulun and Issachar} **H** lacks *and Issachar.*
33:26 {God of Israel.} **H** *of Jeshurun,* a term of endearment for Israel.
34: 2 {the Mediterranean Sea} **H** *the western sea.*
34: 6 {He was buried} **H** *He buried him,* that is, "The LORD buried him." Samaritan Pentateuch and some Greek manuscripts read *They buried him.*
Jos 1: 4 {the Mediterranean Sea} **H** *the Great Sea.*
2: 1 {at Acacia.} **H** *Shittim.*
2:10 {the Red Sea} **H** *sea of reeds.*
2:10 {you completely destroyed.} The **H** term used here refers to the complete consecration of things or people to the LORD, either by destroying them or by giving them as an offering.
3: 1 {Israelites left Acacia} **H** *Shittim.*
3: 4 {half mile} **H** *about 2,000 cubits* [900 meters].
3:16 {Dead Sea} **H** *the sea of the Arabah, the Salt Sea.*
4:16 {of the Covenant} **H** *Ark of the Testimony.*
4:19 {exodus from Egypt.} **H** *the tenth day of the first month.* This day of the **H** lunar calendar occurs in late March or early April.
4:23 {the Red Sea} **H** *sea of reeds.*
5: 1 {the Mediterranean coast} **H** *along the sea.*
5: 9 {been called Gilgal} *Gilgal* sounds like the **H** word *galal,* meaning "to roll."
5:10 {exodus from Egypt.} **H** *the fourteenth day of the first month.* This day of the **H** lunar calendar occurs in late March or early April.
6:17 {be completely destroyed} The **H** term used here refers to the complete consecration of things or people to the LORD, either by destroying them or by giving them as an offering; also in 6:18, 21.
7: 1 {for the LORD.} The **H** term used here refers to the complete consecration of things or people to the LORD, either by destroying them or by giving them as an offering; also in 7:11, 12, 13, 15.
7: 1 {family of Zimri,} As in Greek version (see also 1 Chr 2:6); **H** reads *Zabdi.* Also in 7:17, 18.
7:21 {imported from Babylon,} **H** *Shinar.*
7:21 {hundred silver coins,} **H** *200 shekels of silver,* about 5 pounds or 2.3 kilograms in weight.
7:21 {than a pound.} **H** *50 shekels,* about 20 ounces or 570 grams in weight.
7:26 {Valley of Trouble} **H** *valley of Achor.*
8:14 {the Jordan Valley.} **H** *the Arabah.*
8:26 {was completely destroyed.} The **H** term used here refers to the complete consecration of things or people to the LORD, either by destroying them or by giving them as an offering.
9: 1 {the western foothills,} **H** *the Shephelah.*
9: 1 {the Mediterranean Sea} **H** *the Great Sea.*
10: 1 {and completely destroyed} The **H** term used here refers to the complete consecration of things or people to the LORD, either by destroying them or by giving them as an offering; also in 10:28, 35, 37, 39, 40.
10:40 {the western foothills,} **H** *the Shephelah.*
11: 2 {the Jordan Valley} **H** *the Arabah;* also in 11:16.
11: 2 {south of Galilee} **H** *of Kinnereth.*
11: 2 {the western foothills} **H** *the Shephelah;* also in 11:16.
11:11 {Israelites completely destroyed} The **H** term used here refers to the complete consecration of things or people to the LORD, either by destroying them or by giving them as an offering; also in 11:12, 20, 21.
12: 1 {the Jordan Valley.} **H** *the Arabah;* also in 12:3, 8.
12: 3 {Sea of Galilee} **H** *sea of Kinnereth.*
12: 3 {the Dead Sea,} **H** *the sea of the Arabah, the Salt Sea.*
12: 8 {the western foothills,} **H** *the Shephelah.*
12:23 {city of Naphoth-dor} **H** *Naphath-dor,* a variant name for Naphoth-dor.
13:27 {Sea of Galilee.} **H** *sea of Kinnereth.*
15: 2 {the Dead Sea,} **H** *the Salt Sea;* also in 15:5.
15: 3 {of Scorpion Pass} **H** *Akrabbim.*
15: 4 {the Mediterranean Sea.} **H** *the sea;* also in 15:11.
15: 4 {This was their} **H** *your.*
15:12 {the Mediterranean Sea.} **H** *the Great Sea;* also in 15:47.
15:33 {the western foothills} **H** *the Shephelah.*
16: 2 {(that is, Luz)} As in Greek version (also see 18:13); **H** reads *From Bethel to Luz.*
16: 3 {the Mediterranean Sea.} **H** *the sea;* also in 16:6, 8.
17: 9 {the Mediterranean Sea.} **H** *the sea;* also in 17:10.
17:11 {Beth-shan,} **H** *Beth-shean,* a variant name for Beth-shan; also in 17:16.
17:11 {(that is, Naphoth-dor),} The meaning of the **H** here is uncertain.
18: 1 {up the Tabernacle.} **H** *Tent of Meeting.*
18:15 {it ran westward} Or *it went to Ephron, and.* The meaning of the **H** is uncertain.
18:18 {the Jordan Valley.} **H** *the Arabah.*
18:19 {the Dead Sea,} **H** *Salt Sea.*
18:28 {Gibeah, and Kiriath-jearim} As in Greek version; **H** reads *Kiriath.*
19:28 {Abdon,} As in some **H** manuscripts (see also 21:30); most Hebrew manuscripts read *Ebron.*
19:28 {Abdon,} As in some Hebrew manuscripts (see also 21:30); most **H** manuscripts read *Ebron.*
19:29 {the Mediterranean Sea} **H** *the sea.*
19:34 {the Jordan River} **H** *and Judah at the Jordan River.*
19:47 {town of Laish.} **H** *Leshem,* another name for Laish.
19:51 {of the Tabernacle} **H** *Tent of Meeting.*
21:36 {received Bezer, Jahaz,} **H** *Jahzah,* a variant name for Jahaz.
22:20 {for the LORD} The **H** term used here refers to the complete consecration of things or people to the LORD, either by destroying them or by giving them as an offering.
22:34 {the altar "Witness,"} **H** *edh.* Some manuscripts lack this word.
23: 4 {the Mediterranean Sea} **H** *the Great Sea.*
24: 2 {the Euphrates River,} **H** *the river;* also in 24:3, 14, 15.
24: 6 {the Red Sea,} **H** *sea of reeds.*
24:32 {pieces of silver.} **H** *100 kesitahs;* the value or weight of the kesitah is no longer known.
Jdg 1: 9 {the western foothills.} **H** *the Shephelah.*
1:16 {Judah left Jericho,} **H** *the city of palms.*
1:17 {they completely destroyed} The **H** term used here refers to the complete consecration of things or people to the LORD, either by destroying them or by giving them as an offering.
1:27 {living in Beth-shan,} **H** *Beth-shean,* a variant name for Beth-shan.
1:36 {from Scorpion Pass} **H** *Akrabbim.*
2: 5 {the place "Weeping,"} **H** *Bokim.*
2: 9 {inherited, at Timnath-serah} **H** *Timnath-heres,* a variant name for Timnath-serah.
3:13 {possession of Jericho.} **H** *the city of palms.*
3:16 {was eighteen inches} **H** *1 cubit* [45 centimeters].
5:11 {the village musicians} The meaning of the **H** is uncertain.
6:19 {half a bushel} **H** *1 ephah* [18 liters].
6:24 {LORD Is Peace."} **H** *Yahweh Shalom.*
7: 3 {afraid may leave} **H** *leave Mount Gilead.* The identity of Mount Gilead is uncertain in this context. It is perhaps used here as another name for Mount Gilboa.
8: 8 {up to Peniel} **H** *Penuel,* a variant name for Peniel; also in 8:9, 17.
8:26 {was forty-three pounds,} **H** *1,700 shekels* [19.4 kilograms].
8:29 {Then Gideon} **H** *Jerubbaal;* see 6:32.

9: 1 {One day Gideon's} **H** *Jerubbaal's* (see 6:32); also in 9:2, 24.
9: 6 {beside the pillar} The meaning of the **H** is uncertain.
9:16 {right by Gideon} **H** *Jerubbaal* (see 6:32); also in 9:19, 28, 57.
9:23 {stirred up trouble} **H** *sent a disturbing spirit.*
9:28 {descendant of Shechem!} **H** *Who is Shechem?*
9:29 {I would say} As in Greek version; **H** reads *And he said.*
9:31 {Abimelech in Arumah,} **H** *Tormah;* see 9:41.
9:37 {the Diviners' Oak.} **H** *Elon-meonenim.*
9:46 {temple of Baal-berith.} **H** *El-berith,* another name for Baal-berith; compare 9:4.
10: 4 {Towns of Jair.} **H** *Havvoth-jair.*
11:16 {the Red Sea,} **H** *sea of reeds.*
14:15 {On the fourth} As in Greek version; **H** reads *seventh.*
15:17 {named Jawbone Hill.} **H** *Ramath-lehi.*
15:19 {Who Cried Out,"} **H** *En-hakkore.*
16: 5 {eleven hundred pieces} **H** *1,100 shekels,* about 28 pounds or 12.5 kilograms in weight.
16:13 {the loom shuttle,} As in Greek version; **H** lacks *on your loom and tighten it with the loom shuttle.*
17: 2 {eleven hundred pieces} **H** *1,100 shekels,* about 28 pounds or 12.5 kilograms in weight.
17:10 {you ten pieces} **H** *10 shekels,* about 4 ounces or 114 grams in weight.
18:30 {descendant of Moses,} As in an ancient **H** tradition, some Greek manuscripts, and Latin Vulgate; Masoretic Text reads *of Manasseh.*
20:10 {revenge on Gibeah} **H** *Geba,* in this case, a variant for Gibeah; also in 20:33.
21:11 {said. "Completely destroy} The **H** term used here refers to the complete consecration of things or people to the LORD, either by destroying them or by giving them as an offering.
Ru 2:17 {half a bushel.} **H** *about an ephah* [18 liters].
2:20 {your dead husband.} **H** *to the living and to the dead.*
3:15 {six scoops} **H** *six measures,* an unknown quantity.
3:15 {Then Boaz} Most **H** manuscripts read *he;* many Hebrew manuscripts, Syriac version, and Latin Vulgate read *she.*
3:15 {back. Then Boaz} Most Hebrew manuscripts read *he;* many **H** manuscripts, Syriac version, and Latin Vulgate read *she.*
1Sa 1: 1 {in Ramah} **H** *Ramathaim-zophim;* compare 1:19.
1: 5 {special portion} Or *a double portion.* The meaning of the **H** is uncertain.
1: 7 {to the Tabernacle.} **H** *the house of the LORD;* also in 1:24.
1: 9 {to the Tabernacle} **H** *the Temple of the LORD.*
1:20 {named him Samuel,} *Samuel* sounds like the **H** term for "asked of God" or "heard by God."
1:24 {a three-year-old bull} As in Dead Sea Scrolls, Greek and Syriac versions; **H** reads *3 bulls.*
1:24 {half a bushel} **H** *and an ephah* [18 liters].
2:18 {of a priest.} **H** *He wore a linen ephod.*
2:20 {to the LORD.} As in Greek version; **H** reads *this one she requested of the LORD in prayer.*
2:22 {of the Tabernacle.} **H** *Tent of Meeting.* Some manuscripts lack this entire sentence.
2:28 {your ancestor Aaron} **H** *your father.*
2:28 {the priestly garments} **H** *an ephod.*
2:30 {tribe of Levi} **H** *that your house and your father's house.*
3: 3 {in the Tabernacle} **H** *the Temple of the LORD.*
3:13 {are blaspheming God} As in Greek version; **H** reads *his sons have made themselves contemptible.*
3:15 {of the Tabernacle} **H** *the house of the LORD.*
6:19 {killed seventy men} As in a few **H** manuscripts; most **H** manuscripts and Greek version read *50,070 men.* Perhaps the text should be understood to read *the LORD killed 70 men and 50 oxen.*
7:12 {Jeshanah.} As in Greek version; **H** reads *Shen.*
8:16 {of your cattle} As in Greek version; **H** reads *young men.*
9: 8 {small silver piece.} **H** *1/4 shekel of silver,* about 0.1 ounces or 3 grams in weight.
9:25 {for him there.} As in Greek version; **H** reads *and talked with him there.*
10: 5 {Gibeah of God,} **H** *Gibeath-elohim.*
10:12 {become a prophet."} **H** *responded, "Who is their father?"*
10:20 {Benjamin was chosen.} **H** *chosen by lot;* also in 10:21.
11: 1 {month later,} As in Greek version; **H** lacks *About a month later.*
12: 8 {the Israelites were} **H** *When Jacob was.*
12:11 {Gideon,} **H** *Jerubbaal,* another name for Gideon; see Judg 7:1.
12:11 {Barak,} As in Greek and Syriac versions; **H** reads *Bedan.*
13: 1 {Saul was thirty} As in a few Greek manuscripts; the number is missing in the **H**.
13: 1 {for forty-two years.} **H** *reigned…and two;* the number is incomplete in the Hebrew. Compare Acts 13:21.
13: 1 {for forty-two years.} Hebrew *reigned…and two;* the number is incomplete in the **H**. Compare Acts 13:21.
13: 5 {of three thousand} As in Greek and Syriac versions; **H** reads *30,000.*
13:15 {land of Benjamin.} As in Greek version; **H** reads *Samuel left Gilgal and went to Gibeah in the land of Benjamin.*
13:20 {axes, or sickles,} As in Greek version; **H** reads *or plowshares.*
13:21 {ounce of silver} **H** *1 pim* [8 grams].
13:21 {of an ounce} **H** *1/3 of a shekel* [4 grams].
14:14 {half an acre.} **H** *half a yoke;* a "yoke" was the amount of land plowed by a pair of yoked oxen in one day.
14:18 {of the Israelites.} As in some Greek manuscripts; **H** reads *"Bring the Ark of God." For at that time the Ark of God was with the Israelites.*
14:19 {let's get going!"} **H** *Withdraw your hand.*
14:41 {Saul were chosen} **H** *chosen by lot.*
14:42 {said, "Now choose} **H** *draw lots.*
14:49 {included Jonathan, Ishbosheth,} **H** *Ishvi,* a variant name for Ishbosheth; also known as Eshbaal.
15: 3 {and completely destroy} The **H** term used here refers to the complete consecration of things or people to the LORD, either by destroying them or by giving them as an offering; also in 15:8, 9, 15, 18, 20, 21.
17: 4 {over nine feet} **H** *6 cubits* [9 feet or 2.7 meters] *and 1 span* [9 inches or 23 centimeters]; Greek version reads *4 cubits* [6 feet or 1.8 meters] *and 1 span,* about 6.75 feet or 2 meters in length.
17: 5 {weighed 125 pounds.} **H** *5,000 shekels* [57 kilograms].
17: 7 {weighed fifteen pounds.} **H** *600 shekels* [6.8 kilograms].
17:17 {"Take this half-bushel} **H** *ephah* [18 liters].
17:18 {letter from them.} **H** *and take their pledge.*
17:52 {far as Gath} As in some Greek manuscripts; **H** reads *a valley.*
19:13 {took an idol} **H** *teraphim;* also in 19:16.
20:16 {covenant with David,} **H** *with the house of David.*
20:19 {the stone pile.} **H** *the stone Ezel.* The meaning of the **H** is uncertain.
20:25 {sitting opposite him} As in Greek version; **H** reads *with Jonathan standing.*
20:30 {of a whore!"} **H** *You son of a perverse and rebellious woman.*
20:41 {the stone pile.} As in Greek version; **H** reads *near the south edge.*
21: 7 {for ceremonial purification.} **H** *was detained before the LORD.*
23:28 {Rock of Escape.} **H** *Sela-hammahlekoth.*
25: 1 {wilderness of Maon.} As in Greek version; **H** reads *Paran.*
25:18 {nearly a bushel} **H** *5 seahs* [30 liters].
25:37 {had a stroke,} **H** *his heart failed him.*
28: 6 {by sacred lots} **H** *by Urim.*
2Sa 2:16 {Field of Swords.} **H** *Helkath-hazzurim.*
2:29 {the Jordan Valley.} **H** *the Arabah.*
2:29 {through the morning,} Or *continued on through the Bithron.* The meaning of the **H** is uncertain.
3:15 {her husband Palti} As in 1 Sam 25:44; **H** reads *Paltiel,* a variant name for Palti.
3:29 {sores or leprosy} Or *or a contagious skin disease.* The **H** word used here can describe various skin diseases.
3:29 {walks on crutches} Or *who is effeminate;* **H** reads *who handles a spindle.*
4: 7 {the Jordan Valley} **H** *the Arabah.*
5: 9 {at the Millo} Or *the supporting terraces.* The meaning of the **H** is uncertain.
5:14 {in Jerusalem: Shimea,} As in parallel text at 1 Chr 3:5; **H** reads *Shammua,* a variant name for Shimea.
5:25 {way from Gibeon} As in Greek version (see also 1 Chr 14:16); **H** reads *Geba.*
6: 5 {might, singing songs} As in Greek version (see also 1 Chr 13:8); **H** reads *cypress trees.*
6:14 {a priestly tunic.} **H** *a linen ephod.*
6:19 {cake of dates,} Or *a portion of meat.* The meaning of the **H** is uncertain.
7:19 {everyone this way,} The meaning of the **H** is uncertain.
8: 1 {their largest city.} **H** *by conquering Metheg-ammah,* a name which means "the bridle," possibly referring to the size of the city or the tribute money taken from it. Compare 1 Chr 18:1.
8: 8 {cities of Tebah} As in some Greek manuscripts (see also 1 Chr 18:8); **H** reads *Betah.*
8:12 {Edom,} As in a few **H** manuscripts and Greek and Syriac versions (see also 8:14; 1 Chr 18:11); most **H** manuscripts read *Aram.*
8:13 {eighteen thousand Edomites} As in a few **H** manuscripts and Greek and Syriac versions (see also 8:14; 1 Chr 18:12); most **H** manuscripts read *Arameans.*
8:18 {the king's bodyguard.} **H** *of the Kerethites and Pelethites.*
8:18 {as priestly leaders.} **H** *David's sons were priests;* compare parallel text at 1 Chr 18:17.
10:16 {the Euphrates River.} **H** *the river.*
11:21 {son Abimelech killed} **H** *Was not Abimelech son of Jerubbesheth killed.*
12:30 {seventy-five pounds.} **H** *1 talent* [34 kilograms].
13: 3 {David's brother Shimea.} **H** *Shimeah* (also in 13:32), a variant name for Shimea; compare 1 Chr 2:13.
13:18 {long, beautiful robe,} Or *a robe with sleeves,* or *an ornamented robe.* The meaning of the **H** is uncertain.
13:34 {the Horonaim road} As in Greek version; **H** reads *from the road behind him.*
14:26 {to five pounds!} **H** *200 shekels* [2.3 kilograms] *by the royal standard.*
15: 7 {After four years,} As in Greek and Syriac versions; **H** reads *40 years.*
15:18 {the king's bodyguard.} **H** *the Kerethites and Pelethites.*
15:20 {love and faithfulness.} As in Greek version; **H** reads *and may unfailing love and faithfulness go with you.*
15:27 {the priest, "Look,} As in Greek version; **H** reads *Are you a seer?* or *Do you see?*
15:27 {You and Abiathar} **H** lacks *and Abiathar;* compare 15:29.
15:28 {the Jordan River} **H** *at the crossing points of the wilderness.*
16:11 {relative of Saul} **H** *this Benjaminite.*
16:14 {the Jordan River.} As in Greek version (see also 17:16); **H** reads *when they reached their destination.*
17: 3 {that you seek.} As in Greek version; **H** reads *like the return of all is the man whom you seek.*
17:16 {the Jordan River} **H** *at the crossing points of the wilderness.*
17:25 {Jether,} **H** *Ithra,* a variant name for Jether.
17:25 {an Ishmaelite.} As in some Greek manuscripts (see also 1 Chr 2:17); **H** reads *an Israelite.*
18:11 {pieces of silver} **H** *10 shekels of silver,* about 4 ounces or 114 grams in weight.
18:12 {pieces of silver,} **H** *1,000 shekels,* about 25 pounds or 11.4 kilograms in weight.
19:20 {in all Israel} **H** *the house of Joseph.*
20: 7 {king's own bodyguard.} **H** *the Kerethites and Pelethites;* also in 20:23.
20:24 {Adoniram} As in Greek version (see also 1 Kgs 4:6; 5:14); **H** reads *Adoram.*
21: 6 {of the LORD.} As in Greek version (see also 21:9); **H** reads *at Gibeah of Saul, the chosen of the LORD.*
21: 8 {Saul's daughter Merab,} As in a few **H** and Greek manuscripts and Syriac version (see also 1 Sam 18:19); most **H** manuscripts read *Michal.*
21:16 {of the giants} As in Greek version; **H** reads *a descendant of the Rephaites;* also in 21:18, 20, 22.
21:16 {seven pounds,} **H** *300 shekels* [3.4 kilograms].
21:19 {son of Jair} As in parallel text at 1 Chr 20:5; **H** reads *son of Jaare-oregim.*
21:19 {Goliath of Gath.} As in parallel text at 1 Chr 20:5; **H** reads *killed Goliath of Gath.*
21:21 {Shimea.} As in parallel text at 1 Chr 20:7; **H** reads *Shimei,* a variant name for Shimea.
22: 6 {The grave} **H** *Sheol.*
22:11 {a mighty angel,} **H** *cherub.*
22:11 {soaring} As in some **H** manuscripts (see also Ps 18:10); other **H** manuscripts read *appearing.*
22:36 {your help} As in Dead Sea Scrolls; most **H** manuscripts read *your answering.*
23: 8 {Jashobeam the Hacmonite,} As in parallel text at 1 Chr 11:11; **H** reads *Josheb-basshebeth the Tahkemonite.*
23: 8 {a single battle.} As in some Greek manuscripts (see also 1 Chr 11:11); the **H** is uncertain, though it might be rendered *the Three. It was Adino the Eznite who killed eight hundred men at one time.*
23:18 {of the Thirty.} As in a few **H** manuscripts and Syriac version; most **H** manuscripts read *the Three.*
23:19 {of the Thirty} As in Syriac version; **H** reads *the Three.*
23:26 {Helez from Pelon} As in parallel text at 1 Chr 11:27 (see also 1 Chr 27:10); **H** reads *from Palti.*
23:27 {Sibbecai} As in some Greek manuscripts (see also 1 Chr 11:29); **H** reads *Mebunnai.*
23:29 {Heled} As in some **H** manuscripts (see also 1 Chr 11:30); most **H** manuscripts read *Heleb.*
23:29 {Ithai} As in parallel text at 1 Chr 11:31; **H** reads *Ittai.*
23:30 {Hurai} As in some Greek manuscripts (see also 1 Chr 11:32); **H** reads *Hiddai.*
23:33 {son of Shagee} As in parallel text at 1 Chr 11:34; **H** reads *Jonathan, Shammah;* some Greek manuscripts read *Jonathan son of Shammah.*
24:13 {you choose three} As in Greek version (see also 1 Chr 21:12); **H** reads *seven.*
24:24 {pieces of silver} **H** *50 shekels of silver,* about 20 ounces or 570 grams in weight.
1Ki 1:25 {of the army,} As in Greek version; **H** reads *invited the commanders of the army.*
1:38 {the king's bodyguard} **H** *the Kerethites and Pelethites;* also in 1:44.
1:52 {not be harmed.} **H** *not a hair on his head will be touched.*
4:11 {Ben-abinadab, in Naphoth-dor.} **H** *Naphath-dor,* a variant name for Naphoth-dor.
4:12 {all of Beth-shan} **H** *Beth-shean,* a variant name for Beth-shan; also in 4:12b.
4:19 {land of Judah.} As in some Greek manuscripts; **H** lacks *of Judah.* The meaning of the **H** is uncertain.
4:21 {the Euphrates River} **H** *the river;* also in 4:24.
4:22 {bushels of meal,} **H** *30 cors* [5.5 kiloliters] *of choice flour and 60 cors* [11 kiloliters] *of meal.*
4:26 {had four thousand} As in some Greek manuscripts (see also 2 Chr 9:25); **H** reads *40,000.*
5:11 {100,000 bushels} **H** *20,000 cors* [3,640 kiloliters].
5:11 {110,000 gallons} As in Greek version, which reads *20,000 baths* [420 kiloliters] (see also 2 Chr 2:10); **H** reads *20 cors,* about 800 gallons or 3.6 kiloliters in volume.
5:16 {thirty-six hundred} As in some Greek manuscripts (see also 2 Chr 2:2, 18); **H** reads *3,300.*

6: 1 {in midspring,} **H** *in the month of Ziv, which is the second month.* This month of the **H** lunar calendar usually occurs in April and May.
6: 2 {and 45 feet high.} **H** *60 cubits* [27 meters] *long, 20 cubits* [9 meters] *wide, and 30 cubits* [13.5 meters] *high.* In this chapter, the distance measures are calculated from the **H** cubit at a ratio of 18 inches or 45 centimeters per cubit.
6: 8 {the bottom floor} As in Greek version; **H** reads *middle floor.*
6:20 {made of cedar.} Or *overlaid the altar with cedar.* The meaning of the **H** is uncertain.
6:37 {laid in midspring} **H** *in the month of Ziv.* This month of the **H** lunar calendar usually occurs in April and May.
6:38 {detail by midautumn} **H** *in the month of Bul, which is the eighth month.* This month of the **H** lunar calendar usually occurs in October and November.
7: 2 {and 45 feet high.} **H** *100 cubits* [45 meters] *long, 50 cubits* [22.5 meters] *wide, and 30 cubits* [13.5 meters] *high.* In this chapter, the distance measures are calculated from the **H** cubit at a ratio of 18 inches or 45 centimeters per cubit.
7: 7 {floor to ceiling.} As in Syriac version and Latin Vulgate; **H** reads *from floor to floor.*
7:13 {man named Huram} **H** *Hiram* (also in 7:40, 45); compare 2 Chr 2:13. This is not the same person mentioned in 5:1.
7:24 {gourds per foot} Or *20 gourds per meter;* **H** reads *10 per cubit.*
7:26 {about three inches} **H** *a handbreadth* [8 centimeters].
7:26 {about 11,000 gallons} **H** *2,000 baths* [42 kiloliters].
7:35 {rim 9 inches wide.} **H** *half a cubit wide* [22.5 centimeters].
7:38 {hold 220 gallons} **H** *40 baths* [840 liters].
8: 2 {in early autumn.} **H** *at the festival in the month Ethanim, which is the seventh month.* The Festival of Shelters began on the fifteenth day of the seventh month on the **H** lunar calendar....
8: 4 {with the Tabernacle} **H** *Tent of Meeting.*
8: 9 {at Mount Sinai,} **H** *at Horeb,* another name for Sinai.
8:65 {Festival of Shelters} **H** *the festival;* see note on 8:2.
8:65 {Festival of Shelters.} **H** *seven days and seven days, fourteen days;* compare parallel text at 2 Chr 7:8-10.
8:66 {festival was over,} **H** *On the eighth day,* probably referring to the day following the seven-day Festival of Shelters; compare parallel text at 2 Chr 7:9-10.
9:14 {nine thousand pounds} **H** *120 talents* [4 metric tons].
9:21 {not completely destroyed.} The **H** term used here refers to the complete consecration of things or people to the LORD, either by destroying them or by giving them as an offering.
9:26 {port near Elath} As in Greek version (see also 2 Kgs 14:22; 16:6); **H** reads *Eloth.*
9:26 {the Red Sea.} **H** *sea of reeds.*
9:28 {some sixteen tons} **H** *420 talents* [14 metric tons].
10:10 {nine thousand pounds} **H** *120 talents* [4 metric tons].
10:14 {twenty-five tons} **H** *666 talents* [23 metric tons].
10:16 {over fifteen pounds} **H** *600 shekels* [6.8 kilograms].
10:17 {nearly four pounds} **H** *3 minas* [1.8 kilograms].
10:22 {of trading ships} **H** *fleet of ships of Tarshish.*
10:27 {foothills of Judah.} **H** *the Shephelah.*
10:28 {and from Cilicia} **H** *Kue,* probably another name for Cilicia.
10:29 {pieces of silver,} **H** *600 shekels of silver,* about 15 pounds or 6.8 kilograms in weight.
10:29 {pieces of silver.} **H** *150 [shekels],* about 3.8 pounds or 1.7 kilograms in weight.
11: 5 {Sidonians, and Molech,} **H** *Milcom,* a variant name for Molech; also in 11:33.
11:28 {Ephraim and Manasseh.} **H** *from the house of Joseph.*
11:36 {continue to reign} **H** *will continue to have a lamp.*
12: 2 {returned from Egypt,} As in Greek version and Latin Vulgate (see also 2 Chr 10:2); **H** reads *he lived in Egypt.*
12:18 {Rehoboam sent Adoniram,} As in some Greek manuscripts and Syriac version (see also 4:6; 5:14); **H** reads *Adoram.*
12:25 {town of Peniel.} **H** *Penuel,* a variant name for Peniel.
12:32 {day in midautumn,} **H** *on the fifteenth day of the eighth month* (also in 12:33). This day of the **H** lunar calendar occurs in late October or early November, exactly one month after the annual Festival of Shelters in Judah (see Lev 23:34).
14:15 {the Euphrates River,} **H** *the river.*
15: 2 {daughter of Absalom.} **H** *Abishalom* (also in 15:10), a variant name for Absalom; compare 2 Chr 11:20.
15: 4 {dynasty to continue,} **H** *gave him a lamp in Jerusalem.*
15: 6 {Abijam and Jeroboam} As in a few **H** manuscripts; most **H** manuscripts read *between Rehoboam and Jeroboam.*
15:10 {years. His grandmother} **H** *his mother* (also in 15:13); compare 15:2.
16:24 {pounds of silver.} **H** *for 2 talents* [68 kilograms] *of silver.*
18:31 {tribes of Israel,} **H** *each of the tribes of the sons of Jacob to whom the LORD had said, "Your name will be Israel."*
18:32 {about three gallons.} **H** *2 seahs* [12 liters] *of seed.*
18:36 {Isaac, and Jacob,} **H** *and Israel.*
19: 8 {to Mount Sinai,} **H** *Horeb,* another name for Sinai.
20:39 {of seventy-five pounds} **H** *1 talent* [34 kilograms].
20:42 {must be destroyed,} The **H** term used here refers to the complete consecration of things or people to the LORD, either by destroying them or by giving them as an offering.
21:10 {Find two scoundrels} **H** *two sons of Belial;* also in 21:13.
22:48 {of trading ships} **H** *fleet of ships of Tarshish.*
2Ki 1:17 {his brother Joram} **H** *Jehoram,* a variant name for Joram.
2: 9 {your rightful successor."} **H** *Let me inherit a double share of your spirit.*
2:15 {become Elijah's successor!"} **H** *The spirit of Elijah rests upon Elisha.*
3: 1 {Ahab's son Joram} **H** *Jehoram,* a variant name for Joram; also in 3:6.
3:11 {Elijah's personal assistant.} **H** *He used to pour water on the hands of Elijah.*
3:25 {came under attack.} **H** *until only Kir-hareseth was left, with its stones, but the slingers surrounded and attacked it.*
4:42 {group of prophets} **H** *to the people;* also in 4:43.
5: 1 {suffered from leprosy.} Or *from a contagious skin disease.* The **H** word used here and throughout this passage can describe various skin diseases.
5: 5 {pounds of gold,} **H** *10 talents* [340 kilograms] *of silver, 6,000 shekels* [68 kilograms] *of gold.*
5:22 {would like 75 pounds} **H** *1 talent* [34 kilograms].
5:23 {take 150 pounds} **H** *2 talents* [68 kilograms].
6:25 {about two ounces} **H** *sold for 80 shekels* [0.9 kilograms] *of silver, and 1/4 of a cab* [0.3 liters] *of dove's dung cost 5 shekels* [57 grams]. *Dove's dung* may be a variety of wild vegetable.
6:33 {And the king} **H** *he.*
7: 1 {ounce of silver,} **H** *1 seah* [6 liters] *of fine flour will cost 1 shekel* [11 grams]; also in 7:16, 18.
7: 1 {ounce of silver.} **H** *2 seahs* [12 liters] *of barley grain will cost 1 shekel* [11 grams]; also in 7:16, 18.
7: 3 {men with leprosy} Or *with a contagious skin disease.* The **H** word used here and throughout this passage can describe various skin diseases.
8:11 {stared at Hazael} **H** *He stared at him.*
8:13 {nobody like me} **H** *a dog.*
8:19 {to rule forever.} **H** *promised to give a lamp to David and his descendants forever.*
8:21 {So Jehoram} **H** *Joram,* a variant name for Jehoram; also in 8:23, 24.
9:15 {But Joram} **H** *Jehoram,* a variant name for Joram; also in 9:17, 21, 22, 23, 24.
10: 1 {of the city,} As in some Greek manuscripts and Latin Vulgate (see also 10:6); **H** reads *of Jezreel.*
10:25 {into the fortress} **H** *city.*
11: 2 {of King Jehoram,} **H** *Joram,* a variant name for Jehoram.
11:21 {Joash} **H** *Jehoash,* a variant name for Joash.
12: 1 {Joash} **H** *Jehoash,* a variant name for Joash; also in 12:2, 4, 6, 7, 18.
12:21 {assassins were Jozacar} As in Greek and Syriac versions; **H** reads *Jozabad;* compare parallel text at 2 Chr 24:26.
13: 9 {his son Jehoash} **H** *Joash,* a variant name for Jehoash; also in 13:10, 12, 13, 14, 25.
14: 1 {of King Jehoash} **H** *Joash,* a variant name for Jehoash; also in 14:13, 23, 27.
14:13 {six hundred feet} **H** *400 cubits* [180 meters].
14:21 {sixteen-year-old son, Uzziah,} **H** *Azariah,* a variant name for Uzziah.
14:25 {the Dead Sea,} **H** *the sea of the Arabah.*
15: 1 {Uzziah} **H** *Azariah,* a variant name for Uzziah; also in 15:6, 7, 8, 17, 23, 27.
15: 5 {king with leprosy,} Or *with a contagious skin disease.* The **H** word used here and throughout this passage can describe various skin diseases.
15:16 {town of Tappuah} As in some Greek manuscripts; **H** reads *Tiphsah.*
15:19 {Then King Tiglath-pileser} **H** *Pul,* another name for Tiglath-pileser.
15:19 {thirty-seven tons} **H** *1,000 talents* [34 metric tons].
15:20 {pay twenty ounces} **H** *50 shekels* [570 grams].
16: 6 {king of Edom} As in Latin Vulgate; **H** reads *Rezin king of Aram.*
16: 6 {Edom.} As in Latin Vulgate; **H** reads *Aram.*
16: 6 {and sent Edomites} As in marginal *Qere* reading of the Masoretic Text, Greek version, and Latin Vulgate; **H** reads *Arameans.*
16: 7 {and your vassal.} **H** *your son.*
16:18 {the Sabbath day,} The meaning of the **H** is uncertain.
17:26 {towns of Israel} **H** *of Samaria;* also in 17:29.
18: 2 {mother was Abijah,} As in parallel text at 2 Chr 29:1; **H** reads *Abi,* a variant name for Abijah.
18: 4 {was called Nehushtan.} *Nehushtan* sounds like the **H** terms that mean "snake," "bronze," and "unclean thing."
18:14 {ton of gold.} **H** *300 talents* [10 metric tons] *of silver and 30 talents* [1 metric ton] *of gold.*
19: 9 {Tirhakah of Ethiopia} **H** *of Cush.*
19:35 {the surviving Assyrians} **H** *When they.*
23:13 {and for Molech,} **H** *Milcom,* a variant name for Molech.
23:16 {man of God} As in Greek version; **H** lacks *as Jeroboam stood beside the altar at the festival. Then Josiah turned and looked up at the tomb of the man of God.*
23:33 {75 pounds of gold} **H** *100 talents* [3.4 metric tons] *of silver and 1 talent* [34 kilograms] *of gold.*
25: 1 {So on January 15,} **H** *on the tenth day of the tenth month,* of the **H** calendar. A number of events in 2 Kings can be cross-checked with dates in surviving Babylonian records and related accurately to our modern calendar. This event occurred on January 15, 588 B.C.
25: 3 {Zedekiah's eleventh year,} **H** *By the ninth day,* that is, "of the fourth month of Zedekiah's eleventh year" (compare Jer 52:6 and the note there). This event of the **H** lunar calendar occurred on July 18, 586 B.C.; also see note on 25:1.
25: 4 {the Jordan Valley.} **H** *the Arabah.*
25: 8 {of that year,} **H** *On the seventh day of the fifth month,* of the **H** calendar. This day was August 14, 586 B.C.; also see note on 25:1.
25:17 {pillars was 27 feet} **H** *18 cubits* [8.1 meters].
25:17 {was 7 1/2 feet} As in parallel texts at 1 Kgs 7:16, 2 Chr 3:15, and Jer 52:22, all of which read *5 cubits* [2.3 meters]; **H** reads *3 cubits,* which is 4.5 feet or 1.4 meters.
25:25 {of that year,} **H** *in the seventh month,* of the **H** calendar. This month occurred in October and November 586 B.C.
25:27 {of that year.} **H** *on the twenty-seventh day of the twelfth month,* of the **H** calendar. This day was April 2, 560 B.C.; also see note on 25:1.
1Ch 1: 4 {of Noah were} As in Greek version (see also Gen 5:3-32); **H** lacks *The sons of Noah were.*
1: 6 {were Ashkenaz, Riphath,} As in some **H** manuscripts and Greek version (see also Gen 10:3); most **H** manuscripts read *Diphath.*
1:12 {the Philistines came.} **H** *Casluhites, from whom the Philistines came, Caphtorites.* See Jer 47:4; Amos 9:7.
1:17 {of Aram were} As in one **H** manuscript and some Greek manuscripts (see also Gen 10:23); most **H** manuscripts lack *The descendants of Aram were.*
1:17 {Gether, and Mash.} As in parallel text at Gen 10:23; **H** reads *and Meshech.*
1:22 {Obal,} As in some **H** manuscripts and Syriac version (see also Gen 10:28); most Hebrew manuscripts read *Ebal.*
1:22 {Obal,} As in some Hebrew manuscripts and Syriac version (see also Gen 10:28); most **H** manuscripts read *Ebal.*
1:36 {Zepho,} As in many **H** manuscripts and a few Greek manuscripts (see also Gen 36:11); most **H** manuscripts read *Zephi.*
1:36 {Timna.} As in some Greek manuscripts (see also Gen 36:12); **H** reads *Kenaz, Timna, and Amalek.*
1:39 {Hori and Heman.} As in parallel text at Gen 36:22; **H** reads *and Homam.*
1:40 {Alvan,} As in many **H** manuscripts and a few Greek manuscripts (see also Gen 36:23); most **H** manuscripts read *Alian.*
1:40 {Shepho,} As in some **H** manuscripts (see also Gen 36:23); most **H** manuscripts read *Shephi.*
1:41 {Hemdan,} As in many **H** manuscripts and some Greek manuscripts (see also Gen 36:26); most **H** manuscripts read *Hamran.*
1:42 {Akan.} As in many **H** and Greek manuscripts (see also Gen 36:27); most **H** manuscripts read *Jaakan.*
1:42 {sons of Dishan} **H** *Dishon;* compare 1:38 and parallel text at Gen 36:28.
1:48 {the Euphrates River} **H** *the river.*
1:50 {Pau.} As in many **H** manuscripts, some Greek manuscripts, Syriac version, and Latin Vulgate (see also Gen 36:39); most **H** manuscripts read *Pai.*
1:51 {were Timna, Alvah,} As in parallel text at Gen 36:40; **H** reads *Aliah.*
2: 6 {Calcol, and Darda} As in many **H** manuscripts, some Greek manuscripts, and Syriac version (see also 1 Kgs 4:31); **H** reads *Dara.*
2: 7 {Achan} **H** *Achar;* compare Josh 7:1. *Achar* means "disaster."
2: 7 {for the LORD.} The **H** term used here refers to the complete consecration of things or people to the LORD, either by destroying them or by giving them as an offering.
2: 9 {Ram, and Caleb.} **H** *Kelubai,* a variant name for Caleb; compare 2:18.
2:11 {father of Salmon.} As in Greek version (see also Ruth 4:21); **H** reads *Salma.*
2:19 {Caleb married Ephrathah,} **H** *Ephrath,* a variant name for Ephrathah; compare 2:50 and 4:4.
2:42 {father of Hebron.} The meaning of the **H** is uncertain.
3: 1 {second was Kileab,} As in parallel text at 2 Sam 3:3; **H** reads *Daniel.*
3: 5 {and Solomon. Bathsheba,} **H** *Bathshua,* a variant name for Bathsheba.
3: 6 {sons: Ibhar, Elishua,} As in some **H** and Greek manuscripts (see also 14:5-7 and 2 Sam 5:15); most **H** manuscripts read *Elishama.*

3: 6 {Elpelet,} **H** *Eliphelet;* compare parallel text at 14:5-7.
3: 11 {Jehoram,} **H** *Joram,* a variant name for Jehoram.
3: 12 {Amaziah, Uzziah,} **H** *Azariah,* a variant name for Uzziah.
3: 15 {third), and Jehoahaz} **H** *Shallum,* another name for Jehoahaz.
3: 16 {his uncle Zedekiah.} **H** *The descendants of Jehoiakim were his son Jeconiah* [a variant name for Jehoiachin] *and his son Zedekiah.*
3: 17 {sons of Jehoiachin,} **H** *Jeconiah,* a variant name for Jehoiachin.
4: 3 {The descendants of} As in Greek version; **H** reads *father of.* The meaning of the **H** is uncertain.
4: 9 {named him Jabez} *Jabez* sounds like a **H** term meaning "distress" or "pain."
4: 13 {Hathath and Meonothai.} As in some Greek manuscripts and Latin Vulgate; **H** lacks *and Meonothai.*
4: 33 {away as Baalath.} As in some Greek manuscripts (see also Josh 19:8); **H** reads *Baal.*
4: 41 {and completely destroyed} The **H** term used here refers to the complete consecration of things or people to the LORD, either by destroying them or by giving them as an offering.
5: 6 {by King Tiglath-pileser} **H** *Tilgath-pilneser,* a variant name for Tiglath-pileser; also in 5:26.
6: 16 {Levi were Gershon,} **H** *Gershom,* a variant name for Gershon (see 6:1); also in 6:17, 20, 43, 62, 71.
6: 23 {Elkanah, Abiasaph,} **H** *Ebiasaph,* a variant name for Abiasaph (also in 6:37); compare parallel text at Exod 6:24.
6: 27 {Elkanah, and Samuel.} As in some Greek manuscripts (see also 6:33-34); **H** lacks *and Samuel.*
6: 28 {Samuel were Joel} As in some Greek manuscripts and the Syriac version (see also 6:33 and 1 Sam 8:2); **H** lacks *Joel.*
6: 32 {at the Tabernacle} **H** *the Tabernacle, the Tent of Meeting.*
6: 39 {clan of Gershon.} **H** lacks *from the clan of Gershon;* see 6:43.
6: 58 {Holon,} As in parallel text at Josh 21:15; **H** reads *Hilen.*
6: 59 {Ain,} As in parallel text at Josh 21:16; **H** reads *Ashan.*
6: 59 {Juttah,} As in Syriac version (see also Josh 21:16); **H** lacks *Juttah.*
6: 60 {were given Gibeon,} As in parallel text at Josh 21:17; **H** lacks *Gibeon.*
6: 77 {of Jokneam, Kartah,} As in Greek version (see also Josh 21:34); **H** lacks *Jokneam, Kartah.*
6: 78 {desert town), Jahaz,} **H** *Jahzah,* a variant name for Jahaz.
7: 13 {Jahzeel,} As in parallel text at Gen 46:24; **H** reads *Jahziel,* a variant name for Jahzeel.
7: 13 {Shillem.} As in some **H** and Greek manuscripts (see also Gen 46:24; Num 26:49); most **H** manuscripts read *Shallum.*
7: 23 {named him Beriah} *Beriah* sounds like a **H** term meaning "tragedy" or "misfortune."
7: 29 {towns of Beth-shan,} **H** *Beth-shean,* a variant name for Beth-shan.
8: 29 {Jeiel} As in some Greek manuscripts (see also 9:35); **H** lacks *Jeiel.*
8: 30 {Kish, Baal, Ner,} As in some Greek manuscripts (see also 9:36); **H** lacks *Ner.*
8: 31 {Gedor, Ahio, Zechariah,} As in parallel text at 9:37; **H** reads *Zeker,* a variant name for Zechariah.
8: 32 {father of Shimeam.} As in parallel text at 9:38; **H** reads *Shimeah,* a variant name for Shimeam.
8: 35 {Pithon, Melech, Tahrea,} As in parallel text at 9:41; **H** reads *Tarea,* a variant name for Tahrea.
8: 36 {father of Jadah.} As in parallel text at 9:42; **H** reads *Jehoaddah,* a variant name for Jadah.
8: 37 {father of Rephaiah.} As in parallel text at 9:43; **H** reads *Raphah,* a variant name for Rephaiah.
9: 19 {descendant of Abiasaph,} **H** *Ebiasaph,* a variant name for Abiasaph; compare Exod 6:24.
9: 21 {to the Tabernacle.} **H** *Tent of Meeting.*
9: 41 {Tahrea, and Ahaz.} As in Syriac version and Latin Vulgate (see also 8:35); **H** lacks *and Ahaz.*
9: 42 {Jadah.} As in some **H** manuscripts and Greek version (see also 8:36); **H** reads *Jarah.*
11: 8 {from the Millo} Or *the supporting terraces.* The meaning of the **H** is uncertain.
11: 11 {among David's men.} As in some Greek manuscripts (see also 2 Sam 23:8); **H** *commander of the Thirty,* or *commander of the captains.*
11: 12 {son of Dodai,} As in parallel text at 2 Sam 23:9 (see also 1 Chr 27:4); **H** reads *Dodo,* a variant name for Dodai.
11: 20 {of the Thirty.} As in Syriac version; **H** reads *the Three;* also in 11:21.
11: 23 {a half feet} **H** *5 cubits* [2.3 meters].
11: 27 {Shammah from Harod;} As in parallel text at 2 Sam 23:25; **H** reads *Shammoth from Haror.*
11: 29 {Zalmon} As in parallel text at 2 Sam 23:28; **H** reads *Ilai.*
11: 32 {Abi-albon} As in parallel text at 2 Sam 23:31; **H** reads *Abiel.*
11: 33 {Azmaveth from Bahurim} As in parallel text at 2 Sam 23:31; **H** reads *Baharum.*
11: 34 {sons of Jashen} As in parallel text at 2 Sam 23:32; **H** reads *sons of Hashem.*
11: 35 {son of Sharar} As in parallel text at 2 Sam 23:33; **H** reads *son of Sacar.*
11: 37 {Paarai} As in parallel text at 2 Sam 23:35; **H** reads *Naarai.*
13: 5 {to the other,} **H** *from the Shihor of Egypt to Lebo-hamath.*
13: 9 {floor of Nacon,} As in parallel text at 2 Sam 6:6; **H** reads *Kidon.*
14: 4 {in Jerusalem: Shimea,} **H** *Shammua,* a variant name for Shimea; compare 3:5.
14: 7 {Elishama, Eliada,} **H** *Beeliada,* a variant name for Eliada; compare 3:8 and parallel text at 2 Sam 5:16.
14: 12 {abandoned their idols} **H** *their gods;* compare parallel text at 2 Sam 5:21.
15: 4 {are the priests} **H** *descendants of Aaron.*
15: 7 {clan of Gershon,} **H** *Gershom,* a variant name for Gershon.
15: 20 {play the lyres.} **H** adds *according to Alamoth,* which is probably a musical term. The meaning of the **H** is uncertain.
15: 21 {play the harps.} **H** adds *according to the Sheminith,* which is probably a musical term. The meaning of the **H** is uncertain.
15: 27 {a priestly tunic.} **H** *a linen ephod.*
16: 3 {cake of dates,} Or *a portion of meat.* The meaning of the **H** is uncertain.
16: 15 {by his covenant} As in some Greek manuscripts (see also Ps 105:8); **H** reads *Remember his covenant forever.*
17: 6 {to Israel's leaders,} As in Greek version (see also 2 Sam 7:7); **H** reads *judges.*
17: 17 {someone very great,} The meaning of the **H** is uncertain.
18: 3 {far as Hamath,} The meaning of the **H** is uncertain.
18: 8 {cities of Tebah} **H** reads *Tibhath,* a variant name for Tebah; compare parallel text at 2 Sam 8:8.
18: 9 {When King Toi} As in parallel text at 2 Sam 8:9; **H** reads *Tou;* also in 18:10.
18: 10 {his son Joram} As in parallel text at 2 Sam 8:10; **H** reads *Hadoram,* a variant name for Joram.
18: 16 {Ahimelech} As in some **H** manuscripts, Syriac version, and Latin Vulgate (see also 2 Sam 8:17); most **H** manuscripts read *Abimelech.*
18: 16 {the priests. Seraiah} As in parallel text at 2 Sam 8:17; **H** reads *Shavsha.*
18: 17 {the king's bodyguard.} **H** *of the Kerethites and Pelethites.*
19: 1 {his son Hanun} **H** lacks *Hanun;* compare parallel text at 2 Sam 10:1.
19: 6 {sent thirty-eight tons} **H** *1,000 talents* [34 metric tons].
19: 16 {the Euphrates River.} **H** *the river.*
19: 16 {command of Shobach,} As in parallel text at 2 Sam 10:16; **H** reads *Shophach;* also in 19:18.
20: 2 {about seventy-five pounds.} **H** *1 talent* [34 kilograms].
20: 3 {picks, and axes.} As in parallel text at 2 Sam 12:31; **H** reads *and saws.*
20: 4 {Hushah killed Saph,} As in parallel text at 2 Sam 21:18; **H** reads *Sippai.*
20: 4 {of the giants,} **H** *descendant of the Rephaites;* also in 20:6, 8.
21: 15 {floor of Araunah} As in parallel text at 2 Sam 24:16; **H** reads *Ornan,* another name for Araunah; also in 21:18-28.
21: 25 {pieces of gold} **H** *600 shekels of gold,* about 15 pounds or 6.8 kilograms in weight.
22: 9 {will be Solomon,} *Solomon* sounds like and is probably derived from the **H** word for "peace."
22: 14 {tons of silver,} **H** *100,000 talents* [3,400 metric tons] *of gold, 1,000,000 talents* [34,000 metric tons] *of silver.*
23: 7 {descent from Libni} **H** *Ladan* (also in 23:8-9), another name for Libni; compare 6:17.
23: 10 {were Jahath, Ziza,} As in Greek version and Latin Vulgate (see also 23:11); **H** reads *Zina.*
23: 32 {and the Temple} **H** *the Tent of Meeting and the sanctuary.*
24: 20 {leader was Shebuel.} **H** *Shubael* (also in 24:20b), a variant name for Shebuel; compare 23:16 and 26:24.
24: 22 {leader was Shelomith.} **H** *Shelomoth* (also in 24:22b), a variant name for Shelomith; compare 23:18.
24: 23 {was the leader,} **H** *From the descendants of Jeriah;* compare 23:19.
25: 3 {Zeri, Jeshaiah, Shimei,} As in one **H** manuscript and some Greek manuscripts (see also 25:17); most **H** manuscripts lack *Shimei.*
25: 4 {Mattaniah, Uzziel, Shubael,} **H** *Shebuel,* a variant name for Shubael; compare 25:20.
25: 9 {sons and relatives.} As in Greek version; **H** lacks *and twelve of his sons and relatives.*
25: 11 {fell to Zeri} **H** *Izri,* a variant name for Zeri; compare 25:3.
25: 14 {fell to Asarelah} **H** *Jesharelah,* a variant name for Asarelah; compare 25:2.
25: 18 {fell to Uzziel} **H** *Azarel,* a variant name for Uzziel; compare 25:4.
25: 22 {fell to Jerimoth} **H** *Jeremoth,* a variant name for Jerimoth; compare 25:4.
25: 24 {fell to Joshbekashah} **H** *Joshbekasha,* a variant name for Joshbekashah; compare 25:4.
25: 29 {fell to Geddalti} **H** *Giddalti,* a variant name for Geddalti; compare 25:4.
26: 14 {went to Meshelemiah} **H** *Shelemiah,* a variant name for Meshelemiah; compare 26:2.
26: 16 {to the Temple.} Or *the gate of Shalleketh on the upper road* (also in 26:18). The meaning of the **H** is uncertain.
26: 18 {to the courtyard.} Or *the colonnade.* The meaning of the **H** is uncertain.
26: 21 {family of Libni} **H** *Ladan,* another name for Libni; compare 6:17.
26: 21 {of Gershon, Jehiel} **H** *Jehieli* (also in 26:22), a variant name for Jehiel; compare 23:8.
26: 31 {Hebron came Jeriah,} **H** *Jerijah,* a variant name for Jeriah; compare 23:19.
27: 8 {Shammah} **H** *Shamhuth,* another name for Shammah; compare 11:27 and 2 Sam 23:25.
27: 15 {Heled,} **H** *Heldai,* a variant name for Heled; compare 11:30 and 2 Sam 23:29.
27: 21 {Manasseh (east)} **H** *in Gilead.*
27: 28 {foothills of Judah.} **H** *the Shephelah.*
29: 4 {tons of gold} **H** *3,000 talents* [102 metric tons] *of gold.*
29: 4 {of refined silver} **H** *7,000 talents* [238 metric tons] *of silver.*
29: 7 {tons of gold,} **H** *5,000 talents* [170 metric tons] *of gold.*
29: 7 {10,000 gold coins,} **H** *10,000 darics* [a Persian coin] *of gold,* about 185 pounds or 84 kilograms in weight.
29: 7 {tons of silver,} **H** *10,000 talents* [340 metric tons] *of silver.*
29: 7 {tons of bronze,} **H** *18,000 talents* [612 metric tons] *of bronze.*
29: 7 {tons of iron.} **H** *100,000 talents* [3,400 metric tons] *of iron.*
2Ch 1: 3 {where God's Tabernacle} **H** *Tent of Meeting;* also in 1:6, 13.
1: 15 {foothills of Judah.} **H** *the Shephelah.*
1: 16 {and from Cilicia} **H** *Kue,* probably another name for Cilicia.
1: 17 {pieces of silver,} **H** *600 shekels of silver,* about 15 pounds or 6.8 kilograms in weight.
1: 17 {pieces of silver.} **H** *150 shekels,* about 3.8 pounds or 1.7 kilograms in weight.
2: 3 {to King Hiram} **H** *Huram,* a variant name for Hiram; also in 2:11, 12.
2: 8 {cypress, and almug} **H** *algum;* compare 9:10-11 and parallel text at 1 Kgs 10:11-12.
2: 10 {bushels of barley,} **H** *20,000 cors* [3,640 kiloliters] *of crushed wheat, 20,000 cors of barley.*
2: 10 {of olive oil.} **H** *20,000 baths* [420 kiloliters] *of wine, and 20,000 baths of olive oil.*
3: 1 {floor of Araunah} **H** reads *Ornan,* another name for Araunah; compare 2 Sam 24:16.
3: 2 {began in midspring,} **H** *on the second day of the second month.* This day of the **H** lunar calendar occurs in April or early May.
3: 3 {thirty feet wide.} **H** *60 cubits* [27 meters] *long and 20 cubits* [9 meters] *wide.* In this chapter, the distance measures are calculated from the **H** cubit at a ratio of 18 inches or 45 centimeters per cubit.
3: 4 {was thirty feet} As in some Greek and Syriac manuscripts, which read *20 cubits* [9 meters]; **H** reads *120 cubits,* which is 180 feet or 54 meters.
3: 8 {about twenty-three tons} **H** *600 talents* [20.4 metric tons].
3: 9 {about twenty ounces} **H** *50 shekels* [570 grams].
3: 15 {that were 27 feet} As in Syriac version (see also 1 Kgs 7:15; 2 Kgs 25:17; Jer 52:21), which reads *18 cubits* [8.1 meters]; **H** reads *35 cubits,* which is 52.5 feet or 15.8 meters.
4: 1 {and 15 feet high.} **H** *20 cubits* [9 meters] *long, 20 cubits wide, and 10 cubits* [4.5 meters] *high.* In this chapter, the distance measures are calculated from the **H** cubit at a ratio of 18 inches or 45 centimeters per cubit.
4: 3 {oxen per foot} Or *20 oxen per meter;* **H** reads *10 per cubit.*
4: 5 {about three inches} **H** *a handbreadth* [8 centimeters].
4: 5 {about 16,500 gallons} **H** *3,000 baths* [63 kiloliters].
4: 17 {Succoth and Zarethan.} As in parallel text at 1 Kgs 7:46; **H** reads *Zeredah.*
5: 3 {in early autumn.} **H** *at the festival that is in the seventh month.* The Festival of Shelters began on the fifteenth day of the seventh month of the **H** lunar calendar. This occurs on our calendar in late September or early October.
5: 5 {the special tent} **H** *Tent of Meeting.*
5: 10 {at Mount Sinai,} **H** *Horeb,* another name for Sinai.
6: 13 {4 1/2 feet high} **H** *5 cubits* [2.3 meters] *long, 5 cubits wide, and 3 cubits* [1.4 meters] *high.*
7: 8 {Festival of Shelters} **H** *the festival* (also in 7:9); see note on 5:3.
7: 10 {of the celebration,} **H** *Then on the twenty-seventh day of the seventh month.* This day of the **H** lunar calendar occurs in late September or early October.
8: 2 {that King Hiram} **H** *Huram,* a variant name for Hiram; also in 8:18.
8: 17 {Ezion-geber and Elath,} As in Greek version (see also 2 Kgs 14:22; 16:6); **H** reads *Eloth.*
8: 17 {the Red Sea.} **H** *the sea.*
8: 18 {almost seventeen tons} **H** *450 talents* [15.3 metric tons].
9: 9 {nine thousand pounds} **H** *120 talents* [4 metric tons].
9: 10 {of almug wood} **H** *algum wood* (also in 9:11); compare parallel text at 1 Kgs 10:11-12.

9:11 {to make steps} Or *gateways.* The meaning of the **H** is uncertain.
9:13 {about 25 tons} **H** *666 talents* [23 metric tons].
9:15 {containing over 15 pounds} **H** *600 shekels* [6.8 kilograms].
9:16 {about 7 1/2 pounds} **H** *300 shekels* [3.4 kilograms].
9:21 {of trading ships} **H** *fleet of ships that could sail to Tarshish.*
9:21 {sent by Hiram.} **H** *Huram,* a variant name for Hiram.
9:26 {the Euphrates River} **H** *the river.*
9:27 {foothills of Judah.} **H** *the Shephelah.*
10:18 {Rehoboam sent Adoniram,} **H** *Hadoram,* a variant name for Adoniram; compare 1 Kgs 4:6; 5:14; 12:18.
12:3 {Sukkites, and Ethiopians.} **H** *and Cushites.*
13:2 {mother was Maacah,} As in most Greek manuscripts and Syriac version (see also 2 Chr 11:20-21; 1 Kgs 15:2); **H** reads *Micaiah.*
13:5 {an unbreakable covenant} **H** *a covenant of salt.*
14:9 {Once an Ethiopian} **H** *a Cushite.*
14:9 {a million men} Or *an army of thousands and thousands;* **H** reads *an army of a thousand thousands.*
14:12 {defeated the Ethiopians} **H** *Cushites;* also in 14:13.
15:8 {Azariah the prophet,} As in Syriac version and Latin Vulgate (see also 15:1); **H** reads *from Oded the prophet.*
15:10 {in late spring,} **H** *in the third month.* This month of the **H** lunar calendar usually occurs in May and June.
16:4 {Ijon, Dan, Abel-beth-maacah,} As in parallel text at 1 Kgs 15:20; **H** reads *Abel-maim,* another name for Abel-beth-maacah.
16:8 {to the Ethiopians} **H** *Cushites.*
17:3 {father's early years} Some **H** manuscripts read *the example of his father, David.*
20:1 {of the Meunites} As in some Greek manuscripts (see also 26:7); **H** reads *Ammonites.*
20:2 {army from Edom} As in one **H** manuscript; most **H** manuscripts and ancient versions read *Aram.*
20:2 {the Dead Sea.} **H** *the sea.*
20:25 {of equipment, clothing,} As in some **H** manuscripts and Latin Vulgate; most **H** manuscripts read *corpses.*
20:26 {Valley of Blessing,} **H** *valley of Beracah.*
20:36 {of trading ships} **H** *fleet of ships that could go to Tarshish.*
20:37 {out to sea.} **H** *never set sail for Tarshish.*
21:7 {to rule forever.} **H** *promised to give a lamp to David and his descendants forever.*
21:16 {near the Ethiopians,} **H** *the Cushites.*
21:17 {youngest son, Ahaziah,} **H** *Jehoahaz,* a variant name for Ahaziah; compare 22:1.
22:2 {Ahaziah was twenty-two} As in some Greek manuscripts and Syriac version (see also 2 Kgs 8:26); **H** reads *forty-two.*
22:5 {with King Joram,} **H** *Jehoram,* a variant name for Joram; also in 22:6, 7.
22:6 {and King Ahaziah} Some **H** manuscripts, Greek and Syriac versions, and Latin Vulgate (see also 2 Kgs 8:29); most **H** manuscripts read *Azariah.*
22:8 {and Ahaziah's relatives} As in Greek version (see also 2 Kgs 10:13); **H** reads *and sons of the brothers of Ahaziah.*
22:11 {Ahaziah's sister Jehosheba,} As in parallel text at 2 Kgs 11:2; **H** reads *Jehoshabeath,* a variant name for Jehosheba.
24:6 {of the Covenant.} **H** *Tent of the Testimony.*
24:26 {assassins were Jozacar,} **H** *Zabad;* compare parallel text at 2 Kgs 12:21, and see note there.
24:26 {woman named Shomer.} As in parallel text at 2 Kgs 12:21; **H** reads *Shimrith.*
25:1 {Jehoaddin,} As in parallel text at 2 Kgs 14:2; **H** reads *Jehoaddan,* a variant name for Jehoaddin.
25:6 {about 7,500 pounds} **H** *100 talents* [3.4 metric tons].
25:17 {Israel's king Jehoash,} **H** *Joash,* a variant name for Jehoash; also in 25:18, 21, 23, 25.
25:23 {six hundred feet} **H** *400 cubits* [180 meters].
25:28 {City of David.} As in some **H** manuscripts and other ancient versions (see also 2 Kgs 14:20); most **H** manuscripts read *the city of Judah.*
26:2 {town of Elath} As in Greek version (see also 2 Kgs 14:22; 16:6); **H** reads *Eloth.*
26:7 {Arabs of Gur} As in Greek version; **H** reads *Gur-baal.*
26:8 {The Meunites} As in Greek version; **H** reads *Ammonites.* Compare 26:7.
26:10 {foothills of Judah} **H** *the Shephelah.*
26:19 {LORD's Temple, leprosy} Or *a contagious skin disease.* The **H** word used here and throughout this passage can describe various skin diseases.
27:5 {of 7,500 pounds} **H** *100 talents* [3.4 metric tons].
27:5 {bushels of barley.} **H** *10,000 cors* [1,820 kiloliters] *of wheat, and 10,000 cors of barley.*
28:12 {leaders of Israel} **H** *Ephraim,* referring to the northern kingdom of Israel.
28:18 {foothills of Judah} **H** *the Shephelah.*
28:19 {Ahaz of Judah,} **H** *of Israel.*
28:20 {when King Tiglath-pileser} **H** *Tilgath-pilneser,* a variant name for Tiglath-pileser.
29:17 {in early spring,} **H** *on the first day of the first month.* This day of the **H** lunar calendar occurs in March or early April.
30:2 {Passover in midspring.} **H** *in the second month.* This month of the **H** lunar calendar usually occurs in April and May.
30:3 {in early spring,} **H** *in the first month.* This month of the **H** lunar calendar usually occurs in March and April.
30:13 {Jerusalem in midspring} **H** *in the second month.* This month of the **H** lunar calendar usually occurs in April and May.
30:15 {day in midspring,} **H** *On the fourteenth day of the second month.* This day of the **H** lunar calendar occurs in late April or early May.
31:7 {in late spring,} **H** *in the third month.* This month of the **H** lunar calendar usually occurs in May and June.
31:7 {until early autumn.} **H** *in the seventh month.* This month of the **H** lunar calendar usually occurs in September and October.
34:20 {son of Micaiah,} As in parallel text at 2 Kgs 22:12; **H** reads *Abdon son of Micah.*
34:22 {grandson of Harhas,} As in parallel text at 2 Kgs 22:14; **H** reads *son of Tokhath, son of Hasrah.*
35:1 {in early spring.} **H** *on the fourteenth day of the first month.* This day of the **H** lunar calendar occurs in late March or early April.
36:2 {Jehoahaz} **H** *Joahaz,* a variant name for Jehoahaz; also in 36:4.
36:3 {75 pounds of gold.} **H** *100 talents* [3.4 metric tons] *of silver and 1 talent* [34 kilograms] *of gold.*
36:9 {Jehoiachin was eighteen} As in one **H** manuscript, some Greek manuscripts, and Syriac version (see also 2 Kgs 24:8); most **H** manuscripts read *eight.*
36:10 {appointed Jehoiachin's uncle,} As in parallel text at 2 Kgs 24:17; **H** reads *brother,* or *relative.*

Ezr 1:8 {returning to Judah.} **H** *Sheshbazzar, the prince of Judah.*
1:9 {silver censers} The meaning of this **H** word is uncertain.
2:24 {people of Beth-azmaveth} As in parallel text at Neh 7:28; **H** reads *Azmaveth.*
2:25 {peoples of Kiriath-jearim,} As in some **H** manuscripts and Greek version (see also Neh 7:29); **H** reads *Kiriath-arim.*
2:46 {Hagab, Shalmai,} As in the marginal *Qere* reading of the Masoretic Text (see also Neh 7:48); **H** text reads *Shamlai.*
2:55 {Sotai, Sophereth,} As in parallel text at Neh 7:57; **H** reads *Hassophereth.*
2:63 {of sacred lots.} **H** *consult the Urim and Thummim about the matter.*
2:69 {61,000 gold coins,} **H** *61,000 darics of gold,* about 1,100 pounds or 500 kilograms in weight.
2:69 {6,250 pounds} **H** *5,000 minas* [3 metric tons].
3:1 {in early autumn,} **H** *in the seventh month.* A number of events in the book of Ezra can be cross-checked with dates in surviving Persian records and related accurately to our modern calendar. This month of the **H** lunar calendar occurred in October and November 537 B.C.
3:2 {son of Jehozadak} **H** *Jozadak,* a variant name for Jehozadak; also in 3:8.
3:6 {of Shelters began,} **H** *On the first day of the seventh month.* This day of the **H** lunar calendar occurs in September or early October. The Festival of Shelters began on the fifteenth day of the seventh month.
3:8 {began in midspring,} **H** *in the second month.* This month of the **H** lunar calendar occurred in April and May 536 B.C.
3:9 {descendants of Hodaviah.} **H** *sons of Judah* (i.e., *bene Yehudah*). *Bene* might also be read here as the proper name Binnui; *Yehudah* is probably another name for Hodaviah. Compare 2:40; Neh 7:43; 1 Esdras 5:58.
4:6 {later when Xerxes} **H** *Ahasuerus,* another name for Xerxes.
6:15 {completed on March 12,} Aramaic *on the third day of the month Adar,* of the **H** calendar. This event occurred on March 12, 515 B.C.; also see note on 3:1.
6:19 {On April 21} **H** *On the fourteenth day of the first month,* of the **H** calendar. This event occurred on April 21, 515 B.C.; also see note on 3:1.
7:8 {Jerusalem in August} **H** *in the fifth month.* This month of the **H** lunar calendar occurred in August and September 458 B.C.
7:9 {Babylon on April 8} **H** *on the first day of the first month,* of the **H** calendar. This event occurred on April 8, 458 B.C.; also see note on 3:1.
7:9 {Jerusalem on August 4,} **H** *on the first day of the fifth month,* of the **H** calendar. This event occurred on August 4, 458 B.C.; also see note on 3:1.
8:5 {family of Zattu} As in some Greek manuscripts (see also 1 Esdras 8:32); **H** lacks *Zattu.*
8:10 {family of Bani} As in some Greek manuscripts (see also 1 Esdras 8:36); **H** lacks *Bani.*
8:13 {who came later} The meaning of the **H** for this phrase is uncertain.
8:26 {24 tons} **H** *650 talents* [22 metric tons].
8:26 {7,500 pounds} **H** *100 talents* [3.4 metric tons].
8:26 {7,500 pounds} **H** *100 talents* [3.4 metric tons].
8:27 {1,000 gold coins,} **H** *1,000 darics,* about 19 pounds or 8.6 kilograms in weight.
8:31 {Canal on April 19} **H** *on the twelfth day of the first month,* of the **H** calendar. This event occurred on April 19, 458 B.C.; see note on 7:9a.
10:6 {spent the night} As in parallel text at 1 Esdras 9:2; **H** reads *He went.*
10:9 {place on December 19,} **H** *on the twentieth day of the ninth month,* of the **H** calendar. This event occurred on December 19, 458 B.C.; also see note on 7:9a.
10:16 {On December 29,} **H** *On the first day of the tenth month,* of the **H** calendar. This event occurred on December 29, 458 B.C.; also see note on 7:9a.
10:17 {the next year} **H** *By the first day of the first month,* of the **H** calendar. This event occurred on March 27, 457 B.C.; also see note on 7:9a.
10:18 {son of Jehozadak} **H** *Jozadak,* a variant name for Jehozadak.
10:25 {Mijamin, Eleazar, Hashabiah,} As in parallel text at 1 Esdras 9:26; **H** reads *Malkijah.*
10:37[-38] {family of Binnui} As in Greek version; **H** reads *Jaasu,* [38]*Bani, Binnui.*
10:44 {by these wives.} Or *and they sent them away with their children.* The meaning of the **H** is uncertain.

Ne 1:1 {King Artaxerxes' reign,} **H** *In the month of Kislev of the twentieth year.* A number of events in the book of Nehemiah can be cross-checked with dates in surviving Persian records and related accurately to our modern calendar. This month of the **H** lunar calendar occurred in November and December 446 B.C. The *twentieth year* probably refers to the reign of King Artaxerxes I; compare 2:1; 5:14.
1:11 {ask the king} **H** *stand before this man.*
2:1 {the following spring,} **H** *In the month of Nisan.* This month of the **H** lunar calendar occurred in April and May 445 B.C.
2:15 {the Kidron Valley} **H** *the valley.*
3:13 {fifteen hundred feet} **H** *1,000 cubits* [450 meters].
3:15 {pool of Siloam} **H** *pool of Shelah,* another name for the pool of Siloam.
3:18 {led by Binnui} As in a few **H** manuscripts, some Greek manuscripts, and Syriac version (see also 3:24; 10:9); most **H** manuscripts read *Bavvai.*
4:12 {and attack us!"} The meaning of the **H** is uncertain.
4:23 {went for water.} **H** *Each his weapon the water.* The meaning of the **H** is uncertain.
5:15 {besides a pound} **H** *40 shekels* [456 grams].
6:2 {of the villages} As in Greek version; **H** reads *at Kephirim.*
6:6 {"Geshem} **H** *Gashmu,* another name for Geshem.
6:15 {So on October 2} **H** *on the twenty-fifth day of the month Elul,* of the **H** calendar. This event occurred on October 2, 445 B.C.; also see note on 1:1.
7:7 {Seraiah,} As in parallel text at Ezra 2:2; **H** reads *Azariah.*
7:7 {Reelaiah,} As in parallel text at Ezra 2:2; **H** reads *Raamiah.*
7:7 {Mispar,} As in parallel text at Ezra 2:2; **H** reads *Mispereth.*
7:7 {Rehum,} As in parallel text at Ezra 2:2; **H** reads *Nehum.*
7:15 {family of Bani} As in parallel text at Ezra 2:10; **H** reads *Binnui.*
7:24 {family of Jorah} As in parallel text at Ezra 2:18; **H** reads *Hariph.*
7:25 {family of Gibbar} As in parallel text at Ezra 2:20; **H** reads *Gibeon.*
7:43 {(descendants of Hodaviah} As in parallel text at Ezra 2:40; **H** reads *Hodevah.*
7:47 {Keros, Siaha,} As in parallel text at Ezra 2:44; **H** reads *Sia.*
7:52 {Besai, Meunim, Nephusim,} As in parallel text at Ezra 2:50; **H** reads *Nephushesim.*
7:54 {Bazluth,} As in parallel text at Ezra 2:52; **H** reads *Bazlith.*
7:57 {Sotai, Sophereth, Peruda,} As in parallel text at Ezra 2:55; **H** reads *Perida.*
7:58 {Jaalah,} As in parallel text at Ezra 2:56; **H** reads *Jaala.*
7:59 {Pokereth-hazzebaim, and Ami.} As in parallel text at Ezra 2:57; **H** reads *Amon.*
7:61 {Tel-harsha, Kerub, Addan,} As in parallel text at Ezra 2:59; **H** reads *Addon.*
7:65 {of sacred lots.} **H** *consult the Urim and Thummim about the matter.*
7:68 {horses, 245 mules,} As in some **H** manuscripts (see also Ezra 2:66); most **H** manuscripts lack this verse.
7:70 {1,000 gold coins,} **H** *1,000 darics of gold,* about 19 pounds or 8.6 kilograms in weight.
7:71 {20,000 gold coins} **H** *20,000 darics of gold,* about 375 pounds or 170 kilograms in weight; also in 7:72.
7:71 {some 2,750 pounds} **H** *2,200 minas* [1.3 metric tons].
7:72 {about 2,500 pounds} **H** *2,000 minas* [1.2 metric tons].
7:73 {Now in midautumn,} **H** *in the seventh month.* This month of the **H** lunar calendar occurred in October and November 445 B.C.
8:2 {So on October 8} **H** *on the first day of the seventh month,* of the **H** calendar. This event occurred on October 8, 445 B.C.; also see note on 1:1.
8:10 {And Nehemiah} **H** *he.*
8:13 {On October 9} **H** *On the second day,* of the seventh month of the **H** calendar. This event occurred on October 9, 445 B.C.; also see notes on 1:1 and 8:2.

8:14 {held that month.} **H** *in the seventh month.* This month of the **H** lunar calendar usually occurs in September and October. See Lev 23:39-43.
8:18 {Then on October 15} **H** *on the eighth day,* of the seventh month of the **H** calendar. This event occurred on October 15, 445 B.C.; also see notes on 1:1 and 8:2.
9: 1 {On October 31} **H** *On the twenty-fourth day of that same month,* the seventh month of the **H** calendar. This event occurred on October 31, 445 B.C.; also see note on 1:1.
9: 3 {about three hours.} **H** *for a quarter of a day.*
9: 9 {the Red Sea.} **H** *sea of reeds.*
10:32 {ounce of silver,} **H** *tax of 1/3 of a shekel* [4 grams].
11: 5 {family of Shelah.} **H** *son of the Shilonite.*
12: 3 {Shecaniah, Harim,} **H** *Rehum;* compare 7:42; 12:15; Ezra 2:39.
12: 4 {Iddo, Ginnethon,} As in some **H** manuscripts and Latin Vulgate (see also 12:16); most **H** manuscripts read *Ginnethoi.*
12: 5 {Miniamin, Moadiah,} **H** *Mijamin, Maadiah;* compare 12:17.
12:11 {father of Johanan.} **H** *Jonathan;* compare 12:22.
12:14 {family of Malluch.} As in Greek version (see also 10:4; 12:2); **H** reads *Malluchi.*
12:14 {family of Shecaniah.} As in many **H** manuscripts, some Greek manuscripts, and Syriac version (see also 12:3); most **H** manuscripts read *Shebaniah.*
12:15 {family of Meremoth.} As in some Greek manuscripts (see also 12:3); **H** reads *Meraioth.*
12:17 {was also a} **H** lacks the name of this family leader.
12:20 {family of Sallu.} **H** *Sallai;* compare 12:7.
12:22 {Darius II of Persia,} **H** *Darius the Persian.*
12:23 {Johanan, the grandson} **H** *son;* compare 12:10-11.
12:24 {Sherebiah, Jeshua, Binnui,} **H** *son of* (i.e., *ben*), which should probably be read here as the proper name Binnui; compare Ezra 3:9 and the note there.
12:26 {son of Jehozadak,} **H** *Jozadak,* a variant name for Jehozadak.
12:31 {choirs proceeded southward} **H** *to the right.*
12:38 {choir went northward} **H** *to the left.*
13:19 {every Friday evening,} **H** *on the day before the Sabbath.*
13:28 {sons of Joiada} **H** *Jehoiada,* a variant name for Joiada.
Est 1: 1 {of King Xerxes,} **H** *Ahasuerus,* another name for Xerxes; also throughout the book of Esther.
1: 1 {India to Ethiopia.} **H** *to Cush.*
1: 4 {lasted six months} **H** *180 days.*
2: 6 {with King Jehoiachin} **H** *Jeconiah,* a variant name for Jehoiachin.
2:15 {was Esther's turn} **H** *the turn of Esther, the daughter of Abihail, who was Mordecai's uncle, who had adopted her.*
2:16 {in early winter} **H** *in the tenth month, the month of Tebeth.* A number of events in the book of Esther can be cross-checked with dates in surviving Persian records and related accurately to our modern calendar. This month of the **H** lunar calendar occurred in December 479 B.C. and January 478 B.C.
2:19 {the second harem} The meaning of the **H** is uncertain.
2:21 {king's eunuchs, Bigthana} **H** *Bigthan;* compare 6:2.
3: 7 {month of April,} **H** *in the first month, the month of Nisan.* This month of the **H** lunar calendar occurred in April and May 474 B.C.; also see note on 2:16.
3: 7 {a year later.} As in Greek version, which reads *the thirteenth day of the twelfth month, the month of Adar* (see also 3:13). **H** reads *in the twelfth month,* of the **H** calendar. The date selected was March 7, 473 B.C.; also see note on 2:16.
3: 9 {give 375 tons} **H** *10,000 talents* [340 metric tons].
3:12 {On April 17} **H** *On the thirteenth day of the first month,* of the **H** calendar. This event occurred on April 17, 474 B.C.; also see note on 2:16.
3:13 {later on March 7.} **H** *on the thirteenth day of the twelfth month, the month of Adar,* of the **H** calendar. The date selected was March 7, 473 B.C.; also see note on 2:16.
5:14 {stands seventy-five feet} **H** *50 cubits* [22.5 meters].
7: 9 {stands seventy-five feet} **H** *50 cubits* [22.5 meters].
8: 9 {So on June 25} **H** *on the twenty-third day of the third month, the month of Sivan,* of the **H** calendar. This event occurred on June 25, 474 B.C.; also see note on 2:16.
8: 9 {India to Ethiopia.} **H** *to Cush.*
8:12 {the next year.} **H** *the thirteenth day of the twelfth month, the month of Adar,* of the **H** calendar. The date selected was March 7, 473 B.C.; also see note on 2:16.
9: 1 {So on March 7} **H** *on the thirteenth day of the twelfth month, the month of Adar,* of the **H** calendar. This event occurred on March 7, 473 B.C.; also see note on 2:16.
9:15 {together on March 8} **H** *the fourteenth day of the month of Adar,* of the **H** calendar....
9:17 {done on March 7.} **H** *on the thirteenth day of the month of Adar,* of the **H** calendar. This event occurred on March 7, 473 B.C.; also see note on 2:16.
9:17 {the following day} **H** *on the fourteenth day,* of the **H** month of Adar.
9:18 {the third day,} **H** *killing their enemies on the thirteenth day and the fourteenth day, and then rested on the fifteenth day,* of the **H** month of Adar.
9:19 {in late winter,} **H** *on the fourteenth day of the month of Adar.* This day of the **H** lunar calendar occurs in late February or early March.
Job 1: 6 {the angels} **H** *the sons of God.*
2: 1 {the angels} **H** *the sons of God.*
3: 8 {the sea monster} **H** *rouse Leviathan.*
5: 1 {to the angels,} **H** *the holy ones.*
6:27 {orphan into slavery} **H** *even gamble over an orphan.*
7:19 {for a moment} **H** *long enough to swallow my spittle.*
9:13 {forces against him} **H** *The helpers of Rahab,* the name of a mythical sea monster that represents chaos in ancient literature.
9:17 {me without reason,} As in Syriac version; **H** reads *with a storm.*
10:10 {in the womb.} **H** *You poured me out like milk and curdled me like cheese.*
11: 8 {than the underworld} **H** *Sheol.*
15:15 {trust the angels} **H** *the holy ones.*
16:13 {with my blood.} **H** *my gall.*
20:25 {glistens with blood.} **H** *with gall.*
26: 6 {The underworld} **H** *Sheol.*
26:12 {great sea monster.} **H** *Rahab,* the name of a mythical sea monster that represents chaos in ancient literature.
28:19 {Topaz from Ethiopia} **H** *from Cush.*
32: 3 {had condemned God} As in ancient **H** scribal tradition; the Masoretic Text makes no reference to God.
36:33 {his indignant anger.} Or *even the cattle know when a storm is coming.* The meaning of the **H** is uncertain.
38: 7 {all the angels} **H** *sons of God.*
40:15 {the mighty hippopotamus.} **H** *at behemoth.*
41: 1 {catch a crocodile} **H** *Leviathan;* also throughout the following passage.
41:11 {and remain safe} As in Greek version; **H** reads *confront me that I must pay.*
41:13 {layer of armor} As in Greek version; **H** reads *its bridle.*
42:11 {gift of money} **H** *a kesitah;* the value or weight of the kesitah is no longer known.
Ps 2: 6 {my holy city.} **H** *on Zion, my holy mountain.*
3: 2 {Interlude} **H** *Selah.* The meaning of this word is uncertain, though it is probably a musical or literary term. It is rendered *Interlude* throughout the Psalms.
6: T {an eight-stringed instrument.} **H** *with stringed instruments; according to the sheminith.*
7:12 {God} **H** *he.*
8: T {a stringed instrument.} **H** *according to the gittith.*
8: 2 {give you praise.} As in Greek version; **H** reads *to show strength.*
8: 4 {care for us?} **H** *What is man that you should think of him, the son of man that you should care for him?*
8: 5 {lower than God,} Or *a little lower than the angels;* **H** reads *Elohim.*
9:11 {reigns in Jerusalem.} **H** *Zion;* also in 9:14.
9:16 {Quiet Interlude} **H** *Higgaion Selah.* The meaning of this phrase is uncertain.
9:17 {to the grave.} **H** *to Sheol.*
12: T {an eight-stringed instrument.} **H** *according to the sheminith.*
16: 9 {and my mouth} As in Greek version; **H** reads *glory.*
16:10 {among the dead} **H** *in Sheol.*
18: 5 {The grave} **H** *Sheol.*
18:10 {a mighty angel,} **H** *a cherub.*
18:13 {a mighty shout.} As in Greek version (see also 2 Sam 22:14); **H** adds *raining down hail and burning coals.*
20: 1 {God of Israel} **H** *of Jacob.*
20: 2 {you from Jerusalem.} **H** *Zion.*
20: 7 {armies and weapons,} **H** *chariots and horses.*
22:18 {and throw dice} **H** *cast lots.*
24: 6 {God of Israel.} **H** *of Jacob.*
29: 6 {and Mount Hermon} **H** *Sirion,* another name for Mount Hermon.
44: 4 {for your people.} **H** *for Jacob.*
45:12 {princes of Tyre} **H** *The daughter of Tyre.*
46: T {by soprano voices.} **H** *according to alamoth.*
46: 7 {God of Israel} **H** *of Jacob;* also in 46:11.
48: 2 {the holy mountain,} Or *Mount Zion, in the far north;* **H** reads *Mount Zion, the heights of Zaphon.*
48:12 {city of Jerusalem.} **H** *Zion.*
51: 7 {from my sins,} **H** *Purify me with the hyssop branch.*
55:15 {let the grave} **H** *let Sheol.*
58: 7 {in their hands.} Or *Let them be trodden down and wither like grass.* The meaning of the **H** is uncertain.
59:13 {reigns in Israel.} **H** *in Jacob.*
66: 6 {the Red Sea,} **H** *the sea.*
68:31 {let Ethiopia} **H** *Cush.*
69:35 {will save Jerusalem} **H** *Zion.*
72: 5 {May he live} As in Greek version; **H** reads *May they fear you.*
72: 8 {the Euphrates River} **H** *the river.*
74: 2 {And remember Jerusalem,} **H** *Mount Zion.*
74:16 {made the starlight} Or *moon;* **H** reads *light.*
75: 9 {God of Israel.} **H** *of Jacob.*
76: 2 {Jerusalem} **H** *Salem,* another name for Jerusalem.
76: 4 {the everlasting mountains.} As in Greek version; **H** reads *than mountains filled with beasts of prey.*
76:10 {sword of judgment.} The meaning of the **H** is uncertain.
77:16 {the Red Sea} **H** *the waters.*
78:51 {land of Egypt.} **H** *in the tents of Ham.*
79: 7 {your people Israel,} **H** *Jacob.*
80: 1 {who lead Israel} **H** *Joseph.*
80:11 {the Euphrates River.} **H** *west to the sea,...east to the river.*
81: T {a stringed instrument.} **H** *according to the gittith.*
81: 1 {God of Israel.} **H** *of Jacob.*
81: 5 {decree for Israel} **H** *for Joseph.*
84: T {a stringed instrument.} **H** *according to the gittith.*
84: 6 {Valley of Weeping,} **H** *valley of Baca.*
84: 7 {God in Jerusalem.} **H** *Zion.*
84: 8 {O God of Israel.} **H** *of Jacob.*
85: 1 {fortunes of Israel.} **H** *of Jacob.*
86:13 {depths of death} **H** *of Sheol.*
87: 2 {city in Israel.} **H** *He loves the gates of Zion more than all the dwellings of Jacob.*
87: 4 {will record Egypt} **H** *Rahab,* the name of a mythical sea monster that represents chaos in ancient literature. The name is used here as a poetic name for Egypt.
87: 4 {even distant Ethiopia.} **H** *Cush.*
87: 5 {said of Jerusalem,} **H** *Zion.*
89:10 {great sea monster.} **H** *Rahab,* the name of a mythical sea monster that represents chaos in ancient literature.
89:25 {in the east.} **H** *I will set his hand on the sea, his right hand on the rivers.*
94: 7 {God of Israel} **H** *of Jacob.*
97: 8 {Jerusalem} **H** *Zion.*
99: 2 {majesty in Jerusalem,} **H** *Zion.*
99: 4 {righteousness throughout Israel.} **H** *Jacob.*
102:13 {mercy on Jerusalem} **H** *Zion;* also in 102:16.
106: 7 {the Red Sea.} **H** *at the sea, the sea of reeds.*
106: 9 {the Red Sea} **H** *sea of reeds;* also in 106:22.
106:19 {at Mount Sinai} **H** *at Horeb,* another name for Sinai.
106:33 {made Moses angry,} **H** *They embittered his spirit.*
110: 2 {dominion from Jerusalem} **H** *Zion.*
114: 3 {The Red Sea} **H** *the sea;* also in 114:5.
114: 7 {God of Israel.} **H** *of Jacob.*
116: 3 {of the grave} **H** *of Sheol.*
119: 1 {people of integrity,} This psalm is a **H** acrostic poem; there are 22 stanzas, one for each letter of the **H** alphabet. The 8 verses within each stanza begin with the **H** letter of its section.
126: 1 {exiles to Jerusalem,} **H** *Zion.*
129: 5 {who hate Jerusalem} **H** *Zion.*
132: 2 {One of Israel,} **H** *of Jacob;* also in 132:5.
132:13 {has chosen Jerusalem} **H** *Zion.*
134: 3 {you from Jerusalem.} **H** *Zion.*
136:13 {the Red Sea.} **H** *sea of reeds;* also in 136:15.
137: 1 {thought of Jerusalem.} **H** *Zion;* also in 137:3.
139: 8 {of the dead,} **H** *to Sheol.*
146: 5 {God of Israel} **H** *of Jacob.*
146:10 {O Jerusalem,} **H** *Zion.*
149: 2 {O people of Jerusalem,} **H** *Zion.*
Pr 1: 8 {Listen, my child,} **H** *my son;* also in 1:10, 15.
2: 1 {My child,} **H** *My son.*
2:18 {road to hell.} **H** *to the spirits of the dead.*
3: 1 {My child,} **H** *My son;* also in 3:11, 21.
3:12 {corrects a child} **H** *a son.*
4: 1 {My children,} **H** *My sons.*
4:10 {My child,} **H** *My son;* also in 4:20.
4:23 {everything you do.} **H** *for from it flow the springs of life.*
5: 5 {to the grave.} **H** *to Sheol.*
5:15 {with your wife.} **H** *Drink water from your own cistern, flowing water from your own well.*
5:16 {with just anyone?} **H** *Why spill your springs in public, your streams in the streets?*
6: 1 {My child,} **H** *My son.*
7: 2 {most precious possession.} **H** *as the apple of your eye.*
7:27 {to the grave.} **H** *to Sheol.*
8:32 {so, my children,} **H** *my sons.*
9:18 {in the grave.} **H** *in Sheol.*
10: 1 {wise child} **H** *son;* also in 10:1b.
10:10 {reproof promotes peace.} As in Greek version; **H** reads *but babbling fools fall flat on their faces.*
12:26 {to their friends;} Or *The godly are cautious in friendship, or the godly are freed from evil.* The meaning of the **H** is uncertain.
13: 1 {wise child} **H** *son.*
14: 3 {for their backs,} **H** *a rod of pride.*
14:16 {wise are cautious} **H** *The wise fear.*
14:33 {wisdom is not} As in Greek version; **H** lacks *not.*
15:11 {Death and Destruction} **H** *Sheol and Abaddon.*
15:24 {leave the grave} **H** *Sheol.*
17:19 {who speaks boastfully} Or *who builds up defenses;* **H** reads *who makes a high gate.*
17:25 {A foolish child} **H** *son.*
19:13 {A foolish child} **H** *son;* also in 19:27.
20:16 {of a foreigner.} An alternate reading in the **H** text is *the debt of an adulterous woman;* compare 27:13.
20:30 {cleanses away evil;} The meaning of the **H** is uncertain.
21: 6 {deadly trap.} As in Greek version; **H** reads *mist for those who seek death.*
23:14 {them from death.} **H** *from Sheol.*

23:15 {My child,} **H** *My son;* also in 23:19.
23:24 {have wise children.} **H** *a wise son.*
23:27 {woman is treacherous.} **H** *is a narrow well.*
24: 5 {strong man,} As in Greek version; **H** reads *A wise man is strength.*
24:13 {My child,} **H** *My son;* also in 24:21.
26:23 {Smooth} As in Greek version; **H** reads *Burning.*
27:11 {My child,} **H** *My son.*
27:20 {Death and Destruction} **H** *Sheol and Abaddon.*
28:14 {a tender conscience,} **H** *those who fear.*
30: 1 {worn out, O God.} The **H** can also be translated *The man declares this to Ithiel, to Ithiel and to Ucal.*
30:15 {out, "More, more!"} **H** *two daughters who cry out, "Give, give!"*
31:21 {them have warm} As in Greek version; **H** *scarlet.*

Ecc 1: 1 {of the Teacher,} **H** *Koheleth;* this term is rendered "the Teacher" throughout this book.
3:15 {in its turn.} **H** *For God calls the past to account.*
5: 9 {his own profit!} The meaning of the **H** is uncertain.
8:10 {and are praised} As in some **H** manuscripts and Greek version; many **H** manuscripts read *and are forgotten.*
9: 2 {good or bad,} As in Greek and Syriac versions, and Latin Vulgate; **H** lacks *or bad.*
12:12 {But, my child,} **H** *my son.*

SS 1: 1 {*Young Woman:*} The headings identifying the speakers are not in the original text, though the **H** usually gives clues by means of the gender of the person speaking.
1: 6 {done to me!} **H** *My own vineyard I have neglected.*
1: 7 {like a prostitute} **H** *like a veiled woman.*
1: 9 {my beloved one!} **H** *I compare you, my beloved, to a mare among Pharaoh's chariots.*
3:11 {women of Jerusalem.} **H** *Zion.*
6:12 {my beloved one.} Or *among the royal chariots of my people,* or *among the chariots of Amminadab.* The meaning of the **H** is uncertain.
6:13 {lines of dancers?} Or *as you would at the movements of two armies?* or *as you would at the dance of Mahanaim?* The meaning of the **H** is uncertain.
7: 9 {lips and teeth.} As in Greek and Syriac versions and Latin Vulgate; **H** reads *over lips of sleepers.*
8: 9 {off from men.} **H** *If she is a wall, we will build battlements of silver on her; but if she is a door, we will surround her with panels of cedar.*
8:11 {pieces of silver} **H** *1,000 shekels of silver,* about 25 pounds or 11.4 kilograms in weight; also in 8:12.
8:12 {pieces of silver} **H** *200 [shekels],* about 5 pounds or 2.3 kilograms in weight.

Isa 1: 8 {Jerusalem} **H** *The daughter of Zion.*
1:27 {people of Jerusalem} **H** *Zion.*
2: 3 {God of Israel.} **H** *of Jacob;* also in 2:5, 6.
2:16 {great trading ships} **H** *every ship of Tarshish.*
3:16 {women of Jerusalem,} **H** *the daughters of Zion.*
3:26 {gates of Jerusalem} **H** *Zion.*
4: 4 {women of Jerusalem.} **H** *from the daughters of Zion.*
4: 5 {shade for Jerusalem} **H** *Mount Zion.*
5:10 {Ten acres} **H** *A ten yoke,* that is, the area of land plowed by ten teams of oxen in one day.
5:10 {even six gallons} **H** *a bath* [21 liters].
5:10 {only one measure} **H** *A homer* [5 bushels or 182 liters] *of seed will yield only an ephah* [0.5 bushels or 18.2 liters].
5:14 {The grave} **H** *Sheol.*
5:17 {lambs and kids} As in Greek version; **H** reads *strangers.*
7: 2 {allied with Israel} **H** *Ephraim,* referring to the northern kingdom of Israel; also in 7:5, 8, 9, 17.
7:20 {and your people.} **H** *shave off the head, the hair of the legs, and the beard.*
7:23 {pieces of silver,} **H** *1,000 shekels of silver,* about 25 pounds or 11.4 kilograms in weight.
8: 6 {my gentle care} **H** *rejected the gently flowing waters of Shiloah.*
8: 7 {the Euphrates River} **H** *the river.*
8:10 {is with us!} **H** *Immanuel!*
8:17 {people of Israel.} **H** *the house of Jacob.*
9: 9 {people of Israel} **H** *of Ephraim,* referring to the northern kingdom of Israel.
10:20 {Israel and Judah} **H** *and the house of Jacob.*
10:21 {them will return} **H** *Shear-jashub;* see 7:3; 8:18.
10:24 {people in Jerusalem,} **H** *Zion.*
10:27 {from their shoulders.} As in Greek version; **H** reads *The yoke will be broken, for you have grown so fat.*
11: 1 {of David's family} **H** *the line of Jesse.* Jesse was King David's father.
11:10 {to David's throne} **H** *the root of Jesse.*
11:11 {Upper Egypt, Ethiopia,} **H** *Pathros, Cush.*
11:11 {Elam, Babylonia,} **H** *Shinar.*
11:13 {jealousy between Israel} **H** *Ephraim,* referring to the northern kingdom of Israel.
11:15 {the Red Sea.} **H** *sea of Egypt.*
11:15 {the Euphrates River,} **H** *the river.*
12: 6 {people of Jerusalem} **H** *Zion.*
14: 1 {people of Israel.} **H** *the house of Jacob.*
14: 9 {of the dead} **H** *Sheol;* also in 14:15.
14:32 {has built Jerusalem,} **H** *Zion.*
15: 9 {stream near Dibon} As in Dead Sea Scrolls, some Greek manuscripts, and Latin Vulgate; **H** reads *Dimon;* also in 15:9b.
16: 1 {lambs to Jerusalem} **H** *to the daughter of Zion.*
16: 8 {the Dead Sea.} **H** *the sea.*
16:11 {sorrow for Kir-hareseth} **H** *Kir-heres,* a variant name for Kir-hareseth.
17: 3 {cities of Israel} **H** *of Ephraim,* referring to the northern kingdom of Israel.
17: 4 {glory of Israel} **H** *of Jacob.*
18: 1 {land of Ethiopia,} **H** *Cush.*
18: 7 {Almighty in Jerusalem,} **H** *on Mount Zion.*
19:13 {those from Memphis} **H** *Noph.*
19:18 {the Hebrew language.} **H** *the language of Canaan.*
20: 3 {Egypt and Ethiopia.} **H** *Cush;* also in 20:5.
20: 4 {Egyptians and Ethiopians} **H** *Cushites.*
21: 1 {land of Babylonia} **H** *the desert of the sea.*
21: 8 {Then the watchman} As in Dead Sea Scrolls and Syriac version; **H** reads *a lion.*
21:11 {concerning Edom} **H** *Dumah,* which means "silence" or "stillness." It is a wordplay on the word *Edom.*
21:11 {Someone from Edom} **H** *Seir,* another name for Edom.
21:16 {within a year,"} **H** *Within a year, like the years of a hired hand.* Some ancient manuscripts read *Within three years,* as in 16:14.
22: 1 {me concerning Jerusalem} **H** *concerning the Valley of Vision.*
22: 2 {famine and disease.} **H** *killed, but not by sword and not in battle.*
22: 9 {walls of Jerusalem} **H** *the city of David.*
23: 1 {heard in Cyprus} **H** *Kittim;* also in 23:12.
23: 3 {grain from Egypt} **H** *from Shihor,* a branch of the Nile River.
23:11 {out against Phoenicia} **H** *Canaan.*
25: 6 {In Jerusalem,} **H** *On this mountain;* also in 25:10.
27: 9 {purge away Israel's} **H** *Jacob's.*
27:12 {the Euphrates River} **H** *the river.*
28: 1 {drunkards of Israel} **H** *of Ephraim,* referring to the northern kingdom of Israel; also in 28:3.
28:10 {very simple words!} The **H** text for this verse may simply be childish sounds that have no meaning, or perhaps a childish mimicking of the prophet's words. Also in 28:13.
28:15 {dodge the grave.} **H** *Sheol;* also in 28:18.
28:16 {stone in Jerusalem.} **H** *in Zion.*
29: 1 {certain for Ariel,} *Ariel* sounds like a **H** term that means "hearth" or "altar."
29: 7 {fighting against Jerusalem} **H** *Ariel.*
29: 8 {conquest over Jerusalem,} **H** *Mount Zion.*
29:22 {people of Israel,} **H** *of Jacob;* also in 29:23.
30: 7 {the Harmless Dragon.} **H** *Rahab who sits still.* Rahab is the name of a mythical sea monster that represents chaos in ancient literature. The name is used here as a poetic name for Egypt.
33: 1 {for you Assyrians,} **H** *for you, O destroyer...O betrayer.* The **H** text does not specifically name Assyria as the object of this prophecy.
33: 5 {will make Jerusalem} **H** *Zion.*
33:14 {among my people} **H** *in Zion.*
34: 2 {will completely destroy} The **H** term used here refers to the complete consecration of things or people to the LORD, either by destroying them or by giving them as an offering; also in 34:5.
34: 8 {did to Israel.} **H** *to Zion.*
35:10 {return to Jerusalem,} **H** *Zion.*
37: 9 {Tirhakah of Ethiopia} **H** *of Cush.*
37:36 {the surviving Assyrians} **H** *When they.*
41:21 {King of Israel.} **H** *the King of Jacob.*
43: 3 {gave Egypt, Ethiopia,} **H** *Cush.*
43:28 {of complete destruction} The **H** term used here refers to the complete consecration of things or people to the LORD, either by destroying them or by giving them as an offering.
44: 2 {be afraid. O Israel,} **H** *Jeshurun,* a term of endearment for Israel.
45:14 {"The Egyptians, Ethiopians,} **H** *Cushites.*
45:19 {people of Israel} **H** *of Jacob.*
46:13 {to save Jerusalem} **H** *Zion.*
48:20 {people of Israel.} **H** *his servant, Jacob.*
49:14 {Yet Jerusalem} **H** *Zion.*
49:26 {One of Israel.} **H** *of Jacob.*
51: 3 {will comfort Israel} **H** *Zion;* also in 51:16.
51: 9 {of the Nile.} **H** *slew Rahab the dragon.* Rahab is the name of a mythical sea monster that represents chaos in ancient literature. The name is used here as a poetic name for Egypt.
51:11 {return to Jerusalem,} **H** *Zion.*
52: 7 {God of Israel} **H** *of Zion.*
52: 8 {home to Jerusalem.} **H** *to Zion.*
52:14 {they saw him} As in Syriac version; **H** reads *you.*
57: 9 {of the dead,} **H** *into Sheol.*
58: 1 {my people Israel} **H** *Jacob.*
59:20 {come to Jerusalem,} **H** *to Zion.*
59:20 {those in Israel} **H** *in Jacob.*
60:16 {One of Israel.} **H** *of Jacob.*
61: 3 {mourn in Israel,} **H** *in Zion.*
62: 4 {the Godforsaken City} **H** *Azubah,* which means "forsaken."
62: 4 {the Desolate Land.} **H** *Shemamah,* which means "desolate."
62: 4 {of God's Delight} **H** *Hephzibah,* which means "my delight is in her."
62: 4 {Bride of God,} **H** *Beulah,* which means "married."
62:11 {people of Israel,} **H** *Tell the daughter of Zion.*
63:16 {Abraham and Jacob} **H** *Israel.*
65: 9 {people of Israel} **H** *remnant of Jacob.*
66: 8 {the time Jerusalem's} **H** *Zion's.*
66:19 {to the Libyans} As in some Greek manuscripts, which read *Put* [Libya]; **H** reads *Pul.*
66:19 {and Lydians} **H** *Lud.*
66:19 {Tubal and Greece,} **H** *Javan.*

Jer 1: 3 {of that year,} **H** *In the fifth month,* of the **H** calendar. A number of events in Jeremiah can be cross-checked with dates in surviving Babylonian records and related accurately to our modern calendar. This month in the eleventh year of Zedekiah's reign occurred in August and September 586 B.C. Also see 52:12 and the note there.
1:12 {I am watching,} The **H** word for "watching" sounds like the word for "almond tree."
2: 3 {of my children.} **H** *the firstfruits of his harvest.*
2:10 {land of Cyprus} **H** *Kittim.*
2:11 {their glorious God} **H** *their Glory.*
2:16 {cities of Memphis} **H** *Noph.*
2:18 {of the Nile} **H** *of Shihor,* a branch of the Nile River.
2:18 {and the Euphrates} **H** *the river.*
3:12 {words to Israel,} **H** *toward the north.*
3:14 {land of Israel} **H** *to Zion.*
4: 6 {signal toward Jerusalem} **H** *Zion.*
4:31 {of Jerusalem's people} **H** *the daughter of Zion.*
5:20 {announcement to Israel} **H** *to the house of Jacob.*
6: 2 {O Jerusalem,} **H** *Zion.*
6:23 {destroy you, Jerusalem.} **H** *daughter of Zion.*
7:15 {people of Israel.} **H** *of Ephraim,* referring to the northern kingdom of Israel.
8:19 {LORD abandoned Jerusalem} **H** *Zion.*
9:19 {people of Jerusalem} **H** *Zion.*
10:16 {God of Israel} **H** *the Portion of Jacob.*
10:25 {your people Israel,} **H** *Jacob.*
11: 5 {"So be it,} **H** *Amen.*
13: 4 {the Euphrates River.} **H** *Perath;* also in 13:5, 6, 7.
13:23 {Can an Ethiopian} **H** *a Cushite.*
14:19 {really hate Jerusalem} **H** *Zion.*
17:26 {the western foothills} **H** *the Shephelah.*
20: 3 {Lives in Terror.'} **H** *Magor-missabib,* which means "surrounded by terror"; also in 20:10.
21: 2 {us. King Nebuchadnezzar} **H** *Nebuchadrezzar,* a variant name for Nebuchadnezzar; also in 21:7.
22:11 {says about Jehoahaz,} **H** *Shallum,* another name for Jehoahaz.
22:13 {with forced labor.} **H** *by unrighteousness.*
22:20 {of the river.} **H** *in Abarim.*
22:24 {abandon you, Jehoiachin} **H** *Coniah,* a variant name for Jehoiachin; also in 22:28, 30.
22:25 {King Nebuchadnezzar} **H** *Nebuchadrezzar,* a variant name for Nebuchadnezzar.
23: 6 {Is Our Righteousness.'} **H** *Yahweh Tsidqenu.*
23:33 {are the burden!} As in Greek version and Latin Vulgate; **H** reads *What burden?*
24: 1 {After King Nebuchadnezzar} **H** *Nebuchadrezzar,* a variant name for Nebuchadnezzar.
24: 1 {Babylon exiled Jehoiachin} **H** *Jeconiah,* a variant name for Jehoiachin.
25: 1 {when King Nebuchadnezzar} **H** *Nebuchadrezzar,* a variant name for Nebuchadnezzar; also in 25:9.
25: 9 {will completely destroy} The **H** term used here refers to the complete consecration of things or people to the LORD, either by destroying them or by giving them as an offering.
25:26 {king of Babylon} **H** *of Sheshach,* a code name for Babylon.
27: 1 {reign of Zedekiah} As in some **H** manuscripts and Syriac version (see also 27:3, 12); most **H** manuscripts read *Jehoiakim.*
27:20 {he exiled Jehoiachin} **H** *Jeconiah,* a variant name for Jehoiachin.
28: 1 {in late summer} **H** *In the fifth month,* of the **H** calendar. This month in the fourth year of Zedekiah's reign occurred in August and September 593 B.C. Also see note on 1:3.
28: 4 {bring back Jehoiachin} **H** *Jeconiah,* a variant name for Jehoiachin.
28:17 {Two months later,} **H** *In the seventh month of that same year.* See 28:1 and the note there.
29: 2 {after King Jehoiachin,} **H** *Jeconiah,* a variant name for Jehoiachin.
29:21 {over to Nebuchadnezzar} **H** *Nebuchadrezzar,* a variant name for Nebuchadnezzar.
30: 7 {my people Israel.} **H** *Jacob;* also in 30:10b.
30:17 {called an outcast—'Jerusalem} **H** *Zion.*
31: 6 {up to Jerusalem} **H** *Zion;* also in 31:12.
31: 7 {joy for Israel} **H** *Jacob;* also in 31:11.
31:18 {have heard Israel} **H** *Ephraim,* referring to the northern kingdom of Israel; also in 31:20.
31:22 {embrace her God.} **H** *a woman will court a suitor.*
32: 1 {of King Nebuchadnezzar.} **H** *Nebuchadrezzar,* a variant name for Nebuchadnezzar; also in 32:28.
32: 9 {Hanamel seventeen pieces} **H** *17 shekels,* about 7 ounces or 194 grams in weight.
32:44 {foothills of Judah} **H** *the Shephelah.*
33:13 {foothills of Judah,} **H** *the Shephelah.*
33:15 {a righteous descendant,} **H** *a righteous Branch.*
35: 6 {wine, because Jehonadab} **H** *Jonadab,* a variant name for Jehonadab; also in 35:10, 14, 18, 19. See 2 Kgs 10:15.
35:11 {when King Nebuchadnezzar} **H** *Nebuchadrezzar,* a variant name for Nebuchadnezzar.
36: 9 {in late autumn,} **H** *in the ninth month,* of the **H** calendar (also in 36:22). This month in the fifth year of Jehoiakim's reign occurred in November and December 604 B.C. Also see note on 1:3.

37: 1 {Josiah succeeded Jehoiachin} **H** *Coniah,* a variant name for Jehoiachin.
37: 1 {by King Nebuchadrezzar} **H** *Nebuchadrezzar,* a variant name for Nebuchadnezzar.
37: 5 {of Pharaoh Hophra} **H** *army of Pharaoh;* see 44:30.
38: 1 {of Pashhur, Jehucal} **H** *Jucal,* a variant name for Jehucal; see 37:3.
38: 7 {Ebed-melech the Ethiopian,} **H** *the Cushite.*
39: 1 {was in January} **H** *in the tenth month,* of the **H** calendar. A number of events in Jeremiah can be cross-checked with dates in surviving Babylonian records and related accurately to our modern calendar. This event occurred on January 15, 588 B.C.; see 52:4 and the note there.
39: 1 {that King Nebuchadnezzar} **H** *Nebuchadrezzar,* a variant name for Nebuchadnezzar; also in 39:11.
39: 2 {later, on July 18,} **H** *On the ninth day of the fourth month of the eleventh year of Zedekiah.* This event occurred on July 18, 586 B.C.; also see note on 39:1.
39: 4 {the Jordan Valley.} **H** *the Arabah.*
39:16 {Ebed-melech the Ethiopian,} **H** *the Cushite.*
40: 8 {the Netophathite, Jaazaniah} As in parallel text at 2 Kgs 25:23; **H** reads *Jezaniah,* a variant name for Jaazaniah.
41: 1 {But in midautumn,} **H** *in the seventh month,* of the **H** calendar. This month occurred in October and November 586 B.C. Also see note on 39:1.
43:10 {my servant Nebuchadnezzar,} **H** *Nebuchadrezzar,* a variant name for Nebuchadnezzar.
44: 1 {Tahpanhes, and Memphis,} **H** *Noph.*
44:30 {to King Nebuchadnezzar} **H** *Nebuchadrezzar,* a variant name for Nebuchadnezzar.
46: 2 {by King Nebuchadnezzar} **H** *Nebuchadrezzar,* a variant name for Nebuchadnezzar; also in 46:13, 26.
46: 9 {Libya, and Lydia} **H** *Cush, Put, and Lud.*
46:14 {of Migdol, Memphis,} **H** *Noph;* also in 46:19.
46:25 {god of Thebes,} **H** *No.*
46:27 {their exile. Israel} **H** *Jacob.*
47: 4 {colonists from Crete.} **H** *from Caphtor.*
47: 5 {the Mediterranean plain,} **H** *the plain.*
48: 2 {city of Madmen,} *Madmen* sounds like the **H** word for "silence"; it should not be confused with the English word *madmen.*
48:13 {calf at Bethel.} **H** *ashamed when they trusted in Bethel.*
48:21 {Holon and Jahaz} **H** *Jahzah,* a variant name for Jahaz.
48:31 {men of Kir-hareseth.} **H** *Kir-heres,* a variant name for Kir-hareseth; also in 48:36.
48:32 {the Dead Sea,} **H** *the sea of Jazer.*
49: 1 {who worship Molech,} **H** *Milcom,* a variant name for Molech; also in 49:3.
49: 8 {disaster on Edom,} **H** *Esau;* also in 49:10.
49:21 {the Red Sea.} **H** *sea of reeds.*
49:28 {by King Nebuchadnezzar} **H** *Nebuchadrezzar,* a variant name for Nebuchadnezzar; also in 49:30.
50: 5 {way to Jerusalem} **H** *Zion;* also in 50:28.
50:12 {But your homeland} **H** *your mother.*
50:17 {Then King Nebuchadnezzar} **H** *Nebuchadrezzar,* a variant name for Nebuchadnezzar.
50:21 {and completely destroy} The **H** term used here refers to the complete consecration of things or people to the LORD, either by destroying them or by giving them as an offering.
50:40 {just as I} **H** *just as God.*
51: 1 {people of Babylonia.} **H** *of Leb-kamai,* a code name for Babylonia.
51: 3 {be completely destroyed.} The **H** term used here refers to the complete consecration of things or people to the LORD, either by destroying them or by giving them as an offering.
51:10 {announce in Jerusalem} **H** *Zion;* also in 51:24, 35a.
51:19 {God of Israel} **H** *the Portion of Jacob.*
51:34 {"King Nebuchadnezzar} **H** *Nebuchadrezzar,* a variant name for Nebuchadnezzar.
51:41 {"How Babylon} **H** *Sheshach,* a code name for Babylon.
52: 4 {So on January 15,} **H** *on the tenth day of the tenth month,* of the **H** calendar. A number of events in Jeremiah can be cross-checked with dates in surviving Babylonian records and related accurately to our modern calendar. This event occurred on January 15, 588 B.C.
52: 4 {King Nebuchadnezzar} **H** *Nebuchadrezzar,* a variant name for Nebuchadnezzar; also in 52:12, 28, 29, 30.
52: 6 {Zedekiah's eleventh year,} **H** *By the ninth day of the fourth month* [of Zedekiah's eleventh year]. This event of the **H** lunar calendar occurred on July 18, 586 B.C.; also see note on 52:4a.
52: 7 {the Jordan Valley.} **H** *the Arabah.*
52:12 {of that year,} **H** *On the tenth day of the fifth month,* of the **H** calendar. This day was August 17, 586 B.C.; also see note on 52:4a.
52:21 {18 feet in circumference.} **H** *18 cubits* [8.1 meters] *tall and 12 cubits* [5.4 meters] *in circumference.*
52:21 {3 inches thick.} **H** *4 fingers thick* [8 centimeters].
52:22 {was 7 1/2 feet} **H** *5 cubits* [2.3 meters].
52:31 {of that year.} **H** *on the twenty-fifth day of the twelfth month,* of the **H** calendar. This day was March 31, 560 B.C.; also see note on 52:4a.

La 1: 1 {Jerusalem's streets,} Each of the first four chapters of this book is an acrostic, laid out in the order of the **H** alphabet. The first word of each verse begins with a successive **H** letter. Chapters 1, 2, and 4 have one verse for each of the 22 **H** letters. Chapter 3 contains 22 stanzas of three verses each. Though chapter 5 is not an acrostic, it also has 22 verses.
1: 4 {roads to Jerusalem} **H** *Zion;* also in 1:17.
1: 6 {majesty of Jerusalem} **H** *the daughter of Zion.*
1:15 {his beloved city} **H** *the virgin daughter of Judah.*
1:17 {Regarding his people,} **H** *Jacob.*
2: 1 {shadow over Jerusalem.} **H** *the daughter of Zion;* also in 2:8, 10, 18.
2: 1 {to his Temple.} **H** *footstool.*
2: 2 {home in Israel.} **H** *Jacob;* also in 2:3.
2: 2 {walls of Jerusalem.} **H** *the daughter of Judah;* also in 2:5.
2: 4 {on beautiful Jerusalem.} **H** *on the tent of the daughter of Zion.*
2:15 {and insult Jerusalem,} **H** *the daughter of Jerusalem.*
2:18 {Cry aloud} **H** *Their heart cried.*
3:19 {bitter beyond words.} **H** *is wormwood and gall.*
4: 2 {children of Jerusalem,} **H** *sons of Zion.*
4:11 {fire in Jerusalem} **H** *in Zion.*
4:22 {O Jerusalem,} **H** *daughter of Zion.*
5:11 {girls in Jerusalem} **H** *Zion.*
5:18 {For Jerusalem} **H** *Mount Zion.*

Eze 1: 1 {On July 31} **H** *On the fifth day of the fourth month,* of the **H** calendar (also in 1:2). A number of events in Ezekiel can be cross-checked with dates in surviving Babylonian records and related accurately to our modern calendar. This event occurred on July 31, 593 B.C.
1:24 {of the Almighty,} **H** *Shaddai.*
4:10 {eight ounces} **H** *20 shekels* [228 grams].
4:11 {out a jar} **H** *1/6 of a hin,* about 1.3 pints or 0.6 liters.
6:14 {south to Riblah} As in some **H** manuscripts; most **H** manuscripts read *Diblah.*
8: 1 {Then on September 17,} **H** *on the fifth day of the sixth month,* of the **H** calendar. This event occurred on September 17, 592 B.C.; also see note on 1:1.
10:14 {of an ox,} **H** *the face of a cherub;* compare 1:10.
11: 3 {from all harm.} **H** *This city is the pot, and we are the meat.*
11:19 {them tender hearts} **H** *hearts of flesh.*
12:10 {Zedekiah in Jerusalem} **H** *the prince in Jerusalem;* also in 12:12.
19: 7 {in nearby nations} As in Greek version; **H** reads *He consorted with widows.*
20: 1 {On August 14,} **H** *In the fifth month, on the tenth day,* of the **H** calendar. This event occurred on August 14, 591 B.C.; also see note on 1:1.
20:46 {toward the south} **H** *Teman.*
21:10 {beneath its power!} The meaning of the **H** is uncertain.
21:13 {do they have?} The meaning of the **H** is uncertain.
22:25 {Your princes} As in Greek version; **H** reads *prophets.*
24: 1 {On January 15,} **H** *On the tenth day of the tenth month,* of the **H** calendar. This event occurred on January 15, 588 B.C.; also see note on 1:1.
26: 1 {King Jehoiachin's captivity,} **H** *In the eleventh year, on the first day of the month,* of the **H** calendar year. Since an element is missing in the date formula here, scholars have reconstructed this probable reading: *On the first day of the eleventh month, during the twelfth year.* This reading would put this message on February 3, 585 B.C.; also see note on 1:1.
26: 7 {bring King Nebuchadnezzar} **H** *Nebuchadrezzar,* a variant name for Nebuchadnezzar.
27: 6 {coasts of Cyprus.} **H** *Kittim.*
27:10 {Lydia, and Libya} **H** *Paras, Lud, and Put.*
27:13 {Merchants from Greece,} **H** *Javan.*
27:17 {Minnith, early figs,} The meaning of the **H** is uncertain.
27:19 {Greeks from Uzal} **H** *Vedan and Javan from Uzal.* The meaning of the **H** is uncertain.
27:36 {sight of you,} **H** *hiss at you.*
28:14 {mighty angelic guardian.} **H** *guardian cherub;* also in 28:16.
29: 1 {On January 7,} **H** *On the twelfth day of the tenth month,* of the **H** calendar. A number of events in Ezekiel can be cross-checked with dates in surviving Babylonian records and related accurately to our modern calendar. This event occurred on January 7, 587 B.C.
29:10 {border of Ethiopia.} **H** *Cush.*
29:17 {On April 26,} **H** *On the first day of the first month,* of the **H** calendar. This event occurred on April 26, 571 B.C.; also see note on 29:1.
29:18 {of King Nebuchadnezzar} **H** *Nebuchadrezzar,* a variant name for Nebuchadnezzar; also in 29:19.
30: 4 {land of Ethiopia} **H** *Cush;* also in 30:5, 9.
30: 5 {Ethiopia, Libya,} **H** *Put…Kub.* Both *Put* and *Kub* are associated with Libya.
30: 5 {Lydia,} **H** *Lud.*
30:10 {Through King Nebuchadnezzar} **H** *Nebuchadrezzar,* a variant name for Nebuchadnezzar.
30:13 {images at Memphis.} **H** *Noph;* also in 30:16.
30:14 {Zoan, and Thebes,} **H** *No;* also in 30:15, 16.
30:15 {fury on Pelusium,} **H** *Sin;* also in 30:16.
30:17 {Heliopolis and Bubastis} **H** *of Awen and Pi-beseth.*
30:20 {On April 29,} **H** *On the seventh day of the first month,* of the **H** calendar. This event occurred on April 29, 587 B.C.; also see note on 29:1.
31: 1 {On June 21,} **H** *On the first day of the third month,* of the **H** calendar. This event occurred on June 21, 587 B.C.; also see note on 29:1.
31:15 {into the grave,} **H** *to Sheol;* also in 31:16, 17.
32: 1 {On March 3,} **H** *On the first day of the twelfth month,* of the **H** calendar. This event occurred on March 3, 585 B.C.; also see note on 29:1.
32:17 {On March 17,} **H** *On the fifteenth day of the month,* presumably in the twelfth month of the **H** calendar (see 32:1). This would put this message at the end of King Jehoiachin's twelfth year of captivity, on March 17, 585 B.C.; also see note on 29:1. Greek version reads *On the fifteenth day of the first month,* which would put this message on April 27, 586 B.C., at the beginning of Jehoiachin's twelfth year.
32:21 {in the grave} **H** *in Sheol.*
32:27 {to the grave} **H** *to Sheol.*
32:27 {covering their bodies,} The meaning of the **H** phrase here is uncertain.
33:21 {On January 8,} **H** *On the fifth day of the tenth month,* of the **H** calendar. This event occurred on January 8, 585 B.C.; also see note on 29:1.
36:26 {new, obedient heart.} **H** *a heart of flesh.*
37:16 {tribes of Israel.'} **H** *Ephraim's stick, representing Joseph and all the house of Israel.*
38: 5 {Ethiopia, and Libya} **H** *Paras, Cush, and Put.*
38:14 {will rouse yourself.} As in Greek version; **H** reads *then you will know.*
39:11 {the Dead Sea.} **H** *the sea.*
39:25 {of my people} **H** *of Jacob.*
40: 1 {On April 28,} **H** *At the beginning of the year, on the tenth day of the month,* of the **H** calendar. A number of events in Ezekiel can be cross-checked with dates in surviving Babylonian records and related accurately to our modern calendar. This event occurred on April 28, 573 B.C.
40: 5 {was 10 1/2 feet} **H** *6 long cubits* [3.2 meters], *each being a cubit* [18 inches or 45 centimeters] *and a handbreadth* [3 inches or 8 centimeters] *in length.* In this chapter, the distance measures are calculated using the **H** long cubit, which equals 21 inches or 53 centimeters.
40: 6 {10 1/2 feet deep.} Greek version; **H** reads *1 rod* [10.5 feet or 3.2 meters] *deep, and one threshold, one rod deep.*
40: 8 {of the gateway} Many **H** manuscripts add *which faced inward toward the Temple; it was one rod* [10.5 feet or 3.2 meters] *deep. [9]Then he measured the foyer of the gateway,…*
40:14 {was 105 feet.} The meaning of the **H** in this verse is uncertain.
40:43 {three inches} **H** *a handbreadth* [8 centimeters].
40:44 {beside the south} As in Greek version; **H** reads *east.*
41: 1 {10 1/2 feet} **H** *6 cubits* [3.2 meters]. In this chapter, the distance measures are calculated using the **H** long cubit, which equals 21 inches or 53 centimeters.
42: 2 {87 1/2 feet wide.} **H** *100 cubits* [53 meters] *long and 50 cubits* [26.5 meters] *wide.* In this chapter, the distance measures are calculated using the **H** long cubit, which equals 21 inches or 53 centimeters.
42:10 {On the south} As in Greek version; **H** reads *east.*
43:13 {of the altar} **H** *measurements of the altar in long cubits, each being a cubit* [18 inches or 45 centimeters] *and a handbreadth* [3 inches or 8 centimeters] *in length.* In this chapter, the distance measures are calculated using the **H** long cubit, which equals 21 inches or 53 centimeters.
43:13 {9 inches} **H** *1 span* [23 centimeters].
44:29 {anyone sets apart} The **H** term used here refers to the complete consecration of things or people to the LORD, either by destroying them or by giving them as an offering.
45: 1 {6 2/3 miles wide.} Reflecting the Greek reading *25,000 cubits* [13.3 kilometers] *long and 20,000 cubits* [10.6 kilometers] *wide;* **H** reads *25,000 cubits long and 10,000 cubits wide.* Compare 45:3, 5; 48:9. In this chapter, the distance measures are calculated using the **H** long cubit, which equals 21 inches or 53 centimeters.
45: 5 {for their towns.} As in Greek version; **H** reads *They will have as their possession 20 rooms.*
45:10 {liquid volume measures.} **H** *use honest scales, an honest ephah, and an honest bath.*
45:13 {for every sixty} **H** *1/6 of an ephah from each homer of wheat…and of barley.*
45:14 {your olive oil,} **H** *the portion of oil, measured by the bath, is 1/10 of a bath from each cor, which consists of 10 baths or 1 homer, for 10 baths are equivalent to a homer.*
45:18 {each new year,} **H** *On the first day of the first month,* of the **H** calendar. This day of the **H** lunar calendar occurs in late March or early April.
45:24 {of olive oil} **H** *an ephah* [18 liters] *of flour…a hin* [3.8 liters] *of olive oil.*
45:25 {in early autumn,} **H** *the festival which begins on the fifteenth day of the seventh month* (see Lev 23:33). This day of the **H** lunar calendar occurs in late September or October.

46: 5 {of olive oil} **H** *an ephah* [18 liters] *of flour…a hin* [3.8 liters] *of olive oil;* also in 46:7, 11.
46: 14 {of olive oil} **H** *1/6 of an ephah* [2.9 liters] *of flour with 1/3 of a hin* [1.3 liters] *of olive oil.*
46: 17 {every fiftieth year.} **H** *until the Year of Release;* see Lev 25:8-17.
46: 22 {52 1/2 feet wide,} **H** *40 cubits* [21.2 meters] *long and 30 cubits* [15.9 meters] *wide.* The distances are calculated using the **H** long cubit, which equals 21 inches or 53 centimeters.
47: 3 {for 1,750 feet} **H** *1,000 cubits* [530 meters]; also in 47:4, 5. The distances are calculated using the **H** long cubit, which equals 21 inches or 53 centimeters.
47: 8 {the Jordan Valley,} **H** *the Arabah.*
47: 8 {the Dead Sea.} **H** *the sea;* also in 47:10.
47: 10 {fill the Mediterranean} **H** *the great sea;* also in 47:15, 17, 19, 20.
47: 18 {the Dead Sea} **H** *the eastern sea.*
47: 18 {south as Tamar.} As in Greek version; **H** reads *you will measure.*
47: 19 {Meribah at Kadesh} **H** *waters of Meribath-kadesh.*
48: 9 {6 2/3 miles wide.} Reflecting the Greek reading in 45:1: *25,000 cubits* [13.3 kilometers] *long and 20,000 cubits* [10.6 kilometers] *wide;* **H** reads *25,000 cubits long and 10,000 cubits wide.* Compare 45:1-5; 48:10-13. In this chapter, the distance measures are calculated using the **H** long cubit, which equals 21 inches or 53 centimeters.
48: 16 {measure 1 1/2 miles} **H** *4,500 cubits* [2.4 kilometers]; also in 48:30, 32, 33, 34.
48: 17 {for 150 yards} **H** *250 cubits* [133 meters].
48: 28 {Meribah at Kadesh} **H** *waters of Meribath-kadesh.*
48: 28 {to the Mediterranean.} **H** *the great sea.*
48: 35 {be six miles.} **H** *18,000 cubits* [9.6 kilometers].
48: 35 {LORD Is There.'} **H** *Yahweh Shammah.*
Da 1: 2 {land of Babylonia.} **H** *the land of Shinar.*
8: 11[-12] {everything it did.} The meaning of the **H** for these verses is uncertain.
8: 21 {king of Greece,} **H** *of Javan.*
8: 26 {evenings and mornings} **H** *about the evenings and mornings;* compare 8:14.
9: 24 {sets of seven} **H** *70 sevens.*
9: 25 {sets of seven} **H** *Seven sevens plus 62 sevens.*
9: 26 {sets of seven,} **H** *After 62 sevens.*
9: 27 {set of seven,} **H** *for one seven.*
9: 27 {his terrible deeds,} **H** *on the wing of abominations;* the meaning of the **H** is uncertain.
9: 27 {that causes desecration,} **H** *an abomination of desolation.*
10: 4 {On April 23,} **H** *On the twenty-fourth day of the first month.* This event in the book of Daniel can be cross-checked with dates in surviving Persian records and can be related accurately to our modern calendar. This day of the **H** lunar calendar occurred on April 23, 536 B.C.
10: 13 {the spirit prince} **H** *the prince;* also in 10:13c, 20.
10: 13 {of the archangels,} **H** *the chief princes.*
10: 13 {kingdom of Persia.} As in one Greek version; **H** reads *and I was left there with the kings of Persia.* The meaning of the **H** is uncertain.
10: 20 {kingdom of Greece.} **H** *of Javan.*
10: 21 {your spirit prince.} **H** *against these except Michael, your prince.*
11: 1 {standing beside Michael} **H** *him.*
11: 2 {kingdom of Greece.} **H** *of Javan.*
11: 7 {of her relatives} **H** *a branch from her roots.*
11: 30 {from western coastlands} **H** *from Kittim.*
11: 31 {that causes desecration.} **H** *the abomination of desolation.*
11: 43 {Libyans and Ethiopians} **H** *Cushites.*
12: 1 {Michael, the archangel} **H** *the great prince.*
12: 11 {that causes desecration} **H** *the abomination of desolation.*
Hos 1: 1 {Jehoash} **H** *Joash,* a variant name for Jehoash.
2: 2 {now, call Israel} **H** *call your mother.*
2: 15 {Valley of Trouble} **H** *valley of Achor.*
2: 16 {'my master.'} **H** *'my baal.'*
2: 23 {'Not loved.'} **H** *Lo-ruhamah;* see 1:6.
2: 23 {'Not my people,'} **H** *Lo-ammi;* see 1:9.
3: 1 {them choice gifts.} **H** *raisin cakes.*
3: 2 {pieces of silver} **H** *15 shekels of silver,* about 6 ounces or 171 grams in weight.
3: 2 {measure of wine.} As in Greek version, which reads *a homer* [182 liters] *of barley and a measure of wine;* **H** reads *a homer of barley and a lethech* [2.5 bushels or 91 liters] *of barley.*
3: 5 {descendant, their king.} **H** *to David their king.*
4: 4 {is with you!} **H** *Your people are like those with a complaint against the priests.*
4: 7 {They have exchanged} As in Syriac version and an ancient **H** tradition; Masoretic Text reads *I will exchange.*
4: 18 {love for honor.} As in Greek version; the meaning of the **H** is uncertain.
5: 2 {them at Acacia.} **H** *at Shittim.* The meaning of the **H** for this sentence is uncertain.
5: 9 {is certain, Israel} **H** *Ephraim,* referring to the northern kingdom of Israel; also in 5:11, 12, 13, 14.
5: 10 {bad as thieves.} **H** *have become as those who move a boundary marker.*
6: 4 {"O Israel} **H** *Ephraim,* referring to the northern kingdom of Israel.
7: 8 {people of Israel} **H** *Ephraim,* referring to the northern kingdom of Israel; also in 7:11.
7: 12 {their evil ways.} **H** *I will punish them because of what was reported against them in the assembly.*
8: 9 {people of Israel} **H** *Ephraim,* referring to the northern kingdom of Israel; also in 8:11.
9: 8 {God over Israel,} **H** *Ephraim,* referring to the northern kingdom of Israel; also in 9:11, 13, 16.
10: 11 {"Israel} **H** *Ephraim,* referring to the northern kingdom of Israel.
10: 11 {the plow. Israel} **H** *Jacob.*
11: 2 {the more I} As in Greek version; **H** reads *they.*
11: 3 {who taught Israel} **H** *Ephraim,* referring to the northern kingdom of Israel; also in 11:8, 9, 12.
12: 1 {people of Israel} **H** *Ephraim,* referring to the northern kingdom of Israel; also in 12:8, 14.
12: 4 {spoke to him} As in Greek and Syriac versions; **H** reads *to us.*
12: 9 {Festival of Shelters.} **H** *as in the days of your appointed feast.*
13: 10 {Where now is} As in Greek and Syriac versions and Latin Vulgate; **H** reads *I will be.*
14: 8 {"O Israel,} **H** *Ephraim,* referring to the northern kingdom of Israel.
Joel 1: 6 {army of locusts} **H** *A nation.*
2: 1 {trumpet in Jerusalem} **H** *Zion;* also in 2:15, 23.
2: 20 {into the Mediterranean.} **H** *the eastern sea;…the western sea.*
3: 6 {to the Greeks,} **H** *to the peoples of Javan.*
3: 8 {peoples of Arabia,} **H** *to the Sabeans.*
3: 18 {valley of acacias.} **H** *valley of Shittim.*
3: 21 {home in Jerusalem} **H** *Zion.*
Am 1: 1 {son of Jehoash,} **H** *Joash,* a variant name for Jehoash.
1: 15 {And their king} **H** *malcam,* possibly referring to their god Molech.
3: 9 {leaders of Philistia} **H** *Ashdod.*
3: 13 {throughout all Israel,} **H** *the house of Jacob.*
4: 3 {from your fortresses.} **H** *thrown out toward Harmon,* possibly a reference to Mount Hermon.
4: 11 {as I destroyed} **H** *as when God destroyed.*
5: 6 {roar through Israel} **H** *the house of Joseph.*
5: 15 {people who remain.} **H** *on the remnant of Joseph.*
6: 1 {secure in Jerusalem} **H** *Zion.*
6: 6 {that your nation} **H** *Joseph.*
6: 8 {glory of Israel,} **H** *Jacob.*
7: 2 {you relent, Israel} **H** *Jacob;* also in 7:5.
7: 9 {of your ancestors} **H** *of Isaac.*
7: 16 {against my people.} **H** *against the house of Isaac.*
8: 7 {Pride of Israel} **H** *the pride of Jacob.*
9: 2 {of the dead,} **H** *to Sheol.*
9: 7 {than the Ethiopians} **H** *the Cushites.*
9: 7 {Philistines from Crete} **H** *Caphtor.*
9: 8 {family of Israel,} **H** *the house of Jacob.*
Ob 1: 6 {Edom} **H** *Esau;* also in 8b, 9, 18, 19, 21.
1: 10 {relatives in Israel.} **H** *your brother Jacob.*
1: 17 {"But Jerusalem} **H** *Mount Zion.*
1: 17 {people of Israel} **H** *house of Jacob;* also in 18.
1: 19 {foothills of Judah} **H** *the Shephelah.*
1: 20 {in the north} **H** *in Sepharad.*
Jnh 2: 2 {of the dead,} **H** *from Sheol.*
4: 11 {in spiritual darkness,} **H** *people who don't know their right hands from their left.*
Mic 1: 5 {Israel and Judah.} **H** *and Jacob.*
1: 10 {city of Gath} *Gath* sounds like the **H** term for "tell."
1: 11 {people of Zaanan} *Zaanan* sounds like the **H** term for "come out."
1: 12 {people of Maroth} *Maroth* sounds like the **H** term for "bitter."
1: 13 {people of Lachish.} *Lachish* sounds like the **H** term for "team of horses."
1: 13 {you led Jerusalem} **H** *the daughter of Zion.*
1: 15 {people of Mareshah,} *Mareshah* sounds like the **H** term for "conqueror."
1: 15 {And the leaders} **H** *the glory.*
2: 7 {O family of Israel} **H** *house of Jacob.*
4: 2 {God of Israel.} **H** *of Jacob.*
4: 7 {rule from Jerusalem} **H** *Mount Zion.*
4: 10 {people of Jerusalem,} **H** *O daughter of Zion.*
4: 13 {the nations, O Jerusalem!"} **H** *"Rise up and thresh, O daughter of Zion."*
5: 6 {of Nimrod. They} **H** *He.*
5: 7 {left in Israel} **H** *Jacob;* also in 5:8.
6: 5 {journey from Acacia} **H** *Shittim.*
6: 9 {is sending them.} **H** *"Listen to the rod. Who appointed it?"*
6: 10 {in short measures.} **H** *by using the short ephah;* the ephah was a unit for measuring grain.
7: 12 {the Euphrates River,} **H** *the river.*
Na 3: 8 {better than Thebes,} **H** *No-amon;* also in 3:10.
3: 9 {Ethiopia} **H** *Cush.*
Hab 2: 5 {Wealth} As in Dead Sea Scroll 1QpHab; other **H** manuscripts read *Wine.*
2: 5 {wide as death,} **H** *as Sheol.*
3: 1 {the prophet Habakkuk:} **H** adds *according to shigionoth,* probably indicating the musical setting for the prayer.
3: 3 {deserts from Edom} **H** *Teman.*
3: 3 {and Mount Paran.} **H** adds *selah;* also in 3:9, 13. The meaning of this **H** term is uncertain; it is probably a musical or literary term.
3: 16 {way beneath me,} **H** *Decay entered my bones.*
Zep 1: 3 {heaps of rubble,} The meaning of the **H** is uncertain.
1: 5 {they worship Molech,} **H** *Malcam,* another name for Molech; or it could possibly mean *their king.*
1: 7 {chosen their executioners.} **H** *has prepared a sacrifice and sanctified his guests.*
2: 5 {for you Philistines} **H** *Kerethites.*
2: 12 {"You Ethiopians} **H** *Cushites.*
3: 10 {rivers of Ethiopia} **H** *Cush.*
3: 18 {disgraced no more.} The meaning of the **H** for this verse is uncertain.
Hag 1: 1 {On August 29} **H** *On the first day of the sixth month,* of the **H** calendar. A number of events in Haggai can be cross-checked with dates in surviving Persian records and related accurately to our modern calendar. This event occurred on August 29, 520 B.C.
1: 1 {and to Jeshua} **H** *Joshua,* a variant name for Jeshua; also in 1:12, 14.
1: 15 {was on September 21} **H** *on the twenty-fourth day of the sixth month,* of the **H** calendar. This event occurred on September 21, 520 B.C.; also see note on 1:1a.
2: 1 {Then on October 17} **H** *on the twenty-first day of the seventh month,* of the **H** calendar. This event occurred on October 17, 520 B.C.; also see note on 1:1a.
2: 2 {and to Jeshua} **H** *Joshua,* a variant name for Jeshua; also in 2:4.
2: 10 {On December 18} **H** *On the twenty-fourth day of the ninth month,* of the **H** calendar (also in 2:18). This event occurred on December 18, 520 B.C.; also see note on 1:1a.
2: 20 {on December 18} **H** *on the twenty-fourth day of the month;* see note on 2:10.
Zec 1: 1 {In midautumn} **H** *In the eighth month.* A number of events in Zechariah can be cross-checked with dates in surviving Persian records and related accurately to our modern calendar. This month of the **H** lunar calendar occurred in October and November 520 B.C.
1: 7 {Then on February 15} **H** *on the twenty-fourth day of the eleventh month, the month of Shebat,* of the **H** calendar. This event occurred on February 15, 519 B.C.; also see note on 1:1.
1: 16 {Jerusalem.} **H** *and the measuring line will be stretched out over Jerusalem.*
2: 7 {Escape to Jerusalem,} **H** *to Zion.*
2: 8 {most precious possession.} **H** *harms the apple of my eye.*
2: 10 {and rejoice, O Jerusalem,} **H** *O daughter of Zion.*
3: 1 {Jeshua} **H** *Joshua,* a variant name for Jeshua; also in 3:3, 4, 6, 8, 9.
3: 1 {Satan} Or *The Accuser;* **H** reads *The Adversary;* also in 3:2.
3: 9 {with seven facets.} **H** *7 eyes.*
5: 2 {fifteen feet wide.} **H** *20 cubits* [9 meters] *long and 10 cubits* [4.5 meters] *wide.*
5: 6 {for measuring grain,} **H** *an ephah,* about half a bushel or 18 liters; also in 5:7, 8, 9, 10, 11.
5: 6 {with the sins} As in Greek version; **H** reads *the appearance.*
5: 11 {land of Babylonia} **H** *the land of Shinar.*
6: 6 {is going west,} **H** *is going after them.*
6: 8 {of my Spirit} **H** *have given my Spirit rest.*
6: 11 {make a crown} As in Greek and Syriac versions; **H** reads *crowns.*
6: 11 {head of Jeshua} **H** *Joshua,* a variant name for Jeshua.
6: 14 {Heldai,} As in Syriac version (compare 6:10); **H** reads *Helem.*
6: 14 {Jedaiah, and Josiah} As in Syriac version (compare 6:10); **H** reads *Hen.*
7: 1 {On December 7} **H** *On the fourth day of the ninth month, the month of Kislev,* of the **H** calendar. This event occurred on December 7, 518 B.C.; also see note on 1:1.
7: 3 {the Temple's destruction,} **H** *mourn and fast in the fifth month.* This month of the **H** lunar calendar usually occurs in July and August.
7: 5 {in early autumn,} **H** *fasted and mourned in the fifth and seventh months.* The fifth month of the **H** lunar calendar occurs during our months of July and August. The seventh month occurs during September and October; both the Day of Atonement and the Festival of Shelters were celebrated in the seventh month.
7: 7 {foothills of Judah} **H** *the Shephelah.*
8: 19 {autumn, and winter} **H** *in the fourth, fifth, seventh, and tenth months.* The fourth month of the **H** lunar calendar usually occurs in June and July. The fifth month usually occurs in July and August. The seventh month usually occurs in September and October. The tenth month usually occurs in December and January.
9: 1 {the message} **H** *An Oracle: The message.*
9: 1 {land of Aram} **H** *land of Hadrach.*
9: 4 {the Mediterranean Sea.} **H** *the sea.*
9: 7 {clan in Judah.} **H** *and will become a leader in Judah.*
9: 9 {Rejoice greatly, O people} **H** *daughter.*
9: 10 {chariots from Israel} **H** *from Ephraim;* also in 9:13.
9: 10 {the Euphrates River} **H** *the river.*
9: 13 {my arrow! Jerusalem} **H** *Zion.*
9: 13 {against the Greeks.} **H** *the sons of Javan.*
10: 6 {and save Israel} **H** *save the house of Joseph.*
10: 7 {people of Israel} **H** *of Ephraim.*
11: 12 {wages thirty pieces} **H** *30 shekels,* about 12 ounces or 342 grams in weight.
12: 1 {This} **H** *An Oracle: This.*
14: 5 {across to Azal.} The meaning of the **H** is uncertain.

14: 5 {ones with him.} As in Greek version; **H** reads *with you.*
14: 6 {no longer shine,} **H** *there will be no light, no cold or frost.* The meaning of the **H** is uncertain.
14: 8 {toward the Mediterranean,} **H** *half toward the eastern sea and half toward the western sea.*
14:21 {longer be traders} **H** *Canaanites.*
Mal 1: 1 {is the message} **H** *An Oracle: The message.*
1: 7 {defiled the sacrifices} As in Greek version; **H** reads *defiled you.*
2:12 {nation of Israel} **H** *from the tents of Jacob.*
2:15 {you are his.} Or *Did not one God make us and preserve our life and breath?* or *Did not one God make her, both flesh and spirit?* The meaning of the **H** is uncertain.
3:11 {insects and disease.} **H** *from the devourer.*
4: 4 {on Mount Sinai} **H** *Horeb,* another name for Sinai.
4: 6 {hearts of parents} **H** *fathers;* also in 4:6b.
Jn 20:16 {and exclaimed, "Teacher!"} Greek *and said in H, "Rabboni," which means "Teacher."*
Ac 21:40 {own language, Aramaic.} Or *H.*
26:14 {me in Aramaic,} Or *H.*

HEEL (4)

Ge 25:26 {called him Jacob.} *Jacob* means "he grasps the **h**"; this can also figuratively mean "he deceives."
27:36 {name is Jacob,} *Jacob* means "he grasps the **h**"; this can also figuratively mean "he deceives."
35:10 {be called Israel."} *Jacob* means "he grasps the **h**"; this can also figuratively mean "he deceives"; *Israel* means "God struggles" or "one who struggles with God."
Hos 12: 2 {to punish Jacob} *Jacob* means "he grasps at the **h**"; this can also figuratively mean "he deceives."

HEIGHT (2)

Ezr 6: 3 {be ninety feet.} Aramaic *Its **h** will be 60 cubits* [27 meters], *and its width will be 60 cubits.* It is commonly held that this verse should be emended to read: "Its **h** will be 45 feet, its length will be 90 feet, and its width will be 30 feet"; compare 1 Kgs 6:2. The emendation regarding the width is supported by the Syriac version.

HEIGHTS (1)

Ps 48: 2 {the holy mountain,} Or *Mount Zion, in the far north;* Hebrew reads *Mount Zion, the **h** of Zaphon.*

HELDAI (1)

1Ch 27:15 {Heled,} Hebrew *H,* a variant name for Heled; compare 11:30 and 2 Sam 23:29.

HELEB (1)

2Sa 23:29 {Heled} As in some Hebrew manuscripts (see also 1 Chr 11:30); most Hebrew manuscripts read *H.*

HELED (1)

1Ch 27:15 {Heled,} Hebrew *Heldai,* a variant name for **H**; compare 11:30 and 2 Sam 23:29.

HELEM (1)

Zec 6:14 {who gave it—Heldai,} As in Syriac version (compare 6:10); Hebrew reads *H.*

HELIOPOLIS (1)

Jer 43:13 {of the sun} Or *in H.*

HELKATH-HAZZURIM (1)

2Sa 2:16 {Field of Swords.} Hebrew *H.*

HELLENISTS (1)

Ac 11:20 {preaching to Gentiles} Greek *the Greeks;* other manuscripts read *the H.*

HELPER (1)

Ex 18: 4 {son was Eliezer,} *Eliezer* means "God is my **h**."

HELPERS (1)

Job 9:13 {forces against him} Hebrew *The **h** of Rahab,* the name of a mythical sea monster that represents chaos in ancient literature.

HEN (1)

Zec 6:14 {Jedaiah, and Josiah} As in Syriac version (compare 6:10); Hebrew reads *H.*

HEPHZIBAH (1)

Isa 62: 4 {of God's Delight} Hebrew *H,* which means "my delight is in her."

HERB (1)

Lk 11:42 {of your income,} Greek *to tithe the mint and the rue and every **h**.*

HERMON (3)

Ps 29: 6 {and Mount Hermon} Hebrew *Sirion,* another name for Mount **H**.
Eze 27: 5 {cypress from Senir.} Or *H.*
Am 4: 3 {from your fortresses.} Hebrew *thrown out toward Harmon,* possibly a reference to Mount **H**.

HERODIAS (1)

Mk 6:22 {also named Herodias,} Some manuscripts read *the daughter of H herself.*

HESITANTLY (1)

1Sa 15:32 {have been spared!"} Dead Sea Scrolls and Greek version read *Agag arrived **h**, for he thought, "Surely this is the bitterness of death."*

HIDDAI (1)

2Sa 23:30 {Hurai} As in some Greek manuscripts (see also 1 Chr 11:32); Hebrew reads *H.*

HIGGAION (1)

Ps 9:16 {*Quiet Interlude*} Hebrew *H Selah.* The meaning of this phrase is uncertain.

HIGH (2 of 12)

Pr 17:19 {who speaks boastfully} Or *who builds up defenses;* Hebrew reads *who makes a **h** gate.*
Eze 43: 7 {their dead kings.} Or *by raising pillars on their **h** places.*

HILEN (1)

1Ch 6:58 {Holon,} As in parallel text at Josh 21:15; Hebrew reads *H.*

HILL (2)

Jos 5: 3 {Israel at Gibeath-haaraloth.} *Gibeath-haaraloth* means "**h** of foreskins."
Ac 17:22 {before the Council,} Or *in the middle of Mars H;* Greek reads *in the middle of the Areopagus.*

HILLS (1)

SS 2:17 {the rugged mountains.} Or *on the **h** of Bether.*

HIN (16)

Ex 29:40 {quart of wine} Hebrew *1/10 of an ephah* [2 liters] *of fine flour...1/4 of a **h*** [1 liter] *of olive oil...1/4 of a **h** of wine.*
30:24 {and one gallon} Hebrew *500 shekels* [5.7 kilograms] *of cassia, according to the sanctuary shekel, and 1 **h*** [3.8 liters].
Lev 19:36 {must be accurate.} Hebrew *Use an honest ephah* [a measure for dry goods] *and an honest **h*** [a measure for liquids].
23:13 {offer one quart} Hebrew *1/4 of a **h*** [1 liter].
Nu 15: 4 {with one quart} Hebrew *1/4 of a **h*** [1 liter]; also in 15:5.
15: 6 {a half pints} Hebrew *1/3 of a **h*** [1.3 liters]; also in 15:7.
15: 9 {with two quarts} Hebrew *1/2 of a **h*** [2 liters]; also in 15:10.
28: 5 {with one quart} Hebrew *1/4 of a **h*** [1 liter]; also in 28:7.
28:14 {two quarts} Hebrew *1/2 of a **h*** [2 liters].
28:14 {a half pints} Hebrew *1/3 of a **h*** [1.3 liters].
28:14 {and one quart} Hebrew *1/4 of a **h*** [1 liter].
Eze 4:11 {out a jar} Hebrew *1/6 of a **h**,* about 1.3 pints or 0.6 liters.
45:24 {of olive oil} Hebrew *an ephah* [18 liters] *of flour...a **h*** [3.8 liters] *of olive oil.*
46: 5 {of olive oil} Hebrew *an ephah* [18 liters] *of flour...a **h*** [3.8 liters] *of olive oil;* also in 46:7, 11.
46:14 {of olive oil} Hebrew *1/6 of an ephah* [2.9 liters] *of flour with 1/3 of a **h*** [1.3 liters] *of olive oil.*

HIRAM (4)

1Ki 7:13 {man named Huram} Hebrew *H* (also in 7:40, 45); compare 2 Chr 2:13. This is not the same person mentioned in 5:1.
2Ch 2: 3 {to King Hiram} Hebrew *Huram,* a variant name for **H**; also in 2:11, 12.
8: 2 {that King Hiram} Hebrew *Huram,* a variant name for **H**; also in 8:18.
9:21 {Hiram.} Hebrew *Huram,* a variant name for **H**.

HIRED (2)

Isa 21:16 {within a year,"} Hebrew *Within a year, like the years of a **h** hand.* Some ancient manuscripts read *Within three years,* as in 16:14.
Lk 15:21 {called your son.} Some manuscripts add *Please take me on as a **h** man.*

HISS (1)

Eze 27:36 {sight of you,} Hebrew ***h** at you.*

HITTITES (1)

2Sa 24: 6 {land of Tahtim-hodshi} Greek version reads *to Gilead and to Kadesh in the land of the H.*

HODAVIAH (1)

Ezr 3: 9 {descendants of Hodaviah.} Hebrew *sons of Judah* (i.e., *bene Yehudah*). *Bene* might also be read here as the proper name Binnui; *Yehudah* is probably another name for **H**. Compare 2:40; Neh 7:43; 1 Esdras 5:58.

HODEVAH (1)

Ne 7:43 {(descendants of Hodaviah} As in parallel text at Ezra 2:40; Hebrew reads *H.*

HOLINESS (2)

Ro 1: 4 {the Holy Spirit.} Or *the Spirit of **h**.*
2Co 6: 6 {the Holy Spirit.} Or *the **h** of spirit.*

HOLY (19)

Dt 33: 2 {his right hand.} Or *came from myriads of **h** ones, from the south, from his mountain slopes.* The meaning of the Hebrew is uncertain.
Job 5: 1 {to the angels,} Hebrew *the **h** ones.*
15:15 {trust the angels} Hebrew *the **h** ones.*
Ps 2: 6 {my holy city.} Hebrew *on Zion, my **h** mountain.*
16:10 {your godly one} Or *your H One.*
Da 9:24 {Most Holy Place.} Or *the Most H One.*
Hos 11:12 {the Holy One.} Or *and Judah is unruly against God, the faithful H One.*
Mt 3:11 {and with fire.} Or *in the H Spirit and in fire.*
27:51[-53] {to many people.} Or *The earth shook, rocks split apart, tombs opened, and many bodies of godly men and women who had died were raised from the dead. After Jesus' resurrection, they left the cemetery, went into the **h** city of Jerusalem, and appeared to many people.*
Lk 3:16 {and with fire.} Or *in the H Spirit and in fire.*
Ro 11:16 {also be holy.} Greek *If the dough offered as firstfruits is **h**, so is the whole lump.*
2Co 1:12 {have been honest} Some manuscripts read ***h**.*
1Th 5:26 {in Christian love.} Greek *Greet all the brothers with a **h** kiss.*
Tit 3: 5 {the Holy Spirit.} Greek *He saved us through the washing of regeneration and renewing of the H Spirit.*
Heb 3: 1 {belong to God} Greek ***h** brothers.*
Jas 4: 5 {to be faithful} Or *the spirit that God placed within us tends to envy,* or *the H Spirit, whom God has placed within us, opposes our envy.*
1Jn 2:20 {come upon you,} Greek *But you have an anointing from the H One.*
5: 7 {these three witnesses} Some very late manuscripts add *in heaven—the Father, the Word, and the H Spirit, and these three are one. And we have three witnesses on earth.*
Jude 1:20 {the Holy Spirit.} Greek *Pray in the H Spirit.*

HOMAM (1)

1Ch 1:39 {Hori and Heman.} As in parallel text at Gen 36:22; Hebrew reads *and H.*

HOMER (8)

Lev 27:16 {five bushels} Hebrew *1 **h*** [182 liters].
Isa 5:10 {only one measure} Hebrew *A **h*** [5 bushels or 182 liters] *of seed will yield only an ephah* [0.5 bushels or 18.2 liters].
Eze 45:11 {The homer} The ***h*** measures about 40 gallons or 182 liters.
45:13 {for every sixty} Hebrew *1/6 of an ephah from each **h** of wheat...and of barley.*
45:14 {your olive oil,} Hebrew *the portion of oil, measured by the bath, is 1/10 of a bath from each cor, which consists of 10 baths or 1 **h**, for 10 baths are equivalent to a **h**.*
Hos 3: 2 {measure of wine.} As in Greek version, which reads *a **h*** [182 liters] *of barley and a measure of wine;* Hebrew reads *a **h** of barley and a lethech* [2.5 bushels or 91 liters] *of barley.*

HOMERS (1)

Nu 11:32 {than fifty bushels} Hebrew *10 **h*** [1.8 kiloliters].

HOMES (1)

Lk 16: 9 {you in heaven.} Or *Then when you run out at the end of this life, your friends will welcome you into eternal **h**.*

HONEST (5)

Lev 19:36 {must be accurate.} Hebrew *Use an **h** ephah* [a measure for dry goods] *and an **h** hin* [a measure for liquids].
Eze 45:10 {liquid volume measures.} Hebrew *use **h** scales, an **h** ephah, and an **h** bath.*

HONOR (2)

Ge 30:20 {Zebulun,} *Zebulun* probably means "**h**."
1Ti 5:17 {paid well,} Greek *should be worthy of double **h**.*

HONORED (1)

Eph 1:18 {to his people.} Or *realize how much God has been **h** by acquiring his people.*

HOREB (14)

Ex 3: 1 {near Sinai,} Hebrew *H,* another name for Sinai.
17: 6 {Mount Sinai.} Hebrew *H,* another name for Sinai.
33: 6 {Mount Sinai,} Hebrew *H,* another name for Sinai.
Dt 1: 2 {Mount Sinai} Hebrew *H,* another name for Sinai; also in 1:6, 19.
4:10 {Mount Sinai,} Hebrew *H,* another name for Sinai; also in 4:15.
5: 2 {Mount Sinai,} Hebrew *H,* another name for Sinai.

9: 8 {Mount Sinai,} Hebrew ***H***, another name for Sinai.
18:16 {Mount Sinai.} Hebrew ***H***, another name for Sinai.
29: 1 {Mount Sinai.} Hebrew ***H***, another name for Sinai.
1Ki 8: 9 {Mount Sinai,} Hebrew *at **H***, another name for Sinai.
19: 8 {Mount Sinai,} Hebrew ***H***, another name for Sinai.
2Ch 5:10 {Mount Sinai,} Hebrew ***H***, another name for Sinai.
Ps 106:19 {Mount Sinai} Hebrew *at **H***, another name for Sinai.
Mal 4: 4 {Mount Sinai} Hebrew ***H***, another name for Sinai.

HORMAH (2)

Nu 21: 3 {been called Hormah} ***H*** means "destruction."
Jdg 1:17 {was named Hormah.} ***H*** means "destruction."

HORN (2)

Da 3: 7 {the musical instruments,} Aramaic *the **h**, flute, zither, lyre, harp, and other instruments of the musical ensemble.*
3:10 {the musical instruments.} Aramaic *the **h**, flute, zither, lyre, harp, pipes, and other instruments of the musical ensemble;* also in 3:15.

HORNS (1)

Am 6:13 {we take Karnaim} *Karnaim* means "**h**," a term that symbolizes strength.

HORSES (2)

Ps 20: 7 {armies and weapons,} Hebrew *chariots and **h**.*
Mic 1:13 {people of Lachish.} *Lachish* sounds like the Hebrew term for "team of **h**."

HOS (7)

Mt 2:15 {out of Egypt."} **H** 11:1.
9:13 {want your sacrifices.'} **H** 6:6.
12: 7 {want your sacrifices.'} **H** 6:6.
Ro 9:25 {not love before."} **H** 2:23.
9:26 {the living God.' "} **H** 1:10.
1Co 15:55 {is your sting?"} **H** 13:14.
1Pe 2:10 {received his mercy."} **H** 1:6, 9; 2:23.

HOSANNA (3)

Mt 21: 9 {"Praise God} Greek ***H***, an exclamation of praise that literally means "save now"; also in 21:9b, 15.
Mk 11: 9 {"Praise God!} Greek ***H***, an exclamation of praise that literally means "save now"; also in 11:10.
Jn 12:13 {"Praise God!} Greek ***H***, an exclamation of praise that literally means "save now."

HOSHEA (2)

Nu 13:16 {Joshua.} ***H*** (see 13:8) means "salvation"; *Joshua* means "The LORD is salvation."
Dt 32:44 {Joshua} Hebrew ***H***, a variant name for Joshua.

HOT (1)

Ne 7: 3 {of the day.} Or *Keep the gates of Jerusalem closed until the sun is **h**.*

HOTHAM (1)

1Ch 7:35 {his brother Helem} Possibly another name for ***H***; compare 7:32.

HOUSE (32)

1Sa 1: 7 {to the Tabernacle.} Hebrew *the **h** of the LORD;* also in 1:24.
2:30 {tribe of Levi} Hebrew *that your **h** and your father's **h**.*
3:15 {of the Tabernacle} Hebrew *the **h** of the LORD.*
20:16 {covenant with David,} Hebrew *with the **h** of David.*
2Sa 19:20 {in all Israel} Hebrew *the **h** of Joseph.*
1Ki 11:28 {Ephraim and Manasseh.} Hebrew *from the **h** of Joseph.*
Isa 8:17 {people of Israel.} Hebrew *the **h** of Jacob.*
10:20 {Israel and Judah} Hebrew *and the **h** of Jacob.*
14: 1 {people of Israel.} Hebrew *the **h** of Jacob.*
Jer 5:20 {announcement to Israel} Hebrew *to the **h** of Jacob.*
Eze 37:16 {tribes of Israel.'} Hebrew *Ephraim's stick, representing Joseph and all the **h** of Israel.*
Hos 4:15 {and at Beth-aven.} *Beth-aven* means "**h** of wickedness"; it is being used as another name for Bethel, which means "**h** of God."
5: 8 {cry in Beth-aven} *Beth-aven* means "**h** of wickedness"; it is being used as another name for Bethel, which means "**h** of God."
10: 5 {idol at Beth-aven.} *Beth-aven* means "**h** of wickedness"; it is being used as another name for Bethel, which means "**h** of God."
Am 3:13 {throughout all Israel,} Hebrew *the **h** of Jacob.*
5: 6 {roar through Israel} Hebrew *the **h** of Joseph.*
7:16 {against my people.} Hebrew *against the **h** of Isaac.*
9: 8 {family of Israel,} Hebrew *the **h** of Jacob.*
Ob 1:17 {people of Israel} Hebrew ***h** of Jacob;* also in 18.
Mic 1:10 {people in Beth-leaphrah,} *Beth-leaphrah* means "**h** of dust."
1:11 {people of Beth-ezel} *Beth-ezel* means "adjoining **h**."
2: 7 {O family of Israel} Hebrew ***h** of Jacob.*
Zec 10: 6 {and save Israel} Hebrew *save the **h** of Joseph.*
Lk 1:33 {reign over Israel} Greek *over the **h** of Jacob.*

Jn 2:17 {burns within me."} Or *"Concern for God's **h** will be my undoing."* Ps 69:9.
Ac 5:42 {in their homes,} Greek *from **h** to **h**.*
7:46 {God of Jacob.} Some manuscripts read *the **h** of Jacob.*

HOW (6)

Ps 139:17 {thoughts about me,} Or ***H** precious to me are your thoughts.*
Mt 23:13 {go in yourselves.} Some manuscripts add verse 14, ***H** terrible it will be for you teachers of religious law and you Pharisees. Hypocrites! You shamelessly cheat widows out of their property, and then, to cover up the kind of people you really are, you make long prayers in public. Because of this, your punishment will be the greater.*
Jn 8:57 {have seen Abraham?} Some manuscripts read ***H** can you say Abraham has seen you?*
Eph 1:18 {to his people.} Or *realize **h** much God has been honored by acquiring his people.*
1Th 4: 4 {control your body} Or *will know **h** to take a wife for himself;* Greek reads *will know **h** to possess his own vessel.*

HOZAI (1)

2Ch 33:19 {*of the Seers.*} Or *The Record of **H**.*

HUMAN (6)

Pr 20:27 {the human spirit,} Or *The **h** spirit is the LORD's searchlight.*
Isa 29:13 {learned by rote.} Greek version reads *Their worship is a farce, for they merely teach **h** commands and teachings.*
Da 2:34 {by supernatural means.} Aramaic *not by **h** hands;* also in 2:45.
10:16 {like a man} As in most manuscripts of the Masoretic Text; one manuscript of the Masoretic Text and one Greek version read *Then something that looked like a **h** hand.*
Jn 8:15 {your human limitations,} Or *judge me by **h** standards.*
1Co 3: 4 {are not Christians?} Greek *aren't you merely **h**?*

HUMANITY (1)

Rev 13:18 {of a man.} Or *of **h**.*

HUMBLE (1)

Ps 68:30 {tribute from us.} Or ***H** them until they submit, bringing pieces of silver as tribute.*

HUNDRED (1)

2Sa 23: 8 {a single battle.} As in some Greek manuscripts (see also 1 Chr 11:11); the Hebrew is uncertain, though it might be rendered *the Three. It was Adino the Eznite who killed eight **h** men at one time.*

HUNDREDS (1)

Nu 31:14 {the military commanders} Hebrew *the commanders of thousands, and the commanders of **h**;* also in 31:48, 52, 54.

HURAM (3)

2Ch 2: 3 {to King Hiram} Hebrew ***H***, a variant name for Hiram; also in 2:11, 12.
8: 2 {that King Hiram} Hebrew ***H***, a variant name for Hiram; also in 8:18.
9:21 {sent by Hiram.} Hebrew ***H***, a variant name for Hiram.

HURT (1)

Rev 6: 6 {And don't waste} Or ***h***

HUSBAND (3)

Ge 3:16 {for your husband,} Or *And though you may desire to control your **h**.*
1Ti 3: 2 {to his wife.} Greek *be the **h** of one wife;* also in 3:12.
Tit 1: 6 {to his wife,} Or *have only one wife,* or *be married only once;* Greek reads *be the **h** of one wife.*

HYPOCRITES (1)

Mt 23:13 {go in yourselves.} Some manuscripts add verse 14, *How terrible it will be for you teachers of religious law and you Pharisees. **H**! You shamelessly cheat widows out of their property, and then, to cover up the kind of people you really are, you make long prayers in public. Because of this, your punishment will be the greater.*

HYRAX (2)

Lev 11: 5 {the rock badger} Or *coney,* or ***h***.
Dt 14: 7 {the rock badger.} Or *coney,* or ***h***.

HYRAXES (2)

Ps 104:18 {for rock badgers.} Or *coneys,* or ***h***.
Pr 30:26 {Rock badgers} Or *coneys,* or ***h***.

HYSSOP (1)

Ps 51: 7 {from my sins,} Hebrew *Purify me with the **h** branch.*

I

IBLEAM (1)

2Ki 15:10 {him in public,} Or *at **I**.*

ICONIUM (1)

Ac 14: 1 {In Iconium,} ***I***, as well as *Lystra* and *Derbe* (14:6), were cities in the land now called Turkey.

IDENTIFIED (1 of 3)

2Co 1:21 {firm for Christ.} Or *who has **i** us and you as genuine Christians.*

IDENTIFYING (1)

SS 1: 1 {*Young Woman:*} The headings **i** the speakers are not in the original text, though the Hebrew usually gives clues by means of the gender of the person speaking.

IDENTITY (1)

Jdg 7: 3 {afraid may leave} Hebrew *leave Mount Gilead.* The **i** of Mount Gilead is uncertain in this context. It is perhaps used here as another name for Mount Gilboa.

IDOLS (2)

Lev 17: 7 {to evil spirits} Or *goat **i**.*
1Jn 5:21 {in your hearts.} Greek *keep yourselves from **i**.*

IGNORANCE (1)

1Co 14:38 {not be recognized.} Some manuscripts read *If you are ignorant of this, stay in your **i**.*

IGNORANT (1)

1Co 14:38 {not be recognized.} Some manuscripts read *If you are **i** of this, stay in your ignorance.*

ILAI (1)

1Ch 11:29 {Zalmon} As in parallel text at 2 Sam 23:28; Hebrew reads ***I***.

ILLYRICUM (1)

Ro 15:19 {over into Illyricum.} ***I*** was a region northeast of Italy.

IMAGE (1)

Ge 5: 3 {of his father.} Hebrew *was in his own likeness, after his **i**.*

IMAGES (1)

Am 5:26 {you yourselves made.} Greek version reads *You took up the shrine of Molech, and the star of your god Rephan, and the **i** you made for yourselves.*

IMMANUEL (1)

Isa 8:10 {is with us!} Hebrew ***I**!*

INCLUDE (16)

Mt 16: 2[-3] {of the times!} Several manuscripts do not **i** any of the words in 16:2-3 after *He replied.*
Mk 1: 1 {Son of God.} Some manuscripts do not **i** *the Son of God.*
3:14 {calling them apostles.} Some manuscripts do not **i** *calling them apostles.*
3:32 {brothers and sisters} Some manuscripts do not **i** *and sisters.*
10: 7 {to his wife,} Some manuscripts do not **i** *and is joined to his wife.*
14:68 {a rooster crowed.} Some manuscripts do not **i** *Just then, a rooster crowed.*
16: 8 {frightened to talk.} The most reliable early manuscripts conclude the Gospel of Mark at verse 8. Other manuscripts **i** various endings to the Gospel. Two of the more noteworthy endings are printed here.
Lk 24:12 {what had happened.} Some manuscripts do not **i** this verse.
24:36 {be with you."} Some manuscripts do not **i** *He said, "Peace be with you."*
24:40 {them his feet.} Some manuscripts do not **i** this verse.
24:51 {up to heaven.} Some manuscripts do not **i** *and was taken up to heaven.*
24:52 {worshiped him and} Some manuscripts do not **i** *worshiped him and.*
Jn 11:25 {and the life.} Some manuscripts do not **i** *and the life.*
13:10 {for the feet,} Some manuscripts do not **i** *except for the feet.*

Eph 1: 1 {people in Ephesus,} Some manuscripts do not **i** *in Ephesus.*
Col 1:14 {with his blood} Some manuscripts do not **i** *with his blood.*

INCLUDED (2 of 3)

Lk 22:43[-44] {drops of blood.} These verses are not **i** in many ancient manuscripts.
23:34 {they are doing."} This sentence is not **i** in many ancient manuscripts.

INCOMPLETE (1)

1Sa 13: 1 {for forty-two years.} Hebrew *reigned...and two;* the number is **i** in the Hebrew. Compare Acts 13:21.

INDESCRIBABLE (1)

2Co 9:15 {wonderful for words!} Greek *Thank God for his* ***i*** *gift.*

INFANTS (1)

1Th 2: 7 {as a mother} Some manuscripts read *we were as* ***i*** *among you; we were as a mother.*

INHERIT (1)

2Ki 2: 9 {your rightful successor."} Hebrew *Let me* ***i*** *a double share of your spirit.*

INHERITANCE (2)

1Sa 10: 1 {his people Israel.} Greek version reads *Israel. And you will rule over the LORD's people and save them from their enemies around them. This will be the sign to you that the LORD has appointed you to be leader over his* ***i.***
Eph 1:11 {inheritance from God,} Or *we have become God's* ***i.***

INNER (3)

Ex 27:21 {the Tabernacle.} Hebrew *in the Tent of Meeting, outside of the* ***i*** *curtain, in front of the Testimony.*
Ac 20:22 {the Holy Spirit,} Or *by my spirit,* or *by an* ***i*** *compulsion;* Greek reads *by the spirit.*
2Co 4:16 {our spirits are} Greek *our* ***i*** *being is.*

INNOCENT (1)

Ac 20:26 {blamed on me,} Greek *I am* ***i*** *of the blood of all.*

INSIDE (1)

Ex 25:16 {of the covenant,} Hebrew *place* ***i*** *it the Testimony;* also in 25:21.

INSTRUMENT (1)

1Sa 18: 6 {tambourines and cymbals.} The type of **i** represented by the final word is uncertain.

INSTRUMENTS (4)

Ps 6: T {an eight-stringed instrument.} Hebrew *with stringed* ***i;*** *according to the sheminith.*
Da 3: 5 {and other instruments,} The identification of some of these musical **i** is uncertain.
3: 7 {the musical instruments,} Aramaic *the horn, flute, zither, lyre, harp, and other* ***i*** *of the musical ensemble.*
3:10 {the musical instruments.} Aramaic *the horn, flute, zither, lyre, harp, pipes, and other* ***i*** *of the musical ensemble;* also in 3:15.

INSULTS (1)

Ne 4: 5 {the presence of} Or *for they have thrown* ***i*** *in the face of.*

INTERLUDE (1)

Ps 3: 2 {*Interlude*} Hebrew *Selah.* The meaning of this word is uncertain, though it is probably a musical or literary term. It is rendered ***I*** throughout the Psalms.

INTERPRETATION (1)

2Pe 1:20 {the prophets themselves} Or *is a matter of one's own* ***i.***

INTOXICANTS (1)

1Sa 1:11 {never be cut."} Some manuscripts add *He will drink neither wine nor* ***i.***

INVITED (1)

1Ki 1:25 {of the army,} As in Greek version; Hebrew reads ***i*** *the commanders of the army.*

INVOLVED (1)

Lk 2:49 {my Father's house."} Or *"Didn't you realize that I should be* ***i*** *with my Father's affairs?"*

INWARD (1)

Eze 40: 8 {of the gateway} Many Hebrew manuscripts add *which faced* ***i*** *toward the Temple; it was one rod* [10.5 feet or 3.2 meters] *deep. [9]Then he measured the foyer of the gateway,...*

IOB (1)

Ge 46:13 {Jashub,} As in some Greek manuscripts and Samaritan Pentateuch (see also Num 26:24; 1 Chr 7:1); Hebrew reads ***I.***

ISA (65)

Jer 51:20 {"You} Possibly Cyrus, who was used of God to conquer Babylon. Compare **I** 44:28; 45:1.
Mt 1:23 {be called Immanuel} **I** 7:14; 8:8, 10.
3: 3 {road for him!' "} **I** 40:3.
4:15[-16] {light has shined."} **I** 9:1-2.
8:17 {removed our diseases."} **I** 53:4.
12:18[-21] {all the world."} **I** 42:1-4.
13:14[-15] {me heal them.'} **I** 6:9-10.
15: 8[-9] {own man-made teachings.'} **I** 29:13.
21: 5 {people of Israel,} Greek *Tell the daughter of Zion.* **I** 62:11.
21:13 {den of thieves!"} **I** 56:7; Jer 7:11.
24:29 {will be shaken.} See **I** 13:10; 34:4; Joel 2:10.
Mk 1: 3 {road for him!'} **I** 40:3.
4:12 {and be forgiven.'} **I** 6:9-10.
7: 7 {own man-made teachings.'} **I** 29:13.
9:48 {never goes out.'} **I** 66:24.
11:17 {den of thieves."} **I** 56:7; Jer 7:11.
13:24[-25] {will be shaken.} See **I** 13:10; 34:4; Joel 2:10.
15:27 {side of his.} Some manuscripts add verse 28, *And the Scripture was fulfilled that said, "He was counted among those who were rebels."* See **I** 53:12.
Lk 3: 4[-6] {sent from God.' "} **I** 40:3-5.
4:18[-19] {favor has come.} Or *and to proclaim the acceptable year of the Lord.* **I** 61:1-2.
8:10 {they don't understand.'} **I** 6:9.
19:46 {den of thieves."} **I** 56:7; Jer 7:11.
22:37 {who were rebels.'} **I** 53:12.
Jn 1:23 {the Lord's coming!' "} **I** 40:3.
6:45 {taught by God.'} **I** 54:13.
12:38 {his saving power?"} **I** 53:1.
12:40 {me heal them."} **I** 6:10.
Ac 7:49[-50] {heaven and earth?'} **I** 66:1-2.
8:32[-33] {from the earth."} **I** 53:7-8.
13:34 {promised to David.'} **I** 55:3.
13:47 {of the earth.'} **I** 49:6.
15:16[-18] {known long ago.'} Amos 9:11-12; **I** 45:21.
28:26[-27] {me heal them.'} **I** 6:9-10.
Ro 2:24 {because of you."} **I** 52:5.
3:15[-17] {true peace is."} **I** 59:7-8.
9:27[-28] {and with finality."} **I** 10:22-23.
9:29 {Sodom and Gomorrah."} **I** 1:9.
9:33 {makes them fall.} **I** 8:14.
9:33 {not be disappointed.} Or *will not be put to shame.* **I** 28:16.
10:11 {not be disappointed.} Or *will not be put to shame.* **I** 28:16.
10:15 {bring good news!"} **I** 52:7.
10:16 {believed our message?"} **I** 53:1.
10:20 {asking for me."} **I** 65:1.
10:21 {arguing with me."} **I** 65:2.
11: 8 {do not hear."} Deut 29:4; **I** 29:10.
11:26[-27] {away their sins."} **I** 59:20-21.
11:34 {be his counselor?} See **I** 40:13.
14:11 {allegiance to God.' "} **I** 49:18; 45:23.
15:12 {hopes on him."} **I** 11:10.
15:21 {him will understand."} **I** 52:15.
1Co 1:19 {most brilliant ideas."} **I** 29:14.
2: 9 {who love him."} **I** 64:4.
2:16 {give him counsel?"} **I** 40:13.
14:21 {listen to me,"} **I** 28:11-12.
15:32 {tomorrow we die!"} **I** 22:13.
15:54 {up in victory.} **I** 25:8.
2Co 6: 2 {I helped you."} **I** 49:8.
6:17 {will welcome you.} **I** 52:11; Ezek 20:34.
Gal 4:27 {the other women!"} **I** 54:1.
2Ti 2:19 {from all wickedness."} See **I** 52:11.
Heb 2:13 {has given me."} **I** 8:17-18.
Jas 2:23 {friend of God."} See **I** 41:8.
1Pe 1:24[-25] {will last forever."} **I** 40:6-8.
2: 6 {never be disappointed.} Or *will never be put to shame.* **I** 28:16.
2: 8 {make them fall."} **I** 8:14.

ISAAC (4)

Ge 17:19 {name him Isaac,} ***I*** means "he laughs."
21: 3 {his son Isaac.} ***I*** means "he laughs."
Am 7: 9 {of your ancestors} Hebrew *of* ***I.***
7:16 {against my people.} Hebrew *against the house of* ***I.***

ISAIAH (1)

Isa 8:18 {me have names} ***I*** means "The LORD will save"; *Shear-jashub* means "A remnant will return"; and *Maher-shalal-hash-baz* means "Swift to plunder and quick to spoil."

ISHBOSHETH (1)

1Sa 14:49 {included Jonathan, Ishbosheth,} Hebrew *Ishvi,* a variant name for **I**; also known as Eshbaal.

ISHMAEL (1)

Ge 16:11 {name him Ishmael,} ***I*** means "God hears."

ISHVI (1)

1Sa 14:49 {Ishbosheth,} Hebrew ***I,*** a variant name for Ishbosheth; also known as Eshbaal.

ISLAND (1)

Ac 28:12 {stop was Syracuse,} *Syracuse* was on the **i** of Sicily.

ISRAEL (54)

Ge 32:28 {is now Israel,} ***I*** means "God struggles" or "one who struggles with God."
33:20 {called it El-Elohe-Israel.} *El-Elohe-Israel* means "God, the God of **I**."
34: 7 {against Jacob's family,} Hebrew *in* ***I.***
35:10 {be called Israel."} *Jacob* means "he grasps the heel"; this can also figuratively mean "he deceives"; ***I*** means "God struggles" or "one who struggles with God."
35:21 {Jacob} Hebrew ***I;*** also in 35:22a.
37: 3 {Now Jacob} Hebrew ***I;*** also in 37:13.
43: 6 {another brother?" Jacob} Hebrew ***I;*** also in 43:11.
45:21 {sons of Jacob} Hebrew ***I;*** also in 45:28.
46: 1 {So Jacob} Hebrew ***I;*** also in 46:30.
47:31 {oath, and Jacob} Hebrew ***I.***
48: 8 {Jacob} Hebrew ***I;*** also in 48:10, 11, 13, 14, 21.
49:28 {with which Jacob} Hebrew ***I.***
Ex 1: 1 {sons of Jacob} Hebrew ***I.***
32:13 {Isaac, and Jacob.} Hebrew ***I.***
Lev 16:13 {of the Covenant.} Hebrew *on the Testimony,* referring to the terms of God's covenant with **I**, which were kept in the Ark.
Nu 6:27 {as my people,} Hebrew *will put my name on the people of* ***I.***
Dt 32: 8 {of angelic beings.} As in Dead Sea Scrolls, which read *of the sons of God,* and Greek version, which reads *of the angels of god;* Masoretic Text reads *of the sons of* ***I.***
32:15 {But Israel} Hebrew *Jeshurun,* a term of endearment for **I**.
33: 5 {king in Israel} Hebrew *in Jeshurun,* a term of endearment for **I**.
33:26 {God of Israel.} Hebrew *of Jeshurun,* a term of endearment for **I**.
1Sa 10: 1 {his people Israel.} Greek version reads ***I.*** *And you will rule over the LORD's people and save them from their enemies around them. This will be the sign to you that the LORD has appointed you to be leader over his inheritance.*
14:41 {among the others?"} Greek version adds *If the fault is with me or my son Jonathan, respond with Urim; but if the men of* ***I*** *are at fault, respond with Thummim.*
1Ki 18:31 {tribes of Israel,} Hebrew *each of the tribes of the sons of Jacob to whom the LORD had said, "Your name will be* ***I."***
18:36 {Isaac, and Jacob,} Hebrew *and* ***I.***
1Ch 1:34 {Israel.} ***I*** is the name that God gave to Jacob.
2: 1 {Israel} ***I*** is the name that God gave to Jacob.
5: 1 {Israel} ***I*** is the name that God gave to Jacob.
6:38 {Israel.} ***I*** is the name that God gave to Jacob.
7:29 {Israel} ***I*** is the name that God gave to Jacob.
29:10 {Israel,} ***I*** is the name that God gave to Jacob.
2Ch 28:12 {leaders of Israel} Hebrew *Ephraim,* referring to the northern kingdom of **I**.
28:19 {Ahaz of Judah,} Hebrew *of* ***I.***
30: 6 {Israel,} ***I*** is the name that God gave to Jacob.
Ezr 8:18 {Israel.} ***I*** is the name that God gave to Jacob.
Isa 7: 2 {allied with Israel} Hebrew *Ephraim,* referring to the northern kingdom of **I**; also in 7:5, 8, 9, 17.
9: 9 {people of Israel} Hebrew *of Ephraim,* referring to the northern kingdom of **I**.
11:13 {jealousy between Israel} Hebrew *Ephraim,* referring to the northern kingdom of **I**.
17: 3 {cities of Israel} Hebrew *of Ephraim,* referring to the northern kingdom of **I**.
28: 1 {drunkards of Israel} Hebrew *of Ephraim,* referring to the northern kingdom of **I**; also in 28:3.
44: 2 {be afraid. O Israel,} Hebrew *Jeshurun,* a term of endearment for **I**.
63:16 {Abraham and Jacob} Hebrew ***I.***
Jer 7:15 {people of Israel.} Hebrew *of Ephraim,* referring to the northern kingdom of **I**.
31:18 {have heard Israel} Hebrew *Ephraim,* referring to the northern kingdom of **I**; also in 31:20.
Eze 37:16 {tribes of Israel.'} Hebrew *Ephraim's stick, representing Joseph and all the house of* ***I.***
Hos 5: 9 {is certain, Israel} Hebrew *Ephraim,* referring to the northern kingdom of **I**; also in 5:11, 12, 13, 14.
6: 4 {"O Israel} Hebrew *Ephraim,* referring to the northern kingdom of **I**.
7: 8 {people of Israel} Hebrew *Ephraim,* referring to the northern kingdom of **I**; also in 7:11.
8: 9 {people of Israel} Hebrew *Ephraim,* referring to the northern kingdom of **I**; also in 8:11.
9: 8 {God over Israel,} Hebrew *Ephraim,* referring to the northern kingdom of **I**; also in 9:11, 13, 16.
10:11 {"Israel} Hebrew *Ephraim,* referring to the northern kingdom of **I**.
11: 3 {who taught Israel} Hebrew *Ephraim,* referring to the northern kingdom of **I**; also in 11:8, 9, 12.
12: 1 {people of Israel} Hebrew *Ephraim,* referring to the northern kingdom of **I**; also in 12:8, 14.
14: 8 {"O Israel,} Hebrew *Ephraim,* referring to the northern kingdom of **I**.
Gal 6:16 {people of God.} Greek *the* ***I*** *of God.*

ISRAEL'S (3)
Ge 42: 5 {So Jacob's} Hebrew ***I***.
Nu 1:20[-21] {(Jacob's} Hebrew ***I***.
26: 5 {Jacob's} Hebrew ***I***.

ISRAELITE (3)
Ge 36:31 {kings in Israel} Or *before an **I** king ruled over them.*
2Sa 17:25 {an Ishmaelite.} As in some Greek manuscripts (see also 1 Chr 2:17); Hebrew reads *an **I**.*
1Ch 1:43 {kings in Israel} Or *before an **I** king ruled over them.*

ISRAELITES (3)
1Sa 10:27 {Saul ignored them.} Dead Sea Scroll 4QSam[a] continues: *...He gouged out the right eye of each of the **I** living there, and he didn't allow anyone to come and rescue them. In fact, of all the **I** east of the Jordan, there wasn't a single one whose right eye Nahash had not gouged out....*
14:18 {of the Israelites.} As in some Greek manuscripts; Hebrew reads *"Bring the Ark of God." For at that time the Ark of God was with the **I**.*

ISSACHAR (2)
Ge 30:18 {named him Issachar,} ***I*** sounds like a Hebrew term that means "reward."
Dt 33:18 {Zebulun and Issachar} Hebrew lacks *and **I**.*

ITALY (2)
Ac 28:13 {across to Rhegium.} *Rhegium* was on the southern tip of **I**.
Ro 15:19 {over into Illyricum.} *Illyricum* was a region northeast of **I**.

ITHIEL (2)
Pr 30: 1 {worn out, O God.} The Hebrew can also be translated *The man declares this to **I**, to **I** and to Ucal.*

ITHRA (1)
2Sa 17:25 {father was Jether,} Hebrew ***I***, a variant name for Jether.

ITTAI (1)
2Sa 23:29 {Ithai} As in parallel text at 1 Chr 11:31; Hebrew reads ***I***.

IYE-ABARIM (1)
Nu 33:45 {They left Iye-abarim} As in 33:44; Hebrew reads *Iyim*, another name for **I**.

IYIM (1)
Nu 33:45 {They left Iye-abarim} As in 33:44; Hebrew reads ***I***, another name for Iye-abarim.

IZRI (1)
1Ch 25:11 {fell to Zeri} Hebrew ***I***, a variant name for Zeri; compare 25:3.

J

JAAKAN (1)
1Ch 1:42 {Zaavan, and Akan.} As in many Hebrew and Greek manuscripts (see also Gen 36:27); most Hebrew manuscripts read ***J***.

JAALA (1)
Ne 7:58 {Jaalah,} As in parallel text at Ezra 2:56; Hebrew reads ***J***.

JAARE-OREGIM (1)
2Sa 21:19 {son of Jair} As in parallel text at 1 Chr 20:5; Hebrew reads *son of **J**.*

JAASU (1)
Ezr 10:37[-38] {family of Binnui} As in Greek version; Hebrew reads ***J***, [38]*Bani, Binnui.*

JAAZANIAH (1)
Jer 40: 8 {the Netophathite, Jaazaniah} As in parallel text at 2 Kgs 25:23; Hebrew reads *Jezaniah*, a variant name for **J**.

JABESH-GILEAD (1)
1Sa 10:27 {Saul ignored them.} Dead Sea Scroll 4QSam[a] continues: *...But there were seven thousand men who had escaped from the Ammonites, and they had settled in **J**.*

JABEZ (1)
1Ch 4: 9 {named him Jabez} ***J*** sounds like a Hebrew term meaning "distress" or "pain."

JACOB (71)
Ge 25:26 {called him Jacob.} ***J*** means "he grasps the heel"; this can also figuratively mean "he deceives."
27:36 {name is Jacob,} ***J*** means "he grasps the heel"; this can also figuratively mean "he deceives."
35:10 {be called Israel."} ***J*** means "he grasps the heel"; this can also figuratively mean "he deceives"; *Israel* means "God struggles" or "one who struggles with God."
Dt 33: 4 {assembly of Israel.} Hebrew *of **J**.*
1Sa 12: 8 {the Israelites were} Hebrew *When **J** was.*
1Ki 18:31 {tribes of Israel,} Hebrew *each of the tribes of the sons of **J** to whom the LORD had said, "Your name will be Israel."*
1Ch 1:34 {Israel.} *Israel* is the name that God gave to **J**.
2: 1 {Israel} *Israel* is the name that God gave to **J**.
5: 1 {Israel} *Israel* is the name that God gave to **J**.
6:38 {Israel.} *Israel* is the name that God gave to **J**.
7:29 {Israel} *Israel* is the name that God gave to **J**.
29:10 {Israel,} *Israel* is the name that God gave to **J**.
2Ch 30: 6 {Israel,} *Israel* is the name that God gave to **J**.
Ezr 8:18 {Israel.} *Israel* is the name that God gave to **J**.
Ps 20: 1 {God of Israel} Hebrew *of **J**.*
24: 6 {God of Israel.} Hebrew *of **J**.*
44: 4 {for your people.} Hebrew *for **J**.*
46: 7 {God of Israel} Hebrew *of **J**;* also in 46:11.
59:13 {reigns in Israel.} Hebrew *in **J**.*
75: 9 {God of Israel.} Hebrew *of **J**.*
79: 7 {your people Israel,} Hebrew ***J***.
81: 1 {God of Israel.} Hebrew *of **J**.*
84: 8 {O God of Israel.} Hebrew *of **J**.*
85: 1 {fortunes of Israel.} Hebrew *of **J**.*
87: 2 {city in Israel.} Hebrew *He loves the gates of Zion more than all the dwellings of **J**.*
94: 7 {God of Israel} Hebrew *of **J**.*
99: 4 {righteousness throughout Israel.} Hebrew ***J***.
114: 7 {God of Israel.} Hebrew *of **J**.*
132: 2 {One of Israel,} Hebrew *of **J**;* also in 132:5.
146: 5 {God of Israel} Hebrew *of **J**.*
Isa 2: 3 {God of Israel.} Hebrew *of **J**;* also in 2:5, 6.
8:17 {people of Israel.} Hebrew *the house of **J**.*
10:20 {Israel and Judah} Hebrew *and the house of **J**.*
14: 1 {people of Israel.} Hebrew *the house of **J**.*
17: 4 {glory of Israel} Hebrew *of **J**.*
29:22 {people of Israel,} Hebrew *of **J**;* also in 29:23.
41:21 {King of Israel.} Hebrew *the King of **J**.*
45:19 {people of Israel} Hebrew *of **J**.*
48:20 {people of Israel.} Hebrew *his servant, **J**.*
49:26 {One of Israel.} Hebrew *of **J**.*
58: 1 {my people Israel} Hebrew ***J***.
59:20 {those in Israel} Hebrew *in **J**.*
60:16 {One of Israel.} Hebrew *of **J**.*
65: 9 {people of Israel} Hebrew *remnant of **J**.*
Jer 5:20 {to Israel} Hebrew *to the house of **J**.*
10:16 {God of Israel} Hebrew *the Portion of **J**.*
10:25 {your people Israel,} Hebrew ***J***.
30: 7 {my people Israel.} Hebrew ***J***; also in 30:10b.
31: 7 {joy for Israel} Hebrew ***J***; also in 31:11.
46:27 {their exile. Israel} Hebrew ***J***.
51:19 {God of Israel} Hebrew *the Portion of **J**.*
La 1:17 {Regarding his people,} Hebrew ***J***.
2: 2 {home in Israel.} Hebrew ***J***; also in 2:3.
Eze 39:25 {of my people} Hebrew *of **J**.*
Hos 10:11 {the plow. Israel} Hebrew ***J***.
12: 2 {to punish Jacob} ***J*** means "he grasps at the heel"; this can also figuratively mean "he deceives."
Am 3:13 {throughout all Israel,} Hebrew *the house of **J**.*
6: 8 {glory of Israel,} Hebrew ***J***.
7: 2 {you relent, Israel} Hebrew ***J***; also in 7:5.
8: 7 {Pride of Israel} Hebrew *the pride of **J**.*
9: 8 {family of Israel,} Hebrew *the house of **J**.*
Ob 1:10 {relatives in Israel.} Hebrew *your brother **J**.*
1:17 {people of Israel} Hebrew *house of **J**;* also in 18.
Mic 1: 5 {Israel and Judah.} Hebrew *and **J**.*
2: 7 {O family of Israel} Hebrew *house of **J**.*
4: 2 {God of Israel.} Hebrew *of **J**.*
5: 7 {left in Israel} Hebrew ***J***; also in 5:8.
Mal 2:12 {nation of Israel} Hebrew *from the tents of **J**.*
Lk 1:33 {reign over Israel} Greek *over the house of **J**.*
Ac 7:46 {God of Jacob.} Some manuscripts read *the house of **J**.*
Ro 11:26 {will turn Israel} Greek ***J***.

JACOB'S (2)
Isa 27: 9 {purge away Israel's} Hebrew ***J***.
Jn 1:51 {Son of Man."} See Gen 28:10-17, the account of **J** ladder.

JADAH (1)
1Ch 8:36 {father of Jadah.} As in parallel text at 9:42; Hebrew reads *Jehoaddah*, a variant name for **J**.

JAHAZ (3)
Jos 21:36 {received Bezer, Jahaz,} Hebrew *Jahzah*, a variant name for **J**.
1Ch 6:78 {desert town), Jahaz,} Hebrew *Jahzah*, a variant name for **J**.
Jer 48:21 {Holon and Jahaz} Hebrew *Jahzah*, a variant name for **J**.

JAHZAH (3)
Jos 21:36 {received Bezer, Jahaz,} Hebrew ***J***, a variant name for Jahaz.
1Ch 6:78 {desert town), Jahaz,} Hebrew ***J***, a variant name for Jahaz.
Jer 48:21 {Holon and Jahaz} Hebrew ***J***, a variant name for Jahaz.

JAHZEEL (1)
1Ch 7:13 {Naphtali were Jahzeel,} As in parallel text at Gen 46:24; Hebrew reads *Jahziel*, a variant name for **J**.

JAHZIEL (1)
1Ch 7:13 {Naphtali were Jahzeel,} As in parallel text at Gen 46:24; Hebrew reads ***J***, a variant name for Jahzeel.

JAKEH (1)
Pr 30: 1 {Jakeh. An oracle.} Or *son of **J** from Massa.*

JAKIN (2)
1Ki 7:21 {the north Boaz.} **J** probably means "he establishes"; Boaz probably means "in him is strength."
2Ch 3:17 {the north Boaz.} **J** probably means "he establishes"; Boaz probably means "in him is strength."

JARAH (1)
1Ch 9:42 {father of Jadah.} As in some Hebrew manuscripts and Greek version (see also 8:36); Hebrew reads ***J***.

JAVAN (8)
Isa 66:19 {Tubal and Greece,} Hebrew ***J***.
Eze 27:13 {Merchants from Greece,} Hebrew ***J***.
27:19 {Greeks from Uzal} Hebrew *Vedan and **J** from Uzal.* The meaning of the Hebrew is uncertain.
Da 8:21 {king of Greece,} Hebrew *of **J**.*
10:20 {kingdom of Greece.} Hebrew *of **J**.*
11: 2 {kingdom of Greece.} Hebrew *of **J**.*
Joel 3: 6 {to the Greeks,} Hebrew *to the peoples of **J**.*
Zec 9:13 {against the Greeks.} Hebrew *the sons of **J**.*

JAZER (1)
Jer 48:32 {the Dead Sea,} Hebrew *the sea of **J**.*

JECONIAH (8)
1Ch 3:16 {his uncle Zedekiah.} Hebrew *The descendants of Jehoiakim were his son **J*** [a variant name for Jehoiachin] *and his son Zedekiah.*
3:17 {sons of Jehoiachin,} Hebrew ***J***, a variant name for Jehoiachin.
Est 2: 6 {with King Jehoiachin} Hebrew ***J***, a variant name for Jehoiachin.
Jer 24: 1 {Babylon exiled Jehoiachin} Hebrew ***J***, a variant name for Jehoiachin.
27:20 {he exiled Jehoiachin} Hebrew ***J***, a variant name for Jehoiachin.
28: 4 {bring back Jehoiachin} Hebrew ***J***, a variant name for Jehoiachin.
29: 2 {after King Jehoiachin,} Hebrew ***J***, a variant name for Jehoiachin.
Mt 1:11 {father of Jehoiachin} Greek ***J***; also in 1:12. See 2 Kgs 24:6 and note at 1 Chr 3:16.

JEGAR-SAHADUTHA (1)
Ge 31:47 {language and Galeed} ***J*** means "witness pile" in Aramaic; *Galeed* means "witness pile" in Hebrew.

JEHIEL (1)
1Ch 26:21 {of Gershon, Jehiel} Hebrew *Jehieli* (also in 26:22), a variant name for **J**; compare 23:8.

JEHIELI (1)
1Ch 26:21 {of Gershon, Jehiel} Hebrew ***J*** (also in 26:22), a variant name for Jehiel; compare 23:8.

JEHOADDAH (1)
1Ch 8:36 {father of Jadah.} As in parallel text at 9:42; Hebrew reads ***J***, a variant name for Jadah.

JEHOADDAN (1)
2Ch 25: 1 {mother was Jehoaddin,} As in parallel text at 2 Kgs 14:2; Hebrew reads ***J***, a variant name for Jehoaddin.

JEHOADDIN (1)
2Ch 25: 1 {mother was Jehoaddin,} As in parallel text at 2 Kgs 14:2, Hebrew reads *Jehoaddan*, a variant name for **J**.

JEHOAHAZ (5)
1Ch 3:15 {third), and Jehoahaz} Hebrew *Shallum*, another name for **J**.
2Ch 21:17 {youngest son, Ahaziah,} Hebrew ***J***, a variant name for Ahaziah; compare 22:1.
36: 2 {Jehoahaz} Hebrew *Joahaz*, a variant name for **J**; also in 36:4.
Jer 22:11 {says about Jehoahaz,} Hebrew *Shallum*, another name for **J**.
22:13 {certain for Jehoiakim,} The brother and successor of the exiled **J**.

JEHOASH (7)
2Ki 11:21 {Joash} Hebrew *J*, a variant name for Joash.
12: 1 {Joash} Hebrew *J*, a variant name for Joash; also in 12:2, 4, 6, 7, 18.
13: 9 {his son Jehoash} Hebrew *Joash*, a variant name for **J**; also in 13:10, 12, 13, 14, 25.
14: 1 {of King Jehoash} Hebrew *Joash*, a variant name for **J**; also in 14:13, 23, 27.
2Ch 25:17 {Israel's king Jehoash,} Hebrew *Joash*, a variant name for **J**; also in 25:18, 21, 23, 25.
Hos 1: 1 {Jehoash} Hebrew *Joash*, a variant name for **J**.
Am 1: 1 {Jehoash,} Hebrew *Joash*, a variant name for **J**.

JEHOIACHIN (9)
1Ch 3:16 {his uncle Zedekiah.} Hebrew *The descendants of Jehoiakim were his son Jeconiah* [a variant name for **J**] *and his son Zedekiah.*
3:17 {sons of Jehoiachin,} Hebrew *Jeconiah*, a variant name for **J**.
Est 2: 6 {with King Jehoiachin} Hebrew *Jeconiah*, a variant name for **J**.
Jer 22:24 {abandon you, Jehoiachin} Hebrew *Coniah*, a variant name for **J**; also in 22:28, 30.
24: 1 {Babylon exiled Jehoiachin} Hebrew *Jeconiah*, a variant name for **J**.
27:20 {he exiled Jehoiachin} Hebrew *Jeconiah*, a variant name for **J**.
28: 4 {bring back Jehoiachin} Hebrew *Jeconiah*, a variant name for **J**.
29: 2 {after King Jehoiachin,} Hebrew *Jeconiah*, a variant name for **J**.
37: 1 {Josiah succeeded Jehoiachin} Hebrew *Coniah*, a variant name for **J**.

JEHOIADA (1)
Ne 13:28 {sons of Joiada} Hebrew *J*, a variant name for Joiada.

JEHOIAKIM (2)
1Ch 3:16 {his uncle Zedekiah.} Hebrew *The descendants of **J** were his son Jeconiah* [a variant name for Jehoiachin] *and his son Zedekiah.*
Jer 27: 1 {reign of Zedekiah} As in some Hebrew manuscripts and Syriac version (see also 27:3, 12); most Hebrew manuscripts read *J*.

JEHONADAB (1)
Jer 35: 6 {wine, because Jehonadab} Hebrew *Jonadab*, a variant name for **J**; also in 35:10, 14, 18, 19. See 2 Kgs 10:15.

JEHORAM (7)
2Ki 1:17 {his brother Joram} Hebrew *J*, a variant name for Joram.
3: 1 {Ahab's son Joram} Hebrew *J*, a variant name for Joram; also in 3:6.
8:21 {So Jehoram} Hebrew *Joram*, a variant name for **J**; also in 8:23, 24.
9:15 {But Joram} Hebrew *J*, a variant name for Joram; also in 9:17, 21, 22, 23, 24.
11: 2 {of King Jehoram,} Hebrew *Joram*, a variant name for **J**.
1Ch 3:11 {Jehoram,} Hebrew *Joram*, a variant name for **J**.
2Ch 22: 5 {with King Joram,} Hebrew *J*, a variant name for Joram; also in 22:6, 7.

JEHOSHABEATH (1)
2Ch 22:11 {Ahaziah's sister Jehosheba,} As in parallel text at 2 Kgs 11:2; Hebrew reads *J*, a variant name for Jehosheba.

JEHOSHAPHAT (1)
Joel 3: 2 {Jehoshaphat.} *J* means "the LORD judges."

JEHOSHEBA (1)
2Ch 22:11 {Ahaziah's sister Jehosheba,} As in parallel text at 2 Kgs 11:2; Hebrew reads *Jehoshabeath*, a variant name for **J**.

JEHOVAH (2)
Ex 3:15 {'The LORD,} Hebrew *Yahweh;* traditionally rendered *J*.
6: 3 {the LORD,} Hebrew *Yahweh;* traditionally rendered *J*.

JEHOZADAK (4)
Ezr 3: 2 {son of Jehozadak} Hebrew *Jozadak*, a variant name for **J**; also in 3:8.
5: 2 {son of Jehozadak} Aramaic *Jozadak*, a variant name for **J**.
10:18 {son of Jehozadak} Hebrew *Jozadak*, a variant name for **J**.
Ne 12:26 {son of Jehozadak,} Hebrew *Jozadak*, a variant name for **J**.

JEHUCAL (1)
Jer 38: 1 {of Pashhur, Jehucal} Hebrew *Jucal*, a variant name for **J**; see 37:3.

JEIEL (1)
1Ch 8:29 {Jeiel} As in some Greek manuscripts (see also 9:35); Hebrew lacks *J*.

JER (16)
Ge 10:14 {the Philistines came.} Hebrew *Casluhites, from whom the Philistines came, Caphtorites.* Compare **J** 47:4; Amos 9:7.
2Ki 25: 3 {Zedekiah's eleventh year,} Hebrew *By the ninth day*, that is, "of the fourth month of Zedekiah's eleventh year" (compare **J** 52:6 and the note there). This event of the Hebrew lunar calendar occurred on July 18, 586 B.C.; also see note on 25:1.
25:17 {was 7 1/2 feet} As in parallel texts at 1 Kgs 7:16, 2 Chr 3:15, and **J** 52:22, all of which read *5 cubits* [2.3 meters]; Hebrew reads *3 cubits*, which is 4.5 feet or 1.4 meters.
1Ch 1:12 {the Philistines came.} Hebrew *Casluhites, from whom the Philistines came, Caphtorites.* See **J** 47:4; Amos 9:7.
2Ch 3:15 {that were 27 feet} As in Syriac version (see also 1 Kgs 7:15; 2 Kgs 25:17; **J** 52:21), which reads *18 cubits* [8.1 meters]; Hebrew reads *35 cubits*, which is 52.5 feet or 15.8 meters.
Da 9: 2 {for seventy years.} See **J** 25:11-12; 29:10.
Mt 2:18 {they are dead."} **J** 31:15.
21:13 {den of thieves!"} Isa 56:7; **J** 7:11.
27: 9[-10] {the Lord directed.} Greek *as the Lord directed me.* Zech 11:12-13; **J** 32:6-9.
Mk 8:18 {ears—can't you hear?'} **J** 5:21.
11:17 {den of thieves."} Isa 56:7; **J** 7:11.
Lk 19:46 {den of thieves."} Isa 56:7; **J** 7:11.
1Co 1:31 {Lord has done."} **J** 9:24.
2Co 10:17 {Lord has done."} **J** 9:24.
Heb 8: 8[-12] {remember their sins."} **J** 31:31-34.
10:16[-17] {and lawless deeds."} **J** 31:33-34.

JEREMOTH (1)
1Ch 25:22 {fell to Jerimoth} Hebrew *J*, a variant name for Jerimoth; compare 25:4.

JERIAH (2)
1Ch 24:23 {was the leader,} Hebrew *From the descendants of **J**;* compare 23:19.
26:31 {Hebron came Jeriah,} Hebrew *Jerijah*, a variant name for **J**; compare 23:19.

JERIJAH (1)
1Ch 26:31 {Hebron came Jeriah,} Hebrew *J*, a variant name for Jeriah; compare 23:19.

JERIMOTH (1)
1Ch 25:22 {fell to Jerimoth} Hebrew *Jeremoth*, a variant name for **J**; compare 25:4.

JEROBOAM (2)
1Ki 15: 6 {Abijam and Jeroboam} As in a few Hebrew manuscripts; most Hebrew manuscripts read *between Rehoboam and **J**.*
2Ki 23:16 {man of God} As in Greek version; Hebrew lacks *as **J** stood beside the altar at the festival. Then Josiah turned and looked up at the tomb of the man of God.*

JERUBBAAL (3)
Jdg 8:29 {Then Gideon} Hebrew *J*; see 6:32.
9:16 {right by Gideon} Hebrew *J* (see 6:32); also in 9:19, 28, 57.
1Sa 12:11 {LORD sent Gideon,} Hebrew *J*, another name for Gideon; see Judg 7:1.

JERUBBAAL'S (1)
Jdg 9: 1 {One day Gideon's} Hebrew *J* (see 6:32); also in 9:2, 24.

JERUBBESHETH (1)
2Sa 11:21 {son Abimelech killed} Hebrew *Was not Abimelech son of **J** killed.*

JERUSALEM (8 of 11)
1Ki 15: 4 {dynasty to continue,} Hebrew *gave him a lamp in **J**.*
Ne 7: 3 {of the day.} Or *Keep the gates of **J** closed until the sun is hot.*
Ps 76: 2 {Jerusalem} Hebrew *Salem*, another name for **J**.
La 2:15 {and insult Jerusalem,} Hebrew *the daughter of **J**.*
Eze 12:10 {Zedekiah in Jerusalem} Hebrew *the prince in **J**;* also in 12:12.
Zec 1:16 {reconstruction of Jerusalem.} Hebrew *and the measuring line will be stretched out over **J**.*
Mt 27:51[-53] {to many people.} Or *The earth shook, rocks split apart, tombs opened, and many bodies of godly men and women who had died were raised from the dead. After Jesus' resurrection, they left the cemetery, went into the holy city of **J**, and appeared to many people.*
Ac 18:21 {come back later,} Some manuscripts read *"I must by all means be at **J** for the upcoming festival, but I will come back later."*

JESHANAH (2)
Ne 3: 6 {Old City Gate} Or *The Mishneh Gate*, or *The **J** Gate.*
12:39 {Old City Gate,} Or *the Mishneh Gate*, or *the **J** Gate.*

JESHARELAH (1)
1Ch 25:14 {fell to Asarelah} Hebrew *J*, a variant name for Asarelah; compare 25:2.

JESHIMON (2)
Nu 21:20 {overlooks the wasteland.} Or *overlooks **J**.*
23:28 {overlooking the wasteland.} Or *overlooking **J**.*

JESHUA (4)
Hag 1: 1 {and to Jeshua} Hebrew *Joshua*, a variant name for **J**; also in 1:12, 14.
2: 2 {and to Jeshua} Hebrew *Joshua*, a variant name for **J**; also in 2:4.
Zec 3: 1 {showed me Jeshua} Hebrew *Joshua*, a variant name for **J**; also in 3:3, 4, 6, 8, 9.
6:11 {head of Jeshua} Hebrew *Joshua*, a variant name for **J**.

JESHURUN (4)
Dt 32:15 {But Israel} Hebrew *J*, a term of endearment for Israel.
33: 5 {king in Israel} Hebrew *in **J***, a term of endearment for Israel.
33:26 {God of Israel.} Hebrew *of **J***, a term of endearment for Israel.
Isa 44: 2 {be afraid. O Israel,} Hebrew *J*, a term of endearment for Israel.

JESSE (4)
Isa 11: 1 {of David's family} Hebrew *the line of **J**.* **J** was King David's father.
11:10 {to David's throne} Hebrew *the root of **J**.*
Ro 15:12 {to David's throne} Greek *The root of **J**.*

JESUS (15)
Mt 1:21 {name him Jesus,} *J* means "The LORD saves."
27:16 {man named Barabbas.} Some manuscripts read *J Barabbas;* also in 27:17.
Jn 9:24 {telling the truth,} Or *Give glory to God, not to **J**;* Greek reads *Give glory to God.*
13:23 {at the table.} Greek *was reclining on Jesus' bosom.* The "disciple whom **J** loved" was probably John.
Ac 8:36 {I be baptized?"} Some manuscripts add verse 37, *"You can," Philip answered, "if you believe with all your heart." And the eunuch replied, "I believe that **J** Christ is the Son of God."*
26: 9 {Jesus of Nazareth.} Greek *oppose the name of **J** the Nazarene.*
Ro 16:23 {a Christian brother.} Some manuscripts add verse 24, *May the grace of our Lord **J** Christ be with you all. Amen.*
1Co 5: 4 {of the church,} Or *In the name of the Lord **J**, you are to call a meeting of the church.*
Eph 3:14 {to the Father,} Some manuscripts read *the Father of our Lord **J** Christ.*
2Th 1:12 {Lord, Jesus Christ.} Or *of our God and the Lord **J** Christ.*
Heb 12: 2 {start to finish.} Or *J, the Originator and Perfecter of our faith.*
2Pe 1: 2 {God and Lord,} Or *God and **J** our Lord.*
1Jn 2: 1 {pleases God completely.} Greek *J Christ, the righteous.*
Jude 1: 5 {though the Lord} Some manuscripts read *J*.
Rev 19:10 {witness for Jesus.} Or *is the message confirmed by **J**.*

JESUS' (2)
Mt 27:51[-53] {to many people.} Or *The earth shook, rocks split apart, tombs opened, and many bodies of godly men and women who had died were raised from the dead. After **J** resurrection, they left the cemetery, went into the holy city of Jerusalem, and appeared to many people.*
Jn 13:23 {at the table.} Greek *was reclining on **J** bosom.* The "disciple whom Jesus loved" was probably John.

JETHER (2)
2Sa 17:25 {father was Jether,} Hebrew *Ithra*, a variant name for **J**.
1Ch 7:37 {Shamma, Shilshah, Ithran,} Possibly another name for *J;* compare 7:38.

JETHRO (1)
Ex 3: 1 {his father-in-law, Jethro,} Moses' father-in-law went by two names, **J** and Reuel.

JEW (1)
Gal 3:28 {Jew or Gentile,} Greek *J or Greek.*

JEWISH (7)
Jn 6:41 {Then the people} Greek *J people;* also in 6:52.
8:31 {to the people} Greek *J people;* also in 8:48, 52, 57.

10:19 {things, the people} Greek *J people.*
11:19 {of the people} Greek *J people;* also 11:31, 33, 36, 45, 54.
12:9 {all the people} Greek *J people;* also in 12:11.
18:20 {heard by people} Greek *J people;* also in 18:38.
19:14 {to the people,} Greek *J people;* also in 19:20.

JEWS (1)

Ac 28:28 {will accept it."} Some manuscripts add verse 29, *And when he had said these words, the J departed, greatly disagreeing with each other.*

JEZANIAH (1)

Jer 40:8 {the Netophathite, Jaazaniah} As in parallel text at 2 Kgs 25:23; Hebrew reads ***J***, a variant name for Jaazaniah.

JEZREEL (2)

2Ki 10:1 {of the city,} As in some Greek manuscripts and Latin Vulgate (see also 10:6); Hebrew reads *of J.*
Hos 1:11 {day of Jezreel} ***J*** means "God plants."

JOAB (1)

1Ch 4:14 {Valley of Craftsmen,} Or *J, the father of Ge-harashim.*

JOAHAZ (1)

2Ch 36:2 {Jehoahaz} Hebrew ***J***, a variant name for Jehoahaz; also in 36:4.

JOASH (7)

2Ki 11:21 {Joash} Hebrew *Jehoash,* a variant name for **J**.
12:1 {Joash} Hebrew *Jehoash,* a variant name for **J**; also in 12:2, 4, 6, 7, 18.
13:9 {his son Jehoash} Hebrew ***J***, a variant name for Jehoash; also in 13:10, 12, 13, 14, 25.
14:1 {of King Jehoash} Hebrew ***J***, a variant name for Jehoash; also in 14:13, 23, 27.
2Ch 25:17 {Israel's king Jehoash,} Hebrew ***J***, a variant name for Jehoash; also in 25:18, 21, 23, 25.
Hos 1:1 {Jehoash} Hebrew ***J***, a variant name for Jehoash.
Am 1:1 {Jehoash,} Hebrew ***J***, a variant name for Jehoash.

JOB (1)

1Co 3:19 {their own cleverness."} **J** 5:13.

JOEL (5)

1Ch 6:28 {Samuel were Joel} As in some Greek manuscripts and the Syriac version (see also 6:33 and 1 Sam 8:2); Hebrew lacks ***J***.
Mt 24:29 {will be shaken.} See Isa 13:10; 34:4; **J** 2:10.
Mk 13:24[-25] {will be shaken.} See Isa 13:10; 34:4; **J** 2:10.
Ac 2:17[-21] {will be saved.'} **J** 2:28-32.
Ro 10:13 {will be saved."} **J** 2:32.

JOHN (4)

Mt 16:17 {son of John,} Greek *Simon son of Jonah;* see **J** 1:42; 21:15-17.
Jn 13:23 {at the table.} Greek *was reclining on Jesus' bosom.* The "disciple whom Jesus loved" was probably **J**.
18:9 {you gave me."} See **J** 6:39 and 17:12.
18:32 {he would die.} See **J** 12:32-33.

JOIADA (1)

Ne 13:28 {Joiada} Hebrew *Jehoiada,* a variant name for **J**.

JOINED (3)

Mk 10:7 {to his wife,} Some manuscripts do not include *and is j to his wife.*
Ac 16:10 {So we} Luke, the writer of this book, here **j** Paul and accompanied him on his journey.
1Co 14:33 {the other churches.} The phrase *as in all the other churches* could be **j** to the beginning of 14:34.

JOKNEAM (1)

1Ch 6:77 {of Jokneam, Kartah,} As in Greek version (see also Josh 21:34); Hebrew lacks ***J**, Kartah.*

JONADAB (1)

Jer 35:6 {wine, because Jehonadab} Hebrew ***J***, a variant name for Jehonadab; also in 35:10, 14, 18, 19. See 2 Kgs 10:15.

JONAH (1)

Mt 16:17 {son of John,} Greek *Simon son of J;* see John 1:42; 21:15-17.

JONATHAN (5)

1Sa 14:41 {among the others?"} Greek version adds *If the fault is with me or my son J, respond with Urim; but if the men of Israel are at fault, respond with Thummim.*
20:25 {sitting opposite him} As in Greek version; Hebrew reads *with J standing.*
2Sa 23:33 {son of Shagee} As in parallel text at 1 Chr 11:34; Hebrew reads ***J**, Shammah;* some Greek manuscripts read *J son of Shammah.*
Ne 12:11 {father of Johanan.} Hebrew ***J**;* compare 12:22.

JORAM (9)

2Ki 1:17 {Joram} Hebrew *Jehoram,* a variant name for **J**.
3:1 {Ahab's son Joram} Hebrew *Jehoram,* a variant name for **J**; also in 3:6.
8:21 {So Jehoram} Hebrew ***J***, a variant name for Jehoram; also in 8:23, 24.
9:15 {But Joram} Hebrew *Jehoram,* a variant name for **J**; also in 9:17, 21, 22, 23, 24.
11:2 {Jehoram,} Hebrew ***J***, a variant name for Jehoram.
1Ch 3:11 {Jehoram,} Hebrew ***J***, a variant name for Jehoram.
18:10 {his son Joram} As in parallel text at 2 Sam 8:10; Hebrew reads *Hadoram,* a variant name for **J**.
2Ch 22:5 {with King Joram,} Hebrew *Jehoram,* a variant name for **J**; also in 22:6, 7.
Mt 1:8 {father of Jehoram.} Greek ***J***. See 1 Kgs 22:50 and note at 1 Chr 3:11.

JORDAN (4)

Dt 4:49 {the Dead Sea,} Hebrew *took the Arabah on the east side of the J as far as the sea of the Arabah.*
Jos 19:34 {the Jordan River} Hebrew *and Judah at the J River.*
1Sa 10:27 {Saul ignored them.} Dead Sea Scroll 4QSam[a] continues: *Nahash, king of the Ammonites, had been grievously oppressing the Gadites and Reubenites who lived east of the J River.... of all the Israelites east of the J, there wasn't a single one whose right eye Nahash had not gouged out....*

JOSEPH (10)

Ge 30:24 {named him Joseph,} ***J*** means "may he add."
2Sa 19:20 {in all Israel} Hebrew *the house of J.*
1Ki 11:28 {Ephraim and Manasseh.} Hebrew *from the house of J.*
Ps 80:1 {who lead Israel} Hebrew ***J***.
81:5 {decree for Israel} Hebrew *for J.*
Eze 37:16 {tribes of Israel.'} Hebrew *Ephraim's stick, representing J and all the house of Israel.*
Am 5:6 {roar through Israel} Hebrew *the house of J.*
5:15 {people who remain.} Hebrew *on the remnant of J.*
6:6 {that your nation} Hebrew ***J***.
Zec 10:6 {and save Israel} Hebrew *save the house of J.*

JOSEPH'S (2)

Ge 46:27 {had two sons} Greek version reads *nine sons,* probably including **J** grandsons through Ephraim and Manasseh (see 1 Chr 7:14-20).
Eze 47:13 {shares of land.} A share of land for each of **J** two oldest sons, Ephraim and Manasseh.

JOSES (2)

Mk 6:3 {of James, Joseph,} Greek ***J**;* see Matt 13:55.
15:40 {and of Joseph} Greek ***J**;* also in 15:47. See Matt 27:56.

JOSH (7)

1Ch 2:7 {Achan} Hebrew *Achar;* compare **J** 7:1. *Achar* means "disaster."
4:33 {away as Baalath.} As in some Greek manuscripts (see also **J** 19:8); Hebrew reads *Baal.*
6:58 {Holon,} As in parallel text at **J** 21:15; Hebrew reads *Hilen.*
6:59 {Ain,} As in parallel text at **J** 21:16; Hebrew reads *Ashan.*
6:59 {Juttah,} As in Syriac version (see also **J** 21:16); Hebrew lacks *Juttah.*
6:60 {were given Gibeon,} As in parallel text at **J** 21:17; Hebrew lacks *Gibeon.*
6:77 {of Jokneam, Kartah,} As in Greek version (see also **J** 21:34); Hebrew lacks *Jokneam, Kartah.*

JOSHBEKASHA (1)

1Ch 25:24 {fell to Joshbekashah} Hebrew ***J***, a variant name for Joshbekashah; compare 25:4.

JOSHBEKASHAH (1)

1Ch 25:24 {fell to Joshbekashah} Hebrew *Joshbekasha,* a variant name for **J**; compare 25:4.

JOSHEB-BASSHEBETH (1)

2Sa 23:8 {Jashobeam the Hacmonite,} As in parallel text at 1 Chr 11:11; Hebrew reads *J the Tahkemonite.*

JOSHUA (6)

Nu 13:16 {name to Joshua.} *Hoshea* (see 13:8) means "salvation"; ***J*** means "The LORD is salvation."
Dt 32:44 {came with Joshua} Hebrew *Hoshea,* a variant name for **J**.
Hag 1:1 {and to Jeshua} Hebrew ***J***, a variant name for Jeshua; also in 1:12, 14.
2:2 {and to Jeshua} Hebrew ***J***, a variant name for Jeshua; also in 2:4.
Zec 3:1 {showed me Jeshua} Hebrew ***J***, a variant name for Jeshua; also in 3:3, 4, 6, 8, 9.
6:11 {Jeshua} Hebrew ***J***, a variant name for Jeshua.

JOSIAH (1)

2Ki 23:16 {man of God} As in Greek version; Hebrew lacks *as Jeroboam stood beside the altar at the festival. Then J turned and looked up at the tomb of the man of God.*

JOURNEY (1 of 2)

Ac 1:12 {the half mile} Greek *a Sabbath day's j.*

JOZABAD (1)

2Ki 12:21 {assassins were Jozacar} As in Greek and Syriac versions; Hebrew reads ***J**;* compare parallel text at 2 Chr 24:26.

JOZADAK (4)

Ezr 3:2 {son of Jehozadak} Hebrew ***J***, a variant name for Jehozadak; also in 3:8.
5:2 {son of Jehozadak} Aramaic ***J***, a variant name for Jehozadak.
10:18 {son of Jehozadak} Hebrew ***J***, a variant name for Jehozadak.
Ne 12:26 {son of Jehozadak,} Hebrew ***J***, a variant name for Jehozadak.

JUCAL (1)

Jer 38:1 {of Pashhur, Jehucal} Hebrew ***J***, a variant name for Jehucal; see 37:3.

JUDAH (13)

Ge 29:35 {named him Judah,} ***J*** sounds like the Hebrew term for "praise."
Jos 19:34 {the Jordan River} Hebrew *and J at the Jordan River.*
2Sa 6:2 {Baalah of Judah} *Baalah of J* is another name for Kiriath-jearim; compare 1 Chr 13:6.
1Ki 4:19 {land of Judah.} As in some Greek manuscripts; Hebrew lacks *of J.* The meaning of the Hebrew is uncertain.
12:32 {day in midautumn,} Hebrew *on the fifteenth day of the eighth month* (also in 12:33). This day of the Hebrew lunar calendar occurs in late October or early November, exactly one month after the annual Festival of Shelters in **J** (see Lev 23:34).
1Ch 5:2 {for the nation,} Or *and from J came a prince.*
2Ch 25:28 {City of David.} As in some Hebrew manuscripts and other ancient versions (see also 2 Kgs 14:20); most Hebrew manuscripts read *the city of J.*
Ezr 1:8 {returning to Judah.} Hebrew *Sheshbazzar, the prince of J.*
3:9 {descendants of Hodaviah.} Hebrew *sons of J* (i.e., *bene Yehudah*). *Bene* might also be read here as the proper name Binnui; *Yehudah* is probably another name for Hodaviah. Compare 2:40; Neh 7:43; 1 Esdras 5:58.
La 1:15 {his beloved city} Hebrew *the virgin daughter of J.*
2:2 {walls of Jerusalem.} Hebrew *the daughter of J;* also in 2:5.
Hos 11:12 {the Holy One.} Or *and J is unruly against God, the faithful Holy One.*
Zec 9:7 {clan in Judah.} Hebrew *and will become a leader in J.*

JUDG (1)

1Sa 12:11 {LORD sent Gideon,} Hebrew *Jerubbaal,* another name for Gideon; see **J** 7:1.

JUDGE (4)

Ge 16:5 {this to me!} Hebrew *Let the LORD j between you and me.*
30:6 {named him Dan,} *Dan* is a play on the Hebrew term meaning "to vindicate" or "to **j**."
Mt 7:2 {you treat them.} Or *For God will treat you as you treat others;* Greek reads *For with the judgment you j you will be judged.*
Jn 8:15 {your human limitations,} Or *j me by human standards.*

JUDGED (2)

Mt 7:2 {you treat them.} Or *For God will treat you as you treat others;* Greek reads *For with the judgment you judge you will be j.*
Ac 24:6 {we arrested him.} Some manuscripts add *We would have j him by our law, [7]but Lysias, the commander of the garrison, came and took him violently away from us, [8]commanding his accusers to come before you.*

JUDGES (9)

Ex 21:6 {him before God.} Or *before the j.*
22:8 {not found, God} Or *the j.*
22:9 {come before God} Or *before the j.*
22:9 {whom God declares} Or *whom the j declare.*
22:28 {not blaspheme God} Or *Do not revile your j.*
1Sa 2:25 {another person, God} Or *the j.*
1Ch 17:6 {to Israel's leaders,} As in Greek version (see also 2 Sam 7:7); Hebrew reads *j.*
Da 3:3 {all these officials} Aramaic *the princes, prefects, governors, advisers, counselors, j, magistrates, and all the provincial officials.*
Joel 3:2 {valley of Jehoshaphat.} *Jehoshaphat* means "the LORD **j**."

JUDGMENT (3)

Mt 7:2 {you treat them.} Or *For God will treat you as you treat others;* Greek reads *For with the j you judge you will be judged.*
1Ti 3:6 {make him fall.} Or *he might fall into the same j as the Devil.*

2Pe 2:11 {out disrespectfully against} Greek *never bring blasphemous* ***j*** *from the Lord against.*

JULIA (1)

Ro 16: 7 {Andronicus and Junia,} Or *Junias;* some manuscripts read ***J***.

JUNIAS (1)

Ro 16: 7 {Andronicus and Junia,} Or ***J****;* some manuscripts read *Julia.*

JUST (5)

Jer 50:40 {just as I} Hebrew ***j*** *as God.*
Hab 2: 4 {by their faith.} Or *the* ***j*** *will live by their faithfulness.*
Mk 14:68 {a rooster crowed.} Some manuscripts do not include ***J*** *then, a rooster crowed.*
1Co 5: 6[-7] {can stay pure.} Greek *Don't you realize that even a little leaven spreads quickly through the whole batch of dough? [7]Purge out the old leaven so that you can be a new batch of dough,* ***j*** *as you are already unleavened.*
9:26 {misses his punches.} Or *I am not* ***j*** *shadowboxing.*

JUSTIFIED (1)

Lk 7:35 {who follow it.} Or *But wisdom is* ***j*** *by all her children.*

JUTTAH (1)

1Ch 6:59 {Juttah,} As in Syriac version (see also Josh 21:16); Hebrew lacks ***J***.

K

KADESH (1)

2Sa 24: 6 {land of Tahtim-hodshi} Greek version reads *to Gilead and to* ***K*** *in the land of the Hittites.*

KARNAIM (1)

Am 6:13 {we take Karnaim} ***K*** means "horns," a term that symbolizes strength.

KARTAH (1)

1Ch 6:77 {of Jokneam, Kartah,} As in Greek version (see also Josh 21:34); Hebrew lacks *Jokneam,* ***K***.

KEEP (3)

Ne 7: 3 {of the day.} Or ***K*** *the gates of Jerusalem closed until the sun is hot.*
Heb 11:11 {keep his promise.} Some manuscripts read *It was by faith that Sarah was able to have a child, even though she was too old and barren. Sarah believed that God would* ***k*** *his promise.*
1Jn 5:21 {in your hearts.} Greek ***k*** *yourselves from idols.*

KELUBAI (1)

1Ch 2: 9 {Ram, and Caleb.} Hebrew ***K***, a variant name for Caleb; compare 2:18.

KENAZ (1)

1Ch 1:36 {born to Timna.} As in some Greek manuscripts (see also Gen 36:12); Hebrew reads ***K****, Timna, and Amalek.*

KEPHIRIM (1)

Ne 6: 2 {of the villages} As in Greek version; Hebrew reads *at* ***K***.

KERETHITES (6)

2Sa 8:18 {the king's bodyguard.} Hebrew *of the* ***K*** *and Pelethites.*
15:18 {the king's bodyguard.} Hebrew *the* ***K*** *and Pelethites.*
20: 7 {king's own bodyguard.} Hebrew *the* ***K*** *and Pelethites;* also in 20:23.
1Ki 1:38 {the king's bodyguard} Hebrew *the* ***K*** *and Pelethites;* also in 1:44.
1Ch 18:17 {the king's bodyguard.} Hebrew *of the* ***K*** *and Pelethites.*
Zep 2: 5 {for you Philistines} Hebrew ***K***.

KESITAH (4)

Ge 33:19 {pieces of silver.} Hebrew *100 kesitahs;* the value or weight of the **k** is no longer known.
Jos 24:32 {pieces of silver.} Hebrew *100 kesitahs;* the value or weight of the **k** is no longer known.
Job 42:11 {gift of money} Hebrew *a* ***k****;* the value or weight of the **k** is no longer known.

KESITAHS (2)

Ge 33:19 {pieces of silver.} Hebrew *100* ***k****;* the value or weight of the kesitah is no longer known.
Jos 24:32 {pieces of silver.} Hebrew *100* ***k****;* the value or weight of the kesitah is no longer known.

KGS (35)

2Sa 12:30 {the king's head,} Greek version reads *removed the crown of Milcom;* compare 1 **K** 11:5. Milcom, also called Molech, was the god of the Ammonites.
20:24 {Adoniram} As in Greek version (see also 1 **K** 4:6; 5:14); Hebrew reads *Adoram.*
1Ki 9:26 {port near Elath} As in Greek version (see also 2 **K** 14:22; 16:6); Hebrew reads *Eloth.*
2Ki 25:17 {was 7 1/2 feet} As in parallel texts at 1 **K** 7:16, 2 Chr 3:15, and Jer 52:22, all of which read *5 cubits* [2.3 meters]; Hebrew reads *3 cubits,* which is 4.5 feet or 1.4 meters.
1Ch 2: 6 {Calcol, and Darda} As in many Hebrew manuscripts, some Greek manuscripts, and Syriac version (see also 1 **K** 4:31); Hebrew reads *Dara.*
20: 2 {the king's head,} Greek version and Latin Vulgate read *removed the crown of Milcom;* compare 1 **K** 11:5. Milcom, also called Molech, was the god of the Ammonites.
2Ch 2: 8 {cypress, and almug} Hebrew *algum;* compare 9:10-11 and parallel text at 1 **K** 10:11-12.
3:15 {that were 27 feet} As in Syriac version (see also 1 **K** 7:15; 2 **K** 25:17; Jer 52:21), which reads *18 cubits* [8.1 meters]; Hebrew reads *35 cubits,* which is 52.5 feet or 15.8 meters.
4:17 {Succoth and Zarethan.} As in parallel text at 1 **K** 7:46; Hebrew reads *Zeredah.*
8:17 {Ezion-geber and Elath,} As in Greek version (see also 2 **K** 14:22; 16:6); Hebrew reads *Eloth.*
9:10 {of almug wood} Hebrew *algum wood* (also in 9:11); compare parallel text at 1 **K** 10:11-12.
10:18 {Rehoboam sent Adoniram,} Hebrew *Hadoram,* a variant name for Adoniram; compare 1 **K** 4:6; 5:14; 12:18.
13: 2 {mother was Maacah,} As in most Greek manuscripts and Syriac version (see also 2 Chr 11:20-21; 1 **K** 15:2); Hebrew reads *Micaiah.*
16: 4 {Ijon, Dan, Abel-beth-maacah,} As in parallel text at 1 **K** 15:20; Hebrew reads *Abel-maim,* another name for Abel-beth-maacah.
22: 2 {Ahaziah was twenty-two} As in some Greek manuscripts and Syriac version (see also 2 **K** 8:26); Hebrew reads *forty-two.*
22: 6 {and King Ahaziah} Some Hebrew manuscripts, Greek and Syriac versions, and Latin Vulgate (see also 2 **K** 8:29); most Hebrew manuscripts read *Azariah.*
22: 8 {and Ahaziah's relatives} As in Greek version (see also 2 **K** 10:13); Hebrew reads *and sons of the brothers of Ahaziah.*
22:11 {Ahaziah's sister Jehosheba,} As in parallel text at 2 **K** 11:2; Hebrew reads *Jehoshabeath,* a variant name for Jehosheba.
24:26 {assassins were Jozacar,} Hebrew *Zabad;* compare parallel text at 2 **K** 12:21, and see note there.
24:26 {woman named Shomer.} As in parallel text at 2 **K** 12:21; Hebrew reads *Shimrith.*
25: 1 {mother was Jehoaddin,} As in parallel text at 2 **K** 14:2; Hebrew reads *Jehoaddan,* a variant name for Jehoaddin.
25:28 {City of David.} As in some Hebrew manuscripts and other ancient versions (see also 2 **K** 14:20); most Hebrew manuscripts read *the city of Judah.*
26: 2 {town of Elath} As in Greek version (see also 2 **K** 14:22; 16:6); Hebrew reads *Eloth.*
34:20 {son of Micaiah,} As in parallel text at 2 **K** 22:12; Hebrew reads *Abdon son of Micah.*
34:22 {grandson of Harhas,} As in parallel text at 2 **K** 22:14; Hebrew reads *son of Tokhath, son of Hasrah.*
36: 9 {Jehoiachin was eighteen} As in one Hebrew manuscript, some Greek manuscripts, and Syriac version (see also 2 **K** 24:8); most Hebrew manuscripts read *eight.*
36:10 {appointed Jehoiachin's uncle,} As in parallel text at 2 **K** 24:17; Hebrew reads *brother,* or *relative.*
Ezr 6: 3 {be ninety feet.} Aramaic *Its height will be 60 cubits* [27 meters], *and its width will be 60 cubits.* It is commonly held that this verse should be emended to read: "Its height will be 45 feet, its length will be 90 feet, and its width will be 30 feet"; compare 1 **K** 6:2. The emendation regarding the width is supported by the Syriac version.
Jer 35: 6 {wine, because Jehonadab} Hebrew *Jonadab,* a variant name for Jehonadab; also in 35:10, 14, 18, 19. See 2 **K** 10:15.
40: 8 {the Netophathite, Jaazaniah} As in parallel text at 2 **K** 25:23; Hebrew reads *Jezaniah,* a variant name for Jaazaniah.
Mt 1: 8 {father of Jehoram.} Greek *Joram.* See 1 **K** 22:50 and note at 1 Chr 3:11.
1:11 {father of Jehoiachin} Greek *Jeconiah;* also in 1:12. See 2 **K** 24:6 and note at 1 Chr 3:16.
Ro 11: 3 {kill me, too."} 1 **K** 19:10, 14.
11: 4 {down to Baal!"} 1 **K** 19:18.

KIBROTH-HATTAAVAH (1)

Dt 9:22 {and Kibroth-hattaavah.} ***K*** means "graves of craving." See Num 11:31-34.

KICK (1)

Ac 26:14 {against my will.} Greek *It is hard for you to* ***k*** *against the oxgoads.*

KIDON (1)

1Ch 13: 9 {floor of Nacon,} As in parallel text at 2 Sam 6:6; Hebrew reads ***K***.

KILLED (2 of 5)

2Sa 21:19 {Goliath of Gath.} As in parallel text at 1 Chr 20:5; Hebrew reads ***k*** *Goliath of Gath.*
Isa 22: 2 {famine and disease.} Hebrew ***k****, but not by sword and not in battle.*

KILLING (1)

Est 9:18 {the third day,} Hebrew ***k*** *their enemies on the thirteenth day and the fourteenth day, and then rested on the fifteenth day,* of the Hebrew month of Adar.

KIND (2)

Mt 17:20 {would be impossible."} Some manuscripts add verse 21, *But this* ***k*** *of demon won't leave unless you have prayed and fasted.*
23:13 {go in yourselves.} Some manuscripts add verse 14, *How terrible it will be for you teachers of religious law and you Pharisees. Hypocrites! You shamelessly cheat widows out of their property, and then, to cover up the* ***k*** *of people you really are, you make long prayers in public. Because of this, your punishment will be the greater.*

KINDS (1 of 3)

Rev 22: 2 {crops of fruit,} Or *12* ***k*** *of fruit.*

KING (17 of 26)

Ge 36:31 {kings in Israel} Or *before an Israelite* ***k*** *ruled over them.*
1Sa 10:27 {Saul ignored them.} Dead Sea Scroll 4QSam[a] continues: *Nahash,* ***k*** *of the Ammonites, had been grievously oppressing the Gadites…*
2Ki 16: 6 {king of Edom} As in Latin Vulgate; Hebrew reads *Rezin* ***k*** *of Aram.*
17: 4 {So of Egypt} Or *by asking the* ***k*** *of Egypt at Sais.*
1Ch 1:43 {kings in Israel} Or *before an Israelite* ***k*** *ruled over them.*
Pr 31: 1 {Lemuel, an oracle} Or *of Lemuel,* ***k*** *of Massa.*
Ecc 10:16 {is a child} Or *whose* ***k*** *is a servant.*
SS 1: 4 {bedroom, O my king.} Or *The* ***k*** *has brought me into his bedroom.*
Isa 11: 1 {of David's family} Hebrew *the line of Jesse.* Jesse was **K** David's father.
41:21 {King of Israel.} Hebrew *the* ***K*** *of Jacob.*
57: 9 {perfume to Molech} Or *to the* ***k***.
Hos 3: 5 {descendant, their king.} Hebrew *to David their* ***k***.
Zep 1: 5 {they worship Molech,} Hebrew *Malcam,* another name for Molech; or it could possibly mean *their* ***k***.
Ac 12: 1 {King Herod Agrippa} Greek *Herod the* ***k***. He was the nephew of Herod Antipas and a grandson of Herod the Great.
25:13 {his sister, Bernice,} Greek *Agrippa the* ***k*** *and Bernice arrived.*
Rev 15: 3 {of the nations.} Some manuscripts read ***K*** *of the ages;* other manuscripts read ***K*** *of the saints.*

KINGDOM (4 of 21)

Mt 6:13 {the evil one.} Or *from evil.* Some manuscripts add *For yours is the* ***k*** *and the power and the glory forever. Amen.*
11:12 {people attack it.} Or *until now, eager multitudes have been pressing into the* ***K*** *of Heaven.*
12:29 {house be robbed!} Or *One cannot rob Satan's* ***k*** *without first tying him up. Only then can his demons be cast out.*
Mk 3:27 {house be robbed!} Or *One cannot rob Satan's* ***k*** *without first tying him up. Only then can his demons be cast out.*

KINGS (1 of 2)

Da 10:13 {kingdom of Persia.} As in one Greek version; Hebrew reads *and I was left there with the* ***k*** *of Persia.* The meaning of the Hebrew is uncertain.

KINNERETH (5)

Nu 34:11 {Sea of Galilee,} Hebrew *sea of* ***K***.
Dt 3:17 {the Dead Sea,} Hebrew *from* ***K*** *to the sea of the Arabah, the Salt Sea.*
Jos 11: 2 {south of Galilee} Hebrew *of* ***K***.
12: 3 {Sea of Galilee} Hebrew *sea of* ***K***.
13:27 {Sea of Galilee.} Hebrew *sea of* ***K***.

KIPPUR (1)

Ac 27: 9 {in the fall,} Greek *because the fast was now already gone by.* This fast happened on the Day of Atonement (*Yom* ***K***), which occurred in late September or early October.

KIR-HARESETH (3)

2Ki 3:25 {came under attack.} Hebrew *until only* ***K*** *was left, with its stones, but the slingers surrounded and attacked it.*
Isa 16:11 {sorrow for Kir-hareseth} Hebrew *Kir-heres,* a variant name for **K**.
Jer 48:31 {men of Kir-hareseth.} Hebrew *Kir-heres,* a variant name for **K**; also in 48:36.

KIR-HERES (2)

Isa 16:11 {sorrow for Kir-hareseth} Hebrew *K*, a variant name for Kir-hareseth.
Jer 48:31 {men of Kir-hareseth.} Hebrew *K*, a variant name for Kir-hareseth; also in 48:36.

KIRIATH (1)

Jos 18:28 {Gibeah, and Kiriath-jearim} As in Greek version; Hebrew reads *K*.

KIRIATH-ARIM (1)

Ezr 2:25 {peoples of Kiriath-jearim,} As in some Hebrew manuscripts and Greek version (see also Neh 7:29); Hebrew reads *K*.

KIRIATH-JEARIM (1)

2Sa 6: 2 {Baalah of Judah} *Baalah of Judah* is another name for **K**; compare 1 Chr 13:6.

KISLEV (2)

Ne 1: 1 {King Artaxerxes' reign,} Hebrew *In the month of K of the twentieth year....*
Zec 7: 1 {On December 7} Hebrew *On the fourth day of the ninth month, the month of K,* of the Hebrew calendar....

KISS (5)

Ro 16:16 {in Christian love.} Greek *with a sacred **k**.*
1Co 16:20 {in Christian love.} Greek *with a sacred **k**.*
2Co 13:12 {in Christian love.} Greek *with a sacred **k**.*
1Th 5:26 {in Christian love.} Greek *Greet all the brothers with a holy **k**.*
1Pe 5:14 {in Christian love.} Greek *with a **k** of love.*

KITTIM (5)

Nu 24:24 {coasts of Cyprus} Hebrew *K*.
Isa 23: 1 {heard in Cyprus} Hebrew *K*; also in 23:12.
Jer 2:10 {land of Cyprus} Hebrew *K*.
Eze 27: 6 {coasts of Cyprus.} Hebrew *K*.
Da 11:30 {from western coastlands} Hebrew *from K*.

KNOW (10)

Job 36:33 {his indignant anger.} Or *even the cattle **k** when a storm is coming.* The meaning of the Hebrew is uncertain.
Ps 56: 9 {on my side.} Or *By this I will **k** that God is on my side.*
Eze 38:14 {will rouse yourself.} As in Greek version; Hebrew reads *then you will **k**.*
Jnh 4:11 {in spiritual darkness,} Hebrew *people who don't **k** their right hands from their left.*
Jn 14: 7 {my Father is.} Some manuscripts read *If you really have known me, you will **k** who my Father is.*
Ro 8:28 {to work together} Some manuscripts read *And we **k** that everything works together.*
2Co 12: 2 {I} Greek *I **k** a man in Christ who.*
1Th 4: 4 {control your body} Or *will **k** how to take a wife for himself;* Greek reads *will **k** how to possess his own vessel.*
Jas 1:19 {Dear friends,} Greek *K this, my beloved brothers.*

KNOWN (17)

Ge 33:19 {pieces of silver.} Hebrew *100 kesitahs;* the value or weight of the kesitah is no longer **k**.
Jos 24:32 {pieces of silver.} Hebrew *100 kesitahs;* the value or weight of the kesitah is no longer **k**.
1Sa 14:49 {included Jonathan, Ishbosheth,} Hebrew *Ishvi,* a variant name for Ishbosheth; also **k** as Eshbaal.
2Sa 2: 8 {Saul's son Ishbosheth.} Also **k** as *Eshbaal.*
3: 7 {One day Ishbosheth,} Also **k** as *Eshbaal.*
4: 1 {When Ishbosheth} Also **k** as *Eshbaal.*
4: 4 {son named Mephibosheth,} Also **k** as *Meribbaal.*
9: 6 {name was Mephibosheth} Also **k** as *Meribbaal.*
16: 1 {servant of Mephibosheth,} Also **k** as *Meribbaal.*
19:24 {Now Mephibosheth,} Also **k** as *Meribbaal.*
21: 7 {Jonathan's son Mephibosheth,} Also **k** as *Meribbaal.*
1Ki 14:31 {his son Abijam} Also **k** as *Abijah.*
15: 1 {Abijam} Also **k** as *Abijah.*
Job 42:11 {gift of money} Hebrew *a kesitah;* the value or weight of the kesitah is no longer **k**.
Jn 14: 7 {my Father is.} Some manuscripts read *If you really have **k** me, you will know who my Father is.*
Ac 19:24 {Greek goddess Artemis.} *Artemis* is otherwise **k** as Diana.
Ro 1:18 {away from themselves.} Or *who prevent the truth from being **k**.*

KODRANTES (1)

Mk 12:42 {in two pennies.} Greek *2 lepta, which is a **k**.*

KOHELETH (1)

Ecc 1: 1 {of the Teacher,} Hebrew *K;* this term is rendered "the Teacher" throughout this book.

KOROUS (2)

Lk 16: 7 {eight hundred bushels.} Greek *100 **k**...80 [**k**].*

KUB (2)

Eze 30: 5 {Ethiopia, Libya,} Hebrew *Put...K.* Both *Put* and *K* are associated with Libya.

KUE (2)

1Ki 10:28 {and from Cilicia} Hebrew *K*, probably another name for Cilicia.
2Ch 1:16 {and from Cilicia} Hebrew *K*, probably another name for Cilicia.

KYRIA (1)

2Jn 1: 1 {to her children,} Or *the church God has chosen and her members,* or *the chosen K and her children.*

L

LABOR (2)

Ps 29: 9 {twists mighty oaks} Or *causes the deer to writhe in **l**.*
Mt 20: 2 {normal daily wage} Greek *a denarius,* the payment for a full day's **l**; also in 20:9, 10, 13.

LACHISH (1)

Mic 1:13 {people of Lachish.} *L* sounds like the Hebrew term for "team of horses."

LACK (7)

Jos 8:17 {Ai or Bethel} Some manuscripts **l** *or Bethel.*
22:34 {the altar "Witness,"} Hebrew *edh.* Some manuscripts **l** this word.
1Sa 2:22 {of the Tabernacle.} Hebrew *Tent of Meeting.* Some manuscripts **l** this entire sentence.
23:11 {me to him?} Some manuscripts **l** the first sentence of 23:11.
1Ch 1:17 {of Aram were} As in one Hebrew manuscript and some Greek manuscripts (see also Gen 10:23); most Hebrew manuscripts **l** *The descendants of Aram were.*
25: 3 {Zeri, Jeshaiah, Shimei,} As in one Hebrew manuscript and some Greek manuscripts (see also 25:17); most Hebrew manuscripts **l** *Shimei.*
Ne 7:68 {horses, 245 mules,} As in some Hebrew manuscripts (see also Ezra 2:66); most Hebrew manuscripts **l** this verse.

LACKS (27)

Lev 6: 6 {value in silver.} Or *and the animal must be of the proper value;* Hebrew **l** *in silver;* compare 5:15.
Nu 26:40 {their ancestor Ard.} As in Samaritan Pentateuch, some Greek manuscripts, and Latin Vulgate; Hebrew **l** *named after their ancestor Ard.*
Dt 33: 6 {tribe of Reuben:} Hebrew **l** *Moses said this about the tribe of Reuben.*
33:18 {Zebulun and Issachar} Hebrew **l** *and Issachar.*
Jdg 16:13 {the loom shuttle,} As in Greek version; Hebrew **l** *on your loom and tighten it with the loom shuttle.*
1Sa 11: 1 {month later,} As in Greek version; Hebrew **l** *About a month later.*
2Sa 15:27 {You and Abiathar} Hebrew **l** *and Abiathar;* compare 15:29.
1Ki 4:19 {land of Judah.} As in some Greek manuscripts; Hebrew **l** *of Judah.* The meaning of the Hebrew is uncertain.
2Ki 23:16 {man of God} As in Greek version; Hebrew **l** *as Jeroboam stood beside the altar at the festival. Then Josiah turned and looked up at the tomb of the man of God.*
1Ch 1: 4 {of Noah were} As in Greek version (see also Gen 5:3-32); Hebrew **l** *The sons of Noah were.*
4:13 {Hathath and Meonothai.} As in some Greek manuscripts and Latin Vulgate; Hebrew **l** *and Meonothai.*
6:27 {Elkanah, and Samuel.} As in some Greek manuscripts (see also 6:33-34); Hebrew **l** *and Samuel.*
6:28 {Samuel were Joel} As in some Greek manuscripts and the Syriac version (see also 6:33 and 1 Sam 8:2); Hebrew **l** *Joel.*
6:39 {clan of Gershon.} Hebrew **l** *from the clan of Gershon;* see 6:43.
6:59 {Juttah,} As in Syriac version (see also Josh 21:16); Hebrew **l** *Juttah.*
6:60 {were given Gibeon,} As in parallel text at Josh 21:17; Hebrew **l** *Gibeon.*
6:77 {of Jokneam, Kartah,} As in Greek version (see also Josh 21:34); Hebrew **l** *Jokneam, Kartah.*
8:29 {Jeiel} As in some Greek manuscripts (see also 9:35); Hebrew **l** *Jeiel.*
8:30 {Kish, Baal, Ner,} As in some Greek manuscripts (see also 9:36); Hebrew **l** *Ner.*
9:41 {Tahrea, and Ahaz.} As in Syriac version and Latin Vulgate (see also 8:35); Hebrew **l** *and Ahaz.*
19: 1 {his son Hanun} Hebrew **l** *Hanun;* compare parallel text at 2 Sam 10:1.
25: 9 {sons and relatives.} As in Greek version; Hebrew **l** *and twelve of his sons and relatives.*
Ezr 8: 5 {family of Zattu} As in some Greek manuscripts (see also 1 Esdras 8:32); Hebrew **l** *Zattu.*
8:10 {family of Bani} As in some Greek manuscripts (see also 1 Esdras 8:36); Hebrew **l** *Bani.*
Ne 12:17 {was also a} Hebrew **l** the name of this family leader.
Pr 14:33 {wisdom is not} As in Greek version; Hebrew **l** *not.*
Ecc 9: 2 {good or bad,} As in Greek and Syriac versions, and Latin Vulgate; Hebrew **l** *or bad.*

LADAN (2)

1Ch 23: 7 {descent from Libni} Hebrew *L* (also in 23:8-9), another name for Libni; compare 6:17.
26:21 {family of Libni} Hebrew *L,* another name for Libni; compare 6:17.

LADDER (1)

Jn 1:51 {Son of Man."} See Gen 28:10-17, the account of Jacob's **l**.

LAID (1 of 2)

Php 2: 7 {made himself nothing;} Or *He **l** aside his mighty power and glory.*

LAISH (1)

Jos 19:47 {town of Laish.} Hebrew *Leshem,* another name for **L**.

LAKE (1)

Lk 5: 1 {Sea of Galilee,} Greek *L Gennesaret,* another name for the Sea of Galilee.

LAMP (4)

1Ki 11:36 {continue to reign} Hebrew *will continue to have a **l**.*
15: 4 {dynasty to continue,} Hebrew *gave him a **l** in Jerusalem.*
2Ki 8:19 {to rule forever.} Hebrew *promised to give a **l** to David and his descendants forever.*
2Ch 21: 7 {to rule forever.} Hebrew *promised to give a **l** to David and his descendants forever.*

LAND (8 of 20)

Ge 47:21 {servants to Pharaoh.} As in Greek version and Samaritan Pentateuch; Hebrew reads *He moved the people into the towns throughout the **l** of Egypt.*
48:22 {an extra portion} Or *give you the ridge of **l**.* The meaning of the Hebrew is uncertain.
Lev 4:27 {citizens of Israel} Hebrew *people of the **l**.*
Jdg 9:37 {from the hills.} Or *the center of the **l**.*
1Sa 5: 6 {tumors.} Greek version and Latin Vulgate read *tumors. And rats appeared in their **l**, and death and destruction were throughout the city.*
2Ki 2:21 {death or infertility.} Or *or make the **l** unproductive.*
Zep 1:18 {people on earth.} Or *the people living in the **l**.*
Zec 9:10 {of the earth.} Or *the end of the **l**.*

LANGUAGE (3)

Ps 19: 3 {in the skies;} Or *There is no speech or **l** where their voice is not heard.*
Isa 19:18 {the Hebrew language.} Hebrew *the **l** of Canaan.*
1Co 2:13 {explain spiritual truths.} Or *explaining spiritual truths in spiritual **l**,* or *explaining spiritual truths to spiritual people.*

LANGUAGES (1)

1Co 14: 2 {speak in tongues,} Or *in unknown **l**;* also in 14:4, 5, 13, 14, 18, 22, 28, 39.

LAST (7)

Ps 145:13 {all he does.} The **l** two lines of 145:13 are not found in many of the ancient manuscripts.
Mt 19:30 {the greatest then.} Greek *But many who are first will be **l**; and the **l**, first.*
Mk 10:31 {the greatest then.} Greek *But many who are first will be **l**; and the **l**, first.*
Lk 13:30 {be despised then.} Greek *Some are **l** who will be first, and some are first who will be **l**.*

LATE (2 of 21)

Mt 27:35 {by throwing dice.} Greek *by casting lots.* A few **l** manuscripts add *This fulfilled the word of the prophet: "They divided my clothes among themselves and cast lots for my robe."* See Ps 22:18.
1Jn 5: 7 {these three witnesses} Some very **l** manuscripts add *in heaven—the Father, the Word, and the Holy Spirit, and these three are one. And we have three witnesses on earth.*

LATIN (31)

Nu 2:14[-15] {son of Deuel} As in many Hebrew manuscripts, Samaritan Pentateuch, and **L** Vulgate (see also 1:14); most Hebrew manuscripts read *son of Reuel.*
26:23 {its ancestor Puah.} As in Samaritan Pentateuch, Greek and Syriac versions, and **L** Vulgate (see also 1 Chr 7:1); Hebrew reads *The Punite clan, named after its ancestor Puvah.*

26:39 {its ancestor Shupham.} As in some Hebrew manuscripts, Samaritan Pentateuch, Greek and Syriac versions, and **L** Vulgate; most Hebrew manuscripts read *Shephupham.*
26:40 {their ancestor Ard.} As in Samaritan Pentateuch, some Greek manuscripts, and **L** Vulgate; Hebrew lacks *named after their ancestor Ard.*
Jdg 1:14 {she urged him} Greek version and **L** Vulgate read *he urged her.*
18:30 {descendant of Moses,} As in an ancient Hebrew tradition, some Greek manuscripts, and **L** Vulgate; Masoretic Text reads *of Manasseh.*
Ru 3:15 {back. Then Boaz} Most Hebrew manuscripts read *he;* many Hebrew manuscripts, Syriac version, and **L** Vulgate read *she.*
1Sa 5:6 {plague of tumors.} Greek version and **L** Vulgate read *tumors. And rats appeared in their land, and death and destruction were throughout the city.*
1Ki 7:7 {floor to ceiling.} As in Syriac version and **L** Vulgate; Hebrew reads *from floor to floor.*
12:2 {returned from Egypt,} As in Greek version and **L** Vulgate (see also 2 Chr 10:2); Hebrew reads *he lived in Egypt.*
2Ki 10:1 {of the city,} As in some Greek manuscripts and **L** Vulgate (see also 10:6); Hebrew reads *of Jezreel.*
16:6 {king of Edom} As in **L** Vulgate; Hebrew reads *Rezin king of Aram.*
16:6 {Elath for Edom.} As in **L** Vulgate; Hebrew reads *Aram.*
16:6 {and sent Edomites} As in marginal *Qere* reading of the Masoretic Text, Greek version, and **L** Vulgate; Hebrew reads *Arameans.*
1Ch 1:50 {city of Pau.} As in many Hebrew manuscripts, some Greek manuscripts, Syriac version, and **L** Vulgate (see also Gen 36:39); most Hebrew manuscripts read *Pai.*
4:13 {Hathath and Meonothai.} As in some Greek manuscripts and **L** Vulgate; Hebrew lacks *and Meonothai.*
9:41 {Tahrea, and Ahaz.} As in Syriac version and **L** Vulgate (see also 8:35); Hebrew lacks *and Ahaz.*
18:16 {Ahitub and Ahimelech} As in some Hebrew manuscripts, Syriac version, and **L** Vulgate (see also 2 Sam 8:17); most Hebrew manuscripts read *Abimelech.*
20:2 {the king's head,} Greek version and **L** Vulgate read *removed the crown of Milcom;* compare 1 Kgs 11:5. Milcom, also called Molech, was the god of the Ammonites.
23:10 {were Jahath, Ziza,} As in Greek version and **L** Vulgate (see also 23:11); Hebrew reads *Zina.*
2Ch 15:8 {Azariah the prophet,} As in Syriac version and **L** Vulgate (see also 15:1); Hebrew reads *from Oded the prophet.*
20:25 {of equipment, clothing,} As in some Hebrew manuscripts and **L** Vulgate; most Hebrew manuscripts read *corpses.*
22:6 {and King Ahaziah} Some Hebrew manuscripts, Greek and Syriac versions, and **L** Vulgate (see also 2 Kgs 8:29); most Hebrew manuscripts read *Azariah.*
Ne 12:4 {Iddo, Ginnethon,} As in some Hebrew manuscripts and **L** Vulgate (see also 12:16); most Hebrew manuscripts read *Ginnethoi.*
Ecc 9:2 {good or bad,} As in Greek and Syriac versions, and **L** Vulgate; Hebrew lacks *or bad.*
SS 7:9 {lips and teeth.} As in Greek and Syriac versions and **L** Vulgate; Hebrew reads *over lips of sleepers.*
Isa 15:9 {stream near Dibon} As in Dead Sea Scrolls, some Greek manuscripts, and **L** Vulgate; Hebrew reads *Dimon;* also in 15:9b.
49:24 {that a tyrant} As in Dead Sea Scrolls, Syriac version, and **L** Vulgate (also see 49:25); Masoretic Text reads *a righteous person.*
Jer 23:33 {are the burden!} As in Greek version and **L** Vulgate; Hebrew reads *What burden?*
Hos 13:10 {Where now is} As in Greek and Syriac versions and **L** Vulgate; Hebrew reads *I will be.*
Lk 23:33 {called The Skull.} Sometimes rendered *Calvary,* which comes from the **L** word for "skull."

LAUGHS (2)

Ge 17:19 {name him Isaac,} *Isaac* means "he **l**."
21:3 {his son Isaac.} *Isaac* means "he **l**."

LAW (6)

Mt 23:13 {go in yourselves.} Some manuscripts add verse 14, *How terrible it will be for you teachers of religious **l** and you Pharisees. Hypocrites! You shamelessly cheat widows out of their property, and then, to cover up the kind of people you really are, you make long prayers in public. Because of this, your punishment will be the greater.*
Ac 7:53 {hands of angels.} Greek *received the **L** as it was ordained by angels.*
24:6 {we arrested him.} Some manuscripts add *We would have judged him by our **l**, [7]but Lysias, the commander of the garrison, came and took him violently away from us, [8]commanding his accusers to come before you.*
Ro 8:2 {For the power} Greek *the **l**;* also in 8:2b.
1Co 9:21 {the Jewish law,} Greek *those without the **l**.*
14:21 {in the Scriptures,} Greek *in the **l**.*

LEADER (2 of 3)

1Sa 10:1 {his people Israel.} Greek version reads *Israel. And you will rule over the LORD's people and save them from their enemies around them. This will be the sign to you that the LORD has appointed you to be **l** over his inheritance.*
Zec 9:7 {clan in Judah.} Hebrew *and will become a **l** in Judah.*

LEADING (1)

Ac 17:4 {of the city.} Some manuscripts read *many of the wives of the **l** men.*

LEADS (1)

Mt 7:13 {highway to hell} Greek *The way that **l** to destruction.*

LEARN (1)

1Co 4:6 {to the Scriptures,} Or *You must **l** not to go beyond "what is written," so that.*

LEATHERWORKERS (1)

Ac 18:3 {they were tentmakers} Or **l**.

LEAVE (2)

Jdg 7:3 {afraid may leave} Hebrew ***l** Mount Gilead.* The identity of Mount Gilead is uncertain in this context. It is perhaps used here as another name for Mount Gilboa.
Mt 17:20 {would be impossible."} Some manuscripts add verse 21, *But this kind of demon won't **l** unless you have prayed and fasted.*

LEAVEN (3)

1Co 5:6[-7] {can stay pure.} Greek *Don't you realize that even a little **l** spreads quickly through the whole batch of dough? [7]Purge out the old **l** so that you can be a new batch of dough, just as you are already unleavened.*
5:8 {the old bread} Greek *not with old **l**.*

LEB-KAMAI (1)

Jer 51:1 {people of Babylonia.} Hebrew *of **L**,* a code name for Babylonia.

LEBO-HAMATH (1)

1Ch 13:5 {to the other,} Hebrew *from the Shihor of Egypt to **L**.*

LEFT (7)

1Sa 13:15 {land of Benjamin.} As in Greek version; Hebrew reads *Samuel **l** Gilgal and went to Gibeah in the land of Benjamin.*
2Ki 3:25 {came under attack.} Hebrew *until only Kir-hareseth was **l**, with its stones, but the slingers surrounded and attacked it.*
Ne 12:38 {choir went northward} Hebrew *to the **l**.*
Da 10:13 {kingdom of Persia.} As in one Greek version; Hebrew reads *and I was **l** there with the kings of Persia.* The meaning of the Hebrew is uncertain.
Jnh 4:11 {in spiritual darkness,} Hebrew *people who don't know their right hands from their **l**.*
Mt 27:51[-53] {to many people.} Or *The earth shook, rocks split apart, tombs opened, and many bodies of godly men and women who had died were raised from the dead. After Jesus' resurrection, they **l** the cemetery, went into the holy city of Jerusalem, and appeared to many people.*
Lk 17:35 {the other left.} Some manuscripts add verse 36, *Two men will be working in the field; one will be taken, the other **l**.*

LEGIONS (1)

Mt 26:53 {Father for thousands} Greek [12**l**.]

LEGS (1)

Isa 7:20 {and your people.} Hebrew *shave off the head, the hair of the **l**, and the beard.*

LEPROSY (8)

Lev 13:2 {contagious skin disease,} Traditionally rendered **l**. The Hebrew word used throughout this passage is used to describe various skin diseases.
13:47 {an infectious mildew} Traditionally rendered **l**. The Hebrew term used throughout this passage is the same term used for the various skin diseases described in 13:1-46.
14:2 {contagious skin disease.} Traditionally rendered **l**. See note at 13:2.
14:34 {an infectious mildew.} Traditionally rendered **l**. See note at 13:47.
14:54 {contagious skin disease} Traditionally rendered **l**. See notes at 13:2 and 13:47.
22:4 {contagious skin disease} Traditionally rendered **l**. See note at 13:2.
Nu 5:2 {contagious skin disease} Traditionally rendered **l**. The Hebrew word used here describes various skin diseases.
Dt 24:8 {contagious skin diseases} Traditonally rendered **l**. The Hebrew word used here can describe various skin diseases.

LEPTA (2)

Mk 12:42 {in two pennies.} Greek *2 **l**, which is a kodrantes.*
Lk 21:2 {in two pennies.} Greek *2 **l**.*

LESHEM (1)

Jos 19:47 {town of Laish.} Hebrew ***L**,* another name for Laish.

LETHECH (1)

Hos 3:2 {measure of wine.} As in Greek version, which reads *a homer* [182 liters] *of barley and a measure of wine;* Hebrew reads *a homer of barley and a **l*** [2.5 bushels or 91 liters] *of barley.*

LEV (24)

Ex 23:16 {the Final Harvest} This was later called the Festival of Shelters; see **L** 23:33-36.
34:22 {the Final Harvest} This was later called the Festival of Shelters; see **L** 23:33-36.
1Ki 12:32 {day in midautumn,} Hebrew *on the fifteenth day of the eighth month* (also in 12:33). This day of the Hebrew lunar calendar occurs in late October or early November, exactly one month after the annual Festival of Shelters in Judah (see **L** 23:34).
Ne 8:14 {held that month.} Hebrew *in the seventh month.* This month of the Hebrew lunar calendar usually occurs in September and October. See **L** 23:39-43.
Eze 45:25 {in early autumn,} Hebrew *the festival which begins on the fifteenth day of the seventh month* (see **L** 23:33). This day of the Hebrew lunar calendar occurs in late September or October.
46:17 {every fiftieth year.} Hebrew *until the Year of Release;* see **L** 25:8-17.
Mt 5:38 {who did it.'} Greek *'An eye for an eye and a tooth for a tooth.'* Exod 21:24; **L** 24:20; Deut 19:21.
5:43 {'Love your neighbor'} **L** 19:18.
15:4 {put to death.'} Exod 20:12; 21:17; **L** 20:9; Deut 5:16.
19:18[-19] {neighbor as yourself.'} Exod 20:12-16; **L** 19:18; Deut 5:16-20.
22:39 {neighbor as yourself.'} **L** 19:18.
Mk 7:10 {put to death.'} Exod 20:12; 21:17; **L** 20:9; Deut 5:16.
12:31 {neighbor as yourself.'} **L** 19:18.
Lk 2:24 {two young pigeons."} **L** 12:8.
10:27 {neighbor as yourself.' "} Deut 6:5; **L** 19:18.
Ac 2:1 {after Jesus' resurrection,} Greek *When the day of Pentecost arrived.* This annual celebration came 50 days after the Passover ceremonies. See **L** 23:16.
3:23 {and utterly destroyed.'} Deut 18:19; **L** 23:29.
Ro 10:5 {of its commands.} **L** 18:5.
13:9 {neighbor as yourself."} **L** 19:18.
2Co 6:16 {be my people.} **L** 26:12; Ezek 37:27.
Gal 3:12 {of its commands."} **L** 18:5.
5:14 {neighbor as yourself."} **L** 19:18.
Jas 2:8 {neighbor as yourself."} **L** 19:18.
1Pe 1:16 {I am holy."} **L** 11:44-45; 19:2; 20:7.

LEVI (1)

Ge 29:34 {Levi,} ***L*** sounds like a Hebrew term that means "being attached" or "feeling affection for."

LEVIATHAN (2)

Job 3:8 {the sea monster} Hebrew *rouse **L**.*
41:1 {catch a crocodile} Hebrew ***L**;* also throughout the following passage.

LEVITE (1)

Lk 10:32 {A Temple assistant} Greek *A **L**.*

LEVITES (1)

Jn 1:19 {and Temple assistants} Greek *and **L**.*

LIBNI (2)

1Ch 23:7 {descent from Libni} Hebrew *Ladan* (also in 23:8-9), another name for **L**; compare 6:17.
26:21 {family of Libni} Hebrew *Ladan,* another name for **L**; compare 6:17.

LIBYA (2)

Isa 66:19 {to the Libyans} As in some Greek manuscripts, which read *Put* [**L**]; Hebrew reads *Pul.*
Eze 30:5 {Ethiopia, Libya,} Hebrew *Put...Kub.* Both *Put* and *Kub* are associated with **L**.

LIFE (12)

Ge 3:20 {his wife Eve,} *Eve* sounds like a Hebrew term that means "to give **l**."
Ps 49:7 {themselves from death} Or *no one can redeem the **l** of another.*
Pr 4:23 {everything you do.} Hebrew *for from it flow the springs of **l**.*
Mal 2:15 {you are his.} Or *Did not one God make us and preserve our **l** and breath?* or *Did not one God make her, both flesh and spirit?* The meaning of the Hebrew is uncertain.

Mt 16:26 {your own soul} Or *your l;* also in 16:26b.
18: 8 {to enter heaven} Greek *enter l;* also in 18:9.
Mk 8:36 {your own soul} Or *your l;* also in 8:37.
9:43 {to enter heaven} Greek *enter l;* also in 9:45.
Lk 16: 9 {you in heaven.} Or *Then when you run out at the end of this l, your friends will welcome you into eternal homes.*
Jn 11:25 {and the life.} Some manuscripts do not include *and the l.*
Ro 8:10 {spirit is alive} Or *the Spirit will bring you eternal l.*
1Co 7:26 {the present crisis,} Or *pressures of l.*

LIFTED (3)

Ex 17:16 {throne, so now} Or *Hands have been l up to the LORD's throne, and now.*
Eze 3:12 {in his place!)} A likely reading for this verse is *Then the Spirit l me up, and as the glory of the LORD rose from its place, I heard behind me a loud rumbling sound.*
Jn 3:14 {on a pole,} Greek *must be l up.*

LIGHT (2)

Ps 74:16 {made the starlight} Or *moon;* Hebrew reads *l.*
Zec 14: 6 {no longer shine,} Hebrew *there will be no l, no cold or frost.* The meaning of the Hebrew is uncertain.

LIGHTS (1)

Jas 1:17 {all heaven's lights.} Greek *from above, from the Father of l.*

LIKENESS (2)

Ge 5: 3 {of his father.} Hebrew *was in his own l, after his image.*
Php 2: 7 {in human form.} Greek *he was born in the l of men and was found in appearance as a man.*

LINE (2)

Isa 11: 1 {of David's family} Hebrew *the l of Jesse.* Jesse was King David's father.
Zec 1:16 {reconstruction of Jerusalem.} Hebrew *and the measuring l will be stretched out over Jerusalem.*

LINEN (3)

1Sa 2:18 {of a priest.} Hebrew *He wore a l ephod.*
2Sa 6:14 {a priestly tunic.} Hebrew *a l ephod.*
1Ch 15:27 {a priestly tunic.} Hebrew *a l ephod.*

LION (2)

Isa 21: 8 {Then the watchman} As in Dead Sea Scrolls and Syriac version; Hebrew reads *a l.*
2Ti 4:17 {from certain death.} Greek *from the mouth of a l.*

LISTEN (2)

Mic 6: 9 {is sending them.} Hebrew *"L to the rod. Who appointed it?"*
Mk 7:15 {say and do!} Some manuscripts add verse 16, *Anyone who is willing to hear should l and understand.*

LISTENED (1)

Heb 4: 2 {God told them.} Some manuscripts read *they didn't share the faith of those who l [to God].*

LITERALLY (4)

Mt 5:22 {friend, 'You idiot,'} L *'Raca,'* an Aramaic term of contempt.
21: 9 {"Praise God} Greek *Hosanna,* an exclamation of praise that l means "save now"; also in 21:9b, 15.
Mk 11: 9 {"Praise God!} Greek *Hosanna,* an exclamation of praise that l means "save now"; also in 11:10.
Jn 12:13 {"Praise God!} Greek *Hosanna,* an exclamation of praise that l means "save now."

LITERARY (2)

Ps 3: 2 {Interlude} Hebrew *Selah.* The meaning of this word is uncertain, though it is probably a musical or l term. It is rendered *Interlude* throughout the Psalms.
Hab 3: 3 {and Mount Paran.} Hebrew adds *selah;* also in 3:9, 13. The meaning of this Hebrew term is uncertain; it is probably a musical or l term.

LITRA (1)

Jn 12: 3 {twelve-ounce jar} Greek *took 1 l* [327 grams].

LITRAS (1)

Jn 19:39 {about seventy-five pounds} Greek *100 l* [32.7 kilograms].

LITTLE (6)

Ge 19:22 {known as Zoar.} *Zoar* means "l."
Ps 8: 5 {lower than God,} Or *a l lower than the angels;* Hebrew reads *Elohim.*
Eze 20:31 {burned as sacrifices,} Or *and make your l children pass through the fire.*
Mk 5:41 {little girl!"} Greek text uses Aramaic *"Talitha cumi"* and then translates it as "Get up, l girl."

Ac 26:28 {Christian so quickly?"} Or *"A l more, and your arguments would make me a Christian."*
1Co 5: 6[-7] {can stay pure.} Greek *Don't you realize that even a l leaven spreads quickly through the whole batch of dough? [7]Purge out the old leaven so that you can be a new batch of dough, just as you are already unleavened.*

LIVE (4)

Ge 9:27 {prosperity of Shem;} Hebrew *may he l in the tents of Shem.*
Hos 3: 3 {even with me.} Or *and I will l with you.*
Hab 2: 4 {by their faith.} Or *the just will l by their faithfulness.*
Heb 12: 9 {and live forever} Or *really l.*

LIVED (4)

Ge 11:12[-13] {sons and daughters.} Greek version reads *[12]When Arphaxad was 135 years old, his son Cainan was born. [13]After the birth of Cainan, Arphaxad l another 430 years and had other sons and daughters, and then he died. When Cainan was 130 years old, his son Shelah was born. After the birth of Shelah, Cainan l another 330 years and had other sons and daughters, and then he died.*
1Sa 10:27 {Saul ignored them.} Dead Sea Scroll 4QSam[a] continues: *Nahash, king of the Ammonites, had been grievously oppressing the Gadites and Reubenites who l east of the Jordan River....*
1Ki 12: 2 {returned from Egypt,} As in Greek version and Latin Vulgate (see also 2 Chr 10:2); Hebrew reads *he l in Egypt.*

LIVES (3)

Ge 41:45 {renamed him Zaphenath-paneah} *Zaphenath-paneah* probably means "God speaks and l."
Lk 9:55 {and rebuked them.} Some manuscripts add *And he said, "You don't realize what your hearts are like. [56]For the Son of Man has not come to destroy men's l, but to save them."*
Jn 3:13 {Son of Man,} Some manuscripts add *who l in heaven.*

LIVING (6)

Ge 16:14 {was named Beer-lahairoi,} *Beer-lahairoi* means "well of the L One who sees me."
Ru 2:20 {dead husband.} Hebrew *to the l and to the dead.*
1Sa 10:27 {Saul ignored them.} Dead Sea Scroll 4QSam[a] continues: *...He gouged out the right eye of each of the Israelites l there, and he didn't allow anyone to come and rescue them....*
Zep 1:18 {people on earth.} Or *the people l in the land.*
Lk 23:31 {it is dry?} Or *If these things are done to me, the l tree, what will happen to you, the dry tree?*
Jn 7:37[-38] {out from within."} Or *"Let anyone who is thirsty come to me and drink. [38]For the Scriptures declare that rivers of l water will flow from the heart of those who believe in me."*

LO-AMMI (1)

Hos 2:23 {'Not my people,'} Hebrew *L;* see 1:9.

LO-DEBAR (1)

Am 6:13 {conquest of Lo-debar.} *L* means "nothing."

LO-RUHAMAH (1)

Hos 2:23 {'Not loved.'} Hebrew *L;* see 1:6.

LOG (1)

Lev 14:10 {of a pint} Hebrew *1 l* [0.3 liters]; also in 14:21.

LONG (3 of 32)

Job 7:19 {for a moment} Hebrew *l enough to swallow my spittle.*
Mt 23:13 {go in yourselves.} Some manuscripts add verse 14, *How terrible it will be for you teachers of religious law and you Pharisees. Hypocrites! You shamelessly cheat widows out of their property, and then, to cover up the kind of people you really are, you make l prayers in public. Because of this, your punishment will be the greater.*
1Co 11: 6 {wear a covering.} Or *then she should have l hair.*

LONGER (1 of 4)

2Sa 13:39 {his son Absalom.} Or *no l felt a need to go out after Absalom.*

LOOK (3)

Ge 29:32 {named him Reuben,} *Reuben* means "L, a son!" It also sounds like the Hebrew for "He has seen my misery."
SS 4: 8 {bride. Come down} Or *L down.*
2Co 10: 7 {basis of appearance.} Or *L at the obvious facts.*

LOOKED (4)

2Ki 23:16 {man of God} As in Greek version; Hebrew lacks *as Jeroboam stood beside the altar at the festival. Then Josiah turned and l up at the tomb of the man of God.*

Da 10:16 {like a man} As in most manuscripts of the Masoretic Text; one manuscript of the Masoretic Text and one Greek version read *Then something that l like a human hand.*
Rev 1:13 {Son of Man.} Or *one who l like a man;* Greek reads *one like a son of man.*
14:14 {Son of Man} Or *one who l like a man;* Greek reads *one like a son of man.*

LOOM (2)

Jdg 16:13 {the loom shuttle,} As in Greek version; Hebrew lacks *on your l and tighten it with the l shuttle.*

LORD (15 of 16)

Lk 4:18[-19] {favor has come.} Or *and to proclaim the acceptable year of the L.* Isa 61:1-2.
20:37 {to the Lord} Greek *when he wrote about the burning bush, he referred to the L.*
Jn 4: 1 {Jesus} Some manuscripts read *The L.*
5: 3 {on the porches.} Some manuscripts add *waiting for a certain movement of the water, [4]for an angel of the L came from time to time and stirred up the water. And the first person to step down into it afterward was healed.*
Ro 16:23 {a Christian brother.} Some manuscripts add verse 24, *May the grace of our L Jesus Christ be with you all. Amen.*
1Co 5: 4 {of the church,} Or *In the name of the L Jesus, you are to call a meeting of the church.*
7:39 {to the Lord.} Or *but only to a Christian;* Greek reads *but only in the L.*
10: 9 {we put Christ} Some manuscripts read *the L.*
2Co 1:24 {faith into practice.} Greek *want to l it over your faith.*
Eph 3:14 {to the Father,} Some manuscripts read *the Father of our L Jesus Christ.*
Php 1:14 {of the Christians} Greek *brothers in the L.*
2:29 {with Christian love} Greek *in the L.*
2Th 1:12 {Lord, Jesus Christ.} Or *of our God and the L Jesus Christ.*
2Pe 1: 2 {God and Lord,} Or *God and Jesus our L.*
2:11 {out disrespectfully against} Greek *never bring blasphemous judgment from the L against.*

LORD'S (1 of 2)

1Co 11:29 {body of Christ,} Greek *the body;* some manuscripts read *the L body.*

LORD* (28 of 57)

Ge 10: 9 {the LORD's sight.} Hebrew *a mighty hunter before the L;* also in 10:9b.
16: 5 {this to me!} Hebrew *Let the L judge between you and me.*
Ex 16:33 {a sacred place} Hebrew *before the L.*
Nu 13:16 {name to Joshua.} *Hoshea* (see 13:8) means "salvation"; *Joshua* means "The L is salvation."
Dt 6: 4 {the LORD alone.} Or *The L our God is one L,* or *The L our God, the L is one,* or *The L is our God, the L is one.*
34: 6 {He was buried} Hebrew *He buried him,* that is, "The L buried him." Samaritan Pentateuch and some Greek manuscripts read *They buried him.*
1Sa 1: 7 {to the Tabernacle.} Hebrew *the house of the L;* also in 1:24.
1: 9 {to the Tabernacle} Hebrew *the Temple of the L.*
2:20 {to the LORD.} As in Greek version; Hebrew reads *this one she requested of the L in prayer.*
3: 3 {in the Tabernacle} Hebrew *the Temple of the L.*
3:15 {of the Tabernacle} Hebrew *the house of the L.*
10: 1 {his people Israel.} Greek version reads *Israel. And you will rule over the LORD's people and save them from their enemies around them. This will be the sign to you that the L has appointed you to be leader over his inheritance.*
21: 7 {for ceremonial purification.} Hebrew *was detained before the L.*
2Sa 21: 6 {of the LORD.} As in Greek version (see also 21:9); Hebrew reads *at Gibeah of Saul, the chosen of the L.*
1Ki 18:31 {tribes of Israel,} Hebrew *each of the tribes of the sons of Jacob to whom the L had said, "Your name will be Israel."*
2Ch 30:21 {by loud instruments.} Or *sang to the L with all their strength.*
Ps 112: 4 {They are} Greek version reads *The L is.*
Isa 8:18 {me have names} *Isaiah* means "The L will save"; *Shear-jashub* means "A remnant will return"; and *Maher-shalal-hash-baz* means "Swift to plunder and quick to spoil."
61: 2 {favor has come,} Or *to proclaim the acceptable year of the L.*
Eze 3:12 {in his place!)} A likely reading for this verse is *Then the Spirit lifted me up, and as the glory of the L rose from its place, I heard behind me a loud rumbling sound.*
44:29 {anyone sets apart} The Hebrew term used here refers to the complete consecration of things or people to the L, either by destroying them or by giving them as an offering.
Joel 3: 2 {Jehoshaphat.} *Jehoshaphat* means "the L judges."
Mt 1:21 {name him Jesus,} *Jesus* means "The L saves."

LORD'S* (4)

Ex 17:16 {throne, so now} Or *Hands have been lifted up to the L throne, and now.*
Lev 16: 1 {LORD had commanded.} Hebrew *when they approached the L presence;* compare 10:1.
1Sa 10: 1 {his people Israel.} Greek version reads *Israel. And you will rule over the L people and save them from their enemies around them. This will be the sign to you that the LORD has appointed you to be leader over his inheritance.*
Pr 20:27 {the human spirit,} Or *The human spirit is the L searchlight.*

LOST (1)

Mt 18:10 {my heavenly Father.} Some manuscripts add verse 11, *And I, the Son of Man, have come to save the l.*

LOT (2)

1Sa 10:20 {Benjamin was chosen.} Hebrew *chosen by l;* also in 10:21.
14:41 {Saul were chosen} Hebrew *chosen by l.*

LOTS (7)

1Sa 14:42 {said, "Now choose} Hebrew *draw l.*
Ps 22:18 {and throw dice} Hebrew *cast l.*
Mt 27:35 {by throwing dice.} Greek *by casting l.* A few late manuscripts add *This fulfilled the word of the prophet: "They divided my clothes among themselves and cast l for my robe."* See Ps 22:18.
Mk 15:24 {clothes, throwing dice} Greek *casting l.* See Ps 22:18.
Lk 23:34 {by throwing dice.} Greek *by casting l.* See Ps 22:18.
Jn 19:24 {but throw dice} Greek *cast l.*

LOUD (1)

Eze 3:12 {in his place!)} A likely reading for this verse is *Then the Spirit lifted me up, and as the glory of the LORD rose from its place, I heard behind me a l rumbling sound.*

LOVE (9)

2Sa 15:20 {love and faithfulness.} As in Greek version; Hebrew reads *and may unfailing l and faithfulness go with you.*
SS 2: 7 {time is right.} Or *not to awaken l until it is ready.*
3: 5 {time is right.} Or *not to awaken l until it is ready.*
8: 4 {time is right.} Or *not to awaken l until it is ready.*
2Co 8: 7 {love for us} Some manuscripts read *l from us to you.*
Heb 13: 1 {true Christian love.} Greek *with brotherly l.*
1Pe 5:14 {in Christian love.} Greek *with a kiss of l.*
1Jn 4:19 {love each other} Or *We l him;* Greek reads *We l.*

LOVED (2)

Jn 13: 1 {of his love.} Or *He l his disciples to the very end.*
13:23 {at the table.} Greek *was reclining on Jesus' bosom.* The "disciple whom Jesus l" was probably John.

LOVES (1)

Ps 87: 2 {city in Israel.} Hebrew *He l the gates of Zion more than all the dwellings of Jacob.*

LOWER (1)

Ps 8: 5 {lower than God,} Or *a little l than the angels;* Hebrew reads *Elohim.*

LOWEST (1)

Eph 4: 9 {which we live.} Or *to the l parts of the earth.*

LOYAL (1)

Php 4: 3 {my true teammate,} Greek *true yokefellow,* or *l Syzygus.*

LUD (4)

Isa 66:19 {and Lydians} Hebrew *L.*
Jer 46: 9 {Libya, and Lydia} Hebrew *Cush, Put, and L.*
Eze 27:10 {Lydia, and Libya} Hebrew *Paras, L, and Put.*
30: 5 {Lydia,} Hebrew *L.*

LUKE (6)

Mt 8:28 {of the Gadarenes,} Some manuscripts read *Gerasenes;* other manuscripts read *Gergesenes.* See Mark 5:1; **L** 8:26.
Mk 5: 1 {of the Gerasenes.} Some manuscripts read *Gadarenes;* others read *Gergesenes.* See Matt 8:28; **L** 8:26.
Ac 1: 1 {my first book} The reference is to the book of **L**.
16:10 {So we} **L**, the writer of this book, here joined Paul and accompanied him on his journey.
1Co 7:10 {from the Lord.} See Matt 5:32; 19:9; Mark 10:11-12; **L** 16:18.
1Ti 5:18 {deserve their pay!"} Deut 25:4; **L** 10:7.

LUMP (1)

Ro 11:16 {also be holy.} Greek *If the dough offered as firstfruits is holy, so is the whole l.*

LUZ (1)

Jos 16: 2 {(that is, Luz)} As in Greek version (also see 18:13); Hebrew reads *From Bethel to L.*

LYRE (2)

Da 3: 7 {the musical instruments,} Aramaic *the horn, flute, zither, l, harp, and other instruments of the musical ensemble.*
3:10 {the musical instruments.} Aramaic *the horn, flute, zither, l, harp, pipes, and other instruments of the musical ensemble;* also in 3:15.

LYSIAS (1)

Ac 24: 6 {we arrested him.} Some manuscripts add *We would have judged him by our law, [7]but L, the commander of the garrison, came and took him violently away from us, [8]commanding his accusers to come before you.*

LYSTRA (1)

Ac 14: 1 {In Iconium,} *Iconium,* as well as **L** and *Derbe* (14:6), were cities in the land now called Turkey.

M

MAADIAH (1)

Ne 12: 5 {Miniamin, Moadiah,} Hebrew *Mijamin, M;* compare 12:17.

MACEDONIA (2)

Ro 15:26 {believers in Greece} Greek *M and Achaia,* the northern and southern regions of Greece.
1Th 1: 7 {Christians in Greece.} Greek *M and Achaia,* the northern and southern regions of Greece; also in 1:8.

MADE (9)

Lev 8:15 {atonement for it.} Or *that atonement may be m on it.*
1Sa 3:13 {are blaspheming God} As in Greek version; Hebrew reads *his sons have m themselves contemptible.*
2Ki 1: 8 {hairy man,} Or *He was wearing clothing m of hair.*
17:17 {in the fire.} Or *They even m their sons and daughters pass through the fire.*
21: 6 {in the fire.} Or *even m his son pass through the fire.*
2Ch 20:35 {very wicked man.} Or *who m him do what was wrong.*
33: 6 {in the fire} Or *even m his sons pass through the fire.*
Am 5:26 {you yourselves made.} Greek version reads *You took up the shrine of Molech, and the star of your god Rephan, and the images you m for yourselves.*
Heb 2: 7 {glory and honor.} Some manuscripts add *You put him in charge of everything you m.*

MADMEN (2)

Jer 48: 2 {city of Madmen,} *M* sounds like the Hebrew word for "silence"; it should not be confused with the English word *m.*

MAGI (1)

Mt 2: 1 {some wise men} Or *royal astrologers,* Greek *m;* also in 2:7, 16.

MAGISTRATES (1)

Da 3: 3 {all these officials} Aramaic *the princes, prefects, governors, advisers, counselors, judges, m, and all the provincial officials.*

MAGOR-MISSABIB (1)

Jer 20: 3 {Lives in Terror.'} Hebrew *M,* which means "surrounded by terror"; also in 20:10.

MAHANAIM (2)

Ge 32: 2 {the place Mahanaim.} *M* means "two camps."
SS 6:13 {lines of dancers?} Or *as you would at the movements of two armies?* or *as you would at the dance of M?* The meaning of the Hebrew is uncertain.

MAHANEH-DAN (1)

Jdg 18:12 {is called Mahaneh-dan} *M* means "the camp of Dan."

MAHER-SHALAL-HASH-BAZ (2)

Isa 8: 1 {on it: Maher-shalal-hash-baz.} *M* means "Swift to plunder and quick to spoil."
8:18 {me have names} *Isaiah* means "The LORD will save"; *Shear-jashub* means "A remnant will return"; and *M* means "Swift to plunder and quick to spoil."

MAJESTIC (1)

Lev 23:40 {from citrus trees,} Or *fruit from m trees.*

MAJOR (1)

Ac 18: 1 {went to Corinth.} *Athens* and *Corinth* were **m** cities in Achaia, the region on the southern end of the Greek peninsula.

MAKE (9)

Ge 24: 3 {"Swear} Hebrew *Put your hand under my thigh, and I will m you swear.*
Dt 18:10 {a burnt offering.} Or *never m your son or daughter pass through the fire.*
2Ki 2:21 {death or infertility.} Or *or m the land unproductive.*
23:10 {in the fire} Or *to m a son or daughter pass through the fire.*
Eze 20:31 {burned as sacrifices,} Or *and m your little children pass through the fire.*
Mal 2:15 {you are his.} Or *Did not one God m us and preserve our life and breath?* or *Did not one God m her, both flesh and spirit?* The meaning of the Hebrew is uncertain.
Mt 23:13 {go in yourselves.} Some manuscripts add verse 14, *How terrible it will be for you teachers of religious law and you Pharisees. Hypocrites! You shamelessly cheat widows out of their property, and then, to cover up the kind of people you really are, you m long prayers in public. Because of this, your punishment will be the greater.*
Ac 26:28 {Christian so quickly?"} Or *"A little more, and your arguments would m me a Christian."*

MAKES (3)

Job 32: 3 {had condemned God} As in ancient Hebrew scribal tradition; the Masoretic Text **m** no reference to God.
Pr 17:19 {who speaks boastfully} Or *who builds up defenses;* Hebrew reads *who m a high gate.*
Heb 9:16 {is dead.} Or *Now when someone m a covenant, it is necessary to ratify it with the death of a sacrifice.*

MAKING (3)

Ex 5:21 {situation with Pharaoh} Hebrew *for m us a stench in the nostrils of Pharaoh.*
2Ki 16: 3 {in the fire.} Or *even m his son pass through the fire.*
2Ch 28: 3 {in the fire.} Or *even m his sons pass through the fire.*

MAL (7)

Mt 11:10 {way before you.'} **M** 3:1.
11:14 {said would come.} See **M** 4:5.
Mk 1: 2 {prepare your way.} **M** 3:1.
Lk 1:17 {accept godly wisdom."} See **M** 4:5-6.
7:27 {way before you.'} **M** 3:1.
Jn 1:21 {you the Prophet?"} See Deut 18:15, 18; **M** 4:5-6.
Ro 9:13 {I rejected Esau."} **M** 1:2-3.

MALACHI (1)

Mal 1: 1 {the prophet Malachi.} *M* means "my messenger."

MALCAM (2)

Am 1:15 {And their king} Hebrew *m,* possibly referring to their god Molech.
Zep 1: 5 {they worship Molech,} Hebrew *M,* another name for Molech; or it could possibly mean *their king.*

MALE (1)

Zec 10: 3 {punish these leaders.} Or *these m goats.*

MALES (1)

Ac 4: 4 {women and children.} Greek *5,000 adult m.*

MALKIJAH (1)

Ezr 10:25 {Mijamin, Eleazar, Hashabiah,} As in parallel text at 1 Esdras 9:26; Hebrew reads *M.*

MALLUCHI (1)

Ne 12:14 {family of Malluch.} As in Greek version (see also 10:4; 12:2); Hebrew reads *M.*

MAN (31)

Ge 1:26 {us make people} Hebrew *m;* also in 1:27.
2:19 {them to Adam} Hebrew *the m,* and so throughout this chapter.
3: 9 {called to Adam,} Hebrew *the m,* and so throughout this chapter.
4: 1 {Now Adam} Hebrew *the m.*
5: 1 {God created people,} Hebrew *m.*
5: 2 {called them "human."} Hebrew *m.*
2Sa 17: 3 {that you seek.} As in Greek version; Hebrew reads *like the return of all is the m whom you seek.*
2Ki 23:16 {man of God} As in Greek version; Hebrew lacks *as Jeroboam stood beside the altar at the festival. Then Josiah turned and looked up at the tomb of the m of God.*
Ne 1:11 {ask the king} Hebrew *stand before this m.*

Ps 8: 4 {care for us?} Hebrew *What is **m** that you should think of him, the son of **m** that you should care for him?*
Pr 21:12 {The Righteous One} Or *The righteous **m**.*
24: 5 {strong man,} As in Greek version; Hebrew reads *A wise **m** is strength.*
30: 1 {worn out, O God.} The Hebrew can also be translated *The **m** declares this to Ithiel, to Ithiel and to Ucal.*
Da 7:13 {a man} Or *a Son of **M**;* Aramaic reads *a son of **m**.*
Mt 18:10 {my heavenly Father.} Some manuscripts add verse 11, *And I, the Son of **M**, have come to save the lost.*
19: 9 {has been unfaithful.} Some manuscripts add *And the **m** who marries a divorced woman commits adultery.*
Lk 9:55 {and rebuked them.} Some manuscripts add *And he said, "You don't realize what your hearts are like. [56]For the Son of **M** has not come to destroy men's lives, but to save them."*
15:21 {called your son.} Some manuscripts add *Please take me on as a hired **m**.*
17:30 {of Man returns.} Or *on the day the Son of **M** is revealed.*
Jn 13:32 {God will bring} Some manuscripts read *And if God is glorified in him [the Son of **M**], God will bring.*
2Co 12: 2 {I} Greek *I know a **m** in Christ who.*
Gal 6: 1 {if a Christian} Greek *Brothers, if a **m**.*
Php 2: 7 {in human form.} Greek *he was born in the likeness of men and was found in appearance as a **m**.*
1Ti 5: 9 {to her husband.} Greek *was the wife of one **m**.*
Heb 2: 6 {son of man} Or *Son of **M**.*
Rev 1:13 {Son of Man.} Or *one who looked like a **m**;* Greek reads *one like a son of **m**.*
14:14 {Son of Man} Or *one who looked like a **m**;* Greek reads *one like a son of **m**.*

MANASSEH (2 of 4)

Ge 41:51 {older son Manasseh,} ***M*** sounds like a Hebrew term that means "causing to forget."
Jdg 18:30 {descendant of Moses,} As in an ancient Hebrew tradition, some Greek manuscripts, and Latin Vulgate; Masoretic Text reads *of **M**.*

MANIFEST (1)

Ro 1:19 {to them instinctively.} Greek *is **m** in them.*

MANNA (1)

Ex 16:31 {manna.} ***M*** means "What is it?" See 16:15.

MANUSCRIPT (5)

1Ch 1:17 {of Aram were} As in one Hebrew **m** and some Greek manuscripts (see also Gen 10:23); most Hebrew manuscripts lack *The descendants of Aram were.*
25: 3 {Zeri, Jeshaiah, Shimei,} As in one Hebrew **m** and some Greek manuscripts (see also 25:17); most Hebrew manuscripts lack *Shimei.*
2Ch 20: 2 {army from Edom} As in one Hebrew **m**; most Hebrew manuscripts and ancient versions read *Aram.*
36: 9 {Jehoiachin was eighteen} As in one Hebrew **m**, some Greek manuscripts, and Syriac version (see also 2 Kgs 24:8); most Hebrew manuscripts read *eight.*
Da 10:16 {like a man} As in most manuscripts of the Masoretic Text; one **m** of the Masoretic Text and one Greek version read *Then something that looked like a human hand.*

MANUSCRIPTS (286)

Ge 10: 4 {Rodanim.} As in some Hebrew **m** and Greek version (see also 1 Chr 1:7); most Hebrew **m** read *Dodanim.*
36:39 {Baal-hanan died, Hadad} As in some Hebrew **m**, Samaritan Pentateuch, and Syriac version (see also 1 Chr 1:50); most Hebrew **m** read *Hadar.*
46:13 {Jashub,} As in some Greek **m** and Samaritan Pentateuch (see also Num 26:24; 1 Chr 7:1); Hebrew reads *Iob.*
Nu 2:14[-15] {son of Deuel} As in many Hebrew **m**, Samaritan Pentateuch, and Latin Vulgate (see also 1:14); most Hebrew **m** read *son of Reuel.*
3:28 {There were 8,600} Some Greek **m** read *8,300;* see total in 3:39.
26:39 {its ancestor Shupham.} As in some Hebrew **m**, Samaritan Pentateuch, Greek and Syriac versions, and Latin Vulgate; most Hebrew **m** read *Shephupham.*
26:40 {their ancestor Ard.} As in Samaritan Pentateuch, some Greek **m**, and Latin Vulgate; Hebrew lacks *named after their ancestor Ard.*
Dt 34: 6 {He was buried} Hebrew *He buried him,* that is, "The LORD buried him." Samaritan Pentateuch and some Greek **m** read *They buried him.*
Jos 8:17 {Ai or Bethel} Some **m** lack *or Bethel.*
15:18 {she urged him} Some Greek **m** read *Othniel urged her.*
19:28 {Abdon,} As in some Hebrew **m** (see also 21:30); most Hebrew **m** read *Ebron.*
22:34 {the altar "Witness,"} Hebrew *edh.* Some **m** lack this word.
Jdg 18:30 {descendant of Moses,} As in an ancient Hebrew tradition, some Greek **m**, and Latin Vulgate; Masoretic Text reads *of Manasseh.*
Ru 3:15 {back. Then Boaz} Most Hebrew **m** read *he;* many Hebrew **m**, Syriac version, and Latin Vulgate read *she.*
1Sa 1:11 {never be cut."} Some **m** add *He will drink neither wine nor intoxicants.*
1:22 {the LORD permanently."} Some **m** add *I will offer him as a Nazirite for all time.*
2:22 {of the Tabernacle.} Hebrew *Tent of Meeting.* Some **m** lack this entire sentence.
6:19 {killed seventy men} As in a few Hebrew **m**; most Hebrew **m** and Greek version read *50,070 men.* Perhaps the text should be understood to read *the LORD killed 70 men and 50 oxen.*
13: 1 {Saul was thirty} As in a few Greek **m**; the number is missing in the Hebrew.
14:18 {of the Israelites.} As in some Greek **m**; Hebrew reads *"Bring the Ark of God." For at that time the Ark of God was with the Israelites.*
17:52 {far as Gath} As in some Greek **m**; Hebrew reads *a valley.*
23:11 {me to him?} Some **m** lack the first sentence of 23:11.
2Sa 8: 8 {cities of Tebah} As in some Greek **m** (see also 1 Chr 18:8); Hebrew reads *Betah.*
8:12 {Edom,} As in a few Hebrew **m** and Greek and Syriac versions (see also 8:14; 1 Chr 18:11); most Hebrew **m** read *Aram.*
8:13 {eighteen thousand Edomites} As in a few Hebrew **m** and Greek and Syriac versions (see also 8:14; 1 Chr 18:12); most Hebrew **m** read *Arameans.*
10:18 {forty thousand horsemen,} Some Greek **m** read *foot soldiers;* compare parallel text at 1 Chr 19:18.
17:25 {an Ishmaelite.} As in some Greek **m** (see also 1 Chr 2:17); Hebrew reads *an Israelite.*
21: 8 {Saul's daughter Merab,} As in a few Hebrew and Greek **m** and Syriac version (see also 1 Sam 18:19); most Hebrew **m** read *Michal.*
22:11 {soaring} As in some Hebrew **m** (see also Ps 18:10); other Hebrew **m** read *appearing.*
22:36 {your help} As in Dead Sea Scrolls; most Hebrew **m** read *your answering.*
23: 8 {a single battle.} As in some Greek **m** (see also 1 Chr 11:11); the Hebrew is uncertain, though it might be rendered *the Three. It was Adino the Eznite who killed eight hundred men at one time.*
23:18 {of the Thirty.} As in a few Hebrew **m** and Syriac version; most Hebrew **m** read *the Three.*
23:27 {Sibbecai} As in some Greek **m** (see also 1 Chr 11:29); Hebrew reads *Mebunnai.*
23:29 {Heled} As in some Hebrew **m** (see also 1 Chr 11:30); most Hebrew **m** read *Heleb.*
23:30 {Hurai} As in some Greek **m** (see also 1 Chr 11:32); Hebrew reads *Hiddai.*
23:33 {son of Shagee} As in parallel text at 1 Chr 11:34; Hebrew reads *Jonathan, Shammah;* some Greek **m** read *Jonathan son of Shammah.*
1Ki 4:19 {land of Judah.} As in some Greek **m**; Hebrew lacks *of Judah.* The meaning of the Hebrew is uncertain.
4:26 {had four thousand} As in some Greek **m** (see also 2 Chr 9:25); Hebrew reads *40,000.*
5:16 {and thirty-six hundred} As in some Greek **m** (see also 2 Chr 2:2, 18); Hebrew reads *3,300.*
12:18 {Rehoboam sent Adoniram,} As in some Greek **m** and Syriac version (see also 4:6; 5:14); Hebrew reads *Adoram.*
15: 6 {Abijam and Jeroboam} As in a few Hebrew **m**; most Hebrew **m** read *between Rehoboam and Jeroboam.*
2Ki 10: 1 {of the city,} As in some Greek **m** and Latin Vulgate (see also 10:6); Hebrew reads *of Jezreel.*
15:16 {town of Tappuah} As in some Greek **m**; Hebrew reads *Tiphsah.*
1Ch 1: 6 {were Ashkenaz, Riphath,} As in some Hebrew **m** and Greek version (see also Gen 10:3); most Hebrew **m** read *Diphath.*
1:17 {of Aram were} As in one Hebrew manuscript and some Greek **m** (see also Gen 10:23); most Hebrew **m** lack *The descendants of Aram were.*
1:22 {Obal,} As in some Hebrew **m** and Syriac version (see also Gen 10:28); most Hebrew **m** read *Ebal.*
1:24 {Shem: Arphaxad, Shelah,} Some Greek **m** read *Arphaxad, Cainan, Shelah.* See notes on Gen 10:24 and 11:12-13.
1:36 {Zepho,} As in many Hebrew **m** and a few Greek **m** (see also Gen 36:11); most Hebrew **m** read *Zephi.*
1:36 {born to Timna.} As in some Greek **m** (see also Gen 36:12); Hebrew reads *Kenaz, Timna, and Amalek.*
1:40 {Alvan,} As in many Hebrew **m** and a few Greek **m** (see also Gen 36:23); most Hebrew **m** read *Alian.*
1:40 {Shepho,} As in some Hebrew **m** (see also Gen 36:23); most Hebrew **m** read *Shephi.*
1:41 {Hemdan,} As in many Hebrew **m** and some Greek **m** (see also Gen 36:26); most Hebrew **m** read *Hamran.*
1:42 {Akan.} As in many Hebrew and Greek **m** (see also Gen 36:27); most Hebrew **m** read *Jaakan.*
1:50 {city of Pau.} As in many Hebrew **m**, some Greek **m**, Syriac version, and Latin Vulgate (see also Gen 36:39); most Hebrew **m** read *Pai.*
2: 6 {Darda} As in many Hebrew **m**, some Greek **m**, and Syriac version (see also 1 Kgs 4:31); Hebrew reads *Dara.*
3: 6 {Elishua,} As in some Hebrew and Greek **m** (see also 14:5-7 and 2 Sam 5:15); most Hebrew **m** read *Elishama.*
4:13 {Hathath and Meonothai.} As in some Greek **m** and Latin Vulgate; Hebrew lacks *and Meonothai.*
4:33 {away as Baalath.} As in some Greek **m** (see also Josh 19:8); Hebrew reads *Baal.*
6:27 {Elkanah, and Samuel.} As in some Greek **m** (see also 6:33-34); Hebrew lacks *and Samuel.*
6:28 {Samuel were Joel} As in some Greek **m** and the Syriac version (see also 6:33 and 1 Sam 8:2); Hebrew lacks *Joel.*
7:13 {Shillem.} As in some Hebrew and Greek **m** (see also Gen 46:24; Num 26:49); most Hebrew **m** read *Shallum.*
8:29 {Jeiel} As in some Greek **m** (see also 9:35); Hebrew lacks *Jeiel.*
8:30 {Kish, Baal, Ner,} As in some Greek **m** (see also 9:36); Hebrew lacks *Ner.*
9:42 {father of Jadah.} As in some Hebrew **m** and Greek version (see also 8:36); Hebrew reads *Jarah.*
11:11 {among David's men.} As in some Greek **m** (see also 2 Sam 23:8); Hebrew *commander of the Thirty,* or *commander of the captains.*
16:15 {by his covenant} As in some Greek **m** (see also Ps 105:8); Hebrew reads *Remember his covenant forever.*
18:16 {Ahitub and Ahimelech} As in some Hebrew **m**, Syriac version, and Latin Vulgate (see also 2 Sam 8:17); most Hebrew **m** read *Abimelech.*
25: 3 {Shimei,} As in one Hebrew manuscript and some Greek **m** (see also 25:17); most Hebrew **m** lack *Shimei.*
2Ch 3: 4 {was thirty feet} As in some Greek and Syriac **m**, which read *20 cubits* [9 meters]; Hebrew reads *120 cubits,* which is 180 feet or 54 meters.
13: 2 {mother was Maacah,} As in most Greek **m** and Syriac version (see also 2 Chr 11:20-21; 1 Kgs 15:2); Hebrew reads *Micaiah.*
17: 3 {father's early years} Some Hebrew **m** read *the example of his father, David.*
20: 1 {of the Meunites} As in some Greek **m** (see also 26:7); Hebrew reads *Ammonites.*
20: 2 {army from Edom} As in one Hebrew manuscript; most Hebrew **m** and ancient versions read *Aram.*
20:25 {of equipment, clothing,} As in some Hebrew **m** and Latin Vulgate; most Hebrew **m** read *corpses.*
22: 2 {Ahaziah was twenty-two} As in some Greek **m** and Syriac version (see also 2 Kgs 8:26); Hebrew reads *forty-two.*
22: 6 {and King Ahaziah} Some Hebrew **m**, Greek and Syriac versions, and Latin Vulgate (see also 2 Kgs 8:29); most Hebrew **m** read *Azariah.*
25:28 {City of David.} As in some Hebrew **m** and other ancient versions (see also 2 Kgs 14:20); most Hebrew **m** read *the city of Judah.*
36: 9 {Jehoiachin was eighteen} As in one Hebrew manuscript, some Greek **m**, and Syriac version (see also 2 Kgs 24:8); most Hebrew **m** read *eight.*
Ezr 2:25 {peoples of Kiriath-jearim,} As in some Hebrew **m** and Greek version (see also Neh 7:29); Hebrew reads *Kiriath-arim.*
8: 5 {family of Zattu} As in some Greek **m** (see also 1 Esdras 8:32); Hebrew lacks *Zattu.*
8:10 {family of Bani} As in some Greek **m** (see also 1 Esdras 8:36); Hebrew lacks *Bani.*
Ne 3:18 {led by Binnui} As in a few Hebrew **m**, some Greek **m**, and Syriac version (see also 3:24; 10:9); most Hebrew **m** read *Bavvai.*
7:68 {horses, 245 mules,} As in some Hebrew **m** (see also Ezra 2:66); most Hebrew **m** lack this verse.
12: 4 {Iddo, Ginnethon,} As in some Hebrew **m** and Latin Vulgate (see also 12:16); most Hebrew **m** read *Ginnethoi.*
12:14 {family of Shecaniah.} As in many Hebrew **m**, some Greek **m**, and Syriac version (see also 12:3); most Hebrew **m** read *Shebaniah.*
12:15 {family of Meremoth.} As in some Greek **m** (see also 12:3); Hebrew reads *Meraioth.*
Ps 119:37 {through your word.} Some **m** read *in your ways.*
144: 2 {subdues the nations} Some **m** read *my people.*
145: 5 {I will meditate} Some **m** read *They will speak.*
145:13 {all he does.} The last two lines of 145:13 are not found in many of the ancient **m**.
Ecc 8:10 {are praised} As in some Hebrew **m** and Greek version; many Hebrew **m** read *and are forgotten.*
Isa 15: 9 {Dibon} As in Dead Sea Scrolls, some Greek **m**, and Latin Vulgate; Hebrew reads *Dimon;*...
21:16 {within a year,"} Hebrew *Within a year, like the years of a hired hand.* Some ancient **m** read *Within three years,* as in 16:14.
66:19 {to the Libyans} As in some Greek **m**, which read *Put* [Libya]; Hebrew reads *Pul.*
Jer 27: 1 {reign of Zedekiah} As in some Hebrew **m** and Syriac version (see also 27:3, 12); most Hebrew **m** read *Jehoiakim.*
Eze 6:14 {south to Riblah} As in some Hebrew **m**; most Hebrew **m** read *Diblah.*
16:57 {by Edom} Many ancient **m** read *Aram.*
27:16 {"Aram} Some **m** read *Edom.*
40: 8 {of the gateway} Many Hebrew **m** add *which faced inward toward the Temple; it was one rod* [10.5 feet or 3.2 meters] *deep. [9]Then he measured the foyer of the gateway,...*

Da 10:16 {like a man} As in most **m** of the Masoretic Text; one manuscript of the Masoretic Text and one Greek version read *Then something that looked like a human hand.*
Hab 2: 5 {Wealth} As in Dead Sea Scroll 1QpHab; other Hebrew **m** read *Wine.*
Mt 5:22 {angry with someone,} Some **m** add *without cause.*
5:44 {love your enemies!} Some **m** add *Bless those who curse you, do good to those who hate you.*
6:13 {the evil one.} Or *from evil.* Some **m** add *For yours is the kingdom and the power and the glory forever. Amen.*
8:28 {of the Gadarenes,} Some **m** read *Gerasenes;* other **m** read *Gergesenes.* See Mark 5:1; Luke 8:26.
16: 2[-3] {of the times!} Several **m** do not include any of the words in 16:2-3 after *He replied.*
17:20 {would be impossible."} Some **m** add verse 21, *But this kind of demon won't leave unless you have prayed and fasted.*
18:10 {my heavenly Father.} Some **m** add verse 11, *And I, the Son of Man, have come to save the lost.*
19: 9 {has been unfaithful.} Some **m** add *And the man who marries a divorced woman commits adultery.*
19:16 {this question: "Teacher,} Some **m** read *Good Teacher.*
21:44 {whom it falls.} This verse is omitted in some early **m**.
23:13 {go in yourselves.} Some **m** add verse 14, *How terrible it will be for you teachers of religious law and you Pharisees. Hypocrites! You shamelessly cheat widows out of their property, and then, to cover up the kind of people you really are, you make long prayers in public. Because of this, your punishment will be the greater.*
24:36 {the Son himself.} Some **m** omit the phrase *or the Son himself.*
26:28 {seals the covenant} Some **m** read *the new covenant.*
27:16 {man named Barabbas.} Some **m** read *Jesus Barabbas;* also in 27:17.
27:35 {by throwing dice.} Greek *by casting lots.* A few late **m** add *This fulfilled the word of the prophet: "They divided my clothes among themselves and cast lots for my robe."* See Ps 22:18.
27:49 {and save him."} Some **m** add *And another took a spear and pierced his side, and out came water and blood.*
Mk 1: 1 {Son of God.} Some **m** do not include *the Son of God.*
1:41 {Moved with pity,} Some **m** read *Moved with anger.*
3:14 {calling them apostles.} Some **m** do not include *calling them apostles.*
3:32 {brothers and sisters} Some **m** do not include *and sisters.*
5: 1 {of the Gerasenes.} Some **m** read *Gadarenes;* others read *Gergesenes.* See Matt 8:28; Luke 8:26.
6:14 {Some were saying,} Some **m** read *He was saying.*
6:22 {also named Herodias,} Some **m** read *the daughter of Herodias herself.*
7: 4 {pitchers, and kettles.} Some Greek **m** add *and dining couches.*
7:15 {say and do!} Some **m** add verse 16, *Anyone who is willing to hear should listen and understand.*
7:24 {region of Tyre.} Some Greek **m** add *and Sidon.*
9:29 {only by prayer.} Some **m** add *and fasting.*
9:43 {with two hands.} Some **m** add verse 44 (which is identical with 9:48).
9:45 {with two feet.} Some **m** add verse 46 (which is identical with 9:48).
9:49 {purified with fire.} Greek *salted with fire.* Some **m** add *and every sacrifice will be salted with salt.*
10: 7 {to his wife,} Some **m** do not include *and is joined to his wife.*
10:24 {is very hard} Some **m** add *for those who trust in riches.*
11:19 {and the disciples} Greek *they;* some **m** read *he.*
11:25 {your sins, too.} Some **m** add verse 26, *But if you do not forgive, neither will your Father who is in heaven forgive your sins.*
13:33 {and keep watch.} Some **m** add *and pray.*
14:24 {the covenant} Some **m** read *the new covenant.*
14:68 {a rooster crowed.} Some **m** do not include *Just then, a rooster crowed.*
15:27 {side of his.} Some **m** add verse 28, *And the Scripture was fulfilled that said, "He was counted among those who were rebels."* See Isa 53:12.
16: 8 {frightened to talk.} The most reliable early **m** conclude the Gospel of Mark at verse 8. Other **m** include various endings to the Gospel. Two of the more noteworthy endings are printed here.
16:17 {speak new languages.} Or *new tongues;* some **m** omit *new.*
Lk 1:28 {is with you!} Some **m** add *Blessed are you among women.*
2:14 {whom God favors.} Or *and peace on earth for all those pleasing God;* some **m** read *and peace on earth, goodwill among people.*
3:22 {pleased with you.} Some **m** read *and today I have become your Father.*
4:44 {synagogues throughout Judea.} Some **m** read *Galilee.*
8:26 {of the Gerasenes,} Some **m** read *Gadarenes;* other **m** read *Gergesenes.* See Matt 8:28; Mark 5:1.
8:43 {had on doctors} Some **m** omit *She had spent everything she had on doctors.*
9:35 {my Chosen One.} Some **m** read *This is my beloved Son.*
9:54 {burn them up} Some **m** add *as Elijah did.*
9:55 {and rebuked them.} Some **m** add *And he said, "You don't realize what your hearts are like.* [56]*For the Son of Man has not come to destroy men's lives, but to save them."*
10: 1 {now chose seventy-two} Some **m** read *70;* also in 10:17.
11: 2[-4] {yield to temptation.} Some **m** add additional portions of the Lord's Prayer as it reads in Matt 6:9-13.
11:11 {your children ask} Some **m** add *for bread, do you give them a stone? Or if they ask.*
14: 5 {If your son} Some **m** read *donkey.*
15:21 {called your son.} Some **m** add *Please take me on as a hired man.*
17:35 {the other left.} Some **m** add verse 36, *Two men will be working in the field; one will be taken, the other left.*
22:19[-20] {out for you.} Some **m** omit 22:19b-20, *given for you…I will pour out for you.*
22:43[-44] {drops of blood.} These verses are not included in many ancient **m**.
23:16 {will release him."} Some **m** add verse 17, *For it was necessary for him to release one [prisoner] for them during the feast.*
23:34 {they are doing."} This sentence is not included in many ancient **m**.
24:12 {what had happened.} Some **m** do not include this verse.
24:36 {be with you."} Some **m** do not include *He said, "Peace be with you."*
24:40 {them his feet.} Some **m** do not include this verse.
24:51 {up to heaven.} Some **m** do not include *and was taken up to heaven.*
24:52 {worshiped him and} Some **m** do not include *worshiped him and.*
Jn 1:18 {is himself God,} Some **m** read *his one and only Son.*
1:34 {Son of God.} Some **m** read *the chosen One of God.*
3:13 {Son of Man,} Some **m** add *who lives in heaven.*
3:31 {come from heaven.} Some **m** omit *but he has come from heaven.*
4: 1 {Jesus} Some **m** read *The Lord.*
5: 2 {pool of Bethesda,} Some **m** read *Beth-zatha;* other **m** read *Bethsaida.*
5: 3 {on the porches.} Some **m** add *waiting for a certain movement of the water,* [4]*for an angel of the Lord came from time to time and stirred up the water. And the first person to step down into it afterward was healed.*
7: 8 {am not yet} Some **m** omit *yet.*
8:39 {his good example.} Some **m** read *if you are children of Abraham, follow his example.*
8:57 {have seen Abraham?} Some **m** read *How can you say Abraham has seen you?*
9:35 {Son of Man} Some **m** read *the Son of God.*
11:25 {and the life.} Some **m** do not include *and the life.*
13:10 {for the feet,} Some **m** do not include *except for the feet.*
13:32 {God will bring} Some **m** read *And if God is glorified in him [the Son of Man], God will bring.*
14: 7 {my Father is.} Some **m** read *If you really have known me, you will know who my Father is.*
20:31 {you may believe} Some **m** read *may continue to believe.*
Ac 7:46 {God of Jacob.} Some **m** read *the house of Jacob.*
8:36 {I be baptized?"} Some **m** add verse 37, *"You can," Philip answered, "if you believe with all your heart." And the eunuch replied, "I believe that Jesus Christ is the Son of God."*
11:20 {preaching to Gentiles} Greek *the Greeks;* other **m** read *the Hellenists.*
13:18 {up with them} Other **m** read *He cared for them;* compare Deut 1:31.
15:33 {had sent them.} Some **m** add verse 34, *But Silas decided to stay there.*
17: 4 {of the city.} Some **m** read *many of the wives of the leading men.*
18:21 {come back later,} Some **m** read *"I must by all means be at Jerusalem for the upcoming festival, but I will come back later."*
24: 6 {we arrested him.} Some **m** add *We would have judged him by our law,* [7]*but Lysias, the commander of the garrison, came and took him violently away from us,* [8]*commanding his accusers to come before you.*
27:16 {island named Cauda,} Some **m** read *Clauda.*
28:28 {will accept it."} Some **m** add verse 29, *And when he had said these words, the Jews departed, greatly disagreeing with each other.*
Ro 8: 2 {has freed you} Some **m** read *me.*
8:28 {to work together} Some **m** read *And we know that everything works together.*
11:31 {But someday they} Some **m** read *But now they;* other **m** read *But they.*
16: 7 {Andronicus and Junia,} Or *Junias;* some **m** read *Julia.*
16:23 {a Christian brother.} Some **m** add verse 24, *May the grace of our Lord Jesus Christ be with you all. Amen.*
1Co 2: 1 {you God's message.} Greek *mystery;* other **m** read *testimony.*
10: 9 {we put Christ} Some **m** read *the Lord.*
11:24 {which is given} Some **m** read *broken.*
11:29 {body of Christ,} Greek *the body;* some **m** read *the Lord's body.*
13: 3 {boast about it;} Some **m** read *and even gave my body to be burned.*
14:35 {in church meetings.} Some **m** place verses 34-35 after 14:40.
14:38 {not be recognized.} Some **m** read *If you are ignorant of this, stay in your ignorance.*
16:24 {in Christ Jesus.} Some **m** add *Amen.*
2Co 1:12 {have been honest} Some **m** read *holy.*
3: 2 {written in our} Some **m** read *your.*
8: 7 {love for us} Some **m** read *love from us to you.*
Eph 1: 1 {people in Ephesus,} Some **m** do not include *in Ephesus.*
3:14 {to the Father,} Some **m** read *the Father of our Lord Jesus Christ.*
Php 3: 3 {in the Spirit} Or *in spirit;* some **m** read *worship by the Spirit of God.*
3:13 {I should be,} Some **m** read *I am not all I should be.*
Col 1: 7 {in your place.} Greek *he is ministering on your behalf;* other **m** read *he is ministering on our behalf.*
1:14 {with his blood} Some **m** do not include *with his blood.*
3: 4 {who is your} Some **m** read *our.*
1Th 2: 7 {as a mother} Some **m** read *we were as infants among you; we were as a mother.*
2Th 2:13 {among the first} Some **m** read *God chose you from the very beginning.*
1Ti 3:16 {Christ} Greek *Who;* some **m** read *God.*
4:10 {and suffer much} Some **m** read *and strive.*
Heb 2: 7 {glory and honor.} Some **m** add *You put him in charge of everything you made.*
4: 2 {God told them.} Some **m** read *they didn't share the faith of those who listened [to God].*
11:11 {keep his promise.} Some **m** read *It was by faith that Sarah was able to have a child, even though she was too old and barren. Sarah believed that God would keep his promise.*
1Pe 1:22 {all your hearts.} Some **m** read *with a pure heart.*
2Pe 2: 4 {in gloomy caves} Some **m** read *chains of gloom.*
2:15 {son of Beor,} Other **m** read *Bosor.*
3:10 {exposed to judgment.} Some **m** read *will be burned up.*
1Jn 1: 4 {so that our} Some **m** read *your.*
5: 7 {these three witnesses} Some very late **m** add *in heaven—the Father, the Word, and the Holy Spirit, and these three are one. And we have three witnesses on earth.*
2Jn 1: 8 {for which we} Some **m** read *you.*
Jude 1: 5 {though the Lord} Some **m** read *Jesus.*
Rev 5:10 {they will reign} Some **m** read *they are reigning.*
12:18 {Then he stood} Some **m** read *Then I stood,* and some translations put this entire sentence into 13:1.
13:18 {number is 666.} Some **m** read *616.*
15: 3 {of the nations.} Some **m** read *King of the ages;* other **m** read *King of the saints.*
15: 6 {spotless white linen} Some **m** read *in bright and sparkling stone.*
21: 3 {be with them.} Some **m** read *God himself will be with them, their God.*

MANY (8 of 23)

Ge 17: 5 {known as Abraham,} *Abram* means "exalted father"; *Abraham* means "father of **m**."
37: 3 {gift—a beautiful robe.} Traditionally rendered *a coat of **m** colors.* The exact meaning of the Hebrew is uncertain.
Mt 19:30 {the greatest then.} Greek *But **m** who are first will be last; and the last, first.*
27:51[-53] {to many people.} Or *The earth shook, rocks split apart, tombs opened, and **m** bodies of godly men and women who had died were raised from the dead. After Jesus' resurrection, they left the cemetery, went into the holy city of Jerusalem, and appeared to **m** people.*
Mk 10:31 {the greatest then.} Greek *But **m** who are first will be last; and the last, first.*
Lk 17:25 {must suffer terribly} Or *suffer **m** things.*
Ac 17: 4 {of the city.} Some manuscripts read ***m** of the wives of the leading men.*

MARA (1)

Ru 1:20 {call me Mara,} *Naomi* means "pleasant"; ***M*** means "bitter."

MARANA (1)

1Co 16:22 {Our Lord, come!} From Aramaic, ***M** tha.*

MARE (1)

SS 1: 9 {my beloved one!} Hebrew *I compare you, my beloved, to a **m** among Pharaoh's chariots.*

MARESHAH (2)

2Ch 14:10 {north of Mareshah.} Or *in the Zephathah Valley near **M**.*
Mic 1:15 {people of Mareshah,} ***M*** sounds like the Hebrew term for "conqueror."

MARGINAL (3)

1Ki 9:18 {Baalath, and Tamar} The **m** *Qere* reading of the Masoretic Text reads *Tadmor.*

2Ki 16: 6 {and sent Edomites} As in **m** *Qere* reading of the Masoretic Text, Greek version, and Latin Vulgate; Hebrew reads *Arameans.*
Ezr 2:46 {Hagab, Shalmai,} As in the **m** *Qere* reading of the Masoretic Text (see also Neh 7:48); Hebrew text reads *Shamlai.*

MARK (4)

Mt 8:28 {of the Gadarenes,} Some manuscripts read *Gerasenes;* other manuscripts read *Gergesenes.* See **M** 5:1; Luke 8:26.
Mk 16: 8 {frightened to talk.} The most reliable early manuscripts conclude the Gospel of **M** at verse 8. Other manuscripts include various endings to the Gospel. Two of the more noteworthy endings are printed here.
Lk 8:26 {of the Gerasenes,} Some manuscripts read *Gadarenes;* other manuscripts read *Gergesenes.* See Matt 8:28; **M** 5:1.
1Co 7:10 {from the Lord.} See Matt 5:32; 19:9; **M** 10:11-12; Luke 16:18.

MARKER (1)

Hos 5:10 {bad as thieves.} Hebrew *have become as those who move a boundary **m**.*

MAROTH (1)

Mic 1:12 {people of Maroth} ***M*** sounds like the Hebrew term for "bitter."

MARRIED (2)

Isa 62: 4 {Bride of God,} Hebrew *Beulah,* which means "**m**."
Tit 1: 6 {to his wife,} Or *have only one wife,* or *be **m** only once;* Greek reads *be the husband of one wife.*

MARRIES (1)

Mt 19: 9 {has been unfaithful.} Some manuscripts add *And the man who **m** a divorced woman commits adultery.*

MARS (1)

Ac 17:22 {before the Council,} Or *in the middle of **M** Hill;* Greek reads *in the middle of the Areopagus.*

MASORETIC (16)

Dt 31: 1 {had finished saying} As in Dead Sea Scrolls and Greek version; **M** Text reads *Moses went and spoke.*
32: 8 {of angelic beings.} As in Dead Sea Scrolls, which read *of the sons of God,* and Greek version, which reads *of the angels of god;* **M** Text reads *of the sons of Israel.*
32:43 {God worship him,} As in Dead Sea Scrolls and Greek version; **M** Text reads *Rejoice with his people, O nations.*
Jdg 18:30 {descendant of Moses,} As in an ancient Hebrew tradition, some Greek manuscripts, and Latin Vulgate; **M** Text reads *of Manasseh.*
1Sa 2:33 {a violent death.} As in Dead Sea Scrolls, which read *die by the sword;* **M** Text reads *die like mortals.*
1Ki 9:18 {Baalath, and Tamar} The marginal *Qere* reading of the **M** Text reads *Tadmor.*
2Ki 16: 6 {and sent Edomites} As in marginal *Qere* reading of the **M** Text, Greek version, and Latin Vulgate; Hebrew reads *Arameans.*
Ezr 2:46 {Hagab, Shalmai,} As in the marginal *Qere* reading of the **M** Text (see also Neh 7:48); Hebrew text reads *Shamlai.*
Job 32: 3 {had condemned God} As in ancient Hebrew scribal tradition; the **M** Text makes no reference to God.
Isa 33: 8 {made before witnesses.} As in Dead Sea Scrolls; **M** Text reads *care nothing for the cities.*
45: 2 {level the mountains.} As in Dead Sea Scrolls and Greek version; **M** Text reads *the swellings.*
49:12 {south as Egypt.} As in Dead Sea Scrolls, which read *from the region of Aswan,* which is in southern Egypt. **M** Text reads *from the region of Sinim.*
49:24 {that a tyrant} As in Dead Sea Scrolls, Syriac version, and Latin Vulgate (also see 49:25); **M** Text reads *a righteous person.*
Da 10:16 {like a man} As in most manuscripts of the **M** Text; one manuscript of the **M** Text and one Greek version read *Then something that looked like a human hand.*
Hos 4: 7 {They have exchanged} As in Syriac version and an ancient Hebrew tradition; **M** Text reads *I will exchange.*

MASSA (2)

Pr 30: 1 {Jakeh. An oracle.} Or *son of Jakeh from **M**.*
31: 1 {Lemuel, an oracle} Or *of Lemuel, king of **M**.*

MASSAH (1)

Dt 9:22 {Massah,} ***M*** means "place of testing." See Exod 17:1-7.

MASTER (2)

Ge 24: 9 {solemn oath} Hebrew *put his hand under the thigh of Abraham his **m** and swore an oath.*
Mt 23: 7 {being called 'Rabbi.'} *Rabbi,* from Aramaic, means "**m**" or "teacher."

MATT (6)

Mk 5: 1 {of the Gerasenes.} Some manuscripts read *Gadarenes;* others read *Gergesenes.* See **M** 8:28; Luke 8:26.
6: 3 {of James, Joseph,} Greek *Joses;* see **M** 13:55.
15:40 {and of Joseph} Greek *Joses;* also in 15:47. See **M** 27:56.
Lk 8:26 {of the Gerasenes,} Some manuscripts read *Gadarenes;* other manuscripts read *Gergesenes.* See **M** 8:28; Mark 5:1.
11: 2[-4] {yield to temptation.} Some manuscripts add additional portions of the Lord's Prayer as it reads in **M** 6:9-13.
1Co 7:10 {from the Lord.} See **M** 5:32; 19:9; Mark 10:11-12; Luke 16:18.

MATTER (3)

Ezr 2:63 {of sacred lots.} Hebrew *consult the Urim and Thummim about the **m**.*
Ne 7:65 {of sacred lots.} Hebrew *consult the Urim and Thummim about the **m**.*
2Pe 1:20 {the prophets themselves} Or *is a **m** of one's own interpretation.*

MATURE (1)

Col 1:28 {to God, perfect} Or ***m**.*

ME-NEPHTOAH (2)

Jos 15: 9 {waters of Nephtoah,} Or *the spring at **M**.*
18:15 {waters of Nephtoah,} Or *the spring at **M**.*

MEAN (12)

Ge 4: 1 {birth to Cain,} *Cain* sounds like a Hebrew term that can **m** "bring forth" or "acquire."
4:25 {named him Seth,} *Seth* probably means "granted"; the name may also **m** "appointed."
5:29 {his son Noah,} *Noah* sounds like a Hebrew term that can **m** "relief" or "comfort."
25:26 {called him Jacob.} *Jacob* means "he grasps the heel"; this can also figuratively **m** "he deceives."
26:33 {the well "Oath,"} Hebrew *Shibah,* which can **m** "oath" or "seven."
27:36 {name is Jacob,} *Jacob* means "he grasps the heel"; this can also figuratively **m** "he deceives."
35:10 {be called Israel."} *Jacob* means "he grasps the heel"; this can also figuratively **m** "he deceives"; *Israel* means "God struggles" or "one who struggles with God."
2Ki 18: 4 {was called Nehushtan.} *Nehushtan* sounds like the Hebrew terms that **m** "snake," "bronze," and "unclean thing."
Hos 12: 2 {to punish Jacob} *Jacob* means "he grasps at the heel"; this can also figuratively **m** "he deceives."
Zep 1: 5 {they worship Molech,} Hebrew *Malcam,* another name for Molech; or it could possibly **m** *their king.*
Jn 1:42 {(which means Peter} The names *Cephas* and *Peter* both **m** "rock."
Ac 9:36 {Greek is Dorcas} The names *Tabitha* in Aramaic and *Dorcas* in Greek both **m** "gazelle."

MEANING (79)

Ge 25:18 {to one another.} The **m** of the Hebrew is uncertain.
29:17 {had pretty eyes,} Or *dull eyes.* The **m** of the Hebrew is uncertain.
30: 6 {named him Dan,} *Dan* is a play on the Hebrew term **m** "to vindicate" or "to judge."
37: 3 {gift—a beautiful robe.} Traditionally rendered *a coat of many colors.* The exact **m** of the Hebrew is uncertain.
48:22 {an extra portion} Or *give you the ridge of land.* The **m** of the Hebrew is uncertain.
Ex 28:32 {a woven collar} The **m** of the Hebrew is uncertain.
39:23 {a woven collar,} The **m** of the Hebrew is uncertain.
Lev 1:16 {and the feathers} Or *the crop and its contents.* The **m** of the Hebrew is uncertain.
6:21 {mixed and broken} The **m** of this Hebrew term is uncertain.
21: 4 {among his relatives,} The **m** of the Hebrew is uncertain.
Nu 21:30 {Nophah and Medeba.} Or *until fire spread to Medeba.* The **m** of the Hebrew is uncertain.
Dt 7:20 {will send hornets} Or *will spread panic,* or *will send a plague.* The **m** of the Hebrew is uncertain.
32: 5 {really his children?} The **m** of the Hebrew is uncertain.
32:26 {to scatter them,} As in Greek version; the **m** of the Hebrew is uncertain.
32:31 {even they recognize.} The **m** of the Hebrew is uncertain. Greek version reads *our enemies are fools.*
33: 2 {his right hand.} Or *came from myriads of holy ones, from the south, from his mountain slopes.* The **m** of the Hebrew is uncertain.
Jos 5: 9 {been called Gilgal} *Gilgal* sounds like the Hebrew word *galal,* **m** "to roll."
17:11 {(that is, Naphoth-dor),} The **m** of the Hebrew here is uncertain.
18:15 {it ran westward} Or *it went to Ephron, and.* The **m** of the Hebrew is uncertain.
Jdg 5:11 {the village musicians} The **m** of the Hebrew is uncertain.
9: 6 {beside the pillar} The **m** of the Hebrew is uncertain.
1Sa 1: 5 {special portion} Or *a double portion.* The **m** of the Hebrew is uncertain.
20:19 {the stone pile.} Hebrew *the stone Ezel.* The **m** of the Hebrew is uncertain.
2Sa 2:29 {through the morning,} Or *continued on through the Bithron.* The **m** of the Hebrew is uncertain.
5: 8 {enter the house."} The **m** of this saying is uncertain.
5: 9 {at the Millo} Or *the supporting terraces.* The **m** of the Hebrew is uncertain.
6:19 {cake of dates,} Or *a portion of meat.* The **m** of the Hebrew is uncertain.
7:19 {everyone this way,} The **m** of the Hebrew is uncertain.
13:18 {long, beautiful robe,} Or *a robe with sleeves,* or *an ornamented robe.* The **m** of the Hebrew is uncertain.
1Ki 4:19 {land of Judah.} As in some Greek manuscripts; Hebrew lacks *of Judah.* The **m** of the Hebrew is uncertain.
6:20 {made of cedar.} Or *overlaid the altar with cedar.* The **m** of the Hebrew is uncertain.
2Ki 16:18 {the Sabbath day,} The **m** of the Hebrew is uncertain.
1Ch 2:42 {father of Hebron.} The **m** of the Hebrew is uncertain.
4: 3 {The descendants of} As in Greek version; Hebrew reads *father of.* The **m** of the Hebrew is uncertain.
4: 9 {named him Jabez} *Jabez* sounds like a Hebrew term **m** "distress" or "pain."
7:23 {named him Beriah} *Beriah* sounds like a Hebrew term **m** "tragedy" or "misfortune."
11: 8 {from the Millo} Or *the supporting terraces.* The **m** of the Hebrew is uncertain.
15:20 {play the lyres.} Hebrew adds *according to Alamoth,* which is probably a musical term. The **m** of the Hebrew is uncertain.
15:21 {play the harps.} Hebrew adds *according to the Sheminith,* which is probably a musical term. The **m** of the Hebrew is uncertain.
16: 3 {cake of dates,} Or *a portion of meat.* The **m** of the Hebrew is uncertain.
17:17 {someone very great,} The **m** of the Hebrew is uncertain.
18: 3 {far as Hamath,} The **m** of the Hebrew is uncertain.
26:16 {to the Temple.} Or *the gate of Shalleketh on the upper road* (also in 26:18). The **m** of the Hebrew is uncertain.
26:18 {to the courtyard.} Or *the colonnade.* The **m** of the Hebrew is uncertain.
2Ch 9:11 {to make steps} Or *gateways.* The **m** of the Hebrew is uncertain.
Ezr 1: 9 {silver censers} The **m** of this Hebrew word is uncertain.
8:13 {who came later} The **m** of the Hebrew for this phrase is uncertain.
10:44 {by these wives.} Or *and they sent them away with their children.* The **m** of the Hebrew is uncertain.
Ne 4:12 {and attack us!"} The **m** of the Hebrew is uncertain.
4:23 {went for water.} Hebrew *Each his weapon the water.* The **m** of the Hebrew is uncertain.
Est 2:19 {the second harem} The **m** of the Hebrew is uncertain.
Job 36:33 {his indignant anger.} Or *even the cattle know when a storm is coming.* The **m** of the Hebrew is uncertain.
Ps 3: 2 {Interlude} Hebrew *Selah.* The **m** of this word is uncertain, though it is probably a musical or literary term. It is rendered *Interlude* throughout the Psalms.
9:16 {Quiet Interlude} Hebrew *Higgaion Selah.* The **m** of this phrase is uncertain.
58: 7 {in their hands.} Or *Let them be trodden down and wither like grass.* The **m** of the Hebrew is uncertain.
76:10 {sword of judgment.} The **m** of the Hebrew is uncertain.
Pr 12:26 {to their friends;} Or *The godly are cautious in friendship,* or *the godly are freed from evil.* The **m** of the Hebrew is uncertain.
20:30 {cleanses away evil;} The **m** of the Hebrew is uncertain.
Ecc 5: 9 {own profit!} The **m** of the Hebrew is uncertain.
SS 6:12 {my beloved one.} Or *among the royal chariots of my people,* or *among the chariots of Amminadab.* The **m** of the Hebrew is uncertain.
6:13 {lines of dancers?} Or *as you would at the movements of two armies?* or *as you would at the dance of Mahanaim?* The **m** of the Hebrew is uncertain.
Isa 28:10 {very simple words!} The Hebrew text for this verse may simply be childish sounds that have no **m**, or perhaps a childish mimicking of the prophet's words. Also in 28:13.

Eze 21:10 {beneath its power!} The **m** of the Hebrew is uncertain.
21:13 {do they have?} The **m** of the Hebrew is uncertain.
27:17 {Minnith, early figs,} The **m** of the Hebrew is uncertain.
27:19 {Greeks from Uzal} Hebrew *Vedan and Javan from Uzal.* The **m** of the Hebrew is uncertain.
32:27 {covering their bodies,} The **m** of the Hebrew phrase here is uncertain.
40:14 {was 105 feet.} The **m** of the Hebrew in this verse is uncertain.
Da 8:11[-12] {everything it did.} The **m** of the Hebrew for these verses is uncertain.
9:27 {his terrible deeds,} Hebrew *on the wing of abominations;* the **m** of the Hebrew is uncertain.
10:13 {kingdom of Persia.} As in one Greek version; Hebrew reads *and I was left there with the kings of Persia.* The **m** of the Hebrew is uncertain.
Hos 4:18 {love for honor.} As in Greek version; the **m** of the Hebrew is uncertain.
5:2 {them at Acacia.} Hebrew *at Shittim.* The **m** of the Hebrew for this sentence is uncertain.
Hab 3:3 {and Mount Paran.} Hebrew adds *selah;* also in 3:9, 13. The **m** of this Hebrew term is uncertain; it is probably a musical or literary term.
Zep 1:3 {heaps of rubble,} The **m** of the Hebrew is uncertain.
3:18 {disgraced no more.} The **m** of the Hebrew for this verse is uncertain.
Zec 14:5 {across to Azal.} The **m** of the Hebrew is uncertain.
14:6 {no longer shine,} Hebrew *there will be no light, no cold or frost.* The **m** of the Hebrew is uncertain.
Mal 2:15 {you are his.} Or *Did not one God make us and preserve our life and breath?* or *Did not one God make her, both flesh and spirit?* The **m** of the Hebrew is uncertain.

MEANS (114)

Ge 3:20 {his wife Eve,} *Eve* sounds like a Hebrew term that **m** "to give life."
4:16 {land of Nod,} *Nod* **m** "wandering."
4:25 {named him Seth,} *Seth* probably **m** "granted"; the name may also mean "appointed."
11:9 {was called Babel,} *Babel* sounds like a Hebrew term that **m** "confusion."
16:11 {name him Ishmael,} *Ishmael* **m** "God hears."
16:14 {was named Beer-lahairoi,} *Beer-lahairoi* **m** "well of the Living One who sees me."
17:5 {known as Abraham,} *Abram* **m** "exalted father"; *Abraham* **m** "father of many."
17:15 {call her Sarah.} *Sarah* **m** "princess."
17:19 {name him Isaac,} *Isaac* **m** "he laughs."
19:22 {known as Zoar.} *Zoar* **m** "little."
19:37 {named him Moab.} *Moab* sounds like a Hebrew term that **m** "from father."
19:38 {named him Ben-ammi.} *Ben-ammi* **m** "son of my people."
21:3 {his son Isaac.} *Isaac* **m** "he laughs."
24:10 {traveled to Aram-naharaim} *Aram-naharaim* **m** "Aram of the two rivers," thought to have been located between the Euphrates and Balih Rivers in northwestern Mesopotamia.
25:25 {called him Esau.} *Esau* sounds like a Hebrew term that **m** "hair."
25:26 {called him Jacob.} *Jacob* **m** "he grasps the heel"; this can also figuratively mean "he deceives."
27:36 {name is Jacob,} *Jacob* **m** "he grasps the heel"; this can also figuratively mean "he deceives."
29:32 {named him Reuben,} *Reuben* **m** "Look, a son!" It also sounds like the Hebrew for "He has seen my misery."
29:33 {named him Simeon,} *Simeon* probably **m** "one who hears."
29:34 {named him Levi,} *Levi* sounds like a Hebrew term that **m** "being attached" or "feeling affection for."
30:8 {named him Naphtali,} *Naphtali* **m** "my struggle."
30:11 {named him Gad,} *Gad* **m** "good fortune."
30:13 {named him Asher,} *Asher* **m** "happy."
30:18 {named him Issachar,} *Issachar* sounds like a Hebrew term that **m** "reward."
30:20 {named him Zebulun,} *Zebulun* probably **m** "honor."
30:24 {named him Joseph,} *Joseph* **m** "may he add."
31:47 {language and Galeed} *Jegar-sahadutha* **m** "witness pile" in Aramaic; *Galeed* **m** "witness pile" in Hebrew.
31:49 {also called Mizpah,} *Mizpah* **m** "watchtower."
32:2 {the place Mahanaim.} *Mahanaim* **m** "two camps."
32:28 {is now Israel,} *Israel* **m** "God struggles" or "one who struggles with God."
33:17 {was named Succoth.} *Succoth* **m** "shelters."
33:20 {called it El-Elohe-Israel.} *El-Elohe-Israel* **m** "God, the God of Israel."
35:7 {named it El-bethel,} *El-bethel* **m** "the God of Bethel."
35:10 {be called Israel."} *Jacob* **m** "he grasps the heel"; this can also figuratively mean "he deceives"; *Israel* **m** "God struggles" or "one who struggles with God."
35:18 {called him Benjamin.} *Ben-oni* **m** "son of my sorrow"; *Benjamin* **m** "son of my right hand."
38:29 {was called Perez.} *Perez* **m** "breaking out."
38:30 {was named Zerah.} *Zerah* **m** "scarlet" or "brightness."
41:45 {renamed him Zaphenath-paneah} *Zaphenath-paneah* probably **m** "God speaks and lives."
41:51 {older son Manasseh,} *Manasseh* sounds like a Hebrew term that **m** "causing to forget."
41:52 {second son Ephraim,} *Ephraim* sounds like a Hebrew term that **m** "fruitful."
50:11 {the place Abel-mizraim,} *Abel-mizraim* **m** "mourning of the Egyptians."
Ex 2:10 {named him Moses,} *Moses* sounds like a Hebrew term that **m** "to draw out."
2:22 {named him Gershom,} *Gershom* sounds like a Hebrew term that **m** "a stranger here."
16:31 {known as manna.} *Manna* **m** "What is it?" See 16:15.
18:3 {son was Gershom,} *Gershom* sounds like a Hebrew term that **m** "a stranger here."
18:4 {son was Eliezer,} *Eliezer* **m** "God is my helper."
Lev 16:8 {be the scapegoat.} Hebrew *azazel,* which in this context **m** "the goat of removal"; also in 16:10, 26.
Nu 13:16 {name to Joshua.} *Hoshea* (see 13:8) **m** "salvation"; *Joshua* **m** "The LORD is salvation."
20:13 {waters of Meribah,} *Meribah* **m** "arguing."
21:3 {been called Hormah} *Hormah* **m** "destruction."
21:16 {traveled to Beer,} *Beer* **m** "well."
Dt 9:22 {Taberah,} *Taberah* **m** "place of burning." See Num 11:1-3.
9:22 {Massah,} *Massah* **m** "place of testing." See Exod 17:1-7.
9:22 {Kibroth-hattaavah.} *Kibroth-hattaavah* **m** "graves of craving." See Num 11:31-34.
23:4 {Pethor in Aram-naharaim} *Aram-naharaim* **m** "Aram of the two rivers," thought to have been located between the Euphrates and Balih Rivers in northwestern Mesopotamia.
Jos 5:3 {Israel at Gibeath-haaraloth.} *Gibeath-haaraloth* **m** "hill of foreskins."
8:28 {So Ai} *Ai* **m** "ruin."
Jdg 1:17 {was named Hormah.} *Hormah* **m** "destruction."
3:8 {Cushan-rishathaim of Aram-naharaim.} *Aram-naharaim* **m** "Aram of the two rivers," thought to have been located between the Euphrates and Balih Rivers in northwestern Mesopotamia.
18:12 {is called Mahaneh-dan} *Mahaneh-dan* **m** "the camp of Dan."
Ru 1:20 {call me Mara,} *Naomi* **m** "pleasant"; *Mara* **m** "bitter."
1Sa 25:25 {his name suggests.} The name *Nabal* **m** "fool."
2Sa 8:1 {their largest city.} Hebrew *by conquering Metheg-ammah,* a name which **m** "the bridle," possibly referring to the size of the city or the tribute money taken from it. Compare 1 Chr 18:1.
1Ki 7:21 {the north Boaz.} Jakin probably **m** "he establishes"; Boaz probably **m** "in him is strength."
1Ch 2:7 {Achan} Hebrew *Achar;* compare Josh 7:1. *Achar* **m** "disaster."
2Ch 3:17 {the north Boaz.} Jakin probably **m** "he establishes"; Boaz probably **m** "in him is strength."
SS 1:1 {*Young Woman:*} The headings identifying the speakers are not in the original text, though the Hebrew usually gives clues by **m** of the gender of the person speaking.
Isa 7:3 {your son Shear-jashub.} *Shear-jashub* **m** "A remnant will return."
8:1 {on it: Maher-shalal-hash-baz.} *Maher-shalal-hash-baz* **m** "Swift to plunder and quick to spoil."
8:18 {have names} *Isaiah* **m** "The LORD will save"; *Shear-jashub* **m** "A remnant will return"; and *Maher-shalal-hash-baz* **m** "Swift to plunder and quick to spoil."
21:11 {me concerning Edom} Hebrew *Dumah,* which **m** "silence" or "stillness." It is a wordplay on the word *Edom.*
29:1 {certain for Ariel,} *Ariel* sounds like a Hebrew term that **m** "hearth" or "altar."
62:4 {the Godforsaken City} Hebrew *Azubah,* which **m** "forsaken."
62:4 {the Desolate Land.} Hebrew *Shemamah,* which **m** "desolate."
62:4 {of God's Delight} Hebrew *Hephzibah,* which **m** "my delight is in her."
62:4 {Bride of God,} Hebrew *Beulah,* which **m** "married."
Jer 20:3 {Lives in Terror.'} Hebrew *Magor-missabib,* which **m** "surrounded by terror"; also in 20:10.
Hos 1:11 {day of Jezreel} *Jezreel* **m** "God plants."
4:15 {and at Beth-aven.} *Beth-aven* **m** "house of wickedness"; it is being used as another name for Bethel, which **m** "house of God."
5:8 {cry in Beth-aven} *Beth-aven* **m** "house of wickedness"; it is being used as another name for Bethel, which **m** "house of God."
10:5 {idol at Beth-aven.} *Beth-aven* **m** "house of wickedness"; it is being used as another name for Bethel, which **m** "house of God."
12:2 {to punish Jacob} *Jacob* **m** "he grasps at the heel"; this can also figuratively mean "he deceives."
Joel 3:2 {valley of Jehoshaphat.} *Jehoshaphat* **m** "the LORD judges."
Am 1:5 {valley of Aven.} *Aven* **m** "wickedness."
6:13 {Lo-debar.} *Lo-debar* **m** "nothing."
6:13 {Karnaim} *Karnaim* **m** "horns," a term that symbolizes strength.
Mic 1:10 {people in Beth-leaphrah,} *Beth-leaphrah* **m** "house of dust."
1:11 {people of Shaphir,} *Shaphir* **m** "pleasant."
1:11 {people of Beth-ezel} *Beth-ezel* **m** "adjoining house."
1:14 {town of Aczib} *Aczib* **m** "deception."
Mal 1:1 {the prophet Malachi.} *Malachi* **m** "my messenger."
Mt 1:21 {name him Jesus,} *Jesus* **m** "The LORD saves."
16:18 {you are Peter,} *Peter* **m** "stone" or "rock."
21:9 {"Praise God} Greek *Hosanna,* an exclamation of praise that literally **m** "save now"; also in 21:9b, 15.
23:7 {being called 'Rabbi.'} *Rabbi,* from Aramaic, **m** "master" or "teacher."
Mk 3:17 {"Sons of Thunder"} Greek *whom he named Boanerges, which* **m** *Sons of Thunder.*
11:9 {"Praise God!} Greek *Hosanna,* an exclamation of praise that literally **m** "save now"; also in 11:10.
Jn 12:13 {"Praise God!} Greek *Hosanna,* an exclamation of praise that literally **m** "save now."
20:16 {and exclaimed, "Teacher!"} Greek *and said in Hebrew, "Rabboni," which* **m** *"Teacher."*
Ac 18:21 {come back later,} Some manuscripts read *"I must by all* **m** *be at Jerusalem for the upcoming festival, but I will come back later."*
Phm 1:11 {Onesimus} *Onesimus* **m** "useful."

MEASURED (3)

Lev 27:25 {standard sanctuary shekel.} Hebrew **m** *according to the sanctuary shekel, 20 gerahs to each shekel.* Each sanctuary shekel was about 0.4 ounces or 11 grams in weight.
Eze 40:8 {of the gateway} Many Hebrew manuscripts add *which faced inward toward the Temple; it was one rod* [10.5 feet or 3.2 meters] *deep.* [9]*Then he* **m** *the foyer of the gateway,...*
45:14 {your olive oil,} Hebrew *the portion of oil,* **m** *by the bath, is 1/10 of a bath from each cor, which consists of 10 baths or 1 homer, for 10 baths are equivalent to a homer.*

MEASUREMENTS (1)

Eze 43:13 {of the altar} Hebrew **m** *of the altar in long cubits, each being a cubit* [18 inches or 45 centimeters] *and a handbreadth* [3 inches or 8 centimeters] *in length.* In this chapter, the distance measures are calculated using the Hebrew long cubit, which equals 21 inches or 53 centimeters.

MEASURES (4 of 21)

Ru 3:15 {six scoops} Hebrew *six* **m**, an unknown quantity.
Mt 13:33 {a large amount} Greek *3* **m**.
Lk 13:21 {a large amount} Greek *3* **m**.
Jn 2:6 {thirty gallons} Greek *2 or 3* **m** [75 to 113 liters].

MEASURING (2)

Mic 6:10 {in short measures.} Hebrew *by using the short ephah;* the ephah was a unit for **m** grain.
Zec 1:16 {reconstruction of Jerusalem.} Hebrew *and the* **m** *line will be stretched out over Jerusalem.*

MEAT (3)

2Sa 6:19 {cake of dates,} Or *a portion of* **m**. The meaning of the Hebrew is uncertain.
1Ch 16:3 {cake of dates,} Or *a portion of* **m**. The meaning of the Hebrew is uncertain.
Eze 11:3 {from all harm.} Hebrew *This city is the pot, and we are the* **m**.

MEBUNNAI (1)

2Sa 23:27 {Sibbecai} As in some Greek manuscripts (see also 1 Chr 11:29); Hebrew reads **M**.

MEETING (56)

Ex 27:21 {in the Tabernacle.} Hebrew *in the Tent of* **M**, *outside of the inner curtain, in front of the Testimony.*
28:43 {enter the Tabernacle} Hebrew *Tent of* **M**.
29:4 {of the Tabernacle,} Hebrew *Tent of* **M**; also in 29:10, 11, 30, 32, 42, 44.
30:16 {of the Tabernacle.} Hebrew *Tent of* **M**; also in 30:18, 20, 26, 36.
31:7 {of the Covenant;} Hebrew *the Tent of* **M**; *the Ark of the Testimony.*
35:21 {for the Tabernacle} Hebrew *Tent of* **M**.
38:8 {of the Tabernacle.} Hebrew *Tent of* **M**; also in 38:30.
39:32 {last the Tabernacle} Hebrew *the Tabernacle, the Tent of* **M**; also in 39:40.
40:2 {up the Tabernacle} Hebrew *the Tabernacle, the Tent of* **M**; also in 40:6, 29.
40:7 {between the Tabernacle} Hebrew *Tent of* **M**; also in 40:12, 22, 24, 26, 30, 32, 34, 35.
Lev 1:1 {from the Tabernacle} Hebrew *Tent of* **M**; also in 1:3, 5.
3:2 {of the Tabernacle.} Hebrew *Tent of* **M**; also in 3:8, 13.
4:4 {of the Tabernacle,} Hebrew *Tent of* **M**; also in 4:5, 7, 14, 16, 18.
6:16 {of the Tabernacle.} Hebrew *Tent of* **M**; also in 6:26, 30.
8:3 {of the Tabernacle.} Hebrew *Tent of* **M**; also in 8:4, 31, 33, 35.

9: 5 {of the Tabernacle,} Hebrew *Tent of M;* also in 9:23.
10: 7 {of the Tabernacle,} Hebrew *Tent of M;* also in 10:9.
12: 6 {of the Tabernacle.} Hebrew *Tent of M.*
14: 11 {of the Tabernacle.} Hebrew *Tent of M;* also in 14:23.
15: 14 {of the Tabernacle} Hebrew *Tent of M;* also in 15:29.
16: 7 {of the Tabernacle.} Hebrew *Tent of M;* also in 16:16, 17, 20, 23, 33.
17: 4 {of the Tabernacle} Hebrew *Tent of M;* also in 17:5, 6, 9.
19: 21 {of the Tabernacle.} Hebrew *Tent of M.*
24: 3 {in the Tabernacle} Hebrew *the curtain of the Testimony in the Tent of M.*
Nu 1: 1 {in the Tabernacle} Hebrew *Tent of M.*
2: 2 {banners. The Tabernacle} Hebrew *Tent of M;* also in 2:17.
3: 7 {around the Tabernacle.} Hebrew *around the Tent of M, doing service at the Tabernacle.*
3: 8 {the sacred tent,} Hebrew *Tent of M.*
3: 38 {toward the sunrise} Hebrew *toward the sunrise, in front of the Tent of M.*
4: 3 {in the Tabernacle.} Hebrew *Tent of M;* also in 4:4, 15, 23, 25, 28, 30, 31, 33, 35, 37, 39, 41, 43, 47.
6: 10 {of the Tabernacle.} Hebrew *Tent of M;* also in 6:13, 18.
7: 5 {of the Tabernacle.} Hebrew *Tent of M;* also in 7:89.
8: 9 {of the Tabernacle.} Hebrew *Tent of M;* also in 8:15, 19, 22, 24, 26.
10: 3 {of the Tabernacle.} Hebrew *Tent of M.*
11: 16 {to the Tabernacle} Hebrew *Tent of M.*
12: 4 {to the Tabernacle,} Hebrew *Tent of M.*
14: 10 {above the Tabernacle.} Hebrew *Tent of M.*
16: 18 {of the Tabernacle} Hebrew *Tent of M;* also in 16:19, 42, 43, 50.
17: 4 {of the Covenant,} Hebrew *in the Tent of M before the Testimony.*
18: 4 {of the Tabernacle,} Hebrew *Tent of M;* also in 18:6, 21, 22, 23, 31.
19: 4 {of the Tabernacle.} Hebrew *Tent of M.*
20: 6 {of the Tabernacle,} Hebrew *Tent of M.*
25: 6 {of the Tabernacle.} Hebrew *Tent of M.*
27: 2 {of the Tabernacle.} Hebrew *Tent of M.*
31: 54 {to the Tabernacle} Hebrew *Tent of M.*
Dt 31: 14 {to the Tabernacle,} Hebrew *Tent of M;* also in 31:14b.
Jos 18: 1 {up the Tabernacle.} Hebrew *Tent of M.*
19: 51 {of the Tabernacle} Hebrew *Tent of M.*
1Sa 2: 22 {of the Tabernacle.} Hebrew *Tent of M.* Some manuscripts lack this entire sentence.
1Ki 8: 4 {with the Tabernacle} Hebrew *Tent of M.*
1Ch 6: 32 {at the Tabernacle} Hebrew *the Tabernacle, the Tent of M.*
9: 21 {to the Tabernacle.} Hebrew *Tent of M.*
23: 32 {and the Temple} Hebrew *the Tent of M and the sanctuary.*
2Ch 1: 3 {where God's Tabernacle} Hebrew *Tent of M;* also in 1:6, 13.
5: 5 {the special tent} Hebrew *Tent of M.*
1Co 5: 4 {of the church,} Or *In the name of the Lord Jesus, you are to call a m of the church.*

MEMBERS (2)

2Jn 1: 1 {to her children,} Or *the church God has chosen and her m,* or *the chosen Kyria and her children.*
1: 13 {of your sister,} Or *from the m of your sister church.*

MEMPHIS (1)

Hos 9: 6 {by Egypt. Memphis} **M** was the capital of northern Egypt.

MEN (15)

Nu 1: 20[-21] {clan and family} In the Hebrew text, *number of m . . . family* is repeated in 1:22, 24, 26, 28, 30, 32, 34, 36, 38, 40, 42.
1Sa 6: 19 {killed seventy men} As in a few Hebrew manuscripts; most Hebrew manuscripts and Greek version read *50,070 m.* Perhaps the text should be understood to read *the LORD killed 70 m and 50 oxen.*
8: 16 {of your cattle} As in Greek version; Hebrew reads *young m.*
10: 27 {Saul ignored them.} Dead Sea Scroll 4QSam[a] continues: *. . . But there were seven thousand m who had escaped from the Ammonites, and they had settled in Jabesh-gilead.*
14: 41 {among the others?"} Greek version adds *If the fault is with me or my son Jonathan, respond with Urim; but if the m of Israel are at fault, respond with Thummim.*
2Sa 23: 8 {a single battle.} As in some Greek manuscripts (see also 1 Chr 11:11); the Hebrew is uncertain, though it might be rendered *the Three. It was Adino the Eznite who killed eight hundred m at one time.*
2Ch 26: 15 {and hurl stones} Or *designed by brilliant m to protect those who shot arrows and stones.*
Mt 2: 16 {two years earlier.} Or *according to the time he calculated from the wise m.*
27: 51[-53] {to many people.} Or *The earth shook, rocks split apart, tombs opened, and many bodies of godly m and women who had died were raised from the dead. After Jesus' resurrection, they left the cemetery, went into the holy city of Jerusalem, and appeared to many people.*
Lk 17: 35 {the other left.} Some manuscripts add verse 36, *Two m will be working in the field; one will be taken, the other left.*
Ac 11: 3 {home of Gentiles} Greek *of uncircumcised m.*
14: 15 {"Friends,} Greek *M.*
17: 4 {of the city.} Some manuscripts read *many of the wives of the leading m.*
Php 2: 7 {human form.} Greek *he was born in the likeness of m and was found in appearance as a man.*

MEN'S (1)

Lk 9: 55 {and rebuked them.} Some manuscripts add *And he said, "You don't realize what your hearts are like. [56]For the Son of Man has not come to destroy m lives, but to save them."*

MENSTRUATING (1)

Lev 20: 18 {from a hemorrhage,} Or *a woman who is m.*

MENTIONED (3)

1Ki 7: 13 {man named Huram} Hebrew *Hiram* (also in 7:40, 45); compare 2 Chr 2:13. This is not the same person **m** in 5:1.
Joel 1: 4 {the stripping locusts,} The precise identification of the four kinds of locusts **m** here is uncertain.
2: 25 {the hopping locusts.} The precise identification of the four kinds of locusts **m** here is uncertain.

MEONOTHAI (1)

1Ch 4: 13 {and Meonothai.} As in some Greek manuscripts and Latin Vulgate; Hebrew lacks *and M.*

MERAIOTH (1)

Ne 12: 15 {family of Meremoth.} As in some Greek manuscripts (see also 12:3); Hebrew reads *M.*

MERCHANT (1)

Lev 19: 16 {among your people.} Hebrew *Do not act as a m toward your own people.*

MERCY (1)

Jude 1: 23 {by their sins.} Greek *m, hating even the clothing stained by the flesh.*

MERELY (2)

Isa 29: 13 {learned by rote.} Greek version reads *Their worship is a farce, for they m teach human commands and teachings.*
1Co 3: 4 {are not Christians?} Greek *aren't you m human?*

MERIBAH (1)

Nu 20: 13 {waters of Meribah,} *M* means "arguing."

MERIBATH-KADESH (4)

Nu 27: 14 {Meribah at Kadesh} Hebrew *waters of M.*
Dt 32: 51 {Meribah at Kadesh} Hebrew *waters of M.*
Eze 47: 19 {Meribah at Kadesh} Hebrew *waters of M.*
48: 28 {Meribah at Kadesh} Hebrew *waters of M.*

MERIBBAAL (5)

2Sa 4: 4 {son named Mephibosheth,} Also known as *M.*
9: 6 {name was Mephibosheth} Also known as *M.*
16: 1 {servant of Mephibosheth,} Also known as *M.*
19: 24 {Now Mephibosheth,} Also known as *M.*
21: 7 {Jonathan's son Mephibosheth,} Also known as *M.*

MESHECH (1)

1Ch 1: 17 {Gether, and Mash.} As in parallel text at Gen 10:23; Hebrew reads *and M.*

MESHELEMIAH (1)

1Ch 26: 14 {went to Meshelemiah} Hebrew *Shelemiah,* a variant name for **M**; compare 26:2.

MESSAGE (3 of 6)

Zec 9: 1 {is the message} Hebrew *An Oracle: The m.*
Mal 1: 1 {is the message} Hebrew *An Oracle: The m.*
Rev 19: 10 {witness for Jesus.} Or *is the m confirmed by Jesus.*

MESSENGER (3)

Mal 1: 1 {the prophet Malachi.} *Malachi* means "my **m**."
Rev 2: 1 {the angel of} Or *the m for;* also in 2:8, 12, 18.
3: 1 {the angel of} Or *the m for;* also in 3:7, 14.

MESSENGERS (1)

Rev 1: 20 {the angels of} Or *the m for.*

METHEG-AMMAH (1)

2Sa 8: 1 {their largest city.} Hebrew *by conquering M,* a name which means "the bridle," possibly referring to the size of the city or the tribute money taken from it. Compare 1 Chr 18:1.

MIC (3)

Jer 26: 18 {Temple now stands.'} **M** 3:12.
Mt 2: 6 {my people Israel.'} **M** 5:2; 2 Sam 5:2.
Jn 7: 42 {David was born."} See **M** 5:2.

MICAH (1)

2Ch 34: 20 {son of Micaiah,} As in parallel text at 2 Kgs 22:12; Hebrew reads *Abdon son of M.*

MICAIAH (1)

2Ch 13: 2 {mother was Maacah,} As in most Greek manuscripts and Syriac version (see also 2 Chr 11:20-21; 1 Kgs 15:2); Hebrew reads *M.*

MICHAEL (1)

Da 10: 21 {your spirit prince.} Hebrew *against these except M, your prince.*

MICHAL (1)

2Sa 21: 8 {Saul's daughter Merab,} As in a few Hebrew and Greek manuscripts and Syriac version (see also 1 Sam 18:19); most Hebrew manuscripts read *M.*

MIDDLE (3)

1Ki 6: 8 {the bottom floor} As in Greek version; Hebrew reads *m floor.*
Ac 17: 22 {before the Council,} Or *in the m of Mars Hill;* Greek reads *in the m of the Areopagus.*

MIDIANITES (1)

Ge 37: 28 {when the traders} Hebrew *M;* also in 37:36.

MIGHTY (2)

Ge 10: 9 {the LORD's sight.} Hebrew *a m hunter before the LORD;* also in 10:9b.
Php 2: 7 {made himself nothing;} Or *He laid aside his m power and glory.*

MIJAMIN (1)

Ne 12: 5 {Miniamin, Moadiah,} Hebrew *M, Maadiah;* compare 12:17.

MILCOM (7)

2Sa 12: 30 {the king's head,} Greek version reads *removed the crown of M;* compare 1 Kgs 11:5. **M**, also called Molech, was the god of the Ammonites.
1Ki 11: 5 {Sidonians, and Molech,} Hebrew *M,* a variant name for Molech; also in 11:33.
2Ki 23: 13 {and for Molech,} Hebrew *M,* a variant name for Molech.
1Ch 20: 2 {the king's head,} Greek version and Latin Vulgate read *removed the crown of M;* compare 1 Kgs 11:5. **M**, also called Molech, was the god of the Ammonites.
Jer 49: 1 {who worship Molech,} Hebrew *M,* a variant name for Molech; also in 49:3.

MILION (1)

Mt 5: 41 {for a mile,} Greek *m* [4,854 feet or 1,478 meters].

MILK (1)

Job 10: 10 {in the womb.} Hebrew *You poured me out like m and curdled me like cheese.*

MINAS (5)

1Ki 10: 17 {nearly four pounds} Hebrew *3 m* [1.8 kilograms].
Ezr 2: 69 {6,250 pounds} Hebrew *5,000 m* [3 metric tons].
Ne 7: 71 {2,750 pounds} Hebrew *2,200 m* [1.3 metric tons].
7: 72 {2,500 pounds} Hebrew *2,000 m* [1.2 metric tons].
Lk 19: 13 {pounds of silver} Greek *10 m;* 1 mina was worth about 3 months' wages.

MINISTERING (2)

Col 1: 7 {in your place.} Greek *he is m on your behalf;* other manuscripts read *he is m on our behalf.*

MINT (2)

Mt 23: 23 {of your income,} Greek *to tithe the m, the dill, and the cumin.*
Lk 11: 42 {of your income,} Greek *to tithe the m and the rue and every herb.*

MIRROR (1)

2Co 3: 18 {that brightly reflect} Or *so that we can see in a m.*

MISERY (1)

Ge 29: 32 {named him Reuben,} *Reuben* means "Look, a son!" It also sounds like the Hebrew for "He has seen my **m**."

MISFORTUNE (1)

1Ch 7: 23 {named him Beriah} *Beriah* sounds like a Hebrew term meaning "tragedy" or "**m**."

MISHNEH (2)

Ne 3: 6 {Old City Gate} Or *The M Gate,* or *The Jeshanah Gate.*

12:39 {Old City Gate,} Or *the **M** Gate,* or *the Jeshanah Gate.*

MISPERETH (1)
Ne 7: 7 {Mordecai, Bilshan, Mispar,} As in parallel text at Ezra 2:2; Hebrew reads ***M.***

MIST (1)
Pr 21: 6 {deadly trap.} As in Greek version; Hebrew reads ***m** for those who seek death.*

MIZPAH (1)
Ge 31:49 {also called Mizpah,} ***M*** means "watchtower."

MOAB (1)
Ge 19:37 {named him Moab.} ***M*** sounds like a Hebrew term that means "from father."

MOAT (1)
Da 9:25 {and strong defenses,} Or *and a **m**,* or *and trenches.*

MOLECH (8)
2Sa 12:30 {the king's head,} Greek version reads *removed the crown of Milcom;* compare 1 Kgs 11:5. Milcom, also called **M**, was the god of the Ammonites.
1Ki 11: 5 {Sidonians, and Molech,} Hebrew *Milcom,* a variant name for **M**; also in 11:33.
2Ki 23:13 {and for Molech,} Hebrew *Milcom,* a variant name for **M**.
1Ch 20: 2 {the king's head,} Greek version and Latin Vulgate read *removed the crown of Milcom;* compare 1 Kgs 11:5. Milcom, also called **M**, was the god of the Ammonites.
Jer 49: 1 {who worship Molech,} Hebrew *Milcom,* a variant name for **M**; also in 49:3.
Am 1:15 {And their king} Hebrew *malcam,* possibly referring to their god **M**.
5:26 {you yourselves made.} Greek version reads *You took up the shrine of **M**, and the star of your god Rephan, and the images you made for yourselves.*
Zep 1: 5 {they worship Molech,} Hebrew *Malcam,* another name for **M**; or it could possibly mean *their king.*

MONTH (149 of 191)
Ge 8: 4 {the flood began,} Hebrew *on the seventeenth day of the seventh **m**;* see 7:11.
8: 5 {half months later,} Hebrew *On the first day of the tenth **m**;* see 7:11 and note on 8:4.
8:13 {the flood began,} Hebrew *on the first day of the first **m**;* see 7:11.
8:14 {months went by,} Hebrew *The twenty-seventh day of the second **m** arrived;* see note on 8:13.
Ex 13: 4 {in early spring} Hebrew *in the **m** of Abib.…*
16: 1 {after leaving Egypt.} Hebrew *on the fifteenth day of the second **m**.…*
19: 1 {they left Egypt.} Hebrew *in the third **m**…on the very day,* i.e., two lunar months to the day after leaving Egypt.…
23:15 {in early spring,} Hebrew *in the **m** of Abib.…*
34:18 {in early spring,} Hebrew *in the **m** of Abib.…*
40: 2 {new year.} Hebrew *the first day of the first **m**.…*
40:17 {the new year.} Hebrew *the first day of the first **m**, in the second year.* See note on 40:2b.
Lev 16:29 {in early autumn,} Hebrew *On the tenth day of the seventh **m**.…*
23: 5 {in early spring.} Hebrew *on the fourteenth day of the first **m**.* This day of the Hebrew lunar calendar occurs in late March or early April.
23: 6 {the Passover celebration,} Hebrew *On the fifteenth day of the same **m**.*
23:24 {in early autumn,} Hebrew *On the first day of the seventh **m**.…*
23:27 {Festival of Trumpets.} Hebrew *on the tenth day of the seventh **m**;* see 23:24 and the note there.
23:32 {Day of Atonement} Hebrew *the evening of the ninth day of the **m**;…*
23:34 {Day of Atonement.} Hebrew *on the fifteenth day of the seventh **m**;* see 23:24, 27 and the notes there.
23:39 {Festival of Shelters,} Hebrew *on the fifteenth day of the seventh **m**;* see 23:24 and the note there.
25: 9 {the fiftieth year,} Hebrew *on the tenth day of the seventh **m**, on the Day of Atonement;…*
Nu 1: 1 {day in midspring,} Hebrew *On the first day of the second **m**.…*
1:18 {that very day.} Hebrew *on the first day of the second **m**;* see 1:1.
9: 1 {in early spring,} Hebrew *in the first **m**.…*
9: 3 {in early spring.} Hebrew *on the fourteenth day of the first **m**.…*
9: 5 {the appointed day.} Hebrew *on the fourteenth day of the first **m**;* see note on 9:3.
9:11 {one month later,} Hebrew *on the fourteenth day of the second **m**.…*
10:11 {day in midspring,} Hebrew *On the twentieth day of the second **m**.…*
20: 1 {In early spring} Hebrew *In the first **m**.…*
28:16 {in early spring,} Hebrew *On the fourteenth day of the first **m**.…*
29: 1 {in early autumn} Hebrew *on the first day of the seventh **m**.…*
29: 7 {"Ten days later,} Hebrew *On the tenth day of the seventh **m**;* see 29:1 and the note there.
29:12 {"Five days later,} Hebrew *On the fifteenth day of the seventh **m**;* see 29:1, 7 and the notes there.
33: 3 {in early spring.} Hebrew *on the fifteenth day of the first **m**.…*
33:38 {day in midsummer,} Hebrew *on the first day of the fifth **m**.…*
Dt 1: 3 {day in midwinter,} Hebrew *on the first day of the eleventh **m**.…*
16: 1 {in early spring,} Hebrew *in the **m** of Abib.…*
Jos 4:19 {Egypt.} Hebrew *the tenth day of the first **m**.…*
5:10 {exodus from Egypt.} Hebrew *the fourteenth day of the first **m**.…*
1Sa 11: 1 {month later,} As in Greek version; Hebrew lacks *About a **m** later.*
1Ki 6: 1 {was in midspring,} Hebrew *in the **m** of Ziv, which is the second **m**.…*
6:37 {laid in midspring} Hebrew *in the **m** of Ziv.…*
6:38 {detail by midautumn} Hebrew *in the **m** of Bul, which is the eighth **m**.…*
8: 2 {in early autumn.} Hebrew *at the festival in the **m** Ethanim, which is the seventh **m**.…*
12:32 {day in midautumn,} Hebrew *on the fifteenth day of the eighth **m*** (also in 12:33).…
2Ki 25: 1 {So on January 15,} Hebrew *on the tenth day of the tenth **m**,* of the Hebrew calendar.…
25: 3 {Zedekiah's eleventh year,} Hebrew *By the ninth day,* that is, "of the fourth **m** of Zedekiah's eleventh year"…
25: 8 {of that year,} Hebrew *On the seventh day of the fifth **m**,* of the Hebrew calendar.…
25:25 {of that year,} Hebrew *in the seventh **m**,* of the Hebrew calendar.…
25:27 {of that year.} Hebrew *on the twenty-seventh day of the twelfth **m**,* of the Hebrew calendar.…
2Ch 3: 2 {began in midspring,} Hebrew *on the second day of the second **m**.…*
5: 3 {in early autumn.} Hebrew *at the festival that is in the seventh **m**.…*
7:10 {of the celebration,} Hebrew *Then on the twenty-seventh day of the seventh **m**.…*
15:10 {in late spring,} Hebrew *in the third **m**.…*
29:17 {in early spring,} Hebrew *on the first day of the first **m**.…*
30: 2 {in midspring.} Hebrew *in the second **m**.…*
30: 3 {in early spring,} Hebrew *in the first **m**.…*
30:13 {in midspring} Hebrew *in the second **m**.…*
30:15 {day in midspring,} Hebrew *On the fourteenth day of the second **m**.…*
31: 7 {in late spring,} Hebrew *in the third **m**.…*
31: 7 {until early autumn.} Hebrew *in the seventh **m**.…*
35: 1 {in early spring.} Hebrew *on the fourteenth day of the first **m**.…*
Ezr 3: 1 {in early autumn,} Hebrew *in the seventh **m**.…*
3: 6 {of Shelters began,} Hebrew *On the first day of the seventh **m**.…*
3: 8 {began in midspring,} Hebrew *in the second **m**.…*
6:15 {completed on March 12,} Aramaic *on the third day of the **m** Adar,* of the Hebrew calendar.…
6:19 {On April 21} Hebrew *On the fourteenth day of the first **m**,* of the Hebrew calendar.…
7: 8 {Jerusalem in August} Hebrew *in the fifth **m**.…*
7: 9 {Babylon on April 8} Hebrew *on the first day of the first **m**,* of the Hebrew calendar.…
7: 9 {Jerusalem on August 4,} Hebrew *on the first day of the fifth **m**,* of the Hebrew calendar.…
8:31 {Canal on April 19} Hebrew *on the twelfth day of the first **m**,* of the Hebrew calendar.…
10: 9 {place on December 19,} Hebrew *on the twentieth day of the ninth **m**,* of the Hebrew calendar.…
10:16 {name. On December 29,} Hebrew *On the first day of the tenth **m**,* of the Hebrew calendar.…
10:17 {the next year} Hebrew *By the first day of the first **m**,* of the Hebrew calendar.…
Ne 1: 1 {King Artaxerxes' reign,} Hebrew *In the **m** of Kislev of the twentieth year.…*
2: 1 {following spring,} Hebrew *In the **m** of Nisan.…*
6:15 {So on October 2} Hebrew *on the twenty-fifth day of the **m** Elul,* of the Hebrew calendar.…
7:73 {Now in midautumn,} Hebrew *in the seventh **m**.…*
8: 2 {So on October 8} Hebrew *on the first day of the seventh **m**,* of the Hebrew calendar.…
8:13 {On October 9} Hebrew *On the second day,* of the seventh **m** of the Hebrew calendar.…
8:14 {held that month.} Hebrew *in the seventh **m**.…*
8:18 {Then on October 15} Hebrew *on the eighth day,* of the seventh **m** of the Hebrew calendar.…
9: 1 {On October 31} Hebrew *On the twenty-fourth day of that same **m**,* the seventh **m** of the Hebrew calendar.…
Est 2:16 {in early winter} Hebrew *in the tenth **m**, the **m** of Tebeth.…*
3: 7 {month of April,} Hebrew *in the first **m**, the **m** of Nisan.…*
3: 7 {a year later.} As in Greek version, which reads *the thirteenth day of the twelfth **m**, the **m** of Adar* (see also 3:13). Hebrew reads *in the twelfth **m**,* of the Hebrew calendar.…
3:12 {On April 17} Hebrew *On the thirteenth day of the first **m**,* of the Hebrew calendar.…
3:13 {later on March 7.} Hebrew *on the thirteenth day of the twelfth **m**, the **m** of Adar,* of the Hebrew calendar. …
8: 9 {So on June 25} Hebrew *on the twenty-third day of the third **m**, the **m** of Sivan,* of the Hebrew calendar.…
8:12 {the next year.} Hebrew *the thirteenth day of the twelfth **m**, the **m** of Adar,* of the Hebrew calendar.…
9: 1 {So on March 7} Hebrew *on the thirteenth day of the twelfth **m**, the **m** of Adar,* of the Hebrew calendar.…
9:15 {together on March 8} Hebrew *the fourteenth day of the **m** of Adar,* of the Hebrew calendar.…
9:17 {done on March 7.} Hebrew *on the thirteenth day of the **m** of Adar,* of the Hebrew calendar.…
9:17 {the following day} Hebrew *on the fourteenth day,* of the Hebrew **m** of Adar.
9:18 {the third day,} Hebrew *killing their enemies on the thirteenth day and the fourteenth day, and then rested on the fifteenth day,* of the Hebrew **m** of Adar.
9:19 {in late winter,} Hebrew *on the fourteenth day of the **m** of Adar.…*
Jer 1: 3 {of that year,} Hebrew *In the fifth **m**,* of the Hebrew calendar.…
28: 1 {in late summer} Hebrew *In the fifth **m**,* of the Hebrew calendar.…
28:17 {Two months later,} Hebrew *In the seventh **m** of that same year.* See 28:1 and the note there.
36: 9 {in late autumn,} Hebrew *in the ninth **m**,* of the Hebrew calendar (also in 36:22).…
39: 1 {was in January} Hebrew *in the tenth **m**,* of the Hebrew calendar.…
39: 2 {later, on July 18,} Hebrew *On the ninth day of the fourth **m** of the eleventh year of Zedekiah.…*
41: 1 {But in midautumn,} Hebrew *in the seventh **m**,* of the Hebrew calendar.…
52: 4 {So on January 15,} Hebrew *on the tenth day of the tenth **m**,* of the Hebrew calendar.…
52: 6 {Zedekiah's eleventh year,} Hebrew *By the ninth day of the fourth **m*** [of Zedekiah's eleventh year].…
52:12 {of that year,} Hebrew *On the tenth day of the fifth **m**,* of the Hebrew calendar.…
52:31 {of that year.} Hebrew *on the twenty-fifth day of the twelfth **m**,* of the Hebrew calendar.…
Eze 1: 1 {On July 31} Hebrew *On the fifth day of the fourth **m**,* of the Hebrew calendar (also in 1:2).…
8: 1 {Then on September 17,} Hebrew *on the fifth day of the sixth **m**,* of the Hebrew calendar.…
20: 1 {On August 14,} Hebrew *In the fifth **m**, on the tenth day,* of the Hebrew calendar.…
24: 1 {On January 15,} Hebrew *On the tenth day of the tenth **m**,* of the Hebrew calendar.…
26: 1 {King Jehoiachin's captivity,} Hebrew *In the eleventh year, on the first day of the **m**,* of the Hebrew calendar year. Since an element is missing in the date formula here, scholars have reconstructed this probable reading: *On the first day of the eleventh **m**, during the twelfth year.* This reading would put this message on February 3, 585 B.C.; also see note on 1:1.
29: 1 {On January 7,} Hebrew *On the twelfth day of the tenth **m**,* of the Hebrew calendar.…
29:17 {On April 26,} Hebrew *On the first day of the first **m**,* of the Hebrew calendar.…
30:20 {On April 29,} Hebrew *On the seventh day of the first **m**,* of the Hebrew calendar.…
31: 1 {On June 21,} Hebrew *On the first day of the third **m**,* of the Hebrew calendar.…
32: 1 {On March 3,} Hebrew *On the first day of the twelfth **m**,* of the Hebrew calendar.…
32:17 {On March 17,} Hebrew *On the fifteenth day of the **m**,* presumably in the twelfth **m** of the Hebrew calendar (see 32:1). This would put this message at the end of King Jehoiachin's twelfth year of captivity, on March 17, 585 B.C.; also see note on 29:1. Greek version reads *On the fifteenth day of the first **m**,* which would put this message on April 27, 586 B.C., at the beginning of Jehoiachin's twelfth year.
33:21 {On January 8,} Hebrew *On the fifth day of the tenth **m**,* of the Hebrew calendar.…
40: 1 {On April 28,} Hebrew *At the beginning of the year, on the tenth day of the **m**,…*
45:18 {each new year,} Hebrew *On the first day of the first **m**,* of the Hebrew calendar.…
45:25 {in early autumn,} Hebrew *the festival which begins on the fifteenth day of the seventh **m**.…*
Da 10: 4 {On April 23,} Hebrew *On the twenty-fourth day of the first **m**.…*
Hag 1: 1 {On August 29} Hebrew *On the first day of the sixth **m**,* of the Hebrew calendar.…
1:15 {was on September 21} Hebrew *on the twenty-fourth day of the sixth **m**,* of the Hebrew calendar.…
2: 1 {Then on October 17} Hebrew *on the twenty-first day of the seventh **m**,* of the Hebrew calendar.…
2:10 {On December 18} Hebrew *On the twenty-fourth day of the ninth **m**,* of the Hebrew calendar…
2:20 {on December 18} Hebrew *on the twenty-fourth day of the **m**;* see note on 2:10.
Zec 1: 1 {In midautumn} Hebrew *In the eighth **m**.…*
1: 7 {Then on February 15} Hebrew *on the twenty-fourth day of the eleventh **m**, the **m** of Shebat,* of the Hebrew calendar.…
7: 1 {On December 7} Hebrew *On the fourth day of the ninth **m**, the **m** of Kislev,…*
7: 3 {the Temple's destruction,} Hebrew *mourn and fast in the fifth **m**.…*
7: 5 {in early autumn,} Hebrew *fasted and mourned in the fifth and seventh months.…*

8:19 {autumn, and winter} Hebrew *in the fourth, fifth, seventh, and tenth months....*

MONTHS (3 of 4)

Ex 19: 1 {they left Egypt.} Hebrew *in the third month...on the very day,* i.e., two lunar **m** to the day after leaving Egypt....
Zec 7: 5 {in early autumn,} Hebrew *fasted and mourned in the fifth and seventh* ***m****....*
8:19 {autumn, and winter} Hebrew *in the fourth, fifth, seventh, and tenth* ***m****....*

MOON (1)

Ps 74:16 {made the starlight} Or *m;* Hebrew reads *light.*

MORDECAI'S (1)

Est 2:15 {was Esther's turn} Hebrew *the turn of Esther, the daughter of Abihail, who was* ***M*** *uncle, who had adopted her.*

MORE (2 of 3)

Ps 87: 2 {city in Israel.} Hebrew *He loves the gates of Zion* ***m*** *than all the dwellings of Jacob.*
Ac 26:28 {Christian so quickly?"} Or *"A little* ***m****, and your arguments would make me a Christian."*

MORNING (2)

Lk 24: 1 {on Sunday morning} Greek *But on the first day of the week, very early in the* ***m****.*
2Pe 1:19 {in your hearts.} Or *until the day dawns and the* ***m*** *star rises in your hearts.*

MORTALS (1)

1Sa 2:33 {a violent death.} As in Dead Sea Scrolls, which read *die by the sword;* Masoretic Text reads *die like* ***m****.*

MOSES (3)

Ex 2:10 {named him Moses,} ***M*** sounds like a Hebrew term that means "to draw out."
Dt 31: 1 {had finished saying} As in Dead Sea Scrolls and Greek version; Masoretic Text reads ***M*** *went and spoke.*
33: 6 {tribe of Reuben:} Hebrew lacks ***M*** *said this about the tribe of Reuben.*

MOSES' (2)

Ex 3: 1 {his father-in-law, Jethro,} **M** father-in-law went by two names, Jethro and Reuel.
4:24 {LORD confronted Moses} Or *confronted* ***M*** *son;* Hebrew reads *confronted him.*

MOTHER (4)

1Ki 15:10 {years. His grandmother} Hebrew *his* ***m*** (also in 15:13); compare 15:2.
Jer 50:12 {But your homeland} Hebrew *your* ***m****.*
Hos 2: 2 {now, call Israel} Hebrew *call your* ***m****.*
1Th 2: 7 {as a mother} Some manuscripts read *we were as infants among you; we were as a* ***m****.*

MOTHERS (1)

1Ti 2:15 {saved through childbearing} Or *will be saved by accepting their role as* ***m****,* or *will be saved by the birth of the Child.*

MOUNT (15)

Dt 4:48 {to Mount Sirion,} As in Syriac version (see also 3:9); Hebrew reads ***M*** *Sion.*
Jdg 7: 3 {afraid may leave} Hebrew *leave* ***M*** *Gilead.* The identity of **M** Gilead is uncertain in this context. It is perhaps used here as another name for **M** Gilboa.
Ps 29: 6 {and Mount Hermon} Hebrew *Sirion,* another name for **M** Hermon.
48: 2 {the holy mountain,} Or ***M*** *Zion, in the far north;* Hebrew reads ***M*** *Zion, the heights of Zaphon.*
74: 2 {And remember Jerusalem,} Hebrew ***M*** *Zion.*
Isa 4: 5 {shade for Jerusalem} Hebrew ***M*** *Zion.*
18: 7 {Almighty in Jerusalem,} Hebrew *on* ***M*** *Zion.*
29: 8 {conquest over Jerusalem,} Hebrew ***M*** *Zion.*
La 5:18 {For Jerusalem} Hebrew ***M*** *Zion.*
Am 4: 3 {from your fortresses.} Hebrew *thrown out toward Harmon,* possibly a reference to **M** Hermon.
Ob 1:17 {"But Jerusalem} Hebrew ***M*** *Zion.*
Mic 4: 7 {rule from Jerusalem} Hebrew ***M*** *Zion.*

MOUNTAIN (4)

Dt 33: 2 {his right hand.} Or *came from myriads of holy ones, from the south, from his* ***m*** *slopes.* The meaning of the Hebrew is uncertain.
Ps 2: 6 {my holy city.} Hebrew *on Zion, my holy* ***m****.*
Isa 25: 6 {In Jerusalem,} Hebrew *On this* ***m****;* also in 25:10.
Jn 4:20 {at Mount Gerizim,} Greek *on this* ***m****.*

MOUNTAINS (4)

Nu 27:12 {of the river,} Hebrew *the* ***m*** *of Abarim.*
33:47 {of the river,} Hebrew *the* ***m*** *of Abarim;* also in 33:48.
Dt 32:49 {of the river,} Hebrew *the* ***m*** *of Abarim.*
Ps 76: 4 {the everlasting mountains.} As in Greek version; Hebrew reads *than* ***m*** *filled with beasts of prey.*

MOURN (1)

Zec 7: 3 {the Temple's destruction,} Hebrew ***m*** *and fast in the fifth month.* This month of the Hebrew lunar calendar usually occurs in July and August.

MOURNED (1)

Zec 7: 5 {in early autumn,} Hebrew *fasted and* ***m*** *in the fifth and seventh months....*

MOURNING (1)

Ge 50:11 {the place Abel-mizraim,} *Abel-mizraim* means "**m** of the Egyptians."

MOUTH (2)

Mt 15:11 {say and do.} Or *what comes out of the* ***m*** *defiles a person.*
2Ti 4:17 {from certain death.} Greek *from the* ***m*** *of a lion.*

MOVE (1)

Hos 5:10 {bad as thieves.} Hebrew *have become as those who* ***m*** *a boundary marker.*

MOVED (2)

Ge 47:21 {servants to Pharaoh.} As in Greek version and Samaritan Pentateuch; Hebrew reads *He* ***m*** *the people into the towns throughout the land of Egypt.*
Mk 1:41 {Moved with pity,} Some manuscripts read ***M*** *with anger.*

MOVEMENT (1)

Jn 5: 3 {on the porches.} Some manuscripts add *waiting for a certain* ***m*** *of the water, [4]for an angel of the Lord came from time to time and stirred up the water. And the first person to step down into it afterward was healed.*

MOVEMENTS (1)

SS 6:13 {lines of dancers?} Or *as you would at the* ***m*** *of two armies?* or *as you would at the dance of Mahanaim?* The meaning of the Hebrew is uncertain.

MUCH (1)

Eph 1:18 {to his people.} Or *realize how* ***m*** *God has been honored by acquiring his people.*

MULTITUDES (1)

Mt 11:12 {people attack it.} Or *until now, eager* ***m*** *have been pressing into the Kingdom of Heaven.*

MURDERED (1)

1Ki 2: 5 {time of peace,} Or *He* ***m*** *them during a time of peace as revenge for deaths they had caused in time of war.*

MUSICAL (8)

1Ch 15:20 {play the lyres.} Hebrew adds *according to Alamoth,* which is probably a **m** term. The meaning of the Hebrew is uncertain.
15:21 {play the harps.} Hebrew adds *according to the Sheminith,* which is probably a **m** term. The meaning of the Hebrew is uncertain.
Ps 3: 2 {Interlude} Hebrew *Selah.* The meaning of this word is uncertain, though it is probably a **m** or literary term. It is rendered *Interlude* throughout the Psalms.
Da 3: 5 {and other instruments,} The identification of some of these **m** instruments is uncertain.
3: 7 {the musical instruments,} Aramaic *the horn, flute, zither, lyre, harp, and other instruments of the* ***m*** *ensemble.*
3:10 {the musical instruments.} Aramaic *the horn, flute, zither, lyre, harp, pipes, and other instruments of the* ***m*** *ensemble;* also in 3:15.
Hab 3: 1 {the prophet Habakkuk:} Hebrew adds *according to shigionoth,* probably indicating the **m** setting for the prayer.
3: 3 {and Mount Paran.} Hebrew adds *selah;* also in 3:9, 13. The meaning of this Hebrew term is uncertain; it is probably a **m** or literary term.

MUZUR (4)

1Ki 10:28 {imported from Egypt} Possibly ***M****,* a district near Cilicia; also in 10:29.
2Ki 7: 6 {Hittites and Egyptians} Possibly *and the people of* ***M****,* a district near Cilicia.
2Ch 1:16 {imported from Egypt} Possibly ***M****,* a district near Cilicia; also in 1:17.
9:28 {imported from Egypt} Possibly ***M****,* a district near Cilicia.

MYRIADS (1)

Dt 33: 2 {his right hand.} Or *came from* ***m*** *of holy ones, from the south, from his mountain slopes.* The meaning of the Hebrew is uncertain.

MYSIA (1)

Ac 16: 6[-7] {province of Bithynia,} *Phrygia, Galatia, Asia,* ***M****,* and *Bithynia* were all districts in the land now called Turkey.

MYSTERY (3)

1Co 2: 1 {God's message.} Greek ***m****;* other manuscripts read *testimony.*
2: 7 {wisdom of God,} Greek *we speak God's wisdom in a* ***m****.*
Eph 6:19 {the Gentiles, too.} Greek *explain the* ***m*** *of the gospel.*

MYTHICAL (6)

Job 9:13 {forces against him} Hebrew *The helpers of Rahab,* the name of a **m** sea monster that represents chaos in ancient literature.
26:12 {great sea monster.} Hebrew *Rahab,* the name of a **m** sea monster that represents chaos in ancient literature.
Ps 87: 4 {will record Egypt} Hebrew *Rahab,* the name of a **m** sea monster that represents chaos in ancient literature. The name is used here as a poetic name for Egypt.
89:10 {great sea monster.} Hebrew *Rahab,* the name of a **m** sea monster that represents chaos in ancient literature.
Isa 30: 7 {the Harmless Dragon.} Hebrew *Rahab who sits still.* Rahab is the name of a **m** sea monster that represents chaos in ancient literature. The name is used here as a poetic name for Egypt.
51: 9 {of the Nile.} Hebrew *slew Rahab the dragon.* Rahab is the name of a **m** sea monster that represents chaos in ancient literature. The name is used here as a poetic name for Egypt.

MYTHS (1)

1Ti 1: 4 {and spiritual pedigrees.} Greek *in* ***m*** *and endless genealogies, which cause speculation.*

N

NAARAI (1)

1Ch 11:37 {Paarai} As in parallel text at 2 Sam 23:35; Hebrew reads *N.*

NABAL (1)

1Sa 25:25 {his name suggests.} The name *N* means "fool."

NAHASH (2)

1Sa 10:27 {Saul ignored them.} Dead Sea Scroll 4QSam[a] continues: *N, king of the Ammonites, had been grievously oppressing the Gadites and Reubenites who lived east of the Jordan River....of all the Israelites east of the Jordan, there wasn't a single one whose right eye N had not gouged out....*

NAME (217)

Ge 4:25 {named him Seth,} *Seth* probably means "granted"; the **n** may also mean "appointed."
32:31 {he left Peniel,} Hebrew *Penuel,* a variant **n** for Peniel.
36:26 {sons of Dishon} Hebrew *Dishan,* a variant **n** for Dishon; compare 36:21, 28.
Ex 3: 1 {wilderness near Sinai,} Hebrew *Horeb,* another **n** for Sinai.
17: 6 {Mount Sinai.} Hebrew *Horeb,* another **n** for Sinai.
33: 6 {left Mount Sinai,} Hebrew *Horeb,* another **n** for Sinai.
Nu 6:27 {as my people,} Hebrew *will put my n on the people of Israel.*
33:45 {They left Iye-abarim} As in 33:44; Hebrew reads *Iyim,* another **n** for Iye-abarim.
Dt 1: 2 {from Mount Sinai} Hebrew *Horeb,* another **n** for Sinai; also in 1:6, 19.
4:10 {at Mount Sinai,} Hebrew *Horeb,* another **n** for Sinai; also in 4:15.
5: 2 {at Mount Sinai,} Hebrew *Horeb,* another **n** for Sinai.
9: 8 {at Mount Sinai,} Hebrew *Horeb,* another **n** for Sinai.
18:16 {at Mount Sinai.} Hebrew *Horeb,* another **n** for Sinai.
29: 1 {at Mount Sinai.} Hebrew *Horeb,* another **n** for Sinai.
32:44 {came with Joshua} Hebrew *Hoshea,* a variant **n** for Joshua.
Jos 12:23 {city of Naphoth-dor} Hebrew *Naphath-dor,* a variant **n** for Naphoth-dor.
17:11 {to Manasseh: Beth-shan,} Hebrew *Beth-shean,* a variant **n** for Beth-shan; also in 17:16.
19:47 {town of Laish.} Hebrew *Leshem,* another **n** for Laish.
21:36 {received Bezer, Jahaz,} Hebrew *Jahzah,* a variant **n** for Jahaz.
Jdg 1:27 {living in Beth-shan,} Hebrew *Beth-shean,* a variant **n** for Beth-shan.
2: 9 {inherited, at Timnath-serah} Hebrew *Timnath-heres,* a variant **n** for Timnath-serah.
7: 3 {afraid may leave} Hebrew *leave Mount Gilead.* The identity of Mount Gilead is uncertain in this context. It is perhaps used here as another **n** for Mount Gilboa.

8: 8 {up to Peniel} Hebrew *Penuel,* a variant **n** for Peniel; also in 8:9, 17.
9:46 {temple of Baal-berith.} Hebrew *El-berith,* another **n** for Baal-berith; compare 9:4.
1Sa 12:11 {LORD sent Gideon,} Hebrew *Jerubbaal,* another **n** for Gideon; see Judg 7:1.
14:49 {included Jonathan, Ishbosheth,} Hebrew *Ishvi,* a variant **n** for Ishbosheth; also known as Eshbaal.
25:25 {his name suggests.} The **n** *Nabal* means "fool."
2Sa 3:15 {her husband Palti} As in 1 Sam 25:44; Hebrew reads *Paltiel,* a variant **n** for Palti.
5:14 {in Jerusalem: Shimea,} As in parallel text at 1 Chr 3:5; Hebrew reads *Shammua,* a variant **n** for Shimea.
6: 2 {Baalah of Judah} *Baalah of Judah* is another **n** for Kiriath-jearim; compare 1 Chr 13:6.
8: 1 {their largest city.} Hebrew *by conquering Metheg-ammah,* a **n** which means "the bridle," possibly referring to the size of the city or the tribute money taken from it. Compare 1 Chr 18:1.
13: 3 {David's brother Shimea.} Hebrew *Shimeah* (also in 13:32), a variant **n** for Shimea; compare 1 Chr 2:13.
17:25 {father was Jether,} Hebrew *Ithra,* a variant **n** for Jether.
21:21 {David's brother Shimea.} As in parallel text at 1 Chr 20:7; Hebrew reads *Shimei,* a variant **n** for Shimea.
1Ki 1: 9 {stone of Zoheleth} Or *to the Serpent's Stone;* Greek version supports reading *Zoheleth* as a proper **n**.
4:11 {Ben-abinadab, in Naphoth-dor.} Hebrew *Naphath-dor,* a variant **n** for Naphoth-dor.
4:12 {all of Beth-shan} Hebrew *Beth-shean,* a variant **n** for Beth-shan; also in 4:12b.
8: 9 {at Mount Sinai,} Hebrew *at Horeb,* another **n** for Sinai.
10:28 {and from Cilicia} Hebrew *Kue,* probably another **n** for Cilicia.
11: 5 {Sidonians, and Molech,} Hebrew *Milcom,* a variant **n** for Molech; also in 11:33.
12:25 {town of Peniel.} Hebrew *Penuel,* a variant **n** for Peniel.
15: 2 {Absalom.} Hebrew *Abishalom* (also in 15:10), a variant **n** for Absalom; compare 2 Chr 11:20.
18:31 {tribes of Israel,} Hebrew *each of the tribes of the sons of Jacob to whom the LORD had said, "Your* **n** *will be Israel."*
19: 8 {to Mount Sinai,} Hebrew *Horeb,* another **n** for Sinai.
2Ki 1:17 {Joram} Hebrew *Jehoram,* a variant **n** for Joram.
3: 1 {Ahab's son Joram} Hebrew *Jehoram,* a variant **n** for Joram; also in 3:6.
8:21 {So Jehoram} Hebrew *Joram,* a variant **n** for Jehoram; also in 8:23, 24.
9:15 {But Joram} Hebrew *Jehoram,* a variant **n** for Joram; also in 9:17, 21, 22, 23, 24.
11: 2 {of King Jehoram,} Hebrew *Joram,* a variant **n** for Jehoram.
11:21 {Joash} Hebrew *Jehoash,* a variant **n** for Joash.
12: 1 {Joash} Hebrew *Jehoash,* a variant **n** for Joash; also in 12:2, 4, 6, 7, 18.
13: 9 {his son Jehoash} Hebrew *Joash,* a variant **n** for Jehoash; also in 13:10, 12, 13, 14, 25.
14: 1 {of King Jehoash} Hebrew *Joash,* a variant **n** for Jehoash; also in 14:13, 23, 27.
14:21 {sixteen-year-old son, Uzziah,} Hebrew *Azariah,* a variant **n** for Uzziah.
15: 1 {Uzziah} Hebrew *Azariah,* a variant **n** for Uzziah; also in 15:6, 7, 8, 17, 23, 27.
15:19 {Then King Tiglath-pileser} Hebrew *Pul,* another **n** for Tiglath-pileser.
18: 2 {mother was Abijah,} As in parallel text at 2 Chr 29:1; Hebrew reads *Abi,* a variant **n** for Abijah.
23:13 {and for Molech,} Hebrew *Milcom,* a variant **n** for Molech.
1Ch 1:34 {Esau and Israel.} *Israel* is the **n** that God gave to Jacob.
2: 1 {sons of Israel} *Israel* is the **n** that God gave to Jacob.
2: 9 {Ram, and Caleb.} Hebrew *Kelubai,* a variant **n** for Caleb; compare 2:18.
2:19 {Caleb married Ephrathah,} Hebrew *Ephrath,* a variant **n** for Ephrathah; compare 2:50 and 4:4.
3: 5 {and Solomon. Bathsheba,} Hebrew *Bathshua,* a variant **n** for Bathsheba.
3:11 {Jehoram,} Hebrew *Joram,* a variant **n** for Jehoram.
3:12 {Amaziah, Uzziah,} Hebrew *Azariah,* a variant **n** for Uzziah.
3:15 {third), and Jehoahaz} Hebrew *Shallum,* another **n** for Jehoahaz.
3:16 {his uncle Zedekiah.} Hebrew *The descendants of Jehoiakim were his son Jeconiah* [a variant **n** for Jehoiachin] *and his son Zedekiah.*
3:17 {sons of Jehoiachin,} Hebrew *Jeconiah,* a variant **n** for Jehoiachin.
5: 1 {son of Israel} *Israel* is the **n** that God gave to Jacob.
5: 6 {by King Tiglath-pileser} Hebrew *Tilgath-pilneser,* a variant **n** for Tiglath-pileser; also in 5:26.
6:16 {Levi were Gershon,} Hebrew *Gershom,* a variant **n** for Gershon (see 6:1); also in 6:17, 20, 43, 62, 71.
6:23 {Elkanah, Abiasaph,} Hebrew *Ebiasaph,* a variant **n** for Abiasaph (also in 6:37); compare parallel text at Exod 6:24.
6:38 {Levi, and Israel.} *Israel* is the **n** that God gave to Jacob.
6:78 {desert town), Jahaz,} Hebrew *Jahzah,* a variant **n** for Jahaz.
7:13 {Naphtali were Jahzeel,} As in parallel text at Gen 46:24; Hebrew reads *Jahziel,* a variant **n** for Jahzeel.
7:29 {Beth-shan,} Hebrew *Beth-shean,* a variant **n** for Beth-shan.
7:29 {son of Israel} *Israel* is the **n** that God gave to Jacob.
7:35 {his brother Helem} Possibly another **n** for *Hotham;* compare 7:32.
7:37 {Shamma, Shilshah, Ithran,} Possibly another **n** for *Jether;* compare 7:38.
8:31 {Gedor, Ahio, Zechariah,} As in parallel text at 9:37; Hebrew reads *Zeker,* a variant **n** for Zechariah.
8:32 {father of Shimeam.} As in parallel text at 9:38; Hebrew reads *Shimeah,* a variant **n** for Shimeam.
8:35 {Pithon, Melech, Tahrea,} As in parallel text at 9:41; Hebrew reads *Tarea,* a variant **n** for Tahrea.
8:36 {father of Jadah.} As in parallel text at 9:42; Hebrew reads *Jehoaddah,* a variant **n** for Jadah.
8:37 {father of Rephaiah.} As in parallel text at 9:43; Hebrew reads *Raphah,* a variant **n** for Rephaiah.
9:19 {descendant of Abiasaph,} Hebrew *Ebiasaph,* a variant **n** for Abiasaph; compare Exod 6:24.
11:12 {son of Dodai,} As in parallel text at 2 Sam 23:9 (see also 1 Chr 27:4); Hebrew reads *Dodo,* a variant **n** for Dodai.
14: 4 {in Jerusalem: Shimea,} Hebrew *Shammua,* a variant **n** for Shimea; compare 3:5.
14: 7 {Eliada,} Hebrew *Beeliada,* a variant **n** for Eliada; compare 3:8 and parallel text at 2 Sam 5:16.
15: 7 {clan of Gershon,} Hebrew *Gershom,* a variant **n** for Gershon.
18: 8 {cities of Tebah} Hebrew reads *Tibhath,* a variant **n** for Tebah; compare parallel text at 2 Sam 8:8.
18:10 {his son Joram} As in parallel text at 2 Sam 8:10; Hebrew reads *Hadoram,* a variant **n** for Joram.
21:15 {floor of Araunah} As in parallel text at 2 Sam 24:16; Hebrew reads *Ornan,* another **n** for Araunah; also in 21:18-28.
23: 7 {descent from Libni} Hebrew *Ladan* (also in 23:8-9), another **n** for Libni; compare 6:17.
24:20 {leader was Shebuel.} Hebrew *Shubael* (also in 24:20b), a variant **n** for Shebuel; compare 23:16 and 26:24.
24:22 {leader was Shelomith.} Hebrew *Shelomoth* (also in 24:22b), a variant **n** for Shelomith; compare 23:18.
25: 4 {Mattaniah, Uzziel, Shubael,} Hebrew *Shebuel,* a variant **n** for Shubael; compare 25:20.
25:11 {fell to Zeri} Hebrew *Izri,* a variant **n** for Zeri; compare 25:3.
25:14 {fell to Asarelah} Hebrew *Jesharelah,* a variant **n** for Asarelah; compare 25:2.
25:18 {fell to Uzziel} Hebrew *Azarel,* a variant **n** for Uzziel; compare 25:4.
25:22 {fell to Jerimoth} Hebrew *Jeremoth,* a variant **n** for Jerimoth; compare 25:4.
25:24 {fell to Joshbekashah} Hebrew *Joshbekasha,* a variant **n** for Joshbekashah; compare 25:4.
25:29 {fell to Geddalti} Hebrew *Giddalti,* a variant **n** for Geddalti; compare 25:4.
26:14 {went to Meshelemiah} Hebrew *Shelemiah,* a variant **n** for Meshelemiah; compare 26:2.
26:21 {family of Libni} Hebrew *Ladan,* another **n** for Libni; compare 6:17.
26:21 {of Gershon, Jehiel} Hebrew *Jehieli* (also in 26:22), a variant **n** for Jehiel; compare 23:8.
26:31 {Hebron came Jeriah,} Hebrew *Jerijah,* a variant **n** for Jeriah; compare 23:19.
27: 8 {Shammah} Hebrew *Shamhuth,* another **n** for Shammah; compare 11:27 and 2 Sam 23:25.
27:15 {Heled,} Hebrew *Heldai,* a variant **n** for Heled; compare 11:30 and 2 Sam 23:29.
29:10 {our ancestor Israel,} *Israel* is the **n** that God gave to Jacob.
2Ch 1:16 {and from Cilicia} Hebrew *Kue,* probably another **n** for Cilicia.
2: 3 {to King Hiram} Hebrew *Huram,* a variant **n** for Hiram; also in 2:11, 12.
3: 1 {floor of Araunah} Hebrew reads *Ornan,* another **n** for Araunah; compare 2 Sam 24:16.
5:10 {at Mount Sinai,} Hebrew *Horeb,* another **n** for Sinai.
8: 2 {that King Hiram} Hebrew *Huram,* a variant **n** for Hiram; also in 8:18.
9:21 {sent by Hiram.} Hebrew *Huram,* a variant **n** for Hiram.
10:18 {Adoniram,} Hebrew *Hadoram,* a variant **n** for Adoniram; compare 1 Kgs 4:6; 5:14; 12:18.
16: 4 {Ijon, Dan, Abel-beth-maacah,} As in parallel text at 1 Kgs 15:20; Hebrew reads *Abel-maim,* another **n** for Abel-beth-maacah.
21:17 {youngest son, Ahaziah,} Hebrew *Jehoahaz,* a variant **n** for Ahaziah; compare 22:1.
22: 5 {with King Joram,} Hebrew *Jehoram,* a variant **n** for Joram; also in 22:6, 7.
22:11 {Ahaziah's sister Jehosheba,} As in parallel text at 2 Kgs 11:2; Hebrew reads *Jehoshabeath,* a variant **n** for Jehosheba.
25: 1 {mother was Jehoaddin,} As in parallel text at 2 Kgs 14:2; Hebrew reads *Jehoaddan,* a variant **n** for Jehoaddin.
25:17 {Israel's king Jehoash,} Hebrew *Joash,* a variant **n** for Jehoash; also in 25:18, 21, 23, 25.
28:20 {when King Tiglath-pileser} Hebrew *Tilgath-pilneser,* a variant **n** for Tiglath-pileser.
30: 6 {Isaac, and Israel,} *Israel* is the **n** that God gave to Jacob.
36: 2 {Jehoahaz} Hebrew *Joahaz,* a variant **n** for Jehoahaz; also in 36:4.
Ezr 3: 2 {son of Jehozadak} Hebrew *Jozadak,* a variant **n** for Jehozadak; also in 3:8.
3: 9 {descendants of Hodaviah.} Hebrew *sons of Judah* (i.e., *bene Yehudah*). *Bene* might also be read here as the proper **n** Binnui; *Yehudah* is probably another **n** for Hodaviah. Compare 2:40; Neh 7:43; 1 Esdras 5:58.
4: 6 {later when Xerxes} Hebrew *Ahasuerus,* another **n** for Xerxes.
4:10 {and noble Ashurbanipal} Aramaic *Osnappar,* another **n** for Ashurbanipal.
5: 2 {son of Jehozadak} Aramaic *Jozadak,* a variant **n** for Jehozadak.
8:18 {son of Israel.} *Israel* is the **n** that God gave to Jacob.
10:18 {son of Jehozadak} Hebrew *Jozadak,* a variant **n** for Jehozadak.
Ne 3:15 {pool of Siloam} Hebrew *pool of Shelah,* another **n** for the pool of Siloam.
6: 6 {"Geshem} Hebrew *Gashmu,* another **n** for Geshem.
12:17 {was also a} Hebrew lacks the **n** of this family leader.
12:24 {Sherebiah, Jeshua, Binnui,} Hebrew *son of* (i.e., *ben*), which should probably be read here as the proper **n** Binnui; compare Ezra 3:9 and the note there.
12:26 {son of Jehozadak,} Hebrew *Jozadak,* a variant **n** for Jehozadak.
13:28 {sons of Joiada} Hebrew *Jehoiada,* a variant **n** for Joiada.
Est 1: 1 {of King Xerxes,} Hebrew *Ahasuerus,* another **n** for Xerxes; also throughout the book of Esther.
2: 6 {with King Jehoiachin} Hebrew *Jeconiah,* a variant **n** for Jehoiachin.
Job 9:13 {forces against him} Hebrew *The helpers of Rahab,* the **n** of a mythical sea monster that represents chaos in ancient literature.
26:12 {great sea monster.} Hebrew *Rahab,* the **n** of a mythical sea monster that represents chaos in ancient literature.
Ps 29: 6 {and Mount Hermon} Hebrew *Sirion,* another **n** for Mount Hermon.
76: 2 {Jerusalem} Hebrew *Salem,* another **n** for Jerusalem.
87: 4 {will record Egypt} Hebrew *Rahab,* the **n** of a mythical sea monster that represents chaos in ancient literature. The **n** is used here as a poetic **n** for Egypt.
89:10 {great sea monster.} Hebrew *Rahab,* the **n** of a mythical sea monster that represents chaos in ancient literature.
106:19 {at Mount Sinai} Hebrew *at Horeb,* another **n** for Sinai.
Isa 16:11 {sorrow for Kir-hareseth} Hebrew *Kir-heres,* a variant **n** for Kir-hareseth.
21:11 {Someone from Edom} Hebrew *Seir,* another **n** for Edom.
30: 7 {the Harmless Dragon.} Hebrew *Rahab who sits still.* Rahab is the **n** of a mythical sea monster that represents chaos in ancient literature. The **n** is used here as a poetic **n** for Egypt.
33: 1 {for you Assyrians,} Hebrew *for you, O destroyer...O betrayer.* The Hebrew text does not specifically **n** Assyria as the object of this prophecy.
51: 9 {of the Nile.} Hebrew *slew Rahab the dragon.* Rahab is the **n** of a mythical sea monster that represents chaos in ancient literature. The **n** is used here as a poetic **n** for Egypt.
Jer 21: 2 {us. King Nebuchadnezzar} Hebrew *Nebuchadrezzar,* a variant **n** for Nebuchadnezzar; also in 21:7.
22:11 {says about Jehoahaz,} Hebrew *Shallum,* another **n** for Jehoahaz.
22:24 {abandon you, Jehoiachin} Hebrew *Coniah,* a variant **n** for Jehoiachin; also in 22:28, 30.
22:25 {afraid—to King Nebuchadnezzar} Hebrew *Nebuchadrezzar,* a variant **n** for Nebuchadnezzar.
24: 1 {After King Nebuchadnezzar} Hebrew *Nebuchadrezzar,* a variant **n** for Nebuchadnezzar.
24: 1 {Babylon exiled Jehoiachin} Hebrew *Jeconiah,* a variant **n** for Jehoiachin.
25: 1 {when King Nebuchadnezzar} Hebrew *Nebuchadrezzar,* a variant **n** for Nebuchadnezzar; also in 25:9.
25:26 {king of Babylon} Hebrew *of Sheshach,* a code **n** for Babylon.
27:20 {he exiled Jehoiachin} Hebrew *Jeconiah,* a variant **n** for Jehoiachin.
28: 4 {bring back Jehoiachin} Hebrew *Jeconiah,* a variant **n** for Jehoiachin.
29: 2 {after King Jehoiachin,} Hebrew *Jeconiah,* a variant **n** for Jehoiachin.
29:21 {over to Nebuchadnezzar} Hebrew *Nebuchadrezzar,* a variant **n** for Nebuchadnezzar.
32: 1 {of King Nebuchadnezzar.} Hebrew *Nebuchadrezzar,* a variant **n** for Nebuchadnezzar; also in 32:28.

35: 6 {wine, because Jehonadab} Hebrew *Jonadab,* a variant **n** for Jehonadab; also in 35:10, 14, 18, 19. See 2 Kgs 10:15.
35:11 {when King Nebuchadnezzar} Hebrew *Nebuchadrezzar,* a variant **n** for Nebuchadnezzar.
37: 1 {Josiah succeeded Jehoiachin} Hebrew *Coniah,* a variant **n** for Jehoiachin.
37: 1 {by King Nebuchadnezzar} Hebrew *Nebuchadrezzar,* a variant **n** for Nebuchadnezzar.
38: 1 {of Pashhur, Jehucal} Hebrew *Jucal,* a variant **n** for Jehucal; see 37:3.
39: 1 {that King Nebuchadnezzar} Hebrew *Nebuchadrezzar,* a variant **n** for Nebuchadnezzar; also in 39:11.
40: 8 {the Netophathite, Jaazaniah} As in parallel text at 2 Kgs 25:23; Hebrew reads *Jezaniah,* a variant **n** for Jaazaniah.
43:10 {my servant Nebuchadnezzar,} Hebrew *Nebuchadrezzar,* a variant **n** for Nebuchadnezzar.
44:30 {to King Nebuchadnezzar} Hebrew *Nebuchadrezzar,* a variant **n** for Nebuchadnezzar.
46: 2 {by King Nebuchadnezzar} Hebrew *Nebuchadrezzar,* a variant **n** for Nebuchadnezzar; also in 46:13, 26.
48:21 {Holon and Jahaz} Hebrew *Jahzah,* a variant **n** for Jahaz.
48:31 {men of Kir-hareseth.} Hebrew *Kir-heres,* a variant **n** for Kir-hareseth; also in 48:36.
49: 1 {who worship Molech,} Hebrew *Milcom,* a variant **n** for Molech; also in 49:3.
49:28 {by King Nebuchadnezzar} Hebrew *Nebuchadrezzar,* a variant **n** for Nebuchadnezzar; also in 49:30.
50:17 {Then King Nebuchadnezzar} Hebrew *Nebuchadrezzar,* a variant **n** for Nebuchadnezzar.
51: 1 {people of Babylonia.} Hebrew *of Leb-kamai,* a code **n** for Babylonia.
51:34 {"King Nebuchadnezzar} Hebrew *Nebuchadrezzar,* a variant **n** for Nebuchadnezzar.
51:41 {"How Babylon} Hebrew *Sheshach,* a code **n** for Babylon.
52: 4 {reign, King Nebuchadnezzar} Hebrew *Nebuchadrezzar,* a variant **n** for Nebuchadnezzar; also in 52:12, 28, 29, 30.
Eze 26: 7 {bring King Nebuchadnezzar} Hebrew *Nebuchadrezzar,* a variant **n** for Nebuchadnezzar.
29:18 {of King Nebuchadnezzar} Hebrew *Nebuchadrezzar,* a variant **n** for Nebuchadnezzar; also in 29:19.
30:10 {Through King Nebuchadnezzar} Hebrew *Nebuchadrezzar,* a variant **n** for Nebuchadnezzar.
Hos 1: 1 {son of Jehoash} Hebrew *Joash,* a variant **n** for Jehoash.
4:15 {and at Beth-aven.} *Beth-aven* means "house of wickedness"; it is being used as another **n** for Bethel, which means "house of God."
5: 8 {cry in Beth-aven} *Beth-aven* means "house of wickedness"; it is being used as another **n** for Bethel, which means "house of God."
10: 5 {idol at Beth-aven.} *Beth-aven* means "house of wickedness"; it is being used as another **n** for Bethel, which means "house of God."
Am 1: 1 {son of Jehoash,} Hebrew *Joash,* a variant **n** for Jehoash.
Zep 1: 5 {they worship Molech,} Hebrew *Malcam,* another **n** for Molech; or it could possibly mean *their king.*
Hag 1: 1 {and to Jeshua} Hebrew *Joshua,* a variant **n** for Jeshua; also in 1:12, 14.
2: 2 {and to Jeshua} Hebrew *Joshua,* a variant **n** for Jeshua; also in 2:4.
Zec 3: 1 {showed me Jeshua} Hebrew *Joshua,* a variant **n** for Jeshua; also in 3:3, 4, 6, 8, 9.
6:11 {Jeshua} Hebrew *Joshua,* a variant **n** for Jeshua.
Mal 4: 4 {on Mount Sinai} Hebrew *Horeb,* another **n** for Sinai.
Mt 10:41 {speaks for God,} Greek *welcome a prophet in the **n** of a prophet.*
18:20 {they are mine,} Greek *gather together in my **n**.*
Mk 13: 6 {be the Messiah.} Greek ***n**, saying, 'I am.'*
Lk 5: 1 {Sea of Galilee,} Greek *Lake Gennesaret,* another **n** for the Sea of Galilee.
21: 8 {be the Messiah} Greek ***n**, saying, 'I am.'*
Jn 12:31 {of this world} *The prince of this world* is a **n** for Satan.
17:12 {kept them safe.} Greek *I have kept in your **n** those whom you have given me.*
21: 1 {Sea of Galilee.} Greek *Sea of Tiberias,* another **n** for the Sea of Galilee.
Ac 26: 9 {Jesus of Nazareth.} Greek *oppose the **n** of Jesus the Nazarene.*
1Co 5: 4 {of the church,} Or *In the **n** of the Lord Jesus, you are to call a meeting of the church.*
1Pe 5:13 {here in Rome} Greek *The elect one in Babylon.* Babylon was probably a code **n** for Rome.
3Jn 1: 7 {for the Lord} Greek *the N.*

NAMED (3)
Nu 26:23 {its ancestor Puah.} As in Samaritan Pentateuch, Greek and Syriac versions, and Latin Vulgate (see also 1 Chr 7:1); Hebrew reads *The Punite clan, **n** after its ancestor Puvah.*
26:40 {their ancestor Ard.} As in Samaritan Pentateuch, some Greek manuscripts, and Latin Vulgate; Hebrew lacks ***n** after their ancestor Ard.*
Mk 3:17 {"Sons of Thunder"} Greek *whom he **n** Boanerges, which means Sons of Thunder.*

NAOMI (1)
Ru 1:20 {call me Mara,} *N* means "pleasant"; *Mara* means "bitter."

NAPHATH-DOR (2)
Jos 12:23 {city of Naphoth-dor} Hebrew *N,* a variant name for Naphoth-dor.
1Ki 4:11 {Ben-abinadab, in Naphoth-dor.} Hebrew *N,* a variant name for Naphoth-dor.

NAPHOTH-DOR (2)
Jos 12:23 {city of Naphoth-dor} Hebrew *Naphath-dor,* a variant name for **N**.
1Ki 4:11 {Ben-abinadab, in Naphoth-dor.} Hebrew *Naphath-dor,* a variant name for **N**.

NAPHTALI (1)
Ge 30: 8 {named him Naphtali,} *N* means "my struggle."

NARD (1)
Mk 14: 3 {of expensive perfume.} Greek *an alabaster jar of expensive ointment, pure **n**.*

NARROW (1)
Pr 23:27 {woman is treacherous.} Hebrew *is a **n** well.*

NATION (4)
Joel 1: 6 {army of locusts} Hebrew *A **n**.*
Mt 24:34 {you, this generation} Or *this age,* or *this **n**.*
Mk 13:30 {you, this generation} Or *this age,* or *this **n**.*
Lk 21:32 {you, this generation} Or *this age,* or *this **n**.*

NATIONS (1)
Dt 32:43 {God worship him,} As in Dead Sea Scrolls and Greek version; Masoretic Text reads *Rejoice with his people, O **n**.*

NAZARENE (1)
Ac 26: 9 {Jesus of Nazareth.} Greek *oppose the name of Jesus the N.*

NAZIRITE (1)
1Sa 1:22 {the LORD permanently."} Some manuscripts add *I will offer him as a N for all time.*

NEBUCHADNEZZAR (19 of 20)
Jer 21: 2 {King Nebuchadnezzar} Hebrew *Nebuchadrezzar,* a variant name for **N**; also in 21:7.
22:25 {King Nebuchadnezzar} Hebrew *Nebuchadrezzar,* a variant name for **N**.
24: 1 {King Nebuchadnezzar} Hebrew *Nebuchadrezzar,* a variant name for **N**.
25: 1 {King Nebuchadnezzar} Hebrew *Nebuchadrezzar,* a variant name for **N**; also in 25:9.
29:21 {Nebuchadnezzar} Hebrew *Nebuchadrezzar,* a variant name for **N**.
32: 1 {Nebuchadnezzar.} Hebrew *Nebuchadrezzar,* a variant name for **N**; also in 32:28.
35:11 {King Nebuchadnezzar} Hebrew *Nebuchadrezzar,* a variant name for **N**.
37: 1 {King Nebuchadnezzar} Hebrew *Nebuchadrezzar,* a variant name for **N**.
39: 1 {King Nebuchadnezzar} Hebrew *Nebuchadrezzar,* a variant name for **N**; also in 39:11.
43:10 {Nebuchadnezzar,} Hebrew *Nebuchadrezzar,* a variant name for **N**.
44:30 {King Nebuchadnezzar} Hebrew *Nebuchadrezzar,* a variant name for **N**.
46: 2 {King Nebuchadnezzar} Hebrew *Nebuchadrezzar,* a variant name for **N**; also in 46:13, 26.
49:28 {King Nebuchadnezzar} Hebrew *Nebuchadrezzar,* a variant name for **N**; also in 49:30.
50:17 {King Nebuchadnezzar} Hebrew *Nebuchadrezzar,* a variant name for **N**.
51:34 {Nebuchadnezzar} Hebrew *Nebuchadrezzar,* a variant name for **N**.
52: 4 {King Nebuchadnezzar} Hebrew *Nebuchadrezzar,* a variant name for **N**; also in 52:12, 28, 29, 30.
Eze 26: 7 {King Nebuchadnezzar} Hebrew *Nebuchadrezzar,* a variant name for **N**.
29:18 {King Nebuchadnezzar} Hebrew *Nebuchadrezzar,* a variant name for **N**; also in 29:19.
30:10 {King Nebuchadnezzar} Hebrew *Nebuchadrezzar,* a variant name for **N**.

NEBUCHADREZZAR (19)
Jer 21: 2 {King Nebuchadnezzar} Hebrew *N,* a variant name for Nebuchadnezzar; also in 21:7.
22:25 {King Nebuchadnezzar} Hebrew *N,* a variant name for Nebuchadnezzar.
24: 1 {After King Nebuchadnezzar} Hebrew *N,* a variant name for Nebuchadnezzar.
25: 1 {when King Nebuchadnezzar} Hebrew *N,* a variant name for Nebuchadnezzar; also in 25:9.
29:21 {over to Nebuchadnezzar} Hebrew *N,* a variant name for Nebuchadnezzar.
32: 1 {of King Nebuchadnezzar.} Hebrew *N,* a variant name for Nebuchadnezzar; also in 32:28.
35:11 {when King Nebuchadnezzar} Hebrew *N,* a variant name for Nebuchadnezzar.
37: 1 {by King Nebuchadnezzar} Hebrew *N,* a variant name for Nebuchadnezzar.
39: 1 {that King Nebuchadnezzar} Hebrew *N,* a variant name for Nebuchadnezzar; also in 39:11.
43:10 {my servant Nebuchadnezzar,} Hebrew *N,* a variant name for Nebuchadnezzar.
44:30 {to King Nebuchadnezzar} Hebrew *N,* a variant name for Nebuchadnezzar.
46: 2 {by King Nebuchadnezzar} Hebrew *N,* a variant name for Nebuchadnezzar; also in 46:13, 26.
49:28 {by King Nebuchadnezzar} Hebrew *N,* a variant name for Nebuchadnezzar; also in 49:30.
50:17 {Then King Nebuchadnezzar} Hebrew *N,* a variant name for Nebuchadnezzar.
51:34 {"King Nebuchadnezzar} Hebrew *N,* a variant name for Nebuchadnezzar.
52: 4 {Nebuchadnezzar} Hebrew *N,* a variant name for Nebuchadnezzar; also in 52:12, 28, 29, 30.
Eze 26: 7 {bring King Nebuchadnezzar} Hebrew *N,* a variant name for Nebuchadnezzar.
29:18 {of King Nebuchadnezzar} Hebrew *N,* a variant name for Nebuchadnezzar; also in 29:19.
30:10 {Through King Nebuchadnezzar} Hebrew *N,* a variant name for Nebuchadnezzar.

NECESSARY (2)
Lk 23:16 {will release him."} Some manuscripts add verse 17, *For it was **n** for him to release one [prisoner] for them during the feast.*
Heb 9:16 {is dead.} Or *Now when someone makes a covenant, it is **n** to ratify it with the death of a sacrifice.*

NEED (2)
2Sa 13:39 {his son Absalom.} Or *no longer felt a **n** to go out after Absalom.*
Jn 16:30 {tell you anything.} Or *don't **n** that anyone should ask you anything.*

NEGLECTED (1)
SS 1: 6 {done to me!} Hebrew *My own vineyard I have **n**.*

NEH (5)
Ezr 2:24 {people of Beth-azmaveth} As in parallel text at **N** 7:28; Hebrew reads *Azmaveth.*
2:25 {peoples of Kiriath-jearim,} As in some Hebrew manuscripts and Greek version (see also **N** 7:29); Hebrew reads *Kiriath-arim.*
2:46 {Hagab, Shalmai,} As in the marginal *Qere* reading of the Masoretic Text (see also **N** 7:48); Hebrew text reads *Shamlai.*
2:55 {Sotai, Sophereth,} As in parallel text at **N** 7:57; Hebrew reads *Hassophereth.*
3: 9 {descendants of Hodaviah.} Hebrew *sons of Judah* (i.e., *bene Yehudah*). *Bene* might also be read here as the proper name Binnui; *Yehudah* is probably another name for Hodaviah. Compare 2:40; **N** 7:43; 1 Esdras 5:58.

NEHUM (1)
Ne 7: 7 {Bigvai, Rehum,} As in parallel text at Ezra 2:2; Hebrew reads *N.*

NEHUSHTAN (1)
2Ki 18: 4 {Nehushtan.} *N* sounds like the Hebrew terms that mean "snake," "bronze," and "unclean thing."

NEITHER (2)
1Sa 1:11 {never be cut."} Some manuscripts add *He will drink **n** wine nor intoxicants.*
Mk 11:25 {your sins, too.} Some manuscripts add verse 26, *But if you do not forgive, **n** will your Father who is in heaven forgive your sins.*

NEPHILIM (2)
Ge 6: 4 {even afterward, giants} Hebrew *N.*
Nu 13:33 {even saw giants} Hebrew ***n**.*

NEPHUSHESIM (1)
Ne 7:52 {Besai, Meunim, Nephusim,} As in parallel text at Ezra 2:50; Hebrew reads *N.*

NER (1)
1Ch 8:30 {Kish, Baal, Ner,} As in some Greek manuscripts (see also 9:36); Hebrew lacks *N.*

NERGAL-SHAREZER (1)
Jer 39: 3 {Samgar, and Nebo-sarsekim,} Or *N, Samgar-nebo, Sarsekim.*

NEVER (4)
Dt 18:10 {a burnt offering.} Or ***n** make your son or daughter pass through the fire.*
2Ch 20:37 {out to sea.} Hebrew ***n** set sail for Tarshish.*
1Pe 2: 6 {never be disappointed.} Or *will **n** be put to shame.* Isa 28:16.
2Pe 2:11 {out disrespectfully against} Greek ***n** bring blasphemous judgment from the Lord against.*

NEW (5)
Mt 26:28 {seals the covenant} Some manuscripts read *the **n** covenant.*
Mk 14:24 {sealing the covenant} Some manuscripts read *the **n** covenant.*
16:17 {speak new languages.} Or ***n** tongues;* some manuscripts omit ***n***.
1Co 5: 6[-7] {can stay pure.} Greek *Don't you realize that even a little leaven spreads quickly through the whole batch of dough? [7]Purge out the old leaven so that you can be a **n** batch of dough, just as you are already unleavened.*

NEWS (1)
Eph 6:15 {be fully prepared.} Or *For shoes, put on the readiness to preach the Good **N** of peace with God.*

NEXT (1)
Mt 27:62 {the Passover ceremonies} Or *On the **n** day, which is after the Preparation.*

NIGER (1)
Ac 13: 1 {"the black man"} Greek *who was called **N**.*

NIGHT (2)
Mt 14:25 {in the morning} Greek *In the fourth watch of the **n**.*
Mk 6:48 {in the morning} Greek *About the fourth watch of the **n**.*

NINE (1)
Ge 46:27 {had two sons} Greek version reads ***n** sons,* probably including Joseph's grandsons through Ephraim and Manasseh (see 1 Chr 7:14-20).

NINTH (8)
Lev 23:32 {Day of Atonement} Hebrew *the evening of the **n** day of the month;* see 23:24, 27 and the notes there.
2Ki 25: 3 {Zedekiah's eleventh year,} Hebrew *By the **n** day,* that is, "of the fourth month of Zedekiah's eleventh year"...
Ezr 10: 9 {place on December 19,} Hebrew *on the twentieth day of the **n** month,* of the Hebrew calendar....
Jer 36: 9 {in late autumn,} Hebrew *in the **n** month,* of the Hebrew calendar (also in 36:22)....
39: 2 {later, on July 18,} Hebrew *On the **n** day of the fourth month of the eleventh year of Zedekiah....*
52: 6 {eleventh year,} Hebrew *By the **n** day of the fourth month* [of Zedekiah's eleventh year]....
Hag 2:10 {On December 18} Hebrew *On the twenty-fourth day of the **n** month,* of the Hebrew calendar...
Zec 7: 1 {On December 7} Hebrew *On the fourth day of the **n** month, the month of Kislev,...*

NISAN (2)
Ne 2: 1 {following spring,} Hebrew *In the month of **N**....*
Est 3: 7 {month of April,} Hebrew *in the first month, the month of **N**....*

NISSI (1)
Ex 17:15 {Is My Banner."} Hebrew *Yahweh **N**.*

NO (1)
Jer 46:25 {god of Thebes,} Hebrew ***N**.*

NO-AMON (1)
Na 3: 8 {better than Thebes,} Hebrew ***N**;* also in 3:10.

NOAH (2)
Ge 5:29 {his son Noah,} ***N*** sounds like a Hebrew term that can mean "relief" or "comfort."
1Ch 1: 4 {of Noah were} As in Greek version (see also Gen 5:3-32); Hebrew lacks *The sons of **N** were.*

NOD (1)
Ge 4:16 {land of Nod,} ***N*** means "wandering."

NOON (1)
Ac 8:26 {him, "Go south} Or *Go at **n**.*

NOPH (5)
Isa 19:13 {those from Memphis} Hebrew ***N**.*
Jer 2:16 {cities of Memphis} Hebrew ***N**.*
44: 1 {Tahpanhes, and Memphis,} Hebrew ***N**.*
46:14 {of Migdol, Memphis,} Hebrew ***N**;* also in 46:19.
Eze 30:13 {images at Memphis.} Hebrew ***N**;* also in 30:16.

NORTH (2)
Ps 48: 2 {the holy mountain,} Or *Mount Zion, in the far **n**;* Hebrew reads *Mount Zion, the heights of Zaphon.*
Jer 3:12 {words to Israel,} Hebrew *toward the **n**.*

NOSTRILS (1)
Ex 5:21 {situation with Pharaoh} Hebrew *for making us a stench in the **n** of Pharaoh.*

NOTHING (4)
Isa 33: 8 {made before witnesses.} As in Dead Sea Scrolls; Masoretic Text reads *care **n** for the cities.*
Am 6:13 {conquest of Lo-debar.} *Lo-debar* means "**n**."
Mt 25:29 {who are unfaithful,} Or *who have **n**.*
Lk 19:26 {who are unfaithful,} Or *who have **n**.*

NUM (9)
Ge 15:18 {of Egypt} Hebrew *the river of Egypt,* referring either to an eastern branch of the Nile River or to the brook of Egypt in the Sinai (see **N** 34:5).
46:13 {Jashub,} As in some Greek manuscripts and Samaritan Pentateuch (see also **N** 26:24; 1 Chr 7:1); Hebrew reads *Iob.*
46:16 {Gad were Zephon,} As in Greek version and Samaritan Pentateuch (see also **N** 26:15); Hebrew reads *Ziphion.*
Dt 9:22 {angry at Taberah,} *Taberah* means "place of burning." See **N** 11:1-3.
9:22 {and Kibroth-hattaavah.} *Kibroth-hattaavah* means "graves of craving." See **N** 11:31-34.
1Ch 7:13 {Jezer, and Shillem.} As in some Hebrew and Greek manuscripts (see also Gen 46:24; **N** 26:49); most Hebrew manuscripts read *Shallum.*
Mt 5:33 {to the Lord.'} **N** 30:2.
Jn 19:36 {will be broken,"} Exod 12:46; **N** 9:12; Ps 34:20.
2Ti 2:19 {who are his,"} **N** 16:5.

NUMBER (3 of 15)
Nu 1:20[-21] {clan and family} In the Hebrew text, ***n** of men...family* is repeated in 1:22, 24, 26, 28, 30, 32, 34, 36, 38, 40, 42.
1Sa 13: 1 {Saul was thirty} As in a few Greek manuscripts; the **n** is missing in the Hebrew.
13: 1 {for forty-two years.} Hebrew *reigned...and two;* the **n** is incomplete in the Hebrew. Compare Acts 13:21.

O

OATH (2)
Ge 24: 9 {solemn oath} Hebrew *put his hand under the thigh of Abraham his master and swore an **o**.*
26:33 {the well "Oath,"} Hebrew *Shibah,* which can mean "**o**" or "seven."

OBEY (1)
Ge 49:10 {whom it belongs,} Or *until tribute is brought to him and the peoples **o**;* traditionally rendered *until Shiloh comes.*

OBJECT (1)
Isa 33: 1 {for you Assyrians,} Hebrew *for you, O destroyer...O betrayer.* The Hebrew text does not specifically name Assyria as the **o** of this prophecy.

OBVIOUS (1)
2Co 10: 7 {basis of appearance.} Or *Look at the **o** facts.*

ODED (1)
2Ch 15: 8 {Azariah the prophet,} As in Syriac version and Latin Vulgate (see also 15:1); Hebrew reads *from **O** the prophet.*

OFF (3)
Isa 7:20 {and your people.} Hebrew *shave **o** the head, the hair of the legs, and the beard.*
Gal 5:12 {would mutilate themselves.} Or *castrate themselves;* Greek reads *cut themselves **o**.*
2Pe 1:14 {to die.} Greek *I must soon put **o** this earthly tent.*

OFFER (1)
1Sa 1:22 {the LORD permanently."} Some manuscripts add *I will **o** him as a Nazirite for all time.*

OFFERED (1)
Ro 11:16 {also be holy.} Greek *If the dough **o** as firstfruits is holy, so is the whole lump.*

OFFERING (29)
Lev 27:21 {specially set apart} The Hebrew term used here refers to the complete consecration of things or people to the LORD, either by destroying them or by giving them as an **o**; also in 27:28, 29.
Nu 18:14 {for the LORD} The Hebrew term used here refers to the complete consecration of things or people to the LORD, either by destroying them or by giving them as an **o**.
21: 2 {will completely destroy} The Hebrew term used here refers to the complete consecration of things or people to the LORD, either by destroying them or by giving them as an **o**; also in 21:3.
Dt 2:34 {and completely destroyed} The Hebrew term used here refers to the complete consecration of things or people to the LORD, either by destroying them or by giving them as an **o**.
3: 6 {We completely destroyed} The Hebrew term used here refers to the complete consecration of things or people to the LORD, either by destroying them or by giving them as an **o**.
7: 2 {must completely destroy} The Hebrew term used here refers to the complete consecration of things or people to the LORD, either by destroying them or by giving them as an **o**; also in 7:26.
13:15 {and completely destroy} The Hebrew term used here refers to the complete consecration of things or people to the LORD, either by destroying them or by giving them as an **o**; also in 13:17.
20:17 {must completely destroy} The Hebrew term used here refers to the complete consecration of things or people to the LORD, either by destroying them or by giving them as an **o**.
Jos 2:10 {you completely destroyed.} The Hebrew term used here refers to the complete consecration of things or people to the LORD, either by destroying them or by giving them as an **o**.
6:17 {be completely destroyed} The Hebrew term used here refers to the complete consecration of things or people to the LORD, either by destroying them or by giving them as an **o**; also in 6:18, 21.
7: 1 {for the LORD.} The Hebrew term used here refers to the complete consecration of things or people to the LORD, either by destroying them or by giving them as an **o**; also in 7:11, 12, 13, 15.
8:26 {was completely destroyed.} The Hebrew term used here refers to the complete consecration of things or people to the LORD, either by destroying them or by giving them as an **o**.
10: 1 {and completely destroyed} The Hebrew term used here refers to the complete consecration of things or people to the LORD, either by destroying them or by giving them as an **o**; also in 10:28, 35, 37, 39, 40.
11:11 {Israelites completely destroyed} The Hebrew term used here refers to the complete consecration of things or people to the LORD, either by destroying them or by giving them as an **o**; also in 11:12, 20, 21.
22:20 {for the LORD} The Hebrew term used here refers to the complete consecration of things or people to the LORD, either by destroying them or by giving them as an **o**.
Jdg 1:17 {they completely destroyed} The Hebrew term used here refers to the complete consecration of things or people to the LORD, either by destroying them or by giving them as an **o**.
21:11 {said. "Completely destroy} The Hebrew term used here refers to the complete consecration of things or people to the LORD, either by destroying them or by giving them as an **o**.
1Sa 15: 3 {and completely destroy} The Hebrew term used here refers to the complete consecration of things or people to the LORD, either by destroying them or by giving them as an **o**; also in 15:8, 9, 15, 18, 20, 21.
1Ki 9:21 {not completely destroyed.} The Hebrew term used here refers to the complete consecration of things or people to the LORD, either by destroying them or by giving them as an **o**.
20:42 {must be destroyed,} The Hebrew term used here refers to the complete consecration of things or people to the LORD, either by destroying them or by giving them as an **o**.
1Ch 2: 7 {for the LORD.} The Hebrew term used here refers to the complete consecration of things or people to the LORD, either by destroying them or by giving them as an **o**.
4:41 {and completely destroyed} The Hebrew term used here refers to the complete consecration of things or people to the LORD, either by destroying them or by giving them as an **o**.
Isa 34: 2 {will completely destroy} The Hebrew term used here refers to the complete consecration of things or people to the LORD, either by destroying them or by giving them as an **o**; also in 34:5.
43:28 {of complete destruction} The Hebrew term used here refers to the complete consecration of things or people to the LORD, either by destroying them or by giving them as an **o**.
Jer 25: 9 {will completely destroy} The Hebrew term used here refers to the complete consecration of things or people to the LORD, either by destroying them or by giving them as an **o**.
50:21 {and completely destroy} The Hebrew term used here refers to the complete consecration of things or people to the LORD, either by destroying them or by giving them as an **o**.
51: 3 {be completely destroyed.} The Hebrew term used here refers to the complete consecration of things or people to the LORD, either by destroying them or by giving them as an **o**.
Eze 44:29 {anyone sets apart} The Hebrew term used here refers to the complete consecration of things or people to the LORD, either by destroying them or by giving them as an **o**.
2Co 9: 1 {Christians in Jerusalem.} Greek *about the **o** for the saints.*

OFFICIALS (1)
Da 3: 3 {all these officials} Aramaic *the princes, prefects, governors, advisers, counselors, judges, magistrates, and all the provincial **o**.*

OFFSPRING (1)

Rev 22:16 {to his throne.} Greek *I am the root and **o** of David.*

OINTMENT (1)

Mk 14: 3 {of expensive perfume.} Greek *an alabaster jar of expensive **o**, pure nard.*

OLD (5)

Ge 11:12[-13] {sons and daughters.} Greek version reads [12]*When Arphaxad was 135 years **o**, his son Cainan was born.* [13]*After the birth of Cainan, Arphaxad lived another 430 years and had other sons and daughters, and then he died. When Cainan was 130 years **o**, his son Shelah was born. After the birth of Shelah, Cainan lived another 330 years and had other sons and daughters, and then he died.*
1Co 5: 6[-7] {can stay pure.} Greek *Don't you realize that even a little leaven spreads quickly through the whole batch of dough?* [7]*Purge out the **o** leaven so that you can be a new batch of dough, just as you are already unleavened.*
5: 8 {the old bread} Greek *not with **o** leaven.*
Heb 11:11 {keep his promise.} Some manuscripts read *It was by faith that Sarah was able to have a child, even though she was too **o** and barren. Sarah believed that God would keep his promise.*

OLDER (1)

Ge 10:21 {brother of Japheth.} Or *Shem, whose **o** brother was Japheth.*

OMER (2)

Ex 16:16 {up two quarts} Hebrew *1 **o*** [2 liters]; also in 16:18, 32, 33.
16:36 {about two quarts.)} Hebrew *An **o** is one tenth of an ephah.*

OMERS (1)

Ex 16:22 {the ground—four quarts} Hebrew *2 **o*** [4 liters].

OMIT (6)

Mt 24:36 {the Son himself.} Some manuscripts **o** the phrase *or the Son himself.*
Mk 16:17 {speak new languages.} Or *new tongues;* some manuscripts **o** *new.*
Lk 8:43 {had on doctors} Some manuscripts **o** *She had spent everything she had on doctors.*
22:19[-20] {out for you.} Some manuscripts **o** 22:19b-20, *given for you…I will pour out for you.*
Jn 3:31 {come from heaven.} Some manuscripts **o** *but he has come from heaven.*
7: 8 {am not yet} Some manuscripts **o** *yet.*

OMITTED (1)

Mt 21:44 {whom it falls.} This verse is **o** in some early manuscripts.

ONCE (1)

Tit 1: 6 {to his wife,} Or *have only one wife,* or *be married only **o**;* Greek reads *be the husband of one wife.*

ONE (53 of 65)

Ge 16:14 {was named Beer-lahairoi,} *Beer-lahairoi* means "well of the Living **O** who sees me."
29:33 {named him Simeon,} *Simeon* probably means "**o** who hears."
32:28 {is now Israel,} *Israel* means "God struggles" or "**o** who struggles with God."
35:10 {be called Israel."} *Jacob* means "he grasps the heel"; this can also figuratively mean "he deceives"; *Israel* means "God struggles" or "**o** who struggles with God."
Ex 16:36 {about two quarts.)} Hebrew *An omer is **o** tenth of an ephah.*
Dt 6: 4 {the LORD alone.} Or *The LORD our God is **o** LORD,* or *The LORD our God, the LORD is **o**,* or *The LORD is our God, the LORD is **o**.*
1Sa 2:20 {to the LORD.} As in Greek version; Hebrew reads *this **o** she requested of the LORD in prayer.*
10:27 {Saul ignored them.} Dead Sea Scroll 4QSam[a] continues: *In fact, of all the Israelites east of the Jordan, there wasn't a single **o** whose right eye Nahash had not gouged out.…*
2Sa 23: 8 {a single battle.} As in some Greek manuscripts (see also 1 Chr 11:11); the Hebrew is uncertain, though it might be rendered *the Three. It was Adino the Eznite who killed eight hundred men at **o** time.*
Ps 16:10 {your godly one} Or *your Holy **O**.*
49: 7 {themselves from death} Or *no **o** can redeem the life of another.*
Eze 40: 6 {10 1/2 feet deep.} Greek version; Hebrew reads *1 rod* [10.5 feet or 3.2 meters] *deep, and **o** threshold, **o** rod deep.*
40: 8 {of the gateway} Many Hebrew manuscripts add *which faced inward toward the Temple; it was **o** rod* [10.5 feet or 3.2 meters] *deep.* [9]*Then he measured the foyer of the gateway,…*
Da 9:24 {Most Holy Place.} Or *the Most Holy **O**.*
9:25 {the Anointed One} Or *an anointed **o**.*
9:27 {set of seven,} Hebrew *for **o** seven.*
10:13 {kingdom of Persia.} As in **o** Greek version; Hebrew reads *and I was left there with the kings of Persia.* The meaning of the Hebrew is uncertain.
Hos 11:12 {the Holy One.} Or *and Judah is unruly against God, the faithful Holy **O**.*
Mal 2:15 {you are his.} Or *Did not **o** God make us and preserve our life and breath?* or *Did not **o** God make her, both flesh and spirit?* The meaning of the Hebrew is uncertain.
Mt 5:37 {something is wrong.} Or *Anything beyond this is from the evil **o**.*
12:29 {house be robbed!} Or ***O** cannot rob Satan's kingdom without first tying him up. Only then can his demons be cast out.*
26:23 {with me now} Or *The **o** who has dipped his hand in the bowl with me.*
Mk 3:27 {house be robbed!} Or ***O** cannot rob Satan's kingdom without first tying him up. Only then can his demons be cast out.*
14:20 {with me now.} Or ***o** who is dipping bread into the bowl with me.*
Lk 11:21 {For when Satan,} Greek *the strong **o**.*
17:35 {the other left.} Some manuscripts add verse 36, *Two men will be working in the field; **o** will be taken, the other left.*
23:16 {will release him."} Some manuscripts add verse 17, *For it was necessary for him to release **o** [prisoner] for them during the feast.*
Jn 1:18 {is himself God,} Some manuscripts read *his **o** and only Son.*
1:34 {Son of God.} Some manuscripts read *the chosen **O** of God.*
4:26 {am the Messiah!"} Greek *"I am, the **o** speaking to you."*
11:16 {nicknamed the Twin,} Greek *the **o** who was called Didymus.*
20:24 {(nicknamed the Twin} Greek *the **o** who was called Didymus.*
21: 2 {(nicknamed the Twin} Greek *the **o** who was called Didymus.*
1Co 6: 6 {instead, one Christian} Greek ***o** brother.*
12:13 {the same Spirit.} Greek *we were all given **o** Spirit to drink.*
2Co 5:14 {used to live.} Greek *Since **o** died on behalf of all, then all died.*
Eph 6:16 {you by Satan.} Greek *by the evil **o**.*
1Ti 3: 2 {to his wife.} Greek *be the husband of **o** wife;* also in 3:12.
5: 9 {to her husband.} Greek *was the wife of **o** man.*
Tit 1: 6 {to his wife,} Or *have only **o** wife,* or *be married only once;* Greek reads *be the husband of **o** wife.*
1Pe 5:13 {here in Rome} Greek *The elect **o** in Babylon.* Babylon was probably a code name for Rome.
1Jn 2:20 {come upon you,} Greek *But you have an anointing from the Holy **O**.*
5: 7 {these three witnesses} Some very late manuscripts add *in heaven—the Father, the Word, and the Holy Spirit, and these three are **o**. And we have three witnesses on earth.*
Rev 1:13 {Son of Man.} Or ***o** who looked like a man;* Greek reads ***o** like a son of man.*
14:14 {Son of Man} Or ***o** who looked like a man;* Greek reads ***o** like a son of man.*

ONE'S (1)

2Pe 1:20 {the prophets themselves} Or *is a matter of **o** own interpretation.*

ONES (5)

Dt 33: 2 {his right hand.} Or *came from myriads of holy **o**, from the south, from his mountain slopes.* The meaning of the Hebrew is uncertain.
Job 5: 1 {to the angels,} Hebrew *the holy **o**.*
15:15 {trust the angels} Hebrew *the holy **o**.*
2Pe 2:10 {the glorious ones} *The glorious **o*** are probably evil angels; also in 2:11.
Jude 1: 8 {the glorious ones.} *The glorious **o*** are probably evil angels.

ONESIMUS (1)

Phm 1:11 {Onesimus} ***O*** means "useful."

ONLY (9)

2Ki 3:25 {came under attack.} Hebrew *until **o** Kir-hareseth was left, with its stones, but the slingers surrounded and attacked it.*
Isa 5:10 {only one measure} Hebrew *A homer* [5 bushels or 182 liters] *of seed will yield **o** an ephah* [0.5 bushels or 18.2 liters].
Mt 12:29 {house be robbed!} Or *One cannot rob Satan's kingdom without first tying him up. **O** then can his demons be cast out.*
Mk 3:27 {house be robbed!} Or *One cannot rob Satan's kingdom without first tying him up. **O** then can his demons be cast out.*
Jn 1:18 {is himself God,} Some manuscripts read *his one and **o** Son.*
1Co 7:39 {to the Lord.} Or *but **o** to a Christian;* Greek reads *but **o** in the Lord.*
Tit 1: 6 {to his wife,} Or *have **o** one wife,* or *be married **o** once;* Greek reads *be the husband of one wife.*

OPENED (2)

Mt 27:51[-53] {to many people.} Or *The earth shook, rocks split apart, tombs **o**, and many bodies of godly men and women who had died were raised from the dead. After Jesus' resurrection, they left the cemetery, went into the holy city of Jerusalem, and appeared to many people.*
Mk 7:34 {"Be opened!"} Greek text uses Aramaic *"Ephphatha"* and then translates it as "Be **o**."

OPPOSE (1)

Ac 26: 9 {Jesus of Nazareth.} Greek ***o** the name of Jesus the Nazarene.*

OPPOSES (1)

Jas 4: 5 {to be faithful} Or *the spirit that God placed within us tends to envy,* or *the Holy Spirit, whom God has placed within us, **o** our envy.*

OPPRESSING (1)

1Sa 10:27 {Saul ignored them.} Dead Sea Scroll 4QSam[a] continues: *Nahash, king of the Ammonites, had been grievously **o** the Gadites and Reubenites…*

OR (597 of 774)

Ge 1: 1 {beginning God created} **O** *In the beginning when God created,* **o** *When God began to create.*
2:21 {of Adam's ribs} **O** *took a part of Adam's side.*
3:16 {for your husband,} **O** *And though you may desire to control your husband.*
4: 1 {birth to Cain,} *Cain* sounds like a Hebrew term that can mean "bring forth" **o** "acquire."
4: 1 {have brought forth} **O** *I have acquired.*
4:13 {LORD, "My punishment} **O** *My sin.*
4:18 {the father of} **O** *the ancestor of,* and so throughout the verse.
5: 3 {Seth was born,} **O** *his son, the ancestor of Seth, was born;* similarly in 5:6, 9, 12, 15, 18, 21, 25.
5: 4 {birth of Seth,} **O** *After the birth of his ancestor of Seth;* similarly in 5:7, 10, 13, 16, 19, 22, 26.
5:29 {his son Noah,} *Noah* sounds like a Hebrew term that can mean "relief" **o** "comfort."
10: 6 {were Cush, Mizraim,} **O** *Egypt;* also in 10:13.
10:21 {brother of Japheth.} **O** *Shem, whose older brother was Japheth.*
11:12 {Shelah was born.} **O** *his son, the ancestor of Shelah, was born;* similarly in 11:14, 16, 18, 20, 22, 24.
26:33 {the well "Oath,"} Hebrew *Shibah,* which can mean "oath" **o** "seven."
29:17 {had pretty eyes,} **O** *dull eyes.* The meaning of the Hebrew is uncertain.
29:34 {named him Levi,} *Levi* sounds like a Hebrew term that means "being attached" **o** "feeling affection for."
30: 6 {named him Dan,} *Dan* is a play on the Hebrew term meaning "to vindicate" **o** "to judge."
32:28 {is now Israel,} *Israel* means "God struggles" **o** "one who struggles with God."
35:10 {be called Israel."} *Jacob* means "he grasps the heel"; this can also figuratively mean "he deceives"; *Israel* means "God struggles" **o** "one who struggles with God."
36:31 {kings in Israel} **O** *before an Israelite king ruled over them.*
38:30 {was named Zerah.} *Zerah* means "scarlet" **o** "brightness."
48:22 {an extra portion} **O** *give you the ridge of land.* The meaning of the Hebrew is uncertain.
49:10 {whom it belongs,} **O** *until tribute is brought to him and the peoples obey;* traditionally rendered *until Shiloh comes.*
49:14 {among the sheepfolds.} **O** *saddlebags,* **o** *hearths.*
Ex 3:14 {WHO ALWAYS IS.} **O** *I AM WHO I AM,* **o** *I WILL BE WHAT I WILL BE.*
4: 6 {snow with leprosy.} **O** *with a contagious skin disease.* The Hebrew word used here can describe various skin diseases.
4:24 {LORD confronted Moses} **O** *confronted Moses' son;* Hebrew reads *confronted him.*
17:16 {throne, so now} **O** *Hands have been lifted up to the LORD's throne, and now.*
21: 6 {him before God.} **O** *before the judges.*
22: 8 {not found, God} **O** *the judges.*
22: 9 {come before God} **O** *before the judges.*
22: 9 {whom God declares} **O** *whom the judges declare.*
22:28 {not blaspheme God} **O** *Do not revile your judges.*
23:16 {Festival of Harvest,} **O** *Festival of Weeks.*
25:22 {of the Covenant.} **O** *Ark of the Testimony.*
26:33 {of the Covenant} **O** *Ark of the Testimony;* also in 26:34.
30: 6 {of the Covenant.} **O** *Ark of the Testimony;* also in 30:26, 36.
34:22 {Festival of Harvest} **O** *Festival of Weeks.*
39:35 {of the Covenant} **O** *Ark of the Testimony.*
40: 3 {of the Covenant} **O** *Ark of the Testimony;* also in 40:5, 21.
Lev 1:16 {and the feathers} **O** *the crop and its contents.* The meaning of the Hebrew is uncertain.
6: 6 {value in silver.} **O** *and the animal must be of the proper value;* Hebrew lacks *in silver;* compare 5:15.
8:15 {atonement for it.} **O** *that atonement may be made on it.*

9: 4 {take a bull} **O** *cow;* also in 9:18, 19.
10: 6 {hair hang loose} **O** *by uncovering your heads.*
11: 5 {the rock badger} **O** *coney,* **o** *hyrax.*
13:45 {to hang loose.} **O** *and uncover their heads.*
17: 3 {sacrifices a bull} **O** *cow.*
17: 7 {to evil spirits} **O** *goat idols.*
20:18 {from a hemorrhage,} **O** *a woman who is menstruating.*
21:10 {hair hang loose} **O** *uncover his head.*
22:23 {If the bull} **O** *cow;* also in 22:27.
23:40 {from citrus trees,} **O** *fruit from majestic trees.*
27:16 {area that produces} **O** *requires.*
Nu 1:50 {of the Covenant,} **O** *Tabernacle of the Testimony;* also in 1:53.
4: 5 {of the Covenant} **O** *Ark of the Testimony.*
7:89 {of the Covenant.} **O** *Ark of the Testimony.*
10:11 {of the Covenant.} **O** *Tabernacle of the Testimony.*
11:31 {above the ground.} **O** *there were quail 3 feet* [2 cubits **o** 90 centimeters] *deep on the ground.*
12:10 {snow with leprosy.} **O** *with a contagious skin disease.* The Hebrew word used here can describe various skin diseases.
17: 7 {of the Covenant.} **O** *Tabernacle of the Testimony;* also in 17:8.
18: 2 {of the Covenant.} **O** *Tabernacle of the Testimony.*
21:20 {overlooks the wasteland.} **O** *overlooks Jeshimon.*
21:24 {Ammonites was fortified.} **O** *because the terrain of the Ammonite frontier was rugged;* Hebrew *because the boundary of the Ammonites was strong.*
21:30 {Nophah and Medeba.} **O** *until fire spread to Medeba.* The meaning of the Hebrew is uncertain.
22: 5 {land of Pethor} **O** *who was at Pethor in the land of the Amavites.*
23:28 {overlooking the wasteland.} **O** *overlooking Jeshimon.*
28:26 {Festival of Harvest,} **O** *Festival of Weeks.*
Dt 4:33 {voice of God} **O** *voice of a god.*
6: 4 {the LORD alone.} **O** *The LORD our God is one LORD,* **o** *The LORD our God, the LORD is one,* **o** *The LORD is our God, the LORD is one.*
7:20 {will send hornets} **O** *will spread panic,* **o** *will send a plague.* The meaning of the Hebrew is uncertain.
10: 6 {people of Jaakan} **O** *set out from Beeroth of Bene-jaakan.*
14: 7 {the rock badger.} **O** *coney,* **o** *hyrax.*
16:10 {Festival of Harvest} **O** *Festival of Weeks;* also in 16:16.
18:10 {a burnt offering.} **O** *never make your son* **o** *daughter pass through the fire.*
32:36 {his mind about} **O** *will take revenge for.*
33: 2 {his right hand.} **O** *came from myriads of holy ones, from the south, from his mountain slopes.* The meaning of the Hebrew is uncertain.
Jos 7: 5 {as the quarries,} **O** *as far as Shebarim.*
7:21 {hundred silver coins,} Hebrew *200 shekels of silver,* about 5 pounds **o** 2.3 kilograms in weight.
8:17 {Ai or Bethel} Some manuscripts lack **o** *Bethel.*
8:32 {of the altar.} **O** *onto stones.*
10:13 {*Book of Jashar*} **O** *The Book of the Upright.*
13:26 {Mahanaim to Lo-debar.} **O** *to the territory of Debir.*
15: 9 {waters of Nephtoah,} **O** *the spring at Me-nephtoah.*
18:15 {it ran westward} **O** *it went to Ephron, and.* The meaning of the Hebrew is uncertain.
18:15 {waters of Nephtoah,} **O** *the spring at Me-nephtoah.*
Jdg 4:11 {of Moses' brother-in-law} **O** *father-in-law.*
9:37 {from the hills.} **O** *the center of the land.*
Ru 1:21 {me to suffer} **O** *has testified against me.*
1Sa 1: 5 {special portion} **O** *a double portion.* The meaning of the Hebrew is uncertain.
1:20 {named him Samuel,} *Samuel* sounds like the Hebrew term for "asked of God" **o** "heard by God."
1:28 {And they} **O** *he.*
2:25 {another person, God} **O** *the judges.*
4: 3 {with us, it} **O** *he.*
4: 7 {"The gods have} **O** *A god has.*
5:11 {country, or it} **O** *he.*
13:20 {axes, or sickles,} As in Greek version; Hebrew reads **o** *plowshares.*
14:41 {among the others?"} Greek version adds *If the fault is with me* **o** *my son Jonathan, respond with Urim; but if the men of Israel are at fault, respond with Thummim.*
18:19 {So} **O** *But.*
28:13 {see a god} **O** *gods.*
2Sa 1:18 {*Book of Jashar.*} **O** *The Book of the Upright.*
2:29 {through the morning,} **O** *continued on through the Bithron.* The meaning of the Hebrew is uncertain.
3:29 {sores or leprosy} **O** **o** *a contagious skin disease.* The Hebrew word used here can describe various skin diseases.
3:29 {walks on crutches} **O** *who is effeminate;* Hebrew reads *who handles a spindle.*
5: 9 {at the Millo} **O** *the supporting terraces.* The meaning of the Hebrew is uncertain.
6:19 {cake of dates,} **O** *a portion of meat.* The meaning of the Hebrew is uncertain.
11:11 {living in tents,} **O** *at Succoth.*
12:27 {its water supply.} **O** *captured the city of water.*
13:18 {long, beautiful robe,} **O** *a robe with sleeves,* **o** *an ornamented robe.* The meaning of the Hebrew is uncertain.
13:39 {his son Absalom.} **O** *no longer felt a need to go out after Absalom.*
15:27 {the priest, "Look,} As in Greek version; Hebrew reads *Are you a seer?* **o** *Do you see?*
23:30 {from Nahale-gaash} **O** *from the ravines of Gaash.*
1Ki 1: 5 {chariots and horses} **O** *and charioteers.*
1: 9 {stone of Zoheleth} **O** *to the Serpent's Stone;* Greek version supports reading *Zoheleth* as a proper name.
2: 5 {time of peace,} **O** *He murdered them during a time of peace as revenge for deaths they had caused in time of war.*
4:26 {twelve thousand horses.} **O** *12,000 charioteers.*
6:20 {made of cedar.} **O** *overlaid the altar with cedar.* The meaning of the Hebrew is uncertain.
7:24 {gourds per foot} **O** *20 gourds per meter;* Hebrew reads *10 per cubit.*
9:15 {palace, the Millo,} **O** *the supporting terraces;* also in 9:24.
9:19 {chariots and horses} **O** *and charioteers.*
10:22 {apes, and peacocks.} **O** *and baboons.*
10:26 {twelve thousand horses.} **O** *12,000 charioteers.*
11:27 {rebuilding the Millo} **O** *the supporting terraces.*
20:12 {in their tents.} **O** *in Succoth;* also in 20:16.
2Ki 1: 8 {hairy man,} **O** *He was wearing clothing made of hair.*
2:21 {death or infertility.} **O** **o** *make the land unproductive.*
5: 1 {suffered from leprosy.} **O** *from a contagious skin disease.* The Hebrew word used here and throughout this passage can describe various skin diseases.
7: 3 {men with leprosy} **O** *with a contagious skin disease.* The Hebrew word used here and throughout this passage can describe various skin diseases.
14:28 {belonged to Judah,} **O** *to Yaudi.*
15: 5 {king with leprosy,} **O** *with a contagious skin disease.* The Hebrew word used here and throughout this passage can describe various skin diseases.
15:10 {him in public,} **O** *at Ibleam.*
16: 3 {in the fire.} **O** *even making his son pass through the fire.*
17: 4 {So of Egypt} **O** *by asking the king of Egypt at Sais.*
17:17 {in the fire.} **O** *They even made their sons and daughters pass through the fire.*
18:24 {chariots and horsemen} **O** *and charioteers.*
21: 6 {in the fire.} **O** *even made his son pass through the fire.*
22:14 {newer Mishneh section} **O** *the Second Quarter,* a newer section of Jerusalem.
23:10 {in the fire} **O** *to make a son* **o** *daughter pass through the fire.*
24: 2 {bands of Babylonian,} **O** *Chaldean.*
25: 4 {by the Babylonians,} **O** *the Chaldeans;* also in 25:5, 13, 25, 26.
25:10 {the entire Babylonian} **O** *Chaldean;* also in 25:24.
1Ch 1: 8 {were Cush, Mizraim,} **O** *Egypt;* also in 1:11.
1:43 {kings in Israel} **O** *before an Israelite king ruled over them.*
2:23 {Towns of Jair} **O** *captured Havvoth-jair.*
2:24 {(the father of} **O** *the founder of;* also in 2:42, 45, 49-52 and perhaps other instances where the text reads *the father of.*
2:55 {family of Recab.} **O** *the founder of Beth-recab.*
4: 4 {(the father of} **O** *the founder of;* also in 4:12, 14, 17-18, and perhaps other instances where the text reads *the father of.*
4: 9 {named him Jabez} *Jabez* sounds like a Hebrew term meaning "distress" **o** "pain."
4:14 {Valley of Craftsmen,} **O** *Joab, the father of Ge-harashim.*
5: 2 {for the nation,} **O** *and from Judah came a prince.*
7:23 {named him Beriah} *Beriah* sounds like a Hebrew term meaning "tragedy" **o** "misfortune."
8:29 {(the father of} **O** *the founder of.*
9:35 {(the father of} **O** *the founder of.*
11: 8 {from the Millo} **O** *the supporting terraces.* The meaning of the Hebrew is uncertain.
11:11 {among David's men.} As in some Greek manuscripts (see also 2 Sam 23:8); Hebrew *commander of the Thirty,* **o** *commander of the captains.*
11:32 {from near Nahale-gaash} **O** *from the ravines of Gaash.*
16: 3 {cake of dates,} **O** *a portion of meat.* The meaning of the Hebrew is uncertain.
26:16 {to the Temple.} **O** *the gate of Shalleketh on the upper road* (also in 26:18). The meaning of the Hebrew is uncertain.
26:18 {to the courtyard.} **O** *the colonnade.* The meaning of the Hebrew is uncertain.
28:12 {had in mind} **O** *the plans of the spirit that was with him.*
28:19 {of the LORD.} **O** *was written under the direction of the LORD.*
2Ch 1:14 {twelve thousand horses.} **O** *12,000 charioteers.*
4: 3 {oxen per foot} **O** *20 oxen per meter;* Hebrew reads *10 per cubit.*
6:42 {your servant David.} **O** *Remember the faithfulness of your servant David.*
8: 6 {chariots and horses} **O** *and charioteers.*
9:11 {to make steps} **O** *gateways.* The meaning of the Hebrew is uncertain.
9:21 {apes, and peacocks.} **O** *and baboons.*
9:25 {twelve thousand horses.} **O** *12,000 charioteers.*
14: 9 {a million men} **O** *an army of thousands and thousands;* Hebrew reads *an army of a thousand thousands.*
14:10 {north of Mareshah.} **O** *in the Zephathah Valley near Mareshah.*
16: 8 {chariots and horsemen} **O** *and charioteers.*
20:35 {very wicked man.} **O** *who made him do what was wrong.*
26:15 {and hurl stones} **O** *designed by brilliant men to protect those who shot arrows and stones.*
26:19 {LORD's Temple, leprosy} **O** *a contagious skin disease.* The Hebrew word used here and throughout this passage can describe various skin diseases.
28: 3 {in the fire.} **O** *even making his sons pass through the fire.*
30:21 {by loud instruments.} **O** *sang to the LORD with all their strength.*
32: 5 {reinforced the Millo} **O** *the supporting terraces.*
33: 6 {in the fire} **O** *even made his sons pass through the fire.*
33:19 {*of the Seers.*} **O** *The Record of Hozai.*
34:22 {newer Mishneh section} **O** *the Second Quarter,* a newer section of Jerusalem.
36: 7 {in his palace} **O** *temple.*
36:10 {appointed Jehoiachin's uncle,} As in parallel text at 2 Kgs 24:17; Hebrew reads *brother,* **o** *relative.*
36:17 {them. The Babylonians} **O** *Chaldeans.*
36:19 {everything of value.} **O** *destroyed all the valuable Temple utensils.*
Ezr 7: 1 {was the son} **O** *descendant;* see 1 Chr 6:14.
7: 3 {of Azariah, son} **O** *descendant;* see 1 Chr 6:6-10.
10:44 {by these wives.} **O** *and they sent them away with their children.* The meaning of the Hebrew is uncertain.
Ne 2:13 {the Jackal's Well,} **O** *Serpent's Well.*
3: 6 {Old City Gate} **O** *The Mishneh Gate,* **o** *The Jeshanah Gate.*
3: 8 {They left out} **O** *They restored.*
4: 5 {the presence of} **O** *for they have thrown insults in the face of.*
7: 3 {of the day.} **O** *Keep the gates of Jerusalem closed until the sun is hot.*
9:38 {of all this,} **O** *Because of all this.*
11:35 {Valley of Craftsmen.} **O** *and Ge-harashim.*
12:39 {Old City Gate,} **O** *the Mishneh Gate,* **o** *the Jeshanah Gate.*
Est 2:14 {the second harem,} **O** *to another part of the harem.*
2:23 {on a gallows.} **O** *on a pole.*
5:14 {up a gallows} **O** *a pole.*
6: 4 {from the gallows} **O** *from the pole.*
7: 9 {up a gallows} **O** *a pole;* also in 7:10.
8: 7 {on the gallows} **O** *on the pole.*
9:13 {from the gallows.} **O** *the pole;* also in 9:14, 25.
Job 4:15 {A spirit} **O** *wind.*
9: 3 {God to court,} **O** *If God wanted to take a person to court.*
9:20 {am blameless, it} **O** *he.*
11:12 {bear human offspring} **O** *bear a tame colt.*
19:26 {will see God} **O** *without my body I will see God.*
34:14 {back his spirit} **O** *his Spirit.*
36:33 {his indignant anger.} **O** *even the cattle know when a storm is coming.* The meaning of the Hebrew is uncertain.
Ps 2: 7 {are my son.} **O** *Son;* also in 2:12.
2: 7 {become your Father.} **O** *Today I reveal you as my son.*
8: 5 {lower than God,} **O** *a little lower than the angels;* Hebrew reads *Elohim.*
16:10 {your godly one} **O** *your Holy One.*
19: 3 {in the skies;} **O** *There is no speech* **o** *language where their voice is not heard.*
23: 4 {valley of death,} **O** *the darkest valley.*
29: 9 {twists mighty oaks} **O** *causes the deer to writhe in labor.*
31:10 {Misery} **O** *Sin.*
45: 6 {Your throne, O God,} **O** *Your divine throne.*
48: 2 {the holy mountain,} **O** *Mount Zion, in the far north;* Hebrew reads *Mount Zion, the heights of Zaphon.*
49: 7 {themselves from death} **O** *no one can redeem the life of another.*
56: 9 {on my side.} **O** *By this I will know that God is on my side.*
58: 7 {in their hands.} **O** *Let them be trodden down and wither like grass.* The meaning of the Hebrew is uncertain.
59:15 {to sleep unsatisfied.} **O** *and growl if they don't get enough.*
60: 6 {by his holiness} **O** *in his sanctuary.*
68:30 {tribute from us.} **O** *Humble them until they submit, bringing pieces of silver as tribute.*
74:16 {made the starlight} **O** *moon;* Hebrew reads *light.*
104:18 {for rock badgers.} **O** *coneys,* **o** *hyraxes.*
108: 7 {by his holiness} **O** *in his sanctuary.*
139:17 {thoughts about me,} **O** *How precious to me are your thoughts.*
Pr 12:26 {to their friends;} **O** *The godly are cautious in friendship,* **o** *the godly are freed from evil.* The meaning of the Hebrew is uncertain.
17:19 {who speaks boastfully} **O** *who builds up defenses;* Hebrew reads *who makes a high gate.*
20:27 {the human spirit,} **O** *The human spirit is the LORD's searchlight.*

21:12 {The Righteous One} **O** *The righteous man.*
30: 1 {Jakeh. An oracle.} **O** *son of Jakeh from Massa.*
30:26 {Rock badgers} **O** *coneys,* **o** *hyraxes.*
31: 1 {Lemuel, an oracle} **O** *of Lemuel, king of Massa.*
Ecc 3:19 {the same air,} **O** *both have the same spirit.*
9: 2 {good or bad,} As in Greek and Syriac versions, and Latin Vulgate; Hebrew lacks **o** *bad.*
10:16 {is a child} **O** *whose king is a servant.*
SS 1: 4 {bedroom, O my king.} **O** *The king has brought me into his bedroom.*
2: 7 {time is right.} **O** *not to awaken love until it is ready.*
2:17 {the rugged mountains.} **O** *on the hills of Bether.*
3: 5 {time is right.} **O** *not to awaken love until it is ready.*
4: 8 {bride. Come down} **O** *Look down.*
6:12 {my beloved one.} **O** *among the royal chariots of my people,* **o** *among the chariots of Amminadab.* The meaning of the Hebrew is uncertain.
6:13 {lines of dancers?} **O** *as you would at the movements of two armies?* **o** *as you would at the dance of Mahanaim?* The meaning of the Hebrew is uncertain.
7:11 {among the wildflowers.} **O** *in the villages.*
8: 4 {time is right.} **O** *not to awaken love until it is ready.*
Isa 7:14 {Look! The virgin} **O** *young woman.*
9: 6 {titles: Wonderful Counselor,} **O** *Wonderful, Counselor.*
9:20 {their own children.} **O** *eat their own arms.*
21:11 {me concerning Edom} Hebrew *Dumah,* which means "silence" **o** "stillness." It is a wordplay on the word *Edom.*
23:13 {land of Babylonia} **O** *Chaldea.*
28:10 {very simple words!} The Hebrew text for this verse may simply be childish sounds that have no meaning, **o** perhaps a childish mimicking of the prophet's words. Also in 28:13.
29: 1 {certain for Ariel,} *Ariel* sounds like a Hebrew term that means "hearth" **o** "altar."
36: 9 {chariots and horsemen} **O** *and charioteers.*
43:14 {And the Babylonians} **O** *Chaldeans.*
47: 1 {daughter of Babylonia,} **O** *Chaldea;* also in 47:5.
48:14 {destroying the Babylonian} **O** *Chaldean.*
48:20 {and the Babylonians,} **O** *the Chaldeans.*
52:15 {will again startle} **O** *cleanse.*
53: 4 {was our sorrows} **O** *Yet it was our sicknesses he carried; it was our diseases.*
57: 9 {perfume to Molech} **O** *to the king.*
61: 2 {favor has come,} **O** *to proclaim the acceptable year of the Lord.*
Jer 9:26 {in distant places,} **O** *the people who clip the corners of their hair.*
21: 4 {and the Babylonians} **O** *Chaldeans;* also in 21:9.
22:25 {the mighty Babylonian} **O** *Chaldean.*
24: 5 {of the Babylonians.} **O** *Chaldeans.*
25:12 {of the Babylonians} **O** *Chaldeans.*
25:23 {in distant places.} **O** *who clip the corners of their hair.*
32: 4 {by the Babylonians} **O** *Chaldeans;* also in 32:5, 24, 25, 28, 29, 43.
32: 9 {Hanamel seventeen pieces} Hebrew *17 shekels,* about 7 ounces **o** 194 grams in weight.
33: 5 {the Babylonians} **O** *Chaldeans.*
35:11 {of the Babylonian} **O** *Chaldean.*
37: 5 {When the Babylonian} **O** *Chaldean;* also in 37:10, 11.
37: 8 {Then the Babylonians} **O** *Chaldeans;* also in 37:9, 13.
38: 2 {to the Babylonians} **O** *Chaldeans;* also in 38:18, 19, 23.
39: 3 {Samgar, and Nebo-sarsekim,} **O** *Nergal-sharezer, Samgar-nebo, Sarsekim.*
39: 5 {But the Babylonians} **O** *Chaldeans;* also in 39:8.
40: 9 {to the Babylonians.} **O** *Chaldeans;* also in 40:10.
41: 3 {officials and Babylonian} **O** *Chaldean.*
41:16 {and palace officials.} **O** *eunuchs.*
41:18 {what the Babylonians} **O** *Chaldeans.*
43: 3 {by the Babylonians} **O** *Chaldeans.*
43:13 {of the sun} **O** *in Heliopolis.*
48: 6 {in the wilderness!} **O** *Be like* [the town of] *Aroer in the wilderness.*
49:32 {in distant places.} **O** *who clip the corners of their hair.*
50: 1 {of the Babylonians.} **O** *Chaldeans;* also in 50:8, 25, 35, 45.
50:10 {Babylonia} **O** *Chaldea.*
51: 4 {of the Babylonians,} **O** *Chaldeans;* also in 51:54.
51:24 {people of Babylonia} **O** *Chaldea;* also in 51:35.
52: 7 {by the Babylonians,} **O** *Chaldeans;* also in 50:8, 17.
52:14 {the entire Babylonian} **O** *Chaldean.*
La 4: 6 {The guilt} **O** *punishment.*
5:16 {The garlands have} **O** *The crown has.*
Eze 1: 1 {my thirtieth year,} **O** *in the thirtieth year.*
1: 3 {of the Babylonians,} **O** *Chaldeans.*
11:24 {again to Babylonia,} **O** *Chaldea.*
12:13 {of the Babylonians,} **O** *Chaldeans.*
16:29 {land of Babylonia} **O** *Chaldea.*
20:31 {burned as sacrifices,} **O** *and make your little children pass through the fire.*
23:14 {wall—pictures of Babylonian} **O** *Chaldean.*
23:15 {land of Babylonia.} **O** *Chaldea;* also in 23:16.
27: 5 {cypress from Senir.} **O** *Hermon.*
30:17 {and the women} **O** *her cities.*
43: 7 {their dead kings.} **O** *by raising pillars on their high places.*

Da 1: 4 {of the Babylonians.} **O** *of the Chaldeans.*
2: 2 {sorcerers, and astrologers,} **O** *Chaldeans;* also in 2:4, 5, 10.
4: 7 {magicians, enchanters, astrologers,} **O** *Chaldeans.*
5: 7 {the enchanters, astrologers,} **O** *Chaldeans;* also in 5:11.
5:30 {Belshazzar, the Babylonian} **O** *Chaldean.*
6:28 {Cyrus the Persian.} **O** *of Darius, that is, the reign of Cyrus the Persian.*
7:13 {like a man} **O** *a Son of Man;* Aramaic reads *a son of man.*
8: 2 {the Ulai River.} **O** *the Ulai Gate;* also in 8:16.
8: 3 {beside the river.} **O** *the gate;* also in 8:6.
9: 1 {of the Babylonians.} **O** *the Chaldeans.*
9:24 {Most Holy Place.} **O** *the Most Holy One.*
9:25 {the Anointed One} **O** *an anointed one.*
9:25 {and strong defenses,} **O** *and a moat,* **o** *and trenches.*
11:39 {as their reward.} **O** *at a price.*
Hos 1: 2 {marry a prostitute,} **O** *a promiscuous woman.*
3: 3 {even with me.} **O** *and I will live with you.*
11:12 {the Holy One.} **O** *and Judah is unruly against God, the faithful Holy One.*
Ob 1:21 {go up to} **O** *from.*
Mic 2: 4 {who betrayed us.} **O** *to those who took us captive.*
7:13 {But the land} **O** *earth.*
Hab 1: 6 {up the Babylonians} **O** *Chaldeans.*
2: 4 {by their faith.} **O** *the just will live by their faithfulness.*
3: 3 {and Mount Paran.} Hebrew adds *selah;* also in 3:9, 13. The meaning of this Hebrew term is uncertain; it is probably a musical **o** literary term.
3: 4 {his awesome power.} **O** *He veils his awesome power.*
3:19 {as a deer} **O** *will give me the speed of a deer.*
Zep 1: 5 {they worship Molech,} Hebrew *Malcam,* another name for Molech; **o** it could possibly mean *their king.*
1:10 {newer Mishneh section} **O** *the Second Quarter,* a newer section of Jerusalem.
1:18 {people on earth.} **O** *the people living in the land.*
Zec 3: 1 {Satan} **O** *The Accuser;* Hebrew reads *The Adversary;* also in 3:2.
6: 5 {the four spirits} **O** *the four winds.*
6:13 {from his throne,} **O** *There will be a priest by his throne.*
7: 2 {Sharezer and Regemmelech,} **O** *Bethel-sharezer had sent Regemmelech.*
9:10 {of the earth.} **O** *the end of the land.*
10: 3 {punish these leaders.} **O** *these male goats.*
10:11 {sea of distress,} **O** *the sea of Egypt,* referring to the Red Sea.
13: 6 {on your chest} **O** *scars between your hands.*
14: 6 {no longer shine,} Hebrew *there will be no light, no cold* **o** *frost.* The meaning of the Hebrew is uncertain.
Mal 2:15 {you are his.} **O** *Did not one God make us and preserve our life and breath?* **o** *Did not one God make her, both flesh and spirit?* The meaning of the Hebrew is uncertain.
4: 2 {in his wings.} **O** *the sun of righteousness will rise with healing in its wings.*
Mt 1: 8 {was the father} **O** *ancestor;* also in 1:11.
2: 1 {some wise men} **O** *royal astrologers,* Greek *magi;* also in 2:7, 16.
2: 2 {as it arose,} **O** *in the east.*
2:16 {two years earlier.} **O** *according to the time he calculated from the wise men.*
3: 2 {Heaven is near.} **O** *has come,* **o** *is coming soon.*
3:11 {"I baptize with} **O** *in.*
3:11 {and with fire.} **O** *in the Holy Spirit and in fire.*
3:15 {that is right.} **O** *we must fulfill all righteousness.*
4:17 {Heaven is near.} **O** *has come,* **o** *is coming soon.*
5:37 {something is wrong.} **O** *Anything beyond this is from the evil one.*
6:11 {food for today,} **O** *for tomorrow.*
6:13 {the evil one.} **O** *from evil.* Some manuscripts add *For yours is the kingdom and the power and the glory forever. Amen.*
7: 2 {you treat them.} **O** *For God will treat you as you treat others;* Greek reads *For with the judgment you judge you will be judged.*
7:23 {did were unauthorized.} **O** *unlawful.*
10: 7 {Heaven is near.} **O** *has come,* **o** *is coming soon.*
10:10 {to be fed.} **O** *the worker is worthy of support.*
11: 6 {offended by me.} **O** *who don't fall away because of me.*
11:12 {people attack it.} **O** *until now, eager multitudes have been pressing into the Kingdom of Heaven.*
12:29 {house be robbed!} **O** *One cannot rob Satan's kingdom without first tying him up. Only then can his demons be cast out.*
15:11 {say and do.} **O** *what comes out of the mouth defiles a person.*
16:18 {you are Peter,} *Peter* means "stone" **o** "rock."
16:26 {your own soul} **O** *your life;* also in 16:26b.
17: 4 {shrines,} **O** *shelters;* Greek reads *tabernacles.*
18:22 {"seventy times seven!} **O** *77 times.*
21:23 {from the Temple?} **O** *By whose authority do you do these things?*
23: 7 {being called 'Rabbi.'} *Rabbi,* from Aramaic, means "master" **o** "teacher."
24: 3 {of the world} **O** *the age.*
24:34 {this generation} **O** *this age,* **o** *this nation.*
24:36 {the Son himself.} Some manuscripts omit the phrase **o** *the Son himself.*

25: 1 {of ten bridesmaids} **O** *virgins;* also in 25:7, 11.
25:29 {who are unfaithful,} **O** *who have nothing.*
26:23 {with me now} **O** *The one who has dipped his hand in the bowl with me.*
26:45 {sleeping? Still resting?} **O** *Sleep on, take your rest.*
27: 9 {"They took} **O** *I took.*
27:51[-53] {to many people.} **O** *The earth shook, rocks split apart, tombs opened, and many bodies of godly men and women who had died were raised from the dead. After Jesus' resurrection, they left the cemetery, went into the holy city of Jerusalem, and appeared to many people.*
27:62 {the Passover ceremonies} **O** *On the next day, which is after the Preparation.*
Mk 1: 8 {baptize you with} **O** *in;* also in 1:8b.
3:27 {house be robbed!} **O** *One cannot rob Satan's kingdom without first tying him up. Only then can his demons be cast out.*
8:32 {things like that.} **O** *and began to correct him.*
8:36 {your own soul} **O** *your life;* also in 8:37.
9: 5 {make three shrines} **O** *shelters;* Greek reads *tabernacles.*
9:18 {and become rigid.} **O** *become weak.*
10:52 {down the road.} **O** *on the way.*
11:28 {from the Temple?} **O** *By whose authority do you do these things?*
13: 9 {them about me.} **O** *This will be your testimony against them.*
13:30 {this generation} **O** *this age,* **o** *this nation.*
14:20 {with me now.} **O** *one who is dipping bread into the bowl with me.*
14:41 {sleeping? Still resting?} **O** *Sleep on, take your rest.*
16:17 {speak new languages.} **O** *new tongues;* some manuscripts omit *new.*
Lk 1: 1 {that took place} **O** *have been fulfilled.*
1:15 {before his birth.} **O** *even from birth.*
2:14 {whom God favors.} **O** *and peace on earth for all those pleasing God;* some manuscripts read *and peace on earth, goodwill among people.*
2:49 {my Father's house."} **O** *"Didn't you realize that I should be involved with my Father's affairs?"*
3:16 {"I baptize with} **O** *in.*
3:16 {and with fire.} **O** *in the Holy Spirit and in fire.*
4:18[-19] {favor has come.} **O** *and to proclaim the acceptable year of the Lord.* Isa 61:1-2.
7:23 {offended by me.} **O** *who don't fall away because of me.*
7:29 {plan was right,} **O** *praised God.*
7:35 {who follow it.} **O** *But wisdom is justified by all her children.*
9:33 {make three shrines} **O** *shelters;* Greek reads *tabernacles.*
11: 8 {won't be damaged.} Greek *in order to avoid shame,* **o** *because of [your] persistence.*
11:11 {your children ask} Some manuscripts add *for bread, do you give them a stone?* **O** *if they ask.*
12:38 {just before dawn.} Greek *in the second* **o** *third watch.*
16: 9 {you in heaven.} **O** *Then when you run out at the end of this life, your friends will welcome you into eternal homes.*
17:20 {with visible signs.} **O** *by your speculations.*
17:21 {is among you.} **O** *within you.*
17:25 {must suffer terribly} **O** *suffer many things.*
17:30 {of Man returns.} **O** *on the day the Son of Man is revealed.*
19:26 {who are unfaithful,} **O** *who have nothing.*
20: 2 {from the Temple?} **O** *By whose authority do you do these things?*
21:32 {this generation} **O** *this age,* **o** *this nation.*
23:31 {it is dry?} **O** *If these things are done to me, the living tree, what will happen to you, the dry tree?*
23:47 {man was innocent.} **O** *righteous.*
Jn 1:26 {"I baptize with} **O** *in;* also in 1:31, 33.
2: 6 {to thirty gallons} Greek *2* **o** *3 measures* [75 to 113 liters].
2:17 {burns within me."} **O** *"Concern for God's house will be my undoing."* Ps 69:9.
3: 3 {are born again,} **O** *born from above;* also in 3:7.
3: 5 {and the Spirit.} **O** *spirit.* The Greek word for *Spirit* can also be translated *wind;* see 3:8.
6:19 {or four miles} Greek *25* **o** *30 stadia* [4.6 **o** 5.5 kilometers].
7:37[-38] {out from within."} **O** *"Let anyone who is thirsty come to me and drink. [38]For the Scriptures declare that rivers of living water will flow from the heart of those who believe in me."*
8:15 {your human limitations,} **O** *judge me by human standards.*
8:25 {claimed to be.} **O** *"Why do I speak to you at all?"*
8:58 {was even born!"} **O** *"Truly, truly, before Abraham was, I am."*
9:24 {telling the truth,} **O** *Give glory to God, not to Jesus;* Greek reads *Give glory to God.*
10:22 {Hanukkah.} **O** *the Dedication Celebration.*
13: 1 {of his love.} **O** *He loved his disciples to the very end.*
14:16 {another Counselor,} **O** *Comforter,* **o** *Encourager,* **o** *Advocate.* Greek *Paraclete;* also in 14:26.
15:26 {the Counselor} **O** *Comforter,* **o** *Encourager,* **o** *Advocate.* Greek *Paraclete.*
16: 7 {the Counselor} **O** *Comforter,* **o** *Encourager,* **o** *Advocate.* Greek *Paraclete.*
16:30 {tell you anything.} **O** *don't need that anyone should ask you anything.*

Ac 1: 5 {John baptized with} **O** *in;* also in 1:5b.
2: 4 {in other languages,} **O** *in other tongues.*
8: 26 {him, "Go south} **O** *Go at noon.*
11: 8 {our Jewish laws.} Greek *anything common* **o** *unclean.*
11: 16 {'John baptized with} **O** *in;* also in 11:16b.
13: 33 {become your Father.} **O** *Today I reveal you as my Son.* Ps 2:7.
17: 5 {to the crowd.} **O** *the city council.*
17: 22 {before the Council,} **O** *in the middle of Mars Hill;* Greek reads *in the middle of the Areopagus.*
18: 3 {they were tentmakers} **O** *leatherworkers.*
19: 21 {the Holy Spirit} **O** *purposed in his spirit.*
20: 22 {the Holy Spirit,} **O** *by my spirit,* **o** *by an inner compulsion;* Greek reads *by the spirit.*
21: 40 {own language, Aramaic.} **O** *Hebrew.*
26: 14 {me in Aramaic,} **O** *Hebrew.*
26: 28 {Christian so quickly?"} **O** *"A little more, and your arguments would make me a Christian."*
28: 30 {own rented house.} **O** *at his own expense.*
Ro 1: 4 {the Holy Spirit.} **O** *the Spirit of holiness.*
1: 9 {all my heart} **O** *in my spirit.*
1: 18 {away from themselves.} **O** *who prevent the truth from being known.*
6: 12 {way you live;} **O** *Do not let sin reign in your body, which is subject to death.*
8: 4 {accomplished for us} **O** *accomplished by us.*
8: 10 {spirit is alive} **O** *the Spirit will bring you eternal life.*
9: 5 {eternal praise! Amen.} **O** *May God, who rules over everything, be praised forever. Amen.*
9: 33 {not be disappointed.} **O** *will not be put to shame.* Isa 28:16.
10: 4 {the whole purpose} **O** *the end.*
10: 11 {not be disappointed.} **O** *will not be put to shame.* Isa 28:16.
16: 7 {Andronicus and Junia,} **O** *Junias;* some manuscripts read *Julia.*
16: 7 {my relatives,} **O** *compatriots;* also in 16:21.
16: 11 {Herodion, my relative.} **O** *compatriot.*
1Co 2: 13 {explain spiritual truths.} **O** *explaining spiritual truths in spiritual language,* **o** *explaining spiritual truths to spiritual people.*
3: 16 {God lives in} **O** *among.*
4: 6 {to the Scriptures,} **O** *You must learn not to go beyond "what is written," so that.*
5: 3 {in the Spirit.} **O** *in spirit.*
5: 4 {of the church,} **O** *In the name of the Lord Jesus, you are to call a meeting of the church.*
5: 5 {will be destroyed} **O** *so that he will die;* Greek reads *for the destruction of the flesh.*
6: 11 {been washed away,} **O** *you have been cleansed.*
7: 26 {the present crisis,} **O** *pressures of life.*
7: 39 {to the Lord.} **O** *but only to a Christian;* Greek reads *but only in the Lord.*
9: 26 {misses his punches.} **O** *I am not just shadowboxing.*
11: 6 {a covering.} **O** *then she should have long hair.*
12: 10 {in unknown languages,} **O** *in tongues;* also in 12:28, 30.
13: 8 {in unknown languages} **O** *in tongues.*
14: 2 {speak in tongues,} **O** *in unknown languages;* also in 14:4, 5, 13, 14, 18, 22, 28, 39.
14: 6 {an unknown language,} **O** *in tongues;* also in 14:19, 23, 26, 27.
14: 15 {in the spirit,} **O** *in the Spirit;* also in 14:15b, 16.
2Co 1: 21 {firm for Christ.} **O** *who has identified us and you as genuine Christians.*
3: 18 {that brightly reflect} **O** *so that we can see in a mirror.*
5: 14 {love controls us.} **O** *urges us on.*
6: 1 {As God's partners,} **O** *As we work together.*
6: 6 {the Holy Spirit.} **O** *the holiness of spirit.*
10: 7 {basis of appearance.} **O** *Look at the obvious facts.*
13: 5 {is among you,} **O** *in you.*
Gal 1: 16 {Son to me} **O** *in me.*
3: 28 {Jew or Gentile,} Greek *Jew* **o** *Greek.*
5: 12 {would mutilate themselves.} **O** *castrate themselves;* Greek reads *cut themselves off.*
6: 14 {of that cross,} **O** *Because of him.*
Eph 1: 11 {inheritance from God,} **O** *we have become God's inheritance.*
1: 18 {to his people.} **O** *realize how much God has been honored by acquiring his people.*
4: 9 {which we live.} **O** *to the lowest parts of the earth.*
6: 15 {be fully prepared.} **O** *For shoes, put on the readiness to preach the Good News of peace with God.*
Php 2: 7 {made himself nothing;} **O** *He laid aside his mighty power and glory.*
3: 3 {in the Spirit} **O** *in spirit;* some manuscripts read *worship by the Spirit of God.*
3: 14 {up to heaven.} **O** *from heaven.*
4: 3 {my true teammate,} Greek *true yokefellow,* **o** *loyal Syzygus.*
Col 1: 28 {to God, perfect} **O** *mature.*
2: 8 {of this world,} **O** *from the basic principles of this world;* also in 2:20.
1Th 4: 4 {control your body} **O** *will know how to take a wife for himself;* Greek reads *will know how to possess his own vessel.*
2Th 1: 12 {Lord, Jesus Christ.} **O** *of our God and the Lord Jesus Christ.*
3: 3 {the evil one.} **O** *from evil.*
1Ti 2: 15 {saved through childbearing} **O** *will be saved by accepting their role as mothers,* **o** *will be saved by the birth of the Child.*
3: 6 {make him fall.} **O** *he might fall into the same judgment as the Devil.*
3: 11 {their wives} **O** *the women deacons.* The Greek word can be translated *women* **o** *wives.*
3: 16 {by the Spirit.} **O** *in his spirit.*
5: 1 {an older man,} **O** *an elder.*
5: 7 {widows you support} **O** *so the church;* Greek reads *so they.*
2Ti 1: 12 {entrusted to him} **O** *what has been entrusted to me.*
Tit 1: 6 {to his wife,} **O** *have only one wife,* **o** *be married only once;* Greek reads *be the husband of one wife.*
Heb 1: 5 {become your Father.} **O** *Today I reveal you as my Son.* Ps 2:7.
2: 3 {was passed on} **O** *and confirmed.*
2: 6 {son of man} **O** *Son of Man.*
4: 9 {special rest} **O** *Sabbath rest.*
5: 5 {become your Father.} **O** *Today I reveal you as my Son.* Ps 2:7.
5: 12 {about the Scriptures.} **O** *about the oracles of God.*
6: 1 {basics of Christianity} **O** *the basics about Christ.*
7: 25 {forever, to save} **O** *able to save completely.*
9: 16 {wrote the will} **O** *covenant.*
9: 16 {is dead.} **O** *Now when someone makes a covenant, it is necessary to ratify it with the death of a sacrifice.*
12: 2 {start to finish.} **O** *Jesus, the Originator and Perfecter of our faith.*
12: 9 {and live forever} **O** *really live.*
Jas 4: 5 {to be faithful} **O** *the spirit that God placed within us tends to envy,* **o** *the Holy Spirit, whom God has placed within us, opposes our envy.*
5: 3 {flesh in hell.} **O** *will eat your flesh like fire.*
1Pe 1: 6 {be truly glad!} **O** *So you are truly glad.*
2: 6 {never be disappointed.} **O** *will never be put to shame.* Isa 28:16.
2: 12 {judge the world.} **O** *on the day of visitation.*
3: 18 {in the Spirit.} **O** *spirit.*
3: 21 {to God from} **O** *for.*
2Pe 1: 2 {God and Lord,} **O** *God and Jesus our Lord.*
1: 19 {in your hearts.} **O** *until the day dawns and the morning star rises in your hearts.*
1: 20 {the prophets themselves} **O** *is a matter of one's own interpretation.*
1Jn 4: 19 {love each other} **O** *We love him;* Greek reads *We love.*
2Jn 1: 1 {to her children,} **O** *the church God has chosen and her members,* **o** *the chosen Kyria and her children.*
1: 13 {of your sister,} **O** *from the members of your sister church.*
Jude 1: 12 {can shipwreck you.} **O** *they are contaminants among you,* **o** *they are stains.*
Rev 1: 1 {revelation from} **O** *of.*
1: 10 {in the Spirit.} **O** *in spirit.*
1: 13 {Son of Man.} **O** *one who looked like a man;* Greek reads *one like a son of man.*
1: 20 {the angels of} **O** *the messengers for.*
2: 1 {the angel of} **O** *the messenger for;* also in 2:8, 12, 18.
3: 1 {the angel of} **O** *the messenger for;* also in 3:7, 14.
3: 14 {witness, the ruler} **O** *the source.*
4: 2 {in the Spirit,} **O** *in spirit.*
6: 6 {And don't waste} **O** *hurt*
13: 18 {of a man.} **O** *of humanity.*
14: 14 {Son of Man} **O** *one who looked like a man;* Greek reads *one like a son of man.*
17: 3 {me in spirit} **O** *in the Spirit.*
19: 10 {witness for Jesus.} **O** *is the message confirmed by Jesus.*
21: 10 {me in spirit} **O** *in the Spirit.*
22: 2 {crops of fruit,} **O** *12 kinds of fruit.*

ORACLE (3)

Zec 9: 1 {is the message} Hebrew *An O: The message.*
12: 1 {This} Hebrew *An O: This.*
Mal 1: 1 {is the message} Hebrew *An O: The message.*

ORACLES (2)

Ro 3: 2 {revelation of God.} Greek *the* **o** *of God.*
Heb 5: 12 {about the Scriptures.} Or *about the* **o** *of God.*

ORATOR (1)

Ac 24: 1 {and the lawyer} Greek *some elders and an* **o.**

ORDAINED (1)

Ac 7: 53 {hands of angels.} Greek *received the Law as it was* **o** *by angels.*

ORDER (2 of 3)

Lk 11: 8 {won't be damaged.} Greek *in* **o** *to avoid shame,* or *because of [your] persistence.*
Heb 7: 11 {Levi and Aaron?} Greek *according to the* **o** *of Aaron.*

ORIGINATOR (1)

Heb 12: 2 {start to finish.} Or *Jesus, the* **O** *and Perfecter of our faith.*

ORNAMENTED (1)

2Sa 13: 18 {long, beautiful robe,} Or *a robe with sleeves,* or *an* **o** *robe.* The meaning of the Hebrew is uncertain.

ORNAN (2)

1Ch 21: 15 {floor of Araunah} As in parallel text at 2 Sam 24:16; Hebrew reads ***O***, another name for Araunah; also in 21:18-28.
2Ch 3: 1 {floor of Araunah} Hebrew reads ***O***, another name for Araunah; compare 2 Sam 24:16.

OSNAPPAR (1)

Ezr 4: 10 {and noble Ashurbanipal} Aramaic ***O***, another name for Ashurbanipal.

OTHNIEL (1)

Jos 15: 18 {she urged him} Some Greek manuscripts read ***O*** *urged her.*

OUTSIDE (1)

Ex 27: 21 {in the Tabernacle.} Hebrew *in the Tent of Meeting,* **o** *of the inner curtain, in front of the Testimony.*

OVERLAID (1)

1Ki 6: 20 {made of cedar.} Or **o** *the altar with cedar.* The meaning of the Hebrew is uncertain.

OVERSEER (2)

1Ti 3: 1 {be an elder,} Greek **o**; also in 3:2.
Tit 1: 7 {An elder} Greek **o.**

OVERSEERS (2)

Ac 20: 28 {you as elders.} Greek **o.**
Php 1: 1 {to the elders} Greek **o.**

OWN (7 of 11)

Ge 5: 3 {of his father.} Hebrew *was in his* **o** *likeness, after his image.*
Lev 19: 16 {among your people.} Hebrew *Do not act as a merchant toward your* **o** *people.*
Pr 5: 15 {with your wife.} Hebrew *Drink water from your* **o** *cistern, flowing water from your* **o** *well.*
SS 1: 6 {done to me!} Hebrew *My* **o** *vineyard I have neglected.*
1Th 4: 4 {control your body} Or *will know how to take a wife for himself;* Greek reads *will know how to possess his* **o** *vessel.*
2Pe 1: 20 {the prophets themselves} Or *is a matter of one's* **o** *interpretation.*

OXEN (1 of 4)

1Sa 6: 19 {killed seventy men} As in a few Hebrew manuscripts; most Hebrew manuscripts and Greek version read *50,070 men.* Perhaps the text should be understood to read *the LORD killed 70 men and 50* **o.**

OXGOADS (1)

Ac 26: 14 {against my will.} Greek *It is hard for you to kick against the* **o.**

P

PAI (1)

1Ch 1: 50 {city of Pau.} As in many Hebrew manuscripts, some Greek manuscripts, Syriac version, and Latin Vulgate (see also Gen 36:39); most Hebrew manuscripts read ***P***.

PAIN (1)

1Ch 4: 9 {named him Jabez} *Jabez* sounds like a Hebrew term meaning "distress" or "**p.**"

PALMS (2)

Jdg 1: 16 {Judah left Jericho,} Hebrew *the city of* **p.**
3: 13 {possession of Jericho.} Hebrew *the city of* **p.**

PALTI (2)

2Sa 3: 15 {her husband Palti} As in 1 Sam 25:44; Hebrew reads *Paltiel,* a variant name for **P.**
23: 26 {Helez from Pelon} As in parallel text at 1 Chr 11:27 (see also 1 Chr 27:10); Hebrew reads *from* ***P***.

PALTIEL (1)

2Sa 3: 15 {her husband Palti} As in 1 Sam 25:44; Hebrew reads ***P***, a variant name for Palti.

PAMPHYLIA (1)

Ac 13: 13[-14] {Antioch of Pisidia.} ***P*** and *Pisidia* were districts in the land now called Turkey.

PANELS (1)

SS 8: 9 {off from men.} Hebrew *If she is a wall, we will build battlements of silver on her; but if she is a door, we will surround her with* **p** *of cedar.*

PANIC (1)

Dt 7:20 {will send hornets} Or *will spread* **p**, or *will send a plague.* The meaning of the Hebrew is uncertain.

PARACLETE (3)

Jn 14:16 {you another Counselor,} Or *Comforter,* or *Encourager,* or *Advocate.* Greek ***P;*** also in 14:26.
15:26 {you the Counselor} Or *Comforter,* or *Encourager,* or *Advocate.* Greek ***P.***
16: 7 {don't, the Counselor} Or *Comforter,* or *Encourager,* or *Advocate.* Greek ***P.***

PARALLEL (82)

2Sa 5:14 {in Jerusalem: Shimea,} As in **p** text at 1 Chr 3:5; Hebrew reads *Shammua,* a variant name for Shimea.
8:18 {as priestly leaders.} Hebrew *David's sons were priests;* compare **p** text at 1 Chr 18:17.
10:18 {forty thousand horsemen,} Some Greek manuscripts read *foot soldiers;* compare **p** text at 1 Chr 19:18.
21:19 {son of Jair} As in **p** text at 1 Chr 20:5; Hebrew reads *son of Jaare-oregim.*
21:19 {Goliath of Gath.} As in **p** text at 1 Chr 20:5; Hebrew reads *killed Goliath of Gath.*
21:21 {David's brother Shimea.} As in **p** text at 1 Chr 20:7; Hebrew reads *Shimei,* a variant name for Shimea.
23: 8 {Jashobeam the Hacmonite,} As in **p** text at 1 Chr 11:11; Hebrew reads *Josheb-basshebeth the Tahkemonite.*
23:26 {Helez from Pelon} As in **p** text at 1 Chr 11:27 (see also 1 Chr 27:10); Hebrew reads *from Palti.*
23:29 {Ithai} As in **p** text at 1 Chr 11:31; Hebrew reads *Ittai.*
23:33 {son of Shagee} As in **p** text at 1 Chr 11:34; Hebrew reads *Jonathan, Shammah;* some Greek manuscripts read *Jonathan son of Shammah.*
1Ki 8:65 {Festival of Shelters.} Hebrew *seven days and seven days, fourteen days;* compare **p** text at 2 Chr 7:8-10.
8:66 {festival was over,} Hebrew *On the eighth day,* probably referring to the day following the seven-day Festival of Shelters; compare **p** text at 2 Chr 7:9-10.
2Ki 12:21 {assassins were Jozacar} As in Greek and Syriac versions; Hebrew reads *Jozabad;* compare **p** text at 2 Chr 24:26.
18: 2 {mother was Abijah,} As in **p** text at 2 Chr 29:1; Hebrew reads *Abi,* a variant name for Abijah.
25:17 {was 7 1/2 feet} As in **p** texts at 1 Kgs 7:16, 2 Chr 3:15, and Jer 52:22, all of which read *5 cubits* [2.3 meters]; Hebrew reads *3 cubits,* which is 4.5 feet or 1.4 meters.
1Ch 1:17 {Gether, and Mash.} As in **p** text at Gen 10:23; Hebrew reads *and Meshech.*
1:39 {Hori and Heman.} As in **p** text at Gen 36:22; Hebrew reads *and Homam.*
1:42 {sons of Dishan} Hebrew *Dishon;* compare 1:38 and **p** text at Gen 36:28.
1:51 {were Timna, Alvah,} As in **p** text at Gen 36:40; Hebrew reads *Aliah.*
3: 1 {second was Kileab,} As in **p** text at 2 Sam 3:3; Hebrew reads *Daniel.*
3: 6 {Elpelet,} Hebrew *Eliphelet;* compare **p** text at 14:5-7.
6:23 {Elkanah, Abiasaph,} Hebrew *Ebiasaph,* a variant name for Abiasaph (also in 6:37); compare **p** text at Exod 6:24.
6:58 {Holon,} As in **p** text at Josh 21:15; Hebrew reads *Hilen.*
6:59 {Ain,} As in **p** text at Josh 21:16; Hebrew reads *Ashan.*
6:60 {were given Gibeon,} As in **p** text at Josh 21:17; Hebrew lacks *Gibeon.*
7:13 {Naphtali were Jahzeel,} As in **p** text at Gen 46:24; Hebrew reads *Jahziel,* a variant name for Jahzeel.
8:31 {Gedor, Ahio, Zechariah,} As in **p** text at 9:37; Hebrew reads *Zeker,* a variant name for Zechariah.
8:32 {father of Shimeam.} As in **p** text at 9:38; Hebrew reads *Shimeah,* a variant name for Shimeam.
8:35 {Pithon, Melech, Tahrea,} As in **p** text at 9:41; Hebrew reads *Tarea,* a variant name for Tahrea.
8:36 {father of Jadah.} As in **p** text at 9:42; Hebrew reads *Jehoaddah,* a variant name for Jadah.
8:37 {father of Rephaiah.} As in **p** text at 9:43; Hebrew reads *Raphah,* a variant name for Rephaiah.
11:12 {son of Dodai,} As in **p** text at 2 Sam 23:9 (see also 1 Chr 27:4); Hebrew reads *Dodo,* a variant name for Dodai.
11:27 {Shammah from Harod;} As in **p** text at 2 Sam 23:25; Hebrew reads *Shammoth from Haror.*
11:29 {Zalmon} As in **p** text at 2 Sam 23:28; Hebrew reads *Ilai.*
11:32 {Abi-albon} As in **p** text at 2 Sam 23:31; Hebrew reads *Abiel.*
11:33 {Azmaveth from Bahurim} As in **p** text at 2 Sam 23:31; Hebrew reads *Baharum.*
11:34 {sons of Jashen} As in **p** text at 2 Sam 23:32; Hebrew reads *sons of Hashem.*
11:35 {son of Sharar} As in **p** text at 2 Sam 23:33; Hebrew reads *son of Sacar.*
11:37 {Paarai} As in **p** text at 2 Sam 23:35; Hebrew reads *Naarai.*
13: 9 {floor of Nacon,} As in **p** text at 2 Sam 6:6; Hebrew reads *Kidon.*
14: 7 {Elishama, Eliada,} Hebrew *Beeliada,* a variant name for Eliada; compare 3:8 and **p** text at 2 Sam 5:16.
14:12 {abandoned their idols} Hebrew *their gods;* compare **p** text at 2 Sam 5:21.
18: 8 {cities of Tebah} Hebrew reads *Tibhath,* a variant name for Tebah; compare **p** text at 2 Sam 8:8.
18: 9 {When King Toi} As in **p** text at 2 Sam 8:9; Hebrew reads *Tou;* also in 18:10.
18:10 {his son Joram} As in **p** text at 2 Sam 8:10; Hebrew reads *Hadoram,* a variant name for Joram.
18:16 {the priests. Seraiah} As in **p** text at 2 Sam 8:17; Hebrew reads *Shavsha.*
19: 1 {his son Hanun} Hebrew lacks *Hanun;* compare **p** text at 2 Sam 10:1.
19:16 {command of Shobach,} As in **p** text at 2 Sam 10:16; Hebrew reads *Shophach;* also in 19:18.
20: 3 {picks, and axes.} As in **p** text at 2 Sam 12:31; Hebrew reads *and saws.*
20: 4 {Hushah killed Saph,} As in **p** text at 2 Sam 21:18; Hebrew reads *Sippai.*
21:15 {floor of Araunah} As in **p** text at 2 Sam 24:16; Hebrew reads *Ornan,* another name for Araunah; also in 21:18-28.
2Ch 2: 8 {cypress, and almug} Hebrew *algum;* compare 9:10-11 and **p** text at 1 Kgs 10:11-12.
4:17 {Succoth and Zarethan.} As in **p** text at 1 Kgs 7:46; Hebrew reads *Zeredah.*
9:10 {of almug wood} Hebrew *algum wood* (also in 9:11); compare **p** text at 1 Kgs 10:11-12.
16: 4 {Ijon, Dan, Abel-beth-maacah,} As in **p** text at 1 Kgs 15:20; Hebrew reads *Abel-maim,* another name for Abel-beth-maacah.
22:11 {Ahaziah's sister Jehosheba,} As in **p** text at 2 Kgs 11:2; Hebrew reads *Jehoshabeath,* a variant name for Jehosheba.
24:26 {assassins were Jozacar,} Hebrew *Zabad;* compare **p** text at 2 Kgs 12:21, and see note there.
24:26 {woman named Shomer.} As in **p** text at 2 Kgs 12:21; Hebrew reads *Shimrith.*
25: 1 {mother was Jehoaddin,} As in **p** text at 2 Kgs 14:2; Hebrew reads *Jehoaddan,* a variant name for Jehoaddin.
34:20 {son of Micaiah,} As in **p** text at 2 Kgs 22:12; Hebrew reads *Abdon son of Micah.*
34:22 {grandson of Harhas,} As in **p** text at 2 Kgs 22:14; Hebrew reads *son of Tokhath, son of Hasrah.*
36:10 {appointed Jehoiachin's uncle,} As in **p** text at 2 Kgs 24:17; Hebrew reads *brother,* or *relative.*
Ezr 2:24 {people of Beth-azmaveth} As in **p** text at Neh 7:28; Hebrew reads *Azmaveth.*
2:55 {Sotai, Sophereth,} As in **p** text at Neh 7:57; Hebrew reads *Hassophereth.*
10: 6 {spent the night} As in **p** text at 1 Esdras 9:2; Hebrew reads *He went.*
10:25 {Mijamin, Eleazar, Hashabiah,} As in **p** text at 1 Esdras 9:26; Hebrew reads *Malkijah.*
Ne 7: 7 {Jeshua, Nehemiah, Seraiah,} As in **p** text at Ezra 2:2; Hebrew reads *Azariah.*
7: 7 {Reelaiah,} As in **p** text at Ezra 2:2; Hebrew reads *Raamiah.*
7: 7 {Mordecai, Bilshan, Mispar,} As in **p** text at Ezra 2:2; Hebrew reads *Mispereth.*
7: 7 {Bigvai, Rehum,} As in **p** text at Ezra 2:2; Hebrew reads *Nehum.*
7:15 {family of Bani} As in **p** text at Ezra 2:10; Hebrew reads *Binnui.*
7:24 {family of Jorah} As in **p** text at Ezra 2:18; Hebrew reads *Hariph.*
7:25 {family of Gibbar} As in **p** text at Ezra 2:20; Hebrew reads *Gibeon.*
7:43 {(descendants of Hodaviah} As in **p** text at Ezra 2:40; Hebrew reads *Hodevah.*
7:47 {Keros, Siaha,} As in **p** text at Ezra 2:44; Hebrew reads *Sia.*
7:52 {Besai, Meunim, Nephusim,} As in **p** text at Ezra 2:50; Hebrew reads *Nephushesim.*
7:54 {Bazluth,} As in **p** text at Ezra 2:52; Hebrew reads *Bazlith.*
7:57 {Sotai, Sophereth, Peruda,} As in **p** text at Ezra 2:55; Hebrew reads *Perida.*
7:58 {Jaalah,} As in **p** text at Ezra 2:56; Hebrew reads *Jaala.*
7:59 {Pokereth-hazzebaim, and Ami.} As in **p** text at Ezra 2:57; Hebrew reads *Amon.*
7:61 {Tel-harsha, Kerub, Addan,} As in **p** text at Ezra 2:59; Hebrew reads *Addon.*
Jer 40: 8 {the Netophathite, Jaazaniah} As in **p** text at 2 Kgs 25:23; Hebrew reads *Jezaniah,* a variant name for Jaazaniah.

PARAN (1)

1Sa 25: 1 {wilderness of Maon.} As in Greek version; Hebrew reads ***P.***

PARAS (2)

Eze 27:10 {Lydia, and Libya} Hebrew ***P,*** *Lud, and Put.*
38: 5 {Ethiopia, and Libya} Hebrew ***P,*** *Cush, and Put.*

PARCHMENTS (1)

2Ti 4:13 {especially my papers.} Greek *especially the* ***p.***

PARSIN (1)

Da 5:28 {*Parsin*} Aramaic *Peres,* the singular of ***P.***

PART (2)

Ge 2:21 {of Adam's ribs} Or *took a* ***p*** *of Adam's side.*
Est 2:14 {the second harem,} Or *to another* ***p*** *of the harem.*

PARTS (1)

Eph 4: 9 {which we live.} Or *to the lowest* ***p*** *of the earth.*

PASS (8)

Dt 18:10 {a burnt offering.} Or *never make your son or daughter* ***p*** *through the fire.*
2Ki 16: 3 {in the fire.} Or *even making his son* ***p*** *through the fire.*
17:17 {in the fire.} Or *They even made their sons and daughters* ***p*** *through the fire.*
21: 6 {in the fire.} Or *even made his son* ***p*** *through the fire.*
23:10 {in the fire} Or *to make a son or daughter* ***p*** *through the fire.*
2Ch 28: 3 {in the fire.} Or *even making his sons* ***p*** *through the fire.*
33: 6 {in the fire} Or *even made his sons* ***p*** *through the fire.*
Eze 20:31 {burned as sacrifices,} Or *and make your little children* ***p*** *through the fire.*

PASSAGE (7)

Lev 13: 2 {contagious skin disease,} Traditionally rendered *leprosy.* The Hebrew word used throughout this **p** is used to describe various skin diseases.
13:47 {an infectious mildew} Traditionally rendered *leprosy.* The Hebrew term used throughout this **p** is the same term used for the various skin diseases described in 13:1-46.
2Ki 5: 1 {suffered from leprosy.} Or *from a contagious skin disease.* The Hebrew word used here and throughout this **p** can describe various skin diseases.
7: 3 {men with leprosy} Or *with a contagious skin disease.* The Hebrew word used here and throughout this **p** can describe various skin diseases.
15: 5 {king with leprosy,} Or *with a contagious skin disease.* The Hebrew word used here and throughout this **p** can describe various skin diseases.
2Ch 26:19 {LORD's Temple, leprosy} Or *a contagious skin disease.* The Hebrew word used here and throughout this **p** can describe various skin diseases.
Job 41: 1 {catch a crocodile} Hebrew *Leviathan;* also throughout the following **p.**

PASSOVER (1)

Ac 2: 1 {after Jesus' resurrection,} Greek *When the day of Pentecost arrived.* This annual celebration came 50 days after the **P** ceremonies. See Lev 23:16.

PAST (1)

Ecc 3:15 {in its turn.} Hebrew *For God calls the* ***p*** *to account.*

PATHROS (1)

Isa 11:11 {Upper Egypt, Ethiopia,} Hebrew ***P,*** *Cush.*

PAUL (2)

Ac 7:58 {man named Saul.} *Saul* is later called **P**; see 13:9.
16:10 {So we} Luke, the writer of this book, here joined **P** and accompanied him on his journey.

PAY (1)

Job 41:11 {and remain safe} As in Greek version; Hebrew reads *confront me that I must* ***p.***

PAYMENT (1)

Mt 20: 2 {normal daily wage} Greek *a denarius,* the **p** for a full day's labor; also in 20:9, 10, 13.

PEACE (6)

1Ki 2: 5 {time of peace,} Or *He murdered them during a time of* ***p*** *as revenge for deaths they had caused in time of war.*
1Ch 22: 9 {will be Solomon,} *Solomon* sounds like and is probably derived from the Hebrew word for "**p.**"
Lk 2:14 {whom God favors.} Or *and* ***p*** *on earth for all those pleasing God;* some manuscripts read *and* ***p*** *on earth, goodwill among people.*
24:36 {be with you."} Some manuscripts do not include *He said, "****P*** *be with you."*
Eph 6:15 {be fully prepared.} Or *For shoes, put on the readiness to preach the Good News of* ***p*** *with God.*

PELETHITES (5)

2Sa 8:18 {the king's bodyguard.} Hebrew *of the Kerethites and* ***P.***
15:18 {the king's bodyguard.} Hebrew *the Kerethites and* ***P.***

20: 7 {king's own bodyguard.} Hebrew *the Kerethites and **P**;* also in 20:23.
1Ki 1:38 {the king's bodyguard} Hebrew *the Kerethites and **P**;* also in 1:44.
1Ch 18:17 {the king's bodyguard.} Hebrew *of the Kerethites and **P**.*

PENIEL (3)

Ge 32:31 {he left Peniel,} Hebrew *Penuel,* a variant name for **P**.
Jdg 8: 8 {up to Peniel} Hebrew *Penuel,* a variant name for **P**; also in 8:9, 17.
1Ki 12:25 {town of Peniel.} Hebrew *Penuel,* a variant name for **P**.

PENINSULA (4)

Ac 18: 1 {went to Corinth.} *Athens* and *Corinth* were major cities in Achaia, the region on the southern end of the Greek **p**.
1Co 16:15 {Christians in Greece,} Greek *were the firstfruits in Achaia,* the southern region of the Greek **p**.
2Co 1: 1 {Christians throughout Greece.} Greek *Achaia,* the southern region of the Greek **p**.
9: 2 {Christians in Greece} Greek *Achaia,* the southern region of the Greek **p**.

PENTATEUCH (11)

Ge 36:39 {Baal-hanan died, Hadad} As in some Hebrew manuscripts, Samaritan **P**, and Syriac version (see also 1 Chr 1:50); most Hebrew manuscripts read *Hadar.*
46:13 {Puah,} As in Syriac version and Samaritan **P** (see also 1 Chr 7:1); Hebrew reads *Puvah.*
46:13 {Jashub,} As in some Greek manuscripts and Samaritan **P** (see also Num 26:24; 1 Chr 7:1); Hebrew reads *Iob.*
46:16 {Gad were Zephon,} As in Greek version and Samaritan **P** (see also Num 26:15); Hebrew reads *Ziphion.*
47:21 {servants to Pharaoh.} As in Greek version and Samaritan **P**; Hebrew reads *He moved the people into the towns throughout the land of Egypt.*
Nu 2:14[-15] {son of Deuel} As in many Hebrew manuscripts, Samaritan **P**, and Latin Vulgate (see also 1:14); most Hebrew manuscripts read *son of Reuel.*
26:17 {its ancestor Arodi.} As in Samaritan **P** and Syriac version (see also Gen 46:16); Hebrew reads *Arod.*
26:23 {its ancestor Puah.} As in Samaritan **P**, Greek and Syriac versions, and Latin Vulgate (see also 1 Chr 7:1); Hebrew reads *The Punite clan, named after its ancestor Puvah.*
26:39 {its ancestor Shupham.} As in some Hebrew manuscripts, Samaritan **P**, Greek and Syriac versions, and Latin Vulgate; most Hebrew manuscripts read *Shephupham.*
26:40 {their ancestor Ard.} As in Samaritan **P**, some Greek manuscripts, and Latin Vulgate; Hebrew lacks *named after their ancestor Ard.*
Dt 34: 6 {He was buried} Hebrew *He buried him,* that is, "The LORD buried him." Samaritan **P** and some Greek manuscripts read *They buried him.*

PENTECOST (1)

Ac 2: 1 {after Jesus' resurrection,} Greek *When the day of **P** arrived.* This annual celebration came 50 days after the Passover ceremonies. See Lev 23:16.

PENUEL (3)

Ge 32:31 {he left Peniel,} Hebrew ***P**,* a variant name for Peniel.
Jdg 8: 8 {up to Peniel} Hebrew ***P**,* a variant name for Peniel; also in 8:9, 17.
1Ki 12:25 {town of Peniel.} Hebrew ***P**,* a variant name for Peniel.

PEOPLE (58)

Ge 19:38 {named him Ben-ammi.} *Ben-ammi* means "son of my **p**."
47:21 {servants to Pharaoh.} As in Greek version and Samaritan Pentateuch; Hebrew reads *He moved the **p** into the towns throughout the land of Egypt.*
Lev 4:27 {citizens of Israel} Hebrew ***p** of the land.*
19:16 {among your people.} Hebrew *Do not act as a merchant toward your own **p**.*
27:21 {specially set apart} The Hebrew term used here refers to the complete consecration of things or **p** to the LORD, either by destroying them or by giving them as an offering; also in 27:28, 29.
Nu 6:27 {as my people,} Hebrew *will put my name on the **p** of Israel.*
18:14 {for the LORD} The Hebrew term used here refers to the complete consecration of things or **p** to the LORD, either by destroying them or by giving them as an offering.
21: 2 {will completely destroy} The Hebrew term used here refers to the complete consecration of things or **p** to the LORD, either by destroying them or by giving them as an offering; also in 21:3.
Dt 2:34 {and completely destroyed} The Hebrew term used here refers to the complete consecration of things or **p** to the LORD, either by destroying them or by giving them as an offering.
3: 6 {We completely destroyed} The Hebrew term used here refers to the complete consecration of things or **p** to the LORD, either by destroying them or by giving them as an offering.
7: 2 {must completely destroy} The Hebrew term used here refers to the complete consecration of things or **p** to the LORD, either by destroying them or by giving them as an offering; also in 7:26.
13:15 {and completely destroy} The Hebrew term used here refers to the complete consecration of things or **p** to the LORD, either by destroying them or by giving them as an offering; also in 13:17.
20:17 {must completely destroy} The Hebrew term used here refers to the complete consecration of things or **p** to the LORD, either by destroying them or by giving them as an offering.
32:43 {God worship him,} As in Dead Sea Scrolls and Greek version; Masoretic Text reads *Rejoice with his **p**, O nations.*
Jos 2:10 {you completely destroyed.} The Hebrew term used here refers to the complete consecration of things or **p** to the LORD, either by destroying them or by giving them as an offering.
6:17 {be completely destroyed} The Hebrew term used here refers to the complete consecration of things or **p** to the LORD, either by destroying them or by giving them as an offering; also in 6:18, 21.
7: 1 {for the LORD.} The Hebrew term used here refers to the complete consecration of things or **p** to the LORD, either by destroying them or by giving them as an offering; also in 7:11, 12, 13, 15.
8:26 {was completely destroyed.} The Hebrew term used here refers to the complete consecration of things or **p** to the LORD, either by destroying them or by giving them as an offering.
10: 1 {and completely destroyed} The Hebrew term used here refers to the complete consecration of things or **p** to the LORD, either by destroying them or by giving them as an offering; also in 10:28, 35, 37, 39, 40.
11:11 {Israelites completely destroyed} The Hebrew term used here refers to the complete consecration of things or **p** to the LORD, either by destroying them or by giving them as an offering; also in 11:12, 20, 21.
22:20 {for the LORD} The Hebrew term used here refers to the complete consecration of things or **p** to the LORD, either by destroying them or by giving them as an offering.
Jdg 1:17 {they completely destroyed} The Hebrew term used here refers to the complete consecration of things or **p** to the LORD, either by destroying them or by giving them as an offering.
21:11 {said. "Completely destroy} The Hebrew term used here refers to the complete consecration of things or **p** to the LORD, either by destroying them or by giving them as an offering.
1Sa 10: 1 {his people Israel.} Greek version reads *Israel. And you will rule over the LORD's **p** and save them from their enemies around them. This will be the sign to you that the LORD has appointed you to be leader over his inheritance.*
15: 3 {destroy} The Hebrew term used here refers to the complete consecration of things or **p** to the LORD, either by destroying them or by giving them as an offering; also in 15:8, 9, 15, 18, 20, 21.
1Ki 9:21 {not completely destroyed.} The Hebrew term used here refers to the complete consecration of things or **p** to the LORD, either by destroying them or by giving them as an offering.
20:42 {must be destroyed,} The Hebrew term used here refers to the complete consecration of things or **p** to the LORD, either by destroying them or by giving them as an offering.
2Ki 4:42 {group of prophets} Hebrew *to the **p**;* also in 4:43.
7: 6 {Hittites and Egyptians} Possibly *and the **p** of Muzur,* a district near Cilicia.
1Ch 2: 7 {for the LORD.} The Hebrew term used here refers to the complete consecration of things or **p** to the LORD, either by destroying them or by giving them as an offering.
4:41 {and completely destroyed} The Hebrew term used here refers to the complete consecration of things or **p** to the LORD, either by destroying them or by giving them as an offering.
Ps 144: 2 {the nations} Some manuscripts read *my **p**.*
SS 6:12 {my beloved one.} Or *among the royal chariots of my **p**,* or *among the chariots of Amminadab.* The meaning of the Hebrew is uncertain.
Isa 34: 2 {will completely destroy} The Hebrew term used here refers to the complete consecration of things or **p** to the LORD, either by destroying them or by giving them as an offering; also in 34:5.
43:28 {of complete destruction} The Hebrew term used here refers to the complete consecration of things or **p** to the LORD, either by destroying them or by giving them as an offering.
Jer 9:26 {in distant places,} Or *the **p** who clip the corners of their hair.*
25: 9 {will completely destroy} The Hebrew term used here refers to the complete consecration of things or **p** to the LORD, either by destroying them or by giving them as an offering.
50:21 {and completely destroy} The Hebrew term used here refers to the complete consecration of things or **p** to the LORD, either by destroying them or by giving them as an offering.
51: 3 {be completely destroyed.} The Hebrew term used here refers to the complete consecration of things or **p** to the LORD, either by destroying them or by giving them as an offering.
Eze 44:29 {anyone sets apart} The Hebrew term used here refers to the complete consecration of things or **p** to the LORD, either by destroying them or by giving them as an offering.
Hos 4: 4 {is with you!} Hebrew *Your **p** are like those with a complaint against the priests.*
Jnh 4:11 {in spiritual darkness,} Hebrew ***p** who don't know their right hands from their left.*
Zep 1:18 {people on earth.} Or *the **p** living in the land.*
Mt 23:13 {go in yourselves.} Some manuscripts add verse 14, *How terrible it will be for you teachers of religious law and you Pharisees. Hypocrites! You shamelessly cheat widows out of their property, and then, to cover up the kind of **p** you really are, you make long prayers in public. Because of this, your punishment will be the greater.*
27:51[-53] {to many people.} Or *The earth shook, rocks split apart, tombs opened, and many bodies of godly men and women who had died were raised from the dead. After Jesus' resurrection, they left the cemetery, went into the holy city of Jerusalem, and appeared to many **p**.*
Lk 2:14 {whom God favors.} Or *and peace on earth for all those pleasing God;* some manuscripts read *and peace on earth, goodwill among **p**.*
Jn 6:41 {Then the people} Greek *Jewish **p**;* also in 6:52.
8:31 {to the people} Greek *Jewish **p**;* also in 8:48, 52, 57.
10:19 {things, the people} Greek *Jewish **p**.*
11:19 {of the people} Greek *Jewish **p**;* also 11:31, 33, 36, 45, 54.
12: 9 {all the people} Greek *Jewish **p**;* also in 12:11.
18:20 {heard by people} Greek *Jewish **p**;* also in 18:38.
19:14 {to the people,} Greek *Jewish **p**;* also in 19:20.
Ac 10:41 {the general public,} Greek *the **p**.*
1Co 2:13 {explain spiritual truths.} Or *explaining spiritual truths in spiritual language,* or *explaining spiritual truths to spiritual **p**.*
7:23 {by the world.} Greek *don't become slaves of **p**.*
13: 1 {or on earth} Greek *in tongues of **p** and angels.*
Eph 1:18 {to his people.} Or *realize how much God has been honored by acquiring his **p**.*

PEOPLES (2)

Ge 49:10 {whom it belongs,} Or *until tribute is brought to him and the **p** obey;* traditionally rendered *until Shiloh comes.*
Joel 3: 6 {to the Greeks,} Hebrew *to the **p** of Javan.*

PERATH (1)

Jer 13: 4 {the Euphrates River.} Hebrew ***P**;* also in 13:5, 6, 7.

PERES (1)

Da 5:28 {*Parsin*} Aramaic ***P**,* the singular of *Parsin.*

PEREZ (1)

Ge 38:29 {was called Perez.} ***P*** means "breaking out."

PERFECTER (1)

Heb 12: 2 {start to finish.} Or *Jesus, the Originator and **P** of our faith.*

PERHAPS (5)

Jdg 7: 3 {afraid may leave} Hebrew *leave Mount Gilead.* The identity of Mount Gilead is uncertain in this context. It is **p** used here as another name for Mount Gilboa.
1Sa 6:19 {killed seventy men} As in a few Hebrew manuscripts; most Hebrew manuscripts and Greek version read *50,070 men.* **P** the text should be understood to read *the LORD killed 70 men and 50 oxen.*
1Ch 2:24 {(the father of} Or *the founder of;* also in 2:42, 45, 49-52 and **p** other instances where the text reads *the father of.*
4: 4 {(the father of} Or *the founder of;* also in 4:12, 14, 17-18, and **p** other instances where the text reads *the father of.*
Isa 28:10 {very simple words!} The Hebrew text for this verse may simply be childish sounds that have no meaning, or **p** a childish mimicking of the prophet's words. Also in 28:13.

PERIDA (1)

Ne 7:57 {Sotai, Sophereth, Peruda,} As in parallel text at Ezra 2:55; Hebrew reads ***P**.*

PERSIA (5)

Ezr 5:13 {Cyrus of Babylon,} King Cyrus of **P** is here identified as the king of Babylon because **P** had conquered the Babylonian Empire.
6:22 {king of Assyria} King Cyrus of **P** is here identified as the king of Assyria because **P** had conquered the Babylonian Empire, which included the earlier Assyrian Empire.
Da 10:13 {kingdom of Persia.} As in one Greek version; Hebrew reads *and I was left there with the kings of **P**.* The meaning of the Hebrew is uncertain.

PERSIAN (9)

1Ch 29: 7 {10,000 gold coins,} Hebrew *10,000 darics* [a **P** coin] *of gold,* about 185 pounds or 84 kilograms in weight.

Ezr 3: 1 {in early autumn,} Hebrew *in the seventh month.* A number of events in the book of Ezra can be cross-checked with dates in surviving **P** records and related accurately to our modern calendar. This month of the Hebrew lunar calendar occurred in October and November 537 B.C.

Ne 1: 1 {King Artaxerxes' reign,} Hebrew *In the month of Kislev of the twentieth year.* A number of events in the book of Nehemiah can be cross-checked with dates in surviving **P** records and related accurately to our modern calendar. This month of the Hebrew lunar calendar occurred in November and December 446 B.C. The *twentieth year* probably refers to the reign of King Artaxerxes I; compare 2:1; 5:14.

12:22 {Darius II of Persia,} Hebrew *Darius the P.*

Est 2:16 {in early winter} Hebrew *in the tenth month, the month of Tebeth.* A number of events in the book of Esther can be cross-checked with dates in surviving **P** records and related accurately to our modern calendar. This month of the Hebrew lunar calendar occurred in December 479 B.C. and January 478 B.C.

Da 6:28 {Cyrus the Persian.} Or *of Darius, that is, the reign of Cyrus the P.*

10: 4 {On April 23,} Hebrew *On the twenty-fourth day of the first month.* This event in the book of Daniel can be cross-checked with dates in surviving **P** records and can be related accurately to our modern calendar. This day of the Hebrew lunar calendar occurred on April 23, 536 B.C.

Hag 1: 1 {On August 29} Hebrew *On the first day of the sixth month,* of the Hebrew calendar. A number of events in Haggai can be cross-checked with dates in surviving **P** records and related accurately to our modern calendar. This event occurred on August 29, 520 B.C.

Zec 1: 1 {In midautumn} Hebrew *In the eighth month.* A number of events in Zechariah can be cross-checked with dates in surviving **P** records and related accurately to our modern calendar. This month of the Hebrew lunar calendar occurred in October and November 520 B.C.

PERSIANS (1)

Da 5:30 {king, was killed.} The **P** and Medes conquered Babylon in October 539 B.C.

PERSISTENCE (1)

Lk 11: 8 {won't be damaged.} Greek *in order to avoid shame,* or *because of [your] p.*

PERSON (10)

Ex 38:26 {ounce of silver} Hebrew *1 beka* [6 grams] *per p, that is, half a shekel, according to the sanctuary shekel.*

1Ki 7:13 {man named Huram} Hebrew *Hiram* (also in 7:40, 45); compare 2 Chr 2:13. This is not the same **p** mentioned in 5:1.

Job 9: 3 {God to court,} Or *If God wanted to take a p to court.*

SS 1: 1 {*Young Woman:*} The headings identifying the speakers are not in the original text, though the Hebrew usually gives clues by means of the gender of the **p** speaking.

Isa 49:24 {that a tyrant} As in Dead Sea Scrolls, Syriac version, and Latin Vulgate (also see 49:25); Masoretic Text reads *a righteous p.*

Mt 1: 7 {father of Asaph.} *Asaph* is the same **p** as Asa; also in 1:8. See 1 Chr 3:10.

1:10 {father of Amos.} *Amos* is the same **p** as Amon. See 1 Chr 3:14.

15:11 {say and do.} Or *what comes out of the mouth defiles a p.*

Lk 3:33 {son of Arni.} *Arni* is the same **p** as Ram; see 1 Chr 2:9-10.

Jn 5: 3 {on the porches.} Some manuscripts add *waiting for a certain movement of the water, [4]for an angel of the Lord came from time to time and stirred up the water. And the first p to step down into it afterward was healed.*

PERVERSE (1)

1Sa 20:30 {of a whore!"} Hebrew *You son of a p and rebellious woman.*

PETER (4)

Mt 16:18 {you are Peter,} ***P*** means "stone" or "rock."

Mk 1:16 {he saw Simon} *Simon* is called ***P*** in 3:16 and thereafter.

Lk 5: 3 {Jesus asked Simon,} *Simon* is called ***P*** in 6:14 and thereafter.

Jn 1:42 {(which means Peter} The names *Cephas* and ***P*** both mean "rock."

PETHOR (1)

Nu 22: 5 {land of Pethor} Or *who was at P in the land of the Amavites.*

PHARAOH (2)

Ex 5:21 {situation with Pharaoh} Hebrew *for making us a stench in the nostrils of P.*

Jer 37: 5 {of Pharaoh Hophra} Hebrew *army of P;* see 44:30.

PHARAOH'S (1)

SS 1: 9 {my beloved one!} Hebrew *I compare you, my beloved, to a mare among P chariots.*

PHARISEES (2)

Mt 23:13 {go in yourselves.} Some manuscripts add verse 14, *How terrible it will be for you teachers of religious law and you P. Hypocrites! You shamelessly cheat widows out of their property, and then, to cover up the kind of people you really are, you make long prayers in public. Because of this, your punishment will be the greater.*

Mk 2:16 {who were Pharisees} Greek *the scribes of the P.*

PHILIP (1)

Ac 8:36 {I be baptized?"} Some manuscripts add verse 37, *"You can," P answered, "if you believe with all your heart." And the eunuch replied, "I believe that Jesus Christ is the Son of God."*

PHILISTINES (3)

Ge 10:14 {the Philistines came.} Hebrew *Casluhites, from whom the P came, Caphtorites.* Compare Jer 47:4; Amos 9:7.

Ex 23:31 {the Mediterranean Sea,} Hebrew *from the sea of reeds to the sea of the P.*

1Ch 1:12 {the Philistines came.} Hebrew *Casluhites, from whom the P came, Caphtorites.* See Jer 47:4; Amos 9:7.

PHRASE (5)

Ezr 8:13 {who came later} The meaning of the Hebrew for this **p** is uncertain.

Ps 9:16 {Quiet Interlude} Hebrew *Higgaion Selah.* The meaning of this **p** is uncertain.

Eze 32:27 {covering their bodies,} The meaning of the Hebrew **p** here is uncertain.

Mt 24:36 {the Son himself.} Some manuscripts omit the **p** *or the Son himself.*

1Co 14:33 {the other churches.} The **p** *as in all the other churches* could be joined to the beginning of 14:34.

PHRYGIA (1)

Ac 16: 6[-7] {province of Bithynia,} ***P****, Galatia, Asia, Mysia,* and *Bithynia* were all districts in the land now called Turkey.

PHYLACTERIES (1)

Mt 23: 5 {Scripture verses inside,} Greek *They enlarge their p.*

PI-BESETH (1)

Eze 30:17 {Heliopolis and Bubastis} Hebrew *of Awen and P.*

PIECES (2)

Ps 68:30 {tribute from us.} Or *Humble them until they submit, bringing p of silver as tribute.*

Ac 19:19 {several million dollars.} Greek *50,000 p of silver,* each of which was the equivalent of a day's wage.

PIERCED (1)

Mt 27:49 {and save him."} Some manuscripts add *And another took a spear and p his side, and out came water and blood.*

PILE (2)

Ge 31:47 {language and Galeed} *Jegar-sahadutha* means "witness **p**" in Aramaic; *Galeed* means "witness **p**" in Hebrew.

PILLARS (1)

Eze 43: 7 {their dead kings.} Or *by raising p on their high places.*

PIM (1)

1Sa 13:21 {ounce of silver} Hebrew *1 p* [8 grams].

PINTS (1)

Eze 4:11 {out a jar} Hebrew *1/6 of a hin,* about 1.3 **p** or 0.6 liters.

PIPES (1)

Da 3:10 {the musical instruments.} Aramaic *the horn, flute, zither, lyre, harp, p, and other instruments of the musical ensemble;* also in 3:15.

PISIDIA (1)

Ac 13:13[-14] {Antioch of Pisidia.} *Pamphylia* and ***P*** were districts in the land now called Turkey.

PLACE (5)

Ex 25:16 {of the covenant,} Hebrew *p inside it the Testimony;* also in 25:21.

Dt 9:22 {Taberah,} *Taberah* means "**p** of burning." See Num 11:1-3.

9:22 {Massah,} *Massah* means "**p** of testing." See Exod 17:1-7.

Eze 3:12 {in his place!)} A likely reading for this verse is *Then the Spirit lifted me up, and as the glory of the LORD rose from its p, I heard behind me a loud rumbling sound.*

1Co 14:35 {in church meetings.} Some manuscripts **p** verses 34-35 after 14:40.

PLACED (2)

Jas 4: 5 {to be faithful} Or *the spirit that God p within us tends to envy,* or *the Holy Spirit, whom God has p within us, opposes our envy.*

PLACES (1)

Eze 43: 7 {their dead kings.} Or *by raising pillars on their high p.*

PLAGUE (1)

Dt 7:20 {will send hornets} Or *will spread panic,* or *will send a p.* The meaning of the Hebrew is uncertain.

PLAIN (1)

Jer 47: 5 {the Mediterranean plain,} Hebrew *the p.*

PLANS (1)

1Ch 28:12 {had in mind} Or *the p of the spirit that was with him.*

PLANTS (1)

Hos 1:11 {day of Jezreel} *Jezreel* means "God **p**."

PLATTER (1)

Nu 7:13 {about 1 3/4 pounds.} Hebrew *silver p weighing 130 shekels* [1.5 kilograms] *and a silver basin weighing 70 shekels* [0.8 kilograms], *according to the sanctuary shekel;* also in 7:19, 25, 31, 37, 43, 49, 55, 61, 67, 73, 79, 85.

PLAY (1)

Ge 30: 6 {named him Dan,} *Dan* is a **p** on the Hebrew term meaning "to vindicate" or "to judge."

PLEASANT (2)

Ru 1:20 {call me Mara,} *Naomi* means "**p**"; *Mara* means "bitter."

Mic 1:11 {people of Shaphir,} *Shaphir* means "**p**."

PLEASE (1)

Lk 15:21 {called your son.} Some manuscripts add ***P*** *take me on as a hired man.*

PLEASING (1)

Lk 2:14 {whom God favors.} Or *and peace on earth for all those p God;* some manuscripts read *and peace on earth, goodwill among people.*

PLEASURE (1)

Hab 2: 4 {lives are crooked;} Greek version reads *I will have no p in anyone who turns away.*

PLEDGE (1)

1Sa 17:18 {letter from them.} Hebrew *and take their p.*

PLOWED (2)

1Sa 14:14 {half an acre.} Hebrew *half a yoke;* a "yoke" was the amount of land **p** by a pair of yoked oxen in one day.

Isa 5:10 {Ten acres} Hebrew *A ten yoke,* that is, the area of land **p** by ten teams of oxen in one day.

PLOWSHARES (1)

1Sa 13:20 {axes, or sickles,} As in Greek version; Hebrew reads *or p.*

PLUNDER (2)

Isa 8: 1 {on it: Maher-shalal-hash-baz.} *Maher-shalal-hash-baz* means "Swift to **p** and quick to spoil."

8:18 {me have names} *Isaiah* means "The LORD will save"; *Shear-jashub* means "A remnant will return"; and *Maher-shalal-hash-baz* means "Swift to **p** and quick to spoil."

PLURAL (1)

Jn 3: 7 {statement that you} The Greek word for *you* is **p**; also in 3:12.

PLUS (1)

Da 9:25 {sets of seven} Hebrew *Seven sevens p 62 sevens.*

POINTS (2)
2Sa 15:28 {the Jordan River} Hebrew *at the crossing* **p** *of the wilderness.*
17:16 {the Jordan River} Hebrew *at the crossing* **p** *of the wilderness.*

POLE (6)
Est 2:23 {on a gallows.} Or *on a* **p**.
5:14 {up a gallows} Or *a* **p**.
6:4 {from the gallows} Or *from the* **p**.
7:9 {up a gallows} Or *a* **p**; also in 7:10.
8:7 {on the gallows} Or *on the* **p**.
9:13 {from the gallows.} Or *the* **p**; also in 9:14, 25.

POLLUX (1)
Ac 28:11 {the twin gods} The *twin gods* were the Roman gods Castor and **P**.

POOL (2)
Ne 3:15 {pool of Siloam} Hebrew **p** *of Shelah,* another name for the **p** of Siloam.

POOR (1)
Mt 5:3 {need for him,} Greek *the* **p** *in spirit.*

PORTION (6)
1Sa 1:5 {special portion} Or *a double* **p**. The meaning of the Hebrew is uncertain.
2Sa 6:19 {cake of dates,} Or *a* **p** *of meat.* The meaning of the Hebrew is uncertain.
1Ch 16:3 {cake of dates,} Or *a* **p** *of meat.* The meaning of the Hebrew is uncertain.
Jer 10:16 {God of Israel} Hebrew *the* **P** *of Jacob.*
51:19 {God of Israel} Hebrew *the* **P** *of Jacob.*
Eze 45:14 {your olive oil,} Hebrew *the* **p** *of oil, measured by the bath, is 1/10 of a bath from each cor, which consists of 10 baths or 1 homer, for 10 baths are equivalent to a homer.*

PORTIONS (1)
Lk 11:2[-4] {yield to temptation.} Some manuscripts add additional **p** of the Lord's Prayer as it reads in Matt 6:9-13.

POSSESS (1)
1Th 4:4 {control your body} Or *will know how to take a wife for himself;* Greek reads *will know how to* **p** *his own vessel.*

POSSESSION (1)
Eze 45:5 {for their towns.} As in Greek version; Hebrew reads *They will have as their* **p** *20 rooms.*

POSSIBLY (12)
2Sa 8:1 {their largest city.} Hebrew *by conquering Metheg-ammah,* a name which means "the bridle," **p** referring to the size of the city or the tribute money taken from it. Compare 1 Chr 18:1.
1Ki 10:28 {imported from Egypt} **P** *Muzur,* a district near Cilicia; also in 10:29.
2Ki 7:6 {Hittites and Egyptians} **P** *and the people of Muzur,* a district near Cilicia.
1Ch 7:35 {his brother Helem} **P** another name for *Hotham;* compare 7:32.
7:37 {Shamma, Shilshah, Ithran,} **P** another name for *Jether;* compare 7:38.
8:3 {Addar, Gera, Abihud,} **P** *Gera the father of Ehud;* compare 8:6.
2Ch 1:16 {imported from Egypt} **P** *Muzur,* a district near Cilicia; also in 1:17.
9:28 {imported from Egypt} **P** *Muzur,* a district near Cilicia.
Jer 51:20 {"You} **P** Cyrus, who was used of God to conquer Babylon. Compare Isa 44:28; 45:1.
Am 1:15 {And their king} Hebrew *malcam,* **p** referring to their god Molech.
4:3 {from your fortresses.} Hebrew *thrown out toward Harmon,* **p** a reference to Mount Hermon.
Zep 1:5 {they worship Molech,} Hebrew *Malcam,* another name for Molech; or it could **p** mean *their king.*

POT (1)
Eze 11:3 {from all harm.} Hebrew *This city is the* **p**, *and we are the meat.*

POUR (2)
2Ki 3:11 {Elijah's personal assistant.} Hebrew *He used to* **p** *water on the hands of Elijah.*
Lk 22:19[-20] {out for you.} Some manuscripts omit 22:19b-20, *given for you... I will* **p** *out for you.*

POURED (1)
Job 10:10 {in the womb.} Hebrew *You* **p** *me out like milk and curdled me like cheese.*

POWER (4)
Hab 3:4 {his awesome power.} Or *He veils his awesome* **p**.
Mt 6:13 {the evil one.} Or *from evil.* Some manuscripts add *For yours is the kingdom and the* **p** *and the glory forever. Amen.*
1Co 15:24 {of every kind.} Greek *every ruler and every authority and* **p**.
Php 2:7 {made himself nothing;} Or *He laid aside his mighty* **p** *and glory.*

PRAETORIUM (1)
Mk 15:16 {into their headquarters} Greek *the courtyard, which is the* **p**.

PRAISE (4)
Ge 29:35 {named him Judah,} *Judah* sounds like the Hebrew term for "**p**."
Mt 21:9 {"Praise God} Greek *Hosanna,* an exclamation of **p** that literally means "save now"; also in 21:9b, 15.
Mk 11:9 {"Praise God!} Greek *Hosanna,* an exclamation of **p** that literally means "save now"; also in 11:10.
Jn 12:13 {"Praise God!} Greek *Hosanna,* an exclamation of **p** that literally means "save now."

PRAISED (2)
Lk 7:29 {plan was right,} Or **p** *God.*
Ro 9:5 {eternal praise! Amen.} Or *May God, who rules over everything, be* **p** *forever. Amen.*

PRAY (2)
Mk 13:33 {and keep watch.} Some manuscripts add *and* **p**.
Jude 1:20 {the Holy Spirit.} Greek **P** *in the Holy Spirit.*

PRAYED (1)
Mt 17:20 {would be impossible."} Some manuscripts add verse 21, *But this kind of demon won't leave unless you have* **p** *and fasted.*

PRAYER (3)
1Sa 2:20 {to the LORD.} As in Greek version; Hebrew reads *this one she requested of the LORD in* **p**.
Hab 3:1 {the prophet Habakkuk:} Hebrew adds *according to shigionoth,* probably indicating the musical setting for the **p**.
Lk 11:2[-4] {yield to temptation.} Some manuscripts add additional portions of the Lord's **P** as it reads in Matt 6:9-13.

PRAYERS (1)
Mt 23:13 {go in yourselves.} Some manuscripts add verse 14, *How terrible it will be for you teachers of religious law and you Pharisees. Hypocrites! You shamelessly cheat widows out of their property, and then, to cover up the kind of people you really are, you make long* **p** *in public. Because of this, your punishment will be the greater.*

PREACH (1)
Eph 6:15 {be fully prepared.} Or *For shoes, put on the readiness to* **p** *the Good News of peace with God.*

PREACHING (2)
Mk 1:4 {to be forgiven.} Greek **p** *a baptism of repentance for the forgiveness of sins.*
Lk 3:3 {to be forgiven.} Greek **p** *a baptism of repentance for the forgiveness of sins.*

PRECIOUS (1)
Ps 139:17 {thoughts about me,} Or *How* **p** *to me are your thoughts.*

PRECISE (2)
Joel 1:4 {the stripping locusts,} The **p** identification of the four kinds of locusts mentioned here is uncertain.
2:25 {the hopping locusts.} The **p** identification of the four kinds of locusts mentioned here is uncertain.

PREFECTS (1)
Da 3:3 {all these officials} Aramaic *the princes,* **p**, *governors, advisers, counselors, judges, magistrates, and all the provincial officials.*

PREPARATION (3)
Mt 27:62 {the Passover ceremonies} Or *On the next day, which is after the* **P**.
Mk 15:42 {day of preparation,} Greek *on the day of* **p**.
Lk 23:54 {day of preparation} Greek *on the day of* **p**.

PREPARED (1)
Zep 1:7 {chosen their executioners.} Hebrew *has* **p** *a sacrifice and sanctified his guests.*

PRESENCE (1)
Lev 16:1 {LORD had commanded.} Hebrew *when they approached the LORD's* **p**; compare 10:1.

PRESERVE (1)
Mal 2:15 {you are his.} Or *Did not one God make us and* **p** *our life and breath?* or *Did not one God make her, both flesh and spirit?* The meaning of the Hebrew is uncertain.

PRESSING (1)
Mt 11:12 {people attack it.} Or *until now, eager multitudes have been* **p** *into the Kingdom of Heaven.*

PRESSURES (1)
1Co 7:26 {the present crisis,} Or **p** *of life.*

PRESUMABLY (1)
Eze 32:17 {On March 17,} Hebrew *On the fifteenth day of the month,* **p** in the twelfth month of the Hebrew calendar (see 32:1). This would put this message at the end of King Jehoiachin's twelfth year of captivity, on March 17, 585 B.C.; also see note on 29:1. Greek version reads *On the fifteenth day of the first month,* which would put this message on April 27, 586 B.C., at the beginning of Jehoiachin's twelfth year.

PREVENT (1)
Ro 1:18 {away from themselves.} Or *who* **p** *the truth from being known.*

PREY (1)
Ps 76:4 {the everlasting mountains.} As in Greek version; Hebrew reads *than mountains filled with beasts of* **p**.

PRICE (1)
Da 11:39 {as their reward.} Or *at a* **p**.

PRIDE (2)
Pr 14:3 {for their backs,} Hebrew *a rod of* **p**.
Am 8:7 {Pride of Israel} Hebrew *the* **p** *of Jacob.*

PRIEST (1)
Zec 6:13 {from his throne,} Or *There will be a* **p** *by his throne.*

PRIESTS (2)
2Sa 8:18 {as priestly leaders.} Hebrew *David's sons were* **p**; compare parallel text at 1 Chr 18:17.
Hos 4:4 {is with you!} Hebrew *Your people are like those with a complaint against the* **p**.

PRINCE (7)
1Ch 5:2 {for the nation,} Or *and from Judah came a* **p**.
Ezr 1:8 {returning to Judah.} Hebrew *Sheshbazzar, the* **p** *of Judah.*
Eze 12:10 {Zedekiah in Jerusalem} Hebrew *the* **p** *in Jerusalem;* also in 12:12.
Da 10:13 {the spirit prince} Hebrew *the* **p**; also in 10:13c, 20.
10:21 {your spirit prince.} Hebrew *against these except Michael, your* **p**.
12:1 {Michael, the archangel} Hebrew *the great* **p**.
Jn 12:31 {of this world} *The* **p** *of this world* is a name for Satan.

PRINCES (2)
Da 3:3 {all these officials} Aramaic *the* **p**, *prefects, governors, advisers, counselors, judges, magistrates, and all the provincial officials.*
10:13 {of the archangels,} Hebrew *the chief* **p**.

PRINCESS (1)
Ge 17:15 {call her Sarah.} *Sarah* means "**p**."

PRINCIPLES (1)
Col 2:8 {of this world,} Or *from the basic* **p** *of this world;* also in 2:20.

PRISONER (1)
Lk 23:16 {will release him."} Some manuscripts add verse 17, *For it was necessary for him to release one* **[p]** *for them during the feast.*

PROBABLE (1)
Eze 26:1 {King Jehoiachin's captivity,} Hebrew *In the eleventh year, on the first day of the month,* of the Hebrew calendar year. Since an element is missing in the date formula here, scholars have reconstructed this **p** reading: *On the first day of the eleventh month, during the twelfth year.* This reading would put this message on February 3, 585 B.C.; also see note on 1:1.

PROBABLY (25)
Ge 4:25 {named him Seth,} *Seth* **p** means "granted"; the name may also mean "appointed."
29:33 {named him Simeon,} *Simeon* **p** means "one who hears."
30:20 {named him Zebulun,} *Zebulun* **p** means "honor."
41:45 {renamed him Zaphenath-paneah} *Zaphenath-paneah* **p** means "God speaks and lives."
46:27 {had two sons} Greek version reads *nine sons,* **p** including Joseph's grandsons through Ephraim and Manasseh (see 1 Chr 7:14-20).

1Ki 7:21 {the north Boaz.} Jakin **p** means "he establishes"; Boaz **p** means "in him is strength."
8:66 {festival was over,} Hebrew *On the eighth day,* **p** referring to the day following the seven-day Festival of Shelters; compare parallel text at 2 Chr 7:9-10.
10:28 {and from Cilicia} Hebrew *Kue,* **p** another name for Cilicia.
1Ch 15:20 {play the lyres.} Hebrew adds *according to Alamoth,* which is **p** a musical term. The meaning of the Hebrew is uncertain.
15:21 {play the harps.} Hebrew adds *according to the Sheminith,* which is **p** a musical term. The meaning of the Hebrew is uncertain.
22: 9 {will be Solomon,} *Solomon* sounds like and is **p** derived from the Hebrew word for "peace."
2Ch 1:16 {and from Cilicia} Hebrew *Kue,* **p** another name for Cilicia.
3:17 {the north Boaz.} Jakin **p** means "he establishes"; Boaz **p** means "in him is strength."
Ezr 3: 9 {descendants of Hodaviah.} Hebrew *sons of Judah* (i.e., *bene Yehudah*). *Bene* might also be read here as the proper name Binnui; *Yehudah* is **p** another name for Hodaviah. Compare 2:40; Neh 7:43; 1 Esdras 5:58.
Ne 1: 1 {King Artaxerxes' reign,} Hebrew *In the month of Kislev of the twentieth year.* A number of events in the book of Nehemiah can be cross-checked with dates in surviving Persian records and related accurately to our modern calendar. This month of the Hebrew lunar calendar occurred in November and December 446 B.C. The *twentieth year* **p** refers to the reign of King Artaxerxes I; compare 2:1; 5:14.
12:24 {Sherebiah, Jeshua, Binnui,} Hebrew *son of* (i.e., *ben*), which should **p** be read here as the proper name Binnui; compare Ezra 3:9 and the note there.
Ps 3: 2 {Interlude} Hebrew *Selah.* The meaning of this word is uncertain, though it is **p** a musical or literary term. It is rendered *Interlude* throughout the Psalms.
Hab 3: 1 {the prophet Habakkuk:} Hebrew adds *according to shigionoth,* **p** indicating the musical setting for the prayer.
3: 3 {and Mount Paran.} Hebrew adds *selah;* also in 3:9, 13. The meaning of this Hebrew term is uncertain; it is **p** a musical or literary term.
Jn 13:23 {at the table.} Greek *was reclining on Jesus' bosom.* The "disciple whom Jesus loved" was **p** John.
1Pe 5:13 {here in Rome} Greek *The elect one in Babylon.* Babylon was **p** a code name for Rome.
2Pe 2:10 {the glorious ones} *The glorious ones* are **p** evil angels; also in 2:11.
Jude 1: 8 {the glorious ones.} *The glorious ones* are **p** evil angels.

PROCLAIM (2)
Isa 61: 2 {favor has come,} Or *to* **p** *the acceptable year of the LORD.*
Lk 4:18[-19] {favor has come.} Or *and to* **p** *the acceptable year of the Lord.* Isa 61:1-2.

PROMISCUOUS (1)
Hos 1: 2 {marry a prostitute,} Or *a* **p** *woman.*

PROMISE (1)
Heb 11:11 {keep his promise.} Some manuscripts read *It was by faith that Sarah was able to have a child, even though she was too old and barren. Sarah believed that God would keep his* **p**.

PROMISED (2)
2Ki 8:19 {to rule forever.} Hebrew **p** *to give a lamp to David and his descendants forever.*
2Ch 21: 7 {to rule forever.} Hebrew **p** *to give a lamp to David and his descendants forever.*

PROPER (4)
Lev 6: 6 {value in silver.} Or *and the animal must be of the* **p** *value;* Hebrew lacks *in silver;* compare 5:15.
1Ki 1: 9 {stone of Zoheleth} Or *to the Serpent's Stone;* Greek version supports reading *Zoheleth* as a **p** name.
Ezr 3: 9 {descendants of Hodaviah.} Hebrew *sons of Judah* (i.e., *bene Yehudah*). *Bene* might also be read here as the **p** name Binnui; *Yehudah* is probably another name for Hodaviah. Compare 2:40; Neh 7:43; 1 Esdras 5:58.
Ne 12:24 {Sherebiah, Jeshua, Binnui,} Hebrew *son of* (i.e., *ben*), which should probably be read here as the **p** name Binnui; compare Ezra 3:9 and the note there.

PROPERTY (1)
Mt 23:13 {go in yourselves.} Some manuscripts add verse 14, *How terrible it will be for you teachers of religious law and you Pharisees. Hypocrites! You shamelessly cheat widows out of their* **p**, *and then, to cover up the kind of people you really are, you make long prayers in public. Because of this, your punishment will be the greater.*

PROPHECY (1)
Isa 33: 1 {for you Assyrians,} Hebrew *for you, O destroyer…O betrayer.* The Hebrew text does not specifically name Assyria as the object of this **p**.

PROPHET (4)
2Ch 15: 8 {Azariah the prophet,} As in Syriac version and Latin Vulgate (see also 15:1); Hebrew reads *from Oded the* **p**.
Mt 10:41 {speaks for God,} Greek *welcome a* **p** *in the name of a* **p**.
27:35 {by throwing dice.} Greek *by casting lots.* A few late manuscripts add *This fulfilled the word of the* **p**: *"They divided my clothes among themselves and cast lots for my robe."* See Ps 22:18.

PROPHET'S (1)
Isa 28:10 {very simple words!} The Hebrew text for this verse may simply be childish sounds that have no meaning, or perhaps a childish mimicking of the **p** words. Also in 28:13.

PROPHETIC (1)
Ro 16:26 {as the prophets} Greek *the* **p** *writings.*

PROPHETS (1)
Eze 22:25 {Your princes} As in Greek version; Hebrew reads **p**.

PROSTITUTE (1)
Ge 38:21 {find the prostitute} Hebrew *shrine* **p**; also in 38:21b, 22.

PROTECT (1)
2Ch 26:15 {and hurl stones} Or *designed by brilliant men to* **p** *those who shot arrows and stones.*

PROV (6)
Ro 12:20 {done to you."} Greek *and you will heap burning coals on their heads.* **P** 25:21-22.
Heb 12: 5[-6] {as his children."} **P** 3:11-12.
Jas 4: 6 {to the humble."} **P** 3:34.
1Pe 4:18 {and sinners have?"} **P** 11:31.
5: 5 {to the humble."} **P** 3:34.
2Pe 2:22 {to its vomit,"} **P** 26:11.

PROVINCE (1)
1Co 16:19 {province of Asia} *Asia* was a Roman **p** in what is now western Turkey.

PROVINCIAL (1)
Da 3: 3 {all these officials} Aramaic *the princes, prefects, governors, advisers, counselors, judges, magistrates, and all the* **p** *officials.*

PS (73)
2Sa 22:11 {soaring} As in some Hebrew manuscripts (see also **P** 18:10); other Hebrew manuscripts read *appearing.*
1Ch 16:15 {by his covenant} As in some Greek manuscripts (see also **P** 105:8); Hebrew reads *Remember his covenant forever.*
Mt 4: 6 {on a stone.'} **P** 91:11-12.
13:35 {of the world."} **P** 78:2.
21:16 {give you praise.'} **P** 8:2.
21:42 {marvelous to see.'} **P** 118:22-23.
22:44 {beneath your feet.'} **P** 110:1.
23:39 {of the Lord!'} **P** 118:26.
26:64 {clouds of heaven."} See **P** 110:1; Dan 7:13.
27:35 {by throwing dice.} Greek *by casting lots.* A few late manuscripts add *This fulfilled the word of the prophet: "They divided my clothes among themselves and cast lots for my robe."* See **P** 22:18.
27:46 {you forsaken me?"} **P** 22:1.
Mk 12:10[-11] {marvelous to see.'} **P** 118:22-23.
12:36 {beneath your feet.'} **P** 110:1.
14:62 {clouds of heaven."} See **P** 110:1; Dan 7:13.
15:24 {clothes, throwing dice} Greek *casting lots.* See **P** 22:18.
15:34 {you forsaken me?"} **P** 22:1.
Lk 4:10[-11] {on a stone.'} **P** 91:11-12.
13:35 {of the Lord!'} **P** 118:26.
20:17 {become the cornerstone.'} **P** 118:22.
20:42[-43] {under your feet.'} **P** 110:1.
22:69 {place of power."} See **P** 110:1.
23:34 {by throwing dice.} Greek *by casting lots.* See **P** 22:18.
23:46 {into your hands!"} **P** 31:5.
Jn 2:17 {burns within me."} Or *"Concern for God's house will be my undoing."* **P** 69:9.
6:31 {heaven to eat.'} Exod 16:4; **P** 78:24.
10:34 {you are gods!'} **P** 82:6.
12:13 {King of Israel!"} **P** 118:25-26; Zeph 3:15.
13:18 {turned against me,'} **P** 41:9.
19:24 {for my robe."} **P** 22:18.
19:36 {will be broken,"} Exod 12:46; Num 9:12; **P** 34:20.
Ac 2:25[-28] {in your presence.'} **P** 16:8-11.
2:34[-35] {under your feet.'} **P** 110:1.
4:11 {become the cornerstone.'} **P** 118:22.
4:25[-26] {against his Messiah.'} **P** 2:1-2.
13:33 {become your Father.} Or *Today I reveal you as my Son.* **P** 2:7.
13:35 {in the grave.'} **P** 16:10.
Ro 3: 4 {case in court."} **P** 51:4.
3:14 {cursing and bitterness."} **P** 10:7.
3:18 {to restrain them."} **P** 36:1.
4: 7[-8] {by the Lord."} **P** 32:1-2.
8:36 {slaughtered like sheep."} **P** 44:22.
10:18 {all the world."} **P** 19:4.
11: 9[-10] {weaker and weaker."} **P** 69:22-23.
15: 3 {also insulting me."} **P** 69:9.
15: 9 {to your name."} **P** 18:49.
15:11 {of the earth."} **P** 117:1.
1Co 3:20 {they are worthless."} **P** 94:11.
10:26 {everything in it."} **P** 24:1.
15:27 {over all things."} **P** 8:6.
2Co 4:13 {so I speak."} **P** 116:10.
9: 9 {never be forgotten."} **P** 112:9.
Eph 4: 8 {to his people."} **P** 68:18.
4:26 {control over you."} **P** 4:4.
Heb 1: 5 {become your Father.} Or *Today I reveal you as my Son.* **P** 2:7.
1: 7 {of flaming fire."} **P** 104:4.
1: 8[-9] {on anyone else."} **P** 45:6-7.
1:10[-12] {never grow old."} **P** 102:25-27.
1:13 {under your feet."} **P** 110:1.
2: 6[-8] {over all things."} **P** 8:4-6.
2:12 {brothers and sisters.} Greek *my brothers.* **P** 22:22.
3: 7[-11] {place of rest.' "} **P** 95:7-11.
3:15 {when they rebelled."} **P** 95:7-8.
4: 3 {place of rest,' "} **P** 95:11.
4: 5 {place of rest."} **P** 95:11.
4: 7 {hearts against him."} **P** 95:7-8.
5: 5 {become your Father.} Or *Today I reveal you as my Son.* **P** 2:7.
5: 6 {line of Melchizedek."} **P** 110:4.
7:17 {line of Melchizedek."} **P** 110:4.
7:21 {a priest forever.' "} **P** 110:4.
10: 5[-7] {in the Scriptures.' "} **P** 40:6-8.
13: 6 {do to me?"} **P** 118:6.
1Pe 2: 7 {become the cornerstone."} **P** 118:22.
3:10[-12] {who do evil."} **P** 34:12-16.

PSALM (1)
Ps 119: 1 {people of integrity,} This **p** is a Hebrew acrostic poem; there are 22 stanzas, one for each letter of the Hebrew alphabet. The 8 verses within each stanza begin with the Hebrew letter of its section.

PSALMS (1)
Ps 3: 2 {Interlude} Hebrew *Selah.* The meaning of this word is uncertain, though it is probably a musical or literary term. It is rendered *Interlude* throughout the **P**.

PSS (8)
Mt 21: 9 {in highest heaven!"} **P** 118:25-26; 148:1.
Mk 11: 9[-10] {in highest heaven!"} **P** 118:25-26; 148:1.
Lk 19:38 {in highest heaven!"} **P** 118:26; 148:1.
Jn 15:25 {me without cause.'} **P** 35:19; 69:4.
19:28 {"I am thirsty."} See **P** 22:15; 69:21.
Ac 1:20 {to someone else.'} **P** 69:25; 109:8.
Ro 3:10[-12] {not even one."} **P** 14:1-3; 53:1-3.
3:13 {from their lips."} **P** 5:9; 140:3.

PUBLIC (2)
Pr 5:16 {with just anyone?} Hebrew *Why spill your springs in* **p**, *your streams in the streets?*
Mt 23:13 {go in yourselves.} Some manuscripts add verse 14, *How terrible it will be for you teachers of religious law and you Pharisees. Hypocrites! You shamelessly cheat widows out of their property, and then, to cover up the kind of people you really are, you make long prayers in* **p**. *Because of this, your punishment will be the greater.*

PUL (2)
2Ki 15:19 {Then King Tiglath-pileser} Hebrew ***P***, another name for Tiglath-pileser.
Isa 66:19 {to the Libyans} As in some Greek manuscripts, which read *Put* [Libya]; Hebrew reads ***P***.

PUNISH (1)
Hos 7:12 {their evil ways.} Hebrew *I will* **p** *them because of what was reported against them in the assembly.*

PUNISHMENT (2)
La 4: 6 {The guilt} Or **p**.
Mt 23:13 {go in yourselves.} Some manuscripts add verse 14, *How terrible it will be for you teachers of religious law and you Pharisees. Hypocrites! You shamelessly cheat widows out of their property, and then, to cover up the kind of people you really are, you make long prayers in public. Because of this, your* **p** *will be the greater.*

PUNITE (1)
Nu 26:23 {its ancestor Puah.} As in Samaritan Pentateuch, Greek and Syriac versions, and Latin Vulgate (see also 1 Chr 7:1); Hebrew reads *The* **P** *clan, named after its ancestor Puvah.*

PURE (3)
Ex 30:23 {myrrh, 6 1/4 pounds} Hebrew *500 shekels* [5.7 kilograms] *of* **p** *myrrh, 250 shekels* [2.9 kilograms].
Mk 14: 3 {of expensive perfume.} Greek *an alabaster jar of expensive ointment,* **p** *nard.*
1Pe 1:22 {all your hearts.} Some manuscripts read *with a* **p** *heart.*

PURIFY (1)
Ps 51: 7 {from my sins,} Hebrew **P** *me with the hyssop branch.*

PURPOSED (1)
Ac 19:21 {the Holy Spirit} Or **p** *in his spirit.*

PUT (20)
Ge 24: 3 {"Swear} Hebrew **P** *your hand under my thigh, and I will make you swear.*
24: 9 {solemn oath} Hebrew **p** *his hand under the thigh of Abraham his master and swore an oath.*
Nu 6:27 {as my people,} Hebrew *will* **p** *my name on the people of Israel.*
Isa 66:19 {to the Libyans} As in some Greek manuscripts, which read **P** [Libya]; Hebrew reads *Pul.*
Jer 46: 9 {Libya, and Lydia} Hebrew *Cush, P, and Lud.*
Eze 26: 1 {King Jehoiachin's captivity,} Hebrew *In the eleventh year, on the first day of the month,* of the Hebrew calendar year. Since an element is missing in the date formula here, scholars have reconstructed this probable reading: *On the first day of the eleventh month, during the twelfth year.* This reading would **p** this message on February 3, 585 B.C.; also see note on 1:1.
27:10 {Lydia, and Libya} Hebrew *Paras, Lud, and* **P**.
30: 5 {Ethiopia, Libya,} Hebrew **P***...Kub.* Both **P** and *Kub* are associated with Libya.
32:17 {On March 17,} Hebrew *On the fifteenth day of the month,* presumably in the twelfth month of the Hebrew calendar (see 32:1). This would **p** this message at the end of King Jehoiachin's twelfth year of captivity, on March 17, 585 B.C.; also see note on 29:1. Greek version reads *On the fifteenth day of the first month,* which would **p** this message on April 27, 586 B.C., at the beginning of Jehoiachin's twelfth year.
38: 5 {Ethiopia, and Libya} Hebrew *Paras, Cush, and* **P**.
Ro 8:13 {turn from it} Greek **p** *it to death.*
9:33 {not be disappointed.} Or *will not be* **p** *to shame.* Isa 28:16.
10:11 {not be disappointed.} Or *will not be* **p** *to shame.* Isa 28:16.
Eph 6:15 {be fully prepared.} Or *For shoes,* **p** *on the readiness to preach the Good News of peace with God.*
Heb 2: 7 {glory and honor.} Some manuscripts add *You* **p** *him in charge of everything you made.*
1Pe 2: 6 {never be disappointed.} Or *will never be* **p** *to shame.* Isa 28:16.
2Pe 1:14 {soon to die.} Greek *I must soon* **p** *off this earthly tent.*
Rev 12:18 {Then he stood} Some manuscripts read *Then I stood,* and some translations **p** this entire sentence into 13:1.

PUVAH (2)
Ge 46:13 {were Tola, Puah,} As in Syriac version and Samaritan Pentateuch (see also 1 Chr 7:1); Hebrew reads **P**.
Nu 26:23 {its ancestor Puah.} As in Samaritan Pentateuch, Greek and Syriac versions, and Latin Vulgate (see also 1 Chr 7:1); Hebrew reads *The Punite clan, named after its ancestor* **P**.

Q

QERE (3)
1Ki 9:18 {Baalath, and Tamar} The marginal **Q** reading of the Masoretic Text reads *Tadmor.*
2Ki 16: 6 {and sent Edomites} As in marginal **Q** reading of the Masoretic Text, Greek version, and Latin Vulgate; Hebrew reads *Arameans.*
Ezr 2:46 {Hagab, Shalmai,} As in the marginal **Q** reading of the Masoretic Text (see also Neh 7:48); Hebrew text reads *Shamlai.*

QUAIL (1)
Nu 11:31 {above the ground.} Or *there were* **q** *3 feet* [2 cubits or 90 centimeters] *deep on the ground.*

QUANTITY (1)
Ru 3:15 {out six scoops} Hebrew *six measures,* an unknown **q**.

QUARTER (4)
2Ki 22:14 {newer Mishneh section} Or *the Second* **Q**, a newer section of Jerusalem.
2Ch 34:22 {newer Mishneh section} Or *the Second* **Q**, a newer section of Jerusalem.
Ne 9: 3 {about three hours.} Hebrew *for a* **q** *of a day.*
Zep 1:10 {newer Mishneh section} Or *the Second* **Q**, a newer section of Jerusalem.

QUARTS (1)
Ge 18: 6 {Get three measures} Hebrew *3 seahs,* about 15 **q** or 18 liters.

QUEEN (3)
Mt 12:42 {queen of Sheba} Greek *The* **q** *of the south.*
Lk 11:31 {queen of Sheba} Greek *the* **q** *of the south.*
Ac 8:27 {queen of Ethiopia.} Greek *under the Candace, the* **q** *of Ethiopia.*

QUICK (2)
Isa 8: 1 {on it: Maher-shalal-hash-baz.} *Maher-shalal-hash-baz* means "Swift to plunder and **q** to spoil."
8:18 {me have names} *Isaiah* means "The LORD will save"; *Shear-jashub* means "A remnant will return"; and *Maher-shalal-hash-baz* means "Swift to plunder and **q** to spoil."

QUICKLY (1)
1Co 5: 6[-7] {can stay pure.} Greek *Don't you realize that even a little leaven spreads* **q** *through the whole batch of dough?* [7]*Purge out the old leaven so that you can be a new batch of dough, as you are already unleavened.*

QUOTATION (2)
Gal 2:16 {obeying the law."} Some translators hold that the **q** extends through verse 14; others through verse 16; and still others through verse 21.
Jude 1:14[-15] {spoken against him."} The **q** comes from the Apocrypha: Enoch 1:9.

R

RAAMIAH (1)
Ne 7: 7 {Reelaiah,} As in parallel text at Ezra 2:2; Hebrew reads **R**.

RABBI (1)
Mt 23: 7 {being called 'Rabbi.'} **R**, from Aramaic, means "master" or "teacher."

RABBONI (1)
Jn 20:16 {and exclaimed, "Teacher!"} Greek *and said in Hebrew, "R," which means "Teacher."*

RACA (1)
Mt 5:22 {friend, 'You idiot,'} Literally '**R**,' an Aramaic term of contempt.

RAHAB (8)
Job 9:13 {forces against him} Hebrew *The helpers of* **R**, the name of a mythical sea monster that represents chaos in ancient literature.
26:12 {great sea monster.} Hebrew **R**, the name of a mythical sea monster that represents chaos in ancient literature.
Ps 87: 4 {will record Egypt} Hebrew **R**, the name of a mythical sea monster that represents chaos in ancient literature. The name is used here as a poetic name for Egypt.
89:10 {great sea monster.} Hebrew **R**, the name of a mythical sea monster that represents chaos in ancient literature.
Isa 30: 7 {the Harmless Dragon.} Hebrew **R** *who sits still.* **R** is the name of a mythical sea monster that represents chaos in ancient literature. The name is used here as a poetic name for Egypt.
51: 9 {of the Nile.} Hebrew *slew* **R** *the dragon.* **R** is the name of a mythical sea monster that represents chaos in ancient literature. The name is used here as a poetic name for Egypt.

RAINING (1)
Ps 18:13 {a mighty shout.} As in Greek version (see also 2 Sam 22:14); Hebrew adds **r** *down hail and burning coals.*

RAISED (1)
Mt 27:51[-53] {to many people.} Or *The earth shook, rocks split apart, tombs opened, and many bodies of godly men and women who had died were* **r** *from the dead. After Jesus' resurrection, they left the cemetery, went into the holy city of Jerusalem, and appeared to many people.*

RAISIN (1)
Hos 3: 1 {them choice gifts.} Hebrew **r** *cakes.*

RAISING (1)
Eze 43: 7 {their dead kings.} Or *by* **r** *pillars on their high places.*

RAM (1)
Lk 3:33 {son of Arni.} *Arni* is the same person as **R**; see 1 Chr 2:9-10.

RAMATH-LEHI (1)
Jdg 15:17 {named Jawbone Hill.} Hebrew **R**.

RAMATHAIM-ZOPHIM (1)
1Sa 1: 1 {lived in Ramah} Hebrew **R**; compare 1:19.

RAPHAH (1)
1Ch 8:37 {father of Rephaiah.} As in parallel text at 9:43; Hebrew reads **R**, a variant name for Rephaiah.

RATIFY (1)
Heb 9:16 {is dead.} Or *Now when someone makes a covenant, it is necessary to* **r** *it with the death of a sacrifice.*

RATS (1)
1Sa 5: 6 {plague of tumors.} Greek version and Latin Vulgate read *tumors. And* **r** *appeared in their land, and death and destruction were throughout the city.*

RAVINES (2)
2Sa 23:30 {from Nahale-gaash} Or *from the* **r** *of Gaash.*
1Ch 11:32 {from near Nahale-gaash} Or *from the* **r** *of Gaash.*

REACHED (1)
2Sa 16:14 {the Jordan River.} As in Greek version (see also 17:16); Hebrew reads *when they* **r** *their destination.*

READ (147)
Ge 10: 4 {Kittim, and Rodanim.} As in some Hebrew manuscripts and Greek version (see also 1 Chr 1:7); most Hebrew manuscripts **r** *Dodanim.*
11:32 {for 205 years} Some ancient versions **r** *145 years;* compare 11:26; 12:4.
36:39 {Baal-hanan died, Hadad} As in some Hebrew manuscripts, Samaritan Pentateuch, and Syriac version (see also 1 Chr 1:50); most Hebrew manuscripts **r** *Hadar.*
Ex 1: 5 {Jacob had seventy} Dead Sea Scrolls and Greek version **r** *seventy-five;* see notes on Gen 46:27.
Nu 2:14[-15] {son of Deuel} As in many Hebrew manuscripts, Samaritan Pentateuch, and Latin Vulgate (see also 1:14); most Hebrew manuscripts **r** *son of Reuel.*
3:28 {There were 8,600} Some Greek manuscripts **r** *8,300;* see total in 3:39.
26:39 {its ancestor Shupham.} As in some Hebrew manuscripts, Samaritan Pentateuch, Greek and Syriac versions, and Latin Vulgate; most Hebrew manuscripts **r** *Shephupham.*
Dt 32: 8 {of angelic beings.} As in Dead Sea Scrolls, which **r** *of the sons of God,* and Greek version, which reads *of the angels of god;* Masoretic Text reads *of the sons of Israel.*
34: 6 {He was buried} Hebrew *He buried him,* that is, "The LORD buried him." Samaritan Pentateuch and some Greek manuscripts **r** *They buried him.*
Jos 15:18 {she urged him} Some Greek manuscripts **r** *Othniel urged her.*
19:28 {Abdon,} As in some Hebrew manuscripts (see also 21:30); most Hebrew manuscripts **r** *Ebron.*
Jdg 1:14 {she urged him} Greek version and Latin Vulgate **r** *he urged her.*
Ru 3:15 {Then Boaz} Most Hebrew manuscripts **r** *he;* many Hebrew manuscripts, Syriac version, and Latin Vulgate **r** *she.*
1Sa 2:33 {a violent death.} As in Dead Sea Scrolls, which **r** *die by the sword;* Masoretic Text reads *die like mortals.*
5: 6 {plague of tumors.} Greek version and Latin Vulgate **r** *tumors. And rats appeared in their land, and death and destruction were throughout the city.*
6:19 {killed seventy men} As in a few Hebrew manuscripts; most Hebrew manuscripts and Greek version **r** *50,070 men.* Perhaps the text should be understood to **r** *the LORD killed 70 men and 50 oxen.*
11: 8 {addition to 30,000} Dead Sea Scrolls and Greek version **r** *70,000.*
12:11 {Jephthah, and Samuel} Greek and Syriac versions **r** *Samson.*
15:32 {have been spared!"} Dead Sea Scrolls and Greek version **r** *Agag arrived hesitantly, for he thought, "Surely this is the bitterness of death."*
2Sa 8:12 {Edom,} As in a few Hebrew manuscripts and Greek and Syriac versions (see also 8:14; 1 Chr 18:11); most Hebrew manuscripts **r** *Aram.*
8:13 {eighteen thousand Edomites} As in a few Hebrew manuscripts and Greek and Syriac versions (see also 8:14; 1 Chr 18:12); most Hebrew manuscripts **r** *Arameans.*

10:18 {forty thousand horsemen,} Some Greek manuscripts **r** *foot soldiers;* compare parallel text at 1 Chr 19:18.
21: 8 {Saul's daughter Merab,} As in a few Hebrew and Greek manuscripts and Syriac version (see also 1 Sam 18:19); most Hebrew manuscripts **r** *Michal.*
22:11 {soaring} As in some Hebrew manuscripts (see also Ps 18:10); other Hebrew manuscripts **r** *appearing.*
22:36 {your help} As in Dead Sea Scrolls; most Hebrew manuscripts **r** *your answering.*
23:18 {of the Thirty.} As in a few Hebrew manuscripts and Syriac version; most Hebrew manuscripts **r** *the Three.*
23:29 {Heled} As in some Hebrew manuscripts (see also 1 Chr 11:30); most Hebrew manuscripts **r** *Heleb.*
23:33 {son of Shagee} As in parallel text at 1 Chr 11:34; Hebrew reads *Jonathan, Shammah;* some Greek manuscripts **r** *Jonathan son of Shammah.*
1Ki 15: 6 {Abijam and Jeroboam} As in a few Hebrew manuscripts; most Hebrew manuscripts **r** *between Rehoboam and Jeroboam.*
2Ki 25:17 {was 7 1/2 feet} As in parallel texts at 1 Kgs 7:16, 2 Chr 3:15, and Jer 52:22, all of which **r** *5 cubits* [2.3 meters]; Hebrew reads *3 cubits,* which is 4.5 feet or 1.4 meters.
1Ch 1: 6 {were Ashkenaz, Riphath,} As in some Hebrew manuscripts and Greek version (see also Gen 10:3); most Hebrew manuscripts **r** *Diphath.*
1:22 {Obal,} As in some Hebrew manuscripts and Syriac version (see also Gen 10:28); most Hebrew manuscripts **r** *Ebal.*
1:24 {Shem: Arphaxad, Shelah,} Some Greek manuscripts **r** *Arphaxad, Cainan, Shelah.* See notes on Gen 10:24 and 11:12-13.
1:36 {Zepho,} As in many Hebrew manuscripts and a few Greek manuscripts (see also Gen 36:11); most Hebrew manuscripts **r** *Zephi.*
1:40 {Alvan,} As in many Hebrew manuscripts and a few Greek manuscripts (see also Gen 36:23); most Hebrew manuscripts **r** *Alian.*
1:40 {Shepho,} As in some Hebrew manuscripts (see also Gen 36:23); most Hebrew manuscripts **r** *Shephi.*
1:41 {Dishon were Hemdan,} As in many Hebrew manuscripts and some Greek manuscripts (see also Gen 36:26); most Hebrew manuscripts **r** *Hamran.*
1:42 {Zaavan, and Akan.} As in many Hebrew and Greek manuscripts (see also Gen 36:27); most Hebrew manuscripts **r** *Jaakan.*
1:50 {city of Pau.} As in many Hebrew manuscripts, some Greek manuscripts, Syriac version, and Latin Vulgate (see also Gen 36:39); most Hebrew manuscripts **r** *Pai.*
3: 6 {sons: Ibhar, Elishua,} As in some Hebrew and Greek manuscripts (see also 14:5-7 and 2 Sam 5:15); most Hebrew manuscripts **r** *Elishama.*
7:13 {Jezer, and Shillem.} As in some Hebrew and Greek manuscripts (see also Gen 46:24; Num 26:49); most Hebrew manuscripts **r** *Shallum.*
18:16 {Ahimelech} As in some Hebrew manuscripts, Syriac version, and Latin Vulgate (see also 2 Sam 8:17); most Hebrew manuscripts **r** *Abimelech.*
20: 2 {the king's head,} Greek version and Latin Vulgate **r** *removed the crown of Milcom;* compare 1 Kgs 11:5. Milcom, also called Molech, was the god of the Ammonites.
2Ch 3: 4 {was thirty feet} As in some Greek and Syriac manuscripts, which **r** *20 cubits* [9 meters]; Hebrew reads *120 cubits,* which is 180 feet or 54 meters.
17: 3 {father's early years} Some Hebrew manuscripts **r** *the example of his father, David.*
20: 2 {army from Edom} As in one Hebrew manuscript; most Hebrew manuscripts and ancient versions **r** *Aram.*
20:25 {of equipment, clothing,} As in some Hebrew manuscripts and Latin Vulgate; most Hebrew manuscripts **r** *corpses.*
22: 6 {and King Ahaziah} Some Hebrew manuscripts, Greek and Syriac versions, and Latin Vulgate (see also 2 Kgs 8:29); most Hebrew manuscripts **r** *Azariah.*
25:28 {City of David.} As in some Hebrew manuscripts and other ancient versions (see also 2 Kgs 14:20); most Hebrew manuscripts **r** *the city of Judah.*
36: 9 {Jehoiachin was eighteen} As in one Hebrew manuscript, some Greek manuscripts, and Syriac version (see also 2 Kgs 24:8); most Hebrew manuscripts **r** *eight.*
Ezr 3: 9 {descendants of Hodaviah.} Hebrew *sons of Judah* (i.e., *bene Yehudah*). *Bene* might also be **r** here as the proper name Binnui; *Yehudah* is probably another name for Hodaviah. Compare 2:40; Neh 7:43, 1 Esdras 5:58.
6: 3 {be ninety feet.} Aramaic *Its height will be 60 cubits* [27 meters], *and its width will be 60 cubits.* It is commonly held that this verse should be emended to **r**: "Its height will be 45 feet, its length will be 90 feet, and its width will be 30 feet"; compare 1 Kgs 6:2. The emendation regarding the width is supported by the Syriac version.
Ne 3:18 {Binnui} As in a few Hebrew manuscripts, some Greek manuscripts, and Syriac version (see also 3:24; 10:9); most Hebrew manuscripts **r** *Bavvai.*
12: 4 {Iddo, Ginnethon,} As in some Hebrew manuscripts and Latin Vulgate (see also 12:16); most Hebrew manuscripts **r** *Ginnethoi.*
12:14 {family of Shecaniah.} As in many Hebrew manuscripts, some Greek manuscripts, and Syriac version (see also 12:3); most Hebrew manuscripts **r** *Shebaniah.*
12:24 {Sherebiah, Jeshua, Binnui,} Hebrew *son of* (i.e., *ben*), which should probably be **r** here as the proper name Binnui; compare Ezra 3:9 and the note there.
Ps 119:37 {through your word.} Some manuscripts **r** *in your ways.*
144: 2 {subdues the nations} Some manuscripts **r** *my people.*
145: 5 {I will meditate} Some manuscripts **r** *They will speak.*
Ecc 8:10 {and are praised} As in some Hebrew manuscripts and Greek version; many Hebrew manuscripts **r** *and are forgotten.*
Isa 21:16 {within a year,"} Hebrew *Within a year, like the years of a hired hand.* Some ancient manuscripts **r** *Within three years,* as in 16:14.
49:12 {south as Egypt.} As in Dead Sea Scrolls, which **r** *from the region of Aswan,* which is in southern Egypt. Masoretic Text reads *from the region of Sinim.*
66:19 {to the Libyans} As in some Greek manuscripts, which **r** *Put* [Libya]; Hebrew reads *Pul.*
Jer 27: 1 {reign of Zedekiah} As in some Hebrew manuscripts and Syriac version (see also 27:3, 12); most Hebrew manuscripts **r** *Jehoiakim.*
Eze 6:14 {south to Riblah} As in some Hebrew manuscripts; most Hebrew manuscripts **r** *Diblah.*
16:57 {is scorned—by Edom} Many ancient manuscripts **r** *Aram.*
27:16 {"Aram} Some manuscripts **r** *Edom.*
Da 10:16 {like a man} As in most manuscripts of the Masoretic Text; one manuscript of the Masoretic Text and one Greek version **r** *Then something that looked like a human hand.*
Hab 2: 5 {Wealth} As in Dead Sea Scroll 1QpHab; other Hebrew manuscripts **r** *Wine.*
Mt 8:28 {of the Gadarenes,} Some manuscripts **r** *Gerasenes;* other manuscripts **r** *Gergesenes.* See Mark 5:1; Luke 8:26.
19:16 {this question: "Teacher,} Some manuscripts **r** *Good Teacher.*
26:28 {seals the covenant} Some manuscripts **r** *the new covenant.*
27:16 {man named Barabbas.} Some manuscripts **r** *Jesus Barabbas;* also in 27:17.
Mk 1:41 {Moved with pity,} Some manuscripts **r** *Moved with anger.*
5: 1 {of the Gerasenes.} Some manuscripts **r** *Gadarenes;* others **r** *Gergesenes.* See Matt 8:28; Luke 8:26.
6:14 {Some were saying,} Some manuscripts **r** *He was saying.*
6:22 {also named Herodias,} Some manuscripts **r** *the daughter of Herodias herself.*
11:19 {and the disciples} Greek *they;* some manuscripts **r** *he.*
14:24 {sealing the covenant} Some manuscripts **r** *the new covenant.*
Lk 2:14 {whom God favors.} Or *and peace on earth for all those pleasing God;* some manuscripts **r** *and peace on earth, goodwill among people.*
3:22 {pleased with you.} Some manuscripts **r** *and today I have become your Father.*
4:44 {synagogues throughout Judea.} Some manuscripts **r** *Galilee.*
8:26 {of the Gerasenes,} Some manuscripts **r** *Gadarenes;* other manuscripts **r** *Gergesenes.* See Matt 8:28; Mark 5:1.
9:35 {my Chosen One.} Some manuscripts **r** *This is my beloved Son.*
10: 1 {now chose seventy-two} Some manuscripts **r** *70;* also in 10:17.
14: 5 {If your son} Some manuscripts **r** *donkey.*
Jn 1:18 {is himself God,} Some manuscripts **r** *his one and only Son.*
1:34 {Son of God.} Some manuscripts **r** *the chosen One of God.*
4: 1 {Jesus} Some manuscripts **r** *The Lord.*
5: 2 {pool of Bethesda,} Some manuscripts **r** *Beth-zatha;* other manuscripts **r** *Bethsaida.*
8:39 {his good example.} Some manuscripts **r** *if you are children of Abraham, follow his example.*
8:57 {have seen Abraham?} Some manuscripts **r** *How can you say Abraham has seen you?*
9:35 {Son of Man} Some manuscripts **r** *the Son of God.*
13:32 {God will bring} Some manuscripts **r** *And if God is glorified in him [the Son of Man], God will bring.*
14: 7 {my Father is.} Some manuscripts **r** *If you really have known me, you will know who my Father is.*
20:31 {you may believe} Some manuscripts **r** *may continue to believe.*
Ac 7:46 {God of Jacob.} Some manuscripts **r** *the house of Jacob.*
11:20 {preaching to Gentiles} Greek *the Greeks;* other manuscripts **r** *the Hellenists.*
13:18 {up with them} Other manuscripts **r** *He cared for them;* compare Deut 1:31.
17: 4 {of the city.} Some manuscripts **r** *many of the wives of the leading men.*
18:21 {come back later,} Some manuscripts **r** *"I must by all means be at Jerusalem for the upcoming festival, but I will come back later."*
27:16 {island named Cauda,} Some manuscripts **r** *Clauda.*
Ro 8: 2 {has freed you} Some manuscripts **r** *me.*
8:28 {to work together} Some manuscripts **r** *And we know that everything works together.*
11:31 {But someday they} Some manuscripts **r** *But now they;* other manuscripts **r** *But they.*
16: 7 {Andronicus and Junia,} Or *Junias;* some manuscripts **r** *Julia.*
1Co 2: 1 {you God's message.} Greek *mystery;* other manuscripts **r** *testimony.*
10: 9 {we put Christ} Some manuscripts **r** *the Lord.*
11:24 {which is given} Some manuscripts **r** *broken.*
11:29 {body of Christ,} Greek *the body;* some manuscripts **r** *the Lord's body.*
13: 3 {boast about it;} Some manuscripts **r** *and even gave my body to be burned.*
14:38 {not be recognized.} Some manuscripts **r** *If you are ignorant of this, stay in your ignorance.*
2Co 1:12 {have been honest} Some manuscripts **r** *holy.*
3: 2 {written in our} Some manuscripts **r** *your.*
8: 7 {love for us} Some manuscripts **r** *love from us to you.*
Eph 3:14 {to the Father,} Some manuscripts **r** *the Father of our Lord Jesus Christ.*
Php 3: 3 {in the Spirit} Or *in spirit;* some manuscripts **r** *worship by the Spirit of God.*
3:13 {I should be,} Some manuscripts **r** *I am not all I should be.*
Col 1: 7 {in your place.} Greek *he is ministering on your behalf;* other manuscripts **r** *he is ministering on our behalf.*
3: 4 {who is your} Some manuscripts **r** *our.*
1Th 2: 7 {as a mother} Some manuscripts **r** *we were as infants among you; we were as a mother.*
2Th 2:13 {among the first} Some manuscripts **r** *God chose you from the very beginning.*
1Ti 3:16 {Christ} Greek *Who;* some manuscripts **r** *God.*
4:10 {and suffer much} Some manuscripts **r** *and strive.*
Heb 4: 2 {God told them.} Some manuscripts **r** *they didn't share the faith of those who listened [to God].*
11:11 {keep his promise.} Some manuscripts **r** *It was by faith that Sarah was able to have a child, even though she was too old and barren. Sarah believed that God would keep his promise.*
1Pe 1:22 {all your hearts.} Some manuscripts **r** *with a pure heart.*
2Pe 2: 4 {in gloomy caves} Some manuscripts **r** *chains of gloom.*
2:15 {son of Beor,} Other manuscripts **r** *Bosor.*
3:10 {exposed to judgment.} Some manuscripts **r** *will be burned up.*
1Jn 1: 4 {so that our} Some manuscripts **r** *your.*
2Jn 1: 8 {for which we} Some manuscripts **r** *you.*
Jude 1: 5 {though the Lord} Some manuscripts **r** *Jesus.*
Rev 5:10 {they will reign} Some manuscripts **r** *they are reigning.*
12:18 {Then he stood} Some manuscripts **r** *Then I stood,* and some translations put this entire sentence into 13:1.
13:18 {number is 666.} Some manuscripts **r** *616.*
15: 3 {of the nations.} Some manuscripts **r** *King of the ages;* other manuscripts **r** *King of the saints.*
15: 6 {spotless white linen} Some manuscripts **r** *in bright and sparkling stone.*
21: 3 {be with them.} Some manuscripts **r** *God himself will be with them, their God.*

READINESS (1)

Eph 6:15 {be fully prepared.} Or *For shoes, put on the* **r** *to preach the Good News of peace with God.*

READING (10)

1Ki 1: 9 {stone of Zoheleth} Or *to the Serpent's Stone;* Greek version supports **r** *Zoheleth* as a proper name.
9:18 {Baalath, and Tamar} The marginal *Qere* **r** of the Masoretic Text reads *Tadmor.*
2Ki 16: 6 {and sent Edomites} As in marginal *Qere* **r** of the Masoretic Text, Greek version, and Latin Vulgate; Hebrew reads *Arameans.*
Ezr 2:46 {Hagab, Shalmai,} As in the marginal *Qere* **r** of the Masoretic Text (see also Neh 7:48); Hebrew text reads *Shamlai.*
Pr 20:16 {of a foreigner.} An alternate **r** in the Hebrew text is *the debt of an adulterous woman;* compare 27:13.
Eze 3:12 {in his place!)} A likely **r** for this verse is *Then the Spirit lifted me up, and as the glory of the LORD rose from its place, I heard behind me a loud rumbling sound.*
26: 1 {King Jehoiachin's captivity,} Hebrew *In the eleventh year, on the first day of the month,* of the Hebrew calendar year. Since an element is missing in the date formula here, scholars have reconstructed this probable **r**: *On the first day of the eleventh month, during the twelfth year.* This **r** would put this message on February 3, 585 B.C.; also see note on 1:1.
45: 1 {6 2/3 miles wide.} Reflecting the Greek **r** *25,000 cubits* [13.3 kilometers] *long and 20,000 cubits* [10.6 kilometers] *wide;* Hebrew reads *25,000 cubits long and 10,000 cubits wide.* Compare 45:3, 5; 48:9. In this chapter, the distance measures are calculated using the Hebrew long cubit, which equals 21 inches or 53 centimeters.

48: 9 {6 2/3 miles wide.} Reflecting the Greek **r** in 45:1: *25,000 cubits* [13.3 kilometers] *long and 20,000 cubits* [10.6 kilometers] *wide;* Hebrew reads *25,000 cubits long and 10,000 cubits wide.* Compare 45:1-5; 48:10-13. In this chapter, the distance measures are calculated using the Hebrew long cubit, which equals 21 inches or 53 centimeters.

READS (273)

Ge 1:26 {livestock, wild animals,} As in Syriac version; Hebrew **r** *all the earth.*
10:24 {father of Shelah,} Greek version **r** *Arphaxad was the father of Cainan, Cainan was the father of Shelah.*
11:12[-13] {sons and daughters.} Greek version **r** [12]*When Arphaxad was 135 years old, his son Cainan was born.* [13]*After the birth of Cainan, Arphaxad lived another 430 years and had other sons and daughters, and then he died. When Cainan was 130 years old, his son Shelah was born. After the birth of Shelah, Cainan lived another 330 years and had other sons and daughters, and then he died.*
46:13 {Puah,} As in Syriac version and Samaritan Pentateuch (see also 1 Chr 7:1); Hebrew **r** *Puvah.*
46:13 {Jashub,} As in some Greek manuscripts and Samaritan Pentateuch (see also Num 26:24; 1 Chr 7:1); Hebrew **r** *Iob.*
46:16 {Zephon,} As in Greek version and Samaritan Pentateuch (see also Num 26:15); Hebrew **r** *Ziphion.*
46:27 {had two sons} Greek version **r** *nine sons,* probably including Joseph's grandsons through Ephraim and Manasseh (see 1 Chr 7:14-20).
46:27 {there were seventy} Greek version **r** *seventy-five;* see note on Exod 1:5.
47:21 {servants to Pharaoh.} As in Greek version and Samaritan Pentateuch; Hebrew **r** *He moved the people into the towns throughout the land of Egypt.*
47:31 {on his staff.} As in Greek version; Hebrew **r** *bowed in worship at the head of his bed.*

Ex 4:24 {LORD confronted Moses} Or *confronted Moses' son;* Hebrew **r** *confronted him.*

Nu 26:17 {its ancestor Arodi.} As in Samaritan Pentateuch and Syriac version (see also Gen 46:16); Hebrew **r** *Arod.*
26:23 {its ancestor Puah.} As in Samaritan Pentateuch, Greek and Syriac versions, and Latin Vulgate (see also 1 Chr 7:1); Hebrew **r** *The Punite clan, named after its ancestor Puvah.*
33:45 {They left Iye-abarim} As in 33:44; Hebrew **r** *Iyim,* another name for Iye-abarim.

Dt 4:48 {to Mount Sirion,} As in Syriac version (see also 3:9); Hebrew **r** *Mount Sion.*
31: 1 {had finished saying} As in Dead Sea Scrolls and Greek version; Masoretic Text **r** *Moses went and spoke.*
32: 8 {of angelic beings.} As in Dead Sea Scrolls, which read *of the sons of God,* and Greek version, which **r** *of the angels of god;* Masoretic Text **r** *of the sons of Israel.*
32:31 {even they recognize.} The meaning of the Hebrew is uncertain. Greek version **r** *our enemies are fools.*
32:43 {God worship him,} As in Dead Sea Scrolls and Greek version; Masoretic Text **r** *Rejoice with his people, O nations.*
33: 2 {dawned upon us} As in Greek and Syriac versions; Hebrew **r** *upon them.*

Jos 7: 1 {family of Zimri,} As in Greek version (see also 1 Chr 2:6); Hebrew **r** *Zabdi.* Also in 7:17, 18.
12:23 {Goyim in Gilgal} Greek version **r** *Goyim in Galilee.*
16: 2 {(that is, Luz)} As in Greek version (also see 18:13); Hebrew **r** *From Bethel to Luz.*
18:28 {Gibeah, and Kiriath-jearim} As in Greek version; Hebrew **r** *Kiriath.*

Jdg 9:29 {I would say} As in Greek version; Hebrew **r** *And he said.*
14:15 {On the fourth} As in Greek version; Hebrew **r** *seventh.*
18:30 {descendant of Moses,} As in an ancient Hebrew tradition, some Greek manuscripts, and Latin Vulgate; Masoretic Text **r** *of Manasseh.*

1Sa 1:24 {a three-year-old bull} As in Dead Sea Scrolls, Greek and Syriac versions; Hebrew **r** *3 bulls.*
2:20 {to the LORD.} As in Greek version; Hebrew **r** *this one she requested of the LORD in prayer.*
2:33 {a violent death.} As in Dead Sea Scrolls, which read *die by the sword;* Masoretic Text **r** *die like mortals.*
3:13 {are blaspheming God} As in Greek version; Hebrew **r** *his sons have made themselves contemptible.*
7:12 {Mizpah and Jeshanah.} As in Greek version; Hebrew **r** *Shen.*
8:16 {of your cattle} As in Greek version; Hebrew **r** *young men.*
9:25 {for him there.} As in Greek version; Hebrew **r** *and talked with him there.*
10: 1 {his people Israel.} Greek version **r** *Israel. And you will rule over the LORD's people and save them from their enemies around them. This will be the sign to you that the LORD has appointed you to be leader over his inheritance.*
12:11 {Barak,} As in Greek and Syriac versions; Hebrew **r** *Bedan.*
13: 5 {of three thousand} As in Greek and Syriac versions; Hebrew **r** *30,000.*
13:15 {land of Benjamin.} As in Greek version; Hebrew **r** *Samuel left Gilgal and went to Gibeah in the land of Benjamin.*
13:20 {axes, or sickles,} As in Greek version; Hebrew **r** *or plowshares.*
14:18 {of the Israelites.} As in some Greek manuscripts; Hebrew **r** *"Bring the Ark of God." For at that time the Ark of God was with the Israelites.*
17: 4 {over nine feet} Hebrew *6 cubits* [9 feet or 2.7 meters] *and 1 span* [9 inches or 23 centimeters]; Greek version **r** *4 cubits* [6 feet or 1.8 meters] *and 1 span,* about 6.75 feet or 2 meters in length.
17:52 {far as Gath} As in some Greek manuscripts; Hebrew **r** *a valley.*
20:25 {sitting opposite him} As in Greek version; Hebrew **r** *with Jonathan standing.*
20:41 {the stone pile.} As in Greek version; Hebrew **r** *near the south edge.*
25: 1 {wilderness of Maon.} As in Greek version; Hebrew **r** *Paran.*
30:29 {Racal,} Greek version **r** *Carmel.*

2Sa 3:15 {her husband Palti} As in 1 Sam 25:44; Hebrew **r** *Paltiel,* a variant name for Palti.
3:29 {walks on crutches} Or *who is effeminate;* Hebrew **r** *who handles a spindle.*
5:14 {in Jerusalem: Shimea,} As in parallel text at 1 Chr 3:5; Hebrew **r** *Shammua,* a variant name for Shimea.
5:25 {way from Gibeon} As in Greek version (see also 1 Chr 14:16); Hebrew **r** *Geba.*
6: 5 {might, singing songs} As in Greek version (see also 1 Chr 13:8); Hebrew **r** *cypress trees.*
8: 4 {seventeen hundred charioteers} Greek version **r** *1,000 chariots and 7,000 charioteers;* compare 1 Chr 18:4.
8: 8 {cities of Tebah} As in some Greek manuscripts (see also 1 Chr 18:8); Hebrew **r** *Betah.*
12:30 {the king's head,} Greek version **r** *removed the crown of Milcom;* compare 1 Kgs 11:5. Milcom, also called Molech, was the god of the Ammonites.
13:34 {the Horonaim road} As in Greek version; Hebrew **r** *from the road behind him.*
15: 7 {After four years,} As in Greek and Syriac versions; Hebrew **r** *40 years.*
15:20 {love and faithfulness.} As in Greek version; Hebrew **r** *and may unfailing love and faithfulness go with you.*
15:27 {the priest, "Look,} As in Greek version; Hebrew **r** *Are you a seer?* or *Do you see?*
16:14 {the Jordan River.} As in Greek version (see also 17:16); Hebrew **r** *when they reached their destination.*
17: 3 {that you seek.} As in Greek version; Hebrew **r** *like the return of all is the man whom you seek.*
17:25 {an Ishmaelite.} As in some Greek manuscripts (see also 1 Chr 2:17); Hebrew **r** *an Israelite.*
20:24 {Adoniram} As in Greek version (see also 1 Kgs 4:6; 5:14); Hebrew **r** *Adoram.*
21: 6 {of the LORD.} As in Greek version (see also 21:9); Hebrew **r** *at Gibeah of Saul, the chosen of the LORD.*
21:16 {of the giants} As in Greek version; Hebrew **r** *a descendant of the Rephaites;* also in 21:18, 20, 22.
21:19 {son of Jair} As in parallel text at 1 Chr 20:5; Hebrew **r** *son of Jaare-oregim.*
21:19 {Goliath of Gath.} As in parallel text at 1 Chr 20:5; Hebrew **r** *killed Goliath of Gath.*
21:21 {David's brother Shimea.} As in parallel text at 1 Chr 20:7; Hebrew **r** *Shimei,* a variant name for Shimea.
23: 8 {Jashobeam the Hacmonite,} As in parallel text at 1 Chr 11:11; Hebrew **r** *Josheb-basshebeth the Tahkemonite.*
23:19 {Thirty} As in Syriac version; Hebrew **r** *the Three.*
23:26 {Helez from Pelon} As in parallel text at 1 Chr 11:27 (see also 1 Chr 27:10); Hebrew **r** *from Palti.*
23:27 {Sibbecai} As in some Greek manuscripts (see also 1 Chr 11:29); Hebrew **r** *Mebunnai.*
23:29 {Ithai} As in parallel text at 1 Chr 11:31; Hebrew **r** *Ittai.*
23:30 {Hurai} As in some Greek manuscripts (see also 1 Chr 11:32); Hebrew **r** *Hiddai.*
23:33 {son of Shagee} As in parallel text at 1 Chr 11:34; Hebrew **r** *Jonathan, Shammah;* some Greek manuscripts read *Jonathan son of Shammah.*
24: 6 {land of Tahtim-hodshi} Greek version **r** *to Gilead and to Kadesh in the land of the Hittites.*
24:13 {you choose three} As in Greek version (see also 1 Chr 21:12); Hebrew **r** *seven.*

1Ki 1:25 {of the army,} As in Greek version; Hebrew **r** *invited the commanders of the army.*
4:19 {land of Gilead,} Greek version **r** *of Gad;* compare 4:13.
4:26 {had four thousand} As in some Greek manuscripts (see also 2 Chr 9:25); Hebrew **r** *40,000.*
5:11 {and 110,000 gallons} As in Greek version, which **r** *20,000 baths* [420 kiloliters] (see also 2 Chr 2:10); Hebrew **r** *20 cors,* about 800 gallons or 3.6 kiloliters in volume.
5:16 {and thirty-six hundred} As in some Greek manuscripts (see also 2 Chr 2:2, 18); Hebrew **r** *3,300.*
6: 8 {the bottom floor} As in Greek version; Hebrew **r** *middle floor.*
7: 7 {floor to ceiling.} As in Syriac version and Latin Vulgate; Hebrew **r** *from floor to floor.*
7:24 {gourds per foot} Or *20 gourds per meter;* Hebrew **r** *10 per cubit.*
9:18 {Baalath, and Tamar} The marginal *Qere* reading of the Masoretic Text **r** *Tadmor.*
9:26 {port near Elath} As in Greek version (see also 2 Kgs 14:22; 16:6); Hebrew **r** *Eloth.*
12: 2 {returned from Egypt,} As in Greek version and Latin Vulgate (see also 2 Chr 10:2); Hebrew **r** *he lived in Egypt.*
12:18 {Rehoboam sent Adoniram,} As in some Greek manuscripts and Syriac version (see also 4:6; 5:14); Hebrew **r** *Adoram.*

2Ki 8:21 {town of Zair.} Greek version **r** *Seir.*
10: 1 {of the city,} As in some Greek manuscripts and Latin Vulgate (see also 10:6); Hebrew **r** *of Jezreel.*
12:21 {assassins were Jozacar} As in Greek and Syriac versions; Hebrew **r** *Jozabad;* compare parallel text at 2 Chr 24:26.
15:16 {town of Tappuah} As in some Greek manuscripts; Hebrew **r** *Tiphsah.*
16: 6 {king of Edom} As in Latin Vulgate; Hebrew **r** *Rezin king of Aram.*
16: 6 {Elath for Edom.} As in Latin Vulgate; Hebrew **r** *Aram.*
16: 6 {and sent Edomites} As in marginal *Qere* reading of the Masoretic Text, Greek version, and Latin Vulgate; Hebrew **r** *Arameans.*
18: 2 {mother was Abijah,} As in parallel text at 2 Chr 29:1; Hebrew **r** *Abi,* a variant name for Abijah.
25:17 {was 7 1/2 feet} As in parallel texts at 1 Kgs 7:16, 2 Chr 3:15, and Jer 52:22, all of which read *5 cubits* [2.3 meters]; Hebrew **r** *3 cubits,* which is 4.5 feet or 1.4 meters.

1Ch 1:17 {Gether, and Mash.} As in parallel text at Gen 10:23; Hebrew **r** *and Meshech.*
1:36 {Timna,} As in some Greek manuscripts (see also Gen 36:12); Hebrew **r** *Kenaz, Timna, and Amalek.*
1:39 {Hori and Heman.} As in parallel text at Gen 36:22; Hebrew **r** *and Homam.*
1:51 {were Timna, Alvah,} As in parallel text at Gen 36:40; Hebrew **r** *Aliah.*
2: 6 {Calcol, and Darda} As in many Hebrew manuscripts, some Greek manuscripts, and Syriac version (see also 1 Kgs 4:31); Hebrew **r** *Dara.*
2:11 {father of Salmon.} As in Greek version (see also Ruth 4:21); Hebrew **r** *Salma.*
2:24 {(the father of} Or *the founder of;* also in 2:42, 45, 49-52 and perhaps other instances where the text **r** *the father of.*
3: 1 {second was Kileab,} As in parallel text at 2 Sam 3:3; Hebrew **r** *Daniel.*
4: 3 {The descendants of} As in Greek version; Hebrew **r** *father of.* The meaning of the Hebrew is uncertain.
4: 4 {(the father of} Or *the founder of;* also in 4:12, 14, 17-18, and perhaps other instances where the text **r** *the father of.*
4:33 {away as Baalath.} As in some Greek manuscripts (see also Josh 19:8); Hebrew **r** *Baal.*
6:58 {Holon,} As in parallel text at Josh 21:15; Hebrew **r** *Hilen.*
6:59 {Ain,} As in parallel text at Josh 21:16; Hebrew **r** *Ashan.*
7:13 {Naphtali were Jahzeel,} As in parallel text at Gen 46:24; Hebrew **r** *Jahziel,* a variant name for Jahzeel.
8:31 {Gedor, Ahio, Zechariah,} As in parallel text at 9:37; Hebrew **r** *Zeker,* a variant name for Zechariah.
8:32 {father of Shimeam.} As in parallel text at 9:38; Hebrew **r** *Shimeah,* a variant name for Shimeam.
8:35 {Pithon, Melech, Tahrea,} As in parallel text at 9:41; Hebrew **r** *Tarea,* a variant name for Tahrea.
8:36 {father of Jadah.} As in parallel text at 9:42; Hebrew **r** *Jehoaddah,* a variant name for Jadah.
8:37 {father of Rephaiah.} As in parallel text at 9:43; Hebrew **r** *Raphah,* a variant name for Rephaiah.
9:42 {father of Jadah.} As in some Hebrew manuscripts and Greek version (see also 8:36); Hebrew **r** *Jarah.*
11:12 {son of Dodai,} As in parallel text at 2 Sam 23:9 (see also 1 Chr 27:4); Hebrew **r** *Dodo,* a variant name for Dodai.
11:20 {of the Thirty.} As in Syriac version; Hebrew **r** *the Three;* also in 11:21.
11:27 {Shammah from Harod;} As in parallel text at 2 Sam 23:25; Hebrew **r** *Shammoth from Haror.*
11:29 {Zalmon} As in parallel text at 2 Sam 23:28; Hebrew **r** *Ilai.*
11:32 {Abi-albon} As in parallel text at 2 Sam 23:31; Hebrew **r** *Abiel.*
11:33 {Azmaveth from Bahurim} As in parallel text at 2 Sam 23:31; Hebrew **r** *Baharum.*
11:34 {sons of Jashen} As in parallel text at 2 Sam 23:32; Hebrew **r** *sons of Hashem.*
11:35 {son of Sharar} As in parallel text at 2 Sam 23:33; Hebrew **r** *son of Sacar.*
11:37 {Paarai} As in parallel text at 2 Sam 23:35; Hebrew **r** *Naarai.*
13: 9 {floor of Nacon,} As in parallel text at 2 Sam 6:6; Hebrew **r** *Kidon.*
16:15 {by his covenant} As in some Greek manuscripts (see also Ps 105:8); Hebrew **r** *Remember his covenant forever.*

17: 6 {to Israel's leaders,} As in Greek version (see also 2 Sam 7:7); Hebrew **r** *judges.*

18: 8 {Tebah} Hebrew **r** *Tibhath,* a variant name for Tebah; compare parallel text at 2 Sam 8:8.

18: 9 {When King Toi} As in parallel text at 2 Sam 8:9; Hebrew **r** *Tou;* also in 18:10.

18:10 {his son Joram} As in parallel text at 2 Sam 8:10; Hebrew **r** *Hadoram,* a variant name for Joram.

18:16 {the priests. Seraiah} As in parallel text at 2 Sam 8:17; Hebrew **r** *Shavsha.*

19:16 {command of Shobach,} As in parallel text at 2 Sam 10:16; Hebrew **r** *Shophach;* also in 19:18.

20: 3 {picks, and axes.} As in parallel text at 2 Sam 12:31; Hebrew **r** *and saws.*

20: 4 {Hushah killed Saph,} As in parallel text at 2 Sam 21:18; Hebrew **r** *Sippai.*

21:15 {floor of Araunah} As in parallel text at 2 Sam 24:16; Hebrew **r** *Ornan,* another name for Araunah; also in 21:18-28.

23:10 {were Jahath, Ziza,} As in Greek version and Latin Vulgate (see also 23:11); Hebrew **r** *Zina.*

2Ch 3: 1 {floor of Araunah} Hebrew **r** *Ornan,* another name for Araunah; compare 2 Sam 24:16.

3: 4 {was thirty feet} As in some Greek and Syriac manuscripts, which read *20 cubits* [9 meters]; Hebrew **r** *120 cubits,* which is 180 feet or 54 meters.

3:15 {that were 27 feet} As in Syriac version (see also 1 Kgs 7:15; 2 Kgs 25:17; Jer 52:21), which **r** *18 cubits* [8.1 meters]; Hebrew **r** *35 cubits,* which is 52.5 feet or 15.8 meters.

4: 3 {oxen per foot} Or *20 oxen per meter;* Hebrew **r** *10 per cubit.*

4:17 {Succoth and Zarethan.} As in parallel text at 1 Kgs 7:46; Hebrew **r** *Zeredah.*

8:17 {Ezion-geber and Elath,} As in Greek version (see also 2 Kgs 14:22; 16:6); Hebrew **r** *Eloth.*

13: 2 {mother was Maacah,} As in most Greek manuscripts and Syriac version (see also 2 Chr 11:20-21; 1 Kgs 15:2); Hebrew **r** *Micaiah.*

14: 9 {a million men} Or *an army of thousands and thousands;* Hebrew **r** *an army of a thousand thousands.*

15: 8 {Azariah the prophet,} As in Syriac version and Latin Vulgate (see also 15:1); Hebrew **r** *from Oded the prophet.*

16: 4 {Ijon, Dan, Abel-beth-maacah,} As in parallel text at 1 Kgs 15:20; Hebrew **r** *Abel-maim,* another name for Abel-beth-maacah.

20: 1 {of the Meunites} As in some Greek manuscripts (see also 26:7); Hebrew **r** *Ammonites.*

22: 2 {Ahaziah was twenty-two} As in some Greek manuscripts and Syriac version (see also 2 Kgs 8:26); Hebrew **r** *forty-two.*

22: 8 {and Ahaziah's relatives} As in Greek version (see also 2 Kgs 10:13); Hebrew **r** *and sons of the brothers of Ahaziah.*

22:11 {Ahaziah's sister Jehosheba,} As in parallel text at 2 Kgs 11:2; Hebrew **r** *Jehoshabeath,* a variant name for Jehosheba.

24:26 {woman named Shomer.} As in parallel text at 2 Kgs 12:21; Hebrew **r** *Shimrith.*

25: 1 {mother was Jehoaddin,} As in parallel text at 2 Kgs 14:2; Hebrew **r** *Jehoaddan,* a variant name for Jehoaddin.

26: 2 {town of Elath} As in Greek version (see also 2 Kgs 14:22; 16:6); Hebrew **r** *Eloth.*

26: 7 {Arabs of Gur} As in Greek version; Hebrew **r** *Gur-baal.*

26: 8 {The Meunites} As in Greek version; Hebrew **r** *Ammonites.* Compare 26:7.

34:20 {son of Micaiah,} As in parallel text at 2 Kgs 22:12; Hebrew **r** *Abdon son of Micah.*

34:22 {grandson of Harhas,} As in parallel text at 2 Kgs 22:14; Hebrew **r** *son of Tokhath, son of Hasrah.*

36:10 {appointed Jehoiachin's uncle,} As in parallel text at 2 Kgs 24:17; Hebrew **r** *brother,* or *relative.*

Ezr 2:24 {people of Beth-azmaveth} As in parallel text at Neh 7:28; Hebrew **r** *Azmaveth.*

2:25 {peoples of Kiriath-jearim,} As in some Hebrew manuscripts and Greek version (see also Neh 7:29); Hebrew **r** *Kiriath-arim.*

2:46 {Hagab, Shalmai,} As in the marginal *Qere* reading of the Masoretic Text (see also Neh 7:48); Hebrew text **r** *Shamlai.*

2:55 {Sotai, Sophereth,} As in parallel text at Neh 7:57; Hebrew **r** *Hassophereth.*

10: 6 {spent the night} As in parallel text at 1 Esdras 9:2; Hebrew **r** *He went.*

10:25 {Mijamin, Eleazar, Hashabiah,} As in parallel text at 1 Esdras 9:26; Hebrew **r** *Malkijah.*

10:37[-38] {family of Binnui} As in Greek version; Hebrew **r** *Jaasu,* [38]*Bani, Binnui.*

Ne 6: 2 {of the villages} As in Greek version; Hebrew **r** *at Kephirim.*

7: 7 {Seraiah,} As in parallel text at Ezra 2:2; Hebrew **r** *Azariah.*

7: 7 {Reelaiah,} As in parallel text at Ezra 2:2; Hebrew **r** *Raamiah.*

7: 7 {Mispar,} As in parallel text at Ezra 2:2; Hebrew **r** *Mispereth.*

7: 7 {Rehum,} As in parallel text at Ezra 2:2; Hebrew **r** *Nehum.*

7:15 {Bani} As in parallel text at Ezra 2:10; Hebrew **r** *Binnui.*

7:24 {Jorah} As in parallel text at Ezra 2:18; Hebrew **r** *Hariph.*

7:25 {Gibbar} As in parallel text at Ezra 2:20; Hebrew **r** *Gibeon.*

7:43 {Hodaviah} As in parallel text at Ezra 2:40; Hebrew **r** *Hodevah.*

7:47 {Siaha,} As in parallel text at Ezra 2:44; Hebrew **r** *Sia.*

7:52 {Nephusim,} As in parallel text at Ezra 2:50; Hebrew **r** *Nephushesim.*

7:54 {Bazluth,} As in parallel text at Ezra 2:52; Hebrew **r** *Bazlith.*

7:57 {Peruda,} As in parallel text at Ezra 2:55; Hebrew **r** *Perida.*

7:58 {Jaalah,} As in parallel text at Ezra 2:56; Hebrew **r** *Jaala.*

7:59 {Pokereth-hazzebaim, and Ami.} As in parallel text at Ezra 2:57; Hebrew **r** *Amon.*

7:61 {Tel-harsha, Kerub, Addan,} As in parallel text at Ezra 2:59; Hebrew **r** *Addon.*

12:14 {family of Malluch.} As in Greek version (see also 10:4; 12:2); Hebrew **r** *Malluchi.*

12:15 {family of Meremoth.} As in some Greek manuscripts (see also 12:3); Hebrew **r** *Meraioth.*

Est 3: 7 {a year later.} As in Greek version, which **r** *the thirteenth day of the twelfth month, the month of Adar* (see also 3:13). Hebrew **r** *in the twelfth month,* of the Hebrew calendar. The date selected was March 7, 473 B.C.; also see note on 2:16.

Job 9:17 {me without reason,} As in Syriac version; Hebrew **r** *with a storm.*

15:23 {'Where is it?'} Greek version **r** *He is appointed to be food for a vulture.*

41:11 {and remain safe} As in Greek version; Hebrew **r** *confront me that I must pay.*

41:13 {layer of armor} As in Greek version; Hebrew **r** *its bridle.*

Ps 8: 2 {give you praise.} As in Greek version; Hebrew **r** *to show strength.*

8: 5 {lower than God,} Or *a little lower than the angels;* Hebrew **r** *Elohim.*

16: 9 {and my mouth} As in Greek version; Hebrew **r** *glory.*

48: 2 {the holy mountain,} Or *Mount Zion, in the far north;* Hebrew **r** *Mount Zion, the heights of Zaphon.*

72: 5 {May he live} As in Greek version; Hebrew **r** *May they fear you.*

74:16 {made the starlight} Or *moon;* Hebrew **r** *light.*

76: 4 {the everlasting mountains.} As in Greek version; Hebrew **r** *than mountains filled with beasts of prey.*

112: 4 {They are} Greek version **r** *The LORD is.*

Pr 10:10 {reproof promotes peace.} As in Greek version; Hebrew **r** *but babbling fools fall flat on their faces.*

17:19 {who speaks boastfully} Or *who builds up defenses;* Hebrew **r** *who makes a high gate.*

21: 6 {deadly trap.} As in Greek version; Hebrew **r** *mist for those who seek death.*

24: 5 {strong man,} As in Greek version; Hebrew **r** *A wise man is strength.*

26:23 {Smooth} As in Greek version; Hebrew **r** *Burning.*

SS 7: 9 {lips and teeth.} As in Greek and Syriac versions and Latin Vulgate; Hebrew **r** *over lips of sleepers.*

Isa 5:17 {lambs and kids} As in Greek version; Hebrew **r** *strangers.*

10:27 {from their shoulders.} As in Greek version; Hebrew **r** *The yoke will be broken, for you have grown so fat.*

15: 9 {stream near Dibon} As in Dead Sea Scrolls, some Greek manuscripts, and Latin Vulgate; Hebrew **r** *Dimon;* also in 15:9b.

21: 8 {Then the watchman} As in Dead Sea Scrolls and Syriac version; Hebrew **r** *a lion.*

28:16 {run away again.} Greek version **r** *Anyone who believes in him will not be disappointed.*

29:13 {learned by rote.} Greek version **r** *Their worship is a farce, for they merely teach human commands and teachings.*

33: 8 {made before witnesses.} As in Dead Sea Scrolls; Masoretic Text **r** *care nothing for the cities.*

45: 2 {level the mountains.} As in Dead Sea Scrolls and Greek version; Masoretic Text **r** *the swellings.*

49:12 {south as Egypt.} As in Dead Sea Scrolls, which read *from the region of Aswan,* which is in southern Egypt. Masoretic Text **r** *from the region of Sinim.*

49:24 {that a tyrant} As in Dead Sea Scrolls, Syriac version, and Latin Vulgate (also see 49:25); Masoretic Text **r** *a righteous person.*

52:14 {they saw him} As in Syriac version; Hebrew **r** *you.*

61: 1 {will be freed.} Greek version **r** *and the blind will see.*

66:19 {to the Libyans} As in some Greek manuscripts, which read *Put* [Libya]; Hebrew **r** *Pul.*

Jer 23:33 {are the burden!} As in Greek version and Latin Vulgate; Hebrew **r** *What burden?*

40: 8 {the Netophathite, Jaazaniah} As in parallel text at 2 Kgs 25:23; Hebrew **r** *Jezaniah,* a variant name for Jaazaniah.

42: 1 {Kareah and Jezaniah} Greek version **r** *Azariah;* compare 43:2.

48: 4 {will cry out.} Greek version **r** *Her cries are heard as far away as Zoar.*

Eze 19: 7 {in nearby nations} As in Greek version; Hebrew **r** *He consorted with widows.*

22:25 {Your princes} As in Greek version; Hebrew **r** *prophets.*

27:15 {you from Dedan.} Greek version **r** *Rhodes.*

32:17 {On March 17,} Hebrew *On the fifteenth day of the month,* presumably in the twelfth month of the Hebrew calendar (see 32:1). This would put this message at the end of King Jehoiachin's twelfth year of captivity, on March 17, 585 B.C.; also see note on 29:1. Greek version **r** *On the fifteenth day of the first month,* which would put this message on April 27, 586 B.C., at the beginning of Jehoiachin's twelfth year.

38:14 {will rouse yourself.} As in Greek version; Hebrew **r** *then you will know.*

40: 6 {10 1/2 feet deep.} Greek version; Hebrew **r** *1 rod* [10.5 feet or 3.2 meters] *deep, and one threshold, one rod deep.*

40:44 {beside the south} As in Greek version; Hebrew **r** *east.*

42:10 {On the south} As in Greek version; Hebrew **r** *east.*

45: 1 {6 2/3 miles wide.} Reflecting the Greek reading *25,000 cubits* [13.3 kilometers] *long and 20,000 cubits* [10.6 kilometers] *wide;* Hebrew **r** *25,000 cubits long and 10,000 cubits wide.* Compare 45:3, 5; 48:9. In this chapter, the distance measures are calculated using the Hebrew long cubit, which equals 21 inches or 53 centimeters.

45: 5 {for their towns.} As in Greek version; Hebrew **r** *They will have as their possession 20 rooms.*

47:18 {south as Tamar.} As in Greek version; Hebrew **r** *you will measure.*

48: 9 {6 2/3 miles wide.} Reflecting the Greek reading in 45:1: *25,000 cubits* [13.3 kilometers] *long and 20,000 cubits* [10.6 kilometers] *wide;* Hebrew **r** *25,000 cubits long and 10,000 cubits wide.* Compare 45:1-5; 48:10-13. In this chapter, the distance measures are calculated using the Hebrew long cubit, which equals 21 inches or 53 centimeters.

Da 7:13 {like a man} Or *a Son of Man;* Aramaic **r** *a son of man.*

10:13 {kingdom of Persia.} As in one Greek version; Hebrew **r** *and I was left there with the kings of Persia.* The meaning of the Hebrew is uncertain.

Hos 3: 2 {measure of wine.} As in Greek version, which **r** *a homer* [182 liters] *of barley and a measure of wine;* Hebrew **r** *a homer of barley and a lethech* [2.5 bushels or 91 liters] *of barley.*

4: 7 {They have exchanged} As in Syriac version and an ancient Hebrew tradition; Masoretic Text **r** *I will exchange.*

11: 2 {the more I} As in Greek version; Hebrew **r** *they.*

12: 4 {spoke to him} As in Greek and Syriac versions; Hebrew **r** *to us.*

13:10 {Where now is} As in Greek and Syriac versions and Latin Vulgate; Hebrew **r** *I will be.*

Am 5:26 {you yourselves made.} Greek version **r** *You took up the shrine of Molech, and the star of your god Rephan, and the images you made for yourselves.*

Mic 1:10 {weep at all.} Greek version **r** *weep not in Acco.*

Hab 2: 4 {lives are crooked;} Greek version **r** *I will have no pleasure in anyone who turns away.*

Zec 3: 1 {Satan} Or *The Accuser;* Hebrew **r** *The Adversary;* also in 3:2.

5: 6 {with the sins} As in Greek version; Hebrew **r** *the appearance.*

6:11 {make a crown} As in Greek and Syriac versions; Hebrew **r** *crowns.*

6:14 {Heldai,} As in Syriac version (compare 6:10); Hebrew **r** *Helem.*

6:14 {Jedaiah, and Josiah} As in Syriac version (compare 6:10); Hebrew **r** *Hen.*

11:13 {to the potters} Syriac version **r** *into the treasury;* also in 11:13b.

14: 5 {ones with him.} As in Greek version; Hebrew **r** *with you.*

Mal 1: 7 {defiled the sacrifices} As in Greek version; Hebrew **r** *defiled you.*

Mt 7: 2 {you treat them.} Or *For God will treat you as you treat others;* Greek **r** *For with the judgment you judge you will be judged.*

17: 4 {make three shrines,} Or *shelters;* Greek **r** *tabernacles.*

Mk 9: 5 {make three shrines} Or *shelters;* Greek **r** *tabernacles.*

Lk 9:33 {make three shrines} Or *shelters;* Greek **r** *tabernacles.*

11: 2[-4] {yield to temptation.} Some manuscripts add additional portions of the Lord's Prayer as it **r** in Matt 6:9-13.

Jn 9:24 {telling the truth,} Or *Give glory to God, not to Jesus;* Greek **r** *Give glory to God.*

Ac 17:22 {before the Council,} Or *in the middle of Mars Hill;* Greek **r** *in the middle of the Areopagus.*

20:22 {the Holy Spirit,} Or *by my spirit,* or *by an inner compulsion;* Greek **r** *by the spirit.*

1Co 5: 5 {will be destroyed} Or *so that he will die;* Greek **r** *for the destruction of the flesh.*

7:39 {to the Lord.} Or *but only to a Christian;* Greek **r** *but only in the Lord.*

Gal 5:12 {would mutilate themselves.} Or *castrate themselves;* Greek **r** *cut themselves off.*

1Th 4: 4 {control your body} Or *will know how to take a wife for himself;* Greek **r** *will know how to possess his own vessel.*

1Ti 5: 7 {widows you support} Or *so the church;* Greek **r** *so they.*

Tit 1: 6 {to his wife,} Or *have only one wife,* or *be married only once;* Greek **r** *be the husband of one wife.*

1Jn 4:19 {love each other} Or *We love him;* Greek **r** *We love.*
Rev 1:13 {Son of Man.} Or *one who looked like a man;* Greek **r** *one like a son of man.*
14:14 {Son of Man} Or *one who looked like a man;* Greek **r** *one like a son of man.*

READY (3)

SS 2: 7 {time is right.} Or *not to awaken love until it is* **r.**
3: 5 {time is right.} Or *not to awaken love until it is* **r.**
8: 4 {time is right.} Or *not to awaken love until it is* **r.**

REALIZE (4)

Lk 2:49 {my Father's house."} Or *"Didn't you* **r** *that I should be involved with my Father's affairs?"*
9:55 {and rebuked them.} Some manuscripts add *And he said, "You don't* **r** *what your hearts are like.* [56]*For the Son of Man has not come to destroy men's lives, but to save them."*
1Co 5: 6[-7] {can stay pure.} Greek *Don't you* **r** *that even a little leaven spreads quickly through the whole batch of dough?* [7]*Purge out the old leaven so that you can be a new batch of dough, just as you are already unleavened.*
Eph 1:18 {to his people.} Or **r** *how much God has been honored by acquiring his people.*

REALLY (3)

Mt 23:13 {go in yourselves.} Some manuscripts add verse 14, *How terrible it will be for you teachers of religious law and you Pharisees. Hypocrites! You shamelessly cheat widows out of their property, and then, to cover up the kind of people you* **r** *are, you make long prayers in public. Because of this, your punishment will be the greater.*
Jn 14: 7 {my Father is.} Some manuscripts read *If you* **r** *have known me, you will know who my Father is.*
Heb 12: 9 {and live forever} Or **r** *live.*

REBELLIOUS (1)

1Sa 20:30 {of a whore!"} Hebrew *You son of a perverse and* **r** *woman.*

REBELS (1)

Mk 15:27 {side of his.} Some manuscripts add verse 28, *And the Scripture was fulfilled that said, "He was counted among those who were* **r."** See Isa 53:12.

RECEIVED (1)

Ac 7:53 {hands of angels.} Greek **r** *the Law as it was ordained by angels.*

RECKONING (1)

Da 1: 1 {reign in Judah,} The third year of Jehoiakim's reign, according to the Babylonian system of **r**, was 605 B.C.

RECLINING (1)

Jn 13:23 {at the table.} Greek *was* **r** *on Jesus' bosom.* The "disciple whom Jesus loved" was probably John.

RED (1)

Zec 10:11 {sea of distress,} Or *the sea of Egypt,* referring to the **R** Sea.

REDEEM (1)

Ps 49: 7 {themselves from death} Or *no one can* **r** *the life of another.*

REEDS (20)

Ex 10:19 {the Red Sea.} Hebrew *sea of* **r.**
13:18 {the Red Sea,} Hebrew *sea of* **r.**
15: 4 {the Red Sea.} Hebrew *sea of* **r;** also in 15:22.
23:31 {the Mediterranean Sea,} Hebrew *from the sea of* **r** *to the sea of the Philistines.*
Nu 14:25 {the Red Sea.} Hebrew *sea of* **r.**
21: 4 {the Red Sea} Hebrew *sea of* **r.**
33:10 {the Red Sea.} Hebrew *sea of* **r;** also in 33:11.
Dt 1:40 {the Red Sea.} Hebrew *sea of* **r.**
2: 1 {the Red Sea,} Hebrew *sea of* **r.**
11: 4 {the Red Sea} Hebrew *sea of* **r.**
Jos 2:10 {the Red Sea} Hebrew *sea of* **r.**
4:23 {the Red Sea} Hebrew *sea of* **r.**
24: 6 {the Red Sea,} Hebrew *sea of* **r.**
Jdg 11:16 {the Red Sea,} Hebrew *sea of* **r.**
1Ki 9:26 {the Red Sea.} Hebrew *sea of* **r.**
Ne 9: 9 {the Red Sea.} Hebrew *sea of* **r.**
Ps 106: 7 {the Red Sea.} Hebrew *at the sea, the sea of* **r.**
106: 9 {the Red Sea} Hebrew *sea of* **r;** also in 106:22.
136:13 {the Red Sea.} Hebrew *sea of* **r;** also in 136:15.
Jer 49:21 {the Red Sea.} Hebrew *sea of* **r.**

REGEMMELECH (1)

Zec 7: 2 {Sharezer and Regemmelech,} Or *Bethel-sharezer had sent* **R.**

REGENERATION (2)

Mt 19:28 {in the Kingdom,} Greek *in the* **r.**
Tit 3: 5 {the Holy Spirit.} Greek *He saved us through the washing of* **r** *and renewing of the Holy Spirit.*

REGION (8)

Isa 49:12 {south as Egypt.} As in Dead Sea Scrolls, which read *from the* **r** *of Aswan,* which is in southern Egypt. Masoretic Text reads *from the* **r** *of Sinim.*
Ac 7: 2 {moved to Haran.} *Mesopotamia* was the **r** now called Iraq. *Haran* was a city in what is now called Syria.
18: 1 {went to Corinth.} *Athens* and *Corinth* were major cities in Achaia, the **r** on the southern end of the Greek peninsula.
Ro 15:19 {over into Illyricum.} *Illyricum* was a **r** northeast of Italy.
1Co 16:15 {Christians in Greece,} Greek *were the firstfruits in Achaia,* the southern **r** of the Greek peninsula.
2Co 1: 1 {Christians throughout Greece.} Greek *Achaia,* the southern **r** of the Greek peninsula.
9: 2 {Christians in Greece} Greek *Achaia,* the southern **r** of the Greek peninsula.

REGIONS (2)

Ro 15:26 {believers in Greece} Greek *Macedonia and Achaia,* the northern and southern **r** of Greece.
1Th 1: 7 {Christians in Greece.} Greek *Macedonia and Achaia,* the northern and southern **r** of Greece; also in 1:8.

REHOBOAM (1)

1Ki 15: 6 {Abijam and Jeroboam} As in a few Hebrew manuscripts; most Hebrew manuscripts read *between* **R** *and Jeroboam.*

REHOBOTH (1)

Ge 26:22 {it "Room Enough,"} Hebrew **R.**

REHUM (1)

Ne 12: 3 {Shecaniah, Harim,} Hebrew **R;** compare 7:42; 12:15; Ezra 2:39.

REIGN (1 of 25)

Ro 6:12 {way you live;} Or *Do not let sin* **r** *in your body, which is subject to death.*

REIGNING (1)

Rev 5:10 {they will reign} Some manuscripts read *they are* **r.**

REJECTED (1)

Isa 8: 6 {my gentle care} Hebrew **r** *the gently flowing waters of Shiloah.*

REJOICE (1)

Dt 32:43 {God worship him,} As in Dead Sea Scrolls and Greek version; Masoretic Text reads **R** *with his people, O nations.*

RELATIVE (1)

2Ch 36:10 {appointed Jehoiachin's uncle,} As in parallel text at 2 Kgs 24:17; Hebrew reads *brother,* or **r.**

RELATIVES (1)

1Ch 25: 9 {sons and relatives.} As in Greek version; Hebrew lacks *and twelve of his sons and* **r.**

RELEASE (2)

Eze 46:17 {every fiftieth year.} Hebrew *until the Year of* **R;** see Lev 25:8-17.
Lk 23:16 {will release him."} Some manuscripts add verse 17, *For it was necessary for him to* **r** *one [prisoner] for them during the feast.*

RELIABLE (1)

Mk 16: 8 {frightened to talk.} The most **r** early manuscripts conclude the Gospel of Mark at verse 8. Other manuscripts include various endings to the Gospel. Two of the more noteworthy endings are printed here.

RELIEF (1)

Ge 5:29 {his son Noah,} *Noah* sounds like a Hebrew term that can mean "**r**" or "comfort."

RELIGIOUS (1)

Mt 23:13 {go in yourselves.} Some manuscripts add verse 14, *How terrible it will be for you teachers of* **r** *law and you Pharisees. Hypocrites! You shamelessly cheat widows out of their property, and then, to cover up the kind of people you really are, you make long prayers in public. Because of this, your punishment will be the greater.*

REMEMBER (2)

1Ch 16:15 {by his covenant} As in some Greek manuscripts (see also Ps 105:8); Hebrew reads **R** *his covenant forever.*
2Ch 6:42 {your servant David.} Or **R** *the faithfulness of your servant David.*

REMNANT (5)

Isa 7: 3 {your son Shear-jashub.} *Shear-jashub* means "A **r** will return."
8:18 {me have names} *Isaiah* means "The LORD will save"; *Shear-jashub* means "A **r** will return"; and *Maher-shalal-hash-baz* means "Swift to plunder and quick to spoil."
65: 9 {people of Israel} Hebrew **r** *of Jacob.*
Am 5:15 {people who remain.} Hebrew *on the* **r** *of Joseph.*
Ro 11: 5 {God. A few} Greek *A* **r.**

REMOVAL (1)

Lev 16: 8 {be the scapegoat.} Hebrew *azazel,* which in this context means "the goat of **r**"; also in 16:10, 26.

REMOVED (2)

2Sa 12:30 {the king's head,} Greek version reads **r** *the crown of Milcom;* compare 1 Kgs 11:5. Milcom, also called Molech, was the god of the Ammonites.
1Ch 20: 2 {the king's head,} Greek version and Latin Vulgate read **r** *the crown of Milcom;* compare 1 Kgs 11:5. Milcom, also called Molech, was the god of the Ammonites.

RENDERED (17)

Ge 6:14 {"Make a boat} Traditionally **r** *an ark.*
37: 3 {gift—a beautiful robe.} Traditionally **r** *a coat of many colors.* The exact meaning of the Hebrew is uncertain.
49:10 {whom it belongs,} Or *until tribute is brought to him and the peoples obey;* traditionally **r** *until Shiloh comes.*
Ex 3:15 {'The LORD,} Hebrew *Yahweh;* traditionally **r** *Jehovah.*
6: 3 {the LORD,} Hebrew *Yahweh;* traditionally **r** *Jehovah.*
Lev 13: 2 {contagious skin disease,} Traditionally **r** *leprosy.* The Hebrew word used throughout this passage is used to describe various skin diseases.
13:47 {an infectious mildew} Traditionally **r** *leprosy.* The Hebrew term used throughout this passage is the same term used for the various skin diseases described in 13:1-46.
14: 2 {contagious skin disease.} Traditionally **r** *leprosy.* See note at 13:2.
14:34 {an infectious mildew.} Traditionally **r** *leprosy.* See note at 13:47.
14:54 {contagious skin disease} Traditionally **r** *leprosy.* See notes at 13:2 and 13:47.
22: 4 {contagious skin disease} Traditionally **r** *leprosy.* See note at 13:2.
Nu 5: 2 {contagious skin disease} Traditionally **r** *leprosy.* The Hebrew word used here describes various skin diseases.
Dt 24: 8 {contagious skin diseases} Traditionally **r** *leprosy.* The Hebrew word used here can describe various skin diseases.
2Sa 23: 8 {a single battle.} As in some Greek manuscripts (see also 1 Chr 11:11); the Hebrew is uncertain, though it might be **r** *the Three. It was Adino the Eznite who killed eight hundred men at one time.*
Ps 3: 2 {Interlude} Hebrew *Selah.* The meaning of this word is uncertain, though it is probably a musical or literary term. It is **r** *Interlude* throughout the Psalms.
Ecc 1: 1 {of the Teacher,} Hebrew *Koheleth;* this term is **r** "the Teacher" throughout this book.
Lk 23:33 {called The Skull.} Sometimes **r** *Calvary,* which comes from the Latin word for "skull."

RENEWING (1)

Tit 3: 5 {the Holy Spirit.} Greek *He saved us through the washing of regeneration and* **r** *of the Holy Spirit.*

REPEATED (1)

Nu 1:20[-21] {clan and family} In the Hebrew text, *number of men…family* is **r** in 1:22, 24, 26, 28, 30, 32, 34, 36, 38, 40, 42.

REPENT (1)

Ac 17:30 {turn to him.} Greek *everywhere to* **r.**

REPENTANCE (2)

Mk 1: 4 {to be forgiven.} Greek *preaching a baptism of* **r** *for the forgiveness of sins.*
Lk 3: 3 {to be forgiven.} Greek *preaching a baptism of* **r** *for the forgiveness of sins.*

REPHAIAH (1)

1Ch 8:37 {father of Rephaiah.} As in parallel text at 9:43; Hebrew reads *Raphah,* a variant name for **R.**

REPHAITES (2)

2Sa 21:16 {of the giants} As in Greek version; Hebrew reads *a descendant of the* **R;** also in 21:18, 20, 22.
1Ch 20: 4 {of the giants,} Hebrew *descendant of the* **R;** also in 20:6, 8.

REPHAN (1)

Am 5:26 {you yourselves made.} Greek version reads *You took up the shrine of Molech, and the star of your god **R**, and the images you made for yourselves.*

REPLIED (2)

Mt 16: 2[-3] {of the times!} Several manuscripts do not include any of the words in 16:2-3 after *He **r**.*
Ac 8:36 {I be baptized?"} Some manuscripts add verse 37, *"You can," Philip answered, "if you believe with all your heart." And the eunuch **r**, "I believe that Jesus Christ is the Son of God."*

REPORTED (1)

Hos 7:12 {their evil ways.} Hebrew *I will punish them because of what was **r** against them in the assembly.*

REPRESENTING (1)

Eze 37:16 {tribes of Israel.'} Hebrew *Ephraim's stick, **r** Joseph and all the house of Israel.*

REQUESTED (1)

1Sa 2:20 {to the LORD.} As in Greek version; Hebrew reads *this one she **r** of the LORD in prayer.*

REQUIRES (1)

Lev 27:16 {area that produces} Or ***r**.*

RESCUE (1)

1Sa 10:27 {Saul ignored them.} Dead Sea Scroll 4QSam[a] continues: *He gouged out the right eye of each of the Israelites living there, and he didn't allow anyone to come and **r** them....*

RESIN (1)

Nu 11: 7 {yellow in color.} Hebrew *the color of gum **r**.*

RESPOND (2)

1Sa 14:41 {among the others?"} Greek version adds *If the fault is with me or my son Jonathan, **r** with Urim; but if the men of Israel are at fault, **r** with Thummim.*

RESPONDED (1)

1Sa 10:12 {become a prophet."} Hebrew ***r**, "Who is their father?"*

REST (4)

Zec 6: 8 {of my Spirit} Hebrew *have given my Spirit **r**.*
Mt 26:45 {sleeping? Still resting?} Or *Sleep on, take your **r**.*
Mk 14:41 {sleeping? Still resting?} Or *Sleep on, take your **r**.*
Heb 4: 9 {special rest} Or *Sabbath **r**.*

RESTED (1)

Est 9:18 {the third day,} Hebrew *killing their enemies on the thirteenth day and the fourteenth day, and then **r** on the fifteenth day,* of the Hebrew month of Adar.

RESTORED (1)

Ne 3: 8 {They left out} Or *They **r**.*

RESTS (1)

2Ki 2:15 {become Elijah's successor!"} Hebrew *The spirit of Elijah **r** upon Elisha.*

RESURRECTION (1)

Mt 27:51[-53] {to many people.} Or *The earth shook, rocks split apart, tombs opened, and many bodies of godly men and women who had died were raised from the dead. After Jesus' **r**, they left the cemetery, went into the holy city of Jerusalem, and appeared to many people.*

RETURN (3)

2Sa 17: 3 {that you seek.} As in Greek version; Hebrew reads *like the **r** of all is the man whom you seek.*
Isa 7: 3 {your son Shear-jashub.} *Shear-jashub* means "A remnant will **r**."
8:18 {me have names} *Isaiah* means "The LORD will save"; *Shear-jashub* means "A remnant will **r**"; and *Maher-shalal-hash-baz* means "Swift to plunder and quick to spoil."

REUBEN (2)

Ge 29:32 {named him Reuben,} ***R*** means "Look, a son!" It also sounds like the Hebrew for "He has seen my misery."
Dt 33: 6 {tribe of Reuben:} Hebrew lacks *Moses said this about the tribe of **R**.*

REUBENITES (1)

1Sa 10:27 {Saul ignored them.} Dead Sea Scroll 4QSam[a] continues: *Nahash, king of the Ammonites, had been grievously oppressing the Gadites and **R**...*

REUEL (2)

Ex 3: 1 {his father-in-law, Jethro,} Moses' father-in-law went by two names, Jethro and **R**.
Nu 2:14[-15] {son of Deuel} As in many Hebrew manuscripts, Samaritan Pentateuch, and Latin Vulgate (see also 1:14); most Hebrew manuscripts read *son of **R**.*

REVEAL (4)

Ps 2: 7 {become your Father.} Or *Today I **r** you as my son.*
Ac 13:33 {become your Father.} Or *Today I **r** you as my Son.* Ps 2:7.
Heb 1: 5 {become your Father.} Or *Today I **r** you as my Son.* Ps 2:7.
5: 5 {become your Father.} Or *Today I **r** you as my Son.* Ps 2:7.

REVEALED (1)

Lk 17:30 {of Man returns.} Or *on the day the Son of Man is **r**.*

REVENGE (2)

Dt 32:36 {his mind about} Or *will take **r** for.*
1Ki 2: 5 {time of peace,} Or *He murdered them during a time of peace as **r** for deaths they had caused in time of war.*

REVILE (1)

Ex 22:28 {not blaspheme God} Or *Do not **r** your judges.*

REWARD (1)

Ge 30:18 {named him Issachar,} *Issachar* sounds like a Hebrew term that means "**r**."

REZIN (1)

2Ki 16: 6 {king of Edom} As in Latin Vulgate; Hebrew reads ***R** king of Aram.*

RHEGIUM (1)

Ac 28:13 {across to Rhegium.} ***R*** was on the southern tip of Italy.

RHODES (1)

Eze 27:15 {you from Dedan.} Greek version reads ***R**.*

RICHES (1)

Mk 10:24 {is very hard} Some manuscripts add *for those who trust in **r**.*

RIDGE (1)

Ge 48:22 {an extra portion} Or *give you the **r** of land.* The meaning of the Hebrew is uncertain.

RIGHT (8)

Ge 35:18 {called him Benjamin.} *Ben-oni* means "son of my sorrow"; *Benjamin* means "son of my **r** hand."
1Sa 10:27 {Saul ignored them.} Dead Sea Scroll 4QSam[a] continues: *...He gouged out the **r** eye of each of the Israelites living there, and he didn't allow anyone to come and rescue them. In fact, of all the Israelites east of the Jordan, there wasn't a single one whose **r** eye Nahash had not gouged out....*
Ne 12:31 {choirs proceeded southward} Hebrew *to the **r**.*
Ps 89:25 {in the east.} Hebrew *I will set his hand on the sea, his **r** hand on the rivers.*
Jnh 4:11 {in spiritual darkness,} Hebrew *people who don't know their **r** hands from their left.*
Mt 5:29 {your good eye} Greek *your **r** eye.*
5:30 {your stronger hand} Greek *your **r** hand.*

RIGHTEOUS (5)

Pr 21:12 {The Righteous One} Or *The **r** man.*
Isa 49:24 {that a tyrant} As in Dead Sea Scrolls, Syriac version, and Latin Vulgate (also see 49:25); Masoretic Text reads *a **r** person.*
Jer 33:15 {a righteous descendant,} Hebrew *a **r** Branch.*
Lk 23:47 {man was innocent.} Or ***r**.*
1Jn 2: 1 {pleases God completely.} Greek *Jesus Christ, the **r**.*

RIGHTEOUSNESS (4)

Mal 4: 2 {in his wings.} Or *the sun of **r** will rise with healing in its wings.*
Mt 3:15 {that is right.} Or *we must fulfill all **r**.*
2Co 9:10 {harvest of generosity} Greek ***r**.*
Php 1:11 {of your salvation} Greek *the fruit of **r**.*

RISE (2)

Mic 4:13 {the nations, O Jerusalem!"} Hebrew *"**R** up and thresh, O daughter of Zion."*
Mal 4: 2 {in his wings.} Or *the sun of righteousness will **r** with healing in its wings.*

RISES (1)

2Pe 1:19 {in your hearts.} Or *until the day dawns and the morning star **r** in your hearts.*

RIVER (24)

Ge 15:18 {border of Egypt} Hebrew *the **r** of Egypt,* referring either to an eastern branch of the Nile **R** or to the brook of Egypt in the Sinai (see Num 34:5).
36:37 {the Euphrates River} Hebrew *the **r**.*
Ex 23:31 {the Euphrates River.} Hebrew *the **r**.*
Nu 22: 5 {the Euphrates River.} Hebrew *the **r**.*
Jos 19:34 {the Jordan River} Hebrew *and Judah at the Jordan **R**.*
24: 2 {the Euphrates River,} Hebrew *the **r**;* also in 24:3, 14, 15.
1Sa 10:27 {Saul ignored them.} Dead Sea Scroll 4QSam[a] continues: *Nahash, king of the Ammonites, had been grievously oppressing the Gadites and Reubenites who lived east of the Jordan **R**....*
2Sa 10:16 {the Euphrates River.} Hebrew *the **r**.*
1Ki 4:21 {the Euphrates River} Hebrew *the **r**;* also in 4:24.
14:15 {the Euphrates River,} Hebrew *the **r**.*
1Ch 1:48 {the Euphrates River} Hebrew *the **r**.*
19:16 {the Euphrates River.} Hebrew *the **r**.*
2Ch 9:26 {the Euphrates River} Hebrew *the **r**.*
Ps 72: 8 {the Euphrates River} Hebrew *the **r**.*
80:11 {the Euphrates River.} Hebrew *west to the sea,...east to the **r**.*
Isa 8: 7 {the Euphrates River} Hebrew *the **r**.*
11:15 {the Euphrates River,} Hebrew *the **r**.*
23: 3 {grain from Egypt} Hebrew *from Shihor,* a branch of the Nile **R**.
27:12 {the Euphrates River} Hebrew *the **r**.*
Jer 2:18 {of the Nile} Hebrew *of Shihor,* a branch of the Nile **R**.
2:18 {and the Euphrates} Hebrew *the **r**.*
Mic 7:12 {the Euphrates River,} Hebrew *the **r**.*
Zec 9:10 {the Euphrates River} Hebrew *the **r**.*

RIVERS (8)

Ge 24:10 {traveled to Aram-naharaim} *Aram-naharaim* means "Aram of the two **r**," thought to have been located between the Euphrates and Balih **R** in northwestern Mesopotamia.
Dt 23: 4 {Pethor in Aram-naharaim} *Aram-naharaim* means "Aram of the two **r**," thought to have been located between the Euphrates and Balih **R** in northwestern Mesopotamia.
Jdg 3: 8 {Cushan-rishathaim of Aram-naharaim.} *Aram-naharaim* means "Aram of the two **r**," thought to have been located between the Euphrates and Balih **R** in northwestern Mesopotamia.
Ps 89:25 {in the east.} Hebrew *I will set his hand on the sea, his right hand on the **r**.*
Jn 7:37[-38] {out from within."} Or *"Let anyone who is thirsty come to me and drink. [38]For the Scriptures declare that **r** of living water will flow from the heart of those who believe in me."*

ROAD (2)

2Sa 13:34 {the Horonaim road} As in Greek version; Hebrew reads *from the **r** behind him.*
1Ch 26:16 {to the Temple.} Or *the gate of Shalleketh on the upper **r*** (also in 26:18). The meaning of the Hebrew is uncertain.

ROB (2)

Mt 12:29 {house be robbed!} Or *One cannot **r** Satan's kingdom without first tying him up. Only then can his demons be cast out.*
Mk 3:27 {house be robbed!} Or *One cannot **r** Satan's kingdom without first tying him up. Only then can his demons be cast out.*

ROBE (3)

2Sa 13:18 {long, beautiful robe,} Or *a **r** with sleeves,* or *an ornamented **r**.* The meaning of the Hebrew is uncertain.
Mt 27:35 {by throwing dice.} Greek *by casting lots.* A few late manuscripts add *This fulfilled the word of the prophet: "They divided my clothes among themselves and cast lots for my **r**."* See Ps 22:18.

ROCK (2)

Mt 16:18 {you are Peter,} *Peter* means "stone" or "**r**."
Jn 1:42 {(which means Peter} The names *Cephas* and *Peter* both mean "**r**."

ROCKS (1)

Mt 27:51[-53] {to many people.} Or *The earth shook, **r** split apart, tombs opened, and many bodies of godly men and women who had died were raised from the dead. After Jesus' resurrection, they left the cemetery, went into the holy city of Jerusalem, and appeared to many people.*

ROD (5)

Pr 14: 3 {for their backs,} Hebrew *a **r** of pride.*
Eze 40: 6 {10 1/2 feet deep.} Greek version; Hebrew reads *1 **r*** [10.5 feet or 3.2 meters] *deep, and one threshold, one **r** deep.*
40: 8 {of the gateway} Many Hebrew manuscripts add *which faced inward toward the Temple; it was one **r*** [10.5 feet or 3.2 meters] *deep. [9]Then he measured the foyer of the gateway,...*

Mic 6: 9 {is sending them.} Hebrew *"Listen to the r. Who appointed it?"*

ROLE (1)
1Ti 2:15 {saved through childbearing} Or *will be saved by accepting their r as mothers,* or *will be saved by the birth of the Child.*

ROLL (1)
Jos 5: 9 {been called Gilgal} *Gilgal* sounds like the Hebrew word *galal,* meaning "to **r**."

ROMAN (2)
Ac 28:11 {the twin gods} The *twin gods* were the **R** gods Castor and Pollux.
1Co 16:19 {province of Asia} *Asia* was a **R** province in what is now western Turkey.

ROME (3)
Ac 28:15 {at the Forum} *The Forum* was about 43 miles (70 kilometers) from **R**.
28:15 {The Three Taverns.} *The Three Taverns* was about 35 miles (57 kilometers) from **R**.
1Pe 5:13 {here in Rome} Greek *The elect one in Babylon.* Babylon was probably a code name for **R**.

ROOF (3)
Mt 24:17 {outside the house} Greek *on the r.*
Mk 13:15 {outside the house} Greek *on the r.*
Lk 17:31 {outside the house} Greek *on the r.*

ROOMS (1)
Eze 45: 5 {for their towns.} As in Greek version; Hebrew reads *They will have as their possession 20 r.*

ROOSTER (1)
Mk 14:68 {a rooster crowed.} Some manuscripts do not include *Just then, a r crowed.*

ROOT (4)
Isa 11:10 {to David's throne} Hebrew *the r of Jesse.*
Ro 15:12 {to David's throne} Greek *The r of Jesse.*
Rev 5: 5 {to David's throne,} Greek *the r of David.*
22:16 {to his throne.} Greek *I am the r and offspring of David.*

ROOTS (1)
Da 11: 7 {of her relatives} Hebrew *a branch from her r.*

ROSE (1)
Eze 3:12 {in his place!)} A likely reading for this verse is *Then the Spirit lifted me up, and as the glory of the LORD r from its place, I heard behind me a loud rumbling sound.*

ROUSE (1)
Job 3: 8 {the sea monster} Hebrew *r Leviathan.*

ROYAL (3)
2Sa 14:26 {to five pounds!} Hebrew *200 shekels* [2.3 kilograms] *by the r standard.*
SS 6:12 {my beloved one.} Or *among the r chariots of my people,* or *among the chariots of Amminadab.* The meaning of the Hebrew is uncertain.
Mt 2: 1 {some wise men} Or *r astrologers,* Greek *magi;* also in 2:7, 16.

RUE (1)
Lk 11:42 {of your income,} Greek *to tithe the mint and the r and every herb.*

RUGGED (1)
Nu 21:24 {Ammonites was fortified.} Or *because the terrain of the Ammonite frontier was r;* Hebrew *because the boundary of the Ammonites was strong.*

RUIN (1)
Jos 8:28 {So Ai} *Ai* means "**r**."

RULE (1)
1Sa 10: 1 {his people Israel.} Greek version reads *Israel. And you will r over the LORD's people and save them from their enemies around them. This will be the sign to you that the LORD has appointed you to be leader over his inheritance.*

RULED (2)
Ge 36:31 {kings in Israel} Or *before an Israelite king r over them.*
1Ch 1:43 {kings in Israel} Or *before an Israelite king r over them.*

RULER (1)
1Co 15:24 {of every kind.} Greek *every r and every authority and power.*

RULERS (2)
Mt 14: 1 {When Herod Antipas} Greek *Herod the tetrarch.* He was a son of King Herod and was one of four **r** in Palestine.
Lk 9: 7 {reached Herod Antipas,} Greek *Herod the tetrarch.* He was a son of King Herod and was one of four **r** in Palestine.

RULES (1)
Ro 9: 5 {eternal praise! Amen.} Or *May God, who r over everything, be praised forever. Amen.*

RUMBLING (1)
Eze 3:12 {in his place!)} A likely reading for this verse is *Then the Spirit lifted me up, and as the glory of the LORD rose from its place, I heard behind me a loud r sound.*

RUN (1)
Lk 16: 9 {you in heaven.} Or *Then when you r out at the end of this life, your friends will welcome you into eternal homes.*

RUTH (2)
1Ch 2:11 {father of Salmon.} As in Greek version (see also **R** 4:21); Hebrew reads *Salma.*
Lk 3:32 {son of Salmon.} Greek *Sala;* see **R** 4:22.

S

SABBATH (4)
Ne 13:19 {every Friday evening,} Hebrew *on the day before the S.*
Mt 28: 1 {on Sunday morning,} Greek *After the S, on the first day of the week.*
Ac 1:12 {the half mile} Greek *a S day's journey.*
Heb 4: 9 {special rest} Or *S rest.*

SABEANS (1)
Joel 3: 8 {peoples of Arabia,} Hebrew *to the S.*

SACAR (1)
1Ch 11:35 {son of Sharar} As in parallel text at 2 Sam 23:33; Hebrew reads *son of S.*

SACRED (4)
Mt 7: 6 {to unholy people.} Greek *Don't give the s to dogs.*
Ro 16:16 {in Christian love.} Greek *with a s kiss.*
1Co 16:20 {in Christian love.} Greek *with a s kiss.*
2Co 13:12 {in Christian love.} Greek *with a s kiss.*

SACRIFICE (3)
Zep 1: 7 {chosen their executioners.} Hebrew *has prepared a s and sanctified his guests.*
Mk 9:49 {purified with fire.} Greek *salted with fire.* Some manuscripts add *and every s will be salted with salt.*
Heb 9:16 {is dead.} Or *Now when someone makes a covenant, it is necessary to ratify it with the death of a s.*

SADDLEBAGS (1)
Ge 49:14 {among the sheepfolds.} Or *s,* or *hearths.*

SAIL (2)
2Ch 9:21 {of trading ships} Hebrew *fleet of ships that could s to Tarshish.*
20:37 {out to sea.} Hebrew *never set s for Tarshish.*

SAINTS (3)
2Co 9: 1 {Christians in Jerusalem.} Greek *about the offering for the s.*
1Ti 5:10 {other Christians humbly?} Greek *Has she washed the feet of s?*
Rev 15: 3 {of the nations.} Some manuscripts read *King of the ages;* other manuscripts read *King of the s.*

SAIS (1)
2Ki 17: 4 {So of Egypt} Or *by asking the king of Egypt at S.*

SALA (1)
Lk 3:32 {son of Salmon.} Greek *S;* see Ruth 4:22.

SALEM (1)
Ps 76: 2 {Jerusalem} Hebrew *S,* another name for Jerusalem.

SALLAI (1)
Ne 12:20 {family of Sallu.} Hebrew *S;* compare 12:7.

SALMA (1)
1Ch 2:11 {father of Salmon.} As in Greek version (see also Ruth 4:21); Hebrew reads *S.*

SALT (10)
Ge 14: 3 {the Dead Sea} Hebrew *S Sea.*
Nu 18:19 {an unbreakable covenant} Hebrew *a covenant of s.*
34: 3 {the Dead Sea.} Hebrew *S Sea;* also in 34:12.
Dt 3:17 {the Dead Sea,} Hebrew *from Kinnereth to the sea of the Arabah, the S Sea.*
Jos 3:16 {the Dead Sea} Hebrew *the sea of the Arabah, the S Sea.*
12: 3 {the Dead Sea,} Hebrew *the sea of the Arabah, the S Sea.*
15: 2 {the Dead Sea,} Hebrew *the S Sea;* also in 15:5.
18:19 {the Dead Sea,} Hebrew *S Sea.*
2Ch 13: 5 {an unbreakable covenant} Hebrew *a covenant of s.*
Mk 9:49 {purified with fire.} Greek *salted with fire.* Some manuscripts add *and every sacrifice will be salted with s.*

SALTED (2)
Mk 9:49 {purified with fire.} Greek *s with fire.* Some manuscripts add *and every sacrifice will be s with salt.*

SALVATION (2)
Nu 13:16 {name to Joshua.} *Hoshea* (see 13:8) means "s"; *Joshua* means "The LORD is s."

SAM (36)
2Sa 3:15 {her husband Palti} As in 1S 25:44; Hebrew reads *Paltiel,* a variant name for Palti.
21: 8 {Saul's daughter Merab,} As in a few Hebrew and Greek manuscripts and Syriac version (see also 1 S 18:19); most Hebrew manuscripts read *Michal.*
1Ch 3: 1 {second was Kileab,} As in parallel text at 2S 3:3; Hebrew reads *Daniel.*
3: 6 {sons: Ibhar, Elishua,} As in some Hebrew and Greek manuscripts (see also 14:5-7 and 2S 5:15); most Hebrew manuscripts read *Elishama.*
6:28 {Samuel were Joel} As in some Greek manuscripts and the Syriac version (see also 6:33 and 1S 8:2); Hebrew lacks *Joel.*
11:11 {among David's men.} As in some Greek manuscripts (see also 2S 23:8); Hebrew *commander of the Thirty,* or *commander of the captains.*
11:12 {son of Dodai,} As in parallel text at 2S 23:9 (see also 1 Chr 27:4); Hebrew reads *Dodo,* a variant name for Dodai.
11:27 {Shammah from Harod;} As in parallel text at 2S 23:25; Hebrew reads *Shammoth from Haror.*
11:29 {Zalmon} As in parallel text at 2S 23:28; Hebrew reads *Ilai.*
11:32 {Abi-albon} As in parallel text at 2S 23:31; Hebrew reads *Abiel.*
11:33 {Azmaveth from Bahurim} As in parallel text at 2 S 23:31; Hebrew reads *Baharum.*
11:34 {sons of Jashen} As in parallel text at 2S 23:32; Hebrew reads *sons of Hashem.*
11:35 {son of Sharar} As in parallel text at 2S 23:33; Hebrew reads *son of Sacar.*
11:37 {Paarai} As in parallel text at 2S 23:35; Hebrew reads *Naarai.*
13: 9 {floor of Nacon,} As in parallel text at 2S 6:6; Hebrew reads *Kidon.*
14: 7 {Elishama, Eliada,} Hebrew *Beeliada,* a variant name for Eliada; compare 3:8 and parallel text at 2 S 5:16.
14:12 {abandoned their idols} Hebrew *their gods;* compare parallel text at 2 S 5:21.
17: 6 {to Israel's leaders,} As in Greek version (see also 2 S 7:7); Hebrew reads *judges.*
18: 8 {cities of Tebah} Hebrew reads *Tibhath,* a variant name for Tebah; compare parallel text at 2S 8:8.
18: 9 {When King Toi} As in parallel text at 2S 8:9; Hebrew reads *Tou;* also in 18:10.
18:10 {his son Joram} As in parallel text at 2S 8:10; Hebrew reads *Hadoram,* a variant name for Joram.
18:16 {Ahimelech} As in some Hebrew manuscripts, Syriac version, and Latin Vulgate (see also 2S 8:17); most Hebrew manuscripts read *Abimelech.*
18:16 {Seraiah} As in parallel text at 2S 8:17; Hebrew reads *Shavsha.*
19: 1 {his son Hanun} Hebrew lacks *Hanun;* compare parallel text at 2S 10:1.
19:16 {command of Shobach,} As in parallel text at 2S 10:16; Hebrew reads *Shophach;* also in 19:18.
20: 3 {picks, and axes.} As in parallel text at 2S 12:31; Hebrew reads *and saws.*
20: 4 {Hushah killed Saph,} As in parallel text at 2S 21:18; Hebrew reads *Sippai.*
21:15 {floor of Araunah} As in parallel text at 2S 24:16; Hebrew reads *Ornan,* another name for Araunah; also in 21:18-28.
27: 8 {Shammah} Hebrew *Shamhuth,* another name for Shammah; compare 11:27 and 2S 23:25.
27:15 {Heled,} Hebrew *Heldai,* a variant name for Heled; compare 11:30 and 2S 23:29.
2Ch 3: 1 {floor of Araunah} Hebrew reads *Ornan,* another name for Araunah; compare 2S 24:16.
Ps 18:13 {a mighty shout.} As in Greek version (see also 2 S 22:14); Hebrew adds *raining down hail and burning coals.*
Mt 2: 6 {my people Israel.'} Mic 5:2; 2S 5:2.
Ac 13:22 {want him to.'} 1S 13:14.

2Co 6:18 {the Lord Almighty.} 2**S** 7:14.
Heb 1: 5 {be my Son."} 2**S** 7:14.

SAMARIA (1)

2Ki 17:26 {towns of Israel} Hebrew *of S;* also in 17:29.

SAMARITAN (11)

Ge 36:39 {Baal-hanan died, Hadad} As in some Hebrew manuscripts, **S** Pentateuch, and Syriac version (see also 1 Chr 1:50); most Hebrew manuscripts read *Hadar.*
46:13 {Puah,} As in Syriac version and **S** Pentateuch (see also 1 Chr 7:1); Hebrew reads *Puvah.*
46:13 {Jashub,} As in some Greek manuscripts and **S** Pentateuch (see also Num 26:24; 1 Chr 7:1); Hebrew reads *Iob.*
46:16 {Zephon,} As in Greek version and **S** Pentateuch (see also Num 26:15); Hebrew reads *Ziphion.*
47:21 {servants to Pharaoh.} As in Greek version and **S** Pentateuch; Hebrew reads *He moved the people into the towns throughout the land of Egypt.*
Nu 2:14[-15] {son of Deuel} As in many Hebrew manuscripts, **S** Pentateuch, and Latin Vulgate (see also 1:14); most Hebrew manuscripts read *son of Reuel.*
26:17 {its ancestor Arodi.} As in **S** Pentateuch and Syriac version (see also Gen 46:16); Hebrew reads *Arod.*
26:23 {its ancestor Puah.} As in **S** Pentateuch, Greek and Syriac versions, and Latin Vulgate (see also 1 Chr 7:1); Hebrew reads *The Punite clan, named after its ancestor Puvah.*
26:39 {its ancestor Shupham.} As in some Hebrew manuscripts, **S** Pentateuch, Greek and Syriac versions, and Latin Vulgate; most Hebrew manuscripts read *Shephupham.*
26:40 {their ancestor Ard.} As in **S** Pentateuch, some Greek manuscripts, and Latin Vulgate; Hebrew lacks *named after their ancestor Ard.*
Dt 34: 6 {He was buried} Hebrew *He buried him,* that is, "The LORD buried him." **S** Pentateuch and some Greek manuscripts read *They buried him.*

SAME (11)

Lev 13:47 {an infectious mildew} Traditionally rendered *leprosy.* The Hebrew term used throughout this passage is the **s** term used for the various skin diseases described in 13:1-46.
23: 6 {the Passover celebration,} Hebrew *On the fifteenth day of the s month.*
1Ki 7:13 {man named Huram} Hebrew *Hiram* (also in 7:40, 45); compare 2 Chr 2:13. This is not the **s** person mentioned in 5:1.
Ne 9: 1 {On October 31} Hebrew *On the twenty-fourth day of that s month,* the seventh month of the Hebrew calendar. This event occurred on October 31, 445 B.C.; also see note on 1:1.
Ecc 3:19 {the same air,} Or *both have the s spirit.*
Jer 28:17 {Two months later,} Hebrew *In the seventh month of that s year.* See 28:1 and the note there.
Mt 1: 7 {father of Asaph.} *Asaph* is the **s** person as Asa; also in 1:8. See 1 Chr 3:10.
1:10 {father of Amos.} *Amos* is the **s** person as Amon. See 1 Chr 3:14.
Lk 3:33 {son of Arni.} *Arni* is the **s** person as Ram; see 1 Chr 2:9-10.
1Ti 3: 6 {make him fall.} Or *he might fall into the s judgment as the Devil.*
Rev 4: 5 {the seven spirits} See 1:4 and 3:1, where the **s** expression is translated *the sevenfold Spirit.*

SAMGAR-NEBO (1)

Jer 39: 3 {Samgar, and Nebo-sarsekim,} Or *Nergal-sharezer, S, Sarsekim.*

SAMSON (1)

1Sa 12:11 {Jephthah, and Samuel} Greek and Syriac versions read *S.*

SAMUEL (3)

1Sa 1:20 {named him Samuel,} *S* sounds like the Hebrew term for "asked of God" or "heard by God."
13:15 {land of Benjamin.} As in Greek version; Hebrew reads *S left Gilgal and went to Gibeah in the land of Benjamin.*
1Ch 6:27 {Elkanah, and Samuel.} As in some Greek manuscripts (see also 6:33-34); Hebrew lacks *and S.*

SANCTIFIED (1)

Zep 1: 7 {chosen their executioners.} Hebrew *has prepared a sacrifice and s his guests.*

SANCTUARY (3 of 16)

1Ch 23:32 {and the Temple} Hebrew *the Tent of Meeting and the s.*
Ps 60: 6 {by his holiness} Or *in his s.*
108: 7 {by his holiness} Or *in his s.*

SANDALS (5)

Mt 3:11 {be his slave.} Greek *to carry his s.*
Mk 1: 7 {be his slave.} Greek *to stoop down and untie his s.*
Lk 3:16 {be his slave.} Greek *to untie his s.*
Jn 1:27 {be his slave.} Greek *to untie his s.*
Ac 13:25 {be his slave.} Greek *to untie his s.*

SANG (1)

2Ch 30:21 {by loud instruments.} Or *s to the LORD with all their strength.*

SANHEDRIN (11)

Mt 26:59 {entire high council} Greek *the S.*
Mk 14:55 {entire high council} Greek *the S.*
15: 1 {entire high council} Greek *the S;* also in 15:43.
Lk 22:66 {this high council,} Greek *before their S.*
Jn 11:47 {the high council} Greek *the S.*
Ac 4:15 {the council chamber} Greek *the S.*
5:21 {the high council,} Greek *S;* also in 5:27, 41.
6:12 {the high council.} Greek *S;* also in 6:15.
22:30 {Jewish high council.} Greek *S.*
23: 1 {the high council,} Greek *S;* also in 23:6, 15, 20, 28.
24:20 {Jewish high council} Greek *S.*

SARAH (3)

Ge 17:15 {call her Sarah.} *S* means "princess."
Heb 11:11 {keep his promise.} Some manuscripts read *It was by faith that S was able to have a child, even though she was too old and barren. S believed that God would keep his promise.*

SARSEKIM (1)

Jer 39: 3 {Samgar, and Nebo-sarsekim,} Or *Nergal-sharezer, Samgar-nebo, S.*

SAT (1)

Mt 21: 7 {sat on it.} Greek *over them, and he s on them.*

SATAN (1)

Jn 12:31 {of this world} *The prince of this world* is a name for **S**.

SATAN'S (2)

Mt 12:29 {house be robbed!} Or *One cannot rob S kingdom without first tying him up. Only then can his demons be cast out.*
Mk 3:27 {house be robbed!} Or *One cannot rob S kingdom without first tying him up. Only then can his demons be cast out.*

SAUL (2)

2Sa 21: 6 {of the LORD.} As in Greek version (see also 21:9); Hebrew reads *at Gibeah of S, the chosen of the LORD.*
Ac 7:58 {man named Saul.} *S* is later called Paul; see 13:9.

SAVE (9)

1Sa 10: 1 {his people Israel.} Greek version reads *Israel. And you will rule over the LORD's people and s them from their enemies around them. This will be the sign to you that the LORD has appointed you to be leader over his inheritance.*
Isa 8:18 {me have names} *Isaiah* means "The LORD will s"; *Shear-jashub* means "A remnant will return"; and *Maher-shalal-hash-baz* means "Swift to plunder and quick to spoil."
Zec 10: 6 {and save Israel} Hebrew *s the house of Joseph.*
Mt 18:10 {my heavenly Father.} Some manuscripts add verse 11, *And I, the Son of Man, have come to s the lost.*
21: 9 {"Praise God} Greek *Hosanna,* an exclamation of praise that literally means "**s** now"; also in 21:9b, 15.
Mk 11: 9 {"Praise God!} Greek *Hosanna,* an exclamation of praise that literally means "**s** now"; also in 11:10.
Lk 9:55 {and rebuked them.} Some manuscripts add *And he said, "You don't realize what your hearts are like. [56]For the Son of Man has not come to destroy men's lives, but to s them."*
Jn 12:13 {"Praise God!} Greek *Hosanna,* an exclamation of praise that literally means "**s** now."
Heb 7:25 {forever, to save} Or *able to s completely.*

SAVED (4)

1Ti 2:15 {saved through childbearing} Or *will be s by accepting their role as mothers,* or *will be s by the birth of the Child.*
Tit 3: 5 {the Holy Spirit.} Greek *He s us through the washing of regeneration and renewing of the Holy Spirit.*
1Pe 3:20 {that terrible flood.} Greek *s through water.*

SAVES (1)

Mt 1:21 {name him Jesus,} *Jesus* means "The LORD **s**."

SAWS (1)

1Ch 20: 3 {picks, and axes.} As in parallel text at 2 Sam 12:31; Hebrew reads *and s.*

SAYING (1)

2Sa 5: 8 {enter the house."} The meaning of this **s** is uncertain.

SCALES (1)

Eze 45:10 {liquid volume measures.} Hebrew *use honest s, an honest ephah, and an honest bath.*

SCARLET (2)

Ge 38:30 {was named Zerah.} *Zerah* means "**s**" or "brightness."
Pr 31:21 {them have warm} As in Greek version; Hebrew *s.*

SCARS (1)

Zec 13: 6 {on your chest} Or *s between your hands.*

SCHOLARS (1)

Eze 26: 1 {King Jehoiachin's captivity,} Hebrew *In the eleventh year, on the first day of the month,* of the Hebrew calendar year. Since an element is missing in the date formula here, **s** have reconstructed this probable reading: *On the first day of the eleventh month, during the twelfth year.* This reading would put this message on February 3, 585 B.C.; also see note on 1:1.

SCRIBAL (1)

Job 32: 3 {had condemned God} As in ancient Hebrew **s** tradition; the Masoretic Text makes no reference to God.

SCRIBES (1)

Mk 2:16 {who were Pharisees} Greek *the s of the Pharisees.*

SCRIPTURE (1)

Mk 15:27 {side of his.} Some manuscripts add verse 28, *And the S was fulfilled that said, "He was counted among those who were rebels."* See Isa 53:12.

SCRIPTURES (2)

Mt 22:31 {died, God said,} Greek *in the S? God said.*
Jn 7:37[-38] {out from within."} Or *"Let anyone who is thirsty come to me and drink. [38]For the S declare that rivers of living water will flow from the heart of those who believe in me."*

SCROLL (2)

1Sa 10:27 {Saul ignored them.} Dead Sea **S** 4QSam[a] continues: *Nahash, king of the Ammonites, had been grievously oppressing the Gadites…*
Hab 2: 5 {Wealth} As in Dead Sea **S** 1QpHab; other Hebrew manuscripts read *Wine.*

SCROLLS (15)

Ex 1: 5 {Jacob had seventy} Dead Sea **S** and Greek version read *seventy-five;* see notes on Gen 46:27.
Dt 31: 1 {had finished saying} As in Dead Sea **S** and Greek version; Masoretic Text reads *Moses went and spoke.*
32: 8 {of angelic beings.} As in Dead Sea **S**, which read *of the sons of God,* and Greek version, which reads *of the angels of god;* Masoretic Text reads *of the sons of Israel.*
32:43 {God worship him,} As in Dead Sea **S** and Greek version; Masoretic Text reads *Rejoice with his people, O nations.*
1Sa 1:24 {a three-year-old bull} As in Dead Sea **S**, Greek and Syriac versions; Hebrew reads *3 bulls.*
2:33 {a violent death.} As in Dead Sea **S**, which read *die by the sword;* Masoretic Text reads *die like mortals.*
11: 8 {addition to 30,000} Dead Sea **S** and Greek version read *70,000.*
15:32 {have been spared!"} Dead Sea **S** and Greek version read *Agag arrived hesitantly, for he thought, "Surely this is the bitterness of death."*
2Sa 22:36 {your help} As in Dead Sea **S**; most Hebrew manuscripts read *your answering.*
Isa 15: 9 {stream near Dibon} As in Dead Sea **S**, some Greek manuscripts, and Latin Vulgate; Hebrew reads *Dimon;* also in 15:9b.
21: 8 {Then the watchman} As in Dead Sea **S** and Syriac version; Hebrew reads *a lion.*
33: 8 {made before witnesses.} As in Dead Sea **S**; Masoretic Text reads *care nothing for the cities.*
45: 2 {level the mountains.} As in Dead Sea **S** and Greek version; Masoretic Text reads *the swellings.*
49:12 {south as Egypt.} As in Dead Sea **S**, which read *from the region of Aswan,* which is in southern Egypt. Masoretic Text reads *from the region of Sinim.*
49:24 {that a tyrant} As in Dead Sea **S**, Syriac version, and Latin Vulgate (also see 49:25); Masoretic Text reads *a righteous person.*

SCYTHIAN (1)

Col 3:11 {uncircumcised, barbaric, uncivilized,} Greek *Barbarian, S.*

SEA (101)

Ge 14: 3 {the Dead Sea} Hebrew *Salt S.*
Ex 1: 5 {Jacob had seventy} Dead **S** Scrolls and Greek version read *seventy-five;* see notes on Gen 46:27.
10:19 {the Red Sea.} Hebrew *s of reeds.*
13:18 {the Red Sea,} Hebrew *s of reeds.*

15: 4 {the Red Sea.} Hebrew *s of reeds;* also in 15:22.
23:31 {the Mediterranean Sea,} Hebrew *from the s of reeds to the s of the Philistines.*
Nu 13:29 {the Mediterranean Sea} Hebrew *the s.*
14:25 {the Red Sea.} Hebrew *s of reeds.*
21: 4 {the Red Sea} Hebrew *s of reeds.*
33: 8 {the Red Sea} Hebrew *the s.*
33:10 {the Red Sea.} Hebrew *s of reeds;* also in 33:11.
34: 3 {the Dead Sea.} Hebrew *Salt S;* also in 34:12.
34: 5 {the Mediterranean Sea.} Hebrew *the s;* also in 34:6, 7.
34:11 {Sea of Galilee,} Hebrew *s of Kinnereth.*
Dt 1:40 {the Red Sea.} Hebrew *s of reeds.*
2: 1 {the Red Sea,} Hebrew *s of reeds.*
3:17 {the Dead Sea,} Hebrew *from Kinnereth to the s of the Arabah, the Salt S.*
4:49 {the Dead Sea,} Hebrew *took the Arabah on the east side of the Jordan as far as the s of the Arabah.*
11: 4 {the Red Sea} Hebrew *s of reeds.*
11:24 {in the west.} Hebrew *to the western s.*
31: 1 {had finished saying} As in Dead S Scrolls and Greek version; Masoretic Text reads *Moses went and spoke.*
32: 8 {of angelic beings.} As in Dead S Scrolls, which read *of the sons of God,* and Greek version, which reads *of the angels of god;* Masoretic Text reads *of the sons of Israel.*
32:43 {God worship him,} As in Dead S Scrolls and Greek version; Masoretic Text reads *Rejoice with his people, O nations.*
34: 2 {the Mediterranean Sea} Hebrew *the western s.*
Jos 1: 4 {the Mediterranean Sea} Hebrew *the Great S.*
2:10 {the Red Sea} Hebrew *s of reeds.*
3:16 {the Dead Sea} Hebrew *the s of the Arabah, the Salt S.*
4:23 {the Red Sea} Hebrew *s of reeds.*
5: 1 {the Mediterranean coast} Hebrew *along the s.*
9: 1 {the Mediterranean Sea} Hebrew *the Great S.*
12: 3 {Sea of Galilee} Hebrew *s of Kinnereth.*
12: 3 {the Dead Sea,} Hebrew *the s of the Arabah, the Salt S.*
13:27 {Sea of Galilee.} Hebrew *s of Kinnereth.*
15: 2 {the Dead Sea,} Hebrew *the Salt S;* also in 15:5.
15: 4 {the Mediterranean Sea.} Hebrew *the s;* also in 15:11.
15:12 {the Mediterranean Sea.} Hebrew *the Great S;* also in 15:47.
16: 3 {the Mediterranean Sea.} Hebrew *the s;* also in 16:6, 8.
17: 9 {the Mediterranean Sea.} Hebrew *the s;* also in 17:10.
18:19 {the Dead Sea,} Hebrew *Salt S.*
19:29 {the Mediterranean Sea} Hebrew *the s.*
23: 4 {the Mediterranean Sea} Hebrew *the Great S.*
24: 6 {the Red Sea,} Hebrew *s of reeds.*
Jdg 11:16 {the Red Sea,} Hebrew *s of reeds.*
1Sa 1:24 {a three-year-old bull} As in Dead S Scrolls, Greek and Syriac versions; Hebrew reads *3 bulls.*
2:33 {a violent death.} As in Dead S Scrolls, which read *die by the sword;* Masoretic Text reads *die like mortals.*
10:27 {Saul ignored them.} Dead S Scroll 4QSam[a] continues: *Nahash, king of the Ammonites, had been grievously oppressing the Gadites…*
11: 8 {addition to 30,000} Dead S Scrolls and Greek version read *70,000.*
15:32 {have been spared!"} Dead S Scrolls and Greek version read *Agag arrived hesitantly, for he thought, "Surely this is the bitterness of death."*
2Sa 22:36 {your help} As in Dead S Scrolls; most Hebrew manuscripts read *your answering.*
1Ki 9:26 {the Red Sea.} Hebrew *s of reeds.*
2Ki 14:25 {the Dead Sea,} Hebrew *the s of the Arabah.*
2Ch 8:17 {the Red Sea.} Hebrew *the s.*
20: 2 {the Dead Sea.} Hebrew *the s.*
Ne 9: 9 {the Red Sea.} Hebrew *s of reeds.*
Job 9:13 {forces against him} Hebrew *The helpers of Rahab,* the name of a mythical s monster that represents chaos in ancient literature.
26:12 {great sea monster.} Hebrew *Rahab,* the name of a mythical s monster that represents chaos in ancient literature.
Ps 66: 6 {the Red Sea,} Hebrew *the s.*
80:11 {the Euphrates River.} Hebrew *west to the s,…east to the river.*
87: 4 {will record Egypt} Hebrew *Rahab,* the name of a mythical s monster that represents chaos in ancient literature. The name is used here as a poetic name for Egypt.
89:10 {great sea monster.} Hebrew *Rahab,* the name of a mythical s monster that represents chaos in ancient literature.
89:25 {in the east.} Hebrew *I will set his hand on the s, his right hand on the rivers.*
106: 7 {the Red Sea.} Hebrew *at the s, the s of reeds.*
106: 9 {the Red Sea} Hebrew *s of reeds;* also in 106:22.
114: 3 {The Red Sea} Hebrew *the s;* also in 114:5.
136:13 {the Red Sea.} Hebrew *s of reeds;* also in 136:15.
Isa 11:15 {the Red Sea.} Hebrew *s of Egypt.*
15: 9 {stream near Dibon} As in Dead S Scrolls, some Greek manuscripts, and Latin Vulgate; Hebrew reads *Dimon;* also in 15:9b.
16: 8 {the Dead Sea.} Hebrew *the s.*
21: 1 {land of Babylonia} Hebrew *the desert of the s.*
21: 8 {Then the watchman} As in Dead S Scrolls and Syriac version; Hebrew reads *a lion.*
30: 7 {the Harmless Dragon.} Hebrew *Rahab who sits still.* Rahab is the name of a mythical s monster that represents chaos in ancient literature. The name is used here as a poetic name for Egypt.
33: 8 {made before witnesses.} As in Dead S Scrolls; Masoretic Text reads *care nothing for the cities.*
45: 2 {level the mountains.} As in Dead S Scrolls and Greek version; Masoretic Text reads *the swellings.*
49:12 {south as Egypt.} As in Dead S Scrolls, which read *from the region of Aswan,* which is in southern Egypt. Masoretic Text reads *from the region of Sinim.*
49:24 {that a tyrant} As in Dead S Scrolls, Syriac version, and Latin Vulgate (also see 49:25); Masoretic Text reads *a righteous person.*
51: 9 {of the Nile.} Hebrew *slew Rahab the dragon.* Rahab is the name of a mythical s monster that represents chaos in ancient literature. The name is used here as a poetic name for Egypt.
Jer 48:32 {the Dead Sea,} Hebrew *the s of Jazer.*
49:21 {the Red Sea.} Hebrew *s of reeds.*
Eze 39:11 {the Dead Sea.} Hebrew *the s.*
47: 8 {the Dead Sea.} Hebrew *the s;* also in 47:10.
47:10 {fill the Mediterranean} Hebrew *the great s;* also in 47:15, 17, 19, 20.
47:18 {the Dead Sea} Hebrew *the eastern s.*
48:28 {to the Mediterranean.} Hebrew *the great s.*
Joel 2:20 {into the Mediterranean.} Hebrew *the eastern s;…the western s.*
Hab 2: 5 {Wealth} As in Dead S Scroll 1QpHab; other Hebrew manuscripts read *Wine.*
Zec 9: 4 {the Mediterranean Sea.} Hebrew *the s.*
10:11 {sea of distress,} Or *the s of Egypt,* referring to the Red S.
14: 8 {toward the Mediterranean,} Hebrew *half toward the eastern s and half toward the western s.*
Lk 5: 1 {Sea of Galilee,} Greek *Lake Gennesaret,* another name for the S of Galilee.
Jn 21: 1 {Sea of Galilee.} Greek *S of Tiberias,* another name for the S of Galilee.
Ac 27:27 {Sea of Adria,} The *S of Adria* is in the central Mediterranean; it is not to be confused with the Adriatic S.

SEAH (1)

2Ki 7: 1 {ounce of silver,} Hebrew *1 s* [6 liters] *of fine flour will cost 1 shekel* [11 grams]; also in 7:16, 18.

SEAHS (4)

Ge 18: 6 {Get three measures} Hebrew *3 s,* about 15 quarts or 18 liters.
1Sa 25:18 {nearly a bushel} Hebrew *5 s* [30 liters].
1Ki 18:32 {about three gallons.} Hebrew *2 s* [12 liters] *of seed.*
2Ki 7: 1 {ounce of silver.} Hebrew *2 s* [12 liters] *of barley grain will cost 1 shekel* [11 grams]; also in 7:16, 18.

SEARCHLIGHT (1)

Pr 20:27 {the human spirit,} Or *The human spirit is the LORD's s.*

SEARED (1)

1Ti 4: 2 {consciences are dead.} Greek *are s.*

SEASON (1)

Da 7:12 {a while longer.} Aramaic *for a s and a time.*

SECOND (20)

Ge 8:14 {months went by,} Hebrew *The twenty-seventh day of the s month arrived;* see note on 8:13.
Ex 16: 1 {after leaving Egypt.} Hebrew *on the fifteenth day of the s month.* The Exodus had occurred on the fourteenth day of the first month (see 12:6).
40:17 {the new year.} Hebrew *the first day of the first month, in the s year.* See note on 40:2b.
Nu 1: 1 {day in midspring,} Hebrew *On the first day of the s month.* This day of the Hebrew lunar calendar occurs in April or early May.
1:18 {that very day.} Hebrew *on the first day of the s month;* see 1:1.
9:11 {one month later,} Hebrew *on the fourteenth day of the s month.* This day of the Hebrew lunar calendar occurs in late April or early May.
10:11 {day in midspring,} Hebrew *On the twentieth day of the s month.* This day of the Hebrew lunar calendar occurs in late April or early May.
1Ki 6: 1 {was in midspring,} Hebrew *in the month of Ziv, which is the s month.* This month of the Hebrew lunar calendar usually occurs in April and May.
2Ki 22:14 {newer Mishneh section} Or *the S Quarter,* a newer section of Jerusalem.
2Ch 3: 2 {began in midspring,} Hebrew *on the s day of the s month.* This day of the Hebrew lunar calendar occurs in April or early May.
30: 2 {Passover in midspring.} Hebrew *in the s month.* This month of the Hebrew lunar calendar usually occurs in April and May.
30:13 {Jerusalem in midspring} Hebrew *in the s month.* This month of the Hebrew lunar calendar usually occurs in April and May.
30:15 {day in midspring,} Hebrew *On the fourteenth day of the s month.* This day of the Hebrew lunar calendar occurs in late April or early May.
34:22 {newer Mishneh section} Or *the S Quarter,* a newer section of Jerusalem.
Ezr 3: 8 {began in midspring,} Hebrew *in the s month.* This month of the Hebrew lunar calendar occurred in April and May 536 B.C.
Ne 8:13 {On October 9} Hebrew *On the s day,* of the seventh month of the Hebrew calendar. This event occurred on October 9, 445 B.C.; also see notes on 1:1 and 8:2.
Da 2: 1 {of his reign,} The s year of Nebuchadnezzar's reign was 604 B.C.
Zep 1:10 {newer Mishneh section} Or *the S Quarter,* a newer section of Jerusalem.
Lk 12:38 {just before dawn.} Greek *in the s or third watch.*

SECT (1)

Ac 28:22 {about these Christians} Greek *this s.*

SECTION (4)

2Ki 22:14 {newer Mishneh section} Or *the Second Quarter,* a newer s of Jerusalem.
2Ch 34:22 {newer Mishneh section} Or *the Second Quarter,* a newer s of Jerusalem.
Ps 119: 1 {people of integrity,} This psalm is a Hebrew acrostic poem; there are 22 stanzas, one for each letter of the Hebrew alphabet. The 8 verses within each stanza begin with the Hebrew letter of its s.
Zep 1:10 {newer Mishneh section} Or *the Second Quarter,* a newer s of Jerusalem.

SEE (262)

Ge 8: 4 {the flood began,} Hebrew *on the seventeenth day of the seventh month;* s 7:11.
8: 5 {half months later,} Hebrew *On the first day of the tenth month;* s 7:11 and note on 8:4.
8:13 {the flood began,} Hebrew *on the first day of the first month;* s 7:11.
8:14 {months went by,} Hebrew *The twenty-seventh day of the second month arrived;* s note on 8:13.
10: 4 {Kittim, and Rodanim.} As in some Hebrew manuscripts and Greek version (s also 1 Chr 1:7); most Hebrew manuscripts read *Dodanim.*
14: 8 {the Dead Sea} Hebrew *in Siddim Valley;* s 14:3.
15:18 {border of Egypt} Hebrew *the river of Egypt,* referring either to an eastern branch of the Nile River or to the brook of Egypt in the Sinai (s Num 34:5).
36:39 {Baal-hanan died, Hadad} As in some Hebrew manuscripts, Samaritan Pentateuch, and Syriac version (s also 1 Chr 1:50); most Hebrew manuscripts read *Hadar.*
46:13 {Puah,} As in Syriac version and Samaritan Pentateuch (s also 1 Chr 7:1); Hebrew reads *Puvah.*
46:13 {Jashub,} As in some Greek manuscripts and Samaritan Pentateuch (s also Num 26:24; 1 Chr 7:1); Hebrew reads *Iob.*
46:16 {Zephon,} As in Greek version and Samaritan Pentateuch (s also Num 26:15); Hebrew reads *Ziphion.*
46:27 {had two sons} Greek version reads *nine sons,* probably including Joseph's grandsons through Ephraim and Manasseh (s 1 Chr 7:14-20).
46:27 {there were seventy} Greek version reads *seventy-five;* s note on Exod 1:5.
Ex 1: 5 {Jacob had seventy} Dead Sea Scrolls and Greek version read *seventy-five;* s notes on Gen 46:27.
16: 1 {after leaving Egypt.} Hebrew *on the fifteenth day of the second month.* The Exodus had occurred on the fourteenth day of the first month (s 12:6).
16:31 {known as manna.} *Manna* means "What is it?" S 16:15.
23:16 {the Final Harvest} This was later called the Festival of Shelters; s Lev 23:33-36.
34:22 {the Final Harvest} This was later called the Festival of Shelters; s Lev 23:33-36.
40:17 {the new year.} Hebrew *the first day of the first month, in the second year.* S note on 40:2b.
Lev 14: 2 {contagious skin disease.} Traditionally rendered *leprosy.* S note at 13:2.
14:34 {an infectious mildew.} Traditionally rendered *leprosy.* S note at 13:47.
14:54 {contagious skin disease} Traditionally rendered *leprosy.* S notes at 13:2 and 13:47.
22: 4 {contagious skin disease} Traditionally rendered *leprosy.* S note at 13:2.
23:27 {Festival of Trumpets.} Hebrew *on the tenth day of the seventh month;* s 23:24 and the note there.
23:32 {Day of Atonement} Hebrew *the evening of the ninth day of the month;* s 23:24, 27 and the notes there.
23:34 {Day of Atonement.} Hebrew *on the fifteenth day of the seventh month;* s 23:24, 27 and the notes there.
23:39 {Festival of Shelters,} Hebrew *on the fifteenth day of the seventh month;* s 23:24 and the note there.
25: 9 {the fiftieth year,} Hebrew *on the tenth day of the seventh month, on the Day of Atonement;* s 23:27 and the note there.
Nu 1:18 {that very day.} Hebrew *on the first day of the second month;* s 1:1.
2:14[-15] {son of Deuel} As in many Hebrew manuscripts, Samaritan Pentateuch, and Latin Vulgate (s also 1:14); most Hebrew manuscripts read *son of Reuel.*

3:28 {There were 8,600} Some Greek manuscripts read *8,300;* **s** total in 3:39.
9: 5 {the appointed day.} Hebrew *on the fourteenth day of the first month;* **s** note on 9:3.
13:16 {name to Joshua.} *Hoshea* (**s** 13:8) means "salvation"; *Joshua* means "The LORD is salvation."
26:17 {its ancestor Arodi.} As in Samaritan Pentateuch and Syriac version (**s** also Gen 46:16); Hebrew reads *Arod.*
26:23 {its ancestor Puah.} As in Samaritan Pentateuch, Greek and Syriac versions, and Latin Vulgate (**s** also 1 Chr 7:1); Hebrew reads *The Punite clan, named after its ancestor Puvah.*
29: 7 {"Ten days later,} Hebrew *On the tenth day of the seventh month;* **s** 29:1 and the note there.
29:12 {"Five days later,} Hebrew *On the fifteenth day of the seventh month;* **s** 29:1, 7 and the notes there.
Dt 4:48 {to Mount Sirion,} As in Syriac version (**s** also 3:9); Hebrew reads *Mount Sion.*
9:22 {Taberah,} *Taberah* means "place of burning." **S** Num 11:1-3.
9:22 {Massah,} *Massah* means "place of testing." **S** Exod 17:1-7.
9:22 {and Kibroth-hattaavah.} *Kibroth-hattaavah* means "graves of craving." **S** Num 11:31-34.
33: 8 {the sacred lots} Hebrew *given your Thummim and Urim.* **S** Exod 28:30.
Jos 7: 1 {family of Zimri,} As in Greek version (**s** also 1 Chr 2:6); Hebrew reads *Zabdi.* Also in 7:17, 18.
16: 2 {(that is, Luz)} As in Greek version (also **s** 18:13); Hebrew reads *From Bethel to Luz.*
19:28 {Abdon,} As in some Hebrew manuscripts (**s** also 21:30); most Hebrew manuscripts read *Ebron.*
Jdg 8:29 {Then Gideon} Hebrew *Jerubbaal;* **s** 6:32.
9: 1 {One day Gideon's} Hebrew *Jerubbaal's* (**s** 6:32); also in 9:2, 24.
9:16 {right by Gideon} Hebrew *Jerubbaal* (**s** 6:32); also in 9:19, 28, 57.
9:31 {Abimelech in Arumah,} Hebrew *Tormah;* **s** 9:41.
1Sa 12:11 {LORD sent Gideon,} Hebrew *Jerubbaal,* another name for Gideon; **s** Judg 7:1.
2Sa 5:25 {way from Gibeon} As in Greek version (**s** also 1 Chr 14:16); Hebrew reads *Geba.*
6: 5 {might, singing songs} As in Greek version (**s** also 1 Chr 13:8); Hebrew reads *cypress trees.*
8: 8 {cities of Tebah} As in some Greek manuscripts (**s** also 1 Chr 18:8); Hebrew reads *Betah.*
8:12 {Edom,} As in a few Hebrew manuscripts and Greek and Syriac versions (**s** also 8:14; 1 Chr 18:11); most Hebrew manuscripts read *Aram.*
8:13 {eighteen thousand Edomites} As in a few Hebrew manuscripts and Greek and Syriac versions (**s** also 8:14; 1 Chr 18:12); most Hebrew manuscripts read *Arameans.*
15:27 {the priest, "Look,} As in Greek version; Hebrew reads *Are you a seer?* or *Do you* **s***?*
16:14 {the Jordan River.} As in Greek version (**s** also 17:16); Hebrew reads *when they reached their destination.*
17:25 {an Ishmaelite.} As in some Greek manuscripts (**s** also 1 Chr 2:17); Hebrew reads *an Israelite.*
20:24 {Adoniram} As in Greek version (**s** also 1 Kgs 4:6; 5:14); Hebrew reads *Adoram.*
21: 6 {of the LORD.} As in Greek version (**s** also 21:9); Hebrew reads *at Gibeah of Saul, the chosen of the LORD.*
21: 8 {Saul's daughter Merab,} As in a few Hebrew and Greek manuscripts and Syriac version (**s** also 1 Sam 18:19); most Hebrew manuscripts read *Michal.*
22:11 {soaring} As in some Hebrew manuscripts (**s** also Ps 18:10); other Hebrew manuscripts read *appearing.*
23: 8 {a single battle.} As in some Greek manuscripts (**s** also 1 Chr 11:11); the Hebrew is uncertain, though it might be rendered *the Three. It was Adino the Eznite who killed eight hundred men at one time.*
23:26 {from Pelon} As in parallel text at 1 Chr 11:27 (**s** also 1 Chr 27:10); Hebrew reads *from Palti.*
23:27 {Sibbecai} As in some Greek manuscripts (**s** also 1 Chr 11:29); Hebrew reads *Mebunnai.*
23:29 {Heled} As in some Hebrew manuscripts (**s** also 1 Chr 11:30); most Hebrew manuscripts read *Heleb.*
23:30 {Hurai} As in some Greek manuscripts (**s** also 1 Chr 11:32); Hebrew reads *Hiddai.*
24:13 {you choose three} As in Greek version (**s** also 1 Chr 21:12); Hebrew reads *seven.*
1Ki 4:26 {four thousand} As in some Greek manuscripts (**s** also 2 Chr 9:25); Hebrew reads *40,000.*
5:11 {and 110,000 gallons} As in Greek version, which reads *20,000 baths* [420 kiloliters] (**s** also 2 Chr 2:10); Hebrew reads *20 cors,* about 800 gallons or 3.6 kiloliters in volume.
5:16 {and thirty-six hundred} As in some Greek manuscripts (**s** also 2 Chr 2:2, 18); Hebrew reads *3,300.*
8:65 {Festival of Shelters} Hebrew *the festival;* **s** note on 8:2.
9:26 {port near Elath} As in Greek version (**s** also 2 Kgs 14:22; 16:6); Hebrew reads *Eloth.*
12: 2 {returned from Egypt,} As in Greek version and Latin Vulgate (**s** also 2 Chr 10:2); Hebrew reads *he lived in Egypt.*
12:18 {Rehoboam sent Adoniram,} As in some Greek manuscripts and Syriac version (**s** also 4:6; 5:14); Hebrew reads *Adoram.*
12:32 {day in midautumn,} Hebrew *on the fifteenth day of the eighth month* (also in 12:33). This day of the Hebrew lunar calendar occurs in late October or early November, exactly one month after the annual Festival of Shelters in Judah (**s** Lev 23:34).
2Ki 10: 1 {of the city,} As in some Greek manuscripts and Latin Vulgate (**s** also 10:6); Hebrew reads *of Jezreel.*
25: 3 {Zedekiah's eleventh year,} Hebrew *By the ninth day,* that is, "of the fourth month of Zedekiah's eleventh year" (compare Jer 52:6 and the note there). This event of the Hebrew lunar calendar occurred on July 18, 586 B.C.; also **s** note on 25:1.
25: 8 {of that year,} Hebrew *On the seventh day of the fifth month,* of the Hebrew calendar. This day was August 14, 586 B.C.; also **s** note on 25:1.
25:27 {of that year.} Hebrew *on the twenty-seventh day of the twelfth month,* of the Hebrew calendar. This day was April 2, 560 B.C.; also **s** note on 25:1.
1Ch 1: 4 {of Noah were} As in Greek version (**s** also Gen 5:3-32); Hebrew lacks *The sons of Noah were.*
1: 6 {were Ashkenaz, Riphath,} As in some Hebrew manuscripts and Greek version (**s** also Gen 10:3); most Hebrew manuscripts read *Diphath.*
1:12 {the Philistines came.} Hebrew *Casluhites, from whom the Philistines came, Caphtorites.* **S** Jer 47:4; Amos 9:7.
1:17 {of Aram were} As in one Hebrew manuscript and some Greek manuscripts (**s** also Gen 10:23); most Hebrew manuscripts lack *The descendants of Aram were.*
1:22 {Obal,} As in some Hebrew manuscripts and Syriac version (**s** also Gen 10:28); most Hebrew manuscripts read *Ebal.*
1:24 {Shelah,} Some Greek manuscripts read *Arphaxad, Cainan, Shelah.* **S** notes on Gen 10:24 and 11:12-13.
1:36 {Zepho,} As in many Hebrew manuscripts and a few Greek manuscripts (**s** also Gen 36:11); most Hebrew manuscripts read *Zephi.*
1:36 {born to Timna.} As in some Greek manuscripts (**s** also Gen 36:12); Hebrew reads *Kenaz, Timna, and Amalek.*
1:40 {Alvan,} As in many Hebrew manuscripts and a few Greek manuscripts (**s** also Gen 36:23); most Hebrew manuscripts read *Alian.*
1:40 {Shepho,} As in some Hebrew manuscripts (**s** also Gen 36:23); most Hebrew manuscripts read *Shephi.*
1:41 {Dishon were Hemdan,} As in many Hebrew manuscripts and some Greek manuscripts (**s** also Gen 36:26); most Hebrew manuscripts read *Hamran.*
1:42 {Zaavan, and Akan.} As in many Hebrew and Greek manuscripts (**s** also Gen 36:27); most Hebrew manuscripts read *Jaakan.*
1:50 {city of Pau.} As in many Hebrew manuscripts, some Greek manuscripts, Syriac version, and Latin Vulgate (**s** also Gen 36:39); most Hebrew manuscripts read *Pai.*
2: 6 {Calcol, and Darda} As in many Hebrew manuscripts, some Greek manuscripts, and Syriac version (**s** also 1 Kgs 4:31); Hebrew reads *Dara.*
2:11 {father of Salmon.} As in Greek version (**s** also Ruth 4:21); Hebrew reads *Salma.*
3: 6 {sons: Ibhar, Elishua,} As in some Hebrew and Greek manuscripts (**s** also 14:5-7 and 2 Sam 5:15); most Hebrew manuscripts read *Elishama.*
4:33 {away as Baalath.} As in some Greek manuscripts (**s** also Josh 19:8); Hebrew reads *Baal.*
6:16 {Levi were Gershon,} Hebrew *Gershom,* a variant name for Gershon (**s** 6:1); also in 6:17, 20, 43, 62, 71.
6:27 {Elkanah, and Samuel.} As in some Greek manuscripts (**s** also 6:33-34); Hebrew lacks *and Samuel.*
6:28 {Samuel were Joel} As in some Greek manuscripts and the Syriac version (**s** also 6:33 and 1 Sam 8:2); Hebrew lacks *Joel.*
6:39 {clan of Gershon.} Hebrew lacks *from the clan of Gershon;* **s** 6:43.
6:59 {Juttah,} As in Syriac version (**s** also Josh 21:16); Hebrew lacks *Juttah.*
6:77 {of Jokneam, Kartah,} As in Greek version (**s** also Josh 21:34); Hebrew lacks *Jokneam, Kartah.*
7:13 {Jezer, and Shillem.} As in some Hebrew and Greek manuscripts (**s** also Gen 46:24; Num 26:49); most Hebrew manuscripts read *Shallum.*
8:29 {Jeiel} As in some Greek manuscripts (**s** also 9:35); Hebrew lacks *Jeiel.*
8:30 {Kish, Baal, Ner,} As in some Greek manuscripts (**s** also 9:36); Hebrew lacks *Ner.*
9:41 {Tahrea, and Ahaz.} As in Syriac version and Latin Vulgate (**s** also 8:35); Hebrew lacks *and Ahaz.*
9:42 {father of Jadah.} As in some Hebrew manuscripts and Greek version (**s** also 8:36); Hebrew reads *Jarah.*
11:11 {among David's men.} As in some Greek manuscripts (**s** also 2 Sam 23:8); Hebrew *commander of the Thirty,* or *commander of the captains.*
11:12 {son of Dodai,} As in parallel text at 2 Sam 23:9 (**s** also 1 Chr 27:4); Hebrew reads *Dodo,* a variant name for Dodai.
16:15 {by his covenant} As in some Greek manuscripts (**s** also Ps 105:8); Hebrew reads *Remember his covenant forever.*
17: 6 {to Israel's leaders,} As in Greek version (**s** also 2 Sam 7:7); Hebrew reads *judges.*
18:16 {Ahitub and Ahimelech} As in some Hebrew manuscripts, Syriac version, and Latin Vulgate (**s** also 2 Sam 8:17); most Hebrew manuscripts read *Abimelech.*
23:10 {were Jahath, Ziza,} As in Greek version and Latin Vulgate (**s** also 23:11); Hebrew reads *Zina.*
25: 3 {Zeri, Jeshaiah, Shimei,} As in one Hebrew manuscript and some Greek manuscripts (**s** also 25:17); most Hebrew manuscripts lack *Shimei.*
2Ch 3:15 {that were 27 feet} As in Syriac version (**s** also 1 Kgs 7:15; 2 Kgs 25:17; Jer 52:21), which reads *18 cubits* [8.1 meters]; Hebrew reads *35 cubits,* which is 52.5 feet or 15.8 meters.
7: 8 {Festival of Shelters} Hebrew *the festival* (also in 7:9); **s** note on 5:3.
8:17 {Ezion-geber and Elath,} As in Greek version (**s** also 2 Kgs 14:22; 16:6); Hebrew reads *Eloth.*
13: 2 {mother was Maacah,} As in most Greek manuscripts and Syriac version (**s** also 2 Chr 11:20-21; 1 Kgs 15:2); Hebrew reads *Micaiah.*
15: 8 {Azariah the prophet,} As in Syriac version and Latin Vulgate (**s** also 15:1); Hebrew reads *from Oded the prophet.*
20: 1 {of the Meunites} As in some Greek manuscripts (**s** also 26:7); Hebrew reads *Ammonites.*
22: 2 {Ahaziah was twenty-two} As in some Greek manuscripts and Syriac version (**s** also 2 Kgs 8:26); Hebrew reads *forty-two.*
22: 6 {and King Ahaziah} Some Hebrew manuscripts, Greek and Syriac versions, and Latin Vulgate (**s** also 2 Kgs 8:29); most Hebrew manuscripts read *Azariah.*
22: 8 {and Ahaziah's relatives} As in Greek version (**s** also 2 Kgs 10:13); Hebrew reads *and sons of the brothers of Ahaziah.*
24:26 {assassins were Jozacar,} Hebrew *Zabad;* compare parallel text at 2 Kgs 12:21, and **s** note there.
25:28 {City of David.} As in some Hebrew manuscripts and other ancient versions (**s** also 2 Kgs 14:20); most Hebrew manuscripts read *the city of Judah.*
26: 2 {town of Elath} As in Greek version (**s** also 2 Kgs 14:22; 16:6); Hebrew reads *Eloth.*
36: 9 {Jehoiachin was eighteen} As in one Hebrew manuscript, some Greek manuscripts, and Syriac version (**s** also 2 Kgs 24:8); most Hebrew manuscripts read *eight.*
Ezr 2:25 {peoples of Kiriath-jearim,} As in some Hebrew manuscripts and Greek version (**s** also Neh 7:29); Hebrew reads *Kiriath-arim.*
2:46 {Hagab, Shalmai,} As in the marginal *Qere* reading of the Masoretic Text (**s** also Neh 7:48); Hebrew text reads *Shamlai.*
6:15 {completed on March 12,} Aramaic *on the third day of the month Adar,* of the Hebrew calendar. This event occurred on March 12, 515 B.C.; also **s** note on 3:1.
6:19 {On April 21} Hebrew *On the fourteenth day of the first month,* of the Hebrew calendar. This event occurred on April 21, 515 B.C.; also **s** note on 3:1.
7: 1 {was the son} Or *descendant;* **s** 1 Chr 6:14.
7: 3 {of Azariah, son} Or *descendant;* **s** 1 Chr 6:6-10.
7: 9 {Babylon on April 8} Hebrew *on the first day of the first month,* of the Hebrew calendar. This event occurred on April 8, 458 B.C.; also **s** note on 3:1.
7: 9 {on August 4,} Hebrew *on the first day of the fifth month,* of the Hebrew calendar. This event occurred on August 4, 458 B.C.; also **s** note on 3:1.
8: 5 {family of Zattu} As in some Greek manuscripts (**s** also 1 Esdras 8:32); Hebrew lacks *Zattu.*
8:10 {family of Bani} As in some Greek manuscripts (**s** also 1 Esdras 8:36); Hebrew lacks *Bani.*
8:31 {Canal on April 19} Hebrew *on the twelfth day of the first month,* of the Hebrew calendar. This event occurred on April 19, 458 B.C.; **s** note on 7:9a.
10: 9 {place on December 19,} Hebrew *on the twentieth day of the ninth month,* of the Hebrew calendar. This event occurred on December 19, 458 B.C.; also **s** note on 7:9a.
10:16 {name. On December 29,} Hebrew *On the first day of the tenth month,* of the Hebrew calendar. This event occurred on December 29, 458 B.C.; also **s** note on 7:9a.
10:17 {the next year} Hebrew *By the first day of the first month,* of the Hebrew calendar. This event occurred on March 27, 457 B.C.; also **s** note on 7:9a.
Ne 3:18 {Binnui} As in a few Hebrew manuscripts, some Greek manuscripts, and Syriac version (**s** also 3:24; 10:9); most Hebrew manuscripts read *Bavvai.*
6:15 {So on October 2} Hebrew *on the twenty-fifth day of the month Elul,* of the Hebrew calendar. This event occurred on October 2, 445 B.C.; also **s** note on 1:1.
7:68 {horses, 245 mules,} As in some Hebrew manuscripts (**s** also Ezra 2:66); most Hebrew manuscripts lack this verse.
8: 2 {So on October 8} Hebrew *on the first day of the seventh month,* of the Hebrew calendar. This event occurred on October 8, 445 B.C.; also **s** note on 1:1.
8:13 {On October 9} Hebrew *On the second day,* of the seventh month of the Hebrew calendar. This event occurred on October 9, 445 B.C.; also **s** notes on 1:1 and 8:2.

8:14 {held that month.} Hebrew *in the seventh month.* This month of the Hebrew lunar calendar usually occurs in September and October. **S** Lev 23:39-43.
8:18 {Then on October 15} Hebrew *on the eighth day,* of the seventh month of the Hebrew calendar. This event occurred on October 15, 445 B.C.; also **s** notes on 1:1 and 8:2.
9: 1 {On October 31} Hebrew *On the twenty-fourth day of that same month,* the seventh month of the Hebrew calendar. This event occurred on October 31, 445 B.C.; also **s** note on 1:1.
12: 4 {Iddo, Ginnethon,} As in some Hebrew manuscripts and Latin Vulgate (**s** also 12:16); most Hebrew manuscripts read *Ginnethoi.*
12:14 {family of Malluch.} As in Greek version (**s** also 10:4; 12:2); Hebrew reads *Malluchi.*
12:14 {family of Shecaniah.} As in many Hebrew manuscripts, some Greek manuscripts, and Syriac version (**s** also 12:3); most Hebrew manuscripts read *Shebaniah.*
12:15 {family of Meremoth.} As in some Greek manuscripts (**s** also 12:3); Hebrew reads *Meraioth.*
Est 3: 7 {month of April,} Hebrew *in the first month, the month of Nisan.* This month of the Hebrew lunar calendar occurred in April and May 474 B.C.; also **s** note on 2:16.
3: 7 {a year later.} As in Greek version, which reads *the thirteenth day of the twelfth month, the month of Adar* (**s** also 3:13). Hebrew reads *in the twelfth month,* of the Hebrew calendar. The date selected was March 7, 473 B.C.; also **s** note on 2:16.
3:12 {On April 17} Hebrew *On the thirteenth day of the first month,* of the Hebrew calendar. This event occurred on April 17, 474 B.C.; also **s** note on 2:16.
3:13 {later on March 7.} Hebrew *on the thirteenth day of the twelfth month, the month of Adar,* of the Hebrew calendar. The date selected was March 7, 473 B.C.; also **s** note on 2:16.
8: 9 {So on June 25} Hebrew *on the twenty-third day of the third month, the month of Sivan,* of the Hebrew calendar. This event occurred on June 25, 474 B.C.; also **s** note on 2:16.
8:12 {the next year.} Hebrew *the thirteenth day of the twelfth month, the month of Adar,* of the Hebrew calendar. The date selected was March 7, 473 B.C.; also **s** note on 2:16.
9: 1 {So on March 7} Hebrew *on the thirteenth day of the twelfth month, the month of Adar,* of the Hebrew calendar. This event occurred on March 7, 473 B.C.; also **s** note on 2:16.
9:15 {together on March 8} Hebrew *the fourteenth day of the month of Adar,* of the Hebrew calendar. This event occurred on March 8, 473 B.C.; also **s** note on 2:16.
9:17 {March 7.} Hebrew *on the thirteenth day of the month of Adar,* of the Hebrew calendar. This event occurred on March 7, 473 B.C.; also **s** note on 2:16.
Job 19:26 {will see God} Or *without my body I will s God.*
Ps 18:13 {a mighty shout.} As in Greek version (**s** also 2 Sam 22:14); Hebrew adds *raining down hail and burning coals.*
Isa 10:21 {them will return} Hebrew *Shear-jashub;* **s** 7:3; 8:18.
49:24 {that a tyrant} As in Dead Sea Scrolls, Syriac version, and Latin Vulgate (also **s** 49:25); Masoretic Text reads *a righteous person.*
61: 1 {freed.} Greek version reads *and the blind will s.*
Jer 1: 3 {of that year,} Hebrew *In the fifth month,* of the Hebrew calendar. A number of events in Jeremiah can be cross-checked with dates in surviving Babylonian records and related accurately to our modern calendar. This month in the eleventh year of Zedekiah's reign occurred in August and September 586 B.C. Also **s** 52:12 and the note there.
27: 1 {reign of Zedekiah} As in some Hebrew manuscripts and Syriac version (**s** also 27:3, 12); most Hebrew manuscripts read *Jehoiakim.*
28: 1 {in late summer} Hebrew *In the fifth month,* of the Hebrew calendar. This month in the fourth year of Zedekiah's reign occurred in August and September 593 B.C. Also **s** note on 1:3.
28:17 {Two months later,} Hebrew *In the seventh month of that same year.* **S** 28:1 and the note there.
35: 6 {wine, because Jehonadab} Hebrew *Jonadab,* a variant name for Jehonadab; also in 35:10, 14, 18, 19. **S** 2 Kgs 10:15.
36: 9 {in late autumn,} Hebrew *in the ninth month,* of the Hebrew calendar (also in 36:22). This month in the fifth year of Jehoiakim's reign occurred in November and December 604 B.C. Also **s** note on 1:3.
37: 5 {of Pharaoh Hophra} Hebrew *army of Pharaoh;* **s** 44:30.
38: 1 {of Pashhur, Jehucal} Hebrew *Jucal,* a variant name for Jehucal; **s** 37:3.
39: 1 {was in January} Hebrew *in the tenth month,* of the Hebrew calendar. A number of events in Jeremiah can be cross-checked with dates in surviving Babylonian records and related accurately to our modern calendar. This event occurred on January 15, 588 B.C.; **s** 52:4 and the note there.
39: 2 {later, on July 18,} Hebrew *On the ninth day of the fourth month of the eleventh year of Zedekiah.* This event occurred on July 18, 586 B.C.; also **s** note on 39:1.
41: 1 {But in midautumn,} Hebrew *in the seventh month,* of the Hebrew calendar. This month occurred in October and November 586 B.C. Also **s** note on 39:1.
52: 6 {Zedekiah's eleventh year,} Hebrew *By the ninth day of the fourth month* [of Zedekiah's eleventh year]. This event of the Hebrew lunar calendar occurred on July 18, 586 B.C.; also **s** note on 52:4a.
52:12 {of that year,} Hebrew *On the tenth day of the fifth month,* of the Hebrew calendar. This day was August 17, 586 B.C.; also **s** note on 52:4a.
52:31 {of that year.} Hebrew *on the twenty-fifth day of the twelfth month,* of the Hebrew calendar. This day was March 31, 560 B.C.; also **s** note on 52:4a.
Eze 8: 1 {Then on September 17,} Hebrew *on the fifth day of the sixth month,* of the Hebrew calendar. This event occurred on September 17, 592 B.C.; also **s** note on 1:1.
20: 1 {On August 14,} Hebrew *In the fifth month, on the tenth day,* of the Hebrew calendar. This event occurred on August 14, 591 B.C.; also **s** note on 1:1.
24: 1 {On January 15,} Hebrew *On the tenth day of the tenth month,* of the Hebrew calendar. This event occurred on January 15, 588 B.C.; also **s** note on 1:1.
26: 1 {King Jehoiachin's captivity,} Hebrew *In the eleventh year, on the first day of the month,* of the Hebrew calendar year. Since an element is missing in the date formula here, scholars have reconstructed this probable reading: *On the first day of the eleventh month, during the twelfth year.* This reading would put this message on February 3, 585 B.C.; also **s** note on 1:1.
29:17 {On April 26,} Hebrew *On the first day of the first month,* of the Hebrew calendar. This event occurred on April 26, 571 B.C.; also **s** note on 29:1.
30:20 {On April 29,} Hebrew *On the seventh day of the first month,* of the Hebrew calendar. This event occurred on April 29, 587 B.C.; also **s** note on 29:1.
31: 1 {On June 21,} Hebrew *On the first day of the third month,* of the Hebrew calendar. This event occurred on June 21, 587 B.C.; also **s** note on 29:1.
32: 1 {On March 3,} Hebrew *On the first day of the twelfth month,* of the Hebrew calendar. This event occurred on March 3, 585 B.C.; also **s** note on 29:1.
32:17 {On March 17,} Hebrew *On the fifteenth day of the month,* presumably in the twelfth month of the Hebrew calendar (**s** 32:1). This would put this message at the end of King Jehoiachin's twelfth year of captivity, on March 17, 585 B.C.; also **s** note on 29:1. Greek version reads *On the fifteenth day of the first month,* which would put this message on April 27, 586 B.C., at the beginning of Jehoiachin's twelfth year.
33:21 {On January 8,} Hebrew *On the fifth day of the tenth month,* of the Hebrew calendar. This event occurred on January 8, 585 B.C.; also **s** note on 29:1.
45:25 {in early autumn,} Hebrew *the festival which begins on the fifteenth day of the seventh month* (**s** Lev 23:33). This day of the Hebrew lunar calendar occurs in late September or October.
46:17 {every fiftieth year.} Hebrew *until the Year of Release;* **s** Lev 25:8-17.
48:13 {6 2/3 miles wide.} **S** note on 48:9.
Da 9: 2 {for seventy years.} **S** Jer 25:11-12; 29:10.
Hos 2:23 {'Not loved.'} Hebrew *Lo-ruhamah;* **s** 1:6.
2:23 {'Not my people,'} Hebrew *Lo-ammi;* **s** 1:9.
10: 8 {shrines of Aven,} *Aven* is a reference to Beth-aven; **s** 10:5 and the note there.
Hag 1:15 {was on September 21} Hebrew *on the twenty-fourth day of the sixth month,* of the Hebrew calendar. This event occurred on September 21, 520 B.C.; also **s** note on 1:1a.
2: 1 {Then on October 17} Hebrew *on the twenty-first day of the seventh month,* of the Hebrew calendar. This event occurred on October 17, 520 B.C.; also **s** note on 1:1a.
2:10 {On December 18} Hebrew *On the twenty-fourth day of the ninth month,* of the Hebrew calendar (also in 2:18). This event occurred on December 18, 520 B.C.; also **s** note on 1:1a.
2:20 {on December 18} Hebrew *on the twenty-fourth day of the month;* **s** note on 2:10.
Zec 1: 7 {Then on February 15} Hebrew *on the twenty-fourth day of the eleventh month, the month of Shebat,* of the Hebrew calendar. This event occurred on February 15, 519 B.C.; also **s** note on 1:1.
7: 1 {On December 7} Hebrew *On the fourth day of the ninth month, the month of Kislev,* of the Hebrew calendar. This event occurred on December 7, 518 B.C.; also **s** note on 1:1.
Mt 1: 3 {father of Ram.} Greek *Aram;* also in 1:4. **S** 1 Chr 2:9-10.
1: 7 {father of Asaph.} *Asaph* is the same person as Asa; also in 1:8. **S** 1 Chr 3:10.
1: 8 {father of Jehoram.} Greek *Joram.* **S** 1 Kgs 22:50 and note at 1 Chr 3:11.
1:10 {father of Amos.} *Amos* is the same person as Amon. **S** 1 Chr 3:14.
1:11 {father of Jehoiachin} Greek *Jeconiah;* also in 1:12. **S** 2 Kgs 24:6 and note at 1 Chr 3:16.
8:28 {of the Gadarenes,} Some manuscripts read *Gerasenes;* other manuscripts read *Gergesenes.* **S** Mark 5:1; Luke 8:26.
11:14 {said would come.} **S** Mal 4:5.
16:17 {son of John,} Greek *Simon son of Jonah;* **s** John 1:42; 21:15-17.
24:15 {that causes desecration} Greek *the abomination of desolation.* **S** Dan 9:27; 11:31; 12:11.
24:29 {will be shaken.} **S** Isa 13:10; 34:4; Joel 2:10.
24:30 {and great glory.} **S** Dan 7:13.
26:64 {clouds of heaven."} **S** Ps 110:1; Dan 7:13.
27:35 {by throwing dice.} Greek *by casting lots.* A few late manuscripts add *This fulfilled the word of the prophet: "They divided my clothes among themselves and cast lots for my robe."* **S** Ps 22:18.
Mk 5: 1 {of the Gerasenes.} Some manuscripts read *Gadarenes;* others read *Gergesenes.* **S** Matt 8:28; Luke 8:26.
6: 3 {of James, Joseph,} Greek *Joses;* **s** Matt 13:55.
13:14 {that causes desecration} Greek *the abomination of desolation.* **S** Dan 9:27; 11:31; 12:11.
13:24[-25] {will be shaken.} **S** Isa 13:10; 34:4; Joel 2:10.
13:26 {power and glory.} **S** Dan 7:13.
14:62 {clouds of heaven."} **S** Ps 110:1; Dan 7:13.
15:24 {clothes, throwing dice} Greek *casting lots.* **S** Ps 22:18.
15:27 {side of his.} Some manuscripts add verse 28, *And the Scripture was fulfilled that said, "He was counted among those who were rebels."* **S** Isa 53:12.
15:40 {and of Joseph} Greek *Joses;* also in 15:47. **S** Matt 27:56.
Lk 1:17 {accept godly wisdom."} **S** Mal 4:5-6.
3:32 {son of Salmon.} Greek *Sala;* **s** Ruth 4:22.
3:33 {son of Arni.} *Arni* is the same person as Ram; **s** 1 Chr 2:9-10.
3:38 {son of Enosh.} Greek *Enos;* **s** Gen 5:6.
8:26 {of the Gerasenes,} Some manuscripts read *Gadarenes;* other manuscripts read *Gergesenes.* **S** Matt 8:28; Mark 5:1.
21:27 {and great glory.} **S** Dan 7:13.
22:69 {place of power."} **S** Ps 110:1.
23:34 {by throwing dice.} Greek *by casting lots.* **S** Ps 22:18.
Jn 1:21 {you the Prophet?"} **S** Deut 18:15, 18; Mal 4:5-6.
1:51 {Son of Man."} **S** Gen 28:10-17, the account of Jacob's ladder.
2: 1 {The next day} Greek *On the third day;* **s** 1:35, 43.
3: 5 {and the Spirit.} Or *spirit.* The Greek word for *Spirit* can also be translated *wind;* **s** 3:8.
6:14 {is the Prophet} **S** Deut 18:15, 18.
7:40 {is the Prophet."} **S** Deut 18:15, 18.
7:42 {David was born."} **S** Mic 5:2.
8:17 {accepted as fact.} **S** Deut 19:15.
18: 9 {you gave me."} **S** John 6:39 and 17:12.
18:32 {he would die.} **S** John 12:32-33.
19:28 {"I am thirsty."} **S** Pss 22:15; 69:21.
Ac 2: 1 {after Jesus' resurrection,} Greek *When the day of Pentecost arrived.* This annual celebration came 50 days after the Passover ceremonies. **S** Lev 23:16.
7:58 {man named Saul.} *Saul* is later called Paul; **s** 13:9.
Ro 11:34 {be his counselor?} **S** Isa 40:13.
1Co 7:10 {from the Lord.} **S** Matt 5:32; 19:9; Mark 10:11-12; Luke 16:18.
13:12 {with perfect clarity.} Greek *s face to face.*
2Co 3:18 {that brightly reflect} Or *so that we can s in a mirror.*
8:19 {offering to Jerusalem} **S** 1 Cor 16:3-4.
Gal 3:16 {and his child.} Greek *seed;* also in 3:16c, 19. **S** Gen 12:7.
4:22 {his freeborn wife.} **S** Gen 16:15; 21:2-3.
2Ti 2:19 {from all wickedness."} **S** Isa 52:11.
Jas 2:23 {friend of God."} **S** Isa 41:8.
Rev 4: 5 {the seven spirits} **S** 1:4 and 3:1, where the same expression is translated *the sevenfold Spirit.*
5: 6 {the seven spirits} **S** note on 4:5.
12:14 {from the dragon} Greek *the serpent;* also in 12:15. **S** 12:9.

SEED (10)

Ge 12: 7 {to your offspring.} Hebrew *s.*
13:15 {and your offspring} Hebrew *s.*
17: 7 {and your offspring} Hebrew *s;* also in 17:8.
22:18 {through your descendants,} Hebrew *s.*
24: 7 {to my offspring.} Hebrew *s.*
26: 4 {through your descendants} Hebrew *s.*
28:14 {and your descendants.} Hebrew *s.*
1Ki 18:32 {about three gallons.} Hebrew *2 seahs* [12 liters] *of s.*
Isa 5:10 {only one measure} Hebrew *A homer* [5 bushels or 182 liters] *of s will yield only an ephah* [0.5 bushels or 18.2 liters].
Gal 3:16 {and his child.} Greek *s;* also in 3:16c, 19. See Gen 12:7.

SEEDS (1)

Gal 3:16 {to his children,} Greek *s.*

SEEK (2)

2Sa 17: 3 {that you seek.} As in Greek version; Hebrew reads *like the return of all is the man whom you s.*
Pr 21: 6 {deadly trap.} As in Greek version; Hebrew reads *mist for those who s death.*

SEEN (2)
Ge 29:32 {named him Reuben,} *Reuben* means "Look, a son!" It also sounds like the Hebrew for "He has s my misery."
Jn 8:57 {have seen Abraham?} Some manuscripts read *How can you say Abraham has s you?*

SEER (1)
2Sa 15:27 {the priest, "Look,} As in Greek version; Hebrew reads *Are you a s?* or *Do you see?*

SEES (1)
Ge 16:14 {was named Beer-lahairoi,} *Beer-lahairoi* means "well of the Living One who s me."

SEIR (2)
2Ki 8:21 {town of Zair.} Greek version reads *S.*
Isa 21:11 {Someone from Edom} Hebrew *S,* another name for Edom.

SELA-HAMMAHLEKOTH (1)
1Sa 23:28 {Rock of Escape.} Hebrew *S.*

SELAH (3)
Ps 3:2 {*Interlude*} Hebrew *S.* The meaning of this word is uncertain, though it is probably a musical or literary term. It is rendered *Interlude* throughout the Psalms.
9:16 {*Quiet Interlude*} Hebrew *Higgaion S.* The meaning of this phrase is uncertain.
Hab 3:3 {and Mount Paran.} Hebrew adds *s;* also in 3:9, 13. The meaning of this Hebrew term is uncertain; it is probably a musical or literary term.

SEND (1)
Dt 7:20 {will send hornets} Or *will spread panic,* or *will s a plague.* The meaning of the Hebrew is uncertain.

SENT (3)
Jdg 9:23 {stirred up trouble} Hebrew *s a disturbing spirit.*
Ezr 10:44 {by these wives.} Or *and they s them away with their children.* The meaning of the Hebrew is uncertain.
Zec 7:2 {Sharezer and Regemmelech,} Or *Bethel-sharezer had s Regemmelech.*

SENTENCE (5)
1Sa 2:22 {of the Tabernacle.} Hebrew *Tent of Meeting.* Some manuscripts lack this entire s.
23:11 {me to him?} Some manuscripts lack the first s of 23:11.
Hos 5:2 {them at Acacia.} Hebrew *at Shittim.* The meaning of the Hebrew for this s is uncertain.
Lk 23:34 {they are doing."} This s is not included in many ancient manuscripts.
Rev 12:18 {Then he stood} Some manuscripts read *Then I stood,* and some translations put this entire s into 13:1.

SEPHARAD (1)
Ob 1:20 {in the north} Hebrew *in S.*

SERPENT (1)
Rev 12:14 {from the dragon} Greek *the s;* also in 12:15. See 12:9.

SERPENT'S (2)
1Ki 1:9 {stone of Zoheleth} Or *to the S Stone;* Greek version supports reading *Zoheleth* as a proper name.
Ne 2:13 {the Jackal's Well,} Or *S Well.*

SERVANT (3)
2Ch 6:42 {your servant David.} Or *Remember the faithfulness of your s David.*
Ecc 10:16 {is a child} Or *whose king is a s.*
Isa 48:20 {people of Israel.} Hebrew *his s, Jacob.*

SERVICE (1)
Nu 3:7 {around the Tabernacle.} Hebrew *around the Tent of Meeting, doing s at the Tabernacle.*

SET (3)
Dt 10:6 {people of Jaakan} Or *s out from Beeroth of Bene-jaakan.*
2Ch 20:37 {out to sea.} Hebrew *never s sail for Tarshish.*
Ps 89:25 {in the east.} Hebrew *I will s his hand on the sea, his right hand on the rivers.*

SETH (3)
Ge 4:25 {named him Seth,} *S* probably means "granted"; the name may also mean "appointed."
5:3 {Seth was born,} Or *his son, the ancestor of S, was born;* similarly in 5:6, 9, 12, 15, 18, 21, 25.
5:4 {birth of Seth,} Or *After the birth of this ancestor of S;* similarly in 5:7, 10, 13, 16, 19, 22, 26.

SETTING (1)
Hab 3:1 {the prophet Habakkuk:} Hebrew adds *according to shigionoth,* probably indicating the musical s for the prayer.

SETTLED (1)
1Sa 10:27 {Saul ignored them.} Dead Sea Scroll 4QSam[a] continues: *...But there were seven thousand men who had escaped from the Ammonites, and they had s in Jabesh-gilead.*

SEVEN (9)
Ge 26:33 {the well "Oath,"} Hebrew *Shibah,* which can mean "oath" or "s."
1Sa 10:27 {Saul ignored them.} Dead Sea Scroll 4QSam[a] continues: *...But there were s thousand men who had escaped from the Ammonites, and they had settled in Jabesh-gilead.*
2Sa 24:13 {you choose three} As in Greek version (see also 1 Chr 21:12); Hebrew reads *s.*
1Ki 8:65 {Festival of Shelters.} Hebrew *s days and s days, fourteen days;* compare parallel text at 2 Chr 7:8-10.
Da 9:25 {sets of seven} Hebrew *S sevens plus 62 sevens.*
9:27 {set of seven,} Hebrew *for one s.*
Rev 1:4 {the sevenfold Spirit} Greek *the s spirits.*
3:1 {the sevenfold Spirit} Greek *the s spirits.*

SEVEN-DAY (1)
1Ki 8:66 {festival was over,} Hebrew *On the eighth day,* probably referring to the day following the s Festival of Shelters; compare parallel text at 2 Chr 7:9-10.

SEVENFOLD (1)
Rev 4:5 {the seven spirits} See 1:4 and 3:1, where the same expression is translated *the s Spirit.*

SEVENS (4)
Da 9:24 {sets of seven} Hebrew *70 s.*
9:25 {sets of seven} Hebrew *Seven s plus 62 s.*
9:26 {sets of seven,} Hebrew *After 62 s.*

SEVENTEENTH (1)
Ge 8:4 {the flood began,} Hebrew *on the s day of the seventh month;* see 7:11.

SEVENTH (39)
Ge 8:4 {the flood began,} Hebrew *on the seventeenth day of the s month;* see 7:11.
Lev 16:29 {in early autumn,} Hebrew *On the tenth day of the s month.* This day of the Hebrew lunar calendar occurs in September or early October.
23:24 {in early autumn,} Hebrew *On the first day of the s month.* This day of the Hebrew lunar calendar occurs in September or early October.
23:27 {Festival of Trumpets.} Hebrew *on the tenth day of the s month;* see 23:24 and the note there.
23:34 {Day of Atonement.} Hebrew *on the fifteenth day of the s month;* see 23:24, 27 and the notes there.
23:39 {Festival of Shelters,} Hebrew *on the fifteenth day of the s month;* see 23:24 and the note there.
25:9 {the fiftieth year,} Hebrew *on the tenth day of the s month, on the Day of Atonement;* see 23:27 and the note there.
Nu 29:1 {in early autumn} Hebrew *on the first day of the s month.* This day of the Hebrew lunar calendar occurs in September or early October.
29:7 {"Ten days later,} Hebrew *On the tenth day of the s month;* see 29:1 and the note there.
29:12 {"Five days later,} Hebrew *On the fifteenth day of the s month;* see 29:1, 7 and the notes there.
Jdg 14:15 {On the fourth} As in Greek version; Hebrew reads *s.*
1Ki 8:2 {in early autumn.} Hebrew *at the festival in the month Ethanim, which is the s month.* The Festival of Shelters began on the fifteenth day of the s month on the Hebrew lunar calendar. This occurs on our calendar in late September or early October.
2Ki 25:8 {of that year,} Hebrew *On the s day of the fifth month,* of the Hebrew calendar. This day was August 14, 586 B.C.; also see note on 25:1.
25:25 {of that year,} Hebrew *in the s month,* of the Hebrew calendar. This month occurred in October and November 586 B.C.
2Ch 5:3 {in early autumn.} Hebrew *at the festival that is in the s month.* The Festival of Shelters began on the fifteenth day of the s month of the Hebrew lunar calendar. This occurs on our calendar in late September or early October.
7:10 {of the celebration,} Hebrew *Then on the twenty-seventh day of the s month.* This day of the Hebrew lunar calendar occurs in late September or early October.
31:7 {until early autumn.} Hebrew *in the s month.* This month of the Hebrew lunar calendar usually occurs in September and October.
Ezr 3:1 {in early autumn,} Hebrew *in the s month.* A number of events in the book of Ezra can be cross-checked with dates in surviving Persian records and related accurately to our modern calendar. This month of the Hebrew lunar calendar occurred in October and November 537 B.C.
3:6 {of Shelters began,} Hebrew *On the first day of the s month.* This day of the Hebrew lunar calendar occurs in September or early October. The Festival of Shelters began on the fifteenth day of the s month.
Ne 7:73 {Now in midautumn,} Hebrew *in the s month.* This month of the Hebrew lunar calendar occurred in October and November 445 B.C.
8:2 {So on October 8} Hebrew *on the first day of the s month,* of the Hebrew calendar. This event occurred on October 8, 445 B.C.; also see note on 1:1.
8:13 {On October 9} Hebrew *On the second day,* of the s month of the Hebrew calendar. This event occurred on October 9, 445 B.C.; also see notes on 1:1 and 8:2.
8:14 {held that month.} Hebrew *in the s month.* This month of the Hebrew lunar calendar usually occurs in September and October. See Lev 23:39-43.
8:18 {Then on October 15} Hebrew *on the eighth day,* of the s month of the Hebrew calendar. This event occurred on October 15, 445 B.C.; also see notes on 1:1 and 8:2.
9:1 {On October 31} Hebrew *On the twenty-fourth day of that same month,* the s month of the Hebrew calendar. This event occurred on October 31, 445 B.C.; also see note on 1:1.
Jer 28:17 {Two months later,} Hebrew *In the s month of that same year.* See 28:1 and the note there.
41:1 {But in midautumn,} Hebrew *in the s month,* of the Hebrew calendar. This month occurred in October and November 586 B.C. Also see note on 39:1.
52:28 {of Nebuchadnezzar's reign} This exile in the s year of Nebuchadnezzar's reign occurred in 597 B.C.
Eze 30:20 {On April 29,} Hebrew *On the s day of the first month,* of the Hebrew calendar. This event occurred on April 29, 587 B.C.; also see note on 29:1.
45:25 {in early autumn,} Hebrew *the festival which begins on the fifteenth day of the s month* (see Lev 23:33). This day of the Hebrew lunar calendar occurs in late September or October.
Hag 2:1 {Then on October 17} Hebrew *on the twenty-first day of the s month,* of the Hebrew calendar. This event occurred on October 17, 520 B.C.; also see note on 1:1a.
Zec 7:5 {in early autumn,} Hebrew *fasted and mourned in the fifth and s months.* The fifth month of the Hebrew lunar calendar occurs during our months of July and August. The s month occurs during September and October; both the Day of Atonement and the Festival of Shelters were celebrated in the s month.
8:19 {autumn, and winter} Hebrew *in the fourth, fifth, s, and tenth months.* The fourth month of the Hebrew lunar calendar usually occurs in June and July. The fifth month usually occurs in July and August. The s month usually occurs in September and October. The tenth month usually occurs in December and January.

SEVENTY-FIVE (2)
Ge 46:27 {there were seventy} Greek version reads *s;* see note on Exod 1:5.
Ex 1:5 {Jacob had seventy} Dead Sea Scrolls and Greek version read *s;* see notes on Gen 46:27.

SEVERAL (1)
Mt 16:2[-3] {of the times!} S manuscripts do not include any of the words in 16:2-3 after *He replied.*

SHADDAI (2)
Ex 6:3 {as God Almighty,} Hebrew *El S.*
Eze 1:24 {of the Almighty,} Hebrew *S.*

SHADOWBOXING (1)
1Co 9:26 {misses his punches.} Or *I am not just s.*

SHALLEKETH (1)
1Ch 26:16 {to the Temple.} Or *the gate of S on the upper road* (also in 26:18). The meaning of the Hebrew is uncertain.

SHALLUM (3)
1Ch 3:15 {third), and Jehoahaz} Hebrew *S,* another name for Jehoahaz.
7:13 {Jezer, and Shillem.} As in some Hebrew and Greek manuscripts (see also Gen 46:24; Num 26:49); most Hebrew manuscripts read *S.*
Jer 22:11 {says about Jehoahaz,} Hebrew *S,* another name for Jehoahaz.

SHALOM (1)
Jdg 6:24 {LORD Is Peace."} Hebrew *Yahweh S.*

SHAME (4)
Lk 11:8 {won't be damaged.} Greek *in order to avoid s,* or *because of [your] persistence.*
Ro 9:33 {not be disappointed.} Or *will not be put to s.* Isa 28:16.

10:11 {not be disappointed.} Or *will not be put to s.* Isa 28:16.
1Pe 2:6 {never be disappointed.} Or *will never be put to s.* Isa 28:16.

SHAMELESSLY (1)

Mt 23:13 {go in yourselves.} Some manuscripts add verse 14, *How terrible it will be for you teachers of religious law and you Pharisees. Hypocrites! You s cheat widows out of their property, and then, to cover up the kind of people you really are, you make long prayers in public. Because of this, your punishment will be the greater.*

SHAMHUTH (1)

1Ch 27:8 {Shammah} Hebrew *S*, another name for Shammah; compare 11:27 and 2 Sam 23:25.

SHAMLAI (1)

Ezr 2:46 {Hagab, Shalmai,} As in the marginal *Qere* reading of the Masoretic Text (see also Neh 7:48); Hebrew text reads *S*.

SHAMMAH (4)

2Sa 23:33 {son of Shagee} As in parallel text at 1 Chr 11:34; Hebrew reads *Jonathan, S;* some Greek manuscripts read *Jonathan son of S.*
1Ch 27:8 {Shammah} Hebrew *Shamhuth*, another name for S; compare 11:27 and 2 Sam 23:25.
Eze 48:35 {LORD Is There.'} Hebrew *Yahweh S.*

SHAMMOTH (1)

1Ch 11:27 {Shammah from Harod;} As in parallel text at 2 Sam 23:25; Hebrew reads *S from Haror.*

SHAMMUA (2)

2Sa 5:14 {in Jerusalem: Shimea,} As in parallel text at 1 Chr 3:5; Hebrew reads *S*, a variant name for Shimea.
1Ch 14:4 {in Jerusalem: Shimea,} Hebrew *S*, a variant name for Shimea; compare 3:5.

SHAPHIR (1)

Mic 1:11 {people of Shaphir,} *S* means "pleasant."

SHARE (3)

2Ki 2:9 {your rightful successor."} Hebrew *Let me inherit a double s of your spirit.*
Eze 47:13 {shares of land.} As of land for each of Joseph's two oldest sons, Ephraim and Manasseh.
Heb 4:2 {God told them.} Some manuscripts read *they didn't s the faith of those who listened [to God].*

SHAVE (1)

Isa 7:20 {and your people.} Hebrew *s off the head, the hair of the legs, and the beard.*

SHAVSHA (1)

1Ch 18:16 {the priests. Seraiah} As in parallel text at 2 Sam 8:17; Hebrew reads *S.*

SHEAR-JASHUB (3)

Isa 7:3 {your son Shear-jashub.} *S* means "A remnant will return."
8:18 {me have names} *Isaiah* means "The LORD will save"; *S* means "A remnant will return"; and *Maher-shalal-hash-baz* means "Swift to plunder and quick to spoil."
10:21 {them will return} Hebrew *S;* see 7:3; 8:18.

SHEBANIAH (1)

Ne 12:14 {Shecaniah.} As in many Hebrew manuscripts, some Greek manuscripts, and Syriac version (see also 12:3); most Hebrew manuscripts read *S.*

SHEBARIM (1)

Jos 7:5 {as the quarries,} Or *as far as S.*

SHEBAT (1)

Zec 1:7 {Then on February 15} Hebrew *on the twenty-fourth day of the eleventh month, the month of S,* of the Hebrew calendar. This event occurred on February 15, 519 B.C.; also see note on 1:1.

SHEBUEL (2)

1Ch 24:20 {leader was Shebuel.} Hebrew *Shubael* (also in 24:20b), a variant name for S; compare 23:16 and 26:24.
25:4 {Mattaniah, Uzziel, Shubael,} Hebrew *S*, a variant name for Shubael; compare 25:20.

SHECHEM (1)

Jdg 9:28 {descendant of Shechem!} Hebrew *Who is S?*

SHEKEL (26)

Ge 24:22 {large gold bracelets} Hebrew *a gold nose-ring weighing a half s* [0.2 ounces or 6 grams] *and two gold bracelets weighing 10 shekels* [4 ounces or 114 grams].
Ex 30:13 {of an ounce} Hebrew *half a s* [6 grams], *according to the sanctuary s, 20 gerahs to each s.*
30:24 {and one gallon} Hebrew *500 shekels* [5.7 kilograms] *of cassia, according to the sanctuary s, and 1 hin* [3.8 liters].
38:24 {about 2,200 pounds,} Hebrew *29 talents* [2,175 pounds or 986 kilograms] *and 730 shekels* [18.3 pounds or 8.3 kilograms], *according to the sanctuary s.*
38:25 {about 7,545 pounds.} Hebrew *100 talents* [7,500 pounds or 3,400 kilograms] *and 1,775 shekels* [44.4 pounds or 20.2 kilograms], *according to the sanctuary s.*
38:26 {ounce of silver} Hebrew *1 beka* [6 grams] *per person, that is, half a s, according to the sanctuary s.*
Lev 5:15 {standard sanctuary shekel.} Each sanctuary s was about 0.4 ounces or 11 grams in weight.
27:3 {pieces of silver} Hebrew *50 shekels of silver, according to the standard sanctuary s,* each about 0.4 ounces or 11 grams in weight. The term *shekels* also appears in 27:4, 5, 6, 7, 16.
27:25 {standard sanctuary shekel.} Hebrew *measured according to the sanctuary s, 20 gerahs to each s.* Each sanctuary s was about 0.4 ounces or 11 grams in weight.
Nu 3:47 {standard sanctuary shekel.} Hebrew *5 shekels* [2 ounces or 57 grams] *apiece, according to the sanctuary s, 20 gerahs to each s.*
3:50 {pounds in weight.} Hebrew *1,365 shekels* [15.5 kilograms], *according to the sanctuary s.*
7:13 {about 1 3/4 pounds.} Hebrew *silver platter weighing 130 shekels* [1.5 kilograms] *and a silver basin weighing 70 shekels* [0.8 kilograms], *according to the sanctuary s;* also in 7:19, 25, 31, 37, 43, 49, 55, 61, 67, 73, 79, 85.
18:16 {standard sanctuary shekel.} Hebrew *5 shekels* [about 2 ounces or 57 grams] *of silver, according to the sanctuary s, 20 gerahs to each s.*
1Sa 9:8 {small silver piece.} Hebrew *1/4 s of silver,* about 0.1 ounces or 3 grams in weight.
13:21 {of an ounce} Hebrew *1/3 of a s* [4 grams].
2Ki 7:1 {ounce of silver,} Hebrew *1 seah* [6 liters] *of fine flour will cost 1 s* [11 grams]; also in 7:16, 18.
7:1 {ounce of silver.} Hebrew *2 seahs* [12 liters] *of barley grain will cost 1 s* [11 grams]; also in 7:16, 18.
Ne 10:32 {ounce of silver,} Hebrew *tax of 1/3 of a s* [4 grams].
Eze 45:12 {the silver shekel.} The s weighs about 0.4 ounces or 11 grams.

SHEKELS (61)

Ge 20:16 {pieces of silver} Hebrew *1,000 s of silver,* about 25 pounds or 11.4 kilograms in weight.
23:15 {four hundred pieces} Hebrew *400 s,* about 10 pounds or 4.6 kilograms in weight; also in 23:16.
24:22 {large gold bracelets} Hebrew *a gold nose-ring weighing a half shekel* [0.2 ounces or 6 grams] *and two gold bracelets weighing 10 s* [4 ounces or 114 grams].
37:28 {for twenty pieces} Hebrew *20 s,* about 8 ounces or 228 grams in weight.
45:22 {three hundred pieces} Hebrew *300 s,* about 7.5 pounds or 3.4 kilograms in weight.
Ex 21:32 {thirty silver coins} Hebrew *30 s of silver,* about 12 ounces or 342 grams in weight.
30:23 {myrrh, 6 1/4 pounds} Hebrew *500 s* [5.7 kilograms] *of pure myrrh, 250 s* [2.9 kilograms].
30:24 {and one gallon} Hebrew *500 s* [5.7 kilograms] *of cassia, according to the sanctuary shekel, and 1 hin* [3.8 liters].
38:24 {about 2,200 pounds,} Hebrew *29 talents* [2,175 pounds or 986 kilograms] *and 730 s* [18.3 pounds or 8.3 kilograms], *according to the sanctuary shekel.*
38:25 {about 7,545 pounds.} Hebrew *100 talents* [7,500 pounds or 3,400 kilograms] *and 1,775 s* [44.4 pounds or 20.2 kilograms], *according to the sanctuary shekel.*
38:28 {about 45 pounds,} Hebrew *1,775 s* [20.2 kilograms].
38:29 {brought 5,310 pounds} Hebrew *70 talents* [5,250 pounds or 2,380 kilograms] *and 2,400 s* [60 pounds or 27.4 kilograms].
Lev 27:3 {pieces of silver} Hebrew *50 s of silver, according to the standard sanctuary shekel,* each about 0.4 ounces or 11 grams in weight. The term *s* also appears in 27:4, 5, 6, 7, 16.
Nu 3:47 {standard sanctuary shekel.} Hebrew *5 s* [2 ounces or 57 grams] *apiece, according to the sanctuary shekel, 20 gerahs to each shekel.*
3:50 {pounds in weight.} Hebrew *1,365 s* [15.5 kilograms], *according to the sanctuary shekel.*
7:13 {about 1 3/4 pounds.} Hebrew *silver platter weighing 130 s* [1.5 kilograms] *and a silver basin weighing 70 s* [0.8 kilograms], *according to the sanctuary shekel;* also in 7:19, 25, 31, 37, 43, 49, 55, 61, 67, 73, 79, 85.
7:14 {about four ounces,} Hebrew *10 s* [114 grams]; also in 7:20, 26, 32, 38, 44, 50, 56, 62, 68, 74, 80, 86.
7:85 {weighed about 60 pounds,} Hebrew *2,400 s* [27.4 kilograms].
7:86 {about three pounds,} Hebrew *120 s* [1.4 kilograms].
18:16 {standard sanctuary shekel.} Hebrew *5 s* [about 2 ounces or 57 grams] *of silver, according to the sanctuary shekel, 20 gerahs to each shekel.*
31:52 {about 420 pounds.} Hebrew *16,750 s* [191 kilograms].
Dt 22:19 {pieces of silver,} Hebrew *100 s of silver,* about 2.5 pounds or 1.1 kilograms in weight.
22:29 {pieces of silver} Hebrew *50 s of silver,* about 1.25 pounds or 570 grams in weight.
Jos 7:21 {hundred silver coins,} Hebrew *200 s of silver,* about 5 pounds or 2.3 kilograms in weight.
7:21 {than a pound.} Hebrew *50 s,* about 20 ounces or 570 grams in weight.
Jdg 8:26 {was forty-three pounds,} Hebrew *1,700 s* [19.4 kilograms].
16:5 {eleven hundred pieces} Hebrew *1,100 s,* about 28 pounds or 12.5 kilograms in weight.
17:2 {eleven hundred pieces} Hebrew *1,100 s,* about 28 pounds or 12.5 kilograms in weight.
17:10 {you ten pieces} Hebrew *10 s,* about 4 ounces or 114 grams in weight.
1Sa 17:5 {weighed 125 pounds.} Hebrew *5,000 s* [57 kilograms].
17:7 {weighed fifteen pounds.} Hebrew *600 s* [6.8 kilograms].
2Sa 14:26 {to five pounds!} Hebrew *200 s* [2.3 kilograms] *by the royal standard.*
18:11 {pieces of silver} Hebrew *10 s of silver,* about 4 ounces or 114 grams in weight.
18:12 {pieces of silver,} Hebrew *1,000 s,* about 25 pounds or 11.4 kilograms in weight.
21:16 {than seven pounds,} Hebrew *300 s* [3.4 kilograms].
24:24 {pieces of silver} Hebrew *50 s of silver,* about 20 ounces or 570 grams in weight.
1Ki 10:16 {over fifteen pounds} Hebrew *600 s* [6.8 kilograms].
10:29 {pieces of silver,} Hebrew *600 s of silver,* about 15 pounds or 6.8 kilograms in weight.
10:29 {pieces of silver.} Hebrew *150 [s],* about 3.8 pounds or 1.7 kilograms in weight.
2Ki 5:5 {pounds of gold,} Hebrew *10 talents* [340 kilograms] *of silver, 6,000 s* [68 kilograms] *of gold.*
6:25 {about two ounces} Hebrew *sold for 80 s* [0.9 kilograms] *of silver, and 1/4 of a cab* [0.3 liters] *of dove's dung cost 5 s* [57 grams]. *Dove's dung* may be a variety of wild vegetable.
15:20 {pay twenty ounces} Hebrew *50 s* [570 grams].
1Ch 21:25 {pieces of gold} Hebrew *600 s of gold,* about 15 pounds or 6.8 kilograms in weight.
2Ch 1:17 {pieces of silver,} Hebrew *600 s of silver,* about 15 pounds or 6.8 kilograms in weight.
1:17 {pieces of silver.} Hebrew *150 s,* about 3.8 pounds or 1.7 kilograms in weight.
3:9 {about twenty ounces} Hebrew *50 s* [570 grams].
9:15 {containing over 15 pounds} Hebrew *600 s* [6.8 kilograms].
9:16 {about 7 1/2 pounds} Hebrew *300 s* [3.4 kilograms].
Ne 5:15 {besides a pound} Hebrew *40 s* [456 grams].
SS 8:11 {pieces of silver} Hebrew *1,000 s of silver,* about 25 pounds or 11.4 kilograms in weight; also in 8:12.
8:12 {pieces of silver} Hebrew *200 [s],* about 5 pounds or 2.3 kilograms in weight.
Isa 7:23 {pieces of silver,} Hebrew *1,000 s of silver,* about 25 pounds or 11.4 kilograms in weight.
Jer 32:9 {Hanamel seventeen pieces} Hebrew *17 s,* about 7 ounces or 194 grams in weight.
Eze 4:10 {eight ounces} Hebrew *20 s* [228 grams].
45:12 {to one mina.} Elsewhere the mina is equated to 50 s.
Hos 3:2 {pieces of silver} Hebrew *15 s of silver,* about 6 ounces or 171 grams in weight.
Zec 11:12 {wages thirty pieces} Hebrew *30 s,* about 12 ounces or 342 grams in weight.

SHELAH (6)

Ge 10:24 {father of Shelah,} Greek version reads *Arphaxad was the father of Cainan, Cainan was the father of S.*
11:12 {Shelah was born.} Or *his son, the ancestor of S, was born;* similarly in 11:14, 16, 18, 20, 22, 24.
11:12[-13] {sons and daughters.} Greek version reads [12]*When Arphaxad was 135 years old, his son Cainan was born.* [13]*After the birth of Cainan, Arphaxad lived another 430 years and had other sons and daughters, and then he died. When Cainan was 130 years old, his son S was born. After the birth of S, Cainan lived another 330 years and had other sons and daughters, and then he died.*
1Ch 1:24 {Shem: Arphaxad, Shelah,} Some Greek manuscripts read *Arphaxad, Cainan, S.* See notes on Gen 10:24 and 11:12-13.
Ne 3:15 {pool of Siloam} Hebrew *pool of S,* another name for the pool of Siloam.

SHELEMIAH (1)

1Ch 26:14 {went to Meshelemiah} Hebrew *S*, a variant name for Meshelemiah; compare 26:2.

SHELOMITH (1)

1Ch 24:22 {leader was Shelomith.} Hebrew *Shelomoth* (also in 24:22b), a variant name for S; compare 23:18.

SHELOMOTH (1)

1Ch 24:22 {leader was Shelomith.} Hebrew *S* (also in 24:22b), a variant name for Shelomith; compare 23:18.

SHELTERS (12)

Ge 33:17 {was named Succoth.} *Succoth* means "s."
Mt 17: 4 {three shrines,} Or *s;* Greek reads *tabernacles.*
Mk 9: 5 {three shrines} Or *s;* Greek reads *tabernacles.*
Lk 9:33 {three shrines} Or *s;* Greek reads *tabernacles.*

SHEM (2)

Ge 9:27 {prosperity of Shem;} Hebrew *may he live in the tents of S.*
10:21 {brother of Japheth.} Or *S, whose older brother was Japheth.*

SHEMAMAH (1)

Isa 62: 4 {the Desolate Land.} Hebrew *S,* which means "desolate."

SHEMINITH (3)

1Ch 15:21 {play the harps.} Hebrew adds *according to the S,* which is probably a musical term. The meaning of the Hebrew is uncertain.
Ps 6: T {an eight-stringed instrument.} Hebrew *with stringed instruments; according to the s.*
12: T {an eight-stringed instrument.} Hebrew *according to the s.*

SHEN (1)

1Sa 7:12 {Mizpah and Jeshanah.} As in Greek version; Hebrew reads *S.*

SHEOL (28)

Dt 32:22 {of the grave.} Hebrew *of S.*
2Sa 22: 6 {The grave} Hebrew *S.*
Job 11: 8 {than the underworld} Hebrew *S.*
26: 6 {The underworld} Hebrew *S.*
Ps 9:17 {to the grave.} Hebrew *to S.*
16:10 {among the dead} Hebrew *in S.*
18: 5 {The grave} Hebrew *S.*
55:15 {let the grave} Hebrew *let S.*
86:13 {depths of death} Hebrew *of S.*
116: 3 {of the grave} Hebrew *of S.*
139: 8 {of the dead,} Hebrew *to S.*
Pr 5: 5 {to the grave.} Hebrew *to S.*
7:27 {to the grave.} Hebrew *to S.*
9:18 {in the grave.} Hebrew *in S.*
15:11 {Death and Destruction} Hebrew *S and Abaddon.*
15:24 {leave the grave} Hebrew *S.*
23:14 {them from death.} Hebrew *from S.*
27:20 {Death and Destruction} Hebrew *S and Abaddon.*
Isa 5:14 {The grave} Hebrew *S.*
14: 9 {of the dead} Hebrew *S;* also in 14:15.
28:15 {dodge the grave.} Hebrew *S;* also in 28:18.
57: 9 {of the dead,} Hebrew *into S.*
Eze 31:15 {into the grave,} Hebrew *to S;* also in 31:16, 17.
32:21 {in the grave} Hebrew *in S.*
32:27 {to the grave} Hebrew *to S.*
Am 9: 2 {of the dead,} Hebrew *to S.*
Jnh 2: 2 {of the dead,} Hebrew *from S.*
Hab 2: 5 {wide as death,} Hebrew *as S.*

SHEPHELAH (18)

Dt 1: 7 {the western foothills,} Hebrew *the S.*
Jos 9: 1 {the western foothills,} Hebrew *the S.*
10:40 {the western foothills,} Hebrew *the S.*
11: 2 {the western foothills} Hebrew *the S;* also in 11:16.
12: 8 {the western foothills,} Hebrew *the S.*
15:33 {the western foothills} Hebrew *the S.*
Jdg 1: 9 {the western foothills.} Hebrew *the S.*
1Ki 10:27 {foothills of Judah.} Hebrew *the S.*
1Ch 27:28 {foothills of Judah.} Hebrew *the S.*
2Ch 1:15 {foothills of Judah.} Hebrew *the S.*
9:27 {foothills of Judah.} Hebrew *the S.*
26:10 {foothills of Judah} Hebrew *the S.*
28:18 {foothills of Judah} Hebrew *the S.*
Jer 17:26 {the western foothills} Hebrew *the S.*
32:44 {foothills of Judah} Hebrew *the S.*
33:13 {foothills of Judah,} Hebrew *the S.*
Ob 1:19 {foothills of Judah} Hebrew *the S.*
Zec 7: 7 {foothills of Judah} Hebrew *the S.*

SHEPHI (1)

1Ch 1:40 {Manahath, Ebal, Shepho,} As in some Hebrew manuscripts (see also Gen 36:23); most Hebrew manuscripts read *S.*

SHEPHUPHAM (1)

Nu 26:39 {its ancestor Shupham.} As in some Hebrew manuscripts, Samaritan Pentateuch, Greek and Syriac versions, and Latin Vulgate; most Hebrew manuscripts read *S.*

SHESHACH (2)

Jer 25:26 {king of Babylon} Hebrew *of S,* a code name for Babylon.
51:41 {"How Babylon} Hebrew *S,* a code name for Babylon.

SHESHBAZZAR (1)

Ezr 1: 8 {returning to Judah.} Hebrew *S, the prince of Judah.*

SHIBAH (1)

Ge 26:33 {the well "Oath,"} Hebrew *S,* which can mean "oath" or "seven."

SHIGIONOTH (1)

Hab 3: 1 {the prophet Habakkuk:} Hebrew adds *according to s,* probably indicating the musical setting for the prayer.

SHIHOR (3)

1Ch 13: 5 {to the other,} Hebrew *from the S of Egypt to Lebo-hamath.*
Isa 23: 3 {grain from Egypt} Hebrew *from S,* a branch of the Nile River.
Jer 2:18 {of the Nile} Hebrew *of S,* a branch of the Nile River.

SHILOAH (1)

Isa 8: 6 {my gentle care} Hebrew *rejected the gently flowing waters of S.*

SHILOH (1)

Ge 49:10 {whom it belongs,} Or *until tribute is brought to him and the peoples obey;* traditionally rendered *until S comes.*

SHILONITE (1)

Ne 11: 5 {family of Shelah.} Hebrew *son of the S.*

SHIMEA (4)

2Sa 5:14 {in Jerusalem: Shimea,} As in parallel text at 1 Chr 3:5; Hebrew reads *Shammua,* a variant name for S.
13: 3 {David's brother Shimea.} Hebrew *Shimeah* (also in 13:32), a variant name for S; compare 1 Chr 2:13.
21:21 {David's brother Shimea.} As in parallel text at 1 Chr 20:7; Hebrew reads *Shimei,* a variant name for S.
1Ch 14: 4 {in Jerusalem: Shimea,} Hebrew *Shammua,* a variant name for S; compare 3:5.

SHIMEAH (2)

2Sa 13: 3 {David's brother Shimea.} Hebrew *S* (also in 13:32), a variant name for Shimea; compare 1 Chr 2:13.
1Ch 8:32 {father of Shimeam.} As in parallel text at 9:38; Hebrew reads *S,* a variant name for Shimeam.

SHIMEAM (1)

1Ch 8:32 {father of Shimeam.} As in parallel text at 9:38; Hebrew reads *Shimeah,* a variant name for S.

SHIMEI (2)

2Sa 21:21 {David's brother Shimea.} As in parallel text at 1 Chr 20:7; Hebrew reads *S,* a variant name for Shimea.
1Ch 25: 3 {Zeri, Jeshaiah, Shimei,} As in one Hebrew manuscript and some Greek manuscripts (see also 25:17); most Hebrew manuscripts lack *S.*

SHIMRITH (1)

2Ch 24:26 {woman named Shomer.} As in parallel text at 2 Kgs 12:21; Hebrew reads *S.*

SHINAR (7)

Ge 10:10 {land of Babylonia,} Hebrew *S.*
11: 2 {land of Babylonia} Hebrew *S.*
14: 1 {Amraphel of Babylonia,} Hebrew *S;* also in 14:9.
Jos 7:21 {imported from Babylon,} Hebrew *S.*
Isa 11:11 {Elam, Babylonia,} Hebrew *S.*
Da 1: 2 {land of Babylonia.} Hebrew *the land of S.*
Zec 5:11 {land of Babylonia} Hebrew *the land of S.*

SHIP (1)

Isa 2:16 {great trading ships} Hebrew *every s of Tarshish.*

SHIPS (4)

1Ki 10:22 {of trading ships} Hebrew *fleet of s of Tarshish.*
22:48 {of trading ships} Hebrew *fleet of s of Tarshish.*
2Ch 9:21 {of trading ships} Hebrew *fleet of s that could sail to Tarshish.*
20:36 {of trading ships} Hebrew *fleet of s that could go to Tarshish.*

SHITTIM (6)

Nu 25: 1 {camped at Acacia,} Hebrew *S.*
Jos 2: 1 {camp at Acacia.} Hebrew *S.*
3: 1 {Israelites left Acacia} Hebrew *S.*
Hos 5: 2 {them at Acacia.} Hebrew *at S.* The meaning of the Hebrew for this sentence is uncertain.
Joel 3:18 {valley of acacias.} Hebrew *valley of S.*
Mic 6: 5 {journey from Acacia} Hebrew *S.*

SHOES (1)

Eph 6:15 {be fully prepared.} Or *For s, put on the readiness to preach the Good News of peace with God.*

SHOOK (1)

Mt 27:51[-53] {to many people.} Or *The earth s, rocks split apart, tombs opened, and many bodies of godly men and women who had died were raised from the dead. After Jesus' resurrection, they left the cemetery, went into the holy city of Jerusalem, and appeared to many people.*

SHOPHACH (1)

1Ch 19:16 {command of Shobach,} As in parallel text at 2 Sam 10:16; Hebrew reads *S;* also in 19:18.

SHORT (1)

Mic 6:10 {in short measures.} Hebrew *by using the s ephah;* the ephah was a unit for measuring grain.

SHOT (1)

2Ch 26:15 {and hurl stones} Or *designed by brilliant men to protect those who s arrows and stones.*

SHOW (1)

Ps 8: 2 {give you praise.} As in Greek version; Hebrew reads *to s strength.*

SHRINE (2)

Ge 38:21 {find the prostitute} Hebrew *s prostitute;* also in 38:21b, 22.
Am 5:26 {you yourselves made.} Greek version reads *You took up the s of Molech, and the star of your god Rephan, and the images you made for yourselves.*

SHUBAEL (2)

1Ch 24:20 {leader was Shebuel.} Hebrew *S* (also in 24:20b), a variant name for Shebuel; compare 23:16 and 26:24.
25: 4 {Mattaniah, Uzziel, Shubael,} Hebrew *Shebuel,* a variant name for S; compare 25:20.

SHUTTLE (1)

Jdg 16:13 {the loom shuttle,} As in Greek version; Hebrew lacks *on your loom and tighten it with the loom s.*

SIA (1)

Ne 7:47 {Keros, Siaha,} As in parallel text at Ezra 2:44; Hebrew reads *S.*

SICILY (1)

Ac 28:12 {stop was Syracuse,} *Syracuse* was on the island of S.

SICKNESSES (1)

Isa 53: 4 {was our sorrows} Or *Yet it was our s he carried; it was our diseases.*

SIDDIM (1)

Ge 14: 8 {the Dead Sea} Hebrew *in S Valley;* see 14:3.

SIDE (4)

Ge 2:21 {of Adam's ribs} Or *took a part of Adam's s.*
Dt 4:49 {the Dead Sea,} Hebrew *took the Arabah on the east s of the Jordan as far as the sea of the Arabah.*
Ps 56: 9 {on my side.} Or *By this I will know that God is on my s.*
Mt 27:49 {and save him."} Some manuscripts add *And another took a spear and pierced his s, and out came water and blood.*

SIDON (1)

Mk 7:24 {region of Tyre.} Some Greek manuscripts add *and S.*

SIGN (1)

1Sa 10: 1 {his people Israel.} Greek version reads *Israel. And you will rule over the LORD's people and save them from their enemies around them. This will be the s to you that the LORD has appointed you to be leader over his inheritance.*

SILAS (1)

Ac 15:33 {had sent them.} Some manuscripts add verse 34, *But S decided to stay there.*

SILENCE (2)

Isa 21:11 {me concerning Edom} Hebrew *Dumah,* which means "s" or "stillness." It is a wordplay on the word *Edom.*
Jer 48: 2 {city of Madmen,} *Madmen* sounds like the Hebrew word for "s"; it should not be confused with the English word *madmen.*

SILOAM (1)

Ne 3:15 {pool of Siloam} Hebrew *pool of Shelah,* another name for the pool of S.

SILVANUS (4)
2Co 1:19 {Silas,} Greek *S.*
1Th 1: 1 {from Paul, Silas,} Greek *S.*
2Th 1: 1 {from Paul, Silas,} Greek *S.*
1Pe 5:12 {help of Silas,} Greek *S.*

SIMEON (2)
Ge 29:33 {named him Simeon,} *S* probably means "one who hears."
2Pe 1: 1 {is from Simon} Greek *S.*

SIMILARLY (3)
Ge 5: 3 {Seth was born,} Or *his son, the ancestor of Seth, was born;* s in 5:6, 9, 12, 15, 18, 21, 25.
5: 4 {birth of Seth,} Or *After the birth of this ancestor of Seth;* s in 5:7, 10, 13, 16, 19, 22, 26.
11:12 {Shelah was born.} Or *his son, the ancestor of Shelah, was born;* s in 11:14, 16, 18, 20, 22, 24.

SIMON (6)
Mt 16:17 {son of John,} Greek *S son of Jonah;* see John 1:42; 21:15-17.
17:25 {you think, Peter} Greek *S.*
Mk 1:16 {he saw Simon} *S* is called *Peter* in 3:16 and thereafter.
Lk 5: 3 {Jesus asked Simon,} *S* is called *Peter* in 6:14 and thereafter.
24:34 {appeared to Peter} Greek *S.*
Ac 15:14 {Peter} Greek *S.*

SIMPLY (1)
Isa 28:10 {very simple words!} The Hebrew text for this verse may s be childish sounds that have no meaning, or perhaps a childish mimicking of the prophet's words. Also in 28:13.

SIN (7)
Ge 4:13 {LORD, "My punishment} Or *My s.*
Ex 16: 1 {Sin} Not to be confused with the English word *s.*
17: 1 {Sin} Not to be confused with the English word *s.*
Nu 33:11 {Sin} Not to be confused with the English word *s.*
Ps 31:10 {Misery} Or *S.*
Eze 30:15 {fury on Pelusium,} Hebrew *S;* also in 30:16.
Ro 6:12 {way you live;} Or *Do not let s reign in your body, which is subject to death.*

SINGULAR (1)
Da 5:28 {*Parsin*} Aramaic *Peres,* the s of *Parsin.*

SINIM (1)
Isa 49:12 {south as Egypt.} As in Dead Sea Scrolls, which read *from the region of Aswan,* which is in southern Egypt. Masoretic Text reads *from the region of S.*

SINNERS (3)
Mt 9:11 {with such scum} Greek *with tax collectors and s.*
Mk 2:16 {with such scum} Greek *with tax collectors and s.*
Lk 5:30 {with such scum} Greek *with tax collectors and s.*

SINS (3)
Mk 1: 4 {to be forgiven.} Greek *preaching a baptism of repentance for the forgiveness of s.*
11:25 {your sins, too.} Some manuscripts add verse 26, *But if you do not forgive, neither will your Father who is in heaven forgive your s.*
Lk 3: 3 {to be forgiven.} Greek *preaching a baptism of repentance for the forgiveness of s.*

SION (1)
Dt 4:48 {to Mount Sirion,} As in Syriac version (see also 3:9); Hebrew reads *Mount S.*

SIPPAI (1)
1Ch 20: 4 {Hushah killed Saph,} As in parallel text at 2 Sam 21:18; Hebrew reads *S.*

SIRION (1)
Ps 29: 6 {and Mount Hermon} Hebrew *S,* another name for Mount Hermon.

SISTER (2)
1Co 9: 5 {Christian wife} Greek *a s, a wife.*
2Jn 1:13 {of your sister,} Or *from the members of your s church.*

SISTERS (1)
Mk 3:32 {brothers and sisters} Some manuscripts do not include *and s.*

SITNAH (1)
Ge 26:21 {named it "Opposition."} Hebrew *S.*

SITS (1)
Isa 30: 7 {the Harmless Dragon.} Hebrew *Rahab who s still.* Rahab is the name of a mythical sea monster that represents chaos in ancient literature. The name is used here as a poetic name for Egypt.

SIVAN (1)
Est 8: 9 {So on June 25} Hebrew *on the twenty-third day of the third month, the month of S,* of the Hebrew calendar. This event occurred on June 25, 474 B.C.; also see note on 2:16.

SIX (1)
Ru 3:15 {out six scoops} Hebrew *s measures,* an unknown quantity.

SIXTH (3)
Eze 8: 1 {Then on September 17,} Hebrew *on the fifth day of the s month,* of the Hebrew calendar. This event occurred on September 17, 592 B.C.; also see note on 1:1.
Hag 1: 1 {On August 29} Hebrew *On the first day of the s month,* of the Hebrew calendar. A number of events in Haggai can be cross-checked with dates in surviving Persian records and related accurately to our modern calendar. This event occurred on August 29, 520 B.C.
1:15 {was on September 21} Hebrew *on the twenty-fourth day of the s month,* of the Hebrew calendar. This event occurred on September 21, 520 B.C.; also see note on 1:1a.

SIZE (1)
2Sa 8: 1 {their largest city.} Hebrew *by conquering Metheg-ammah,* a name which means "the bridle," possibly referring to the s of the city or the tribute money taken from it. Compare 1 Chr 18:1.

SKIN (18)
Ex 4: 6 {snow with leprosy.} Or *with a contagious s disease.* The Hebrew word used here can describe various s diseases.
Lev 13: 2 {contagious skin disease,} Traditionally rendered *leprosy.* The Hebrew word used throughout this passage is used to describe various s diseases.
13:47 {an infectious mildew} Traditionally rendered *leprosy.* The Hebrew term used throughout this passage is the same term used for the various s diseases described in 13:1-46.
Nu 5: 2 {contagious skin disease} Traditionally rendered *leprosy.* The Hebrew word used here describes various s diseases.
12:10 {snow with leprosy.} Or *with a contagious s disease.* The Hebrew word used here can describe various s diseases.
Dt 24: 8 {contagious skin diseases} Traditonally rendered *leprosy.* The Hebrew word used here can describe various s diseases.
2Sa 3:29 {sores or leprosy} Or *or a contagious s disease.* The Hebrew word used here can describe various s diseases.
2Ki 5: 1 {suffered from leprosy.} Or *from a contagious s disease.* The Hebrew word used here and throughout this passage can describe various s diseases.
7: 3 {men with leprosy} Or *with a contagious s disease.* The Hebrew word used here and throughout this passage can describe various s diseases.
15: 5 {king with leprosy,} Or *with a contagious s disease.* The Hebrew word used here and throughout this passage can describe various s diseases.
2Ch 26:19 {LORD's Temple, leprosy} Or *a contagious s disease.* The Hebrew word used here and throughout this passage can describe various s diseases.

SKULL (1)
Lk 23:33 {called The Skull.} Sometimes rendered *Calvary,* which comes from the Latin word for "s."

SLAVES (1)
1Co 7:23 {by the world.} Greek *don't become s of people.*

SLEEP (2)
Mt 26:45 {sleeping? Still resting?} Or *S on, take your rest.*
Mk 14:41 {sleeping? Still resting?} Or *S on, take your rest.*

SLEEPERS (1)
SS 7: 9 {lips and teeth.} As in Greek and Syriac versions and Latin Vulgate; Hebrew reads *over lips of s.*

SLEEVES (1)
2Sa 13:18 {long, beautiful robe,} Or *a robe with s,* or *an ornamented robe.* The meaning of the Hebrew is uncertain.

SLEW (1)
Isa 51: 9 {of the Nile.} Hebrew *s Rahab the dragon.* Rahab is the name of a mythical sea monster that represents chaos in ancient literature. The name is used here as a poetic name for Egypt.

SLINGERS (1)
2Ki 3:25 {came under attack.} Hebrew *until only Kir-hareseth was left, with its stones, but the s surrounded and attacked it.*

SLOPES (1)
Dt 33: 2 {his right hand.} Or *came from myriads of holy ones, from the south, from his mountain s.* The meaning of the Hebrew is uncertain.

SNAKE (1)
2Ki 18: 4 {was called Nehushtan.} *Nehushtan* sounds like the Hebrew terms that mean "s," "bronze," and "unclean thing."

SOLD (1)
2Ki 6:25 {about two ounces} Hebrew *s for 80 shekels* [0.9 kilograms] *of silver, and 1/4 of a cab* [0.3 liters] *of dove's dung cost 5 shekels* [57 grams]. *Dove's dung* may be a variety of wild vegetable.

SOLDIERS (1)
2Sa 10:18 {forty thousand horsemen,} Some Greek manuscripts read *foot s;* compare parallel text at 1 Chr 19:18.

SOLOMON (1)
1Ch 22: 9 {will be Solomon,} *S* sounds like and is probably derived from the Hebrew word for "peace."

SOMEONE (1)
Heb 9:16 {is dead.} Or *Now when s makes a covenant, it is necessary to ratify it with the death of a sacrifice.*

SOMETHING (1)
Da 10:16 {like a man} As in most manuscripts of the Masoretic Text; one manuscript of the Masoretic Text and one Greek version read *Then s that looked like a human hand.*

SOMETIMES (1)
Lk 23:33 {called The Skull.} S rendered *Calvary,* which comes from the Latin word for "skull."

SON (73)
Ge 5: 3 {Seth was born,} Or *his s, the ancestor of Seth, was born;* similarly in 5:6, 9, 12, 15, 18, 21, 25.
11:12 {Shelah was born.} Or *his s, the ancestor of Shelah, was born;* similarly in 11:14, 16, 18, 20, 22, 24.
11:12[-13] {sons and daughters.} Greek version reads [12]*When Arphaxad was 135 years old, his s Cainan was born.* [13]*After the birth of Cainan, Arphaxad lived another 430 years and had other sons and daughters, and then he died. When Cainan was 130 years old, his s Shelah was born. After the birth of Shelah, Cainan lived another 330 years and had other sons and daughters, and then he died.*
19:38 {named him Ben-ammi.} *Ben-ammi* means "s of my people."
29:32 {named him Reuben,} *Reuben* means "Look, a s!" It also sounds like the Hebrew for "He has seen my misery."
35:18 {called him Benjamin.} *Ben-oni* means "s of my sorrow"; *Benjamin* means "s of my right hand."
Ex 4:24 {LORD confronted Moses} Or *confronted Moses' s;* Hebrew reads *confronted him.*
Nu 2:14[-15] {son of Deuel} As in many Hebrew manuscripts, Samaritan Pentateuch, and Latin Vulgate (see also 1:14); most Hebrew manuscripts read *s of Reuel.*
Dt 18:10 {a burnt offering.} Or *never make your s or daughter pass through the fire.*
1Sa 14:41 {among the others?"} Greek version adds *If the fault is with me or my s Jonathan, respond with Urim; but if the men of Israel are at fault, respond with Thummim.*
20:30 {of a whore!"} Hebrew *You s of a perverse and rebellious woman.*
2Sa 11:21 {son Abimelech killed} Hebrew *Was not Abimelech s of Jerubbesheth killed.*
21:19 {son of Jair} As in parallel text at 1 Chr 20:5; Hebrew reads *s of Jaare-oregim.*
23:33 {son of Shagee} As in parallel text at 1 Chr 11:34; Hebrew reads *Jonathan, Shammah;* some Greek manuscripts read *Jonathan s of Shammah.*
2Ki 16: 3 {in the fire.} Or *even making his s pass through the fire.*
16: 7 {and your vassal.} Hebrew *your s.*
21: 6 {in the fire.} Or *even made his s pass through the fire.*
23:10 {in the fire} Or *to make a s or daughter pass through the fire.*
1Ch 3:16 {his uncle Zedekiah.} Hebrew *The descendants of Jehoiakim were his s Jeconiah* [a variant name for Jehoiachin] *and his s Zedekiah.*
11:35 {son of Sharar} As in parallel text at 2 Sam 23:33; Hebrew reads *s of Sacar.*
2Ch 34:20 {son of Micaiah,} As in parallel text at 2 Kgs 22:12; Hebrew reads *Abdon s of Micah.*

34:22 {grandson of Harhas,} As in parallel text at 2 Kgs 22:14; Hebrew reads *s of Tokhath, s of Hasrah.*
Ne 11:5 {family of Shelah.} Hebrew *s of the Shilonite.*
12:23 {Johanan, the grandson} Hebrew *s;* compare 12:10-11.
12:24 {Sherebiah, Jeshua, Binnui,} Hebrew *s of* (i.e., *ben*), which should probably be read here as the proper name Binnui; compare Ezra 3:9 and the note there.
Ps 2:7 {are my son.} Or *S;* also in 2:12.
2:7 {become your Father.} Or *Today I reveal you as my s.*
8:4 {care for us?} Hebrew *What is man that you should think of him, the s of man that you should care for him?*
Pr 1:8 {Listen, my child,} Hebrew *my s;* also in 1:10, 15.
2:1 {My child,} Hebrew *My s.*
3:1 {My child,} Hebrew *My s;* also in 3:11, 21.
3:12 {corrects a child} Hebrew *a s.*
4:10 {My child,} Hebrew *My s;* also in 4:20.
6:1 {My child,} Hebrew *My s.*
10:1 {wise child} Hebrew *s;* also in 10:1b.
13:1 {wise child} Hebrew *s.*
17:25 {A foolish child} Hebrew *s.*
19:13 {A foolish child} Hebrew *s;* also in 19:27.
23:15 {My child,} Hebrew *My s;* also in 23:19.
23:24 {have wise children.} Hebrew *a wise s.*
24:13 {My child,} Hebrew *My s;* also in 24:21.
27:11 {My child,} Hebrew *My s.*
30:1 {Jakeh. An oracle.} Or *s of Jakeh from Massa.*
Ecc 12:12 {But, my child,} Hebrew *my s.*
Da 3:25 {a divine being} Aramaic *like a s of the gods.*
5:22 {are his successor,} Aramaic *s.*
7:13 {like a man} Or *a S of Man;* Aramaic reads *a s of man.*
Mt 14:1 {When Herod Antipas} Greek *Herod the tetrarch.* He was a **s** of King Herod and was one of four rulers in Palestine.
16:17 {son of John,} Greek *Simon s of Jonah;* see John 1:42; 21:15-17.
18:10 {my heavenly Father.} Some manuscripts add verse 11, *And I, the S of Man, have come to save the lost.*
24:36 {the Son himself.} Some manuscripts omit the phrase *or the S himself.*
Mk 1:1 {Son of God.} Some manuscripts do not include *the S of God.*
Lk 3:1 {Antipas was ruler} Greek *Herod was tetrarch.* Herod Antipas was a **s** of King Herod.
9:7 {reached Herod Antipas,} Greek *Herod the tetrarch.* He was a **s** of King Herod and was one of four rulers in Palestine.
9:35 {my Chosen One.} Some manuscripts read *This is my beloved S.*
9:55 {and rebuked them.} Some manuscripts add *And he said, "You don't realize what your hearts are like. [56]For the S of Man has not come to destroy men's lives, but to save them."*
17:30 {of Man returns.} Or *on the day the S of Man is revealed.*
Jn 1:18 {is himself God,} Some manuscripts read *his one and only S.*
9:35 {Son of Man} Some manuscripts read *the S of God.*
13:32 {God will bring} Some manuscripts read *And if God is glorified in him [the S of Man], God will bring.*
Ac 8:36 {I be baptized?"} Some manuscripts add verse 37, *"You can," Philip answered, "if you believe with all your heart." And the eunuch replied, "I believe that Jesus Christ is the S of God."*
13:33 {become your Father.} Or *Today I reveal you as my S.* Ps 2:7.
2Th 2:3 {who brings destruction.} Greek *the s of destruction.*
Heb 1:5 {become your Father.} Or *Today I reveal you as my S.* Ps 2:7.
2:6 {son of man} Or *S of Man.*
5:5 {become your Father.} Or *Today I reveal you as my S.* Ps 2:7.
Rev 1:13 {Son of Man.} Or *one who looked like a man;* Greek reads *one like a s of man.*
14:14 {Son of Man} Or *one who looked like a man;* Greek reads *one like a s of man.*

SONS (26)

Ge 11:12[-13] {sons and daughters.} Greek version reads *[12]When Arphaxad was 135 years old, his son Cainan was born. [13]After the birth of Cainan, Arphaxad lived another 430 years and had other s and daughters, and then he died. When Cainan was 130 years old, his son Shelah was born. After the birth of Shelah, Cainan lived another 330 years and had other s and daughters, and then he died.*
46:27 {had two sons} Greek version reads *nine s,* probably including Joseph's grandsons through Ephraim and Manasseh (see 1 Chr 7:14-20).
Dt 32:8 {of angelic beings.} As in Dead Sea Scrolls, which read *of the s of God,* and Greek version, which reads *of the angels of god;* Masoretic Text reads *of the s of Israel.*
1Sa 3:13 {are blaspheming God} As in Greek version; Hebrew reads *his s have made themselves contemptible.*
2Sa 8:18 {as priestly leaders.} Hebrew *David's s were priests;* compare parallel text at 1 Chr 18:17.
1Ki 18:31 {tribes of Israel,} Hebrew *each of the tribes of the s of Jacob to whom the LORD had said, "Your name will be Israel."*
21:10 {Find two scoundrels} Hebrew *two s of Belial;* also in 21:13.
2Ki 17:17 {in the fire.} Or *They even made their s and daughters pass through the fire.*
1Ch 1:4 {of Noah were} As in Greek version (see also Gen 5:3-32); Hebrew lacks *The s of Noah were.*
11:34 {sons of Jashen} As in parallel text at 2 Sam 23:32; Hebrew reads *s of Hashem.*
25:9 {sons and relatives.} As in Greek version; Hebrew lacks *and twelve of his s and relatives.*
2Ch 22:8 {and Ahaziah's relatives} As in Greek version (see also 2 Kgs 10:13); Hebrew reads *and s of the brothers of Ahaziah.*
28:3 {in the fire.} Or *even making his s pass through the fire.*
33:6 {in the fire} Or *even made his s pass through the fire.*
Ezr 3:9 {descendants of Hodaviah.} Hebrew *s of Judah* (i.e., *bene Yehudah*). *Bene* might also be read here as the proper name Binnui; *Yehudah* is probably another name for Hodaviah. Compare 2:40; Neh 7:43; 1 Esdras 5:58.
Job 1:6 {the angels} Hebrew *the s of God.*
2:1 {the angels} Hebrew *the s of God.*
38:7 {all the angels} Hebrew *s of God.*
Pr 4:1 {My children,} Hebrew *My s.*
8:32 {so, my children,} Hebrew *my s.*
La 4:2 {children of Jerusalem,} Hebrew *s of Zion.*
Eze 47:13 {shares of land.} A share of land for each of Joseph's two oldest **s**, Ephraim and Manasseh.
Zec 9:13 {against the Greeks.} Hebrew *the s of Javan.*
Mk 3:17 {"Sons of Thunder"} Greek *whom he named Boanerges, which means S of Thunder.*

SOON (4)

Mt 3:2 {Heaven is near.} Or *has come,* or *is coming s.*
4:17 {Heaven is near.} Or *has come,* or *is coming s.*
10:7 {Heaven is near.} Or *has come,* or *is coming s.*
2Pe 1:14 {soon to die.} Greek *I must s put off this earthly tent.*

SORROW (1)

Ge 35:18 {called him Benjamin.} *Ben-oni* means "son of my **s**"; *Benjamin* means "son of my right hand."

SOUND (1)

Eze 3:12 {in his place!)} A likely reading for this verse is *Then the Spirit lifted me up, and as the glory of the LORD rose from its place, I heard behind me a loud rumbling s.*

SOUNDS (30)

Ge 3:20 {his wife Eve,} *Eve* **s** like a Hebrew term that means "to give life."
4:1 {birth to Cain,} *Cain* **s** like a Hebrew term that can mean "bring forth" or "acquire."
5:29 {his son Noah,} *Noah* **s** like a Hebrew term that can mean "relief" or "comfort."
11:9 {was called Babel,} *Babel* **s** like a Hebrew term that means "confusion."
19:37 {named him Moab.} *Moab* **s** like a Hebrew term that means "from father."
25:25 {called him Esau.} *Esau* **s** like a Hebrew term that means "hair."
29:32 {named him Reuben,} *Reuben* means "Look, a son!" It also **s** like the Hebrew for "He has seen my misery."
29:34 {named him Levi,} *Levi* **s** like a Hebrew term that means "being attached" or "feeling affection for."
29:35 {named him Judah,} *Judah* **s** like the Hebrew term for "praise."
30:18 {named him Issachar,} *Issachar* **s** like a Hebrew term that means "reward."
41:51 {older son Manasseh,} *Manasseh* **s** like a Hebrew term that means "causing to forget."
41:52 {second son Ephraim,} *Ephraim* **s** like a Hebrew term that means "fruitful."
Ex 2:10 {named him Moses,} *Moses* **s** like a Hebrew term that means "to draw out."
2:22 {named him Gershom,} *Gershom* **s** like a Hebrew term that means "a stranger here."
18:3 {son was Gershom,} *Gershom* **s** like a Hebrew term that means "a stranger here."
Jos 5:9 {been called Gilgal} *Gilgal* **s** like the Hebrew word *galal,* meaning "to roll."
1Sa 1:20 {named him Samuel,} *Samuel* **s** like the Hebrew term for "asked of God" or "heard by God."
2Ki 18:4 {was called Nehushtan.} *Nehushtan* **s** like the Hebrew terms that mean "snake," "bronze," and "unclean thing."
1Ch 4:9 {named him Jabez} *Jabez* **s** like a Hebrew term meaning "distress" or "pain."
7:23 {named him Beriah} *Beriah* **s** like a Hebrew term meaning "tragedy" or "misfortune."
22:9 {will be Solomon,} *Solomon* **s** like and is probably derived from the Hebrew word for "peace."
Isa 28:10 {very simple words!} The Hebrew text for this verse may simply be childish **s** that have no meaning, or perhaps a childish mimicking of the prophet's words. Also in 28:13.
29:1 {certain for Ariel,} *Ariel* **s** like a Hebrew term that means "hearth" or "altar."
Jer 1:12 {I am watching,} The Hebrew word for "watching" **s** like the word for "almond tree."
48:2 {city of Madmen,} *Madmen* **s** like the Hebrew word for "silence"; it should not be confused with the English word *madmen.*
Mic 1:10 {city of Gath} *Gath* **s** like the Hebrew term for "tell."
1:11 {people of Zaanan} *Zaanan* **s** like the Hebrew term for "come out."
1:12 {people of Maroth} *Maroth* **s** like the Hebrew term for "bitter."
1:13 {people of Lachish.} *Lachish* **s** like the Hebrew term for "team of horses."
1:15 {people of Mareshah,} *Mareshah* **s** like the Hebrew term for "conqueror."

SOURCE (1)

Rev 3:14 {witness, the ruler} Or *the s.*

SOUTH (4)

Dt 33:2 {his right hand.} Or *came from myriads of holy ones, from the s, from his mountain slopes.* The meaning of the Hebrew is uncertain.
1Sa 20:41 {the stone pile.} As in Greek version; Hebrew reads *near the s edge.*
Mt 12:42 {queen of Sheba} Greek *The queen of the s.*
Lk 11:31 {queen of Sheba} Greek *the queen of the s.*

SOUTHERN (8)

Isa 49:12 {south as Egypt.} As in Dead Sea Scrolls, which read *from the region of Aswan,* which is in **s** Egypt. Masoretic Text reads *from the region of Sinim.*
Ac 18:1 {went to Corinth.} *Athens* and *Corinth* were major cities in Achaia, the region on the **s** end of the Greek peninsula.
28:13 {across to Rhegium.} *Rhegium* was on the **s** tip of Italy.
Ro 15:26 {believers in Greece} Greek *Macedonia and Achaia,* the northern and **s** regions of Greece.
1Co 16:15 {Christians in Greece,} Greek *were the firstfruits in Achaia,* the **s** region of the Greek peninsula.
2Co 1:1 {Christians throughout Greece.} Greek *Achaia,* the **s** region of the Greek peninsula.
9:2 {Christians in Greece} Greek *Achaia,* the **s** region of the Greek peninsula.
1Th 1:7 {Christians in Greece.} Greek *Macedonia and Achaia,* the northern and **s** regions of Greece; also in 1:8.

SPAN (5)

Ex 28:16 {pouch nine inches} Hebrew *1 s* [23 centimeters].
39:9 {pouch, nine inches} Hebrew *1 s* [23 centimeters].
1Sa 17:4 {over nine feet} Hebrew *6 cubits* [9 feet or 2.7 meters] *and 1 s* [9 inches or 23 centimeters]; Greek version reads *4 cubits* [6 feet or 1.8 meters] *and 1 s,* about 6.75 feet or 2 meters in length.
Eze 43:13 {a curb 9 inches} Hebrew *1 s* [23 centimeters].

SPARKLING (1)

Rev 15:6 {spotless white linen} Some manuscripts read *in bright and s stone.*

SPEAK (3)

Ps 145:5 {I will meditate} Some manuscripts read *They will s.*
Jn 8:25 {claimed to be.} Or *"Why do I s to you at all?"*
1Co 2:7 {wisdom of God,} Greek *we s God's wisdom in a mystery.*

SPEAKERS (1)

SS 1:1 {*Young Woman:*} The headings identifying the **s** are not in the original text, though the Hebrew usually gives clues by means of the gender of the person speaking.

SPEAKING (2)

SS 1:1 {*Young Woman:*} The headings identifying the speakers are not in the original text, though the Hebrew usually gives clues by means of the gender of the person **s**.
Jn 4:26 {am the Messiah!"} Greek *"I am, the one s to you."*

SPEAKS (1)

Ge 41:45 {renamed him Zaphenath-paneah} *Zaphenath-paneah* probably means "God **s** and lives."

SPEAR (1)

Mt 27:49 {and save him."} Some manuscripts add *And another took a s and pierced his side, and out came water and blood.*

SPECIFICALLY (1)

Isa 33:1 {for you Assyrians,} Hebrew *for you, O destroyer...O betrayer.* The Hebrew text does not **s** name Assyria as the object of this prophecy.

SPECULATION (1)

1Ti 1: 4 {and spiritual pedigrees.} Greek *in myths and endless genealogies, which cause s.*

SPECULATIONS (1)

Lk 17:20 {with visible signs.} Or *by your s.*

SPEECH (1)

Ps 19: 3 {in the skies;} Or *There is no s or language where their voice is not heard.*

SPEED (1)

Hab 3:19 {as a deer} Or *will give me the s of a deer.*

SPENT (1)

Lk 8:43 {had on doctors} Some manuscripts omit *She had s everything she had on doctors.*

SPILL (1)

Pr 5:16 {with just anyone?} Hebrew *Why s your springs in public, your streams in the streets?*

SPINDLE (1)

2Sa 3:29 {walks on crutches} Or *who is effeminate;* Hebrew reads *who handles a s.*

SPIRIT (41)

Jdg 9:23 {stirred up trouble} Hebrew *sent a disturbing s.*
2Ki 2: 9 {your rightful successor."} Hebrew *Let me inherit a double share of your s.*
2:15 {become Elijah's successor!"} Hebrew *The s of Elijah rests upon Elisha.*
1Ch 28:12 {had in mind} Or *the plans of the s that was with him.*
Job 34:14 {back his spirit} Or *his S.*
Ps 106:33 {made Moses angry,} Hebrew *They embittered his s.*
Pr 20:27 {the human spirit,} Or *The human s is the LORD's searchlight.*
Ecc 3:19 {the same air,} Or *both have the same s.*
Eze 3:12 {in his place!)} A likely reading for this verse is *Then the S lifted me up, and as the glory of the LORD rose from its place, I heard behind me a loud rumbling sound.*
Zec 6: 8 {of my Spirit} Hebrew *have given my S rest.*
Mal 2:15 {you are his.} Or *Did not one God make us and preserve our life and breath?* or *Did not one God make her, both flesh and s?* The meaning of the Hebrew is uncertain.
Mt 3:11 {and with fire.} Or *in the Holy S and in fire.*
5: 3 {need for him,} Greek *the poor in s.*
Lk 3:16 {and with fire.} Or *in the Holy S and in fire.*
Jn 3: 5 {and the Spirit.} Or *s.* The Greek word for S can also be translated *wind;* see 3:8.
Ac 19:21 {the Holy Spirit} Or *purposed in his s.*
20:22 {the Holy Spirit,} Or *by my s,* or *by an inner compulsion;* Greek reads *by the s.*
Ro 1: 4 {the Holy Spirit.} Or *the S of holiness.*
1: 9 {all my heart} Or *in my s.*
8:10 {spirit is alive} Or *the S will bring you eternal life.*
1Co 5: 3 {in the Spirit.} Or *in s.*
5: 5 {and he himself} Greek *and the s.*
12:13 {the same Spirit.} Greek *we were all given one S to drink.*
14:15 {in the spirit,} Or *in the S;* also in 14:15b, 16.
2Co 6: 6 {the Holy Spirit.} Or *the holiness of s.*
Php 3: 3 {in the Spirit} Or *in s;* some manuscripts read *worship by the S of God.*
1Ti 3:16 {by the Spirit.} Or *in his s.*
Tit 3: 5 {the Holy Spirit.} Greek *He saved us through the washing of regeneration and renewing of the Holy S.*
Jas 4: 5 {to be faithful} Or *the s that God placed within us tends to envy,* or *the Holy S, whom God has placed within us, opposes our envy.*
1Pe 3:18 {in the Spirit.} Or *s.*
1Jn 5: 7 {these three witnesses} Some very late manuscripts add *in heaven—the Father, the Word, and the Holy S, and these three are one. And we have three witnesses on earth.*
Jude 1:20 {the Holy Spirit.} Greek *Pray in the Holy S.*
Rev 1:10 {in the Spirit.} Or *in s.*
4: 2 {in the Spirit,} Or *in s.*
4: 5 {the seven spirits} See 1:4 and 3:1, where the same expression is translated *the sevenfold S.*
17: 3 {me in spirit} Or *in the S.*
21:10 {me in spirit} Or *in the S.*

SPIRITS (3)

Pr 2:18 {road to hell.} Hebrew *to the s of the dead.*
Rev 1: 4 {the sevenfold Spirit} Greek *the seven s.*
3: 1 {the sevenfold Spirit} Greek *the seven s.*

SPIRITUAL (5)

1Co 2:13 {explain spiritual truths.} Or *explaining s truths in s language,* or *explaining s truths to s people.*
10: 3 {the same miraculous} Greek *s;* also in 10:4.

SPITTLE (1)

Job 7:19 {for a moment} Hebrew *long enough to swallow my s.*

SPLIT (1)

Mt 27:51[-53] {to many people.} Or *The earth shook, rocks s apart, tombs opened, and many bodies of godly men and women who had died were raised from the dead. After Jesus' resurrection, they left the cemetery, went into the holy city of Jerusalem, and appeared to many people.*

SPOIL (2)

Isa 8: 1 {on it: Maher-shalal-hash-baz.} *Maher-shalal-hash-baz* means "Swift to plunder and quick to s."
8:18 {me have names} *Isaiah* means "The LORD will save"; *Shear-jashub* means "A remnant will return"; and *Maher-shalal-hash-baz* means "Swift to plunder and quick to s."

SPOKE (1)

Dt 31: 1 {had finished saying} As in Dead Sea Scrolls and Greek version; Masoretic Text reads *Moses went and s.*

SPREAD (2)

Nu 21:30 {Nophah and Medeba.} Or *until fire s to Medeba.* The meaning of the Hebrew is uncertain.
Dt 7:20 {will send hornets} Or *will s panic,* or *will send a plague.* The meaning of the Hebrew is uncertain.

SPREADS (1)

1Co 5: 6[-7] {can stay pure.} Greek *Don't you realize that even a little leaven s quickly through the whole batch of dough? [7]Purge out the old leaven so that you can be a new batch of dough, just as you are already unleavened.*

SPRING (2)

Jos 15: 9 {waters of Nephtoah,} Or *the s at Me-nephtoah.*
18:15 {waters of Nephtoah,} Or *the s at Me-nephtoah.*

SPRINGS (2)

Pr 4:23 {everything you do.} Hebrew *for from it flow the s of life.*
5:16 {with just anyone?} Hebrew *Why spill your s in public, your streams in the streets?*

SQUARE (2)

Ex 30: 2 {three feet high,} Hebrew *1 cubit* [45 centimeters] *s and 2 cubits* [90 centimeters] *high.*
38: 1 {4 1/2 feet high.} Hebrew *5 cubits* [2.3 meters] *s at the top, and 3 cubits* [1.4 meters] *high.* In this chapter, the distance measures are calculated from the Hebrew cubit at a ratio of 18 inches or 45 centimeters per cubit.

STADIA (5)

Lk 24:13 {Emmaus, seven miles} Greek *60 s* [11.1 kilometers].
Jn 6:19 {or four miles} Greek *25 or 30 s* [4.6 or 5.5 kilometers].
11:18 {a few miles} Greek *was about 15 s* [about 2.8 kilometers].
Rev 14:20 {about 180 miles} Greek *1,600 s* [296 kilometers].
21:16 {each 1,400 miles.} Greek *12,000 s* [2,220 kilometers].

STAINED (1)

Jude 1:23 {by their sins.} Greek *mercy, hating even the clothing s by the flesh.*

STAINS (1)

Jude 1:12 {can shipwreck you.} Or *they are contaminants among you,* or *they are s.*

STAND (1)

Ne 1:11 {ask the king} Hebrew *s before this man.*

STANDARD (2)

Lev 27: 3 {pieces of silver} Hebrew *50 shekels of silver, according to the s sanctuary shekel,* each about 0.4 ounces or 11 grams in weight. The term *shekels* also appears in 27:4, 5, 6, 7, 16.
2Sa 14:26 {to five pounds!} Hebrew *200 shekels* [2.3 kilograms] *by the royal s.*

STANDARDS (1)

Jn 8:15 {your human limitations,} Or *judge me by human s.*

STANDING (1)

1Sa 20:25 {sitting opposite him} As in Greek version; Hebrew reads *with Jonathan s.*

STANZA (1)

Ps 119: 1 {people of integrity,} This psalm is a Hebrew acrostic poem; there are 22 stanzas, one for each letter of the Hebrew alphabet. The 8 verses within each **s** begin with the Hebrew letter of its section.

STANZAS (2)

Ps 119: 1 {people of integrity,} This psalm is a Hebrew acrostic poem; there are 22 **s**, one for each letter of the Hebrew alphabet. The 8 verses within each stanza begin with the Hebrew letter of its section.
La 1: 1 {Jerusalem's streets,} Each of the first four chapters of this book is an acrostic, laid out in the order of the Hebrew alphabet. The first word of each verse begins with a successive Hebrew letter. Chapters 1, 2, and 4 have one verse for each of the 22 Hebrew letters. Chapter 3 contains 22 **s** of three verses each. Though chapter 5 is not an acrostic, it also has 22 verses.

STAR (2)

Am 5:26 {you yourselves made.} Greek version reads *You took up the shrine of Molech, and the s of your god Rephan, and the images you made for yourselves.*
2Pe 1:19 {in your hearts.} Or *until the day dawns and the morning s rises in your hearts.*

STARED (1)

2Ki 8:11 {stared at Hazael} Hebrew *He s at him.*

STAY (2)

Ac 15:33 {had sent them.} Some manuscripts add verse 34, *But Silas decided to s there.*
1Co 14:38 {not be recognized.} Some manuscripts read *If you are ignorant of this, s in your ignorance.*

STENCH (1)

Ex 5:21 {situation with Pharaoh} Hebrew *for making us a s in the nostrils of Pharaoh.*

STEP (1)

Jn 5: 3 {on the porches.} Some manuscripts add *waiting for a certain movement of the water, [4]for an angel of the Lord came from time to time and stirred up the water. And the first person to s down into it afterward was healed.*

STEWARDSHIP (1)

1Ti 1: 4 {faith in God.} Greek *a s of God in faith.*

STICK (1)

Eze 37:16 {tribes of Israel.'} Hebrew *Ephraim's s, representing Joseph and all the house of Israel.*

STILL (2)

Isa 30: 7 {the Harmless Dragon.} Hebrew *Rahab who sits s.* Rahab is the name of a mythical sea monster that represents chaos in ancient literature. The name is used here as a poetic name for Egypt.
Gal 2:16 {obeying the law."} Some translators hold that the quotation extends through verse 14; others through verse 16; and **s** others through verse 21.

STILLNESS (1)

Isa 21:11 {me concerning Edom} Hebrew *Dumah,* which means "silence" or "s." It is a wordplay on the word *Edom.*

STIRRED (1)

Jn 5: 3 {on the porches.} Some manuscripts add *waiting for a certain movement of the water, [4]for an angel of the Lord came from time to time and s up the water. And the first person to step down into it afterward was healed.*

STONE (5)

1Sa 20:19 {the stone pile.} Hebrew *the s Ezel.* The meaning of the Hebrew is uncertain.
1Ki 1: 9 {stone of Zoheleth} Or *to the Serpent's S;* Greek version supports reading *Zoheleth* as a proper name.
Mt 16:18 {you are Peter,} *Peter* means "s" or "rock."
Lk 11:11 {your children ask} Some manuscripts add *for bread, do you give them a s? Or if they ask.*
Rev 15: 6 {spotless white linen} Some manuscripts read *in bright and sparkling s.*

STONES (3)

Jos 8:32 {of the altar.} Or *onto s.*
2Ki 3:25 {came under attack.} Hebrew *until only Kir-hareseth was left, with its s, but the slingers surrounded and attacked it.*
2Ch 26:15 {and hurl stones} Or *designed by brilliant men to protect those who shot arrows and s.*

STOOD (2)

2Ki 23:16 {man of God} As in Greek version; Hebrew lacks *as Jeroboam s beside the altar at the festival. Then Josiah turned and looked up at the tomb of the man of God.*
Rev 12:18 {Then he stood} Some manuscripts read *Then I s,* and some translations put this entire sentence into 13:1.

STOOP (1)

Mk 1: 7 {be his slave.} Greek *to s down and untie his sandals.*

STORM (2)

Job 9:17 {me without reason,} As in Syriac version; Hebrew reads *with a s.*
36:33 {his indignant anger.} Or *even the cattle know when a s is coming.* The meaning of the Hebrew is uncertain.

STORY (2)

Mt 25:15 {bags of gold} Greek *talents;* also throughout the s. A talent is equal to 75 pounds or 34 kilograms.
Mk 12:26 {said to Moses,} Greek *in the s of the bush? God said to him.*

STRANGER (2)

Ex 2:22 {named him Gershom,} *Gershom* sounds like a Hebrew term that means "a s here."
18: 3 {son was Gershom,} *Gershom* sounds like a Hebrew term that means "a s here."

STRANGERS (1)

Isa 5:17 {lambs and kids} As in Greek version; Hebrew reads *s.*

STREAMS (1)

Pr 5:16 {with just anyone?} Hebrew *Why spill your springs in public, your s in the streets?*

STREETS (1)

Pr 5:16 {with just anyone?} Hebrew *Why spill your springs in public, your streams in the s?*

STRENGTH (6)

1Ki 7:21 {the north Boaz.} Jakin probably means "he establishes"; Boaz probably means "in him is s."
2Ch 3:17 {the north Boaz.} Jakin probably means "he establishes"; Boaz probably means "in him is s."
30:21 {by loud instruments.} Or *sang to the LORD with all their s.*
Ps 8: 2 {give you praise.} As in Greek version; Hebrew reads *to show s.*
Pr 24: 5 {strong man,} As in Greek version; Hebrew reads *A wise man is s.*
Am 6:13 {we take Karnaim} *Karnaim* means "horns," a term that symbolizes s.

STRETCHED (1)

Zec 1:16 {reconstruction of Jerusalem.} Hebrew *and the measuring line will be s out over Jerusalem.*

STRINGED (1)

Ps 6: T {an eight-stringed instrument.} Hebrew *with s instruments; according to the sheminith.*

STRIVE (1)

1Ti 4:10 {and suffer much} Some manuscripts read *and s.*

STRONG (2)

Nu 21:24 {Ammonites was fortified.} Or *because the terrain of the Ammonite frontier was rugged;* Hebrew *because the boundary of the Ammonites was s.*
Lk 11:21 {For when Satan,} Greek *the s one.*

STRUGGLE (1)

Ge 30: 8 {named him Naphtali,} *Naphtali* means "my s."

STRUGGLES (4)

Ge 32:28 {is now Israel,} *Israel* means "God s" or "one who s with God."
35:10 {be called Israel."} *Jacob* means "he grasps the heel"; this can also figuratively mean "he deceives"; *Israel* means "God s" or "one who s with God."

SUBJECT (1)

Ro 6:12 {way you live;} Or *Do not let sin reign in your body, which is s to death.*

SUBMIT (1)

Ps 68:30 {tribute from us.} Or *Humble them until they s, bringing pieces of silver as tribute.*

SUCCESSIVE (1)

La 1: 1 {Jerusalem's streets,} Each of the first four chapters of this book is an acrostic, laid out in the order of the Hebrew alphabet. The first word of each verse begins with a s Hebrew letter. Chapters 1, 2, and 4 have one verse for each of the 22 Hebrew letters. Chapter 3 contains 22 stanzas of three verses each. Though chapter 5 is not an acrostic, it also has 22 verses.

SUCCESSOR (1)

Jer 22:13 {certain for Jehoiakim,} The brother and s of the exiled Jehoahaz.

SUCCOTH (3)

Ge 33:17 {was named Succoth.} *S* means "shelters."
2Sa 11:11 {living in tents,} Or *at S.*
1Ki 20:12 {in their tents.} Or *in S;* also in 20:16.

SUFFER (1)

Lk 17:25 {must suffer terribly} Or *s many things.*

SUITOR (1)

Jer 31:22 {embrace her God.} Hebrew *a woman will court a s.*

SUN (2)

Ne 7: 3 {of the day.} Or *Keep the gates of Jerusalem closed until the s is hot.*
Mal 4: 2 {in his wings.} Or *the s of righteousness will rise with healing in its wings.*

SUNRISE (1)

Nu 3:38 {toward the sunrise} Hebrew *toward the s, in front of the Tent of Meeting.*

SUPPORT (1)

Mt 10:10 {to be fed.} Or *the worker is worthy of s.*

SUPPORTED (1)

Ezr 6: 3 {be ninety feet.} Aramaic *Its height will be 60 cubits* [27 meters], *and its width will be 60 cubits.* It is commonly held that this verse should be emended to read: "Its height will be 45 feet, its length will be 90 feet, and its width will be 30 feet"; compare 1 Kgs 6:2. The emendation regarding the width is s by the Syriac version.

SUPPORTING (5)

2Sa 5: 9 {at the Millo} Or *the s terraces.* The meaning of the Hebrew is uncertain.
1Ki 9:15 {palace, the Millo,} Or *the s terraces;* also in 9:24.
11:27 {rebuilding the Millo} Or *the s terraces.*
1Ch 11: 8 {from the Millo} Or *the s terraces.* The meaning of the Hebrew is uncertain.
2Ch 32: 5 {reinforced the Millo} Or *the s terraces.*

SUPPORTS (1)

1Ki 1: 9 {stone of Zoheleth} Or *to the Serpent's Stone;* Greek version s reading *Zoheleth* as a proper name.

SURELY (1)

1Sa 15:32 {have been spared!"} Dead Sea Scrolls and Greek version read *Agag arrived hesitantly, for he thought, "S this is the bitterness of death."*

SURROUND (1)

SS 8: 9 {off from men.} Hebrew *If she is a wall, we will build battlements of silver on her; but if she is a door, we will s her with panels of cedar.*

SURROUNDED (2)

2Ki 3:25 {came under attack.} Hebrew *until only Kir-hareseth was left, with its stones, but the slingers s and attacked it.*
Jer 20: 3 {Lives in Terror.'} Hebrew *Magor-missabib,* which means "s by terror"; also in 20:10.

SWALLOW (1)

Job 7:19 {for a moment} Hebrew *long enough to s my spittle.*

SWEAR (1)

Ge 24: 3 {"Swear} Hebrew *Put your hand under my thigh, and I will make you s.*

SWELL (2)

Nu 5:21 {makes you infertile.} Hebrew *when he causes your thigh to waste away and your abdomen to s.*
5:27 {will become infertile,} Hebrew *Her body will s and her thigh will waste away.*

SWELLINGS (1)

Isa 45: 2 {level the mountains.} As in Dead Sea Scrolls and Greek version; Masoretic Text reads *the s.*

SWELLS (1)

Nu 5:22 {make you infertile.} Hebrew *enter your body so that your abdomen s and your thigh wastes away.*

SWIFT (2)

Isa 8: 1 {on it: Maher-shalal-hash-baz.} *Maher-shalal-hash-baz* means "S to plunder and quick to spoil."
8:18 {me have names} *Isaiah* means "The LORD will save"; *Shear-jashub* means "A remnant will return"; and *Maher-shalal-hash-baz* means "S to plunder and quick to spoil."

SWORD (2)

1Sa 2:33 {a violent death.} As in Dead Sea Scrolls, which read *die by the s;* Masoretic Text reads *die like mortals.*
Isa 22: 2 {famine and disease.} Hebrew *killed, but not by s and not in battle.*

SWORE (1)

Ge 24: 9 {solemn oath} Hebrew *put his hand under the thigh of Abraham his master and s an oath.*

SYMBOLIZES (1)

Am 6:13 {we take Karnaim} *Karnaim* means "horns," a term that s strength.

SYNAGOGUE (1)

Jas 2: 2 {into your meeting} Greek *s.*

SYRACUSE (1)

Ac 28:12 {stop was Syracuse,} *S* was on the island of Sicily.

SYRIA (1)

Ac 7: 2 {moved to Haran.} *Mesopotamia* was the region now called Iraq. *Haran* was a city in what is now called S.

SYRIAC (54)

Ge 1:26 {livestock, wild animals,} As in S version; Hebrew reads *all the earth.*
36:39 {Baal-hanan died, Hadad} As in some Hebrew manuscripts, Samaritan Pentateuch, and S version (see also 1 Chr 1:50); most Hebrew manuscripts read *Hadar.*
46:13 {were Tola, Puah,} As in S version and Samaritan Pentateuch (see also 1 Chr 7:1); Hebrew reads *Puvah.*
Nu 26:17 {its ancestor Arodi.} As in Samaritan Pentateuch and S version (see also Gen 46:16); Hebrew reads *Arod.*
26:23 {its ancestor Puah.} As in Samaritan Pentateuch, Greek and S versions, and Latin Vulgate (see also 1 Chr 7:1); Hebrew reads *The Punite clan, named after its ancestor Puvah.*
26:39 {its ancestor Shupham.} As in some Hebrew manuscripts, Samaritan Pentateuch, Greek and S versions, and Latin Vulgate; most Hebrew manuscripts read *Shephupham.*
Dt 4:48 {to Mount Sirion,} As in S version (see also 3:9); Hebrew reads *Mount Sion.*
33: 2 {dawned upon us} As in Greek and S versions; Hebrew reads *upon them.*
Ru 3:15 {back. Then Boaz} Most Hebrew manuscripts read *he;* many Hebrew manuscripts, S version, and Latin Vulgate read *she.*
1Sa 1:24 {a three-year-old bull} As in Dead Sea Scrolls, Greek and S versions; Hebrew reads *3 bulls.*
12:11 {Barak,} As in Greek and S versions; Hebrew reads *Bedan.*
12:11 {Samuel} Greek and S versions read *Samson.*
13: 5 {of three thousand} As in Greek and S versions; Hebrew reads *30,000.*
2Sa 8:12 {Edom,} As in a few Hebrew manuscripts and Greek and S versions (see also 8:14; 1 Chr 18:11); most Hebrew manuscripts read *Aram.*
8:13 {eighteen thousand Edomites} As in a few Hebrew manuscripts and Greek and S versions (see also 8:14; 1 Chr 18:12); most Hebrew manuscripts read *Arameans.*
15: 7 {After four years,} As in Greek and S versions; Hebrew reads *40 years.*
21: 8 {Saul's daughter Merab,} As in a few Hebrew and Greek manuscripts and S version (see also 1 Sam 18:19); most Hebrew manuscripts read *Michal.*
23:18 {of the Thirty.} As in a few Hebrew manuscripts and S version; most Hebrew manuscripts read *the Three.*
23:19 {of the Thirty} As in S version; Hebrew reads *the Three.*
1Ki 7: 7 {floor to ceiling.} As in S version and Latin Vulgate; Hebrew reads *from floor to floor.*
12:18 {Rehoboam sent Adoniram,} As in some Greek manuscripts and S version (see also 4:6; 5:14); Hebrew reads *Adoram.*
2Ki 12:21 {assassins were Jozacar} As in Greek and S versions; Hebrew reads *Jozabad;* compare parallel text at 2 Chr 24:26.
1Ch 1:22 {Obal,} As in some Hebrew manuscripts and S version (see also Gen 10:28); most Hebrew manuscripts read *Ebal.*
1:50 {city of Pau.} As in many Hebrew manuscripts, some Greek manuscripts, S version, and Latin Vulgate (see also Gen 36:39); most Hebrew manuscripts read *Pai.*
2: 6 {Calcol, and Darda} As in many Hebrew manuscripts, some Greek manuscripts, and S version (see also 1 Kgs 4:31); Hebrew reads *Dara.*
6:28 {Samuel were Joel} As in some Greek manuscripts and the S version (see also 6:33 and 1 Sam 8:2); Hebrew lacks *Joel.*
6:59 {Juttah,} As in S version (see also Josh 21:16); Hebrew lacks *Juttah.*
9:41 {Tahrea, and Ahaz.} As in S version and Latin Vulgate (see also 8:35); Hebrew lacks *and Ahaz.*

11:20 {of the Thirty.} As in **S** version; Hebrew reads *the Three;* also in 11:21.
18:16 {Ahitub and Ahimelech} As in some Hebrew manuscripts, **S** version, and Latin Vulgate (see also 2 Sam 8:17); most Hebrew manuscripts read *Abimelech.*
2Ch 3: 4 {was thirty feet} As in some Greek and **S** manuscripts, which read *20 cubits* [9 meters]; Hebrew reads *120 cubits,* which is 180 feet or 54 meters.
3:15 {that were 27 feet} As in **S** version (see also 1 Kgs 7:15; 2 Kgs 25:17; Jer 52:21), which reads *18 cubits* [8.1 meters]; Hebrew reads *35 cubits,* which is 52.5 feet or 15.8 meters.
13: 2 {mother was Maacah,} As in most Greek manuscripts and **S** version (see also 2 Chr 11:20-21; 1 Kgs 15:2); Hebrew reads *Micaiah.*
15: 8 {Azariah the prophet,} As in **S** version and Latin Vulgate (see also 15:1); Hebrew reads *from Oded the prophet.*
22: 2 {Ahaziah was twenty-two} As in some Greek manuscripts and **S** version (see also 2 Kgs 8:26); Hebrew reads *forty-two.*
22: 6 {and King Ahaziah} Some Hebrew manuscripts, Greek and **S** versions, and Latin Vulgate (see also 2 Kgs 8:29); most Hebrew manuscripts read *Azariah.*
36: 9 {Jehoiachin was eighteen} As in one Hebrew manuscript, some Greek manuscripts, and **S** version (see also 2 Kgs 24:8); most Hebrew manuscripts read *eight.*
Ezr 6: 3 {be ninety feet.} Aramaic *Its height will be 60 cubits* [27 meters], *and its width will be 60 cubits.* It is commonly held that this verse should be emended to read: "Its height will be 45 feet, its length will be 90 feet, and its width will be 30 feet"; compare 1 Kgs 6:2. The emendation regarding the width is supported by the **S** version.
Ne 3:18 {led by Binnui} As in a few Hebrew manuscripts, some Greek manuscripts, and **S** version (see also 3:24; 10:9); most Hebrew manuscripts read *Bavvai.*
12:14 {family of Shecaniah.} As in many Hebrew manuscripts, some Greek manuscripts, and **S** version (see also 12:3); most Hebrew manuscripts read *Shebaniah.*
Job 9:17 {me without reason,} As in **S** version; Hebrew reads *with a storm.*
Ecc 9: 2 {good or bad,} As in Greek and **S** versions, and Latin Vulgate; Hebrew lacks *or bad.*
SS 7: 9 {lips and teeth.} As in Greek and **S** versions and Latin Vulgate; Hebrew reads *over lips of sleepers.*
Isa 21: 8 {Then the watchman} As in Dead Sea Scrolls and **S** version; Hebrew reads *a lion.*
49:24 {that a tyrant} As in Dead Sea Scrolls, **S** version, and Latin Vulgate (also see 49:25); Masoretic Text reads *a righteous person.*
52:14 {they saw him} As in **S** version; Hebrew reads *you.*
Jer 27: 1 {reign of Zedekiah} As in some Hebrew manuscripts and **S** version (see also 27:3, 12); most Hebrew manuscripts read *Jehoiakim.*
Hos 4: 7 {They have exchanged} As in **S** version and an ancient Hebrew tradition; Masoretic Text reads *I will exchange.*
12: 4 {spoke to him} As in Greek and **S** versions; Hebrew reads *to us.*
13:10 {Where now is} As in Greek and **S** versions and Latin Vulgate; Hebrew reads *I will be.*
Zec 6:11 {make a crown} As in Greek and **S** versions; Hebrew reads *crowns.*
6:14 {Heldai,} As in **S** version (compare 6:10); Hebrew reads *Helem.*
6:14 {Jedaiah, and Josiah} As in **S** version (compare 6:10); Hebrew reads *Hen.*
11:13 {to the potters} **S** version reads *into the treasury;* also in 11:13b.

SYZYGUS (1)

Php 4: 3 {my true teammate,} Greek *true yokefellow,* or *loyal* **S***.*

T

TABERAH (1)

Dt 9:22 {angry at Taberah,} ***T*** means "place of burning." See Num 11:1-3.

TABERNACLE (11)

Ex 38:21 {of the Covenant.} Hebrew *the* ***T****, the* ***T*** *of the Testimony.*
39:32 {last the Tabernacle} Hebrew *the* ***T****, the Tent of Meeting;* also in 39:40.
40: 2 {up the Tabernacle} Hebrew *the* ***T****, the Tent of Meeting;* also in 40:6, 29.
Nu 1:50 {of the Covenant,} Or ***T*** *of the Testimony;* also in 1:53.
3: 7 {around the Tabernacle.} Hebrew *around the Tent of Meeting, doing service at the* ***T****.*
9:15 {cloud covered it.} Hebrew *covered the* ***T****, the Tent of the Testimony.*
10:11 {of the Covenant.} Or ***T*** *of the Testimony.*
17: 7 {of the Covenant.} Or ***T*** *of the Testimony;* also in 17:8.
18: 2 {of the Covenant.} Or ***T*** *of the Testimony.*
1Ch 6:32 {at the Tabernacle} Hebrew *the* ***T****, the Tent of Meeting.*

TABERNACLES (3)

Mt 17: 4 {make three shrines,} Or *shelters;* Greek reads **t***.*
Mk 9: 5 {make three shrines} Or *shelters;* Greek reads **t***.*
Lk 9:33 {make three shrines} Or *shelters;* Greek reads **t***.*

TABITHA (1)

Ac 9:36 {Greek is Dorcas} The names ***T*** in Aramaic and *Dorcas* in Greek both mean "gazelle."

TADMOR (1)

1Ki 9:18 {Baalath, and Tamar} The marginal *Qere* reading of the Masoretic Text reads ***T****.*

TAHKEMONITE (1)

2Sa 23: 8 {Jashobeam the Hacmonite,} As in parallel text at 1 Chr 11:11; Hebrew reads *Josheb-basshebeth the* ***T****.*

TAHREA (1)

1Ch 8:35 {Pithon, Melech, Tahrea,} As in parallel text at 9:41; Hebrew reads *Tarea,* a variant name for **T**.

TAKE (8)

Dt 32:36 {his mind about} Or *will* **t** *revenge for.*
1Sa 17:18 {letter from them.} Hebrew *and* **t** *their pledge.*
Job 9: 3 {God to court,} Or *If God wanted to* **t** *a person to court.*
Mt 26:45 {sleeping? Still resting?} Or *Sleep on,* **t** *your rest.*
Mk 14:41 {sleeping? Still resting?} Or *Sleep on,* **t** *your rest.*
Lk 15:21 {called your son.} Some manuscripts add *Please* **t** *me on as a hired man.*
1Th 4: 4 {control your body} Or *will know how to* **t** *a wife for himself;* Greek reads *will know how to possess his own vessel.*
2Ti 3: 6 {the confidence of} Greek *and* **t** *captive.*

TAKEN (3)

2Sa 8: 1 {their largest city.} Hebrew *by conquering Metheg-ammah,* a name which means "the bridle," possibly referring to the size of the city or the tribute money **t** from it. Compare 1 Chr 18:1.
Lk 17:35 {the other left.} Some manuscripts add verse 36, *Two men will be working in the field; one will be* **t***, the other left.*
24:51 {up to heaven.} Some manuscripts do not include *and was* **t** *up to heaven.*

TALENT (11)

Ex 25:39 {need seventy-five pounds} Hebrew *1* **t** [34 kilograms].
37:24 {from seventy-five pounds} Hebrew *1* **t** [34 kilograms].
38:27 {for each base.} Hebrew *100 talents* [3,400 kilograms] *of silver, 1* **t** [34 kilograms] *for each base.*
2Sa 12:30 {about seventy-five pounds.} Hebrew *1* **t** [34 kilograms].
1Ki 20:39 {of seventy-five pounds} Hebrew *1* **t** [34 kilograms].
2Ki 5:22 {would like 75 pounds} Hebrew *1* **t** [34 kilograms].
23:33 {75 pounds of gold} Hebrew *100 talents* [3.4 metric tons] *of silver and 1* **t** [34 kilograms] *of gold.*
1Ch 20: 2 {about seventy-five pounds.} Hebrew *1* **t** [34 kilograms].
2Ch 36: 3 {75 pounds of gold.} Hebrew *100 talents* [3.4 metric tons] *of silver and 1* **t** [34 kilograms] *of gold.*
Mt 25:15 {bags of gold} Greek *talents;* also throughout the story. A **t** is equal to 75 pounds or 34 kilograms.
Rev 16:21 {weighing seventy-five pounds} Greek *1* **t** [34 kilograms].

TALENTS (38)

Ex 38:24 {about 2,200 pounds,} Hebrew *29* **t** [2,175 pounds or 986 kilograms] *and 730 shekels* [18.3 pounds or 8.3 kilograms], *according to the sanctuary shekel.*
38:25 {about 7,545 pounds.} Hebrew *100* **t** [7,500 pounds or 3,400 kilograms] *and 1,775 shekels* [44.4 pounds or 20.2 kilograms], *according to the sanctuary shekel.*
38:27 {for each base.} Hebrew *100* **t** [3,400 kilograms] *of silver, 1 talent* [34 kilograms] *for each base.*
38:29 {brought 5,310 pounds} Hebrew *70* **t** [5,250 pounds or 2,380 kilograms] *and 2,400 shekels* [60 pounds or 27.4 kilograms].
1Ki 9:14 {nine thousand pounds} Hebrew *120* **t** [4 metric tons].
9:28 {some sixteen tons} Hebrew *420* **t** [14 metric tons].
10:10 {nine thousand pounds} Hebrew *120* **t** [4 metric tons].
10:14 {about twenty-five tons} Hebrew *666* **t** [23 metric tons].
16:24 {pounds of silver.} Hebrew *for 2* **t** [68 kilograms] *of silver.*
2Ki 5: 5 {pounds of gold,} Hebrew *10* **t** [340 kilograms] *of silver, 6,000 shekels* [68 kilograms] *of gold.*
5:23 {take 150 pounds} Hebrew *2* **t** [68 kilograms].
15:19 {him thirty-seven tons} Hebrew *1,000* **t** [34 metric tons].
18:14 {ton of gold.} Hebrew *300* **t** [10 metric tons] *of silver and 30* **t** [1 metric ton] *of gold.*
23:33 {75 pounds of gold} Hebrew *100* **t** [3.4 metric tons] *of silver and 1 talent* [34 kilograms] *of gold.*
1Ch 19: 6 {sent thirty-eight tons} Hebrew *1,000* **t** [34 metric tons].
22:14 {tons of silver,} Hebrew *100,000* **t** [3,400 metric tons] *of gold, 1,000,000* **t** [34,000 metric tons] *of silver.*
29: 4 {tons of gold} Hebrew *3,000* **t** [102 metric tons] *of gold.*
29: 4 {of refined silver} Hebrew *7,000* **t** [238 metric tons] *of silver.*
29: 7 {tons of gold,} Hebrew *5,000* **t** [170 metric tons] *of gold.*
29: 7 {tons of silver,} Hebrew *10,000* **t** [340 metric tons] *of silver.*
29: 7 {tons of bronze,} Hebrew *18,000* **t** [612 metric tons] *of bronze.*
29: 7 {tons of iron.} Hebrew *100,000* **t** [3,400 metric tons] *of iron.*
2Ch 3: 8 {about twenty-three tons} Hebrew *600* **t** [20.4 metric tons].
8:18 {almost seventeen tons} Hebrew *450* **t** [15.3 metric tons].
9: 9 {nine thousand pounds} Hebrew *120* **t** [4 metric tons].
9:13 {received about 25 tons} Hebrew *666* **t** [23 metric tons].
25: 6 {about 7,500 pounds} Hebrew *100* **t** [3.4 metric tons].
27: 5 {of 7,500 pounds} Hebrew *100* **t** [3.4 metric tons].
36: 3 {75 pounds of gold.} Hebrew *100* **t** [3.4 metric tons] *of silver and 1 talent* [34 kilograms] *of gold.*
Ezr 7:22 {to 7,500 pounds} Aramaic *100* **t** [3.4 metric tons].
8:26 {24 tons} Hebrew *650* **t** [22 metric tons].
8:26 {7,500 pounds} Hebrew *100* **t** [3.4 metric tons].
8:26 {7,500 pounds} Hebrew *100* **t** [3.4 metric tons].
Est 3: 9 {give 375 tons} Hebrew *10,000* **t** [340 metric tons].
Mt 18:24 {millions of dollars.} Greek *10,000* **t***.*
25:15 {bags of gold} Greek **t***;* also throughout the story. A talent is equal to 75 pounds or 34 kilograms.

TALITHA (1)

Mk 5:41 {up, little girl!"} Greek text uses Aramaic *"***T** *cumi"* and then translates it as "Get up, little girl."

TALKED (1)

1Sa 9:25 {for him there.} As in Greek version; Hebrew reads *and* **t** *with him there.*

TALL (2)

Jer 52:21 {18 feet in circumference.} Hebrew *18 cubits* [8.1 meters] **t** *and 12 cubits* [5.4 meters] *in circumference.*
Da 3: 1 {nine feet wide} Aramaic *60 cubits* [27 meters] **t** *and 6 cubits* [2.7 meters] *wide.*

TAME (1)

Job 11:12 {bear human offspring} Or *bear a* **t** *colt.*

TAREA (1)

1Ch 8:35 {Pithon, Melech, Tahrea,} As in parallel text at 9:41; Hebrew reads ***T****,* a variant name for Tahrea.

TARSHISH (6)

1Ki 10:22 {of trading ships} Hebrew *fleet of ships of* ***T****.*
22:48 {of trading ships} Hebrew *fleet of ships of* ***T****.*
2Ch 9:21 {of trading ships} Hebrew *fleet of ships that could sail to* ***T****.*
20:36 {of trading ships} Hebrew *fleet of ships that could go to* ***T****.*
20:37 {out to sea.} Hebrew *never set sail for* ***T****.*
Isa 2:16 {great trading ships} Hebrew *every ship of* ***T****.*

TARTAROS (1)

2Pe 2: 4 {them into hell,} Greek ***T****.*

TAVERNS (1)

Ac 28:15 {The Three Taverns.} *The Three* **t** was about 35 miles (57 kilometers) from Rome.

TAX (4)

Ne 10:32 {ounce of silver,} Hebrew **t** *of 1/3 of a shekel* [4 grams].
Mt 9:11 {with such scum} Greek *with* **t** *collectors and sinners.*
Mk 2:16 {with such scum} Greek *with* **t** *collectors and sinners.*
Lk 5:30 {with such scum} Greek *with* **t** *collectors and sinners.*

TEACH (1)

Isa 29:13 {learned by rote.} Greek version reads *Their worship is a farce, for they merely* **t** *human commands and teachings.*

TEACHER (4)
Ecc 1: 1 {of the Teacher,} Hebrew *Koheleth;* this term is rendered "the **T**" throughout this book.
Mt 19:16 {this question: "Teacher,} Some manuscripts read *Good **T**.*
23: 7 {being called 'Rabbi.'} *Rabbi,* from Aramaic, means "master" or "**t**."
Jn 20:16 {and exclaimed, "Teacher!"} Greek *and said in Hebrew, "Rabboni," which means "**T**."*

TEACHERS (1)
Mt 23:13 {go in yourselves.} Some manuscripts add verse 14, *How terrible it will be for you **t** of religious law and you Pharisees. Hypocrites! You shamelessly cheat widows out of their property, and then, to cover up the kind of people you really are, you make long prayers in public. Because of this, your punishment will be the greater.*

TEACHINGS (1)
Isa 29:13 {learned by rote.} Greek version reads *Their worship is a farce, for they merely teach human commands and **t**.*

TEAM (1)
Mic 1:13 {people of Lachish.} *Lachish* sounds like the Hebrew term for "**t** of horses."

TEAMS (1)
Isa 5:10 {Ten acres} Hebrew *A ten yoke,* that is, the area of land plowed by ten **t** of oxen in one day.

TEBAH (1)
1Ch 18: 8 {cities of Tebah} Hebrew reads *Tibhath,* a variant name for **T**; compare parallel text at 2 Sam 8:8.

TEBETH (1)
Est 2:16 {in early winter} Hebrew *in the tenth month, the month of **T**.* A number of events in the book of Esther can be cross-checked with dates in surviving Persian records and related accurately to our modern calendar. This month of the Hebrew lunar calendar occurred in December 479 B.C. and January 478 B.C.

TEETH (1)
Ac 7:54 {fists in rage.} Greek *they were grinding their **t** against him.*

TELL (3)
Isa 62:11 {people of Israel,} Hebrew ***T** the daughter of Zion.*
Mic 1:10 {city of Gath} *Gath* sounds like the Hebrew term for "**t**."
Mt 21: 5 {people of Israel,} Greek ***T** the daughter of Zion.* Isa 62:11.

TEMAN (2)
Eze 20:46 {toward the south} Hebrew ***T**.*
Hab 3: 3 {deserts from Edom} Hebrew ***T**.*

TEMPLE (5)
1Sa 1: 9 {to the Tabernacle} Hebrew *the **T** of the LORD.*
3: 3 {in the Tabernacle} Hebrew *the **T** of the LORD.*
2Ch 36: 7 {in his palace} Or ***t**.*
36:19 {everything of value.} Or *destroyed all the valuable **T** utensils.*
Eze 40: 8 {of the gateway} Many Hebrew manuscripts add *which faced inward toward the **T**; it was one rod* [10.5 feet or 3.2 meters] *deep. [9]Then he measured the foyer of the gateway,...*

TEMPTER (1)
Mt 4: 3 {Then the Devil} Greek *the **t**.*

TEN (2)
Isa 5:10 {Ten acres} Hebrew *A **t** yoke,* that is, the area of land plowed by **t** teams of oxen in one day.

TENDS (1)
Jas 4: 5 {to be faithful} Or *the spirit that God placed within us **t** to envy,* or *the Holy Spirit, whom God has placed within us, opposes our envy.*

TENT (63)
Ex 27:21 {in the Tabernacle.} Hebrew *in the **T** of Meeting, outside of the inner curtain, in front of the Testimony.*
28:43 {enter the Tabernacle} Hebrew ***T** of Meeting.*
29: 4 {of the Tabernacle,} Hebrew ***T** of Meeting;* also in 29:10, 11, 30, 32, 42, 44.
30:16 {of the Tabernacle.} Hebrew ***T** of Meeting;* also in 30:18, 20, 26, 36.
31: 7 {of the Covenant;} Hebrew *the **T** of Meeting; the Ark of the Testimony.*
35:21 {for the Tabernacle} Hebrew ***T** of Meeting.*
38: 8 {of the Tabernacle.} Hebrew ***T** of Meeting;* also in 38:30.
39:32 {last the Tabernacle} Hebrew *the Tabernacle, the **T** of Meeting;* also in 39:40.
40: 2 {up the Tabernacle} Hebrew *the Tabernacle, the **T** of Meeting;* also in 40:6, 29.
40: 7 {between the Tabernacle} Hebrew ***T** of Meeting;* also in 40:12, 22, 24, 26, 30, 32, 34, 35.
Lev 1: 1 {from the Tabernacle} Hebrew ***T** of Meeting;* also in 1:3, 5.
3: 2 {of the Tabernacle.} Hebrew ***T** of Meeting;* also in 3:8, 13.
4: 4 {of the Tabernacle,} Hebrew ***T** of Meeting;* also in 4:5, 7, 14, 16, 18.
6:16 {of the Tabernacle.} Hebrew ***T** of Meeting;* also in 6:26, 30.
8: 3 {of the Tabernacle.} Hebrew ***T** of Meeting;* also in 8:4, 31, 33, 35.
9: 5 {of the Tabernacle,} Hebrew ***T** of Meeting;* also in 9:23.
10: 7 {of the Tabernacle.} Hebrew ***T** of Meeting;* also in 10:9.
12: 6 {of the Tabernacle.} Hebrew ***T** of Meeting.*
14:11 {of the Tabernacle.} Hebrew ***T** of Meeting;* also in 14:23.
15:14 {of the Tabernacle} Hebrew ***T** of Meeting;* also in 15:29.
16: 7 {of the Tabernacle.} Hebrew ***T** of Meeting;* also in 16:16, 17, 20, 23, 33.
17: 4 {of the Tabernacle.} Hebrew ***T** of Meeting;* also in 17:5, 6, 9.
19:21 {of the Tabernacle.} Hebrew ***T** of Meeting.*
24: 3 {in the Tabernacle} Hebrew *the curtain of the Testimony in the **T** of Meeting.*
Nu 1: 1 {in the Tabernacle} Hebrew ***T** of Meeting.*
2: 2 {banners. The Tabernacle} Hebrew ***T** of Meeting;* also in 2:17.
3: 7 {around the Tabernacle.} Hebrew *around the **T** of Meeting, doing service at the Tabernacle.*
3: 8 {the sacred tent,} Hebrew ***T** of Meeting.*
3:38 {toward the sunrise} Hebrew *toward the sunrise, in front of the **T** of Meeting.*
4: 3 {in the Tabernacle} Hebrew ***T** of Meeting;* also in 4:4, 15, 23, 25, 28, 30, 31, 33, 35, 37, 39, 41, 43, 47.
6:10 {of the Tabernacle.} Hebrew ***T** of Meeting;* also in 6:13, 18.
7: 5 {of the Tabernacle.} Hebrew ***T** of Meeting;* also in 7:89.
8: 9 {of the Tabernacle.} Hebrew ***T** of Meeting;* also in 8:15, 19, 22, 24, 26.
9:15 {cloud covered it.} Hebrew *covered the Tabernacle, the **T** of the Testimony.*
10: 3 {of the Tabernacle.} Hebrew ***T** of Meeting.*
11:16 {to the Tabernacle} Hebrew ***T** of Meeting.*
11:24 {around the Tabernacle.} Hebrew *the **t**;* also in 11:26.
12: 4 {to the Tabernacle,} Hebrew ***T** of Meeting.*
12: 5 {of the Tabernacle.} Hebrew *the **t**;* also in 12:10.
14:10 {above the Tabernacle.} Hebrew ***T** of Meeting.*
16:18 {of the Tabernacle} Hebrew ***T** of Meeting;* also in 16:19, 42, 43, 50.
17: 4 {of the Covenant,} Hebrew *in the **T** of Meeting before the Testimony.*
18: 4 {of the Tabernacle,} Hebrew ***T** of Meeting;* also in 18:6, 21, 22, 23, 31.
19: 4 {of the Tabernacle.} Hebrew ***T** of Meeting.*
20: 6 {of the Tabernacle,} Hebrew ***T** of Meeting.*
25: 6 {of the Tabernacle.} Hebrew ***T** of Meeting.*
27: 2 {of the Tabernacle.} Hebrew ***T** of Meeting.*
31:54 {to the Tabernacle} Hebrew ***T** of Meeting.*
Dt 31:14 {to the Tabernacle,} Hebrew ***T** of Meeting;* also in 31:14b.
Jos 18: 1 {up the Tabernacle.} Hebrew ***T** of Meeting.*
19:51 {of the Tabernacle} Hebrew ***T** of Meeting.*
1Sa 2:22 {of the Tabernacle.} Hebrew ***T** of Meeting.* Some manuscripts lack this entire sentence.
1Ki 8: 4 {with the Tabernacle} Hebrew ***T** of Meeting.*
1Ch 6:32 {at the Tabernacle} Hebrew *the Tabernacle, the **T** of Meeting.*
9:21 {to the Tabernacle.} Hebrew ***T** of Meeting.*
23:32 {and the Temple} Hebrew *the **T** of Meeting and the sanctuary.*
2Ch 1: 3 {where God's Tabernacle} Hebrew ***T** of Meeting;* also in 1:6, 13.
5: 5 {the special tent} Hebrew ***T** of Meeting.*
24: 6 {of the Covenant.} Hebrew ***T** of the Testimony.*
La 2: 4 {on beautiful Jerusalem.} Hebrew *on the **t** of the daughter of Zion.*
Ac 7:44 {carried the Tabernacle} Greek *the **t** of witness.*
Heb 9: 6 {the first room} Greek *first **t**;* also in 9:8.
2Pe 1:14 {soon to die.} Greek *I must soon put off this earthly **t**.*

TENTH (24)
Ge 8: 5 {half months later,} Hebrew *On the first day of the **t** month;* see 7:11 and note on 8:4.
Ex 16:36 {about two quarts.)} Hebrew *An omer is one **t** of an ephah.*
Lev 16:29 {in early autumn,} Hebrew *On the **t** day of the seventh month.* This day of the Hebrew lunar calendar occurs in September or early October.
23:27 {Festival of Trumpets.} Hebrew *on the **t** day of the seventh month;* see 23:24 and the note there.
25: 9 {the fiftieth year,} Hebrew *on the **t** day of the seventh month, on the Day of Atonement;* see 23:27 and the note there.
Nu 29: 7 {"Ten days later,} Hebrew *On the **t** day of the seventh month;* see 29:1 and the note there.
Jos 4:19 {exodus from Egypt.} Hebrew *the **t** day of the first month.* This day of the Hebrew lunar calendar occurs in late March or early April.
2Ki 25: 1 {So on January 15,} Hebrew *on the **t** day of the **t** month,* of the Hebrew calendar. A number of events in 2 Kings can be cross-checked with dates in surviving Babylonian records and related accurately to our modern calendar. This event occurred on January 15, 588 B.C.
Ezr 10:16 {name. On December 29,} Hebrew *On the first day of the **t** month,* of the Hebrew calendar. This event occurred on December 29, 458 B.C.; also see note on 7:9a.
Est 2:16 {in early winter} Hebrew *in the **t** month, the month of Tebeth.* A number of events in the book of Esther can be cross-checked with dates in surviving Persian records and related accurately to our modern calendar. This month of the Hebrew lunar calendar occurred in December 479 B.C. and January 478 B.C.
Jer 32: 1 {reign of Zedekiah,} The **t** year of Zedekiah's reign and the eighteenth year of Nebuchadnezzar's reign was 587 B.C.
39: 1 {was in January} Hebrew *in the **t** month,* of the Hebrew calendar. A number of events in Jeremiah can be cross-checked with dates in surviving Babylonian records and related accurately to our modern calendar. This event occurred on January 15, 588 B.C.; see 52:4 and the note there.
52: 4 {So on January 15,} Hebrew *on the **t** day of the **t** month,* of the Hebrew calendar. A number of events in Jeremiah can be cross-checked with dates in surviving Babylonian records and related accurately to our modern calendar. This event occurred on January 15, 588 B.C.
52:12 {of that year,} Hebrew *On the **t** day of the fifth month,* of the Hebrew calendar. This day was August 17, 586 B.C.; also see note on 52:4a.
Eze 20: 1 {On August 14,} Hebrew *In the fifth month, on the **t** day,* of the Hebrew calendar. This event occurred on August 14, 591 B.C.; also see note on 1:1.
24: 1 {On January 15,} Hebrew *On the **t** day of the **t** month,* of the Hebrew calendar. This event occurred on January 15, 588 B.C.; also see note on 1:1.
29: 1 {On January 7,} Hebrew *On the twelfth day of the **t** month,* of the Hebrew calendar. A number of events in Ezekiel can be cross-checked with dates in surviving Babylonian records and related accurately to our modern calendar. This event occurred on January 7, 587 B.C.
33:21 {On January 8,} Hebrew *On the fifth day of the **t** month,* of the Hebrew calendar. This event occurred on January 8, 585 B.C.; also see note on 29:1.
40: 1 {On April 28,} Hebrew *At the beginning of the year, on the **t** day of the month,* of the Hebrew calendar. A number of events in Ezekiel can be cross-checked with dates in surviving Babylonian records and related accurately to our modern calendar. This event occurred on April 28, 573 B.C.
Zec 8:19 {autumn, and winter} Hebrew *in the fourth, fifth, seventh, and **t** months.* The fourth month of the Hebrew lunar calendar usually occurs in June and July. The fifth month usually occurs in July and August. The seventh month usually occurs in September and October. The **t** month usually occurs in December and January.

TENTS (3)
Ge 9:27 {prosperity of Shem;} Hebrew *may he live in the **t** of Shem.*
Ps 78:51 {land of Egypt.} Hebrew *in the **t** of Ham.*
Mal 2:12 {nation of Israel} Hebrew *from the **t** of Jacob.*

TERAPHIM (1)
1Sa 19:13 {took an idol} Hebrew ***t**;* also in 19:16.

TERM (71)
Ge 3:20 {his wife Eve,} *Eve* sounds like a Hebrew **t** that means "to give life."
4: 1 {birth to Cain,} *Cain* sounds like a Hebrew **t** that can mean "bring forth" or "acquire."
5:29 {his son Noah,} *Noah* sounds like a Hebrew **t** that can mean "relief" or "comfort."
11: 9 {was called Babel,} *Babel* sounds like a Hebrew **t** that means "confusion."
19:37 {named him Moab.} *Moab* sounds like a Hebrew **t** that means "from father."
25:25 {called him Esau.} *Esau* sounds like a Hebrew **t** that means "hair."
29:34 {named him Levi,} *Levi* sounds like a Hebrew **t** that means "being attached" or "feeling affection for."
29:35 {named him Judah,} *Judah* sounds like the Hebrew **t** for "praise."
30: 6 {named him Dan,} *Dan* is a play on the Hebrew **t** meaning "to vindicate" or "to judge."
30:18 {named him Issachar,} *Issachar* sounds like a Hebrew **t** that means "reward."
41:51 {older son Manasseh,} *Manasseh* sounds like a Hebrew **t** that means "causing to forget."
41:52 {second son Ephraim,} *Ephraim* sounds like a Hebrew **t** that means "fruitful."

Ex 2:10 {named him Moses,} *Moses* sounds like a Hebrew **t** that means "to draw out."
2:22 {named him Gershom,} *Gershom* sounds like a Hebrew **t** that means "a stranger here."
18:3 {son was Gershom,} *Gershom* sounds like a Hebrew **t** that means "a stranger here."
Lev 6:21 {mixed and broken} The meaning of this Hebrew **t** is uncertain.
13:47 {an infectious mildew} Traditionally rendered *leprosy.* The Hebrew **t** used throughout this passage is the same **t** used for the various skin diseases described in 13:1-46.
27:3 {pieces of silver} Hebrew *50 shekels of silver, according to the standard sanctuary shekel,* each about 0.4 ounces or 11 grams in weight. The **t** *shekels* also appears in 27:4, 5, 6, 7, 16.
27:21 {specially set apart} The Hebrew **t** used here refers to the complete consecration of things or people to the LORD, either by destroying them or by giving them as an offering; also in 27:28, 29.
Nu 18:14 {for the LORD} The Hebrew **t** used here refers to the complete consecration of things or people to the LORD, either by destroying them or by giving them as an offering.
21:2 {will completely destroy} The Hebrew **t** used here refers to the complete consecration of things or people to the LORD, either by destroying them or by giving them as an offering; also in 21:3.
Dt 2:34 {and completely destroyed} The Hebrew **t** used here refers to the complete consecration of things or people to the LORD, either by destroying them or by giving them as an offering.
3:6 {We completely destroyed} The Hebrew **t** used here refers to the complete consecration of things or people to the LORD, either by destroying them or by giving them as an offering.
7:2 {must completely destroy} The Hebrew **t** used here refers to the complete consecration of things or people to the LORD, either by destroying them or by giving them as an offering; also in 7:26.
13:15 {and completely destroy} The Hebrew **t** used here refers to the complete consecration of things or people to the LORD, either by destroying them or by giving them as an offering; also in 13:17.
20:17 {must completely destroy} The Hebrew **t** used here refers to the complete consecration of things or people to the LORD, either by destroying them or by giving them as an offering.
32:15 {But Israel} Hebrew *Jeshurun,* a **t** of endearment for Israel.
33:5 {king in Israel} Hebrew *in Jeshurun,* a **t** of endearment for Israel.
33:26 {God of Israel.} Hebrew *of Jeshurun,* a **t** of endearment for Israel.
Jos 2:10 {you completely destroyed.} The Hebrew **t** used here refers to the complete consecration of things or people to the LORD, either by destroying them or by giving them as an offering.
6:17 {be completely destroyed} The Hebrew **t** used here refers to the complete consecration of things or people to the LORD, either by destroying them or by giving them as an offering; also in 6:18, 21.
7:1 {for the LORD.} The Hebrew **t** used here refers to the complete consecration of things or people to the LORD, either by destroying them or by giving them as an offering; also in 7:11, 12, 13, 15.
8:26 {was completely destroyed.} The Hebrew **t** used here refers to the complete consecration of things or people to the LORD, either by destroying them or by giving them as an offering.
10:1 {and completely destroyed} The Hebrew **t** used here refers to the complete consecration of things or people to the LORD, either by destroying them or by giving them as an offering; also in 10:28, 35, 37, 39, 40.
11:11 {Israelites completely destroyed} The Hebrew **t** used here refers to the complete consecration of things or people to the LORD, either by destroying them or by giving them as an offering; also in 11:12, 20, 21.
22:20 {for the LORD} The Hebrew **t** used here refers to the complete consecration of things or people to the LORD, either by destroying them or by giving them as an offering.
Jdg 1:17 {they completely destroyed} The Hebrew **t** used here refers to the complete consecration of things or people to the LORD, either by destroying them or by giving them as an offering.
21:11 {said. "Completely destroy} The Hebrew **t** used here refers to the complete consecration of things or people to the LORD, either by destroying them or by giving them as an offering.
1Sa 1:20 {named him Samuel,} *Samuel* sounds like the Hebrew **t** for "asked of God" or "heard by God."
15:3 {and completely destroy} The Hebrew **t** used here refers to the complete consecration of things or people to the LORD, either by destroying them or by giving them as an offering; also in 15:8, 9, 15, 18, 20, 21.
1Ki 9:21 {not completely destroyed.} The Hebrew **t** used here refers to the complete consecration of things or people to the LORD, either by destroying them or by giving them as an offering.
20:42 {must be destroyed,} The Hebrew **t** used here refers to the complete consecration of things or people to the LORD, either by destroying them or by giving them as an offering.
1Ch 2:7 {for the LORD.} The Hebrew **t** used here refers to the complete consecration of things or people to the LORD, either by destroying them or by giving them as an offering.
4:9 {named him Jabez} *Jabez* sounds like a Hebrew **t** meaning "distress" or "pain."
4:41 {and completely destroyed} The Hebrew **t** used here refers to the complete consecration of things or people to the LORD, either by destroying them or by giving them as an offering.
7:23 {named him Beriah} *Beriah* sounds like a Hebrew **t** meaning "tragedy" or "misfortune."
15:20 {play the lyres.} Hebrew adds *according to Alamoth,* which is probably a musical **t**. The meaning of the Hebrew is uncertain.
15:21 {play the harps.} Hebrew adds *according to the Sheminith,* which is probably a musical **t**. The meaning of the Hebrew is uncertain.
Ps 3:2 {*Interlude*} Hebrew *Selah.* The meaning of this word is uncertain, though it is probably a musical or literary **t**. It is rendered *Interlude* throughout the Psalms.
Ecc 1:1 {of the Teacher,} Hebrew *Koheleth;* this **t** is rendered "the Teacher" throughout this book.
Isa 29:1 {certain for Ariel,} *Ariel* sounds like a Hebrew **t** that means "hearth" or "altar."
34:2 {will completely destroy} The Hebrew **t** used here refers to the complete consecration of things or people to the LORD, either by destroying them or by giving them as an offering; also in 34:5.
43:28 {of complete destruction} The Hebrew **t** used here refers to the complete consecration of things or people to the LORD, either by destroying them or by giving them as an offering.
44:2 {be afraid. O Israel,} Hebrew *Jeshurun,* a **t** of endearment for Israel.
Jer 25:9 {will completely destroy} The Hebrew **t** used here refers to the complete consecration of things or people to the LORD, either by destroying them or by giving them as an offering.
50:21 {and completely destroy} The Hebrew **t** used here refers to the complete consecration of things or people to the LORD, either by destroying them or by giving them as an offering.
51:3 {be completely destroyed.} The Hebrew **t** used here refers to the complete consecration of things or people to the LORD, either by destroying them or by giving them as an offering.
Eze 44:29 {anyone sets apart} The Hebrew **t** used here refers to the complete consecration of things or people to the LORD, either by destroying them or by giving them as an offering.
Am 6:13 {we take Karnaim} *Karnaim* means "horns," a **t** that symbolizes strength.
Mic 1:10 {Gath} *Gath* sounds like the Hebrew **t** for "tell."
1:11 {people of Zaanan} *Zaanan* sounds like the Hebrew **t** for "come out."
1:12 {people of Maroth} *Maroth* sounds like the Hebrew **t** for "bitter."
1:13 {people of Lachish.} *Lachish* sounds like the Hebrew **t** for "team of horses."
1:15 {people of Mareshah,} *Mareshah* sounds like the Hebrew **t** for "conqueror."
Hab 3:3 {and Mount Paran.} Hebrew adds *selah;* also in 3:9, 13. The meaning of this Hebrew **t** is uncertain; it is probably a musical or literary **t**.
Mt 5:22 {friend, 'You idiot,'} Literally *'Raca,'* an Aramaic **t** of contempt.
Mk 14:36 {"Abba,} *Abba* is an Aramaic **t** for "father."
Ro 8:15 {"Father, dear Father."} Greek *"Abba, Father." Abba* is an Aramaic **t** for "father."
Gal 4:6 {your dear Father.} Greek *into your hearts, crying, "Abba, Father."* Abba is an Aramaic **t** for "Father."

TERMS (2)

Lev 16:13 {of the Covenant.} Hebrew *on the Testimony,* referring to the **t** of God's covenant with Israel, which were kept in the Ark.
2Ki 18:4 {was called Nehushtan.} *Nehushtan* sounds like the Hebrew **t** that mean "snake," "bronze," and "unclean thing."

TERRACES (5)

2Sa 5:9 {at the Millo} Or *the supporting t.* The meaning of the Hebrew is uncertain.
1Ki 9:15 {the Millo,} Or *the supporting t;* also in 9:24.
11:27 {rebuilding the Millo} Or *the supporting t.*
1Ch 11:8 {from the Millo} Or *the supporting t.* The meaning of the Hebrew is uncertain.
2Ch 32:5 {reinforced the Millo} Or *the supporting t.*

TERRAIN (1)

Nu 21:24 {Ammonites was fortified.} Or *because the t of the Ammonite frontier was rugged;* Hebrew *because the boundary of the Ammonites was strong.*

TERRIBLE (1)

Mt 23:13 {go in yourselves.} Some manuscripts add verse 14, *How t it will be for you teachers of religious law and you Pharisees. Hypocrites! You shamelessly cheat widows out of their property, and then, to cover up the kind of people you really are, you make long prayers in public. Because of this, your punishment will be the greater.*

TERRITORY (1)

Jos 13:26 {Mahanaim to Lo-debar.} Or *to the t of Debir.*

TERROR (1)

Jer 20:3 {Lives in Terror.'} Hebrew *Magor-missabib,* which means "surrounded by **t**"; also in 20:10.

TESTIFIED (1)

Ru 1:21 {me to suffer} Or *has t against me.*

TESTIMONY (29)

Ex 16:34 {of the Covenant.} Hebrew *in front of the T.*
25:16 {of the covenant,} Hebrew *place inside it the T;* also in 25:21.
25:22 {of the Covenant.} Or *Ark of the T.*
26:33 {of the Covenant} Or *Ark of the T;* also in 26:34.
27:21 {in the Tabernacle.} Hebrew *in the Tent of Meeting, outside of the inner curtain, in front of the T.*
30:6 {of the Covenant.} Or *Ark of the T;* also in 30:26, 36.
31:7 {of the Covenant;} Hebrew *the Tent of Meeting; the Ark of the T.*
31:18 {of the covenant,} Hebrew *the T.*
32:15 {of the covenant.} Hebrew *the T.*
34:29 {of the covenant,} Hebrew *the T.*
38:21 {of the Covenant.} Hebrew *the Tabernacle, the Tabernacle of the T.*
39:35 {of the Covenant} Or *Ark of the T.*
40:3 {of the Covenant} Or *Ark of the T;* also in 40:5, 21.
40:20 {of the covenant,} Hebrew *the T.*
Lev 16:13 {of the Covenant.} Hebrew *on the T,* referring to the terms of God's covenant with Israel, which were kept in the Ark.
24:3 {in the Tabernacle} Hebrew *the curtain of the T in the Tent of Meeting.*
Nu 1:50 {of the Covenant,} Or *Tabernacle of the T;* also in 1:53.
4:5 {of the Covenant} Or *Ark of the T.*
7:89 {of the Covenant.} Or *Ark of the T.*
9:15 {cloud covered it.} Hebrew *covered the Tabernacle, the Tent of the T.*
10:11 {of the Covenant.} Or *Tabernacle of the T.*
17:4 {of the Covenant,} Hebrew *in the Tent of Meeting before the T.*
17:7 {of the Covenant.} Or *Tabernacle of the T;* also in 17:8.
17:10 {of the Covenant} Hebrew *before the T.*
18:2 {of the Covenant.} Or *Tabernacle of the T.*
Jos 4:16 {of the Covenant.} Hebrew *Ark of the T.*
2Ch 24:6 {of the Covenant.} Hebrew *Tent of the T.*
Mk 13:9 {them about me.} Or *This will be your t against them.*
1Co 2:1 {you God's message.} Greek *mystery;* other manuscripts read *t.*

TESTING (1)

Dt 9:22 {Massah,} *Massah* means "place of **t**." See Exod 17:1-7.

TETRARCH (5)

Mt 14:1 {When Herod Antipas} Greek *Herod the t.* He was a son of King Herod and was one of four rulers in Palestine.
Lk 3:1 {Antipas was ruler} Greek *Herod was t.* Herod Antipas was a son of King Herod.
3:1 {Philip was ruler} Greek *t;* also in 3:1c, 19.
9:7 {reached Herod Antipas,} Greek *Herod the t.* He was a son of King Herod and was one of four rulers in Palestine.
Ac 13:1 {King Herod Antipas} Greek *Herod the t.*

TEXT (112)

Nu 1:20[-21] {clan and family} In the Hebrew **t**, *number of men…family* is repeated in 1:22, 24, 26, 28, 30, 32, 34, 36, 38, 40, 42.
Dt 31:1 {had finished saying} As in Dead Sea Scrolls and Greek version; Masoretic **T** reads *Moses went and spoke.*
32:8 {of angelic beings.} As in Dead Sea Scrolls, which read *of the sons of God,* and Greek version, which reads *of the angels of god;* Masoretic **T** reads *of the sons of Israel.*
32:43 {God worship him,} As in Dead Sea Scrolls and Greek version; Masoretic **T** reads *Rejoice with his people, O nations.*
Jdg 18:30 {descendant of Moses,} As in an ancient Hebrew tradition, some Greek manuscripts, and Latin Vulgate; Masoretic **T** reads *of Manasseh.*
1Sa 2:33 {a violent death.} As in Dead Sea Scrolls, which read *die by the sword;* Masoretic **T** reads *die like mortals.*
6:19 {killed seventy men} As in a few Hebrew manuscripts; most Hebrew manuscripts and Greek version read *50,070 men.* Perhaps the **t** should be understood to read *the LORD killed 70 men and 50 oxen.*
2Sa 5:14 {in Jerusalem: Shimea,} As in parallel **t** at 1 Chr 3:5; Hebrew reads *Shammua,* a variant name for Shimea.
8:18 {as priestly leaders.} Hebrew *David's sons were priests;* compare parallel **t** at 1 Chr 18:17.

10:18 {forty thousand horsemen,} Some Greek manuscripts read *foot soldiers;* compare parallel t at 1 Chr 19:18.
21:19 {son of Jair} As in parallel t at 1 Chr 20:5; Hebrew reads *son of Jaare-oregim.*
21:19 {Goliath of Gath.} As in parallel t at 1 Chr 20:5; Hebrew reads *killed Goliath of Gath.*
21:21 {David's brother Shimea.} As in parallel t at 1 Chr 20:7; Hebrew reads *Shimei,* a variant name for Shimea.
23: 8 {Jashobeam the Hacmonite,} As in parallel t at 1 Chr 11:11; Hebrew reads *Josheb-basshebeth the Tahkemonite.*
23:26 {Helez from Pelon} As in parallel t at 1 Chr 11:27 (see also 1 Chr 27:10); Hebrew reads *from Palti.*
23:29 {Ithai} As in parallel t at 1 Chr 11:31; Hebrew reads *Ittai.*
23:33 {son of Shagee} As in parallel t at 1 Chr 11:34; Hebrew reads *Jonathan, Shammah;* some Greek manuscripts read *Jonathan son of Shammah.*
1Ki 8:65 {Festival of Shelters.} Hebrew *seven days and seven days, fourteen days;* compare parallel t at 2 Chr 7:8-10.
8:66 {festival was over,} Hebrew *On the eighth day,* probably referring to the day following the seven-day Festival of Shelters; compare parallel t at 2 Chr 7:9-10.
9:18 {Baalath, and Tamar} The marginal *Qere* reading of the Masoretic T reads *Tadmor.*
2Ki 12:21 {assassins were Jozacar} As in Greek and Syriac versions; Hebrew reads *Jozabad;* compare parallel t at 2 Chr 24:26.
16: 6 {and sent Edomites} As in marginal *Qere* reading of the Masoretic T, Greek version, and Latin Vulgate; Hebrew reads *Arameans.*
18: 2 {mother was Abijah,} As in parallel t at 2 Chr 29:1; Hebrew reads *Abi,* a variant name for Abijah.
1Ch 1:17 {Gether, and Mash.} As in parallel t at Gen 10:23; Hebrew reads *and Meshech.*
1:39 {Hori and Heman.} As in parallel t at Gen 36:22; Hebrew reads *and Homam.*
1:42 {sons of Dishan} Hebrew *Dishon;* compare 1:38 and parallel t at Gen 36:28.
1:51 {were Timna, Alvah,} As in parallel t at Gen 36:40; Hebrew reads *Aliah.*
2:24 {(the father of} Or *the founder of;* also in 2:42, 45, 49-52 and perhaps other instances where the t reads *the father of.*
3: 1 {second was Kileab,} As in parallel t at 2 Sam 3:3; Hebrew reads *Daniel.*
3: 6 {Elpelet,} Hebrew *Eliphelet;* compare parallel t at 14:5-7.
4: 4 {(the father of} Or *the founder of;* also in 4:12, 14, 17-18, and perhaps other instances where the t reads *the father of.*
6:23 {Elkanah, Abiasaph,} Hebrew *Ebiasaph,* a variant name for Abiasaph (also in 6:37); compare parallel t at Exod 6:24.
6:58 {Holon,} As in parallel t at Josh 21:15; Hebrew reads *Hilen.*
6:59 {Ain,} As in parallel t at Josh 21:16; Hebrew reads *Ashan.*
6:60 {were given Gibeon,} As in parallel t at Josh 21:17; Hebrew lacks *Gibeon.*
7:13 {Naphtali were Jahzeel,} As in parallel t at Gen 46:24; Hebrew reads *Jahziel,* a variant name for Jahzeel.
8:31 {Gedor, Ahio, Zechariah,} As in parallel t at 9:37; Hebrew reads *Zeker,* a variant name for Zechariah.
8:32 {father of Shimeam.} As in parallel t at 9:38; Hebrew reads *Shimeah,* a variant name for Shimeam.
8:35 {Pithon, Melech, Tahrea,} As in parallel t at 9:41; Hebrew reads *Tarea,* a variant name for Tahrea.
8:36 {father of Jadah.} As in parallel t at 9:42; Hebrew reads *Jehoaddah,* a variant name for Jadah.
8:37 {father of Rephaiah.} As in parallel t at 9:43; Hebrew reads *Raphah,* a variant name for Rephaiah.
11:12 {son of Dodai,} As in parallel t at 2 Sam 23:9 (see also 1 Chr 27:4); Hebrew reads *Dodo,* a variant name for Dodai.
11:27 {Shammah from Harod;} As in parallel t at 2 Sam 23:25; Hebrew reads *Shammoth from Haror.*
11:29 {Zalmon} As in parallel t at 2 Sam 23:28; Hebrew reads *Ilai.*
11:32 {Abi-albon} As in parallel t at 2 Sam 23:31; Hebrew reads *Abiel.*
11:33 {Azmaveth from Bahurim} As in parallel t at 2 Sam 23:31; Hebrew reads *Baharum.*
11:34 {sons of Jashen} As in parallel t at 2 Sam 23:32; Hebrew reads *sons of Hashem.*
11:35 {son of Sharar} As in parallel t at 2 Sam 23:33; Hebrew reads *son of Sacar.*
11:37 {Paarai} As in parallel t at 2 Sam 23:35; Hebrew reads *Naarai.*
13: 9 {floor of Nacon,} As in parallel t at 2 Sam 6:6; Hebrew reads *Kidon.*
14: 7 {Elishama, Eliada,} Hebrew *Beeliada,* a variant name for Eliada; compare 3:8 and parallel t at 2 Sam 5:16.
14:12 {abandoned their idols} Hebrew *their gods;* compare parallel t at 2 Sam 5:21.
18: 8 {cities of Tebah} Hebrew reads *Tibhath,* a variant name for Tebah; compare parallel t at 2 Sam 8:8.
18: 9 {When King Toi} As in parallel t at 2 Sam 8:9; Hebrew reads *Tou;* also in 18:10.
18:10 {his son Joram} As in parallel t at 2 Sam 8:10; Hebrew reads *Hadoram,* a variant name for Joram.
18:16 {the priests. Seraiah} As in parallel t at 2 Sam 8:17; Hebrew reads *Shavsha.*
19: 1 {his son Hanun} Hebrew lacks *Hanun;* compare parallel t at 2 Sam 10:1.
19:16 {command of Shobach,} As in parallel t at 2 Sam 10:16; Hebrew reads *Shophach;* also in 19:18.
20: 3 {picks, and axes.} As in parallel t at 2 Sam 12:31; Hebrew reads *and saws.*
20: 4 {Hushah killed Saph,} As in parallel t at 2 Sam 21:18; Hebrew reads *Sippai.*
21:15 {floor of Araunah} As in parallel t at 2 Sam 24:16; Hebrew reads *Ornan,* another name for Araunah; also in 21:18-28.
2Ch 2: 8 {cypress, and almug} Hebrew *algum;* compare 9:10-11 and parallel t at 1 Kgs 10:11-12.
4:17 {Succoth and Zarethan.} As in parallel t at 1 Kgs 7:46; Hebrew reads *Zeredah.*
9:10 {of almug wood} Hebrew *algum wood* (also in 9:11); compare parallel t at 1 Kgs 10:11-12.
16: 4 {Ijon, Dan, Abel-beth-maacah,} As in parallel t at 1 Kgs 15:20; Hebrew reads *Abel-maim,* another name for Abel-beth-maacah.
22:11 {Ahaziah's sister Jehosheba,} As in parallel t at 2 Kgs 11:2; Hebrew reads *Jehoshabeath,* a variant name for Jehosheba.
24:26 {assassins were Jozacar,} Hebrew *Zabad;* compare parallel t at 2 Kgs 12:21, and see note there.
24:26 {woman named Shomer.} As in parallel t at 2 Kgs 12:21; Hebrew reads *Shimrith.*
25: 1 {mother was Jehoaddin,} As in parallel t at 2 Kgs 14:2; Hebrew reads *Jehoaddan,* a variant name for Jehoaddin.
34:20 {son of Micaiah,} As in parallel t at 2 Kgs 22:12; Hebrew reads *Abdon son of Micah.*
34:22 {grandson of Harhas,} As in parallel t at 2 Kgs 22:14; Hebrew reads *son of Tokhath, son of Hasrah.*
36:10 {appointed Jehoiachin's uncle,} As in parallel t at 2 Kgs 24:17; Hebrew reads *brother,* or *relative.*
Ezr 2:24 {people of Beth-azmaveth} As in parallel t at Neh 7:28; Hebrew reads *Azmaveth.*
2:46 {Hagab, Shalmai,} As in the marginal *Qere* reading of the Masoretic T (see also Neh 7:48); Hebrew t reads *Shamlai.*
2:55 {Sotai, Sophereth,} As in parallel t at Neh 7:57; Hebrew reads *Hassophereth.*
4: 8 {Rehum} The original t of 4:8—6:18 is in Aramaic.
7:12 {"Greetings} The original t of 7:12-26 is in Aramaic.
10: 6 {spent the night} As in parallel t at 1 Esdras 9:2; Hebrew reads *He went.*
10:25 {Mijamin, Eleazar, Hashabiah,} As in parallel t at 1 Esdras 9:26; Hebrew reads *Malkijah.*
Ne 7: 7 {Jeshua, Nehemiah, Seraiah,} As in parallel t at Ezra 2:2; Hebrew reads *Azariah.*
7: 7 {Reelaiah,} As in parallel t at Ezra 2:2; Hebrew reads *Raamiah.*
7: 7 {Mordecai, Bilshan, Mispar,} As in parallel t at Ezra 2:2; Hebrew reads *Mispereth.*
7: 7 {Bigvai, Rehum,} As in parallel t at Ezra 2:2; Hebrew reads *Nehum.*
7:15 {family of Bani} As in parallel t at Ezra 2:10; Hebrew reads *Binnui.*
7:24 {family of Jorah} As in parallel t at Ezra 2:18; Hebrew reads *Hariph.*
7:25 {family of Gibbar} As in parallel t at Ezra 2:20; Hebrew reads *Gibeon.*
7:43 {(descendants of Hodaviah} As in parallel t at Ezra 2:40; Hebrew reads *Hodevah.*
7:47 {Keros, Siaha,} As in parallel t at Ezra 2:44; Hebrew reads *Sia.*
7:52 {Besai, Meunim, Nephusim,} As in parallel t at Ezra 2:50; Hebrew reads *Nephushesim.*
7:54 {Bazluth,} As in parallel t at Ezra 2:52; Hebrew reads *Bazlith.*
7:57 {Sotai, Sophereth, Peruda,} As in parallel t at Ezra 2:55; Hebrew reads *Perida.*
7:58 {Jaalah,} As in parallel t at Ezra 2:56; Hebrew reads *Jaala.*
7:59 {Pokereth-hazzebaim, and Ami.} As in parallel t at Ezra 2:57; Hebrew reads *Amon.*
7:61 {Tel-harsha, Kerub, Addan,} As in parallel t at Ezra 2:59; Hebrew reads *Addon.*
Job 32: 3 {had condemned God} As in ancient Hebrew scribal tradition; the Masoretic T makes no reference to God.
Pr 20:16 {of a foreigner.} An alternate reading in the Hebrew t is *the debt of an adulterous woman;* compare 27:13.
SS 1: 1 {*Young Woman:*} The headings identifying the speakers are not in the original t, though the Hebrew usually gives clues by means of the gender of the person speaking.
Isa 28:10 {very simple words!} The Hebrew t for this verse may simply be childish sounds that have no meaning, or perhaps a childish mimicking of the prophet's words. Also in 28:13.
33: 1 {for you Assyrians,} Hebrew *for you, O destroyer...O betrayer.* The Hebrew t does not specifically name Assyria as the object of this prophecy.
33: 8 {made before witnesses.} As in Dead Sea Scrolls; Masoretic T reads *care nothing for the cities.*
45: 2 {level the mountains.} As in Dead Sea Scrolls and Greek version; Masoretic T reads *the swellings.*
49:12 {south as Egypt.} As in Dead Sea Scrolls, which read *from the region of Aswan,* which is in southern Egypt. Masoretic T reads *from the region of Sinim.*
49:24 {that a tyrant} As in Dead Sea Scrolls, Syriac version, and Latin Vulgate (also see 49:25); Masoretic T reads *a righteous person.*
Jer 10:11 {from the earth."} The original t of this verse is in Aramaic.
40: 8 {the Netophathite, Jaazaniah} As in parallel t at 2 Kgs 25:23; Hebrew reads *Jezaniah,* a variant name for Jaazaniah.
Da 2: 4 {king in Aramaic,} The original t from this point through chapter 7 is in Aramaic.
10:16 {like a man} As in most manuscripts of the Masoretic T; one manuscript of the Masoretic T and one Greek version read *Then something that looked like a human hand.*
Hos 4: 7 {They have exchanged} As in Syriac version and an ancient Hebrew tradition; Masoretic T reads *I will exchange.*
Mk 5:41 {up, little girl!"} Greek t uses Aramaic *"Talitha cumi"* and then translates it as "Get up, little girl."
7:34 {"Be opened!"} Greek t uses Aramaic *"Ephphatha"* and then translates it as "Be opened."

TEXTS (1)

2Ki 25:17 {was 7 1/2 feet} As in parallel t at 1 Kgs 7:16, 2 Chr 3:15, and Jer 52:22, all of which read *5 cubits* [2.3 meters]; Hebrew reads *3 cubits,* which is 4.5 feet or 1.4 meters.

THA (1)

1Co 16:22 {Our Lord, come!} From Aramaic, *Marana t.*

THAN (3)

Ps 8: 5 {lower than God,} Or *a little lower t the angels;* Hebrew reads *Elohim.*
76: 4 {the everlasting mountains.} As in Greek version; Hebrew reads *t mountains filled with beasts of prey.*
87: 2 {city in Israel.} Hebrew *He loves the gates of Zion more t all the dwellings of Jacob.*

THANK (1)

2Co 9:15 {wonderful for words!} Greek *T God for his indescribable gift.*

THEREAFTER (2)

Mk 1:16 {he saw Simon} *Simon* is called *Peter* in 3:16 and t.
Lk 5: 3 {Jesus asked Simon,} *Simon* is called *Peter* in 6:14 and t.

THEREFORE (1)

Lk 11:49 {said about you:} Greek *T, the wisdom of God said.*

THICK (1)

Jer 52:21 {walls 3 inches thick.} Hebrew *4 fingers t* [8 centimeters].

THIGH (5)

Ge 24: 3 {"Swear} Hebrew *Put your hand under my t, and I will make you swear.*
24: 9 {solemn oath} Hebrew *put his hand under the t of Abraham his master and swore an oath.*
Nu 5:21 {makes you infertile.} Hebrew *when he causes your t to waste away and your abdomen to swell.*
5:22 {make you infertile.} Hebrew *enter your body so that your abdomen swells and your t wastes away.*
5:27 {will become infertile,} Hebrew *Her body will swell and her t will waste away.*

THING (1)

2Ki 18: 4 {was called Nehushtan.} *Nehushtan* sounds like the Hebrew terms that mean "snake," "bronze," and "unclean t."

THINGS (33)

Lev 27:21 {specially set apart} The Hebrew term used here refers to the complete consecration of t or people to the LORD, either by destroying them or by giving them as an offering; also in 27:28, 29.
Nu 18:14 {for the LORD} The Hebrew term used here refers to the complete consecration of t or people to the LORD, either by destroying them or by giving them as an offering.
21: 2 {will completely destroy} The Hebrew term used here refers to the complete consecration of t or people to the LORD, either by destroying them or by giving them as an offering; also in 21:3.
Dt 2:34 {and completely destroyed} The Hebrew term used here refers to the complete consecration of t or people to the LORD, either by destroying them or by giving them as an offering.
3: 6 {We completely destroyed} The Hebrew term used here refers to the complete consecration of t or people to the LORD, either by destroying them or by giving them as an offering.

7: 2 {must completely destroy} The Hebrew term used here refers to the complete consecration of **t** or people to the LORD, either by destroying them or by giving them as an offering; also in 7:26.
13:15 {and completely destroy} The Hebrew term used here refers to the complete consecration of **t** or people to the LORD, either by destroying them or by giving them as an offering; also in 13:17.
20:17 {must completely destroy} The Hebrew term used here refers to the complete consecration of **t** or people to the LORD, either by destroying them or by giving them as an offering.
Jos 2:10 {you completely destroyed.} The Hebrew term used here refers to the complete consecration of **t** or people to the LORD, either by destroying them or by giving them as an offering.
6:17 {be completely destroyed} The Hebrew term used here refers to the complete consecration of **t** or people to the LORD, either by destroying them or by giving them as an offering; also in 6:18, 21.
7: 1 {for the LORD.} The Hebrew term used here refers to the complete consecration of **t** or people to the LORD, either by destroying them or by giving them as an offering; also in 7:11, 12, 13, 15.
8:26 {was completely destroyed.} The Hebrew term used here refers to the complete consecration of **t** or people to the LORD, either by destroying them or by giving them as an offering.
10: 1 {destroyed} The Hebrew term used here refers to the complete consecration of **t** or people to the LORD, either by destroying them or by giving them as an offering; also in 10:28, 35, 37, 39, 40.
11:11 {destroyed} The Hebrew term used here refers to the complete consecration of **t** or people to the LORD, either by destroying them or by giving them as an offering; also in 11:12, 20, 21.
22:20 {for the LORD} The Hebrew term used here refers to the complete consecration of **t** or people to the LORD, either by destroying them or by giving them as an offering.
Jdg 1:17 {they completely destroyed} The Hebrew term used here refers to the complete consecration of **t** or people to the LORD, either by destroying them or by giving them as an offering.
21:11 {said. "Completely destroy} The Hebrew term used here refers to the complete consecration of **t** or people to the LORD, either by destroying them or by giving them as an offering.
1Sa 15: 3 {destroy} The Hebrew term used here refers to the complete consecration of **t** or people to the LORD, either by destroying them or by giving them as an offering; also in 15:8, 9, 15, 18, 20, 21.
1Ki 9:21 {not completely destroyed.} The Hebrew term used here refers to the complete consecration of **t** or people to the LORD, either by destroying them or by giving them as an offering.
20:42 {must be destroyed,} The Hebrew term used here refers to the complete consecration of **t** or people to the LORD, either by destroying them or by giving them as an offering.
1Ch 2: 7 {for the LORD.} The Hebrew term used here refers to the complete consecration of **t** or people to the LORD, either by destroying them or by giving them as an offering.
4:41 {and completely destroyed} The Hebrew term used here refers to the complete consecration of **t** or people to the LORD, either by destroying them or by giving them as an offering.
Isa 34: 2 {will completely destroy} The Hebrew term used here refers to the complete consecration of **t** or people to the LORD, either by destroying them or by giving them as an offering; also in 34:5.
43:28 {of complete destruction} The Hebrew term used here refers to the complete consecration of **t** or people to the LORD, either by destroying them or by giving them as an offering.
Jer 25: 9 {will completely destroy} The Hebrew term used here refers to the complete consecration of **t** or people to the LORD, either by destroying them or by giving them as an offering.
50:21 {and completely destroy} The Hebrew term used here refers to the complete consecration of **t** or people to the LORD, either by destroying them or by giving them as an offering.
51: 3 {be completely destroyed.} The Hebrew term used here refers to the complete consecration of **t** or people to the LORD, either by destroying them or by giving them as an offering.
Eze 44:29 {anyone sets apart} The Hebrew term used here refers to the complete consecration of **t** or people to the LORD, either by destroying them or by giving them as an offering.
Mt 21:23 {from the Temple?} Or *By whose authority do you do these **t**?*
Mk 11:28 {from the Temple?} Or *By whose authority do you do these **t**?*
Lk 17:25 {must suffer terribly} Or *suffer many **t**.*
20: 2 {from the Temple?} Or *By whose authority do you do these **t**?*
23:31 {it is dry?} Or *If these **t** are done to me, the living tree, what will happen to you, the dry tree?*

THINK (1)

Ps 8: 4 {care for us?} Hebrew *What is man that you should **t** of him, the son of man that you should care for him?*

THIRD (9)

Ex 19: 1 {they left Egypt.} Hebrew *in the **t** month…on the very day,* i.e., two lunar months to the day after leaving Egypt.…
2Ch 15:10 {in late spring,} Hebrew *in the **t** month.* This month of the Hebrew lunar calendar usually occurs in May and June.
31: 7 {in late spring,} Hebrew *in the **t** month.* This month of the Hebrew lunar calendar usually occurs in May and June.
Ezr 6:15 {completed on March 12,} Aramaic *on the **t** day of the month Adar,* of the Hebrew calendar. This event occurred on March 12, 515 B.C.; also see note on 3:1.
Est 8: 9 {So on June 25} Hebrew *on the twenty-third day of the **t** month, the month of Sivan,* of the Hebrew calendar. This event occurred on June 25, 474 B.C.; also see note on 2:16.
Eze 31: 1 {On June 21,} Hebrew *On the first day of the **t** month,* of the Hebrew calendar. This event occurred on June 21, 587 B.C.; also see note on 29:1.
Da 1: 1 {reign in Judah,} The **t** year of Jehoiakim's reign, according to the Babylonian system of reckoning, was 605 B.C.
Lk 12:38 {just before dawn.} Greek *in the second or **t** watch.*
Jn 2: 1 {The next day} Greek *On the **t** day;* see 1:35, 43.

THIRSTY (1)

Jn 7:37[-38] {out from within."} Or *"Let anyone who is **t** come to me and drink. [38]For the Scriptures declare that rivers of living water will flow from the heart of those who believe in me."*

THIRTEENTH (9)

Est 3: 7 {a year later.} As in Greek version, which reads *the **t** day of the twelfth month, the month of Adar* (see also 3:13). Hebrew reads *in the twelfth month,* of the Hebrew calendar. The date selected was March 7, 473 B.C.; also see note on 2:16.
3:12 {On April 17} Hebrew *On the **t** day of the first month,* of the Hebrew calendar. This event occurred on April 17, 474 B.C.; also see note on 2:16.
3:13 {later on March 7.} Hebrew *on the **t** day of the twelfth month, the month of Adar,* of the Hebrew calendar. The date selected was March 7, 473 B.C.; also see note on 2:16.
8:12 {the next year.} Hebrew *the **t** day of the twelfth month, the month of Adar,* of the Hebrew calendar. The date selected was March 7, 473 B.C.; also see note on 2:16.
9: 1 {So on March 7} Hebrew *on the **t** day of the twelfth month, the month of Adar,* of the Hebrew calendar. This event occurred on March 7, 473 B.C.; also see note on 2:16.
9:17 {done on March 7.} Hebrew *on the **t** day of the month of Adar,* of the Hebrew calendar. This event occurred on March 7, 473 B.C.; also see note on 2:16.
9:18 {the third day,} Hebrew *killing their enemies on the **t** day and the fourteenth day, and then rested on the fifteenth day,* of the Hebrew month of Adar.
Jer 1: 2 {reign in Judah.} The **t** year of Josiah's reign was 626 B.C.
25: 3 {son of Amon,} The **t** year of Josiah's reign was 626 B.C.

THIRTIETH (1)

Eze 1: 1 {my thirtieth year,} Or *in the **t** year.*

THIRTY (1)

1Ch 11:11 {among David's men.} As in some Greek manuscripts (see also 2 Sam 23:8); Hebrew *commander of the **T**,* or *commander of the captains.*

THIRTY-SECOND (1)

Ne 13: 6 {Artaxerxes of Babylon,} The **t** year of Artaxerxes was 433 B.C.

THOUGH (2 of 6)

Ge 3:16 {for your husband,} Or *And **t** you may desire to control your husband.*
Heb 11:11 {keep his promise.} Some manuscripts read *It was by faith that Sarah was able to have a child, even **t** she was too old and barren. Sarah believed that God would keep his promise.*

THOUGHT (4)

Ge 24:10 {traveled to Aram-naharaim} *Aram-naharaim* means "Aram of the two rivers," **t** to have been located between the Euphrates and Balih Rivers in northwestern Mesopotamia.
Dt 23: 4 {Pethor in Aram-naharaim} *Aram-naharaim* means "Aram of the two rivers," **t** to have been located between the Euphrates and Balih Rivers in northwestern Mesopotamia.
Jdg 3: 8 {Cushan-rishathaim of Aram-naharaim.} *Aram-naharaim* means "Aram of the two rivers," **t** to have been located between the Euphrates and Balih Rivers in northwestern Mesopotamia.
1Sa 15:32 {have been spared!"} Dead Sea Scrolls and Greek version read *Agag arrived hesitantly, for he **t**, "Surely this is the bitterness of death."*

THOUGHTS (1)

Ps 139:17 {thoughts about me,} Or *How precious to me are your **t**.*

THOUSAND (2)

1Sa 10:27 {Saul ignored them.} Dead Sea Scroll 4QSam[a] continues: *…But there were seven **t** men who had escaped from the Ammonites, and they had settled in Jabesh-gilead.*
2Ch 14: 9 {a million men} Or *an army of thousands and thousands;* Hebrew reads *an army of a **t** thousands.*

THOUSANDS (4)

Nu 31:14 {the military commanders} Hebrew *the commanders of **t**, and the commanders of hundreds;* also in 31:48, 52, 54.
2Ch 14: 9 {a million men} Or *an army of **t** and **t**;* Hebrew reads *an army of a thousand **t**.*

THREE (9)

2Sa 23: 8 {a single battle.} As in some Greek manuscripts (see also 1 Chr 11:11); the Hebrew is uncertain, though it might be rendered *the **T**. It was Adino the Eznite who killed eight hundred men at one time.*
23:18 {of the Thirty.} As in a few Hebrew manuscripts and Syriac version; most Hebrew manuscripts read *the **T**.*
23:19 {of the Thirty} As in Syriac version; Hebrew reads *the **T**.*
1Ch 11:20 {of the Thirty.} As in Syriac version; Hebrew reads *the **T**;* also in 11:21.
Isa 21:16 {within a year,"} Hebrew *Within a year, like the years of a hired hand.* Some ancient manuscripts read *Within **t** years,* as in 16:14.
La 1: 1 {Jerusalem's streets,} Each of the first four chapters of this book is an acrostic, laid out in the order of the Hebrew alphabet. The first word of each verse begins with a successive Hebrew letter. Chapters 1, 2, and 4 have one verse for each of the 22 Hebrew letters. Chapter 3 contains 22 stanzas of **t** verses each. Though chapter 5 is not an acrostic, it also has 22 verses.
Ac 28:15 {The Three Taverns.} *The **T** Taverns* was about 35 miles (57 kilometers) from Rome.
1Jn 5: 7 {these three witnesses} Some very late manuscripts add *in heaven—the Father, the Word, and the Holy Spirit, and these **t** are one. And we have **t** witnesses on earth.*

THRESH (1)

Mic 4:13 {the nations, O Jerusalem!"} Hebrew *"Rise up and **t**, O daughter of Zion."*

THRESHOLD (1)

Eze 40: 6 {10 1/2 feet deep.} Greek version; Hebrew reads *1 rod* [10.5 feet or 3.2 meters] *deep, and one **t**, one rod deep.*

THRONE (3)

Ex 17:16 {throne, so now} Or *Hands have been lifted up to the LORD's **t**, and now.*
Ps 45: 6 {Your throne, O God,} Or *Your divine **t**.*
Zec 6:13 {from his throne,} Or *There will be a priest by his **t**.*

THROUGH (17)

Ge 46:27 {had two sons} Greek version reads *nine sons,* probably including Joseph's grandsons **t** Ephraim and Manasseh (see 1 Chr 7:14-20).
Dt 18:10 {a burnt offering.} Or *never make your son or daughter pass **t** the fire.*
2Sa 2:29 {through the morning,} Or *continued on **t** the Bithron.* The meaning of the Hebrew is uncertain.
2Ki 16: 3 {in the fire.} Or *even making his son pass **t** the fire.*
17:17 {in the fire.} Or *They even made their sons and daughters pass **t** the fire.*
21: 6 {in the fire.} Or *even made his son pass **t** the fire.*
23:10 {in the fire} Or *to make a son or daughter pass **t** the fire.*
2Ch 28: 3 {in the fire.} Or *even making his sons pass **t** the fire.*
33: 6 {in the fire} Or *even made his sons pass **t** the fire.*
Eze 20:31 {burned as sacrifices,} Or *and make your little children pass **t** the fire.*
Da 2: 4 {king in Aramaic,} The original text from this point **t** chapter 7 is in Aramaic.
1Co 5: 6[-7] {can stay pure.} Greek *Don't you realize that even a little leaven spreads quickly **t** the whole batch of dough? [7]Purge out the old leaven so that you can be a new batch of dough, just as you are already unleavened.*
Gal 2:16 {obeying the law."} Some translators hold that the quotation extends **t** verse 14; others **t** verse 16; and still others **t** verse 21.
Tit 3: 5 {the Holy Spirit.} Greek *He saved us **t** the washing of regeneration and renewing of the Holy Spirit.*
1Pe 3:20 {that terrible flood.} Greek *saved **t** water.*

THROUGHOUT (16)
Ge 2:19 {Adam} Hebrew *the man,* and so **t** this chapter.
3: 9 {Adam,} Hebrew *the man,* and so **t** this chapter.
4:18 {the father of} Or *the ancestor of,* and so **t** the verse.
47:21 {servants to Pharaoh.} As in Greek version and Samaritan Pentateuch; Hebrew reads *He moved the people into the towns* **t** *the land of Egypt.*
Lev 13: 2 {contagious skin disease,} Traditionally rendered *leprosy.* The Hebrew word used **t** this passage is used to describe various skin diseases.
13:47 {an infectious mildew} Traditionally rendered *leprosy.* The Hebrew term used **t** this passage is the same term used for the various skin diseases described in 13:1-46.
1Sa 5: 6 {plague of tumors.} Greek version and Latin Vulgate read *tumors. And rats appeared in their land, and death and destruction were* **t** *the city.*
2Ki 5: 1 {suffered from leprosy.} Or *from a contagious skin disease.* The Hebrew word used here and **t** this passage can describe various skin diseases.
7: 3 {men with leprosy} Or *with a contagious skin disease.* The Hebrew word used here and **t** this passage can describe various skin diseases.
15: 5 {king with leprosy,} Or *with a contagious skin disease.* The Hebrew word used here and **t** this passage can describe various skin diseases.
2Ch 26:19 {LORD's Temple, leprosy} Or *a contagious skin disease.* The Hebrew word used here and **t** this passage can describe various skin diseases.
Est 1: 1 {of King Xerxes,} Hebrew *Ahasuerus,* another name for Xerxes; also **t** the book of Esther.
Job 41: 1 {catch a crocodile} Hebrew *Leviathan;* also **t** the following passage.
Ps 3: 2 {Interlude} Hebrew *Selah.* The meaning of this word is uncertain, though it is probably a musical or literary term. It is rendered *Interlude* **t** the Psalms.
Ecc 1: 1 {of the Teacher,} Hebrew *Koheleth;* this term is rendered "the Teacher" **t** this book.
Mt 25:15 {bags of gold} Greek *talents;* also **t** the story. A talent is equal to 75 pounds or 34 kilograms.

THROWN (2)
Ne 4: 5 {the presence of} Or *for they have* **t** *insults in the face of.*
Am 4: 3 {from your fortresses.} Hebrew **t** *out toward Harmon,* possibly a reference to Mount Hermon.

THUMMIM (4)
Dt 33: 8 {the sacred lots} Hebrew *given your* **T** *and Urim.* See Exod 28:30.
1Sa 14:41 {among the others?"} Greek version adds *If the fault is with me or my son Jonathan, respond with Urim; but if the men of Israel are at fault, respond with* **T**.
Ezr 2:63 {of sacred lots.} Hebrew *consult the Urim and* **T** *about the matter.*
Ne 7:65 {of sacred lots.} Hebrew *consult the Urim and* **T** *about the matter.*

THUNDER (1)
Mk 3:17 {"Sons of Thunder"} Greek *whom he named Boanerges, which means Sons of* **T**.

TIBERIAS (1)
Jn 21: 1 {Sea of Galilee.} Greek *Sea of* **T**, another name for the Sea of Galilee.

TIBHATH (1)
1Ch 18: 8 {cities of Tebah} Hebrew reads **T**, a variant name for Tebah; compare parallel text at 2 Sam 8:8.

TIGHTEN (1)
Jdg 16:13 {the loom shuttle,} As in Greek version; Hebrew lacks *on your loom and* **t** *it with the loom shuttle.*

TIGLATH-PILESER (3)
2Ki 15:19 {Then King Tiglath-pileser} Hebrew *Pul,* another name for **T**.
1Ch 5: 6 {by King Tiglath-pileser} Hebrew *Tilgath-pilneser,* a variant name for **T**; also in 5:26.
2Ch 28:20 {when King Tiglath-pileser} Hebrew *Tilgath-pilneser,* a variant name for **T**.

TILGATH-PILNESER (2)
1Ch 5: 6 {by King Tiglath-pileser} Hebrew **T**, a variant name for Tiglath-pileser; also in 5:26.
2Ch 28:20 {when King Tiglath-pileser} Hebrew **T**, a variant name for Tiglath-pileser.

TIME (9)
1Sa 1:22 {the LORD permanently."} Some manuscripts add *I will offer him as a Nazirite for all* **t**.
14:18 {of the Israelites.} As in some Greek manuscripts; Hebrew reads *"Bring the Ark of God." For at that* **t** *the Ark of God was with the Israelites.*
2Sa 23: 8 {a single battle.} As in some Greek manuscripts (see also 1 Chr 11:11); the Hebrew is uncertain, though it might be rendered *the Three. It was Adino the Eznite who killed eight hundred men at one* **t**.
1Ki 2: 5 {time of peace,} Or *He murdered them during a* **t** *of peace as revenge for deaths they had caused in* **t** *of war.*
Da 7:12 {a while longer.} Aramaic *for a season and a* **t**.
Mt 2:16 {two years earlier.} Or *according to the* **t** *he calculated from the wise men.*
Jn 5: 3 {on the porches.} Some manuscripts add *waiting for a certain movement of the water, [4]for an angel of the Lord came from* **t** *to* **t** *and stirred up the water. And the first person to step down into it afterward was healed.*

TIMES (1)
Mt 18:22 {"seventy times seven!} Or *77* **t**.

TIMNA (1)
1Ch 1:36 {born to Timna.} As in some Greek manuscripts (see also Gen 36:12); Hebrew reads *Kenaz,* **T**, *and Amalek.*

TIMNATH-HERES (1)
Jdg 2: 9 {inherited, at Timnath-serah} Hebrew **T**, a variant name for Timnath-serah.

TIMNATH-SERAH (1)
Jdg 2: 9 {inherited, at Timnath-serah} Hebrew *Timnath-heres,* a variant name for **T**.

TIP (1)
Ac 28:13 {across to Rhegium.} *Rhegium* was on the southern **t** of Italy.

TIPHSAH (1)
2Ki 15:16 {town of Tappuah} As in some Greek manuscripts; Hebrew reads **T**.

TITHE (2)
Mt 23:23 {of your income,} Greek *to* **t** *the mint, the dill, and the cumin.*
Lk 11:42 {of your income,} Greek *to* **t** *the mint and the rue and every herb.*

TODAY (5)
Ps 2: 7 {become your Father.} Or **T** *I reveal you as my son.*
Lk 3:22 {pleased with you.} Some manuscripts read *and* **t** *I have become your Father.*
Ac 13:33 {become your Father.} Or **T** *I reveal you as my Son.* Ps 2:7.
Heb 1: 5 {become your Father.} Or **T** *I reveal you as my Son.* Ps 2:7.
5: 5 {become your Father.} Or **T** *I reveal you as my Son.* Ps 2:7.

TOGETHER (3)
Mt 18:20 {they are mine,} Greek *gather* **t** *in my name.*
Ro 8:28 {to work together} Some manuscripts read *And we know that everything works* **t**.
2Co 6: 1 {As God's partners,} Or *As we work* **t**.

TOKHATH (1)
2Ch 34:22 {grandson of Harhas,} As in parallel text at 2 Kgs 22:14; Hebrew reads *son of* **T**, *son of Hasrah.*

TOMB (1)
2Ki 23:16 {man of God} As in Greek version; Hebrew lacks *as Jeroboam stood beside the altar at the festival. Then Josiah turned and looked up at the* **t** *of the man of God.*

TOMBS (1)
Mt 27:51[-53] {to many people.} Or *The earth shook, rocks split apart,* **t** *opened, and many bodies of godly men and women who had died were raised from the dead. After Jesus' resurrection, they left the cemetery, went into the holy city of Jerusalem, and appeared to many people.*

TOMORROW (1)
Mt 6:11 {food for today,} Or *for* **t**.

TONGUES (6)
Mk 16:17 {speak new languages.} Or *new* **t**; some manuscripts omit *new.*
Ac 2: 4 {in other languages,} Or *in other* **t**.
1Co 12:10 {in unknown languages,} Or *in* **t**; also in 12:28, 30.
13: 1 {or on earth} Greek *in* **t** *of people and angels.*
13: 8 {in unknown languages} Or *in* **t**.
14: 6 {an unknown language,} Or *in* **t**; also in 14:19, 23, 26, 27.

TOOK (8)
Ge 2:21 {of Adam's ribs} Or **t** *a part of Adam's side.*
Dt 4:49 {the Dead Sea,} Hebrew **t** *the Arabah on the east side of the Jordan as far as the sea of the Arabah.*
Am 5:26 {you yourselves made.} Greek version reads *You* **t** *up the shrine of Molech, and the star of your god Rephan, and the images you made for yourselves.*
Mic 2: 4 {who betrayed us.} Or *to those who* **t** *us captive.*
Mt 27: 9 {"They took} Or *I* **t**.
27:49 {and save him."} Some manuscripts add *And another* **t** *a spear and pierced his side, and out came water and blood.*
Jn 12: 3 {twelve-ounce jar} Greek **t** *1 litra* [327 grams].
Ac 24: 6 {we arrested him.} Some manuscripts add *We would have judged him by our law, [7]but Lysias, the commander of the garrison, came and* **t** *him violently away from us, [8]commanding his accusers to come before you.*

TOOTH (2)
Mt 5:38 {who did it.'} Greek *'An eye for an eye and a* **t** *for a* **t**.*'* Exod 21:24; Lev 24:20; Deut 19:21.

TOP (1)
Ex 38: 1 {4 1/2 feet high.} Hebrew *5 cubits* [2.3 meters] *square at the* **t**, *and 3 cubits* [1.4 meters] *high.* In this chapter, the distance measures are calculated from the Hebrew cubit at a ratio of 18 inches or 45 centimeters per cubit.

TORMAH (1)
Jdg 9:31 {Abimelech in Arumah,} Hebrew **T**; see 9:41.

TOTAL (1)
Nu 3:28 {There were 8,600} Some Greek manuscripts read *8,300;* see **t** in 3:39.

TOU (1)
1Ch 18: 9 {When King Toi} As in parallel text at 2 Sam 8:9; Hebrew reads **T**; also in 18:10.

TOUCHED (1)
1Ki 1:52 {not be harmed.} Hebrew *not a hair on his head will be* **t**.

TOWARD (7)
Lev 19:16 {among your people.} Hebrew *Do not act as a merchant* **t** *your own people.*
Nu 3:38 {toward the sunrise} Hebrew **t** *the sunrise, in front of the Tent of Meeting.*
Jer 3:12 {words to Israel,} Hebrew **t** *the north.*
Eze 40: 8 {of the gateway} Many Hebrew manuscripts add *which faced inward* **t** *the Temple; it was one rod* [10.5 feet or 3.2 meters] *deep. [9]Then he measured the foyer of the gateway,…*
Am 4: 3 {from your fortresses.} Hebrew *thrown out* **t** *Harmon,* possibly a reference to Mount Hermon.
Zec 14: 8 {toward the Mediterranean,} Hebrew *half* **t** *the eastern sea and half* **t** *the western sea.*

TOWN (1)
Jer 48: 6 {in the wilderness!} Or *Be like* [the **t** of] *Aroer in the wilderness.*

TOWNS (1)
Ge 47:21 {servants to Pharaoh.} As in Greek version and Samaritan Pentateuch; Hebrew reads *He moved the people into the* **t** *throughout the land of Egypt.*

TRADITION (3)
Jdg 18:30 {descendant of Moses,} As in an ancient Hebrew **t**, some Greek manuscripts, and Latin Vulgate; Masoretic Text reads *of Manasseh.*
Job 32: 3 {had condemned God} As in ancient Hebrew scribal **t**; the Masoretic Text makes no reference to God.
Hos 4: 7 {They have exchanged} As in Syriac version and an ancient Hebrew **t**; Masoretic Text reads *I will exchange.*

TRADITIONALLY (13)
Ge 6:14 {"Make a boat} **T** rendered *an ark.*
37: 3 {gift—a beautiful robe.} **T** rendered *a coat of many colors.* The exact meaning of the Hebrew is uncertain.
49:10 {whom it belongs,} Or *until tribute is brought to him and the peoples obey;* **t** rendered *until Shiloh comes.*
Ex 3:15 {'The LORD,} Hebrew *Yahweh;* **t** rendered *Jehovah.*
6: 3 {the LORD,} Hebrew *Yahweh;* **t** rendered *Jehovah.*
Lev 13: 2 {contagious skin disease,} **T** rendered *leprosy.* The Hebrew word used throughout this passage is used to describe various skin diseases.
13:47 {an infectious mildew} **T** rendered *leprosy.* The Hebrew term used throughout this passage is the same term used for the various skin diseases described in 13:1-46.
14: 2 {contagious skin disease.} **T** rendered *leprosy.* See note at 13:2.
14:34 {an infectious mildew.} **T** rendered *leprosy.* See note at 13:47.
14:54 {contagious skin disease} **T** rendered *leprosy.* See notes at 13:2 and 13:47.
22: 4 {contagious skin disease} **T** rendered *leprosy.* See note at 13:2.
Nu 5: 2 {contagious skin disease} **T** rendered *leprosy.* The Hebrew word used here describes various skin diseases.
Lk 14: 2 {legs were swollen.} **T** translated *who had dropsy.*

TRADITONALLY (1)

Dt 24: 8 {contagious skin diseases} **T** rendered *leprosy.* The Hebrew word used here can describe various skin diseases.

TRAGEDY (1)

1Ch 7:23 {named him Beriah} *Beriah* sounds like a Hebrew term meaning "**t**" or "misfortune."

TRANSLATED (5)

Pr 30: 1 {worn out, O God.} The Hebrew can also be **t** *The man declares this to Ithiel, to Ithiel and to Ucal.*
Lk 14: 2 {legs were swollen.} Traditionally **t** *who had dropsy.*
Jn 3: 5 {and the Spirit.} Or *spirit.* The Greek word for *Spirit* can also be **t** *wind;* see 3:8.
1Ti 3:11 {way, their wives} Or *the women deacons.* The Greek word can be **t** *women* or *wives.*
Rev 4: 5 {the seven spirits} See 1:4 and 3:1, where the same expression is **t** *the sevenfold Spirit.*

TRANSLATES (2)

Mk 5:41 {up, little girl!"} Greek text uses Aramaic *"Talitha cumi"* and then **t** it as "Get up, little girl."
7:34 {commanded, "Be opened!"} Greek text uses Aramaic *"Ephphatha"* and then **t** it as "Be opened."

TRANSLATIONS (1)

Rev 12:18 {Then he stood} Some manuscripts read *Then I stood,* and some **t** put this entire sentence into 13:1.

TRANSLATORS (1)

Gal 2:16 {obeying the law."} Some **t** hold that the quotation extends through verse 14; others through verse 16; and still others through verse 21.

TREASURE (1)

2Co 4: 7 {our weak bodies.} Greek *But we have this* **t** *in earthen vessels.*

TREASURY (1)

Zec 11:13 {to the potters} Syriac version reads *into the* **t**; also in 11:13b.

TREAT (2)

Mt 7: 2 {you treat them.} Or *For God will* **t** *you as you* **t** *others;* Greek reads *For with the judgment you judge you will be judged.*

TREE (3)

Jer 1:12 {I am watching,} The Hebrew word for "watching" sounds like the word for "almond **t**."
Lk 23:31 {it is dry?} Or *If these things are done to me, the living* **t**, *what will happen to you, the dry* **t**?

TREES (2)

Lev 23:40 {from citrus trees,} Or *fruit from majestic* **t**.
2Sa 6: 5 {might, singing songs} As in Greek version (see also 1 Chr 13:8); Hebrew reads *cypress* **t**.

TRENCHES (1)

Da 9:25 {and strong defenses,} Or *and a moat,* or *and* **t**.

TRIBE (1)

Dt 33: 6 {tribe of Reuben:} Hebrew lacks *Moses said this about the* **t** *of Reuben.*

TRIBES (2)

1Ki 18:31 {tribes of Israel,} Hebrew *each of the* **t** *of the sons of Jacob to whom the* LORD *had said, "Your name will be Israel."*
Jas 1: 1 {among the nations.} Greek *To the twelve* **t** *in the dispersion.*

TRIBUTE (3)

Ge 49:10 {whom it belongs,} Or *until* **t** *is brought to him and the peoples obey;* traditionally rendered *until Shiloh comes.*
2Sa 8: 1 {their largest city.} Hebrew *by conquering Metheg-ammah,* a name which means "the bridle," possibly referring to the size of the city or the **t** money taken from it. Compare 1 Chr 18:1.
Ps 68:30 {tribute from us.} Or *Humble them until they submit, bringing pieces of silver as* **t**.

TRODDEN (1)

Ps 58: 7 {in their hands.} Or *Let them be* **t** *down and wither like grass.* The meaning of the Hebrew is uncertain.

TROPHIMUS (1)

Ac 21:29 {Gentile from Ephesus,} Greek **T**, *the Ephesian.*

TRUE (1)

Php 4: 3 {my true teammate,} Greek **t** *yokefellow,* or *loyal Syzygus.*

TRULY (3)

Jn 8:58 {was even born!"} Or *"T, t, before Abraham was, I am."*
1Pe 1: 6 {be truly glad!} Or *So you are* **t** *glad.*

TRUST (1)

Mk 10:24 {is very hard} Some manuscripts add *for those who* **t** *in riches.*

TRUSTED (1)

Jer 48:13 {calf at Bethel.} Hebrew *ashamed when they* **t** *in Bethel.*

TRUTH (2)

Jn 1:14 {love and faithfulness.} Greek *grace and* **t**; also in 1:17.
Ro 1:18 {away from themselves.} Or *who prevent the* **t** *from being known.*

TRUTHS (2)

1Co 2:13 {explain spiritual truths.} Or *explaining spiritual* **t** *in spiritual language,* or *explaining spiritual* **t** *to spiritual people.*

TSIDQENU (1)

Jer 23: 6 {Is Our Righteousness.'} Hebrew *Yahweh* **T**.

TUMORS (1)

1Sa 5: 6 {plague of tumors.} Greek version and Latin Vulgate read **t**. *And rats appeared in their land, and death and destruction were throughout the city.*

TURKEY (4)

Ac 13:13[-14] {Antioch of Pisidia.} *Pamphylia* and *Pisidia* were districts in the land now called **T**.
14: 1 {In Iconium,} *Iconium,* as well as *Lystra* and *Derbe* (14:6), were cities in the land now called **T**.
16: 6[-7] {province of Bithynia,} *Phrygia, Galatia, Asia, Mysia,* and *Bithynia* were all districts in the land now called **T**.
1Co 16:19 {province of Asia} *Asia* was a Roman province in what is now western **T**.

TURN (1)

Est 2:15 {was Esther's turn} Hebrew *the* **t** *of Esther, the daughter of Abihail, who was Mordecai's uncle, who had adopted her.*

TURNED (1)

2Ki 23:16 {man of God} As in Greek version; Hebrew lacks *as Jeroboam stood beside the altar at the festival. Then Josiah* **t** *and looked up at the tomb of the man of God.*

TURNS (1)

Hab 2: 4 {lives are crooked;} Greek version reads *I will have no pleasure in anyone who* **t** *away.*

TWELFTH (14)

2Ki 25:27 {of that year.} Hebrew *on the twenty-seventh day of the* **t** *month,* of the Hebrew calendar. This day was April 2, 560 B.C.; also see note on 25:1.
Ezr 8:31 {Canal on April 19} Hebrew *on the* **t** *day of the first month,* of the Hebrew calendar. This event occurred on April 19, 458 B.C.; see note on 7:9a.
Est 3: 7 {a year later.} As in Greek version, which reads *the thirteenth day of the* **t** *month, the month of Adar* (see also 3:13). Hebrew reads *in the* **t** *month,* of the Hebrew calendar. The date selected was March 7, 473 B.C.; also see note on 2:16.
3:13 {later on March 7.} Hebrew *on the thirteenth day of the* **t** *month, the month of Adar,* of the Hebrew calendar. The date selected was March 7, 473 B.C.; also see note on 2:16.
8:12 {the next year.} Hebrew *the thirteenth day of the* **t** *month, the month of Adar,* of the Hebrew calendar. The date selected was March 7, 473 B.C.; also see note on 2:16.
9: 1 {So on March 7} Hebrew *on the thirteenth day of the* **t** *month, the month of Adar,* of the Hebrew calendar. This event occurred on March 7, 473 B.C.; also see note on 2:16.
Jer 52:31 {of that year.} Hebrew *on the twenty-fifth day of the* **t** *month,* of the Hebrew calendar. This day was March 31, 560 B.C.; also see note on 52:4a.
Eze 26: 1 {King Jehoiachin's captivity,} Hebrew *In the eleventh year, on the first day of the month,* of the Hebrew calendar year. Since an element is missing in the date formula here, scholars have reconstructed this probable reading: *On the first day of the eleventh month, during the* **t** *year.* This reading would put this message on February 3, 585 B.C.; also see note on 1:1.
29: 1 {On January 7,} Hebrew *On the* **t** *day of the tenth month,* of the Hebrew calendar. A number of events in Ezekiel can be cross-checked with dates in surviving Babylonian records and related accurately to our modern calendar. This event occurred on January 7, 587 B.C.
32: 1 {On March 3,} Hebrew *On the first day of the* **t** *month,* of the Hebrew calendar. This event occurred on March 3, 585 B.C.; also see note on 29:1.
32:17 {On March 17,} Hebrew *On the fifteenth day of the month,* presumably in the **t** month of the Hebrew calendar (see 32:1). This would put this message at the end of King Jehoiachin's **t** year of captivity, on March 17, 585 B.C.; also see note on 29:1. Greek version reads *On the fifteenth day of the first month,* which would put this message on April 27, 586 B.C., at the beginning of Jehoiachin's **t** year.

TWELVE (2)

1Ch 25: 9 {sons and relatives.} As in Greek version; Hebrew lacks *and* **t** *of his sons and relatives.*
Jas 1: 1 {among the nations.} Greek *To the* **t** *tribes in the dispersion.*

TWENTIETH (4)

Nu 10:11 {day in midspring,} Hebrew *On the* **t** *day of the second month.* This day of the Hebrew lunar calendar occurs in late April or early May.
Ezr 10: 9 {place on December 19,} Hebrew *on the* **t** *day of the ninth month,* of the Hebrew calendar. This event occurred on December 19, 458 B.C.; also see note on 7:9a.
Ne 1: 1 {King Artaxerxes' reign,} Hebrew *In the month of Kislev of the* **t** *year.* A number of events in the book of Nehemiah can be cross-checked with dates in surviving Persian records and related accurately to our modern calendar. This month of the Hebrew lunar calendar occurred in November and December 446 B.C. The **t** *year* probably refers to the reign of King Artaxerxes I; compare 2:1; 5:14.

TWENTY-FIFTH (2)

Ne 6:15 {So on October 2} Hebrew *on the* **t** *day of the month Elul,* of the Hebrew calendar. This event occurred on October 2, 445 B.C.; also see note on 1:1.
Jer 52:31 {of that year.} Hebrew *on the* **t** *day of the twelfth month,* of the Hebrew calendar. This day was March 31, 560 B.C.; also see note on 52:4a.

TWENTY-FIRST (1)

Hag 2: 1 {Then on October 17} Hebrew *on the* **t** *day of the seventh month,* of the Hebrew calendar. This event occurred on October 17, 520 B.C.; also see note on 1:1a.

TWENTY-FOURTH (6)

Ne 9: 1 {On October 31} Hebrew *On the* **t** *day of that same month,* the seventh month of the Hebrew calendar. This event occurred on October 31, 445 B.C.; also see note on 1:1.
Da 10: 4 {On April 23,} Hebrew *On the* **t** *day of the first month.* This event in the book of Daniel can be cross-checked with dates in surviving Persian records and can be related accurately to our modern calendar. This day of the Hebrew lunar calendar occurred on April 23, 536 B.C.
Hag 1:15 {was on September 21} Hebrew *on the* **t** *day of the sixth month,* of the Hebrew calendar. This event occurred on September 21, 520 B.C.; also see note on 1:1a.
2:10 {On December 18} Hebrew *On the* **t** *day of the ninth month,* of the Hebrew calendar (also in 2:18). This event occurred on December 18, 520 B.C.; also see note on 1:1a.
2:20 {on December 18} Hebrew *on the* **t** *day of the month;* see note on 2:10.
Zec 1: 7 {Then on February 15} Hebrew *on the* **t** *day of the eleventh month, the month of Shebat,* of the Hebrew calendar. This event occurred on February 15, 519 B.C.; also see note on 1:1.

TWENTY-SEVENTH (3)

Ge 8:14 {months went by,} Hebrew *The* **t** *day of the second month arrived;* see note on 8:13.
2Ki 25:27 {of that year.} Hebrew *on the* **t** *day of the twelfth month,* of the Hebrew calendar. This day was April 2, 560 B.C.; also see note on 25:1.
2Ch 7:10 {of the celebration,} Hebrew *Then on the* **t** *day of the seventh month.* This day of the Hebrew lunar calendar occurs in late September or early October.

TWENTY-THIRD (2)

Est 8: 9 {So on June 25} Hebrew *on the* **t** *day of the third month, the month of Sivan,* of the Hebrew calendar. This event occurred on June 25, 474 B.C.; also see note on 2:16.
Jer 52:30 {his twenty-third year} This exile in the **t** year of Nebuchadnezzar's reign occurred in 581 B.C.

TWIN (1)

Ac 28:11 {the twin gods} The **t** *gods* were the Roman gods Castor and Pollux.

TWO (15)

Ge 24:10 {traveled to Aram-naharaim} *Aram-naharaim* means "Aram of the **t** rivers," thought to have been located between the Euphrates and Balih Rivers in northwestern Mesopotamia.
24:22 {large gold bracelets} Hebrew *a gold nose-ring weighing a half shekel* [0.2 ounces or 6 grams] *and* ***t*** *gold bracelets weighing 10 shekels* [4 ounces or 114 grams].
32: 2 {the place Mahanaim.} *Mahanaim* means "**t** camps."
Ex 3: 1 {his father-in-law, Jethro,} Moses' father-in-law went by **t** names, Jethro and Reuel.
19: 1 {they left Egypt.} Hebrew *in the third month…on the very day,* i.e., **t** lunar months to the day after leaving Egypt. This day of the Hebrew lunar calendar occurs in late May or early June; compare note on 13:4.
Dt 23: 4 {Pethor in Aram-naharaim} *Aram-naharaim* means "Aram of the **t** rivers," thought to have been located between the Euphrates and Balih Rivers in northwestern Mesopotamia.
Jdg 3: 8 {Cushan-rishathaim of Aram-naharaim.} *Aram-naharaim* means "Aram of the **t** rivers," thought to have been located between the Euphrates and Balih Rivers in northwestern Mesopotamia.
1Sa 13: 1 {for forty-two years.} Hebrew *reigned…and* ***t;*** the number is incomplete in the Hebrew. Compare Acts 13:21.
1Ki 21:10 {Find two scoundrels} Hebrew ***t*** *sons of Belial;* also in 21:13.
Ps 145:13 {all he does.} The last **t** lines of 145:13 are not found in many of the ancient manuscripts.
Pr 30:15 {out, "More, more!"} Hebrew ***t*** *daughters who cry out, "Give, give!"*
SS 6:13 {lines of dancers?} Or *as you would at the movements of* ***t*** *armies? or as you would at the dance of Mahanaim?* The meaning of the Hebrew is uncertain.
Eze 47:13 {shares of land.} A share of land for each of Joseph's **t** oldest sons, Ephraim and Manasseh.
Mk 16: 8 {frightened to talk.} The most reliable early manuscripts conclude the Gospel of Mark at verse 8. Other manuscripts include various endings to the Gospel. **T** of the more noteworthy endings are printed here.
Lk 17:35 {the other left.} Some manuscripts add verse 36, ***T*** *men will be working in the field; one will be taken, the other left.*

TYING (2)

Mt 12:29 {house be robbed!} Or *One cannot rob Satan's kingdom without first* ***t*** *him up. Only then can his demons be cast out.*
Mk 3:27 {house be robbed!} Or *One cannot rob Satan's kingdom without first* ***t*** *him up. Only then can his demons be cast out.*

TYPE (1)

1Sa 18: 6 {tambourines and cymbals.} The **t** of instrument represented by the final word is uncertain.

TYRE (1)

Ps 45:12 {princes of Tyre} Hebrew *The daughter of* ***T.***

U

UCAL (1)

Pr 30: 1 {worn out, O God.} The Hebrew can also be translated *The man declares this to Ithiel, to Ithiel and to U.*

ULAI (1)

Da 8: 2 {the Ulai River.} Or *the* ***U*** *Gate;* also in 8:16.

UNCERTAIN (87)

Ge 25:18 {to one another.} The meaning of the Hebrew is **u.**
29:17 {had pretty eyes,} Or *dull eyes.* The meaning of the Hebrew is **u.**
37: 3 {gift—a beautiful robe.} Traditionally rendered *a coat of many colors.* The exact meaning of the Hebrew is **u.**
48:22 {an extra portion} Or *give you the ridge of land.* The meaning of the Hebrew is **u.**
Ex 28:17 {rows of gemstones} The identification of some of these gemstones is **u.**
28:32 {a woven collar} The meaning of the Hebrew is **u.**
39:10 {rows of gemstones} The identification of some of these gemstones is **u.**
39:23 {a woven collar,} The meaning of the Hebrew is **u.**
Lev 1:16 {and the feathers} Or *the crop and its contents.* The meaning of the Hebrew is **u.**
6:21 {mixed and broken} The meaning of this Hebrew term is **u.**
11: 4 {animals named here} The identification of some of the animals, birds, and insects in this chapter is **u.**
21: 4 {among his relatives,} The meaning of the Hebrew is **u.**
Nu 21:30 {Nophah and Medeba.} Or *until fire spread to Medeba.* The meaning of the Hebrew is **u.**
Dt 7:20 {will send hornets} Or *will spread panic,* or *will send a plague.* The meaning of the Hebrew is **u.**
14: 4 {are the animals} The identification of some of the animals and birds listed in this chapter is **u.**
32: 5 {really his children?} The meaning of the Hebrew is **u.**
32:26 {to scatter them,} As in Greek version; the meaning of the Hebrew is **u.**
32:31 {even they recognize.} The meaning of the Hebrew is **u.** Greek version reads *our enemies are fools.*
33: 2 {his right hand.} Or *came from myriads of holy ones, from the south, from his mountain slopes.* The meaning of the Hebrew is **u.**
Jos 17:11 {(that is, Naphoth-dor),} The meaning of the Hebrew here is **u.**
18:15 {it ran westward} Or *it went to Ephron, and.* The meaning of the Hebrew is **u.**
Jdg 5:11 {the village musicians} The meaning of the Hebrew is **u.**
7: 3 {afraid may leave} Hebrew *leave Mount Gilead.* The identity of Mount Gilead is **u** in this context. It is perhaps used here as another name for Mount Gilboa.
9: 6 {beside the pillar} The meaning of the Hebrew is **u.**
1Sa 1: 5 {special portion} Or *a double portion.* The meaning of the Hebrew is **u.**
18: 6 {tambourines and cymbals.} The type of instrument represented by the final word is **u.**
20:19 {the stone pile.} Hebrew *the stone Ezel.* The meaning of the Hebrew is **u.**
2Sa 2:29 {through the morning,} Or *continued on through the Bithron.* The meaning of the Hebrew is **u.**
5: 8 {enter the house."} The meaning of this saying is **u.**
5: 9 {at the Millo} Or *the supporting terraces.* The meaning of the Hebrew is **u.**
6:19 {cake of dates,} Or *a portion of meat.* The meaning of the Hebrew is **u.**
7:19 {everyone this way,} The meaning of the Hebrew is **u.**
13:18 {long, beautiful robe,} Or *a robe with sleeves,* or *an ornamented robe.* The meaning of the Hebrew is **u.**
23: 8 {a single battle.} As in some Greek manuscripts (see also 1 Chr 11:11); the Hebrew is **u,** though it might be rendered *the Three. It was Adino the Eznite who killed eight hundred men at one time.*
1Ki 4:19 {land of Judah.} As in some Greek manuscripts; Hebrew lacks *of Judah.* The meaning of the Hebrew is **u.**
6:20 {made of cedar.} Or *overlaid the altar with cedar.* The meaning of the Hebrew is **u.**
2Ki 16:18 {the Sabbath day,} The meaning of the Hebrew is **u.**
1Ch 2:42 {father of Hebron.} The meaning of the Hebrew is **u.**
4: 3 {The descendants of} As in Greek version; Hebrew reads *father of.* The meaning of the Hebrew is **u.**
11: 8 {from the Millo} Or *the supporting terraces.* The meaning of the Hebrew is **u.**
15:20 {play the lyres.} Hebrew adds *according to Alamoth,* which is probably a musical term. The meaning of the Hebrew is **u.**
15:21 {play the harps.} Hebrew adds *according to the Sheminith,* which is probably a musical term. The meaning of the Hebrew is **u.**
16: 3 {cake of dates,} Or *a portion of meat.* The meaning of the Hebrew is **u.**
17:17 {someone very great,} The meaning of the Hebrew is **u.**
18: 3 {far as Hamath,} The meaning of the Hebrew is **u.**
26:16 {to the Temple.} Or *the gate of Shalleketh on the upper road* (also in 26:18). The meaning of the Hebrew is **u.**
26:18 {to the courtyard.} Or *the colonnade.* The meaning of the Hebrew is **u.**
2Ch 9:11 {to make steps} Or *gateways.* The meaning of the Hebrew is **u.**
Ezr 1: 9 {silver censers} The meaning of this Hebrew word is **u.**
8:13 {who came later} The meaning of the Hebrew for this phrase is **u.**
10:44 {by these wives.} Or *and they sent them away with their children.* The meaning of the Hebrew is **u.**
Ne 4:12 {and attack us!"} The meaning of the Hebrew is **u.**
4:23 {went for water.} Hebrew *Each his weapon the water.* The meaning of the Hebrew is **u.**
Est 2:19 {the second harem} The meaning of the Hebrew is **u.**
Job 36:33 {his indignant anger.} Or *even the cattle know when a storm is coming.* The meaning of the Hebrew is **u.**
Ps 3: 2 {Interlude} Hebrew *Selah.* The meaning of this word is **u,** though it is probably a musical or literary term. It is rendered *Interlude* throughout the Psalms.
9:16 {Quiet Interlude} Hebrew *Higgaion Selah.* The meaning of this phrase is **u.**
58: 7 {in their hands.} Or *Let them be trodden down and wither like grass.* The meaning of the Hebrew is **u.**
76:10 {sword of judgment.} The meaning of the Hebrew is **u.**
Pr 12:26 {to their friends;} Or *The godly are cautious in friendship,* or *the godly are freed from evil.* The meaning of the Hebrew is **u.**
20:30 {cleanses away evil;} The meaning of the Hebrew is **u.**
Ecc 5: 9 {his own profit!} The meaning of the Hebrew is **u.**
SS 6:12 {my beloved one.} Or *among the royal chariots of my people,* or *among the chariots of Amminadab.* The meaning of the Hebrew is **u.**
6:13 {lines of dancers?} Or *as you would at the movements of two armies?* or *as you would at the dance of Mahanaim?* The meaning of the Hebrew is **u.**
Isa 34:11 {and the raven.} The identification of some of these birds is **u.**
Jer 8: 7 {and the crane.} The identification of some of these birds is **u.**
Eze 21:10 {beneath its power!} The meaning of the Hebrew is **u.**
21:13 {do they have?} The meaning of the Hebrew is **u.**
27:17 {Minnith, early figs,} The meaning of the Hebrew is **u.**
27:19 {Greeks from Uzal} Hebrew *Vedan and Javan from Uzal.* The meaning of the Hebrew is **u.**
28:13 {every precious stone} The identification of some of these gemstones is **u.**
32:27 {covering their bodies,} The meaning of the Hebrew phrase here is **u.**
40:14 {was 105 feet.} The meaning of the Hebrew in this verse is **u.**
Da 3: 5 {and other instruments,} The identification of some of these musical instruments is **u.**
8:11[-12] {everything it did.} The meaning of the Hebrew for these verses is **u.**
9:27 {his terrible deeds,} Hebrew *on the wing of abominations;* the meaning of the Hebrew is **u.**
10:13 {kingdom of Persia.} As in one Greek version; Hebrew reads *and I was left there with the kings of Persia.* The meaning of the Hebrew is **u.**
Hos 4:18 {love for honor.} As in Greek version; the meaning of the Hebrew is **u.**
5: 2 {them at Acacia.} Hebrew *at Shittim.* The meaning of the Hebrew for this sentence is **u.**
Joel 1: 4 {the stripping locusts,} The precise identification of the four kinds of locusts mentioned here is **u.**
2:25 {the hopping locusts.} The precise identification of the four kinds of locusts mentioned here is **u.**
Hab 3: 3 {and Mount Paran.} Hebrew adds *selah;* also in 3:9, 13. The meaning of this Hebrew term is **u;** it is probably a musical or literary term.
Zep 1: 3 {heaps of rubble,} The meaning of the Hebrew is **u.**
3:18 {disgraced no more.} The meaning of the Hebrew for this verse is **u.**
Zec 14: 5 {across to Azal.} The meaning of the Hebrew is **u.**
14: 6 {no longer shine,} Hebrew *there will be no light, no cold or frost.* The meaning of the Hebrew is **u.**
Mal 2:15 {you are his.} Or *Did not one God make us and preserve our life and breath?* or *Did not one God make her, both flesh and spirit?* The meaning of the Hebrew is **u.**

UNCIRCUMCISED (2)

Lev 19:23 {consider it forbidden.} Hebrew *consider it* ***u.***
Ac 11: 3 {home of Gentiles} Greek *of* ***u*** *men.*

UNCLE (1)

Est 2:15 {was Esther's turn} Hebrew *the turn of Esther, the daughter of Abihail, who was Mordecai's* ***u,*** *who had adopted her.*

UNCLEAN (5)

2Ki 18: 4 {was called Nehushtan.} *Nehushtan* sounds like the Hebrew terms that mean "snake," "bronze," and "**u** thing."
Ac 10:14 {our Jewish laws.} Greek *anything common and* ***u.***
10:15 {say it isn't."} Greek *"What God calls clean you must not call* ***u.****"*
11: 8 {our Jewish laws.} Greek *anything common or* ***u.***
11: 9 {say it isn't.'} Greek *'What God calls clean you must not call* ***u.****'*

UNCOVER (2)

Lev 13:45 {to hang loose.} Or *and* ***u*** *their heads.*
21:10 {hair hang loose} Or ***u*** *his head.*

UNCOVERING (1)

Lev 10: 6 {hair hang loose} Or *by* ***u*** *your heads.*

UNDER (4)

Ge 24: 3 {"Swear} Hebrew *Put your hand* ***u*** *my thigh, and I will make you swear.*
24: 9 {solemn oath} Hebrew *put his hand* ***u*** *the thigh of Abraham his master and swore an oath.*
1Ch 28:19 {of the LORD.} Or *was written* ***u*** *the direction of the LORD.*
Ac 8:27 {queen of Ethiopia.} Greek ***u*** *the Candace, the queen of Ethiopia.*

UNDERSTAND (1)

Mk 7:15 {say and do!} Some manuscripts add verse 16, *Anyone who is willing to hear should listen and **u**.*

UNDERSTOOD (1)

1Sa 6:19 {killed seventy men} As in a few Hebrew manuscripts; most Hebrew manuscripts and Greek version read *50,070 men.* Perhaps the text should be **u** to read *the LORD killed 70 men and 50 oxen.*

UNDOING (1)

Jn 2:17 {burns within me."} Or *"Concern for God's house will be my **u**."* Ps 69:9.

UNFAILING (1)

2Sa 15:20 {love and faithfulness.} As in Greek version; Hebrew reads *and may **u** love and faithfulness go with you.*

UNIT (1)

Mic 6:10 {in short measures.} Hebrew *by using the short ephah;* the ephah was a **u** for measuring grain.

UNKNOWN (2)

Ru 3:15 {out six scoops} Hebrew *six measures,* an **u** quantity.
1Co 14: 2 {speak in tongues,} Or *in **u** languages;* also in 14:4, 5, 13, 14, 18, 22, 28, 39.

UNLAWFUL (1)

Mt 7:23 {did were unauthorized.} Or *u.*

UNLEAVENED (4)

Ac 12: 3 {the Passover celebration} Greek *the days of **u** bread.*
20: 6 {the Passover season} Greek *the days of **u** bread.*
1Co 5: 6[-7] {can stay pure.} Greek *Don't you realize that even a little leaven spreads quickly through the whole batch of dough? [7]Purge out the old leaven so that you can be a new batch of dough, just as you are already **u**.*
5: 8 {the new bread} Greek *but with **u** [bread].*

UNLESS (1)

Mt 17:20 {would be impossible."} Some manuscripts add verse 21, *But this kind of demon won't leave **u** you have prayed and fasted.*

UNPRODUCTIVE (1)

2Ki 2:21 {death or infertility.} Or *or make the land **u**.*

UNRIGHTEOUSNESS (1)

Jer 22:13 {with forced labor.} Hebrew *by **u**.*

UNRULY (1)

Hos 11:12 {the Holy One.} Or *and Judah is **u** against God, the faithful Holy One.*

UNTIE (4)

Mk 1: 7 {be his slave.} Greek *to stoop down and **u** his sandals.*
Lk 3:16 {be his slave.} Greek *to **u** his sandals.*
Jn 1:27 {be his slave.} Greek *to **u** his sandals.*
Ac 13:25 {be his slave.} Greek *to **u** his sandals.*

UNTIL (12)

Ge 49:10 {whom it belongs,} Or ***u** tribute is brought to him and the peoples obey;* traditionally rendered ***u** Shiloh comes.*
Nu 21:30 {Nophah and Medeba.} Or ***u** fire spread to Medeba.* The meaning of the Hebrew is uncertain.
2Ki 3:25 {came under attack.} Hebrew ***u** only Kir-hareseth was left, with its stones, but the slingers surrounded and attacked it.*
Ne 7: 3 {of the day.} Or *Keep the gates of Jerusalem closed **u** the sun is hot.*
Ps 68:30 {tribute from us.} Or *Humble them **u** they submit, bringing pieces of silver as tribute.*
SS 2: 7 {time is right.} Or *not to awaken love **u** it is ready.*
3: 5 {time is right.} Or *not to awaken love **u** it is ready.*
8: 4 {time is right.} Or *not to awaken love **u** it is ready.*
Eze 46:17 {every fiftieth year.} Hebrew ***u** the Year of Release;* see Lev 25:8-17.
Mt 11:12 {people attack it.} Or ***u** now, eager multitudes have been pressing into the Kingdom of Heaven.*
2Pe 1:19 {in your hearts.} Or ***u** the day dawns and the morning star rises in your hearts.*

UPCOMING (1)

Ac 18:21 {come back later,} Some manuscripts read *"I must by all means be at Jerusalem for the **u** festival, but I will come back later."*

UPPER (1)

1Ch 26:16 {to the Temple.} Or *the gate of Shalleketh on the **u** road* (also in 26:18). The meaning of the Hebrew is uncertain.

UPRIGHT (2)

Jos 10:13 {*Book of Jashar*} Or *The Book of the **U**.*
2Sa 1:18 {*Book of Jashar.*} Or *The Book of the **U**.*

URGED (2)

Jos 15:18 {she urged him} Some Greek manuscripts read *Othniel **u** her.*
Jdg 1:14 {she urged him} Greek version and Latin Vulgate read *he **u** her.*

URGES (1)

2Co 5:14 {love controls us.} Or ***u** us on.*

URIM (6)

Nu 27:21 {of sacred lots.} Hebrew *of the **U**.*
Dt 33: 8 {the sacred lots} Hebrew *given your Thummim and **U**.* See Exod 28:30.
1Sa 14:41 {among the others?"} Greek version adds *If the fault is with me or my son Jonathan, respond with **U**; but if the men of Israel are at fault, respond with Thummim.*
28: 6 {by sacred lots} Hebrew *by **U**.*
Ezr 2:63 {of sacred lots.} Hebrew *consult the **U** and Thummim about the matter.*
Ne 7:65 {of sacred lots.} Hebrew *consult the **U** and Thummim about the matter.*

USE (2)

Lev 19:36 {must be accurate.} Hebrew ***U** an honest ephah* [a measure for dry goods] *and an honest hin* [a measure for liquids].
Eze 45:10 {liquid volume measures.} Hebrew ***u** honest scales, an honest ephah, and an honest bath.*

USEFUL (1)

Phm 1:11 {Onesimus} *Onesimus* means "**u**."

UTENSILS (1)

2Ch 36:19 {everything of value.} Or *destroyed all the valuable Temple **u**.*

UZZIAH (3)

2Ki 14:21 {sixteen-year-old son, Uzziah,} Hebrew *Azariah,* a variant name for **U**.
15: 1 {Uzziah} Hebrew *Azariah,* a variant name for **U**; also in 15:6, 7, 8, 17, 23, 27.
1Ch 3:12 {Amaziah, Uzziah,} Hebrew *Azariah,* a variant name for **U**.

UZZIEL (1)

1Ch 25:18 {fell to Uzziel} Hebrew *Azarel,* a variant name for **U**; compare 25:4.

V

VALLEY (11)

Ge 14: 8 {the Dead Sea} Hebrew *in Siddim **V**;* see 14:3.
Jos 7:26 {Valley of Trouble} Hebrew ***v** of Achor.*
1Sa 17:52 {far as Gath} As in some Greek manuscripts; Hebrew reads *a **v**.*
2Ch 14:10 {north of Mareshah.} Or *in the Zephathah **V** near Mareshah.*
20:26 {Valley of Blessing,} Hebrew ***v** of Beracah.*
Ne 2:15 {the Kidron Valley} Hebrew *the **v**.*
Ps 23: 4 {valley of death,} Or *the darkest **v**.*
84: 6 {Valley of Weeping,} Hebrew ***v** of Baca.*
Isa 22: 1 {me concerning Jerusalem} Hebrew *concerning the **V** of Vision.*
Hos 2:15 {Valley of Trouble} Hebrew ***v** of Achor.*
Joel 3:18 {valley of acacias.} Hebrew ***v** of Shittim.*

VALUABLE (1)

2Ch 36:19 {everything of value.} Or *destroyed all the **v** Temple utensils.*

VALUE (4)

Ge 33:19 {pieces of silver.} Hebrew *100 kesitahs;* the **v** or weight of the kesitah is no longer known.
Lev 6: 6 {value in silver.} Or *and the animal must be of the proper **v**;* Hebrew lacks *in silver;* compare 5:15.
Jos 24:32 {pieces of silver.} Hebrew *100 kesitahs;* the **v** or weight of the kesitah is no longer known.
Job 42:11 {gift of money} Hebrew *a kesitah;* the **v** or weight of the kesitah is no longer known.

VARIANT (127)

Ge 32:31 {Peniel,} Hebrew *Penuel,* a **v** name for Peniel.
36:26 {sons of Dishon} Hebrew *Dishan,* a **v** name for Dishon; compare 36:21, 28.
Dt 32:44 {Joshua} Hebrew *Hoshea,* a **v** name for Joshua.
Jos 12:23 {city of Naphoth-dor} Hebrew *Naphath-dor,* a **v** name for Naphoth-dor.
17:11 {to Manasseh: Beth-shan,} Hebrew *Beth-shean,* a **v** name for Beth-shan; also in 17:16.
21:36 {received Bezer, Jahaz,} Hebrew *Jahzah,* a **v** name for Jahaz.
Jdg 1:27 {living in Beth-shan,} Hebrew *Beth-shean,* a **v** name for Beth-shan.
2: 9 {inherited, at Timnath-serah} Hebrew *Timnath-heres,* a **v** name for Timnath-serah.
8: 8 {up to Peniel} Hebrew *Penuel,* a **v** name for Peniel; also in 8:9, 17.
20:10 {revenge on Gibeah} Hebrew *Geba,* in this case, a **v** for Gibeah; also in 20:33.
1Sa 14:49 {included Jonathan, Ishbosheth,} Hebrew *Ishvi,* a **v** name for Ishbosheth; also known as Eshbaal.
2Sa 3:15 {her husband Palti} As in 1 Sam 25:44; Hebrew reads *Paltiel,* a **v** name for Palti.
5:14 {in Jerusalem: Shimea,} As in parallel text at 1 Chr 3:5; Hebrew reads *Shammua,* a **v** name for Shimea.
13: 3 {David's brother Shimea.} Hebrew *Shimeah* (also in 13:32), a **v** name for Shimea; compare 1 Chr 2:13.
17:25 {father was Jether,} Hebrew *Ithra,* a **v** name for Jether.
21:21 {David's brother Shimea.} As in parallel text at 1 Chr 20:7; Hebrew reads *Shimei,* a **v** name for Shimea.
1Ki 4:11 {Ben-abinadab, in Naphoth-dor.} Hebrew *Naphath-dor,* a **v** name for Naphoth-dor.
4:12 {all of Beth-shan} Hebrew *Beth-shean,* a **v** name for Beth-shan; also in 4:12b.
11: 5 {Sidonians, and Molech,} Hebrew *Milcom,* a **v** name for Molech; also in 11:33.
12:25 {town of Peniel.} Hebrew *Penuel,* a **v** name for Peniel.
15: 2 {daughter of Absalom.} Hebrew *Abishalom* (also in 15:10), a **v** name for Absalom; compare 2 Chr 11:20.
2Ki 1:17 {his brother Joram} Hebrew *Jehoram,* a **v** name for Joram.
3: 1 {Ahab's son Joram} Hebrew *Jehoram,* a **v** name for Joram; also in 3:6.
8:21 {So Jehoram} Hebrew *Joram,* a **v** name for Jehoram; also in 8:23, 24.
9:15 {But Joram} Hebrew *Jehoram,* a **v** name for Joram; also in 9:17, 21, 22, 23, 24.
11: 2 {of King Jehoram,} Hebrew *Joram,* a **v** name for Jehoram.
11:21 {Joash} Hebrew *Jehoash,* a **v** name for Joash.
12: 1 {Joash} Hebrew *Jehoash,* a **v** name for Joash; also in 12:2, 4, 6, 7, 18.
13: 9 {his son Jehoash} Hebrew *Joash,* a **v** name for Jehoash; also in 13:10, 12, 13, 14, 25.
14: 1 {of King Jehoash} Hebrew *Joash,* a **v** name for Jehoash; also in 14:13, 23, 27.
14:21 {sixteen-year-old son, Uzziah,} Hebrew *Azariah,* a **v** name for Uzziah.
15: 1 {Uzziah} Hebrew *Azariah,* a **v** name for Uzziah; also in 15:6, 7, 8, 17, 23, 27.
18: 2 {mother was Abijah,} As in parallel text at 2 Chr 29:1; Hebrew reads *Abi,* a **v** name for Abijah.
23:13 {and for Molech,} Hebrew *Milcom,* a **v** name for Molech.
1Ch 2: 9 {Ram, and Caleb.} Hebrew *Kelubai,* a **v** name for Caleb; compare 2:18.
2:19 {Caleb married Ephrathah,} Hebrew *Ephrath,* a **v** name for Ephrathah; compare 2:50 and 4:4.
3: 5 {and Solomon. Bathsheba,} Hebrew *Bathshua,* a **v** name for Bathsheba.
3:11 {Jehoram,} Hebrew *Joram,* a **v** name for Jehoram.
3:12 {Uzziah,} Hebrew *Azariah,* a **v** name for Uzziah.
3:16 {his uncle Zedekiah.} Hebrew *The descendants of Jehoiakim were his son Jeconiah* [a **v** name for Jehoiachin] *and his son Zedekiah.*
3:17 {sons of Jehoiachin,} Hebrew *Jeconiah,* a **v** name for Jehoiachin.
5: 6 {by King Tiglath-pileser} Hebrew *Tilgath-pilneser,* a **v** name for Tiglath-pileser; also in 5:26.
6:16 {Levi were Gershon,} Hebrew *Gershom,* a **v** name for Gershon (see 6:1); also in 6:17, 20, 43, 62, 71.
6:23 {Elkanah, Abiasaph,} Hebrew *Ebiasaph,* a **v** name for Abiasaph (also in 6:37); compare parallel text at Exod 6:24.
6:78 {Jahaz,} Hebrew *Jahzah,* a **v** name for Jahaz.
7:13 {Naphtali were Jahzeel,} As in parallel text at Gen 46:24; Hebrew reads *Jahziel,* a **v** name for Jahzeel.
7:29 {towns of Beth-shan,} Hebrew *Beth-shean,* a **v** name for Beth-shan.
8:31 {Gedor, Ahio, Zechariah,} As in parallel text at 9:37; Hebrew reads *Zeker,* a **v** name for Zechariah.
8:32 {father of Shimeam.} As in parallel text at 9:38; Hebrew reads *Shimeah,* a **v** name for Shimeam.
8:35 {Pithon, Melech, Tahrea,} As in parallel text at 9:41; Hebrew reads *Tarea,* a **v** name for Tahrea.
8:36 {father of Jadah.} As in parallel text at 9:42; Hebrew reads *Jehoaddah,* a **v** name for Jadah.
8:37 {father of Rephaiah.} As in parallel text at 9:43; Hebrew reads *Raphah,* a **v** name for Rephaiah.
9:19 {descendant of Abiasaph,} Hebrew *Ebiasaph,* a **v** name for Abiasaph; compare Exod 6:24.
11:12 {son of Dodai,} As in parallel text at 2 Sam 23:9 (see also 1 Chr 27:4); Hebrew reads *Dodo,* a **v** name for Dodai.
14: 4 {in Jerusalem: Shimea,} Hebrew *Shammua,* a **v** name for Shimea; compare 3:5.
14: 7 {Elishama, Eliada,} Hebrew *Beeliada,* a **v** name for Eliada; compare 3:8 and parallel text at 2 Sam 5:16.

15: 7 {clan of Gershon,} Hebrew *Gershom,* a **v** name for Gershon.
18: 8 {cities of Tebah} Hebrew reads *Tibhath,* a **v** name for Tebah; compare parallel text at 2 Sam 8:8.
18: 10 {his son Joram} As in parallel text at 2 Sam 8:10; Hebrew reads *Hadoram,* a **v** name for Joram.
24: 20 {leader was Shebuel.} Hebrew *Shubael* (also in 24:20b), a **v** name for Shebuel; compare 23:16 and 26:24.
24: 22 {leader was Shelomith.} Hebrew *Shelomoth* (also in 24:22b), a **v** name for Shelomith; compare 23:18.
25: 4 {Mattaniah, Uzziel, Shubael,} Hebrew *Shebuel,* a **v** name for Shubael; compare 25:20.
25: 11 {fell to Zeri} Hebrew *Izri,* a **v** name for Zeri; compare 25:3.
25: 14 {fell to Asarelah} Hebrew *Jesharelah,* a **v** name for Asarelah; compare 25:2.
25: 18 {fell to Uzziel} Hebrew *Azarel,* a **v** name for Uzziel; compare 25:4.
25: 22 {fell to Jerimoth} Hebrew *Jeremoth,* a **v** name for Jerimoth; compare 25:4.
25: 24 {fell to Joshbekashah} Hebrew *Joshbekasha,* a **v** name for Joshbekashah; compare 25:4.
25: 29 {fell to Geddalti} Hebrew *Giddalti,* a **v** name for Geddalti; compare 25:4.
26: 14 {went to Meshelemiah} Hebrew *Shelemiah,* a **v** name for Meshelemiah; compare 26:2.
26: 21 {of Gershon, Jehiel} Hebrew *Jehieli* (also in 26:22), a **v** name for Jehiel; compare 23:8.
26: 31 {Hebron came Jeriah,} Hebrew *Jerijah,* a **v** name for Jeriah; compare 23:19.
27: 15 {Heled,} Hebrew *Heldai,* a **v** name for Heled; compare 11:30 and 2 Sam 23:29.
2Ch 2: 3 {to King Hiram} Hebrew *Huram,* a **v** name for Hiram; also in 2:11, 12.
8: 2 {that King Hiram} Hebrew *Huram,* a **v** name for Hiram; also in 8:18.
9: 21 {sent by Hiram.} Hebrew *Huram,* a **v** name for Hiram.
10: 18 {Rehoboam sent Adoniram,} Hebrew *Hadoram,* a **v** name for Adoniram; compare 1 Kgs 4:6; 5:14; 12:18.
21: 17 {youngest son, Ahaziah,} Hebrew *Jehoahaz,* a **v** name for Ahaziah; compare 22:1.
22: 5 {with King Joram,} Hebrew *Jehoram,* a **v** name for Joram; also in 22:6, 7.
22: 11 {Ahaziah's sister Jehosheba,} As in parallel text at 2 Kgs 11:2; Hebrew reads *Jehoshabeath,* a **v** name for Jehosheba.
25: 1 {mother was Jehoaddin,} As in parallel text at 2 Kgs 14:2; Hebrew reads *Jehoaddan,* a **v** name for Jehoaddin.
25: 17 {Israel's king Jehoash,} Hebrew *Joash,* a **v** name for Jehoash; also in 25:18, 21, 23, 25.
28: 20 {when King Tiglath-pileser} Hebrew *Tilgath-pilneser,* a **v** name for Tiglath-pileser.
36: 2 {Jehoahaz} Hebrew *Joahaz,* a **v** name for Jehoahaz; also in 36:4.
Ezr 3: 2 {son of Jehozadak} Hebrew *Jozadak,* a **v** name for Jehozadak; also in 3:8.
5: 2 {son of Jehozadak} Aramaic *Jozadak,* a **v** name for Jehozadak.
10: 18 {son of Jehozadak} Hebrew *Jozadak,* a **v** name for Jehozadak.
Ne 12: 26 {son of Jehozadak,} Hebrew *Jozadak,* a **v** name for Jehozadak.
13: 28 {sons of Joiada} Hebrew *Jehoiada,* a **v** name for Joiada.
Est 2: 6 {with King Jehoiachin} Hebrew *Jeconiah,* a **v** name for Jehoiachin.
Isa 16: 11 {sorrow for Kir-hareseth} Hebrew *Kir-heres,* a **v** name for Kir-hareseth.
Jer 21: 2 {us. King Nebuchadnezzar} Hebrew *Nebuchadrezzar,* a **v** name for Nebuchadnezzar; also in 21:7.
22: 24 {abandon you, Jehoiachin} Hebrew *Coniah,* a **v** name for Jehoiachin; also in 22:28, 30.
22: 25 {afraid—to King Nebuchadnezzar} Hebrew *Nebuchadrezzar,* a **v** name for Nebuchadnezzar.
24: 1 {After King Nebuchadnezzar} Hebrew *Nebuchadrezzar,* a **v** name for Nebuchadnezzar.
24: 1 {Babylon exiled Jehoiachin} Hebrew *Jeconiah,* a **v** name for Jehoiachin.
25: 1 {when King Nebuchadnezzar} Hebrew *Nebuchadrezzar,* a **v** name for Nebuchadnezzar; also in 25:9.
27: 20 {he exiled Jehoiachin} Hebrew *Jeconiah,* a **v** name for Jehoiachin.
28: 4 {bring back Jehoiachin} Hebrew *Jeconiah,* a **v** name for Jehoiachin.
29: 2 {after King Jehoiachin,} Hebrew *Jeconiah,* a **v** name for Jehoiachin.
29: 21 {over to Nebuchadnezzar} Hebrew *Nebuchadrezzar,* a **v** name for Nebuchadnezzar.
32: 1 {of King Nebuchadnezzar.} Hebrew *Nebuchadrezzar,* a **v** name for Nebuchadnezzar; also in 32:28.
35: 6 {wine, because Jehonadab} Hebrew *Jonadab,* a **v** name for Jehonadab; also in 35:10, 14, 18, 19. See 2 Kgs 10:15.
35: 11 {when King Nebuchadnezzar} Hebrew *Nebuchadrezzar,* a **v** name for Nebuchadnezzar.
37: 1 {Josiah succeeded Jehoiachin} Hebrew *Coniah,* a **v** name for Jehoiachin.
37: 1 {by King Nebuchadnezzar} Hebrew *Nebuchadrezzar,* a **v** name for Nebuchadnezzar.
38: 1 {of Pashhur, Jehucal} Hebrew *Jucal,* a **v** name for Jehucal; see 37:3.
39: 1 {that King Nebuchadnezzar} Hebrew *Nebuchadrezzar,* a **v** name for Nebuchadnezzar; also in 39:11.
40: 8 {the Netophathite, Jaazaniah} As in parallel text at 2 Kgs 25:23; Hebrew reads *Jezaniah,* a **v** name for Jaazaniah.
43: 10 {my servant Nebuchadnezzar,} Hebrew *Nebuchadrezzar,* a **v** name for Nebuchadnezzar.
44: 30 {to King Nebuchadnezzar} Hebrew *Nebuchadrezzar,* a **v** name for Nebuchadnezzar.
46: 2 {by King Nebuchadnezzar} Hebrew *Nebuchadrezzar,* a **v** name for Nebuchadnezzar; also in 46:13, 26.
48: 21 {Holon and Jahaz} Hebrew *Jahzah,* a **v** name for Jahaz.
48: 31 {men of Kir-hareseth.} Hebrew *Kir-heres,* a **v** name for Kir-hareseth; also in 48:36.
49: 1 {who worship Molech,} Hebrew *Milcom,* a **v** name for Molech; also in 49:3.
49: 28 {by King Nebuchadnezzar} Hebrew *Nebuchadrezzar,* a **v** name for Nebuchadnezzar; also in 49:30.
50: 17 {Then King Nebuchadnezzar} Hebrew *Nebuchadrezzar,* a **v** name for Nebuchadnezzar.
51: 34 {"King Nebuchadnezzar} Hebrew *Nebuchadrezzar,* a **v** name for Nebuchadnezzar.
52: 4 {reign, King Nebuchadnezzar} Hebrew *Nebuchadrezzar,* a **v** name for Nebuchadnezzar; also in 52:12, 28, 29, 30.
Eze 26: 7 {bring King Nebuchadnezzar} Hebrew *Nebuchadrezzar,* a **v** name for Nebuchadnezzar.
29: 18 {of King Nebuchadnezzar} Hebrew *Nebuchadrezzar,* a **v** name for Nebuchadnezzar; also in 29:19.
30: 10 {Through King Nebuchadnezzar} Hebrew *Nebuchadrezzar,* a **v** name for Nebuchadnezzar.
Hos 1: 1 {son of Jehoash} Hebrew *Joash,* a **v** name for Jehoash.
Am 1: 1 {son of Jehoash,} Hebrew *Joash,* a **v** name for Jehoash.
Hag 1: 1 {and to Jeshua} Hebrew *Joshua,* a **v** name for Jeshua; also in 1:12, 14.
2: 2 {and to Jeshua} Hebrew *Joshua,* a **v** name for Jeshua; also in 2:4.
Zec 3: 1 {showed me Jeshua} Hebrew *Joshua,* a **v** name for Jeshua; also in 3:3, 4, 6, 8, 9.
6: 11 {head of Jeshua} Hebrew *Joshua,* a **v** name for Jeshua.

VARIETY (1)

2Ki 6: 25 {about two ounces} Hebrew *sold for 80 shekels* [0.9 kilograms] *of silver, and 1/4 of a cab* [0.3 liters] *of dove's dung cost 5 shekels* [57 grams]. *Dove's dung* may be a **v** of wild vegetable.

VARIOUS (12)

Ex 4: 6 {snow with leprosy.} Or *with a contagious skin disease.* The Hebrew word used here can describe **v** skin diseases.
Lev 13: 2 {contagious skin disease,} Traditionally rendered *leprosy.* The Hebrew word used throughout this passage is used to describe **v** skin diseases.
13: 47 {an infectious mildew} Traditionally rendered *leprosy.* The Hebrew term used throughout this passage is the same term used for the **v** skin diseases described in 13:1-46.
Nu 5: 2 {contagious skin disease} Traditionally rendered *leprosy.* The Hebrew word used here describes **v** skin diseases.
12: 10 {snow with leprosy.} Or *with a contagious skin disease.* The Hebrew word used here can describe **v** skin diseases.
Dt 24: 8 {contagious skin diseases} Traditonally rendered *leprosy.* The Hebrew word used here can describe **v** skin diseases.
2Sa 3: 29 {sores or leprosy} Or *or a contagious skin disease.* The Hebrew word used here can describe **v** skin diseases.
2Ki 5: 1 {suffered from leprosy.} Or *from a contagious skin disease.* The Hebrew word used here and throughout this passage can describe **v** skin diseases.
7: 3 {men with leprosy} Or *with a contagious skin disease.* The Hebrew word used here and throughout this passage can describe **v** skin diseases.
15: 5 {king with leprosy,} Or *with a contagious skin disease.* The Hebrew word used here and throughout this passage can describe **v** skin diseases.
2Ch 26: 19 {LORD's Temple, leprosy} Or *a contagious skin disease.* The Hebrew word used here and throughout this passage can describe **v** skin diseases.
Mk 16: 8 {frightened to talk.} The most reliable early manuscripts conclude the Gospel of Mark at verse 8. Other manuscripts include **v** endings to the Gospel. Two of the more noteworthy endings are printed here.

VEDAN (1)

Eze 27: 19 {Greeks from Uzal} Hebrew *V and Javan from Uzal.* The meaning of the Hebrew is uncertain.

VEGETABLE (1)

2Ki 6: 25 {about two ounces} Hebrew *sold for 80 shekels* [0.9 kilograms] *of silver, and 1/4 of a cab* [0.3 liters] *of dove's dung cost 5 shekels* [57 grams]. *Dove's dung* may be a variety of wild **v**.

VEILED (1)

SS 1: 7 {like a prostitute} Hebrew *like a v woman.*

VEILS (1)

Hab 3: 4 {his awesome power.} Or *He v his awesome power.*

VERSE (25 of 31)

Ezr 6: 3 {be ninety feet.} Aramaic *Its height will be 60 cubits* [27 meters], *and its width will be 60 cubits.* It is commonly held that this **v** should be emended to read: "Its height will be 45 feet, its length will be 90 feet, and its width will be 30 feet"; compare 1 Kgs 6:2. The emendation regarding the width is supported by the Syriac version.
Ne 7: 68 {horses, 245 mules,} As in some Hebrew manuscripts (see also Ezra 2:66); most Hebrew manuscripts lack this **v**.
Jer 10: 11 {from the earth."} The original text of this **v** is in Aramaic.
Eze 3: 12 {in his place!)} A likely reading for this **v** is *Then the Spirit lifted me up, and as the glory of the LORD rose from its place, I heard behind me a loud rumbling sound.*
40: 14 {was 105 feet.} The meaning of the Hebrew in this **v** is uncertain.
Zep 3: 18 {disgraced no more.} The meaning of the Hebrew for this **v** is uncertain.
Mt 17: 20 {would be impossible."} Some manuscripts add **v** 21, *But this kind of demon won't leave unless you have prayed and fasted.*
18: 10 {my heavenly Father.} Some manuscripts add **v** 11, *And I, the Son of Man, have come to save the lost.*
21: 44 {whom it falls.} This **v** is omitted in some early manuscripts.
23: 13 {go in yourselves.} Some manuscripts add **v** 14, *How terrible it will be for you teachers of religious law and you Pharisees. Hypocrites! You shamelessly cheat widows out of their property, and then, to cover up the kind of people you really are, you make long prayers in public. Because of this, your punishment will be the greater.*
Mk 7: 15 {say and do!} Some manuscripts add **v** 16, *Anyone who is willing to hear should listen and understand.*
9: 43 {with two hands.} Some manuscripts add **v** 44 (which is identical with 9:48).
9: 45 {with two feet.} Some manuscripts add **v** 46 (which is identical with 9:48).
11: 25 {your sins, too.} Some manuscripts add **v** 26, *But if you do not forgive, neither will your Father who is in heaven forgive your sins.*
15: 27 {side of his.} Some manuscripts add **v** 28, *And the Scripture was fulfilled that said, "He was counted among those who were rebels."* See Isa 53:12.
16: 8 {frightened to talk.} The most reliable early manuscripts conclude the Gospel of Mark at **v** 8. Other manuscripts include various endings to the Gospel. Two of the more noteworthy endings are printed here.
Lk 17: 35 {the other left.} Some manuscripts add **v** 36, *Two men will be working in the field; one will be taken, the other left.*
23: 16 {will release him."} Some manuscripts add **v** 17, *For it was necessary for him to release one [prisoner] for them during the feast.*
24: 12 {what had happened.} Some manuscripts do not include this **v**.
24: 40 {them his feet.} Some manuscripts do not include this **v**.
Ac 8: 36 {I be baptized?"} Some manuscripts add **v** 37, *"You can," Philip answered, "if you believe with all your heart." And the eunuch replied, "I believe that Jesus Christ is the Son of God."*
15: 33 {had sent them.} Some manuscripts add **v** 34, *But Silas decided to stay there.*
28: 28 {will accept it."} Some manuscripts add **v** 29, *And when he had said these words, the Jews departed, greatly disagreeing with each other.*
Ro 16: 23 {a Christian brother.} Some manuscripts add **v** 24, *May the grace of our Lord Jesus Christ be with you all. Amen.*

VERSES (3 of 6)

Da 8: 11[-12] {everything it did.} The meaning of the Hebrew for these **v** is uncertain.
Lk 22: 43[-44] {drops of blood.} These **v** are not included in many ancient manuscripts.
1Co 14: 35 {in church meetings.} Some manuscripts place **v** 34-35 after 14:40.

VERSION (168)

Ge 1: 26 {livestock, wild animals,} As in Syriac **v**; Hebrew reads *all the earth.*
10: 4 {Kittim, and Rodanim.} As in some Hebrew manuscripts and Greek **v** (see also 1 Chr 1:7); most Hebrew manuscripts read *Dodanim.*

10:24 {father of Shelah,} Greek v reads *Arphaxad was the father of Cainan, Cainan was the father of Shelah.*
11:12[-13] {sons and daughters.} Greek v reads [12]*When Arphaxad was 135 years old, his son Cainan was born.* [13]*After the birth of Cainan, Arphaxad lived another 430 years and had other sons and daughters, and then he died. When Cainan was 130 years old, his son Shelah was born. After the birth of Shelah, Cainan lived another 330 years and had other sons and daughters, and then he died.*
36:39 {Hadad} As in some Hebrew manuscripts, Samaritan Pentateuch, and Syriac v (see also 1 Chr 1:50); most Hebrew manuscripts read *Hadar.*
46:13 {Puah,} As in Syriac v and Samaritan Pentateuch (see also 1 Chr 7:1); Hebrew reads *Puvah.*
46:16 {Gad were Zephon,} As in Greek v and Samaritan Pentateuch (see also Num 26:15); Hebrew reads *Ziphion.*
46:27 {had two sons} Greek v reads *nine sons,* probably including Joseph's grandsons through Ephraim and Manasseh (see 1 Chr 7:14-20).
46:27 {there were seventy} Greek v reads *seventy-five;* see note on Exod 1:5.
47:21 {servants to Pharaoh.} As in Greek v and Samaritan Pentateuch; Hebrew reads *He moved the people into the towns throughout the land of Egypt.*
47:31 {on his staff.} As in Greek v; Hebrew reads *bowed in worship at the head of his bed.*

Ex 1: 5 {Jacob had seventy} Dead Sea Scrolls and Greek v read *seventy-five;* see notes on Gen 46:27.

Nu 26:17 {its ancestor Arodi.} As in Samaritan Pentateuch and Syriac v (see also Gen 46:16); Hebrew reads *Arod.*

Dt 4:48 {to Mount Sirion,} As in Syriac v (see also 3:9); Hebrew reads *Mount Sion.*
31: 1 {had finished saying} As in Dead Sea Scrolls and Greek v; Masoretic Text reads *Moses went and spoke.*
32: 8 {of angelic beings.} As in Dead Sea Scrolls, which read *of the sons of God,* and Greek v, which reads *of the angels of god;* Masoretic Text reads *of the sons of Israel.*
32:26 {to scatter them,} As in Greek v; the meaning of the Hebrew is uncertain.
32:31 {even they recognize.} The meaning of the Hebrew is uncertain. Greek v reads *our enemies are fools.*
32:43 {God worship him,} As in Dead Sea Scrolls and Greek v; Masoretic Text reads *Rejoice with his people, O nations.*

Jos 7: 1 {family of Zimri,} As in Greek v (see also 1 Chr 2:6); Hebrew reads *Zabdi.* Also in 7:17, 18.
12:23 {Goyim in Gilgal} Greek v reads *Goyim in Galilee.*
16: 2 {(that is, Luz)} As in Greek v (also see 18:13); Hebrew reads *From Bethel to Luz.*
18:28 {Gibeah, and Kiriath-jearim} As in Greek v; Hebrew reads *Kiriath.*

Jdg 1:14 {she urged him} Greek v and Latin Vulgate read *he urged her.*
9:29 {I would say} As in Greek v; Hebrew reads *And he said.*
14:15 {On the fourth} As in Greek v; Hebrew reads *seventh.*
16:13 {the loom shuttle,} As in Greek v; Hebrew lacks *on your loom and tighten it with the loom shuttle.*
19:28 {was no answer.} Greek v adds *for she was dead.*

Ru 3:15 {back. Then Boaz} Most Hebrew manuscripts read *he;* many Hebrew manuscripts, Syriac v, and Latin Vulgate read *she.*

1Sa 2:20 {to the LORD.} As in Greek v; Hebrew reads *this one she requested of the LORD in prayer.*
3:13 {are blaspheming God} As in Greek v; Hebrew reads *his sons have made themselves contemptible.*
5: 6 {plague of tumors.} Greek v and Latin Vulgate read *tumors. And rats appeared in their land, and death and destruction were throughout the city.*
6:19 {seventy men} As in a few Hebrew manuscripts; most Hebrew manuscripts and Greek v read *50,070 men.* Perhaps the text should be understood to read *the LORD killed 70 men and 50 oxen.*
7:12 {Mizpah and Jeshanah.} As in Greek v; Hebrew reads *Shen.*
8:16 {of your cattle} As in Greek v; Hebrew reads *young men.*
9:25 {for him there.} As in Greek v; Hebrew reads *and talked with him there.*
10: 1 {his people Israel.} Greek v reads *Israel. And you will rule over the LORD's people and save them from their enemies around them. This will be the sign to you that the LORD has appointed you to be leader over his inheritance.*
11: 1 {month later,} As in Greek v; Hebrew lacks *About a month later.*
11: 8 {addition to 30,000} Dead Sea Scrolls and Greek v read *70,000.*
13:15 {land of Benjamin.} As in Greek v; Hebrew reads *Samuel left Gilgal and went to Gibeah in the land of Benjamin.*
13:20 {axes, or sickles,} As in Greek v; Hebrew reads *or plowshares.*
14:41 {among the others?"} Greek v adds *If the fault is with me or my son Jonathan, respond with Urim; but if the men of Israel are at fault, respond with Thummim.*
15:32 {have been spared!"} Dead Sea Scrolls and Greek v read *Agag arrived hesitantly, for he thought, "Surely this is the bitterness of death."*
17: 4 {over nine feet} Hebrew *6 cubits* [9 feet or 2.7 meters] *and 1 span* [9 inches or 23 centimeters]; Greek v reads *4 cubits* [6 feet or 1.8 meters] *and 1 span,* about 6.75 feet or 2 meters in length.
20:25 {sitting opposite him} As in Greek v; Hebrew reads *with Jonathan standing.*
20:41 {the stone pile.} As in Greek v; Hebrew reads *near the south edge.*
25: 1 {wilderness of Maon.} As in Greek v; Hebrew reads *Paran.*
30:29 {Racal,} Greek v reads *Carmel.*

2Sa 5:25 {way from Gibeon} As in Greek v (see also 1 Chr 14:16); Hebrew reads *Geba.*
6: 5 {might, singing songs} As in Greek v (see also 1 Chr 13:8); Hebrew reads *cypress trees.*
8: 4 {seventeen hundred charioteers} Greek v reads *1,000 chariots and 7,000 charioteers;* compare 1 Chr 18:4.
12:30 {the king's head,} Greek v reads *removed the crown of Milcom;* compare 1 Kgs 11:5. Milcom, also called Molech, was the god of the Ammonites.
13:34 {the Horonaim road} As in Greek v; Hebrew reads *from the road behind him.*
15:20 {love and faithfulness.} As in Greek v; Hebrew reads *and may unfailing love and faithfulness go with you.*
15:27 {the priest, "Look,} As in Greek v; Hebrew reads *Are you a seer?* or *Do you see?*
16:14 {the Jordan River.} As in Greek v (see also 17:16); Hebrew reads *when they reached their destination.*
17: 3 {that you seek.} As in Greek v; Hebrew reads *like the return of all is the man whom you seek.*
20:24 {Adoniram} As in Greek v (see also 1 Kgs 4:6; 5:14); Hebrew reads *Adoram.*
21: 6 {of the LORD.} As in Greek v (see also 21:9); Hebrew reads *at Gibeah of Saul, the chosen of the LORD.*
21: 8 {Saul's daughter Merab,} As in a few Hebrew and Greek manuscripts and Syriac v (see also 1 Sam 18:19); most Hebrew manuscripts read *Michal.*
21:16 {of the giants} As in Greek v; Hebrew reads *a descendant of the Rephaites;* also in 21:18, 20, 22.
23:18 {of the Thirty.} As in a few Hebrew manuscripts and Syriac v; most Hebrew manuscripts read *the Three.*
23:19 {Thirty} As in Syriac v; Hebrew reads *the Three.*
24: 6 {land of Tahtim-hodshi} Greek v reads *to Gilead and to Kadesh in the land of the Hittites.*
24:13 {you choose three} As in Greek v (see also 1 Chr 21:12); Hebrew reads *seven.*

1Ki 1: 9 {stone of Zoheleth} Or *to the Serpent's Stone;* Greek v supports reading *Zoheleth* as a proper name.
1:25 {of the army,} As in Greek v; Hebrew reads *invited the commanders of the army.*
4:19 {of Gilead,} Greek v reads *of Gad;* compare 4:13.
5:11 {and 110,000 gallons} As in Greek v, which reads *20,000 baths* [420 kiloliters] (see also 2 Chr 2:10); Hebrew reads *20 cors,* about 800 gallons or 3.6 kiloliters in volume.
6: 8 {the bottom floor} As in Greek v; Hebrew reads *middle floor.*
7: 7 {floor to ceiling.} As in Syriac v and Latin Vulgate; Hebrew reads *from floor to floor.*
9:26 {port near Elath} As in Greek v (see also 2 Kgs 14:22; 16:6); Hebrew reads *Eloth.*
12: 2 {returned from Egypt,} As in Greek v and Latin Vulgate (see also 2 Chr 10:2); Hebrew reads *he lived in Egypt.*
12:18 {Rehoboam sent Adoniram,} As in some Greek manuscripts and Syriac v (see also 4:6; 5:14); Hebrew reads *Adoram.*

2Ki 8:21 {town of Zair.} Greek v reads *Seir.*
16: 6 {and sent Edomites} As in marginal *Qere* reading of the Masoretic Text, Greek v, and Latin Vulgate; Hebrew reads *Arameans.*
23:16 {man of God} As in Greek v; Hebrew lacks *as Jeroboam stood beside the altar at the festival. Then Josiah turned and looked up at the tomb of the man of God.*

1Ch 1: 4 {of Noah were} As in Greek v (see also Gen 5:3-32); Hebrew lacks *The sons of Noah were.*
1: 6 {were Ashkenaz, Riphath,} As in some Hebrew manuscripts and Greek v (see also Gen 10:3); most Hebrew manuscripts read *Diphath.*
1:22 {Obal,} As in some Hebrew manuscripts and Syriac v (see also Gen 10:28); most Hebrew manuscripts read *Ebal.*
1:50 {city of Pau.} As in many Hebrew manuscripts, some Greek manuscripts, Syriac v, and Latin Vulgate (see also Gen 36:39); most Hebrew manuscripts read *Pai.*
2: 6 {Calcol, and Darda} As in many Hebrew manuscripts, some Greek manuscripts, and Syriac v (see also 1 Kgs 4:31); Hebrew reads *Dara.*
2:11 {father of Salmon.} As in Greek v (see also Ruth 4:21); Hebrew reads *Salma.*
4: 3 {The descendants of} As in Greek v; Hebrew reads *father of.* The meaning of the Hebrew is uncertain.
6:28 {Samuel were Joel} As in some Greek manuscripts and the Syriac v (see also 6:33 and 1 Sam 8:2); Hebrew lacks *Joel.*
6:59 {Juttah,} As in Syriac v (see also Josh 21:16); Hebrew lacks *Juttah.*
6:77 {of Jokneam, Kartah,} As in Greek v (see also Josh 21:34); Hebrew lacks *Jokneam, Kartah.*
9:41 {Tahrea, and Ahaz.} As in Syriac v and Latin Vulgate (see also 8:35); Hebrew lacks *and Ahaz.*
9:42 {father of Jadah.} As in some Hebrew manuscripts and Greek v (see also 8:36); Hebrew reads *Jarah.*
11:20 {of the Thirty.} As in Syriac v; Hebrew reads *the Three;* also in 11:21.
17: 6 {to Israel's leaders,} As in Greek v (see also 2 Sam 7:7); Hebrew reads *judges.*
18:16 {Ahitub and Ahimelech} As in some Hebrew manuscripts, Syriac v, and Latin Vulgate (see also 2 Sam 8:17); most Hebrew manuscripts read *Abimelech.*
20: 2 {the king's head,} Greek v and Latin Vulgate read *removed the crown of Milcom;* compare 1 Kgs 11:5. Milcom, also called Molech, was the god of the Ammonites.
23:10 {were Jahath, Ziza,} As in Greek v and Latin Vulgate (see also 23:11); Hebrew reads *Zina.*
25: 9 {sons and relatives.} As in Greek v; Hebrew lacks *and twelve of his sons and relatives.*

2Ch 3:15 {that were 27 feet} As in Syriac v (see also 1 Kgs 7:15; 2 Kgs 25:17; Jer 52:21), which reads *18 cubits* [8.1 meters]; Hebrew reads *35 cubits,* which is 52.5 feet or 15.8 meters.
8:17 {Ezion-geber and Elath,} As in Greek v (see also 2 Kgs 14:22; 16:6); Hebrew reads *Eloth.*
13: 2 {mother was Maacah,} As in most Greek manuscripts and Syriac v (see also 2 Chr 11:20-21; 1 Kgs 15:2); Hebrew reads *Micaiah.*
15: 8 {Azariah the prophet,} As in Syriac v and Latin Vulgate (see also 15:1); Hebrew reads *from Oded the prophet.*
22: 2 {Ahaziah was twenty-two} As in some Greek manuscripts and Syriac v (see also 2 Kgs 8:26); Hebrew reads *forty-two.*
22: 8 {and Ahaziah's relatives} As in Greek v (see also 2 Kgs 10:13); Hebrew reads *and sons of the brothers of Ahaziah.*
26: 2 {town of Elath} As in Greek v (see also 2 Kgs 14:22; 16:6); Hebrew reads *Eloth.*
26: 7 {Arabs of Gur} As in Greek v; Hebrew reads *Gur-baal.*
26: 8 {The Meunites} As in Greek v; Hebrew reads *Ammonites.* Compare 26:7.
36: 9 {Jehoiachin was eighteen} As in one Hebrew manuscript, some Greek manuscripts, and Syriac v (see also 2 Kgs 24:8); most Hebrew manuscripts read *eight.*

Ezr 2:25 {peoples of Kiriath-jearim,} As in some Hebrew manuscripts and Greek v (see also Neh 7:29); Hebrew reads *Kiriath-arim.*
6: 3 {be ninety feet.} Aramaic *Its height will be 60 cubits* [27 meters], *and its width will be 60 cubits.* It is commonly held that this verse should be emended to read: "Its height will be 45 feet, its length will be 90 feet, and its width will be 30 feet"; compare 1 Kgs 6:2. The emendation regarding the width is supported by the Syriac v.
10:37[-38] {family of Binnui} As in Greek v; Hebrew reads *Jaasu,* [38]*Bani, Binnui.*

Ne 3:18 {led by Binnui} As in a few Hebrew manuscripts, some Greek manuscripts, and Syriac v (see also 3:24; 10:9); most Hebrew manuscripts read *Bavvai.*
6: 2 {of the villages} As in Greek v; Hebrew reads *at Kephirim.*
12:14 {family of Malluch.} As in Greek v (see also 10:4; 12:2); Hebrew reads *Malluchi.*
12:14 {family of Shecaniah.} As in many Hebrew manuscripts, some Greek manuscripts, and Syriac v (see also 12:3); most Hebrew manuscripts read *Shebaniah.*

Est 3: 7 {a year later.} As in Greek v, which reads *the thirteenth day of the twelfth month, the month of Adar* (see also 3:13). Hebrew reads *in the twelfth month,* of the Hebrew calendar. The date selected was March 7, 473 B.C.; also see note on 2:16.

Job 9:17 {me without reason,} As in Syriac v; Hebrew reads *with a storm.*
15:23 {'Where is it?'} Greek v reads *He is appointed to be food for a vulture.*
41:11 {and remain safe} As in Greek v; Hebrew reads *confront me that I must pay.*
41:13 {layer of armor} As in Greek v; Hebrew reads *its bridle.*

Ps 8: 2 {give you praise.} As in Greek v; Hebrew reads *to show strength.*
16: 9 {and my mouth} As in Greek v; Hebrew reads *glory.*
18:13 {a mighty shout.} As in Greek v (see also 2 Sam 22:14); Hebrew adds *raining down hail and burning coals.*
72: 5 {May he live} As in Greek v; Hebrew reads *May they fear you.*
76: 4 {everlasting mountains.} As in Greek v; Hebrew reads *than mountains filled with beasts of prey.*
112: 4 {They are} Greek v reads *The LORD is.*

Pr 10:10 {reproof promotes peace.} As in Greek v; Hebrew reads *but babbling fools fall flat on their faces.*
14:33 {wisdom is not} As in Greek v; Hebrew lacks *not.*
21: 6 {deadly trap.} As in Greek v; Hebrew reads *mist for those who seek death.*
24: 5 {strong man,} As in Greek v; Hebrew reads *A wise man is strength.*

26:23 {Smooth} As in Greek **v**; Hebrew reads *Burning.*
31:21 {them have warm} As in Greek **v**; Hebrew *scarlet.*
Ecc 8:10 {and are praised} As in some Hebrew manuscripts and Greek **v**; many Hebrew manuscripts read *and are forgotten.*
Isa 5:17 {lambs and kids} As in Greek **v**; Hebrew reads *strangers.*
10:27 {from their shoulders.} As in Greek **v**; Hebrew reads *The yoke will be broken, for you have grown so fat.*
21: 8 {Then the watchman} As in Dead Sea Scrolls and Syriac **v**; Hebrew reads *a lion.*
28:16 {run away again.} Greek **v** reads *Anyone who believes in him will not be disappointed.*
29:13 {learned by rote.} Greek **v** reads *Their worship is a farce, for they merely teach human commands and teachings.*
45: 2 {level the mountains.} As in Dead Sea Scrolls and Greek **v**; Masoretic Text reads *the swellings.*
49:24 {that a tyrant} As in Dead Sea Scrolls, Syriac **v**, and Latin Vulgate (also see 49:25); Masoretic Text reads *a righteous person.*
52:14 {they saw him} As in Syriac **v**; Hebrew reads *you.*
61: 1 {freed.} Greek **v** reads *and the blind will see.*
Jer 23:33 {are the burden!} As in Greek **v** and Latin Vulgate; Hebrew reads *What burden?*
27: 1 {reign of Zedekiah} As in some Hebrew manuscripts and Syriac **v** (see also 27:3, 12); most Hebrew manuscripts read *Jehoiakim.*
42: 1 {Kareah and Jezaniah} Greek **v** reads *Azariah;* compare 43:2.
48: 4 {will cry out.} Greek **v** reads *Her cries are heard as far away as Zoar.*
Eze 19: 7 {in nearby nations} As in Greek **v**; Hebrew reads *He consorted with widows.*
22:25 {Your princes} As in Greek **v**; Hebrew reads *prophets.*
27:15 {you from Dedan.} Greek **v** reads *Rhodes.*
32:17 {On March 17,} Hebrew *On the fifteenth day of the month,* presumably in the twelfth month of the Hebrew calendar (see 32:1). This would put this message at the end of King Jehoiachin's twelfth year of captivity, on March 17, 585 B.C.; also see note on 29:1. Greek **v** reads *On the fifteenth day of the first month,* which would put this message on April 27, 586 B.C., at the beginning of Jehoiachin's twelfth year.
38:14 {will rouse yourself.} As in Greek **v**; Hebrew reads *then you will know.*
40: 6 {10 1/2 feet deep.} Greek **v**; Hebrew reads *1 rod* [10.5 feet or 3.2 meters] *deep, and one threshold, one rod deep.*
40:44 {beside the south} As in Greek **v**; Hebrew reads *east.*
42:10 {On the south} As in Greek **v**; Hebrew reads *east.*
45: 5 {for their towns.} As in Greek **v**; Hebrew reads *They will have as their possession 20 rooms.*
47:18 {south as Tamar.} As in Greek **v**; Hebrew reads *you will measure.*
Da 10:13 {kingdom of Persia.} As in one Greek **v**; Hebrew reads *and I was left there with the kings of Persia.* The meaning of the Hebrew is uncertain.
10:16 {like a man} As in most manuscripts of the Masoretic Text; one manuscript of the Masoretic Text and one Greek **v** read *Then something that looked like a human hand.*
Hos 3: 2 {measure of wine.} As in Greek **v**, which reads *a homer* [182 liters] *of barley and a measure of wine;* Hebrew reads *a homer of barley and a lethech* [2.5 bushels or 91 liters] *of barley.*
4: 7 {They have exchanged} As in Syriac **v** and an ancient Hebrew tradition; Masoretic Text reads *I will exchange.*
4:18 {love for honor.} As in Greek **v**; the meaning of the Hebrew is uncertain.
11: 2 {the more I} As in Greek **v**; Hebrew reads *they.*
Am 5:26 {you yourselves made.} Greek **v** reads *You took up the shrine of Molech, and the star of your god Rephan, and the images you made for yourselves.*
Mic 1:10 {weep at all.} Greek **v** reads *weep not in Acco.*
Hab 2: 4 {lives are crooked;} Greek **v** reads *I will have no pleasure in anyone who turns away.*
Zec 5: 6 {with the sins} As in Greek **v**; Hebrew reads *the appearance.*
6:14 {Heldai,} As in Syriac **v** (compare 6:10); Hebrew reads *Helem.*
6:14 {Jedaiah, and Josiah} As in Syriac **v** (compare 6:10); Hebrew reads *Hen.*
11:13 {to the potters} Syriac **v** reads *into the treasury;* also in 11:13b.
14: 5 {ones with him.} As in Greek **v**; Hebrew reads *with you.*
Mal 1: 7 {defiled the sacrifices} As in Greek **v**; Hebrew reads *defiled you.*

VERSIONS (20)

Ge 11:32 {for 205 years} Some ancient **v** read *145 years;* compare 11:26; 12:4.
Nu 26:23 {its ancestor Puah.} As in Samaritan Pentateuch, Greek and Syriac **v**, and Latin Vulgate (see also 1 Chr 7:1); Hebrew reads *The Punite clan, named after its ancestor Puvah.*
26:39 {its ancestor Shupham.} As in some Hebrew manuscripts, Samaritan Pentateuch, Greek and Syriac **v**, and Latin Vulgate; most Hebrew manuscripts read *Shephupham.*
Dt 33: 2 {dawned upon us} As in Greek and Syriac **v**; Hebrew reads *upon them.*
1Sa 1:24 {a three-year-old bull} As in Dead Sea Scrolls, Greek and Syriac **v**; Hebrew reads *3 bulls.*
12:11 {Barak,} As in Greek and Syriac **v**; Hebrew reads *Bedan.*
12:11 {Jephthah, and Samuel} Greek and Syriac **v** read *Samson.*
13: 5 {of three thousand} As in Greek and Syriac **v**; Hebrew reads *30,000.*
2Sa 8:12 {Edom,} As in a few Hebrew manuscripts and Greek and Syriac **v** (see also 8:14; 1 Chr 18:11); most Hebrew manuscripts read *Aram.*
8:13 {eighteen thousand Edomites} As in a few Hebrew manuscripts and Greek and Syriac **v** (see also 8:14; 1 Chr 18:12); most Hebrew manuscripts read *Arameans.*
15: 7 {After four years,} As in Greek and Syriac **v**; Hebrew reads *40 years.*
2Ki 12:21 {assassins were Jozacar} As in Greek and Syriac **v**; Hebrew reads *Jozabad;* compare parallel text at 2 Chr 24:26.
2Ch 20: 2 {army from Edom} As in one Hebrew manuscript; most Hebrew manuscripts and ancient **v** read *Aram.*
22: 6 {and King Ahaziah} Some Hebrew manuscripts, Greek and Syriac **v**, and Latin Vulgate (see also 2 Kgs 8:29); most Hebrew manuscripts read *Azariah.*
25:28 {City of David.} As in some Hebrew manuscripts and other ancient **v** (see also 2 Kgs 14:20); most Hebrew manuscripts read *the city of Judah.*
Ecc 9: 2 {good or bad,} As in Greek and Syriac **v**, and Latin Vulgate; Hebrew lacks *or bad.*
SS 7: 9 {lips and teeth.} As in Greek and Syriac **v** and Latin Vulgate; Hebrew reads *over lips of sleepers.*
Hos 12: 4 {spoke to him} As in Greek and Syriac **v**; Hebrew reads *to us.*
13:10 {Where now is} As in Greek and Syriac **v** and Latin Vulgate; Hebrew reads *I will be.*
Zec 6:11 {make a crown} As in Greek and Syriac **v**; Hebrew reads *crowns.*

VERY (5)

Ex 19: 1 {they left Egypt.} Hebrew *in the third month…on the **v** day,* i.e., two lunar months to the day after leaving Egypt. This day of the Hebrew lunar calendar occurs in late May or early June; compare note on 13:4.
Lk 24: 1 {on Sunday morning} Greek *But on the first day of the week, **v** early in the morning.*
Jn 13: 1 {of his love.} Or *He loved his disciples to the **v** end.*
2Th 2:13 {among the first} Some manuscripts read *God chose you from the **v** beginning.*
1Jn 5: 7 {these three witnesses} Some **v** late manuscripts add *in heaven—the Father, the Word, and the Holy Spirit, and these three are one. And we have three witnesses on earth.*

VESSEL (1)

1Th 4: 4 {control your body} Or *will know how to take a wife for himself;* Greek reads *will know how to possess his own **v**.*

VESSELS (1)

2Co 4: 7 {our weak bodies.} Greek *But we have this treasure in earthen **v**.*

VILLAGES (1)

SS 7:11 {among the wildflowers.} Or *in the **v**.*

VINDICATE (1)

Ge 30: 6 {named him Dan,} *Dan* is a play on the Hebrew term meaning "to **v**" or "to judge."

VINEYARD (1)

SS 1: 6 {done to me!} Hebrew *My own **v** I have neglected.*

VIOLENTLY (1)

Ac 24: 6 {we arrested him.} Some manuscripts add *We would have judged him by our law, 7but Lysias, the commander of the garrison, came and took him **v** away from us, 8commanding his accusers to come before you.*

VIRGIN (2)

La 1:15 {his beloved city} Hebrew *the **v** daughter of Judah.*
2Co 11: 2 {pure bride} Greek *a **v**.*

VIRGINS (2)

Mt 25: 1 {of ten bridesmaids} Or ***v**;* also in 25:7, 11.
Rev 14: 4 {pure as virgins,} Greek *they are **v** who have not defiled themselves with women.*

VISION (1)

Isa 22: 1 {me concerning Jerusalem} Hebrew *concerning the Valley of **V**.*

VISITATION (1)

1Pe 2:12 {judge the world.} Or *on the day of **v**.*

VOICE (2)

Dt 4:33 {voice of God} Or ***v** of a god.*
Ps 19: 3 {in the skies;} Or *There is no speech or language where their **v** is not heard.*

VOLUME (1)

1Ki 5:11 {and 110,000 gallons} As in Greek version, which reads *20,000 baths* [420 kiloliters] (see also 2 Chr 2:10); Hebrew reads *20 cors,* about 800 gallons or 3.6 kiloliters in **v**.

VULGATE (30)

Nu 2:14[-15] {son of Deuel} As in many Hebrew manuscripts, Samaritan Pentateuch, and Latin **V** (see also 1:14); most Hebrew manuscripts read *son of Reuel.*
26:23 {its ancestor Puah.} As in Samaritan Pentateuch, Greek and Syriac versions, and Latin **V** (see also 1 Chr 7:1); Hebrew reads *The Punite clan, named after its ancestor Puvah.*
26:39 {its ancestor Shupham.} As in some Hebrew manuscripts, Samaritan Pentateuch, Greek and Syriac versions, and Latin **V**; most Hebrew manuscripts read *Shephupham.*
26:40 {their ancestor Ard.} As in Samaritan Pentateuch, some Greek manuscripts, and Latin **V**; Hebrew lacks *named after their ancestor Ard.*
Jdg 1:14 {she urged him} Greek version and Latin **V** read *he urged her.*
18:30 {descendant of Moses,} As in an ancient Hebrew tradition, some Greek manuscripts, and Latin **V**; Masoretic Text reads *of Manasseh.*
Ru 3:15 {back. Then Boaz} Most Hebrew manuscripts read *he;* many Hebrew manuscripts, Syriac version, and Latin **V** read *she.*
1Sa 5: 6 {plague of tumors.} Greek version and Latin **V** read *tumors. And rats appeared in their land, and death and destruction were throughout the city.*
1Ki 7: 7 {floor to ceiling.} As in Syriac version and Latin **V**; Hebrew reads *from floor to floor.*
12: 2 {returned from Egypt,} As in Greek version and Latin **V** (see also 2 Chr 10:2); Hebrew reads *he lived in Egypt.*
2Ki 10: 1 {of the city,} As in some Greek manuscripts and Latin **V** (see also 10:6); Hebrew reads *of Jezreel.*
16: 6 {king of Edom} As in Latin **V**; Hebrew reads *Rezin king of Aram.*
16: 6 {Elath for Edom.} As in Latin **V**; Hebrew reads *Aram.*
16: 6 {and sent Edomites} As in marginal *Qere* reading of the Masoretic Text, Greek version, and Latin **V**; Hebrew reads *Arameans.*
1Ch 1:50 {city of Pau.} As in many Hebrew manuscripts, some Greek manuscripts, Syriac version, and Latin **V** (see also Gen 36:39); most Hebrew manuscripts read *Pai.*
4:13 {Hathath and Meonothai.} As in some Greek manuscripts and Latin **V**; Hebrew lacks *and Meonothai.*
9:41 {Tahrea, and Ahaz.} As in Syriac version and Latin **V** (see also 8:35); Hebrew lacks *and Ahaz.*
18:16 {Ahitub and Ahimelech} As in some Hebrew manuscripts, Syriac version, and Latin **V** (see also 2 Sam 8:17); most Hebrew manuscripts read *Abimelech.*
20: 2 {the king's head,} Greek version and Latin **V** read *removed the crown of Milcom;* compare 1 Kgs 11:5. Milcom, also called Molech, was the god of the Ammonites.
23:10 {were Jahath, Ziza,} As in Greek version and Latin **V** (see also 23:11); Hebrew reads *Zina.*
2Ch 15: 8 {Azariah the prophet,} As in Syriac version and Latin **V** (see also 15:1); Hebrew reads *from Oded the prophet.*
20:25 {of equipment, clothing,} As in some Hebrew manuscripts and Latin **V**; most Hebrew manuscripts read *corpses.*
22: 6 {and King Ahaziah} Some Hebrew manuscripts, Greek and Syriac versions, and Latin **V** (see also 2 Kgs 8:29); most Hebrew manuscripts read *Azariah.*
Ne 12: 4 {Iddo, Ginnethon,} As in some Hebrew manuscripts and Latin **V** (see also 12:16); most Hebrew manuscripts read *Ginnethoi.*
Ecc 9: 2 {good or bad,} As in Greek and Syriac versions, and Latin **V**; Hebrew lacks *or bad.*
SS 7: 9 {lips and teeth.} As in Greek and Syriac versions and Latin **V**; Hebrew reads *over lips of sleepers.*
Isa 15: 9 {stream near Dibon} As in Dead Sea Scrolls, some Greek manuscripts, and Latin **V**; Hebrew reads *Dimon;* also in 15:9b.
49:24 {that a tyrant} As in Dead Sea Scrolls, Syriac version, and Latin **V** (also see 49:25); Masoretic Text reads *a righteous person.*
Jer 23:33 {are the burden!} As in Greek version and Latin **V**; Hebrew reads *What burden?*
Hos 13:10 {Where now is} As in Greek and Syriac versions and Latin **V**; Hebrew reads *I will be.*

VULTURE (1)

Job 15:23 {'Where is it?'} Greek version reads *He is appointed to be food for a **v**.*

VULTURES (2)
Mt 24:28 {end is near.} Greek *Wherever the carcass is, the* **v** *gather.*
Lk 17:37 {end is near."} Greek *Wherever the carcass is, the* **v** *gather.*

W

WAGE (9)
Mt 18:28 {few thousand dollars.} Greek *100 denarii.* A denarius was the equivalent of a full day's **w**.
Mk 6:37 {a small fortune} Greek *200 denarii.* A denarius was the equivalent of a full day's **w**.
14: 5 {small fortune} Greek *300 denarii.* A denarius was the equivalent of a full day's **w**.
Lk 7:41 {pieces of silver} Greek *500 denarii.* A denarius was the equivalent of a full day's **w**.
10:35 {pieces of silver} Greek *2 denarii.* A denarius was the equivalent of a full day's **w**.
15: 8 {valuable silver coins} Greek *10 drachmas.* A drachma was the equivalent of a full day's **w**.
Jn 6: 7 {small fortune} Greek *200 denarii.* A denarius was the equivalent of a full day's **w**.
12: 5 {small fortune.} Greek *300 denarii.* A denarius was equivalent to a full day's **w**.
Ac 19:19 {several million dollars.} Greek *50,000 pieces of silver,* each of which was the equivalent of a day's **w**.

WAGES (1)
Lk 19:13 {pounds of silver} Greek *10 minas;* 1 mina was worth about 3 months' **w**.

WAITING (1)
Jn 5: 3 {on the porches.} Some manuscripts add **w** *for a certain movement of the water, [4]for an angel of the Lord came from time to time and stirred up the water. And the first person to step down into it afterward was healed.*

WALL (1)
SS 8: 9 {off from men.} Hebrew *If she is a* **w**, *we will build battlements of silver on her; but if she is a door, we will surround her with panels of cedar.*

WANDERING (1)
Ge 4:16 {land of Nod,} *Nod* means "**w**."

WANT (1)
2Co 1:24 {faith into practice.} Greek **w** *to lord it over your faith.*

WANTED (1)
Job 9: 3 {God to court,} Or *If God* **w** *to take a person to court.*

WAR (1)
1Ki 2: 5 {time of peace,} Or *He murdered them during a time of peace as revenge for deaths they had caused in time of* **w**.

WASHED (2)
Mk 7: 3 {their cupped hands,} Greek **w** *with the fist.*
1Ti 5:10 {other Christians humbly?} Greek *Has she* **w** *the feet of saints?*

WASHING (2)
Eph 5:26 {and God's word.} Greek *having cleansed her by the* **w** *of water with the word.*
Tit 3: 5 {the Holy Spirit.} Greek *He saved us through the* **w** *of regeneration and renewing of the Holy Spirit.*

WASTE (2)
Nu 5:21 {makes you infertile.} Hebrew *when he causes your thigh to* **w** *away and your abdomen to swell.*
5:27 {will become infertile,} Hebrew *Her body will swell and her thigh will* **w** *away.*

WASTES (1)
Nu 5:22 {make you infertile.} Hebrew *enter your body so that your abdomen swells and your thigh* **w** *away.*

WATCH (3)
Mt 14:25 {in the morning} Greek *In the fourth* **w** *of the night.*
Mk 6:48 {in the morning} Greek *About the fourth* **w** *of the night.*
Lk 12:38 {just before dawn.} Greek *in the second or third* **w**.

WATCHER (1)
Da 4:13 {saw a messenger,} Aramaic *a* **w**; also in 4:23.

WATCHERS (1)
Da 4:17 {by the messengers} Aramaic *the* **w**.

WATCHING (1)
Jer 1:12 {I am watching,} The Hebrew word for "**w**" sounds like the word for "almond tree."

WATCHTOWER (1)
Ge 31:49 {also called Mizpah,} *Mizpah* means "**w**."

WATER (12)
2Sa 12:27 {its water supply.} Or *captured the city of* **w**.
2Ki 3:11 {Elijah's personal assistant.} Hebrew *He used to pour* **w** *on the hands of Elijah.*
Ne 4:23 {went for water.} Hebrew *Each his weapon the* **w**. The meaning of the Hebrew is uncertain.
Pr 5:15 {with your wife.} Hebrew *Drink* **w** *from your own cistern, flowing* **w** *from your own well.*
Mt 27:49 {and save him."} Some manuscripts add *And another took a spear and pierced his side, and out came* **w** *and blood.*
Jn 5: 3 {on the porches.} Some manuscripts add *waiting for a certain movement of the* **w**, *[4]for an angel of the Lord came from time to time and stirred up the* **w**. *And the first person to step down into it afterward was healed.*
7:37[-38] {out from within."} Or *"Let anyone who is thirsty come to me and drink. [38]For the Scriptures declare that rivers of living* **w** *will flow from the heart of those who believe in me."*
Eph 5:26 {and God's word.} Greek *having cleansed her by the washing of* **w** *with the word.*
1Pe 3:20 {that terrible flood.} Greek *saved through* **w**.
1Jn 5: 6 {on the cross} Greek *This is he who came by* **w** *and blood.*

WATERS (6)
Nu 27:14 {Meribah at Kadesh} Hebrew **w** *of Meribath-kadesh.*
Dt 32:51 {Meribah at Kadesh} Hebrew **w** *of Meribath-kadesh.*
Ps 77:16 {the Red Sea} Hebrew *the* **w**.
Isa 8: 6 {my gentle care} Hebrew *rejected the gently flowing* **w** *of Shiloah.*
Eze 47:19 {Meribah at Kadesh} Hebrew **w** *of Meribath-kadesh.*
48:28 {Meribah at Kadesh} Hebrew **w** *of Meribath-kadesh.*

WAY (2)
Mt 7:13 {highway to hell} Greek *The* **w** *that leads to destruction.*
Mk 10:52 {down the road.} Or *on the* **w**.

WAYS (1)
Ps 119:37 {through your word.} Some manuscripts read *in your* **w**.

WEAK (1)
Mk 9:18 {and become rigid.} Or *become* **w**.

WEAPON (1)
Ne 4:23 {went for water.} Hebrew *Each his* **w** *the water.* The meaning of the Hebrew is uncertain.

WEARING (1)
2Ki 1: 8 {hairy man,} Or *He was* **w** *clothing made of hair.*

WEEK (5)
Mt 28: 1 {on Sunday morning,} Greek *After the Sabbath, on the first day of the* **w**.
Mk 16: 2 {on Sunday morning,} Greek *on the first day of the* **w**; also in 16:9.
Lk 24: 1 {on Sunday morning} Greek *But on the first day of the* **w**, *very early in the morning.*
Jn 20: 1 {Early Sunday morning,} Greek *On the first day of the* **w**.
1Co 16: 2 {every Lord's Day,} Greek *every first day of the* **w**.

WEEKS (4)
Ex 23:16 {Festival of Harvest,} Or *Festival of* **W**.
34:22 {Festival of Harvest} Or *Festival of* **W**.
Nu 28:26 {Festival of Harvest,} Or *Festival of* **W**.
Dt 16:10 {Festival of Harvest} Or *Festival of* **W**, also in 16:16.

WEEP (1)
Mic 1:10 {weep at all.} Greek version reads **w** *not in Acco.*

WEIGHING (4)
Ge 24:22 {large gold bracelets} Hebrew *a gold nose-ring* **w** *a half shekel* [0.2 ounces or 6 grams] *and two gold bracelets* **w** *10 shekels* [4 ounces or 114 grams].
Nu 7:13 {about 1 3/4 pounds.} Hebrew *silver platter* **w** *130 shekels* [1.5 kilograms] *and a silver basin* **w** *70 shekels* [0.8 kilograms], *according to the sanctuary shekel;* also in 7:19, 25, 31, 37, 43, 49, 55, 61, 67, 73, 79, 85.

WEIGHS (1)
Eze 45:12 {the silver shekel.} The shekel **w** about 0.4 ounces or 11 grams.

WELCOME (2)
Mt 10:41 {speaks for God,} Greek **w** *a prophet in the name of a prophet.*
Lk 16: 9 {you in heaven.} Or *Then when you run out at the end of this life, your friends will* **w** *you into eternal homes.*

WELL (6)
Ge 16:14 {was named Beer-lahairoi,} *Beer-lahairoi* means "**w** of the Living One who sees me."
Nu 21:16 {traveled to Beer,} *Beer* means "**w**."
Ne 2:13 {the Jackal's Well,} Or *Serpent's* **W**.
Pr 5:15 {with your wife.} Hebrew *Drink water from your own cistern, flowing water from your own* **w**.
23:27 {woman is treacherous.} Hebrew *is a narrow* **w**.
Ac 14: 1 {In Iconium,} *Iconium,* as **w** as *Lystra* and *Derbe* (14:6), were cities in the land now called Turkey.

WEST (1)
Ps 80:11 {the Euphrates River.} Hebrew **w** *to the sea,...east to the river.*

WESTERN (5)
Dt 11:24 {in the west.} Hebrew *to the* **w** *sea.*
34: 2 {the Mediterranean Sea} Hebrew *the* **w** *sea.*
Joel 2:20 {into the Mediterranean.} Hebrew *the eastern sea;...the* **w** *sea.*
Zec 14: 8 {toward the Mediterranean,} Hebrew *half toward the eastern sea and half toward the* **w** *sea.*
1Co 16:19 {province of Asia} *Asia* was a Roman province in what is now **w** Turkey.

WHERE (4)
1Ch 2:24 {(the father of} Or *the founder of;* also in 2:42, 45, 49-52 and perhaps other instances **w** the text reads *the father of.*
4: 4 {(the father of} Or *the founder of;* also in 4:12, 14, 17-18, and perhaps other instances **w** the text reads *the father of.*
Ps 19: 3 {in the skies;} Or *There is no speech or language* **w** *their voice is not heard.*
Rev 4: 5 {the seven spirits} See 1:4 and 3:1, **w** the same expression is translated *the sevenfold Spirit.*

WHEREVER (2)
Mt 24:28 {end is near.} Greek **W** *the carcass is, the vultures gather.*
Lk 17:37 {end is near."} Greek **W** *the carcass is, the vultures gather.*

WHOLE (2)
Ro 11:16 {also be holy.} Greek *If the dough offered as firstfruits is holy, so is the* **w** *lump.*
1Co 5: 6[-7] {can stay pure.} Greek *Don't you realize that even a little leaven spreads quickly through the* **w** *batch of dough? [7]Purge out the old leaven so that you can be a new batch of dough, just as you are already unleavened.*

WHY (2)
Pr 5:16 {with just anyone?} Hebrew **W** *spill your springs in public, your streams in the streets?*
Jn 8:25 {claimed to be.} Or *"***W** *do I speak to you at all?"*

WICKEDNESS (4)
Hos 4:15 {and at Beth-aven.} *Beth-aven* means "house of **w**"; it is being used as another name for Bethel, which means "house of God."
5: 8 {cry in Beth-aven} *Beth-aven* means "house of **w**"; it is being used as another name for Bethel, which means "house of God."
10: 5 {idol at Beth-aven.} *Beth-aven* means "house of **w**"; it is being used as another name for Bethel, which means "house of God."
Am 1: 5 {valley of Aven.} *Aven* means "**w**."

WIDOWS (2)
Eze 19: 7 {in nearby nations} As in Greek version; Hebrew reads *He consorted with* **w**.
Mt 23:13 {go in yourselves.} Some manuscripts add verse 14, *How terrible it will be for you teachers of religious law and you Pharisees. Hypocrites! You shamelessly cheat* **w** *out of their property, and then, to cover up the kind of people you really are, you make long prayers in public. Because of this, your punishment will be the greater.*

WIDTH (3)
Ezr 6: 3 {be ninety feet.} Aramaic *Its height will be 60 cubits* [27 meters], *and its* **w** *will be 60 cubits.* It is commonly held that this verse should be emended to read: "Its height will be 45 feet, its length will be 90 feet, and its **w** will be 30 feet"; compare 1 Kgs 6:2. The emendation regarding the **w** is supported by the Syriac version.

WIFE (7)
Mk 10: 7 {to his wife,} Some manuscripts do not include *and is joined to his* **w**.
1Co 9: 5 {Christian wife} Greek *a sister, a* **w**.

1Th 4: 4 {control your body} Or *will know how to take a* **w** *for himself;* Greek reads *will know how to possess his own vessel.*
1Ti 3: 2 {to his wife.} Greek *be the husband of one* **w**; also in 3:12.
5: 9 {to her husband.} Greek *was the* **w** *of one man.*
Tit 1: 6 {to his wife,} Or *have only one* **w**, or *be married only once;* Greek reads *be the husband of one* **w**.

WILD (2)
2Ki 6:25 {about two ounces} Hebrew *sold for 80 shekels* [0.9 kilograms] *of silver, and 1/4 of a cab* [0.3 liters] *of dove's dung cost 5 shekels* [57 grams]. *Dove's dung* may be a variety of **w** vegetable.
1Co 15:32 {men of Ephesus} Greek *fighting* **w** *beasts in Ephesus.*

WILDERNESS (3)
2Sa 15:28 {the Jordan River} Hebrew *at the crossing points of the* **w**.
17:16 {the Jordan River} Hebrew *at the crossing points of the* **w**.
Jer 48: 6 {in the wilderness!} Or *Be like* [the town of] *Aroer in the* **w**.

WILLING (1)
Mk 7:15 {say and do!} Some manuscripts add verse 16, *Anyone who is* **w** *to hear should listen and understand.*

WIND (2)
Job 4:15 {A spirit} Or **w**.
Jn 3: 5 {and the Spirit.} Or *spirit.* The Greek word for *Spirit* can also be translated **w**; see 3:8.

WINDS (1)
Zec 6: 5 {the four spirits} Or *the four* **w**.

WINE (6)
Ex 29:40 {quart of wine} Hebrew *1/10 of an ephah* [2 liters] *of fine flour . . . 1/4 of a hin* [1 liter] *of olive oil . . . 1/4 of a hin of* **w**.
1Sa 1:11 {never be cut."} Some manuscripts add *He will drink neither* **w** *nor intoxicants.*
2Ch 2:10 {of olive oil.} Hebrew *20,000 baths* [420 kiloliters] *of* **w**, *and 20,000 baths of olive oil.*
Ezr 7:22 {of olive oil,} Aramaic *100 baths* [2.1 kiloliters] *of* **w**, *100 baths of olive oil.*
Hos 3: 2 {measure of wine.} As in Greek version, which reads *a homer* [182 liters] *of barley and a measure of* **w**; Hebrew reads *a homer of barley and a lethech* [2.5 bushels or 91 liters] *of barley.*
Hab 2: 5 {Wealth} As in Dead Sea Scroll 1QpHab; other Hebrew manuscripts read **W**.

WING (1)
Da 9:27 {his terrible deeds,} Hebrew *on the* **w** *of abominations;* the meaning of the Hebrew is uncertain.

WINGS (1)
Mal 4: 2 {in his wings.} Or *the sun of righteousness will rise with healing in its* **w**.

WISDOM (3)
Lk 7:35 {who follow it.} Or *But* **w** *is justified by all her children.*
11:49 {said about you:} Greek *Therefore, the* **w** *of God said.*
1Co 2: 7 {wisdom of God,} Greek *we speak God's* **w** *in a mystery.*

WISE (4)
Pr 14:16 {wise are cautious} Hebrew *The* **w** *fear.*
23:24 {have wise children.} Hebrew *a* **w** *son.*
24: 5 {strong man,} As in Greek version; Hebrew reads *A* **w** *man is strength.*
Mt 2:16 {two years earlier.} Or *according to the time he calculated from the* **w** *men.*

WITHDRAW (1)
1Sa 14:19 {let's get going!"} Hebrew **W** *your hand.*

WITHER (1)
Ps 58: 7 {in their hands.} Or *Let them be trodden down and* **w** *like grass.* The meaning of the Hebrew is uncertain.

WITHIN (6)
Ps 119: 1 {people of integrity,} This psalm is a Hebrew acrostic poem; there are 22 stanzas, one for each letter of the Hebrew alphabet. The 8 verses **w** each stanza begin with the Hebrew letter of its section.
Isa 21:16 {within a year,"} Hebrew **W** *a year, like the years of a hired hand.* Some ancient manuscripts read **W** *three years,* as in 16:14.
Lk 17:21 {is among you.} Or **w** *you.*
Jas 4: 5 {to be faithful} Or *the spirit that God placed* **w** *us tends to envy,* or *the Holy Spirit, whom God has placed* **w** *us, opposes our envy.*

WITHOUT (5)
Job 19:26 {will see God} Or **w** *my body I will see God.*
Mt 5:22 {angry with someone,} Some manuscripts add **w** *cause.*
12:29 {house be robbed!} Or *One cannot rob Satan's kingdom* **w** *first tying him up. Only then can his demons be cast out.*
Mk 3:27 {house be robbed!} Or *One cannot rob Satan's kingdom* **w** *first tying him up. Only then can his demons be cast out.*
1Co 9:21 {the Jewish law,} Greek *those* **w** *the law.*

WITNESS (3)
Ge 31:47 {language and Galeed} *Jegar-sahadutha* means "**w** pile" in Aramaic; *Galeed* means "**w** pile" in Hebrew.
Ac 7:44 {carried the Tabernacle} Greek *the tent of* **w**.

WITNESSES (1)
1Jn 5: 7 {these three witnesses} Some very late manuscripts add *in heaven—the Father, the Word, and the Holy Spirit, and these three are one. And we have three* **w** *on earth.*

WIVES (2)
Ac 17: 4 {of the city.} Some manuscripts read *many of the* **w** *of the leading men.*
1Ti 3:11 {way, their wives} Or *the women deacons.* The Greek word can be translated *women* or **w**.

WOMAN (9)
Lev 20:18 {from a hemorrhage,} Or *a* **w** *who is menstruating.*
1Sa 20:30 {of a whore!"} Hebrew *You son of a perverse and rebellious* **w**.
Pr 20:16 {of a foreigner.} An alternate reading in the Hebrew text is *the debt of an adulterous* **w**; compare 27:13.
SS 1: 7 {like a prostitute} Hebrew *like a veiled* **w**.
Isa 7:14 {Look! The virgin} Or *young* **w**.
Jer 31:22 {embrace her God.} Hebrew *a* **w** *will court a suitor.*
Hos 1: 2 {marry a prostitute,} Or *a promiscuous* **w**.
Mt 19: 9 {has been unfaithful.} Some manuscripts add *And the man who marries a divorced* **w** *commits adultery.*
Lk 13:16 {this dear woman} Greek *this* **w**, *a daughter of Abraham.*

WOMEN (5)
Mt 27:51[-53] {to many people.} Or *The earth shook, rocks split apart, tombs opened, and many bodies of godly men and* **w** *who had died were raised from the dead. After Jesus' resurrection, they left the cemetery, went into the holy city of Jerusalem, and appeared to many people.*
Lk 1:28 {is with you!} Some manuscripts add *Blessed are you among* **w**.
1Ti 3:11 {way, their wives} Or *the* **w** *deacons.* The Greek word can be translated **w** or *wives.*
Rev 14: 4 {pure as virgins,} Greek *they are virgins who have not defiled themselves with* **w**.

WONDERFUL (1)
Isa 9: 6 {titles: Wonderful Counselor,} Or **W**, *Counselor.*

WOOD (1)
2Ch 9:10 {of almug wood} Hebrew *algum* **w** (also in 9:11); compare parallel text at 1 Kgs 10:11-12.

WORD (32)
Ex 4: 6 {snow with leprosy.} Or *with a contagious skin disease.* The Hebrew **w** used here can describe various skin diseases.
16: 1 {Sin} Not to be confused with the English **w** *sin.*
17: 1 {Sin} Not to be confused with the English **w** *sin.*
Lev 13: 2 {contagious skin disease,} Traditionally rendered *leprosy.* The Hebrew **w** used throughout this passage is used to describe various skin diseases.
Nu 5: 2 {contagious skin disease} Traditionally rendered *leprosy.* The Hebrew **w** used here describes various skin diseases.
12:10 {snow with leprosy.} Or *with a contagious skin disease.* The Hebrew **w** used here can describe various skin diseases.
33:11 {Sin} Not to be confused with the English **w** *sin.*
Dt 24: 8 {contagious skin diseases} Traditonally rendered *leprosy.* The Hebrew **w** used here can describe various skin diseases.
Jos 5: 9 {been called Gilgal} *Gilgal* sounds like the Hebrew **w** *galal,* meaning "to roll."
22:34 {the altar "Witness,"} Hebrew *edh.* Some manuscripts lack this **w**.
1Sa 18: 6 {tambourines and cymbals.} The type of instrument represented by the final **w** is uncertain.
2Sa 3:29 {sores or leprosy} Or *or a contagious skin disease.* The Hebrew **w** used here can describe various skin diseases.
2Ki 5: 1 {suffered from leprosy.} Or *from a contagious skin disease.* The Hebrew **w** used here and throughout this passage can describe various skin diseases.
7: 3 {men with leprosy} Or *with a contagious skin disease.* The Hebrew **w** used here and throughout this passage can describe various skin diseases.
15: 5 {king with leprosy,} Or *with a contagious skin disease.* The Hebrew **w** used here and throughout this passage can describe various skin diseases.
1Ch 22: 9 {will be Solomon,} *Solomon* sounds like and is probably derived from the Hebrew **w** for "peace."
2Ch 26:19 {LORD's Temple, leprosy} Or *a contagious skin disease.* The Hebrew **w** used here and throughout this passage can describe various skin diseases.
Ezr 1: 9 {silver censers} The meaning of this Hebrew **w** is uncertain.
Ps 3: 2 {Interlude} Hebrew *Selah.* The meaning of this **w** is uncertain, though it is probably a musical or literary term. It is rendered *Interlude* throughout the Psalms.
Isa 21:11 {me concerning Edom} Hebrew *Dumah,* which means "silence" or "stillness." It is a wordplay on the **w** *Edom.*
Jer 1:12 {I am watching,} The Hebrew **w** for "watching" sounds like the **w** for "almond tree."
48: 2 {city of Madmen,} *Madmen* sounds like the Hebrew **w** for "silence"; it should not be confused with the English **w** *madmen.*
La 1: 1 {Jerusalem's streets,} Each of the first four chapters of this book is an acrostic, laid out in the order of the Hebrew alphabet. The first **w** of each verse begins with a successive Hebrew letter. Chapters 1, 2, and 4 have one verse for each of the 22 Hebrew letters. Chapter 3 contains 22 stanzas of three verses each. Though chapter 5 is not an acrostic, it also has 22 verses.
Mt 27:35 {by throwing dice.} Greek *by casting lots.* A few late manuscripts add *This fulfilled the* **w** *of the prophet: "They divided my clothes among themselves and cast lots for my robe."* See Ps 22:18.
Lk 23:33 {called The Skull.} Sometimes rendered *Calvary,* which comes from the Latin **w** for "skull."
Jn 3: 5 {and the Spirit.} Or *spirit.* The Greek **w** for *Spirit* can also be translated *wind;* see 3:8.
3: 7 {statement that you} The Greek **w** for *you* is plural; also in 3:12.
Eph 5:26 {and God's word.} Greek *having cleansed her by the washing of water with the* **w**.
1Ti 3:11 {way, their wives} Or *the women deacons.* The Greek **w** can be translated *women* or *wives.*
1Jn 5: 7 {these three witnesses} Some very late manuscripts add *in heaven—the Father, the* **W**, *and the Holy Spirit, and these three are one. And we have three witnesses on earth.*

WORDPLAY (1)
Isa 21:11 {me concerning Edom} Hebrew *Dumah,* which means "silence" or "stillness." It is a **w** on the word *Edom.*

WORDS (3)
Isa 28:10 {very simple words!} The Hebrew text for this verse may simply be childish sounds that have no meaning, or perhaps a childish mimicking of the prophet's **w**. Also in 28:13.
Mt 16: 2[-3] {of the times!} Several manuscripts do not include any of the **w** in 16:2-3 after *He replied.*
Ac 28:28 {will accept it."} Some manuscripts add verse 29, *And when he had said these* **w**, *the Jews departed, greatly disagreeing with each other.*

WORE (1)
1Sa 2:18 {of a priest.} Hebrew *He* **w** *a linen ephod.*

WORK (1)
2Co 6: 1 {As God's partners,} Or *As we* **w** *together.*

WORKER (1)
Mt 10:10 {to be fed.} Or *the* **w** *is worthy of support.*

WORKING (1)
Lk 17:35 {the other left.} Some manuscripts add verse 36, *Two men will be* **w** *in the field; one will be taken, the other left.*

WORKS (1)
Ro 8:28 {to work together} Some manuscripts read *And we know that everything* **w** *together.*

WORLD (2)
Jn 12:31 {of this world} *The prince of this* **w** *is a name for Satan.*
Col 2: 8 {of this world,} Or *from the basic principles of this* **w**; also in 2:20.

WORMWOOD (2)
La 3:19 {bitter beyond words.} Hebrew *is* **w** *and gall.*
Rev 8:11 {star was Bitterness.} Greek **W**.

WORSHIP (3)
Ge 47:31 {on his staff.} As in Greek version; Hebrew reads *bowed in* **w** *at the head of his bed.*

Isa 29:13 {learned by rote.} Greek version reads *Their w is a farce, for they merely teach human commands and teachings.*
Php 3:3 {in the Spirit} Or *in spirit;* some manuscripts read *w by the Spirit of God.*

WORSHIPED (1)

Lk 24:52 {worshiped him and} Some manuscripts do not include *w him and.*

WORTH (1)

Lk 19:13 {pounds of silver} Greek *10 minas;* 1 mina was w about 3 months' wages.

WORTHY (2)

Mt 10:10 {to be fed.} Or *the worker is w of support.*
1Ti 5:17 {be paid well,} Greek *should be w of double honor.*

WRITER (1)

Ac 16:10 {So we} Luke, the w of this book, here joined Paul and accompanied him on his journey.

WRITHE (1)

Ps 29:9 {twists mighty oaks} Or *causes the deer to w in labor.*

WRITINGS (1)

Ro 16:26 {as the prophets} Greek *the prophetic w.*

WRITTEN (2)

1Ch 28:19 {of the LORD.} Or *was w under the direction of the LORD.*
1Co 4:6 {to the Scriptures,} Or *You must learn not to go beyond "what is w," so that.*

WRONG (1)

2Ch 20:35 {very wicked man.} Or *who made him do what was w.*

WROTE (1)

Lk 20:37 {to the Lord} Greek *when he w about the burning bush, he referred to the Lord.*

X

XERXES (2)

Ezr 4:6 {later when Xerxes} Hebrew *Ahasuerus,* another name for **X.**
Est 1:1 {of King Xerxes,} Hebrew *Ahasuerus,* another name for **X**; also throughout the book of Esther.

Y

YAHWEH (7)

Ge 22:14 {LORD Will Provide."} Hebrew ***Y*** *Yir'eh.*
Ex 3:15 {'The LORD,} Hebrew ***Y;*** traditionally rendered *Jehovah.*
6:3 {the LORD,} Hebrew ***Y;*** traditionally rendered *Jehovah.*
17:15 {Is My Banner."} Hebrew ***Y*** *Nissi.*
Jdg 6:24 {LORD Is Peace."} Hebrew ***Y*** *Shalom.*
Jer 23:6 {Is Our Righteousness.'} Hebrew ***Y*** *Tsidqenu.*
Eze 48:35 {LORD Is There.'} Hebrew ***Y*** *Shammah.*

YAUDI (1)

2Ki 14:28 {belonged to Judah,} Or *to* ***Y.***

YEAR (41)

Ex 40:17 {the new year.} Hebrew *the first day of the first month, in the second y.* See note on 40:2b.
2Ki 25:3 {Zedekiah's eleventh year,} Hebrew *By the ninth day,* that is, "of the fourth month of Zedekiah's eleventh y" (compare Jer 52:6 and the note there). This event of the Hebrew lunar calendar occurred on July 18, 586 B.C.; also see note on 25:1.
2Ch 36:22 {Cyrus of Persia,} The first y of Cyrus's reign was 538 B.C.
Ezr 1:1 {Cyrus of Persia,} The first y of Cyrus's reign was 538 B.C.
Ne 1:1 {King Artaxerxes' reign,} Hebrew *In the month of Kislev of the twentieth y.* A number of events in the book of Nehemiah can be cross-checked with dates in surviving Persian records and related accurately to our modern calendar. This month of the Hebrew lunar calendar occurred in November and December 446 B.C. The *twentieth y* probably refers to the reign of King Artaxerxes I; compare 2:1; 5:14.
13:6 {Artaxerxes of Babylon,} The thirty-second y of Artaxerxes was 433 B.C.
Isa 21:16 {within a year,"} Hebrew *Within a y, like the years of a hired hand.* Some ancient manuscripts read *Within three years,* as in 16:14.
61:2 {favor has come,} Or *to proclaim the acceptable y of the LORD.*
Jer 1:2 {reign in Judah.} The thirteenth y of Josiah's reign was 626 B.C.
1:3 {of that year,} Hebrew *In the fifth month,* of the Hebrew calendar. A number of events in Jeremiah can be cross-checked with dates in surviving Babylonian records and related accurately to our modern calendar. This month in the eleventh y of Zedekiah's reign occurred in August and September 586 B.C. Also see 52:12 and the note there.
25:1 {of Jehoiakim's reign} The fourth y of Jehoiakim's reign and the first y of Nebuchadnezzar's reign was 605 B.C.
25:3 {son of Amon,} The thirteenth y of Josiah's reign was 626 B.C.
26:1 {son of Josiah,} The first y of Jehoiakim's reign was 608 B.C.
28:1 {in late summer} Hebrew *In the fifth month,* of the Hebrew calendar. This month in the fourth y of Zedekiah's reign occurred in August and September 593 B.C. Also see note on 1:3.
28:17 {Two months later,} Hebrew *In the seventh month of that same y.* See 28:1 and the note there.
32:1 {reign of Zedekiah,} The tenth y of Zedekiah's reign and the eighteenth y of Nebuchadnezzar's reign was 587 B.C.
36:1 {king in Judah,} The fourth y of Jehoiakim's reign was 605 B.C.
36:9 {in late autumn,} Hebrew *in the ninth month,* of the Hebrew calendar (also in 36:22). This month in the fifth y of Jehoiakim's reign occurred in November and December 604 B.C. Also see note on 1:3.
39:2 {later, on July 18,} Hebrew *On the ninth day of the fourth month of the eleventh y of Zedekiah.* This event occurred on July 18, 586 B.C.; also see note on 39:1.
45:1 {son of Josiah,} The fourth y of Jehoiakim's reign was 605 B.C.
46:2 {son of Josiah,} The fourth y of Jehoiakim's reign was 605 B.C.
51:59 {of Zedekiah's reign.} The fourth y of Zedekiah's reign was 593 B.C.
52:6 {Zedekiah's eleventh year,} Hebrew *By the ninth day of the fourth month* [of Zedekiah's eleventh y]. This event of the Hebrew lunar calendar occurred on July 18, 586 B.C.; also see note on 52:4a.
52:28 {of Nebuchadnezzar's reign} This exile in the seventh y of Nebuchadnezzar's reign occurred in 597 B.C.
52:29 {Nebuchadnezzar's eighteenth year} This exile in the eighteenth y of Nebuchadnezzar's reign occurred in 586 B.C.
52:30 {his twenty-third year} This exile in the twenty-third y of Nebuchadnezzar's reign occurred in 581 B.C.
Eze 1:1 {my thirtieth year,} Or *in the thirtieth y.*
26:1 {King Jehoiachin's captivity,} Hebrew *In the eleventh y, on the first day of the month,* of the Hebrew calendar y. Since an element is missing in the date formula here, scholars have reconstructed this probable reading: *On the first day of the eleventh month, during the twelfth y.* This reading would put this message on February 3, 585 B.C.;...
32:17 {On March 17,} Hebrew *On the fifteenth day of the month,* presumably in the twelfth month of the Hebrew calendar (see 32:1). This would put this message at the end of King Jehoiachin's twelfth y of captivity, on March 17, 585 B.C.; also see note on 29:1. Greek version reads *On the fifteenth day of the first month,* which would put this message on April 27, 586 B.C., at the beginning of Jehoiachin's twelfth y.
40:1 {On April 28,} Hebrew *At the beginning of the y, on the tenth day of the month,* of the Hebrew calendar. A number of events in Ezekiel can be cross-checked with dates in surviving Babylonian records and related accurately to our modern calendar. This event occurred on April 28, 573 B.C.
46:17 {every fiftieth year.} Hebrew *until the Y of Release;* see Lev 25:8-17.
Da 1:1 {reign in Judah,} The third y of Jehoiakim's reign, according to the Babylonian system of reckoning, was 605 B.C.
1:21 {King Cyrus's reign.} The first y of Cyrus's reign was 538 B.C.
2:1 {of his reign,} The second y of Nebuchadnezzar's reign was 604 B.C.
Lk 4:18[-19] {favor has come.} Or *and to proclaim the acceptable y of the Lord.* Isa 61:1-2.

YEARS (8)

Ge 11:12[-13] {sons and daughters.} Greek version reads [12]*When Arphaxad was 135 y old, his son Cainan was born.* [13]*After the birth of Cainan, Arphaxad lived another 430 y and had other sons and daughters, and then he died. When Cainan was 130 y old, his son Shelah was born. After the birth of Shelah, Cainan lived another 330 y and had other sons and daughters, and then he died.*
11:32 {for 205 years} Some ancient versions read *145 y;* compare 11:26; 12:4.
2Sa 15:7 {After four years,} As in Greek and Syriac versions; Hebrew reads *40 y.*
Isa 21:16 {within a year,"} Hebrew *Within a year, like the y of a hired hand.* Some ancient manuscripts read *Within three y,* as in 16:14.

YEHUDAH (2)

Ezr 3:9 {descendants of Hodaviah.} Hebrew *sons of Judah* (i.e., *bene Y*). *Bene* might also be read here as the proper name Binnui; *Y* is probably another name for Hodaviah. Compare 2:40; Neh 7:43; 1 Esdras 5:58.

YET (2)

Isa 53:4 {was our sorrows} Or *Y it was our sicknesses he carried; it was our diseases.*
Jn 7:8 {am not yet} Some manuscripts omit y.

YIELD (1)

Isa 5:10 {only one measure} Hebrew *A homer* [5 bushels or 182 liters] *of seed will y only an ephah* [0.5 bushels or 18.2 liters].

YIR'EH (1)

Ge 22:14 {LORD Will Provide."} Hebrew *Yahweh* ***Y.***

YOKE (4)

1Sa 14:14 {half an acre.} Hebrew *half a y;* a "y" was the amount of land plowed by a pair of yoked oxen in one day.
Isa 5:10 {Ten acres} Hebrew *A ten y,* that is, the area of land plowed by ten teams of oxen in one day.
10:27 {from their shoulders.} As in Greek version; Hebrew reads *The y will be broken, for you have grown so fat.*

YOKED (1)

1Sa 14:14 {half an acre.} Hebrew *half a yoke;* a "yoke" was the amount of land plowed by a pair of y oxen in one day.

YOKEFELLOW (1)

Php 4:3 {my true teammate,} Greek *true y,* or *loyal Syzygus.*

YOM (1)

Ac 27:9 {in the fall,} Greek *because the fast was now already gone by.* This fast happened on the Day of Atonement (*Y Kippur*), which occurred in late September or early October.

YOUNG (2)

1Sa 8:16 {of your cattle} As in Greek version; Hebrew reads *y men.*
Isa 7:14 {Look! The virgin} Or *y woman.*

Z

ZAANAN (1)

Mic 1:11 {people of Zaanan} **Z** sounds like the Hebrew term for "come out."

ZABAD (1)

2Ch 24:26 {assassins were Jozacar,} Hebrew **Z**; compare parallel text at 2 Kgs 12:21, and see note there.

ZABDI (1)

Jos 7:1 {family of Zimri,} As in Greek version (see also 1 Chr 2:6); Hebrew reads **Z.** Also in 7:17, 18.

ZAPHENATH-PANEAH (1)

Ge 41:45 {renamed him Zaphenath-paneah} **Z** probably means "God speaks and lives."

ZAPHON (1)

Ps 48:2 {the holy mountain,} Or *Mount Zion, in the far north;* Hebrew reads *Mount Zion, the heights of* ***Z.***

ZATTU (1)

Ezr 8:5 {family of Zattu} As in some Greek manuscripts (see also 1 Esdras 8:32); Hebrew lacks **Z.**

ZEBULUN (1)

Ge 30:20 {named him Zebulun,} **Z** probably means "honor."

ZECH (7)

Mt 21:5 {a donkey's colt.' "} **Z** 9:9.
26:31 {will be scattered.'} **Z** 13:7.
27:9[-10] {the Lord directed.} Greek *as the Lord directed me.* **Z** 11:12-13; Jer 32:6-9.
Mk 14:27 {will be scattered.'} **Z** 13:7.

Jn 12:15 {a donkey's colt."} **Z** 9:9.
19:37 {whom they pierced."} **Z** 12:10.
Eph 4:25 {neighbor the truth"} **Z** 8:16.

ZECHARIAH (2)

1Ch 8:31 {Gedor, Ahio, Zechariah,} As in parallel text at 9:37; Hebrew reads *Zeker,* a variant name for **Z**.
Zec 1: 1 {In midautumn} Hebrew *In the eighth month.* A number of events in **Z** can be cross-checked with dates in surviving Persian records and related accurately to our modern calendar. This month of the Hebrew lunar calendar occurred in October and November 520 B.C.

ZEDEKIAH (2)

1Ch 3:16 {his uncle Zedekiah.} Hebrew *The descendants of Jehoiakim were his son Jeconiah* [a variant name for Jehoiachin] *and his son* **Z**.
Jer 39: 2 {later, on July 18,} Hebrew *On the ninth day of the fourth month of the eleventh year of* **Z**. This event occurred on July 18, 586 B.C.; also see note on 39:1.

ZEDEKIAH'S (6)

2Ki 25: 3 {Zedekiah's eleventh year,} Hebrew *By the ninth day,* that is, "of the fourth month of **Z** eleventh year" (compare Jer 52:6 and the note there). This event of the Hebrew lunar calendar occurred on July 18, 586 B.C.; also see note on 25:1.
Jer 1: 3 {of that year,} Hebrew *In the fifth month,* of the Hebrew calendar. A number of events in Jeremiah can be cross-checked with dates in surviving Babylonian records and related accurately to our modern calendar. This month in the eleventh year of **Z** reign occurred in August and September 586 B.C. Also see 52:12 and the note there.
28: 1 {in late summer} Hebrew *In the fifth month,* of the Hebrew calendar. This month in the fourth year of **Z** reign occurred in August and September 593 B.C. Also see note on 1:3.
32: 1 {reign of Zedekiah,} The tenth year of **Z** reign and the eighteenth year of Nebuchadnezzar's reign was 587 B.C.
51:59 {of Zedekiah's reign.} The fourth year of **Z** reign was 593 B.C.
52: 6 {Zedekiah's eleventh year,} Hebrew *By the ninth day of the fourth month* [of **Z** eleventh year]. This event of the Hebrew lunar calendar occurred on July 18, 586 B.C.; also see note on 52:4a.

ZEKER (1)

1Ch 8:31 {Gedor, Ahio, Zechariah,} As in parallel text at 9:37; Hebrew reads **Z**, a variant name for Zechariah.

ZEPH (1)

Jn 12:13 {King of Israel!"} Ps 118:25-26; **Z** 3:15.

ZEPHATHAH (1)

2Ch 14:10 {north of Mareshah.} Or *in the* **Z** *Valley near Mareshah.*

ZEPHI (1)

1Ch 1:36 {Teman, Omar, Zepho,} As in many Hebrew manuscripts and a few Greek manuscripts (see also Gen 36:11); most Hebrew manuscripts read **Z**.

ZERAH (1)

Ge 38:30 {was named Zerah.} **Z** means "scarlet" or "brightness."

ZEREDAH (1)

2Ch 4:17 {Succoth and Zarethan.} As in parallel text at 1 Kgs 7:46; Hebrew reads **Z**.

ZERI (1)

1Ch 25:11 {fell to Zeri} Hebrew *Izri,* a variant name for **Z**; compare 25:3.

ZINA (1)

1Ch 23:10 {were Jahath, Ziza,} As in Greek version and Latin Vulgate (see also 23:11); Hebrew reads **Z**.

ZION (86)

Ps 2: 6 {my holy city.} Hebrew *on* **Z**, *my holy mountain.*
9:11 {reigns in Jerusalem.} Hebrew **Z**; also in 9:14.
20: 2 {you from Jerusalem.} Hebrew **Z**.
48: 2 {the holy mountain,} Or *Mount* **Z**, *in the far north;* Hebrew reads *Mount* **Z**, *the heights of Zaphon.*
48:12 {city of Jerusalem.} Hebrew **Z**.
69:35 {will save Jerusalem} Hebrew **Z**.
74: 2 {And remember Jerusalem,} Hebrew *Mount* **Z**.
84: 7 {God in Jerusalem.} Hebrew **Z**.
87: 2 {city in Israel.} Hebrew *He loves the gates of* **Z** *more than all the dwellings of Jacob.*
87: 5 {said of Jerusalem,} Hebrew **Z**.
97: 8 {Jerusalem} Hebrew **Z**.
99: 2 {majesty in Jerusalem,} Hebrew **Z**.
102:13 {mercy on Jerusalem} Hebrew **Z**; also in 102:16.
110: 2 {dominion from Jerusalem} Hebrew **Z**.
126: 1 {exiles to Jerusalem,} Hebrew **Z**.
129: 5 {who hate Jerusalem} Hebrew **Z**.
132:13 {has chosen Jerusalem} Hebrew **Z**.
134: 3 {you from Jerusalem.} Hebrew **Z**.
137: 1 {thought of Jerusalem.} Hebrew **Z**; also in 137:3.
146:10 {O Jerusalem,} Hebrew **Z**.
149: 2 {O people of Jerusalem,} Hebrew **Z**.
SS 3:11 {women of Jerusalem.} Hebrew **Z**.
Isa 1: 8 {Jerusalem} Hebrew *The daughter of* **Z**.
1:27 {people of Jerusalem} Hebrew **Z**.
3:16 {women of Jerusalem,} Hebrew *the daughters of* **Z**.
3:26 {gates of Jerusalem} Hebrew **Z**.
4: 4 {women of Jerusalem.} Hebrew *from the daughters of* **Z**.
4: 5 {shade for Jerusalem} Hebrew *Mount* **Z**.
10:24 {people in Jerusalem,} Hebrew **Z**.
12: 6 {people of Jerusalem} Hebrew **Z**.
14:32 {has built Jerusalem,} Hebrew **Z**.
16: 1 {lambs to Jerusalem} Hebrew *to the daughter of* **Z**.
18: 7 {Almighty in Jerusalem,} Hebrew *on Mount* **Z**.
28:16 {stone in Jerusalem.} Hebrew *in* **Z**.
29: 8 {conquest over Jerusalem,} Hebrew *Mount* **Z**.
33: 5 {will make Jerusalem} Hebrew **Z**.
33:14 {among my people} Hebrew *in* **Z**.
34: 8 {did to Israel.} Hebrew *to* **Z**.
35:10 {return to Jerusalem,} Hebrew **Z**.
46:13 {to save Jerusalem} Hebrew **Z**.
49:14 {Yet Jerusalem} Hebrew **Z**.
51: 3 {will comfort Israel} Hebrew **Z**; also in 51:16.
51:11 {return to Jerusalem,} Hebrew **Z**.
52: 7 {God of Israel} Hebrew *of* **Z**.
52: 8 {home to Jerusalem.} Hebrew *to* **Z**.
59:20 {come to Jerusalem,} Hebrew *to* **Z**.
61: 3 {mourn in Israel,} Hebrew *in* **Z**.
62:11 {people of Israel,} Hebrew *Tell the daughter of* **Z**.
Jer 3:14 {land of Israel} Hebrew *to* **Z**.
4: 6 {signal toward Jerusalem} Hebrew **Z**.
4:31 {of Jerusalem's people} Hebrew *the daughter of* **Z**.
6: 2 {O Jerusalem,} Hebrew **Z**.
6:23 {destroy you, Jerusalem.} Hebrew *daughter of* **Z**.
8:19 {LORD abandoned Jerusalem} Hebrew **Z**.
9:19 {people of Jerusalem} Hebrew **Z**.
14:19 {really hate Jerusalem} Hebrew **Z**.
30:17 {called an outcast—'Jerusalem} Hebrew **Z**.
31: 6 {up to Jerusalem} Hebrew **Z**; also in 31:12.
50: 5 {way to Jerusalem} Hebrew **Z**; also in 50:28.
51:10 {announce in Jerusalem} Hebrew **Z**; also in 51:24, 35a.
La 1: 4 {roads to Jerusalem} Hebrew **Z**; also in 1:17.
1: 6 {majesty of Jerusalem} Hebrew *the daughter of* **Z**.
2: 1 {shadow over Jerusalem.} Hebrew *the daughter of* **Z**; also in 2:8, 10, 18.
2: 4 {on beautiful Jerusalem.} Hebrew *on the tent of the daughter of* **Z**.
4: 2 {children of Jerusalem,} Hebrew *sons of* **Z**.
4:11 {fire in Jerusalem} Hebrew *in* **Z**.
4:22 {O Jerusalem,} Hebrew *daughter of* **Z**.
5:11 {girls in Jerusalem} Hebrew **Z**.
5:18 {For Jerusalem} Hebrew *Mount* **Z**.
Joel 2: 1 {trumpet in Jerusalem} Hebrew **Z**; also in 2:15, 23.
3:21 {home in Jerusalem} Hebrew **Z**.
Am 6: 1 {secure in Jerusalem} Hebrew **Z**.
Ob 1:17 {"But Jerusalem} Hebrew *Mount* **Z**.
Mic 1:13 {you led Jerusalem} Hebrew *the daughter of* **Z**.
4: 7 {rule from Jerusalem} Hebrew *Mount* **Z**.
4:10 {people of Jerusalem,} Hebrew *O daughter of* **Z**.
4:13 {the nations, O Jerusalem!"} Hebrew *"Rise up and thresh, O daughter of* **Z**."
Zec 2: 7 {Escape to Jerusalem,} Hebrew *to* **Z**.
2:10 {and rejoice, O Jerusalem,} Hebrew *O daughter of* **Z**.
9:13 {my arrow! Jerusalem} Hebrew **Z**.
Mt 21: 5 {people of Israel,} Greek *Tell the daughter of* **Z**. Isa 62:11.
Jn 12:15 {people of Israel.} Greek *daughter of* **Z**.
Ro 9:33 {stone in Jerusalem} Greek *in* **Z**.
11:26 {come from Jerusalem,} Greek *from* **Z**.
1Pe 2: 6 {stone in Jerusalem,} Greek *in* **Z**.

ZION'S (1)

Isa 66: 8 {the time Jerusalem's} Hebrew **Z**.

ZIPHION (1)

Ge 46:16 {Gad were Zephon,} As in Greek version and Samaritan Pentateuch (see also Num 26:15); Hebrew reads **Z**.

ZITHER (2)

Da 3: 7 {the musical instruments,} Aramaic *the horn, flute, z, lyre, harp, and other instruments of the musical ensemble.*
3:10 {the musical instruments.} Aramaic *the horn, flute, z, lyre, harp, pipes, and other instruments of the musical ensemble;* also in 3:15.

ZIV (2)

1Ki 6: 1 {was in midspring,} Hebrew *in the month of* **Z**, *which is the second month.* This month of the Hebrew lunar calendar usually occurs in April and May.
6:37 {laid in midspring} Hebrew *in the month of* **Z**. This month of the Hebrew lunar calendar usually occurs in April and May.

ZOAR (2)

Ge 19:22 {known as Zoar.} **Z** means "little."
Jer 48: 4 {will cry out.} Greek version reads *Her cries are heard as far away as* **Z**.

ZOHELETH (1)

1Ki 1: 9 {stone of Zoheleth} Or *to the Serpent's Stone;* Greek version supports reading **Z** as a proper name.